THE AMERICAN HISTORICAL ASSOCIATION'S

Guide to Historical Literature

THE AMERICAN HISTORICAL ASSOCIATION'S

Guide to
Historical Literature

THIRD EDITION

General Editor
Mary Beth Norton

Associate Editor
Pamela Gerardi

VOLUME ONE

New York   Oxford
OXFORD UNIVERSITY PRESS
1995

Oxford University Press

Oxford   New York
Athens   Auckland   Bangkok   Bombay
Calcutta   Cape Town   Dar es Salaam   Delhi
Florence   Hong Kong   Istanbul   Karachi
Kuala Lumpur   Madras   Madrid   Melbourne
Mexico City   Nairobi   Paris   Singapore
Taipei   Tokyo   Toronto

and associated companies in
Berlin   Ibadan

Published by Oxford University Press, Inc.,
200 Madison Avenue, New York, NY 10016

Oxford is a registered trademark of Oxford University Press

Library of Congress Cataloging-in-Publication Data

The American Historical Association's guide to historical literature /
general editor, Mary Beth Norton ; associate editor, Pamela Gerardi.
—3rd ed.
p.   cm.
Contains nearly 27,000 annotated citations (primarily to English
language works) divided into forty-eight sections; citations refer
chiefly to works published between 1961 and 1992.
Includes indexes.
1. History—Bibliography. 2. Bibliography—Best books—History.
I. Norton, Mary Beth. II. Gerardi, Pamela, 1956– . III. American
Historical Association. IV. Title: Guide to historical literature.
Z6201.A55 1995   [D20]   016.9—dc20   94-36720   CIP

ISBN 0-19-509952-4 (vol. 1)
ISBN 0-19-505727-9 (2-vol. set)

Printing (last digit): 9 8 7 6 5 4 3 2 1
Printed in the United States of America
on acid-free paper

CONTENTS

PREFACE

The publication of this edition of *The American Historical Association's Guide to Historical Literature* represents the culmination of over a decade of work by an extremely dedicated group of scholars. The AHA began discussing the compilation of this new *Guide* in 1983, over twenty years after the publication of the previous edition and over fifty years after the publication of the first in 1931. Planning did not begin in earnest, however, until 1985, when Mary Beth Norton, professor of history at Cornell University and newly elected AHA vice president for research, asked the Association for the Bibliography of History to study the feasibility of compiling a new *Guide*. Completed the following year, the study systematically examined various options and recommended the parameters under which this edition has been produced. With authorization from the AHA's governing Council, Professor Norton and the AHA staff then proceeded in 1987 to solicit proposals from potential publishers and institutional co-sponsors; a review of responses culminated in agreements with Oxford University Press and the Department of History at the University of Maryland.

That same year the AHA's Council appointed John Higham, The Johns Hopkins University, as general editor of the *Guide* and, with his concurrence, a board of editors. In consultation with the board, Professor Higham refined the structure of the *Guide*, recruited section editors, and provided the direction for the project prior to its startup in 1990. By that time, however, because of a variety of delays in the project, he was unable to continue with the project, and Council appointed Professor Norton as his successor. In early 1991, a national search culminated in the hiring of Pamela Gerardi as the associate editor, the project's only full-time staff member, and the project office at College Park opened shortly thereafter.

The complexity of the task that Drs. Norton and Gerardi undertook is illustrated by the fact that over five hundred historians, consultants, and graduate students have taken part in various stages of the project. Not only have they successfully orchestrated this mobilization of historical expertise, but they have done so with an enviable grace and ease. On behalf of the AHA, I thank them for their commitment to this project—without them there simply would be no *Guide*. Also deserving special recognition are John Higham, the founding general editor; Richard T. Vann, Professor Norton's successor as AHA vice president for research; Richard Price, then chair of the history department at College Park, and his successor Clifford Foust; John Smith, director of academic computing at the University of Maryland, and Ronald F. E. Weissman, his predecessor; Joyce Duncan Falk, author of the ABH's feasibility study and bibliographic consultant to the project; David Myers, consultant on library needs from the Library of Congress; and James B. Gardner, AHA deputy executive director and staff liaison with the project. We also thank the Association for the Bibliography of History for its invaluable advice and the AHA's Research Division for its continuing support. And, of course, we appreciate the many long hours devoted to the project by the fourteen members of the board of editors, the fifty-six section editors, and the more than four hundred contributors whose names are listed elsewhere. Last but not least we thank the graduate students of the Department of History, University of Maryland, College Park, who performed the many tasks of compiling, verifying, and indexing the volumes: E. Susan Barber, Christopher Jed Coffin, Cynthia Kennedy-Hafllet, David L. Hostetter, R. Matthew Ives,

Lori Jancik, Andrew Laas, Amy Masciola, Franklin Noll, Edwin Thomas Schock, Jr., Marie Schwartz, Donna B. Shear, Diana Snigurowicz, Cynthia L. Vitere, and Frederick B. Wynn, Jr.

None of this would have been possible without outside funding; the compilation of a new *Guide* was simply too costly a project for the AHA to undertake alone. The Rockefeller Foundation provided financial assistance for initial planning, but the key to launching this ambitious project was the support of the National Endowment for the Humanities, which provided both outright funds and federal matching support for the duration of the project. With that core funding in place, the Rockefeller Foundation, the Andrew W. Mellon Foundation, and the Henry Luce Foundation generously provided the necessary matching funds. Also critical to funding was cost sharing by the University of Maryland, which not only provided office space and the necessary computer hardware but also absorbed a significant portion of the administrative costs. To all of the above, the American Historical Association extends its sincere thanks. We are proud to have been the sponsor of this truly impressive demonstration of scholarly collaboration.

Thomas C. Holt
University of Chicago
President, American Historical Association

INTRODUCTION

In the third edition of its *Guide to Historical Literature*, the American Historical Association's purpose is the same that directed the production of the first and second editions in 1931 and 1961: the selection and listing, with appropriate commentary, of the finest and most useful books and articles available in every field of historical scholarship. This edition of the *Guide*, an entirely new and reconceptualized work, provides professional historians, librarians, students, and all others interested in history with a critical overview of the best contemporary historical scholarship. Its systematic survey of all fields of history offers access to the scholarly literature unmatched by any other single reference work.

BACKGROUND

The American Historical Association undertook the task of creating a new edition of the *Guide* because of its conviction that the frequently lamented fragmentation of the once unified discipline of history could be overcome through cooperative and concentrated effort. This two-volume work results from the collaboration of more than four hundred historians, who have contributed their insights to the selection and annotation of the listed items. Scholars familiar with the best research on history in their own fields have chosen and evaluated those articles and books that most successfully introduce others to the study of key issues. Section editors have also contributed brief essays summarizing the history and development of their areas of scholarly inquiry.

The *Guide to Historical Literature* is not a comprehensive ongoing bibliography similar to those produced by a number of other scholarly organizations. Instead, it combines qualitative selectivity, inclusive breadth, and intellectual integration. Although the *Guide* is too selective to serve established scholars in their own fields of specialization, it supplies all its users with information about works on unfamiliar topics and thus fosters the development of broader, more comparative perspectives. By making authoritative references readily available and by situating them within a comprehensible matrix of related inquiries, the *Guide* serves a unifying function and helps to regain the synthetic vision that historians have feared had been lost. The space limitations of the *Guide* and the need for breadth necessarily excludes many fine works of scholarship. Section editors faced a difficult task in selecting appropriate works to produce a balanced and unified list.

The board of editors identified three user needs that have governed the selection of items for this edition of the *Guide to Historical Literature*: first, the need for reliable syntheses and reference works that provide entry into a historical field; second, the need to know the most highly esteemed works that set the standards of excellence (in the various fields of history); and, third, the need to explore the major alternative interpretations represented in current scholarly debate.

Three further considerations have determined the context and organization of the *Guide*. This work lists only printed materials, the great majority of them monographic or synthetic secondary works, because interested researchers can use such titles to locate more specialized primary and secondary sources if they so desire. It also gives strong although not exclusive preference to titles available in English. Since English-speaking nonspecialists in any given field constitute the primary audience for the listings in the *Guide*, it seemed essential that most of the titles identified herein be accessible to most of the readers of these volumes. People with facility in languages other than English can use the cited works to locate more specialized titles in those languages. Finally, the third edition of the *Guide*, like its predecessors, is organized primarily along regional, national, and chronological lines, since historians ordinarily work within a temporal and spatial matrix. The extensive index and listings of cross-references within each subsection give access to materials that span different times and places.

EDITORIAL PRINCIPLES AND PRACTICES

The *Guide to Historical Literature* contains 26,926 bibliographic citations and is divided into forty-eight sections. Each section comprises an introductory essay, a guide to contents, and an annotated bibliography. The section editors were given wide latitude in the arrangement of the bibliographies. Most sections begin with a list of reference works and general studies and then proceed in an arrangement designed specifically for the material in that field. Individual items are arranged alphabetically within the subsections. To maximize the number of citations that could be included in the *Guide*, the appearance of a single bibliographic item in more than one section was strongly discouraged and expressly forbidden within a single section. Thus items that are equally appropriate to more than one list were generally assigned to only one. Users of this *Guide* should consult the general table of contents in volume I and the "guides to contents" at the beginning of each section to facilitate locating studies on a subject that may be spread over several subsections within a section or over two or three sections. The subject index will, of course, aid the user in finer topical searches.

The editorial office has made every effort to verify the bibliographic information provided, by consulting *Books in Print* and the various library catalogs available through the Internet. Confusing and contradictory citations abound out there in the ether, however, and the editors, with the aid of the section editors and contributors, have provided the most reasonable and accurate citation based on the information available. The editorial office had no reasonable or efficient facility for checking article titles. Thus they appear as they were submitted to the office.

Most editors concentrated on works published since 1961 when the last edition of the *Guide* was published. The official cut-off date for works included in this edition was 1992, although a few works published after that date are included.

The *Guide*'s editors chose to list the most recent American editions of items proposed whenever possible, since these are the most readily available in the United States. When works were more recently published outside the United States, they were preferred only if the U.S. publication was out of print or if they represented a newer edition.

Bibliographic citations include the following information:

- CITATION NUMBER. Each bibliographic item has been assigned a unique citation number, consisting of the section number followed by the number of the item in the section bibliography.
- NAME OF AUTHOR OR EDITOR OF WORK CITED. Names are given in normal order: given name–family name for Western names; family name–given name for some Asian names. In all instances, forms of names known to be preferred by individual authors and editors are used. If an author's work has been edited or translated, the name of the editor or translator follows the book title.
- TITLE OF WORK CITED. Titles of articles and books are given in full. Changes in book titles between editions or reprints are usually noted in the annotation.
- EDITION. The edition of the work cited or date of publication for a reprinted work follows the title of a book.

- JOURNAL TITLES. Journal titles are abbreviated to the main title.
- PAGE NUMBERS. Inclusive page numbers are given for an article in a journal or a book.
- PUBLICATION DATA. For books, the place of publication, the name of the publisher, and the date of publication are cited. Publishers' names are usually given in abbreviated forms.
- SERIES TITLE. Series titles were kept to a minimum; only those associated with institutes, societies, associations, programs, or departments and those for series shelved together in libraries are included.
- ISBN or ISSN. International Standard Book/Serial numbers have been provided wherever possible. ISBNs for paperbacks are indicated by (pbk); numbers without a following designation identify clothbound editions.
- ANNOTATION. Each citation includes an annotation. To conserve space, contributors were asked to keep their comments brief, averaging thirty words in length, and to make them in a highly compressed form, using sentence fragments and minimum punctuation and capitalization. Annotations were submitted by over four hundred section editors and contributors; the editorial office made every effort to ensure that the annotations would be understandable to the nonspecialist but kept stylistic editing to a minimum, smoothing out only the most jarring stylistic shifts. The user will therefore find wide variations in style and content in sections with many contributors. *The opinions expressed in the annotations are those of the contributors and do not represent the official opinions of the American Historical Association or of Oxford University Press.* Annotations occasionally refer to another item cited in the *Guide*. These cross-references are indicated by the author's last name and the citation number for the item.
- CONTRIBUTORS' INITIALS. Each annotation is followed by the initials of the contributor(s). A key to contributors' initials follows the "guide to contents" at the beginning of each section bibliography.

Some subsections are followed by "see also" cross-references. These references are listed by citation number, followed by author and main title.

Following the bibliographies in volume 2 is a list of journals that provides the full title and ISSN of journals that focus on publishing articles in history. The journals list, like the bibliography, is selective and is intended only to provide a starting place for the nonspecialist. Volume 2 also contains the indexes for both volumes: an author index and a subject index.

ACKNOWLEDGMENTS

The process of producing a new edition of the *Guide to Historical Literature* has been an enlightening, daunting, exacting, and yet endlessly fascinating experience, and we, the editors, have enjoyed working with the American Historical Association and with Oxford University Press to produce these volumes. We would like to express our personal thanks to the many historians who advised us on the selection of section editors, consultants, and contributors; to the Department of History at Cornell University for facilitating many administrative tasks; to the members of the board of editors for their sage advice and unswerving interest; to Jim Gardner, deputy executive director at the AHA, for his involvement in the project since its inception and for his constant support throughout; and finally to the section editors, who found themselves in the midst of a project larger than they had anticipated but who rose to the occasion beautifully.

Mary Beth Norton
Pamela Gerardi

CONTRIBUTORS AND CONSULTANTS

HOWARD E. ADELMAN
Associate Professor of Jewish Studies, Smith College

HUGH L. AGNEW
Associate Professor of History and International Affairs,
George Washington University

JAMES SMITH ALLEN
Professor of History, Southern Illinois University,
Carbondale

THOMAS T. ALLSEN
Associate Professor of History, Trenton State College

CHARLES AMBLER
Associate Professor of History, University of Texas, El
Paso

DAVID M. ANDERSON
Senior Lecturer in the History of Africa, School of
Oriental and African Studies, University of London

CELIA S. APPLEGATE
Associate Professor of History, University of Rochester

LORRAINE C. ATTREED
Associate Professor of History, College of the Holy Cross

WILLIAM S. ATWELL
Professor and Chair of History, Hobart and William
Smith Colleges

JÁNOS M. BAK
Professor of History, Emeritus, University of British
Columbia; Professor of Medieval Studies, Central
European University, Budapest

IVO BANAC
Professor of History, Yale University

LUCY G. BARBER
Ph.D. Candidate, Department of History, Brown
University

ANNE L. BARSTOW
Professor of History, State University of New York,
College at Old Westbury

ISRAEL BARTAL
Associate Professor of Jewish History, The Hebrew
University, Jerusalem

JOSEF J. BARTON
Associate Professor of History; Associate Professor of
Urban Affairs, Northwestern University

DANIEL A. BAUGH
Professor of History, Cornell University

ROGER B. BECK
Associate Professor of History, Eastern Illinois University

MARGUERITE F. BEEBY
Instructor, Department of History, University of West
Florida, Pensacola

GORDON M. BERGER
Professor of History, University of Southern California

LENARD R. BERLANSTEIN
Professor of History, University of Virginia

ELEZ BIBERAJ
Chief, Albanian Service, Voice of America

RICHARD A. BILLOWS
Associate Professor of History, Columbia University

WILLIAM LEE BLACKWOOD
Ph.D. Candidate, Department of History, Yale
University

DAVID L. BLANK
Associate Professor of Classics, University of California,
Los Angeles

GORDON C. BOND
Professor of History and Dean, College of Liberal Arts,
Auburn University

KARL S. BOTTIGHEIMER
Associate Professor of History, State University of New
York, Stony Brook

JOHN BOWER
Lecturer, Department of Sociology and Anthropology,
University of Minnesota, Duluth; Professor, Emeritus,
Iowa State University

JAMES BOYDEN
Assistant Professor of History, Tulane University

JOHN W. BOYER
Professor of History, University of Chicago

JOSEPH C. BRADLEY
Professor of History, University of Tulsa

THOMAS A. BRADY, JR.
Professor of History, University of California, Berkeley

KINLEY J. BRAUER
Professor of History, University of Minnesota

DAVID L. BROWMAN
Chairman, Archaeology, Washington University

SHELBY BROWN
Research Associate, Institute of Archaeology, University
of California, Los Angeles

VICTORIA BISSELL BROWN
Associate Professor of History, Grinnell College

JOHN BUCKLER
Professor of History, University of Illinois, Urbana-
Champaign

SUZANNE BURKHOLDER
Associate Professor of History, St. Louis College of
Pharmacy

STANLEY M. BURSTEIN
Professor of History, California State University, Los
Angeles

JON BUTLER
William Robertson Coe Professor of American Studies
and History, Yale University

DAVID L. CARLTON
Associate Professor of History, Vanderbilt University

JEAN-CLAUDE CARON
Chargé de Cours, Université de Paris VIII, Saint-Denis

THOMAS H. CARPENTER
Professor of Art History and Humanities, Virginia
Polytechnic Institute and State University

NOEL D. CARY
Associate Professor of History, College of the Holy Cross

JAMES H. CASSEDY
Editor, *Bibliography of the History of Medicine*, National
Library of Medicine

ANDREW R. L. CAYTON
Professor of History, Miami University

JONATHAN G. CEDARBAUM
Ph.D. Candidate, Department of History, Yale
University

JOHN W. CELL
Professor of History, Duke University

JACK R. CENSER
Professor of History, George Mason University

PAUL E. CERUZZI
Curator, Department of Space History, National Air and
Space Museum, Smithsonian Institution

JOHN W. CHAFFEE
Associate Professor and Chair of History, State
University of New York, Binghamton

DAVID CHERRY
Assistant Professor of History, Montana State University

HENRY C. CLARK
Associate Professor of History, Canisius College

JENNY S. CLAY
Professor of Classics, University of Virginia

RICHARD CLOGG
Associate Fellow, St. Antony's College, Oxford

DONALD STEPHEN CLOYD
Rochester, New York

MORDECHAI COGAN
Professor of Biblical History, The Hebrew University,
Jerusalem

MARK R. COHEN
Professor of Near Eastern Studies, Princeton University

THOMAS COHEN
Assistant Professor of History, The Catholic University
of America

LORI E. COLE
Assistant Professor of History, University of Maine at
Machais

DONALD E. COLLINS
Ph.D. Candidate, Department of History, Carnegie
Mellon University

FRANK F. CONLON
Professor of History and South Asian Studies, University
of Washington, Seattle

JOHN J. CONTRENI
Professor of History, Purdue University

NOBLE DAVID COOK
Professor of History, Florida International University,
Miami

PATRICIA A. COOPER
Associate Professor of History and Women's Studies,
University of Kentucky

WILLIAM J. COURTENAY
Professor of History, University of Wisconsin, Madison

RICHARD J. CRAMPTON
Lecturer in East European History and Fellow, St.
Edmund Hall, Oxford

GARY W. CRAWFORD
Professor and Chair of Anthropology, University of
Toronto

MICHAEL J. CROWE
Professor, Program of Liberal Studies, University of
Notre Dame

ALEXANDER DALLIN
Raymond A. Spruance Professor of International History, Stanford University

GREGORY N. DAUGHERTY
Associate Professor of Classics, Randolph-Macon College

ANGELA E. DAVIS
Winnipeg, Manitoba

DEVIN A. DeWEESE
Associate Professor of Central Eurasian Studies, Indiana University

DONALD DENOON
Professor of Pacific Islands History, Australian National University, Canberra

GEORGI M. DERLUGUIAN
Research Associate, Fernand Braudel Center for the Study of Economies, Historical Systems, and Civilizations, State University of New York, Binghamton

LIUBOV G. DERLUGUIAN
Junior Researcher, Institute of Orientalistics, Russia's Academy of Sciences, Moscow

WILLIAM F. DEVERELL
Assistant Professor of History, University of California, San Diego

BARBARA B. DIEFENDORF
Professor of History, Boston University

MICHAEL DINTENFASS
Associate Professor of History and Urban Social Institutions, University of Wisconsin, Milwaukee

JOHN J. DOBBINS
Associate Professor of Classical Art and Archaeology, McIntire Department of Art, University of Virginia

WILLIAM M. DOYLE
Assistant Professor of Economics, University of Dallas

MICHAEL ROBERT DROMPP
Associate Professor of History, Rhodes College

ALASTAIR C. DUKE
Reader, Department of History, University of Southampton

TOM DUNNE
Statutory Lecturer in Irish History, Faculty of Arts, University College, Cork

RUTH W. DUNNELL
Storer Assistant Professor of Asian History, Kenyon College

CARTER J. ECKERT
Professor of Korean History, Harvard University

ELIZABETH A. ELDREDGE
Assistant Professor of History, Michigan State University

RICHARD ELPHICK
Professor of History, Wesleyan University

GEORGE N. EMERY
Associate Professor of History, University of Western Ontario

ELIZABETH ENDICOTT-WEST
Simsbury, Connecticut

STANLEY L. ENGERMAN
John H. Munro Professor of Economics and Professor of History, University of Rochester

NORA FAIRES
Associate Professor of History, University of Michigan, Flint

MARJORIE M. FARRAR
Chestnut Hill, Massachusetts

ANDREA FELDMAN
Ph.D. Candidate, Department of History, Yale University

DANIEL FELLER
Associate Professor of History, University of New Mexico

PHYLLIS F. FIELD
Associate Professor of History, Ohio University

LORENZ J. FIRSCHING
Associate Professor of History, Broome Community College

DAVID E. FISHMAN
Assistant Professor of History, Jewish Theological Seminary of America

IAN CHRISTOPHER FLETCHER
Assistant Professor of History, Georgia State University

HONORE C. FORSTER
Research Officer, Division of Pacific and Asian History, Australian National University, Canberra

RENÉE FOSSETT
Ph.D. Candidate, Department of History, University of Manitoba

SIMON C. FRANKLIN
Lecturer in Slavonic Studies, Clare College, Cambridge

GLADYS FRANTZ-MURPHY
Associate Professor of History, Regis University, Denver

JOHN B. FREED
Distinguished Professor of History, Illinois State University

PAUL H. FREEDMAN

Professor of History, Vanderbilt University

GREGORY L. FREEZE
Professor and Chair of History, Brandeis University

CHRISTOPHER R. FRIEDRICHS
Associate Professor of History, University of British
Columbia

RACHEL G. FUCHS
Professor of History, Arizona State University

DONNA R. GABACCIA
Charles Stone Professor of American History, University
of North Carolina, Charlotte

LYDIA M. GARNER
Assistant Professor of History, Southwest Texas State
University

GENE R. GARTHWAITE
Professor and Chair of History, Dartmouth College

PATRICK J. GEARY
Professor of History and Director, Center for Medieval
and Renaissance Studies, University of California, Los
Angeles

PAMELA GERARDI
Associate Editor, *Guide to Historical Literature*

LIETTE P. GIDLOW
Ph.D. Candidate, Department of History, Cornell
University

MARC JASON GILBERT
Professor of History, North Georgia College

RICHARD M. GOLDEN
Professor of History, Clemson University

ARTHUR GOLDSCHMIDT, JR.
Professor of Middle East History, Pennsylvania State
University

DENA GOODMAN
Associate Professor of History, Louisiana State
University

BERTRAM M. GORDON
Professor and Chair of History, Mills College

STEPHEN S. GOSCH
Professor of History, University of Wisconsin, Eau Claire

PAMELA S. GOSSIN
Visiting Assistant Professor of History of Science,
University of Oklahoma

DENNIS GRAFFLIN
Associate Professor and Chair of History, Bates College

LOREN R. GRAHAM
Professor of History, Massachusetts Institute of
Technology and Harvard University

MOTT T. GREENE
John B. Magee Distinguished Professor of Science and
Values, University of Puget Sound

PETER N. GREGORY
Professor of Religious Studies, University of Illinois,
Urbana-Champaign

ROBERT K. GRIFFITH, JR.
Pawtucket, Rhode Island

JO-ANN GROSS
Associate Professor, Department of History, Trenton
State College

CARL J. GUARNERI
Professor of History, St. Mary's College of California

JEFFREY S. GUROCK
Libby M. Klaperman Professor of Jewish History,
Yeshiva University

MARK VON HAGEN
Associate Professor of History, Columbia University

PETER L. HAHN
Assistant Professor of History, Ohio State University;
Associate Editor, *Diplomatic History*

STEVEN H. HAHN
Professor of History, University of California, San Diego

BERT S. HALL
Associate Professor, Institute for the History and
Philosophy of Science and Technology, University of
Toronto

CHRISTOPHER S. HAMLIN
Associate Professor of History, University of Notre
Dame

THOMAS D. HAMM
Curator and Associate Professor of History, Earlham
College

CAROLINE HANNAWAY
Philadelphia, Pennsylvania

PATRICK J. HARRIGAN
Professor of History, University of Waterloo

EDWARD M. HARRIS
Professor of Classics, Brooklyn College and The
Graduate School, City University of New York

JAMES F. HARRIS
Professor of History, University of Maryland, College
Park

CHARLES HARTMAN
Professor of East Asian Studies, State University of New
York, Albany

ROBERT A. HATCH
Associate Professor of History, University of Florida

STEVEN C. HAUSE
Professor of History, University of Missouri, St. Louis

JOHN N. HAWKINS
Dean, International Studies and Overseas Programs, University of California, Los Angeles

PETER HAYES
Professor of History and German; Alfred W. Chase Professor of Business Institutions, Northwestern University

CHARLES W. HEDRICK
Associate Professor of History, University of California, Santa Cruz

MARY W. HELMS
Professor of Anthropology, University of North Carolina, Greensboro

DAVID P. HENIGE
African Studies Bibliographer, Memorial Library, University of Wisconsin, Madison

SANDRA HERBERT
Professor of History, University of Maryland, Baltimore County

JOHN S. HILL
Assistant Professor of History, Ohio State University

JOHN HINSHAW
Ph.D. Candidate, Department of History, Carnegie Mellon University

KEITH A. HITCHINS
Professor of History, University of Illinois, Urbana-Champaign

STEVEN L. HOCH
Associate Professor of History, University of Iowa

PHILIP T. HOFFMAN
Associate Professor of History and Social Science, Division of Humanities and Social Sciences, California Institute of Technology

DANIEL U. HOLBROOK
Ph.D. Candidate, Department of History, Carnegie Mellon University

MACK P. HOLT
Associate Professor of History, George Mason University

EVELYN HU-DEHART
Professor of History, University of Colorado, Boulder

BRADY A. HUGHES
Shippensburg, Pennsylvania

SARAH S. HUGHES
Associate Professor of History, Shippensburg University

NANCY ROSE HUNT
Assistant Professor of History, University of Arizona

PAULA E. HYMAN
Professor of History, Yale University

ROBERT P. HYMES
Assistant Professor of History, Columbia University

CHARLES W. INGRAO
Professor of History, Purdue University

PAUL B. ISRAEL
Associate Editor, Thomas A. Edison Papers, Rutgers University

NATALIE K. ISSER
Professor of History, Pennsylvania State University, Ogontz

DONALD C. JACKSON
Assistant Professor of History, Lafayette College

ESTHER JACOBSON
Maude I. Kerns Professor of Oriental Art, University of Oregon

DAVID JARDINI
Ph.D. Candidate, Department of History, Carnegie Mellon University

KRISTINE L. JONES
Resident Director, Council on International Educational Exchange, Dominican Republic

CHRISTOPHER M. JOYCE
Ph.D. Candidate, College of William and Mary

RICHARD W. KAEUPER
Professor of History, University of Rochester

CEMAL KAFADAR
Associate Professor of History, Harvard University

SUSAN C. KARANT-NUNN
Professor of History, Portland State University

RUTH M. KARRAS
Assistant Professor of History, University of Pennsylvania

DAVID N. KEIGHTLEY
Professor and Chair of History, University of California, Berkeley

KENNETH W. KELLER
Professor of History, Mary Baldwin College

WILLIAM KEYLOR
Professor and Chair of History, Boston University

PHILIP S. KHOURY
Dean, School of Humanities and Social Science; Professor of History, Massachusetts Institute of Technology

SHARON E. KINGSLAND
Professor of History, Department of History of Sciences, The Johns Hopkins University

PATRICK V. KIRCH
Professor of Anthropology, University of California, Berkeley

NICHOLAS M. KLIMENT
Instructor in Religion; Assistant School Minister, Phillips Exeter Academy

WILBUR R. KNORR
Professor of History and Philosophy of Science, Stanford University

JONATHAN B. KNUDSEN
Professor and Chair of History, Wellesley College

PHILIP L. KOHL
Professor of Anthropology, Wellesley College

NANCY SHIELDS KOLLMANN
Associate Professor of History, Stanford University

GARY J. KORNBLITH
Associate Professor of History, Oberlin College

MÁRIA M. KOVÁCS
Assistant Professor of History, University of Wisconsin, Madison

P. DAVID KOVACS
Professor of Classics, University of Virginia, Charlottesville

SHELDON KRIMSKY
Professor and Chair, Department of Urban and Environmental Policy, Tufts University

PETER KRÜGER
Professor of Modern History, University of Marburg

BONNELYN YOUNG KUNZE
Adjunct Professor of History, LeMoyne College, Colgate Rochester Divinity School

HIROAKI KUROMIYA
Associate Professor of History, Indiana University

HOWARD I. KUSHNER
Professor of History, San Diego State University

JOHN T. LANDRY
Ph.D. Candidate, Department of History, Brown University

ERICK D. LANGER
Associate Professor of History, Carnegie Mellon University

JOSEPH J. LAUER
Africana Bibliographer, Library, Michigan State University

ROBIN LAW
Professor of African History, University of Stirling

DAVID E. LEARY
Dean of Arts and Sciences; Professor of Psychology, University of Richmond

LOYD E. LEE
Professor of History, State University of New York, New Paltz

HARTMUT LEHMANN
Director, Max-Planck-Institut für Geschichte, Göttingen

BRIAN P. LEVACK
Professor and Chair of History, University of Texas, Austin

MIRIAM R. LEVIN
Assistant Professor of History, Case Western Reserve University

ALLAN G. LEVINE
Ph.D., Department of History, St. John's Ravenscourt School, Winnipeg, Manitoba

ROBERT M. LEVINE
Professor of History, University of Miami

EUGENE D. LEVY
Associate Professor of History, Carnegie Mellon University

JANET E. LEVY
Associate Professor of Anthropology, Department of Sociology, Anthropology, and Social Work, University of North Carolina, Charlotte

YOUNG ICK LEW
Professor of History, Hallym University

EARL LEWIS
Associate Professor of History and Afroamerican and African Studies, University of Michigan

THEODORE C. LIAZOS
Ph.D. Candidate, Department of History, Yale University

MARY LINDEMANN
Associate Professor of History, Carnegie Mellon University

DEBRA J. LINDSAY
Postdoctoral Fellow, Social Science and Humanistic Research College, University of Manitoba

JENNIFER M. LLOYD
Instructor, Department of History, State University of New York, Brockport

CRAIG A. LOCKARD
Professor of History, Department of Social Change and Development, University of Wisconsin, Green Bay

RALPH P. LOCKE
Professor of Musicology, Eastman School of Music, University of Rochester

F. BULLITT LOWRY
Associate Professor of History, University of North
Texas

DAVID E. LUDDEN
Associate Professor of History, University of
Pennsylvania

KENNETH M. LUDMERER
Professor of History and of Medicine, Washington
University, St. Louis

KEITH P. LURIA
Associate Professor of History, North Carolina State
University

OLIVER MACDONAGH
Research Professor of History, Australian Catholic
University

PAMELA E. MACK
Associate Professor of History, Clemson University

DAVID MACKENZIE
Professor of History, University of North Carolina,
Greensboro

PATRICK MANNING
College of Arts and Sciences Distinguished Professor of
History and African-American Studies, Northeastern
University

BEATRICE FORBES MANZ
Associate Professor of History, Tufts University

ALAN I. MARCUS
Professor of History and Director, Center for Historical
Studies of Technology and Science, Iowa State
University

GARY J. MARKER
Associate Professor of History, State University of New
York, Stony Brook

HARVEY MARKOWITZ
Lecturer, Department of Anthropology, Indiana
University

SALLY MARKS
Providence, Rhode Island

JEAN-PIERRE MARTIN
University of Aix-en-Provence

PHYLLIS M. MARTIN
Associate Professor of History, Indiana University

PHILIP MATTAR
Executive Director, Institute for Palestine Studies;
Coeditor, *Encyclopedia of the Modern Middle East*

IAIN MCCALMAN
Professor and Associate Director, Humanities Research
Centre, Australian National University, Canberra

TERRENCE J. MCDONALD
Associate Professor of History, University of Michigan

E. ANN MCDOUGALL
Associate Professor of History, University of Alberta

RODERICK J. MCINTOSH
Professor of Anthropology, Rice University

BRIAN J. C. MCKERCHER
Associate Professor of History, Royal Military College of
Canada

SALLY G. MCMILLEN
Associate Professor of History, Davidson College

JOHN A. MEARS
Associate Professor of History, Southern Methodist
University

EZRA MENDELSOHN
The Hebrew University, Jerusalem

RALPH R. MENNING
Assistant Professor of History, Heidelberg College

MICHAEL F. METCALF
Professor of Scandinavian History, University of
Minnesota

JON D. MIKALSON
Professor of Classics, University of Virginia

DAVID HARRY MILLER
Professor, Emeritus, University of Oklahoma

RICHARD L. MILLETT
Professor of History, Southern Illinois University,
Edwardsville

CLYDE A. MILNER II
Professor of History, Utah State University; Editor,
Western Historical Quarterly

ARTHUR P. MOLELLA
Chair, History of Science and Technology Department,
Museum of American History, Smithsonian Institution

ERIC H. MONKKONEN
Professor of History, University of California, Los
Angeles

E. WILLIAM MONTER
Professor of History, Northwestern University

ANDREW M. T. MOORE
Associate Dean, Graduate School, Yale University

EDWARD T. MORMAN
Librarian, Institute of the History of Medicine, The
Johns Hopkins University

MARK MOTLEY
Assistant Professor of Education and of History,
University of Rochester

JAMES D. MUHLY
Professor of Ancient Near Eastern History, Department of Asian and Middle Eastern Studies, University of Pennsylvania

DIANA MURIN
Research Assistant, Classical Studies, Trinity University

TERESA A. MURPHY
Associate Professor of American Studies, The George Washington University

ALEXANDER C. MURRAY
Associate Professor of History, University of Toronto, Mississauga

DOROTHY NELKIN
University Professor, Sociology Department and School of Law, New York University

LYNN A. NELSON
Ph.D. Candidate, Department of History, College of William and Mary

DAVID S. NEWBURY
Associate Professor of History, University of North Carolina, Chapel Hill

RICHARD S. NEWELL
Professor of History, University of Northern Iowa

EDGAR NEWMAN
Associate Professor of History, New Mexico State University, Las Cruces

THOMAS F. X. NOBLE
Associate Professor of History, University of Virgina

DAVID NORTHRUP
Professor of History, Boston College

WILLIAM L. OCHSENWALD
Professor of History, Virginia Polytechnic Institute and State University

DAVID O'CONNOR
Curator, Egyptian Section, The University Museum; Professor of Egyptology, Department of Asian and Middle Eastern Studies, University of Pennsylvania

KAREN OFFEN
Affiliated Scholar, Institute for Research on Women and Gender, Stanford University

PHILIP K. OLDENBURG
Adjunct Assistant Professor of Political Science, Columbia University

ERIK N. OLSSEN
Professor of History, University of Otago

DUANE J. OSHEIM
Professor of History, University of Virginia

KATHARINE PARK
William R. Kenan, Jr., Professor of History, Wellesley College

K. DAVID PATTERSON
Professor of History, University of North Carolina, Charlotte

HARRY W. PAUL
Professor of History, University of Florida, Gainsville

KENNETH PENNINGTON
Professor of History, Syracuse University

DUNCAN M. PERRY
Director, Analytical Research Department and Editor-in-Chief, *RFE/RL Research Report*, Radio Free Europe/Radio Liberty Research Institute, Munich

CARLA RAHN PHILLIPS
Professor of History, University of Minnesota

WILLIAM D. PHILLIPS, JR.
Professor of History, University of Minnesota

G. KURT PIEHLER
Research Fellow, Rutgers Center for Historical Analysis

UTA G. POIGER
Ph.D. Candidate, Department of History, Brown University

JANET L. POLASKY
Associate Professor of History, University of New Hampshire

LINDA A. POLLOCK
Professor of History, Tulane University

GREGORY L. POSSEHL
Professor of Anthropology, University of Pennsylvania

D. T. POTTS
Edwin Cuthbert Hall Professor of Middle Eastern Archaeology, School of Archaeology, The University of Sydney

JAMES F. POWERS
Professor of History, College of the Holy Cross

DONALD J. RALEIGH
Professor of History, University of North Carolina, Chapel Hill

DAVID A. RAWSON
Ph.D. Candidate, Department of History, College of William and Mary

PEEP PETER REBANE
Associate Professor of History, Penn State University, Ogontz

WILLIAM W. REGISTER, JR.
Assistant Professor of History, University of the South

SUSAN M. REVERBY
Luella LeMar Associate Professor, Women's Studies Program, Wellesley College

TERRY S. REYNOLDS
Chair, Department of Social Sciences, Michigan Technological University

NORMAN RICH
Professor of History, Emeritus, Brown University

JONATHAN S. C. RILEY-SMITH
Professor of History, Royal Holloway University of London

RICHARD ROBERTS
Associate Professor of History, Stanford University

DAVID ROBINSON
University Distinguished Professor of History and African Studies, Michigan State University

MICHAEL ROBINSON
Associate Professor of History, University of Southern California

THOMAS ROBISHEAUX
Associate Professor of History, Duke University

ALAN J. ROCKE
Professor of History, Case Western Reserve University

ARON RODRIGUE
Associate Professor of History, Stanford University

ALEX ROLAND
Professor of History, Duke University

WILLIAM G. ROSENBERG
Professor of History, University of Michigan

MORRIS ROSSABI
Professor of History, City University of New York

JACQUES ROUILLARD
Professor of History, Université de Montréal

DON K. ROWNEY
Professor of History, Bowling Green State University

MIECZYSŁAW ROZBICKI
Ph.D. Candidate, Department of History, Yale University

ANN POTTINGER SAAB
Professor of History, University of North Carolina, Greensboro

JOHN SCARBOROUGH
Professor of the History of Pharmacy and Medicine; Professor of Classics, University of Wisconsin, Madison

ULI SCHAMILOGLU
Associate Professor of Central Asian Studies, Department of Slavic Languages, University of Wisconsin, Madison

T. PHILIP SCHOFIELD
Lecturer in Laws, University College, London

SUSAN SCHROEDER
Associate Professor of History, Loyola University of Chicago

STEPHEN SCHUKER
William W. Corcoran Professor of History, University of Virginia

BRUCE E. SEELY
Associate Professor of History, Department of Social Sciences, Michigan Technological University; Secretary, Society for the History of Technology

GRACE SEIBERLING
Associate Professor of Art History and Visual and Cultural Studies, University of Rochester

MARLÈNE SHAMAY
Ingénieur d'Études, École des Hautes Études en Sciences Sociales

MICHAEL H. SHANK
Associate Professor of the History of Science, University of Wisconsin, Madison

LEWIS SIEGELBAUM
Professor of History, Michigan State University

REEVA S. SIMON
Assistant Director, Middle East Institute, Columbia University

DANIEL SCOTT SMITH
Professor of History, University of Illinois at Chicago

JOHN K. SMITH
Assistant Professor of History, Lehigh University

ROBERT W. SMITH, JR.
Ph.D. Candidate, College of William and Mary

JAY L. SPAULDING
Associate Professor of History, Kean College of New Jersey

THOMAS T. SPEAR
Professor of History, University of Wisconsin, Madison

JONATHAN SPERBER
Professor of History, University of Missouri, Columbia

ELLIOT SPERLING
Associate Professor of Central Eurasian Studies, Indiana University

DARREN M. STALOFF
Assistant Professor of History, City College of New York

PETER STANSKY
Frances and Charles Field Professor of History, Stanford University

DARWIN H. STAPLETON
Director, Rockefeller Archive Center

RICHARD STITES
Professor of History, Georgetown University

FIONA HARRIS STOERTZ
Ph.D. Candidate, Department of History, University of
California, Santa Barbara

JUDITH F. STONE
Associate Professor of History, Western Michigan
University

KENNETH R. STOW
Professor of Jewish History, Haifa University

DONA S. STRALEY
Associate Professor and Middle East Studies Librarian,
Ohio State University

JON T. SUMIDA
Associate Professor of History, University of Maryland,
College Park

RONALD GRIGOR SUNY
Alex Manoqgian Professor of Modern Armenian History,
University of Michigan

DAVID G. SWEET
Associate Professor of History, University of California,
Santa Cruz

LLOYD S. SWENSON, JR.
Professor of History, University of Houston

ALICE-MARY TALBOT
Advisor for Hagiography, Dumbarton Oaks

M. BROOK TAYLOR
Associate Professor of History, Mount Saint Vincent
University

CAROL G. THOMAS
Professor of History, University of Washington

GORDON C. THOMASSON
Assistant Professor of World History, Broome
Community College

F.M.L. THOMPSON
Professor of History, Emeritus, University of London

JOHN K. THORNTON
Associate Professor of History, Millersville University of
Pennsylvania

ROBERT L. THORP
Associate Professor of Chinese Art and Archaeology,
Washington University

HOYT CLEVELAND TILLMAN
Professor of History, Arizona State University

MARGO TODD
Associate Professor of History, Vanderbilt University

AVIEZER TUCKER
Research grantee, Research Support Scheme, Central
European University, Prague

JUDITH E. TUCKER
Associate Professor of History, Georgetown University

MARY EVELYN TUCKER
Associate Professor of Religion, Bucknell University,
Lewisburg

CAROL URNESS
Curator and Professor, James Ford Bell Library,
University of Minnesota

LUCETTE VALENSI
Directeur d'Études, École des Hautes Études en Sciences
Sociales

STEVEN BÉLA VÁRDY
Professor of History and Director, History Forum,
Duquesne University

LYNNE VIOLA
Associate Professor of History, University of Toronto

JOHN O. VOLL
Professor of History, University of New Hampshire

BARBARA A. VOYTEK
Executive Director, Center for Slavic and East European
Studies, University of California, Berkeley

JOHAN DE VRIES
Professor of History, Catholic University of Tilburg

HARUKO WAKABAYASHI
Ph.D. Candidate, East Asian Studies, Princeton
University

ROBERT W. WALLACE
Associate Professor of Classics, Northwestern University

IMMANUEL WALLERSTEIN
Director, Fernand Braudel Center for the Study of
Economics, Historical Systems, and Civilizations, State
University of New York, Binghamton

MARGARET WASHINGTON
Professor of History, Cornell University

MATTHEW W. WATERS
Ph.D. Candidate, Graduate Group in Ancient History,
University of Pennsylvania

DAVID J. WEBER
Robert and Nancy Dedman Professor of History,
Dedman College, Southern Methodist University

PETER S. WELLS
Professor of Anthropology, University of Minnesota

RICHARD F. WETZELL
Assistant Professor of History, University of Maryland, College Park

DOUGLAS WHEELER
Professor of History, University of New Hampshire

STEPHEN D. WHITE
Asa G. Candler Professor of Medieval History, Emory University

MERRY E. WIESNER-HANKS
Associate Professor of History, University of Wisconsin, Milwaukee

KATHLEEN WILSON
Assistant Professor of History, State University of New York, Stony Brook

MARY C. WILSON
Associate Professor of History; Director, Near Eastern Studies Program, University of Massachusetts, Amherst

JUDITH WISHNIA
Associate Professor of History, State University of New York, Stony Brook

JOHN E. WOODS
Professor of History, University of Chicago

EDWARD V. WOODWARD
University of Florida

WILLIAM H. WORGER
Associate Professor of History, University of California, Los Angeles

BERNARD B. YAMRON
Ph.D. Candidate, Department of History, Brown University

ANAND A. YANG
Professor and Chair of History, University of Utah

ROBERT J. YOUNG
Professor of History, University of Winnipeg

KRISTIN E. S. ZAPALAC
Assistant Professor of History, Washington University

THE AMERICAN HISTORICAL ASSOCIATION'S

Guide to Historical Literature

RICHARD T. VANN

Theory and Practice in Historical Study

The thirty-odd years since the publication of the second edition of this *Guide* have been the best and the worst of times for historians. More are professionally employed in teaching and writing history than ever before; historical scholarship has reached new heights of scope and sophistication; and the public's interest in the past, even in such degraded forms as the docudrama or the bodice-ripper historical novel, seems insatiable. Yet never have so many—including some historians—questioned the very foundations of historiography. How can any statement about the past be confirmed when we cannot produce the past for examination? Is the claim to make objective statements about the past only a "noble dream"? If, as logicians tell us, explanations must make reference to laws, and explanation, causation, and prediction are conceptually inseparable, what entitles the historian to claim to have explained anything? And is there even an integral "history" any more, rather than a congeries of separate fields of investigation, many of which are more closely related to other social sciences than to history as traditionally conceived? As the second millennium of the common era ends, postmodernism appears to proclaim, with Michel Foucault, the end also of historical consciousness—a transitory moment in thought, now played out.

The paradox inherent in such a claim—only historical consciousness could discern the death of historical consciousness—does not bother postmodernists, who revel in such ironies; but it may suggest to others that reports of that death have been exaggerated. This first section of the new *Guide* is devoted to fundamental questions about historical thinking, writing, and teaching. Some have been raised by philosophers of history—a small minority to be found in the soft tissues of a few philosophy departments. Others have come from historically minded social scientists and humanists, but most have arisen within the community of historians; and it is this self-understanding that is most important.

History has two mandates: to get the facts right and to make sense. The history of historiography is to a large degree a development of the ability to get the facts right. The ancillary studies have helped make this possible. Forged charters, for example, were freely concocted in the Middle Ages, and examples of their successful detection are at least five hundred years old. Less dramatic but of fundamental importance has been the incremental increase in our ability to read the handwriting of our ancestors. Early historians were bedeviled by the confusion of calendars in different ancient cultures, so the establishment of a relatively secure comparative chronology is a humble and often unacknowledged advance in the human sciences. In more recent times historians have expanded the range of artifacts that can serve as evidence and have mastered new techniques for evaluating the testimony of oral witnesses—the oldest historical source of all—and of literary texts (the still controversial insights of psychoanalysis have been important here).

Historians who write about historiography often evoke the imagery of apprenticeship and craftsmanship. Learning such techniques has been taken to be the hallmark of this craft knowledge; indeed, when under pressure from philosophers to explain themselves, many historians have treated historiography as something like a medieval "mystery"— a guild pursuit whose practices are, if not ineffable, at least inaccessible to those without the proper professional training (which is certainly organized on craft-guild lines by those medieval survivals, the modern universities).

No one can reasonably doubt that historians have worked out methods that make it unlikely they will be grossly deceived for very long on most purely factual questions. A chronicle, however—a mere assemblage of facts in chronological order—is not a history. When historians select the facts and construct an account, they exercise judgment, but it is judgment subject to criticism, freely offered by fellow historians but also by scholars outside the discipline.

Reflection on the way historians make sense of the facts has taken two conventionally distinguished forms: analytical (or critical) and substantive (or speculative) philosophy of history. This distinction cannot be drawn sharply, since ways of making sense are implicated in the establishment of the facts; but it does point to some family resemblances between two styles of philosophizing.

There are two founding texts of modern analytical philosophy of history: Carl Hempel's article "The Function of General Laws in History," attempting to assimilate historical explanation to the model of the most advanced natural sciences (reprinted in Gardiner 1.54), and R. G. Collingwood's *The Idea of History* (1.280), which argues for the irreducible difference between history and natural science. Few people believed Hempel's claim that historians, when studying events, make at least an "explanation sketch" by adducing laws specifying that, given certain initial conditions, events of that type will occur. No such laws could be identified, and the claim ran counter to the traditional preoccupation of historians to explain particular, if not unique, situations. Hempel (in Dray, 1.242) retreated from his earlier position; but the ideal of "scientific history" did not disappear. In fact much of the innovative history of the past generation has been inspired by an ambition to bring historical explanation closer to that thought to be characteristic of natural sciences. The "new" economic history explicitly drew on a Hempelian conception of science, since its econometric models allowed for the manipulation of variables to produce quasi-experimental results. Comparative history, too, relies on a logic in which the typical is established analogously to the experimental control of variables so that the significance of the unusual can emerge.

Even though the ideal of a "unified science" may never be realized, as advocates of the autonomy of history insist, history would be unintelligible without some generalizations and general terms. Nevertheless, the emphasis of most historical research still falls upon the particular (not the unique). Much of the thinking represented in this section is devoted to working out the implications of this necessary and, at best, productive tension between the general and the particular.

The great philosopher of understanding the particular was Collingwood, the only philosopher of history with extensive experience as a practicing historian (of Roman Britain). He conceived history as composed of episodes, with the historian trying to understand the reasons for the actions performed in them. This must be done, he maintained, by grasping the problem that the historical actor was trying to solve and reenacting in one's mind the reasoning that led to the action. This procedure yields historical knowledge (Collingwood was not a skeptic or a relativist), since the reasonings of historical agents can be recovered in much the same way that one works through a Euclidean geometrical proof.

Collingwood's arguments, like those of Hempel, were attacked by a swarm of critics (many of whom reacted only to *The Idea of History*, without realizing that it can only be understood in the context of Collingwood's attempted philosophical system). He was charged with underestimating the importance of material factors and of supposing that historical actors were always reasonable calculators instead of passionate beings (the latter charge betraying incomprehension of Collingwood's dialectic of mind). Refinements and adjustments of Collingwood's position, generically called "rational explanation," are eminently appropriate in political and diplomatic history; they also underlie some work in intellectual history and history of the arts, and they play an essential role in psychohistorical biographies (since to detect irrational behavior it is necessary to know what rational courses of action are available). Analytical philosophy of history thus is not remote from the concerns of practicing historians.

In recent years the focus of philosophical interest in history has largely shifted from preoccupation with causation, explanation, determinism, and moral judgments to the language historians use and the stories they tell. Here the most influential, and certainly the most controversial, book was Hayden White's *Metahistory* (1.334)—part theory of historical narrative, part study and defense of substantive philosophy of history, and part reading of great historians of the nineteenth century. When philosophers grew less inclined to give methodological lectures and commenced to think about actual historical practice, one of their principal concerns was showing how narratives could explain. Many historians took comfort from this recognition that their traditional art of arranging events into a compelling story did not mean that they were mere fabulists, condemned to perpetual anecdotage. But White, and those analysts of discourse who followed him, supplied somewhat cold comfort, because they purported to show that historical events could support *any number* of narratives—even narratives of quite different sorts. (As White has mischievously pointed out, Fogel and Engerman's *Time on the Cross* emplotted African American slavery as a comedy.) Rather than confronting a field of data, historians, White argued, make an essentially poetic (and moral) choice to configure this field—to establish what will count as data.

Such writers raised the specter of relativism in a new way, forcing historians to confront the problem of comparing possible narratives, each of which might be composed entirely of true statements. The freedom to narrate on this argument would be purchased at the price of abandoning any way to discredit alternate narratives by an appeal to the evidence. This is a price few historians, ever desirous of hanging on to the privileges of both art and science, have been reluctant to pay. Whether they have to pay it has become the most controverted question in the past few years.

"Metahistory," for White, is another name for substantive philosophy of history, which has during the past twenty years unexpectedly risen from the dustbin of historiography. It has evidently survived the charge by Karl Popper (1.169) that all substantive philosophies of history must be false. The great nineteenth-century systems of Hegel and Marx have not necessarily revived, and though Vico has enjoyed a great vogue, it has been primarily Vico the rhetorician rather than the theorist of cycles. Nor has the reputation of Toynbee, Spengler, or Voegelin greatly improved among professional historians—though new books about them continue to appear. The mandate to make sense of the facts, however, remains, and discourse theory has presented a new freedom to narrate to historians bold enough to take it. It is doubtful that historians have ever operated without at least some sense, however tacit, of the historical process as a whole—whether this be the dialectical vision of Marxism, the neo-Hegelianism that sees liberal democratic institutions as an inevitable goal (much invoked after the "winning" of the cold war), a view of history as subject to the providence of God, or simply a sense of national destiny. (It would be barely possible to hold all four of these views, in fact.) Progress, though perhaps it will never again be reverenced as it was in Victorian Britain, has reemerged in modern social science as modernization theory—much criticized, seldom exorcised. The development of world-systems theories, and increasing interest in world history generally, has sent some historians back to the ideals and practice of universal history.

The fact that history in the past thirty years has undergone unprecedented philosophical scrutiny and has seen its most cherished convictions attacked is a sign it is healthy, not moribund. No brief summary can do full justice to the diversity of viewpoints, which this section of the *Guide* has attempted to represent.

A few words should be said about this section's organization. It begins with a selection of the best introductory works in both historiography and philosophy of history. These raise the issues that figure throughout the remaining sections. Next comes the array of the old and new ancillary studies required by historiography—some of which any aspiring historian must learn. Classic and modern works in the substantive and analytical philosophy of history follow, laying out in more or less abstract terms the issues involved in historical work. The import of these for the variety of histories produced today is exhibited in the fifth part on the branches of history. The books and articles in the final section explore the implications of these various arguments for teaching history—at every level from middle school to graduate school.

The characteristic vehicle for works in philosophy of history is the article rather than the book. Many books included here are anthologies, usually containing articles on a number of different questions. Since most arguments implicate others (for example, it is hard to believe in the appropriateness of moral judgments if you believe in determinism), there is a certain degree of arbitrariness about where some of the entries are placed. This can be remedied by using the index, whose listings will reveal the full range of views on any particular issue.

Entries are arranged under the following headings:

General Introductions
Handbooks on Method
Surveys of Historiography
Biographies
Philosophy of History
Reference Works

Ancillary Studies
Chronology
Diplomatics
Palaeography
Numismatics
Archaeology
Linguistics
Geography
Quantitative Methods
Oral History
History and Memory

Substantive Philosophies of History
Reflections on History
Uses of History
Time and Periodization
The Historical Process
Great Individuals

Analytical Philosophies of History
Laws and Causal Explanation
Rational Explanation
Evidence
Constructionism
Realism
Narrative
Rhetorical Analyses
Objectivity and Relativism

The Branches of History
Introductions
Comparative History
Economic History
History of the Family
Demographic History
Social History
Cultural History
Intellectual History
History of the Arts
Psychohistory and Biography
Women's History
Political and Diplomatic History
Local History
History of Science

Teaching History

[Contributors: AT = Aviezer Tucker, CKF = Carole K. Fink, GKP = G. Kurt Piehler, LPG = Liette P. Gidlow, RTV = Richard T. Vann]

GENERAL INTRODUCTIONS

Handbooks on Method

1.1 Jacques Barzun and Henry F. Graff. *The modern researcher.* 5th ed. Boston: Houghton-Mifflin, 1992. ISBN 0-395-64494-1. ▸ Helpful at all levels of research, from how to take (and organize) notes to tips on good writing and organization of finished product. [RTV]

1.2 Richard E. Beringer. *Historical analysis: contemporary approaches to Clio's craft.* 1978 ed. Malabar, Fla.: Krieger, 1986. ISBN 0-89874-751-1. ▸ Good nonpatronizing introduction to variety of contemporary techniques used in historical analysis, each

exemplified by short sample from nineteenth-century American history. Intended for history majors and beginning graduate students. [RTV]

1.3 Ernst Bernheim. *Lehrbuch der historischen Methode und der Geschichtsphilosophie: mit Nachweis der wichtigsten Quellen und Hilfsmittel zum Studien der Geschichte.* 6th ed. Leipzig: Duncker & Humblot, 1908. ▸ Classic work combining treatment of source criticism and auxiliary sciences for historians with introduction to problems in philosophy of history. [RTV]

1.4 Marc Bloch. *The historian's craft.* 1953 ed. Peter Putnam, trans. Joseph Reese Strayer, Introduction. Manchester: Manchester University Press, 1984. ISBN 0-7190-0664-3. ▸ Introduction to historical methods by master craftsman, rich with example and reminiscence; strongest on criticism and handling of evidence. Argues historians must command vast knowledge of present. [RTV]

1.5 G. Kitson Clark. *The critical historian.* New York: Basic Books, 1967. ▸ Aimed at making users of history aware of pitfalls in establishing what happened and how historians think. Especially pertinent on evaluating evidence. Common sense approach. [RTV]

1.6 L. P. Curtis, Jr., ed. *The historian's workshop: original essays by sixteen historians.* 1970 ed. New York: Garland, 1985. ISBN 0-8240-6357-0 (pbk). ▸ Collection reveals idiosyncratic methods used by many historians and reveals large gap between manuals of historical method and actual practice. Based on narrow sample of historians: all men, almost half from editor's university. [RTV]

1.7 James West Davidson and Mark H. Lytle. *After the fact: the art of historical detection.* 2d ed. New York: Knopf; distributed by Random House, 1986. ISBN 0-394-55287-3 (cl), 0-394-35475-3 (pbk). ▸ Entertaining introduction presenting cases that resemble detective stories, embellished with anecdotes and photographs, and emphasizing how historians select and evaluate various types of evidence. [AT]

1.8 Geoffrey R. Elton. *The practice of history.* 1967 ed. New York: Crowell, 1970. ▸ Brisk introduction stoutly defending autonomy of history, historical realism, and empirical methods (defined as reading everything that might conceivably be pertinent). Skeptical toward borrowing from social science and vogue of social history. [RTV]

1.9 J. H. Hexter. *The history primer.* New York: Basic Books, 1971. ISBN 0-465-03027-0. ▸ Misconceived attack on covering law theory of explanation, confused with rules for games, but valuable for treatment of historical tempo, constitutive role of rhetoric in historiography, and relationship of historians' general knowledge to research. [RTV]

1.10 Homer C. Hockett. *The critical method in historical research and writing.* 1955 ed. New York: Macmillan, 1970. ▸ Standard reference work on both research methods and presentation of results. Though first published in 1931, sections on citation and bibliographies still valuable. [RTV]

1.11 Georg G. Iggers and Harold T. Parker, eds. *International handbook of historical studies: contemporary research and theory.* Westport, Conn.: Greenwood, 1979. ISBN 0-313-21367-4. ▸ Notable for international roster of contributors and inclusion of theory and practice. Articles on specialized branches of history as well as historiography of North and South America, Europe, Asia, and sub-Saharan Africa. [RTV]

1.12 Charles Victor Langlois and Charles Seignobos. *Introduction to the study of history.* G. G. Berry, trans. New York: Barnes & Noble, 1966. ▸ Comprehensive, long considered near definitive, account of historical criticism and synthesis representing nineteenth-century scholarship. Emphasis entirely on written documents and on political and constitutional history. [RTV]

1.13 Savoie Lottinville. *The rhetoric of history.* Norman: University of Oklahoma Press, 1976. ISBN 0-8061-1330-8. ▸ Not a formal rhetorical analysis, but helpful advice from university press editor on how to write (and publish) historical syntheses, reviews, and bibliographies. Techniques of novel-writing recommended for historical narratives. [RTV]

1.14 Henri-Irenée Marrou. *The meaning of history.* Robert J. Olsen, trans. Baltimore: Helicon, 1966. ▸ Still best introduction to study of history. Comprehensive treatment of conditions of historical knowledge, inferences from evidence, explanation, concepts, and usefulness of history. Translation of *De la connaissance historique.* [RTV]

1.15 Robin W. Winks, comp. *The historian as detective: essays on evidence.* New York: Harper & Row, 1969. ▸ Anthology amusingly pursuing analogy between historical and criminal investigations: evidence and inference, vigilante justice, habeas corpus, adversarial methods, and verdicts. [AT]

Surveys of Historiography

1.16 Geoffrey Barraclough. *Main trends in history.* Rev. ed. Michael Burns, revisions. New York: Holmes & Meier, 1991. ISBN 0-8419-1287-4 (cl), 0-8419-1062-6 (pbk). ▸ Wide-ranging survey of current historiography, raising both conceptual problems and national peculiarities. Particularly notable for material on Third World historiography and author's resolute avoidance of blandness. [RTV]

1.17 Ernst Breisach. *Historiography ancient, medieval, and modern.* Chicago: University of Chicago Press, 1983. ISBN 0-226-07274-6 (cl), 0-226-07275-4 (pbk). ▸ First comprehensive history of historiography in almost fifty years. Largely confined to Greece, Rome, and western Europe; organized nationally until modern times, then by other specialized fields. [RTV]

1.18 Donald E. Brown. *Hierarchy, history, and human nature: the social origins of historical consciousness.* Tucson: University of Arizona Press, 1988. ISBN 0-8165-1060-1. ▸ Unusual comparative history of historiography. Argues that open elites and social mobility promote sound historiography (i.e., modern academic history) while castes stifle it. Based on comparison of China, India, Southeast Asia, and the West. [RTV]

1.19 Peter Burke, ed. *New perspectives on historical writing.* University Park: Pennsylvania State University Press, 1992. ISBN 0-271-00827-X (cl), 0-271-00834-2 (pbk). ▸ Misleadingly titled: mostly British and European historians discuss with infectious enthusiasm latest subjects of historical inquiry—microhistory, reading, images, the body—and give new perspectives on politics, diplomacy, and society. [RTV]

1.20 Herbert Butterfield. *Man on his past: the study of the history of historical scholarship.* 1955 ed. London: Cambridge University Press, 1969. ISBN 0-521-09567-0. ▸ Important for treatment of development of techniques of historiography rather than changes in conceptions of past. Particular emphasis on German historical school in Göttingen and achievement of Ranke. [RTV]

1.21 Herbert Butterfield. *The origins of history.* Adam Watson, ed. London: Methuen, 1981. ISBN 0-413-48370-3. ▸ History of historical thinking, not scholarship: how and why it arose in some cultures (e.g., Hittite, Chinese) and not others. Explanations sought in religious and intellectual life, not in social structure. [RTV]

1.22 John Clive. *Not by fact alone: essays on the writing and reading of history.* 1989 ed. Boston: Houghton-Mifflin, 1991. ISBN 0-395-56755-6. ▸ Collected lectures, book reviews, and occasional pieces that make the case—with learning, humor, and sprightly writing—that great eighteenth- and nineteenth-century historians still have much to teach us. [RTV]

1.23 Marcus Cunliffe and Robert W. Winks, eds. *Pastmasters: some essays on American historians.* 1969 ed. Westport, Conn.: Greenwood, 1979. ▸ Studies of thirteen historians of the United States by eight American and five English historians. Sympathetic biographies, often severe criticism of works, amounting to good introduction to history of American historiography. [RTV]

1.24 Felix Gilbert and Stephen R. Graubard, eds. *Historical studies today.* New York: Norton, 1972. ISBN 0-393-05453-5 (cl), 0-393-09402-2 (pbk). ▸ "Today" was a quarter-century ago, but historiography develops slowly and many essays still useful. All-star roster from France, United Kingdom, and United States; treatment of specialized histories and ancillary disciplines. [RTV]

1.25 John Higham. *History: professional scholarship in America.* Rev. ed. Baltimore: Johns Hopkins University Press, 1989. ISBN 0-8018-3952-1 (pbk). ▸ Revision of main narrative in Higham et al. 1.26. [RTV]

1.26 John Higham, Leonard Krieger, and Felix Gilbert. *History.* 1965 ed. New York: Garland, 1985. ISBN 0-8240-6364-3. ▸ Comprehensive, slightly complacent discussion of American historical profession in twentieth century. Includes discussion of historians of Europe (Krieger) and comparison of American and European historians (Gilbert). Main narrative updated in Higham 1.25. [RTV]

1.27 Gertrude Himmelfarb. *The new history and the old.* Cambridge, Mass.: Belknap, 1987. ISBN 0-674-61580-8 (cl), 0-674-61581-6 (pbk). ▸ Collection of essays, written at various times, supporting old political and intellectual history against social history and history of *mentalités.* Shrewd, humane, well written, but underargued and occasionally uninformed. [RTV]

1.28 Georg G. Iggers. *New directions in European historiography.* Rev. ed. Middletown, Conn.: Wesleyan University Press; distributed by Harper & Row, 1984. ISBN 0-8195-6097-9 (cl), 0-8195-6071-5 (pbk). ▸ Survey of German and French historical thinking in twentieth century. Sees increasing "scientization" of history. Especially good on German developments after Fischer controversy (see 47.375), French Annales school, and modern social history. Only slightly revised from 1975 edition. [JFH]

1.29 Michael G. Kammen, ed. *The past before us: contemporary historical writing in the United States.* Ithaca, N.Y.: Cornell University Press, 1980. ISBN 0-8014-1224-2. ▸ Twenty American historians take stock of what happened in and to discipline in 1970s, by geographical area and subspecialties. Job crisis induced some pessimism, but most contributors were well satisfied by developments in the field. [RTV]

1.30 J. P. Kenyon. *The history men: the historical profession in England since the Renaissance.* 1983 ed. Pittsburgh: University of Pittsburgh Press, 1984. ISBN 0-8229-5900-3 (pbk). ▸ Spirited and witty tour through English historiography from amateurism to professional status, with thumbnail biographies of great and near-great historians. Unusual emphasis on curricula, textbooks, and sales of history books. [RTV]

1.31 Theodore K. Rabb and Robert I. Rotberg, eds. *The new history: the 1980's and beyond; studies in interdisciplinary history.* Princeton: Princeton University Press, 1982. ISBN 0-691-05370-7 (cl), 0-691-00794-2 (pbk). ▸ "New" histories have appeared since 1910, but this symposium goes beyond state-of-the-field reviews to raise prescriptive questions, thus suggesting desirable future developments of historiography. [RTV]

1.32 Lawrence Stone. *The past and the present revisited.* New York: Routledge & Kegan Paul, 1987. ISBN 0-7102-1253-4 (cl), 0-7102-1193-7 (pbk). ▸ Collected essays and reviews championing new social history and suggesting influence of social anthropology and revival of narrative characterized 1980s. Discriminating accounts of most themes in social and cultural history. [RTV]

1.33 James Westfall Thompson and Bernard J. Holm. *A history of historical writing.* 1942 ed. 2 vols. Gloucester, Mass.: Smith, 1967. ▸ Strongest where similar works are weakest: medieval, Syrian, Armenian, and Persian historiography. Other sections also worth reading. [RTV]

1.34 C. Vann Woodward. *The future of the past.* New York: Oxford University Press, 1989. ISBN 0-19-505744-9. ▸ Urbane reflections on fortunes of history in United States over past twenty-five years; guarded welcome to cliometrics and historical fiction. View from top of profession by distinguished practitioner. [RTV]

Biographies

1.35 Henry Abelove et al., eds. *Visions of history.* New York: Pantheon, 1983. ISBN 0-394-53046-2 (cl), 0-394-72200-0 (pbk). ▸ Interviews with thirteen American, English, and Israeli radical historians, providing unusual autobiographical insights not only into their work but also into their struggles in and with academic establishments. [RTV]

1.36 Roland Barthes. *Michelet.* Richard Howard, trans. Berkeley: University of California Press, 1992. ISBN 0-520-07826-8. ▸ Just skeleton of a biography then excerpts from Michelet's writings. Preceded by brilliant if sometimes weird prefaces by Barthes. Classic literary readings of historical texts. Translation of *Michelet par lui-même* (1954). [RTV]

1.37 Ray Allen Billington. *Frederick Jackson Turner: historian, scholar, teacher.* New York: Oxford University Press, 1973. ISBN 0-19-501609-2. ▸ Monumental biography achieving near-definitive status. Unusual concentration on quotidian details of college teaching and administration, adduced as partial explanation for Turner's meager though fertile publications. [RTV]

1.38 David Cannadine. *G. M. Trevelyan: a life in history.* 1992 ed. New York: Norton, 1993. ISBN 0-393-03528-X. ▸ Most famous English historian of early twentieth century vigorously and entertainingly defended from Kenyon (1.30) and others, together with defense of history as preeminently a literary art. [RTV]

1.39 John Clive. *Macaulay: the shaping of the historian.* 1973 ed. Cambridge, Mass.: Belknap, 1987. ISBN 0-694-54005-0 (pbk). ▸ Leisurely but ultimately engaging account of early life of great whig historian. Emphasis on extent of learning as well as political experience that went into Macaulay's preparation for his *History.* [RTV]

1.40 Linda Colley. *Lewis Namier.* New York: St. Martin's, 1989. ISBN 0-312-02854-7. ▸ Namier was unusual among historians in having an interesting life and attracting two biographers. Shorter than Julia Namier's brilliant personal memoir, but more focused on his historical work. [RTV]

1.41 Carol Fink. *Marc Bloch: a life in history.* 1989 ed. Cambridge: Cambridge University Press, 1991. ISBN 0-521-37300-X (cl), 0-521-40671-4 (pbk). ▸ Straightforward study, avoiding hagiography, of historian who united heroism in life and pathbreaking scholarship. Good treatment of sometimes arcane twists of French academic politics. [RTV]

1.42 William H. McNeill. *Arnold J. Toynbee: a life.* New York: Oxford University Press, 1989. ISBN 0-19-505863-1 (cl), 0-19-506335-X (pbk). ▸ Penetrating biography illuminating stages of Toynbee's career and intellectual development. Accounts for discontinuity between first six and remaining volumes of *A Study of History* (1.180) and stages of Toynbee's religiosity. [RTV]

1.43 Arthur Mitzman. *Michelet, historian: rebirth and romanticism in nineteenth-century France.* New Haven: Yale University Press, 1990. ISBN 0-300-04551-4. ▸ Sacrifices brilliant "literary" readings of Michelet for psychobiographical reconstruction of his life, yielding best biography in English. Revealing insights on nineteenth-century French intellectual life. [RTV]

1.44 Ellen Nore. *Charles A. Beard: an intellectual biography.* Carbondale: Southern Illinois University Press, 1983. ISBN 0-8093-1078-3. ▸ Sympathetic but not uncritical exploration of Beard's career, especially as urban historian and planner and political activist. Sparse on personal details (Beard destroyed most of his letters). [RTV]

1.45 Gregory M. Pfitzer. *Samuel Eliot Morison's historical world: in quest of a new Parkman.* Boston: Northeastern University Press, 1991. ISBN 1-55553-101-6. ▸ Illuminates Morison's career by rich archival research and by counterposing him to many other influential historians of his time. Particularly interesting on tension between academic history and writing for general public. [RTV]

1.46 John Herbert Roper. *C. Vann Woodward: southerner.* Athens: University of Georgia Press, 1987. ISBN 0-8203-0933-8. ▸ Though marred by some factual errors and eccentric interpretations, locates Woodward in progressivist tradition (from Macaulay through Beard) and shows tension between political activism and ironic approach to history. [RTV]

1.47 Ernest Samuels. *Henry Adams.* Cambridge, Mass.: Belknap, 1989. ISBN 0-674-38735-X. ▸ Abridgment of classic three-volume biography, perhaps best and certainly most copious of an historian. Sensitive to complex personality of would-be scientific historian who became twentieth-century prophet. [RTV]

1.48 Charlotte Watkins Smith. *Carl Becker: on history and the climate of opinion.* Ithaca, N.Y.: Cornell University Press, 1956. ▸ Particularly valuable for chapters 4 and 5, giving Becker's views on art of writing history and account of how he actually wrote and revised. [RTV]

1.49 Theodore H. Von Laue. *Leopold Ranke: the formative years.* 1950 ed. New York: Johnson Reprint, 1970. ▸ Covers first forty-one of Ranke's ninety-one years, but convincingly argues that historian's basic ideas were in place by 1836. Best study in English of virtual founder of modern academic historiography. [RTV]

Philosophy of History

1.50 Raymond Aron. *Introduction to the philosophy of history: an essay on the limits of historical objectivity.* George J. Irwin, trans. Boston: Beacon, 1961. ▸ Introduction only in sense of treating first principles. Questions whether universally valid objective science of history is possible and how it might contribute to human understanding. [AT]

1.51 E. H. Carr. *What is history? The George Macaulay Trevelyan lectures.* 2d ed. R. W. Davis, ed. London: Macmillan, 1986. ISBN 0-333-38956-5. ▸ Vigorous if not always sophisticated presentation of main issues in analytical philosophy of history by prominent historian of Soviet Union. Advocates moderate relativism. Author's experience as historian compensates for his occasional philosophical naiveté. [AT]

1.52 Alan Donagan and Barbara L. Donagan, eds. *Philosophy of history.* New York: Macmillan, 1965. ▸ Excerpts from classical, analytical, and substantive philosophers of history; three on Christian interpretations of history. Section on Marx offers particularly deft introduction to historical materialism. [AT]

1.53 William H. Dray. *Philosophy of history.* Englewood Cliffs, N.J.: Prentice-Hall, 1964. ▸ Updated edition of this standard introduction is promised; still one of best. Three examples of substantive philosophies and excellent discussion of issues in analytical philosophy, including continental sources. [AT]

1.54   Patrick L. Gardiner, ed. *Theories of history.* 1959 ed. New York: Free Press, 1966. ▸ Best introductory anthology. Well-chosen excerpts from substantive (Vico through Toynbee) and analytical philosophy of history and useful introductory comments. Includes Hempel's founding text (see section introduction). [RTV]

1.55   Rolf Gruner. "The concept of speculative philosophy of history." *Metaphilosophy* 3 (1972) 283–300. ISSN 0026-1068. ▸ Has history pattern, value, or purpose? Thinking about any of these questions constitutes speculative philosophy of history. Almost everyone has one. [AT]

1.56   B. A. Haddock. *An introduction to historical thought.* London: Arnold, 1980. ISBN 0-7131-6323-2 (cl), 0-7131-6324-0 (pbk). ▸ Treats early modern philosophical historians, then Vico, Herder, Hegel, Marx, and Comte. No startling insights, but emphasis on thought rather than technique makes good introduction. [RTV]

1.57   Keith Jenkins. *Re-thinking history.* New York: Routledge, 1991. ISBN 0-415-06778-2. ▸ First postmodernist introduction to history; disputes premises of all previous works from consistent relativistic standpoint. Aimed at beginners but usefully presents viewpoints most historians regard as subjectivist or nihilist. [RTV]

1.58   Leonard Krieger. *Time's reasons: philosophies of history old and new.* Chicago: University of Chicago Press, 1989. ISBN 0-226-45300-6. ▸ Excellent introductions to philosophy of history (especially substantive) and history of historiography, knit together by concern to reappraise history in light of poststructuralist and other challenges. Emphasizes that history must make sense. [RTV]

1.59   John Lukacs. *Historical consciousness, or, the remembered past.* Rev. ed. New York: Schocken, 1985. ISBN 0-8052-0730-9 (pbk). ▸ Provocative, somewhat opinionated, extended meditation on historical consciousness as (distinctively Western) remembrance of the past. Idiosyncratic history of historiography and discursive treatment of historical concepts. [RTV]

1.60   Frank Edward Manuel. *Shapes of philosophical history.* Stanford, Calif.: Stanford University Press, 1965. ▸ History of substantive philosophies of history from antiquity through nineteenth century. Overstates contrast between classical cyclical and linear Christian theories. [AT]

1.61   Bruce Mazlish. *The riddle of history: the great speculators from Vico to Freud.* New York: Harper & Row, 1966. ▸ Sometimes insightful, occasionally jejune chapters introducing all important figures. Particularly interesting in treating Freud as substantive philosopher of history. [AT]

1.62   Friedrich Meinecke. *Historism: the rise of a new historical outlook.* J. E. Anderson, trans. New York: Herder & Herder, 1972. ▸ Slights sixteenth-century contributions to rise of historism, but this account of its development from Shaftesbury, Leibniz, Vico, Montesquieu, and Voltaire to its flowering in Möser, Herder, and Goethe, remains unsurpassed. [RTV]

1.63   W. H. Walsh. *An introduction to the philosophy of history.* 3d rev. ed. New York: Harper & Row, 1967. ▸ Early introductory work; still valuable for discussion of colligation (how historians bring things together) and for discussions of some great systems of issues in analytical philosophy. Unusually lucid style. [AT]

Reference Works

1.64   *Bibliography of works in the philosophy of history.* 9 vols. to date. The Hague and Middletown, Conn.: Mouton and Wesleyan University Press, 1961. (*History and theory,* Beiheft, 1, 3, 7, 10, 12, 13, 18, 23, 28.) ISSN 0018-2656. ▸ Not exhaustive; covers works in Western European languages (also Eastern European language works if accompanied by summary in Western Euro-

pean language). Covers works published 1500–1800, 1945–87. [RTV]

1.65   Otto Brunner, Werner Conze, and Reinhart Koselleck, eds. *Geschichtliche Grundbegriffe: historisches Lexikon zur politische-sozialen Sprache in Deutschland.* 7 vols. Stuttgart: Ernst Klett, 1972–. ISBN 3-12-903850-7 (v. 1), 3-12-903860-4 (v. 2), 3-12-903870-1 (v. 3), 3-12-903880-9 (v. 4), 3-12-903890-6 (v. 5), 3-12-903900-7 (v. 6), 3-12-903912-0 (v. 7). ▸ Extraordinarily thorough articles (averaging fifty pages) provide synchronic analyses of political and social language, situation, and time and diachronic analyses of continuity, alteration, and innovation in these vocabularies. [RTV]

1.66   Paul Edwards, ed. *Encyclopedia of philosophy.* 1967 ed. 8 vols. in 4. New York: Macmillan, 1972. ▸ Standard encyclopedia of philosophy in English with articles both on individual thinkers and philosophical topics. Article on philosophy of history by Dray offers good short introduction. [AT]

1.67   Harry Ritter. *Dictionary of concepts in history.* Westport, Conn.: Greenwood, 1986. ISBN 0-313-22700-4, ISSN 0730-3335. ▸ Handy compilation of short articles on many terms used in historical writing, such as crisis and mercantilism, with directions for further reading. [RTV]

1.68   David L. Sills, ed. *International encyclopedia of the social sciences.* 19 vols. New York: Macmillan, 1968–91. ISBN 0-02-895510-2 (v. 18), 0-02-928751-0 (v. 19.1), 0-02-897395-X (v. 19.2). ▸ Mostly devoted to articles on institutions and practices, although some on a few important thinkers included. Many of interest to historians; index, biographical supplement, and entire volume of quotations. [RTV]

1.69   James Trager. *The people's chronology: a year-by-year record of human events from prehistory to the present.* Rev. ed. New York: Holt, 1992. ISBN 0-8050-1786-0. ▸ Most complete chronicle of historical happenings, both in temporal and geographical extent and breadth of coverage. Treats economic and cultural life as well as political and diplomatic history. [RTV]

1.70   Bruce Wetterau, comp. *Macmillan concise dictionary of world history.* 1983 ed. New York: Collier, 1986. ISBN 0-02-626110-3 (cl, 1983), 0-02-082410-6 (pbk). ▸ Contains a few articles on institutions and concepts, but valuable mostly for comprehensive coverage of people and places. Closer than most to covering all of world history. [RTV]

1.71   Philip P. Wiener, ed. *Dictionary of the history of ideas: studies of selected pivotal ideas.* 1973 ed. 5 vols. New York: Scribner's, 1980. ISBN 0-684-16418-3 (set, pbk). ▸ Organized through Lovejoy's conception of unit ideas (1.434), whose development is traced through time. Useful entries with full bibliographies by experts. Article on historicism (historism) by Iggers particularly good. [RTV]

ANCILLARY STUDIES

1.72   V. H. Galbraith. *An introduction to the study of history.* London: Watts, 1964. ▸ Focuses almost entirely on English medieval history, but gives good general survey of all ancillary studies (e.g., chronology, archaeology, geography), spiced with opinionated and witty asides. [RTV]

Chronology

1.73   Sherrard B. Burnaby. *Elements of the Jewish and Muhammadan calendars with rules and tables and explanatory notes on the Julian and Georgian calendars.* London: Bell, 1901. ▸ Contains tables for converting dates from early seventh century to fourth millennium between Muslim, Jewish, and Christian (Gregorian) calendars. [RTV]

1.74   Christopher R. Cheney, ed. *Handbook of dates for students* *of English history.* 1945 corr. ed. London: Royal Historical Society, 1991. (Royal Historical Society, Guides and handbooks, 4.) ISBN 0-901050-10-5. ▸ Useful for lists of popes, saints' days, all possible days for Easter, English rulers, as well as reconciling Julian and Gregorian calendars. [RTV]

1.75 James William Johnson. "Chronological writing: its concepts and development." *History and theory* 2.2 (1962) 124–45. ISSN 0018-2656. ▸ Distinguishes between chronologies and history; chronology is not limited to human experience and events, yet it influences historical concepts and frameworks. Examples from history of chronology are discussed. [AT]

1.76 C. H. Philips, ed. *Handbook of Oriental history.* 1951 ed. London: Royal Historical Society, 1963. (Royal Historical Society, Guides and handbooks, 6.) ▸ Covers Near Eastern countries as well as South and East Asia. Guides to harmonizing Oriental and Muslim calendars with Gregorian one and to transliterating names from Asian languages. [RTV]

1.77 G. J. Whitrow. *Time in history: the evolution of our general awareness of time and temporal perspective.* Oxford: Oxford University Press, 1988. ISBN 0-19-215361-7. ▸ Intriguing account of conceptions of time and ways of measuring since prehistory. Particularly interesting on political and religious context for calendars and on development of timepieces. [RTV]

1.78 Donald J. Wilcox. *The measure of times past: pre-Newtonian chronologies and the rhetoric of relative time.* Chicago: University of Chicago Press, 1987. ISBN 0-226-89721-4 (cl), 0-226-89722-2 (pbk). ▸ Important reminder that modern chronology based on absolute time is less than 400 years old and that relative time-schemes employed by ancient, medieval, and Renaissance historians avoid some problems created by absolute chronology. [RTV]

Diplomatics

1.79 John Carter and Graham Pollard. *An enquiry into the nature of certain nineteenth-century pamphlets.* 2d ed. Newcastle, Del.: Oak Knoll, 1992. ISBN 0-938768-31-X. ▸ Detective-story-like exposure of some forgeries of British bibliophile T. J. Wise, through examination of nineteenth-century paper, ink, and typography as well as provenance. Virtual how-to manual, if faced with authenticating possibly spurious material. [RTV]

1.80 Arthur Giry. *Manuel de diplomatique: diplômes et chartes, chronologie technique, éléments critiques et parties constitutives de la teneur des chartes, les chancelleries, les actes privés.* 1894 ed. New York: Franklin, 1965. ▸ Summarizes work on structure, dating, sealing, and legal force of charters and papal bulls. No comparable English-language book. [RTV]

1.81 Wilson R. Harrison. *Suspect documents: their scientific examination.* 1958 ed. Chicago: Nelson-Hall, 1981. ▸ Written by forensic expert on forgeries; especially useful for illustrated chapter on forged typescripts and methods of dating documents. [RTV]

Palaeography

1.82 Michelle P. Brown. *A guide to Western historical scripts from antiquity to 1600.* Toronto: University of Toronto Press, 1990. ISBN 0-8020-5866-3. ▸ Valuable illustrations of scripts and facing-page transcriptions. Emphasis on scripts in use in France and England. [RTV]

1.83 Paul J. G. Lehman, ed. *Zur Paläographie und Handschriftenkunde.* Munich: Beck, 1909. ▸ Still fullest discussion of Latin handwriting and palaeography, giving history of latter. [RTV]

Numismatics

1.84 R.A.G. Carson. *Coins of the world.* New York: Harper & Row, 1962. ▸ Helpful mainly in identifying coinage (sixty-four pages of plates, some 2,000 coins illustrated). Good discussion of formal properties of coins, but little attention to historical context. [RTV]

1.85 Ferdinand Friedensburg. *Die Münze in der Kulturgeschichte.* 2d ed. Berlin: Weidmann, 1926. ▸ Systematic and exhaustive treatment of coins as historical evidence and role of coinage in economic and cultural life. [RTV]

1.86 Philip Grierson. *Numismatics.* London: Oxford University Press, 1975. ISBN 0-19-885098-0 (cl), 0-19-888098-7 (pbk). ▸ Best short introduction for historians for its emphasis on political and economic context of coinage. Also treats tokens, medals, and banknotes. Relatively few illustrations. [RTV]

Archaeology

1.87 David Percy Dymond. *Archaeology for the historian.* London: Historical Association, 1967. ▸ Good brief general introduction, though focusing on English materials. [RTV]

1.88 Ian Hodder. *Reading the past: current approaches to interpretation in archaeology.* 2d ed. New York: Cambridge University Press, 1991. ISBN 0-521-32743-1 (cl), 0-521-33960-X (pbk). ▸ Counters effort to discover archaeological laws and advocates bringing history and social anthropology to bear on archaeology. Useful chapters on historical archaeology and Marxist archaeology. [RTV]

1.89 Jaroslav Malina and Zdeněk Vašíček. *Archaeology, yesterday and today: the development of archaeology in the sciences and humanities.* Marek Zvelebil, ed. and trans. Cambridge: Cambridge University Press, 1990. ISBN 0-521-26621-1 (cl), 0-521-31977-3 (pbk). ▸ Encyclopedic account of development of archaeology, relating it to all human and most physical sciences. Good treatment of current schools of archaeology and of concept formation in discipline. [RTV]

1.90 Robert L. Schuyler, ed. *Historical archaeology: a guide to substantive and theoretical contributions.* Farmingdale, N.Y.: Baywood, 1978. ISBN 0-89503-008-X. ▸ Provides some theoretical contributions, but mainly supplies concrete examples of how archaeology can illuminate historical problems and vice versa. [RTV]

1.91 Stanley A. South. *Method and theory in historical archeology.* New York: Academic Press, 1977. ISBN 0-12-655750-0. ▸ Scientistic manifesto against particularism. Argument that pattern recognition is needed to achieve archaeological science; requires quantification to predictably test ideas of human past. Ample illustrations, cute graphics. [RTV]

Linguistics

1.92 Antoine Meillet. *The comparative method in historical linguistics.* 1967 ed. Gordon B. Ford, Jr., trans. Paris: Librairie Honoré Champion, 1970. ▸ Valuable not only for suggestions for uses of historical linguistics for historians, but also as source for theories of comparative methods put forward by Bloch 1.4. [RTV]

1.93 Nancy S. Struever. "The study of language and the study of history." *New literary history* 4 (1974) 401–15. ISSN 0028-6087. ▸ Early, influential programmatic article calling for historians to avail themselves of sociolinguistics and structural linguistics. Latter's emphasis on unconscious deep structures offers possible basis for comparative history. [RTV]

1.94 Lawrence D. Walker. "A note on historical linguistics and Marc Bloch's comparative method." *History and theory* 19.2 (1980) 154–64. ISSN 0018-2656. ▸ Clarifies Bloch's comparative method by showing its borrowings from Meillet's historical linguistics (1.92). It was regressive (starting from most modern appearance of phenomenon) and used ideal types. [RTV]

Geography

1.95 Alan R. H. Baker and Mark Billinge, eds. *Period and place: research methods in historical geography.* New York: Cambridge University Press, 1982. ISBN 0-521-24272-X. ▸ Heterogeneous collection of short articles, covering historical geography over most of world, with a few theoretical essays on method and interpretation, revealing no consensus among historical geographers. [RTV]

1.96 Alan R. H. Baker and Derek Gregory, eds. *Explorations in historical geography.* New York: Cambridge University Press, 1984. ISBN 0-521-24968-6. ▸ Shows uses for historians by going well beyond traditional geography. Analyses of Annales school, Industrial Revolution, medieval village communities, and class structure. [RTV]

1.97 Lucien Febvre. *A geographical introduction to history.* E. G. Mountford and J. H. Paxton, trans. Westport, Conn.: Greenwood, 1974. ISBN 0-8371-6710-8. ▸ Constructs *histoire totale* for human societies, based on extensive discussion of constraints set and possibilities opened by geography for human societies. Outlines program for Annales school. [RTV]

1.98 Robert David Sack. *Human territoriality: its theory and history.* New York: Cambridge University Press, 1986. ISBN 0-521-26614-9 (cl), 0-521-31180-2 (pbk). ▸ Counters theorists of territorial imperative by applying territorial theory to historical examples (Roman Catholic church, development of United States). Some hair-raising historical generalizations; also some valuable insights. [RTV]

1.99 David Ward, ed. *Geographic perspectives on America's past: readings on the historical geography of the United States.* New York: Oxford University Press, 1979. ISBN 0-19-502353-6. ▸ A few somewhat theoretical essays, but mostly examples exhibiting geographical influences on American society from colonial times to present. [RTV]

Quantitative Methods

1.100 William O. Aydelotte, Allan G. Bogue, and Robert William Fogel, eds. *The dimensions of quantitative research in history.* Princeton: Princeton University Press, 1972. ISBN 0-691-07544-1. ▸ Long introduction claims quantitative methods can at least approach truth and advocates possible applications, especially in political history. Nine articles then illustrate methods as applied. [RTV]

1.101 Jacques Barzun. *Clio and the doctors: psycho-history, quanto-history, and history.* Chicago: University of Chicago Press, 1974. ISBN 0-226-038491-0. ▸ Attack on these two methods: neither are truly new, both jargon-ridden. Psychohistory suffers from diversity in methods, devious use of evidence, and uncertain transition from individual to social; quantification is excessively abstract. [RTV]

1.102 Charles M. Dollar and Richard J. Jensen. *Historian's guide to statistics: quantitative analysis and historical research.* New York: Holt, Rinehart & Winston, 1971. ISBN 0-03-078020-9. ▸ Best introduction when first published. Revision needed and extremely desirable. [RTV]

1.103 Roderick Floud. *An introduction to quantitative methods for historians.* 2d ed. London: Methuen, 1979. ISBN 0-416-71660-1 (cl), 0-416-71670-9 (pbk). ▸ Chapter on computing still in palaeotechnic (punch-card) era; otherwise excellent introduction, especially in its sensitivity to typical historical problems (time series, too much, too little, or spotty data). [RTV]

1.104 Robert William Fogel. "The limits of quantitative methods in history." *American historical review* 80.2 (1975) 329–65. ISSN 0002-8762. ▸ Despite title, little about limitations by advocate of quantitative methods, who now believes such methods will not make history scientific. Suggests how graduate schools can train quantitative historians. [RTV]

1.105 Loren Haskins and Kirk Jeffrey. *Understanding quantitative history.* Cambridge, Mass.: MIT Press, 1990. ISBN 0-262-08190-3. ▸ Guide to understanding for undergraduates and other beginners; little direction for beginning practitioners. Includes examples (all from United States history) and questions testing comprehension of statistical concepts and presentation. Very few mathematical formulas. [RTV]

1.106 Konrad H. Jarausch and Kenneth A. Hardy. *Quantitative methods for historians: a guide to research, data, and statistics.* Chapel Hill: University of North Carolina Press, 1991. ISBN 0-8078-1947-6 (cl), 0-8078-4309-1 (pbk). ▸ Basically up-to-date manual for researchers, calling for acceptance of both qualitative and quantitative methods. Chapters on scope and role of quantitative history. [RTV]

1.107 Don Karl Rowney and James Q. Graham, Jr., eds. *Quantitative history: selected readings in the quantitative analysis of historical data.* Homewood, Ill.: Dorsey, 1969. ▸ Early fruits of quantitative history, most using elementary statistical techniques and thus accessible to most historians. Examples from United States, West European, and Japanese political, social, economic, and demographic history. [RTV]

1.108 *Studies in quantitative history and the logic of the social sciences.* Middletown, Conn.: Wesleyan University Press, 1969. (*History and theory*, Beiheft, 9.) ISSN 0018-2656. ▸ Theoretical essays comparing quantitative history with other approaches in cultural history and demography; also unusually sophisticated article on counterfactuals. [RTV]

Oral History

1.109 Barbara Allen and William Lynwood Montell. *From memory to history: using oral sources in local historical research.* Nashville: American Association for State and Local History Press, 1981. ISBN 0-910050-51-1. ▸ Concentrates on epistemology of oral history; how to test for validity and detect "submerged forms of truth." Long case study illustrates interweaving of oral sources and documents. [RTV]

1.110 Willa K. Baum. *Transcribing and editing oral history.* Nashville: American Association for State and Local History Press, 1977. ISBN 0-910050-26-0. ▸ Concerned only with this stage of oral history process, but gives complete instructions and suggestions, together with illustrations of edited tapes. Comes with especially useful 33 1/3 rpm record that can be compared with edited transcript. [RTV]

1.111 Michael Frisch. *A shared authority: essays on the craft and meaning of oral and public history.* Albany: State University of New York Press, 1990. ISBN 0-7914-0132-4 (cl), 0-7914-0133-2 (pbk). ▸ Collection of articles, rather than manual, thoughtfully questioning how oral and public history fit into historical discourse and power relationships in our society. [RTV]

1.112 Louis Gottschalk, Clyde Kluckhohn, and Robert Angell. *The use of personal documents in history, anthropology, and sociology.* New York: Social Science Research Council, 1945. (Social Science Research Council, Bulletin, 53.) ▸ Interdisciplinary perspectives; essay on history emphasizing source criticism; those on sociology and anthropology open possibilities for expanding scope of historiography. Defines personal documents as those revealing personality of authors. [RTV]

1.113 David P. Henige. *Oral historiography.* New York: Longman, 1982. ISBN 0-582-64364-3 (cl), 0-582-64363-5 (pbk). ▸ Emphasizes how oral historians add to stock of historical evidence. Focuses on interviewing in preliterate African societies as only way of reconstructing their histories. [RTV]

1.114 Anthony Seldon and Joanna Pappworth. *By word of mouth: "elite" oral history.* New York: Methuen, 1983. ISBN 0-416-33020-7 (cl), 0-416-36740-2 (pbk). ▸ From questionnaires to biographers and contemporary historians, gives many tips on interview methods and critique as well as defense of oral history, with examples. Supplements more usual oral histories of ordinary people. Also useful for archivists. [RTV]

1.115 Paul Thompson. *The voice of the past: oral history.* 2d ed. Oxford: Oxford University Press, 1988. ISBN 0-19-219230-2 (cl), 0-19-289216-9 (pbk). ▸ Sets suggestions about oral-history techniques in context of philosophy and of history of historiography, giving unique insight into historical methods. Good discussion of oral history projects. [RTV]

1.116 Jan Vansina. *Oral tradition as history.* Madison: University of Wisconsin Press, 1985. ISBN 0-299-10210-6 (cl), 0-299-10214-9 (pbk). ▸ Oral tradition an hypothesis, irreplaceable but requiring special techniques. Based on premise that all humans everywhere think and recall in identical fashion. Essentially revision of classic *Oral Tradition* (1959), now emphasizing communication. [RTV]

History and Memory

1.117 Susan Porter Benson, Stephen Brier, and Roy Rosenzweig, eds. *Presenting the past: essays on history and the public.* Philadelphia: Temple University Press, 1986. ISBN 0-87722-406-4 (cl), 0-87722-413-7 (pbk). ▸ Wide-ranging essays, from left-wing perspective, on modes of presenting history to wider public (novels, films, magazines, museums) and enlisting public in historiographical projects. [RTV]

1.118 John Bodnar. *Remaking America: public memory, commemoration, and patriotism in the twentieth century.* Princeton: Princeton University Press, 1992. ISBN 0-691-04783-9. ▸ Much shorter but covers similar ground as Kammen 1.123 with emphasis on last 100 years. Focuses primarily on differences between "vernacular" collective memory held by ordinary people and public memory resulting from commemorative activities arranged by elites. [RTV]

1.119 Edward S. Casey. *Remembering: a phenomenological study.* Bloomington: Indiana University Press, 1987. ISBN 0-253-34942-7 (cl), 0-253-20409-7 (pbk). ▸ Best philosophical analysis with profound implications for history. Subtle insights mostly on way individuals remember, but some attention to written remembrances and to commemorations. [RTV]

1.120 Mary Douglas. *How institutions think.* Syracuse, N.Y.: Syracuse University Press, 1986. ▸ Short, pungent, witty lectures on ideology, *mentalités*, and collective memory. Chapters 6 and 7 particularly relevant; show, with illustrations, why some things are remembered and how institutions mandate forgetting others. [RTV]

1.121 Maurice Halbwachs. *On collective memory.* Lewis A. Coser, ed. and trans. Chicago: University of Chicago Press, 1992. ISBN 0-226-11594-1 (cl), 0-226-11596-8 (pbk). ▸ Brilliant pioneering study locating collective memory in present concerns of family, religious groups, and social classes. Individual memory exists only in dreams. Partial translation of *Cadres sociaux de la mémoire* and *La topographie légendaire des évangiles en terre sainte.* [RTV]

1.122 Eric Hobsbawm and Terence Ranger, eds. *The invention of tradition.* 1983 ed. Cambridge: Cambridge University Press, 1992. ISBN 0-521-43773-3 (pbk). ▸ Wide-ranging essays on relationship between origins of officially sponsored rituals (e.g., those of British monarchy) and popular traditions. Most on Europe, but African and Indian examples also considered. [RTV]

1.123 Michael Kammen. *Mystic chords of memory: the transformation of tradition in American culture.* New York: Knopf, 1991. ISBN 0-394-57769-8. ▸ Monumental study of representations and conceptions of American past since early nineteenth century, with illuminating comparative perspective and attention to class (though less on gender) differences in historical memory. [RTV]

1.124 Lawrence L. Langer. *Holocaust testimonies: the ruins of memory.* New Haven: Yale University Press, 1991. ISBN 0-300-04966-8. ▸ Based on videotaped recollections of Holocaust survivors. Perceptively shows how pain of "deep memories"— almost reliving events—drives survivors into orderly chronological but less authentic "common memory." [RTV]

1.125 Jacques Le Goff. *History and memory.* Steven Rendall and Elizabeth Claman, trans. New York: Columbia University Press, 1992. ISBN 0-231-07590-1. ▸ History of historiography as gradual process of emancipation from dependence on memory; modern historiography thus problematizes memory as it aspires to serve as purified, socially accessible form of it. [RTV]

1.126 Bernard Lewis. *History—remembered, recovered, invented.* Princeton: Princeton University Press, 1975. ISBN 0-691-03547-4. ▸ Great learning in small compass. Intriguing examples of forgotten incidents resurrected for nationalistic purposes. Less emphasis on collective memory or historical investigation than on array of fabricated and tendentious histories. [RTV]

1.127 George Lipsitz. *Time passages: collective memory and American popular culture.* Minneapolis: University of Minnesota Press, 1990. ISBN 0-8166-1805-4 (cl), 0-8166-1806-2 (pbk). ▸ Provocative application of techniques of cultural studies to American historical memory after 1945. Argues, controversially, that popular television, music, film, and novels may contain historical insights superior to academic history. [RTV]

1.128 Howard Schuman and Jacqueline Scott. "Generations and collective memory." *American sociological review* 54 (1989) 374–97. ISSN 0003-1224. ▸ One of few empirical studies of how historical events are recalled; those occurring in teens and early twenties of survey respondents were most vividly remembered. [RTV]

1.129 Barry Schwartz. "The social context of commemoration: a study in collective memory." *Social forces* 61.2 (1982) 374–97. ISSN 0037-7732. ▸ Important corrective to presentism of Halbwachs 1.121, contending that, taken to extremes, all historical continuity would be lost and that construction of past must be compound of persistence and change. [RTV]

1.130 Pierre Vidal-Naquet. *Assassins of memory: essays on the denial of the Holocaust.* Jeffrey Mehlmann, trans. New York: Columbia University Press, 1992. ISBN 0-231-07458-1. ▸ Author, a Holocaust survivor, attacks revisionist deniers of Holocaust by vindicating memory and making novel attack on rhetorical and constructionist analyses of historiography used by revisionists as irredeemably relativistic. [RTV]

SUBSTANTIVE PHILOSOPHIES OF HISTORY

1.131 Louis Althusser and Étienne Balibar. *Reading "Capital."* 1970 ed. Ben Brewster, trans. London: Verso, 1979. ISBN 0-902308-56-4. ▸ Pathbreaking effort (influenced by structuralism) to purge Marxism of historicism and humanism and criticize empiricist historiography. Dense text with much technical language, but extremely influential. [RTV]

1.132 Perry Anderson. *Arguments within English Marxism.* London: New Left Books, 1980. ISBN 0-86091-030-X (cl), 0-86091-727-4 (pbk). ▸ Interesting for prominence of historians and emphasis on historiography within English Marxism. Criticizes Thompson 1.178 without embracing Althusser and Balibar 1.131. Like Thompson, stronger on historiography than philosophy of history. [RTV]

1.133 Raymond Aron. *The dawn of universal history.* Dorothy Pickles, trans. New York: Praeger, 1961. ‣ Twentieth century marks beginning of "universal history," plagued by national and imperialist conflicts. Contends West may yet prove its greatness by curing infantile disease of modernism. [AT]

1.134 Augustine, Saint. *Concerning the city of God against the pagans.* Henry Bettenson, trans. David Knowles, Introduction. Harmondsworth: Penguin, 1984. ISBN 0-14-044426-2. ‣ Foundational text of Christian philosophy of history. Sack of Rome not owing to christianization of empire; earthly and heavenly cities will live inextricably until final judgment; this is sole significance of history. [AT]

1.135 Isaiah Berlin. *Vico and Herder: two studies in the history of ideas.* New York: Vintage, 1977. ISBN 0-394-72250-7. ‣ Using skills of analytical philosopher, untangles some of contradictions and complexities of these two notoriously difficult thinkers, thus elucidating their philosophies of history. [RTV]

1.136 George Allen Cohen. *Karl Marx's theory of history: a defence.* Princeton: Princeton University Press, 1978. ISBN 0-691-07175-6. ‣ Ingenious effort to employ tools of analytical philosophy to clarify and defend Marx's emphasis on determination by developments in technology. True to Marx, but unconvincing to most Marxists. [RTV]

1.137 Kins Collins. "Marx on the English agricultural revolution: theory and evidence." *History and theory* 6.3 (1967) 351–81. ISSN 0018-2656. ‣ Rare attempt at systematic comparison of Marxian theory and historiography with current knowledge. Shows where subsequent research has corrected many of Marx's claims. Argues whole theory disproven by refutation of any single claim. [RTV]

1.138 Auguste Comte. *August Comte and positivism: the essential writings.* Gertrud Lenzer, ed. New York: Harper & Row, 1975. ISBN 0-06-131827-2. ‣ Intelligently chosen, extensive excerpts illustrating both first and second systems (facts and laws) of positivism. Hierarchy of positive sciences relegates history to discovery of discrete facts; sociologists then induce laws covering them. [RTV]

1.139 Frank Cunningham. "Practice and some muddles about the methodology of historical materialism." *Canadian journal of philosophy* 3.4 (1973) 235–48. ISSN 0045-5091. ‣ Distinguishes Marxian view of individual, praxis, determinism, and primacy of economic forces; failure to make distinctions has led Sartre (and some Marxists) into confusion. [AT]

1.140 Roy Enfield. "Marx and historical laws." *History and theory* 15.3 (1976) 267–77. ISSN 0018-2656. ‣ Clear exposition of Marx's conception of the stages of historical development; especially notable for discussion of why capitalism did not emerge in antiquity but had to be preceded by feudalism. [RTV]

1.141 Haskell Fain. *Between philosophy and history: the resurrection of speculative philosophy of history within the analytic tradition.* Princeton: Princeton University Press, 1970. ISBN 0-691-07158-6. ‣ Argues analytical philosophy of history cannot entirely account for historical practice; considerations of how historical facts fit together essential and lead in direction of substantive philosophies of history. [RTV]

1.142 John Farrenkopf. "Hegel, Spengler, and the enigma of world history: progress or decline?" *Clio* 19.4 (1990) 331–44. ISSN 0884-2043. ‣ Attempted rehabilitation of Spengler 1.173 by systematic contrast with rationalism, progressivism, and Eurocentrism of Hegel, judged inappropriate to modern consciousness. Overly simple in places, but provides rationale for Spengler revival. [RTV]

1.143 Francis Fukuyama. *The end of history and the last man.* New York: Free Press, 1992. ISBN 0-02-910975-2. ‣ Modern

right-wing Hegelian speculations on conclusion of cold war. Exhibits some of Hegel's limitations (particularly Eurocentrism) and has little philosophical depth, but provocative reworking of thesis that liberal national state is telos of history. [RTV]

1.144 William A. Galston. *Kant and the problem of history.* Chicago: University of Chicago Press, 1975. ISBN 0-226-28044-6. ‣ Most comprehensive and penetrating commentary on essays on history, but limitation to those leaves question whether Kant's philosophy of history can be fitted into overall system. [RTV]

1.145 Edward T. Gargan, ed. *The intent of Toynbee's history: a cooperative appraisal.* Arnold J. Toynbee, Preface. Chicago: Loyola University Press, 1961. ‣ Symposium predictably exhibiting sharp criticism from specialists on Toynbee's treatment of their specialties (1.180), more favorable comments from Voegelin, McNeill, and others sympathetic to universal history. Volume 12 of Toynbee responds to these. [RTV]

1.146 Pieter Geyl. *Debates with historians.* 1962 ed. Glasgow: Collins, 1974. ‣ Four essays on Toynbee, tracking development of *A Study of History* (1.180) and constituting one of best critiques. Also includes essays on great nineteenth-century historians and on historical inevitability. [RTV]

1.147 Jürgen Habermas. "Towards a reconstruction of historical materialism." *Theory and society* 2.3 (1975) 287–300. ISSN 0304-2421. ‣ Attack on conceptual problems in historical materialism's explanation of social evolution. Abstract principles of organization needed to comprehend innovations and limits of institutional change. [AT]

1.148 G.W.F. Hegel. *Lectures on the philosophy of world history, introduction: reason in history.* 1975 ed. Johannes Hoffmeister, ed. H. B. Nisbet, trans. New York: Cambridge University Press, 1980. ISBN 0-521-20566-2 (cl, 1975), 0-521-28145-8 (pbk). ‣ Superior translation of introduction to this basic text of Hegel's philosophy of history. Sets forth fundamental idea that if history is regarded rationally, its rationality will be seen through play of human passion. [AT]

1.149 G.W.F. Hegel. *The philosophy of history.* 1956 rev. ed. J. Sibree, trans. C. J. Friedrich, Introduction. Magnolia, Mass.: Smith, 1970. ISBN 0-486-20112-0. ‣ Conceives history as spirit's coming to full self-consciousness in Germanic world after its East-to-West transit from China. Historical progress analyzed in relation to geography and historical figures of world. Only English translation in print of full work; originally published in 1899. [AT]

1.150 J. G. Herder. *J.G. Herder on social and political culture.* F. M. Barnard, ed. Cambridge: Cambridge University Press, 1969. ISBN 0-521-07336-7. ‣ Best introduction to Herder's philosophy of history from entire corpus of his work, including only English translation from *Yet Another Philosophy of History* and fine editorial introduction. [RTV]

1.151 Paul Q. Hirst. *Marxism and historical writing.* Boston: Routledge & Kegan Paul, 1985. ISBN 0-7100-9925-8. ‣ Latest round in theoretical English historians' discussion of Marxist historiography. Takes position distinct from Althusser and Balibar 1.131 and critical of Anderson 1.132 and Thompson 1.178. Irenic, as these things go. [RTV]

1.152 H. Stuart Hughes. *Oswald Spengler.* 1952 ed. New Brunswick, N.J.: Transaction, 1992. ISBN 1-56000-576-9. ‣ Author claims Spengler's relevance greater than ever, notwithstanding his deviations from usual historiographical principles. More an intellectual history than analysis of *The Decline of the West* (1.173). [RTV]

1.153 Richard Johnson et al. *Making histories: studies in history-writing and politics.* Minneapolis: University of Minnesota Press, 1982. ISBN 0-8166-1164-5 (cl), 0-8166-1165-3 (pbk). ‣ History of

English historiography approached as cultural studies with particular emphasis on fortunes of Marxist historical writing. Acute study of relationships between political activism and historiography. [RTV]

1.154 Immanuel Kant. *On history*. Lewis White Beck, ed. and trans. Robert Anchor and Emil L. Fackenheim, trans. New York: Macmillan, 1963. ISBN 0-02-307860-X. ▸ Collection of all Kant's important essays on history. Collectively develops thesis that pure empirical history displays apparent disorder; but philosophical minds can discern order and progress through discovery of constant natural laws that direct humanity to completed rational end. [RTV]

1.155 Ibn Khaldûn. *The Muqaddimah: an introduction to history*. Abr. ed. N. J. Dawood, ed. Franz Rosenthal, trans. Princeton: Princeton University Press, 1967. ISBN 0-691-09946-4 (cl), 0-691-01754-9 (pbk). ▸ Excerpts from massive late Arab philosophy of history, dealing with method, geography, culture, economics, public finance, population, society and state, religion and politics, and knowledge and society. [AT]

1.156 Yves Lacoste. *Ibn Khaldûn: the birth of history and the past of the Third World*. David Macey, trans. London: Verso, 1984. ISBN 0-86091-084-9 (cl), 0-86091-789-4 (pbk). ▸ Provocative if somewhat anachronistic interpretation of Ibn Khaldûn as founder of scientific history and first theorist of underdevelopment. Emphasizes Ibn Khaldûn's interest in material conditions and dialectical character of his thought. [RTV]

1.157 Muhsin Mahdi. *Ibn Khaldûn's philosophy of history: a study in the philosophic foundation of the science of culture*. 1957 ed. Chicago: University of Chicago Press, 1964. ▸ Places Ibn Khaldûn in tradition of Islamic Platonism. His science of culture practical rather than theoretical, requiring universal scope. Despite similarities to modern thought, philosophical foundations are quite different. [RTV]

1.158 Herbert Marcuse. *Reason and revolution: Hegel and the rise of social theory*. 1955 2d ed. Atlantic Highlands, N.J.: Humanities, 1989. ISBN 0-391-02999-1. ▸ Celebration of Hegel's power of the negative in social thought, as contrasted to implicit conservatism of positivism dominant in American social sciences. Unusual combination of complex analysis and passion. [RTV]

1.159 Karl Marx and Friedrich Engels. *The Marx-Engels reader*. 2d ed. Robert C. Tucker, ed. New York: Norton, 1978. ISBN 0-393-05684-8 (cl), 0-393-09040-X (pbk). ▸ Contains more of Marx's historical writings than any other anthology, including 150 pages of *Kapital* and substantial chunks of the *Grundrisse*, *Eighteenth Brumaire*, and *German Ideology* with long helpful editorial introduction. [RTV]

1.160 C. T. McIntire and Marvin Perry, eds. *Toynbee: reappraisals*. Toronto: University of Toronto Press, 1989. ISBN 0-8020-5785-3. ▸ Publication indicates continuing interest in Toynbee. Two biographical essays, some appreciations of Toynbee's project, and more negative treatments of Toynbee on Russian, United States, and (especially) Jewish history. [RTV]

1.161 Stephen A. McKnight, ed. *Eric Voegelin's search for order in history*. Rev. ed. Lanham, Md.: University Press of America, 1987. ISBN 0-8191-6557-3 (pbk). ▸ Series of articles on Voegelin's political theory and philosophy of history, sympathetic but not uncritical, especially of Voegelin's reading of Christianity and Hebrew Bible (1.184). [RTV]

1.162 Gregor McLennan. *Marxism and the methodologies of history*. London: New Left Books, 1981. ISBN 0-86091-045-8 (cl), 0-86091-743-6 (pbk). ▸ Thorough and nonpolemical account not only of issues in historical materialism, but also of many issues in contemporary philosophy of history. Particularly interesting in revealing politics of philosophy of history. [RTV]

1.163 M. F. Ashley Montagu, ed. *Toynbee and history: critical essays and reviews*. Boston: Porter Sargent, 1956. ▸ Compendium of twenty-nine reviews, most appearing after publication of volume 10 of *A Study of History* (1.180). Specialists consider work from many angles, most professing admiration for everything except material falling within their own specialties. [RTV]

1.164 Ernst Nolte. "The relationship between 'bourgeois' and 'Marxist' historiography." *History and theory* 14.1 (1975) 57–73. ISSN 0018-2656. ▸ Real difference is between independent and state-sponsored Marxist historiography, rather than between Marxist and bourgeois, since both of these can be independent, whereas state-sponsored Marxism is ideology. [AT]

1.165 George Dennis O'Brien. *Hegel on reason and history: a contemporary interpretation*. Chicago: University of Chicago Press, 1975. ISBN 0-226-61646-0. ▸ Skillful commentary on and reconstruction of text and argument (Hegel 1.149), emphasizing need to construe Hegelian language in light of other works. Shows subtlety of Hegel's employment of dialectic. [RTV]

1.166 José Ortega y Gasset. *An interpretation of universal history*. Mildred Adams, trans. New York: Norton, 1973. ISBN 0-393-05478-0. ▸ Text of lectures on Toynbee's *A Study of History* (1.180) in which decline of Roman empire furnished most important theme. Sympathetic to Toynbee's project, but advances criticism based on alternative view of universal history. [RTV]

1.167 Robert L. Perkins, ed. *History and system: Hegel's philosophy of history*. Albany: State University of New York Press, 1984. ISBN 0-87395-814-4 (cl), 0-87395-815-2 (pbk). ▸ Symposium treating absolute spirit, dialectic, and freedom in various Hegelian texts, each article followed by comment. Wide range of views expressed, making volume useful introduction. [RTV]

1.168 Leon Pompa. *Vico: a study of the "New Science."* 2d ed. New York: Cambridge University Press, 1990. ISBN 0-521-38217-3 (cl), 0-521-38871-6 (pbk). ▸ Reacting against humanist emphasis, argues that Vico intended "science" to be taken seriously— a humanistic science, but one that meets criteria for scientific knowledge. [RTV]

1.169 Karl Raimund Popper. *The poverty of historicism*. 1961 3d ed. New York: Harper & Row, 1964. ▸ Classic attack on possibility of any valid substantive philosophy of history. As future human discoveries cannot be predicted, course of history open and beliefs in historical inevitability must lead to totalitarianism. [RTV]

1.170 S. H. Rigby. *Marxism and history: a critical introduction*. New York: St. Martin's, 1987. ISBN 0-312-00921-6. ▸ Helpful guide through massive secondary literature, emphasizing whether productive forces are determinative in history (proposing an alternative) and utility of base-and-superstructure model of culture. [RTV]

1.171 Ellis Sandoz, ed. *Eric Voegelin's significance for the modern mind*. Baton Rouge: Louisiana State University Press, 1991. ISBN 0-8071-1588-6. ▸ Somewhat reverential symposium convened shortly after Voegelin's death giving good sample of writings about him. Particularly useful articles on his new science of history and on mystical element in his thought. [RTV]

1.172 Friedrich von Schiller. "The nature and value of universal history: an inaugural lecture (1789)." Louis O. Mink, trans. *History and theory* 11.3 (1972) 321–34. ISSN 0018-2656. ▸ Adapts Kant's teleological view of history (1.154) as tending toward human perfection, but shows much greater historical knowledge. Historian also needs philosophy for deducing facts where evidence fails. [RTV]

1.173 Oswald Spengler. *The decline of the West*. Abr. ed. Helmut Werner, ed. New York: Oxford University Press, 1991. ISBN 0-19-506751-7 (cl), 0-19-506634-0 (pbk). ▸ Influential interpretation of history of civilizations based on biological analogy of life cycle of organism: Western civilization has exhausted energies of its Faustian period and is doomed to be superseded. [RTV]

1.174 Walter T. Stace. *The philosophy of Hegel: a systematic exposition.* New York: Dover, 1955. ▸ Hegel made, if not simple, at least largely comprehensible. Somewhat simplified, but clearest exposition of whole system; required reading to make his philosophy of history fully intelligible. [RTV]

1.175 Arline Reilein Standley. *Auguste Comte.* Boston: Twayne, 1981. ISBN 0-8057-6467-4. ▸ Best short introduction to Comte's thought; somewhat oversimplified. Most emphasis given to Comte as founder of sociology, though chapter 3 discusses Comte's conception of social dynamics. [RTV]

1.176 W. A. Suchting. "Marx, Popper, and 'historicism.'" *Inquiry* 15 (1972) 235–66. ISSN 0020-174X. ▸ Lucid reformulation of Marxian theory in light of Popper's criticisms of "historicism," which are also clarified. Concludes Marx was not an "historicist" since he neither prophesied nor believed in historical inevitability. [RTV]

1.177 Giorgio Tagliacozzo and Donald Phillip Verene, eds. *Giambattista Vico's science of humanity.* Baltimore: Johns Hopkins University Press, 1976. ISBN 0-8018-1720-X. ▸ Parts 1 and 2 offer several penetrating interpretations, some philosophical and others literary; remainder suffers from "precursoritis," picturing Vico as forerunner of almost all modern thought. [RTV]

1.178 E. P. Thompson. *The poverty of theory and other essays.* New York: Monthly Review Press, 1978. ISBN 0-85345-489-2 (cl), 0-85345-491-4 (pbk). ▸ Important statement of Anglo-Marxism, defending historians' practice and "discourse of the proof" (empirical methods) against Althusser and Balibar 1.131. Vigorous polemic for indigenous English radical tradition as guide to historical work. [RTV]

1.179 Jerzy Topolski. *Historical explanation in the light of the Marxist theory of the historical process.* Amherst: State University of New York, Council on International Studies, 1978. (Special studies series, 102.) ▸ Rare encounter on this subject between Western (Buffalo) academics and Eastern European (Poznań) scholars. Marxist answers to Popper 1.169 with rejoinders from Buffalo participants in colloquium. [AT]

1.180 Arnold J. Toynbee. *A study of history.* 12 vols. New York: Oxford University Press, 1935–61. ▸ Grand scheme of history conceived on quasi-empiricist lines: civilizations (defined largely by religion) are only units of study; all but Western one have fallen after characteristic pattern of expansion and contraction. View of universal history leads to convergence of all religions. Abridged edition (vols. 1–10) also available (Oxford, 1960). [AT]

1.181 Peter Urbach. "Is any of Popper's arguments against historicism valid?" *British journal for the philosophy of science* 29.2 (1978) 117–30. ISSN 0007-0882. ▸ Meticulous examination of Popper's arguments against what he called historicism (1.169). Concludes none are valid; unity of natural and social science therefore upheld. [AT]

1.182 Donald Phillip Verene. *Vico's science of imagination.* Ithaca, N.Y.: Cornell University Press, 1981. ISBN 0-8014-1391-5. ▸ Good example of hermeneutic reading of Vico. Claims Vico's theory of imagination is key to text—both imagination displayed by primitive humankind and recollective imagination allowing understanding of imaginative origins of humanity. [RTV]

1.183 Giambattista Vico. *The new science of Giambattista Vico: with practice of the new science.* 3d ed. Thomas Goddard Bergin and Max Harold Frisch, trans. Ithaca, N.Y.: Cornell University Press, 1984. ISBN 0-8014-9265-3. ▸ Cyclical pattern of profane history (ages of gods, heroes, and men) with tropes characteristic

of their mentalities. Foreshadows modern hermeneutics, social anthropology, philology, rhetoric, and historicism. [AT]

1.184 Eric Voegelin. *Order and history.* 5 vols. Baton Rouge: Louisiana State University Press, 1956–87. ISBN 0-8071-0818-9 (v. 1), 0-8071-0818-7 (v. 2), 0-8071-0820-0 (v. 3), 0-8071-0081-1 (v. 4), 0-8071-1414-6 (v. 5). ▸ History of order that endows existence with meaning and finds systematic forms that express it in five cultures: ancient empires, Chosen People, polis, Hellenic world and Christianity, and modern world-gnostic order. [AT]

1.185 François Marie Arouet de Voltaire. "Essay on the customs and the spirit of nations." In *The age of Louis XIV and other selected writings.* 1963 ed. J. H. Brumfitt, ed., pp. 240–311. New York: Twayne, 1965. ▸ Abridgment of influential work, first to use phrase "philosophy of history." Foreshadowed emphasis on cultural and universal history (includes chapters on China and India, unlike previous Western histories). [RTV]

1.186 Eugene Webb. *Eric Voegelin, philosopher of history.* Seattle: University of Washington Press, 1981. ISBN 0-295-95759-X. ▸ Dedicated to Voegelin, offers sympathetic and lucid explication of his philosophy of history and thoughts on political theory, showing how difficult it is for ordinary categories to capture it. [RTV]

1.187 Burleigh Taylor Wilkins. *Hegel's philosophy of history.* Ithaca, N.Y.: Cornell University Press, 1974. ISBN 0-8014-0819-9. ▸ Schematic outline of Hegel's philosophy of history (1.149), emphasizing that empirical historical research is essential starting point. Less successful in attempting to relate Hegel's philosophy of history to his logic. [RTV]

1.188 Yirmiahu Yovel. *Kant and the philosophy of history.* 1980 ed. Princeton: Princeton University Press, 1989. ISBN 0-691-07225-6 (cl, 1980), 0-691-02056-6 (pbk). ▸ Important for reconstruction of Kant's understanding of history from his major works. History conceived as arena of reason, displayed as moral teleology and progress. Also discusses Kant's philosophy of history as critical system. [AT]

Reflections on History

1.189 Richard James Blackburn. *The vampire of reason: an essay in the philosophy of history.* New York: Verso, 1990. ISBN 0-86091-257-4 (cl), 0-86091-972-6 (pbk). ▸ Ambitious attempt to sketch post-Marxian philosophy of history that would be dialectical and take account of geopolitical realities (demographic as well as power-political) and nature as active force. [RTV]

1.190 Kenneth Elliott Bock. *Human nature and history: a response to sociobiology.* New York: Columbia University Press, 1980. ISBN 0-231-05078-X (cl), 0-231-05079-8 (pbk). ▸ Strong critique by historian. Task of human sciences is to explicate social and cultural differences, best done through historical comparisons, not by comparative biology or ethnology. [AT]

1.191 Jacob Burckhardt. *Force and freedom.* New ed. James Hastings Nichols, ed. New York: Pantheon, 1964. ▸ Interpretation of history as determined by interrelationship of religion, culture, and state. Reflections also on crises, great men, and fortune and misfortune in history. Poor translation of *Weltgeschichtliche Betrachtungen.* [RTV]

1.192 Kenneth Burke. *Attitudes toward history.* 3d ed. Berkeley: University of California Press, 1984. ISBN 0-520-04145-3 (cl), 0-520-04148-8 (pbk). ▸ Attitudes express literary forms or poetic images. Western history figured as five-act drama: evangelical Christianity, medieval synthesis, Protestantism, early capitalism, and collectivism. Quirky, suggestive, often brilliant. [AT]

1.193 Paul A. Colinvaux. *The fates of nations: a biological theory of history.* New York: Simon & Schuster, 1980. ISBN 0-671-25204-6. ▸ Malthusian perspectives, Toynbean scope. Clearly reveals strengths and weaknesses of sociobiological approach: provocative arguments weakly supported by facts (no footnotes) and overemphasis on demography, conceived deterministically. [RTV]

1.194 M. C. D'Arcy. *The meaning and matter of history: a Christian view.* 1959 ed. New York: Meridian, 1961. ▸ Stipulating truth of Christianity, examines its possible contribution to substantive philosophies of history. Eschatology, other-worldliness, and providence in tension; chief Christian insight is supreme worth of individual lives. [RTV]

1.195 Mircea Eliade. *Cosmos and history: the myth of the eternal return.* 1959 ed. New York: Garland, 1985. ISBN 0-8240-6360-0. ▸ Suggestive account of origins of historical consciousness (said to be absent in primitive societies). Manifest terror of history allayed by annual cycle of festivals in which archetypes remodel accounts of events. [RTV]

1.196 M. I. Finley. *The use and abuse of history.* 1975 rev. ed. London: Penguin, 1990. ISBN 0-14-013443-3 (pbk). ▸ Collected essays by great social historian. Most pertinent are discussions of relationship between myth and history in Greek thought and role of generalizations in ancient history. [RTV]

1.197 Karl Jaspers. *The origin and goal of history.* Michael Bullock, trans. New Haven: Yale University Press, 1953. ▸ Existentialist philosophy of history. After surveying prehistory and noteworthy treatment of axial period (800–200 BCE), pleads for universal history oriented toward future, in which Europe will have lost its predominance. [RTV]

1.198 Karl Löwith. *Meaning in history.* 1949 ed. Chicago: University of Chicago Press, 1964. ▸ Vindicates genre of religious interpretations of history, since all views of overall meaning to history are theological. These traced backwards from Burckhardt to Bible. Such views cannot be confirmed by philosophy, but neither can questions of meaning be suppressed. [RTV]

1.199 C. T. McIntire, ed. *God, history, and historians: an anthology of modern Christian views on history.* New York: Oxford University Press, 1977. ISBN 0-19-502203-3 (cl), 0-19-502204-1 (pbk). ▸ Anthology representing most of best writing on Christian theology of history, providence and historical laws, and influence Christianity should have on historical practice. All shades of Christian belief included. [RTV]

1.200 Jan Patocka. *Essais hérétiques sur la philosophie de l'histoire.* Erika Abrams, trans. Paris: Verdier, 1981. ISBN 2-86432-014-2. ▸ Unusual interpretation of Western civilization as rising from Greek origins to height in medieval Holy Roman Empire, then suffering post-Renaissance decline. Advocates sacrifice to transcend productionist antihuman metaphysics (i.e., Marxism). [AT]

Uses of History

1.201 Richard E. Neustadt and Ernest R. May. *Thinking in time: the uses of history for decision-makers.* 1986 ed. New York: Free Press, 1988. ISBN 0-02-922790-9 (cl, 1986), 0-02-922791-7 (pbk). ▸ Intriguing answers to questions about uses of history. Exploration of how American statesmen since World War II were influenced by historical analogies with suggestions for fruitful use of analogy in policy making. [RTV]

1.202 Friedrich Nietzsche. *On the advantage and disadvantage of history for life.* Peter Preuss, trans. Indianapolis: Hackett, 1980. ISBN 0-915144-95-6 (cl), 0-915144-94-8 (pbk). ▸ Early essay expounding necessity of history and its perversion by nineteenth-century historical scholarship. Argues historical facts must be assimilated into present life, not merely objectively uncovered and unexplained. [RTV]

Time and Periodization

1.203 Fernand Braudel. *On history.* Sarah Matthews, trans. Chicago: University of Chicago Press, 1980. ISBN 0-226-07150-2. ▸ Collection of essays and reviews, including classic exposition of historians' time spans: short (event, individual), conjuncture (focusing on cycles, longer spans of time), and *longue durée* (relationship between society and structures, e.g., geology, biology). Repetitious but essential for understanding Annales approach to history. [RTV]

1.204 John R. Hall. "The time of history and the history of times." *History and theory* 19.2 (1980) 113–31. ISSN 0018-2656. ▸ Most comprehensive analysis of various theories of historical time: Braudel's three levels (1.203), Althusser's attempt to link temporal with social levels (1.131), and phenomenology of time. [RTV]

1.205 *History and the concept of time.* Middletown, Conn.: Wesleyan University Press, 1966. (*History and theory,* Beiheft, 6.) ISSN 0018-2656. ▸ Important collection of essays. Momigliano debunks Greek cyclical-Christian linear view of time; Starr discusses historical and philosophical time; Eisenstein, conceptions of time inculcated by printing; and Kracauer, time and eschatology. [AT]

1.206 Hans Jaeger. "Generations in history." *History and theory* 24.3 (1985) 273–92. ISSN 0018-2656. ▸ Analysis of generational change offers new insights into history. Clear in intellectual and art history, less distinguishable in economic, social, and political history. Relationship of generations needs to be articulated theoretically. [AT]

1.207 Emmanuel Le Roy Ladurie. "History that stands still." In *The mind and method of the historian.* Siân Reynolds and Ben Reynolds, trans. Chicago: University of Chicago Press, 1981. ISBN 0-226-47326-0 (cl), 0-226-47325-2 (pbk). ▸ Best short example (France, 1320–1720) of history in *longue durée*, because population oscillated around norm and there were no great technological breakthroughs. No discussion of politics, religion, or intellectual change. [RTV]

1.208 Wolfgang von Leyden. "History and the concept of relative time." *History and theory* 2.3 (1962) 263–85. ISSN 0018-2656. ▸ Strong challenge to concept of objective universal historical time. Argues each phenomenon context-dependent and each epoch has different concept of historical moments in time. [AT]

1.209 John T. Marcus. "Time and the sense of history: West and East." *Comparative studies in society and history* 3.2 (1961) 123–39. ISSN 0010-4175. ▸ Progress depends on historical consciousness as leading to action. Western civilization influenced rest of world by allowing coexistence and convergence of local essences and goals with material phenomena. [AT]

1.210 Nathan Rotenstreich. *Time and meaning in history.* Boston: Reidel; distributed by Kluwer Academic, 1987. ISBN 90-277-2467-9. ▸ Subtle but reasonably accessible phenomenological discussion of time and the meanings attributed to temporality through human actions, both as figuring in history and as reconstructed by historical research. [RTV]

1.211 Ulysses Santamaria and Anne M. Bailey. "A note on Braudel's structure as a duration." *History and theory* 23.1 (1984) 78–83. ISSN 0018-2656. ▸ Critical study of Braudel's three durations: event, conjuncture, *longue durée*. Sees relationship and possible contradiction between *longue durée* and conjunctural durations and short-term events as problematic and requiring further theorization from Annales school. [AT]

1.212 Peter H. Smith. "Time as a historical construct." *Historical methods* 17.4 (1984) 182–91. ISSN 0161-5440. ▸ Necessary corrective to excessively metaphysical views. Discussion of statistical and quantitative methods in generational and event-time series and causal analysis. [AT]

1.213 Robert C. Stalnaker. "Events, periods, and institutions in historians' language." *History and theory* 6.2 (1967) 159–79. ISSN 0018-2656. ▸ Sensible analysis of propriety of using holistic words like Renaissance or English Revolution since such names have no clear referent. Argues general statements employing them can be reconciled with evidence and must be evaluated on case-by-case basis. [AT]

The Historical Process

1.214 Cyril Edwin Black. *The dynamics of modernization: a study in comparative history.* New York: Harper & Row, 1966. ▸ Standard work. After consideration of epistemological problems of comparative history, proposes typology of modernization, emphasizing importance of political leadership and power of developed countries to affect modernization in Third World. [RTV]

1.215 Herbert Butterfield. *The Whig interpretation of history.* 1931 ed. New York: AMS Press, 1978. ISBN 0-404-14515-9. ▸ Directed specifically to English constitutional history, but applicable to all historical practice that works backward from present to document gradual progress. Classic attack on presentism. [RTV]

1.216 Rushton Coulborn. "Structure and process in the rise and fall of civilized societies." *Comparative studies in society and history* 8.4 (1966) 404–31. ISSN 0010-4175. ▸ Noteworthy contemporary three-stage theory: ages of faith, reason, and fulfillment. No inevitable tendency to decline or to revive; revivals usually made possible by religious leadership, far more effectively than political. [RTV]

1.217 David L. Hull. "In defense of presentism." *History and theory* 18.1 (1979) 1–15. ISSN 0018-2656. ▸ Historians must understand present to reconstruct past, since they depend on present language and concepts for historical understanding. Stimulating argument against understanding past "for its own sake." [RTV]

1.218 George Modelski. "The long cycle of global politics and the nation-state." *Comparative studies in society and history* 20.2 (1978) 214–35. ISSN 0010-4175. ▸ Absence of world empires does not imply lack of world political system. Modern system dates from ca. 1500 and controlled successively by Portugal, Netherlands, Britain, and United States. Good description of cycles of growth and decay. [RTV]

1.219 Barrington Moore, Jr. "On the notions of progress, revolution, and freedom." *Ethics* 72.2 (1962) 106–19. ISSN 0014-1704. ▸ Denies these terms are so value-laden as to be useless. Progress can be measured in technology and perhaps in growth of freedom. Prospects for such progress are dim as neither liberalism nor Marxism can guarantee it. [RTV]

1.220 Reinhold Niebuhr. *Faith and history: a comparison of Christian and modern views of history.* 1949 ed. New York: Macmillan, 1987. ▸ Powerful critique of idea of progress in both Western bourgeois and Marxist versions. Christian perspective on history important as preserving sense of mystery and holding all human social formations under judgment. [RTV]

1.221 Robert A. Nisbet. *History of the idea of progress.* New York: Basic Books, 1980. ISBN 0-465-03025-4. ▸ History of and apologia for idea, wherever in Western tradition traces of it are found. Rests largely on secondary works; notable for vigorous defense of Western tradition. [RTV]

1.222 Lester M. Salamon. "Comparative history and the theory of modernization." *World politics* 23.1 (1970) 83–103. ISSN 0043-8871. ▸ Examines Black 1.214 and Moore 1.219 models of modernization for economy, originality, and predictive power (rigor, combinatorial richness, and organizing capacity). On these desiderata for any comparative history, Moore comes off best. [RTV]

1.223 Randolph Starn. "Meaning-levels in the theme of historical decline." *History and theory* 14.1 (1975) 1–31. ISSN 0018-2656. ▸ Decline (originally value-free concept) came to connote movement from better to worse values. Now implies interplay of ethical norms and contrast of ideal and subsequent states, whether steady or in cyclical or spiral movement. [RTV]

1.224 Peter N. Stearns. "Modernization and social history: some suggestions, and a muted cheer." *Journal of social history* 14.2 (1980) 189–209. ISSN 0022-4529. ▸ Nuanced defense against charges of Eurocentrism, teleology, static character, and effacement of regional and sectoral differences. Modernization theory particularly useful for teaching, but also still valuable for research. [RTV]

1.225 Garry W. Trompf. *The idea of historical recurrence in Western thought: from antiquity to the Reformation.* Berkeley: University of California Press, 1979. ISBN 0-520-03479-1. ▸ Comprehensive, subtle treatment of recurrence in classical and Christian thought. Cycles, reenactment, and typology carefully distinguished. Antidote to oversimplified linear versus cyclical formulations. [RTV]

Great Individuals

1.226 Thomas Carlyle. *On heroes, hero-worship, and the heroic in history.* 1841 ed. Berkeley: University of California Press, 1992. ▸ Tumultuous barrage of language brilliantly expounds view of history as biography of great men (and gods). Heroes of religion, poetry, even criticism, and more usual political figures (Cromwell, Napoleon, and revolutionaries). [RTV]

1.227 Sidney Hook. *The hero in history: a study in limitation and possibility.* 1955 ed. Arnold Beichman, Introduction. New Brunswick, N.J.: Transaction, 1992. ISBN 0-88738-428-5. ▸ Wide-ranging discussion of great-man theories, including geniuses in arts as well as great political or military leaders. Distinguishes eventful from event-making people; latter very rare (Lenin an example). [RTV]

1.228 Georgii Valentinovich Plekhanov. *The role of the individual in history.* 1940 ed. London: Lawrence & Wishart, 1976. ▸ Marxism not incompatible with belief great men play significant role in history; places emphasis on social setting that defines greatness. Fails to explain how individuals achieve greatness. First published 1898 in *Nauchnoye obozrenie* under *nom de plume* of A. Kirsanov. [RTV]

1.229 Nathan Rotenstreich. "Individuals, great men, and historical determination." *Social research* 38.1 (1971) 139–65. ISSN 0037-783X. ▸ History neither the product of outstanding individuals nor of impersonal forces, so Carlyle 1.226 and Plekhanov 1.228 exaggerated in opposite ways. In histories of literature, philosophy, and art, individuals are irreplaceable, whereas this is less certain for generals or statesmen. [RTV]

ANALYTICAL PHILOSOPHIES OF HISTORY
Laws and Causal Explanation

1.230 Lee Benson and Cushing Strout. "Causation and the American Civil War: two approaches." *History and theory* 1.2 (1961) 163–85. ISSN 0018-2656. ▸ Examination of explanations of causes. Benson devises four logical principles that should govern historical explanation. Strout, in convincing narrative, regards historical causes as reasons and purposes. [AT]

1.231 Isaiah Berlin. *Historical inevitability.* New York: Oxford University Press, 1955. ▸ Strong defense of ordinary historical language. It inevitably conveys moral valuations and causal implication. Limited sphere of human freedom thus justifies moral judgments. [RTV]

1.232 Isaiah Berlin. "History and theory: the concept of scientific history." *History and theory* 1.1 (1960) 1–31. ISSN 0018-2656. ‣ States case against scientific history: unlike science, history individuates events, does not generalize from them; historian projects experience on past rather than using ideal types (models), and emphasizes facts, not theories. [AT]

1.233 G. H. Bousquet. "Le hasard, son rôle dans l'histoire des sociétés." *Annales: économies, sociétés, civilisations* 22 (1967) 419–28. ISSN 0395-2649. ‣ Interesting analysis of examples from religious and political history in which delicate balance of forces allows random events, such as changes in weather, to determine outcome of conflicts. [AT]

1.234 F. H. Bradley. *The presuppositions of critical history.* 1935 ed. Lionel Rubinoff, ed. Chicago: Quadrangle, 1968. ‣ First book (1874) by British idealist discussing possibility of historical knowledge. Departs from Hume and Hegel (1.149); concurs with positivism and Tübingen school of biblical historiography. [AT]

1.235 May I. Brodbeck, comp. *Readings in the philosophy of the social sciences.* New York: Macmillan, 1968. ‣ Extensive anthology from classics to contemporaries, slanted toward positivism but treating great variety of problems from several viewpoints. [AT]

1.236 David Carr et al., eds. *La philosophie de l'histoire et la pratique historienne d'aujourd'hui/Philosophy of history and contemporary historiography.* Ottawa: University of Ottawa Press, 1982. ISBN 2-7603-1033-7. ‣ Symposium featuring stellar cast of philosophers and historians. Many topics covered; central discussion of contrast between and explication of old and new history. [AT]

1.237 L. B. Cebik. "Concepts, laws, and the resurrection of ideal types." *Philosophy of the social sciences* 1.1 (1971) 65–81. ISSN 0048-3931. ‣ Polemic against Watkins 1.296. Differentiates concepts (as in explanatory models) from scientific covering laws, as basis for causal explanations, in terms of use, justification, and proposal. [AT]

1.238 T. A. Climo and P.G.A. Howells. "Possible worlds in historical explanation." *History and theory* 15.1 (1976) 1–20. ISSN 0018-2656. ‣ Valiant effort to sort out three theories of causality: regularity, traditional counterfactual, and possible-world semantic counterfactual analysis. Uses historical examples to prove superiority of last. [AT]

1.239 Paul Keith Conkin. "Causation revisited." *History and theory* 13.1 (1974) 1–20. ISSN 0018-2656. ‣ Useful warning by historian against forcing analysis of causes further than limited evidence warrants. Historians can seldom even identify sufficient causes, much less distinguish among necessary ones. [RTV]

1.240 Alan Donagan. "Historical explanation: the Popper-Hempel theory reconsidered." *History and theory* 4.1 (1964) 3–26. ISSN 0018-2656. ‣ Careful and generous summary of covering-law position, which is then rejected because no genuine covering laws exist, yet historians can give causal (deductive) explanations. [AT]

1.241 William H. Dray. *Perspectives on history.* Boston: Routledge & Kegan Paul, 1980. ISBN 0-7100-0569-5 (cl), 0-7100-0570-9 (pbk). ‣ Articles on both substantive and analytical philosophy of history; those on truth of historical accounts and distinguishing causes from conditions in controversy over Taylor's *The Origins of the Second World War* (48.186) particularly valuable. [AT]

1.242 William H. Dray, ed. *Philosophical analysis and history.* 1966 ed. Westport, Conn.: Greenwood, 1978. ISBN 0-313-20068-8. ‣ Anthology of majority of best articles in analytical philosophy of history written before 1966. Summarizes (and in effect buries) controversy over covering laws without anticipating interest in narrative. Includes Hempel's qualification of earlier position. [AT]

1.243 Evan Fales. "Uniqueness and historical laws." *Philosophy of science* 47.2 (1980) 260–76. ISSN 0031-8248. ‣ Analytical defense of nontrivial uniqueness of historical events, and cogent attack on reducing reasons to causes or social formations to individuals that compose them. [AT]

1.244 Patrick L. Gardiner. *The nature of historical explanation.* 1968 ed. New York: Oxford University Press, 1978. ISBN 0-19-824599-8 (pbk). ‣ Ordinary-language philosophy applied for first time to philosophy of history. Explores and clarifies usually vague concept of explanation; discusses causation and determinism. [RTV]

1.245 Gordon Graham. *Historical explanation reconsidered.* Aberdeen: Aberdeen University Press; distributed by Humanities Press, 1983. ISBN 0-08-028495-7 (cl), 0-08-028478-7 (pbk). ‣ Brisk attempt to dispose of covering-law controversy. Carl Hempel (in Gardiner 1.54) and Morton White 1.274 confused relationship between philosophy and its objects and failed to see historical explanation poses few philosophical problems. [AT]

1.246 Michael Hammond. "Weighing causes in historical explanation." *Theoria* 43 (1977) 103–28. ISSN 0040-5825. ‣ Cause important if anything with same causal weight was unlikely and if without that cause events would not have occurred. Weighing of causes makes sense only at fairly crude level. Good analysis of historical arguments. [AT]

1.247 Geoffrey Hawthorn. *Plausible worlds: possibility and understanding in history and the social sciences.* New York: Cambridge University Press, 1991. ISBN 0-521-40359-6. ‣ Examines counterfactuals in art and political and demographic history, concluding there are no rules stipulating which to accept and that only practical judgment on case-by-case basis can decide. [RTV]

1.248 Sidney Hook, ed. *Philosophy and history.* New York: New York University Press, 1963. ‣ Proceedings of conference held when activity in philosophy of history particularly intense. Almost all positions in analytical philosophy of history represented by field's major scholars. [AT]

1.249 Wilhelm von Humboldt. "On the historian's task." *History and theory* 6.1 (1967) 57–71. ISSN 0018-2656. ‣ Classic 1821 essay proscribing simple narration of events (contra Leopold von Ranke). Intuiting ideas needed to connect disjointed fragments of events to discover determining forces and historical truth. [AT]

1.250 Carey B. Joynt and Nicholas Rescher. "The problem of uniqueness in history." *History and theory* 1.2 (1961) 150–62. ISSN 0018-2656. ‣ Clear and influential article giving due weight to historians' interest in the particular, but showing that they are consumers, rather than producers, of generalizations needed to make sense of events. [AT]

1.251 Marvin Levich. "Disagreement and controversy in history." *History and theory* 2.1 (1962) 41–51. ISSN 0018-2656. ‣ Important, often overlooked issue. Disagreements among historians not usually about facts, but about explanation types: anticipatory, causal, or stylistic. Value-laden positions of historians determine choice of explanation type. [AT]

1.252 Thomas T. Lewis. "Karl Popper's situation logic and the covering law model of historical explanation." *Clio* 10.3 (1981) 291–303. ISSN 0884-2043. ‣ Shows importance of Popper's conception of laws and trends and logic of situation (1.169); argues latter is close to position of Dray (1.282). See comment by Dray and Lewis, in the same volume, 305–21. [AT]

1.253 Maurice Mandelbaum. *The anatomy of historical knowledge.* Baltimore: Johns Hopkins University Press, 1977. ISBN 0-8018-1929-6. ‣ Emphasis on variety of historical work (usually ignored by philosophers), some general, others specialized (e.g., art historical). Explanation not the same for all; part-whole relationships often more important than sequential relationships. [RTV]

1.254 Maurice Mandelbaum. "Historical explanation: the problem of 'covering laws.'" *History and theory* 1.3 (1961) 229–42. ISSN 0018-2656. ▸ Thoughtful attempt to satisfy criteria for scientific endeavor while accommodating historical practice. Points out covering laws need not be as ambitious as uniform sequences of events, and that historians seldom go beyond establishing sufficient conditions for events. [AT]

1.255 Juha Manninen and Tuomela Raimo, eds. *Essays on explanation and understanding: studies in the foundations of humanities and social sciences.* Boston: Reidel, 1976. ISBN 90-277-0592-5. ▸ Comprehensive anthology analyzing important work of von Wright (1.298), who contributes rejoinder. Major issues are intentionality, teleology, historical understanding, causality, and explanation of human actions. [AT]

1.256 Raymond Martin. *The past within us: an empirical approach to philosophy of history.* Princeton: Princeton University Press, 1989. ISBN 0-691-07341-4. ▸ Especially useful for three extended case histories of historical controversies, asking how historians choose best explanations. Concludes no definitive decision rules; historians' trained judgment required. [AT]

1.257 C. T. McIntire and Ronald A. Wells, eds. *History and historical understanding.* Grand Rapids, Mich.: Eerdmans, 1984. ISBN 0-8028-0030-0. ▸ Essays on whether being a Christian should make any difference to one's historical practice—for example, in biblical history or studying French Revolution. Familiar topics addressed from variety of Christian perspectives. [AT]

1.258 Richard W. Miller. *Fact and method: explanation, confirmation, and reality in the natural and social sciences.* Princeton: Princeton University Press, 1987. ISBN 0-691-07318-X (cl), 0-691-02045-0 (pbk). ▸ Proposes alternative to positivist notions of unity of scientific knowledge. Sciences differ; history is one since underlying causes can be specified according to rules of each science. [AT]

1.259 Louis O. Mink. *Historical understanding.* Brian Fay, Eugene O. Golob, and Richard T. Vann, eds. Ithaca, N.Y.: Cornell University Press, 1987. ISBN 0-8014-1983-2. ▸ Collection of thoughtful, beautifully written articles on main problems of contemporary philosophy of history: autonomy of historical and other modes of understanding, narratives as explanations, history and myth, and events and evidence. [AT]

1.260 Fred D. Newman. *Explanation by description: an essay on historical methodology.* The Hague: Mouton, 1968. ▸ Short, lucid essay arguing that description is necessary in history, but is not inconsistent with employment of laws, which can be borrowed from any other science. [RTV]

1.261 Sten Sparre Nilson. "Covering laws in historical practice." *Inquiry* 14.4 (1971) 445–63. ISSN 0020-174X. ▸ Notices that historians don't always explain by showing what was expected; they often say events occurred by chance or through unpredictable activities of extraordinary individuals. [RTV]

1.262 Sten Sparre Nilson. "On the logic of historical explanation." *Theoria* 36.1 (1970) 65–81. ISSN 0040-5825. ▸ Interesting attempt at logical explication of how historians assign relative causal importance among necessary conditions in history. Analyzes historical problems and reduces causal importance to necessary and sufficient probabilistic conditions. For response to criticisms see *Theoria* 37 (1971) 15–20. [AT]

1.263 Donald Ostrowski. "A typology of historical theories." *Diogenes* 129 (1985) 127–45. ISSN 0012-303X. ▸ Good for sorting out historical arguments. Eight positions of historians distinguished on basis of following criteria: idealist versus materialist,

objectivism versus subjectivism, and contemplators versus activists. [AT]

1.264 Henry M. Pachter. "Defining an event: prolegomenon to any future philosophy of history." *Social research* 41.3 (1974) 439–66. ISSN 0037-783X. ▸ Pioneering effort at definition. Magnitude of events determines appropriate degree of generalization: cause for individual occurrence, explanation for middle level, and covering laws for grand scale. [AT]

1.265 John Passmore. "Explanation in everyday life, in science, and in history." *History and theory* 2.2 (1962) 105–23. ISSN 0018-2656. ▸ Valuable and accessible discussion of explanation. Scientific and everyday explanations do not share logical form, but both remove puzzlement. Distinguishable by criteria and degree of rigor applied to inquiry. Historical explanations generally resemble everyday ones. [AT]

1.266 John Passmore. "History, the individual, and inevitability." *Philosophical review* 68 (1959) 93–102. ISSN 0031-8108. ▸ Sensible stand against philosophical extremes; claims Popper 1.169 and Berlin 1.231 went too far in attacking monism and determinism, since everyday experience shows unreasonableness of treating groups as abstract concepts and attributing total freedom to humans. [AT]

1.267 *Philosophy of history.* La Salle, Ill.: Open Court for the Hegeler Institute, 1969. (Monist, 53.) ISSN 0026-9662. ▸ Special issue on philosophy of history with articles by Smith on time and existence, Cebik on colligation and writing history, Donagan on explanation and verification, and also on Collingwood and history as behavioral science. [AT]

1.268 Terry Pinkard. "Historical explanation and the grammar of theories." *Philosophy of the social sciences* 8 (1978) 227–40. ISSN 0048-3931. ▸ History has a different grammar (i.e., way its concepts are constructed) from natural science. Systematic narrative redescription of events in a chronicle is paradigmatic historical explanation. [RTV]

1.269 Leon Pompa and William H. Dray, eds. *Substance and form in history.* Edinburgh: Edinburgh University Press, 1981. ISBN 0-85224-413-4. ▸ Unusually coherent Festschrift (for W. H. Walsh) contains six articles on substantive philosophy of history (mostly on Hegel 1.148, 1.149) and six on analytical (on colligation, Collingwood 1.280, rational explanation, and truth and fact). [AT]

1.270 George A. Reisch. "Chaos, history, and narrative." *History and theory* 30.1 (1991) 1–20. ISSN 0018-2656. ▸ Novel critique of covering-law theories of historical explanation; they fail because initial conditions never completely known and final states (over historically interesting periods of time) very sensitive to minute variations in initial conditions. [RTV]

1.271 Paul Arthur Schilpp, ed. *The philosophy of Karl Popper.* 2 vols. LaSalle, Ill.: Open Court, 1974. ISBN 0-87548-141-8 (v. 1), 0-87548-142-6 (v. 2). ▸ Anthology of relevant articles on relationship between Popper's philosophies of history and of science; his sense of historicism; and determinism, explanation in history, and interpretation. [AT]

1.272 Robert C. Stover. *The nature of historical thinking.* Chapel Hill: University of North Carolina Press, 1967. ▸ Argues historians seek both natural-order intelligibility (as in natural sciences) and perspective from practical experience. Neither necessarily preferable; although not incompatible, neither reducible to the other. [RTV]

1.273 Ludwig Von Mises. *Theory and history.* 1957 ed. New York: Garland, 1984. ▸ Well-known *laissez-faire* economist works out coherent and challenging philosophy of history and the social sciences on libertarian, free-market principles. [AT]

1.274 Morton White. *Foundations of historical knowledge.* 1965 ed. Westport, Conn.: Greenwood, 1982. ISBN 0-313-23479-5. ‣ Mature and sophisticated statement of covering-law positivistic model of historical explanation. Covering laws may be unknown, deductive, or inductive. Historical factual and value statements and narratives also discussed. [AT]

1.275 Burleigh Taylor Wilkins. *Has history any meaning? A critique of Popper's philosophy of history.* Ithaca, N.Y.: Cornell University Press, 1978. ISBN 0-8014-1187-4. ‣ Thoughtful, sympathetic critique of Popper 1.169. Accepts part of covering-law theory, but denies such laws need be trivial; also believes in possibility of a theory of history. [RTV]

1.276 Wilhelm Windelband. "On history and natural science." Guy Oakes, Introduction. *History and theory* 19.2 (1980) 165–85. ISSN 0018-2656. ‣ Publication of 1894 address, source of classic distinction between nomothetic (natural science) and idiographic (particularizing, including historical) methods, made to defend against positivist limitations on philosophy. [AT]

Rational Explanation

1.277 Howard Adelman. "Rational explanation reconsidered: case studies and the Hempel-Dray model." *History and theory* 13.3 (1974) 208–24. ISSN 0018-2656. ‣ Performs feat of amalgamating two rival theorists, both of whom view explanation as rational choice among alternatives by agent. But agents usually decide whether to perform a certain action, not pick out one action among possible alternatives, and this is what requires explanation. [AT]

1.278 Ronald F. Atkinson. *Knowledge and explanation in history: an introduction to the philosophy of history.* Ithaca, N.Y.: Cornell University Press, 1978. ISBN 0-8014-1116-5 (cl), 0-8014-9171-1 (pbk). ‣ Defends narrative and rational explanations against covering laws and objectivity from antirelativistic perspective. Stresses plurality of causes of events. Fair summaries of major issues. [AT]

1.279 F. M. Barnard. "Accounting for actions: causality and teleology." *History and theory* 20.3 (1981) 291–312. ISSN 0018-2656. ‣ Comprehensive support for Collingwood's theory of historical understanding and causality (1.280), revising problematic aspects (re-enactment), proving consistency with teleologies, and claiming there are no better alternatives. [AT]

1.280 R. G. Collingwood. *The idea of history.* Rev. ed. W. J. van der Dussen, ed. Oxford: Clarendon, 1993. ISBN 0-19-823957-2. ‣ History of historiography as progressing toward conception of history elaborated in final section. Poses questions of evidence, aimed at explanation by rethinking thoughts of historical agents. Essential work. [RTV]

1.281 Alan Donagan. *The later philosophy of R. G. Collingwood.* Oxford: Clarendon, 1962. ‣ Chapters 8 (scientific history) and 9 (philosophy of history) relevant. Argues Collingwood's philosophy of history consistent throughout career, despite revolutionary changes in his later thinking about metaphysics, religion, and aesthetics. [AT]

1.282 William H. Dray. *Laws and explanation in history.* London: Oxford University Press, 1957. ‣ Classic response to Hempel's theory (in Gardiner 1.54); argues historical explanation need not involve laws. It is sufficient to reconstruct reasons why agents took actions. [RTV]

1.283 W. J. van der Dussen. *History as a science: the philosophy of R. G. Collingwood.* Boston: Nijhoff, 1981. ISBN 90-247-2453-8. ‣ Fullest intellectual biography and reconsideration of *The Idea of History* (1.280) using previously unavailable materials illuminating Collingwood's experience as archaeologist and historian. [RTV]

1.284 Hans-Georg Gadamer. *Truth and method.* 2d rev. ed. Donald Marshall and Joel C. Weinsheimer, trans. New York: Crossroad, 1989. ISBN 0-8264-0401-4. ‣ Classic of hermeneutics defines truth as artistic experience; questions what kinds of truth and insight understanding can convey. Answer proposed through hermeneutic study of Leopold von Ranke, J. G. Droysen, Wilhelm Dilthey, Edmund Husserl, and Martin Heidegger. [AT]

1.285 Leon J. Goldstein. *Historical knowing.* Austin: University of Texas Press, 1976. ISBN 0-292-73002-0. ‣ Distinctive idealist argument. Many examples show history is licit way of getting knowledge; philosophers challenged to account for this. Emphasis on historians' research process, not on literary presentation. [RTV]

1.286 Gilbert H. Harman. "Knowledge, reasons, and causes." *Journal of philosophy* 67.21 (1970) 841–55. ISSN 0022-362X. ‣ Explanation by reasons not necessarily causal explanation, nor deterministic. Advances functional account of reasoning; purpose is to gain knowledge. [AT]

1.287 K. E. Jones. "Rational explanation and historical practice." *Philosophy* 58.226 (1983) 528–34. ISSN 0031-8191. ‣ Based on close study of historical practice, concludes that historians often do not use rational explanations based on agents' intentionality and reasoning. Supporters of this theory should call for reform of historiography, not claim to explain it. [AT]

1.288 Michael Krausz, ed. *Critical essays on the philosophy of R.G. Collingwood.* Oxford: Oxford University Press, 1972. ISBN 0-19-824378-2. ‣ Collection of essays treating various aspects of Collingwood's attempt at systematic philosophy. Particularly interesting for historians are those treating Collingwood's idea of reenactment as key to historical understanding. [AT]

1.289 Wolfgang von Leyden. "Categories of historical understanding." *History and theory* 23.1 (1984) 53–77. ISSN 0018-2656. ‣ Good survey suggesting six categories to distinguish balanced from tendentious historical narratives: real past, logical primacy of historical knowledge, imaginative construction of the past, new evidence, independent viewpoint, and modern critical interpretation. [AT]

1.290 Rex Martin. *Historical explanation: re-enactment and practical inference.* Ithaca, N.Y.: Cornell University Press, 1977. ISBN 0-8014-1084-3. ‣ In tradition of Collingwood, attempts to find mediating position between human nature and historicism, covering laws and *Verstehen.* Critical of sweeping universal generalizations. [AT]

1.291 Louis O. Mink. *Mind, history, and dialectic: the philosophy of R. G. Collingwood.* 1969 ed. Middletown, Conn.: Wesleyan University Press, 1987. ISBN 0-8195-6178-9. ‣ Reconstruction of Collingwood's philosophy, correcting impressions gained from reading *The Idea of History* (1.280) alone and stressing dialectical nature of Collingwood's thought. Rethinks rather than repeats Collingwood's philosophy; clarifies many of its difficulties. [RTV]

1.292 Michael Joseph Oakeshott. *On history and other essays.* Totowa, N.J.: Barnes & Noble, 1983. ISBN 0-389-20355-6. ‣ Attempt by influential idealist philosopher to vindicate distinctive historical understanding of historical past. Historians must present reliable relation of events, not subsume them causally under general laws. [AT]

1.293 William Outhwaite. *Understanding social life: the method called Verstehen.* 2d ed. Lewes, England: Stroud, 1986. ISBN 0-9504400-4-3. ‣ History of concept from origins to current usages. Usefully specifies relationship of understanding to hermeneutics, dialectic, meaning, and subjectivity. [AT]

1.294 Nathan Rotenstreich. *Philosophy, history, and politics: studies in contemporary English philosophy of history.* The Hague: Nijhoff, 1976. ISBN 90-247-1743-4. ‣ Essays on Collingwood

1.280, stressing tension between historicism and independent status of philosophy; on Berlin 1.231; Oakeshott 1.292 on tradition and politics; and Popper's change from substantive to analytical philosophy of history. Judicious mixture of description, analysis, and criticism. [RTV]

1.295 Charles Taylor. "Understanding in human science." *Review of metaphysics* 34.1 (1980) 25–38. ISSN 0034-6632. ▸ Clearly argued attempt to sustain distinction between natural and social sciences, based on modes of understanding. Human sciences require array of skills acquired only through life experience. [AT]

1.296 J.W.N. Watkins. "Ideal types and historical explanation." In *Philosophy of social explanation.* Alan Ryan, ed., pp. 82–104. Oxford: Oxford University Press, 1973. ISBN 0-19-875025-0. ▸ Helpful discussion of Max Weber's two notions of ideal types. First, unworkable; second, focusing on rational individual action, particularly valuable for explanation in principle (as opposed to colligation or explanation in detail). [AT]

1.297 David A. White. "Imagination and description: Collingwood and the historical consciousness." *Clio* 1 (1972) 14–28. ISSN 0884-2043. ▸ Collingwood's difficult concept of *a priori* imagination explained and illustrated by comparisons with Tacitus and Proust. Artistic style of historical description appropriate for narrative technique. [AT]

1.298 G. Henrik von Wright. *Explanation and understanding.* Ithaca, N.Y.: Cornell University Press, 1971. ISBN 0-8014-0644-7. ▸ Important analytical answer to hermeneutics. Discussions of teleology, understanding, causal explanation, intentional explanation, philosophy of action, rules and norms as motivational explanation, and historicism. [AT]

Evidence

1.299 Vernon K. Dibble. "Four types of inference from documents to events." *History and theory* 3.2 (1964) 203–19. ISSN 0018-2656. ▸ Documents can be testimony, social bookkeeping, correlates, or direct indicators. Testimony and social bookkeeping differ in source and technique, correlates and direct indicators differ in technique alone. All four must be mastered. [RTV]

1.300 B. C. Hurst. "The myth of historical evidence." *History and theory* 20.3 (1981) 278–90. ISSN 0018-2656. ▸ Provocative attack on notion of conclusive evidence. Choice between competing claims (narratives) about past events determined by network of other assumptions about past and predictive power connected to those assumptions. [AT]

1.301 Carey B. Joynt and Nicholas Rescher. "Evidence in history and the law." *Journal of philosophy* 56.15 (1959) 561–77. ISSN 0022-362X. ▸ Good philosophical treatment of similarities and differences. Historians' only goal is truth, which allows a weaker standard for admissibility of evidence and different modes of analysis. [RTV]

1.302 John Lange. "The argument from silence." *History and theory* 5.3 (1966) 288–301. ISSN 0018-2656. ▸ Sole treatment of this common historical argument which can only be probabilistic and seldom rationally and never logically conclusive. Depends mainly on estimates of likelihood of documents being available in given case. [RTV]

1.303 John D. Milligram. "The treatment of an historical source." *History and theory* 18.2 (1979) 177–96. ISSN 0018-2656. ▸ Helpful discussion of practical steps that working historians should use in evaluating historical source seeming to contradict accepted historical accounts. [AT]

Constructionism

1.304 *The constitution of the historical past.* Middletown, Conn.: Wesleyan University Press, 1977. (*History and theory,* Beiheft, 16.) ISSN 0018-2656. ▸ Three articles stating constructionist position, holding not just that historians must construct theories to account for evidence, but that since real past not observable, it cannot influence historical knowledge. [RTV]

1.305 Benedetto Croce. *History: its theory and practice.* 1920 ed. Douglas Ainslie, trans. New York: Russell & Russell, 1960. ▸ Source of renowned idealist maxims "all history is contemporary history" and "all history is the history of thought." Influenced by Giambattista Vico and G.W.F. Hegel, and influential on Collingwood (1.280). [AT]

1.306 Jack W. Meiland. *Scepticism and historical knowledge.* New York: Random House, 1965. ▸ Most thoroughgoing (and extreme) formulation of constructionist view of history, based on arguments that historical knowledge is impossible. Croce 1.305 and Oakeshott 1.292 claimed as constructionists; skepticism distinguished from relativism, which is rejected. [RTV]

Realism

1.307 Harriet Gilliam. "The dialectics of realism and idealism in modern historiographic theory." *History and theory* 15.3 (1976) 231–56. ISSN 0018-2656. ▸ Positions not as completely opposed as usually believed; on most questions they borrow from one another, addressing common issues and sharing epistemological presuppositions. Contribution to essential ongoing dialogue. [RTV]

1.308 Adrian Kuzminski. "Defending historical realism." *History and theory* 18.3 (1979) 316–49. ISSN 0018-2656. ▸ Defends Leopold von Ranke's version of historical truth against relativism and structuralism, claiming these offer no alternative methodological advantages. Instead author suggests faith in power of historical evidence. [AT]

1.309 C. Behan McCullagh. *Justifying historical descriptions.* New York: Cambridge University Press, 1984. ISBN 0-521-26722-6 (cl), 0-521-31830-0 (pbk). ▸ Lucidly advances four empiricist assumptions about reality and knowledge of it, founding case for justification, defined as giving logical conditions under which people are warranted in believing historical descriptions to be true. [AT]

1.310 Murray G. Murphey. *Our knowledge of the historical past.* Indianapolis: Bobbs-Merrill, 1973. ISBN 0-672-61269-0. ▸ Sophisticated defense of historical realism: George Washington is as real as the electron, both being required to account for present traces. Realism "more natural" than pragmatism or constructivism. [RTV]

1.311 Michael Moissey Postan. *Fact and relevance: essays on historical method.* Cambridge: Cambridge University Press, 1971. ISBN 0-521-07841-5. ▸ Witty and graceful essays on interrelations between history and social sciences, advocating non-Marxist scientific approach and attacking idealist interpretations of history. [AT]

Narrative

1.312 F. R. Ankersmit, ed. *Knowing and telling history: the Anglo-Saxon debate.* Middletown, Conn.: Wesleyan University Press, 1986. (*History and theory,* Beiheft, 25.) ISSN 0018-2656. ▸ Instructive confrontation between the knowers, neopositivist Murphey and idealist Goldstein, versus the tellers, Ankersmit, advocate of narrative, and Cebik, proposing typology of narratives. [AT]

1.313 C. J. Arthur. "On the historical understanding." *History and theory* 7.2 (1968) 205–16. ISSN 0018-2656. ▸ Attempts, against

Gallie 1.320, to reassert importance of laws in narrative understanding of history. Interest in connective events, aside from outcome of story, requires generalizations; so history more than art. [AT]

1.314 Robert H. Canary and Henry Kozicki, eds. *The writing of history: literary form and historical understanding.* Madison: University of Wisconsin Press, 1978. ISBN 0-299-07570-2. ▸ Important collection on history and literature, especially Gossman; historical texts as literary artifacts (H. White); and narrative form as cognitive instrument (Mink). [AT]

1.315 David Carr. *Time, narrative, and history.* 1986 ed. Bloomington: Indiana University Press, 1991. ISBN 0-253-36024-2 (cl, 1986), 0-253-20603-0 (pbk). ▸ Accepts importance of narrative, but denies it is just constructed by historian. Individual and social time have narrative (historical) forms; therefore story, storyteller, and audience isomorphic and narratives not simply imposed upon flux of events. [AT]

1.316 Philippe Carrard. *Poetics of the new history: French historical discourse from Braudel to Chartier.* Baltimore: Johns Hopkins University Press, 1992. ISBN 0-8018-4254-9. ▸ Exemplary rhetorical analysis of positivism, and paradigms that aspired to replace it. Shows new historians, though heterogeneous in style, deploy (perhaps without fully realizing it) new kinds of textualization. [RTV]

1.317 Noël Carroll. "Interpretation, history, and narrative." *Monist* 73.2 (1990) 134–66. ISSN 0026-9662. ▸ Best philosophical critique of White's *Metahistory* (1.334). Claims selectivity (fact that events can figure in different stories and that no account can be literal and total representation of past) does not warrant claim that historical narratives are fictive. [RTV]

1.318 L. B. Cebik. "Narrative and argument." *Clio* 1.1 (1971) 7–25. ISSN 0884-2043. ▸ Ambitious attempt to define narratives (fictional and historical) and to clarify their relationship to causality, arguments (distinguishable though compatible), and nonnarrative elements in histories. [RTV]

1.319 Arthur Coleman Danto. *Narration and knowledge: including the integral text of analytical philosophy of history.* New York: Columbia University Press, 1985. ISBN 0-231-06116-1 (cl), 0-231-06117-X (pbk). ▸ Valuable treatment of many problems in philosophy of history; especially useful for concept of narrative sentences as distinctive to historiography. [AT]

1.320 W. H. Gallie. *Philosophy and the historical understanding.* 2d ed. New York: Schocken, 1968. ▸ First extended philosophical analysis of narrative. Aims at understanding history rather than verifying historians' claims to truth. Understanding achieved by following story to outcome; generalizations only appear when something in sequence unintelligible. [AT]

1.321 J. L. Gorman. *The expression of historical knowledge.* Edinburgh: Edinburgh University Press, 1982. ISBN 0-85224-427-4. ▸ Original treatment of problems in narration, relevance, and epistemology. History is self-understanding; ultimate foundation for historical knowledge can be found in Giambattista Vico, as interpreted by Pompa 1.168. [AT]

1.322 David L. Hull. "Central subjects and historical narratives." *History and theory* 14.3 (1975) 253–74. ISSN 0018-2656. ▸ Rare philosophical formal analysis of narrative. Since history cannot explain by invoking covering laws characteristic of developed sciences, it uses narrative, for which historical subject, providing unity and continuity, must be posited. [AT]

1.323 T. Carlos Jacques. "The primacy of narrative in historical understanding." *Clio* 19.3 (1990) 197–214. ISSN 0884-2043. ▸ Searching critique arguing, contra Mink 1.259, all modes of comprehension are varieties of configuration; narrative is nec-

essary condition for truth value as well as meaningfulness of historical beliefs. [RTV]

1.324 David Konstan. "The function of narrative in Hayden White's *Metahistory*." *Clio* 11.1 (1981) 65–78. ISSN 0884-2043. ▸ Supports White 1.334 by rereading chapters on historians and philosophers of history as narratives, essentially composed of conflicting motives. Allows for reintroduction of nonnarrative discourse and more logical basis for association of typologies. [RTV]

1.325 A. R. Louch. "History as narrative." *History and theory* 8.1 (1969) 54–70. ISSN 0018-2656. ▸ Extreme narrativist position; narratives not merely incidental but essential for historical explanation; necessary to fill in gaps in knowledge to explain change. Narratives limited by chronology of events and need for factual accuracy; never achieve ideal of correspondence to reality. [AT]

1.326 Donald N. McCloskey. "History, differential equations, and the problem of narration." *History and theory* 30.1 (1991) 21–36. ISSN 0018-2656. ▸ Novel approach to comparison between technical scientific and literary reasoning. Both engineers and historians use metaphors and stories, connected by themes—for both, time. Nonlinear differential equations chaotic, like history, making narration difficult. [RTV]

1.327 *Metahistory: six critiques.* Middletown, Conn.: Wesleyan University Press, 1980. (*History and theory*, Beiheft, 19.) ISSN 0018-2656. ▸ Three sympathetic articles, defending role of rhetoric and linking to humanism (Kellner); three critiques, questioning presuppositions (Mandelbaum), proposing a "Collingwoodian" theory of narrative (Golob), and pointing out implicit psychology (Pomper). [AT]

1.328 Dale H. Porter. *The emergence of the past: a theory of historical explanation.* Chicago: University of Chicago Press, 1981. ISBN 0-226-67550-5. ▸ Rare philosophical text by working historian. Rich with examples, original in approach, which shows how explicit use of plots, subplots, and constitution of events makes story into explanatory narrative. [AT]

1.329 Paul Ricoeur. *Time and narrative.* 3 vols. Kathleen McLaughlin and David Pellauer, trans. Chicago: University of Chicago Press, 1984–88. ISBN 0-226-71331-8 (v. 1), 0-226-71333-4 (v. 2), 0-226-71335-0 (v. 3). ▸ Despite tediously exhaustive treatment of all previous theories, a must for anyone seriously interested in narrative. Volumes 1 (noteworthy for brilliant discussion of St. Augustine) and 3 focus on history. [AT]

1.330 Cushing Strout. *The veracious imagination: essays on American history, literature, and biography.* Middletown, Conn.: Wesleyan University Press; distributed by Columbia University Press, 1981. ISBN 0-8195-5048-5. ▸ Situates narrative explanation between positivism and postmodernism, arguing that imaginary and real have no borders, though some interpretations less legitimate than others. [AT]

1.331 Jerzy Topolski. "Truth conditions of historical narratives." *History and theory* 20.1 (1980) 47–60. ISSN 0018-2656. ▸ Special truth claims are made in historical narratives; truth of parts does not entail truth of whole; whole may be true though it has false parts; greater proportion of truthful statements does not entail greater truth. [AT]

1.332 Jerzy Topolski, ed. *Narration and explanation: contributions to methodology of the historical research.* Atlanta: Rodopi, 1990. ISBN 90-5183-155-2. ▸ Collection of essays taking narrative to be key problem in philosophy of history and considering various aspects of it, especially—and surprisingly—with reference to Marxism. [RTV]

1.333 Hayden V. White. *The content of the form: narrative dis-*

course and historical representation. Baltimore: Johns Hopkins University Press, 1987. ISBN 0-8018-2937-2. ▸ Essays, 1979–85, focused mainly on narrative: how it represents; its place in theory of history; views of Jameson 1.348, Michel Foucault, and Ricoeur 1.329; and politics of historical interpretation. [AT]

1.334 Hayden V. White. *Metahistory: the historical imagination in nineteenth-century Europe.* 1973 ed. Baltimore: Johns Hopkins University Press, 1975. ISBN 0-8018-1469-3 (cl, 1973), 0-8018-1761-7 (pbk). ▸ Formidable, extremely influential work presenting readings of four nineteenth-century historians, three philosophers of history, and theory of historical writing analyzed by choice of tropes, genres, modes of argument, and ideological implication. [RTV]

1.335 Hayden V. White. *Tropics of discourse: essays in cultural criticism.* 1978 ed. Baltimore: Johns Hopkins University Press, 1985. ISBN 0-8018-2127-4 (cl, 1978), 0-8018-2741-8 (pbk). ▸ Stimulating essays, 1966–76, beginning with "The Burden of History," critique of bad faith in contemporary historiography and developing tropological theory of historiography, especially in intellectual history. [AT]

Rhetorical Analyses

1.336 F. R. Ankersmit. "Historiography and postmodernism." *History and theory* 28.2 (1989) 137–53. ISSN 0018-2656. ▸ Controversial manifesto. Historiographical viewpoint and language used to express it do not intersect the past; therefore historiography shares opacity of art. Texts bear indefinite number of interpretations, so historical debates will remain unsettled. [RTV]

1.337 F. R. Ankersmit. *Narrative logic: a semantic analysis of the historian's language.* The Hague: Nijhoff; distributed by Kluwer, 1983. ISBN 90-247-2731-6. ▸ Historical texts are interpretations of past, supported by but never mirrors of the past. Point of view precedes our knowledge of individual things. Narratives and metaphors can be explanations. [AT]

1.338 Derek Attridge, Geoff Bennington, and Robert Young, eds. *Post-structuralism and the question of history.* New York: Cambridge University Press, 1987. ISBN 0-521-32759-8. ▸ Despite its critique of structuralism, poststructuralism has been reproached as ahistorical. Collected essays wrestle with issue that crisis of historicity itself implicated in poststructuralism, not absence of history. [RTV]

1.339 Stephen Bann. *The clothing of Clio: a study of the representation of history in nineteenth-century Britain and France.* New York: Cambridge University Press, 1984. ISBN 0-521-25616-X. ▸ Valuable recovery of side of nineteenth-century historiography repressed by Meinecke's standard account (1.62) through reading of Prosper de Barante, Augustin Thierry, Jules Michelet, and Walter Scott. Tropological treatment of ironies of realism. [RTV]

1.340 Roland Barthes. "An introduction to the structural analysis of narrative." *New literary history* 6.2 (1975) 237–72. ISSN 0028-6087. ▸ Good introduction to French discourse theory. Concentrates on codes that identify a narrative to reader; claims bourgeois society prefers narrators who (like most historical writers) conceal fictive element in narratives. [RTV]

1.341 Michel de Certeau. *The writing of history.* Tom Conley, trans. New York: Columbia University Press, 1988. ISBN 0-231-05574-9. ▸ Traces historiography to obsession with death, and exemplifies a kind of critical history à la Nietzsche that both analyzes and transcends rhetoric of history. Difficult style, diverse chapters, mind-bending insights. [RTV]

1.342 Sande M. Cohen. *Historical culture: on the recoding of an academic discipline.* 1986 ed. Berkeley: University of California Press, 1988. ISBN 0-520-05565-9 (cl, 1986), 0-520-06453-4 (pbk). ▸ Narrative essential to historiography, but makes readers passive

and distracted from contemporary problems. Academic history should thus be abandoned. Anarchist and anticapitalist standpoint; prose deliberately difficult, but some brilliant semiological readings of histories. [RTV]

1.343 Thomas M. DePietro. "Literary criticism as history: the example of Auerbach's *Mimesis.*" *Clio* 8 (1979) 377–87. ISSN 0884-2043. ▸ *Mimesis* an attempt to understand texts as part of world, constituting self-understanding of humans and their society. Explores boundary between literary criticism and history, treated as permeable. [AT]

1.344 Johann Gustav Droysen. *Outline of the principles of history (Grundriss der Historik).* 1966 ed. E. Benjamin Andrews, trans. Boston: Ginn, 1970. ▸ Searching critique of nineteenth-century German historical tradition, emphasizing rootedness of history within present concerns as well as present evidence, problems of presentation, interpretation versus criticism of historical facts. Also available in photocopy from Ann Arbor: University Microfilms International. [RTV]

1.345 Peter Gay. *Style in history.* 1974 ed. New York: Norton, 1988. ISBN 0-393-30558-9. ▸ Instructive contrast with White 1.333. Approaches subject from perspectival realism; historians' techniques similar to those of poets and novelists, but primary loyalty to truth (i.e., facticity). Order and selection of events in narrative found, not made. [RTV]

1.346 Lionel Gossman. *Between history and literature.* Cambridge, Mass.: Harvard University Press, 1990. ISBN 0-674-06815-7. ▸ Judicious essays in disputed territory: history of literature, rhetorical analysis of historians (Augustin Thierry and Jules Michelet), and attempt to distinguish history from literature, relying on professional standards of historians. [RTV]

1.347 Jean E. Howard. "Towards a postmodern, politically committed historical practice." In *Uses of history: Marxism, postmodernism, and the Renaissance.* Francis Barker, Peter Hulme, and Margaret Iverson, eds., pp. 101–22. New York: Manchester University Press; distributed by St. Martin's, 1991. ISBN 0-7190-3512-0. ▸ Takes up problem of how to incorporate insights of postmodernism (such as rejection of objectivity and locality of knowledge) with emancipatory feminist political program in producing histories. [RTV]

1.348 Fredric Jameson. *The political unconscious: narrative as a socially symbolic act.* Ithaca, N.Y.: Cornell University Press, 1981. ISBN 0-8014-1233-1 (cl), 0-8014-9222-X (pbk). ▸ Difficult but rewarding philosophical-aesthetic, Marxist-historicist attempt to study interpretive categories of texts as between ideology and utopia or instrumentalist and communal reading. [AT]

1.349 Hans Kellner. *Language and historical representation: getting the story crooked.* Madison: University of Wisconsin Press, 1989. ISBN 0-299-12050-3 (cl), 0-299-12054-6 (pbk). ▸ Often brilliant, always provocative essays exemplifying insights gained from discourse analysis applied to historical texts. Sources for historians not only linguistically mediated, but also constrained by rhetoric and language. [AT]

1.350 Dominick LaCapra. *History and criticism.* Ithaca, N.Y.: Cornell University Press, 1985. ISBN 0-8014-1788-0. ▸ Stimulating critique of current historiography, especially complacent evocation of it as a craft. Considers boundaries of history and fiction and resists subsumption of intellectual history into history of *mentalités.* [RTV]

1.351 Marie-Rose Logan and John F. Logan, eds. *Rethinking history: time, myth, and writing.* New Haven: Yale University Press, 1980. ISSN 0044-0078. ▸ Anthology, including essays on patterns of memory, fiction as history/history as fiction, and politics of historical discourse. [AT]

1.352 *The representation of historical events.* Middletown, Conn.:

Wesleyan University Press, 1987. (*History and theory*, Beiheft, 26.4.) ISSN 0018-2656. ‣ Collection of essays about relations between historical writing and history and meaning of historical truth in light of recent narrativist, structuralist, poststructuralist, and postmodernist theories. [AT]

1.353 Brian Stock. *Listening for the text: on the uses of the past.* Baltimore: Johns Hopkins University Press, 1990. ISBN 0-8018-3903-3. ‣ Collection of theoretical articles on relationship of literary theory to historiography and social history and case studies of textual communities. Acknowledges value of linguistic approaches without making history exclusively textual. [RTV]

1.354 Paul Veyne. *Writing history: essay on historical epistemology.* Mina Moore-Rinvolucri, trans. Middletown, Conn.: Wesleyan University Press, 1984. ISBN 0-8195-5067-1 (cl), 0-8195-6076-6 (pbk). ‣ Deflates any scientific pretensions of history, which has neither laws nor methods. Practice of history more difficult than it seems, as broad historical culture required for any success. Quirky, funny; eccentric translation. [RTV]

1.355 Elazar Weinryb. "'If we write novels so, how shall we write history?'" *Clio* 17.3 (1988) 265–81. ISSN 0884-2043. ‣ Ricoeur's games with time (1.329) are constantly played in historiography as in fiction: prolepsis, flashbacks, repetitions, accelerations, and decelerations. Concludes formal elements of writing cannot distinguish histories from novels. [RTV]

1.356 Robert Young. *White mythologies: writing history and the West.* New York: Routledge, 1990. ISBN 0-415-05371-4 (cl), 0-415-05372-2 (pbk). ‣ Unusually lucid poststructuralist discussion of theory and history in French and French-inspired contemporary writers. Opposition between terms dissolved; colonialism key to analysis. [RTV]

1.357 Perez Zagorin. "Historiography and postmodernism: reconsiderations." *History and theory* 29.3 (1990) 263–74. ISSN 0018-2656. ‣ Ankersmit's postmodernist view (1.336) contravenes feelings historians have about their discipline. Treating history aesthetically severs its connection with past reality. Reply by Ankersmit in same issue (pp. 275–96). [RTV]

Objectivity and Relativism

1.358 Carl L. Becker. *Everyman his own historian: essays on history and politics.* Chicago: Quadrangle, 1966. ‣ Famous title essay demonstrates historical practices in everyday life and power of everyday life to influence historical perspectives; also remarkable fictive essay on "the spirit of '76" and subjects as disparate as Marxism and Kansas. [RTV]

1.359 William H. Dray. *On history and philosophers of history.* New York: Brill, 1989. ISBN 90-04-09000-2, ISSN 0922-6001. ‣ Distinguished by attention to topics important to historians (point of view, importance of topic, value judgments, colligation) but usually slighted by philosophers. New papers on realism and presentism. Precise, sensible work. [RTV]

1.360 W. J. van der Dussen and Lionel Rubinoff, eds. *Objectivity, method, and point of view: essays in the philosophy of history.* New York: Brill, 1991. ISBN 90-04-09411-3, ISSN 0922-6001. ‣ Especially valuable in this collection are Christianson on patterns of historical conceptualization, Krausz on ontology in historical practice, Pompa on values and history, and Dray's comments on each essay. [RTV]

1.361 J. L. Gorman. "Objectivity and truth in history." *Inquiry* 17 (1974) 373–97. ISSN 0020-174X. ‣ Ingenious example shows account riddled with factual errors is more objective than one with only true statements tendentiously chosen. Objectivity is a matter of selectivity; rational standards of relevance essential. [RTV]

1.362 Thomas L. Haskell. "Objectivity is not neutrality: rhetoric

vs. practice in Peter Novick's *That Noble Dream.*" *History and theory* 29.2 (1990) 129–57. ISSN 0018-2656. ‣ Novick 1.369 demonstrates objectivity is detachment while denying its possibility. Goal of objectivity allows historians to produce criteria for evaluating historical accounts without withdrawing from life. [RTV]

1.363 John Higham. "Beyond consensus: the historian as moral critic." *American historical review* 67 (1962) 609–25. ISSN 0002-8762. ‣ Influential critique of pragmatic progressive and consensus schools of American historians; calls for renewal of moral passion among historians, appraising quality of life and particular choices by historical actors. [RTV]

1.364 Maurice Mandelbaum. *Philosophy, history, and the sciences: selected critical essays.* Baltimore: Johns Hopkins University Press, 1984. ISBN 0-8018-3112-1. ‣ Sections 2 and 4 devoted to methodology and interpretation of history, defending objectivity against rhetorical relativism and proposing sensible methodological rules for conducting intellectual history. [AT]

1.365 Maurice Mandelbaum. *The problem of historical knowledge: an answer to relativism.* 1938 ed. New York: Harper & Row, 1967. ‣ Pioneering study. First part confronts relativist and counterrelativist theorists; arguments of latter rejected, but relativism judged to be self-refuting and wrong in believing selection of facts entails value judgments. [RTV]

1.366 John T. Marcus. *Sub specie historiae: essays in the manifestation of historical and moral consciousness.* Cranbury, N.J.: Associated University Presses, 1980. ISBN 0-8386-2057-4. ‣ Modest attempt to reconnect our sense of history and moral vision, not to support any particular values, but to preserve moral sensibility. Draws on Chinese and Indian materials as well as Western. [RTV]

1.367 Wolfgang J. Mommsen. "Social conditioning and social relevance of historical judgments." In *Historical consciousness and political action: essays.* Robert Kimber and Rita Kimber, trans., pp. 19–35. Middletown, Conn.: Wesleyan University Press, 1978. (*History and theory*, Beiheft, 17.) ISSN 0018-2656. ‣ Vigorous defense of historical accounts as subjective and value-dependent; desirable because this is a necessary condition for full-blooded, interesting historical judgments and perspectives. [AT]

1.368 Terrence Murphy. "Lord Acton and the question of moral judgments in history: the development of his position." *Catholic historical review* 70.2 (1984) 225–50. ISSN 0008-8080. ‣ Usefully traces how Acton, believing power tended to corrupt, came to judge individuals by severe and unchanging moral standards, especially seeking examples of corruption and persecution by popes and saints. [RTV]

1.369 Peter Novick. *That noble dream: the "objectivity question" and the American historical profession.* New York: Cambridge University Press, 1988. ISBN 0-521-34328-3 (cl), 0-521-35745-4 (pbk). ‣ Excellent history of conceptions of objectivity since 1884 by American professional historians, revealing them to be usually inept theorizers. Treats objectivity as not only contested but essentially meaningless predicate. [RTV]

1.370 Adrian Oldfield. "Moral judgments in history." *History and theory* 20.3 (1981) 260–77. ISSN 0018-2656. ‣ Historians who deny they should make moral judgments have failed to distinguish moral from other sorts of judgments. Moral interpretation may aid understanding past, and historians' duty to educate must include moral issues. [RTV]

1.371 *The ontology of history.* LaSalle, Ill.: Hegeler Institute, 1991. (Monist, 74.) ISSN 0026-9662. ‣ Particularly interesting are articles by Martin on intelligibility, Mathien on moral judgments, and Flynn on Michel Foucault's conception of history. [RTV]

1.372 Hilary Putnam. "Reason and history." In *Reason, truth, and history,* pp. 150–73. New York: Cambridge University Press, 1981. ISBN 0-521-23035-7 (cl), 0-521-29776-1 (pbk). ‣ Cogent philosophical defense of possibility of rational moral choices and exposure of self-refuting character of total relativism. [RTV]

1.373 Adam Schaff. *History and truth.* New York: Pergamon, 1976. ISBN 0-08-020579-8 (cl), 0-08-020595-X (flexi). ▸ Nondogmatic Marxist explores why historians have different visions of same facts. Historians can achieve truth although their class position always influences them. [AT]

1.374 Bernard W. Sheehan. "The problem of moral judgments in history." *South Atlantic quarterly* 84.1 (1985) 37–50. ISSN 0038-2876. ▸ Making moral judgments essential, but risky; guiding principle should be "even erroneous conscience binds"—past agents can only be judged by moral standards of their culture. To think otherwise entails culture-denying atomism. [RTV]

1.375 Alfred Stern. *Philosophy of history and the problem of values.* The Hague: Mouton, 1962. ▸ Most thorough exploration of problem; takes basically historicist stance (moral judgments impermissible because no absolute criteria exist) but defends judgments of importance. Historians should judge as best they can though future ages will differ. [RTV]

1.376 Max Weber. "Science as a vocation." In *From Max Weber: essays in sociology.* Rev. ed. Hans H. Gerth and C. Wright Mills, eds. and trans., pp. 129–56. London: Routledge, 1991. ISBN 0-415-06056-7. ▸ Classic statement of ideal of value-free social science, not so much argued for as invoked. Valuable insights into German and American academic careers. [RTV]

THE BRANCHES OF HISTORY

Introductions

1.377 Juliet Gardiner, ed. *What is history today?* Atlantic Highlands, N.J.: Humanities International, 1988. ISBN 0-391-03569-X (cl), 0-391-03570-3 (pbk). ▸ Brief statements by practitioners of various kinds of history with suggestions for further reading (mostly substantive). Brevity allows little argumentation, but breadth of contributors illustrates pluralism in historiography today. [RTV]

Comparative History

1.378 Marc Bloch. "Toward a comparative history of European societies." In *Enterprise and secular change: readings in economic history.* Frederic Chapin Lane, ed., pp. 494–521. Homewood, Ill.: Irwin, 1953. ▸ Classic manifesto. Comparison no panacea, but valuable between unrelated societies and especially in related ones to reveal and show causes of similar developments and explain different developments from similar origins. [RTV]

1.379 Raymond Grew. "The case for comparing histories." *American historical review* 85.3 (1980) 763–78. ISSN 0002-8762. ▸ Unusual empirical analysis of 500 manuscripts submitted to *Comparative Studies* reveals new subjects opened by comparative studies. Intersection of social structure and culture promising area; comparison facilitated by developed theories. [RTV]

1.380 Jürgen Habermas. "History and evolution." David J. Parent, trans. *Telos* 39 (1979) 5–44. ISSN 0090-6514. ▸ Theory of social evolution cannot be combined with history writing, which is different from research and which must assume narrative form; can be used, however, to evaluate competing theories in same phenomenal field. [RTV]

1.381 Alette Olin Hill and Boyd H. Hill, Jr. "AHR forum: Marc Bloch and comparative history." William H. Sewell, Jr., and Sylvia L. Thrupp, respondents. *American historical review* 85.4 (1980) 828–53. ISSN 0002-8762. ▸ Bloch drew inspiration from comparative linguistics, only partly understood. Comparisons should be among all comparable units, not only two. Objections: historians should not try to reconstruct original society; languages and societies differ too much. [RTV]

1.382 William H. Sewell, Jr. "Marc Bloch and the logic of comparative history." *History and theory* 6.2 (1967) 208–18. ISSN 0018-2656. ▸ Best analysis. Comparative history tests whether association of phenomena and antecedent conditions usual or exceptional. Units compared can be any social systems, not necessarily proximate in time or space. Method only tests, not suggests, hypotheses. [RTV]

1.383 Theda Skocpol and Margaret Somers. "The uses of comparative history in macrosocial inquiry." *Comparative studies in society and history* 22.2 (1980) 174–97. ISSN 0010-4175. ▸ Previous discussions have collapsed comparative history into single methodological logic, but there are three complementary ones: macro-causal analysis, parallel demonstration of theory, and contrast of contexts. Examples of each discussed. Valuable sociological perspectives. [RTV]

1.384 Peter J. Taylor. "The poverty of international comparisons: some methodological lessons from world-systems analysis." *Studies in comparative international development* 22.1 (1987) 12–39. ISSN 0039-3606. ▸ Quantitative comparisons of democracy and war have been trivial (no significant correlations of propensity to war with anything else have been found). More significant results demand consideration of systems, not isolated units. [RTV]

1.385 Frederick J. Teggart. *Rome and China: a study of correlations in historical events.* 1939 ed. Westport, Conn.: Greenwood, 1983. ISBN 0-313-24061-2. ▸ Pioneering attempt at scientific history: comparison of Roman and Chinese history between 58 BCE and 107 CE shows correlations between wars and barbarian incursions. Attempt to establish cause of correlations less successful. [RTV]

1.386 Frederick J. Teggart. *Theory and processes of history.* 1941 ed. Berkeley: University of California Press, 1977. ISBN 0-520-03176-8 (pbk). ▸ Seldom-heeded call for historians to cease writing mere narratives and turn their study into real science. This would inevitably lead to making history comparative in method and worldwide in scope. [RTV]

1.387 Charles Tilly. *Big structures, large processes, huge comparisons.* New York: Russell Sage Foundation, 1984. ISBN 0-87154-879-8. ▸ Breezy style, serious content. Logic of comparisons; criticizes "pernicious principles" derived from nineteenth-century bourgeois thought, hypostatizing society, social change through stages, mental events causing social behavior, differentiation leading to advancement, and disorder through rapid social change. [RTV]

1.388 A. A. Van den Braembussche. "Historical explanation and comparative method: towards a theory of the history of society." *History and theory* 28.1 (1989) 1–24. ISSN 0018-2656. ▸ Supports pragmatic philosophy of history focusing on growth of historical scholarship; thus plurality of shades of meaning possible in historical explanation and dichotomy between global and particular cannot be sustained. [RTV]

Economic History

1.389 Ralph L. Andreano, ed. *The new economic history: recent papers on methodology.* New York: Wiley, 1970. ISBN 0-471-02902-5 (cl), 0-471-02903-3 (pbk). ▸ Seven articles give good sampling of viewpoints; some introduce then-new approaches of retrospective econometrics, which others criticize for application of irrelevant models to history and choice of subjects by accessibility of sources. [RTV]

1.390 D. C. Coleman. *History and the economic past: an account of the rise and decline of economic history in Britain.* New York: Oxford University Press, 1987. ISBN 0-19-828305-9. ▸ History of economic history in Britain and critique by prominent scholar. Laments institutional and pedagogical separation of economics from history: some economic historians innumerate, others achieve statistical rigor by leaving out institutional factors. [RTV]

1.391 Alexander J. Field, ed. *The future of economic history.* Boston: Nijhoff-Kluwer; distributed by Kluwer-Academic, 1987. ISBN 0-89838-217-3. ▸ Declares cliometrics revolution dead—partly through its own successes, partly because it depended on buoyant economy that will not return. Sees new direction away from *a priori* theoreticism, back to more descriptive tradition. [RTV]

1.392 Robert William Fogel. "Historiography and retrospective econometrics." *History and theory* 9.3 (1970) 245–64. ISSN 0018-2656. ▸ Survey of range of cliometric studies and their special problems. Counterfactuals essential if history to have explanatory power; only real problem they pose is determining correct descriptive equation. [RTV]

1.393 Robert William Fogel. *Railroads and American economic growth: essays in econometric history.* 1964 ed. Baltimore: Johns Hopkins University Press, 1970. ISBN 0-8018-0201-6 (cl), 0-8018-1148-1 (pbk). ▸ Classic case study in retrospective econometrics: what would United States Gross National Product have been in 1890 without railroads? (Answer: almost the same.) Based on Hempelian model of explanation (in Gardiner 1.54) with elaborate computations of counterfactual railroadless United States. [RTV]

1.394 O. F. Hamouda and B. B. Price. *Verification in economics and history: a sequel to "scientifization."* New York: Routledge, 1991. ISBN 0-415-05336-6. ▸ Attacks notion that economic or historical phenomena can only be explained by comparing quantifiable theory with facts—which are themselves theory-laden. History not determined, so causal explanation through laws often inappropriate. [RTV]

1.395 Peter D. McClelland. *Causal explanation and model building in history, economics, and the new economic history.* Ithaca, N.Y.: Cornell University Press, 1975. ISBN 0-8014-0929-2. ▸ Excellent treatment of logic and accomplishments of new economic history, analysis of short-run patterns of undramatic change. Discussion of models (Weber unaccountably omitted) and causal explanation less satisfactory. [AT]

1.396 Pierre Vilar. "Pour une meilleure compréhension entre économistes et historiens: 'histoire quantitative' ou économétrie retrospective?" *Revue historique* 233.2 (1965) 293–312. ISSN 0035-3264. ▸ Leading French economic historian responds to claim that history is ancillary to economics. Much of retrospective econometrics hindered by uncertain data; history as necessary for it as vice versa. [RTV]

History of the Family

1.397 John Demos. "Digging up family history: myths, realities, and works in progress." In *Past, present, and personal: the family and the life course in American history*, pp. 3–23. New York: Oxford University Press, 1986. ISBN 0-19-503777-4. ▸ Nontechnical introduction to history of the family, using mostly American scholarship. Discusses demography, family structure, life cycle, and emotions in the past, illustrated by episodes from author's career. [RTV]

1.398 "Family history at the crossroads: linking familial and historical change." *Journal of family history* 12.1–3 (1987) 263–330. ISSN 0363-1990. ▸ Valuable articles by Laslett, Wheaton, and Charles and Louise Tilly explore relations between family history, women's history, and French and American social history. Attacks modernization theory of family history. [RTV]

1.399 Rayna Rapp, Ellen Ross, and Renate Bridenthal. "Examining family history." *Feminist studies* 5.1 (1979) 174–200. ISSN 0046-3663. ▸ Three critiques focusing on relationship of family to

wider society. Contends family one mode of social reproduction (among others). Argues social theories (role theory), social dynamics (consensus within families), and emotional isolation of women have obscured women's position. [RTV]

Demographic History

1.400 David Coleman and Roger Schofield, eds. *The state of population theory: forward from Malthus.* New York: Blackwell, 1986. ISBN 0-631-13975-3. ▸ Particularly interesting articles on Malthus by Wrigley and Stone, and good appraisal of state of population theory by editors, situating present and suggesting future direction of demographic history. [RTV]

1.401 Thomas Henry Hollingsworth. *Historical demography.* New York: Cambridge University Press for Sources of History, 1976. ISBN 0-521-21454-8 (cl), 0-521-29154-2 (pbk). ▸ Cross-cultural survey of evidence available to demographic historians and advantages, as well as perils, of using it. Also gives clear definitions of basic demographic vocabulary. [RTV]

1.402 Kenneth W. Wachter, Peter Laslett, and Eugene A. Hammel. *Statistical studies of historical social structure.* New York: Academic Press, 1978. ISBN 0-12-729150-4. ▸ Collection of computerized simulations dealing with various questions about household and population structure. Valuable suggestions on how typicality of randomly surviving documents can be assessed through simulation. [RTV]

1.403 J. Dennis Willigan and Katherine A. Lynch. *Sources and methods of historical demography.* New York: Academic Press, 1982. ISBN 0-12-757020-9 (cl), 0-12-757022-5 (pbk). ▸ Brief history of field, extensive guide to sources, including non-Western ones; techniques of analysis, statistical tools, and major interpretive schemes, including relationship of historical demography to total history. [RTV]

Social History

1.404 Philip Abrams. *Historical sociology.* Ithaca, N.Y.: Cornell University Press, 1982. ISBN 0-8014-1578-0 (cl), 0-8014-9243-2 (pbk). ▸ Useful theoretical essays and historical chapters. Argues not just for reciprocal influences, but for abolition of disciplinary boundaries; resulting unified discipline of historical sociology would grapple with problem of human agency. [RTV]

1.405 Peter Burke. *History and social theory.* Ithaca, N.Y.: Cornell University Press, 1992. ISBN 0-8014-2861-0 (cl), 0-8014-8100-7 (pbk). ▸ Genial and accessible though bland introduction not just to great social theorists, but also cultural theory, psychology, women's history, "new historicism" in literary criticism, and rhetoric of historiography. [RTV]

1.406 Geoff Eley and Keith Nield. "Why does social history ignore politics?" *Social history* 5.1 (1980) 249–71. ISSN 0307-1022. ▸ Penetrating comparative study of labor history in Britain and Germany, warning against spread of British overemphasis of culture at expense of politics. Each author takes history of labor movement of other as normative. [RTV]

1.407 James A. Henretta. "Social history as lived and written." Darrett B. Rutman and Robert F. Berkhofer, Jr., Commentators. *American historical review* 84.5 (1979) 1293–1333. ISSN 0002-8762. ▸ Compares American to Annales and English Marxist social history to bring it greater theoretical coherence. French and British models cannot simply be imitated, since American culture has no mass socialist tradition or grounds for pessimism. [RTV]

1.408 *History and sociology.* London: Routledge & Kegan Paul, 1976. (*British journal of sociology*, 27.) ISSN 0007-1315. ▸ Good contributions by Jones, Laslett, Wallerstein, Thompson, and others. Easy accommodation of disciplines discounted; history borrows from sociology only if history (wrongly) conceived as untheoretical. [RTV]

1.409 "History and the social sciences: progress and prospects." *American behavioral scientist* 21 (1977). ISSN 0002-7642. ▸ Consideration of whether history has (or can) become social science from specialists in variety of disciplines. Good treatment of methodologies, though seldom aware of philosophical critiques of logical empiricism or positivism. [RTV]

1.410 Tony Judt. "A clown in regal purple: social history and the historians." *History workshop* 7 (1979) 64–94. ISSN 0309-2984. ▸ Blunt assault on contemporary American (and some French) social history for neglect of politics and failure to focus on significant problems, thus drifting into fetishism of method without theory. [RTV]

1.411 Jacques Le Goff and Pierre Nora, eds. *Constructing the past: essays in historical methodology.* Colin Lucas, Introduction. David Denby and Martin Thom, trans. Cambridge: Cambridge University Press, 1985. ISBN 0-521-25976-2. ▸ Best introduction to new social history French-style, chiefly but not exclusively from Annales writers. Articles illustrate methods, while introduction emphasizes politics of French historical profession. [RTV]

1.412 Seymour Martin Lipset and Richard Hofstadter, eds. *Sociology and history: methods.* New York: Basic Books, 1968. ▸ Volume exemplifies various quantitative techniques in essays on American social, political, and religious history following three not particularly penetrating methodological essays on relationships between disciplines. [RTV]

1.413 Christopher Lloyd. *Explanation in social history.* New York: Blackwell, 1986. ISBN 0-631-13113-2. ▸ Exhaustive overview of theories of explanation to bring history into unified social science. Explanation must be causal and modeled on natural sciences; history must allow for both agency and institutional constraints. [RTV]

1.414 Dennis Smith. "Social history and sociology—more than just good friends." *Sociological review,* n.s. 1 (1982) 286–308. ISSN 0038-0261. ▸ Cheerful account of how convergence of two fields has been obscured by recent preoccupation with structuralism. Historians now less prone to ad hoc appropriations of decontextualized theory; some sociologists recognize problems of analyzing historical data. [RTV]

1.415 Peter N. Stearns. "Social history and history: a progress report." *Journal of social history* 19.2 (1985) 319–34. ISSN 0022-4529. ▸ Survey of recent developments and response to critics such as Elton 1.8, Himmelfarb 1.27, and Judt 1.410. Suggests areas—world, diplomatic, and military history—to be reexamined if social historians assume responsibility for whole discipline. [RTV]

1.416 Arthur L. Stinchcombe. *Theoretical methods in social history.* New York: Academic Press, 1978. ISBN 0-12-672250-1. ▸ Sharp, iconoclastic argument that social theory not applicable to historical materials, but history used to develop theory. Progress is development of deep analogies between events and institutions; immersion in historical facts, not broadest generalizations, required. [RTV]

1.417 Richard T. Vann. "The rhetoric of social history." *Journal of social history* 10 (1976) 221–36. ISSN 0022-4529. ▸ Applies traditional rhetorical categories to social histories, taking up rhetoric of graphics and statistical tables as well as characteristic plot structures. [RTV]

1.418 Olivier Zunz, ed. *Reliving the past: the worlds of social history.* Chapel Hill: University of North Carolina Press, 1985. ISBN 0-8078-1658-2 (cl), 0-8078-4137-4 (pbk). ▸ Useful collected articles expanding scope of social history beyond United States and Europe. Writers on Latin American, Kenyan, and Chinese social

history question whether categories developed in Europe or United States are appropriate. [RTV]

Cultural History

1.419 Roger Chartier. *Cultural history: between practices and representations.* Lydia G. Cochrane, trans. Ithaca, N.Y.: Cornell University Press, 1988. ISBN 0-8014-2223-X. ▸ Collected essays giving critical exposition of *histoire des mentalités*, distinguishing it from varieties of intellectual history. Emphasis on French scholarship, but well acquainted with American and German. [RTV]

1.420 Clifford Geertz. *The interpretation of cultures: selected essays.* New York: Basic Books, 1973. ISBN 0-465-03425-X (cl), 0-465-09719-7 (pbk). ▸ First and last of these selected essays, "Thick Description" and "Balinese Cock Fight," have been enormously influential on American cultural historians in emphasizing cultural semantics or how cultures symbolize themselves. [RTV]

1.421 Clifford Geertz. *Local knowledge: further essays in interpretive anthropology.* New York: Basic Books, 1983. ISBN 0-465-04158-2. ▸ Proposes hermeneutic circle as essential in understanding cultures; this means continual alternation between examining general form of a people's life and specific vehicles in which that form is embodied. [RTV]

1.422 Carlo Ginzburg. *Clues, myths, and historical method.* John Tedeschi and Anne C. Tedeschi, trans. Baltimore: Johns Hopkins University Press, 1989. ISBN 0-8018-3458-9. ▸ Hugely, sometimes wearyingly, erudite collected essays, but out of welter of detail emerges fascinating meditation on how to move from detail (e.g., iconography, fingerprints) to deeper morphological structures of consciousness. [RTV]

1.423 Lynn Hunt, ed. *The new cultural history: essays.* Berkeley: University of California Press, 1989. ISBN 0-520-06428-3 (cl), 0-520-06429-1 (pbk). ▸ Informative introduction and articles illustrating marriage of new literary techniques and approaches to cultures treated as complex texts. Half critiques of leading theorists, half case studies. [RTV]

1.424 T. J. Jackson Lears. "The concept of cultural hegemony: problems and possibilities." *American historical review* 90.3 (1985) 567–93. ISSN 0002-8762. ▸ Sympathetic examination of Antonio Gramsci's concept as applied to American history. Stresses Gramsci's openness to concrete details of social life. Hegemony not just social control; hegemonic institutions have utopian possibilities. [RTV]

Intellectual History

1.425 George Boas. *The history of ideas: an introduction.* New York: Scribner's, 1969. ▸ Lucid discussion of nature of ideas, why they change (mostly for emotional reasons, although other sources of new ideas are suggested), role of metaphor, social contexts of ideas, and periodization. [RTV]

1.426 Thomas Bredsdorff. "Lovejoy's idea of 'idea.'" *New literary history* 8.2 (1977) 1954–211. ISSN 0028-6087. ▸ Thoroughgoing reconstruction and convincing reformulation of Lovejoy's principles (1.434) in light of his practice, providing missing causal claim: ideas are caused by other ideas. [RTV]

1.427 André Burguière. "The fate of the history of *mentalités* in the Annales." *Comparative studies in society and history* 24.3 (1982) 424–37. ISSN 0010-4175. ▸ Marc Bloch and Lucien Febvre conceived mentalities differently: for Bloch, structures of (largely unconscious) collective attitudes; for Febvre, configurations of individual thought. Move toward anthropological history has caused Bloch's view to prevail. [RTV]

1.428 John Patrick Diggins. "The oyster and the pearl: the problem of contextualism in intellectual history." *History and theory* 23.2 (1984) 151–69. ISSN 0018-2656. ‣ Presents paradoxical historiographical position: despite current orthodoxy of contextualism, text may arise more from internal reflection than social conditioning; depth of knowledge of some thinkers surpasses available epistemology or paradigms of discourse. [RTV]

1.429 Michael A. Gismondi. "'The gift of theory': a critique of the *Histoire des mentalités*." *Social history* 10.2 (1985) 211–30. ISSN 0307-1022. ‣ Criticizes Annales historians of mentalities for diminishing rational agency in history, importing functionalist modernization theories, and obscuring differences in attitudes of different social classes. [RTV]

1.430 Donald R. Kelley, ed. *The history of ideas: canon and variations*. Rochester, N.Y.: University of Rochester Press, 1990. ISBN 1-878822-00-4. ‣ Much about Lovejoy; various useful articles defining present state of history of ideas (especially by Krieger) and calling for various improvements (such as reliance on semantics suggested by Kvastad). [RTV]

1.431 Reinhart Koselleck. *Futures past: on the semantics of historical time*. Keith Tribe, trans. Boston: MIT Press, 1985. ISBN 0-262-11100-4. ‣ Rich display of results achievable by history of ideas in hands of a master. Traces change over time in meaning of important concepts for historiography and changing conceptions of time itself. [RTV]

1.432 Dominick LaCapra. *Rethinking intellectual history: texts, contexts, language*. Ithaca, N.Y.: Cornell University Press, 1983. ISBN 0-8014-1587-X (cl), 0-8014-9886-4 (pbk). ‣ Collected essays advocating and illustrating dialogical alternative to documentary approach, which stresses performative analysis of relationship between language of text and that of context in leading modern thinkers. Difficult style but worth reader's effort. [RTV]

1.433 Dominick LaCapra and Steven L. Kaplan, eds. *Modern European intellectual history: reappraisals and new perspectives*. Ithaca, N.Y.: Cornell University Press, 1982. ISBN 0-8014-1470-9 (cl), 0-8014-9881-3 (pbk). ‣ Best introduction to theoretical challenges facing intellectual history from French structuralism and poststructuralism and German hermeneutics. Also readings of classic texts. [RTV]

1.434 Arthur O. Lovejoy. *The great chain of being: a study of the history of an idea*. 1936 ed. New York: Harper & Row, 1960. ‣ First chapter contains best statement of theory of unit ideas (plentitude, continuity, and gradation) as proper subject for history of ideas; remainder is classic exhibition of his method at work. Surprisingly undated. [RTV]

1.435 Leo Strauss. *Persecution and the art of writing*. 1952 ed. Chicago: University of Chicago Press, 1988. ISBN 0-226-77711-1 (pbk). ‣ Provocative argument that virtually all philosophers had reason to fear if their doctrines were unambiguously set forth; hence careful study of form and contradictions is needed for their true (esoteric) meaning to emerge. [RTV]

1.436 James Tully, ed. *Meaning and context: Quentin Skinner and his critics*. Princeton: Princeton University Press, 1988. ISBN 0-691-07796-7 (cl), 0-691-02301-8 (pbk). ‣ Reprints five Skinner articles, articulating influential claim that historians must confine themselves to recovering what ideas meant to their authors. Seven critiques and Skinner's rejoinder. Lively collection on fundamental methodological issue. [RTV]

1.437 W. H. Walsh. "The causation of ideas." *History and theory* 14.2 (1975) 186–99. ISSN 0018-2656. ‣ Thoughtful philosophical analysis of important problem. Only rough causal laws achievable, linking acknowledged (or more often unacknowledged) clusters of assumptions resulting from social conditions with types of states of mind. [RTV]

History of the Arts

1.438 Svetlana Alpers. "Is art history?" *Daedalus* 106.3 (1977) 1–13. ISSN 0011-5266. ‣ Masterly survey of state of the field, focusing especially on works placing individual artworks in historical context. Recommends directions for further research. [RTV]

1.439 Timothy Bahti. *Allegories of history: literary historiography after Hegel*. Baltimore: Johns Hopkins University Press, 1992. ISBN 0-8018-4342-1. ‣ Antihistorical historiography; after describing nineteenth-century German historical profession, discusses historicism in its various guises and dreams of "the unknown nothing of literature's being known otherwise" than historically. [RTV]

1.440 Hans Belting. *The end of the history of art?* Christopher S. Wood, trans. Chicago: University of Chicago Press, 1987. ISBN 0-226-04217-0. ‣ Stimulating essay that briefly lays out issues in "crisis" in art history: what constitutes artwork, relation of art to its history, availability of any master narrative to comprehend both modern and traditional, and place of iconology and social history. [RTV]

1.441 Rosalie L. Colie. "Literature and history." In *Relations of literary study: essays on interdisciplinary contributions*. James Thorpe, ed., pp. 1–26. New York: Modern Language Association of America, 1967. ‣ Lucid, learned discussion of history as ancillary to literary understanding: style, originality, genre, and context. Also evaluates contributions of many intellectual histories to understanding of English Renaissance literature. [RTV]

1.442 *Critical challenges: the Bellagio symposium*. Charlottesville: University Press of Virginia, 1975. (*New literary history*, 7.) ISSN 0028-6087. ‣ Five essays on literary history, dealing with methodology, conceptualization of change (White), and interpretation (Starobinski and Skinner). [RTV]

1.443 Ernst H. Gombrich. *Ideals and idols: essays on values in history and in art*. Oxford: Phaidon, 1979. ISBN 0-7148-2009-1. ‣ Influential critiques; like Popper 1.169, attacks intellectual history and attempts to link art with a *Zeitgeist*; defends canons in art and claims judgments of artistic value are true, not mere statements of preferences. [RTV]

1.444 Robert Hodge. *Literature as discourse: textual strategies in English and history*. Cambridge: Polity, 1990. ISBN 0-7456-0479-X. ‣ Good introduction to "social semiotics" or cultural production of meaning. Mostly addressed to students of English, but last two chapters address realistic fictions as historical sources and desired interpenetration of history and literature. [RTV]

1.445 Michael Ann Holly. *Panofsky and the foundation of art history*. Ithaca, N.Y.: Cornell University Press, 1984. ISBN 0-8014-1614-0. ‣ Examines art historical practice through analysis of early essays of probably most influential twentieth-century figure. Favored technique, iconology, should go beyond iconography to reveal worldview of period. [RTV]

1.446 George Kubler. *The shape of time: remarks on the history of things*. New Haven: Yale University Press, 1962. ISBN 0-300-00643-8 (cl), 0-300-00144-4 (pbk). ‣ Provocative, aphoristic essay situating art history in "history of things." Fascinating thoughts on periodization and on different durations within history. Advocates understanding historical sequences of continuous change rather than focusing on "styles." [RTV]

1.447 John E. O'Connor, ed. *Image as artifact: the historical analysis of film and television*. Malabar, Fla.: Krieger, 1990. ISBN 0-89464-312-6 (cl), 0-89464-313-4 (pbk). ‣ Useful compendium with proposed methodology for gathering information about moving-image documents: film and television as historical representations, as evidence for social historians, and as primary sources. Includes case study and primer of visual language. [RTV]

1.448 Donald Preziosi. *Rethinking art history: meditations on a coy science.* New Haven: Yale University Press, 1989. ISBN 0-300-04462-3. ▸ Set of interlinked essays on "crisis" in the discipline; particularly insightful chapters on impact of photography for art historians, social history of art, and problem of origins of art. [RTV]

1.449 Mark Roskill. *What is art history?* 2d ed. Amherst: University of Massachusetts Press, 1989. ISBN 0-87023-675-X. ▸ Introduction via series of art historical problems: attribution, collaboration, modes of display, iconography, detection of forgery, interpretation of nonrepresentational art. Lucid, unpretentious writing. [RTV]

1.450 Siegfried J. Schmidt. "Problems of empirical research in literary history: notes on the observation problem in literary science." *New literary history* 8.2 (1977) 213–23. ISSN 0028-6087. ▸ Challenging project for literary science against more customary hermeneutics. It deals not with isolated texts but with literary communication and is problem oriented, treating only questions potentially soluble by observation. [RTV]

1.451 Paul Smith, ed. *The historian and film.* New York: Cambridge University Press, 1976. ISBN 0-521-20992-7. ▸ Pathbreaking set of essays; mostly English contributors, but France, United States, and Netherlands also represented. Films (including newsreels) as evidence, historians as filmmakers, and films in teaching among topics discussed. [RTV]

1.452 R. H. Tawney. "Social history and literature." In *The radical tradition: twelve essays on politics, education, and literature.* Rita Hinden, ed., pp. 183–209. New York: Pantheon, 1964. ▸ Although stating "we know next to nothing" about relationships of economic conditions to artistic accomplishments, gives a lively background to Shakespearean and romantic England, written with customary elegance. [RTV]

1.453 Brook Thomas. *The new historicism and other old-fashioned topics.* Princeton: Princeton University Press, 1991. ISBN 0-691-06893-3 (cl), 0-691-01507-4 (pbk). ▸ Collected essays offering sympathetic although critical account, especially interesting in exploring connections of new to old historicism and to its political context. [RTV]

1.454 Giorgio Vasari. *The lives of the artists.* Julia Conaway Bondanella and Peter Bondanella, trans. New York: Oxford University Press, 1991. ISBN 0-19-281754-X. ▸ Foundational text for art history; arrangement of biographies presents progress in art as increasing approximation of skills in representing nature achieved by classical artists. [RTV]

1.455 H. Aram Veeser, ed. *The new historicism.* New York: Routledge, 1989. ISBN 0-415-90069-7 (cl), 0-415-90070-0 (pbk). ▸ Anthology of articles defending and debating important new approach to literary history which transgresses all boundaries in human sciences, treats noncanonical texts as seriously as classics, and emphasizes politics of literature. [RTV]

1.456 Geoffrey Waite. "Lenin in Las Meninas: an essay in historical-materialist vision." *History and theory* 25.2 (1986) 248–85. ISSN 0018-2656. ▸ Offbeat Marxist essay imagines Lenin's seeing the painting and noting abyss between culture and material conditions, emphasizing paradox of literary and art historians' *siglo d'oro* and decline in Spanish economy and political and social life. [RTV]

1.457 Heinrich Wölfflin. *Principles of art history: the problem of the development of style in later art.* Marie D. Hottinger, trans. New York: Dover, 1950. ▸ Most important for "categories of beholding": linear versus painterly; plane surface versus recessional depth; closed versus open form; multiple versus uniform unity; and absolute versus relative clarity. Formalistic but approaches theory of aesthetic reception. [RTV]

Psychohistory and Biography

1.458 James William Anderson. "The methodology of psychological biography." *Journal of interdisciplinary history* 11.3 (1981) 455–75. ISSN 0022-1953. ▸ Candidly faces weaknesses of psychobiography, defined as reductionism, inflated hopes, disparagement of subjects, anachronism of concepts, inadequate psychological theory, and absence of subject. Suggestions for and examples of remedies. [RTV]

1.459 Zevedei Barbu. *Problems of historical psychology.* 1960 ed. Westport, Conn.: Greenwood, 1976. ISBN 0-8371-8476-2. ▸ Unusual in being influenced by anthropology rather than psychoanalysis. Projects historical-social psychology discussing how historical circumstances affect perception, emotional climate, and national character (ancient Greek and English). [RTV]

1.460 Norman Oliver Brown. *Life against death: the psychoanalytical meaning of history.* 2d ed. Christopher Lasch, Introduction. Middletown, Conn.: Wesleyan University Press; distributed by Harper & Row, 1985. ISBN 0-8195-5148-1 (cl), 0-8195-6144-4 (pbk). ▸ Development of Freud's metahistorical works in radical direction, emphasizing irreducible opposition of Eros and Thanatos and suggesting salvation in abolition of repression and polymorphous perversity. Apollonian form, Dionysian contents. [RTV]

1.461 Richard L. Bushman. "On the uses of psychology: conflict and conciliation in Benjamin Franklin." *History and theory* 5.3 (1966) 227–40. ISSN 0018-2656. ▸ Psychology provides no source of automatic diagnosis, but can enhance historian's sensitivity to patterns of character. Brilliantly illustrated by Franklin's anxiety over getting supplies and skill in getting them while withdrawing from hostilities. [RTV]

1.462 Leon Edel. *Writing lives: principia biographica.* New York: Norton, 1984. ISBN 0-393-01882-2. ▸ Leading literary biographer ruminates on his craft, chiding fellow biographers for neglecting anthropology and psychoanalysis. Biographies should not be chronologically organized, but free to follow sinuosities of memory. [RTV]

1.463 Sigmund Freud. *Moses and monotheism.* 1939 ed. Katherine Jones, trans. New York: Vintage, 1967. ▸ Final development of Freud's speculations. Asserts Moses and monotheism were Egyptian, Hebrews killed Moses, Judaism was repressed memory of deed, Christianity admitted its deicide. [RTV]

1.464 Sigmund Freud. *Totem and taboo: resemblances between the psychic lives of savages and neurotics.* 1946 ed. A. A. Brill, trans. New York: Vintage, 1961. ▸ Pre–World War I exposition of Freud's psychohistorical universal history, based on claim that taboos and totemic animals can be explained by primal patricide and inherited mutual guilt of brothers who committed it. [RTV]

1.465 Peter Gay. *Freud for historians.* New York: Oxford University Press, 1985. ISBN 0-19-503586-0. ▸ Argues that historians should use psychoanalytic concepts (not just Freud). Case for scientific status of psychoanalysis unconvincing, but persuasive argument for insights technique offers. [RTV]

1.466 Peter Loewenberg. *Decoding the past: the psychohistorical approach.* New York: Knopf; distributed by Random House, 1983. ISBN 0-394-48152-6. ▸ After overview of psychohistory, presents remarkable psychoanalytic study of graduate school and academy, suggesting unconscious roots both of acceptance of and resistance to adopting psychoanalytic theories. [RTV]

1.467 Herbert Marcuse. *Eros and civilization: a philosophical inquiry into Freud.* Rev. ed. Boston: Beacon, 1974. ISBN 0-8070-1555-5 (pbk). ▸ Attempt to recover later, metahistorical Freud and its political import. Claims late capitalism exacts surplus repression and diffuses revolutionary energy with repressive desublimation. Profound sketch of how Marx might have read Freud. [RTV]

1.468 Bruce Mazlish. "What is psycho-history?" *Transactions of the Royal Historical Society*, Fifth series, 21 (1971) 79–99. ISSN 0-901050-05-9. ▸ Early, influential definition. Prefers "psychosocial" history, emphasizing psychology of social groups rather than biography. As example: proposes analysis of 1960s radical youth as traumatized by atomic arms race. [RTV]

1.469 David Novarr. *The lines of life: theories of biography, 1880–1970.* West Lafayette, Ind.: Purdue University Press, 1986. ISBN 0-911198-79-2. ▸ Essentially an annotated bibliography, thus good introduction to these theories, though sometimes frustrating because of brevity of treatment given even major figures. Largely concerned with literary biography. [RTV]

1.470 Philip Pomper. *The structure of mind in history: five major figures in psychohistory.* New York: Columbia University Press, 1985. ISBN 0-231-06064-5. ▸ Good comparative study of five psychohistorians—Freud, Erik Erikson, Herbert Marcuse, Norman Oliver Brown, and Robert J. Lifton—placing them in tradition of substantive philosophies of history. Each has distinctive architectonic of unconscious mind. [RTV]

1.471 William McKinley Runyan. *Life histories and psychobiography.* New York: Oxford University Press, 1982. ISBN 0-19-503189-x. ▸ Particularly valuable in confronting issue of alternate explanations of lives (e.g., why Van Gogh cut off his ear) and evaluating merits of case studies, idiographic methods, and those of psychohistory. [RTV]

1.472 David E. Stannard. *Shrinking history: on Freud and the failure of psychohistory.* New York: Oxford University Press, 1980. ISBN 0-19-502735-3. ▸ Fullest statement of antipsychohistory case. Musters familiar array of arguments against entire body of psychoanalytic theory; since it fails, psychohistory must also be misconceived. Explanation for historians' continued interest: they have been taken in. [RTV]

1.473 Cushing Strout. "Ego psychology and the historian." *History and theory* 7.3 (1968) 281–97. ISSN 0018-2656. ▸ Sensible advocacy of ego psychology as particularly useful for biography of creative and conflicted leaders. Phenomenologically descriptive rather than causally explanatory, it mediates between Freud's naturalism and Collingwood's idealism (1.280), relating conscious to unconscious motives. [RTV]

1.474 Fred Weinstein. *History and theory after the fall: an essay on interpretation.* Chicago: University of Chicago Press, 1990. ISBN 0-226-88606-9. ▸ Latest reappraisal of psychohistory and social theory in light of narrativist challenge to objectivity and great diversity in psychoanalytic theory. Concludes truthful interpretations can be achieved using latest conceptual tools. [RTV]

Women's History

1.475 Gisela Bock. "Women's history and gender history: aspects of an international debate." *Gender and history* 1.1 (1989) 7–30. ▸ Thoughtful appraisal emphasizing that not all women have same history (so intragender conflicts must be studied), gender must comprehend even what seems biological, and gender-encompassing rather than gender-neutral discourse needed. [RTV]

1.476 Berenice A. Carroll, ed. *Liberating women's history: theoretical and critical essays.* Urbana: University of Illinois Press, 1976. ISBN 0-252-00441-8 (cl), 0-252-00569-4 (pbk). ▸ Lengthy anthology with both substantive and theoretical articles and critiques of classics in women's history, representing good cross section of views at early stage of development of field. [RTV]

1.477 Elizabeth Fox-Genovese. "Placing women's history in

history." *New Left review* 33 (1982) 5–29. ISSN 0028-6060. ▸ Women's history more advanced in America than Europe, but lacks adequate theory. Warns against constructing alternate "herstory," reproducing women as "other," and ahistorical employment of patriarchy as a category. [RTV]

1.478 Joan Kelly. *Women, history, and theory: the essays of Joan Kelly.* 1984 ed. Chicago: University of Chicago Press, 1986. ISBN 0-226-43027-8 (cl, 1984), 0-226-43028-6 (pbk). ▸ Important theoretical essays tracing the consequences of making women central historical subjects. Reconceives social relations of the sexes, periodization, traditional Marxism, history of the family. [RTV]

1.479 Gerda Lerner. *The majority finds its past: placing women in history.* New York: Oxford University Press, 1979. ISBN 0-19-502597-0. ▸ Eight substantive and four programmatic essays, latter perhaps most valuable as benchmark to measure subsequent developments in field. Autobiographical introduction valuable contribution to history of historiography. [RTV]

1.480 Denise Riley. *"Am I that name?" Feminism and the category of "women" in history.* Minneapolis: University of Minnesota Press, 1988. ISBN 0-8166-1730-9 (cl), 0-8166-1731-7 (pbk). ▸ Examination of conditions in which "woman" and "women" become active and appropriate categories in history, illustrated by women's writing in early modern England and campaign for vote. [RTV]

1.481 Joan Wallach Scott. *Gender and the politics of history.* New York: Columbia University Press, 1988. ISBN 0-231-06554-x (cl), 0-231-06555-8 (pbk). ▸ Searching critique of women's history as incorporated in social history (thus occluding gender) or as "herstory" (marginalizing women). Argument for rethinking along poststructuralist lines strengthened by case studies, especially of Sears case. [RTV]

Political and Diplomatic History

1.482 William O. Aydelotte, ed. *The history of parliamentary behavior.* Princeton: Princeton University Press, 1977. ISBN 0-691-0524205. ▸ Articles show development of quantitative techniques for studying legislators' backgrounds and decision making. Methods range from simple tables and diagrams to complicated models and computer simulations. Lucid throughout. [LPG]

1.483 Lee Benson et al., eds. *American political behavior: historical essays and readings.* New York: Harper & Row, 1974. ISBN 0-06-040636-4. ▸ Collection of articles reviewing behavioral revolution in political historiography; asserts that history is a social science. Conceptual essays introduce each subject section; selected readings then demonstrate techniques in accessible fashion. [LPG]

1.484 Lee Benson, ed. and comp. *Toward the scientific study of history: selected essays of Lee Benson.* Philadelphia: Lippincott, 1972. ISBN 0-397-47265-x (cl), 0-397-47233-4 (pbk). ▸ Collection of essays by founding "new political historian" showing development of his thought. Argues consistently for system and logic in historical method. Thoughtful treatment of problems of verification, causation, and generalization. [LPG]

1.485 Allan G. Bogue. *Clio and the bitch goddess: quantification in American political history.* Beverly Hills, Calif.: Sage, 1983. ISBN 0-8039-2089-x (cl), 0-8039-2090-3 (pbk). ▸ Collection of essays, some previously published, providing periodic reappraisals of state of social science history. Focuses on development of institutional supports such as quantitative data archives and journals. Reads easily. [LPG]

1.486 Allan G. Bogue, ed. *Emerging theoretical models in social and political history.* Beverly Hills, Calif.: Sage, 1973. ISBN 0-8039-0321-9. ▸ Accessible collection of essays evaluating progress and problems of using models and theory in economic, political, and social history. Includes attempts at transnational model building. [LPG]

1.487 Gordon A. Craig. "The historian and the study of international relations." *American historical review* 88.1 (1983) 1–11. ISSN 0002-8762. ‣ Ponders neglected state of diplomatic history and advances suggestions for renaissance: greater use of theory (learned mainly from political science) and cultivation of style, given public's continued interest. [RTV]

1.488 Jorge I. Dominguez. "Consensus and divergence: the state of the literature on inter-American relations in the 1970s." *Latin American historical review* 13.1 (1978) 87–126. ISSN 0023-8791. ‣ Selective but broad examination of major trends in both United States and Latin American historiography dealing with 1970s. Offers critique of various methods of analysis used by scholars of region, e.g., liberal, strategic, dependency, bureaucratic, and political system perspectives. [GKP]

1.489 Ronald Dryer. "Perception of state-intervention in diplomatic history: a case for an interdisciplinary approach between history and political science." *Millennium* 12.3 (1983) 260–75. ISSN 0305-8298. ‣ Model interdisciplinary approach using perception theory as way to examine decision making by individuals, organizations, and states. [GKP]

1.490 Geoffrey R. Elton. *Political history: principles and practice.* New York: Basic Books, 1970. ISBN 0-465-05894-9. ‣ Vigorous defense of political history as story of power in society. Must learn from social history or history of law or ideas, but also preserve its distinctive set of questions and narrative structure. [RTV]

1.491 Michael G. Fry and Arthur N. Gilbert. "A historian and linkage politics: Arno Mayer." *International studies quarterly* 26.3 (1982) 425–44. ISSN 0020-8833. ‣ Favorable but thoughtful examination of Mayer's theories along with thoughtful examination of relationship between diplomatic history and internal social forces. [GKP]

1.492 Gerald K. Haines and J. Samuel Walker, eds. *American foreign relations: a historiographical review.* Westport, Conn.: Greenwood, 1981. ISBN 0-313-21061-6. ‣ Sixteen essays of varying quality that examine major approaches in United States foreign policy from revolutionary era to cold war. McMahon's essay on literature of United States relations with Asia particularly useful. [GKP]

1.493 Andreas Hillgruber. "Methodologie und Theorie der Geschichte der internationalen Beziehungen." *Geschichte in Wissenschaft und Unterricht* 27.4 (1976) 193–210. ISSN 0016-9056. ‣ Dated but useful essay comparing Soviet and Western historiography on such issues as primacy of internal policy, ideological discontinuity in foreign policy, international systems analysis, and nature of coexistence. [GKP]

1.494 Michael H. Hunt. "The long crisis in U.S. diplomatic history: coming to closure." *Diplomatic history* 16.2 (1992) 115–40. ISSN 0145-2096. ‣ Probing critique of realist, progressive, and comparative approaches to diplomatic history. Emphasizes need to continue multiarchival research and to take account of nongovernmental factors in shaping state relations and policy making. [GKP]

1.495 Akira Iriye. "Culture and power: international relations as intercultural relations." *Diplomatic history* 3.2 (1979) 115–28. ISSN 0145-2096. ‣ Influential statement urging cultural systems approach in study of international relations. Perceptive insights into how divergent cultural interpretations of power can influence foreign policy perceptions and actions of nations. [GKP]

1.496 Whittle Johnston. "E. H. Carr's theory of international relations: a critique." *Journal of politics* 29.4 (1967) 861–84. ISSN 0022-3816. ‣ Examines evolution of Carr's theories of history and international relations exposing tension between idealistic striv-

ing for conjuncture between reason and morality and his ultimate acceptance of relativist doctrine of harmony of interests. [CKF/ GKP]

1.497 Paul Gordon Lauren, ed. *Diplomacy: new approaches in history, theory, and policy.* New York: Free Press, 1979. ISBN 0-02-918070-8. ‣ Collected essays treating theory of diplomatic history, including comparative and quantitative methods, case studies, and relationship of history and policy making. Shows new thinking in supposedly old-fashioned branch of history. [RTV]

1.498 Seymour Martin Lipset, ed. *Politics and the social sciences.* New York: Oxford University Press, 1969. ‣ Survey of methodological, theoretical borrowings by political scientists from history, anthropology, sociology, economics, psychology, and statistics; two essays explicitly historical. Introductory text. [LPG]

1.499 Gerhard Loewenberg, Samuel C. Patterson, and Malcom E. Jewell, eds. *Handbook of legislative research.* Cambridge, Mass.: Harvard University Press, 1985. ISBN 0-674-37075-9. ‣ Collection of essays forming exhaustive "stock-taking" of research on legislatures, including institutional processes, legislators, and constituencies; two explicitly historical essays. Comparative approach nonetheless reflects emphasis in literature on American institutions. [LPG]

1.500 Charles S. Maier. "Marking time: the historiography of international relations." In *The past before us: contemporary historical writings in the United States.* Michael G. Kammen, ed., pp. 355–87. Ithaca, N.Y.: Cornell University Press, 1980. ISBN 0-8014-1224-2. ‣ Pessimistic assessment of literature and field arguing for international systems approach that takes into account such domestic variables as class, culture, and ethnicity. For rejoinders, see symposium in *Diplomatic History* 5.4 (1981) 353–82. [GKP]

1.501 Thomas G. Patterson et al. "A round table: explaining the history of American foreign relations." *Journal of American history* 77.1 (1990) 93–182. ISSN 0021-8723. ‣ Nine superb analytical essays examining major historiographical themes used by historians of American foreign policy. Essays by Rosenberg on gender and Immerman on psychology particularly informative. [GKP]

1.502 Giovanni Sartori. *Parties and party systems: a framework for analysis.* Cambridge: Cambridge University Press, 1976. ISBN 0-521-21238-3 (cl), 0-521-29106-2 (pbk). ‣ Definitive guide to defining and classifying political parties and party systems. Meticulously argued; thorough coverage of literature. Truly comparative approach. [LPG]

1.503 Joel H. Silbey, Allan G. Bogue, and William H. Flanigan, eds. *The history of American electoral behavior.* Princeton: Princeton University Press, 1978. ISBN 0-691-07590-5 (cl), 0-691-10062-4 (pbk). ‣ Good essays demonstrating how quantitative methods can be applied to studies of popular voting behavior and policy outcomes. Most essays assume familiarity with regression and other statistical techniques. [LPG]

1.504 Lawrence S. Wittner. "Peace movements and foreign policy: the challenge to diplomatic historians." *Diplomatic history* 11.4 (1987) 355–70. ISSN 0145-2096. ‣ Examination of development of peace research and peace movement emphasizing need for historians to challenge realist assumptions of war as inevitable element in foreign policy. [GKP]

SEE ALSO

40.603 Michael J. Hogan and Thomas G. Paterson, eds. *Explaining the history of American foreign relations.*

Local History

1.505 H.P.R. Finberg and V.H.T. Skipp. *Local history: objective and pursuit.* 1967 ed. Newton Abbot, England: David & Charles, 1973. ISBN 0-7153-4159-6. ‣ Leading English local historians survey and defend field; few methodological tips, much reflection on relationship between historical microcosm and macrocosm. [RTV]

1.506 Carol Kammen. *On doing local history: reflections on what local historians do, why, and what it means.* Nashville: American Association for State and Local History Press, 1986. ISBN 0-910050-81-3. ‣ Not how-to manual, rather thoughtful history of local history and discussion of evidence, interpretation, projects, writing, and amateur versus professional history. [RTV]

History of Science

1.507 Joseph Agassi. *Towards an historiography of science.* 1963 ed. Middletown, Conn.: Wesleyan University Press, 1967. (*History and theory*, Beiheft, 2.) ISSN 0018-2656. ‣ Undertakes to correct most historians of science. Advocates Popper's approach, allowing recognition of valuable errors, and avoids being wise after event, unlike inductivist approach which sees smooth process of factual and conventional discovery. [RTV]

1.508 R. M. Burian. "More than a marriage of convenience: on the inextricability of history and philosophy of science." *Philosophy of science* 44.1 (1977) 1–42. ISSN 0031-8248. ‣ Strong case to unite the two. Philosophy of science must take into account historical context in rational reconstruction of explanation or theory. Theories develop historically; historians might usefully apply and test philosophical theories about science. [RTV]

1.509 Michael J. Crowe. "Ten misconceptions about mathematics and its history." In *History and philosophy of modern mathematics.* William Aspray and Philip Kitcher, eds., pp. 260–77. Minneapolis: University of Minnesota Press, 1988. ISBN 0-8166-1566-7 (cl), 0-8166-1567-5 (pbk). ‣ Entertaining, iconoclastic essay denies mathematics is deductive, provides certain knowledge, cumulative, and always correct. Its proofs neither unproblematic nor decisively falsifiable; standards of rigor change, and structure does not reflect its history. [RTV]

1.510 Paul Feyerabend. *Against method.* Rev. ed. London: Verso, 1988. ISBN 0-86091-222-1 (cl), 0-86091-934-X (pbk). ‣ Takes constructionist view of science to its logical conclusion and claims there is no normative scientific method. Attacks conventional interpretation of episodes from history (especially Copernicus, Galileo, and the church) to support his claims. [RTV]

1.511 Maurice A. Finocchiaro. *History of science as explanation.* Detroit: Wayne State University Press, 1973. ISBN 0-8143-1480-5. ‣ Unusual for extensive analysis of whole works in history of science (by Koyré 4.92 and Henry Guerlac); argues for distinction of context of discovery versus that of justification with former basis of history of science. [RTV]

1.512 G. Nigel Gilbert and Michael Mulkey. "Experiments are the key: participants' histories and historians' histories of science." *Isis* 75 (1984) 105–25. ISSN 0021-1753. ‣ Penetrating critique of historians of science who present science as created by great scientists and validated by key experiments. Argues no objective criteria for these conclusions since they rely on participants' reconstructions, which are too unreliable to tell what really happened. Followed by critique by Steven Shapin, pp. 125–31. [RTV]

1.513 David L. Hull. *Science as a process: an evolutionary account of the social and conceptual development of science.* Chicago: University of Chicago Press, 1988. ISBN 0-226-36050-4. ‣ Institutional and conceptual history of branch of biology, raising all problems associated with internalist versus externalist views of science. Remarkable combination of history and philosophy of science. [RTV]

1.514 M. D. King. "Reason, tradition, and the progressiveness of science." *History and theory* 10.1 (1971) 3–32. ISSN 0018-2656.

‣ Agrees with Kuhn 1.516 that product and process of production of scientific knowledge resist complete rationalization, but argues Kuhn erred in replacing epistemology with sociology to retain notion of scientific progress. [RTV]

1.515 Thomas S. Kuhn. *The essential tension: selected studies in scientific tradition and change.* Chicago: University of Chicago Press, 1977. ISBN 0-266-45805-9 (cl), 0-266-45806-7 (pbk). ‣ First chapter of most interest to theory of history; argues history of science and philosophy of science may be mutually exclusive. Distinctive mental acts of historians are puzzle solving and explaining through showing patterns of facts. [RTV]

1.516 Thomas S. Kuhn. *The structure of scientific revolutions.* 2d ed. Chicago: University of Chicago Press, 1970. ISBN 0-226-45804-0. ‣ Argues science not a cumulative march toward truth, but proceeds discontinuously, in "paradigm shifts" in which normal scientific practice is challenged, then reorganized. Influential in all branches of history. [RTV]

1.517 Imre Lakatos. "History of science and its rational reconstruction." In *PSA 1970: proceedings of the 1970 biennial meetings, Philosophy of Science Association.* Roger Buck and Robert J. Cohen, eds., pp. 91–136. Dordrecht: Reidel, 1970. (Boston University studies in the philosophy of science, 8.) ISSN 0068-0346. ‣ Good condensed statement of conception of "internalist" history of science as research programs, progressive when predicting novel facts and allowing rational reconstruction of scientific practice and change, stagnant when new facts outrun theories. Followed by comments of Kuhn and others. [RTV]

1.518 Larry Laudan et al. "Scientific change: philosophical models and historical research." *Synthese* 69.2 (1986) 141–223. ISSN 0039-7857. ‣ Radical review of theories. Assumes positivism and whig approach are discredited, but Kuhn 1.516 and others have not tested theories systematically against historical evidence. Concludes with lengthy, precise formulation of theories to facilitate such testing. [RTV]

1.519 Ernest Nagel. "Teleology revisited." In *Teleology revisited and other essays in the philosophy and history of science,* pp. 275–316. New York: Columbia University Press, 1979. ISBN 0-231-04504-2. ‣ Careful discussion of teleological language; laws and theories of biology may be reducible to those of physical sciences, since teleological explanations not in principle obscure or objectionable. [RTV]

1.520 Roger H. Stuewer, ed. *Historical and philosophical perspectives of science.* Minneapolis: University of Minnesota Press, 1970. ISBN 0-8166-0592-0. ‣ Important papers by Thackray, analyzing historiography of science and calling for external approaches, and by Hesse and Rosen, defending internal historiography as applied to Copernicus and seventeenth-century science. [RTV]

1.521 Bob Young. "Science *is* social relations." *Radical science journal* 5 (1977) 65–129. ISSN 0305-0963. ‣ Written from updated Marxist perspective pushing analogy between production of commodities and of scientific knowledge. Claims natural science always implicated in ideology; stronger on demystification than on recommended practices. [RTV]

TEACHING HISTORY

1.522 Martin Ballard, ed. *New movements in the study and teaching of history.* Bloomington: Indiana University Press, 1970. ISBN 0-253-34020-9. ‣ Survey of new directions in historiography, ca. 1970, followed by six articles on teachers' opportunities: projects, exams, original sources, curriculum, and applications of Piaget's psychological theories. [RTV]

1.523 Volker R. Berghahn and Hanna Schissler, eds. *Perceptions of history: international textbook research on Britain, Germany, and the United States.* New York: Berg; distributed by St. Martin's, 1987. ISBN 0-85496-526-2. ‣ Best articles show how textbooks of these countries portray national histories of others or compare how these deal with their own histories. Suggestions for eliminating cultural biases advanced. [RTV]

1.524   Stephen Botein et al., eds. *Experiments in history teaching.* Cambridge, Mass.: Press of Langdon Associates for Harvard-Danforth Center for Teaching and Learning, 1977. ▸ More than seventy-five New England history teachers exchange ideas, teaching aids, syllabi in cultural artifacts, community history, psychohistory, quantitative methods, and history of ordinary people. High school and community college teachers particularly innovative. [RTV]

1.525   W. H. Burston and D. Thompson, eds. *Studies in the nature and teaching of history.* New York: Humanities Press, 1967. ▸ Useful collection of articles interpreting various issues in philosophy of history, but most notable for two articles on psychology of history teaching. [RTV]

1.526   A. K. Dickinson, P. J. Lee, and P. J. Rogers. *Learning history.* London: Heinemann Educational Books, 1984. ISBN 0-435-80288-7 (cl), 0-435-80289-5 (pbk). ▸ Articles examining issues in teaching on unusually high theoretical level: empathy and imagination, modes of comprehension, and psychological development of students together with articles on assessment and on visual aids. [RTV]

1.527   Marc Ferro. *The use and abuse of history: or how the past is taught.* 1981 ed. Boston: Routledge & Kegan Paul, 1984. ISBN 0-7100-9658-5. ▸ Survey of history teaching, largely in Eastern Europe and Third World. Concludes universal history, even Marxist, is European mirage; rest of world seen only in European light. Better mode of comprehension, not more facts, needed. [RTV]

1.528   Incorporated Association of Assistant Masters in Secondary Schools. *The teaching of history in secondary schools.* 4th ed. New York: Cambridge University Press, 1975. ISBN 0-521-20568-9. ▸ Mostly directed toward teaching young British teens, but chapters on methods and aids of general interest. Good advice on last-minute preparation, use of blackboard, how to tap into potential interest in history. [RTV]

1.529   *The philosophy of history teaching.* Middletown, Conn.: Wesleyan University Press, 1983. (*History and theory*, Beiheft, 22.) ISSN 0018-2656. ▸ International symposium examines claims that conceptual grasp of history as form of knowledge preferable to content-based curriculum for adolescents. History teaching should aim at developing skill in empathetic understanding of past actions. [RTV]

1.530   James B. M. Schick. *Teaching history with a computer: a complete guide for college professors.* Chicago: Lyceum, 1990. ISBN 0-925065-32-3 (pbk). ▸ Refreshing reasons not to use computers introduce reference guide emphasizing available software for simulations, data management, games, and programing (in Basic). Nontechnical writing, often humorous. [RTV]

1.531   Paul L. Ward. *A style of history for beginners.* Washington, D.C.: Service Center for Teachers of History, 1959. (Service Center for Teachers of History, 22.) ▸ Teaching beginners should emphasize evidence (acquired through reading in sources), how evidence can support coherent narrative (with emphasis on chronological charts), and how to make living, human story. [RTV]

PATTY JO WATSON

Prehistory

Modern archaeology is a highly eclectic discipline. Archaeologists use physics, chemistry, biology, and various statistical means to date, analyze, and describe their finds, while interpreting and discussing them within a wide variety of frameworks drawn from the social sciences, the natural sciences, and the humanities. An individual practitioner must know something about topics as diverse as geomorphology, mineralogy, and sedimentology; satellite imagery; scanning electron microscopy; oxygen isotope analysis of deep sea cores; plant and animal ecology; subsistence technology, economics, alliance or warfare principles, and the symbolic-structuralist systems common to ethnographically documented human groups; principles of design and stylistic analysis; information theory; Marxist theory; and philosophy of science. And, of course, most archaeologists also learn how to excavate, document, and conserve cultural remains from the near or remote past. To launch, carry out, and complete an archaeological excavation project, a scholar must write successful grant proposals, perform and oversee fieldwork that usually takes place in fairly demanding physical circumstances (too hot, too cold, too dry, too wet, too windy, too far from contemporary roads or paths or lodgings or supplies; insect-ridden; politically complex and/or dangerous, etc.), and maintain good working relationships with and among a variegated interdisciplinary group of collaborators.

Not all modern archaeologists dig, however, and some do not even do research. In nearly every nation-state there are archaeological administrators whose task it is to inventory or otherwise define archaeological sites or materials and then protect them. These same administrators are sometimes but not always charged with interpreting cultural resources to the public, and hence they may be in charge of or linked to museums and other repositories where research on archaeologically obtained materials takes place.

From a more traditional perspective, contemporary archaeology may be divided into prehistoric and historic domains, or into natural scientific, social scientific, and humanistic branches. Classical archaeology—the study of ancient Greece, Rome, their antecedents, and those portions of the world affected by their economic and military activities—is usually approached via the humanities. Prehistoric archaeology—that part of the human past undocumented by written records—is usually approached via the natural and social sciences (especially anthropology). These divisions arose because they placed the focus of scholarship upon what seemed to be the most relevant subject matter and intellectual frameworks. This has resulted in a dichotomizing of archaeological fieldwork training and theoretical orientation that is often unfortunate.

At present, prehistoric archaeology in North America is predominantly viewed and taught as a branch of anthropology; in Latin America as a branch of history; in England as culture history, social history, or social theory; in much of continental Europe, Africa, and Asia as natural science for Pleistocene and Early Holocene prehistory and as cultural or social history once agriculture and/or pottery appear.

In many modern nation-states, archaeology and archaeologists operate within a variety of highly charged political contexts (see, e.g., 2.4), and one of the prominent themes within contemporary archaeological theory is how to accommodate the overt politicization of the field (see Hodder 2.5; Preucel 2.6). Another prominent theme is the ubiquitous destruction of the prehistoric archaeological record by all those forces that are so rapidly and profoundly altering not only the face of the earth but also its subterranean attributes. Urban and suburban sprawl, the continual expansion of national and international communication systems and of economic exploration and exploitation above ground and below, and mass landscape destruction concomitant with modern warfare, are all factors that have recently reached a global pitch and intensity previously unwitnessed, even locally. Most countries have some archaeological conservation regulations on the books, but these are rarely sufficient to ensure the survival of representative portions of the archaeological record. In such circumstances, well-documented public and private collections made during the nineteenth and early twentieth centuries have become increasingly precious and are attracting more detailed scholarly attention than at any time since archaeology emerged as a formal discipline some one hundred and fifty years ago (Hodder 2.5).

For the purposes of this section, the coverage of prehistory starts with the Neolithic and ends when documentation (ancient history) begins. This is some time in the Late Bronze and Iron ages over much of the Old World (some 2000 to 4000 years ago), and in the ancient or modern colonialist eras elsewhere (e.g., Roman invasion of western Europe or European invasion of Oceania and the Americas).

Excavation, analysis, and interpretation with the aid of natural science techniques plus ethnography and ethnohistory inform us about regional versions of such major transformations as the origins of agriculture and pastoralism, of urbanized state-based civilizations (see Africa, West Asia, Central Asia, South Asia, and East Asia subsections here), and the impact of those developments on areas peripheral to them (see European subsection). Archaeologists have also learned when human populations reached and settled the major land masses of the globe. At the other end of the interpretive scale, they are also sometimes able to reveal minute particulars of individual human lives or even single events in those lives centuries or millennia ago.

As a field science, prehistoric archaeology is exacting, requiring meticulous and unrelenting attention to the details of provenance and context for every category or topic investigated (Fagan 2.2, 2.3; Sharer and Ashmore 2.7; Thomas 2.8). But, like other forms of historical scholarship, it can be enormously rewarding. And it is the only means we can employ to learn about the 99.99 percent of the human story that began more than three million years ago and ran its course leaving none but archaeological records. The relevant scholarly literature, although small compared to the immense scope of its subject matter, is both extensive and diverse. The following bibliography, although limited in size, includes surveys, bibliographies, and journals that will guide the reader more deeply into the fascinating realms of world prehistory.

Entries are arranged under the following headings:

History, Theory, and Method

Africa

Ancient Egypt and the Near East

Central Asia

South Asia

China

Southeast Asia, Japan, and Korea

Australia, New Zealand, and Oceania

Eastern Europe

Northern and Western Europe and England

North America

Mesoamerica and South America

[Contributors: AMTM = Andrew M. T. Moore, BAV = Barbara A. Voytek, DLB = David L. Browman, GLP = Gregory L. Possehl, GWC = Gary W. Crawford, JB = John Bower, JEL = Janet E. Levy, PJW = Patty Jo Watson, PLK = Philip L. Kohl, PVK = Patrick V. Kirch, RLT = Robert L. Thorp]

HISTORY, THEORY, AND METHOD

2.1 Glyn Daniel. *150 years of archaeology.* 2d ed. London: Duckworth, 1975. ISBN 0-7156-0775-8. ▸ Standard treatment of history of archaeology in southern and western Asia and Europe by well-known British archaeologist and long-time editor of journal *Antiquity.* Complements Trigger 2.9. [PJW]

2.2 Brian M. Fagan. *In the beginning.* 8th ed. New York: HarperCollins, 1994. ISBN 0-673-52335-7. ▸ Good overview of contemporary archaeological methods and techniques with more emphasis on Old World archaeology than either Sharer and Ashmore 2.7 or Thomas 2.8. By British archaeologist who specialized in West African Iron Age archaeology. [PJW]

2.3 Brian M. Fagan. *People of the earth: an introduction to world prehistory.* 7th ed. New York: HarperCollins, 1992. ISBN 0-673-52167-2 (pbk). ▸ Authoritative summary of world prehistory with emphasis on Old World. Successive editions keep contents reasonably up to date. [PJW]

2.4 Joan M. Gero and Margaret W. Conkey, eds. *Engendering archaeology: women and prehistory.* Oxford: Blackwell, 1991. ISBN 0-631-16505-3 (cl), 0-631-17501-6 (pbk). ▸ First book to bring together case studies explicitly addressing gender (especially roles of women in prehistoric past). Each chapter addresses specific site or time period in the Americas, Europe, and Australia. Well written and thought provoking. [PJW]

2.5 Ian Hodder. *Reading the past: current approaches to interpretation in archaeology.* 2d ed. Cambridge: Cambridge University Press, 1991. ISBN 0-521-32743-1 (cl), 0-521-33960-X (pbk). ▸ Clearest overview of various postmodernist (postprocessualist) views about archaeology: theory, goals, methods, and practice. Well-written account by highly influential postprocessualist. [PJW]

2.6 Robert W. Preucel, ed. *Processual and postprocessual archaeologies: multiple ways of knowing the past.* Carbondale: University of Illinois, Center for Archaeological Investigations, 1991. (Occasional paper, 10.) ISBN 0-88104-074-6. ▸ Collection of twenty-one papers with introductory chapter by proponents, opponents, and onlookers concerning postmodernist themes in contemporary archaeology. Good introduction to spectrum of theoretical discussions in European American archaeological theory. [PJW]

2.7 Robert J. Sharer and Wendy Ashmore. *Archaeology: discovering our past.* 2d ed. Mountain View, Calif.: Mayfield, 1992. ISBN 1-55934-041-X. ▸ Excellent textbook by two experts in ancient

Mesoamerica who represent archaeology with emphasis on its relationship to history. Well illustrated, several color plates. [PJW]

2.8 David Hurst Thomas. *Archaeology.* 2d ed. New York: Holt, Reinhart & Winston, 1989. ISBN 0-03-019926-3. ▸ Good coverage of contemporary archaeology in lively textbook format by prominent archaeologist with broad expertise in prehistoric archaeology in both eastern and western United States. Stresses scientific aspects of archaeological theory and method. [PJW]

2.9 Bruce G. Trigger. *A history of archaeological thought.* Cambridge: Cambridge University Press, 1989. ISBN 0-521-32878-0 (cl), 0-521-33818-2 (pbk). ▸ Substantive and authoritative account of archaeological theory, ancient times to present. Considerable attention to eastern Europe and former Soviet Union as well as western Europe, United States, and Australia. [PJW]

2.10 Mortimer Wheeler. *Archaeology from the earth.* London: Oxford University Press, 1954. ▸ Classic text on archaeological field methods and techniques by flamboyant and virtuoso excavator, founder of Institute of Archaeology, University of London, and specialist in Romano-British and Indian Bronze Age archaeology. Witty, well-written discussion of archaeological excavation; still a must for all students of the discipline. [PJW]

AFRICA

2.11 John Bower and David Lubell, eds. *Prehistoric cultures and environments in the late Quaternary of Africa.* Oxford: British Archaeological Reports, 1988. (British archaeological reports, International series, 405. Cambridge monographs in African archaeology, 26.) ISBN 0-86054-520-2 (pbk). ▸ Best available study on pan-African scale of cultural responses to changing environments throughout Africa, ca. 18,000 BCE to 1000 CE. Selected case studies of cultural adaptation in each major geographic division of the continent. Attention to methods of investigation as well as results of inquiry. Methodologically important work. [JB]

2.12 J. Desmond Clark and Steven A. Brandt, eds. *From hunters to farmers: the causes and consequences of food production in Africa.* Berkeley: University of California Press, 1984. ISBN 0-520-04574-2. ▸ Best available pan-African study of beginnings of agriculture and livestock herding in Africa. Treats linguistic and archaeological evidence for early use of domesticated plants and animals, environmental contexts, and social and ecological outcomes of Neolithic in Africa. Useful introduction. [JB]

2.13 Angela E. Close, ed. *Prehistory of arid North Africa; essays in honor of Fred Wendorf.* Dallas: Southern Methodist University Press, 1987. ISBN 0-87074-222-1 (cl), 0-87074-223-X (pbk). ▸ State-of-the-art regional coverage of late prehistoric peoples, cultures, and environments of Saharan desert and adjoining zones. Emphasis on human response to environmental change. Topics range from early food production to beginnings of metallurgy. Aimed largely at specialist audience. [JB]

2.14 Graham Connah. *African civilizations: precolonial cities and states in tropical Africa, an archaeological perspective.* Cambridge: Cambridge University Press, 1987. ISBN 0-521-26666-1 (cl), 0-521-31992-7 (pbk). ▸ Up-to-date introductory overview; comparative study of early African civilizations in various geographic settings. Recognizes social stratification as primary development in each instance. Attributes stratification to differential control of land. For nonspecialist audience. [JB]

2.15 James Denbow. "Congo to Kalahari: data and hypotheses about the political economy of the western stream of the early Iron Age." *African archaeological review* 8 (1990) 139–76. ISSN 0263-0338. ▸ Technical, specialist study of spread of Bantu-speaking peoples from West Central Africa to southern Africa, using archaeological and linguistic evidence for diffusion of early ceramics, metallurgy, and food production. Focus on economic and political consequences of interaction between farmers and hunter-gatherers. [JB]

2.16 Randi Haaland. *Socio-economic differentiation in the Neolithic Sudan.* Oxford: British Archaeological Reports, 1987. (British archaeological reports, International series, 350. Cambridge monographs in African archaeology, 20.) ISBN 0-86054-453. ‣ Sophisticated, accessible analysis of origins of food production in Khartoum (Sudan) region. Considers archaeological and ethnological evidence bearing on early plant cultivation and livestock herding. Proposes major changes in role of women as result of shift from hunting-gathering to food production. [JB]

2.17 Thomas N. Huffman. "Ceramics, settlements, and late Iron Age migrations." *African archaeological review* 7 (1989) 155–82. ISSN 0263-0338. ‣ Discussion of migrations of Bantu-speaking peoples in central and southern Africa since about 1000 CE. State-of-the-art review and substantial revision of previous interpretations of late Iron Age pottery distributions and relation to Bantu-language groups. Difficult for nonspecialist. [JB]

2.18 Richard G. Klein, ed. *Southern African prehistory and paleoenvironments.* Rotterdam: Balkema, 1984. ISBN 90-6191-097-8. ‣ Selected coverage of southern African prehistory. Includes articles on large mammal faunas and their environmental implications (Klein), on later Stone Age peoples and their descendants (Deacon), and on Iron Age south of Zambezi River (Maggs). [JB]

2.19 Raymond Lanfranchi and Bernard Clist, eds. *Aux origines de l'Afrique centrale.* Paris: Sepia, 1991. ISBN 2-907888-11-0. ‣ General survey of prehistory of central Africa. Includes sections on present and ancient environments, linguistics, and overview of region's cultural history by stages, Stone Age through Iron Age. [JB]

2.20 Susan Keech McIntosh and Roderick James McIntosh. "The early city in West Africa: towards an understanding." *African archaeological review* 2 (1984) 73–98. ISSN 0263-0338. ‣ Methodologically important study of emergence of urban settlements in West Africa. Looks at urbanization as part of regional process of settlement differentiation. Draws heavily on investigations at Jenne-jeno (Mali), but includes comparisons with other centers, such as Tegdaoust and Ife. [JB]

ANCIENT EGYPT AND THE NEAR EAST

2.21 Olivier Aurenche, Jacques Evin, and Francis Hours, eds. *Chronologies du Proche Orient=Chronologies in the Near East; relative chronologies and absolute chronology 16,000–4,000 BP. C.N.R.S. international symposium, Lyon (France), 24–28 November 1986.* 2 vols. Oxford: British Archaeological Reports, 1987. (Centre National de la Recherche Scientifique, Maison de l'Orient Mediterranéen, Archaeological series, 3. British archaeological reports, International series, 379.) ISBN 0-86054-487-7 (set). ‣ Thorough review of later prehistory of Near East for advanced readers. Thirty-seven articles on dating methods, environmental phenomena, and dating of periods and sites. Conference volume on use of radiocarbon method to refine dating of archaeological periods from eastern Mediterranean to Indus Valley. [AMTM]

2.22 Ofer Bar-Yosef and François R. Valla, eds. *The Natufian culture in the Levant.* Ann Arbor: International Monographs in Prehistory, 1991. (International monographs in prehistory, Archaeological series, 1.) ISBN 1-879621-03-7 (cl), 1-879621-01-0 (pbk). ‣ Comprehensive series of detailed studies on hunters and gatherers of late Epipaleolithic. Brings together results of recent research on environment, sites, artifacts, and economy of this significant culture. For readers with some background in prehistory. [AMTM]

2.23 Fekri A. Hassan. "The Predynastic of Egypt." *Journal of world prehistory* 2.2 (1988) 135–85. ISSN 0892-7537. ‣ Compre-

hensive, up-to-date account of important formative period, later prehistory from final prehistoric hunters-gatherers-fishers through early farmers to beginning of civilization. Focus on social and economic organization and rise of the state, ca. 4000–3000 BCE. For general readers and students. [AMTM]

2.24 Elizabeth F. Henrickson and Ingolf Thuesen, eds. *Upon this foundation, the 'Ubaid reconsidered: proceedings from the 'Ubaid symposium, Elsinore May 30th–June 1st 1988.* Copenhagen: Museum Tusculanum Press and University of Copenhagen, Carsten Niebuhr Institute of Ancient Near Eastern Studies, 1989. (Carsten Niebuhr Institute, Publications, 10.) ISBN 87-7289-070-3, ISSN 0902-5499. ‣ Nineteen articles on cultural sequence, settlements, society, and trade in Mesopotamia and contiguous regions. Comprehensive review of recent excavations and research on formative period of civilization. Interesting for development of complex societies in ancient Mesopotamia. [AMTM]

2.25 Michael A. Hoffman. *Egypt before the pharaohs: the prehistoric foundations of Egyptian civilization.* Rev. ed. Austin: University of Texas Press, 1991. ISBN 0-292-72073-4. ‣ Prehistory interpreted through investigations and writings of successive generations of archaeologists. Lively account that blends archaeological interpretation with anecdotes of personalities and fieldwork conditions. Emphasis on Predynastic period. [AMTM]

2.26 James Mellaart. *The Neolithic of the Near East.* New York: Scribner's, 1975. ISBN 0-684-14483-2. ‣ Best general account of later Near Eastern prehistory. Development of villages and farming way of life from eastern Mediterranean to Turkmenia. Comprehensive description of archaeological sites and their contents; stresses human cultural development. For general readers and students. [AMTM]

2.27 Andrew M. T. Moore. *The development of Neolithic societies in the Near East.* Orlando, Fla.: Academic Press, 1985. ISBN 0-12-039904-0 (cl), 0-12-000003-2 (pbk). ‣ Study of indigenous inception of farming and sedentary village life in Levant, Anatolia, Mesopotamia, and Zagros Mountains, its cultural and economic consequences. Review of material evidence from ecological perspective; critical discussion of theories of agricultural beginnings. [AMTM]

2.28 Charles L. Redman. *The rise of civilization: from early farmers to urban society in the ancient Near East.* San Francisco: Freeman, 1978. ISBN 0-7167-0056-5 (cl), 0-7167-0055-7 (pbk). ‣ Good general introductory account of development of agriculture, village life, and urbanism. Emphasis on various theories for beginning of agriculture and emergence of complex societies, stressing systems approach. [AMTM]

2.29 T. Cuyler Young, Philip E. L. Smith, and Peder Mortensen, eds. *The hilly flanks and beyond: essays on the prehistory of southwestern Asia presented to Robert J. Braidwood, November 15, 1982.* Chicago: Oriental Institute, 1983. (Studies in ancient Oriental civilization, 36.) ISBN 0-91898-637-0 (pbk), ISSN 0069-3367. ‣ Eighteen articles on major themes in wide-ranging accounts, treating Epipaleolithic, Neolithic, and Chalcolithic of Southwest Asia. Celebratory volume for Robert J. Braidwood on subjects of his research, especially origins of agriculture and early village life. [AMTM]

CENTRAL ASIA

2.30 Philip L. Kohl. *Central Asia: Paleolithic beginnings to the Iron Age.* Paris: Éditions Recherche sur les Civilisations, 1984. (Éditions Recherche sur les Civilisations, Synthèse, 14.) ISBN 2-86538-071-8. ‣ Best single-volume overview of prehistory of region available in Western language; slightly dated. Synthesis of Central Asian prehistory to early Iron Age. Relates materials to later prehistoric remains from South Asia and ancient Near East. [PLK]

2.31 Philip L. Kohl, ed. *The Bronze Age civilization of Central Asia: recent Soviet discoveries.* William Mandell and Philip L. Kohl, trans. Armonk, N.Y.: Sharpe, 1981. ISBN 0-87332-169-3. ▸ Best collection of translated articles on Soviet archaeology in Central Asia. Illustrates state of Soviet research, ca. 1980. Introduction assesses significance of discoveries and summarizes what is known of Namazga civilization. [PLK]

2.32 Gennadii A. Kosholenko, ed. *Drevneishie gosudarstva kavkaza i srednei Azii* (The most ancient states of Central Asia and the Caucasus). Moscow: Nauka, 1985. ▸ Best summary of Soviet archaeological research on later prehistory and early history of Caucasus and Central Asia. Well illustrated and current through early 1980s. [PLK]

2.33 Giancarlo Ligabue and Sandro Salvatori, eds. *Bactria: an ancient oasis civilization from the sands of Afghanistan.* Venice: Erizso, 1989. ISBN 88-7077-025-7. ▸ Collection of articles by leading international scholars on late Bronze Age civilization of Bactria. Richly illustrated with over a hundred color plates, primarily of objects plundered from Bronze Age cemeteries in northern Afghanistan. [PLK]

2.34 Otar Lordkipanidse. *Archäologie in Georgien: von der Altsteinzeit zum Mittelalter.* Weinheim: VCH Acta Humaniora, 1991. (Quellen und Forschungen zur prähistorischen und provinzialrömischen Archäologie, 5.) ISBN 3-527-17531-8. ▸ Synthesis of prehistory and historical archaeology of Georgia from Old Stone Age to medieval period. Focus on developments within modern political boundaries of Georgia. Most up-to-date single-volume study of prehistory and archaeology in Georgia. Extensive bibliography; profusely illustrated. [PLK]

2.35 Vadim M. Masson and Nikolai I. Merpert, eds. *Eneolit SSSR* (The USSR in the Chalcolithic period). Moscow: Nauka, 1982. ▸ Synthesis of Chalcolithic archaeological remains found throughout former Soviet Union. Materials organized regionally and include Central Asia, Caucasus, Ukraine and Molodova, and southern Russia and Eurasian steppes. Well illustrated, current through late 1970s. [PLK]

2.36 Viktor I. Sarianidi. *Die Kunst des alten Afghanistan; Architektur, Keramik, Siegel: Kunstwerke aus Stein und Metall.* Sabine Grebe, trans. Leipzig: VCH Acta Humaniora, 1986. ISBN 3-527-17561-X. ▸ Profusely illustrated discussion particularly of Bronze Age Bactria and comparison with neighboring regions, particularly Margiana. Favors late dating of materials to second half of second millennium BCE. [PLK]

SEE ALSO
    5.14 Michael Roaf. *Cultural atlas of Mesopotamia and the ancient Near East.*

SOUTH ASIA

2.37 D. P. Agrawal. *The archaeology of India.* 1982 ed. New Delhi: Select Book Service Syndicate, 1984. (Scandinavian Institute of Asia Studies, Monograph series, 46.) ▸ Synthesis of South Asian archaeology, Lower Paleolithic through beginnings of Iron Age. Well illustrated; written by head of India's leading radiocarbon dating laboratory. [GLP]

2.38 Bridget Allchin and F. Raymond Allchin. *The rise of civilization in India and Pakistan.* Cambridge: Cambridge University Press, 1982. ISBN 0-521-24244-4 (cl), 0-521-28550-X (pbk). ▸ Synthesis of South Asian archaeology, Lower Paleolithic through beginnings of Iron Age. Well illustrated; written by husband and wife team with more than forty years' experience in archaeology of subcontinent. Especially strong on South India and Sri Lanka. [GLP]

2.39 F. Raymond Allchin and Norman Hammond, eds. *The archaeology of Afghanistan from earliest times to the Timurid period.*

London: Academic Press, 1978. ISBN 0-12-050440-5. ▸ Excellent papers covering Paleolithic to historical eras. Very good selection of authors; well illustrated; little theory. [GLP]

2.40 A. Ghosh, ed. *An encyclopedia of Indian archaeology.* 1989 ed. 2 vols. Leiden: Brill, 1990. ISBN 90-04-09264-1 (set), 90-04-09262-5 (v. 1), 90-04-09263-3 (v. 2). ▸ Limited, for most part, to modern nation-state of India. Volume 1 organized topically, covers Paleolithic to historic periods; volume 2, gazetteer of archaeological sites of those periods. Major site summaries generally written by excavators or other experts. Moderately well illustrated. [GLP]

2.41 Catherine Jarrige, ed. *South Asian archaeology, 1989.* Madison, Wis.: Prehistory Press, 1992. ISSN 1055-2316. ▸ Publication of 1989 South Asian Archaeology Conference in Paris. Wide range of current material on historical and archaeological topics within South Asian region. Some papers highly specialized, but others general and synthetic and useful to nonspecialists. [GLP]

2.42 Gregory L. Possehl. "Revolution in the urban revolution: the emergence of Indus urbanization." *Annual review of anthropology* 19 (1990) 261–82. ISSN 0084-6570. ▸ Contemporary view of Harappan state formation. Scholarly but accessible discussion of rise of Harappan civilization beginning with origins of agriculture in Baluchistan. Suggests rapid transition to urbanization from 2600 to 2500 BCE after period of gestation lasting several millennia. [GLP]

2.43 H. D. Sankalia. *The prehistory and protohistory of India and Pakistan.* New ed. Poona: Deccan College Post-Graduate and Research Institute, 1974. ▸ Synthesis of South Asian archaeology, Lower Paleolithic through beginnings of Iron Age. Detailed, nearly encyclopedic coverage but little theory. Somewhat dated but very good for sites excavated prior to early 1970s. By one of India's leading archaeologists. [GLP]

2.44 Maurizio Taddei, ed. *South Asian archaeology 1987: proceedings of the ninth International Conference of the Association of South Asian Archaeologists in Western Europe, held in the Fondazione Giorgio Cini, Island of San Giorgio Maggiore, Venice.* 2 vols. Rome: Instituto Italiano per il Medio ed Estremo Oriente, 1990. (Serie Orientale Roma, 66.) ▸ Major papers on all aspects of South Asian archaeology including prehistory and historic archaeology. Wide range of up-to-date material. Some papers highly specialized, others general and synthetic. [GLP]

CHINA

2.45 J. Gunnar Andersson. *Children of the yellow earth: studies in prehistoric China.* E. Classen, trans. Cambridge, Mass.: MIT Press, 1973. ISBN 0-262-51011-1 (pbk). ▸ First-person narrative (written ca. 1934) of early archaeological discoveries in North China, including Peking man, Chou-k'ou-tien site, and Yangshao Neolithic type site. Valuable as documentation of birth of modern archaeology in China. [RLT]

2.46 Herrlee Glessner Creel. *The birth of China: a study of the formative period of Chinese civilization.* 1937 ed. New York: Ungar, 1961. ISBN 0-8044-1205-7 (cl), 0-8044-6093-0 (pbk). ▸ First synthetic account by non-Chinese scholar of Anyang Shang excavations then in progress. Insightful and highly readable. [RLT]

2.47 Albert E. Dien, Nancy T. Price, and Jeffrey K. Riegel, eds. *Prehistory to Western Zhou.* Vol. 2 of *Chinese archaeological abstracts.* Los Angeles: University of California, Institute of Archaeology, 1985. (Monumenta archaeologica, 9). ISBN 0-917956-55-9. ▸ Eighty-nine abstracts of articles from principal Chinese archaeological journals, published 1928–81, on general, prehistoric, and Hsia-Shang topics. Highly selective and variable in detail. [RLT]

2.48 David N. Keightley. *Sources of Shang history: the oracle-bone inscriptions of Bronze Age China.* 1978 ed. Berkeley: University of California Press, 1985. ISBN 0-520-02969-0 (cl), 0-520-05455-5 (pbk). ▸ Seventeen analyses; handbook for earliest epigraphic sources in East Asia, emphasizing their traits, decipherment, dating, and historiographical issues. Rigorous exposition of every topic and issue; judicious presentation of most contested topics. [RLT/DNK]

2.49 David N. Keightley, ed. *The origins of Chinese civilization.* Berkeley: University of California Press, 1983. ISBN 0-520-04229-8 (cl), 0-520-04230-1 (pbk). ▸ Proceedings of 1978 conference; attention to environment and agriculture, cultures and peoples, language and writing, and tribe and state. [RLT]

2.50 Chi Li. *Anyang.* Seattle: University of Washington Press, 1977. ISBN 0-295-95490-5. ▸ Firsthand account of excavations at Anyang (1928–37) and preliminary synthesis of them. Little reference to post-1949 excavations. [RLT]

2.51 William Watson. *Cultural frontiers in ancient East Asia.* Edinburgh: Edinburgh University Press, 1971. ISBN 0-85224-203-4. ▸ Lectures (delivered 1965) on Neolithic and protohistoric cultures with attention to relations among settled and nomadic populations, especially those north-northwest and south-southwest of central North China. Coverage of data now badly out of date, but addresses important issues. [RLT]

2.52 Paul Wheatley. *The pivot of the four quarters: a preliminary enquiry into the origins and character of the ancient Chinese city.* Chicago: Aldine, 1971. ISBN 0-85224-174-7. ▸ Synthesis (through 1968) of data for protohistoric and early historic urbanism in North China applying crosscultural perspective with emphasis on role of ceremonial center. Significant gaps in data; esoteric orthography. [RLT/DNK]

SEE ALSO
10.167 Kwang-chih Chang. *The archaeology of ancient China.*
10.179 Kwang-chih Chang. *Shang civilization.*

SOUTHEAST ASIA, JAPAN, AND KOREA

2.53 C. Melvin Aikens and Takayasu Higuchi. *The prehistory of Japan.* New York: Academic Press, 1982. ISBN 0-12-045280-4. ▸ Narrative summary of Japanese archaeology from Paleolithic period to protohistoric times. Extensive bibliography, primarily of Japanese sources. Archaeological site summaries used as basis for discussion; sidesteps significant debates. Good for beginners. [GWC]

2.54 Gina Lee Barnes. *Protohistoric Yamamoto: archaeology of the first Japanese state.* Ann Arbor: University of Michigan, Museum of Anthropology and Center for Japanese Studies, 1988. (Michigan papers in Japanese studies, 17. Museum of Anthropology, Anthropological papers, 78.) ISBN 0-915703-11-4. ▸ Revised doctoral dissertation taking anthropological-archaeological approach to origin and development of first centralized sociopolitical system (state) in Japan. Includes suggestion that earliest villages within Yamato state are actually latest Yayoi sites. State-of-the-art specialist study. [GWC]

2.55 Gary W. Crawford. *Paleoethnobotany of the Kameda Peninsula Jomon.* Ann Arbor: University of Michigan, Museum of Anthropology and Center for Japanese Studies, 1983. (Museum of Anthropology, Anthropological papers, 73.) ISBN 0-932206-95-6. ▸ Problem-oriented specialist study of subsistence ecology of Jomon culture in Hokkaido, Japan. Includes a brief summary of northern Japanese prehistory and subsistence research. Concludes Jomon subsistence ecology not simple coastal adaptation; draws parallels with North American Eastern Woodlands culture. [GWC]

2.56 Gary W. Crawford. "Plant domestication in East Asia." In *The origins of agriculture: an international perspective.* C. Wesley Cowan and Patty Jo Watson, eds., pp. 7–38. Washington, D.C.: Smithsonian Institution Press, 1992. ISBN 0-87474-990-5 (cl), 0-87474-991-3 (pbk). ▸ Overview of complex East Asian Neolithic including China, Korea, and Japan. Emphasis on plant domestication and environmental history. Archaeological plant remains from northern Japan provide evidential basis for discussion. Good for both specialists and nonspecialists. [GWC]

2.57 Gary W. Crawford and Hiroto Takamiya. "The origins and implications of late prehistoric plant husbandry in northern Japan." *Antiquity* 64 (1990) 889–911. ISSN 0003-598X. ▸ Summary of new understandings about late prehistory of northern Japan including data recovered by authors in Hokkaido relevant to origin and nature of ancestral Ainu culture. [GWC]

2.58 Charles Higham. *The archaeology of mainland Southeast Asia from 10,000 B.C. to the fall of Angkor.* Cambridge: Cambridge University Press, 1989. ISBN 0-521-25523-6 (cl), 0-521-25525-3 (pbk). ▸ Superb summary by author who excavated in Thailand for over two decades bringing personal observations and interpretations to regional prehistory. Thailand emphasized but also Mekong and Red rivers as well as Indian and Chinese relationships with Southeast Asia. Extremely well illustrated. [GWC/DKW]

2.59 J. Edward Kidder, Jr. *Prehistoric Japanese arts: Jomon pottery.* Tokyo: Kodansha, 1968. ▸ Somewhat dated but still very valuable summary of Japanese prehistory. Provides authoritative view of cultural history that is widely accepted, except for some details, by Japanese archaeologists. Superb maps and illustrations. [GWC]

2.60 Jeong-hak Kim. *The prehistory of Korea.* Richard J. Pearson and Kazue Pearson, trans. Honolulu: University Press of Hawaii, 1978. ISBN 0-8248-0552-6. ▸ Best available summary of Korean archaeology in English. Spans Paleolithic through Iron Age. [GWC]

2.61 Shuzo Koyama and David H. Thomas, eds. *Affluent foragers: Pacific coasts, east and west.* Ōsaka, Japan: National Museum of Ethnology, 1981. (Senri ethnological studies, 9.) ▸ Excellent collection of specialist studies, many on Japan; others draw circum-Pacific comparisons. Offers good theoretical perspective. Key essay examines introduction of rice agriculture to Japan; another examines logistics and productivity of nut harvesting, mode of subsistence supposedly critical to Holocene Jomon culture. [GWC]

2.62 Richard J. Pearson, Gina Lee Barnes, and Karl L. Hutterer, eds. *Windows on the Japanese past: studies in archaeology and prehistory.* Ann Arbor: University of Michigan, Center for Japanese Studies, 1986. ISBN 0-939512-23-8 (cl), 0-939512-24-6 (pbk). ▸ Twenty-seven chapters mostly by Japanese authors. Provides important insights on Japanese archaeological methods and on substance of Japanese prehistory. Best read in conjunction with a narrative prehistory of Japan (e.g., 2.53 or 2.59). Five Japanese-English glossaries; extremely useful reference for place, personnel, site, type names, and technical terms. [GWC]

2.63 Shinichiro Takakura. *The Ainu of northern Japan: a study in conquest and acculturation.* John A. Harrison, trans. Philadelphia: American Philosophical Society, 1960. (American Philosophical Society, Transactions, n.s., 5, 50, 4.) ▸ Best political and economic history of Ainu available. Emphasizes history of conflict in north but provides excellent information on Ainu culture. [GWC]

AUSTRALIA, NEW ZEALAND, AND OCEANIA

2.64 Jim Allen and Chris Gosden, eds. *Report of the Lapita Homeland Project.* Canberra: Australian National University, School of Pacific Studies, Department of Prehistory, 1991.

(Department of Prehistory, Occasional papers in prehistory, 20.) ISBN 0-7315-1299-5. ‣ Eighteen papers summarizing results of project defining Pleistocene prehistoric sequence for Melanesia as well as best-documented Lapita period sites yet excavated in southwestern Pacific. Specialist reports with comprehensive data tables. [PVK]

2.65 Peter S. Bellwood. *Man's conquest of the Pacific: the prehistory of Southeast Asia and Oceania.* New York: Oxford University Press, 1979. ISBN 0-19-520103-5. ‣ Massive, well-illustrated overview of archaeology and prehistory of Oceania including islands of Southeast Asia; superb bibliography. Includes summaries of linguistic prehistory and ethnohistory and analysis of probable settlement routes into islands. [PVK/DD/HF]

2.66 Janet Davidson. *The prehistory of New Zealand.* Auckland: Longman Paul, 1984. ISBN 0-582-71793-0 (cl), 0-582-71812-0 (pbk). ‣ Readable, well-illustrated account of archaeology and prehistory of New Zealand by one of country's leading authorities. Includes comprehensive bibliography. [PVK]

2.67 Josephine Flood. *Archaeology of the dreamtime: the story of prehistoric Australia and its people.* Rev. ed. New Haven: Yale University Press, 1990. ISBN 0-300-04924-2. ‣ Comprehensive overview of archaeology and prehistory of Australian continent from first colonization by humans, ca. 40,000 years ago to late prehistoric. Well-written account for nonspecialist. [PVK]

2.68 Rosalind L. Hunter-Anderson, ed. *Recent advances in Micronesian archaeology: selected papers from the Micronesian Archaeology Conference, September 9–12, 1987.* Guam: University of Guam, 1990. (Micronesia, Supplement, 2.) ISSN 0026-279X. ‣ Thirty articles on archaeology, ethnohistory, and physical anthropology. Most comprehensive update of recent archaeological research for Marianas, Palau, Yap, Caroline, and Marshall Island groups. [PVK]

2.69 Jesse D. Jennings, ed. *The prehistory of Polynesia.* Cambridge, Mass.: Harvard University Press, 1979. ISBN 0-674-70060-0. ‣ Fifteen chapters providing comprehensive overview of archaeology and prehistory of various Polynesian island groups. Includes topical reviews of language, physical anthropology, subsistence and ecology, settlement patterns, and voyaging. [PVK]

2.70 Patrick Vinton Kirch. *The evolution of the Polynesian chiefdoms.* Cambridge: Cambridge University Press, 1984. ISBN 0-521-25332-2. ‣ Synthesis of prehistory, archaeology, and comparative ethnography of Polynesian islands. Particular emphasis on development of chiefdom level societies from common ancestral culture over 3,000-year period. [PVK]

2.71 Patrick Vinton Kirch. *Feathered gods and fishhooks: an introduction to Hawaiian archaeology and prehistory.* Honolulu: University of Hawaii Press, 1985. ISBN 0-8248-0981-5. ‣ Comprehensive, well-illustrated overview of archaeology and prehistory of Hawaiian Islands aimed at nonspecialist audience. Includes island-by-island reviews of key sites as well as topical discussions of origins, material culture, settlement pattern, subsistence, and social organization. [PVK]

2.72 Marshall Sahlins and Patrick Vinton Kirch. *Anahulu: the anthropology of history in the kingdom of Hawaii.* Vol. 1: *Historical ethnography.* Vol. 2: *The archaeology of history.* Chicago: University of Chicago Press, 1992. 2 vols. ISBN 0-226-73363-7 (v. 1), 0-226-73364-5 (v. 2). ‣ Definitive account of transformation of Hawaiian kingdom during period 1778–1860; based on collaborative ethnohistorical and archaeological research. Volume 1 by Sahlins, volume 2 by Vinton Kirch. [PVK]

2.73 J. Peter White and James F. O'Connell. *A prehistory of Australia, New Guinea, and Sahul.* Sidney: Academic Press, 1982. ISBN 0-12-746750-5 (cl), 0-12-746730-0 (pbk). ‣ Scholarly overview of prehistoric archaeology of Australian continent and adja-

cent island of New Guinea. More emphasis given to Pleistocene-Paleolithic than to Holocene-Neolithic. [PVK]

EASTERN EUROPE

2.74 David W. Anthony. "The 'Kurgan culture,' Indo-European origins, and the domestication of the horse: a reconsideration." *Current anthropology* 27.4 (1986) 291–313. ISSN 0011-3204. ‣ Compact synthesis of evidence and major points of view in debate on origins of Indo-European-speaking peoples, their material culture, and archaeological manifestation. Provides alternative model based on historical documentation of settling of American West. [BAV]

2.75 Paul M. Dolukhanov. *Ecology and economy in Neolithic eastern Europe.* New York: St. Martin's, 1978. ISBN 0-312-22613-6. ‣ Examination of role of environmental and social factors in prehistory using paleogeographical and archaeological evidence. Russian geographer links Soviet and Western approaches in ecological study of Holocene populations of eastern Europe and Near East. [BAV]

2.76 Jaroslav Malina and Zdeněk Vašíček. *Archaeology yesterday and today: the development of archaeology in the sciences and humanities.* Marek Zvelebil, ed. and trans. Cambridge: Cambridge University Press, 1990. ISBN 0-521-26621-1 (cl), 0-521-31977-3 (pbk). ‣ Archaeological history and theory originally published in Czech. Emphasizes archaeology's historical purpose, a view differing from that held by many Westerners. [BAV]

2.77 J. P. Mallory. *In search of the Indo-Europeans: language, archaeology, and myth.* New York: Thames & Hudson, 1989. ISBN 0-500-05052-X. ‣ Excellent introduction to Indo-European historical studies. Synthesis of most recent research into origins and spread of Indo-Europeans from eastern Europe in earliest Bronze Age; defends older concept of Indo-European homeland in Eurasia (contra Gamkrelidze and Ivanov 9.31). Integrates archaeology with extensive linguistic analysis. See Renfrew 2.79 for alternative perspective based on studies of prehistoric agriculture. [BAV/PBG]

2.78 Sarunas Milisauskas. *European prehistory.* New York: Academic Press, 1978. ISBN 0-12-497950-5. ‣ Extensive survey with emphasis on Central and eastern Europe; excellent introduction to area and archaeology; attempts to humanize archaeological cultures by discussing settlement organization, social and political organization, and ritual organization. [BAV]

2.79 Colin Renfrew. *Archaeology and language: the puzzle of Indo-European origins.* New York: Cambridge University Press, 1988. ISBN 0-521-35432-3. ‣ Noted prehistorian takes on problem of Indo-European origins and ties it to problem of spread of earliest agriculture into Europe. Controversial analysis; see Mallory 2.77 for alternative linguistic approach. [BAV]

2.80 Karel Sklenář. *Archaeology in Central Europe: the first 500 years.* Iris Lewitova, trans. New York: St. Martin's, 1983. ISBN 0-312-04721-5. ‣ Pioneering work on history of archaeological thought and practice in Central Europe. Relates diversity of prehistoric record to its diverse cultural background. [BAV.]

2.81 Ruth Tringham. *Hunters, fishers, and farmers of eastern Europe, 6000–3000 B.C.* London: Hutchinson University Library, 1971. ISBN 0-09-108790-2 (cl), 0-09-108791-0 (pbk). ‣ One of best surveys in English of archaeological record of eastern and southeastern Europe despite out-of-date theory and chronology. [BAV]

2.82 Alasdair W. R. Whittle. *Neolithic Europe: a survey.* Cambridge: Cambridge University Press, 1985. ISBN 0-521-24799-3 (cl), 0-521-29870-X (pbk). ‣ Wide-ranging, interpretive survey that includes East Central and southeastern Europe. Emphasis on Neolithic society and dynamics and theories of social change. [BAV]

NORTHERN AND WESTERN EUROPE
AND ENGLAND

2.83 Graeme Barker. *Prehistoric farming in Europe*. Cambridge: Cambridge University Press, 1985. ISBN 0-521-22810-7 (cl), 0-521-26969-5 (pbk). ‣ Beginnings of farming including theoretical discussion; demographic and ecological implications; changes in technology, plants, and animals from Neolithic through Iron Age. Excellent starting point for nonspecialist. [JEL]

2.84 Richard Bradley. *The social foundations of prehistoric Britain*. London: Longman, 1984. ISBN 0-582-49163-0 (cl), 0-582-49164-9 (pbk). ‣ Development of stratification, integrating economy and ideology, and emphasizing monuments and luxury items as expressions of power. Innovative synthesis focusing on Neolithic and Bronze Age. [JEL]

2.85 Timothy C. Champion et al. *Prehistoric Europe*. London: Academic Press, 1984. ISBN 0-12-167550-5 (cl), 0-12-167552-1 (pbk). ‣ Comprehensive, well-illustrated review. Emphasizes settlement patterns, economy, trade, and cultural change. Paleolithic through early Roman state. [JEL]

2.86 Timothy C. Champion and J. V. S. Megaw, eds. *Settlement and society: aspects of West European prehistory in the first millennium B.C.* New York: St. Martin's, 1985. ISBN 0-312-71317-7. ‣ Relations between Celtic areas of Central and West Europe and Mediterranean. Evaluates written documents and archaeological evidence of settlement, trade, and social organization; mainly for specialists. [JEL]

2.87 Christopher Chippindale. *Stonehenge complete*. 1983 ed. London: Thames & Hudson, 1987. ISBN 0-500-27355-3 (pbk). ‣ History of research, analysis, and popular interpretations of Stonehenge and related megalithic monuments. Reviews archaeological method and theory as well as prehistoric monuments. Magnificently illustrated; superb and enjoyable scholarship. [JEL]

2.88 John M. Coles and Anthony F. Harding. *The Bronze Age in Europe: an introduction to the prehistory of Europe, 2000–700 BC*. New York: St. Martin's, 1979. ISBN 0-312-10597-5. ‣ Detailed coverage of Europe, excluding Greece. Artifact types, chronology, environment, settlement pattern, social organization, and technology. Immense bibliography. [JEL]

2.89 Carole L. Crumley and William H. Marquardt, eds. *Regional dynamics: Burgundian landscapes in historical perspective*. San Diego, Calif.: Academic Press, 1987. ISBN 0-12-198380-3, 0-12-198381-1. ‣ Archaeological and historical data about Iron Age, Gallo-Roman, and early medieval periods. Unusual synthesis of neo-Marxist theory, ecological perspectives, and landscape archaeology. [JEL]

2.90 Margaret R. Ehrenberg. *Women in prehistory*. Norman: University of Oklahoma Press, 1989. ISBN 0-8061-2223-4 (cl), 0-8061-2237-4 (pbk). ‣ Roles and status of women in Europe from Paleolithic through Roman periods based on archaeological and anthropological data. Little discussion of feminist theory, but innovative perspective on traditional evidence. [JEL]

2.91 Stephen J. Shennan. "Trends in the study of later European prehistory." *Annual review of anthropology* 16 (1987) 365–82. ISSN 0084-6570. ‣ Important review of theoretical developments in 1980s emphasizing new approaches in symbolic and Marxist archaeology, critical theory, and world systems models; applications to European archaeology. [JEL]

2.92 Peter S. Wells. *Farms, villages, and cities: commerce and urban origins in late prehistoric Europe*. Ithaca, N.Y.: Cornell University Press, 1984. ISBN 0-8014-1554-3 (cl), 0-8014-9298-X (pbk). ‣ Iron Age and Roman period in Celtic Central and West

Europe. Argues for entrepreneurs as political and economic leaders. Narrow theoretical focus but excellent bibliography and review of archaeological material. [JEL]

NORTH AMERICA

2.93 Tom D. Dillehay and David J. Meltzer, eds. *The first Americans: search and research*. Boca Raton, Fla.: CRC Press, 1991. ISBN 0-8493-8818-X. ‣ Eleven chapters on peopling of Americas by experts on paleoenvironment, archaeology, chronology, and historical events relevant to human antiquity in Western Hemisphere. Introductory and concluding sections draw together individual chapters and specific lessons they offer. Very good overview of problem and status of current solutions. [PJW]

2.94 Brian M. Fagan. *Ancient North America: the archaeology of a continent*. New York: Thames & Hudson, 1991. ISBN 0-500-27606-4. ‣ Summary of North American prehistory by area (Great Plains, Far North, West, Eastern Woodlands) with overview of history of North American archaeology. Separate sections on earliest (Paleo-Indian) and latest periods (European contact and after). Generally authoritative and well illustrated. [PJW]

2.95 Gayle J. Fritz. "Multiple pathways to farming in precontact eastern North America." *Journal of world prehistory* 4.4 (1990) 387–435. ISSN 0892-7537. ‣ Excellent summary of archaeobotanical evidence for beginnings of plant cultivation in pre-Columbian eastern North America with comparative reference to Southwest by authoritative paleoethnobotanist. Good summary chart, map, and bibliography. [PJW]

2.96 Jesse D. Jennings. *The prehistory of North America*. 3d ed. Mountain View, Calif.: Mayfield, 1989. ISBN 0-87484-865-2. ‣ Standard textbook treatment. Comprehensive and authoritative; good basic bibliographies. [PJW]

2.97 Jesse D. Jennings, ed. *Ancient North Americans*. Rev. ed. New York: Freeman, 1983. ISBN 0-7167-1428-0. ‣ Includes summary chapters on prehistoric archaeology of each major geographic region plus chapter on peopling of the Americas. Authoritative and fairly up-to-date accounts with good basic bibliographies by well-known experts. [PJW]

2.98 Gordon R. Willey and Jeremy A. Sabloff. *A history of American archaeology*. 3d ed. New York: Freeman, 1993. ISBN 0-7167-2370-2 (cl), 0-7167-2371-9 (pbk). ‣ Summary of origins and development of archaeology in and about the Americas. Valuable, well-written survey with numerous illustrations and substantial bibliography. [PJW]

MESOAMERICA AND SOUTH AMERICA

2.99 Richard E. W. Adams. *Prehistoric Mesoamerica*. Rev. 2d ed. Norman: University of Oklahoma Press, 1991. ISBN 0-8061-2304-4. ‣ Synthesis of native pre-Columbian civilizations of Mesoamerica. Strongest on highland groups with emphasis on continuities from earlier to later complexes. [DLB]

2.100 Michael D. Coe. *Mexico*. 3d ed. New York: Thames & Hudson, 1984. ISBN 0-500-27257-3 (cl), 0-500-27328-6 (pbk). ‣ Highly readable, short summary of prehistoric civilizations of Mexico; strongest on highland cultures. [DLB]

2.101 T. Patrick Culbert, ed. *Classic Maya political history: hieroglyphic and archaeological evidence*. Cambridge: Cambridge University Press, 1991. ISBN 0-521-39210-1. ‣ Focus on political institutions and evolution of specific centers as well as on general models. Data from hieroglyphic texts and their archaeological settings. Good state-of-the-art summaries of these and related topics in last few chapters. [DLB]

2.102 Richard W. Keatinge, ed. *Peruvian prehistory: an overview of pre-Inca and Inca society*. Cambridge: Cambridge University Press, 1988. ISBN 0-521-25560-0 (cl), 0-521-27555-5 (pbk).

▸ Strong contributions by individual specialists on specific selected prehistoric cultures in Peru. Most useful for earlier major civilizations, such as Chavin. [DLB]

2.103 Luis G. Lumbreras. *The peoples and cultures of ancient Peru.* Betty Jane Meggers, trans. Washington, D.C.: Smithsonian Institution Press; distributed by Braziller, 1974. ISBN 0-87474-146-7 (cl), 0-87474-151-3 (pbk). ▸ Most complete synthesis available of civilizations from earliest peoples through Inca; organized on basis of evolutionary stages rather than fixed chronological units. Especially good coverage of highland cultures. Marxist theoretical arguments for origin of Andean state. [DLB]

2.104 Michael E. Moseley. *The Incas and their ancestors: the archaeology of Peru.* London: Thames & Hudson, 1992. ISBN 0-500-05063-5. ▸ Review of Peruvian prehistory from first entry of humans through Incas. Especially good coverage of coastal groups. [DLB]

2.105 Michael E. Moseley and Alana Cordy-Collins, eds. *The northern dynasties, kingship and statecraft in Chimor: a symposium at Dumbarton Oaks, 12th and 13th October 1985.* Washington, D.C.: Dumbarton Oaks Research Library and Collection, 1990. ISBN 0-88402-180-7. ▸ Focuses on largest, immediately pre-Inca state. Extremely important for understanding which institutions are pan-Peruvian and which specific to Chimu or Inca states and their continuities in early colonial periods. [DLB]

2.106 Anna C. Roosevelt. *Moundbuilders of the Amazon: geophysical archaeology on Marajo Island, Brazil.* San Diego, Calif.: Academic Press, 1991. ISBN 0-12-595348-8. ▸ Includes good section on general developmental sequence of Amazonian prehistory along with solid reconstruction of Marajoara chiefdom. Details employment of geophysical methods in archaeological recovery of cultural evidence in tropics. [DLB]

2.107 Linda Schele and Mary E. Miller. *The blood of kings: dynasty and ritual in Maya art.* Rev. ed. Fort Worth, Tex.: Braziller and Kimball Art Museum, 1986. ISBN 0-8076-1159-X (cl), 0-912804-238 (cl), 0-912804-22-X (pbk). ▸ New interpretations of Mayan kingship based on hieroglyphic texts. Includes emphasis on rituals of state, such as bloodletting, based on artistic evidence. [DLB]

2.108 Gordon R. Willey. *South America.* Vol. 2 of *An introduction to American archaeology.* Englewood Cliffs, N.J.: Prentice-Hall, 1971. ISBN 0-13-477851-0. ▸ Synthesis of all complexes from Isthmus of Panama to Tierra del Fuego. Best source for equitable treatment of prehistoric cultural sequences for South American peoples outside of Peru. Subsequent advances in understanding of chronology have left basic sequences unchanged. [DLB]

KEVIN REILLY AND LYNDA NORENE SHAFFER

World History

The antecedents of world history in the West can be found in some of the cultural traditions of the ancient world. A small "culture-in-between" like the ancient Greek, in the shadow of Egypt and threatened by Persia, developed historical writing as early as Herodotus in the fifth century BCE in order to know the other as well as the self. Then, along the trade and pilgrimage routes of the Eurasian ecumene, Christian and Buddhist travelers and thinkers evolved comparative and even presumed universal views of humankind. Medieval Christianity contributed a theological framework that demanded a single narrative, a providential vision that applied to all people, and a useful tool in universal chronology.

The vast house of Islam combined theological universalism and hemispheric coordination, but it was Islam under siege (by the Mongols and the Spanish in the thirteenth to fourteenth century) that produced a world history. Ibn Khaldûn, from a displaced Spanish family in North Africa, contributed a secular anthropology, a comparative method, and a scientific ideal that was directed toward revealing the causes of Islamic defeat. And in Iran, the victorious Mongol rulers, especially after their conversion to Islam, called on local scholars such as Rashid al-din Fadl Allah. This Jewish convert to Islam, while vizier to the Il-khans in Persia, wrote the *Collection of Histories* which covered almost all of Eurasia from the Franks to the Chinese, thus combining the universalism of Islam and Mongol dominion into a work that might lay claim to be the first global history.

While the expansion of Europe created a single world, well-stocked northern museums, and a comparative method suitable for political and cultural critique (in such figures as Thomas More or Voltaire), the advent of an historical anthropology or global history was remarkably late. Despite early prototypes for historical cultural comparisons in preindustrial Europe (e.g., works of Montesquieu or Vico), it was not until the end of the nineteenth century that Europeans used their hegemony and knowledge of the world to develop the elements of a world history. These elements were the historical anthropology and historical sociology of primarily British and German system builders (foremost among them, Max Weber).

In the twentieth century the historical sociological tradition continued in the work of Oswald Spengler (3.54) and Pitirim Sorokin (3.53) and the Christian providential vision in the work of Arnold J. Toynbee (3.62). But it was not until after World War II that world history emerged as a scholarly subdiscipline of history, one that still included the work of generalists, but was not limited to them. This new world history owed much to the phenomenal growth after the war of area studies programs and institutes, many of which defined their areas (East Asia, Middle East, Latin America, South and Southeast Asia, Africa, etc.), more or less as world historians such as Spengler and Toynbee had defined civilizations. Governments, foundations, and universities funded language study and research at these institutes, vastly increasing our knowledge of the world's various regions, but also aiding the emergence of a world history that was more than the sum of its parts.

Two Canadian American historians working in recent Greek history as World War changed to Cold War created important models of world history in the United States. Both William H. McNeill and L. S. Stavrianos (e.g., 3.47, 3.48, 3.55, 3.57) wrote world history textbooks for the newly globally conscious (post-Sputnik) American schools. In many ways their books created paradigms for world history that continue today. Stavrianos offered a stage theory for human development, drawn from European historical sociology (Marx and Weber) and mid-twentieth century archaeology (V. Gordon Childe) to delineate the technological stages of history: hunting-gathering, agricultural, urban, and industrial. McNeill, in his influential *Rise of the West* (3.47)—which combined scholarly erudition and wide-ranging hypotheses for a general audience— and in his textbooks, offered a model for world history based on increasing human interaction, the "expanding ecumene" of technological diffusion, migration, and cultural (later even microbiological) contact.

It was not until the 1980s that other models began to emerge, two from scholars working on Africa, an area that had received little attention from Stavrianos and McNeill. Philip Curtin (perhaps as much by his teaching at Wisconsin-Madison, and Johns Hopkins as by his important monographs) influenced a generation of Africanists to see Africa's role in world history, to study the Atlantic as a global region, and to develop manageable monographs on topics of trade, migration, and cross-cultural contact across regional "intercommunicating zones."

Another Africanist, the sociologist Immanuel Wallerstein (3.428), developed a very different model of world history, one less concerned with centering attention on areas like Africa, the South Atlantic, and the Indian Ocean, and more concerned with delineating the Marxist dialectic of capitalist development in the core northern European countries at the expense of increasingly remote "peripheries" that were exploited for their labor, resources, and markets. Wallerstein's world-systems theory has proved an extremely influential approach to the study of both the development of capitalism and the history of the Third World. In recent years, however, his model has been criticized for displaying the same Eurocentrism as its Marxist forerunners. Some scholars such as economist Andre Gunder Frank and sociologist Janet Abu-Lughod have rejected the uniqueness of Europe's world system and offer instead an earlier date for capitalism or core-periphery tension: Abu-Lughod (3.405) argues for a thirteenth-century Islamic world trading system; Gunder Frank (3.415) poses an ancient world system.

Wallerstein named the Fernand Braudel Center at Binghamton after the leader of the French Annales school, who founded a world history in France in mid-century that we must account a fifth model (if it were not actually first). Braudel initiated a route to world history as early as 1949 with the publication of his *The Mediterranean and the Mediterranean World of Philip II* (6.26). This two-volume masterpiece made two important contributions to world history. First, it chose as its area of study not France, or even Europe, but a vast region, from North Africa to the Alps, from the Atlantic to the Levant, that encompassed the Mediterranean as its lake. In this way, Braudel taught other historians to move from national history to regional and transregional histories and to explore the way seas and deserts integrated different cultures over vast areas. The work of his student K. N. Chaudhuri (3.37) on the Indian Ocean from Persia to China as a trading and cultural area is instructive in this regard. Second *The Mediter-*

ranean and Braudel's more explicit world history, his three-volume *Civilization and Capitalism* (3.247, 3.345, 3.346) contributed to world history the focus on the *longue durée*. By beginning each of these major works with an examination of the longest historical processes—geology, geography, climate—and then moving gradually to lengthy social processes—food, clothing, housing—Braudel called attention to the vast territorial regions in which these continuities took place. Further, the definition of cultures by the use of butter or oil, camel or wheel, viticulture or transhumance betrayed history's obsession with such transitory phenomena as nations and states. In Braudel's history, politics (some critics argued, even people) flicker fleetingly far from the stage.

In much the way Braudel moved from a new kind of regional history in *The Mediterranean* to a genuine world history, the American Islamic historian Marshall G. S. Hodgson in the 1950s and 1960s developed a history of Islam that assumed hemispheric boundaries and a context of global history for his subject, and, had he lived, would have written an explicit world history, but one in which the Afro-Eurasian landmass rather than Europe would be central. Even his *magnum opus*, *The Venture of Islam* (3.136), which includes much of his work on a future world history, was published posthumously. In *The Venture*, he not only situated Islam in a global context, he redrew that global history, centering it geographically in the middle of Eurasia in the "Nile to Oxus" region and chronologically in the "agrarianate cities" age that lasted until the modern "technical" age beginning around 1800. With this periodization, Hodgson emphasized the vitality of Islam into the period of "gunpowder empires" in the sixteenth to eighteenth centuries, underscoring the limits of European hegemony before 1800.

Such periodizations by Hodgson, his followers, and many other historians of Africa and Asia have often been used to counter a Europe-centered world history that charts a straight line from the Renaissance to the modern world, or posits an ever dynamic West surrounded by a static "traditional" world. This view is most unapologetically expressed by proponents of modernization theory, initiated by C. E. Black's *The Dynamics of Modernization* (3.432). In its extreme form modernization theory has been equivalent to a belief in a single-line historical process, that experienced by the West, and the conviction that westernization was an inevitable and advantageous model for the rest of the world. Recently there have been more subtle works in the tradition of modernization theory (often by political scientists).

Seven models would seem more than sufficient, but the rapid proliferation of works and approaches to world history has continued unabated in recent decades. The newness of the field (the World History Association dates from 1982, its *Journal of World History* from 1990), and growing global interaction, account for its vitality. Like a newly opened country, world history draws its numbers from immigrants. Historians and other social scientists come from various specialties that gain coherence and perspective from comparison, regionalization, or globalization. Only within the last few years have graduate departments initiated programs to train world historians.

So perhaps an eighth model should be added to our list—one that draws on the specialties of the "immigrants" to the field. We might call this the composite world history. This is the encyclopedic survey that is based not so much on a single vision, but on an accumulation of insights from area specialists who attempt to elicit the globally relevant from their areas of expertise. Most college textbooks are produced according to this method, gaining in current expertise what might be lost in coherence. It is also the method of one of the earliest modern world histories, the UNESCO *History of Mankind*, the multivolume international project of the 1950s and 1960s.

The preceding is our modeling of the field rather than a map of any actual intramural walls. Therefore we have chosen other categories for organizing this bibliography, both chronological and topical. The chronological periods are fairly commonplace. We did, however, divide one category geographically in order to separate simultaneous narratives. Thus a section called "Columbian Exchanges and Encounters, 1400–1600" is followed by "Afro-Eurasian Worlds, 1500–1800." Like any narrative, this will obscure some things (e.g., the Portuguese empire), while revealing others (e.g., the creation of an Atlantic world).

The topical categories require greater explanation. In the case of fairly well-established and widely recognized paradigms—modernization theory and world-systems theory—we have borrowed them intact, adding colonialism and imperialism to the latter. Other categories, demography, economy and society, and science and technology, are fairly conventional subdivisions of historical inquiry. Women is similarly a conventional heading, properly expected, though we regret the opportunity consequently lost to integrate women's history into the other topics. Some topics (frontiers, ecology, cross-cultural trade and exchange, and cross-cultural travelers) are preeminently world history topics. These topics reflect both traditional interests and new directions in world history. The rapidity at which the field is evolving, however, precludes any confidence that these will remain the categories of the field. Our only certainty is that future editions of this bibliography will make our list appear a mere beginning.

Entries are arranged under the following headings:

[Contributors: ALB = Anne L. Barstow, BAH = Brady A. Hughes, BFM = Beatrice F. Manz, BL = F. Bullitt Lowry, CAL = Craig A. Lockard, CRP = Carla Rahn Phillips, CU = Carol Urness, DHM = David Harry Miller, GCT = Gordon C. Thomasson, GD = Georgi Derluguian, GFM = Gladys Frantz-Murphy, JAM = John A. Mears, KR = Kevin Reilly, LEL = Loyd E. Lee, LGD = Liubov G. Derluguian, LJF = Lorenz J. Firsching, LMG = Lydia M. Garner, LNS = Lynda Norene Shaffer, LSS = Lloyd S. Swenson, MET = Mary Evelyn Tucker, MJG = Marc Jason Gilbert, PM = Patrick Manning, RBB = Roger B. Beck, SSG = Stephen S. Gosch, SSH = Sarah S. Hughes, WDP = William D. Phillips, Jr.]

REFERENCE WORKS

3.1 Isma'il Ragi Al-Faruqi and David E. Sopher, eds. *Historical atlas of the religions of the world.* New York: Macmillan, 1974. ISBN 0-02-336400-9. ▸ Addresses cross-cultural topics such as use of stimulants in religious practices. Includes chronology. Useful for library collections lacking specialized encyclopedias of major world religions, i.e., *The Encyclopedia of Islam.* [MJG]

3.2 Arthur S. Banks and Center for Comparative Political Research, State University of New York at Binghamton, comps. *Cross-polity time series data.* Cambridge, Mass.: MIT Press, 1971. ISBN 0-262-02071-8. ▸ Useful databank of statistical resources for years 1815–1966. Divided into ten sections, including revenue and episodes of domestic conflict. [MJG]

3.3 Geoffrey Barraclough, ed. *The Times atlas of world history.* 1989 3d ed. Norman Stone, ed. of 3d edition. New York: Hammond, 1991. ISBN 0-7230-0304-1. ▸ Premier atlas of world history. Informed by author's pioneering ecumenical view. [MJG]

3.4 Geoffrey Barraclough, ed. *The Times concise atlas of world history.* 3d ed. Maplewood, N.J.: Hammond, 1988. ISBN 0-7230-0280-0. ▸ Shorter version of 3.3; most of maps from original. [KR]

3.5 Robert Blackey. *Modern revolutions and revolutionists: a bibliography.* Santa Barbara, Calif.: ABC-Clio, 1976. ISBN 0-87436-223-7. ▸ Comprehensive list of works on political upheavals, 1555–1975. [MJG]

3.6 Courtlandt Canby. *The Encyclopedia of historic places.* 2 vols. Gordon Carruth, ed. New York: Facts on File, 1984. ISBN 0-87196-126-1 (set), 0-87196-397-3 (v. 1), 0-87196-125-3 (v. 2). ▸ Standard reference; 100,000 user-friendly entries. [MJG]

3.7 Gérard Chaliand and Jean-Pierre Rageau. *A strategic atlas: comparative geopolitics of the world's powers.* 3d ed. Tony Berrett, trans. New York: Harper & Row, 1992. ISBN 0-06-271554-2 (cl), 0-06-273153-X (pbk). ▸ Effort to overcome Eurocentric bias of most strategic map collections through circular map projections and attention to world beyond Europe. [MJG]

3.8 Ben Crow et al. *The Third World atlas.* 1983 ed. Milton Keynes, England, and Philadelphia: Open University Press, 1988. ISBN 0-335-15015-2 (cl), 0-335-10259-X (pbk). ▸ Corrective to Eurocentric content of most atlases. Produced as part of Open University Third World Studies course. [MJG]

3.9 Gerald Danzer. *Discovering world history through maps and views.* New York: HarperCollins, 1992. ISBN 0-06-500559-7. ▸ Superb loose-leaf instructional atlas with sixty-seven plates prepared for overhead projection. Effective introduction to both cartography and world history. [MJG]

3.10 Diagram Group. *Time lines on file.* New York: Facts on File, 1988. ISBN 0-8160-1897-9. ▸ Useful resource. Removable pages and other features make it valuable aid to teaching as well as research. [MJG]

3.11 Joe D. Dixon and Neil D. Martin, eds. *1982 world history teaching conference; USAF-TR-83-11.* Colorado Springs: United States Air Force Academy, 1983. ▸ Important, valuable collection of papers from conference that played significant role in founding of World History Association. Includes historiography, analytical essays on modernization and world-systems theory, and rationales for teaching world history. [LNS]

3.12 John Drexel, ed. *The Facts on File encyclopedia of the twentieth century.* New York: Facts on File, 1991. ISBN 0-8160-2461-8. ▸ Stands out in crowded field of contemporary encyclopedias and almanacs. Worldwide scope and effective cross-indexing, with bibliographies appended to many entries. [MJG]

3.13 Felipe Fernández-Armesto, ed. *The Times atlas of world exploration: 3,000 years of exploring, explorers, and mapmaking.* K. N. Chaudhuri et al., eds. New York: HarperCollins, 1991. ISBN 0-06-270032-4. ▸ Effort to transcend Eurocentric framework within which many Western scholars have placed world exploration. [MJG]

3.14 G.S.P. Freeman-Grenville. *Chronology of world history: a calendar of events from 3000 B.C. to A.D. 1976.* 2d ed. Totowa, N.J.: Rowman & Littlefield, 1978. ISBN 0-8476-6040-0. ▸ Outstanding treatment of political and military history, but second to *Timetables of History* (3.15) in treatment of cultural affairs. [MJG]

3.15 Bernard Grun. *Timetables of history: a horizontal linkage of people and events.* 3d rev. ed. New York: Simon & Schuster, 1991. ISBN 0-671-74919-6 (cl), 0-671-74271-X (pbk). ▸ Premier chronology of world history. Based on Werner Stein's *Kulturfahrplan.* Examines history and politics, literature and theater, religion and philosophy, visual arts and music, science and growth, and daily life. Eurocentric. [MJG/SSG]

3.16 John Keegan, ed. *The Times atlas of the Second World War.* New York: Harper & Row, 1989. ISBN 0-06-016178-7. ▸ Acclaimed work by leading authority in military history. [MJG]

3.17 Michael Kidron and Ronald Segal. *The new state of the* *world atlas.* 4th ed. New York: Simon & Schuster, 1991. ISBN 0-671-74556-5. ▸ Topical treatment of issues ranging from nuclear proliferation and growth of refugee populations to current status of gay and women's rights. [MJG]

3.18 William L. Langer, ed. *An encyclopedia of world history: ancient, medieval, and modern, chronologically arranged.* 5th rev. ed. Boston: Houghton-Mifflin, 1972. ISBN 0-395-13592-3. ▸ Premier encyclopedia of world history, and indispensable resource. Basic one-volume desk reference, begun as Karl Ploetz's *Epitome of History* over a century ago. Now a handbook in eight chronological parts, more than 1,500 pages; includes eleven helpful tabular appendixes and almost 200 pages of index. [MJG/LSS/SSG]

3.19 Colin McEvedy and Richard Jones. *Atlas of world population history.* New York: Facts on File, 1978. ISBN 0-87196-402-3. ▸ National, regional, continental, and world population data presented in text and graphs. Includes summaries of population trends and annotated bibliography. Use with caution, e.g., Americas before 1500. [MJG/SSG]

3.20 R. I. Moore, ed. *Atlas of world history.* 1987 rev. ed. Chicago: Rand McNally, 1992. ISBN 0-528-83499-3 (cl), 0-528-83498-3 (pbk). ▸ Explores evolution of human communities from isolation to globalism. Most maps have European-American focus, but thoughtful attention given to non-European societies. Attractive color maps and extensive text. [MJG]

3.21 Richard B. Morris and Graham W. Irwin, eds. *Harper encyclopedia of the modern world: a concise reference history from 1760 to the present.* New York: Harper & Row, 1970. ▸ Standard reference. [MJG]

3.22 Kevin Reilly, ed. *World history.* 3d ed. New York: Wiener, 1991. ISBN 1-55876-033-4. ▸ Exemplary syllabi from wide variety of institutions. Indicates conceptualizations of field as well as seminal works. [LNS]

3.23 Martha Ross, comp. *Rulers and governments of the world.* Vol. 1: *Earliest times to 1491.* New York: Bowker, 1977. ISBN 0-85935-051-7 (set), 0-85935-021-5 (v. 1). ▸ Supersedes previous efforts to catalog identities of premodern rulers. [MJG]

3.24 Chris Scarre. *Past worlds: the Times atlas of archeology.* Maplewood, N.J.: Hammond, 1989. ISBN 0-7230-0306-8. ▸ Invaluable resource; 750 maps, illustrations, and superb site reconstructions. Divided into seven chronological sections, concluding with period 650–1800 CE. [MJG]

3.25 Joseph E. Schwartzberg, ed. *A historical atlas of South Asia.* 1978 ed. New York: Oxford University Press, 1992. (Association for Asian Studies, Reference series, 2.) ISBN 0-19-506869-6. ▸ Indispensable, comprehensive resource. Excellent representation of divergent scholarly opinion showing, for example, "Ten Views of the Limits of the Kusana Empire c. 1–300 A.D." Maps show known kingdoms and territorial representations in classical epochs. [GCT]

3.26 Leon E. Selzer and Geographical Research Staff of Columbia University Press with American Geographical Society, eds. *The Columbia Lippincott gazetteer of the world with 1961 supplement.* 1952 ed. New York: Columbia University Press, 1962. ▸ Despite venerable age, single most valuable historical gazetteer. [MJG]

3.27 William R. Shepherd, ed. *Shepherd's historical atlas.* 9th rev. ed. Totowa, N.J.: Barnes & Noble, 1980. ISBN 0-389-20155-3. ▸ Standard reference. Maps of high quality, but most created before 1929. [MJG]

3.28 Bertold Spuler, comp. *Rulers and governments of the world.* 3 vols. John Fletcher, trans. New York: Bowker, 1977. ISBN 0-85935-051-7 (set). ▸ Standard reference to those in power in var-

ious countries and periods, including basic biographical information. German edition, 4 volumes, compiled as 3 volumes for English edition: volume 1 covers period to 1491; volume 2, 1492–29; and volume 3, 1930–75. Translation of *Regenten und Regierungen der Welt.* [MJG]

3.29 Pierre Vidal-Naquet, ed. *The Harper atlas of world history.* New York: Harper & Row, 1987. ISBN 0-06-181884-4. ▸ Some maintain this work is superior to *The Times Atlas of World History* (3.3). Exceptionally clear maps and graphic displays, chronology, extensive text, and well-chosen illustrative material. [MJG]

3.30 W. Warren Wagar. *Books in world history: a guide for teachers and students.* Bloomington: Indiana University Press, 1973. ISBN 0-253-31220-5. ▸ Stimulating introduction to field. Explores variety of teaching strategies and identifies 480 reference works and monographs. [MJG]

3.31 *Webster's new biographical dictionary.* 1983 rev. ed. Springfield, Mass.: Merriam-Webster, 1988. ISBN 0-87779-543-6. ▸ Useful for library collections without specialized regional/national sources such as *The Dictionary of National Biography.* Contains 30,000 entries drawn from all regions and periods. [MJG]

3.32 *Webster's new geographical dictionary.* 1980 ed. Springfield, Mass.: Merriam-Webster, 1988. ISBN 0-87779-446-4. ▸ Standard reference. Real benefits can be derived from using this dictionary alongside much older, but more comprehensive *Columbia Lippincott Gazetteer of the World* (3.26). [MJG]

3.33 Bruce Wetterau. *Macmillan concise dictionary of world history.* 1983 ed. New York: Collier, 1986. ISBN 0-02-626110-3 (cl, 1983), 0-02-082410-6 (pbk). ▸ Contains 17,000 brief, effectively indexed entries. [MJG]

3.34 *The world atlas of archaeology.* Boston: Hall, 1985. ISBN 0-8161-8747-9. ▸ Premier general atlas of ancient world. Informed by Annales school and includes thematic treatments of some topics, e.g., European horse sacrifice. [MJG]

SEE ALSO
36.74 Michael D. Coe et al. *Atlas of ancient America.*

CLASSICS AND GENERAL STUDIES

3.35 Philip Bagby. *Culture and history: prolegomena to the comparative study of civilizations.* 1958 ed. Westport, Conn.: Greenwood, 1976. ISBN 0-8371-8797-4. ▸ Significant comparative study of anthropological and historical presuppositions and methodology. Shows how anthropological idea of culture can be useful to historians in constructing history of civilizations. Originally published in 1958 as criticism of system-building in philosophy of history. [LSS/KR]

3.36 Daniel J. Boorstin. *The discoverers: an illustrated history of man's search to know his world and himself.* 1983 ed. 2 vols. New York: Abrams, 1991. ISBN 0-8109-3207-5 (set). ▸ Four books in one, devoted to natural versus artificial time, explorations in geography, advent of physical sciences, and geneses of social sciences. Originally published in one volume as *The Discoverers* (1983). Precursor to *The Creators* (1992). [LSS]

3.37 K. N. Chaudhuri. *Asia before Europe: economy and civilisation of the Indian Ocean from the rise of Islam to 1750.* Cambridge: Cambridge University Press, 1990. ISBN 0-521-30400-8 (cl), 0-521-31681-2 (pbk). ▸ Does for Indian Ocean what Braudel did for Mediterranean (6.26); vast canvas from Middle East to China. Rich and suggestive detail on "structure" of time and space, food and drink, clothing, "architecture of symbolic power," land, nomadism, and towns and cities. Masterpiece, despite mathematical eccentricities. [KR/LEL]

3.38 Rushton Coulborn. *The origin of civilized societies.* 1959 ed. Princeton: Princeton University Press, 1969. ▸ Bridges archaeology and prehistory with brief comparisons of seven independently originating civilized societies. Uses multivariate analysis and assumes rapid evolutionary responses to threats to cultural survival; position paper for multiple, independent origins of civilized societies in Egypt, Mesopotamia, India, Crete, China, Mesoamerica, and Andes. [LSS]

3.39 Christopher Dawson. *The dynamics of world history.* 1956 ed. John J. Mulloy, ed. La Salle, Ill.: Sugden, 1978. ISBN 0-89385-003-9. ‣ Catholic sociological history, global and providential, with resacralization and European ethnocentrism presumed. Apologetics at their best for mid-twentieth century. Compares visions of Saint Augustine, Edward Gibbon, Karl Marx, H. G. Wells, Oswald Spengler, and Arnold Toynbee. [LSS/KR]

3.40 Anthony Esler. *The human venture: a world history from prehistory to the present.* 2d ed. Englewood Cliffs, N.J.: Prentice-Hall, 1992. ISBN 0-13-430943-X. ‣ Short college text distinguished by broad geographical coverage (including the Pacific) and lively writing style. Available in two volumes as *The Human Venture: The Great Enterprise, a World History to 1500* and *The Human Venture: The Globe Encompassed, a World History since 1500.* [KR]

3.41 John A. Garraty and Peter Gay, eds. *The Columbia history of the world.* 1972 ed. New York: Dorset, 1981. ISBN 0-88029-004-8. ‣ Expanded lectures by forty Columbia University faculty experts covering areas and periods considered comprehensive in New York City in 1960s. Influential overview emphasizing Europe. [LSS]

3.42 Ernest Gellner. *Plough, sword, and book: the structure of human history.* 1988 ed. Chicago: University of Chicago Press, 1989. ISBN 0-226-28701-7. ‣ Application of social anthropology to metahistory. Examines agriculture (i.e., production), armaments (coercion), and information storage (cognition) as titular symbols for cognitive evolution of humankind. Linguistic and ethnographic reflections illuminate prime trends of cultural inheritance of acquired characteristics. [LSS]

3.43 International Commission for a History of the Scientific and Cultural Development of Mankind. *History of mankind: cultural and scientific development.* 6 vols. New York: Harper & Row and Allen & Unwin, 1963-76. ISBN 0-06-013275-2 (v. 2), 0-06-014622-2 (v. 3), 0-06-014993-8 (v. 4), 0-04-900026-8 (v. 5), 0-06-014532-3 (v. 6). ‣ Monumental effort to produce comprehensive cultural history. Invaluable reference work with substantial bibliographies, although often criticized. [LNS]

3.44 William H. McNeill. *Arnold J. Toynbee: a life.* New York: Oxford University Press, 1989. ISBN 0-19-505863-1 (cl), 0-19-506335-X (pbk). ‣ Personal and professional biography of historian who had great influence on writing of world history; finely crafted by his most worthy successor. Reveals Toynbee's remarkable productivity and ideas that motivated him. Concludes Toynbee was better historian, with broader vision, than H. G. Wells or Oswald Spengler. [LNS]

3.45 William H. McNeill. *A history of the human community: prehistory to the present.* 4th ed. Englewood Cliffs, N.J.: Prentice-Hall, 1993. ISBN 0-13-388273-X (one vol. ed.), 0-13-389701-X (v. 1), 0-13-389719-2 (v. 2). ‣ Simplified version of *The Rise of the West,* as college text (developed from earlier secondary school text). Available in two volumes as *A History of the Human Community.* [KR]

3.46 William H. McNeill. *Mythistory and other essays.* Chicago: University of Chicago Press, 1986. ISBN 0-226-56135-6. ‣ Collection of ten essays on historiography, defense of world history, and sketches of other master historians. Based on 1985 presidential address before American Historical Association entitled "Truth, Myth, History, and Historians." [LSS]

3.47 William H. McNeill. *The rise of the West: a history of the human community.* 1963 ed. Chicago: University of Chicago

Press, 1991. ISBN 0-226-56141-0 (pbk). ‣ Brilliant, erudite, and lucid survey that propelled world history to public consciousness and professional legitimacy. In retrospect, emphasis on military technology and cultural diffusion reflected American imperial vision, and slights China and Africa, but still in a class by itself. [KR]

3.48 William H. McNeill. *A world history.* 3d ed. New York: Oxford University Press, 1979. ISBN 0-19-502554-7 (cl), 0-19-502555-5 (pbk). ‣ Abridged version of 3.47, for college and general reader with new folio of plates that illustrate global trends in history of art. [KR]

3.49 Lewis Mumford. *The city in history: its origins, its transformations, and its prospects.* New York: Harcourt, Brace & World, 1961. ‣ History of city in all its symbolism. Limited to Western history and dated, but joy to read and bursting with suggestions. Invaluable tool in considering global history of city, from Palaeolithic sanctuary to postwar suburbia. [KR]

3.50 Carroll Quigley. *The evolution of civilizations: an introduction to historical analysis.* 2d ed. Indianapolis: Liberty, 1979. ISBN 0-913966-56-8 (cl), 0-913966-57-6 (pbk). ‣ First of two studies showing value of applied metahistory for international relations. Followed by *Tragedy and Hope* in 1966 for twentieth century. [LSS]

3.51 Kevin Reilly. *The West and the world: a history of civilization.* 2d ed. New York: Harper & Row, 1989. ISBN 0-06-045346-X (v. 1), 0-06-045347-8 (v. 2). ‣ Historical essays on topical issues (e.g., men and women, love and sex, war and peace, economics and ecology, individual and society) within broad chronological periods. College text. [LNS]

3.52 J. M. Roberts. *The Hutchinson history of the world.* Rev. ed. London: Hutchinson, 1987. ISBN 0-09-126970-9. ‣ One of many incarnations in print and video media of Oxford don's guided tour of global interactions. Emphasizes historical inertia as well as changes provoked by technological progression. [LSS]

3.53 Pitirim Aleksandrovich Sorokin. *Social and cultural dynamics.* 1937-41 ed. 4 vols. New York: Bedminster, 1962. ‣ Masterwork of founder of positivist sociology and comparative study of civilizations, or better, sociocultural supersystems. Analyzes cyclical fluctuations in art, truth, law, ethics, war, and social relationships to describe macroscopically fateful returns of ideational, sensate, and idealistic phases in human developments. Abridged and revised (1957). [LSS]

3.54 Oswald Spengler. *The decline of the West.* 1926-28 ed. 2 vols. Charles Francis Atkinson, ed. and trans. New York: Knopf, 1970. ‣ First of three great works of modern metahistory establishing Oswald Spengler, Arnold Toynbee, and Pitirim Sorokin as most influential scholar-prophets outside of professional academic history. First published 1918. [LSS]

3.55 L. S. Stavrianos. *A global history: from prehistory to the present.* 5th ed. Englewood Cliffs, N.J.: Prentice-Hall, 1991. ISBN 0-13-357005-3. ‣ One of the earliest and most widely used college texts. Emphasizes technological and social changes. Also available as *The World to 1500: A Global History* and *The World since 1500: A Global History.* [KR]

3.56 L. S. Stavrianos. *Global rift: the Third World comes of age.* New York: Morrow, 1981. ISBN 0-688-00656-6 (cl), 0-688-00657-4 (pbk). ‣ Richly documented, unabashedly progressive survey of development of Third World as dependency of capitalist North in world economic system and recent history of resistance and waves of revolution. Effective combination of detailed narrative and sweeping generalization, local and global perspectives. Comprehensive and very readable. [KR]

3.57 L. S. Stavrianos. *Lifelines from our past: a new world history.* 1989 ed. Kevin Reilly, Foreword. Armonk, N.Y.: Sharpe, 1992.

ISBN 1-56324-031-9. ▸ Latest synthesis from prolific rival to William H. McNeill whose global visions have usually emphasized technologies and balkanizations. Humankind progresses through kinship, tributary, and capitalist societies, each of which exhibits four "lifeline" issues—ecology, gender relations, social relations, and war. [LSS]

3.58 Peter N. Stearns. *World history: patterns of change and continuity.* New York: Harper & Row, 1987. ISBN 0-06-046386-4 (pbk). ▸ Short college text organized in broad chronological periods to distinguish characteristics of large civilizations or geographical/cultural areas. [KR]

3.59 Traian Stoianovich. *A study in Balkan civilization.* New York: Knopf, 1967. ▸ Braudellian "total history" of region over *longue durée.* By reconceptualizing history of many diverse cultures of Balkans over millennia, brilliantly shows how world history can break old categories. [KR]

3.60 Frederick J. Teggart. *Theory and processes of history.* 1941 ed. Berkeley: University of California Press, 1977. ISBN 0-520-03176-8 (pbk). ▸ Assessment of methodology and historiography amid growing anthropological consciousness before and after World War I. Argues for scientific-like laws in historical process. Part on processes first published 1918, theory in 1925. Influenced "new history" movement between wars to become more anthropologically sophisticated. [LSS/KR]

3.61 Hugh Thomas. *A history of the world.* Rev. ed. New York: HarperColophon, 1982. ISBN 0-06-090891-2 (pbk). ▸ Idiosyncratic montage in some 700 pages of thematic treatments of six topics: hunter-gatherers, agriculturalists, Renaissance-Reformationists, industrializers, democratizers, and cold warriors. [LSS]

3.62 Arnold J. Toynbee. *A study of history.* 12 vols. New York: Oxford University Press, 1935–61. ▸ Magisterial study by English classicist turned generalist by trauma of World War I. Substitutes societies or civilizations for nation-states as most intelligible units for long-term history. Combines cyclical-secular with linear-sacred assumptions. [LSS]

3.63 Arnold J. Toynbee. *A study of history: abridgement of volumes 1–10.* Abr. ed. 2 vols. D. C. Somervell, ed. London: Oxford University Press, 1947–57. ▸ Careful rewrite and encapsulation of Toynbee's thought. Independently done, but praised by Toynbee and more widely read than ten-volume original. First six volumes condensed in 1939, next four in 1954. [LSS]

3.64 Hendrik Willem Van Loon. *The story of mankind.* 1921 ed. New York: Liveright, 1984. ISBN 0-87140-647-0. ▸ Perhaps most influential world history in popular literature produced between world wars, comparable from 1921 onward with Wells (3.65). Cartoon-illustrated for younger generation. [LSS]

3.65 H. G. Wells. *The outline of history, being a plain history of life and mankind.* Rev. ed. Raymond Postgate and G. P. Wells. Garden City, N.Y.: Doubleday, 1971. ▸ Most popular and influential world history ever published in English. Natural history of culture, with Fabian socialist tints. Finds evolutionary progress threatened by ignorance of masses, being manipulated to kill each other in name of nation-state. First published 1920. [LSS]

3.66 Leslie A. White. *The evolution of culture: the development of civilization to the fall of Rome.* New York: McGraw-Hill, 1959. ▸ Ancient history by anthropologist aiming to illustrate power of concept of culture and of science devoted to its study. [LSS]

3.67 Eric R. Wolf. *Europe and the people without history.* Berkeley: University of California Press, 1982. ISBN 0-520-04459-2 (cl), 0-520-04898-9 (pbk). ▸ How European commercial-industrial development since 1400 resulted from exploitation of American Indians, Africans, and Asians. World-system approach that transcends Eurocentrism, highlights people of periphery. Especially

interesting and controversial on fur trade in Americas. [SSG/PM/LSS]

SEE ALSO
1.203 Fernand Braudel. *On history.*

HUNTING, GATHERING, AND EARLY AGRICULTURAL SOCIETIES

3.68 Bernard G. Campbell. *Humankind emerging.* 6th ed. New York: HarperCollins, 1992. ISBN 0-673-52170-2. ▸ Standard authority on origins and evolution of humankind through appearance of first modern people. Detailed exposition of current scholarship with thoughtful overview of human condition. [JAM]

3.69 J. Desmond Clark and Steven A. Brandt, eds. *From hunters to farmers: the causes and consequences of food production in Africa.* Berkeley: University of California Press, 1984. ISBN 0-520-04574-2. ▸ Wide array of information on fundamental transition throughout continent, viewed as important laboratory for investigating general problem of plant and animal domestication. Examines diversity of cultigens and paucity of animal domesticates within different regional contexts. [JAM]

3.70 Grahame Clarke. *World prehistory in new perspective.* 3d ed. Cambridge: Cambridge University Press, 1977. ISBN 0-521-21506-4 (cl), 0-521-29178-x (pbk). ▸ Balanced coverage of major regions, celebrating human inventiveness and diversity. Discussion includes sub-Saharan Africa, Australia, and Oceania. No conclusion, but exceptionally revealing maps, diagrams, pictures, and charts. [JAM]

3.71 Mark Nathan Cohen. *The food crisis in prehistory: overpopulation and the origins of agriculture.* New Haven: Yale University Press, 1977. ISBN 0-300-02016-3. ▸ Applies theory of population pressure to problem of agricultural origins in Americas as well as Eurasia. Compelling argument for historical parallels in different world regions operating in conjunction with local variables. [JAM]

3.72 Eric Delson, ed. *Ancestors, the hard evidence: proceedings of the symposium held at the American Museum of Natural History, April 6–10, 1984 to mark the opening of the exhibition "Ancestors, Four Million Years of Humanity."* New York: Liss, 1985. ISBN 0-8451-0249-4. ▸ Papers from 1984 symposium summarizing state of palaeoanthropology on basis of fossil remains. Especially good presentations on early hominid evolution and history of Neanderthals. [JAM]

3.73 Brian M. Fagan. *The journey from eden: the peopling of our world.* London: Thames & Hudson, 1990. ISBN 0-500-05057-0. ▸ Defense of hypothesis that fully modern humans evolved in Africa and from there colonized globe. Lucid narrative makes difficult issues accessible. [JAM]

3.74 Brian M. Fagan. *People of the earth: an introduction to world prehistory.* 7th ed. New York: HarperCollins, 1992. ISBN 0-673-52167-2 (pbk). ▸ Straightforward account of human history from earliest hominids to emergence of civilizations. Theory and description nicely balanced with appropriate emphasis on Americas. Chronological tables at beginning of each chapter enhance integration. [JAM]

3.75 J. D. Fage and R. A. Oliver, eds. *Papers in African prehistory.* Cambridge: Cambridge University Press, 1970. ISBN 0-521-07470-3. ▸ Handy collection of reprinted articles drawn largely from *Journal of African History.* Overarching themes delineated in two magisterial surveys by J. Desmond Clark. Specialized essays, ranging from evolution of tsetse fly to classification of Bantu languages, illuminate broader issues. [JAM]

3.76 Stuart J. Ficdel. *Prehistory of the Americas.* 2d ed. Cambridge: Cambridge University Press, 1992. ISBN 0-521-41532-2 (cl), 0-521-42544-1 (pbk). ▸ New World developments from spread of Palaeo-Indians through origins of agriculture to emergence of complex societies. Concise summary of basic problems. [JAM]

3.77 Marija Gimbutas. *The civilization of the goddess: the world of old Europe.* New York: HarperCollins, 1991. ISBN 0-06-250368-5 (cl), 0-06-250337-5 (pbk). ‣ Most recent and definitive volume in distinguished career of controversial archaeologist. Argues for existence of Neolithic goddess-centered culture in prepatriarchal, pre–Indo-European Europe. Profusely illustrated, mapped, and charted. [KR]

3.78 Donald O. Henry. *From foraging to agriculture: the Levant at the end of the Ice Age.* Philadelphia: University of Pennsylvania Press, 1989. ISBN 0-8122-8137-3. ‣ Synthetic work arguing hunter-gatherer groups in Levant were drawn to new resources that demanded intensified and destabilizing exploitation. Critique of universal explanation for origins of agriculture. [JAM]

3.79 Allen W. Johnson and Timothy Earle. *The evolution of human societies: from foraging group to agrarian state.* Stanford, Calif.: Stanford University Press, 1987. ISBN 0-8047-1339-1. ‣ Theoretically integrated overview of current thinking on evolution of economy in society. Combines economic anthropology with cultural ecology and draws on cross-cultural data. Specific examples enrich meaning of systematically developed analytical framework. [JAM]

3.80 Richard Leakey and Roger Lewin. *Origins reconsidered: in search of what makes us human.* New York: Doubleday, 1992. ISBN 0-385-41264-9. ‣ Most recent reflections of renowned palaeoanthropologist and his coauthor concerning fundamental question of how we became human. Readable, highly personal discourse incorporating ideas from various disciplines. [JAM]

3.81 Philip Lieberman. *The biology and evolution of language.* Cambridge, Mass.: Harvard University Press, 1984. ISBN 0-674-07412-2. ‣ Explication of thesis that evolution of human linguistic and cognitive ability is part of general evolutionary process that explains uniqueness of our humanness. Clear summary of fundamental arguments in conclusion. [JAM]

3.82 Betty J. Meggers. *Prehistoric America: an ecological perspective.* 2d ed. New York: Aldine, 1979. ISBN 0-202-33079-6. ‣ Compact review of early cultural development in New World, emphasizing effects of environmental pressures. Reveals stress on parallels between distant regions; strong concluding chapter. [JAM]

3.83 Paul Mellars, ed. *The emergence of modern humans: an archaeological perspective.* Ithaca, N.Y.: Cornell University Press, 1990. ISBN 0-8014-2614-6. ‣ Indispensable treatment of difficult and controversial questions by impressive array of specialists. Regional studies highlight substantial variations in behavioral and technological development, but contributions on general patterns of greatest interest to historians. [JAM]

3.84 John E. Pfeiffer. *The creative explosion: an inquiry into the origins of art and religion.* 1982 ed. Ithaca, N.Y.: Cornell University Press, 1985. ISBN 0-8014-9308-0 (pbk). ‣ Explanation of abrupt appearance of cave art in France and Spain during Upper Palaeolithic. Discusses issue within context of cultural watershed invoking changes in many areas of human endeavor. Drawings and photographs highlight character of this great release of creativity. [JAM]

3.85 Patricia Phillips. *The prehistory of Europe.* Bloomington: Indiana University Press, 1980. ISBN 0-253-11956-1. ‣ Personal view of new theories and advances in knowledge since late 1960s. Chronological presentation from earliest human presence through Iron Age. Evenhanded coverage but lacks integrating vision. [JAM]

3.86 T. Douglas Price and James A. Brown, eds. *Prehistoric hunter-gatherers: the emergence of cultural complexity.* Orlando,

Fla.: Academic Press, 1985. ISBN 0-12-564750-6. ‣ Multiauthored global approach to culture change in diverse societies, challenging traditional forager-farmer dichotomy. Stimulating combination of theoretical discussion and analysis of specific case studies. [JAM]

3.87 Charles A. Reed, ed. *Origins of agriculture.* The Hague: Mouton; distributed by Aldine, 1977. ISBN 90-279-7919-7. ‣ Discussion of complex problem of beginning and spread of early farming by scholars from all parts of world and many disciplines. High quality individual contributions drawn together by editor's introduction and conclusion. [JAM]

3.88 Colin Renfrew, ed. *The explanation of culture change: models in prehistory; proceedings of a meeting of the Research Seminar in Archaeology and Related Subjects held at the University of Sheffield.* London: Duckworth, 1973. ISBN 0-7156-0673-5. ‣ Interdisciplinary set of essays on new approaches and methods. Discussion of underlying concepts and concluding essay dramatizing intellectual battle lines of particular use to historians. [JAM]

3.89 David Rindos. *The origins of agriculture: an evolutionary perspective.* Robert C. Dunnell, Foreword. Orlando, Fla.: Academic Press, 1984. ISBN 0-12-589280-2. ‣ Theoretical model for development and spread of agricultural systems. Successful integration of many scientific studies into readable synthesis. [JAM]

3.90 Robert J. Wenke. *Patterns in prehistory: humankind's first three million years.* 3d ed. New York: Oxford University Press, 1990. ISBN 0-19-506848-3 (cl), 0-19-505522-5 (pbk). ‣ Sound treatment of five central topics: origins of culture, development of modern humans, spread of Pleistocene societies, emergence of agricultural economies, and rise of cultural complexity. Strong in relating archaeological data to broad issues and identifying regularities of human experience. [JAM]

SEE ALSO
2.77 J. P. Mallory. *In search of the Indo-Europeans.*
2.79 Colin Renfrew. *Archaeology and language.*
10.181 Ping-ti Ho. *The cradle of the East.*

URBAN REVOLUTIONS, 3500–1000 BCE

3.91 Robert McC. Adams. *The evolution of urban society: early Mesopotamia and prehispanic Mexico.* Chicago: Aldine, 1966. ‣ Familiar reference comparing two examples treated as variants of single processual pattern. Straightforward analysis emphasizes similarities between them. Worthwhile starting point despite dated scholarship. [JAM]

3.92 Karl W. Butzer. *Early hydraulic civilization in Egypt: a study in cultural ecology.* Chicago: University of Chicago Press, 1976. ISBN 0-226-08634-8 (cl), 0-226-08635-6 (pbk). ‣ Analysis of rise of one complex society based on irrigation farming from perspective of cultural ecology. Highly readable account with good illustrations, strong conclusion, and lengthy bibliography. [JAM]

3.93 Kwang-chih Chang. *Art, myth, and ritual: the path to political authority in ancient China.* Cambridge, Mass.: Harvard University Press, 1983. ISBN 0-674-04807-5 (cl), 0-674-04808-3 (pbk). ‣ Selected lectures and essays by leading expert in early Chinese history. Interdisciplinary discussion of various factors that concentrated political power in hands of ruling elite. Seldom do so few pages yield so much insight. [JAM]

3.94 Nigel Davies. *The ancient kingdoms of Mexico.* London: Lane, 1982. ISBN 0-7139-1245-6. ‣ Synthesis of pre-Hispanic history of Mexico, with special attention to economic and social trends; coverage excludes Maya. Genuinely revealing photographs, elaborate diagrams, and detailed maps augment informative text. [JAM]

3.95 I. M. Diakonoff, ed. *Early antiquity.* Alexander Kirjanov, trans. Chicago: University of Chicago Press, 1991. ISBN 0-226-

14465-8. ‣ First of recent three-volume set by major Soviet historians of antiquity. Comprehensive, accessible synthesis in Marxist tradition for general audience. Topics include periodization, sources, and limitations of traditional Marxist categories. Covers Mesopotamia, Egypt, Hittites, India, and China. [KR]

3.96 Walter A. Fairservis, Jr. *The roots of ancient India.* Chicago: University of Chicago Press, 1975. ISBN 0-226-23429-0 (pbk). ‣ Interpretive framework for holistic understanding of early Indian history based on assumption that its civilization consisted of three components: a great tradition, a little tradition, and a tribal tradition. Especially illuminating introduction for nonspecialist. [JAM]

3.97 Mason Hammond. *The city in the ancient world.* Cambridge, Mass.: Harvard University Press, 1972. ISBN 0-674-13180-0. ‣ General consideration of city and its role in ancient history. Informative discussion with minimal explanatory theory in framework fundamentally oriented toward West. [JAM]

3.98 C. C. Lamberg-Karlovsky and Jeremy A. Sabloff, comps. *The rise and fall of civilizations: modern archaeological approaches to ancient cultures.* Menlo Park, Calif.: Cummings, 1974. ISBN 0-8465-6706-7. ‣ Selected articles by leading authorities with firm theoretical or interpretive positions. Primary emphasis on Mesopotamia and Mesoamerica. Clarification of critical issues in many wide-ranging lists of references. [JAM]

3.99 Charles Keith Maisels. *The emergence of civilization: from hunting and gathering to agriculture, cities, and the state in the Near East.* London: Routledge, 1990. ISBN 0-415-00168-4. ‣ Unusually revealing, up-to-date discussion of key issues raised by crystallization of complex society in ancient Sumer. Immense bibliography reflects extraordinary scholarly achievement. [JAM]

3.100 P.R.S. Moorey, ed. *The origins of civilization.* Oxford: Clarendon, 1979. ISBN 0-19-813198-4. ‣ Integration of fresh research into general surveys of such topics as early development of religion and origins of writing, by distinguished scholars from 1978 Wolfson College lectures at Oxford. Especially interesting are reviews of urban society as it evolved in four contexts: Near East, Europe, China, and Mesoamerica. [JAM]

3.101 Gregory L. Possehl, ed. *Harappan civilization: a contemporary perspective.* Warminster, Pa.: Aris & Philips with American Institute of Indian Studies, 1982. ISBN 0-85668-211-X. ‣ Edited contributions from 1979 international conference held in Kashmir. Strong emphasis on cities and urbanization. Comparative and conceptual essays of particular interest to world historians. [JAM]

3.102 William T. Sanders and Barbara J. Price. *Mesoamerica: the evolution of a civilization.* New York: Random House, 1968. ‣ Theoretical contribution built on substantive data related to one relatively well-documented pristine civilization. Posits principle of critical population mass as condition for rise of cultural complexity; takes ecological approach. Excellent summary in concluding chapters. [JAM]

3.103 Elman R. Service. *Origins of the state and civilization: the process of cultural evolution.* New York: Norton, 1975. ISBN 0-393-05547-7. ‣ Standard reference on early development of political organization in various historical contexts. Comparative study questions theory equating rise of complex societies with maturation of the state. Consciously non-Marxist perspective with set of far-reaching conclusions. [JAM]

SEE ALSO

2.28 Charles L. Redman. *The rise of civilization.*

5.24 Hans J. Nissen. *The early history of the ancient Near East, 9000–2000 B.C.*

6.185 Colin Renfrew. *The emergence of civilisation.*

CLASSICAL TRADITIONS, 1000 BCE–200 CE

3.104 Paul J. Achtemeier, ed. *Harper's Bible dictionary.* San Francisco: Harper & Row, 1985. ISBN 0-06-069862-4 (cl), 0-06-069863-2 (cl, thumb index). ‣ Best one-volume treatment of Hebrew and Christian Bibles and Apocrypha. [GCT]

3.105 William Foxwell Albright. *From the Stone Age to Christianity: monotheism and the historical process.* 1957 2d ed. Baltimore: Johns Hopkins University Press, 1967. ‣ Remarkable, readable one-volume survey; yet to be surpassed. [GCT]

3.106 A. J. Carpenter. "The history of rice in Africa." In *Rice in Africa: proceedings of a conference held at the International Institute of Tropical Agriculture, Ibadan, Nigeria, 7–11 March 1977.* I. W. Buddenhagen and G. J. Persley, eds., pp. 3–10. London: Academic Press, 1978. ISBN 0-12-139350-X. ‣ Important source on ancient Malayo-Polynesian migrations to Madagascar and on movement of Asian rice (*O. sativa*) to Southeast Africa over several centuries BCE. [GCT]

3.107 Janet Coleman. *Ancient and medieval memories: studies in the reconstruction of the past.* Cambridge: Cambridge University Press, 1992. ISBN 0-521-41144-0. ‣ Ancient history and historiography; valuable for understanding use of relevant sources. [GCT]

3.108 Giorgio De Santillana and Hertha von Dechend. *Hamlet's mill: an essay on myth and the frame of time.* 1969 ed. Boston: Godine, 1977. ISBN 0-87923-215-3 (pbk). ‣ Tour-de-force exploration of origins of human knowledge about astronomy and its cultural transmission through media of myth, religion, and ritual. [GCT]

3.109 S. N. Eisenstadt, ed. *The origins and diversity of axial age civilizations.* Albany: State University of New York Press, 1986. ISBN 0-88706-094-3 (cl), 0-88706-096-X (pbk). ‣ Recent update on very important period (600 BCE) within 1000 BCE–200 CE time frame. Elaborates on Jaspers's concept of axial age (3.122). [GCT]

3.110 Josephine Flood. *Archaeology of the dreamtime: the story of prehistoric Australia and its people.* Rev. ed. New Haven: Yale University Press, 1990. ISBN 0-300-04924-2. ‣ Part 5 treats last 2,000 years of prehistory and history. Covers, among other things, evolution of technology and proto-agriculture (predominance of fruit trees at former campsites, etc.). [GCT]

3.111 Theodor H. Gaster. *Thespis: ritual, myth, and drama in the ancient Near East.* 1961 rev. ed. New York: Gordian, 1975. ISBN 0-87752-188-3. ‣ Essential perspective on arts and religions of ancient Near East. [GCT]

3.112 J. R. Hamilton. *Alexander the Great.* 1973 ed. Pittsburgh: University of Pittsburgh Press, 1974. ISBN 0-8229-6084-2. ‣ Careful biography of conqueror and empire builder. [GCT]

3.113 Gerhard Herm. *The Phoenicians: the purple empire of the ancient world.* Caroline Hillier, trans. New York: Morrow, 1975. ISBN 0-688-02908-6. ‣ Analysis of trade and voyaging of early world-traveling (and linking) people. [GCT]

3.114 Hugh Nibley. *The ancient state: the rulers and the ruled.* Donald W. Parry and Stephen D. Ricks, eds. Salt Lake City and Provo, Utah: Deseret Book and Foundation for Ancient Research and Mormon Studies, 1991. ISBN 0-87579-375-4. ‣ Complex comparative studies on origins of ancient state, bringing enormous breadth of primary sources and secondary analysis to bear on such questions as individualism, religion, and politics. [GCT]

3.115 Stuart Piggot. *Ancient Europe from the beginnings of agriculture to classical antiquity: a survey.* 1965 ed. Chicago: Aldine, 1969. ‣ Standard source for ancient Europe. [GCT]

3.116 Robert B. Marks Ridinger. *African archaeology: a selected bibliography.* New York and Toronto: Hall and Macmillan, 1992. ISBN 0-8161-9086-0. ‣ Necessary adjunct to study of ancient

Africa, reflecting virtual neglect of sub-Saharan research compared to more "spectacular" world areas, and consequent scarcity of historical literature. [GCT]

3.117 James M. Robinson, ed. *The Nag Hammadi library in English.* 1988 3d rev. ed. Coptic Gnostic Library Project of the Institute for Antiquity and Christianity, trans. San Francisco: HarperCollins, 1990. ISBN 0-06-066935-7 (pbk). ▸ Essential collection of texts illuminating contact between and syncretism of ancient European, Asian, and African religions, resulting in phenomena called gnosticism. Excellent theoretical commentary. [GCT]

3.118 Karim Sadr. *The development of nomadism in ancient Northeast Africa.* Philadelphia: University of Pennsylvania Press, 1991. ISBN 0-8122-3066-3. ▸ Useful recognition of archaeological bias away from non-Nilotic peoples and societies. Focuses on nomadic peoples and "symbiotic" relationship between nomadic and agricultural societies, 750 BCE to 350–500 CE. [GCT]

3.119 Chester G. Starr. *The influence of sea-power on ancient history.* New York: Oxford University Press, 1989. ISBN 0-19-505666-3 (cl), 0-19-505667-1 (pbk). ▸ Valuable study of interrelationship of oceans, cultural diffusion, and empire in world history. Also treats place of navy in Rome. [GCT]

3.120 Charles D. Trombold, ed. *Ancient road networks and settlement hierarchies in the New World.* Cambridge: Cambridge University Press, 1991. ISBN 0-521-38337-4. ▸ Employs land-use archaeology (cultural geography) to study road-building among South American peoples where there is no evidence of use of wheel. Considers other early social-developmental factors. [GCT]

SEE ALSO
5.13 James B. Pritchard, ed. *Ancient Near Eastern texts relating to the Old Testament.*

CLASSICAL EMPIRES, 500 BCE–500 CE

3.121 Martin Bernal. *The fabrication of ancient Greece, 1785–1985.* Vol. 1 of *Black Athena: the Afroasiatic roots of classical civilization.* New Brunswick, N.J.: Rutgers University Press, 1987. ISBN 0-8135-1276-X (cl), 0-8135-1277-8 (pbk). ▸ Argues roots of classical Greek civilization were in Phoenician and Egyptian civilizations, but those roots were obscured by post-Enlightenment European scholarship, which was racist and antisemitic. Audacious, formidable, and controversial. [KR]

3.122 Karl Jaspers. *Socrates, Buddha, Confucius, and Jesus: the paradigmatic individuals.* 1962 ed. Ralph Manheim, trans. Hannah Arendt, ed. San Diego, Calif.: Harcourt Brace Jovanovich, 1985. ISBN 0-15-683580-0 (pbk). ▸ Introduction of concept of axial age, when philosophical and religious responses to common economic, social, and political problems culminated in world's great religious and philosophical systems. [GFM]

3.123 Jaroslav Krejčí. *Before the European challenge: the great civilizations of Asia and the Middle East.* Albany: State University of New York Press, 1990. ISBN 0-7914-0168-5 (cl), 0-7914-0169-3 (pbk). ▸ Focuses on great religious traditions. Exposition identifies issues; coverage moves from cuneiform tradition through Islam, Hindu, Buddhist, and Confucian societies. Invaluable for teaching global history. [GFM]

3.124 F. E. Peters. *Children of Abraham: Judaism, Christianity, Islam.* Princeton: Princeton University Press, 1983. ISBN 0-691-02030-2 (pbk). ▸ Comparative treatment of scriptures, community, hierarchy, law, liturgy, asceticism, mysticism, and theology of branches of monotheism. For nonspecialist. [GFM]

3.125 F. E. Peters. *The harvest of Hellenism: a history of the Near East from Alexander the Great to the triumph of Christianity.* 1970 ed. New York: Simon & Schuster, 1971. ISBN 0-671-20658-3. ▸ Synthesis of history of Near East from Nile to Himalayas, 338

BCE to 393 CE. Focuses on philosophical and religious traditions. [GFM/KR]

3.126 H. G. Rawlinson. *Intercourse between India and the Western world from the earliest times to the fall of Rome.* 1926 2d ed. New York: Octagon Books, 1971. ISBN 0-374-96721-0. ▸ Cautious, scholarly account of considerable commercial and more limited cultural interaction. Intended to refute contemporaries' overenthusiastic accounts of Indian and Mediterranean influences on each other. [LNS]

3.127 Frederick J. Teggart. *Rome and China: a study of correlations in historical events.* 1939 ed. Westport, Conn.: Greenwood, 1983. ISBN 0-313-24061-2. ▸ Correlates barbarian attacks on Roman frontiers with barbarian warfare on Chinese frontiers. Sees Silk Road as vital to Inner Asian stability. Difficult style; thesis still debated. [GFM]

SEE ALSO
1.18 Donald E. Brown. *Hierarchy, history, and human nature.*
5.542 Donald B. Redford. *Egypt, Canaan, and Israel in ancient times.*
9.61 Samuel N. C. Lieu. *Manichaeism in the later Roman empire and medieval China.*
20.1429 L. D. Reynolds and N. G. Wilson. *Scribes and scholars.*

ECUMENICAL INTEGRATIONS AND EMPIRES, 500–1500

3.128 S.A.M. Adshead. *China in world history.* New York: St. Martin's, 1988. ISBN 0-312-00506-7. ▸ Detailed study of material and cultural foreign influences, foreign relations, and imperial tradition. Especially useful on transmission of material culture. [GFM]

3.129 Karen Armstrong. *Muhammad, a biography of the Prophet.* San Francisco: HarperSanFrancisco, 1992. ISBN 0-06-250014-7. ▸ Incorporates mainstream and fundamental research and interpretations. Puts topic into perspective of world religions and world history. Accessible to nonspecialist audience. [GFM]

3.130 Luce Boulnois. *The Silk Road.* Dennis Chamberlain, trans. New York: Dutton, 1966. ▸ Absorbing account of Chinese silk industry and Central Asian trade routes and nomads involved in international trade. Helpful maps. [GFM]

3.131 Peter Brown. *The world of late antiquity, AD 150–750.* 1971 ed. New York: Norton, 1989. ISBN 0-393-95803-5 (pbk). ▸ Well-illustrated synthesis of evolution of society, culture, and religious thought in ancient Mediterranean during transitional period from Christian to early Islamic times. Breathes life into important and neglected period. [GFM]

3.132 Robert Canfield, ed. *Turko-Persia in historical perspective.* Cambridge: Cambridge University Press, 1991. ISBN 0-521-39094-X. ▸ Essays on history of Iranian and Turkic areas of Central Asia and Middle East. [BFM]

3.133 Geoffrey W. Conrad and Arthur A. Demarest. *Religion and empire: the dynamics of Aztec and Inca expansionism.* Cambridge: Cambridge University Press, 1984. ISBN 0-521-24357-2 (cl), 0-521-31896-3 (pbk). ▸ Separate studies, rather than comparison, but deftly shows how both Aztec and Inca expansions were motivated by religious concerns. Uses "ethnohistorical" documents of sixteenth and seventeenth centuries as well as recent archaeological research; presented in accessible style. [KR]

3.134 Arthur Goldschmidt, Jr. *A concise history of the Middle East.* 4th rev. ed. Boulder: Westview, 1991. ISBN 0-8133-1117-9 (cl), 0-8133-1118-7 (pbk). ▸ Popular, accessible survey of Islamic world, including geographic and historic context of late antiquity from which Islam arose, Prophet Muhammad, Islamic beliefs, and civilization. [GFM]

3.135 René Grousset. *Conqueror of the world.* Marian McKellar and Denis Sinor, trans. New York: Orion, 1967. ▸ Details Chinggis Khan's life based on primary Chinese and Persian sources. Fascinating account of conditions in Central Asia and Mongol beliefs. Definitive biography. [GFM]

3.136 Marshall G. S. Hodgson. *The venture of Islam: conscience and history in a world civilization.* Vol. 1: *The classical age of Islam.* Vol. 2: *The expansion of Islam in the middle periods.* 1974 ed. Chicago: University of Chicago Press, 1977. ISBN 0-226-34677-3 (set), 0-226-34683-8 (v. 1, pbk), 0-226-34684-6 (v. 2, pbk). ▸ History of Islam in context of world history over complete span of Islam in time and space. Includes anthropology, sociology, religious studies, and geography in meaningful paradigm. Volume 2 focuses on religions and cultural and intellectual trends in making of international Islamic order. Some of best coverage of Turkic and Mongol periods. [GFM]

3.137 Emmanuel Le Roy Ladurie. *Times of feast, times of famine: a history of climate since the year 1000.* 1971 ed. Barbara Bray, trans. New York: Farrar, Straus & Giroux, 1988. ISBN 0-374-52122-0. ▸ History of climate focusing on western Europe from medieval times but with reference to evidence available for rest of world. Fascinating example of historian's craft. [GFM]

3.138 Joseph R. Levenson, ed. *European expansion and the counter-example of Asia, 1300–1600.* Englewood Cliffs, N.J.: Prentice-Hall, 1967. ▸ Useful collection of primary and secondary sources that addresses complicated question of why Asian powers (China, in particular) did not create overseas empires and why ultimately they were overtaken by Europe. Considers technology, religion, "spirit," and social structure. [LNS]

3.139 Archibald R. Lewis. *Nomads and Crusaders, AD 1000–1368.* Bloomington: Indiana University Press, 1988. ISBN 0-253-34787-4. ▸ Interpretation that sees Crusades as cause of European success over contemporaries—Asian, Indic, Islamic, Byzantine, Russian—although Europe had no initial advantage. Useful survey of period. [GFM]

3.140 Ferdinand Lot. *The end of the ancient world and the beginnings of the Middle Ages.* 1931 ed. New York: Barnes & Noble, 1966. ISBN 06-131044-1. ▸ Classic interpretation of decline of late Roman cultural economy, society, and polity; Byzantine attempts to revive empire; and rise of papacy and frontier. Suitable for undergraduates. [GFM]

3.141 Harry A. Miskimin. *The economy of early Renaissance Europe, 1300–1460.* 1969 ed. Cambridge: Cambridge University Press, 1975. ISBN 0-521-21017-8 (cl), 0-521-29021-X (pbk). ▸ Topical survey of transition from economy based on subsistence to one based on commerical agriculture and repercussions on social and political organization. Broad implications for economic history in other geographic areas. Suitable for upper level or graduates. [GFM]

3.142 Anthony Reid. *Southeast Asia in the age of commerce, 1450–1680.* Vol. 1: *The lands below the winds.* New Haven: Yale University Press, 1988. ISBN 0-300-03921-2 (v. 1, cl), 0-300-04750-9 (v. 1, pbk). ▸ Multivariate analysis of economic, cultural, and political integration arising from internal stimulus. Burgeoning international trade, enhanced agricultural productivity, and increased population created material and cultural preconditions for political integration. [GFM]

3.143 J. J. Saunders, ed. *The Muslim world on the eve of Europe's expansion.* Englewood Cliffs, N.J.: Prentice-Hall, 1966. ▸ Valuable, informative survey of Muslim world from approximately 1450 to 1550, using selections from primary and secondary sources, regarding situation in Western, Central, South, and Southeast Asia and Muslim parts of Africa. Emphasizes economic and political power of Muslim states; points to religious schism as source of vulnerability. [LNS]

3.144 Lynda Norene Shaffer. *Native Americans before 1492: the moundbuilding centers of the Eastern Woodlands.* Armonk, N.Y.: Sharpe, 1992. ISBN 1-56324-029-7 (cl), 1-56324-030-0 (pbk). ▸ Reconstructs culture extending from Great Lakes to Gulf of Mexico, Great Plains to Appalachian Mountains from archaeology and accounts of early explorers. New perspective on American history. [GFM]

SEE ALSO

7.553 Peter Brown. *The making of late antiquity.*

9.36 Anatoli Mikhailovich Khazanov. *Nomads and the outside world.*

9.138 Christopher I. Beckwith. *The Tibetan empire in Central Asia.*

10.23 Jacques Gernet. *A history of Chinese civilization.*

10.209 Étienne Balazs. *Chinese civilization and bureaucracy.*

10.320 Morris Rossabi, ed. *China among equals.*

10.342 Morris Rossabi. *Khubilai Khan.*

16.43 Kenneth R. Hall. *Maritime trade and state development in early Southeast Asia.*

17.36 Francis E. Peters. *Allah's commonwealth.*

17.93 W. Montgomery Watt. *Muhammad's Mecca.*

17.94 W. Montgomery Watt. *Muhammad.*

19.79 Nehemia Levtzion and J.F.P. Hopkins, eds. *Corpus of early Arabic sources for West African history.*

20.120 Georges Duby. *The early growth of the European economy.*

20.490 David C. Douglas. *The Norman achievement, 1050–1100.*

COLUMBIAN EXCHANGES AND ENCOUNTERS, 1400–1600

3.145 P. M. Ashburn. *The ranks of death: a medical history of the conquest of America.* 1947 ed. Frank D. Ashburn, ed. Philadelphia: Porcupine, 1980. ISBN 0-87991-599-4. ▸ Early treatment of influence of Old World diseases on previously unexposed American Indian populations. [WDP/CRP]

3.146 James Axtell. *After Columbus: essays in the ethnohistory of colonial North America.* New York: Oxford University Press, 1988. ISBN 0-19-505375-3. ▸ Good introduction to important work of ethnohistorian who has published extensively on varieties of interactions between Europeans and American Indians in colonial North America. Extensive scholarship combined with explicit morality and entertaining writing. [WDP/CRP]

3.147 C. R. Boxer. *The Portuguese seaborne empire, 1415–1825.* New York: Knopf, 1969. ▸ Full treatment of Portuguese imperial activities in Africa, Asia, and America. Covers spice trade, religion, slaves, sugar, crown and patronage, and creole societies. Grand narrative by leading scholar. [PM/WDP/CRP]

3.148 Bernadette Bucher. *Icon and conquest: a structural analysis of the illustrations of de Bry's "Great Voyages."* Basia Miller Gulati, trans. Chicago: University of Chicago Press, 1981. ISBN 0-226-07832-9 (pbk). ▸ Examination of early European prints of encounter by structuralist anthropologist, finding they tell more about European than American Indian culture. Well illustrated. Insightful, if a bit formulaic. [KR]

3.149 Pierre Chaunu. *European expansion in the later Middle Ages.* Katharine Bertram, trans. Amsterdam: North Holland; distributed by Elsevier North-Holland, 1979. ISBN 0-444-85132-1. ▸ Comprehensive account of Mediterranean background for European expansion into Africa and America. First published in French in 1969; bibliography not updated for English translation. [WDP/CRP]

3.150 Fredi Chiappelli, ed. *First images of America: the impact of the New World on the Old.* 2 vols. Berkeley: University of California Press, 1976. ISBN 0-520-03010-9. ▸ Extensive collection of studies of literary and artistic impact of Americas on Europe in early colonial period. [WDP/CRP]

3.151 Christopher Columbus. *"The Diario" of Chrisotopher Columbus's first voyage to America, 1492–1493: abstracted by Bartolomé de Las Casas.* Oliver Dunn and James E. Kelley, Jr., eds. and trans. Norman: University of Oklahoma Press, 1989. ISBN 0-8061-2101-7. ‣ Magnificent new edition, with Spanish and English on facing pages, of Las Casas's recension of Columbus's log of his first transatlantic voyage. Essential source for first voyage and initial encounter between Europeans and American Indians. Careful reading distinguishes Columbus's own words from paraphrasing by Las Casas. [WDP/CRP]

3.152 Jeannine Cook, ed. *Columbus and the land of Ayllon: the exploration and settlement of the Southeast.* Valona, Ga.: Lower Altamaha Historical Society–Ayllon, 1992. ISBN 0-9632876-0-5. ‣ Historians, anthropologists, and geographers focus on aspects of exploration, mapping, and colonization of southeastern region of present-day United States by Europeans and Africans. Also includes analyses of responses of American Indians. [WDP/CRP]

3.153 Alfred W. Crosby, Jr. *The Columbian exchange: biological and cultural consequences of 1492.* 1972 ed. Westport, Conn.: Greenwood, 1973. ISBN 0-8371-5821-4 (cl), 0-8371-7228-4 (pbk). ‣ Well-known survey of biology of European contact with Americas. Excellent introduction to impact of diseases on demography and to consequences of exchanges of plants and animals for world history. [WDP/CRP]

3.154 Alfred W. Crosby, Jr. *The Columbian voyages, the Columbian exchange, and their historians.* Washington, D.C.: American Historical Association, 1987. ISBN 0-87229-039-5. ‣ Historiographical survey contrasting romantic, heroic views of Columbus and his enterprise with critical and analytical views. [WDP/CRP]

3.155 William M. Denevan, ed. *The native population of the Americas in 1492.* 2d ed. Madison: University of Wisconsin Press, 1992. ISBN 0-299-13430-X (cl), 0-299-13434-2 (pbk). ‣ Comprehensive collection of speculative but important estimates of pre-Columbian American populations; author's revised total declines to 54 million. Good exercise in comparative method. [PM]

3.156 Bailey W. Diffie. *Prelude to empire: Portugal overseas before Henry the Navigator.* Lincoln: University of Nebraska Press, 1960. ISBN 0-8032-5049-5 (pbk). ‣ Medieval background for Portuguese overseas expansion, stressing internal Portuguese developments and role of Italians in Portuguese naval and maritime enterprise. [WDP/CRP]

3.157 J. H. Elliott. *The Old World and the New, 1492–1650.* 1970 ed. Cambridge: Cambridge University Press, 1992. ISBN 0-521-42709-6 (pbk). ‣ Brief summary by leading English historian of Spanish empire of how Europeans understood and assimilated New World. Study of impact of new ideas, new trading relationships, influx of gold and silver, and new sources of power. [KR]

3.158 Felipe Fernández-Armesto. *Before Columbus: exploration and colonization from the Mediterranean to the Atlantic, 1229–1492.* Philadelphia: University of Pennsylvania Press, 1987. ISBN 0-8122-8083-0. ‣ Indispensable series of essays on aspects of pre-Columbian European expansion in Iberia, Mediterranean, Northwest Africa, and Atlantic islands. Synthesizes vast range of scholarship. [WDP/CRP]

3.159 Felipe Fernández-Armesto. *The Canary Islands after the conquest: the making of a colonial society in the early sixteenth century.* Oxford: Clarendon, 1982. ISBN 0-19-821888-5. ‣ Thorough discussion of economic, political, and social aspects of Spanish settlement in Canary Islands, precursor and practical model for actions in Caribbean islands after 1492. [WDP/CRP]

3.160 Antonello Gerbi. *Nature in the New World: from Christopher Columbus to Gonzalo Fernandez de Oviedo.* Jeremy Moyle, trans. Pittsburgh: University of Pittsburgh Press, 1985. ISBN

0-8229-3516-3. ‣ Good introduction to intellectual history of encounter period. Analyzes thesis of "weakness of America" (idea that natural world of Western Hemisphere did not measure up to Europe's) in earliest chroniclers. [LMG]

3.161 Stephen Greenblatt. *Marvelous possessions: the wonder of the New World.* 1991 ed. Chicago: University of Chicago Press, 1992. ISBN 0-226-30651-8 (cl, 1991), 0-226-30652-6 (pbk). ‣ Leading "new historicism" literary critic mines travelers accounts of Columbus, Bartolemé de Las Casas, Bernal Díaz, and medieval literature. Subjects include Mandeville's *Travels*, connection between wonder and possession, conquest and language, and go-between. Brief but dazzling essays show how different medieval imagination was from our own. [KR]

3.162 Serge Gruzinski. *Painting the conquest: the Mexican Indians and the European Renaissance.* Deke Dusinberre, trans. Paris: Flammarion, 1992. ISBN 2-08-013521-X. ‣ Lavishly illustrated presentation of different visions and mutual influences. Conquest of Mexico was also encounter of two different painting styles and ways of seeing. [KR]

3.163 Henry Hobhouse. *Seeds of change: five plants that transformed mankind.* 1985 ed. New York: Harper & Row, 1986. ISBN 0-06-015631-7. ‣ Account of influence on world history exerted by development of five plants: quinine, potato, sugarcane, cotton, and tea. [WDP/CRP]

3.164 Paul E. Hoffman. *A new Andalusia and a way to the Orient: the American Southeast during the sixteenth century.* Baton Rouge: Louisiana State University Press, 1990. ISBN 0-0871-1552-5. ‣ Soundly researched account of Spanish exploration and settlement in southeastern part of what became United States, with treatment of interactions with native inhabitants and rivalries with European competitors. [WDP/CRP]

3.165 Cecil Jane, ed. and trans. *The four voyages of Columbus: a history in eight documents, including five by Christopher Columbus, in the original Spanish with English translations.* 2 vols. in 1. New York: Dover, 1988. ISBN 0-486-25626-X (pbk). ‣ Originally published in two volumes by Hakluyt Society, includes four letters of Columbus, his memorandum to Ferdinand and Isabella on second voyage, and two contemporary accounts. Excellent introduction and good maps. [KR]

3.166 Miguel León-Portilla, ed. *The broken spears.* 1962 ed. Boston: Beacon, 1992. ISBN 0-8070-5501-8. ‣ Nahuatl-language account of Spanish conquest of Mexico. Accessible, with excellent introduction and notes. Often used in college courses. [KR]

3.167 Jean de Lery. *History of a voyage to the land of Brazil otherwise called America.* Janey Whatley, trans. Berkeley: University of California Press, 1990. ISBN 0-520-06849-1. ‣ Account of author's voyage to Brazil in 1556 and stay among Tupinambi to 1558. Source of valuable historical and ethnographic information. Reveals failure of French attempt to colonize Rio de Janeiro and details of Brazilian Indian life. [LMG]

3.168 Marvin Lunenfeld, ed. *1492: discovery, invasion, encounter; sources and interpretation.* Lexington, Mass.: Heath, 1991. ISBN 0-669-21115-X (pbk). ‣ Comprehensive collection assembling primary and secondary sources bearing on major problems arising from European contact with Americas; includes commentary. [WDP/CRP]

3.169 Alexander Marchant. *From barter to slavery: the economic relations of Portuguese and Indians in the settlement of Brazil, 1500–1580.* 1942 ed. Gloucester, Mass.: Smith, 1966. ‣ Early treatment of economic relations of Portuguese and Brazilian Indians during first century of colonization. Shows events leading to Indian enslavement and decimation by epidemics. [LMG]

3.170 John Mercer. *The Canary Islanders: their prehistory, conquest, and survival.* London: Collings, 1980. ISBN 0-86036-126-8. ‣ Full account of Canary Islands and their people from prehistoric times to present, with emphasis on colonial period beginning in fifteenth century. [WDP/CRP]

3.171 Jerald T. Milanich and Susan Milbrath, eds. *First encounters: Spanish explorations in the Caribbean and the United States, 1492–1570.* Gainesville: University Presses of Florida and Florida Museum of Natural History, 1989. ISBN 0-8130-0946-4 (cl), 0-8130-0947-2 (pbk). ‣ Rare collection; most articles address neglected topic of early contact between Spanish and Indians in Southeast United States, especially Florida, Alabama, and northwestern Georgia. Good introductory material, particularly on Timucua and Coosa Indians, on Spanish expeditions, Indian resistance, trade goods, and missions. Important addition to encounter literature. [LNS]

3.172 Samuel Eliot Morison. *Admiral of the ocean sea: a life of Christopher Columbus.* 1942 ed. 2 vols. New York: Time, 1962. ‣ Pulitzer Prize–winning (1942) romantic biography of Columbus. Both product of and contributor to mythic-heroic image of Columbus; influenced encyclopedias and textbooks in United States. Appeared also in one-volume edition without notes in 1955. [WDP/CRP]

3.173 Samuel Eliot Morison. *The European discovery of America: the northern voyages, A.D. 500–1600.* New York: Oxford University Press, 1971. ISBN 0-19-501377-8. ‣ Erudite but idiosyncratic survey of northern European maritime exploration of North America. Begins with Vikings, focuses on British. [WDP/CRP]

3.174 Samuel Eliot Morison. *The European discovery of America: the southern voyages, A.D. 1492–1616.* 1974 ed. New York: Oxford University Press, 1978. ISBN 0-19-501823-0. ‣ Survey of Spanish, Portuguese, and Italian voyagers in Atlantic and Pacific waters as they charted globe and place of America on it. Contains author's last published reflections on Columbus, whom he studied for decades. [WDP/CRP]

3.175 Samuel Eliot Morison. *The great explorers: the European discovery of America.* 1978 ed. New York: Oxford University Press, 1986. ISBN 0-19-504222-0 (pbk). ‣ Condensation of author's two volumes on European discovery of America (3.173, 3.174). [WDP/CRP]

3.176 J. H. Parry. *The discovery of the sea.* New York: Dial, 1974. ISBN 0-8037-2019-X. ‣ Masterly account surveying maritime history of world. Emphasizes western expansion of fifteenth and sixteenth centuries. Less lavishly illustrated edition available from University of California Press. [WDP/CRP]

3.177 J. H. Parry. *The establishment of European hegemony, 1415–1715: trade and exploration in the age of the Renaissance.* 3d rev. ed. New York: Harper & Row, 1966. ISBN 0-06-131045-X (pbk). ‣ Masterly, brief summary of technologies of discovery, discoverers and their motives, and commercial empires they established worldwide. [LEL]

3.178 William D. Phillips, Jr., and Carla Rahn Phillips. *The worlds of Christopher Columbus.* Cambridge: Cambridge University Press, 1992. ISBN 0-521-35097-2. ‣ Life and times of Columbus, in wide range of relevant contexts, including medieval background for European interest in routes to Asia. Columbus's years in Genoa, Portugal, and Spain before 1492, and his four American voyages receive extensive treatment, as do consequences of increasing global contacts after 1492. [WDP/CRP]

3.179 Kirkpatrick Sale. *The conquest of paradise: Christopher Columbus and the Columbian legacy.* 1990 ed. New York: Plume, 1991. ISBN 0-452-26669-6 (pbk). ‣ Reassessment of discovery and process it unfolded through analysis of Columbus's character and

exploits. Treatment of ecological issues makes this legacy eminently contemporary and controversial. [LMG]

3.180 G. V. Scammell. *The world encompassed: the first European maritime empires, c. 800–1650.* Berkeley: University of California Press, 1981. ISBN 0-520-04422-3. ‣ Major study of European maritime ventures from Middle Ages through early modern period. Chapters on Norse, Hansa, Venetians, Genoese, Portuguese, Spanish, Dutch, French, and English. Excellent annotated bibliography. [WDP/CRP]

3.181 Russell Thornton. *American Indian holocaust and survival: a population history since 1492.* Norman: University of Oklahoma Press, 1987. ISBN 0-8061-2074-6 (cl), 0-8061-2220-X (pbk). ‣ Sober scholarly look at American Indian population history over past 500 years. Good place to enter debate over population numbers. [WDP/CRP]

3.182 Garcilaso de la Vega. *The Florida of the Inca: a history of Adelantado, Hernando de Soto, governor and capitan general of the kingdom of Florida, and of other heroic Spanish and Indian cavaliers.* 1951 ed. John Grier Varner and Jeannette Johnson Varner, trans. Austin: University of Texas Press, 1980. ISBN 0-292-73238-4 (cl), 0-292-72434-9 (pbk). ‣ History of de Soto's expedition through what is now southern part of United States. Written by "the Inca," son of Inca noblewoman and Spanish conquistador, in last decades of sixteenth century. Based on interviews of participants and unpublished written account. Considered less reliable than several published accounts (e.g., Portuguese account of Gentleman of Elvas), but valuable for unique bicultural perspective. [LNS]

3.183 Charles Verlinden. *The beginnings of modern colonization: eleven essays with an introduction.* Yvonne Freccero, trans. Ithaca, N.Y.: Cornell University Press, 1970. ISBN 0-8014-0588-2. ‣ Essays of fundamental importance showing continuity of colonial patterns of Mediterranean origin as they were transplanted into Atlantic areas in fifteenth and sixteenth centuries. Emphasis on Italian role in Portuguese and Spanish expansion. [WDP/CRP]

3.184 Herman J. Viola and Carolyn Margolis. *Seeds of change: a quincentennial commemoration.* Washington, D.C.: Smithsonian Institution, 1991. ISBN 1-56098-035-4 (cl), 1-56098-036-2 (pbk). ‣ Lavishly illustrated companion volume to Smithsonian's celebrated exhibition on biological transformations following 1492. Essays by experts on wide range of topics, including five focuses of exhibition: corn, horse, disease, potato, and sugar. [WDP/CRP]

SEE ALSO
20.347 J.R.S. Phillips. *The medieval expansion of Europe.*
22.98 J. H. Parry. *The age of reconnaissance.*
23.102 Kenneth R. Andrews. *Trade, plunder, and settlement.*
29.347 Luis Vaz de Camœs. *The Lusiads.*
36.289 Serge Gruzinski. *Man-gods in the Mexican highlands.*
36.337 Irving Rouse. *The Tainos.*
36.340 Samuel M. Wilson. *Hispaniola.*
36.437 John Hemming. *Red gold.*
37.90 Colin M. MacLachlan. *Spain's empire in the New World.*
37.96 J. H. Parry. *The Spanish seaborne empire.*
37.98 J. H. Parry, Robert G. Keith, and Michael Francis Jimenez, eds. *New Iberian world.*
37.110 Ruth Pike. *Enterprise and adventure.*
37.114 Louis-André Vigneras. *The discovery of South America and the Andalusian voyages.*
37.144 Lewis Hanke. *The Spanish struggle for justice in the conquest of America.*
37.322 Kenneth R. Andrews. *The Spanish Caribbean.*

AFRO-EURASIAN WORLDS, 1500–1800

3.185 Perry Anderson. *Lineages of the absolute state.* 1974 ed. London: Verso; distributed by Schocken, 1984. ISBN 0-86091-710-X (pbk). ‣ Marxist inquiry into emerging early modern absolutist state out of feudalism in eastern and western Europe and

Russia, with considerations of Ottoman empire and Japan. Skillful blending of theory with empirical detail. [LEL]

3.186 C. R. Boxer. *The Dutch seaborne empire, 1600–1800*. London: Viking, 1989. ISBN 0-14-621600-6 (pbk). ‣ Excellent, brief introduction to interacting social forces creating Dutch commercial hegemony in Europe and world maritime trade in seventeenth century and subsequent decline. Includes East India Company; neglects Japanese trade. [LEL]

3.187 S. N. Eisenstadt. *The political systems of empires*. 1963 ed. New Brunswick, N.J.: Transaction, 1992. ISBN 1-56000-641-2 (pbk). ‣ Pioneering typological worldwide survey of thirty-two political systems from antiquity through absolutist, but especially early modern Eurasia, seeking common features. Predominance of comparison and analysis over narrative makes it unsuitable for beginners. [LEL]

3.188 Holden Furber. *Rival empires of trade in the Orient, 1600–1800*. Minneapolis: University of Minnesota, 1976. ISBN 0-8166-0787-7 (cl), 0-8166-0851-2 (pbk). ‣ Masterly synthesis of western European trading companies and their role throughout Asia. Emphasis on institutions, articles of trade, and Europeans in Asia. [LEL]

3.189 Jack A. Goldstone. *Revolution and rebellion in the early modern world*. Berkeley: University of California Press, 1991. ISBN 0-520-06758-4. ‣ Challenging argument that long-term demographic expansion throughout Eurasia intensified pressure on stagnant economic and social systems, explaining periodic political crises in Europe, Middle East, and China. [LEL]

3.190 Jonathan I. Israel. *Dutch primacy in world trade, 1585–1740*. Oxford: Clarendon, 1989. ISBN 0-19-822729-9 (cl), 0-19-821139-2 (pbk). ‣ Varying fortunes of Netherlands' spectacular, rapid rise to global trade dominance from wars of independence from Spain to peak in 1647–72. World-systems approach, connecting economy to politics and challenging other scholars' views. [LEL]

3.191 J. R. Jones. *Britain and the world, 1649–1815*. Brighton, England, and Atlantic Highlands, N.J.: Harvester and Humanities, 1980. ISBN 0-85527-225-2. ‣ Synthetic study of sea power, diplomacy, and military power, with commercial and business interests supporting Britain's triumph over Dutch as world power and defense of empire against Napoleonic France. General introduction, limited consideration of non-European affairs. [LEL]

3.192 Donald F. Lach. *Asia in the making of Europe*. Vol. 1: *The century of discovery*. Vol 2: *A century of wonder*. Chicago: University of Chicago Press, 1965–78. ISBN 0-226-46751-1 (set), 0-226-46744-9 (v. 1), 0-226-46750-3 (v. 2). ‣ Classic study of reception and impact of Asian culture and social experience in its various forms on European intellectual life. Encyclopedic in scope, richly illustrated mine of information. Analyses and examples from time when Asia opened new horizons for Europe. [LEL]

3.193 Bernard Lewis. *The Muslim discovery of Europe*. New York: Norton, 1982. ISBN 0-393-01529-7 (cl), 0-393-30233-4 (pbk). ‣ Argues that Islamic interest in Europe was virtually nonexistent; much interesting detail. Oversimplifies complexities of Islamic literary, intellectual, and artistic cultures. [LEL]

3.194 P. J. Marshall and Glyndwr Williams. *The great map of mankind: perceptions of new worlds in the age of Enlightenment*. Cambridge, Mass.: Harvard University Press, 1982. ISBN 0-674-36210-1. ‣ Contends that increased contact with non-Western cultures resulted mainly in incomprehension and attitude of superiority by 1800. Limited to English reactions; ignores impact of continental reactions on English thought. [LEL]

3.195 William H. McNeill. *The pursuit of power: technology, armed force, and society since A.D. 1000*. Chicago: University of Chicago Press, 1982. ISBN 0-226-56157-7. ‣ Traces ascendancy of Europe in modern history to commercialized violence which

fostered development of military technologies. Finds process ended with militarized command economies since 1945. Basic study by leading world historian. [LEL]

3.196 M.A.P. Meilink-Roelofsz. *Asian trade and European influence in the Indonesian Archipelago between 1500 and about 1630*. The Hague: Nijhoff, 1962. ‣ Analyzes complex trading networks of Southeast Asia prior to European arrival through Portuguese ascendancy and triumph of Dutch United East Indies Company in seventeenth century. Pathbreaking study showing Asian side of European expansion. [LEL]

3.197 Alan Moorehead. *The fatal impact: an account of the invasion of the South Pacific, 1767–1840*. 1966 ed. Honolulu: Mutual, 1989. ISBN 0-935180-77-X (pbk). ‣ Early synthesis of European contact and conquest of indigenous peoples of Tahiti and Australia, through nineteenth century. More attention to effect on European than on indigenous culture. Short section on Antarctic. Accessible and richly illustrated. [LEL/KR]

3.198 Alan K. Smith. *Creating a world economy: merchant capital, colonialism, and world trade, 1400–1825*. Boulder: Westview, 1991. ISBN 0-8133-1110-1 (cl), 0-8133-1109-8 (pbk). ‣ Narrative survey responding to theorists of global and world-systems history. Stresses social origins of global conditions accounting for rise of global capitalism, especially in Netherlands and England. [LEL]

3.199 Niels Steensgaard. *The Asian trade revolution of the seventeenth century: the East India companies and the decline of the caravan trade*. Chicago: University of Chicago Press, 1974. ISBN 0-226-77138-5 (cl), 0-226-77139-3 (pbk). ‣ Examines Eastern and Western institutional crises to explain importance of fall of Hormuz in 1622 and why Dutch and English companies supplanted their competitors. Revision of author's thesis, *Carracks, Caravans, and Companies*. [LEL]

3.200 James D. Tracy, ed. *The political economy of merchant empires*. Cambridge: Cambridge University Press, 1991. ISBN 0-521-41046-0. ‣ Eleven essays by leading scholars on diverse themes relating to why Europeans achieved global trade hegemony in face of well-organized, powerful rivals. [LEL]

3.201 James D. Tracy, ed. *The rise of merchant empires: long-distance trade in the early modern world, 1350–1750*. Cambridge: Cambridge University Press, 1990. ISBN 0-521-38210-6. ‣ Thirteen essays analyzing European merchant networks, comparisons with Asian counterparts, transatlantic slave trade, trans-Saharan trade, and Central Asian trade. Excellent introduction to current scholarship. [LEL]

SEE ALSO

4.450 David S. Landes. *Revolution in time*.

19.190 John Vogt. *Portuguese rule on the Gold Coast, 1469–1682*.

22.96 Geoffrey Parker. *The military revolution*.

46.363 O.H.K. Spate. *The Pacific since Magellan*.

ATLANTIC WORLDS, 1600–1900

3.202 Robin Blackburn. *The overthrow of colonial slavery, 1776–1848*. London: Verso, 1988. ISBN 0-86091-188-8 (cl), 0-86091-901-3 (pbk). ‣ Study of abolition and emancipation in European colonies of Americas (but not of Africa or Asia). Slavery overthrown for political not economic reasons; abolition reinforced colonial rule in Caribbean, undermined it elsewhere. [PM]

3.203 David Brion Davis. *The problem of slavery in Western culture*. 1966 ed. New York: Oxford University Press, 1988. ISBN 0-19-505639-6 (pbk). ‣ History of ideas on slavery; evolution of antislavery in British and Spanish America, emphasizing Quaker leadership. First of three volumes synthesizing Atlantic intellectual and social history through slavery. [PM]

3.204 W.E.B. Du Bois. *The Negro*. 1915 ed. Herbert Aptheker,

Introduction. Millwood, N.Y.: Kraus-Thomson Organization, 1975. ISBN 0-527-25315-4. ▸ Early and concise but comprehensive view of Africans in world history. Sweeping view of Africa, slave trade, and Americas. [PM]

3.205 P. C. Emmer, ed. *Colonialism and migration: indentured labour before and after slavery.* Dordrecht: Nijhoff; distributed by Kluwer Academic, 1986. ISBN 90-247-3253-0. ▸ Analysis of similarities and differences of two flows of contract labor, each a dimension of European colonialism: servants to slaves, slaves to servants. [PM]

3.206 Joseph E. Harris, ed. *Global dimensions of the African diaspora.* Washington, D.C.: Howard University Press, 1982. ISBN 0-88258-022-1. ▸ Essays on dialectic between diaspora and homeland, especially in culture. Intellectual pan-Africanism. Treats concepts, methods, assimilation and identity, and return. [PM]

3.207 Herbert S. Klein. *African slavery in Latin America and the Caribbean.* New York: Oxford University Press, 1986. ISBN 0-19-503837-1. ▸ Comprehensive survey by region and by century of plantation economy, social life, resistance, and emancipation. Useful for comparisons with slavery in United States and in Africa. [PM]

3.208 Peggy K. Liss. *Atlantic empires: the network of trade and revolution, 1713–1826.* Baltimore: Johns Hopkins University Press, 1983. ISBN 0-8018-2742-6. ▸ Comparisons of United States and Latin America on basis of ideas and economic structure that developed out of web of Atlantic imperial relations during Enlightenment. New World analysis on grand scale. [PM]

3.209 Sidney W. Mintz. *Sweetness and power: the place of sugar in modern history.* 1985 ed. New York: Penguin, 1986. ISBN 0-14-009233-1 (pbk). ▸ Study of sweetness as a habit, inculcated especially among English, giving rise to plantation system and sugary symbols of power. Focuses as much on working-class consumption as on slave production. [PM]

3.210 J. H. Parry. *Trade and dominion: the European overseas empires in the eighteenth century.* New York: Praeger, 1971. ▸ Basic, well-told and illustrated examination of global empires through eyes of administrators at home and abroad; sailors, ships and merchants, trade and wars. Argues for "second age of discovery" culminating in British imperial dominance. [PM/LEL]

3.211 Walter Rodney. *How Europe underdeveloped Africa.* 1981 rev. ed. Washington, D.C.: Howard University Press, 1982. ISBN 0-88258-105-8 (cl), 0-88258-096-5 (pbk). ▸ Concludes slave trade set scene, but real underdevelopment came with colonial era. Passionately nationalist, but sound on details. [PM]

3.212 Eric Williams. *Capitalism and slavery.* 1944 ed. New York: Capricorn, 1966. ▸ Study of slavery and slave trade as source of English fortunes and industrial investment. Sees industry, based on wage labor, as leading force in antislavery movement. Presents economic determinism in compelling language. [PM]

SEE ALSO

19.911 Patrick Manning. *Slavery and African life.*

19.917 Joseph C. Miller. *Way of death.*

22.252 David Eltis. *Economic growth and the ending of the transatlantic slave trade.*

24.444 Roger Anstey. *The Atlantic slave trade and British abolition, 1760–1810.*

24.447 Seymour Drescher. *Econocide.*

INDUSTRIALIZATION AND GLOBAL INTEGRATION, 1700–1900

3.213 Rudolf von Albertini. *European colonial rule, 1880–1940: the impact of the West on India, Southeast Asia, and Africa.* John G. Williamson, trans. Westport, Conn.: Greenwood, 1982. ISBN 0-313-21275-9. ▸ Study of administration, economic development, and rise of Asian and African nationalisms. Rejects dependency and underdevelopment theories; sees administrative and economic dualism as common characteristics of empires. [LJF]

3.214 Lucile H. Brockway. *Science and colonial expansion: the role of the British Royal Botanic Gardens.* New York: Academic Press, 1979. ISBN 0-12-134150-X. ▸ Study of Western development and transfer of economically valuable plants—cinchona, rubber, sisal—in tropics. Argues conscious exploitation underlay botanical research, using world-systems and dependency theories as framework. [LJF]

3.215 Herbert Feis. *Europe, the world's banker, 1870–1914: an account of European foreign investment and the connection of world finance with diplomacy before World War I.* 1930 ed. New York: Kelley, 1974. ISBN 0-678-00044-1. ▸ Classic study of foreign investment in age of imperialism. Liberal critique of political imperialism and defense of free trade. Dated, but still most frequently cited work on subject. [LJF]

3.216 D. K. Fieldhouse. *Economics and empire, 1830–1914.* Ithaca, N.Y.: Cornell University Press, 1973. ISBN 0-8014-0810-5. ▸ Analysis of relationship of imperialism to European industrialization. Critical of Marxist approach, denies economic exploitation was decisive factor in imperialist policies. Sees events in colonies as driving force in imperial policies. [LJF]

3.217 Wolfram Fischer et al., eds. *The emergence of a world economy, 1500–1914: papers of the Ninth International Congress of Economic History.* Vol. 2: *1850–1914.* Wiesbaden: Steiner, 1986. ISBN 3-515-04748-4 (pbk, set), ISSN 0723-5453. ▸ Essays on monetary standards, trade, and transportation, both global and regional/national in perspective. No single, coherent viewpoint, but useful ideas and information on evolution of international markets. [LJF]

3.218 Tom Kemp. *Historical patterns of industrialization.* London: Longman, 1978. ISBN 0-582-48922-9 (cl), 0-582-48923-7 (pbk). ▸ Topical chapters on peasantry, technology, transport, banking, and the state, as well as studies of industrialization in Canada, India, and Japan. Brief with valuable, comparative insights. [KR]

3.219 V. G. Kiernan. *European empires from conquest to collapse, 1815–1960.* Leicester: Leicester University Press with Fontana, 1982. ISBN 0-7185-1228-6. ▸ Military history of colonial expansion and rule. Colonial wars fostered tensions at home and impeded political development in colonies before and after independence. Excellent introduction and synthesis. [LJF]

3.220 V. G. Kiernan. *The lords of human kind: black man, yellow man, and white man in an age of empire.* 1969 ed. New York: Columbia University Press, 1984. ISBN 0-231-05941-8 (pbk). ▸ Classic study of attitudes and behaviors of Europeans and non-Europeans toward each other in era of imperialism. Concludes colonialism led to increasingly virulent European prejudices. [LJF]

3.221 Karl Polanyi. *The great transformation.* 1944 ed. Boston: Beacon, 1985. ISBN 0-8070-5679-0 (pbk). ▸ Detailed analysis of nineteenth-century Europe as epoch of unheard of peace, liberalism, and prosperity. While attributable to new economic system of self-regulating market, new system also responsible for destroying "human and natural substance of society." Classic critique. [GD]

3.222 William Woodruff. *Impact of Western man: a study of Europe's role in the world economy, 1750–1960.* 1966 ed. Washington, D.C.: University Press of America, 1982. ISBN 0-8191-2485-0 (cl), 0-8191-2486-9 (pbk). ▸ Seminal study of Western economic expansion, treating migrations, investment, technological diffusion, transportation, and trade. Stresses benefits of Western attitudes and techniques. [LJF]

SEE ALSO

24.456 Bernard Porter. *The lion's share.*

TWENTIETH CENTURY

3.223 Walter M. Abbott, ed. *The documents of Vatican II: introduction and commentaries by Catholic bishops and experts, responses by Protestant and Orthodox scholars.* 1966 ed. Joseph Gallagher, ed. and trans. Hampton, N.J.: New Century, 1974. ISBN 0-8329-1115-1 (pbk). ▸ Publication in English translation of sixteen official documents of 1963–65 council, which restructured teachings and policy of Roman Catholic church. Includes commentary and some criticism. [BL]

3.224 Richard J. Barnet and Ronald E. Müller. *Global reach: the power of the multinational corporations.* New York: Simon & Schuster, 1974. ISBN 0-671-21835-2 (cl), 0-671-22104-3 (pbk). ▸ Analysis of multinational corporations arguing they are most important force in modern world economy. Charges multinationals with many ills and argues necessity of their social control. Conservative economists attack authors' social bias. [BL]

3.225 Geoffrey Barraclough. *An introduction to contemporary history.* 1964 ed. London: Penguin, 1986. ISBN 0-14-020827-5. ▸ Industrial and social revolutions and new imperialism destroyed Old World; sees 1890–1961 as watershed. Concludes liberal democracy has broken down and power blocs drive new world. [BL]

3.226 Geoffrey Barraclough. *Main trends in history.* Rev. ed. Michael Burns, revisions. New York: Holmes & Meier, 1991. ISBN 0-8419-1287-4 (cl), 0-8419-1062-6 (pbk). ▸ Assesses seven aspects of history since 1945, including crises of historicism, new concepts, ideological influences, impacts of social sciences, area studies, axiological interests, institutions for research, and prospects for a more scientific history. Originally written as UNESCO report amid cold war and decolonialization processes. [LSS]

3.227 Geoffrey Blainey. *The causes of war.* 3d ed. New York: Free Press, 1988. ISBN 0-02-903592-9 (cl), 0-02-903591-0 (pbk). ▸ Analysis of why wars occur and why peace occurs. Discusses many modern events, emphasis on twentieth century. Rebuts standard, popular explanations. [BL]

3.228 David Caute. *The year of the barricades: a journey through 1968.* New York: Harper & Row, 1988. ISBN 0-06-015870-0. ▸ Events of world revolution of 1967–69 in United States, Japan, Western Europe, Poland, Czechoslovakia, and Mexico. Examines New Left, counterculture, black power, antiwar, women's, and workers' movements; counterrevolutionary violence; and coercion. Critical and nostalgic narration. [LGD]

3.229 George M. Foster. *Traditional societies and technological change.* 2d ed. New York: Harper & Row, 1973. ISBN 0-06-042129-0. ▸ Argues modern technology has tended to homogenize culture around world. Earlier title: *Traditional Cultures and the Impact of Technological Change* (1962). [BL]

3.230 Martin Gilbert. *The Holocaust: a history of the Jews of Europe during the Second World War.* 1985 ed. New York: Holt, 1987. ISBN 0-8050-0348-7. ▸ Chronological, chilling account. Encyclopedic, but lacks explanations of events. [BL]

3.231 Henri Grimal. *Decolonization: the British, French, Dutch, and Belgian empires, 1919–1963.* Stephan De Vos, trans. Boulder: Westview, 1978. ISBN 0-89158-732-2. ▸ Encyclopedic narrative with some documents. Focuses on post-1945 experience. [BL]

3.232 Louis J. Halle. *The cold war as history.* 1967 ed. New York: HarperPerennial, 1991. ISBN 0-06-096888-5 (pbk). ▸ Finds cold war result of balance-of-power conflicts, not ideology; created by power vacuum in Eastern Europe after World War II. [BL]

3.233 Freda Harcourt and Francis Robinson. *Twentieth-century history: a select bibliography.* London and New York: Croom Helm and Barnes & Noble, 1979. ISBN 0-06-4925680-X. ▸ Iden-

tifies interpretive scholarship on issues such as technology and urbanization, fascism, and decolonization. Originally prepared as course aid in modern world history at University of London. [MJG]

3.234 B. H. Liddell Hart. *The real war, 1914–1918.* 1930 ed. Boston: Little, Brown, 1963. ▸ Narrative by major figure in modern military history. Focuses on Europe, but notes non-European theaters. [BL]

3.235 Evan Luard. *The years of Western domination, 1945–1955.* Vol. 1 of *A history of the United Nations.* New York: St. Martin's, 1982. ISBN 0-312-38654-0 (v. 1). ▸ Well-balanced narrative with emphasis on territorial activities of central United Nations agency. Liberal, internationalist scholar's interpretation. [BL]

3.236 Charles S. Maier. *Recasting bourgeois Europe: stabilization in France, Germany, and Italy in the decade after World War I.* Princeton: Princeton University Press, 1975. ISBN 0-691-05220-4 (cl), 0-691-10025-X (pbk). ▸ Analysis of post–World War I social structures in western Europe. Finds the war led to less social and economic development in Western Europe than usually claimed. After war, power moved to organized pressure groups concerned with economic self-interest. [BL]

3.237 Octave Mannoni. *Prospero and Caliban: the psychology of colonization.* 1964 2d ed. Pamela Powesland, trans. Ann Arbor: University of Michigan Press, 1990. ISBN 0-472-09430-0 (cl), 0-472-06430-4 (pbk). ▸ Unique, important work focusing on 1947 uprisings in Madagascar (later, Malagasy Republic) to examine psychohistorical relationship between colonizers and colonized. Uses *The Tempest* as metaphor, tracing attitudes of superiority, dependency, and rebellion. [BL/LJF]

3.238 Hans Ruthenberg. *Farming systems in the tropics.* 3d ed. Oxford: Clarendon, 1980. ISBN 0-19-859481-X (cl), 0-19-859482-8 (pbk). ▸ Essential for understanding difference between developing world and high technology systems. [BL]

3.239 John L. Seitz. *The politics of development: an introduction to global issues.* New York: Blackwell, 1988. ISBN 0-631-15746-8 (cl), 0-631-15801-4 (pbk). ▸ Surveys issues of twentieth-century economic development. Present rate of population growth plus industrialism's toxic poisoning puts unprecedented strain on society. Underdeveloped countries are learning to control harmful effects of economic activity, but process is painful. [BL]

3.240 Tony Smith, ed. *The end of the European empire: decolonization after World War II.* Lexington, Mass.: Heath, 1975. ISBN 0-669-93195-0. ▸ Selection of primary and secondary materials assembled for comparative analysis of European decolonization. Ends with section on neocolonialism. Argues that neglected subject of decolonization, which ushered in new period in world history, is as important as often-studied subject of colonization. [LNS]

3.241 C. P. Snow. *The two cultures and a second look: an expanded version of the "Two Cultures and the Scientific Revolution."* 1964 2d ed. London: Cambridge University Press, 1969. ISBN 0-521-09576-X. ▸ Argues that divergence between science and humanities has been disastrous for modern world. [BL]

3.242 Ivar Spector. *The first Russian Revolution: its impact on Asia.* Englewood Cliffs, N.J.: Prentice-Hall, 1962. ▸ Rare but valuable linking of pre–World War I revolutions in Russia, Iran, and the Ottoman empire and the protests in India between 1905 and 1911, billed as antidote to Soviet historiography on Russian Revolution of 1905. Goes beyond Russian impact to provide useful comparative discussion of constitutional struggles that followed Russo-Japanese War. [LNS]

3.243 Michael P. Todaro. *Internal migration in developing countries: a review of theory, evidence, methodology, and research priorities.* Geneva: International Labour Office, 1976. ISBN 92-210-

1599-8 (cl), 92-210-1598-x (pbk). ‣ Excellent research guide and survey of extant population research. [BL]

3.244 Theodore Von Laue. *The world revolution of westernization: the twentieth century in global perspective.* New York: Oxford University Press, 1987. ISBN 0-19-504906-3. ‣ Argues twentieth-century wars and violence are result of westernization and emerging global interdependence, resulting in communism, fascism, Third World dictatorships, and terrorism. [BL]

3.245 Caroline F. Ware, K. M. Panikkar, and J. M. Romein, eds. *The twentieth century.* Vol. 6 of *History of mankind: cultural and scientific development.* United Nations Educational, Scientific, and Cultural Organization (UNESCO): International Commission for a History of the Scientific and Cultural Development of Mankind. New York: Harper & Row, 1966. ‣ Massive cooperative effort to create true world history. Result uneven; authors try too hard to respect all political and social views. [BL]

SEE ALSO
18.363 Frantz Fanon. *The wretched of the earth.*
22.516 Hannah Arendt. *The origins of totalitarianism.*
22.517 Raymond Aron. *The century of total war.*
22.523 Arthur Marwick. *War and social change in the twentieth century.*
22.527 Raymond J. Sontag. *A broken world, 1919–1939.*
22.544 Charles P. Kindleberger. *The world in depression, 1929–1939.*
22.619 Roland N. Stromberg. *After everything.*
40.655 Daniel Yergin. *The prize.*
47.204 Winfried Baumgart. *Imperialism.*
48.225 Peter Calvocoressi, Guy Wint, and John Pritchard. *Total war.*
48.551 Paul Bairoch. *The economic development of the Third World since 1900.*

CROSS-CULTURAL TRADE AND EXCHANGE

3.246 Vimala Begley and Richard Daniel De Puma, eds. *Rome and India: the ancient sea trade.* Madison: University of Wisconsin Press, 1991. ISBN 0-299-12640-4. ‣ Dynamics of Rome-India trade as seen by archaeologists reporting on recent excavations of Roman pottery, coins, bronzes, and glass in southern India and Sri Lanka. Includes articles on naval technology and Red Sea ports. [SSG]

3.247 Fernand Braudel. *The perspective of the world.* Vol. 3 of *Civilization and capitalism, fifteenth–eighteenth century.* 1984 ed. Sian Reynolds, trans. Berkeley: University of California Press, 1992. ISBN 0-520-08116-1 (v. 3). ‣ Study of emergence of four early modern world economies: Europe, Russia, Ottoman empire, and Asia. Discusses how Venice, Antwerp, Genoa, and Amsterdam succeeded one another as dominant capitalist cities. Richly descriptive, Eurocentric approach to cross-cultural trade by greatest of Annales school historians. [SSG]

3.248 Lionel Casson, ed. and trans. *The Periplus Maris Erythraei: text with introduction, translation, and commentary.* Princeton: Princeton University Press, 1989. ISBN 0-691-04060-5. ‣ New translation of first-century handbook for merchants trading in Red Sea and Arabian Sea. Crucial source for information on economies and societies of western Indian Ocean region. Includes useful introduction and appendixes. [SSG]

3.249 M. P. Charlesworth. *Trade routes and commerce of the Roman empire.* 1926 ed. Chicago: Ares, 1986. ISBN 0-89005-444-4 (pbk). ‣ Overview of Roman commerce, including brief chapters on trade with eastern Mediterranean, maritime links to India, and overland routes to Asia. Still useful introduction. [SSG]

3.250 K. N. Chaudhuri. *Trade and civilization in the Indian Ocean: an economic history from the rise of Islam to 1750.* Cambridge: Cambridge University Press, 1985. ISBN 0-521-24226-6

(cl), 0-521-28542-9 (pbk). ‣ Importance of Asian merchants and emporia to maritime trade networks extending from South China Sea to Mediterranean basin. Includes examination of importance of Central Asian caravan routes. Argues for chronological unity over long term. [SSG]

3.251 Philip D. Curtin. *Cross-cultural trade in world history.* 1984 ed. Cambridge: Cambridge University Press, 1985. ISBN 0-521-26319-0 (cl), 0-521-26931-8 (pbk). ‣ Study of how alien merchant settlements facilitated cross-cultural trade from ancient times to nineteenth century. Emphasis on trading communities in Afro-Eurasia prior to 1500. Major contribution to comparative world history. [SSG]

3.252 Ashin Das Gupta and M. N. Pearson, eds. *India and the Indian Ocean, 1500–1800.* Calcutta: Oxford University Press, 1987. ISBN 0-19-561932-3. ‣ Fifteen contributions by specialists on various aspects of Indian Ocean trade. Editors argue for unity of Indian Ocean region in space and time. Successfully transcends Eurocentric framework. [SSG]

3.253 Teobaldi Filesi. *China and Africa in the Middle Ages.* David L. Morison, trans. London: Cass with Central Asian Research Centre, 1972. ISBN 0-7146-2604-X. ‣ Brief account of early Chinese contacts with Africa, emphasizing Ming voyages. Argues Zheng He expeditions undertaken for commercial and diplomatic reasons. Learned overview by Africanist. [SSG]

3.254 Irene M. Franck and David M. Brownstone. *The Silk Road: a history.* New York: Facts on File, 1986. ISBN 0-8160-1122-2. ‣ Overview of Eurasian overland trade routes through Mongol period. Some attention to maritime trade. Semipopular account. [SSG]

3.255 Jan Hogendorn and Marion Johnson. *The shell money of the slave trade.* Cambridge: Cambridge University Press, 1986. ISBN 0-521-32086-0. ‣ Lively case study of unsung dimension of world trade. Cowrie shells from Maldives widely used as currency in Bengal and West Africa; shipments to Europe then West Africa facilitated slave trade and palm-oil trade. [PM]

3.256 George Fadlo Hourani. *Arab seafaring in the Indian Ocean in ancient and early medieval times.* 1951 ed. New York: Octagon Books, 1975. ISBN 0-374-93985-3. ‣ Brief overview of Indian Ocean trade routes and navigation techniques during first millennium CE. Highlights Arab role, but also discusses Persians and Chinese. Valuable survey. [SSG]

3.257 Isidore of Charax. *Parthian stations by Isidore of Charax: an account of the overland trade route between the Levant and India in the first century B.C.* 1914 ed. Wilfred H. Schoff, ed. and trans. Chicago: Ares, 1989. ISBN 0-89005-058-9. ‣ Brief itinerary of caravan route from Antioch to border of India dating from late first century BCE. Edition includes Greek text, maps, and notes. [SSG]

3.258 Xinru Liu. *Ancient India and ancient China: trade and religious exchanges, AD 1–600.* Delhi: Oxford University Press, 1988. ISBN 0-19-562050-X. ‣ Development of commercial and religious interchange between North India and North China during early first millennium CE. Examines Buddhist ideology and institutions as well as items, routes, and structures of trade, including commerce in silk and precious stones. Impressive study based on contemporary Sanskrit and Chinese sources, as well as archaeology. [SSG/LNS]

3.259 J. Innes Miller. *The spice trade of the Roman empire, 29 B.C. to A.D. 641.* Oxford: Clarendon, 1969. ISBN 0-19-814264-1. ‣ Study of emergence of spice trade linking Roman Mediterranean to Southeast Asia. Includes discussion of spice-producing regions, routes, entrepôts, carriers, and terms of trade. Essential source. [SSG]

3.260 Karl Polanyi, Conrad M. Arensberg, and Harry W. Pearson, eds. *Trade and market in the early empires: economies in history* *and theory*. Glencoe, Ill.: Free Press, 1957. ‣ Articles argue for importance of administered or marketless trade in state-controlled ports of trade. Classic statement of substantivist school of trade associated with Polanyi. See recent critical appraisal of substantive school in Curtin 3.251. [SSG]

3.261 Manfred G. Raschke. "New studies in Roman commerce with the East." *Aufstieg und Niedergang der römischen Welt*, Series 2: *Principat*, 9.2 (1978) 604–1378. ISBN 3-11-007175-4. ‣ Monumental study of Roman trade in silk and spices. Chinese "gifts" to steppe nomads as key to westward shipment of silk; Roman importation of spices, not silk, as principal source of its trade deficit. Text followed by 1,800 notes, 4,000 bibliographic entries. Fundamental source. [SSG]

3.262 Shereen Ratnagar. *Encounters: the westerly trade of the Harappa civilization*. Delhi: Oxford University Press, 1981. ISBN 0-19-561253-1. ‣ Study of emergence of maritime trade between Indus Valley and Mesopotamia via Bahrain, ca. 2600 BCE, and how this partly administered, partly free-lance exchange of rarities for bulk goods was central to Harappan economy. [SSG]

3.263 D. S. Richards, ed. *Islam and the trade of Asia: a colloquium*. Oxford and Philadelphia: Cassirer and University of Pennsylvania Press, 1970. ISBN 0-8122-7619-1. ‣ Articles by leading scholars on Eurasian trade, from opening of Rome-China routes to nineteenth century. Discusses role of Islam in facilitating cross-cultural interchange. Especially valuable for commerce in premodern Indian Ocean region. Remains key work for comparativists. [SSG]

3.264 M. Rostovzeff. *Caravan cities*. 1932 ed. D. Talbot Rice and T. Talbot Rice, trans. New York: AMS Press, 1971. ISBN 0-404-05445-5. ‣ Sketches of Petra, Jerash, Palmyra, and Dura Europos during Roman period when all were important to caravan trade. Based on author's travels in 1928. Includes useful introductory essay. [SSG]

3.265 Jeremy A. Sabloff and C. C. Lamberg-Karlovsky, eds. *Ancient civilization and trade*. Albuquerque: University of New Mexico Press, 1975. ISBN 0-8263-0345-5. ‣ Articles by leading authorities from various disciplines on theory of long-distance trade. Includes case studies of Mesopotamia, Shang China, Southeast Asia, and Mayan civilization. Collection indicates continuing influence of substantivist model. See also Curtin 3.251 and Polanyi et al., eds. 3.260. [SSG]

3.266 William Lytle Schurz. *The Manila galleon*. 1939 ed. New York: Dutton, 1959. ‣ Vivid narrative of Spanish galleons that sailed from Manila to Acapulco, 1565–1815. Principal items of trade included Chinese silk, Southeast Asian spices, and Mexican silver. [SSG]

3.267 C.G.F. Simkin. *The traditional trade of Asia*. London: Oxford University Press, 1968. ISBN 0-19-215317-X. ‣ Economist's superb overview of Asian trade, 500 BCE to nineteenth century. Focuses on three trade "triangles": India-Iran-Arabia, India–Central Asia–China, and India–Southeast Asia–China. Includes subjects covered nowhere else, such as Japanese attempted trade at Acapulco in early 1600s. [SSG/LNS]

3.268 Wang Gungwu. "The Nanhai trade: a study of the early history of Chinese trade in the South China Sea." *Journal of the Malayan Branch of the Royal Asiatic Society* 31.2 (1958) 1–133. ‣ Study of expansion of Chinese commerce in southern seas within context of Persian and Arab commercial preeminence. Remarks on "passivity" of Chinese merchants. [SSG/LNS]

3.269 E. H. Warmington. *The commerce between the Roman empire and India*. 2d rev. ed. London and New York: Curzon and Octagon Books, 1974. ISBN 0-374-98250-3. ‣ Study of Roman trade with India during first two centuries CE. Examines land and sea routes, "discovery" of monsoons, items traded, and Roman

trade deficit. Dated owing to dependence on literary sources, as opposed to recent archaeological evidence, but still worth consulting for overview. [SSG]

3.270 Andre Wink. *Al-Hind: the making of the Indo-Islamic world*. Vol. 1: *Early medieval India and the expansion of Islam, 7th–11th centuries*. 2d rev. ed. Leiden: Brill, 1991. ISBN 90-04-09509-8 (set), 90-04-09249-8 (v. 1). ‣ Emergence of Muslim economic supremacy following Arab conquest of Sind and linkage of Indian Ocean to Mediterranean. How unified bimetallic currency and open-trade diasporas in Indian Ocean strengthened Muslim hegemony. Major contribution to Indian Ocean studies. [SSG]

3.271 Ying-shih Yü. *Trade and expansion in Han China: a study in the structure of Sino-barbarian economic relations*. Berkeley: University of California Press, 1967. ‣ Valuable synthesis examining cross-cultural interchange from Chinese perspective. Examines origins of Chinese system of tributary trade in which imperial gifts were exchanged for "barbarian" tribute, and how Chinese tributary system shaped relations with nomads and maritime traders. Many implicit comparisons with Rome. [SSG]

SEE ALSO

9.87 Sechin Jagchid and Van Jay Symons. *Peace, war, and trade along the Great Wall*.

18.206 Bruce Masters. *The origins of Western economic dominance in the Middle East*.

CROSS-CULTURAL TRAVELERS

3.272 Ibrahim A. Abu-Lughod. *Arab rediscovery of Europe: a study in cultural encounters*. Princeton: Princeton University Press, 1963. ‣ Appraisal of modern reemergence of Arab awareness of Europe, 1798–1870. Based partly on travel accounts written by six Arab travelers to Europe, 1820s to 1860s. How Arab travelers were favorably impressed with European political and educational systems. Includes information on twelve post-1870 Arab travelers to Europe. [SSG]

3.273 Thomas J. Assad. *Three Victorian travellers: Burton, Blunt, Doughty*. London: Routledge & Kegan Paul, 1964. ‣ How three Victorian travelers to Middle East represented Arab culture in their writings. Argues all three knew Arab world well but embodied Victorian prejudices. Includes material on other British writers of same period who also traveled in Middle East. [SSG]

3.274 C. Raymond Beazley. *The dawn of modern geography*. 1901–06 ed. 3 vols. New York: Smith, 1949. ‣ Detailed commentary on long-distance travel by medieval Europeans: Christian pilgrims, Jewish travelers, visitors to Mongol capital, merchants, and maritime explorers. Volumes 1 and 3 include Muslim and Chinese travel. Dated but still valuable for reference. [SSG]

3.275 François Bernier. *Travels in the Mogul empire, A.D. 1656–1668*. 1934 2d rev. ed. Archibald Constable, ed. and trans. Vincent A. Smith, ed. Delhi: Low Price Editions, 1989. ISBN 81-85395-12-8. ‣ Observations of India by philosopher who was physician to Aurangzeb (r. 1656–1707) for eight years. Valuable on Mughal court life, Delhi, Agra, and economic and social conditions in India. [SSG]

3.276 Emilii V. Bretschneider. *Mediaeval researches from eastern Asiatic sources: fragments towards the knowledge of the geography and history of central and western Asia from the thirteenth to the seventeenth century*. 1888 ed. 2 vols. London: Routledge & Kegan, 1967. ‣ Translations of Chinese primary sources on Mongols and Muslims in volume 1. Explains Chinese-Mongol map of central and western Asia and includes sources on fifteenth and sixteenth centuries in volume 2. [SSG]

3.277 Richard F. Burton. *Personal narrative of a pilgrimage to al-Madinah and Meccah*. 1893 ed. 2 vols. Isabel Burton, ed. New York: Dover, 1964. ISBN 0-486-21217-3 (v. 1), 0-486-21218-1

(v. 2). ▸ Firsthand account of famous Victorian traveler-explorer's 1853 pilgrimage, in disguise, to Muslim holy places. Enormously informative on Arab-Islamic world and Orientalist sensibilities. [SSG]

3.278   Robert Byron. *The road to Oxiana.* 1950 rev. ed. Paul Fussell, Introduction. New York: Oxford University Press, 1982. ISBN 0-19-503067-2 (pbk). ▸ Record of eleven-month tour of Persia, Afghanistan, and India in 1933–34 by British writer with special interest in premodern architecture in Persia. Fussell (in 3.288) argues this book is among best of British interwar travel accounts. [SSG]

3.279   Mary B. Campbell. *The witness and the other world: exotic European travel writing, 400–1600.* Ithaca, N.Y.: Cornell University Press, 1988. ISBN 0-8014-2137-3. ▸ Literary historian's view of "prehistory" of European travel books. Includes discussion of William of Rubruck, Marco Polo, Sir John Mandeville, Christopher Columbus, and Sir Walter Raleigh. Discusses how transition from impersonal to personal travel writing, seen first in Rubruck, marks beginning of modern genre. Brings new perspective to classic texts. [SSG]

3.280   Lionel Casson. *Travel in the ancient world.* London: Allen & Unwin, 1974. ISBN 0-04-913017-X. ▸ Overview of Roman travel and travelers in Mediterranean region. Includes travel by ancient Egyptians, Mesopotamians, Greeks, Romans, and early Christian pilgrims. Useful survey. [SSG]

3.281   John Chardin. *Travels in Persia, 1673–1677.* 1927 ed. Percy Sykes, Introduction. New York: Dover, 1988. ISBN 0-486-25636-7. ▸ Classic French account of Safavid court at Isfahan. Includes observations of economic and social conditions in Persia as well as Persian flora and fauna. [SSG]

3.282   Christopher Dawson, ed. *Mission to Asia: narratives and letters of the Franciscan missionaries in Mongolia and China in the thirteenth and fourteenth centuries.* 1955 ed. Nun of Stanbrook Abbey, trans. Toronto: University of Toronto Press with Medieval Academy of America, 1980. (Medieval Academy reprints for teaching, 8.) ISBN 0-8020-6436-1 (pbk). ▸ Collection of primary sources, highlighted by narratives written by Franciscan missionaries John of Plano Carpini and William of Rubruck. Both traveled across Central Asia to visit with Mongol khans in thirteenth century and wrote vividly about their observations. [SSG]

3.283   Ross E. Dunn. *The adventures of Ibn Battuta, a Muslim traveller of the fourteenth century.* Berkeley: University of California Press, 1986. ISBN 0-520-057771-6 (cl), 0-520-06743-6 (pbk). ▸ Account of how Ṣūfī devotee and scholar traveled more than 70,000 miles, enjoying Muslim hospitality from Morocco to Mecca, India, China, and West Africa. Vivid illustration of Islamic cultural unity. [SSG]

3.284   J.J.L. Duyvendak. *China's discovery of Africa: lectures given at the University of London on January 22 and 23, 1947.* London: Probsthain, 1949. ▸ Two lectures surveying Chinese knowledge of Western lands, Indian Ocean, and Africa, from Han dynasty to fifteenth-century Ming voyages. Includes brief passages from key primary sources. [SSG]

3.285   Dale F. Eickelman and James Piscatori, eds. *Muslim travellers: pilgrimage, migration, and the religious imagination.* Berkeley: University of California Press, 1990. ISBN 0-520-07019-4 (cl), 0-520-07252-9 (pbk). ▸ Twelve essays on aspects of Muslim travel in various regions of Afro-Eurasia from emergence of Islam to twentieth century. Collection is diffuse but quality of individual chapters is high. [SSG]

3.286   Fa-hsien [Fa Xian]. *The travels of Fa-hsien (399–414 A.D.), or, record of the Buddhistic kingdoms.* 1923 ed. H. A. Giles, trans. Westport, Conn.: Greenwood, 1981. ISBN 0-313-23240-7. ▸ Account of journey overland from Changan, China, through

Central Asia to India and by sea from Sri Lanka back to China (from 399–413 CE), by Chinese Buddhist monk. Earliest Chinese traveler's description of India's Buddhist heartland and maritime route through Straits region of Southeast Asia. [SSG]

3.287   G.S.P. Freeman-Grenville, ed. *The East African coast: select documents from the first to the earlier nineteenth century.* 2d ed. London: Collings, 1975. ISBN 0-901720-85-2. ▸ East African coast as seen by forty travelers over two millennia, with brief excerpts of their descriptions. Valuable collection of key sources. [SSG]

3.288   Paul Fussell, ed. *The Norton book of travel.* New York: Norton, 1987. ISBN 0-393-02481-4. ▸ Anthology devoted mainly to travel writing by males from Britain and United States since eighteenth century. How English-language writers responded to and represented travel in Europe and North America. [SSG]

3.289   Fatma Müge Göçek. *East encounters West: France and the Ottoman empire in the eighteenth century.* New York: Oxford University Press, 1987. ISBN 0-19-504826-1. ▸ Discusses cross-cultural impact of Mehmed Efendi's 1720–21 embassy to Paris, including French enthusiasm for *Turquerie* and early westernization in Ottoman empire. Suggests dignitaries such as Mehmed Efendi (and their large households) were more important source of Ottoman westernization than foreign or minority communities. [LNS]

3.290   Hiuen Tsiang [Hsuan Tsang, Xuan Zang]. *Si-Yu-Ki: Buddhist records of the western world.* 1884 ed. 2 vols. in 1. Samuel Beal, trans. Delhi: Motilal Banarsidass, 1981. ISBN 0-89581-131-6. ▸ Seventh-century Chinese Buddhist monk's account of his journey from Tang capital through Central Asia to India. Includes description of travels in India and return trip. Key source for Central Asian interchange, Buddhism, and India. [SSG]

3.291   R. H. Major, ed. *India in the fifteenth century, being a collection of narratives of voyages to India in the century preceeding the Portuguese discovery of the Cape of Good Hope; from Latin, Persian, Russian, and Italian sources, now first translated into English.* 1857 ed. New Delhi: Asian Educational Service, 1992. ISBN 81-206-0768-6. ▸ Extensive introduction, including lengthy survey of travelers from Mediterranean and Middle East to India beginning with Alexander; extensive commentary on and translation of four fifteenth-century accounts—by a Venetian, a Persian, a Russian, and a Genoese. Provides some intriguing eye-witness descriptions of India and much more material on hazards encountered. [LNS]

3.292   Jeannette Mirsky, ed. *The great Chinese travelers: an anthology.* New York: Pantheon, 1964. ▸ Well-done study of eight Chinese travelers (from about 1000 BCE to eighteenth century) plus five nineteenth-century experts on foreign lands, demonstrating that Europeans were not only ones who sought to explore unknown lands. Includes substantial selections from travelers' accounts and discusses Chinese knowledge of foreign lands. [LNS]

3.293   Leonardo Olschki. *Marco Polo's Asia: an introduction to his "Description of the World" called "Il Milione."* Rev. ed. John A. Scott, trans. Berkeley: University of California Press, 1960. ▸ Essays on aspects of Marco Polo's book. How nature, politics, religions, history, legendary figures, and medicine are represented. Also discusses Polo's itineraries and precursors. Useful supplement to Polo 3.296. [SSG]

3.294   Boies Penrose. *Travel and discovery in the Renaissance, 1420–1620.* 1952 ed. Cambridge, Mass.: Harvard University Press, 1967. ▸ Overview of travel by Europeans to Africa, Americas, and Asia. Older Eurocentric work, still worth consulting as introduction. [SSG]

3.295 Fernão Mendes Pinto. *The travels of Mendes Pinto.* Rebecca D. Catz, ed. and trans. Chicago: University of Chicago Press, 1989. ISBN 0-226-66951-3. ▸ Fascinating blend of fact and fiction by Portuguese merchant adventurer who traveled widely in Asian coastal regions, 1530s to 1550s. Newly translated edition includes valuable introduction and notes. [SSG]

3.296 Marco Polo. *The travels of Marco Polo.* 1958 ed. Ronald Latham, ed. and trans. New York: Abaris, 1982. ISBN 0-89835-058-1. ▸ Scholarly, readable edition with useful introduction and bibliography. For most extensive, authoritative editions of Polo's book see 9.227. [SSG]

3.297 Marco Polo. *The travels of Marco Polo: the complete Yule-Cordier Edition, including the unabridged third edition (1903) of Henry Yule's annotated translation, as revised by Henri Cordier, together with Cordier's later volume of notes and addenda (1920).* 1903 and 1920 eds. 2 vols. New York: Dover, 1993. ISBN 0-486-27586-8 (v. 1), 0-486-27587-6 (v. 2). ▸ Henry Yule's authoritative translation first issued in 1870s; revised and updated by Henri Cordier in 1920. Extensive annotations, splendid illustrations make this book a collector's item. Beautifully reproduced by Dover. Buy it; treasure it. [SSG]

3.298 Jane Robinson. *Wayward women: a guide to women travellers.* New York: Oxford University Press, 1990. ISBN 0-19-212261-4. ▸ List of 400 English-language travel accounts written by women, mainly in nineteenth and twentieth centuries. Includes biographical sketch of each writer, maps, and geographical index. Maintains that men's travel writing concentrates on what and where; women's, on how and why. [SSG]

3.299 Morris Rossabi. *Voyager from Xanadu: Rabban Sauma and the first journey from China to the West.* Tokyo: Kodansha International; distributed by Kodansha America, 1992. ISBN 4-7700-1650-6. ▸ Biography of Chinese Nestorian monk who traveled through Central Asia to Persia, France, and Rome in late thirteenth century. Scholarly treatment of intriguing life of pilgrim and Il-khan envoy to papacy. [SSG]

3.300 Willem van Ruysbroeck. *The mission of Friar William of Rubruck: his journey to the court of the great khan Mongke, 1253–1255.* Peter Jackson, trans. Peter Jackson and David O. Morgan, eds. London: Hakluyt Society, 1990. (Works issued by the Hakluyt Society, Second series, 173.) ISBN 0-904180-29-8. ▸ New translation of report of Franciscan friar who traveled from France across Central Asia to Mongol capital at Qaraqorum in thirteenth century. Edition includes valuable introduction and appendixes. [SSG]

3.301 Muhammad Saffar. *Disorienting encounters: travels of a Moroccan scholar in France in 1845–1846, the voyage of Muhammad as-Saffar.* Susan Gilson Miller, ed. and trans. Berkeley: University of California Press, 1992. ISBN 0-520-07461-0 (cl), 0-520-07462-9 (pbk). ▸ Observations of life in Paris in 1845 made by secretary of Moroccan diplomatic mission. Translator's introduction is insightful discussion of how as-Saffar's experience in France led to "dislocation" in three spheres: time, space, and social relations. [SSG]

3.302 Jonathan D. Spence. *The question of Hu.* 1988 ed. New York: Random House, 1989. ISBN 0-679-72580-6 (pbk). ▸ How Cantonese Catholic accompanied Jesuit missionary to France in 1722, was confined in hospital for insane for eighteen months before returning home in 1726. Learned, sensitive study of cross-cultural travel and interchange. [SSG]

3.303 Jean-Baptiste Tavernier. *Travels in India.* 1925 2d ed. 2 vols. V. Ball, trans. William Crooks, ed. New Delhi, India: Oriental Books; distributed by Munshiram Manoharlal, 1977. ▸ Account of jewel merchant who traveled extensively in Middle East, India, and Southeast Asia, 1630s to 1660s. Observations

about trade routes, Mughal court life, and Indian social and economic conditions especially valuable. First published 1676. [SSG]

3.304 Henry Yule, ed. and trans. *Cathay and the way thither, being a collection of medieval notices of China.* 1914–15 rev. ed. 4 vols. in 2. Henri Cordier, ed. Taipei: Ch'eng Wen, 1972. ▸ Monumental review of European knowledge of China from Greco-Roman period to early seventeenth century. Extracts from key primary sources, some Islamic; extensive commentary. Somewhat dated, but still valuable for reference. [SSG]

SEE ALSO
9.216 Igor de Rachewiltz. *Papal envoys to the great khans.*
10.113 Edwin O. Reischauer, trans. *Ennin's diary.*
10.265 Edwin O. Reischauer. *Ennin's travels in T'ang China.*
10.276 Arthur Waley. *The real "Tripitaka" and other pieces.*
16.67 Thome Pires. *The "Suma Oriental" of Tomé Pires.*
17.50 Edward W. Said. *Orientalism.*
19.197 Umar Al-Naqar. *The pilgrimage tradition in West Africa.*

DEMOGRAPHY

3.305 A. M. Carr-Saunders. *World population: past growth and present trends.* 1936 ed. New York: Barnes & Noble, 1965. ▸ Estimates of population size, growth, migration, fertility and mortality. Benchmark for modern studies. [PM]

3.306 Tertius Chandler. *Four thousand years of urban growth: an historical census.* 2d ed. Lewiston, N.Y.: Mellen, 1987. ISBN 0-88946-207-0. ▸ Eccentric but systematic work containing tables of world cities in each era by estimated population; brief commentary. Useful for teaching. [PM]

3.307 Carlo M. Cipolla. *The economic history of world population.* 7th ed. Harmondsworth: Penguin, 1978. ISBN 0-14-020537-3. ▸ Comparison of agricultural and industrial revolutions, with focus on energy usage, births, and deaths. Compares Europe to world, though data beyond Europe limited. Good bibliography to 1970. [PM]

3.308 Philip D. Curtin. *The Atlantic slave trade: a census.* Madison: University of Wisconsin Press, 1969. ISBN 0-299-05400-4. ▸ Assembled estimates of volume and direction of slave trade, revealing patterns of this second-largest human migration. Set terms for decades of debate and further research. [PM]

3.309 Philip D. Curtin. *Death by migration: Europe's encounter with the tropical world in the nineteenth century.* Cambridge: Cambridge University Press, 1989. ISBN 0-521-37162-7 (cl), 0-521-38922-4 (pbk). ▸ Empirical results, plus fine description of Victorian tropical medicine. For English and French military overseas, mortality dropped sharply in mid-nineteenth century as result of simple public health measures. [PM]

3.310 Kingsley Davis. *The population of India and Pakistan.* 1951 ed. New York: Russell & Russell, 1968. ▸ Remains comprehensive survey of South Asian demography since 1871. Treats births, deaths, migration, caste, religion, and economy. [PM]

3.311 Paul R. Ehrlich. *The population bomb.* 1971 rev. ed. New York: Ballantine, 1978. ISBN 0-345-27773-2. ▸ Alarmist but influential study of global population growth and environmental destruction. Concludes too many people, too little food. [PM]

3.312 James J. Fawcett and Benjamin V. Carino, eds. *Pacific bridges: the new immigration from Asia and the Pacific islands.* Staten Island, N.Y.: Center for Migration Studies, 1987. ISBN 0-934733-10-4 (cl), 0-934733-09-0 (pbk). ▸ Demographic, economic, and social analyses, especially since 1960. Solid studies showing conflicts between state policies and economic motivations. [PM]

3.313 D. V. Glass and D.E.C. Eversley, eds. *Population in history: essays in historical demography.* Chicago: Aldine, 1965.

▸ Essays on patterns and methods of North Atlantic historical demography focusing on population and industrial growth in Europe, plus impact of medicine. Good collection of formative studies. [PM]

3.314 Philip M. Hauser, ed. *World population and development: challenges and prospects.* Syracuse, N.Y.: Syracuse University Press, 1979. ISBN 0-8156-2216-3 (cl), 0-8156-2219-8 (pbk). ▸ Results of United Nations agency studies of populations of "have" and "have-not" nations. Basic-needs approach. [PM]

3.315 B. W. Higman. *Slave populations of the British Caribbean, 1807–1834.* Baltimore: Johns Hopkins University Press, 1984. ISBN 0-8018-3036-2. ▸ Definitive study of population, economy, and health among slaves registered by British officials in years before abolition. Finds wide variety in conditions, yet all with naturally declining population. [PM]

3.316 R. R. Kuczynski. *Demographic survey of the British colonial empire.* 1948–51 ed. 3 vols. Fairfield, N.J.: Kelley, 1977. ISBN 0-678-00740-3. ▸ Concentration on twentieth-century demography; but much evidence on earlier times. Valuable colonial era compendium. Two volumes on Africa, one on Americas, and one on Asia and Europe. [PM]

3.317 Ronald Demos Lee, ed. *Population patterns in the past.* New York: Academic Press, 1977. ISBN 0-12-441850-3. ▸ Sophisticated analyses of individual-level demographic data, with tests of main theories of population change. [PM]

3.318 G. Robina Quale. *Families in context: a world history of population.* Westport, Conn.: Greenwood, 1992. ISBN 0-313-27830-X. ▸ Encyclopedic survey of family size and structure, as related to economic structure, by region and over time. Assembles materials from literatures in history, anthropology, and demography, with focus on growing importance of city life. [PM]

3.319 G. Robina Quale. *A history of marriage systems.* Westport, Conn.: Greenwood, 1988. ISBN 0-313-26010-9. ▸ Survey of marriage patterns from Neolithic to industrial society, drawing on ethnographic and sociological sources. Emphasizes interdependence in marriage as relationship of choice. Evolutionary perspective balanced by emphasis on variety of marriage systems. [PM]

3.320 Brinley Thomas. *Migration and economic growth: a study of Great Britain and the Atlantic economy.* 2d ed. Cambridge: Cambridge University Press, 1973. ISBN 0-521-08566-7. ▸ Pathbreaking study of economic growth in both Britain and America as migrants crossed Atlantic. Formal analysis of "push" and "pull" factors in migration. [PM]

3.321 E. A. Wrigley. *Population and history.* New York: McGraw-Hill, 1969. ▸ Principles and patterns of historical demography, focusing on Europe and, in recent times, Third World countries. Excellent introduction. [PM]

SEE ALSO
19.264 Dennis D. Cordell and Joel W. Gregory, eds. *African population and capitalism.*
19.911 Patrick Manning. *Slavery and African life.*
22.452 Ansley J. Coale and Susan Cotts Watkins, eds. *The decline of fertility in Europe.*
23.271 E. A. Wrigley and Roger Schofield. *The population history of England, 1541–1871.*

ECOLOGY

3.322 Kendall E. Bailes, ed. *Environmental history: critical issues in comparative perspective.* Lanham, Md.: University Press of America for American Society for Environmental History, 1985. ISBN 0-8191-4376-6 (cl), 0-8191-4377-4 (pbk). ▸ Conference papers focusing on environmental history of United States, including American Indians. Additional contributions on Eastern Europe, South America, Japan, and Soviet Union. Some attention to climate and impact of western expansion on ecosystems. [SSG]

3.323 Alfred W. Crosby, Jr. *America's forgotten pandemic: the influenza of 1918.* 1976 ed. Cambridge: Cambridge University Press, 1989. ISBN 0-521-38547-4 (cl), 0-521-38695-0 (pbk). ▸ Examination of "Spanish" influenza pandemic in United States, 1918–19. Includes attention to simultaneous outbreaks of flu in West Africa, Europe, Pacific islands, and Alaska. Originally published as *Epidemic and Peace, 1918.* [SSG]

3.324 Alfred W. Crosby, Jr. *Ecological imperialism: the biological expansion of Europe, 900–1900.* Cambridge: Cambridge University Press, 1986. ISBN 0-521-32009-7 (cl), 0-521-33613-9 (pbk). ▸ How European flora, fauna, and pathogens overwhelmed biota native to temperate regions from Azores to Americas to Australia beginning in tenth century. Includes extended case study of European impact on ecology of New Zealand. [SSG]

3.325 Richard W. Franke and Barbara H. Chasin. *Seeds of famine: ecological destruction and the development dilemma in the West African Sahel.* Totowa, N.J.: Rowman & Allanheld, 1980. ISBN 0-916672-26-3 (cl), 0-86598-053-5 (pbk). ▸ Ecological history explaining complex interdependency of farmers and herders. Shows how commercial peanut production in colonial and postcolonial periods disrupted traditional ecological balance and brought about desiccation and famine. [LNS/KR]

3.326 Johan Goudsblom, E. L. Jones, and Stephen Mennell, eds. *Human history and social process.* Exeter, England: University of Exeter Press, 1989. ISBN 0-85989-332-4. ▸ Collection of essays on long-term social processes, two by Jones on economic growth and two by Goudsblom: "Ecological Regimes and the Rise of Organized Religions" and "The Formation of 'Military-Agrarian Regimes.'" Mennel and Goudsblom introduce and conclude these essays in grand theory; influenced by Norbert Elias. [SSG/KR]

3.327 J. Donald Hughes. *Ecology in ancient civilizations.* Albuquerque: University of New Mexico Press, 1975. ISBN 0-8263-0367-6. ▸ How Greeks, Romans, Jews, and early Christians interacted with ancient Mediterranean ecosystem, shaping present-day Western thinking on environmental issues. Informative on soil, water, agriculture, animals, birds, plants, trees, deforestation, and attitudes toward nature. Brief, useful introductory work. [SSG]

3.328 Miklos Jankovich. *They rode into Europe: the fruitful exchange in the arts of horsemanship between East and West.* 1971 ed. Anthony Dent, trans. New York: Scribner's, 1973. ISBN 0-684-13304-0. ▸ Brief overview of Eurasian horse breeding and horse riding from earliest times to nineteenth century. Eurocentric but informative about equestrian life. Useful maps, well-chosen illustrations. [SSG]

3.329 Kenneth F. Kiple, ed. *The African exchange: toward a biological history of black people.* 1987 ed. Durham, N.C.: Duke University Press, 1988. ISBN 0-8223-0731-6. ▸ Articles on health of blacks, mainly in Americas, 1550–1850. Includes consideration of smallpox, lung disease, lead poisoning, malnourishment, cholera, and hypertension. Adds new dimension to concept of Columbian exchange. [SSG]

3.330 Calvin Martin. *Keepers of the game: Indian-animal relationships and the fur trade.* Berkeley: University of California Press, 1978. ISBN 0-520-03519-4. ▸ Controversial argument that European diseases destroyed indigenous culture of American Indians of eastern Canada, led them to convert to Christianity, plunge into fur trade, and transform woodlands ecosystem. [SSG]

3.331 Mary Kilbourne Matossian. *Poisons of the past: molds, epidemics, and history.* 1989 ed. New Haven: Yale University Press,

1991. ISBN 0-300-03949-2 (cl, 1989), 0-300-05121-2 (pbk).
▸ Examination of fungal poisoning of food crops, especially rye, in early modern Europe, colonial New England, and nineteenth-century Russia. Shows how plant health affected human health, demographic trends, and popular movements. Thought-provoking work. [SSG]

3.332 William H. McNeill. *The human condition: an ecological and historical view.* Princeton: Princeton University Press, 1980. ISBN 0-691-05317-0. ▸ Brief overview of human past arguing central dynamic has been shifting patterns of interaction between microparasites and macroparasites (i.e., exploitive social arrangements). Discusses how rise of cities and development of markets constituted key turning points in human past. Extraordinary synthesis. [SSG]

3.333 William H. McNeill. *Plagues and peoples.* 1976 ed. Garden City, N.Y.: Anchor, 1989. ISBN 0-385-12122-9 (pbk). ▸ Global history of infectious diseases from earliest times to modern era. How disease patterns were altered by agricultural innovation, increased population density, and growing interaction between civilizations. Classic work on disease in world history. [SSG]

3.334 John F. Richards and Richard P. Tucker, eds. *World deforestation in the twentieth century.* Durham, N.C.: Duke University Press, 1988. ISBN 0-8223-0784-7. ▸ Conference volume on acceleration of deforestation in Brazil, sub-Saharan Africa, India, Thailand, Tasmania, and Soviet Union. Contributors find key to destruction of forests in developing countries is not demographic increase, but rather expansion of export agriculture and growth of timber trade. [SSG]

3.335 Redcliffe N. Salaman. *The history and social influence of the potato.* Rev. ed. J. G. Hawkes, ed. Cambridge: Cambridge University Press, 1985. ISBN 0-521-07783-4 (cl), 0-521-31623-5 (pbk). ▸ Traces migration of potato from Andes to Great Britain, with special emphasis on Ireland. Outdated in many respects but, if used carefully, still valuable as storehouse of information. [SSG]

3.336 Robert Sallares. *The ecology of the ancient Greek world.* Ithaca, N.Y.: Cornell University Press, 1991. ISBN 0-8014-2615-4. ▸ Fertile combination of modern historical and demographic techniques and agricultural and ecological perspectives. Considers variables such as long-term climatic change and evolution of nonhuman species. Model for future work. [GCT]

3.337 Richard P. Tucker and John F. Richards, eds. *Global deforestation and the nineteenth-century world economy.* Durham, N.C.: Duke University Press, 1983. ISBN 0-8223-0482-1. ▸ Conference volume addressing widespread deforestation in United States, Philippines, Brazil, India, Burma, China, and African Sahel. Includes appraisal of successful reforestation in Japan. Argues expansion of world economy, rather than demographic growth, led to destruction of forests. [SSG]

3.338 B. L. Turner II et al., eds. *The earth as transformed by human action: global and regional changes in the biosphere over the past 300 years.* Cambridge: Cambridge University Press with Clark University Press, 1990. ISBN 0-521-36357-8 (cl). ▸ Extraordinarily important examination of how human activities have reshaped global environment since beginnings of industrialization. Massive collaborative work by geographers, natural scientists, and historians; rich in data, insights, and hypotheses. [SSG]

3.339 Andrew M. Watson. *Agricultural innovation in the early Islamic world: the diffusion of crops and farming techniques, 700–1100.* Cambridge: Cambridge University Press, 1983. ISBN 0-521-24711-X. ▸ History of diffusion of fifteen plants (including rice, sugar cane, and cotton) domesticated or developed in India, to China prior to 700 and throughout Muslim world and Mediterranean after 700. Separate chapters provide excellent discussion on paths of diffusion, technological advances, and economic

impact. Also discusses negative impact of European production of sugar, cotton, and rice on Muslim fortunes. [LNS]

3.340 Lynn T. White, Jr. "The historic roots of our ecologic crisis." *Science* 155 (10 March 1967) 1202–07. ISSN 0036-8075. ▸ Argues transition from animist nature-worship to Judeo-Christian monotheism in medieval Europe is root of modern Western exploitive attitudes toward nature. Classic article from Eurocentric, idealist perspective. [SSG]

3.341 Karl A. Wittfogel. *Oriental despotism: a comparative study of total power.* 1957 ed. New York: Vintage, 1981. ISBN 0-394-74701-1. ▸ Argues state control of hydraulic agriculture was root of autocratic regimes in premodern Asia, especially China. Influential interpretation, but dismissed by Sinologists as uninformed. [SSG/LNS]

SEE ALSO
4.253 Donald Worster, ed. *The ends of the earth.*
22.247 Noel Deerr. *The history of sugar.*
36.92 William Cronon. *Changes in the land.*

ECONOMY AND SOCIETY

3.342 Michael Adas. *Prophets of rebellion: millenarian protest movements against the European colonial order.* 1979 ed. New York: Cambridge University Press, 1987. ISBN 0-521-33568-X (pbk). ▸ Study of emergence of millennialist anticolonial movements in Java, New Zealand, India, sub-Saharan Africa, and Burma, 1830s to 1930s. How popular uprisings were shaped by relative deprivation, repressive violence, and use of magic. [SSG]

3.343 Jean Baechler, John A. Hall, and Michael Mann, eds. *Europe and the rise of capitalism.* 1988 ed. Oxford: Blackwell, 1990. ISBN 0-631-15006-4 (cl, 1988), 0-631-16942-3 (pbk). ▸ Comparisons of chapters on early modern European economy and preindustrial economic systems in Mughal India, Mamluk Egypt, imperial China, Tokugawa Japan, and tsarist Russia. Historical sociology by neo-Marxists and others. [SSG]

3.344 Paul Bairoch. *Cities and economic development: from the dawn of history to the present.* Christopher Brauder, trans. Chicago: University of Chicago Press, 1988. ISBN 0-226-03465-8 (cl), 0-226-03466-6 (pbk). ▸ Quantitative approach to global urbanization from emergence of first cities onward. Strongest on Europe, but includes data on other major world areas. Full of intriguing hypotheses. [SSG]

3.345 Fernand Braudel. *The structures of everyday life: the limits of the possible.* Vol. 1 of *Civilization and capitalism, 15th–18th century.* 1981 ed. Sian Reynolds, trans. Berkeley: University of California Press, 1992. ISBN 0-520-08114-5 (v. 1). ▸ Study of material life in early modern Europe. Treats demography, food, drink, agriculture, dwellings, clothes, technology, money, and cities. Includes some attention to other civilization areas. Classic Annales school work of great value for Europe, but less so for other regions. [SSG]

3.346 Fernand Braudel. *The wheels of commerce.* Vol. 2 of *Civilization and capitalism, 15th–18th century.* 1982 ed. Sian Reynolds, trans. Berkeley: University of California Press, 1992. ISBN 0-520-08115-3 (v. 2). ▸ How small-scale economic exchange in local settings (economic life) differed from large-scale speculative transactions (capitalism). Sees European capitalism as product of economic and social forces rather than political-military developments. Learned, thought provoking, beautifully illustrated, Eurocentric. [SSG]

3.347 Rushton Coulborn, ed. *Feudalism in history.* 1956 ed. Hamden, Conn.: Archon, 1965. ▸ Case studies of feudalism in western Europe, Japan, China, Mesopotamia, ancient Egypt, India, Byzantine empire, and Russia by leading authorities. Also includes substantial comparative essay by editor. Dated but still useful for reference. [SSG]

3.348 Patricia Crone. *Pre-industrial societies.* Oxford: Blackwell, 1989. ISBN 0-631-15661-5 (cl), 0-631-15662-3 (pbk). ▸ Examination of key features of Eurasian agrarian civilizations from ca. 600 BCE onward. How Europe's failure to create enduring political and economic stability led to industrialization. Outstanding example of large-scale comparative approach. [SSG]

3.349 Philip D. Curtin. *The rise and fall of the plantation complex: essays in Atlantic history.* Cambridge: Cambridge University Press, 1990. ISBN 0-521-37475-8 (cl), 0-521-37616-5 (pbk). ▸ Study of migration of plantation agriculture from medieval Mediterranean to Atlantic islands and American tropics. How African slave trade linked Caribbean plantations to wider world. [SSG]

3.350 Jack Goody. *The Oriental, the ancient, and the primitive: systems of marriage and the family in the pre-industrial societies of Eurasia.* Cambridge: Cambridge University Press, 1990. ISBN 0-521-36574-0 (cl), 0-521-36761-1 (pbk). ▸ Anthropologist's examination of kinship and property in China, India, Near East, and classical Mediterranean. Examines how premodern Eurasian patterns resembled one another and differed from those in sub-Saharan Africa. Major synthesis, controversial point of view. [SSG]

3.351 E. L. Jones. *The European miracle: environments, economies, and geopolitics in the history of Europe and Asia.* 2d ed. Cambridge: Cambridge University Press, 1987. ISBN 0-521-33449-7 (cl), 0-521-33670-8 (pbk). ▸ Comparison of early modern European economic trends and those in Ottoman lands, India, and China. Examines how Europe's industrialization stemmed from its comparatively benign natural environment, distinctive demographic regime, and political fragmentation. [SSG]

3.352 E. L. Jones. *Growth recurring: economic change in world history.* Oxford: Clarendon, 1988. ISBN 0-19-828300-8. ▸ Thought-provoking thesis arguing that tendency toward intensive growth, i.e., increasing per-capita income, was widespread in world long before British Industrial Revolution. Key examples are ancient Athens, Abbasid caliphate, Sung China, Tokugawa Japan, and early modern Europe. [SSG]

3.353 John H. Kautsky. *The politics of aristocratic empires.* Chapel Hill: University of North Carolina Press, 1982. ISBN 0-8078-1502-0. ▸ Comparison of traditional aristocratic empires in global perspective over 5,000 years. Argues imperial China and medieval Europe were special cases in that merchants shared power with aristocrats. Emphasis on generalizations rather than case studies. [SSG]

3.354 Archibald R. Lewis. *Knights and samurai: feudalism in northern France and Japan.* London: Temple Smith, 1974. ISBN 0-8511-7043-9. ▸ Discusses emergence, development, and aftermath of feudalism in northern France and Japan. Brief, insightful contribution to comparative studies. [SSG]

3.355 Ko-yao Ma. *Asian and European feudalism: three studies in comparative history.* Copenhagen: University of Copenhagen East Asian Institute, 1990. (East Asian Institute, Occasional papers, 7.) ▸ Comparison of Chinese and English feudalism; far better on Chinese than on English. Valuable as first such comparison by Chinese scholar. [GFM]

3.356 Barrington Moore, Jr. *Social origins of dictatorship and democracy: lord and peasant in the making of the modern world.* 1966 ed. Boston: Beacon, 1967. ISBN 0-8070-5075-X (pbk). ▸ Study of how landed upper classes and peasantry responded to emergence of commercial and industrial power in England, France, United States, Japan, China, India, Germany, and Russia. Classic con-

tribution to comparative world history by neo-Marxist historical sociologist. [SSG]

3.357 Roland Mousnier. *Peasant uprisings in seventeenth-century France, Russia, and China.* 1970 ed. Brian Pearce, trans. New York: Harper & Row, 1972. ISBN 0-06-131619-9. ▸ Study of how peasant revolts in France, Russia, and China were structured by power of estate system. Argues that in all three cases uprisings were reactions against state power rather than challenges to class exploitation. Also available from Ann Arbor: Books on Demand, University Microfilms International. [SSG]

3.358 Orlando Patterson. *Slavery and social death: a comparative study.* Cambridge, Mass.: Harvard University Press, 1982. ISBN 0-674-81082-1 (cl), 0-674-81083-X (pbk). ▸ Slavery in world historical perspective; comparative study of internal relations of slavery and slavery as institutional process. Attention to process of enslavement, treatment of slaves, and patterns of manumission. Erudite, insightful work of synthesis. [SSG]

3.359 John F. Richards, ed. *Precious metals in the later medieval and early modern world.* Durham, N.C.: Carolina Academic, 1983. ISBN 0-89089-224-5. ▸ Essays on premodern monetary flow in global perspective. Important contributions on Europe, Middle East, Africa, India, East Asia, Southeast Asia, and Americas. [SSG]

3.360 Teodor Shanin, ed. *Peasants and peasant societies: selected readings.* 2d ed. Oxford: Blackwell, 1987. ISBN 0-631-15212-1 (cl), 0-631-15619-4 (pbk). ▸ Short excerpts on key aspects of peasant life, including social structure, economy, culture, and politics. Contributors include numerous historians. Global approach; valuable introduction to field of peasant studies. [SSG]

3.361 Adna Weber. *The growth of cities in the nineteenth century: a study in statistics.* 1899 ed. New York: Greenwood, 1969. ▸ Pioneering work containing data on nineteenth-century urbanization, mainly in United States and Europe. Includes some information on other regions. Still worth consulting. [SSG]

3.362 Eric R. Wolf. *Peasants.* Englewood Cliffs, N.J.: Prentice-Hall, 1966. ISBN 0-13-655456-3. ▸ Leading anthropologist's brief overview of peasant life. Includes examination of economic, social, political, and cultural issues in global, historical perspective. Valuable introduction to peasant studies. [SSG]

3.363 Norman Yoffee and George L. Cowgill, eds. *The collapse of ancient states and civilizations.* Tucson: University of Arizona Press, 1988. ISBN 0-8165-1049-0. ▸ Chapters on Mesopotamia, Rome, Han China, Mayan civilization, Teotihuacán, and role of "barbarians" by historians and social scientists. Includes attention to comparative issues. [SSG]

FRONTIERS

3.364 *Antarctica: the extraordinary history of man's conquest of the frozen continent.* 2d ed. Sydney: Reader's Digest, 1990. ISBN 0-86438-167-0. ▸ From the cover this book appears directed to young readers, but text and illustrations quickly dispel this impression. Fine book that has not received recognition. [CU]

3.365 Talal Asad, ed. *Anthropology and the colonial encounter.* 1973 ed. Atlantic Highlands, N.J.: Humanities, 1988. ISBN 0-391-00391-7. ▸ Examination of effect of encounters between intrusive and indigenous societies on how indigenous cultures are interpreted by representatives of intrusive cultures. Useful antidote to cultural stereotypes. [DHM]

3.366 Pierre Berton. *The Arctic grail: the quest for the North West Passage and the North Pole, 1818–1909.* New York: Viking, 1988. ISBN 0-670-82491-7. ▸ Account of explorations of Polar regions of North America based on manuscript as well as published sources. Interesting and easy to read text; good introduction. [CU]

3.367 Kenneth J. Bertrand. *Americans in Antarctica, 1775–1948.* New York: American Geographical Society, 1971. (American Geographical Society, Special publication, 39.) ▸ Gem of a book; well-documented and written in engaging style. Excellent maps and illustrations. [CU]

3.368 Paul Bohannan and Fred Plog, eds. *Beyond the frontier: social process and cultural change.* Garden City, N.Y.: Natural History for American Museum of Natural History, 1967. ▸ Collection of previously published essays. Useful except for few essays based on Turner thesis (see 40.125). [DHM]

3.369 Frank Debenham. *Antarctica: the story of a continent.* London: Herbert Jenkins, 1959. ▸ Popular book by professor of geography at Cambridge University, member of Robert F. Scott's last expedition, and, later, first director of Scott Polar Institute. [CU]

3.370 Stephen L. Dyson, ed. *Comparative studies in the archaeology of colonialism.* Oxford: British Archaeological Reports, 1985. (British Archaeological Reports international series, 233.) ISBN 0-86054-302-1. ▸ Papers concerning archaeological traces of frontier acculturation. Treats variety of cultures in time and space. [DHM]

3.371 R. Brian Ferguson and Neil L. Whitehead, eds. *War in the tribal zone: expanding states and indigenous warfare.* Santa Fe, N.M.: School of American Research; distributed by University of Washington Press, 1992. ISBN 0-933452-79-9 (cl), 0-933452-80-2 (pbk). ▸ Essays on so-called tribal warfare, considered consequence of intrusion and statist perceptions of tribal peoples conditioned by contact and its consequences. Useful corrective to traditional views. [DHM]

3.372 Dietrich Gerhard. "The frontier in comparative view." *Comparative studies in society and history* 1.3 (1959) 205–29. ISSN 0010-4175. ▸ Discussion of Turner frontier thesis (40.125). Discusses relationship between expansion and transmigration within society and Russian overland and western European transoceanic expansion. [DHM]

3.373 Stanton W. Green and Stephen M. Perlman, eds. *The archaeology of frontiers and boundaries.* Orlando, Fla.: Academic Press, 1985. ISBN 0-12-298780-2. ▸ Addresses theoretical and practical problems concerning archaeological study of frontiers between cultural systems. Explores aspects of problem not usually considered by historians. [DHM]

3.374 Louis Hartz, ed. *The founding of new societies: studies in the history of the United States, Latin America, South Africa, Canada, and Australia.* New York: Harcourt, Brace & World, 1964. ▸ Discussion of fragment theory that frontiers established as fragments of parent societies and reflect their characteristics. Non-Turnerian analysis; applied mainly to frontiers of settlement. [DHM]

3.375 Robert Headland. *Chronological list of Antarctic expeditions and related historical events.* Cambridge: Cambridge University Press, 1989. ISBN 0-521-30903-4. ▸ Revision and update of similar list published in 1958 by Brian Roberts. Includes 3,342 entries, plus maps, references, and an index of some 27,000 entries. Covers period from 700 BC to 1988. Valuable reference work. [CU]

3.376 Herbert Heaton. "Other wests than ours." *Journal of economic history,* Supplement, 6 (1946) 50–62. ISSN 0022-0507. ▸ Discussion of frontiers, greater Europe, and settlement and economy. Precursor to Webb's great frontier thesis (3.402). Contains suggestions for further study. [DHM]

3.377 Andrew Hess. *The forgotten frontier: a history of the sixteenth-century Ibero-African frontier.* Chicago: University of Chicago Press, 1978. (Publication of the Center for Middle Eastern Studies, 10.) ISBN 0-226-33028-1. ▸ Historical and cultural evolution on frontiers of two great empires as they move away from zenith of their power. Contradicts Braudel's view of unitary Mediterranean world (6.26). [GFM]

3.378 Clive Holland. *Arctic exploration and development, c. 500 B.C. to 1915: an encyclopedia.* New York: Garland, 1994. ISBN 0-8240-7648-6. ▸ Provides comprehensive chronological record of expeditions, voyages, and historical events in Arctic from early times to 1915. Chronological divisions further divided by area and nationality of explorers, with commentaries and bibliographical references. Full bibliography and appendices of members of expeditions, maps, general index plus index of ships. Excellent reference book. [CU]

3.379 H.G.R. King, comp. *The Arctic.* Oxford: Clio Press, 1989. (World Bibliographical Series, 99.) ISBN 1-85109-072-X. ▸ Reference work providing introduction to English-language writings on many subjects, from geography, flora and fauna, to prehistory and archaeology, Arctic peoples, literature, arts, etc. Section on voyages and expeditions, with biographies of explorers. Fine annotations. [CU]

3.380 Laurence Patrick Kirwan. *The white road: a survey of polar exploration.* London: Hollis & Carter, 1959. ▸ Remains useful, succinct introduction to explorations of both northern and southern polar regions. Good illustrations and maps. [CU]

3.381 Ladis K. D. Kristof. "The nature of frontiers and boundaries." *Annals of the American Association of Geographers* 49.3, pt. 1 (1959) 269–82. ISSN 0004-5608. ▸ View of frontier as outward-oriented zone and zone of culture contact. Theoretical discussion contributing to clearer definition of frontier concept. [DHM]

3.382 Howard Lamar and Leonard Thompson, eds. *The frontier in history: North America and southern Africa compared.* New Haven: Yale University Press, 1981. ISBN 0-300-02624-2. ▸ Well-planned and executed analytical discussion of specific features of frontiers in paired essays on North America and South Africa. [DHM]

3.383 Owen Lattimore. *Studies in frontier history: collected papers, 1928–1958.* London: Oxford University Press, 1962. ▸ Studies of Inner Asian frontiers between China and Russia, offering non-Turnerian view of frontiers. See especially "Frontiers in History." [DHM]

3.384 Anthony Lemon and Norman Pollock, eds. *Studies in overseas settlement and population.* London: Longman, 1980. ISBN 0-582-48567-3. ▸ Studies on intrusive settlement at European maritime frontiers, mainly in nineteenth century, from sociological perspective. [DHM]

3.385 Clements R. Markham. *The lands of silence: a history of Arctic and Antarctic exploration.* Cambridge: Cambridge University Press, 1921. ▸ After more than seventy years, book is still invaluable for its text, maps, and illustrations. At the age of fourteen, Markham joined Royal Navy; in 1850–51 took part in search for Arctic explorer Sir John Franklin. [CU]

3.386 William H. McNeill. *Europe's steppe frontier, 1500–1800.* Chicago: University of Chicago Press, 1964. ▸ Steppe pastoralism and agricultural colonization in Danubian-Pontic frontier regions shared by Russia, Austria, and Turkey. Topic not widely discussed elsewhere. [DHM]

3.387 William H. McNeill. *The great frontier: freedom and hierarchy in modern times.* Princeton: Princeton University Press, 1983. ISBN 0-691-04658-1. ▸ Discussion of Turner's frontier thesis (40.125) and Webb's great frontier (3.402), focusing on European expansion since 1500. Discusses colonization and settlement, epidemiology, and acculturation, with special concentration on egalitarianism and coercion. [DHM]

3.388 Marvin W. Mikesell. "Comparative studies in frontier history." *Annals of the Association of American Geographers* 50.1 (1960) 62–74. ISSN 0004-5608. ▸ Important work arguing distinction between frontiers of inclusion and frontiers of exclusion, where natives are exterminated or segregated, and between static and dynamic frontiers. [DHM]

3.389 Hugh Robert Mill. *The siege of the South Pole: the story of Antarctic exploration.* London: Alston Rivers, 1905. ▸ Account of Antarctic exploration based on original narratives and on conversations of those who took part. Spritely text, superb illustrations, and large fold-out map. Chapter on early geographical ideas of Antarctica. A classic. [CU]

3.390 David Harry Miller and William W. Savage, Jr., eds. Editor's introduction to *The character and influence of the Indian trade in Wisconsin: a study of the trading post as an institution.* Frederick Jackson Turner, pp. vii–xxxiv. Norman: University of Oklahoma Press, 1977. ISBN 0-8061-1335-9. ▸ Theoretical introduction to comparative frontier studies, together with assessment of Turner thesis (40.125). Examines why Turner frontier thesis not useful in comparative study. [DHM]

3.391 David Harry Miller and Jerome O. Steffen, eds. *The frontier: comparative studies.* Vol. 1. Norman: University of Oklahoma Press, 1977. ISBN 0-8061-1376-6 (v. 1). ▸ Essays on variety of frontier problems in varied geographic and temporal contexts. Intended to stimulate interest in neglected field. [DHM]

3.392 Leslie H. Neatby. *Conquest of the last frontier.* Athens: Ohio University Press, 1966. ▸ Excellent survey covers period from 1853 to 1918. Includes expeditions of Americans Elisha Kent Kane, Charles Francis Hall, George S. Nares, Adolphus W. Greely, and Robert Peary, plus Norwegians Otto Sverdrup and Vilhjalmur Stefansson. [CU]

3.393 A. Grenfell Price. *The Western invasions of the Pacific and its continents: a study of moving frontiers and changing landscapes, 1513–1958.* Oxford: Clarendon, 1963. ▸ Turnerian study of Western intrusion and conquest in Pacific Oceania and along Pacific Rim. Discusses colonization, settlement, and disease. [DHM]

3.394 A. Grenfell Price. *White settlers and native peoples: an historical study of racial contacts between English-speaking whites and aboriginal peoples in the United States, Canada, Australia, and New Zealand.* 1950 ed. Westport, Conn.: Greenwood, 1972. ▸ Examination of effect of white, predominantly Anglo-Celtic, settlement on native peoples in Australian, Canadian, New Zealand, and United States frontier experiences. Discusses destructive acculturation, racism, and cultural trauma and dysfunction. [DHM]

3.395 A. Grenfell Price. *White settlers in the tropics.* New York: American Geographical Society, 1939. (American Geographical Society, Special publication, 23.) ▸ Study of white settlement and racial confrontation in European overseas expansion. Treats environment and problems of acclimatization and acculturation. [DHM]

3.396 Michael Rowlands, Mogens Larsen, and Kristian Kristiansen, eds. *Centre and periphery in the ancient world.* Cambridge: Cambridge University Press, 1987. ISBN 0-521-25103-6. ▸ Important and useful collection of essays applying Wallerstein's core-periphery model (22.275) to study of frontier situations in ancient Near East and Europe. [DHM]

3.397 William W. Savage, Jr., and Stephen I. Thompson, eds. *The frontier: comparative studies.* Vol. 2. Norman: University of Oklahoma Press, 1979. ISBN 0-8061-1514-9 (v. 2). ▸ Essays on frontier topics in various temporal and geographical contexts. Editors offer best existing introduction to literature on frontier studies. [DHM]

3.398 Andrew Bard Schmookler. *The parable of the tribes: the problem of power in social evolution.* 1984 ed. Boston: Houghton-Mifflin, 1986. ISBN 0-395-40005-8 (pbk). ▸ Theoretical discussion of role of power, with particular attention to predicament of

indigenous populations intruded upon by outside powers. Useful corrective to pejorative stereotypes. [DHM]

3.399 Paul F. Sharp. "Three frontiers: some comparative studies of Canadian, American, and Australian settlement." *Pacific historical review* 24.4 (1955) 369–77. ISSN 0030-8684. ▸ Comparative study of frontier expansion in three similar contexts. Discusses applicability of Turner frontier thesis (40.125) in non-American contexts. [DHM]

3.400 John Stewart. *Antarctica: an encyclopedia.* 2 vols. Jefferson, N.C.: McFarland, 1990. ISBN 0-89950-470-1 (set), 0-89950-597-X (v. 1), 0-89950-598-8 (v. 2). ▸ Incorporates geographical features, expeditions, people, scientific subjects, and entries of general interest. Useful and informative for average reader and specialist. Over 1,100 pages of entries, with chronologies of events and expeditions and bibliography. [CU]

3.401 Stephen I. Thompson. *Pioneer colonization: a cross-cultural view.* Reading, Mass.: Addison Wesley, 1973. ▸ Important theoretical and comparative survey of pioneer colonization in variety of geographic and historical contexts. [DHM]

3.402 Walter Prescott Webb. *The great frontier.* 1952 ed. Arnold J. Toynbee, Introduction. Austin: University of Texas Press, 1964. ▸ Analysis of European overseas expansion, ca. 1500–1900; created economic boom in European cities based on exploitation of new lands. Precursor to Wallerstein's world-systems theory (3.428). [DHM]

3.403 George Wolfskill and Stanley Palmer, eds. *Essays on frontiers in world history.* College Station: Texas A&M University Press for University of Texas at Arlington, 1983. ISBN 0-89096-167-0. ▸ Studies of frontiers in South Africa, Americas, and Australasia from sixteenth to nineteenth century. Refers to Webb's great frontier thesis (3.402) and Turner's frontier thesis (40.125). [DHM]

3.404 Walker D. Wyman and Clifton B. Kroeber, eds. *The frontier in perspective.* 1957 ed. Madison: University of Wisconsin Press, 1965. ▸ Application of Turner frontier thesis (40.125) to variety of frontier contexts in space and time. Inadvertently shows inapplicability of Turner to comparative studies. [DHM]

IMPERIALISM, COLONIALISM, AND WORLD-SYSTEMS THEORY

3.405 Janet L. Abu-Lughod. *Before European hegemony: the world system, A.D. 1250–1350.* New York: Oxford University Press, 1989. ISBN 0-19-505886-0 (cl), 0-19-506774-6 (pbk). ▸ Examination of medieval world as interdependent, decentralized world system, stretching from British Isles to Japan. Rise of West possible only because of decline of previous world system in which West played modest role. [GD]

3.406 Samir Amin. *Unequal development: an essay on the social formations of peripheral capitalism.* Brian Pearce, trans. New York: Monthly Review, 1976. ISBN 0-85345-380-2. ▸ Study of historical origins of capitalism on world scale, its fundamental laws, contradictions, and resistances to it, with particular emphasis on Third World. Concludes when historical system is outgrown and superseded, process takes place not from center but from periphery. [GD]

3.407 Giovanni Arrighi. *The geometry of imperialism: the limits of Hobson's paradigm.* 1978 rev. ed. Patrick Camiller, trans. London: Verso; distributed by Schocken, 1983. ISBN 0-86091-766-5. ▸ Comparison of British imperialism with its successors, German and American imperialism. Emergence of multinational capital as insolvable problem for classical definitions of imperialism. Critique of major theories of imperialism (Hobson 22.337, Lenin 22.345). [GD]

3.408 Maurice Aymard, ed. *Dutch capitalism and world capital-*

ism/Capitalisme hollandais et capitalisme mondial. Cambridge and Paris: Cambridge University Press and Éditions de la Maison des Sciences de l'Homme, 1982. ISBN 0-521-23812-9. ▸ Analyses and explanations of Dutch role in seventeenth-century capitalist world economy. Debate between world systems, neoclassical, and Annales approaches. In English and French. [GD]

3.409 Michel Beaud. *A history of capitalism, 1500–1980.* Tom Dickman and Anny Lefebvre, trans. New York: Monthly Review, 1983. ISBN 0-85345-626-7 (cl), 0-85345-627-5 (pbk). ▸ Study of capitalism at five different stages of historical development, reaching its pinnacle with British industrialism and entering into sixth stage of terminal decline after revolution of 1968. Less conservative version of Schumpeterian dialectic (3.477) of creative/destructive forces in rise and inevitable demise of capitalism. [GD]

3.410 Michael L. Budde. *The two churches: Catholicism and capitalism in the world-system.* Durham, N.C.: Duke University Press, 1992. ISBN 0-8223-1229-8. ▸ Study of Roman Catholic Christianity as part of modern capitalist geoculture. Examines cleavages in Catholicism, originally a precapitalist institution, under effects of its stretching over different zones of capitalist world system, from core to peripheries. [GD]

3.411 Christopher Chase-Dunn. *Global formation: structures of the world-economy.* Cambridge, Mass.: Blackwell, 1989. ISBN 1-55786-011-4. ▸ Examination of functioning of "real capitalism" as whole entity at levels of states and world system. Traditional liberal and Marxist views on capitalism and their recent critiques. Structuralist approach to world-systems analysis and quantitative methods seeking to be theoretical synthesis. [GD]

3.412 Daniel Chirot. *Social change in the twentieth century.* New York: Harcourt Brace Jovanovich, 1977. ISBN 0-15-581420-6. ▸ Stimulating interpretation of twentieth-century world history using modified version of world-systems theory. Emphasizes relationship between internal and international social, economic, and political changes. Integrates American, European, Soviet, and Third World developments. [CAL]

3.413 Oliver Cromwell Cox. *The foundations of capitalism.* New York: Philosophical Library, 1959. ▸ Examination of empirical documentation of recurrent institutions and organizing patterns in historical capitalism from Venice to Great Britain. Sees capitalist society as peculiar form of social organization requiring and producing democratic government, urban classes, markets, rationalistic religion, and interstate system. [GD]

3.414 D. K. Fieldhouse. *The colonial empires: a comparative survey from the eighteenth century.* 1966 ed. New York: Dell, 1971. ▸ Classic that resurrected political approach to imperialism. Argues European expansion, 1815–82, was unplanned response to weakness of periphery, and partitions after 1882 were product of European diplomatic rivalries. Dismisses "myth of economic exploitation." [KR]

3.415 Andre Gunder Frank. *World accumulation, 1492–1789.* New York: Monthly Review, 1978. ISBN 0-85345-442-6. ▸ Classic of radical political economy and dependency literature. Examines genesis in sixteenth century of single, all-embracing, albeit unequal and uneven, capitalist formation. Concludes Third World's underdevelopment is logical outcome of production and exchange relations of dependence within global process of capital accumulation. [GD]

3.416 Alexander Gerschenkron. *Economic backwardness in historical perspective: a book of essays.* 1962 ed. New York: Praeger, 1965. ISBN 0-647-22600-3. ▸ Collection of essays exhibiting trademark Russian intelligentsia's easy mix of themes, ranging from economic theory and history of industrialization to literary criticism. Includes famous essay that titles volume. [GD]

3.417 Joshua S. Goldstein. *Long cycles: prosperity and war in the modern age.* New Haven: Yale University Press, 1988. ISBN 0-300-03994-8 (cl), 0-300-04112-8 (pbk). ▸ Analysis of cyclical rhythms in modern world as debate agenda, field of study, and method of historical inquiry. Argues system of war among great powers, economic development, and class relationships strongly influence each other and follow cyclical patterns. [GD]

3.418 John A. Hobson. *Imperialism.* London: Allen & Unwin, 1948. ▸ Study of late nineteenth-century colonial division of world among European states in economic, political and ideological terms. Imperialism as trespassing of "reasonable" borders of modern European nationalism caused by emergence of financial monopolistic groups. Original turn-of-century critique. [GD]

3.419 R. J. Holton. *The transition from feudalism to capitalism.* New York: St. Martin's, 1985. ISBN 0-312-81454-2. ▸ Historical-sociological synthesis debating transition to capitalism as continuation of three intellectual traditions of Adam Smith, Karl Marx, and Max Weber. Argues that capitalism was not inscribed in European past. [GD]

3.420 Peter Kriedte. *Peasants, landlords, and merchant capitalists: Europe and the world economy, 1500–1800.* Volker R. Berghahn, trans. Cambridge: Cambridge University Press, 1983. ISBN 0-521-25755-7 (cl), 0-521-27681-0 (pbk). ▸ Concise survey of main approaches in economic history research. Discusses population, agriculture, crafts and commerce, and proto-industrialization in early modern Europe from perspective of long cycles of economic stagnation and growth. Also treats proliferation of rural manufacturing and colonial expansion as two sides of genesis of capitalism. [GD]

3.421 David S. Landes, ed. *The rise of capitalism.* New York: Macmillan, 1966. ▸ Essays by renowned scholars analyzing problems of formation of capitalism, Protestant ethic, agricultural development, factory organization, roots of economic backwardness, Great Depression, and "mass society" to discover "secret" of European modernization and apply it to Third World development. [GD]

3.422 Angus Maddison. *Dynamic forces in capitalist development: a long-run comparative view.* Oxford: Oxford University Press, 1991. ISBN 0-19-828397-0 (cl), 0-19-828398-9 (pbk). ▸ Explains past two centuries of unprecedented growth in advanced capitalist countries as complex interplay of political, social, and economic factors, in which historical accidents are also important. Critical commentary and statistical evidence argued against theories of major analysts of capitalist process. [GD]

3.423 Roger Owen and Robert Sutcliffe, eds. *Studies in the theory of imperialism.* 1972 ed. Harlow, England: Longman Group, 1981. ISBN 0-582-48753-6. ▸ Wide-ranging collection of essays on theory and history of imperialism, especially in India, Africa, and Latin America. Critique of traditional and new interpretations by mainly Marxist authors. [KR]

3.424 Nathan Rosenberg and L. E. Birdzell, Jr. *How the West grew rich: the economic transformation of the industrial world.* New York: Basic Books, 1986. ISBN 0-465-03108-0. ▸ Study of evolution of key capitalist institutions: market, private property, money and banking, and industry and technologism. Concludes Western success grew from its economy, always more mixed than capitalist, and uniquely open to technological and organizational experiment. [GD]

3.425 Tony Smith. *The pattern of imperialism: the United States, Great Britain, and the late industrializing world since 1815.* Cambridge: Cambridge University Press, 1981. ISBN 0-521-23619-3 (cl), 0-521-28076-1 (pbk). ▸ Political, eclectic approach to imperialism and decolonization. Examples drawn globally, with special attention to Asia and Latin America. Critique of world-systems and Marxist interpretations by political scientist. [KR]

3.426 Paul M. Sweezy et al. *The transition from feudalism to capitalism.* 1976 rev. ed. Rodney Hilton, Introduction. London: Verso; distributed by Schocken, 1978. ISBN 0-86091-701-0. ‣ Study of structures of class, economy, and power in late feudalism. Surveys problems of "prime mover," exogenous and internal factors in emergence of capitalist mode of production discussed by Dobb and Sweezy and many others in famous debate of 1950s. [GD]

3.427 Charles Tilly, ed. *The formation of national states in western Europe.* Princeton: Princeton University Press, 1975. ISBN 0-691-05219-0 (cl), 0-691-00772-1 (pbk). ‣ Collection of studies on different historical aspects of state-building in West. Sees accomplishments of European states as byproducts of drive to monopolize means of violence and of extraction of economic surplus. [GD/LEL]

3.428 Immanuel Wallerstein. *The modern world system.* 3 vols. New York: Academic Press, 1974–89. ISBN 0-12-785925-X (cl, set), 0-12-785926-8 (pbk, set). ‣ Analysis of capitalist world economy, our modern world system, as historical system. Describes cyclical rhythms and secular trends in their historical evolution and thematically: agrarian origins of modern capitalism; struggles for world hegemony; and relations of core, semiperiphery, and periphery of world system. First three volumes cover period 1450 to 1840s, with two more volumes projected. [GD]

3.429 William Woodruff. *The struggle for world power, 1500–1980.* New York: St. Martin's, 1981. ISBN 0-312-76873-7. ‣ Analysis of interstate hegemony and rivalry from Mongol conquests to Reagan presidency. History as moral lesson: shows that, in age of nuclear weapons and degraded environment, abuse of power in interstate relations imperils civilization itself. Densely written world history. [GD]

SEE ALSO
22.236 T. H. Aston and C.H.E. Philpin, eds. *The Brenner debate.*
30.209 Peter Kriedte, Hans Medick, and Jürgen Schlumbohm. *Industrialization before industrialization.*
33.6 T. Iván Berend and György Ránki. *The European periphery and industrialization, 1780–1914.*
47.2 Ludwig Dehio. *The precarious balance.*
47.3 Paul M. Kennedy. *The rise and fall of the great powers.*

MODERNIZATION THEORY

3.430 Reinhard Bendix. *Kings or people: power and the mandate to rule.* Berkeley: University of California Press, 1978. ISBN 0-520-02302-1 (cl), 0-520-04090-2 (pbk). ‣ Historical examination of transition from monarchy to popular mandate in Japan, Russia, Germany, and England by eminent sociologist. Examines types of kingship and dynamics of nation-building; emphasizes trauma of transition. [CAL]

3.431 Reinhard Bendix. *Nation-building and citizenship: studies of our changing social order.* Rev. ed. Berkeley: University of California Press, 1977. ISBN 0-520-02676-4 (cl), 0-520-02761-2 (pbk). ‣ Classic work of comparative development studies. Analyzes transformation of western European societies, preconditions of development in Japan and Germany, and political authority in India. Stresses political institutions and social structures as formative. [CAL]

3.432 Cyril E. Black. *The dynamics of modernization: a study in comparative history.* 1966 ed. New York: Harper & Row, 1967. ISBN 0-06-131321-1. ‣ Seminal work in modernization theory. Finds increased knowledge of natural environment explains transformation of traditional societies to modern ones. Sees seven patterns of change, with country's political order setting pace and scope. Controversial and much debated attempt at comparative history. [BL/CAL]

3.433 Cyril E. Black et al. *The modernization of Japan and Russia: a comparative study.* Glencoe, N.Y.: Free Press, 1975. ISBN 0-02-906850-9. ‣ Multiauthor examination of Japan and Russia's historical evolution toward modernity. Emphasizes political, economic, and social structures and education. Examines preconditions of modernization and comparative patterns. [CAL]

3.434 Daniel Chirot. *Social change in the modern era.* San Diego, Calif.: Harcourt Brace Jovanovich, 1986. ISBN 0-15-581421-4. ‣ Substantial revision and updating of *Social Change in the Twentieth Century* (1977) that blends world-systems and modernization approaches in interpreting world history, 1500 to present. Integrates social, economic, and political developments. [CAL]

3.435 S. N. Eisenstadt, ed. *The Protestant ethic and modernization: a comparative view.* New York: Basic Books, 1968. ‣ Multidisciplinary collection of essays assessing application of Max Weber's Protestant ethic and capitalism thesis in Europe, Americas, and Asia. Some essays emphasize historical patterns. Stresses role of modernizing elites. [CAL]

3.436 Samuel P. Huntington. *Political order in changing societies.* 1968 ed. New Haven: Yale University Press, 1971. ISBN 0-300-01171-7 (pbk). ‣ One of most influential books in modernization literature, by political scientist. Perceives military rule as necessary precondition for development in non-Western societies; stresses inefficiency of democracy and need for order. [CAL/BL]

3.437 John H. Kautsky. *The political consequences of modernization.* 1971 ed. New York: Wiley, 1972. ISBN 0-471-46095-8 (cl), 0-471-46096-6 (pbk). ‣ Influential work explaining political change in terms of modernization. Emphasizes transformation of traditional societies through group conflict, anticolonial movements, revolutions, and industrialization. [CAL]

3.438 Daniel Lerner. *The passing of traditional society: modernizing the Middle East.* 1958 ed. David Riesman, Introduction. New York: Free Press, 1964. ‣ Portrait of variety of Middle Eastern nations rapidly replacing deeply implanted traditional patterns with modern ways of thinking and behaving. Stresses impact of West, but also cultural adaptations unique to region. [CAL]

3.439 Marion J. Levy, Jr. "Contrasting factors in the modernization of China and Japan." *Economic development and cultural change* 2 (1953) 161–97. ISSN 0013-0079. ‣ Influential comparison of nineteenth-century China and Japan in terms of modernizing prerequisites. Emphasizes social structure and centralizing politics as key variables in successful Japanese industrialization and Chinese failure. [CAL]

3.440 Craig Alan Lockard. "Global history, modernization, and the world-system approach: a critique." *The history teacher* 14.4 (1981) 489–516. ISSN 0018-2745. ‣ Examination of value of world-systems and modernization approaches for understanding modern world history. Critiques literature and identifies insights. Argues for replacing Eurocentrism with comprehensive global perspective. [CAL]

3.441 Wilbert E. Moore. *Social change.* 2d ed. Englewood Cliffs, N.J.: Prentice-Hall, 1974. ISBN 0-13-815423-6 (cl), 0-13-815415-5 (pbk). ‣ Classic work by pioneering sociologist, analyzing social change in modern world as part of broader pattern of modernization. Examines and critiques various theories of social change and convergence and divergence of industrial societies. [CAL]

3.442 Wilbert E. Moore. *World modernization: the limits of convergence.* New York: Elsevier, 1979. ISBN 0-444-99062-3. ‣ Argues modernization should be perceived as rationalization of how social life is organized and social activities performed. Challenges emphasis on convergence (increasing global homogeneity) in modernization literature. [CAL]

3.443 Talcott Parsons. *Societies: evolutionary and comparative* *perspectives*. Englewood Cliffs, N.J.: Prentice-Hall, 1966. ▸ Good summary by major intellectual functionalist. Shows influence of modernization theory. Attempts comparative and theoretical overview of society as total system through examination of major historical patterns in ancient world. [CAL]

3.444 W. W. Rostow. *The stages of economic growth: a non-communist manifesto*. 3d ed. Cambridge: Cambridge University Press, 1990. ISBN 0-521-40070-8 (cl), 0-521-40928-4 (pbk). ▸ Seminal and controversial work in modernization literature that generalizes modern world history. Distinguishes five stages of economic growth that characterized advanced industrial nations. Identifies preconditions necessary to development. [CAL]

3.445 W. W. Rostow. *The world economy: history and prospect*. Austin: University of Texas Press, 1978. ISBN 0-292-79008-2. ▸ Trends and cycles in global production and distribution, 1700s to 1970s. Elaborate defense of modernization theory; extension of famous *The Stages of Economic Growth* (3.444). [LJF]

3.446 Dankwart A. Rustow. *A world of nations: problems of political modernization*. Washington, D.C.: Brookings Institution, 1967. ▸ Analysis of political evolution of developing nations leading to modernity. Emphasizes major elements of nationhood, growth of government and participation, and foreign influences. Contrasts early and late modernizing societies. [CAL]

3.447 Milton Singer. *When a great tradition modernizes: an anthropological approach to Indian civilization*. New York: Praeger, 1972. ▸ Offers theory of cultural change based on interaction between Indian classical tradition of brahmanic Hinduism and urban life. Explores coexistence and adaptation of traditional and modern, and effects of urbanization on culture and religion. [CAL]

3.448 Alvin Y. So. *Social change and development: modernization, dependency, and world-systems theories*. Newbury Park, Calif.: Sage, 1990. ISBN 0-8039-3546-3 (cl), 0-8039-3547-1 (pbk). ▸ Stimulating critique and overview of modernization, dependency, and world-system approaches, including both their traditional and contemporary literatures. Excellent introduction to major issues, controversies, and insights, including analytical and explanatory merits of each. [CAL]

3.449 Robert E. Ward and Dankwart A. Rustow, eds. *Political modernization in Japan and Turkey*. Princeton: Princeton University Press, 1964. ISBN 0-691-00004-2. ▸ Classic collection of essays that attempts systematic analysis of historical factors characterizing modernization of these two non-Western societies. Emphasizes economic and political developments, including education, bureaucracy, military, and leadership. [CAL]

3.450 Myron Weiner, ed. *Modernization: the dynamics of growth*. New York: Basic Books, 1966. ▸ Collection of essays by leading scholars of modernization school addressing political, economic, social, and cultural issues. Provides excellent introduction to major parameters of approach. [CAL]

SEE ALSO
  11.59 Gilbert Rozman, ed. *The modernization of China*.

NATIONALISM, ANTICOLONIALISM, SOCIALISM, AND COMMUNISM

3.451 Anouar Abdel-Malek. *Social dialectics*. Vol. 2: *Nationalism and socialism*. Mike Gonzalez, trans. Albany: State University of New York Press, 1981. ISBN 0-87395-501-3 (v. 2). ▸ Typology of national formation in Third World, treating imperialism, national liberation, and socialism. Argues national liberation struggles became main current of anticapitalism, eliminating European Marxist tradition. [LGD]

3.452 Samir Amin. *Class and nation, historically and in the current crisis*. Susan Kaplov, trans. New York: Monthly Review, 1980.

ISBN 0-85345-522-8 (cl), 0-85345-532-6 (pbk). ▸ Discussion of precapitalist historical formations and genesis of capitalist world system. Articulation of classes, nations, and the state. Class and nationality both products and structures of capitalist world system, constituting bases for anticapitalist struggle. [LGD]

3.453 Benedict R. O'G. Anderson. *Imagined communities: reflections on the origin and spread of nationalism*. 2d ed. London: Verso, 1983. ISBN 0-86091-059-8 (cl), 0-86091-759-2 (pbk). ▸ Construction of national consciousness, first in Americas, then in Europe and elsewhere viewed as form of historical discourse of modernity. Claims of nationalisms to be ancient, universal, coherent, and classless are socially created myths of very real power. [LGD]

3.454 Hannah Arendt. *On revolution*. 1963 ed. Harmondsworth: Penguin, 1977. ISBN 0-14-021681-2. ▸ Influential and outspoken philosophical essay on civilizational roots and gravely dangerous consequences of modern revolutions; by leading theorist of totalitarianism, disciple and friend of Karl Jaspers. [LGD]

3.455 John A. Armstrong. *Nations before nationalism*. Chapel Hill: University of North Carolina Press, 1982. ISBN 0-8079-1501-2. ▸ Compares origins of national/ethnic identity for nomadic and sedentary peoples in Christian and Islamic regions as basis for political organization. Key contribution to theory of nationalism. Photocopy available from Ann Arbor: University Microfilms International, 1992. [LEL]

3.456 Giovanni Arrighi, Terence K. Hopkins, and Immanuel Wallerstein. *Antisystemic movements*. London: Verso, 1989. ISBN 0-86091-249-3 (cl), 0-86091-964-1 (pbk). ▸ Analysis of classes and status groups (nation, race, gender, etc.) as two historical bases for social movements challenging capitalist world system (thus, antisystemic). Failure of Social-Democrats, Communists, and nationalists due to their use of national state power for social transformation, which in modern world system can be only global. [LGD]

3.457 Étienne Balibar and Immanuel Wallerstein. *Race, nation, class: ambiguous identities*. Chris Turner, trans. London: Routledge, Chapman & Hall, 1991. ISBN 0-86091-327-9 (cl), 0-86091-542-5 (pbk). ▸ Discussion between French Marxist philosopher and American sociologist of world-systems school. Treats modern racism, its relation to class divisions within capitalism, nationalism, and class struggle, and inherent contradictions of nation-state as transitory historical form. [LGD]

3.458 G. Carter Bentley. *Ethnicity and nationality: a bibliographic guide*. Seattle: University of Washington Press, 1981. (University of Washington, Publications on ethnicity and nationality of the School of International Studies, 3.) ISBN 0-295-95853-7. ▸ Main source of bibliographical information in field of ethnicity and nationality studies. Contains more than 2,300 professionally annotated entries on general, theoretical, and area studies. [LGD]

3.459 Gérard Chaliand. *Revolution in the Third World*. Rev. ed. Diana Johnstone and Tony Berrett, trans. New York: Viking, 1989. ISBN 0-670-82637-5. ▸ Theoretical setting and firsthand accounts of realities of contemporary Third World revolutions and guerrilla movements. Three features common to all victorious antisystemic movements: fusion of nationalism and socialism before taking power, bureaucratic degeneration afterwards, and importance of local civilizational roots. [LGD]

3.460 Fernando Claudin. *The communist movement: from Comintern to Cominform*. 2 vols. Brian Pearce and F. MacDonagh, trans. New York: Monthly Review, 1975. ISBN 0-85345-366-7. ▸ Internal history of international communist movement from inception of Third International to destalinization struggles following 1956 Twentieth Party Congress of Communist Party of the Soviet Union. Antidemocratic degeneration perspective by prominent Spanish ex-Communist. [LGD]

3.461 John Coakley, ed. *The social origins of nationalist movements: the contemporary West European experience*. London: Sage, 1992. ISBN 0-8039-8572-X. ‣ Overview of main theoretical approaches to problem of nationalism and case studies of contemporary West European nationalism (in Spain, Britain, Switzerland) and regionalism (Italy, France) or their absence (Scandinavia). Concludes nationalism, despite predictions, is far from dead in advanced capitalist societies, posing political and theoretical challenges. [LGD]

3.462 Karl Wolfgang Deutsch and William J. Foltz, eds. *Nation-building*. 1963 ed. New York: Atherton, 1966. ‣ Discussion of processes of nation and state formation in modern world, their subjective and objective aspects. Argues modern communications first made nationalism and nation-state possible, but later outgrew and undid them in West and then elsewhere in modernizing world. [LGD]

3.463 John Dunn. *Modern revolutions: an introduction to the analysis of a political phenomenon*. 2d ed. Cambridge: Cambridge University Press, 1989. ISBN 0-521-37176-7 (cl), 0-521-37814-1 (pbk). ‣ Case analysis of all major revolutions in twentieth century, their moving forces and ideological dilemmas. Argues modern revolutions consist of intense political struggles initiated by crises in particular historical societies and terminate in drastic reconstruction of state power that often creates greater injustices. [LGD]

3.464 Jean Elleinstein, ed. *Histoire mondiale des socialismes*. 6 vols. Paris: Colin and Lilas, 1984. ISBN 2-200-37058-X (set), 2-904591-00-1 (set). ‣ One of most complete histories of world socialist movements and ideologies. Numerous illustrations, bibliographies, and indexes. Claims only to supply readers with accessible, exhaustive dossier, allowing them to make own judgments. [LGD]

3.465 Boris Frankel. *The post-industrial utopians*. Madison: University of Wisconsin Press, 1987. ISBN 0-299-10810-4 (cl), 0-299-10814-7 (pbk). ‣ Study of alternative life styles, small-is-beautiful, and green movements in contemporary Western Europe and in Great Britain particularly, their agendas and relations to the state, established parties, and postindustrial economies. [GD]

3.466 Imanuel Geiss. *The pan-African movement: a history of pan-Africanism in America, Europe, and Africa*. Ann Keep, trans. New York: Africana, 1974. ISBN 0-8419-0161-9. ‣ Emergence in nineteenth century and evolution to 1960s of first black emancipation movements in Americas, Africa, and Europe that claimed common ancestry and political future based on race. Detailed account of major figures, organizations, and events. Views pan-Africanism as reaction of modernized African and African American elites to European supremacy. [GD]

3.467 Georges Haupt. *Aspects of international socialism, 1871–1914: essays*. Peter Fawcett, trans. Cambridge: Cambridge University Press, 1986. ISBN 0-521-26259-3. ‣ Encyclopedic study of socialist movement between Marx and Lenin. Concludes socialists from Paris Commune to World War I and Bolshevik Revolution functioned as genuine international community of men and women consciously engaged in common historical task. Fine product of East European dissident Marxism. [LGD]

3.468 Eric J. Hobsbawm. *Nations and nationalism since 1780: programme, myth, reality*. 2d ed. Cambridge: Cambridge University Press, 1992. ISBN 0-521-43961-2. ‣ Discussion of nationalism from "below" and from "above" in revolutionary and liberal traditions, origins in eighteenth century, apogee in 1918–50, and present demise. Argues nationalism should be discussed only in relation to modern nation-state, its centralization drive, and popular resistances. [LGD]

3.469 Eric J. Hobsbawm. *Revolutionaries: contemporary essays*. 1973 ed. New York: Meridian, 1976. ‣ Topics in history of communism, anarchism, and nationalist revolutionary guerrillas, with case studies from Europe and Third World. Critique of non-Marxist theories of revolution (Arendt 3.454, etc.) Western neo-Marxist history by its foremost author. [LGD]

3.470 Edward Hyams. *The millennium postponed: socialism from Sir Thomas More to Mao Tse-tung*. 1973 ed. New York: Taplinger, 1974. ISBN 0-8008-5247-8. ‣ Fairly detailed history of socialism in all its divergent traditions and vigorous liberal critique of socialist millenarianism that, when in power, brings total bureaucratization as inevitable outcome. [LGD]

3.471 Lawrence Kaplan, ed. *Fundamentalism in comparative perspective*. Amherst: University of Massachusetts Press, 1992. ISBN 0-87023-797-7 (cl), 0-87023-798-5 (pbk). ‣ Theoretical problems in study of contemporary religious fundamentalism (not just Islamic), with case studies. Sees desecularization as reaction of civil society in capitalist peripheries to modern state formation and demise of nationalist developmental projects. Part of recent, important shift in studies of religious militancy. [LGD]

3.472 Hans Kohn. *Nationalism, its meaning and history*. 1965 rev. ed. Malabar, Fla.: Krieger, 1982. ISBN 0-89874-479-2 (pbk). ‣ Concise theoretical survey combined with annotated reader, from Machiavelli to Mao. Views nationalism, or loyalty to nation-state, as quintessentially modern phenomenon spreading from eighteenth-century Europe throughout globe and producing countless variations. [LGD]

3.473 George Lichtheim. *A short history of socialism*. 1970 ed. London: Fontana, 1983. ISBN 0-00-654026-0 (pbk). ‣ Overview of antecedents and multiplicity of conflicting currents and sects of socialism, seen as historically conditioned response of intelligentsias and workers to bourgeois individualism formulated in terms of Enlightenment and modernity. [LGD]

3.474 Ronaldo Munck. *The difficult dialogue: Marxism and nationalism*. London: Zed, 1986. ISBN 0-86232-493-9 (cl), 0-86232-494-7 (pbk). ‣ Discussion of nationality question in works of major Marxist thinkers and revolutionaries (Karl Kautsky, Lenin, Mao Tse-tung, Sultan Galiev, Amilcar Cabral, etc.) Survey of Marxist attempts to grapple with enduring power of nationalism as manifestation of nonclass consciousness. [LGD]

3.475 Adam Przeworski. *Capitalism and social democracy*. 1985 ed. New York and Paris: Cambridge University Press and Éditions de la Maison des Sciences de l'Homme, 1986. ISBN 0-521-26742-0 (cl, 1985), 0-521-33656-2 (pbk). ‣ Study in formation and functioning of social-democratic parties in Western Europe, their strategy and tactics, and forms and conditions of class compromise. Although efficient form of managing workers' economic needs in core societies, social democracy never offered alternative to capitalist system. [LGD]

3.476 Cedric J. Robinson. *Black Marxism: the making of the black radical tradition*. London: Zed; distributed by Biblio Distribution Center, 1983. ISBN 0-86232-126-3 (cl), 0-86232-127-1 (pbk). ‣ Study of race, class, and racism in formation of capitalism. Discussion of socialist theory and nationalism. Examines black resistance and radicalism in history, from slave revolts to present. Synthesis of black radicalism and Marxism, loosely defined. [LGD]

3.477 Joseph A. Schumpeter. *Capitalism, socialism, and democracy*. 1950 3d ed. New York: Harper & Row, 1976. ISBN 0-06-090456-9. ‣ Analysis of modern capitalism as economy, political system, and civilization facing test of survival from its own self-destructive successes. Views socialism as sad inevitability of bureaucratic regulation. Masterpiece of twentieth-century social thought and one of few truly consistent conservative critiques of Marxism. [LGD]

3.478 Theda Skocpol. *States and social revolutions: a comparative* *analysis of France, Russia, and China.* Cambridge: Cambridge University Press, 1979. ISBN 0-521-22439-X (cl), 0-521-29499-1 (pbk). ▸ Causal theory of revolutions. Discusses French, Russian, and Chinese revolutions in comparative historical-sociological perspective. Concludes revolutions arise from inability of old imperial states to cope with international defeats and internal social pressures, ultimately making state much stronger and independent of internal classes and foreign powers. [LGD]

3.479 Jane Slaughter and Robert Kern. *European women on the Left: socialism, feminism, and the problems faced by political women, 1880 to the present.* Westport, Conn.: Greenwood, 1981. ISBN 0-313-22543-5. ▸ Analysis of women activists and women's issues in Western and Russian Left (communist, social democratic, anarchist), from Sylvia Pankhurst to Ulrika Meinhof. Concludes well-defined anticapitalist movement since 1880 had strong appeal to women, although often for different reasons than for men. Biographical case studies illuminate main argument. [LGD]

3.480 Louis L. Snyder. *Macro-nationalisms: a history of the pan-movements.* Westport, Conn.: Greenwood, 1984. ISBN 0-313-23191-5. ▸ Comparative study of pan-national (-Slavic, -German, -Arab, -African, etc.) movements. Finds macro- and micro-nationalisms are two peripheries that will never succeed over mainstream nationalism because they do not correspond to nation-states, main political unit of modernity. [LGD]

3.481 Adam B. Ulam. *The Communists: the story of power and lost illusions, 1948–1991.* New York and Toronto: Scribner's and Maxwell Macmillan Canada, 1992. ISBN 0-684-19236-5. ▸ Study of post-1945 apogee, decline, and disintegration of communist movement and states by leading Western Sovietologist. [LGD]

3.482 Eric R. Wolf. *Peasant wars of the twentieth century.* 1969 ed. New York: Harper & Row, 1973. ISBN 0-06-131774-8. ▸ Analysis of revolutionary wars in Mexico, Russia, China, Vietnam, Algeria, and Cuba through prism of peasant class consciousness. Emphasizes importance of "middle" peasants stimulated by North Atlantic capitalism. [LGD]

SEE ALSO
22.380 James H. Billington. *Fire in the minds of men.*
22.389 Ernest Gellner. *Nations and nationalism.*

RELIGION

3.483 Charles J. Adams, ed. *A reader's guide to the great religions.* 2d ed. New York: Free Press, 1977. ISBN 0-02-900240-0. ▸ Thirteen bibliographic essays on religions of world, antiquity to modern times. [ALB/MET]

3.484 Phillip Berryman. *Liberation theology: essential facts about the revolutionary religious movement in Latin America and beyond.* New York: Pantheon, 1987. ISBN 0-394-55241-5 (cl), 0-394-74652-X (pbk). ▸ Concise, cogent survey of historical background, sources of biblical authority, modern evolution, and influence of Marxism. Emphasizes Latin America, but also discusses and compares North American developments. [RBB]

3.485 Peter Bishop and Michael Darton, eds. *The encyclopedia of world faiths: an illustrated survey of the world's living religions.* 1987 ed. New York: Facts on File, 1989. ISBN 0-8160-1860-X. ▸ Interesting narrative essays on all major faiths, plus Baha'i, Jainism, Zoroastrianism, and others; also treats new religious movements and religion in modern world. Authors predominantly British. Useful maps, glossary, bibliography, illustrations, and diagrams. [RBB]

3.486 Lionel Caplan, ed. *Studies in religious fundamentalism.* Albany: State University of New York Press, 1987. ISBN 0-88706-518-X (cl), 0-88706-519-8 (pbk). ▸ Informative essays on fundamentalism in widely diverse traditions—Tamils in Britain, Wahabis in West Africa, Muslims in Egypt, and Sikhs in India.

Thoughtful introduction elucidates difficulties in comparative study of fundamentalism. [RBB]

3.487 John Durant, ed. *Darwinism and divinity: essays on evolution and religious belief.* 1985 ed. New York: Blackwell, 1986. ISBN 0-631-14188-X (cl, 1985), 0-631-15101-X (pbk). ▸ Well-edited, reflective essays on consequences of Charles Darwin's work on religious belief. Two essays display sympathetic bias to creationism, but overall valuable, thought-provoking examination of influential theory of evolution. [RBB]

3.488 Mircea Eliade, ed. *The encyclopedia of religion.* 16 vols. New York and London: Macmillan and Collier Macmillan, 1987. ISBN 0-02-909480-1 (set). ▸ Indispensable tool with comprehensive world coverage, including comparative discussion of many topics. [ALB/MET]

3.489 Charles Wei-hsun Fu and Gerhard E. Spiegler, eds. *Movements and issues in world religions: a sourcebook and analysis of developments since 1945.* 1 vol. to date. Westport, Conn.: Greenwood, 1987–. ISBN 0-313-23238-5 (v. 1). ▸ Scholarly essays examining relationship between religion and social and political change since 1945 in five areas: interreligious conflicts, developing nations, developed nations, Marxism, and Holocaust. Excellent survey in historical context. [RBB]

3.490 Richard Garbe. *India and Christendom: the historical connections between their religions.* Lydia Gillingham Robinson, trans. LaSalle, Ill.: Open Court, 1959. ▸ Comprehensive, scholarly evaluation of controversial topic that once suffered from overenthusiastic devotees discerning dubious linkages. Includes discussion of dispersion of material objects such as rosaries. Fascinating reading. Originally published in German in 1914. [LNS]

3.491 Bruce Grelle and David A. Krueger, eds. *Christianity and capitalism: perspectives on religion, liberalism, and the economy.* Chicago: Center for the Scientific Study of Religion, 1986. ISBN 0-913348-23-6 (cl), 0-913348-24-4 (pbk). ▸ Stimulating essays on issues surrounding religion and human work, global economy, Catholic and Protestant economic ethics, and economic liberalism. Lacks global, multireligions perspective, but valuable introduction. [RBB]

3.492 Paul J. Griffiths, ed. *Christianity through non-Christian eyes.* Maryknoll, N.Y.: Orbis, 1990. ISBN 0-88344-662-6 (cl), 0-88344-661-8 (pbk). ▸ Intriguing, unique, diverse essays by Buddhist, Hindu, Jewish, and Muslim authors whose views of Christianity are sometimes conciliatory, sometimes caustic. Editor's comments and notations enhance readability and understanding. [RBB]

3.493 Eugene C. Hargrove, ed. *Religion and environmental crisis.* Athens: University of Georgia Press, 1986. ISBN 0-8203-0845-5 (cl), 0-8203-0846-3 (pbk). ▸ Readable, original essays introducing environmental ethics and views of nature from various religious traditions, including Greco-Roman worship of Pan, Judaism, Islam, American Indian religions, and liberation, feminist, and process theology. [RBB]

3.494 Joseph Mitsuo Kitagawa. *The quest for human unity: a religious history.* Minneapolis: Fortress, 1990. ISBN 0-8006-2422-X. ▸ Original, thoughtful work by distinguished scholar. Seeks to identify vision of and longing for human unity by studying "inner" and "outer" meanings of religious traditions from most ancient civilizations to present. [RBB]

3.495 Hans Küng et al. *Christianity and the world religions: paths of dialogue with Islam, Hinduism, and Buddhism.* Peter Heinegg, trans. Garden City, N.Y.: Doubleday, 1986. ISBN 0-385-19471-4. ▸ Intellectually ambitious, ecumenical venture. Three scholars each offer four perspectives on their specialties. Prominent Catholic scholar-priest Küng responds from Christian viewpoint.

Challenging, stimulating, and rich in historical and theological detail. Bibliographies. [RBB]

3.496 Bruce B. Lawrence. *Defenders of God: the fundamentalist revolt against the modern age.* San Francisco: Harper & Row, 1989. ISBN 0-06-250509-2. ▸ Groundbreaking, provocative, insightful analysis viewing fundamentalism as ideology, not theology. Seeks to demonstrate multicultural, cross-creedal commonality among certain Israelis, Muslims, and American Protestants. [RBB]

3.497 John McManners. *The Oxford illustrated history of Christianity.* Oxford: Oxford University Press, 1990. ISBN 0-19-822928-3. ▸ Lavishly illustrated, scholarly, and lucid survey of world Christianity from beginnings to twenty-first century. Emphasis on interaction between church and society, shaping and being shaped by world. Maps, chronology, annotated bibliography. [RBB]

3.498 Albert C. Moore. *Iconography of religions: an introduction.* Philadelphia: Fortress, 1977. ISBN 0-8006-0488-1. ▸ Systematic, comprehensive guide to iconography. Illustrations not lavish but useful for recognition and understanding of types and meanings of visual images in religious thought and worship. Primarily Eastern religions and Islam, Judaism, and Christianity. [RBB]

3.499 Stephen Neill. *A history of Christian missions.* 1986 2d ed. Owen Chadwick, ed. Harmondsworth: Penguin, 1990. ISBN 0-14-022736-9 (pbk). ▸ Standard, generally favorable, though not entirely uncritical, narrative account of worldwide Christian expansion and missionary movement that led it, by highly regarded missionary-scholar. All-encompassing and detailed. [RBB]

3.500 Niels C. Nielsen, Jr., et al. *Religions of the world.* 2d ed. New York: St. Martin's, 1988. ISBN 0-312-00308-0. ▸ Accessible history of course of world religions. Well written, researched, organized, and accurate, with quality maps, illustrations, and time lines. Extensive historical framework for each religion. [RBB]

3.501 Geoffrey Parrinder, ed. *World religions: from ancient history to the present.* 1971 ed. New York: Facts on File, 1983. ISBN 0-87196-129-6. ▸ One of best introductions; impressive range of traditions from prehistoric times, Maya, Inca, Africa, Rome, and Greece to Japan, China, and major world religions. Well-illustrated, informative, introductory essay and valuable bibliography. [RBB]

3.502 Frank E. Reynolds and Earle H. Waugh, eds. *Religious encounters with death: insights from the history and anthropology of religions.* University Park: Pennsylvania State University Press, 1977. ISBN 0-271-01229-3. ▸ Study of social context of death rituals and mythological accounts, not speculative individual beliefs and faith in afterlife, in truly diverse cultures. Significant addition to extensive literature on these themes in Christianity. [RBB]

3.503 Ninian Smart. *Worldviews: crosscultural explorations of human beliefs.* New York: Scribner's, 1983. ISBN 0-684-17811-7 (cl), 0-684-17812-5 (pbk). ▸ Readable, original introduction to study of religion through thematic comparisons of six major worldviews. Examples demonstrate author's six dimensions of religion. Argues for polymethodic approach employing several disciplines. [RBB]

3.504 Huston Smith. *Huston Smith: essays on world religions.* M. Darrol Bryant, ed. New York: Paragon House, 1992. ISBN 1-55778-447-7. ▸ Collection of previously published essays by noted scholar. Erudite, intelligible, challenging, original, and truly global; moves easily from Taoism, Zen (Ch'an) Buddhism, and Tibetan Lamas to China, India, and West. [RBB]

3.505 Wilfred Cantwell Smith. *Towards a world theology: faith and the comparative history of religion.* 1981 ed. Maryknoll, N.Y.: Orbis, 1989. ISBN 0-88344-646-4. ▸ Historical and theological arguments for unity of religious experience. New scientifically

based religious consciousness makes it possible to affirm universal nature of spirituality while respecting differences. [ALB/MET]

3.506 Roger N. Walsh. *The spirit of shamanism.* Los Angeles: Tarcher, 1990. ISBN 0-87477-562-0. ▸ Readable introduction in global perspective to nature of shamanism, using recent psychological and anthropological research. Includes comparative references to world religions and historical perspective. Useful for further research. [RBB]

3.507 Arthur F. Wright. *Buddhism in Chinese history.* 1959 ed. Stanford, Calif.: Stanford University Press, 1971. ISBN 0-8047-0546-1 (cl), 0-8047-0548-8 (pbk). ▸ Six essays on Buddhism's introduction to and transformation of Chinese culture. Valuable for students and teachers of world history. [GFM]

WOMEN

3.508 Ester Boserup. *Woman's role in economic development.* 1970 ed. Aldershot, England: Gower, 1986. ISBN 0-566-05139-7. ▸ Study of women's economic roles in Africa, Near East, Asia, and Latin America. Groundbreaking in its analysis of traditional agriculture, polygyny, education, towns, and family migration to industrialized cities. [BAH/SSH]

3.509 Vern L. Bullough, Brenda Shelton, and Sarah Slavin. *The subordinated sex: a history of attitudes toward women.* Rev. ed. Athens: University of Georgia Press, 1988. ISBN 0-8203-1002-6 (cl), 0-8203-1003-4 (pbk). ▸ Survey of male attitudes toward women from prehistory to contemporary times. Introduction to women's history in Eurasia and United States. [BAH/SSH]

3.510 Jane Frances Conners. *Violence against women in the family.* New York: United Nations, 1989. ISBN 92-113-0133-5. ▸ Survey of research primarily on wife abuse. Most research undertaken in Western Europe, North America, Australia, and New Zealand. Sections focus on analysis of violence, governmental responses, and suggested reforms. [BAH/SSH]

3.511 Miranda Davies, comp. *Third World, second sex: women's struggles and national liberation, Third World women speak out.* 2 vols. to date. London: Zed; distributed by Hill, 1983–. ISBN 0-86232-017-8 (v. 1, cl), 0-86232-752-0 (v. 2, cl), 0-86232-029-1 (v. 1, pbk), 0-86232-753-9 (v. 2, pbk). ▸ Collection of documents by activist women from thirty-six Third World countries on participation in revolutions, politics, and labor unions. Organized around issues of violence, rape, prostitution, birth control, and health. [BAH/SSH]

3.512 Mona Etienne and Eleanor Burke Leacock, eds. *Women and colonization: anthropological perspectives.* New York: Praeger, 1980. ISBN 0-03-052586-1 (cl), 0-03-052581-0 (pbk). ▸ Studies of societies in North and South America, Africa, Australia, and Oceania, describing women's lives before colonization and effects of colonization. Insightful, general introduction. [BAH/SSH]

3.513 Nancy Auer Falk and Rita M. Gross, eds. *Unspoken worlds: women's religious lives.* 3d ed. Belmont, Calif.: Wadsworth, 1989. ISBN 0-534-09852-5. ▸ Essays on women's roles in folk religions such as Shinto, Korean shamanism, voodoo, and indigenous American and African religions, as well as charismatic figures from Christianity and Buddhism. [ALB/MET]

3.514 Ernestine Friedl. *Women and men: an anthropologist's view.* 1975 ed. Prospect Heights, Ill.: Waveland, 1984. ISBN 0-88133-040-X. ▸ Examination of sex roles in two types of societies: hunter-gatherer and horticultural. Useful as primer for definitions and concepts. [BAH/SSH]

3.515 Yvonne Yazbeck Haddad and Ellison Banks Findly, eds. *Women, religion, and social change.* Albany: State University of New York, 1985. ISBN 0-88706-068-4 (cl), 0-88706-069-2 (pbk). ▸ Global comparative study of women's role in social change and religion over two millennia. Explores whether women influence religions by preserving values or by initiating change. Concludes during founding stages, women seek change; but in later periods lose influence, support modern revolutions and reforms. [BAH/SSH/RBB]

3.516 Guida M. Jackson. *Women who ruled.* Santa Barbara, Calif.: ABC-Clio, 1990. ISBN 0-87436-560-0. ▸ Global survey of 270 monarchs, *de facto* rulers, and women of influence from 3000 BCE to present. Features readable text, chronology, bibliography, and source list for each entry. [MJG]

3.517 Kumari Jayawardena, ed. *Feminism and nationalism in the Third World.* Rev. ed. New Delhi and London: Kali for Women and Zed; distributed by Biblio, 1986. ISBN 0-86232-264-2 (cl), 0-86232-265-0 (pbk). ▸ Traces rise of indigenous feminism in late nineteenth-century Asia and Middle East as women sought education and political rights. Links feminism to middle-class nationalism and resistance to Western subordination. [BAH/SSH]

3.518 Cheryl Johnson-Odim and Margaret Strobel, eds. *Expanding the boundaries of women's history: essays on women in the Third World.* Bloomington: Indiana University Press for Journal of Women's History, 1992. ISBN 0-253-33097-1 (cl), 0-253-20734-7 (pbk). ▸ Collection of essays describing women's history in non-Western countries in nineteenth and twentieth centuries as discourse between Third World and Western cultures. Examines cross-cultural contact, activism, women workers, and methodology and theory. [BAH/SSH]

3.519 S. Jay Kleinberg, ed. *Retrieving women's history: changing perspectives of the role of women in politics and society.* Oxford: UNESCO; distributed by St. Martin's, 1988. ISBN 0-85496-264-6. ▸ Papers by international scholars identifying theoretical and methodological approaches and areas of investigation including work, family, politics, and ideology-culture-religion. Good regional balance and bibliography. [BAH/SSH]

3.520 Eleanor Burke Leacock, ed. *Myths of male dominance: collected articles on women cross-culturally.* New York: Monthly Review, 1981. ISBN 0-85345-537-6 (cl), 0-85345-538-4 (pbk). ▸ Examination of aboriginal society in Labrador focusing on evolution of women's oppression and arguments for universal male dominance. Argues aboriginal gathering societies changed from egalitarian to patriarchal with Western contact. [BAH/SSH]

3.521 Gerda Lerner. *The creation of patriarchy.* 1986 ed. New York: Oxford University Press, 1987. ISBN 0-19-503996-3 (cl, 1986), 0-19-505185-8 (pbk). ▸ Study of origin of Western women's subordination, linking it to rise of property-conscious agricultural societies. Narratives cover ancient Mesopotamia, Israel, and Greece, and have broad theoretical implications. [BAH/SSH]

3.522 Beverly Lindsay, ed. *Comparative perspectives of Third World women: the impact of race, sex, and class.* New York: Praeger, 1980. ISBN 0-03-046651-2. ▸ Interdisciplinary studies evaluating race and class in political and social institutions oppressing women in Africa, Asia, Caribbean, Latin America, and United States. Focuses on twentieth century. [BAH/SSH]

3.523 Carolyn J. Matthiasson, ed. *Many sisters: women in cross-cultural perspective.* 1974 ed. New York: Free Press, 1979. ISBN 0-02-920320-1 (pbk). ▸ Studies by anthropologists describing gender in thirteen societies. Ranked according to whether women feel inferior, complementary, or superior to men. Good comparative balance among world's regions. [BAH/SSH]

3.524 Chandra Talpade Mohanty, Ann Russo, and Lourdes Torres, eds. *Third World women and the politics of feminism.* Bloomington: Indiana University Press, 1991. ISBN 0-253-33873-5 (cl), 0-253-20632-4 (pbk). ▸ Description of Third World women's engagements with feminism in decolonization, national liberation, state regulation, multinational corporations, and

Western feminism in context of race, class, gender, and sexuality. [BAH/SSH]

3.525 Sandra Morgen, ed. *Gender and anthropology: critical reviews for research and teaching.* Washington, D.C.: American Anthropological Association, 1989. ISBN 0-913167-33-9. ▸ Review of research on evolution, prehistory, archaeology, biology, sexuality, and language, with regional articles on Asia, Southeast Asia, Middle East, Africa, Latin America, Caribbean, and United States minorities. [BAH/SSH]

3.526 Jean F. O'Barr, ed. *Perspectives on power: women in Africa, Asia, and Latin America.* Durham, N.C.: Duke University, Center for International Studies, 1982. (Duke University Center for International Studies, Occasional paper series, 13.) ISBN 0-916994-24-7 (pbk). ▸ Conference papers on Third World women and political power, including summaries of Africa, Asia, and Latin America and case studies of Japan, colonial Africa, Asian textile factories, and Scandinavia. [BAH/SSH]

3.527 Karen M. Offen, Ruth Roach Pierson, and Jane Rendall, eds. *Writing women's history: international perspectives.* Bloomington: Indiana University Press, 1991. ISBN 0-253-34160-4 (cl), 0-253-20651-0 (pbk). ▸ Outstanding introduction to women's history in nineteen countries by scholars from each. Includes most of Europe, Australia, Brazil, India, Japan, and Nigeria, plus seven theoretical essays. [BAH/SSH]

3.528 Carl Olson, ed. *The book of the goddess, past and present: an introduction to her religion.* 1983 ed. New York: Crossroad, 1990. ISBN 0-8245-0689-8 (pbk). ▸ Description of role of goddesses in religions from prehistory to present, including Egyptian, Grecian, Roman, Christian, Hindu, Buddhist, Yoruba, and American Indian. [BAH/SSH]

3.529 Organization of American Historians. *Restoring women to history: teaching packets for integrating women's history into courses on Africa, Asia, Latin America, the Caribbean, and the Middle East.* Rev. ed. Bloomington: Organization of American Historians, 1990. ▸ Despite title, volume's introduction offers important comparative overview of themes in women's history, ranging from personal issues to political power. Four regional sections contain narrative histories and bibliographies. [BAH/SSH]

3.530 Rayna R. Reiter, ed. *Toward an anthropology of women.* New York: Monthly Review, 1975. ISBN 0-85345-372-1. ▸ Path-breaking anthology with often cited articles on evolution and gender; women's gathering labor; and women in Asia, Pacific Islands, Europe, Africa, Latin America, Caribbean, and among native peoples of North America. [BAH/SSH]

3.531 Michelle Zimbalist Rosaldo and Louise Lamphere, eds. *Woman, culture, and society.* Stanford, Calif.: Stanford University Press, 1974. ISBN 0-8047-0850-9 (cl), 0-8047-0851-7 (pbk). ▸ Influential anthropological articles discuss sex roles, ideology of subordination, women's strategies of power, matrifocal organizations, and women with political power. Proposes that women are often associated with nature and men with culture. [BAH/SSH]

3.532 Arvind Sharma, ed. *Women in world religions.* Katherine K. Young, Introduction. Albany: State University of New York Press, 1987. ISBN 0-88706-374-8 (cl), 0-88706-375-6 (pbk). ▸ Introduction and following essay discuss issues surrounding women's role in world religions as revealed in major texts. Remaining essays describe women's roles, actions, thoughts, and experiences in various world religions. Valuable and informative; useful bibliographies. [RBB]

3.533 Filomina Chioma Steady, ed. *The black woman cross-culturally.* 1981 ed. Rochester, Vt.: Schenkman, 1985. ISBN 0-87073-345-1 (cl, 1981), 0-87073-346-X (pbk). ▸ Comparative anthology by thirty-one scholars of black women's history and contemporary lives in Africa, United States, Caribbean, and South America. Introductory overview by editor. [BAH/SSH]

3.534 Evelyne Sullerot. *Woman, society, and change.* Margaret Scotford Archer, trans. New York: McGraw-Hill, 1971. ‣ Comparative study of changes in women's roles worldwide, by French sociologist. Gives evidence on differential treatment of women. Pessimistic about real, lasting change of women's status. [BL]

3.535 Marion Tinling. *Women into the unknown: a sourcebook on women explorers and travelers.* New York: Greenwood, 1989. ISBN 0-313-25328-5. ‣ Brief biographies of more than forty women travelers, mostly from twentieth-century England and United States. Bibliography includes works by many other women travelers. Useful as reference. [SSG]

3.536 United Nations. *The world's women, 1970–1990: trends and statistics.* New York: United Nations, 1991. (Social statistics and indicators, Series K, 8.) ISBN 92-1-161313-2. ‣ Readable statistics on women's demography, families, public life, leadership, education, and training. Indicators available for each country and summarized by region and subregion. [BAH/SSH]

SEE ALSO
2.90 Margaret R. Ehrenberg. *Women in prehistory.*
6.571 Sarah B. Pomeroy. *Goddesses, whores, wives, and slaves.*
24.446 Nupur Chaudhuri and Margaret Strobel, eds. *Western women and imperialism.*

SCIENCE AND TECHNOLOGY

3.537 Michael Adas. *Machines as the measure of men: science, technology, and ideologies of Western dominance.* Ithaca, N.Y.: Cornell University Press, 1989. ISBN 0-8014-2303-1. ‣ Comparative study tracing changes in European attitudes toward "natives" encountered from ca. 1500 to World War I. Concludes rationale for colonialism and imperialism shifts from religious and racial to secular, technological, and quasi-scientific criteria. [LSS]

3.538 Anthony F. Aveni, ed. *World archaeoastronomy.* Cambridge: Cambridge University Press, 1989. ISBN 0-521-34180-9. ‣ Most comprehensive of titles by this author-editor on pre-Columbian and paleoastronomy. Thirty-eight papers selected from second Oxford International Conference on Archaeoastronomy held at Merida, Yucatán, Mexico (1986). [LSS]

3.539 A. K. Bag. *Science and civilization in India.* Vol. 1: *Harappan period (c. 3000 B.C.–1500 B.C.)* New Delhi: Navarang, 1985–. ISBN 81-7013-031-X (v. 1). ‣ Archaeological study beginning with Indus Valley culture in ancient Punjab. Contains nine chapters treating dating, strata, urban layout, crafts, metals, bricks, mathematics, and language. Hopes to start series to parallel Needham's works on China (3.552). [LSS]

3.540 Richard W. Bulliet. *The camel and the wheel.* 1975 ed. New York: Columbia University Press, 1990. ISBN 0-231-07255-X (pbk). ‣ Masterly monograph on ancient mid-Eurasian land transport and long-distance trade. Domestication and introduction of dromedaries in Arabian and Saharan regions in late antiquity displaced wheeled vehicles. [LSS]

3.541 Thomas Francis Carter. *The invention of printing in China and its spread westward.* 2d ed. L. Carrington Goodrich, ed. New York: Ronald, 1955. ‣ Although published decades ago, still one of best sources on origin and dissemination of printing. Discusses China, Europe, and all parts between. [LNS]

3.542 Carlo M. Cipolla. *Before the Industrial Revolution: European society and economy, 1000–1700.* New York: Norton, 1976. ISBN 0-393-05538-8 (cl), 0-393-09255-0 (pbk). ‣ Important background to Western expansion. European socioeconomic development during 700 years of prehistory to industrialization. Blends economic theory and economic history stressing urbanization as prerequisite. [LSS]

3.543 I. Bernard Cohen. *Revolution in science.* Cambridge, Mass.: Belknap, 1985. ISBN 0-674-76777-2. ‣ Historical analysis of concept of scientific revolution over course of four centuries. Discusses historiographical controversies over rapidity and profundity of basic changes in development of about eight sciences since Copernicus. Traditional historian's response to furor aroused by Kuhn 1.516. [LSS]

3.544 Daniel R. Headrick. *The invisible weapon: telecommunications and international politics, 1851–1945.* New York: Oxford University Press, 1991. ISBN 0-19-506273-6. ‣ Third in trilogy of technological histories on worldwide transformations due to new tools and techniques in late nineteenth and early twentieth centuries. Emphasizes financial, political, and socioeconomic aspects of telegraph, submarine cable, wireless radio, and telephone systems, from AT&T to ITT. [LSS]

3.545 Daniel R. Headrick. *The tentacles of progress: technology transfer in the age of imperialism, 1850–1940.* New York: Oxford University Press, 1988. ISBN 0-19-505115-7 (cl), 0-19-505116-5 (pbk). ‣ Seminal study of octopus-like expansion and control of industrial transportation networks, communications grids, civil engineering, plantation agriculture, mining and metals production, technical education, and engineering entrepreneurs worldwide led by the British. [LSS]

3.546 Daniel R. Headrick. *The tools of empire: technology and European imperialism in the nineteenth century.* New York: Oxford University Press, 1981. ISBN 0-19-502831-7 (cl), 0-19-502835-2 (pbk). ‣ Study of steamboats, steamships, opium, quinine, rifles, machine-guns, telegraph, submarine cables, and railroads as prime products of industrial technology that both allowed and stimulated new imperialism. [LSS]

3.547 Georges Ifrah. *From one to zero: a universal history of numbers.* 1985 ed. Lowell Bair, trans. New York: Penguin, 1987. ISBN 0-14-009919-0 (pbk). ‣ Erudite but accessible, truly global history of numbers, as well as some basic mathematics associated with them. Makes clear that our Arabic numbers are Indian and elucidates several apparent contradictions in literature regarding origin of true zero. [LNS]

3.548 David Knight. *Sources for the history of science, 1660–1914.* Ithaca, N.Y.: Cornell University Press, 1975. ISBN 0-8014-0941-1. ‣ Guide to primary and secondary sources and locations of material for two and a half centuries of scientific growth. [LSS]

3.549 Edgardo Marcorini, ed. *The history of science and technology: a narrative chronology.* Vol. 1: *Prehistory to 1900.* Vol. 2: *1900–1970.* 2 vols. New York: Facts on File, 1988. ISBN 0-87196-477-5 (set), 0-87196-475-9 (v. 1), 0-87196-476-7 (v. 2). ‣ Well organized by periods that become briefer as categories become more numerous. Excellent time-line comparisons. Translation from Italian reference work, *Scienza e tecnica* (1975). [LSS]

3.550 Joel Mokyr. *The lever of riches: technological creativity and economic progress.* New York: Oxford University Press, 1990. ISBN 0-19-506113-6. ‣ Economic history balanced by analyses and comparisons of technological change worldwide. Attributes causes and consequences of ongoing industrial revolutions to techniques, microinventions, and macroinventions acting like species in competition and cooperation. [LSS]

3.551 Seyyed Hossein Nasr. *Science and civilization in Islam.* Giorgio de Santillana, Preface. Cambridge, Mass.: Harvard University Press, 1968. ‣ Brief overview of Islamic science and culture, with attempt to raise appreciation in West for Middle East as Islamic civilization. [LSS]

3.552 Joseph Needham. *Science and civilization in China.* 7 vols. to date. Cambridge: Cambridge University Press, 1954–. ISBN 0-521-25076-5 (v. 6). ‣ Unique scholarly project for raising Western appreciation of 3,000-year legacy of Chinese material and moral culture. Twenty volumes projected. [LSS]

3.553 Arnold Pacey. *Technology in world civilization: a thousand-year history.* 1990 ed. Cambridge, Mass.: MIT Press, 1991. ISBN 0-262-16117-6 (cl, 1990), 0-262-66072-5 (pbk). ▸ Highly impressionistic yet insightful work ranging from golden age of Sung China to survival technology, from gunpowder empires to railroad empires, and beyond. Physicist turned historian argues East-West dialectic for technology transfer in attempt to transcend Eurocentrism. [LSS]

3.554 J. R. Partington. *A history of Greek fire and gunpowder.* Frederick Morgan, Foreword. Cambridge: Heffer, 1960. ▸ Dated in some parts, but remains useful source. Discusses origins of gunpowder in China and its spread, carefully distinguishing among several different incendiary substances, not all of which were gunpowder. [LNS]

3.555 Colin A. Ronan. *Science: its history and development among the world's cultures.* New York: Facts on File, 1982. ISBN 0-87196-745-6. ▸ Well-illustrated introduction with separate chapters on Chinese, Indian, Roman, and Islamic knowledge systems. Focus on pure science and major conceptual changes; attempts equal coverage of cultures. Less Eurocentric than most survey texts. [LSS]

3.556 Ina Spiegel-Rosing and Derek de Solla Price, eds. *Science, technology, and society: a cross-disciplinary perspective.* London: Sage, 1977. ISBN 0-8039-9858-9. ▸ International Council for Science Policy Studies (established 1971) called for organization of "science of the sciences," here attempted in three parts: Normative and Professional Contexts; Social Studies of Science (Disciplinary Perspectives); and Science Policy Studies. [LSS]

3.557 René Taton, ed. *History of science.* Vol. 1: *Ancient and medieval science from the beginnings to 1450.* Vol. 2: *Beginnings of modern science, from 1450 to 1800.* Vol. 3: *Science in the nineteenth century.* Vol. 4: *Science in the twentieth century.* 1963–64 ed. 4 vols. A. J. Pomerans, trans. New York: Basic Books, 1964–66. ▸ Includes bibliographies and appendixes on advances in non-European regions. Translation of *Histoire générale des sciences* (1957–64). [LSS]

3.558 Lynn T. White, Jr. *Medieval technology and social change.* New York: Oxford University Press, 1990. ISBN 0-19-520843-9.

▸ Lecture-essays by influential medievalist on long-term changes in European material culture. Chapters on stirrups, plows, and cranks as technological innovations with profound social consequences. [LSS]

3.559 Lynn T. White, Jr. "Tibet, India, and Malaya as sources of Western medieval technology." *American historical review* 65.3 (1960) 515–26. ISSN 0002-8762. ▸ Important article arguing focus on Chinese technology and its dissemination has obscured importance of inventions and ideas from Tibet (verticle axle windmill, hot-air turbine, and ball-and-chain governor), Malaya (blowguns), and India (numbers and positional reckoning, and concept of perpetual motion machine). Suggests most likely source of transmission of Tibetan devices to Italy were thousands of "Tartar" slaves in every major Italian city by about 1450. Demonstrates Arab transmission of Malayan and Indian items. [LNS]

3.560 Trevor I. Williams. *Science: a history of discovery in the twentieth century.* New York: Oxford University Press, 1990. ISBN 0-19-520843-9. ▸ Lavishly illustrated overview of major developments in pure and applied science by fifteen-year periods throughout century. See also his abridgement (with T. K. Derry) of first five volumes of Singer et al., eds. *A History of Technology* (4.369) and his digest of volumes 6 and 7 of *A Short History of Twentieth-Century Technology* (4.425). [LSS]

SEE ALSO

1.516 Thomas S. Kuhn. *The structure of scientific revolutions.*
4.1 William F. Bynum, E. Janet Browne, and Roy Porter, eds. *Dictionary of the history of science.*
4.2 Pietro Corsi and Paul Weindling, eds. *Information sources in the history of science and medicine.*
4.3 Charles Coulston Gillispie et al., eds. *Dictionary of scientific biography.*
4.14 Charles Coulston Gillispie. *The edge of objectivity.*
4.19 Paul T. Durbin, ed. *A guide to the culture of science, technology, and medicine.*
4.21 Helge Kragh. *An introduction to the historiography of science.*
4.23 Robert C. Olby et al., eds. *Companion to the history of modern science.*
4.320 Evelyn Fox Keller. *Reflections on gender and science.*
4.369 Charles Joseph Singer et al., eds. *A history of technology.*

ROBERT K. DEKOSKY

Science, Technology, and Medicine

Interactions among histories of science, technology, and medicine are evident in the scholarship of historians who study these three broad disciplines (e.g., A. B. Davis, *Medicine and Its Technology*, 4.656). Nevertheless, the histories of science, technology, and medicine are pursued essentially independently; each has its own professional organizations, journals, and distinct scholarly evolution. A brief essay cannot exhaustively expose the varied traditions and agendas that have shaped these fields of history into their current forms; possibly the best single source for this is P. T. Durbin, ed., *A Guide to the Culture of Science, Technology, and Medicine* (4.19)—notably the historiographic essays by A. Thackray (science), C. W. Pursell (technology), and G. Brieger (medicine). Here we want to focus on trends that have emerged forcefully within the last quarter century in the literature of all three disciplines and that promise to influence historical interpretation in the foreseeable future.

As in other fields of history, the current views of historians of science, technology, and medicine appear through socioeconomic, political, and cultural lenses that significantly alter the images of thirty years ago. Rich studies of context such as M. R. Smith's *Harpers Ferry Armory and the New Technology* (4.423) testify to this. Moreover, some scholars have moved beyond descriptions of context to contend that human knowledge evolves wholly or partly as a social construction (e.g., S. Shapin and S. Shaffer, *Leviathan and the Air Pump*, 4.99). In developing this interpretation, scholars have been stimulated by recent social history, an historically conscious sociology of science, and a cultural history sensitive to rhetorical and semantic influences on human thought. Anthropological studies have exerted a notable impact on historians of biology, gender, and sexuality. The assertion that the content of knowledge derives from social processes producing consensus—be they political, economic, professional, semantic, gender related, or broadly cultural—provokes praise and damnation as a major historiographic issue now confronting scholars of scientific, technological, and medical histories.

The histories of medicine and technology have eased into socioeconomic modes with less controversy than their scientific counterpart. Indeed, a tradition of viewing medicine as a social science extends back to Hippocrates. When the history of medicine developed into an independent discipline in the mid-twentieth century, its leading practitioner in the United States, Henry Sigerist, pointed to social and cultural contexts of medicine even while concentrating on the history of medical ideas and great men. At mid-century, R. H. Shryock, (*The Development of Modern Medicine*, 4.661) and G. Rosen (*A History of Public Health*, 4.778) vigorously advocated the social history of medicine. Recent studies of the history of medicine both apply the newer social and cultural history to medicine and reflect the heritage of mid-twentieth-century predecessors.

One approach to the history of technology in the early twentieth century illuminated the technical evolution of inventions and manufacturing processes. Scholars such as the American economic historian Abbott Payson Usher and members of the British Newcomen Society wrote histories of this type. But some historians strayed from internal analysis and sought to associate technological change with shifting economic and market conditions (e.g., H. C. Passer, *The Electrical Manufacturers, 1875–1900*, 4.524). Other classical works, such as S. Giedion, *Mechanization Takes Command* (4.406) and L. Mumford, *Technics and Civilization* (4.354), sensitized their readers to the social, economic, and cultural implications of technological change. By the time the Society for the History of Technology (SHOT) formed over three decades ago, dedication to treat the history of technology in full cultural context was evident in the society's decision to name its journal *Technology and Culture*. This aim has invigorated U.S. university programs in the history of technology since that time.

The history of science that developed in post–World War II United States university centers such as Wisconsin, Harvard, and Indiana stressed intellectual and internal dimensions of the Western scientific tradition. During the 1950s and 1960s, the books of Alexandre Koyré were central to higher studies in the discipline (e.g., *From the Closed World to the Infinite Universe*, 4.92). The philosophically and mathematically trained Koyré published studies of Galileo, Copernicus, Kepler, and Newton that swayed interpretation of early modern changes in astronomy, cosmology, and physics. Moreover, these studies appealed to some enthusiastic teachers and students as models for pursuing the history of science. Convinced that Western science was motored by an independent life of the mind, Koyré frequently ignored and occasionally disparaged the socioeconomic factors in scientific history; he even denied that experimental method was crucial in the "scientific revolution" of the sixteenth and seventeenth centuries. His persuasive writings muted the influence of other, now classic works that revealed important social and cultural effects on the scientific enterprise; for instance, R. K. Merton's *Science, Technology, and Society in Seventeenth-Century England* (see I. B. Cohen, 4.84). And Koyré's emphasis on conceptual revolution as the key to scientific change also informed publications treating eighteenth-century chemistry, nineteenth-century Darwinism, and early twentieth-century physics.

By the 1970s and early 1980s, the topography of the history of science was altering swiftly. Pressure from scholars advocating critical roles for magic (F. A. Yates, *Giordano Bruno and the Hermetic Tradition*, 28.70), experimental method (S. Drake, *Galileo at Work*, 4.87), and chemical philosophy (A. G. Debus, *Man and Nature in the Renaissance*, 4.86) combatted the philosophical-mathematical interpretation of the scientific revolution. Powerful currents of sociopolitical analysis (M. C. Jacob, *The Newtonians and the English Revolution, 1689–1720*, 23.324), feminism and environmentalism (C. Merchant, *The Death of Nature*, 4.321), and institutional studies (M. Feingold, *The Mathematicians' Apprenticeship*, 4.88) challenged the autonomy of intellectual constructs and submitted the acceptance of scientific theory to social, economic, political, and cultural criteria.

More recently, similar currents have swept over other topical and chronological aspects of the history of science—chemistry (J. Golinski, *Science as Public Culture*, 4.282), earth sciences (M.J.S. Rudwick, *The Great Devonian Controversy*, 4.239), psychology (K. Danziger, *Constructing the Subject*, 4.278), and biology (G. L. Geison, ed., *Physiology in the American Context, 1850–1940*, 4.207). A common face of scholarly interpretation has resulted. Women's and gender studies—a thriving dimension of recent socioeconomic, political, and cultural analyses of science, technology, and medicine—aptly illustrate this (e.g., M. Rossiter, *Women Scientists in America*, 44.323).

The aggressive and philosophically controversial social constructionist view has animated scholarship in all three areas of science, technology, and medicine. On the general level, its practitioners have radically reassessed the process and role of experimentation in the acquisition of human knowledge (e.g., Latour and Woolgar, *Laboratory Life*, 4.283). In science, citing biology as an example, this approach has seriously affected the historiography of evolutionary biology (Desmond, *The Politics of Evolution*, 24.354). It has exposed the social as well as technical forces that produced a crucial military technology of the Cold War (D. MacKenzie, *Inventing Accuracy*, 4.490). In medicine, F. Delaporte (*Disease and Civilization*, 4.771) has revealed the contribution of social relations to the construction of a disease category. Surely one of the most acute areas of disagreement about social constructionism lies within the history of physics: such works as A. Pickering's *Constructing Quarks* (4.284) seek to show that physical theory is guided more by vested social interests within a scientific community than experimental "discovery" of external reality or the piercing intellects of great minds. But whatever the outcome of its controversies, and whether or not social constructionism emerges triumphant as a philosophy of science, its historical fruitfulness is manifest. Its advocates probably will continue to generate stimulating insights into the histories of science, technology, and medicine in coming years.

The type of scholarship described in previous paragraphs is prominent in the journals, graduate colloquia and seminars, professional meetings, and public expressions of science, technology, and medicine professionals. But other traditional and more recent approaches flourish and remain essential. Studies in ancient and medieval science, technology, and medicine maintain an important place, as they have from the beginning of this century (D. C. Lindberg, *The Beginnings of Western Science*, 4.54). Scholars continue to issue internal and technical analyses of high quality (R. S. Woodbury, *Studies in the History of Machine Tools*, 4.428). Disciplinary investigations remain evident (R. C. Maulitz, *Morbid Appearances*, 4.725). Significant institutional histories enrich the literature (B. Sinclair, *Philadelphia's Philosopher Mechanics*, 4.422). Analyses of national traditions have enlightened science, technology, and medicine scholarship for over a quarter century (M. Ramsey, *Professional and Popular Medicine in France, 1770–1830*, 4.789), and interest in American science, technology, and medicine grows seemingly at an exponential pace (D. J. Kevles, *The Physicists*, 4.135). Scientific biography continues to attract scholars as a rewarding medium for integrating the intellectual and sociological aspects of science, technology, and medicine (R. R. Kline, *Steinmetz*, 4.522). Relations between science, technology, and medicine and religion are yet the objects of study (J. H. Brooke, *Science and Religion*, 4.302). The role of science, technology, and medicine in Western colonialism and imperialism is a rapidly developing area (D. R. Headrick, *The Tools of Empire*, 47.215). Historical investigations of ecology and the environment have already won a significant place in scholarship and surely will expand in coming years (D. Worster, *Nature's Economy*, 4.253).

A half century ago, a few pioneers labored to define and professionalize the histories of science, technology, and medicine. They were predominantly Western white men, many of whom came to their studies with technical training. Today, each of the histories of science, technology, and medicine embodies a large and growing community of scholars, a multitude of subsidiary fields, and numerous specialized journals. Along with this has come demographic change. Many more women now teach and research the history of science, technology, and medicine. The training people bring to their educations and scholarly activities is much more varied, including backgrounds in the biological and physical sciences, mathematics, technology, medicine, history, philosophy, sociology, anthropology, political science, religion, journalism, literature, and fine arts. In ensuing years, this diversity probably will increase all the more as these fields of history steadily internationalize and increasingly reflect the perspectives of scholars with different ethnic, national, and religious origins.

Space limitations required that the bibliography in this section of the *Guide* be representative rather than comprehensive. Therefore, contributors have cited bibliographies covering their specific categories wherever possible and appropriate. In this way, readers can access references to outstanding works that for want of space could not be included in this edition of the *Guide*.

This section does not contain all the *Guide*'s science, technology, and medicine entries. Most medieval Islamic and Byzantine science, technology, and medicine items appear in those sections of the *Guide*. Publications that deal with particular national traditions—especially those emphasizing organization, patronage, and education—are found in the national sections; significant numbers of science, technology, and medicine sources are in the U.S., British, French, German, Italian, Russian, Soviet, Chinese, and Japanese sections. A number of writings on the historiography of science is located in the section on Theory and Practice in Historical Study. The section on World History likewise includes some science, technology, and medicine items. Readers will find the index an essential tool to exploit the *Guide*'s full resources.

ACKNOWLEDGMENTS   *I am grateful to a number of people who aided the effort to organize an up-to-date bibliography covering the vast terrain of the histories of science, technology, and medicine. James Cassedy, Caroline Hannaway, Robert Hudson, and Kenneth Ludmerer furnished invaluable advice on medical categories. Terry Reynolds, John K. Smith, and Miriam Levin provided similar aid in the area of technology. Peter Galison suggested publications for inclusion in several categories. Sharon Kingsland and Robert Hatch merit special thanks for their advice throughout the life of the project.*

[Contributors: AIM = Alan I. Marcus, AJR = Alan J. Rocke, APM = Arthur P. Molella, AR = Alex Roland, BES = Bruce E. Seely, BSH = Bert S. Hall, CH = Caroline Hannaway, CSH = Christopher S. Hamlin, DCJ = Donald C. Jackson, DEL = David E. Leary, DHS = Darwin H. Stapleton, DMH = Derek M. Hirst, DN = Dorothy Nelkin, ETM = Edward T. Morman, FEH = Frederick E. Hoxie, FLC = Frederic L. Cheyette, HM = Harvey Markowitz, JGC = Jonathan G. Cedarbaum, JHC = James H. Cassedy, JKS = John K. Smith, JML = Jennifer M. Lloyd, JS = John Scarborough, JSCRS = Jonathan S. C. Riley-Smith, KML = Kenneth M. Ludmerer, KP = Katharine Park, MHS = Michael H. Shank, MJC = Michael J. Crowe, MLC = Marcia L. Colish, MM = Mark Motley, MRL = Miriam R. Levin, MTG = Mott T. Greene, PBI = Paul B. Israel, PEC = Paul E. Ceruzzi, PEM = Pamela E. Mack, PSG = Pamela S. Gossin, RAH = Robert A. Hatch, RKD = Robert K. DeKosky, RKW = R. K. Webb, SEK = Sharon E. Kingsland, SK = Sheldon Krimsky, SMR = Susan M. Reverby, TSR = Terry S. Reynolds, WJC = William J. Courtenay, WRK = Wilbur R. Knorr]

HISTORY OF SCIENCE

Reference Works

4.1 William F. Bynum, E. Janet Browne, and Roy Porter, eds. *Dictionary of the history of science.* 1981 ed. Princeton: Princeton University Press, 1985. ISBN 0-691-08287-1 (cl, 1981), 0-691-02384-0 (pbk). ▸ Approximately 700 short essays on terms relevant to histories of physical, biological, social, and medical sciences as well as philosophy and sociology of science. Emphasis on last five centuries. [RAH]

4.2 Pietro Corsi and Paul Weindling, eds. *Information sources in the history of science and medicine.* London: Butterworth Scientific, 1983. ISBN 0-408-10764-2. ▸ Bibliographic guide to sources with over twenty topical, bibliographic, and historiographic essays designed to survey and assess the discipline, its issues, historiography, and sources. [RAH]

4.3 Charles Coulston Gillispie et al., eds. *Dictionary of scientific biography.* 1970–81 ed. 16 vols. New York: Scribner's, 1990. ISBN 0-684-16962-2 (set). ▸ Monumental biographical reference for history of science, consisting of entries with useful bibliographies for over 5,000 nonliving scientists worldwide. [RAH]

4.4 *ISIS annual: current bibliography of the history of science and its cultural influences.* Philadelphia: History of Science Society, 1989–. ISSN 0021-1753. ▸ Annual bibliography of works in history of science arranged topically, chronologically, and geographically. Also includes publications on histories of technology and medicine. ISIS is quarterly journal of American History of Science Society. [RAH]

4.5 S. A. Jayawardene, comp. *Reference books for the historian of science: a handlist.* London: Science Museum, 1982. ISBN 0-901805-14-9, ISSN 0262-4818. ▸ Comprehensive listing of bibliographic sources in history of science and related subjects, arranged thematically, geographically, and chronologically. [RAH]

4.6 John Neu, ed. *ISIS cumulative bibliography, 1966–1975: a bibliography of the history of science formed from ISIS critical bibliographies 91–100, indexing literature published from 1965 through 1974.* 2 vols. London: Mansell with History of Science Society,

1980–85. ISBN 0-7201-0550-1 (set), 0-7201-1515-9 (v. 1), 0-7201-1516-7 (v. 2). ‣ Bibliography of history of science and related disciplines based on annual ISIS bibliographies from 1966 to 1975 (4.4). Arranged by personalities, institutions, subjects, civilizations, and periods. [RAH]

4.7 John Neu, ed. *ISIS cumulative bibliography, 1976–1985: a bibliography of the history of science formed from ISIS critical bibliographies 101–110, indexing literature published from 1975 through 1984.* 2 vols. Boston: Hall with History of Science Society, 1989. ISBN 0-8161-9058-5 (v. 1), 0-8161-9069-0 (v. 2). ‣ Bibliography of history of science and related disciplines based on annual ISIS bibliographies (4.4). Arranged by personalities, institutions, subjects, civilizations, and periods. [RAH]

4.8 Magda Whitrow, ed. *ISIS cumulative bibliography: a bibliography of the history of science formed from ISIS critical bibliographies 1–90, 1913–1965.* 6 vols. London: Mansell with History of Science Society, 1971. ISBN 0-7201-0183-2 (v. 1–2), 0-7201-0629-X (v. 3), 0-7201-0547-8 (v. 4–5), 0-7201-1686-4 (v. 6). ‣ Bibliography of history of science and related disciplines based on annual ISIS bibliographies (4.4). Arranged by personalities, institutions, subjects, civilizations, and periods. [RAH]

General Studies

4.9 Joseph Ben-David. *The scientist's role in society: a comparative study.* 1971 ed. Chicago: University of Chicago Press, 1984. ISBN 0-226-04227-8 (cl), 0-226-04221-9 (pbk). ‣ Survey of evolution of scientific role from perspective of sociologist-historian. Particularly useful for comparisons of scientific organization in France, Britain, Germany, and United States since seventeenth century. [RAH]

4.10 J. D. Bernal. *Science in history.* 1969 3d rev. ed. 4 vols. Boston: MIT Press, 1971. ISBN 0-262-02073-4 (v. 1, cl), 0-262-52020-6 (v. 1, pbk). ‣ Classic, somewhat dated survey of broader socioeconomic contexts of science from antiquity to mid-twentieth century. Written by eminent Marxist historian; emphasizes modern period and emergence of social sciences. [RAH]

4.11 Daniel Joseph Boorstin. *The discoverers: an illustrated history of man's search to know his world and himself.* 1983 ed. 2 vols. New York: Abrams, 1991. ISBN 0-8109-3207-5 (set). ‣ Sweeping interpretation of emergence and influence of science and technology. Written for wide audience by Pulitzer prize–winning historian. [RAH]

4.12 R. G. Collingwood. *The idea of nature.* 1945 ed. Westport, Conn.: Greenwood, 1986. ISBN 0-313-25166-5. ‣ Brief but brilliant, classic interpretation of history of idea of nature from antiquity to nineteenth century. [RAH]

4.13 Eduard Jan Dijksterhuis. *The mechanization of the world picture.* C. Dikkshoorn, trans. Oxford: Clarendon, 1961. ‣ Standard survey from antiquity to Newton. Somewhat dated in approach but yet to be replaced for rigor, substance, and scope. [RAH]

4.14 Charles Coulston Gillispie. *The edge of objectivity: an essay in the history of scientific ideas.* 1960 ed. Princeton: Princeton University Press, 1990. ISBN 0-691-02350-6 (pbk). ‣ Engaging interpretation of modern science, seventeenth to nineteenth century, suggesting that science is human activity rooted in measurement rather than in sympathy. [RAH]

4.15 Thomas L. Hankins. *Science and the Enlightenment.* Cambridge: Cambridge University Press, 1985. ISBN 0-521-24349-1 (cl), 0-521-28619-0 (pbk). ‣ Elegantly written survey of role of science in Enlightenment thought with particular emphasis on French developments. [RAH]

4.16 John Marks. *Science and the making of the modern world.* London: Heinemann, 1983. ISBN 0-435-54780-1 (cl), 0-435-54781-X (pbk). ‣ Broad survey of science as global phenomenon, emphasizing social, technological, and political implications of applied science since industrial revolution. [RAH]

4.17 Stephen F. Mason. *A history of the sciences.* 1962 rev. ed. New York: Collier, 1968. ISBN 0-02-093400-9 (pbk). ‣ Broad survey of growth of science from antiquity to present with particular emphasis on period since Newton. [RAH]

4.18 Stephen Toulmin and June Goodfield. *The discovery of time.* 1965 ed. Chicago: University of Chicago Press, 1982. ISBN 0-226-80842-4 (pbk). ‣ Provocative interpretation of role of science in histories of cosmology, natural history to evolution, social sciences, and emergence of history as discipline. [RAH]

Historiography

4.19 Paul T. Durbin, ed. *A guide to the culture of science, technology, and medicine.* 1980 ed. New York: Free Press, 1984. ISBN 0-02-907890-3 (pbk). ‣ Major essays on historiographies of science (Thackray), technology (Pursell), medicine (Brieger), and science policy studies (Crane). Also treats philosophy and sociology of science, technology, and medicine. [RAH]

4.20 Jan Golinski. "The theory of practice and the practice of theory: sociological approaches in the history of science." *ISIS* 81 (1990) 492–505. ISSN 0021-1753. ‣ Overview of recent relationship between sociology of science and history of science. Describes various interpretations of sociologists and historians concerning effects of social relations on historical development of science. [RAH]

4.21 Helge Kragh. *An introduction to the historiography of science.* Cambridge: Cambridge University Press, 1987. ISBN 0-521-33360-1 (cl), 0-521-38921-6 (pbk). ‣ Comprehensive, useful, single-volume survey of history, philosophy, objectives, methods, and historiographic traditions in history of science. [RAH]

4.22 Thomas S. Kuhn. "The history of science." *International encyclopedia of the social sciences.* 19 vols. David L. Sills, ed., vol. 1, pp. 74–83. New York: Macmillan, 1968–. ‣ Classic article—assessment, survey, and manifesto—surveying origins, development, and future of history of science as independent professional discipline. [RAH]

4.23 Robert C. Olby et al., eds. *Companion to the history of modern science.* London: Routledge, 1990. ISBN 0-415-01988-5. ‣ Imposing compilation of sixty-seven chapters treating emergence of science and its influence since 1500 as well as historiographic and interpretive trends in history, philosophy, and sociology of knowledge. [RAH]

Ancient Near East

4.24 A. F. Aveni, ed. *World archaeoastronomy: selected papers from the second Oxford International Conference on Archaeoastronomy, held at Merida, Yucatan, Mexico, 13–17 January 1986.* Cambridge: Cambridge University Press, 1989. ISBN 0-521-34180-9. ‣ Collection of papers from conference on archaeoastronomy, including criticisms of present state and methods of field and reports on current research on Old and New World sites and artifacts. [WRK]

4.25 Marshall Clagett. *Ancient Egyptian science.* Vol. 1: *A source book.* Philadelphia: American Philosophical Society, 1989. (Memoirs of the American Philosophical Society, 184.) ISBN 0-87169-184-1. ‣ Texts with commentary on ancient Egyptian cosmology. [WRK]

4.26 Henri Frankfort et al. *The intellectual adventure of ancient man: an essay on speculative thought in the ancient Near East.* 1946 ed. Chicago: University of Chicago Press, 1977. ISBN 0-226-26008-9. ‣ Description of ancient Egyptian and Mesopotamian mythopoetic interpretations of natural phenomena, in contrast to philosophical approach of later Hellenic culture. [RKD]

4.27   Douglas C. Heggie. *Megalithic science: ancient mathematics and astronomy in northwest Europe.* New York: Thames & Hudson, 1981. ISBN 0-500-05036-8. ▸ Readable, well-documented review of evidence for theories on astronomical and geometric structures from Neolithic Britain and Northwest Europe. Judicious criticism in field fraught with extravagance. [WRK]

4.28   F. R. Hodson, ed. *The place of astronomy in the ancient world: joint symposium of the Royal Society and the British Academy.* London: Oxford University Press for British Academy, 1974. ISBN 0-19-725944-8. ▸ Technical, detailed essays on astronomy in ancient Mesopotamia, Egypt, China, and among Maya and on archaeoastronomy of Neolithic and traditional cultures. [WRK]

4.29   Otto Neugebauer. *The exact sciences in antiquity.* 1957 2d ed. New York: Dover, 1969. ISBN 0-486-22332-2. ▸ Discussion of mathematics and astronomy in ancient Egypt and Mesopotamia, drawing parallels with classical Greece, including Ptolemy. Introductory but technically and historiographically sophisticated study. [WRK]

4.30   A. Leo Oppenheim. "Man and nature in Mesopotamian civilization." In *Dictionary of scientific biography.* Charles Coulston Gillispie et al., eds., vol. 15, pp. 634–66. New York: Scribner's, 1978. ▸ Well-documented summary of cultural, cosmological, and technological aspects of ancient Mesopotamian civilization. [WRK]

4.31   Richard A. Parker. "Egyptian astronomy, astrology, and calendrical reckoning." *Dictionary of scientific biography.* Charles Coulston Gillispie et al., eds., vol. 15, pp. 706–27. New York: Scribner's, 1978. ISBN 0-684-10114-9. ▸ Condensed review of subject with ample references. [WRK]

4.32   Bartel L. van der Waerden and Peter Huber. *Science awakening. Vol. 2: The birth of astronomy.* 1975 4th ed. Princeton: Scholar's Bookshelf, 1988. ▸ Technical, detailed accounts of Egyptian and Mesopotamian astronomy with frequent ingenious, if highly speculative, reconstructions. Completely revised translation of *Die Anfänge der Astronomie.* [WRK]

Ancient Greece and Rome

4.33   Marshall Clagett. *Greek science in antiquity.* 1963 rev. ed. Princeton: Scholar's Bookshelf, 1988. ISBN 0-945726-10-4. ▸ Popular survey covering science from ancient Egypt and Mesopotamia to Latin and Greek science, ca. 600 CE. [WRK]

4.34   David J. Furley. *The Greek cosmologists. Vol. 1: The formation of the atomic theory and its earliest critics.* Cambridge: Cambridge University Press, 1987. ISBN 0-521-33328-8. ▸ Study of pre-Socratic cosmologies with particular reference to atomist theories. Volume 2 will focus on teleological cosmologies of Plato and Aristotle. [WRK]

4.35   Thomas Heath. *A history of Greek mathematics.* 2 vols. Oxford: Clarendon, 1921. ▸ Classic, thorough survey of Greek mathematics. Although now outdated in parts, remains most comprehensive treatment of subject. [MJC]

4.36   Wilbur R. Knorr. *The ancient tradition of geometric problems.* 1986 ed. New York: Dover, 1993. ISBN 0-486-67532-7. ▸ Comprehensive survey of geometric construction in ancient Greek sources with extensive references to current secondary accounts. [WRK]

4.37   G.E.R. Lloyd. *Early Greek science: Thales to Aristotle.* 1970 ed. New York: Norton, 1971. ISBN 0-393-04340-1. ▸ Brief, readable, introductory survey of Greek science, technology, and natural philosophy in Hellenic age. Emphasis on development and criticism of methods. [WRK]

4.38   G.E.R. Lloyd. *Greek science after Aristotle.* New York: Norton, 1973. ISBN 0-393-04371-1 (cl), 0-393-00689-1 (pbk). ▸ Brief, readable, introductory survey of Greek science, technology, and natural philosophy in Hellenistic age. Emphasis on development and criticism of methods. [WRK]

4.39   G.E.R. Lloyd. *The revolutions of wisdom: studies in the claims and practice of ancient Greek science.* Berkeley: University of California Press, 1987. ISBN 0-520-05832-1. ▸ Case studies from Greek natural philosophy, medicine, biology, mathematics, and astronomy on cultural strategies underlying scientific discourse. Profusely detailed on sources and secondary literature. [WRK]

4.40   Otto Neugebauer. *A history of ancient mathematical astronomy.* 3 vols. Berlin: Springer-Verlag, 1975. ISBN 0-387-06995-X (set). ▸ Definitive account, focusing first on Ptolemy's completed astronomical system in *Almagest*, then on historical antecedents in Egypt, Mesopotamia, and Greece, and finally on tradition in later antiquity. [WRK]

4.41   Olaf Pedersen. *A survey of the "Almagest."* Odense: Odense University Press, 1974. (Acta historica scientiarum naturalium et medicinalium, 30.) ISBN 87-7492-087-1. ▸ Detailed historical and technical commentary on Ptolemy's astronomical system. [WRK]

4.42   S. Sambursky. *The physical world of the Greeks.* 1956 ed. Merton Dagut, trans. Princeton: Princeton University Press, 1987. ISBN 0-691-08477-7 (cl), 0-691-02411-1 (pbk). ▸ Survey of ancient Greek physical theories. [WRK]

4.43   William H. Stahl. *Roman science: origins, development, and influence to the later Middle Ages.* Madison: University of Wisconsin Press, 1962. ▸ Standard treatment of science in Roman culture and its influence on later medieval tradition. [RKD]

4.44   Bartel L. van der Waerden. *Science awakening: Egyptian, Babylonian, and Greek mathematics.* 1975 4th ed. Arnold Dresden, trans. Princeton: Scholar's Bookshelf, 1988. ISBN 0-945726-04-X (cl), 0-945726-05-8 (pbk). ▸ Readable, often idiosyncratic, but brilliant survey of ancient Greek mathematics with Egyptian and Mesopotamian precursors. [WRK]

Medieval Science

4.45   Marshall Clagett. *The science of mechanics in the Middle Ages.* 1959 ed. Madison: University of Wisconsin Press, 1979. ISBN 0-299-01900-4. ▸ Indispensable collection of central texts in translation with explanations and commentaries. Typifies author's physics-oriented approach to medieval natural philosophy. [MHS]

4.46   Alistair C. Crombie. *Medieval and early modern science.* 1961 2d ed. 2 vols. Cambridge, Mass.: Harvard University Press, 1967. ▸ History of science from Augustine to Galileo. Argues for continuity of experimental methodology between Middle Ages and seventeenth century. [MHS]

4.47   Pierre Duhem. *Medieval cosmology: theories of infinity, place, time, void, and the plurality of worlds.* Roger Ariew, ed. and trans. Chicago: University of Chicago Press, 1985. ISBN 0-226-16922-7 (cl), 0-226-16923-5 (pbk). ▸ Selections from the pioneering *Système du monde* (1909–16), valuable for summaries of medieval conceptions of cosmos and illustrations of author's historiographical stance. [MHS]

4.48   Wilma George and William Brunsdon Yapp. *The naming of the beasts: natural history in the medieval bestiary.* London: Duckworth, 1991. ISBN 0-7156-2238-2. ▸ Only systematic study of most widely diffused work of moralized natural history in Middle Ages. [MHS]

4.49   Edward Grant. *Much ado about nothing: theories of space and vacuum from the Middle Ages to the Scientific Revolution.* Cambridge: Cambridge University Press, 1981. ISBN 0-521-22983-9. ▸ Detailed conceptual history of Aristotelian tradition and some of its critics, including problems of motion in a void and of possibility of extracosmic infinite void. [MHS]

4.50 Edward Grant. *Physical science in the Middle Ages.* 1971 ed. Cambridge: Cambridge University Press, 1977. ISBN 0-521-21862-4 (cl), 0-521-29294-8 (pbk). ‣ Concise, readable, conceptual survey oriented toward pre-Galilean mechanics. [MHS]

4.51 Edward Grant, ed. *A source book in medieval science.* Cambridge, Mass.: Harvard University Press, 1974. ISBN 0-674-82360-5. ‣ Comprehensive selection of primary sources in translation. One hundred ninety excerpts (fifth to fifteenth century) include, in addition to Latin authors, most influential Arabic, Persian, and Hebrew authors. [MHS]

4.52 Charles Homer Haskins. *Studies in the history of mediaeval science.* 1927 2d ed. New York: Ungar, 1960. ‣ Classic studies of twelfth- and early thirteenth-century translation and reception of Arabic and Greek materials in Latin world and of science at Sicilian court of Frederick II. [MHS]

4.53 Claudia Kren. *Medieval science and technology: a selected, annotated bibliography.* New York: Garland, 1985. ISBN 0-8240-8969-3. ‣ Almost 1,500 well-selected items organized by field. [MHS]

4.54 David C. Lindberg. *The beginnings of Western science: the European scientific tradition in philosophical, religious, and institutional context, 600 B.C. to A.D. 1450.* Chicago: University of Chicago Press, 1992. ISBN 0-226-48230-8 (cl), 0-226-48231-6 (pbk). ‣ Most up-to-date synthesis, combining detailed exposition with new interpretations. Has clarity required for undergraduate surveys and substance needed for graduate student exams. Extensive bibliography. [MHS/WJC]

4.55 David C. Lindberg, ed. *Science in the Middle Ages.* Chicago: University of Chicago Press, 1978. ISBN 0-226-48232-4. ‣ Comprehensive collection focused on Latin world. Transmission of Greek and Arabic learning, philosophical and institutional contexts, and sciences including mathematics, astronomy, optics, motion, medicine, natural history, and magic. [MHS/WJC]

4.56 David C. Lindberg. *Theories of vision from al-Kindi to Kepler.* 1976 ed. Chicago: University of Chicago Press, 1981. ISBN 0-226-48234-0 (cl, 1976), 0-226-48235-9 (pbk). ‣ Synthesizes eight centuries of medieval and early modern optical tradition. Places Kepler's seventeenth-century solution to problem of vision in continuity with medieval contributions. Of interest to scientists and philosophers alike since vision was regarded as paradigm case for understanding sensation more generally. [MHS/MLC]

4.57 Anneliese Maier. *On the threshold of exact science: selected writings of Anneliese Maier on late medieval natural philosophy.* Steven D. Sargent, ed. and trans. Philadelphia: University of Pennsylvania Press, 1982. ISBN 0-8122-7831-3. ‣ Collection of most important papers of influential historian of science. Essays of central historiographical importance for our understanding of differences between fourteenth- and seventeenth-century approaches to natural philosophy. [MHS]

4.58 John Emery Murdoch. *Album of science: antiquity and the Middle Ages.* New York: Scribner's, 1984. ISBN 0-684-15496-X. ‣ Scholarly pictorial history of scientific illustration and diagraming in manuscript tradition. Addresses relationship between text and illustration and pedagogical uses of visual representation. [MHS]

4.59 Karen Meier Reeds. *Botany in medieval and Renaissance universities.* New York: Garland, 1991. ISBN 0-8240-7449-1. ‣ Discussion of teaching of botany, especially at universities of Montpellier and Basel, in relation to medicine, Reformation, and introduction of printing. [MHS]

4.60 Nicholas Steneck. *Science and creation in the Middle Ages: Henry of Langenstein (d. 1397) on Genesis.* Notre Dame, Ind.: University of Notre Dame Press, 1976. ISBN 0-268-01672-0. ‣ In setting context for its specific focus, study provides excellent introduction to full range and key theories of late medieval science and natural philosophy. [MHS]

4.61 Brian Stock. *Myth and science in the twelfth century: a study of Bernard Silvester.* Princeton: Princeton University Press, 1972. ISBN 0-691-05201-8. ‣ Study of Silvester's *Cosmographia* as exemplar of new naturalism and explanatory frameworks ca. 1150. Emphasis on mythopoeic form and context of cosmogony as well as its content and roots. Major figure in school of Chartres. [MHS]

4.62 Katherine H. Tachau. *Vision and certitude in the age of Ockham: optics, epistemology, and the foundations of semantics, 1250–1345.* Leiden: Brill, 1988. ISBN 90-04-08552-1 (pbk). ‣ Sophisticated interdisciplinary study of Oxford natural philosophy and its practitioners from Roger Bacon to William of Ockham. Demonstrates close connection between philosophy, logic, and natural philosophy. [MHS]

4.63 James A. Weisheipl. *The development of physical theory in the Middle Ages.* 1959 ed. Ann Arbor: University of Michigan Press, 1971. ISBN 0-472-06181-X (pbk). ‣ Brief overview focused on thirteenth and fourteenth centuries. Stresses medieval antecedents of Galileo in work of Robert Grosseteste, St. Thomas Aquinas, and Thomas Bradwardine and his colleagues at Merton College, Oxford. [MHS]

SEE ALSO
20.1369 James McEvoy. *The philosophy of Robert Grosseteste.*
20.1376 John Emery Murdoch and Edith Dudley Sylla, eds. *The cultural context of medieval learning.*
20.1384 Marilyn McCord Adams. *William Ockham.*
20.1406 Richard C. Dales. *Medieval discussions of the eternity of the world.*
20.1525 Sabina Flanagan. *Hildegard of Bingen, 1098–1179.*

Astrology, Alchemy, and Magic to 1700

4.64 Nicholas H. Clulee. *John Dee's natural philosophy: between science and religion.* London: Routledge, 1988. ISBN 0-415-00625-2. ‣ Documents alchemist-mathematician's changing attitude toward nature, philosophy, and mathematics. Argues, against Yates 28.70, that his magical outlook was not exclusively tethered to hermeticism and Florentine Neoplatonism. [MHS]

4.65 Suzanne Colnort-Bodet. *Le code alchimique dévoilé: distillateurs, alchimistes, et symbolistes.* Paris: Librairie Honoré Champion, 1989. ISBN 2-85203-071-3. ‣ Uses concept of quintessence to draw tantalizing links between experimental distillation tradition and such seemingly disparate ideas as impetus theory, millenarianism of Spiritual Franciscans, and Newtonian attraction. [MHS]

4.66 Betty Jo Teeter Dobbs. *The foundations of Newton's alchemy, or "the hunting of the greene lyon."* Cambridge: Cambridge University Press, 1975. ISBN 0-521-20786-X. ‣ Demonstrates from manuscripts Newton's pervasive interest in theoretical and experimental transmutation. Argues alchemical views underlay his matter theory and his concept of attractive force. [MHS]

4.67 Robert Halleux. *Les textes alchimiques.* Turnhout, Belgium: Brepols, 1979. ‣ Concise guide to history, historiography, typology, literature, and research problems of medieval alchemy, primarily in Latin West. [MHS]

4.68 E. J. Holmyard. *Alchemy.* 1957 ed. New York: Dover, 1968. ISBN 0-486-26298-7. ‣ Standard English-language survey. Aging but useful introduction to subject, from Greeks through China, Islam, and Latin Middle Ages to early modern Europe. [MHS]

4.69   Richard Kieckhefer. *Magic in the Middle Ages.* Cambridge: Cambridge University Press, 1990. ISBN 0-521-30941-7 (cl), 0-521-31202-7 (pbk). ‣ Best concise overview, suitable for undergraduate courses. Examines natural and demonic magic in connection with high and low culture, science, and religion among other topics. [MHS]

4.70   Claudia Kren. *Alchemy in Europe: a guide to research.* New York: Garland, 1990. ISBN 0-8240-8538-8. ‣ Partially annotated bibliography of more than 500 selected articles and monographs. [MHS]

4.71   Robert P. Multhauf. *The origins of chemistry.* New York: Watts, 1967. ‣ Survey of alchemy and chemistry from antiquity through Latin and Arabic Middle Ages to early eighteenth century, including attention to medical chemistry, industrial and practical chemistry, matter theory, and chemical affinity. [MHS]

4.72   William R. Newman, ed. *The "Summa Perfectionis" of Pseudo-Geber: a critical edition, translation, and study.* Leiden: Brill, 1991. (Collection de travaux de l'Académie Internationale d'Histoire des Sciences, 35.) ISBN 90-04-09464-4, ISSN 0169-7897. ‣ Study of highly influential treatise on alchemy. Reassigns work to Paul of Taranto. Argues *Summa* defends corpuscularian matter theory and non-Aristotelian observational methodology. [MHS]

4.73   John D. North. *Stars, minds, and fate: essays in ancient and medieval cosmology.* London: Hambledon, 1989. ISBN 0-907628-94-X. ‣ Important collection of excellent articles by North, including several on contexts of medieval astrology, medieval understanding of celestial influence, and astrolabe. [MHS]

4.74   Wayne Shumaker. *The occult sciences in the Renaissance: a study in intellectual patterns.* Berkeley: University of California Press, 1972. ISBN 0-520-02021-9 (cl), 0-520-03840-1 (pbk). ‣ General, usually reliable overview of topic by scholar of literature. Surveys astrology, natural magic, witchcraft, alchemy, and Hermetic tradition. [MHS]

4.75   Nathan Sivin. *Chinese alchemy: preliminary studies.* Cambridge, Mass.: Harvard University Press, 1968. ‣ Fundamental study of sixth- and seventh-century Chinese alchemical theory and technique. Emphasizes connections between alchemy and other branches of knowledge. [MHS]

4.76   S. J. Tester. *A history of Western astrology.* Woodbridge, England: Boydell, 1987. ISBN 0-85115-446-8. ‣ Up-to-date, non-technical survey, antiquity to seventeenth century. [MHS]

4.77   Lynn Thorndike. *A history of magic and experimental science.* 8 vols. New York: Columbia University Press, 1923–58. ISBN 0-231-08794-2 (v. 1), 0-231-08795-0 (v. 2), 0-231-08796-9 (v. 3), 0-231-08797-7 (v. 4), 0-231-08798-5 (v. 5), 0-231-08799-3 (v. 6), 0-231-08800-0 (v. 7), 0-231-08801-9 (v. 8). ‣ Quasi-encyclopedic coverage of astrology, alchemy, and magic from antiquity through early modern period. Many quotations and paraphrases from primary sources. Remains useful reference. [MHS]

4.78   D. P. Walker. *Spiritual and demonic magic from Ficino to Campanella.* 1958 ed. Notre Dame, Ind.: University of Notre Dame Press, 1975. ISBN 0-268-01670-4. ‣ Excellent introduction to Renaissance magic and its connections with music, physiology and medicine, astrology, and philosophical assumptions. Claims Tommaso Campanella united two traditions, natural spiritual and demonic, both inimical to religion. [MHS/JML]

SEE ALSO

   28.70 Frances A. Yates. *Giordano Bruno and the hermetic tradition.*

Scientific Revolution of the Sixteenth and Seventeenth Centuries

4.79   Richard J. Blackwell. *Galileo, Bellarmine, and the Bible, including a translation of Foscarini's "Letter on the Motion of the Earth."* Notre Dame, Ind.: University of Notre Dame Press, 1991. ISBN 0-268-01024-2. ‣ Analysis of Galileo affair against background of changing attitudes toward biblical interpretation since Copernicus and Council of Trent. [MHS]

4.80   Marie Boas [Hall]. *The scientific renaissance, 1450–1630.* 1962 ed. New York: Collins, 1972. ISBN 0-06-130583-9. ‣ Survey of impact of Renaissance on first phase of early modern science (to Kepler). Shows eventual decline of influence of ancient authorities on thought about nature. Broadly conceived, highly readable, has aged well. [MHS/MM]

4.81   Edwin Arthur Burtt. *The metaphysical foundations of modern physical science.* 1952 rev. ed. Atlantic Highlands, N.J.: Humanities Press, 1989. ISBN 0-391-01742-X. ‣ Historiographical classic, originally written in 1924. Among first to associate early modern science with new metaphysics based only on entities and causal explanations that meet mathematical criteria. [MHS]

4.82   I. Bernard Cohen. *The birth of a new physics.* Rev. ed. New York: Norton, 1985. ISBN 0-393-01994-2 (cl), 0-393-30045-5 (pbk). ‣ Main developments in history of mechanics (terrestrial and celestial) from Copernicus to Isaac Newton. Very accessible overview; suitable for undergraduates. [MHS]

4.83   I. Bernard Cohen. *The Newtonian revolution, with illustrations of the transformation of scientific ideas.* Cambridge: Cambridge University Press, 1980. ISBN 0-521-22964-2. ‣ Best technical exposition of Newtonianism and its scientific impact. Examines relationship between mathematics and world in Sir Isaac Newton's *Principia* (1687). Isolates distinctive Newtonian style. Proposes theory of scientific change based on concept of transformations. [MHS/DMH]

4.84   I. Bernard Cohen, ed. *Puritanism and the rise of modern science: the Merton thesis.* New Brunswick, N.J.: Rutgers University Press, 1990. ISBN 0-8135-1529-7 (cl), 0-8135-1530-0 (pbk). ‣ Excerpts, old and new critiques, reviews, and analyses of Robert K. Merton's epoch-making contribution to sociology of science: *Science, Technology, and Society in Seventeenth-Century England* (1938). [MHS]

4.85   Peter Dear. *Mersenne and the learning of the schools.* Ithaca, N.Y.: Cornell University Press, 1988. ISBN 0-8014-1875-5. ‣ First major work in English on French mathematician. Shows compatibility of his nonrevolutionary outlook with new ideas. [MHS]

4.86   Allen G. Debus. *Man and nature in the Renaissance.* Cambridge: Cambridge University Press, 1978. ISBN 0-521-21972-8 (cl), 0-521-29328-6 (pbk). ‣ Survey of impact of humanism on science and medicine between fifteenth and seventeenth centuries. Emphasizes tensions between mystical-occult and mathematical-observational outlooks. [MHS]

4.87   Stillman Drake. *Galileo at work: his scientific biography.* Chicago: University of Chicago Press, 1978. ISBN 0-226-16226-5. ‣ Narrative chronology of activities and works, tightly focused on science. Shuns Galileo's philosophical and social contexts, as well as personal history; portrays Galileo as empiricist and experimentalist. [MHS]

4.88   Mordechai Feingold. *The mathematicians' apprenticeship: science, universities, and society in England, 1560–1640.* Cambridge: Cambridge University Press, 1984. ISBN 0-521-25133-8. ‣ Study of role of universities, arguing early modern Oxford and Cambridge played greater role in science than hitherto suspected. Stresses continuities between pre- and post-1640s English science. [MHS]

4.89 Robert G. Frank, Jr. *Harvey and the Oxford physiologists: scientific ideas and social interaction.* Berkeley: University of California Press, 1980. ISBN 0-520-03906-8. ▸ Classic study of early scientific community and transformation of physiology by Oxford-trained natural philosophers in two generations following discovery of circulation of blood. [MHS]

4.90 A. Rupert Hall. *The revolution in science, 1500–1750.* 3d ed. London: Longman, 1983. ISBN 0-582-49133-9. ▸ Reworking of author's classic 1954 textbook. Integrates newer scholarship into unabashedly positivist interpretation of Scientific Revolution as progress of value-free knowledge of nature. [MHS]

4.91 Lynn Sumida Joy. *Gassendi the atomist: advocate of history in an age of science.* Cambridge: Cambridge University Press, 1987. ISBN 0-521-30142-4. ▸ Analysis of French philosopher Pierre Gassendi's humanist-historical method of arguing in philosophy and science as key to both his seventeenth-century success and his subsequent relative neglect. [MHS]

4.92 Alexandre Koyré. *From the closed world to the infinite universe.* 1957 ed. Baltimore: Johns Hopkins University Press, 1979. (Johns Hopkins University Institute of the History of Medicine, Publications, Hideyo Noguchi lectures, Third series, 7.) ISBN 0-8018-0387-0. ▸ Classic history of philosophy approach to changing cosmological concepts of Scientific Revolution (from Nicolaus of Cusa, Copernicus, Giordiano Bruno, and Johann Kepler to Galileo, René Descartes, Gottfried Wilhelm Leibniz, Isaac Newton, and George Berkeley). [MHS]

4.93 Thomas S. Kuhn. *The Copernican revolution: planetary astronomy in the development of Western thought.* 1957 ed. Cambridge, Mass.: Harvard University Press, 1985. ISBN 0-674-17100-4 (cl), 0-674-17103-9 (pbk). ▸ Excellent older introduction to subject, devoted half to Greek and Latin antecedents and half to Copernicus and his impact. Important application of influential theory of change in scientific ideas. Can be updated with Swerdlow and Neugebauer 4.102. [MHS/MM]

4.94 David C. Lindberg and Robert S. Westman, eds. *Reappraisals of the Scientific Revolution.* Cambridge: Cambridge University Press, 1990. ISBN 0-521-34262-7 (cl), 0-521-34804-8 (pbk). ▸ Important collection of revisionist historiographical essays. Reassesses traditional interpretations of Scientific Revolution and highlights marginalized areas such as natural history and emblematics. [MHS]

4.95 David S. Lux. *Patronage and royal science in seventeenth-century France: the Academie de Physique in Caen.* Ithaca, N.Y.: Cornell University Press, 1989. ISBN 0-8014-2334-1. ▸ Rise and demise of provincial scientific academy. Challenges entrenched assumptions about private versus state support for experimental science in relation to emergence of Parisian Académie Royale des Sciences. [MHS]

4.96 Martha Ornstein [Bronfenbrenner]. *The role of scientific societies in the seventeenth century.* 1928 ed. New York: Arno, 1975. ISBN 0-405-06609-0. ▸ Pioneering dissertation, still fundamental overview of subject. European-wide scope, including attention to scientific journals and relations between societies and universities. [MHS]

4.97 Charles E. Raven. *John Ray, naturalist: his life and works.* 1950 2d ed. S. M. Walters, Introduction and annotation. Cambridge: Cambridge University Press, 1986. ISBN 0-521-31083-0 (pbk). ▸ Extraordinarily detailed study of great seventeenth-century naturalist. Religious context of science. [SEK]

4.98 A. I. Sabra. *Theories of light from Descartes to Newton.* Cambridge: Cambridge University Press, 1981. ISBN 0-521-24094-8 (cl), 0-521-28436-8 (pbk). ▸ Philosophical approach to methods and practices of seventeenth-century optics. Excellent analysis of key experiments, debates, and arguments of René Descartes, Pierre de Fermat, Christiaan Huygens, and Sir Isaac Newton. [MHS]

4.99 Steven Shapin and Simon Schaffer. *Leviathan and the air-pump: Hobbes, Boyle, and the experimental life; including a translation of Thomas Hobbes, "Dialogus Physicus de Natura Aeris."* Princeton: Princeton University Press, 1985. ISBN 0-691-08393-2 (cl), 0-691-02432-4 (pbk). ▸ Controversy between Thomas Hobbes and Robert Boyle about alleged experimental production of vacuum. Argues Boyle established experiment as new form of socially constructed persuasion. Historiographical landmark. [MHS]

4.100 William R. Shea. *The magic of numbers and motion: the scientific career of René Descartes.* Canton, Mass.: Science History, 1991. ISBN 0-88135-098-2. ▸ Survey of range of Descartes's natural philosophy. Emphasizes mathematical approach with attention to broader intellectual context, from methodology to Rosicrucian influences. [MHS]

4.101 Alice Stroup. *A company of scientists: botany, patronage, and community in the seventeenth-century Parisian Academy of Sciences.* Berkeley: University of California Press, 1990. ISBN 0-520-05949-2. ▸ Study of academy's members and their research over three decades, as well as ministerial patronage. Less emphasis on wider scientific community involved in their work. [MHS]

4.102 N. M. Swerdlow and Otto Neugebauer. *Mathematical astronomy in Copernicus's "De Revolutionibus."* 2 vols. New York: Springer-Verlag, 1984. ISBN 0-387-90939-7. ▸ Technical exposition of Copernicus's work. Introduction includes best state-of-art summary of links between Copernicus and his Latin and Arabic predecessors. [MHS]

4.103 René Taton and Curtis Wilson, eds. *Planetary astronomy from the Renaissance to the rise of astrophysics.* Part A: *Tycho Brahe to Newton.* Cambridge: Cambridge University Press, 1989. ISBN 0-521-24254-1. ▸ Most detailed, up-to-date collection of topical articles surveying history of early modern astronomy. Illustrations and glossary of terms. [MHS]

4.104 Albert Van Helden. *Measuring the universe: cosmic dimensions from Aristarchus to Halley.* Chicago: University of Chicago Press, 1985. ISBN 0-226-84881-7. ▸ Succinct overview focusing primarily on period from Copernicus to Newton. [MHS]

4.105 William A. Wallace. *Galileo and his sources: the heritage of the Collegio Romano in Galileo's science.* Princeton: Princeton University Press, 1984. ISBN 0-691-08355-X. ▸ Shows how teaching of Jesuit school exposed Galileo to medieval natural philosophical traditions and Aristotelian methodology. [MHS]

4.106 Charles Webster. *The great instauration: science, medicine, and reform, 1626–1660.* 1975 ed. New York: Holmes & Meier, 1976. ISBN 0-8419-0267-4. ▸ Analysis of worldview of mid-seventeenth-century English society with focus on Puritans. Argues Puritans drew convincing connection between economic growth and scientific attitude toward nature. [MHS]

4.107 Richard S. Westfall. *The construction of modern science: mechanisms and mechanics.* 1971 ed. Cambridge: Cambridge University Press, 1977. ISBN 0-521-21863-2 (cl), 0-521-29295-6 (pbk). ▸ Classic, in tradition of intellectual history. Valuable introduction to mechanical vision and practice of main branch of science; stresses mathematization of nature and growth of mechanical philosophy from Johann Kepler and William Harvey to Sir Isaac Newton. Critical bibliography. [MHS/DMH]

4.108 Richard S. Westfall. *Never at rest: a biography of Isaac Newton.* 1980 ed. Cambridge: Cambridge University Press, 1986. ISBN 0-521-27435-4 (pbk). ▸ Outstanding biography of culminating figure of Scientific Revolution. Combines impressive manuscript research with historiographical synthesis and excellent exposition. [MHS]

4.109 W.P.D. Wightman. *Science in a Renaissance society.* London: Hutchinson University Library, 1972. ISBN 0-09-111651-1. ▸ Survey of general trends in period 1450–1620 in northern Europe as well as Italy. Attention to arts, printing, and political theory among other topics. [MHS]

4.110 Joella G. Yoder. *Unrolling time: Christiaan Huygens and the mathematization of nature.* Cambridge: Cambridge University Press, 1988. ISBN 0-521-34140-X. ▸ Best study in English of leading Dutch natural philosopher of seventeenth century. Shows that Huygens's methodology assumes thoroughly symbiotic relationship between mathematics and physical theory. [MHS]

SEE ALSO

23.322 Michael Hunter. *Science and society in Restoration England.*

23.324 Margaret C. Jacob. *The Newtonians and the English Revolution, 1689–1720.*

28.60 Paul Lawrence Rose. *The Italian renaissance of mathematics.*

Mathematics

4.111 Margaret E. Baron. *The origins of the infinitesimal calculus.* 1969 ed. New York: Dover, 1987. ISBN 0-486-65371-4 (pbk). ▸ One of number of excellent studies of development of calculus. Particular attention to period before 1650. [MJC]

4.112 Carl B. Boyer. *A history of mathematics.* 2d ed. Uta C. Merzbach, ed. New York: Wiley, 1989. ISBN 0-471-09763-2. ▸ Excellent survey of history of mathematics from ancient to modern times. One of author's many contributions to history of mathematics. [MJC]

4.113 Robert M. Burton. *The history of mathematics: an introduction.* Boston: Allyn & Bacon, 1985. ISBN 0-205-08095-2. ▸ Useful survey of development of mathematics from antiquity to early twentieth century. Designed for use as textbook. [MJC]

4.114 Ronald Calinger, ed. *Classics of mathematics.* Oak Park, Ill.: Moore, 1982. ISBN 0-935610-13-8. ▸ Contains 133 classic selections from Greeks to twentieth century. Commentaries, including biographical essays, enhance accessibility of selections. [MJC]

4.115 Joseph W. Dauben, ed. *The history of mathematics from antiquity to the present: a selective bibliography.* New York: Garland, 1985. ISBN 0-8240-9284-8. ▸ Listing of 2,384 citations to publications in history of mathematics with some repetition. Selective rather than comprehensive. [MJC]

4.116 John Fauvel and Jeremy Gray, eds. *The history of mathematics: a reader.* Basingstoke: Macmillan Education with Open University, 1987. ISBN 0-333-42790-4 (cl), 0-333-42791-2 (pbk). ▸ Collection of about 350 selections from both primary and secondary works, former dominating. Extensive commentary enhances usefulness. [MJC]

4.117 Morris Kline. *Mathematical thought from antiquity to modern times.* 1972 ed. New York: Oxford University Press, 1990. ISBN 0-19-506135-7 (v. 1). ▸ Extremely thorough survey (1,239 pages) of history of mathematics, by mathematician who has made numerous contributions to field. [MJC]

4.118 Morris Kline. *Mathematics: the loss of certainty.* 1980 ed. New York: Oxford University Press, 1982. ISBN 0-19-502754-X (cl, 1980), 0-19-503085-0 (pbk). ▸ Development of mathematics and philosophy of mathematics from antiquity to present. Argues that, in course of its development, mathematics lost level of certainty long ascribed to it. [MJC]

4.119 Kenneth O. May, comp. *Bibliography and research manual of the history of mathematics.* Toronto: University of Toronto Press, 1973. ISBN 0-8020-1764-9, 0-8020-0047-9 (microfiche). ▸ Approximately 31,000 citations to publications in history of mathematics. Comprehensive listing of secondary works published from 1868 to 1965. [MJC]

4.120 James R. Newman, comp. *The world of mathematics.* 1956 ed. 4 vols. Redmond, Wash.: Tempus, 1988. ISBN 1-55615-149-7 (cl), 1-55615-148-9 (pbk). ▸ Massive, well-chosen collection of materials, both primary and secondary, in history of mathematics. Includes selections on nearly all areas of mathematics along with modest commentary. [MJC]

4.121 Theodore M. Porter. *The rise of statistical thinking, 1820–1900.* Princeton: Princeton University Press, 1986. ISBN 0-691-08416-5. ▸ Survey of emergence in nineteenth century of statistical analysis of scientific and social scientific phenomena. One of number of valuable studies of history of statistical method. [MJC]

4.122 David E. Rowe and John McCleary, eds. *The history of modern mathematics.* Vol. 1: *Ideas and their reception.* Vol. 2: *Institutions and applications.* 2 vols. Boston: Academic Press, 1989. ISBN 0-12-599661-6 (v. 1), 0-12-599661-4 (v. 2). ▸ Twenty-four essays by leading scholars on developments in mathematics after 1800. [MJC]

4.123 John Stillwell. *Mathematics and its history.* New York: Springer-Verlag, 1989. ISBN 0-387-96981-0. ▸ Recent, well-presented history of mathematics from ancient times to present. Strives to provide historical background on areas of mathematics studied by undergraduate mathematics students. [MJC]

4.124 Dirk Struik. *A concise history of mathematics.* 4th rev. ed. New York: Dover, 1987. ISBN 0-486-60255-9 (pbk). ▸ Brief survey of history of mathematics from antiquity to nineteenth century. Retains reputation as valuable treatment. [MJC]

Modern Physics

4.125 Henry A. Boorse and Lloyd Motz, eds. *The world of the atom.* 2 vols. New York: Basic Books, 1966. ISBN 0-465-09251-9 (set). ▸ More than one hundred selections from major publications concerning atomic theory from Lucretius (first century BCE to twentieth century). Some commentary accompanies each selection. [MJC]

4.126 Stephen G. Brush and Lanfranco Belloni, comps. *The history of modern physics: an international bibliography.* New York: Garland, 1983. ISBN 0-8240-9117-5. ▸ Provides 2,073 references, many annotated, to publications on developments in physics from discovery of X-rays (1895) to late twentieth century. [MJC]

4.127 G. N. Cantor. *Optics after Newton: theories of light in Britain and Ireland, 1704–1840.* Manchester: Manchester University Press, 1983. ISBN 0-7190-0938-3. ▸ Very effective, thorough presentation of rise and acceptance of wave theory of light. Treats competing theories in comparable detail and with admirable balance. [MJC]

4.128 D.S.L. Cardwell. *From Watt to Clausius: the rise of thermodynamics in the early industrial age.* Ithaca, N.Y.: Cornell University Press, 1971. ISBN 0-8014-0678-1. ▸ Authoritative treatment of rise of thermodynamics, especially in relation to developments in technology. Extensive attention to theories of heat. [MJC]

4.129 René Dugas. *A history of mechanics.* 1955 ed. J. R. Maddox, trans. London: Routledge & Paul, 1957. ▸ One of few treatments of history of mechanics, especially in period after Sir Isaac Newton. Some discussions sketchy but still standard source. [MJC]

4.130 P. M. Harman. *Energy, force, and matter: the conceptual development of nineteenth-century physics.* Cambridge: Cambridge University Press, 1982. ISBN 0-521-24600-8 (cl), 0-521-28812-6 (pbk). ▸ Tightly packed, authoritative history of physics in nineteenth century. Extensive annotated bibliography. [MJC]

4.131 J. L. Heilbron. *Elements of early modern physics.* Berkeley: University of California Press, 1982. ISBN 0-520-04554-8 (cl), 0-520-04555-6 (pbk). ▸ Excellent introduction to development of physics, including instrumental and institutional bases, seventeenth and eighteenth centuries. Valuable chapter on rise of science of electricity. [MJC]

4.132 J. L. Heilbron and Bruce R. Wheaton, comps. *Literature on the history of physics in the twentieth century.* Berkeley: University of California, Office for the History of Science and Technology, 1981. ISBN 0-918102-05-7 (pbk), ISSN 0145-0379. ▸ Extensive bibliography on development of physics in twentieth century. Unannotated citations arranged in twenty-three broad areas. [MJC]

4.133 R. W. Home, comp. *The history of classical physics: a selected, annotated bibliography.* New York: Garland, 1984. ISBN 0-8240-9067-5. ▸ Provides 1,210 citations, most with helpful annotations, to publications on history of physics from 1700 to 1900. Includes publications in many languages. [MJC]

4.134 Christa Jungnickel and Russell McCormmach. *Intellectual mastery of nature: theoretical physics from Ohm to Einstein.* 2 vols. Chicago: University of Chicago Press, 1986. ISBN 0-226-41581-3 (v. 1), 0-226-41584-8 (v. 2). ▸ Emergence of physics as major discipline from early nineteenth to twentieth century. Concentrates on German physics and includes attention to institutional basis for research in physics. [MJC]

4.135 Daniel J. Kevles. *The physicists: the history of a scientific community in modern America.* 1977 ed. Cambridge, Mass.: Harvard University Press, 1987. ISBN 0-674-66655-0 (pbk). ▸ Emergence of physics community in United States from late nineteenth century to 1970s. Focuses on tension between hierarchical professional structure of science and democratic ideals of nation that sustains scientific activity. [MJC]

4.136 Thomas S. Kuhn. *Black-body theory and the quantum discontinuity, 1894–1912.* 1978 ed. Chicago: University of Chicago Press, 1987. ISBN 0-226-45800-8 (pbk). ▸ Highly regarded study of background and early development of one of chief areas of twentieth-century physics. [MJC]

4.137 William Francis Magie. *A source book in physics.* 1935 ed. Cambridge, Mass.: Harvard University Press, 1969. ▸ Over one hundred selections from key publications in physics from Galileo to early twentieth century. Arranged by subject area; minimal commentary. [MJC]

4.138 Arthur I. Miller. *Albert Einstein's special theory of relativity: emergence (1905) and early interpretation (1905–1911).* Reading, Mass.: Addison-Wesley, Advanced Book Program, 1981. ISBN 0-201-04680-6 (cl), 0-201-04679-2 (pbk). ▸ One of most thorough and accessible accounts of development of special theory of relativity. Extensive bibliography. [MJC]

4.139 Emilio Segrè. *From falling bodies to radio waves: classical physicists and their discoveries.* New York: Freeman, 1984. ISBN 0-7167-1481-7 (cl), 0-7167-1482-5 (pbk). ▸ Most accessible survey of physics in period between Galileo and Einstein. Written by Nobel Prize–winning physicist; includes biographical information on many of physicists treated. [MJC]

4.140 Emilio Segrè. *From X-rays to quarks: modern physicists and their discoveries.* San Francisco: Freeman, 1980. ISBN 0-7167-1146-X (cl), 0-7167-1147-8 (pbk). ▸ Useful, well-illustrated survey of development of physics in twentieth century. Attention to biographies of major physicists. [MJC]

4.141 Edmund T. Whittaker. *A history of the theories of aether and electricity.* 1951–53 rev. ed. 2 vols. Los Angeles: American

Institute of Physics, 1987. (History of modern physics, 1800–1950, 7.) ISBN 0-88318-523-7 (set). ▸ Standard history of contributions to physical understanding of electromagnetism. First volume treats classical (pre-1900) theories; second volume carries story to 1926. [MJC]

Modern Astronomy, Cosmology, and Astrophysics

4.142 Agnes M. Clerke. *A popular history of astronomy during the nineteenth century.* 4th ed. London: Black, 1904. ▸ Elegantly written survey of astronomy from late eighteenth century to 1885. Although outdated in parts, still very valuable resource. [MJC]

4.143 Michael J. Crowe. *The extraterrestrial life debate, 1750–1900: the idea of a plurality of worlds from Kant to Lowell.* 1986 ed. Cambridge: Cambridge University Press, 1988. ISBN 0-521-26305-0 (cl, 1986), 0-521-35986-4 (pbk). ▸ Survey of ideas of extraterrestrial life, concentrating on period, 1750–1900. Treats interactions of astronomy with religion, literature, and philosophy. [MJC]

4.144 David H. DeVorkin, comp. *The history of modern astronomy and astrophysics: a selected, annotated bibliography.* New York: Garland, 1982. ISBN 0-8240-9283-X. ▸ Bibliography of 1,417 publications on history of astronomy and astrophysics in period after 1500. Useful annotations accompany most citations. [MJC]

4.145 Owen Gingerich, ed. *Astrophysics and twentieth-century astronomy to 1950,* Part A. Cambridge: Cambridge University Press, 1984. ISBN 0-521-24256-8. ▸ Essays on birth of astrophysics and development of astronomical observatories and instrumentation by leading experts. Extensively illustrated. [MJC]

4.146 Dieter B. Herrmann. *The history of astronomy from Herschel to Hertzsprung.* Kevin Krisciunas, trans. Cambridge: Cambridge University Press, 1984. ISBN 0-521-25733-6. ▸ Survey of development of astronomy from late eighteenth century to present by German historian of astronomy. Excellent illustrations. [MJC]

4.147 Michael A. Hoskin. *Stellar astronomy: historical studies.* Chalfont St. Giles, England: Science History, 1982. ISBN 0-905193-04-0. ▸ Thorough studies of main developments in stellar and extragalactic astronomy from seventeenth century to formulation of theory of expanding universe. [MJC]

4.148 Karl Hufbauer. *Exploring the sun: solar science since Galileo.* Baltimore: Johns Hopkins University Press, 1991. ISBN 0-8018-4098-8. ▸ Engaging treatment of studies of sun from early observations of sunspots and solar rotation to development of solar physics and chemistry. Extends to present. [MJC]

4.149 Stanley L. Jaki. *The Milky Way: an elusive road for science.* New York: Science History, 1972. ISBN 0-88202-007-2. ▸ Useful survey of ideas of nature and structure of Milky Way from antiquity to twentieth century. Based on extensive reading in sources. [MJC]

4.150 Kenneth R. Lang and Owen Gingerich, eds. *A source book in astronomy and astrophysics, 1900–1975.* Cambridge, Mass.: Harvard University Press, 1979. ISBN 0-674-82200-5. ▸ Collection of 132 well-chosen selections from works of astronomers and astrophysicists. Helpful commentary increases accessibility of selections. [MJC]

4.151 A. Pannekoek. *A history of astronomy.* 1961 ed. New York: Dover, 1989. ISBN 0-486-65994-1. ▸ Discussion of history of astronomy from antiquity to twentieth century by Dutch astronomer. Best single-volume survey of subject. [MJC]

4.152 Harlow Shapley and Helen E. Howarth, eds. *A source book in astronomy, 1500–1900.* 1929 ed. Cambridge, Mass.: Harvard University Press, 1960. ▸ Selections from writings of sixty-four astronomers from Copernicus to end of nineteenth century.

Despite minimal commentary, still standard anthology of primary sources. Also available on microfilm from Palo Alto: Bay Microfilm, 1988. [MJC]

4.153 Otto Struve and Velta Zebergs. *Astronomy of the twentieth century.* New York: Macmillan, 1962. ▸ Useful study of development of astronomy, 1900 to ca. 1960. Covers many areas; special attention to observational astrophysics. [MJC]

Modern Chemistry

4.154 Robert Bud and Gerrylynn K. Roberts. *Science versus practice: chemistry in Victorian Britain.* Manchester: Manchester University Press, 1984. ISBN 0-7190-1070-5. ▸ Discussion of Victorian debate between advocates of chemistry as pure science and advocates of chemistry as applied science. [AJR]

4.155 J.R.R. Christie and Jan Golinski. "The spreading of the word: new directions in the historiography of chemistry, 1600–1800." *History of science* 20 (1982) 235–66. ISSN 0073-2753. ▸ Summary of recent scholarship on seventeenth- and eighteenth-century chemistry. Emphasizes relationship of didactically methodized texts to chemical methods as well as social and institutional forces affecting emergence of modern chemistry. [AJR]

4.156 Maurice P. Crosland. *The Society of Arcueil: a view of French science at the time of Napoleon I.* Cambridge, Mass.: Harvard University Press, 1967. ▸ Influence of informal society, founded by C. L. Berthollet in Paris suburb, on French science (particularly chemistry), ca. 1794–1822. Describes scientific patronage and social relevance of pure science in preindustrial France. [AJR]

4.157 Joseph S. Fruton. *Contrasts in scientific style: research groups in the chemical and biochemical sciences.* Philadelphia: American Philosophical Society, 1990. (Memoirs of the American Philosophical Society, 191.) ISBN 0-87169-191-4, ISSN 0065-9738. ▸ Social, prosopographical, and scientific study of six academic chemical research groups, including Justus Liebig's, in nineteenth and twentieth centuries. Explores factors of bureaucratic structure and scientific style. [AJR]

4.158 Owen Hannaway. *The chemists and the word: the didactic origins of chemistry.* Baltimore: Johns Hopkins University Press, 1975. ISBN 0-8018-1666-1. ▸ Origin of discipline of chemistry around 1600 from encounter between humanist Libavius and hermetic Paracelsians. Pioneering exploration of linguistic and rhetorical features of new chemical textbooks. [AJR]

4.159 Frederic Lawrence Holmes. *Lavoisier and the chemistry of life: an exploration of scientific creativity.* Madison: University of Wisconsin Press, 1985. ISBN 0-299-09980-6. ▸ Detailed examination of French chemist's research in biochemistry and physiology that portrays his scientific creativity. Extensive use of Antoine Lavoisier's copious manuscript notes and drafts of articles. [AJR]

4.160 Karl Hufbauer. *The formation of the German chemical community, 1720–1795.* Berkeley: University of California Press, 1982. ISBN 0-520-04318-9 (cl), 0-520-04415-0 (pbk). ▸ Formation of national chemical community in politically fragmented Germany. Prosopographical and sociohistorical study that also gives good coverage of scientific content of discipline. [AJR]

4.161 Aaron J. Ihde. *The development of modern chemistry.* 1964 ed. New York: Dover, 1984. ISBN 0-486-64235-6 (pbk). ▸ General history of chemistry and chemical technology, 1750 to 1950. Only one-volume monographic treatment of this scope; useful as textbook. Internalist orientation with excellent bibliographies and scores of illustrations. [AJR]

4.162 Jeffrey Allan Johnson. *The kaiser's chemists: science and modernization in imperial Germany.* Chapel Hill: University of North Carolina Press, 1990. ISBN 0-8078-1902-6. ▸ Study of inter-

action among academic, government, and corporate chemistry in Wilhelmine Germany. Advocates model for role of science in context of conservative modernization. [AJR]

4.163 J. R. Partington. *A history of chemistry.* 4 vols. New York: St. Martin's, 1961–70. ▸ Survey of history of chemistry from antiquity to ca. 1900. By far most detailed single work of its kind. Relentlessly internalist (no attention to external factors), handbook-style text, extensive citations to primary and secondary sources. [AJR]

4.164 Colin Archibald Russell, ed. *Recent developments in the history of chemistry.* London: Royal Society of Chemistry, 1985. ISBN 0-85186-917-3. ▸ Twelve topically oriented chapters by nine authors on historical literature regarding chemistry and chemical technology with extensive citations. Best guide to secondary literature published through 1983. [AJR]

4.165 John W. Servos. *Physical chemistry from Ostwald to Pauling: the making of a science in America.* Princeton: Princeton University Press, 1990. ISBN 0-691-08566-8. ▸ Description of rise of physical chemistry in United States, focusing on A. A. Noyes, G. N. Lewis, Linus Pauling, and Wilder Bancroft. Discussion of social and intellectual issues affecting development of a scientific discipline in national context. [AJR]

4.166 Arnold Thackray. *Atoms and powers: an essay on Newtonian matter-theory and the development of chemistry.* Cambridge, Mass.: Harvard University Press, 1970. ISBN 0-674-05257-9. ▸ Study of theories of matter during European Enlightenment from Sir Isaac Newton to John Dalton. [AJR]

4.167 R. Steven Turner. "Justus Liebig versus Prussian chemistry: reflections on early institute building in Germany." *Historical studies in the physical sciences* 13 (1982) 129–62. ISSN 0890-9997. ▸ Study of Liebig's impact on administration of Prussian academic science and disciplinary and institutional growth of chemistry in nineteenth-century Germany. [AJR]

SEE ALSO
11.343 James Reardon-Anderson. *The study of change.*

Biology in the Eighteenth and Nineteenth Centuries

4.168 Edwin Clarke and L. S. Jacyna. *Nineteenth-century origins of neuroscientific concepts.* Berkeley: University of California Press, 1987. ISBN 0-520-05694-9. ▸ Detailed history of key British and European scientific concepts, their revolutionary impact and relation to romantic natural philosophy. Excellent bibliography. Useful reference. [SEK]

4.169 William Coleman. *Biology in the nineteenth century: problems of form, function, and transformation.* 1971 ed. Cambridge: Cambridge University Press, 1977. ISBN 0-521-21861-6 (cl), 0-521-29293-x (pbk). ▸ Survey of cell biology, anatomy, embryology, evolutionary biology, and physiology. Main scientific ideas charted, little on social or institutional context. Bibliographic essay. [SEK]

4.170 Virginia P. Dawson. *Nature's enigma: the problem of the polyp in the letters of Bonnet, Trembley, and Réaumur.* Philadelphia: American Philosophical Society, 1987. (Memoirs of the American Philosophical Society, 174.) ISBN 0-87169-174-4, ISSN 0065-9738. ▸ Chronicle of discovery of the polyp, tiny water animal, in context of Genevan intellectual and religious climate. Detailed description of key experiments in Enlightenment science. [SEK]

4.171 François Delaporte. *Nature's second kingdom: explorations of vegetality in the eighteenth century.* Arthur Goldhammer, trans. Cambridge, Mass.: MIT Press, 1982. ISBN 0-262-04066-2. ▸ Study in tradition of George Canguilhem and Michel Foucault, arguing analogies with animal physiology guided studies of plant nutrition, movement, and generation. [SEK]

4.172 A. Hunter Dupree. *Asa Gray: American botanist, friend of Darwin.* 1959 ed. Baltimore: Johns Hopkins University Press, 1988. ISBN 0-8018-3741-3 (pbk). ▸ Biography of key player in Darwinian debates. Places science in cultural, religious, and political context. Earlier title: *Asa Gray, 1810–1888.* [SEK]

4.173 Catherine Gallagher and Thomas Walter Laqueur, eds. *The making of the modern body: sexuality and society in the nineteenth century.* Berkeley: University of California Press, 1987. ISBN 0-520-05960-3 (cl), 0-520-05961-1 (pbk). ▸ Essays exploring discourse on body and biological construction of femininity in broader cultural and political contexts. History as influenced by anthropological perspectives. [SEK]

4.174 Gerald L. Geison. *Michael Foster and the Cambridge school of physiology: the scientific enterprise in late Victorian society.* Princeton: Princeton University Press, 1978. ISBN 0-691-08197-2. ▸ Study of English physiologists at Cambridge school, 1870–1900, centered on studies of heartbeat. Discusses scientific issues and socioinstitutional influences on group. [SEK]

4.175 Bentley Glass, Owsei Temkin, and William L. Straus, Jr., eds. *Forerunners of Darwin: 1745–1859.* 1959 ed. Baltimore: Johns Hopkins University Press, 1968. ▸ Essays on mathematician (Maupertuis), writer (Diderot), philosophers (Kant, Herder, and Schopenhauer), and naturalist (Lamarck). Treats problems of embryology, fossils, species concept, and transformist ideas. [SEK]

4.176 Anne Harrington. *Medicine, mind, and the double brain: a study in nineteenth-century thought.* Princeton: Princeton University Press, 1987. ISBN 0-691-08465-3. ▸ Detailed discussion of experimental studies of brain asymmetry with secondary themes of cultural significance of concepts of brain polarity and links to phrenology and psychoanalysis. Good bibliography. [SEK]

4.177 Hugo Iltis. *Life of Mendel.* Eden Paul and Cedar Paul, trans. London: Allen & Unwin, 1932. ▸ Useful nontechnical introduction to life and scientific work of founding figure in genetics. [SEK]

4.178 James L. Larson. *Reason and experience: the representation of natural order in the work of Carl von Linne.* Berkeley: University of California Press, 1971. ISBN 0-520-01834-6. ▸ Discussion of formative forces in Linnaeus's botanical classification. Elucidates hierarchy of concepts and definitions underlying eighteenth-century views of natural order. [SEK]

4.179 Timothy Lenoir. *The strategy of life: teleology and mechanics in nineteenth-century German biology.* 1982 ed. Chicago: University of Chicago Press, 1989. ISBN 0-226-47183-7. ▸ Richly detailed analysis of intellectual developments in biology, early to mid-nineteenth century. Important for understanding philosophical developments in science. [SEK]

4.180 Edward Lurie. *Louis Agassiz: a life in science.* 1960 ed. Baltimore: Johns Hopkins University Press, 1988. ISBN 0-8018-3743-x (pbk). ▸ Biography of major figure in nineteenth-century American science, founder of Museum of Comparative Zoology at Harvard University and opponent of Darwinism. [SEK]

4.181 Dorinda Outram. *Georges Cuvier: vocation, science, and authority in post-revolutionary France.* Manchester: Manchester University Press, 1984. ISBN 0-7190-1077-2. ▸ Study of Cuvier's scientific career in social context. Stops short of extended inquiry into his anatomical and taxonomic research. [SEK]

4.182 Judith Overmier. *The history of biology: an annotated bibliography.* New York: Garland, 1989. ISBN 0-8240-9118-3. ▸ Selective, annotated bibliography; excellent initial reference source. [SEK]

4.183 Jacques Roger. *Les sciences de la vie dans la pensée française du dix-huitième siècle: la génération des animaux de Descartes à l'Encyclopédie.* 2d ed. Paris: Colin, 1971. ▸ Standard work for survey of French biology, especially embryology. [SEK]

4.184 G. S. Rousseau, ed. *The languages of Psyche: mind and body in Enlightenment thought.* Berkeley: University of California Press, 1990. (Publications from the Clark Library professorship, UCLA, 12.) ISBN 0-520-07044-5 (cl), 0-520-07119-0 (pbk). ▸ Essays include scientific, medical, philosophical, and literary themes. [SEK]

4.185 Martin J. S. Rudwick. *Scenes from deep time: early pictorial representations of the prehistoric world.* Chicago: University of Chicago Press, 1992. ISBN 0-226-73104-9. ▸ Analyis of scientific illustration and reconstruction of unknown eras in eighteenth and nineteenth centuries. Well illustrated with commentary accessible to nonspecialists. [SEK]

4.186 Aram Vartanian. *Diderot and Descartes: a study in scientific naturalism in the Enlightenment.* 1953 ed. Westport, Conn.: Greenwood, 1975. ISBN 0-8371-8337-5. ▸ Analysis of how Cartesian mechanistic biology became basis of consistently materialistic view of man. Discussion of roles of philosophers, Julien Offray de LaMettrie, Count Buffon, Pierre L. M. de Maupertuis, and Baron d'Holbach. [SEK]

4.187 Mary P. Winsor. *Reading the shape of nature: comparative zoology at the Agassiz Museum.* Chicago: University of Chicago Press, 1991. ISBN 0-226-90214-5 (cl), 0-226-90215-3 (pbk). ▸ Study contrasting careers of Louis and Alexander Agassiz. Scientific issues in classification seen in context of institutional change and broader shifts in American biology. [SEK]

SEE ALSO
22.199 Thomas Walter Laqueur. *Making sex.*

Darwinism and Evolutionary Biology

4.188 Mark B. Adams, ed. *The wellborn science: eugenics in Germany, France, Brazil, and Russia.* New York: Oxford University Press, 1990. ISBN 0-19-505361-3. ▸ Essays demonstrating diversity of eugenics movement worldwide. Essay on Soviet science and politics relevant to controversy involving agrobiologist and ideologue T. D. Lysenko. [SEK]

4.189 Richard W. Burkhardt, Jr. *The spirit of system: Lamarck and evolutionary biology.* Cambridge, Mass.: Harvard University Press, 1977. ISBN 0-674-83317-1. ▸ Study of intellectual context of French naturalist's science, his scientific career, and reasons for failure to make immediate impact. [SEK]

4.190 Hamilton Cravens. *The triumph of evolution: the heredity-environment controversy 1900–1941.* 1978 ed. Baltimore: Johns Hopkins University Press, 1988. ISBN 0-8018-3742-1. ▸ Discussion of debates in biology and social science, especially eugenics, I.Q. testing, and instinct theory. Sees evolutionary ideas as ideology of modernization in America. [SEK]

4.191 Carl N. Degler. *In search of human nature: the decline and revival of Darwinism in American social thought.* New York: Oxford University Press, 1991. ISBN 0-19-506380-5. ▸ Survey of vast literature on acceptance and rejection of arguments in social science for biological basis of human behavior, late nineteenth century to current sociobiology. Anthropology emphasized. [SEK]

4.192 Adrian J. Desmond and James R. Moore. *Darwin.* 1991 ed. New York: Warner, 1992. ISBN 0-446-51589-2. ▸ Definitive biography based on most recent scholarship. Darwin's struggles with Christianity, anxiety over developing evolution thesis, and position in scientific society. [SEK]

4.193 Thomas F. Glick, ed. *The comparative reception of Darwinism.* 1974 ed. Chicago: University of Chicago Press, 1988. ISBN 0-226-29977-5 (pbk). ▸ Case studies on Darwinism in

England, Germany, France, United States, Russia, Netherlands, Spain, Mexico, and Islamic world. Historiographic and bibliographic essays. [SEK]

4.194 John S. Haller. *Outcasts from evolution: scientific attitudes of racial inferiority, 1859–1900.* 1971 ed. New York: McGraw-Hill, 1975. ISBN 0-07-025625-X. ‣ Survey of scientific and medical racism in America. [SEK]

4.195 Richard Hofstadter. *Social Darwinism in American thought.* 1955 rev. ed. Richard Foner, Introduction. Boston: Beacon, 1992. ISBN 0-8070-5461-5 (cl), 0-8070-5503-4 (pbk). ‣ Classic survey of attitudes toward evolution and impact of Herbert Spencer in America, to World War I. Includes discussion of conservative and radical thinkers. [SEK]

4.196 David L. Hull. *Darwin and his critics: the reception of Darwin's theory of evolution by the scientific community.* 1973 ed. Chicago: University of Chicago Press, 1983. ISBN 0-226-36046-6 (pbk). ‣ Set of original reviews of Darwin with lengthy essay on scientific method as relevant to debates on evolution and criticism of Darwin's work. [SEK]

4.197 Daniel J. Kevles. *In the name of eugenics: genetics and the uses of human heredity.* 1985 ed. Berkeley: University of California Press, 1986. ISBN 0-520-05763-5. ‣ Rise and fall of eugenics in Britain and United States. Charts rise of human genetics after World War II to development of recombinant DNA technology. [SEK]

4.198 David Kohn, ed. *The Darwinian heritage.* Princeton: Princeton University Press, 1985. ISBN 0-691-08356-8. ‣ Essays on evolution of Darwin's thought, Victorian context, and comparative reception of Darwinism. Includes historiographic overview of Darwin literature and extensive bibliography. [SEK]

4.199 Ernst Mayr and William B. Provine, eds. *The evolutionary synthesis: perspectives on the unification of biology.* Cambridge, Mass.: Harvard University Press, 1980. ISBN 0-674-27225-0. ‣ Survey of various disciplines in English, European, and American national contexts. Builds picture of modern neo-Darwinism. Includes reminiscences by scientists. [SEK]

4.200 James R. Moore. *The post-Darwinian controversies: a study of the Protestant struggle to come to terms with Darwin in Great Britain and America, 1870–1900.* 1979 ed. Cambridge: Cambridge University Press, 1981. ISBN 0-521-21989-2 (cl, 1979), 0-521-28517-8. ‣ Careful reading of Christian authors responding to Darwinism showing compatibility between evolutionary thought and religion. Challenges stereotype of warfare between science and religion. [SEK]

4.201 James G. Paradis. *T. H. Huxley: man's place in nature.* Lincoln: University of Nebraska Press, 1978. ISBN 0-8032-0917-7. ‣ Career, scientific work, and personal crises of "Darwin's bulldog." [SEK]

4.202 Robert J. Richards. *Darwin and the emergence of evolutionary theories of mind and behavior.* 1987 ed. Chicago: University of Chicago Press, 1989. ISBN 0-226-71199-4 (cl, 1987), 0-226-71200-1 (pbk). ‣ Intellectual history of major thinkers from eighteenth to twentieth century, emphasizing fundamental importance of evolutionary ethics and idea of behavior. Reinterprets Charles Darwin, Herbert Spencer, and post-Darwinian evolutionists. [SEK]

4.203 William Stanton. *The leopard's spots: scientific attitudes toward race in America, 1815–59.* 1960 ed. Chicago: University of Chicago Press, 1982. ISBN 0-226-77124-5. ‣ Discussion of debates about human origins and whether races were distinct species in context of religion and politics leading up to Civil War. [SEK]

SEE ALSO
24.354 Adrian J. Desmond. *The politics of evolution.*
31.262 Alfred Kelly. *The descent of Darwin.*
34.443 Alexander Vucinich. *Darwin in Russian thought.*

Biology in the Twentieth Century

4.204 Garland E. Allen. *Life science in the twentieth century.* 1975 ed. Cambridge: Cambridge University Press, 1979. ISBN 0-521-21864-0 (cl), 0-521-29296-4 (pbk). ‣ Survey of Darwin's impact, rise of experimental science, physiology, genetics, evolutionary synthesis, biochemistry, and molecular biology. [SEK]

4.205 Garland E. Allen. *Thomas Hunt Morgan: the man and his science.* Princeton: Princeton University Press, 1978. ISBN 0-691-08200-6. ‣ Depiction of reception of Mendelism, growth of genetics, and rise of American science to world status, through biography of Nobel prize–winning scientist. [SEK]

4.206 Keith R. Benson, Jane Maienschein, and Ronald Rainger, eds. *The expansion of American biology.* New Brunswick, N.J.: Rutgers University Press, 1991. ISBN 0-8135-1650-1 (cl), 0-8135-1651-X (pbk). ‣ Essays on cytology, reproductive science, paleontology, behavioral sciences, genetics in atomic age, and women in science in early to mid-twentieth century. [SEK]

4.207 Gerald L. Geison, ed. *Physiology in the American context, 1850–1940.* Bethesda, Md.: American Physiological Society; distributed by Williams & Wilkins, 1987. ISBN 0-683-03446-4. ‣ History of institutions, investigative practices, and connections between physiology and wider social concerns. Relationship of physiology to other disciplines. [SEK]

4.208 Donna Haraway. *Primate visions: gender, race, and nature in the world of modern science.* New York: Routledge, 1989. ISBN 0-415-90114-6 (cl), 0-415-90294-0 (pbk). ‣ Feminist exploration of primatology in twentieth century. Concludes with case studies of four contemporary women scientists. Wide-ranging, provocative, often nonlinear narrative. [SEK]

4.209 Jonathan Harwood. *Styles of scientific thought: the German genetics community, 1900–1933.* Chicago: University of Chicago Press, 1992. ISBN 0-226-37881-8 (cl), 0-226-31882-6 (pbk). ‣ Comparison of American and German scientific traditions examining influence of culture on science. Combines historical and sociological analysis to defend idea of national styles in science. [SEK]

4.210 David Joravsky. *The Lysenko affair.* 1970 ed. Chicago: University of Chicago Press, 1986. ISBN 0-226-41031-5 (pbk). ‣ Analysis of evolving interaction of agriculture, natural science, ideology, and political power. Charts reasons for rise and fall of agrobiologist and ideologue T. D. Lysenko in Soviet Union. [SEK]

4.211 Horace Freeland Judson. *The eighth day of creation: makers of the revolution in biology.* 1979 ed. New York: Simon & Schuster, 1980. ISBN 0-671-22540-5 (cl), 0-671-25410-3 (pbk). ‣ Exhaustive account of creation of molecular biology with focus on scientific creativity, based on extensive interviews with scientists. Tells story from scientists' point of view. [SEK]

4.212 Lily E. Kay. *The molecular vision of life: Caltech, the Rockefeller Foundation, and the rise of the new biology.* New York: Oxford University Press, 1992. ISBN 0-19-505812-7. ‣ Relationship between growth of research programs and private patronage. Intellectual developments in molecular biology. Institutional and social context of science to 1950s. [SEK]

4.213 Evelyn Fox Keller. *A feeling for the organism: the life and work of Barbara McClintock.* San Francisco: Freeman, 1983. ISBN 0-7167-1433-7 (cl), 0-7167-1504-X (pbk). ‣ Life and work of Nobel prize–winning maize geneticist. Explores nature of biological thought and women in science. [SEK]

4.214 Kenneth R. Manning. *Black Apollo of science: the life of Ernest Everett Just.* New York: Oxford University Press, 1983. ISBN 0-19-503299-3 (cl), 0-19-503498-8 (pbk). ‣ Study of career of brilliant African American biologist in early twentieth century. Contrasts milieu at University of Chicago, Woods Hole, and Howard University. Discusses importance of foundation support. [SEK]

4.215 Gregg Mitman. *The state of nature: ecology, community, and American social thought, 1900–1950.* Chicago: University of Chicago Press, 1992. ISBN 0-226-53236-4 (cl), 0-226-53237-2 (pbk). ‣ Discussion of growth of animal ecology at Chicago, including study of communities and evolution of sociality and cooperation. Relationship between science and concerns about democracy, social order, and religious belief. [SEK]

4.216 Robert C. Olby. *The path to the double helix.* Seattle: University of Washington Press, 1974. ISBN 0-295-95359-4. ‣ Account of major parallel scientific developments in several fields, leading to James Watson and Francis Crick's discovery of DNA structure. [SEK]

4.217 Philip J. Pauly. *Controlling life: Jacques Loeb and the engineering ideal in biology.* New York: Oxford University Press, 1987. ISBN 0-19-504244-1. ‣ Analysis of Loeb's quest to control development and behavior as exemplar of American engineering mentality. Discussion of image making in science and institutional context. [SEK]

4.218 Ronald Rainger. *An agenda for antiquity: Henry Fairfield Osborn and vertebrate paleontology at the American Museum of Natural History, 1890–1935.* Tuscaloosa: University of Alabama Press, 1991. ISBN 0-8173-0536-x. ‣ How and why Osborn developed leading research center in United States. Combines institutional and intellectual history. [SEK]

4.219 Ronald Rainger, Keith R. Benson, and Jane Maienschein, eds. *The American development of biology.* Philadelphia: University of Pennsylvania Press, 1988. ISBN 0-8122-8092-x. ‣ Essays on professionalization, research centers, and disciplines of ethology, ecology, paleontology, genetics, and cell biology in late nineteenth and early twentieth cenuries. [SEK]

4.220 Jan Sapp. *Where the truth lies: Franz Moewus and the origins of molecular biology.* Cambridge: Cambridge University Press, 1990. ISBN 0-521-36550-3 (cl), 0-521-36751-4 (pbk). ‣ Career of German microbiologist. Dissects scientific process through case study of suspected fraud. Follows Latour and Woolgar 4.283 in arguing for social construction of scientific knowledge. [SEK]

4.221 Charles Webster, ed. *Biology, medicine, and society, 1840–1940.* Cambridge: Cambridge University Press, 1981. ISBN 0-521-23770-x. ‣ Essays exploring issues of policy and politics involving modern biology and medicine. Topics include women's health, infant mortality, ethology, genetics, eugenics, sociobiology, sociopolitical applications of cell theory, psychologists and class, and intelligence testing. [SEK]

Geology and Other Earth Sciences

4.222 Stephen G. Brush and Helmut E. Landsberg. *The history of geophysics and meteorology: an annotated bibliography.* New York: Garland, 1985. ISBN 0-8240-9116-7. ‣ Best bibliography of these fields. Includes much geology and oceanography as well. [MTG]

4.223 Joe D. Burchfield. *Lord Kelvin and the age of the earth.* 1975 ed. Chicago: University of Chicago Press, 1990. ISBN 0-226-08043-9. ‣ History of attempts to establish geological time scale, focusing on late nineteenth-century controversies about age of earth. [MTG]

4.224 Margaret Deacon. *Scientists and the sea, 1650–1950: a study of marine science.* London: Academic Press, 1971. ISBN

0-12-207850-0. ‣ Standard, essential history of oceanography. [MTG]

4.225 Gary S. Dunbar. *The history of modern geography: an annotated bibliography of selected works.* New York: Garland, 1985. ISBN 0-8240-9066-7. ‣ Annotated bibliography; excellent initial reference source. [MTG]

4.226 Robert Marc Friedman. *Appropriating the weather: Vilhelm Bjerknes and the construction of a modern meteorology.* Ithaca, N.Y.: Cornell University Press, 1989. ISBN 0-8014-2062-8. ‣ History of political, social, and scientific issues surrounding development of modern meteorology. [MTG]

4.227 William Glen. *The road to Jaramillo: critical years of the revolution in earth science.* Stanford, Calif.: Stanford University Press, 1982. ISBN 0-8047-1119-4. ‣ History of geomagnetism and sea-floor spreading. Very strong on personalities and institutions. [MTG]

4.228 Mott T. Greene. *Geology in the nineteenth century: changing views of a changing world.* Ithaca, N.Y.: Cornell University Press, 1982. ISBN 0-8014-1467-9. ‣ History of geological theory from late eighteenth to early twentieth century, emphasizing theories of mountain ranges, continents, and oceans. [MTG]

4.229 Anthony Hallam. *Great geological controversies.* 2d ed. New York: Oxford University Press, 1989. ISBN 0-19-858218-8 (cl), 0-19-858219-6 (pbk). ‣ History of geology from late eighteenth century to present through history of major controversies, including age of earth, continental drift, ice ages, and mass extinctions. [MTG]

4.230 John B. Harley and David Woodward, eds. *The history of cartography.* Vol. 1: *Cartography in prehistoric, ancient, and medieval Europe and the Mediterranean.* Vol. 2: *Cartography in the traditional Islamic and South Asian societies.* Chicago: University of Chicago Press, 1987. ISBN 0-226-31633-5. ‣ History of maps as practical tools and as images symbolizing religion and culture. Includes technical analysis and classification types, traditions, and workshops. Catalogs of extant maps, published and manuscript. Additional volumes on age of Renaissance and discovery, age of science, Enlightenment and expansion, nineteenth century, and twentieth century forthcoming. [MTG/FLC]

4.231 G. L. Herries-Davies. *The earth in decay: a history of British geomorphology, 1578–1878.* New York: Elsevier, 1969. ISBN 0-444-19701-x. ‣ Study of landforms over three centuries with attention to religious, philosophical, and scientific issues. [MTG]

4.232 John Imbrie and Katherine Palmer Imbrie. *Ice ages: solving the mystery.* 1978 ed. Cambridge, Mass.: Harvard University Press, 1986. ISBN 0-674-44075-7. ‣ Broad popular history of astronomical theories of ice ages. [MTG]

4.233 Gisela Kutzbach. *The thermal theory of cyclones: a history of meteorological thought in the nineteenth century.* Boston: American Meteorological Society, 1979. ISBN 0-933876-48-3. ‣ Technical history of meteorology with coverage of American and European developments. Contains biographical summaries. [MTG]

4.234 Rachel Laudan. *From mineralogy to geology: the foundations of a science, 1650–1830.* Chicago: University of Chicago Press, 1987. ISBN 0-226-46950-6. ‣ Discussion of emergence of modern geology from mineralogy and natural history in Europe. Studies contrasting national traditions. [MTG]

4.235 Ursula B. Marvin. *Continental drift: the evolution of a concept.* Washington, D.C.: Smithsonian Institution Press; distributed by Braziller, 1973. ISBN 0-87474-129-7. ‣ Popular, well-illustrated history of idea of continental drift since mid-nineteenth century with good coverage of general geology in period. [MTG]

4.236 Henry W. Menard. *The ocean of truth: a personal history of*

global tectonics. Princeton: Princeton University Press, 1986. ISBN 0-691-08414-9. ▸ Candid insider's memoir, by former head of United States Geological Survey, of major shift in geological theory. [MTG]

4.237 Roy Porter. *The earth sciences: an annotated bibliography.* New York: Garland, 1983. ISBN 0-8240-9267-8. ▸ Standard bibliography of history of earth sciences. [MTG]

4.238 Herbert Harold Read. *The granite controversy: geological addresses illustrating the evolution of a disputant.* New York: Interscience, 1957. ▸ Thoughtful analysis of debate and, in more general terms, of character of debate within geology. [MTG]

4.239 Martin J. S. Rudwick. *The great Devonian controversy: the shaping of scientific knowledge among gentlemanly specialists.* Chicago: University of Chicago Press, 1985. ISBN 0-226-73101-4 (cl), 0-226-73102-2 (pbk). ▸ Analysis of geological controversy in early nineteenth-century Britain describing relations among theoretical, social, professional, and institutional dimensions of scientific development. Emphasizes social contribution to knowledge formation. [MTG]

4.240 Martin J. S. Rudwick. *The meaning of fossils: episodes in the history of paleontology.* 1976 2d ed. Chicago: University of Chicago Press, 1985. ISBN 0-226-73103-0 (pbk). ▸ Essays on origins of paleontology, its social and scientific context and cultural and religious implications in Europe, sixteenth to early nineteenth century. Not overly technical. [SEK]

4.241 William Antony S. Sarjeant. *Geologists and the history of geology: an international bibliography from the origins to 1978.* 5 vols. New York: Arno, 1980. ISBN 0-405-10469-3 (set). ▸ Massive bibliography with many cross-indexes. Supplemental volumes 6 and 7 cover 1979–84. [MTG]

4.242 Susan Schlee. *The edge of an unfamiliar world: a history of oceanography.* New York: Dutton, 1973. ISBN 0-525-09673-6. ▸ Well-illustrated scientific, social, and institutional history of oceanography from mid-nineteenth century to 1960s. Emphasizes United States, Britain, and Scandinavia. Also covers political and economic issues. [MTG]

4.243 Cecil J. Schneer, ed. *Two hundred years of geology in America: proceedings of the New Hampshire Bicentennial Conference on the History of Geology.* Hanover, N.H.: University Press of New England for University of New Hampshire, 1979. ISBN 0-87451-160-7. ▸ Collection of papers on aspects of American geology. [MTG]

4.244 James A. Secord. *Controversy in Victorian geology: the Cambrian-Silurian dispute.* 1986 ed. Princeton: Princeton University Press, 1990. ISBN 0-691-08417-3 (cl, 1986), 0-691-02441-3 (pbk). ▸ Exploration of social and institutional history of Victorian earth science through dispute of Sir R. I. Murchison and Professor Adam Sedgwick over boundaries of geologic periods. [MTG]

Ecology and Environmentalism

4.245 Stephen Fox. *The American conservation movement: John Muir and his legacy.* 1981 ed. Madison: University of Wisconsin Press, 1985. ISBN 0-299-10634-9 (pbk). ▸ Biography and history of conservation to 1975. Emphasis on role of amateur radical. Generalizes about meaning of conservation. [SEK]

4.246 Clarence J. Glacken. *Traces on the Rhodian shore: nature and culture in Western thought from ancient times to the end of the eighteenth century.* 1967 ed. Berkeley: University of California Press, 1973. ISBN 0-520-02367-6. ▸ Historical survey of Western environmental thought. [MTG]

4.247 Samuel P. Hays. *Beauty, health, and permanence: environmental politics in the United States, 1955–1985.* 1987 ed. Cam-

bridge: Cambridge University Press, 1989. ISBN 0-521-32428-9 (cl, 1987), 0-521-38928-3 (pbk). ▸ Encyclopedic history of urban environment, public wildlands, pollution, issues of population, resources, and limits to growth. Critical of environmental policy makers. Good general reference. [SEK]

4.248 Sharon E. Kingsland. *Modeling nature: episodes in the history of population ecology.* 1985 ed. Chicago: University of Chicago Press, 1988. ISBN 0-226-43726-4 (cl, 1985), 0-226-43727-2 (pbk). ▸ Discussion of controversy over use of mathematics in ecology and population biology, 1920s to 1970s. Also treats nature of biological reasoning and key concepts in ecology. [SEK]

4.249 Roderick Nash. *Wilderness and the American mind.* 3d ed. New Haven: Yale University Press, 1982. ISBN 0-300-02905-5 (cl), 0-300-02910-1 (pbk). ▸ Extensive history of wilderness preservation. New material added since first 1967 edition on controversies, trends in wilderness preservation, and international perspective. [SEK]

4.250 Thomas Søderqvist. *The ecologists, from merry naturalists to saviours of the nation: a sociologically informed narrative survey of the ecologization of Sweden, 1895–1975.* Stockholm: Almqvist & Wiksell, 1986. ISBN 91-22-00827-6 (pbk). ▸ Study of emergence of ecology as discipline in Sweden. Exemplary study of national science and political context in which ecology affected social order in Sweden. [SEK]

4.251 Ronald C. Tobey. *Saving the prairies: the life cycle of the founding school of American plant ecology, 1895–1955.* Berkeley: University of California Press, 1981. ISBN 0-520-04352-9. ▸ Lucid analysis of rise of grassland ecology with focus on Frederic Clements and Dust Bowl research. Combines straightforward narrative history with sociological analysis. [SEK]

4.252 Douglas R. Weiner. *Models of nature: ecology, conservation, and cultural revolution in Soviet Russia.* Bloomington: Indiana University Press, 1988. ISBN 0-253-33837-9. ▸ Analysis of ecology's growth and decline under Stalin from before revolution to 1930s. Illuminates relation between science, politics, and society in modern world. [SEK]

4.253 Donald Worster. *Nature's economy: a history of ecological ideas.* 1977 ed. Cambridge: Cambridge University Press, 1985. ISBN 0-521-26792-7 (cl), 0-521-31870-X (pbk). ▸ Ranges from Arcadian, imperialist visions of eighteenth century to development of ecological science and environmentalism in twentieth century. Strong political thesis sometimes skews analysis of science. [SEK]

4.254 Donald Worster, ed. *The ends of the earth: perspectives on modern environmental history.* Cambridge: Cambridge University Press, 1988. ISBN 0-521-34365-8 (cl), 0-521-34846-3 (pbk). ▸ Introduction to historiography, approaches, and range of subjects in environmental history. American, Third World, and European case studies. Extensive bibliography. [SEK]

Modern Social Sciences

4.255 Kerry W. Buckley. *Mechanical man: John Broadus Watson and the beginnings of behaviorism.* New York: Guilford, 1989. ISBN 0-89862-744-3. ▸ Analysis of psychologist's experience at University of Chicago, his revolt from psychology, and creation of behaviorism. Sees behaviorism as expression of American modernity and interwar cultural anxiety. Discusses applications in advertising and child rearing. [SEK]

4.256 Martin Bulmer. *The Chicago school of sociology: institutionalization, diversity, and the rise of sociological research.* Chicago: University of Chicago Press, 1984. ISBN 0-226-08004-8. ▸ Description of Chicago school of sociology in early twentieth century, focusing on major figures and social and institutional factors producing empirical social science at University of Chicago. [DEL]

4.257 Hamilton Cravens. "History of the social sciences." In *Historical writing on American science.* 1985 ed. Sally Gregory Kohlstedt and Margaret W. Rossiter, eds., pp. 183–207. Baltimore: Johns Hopkins University Press, 1985. ISBN 0-8018-3438-4 (pbk). ‣ Survey of recent literature on history of social sciences in United States over past 150 years—especially as related to social and political trends associated with democracy, professionalization, and pluralism. [DEL]

4.258 Mary O. Furner. *Advocacy and objectivity: a crisis in the professionalization of American social science, 1865–1905.* Lexington: University Press of Kentucky for Organization of American Historians, 1975. ISBN 0-8131-1309-1. ‣ Analysis of development of social sciences in America—especially economics, sociology, and political science—within context of rapid social change that created demand for professional social services based upon sound, research-supported theory. [DEL]

4.259 Howard Gardner. *The mind's new science: a history of the cognitive revolution.* New York: Basic Books, 1985. ISBN 0-465-04634-7 (cl), 0-465-04635-5 (pbk). ‣ Survey of developments in cognitive science (as rooted in information processing, cybernetics, artificial intelligence, linguistics, anthropology, and neuropsychology) that have radically changed conceptual frameworks and prospects of social sciences. [DEL]

4.260 Marvin Harris. *The rise of anthropological theory: a history of theories of culture.* New York: Crowell, 1968. ISBN 0-690-70322-8. ‣ Survey of history of anthropological theories from Enlightenment to mid-twentieth century. [DEL]

4.261 Thomas L. Haskell. *The emergence of professional social science: the American Social Science Association and the nineteenth-century crisis of authority.* Urbana: University of Illinois Press, 1977. ISBN 0-252-00609-7. ‣ Study of transition from amateur social inquiry to professional social science in United States—emergence of modern discipline of sociology. [DEL]

4.262 Ernest R. Hilgard. *Psychology in America: a historical survey.* San Diego: Harcourt Brace Jovanovich, 1987. ISBN 0-15-539202-6. ‣ Survey of major historical developments in different areas of psychology as well as professional organization of both scholars and practitioners over past century. [DEL]

4.263 Ernest R. Hilgard, David E. Leary, and Gregory R. McGuire. "The history of psychology: a survey and critical assessment." *Annual review of psychology* 42 (1991) 79–107. ISSN 0066-4308. ‣ Review of historiography of psychology, major issues pertaining to history of psychology, and many major books, articles, chapters, and reference works. [DEL]

4.264 Curtis M. Hinsley, Jr. *Savages and scientists: the Smithsonian Institution and the development of American anthropology, 1846–1910.* Washington, D.C.: Smithsonian Institution Press, 1981. ISBN 0-87474-518-7. ‣ Development of American anthropology in relation to interests of major museum, needs of government, and agendas of important early American anthropologists. Vivid portraits of anthropologists Frank Cushing, John Wesley Powell, and James Mooney. [DEL/FEH/HM]

4.265 Robert V. Kemper and John F. S. Phinney. *The history of anthropology: a research bibliography.* New York: Garland, 1977. ISBN 0-8240-9911-7. ‣ Extensive lists of references on history of anthropology and related disciplines. [DEL]

4.266 Anthony Oberschall, ed. *The establishment of empirical sociology: studies in continuity, discontinuity, and institutionalization.* New York: Harper & Row, 1972. ISBN 0-06-044883-0. ‣ Collection of essays treating sources of demand for empirical social research and its professional development in Germany, France, England, and United States. [DEL]

4.267 John M. O'Donnell. *The origins of behaviorism: American psychology, 1870–1920.* New York: New York University Press, 1985. ISBN 0-8147-6162-3 (cl), 0-8147-6165-8 (pbk). ‣ Study of development of distinctively American psychology—a science of conditioned behavior rather than conscious reflection—within academic, economic, and social contexts. [DEL]

4.268 Dorothy Ross. *The origins of American social science.* Cambridge: Cambridge University Press, 1991. ISBN 0-521-35092-1. ‣ American social science from mid-nineteenth century through 1920s (especially history, political science, and sociology). Emphasizes role of ideology of American exceptionalism, model of natural science, and liberal politics. [DEL]

4.269 Elizabeth Scarborough and Laurel Furumoto. *Untold lives: the first generation of American women psychologists.* New York: Columbia University Press, 1987. ISBN 0-231-05154-9. ‣ Experiences of five first-generation women psychologists and collective portrait of entire first generation of women psychologists describing origins, educations, life styles, careers, and contributions. [DEL]

4.270 Raymond Seidelman. *Disenchanted realists: political science and the American crisis, 1884–1984.* Albany: State University of New York Press, 1985. ISBN 0-87395-994-9 (cl), 0-87395-995-7 (pbk). ‣ Development of science of politics from its early association with political liberalism to its eventual professionalization and insulation from realities of politics, power, and protest that gave rise to it. [DEL]

4.271 Frank Spencer. *Piltdown: a scientific forgery.* London: Oxford University Press, 1990. ISBN 0-19-858522-5. ‣ Exhaustive detail on famous hoax. Attempts to solve mystery; chronicles palaeoanthropology in twentieth century. [SEK]

4.272 George J. Stigler. *Essays in the history of economics.* 1965 ed. Chicago: University of Chicago Press, 1967. ‣ Fourteen essays on various aspects of history of economic theory and practice over past several centuries. [DEL]

4.273 George W. Stocking, Jr. *Victorian anthropology.* New York: Free Press, 1987. ISBN 0-02-931550-6. ‣ Emergence of classical evolutionism in 1860s in national, disciplinary, and scientific contexts. [SEK]

4.274 Arthur J. Vidich and Stanford M. Lyman. *American sociology: worldly rejections of religion and their directions.* 1985 ed. New Haven: Yale University Press, 1987. ISBN 0-300-03037-1 (cl, 1985), 0-300-04041-5 (pbk). ‣ History of American sociology focusing on major figures within context of Protestantism, positivism, and progressivism. [DEL]

4.275 Robert I. Watson. *The history of psychology and the behavioral sciences: a bibliographic guide.* New York: Springer, 1978. ISBN 0-8261-2080-6 (cl), 0-8261-2081-4 (pbk). ‣ Extensive lists of references, including references to other bibliographic guides, regarding histories of psychology, psychiatry, psychoanalysis, anthropology, sociology, and other related fields of social, behavioral, and biological sciences. [DEL]

SEE ALSO
26.250 Terry Nichols Clark. *Prophets and patrons.*

Social Relations of Science

4.276 Mario Biagioli. "Galileo the emblem maker." *ISIS* 81 (1990) 230–58. ISSN 0021-1753. ‣ Examination of Galileo's patronage strategy aimed at securing appointment in 1610 as philosopher to Cosimo II de'Medici in Florence. Describes his exploitation of court's fascination with mythology and symbolism. [RKD]

4.277 H. M. Collins. *Changing order: replication and induction in scientific practice, with new afterward.* 1985 ed. Chicago: University of Chicago Press, 1992. ISBN 0-226-11376-0 (pbk). ‣ Social-constructionist interpretation of how scientists conduct and draw conclusions from experiments. Organized around three case studies: replication of TEA-laser, detecting gravitational rotation, and experiments in the paranormal. [RKD]

4.278 Kurt Danziger. *Constructing the subject: historical origins of psychological research.* Cambridge: Cambridge University Press, 1990. ISBN 0-521-36358-6. ‣ Asserts psychologists have imposed quantification on psychology to establish "scientific" identity for discipline and to ally it with power groups (industry, military, educational administrators) in American society. [RKD]

4.279 Paul Forman. "Weimar culture, causality, and quantum theory, 1918–1927: adaptation by German physicists and mathematicians to a hostile intellectual environment." *Historical studies in the physical sciences* 3 (1971) 1–115. ISSN 0890-9997. ‣ Provocative essay exploring relations of quantum theories of German physicists to cultural context of Weimar period. [RKD]

4.280 Peter Galison. *How experiments end.* Chicago: University of Chicago Press, 1987. ISBN 0-226-27914-6 (cl), 0-226-27915-4 (pbk). ‣ Sociological study of experimental practice, recognizing significance of communal negotiating process but arguing for extrasociological "passive elements" that constrain production of scientific knowledge. [RKD]

4.281 James Gleick. *Chaos: making a new science.* 1987 ed. New York: Penguin, 1988. ISBN 0-14-009250-1. ‣ Chronicle of birth of science of chaos out of independent experiments and conceptualizations by individual mathematicians, biologists, and physical scientists. Treats intellectual and sociological aspects of its brief history. [RKD]

4.282 Jan Golinski. *Science as public culture: chemistry and Enlightenment in Britain, 1760–1820.* Cambridge: Cambridge University Press, 1992. ISBN 0-521-39414-7. ‣ Relates development of chemistry in Britain between 1760 and 1820 to rise and subsequent eclipse of forms of civic life characteristic of European Enlightenment. [RKD]

4.283 Bruno Latour and Steve Woolgar. *Laboratory life: the construction of scientific facts.* 1979 ed. Princeton: Princeton University Press, 1986. ISBN 0-691-09418-7 (cl), 0-691-02832-x (pbk). ‣ Anthropological study of biochemical laboratory leading authors to emphasize sociological factors in origin of scientific knowledge and use of rhetorical devices by scientists to defend their views. [RKD]

4.284 Andrew Pickering. *Constructing quarks: a sociological history of particle physics.* Chicago: University of Chicago Press, 1984. ISBN 0-226-66798-7 (cl), 0-226-66799-5 (pbk). ‣ Sociological analysis of high-energy physics, attempting to show scientists guided by social interests within their community. Argues scientific knowledge is socially constructed. [RKD]

Scientific Instruments

4.285 J. A. Bennett. *The divided circle: a history of instruments for astronomy, navigation, and surveying.* Oxford: Phaidon Christie's, 1987. ISBN 0-7148-8038-8. ‣ Well-illustrated narrative account, ancient period through nineteenth century. Instrument-making trade considered as well as context of problems to which instruments were applied. [APM]

4.286 Maurice Daumas. *Scientific instruments of the seventeenth and eighteenth centuries.* 1972 ed. Mary Holbrook, ed. and trans. London: Portman, 1989. ISBN 0-7134-0727-1. ‣ Discussion of mutual stimulation between natural sciences and techniques of instrument making. Importance of industrial, social, and economic contexts. [APM]

4.287 Timothy Lenoir. "Models and instruments in the development of electrophysiology, 1845–1912." *Historical studies in the*

physical and biological sciences 17.1 (1986) 1–54. ISSN 0073-2672. ‣ Electrophysiology as prime example of transformation of physiology from descriptive field to experimental quantitative discipline. Instruments of physiologists Emil DuBois-Reymond and Julius Bernstein provided basis for most influential quantitative theories of electrophysiology. [APM]

4.288 W. E. Knowles Middleton. *Invention of the meteorological instruments.* Baltimore: Johns Hopkins University Press, 1969. ‣ Argues barometer, thermometer, rain gauge, radiosonde, and other such instruments spurred development of meteorology. Surveys seventeenth through twentieth centuries. [APM]

4.289 John D. North. "The astrolabe." *Scientific American* 230.1 (1974) 96–106. ISSN 0036-8733. ‣ Clear, concise explanation of theory behind and many functions of important instrument. Includes diagrams and illustrations of astrolabes in different periods. [BSH]

4.290 John T. Stock and Mary Virginia Orna, eds. *The history and preservation of chemical instrumentation: proceedings of the ACS division of the History of Chemistry Symposium, Chicago, Ill., September 9–10, 1985.* Dordrecht: Reidel; distributed by Kluwer, 1986. ISBN 90-277-2269-2. ‣ Chemical instruments and theory closely interrelated. Strategies for preserving chemical instruments must take into account common industrial practice of discarding older instruments once new ones become available. [APM]

4.291 E.G.R. Taylor. *The mathematical practitioners of Tudor and Stuart England.* 1954 ed. Costa Mesa, Calif.: Knowledge Resources, 1985. ‣ Mathematical knowledge widely diffused among England's instrument makers. Includes extensive biographies of obscure practitioners. [APM]

4.292 Gerard L'E. Turner. *Scientific instruments and experimental philosophy, 1550–1850.* Brookfield, Vt.: Gower, 1990. ISBN 0-86078-280-8. ‣ Evolution of scientific instruments from sixteenth to nineteenth century, especially telescope and microscope. Instruments crucial to advance of scientific thought. Links development of instrumentation to economic and social phenomena. [APM]

4.293 Albert Van Helden. "The invention of the telescope." *Transactions of the American Philosophical Society* 67 (1977). ISSN 0065-9746. ‣ Actual invention of telescope impossible to document, but explores prehistory in England and Italy in late sixteenth century and history in Netherlands thereafter, presenting many original documents. [APM]

4.294 David W. Waters. *The art of navigation in England in Elizabethan and early Stuart times.* 2d ed. 3 vols. Greenwich, England: National Maritime Museum, 1978. ISBN 0-905555-13-9 (set, pbk). ‣ Navigation rooted in both empirical and scientific-mathematical techniques. England slow to pick up navigation from rest of Europe, but entering mercantile period, quickly advanced art and science of subject. Instruments understood in context of contemporary knowledge, especially mathematics. [APM]

4.295 M. Norton Wise. "Mediating machines." *Science in context* 2.1 (1988) 77–113. ISSN 0269-8897. ‣ Instruments mediate social concerns and scientific knowledge. Cites examples of steam engine and electric telegraph bringing "labor value" and industrial interests into physical theories of Lord Kelvin. [APM]

History of the Philosophy of Science

4.296 J. Alberto Coffa. *The semantic tradition from Kant to Carnap: to the Vienna station.* Linda Wessels, ed. Cambridge: Cambridge University Press, 1991. ISBN 0-521-37429-4. ‣ Delineates role of semantic notions in understanding ground of *a priori* knowledge and its relationship to empirical knowledge from early nineteenth century through activities of Vienna circle. [RKD]

4.297 Thomas S. Kuhn. *The structure of scientific revolutions.* 2d ed. Chicago: University of Chicago Press, 1970. ISBN 0-226-45804-0. ‣ Details author's interpretation of historical growth of science, involving replacement of one paradigm by another without conventional sense of progress toward objective truth. [AJR]

4.298 Imre Lakatos and Alan Musgrave, eds. *Criticism and the growth of knowledge.* Cambridge: Cambridge University Press, 1970. ISBN 0-521-07826-1 (cl), 0-521-09623-5 (pbk). ‣ Edited proceedings of 1965 conference assessing and critiquing Kuhn's *Structure of Scientific Revolutions* (4.297) with responses by Kuhn. [AJR]

4.299 Larry Laudan. *Science and hypothesis: historical essays on scientific methodology.* Dordrecht: Reidel; distributed by Kluwer, 1981. (University of Western Ontario series in philosophy of science, 19.) ISBN 90-277-1315-4 (cl), 90-277-1316-2 (pbk). ‣ History of "method of hypothesis" from seventeenth to end of nineteenth century. Emphasizes interaction between ideas of philosophers (theorists of science) and ideas of practicing scientists. [AJR]

4.300 John Losee. *A historical introduction to the philosophy of science.* 2d ed. Oxford: Oxford University Press, 1980. ISBN 0-19-219156-X (cl), 0-19-289143-X (pbk). ‣ Compact history of philosophy of science. Stresses changing interpretations of scientific method. [AJR]

4.301 John A. Schuster and Richard R. Yeo, eds. *The politics and rhetoric of scientific method: historical studies.* Dordrecht: Reidel; distributed by Kluwer, 1986. ISBN 90-277-2152-1. ‣ Discussion of substance and appearance of scientific method. Analyzes how scientists shape it consciously and unconsciously for rhetorical and political purposes. [AJR]

Science and Religion

4.302 John Hedley Brooke. *Science and religion: some historical perspectives.* Cambridge: Cambridge University Press, 1991. ISBN 0-521-23961-3 (cl), 0-521-28374-4 (pbk). ‣ Stimulating essays on historical relationship of religion and science from Copernicus to twentieth century. Superlative bibliographic essay. [RAH/RKW]

4.303 John Dillenberger. *Protestant thought and natural science: a historical interpretation.* 1960 ed. Westport, Conn.: Greenwood, 1977. ISBN 0-8371-9670-1. ‣ Useful but somewhat dated survey of Protestant theology from Copernicus to Darwin, concluding with brief examination of issues in twentieth century. [RAH]

4.304 Amos Funkenstein. *Theology and the scientific imagination: from the Middle Ages to the seventeenth century.* Princeton: Princeton University Press, 1986. ISBN 0-691-08408-4. ‣ Thoughtful interpretation of emergence of secular theology (in physics, history, political theory) as extension of God's traditional attributes—omnipresence, omnipotence, and providence. [RAH]

4.305 Frederick Gregory. *Nature lost? Natural science and the German theological traditions of the nineteenth century.* Cambridge, Mass.: Harvard University Press, 1992. ISBN 0-674-60483-0. ‣ Traces "loss of nature" from theological systems in nineteenth-century German-speaking Europe, suggesting that this "denatured theology" reflected larger cultural shift in epistemology but had little affect on popular religious belief. [RAH]

4.306 R. Hooykaas. *Religion and the rise of modern science.* Grand Rapids, Mich.: Eerdmans, 1972. ISBN 0-8028-1474-3. ‣ Succinct standard study tracing notions of God, nature, reason, and experience from antiquity to scientific and Puritan revolutions. [RAH]

4.307 David C. Lindberg and Ronald L. Numbers, eds. *God and nature: historical essays on the encounter between Christianity and science.* Berkeley: University of California Press, 1986. ISBN 0-520-05538-1 (cl), 0-520-05692-2 (pbk). ‣ Excellent multiauthored col-

lection of essays challenging hypothesis that science and religion have been at war since early modern period. [RAH]

4.308 Richard S. Westfall. *Science and religion in seventeenth-century England.* 1958 ed. Ann Arbor: University of Michigan Press, 1973. ISBN 0-472-06190-9. ‣ Classic study of natural philosophy, religion, and theology. Suggests uncertain belief in final harmony of Christianity and mechanism rooted in equating God's rationality with providence, natural law, and design. [RAH]

Science Policy Studies

4.309 Congressional Research Service, Library of Congress. *Expertise and democratic decisionmaking: a reader.* Washington, D.C.: United States Government Printing Office, 1987. (Committee Print, Background report no. 7, Committee on Science and Technology, U.S. House of Representatives, Ninety-Ninth Congress, Second session, December, 1986.) ‣ Readings on role of experts in democratic society ranging from political theory to contemporary perspectives on technocracy, roles of Congress and executive branch, influence of scientists, and science policy disputes. [DN]

4.310 David Dickson. *The new politics of science.* 1984 ed. Chicago: University of Chicago Press, 1988. ISBN 0-226-14763-0 (pbk). ‣ Analysis of science policy in context of relationships among industry, military, universities, and government. Suggests how perceptions of scientific applications shape science agendas, research results, and applications of knowledge. [DN]

4.311 Yaron Ezrahi. *The descent of Icarus: science and the transformation of contemporary democracy.* Cambridge, Mass.: Harvard University Press, 1990. ISBN 0-674-19828-X. ‣ Science as political resource used by governments to legitimate political authority. Suggests that ironically, this has led to sharp decline in status of science and its influence on state. [DN]

4.312 Sheila Jasanoff. *The fifth branch: science advisers as policymakers.* Cambridge, Mass.: Harvard University Press, 1990. ISBN 0-674-30061-0. ‣ Role of science advisers as fifth branch of government. Describes scientists' activities in Environmental Protection Agency and Food and Drug Administration, analyzing growing influence of scientific and technical information on public policy. [DN]

4.313 Dorothy Nelkin, ed. *Controversy: the politics of technical decisions.* 3d ed. Newbury Park, Calif.: Sage, 1992. ISBN 0-8039-4466-7 (cl), 0-8039-4467-5 (pbk). ‣ Twelve case studies illustrating political priorities, economic interests, moral sentiments, and social values underlying science and technology policy decisions. Introductory essay places science policy in broader social and political context. [DN]

4.314 Robert N. Proctor. *Value-free science? Purity and power in modern knowledge.* Cambridge, Mass.: Harvard University Press, 1991. ISBN 0-674-93170-X. ‣ How image of value neutrality has provided opportunity to influence science. Describes development of value neutrality claims as defensive reaction to increasing involvement of science in practical and political affairs. [DN]

4.315 Bruce L. R. Smith. *American science policy since World War II.* Washington, D.C.: Brookings Institution, 1990. ISBN 0-8157-7998-4 (cl), 0-8157-7997-6 (pbk). ‣ Description of how government support of science relates to technological advances. Assesses change from consensus to conflict in policy formulation as advocates of costly scientific projects compete for limited resources. [DN]

4.316 Vivien Weil and John W. Snapper, eds. *Owning scientific and technical information: value and ethical issues.* New Brunswick, N.J.: Rutgers University Press, 1989. ISBN 0-8135-1454-1 (cl), 0-8135-1455-X (pbk). ‣ Fifteen essays reviewing intellectual property issues associated with contemporary scientific and technological developments. Explores historical, legal, ethical, and economic dimensions. Raises practical and philosophical questions about property rights in science. [DN]

Gender and Science

4.317 Pnina Abir-Am and Dorinda Outram. *Uneasy careers and intimate lives: women in science, 1789–1979.* New Brunswick, N.J.: Rutgers University Press, 1987. ISBN 0-8135-1255-7 (cl), 0-8135-1256-5 (pbk). ▸ Essays examining how women scientists integrated work and private lives; particularly strong on women botanists. Introduction examines impact on women scientists of shift of science from domestic to professional work space. [PEM]

4.318 Sandra Harding. *The science question in feminism.* Ithaca, N.Y.: Cornell University Press, 1986. ISBN 0-8014-1880-1 (cl), 0-8014-9363-3 (pbk). ▸ Argues science shaped by values of society creating it. Not primarily historical study (although using historical case studies), but valuable for categorization of different approaches to feminist critique of science. [PEM]

4.319 G. Kass-Simon and Patricia Farnes, eds. *Women of science: righting the record.* Bloomington: Indiana University Press, 1990. ISBN 0-253-33264-8. ▸ Articles on women in archaeology, geology, astronomy, mathematics, engineering, physics, biology, medical science, chemistry, and crystallography. Somewhat uneven but good start for investigation of women in particular disciplines. [PEM]

4.320 Evelyn Fox Keller. *Reflections on gender and science.* New Haven: Yale University Press, 1985. ISBN 0-300-03291-9 (cl), 0-300-03636-1 (pbk). ▸ Study of how ideas about gender have shap–ed assumptions underlying science, using historical, psychoanalytic, and scientific analyses. Important introduction to feminist analysis of history of science. [PEM]

4.321 Carolyn Merchant. *The death of nature: women, ecology, and the scientific revolution.* 1980 ed. New York: Harper & Row, 1989. ISBN 0-06-250595-5 (pbk). ▸ How Scientific Revolution transformed Western view of nature: respect for mother earth gave way to exploitation (even rape) of nature. Argument sometimes carried too far, but evidence is striking. [PEM]

4.322 David F. Noble. *A world without women: the Christian clerical culture of Western science.* New York: Knopf, 1992. ISBN 0-394-55650-X. ▸ Controversial study of how science came to be male activity, emphasizing role of Catholic church. Focuses on Middle Ages but covers material from early Christian era to nineteenth century. [PEM]

4.323 Margaret W. Rossiter. *Women scientists in America: struggles and strategies to 1940.* Baltimore: Johns Hopkins University Press, 1982. ISBN 0-8018-2443-5 (cl), 0-8018-2509-1 (pbk). ▸ Study of education, employment, and achievements of women scientists in United States in nineteenth and twentieth centuries. Pathbreaking overview and analysis; best starting place for any exploration of women in science. [PEM]

4.324 Cynthia Eagle Russett. *Sexual science: the Victorian construction of womanhood.* Cambridge, Mass.: Harvard University Press, 1989. ISBN 0-674-80290-X. ▸ Examination of theories such as Darwinism and biogenetic law (embryonic development recapitulates evolution) in social control. Emphasizes power of science as weapon in argument about women's proper place. Good synthesis. [PEM]

4.325 Londa L. Schiebinger. "The history and philosophy of women in science: a review essay." *Signs* 12.2 (1987) 305–32. ISSN 0097-9740. ▸ Survey of historical and philosophical issues in women in science. Useful both for bibliography and for overview of different approaches. [PEM]

4.326 Londa L. Schiebinger. *The mind has no sex? Women in the*

origins of modern science. Cambridge, Mass.: Harvard University Press, 1989. ISBN 0-674-57623-3. ▸ Argues women significant in both craft and philosophical traditions of early modern science until new philosophical ideas devalued their capabilities. [PEM]

4.327 Deborah Warner. "Science education for women in antebellum America." *ISIS* 69 (1978) 58–67. ISSN 0021-1753. ▸ Survey of antebellum opportunities for women's scientific education in schools, popular lectures, museums, and printed materials. Describes participation by women as assistants to scientist husbands and as scientists in their own right. [PEM]

Science-Technology Museums, Fairs, and Expositions

4.328 Edward P. Alexander. *Museum masters: their museums and their influence.* Nashville, Tenn.: American Association for State and Local History, 1983. ISBN 0-910050-68-6. ▸ Profiles twelve museum leaders, including William Jackson Hooker of Kew Gardens, George B. Goode of Smithsonian, and Oscar von Miller of Deutsches Museum, founder of the modern science and technology museum. Includes bibliography. [APM]

4.329 John Allwood. *The great exhibitions.* London: Studio Vista, 1977. ISBN 0-289-70792-7. ▸ Handsomely illustrated tour guide to fairs and expositions since 1851. Portrays expositions as national "showoffs" and as bids for international status. [APM]

4.330 Burton Benedict. *The anthropology of world's fairs: San Francisco's Panama Pacific International Exposition of 1915.* London and Berkeley: Scolar and Lowie Museum of Anthropology, 1983. ISBN 0-85967-676-5 (cl), 0-85967-677-3 (pbk). ▸ San Francisco's fair in sociopolitical context of world's fair movement. Portrays world's fairs as rituals, compared to potlatches, and interprets industrial expositions as expressions of nationalism. [APM]

4.331 Carl W. Condit, Melvin Kranzberg, and Robert P. Multhauf, eds. *Museums of technology.* Chicago: University of Chicago Press, 1965. ISSN 0040-165X. ▸ Evolution of museums in Europe and America. Origins traced to international expositions. Special attention to Smithsonian's Museum of History and Technology. [APM]

4.332 Bernard S. Finn. "The museum of science and technology." In *The museum: a reference guide.* Michael Steven Shapiro, ed., pp. 59–83. New York: Greenwood, 1990. ISBN 0-313-23686-0. ▸ Recent changes in museums reflect changes in public perceptions of science and technology. Includes bibliography on European and American science technology museums. Also considers museums in India and other non-Western countries. [APM]

4.333 Paul Greenhalgh. *Ephemeral vistas: the expositions universelles, great exhibitions and world's fairs, 1851–1939.* Manchester: Manchester University Press; distributed by St. Martin's, 1988. ISBN 0-7190-2299-1. ▸ Discussion of fairs as expressions of nationalism and as justification for imperialism and racism. Funding of fairs highly political. Extensive bibliography. [APM]

4.334 Kenneth W. Luckhurst. *The story of exhibitions.* London: Studio, 1951. ▸ International expositions from 1851–1939 with focus on Great (Crystal Palace) Exposition. Fairs placed in rich context of early local industrial displays, trade fairs, and specialized exhibitions. Also available in microfilm from Berkeley: University of California Library Photographic Service, 1981. [APM]

4.335 Robert W. Rydell. *All the world's a fair: visions of empire at American international expositions, 1876–1916.* Chicago: University of Chicago Press, 1984. ISBN 0-226-73239-8. ▸ Analysis of twelve fairs; overt aim to teach public about science, but racism, white supremacy, and imperialism were underlying themes. [APM]

4.336 Brigitte Schroeder-Gudehus, ed. *Industrial society and its museums, 1890–1990: social aspirations and cultural politics.* Philadelphia: Harwood Academic, 1992. ISBN 3-7186-5301-X. ▸ Collection of essays exploring political, social, and corporate roots of industrial museums of twentieth century. Museums became core symbol of industrial corporate culture. [APM]

Science and Literature

4.337 Walter Gratzer, ed. *A literary companion to science.* 1989 ed. New York: Norton, 1990. ISBN 0-393-02836-4. ▸ Over two hundred excerpts of fiction, nonfiction, and poetry featuring scientific work and lives, science and society. Eclectic creative annotations. Predominantly "great men" of modern Europe, some Americans. Negligible attention to women. [PSG]

4.338 N. Katherine Hayles. *Chaos bound: orderly disorder in contemporary literature and science.* Ithaca, N.Y.: Cornell University Press, 1990. ISBN 0-8014-2262-0 (cl), 0-8014-9701-9 (pbk). ▸ Finely crafted postmodern analysis of literature, information theory, chaos science, and culture by president of Society for Literature and Science. Clearly written, powerfully argued, technically masterful. [PSG]

4.339 John Heath-Stubbs and Phillips Salman, eds. *Poems of science.* Harmondsworth: Penguin, 1984. ISBN 0-14-042317-6 (pbk). ▸ Anthology of British and American poetry featuring images, concepts, and commentary on "pure" science from Middle Ages to twentieth century. Organized chronologically, helpful introduction, and some brief annotations. No index. [PSG]

4.340 Greg Myers. *Writing biology: texts in the social construction of scientific knowledge.* Madison: University of Wisconsin Press, 1990. ISBN 0-299-12230-1 (cl), 0-299-12234-4 (pbk). ▸ State-of-art study of rhetoric of science and scientists in social context. Analyzes variety of professional and popular texts. Valuable guide to understanding scientific work and discourse. [PSG]

4.341 Marjorie Hope Nicolson. *Science and imagination.* 1956 ed. Hamden, Conn.: Archon, 1976. ISBN 0-208-01603-1. ▸ Classic study of astronomy and experimental science in literary imagery and themes. Shows new science of seventeenth century changed religion, society, thought, and expression. [PSG]

4.342 Stuart Peterfreund, ed. *Literature and science: theory and practice.* Boston: Northeastern University Press, 1990. ISBN 1-55553-058-3. ▸ Eight important scholars on positivism, patient-physician perceptions, metaphor, cosmology, relations of literary and scientific discourse, optics, and information theory. Sampling of methodologies current in Society for Literature and Science. [PSG]

4.343 Walter Schatzberg, Ronald A. Waite, and Jonathan K. Johnson, eds. *The relations of literature and science: an annotated bibliography of scholarship, 1880-1980.* New York: Modern Language Association of America, 1987. ISBN 0-87352-172-2 (cl), 0-87352-173-0 (pbk). ▸ Citations of studies of authors, topics, and surveys from antiquity to twentieth century; primarily Western literature, science, and pseudoscience. Some medicine and science fiction; omits social sciences, philosophy, and linguistics. [PSG]

HISTORY OF TECHNOLOGY

Reference Works

4.344 "Current bibliography in the history of technology." *Technology and culture* (1959–). ISSN 0040-165X. ▸ Annual list of publications in history of technology arranged chronologically, historiographically, and by technological area. [JKS]

4.345 Stephen H. Cutcliffe, Judith A. Mistichelli, and Christine M. Roysdon. *Technology and values in American civilization: a guide to information sources.* Detroit: Gale Research, 1980. ISBN 0-8103-1475-4. ▸ Extensive annotated bibliography including history of technology in America. [JKS]

4.346 Maurice Daumas, ed. *A history of technology and invention: progress through the ages.* 1969 ed. 3 vols. Eileen B. Hennessy, trans. London: Murray, 1980. ISBN 0-7195-3730-4 (v. 1), 0-7195-3731-2 (v. 2), 0-7195-3732-0 (v. 3). ▸ General survey from origins to 1860, also useful as reference. Two volumes on preindustrial technology. Sections in volume 1 on Asia, Islam, and pre-Columbian America. Best large survey-reference work to date. [JKS]

4.347 Eugene S. Ferguson. *Bibliography of the history of technology.* Cambridge, Mass.: Society for the History of Technology and MIT Press, 1968. (Society for the History of Technology, Monograph series, 5.) ▸ Bibliography of primary and secondary sources providing comprehensive introduction. Thoughtful and insightful annotations. [JKS]

General Studies

4.348 George Basalla. *The evolution of technology.* New York: Cambridge University Press, 1988. ISBN 0-521-22855-7 (cl), 0-521-29681-1 (pbk). ▸ Nonchronological, anthropological treatment of technological history. Uses evolutionary model to separate technological creativity from criteria of selection for widespread use. [JKS]

4.349 D.S.L. Cardwell. *Turning points in Western technology: a study of technology, science, and history.* 1972 ed. Canton, Mass.: Science History, 1991. ISBN 0-88135-069-9 (pbk). ▸ Technology from medieval clock to twentieth-century radio. Shows how technology became more scientific and how science was stimulated by new technology. Story of progress. [JKS]

4.350 T. K. Derry and Trevor I. Williams. *A short history of technology.* 1960 ed. New York: Oxford University Press, 1961. ▸ Survey of technology from earliest times to 1900. Based on Singer, et al., eds. 4.369. Most thorough survey treatment of subject. [JKS]

4.351 Friedrich Klemm. *A history of Western technology.* 1959 ed. Dorothea Waley Singer, trans. Ames: Iowa State University Press, 1991. ISBN 0-8138-0499-X. ▸ Overview of technology from Graeco-Roman antiquity to mid-twentieth century. Primary documents with connecting passages relating technology to culture. [JKS]

4.352 Melvin Kranzberg and Carroll W. Pursell, Jr., eds. *Technology in Western civilization.* 2 vols. New York: Oxford University Press, 1967. ISBN 0-19-500938-X (v. 1). ▸ Essays by prominent scholars covering entire history of technology, but emphasizing post-1750. Twentieth-century material devoted mainly to United States. [JKS]

4.353 Joel Mokyr. *The lever of riches: technological creativity and economic progress.* New York: Oxford University Press, 1990. ISBN 0-19-506113-6. ▸ Short survey from classical antiquity to 1914, followed by analytical chapters on China and Europe, classical and medieval technology, and Industrial Revolution. Economic historian investigates sources of technological innovativeness. [JKS]

4.354 Lewis Mumford. *Technics and civilization.* 1934 ed. San Diego: Harcourt Brace & World, 1963. ISBN 0-15-688254-X. ▸ Classic work inspired by machine age characterization of modern civilization. Traces evolution of mechanization from Middle Ages. Asserts that machine is expression of cultural values. [JKS]

4.355 Arnold Pacey. *The maze of ingenuity: ideas and idealism in the development of technology.* 2d ed. Cambridge, Mass.: MIT Press, 1992. ISBN 0-262-16128-1 (cl), 0-262-66075-X (pbk). ▸ Discussion of technology from eleventh-century cathedral builders to recent times. Selects specific topics to explore thesis that idealistic concerns stimulated technological creativity and promoted social uses of technology. [JKS]

4.356 Arnold Pacey. *Technology in world civilization: a thousand-*

year history. Cambridge, Mass.: MIT Press, 1990. ISBN 0-262-16117-6. ▸ Technology from 700 CE to present. Emphasizes cultural interactions as stimulus for technological creativity. Shows how various cultures, including China, India, and Africa, responded to new techniques. [JKS]

4.357 Gene I. Rochlin, ed. *Scientific technology and social change: readings from "Scientific American."* San Francisco: Freeman, 1974. ISBN 0-7167-0501-X (cl), 0-7167-0500-1 (pbk). ▸ Collection of previously published articles. Not comprehensive but includes excellent contributions. Energy and power generation receive considerable attention. [JKS]

Historiography

4.358 Stephen H. Cutcliffe and Robert C. Post, eds. *In context: history and the history of technology: essays in honor of Melvin Kranzberg.* Bethlehem, Pa.: Lehigh University Press, 1989. ISBN 0-934223-03-3. ▸ Fourteen essays arguing technology must be understood in sociocultural context. Relevant contextual factors include politics, gender, philosophy, and linguistic conventions. [APM]

4.359 Brooke Hindle. *Technology in early America: needs and opportunities for study with a directory of artifact collections by Lucius F. Ellsworth.* Chapel Hill: University of North Carolina Press for Institute of Early American History and Culture, 1966. ▸ Bibliography of American technology before 1850. Argues for crucial role of technology in American history. Asserts "technological enthusiasm" as reason for American dominance in invention. Surveys technological artifact collections in United States. [APM]

4.360 Joan Rothschild, ed. *Machina ex dea: feminist perspectives on technology.* New York: Pergamon, 1983. ISBN 0-08-029404-9 (cl), 0-08-029403-0 (pbk). ▸ Twelve essays on history of technology and feminism. Denies technology is exclusively male domain. Portrays technology as oppressor, yet also possible liberator, of women. [APM]

4.361 John M. Staudenmaier. *Technology's storytellers: reweaving the human fabric.* Cambridge, Mass.: Society for the History of Technology and MIT Press, 1985. ISBN 0-262-19237-3. ▸ Analysis of three decades of articles in journal *Technology and Culture* as indicator of broad trends in historiography of technology. Calls for even more emphasis on sociopolitical context. Includes bibliography. [APM]

Ancient Near East

4.362 R. J. Forbes. *Man, the maker: a history of technology and engineering.* 1950 ed. London: Constable, 1958. ▸ Popularized, serviceable introduction to history of technology and engineering from prehistoric to modern times. [WRK]

4.363 R. J. Forbes. *Studies in ancient technology.* 2d rev. ed. 9 vols. Leiden: Brill, 1964–72. ▸ Detailed studies of ancient and classical technologies—petroleum, alchemy, water supply (volume 1); irrigation, power, land transport (volume 2); cosmetics, food, salts, paints (volume 3); fabrics, washing, dyes, spinning, weaving (volume 4); leather, sugar, glass (volume 5); heating, refrigeration, light (volume 6); geology, mining (volume 7); metallurgy, tools, (volumes 8, 9). [WRK]

4.364 James Hornell. *Water transport: origins and early evolution.* 1946 ed. Newton Abbott, England: David & Charles, 1970. ISBN 0-7153-4860-4. ▸ Primarily anthropological summary of skin and wood craft, mostly in prehistoric and traditional cultures, with some discussion of ancient Egypt and Near East. Amply referenced. [WRK]

4.365 Alfred Lucas. *Ancient Egyptian materials and industries.* 1962 4th rev. ed. J. R. Harris, ed. London: Histories & Mysteries of Man, 1989. ISBN 1-85417-046-5. ▸ Comprehensive survey of Egyptian technical methods with full reference to extant specimens and secondary accounts. Seventeen chapters, alphabetically arranged from adhesives to wood. [WRK]

4.366 P. R. S. Moorey. *Materials and manufacture in ancient Mesopotamia: the evidence of archaeology and art: metals and metalwork, glazed materials, and glass.* Oxford: British Archaeological Reports, 1985. (British Archaeological Reports international series, 237.) ISBN 0-86054-306-4 (pbk). ▸ Comprehensive survey of archaeological evidence with extensive bibliographies. [WRK]

4.367 A. Neuberger. *Technical arts and sciences of the ancients.* 1930 ed. Henry L. Brose, trans. New York: Barnes & Noble, 1969. ▸ Substantial one-volume survey similar in scope to Forbes 4.363. [WRK]

4.368 S. A. Semenov. *Prehistoric technology: an experimental study of the oldest tools and artefacts from traces of manufacture and wear.* 1964 ed. Totowa, N.J.: Barnes & Noble, 1985. ISBN 0-389-20571-0. ▸ Descriptive and experimental studies of bone and stone tools from Palaeolithic and Neolithic periods. [WRK]

4.369 Charles Joseph Singer et al., eds. *A history of technology.* 8 vols. New York: Oxford University Press, 1954–84. ISBN 0-19-858155-6 (v. 6), 0-19-858151-3 (v. 7). 0-19-822905-4 (v. 8). ▸ Comprehensive surveys of prehistoric (volume 1) and ancient Mediterranean (volume 2) technologies. Accounts of ancient time measurement and precision technology included in volume 3. Standard reference work, but now considerably out of date. [WRK/JML]

Ancient Greece and Rome

4.370 Lionel Casson. *The ancient mariners: seafarers and sea fighters of the Mediterranean in ancient times.* 2d ed. Princeton: Princeton University Press, 1991. ISBN 0-691-06836-4 (cl), 0-691-01477-9 (pbk). ▸ Ancient naval history, combining political, military, commercial, and technological analysis. [WRK]

4.371 Raymond Chevallier. *Roman roads.* N. H. Field, trans. Berkeley: University of California Press, 1976. ISBN 0-520-02834-1. ▸ Based on evidence from literature and archaeology, traces function of roads in Rome and Roman society. Relatively limited treatment of construction but superb bibliography. [BES]

4.372 J. J. Coulton. *Ancient Greek architects at work: problems of structure and design.* 1977 ed. Ithaca, N.Y.: Cornell University Press, 1988. ISBN 0-8014-1077-0 (cl, 1977), 0-8014-9234-3 (pbk). ▸ Analysis of early Greek architecture, combining historical perspectives on technology and art. [WRK]

4.373 O.A.W. Dilke. *The Roman land surveyors: an introduction to the agrimensores.* New York: Barnes & Noble, 1971. ISBN 0-389-04165-3. ▸ Describes the activities and technical methods of ancient Roman engineers (*agrimensores*). [WRK]

4.374 A. G. Drachmann. *The mechanical technology of Greek and Roman antiquity: a study of literary sources.* Madison: University of Wisconsin Press, 1963. (Acta historica scientiarum naturalium et medicinalium, 17.) ▸ Critical study of principal Greek and Roman treatises on machine design. [WRK]

4.375 John G. Landels. *Engineering in the ancient world.* 1978 ed. Berkeley: University of California Press, 1981. ISBN 0-520-04127-5 (pbk). ▸ Popularized, well-informed account of power, machine, and transport technologies in ancient Greece and Rome. [WRK]

4.376 John Peter Oleson. *Bronze Age, Greek, and Roman technology: a selected, annotated bibliography.* New York: Garland, 1986. ISBN 0-8240-8677-5. ▸ Excellent initial reference source for history of ancient technology. [RKD]

4.377 John Peter Oleson. *Greek and Roman mechanical water-lifting devices: the history of a technology.* Toronto: University of

Toronto Press, 1984. ISBN 0-8020-5597-4. ‣ Comprehensive survey of extant artifacts and ancient literary accounts of water-power technology. [WRK]

4.378 K. D. White. *Greek and Roman technology.* Ithaca, N.Y.: Cornell University Press, 1984. ISBN 0-8014-1439-3. ‣ Brief survey describing entire range of classical technology, including power technologies, agriculture, building, mining, and transport. Ample citation of other secondary works. [WRK]

Medieval Technology

4.379 Ahmad Y. Al-Hassan and Donald R. Hill. *Islamic technology: an illustrated history.* 1986 ed. Cambridge: Cambridge University Press, 1992. ISBN 0-521-26333-6 (cl, 1986), 0-521-42239-6 (pbk). ‣ Textbook, produced under United Nations auspices, to introduce Western readers to history of Middle Eastern and Islamic technology and engineering. Provides Western-language references wherever possible. [BSH]

4.380 Brian Cotterell and Johan Kamminga. *The mechanics of pre-industrial technology: an introduction to the mechanics of ancient and traditional material culture.* Cambridge: Cambridge University Press, 1990. ISBN 0-521-34194-9. ‣ Clear expositions of ancient and medieval mechanisms, including bows and arrows, crossbows, water mills, transportation, and ships. [BSH]

4.381 Jean Gimpel. *The medieval machine: the Industrial Revolution of the Middle Ages.* 2d ed. Aldershot, England: Wildwood House, 1988. ISBN 0-7045-3098-8. ‣ Overview of technological developments in European Middle Ages. Asserts foundations of modern Western, technologically oriented society lie in Middle Ages rather than Renaissance or English Industrial Revolution. [RKD]

4.382 Donald Hill. *A history of engineering in classical and medieval times.* London: Croom Helm, 1984. ISBN 0-7099-1209-9. ‣ Very perceptive, balanced textbook with excellent references. "Engineering" in title means technology. Only work of its type to give adequate attention to Islamic world. [BSH]

4.383 Albert C. Leighton. *Transport and communication in early medieval Europe, A.D. 500–1100.* New York: Barnes & Noble, 1972. ISBN 0-389-04613-2. ‣ Study of land and water transport in Europe. Finds little continuity with Roman transportation systems. Focuses on vehicles. [BES]

4.384 Robert Mark. *Experiments in Gothic structure.* Cambridge, Mass.: MIT Press, 1982. ISBN 0-262-13170-6 (cl), 0-262-63095-8 (pbk). ‣ Explanation of structural mechanics of Gothic architecture through experimental and mathematical modeling techniques. Reinforces Viollet-le-Duc's theory of structural rationality in Gothic buildings. [BSH]

4.385 George Ovitt, Jr. *The restoration of perfection: labor and technology in medieval culture.* New Brunswick, N.J.: Rutgers University Press, 1987. ISBN 0-8135-1235-2. ‣ Explores changing meanings of work within developing religious framework of medieval thought. Controversial thesis concerning role of women in work. [BSH]

4.386 Theophilus Presbyter. *On divers arts: the foremost medieval treatise on painting, glassmaking, and metalwork.* 1963 ed. Cyril Stanley Smith and John Hawthorne, eds. and trans. New York: Dover, 1979. ISBN 0-486-23784-2. ‣ Theophilus, twelfth-century German Benedictine monk, produced treatise on decorative arts. English translation provides penetrating comprehensive body of explanatory notes; original Latin text not included. [BSH]

4.387 Lynn T. White, Jr. "The historical roots of our ecologic crisis." *Science* 155 (1967) 1203–07. ISSN 0036-8075. ‣ Trenchant, provocative assertion of Western Christianity's ethical role in exploiting and degrading nature. Frequently reprinted and object of many attempted rebuttals, remains powerful if one-sided indictment. [BSH]

4.388 Lynn T. White, Jr. *Medieval technology and social change.* 1962 ed. London: Oxford University Press, 1980. ISBN 0-19-500266-0 (pbk). ‣ Perhaps best read for its narrative rather than its controversial theses. Pioneering work of 1960s remains fundamental introduction with extensive references. [BSH]

4.389 Elspeth Whitney. *Paradise restored: the mechanical arts from antiquity through the thirteenth century.* Philadelphia: American Philosophical Society, 1990. (Transactions of the American Philosophical Society, 80.1.) ISBN 0-87169-801-3, ISSN 0065-9746. ‣ Traces meaning of *artes mechanicae* from late ancient philosophy through high scholasticism, arguing for close relationship between views of technology and technology's social role. [BSH]

SEE ALSO
20.1312 Lynn White, Jr. *Medieval religion and technology.*

Early Modern Technology

4.390 Vannoccio Biringuccio. *The "Pirotechnia" of Vannoccio Biringuccio: the classic sixteenth-century treatise on metals and metallurgy.* 1959 ed. Cyril Stanley Smith and Martha Teach Gnudi, eds. and trans. New York: Dover, 1990. ISBN 0-486-26134-4. ‣ Practical treatise (first published 1540) accompanied by Smith's unrivaled explanatory notes. Describes all crafts that depended on fire, especially metalworking in both fine metals and iron. [BSH]

4.391 William Eamon. "Technology as magic in the late Middle Ages and Renaissance." *Janus* 70 (1983) 171–212. ISSN 0021-4264. ‣ Attempts to distinguish between magic, science, and technology in terms appropriate to late medieval and Renaissance culture. Fundamental for understanding differences between premodern and modern views of technology. [BSH]

4.392 Bertrand Gille. *Engineers of the Renaissance.* Cambridge, Mass.: MIT Press, 1966. ‣ Leonardo da Vinci in context of Renaissance artist-engineers and writers of technological treatises. Excellent manuscript bibliography. [BSH]

4.393 Daryl Hafter. "Artisans, drudges, and the problem of gender in pre-industrial France." In *Science and technology in medieval society.* Pamela O. Long, ed., pp. 71–87. New York: New York Academy of Science, 1985. (Annals of the New York Academy of Science, 441.) ISBN 0-89766-276-8, ISSN 0077-8923. ‣ Concentrates on women in textile industries mainly from fifteenth to eighteenth century. Shows how women were displaced from positions of power and influence during shift toward capital-and technology-intensive modes of production. [BSH]

4.394 Alexander Keller. "Mathematics, mechanics, and the origins of the culture of mechanical inventions." *Minerva* 23 (1985) 348–61. ISSN 0026-4695. ‣ Explores relationship between science, mathematics, and mechanical invention. Concludes mechanical invention not engendered by science or mathematics but arose within its own recognizable culture. [BSH]

4.395 Martin Kemp. *Leonardo da Vinci: artist, scientist, inventor.* New Haven: Yale University Press with South Bank Centre, 1989. ISBN 0-300-04508-5 (cl), 0-300-04509-3 (pbk), 0-300-04563-8 (pbk). ‣ Biography of Leonardo unique in its perceptive attention to his technological investigations. Exceptional also for lack of romanticism for its subject. [BSH]

4.396 Agostino Ramelli. *"The Various and Ingenious Machines" of Agostino Ramelli: a classic sixteenth-century treatise on technology.* 1976 ed. Eugene S. Ferguson and Martha Teach Gnudi, eds. and trans. New York: Dover, 1987. ISBN 0-486-25497-6 (pbk). ‣ English translation of treatise on machinery. Modern notes and explanations provide excellent, wide-ranging introduction to premodern mechanical technology. [BSH]

4.397 Terry S. Reynolds. *Stronger than a hundred men: a history of the vertical water wheel*. Baltimore: Johns Hopkins University Press, 1983. ISBN 0-8018-2554-7. ‣ Fundamental study of prime mover before steam. Explores engineering and scientific interest in water wheels also. Study not confined to early modern period. Excellent references. [BSH]

4.398 John R. T. Schubert. *A history of the British iron and steel industry from c. 450 B.C. to A.D. 1775*. London: Routledge & Kegan Paul, 1957. ‣ Despite age, still fundamental study of early iron production. Noteworthy for clear technical explanations. [BSH]

4.399 Charles Joseph Singer et al., eds. *From the Renaissance to the Industrial Revolution, 1500–1750*. Vol. 3 of *A history of technology*. Oxford: Clarendon, 1957. ISBN 0-19-858107-6. ‣ Venerable encyclopedia of technological history, essential for beginners. Not all volumes have aged as well as this one. Views and bibliographies are necessarily outdated, but essential facts are well presented. [BSH]

SEE ALSO
22.172 Elizabeth L. Eisenstein. *The printing press as an agent of change.*
29.82 David C. Goodman. *Power and penury.*

Modern Technology

4.400 Hugh G. J. Aitken. *Scientific management in action: Taylorism at Watertown Arsenal, 1908–1915*. 1960 ed. Princeton: Princeton University Press, 1985. ISBN 0-691-04241-1 (cl), 0-691-00375-0 (pbk). ‣ Careful analysis of unsuccessful attempt to install Taylor system of scientific management in Watertown Arsenal. Emphasis on social and institutional dynamics that defeated Taylor. [JKS]

4.401 Kendall E. Bailes. *Technology and society under Lenin and Stalin: origins of the Soviet technical intelligensia, 1917–1941*. Princeton: Princeton University Press, 1978. ISBN 0-691-05265-4 (cl), 0-691-10063-2 (pbk). ‣ Focuses on precarious position of former tsarist engineering elite after Russian Revolution. Analysis of interplay of technocratic and communistic ideologies among Soviet engineers. [JKS]

4.402 Daniel Joseph Boorstin. *The Americans: the democratic experience*. Vol. 3 of *The Americans*. 1973 ed. New York: Vintage, 1974. ISBN 0-394-71011-8. ‣ Thematic approach to modern American history. Explores how American democratic society and ideals have shaped technology in nineteenth and twentieth centuries. [JKS]

4.403 Alfred D. Chandler, Jr. *Scale and scope: the dynamics of industrial capitalism*. Cambridge, Mass.: Harvard University Press, 1990. ISBN 0-674-78994-6. ‣ Comparative study of evolution of modern industrial enterprise in United States, Great Britain, and Germany. Develops general model for dynamics of industry structure. Argues social, cultural, and political factors explain national differences. [JKS]

4.404 Alfred D. Chandler, Jr. *The visible hand: the managerial revolution in American business*. Cambridge, Mass.: Belknap, 1977. ISBN 0-674-94051-2 (cl), 0-674-94052-0 (pbk). ‣ Study of rise of big business between 1880 and 1920. New technologies, especially railroads, central to development of modern big business enterprise. Links history of technology and business. [JKS]

4.405 Eugene S. Ferguson. "The American-ness of American technology." *Technology and culture* 20.1 (1979) 3–24. ISSN 0040-165X. ‣ Early American technological precociousness emanated from enthusiasm for technology, risk-taking entrepreneurs, and egalitarian ideals. [JKS]

4.406 Siegfried Giedion. *Mechanization takes command: a contribution to anonymous history*. 1948 ed. New York: Norton, 1969.

ISBN 0-393-00489-9. ‣ Pioneering analysis of mechanization and its effects since 1800. Asserts contributions of anonymous mechanics, inventors, and artisans just as significant in modern civilization as activities of famous politicians, generals, industrialists, etc. [JKS]

4.407 Brooke Hindle and Steven Lubar. *Engines of change: the American Industrial Revolution, 1790–1860*. Washington, D.C.: Smithsonian Institution Press, 1986. ISBN 0-87474-540-3 (cl), 0-87474-539-X (pbk). ‣ Textbook-type survey of transformation of United States from agrarian to industrial nation between Revolutionary and Civil wars. Good summary of recent work. [JKS]

4.408 David A. Hounshell. *From the American system to mass production, 1800–1932: the development of manufacturing technology in the United States*. Baltimore: Johns Hopkins University Press, 1984. ISBN 0-8018-2975-5 (cl), 0-8018-3158-X (pbk). ‣ Origins and evolution of mass production technology in United States. Includes firearms, sewing machines, reapers, bicycles, and automobiles. Final chapter assesses responses to mass production in the 1920s and 1930s. [JKS]

4.409 Thomas P. Hughes. *American genesis: a century of invention and technological enthusiasm, 1870–1970*. 1989 ed. New York: Penguin, 1990. ISBN 0-14-009741-4 (pbk). ‣ Technological systems-building central to modern American history. Focuses on contributions by independent inventors and impact of technological systems on culture and society. Discusses Soviet Union and Germany in 1920s and 1930s. [JKS]

4.410 Reese V. Jenkins. *Images and enterprise: technology and the American photographic industry, 1839 to 1925*. Baltimore: Johns Hopkins University Press, 1975. ISBN 0-8018-3549-6. ‣ Relationship between technology, science, business strategy, and market structure in photographic industry. Includes George Eastman's creation of amateur photography business. [JKS]

4.411 John F. Kasson. *Civilizing the machine: technology and republican values in America, 1776–1900*. 1976 ed. New York: Penguin, 1977. ISBN 0-14-004415-9. ‣ Explores relationship between republican values and development of industrial technology. Five essays on political, intellectual, and aesthetic responses to technology. [JKS]

4.412 David S. Landes. *The unbound Prometheus: technological change and industrial development in western Europe from 1750 to the present*. New York: Cambridge University Press, 1969. ISBN 0-521-07200-X (cl), 0-521-09418-6 (pbk). ‣ Comparative histories of industrialization of Western European countries. Concludes Industrial Revolution initiated era of self-sustaining technological change, and economic growth resulted from accomodation to technological change. [JKS]

4.413 Edwin T. Layton. "Mirror-image twins: the communities of science and technology in nineteenth-century America." *Technology and culture* 12.3 (1971) 562–580. ISSN 0040-165X. ‣ Engineers adopted scientific method but remained separate community from science with different goals and value system. [JKS]

4.414 Alan I. Marcus and Howard P. Segal. *Technology in America: a brief history*. San Diego: Harcourt Brace Jovanovich, 1989. ISBN 0-15-589762-4. ‣ Short history characterizing technological developments as part of larger cultural phenomena. Bibliography follows each chapter. [JKS]

4.415 Judith A. McGaw. *Most wonderful machine: mechanization and social change in Berkshire paper making, 1801–1885*. Princeton: Princeton University Press, 1987. ISBN 0-691-04740-5. ‣ Important work in social history of United States technology asserting that new machines in papermaking did not create new social order in Berkshires. Skillfully interweaves social, business, women's, and technical history. [JKS]

4.416 A. E. Musson and Eric Robinson. *Science and technology* *in the Industrial Revolution.* Toronto: University of Toronto Press, 1969. ISBN 0-8020-1637-5. ‣ Asserts scientific tradition (in concert with craft tradition) influenced Industrial Revolution more profoundly than previously believed. Emphasizes chemical and engineering activities in Great Britain. [RKD]

4.417 Daniel Nelson. *Managers and workers: origins of the new factory system in the United States, 1880–1920.* 1975 ed. Madison: University of Wisconsin Press, 1979. ISBN 0-299-06900-1 (cl, 1975), 0-299-06904-4 (pbk). ‣ Study of transformation of factory by technological innovation and managerial control. Shows key role of scientific management in process. [JKS]

4.418 David F. Noble. *America by design: science, technology, and the rise of corporate capitalism.* 1977 ed. Oxford: Oxford University Press, 1979. ISBN 0-19-502618-7 (pbk). ‣ Corporate capitalism between 1880 and 1920 harnessed historically progressive forces of science and technology to serve corporate needs. Focuses on engineers in engineering societies, academia, and industry. [JKS]

4.419 Carroll W. Pursell, Jr., ed. *Technology in America: a history of individuals and ideas.* 2d ed. Cambridge, Mass.: MIT Press, 1990. ISBN 0-262-66067-9 (cl), 0-262-66049-0 (pbk). ‣ Short biographies of prominent figures in history of American technology. Textbook-level treatment. [JKS]

4.420 Nathan Rosenberg. *Technology and American economic growth.* Armonk, N.Y., and New York: Sharpe and Harper & Row, 1972. ISBN 0-06-131606-7 (cl), 0-87332-104-9 (pbk). ‣ Explores relationship between technological change and long-term growth of economy. Perceptive book by economic historian who understands technology. [JKS]

4.421 Philip Scranton. *Proprietary capitalism: the textile manufacture at Philadelphia, 1800–1885.* Philadelphia: Temple University Press, 1983. ISBN 0-87722-461-7 (pbk). ‣ Analysis of industrial network of firms favoring diversity over standardization and skill over mechanization. Flexible-type production quickly adaptable to changing market conditions and consumer tastes. New social history methodology. [JKS]

4.422 Bruce Sinclair. *Philadelphia's philosopher mechanics: a history of the Franklin Institute, 1824–1865.* Baltimore: Johns Hopkins University Press, 1974. ISBN 0-8018-1636-X. ‣ Evolution of early American technological institution from emphasis on disseminating knowledge to artisans to more specialized and professionalized research institute. [JKS]

4.423 Merritt Roe Smith. *Harpers Ferry armory and the new technology: the challenge of change.* 1977 ed. Ithaca, N.Y.: Cornell University Press, 1980. ISBN 0-8014-0984-5 (cl, 1977), 0-8014-9181-9 (pbk). ‣ Classic study of social dimensions of technological change. Antebellum efforts by military to mechanize gun manufacture and produce firearms with interchangeable parts. Armory at Harpers Ferry rejected new technology because it threatened community structure and values. [JKS]

4.424 Anthony F. C. Wallace. *Rockdale: the growth of an American village in the early Industrial Revolution.* 1978 ed. New York: Norton, 1980. ISBN 0-393-09991-2 (pbk). ‣ Study of Industrial Revolution as experienced by complex of textile manufacturers near Philadelphia, 1825–65. Community study encompassing business, technology, society, and religion. [JKS]

4.425 Trevor I. Williams. *A short history of twentieth-century technology, c. 1900–c. 1950.* New York: Oxford University Press, 1982. ISBN 0-19-858159-9. ‣ Topically organized survey of history of twentieth-century technology. Provides European perspective and gives considerable attention to European developments. [JKS]

4.426 Langdon Winner. *The whale and the reactor: a search for limits in an age of high technology.* Chicago: University of Chicago Press, 1986. ISBN 0-226-90210-2. ‣ Essays on relationship between modern technology and politics and on recent technological issues such as appropriate technology and environment. [JKS]

4.427 George Wise. "A new role for professional scientists: industrial research at General Electric, 1900–1916." *Technology and culture* 21.3 (1980) 408–29. ISSN 0040-165X. ‣ Assertion that industrial researchers are not academics-in-exile. They pursue different type of research with talents different from, not inferior to, those of academic researchers. [JKS]

4.428 Robert S. Woodbury. *Studies in the history of machine tools.* Cambridge, Mass.: MIT Press, 1972. ISBN 0-262-73033-2 (pbk). ‣ Development of four seminal machine tools: gear cutting machine, grinding machine, milling machine, and lathe. Argues machine tool industry fundamental to developments in textile, automobile, and firearms manufacture—indeed triggered Industrial Revolution. [PEC]

SEE ALSO
44.187 David F. Noble. *Forces of production.*
44.652 Walter A. McDougall. *... the heavens and the earth.*
47.215 Daniel R. Headrick. *The tools of empire.*

Agriculture

4.429 Oscar E. Anderson, Jr. *Refrigeration in America: a history of a new technology and its impact.* 1953 ed. Port Washington, N.Y.: Kennikat, 1972. ISBN 0-8046-1621-3. ‣ Development of mechanical refrigeration, refrigeration cars, and frozen foods. [AIM]

4.430 Edward H. Beardsley. *Harry L. Russell and agricultural science in Wisconsin.* Madison: University of Wisconsin Press, 1969. ISBN 0-299-05470-5. ‣ Evolution of leading U.S. institution of agricultural science at University of Wisconsin in late nineteenth century. [AIM]

4.431 Francesca Bray. *Science and civilisation in China.* Vol. 6.2: *Biology and biological technology: agriculture.* London: Cambridge University Press, 1984. ISBN 0-521-25076-5. ‣ Discussion of cropping systems in premodern China, analyzing agricultural implements and dry farming. [AIM]

4.432 David B. Danbom. *The resisted revolution: urban America and the industrialization of agriculture.* Ames: Iowa State University Press, 1979. ISBN 0-8138-0945-2. ‣ Rise of social science engineering that redirected American agriculture to serve urban needs. [AIM]

4.433 Penelope Francks. *Technology and agricultural development in pre-war Japan.* 1983 ed. New Haven: Yale University Press, 1984. ISBN 0-300-02927-6. ‣ Analysis of how economic necessity forced Japan to adopt industrial agriculture. [AIM]

4.434 G. E. Fussell. *The classical tradition in West European farming.* Rutherford, N.J.: Fairleigh Dickinson University Press, 1972. ISBN 0-8386-1090-0. ‣ Survey of agricultural practice in Western Europe from ancient Greece to 1820. Demonstrates continued reverence for Greco-Roman texts into nineteenth century. [AIM]

4.435 G. E. Fussell. *Crop nutrition: science and practice before Liebig.* Lawrence, Kan.: Coronado, 1971. ISBN 0-87291-026-1. ‣ Description of ideas of crop rotation prior to mid-nineteenth century. [AIM]

4.436 Nicholas Goddard. *Harvests of change: the Royal Agricultural Society of England, 1838–1988.* London: Quiller, 1988. ISBN 0-907621-96-1. ‣ Description of Society's leading role in modernizing British agricultural practice. [AIM]

4.437 John Alfred Heitmann. *The modernization of the Louisiana sugar industry, 1830–1910.* Baton Rouge: Louisiana State University Press, 1987. ISBN 0-8071-1324-7. ‣ Study of industry's increasing reliance on new technologies to compete in international markets. Describes impact of those changes on local scientific and technological institutions. [AIM]

4.438 Kenneth Hudson. *Patriotism with profit: British agricultural societies in the eighteenth and nineteenth centuries.* London: Evelyn, 1972. ISBN 0-238-78982-1. ▸ Analysis of how profit motive and patriotism spurred agricultural society formation and spread technological innovations through British agricultural sector. [AIM]

4.439 R. Douglas Hurt. *Agricultural technology in the twentieth century.* Manhattan, Kan.: Sunflower University Press, 1991. ISBN 0-89745-146-5. ▸ Description of types of implements used in twentieth-century American agriculture. [AIM]

4.440 R. Douglas Hurt. *American farm tools: from hand-power to steam-power.* Manhattan, Kan.: Sunflower University Press, 1982. ISBN 0-89745-027-2 (cl), 0-89745-026-4 (pbk). ▸ Convenient survey of agricultural implements in America to about 1900. [AIM]

4.441 John Langdon. *Horses, oxen, and technological innovation: the use of draught animals in English farming from 1066 to 1500.* New York: Cambridge University Press, 1986. ISBN 0-521-26772-2. ▸ Discussion of how shift from oxen to horses as beasts of burden was accompanied by corresponding adoption of new agricultural technologies and implements. [AIM]

4.442 Alan I. Marcus. *Agricultural science and the quest for legitimacy: farmers, agricultural colleges, and experiment stations, 1870–1890.* Ames: Iowa State University Press, 1985. ISBN 0-8138-0083-8. ▸ Creation of agricultural experiment stations and history of agricultural experimentation in United States. Describes rise of professional class of agricultural researchers and teachers. [AIM]

4.443 F.W.J. McCosh. *Boussingault, chemist and agriculturist.* Dordrecht: Reidel; distributed by Kluwer, 1984. ISBN 90-277-1682-X. ▸ Life, work, and disputes of foremost mid-nineteenth-century French agricultural scientist. [AIM]

4.444 J. Sanford Rikoon. *Threshing in the midwest, 1820–1940: a study of traditional culture and technological change.* Bloomington: Indiana University Press, 1988. ISBN 0-253-36047-1. ▸ Discussion of social aspects of threshing prior to adoption of combine. [AIM]

4.445 Jimmy M. Skaggs. *Prime cut: livestock raising and meatpacking in the United States, 1607–1983.* College Station: Texas A&M University Press, 1986. ISBN 0-89096-249-9. ▸ Account of major events in American meatpacking and cattle raising. Contains extensive bibliography. [AIM]

4.446 K. D. White. *Farm equipment of the Roman world.* Cambridge: Cambridge University Press, 1975. ISBN 0-521-20333-3. ▸ Description of farm implements and structures in ancient Rome. [AIM]

4.447 Robert C. Williams. *Fordson, Farmall, and Poppin' Johnny: a history of the farm tractor and its impact on America.* Urbana: University of Illinois Press, 1987. ISBN 0-252-01328-X. ▸ Study of internal combustion engine-driven tractor. Describes changes in American farm life that accompanied changes in technology. [AIM]

4.448 Richard A. Wines. *Fertilizer in America: from waste recycling to resource exploitation.* Philadelphia: Temple University Press, 1985. ISBN 0-87722-374-2. ▸ Description of shift to commercial fertilizers in nineteenth- and twentieth-century United States. [AIM]

SEE ALSO

17.355 Andrew M. Watson. *Agricultural innovation in the early Islamic world.*

Time

4.449 Carlo M. Cipolla. *Clocks and culture, 1300–1700.* 1965 ed. New York: Norton, 1978. ISBN 0-393-00866-5. ▸ Discussion of clocks' integration into European culture and status in China and Japan, seeking cultural explanations for different meanings of time. [BSH]

4.450 David S. Landes. *Revolution in time: clocks and the making of the modern world.* Cambridge, Mass: Belknap, 1984. ISBN 0-674-76800-0. ▸ Uniquely comprehensive, yet readable, treatment of clocks and watches from Middle Ages to present. Especially good on Swiss watch industry's rise and decline as digital watches grew. Splendid bibliography in footnotes. [BSH]

4.451 H. Alan Lloyd. *Some outstanding clocks over seven hundred years.* 1958 ed. Woodbridge, England: Antique Collectors' Club, 1981. ISBN 0-907462-04-9. ▸ Detailed descriptions of selected examples of clockwork mechanisms from fourteenth to twentieth century. Not for beginner. [BSH]

4.452 Samuel L. Macey. *Clocks and the cosmos: time in Western life and thought.* Hamden, Conn.: Archon, 1980. ISBN 0-208-01773-9. ▸ Less about clocks as mechanisms than their changing cultural meaning. Especially strong on time in literary texts from Renaissance to seventeenth century. [BSH]

4.453 Joseph Needham et al. *Heavenly clockwork: the great astronomical clocks of medieval China.* 2d ed. Cambridge: Cambridge University Press, 1986. (Antiquarian Horological Society monographs, 1.) ISBN 0-521-32276-6. ▸ Pioneering study dealing with mechanical astronomical "clock" erected in eleventh-century Beijing. Advances alternative theory on origin of clockwork to that found in Landes 4.450. Excellent references. [BSH]

Mining and Metallurgy

4.454 J. C. Carr and W. Taplin. *History of the British steel industry.* Cambridge, Mass.: Harvard University Press, 1962. ▸ Thorough treatment of British steel industry from Sir Henry Bessemer's steel manufacturing process to 1939 with emphasis on twentieth century. Epilogue covers 1940–60. Treats technological changes within context of general developmental patterns within industry. [BES]

4.455 William T. Hogan, S.J. *Economic history of the iron and steel industry in the United States.* 5 vols. Lexington, Mass.: Heath, 1971. ISBN 0-669-59964-6. ▸ Standard starting point for understanding all aspects of American iron and steel industry by scholar who has devoted his life to its study. Several later volumes continue this work. [BES]

4.456 Larry Lankton. *Cradle to grave: life, work, and death at the Lake Superior copper mines.* New York: Oxford University Press, 1991. ISBN 0-19-506263-9. ▸ Examination of interaction of technology, labor, and business in Lake Superior copper industry from 1840s to 1970s. Emphasizes transition from hand to mechanized procedures, safety issues, and corporate paternalism. [BES]

4.457 Peter M. Molloy, ed. *The history of metal mining and metallurgy: an annotated bibliography.* New York: Garland, 1986. ISBN 0-8240-9065-9. ▸ Provides wonderful entrance into this field. Thorough coverage, including international, with satisfactory annotations. [BES]

4.458 Joseph Needham. *The development of iron and steel technology in China.* 1958 ed. Cambridge: Heffer for Newcomen Society, 1964. ▸ Brief examination of iron and steel in China by leading scholar on technology in China. [BES]

4.459 John Ulric Nef. *The rise of the British coal industry.* 1932 ed. 2 vols. Freeport, N.Y.: Books for Libraries, 1972. ISBN

0-8369-6740-2. ▸ Massive, thorough study of British coal industry to about 1700. Remains point of departure for this area. [BES]

4.460 Norman John Greville Pounds and William N. Parker. *Coal and steel in western Europe: the influence of resources and techniques on production.* Bloomington: Indiana University Press, 1957. ▸ Argues for importance of resources as determinant of industrial leadership in nineteenth-century Europe. Good treatments of technical developments in both iron and steel and coal industries. [BES]

4.461 Clark C. Spence. *Mining engineers and the American West: the lace boot brigade, 1849–1933.* New Haven: Yale University Press, 1970. ISBN 0-300-01224-1. ▸ One of many books on mining in American West, examining emergence of profession of mining engineering. Also treats technical developments and work of United States engineers outside country. [BES]

4.462 Peter Temin. *Iron and steel in nineteenth-century America: an economic inquiry.* Cambridge, Mass.: MIT Press, 1964. ▸ Change in American industry in nineteenth century from perspective of economic historian. Argues technical developments determined by rational cost analysis. Describes technological processes—coke smelting, hot blast, rolling, steel making. [BES]

4.463 R. F. Tylecote. *A history of metallurgy.* 2d ed. London: Institute of Materials, 1992. (Institute of Materials, 498.) ISBN 0-901462-88-8. ▸ Succinct overview of metallurgical developments throughout history, designed to introduce students to field. Good references and illustrations. [BES]

4.464 Anthony F. C. Wallace. *St. Clair: a nineteenth-century coal town's experience with a disaster prone industry.* Howard Robert, Maps and Technical Drawings. New York: Knopf; distributed by Random House, 1987. ISBN 0-394-52867-0. ▸ Examination by anthropologist of town, life and work, politics, corporate power, safety, and unionization. Includes discussion of technical processes of mining. [BES]

4.465 Theodore A. Wertime and James D. Muhly, eds. *The coming of the age of iron.* New Haven: Yale University Press, 1980. ISBN 0-300-02425-8. ▸ Superb collection of papers on ancient metals. Treats iron, bronze, and copper in iron ages of Asia, Africa, South America, and Europe. Wertime has written extensively on history of metallurgy. [BES]

SEE ALSO
44.188 George David Smith. *From monopoly to competition.*

Ground Transportation

4.466 Paul Barrett. *The automobile and urban transit: the formation of public policy in Chicago, 1900–1930.* Philadelphia: Temple University Press, 1983. ISBN 0-87722-294-0. ▸ Best of case studies of urban transportation, examining Chicago's efforts to accommodate, and eventually favor, the automobile. Field still lacks good overview history of urban transportation in United States. [BES]

4.467 Richard W. Bulliet. *The camel and the wheel.* 1975 ed. New York: Columbia University Press, 1990. ISBN 0-231-07234-1 (cl), 0-231-07235-X (pbk). ▸ Study of camel's crucial role in transportation in Middle East, arguing that camel replaced wheel. Challenges Western assumption that level of technological development provides yardstick for determining backwardness of non-Western societies. [BES]

4.468 George W. Hilton and John F. Due. *The electric interurban railways in America.* Stanford, Calif.: Stanford University Press, 1960. ▸ Treats technology and rise of industry; also covers finance, government regulation, freight and passenger traffic, and decline. Short summaries of individual companies and car builders. [BES]

4.469 Maury Klein. *The Union Pacific.* Vol. 1: *Birth of a railroad, 1862–1893.* Vol. 2: *The rebirth, 1894–1969.* 1987 ed. Garden City, N.Y.: Doubleday, 1990. ISBN 0-385-17728-3 (v. 1), 0-385-17735-6 (v. 2). ▸ One of best of many recent examples of histories of individual railroad companies. Examines Union Pacific with advantage of corporate records. [BES]

4.470 Jean Labattut and Wheaton J. Lane, eds. *Highways in our national life: a symposium.* Princeton: Princeton University Press, 1950. ▸ Rare example of useful published symposium papers. Traces historical development of roads and their interconnection with American social, political, and economic life. Reflects optimistic assumptions of 1950s. [BES]

4.471 Albro Martin. *Railroads triumphant: the growth, rejection, and rebirth of a vital American force.* Oxford: Oxford University Press, 1992. ISBN 0-19-503853-3. ▸ Readable overview of interweaving of railroad and American life. Strong views on disaster of government regulation and abilities of railroad management. Author's love of railroads evident. No bibliography. [BES]

4.472 John B. Rae. *The American automobile industry.* 1984 ed. Boston: Twayne, 1985. ISBN 0-8057-9803-X (cl, 1984), 0-8057-9808-0 (pbk). ▸ Thorough introductory survey of automobile industry by leading technological historian. Perhaps too optimistic in tone, traces American accomplishments to problem-plagued modern era. [BES]

4.473 Bruce E. Seely. *Building the American highway system: engineers as policy makers.* Philadelphia: Temple University Press, 1987. ISBN 0-87722-472-2. ▸ Analysis of role of engineers in federal government's Bureau of Public Roads in shaping American highway policy from 1890s through mid-1950s. Focuses on role of technical experts within state-federal relations. [BES]

4.474 John F. Stover. *American railroads.* 1961 ed. Chicago: University of Chicago Press, 1978. ISBN 0-226-77655-7 (cl, 1976), 0-226-77656-5 (pbk). ▸ Book that is closest to general historical overview of American railroads. Still good starting point. [BES]

4.475 George Rogers Taylor. *The transportation revolution, 1815–1860.* 1951 ed. Armonk, N.Y.: Sharpe, 1989. ISBN 0-87332-101-4. ▸ Classic study of development of transportation systems in United States before Civil War, examining new technical systems and their effect on society and economy. [BES]

4.476 James E. Vance, Jr. *Capturing the horizon: the historical geography of transportation since the transportation revolution of the sixteenth century.* New York: Harper & Row, 1986. ISBN 0-06-046805-X. ▸ International overview of transportation development from historical geographer's perspective. Touches on all modes: canals, railroads, highways, urban transit, ocean shipping, and aviation. [BES]

4.477 John H. White, Jr. *The American railroad passenger car.* 1978 ed. 2 vols. Baltimore: Johns Hopkins University Press, 1985. ISBN 0-8018-2743-4 (set, pbk), 0-8018-2722-1 (v. 1, pbk), 0-8018-2747-7 (v. 2, pbk). ▸ Massive definitive history of all aspects of railroad car construction by Smithsonian curator who produced similar volumes on steam locomotives. Loving attention to technical detail; lavishly illustrated. [BES]

SEE ALSO
24.155 H. J. Dyos and Derek H. Aldcroft. *British transport.*
44.179 James J. Flink. *The automobile age.*

Steam Engine and Internal Combustion Technology

4.478 D. B. Barton. *The Cornish beam engine: a survey of its history and development in the mines of Cornwall and Devon from before 1800 to the present day with something of its use elsewhere in Britain and abroad.* 1966 ed. Truro, England: Barton, 1969. ▸ Definitive work on this type of steam engine by writer and publisher of numerous works on mining and technology in Cornwall. Discusses engines, their erection, engine houses, and their use. [BES]

4.479 Lynwood Bryant. "The development of the diesel engine." *Technology and culture* 17.3 (1976) 432–46. ISSN 0040-165X. ▸ Last of four superior articles on technical history of internal combustion engines by Bryant in this journal from 1967–76. Others on Otto engine, four-stroke cycle, thermodynamics, and heat engine development. [BES]

4.480 C. Lyle Cummins. *Internal fire*. Rev. ed. Warrendale, Pa.: Society of Automotive Engineers, 1989. ISBN 0-89883-765-0. ▸ Detailed hardware history tracing historical development of internal combustion engine. Fine drawings and illustrations. Only recent book on this subject. [BES]

4.481 Richard L. Hills. *Power from steam: a history of the stationary steam engine*. Cambridge: Cambridge University Press, 1989. ISBN 0-521-34356-9. ▸ Overview of development of steam power from Thomas Newcomen's atmospheric steam engine through turbine, focusing on interaction of science and technology; fine illustrations, bibliography. [BES]

4.482 Louis C. Hunter. *A history of industrial power in the United States, 1780–1930*. Vol. 2: *Steam power*. Charlottesville: University Press of Virginia for Hagley Museum and Library, 1985. ISBN 0-8139-1044-7 (v. 2). ▸ Massive volume covering development of steam engine in United States to about 1900, including construction, boilers, their use, and their makers. Thorough documentation and illustrations. [BES]

4.483 Svante Lindqvist. *Technology on trial: the introduction of steam power technology into Sweden, 1715–1736*. Uppsala and Stockholm: Uppsala Universitet and Almqvist & Wiksell, 1984. ISBN 91-22-00716-4 (cl), 91-86836-00-5 (pbk), ISSN 0282-1036. ▸ Beautiful book documenting difficulties associated with transfer of Newcomen's steam engine to Sweden. Stresses social as well as technical contexts. Model study. [BES]

4.484 L.T.C. Rolt and John Scott Allen. *The steam engine of Thomas Newcomen*. New York: Science History, 1977. ISBN 0-88202-171-0. ▸ Well-illustrated summary of development of earliest steam engine. Covers technical details, business developments, and spread of engine. [BES]

4.485 G. N. von Tunzelmann. *Steam power and British industrialization to 1960*. Oxford: Clarendon, 1978. ISBN 0-19-828273-7. ▸ Detailed econometric examination of diffusion of steam engine within Britain, focusing on textile industry. Thorough research, fine bibliography. [BES]

Military Technology

4.486 Bernard Brodie and Fawn Brodie. *From cross-bow to H-bomb*. Rev. ed. Bloomington: Indiana University Press, 1973. ISBN 0-253-32490-4 (cl), 0-253-20161-6 (pbk). ▸ Brief review of Western experience by nuclear strategist and historian. Drawn from secondary sources and heavily weighted to developments in science. Mostly descriptive but rich with insights. [AR]

4.487 Martin van Creveld. *Technology and war: from 2000 B.C. to the present*. New York: Free Press, 1989. ISBN 0-02-933151-X. ▸ Survey by military historian drawing from secondary sources. Iconoclastic and suggestive, but erratic in coverage and weak on history of technology. [AR]

4.488 Ludwig Fritz Haber. *The poisonous cloud: chemical warfare in the First World War*. New York: Oxford University Press, 1986. ISBN 0-19-858142-4. ▸ Thoughtful, comprehensive, and reliable overview by son of leading German practitioner. Sensitive to technical and larger social and ethical issues. [AR]

4.489 I. B. Holley, Jr. *Ideas and weapons, exploitation of the aerial weapon by the United States during World War I: a study in the*

relationship of technological advance, military doctrine, and the development of weapons. 1953 ed. Washington, D.C.: Office of Air Force History; distributed by United States General Printing Office, 1983. ISBN 0-912799-11-0. ▸ Seminal study arguing doctrine is essential to successful development and exploitation of new technology. [AR]

4.490 Donald MacKenzie. *Inventing accuracy: a historical sociology of nuclear missile guidance*. Cambridge, Mass: MIT Press, 1990. ISBN 0-262-13258-3. ▸ Social construction of secret and fundamental technology of cold war, based on extensive interviews. Traces United States development in its full complexity, revealing both technical and social forces at work. [AR]

4.491 E. W. Marsden. *Greek and Roman artillery: historical development*. Oxford: Clarendon, 1969. ▸ Rigorous, exhaustive analysis of most thoroughly documented weapons technology of ancient world. Based on close reading of extant texts, published in companion volume. [AR]

4.492 William H. McNeill. *The pursuit of power: technology, armed force, and society since A.D. 1000*. Chicago: University of Chicago Press, 1982. ISBN 0-226-56157-7 (cl), 0-226-56158-5 (pbk). ▸ Rise of West may be explained partly by free enterprise system in Europe which allowed wealth, technology, and political power to reinforce each other. Elegant, persuasive, though presentist viewpoint. [AR]

4.493 John Ulric Nef. *War and human progress: an essay on the rise of industrial civilization*. Cambridge, Mass.: Harvard University Press, 1950. ▸ Rebuttal to Werner Sombart's thesis in *Krieg und Kapitalismus* that war stimulates industrial development. Argues that material progress depends on free exchange of ideas in peacetime. [AR]

4.494 Robert L. O'Connell. *Of arms and men: a history of war, weapons, and aggression*. New York: Oxford University Press, 1989. ISBN 0-19-505359-1. ▸ Survey of primarily Western experience based on conceptualizations from anthropology and sociobiology. Cleverly written and rich with insights, but weak on sustained argumentation. [AR]

4.495 Maurice Pearton. *Diplomacy, war, and technology since 1830*. 1982 ed. Lawrence: University Press of Kansas, 1984. ISBN 0-7006-0254-2 (pbk). ▸ Argues technology reshaped warfare after Napoleon, influencing course of international relations. Avoids technological determinism by detailing varying ways countries selected and exploited new technologies of war. Earlier title: *The Knowledgeable State*. [AR]

4.496 Merritt Roe Smith, ed. *Military enterprise and technological change: perspectives on the American experience*. Cambridge, Mass: MIT Press, 1985. ISBN 0-262-19239-X. ▸ Solid collection of high-quality essays analyzing military technology from wide variety of perspectives and methodologies. Contains two comprehensive reviews of existing literature. [AR]

Naval and Maritime Technology

4.497 Robert Greenhalgh Albion. *Forests and sea power: the timber problem of the Royal Navy, 1652–1862*. 1926 ed. Hamden, Conn.: Archon, 1965. ▸ Early influential appreciation of role of logistics and technology. Exhaustion of indigenous supplies of hardwood and timber by-products shaped British naval policy during country's rise to naval hegemony. [AR]

4.498 Bernard Brodie. *Sea power in the machine age*. 1943 2d ed. New York: Greenwood, 1969. ISBN 0-8371-1445-4. ▸ Treats steam propulsion, iron hulls, armor, rifled guns, mines, torpedoes, submarines, and aviation. Thorough and insightful on evolution of battleship, but underestimates importance of aircraft carrier in World War II. [AR]

4.499 Lionel Casson. *Ships and seamanship in the ancient world*.

1971 ed. Princeton: Princeton University Press, 1986. ISBN 0-691-00215-0 (pbk). ‣ Detailed, authoritative discussion of technology and technique of sailing and rowing, primarily in Mediterranean, from earliest times to Middle Ages. With addenda and corrigenda to 1971 edition. [AR]

4.500 John Francis Guilmartin, Jr. *Gunpowder and galleys: changing technology and Mediterranean warfare at sea in the sixteenth century.* London: Cambridge University Press, 1974. ISBN 0-521-20272-8. ‣ Impact of cannon on galley warfare at dawn of age of sail. Informed, insightful study treating both technical and combat developments. [AR]

4.501 Frederic Chapin Lane. *Venetian ships and shipbuilders of the Renaissance.* 1934 ed. New York: Arno, 1979. ISBN 0-405-10609-2. ‣ Analysis of heart of Mediterranean maritime activity by economic historian. Pioneering study in labor history and history of technology. [AR]

4.502 Elting E. Morison. *Admiral Sims and the modern American navy.* 1942 ed. New York: Russell & Russell, 1968. ‣ Insightful synthesis of technology, personality, and politics. Reformer confronts conservative United States naval establishment in technological revolution around turn of twentieth century. [AR]

4.503 John S. Morison and John F. Coates. *The Athenian trireme: the history and reconstruction of an ancient Greek warship.* Cambridge: Cambridge University Press, 1986. ISBN 0-521-32202-2 (cl), 0-521-31100-4 (pbk). ‣ Recounts modern reconstruction of most famous and mysterious ship type of the ancient Mediterranean. Authoritative account based on wide-ranging research and modern experiments. [AR]

4.504 John H. Pryor. *Geography, technology, and war: studies in the maritime history of the Mediterranean, 649–1571.* New York: Cambridge University Press, 1988. ISBN 0-521-34424-7. ‣ Studies of commercial and military shipping in context of climate and geography. Examines how relationship between ship technology and geography shaped military power in Mediterranean in Middle Ages. Insights into need to study technology in context. [AR/JSCRS]

SEE ALSO
20.95 Richard Unger. *The ship in the medieval economy, 600–1600.*
24.400 Jon Tetsuro Sumida. *In defence of naval supremacy.*

Structural Technology

4.505 David P. Billington. *The tower and the bridge: the new art of structural engineering.* 1983 ed. Princeton: Princeton University Press, 1985. ISBN 0-691-02393-X. ‣ Analysis of structural technologies facilitated by Industrial Revolution using iron, steel, and reinforced concrete. Explores artistic potential of engineering with focus on efficiency, economy, and elegance. [DCJ]

4.506 Carl W. Condit. *American building: materials and techniques from the first colonial settlements to the present.* 2d ed. Chicago: University of Chicago Press, 1982. ISBN 0-226-11448-1 (cl), 0-226-11450-3 (pbk). ‣ Overview of American building arts including bridges, roofs, dams, and skyscrapers. Includes wood, iron, steel, and reinforced concrete structures. Emphasizes relation of architecture and engineering. [DCJ]

4.507 Henry J. Cowan and Peter R. Smith. *The science and technology of building materials.* New York: Van Nostrand Reinhold, 1988. ISBN 0-442-21799-4 (pbk). ‣ Description of physical properties and uses of building materials including wood, stone, metal, reinforced concrete, plastic, glass, and paint. Analyzes historic and contemporary production and erection techniques. [DCJ]

4.508 John Fitchen. *Building construction before mechanization.* Cambridge, Mass.: MIT Press, 1986. ISBN 0-262-06102-3 (cl), 0-262-56047-X (pbk). ‣ Analysis of traditional construction techniques using wood, stone, and earth. Describes social and technical processes of construction before reliance on powerful equipment. [DCJ]

4.509 H. Ward Jandl, ed. *Technology of historic American buildings: studies of the materials, craft processes, and the mechanization of building construction.* Washington, D.C.: Foundation for Preservation Technology for Association for Preservation Technology, 1984. ISBN 0-09-2476-07-4. ‣ Collection of articles, descriptive and analytic, on history of iron builders' hardware, wooden balloon frame, I-beams, cast-iron architecture, terra cotta, metal roofing, and painting technologies. [DCJ]

4.510 David G. McCullough. *The great bridge.* 1972 ed. New York: Simon & Schuster, 1982. ISBN 0-671-45711-X (pbk). ‣ Social, economic, and technological history of John Roebling's Brooklyn Bridge, masterpiece of engineering art. Longest span suspension bridge in world when completed in 1883. [DCJ]

4.511 Mario Salvadori. *Building: the fight against gravity.* New York: Atheneum, 1979. ISBN 0-689-50144-7. ‣ Analysis of forces affecting stability of buildings. Describes basic structural forms such as beams and cables and how earthquakes and winds influence building design. Geared toward nonspecialists. [DCJ]

Hydraulic Technology

4.512 William U. Chandler. *Myth of the TVA: conservation and development in the Tennessee Valley, 1933–1983.* Cambridge, Mass.: Ballinger, 1984. ISBN 0-88410-976-3. ‣ Critiques federal New Deal effort to develop water resources in American South. Analyzes social and economic value of hydroelectric power and flood control projects built by Tennessee Valley Authority. [DCJ]

4.513 Gordon Jackson. *The history and archaeology of ports.* Tadworth, England: World's Work, 1983. ISBN 0-437-07539-7. ‣ Social and economic history of harbor development in Great Britain. Good visual material places subject in greater context of maritime navigation. Discussion of London, Hull, and other ports. [DCJ]

4.514 Lawrence B. Lee. *Reclaiming the American West: an historiography and guide.* Santa Barbara, Calif.: ABC-Clio, 1980. ISBN 0-87436-298-9. ‣ Bibliographic essay and listing of books, articles, and reports on development of irrigated agriculture. Emphasis on role of federal involvement in developing regional water supply systems. [DCJ]

4.515 Norman A. Smith. *A history of dams.* Secaucus, N.J.: Citadel, 1971. ISBN 0-8065-0291-6. ‣ Overview of dam construction techniques from ancient through modern times including timber, earthen, rockfill, masonry, and concrete designs. Discusses role of dams in world economic and social development. [DCJ]

SEE ALSO
38.335 David G. McCullough. *The path between the seas.*

Electrical Technology

4.516 W. A. Atherton. *From compass to computer: a history of electrical and electronics engineering.* San Francisco: San Francisco Press, 1984. ISBN 0-911302-48-4 (cl), 0-911302-49-2 (pbk). ‣ Broad-based survey treating developments on international basis. Based largely on standard secondary sources, but best single-volume work on entire field. [TSR]

4.517 Arthur A. Bright, Jr. *The electric lamp industry: technological change and economic development from 1800 to 1947.* New York: Macmillan, 1949. ‣ Analysis of forces influencing evolution of electric light, especially patents, industrial organization, and government regulation. Combination economic and technological history; still best general account of evolution of electric lamp. [TSR]

4.518   Bernard S. Finn. *The history of electrical technology: an annotated bibliography.* New York: Garland, 1991. ISBN 0-8240-9120-5. ‣ Over 1,500 well-annotated entries organized into several broad fields (general works, communications, power, and miscellaneous) with numerous subfields. Author and subject indexes. [TSR]

4.519   Robert Friedel, Paul Israel, and Bernard S. Finn. *Edison's electric light: biography of an invention.* New Brunswick, N.J.: Rutgers University Press, 1986. ISBN 0-8135-1118-6. ‣ Study of Thomas Edison's development of commercial incandescent lighting system. No more detailed account of evolution of system of inventions available. [TSR]

4.520   Richard F. Hirsh. *Technology and transformation in the American electric utility industry.* Cambridge: Cambridge University Press, 1989. ISBN 0-521-36478-7. ‣ History of industry from 1920s to 1980s. Study of collapse of industry's grow-and-build strategy due to emerging technological stagnation. Based on published sources and extensive interviews. [TSR]

4.521   Thomas P. Hughes. *Networks of power: electrification in Western society, 1880–1930.* Baltimore: Johns Hopkins University Press, 1983. ISBN 0-8018-2873-2. ‣ Masterful comparative study of evolution of electric power systems in Britain, Germany, and United States. Describes how social, political, and economic factors influenced technology and gave rise to significantly different systems. [TSR]

4.522   Ronald R. Kline. *Steinmetz: engineer and socialist.* Baltimore: Johns Hopkins University Press, 1992. ISBN 0-8018-4298-0. ‣ Intellectual biography of well-known electrical engineer set in political, social, scientific, and technological context of Progressive Era. Solid, well-documented example of biographical genre in this area. [TSR]

4.523   David E. Nye. *Electrifying America: social meanings of a new technology, 1880–1940.* Cambridge, Mass.: MIT Press, 1990. ISBN 0-262-14048-9. ‣ Study of how electrical light and power were received in America, how Americans incorporated it into their daily lives, and how American culture shaped and was shaped by new technologies. [TSR]

4.524   Harold Clarence Passer. *The electrical manufacturers, 1875–1900: a study in competition, entrepreneurship, technical change, and economic growth.* Cambridge, Mass.: Harvard University Press, 1953. ‣ Study of firms that manufactured equipment for emerging arc lighting, incandescent lighting, electric motor, and traction industries in United States. Particular attention to role of engineer-entrepreneur. Combines economic and technological history. [TSR]

4.525   Harold L. Pratt. *The electric city: energy and the growth of the Chicago area, 1880–1930.* Chicago: University of Chicago Press, 1991. ISBN 0-226-67075-9. ‣ Detailed study of impact of electric light and power systems on single locality. Excellent analysis of interaction of social values, politics, and electrical technology. [TSR]

4.526   Richard H. Schallenberg. *Bottled energy: electrical engineering and the evolution of chemical energy storage.* Philadelphia: American Philosophical Society, 1982. (Memoirs of the American Philosophical Society, 148.) ISBN 0-87169-148-5 (pbk), ISSN 0065-9738. ‣ Detailed history of chemical storage battery, 1880–1910. Analyzes how engineers and inventors attempted to adapt battery to meet changing social and commercial needs. Solid study, technical in places. [TSR]

Telecommunications

4.527   Hugh G. J. Aitken. *The continuous wave: technology and American radio, 1900–1932.* Princeton: Princeton University Press, 1985. ISBN 0-691-08376-2 (cl), 0-691-02390-5 (pbk).

‣ Examination of political, economic, and technical influences exerted by inventors, corporate strategies, government policy, and military concerns on early development of American radio industry. [PBI]

4.528   Hugh G. J. Aitken. *Syntony and spark: the origins of radio.* 1976 ed. Princeton: Princeton University Press, 1985. ISBN 0-691-08377-0 (cl), 0-691-02392-1 (pbk). ‣ Study of work of radio pioneers Heinrich Hertz, Oliver Lodge, and Guglielmo Marconi. Important contribution to understanding of science-technology relations as well as origins of radio. [PBI]

4.529   Gerald W. Brock. *The telecommunications industry: the dynamics of market structure.* Cambridge, Mass.: Harvard University Press, 1981. ISBN 0-674-87285-1. ‣ Economic history of American telecommunications industry emphasizing market structures and government regulations. Although focusing on American telephony, also includes discussions of telegraphy and radio with some European comparisons. [PBI]

4.530   R. W. Burns. *British television: the formative years.* London: Peregrinus with Science Museum, 1986. ISBN 0-86341-079-0. ‣ Only significant study of early television technology and television industry. Focuses on technical development in Britain and introduction of television service by British Broadcasting Corporation before World War II. [PBI]

4.531   Daniel J. Czitrom. *Media and the American mind: from Morse to McLuhan.* Chapel Hill: University of North Carolina Press, 1982. ISBN 0-8078-1500-4 (cl), 0-8078-4107-2 (pbk). ‣ Cultural history of introduction of three new communications media (telegraph, film, and radio) in United States. Examines history of twentieth-century mass media theory. [PBI]

4.532   Susan J. Douglas. *Inventing American broadcasting, 1899–1922.* Baltimore: Johns Hopkins University Press, 1987. ISBN 0-8018-3387-6. ‣ Examination of ways in which variety of individuals and institutions transformed radio into medium of mass communication. Orientation toward social construction of technology. [PBI]

4.533   Robert W. Garnet. *The telephone enterprise: the evolution of the Bell System's horizontal structure, 1876–1909.* Baltimore: Johns Hopkins University Press, 1985. ISBN 0-8018-2698-5. ‣ Evolution of Bell system with attention to influence of political as well as economic and managerial factors. [PBI]

4.534   Paul Israel. *From machine shop to industrial laboratory: telegraphy and the changing context of American invention, 1830–1920.* Baltimore: Johns Hopkins University Press, 1992. ISBN 0-8018-4379-0. ‣ Use of telegraph industry to examine changing American inventive practice from shop invention to laboratory research. Explores relationship between technology, markets, and industrial structure in nineteenth-century American telegraph industry. [PBI]

4.535   Jeffrey Kieve. *The electric telegraph in the U.K.: a social and economic history.* New York: Barnes & Noble, 1973. ISBN 0-06-493681-3. ‣ Study of development, nationalization, and government operation of telegraph in Great Britain. Remains only significant book on telegraphy outside United States. [PBI]

4.536   Ithiel de Sola Pool, ed. *The social impact of the telephone.* 1977 ed. Cambridge, Mass.: MIT Press, 1981. ISBN 0-262-16066-8 (cl, 1977), 0-262-66048-2 (pbk). ‣ Interdisciplinary collection of essays on influence of telephone technology on American and European societies from its origins to present. [PBI]

4.537   Christopher H. Sterling and John M. Kittross. *Stay tuned: a concise history of American broadcasting.* 2d ed. Belmont, Calif.: Wadsworth, 1990. ISBN 0-534-11904-0 (cl), 0-534-11905-2 (pbk). ‣ Probably best general history of American broadcasting. Provides overview of issues including technological development, stations and systems, marketing and advertising, programing, laws and regulations, and broadcasting's impact on society. [PBI]

4.538 Robert Luther Thompson. *Wiring a continent: the history of the telegraph industry in the United States, 1832–1866.* Princeton: Princeton University Press, 1947. ▸ Remains standard study of early American telegraph industry from its origins through Civil War. [PBI]

Computers and Electronics

4.539 William Aspray et al. *Computing before computers.* Ames: Iowa State University Press, 1990. ISBN 0-8138-0047-1. ▸ Discussion of techniques used for calculation before invention of electronic digital computer in 1940s, including slide rules, planimeters, mechanical adding machines and calculators, punched card equipment, and specialized analog equipment. For nonspecialist. [PEC]

4.540 Ernest Braun and Stuart McDonald. *Revolution in miniature: the history and impact of semiconductor electronics reexplored in an updated and revised second edition.* 2d ed. Cambridge: Cambridge University Press, 1982. ISBN 0-521-24701-2 (cl), 0-521-28903-3 (pbk). ▸ Brief history of invention of transistor and integrated circuit. Examines economic impact on military, commercial, and eventually consumer products. Based on secondary sources and interviews. [PEC]

4.541 James W. Cortada. *A bibliographic guide to the history of computing, computers, and the information processing industry.* Westport, Conn.: Greenwood, 1990. ISBN 0-313-26810-X. ▸ Exhaustive bibliography with some entries lightly annotated. Covers computing industry, major technological developments, and early calculating and punched-card aspects of information processing as well as more recent electronic era. [PEC]

4.542 Charles Eames and Ray Eames. *A computer perspective: background to the computer age.* 1973 ed. Glen Fleck, ed. Cambridge, Mass.: Harvard University Press, 1990. ISBN 0-674-15625-0 (cl, 1973), 0-674-15626-9 (pbk). ▸ Discussion of computing from 1890 to about 1950. Pathbreaking research by I. Bernard Cohen relating computing to social, cultural, and political events. Afterword by Brian Randell on recent developments. [PEC]

4.543 N. Metropolis, J. Howlett, and Gian-Carlo Rota, eds. *A history of computing in the twentieth century: a collection of essays.* 1980 ed. New York: Academic Press, 1985. ISBN 0-12-491650-3. ▸ Proceedings of conference attended by pioneers in computing, 1930–60. Firsthand information with editorial comments. Does not cover early part of century despite title. Discusses European developments. [PEC]

4.544 Kent C. Redmond and Thomas M. Smith. *Project Whirlwind: the history of a pioneer computer.* Bedford, Mass.: Digital, 1980. ISBN 0-932376-09-6. ▸ Monograph describing very influential early computing project. Many later commercial developments in computing originated with Whirlwind. Covers political and managerial aspects of project. [PEC]

4.545 Nancy Stern. *From ENIAC to UNIVAC: an appraisal of the Eckert-Mauchly computers.* Bedford, Mass.: Digital, 1981. ISBN 0-932376-14-2. ▸ Description of building of first electronic computer as special project for military in 1945 by Presper Eckert and John Mauchly. Discusses their attempt to commercialize it with UNIVAC five years later. [PEC]

4.546 Michael R. Williams. *A history of computing technology.* Englewood Cliffs, N.J.: Prentice-Hall, 1985. ISBN 0-13-389917-9. ▸ Overview of principal machines and instruments used for calculation from antiquity to mid-1960s. Wealth of technical detail, but understandable for layperson. Does not cover social, economic, or political context. [PEC]

Chemical Technology

4.547 Fred Aftalion. *A history of the international chemical industry.* Otto Theodor Benfey, trans. Philadelphia: University of Pennsylvania Press, 1991. ISBN 0-8122-8207-8 (cl), 0-8122-1297-5 (pbk). ▸ Only chronologically comprehensive, international survey. Focuses more on industry than technology. Adequately written with material contained nowhere else, but devoid of reference notes and bibliography. [TSR]

4.548 John J. Beer. *The emergence of the German dye industry.* 1959 ed. New York: Arno, 1981. ISBN 0-405-13835-0. ▸ Well-researched classic, still one of best scholarly accounts of emergence of key chemical industry. Focus on Germany but also treats significant developments in Britain, France, and Switzerland. [TSR]

4.549 John L. Enos. *Petroleum, progress, and profits: a history of process innovation.* Cambridge, Mass.: MIT Press, 1962. ▸ Traces key innovations focusing on nature of technological progress. Excellent account of research and development efforts, emergence of new processing technologies, and their advantages and economic impact. [TSR]

4.550 Gustav Anselm Fester. *Die Entwicklung der chemischen Technik bis zu den Anfängen der Grossindustrie: ein technologisch-historischer Versuch.* 1923 ed. Weisbaden: Sandig, 1969. ▸ Excellent general history of earlier chemical technology, an understudied area of historical scholarship in recent period. [TSR]

4.551 Ludwig Fritz Haber. *The chemical industry during the nineteenth century: a study of the economic aspect of applied chemistry in Europe and North America.* Oxford: Clarendon, 1958. ▸ Business, technological, and economic history covering major Western nations, especially Britain and Germany. Focus on sulfuric acid, soda ash, caustic soda, bleaching powder, and coal-tar dyestuffs. Best book covering this period. [TSR]

4.552 Ludwig Fritz Haber. *The chemical industry, 1900–1930: international growth and technological change.* Oxford: Clarendon, 1971. ISBN 0-19-858133-5. ▸ Continuation of 4.551. Exceptionally good at international corporate comparison of Du Pont, Imperial Chemical Industries, and I. G. Farben. Good bibliographical essay. [TSR]

4.553 Williams Haynes. *American chemical industry: a history.* 6 vols. New York: Van Nostrand Reinhold, 1945–54. ▸ Very detailed overview of growth of industry to World War II. Better on economic and organizational elements than on technological history, but nothing on this scale for any other country. Standard, useful, if somewhat celebratory. [TSR]

4.554 Paul M. Hohenberg. *Chemicals in western Europe, 1850–1914: an economic study of technical change.* Chicago: Rand McNally, 1967. ▸ Comparative impact of technical developments, changing factors of production, and price movements on French, German, and Swiss chemical industries. Focuses on how and why Germany surpassed France and Switzerland after 1850. [TSR]

4.555 David A. Hounshell and John Kenly Smith, Jr. *Science and corporate strategy: Du Pont R & D, 1902–1980.* Cambridge: Cambridge University Press, 1988. ISBN 0-521-32767-9. ▸ Excellent institutional history involving single company. Examines company research and development and how it was used to pursue corporate objectives, how it changed in response to changes in corporate environment, and role it played in corporate transformation. [TSR]

4.556 Robert P. Multhauf. *The history of chemical technology: an annotated bibliography.* New York: Garland, 1984. ISBN 0-8240-9255-4. ▸ Over 1,500 entries organized by nation, chemical product, and corporation. Best bibliographical tool for entering field. [TSR]

4.557 John Graham Smith. *The origins and early development of the heavy chemical industry in France.* New York: Oxford University Press, 1979. ISBN 0-19-858136-x. ▸ Detailed study of early sulfuric acid, chlorine bleach, and Leblanc soda production in earliest stages of French chemical industry (1760s to 1820s). Traces interactions among manufacturing technology, science, commercial-economic context. [TSR]

4.558 Peter H. Spitz. *Petrochemicals: the rise of an industry.* New York: Wiley, 1988. ISBN 0-471-95985-0. ▸ Traces shift from coal to petroleum as key feedstock for chemical industry in twentieth century. More popular than scholarly. May be too technical for some readers, but no work covers subject better. [TSR]

4.559 Harold F. Williamson et al. *The American petroleum industry.* 1959–63 ed. 2 vols. Westport, Conn.: Greenwood, 1981. ISBN 0-313-22789-6 (v. 1), 0-313-22790-X (v. 2). ▸ Massive (almost 1,900 pages) economic history covering development of industry and leading firms. Also treats technology from 1859 to 1959. Bibliographies in both volumes. [BES]

Nuclear Weapons and Power

4.560 Brian Balogh. *Chain reaction: expert debate and public participation in American commercial nuclear power, 1945–1975.* Cambridge: Cambridge University Press, 1991. ISBN 0-521-37296-8. ▸ Examination of role of experts in rise and eventual decline of public and private support for commercial nuclear power in United States. [PEC]

4.561 Barton C. Hacker. *The dragon's tail: radiation safety in the Manhattan Project, 1942–1946.* Berkeley: University of California Press, 1987. ISBN 0-520-05852-6. ▸ Examination of steps taken during construction of first atomic bomb to ensure safety from radiation damage. Set tone for subsequent debates on radiation safety in military and civilian spheres. [PEC]

4.562 J. L. Heilbron and Robert W. Seidel. *Lawrence and his laboratory: a history of the Lawrence Berkeley Laboratory.* Berkeley: University of California Press, 1989. ISBN 0-520-06426-7. ▸ Study of forerunner and model for Big Science research labs, weapons labs, and university-military-industrial alliances since World War II. First of planned two-volume study covers events to 1941. [PEC]

4.563 Gregg Herken. *The winning weapon: the atomic bomb in the cold war, 1945–1950; with a new preface.* 1980 ed. Princeton: Princeton University Press, 1988. ISBN 0-691-02286-0 (pbk). ▸ Analysis of why United States could not exploit nuclear weapons monopoly in diplomacy with Soviet Union, for example, during Berlin crisis (1948) and why United States failed to predict speed with which Soviets attained bomb (1949). [PEC]

4.564 Richard G. Hewlett et al. *A history of the United States Atomic Energy Commission.* Vol. 1: *The new world, 1939–1946.* Vol. 2: *Atomic shield, 1947–1952.* Vol. 3: *Atoms for peace and war, 1953–1961: Eisenhower and the Atomic Energy Commission.* 1962–69 (v. 1–2) ed. 3 vols. Berkeley: University of California Press, 1989–90. ISBN 0-520-07186-7 (v. 1), 0-520-07187-5 (v. 2), 0-520-06018-0 (v. 3). ▸ Authoritative official history, begun in 1960s. Authors had access to internal files, correspondence, and classified materials. Covers events leading to development of atomic bomb as well as subsequent history of Atomic Energy Commission. Technical, administrative, and political developments fully covered. [PEC]

4.565 Alwyn McKay. *The making of the atomic age.* Oxford: Oxford University Press, 1984. ISBN 0-19-219193-4 (cl), 0-19-289174-X (pbk). ▸ Concise account of key events and people by physicist with firsthand knowledge of many events described. Covers technical details and roles of key individuals. [PEC]

4.566 Richard Rhodes. *The making of the atomic bomb.* New York: Simon & Schuster, 1988. ISBN 0-671-44133-7 (cl), 0-671-65719-4 (pbk). ▸ Prize-winning comprehensive history of atomic bomb, concentrating on events from mid-1930s to late 1940s. Discusses technical problems and solutions and roles of physicists and politicians in decision to use bomb. [PEC]

4.567 Robert W. Seidel. "Books on the bomb." *ISIS* 81 (1990) 519–37. ISSN 0021-1753. ▸ Annotated bibliography of major works on internal history of atomic bomb and writings covering bomb's social, cultural, and political dimensions. [PEC]

4.568 Spencer R. Weart. *Nuclear fear: a history of images.* 1988 ed. Cambridge, Mass.: Harvard University Press, 1989. ISBN 0-674-62835-7 (cl, 1988), 0-674-62836-5 (pbk). ▸ Analysis of images used by scientists, politicians, engineers, and laypersons to characterize nuclear energy from its discovery in early twentieth century. Sources are popular and scholarly literature, film, television, and popular culture. [PEC]

SEE ALSO
44.816 Paul S. Boyer. *By the bomb's early light.*

Aviation and Space Technology

4.569 Roger Bilstein. *Flight in America, 1900–1983: from the Wrights to the astronauts.* Baltimore: Johns Hopkins University Press, 1984. ISBN 0-8018-2973-9. ▸ Probably best survey of aviation history by author interested in history, not just airplanes. [PEM]

4.570 Edward W. Constant II. *The origins of the turbojet revolution.* Baltimore: Johns Hopkins University Press, 1980. ISBN 0-8018-2222-X. ▸ Analysis of development of jet engine as study of process of technological change. [PEM]

4.571 Joseph J. Corn. *The winged gospel: America's romance with aviation, 1900–1950.* New York: Oxford University Press, 1983. ISBN 0-19-503356-6. ▸ Cultural history of aviation, looking particularly at how aviation was promoted to American public. [PEM]

4.572 Tom D. Crouch. *The bishop's boys: a life of Wilbur and Orville Wright.* 1989 ed. New York: Norton, 1990. ISBN 0-393-02660-4 (cl, 1989), 0-393-30695-x (pbk). ▸ Personal biography of Wright brothers by a leading aviation historian. [PEM]

4.573 James R. Hansen. "Aviation history in the wider view." *Technology and culture* 30.3 (1989) 643–56. ISSN 0040-165X. ▸ Analysis of strengths and weaknesses of literature in aviation history. [PEM]

4.574 Lee Kennett. *The first air war, 1914–1918.* New York: Free Press, 1991. ISBN 0-02-917301-9. ▸ Balanced account of all aspects of use of aviation in World War I. [PEM]

4.575 Clayton R. Koppes. *JPL and the American space program: a history of the Jet Propulsion Laboratory.* New Haven: Yale University Press, 1982. ISBN 0-300-02408-8. ▸ Exemplary study of one of National Air and Space Administration's research centers. Shows how space research was organized; raises important questions about tensions between government science policy and interests of researchers. [PEM]

4.576 John M. Logsdon. *The decision to go to the moon: Project Apollo and the national interest.* 1970 ed. Chicago: University of Chicago Press, 1976. ISBN 0-226-49175-7. ▸ Examination of process by which Kennedy administration made decision to send person to moon. Classic study of politics of space program. [PEM]

4.577 Pamela E. Mack. "Space history." *Technology and culture* 30.3 (1989) 657–65. ISSN 0040-165X. ▸ Survey of literature in space history. [PEM]

4.578 Dominick A. Pisano and Cathleen S. Lewis. *Air and space history: an annotated bibliography.* New York: Garland, 1988. ISBN

0-8240-8543-4. ‣ Over 1,700 entries covering all aspects of aviation and space history. [PEM]

4.579 John B. Rae. *Climb to greatness: the American aircraft industry, 1920–1960.* Cambridge, Mass.: MIT Press, 1968. ‣ Classic survey of aviation as industry rather than as series of technological feats. [PEM]

4.580 Robert W. Smith. *The space telescope: a study of NASA, science, technology, and politics.* Cambridge: Cambridge University Press, 1989. ISBN 0-521-26634-3. ‣ Exemplary case study synthesizing history of science, technology, and policy. Published before launch of space telescope but suggests origins of problems that appeared after launch. [PEM]

Urban Technology

4.581 Ellis L. Armstrong, Suellen M. Hoy, and Michael C. Robinson, eds. *History of public works in the United States, 1776–1976.* Chicago: American Public Works Association, 1976. ISBN 0-917084-03-9. ‣ Thorough, authoritative survey articles about waterways, roads and streets, urban mass transportation, park building, educational facilities, and other public works, including concept and profession of public works. Includes select bibliography. [CSH]

4.582 M. N. Baker (v. 1) and Michael J. Taras (v. 2). *The quest for pure water: the history of water purification from the earliest records to the twentieth century.* 2d ed. 2 vols. New York: American Waterworks Association, 1981. ISBN 0-89867-249-X (set), 0-89867-247-3 (v. 1), 0-89867-248-1 (v. 2). ‣ Thorough invaluable summary of water purification technologies; somewhat underdocumented. [CSH]

4.583 Nelson M. Blake. *Water for the cities: a history of the urban water supply problem in the United States.* Syracuse, N.Y.: Syracuse University Press, 1956. ‣ Examination of how eastern and midwestern cities attempted to establish public water service. Concentrates on political and financial dimensions. [CSH]

4.584 Andre Guillereme. *The age of water: the urban environment in the north of France, A.D. 300–1800.* College Station: Texas A&M University Press, 1988. ISBN 0-89096-270-7. ‣ Provocative exploration of how water—as pagan religious symbol, means of protection, industrial material, and means of sanitation—shaped cities in northern France. [CSH]

4.585 Josef W. Konvitz. *The urban millennium: the city-building process from the early Middle Ages to the present.* Carbondale: Southern Illinois University Press, 1985. ISBN 0-8093-1201-8. ‣ Thematic review of responses of city planners to various incentives to urbanization: political, military, symbolic, and economic. Includes excellent bibliography of secondary sources. [CSH]

4.586 Martin V. Melosi. *Garbage in the cities: refuse, reform, and the environment, 1880–1980.* College Station: Texas A&M University Press, 1981. ISBN 0-89096-119-0. ‣ Study of interaction of urban politics, public sensibility, and technological change on changing modes of refuse removal in American cities. [CSH]

4.587 Public Works Historical Society. *Public works history in the United States.* Suellen M. Hoy and Michael C. Robinson, eds. and comps. Nashville: American Association for State and Local History, 1982. ISBN 0-910050-63-5. ‣ Superb bibliography of secondary sources on United States public works including airports, water and sewage works, public buildings, city planning, flood control, and irrigation works. [CSH]

4.588 Joel A. Tarr and Gabriel Dupuy, eds. *Technology and the rise of the networked city in Europe and America.* Philadelphia: Temple University Press, 1988. ISBN 0-87722-540-0. ‣ Sixteen essays review (and sometimes compare) nineteenth-and twentieth-century development of urban transportation, water supply, waste disposal, energy, and communications systems in France, Germany, Britain, and United States. [CSH]

Biotechnology

4.589 David Bennett, Peter Glasner, and David Travis. *The politics of uncertainty: regulating recombinant DNA research in Britain.* London: Routledge & Kegan Paul, 1986. ISBN 0-7102-0503-1. ‣ Discussion of development and functioning of regulations governing use of recombinant DNA techniques in Britain. Detailed analysis of Genetic Manipulation Advisory Group, conceptualization of risks, and public participation in decisions in United Kingdom. [SK]

4.590 Calestous Juma. *The gene hunters: biotechnology and the scramble for seeds.* Princeton: Princeton University Press, 1989. (African Centre for Technology Studies research series, 1.) ISBN 0-691-04258-6 (cl), 0-691-00378-5 (pbk). ‣ Description of exploitation of plant resources during African colonialism, current place of genetic resources in world agriculture, and biotechnological trends. Suggests African countries may produce cash crops through biotechnology. [SK]

4.591 Jack Ralph Kloppenburg, Jr. *First the seed: the political economy of plant biotechnology, 1492–2000.* Cambridge: Cambridge University Press, 1988. ISBN 0-521-32691-5. ‣ American agriculture viewed through political economy of seed. Development of genetics in agricultural research, breeder rights, and global plant genetic resources. Application of commercial biotechnology to agriculture. [SK]

4.592 Sheldon Krimsky. *Genetic alchemy: the social history of the recombinant DNA controversy.* Cambridge, Mass.: MIT Press, 1982. ISBN 0-262-11083-0 (cl), 0-262-61038-8 (pbk). ‣ Study of origins of recombinant DNA (rDNA) controversy in United States. Discusses Asilomar Conference (1975); rDNA controversy at Cambridge, Massachusetts; different perceptions of risk among scientists; developing rDNA guidelines from National Institutes of Health; and public participation in debate. [SK]

4.593 John Lear. *Recombinant DNA: the untold story.* New York: Crown, 1978. ISBN 0-517-53165-8. ‣ Detailed chronicle of early stages of controversy over laboratory experiments involving genetically modified life forms. Covers Asilomar Conference and early public controversy about creating novel pathogen that could escape laboratory. [SK]

Technology and the Environment

4.594 Eric Ashby and Mary Anderson. *The politics of clean air.* New York: Oxford University Press, 1981. ISBN 0-19-858330-3. ‣ Discussion of efforts to establish government regulation of air pollution in nineteenth-century Britain. Development of smoke-consuming furnaces and alkali inspectorate to enforce acid emission standards in heavy chemicals industry. [CSH]

4.595 Peter A. Coates. *The Trans-Alaska Pipeline controversy: technology, conservation, and the frontier.* Bethlehem, Pa.: Lehigh University Press, 1991. ISBN 0-934223-10-6. ‣ Interdisciplinary environmental history studying cultural, institutional, and material factors involved in pipeline controversy. Integrates environmental history with Alaskan cultural history. [CSH]

4.596 Martin V. Melosi. *Coping with abundance: energy and environment in industrial America.* Philadelphia: Temple University Press, 1985. ISBN 0-87722-372-6. ‣ Survey of United States energy policy, including wood, coal, petroleum, electricity, and nuclear power from 1820. Concentrates on period 1914–80. [CSH]

4.597 John H. Perkins. *Experts and the insecticide crisis: the quest for new pest management strategies.* New York: Plenum, 1982. ISBN

0-306-40770-1. ▸ History of debate over insecticides after ban of DDT. [AIM]

4.598 Nicholas H. Steneck. *The microwave debate.* Cambridge, Mass.: MIT Press, 1984. ISBN 0-262-19230-6. ▸ Examination of controversy over effects of (nonionizing) microwave radiation on human health. Analyzes how public opinion in technical controversies is influenced by media treatment. [CSH]

4.599 Donald Worster. *Rivers of empire: water, aridity, and the growth of the American West.* New York: Pantheon, 1985. ISBN 0-394-51680-X. ▸ Analysis of relations of irrigation policy, land settlement, and political power, drawing on Karl Wittfogel's Oriental despotism thesis (3.341). [CSH]

SEE ALSO
44.211 James Whorton. *Before Silent Spring.*
44.624 Thomas R. Dunlap. *DDT.*

Technical Education and Development of the Engineering Profession

4.600 Göran Ahlström. *Engineers and industrial growth: higher technical education and the engineering profession during the nineteenth and early twentieth centuries: France, Germany, Sweden, and England.* London: Croom Helm, 1982. ISBN 0-7099-0506-8. ▸ Comparative study of engineering education in Britain, France, Germany, and Sweden and relationship between technical education and industrialization. [TSR]

4.601 Frederick B. Artz. *The development of technical education in France, 1500–1850.* Cleveland: Society for the History of Technology, 1966. (Society for the History of Technology, Monograph series, 3.) ▸ Standard account of emergence of technical education in country where it first assumed prominence. Very good at placing growth of technical education in intellectual and social context. [TSR]

4.602 François Bucher. *Architector: the lodge books and sketchbooks of medieval architects.* New York: Abaris, 1979. ISBN 0-913870-47-1. ▸ Short biographies of cathedral and castle builders demarcating social position and suggesting relationships between them. [AIM]

4.603 Daniel Hovey Calhoun. *The American civil engineer: origins and conflict.* Cambridge, Mass.: MIT Press; distributed by Harvard University Press, 1960. ▸ Study of emergence of American engineering from European origins and from experience gained in canal building, especially Erie Canal. Describes ensuing conflicts between construction engineers and West Point graduates. [AIM]

4.604 David F. Channell. *The history of engineering science: an annotated bibliography.* New York: Garland, 1989. ISBN 0-8240-6636-7. ▸ Chapter 4 contains more than one hundred annotated entries on history of engineering education. Good coverage of United States and Britain, but weaker for other regions. [TSR]

4.605 Charles R. Day. *Education for the industrial world: the Écoles d'Arts et Metiers and the rise of French industrial engineering.* Cambridge, Mass.: MIT Press, 1987. ISBN 0-262-04088-3. ▸ Description of how school's graduates achieved great success, particularly in new industrial areas of engineering, despite unprestigious social backgrounds. [AIM]

4.606 George S. Emmerson. *Engineering education: a social history.* New York: Crane Russak, 1973. ISBN 0-8448-0218-2. ▸ Wide-ranging review on international scale with considerable material on nineteenth-century Europe and United States. Often not well documented and sometimes inaccurate, but only international survey of any value. [TSR]

4.607 Jean Gimpel. *The cathedral builders.* 1983 ed. Teresa Waugh, trans. New York: Harper & Row, 1984. ISBN 0-06-

091158-1 (pbk). ▸ Analysis of social situation and pressures on medieval architects. [AIM]

4.608 Kees Gispen. *New profession, old order: engineers and German society, 1815–1914.* Cambridge: Cambridge University Press, 1989. ISBN 0-521-37198-8. ▸ Study of rise of management professionals in Germany. Describes discontent at inability to gain status among industrial capitalists or traditional elites. [AIM]

4.609 Konrad H. Jarausch. *The unfree professions: German lawyers, teachers, and engineers, 1900–1950.* New York: Oxford University Press, 1990. ISBN 0-19-504482-7. ▸ Study of corruption of professional ideal during Nazi era; attributed to economic imperatives. [AIM]

4.610 Melvin Kranzberg, ed. *Technological education—technological style.* San Francisco: San Francisco Press, 1986. ISBN 0-911302-59-X. ▸ Twelve essays on development of technical education primarily in Western Europe and United States. Good comparative perspective; short essays well done with provocative ideas. [TSR]

4.611 Edwin T. Layton. *The revolt of the engineers: social responsibility and the American engineering profession.* 1971 ed. Baltimore: Johns Hopkins University Press, 1986. ISBN 0-8018-3286-1 (cl), 0-8018-3287-X (pbk). ▸ Rise of social responsibility concurrent with professionalism in United States. Crisis of identity in 1920s and 1930s leading to adoption of public service outlook. [AIM]

4.612 A. Michal McMahon. *The making of a profession: a century of electrical engineering in America.* New York: Institute of Electrical & Electronic Engineers, 1984. ISBN 0-87942-173-8. ▸ Analysis of three major American electrical engineering societies in political, industrial, and educational contexts. Uses biographical episodes from careers of individuals such as Charles Proteus Steinmetz, David Sarnoff, and Frederick Terman to illustrate themes. Only modestly successful. [TSR]

4.613 Terry S. Reynolds. *Seventy-five years of progress: a history of the American Institute of Chemical Engineers, 1908–1983.* J. Charles Forman and Larry Resen, eds. New York: American Institute of Chemical Engineers, 1983. ISBN 0-8169-0231-3. ▸ Focus on idea of unit operations and its acceptance as central facet of chemical engineering in United States. [AIM]

4.614 Terry Shinn. *L'École Polytechnique: 1794–1914.* Paris: Presses de la Foundation Nationale des Sciences Politiques, 1980. ISBN 2-7246-0434-2. ▸ History of France's most prestigious engineering school. Relates how it provided social legitimation and reinforced class system in France. [AIM]

4.615 Bruce Sinclair. *A centennial history of the American Society of Mechanical Engineers, 1880–1980.* Toronto: University of Toronto Press for American Society of Mechanical Engineers, 1980. ISBN 0-8020-2380-0. ▸ Focus on social issues and Society's responses to them. Mechanical engineering standardization also major theme. [AIM]

4.616 John Hubbel Weiss. *The making of technological man: the social origins of French engineering education.* Cambridge, Mass.: MIT Press, 1982. ISBN 0-262-23112-3. ▸ Study of backgrounds of graduates of École Centrale des Arts et Manufactures, Paris, 1829–50. Shows prominent construction engineers emerging from middle class. [AIM]

Technology Transfer

4.617 Shannon R. Brown. "The Ewo filature: a study in the transfer of technology to China in the nineteenth century." *Technology and culture* 20 (1979) 550–68. ISSN 0040-165X. ▸ Study of first steam-powered silk factory in China. Failure due to social factors. [DHS]

4.618 Carlo M. Cipolla. "The diffusion of innovations in early modern Europe." *Comparative studies in society and history* 14 (1974) 46–52. ISSN 0010-4175. ▸ Framework for spread of early industrialization. Obstacles to diffusion overcome by migration of skilled craftsmen. [DHS]

4.619 Daniel R. Headrick. *The tentacles of progress: technology transfer in the age of imperialism, 1850–1940.* New York: Oxford University Press, 1988. ISBN 0-19-505115-7 (cl), 0-19-505116-5 (pbk). ▸ Discussion of how colonial powers attempted to modernize and control Asia, Africa, and Latin America with latest innovations: shipping, railroads, telegraphy and radio, sewerage, technical education, etc. India prime example. [DHS]

4.620 Ian Inkster. *Science and technology in history: an approach to industrial development.* New Brunswick, N.J.: Rutgers University Press, 1991. ISBN 0-8135-1689-3. ▸ Global review of economic development based on diffusion of science and technology. Emphasizes role of government; recognizes failures as well as successes. [DHS]

4.621 David J. Jeremy, ed. *International technology transfer: Europe, Japan, and the USA, 1700–1914.* Aldershot, England: Elgar, 1991. ISBN 1-85278-317-6. ▸ Essays on textiles, railroads, iron and steel, shipping, telegraphy and telephony, chemicals, and electrical products. Explores varieties of transfer process and adaptations of new technologies by receiving nations. [DHS]

4.622 David J. Jeremy, ed. *The transfer of international technology: Europe, Japan, and the USA in the twentieth century.* Aldershot, England: Elgar, 1992. ISBN 1-85279-453-9. ▸ Overview of automobile, chemical, computer, petroleum, and textile technologies in age of global transfers. [DHS]

4.623 Eric Robinson. "The early diffusion of steam power." *Journal of economic history* 34.1 (1974) 91–107. ISSN 0022-0507. ▸ British engineers and Newcomen-Watt technology in continental Europe and United States, 1720s to early 1800s. One of several studies of technology transfer in this issue. [DHS]

4.624 Darwin H. Stapleton. *The transfer of early industrial technologies to America.* Philadelphia: American Philosophical Society, 1987. (Memoirs of the American Philosophical Society, 177.) ISBN 0-87169-177-9. ▸ Review of European transplants to seaboard colonies and United States to 1850. Case studies of civil engineering, gunpowder manufacture, and coal-fueled iron making. [DHS]

Gender and Technology

4.625 Ruth Schwartz Cowan. *More work for mother: the ironies of household technology from the open hearth to the microwave.* New York: Basic Books, 1983. ISBN 0-465-04731-9, ISSN 0065-9738. ▸ Best history of technology's impact on American housework. Seeks to understand why technology has not freed women from housework. Excellent overview and analysis including histories of particular household technologies. [PEM]

4.626 Margery W. Davies. *Woman's place is at the typewriter: office work and office workers, 1870–1930.* Philadelphia: Temple University Press, 1982. ISBN 0-87722-291-6 (cl), 0-87722-368-8 (pbk). ▸ Study of women's move into clerical work in late nineteenth-century United States. New technology (e.g., typewriter) and new techniques of scientific management crucial. Radical political framework. [PEM]

4.627 Thomas Dublin. *Women at work: the transformation of work and community in Lowell, Massachusetts, 1826–1860.* New York: Columbia University Press, 1979. ISBN 0-231-04166-7 (cl), 0-231-04167-5 (pbk). ▸ Key study of mostly female workforce in early American textile factories—important in American industrial revolution. Good place to start any investigation of women workers in America or early industrialization. [PEM]

4.628 Sarah Franklin and Maureen McNeil. "Reproductive

futures, recent literature, and current feminist debates on reproductive technologies: review essay." *Feminist studies* 14 (1988) 545–60. ISSN 0046-3663. ▸ Introduction to literature on gender and technology, mostly oriented toward current and future issues but also involving issues and cases of interest to historians. [PEM]

4.629 Sally L. Hacker. *"Doing it the hard way": investigations of gender and technology.* Dorothy E. Smith and Susan M. Turner, eds. Boston: Unwin Hyman, 1990. ISBN 0-04-445434-1 (cl), 0-04-445435-X (pbk). ▸ Papers and interviews by sociologist concerned with issues of technology and gender. Examines women workers at AT&T, women and agribusiness, women and culture of engineering, impact of automation, technology and eroticism. [PEM]

4.630 Barbara A. Hanawalt, ed. *Women and work in preindustrial Europe.* Bloomington: Indiana University Press, 1986. ISBN 0-253-36610-0 (cl), 0-253-20367-8 (pbk). ▸ Useful survey of women's work in medieval and early modern Europe but not primarily oriented toward technology. Articles on work of peasant women, town women, and women who worked in crafts. [PEM]

4.631 Ruth Perry and Lisa Greber. "Women and computers: an introduction." *Signs* 16.1 (1990) 74–101. ISSN 0097-9740. ▸ Valuable introduction to ideas and literature on women and computers, including lengthy section on history of women and computers. [PEM]

4.632 Martha Moore Trescott, ed. *Dynamos and virgins revisited: women and technological change in history: an anthology.* Metuchen, N.J.: Scarecrow, 1979. ISBN 0-8108-1263-0. ▸ Somewhat dated but still useful overview. Includes sections on women's employment, women inventors and scientists, effect of technological change on household, and technology relating to reproduction and child rearing. [PEM]

4.633 Judy Wajcman. *Feminism confronts technology.* University Park: Pennsylvania State University Press, 1991. ISBN 0-271-00801-6 (cl), 0-271-00802-4 (pbk). ▸ Sociologist's overview of interrelationship between technology and gender. Analyses of production, reproductive and domestic technology, and built environment. Not primarily historical, but provides useful theoretical perspective. [PEM]

Technology and Material Culture

4.634 Siegfried Giedion. *Space, time, and architecture: the growth of a new tradition.* 5th ed. Cambridge, Mass.: Harvard University Press, 1967. ▸ Uses changes in architecture to chronicle alterations in consciousness of space and time. Discusses urban development, city planning, universal expositions, industrial towns, and worker housing from Renaissance to World War I. [MRL]

4.635 Francis D. Klingender. *Art and the Industrial Revolution.* Rev. ed. Arthur Elton, ed. New York: Kelley, 1968. ▸ Marxist exploration of role of arts in British Industrial Revolution. Chapters on Joseph Wright of Derby, documentary illustration, the sublime and picturesque, and photographic use by generation of "new-fangled men." [MRL]

4.636 Miriam R. Levin. *When the Eiffel Tower was new: French visions of progress at the centennial of the Revolution.* South Hadley, Mass.: Mount Holyoke College Art Museum; distributed by University of Massachusetts Press, 1989. ISBN 0-87023-673-3 (pbk). ▸ Ideological context of tower's construction, universal expositions of 1889 and 1900, and meaning of images of tower and new consumer technologies in posters, photographs, and prints of Belle Epoch. [MRL]

4.637 Lewis Mumford. *Art and technics.* New York: Columbia University Press, 1952. ▸ Explores relationship between art and technology in industrial era. Moralizing, deeply felt argument in favor of liberal democratic technics. From lectures delivered at Columbia University in 1951. [MRL]

4.638 Miles Orvell. *The real thing: imitation and authenticity in American culture, 1880–1940.* Chapel Hill: University of North Carolina Press, 1989. ISBN 0-8078-1837-2 (cl), 0-8078-4246-X (pbk). ▸ Examination of furnishings, architecture, photography, and literature from 1880s to World War II. Explores interaction of artists with forces of contemporary science and technology. [MRL]

4.639 Nikolaus Pevsner. *The sources of modern architecture and design.* New York: Praeger, 1968. ▸ Discussion of shift in design from handicraft in late nineteenth-century Europe and Britain to industrial design and development of international style. Chapters on art nouveau, art, and industry. Well illustrated. [MRL]

4.640 Alan Trachtenberg. *Brooklyn Bridge: fact and symbol.* 2d ed. Chicago: University of Chicago Press, 1979. ISBN 0-226-81115-8. ▸ Bridge as cultural symbol. Contains less on technical aspects of bridge design and construction than meaning of technology for generation of writers and journalists of Gilded Era. [MRL]

Technology and Literature

4.641 Frederick Amrine, ed. *Literature and science as modes of expression.* Dordrecht: Kluwer, 1989. ISBN 0-7923-0133-1. ▸ Collection of essays. Of particular interest are: Slade, "Conceptualizing Technology in Literary Terms: Some American Examples" and Orvell, "Literature and the Authority of Technology." [MRL]

4.642 Arthur Kroker. *The possessed individual: technology and new French theory.* New York: St. Martin's, 1992. ISBN 0-312-07130-2 (pbk). ▸ Study of theories of French structuralists and poststructuralists with common focus on technology as unifying factor among French intellectuals. Includes Michel Foucault, Roland Barthes, Jean Baudrillard, and Jean Francois Lyotard. [MRL]

4.643 Leo Marx. *Machine in the garden: technology and the pastoral ideal in America.* 1964 ed. London: Oxford University Press, 1977. ISBN 0-19-500738-7. ▸ History of pastoral idea in American literature and role as mediation between art and nature in which machine is integrated, tamed, and made compatible with nature in nineteenth century. [MRL]

4.644 Leo Marx. *The pilot and the passenger: essays on literature, technology, and culture in the United States.* New York: Oxford University Press, 1988. ISBN 0-19-504875-X. ▸ Essays exploring dialectic between American pastoral dream and harsh realities of industrialism. Critiques efforts to solve difficulties of industrial life through appeals to political ideal referencing unblemished nature. [MRL]

4.645 Mary Wollstonecraft Shelley. *Frankenstein, or, the modern Prometheus: the 1818 text with a new preface.* James Rieger, ed. Chicago: University of Chicago Press, 1982. ISBN 0-226-75227-5 (pbk). ▸ Romantic novel about creation of artificial life (man as companion to its inventor). Intriguing themes: love-hate relationship between humans and their inventions, destructiveness of misused technology, and autonomous technology. [MRL]

4.646 Wylie Sypher. *Literature and technology: the alien vision.* 1968 ed. New York: Vintage, 1971. ▸ Study of alienation of individual in society using two developments to structure argument: rise of objective outlook among artists and scientists and mechanization of production that separated worker from product of his labor. [MRL]

4.647 Thomas R. West. *Flesh of steel: literature and the machine in American culture.* Ann Arbor: University Microfilms International Research Press, 1967. ISBN 0-8357-3269-X. ▸ Explores

response of American writers to mechanization of environment. Includes discussions of John Dos Passos, Thorstein Veblen, and Lewis Mumford. Asserts writers evidenced polarity between discipline and energy in their aesthetic and moral attitudes. [MRL]

4.648 Rosalind Williams. *Notes on the underground: an essay on technology, society, and the imagination.* Cambridge, Mass.: MIT Press, 1990. ISBN 0-262-23145-X. ▸ Asserts writers, including Victor Hugo, Charles Dickens, H. G. Wells, and E. M. Forster, turned forbidden depths (sewers, tunnels, mines, subways) into dominant literary theme. Transformed notions of sublime into those of fantastic. [MRL]

HISTORY OF MEDICINE

Reference Works

4.649 Martin Kaufman, Stuart Galishoff, and Todd L. Savitt, eds. *Dictionary of American medical biography.* 2 vols. Westport, Conn.: Greenwood, 1984. ISBN 0-313-21378-X. ▸ Listing of orthodox and irregular contributors to medical practice, knowledge, and institutions from seventeenth century to 1970s. Includes leading health professionals from all states and some who were not necessarily physicians. [JHC]

4.650 Jeremy Norman, ed. *Morton's medical bibliography: an annotated check-list of texts illustrating the history of medicine.* 5th ed. Brookfield, Vt.: Gower, 1991. ISBN 0-566-03630-4, 0-85967-897-0. ▸ Classified guide to landmark publications in various branches, specialties, and sciences of medicine. Heavily emphasizes mainline Western scientific medicine. [JHC]

4.651 United States. Department of Health and Human Services, Public Health Service, National Institutes of Health, National Library of Medicine. *Bibliography of the history of medicine.* Washington, D.C.: United States Government Printing Office, 1965–. ISSN 0067-7280. ▸ Annually published index to current scholarship (1964 onward) in history of medicine and related specialties, branches, and sciences. Covers all countries and principal languages. Classified by geographical areas and historical periods as well as by subject. [JHC]

4.652 United States. National Library of Medicine. *Index-catalogue of the Library of the Surgeon-General's Office, United States Army: Authors and subjects.* 1880–1961 ed. 61 vols. Washington, D.C.: United States Government Printing Office, 1980–83. ISSN 0733-978X. ▸ Comprehensive index to medical monograph literature from invention of printing to 1950. Issued in five series between 1880 and 1961. Limited indexing of periodical literature. Citations from most countries and in principal languages. [JHC]

4.653 John Walton, Paul B. Beeson, and Ronald B. Scott, eds. *The Oxford companion to medicine.* 2 vols. Oxford: Oxford University Press, 1986. ISBN 0-19-261191-7 (set). ▸ Heavily historical encyclopedia-*cum*-dictionary of medical terms, events, personages, specialties, and branches. Emphasizes Great Britain and United States. Subject matter primarily mainstream scientific medicine. [JHC]

General Studies

4.654 Erwin H. Ackerknecht. *A short history of medicine.* Rev. ed. Baltimore: Johns Hopkins University Press, 1982. ISBN 0-8018-2726-4 (pbk). ▸ History of ideas, therapies, and institutions of all periods with emphasis on mainstream Western medicine. Devotes special attention to primitive healing, medical practices in Asia, and pre-Columbian American practices. [JHC]

4.655 James H. Cassedy. *Medicine in America: a short history.* Baltimore: Johns Hopkins University Press, 1991. ISBN 0-8018-4207-7 (cl), 0-8018-4208-5 (pbk). ▸ Examination of American medical distinctiveness between 1600 and present. Five main areas of emphasis: medical orthodoxy, alternative therapies, government role in health, scientific pursuits, and changing health environments. [JHC]

4.656 Audrey B. Davis. *Medicine and its technology: an introduction to the history of medical instruments.* Westport, Conn.: Greenwood, 1981. ISBN 0-313-22807-8. ▸ Wide-ranging survey of medical tools and instruments. Useful introduction with remarkable breadth of scope. [AR]

4.657 John Duffy. *The healers: a history of American medicine.* 1976 ed. Urbana: University of Illinois Press, 1979. ISBN 0-252-00743-3 (pbk). ▸ Medicine in United States from seventeenth to twentieth centuries. Social approach arranged by special topics, relying primarily on experience of selected communities. [JHC]

4.658 Fielding H. Garrison. *An introduction to the history of medicine: with medical chronology, suggestions for study, and bibliographic data.* 1929 4th ed. Philadelphia: Saunders, 1967. ISBN 0-7216-4030-3. ▸ Evolution of scientific medicine from antiquity to twentieth century, chiefly in Western world. Emphasizes "great men" and "firsts" in healing disciplines. Humanistic tradition of medical historiography. [JHC]

4.659 Lois N. Magner. *A history of medicine.* New York: Dekker, 1992. ISBN 0-8247-8673-4. ▸ Introductory survey, overview of Western and Near and Far Eastern medical traditions. Treats both intellectual and social aspects of history of medicine. [RKD]

4.660 Ronald L. Numbers and Darrel W. Amundsen, eds. *Caring and curing: health and medicine in the Western religious traditions.* New York: Macmillan, 1986. ISBN 0-02-919270-6. ▸ Twenty essays on medicine and health care in religious traditions: Jewish, early Christian, medieval Roman Catholic, later Roman Catholic, Eastern Orthodox, African American, and fourteen Protestant sects. [RKD]

4.661 Richard Harrison Shryock. *The development of modern medicine: an interpretation of the social and scientific factors involved.* 1947 rev. ed. Madison: University of Wisconsin Press, 1980. ISBN 0-299-07530-3 (cl), 0-299-07534-6 (pbk). ▸ Survey of mainstream medical developments in western Europe, 1600 to World War II. Special attention to impact in United States. Classic study of social aspects of medicine. [JHC]

4.662 Henry E. Sigerist. *Great doctors: a biographical history of medicine.* 1933 ed. Eden Paul and Cedar Paul, trans. New York: Dover, 1971. ISBN 0-486-22696-4. ▸ Venerable survey of history of medicine through lives and works of "great men." Dated but still useful within its historiographic genre. [RKD]

4.663 Charles Joseph Singer and E. Ashworth Underwood. *A short history of medicine.* 2d ed. Oxford: Clarendon, 1962. ▸ Study of mainstream medicine in West from antiquity to twentieth century with particular emphasis on post-1700 period. Treats scientific developments and social factors. [JHC]

4.664 Charles-Edward Amory Winslow. *The conquest of epidemic disease: a chapter in the history of ideas.* 1943 ed. Madison: University of Wisconsin Press, 1980. ISBN 0-299-08240-7 (cl), 0-299-08244-X (pbk). ▸ Analysis of changing ideas of epidemiology from primitive times to twentieth-century science. Concept of contagion considered in relation to beliefs in metaphysical and environmental influences on infection. [JHC]

Ancient Near East

4.665 J. Worth Estes. *The medical skills of ancient Egypt.* Canton, Mass.: Science History, 1989. ISBN 0-88135-093-1. ▸ Discussion of what *swnw* (physician) did and why, over two thousand years. Particularly good in connecting ancient with modern. Should be read with Manniche 4.668. [JS]

4.666 Paul Ghalioungui. *The house of life, Per Ankh: magic and medical science in ancient Egypt.* 2d ed. Amsterdam: Israel, 1973.

ISBN 90-6078-062-0. ▸ Based firmly on Hermann Grapow's exhaustive studies (in German), competently summarizes what was understood of ancient Egyptian medical practices in early 1970s. With Estes 4.665, gives good account of pharmaceutics. [JS]

4.667 James E. Harris and Edward F. Wente. *An X-ray atlas of the royal mummies.* Chicago: University of Chicago Press, 1980. ISBN 0-226-31745-5. ▸ Surveys what can be learned through modern techniques about diseases in ancient Egypt. Iskander's introductory chapter on mummification perhaps best available in any language. [JS]

4.668 Lise Manniche. *An ancient Egyptian herbal.* Austin: University of Texas Press in cooperation with the British Museum, 1989. ISBN 0-292-70415-1 (pbk). ▸ Together with Estes' medical expertise (4.665), Manniche's Egyptological skills reveal specific herbal lore, accompanied by parallels from later Greek texts, especially Dioscorides. [JS]

Ancient Greece and Rome

4.669 Ralph Jackson. *Doctors and diseases in the Roman empire.* Norman: University of Oklahoma Press, 1988. ISBN 0-8061-2167-X. ▸ Roman imperial medicine packaged generally through archaeology. Supplements Scarborough 4.675 with scholarship since early 1970s. [JS]

4.670 Guido Majno. *The healing hand: man and wound in the ancient world.* Cambridge, Mass.: Harvard University Press, 1975. ISBN 0-674-38330-3. ▸ Although focused on surgery, gives good accounts of myrrh and frankincense and solid summaries of Hippocratic, Hellenistic, and Roman medicine. Ancient Mesopotamia, China, India also included. Sprightly prose. [JS]

4.671 Vivian Nutton. *From Democedes to Harvey: studies in the history of medicine.* London: Variorum, 1988. ISBN 0-86078-225-5. ▸ Fourteen essays reprinted, ten on Galen and related topics in Roman antiquity. Nutton's scholarship fundamental in what we now know of Galen's intellectual context. [JS]

4.672 E. D. Phillips. *Greek medicine.* London: Thames & Hudson, 1973. ISBN 0-500-40021-0. ▸ Graceful survey of Greek medicine from pre-Socratic times through Hellenistic era. Summary of Hippocratic works one of best in English. [JS]

4.673 John M. Riddle. *Dioscorides on pharmacy and medicine.* Austin: University of Texas Press, 1985. ISBN 0-292-71544-7. ▸ Intertwining of drug lore and medicine as practiced in Roman antiquity. Finest study on often overlooked giant of medical history. [JS]

4.674 John Scarborough. *Medical terminologies: classical origins.* Norman: University of Oklahoma Press, 1992. ISBN 0-8061-2443-1. ▸ Greek and Latin in modern guise. Much history intermeshed, featuring ancient Egyptian, Greek, Roman, and late medieval texts. [JS]

4.675 John Scarborough. *Roman medicine.* 1969 ed. Ithaca, N.Y.: Cornell University Press, 1976. ISBN 0-8014-0525-4. ▸ Roman medicine from early Italic and Etruscan times through third century CE. Emphasizes social as well as medical questions that permeate both Greek and Roman medical studies. [JS]

4.676 Wesley D. Smith. *The Hippocratic tradition.* Ithaca, N.Y.: Cornell University Press, 1979. ISBN 0-8014-1209-9. ▸ Begins appropriately with modern Hippocratism, descended directly from ideals and standards created by Galen. Important book seemingly answers Hippocratic question: which Hippocratic works were, indeed, by Hippocrates of Cos? [JS]

4.677 Owsei Temkin. *Galenism: rise and decline of a medical philosophy.* Ithaca, N.Y.: Cornell University Press, 1973. ISBN 0-8014-0774-5. ▸ Galen's life and times together with his long medico-philosophical influences. Best monograph on Galenism as medical philosophy that lasted well into nineteenth century. [JS]

4.678 Owsei Temkin. *Hippocrates in a world of pagans and Christians.* Baltimore: Johns Hopkins University Press, 1991. ISBN 0-8018-4090-2. ▸ Discussion of how neutral Hippocratism survived new world order of Christianity and why Hippocratic medicine remained ideal model (as taught by Galen) throughout Middle Ages and Renaissance. [JS]

4.679 Heinrich von Staden. *Herophilus: the art of medicine in early Alexandria.* Cambridge: Cambridge University Press, 1989. ISBN 0-521-23646-0. ▸ Collection of Greek and Latin texts with extensive commentary on early Hellenistic medicine. Superb introductory chapter on relationship between native Egyptian and Hellenistic Alexandrian medicine and anatomy. [JS]

Medieval Medicine

4.680 Ann G. Carmichael. *Plague and poor in Renaissance Florence.* Cambridge: Cambridge University Press, 1986. ISBN 0-521-26833-8. ▸ Description of appearance, development, and social consequences of sanitary control measures (quarantine, lazarettos, health boards) against epidemic diseases in late medieval and early Renaissance Florence. [RKD]

4.681 Luke E. Demaitre. *Doctor Bernard de Gordon: professor and practitioner.* Toronto: Pontifical Institute of Mediaeval Studies, 1980. (Studies and texts, 51.) ISBN 0-88844-051-0, ISSN 0082-5328. ▸ Description of work of Bernard of Montpellier, famous as teacher and doctor in thirteenth and fourteenth centuries. Provides full bibliographies; guides reader through thicket of editions and texts. [JS]

4.682 Edward J. Kealey. *Medieval medicus: a social history of Anglo-Norman medicine.* Baltimore: Johns Hopkins University Press, 1981. ISBN 0-8018-2533-4. ▸ Examination of court, family, and legal connections of medical practitioners in early twelfth-century England, but little on their studies or techniques. Describes rise of institutional care and early hospital regulations. [RKD]

4.683 Per-Gunnar Ottosson. *Scholastic medicine and philosophy: a study of commentaries on Galen's Tegni, ca. 1300–1450.* Naples: Bibliopolis, 1984. ISBN 88-7088-108-3 (pbk). ▸ Shows importance of early scholastic commentaries (especially on Galen's *Tegni*) in preservation of classical knowledge in early Latin medical texts. [JS]

4.684 Katharine Park. *Doctors and medicine in early Renaissance Florence.* Princeton: Princeton University Press, 1985. ISBN 0-691-08373-8. ▸ Medical organization in fourteenth-century Florence. Stresses variety of medical care, relationship to corporate culture of north Italian city-states, and disruptive effects of plague on patterns of medical recruitment. [JS]

4.685 John M. Riddle. *Contraception and abortion from the ancient world to the Renaissance.* Cambridge, Mass.: Harvard University Press, 1992. ISBN 0-674-16875-5. ▸ History of subject arguing that ancient world possessed effective safe contraceptives and abortifacients. Discusses why body of ancient knowledge was lost during Middle Ages. [RKD]

4.686 Stanley Rubin. *Medieval English medicine.* New York: Barnes & Noble, 1974. ISBN 0-06-496016-1. ▸ Sturdy, much more readable successor to J.H.G. Grattan and Charles Singer's *Anglo-Saxon Magic and Medicine* (1952). Certainly one of best accounts of early English medicine. [JS]

4.687 Nancy G. Siraisi. *Medieval and early Renaissance medicine: an introduction to knowledge and practice.* Chicago: University of Chicago Press, 1990. ISBN 0-226-76129-0 (cl), 0-226-76130-4 (pbk). ▸ Outstanding survey of medicine in western Europe,

especially Italian city-states, from roughly twelfth to fifteenth century. Concentrates on lives, expertise, and associations of medical practitioners. Superb combination of breadth and depth. [RKD/JS/MLC]

4.688 Nancy G. Siraisi. *Taddeo Alderotti and his pupils: two generations of Italian medical learning.* Princeton: Princeton University Press, 1981. ISBN 0-691-05313-8. ▸ Late thirteenth-century teaching and practice of medicine brilliantly evoked directly from the texts. One of fundamental studies on medieval Italian medicine. [JS]

Early Modern Medicine

4.689 Giulia Calvi. *Histories of a plague year: the social and the imaginary in baroque Florence.* Dario Biocca and Bryant T. Ragan, Jr., trans. Berkeley: University of California Press, 1989. ISBN 0-520-05799-6. ▸ Popular and political responses to and interpretations of plague of 1630–33. Interdisciplinary history of mentalities based on archival sources and on semiotics and methods of cultural anthropology. [KP]

4.690 Harold J. Cook. *The decline of the old medical regime in Stuart London.* Ithaca, N.Y.: Cornell University Press, 1986. ISBN 0-8014-1850-X. ▸ History of London College of Physicians from its zenith in 1630s through decline around 1700. Relations between medical practice, intellectual values, and economic and political history. [KP]

4.691 Allen G. Debus. *The chemical philosophy: Paracelsian science and medicine in the sixteenth and seventeenth centuries.* 2 vols. New York: Science History, 1977. ISBN 0-88202-047-1. ▸ Background to and development of Paracelsian tradition in western Europe. Synthetic survey of relevant ideas, authors, and institutions. [KP]

4.692 John Duffy. *Epidemics in colonial America.* 1953 ed. Port Washington, N.Y.: Kennikat, 1972. ISBN 0-8046-1664-7. ▸ Analysis of distribution and extent of principal infectious diseases throughout colonial period, together with prevailing religious beliefs and scientific knowledge pertaining to them. Social, economic, and political effects of outbreaks on colonial development. [JHC]

4.693 Audrey Eccles. *Obstetrics and gynaecology in Tudor and Stuart England.* Kent, Ohio: Kent State University Press, 1982. ISBN 0-87338-270-6. ▸ Study of ideas on obstetrics and generation between 1540 and 1740 as contained in textbooks for practitioners. Useful introduction to both theories of generation and obstetrical practice. [KP]

4.694 Sander L. Gilman. *Sexuality, an illustrated history: representing the sexual in medicine and culture from the Middle Ages to the age of AIDS.* New York: Wiley, 1989. ISBN 0-471-83792-X. ▸ Evolution of Western male constructions of human sexuality as expressed in works of European artists and writers. Six provocative and important chapters devoted to Renaissance and early modern period. [KP]

4.695 Francisco Guerra. *American medical bibliography, 1639–1783.* New York: Harper, 1962. (Yale University, Department of the History of Science and Medicine, 40.) ▸ Medical and health-related material in printed publications of early America. Summarizes content, gives locations of known copies of relevant books, pamphlets, almanacs, newspapers, and other periodicals. [JHC]

4.696 Michael MacDonald. *Mystical bedlam: madness, anxiety, and healing in seventeenth-century England.* 1981 ed. Cambridge: Cambridge University Press, 1983. ISBN 0-521-23170-1 (cl, 1981), 0-521-27382-X (pbk). ▸ Beliefs and practices surrounding mental illness as revealed in medical notes of physician Richard

Napier. Important contribution to history of psychiatry in religious and cultural context. [KP]

4.697   Charles Donald O'Malley. *Andreas Vesalius of Brussels, 1514–1564.* Berkeley: University of California Press, 1964. ‣ Life and work of leading figure in anatomical Renaissance. Classic biography containing much general information about teaching and practice of medicine and about medical patronage and publishing. [KP]

4.698   Walter Pagel. *Paracelsus: an introduction to philosophical medicine in the era of the Renaissance.* 2d rev. ed. Basel: Karger, 1982. ISBN 3-8055-3518-X. ‣ Life and thought of Paracelsus in context of contemporary religious and intellectual history. Classic study of medical and philosophical ideas in sixteenth-century central Europe. [KP]

4.699   David B. Ruderman. *Kabbalah, magic, and science: the cultural universe of a sixteenth-century Jewish physician.* Cambridge, Mass.: Harvard University Press, 1988. ISBN 0-674-49660-4. ‣ Study of intellectual and social world of Italian physician Abraham ben Hananiah Yagel. Intellectual history emphasizing relationships between religion, magic, and science and between Jewish and non-Jewish cultures. [KP]

4.700   Nancy G. Siraisi. *Avicenna in Renaissance Italy: the canon and medical teaching in Italian universities after 1500.* Princeton: Princeton University Press, 1987. ISBN 0-691-05137-2. ‣ Academic medicine in sixteenth-century Italy with emphasis on textual scholarship and relations between medicine and philosophy. Fine-grained textual analysis and intellectual history. [KP]

4.701   Paul Slack. *The impact of the plague in Tudor and Stuart England.* 1985 ed. New York: Oxford University Press, 1990. ISBN 0-19-820213-X. ‣ In-depth examination of incidence and mortality of later plague epidemics, response of public authorities to them, and effects on English culture. [CSH]

4.702   Andrew Wear, Roger K. French, and Ian M. Lonie, eds. *The medical Renaissance of the sixteenth century.* Cambridge: Cambridge University Press, 1985. ISBN 0-521-30112-2. ‣ Essays on medical learning in sixteenth-century Europe with emphasis on academic medicine and role of humanism. Sample of state-of-art intellectual history by leading scholars. [KP]

4.703   Charles Webster, ed. *Health, medicine, and mortality in the sixteenth century.* Cambridge: Cambridge University Press, 1979. ISBN 0-521-22643-0. ‣ Essays on disease, its interpretation, and its treatment with emphasis on English sources and on social and demographic approaches. [KP]

SEE ALSO

22.203 Ian Maclean. *The Renaissance notion of woman.*
37.414 John Tate Lanning. *The Royal Protomedicato.*

Modern Medicine

4.704   Erwin H. Ackerknecht. *Rudolf Virchow: doctor, statesman, and anthropologist.* 1953 ed. New York: Arno, 1981. ISBN 0-405-13832-6. ‣ Analysis of Virchow's multifaceted career and ideas. Classic account of influential German medical thinker, political reformer, and anthropologist. [CH]

4.705   Michael Bliss. *The discovery of insulin.* Chicago: University of Chicago Press, 1982. ISBN 0-226-05897-2 (cl), 0-226-05898-0 (pbk). ‣ Richly textured case study exploring problems posed by isolation and production of insulin. [AR]

4.706   Thomas Neville Bonner. *American doctors and German universities: a chapter in international intellectual relations, 1870–1914.* Lincoln: University of Nebraska Press, 1963. ‣ Examination of historical roots of American medical system in experiences of American medical students at German universities in Ger-

many, Austria-Hungary, and Switzerland. Describes their ambitions and activities after return to United States. [JHC]

4.707   Jeanne L. Brand. *Doctors and the state: the British medical profession and government action in public health, 1870–1912.* Baltimore: Johns Hopkins University Press, 1965. ‣ Examination of role of British medical profession in development of government action for preventive and curative medicine in period leading to program of social medicine. [CH]

4.708   Joan Jacobs Brumberg. *Fasting girls: the emergence of anorexia nervosa as a modern disease.* Cambridge, Mass.: Harvard University Press, 1988. ISBN 0-674-29501-3. ‣ History of disease as "cultural artifact, defined and redefined over time." Reveals biological, psychological, social, intellectual, and economic factors involved with food refusal from Middle Ages to present. [CH]

4.709   William F. Bynum and Roy Porter, eds. *William Hunter and the eighteenth-century medical world.* Cambridge: Cambridge University Press, 1985. ISBN 0-521-26806-0. ‣ Fourteen essays exploring Hunter's career and influence in eighteenth-century medicine. Innovative approaches to topics of medical education, clinical medicine, role of teaching hospitals, anatomy and physiology, and obstetrics. [CH]

4.710   William Coleman. *Yellow fever in the north: the methods of early epidemiology.* Madison: University of Wisconsin Press, 1987. ISBN 0-299-11110-5 (cl), 0-299-11114-8 (pbk). ‣ Uses European outbreaks of yellow fever to assess epidemiological thinking prior to germ theory of disease. Illuminates difficulty of understanding disease origin and transmission in first half of nineteenth century. [CH]

4.711   William Coleman and Frederic Lawrence Holmes, eds. *The investigative enterprise: experimental physiology in nineteenth-century medicine.* Berkeley: University of California Press, 1988. ISBN 0-520-06048-2. ‣ Essays on nineteenth-century experimental physiology, primarily in Germany and France. New emphasis on interplay among research programs, institutional forms, professional careers, medical practice and education, and state interests. [CH]

4.712   John M. Eyler. *Victorian social medicine: the ideas and methods of William Farr.* Baltimore: Johns Hopkins University Press, 1979. ISBN 0-8018-2246-7. ‣ Intellectual biography of prominent public health reformer in Victorian England and pioneering statistician of morbidity and mortality. Analyzes state medicine and social welfare in Britain through case study. [CH]

4.713   Donald Fleming. *William H. Welch and the rise of modern medicine.* 1954 ed. Baltimore: Johns Hopkins University Press, 1987. ISBN 0-8018-3389-2 (pbk). ‣ Description of Welch's role in transformation of late nineteenth- and early twentieth-century American medicine based on European medical theory, method, and educational practice. [JHC]

4.714   Simon Flexner and James Thomas Flexner. *William Henry Welch and the heroic age of American medicine.* New York: Viking, 1941. ‣ Study of transfer of European experimental medicine to America, 1870s to 1930s. Discusses revolutionary reshaping of hospitals, sciences, medical education, and public health and key supportive roles of new philanthropic foundations. [JHC]

4.715   Richard D. French. *Antivivisection and medical science in Victorian society.* Princeton: Princeton University Press, 1975. ISBN 0-691-05226-3 (cl), 0-691-10027-6 (pbk). ‣ Emergence of antivivisection movement in late nineteenth-century England and its implications for medicine and science. Useful exploration of public perceptions of medicine at turning point in development of scientific medicine. [CH]

4.716   Norman Gevitz, ed. *Other healers: unorthodox medicine in the United States.* Baltimore: Johns Hopkins University Press, 1988. ISBN 0-8018-3664-6 (cl), 0-8018-3710-3 (pbk). ‣ Emergence of alternative therapies in nineteenth century and continued manifestations during twentieth century. Essays on homeopathy, water cure, hygiene, chiropractic, faith healing, and other aspects of nonmainstream medicine. [JHC]

4.717 Victoria A. Harden. *Rocky mountain spotted fever: history of a twentieth-century disease.* Baltimore: Johns Hopkins University Press, 1990. ISBN 0-8018-3905-X. ▸ Uses investigation of research into spotted fever to explore larger issues of twentieth-century infectious disease management. [CH]

4.718 Frederic Lawrence Holmes. *Claude Bernard and animal chemistry: the emergence of a scientist.* Cambridge, Mass: Harvard University Press, 1974. ISBN 0-674-13485-0. ▸ Examination of early career of renowned French experimental physiologist and medical philosopher. Thorough detailed account of Bernard's research in 1840s. [CH]

4.719 Lester S. King. *The medical world of the eighteenth century.* 1958 ed. Huntington, N.Y.: Krieger, 1971. ▸ Series of essays discussing medical profession, quackery, medical theory, Hermann Boerhaave's scientific and medical ideas, and development of pathological anatomy. Old-fashioned survey of eighteenth-century medicine in European context. [CH]

4.720 Judith Walzer Leavitt and Ronald L. Numbers, eds. *Sickness and health in America: readings in the history of medicine and public health.* 2d ed. Madison: University of Wisconsin Press, 1985. ISBN 0-299-10270-X (cl), 0-299-10274-2 (pbk). ▸ Selected journal articles by modern authorities and including extensive reading lists. Deals primarily with social aspects of American medicine from colonial period to twentieth century. [JHC]

4.721 Jacques Leonard. *La médecine entre les savoirs et les pouvoirs: histoire intellectuelle et politique de la médecine française au dix-neuvième siècle.* Paris: Montaigne, 1981. ISBN 2-7007-0230-1. ▸ Intellectual and political history of medicine in France from Revolution to beginning of twentieth century. Contribution to understanding role of medicine in French society. [CH]

4.722 John E. Lesch. *Science and medicine in France: the emergence of experimental physiology, 1790–1855.* Cambridge, Mass.: Harvard University Press, 1984. ISBN 0-674-79400-1. ▸ Traces emergence of experimental physiology in France and examines how it was shaped by Parisian scientific and medical milieu. Shows significance of Paris medicine of first half of nineteenth century. [CH]

4.723 G. A. Lindeboom. *Hermann Boerhaave: the man and his work.* London: Methuen, 1968. ▸ Biography of dominant figure in eighteenth-century European medicine. Straightforward examination of life, writings, medical teaching and practice, and scientific ideas. Portrait of Leiden as medical university and location of early bedside teaching. [CH]

4.724 Roy M. MacLeod and Milton Lewis, eds. *Disease, medicine, and empire: perspectives on Western medicine and the experience of European expansion.* London: Routledge, 1988. ISBN 0-415-00685-6. ▸ Collection of essays analyzing legacy of European imperialism in colonial medicine. Treats British empire primarily, but comparative material on French and German colonies also discussed. Pathbreaking work in new area of medical history. [CH]

4.725 Russell C. Maulitz. *Morbid appearances: the anatomy of pathology in the early nineteenth century.* Cambridge: Cambridge University Press, 1987. ISBN 0-521-32828-4. ▸ Rise of pathological anatomy in France and England in early 1800s. Analyzes political and institutional as well as intellectual context. Examines transmission of medical ideas from one culture to another. [CH]

4.726 Genevieve Miller. *The adoption of inoculation for smallpox in England and France.* Philadelphia: University of Pennsylvania Press, 1957. ▸ Factors influencing scientific and public accep-

tance of inoculation in eighteenth century before Edward Jenner's discovery. Contribution to history of preventive medicine. [CH]

4.727 Anne Marie Moulin. *Le dernier langage de la médecine: histoire de l'immunologie de Pasteur au Sida.* Paris: Presses Universitaires de France, 1991. ISBN 2-13-043798-2, ISSN 0753-6216. ▸ Study of effects of development of immunological knowledge on medical understanding and language from historical perspective. [CH]

4.728 Martin S. Pernick. *A calculus of suffering: pain, professionalism, and anesthesia in nineteenth-century America.* New York: Columbia University Press, 1985. ISBN 0-231-05186-7. ▸ Examination of why American physicians reserved anesthesia only for selected patients following its discovery. Fascinating, meticulously documented analysis. [AR]

4.729 Dorothy Porter and Roy Porter. *Patient's progress: doctors and doctoring in eighteenth-century England.* Stanford, Calif.: Stanford University Press, 1989. ISBN 0-8047-1744-3. ▸ Exploration of relationship between sick people and their doctors in premodern era. Analyzes attitudes, treatments, and problems of practice in medical, cultural, and social context. [CH]

4.730 Roy Porter. *Health for sale: quackery in England, 1660–1850.* Manchester: Manchester University Press; distributed by St. Martin's, 1989. ISBN 0-7190-1903-6. ▸ Analysis of medical quackery as part of growth of commercialized marketplace medicine. Innovative survey of understudied topic; includes patient's perspective. [CH]

4.731 Roy Porter and Dorothy Porter. *In sickness and in health: the British experience, 1650–1850.* 1988 ed. New York: Blackwell, 1989. ISBN 1-55786-036-X. ▸ Lay experience of sickness during long eighteenth century. Breaks new ground in rediscovery of attitudes and beliefs about health and illness. [CH]

4.732 Stanley Joel Reiser. *Medicine and the reign of technology.* Cambridge: Cambridge University Press, 1978. ISBN 0-521-21907-8. ▸ Argument that diagnostic technology has pushed patient to periphery of modern medicine. Impressive synthesis in spite of polemical overtones. [AR]

4.733 James C. Riley. *The eighteenth-century campaign to avoid disease.* New York: St. Martin's, 1987. ISBN 0-312-00238-6. ▸ Study of epidemiological thinking in eighteenth century analyzing role of environment and measures to avoid disease. [CH]

4.734 James C. Riley. *Sickness, recovery, and death: a history and forecast of ill health.* Iowa City: University of Iowa Press, 1989. ISBN 0-87745-233-4. ▸ Analysis of trends in ill health from seventeenth to twentieth century using records of health care expenditures. Also projects future human health trends. [CH]

4.735 Charles E. Rosenberg. *The cholera years: the United States in 1832, 1849, and 1866; with a new afterword.* 1962 ed. Chicago: University of Chicago Press, 1987. ISBN 0-226-72679-7 (cl), 0-226-72677-0 (pbk). ▸ Analysis of social impact of century's most feared epidemic disease. Documents decline in belief that divine intervention caused cholera during period of increasing medical knowledge and public sanitary action. [JHC]

4.736 Todd L. Savitt and James Harvey Young, eds. *Disease and distinctiveness in the American South.* Knoxville: University of Tennessee Press, 1988. ISBN 0-87049-572-0. ▸ Historical significance of endemic malaria, hookworm infection, pellagra, and recurring yellow fever in shaping social, intellectual, and economic development of South. Examines slave health and special aspects of southern therapeutics. [JHC]

4.737 Richard Harrison Shryock. *Medicine and society in America, 1660–1860.* 1960 ed. Ithaca, N.Y.: Cornell University Press, 1977. ISBN 0-8014-9093-6. ▸ How American medicine developed from British and European ideas altered by local influences and conditions. Medicine considered in its social as well as professional development. [JHC]

4.738 Reinhard Spree. *Health and social class in imperial Germany: a social history of mortality, morbidity, and inequality.* Stuart McKinnon Evans, trans. Oxford: Berg; distributed by St. Martin's, 1988. ISBN 0-85496-527-0. ‣ Examination of how health care differed among social classes in imperial Germany. [CH]

4.739 Stephen P. Strickland. *Politics, science, and dread disease: a short history of United States medical research policy.* Cambridge, Mass.: Harvard University Press, 1972. ISBN 0-674-68955-0. ‣ Evolution of large-scale federal role, 1930–70. Buildup of National Institutes of Health based on key congressional support and heavy involvement of lobbyists representing private foundations and medical groups. [JHC]

4.740 Virgil J. Vogel. *American Indian medicine.* Norman: University of Oklahoma Press, 1970. ISBN 0-8061-0863-0 (cl), 0-8061-2293-5 (pbk). ‣ Theories, practices, and diseases from first contacts with whites to twentieth century. Special examination of American Indian therapies, including numerous botanical drugs subsequently adopted in modern pharmacology. [JHC]

4.741 John Harley Warner. *The therapeutic perspective: medical practice, knowledge, and identity in America, 1820–1885.* Cambridge, Mass.: Harvard University Press, 1986. ISBN 0-674-88330-6. ‣ Evolution of American medicine from decline of speculative systems to early impact of laboratory science. Differential transformation of orthodox profession in eastern, southern, and midwestern regions. [JHC]

4.742 Paul Weindling. *Health, race, and German politics between national unification and nazism, 1870–1945.* Cambridge: Cambridge University Press, 1989. ISBN 0-521-36381-0. ‣ Analysis of effects of racial ideas in biology, on medical profession, public health, and welfare services. Studies use of eugenics in program of national German reconstruction and effect on medical and scientific aspirations. [CH]

SEE ALSO
26.248 Alain Corbin. *The foul and the fragrant.*
30.155 Barbara Duden. *The woman beneath the skin.*
31.441 Michael H. Kater. *Doctors under Hitler.*
34.449 Susan Gross Solomon and John F. Hutchinson. *Health and society in revolutionary Russia.*

Pharmacy

4.743 David L. Cowen and William H. Helfand. *Pharmacy: an illustrated history.* New York: Abrams, 1990. ISBN 0-8109-1498-0. ‣ Unlike most coffee-table books, offers both readable scholarly text and some gorgeous color plates. Ranges from prehistoric drug lore to molecular genetics. [JS]

4.744 Richard A. Deno, Thomas D. Rowe, and Donald C. Brodie. *The profession of pharmacy: an introductory textbook.* 2d ed. Philadelphia: Lippincott, 1966. ‣ Pharmacy as contrasted with general practice of medicine from medieval times to mid-1950s. Argues pharmacy was separate from medicine from earliest times. [JS]

4.745 Barbara Griggs. *Green pharmacy: a history of herbal medicine.* 1981 ed. New York: Viking, 1982. ISBN 0-670-35434-1. ‣ Very readable study of herbs and herbalism from antiquity to modern times with welcome comparisons between ancient texts and modern herbal practices. Good coverage of primary texts in English and French. [JS]

4.746 Edward Kremers and George Urdang. *Kremers and Urdang's History of Pharmacy.* 4th ed. Glenn Sonnedecker, Revisions. Philadelphia: Lippincott, 1976. ISBN 0-397-52074-3. ‣ Standard English-language survey of history of pharmacy from

ancient times to mid-twentieth century. Particularly strong on modern American and western European pharmacy as distinguished from medicine. [JS]

4.747 Ronald D. Mann. *Modern drug use: an enquiry on historical principles.* Lancaster, Pa.: MTP Press, 1984. ISBN 0-85200-717-5. ‣ Ambitious, succinct survey of phytopharmacology from antiquity through about 1975. Accuracy increases with advances in time: weakest sections treat matters before eighteenth century. [JS]

4.748 John Scarborough, ed. *Folklore and folk medicines.* Madison, Wisc.: American Institute of the History of Pharmacy, 1987. ISBN 0-931292-19-0 (pbk). ‣ Eight essays by seven authors describing fundamental influence of folk medicine in several cultures from ancient Greece to colonial and modern America and Caucasian Armenia. [JS]

4.749 Hermann Schelenz. *Geschichte der Pharmazie.* 1904 ed. Hildesheim: Olms, 1965. ‣ Pharmacy intermixed with medicine until eighteenth century. Still finest, most comprehensive, compact history of pharmacy until about 1890. Sources cited from original texts (Greek, Latin, Arabic, etc.). [JS]

4.750 John P. Swann. *Academic scientists and the pharmaceutical industry: cooperative research in twentieth-century America.* Baltimore: Johns Hopkins University Press, 1988. ISBN 0-8018-3558-5. ‣ Describes evolution of relationship between university researchers and pharmaceutical companies that was crucial to development of pharmaceutical industry in early and mid-twentieth century. [RKD]

Psychiatry

4.751 Anne Digby. *Madness, morality, and medicine: a study of the York Retreat, 1796–1914.* Cambridge: Cambridge University Press, 1985. ISBN 0-521-26067-1. ‣ Case study of institution influential in asylum development in Britain and New England. Retreat known for instigation of moral therapy. [CH]

4.752 Michel Foucault. *Madness and civilization: a history of insanity in the age of reason.* 1965 ed. Richard Howard, trans. New York: Vintage, 1973. ISBN 0-394-71914-X. ‣ History of madness, 1500 to early nineteenth century. Seminal account and inspiration for extensive scholarship in history of psychiatry. [CH]

4.753 Jan Goldstein. *Console and classify: the French psychiatric profession in the nineteenth century.* Cambridge: Cambridge University Press, 1987. ISBN 0-521-32279-0. ‣ Study of legitimation of psychiatry as science and recognition of profession as medical specialty. Explores implications of profession-building for disease definition, patient care, and institutional development in France. [CH]

4.754 Gerald N. Grob. *Mental institutions in America: social policy to 1875.* 1972 ed. New York: Free Press, 1973. ‣ Overview of history of psychiatric hospitals in nineteenth-century United States. [CH]

4.755 Nancy Tomes. *A generous confidence: Thomas Story Kirkbride and the art of asylum-keeping, 1840–1883.* Cambridge: Cambridge University Press, 1984. ISBN 0-521-24172-3. ‣ Social history of medical practice in private nineteenth-century asylum in Philadelphia. Relates history of asylum to intellectual and professional development of American psychiatry. [CH]

SEE ALSO
24.368 Andrew Scull, ed. *Madhouses, mad-doctors, and madmen.*

Nursing

4.756 Karen Buhler-Wilkerson. *False dawn: the rise and decline of public health nursing, 1900–1930.* New York: Garland, 1989.

ISBN 0-8240-4355-3. ▸ Description of professionalization of nursing specialty out of work of "lady visitors." Analyzes divisions between voluntary and state-funded sectors and tensions with public health physicians. [SMR]

4.757 Celia Davies, ed. *Rewriting nursing history.* Totowa, N.J.: Barnes & Noble, 1980. ISBN 0-389-20153-7. ▸ Treats work organization and training of nurses. Emphasizes women's history approach to nursing history. [SMR]

4.758 Darlene Clark Hine. *Black women in white: racial conflict and cooperation in the nursing profession, 1890–1950.* Bloomington: Indiana University Press, 1989. ISBN 0-253-32773-3 (cl), 0-253-20529-8 (pbk). ▸ Discussion of professionalization of American nursing from African American perspective. Treats tensions with white nursing and medicine, economic difficulties, and importance to African American community. [SMR]

4.759 Barbara Melosh. *"The physician's hand": work culture and conflict in American nursing.* Philadelphia: Temple University Press, 1982. ISBN 0-87722-278-9 (cl), 0-87722-290-8 (pbk). ▸ Nursing viewed from labor history perspective. Describes nursing work culture in context of service industry rationalization. How nurses shaped their own work experience and expressed broad and narrow understandings of professionalization. [SMR/JGC]

4.760 Susan Reverby. *Ordered to care: the dilemma of American nursing, 1850–1945.* Cambridge: Cambridge University Press, 1987. ISBN 0-521-25604-6 (cl), 0-521-33565-5 (pbk). ▸ Development of nursing ideology, work conditions, and efforts at reform and professionalization. Focus on class divisions, hospital demands, and tension between caring and autonomy. [SMR]

4.761 Anne Summers. *Angels and citizens: British women as military nurses, 1854–1914.* London: Routledge & Kegan Paul, 1988. ISBN 0-7102-1479-0 (cl), 0-7102-1338-7 (pbk). ▸ Description of nursing reforms that defined nurses as servants of state. Acceptance of soldiering and nursing as claims to citizenship. [SMR]

4.762 Martha Vicinus and Bea Nergaard, eds. *Ever yours, Florence Nightingale: selected letters.* 1989 ed. Cambridge, Mass.: Harvard University Press, 1990. ISBN 0-674-27020-7. ▸ Nightingale's life seen through her letters. Reevaluation of sources of her power and influence on nursing and governmental reform. [SMR]

Evolution of the Modern Hospital

4.763 Erwin H. Ackerknecht. *Medicine at the Paris hospital, 1794–1848.* Baltimore: Johns Hopkins University Press, 1967. ▸ Classic account of centrality of hospital-based medicine to development of Paris clinical school. Delineates factors impinging on rise of clinical medicine. [CH]

4.764 Michel Foucault. *The birth of the clinic: an archeology of medical perception.* 1973 ed. A. M. Sheridan Smith, trans. New York: Vintage, 1975. ISBN 0-394-48321-9 (cl, 1973), 0-394-71097-5 (pbk). ▸ Important, seminal work questioning beliefs and approaches that influenced development of clinical medicine and teaching hospital. Emergence of modern medicine depends on new relationship between words and things, visible and invisible. [CH]

4.765 Lindsay Granshaw and Roy Porter, eds. *The hospital in history.* London: Routledge, 1989. ISBN 0-415-00375-X. ▸ Essays on hospitals from medieval period to mid-twentieth century. Changing perceptions of hospital as institution of pauperism and death to necessary facility for acutely ill. [SMR]

4.766 Guenter B. Risse. *Hospital life in Enlightenment Scotland: care and teaching at the Royal Infirmary of Edinburgh.* Cambridge: Cambridge University Press, 1986. ISBN 0-521-30518-7. ▸ Study of Scottish hospital that institutionalized poor for their own welfare and provided clinical instruction for future medical professionals. Undercuts view of hospitals as houses of death; amplifies origins of hospitals as teaching institutions. [CH]

4.767 Charles E. Rosenberg. *The care of strangers: the rise of America's hospital system.* New York: Basic Books, 1987. ISBN 0-465-00877-1. ▸ Study of evolution of health care institutions, 1800–1920. Focuses on shifting class perceptions of hospitals along with changes in latter's social and medical roles and expanding importance in medical education and research. [JHC]

4.768 Rosemary Stevens. *In sickness and in wealth: American hospitals in the twentieth century.* New York: Basic Books, 1989. ISBN 0-465-03223-0. ▸ Analysis of emergence and shifting roles of modern health care institutions and personnel. Treats interaction of organized curative medicine with scientific and technological innovation, economic forces, philanthropic motivation, professional trends, and governmental regulation. [JHC]

4.769 John D. Thompson and Grace Goldin. *The hospital: a social and architectural history.* New Haven: Yale University Press, 1975. ISBN 0-300-01829-0. ▸ Detailed illustrated overview of structure of hospitals. Describes design elements of healthy environment, privacy, efficiency, and supervision in cultural context. [SMR]

Public Health and Hygiene

4.770 William Coleman. *Death is a social disease: public health and political economy in early industrial France.* Madison: University of Wisconsin Press, 1982. ISBN 0-299-08950-9. ▸ Assessment of development of public health as science in nineteenth-century France. Shows how its architects were influenced by belief in economic liberty. [CH]

4.771 François Delaporte. *Disease and civilization: the cholera in Paris, 1832.* Arthur Goldhammer, trans. Cambridge, Mass.: MIT Press, 1986. ISBN 0-262-04084-0. ▸ Influential case study of how practices and social relations construct a disease category. Emphasizes sociological over biological bases of defining and treating Parisian cholera outbreak of 1832. [CSH]

4.772 John Duffy. *The sanitarians: a history of American public health.* Urbana: University of Illinois Press, 1990. ISBN 0-252-01663-7. ▸ Chronicle of public health efforts in America from colonial times, stressing interaction of politics and medicine. [CSH]

4.773 Richard J. Evans. *Death in Hamburg: society and politics in the cholera years, 1830–1910.* 1987 ed. Harmondsworth: Penguin, 1990. ISBN 0-14-012473-X (pbk). ▸ Study of ways epidemic disease both reflects and affects social relations in community. Examines relationship between devastating cholera of 1892 and Hamburg's government controlled by liberal elite. [CSH]

4.774 S. E. Finer. *The life and times of Sir Edwin Chadwick.* 1952 ed. London: Methuen, 1980. ISBN 0-416-17350-0. ▸ Discussion of political and ideological context of early British public health movement (early to mid-nineteenth century). [CSH]

4.775 Jean-Pierre Goubert. *The conquest of water: the advent of health in the industrial age.* 1986 ed. Andrew Wilson, trans. Princeton: Princeton University Press, 1989. ISBN 0-691-08544-7. ▸ Study of development of scientific and technological knowledge about water and implications for epidemic disease control and public health generally in nineteenth and twentieth centuries. Innovative analysis influenced by Annales school. [CH]

4.776 Christopher Hamlin. *A science of impurity: water analysis in nineteenth-century Britain.* Berkeley: University of California Press, 1990. ISBN 0-520-07088-7. ▸ Study of relationship of science to public health policy, exploring how water scientists adapted their habits of inference to public's demand for certainty. [CSH]

4.777 Margaret Pelling. *Cholera, fever, and English medicine, 1825–1865.* Oxford: Oxford University Press, 1978. ISBN 0-19-821872-9. ‣ Most thorough examination of background and emergence of germ theory of disease, focusing on English public health workers and biomedical scientists. [CSH]

4.778 George Rosen. *A history of public health.* New York: MD Publications, 1958. ‣ Excellent survey of public health (broadly conceived) in Western civilization. Unfortunately underdocumented. [CSH]

4.779 Georges Vigarello. *Concepts of cleanliness: changing attitudes in France since the Middle Ages.* Jean Birrell, trans. Cambridge: Cambridge University Press, 1988. ISBN 0-521-34248-1. ‣ Study of changes in attitudes and perceptions of human cleanliness, health, and hygiene over centuries, accompanied by alterations in moral properties attributed to human body. [CH]

SEE ALSO

24.220 Anthony S. Wohl. *Endangered lives.*
24.369 F. B. Smith. *The people's health, 1830–1910.*
34.447 John F. Hutchinson. *Politics and public health in revolutionary Russia, 1890–1918.*

Medical Education and Development of the Modern Medical Profession

4.780 Thomas Neville Bonner. *To the ends of the earth: women's search for education in medicine.* Cambridge, Mass.: Harvard University Press, 1992. ISBN 0-674-89303-4. ‣ Women's struggles to receive medical education in United States, Britain, Russia, imperial Germany, Austria, and France in late nineteenth century. Comparative approach makes this study extremely valuable. [KML]

4.781 Toby Gelfand. *Professionalizing modern medicine: Paris surgeons and medical science and institutions in the eighteenth century.* Westport, Conn.: Greenwood, 1980. ISBN 0-313-21488-3. ‣ Medical professionalization in France stemming from effect of surgical approach to medicine. Links elevation of status of surgery with development of hospital-based medicine. [CH]

4.782 John S. Haller. *American medicine in transition, 1840–1910.* Urbana: University of Illinois Press, 1981. ISBN 0-252-00806-5. ‣ Intellectual, structural, and functional development of medical profession. Emphasis on therapeutic concepts, introduction of laboratory methods and new knowledge, and emergence of medical establishment. [JHC]

4.783 Joseph F. Kett. *The formation of the American medical profession: the role of institutions, 1780–1860.* 1968 ed. Westport, Conn.: Greenwood, 1980. ISBN 0-313-22428-5. ‣ Development of postrevolutionary professional institutions in framework of changing social aspirations and ideologies. Relationship of emerging medical licensing regulations, schools, and societies to sectarian and pluralistic impulses. [JHC]

4.784 Erna Lesky. *The Vienna Medical School of the nineteenth century.* L. Williams and I. S. Levij, trans. Baltimore: Johns Hopkins University Press, 1976. ISBN 0-8018-1908-3. ‣ Important account of educational practices at influential Vienna Medical School. Teaching practices described subject by subject. Richly detailed history. [KML]

4.785 Irvine Loudon. *Medical care and the general practitioner, 1750–1850.* New York: Oxford University Press, 1986. ISBN 0-19-822793-0. ‣ Investigation of English rank-and-file practitioner's social and economic status, work, patients, and treatment methods over century. Challenges assumptions about professional growth and stability. [CH]

4.786 Kenneth M. Ludmerer. *Learning to heal: the development of American medical education.* New York: Basic Books, 1985. ISBN 0-465-03880-8 (cl), 0-465-03881-6 (pbk). ‣ Creation of modern medical school, teaching hospital, and philosophy of medical education in America. Emphasizes entrepreneurship of academic physicians. Richly grounded in archival sources and placed in cultural and educational context. [KML]

4.787 Ronald L. Numbers, ed. *The education of American physicians: historical essays.* Berkeley: University of California Press, 1980. ISBN 0-520-03611-5. ‣ Important essay collection describing teaching of various scientific and clinical disciplines in America since 1765. Useful shift from traditional institutional approach to medical education. [KML]

4.788 Charles Donald O'Malley, ed. *The history of medical education.* Berkeley: University of California Press, 1970. ISBN 0-520-01578-9. ‣ Useful essay collection treating medical education in Europe, Asia, and Americas. Essays transcend time as well as geographic borders. [KML]

4.789 Matthew Ramsey. *Professional and popular medicine in France, 1770–1830: the social world of medical practice.* Cambridge: Cambridge University Press, 1988. ISBN 0-521-30517-9. ‣ Study of entire range of medical practitioners who flourished in preindustrial and early industrial France. Contribution to understanding transition of medical profession and popular medical culture. [CH]

4.790 William G. Rothstein. *American medical schools and the practice of medicine.* New York: Oxford University Press, 1987. ISBN 0-19-504186-0. ‣ Overview of development of American medical education from colonial times to present. Sensitive to context of changes in medical practice. Especially useful for references to published sources. [KML]

4.791 William G. Rothstein. *American physicians in the nineteenth century: from sects to science.* Baltimore: Johns Hopkins University Press, 1972. ISBN 0-8018-1242-9. ‣ Sociohistorical study of profession as occupational group. Organizational and institutional aspects of emerging regular medical establishment in relation to development and flourishing of competing therapeutic sects. [JHC]

4.792 Richard Harrison Shryock. *Medical licensing in America, 1650–1965.* Ann Arbor: University Microfilms International, 1967. ‣ Comparative study of rise and fall and rise of licensure in United States, discussed in relationship to medical education and the European experience. [ETM]

4.793 Rosemary Stevens. *American medicine and the public interest.* New Haven: Yale University Press, 1971. ISBN 0-300-01419-8 (cl), 0-300-01744-8 (pbk). ‣ Description of history and effects of specialization in medicine in United States. Depicts evolving context of contemporary health and professional crises. [JHC]

SEE ALSO

34.446 Nancy Mandelker Frieden. *Russian physicians in an era of reform and revolution, 1856–1905.*

Health Care Policy

4.794 Ruth Barrington. *Health, medicine, and politics in Ireland, 1900–1970.* Dublin: Institute of Public Administration, 1987. ISBN 0-906980-70-4 (cl), 0-906980-72-0 (pbk). ‣ Description of Irish health policy, integrating role of Catholic church and influence of domestic economics and politics. Serves as useful contrast to British health policy developments during same period. [ETM]

4.795 Ann Beck. *Medicine, tradition, and development in Kenya and Tanzania, 1920–1970.* Waltham, Mass.: Crossroads, 1981. ISBN 0-918456-44-4. ‣ Study of factors in development of medical systems of Kenya and Tanzania. Stresses colonial legacy, postindependence political system, climate and raw materials, and approaches to education. [ETM]

4.796 Ross Danielson. *Cuban medicine.* New Brunswick, N.J.: Transaction, 1979. ISBN 0-87855-114-X. ‣ Survey of entire history of Cuban medicine from first European contacts, but emphasizes period since 1959. Sympathetic to health program of revolutionary regime. [ETM]

4.797 Daniel M. Fox. *Health policies, health politics: the British and American experience, 1911–1965.* Princeton: Princeton University Press, 1986. ISBN 0-691-04733-2. ‣ Contrasts United States with Britain to explain why each country developed own approach to health care rather than why United States failed to adopt British model. [ETM]

4.798 Victoria A. Harden. *Inventing the NIH: federal biomedical research policy, 1887–1937.* Baltimore: Johns Hopkins University Press, 1986. ISBN 0-8018-3071-0. ‣ Pioneering study of role of National Institutes of Health in development of medical research and health policy. [CH]

4.799 J. Rogers Hollingsworth, Jerald Hage, and Robert A. Hanneman. *State intervention in medical care: consequences for Britain, France, Sweden, and the United States, 1890–1970.* Ithaca, N.Y.: Cornell University Press, 1990. ISBN 0-8014-2389-9 (cl), 0-8014-9615-2 (pbk). ‣ Positive assessment of state intervention in health care, based on measures such as mortality rates, per capita costs, and diffusion of innovations. [ETM]

4.800 Frank Honigsbaum. *Health, happiness, and security: the creation of the National Health Service.* London: Routledge, 1989. ISBN 0-415-01739-4. ‣ Concentrates on role of civil servants and cabinet ministers, but examines process as result of conflicts within and between these groups, general practitioners, and medical specialists. [ETM]

4.801 Roger Jeffery. *The politics of health in India.* Berkeley: University of California Press, 1988. ISBN 0-520-05938-7. ‣ Covers British Raj and independence periods. Attempts balance between viewing modernization through technology transfer as unproblematically positive and asserting British imperialism and local elites used health services as means of control. [ETM]

4.802 AnElissa Lucas. *Chinese medical modernization: comparative policy continuities, 1930s–1980s.* New York: Praeger, 1982. ISBN 0-03-059454-5. ‣ Analysis of medical policy from revolution of 1949, Great Leap Forward of late 1950s, and Cultural Revolution of 1960s. Finds no radical change from system of state medicine introduced in 1920s. [ETM]

4.803 Ronald L. Numbers. *Almost persuaded: American physicians and compulsory health insurance, 1912–1920.* Baltimore: Johns Hopkins University Press, 1978. ISBN 0-8018-2052-9. ‣ Authoritative work on first effort toward establishment of national health insurance in United States, following British initiative of 1911. [ETM]

4.804 Paul Starr. *The social transformation of American medicine.* New York: Basic Books, 1982. ISBN 0-465-07934-2 (cl), 0-465-07935-0 (pbk). ‣ Discussion of nineteenth-century origins of late twentieth-century corporate medicine. Examines shifting attitudes toward medical authority and hospitals; describes factors accounting for limited development of public health and rejection of national health insurance. [JHC]

4.805 Robert Bocking Stevens and Rosemary Stevens. *Welfare medicine in America: a case study of Medicaid.* New York: Free Press, 1974. ISBN 0-02-931520-4. ‣ Examination of compromises involved in creating Medicaid and results of first eight years of program. Medicaid's supporters viewed it as first stage of implementing national health insurance in United States. [ETM]

4.806 Malcolm G. Taylor. *Health insurance and Canadian public policy: the seven decisions that created the Canadian Health Insurance System and their outcomes.* 2d ed. Toronto and Kingston, Ont.: Institute of Public Administration of Canada and McGill-Queen's University Press, 1987. (Canadian public administration series, 10.) ISBN 0-7735-0628-4 (cl), 0-7735-0629-2 (pbk). ‣ Detailed analysis of development of Canadian policy, sensitive to peculiarities in Canadian politics and class relations. [ETM]

4.807 Charles Webster. *Problems of health care: the National Health Service before 1957.* London: Her Majesty's Stationary Office, 1988. (The health services since the war, peacetime history, 1.) ISBN 0-11-630942-3. ‣ Commissioned by Labour government of 1970s, examines events and decision making that led to establishment of National Health Service as well as development of Service through mid-1950s. [ETM]

Gender and Medicine

4.808 Rima Apple, ed. *Women, health, and medicine in America: a historical handbook.* New York: Garland, 1990. ISBN 0-8240-8447-0. ‣ Historiographic essays covering diseases, orthodox and alternative health care, politics, and health care providers. Thorough bibliographies and discussions of analytic strengths and limitations on various topics. [SMR]

4.809 Jacques Gélis. *History of childbirth: fertility, pregnancy, and birth in early modern Europe.* Rosemary Morris, trans. Boston: Northeastern University Press, 1991. ISBN 1-55553-102-4 (cl), 1-55553-105-9 (pbk). ‣ Study of cultural beliefs and practices of childbirth through four centuries. Attitudes toward women and nature, children, pregnancy, child rearing, and child mortality. [SMR]

4.810 Ludmilla Jordanova. *Sexual visions: images of gender in science and medicine between the eighteenth and twentieth centuries.* Madison: University of Wisconsin Press, 1989. ISBN 0-299-12290-5. ‣ Medical and scientific focus on gender differences and gendered nature of natural knowledge. Centrality of gender and female body to problematics of European science and medicine. [SMR]

4.811 Judith Walzer Leavitt. *Brought to bed: child-bearing in America, 1750–1950.* New York: Oxford University Press, 1986. ISBN 0-19-503843-6. ‣ Discussion of changes in birthing practices from home to hospital; emphasis on women's versus physician's control in differing contexts. Links women's history and medical history in balanced analysis of shift of birthing site. [SMR]

4.812 Judith Walzer Leavitt, ed. *Women and health in America: historical readings.* Madison: University of Wisconsin Press, 1984. ISBN 0-299-09640-8 (cl), 0-299-09644-0 (pbk). ‣ Classic essays on women's health and women in health professions. Wide-ranging coverage of diseases, reproductive health, professionalization, workers, and health reform. [SMR]

4.813 Regina Markell Morantz-Sanchez. *Sympathy and science: women physicians in American medicine.* New York: Oxford University Press, 1985. ISBN 0-19-503627-1. ‣ Overview of tensions between professionalization and womanhood. Analysis of divisions within women's medical community and strategies for acceptance within profession. [SMR]

Section 5

ERLE LEICHTY

Ancient Near East

The history of the ancient Near East traditionally comprises the study of those civilizations which arose in the geographical area currently occupied by the modern states of Iran, Iraq, Turkey, Syria, Lebanon, Israel, Jordan, and Egypt. In recent years there have been moves to expand that area to include the Arabian peninsula and the Gulf states as well. Chronologically, ancient Near Eastern history is normally seen to start at about 3400 BCE with the invention of writing and to end with the death of Alexander the Great in 323 BCE. The bibliography below contains a few works beyond that date in order to bridge the gap between Alexander and the Muslim conquest.

Ancient Near Eastern history is a relatively young field. Most of the civilizations represented were rediscovered in the nineteenth century through archaeological excavation; the various ancient dead languages were deciphered at about the same time. Early scholars attempted to cope with the whole of the ancient Near East, but the difficulty of the languages and the complexity and quantity of the evidence quickly forced specialization. Egyptology and Biblical studies, for example, are now largely separate and distinct fields. Specialization in general tends to fall along ethnic, linguistic, or geographical lines. Scholars of the ancient Near East are largely trained as philologists and/or archaeologists, reflecting in large measure the current needs of the field: the evaluation and publication of the copious archaeological material and documents already unearthed.

Ancient Near Eastern history is volatile. New evidence has been and is being recovered at an extraordinary pace. Specialists have been and are few in number, too few to absorb the millions of pieces of evidence unearthed. Even a respite from archaeological fieldwork when political relations are cold or broken does not slow the flow of new evidence. Scholars simply turn to the large, unpublished collections in Western museums.

Because of the massive quantity of unpublished and/or new data available, there is a tendency in these ancient Near Eastern fields to publish the evidence rather than to synthesize or interpret it. This is not to say that we cannot or do not write history. The skeletal outline of ancient Near Eastern history is established and is most certainly correct. The details, however, change frequently and will do so for years to come. Thus, studies devoted to history, especially in the form of books and monographs, are relatively rare. New syntheses of the ancient Near East appear every fifteen to twenty years and often two or three at a time. Those histories that attempt to survey the whole of the ancient Near East, even when jointly authored, tend to be less authoritative than those that specialize in a single area. But even the more specialized histories are likely to be spotty because our evidence is uneven and the author's emphasis is usually on his own period of interest. Often the best, most up-to-date syntheses of periods or topics are found in essay collections. To gain an overall view of ancient Near Eastern history, or any single subspecialty, the reader should consult multiple sources.

Mesopotamian history deals with six major populations that migrated into or invaded the Tigris-Euphrates Valley. Three were Semitic: the Akkadians (third millennium), Amorites (second millennium), and the Aramaeans (first millennium). The remaining three were of unknown linguistic affiliation: the Sumerians (third millennium), the Hurrians (second millennium), and the Kassites (second millennium). Several other ethnic groups, such as the Subarians, the Guti, the Lullubi, etc., played lesser roles. After 539 BCE the area was occupied in succession by the Persians, the Greeks, the Parthians, the Sasanians, and finally the Arabs.

A topic that unites all the areas represented in this bibliography is chronology. Specialists work with both relative and absolute chronology. The absolute chronology of Mesopotamia is secure back to 911 BCE, and there is general agreement on a relative chronology before then, but absolute chronology remains the subject of fierce debate because of frequent breaks, "dark ages" in the king lists, year-date formula lists, and other chronographic materials that provide the framework for the chronology of the region. Users of the materials in this bibliography will encounter three basic chronologies, referred to as the high, middle, and low chronologies, that reflect differing interpretations of the various evidence. A good discussion of these chronological problems and possible solutions may be found in M. Rowton's article on chronology in *The Cambridge Ancient History* (5.2, vol. 1.1). A list of kings with absolute dates according to the popular "middle" chronology has been compiled by J. A. Brinkman and can be found at the back of A. L. Oppenheim, *Ancient Mesopotamia* (5.28). The chronologies of Iran, Syria-Palestine, and Anatolia are largely based on the Mesopotamian.

Egyptian chronology is based on the work of Manetho, an Egyptian priest, of the fourth century BCE, who compiled a king list arranged by dynasty. For convenience modern Egyptologists have grouped the dynasties into blocks: Old Kingdom, First Intermediate period, Middle Kingdom, Second Intermediate period, New Kingdom, and so forth. Like Mesopotamia, the relative chronology is generally agreed upon; absolute chronology is debatable. There are several synchronisms with Mesopotamia and Anatolia that limit the manipulation of both the Mesopotamian and Egyptian systems. (For a discussion of Egyptian chronology, see Kitchen 5.538).

Our knowledge of Mesopotamian history is based primarily on written sources in cuneiform script on clay tablets. Most of the tablets are written in Sumerian and Akkadian, but inscriptions in other languages such as Hurrian or Kassite also occur. Since these tablets are virtually indestructible, we are overwhelmed with data. The textual evidence is supplemented by archaeological data; for most periods visual data are meager.

Scholarly literature on ancient Mesopotamia is normally published in English, French, and German, but there is also substantial work in Italian, Hebrew, Russian, Turkish, and Arabic. Scholarly papers are seldom translated into a second modern language. Scholars working in the field normally must master Sumerian and Akkadian and have some knowledge of Arabic and Hebrew as well as English, French, and German. Because of the number of languages needed and the complexity of the ancient languages and writing system, the field has always been dominated by philologists and is difficult for the nonspecialist to access. There are some ongoing projects that will alleviate this, such as the Royal Inscriptions of Mesopotamia project in Toronto and the State Archives of Assyria project in Helsinki. Both projects are producing translations of large corpora of cuneiform texts for the layman.

The last generation of scholars was engaged primarily in the creation of tools: grammars, dictionaries, and sign lists. The choice of topics for study focused on reconstructing a framework for the history of the region and on the recovery of the epic and mythological literature. But there was also a strong focus on topics of interest to Old Testament studies, especially Mesopotamian relations with Syria-Palestine and comparative legal history. The current generation has begun to import methodologies from other disciplines: anthropology, literary criticism, history, etc., and there have also been renewed attempts to integrate the archaeological material and the written records. But the dominant activity remains the publication of primary sources.

Syria-Palestine was a crossroads in antiquity, inhabited and invaded by numerous groups, including Phoenicians, Hebrews, Philistines, Canaanites, Hurrians, Syrians, Aramaeans, and others. Politically the area was often under the rule or influence of one of the great powers: Egypt, Mesopotamia, or the Hittites. When free of foreign rule the area was fractious and riddled with interstate conflict. The chronology of the area is based on synchronisms with Egypt, Anatolia, and Mesopotamia and as such is subject to the same uncertainties and controversies as the chronologies of those regions.

Evidence for the history of this area is both written and archaeological, but uneven. One reason for this is that the major cities of the region are almost all still occupied and cannot be excavated. In the north and east of Syria several very large archives of cuneiform tablets have been found that spotlight particular cities and time periods, notably Mari, Ebla, and Ugarit. There are also several smaller archives. At least six different languages are represented. Archaeological exploration in this area has been largely dictated by salvage needs, but this is now changing. Study of this area is expanding very rapidly. Many scholars who worked in Iran or Iraq have now turned their attention to Syria because of the political situation.

In the south, in the region of Israel and Jordan, no (pre-Roman) written archives have been found despite extensive and widespread archaeological activity. The history of the area is based on the Old Testament and Egyptian, Mesopotamian, and classical sources, supplemented by the archaeological record.

The study of this area is the most populated of any field represented in this section, with thousands of professional and amateur scholars who research and publish in this field. Studies appear in every language (but mostly English, French, and German and now, increasingly, in Hebrew) and for every audience. Although publications both scholarly and popular abound, negotiating the material can be treacherous; political and religious agendas are often evident and pronounced. The nonprofessional will find much stimulating material easily available, but will find it almost impossible to evaluate the secondary or even the primary sources without guidance.

For much of the last century, scholarly research has concentrated on clarifying the background of biblical Israel and its ties to the ancient Near East. Most recent historical work has returned to the analysis of the literary genres of the Bible, while the use of archaeological and anthropological models for the reconstruction of Israelite society forms a second focus of research.

Over the centuries Anatolia was subjected to many migrations and invasions of various ethnic and linguistic groups including the Hittites, Hurrians, Scythians, Cimmerians, Lydians, Lycians, Phrygians, Carians, Persians, and Greeks. The early history of Anatolia is unknown; it is represented by archaeological data only. From the beginning of the second millennium, however, there are substantial archives of clay tablets written in the Old Assyrian dialect of Akkadian. These archives, the records of Assyrian merchants living in Anatolia, provide a reasonably detailed picture of central Anatolia for a one-hundred-year period. For the mid-second millennium, there is a major royal archive of cuneiform tablets from the Hittite capital written in Hittite (an Indo-European language), Hurrian, and Akkadian. These two archives provide the only indigenous sources for Hittite history, the remainder of the historical framework is based on Mesopotamian, Hittite, and classical sources.

Scholarly activity in the field is dominated by archaeological, often salvage, activity and philology. Although Hittite, as the earliest Indo-European language, has drawn the attention of linguists, linguists and philologists still lack the most basic tools. Scholarship in the field focuses mainly on the publication of primary evidence, written and archaeological, and topics that benefit from evidence found in other regions. Articles and books are mostly written in English, French, or German with German predominating.

The history of ancient Iran is very poorly attested, and few scholars work in this field, although the French have been particularly active. There are scattered inscriptions on clay tablets in Proto-Elamite (undeciphered), Elamite (linguistic affinity unknown), Akkadian (Semitic), Sumerian (linguistic affinity unknown), and Old Persian (Indo-European). The earliest people in the area that we can identify are the Elamites. In the ninth century BCE the Medes and Persians migrated into Iran. The early history of the Persian empire is known largely from Mesopotamian and classical sources. The business of the Persian empire was recorded in Aramaic on parchment and is not preserved. There are a few Persian royal inscriptions preserved on stone and clay; the archaeological record is sketchy and the visual data meager.

The chronology of ancient Iran, too, is very unsettled. The archaeological work has been insufficient to establish a firm relative chronology. Absolute chronology is virtually nonexistent before the sixth century BCE. Iran's close interaction with Mesopotamia provides the basic chronology for its history.

Since the Revolution in Iran (1979–1980) archaeological activity has all but ceased, and most scholars with an interest in the area have turned their attention to Inner or South Asia or to Turkey or Syria. But recently there has been a revived interest in the Persian empire.

Unlike the regions of Western Asia, the population of ancient Egypt was generally homogeneous and suffered only one foreign incursion (Hyksos) until the first millennium BCE when Egypt was invaded by Assyria, Babylonia, Persia, Greece, and Rome, followed by Byzantium and the Arabs in the first millennium CE.

Egyptian history is reconstructed from contemporary written sources, archaeological material, and later classical authors. The general outline is established, but details change when new data appear. The ancient Egyptians wrote in three scripts: hieroglyphic, hieratic, and demotic; the latter two were derived from the first. Many inscriptions were written on papyrus in ink and have not survived unless they were in tombs or other dry places. There are also monumental inscriptions carved or painted on stone. The corpus of written data is smaller than in Mesopotamia, but the archaeological material and visual data are extremely rich.

Egyptologists are few in number, but they pretty well span the globe. Most articles are written in English, French, or German, but articles also appear in other European languages and Arabic and Hebrew, and are seldom translated from their original languages. Egyptologists are usually archaeologists or philologists, but some are both. Recently there has been a trend to bring more anthropology into the field. In Egypt the effort to record all of the monumental inscriptions has become more systematic and comprehensive. There is also extensive and ongoing archeological activity.

Current research in Egyptology, from a historical perspective, is noteworthy in several respects. First, there is increasing interest in producing monographs on individual rulers, providing detailed perspectives on motivation and process not possible in more generalized histories. Second, interest in social and economic history is increasing, and the role of archaeology in complementing the meager textual record in this regard is becoming more appreciated; several active field projects are now focused on such issues. Third, the historical significance of the cognitive world of the Egyptians is another developing focus in terms of how the Egyptians' worldview both shaped and was shaped by their activities as a historically documented society.

[Contributors: DO'C = David O'Connor, DTP = D. T. Potts, EL = Erle Leichty, JDM = James D. Muhly, MC = Mordechai Cogan, MWW = Matthew W. Waters, PG = Pamela Gerardi, PLK = Philip L. Kohl]

REGIONAL STUDIES AND REFERENCE WORKS

5.1 Jean Bottéro et al. *The Near East: the early civilizations.* Jean Bottéro, Elena Cassin, and Jean Vercoutter, eds. R. F. Tannen- baum, trans. New York: Delacorte, 1967. ▸ General history of Mesopotamia and Egypt from beginning of civilization to 1500 BCE. Stress on political history. Especially important are Edzard's chapters on Second Intermediate period (1640–1532 BCE), which constitute a summary of his German-language volume. Can be used as textbook. [EL]

5.2 I.E.S. Edwards et al. *The Cambridge ancient history.* 3d ed. 3 vols. in 5 to date. Cambridge: Cambridge University Press, 1970–75. ISBN 0-521-07051-1 (v. 1.1), 0-521-07791-5 (v. 1.2), 0-521-08230-7 (v. 2.2), 0-521-08691-4 (v. 2.2), 0-521-22496-9 (v. 3). ▸ Collection of essays covering ancient world, including Aegean, North Africa, Syria-Palestine, Mesopotamia, Anatolia, and Iran, prehistory to end of second millennium. Volume 3 will cover first millennium (only volume 3.1 now available). Articles vary in quality but offer comprehensive coverage and good bibliography. Best starting place. [PG]

5.3 Henri A. Frankfort et al. *The intellectual adventure of ancient man.* Chicago: University of Chicago Press, 1977. ▸ Excellent introduction to ancient Near East. Attempts to understand psyche of populations. Republished in paperback without chapter on Israel under title *Before Philosophy.* [EL]

5.4 Ignace J. Gelb. *A study of writing.* 2d ed. Chicago: University of Chicago Press, 1963. ISBN 0-226-28605-3 (cl), 0-226-28606-1 (pbk). ▸ Basic, worldwide study of writing systems and their origins. [EL]

5.5 McG. Gibson and Robert D. Biggs, eds. *The organization of power: aspects of bureaucracy in the ancient Near East.* 2d ed. Chicago: University of Chicago, Oriental Institute, 1991. (Studies in ancient Oriental civilization, 46.) ISBN 0-918986-72-9 (pbk). ▸ Collection of essays from informal symposium. Five papers on Ur III period of Mesopotamia offer significant reassessment of that state's administration. Also includes papers on Byzantium and Egypt. [PG]

5.6 A. Kirk Grayson, ed. Royal inscriptions of Mesopotamia. 4 vols. to date. Toronto: University of Toronto Press, 1987–. ▸ Important project publishing, in Akkadian/Sumerian and English translation, royal inscriptions of Mesopotamia. Divided into three series, Early periods, Assyrian periods, and Babylonian periods. Each volume includes general introduction to inscriptions of period covered; introduction for each king included; and introduction to each inscription. Full bibliographies for each document, studies as well as editions. Useful for both specialists and nonspecialists. [PG]

5.7 William W. Hallo and W. Kelly Simpson. *The ancient Near East: a history.* New York: Harcourt Brace Jovanovich, 1971. ISBN 0-15-502755-7. ▸ Simpson on Egypt and Hallo on Mesopotamia provide good brief survey, prehistory to Alexander the Great. Primarily narrative description but some discussion of specific issues, (e.g., early administration and political literature). [DO'C]

5.8 "Keilschrift Bibliographie." In *Orientalia,* n.s. Rome: Pontifical Biblical Institute, 1940–. ▸ Good, comprehensive, annual bibliography of publications on ancient Near Eastern studies, language, literature, history, and archaeology. Includes articles, books, and reviews. Appears somewhat irregularly, but only annual bibliography available. [PG]

5.9 Mogens Trolle Larsen, ed. *Power and propaganda.* Copenhagen: Akademisk Forlag, 1979. (Mesopotamia, 7.) ISBN 87-500-1878-7. ▸ Interesting collection of papers on imperialism and empires, dealing primarily with ancient Near East. [EL]

5.10 Barbara S. Lesko, ed. *Women's earliest records from ancient Egypt and western Asia: proceedings of the Conference on Women in the Ancient Near East.* Atlanta: Scholars Press, 1989. ISBN 1-55540-319-0. ▸ Collection of essays by leading experts, from conference on women in antiquity. Covers many aspects: women in society, in economy, and in art. [DO'C]

5.11 Joseph Naveh. *Early history of the alphabet.* Jerusalem and Leiden: Magnes and Brill, 1982. ISBN 965-223-436-2. ▸ Discussion of origins, development, and spread of alphabet from its West Semitic home to Greece and Rome; richly illustrated. [MC]

5.12 Simo Parpola, ed. *State archives of Assyria.* 8 vols. to date. Helsinki: Helsinki University Press, 1987–. ISBN 951-570-002-7 (set, cl), 951-570-001-9 (set, pbk). ▸ Ambitious series, publishing, in Akkadian and English translation, royal Assyrian archives of Kuyunjik (Nineveh). Volumes focus on genres of text, including astrological reports, correspondence, legal documents, treaties, etc. Each volume includes introduction discussing context, genre, and content of documents. Reliable editions of excellent source material. [PG]

5.13 James B. Pritchard, ed. *Ancient Near Eastern texts relating to the Old Testament.* 3d ed. William Foxwell Albright et al., trans. Princeton: Princeton University Press, 1969. ISBN 0-691-03503-2. ▸ Anthology of Egyptian, Mesopotamian, and Hittite literary, historical, and legal texts in translation. Dated but very useful. Two-volume paperback abridged edition good for classroom use. [EL]

5.14 Michael Roaf. *Cultural atlas of Mesopotamia and the ancient Near East.* New York: Facts on File, 1990. ISBN 0-8160-2218-6. ▸ Profusely illustrated, up-to-date synthesis of prehistory and early history of greater ancient Near East stretching to Central and South Asia, from beginnings of food production to collapse of Persian empire. More than sixty original distribution maps; special illustrations of specific sites particularly valuable. [PLK]

5.15 Hayim Tadmor. "The chronology of the ancient Near East in the second millennium B.C.E." In *The world history of the Jewish people.* Benjamin Mazar, ed., vol. 2, pp. 51–101, 260–69. Tel Aviv: Jewish History Publications, 1970. ▸ Good, mainstream discussion of various, ongoing arguments for setting chronology of second-millennium Near East. Three systems currently in use: high, middle, and low chronologies. See also Rowton in 5.2, vol. I.I. [PG]

5.16 John Van Seters. *In search of history: historiography in the ancient world and the origins of biblical history.* New Haven: Yale University Press, 1983. ISBN 0-300-02877-6. ▸ Study of methods of historical writing in ancient world, with emphasis on origins of biblical historical writing. Valuable, substantial treatment of Egyptian concept of history. Weak on Mesopotamia. [MC/DO'C]

SEE ALSO
3.95 I. M. Diakonoff, ed. *Early antiquity.*
3.363 Norman Yoffee and George L. Cowgill, eds. *The collapse of ancient states and civilizations.*

MESOPOTAMIA

General Studies

5.17 Jean Bottéro. *Mesopotamia: writing, reasoning, and the gods.* Zainab Bahrani and Marc van de Mieroop, trans. Chicago: University of Chicago Press, 1992. ISBN 0-266-06726-2. ▸ Interesting collection of essays on various aspects of field by prominent, senior French Assyriologist. Written with nonspecialist in mind, but valuable for specialists as well. [PG]

5.18 J. A. Brinkman. "Settlement surveys and documentary evidence: regional variation and secular trends in Mesopotamian demography." *Journal of Near Eastern studies* 43.3 (1984) 169–80. ISSN 0022-2968. ▸ Rare demographic study of Mesopotamia, combining archaeological survey with cuneiform data. Outlines problems, questions, and suggestions for future work. [PG]

5.19 Kevin J. Cathcart. "Edward Hincks (1792–1866) and the decipherment of cuneiform writing." *Proceedings of the Irish Bib-lical Association* 7 (1983) 24–43. ▸ Basic discussion of decipherment of cuneiform, based on account of one of the decipherers. [PG]

5.20 J. J. Finkelstein. "Early Mesopotamia, 2500–1000 B.C." In *Propaganda and communication in world history.* Harold Lasswell, Daniel Lerner, and Hans Speier, eds., vol. 1, pp. 50–110. Honolulu: University Press of Hawaii, 1978. ISBN 0-8248-0496-1. ▸ Discussion and evaluation of written sources from Mesopotamia. [EL]

5.21 Horst Klengel. *Kulturgeschichte des alten Vorderasien.* Berlin: Akademie Verlag, 1989. (Veröffentlichungen des Zentralinstituts für alte Geschichte und Archäologie der Akademie der Wissenschaften der DDR, 18.) ISBN 3-05-000577-7, ISSN 0138-3914. ▸ Cultural history of Mesopotamia focusing on society and material culture. Richly illustrated; extensive bibliography. [EL]

5.22 Samuel Noah Kramer. *The Sumerians: the history, culture, and character.* 1963 ed. Chicago: University of Chicago Press, 1971. ISBN 0-226-45237-9 (cl), 0-226-45238-7 (pbk). ▸ Well-written, accessible political and cultural history of Sumer, 4500–1750 BCE, with literary emphasis. Selected translations of Sumerian texts. Best general book on Sumerians. [EL]

5.23 Jørgen Laessøe. *People of ancient Assyria.* London: Routledge & Kegan Paul, 1963. ▸ General history of Assyria concentrating on Hammurabi period (ca. 1800 BCE). Treats Assyria's relations with peoples of Zagros mountains, east of Assyria. [EL]

5.24 Hans J. Nissen. *The early history of the ancient Near East, 9000–2000 B.C.* Elizabeth Lutzeier and Kenneth J. Northcott, trans. Chicago: University of Chicago Press, 1988. ISBN 0-226-58656-1 (cl), 0-226-58658-8 (pbk). ▸ Recent, general political and cultural history of Mesopotamia from development of agriculture to 2000 BCE. Deals primarily with archaeological sources and material culture. Excellent bibliography. [EL]

5.25 David Oates. *Studies in the ancient history of northern Iraq.* London: Oxford University Press for British Academy, 1968. ▸ Series of studies on specific problems. Strong archaeological orientation; treats geography, major cities, and Roman, Parthian, Byzantine, and Sasanian periods in Assyria. [EL]

5.26 Joan Oates. *Babylon.* 1979 ed. New York: Thames & Hudson, 1986. ISBN 0-500-02095-7 (pbk). ▸ Interesting, well-illustrated history of Babylonia and city of Babylon, with chapter on Babylonian legacy. [EL]

5.27 Albert T. E. Olmstead. *History of Assyria.* 1923 ed. Chicago: University of Chicago Press, 1975. ISBN 0-226-62776-4 (pbk). ▸ Classic, dated, but highly detailed history. Still useful for first millennium history, but out of date for earlier periods. [EL]

5.28 A. Leo Oppenheim. *Ancient Mesopotamia: portrait of a dead civilization.* 2d rev. ed. Erica Reiner, Revisions. John A. Brinkman, Appendix. Chicago: University of Chicago Press, 1977. ISBN 0-226-63187-7 (pbk). ▸ Provocative, highly personalized cultural history, with emphasis on first millennium. Widely accepted chronological tables in appendix. Essential reading. [EL]

5.29 J. N. Postgate. *Early Mesopotamia: society and economy at the dawn of history.* 1992 ed. London: Routledge, 1994. ISBN 0-415-00843-3 (cl, 1992), 0-415-11032-7 (pbk). ▸ Very good cultural history of Mesopotamia. Suitable as textbook. [EL]

5.30 Erica Reiner. "How we read cuneiform texts." *Journal of cuneiform studies* 25 (1973) 3–58. ISSN 0022-2968. ▸ Good introduction for nonspecialist to problems of reading Akkadian and reconstructing texts. [PG]

5.31 Georges Roux. *Ancient Iraq.* 2d ed. New York: Penguin, 1980. ISBN 0-14-020828-3 (pbk). ▸ General overview of political history of Mesopotamia, prehistory to Parthian period. Good introductory text for undergraduates. [EL]

5.32 H.W.F. Saggs. *The greatness that was Babylon: a survey of the ancient civilization of the Tigris-Euphrates valley.* 1962 ed. London: Sidgwick & Jackson, 1988. ISBN 0-283-99623-4. ▸ General political and cultural history of Mesopotamia from beginning of civilization to 539 BCE. Large section on everyday life. Good introductory text for undergraduates. [EL]

5.33 H.W.F. Saggs. *The might that was Assyria.* 1984 ed. New York: St. Martin's, 1990. ISBN 0-312-03511-X. ▸ Political and cultural history of Assyria from beginning of civilization to fall of Assyrian empire, 612 BCE. Large section on everyday life. Suitable for undergraduates. [EL]

5.34 Gernot Wilhelm and Diana Stein. *The Hurrians.* Jennifer Barnes, trans. Warminster: Aris & Phillips, 1989. ISBN 0-85668-442-2. ▸ Political and cultural history of Hurrians. Most comprehensive, up-to-date source on Hurrian-speaking peoples. Complete bibliography. [EL]

5.35 C. Leonard Woolley. *A forgotten kingdom, being a record of the results obtained from the excavation of two mounds, Al Chana and Al Mina, in the Turkish Hatay.* New York: Norton, 1968. ▸ History of Alalakh, important kingdom near Aleppo, Syria, during Old Babylonian period (ca. 2000–1595 BCE) and a little later. Crucial for study of Hurrians. [EL]

5.36 Gordon D. Young, ed. *Mari in retrospect: fifty years of Mari and Mari studies.* Winona Lake, Ind.: Eisenbrauns, 1992. ISBN 0-931464-28-5. ▸ Collection of essays summarizing current state of knowledge of Mari, important state in eastern Syria during early second millennium BCE. Extensive bibliography. [EL]

5.37 Paul E. Zimansky. *Ecology and empire: the structure of the Urartian state.* Chicago: University of Chicago, Oriental Institute, 1985. (Studies in ancient Oriental civilization, 41.) ISBN 0-918998-641-9, ISSN 0081-7554. ▸ Only survey of Urartian empire available. Good coverage of linguistic and archaeological evidence. [PG]

Historiography

5.38 Jerrold S. Cooper. "Mesopotamian historical consciousness and the production of monumental art in the third millennium B.C." In *Investigating artistic environments in the ancient Near East.* Ann C. Gunter, ed., pp. 39–52. Washington, D.C.: Smithsonian Institution; distributed by University of Wisconsin Press, 1990. ISBN 0-299-97070-1 (cl), 0-299-97071-X (pbk). ▸ Discussion of relationship between representations and texts on third-millennium BCE monuments and their ideological context. [EL]

5.39 J. J. Finkelstein. "Mesopotamian historiography." *Proceedings of the American Philosophical Society* 107.6 (1963) 461–72. ▸ Fundamental, often cited discussion of Mesopotamian historiography. [PG]

5.40 A. Kirk Grayson. "Histories and historians of the ancient Near East: Assyria and Babylonia." *Orientalia,* n.s., 49.2 (1980) 140–93. ISSN 0030-5367. ▸ Useful, basic typology and discussion of historical documents. [PG]

5.41 Mario Liverani. "Memorandum on the approach to historiographic texts." *Orientalia,* n.s., 42 (1973) 178–94. ▸ Interesting, brief essay with case studies drawing on methodologies of anthropology, linguistics, folklore, and literary criticism. [PG]

5.42 Peter Machinist. "Literature as politics: the Tukulti-Ninurta epic and the Bible." *Catholic biblical quarterly* 38.4 (1976) 455–82. ISSN 0008-7912. ▸ Wide-ranging discussion of historical epic and light it sheds on Assyrian-Babylonian political and cultural relationship. Discusses genre, political and cultural background, audience, and analogous biblical compositions. [PG]

5.43 A. Leo Oppenheim. "Neo-Assyrian and neo-Babylonian empires." In *Propaganda and communication in world history.* Har-

old D. Lasswell, Daniel Lerner, and Hans Speier, eds., vol. 1, pp. 111–44. Honolulu: University Press of Hawaii, 1979. ISBN 0-8248-0496-1. ▸ Study of royal propaganda in first-millennium BCE Mesopotamia. [EL]

5.44 E. A. Speiser. "Ancient Mesopotamia." In *The idea of history in the ancient Near East.* 1955 ed. Robert C. Dentan, ed., pp. 37–76. New Haven: Yale University Press, 1966. ▸ Extended discussion of Mesopotamian conception of history, their history, its rendering, and Mesopotamian documents as source material for the modern scholar. [PG]

5.45 Hayim Tadmor and M. Weinfeld, eds. *History, historiography, and interpretation: studies in biblical and cuneiform literatures.* Jerusalem: Magnus, 1986. ISBN 965-223-459-1 (pbk). ▸ Collection of essays including two surveys of Sumerian and Hittite historiography and others focusing on themes or specific documents. [PG]

Political History

Third Millennium BCE

5.46 Petr Charvát. "Early Ur." *Archiv Orientální* 47.1–2 (1979) 15–20. ISSN 0044-8699. ▸ Discussion of origin and social structure of one of earliest and most important Mesopotamian city-states. [EL]

5.47 Petr Charvát. "Early Ur—war chiefs and kings of Early Dynastic III." *Altorientalische Forschungen* 9 (1982) 43–60. ISSN 0232-8461. ▸ Summary of current knowledge of Sumer in the Early Dynastic III period, ca. 2650–2334 BCE, focusing on city of Ur. [EL]

5.48 Jerrold S. Cooper. *Reconstructing history from ancient inscriptions: the Lagash-Umma border conflict.* 2d ed. Malibu: Undena, 1987. (Sources from the ancient Near East, 2/1.) ISBN 0-89003-059-6. ▸ Account of history's first documented war, end of Early Dynastic period, ca. 2500 BCE. Good discussion of use of inscriptional evidence. [EL]

5.49 Dietz Otto Edzard. "Problèmes de la royauté dans la période présargonique." In *Le palais et la royauté.* Paul Garelli, ed., pp. 141–49. Paris: Geuthner, 1974. ▸ Discussion of kingship in early third millennium BCE. [EL]

5.50 William W. Hallo. "A Sumerian amphictyony." *Journal of cuneiform studies* 14 (1960) 88–114. ISSN 0022-0256. ▸ Discussion of political organization of neo-Sumerian (Ur III) empire, 2112–2004 BCE. [EL]

5.51 Thorkild Jacobsen. "Early political development in Mesopotamia." In *Toward the image of Tammuz and other essays on Mesopotamian history and culture.* William L. Moran, ed., pp. 123–56. Cambridge, Mass.: Harvard University Press, 1970. (Harvard Semitic series, 21.) ISBN 0-674-89810-9. ▸ Expanded development of theory of primitive democracy in Sumer, first presented in 5.52. [EL]

5.52 Thorkild Jacobsen. "Primitive democracy in ancient Mesopotamia." In *Toward the image of Tammuz and other essays on Mesopotamian history and culture.* William L. Moran, ed., pp. 157–70. Cambridge, Mass.: Harvard University Press, 1970. (Harvard Semitic series, 21.) ISBN 0-674-89810-9. ▸ Reprint of 1943 article presenting controversial, much-discussed theory of primitive democracy in Sumer. Discusses origin and development of government in Sumer. [EL]

5.53 Thorkild Jacobsen. "The reign of Ibbi-Suen." In *Toward the image of Tammuz and other essays on Mesopotamian history and culture.* William L. Moran, ed., pp. 173–86. Cambridge, Mass.: Harvard University Press, 1970. (Harvard Semitic series, 21.) ISBN 0-674-89810-9. ▸ Study of collapse of neo-Sumerian (Ur III) empire, 2112–2004 BCE. [EL]

5.54 Tom B. Jones. *The Sumerian problem.* New York: Wiley, 1969. ISBN 0-471-44940-7 (cl), 0-471-44941-5 (pbk). ‣ Excellent summary of evidence for origin of Sumerians. [EL]

5.55 Piotr Steinkeller. "The date of Gudea and his dynasty." *Journal of cuneiform studies* 40.1 (1988) 47–53. ISSN 0022-0256. ‣ Recent attempt to provide firm date for Gudea (ca. 2122), ruler of Lagash, and relate data from city of Lagash to succeeding neo-Sumerian (Ur III) empire, 2112–2004 BCE. [EL]

Second Millennium BCE

5.56 Maurice Birot. *Les chroniques "assyriennes" de Mari.* Paris: Éditions Recherche sur les Civilisations, 1985. (Mari: annales de recherches interdisciplinaires, 4.) ISBN 2-86538-134-3. ‣ Publication of earliest known historical chronicles (ca. 1800 BCE). Fragmentary but shows what may be found in future. [EL]

5.57 John A. Brinkman. "Foreign relations of Babylonia from 1600 to 625 B.C." *American journal of archaeology* 76.3 (1972) 271–81. ISSN 0002-9114. ‣ Excellent summary of Babylonian foreign relations during Kassite and Second Dynasty of Isin periods. Chronological chart. [EL]

5.58 John A. Brinkman. *Materials and studies for Kassite history, I.* Chicago: University of Chicago, Oriental Institute, 1976. ‣ Thorough, annotated catalog of sources for Kassite (Middle Babylonian) history, 1595–1155 BCE. No narrative discussion but contains vast quantity of historical information for a dark age. [EL]

5.59 John A. Brinkman. "Notes on Mesopotamian history in the thirteenth century B.C." *Bibliotheca Orientalis* 27.5–6 (1970) 301–14. ISSN 0291-0054. ‣ Review article of chapter in *The Cambridge Ancient History* (5.2), with substantial discussion of several aspects of history of Babylonia and Assyria during late Kassite period. [EL]

5.60 John A. Brinkman. *A political history of post-Kassite Babylonia, 1158–722 B.C.* Rome: Pontifical Biblical Institute, 1968. (Analecta Orientalia, 43.) ‣ Exhaustive history with catalog of sources. Dense narrative, most detailed source for period. [EL]

5.61 John A. Brinkman. "Ur: the Kassite period and the period of the Assyrian kings." *Orientalia,* n.s., 38.2 (1969) 310–48. ISSN 0030-5367. ‣ Thorough history of city of Ur, 1740–625 BCE. [EL]

5.62 Dominique Charpin. *Données nouvelles sur las chronologie des souverains d'Ešnunna.* Paris: Éditions Recherche sur les Civilisations, 1985. ISBN 2-86538-147-3. ‣ Summary of current knowledge of history of important city of Eshnunna, ca. 1800 BCE. [EL]

5.63 Maria de J. Ellis. "Notes on the chronology of the later Eshnunna dynasty." *Journal of cuneiform studies* 37 (1985) 61–85. ISSN 0022-0256. ‣ Discussion of year dates from important city, ca. 1800 BCE. [EL]

5.64 J. J. Finkelstein. "The genealogy of the Hammurapi dynasty." *Journal of cuneiform studies* 20 (1966) 95–118 and pls. ISSN 0022-0256. ‣ Discussion of origins of Amorite (West Semitic) dynasties of Babylonia and Assyria in early second millennium BCE. Treats sources and especially problems associated with beginning of Assyrian king list. Very important for understanding role of Amorites in Mesopotamia. [EL]

5.65 Ignace J. Gelb. "The early history of the West Semitic peoples." *Journal of cuneiform studies* 15.1 (1961) 27–47. ISSN 0022-0256. ‣ Excellent summary of various migrations of West Semitic peoples into Mesopotamia; particularly good on Amorites. [EL]

5.66 A. Kirk Grayson. "Rivalry over rulership at Ashur: the Puzur-Sin inscription." *Annual review of the Royal Inscriptions of Mesopotamia project* 3 (1985) 9–14. ISSN 0822-2525. ‣ Survey of Assyrian dynastic struggles in early second millennium BCE. [EL]

5.67 William W. Hallo. "The last years of the kings of Isin." *Journal of Near Eastern studies* 18.1 (1959) 54–73. ISSN 0022-2968. ‣ Discussion of end of Isin dynasty, ca. 1794 BCE. [EL]

5.68 Amir Harrak. *Assyria and Hanigalbat: a historical reconstruction of bilateral relations from the middle of the fourteenth to the end of the twelfth centuries B.C.* Hildesheim: Olms, 1987. ISBN 3-487-07948-8. ‣ Most recent, competent study of Assyrian relations with northwestern neighbors, mid-fourteenth to end of twelfth century BCE. [EL]

5.69 Mario Liverani. "The growth of the Assyrian empire in the Habur/Middle Euphrates area: a new paradigm." *State Archives of Assyria bulletin* 2.2 (1988) 81–98. ISSN 1120-4699. ‣ Summary of history of formation of Assyrian empire after 883 BCE. [EL]

5.70 Peter Machinist. "Provincial governance in Middle Assyria and some new texts from Yale." *Assur* 3.2 (1982) 65–101, pls i–iv. ISSN 0145-6334. ‣ Good treatment of organization and governance of Assyrian provinces in fourteenth and thirteenth centuries BCE. [EL]

First Millennium BCE

5.71 Paul-Alain Beaulieu. *The reign of Nabonidus, king of Babylon, 556–539 B.C.* New Haven: Yale University Press, 1989. (Yale Near Eastern researches, 10.) ISBN 0-300-04314-7. ‣ Thorough, up-to-date biography of controversial king of Babylon (556–539 BCE). Best source for period; includes bibliography of previous studies. [EL]

5.72 John A. Brinkman. "Merodach-Baladan II." In *Studies presented to A. Leo Oppenheim, June 7, 1964,* pp. 6–53. Chicago: University of Chicago, Oriental Institute, 1964. ‣ Thorough, detailed study of Chaldean leader, sometime Babylonian king, and scourge of Assyrian rule in Babylonia. [PG]

5.73 John A. Brinkman. *Prelude to empire: Babylonian society and politics, 747–626 B.C.* Philadelphia: The University Museum, Babylonian Fund, 1984. (Occasional publications of the Babylonian Fund, 7.) ISBN 0-934718-62-8. ‣ Well-researched, reliable political history of Babylonia, 747–626 BCE. Extensive bibliography. Best source for neo-Babylonian period. [EL]

5.74 Israel Eph'al. "The western minorities in Babylonia in the sixth to fifth century B.C.: maintenance and cohesion." *Orientalia,* n.s., 47 (1961) 364–78. ISSN 0038-5367. ‣ Interesting discussion of deported populations. [EL]

5.75 Grant Frame. *Babylonia, 689–627 B.C.: a political history.* Istanbul: Nederlands Historisch-Archaeologisch Instituut te Istanbul, 1992. (Uitgaven van het Nederlands Historisch-Archaeologisch Instituut te Istanbul, 69.) ISBN 90-6258-069-6, ISSN 0926-9568. ‣ Thorough, penetrating political history of Babylonia in seventh century BCE. [EL]

5.76 Paul Garelli. "The achievement of Tiglath-pileser III: novelty or continuity?" In *Ah, Assyria . . . : studies in Assyrian history and ancient Near Eastern historiography presented to Hayim Tadmor.* Mordechai Cogan and Israel Eph'al, eds., pp. 46–51. Jerusalem: Magnes and The Hebrew University, 1991. (Scripta Hierosolymitana, 33.) ISSN 0080-8369. ‣ Discussion of reign of Tiglath-pileser III (744–727 BCE) and founding of last Assyrian empire. Explores whether empire was result of deliberate Assyrian policy. [EL]

5.77 Pamela Gerardi. "The Arab campaigns of Assurbanipal: scribal reconstruction of the past." *State Archives of Assyria bulletin* 6.2 (1992) 67–103. ISSN 1120-4699. ‣ Thorough literary analysis of Assyrian king's campaign narratives. [EL]

5.78 A. Kirk Grayson. "Assyria's foreign policy in relation to Egypt in the eighth and seventh centuries B.C." *Journal of the Society for the Study of Egyptian Antiquities* 11.2 (1981) 85–88.

▸ Discussion of Assyria's long-range foreign policy toward Egypt. [EL]

5.79 A. Kirk Grayson. "Assyria's foreign policy in relation to Elam in the eighth and seventh centuries B.C." *Sumer* 42.1–2 (1984) 146–48. ISSN 0081-9271. ▸ Brief discussion of hostile relations between Assyria and her eastern neighbor, Elam, in first millennium BCE. [EL]

5.80 A. Kirk Grayson. "The chronology of the reign of Ashurbanipal." *Zeitschrift für Assyriologie und vorderasiatische Archäologie* 70.2 (1980) 227–45. ISSN 0084-5299. ▸ Basic, useful discussion of the order of events during reign of Assyrian king Ashurbanipal (668–626 BCE). [EL]

5.81 A. Kirk Grayson. "Studies in neo-Assyrian history." *Bibliotheca Orientalis* 33.3–4 (1976) 134–45. ISSN 0006-1913. ▸ Miscellaneous studies of political history of ninth-century BCE Assyria. Not detailed, but supplements corresponding articles in *The Cambridge Ancient History* (5.2). [EL]

5.82 Leo L. Honor. *Sennacherib's invasion of Palestine: a critical sources study.* 1926 ed. New York: AMS Press, 1966. ISBN 0-404-50542-2. ▸ Dated but useful treatment of Sennacherib's campaign(s) in Palestine. Summarizes long-debated question of whether Sennacherib carried out one or two campaigns to region. [EL]

5.83 Wilfred G. Lambert. "The reigns of Ashurnasirpal II and Shalmaneser III: an interpretation." *Iraq* 36.1–2 (1974) 103–10. ISSN 0021-0889. ▸ General overview of Assyrian history, 883–824 BCE, when the great Assyrian empire first began to expand to the West. [EL]

5.84 Erle Leichty. "Esarhaddon's 'Letter to the Gods.'" In *Ah, Assyria . . . : studies in Assyrian history and ancient Near Eastern historiography presented to Hayim Tadmor.* Mordechai Cogan and Israel Eph'al, eds., pp. 52–57. Jerusalem: Magnes and The Hebrew University, 1991. (Scripta Hierosolymitana, 33.) ISSN 0080-8369. ▸ Interesting interpretation of document recording Assyrian king Esarhaddon's campaign against Shubria in 673 BCE. Connects campaign to revenge for murder of his father Sennacherib. [EL]

5.85 Louis D. Levine. "Sennacherib's southern front, 704–689 B.C." *Journal of cuneiform studies* 34.1 (1982) 28–58. ISSN 0022-0256. ▸ Competent analysis of Sennacherib's campaigns against Babylonia and Elam based on analysis of Assyrian king's royal inscriptions. [EL]

5.86 Mario Liverani. *Prestige and interest.* Padua: Sargon, 1990. (History of the ancient Near East, Studies, 1.) ▸ Interesting interpretation of second-millennium international relations, economic and diplomatic, based on reciprocity and redistribution patterns of integration. Poor English (nonnative writer), but worth the trouble. [PG]

5.87 A. R. Millard and Hayim Tadmor. "Adad-nirari III in Syria." *Iraq* 35.1 (1973) 57–64. ISSN 0021-0889. ▸ Discussion of campaigns of Adad-nirari III (810–783 BCE), king of Assyria, in light of new stele fragment. Deals with expansion of Assyria into Syria. [EL]

5.88 Nadav Na'aman. "Chronology and history in the late Assyrian empire (631–619 B.C.)." *Zeitschrift für Assyriologie und vorderasiatische Archäologie* 81.2 (1991) 243–67. ISSN 0084-5299. ▸ Reassessment of seventh-century BCE chronology. Compare Oates 5.90. [EL]

5.89 J. Neumann and Simo Parpola. "Climatic change and the eleventh- to tenth-century eclipse of Assyria and Babylonia." *Journal of Near Eastern studies* 46.3 (1987) 161–82. ISSN 0022-2968. ▸ Discussion of decline of political and military power in Mesopotamia after 1200 BCE. Ties decline to possible climatic changes. [EL]

5.90 Joan Oates. "Assyrian chronology, 631–612 B.C." *Iraq* 27 (1965) 135–59. ISSN 0021-0889. ▸ Study of chronology of last kings and events of Assyrian empire, period fraught with chronological problems. Long considered most probable chronological reconstruction; but now see Na'aman 5.88. [EL]

5.91 A. Leo Oppenheim. "The city of Assur in 714 B.C." *Journal of Near Eastern studies* 19.2 (1960) 133–47. ISSN 0022-2968. ▸ Interesting analysis of Assyrian society based on document, written in form of a letter to the god Assur, describing campaign of Sargon II of Assyria against Urartu in 714 BCE. [EL]

5.92 Simo Parpola. "A letter from Shamash-shumu-ukin to Esarhaddon." *Iraq* 34.1 (1972) 21–34. ISSN 0021-0889. ▸ Excellent study of letter with detailed information on murder of Ashur-nadin-shumi, king of Babylon and son of Assyrian king Sennacherib. Murder a factor in Sennacherib's destruction of Babylon, 689 BCE. [EL]

5.93 Simo Parpola. *Letters from Assyrian scholars to the kings Esarhaddon and Assurbanipal*, Part 2: *Commentary and appendices.* Kevelaer/Neukirchen-Vluyn: Verlag Butzon & Bercker/Neukirchener Verlag. (Alter Orient und Altes Testament, 5/2.) ISBN 3-7666-9326-3, 3-7887-0723-3. ▸ Specialist study of letters from royal archives of Nineveh. Commentary loaded with historical information on neo-Assyrian period. Also contains detailed and important information on royal family, personalities, and palace life. [EL]

5.94 Simo Parpola. "The murderer of Sennacherib." In *Death in Mesopotamia.* Bendt Alster, ed., pp. 171–82. Copenhagen: Akademisk Forlag, 1980. (Mesopotamia, 8.) ISBN 87-500-1946-5. ▸ Fine study of letter unmasking murderer of Assyrian king Sennacherib, subject of much scholarly debate. [EL]

5.95 Julian Reade. "Shalmaneser or Ashurnasirpal in Ararat?" *State Archives of Assyria bulletin* 3.2 (1989) 93–98. ISSN 1120-4699. ▸ Discussion of Assyrian relations with Urartu in ninth century BCE. Treats possible misattribution of military campaign. [EL]

5.96 Ronald H. Sack. *Images of Nebuchadnezzar.* Selinsgrove, Pa.: Susquehanna University Press, 1991. ISBN 0-945636-35-0. ▸ Competent biography of Nebuchadnezzar II, king of Babylon (605–562 BCE). [EL]

5.97 Ronald H. Sack. "Nergal-sharra-uṭur, king of Babylon as seen in the cuneiform, Greek, Latin, and Hebrew sources." *Zeitschrift für Assyriologie und vorderasiatische Archäologie* 68.1 (1978) 129–49. ISSN 0084-5299. ▸ History of reign of Neriglissar, king of Babylon (560–556 BCE). [EL]

5.98 Hayim Tadmor. "The campaigns of Sargon II of Assur: a chronological-historical study." *Journal of cuneiform studies* 12 (1958) 22–40, 77–100. ISSN 0022-0256. ▸ Excellent history of military campaigns of Sargon II of Assyria at end of eighth century BCE. Important for analysis of Sargon's annals. [EL]

5.99 Hayim Tadmor. "The historical inscriptions of Adad-nirari III." *Iraq* 35.2 (1973) 141–50. ISSN 0021-0889. ▸ Offers latest evidence for reign of Adad-nirari III (810–783 BCE), king of Assyria. [EL]

5.100 Hayim Tadmor. "History and ideology in the Assyrian royal inscriptions." In *Assyrian royal inscriptions: new horizons in literary, ideological, and historical analysis.* F. M. Fales, ed., pp. 13–33. Rome: Istituto per l'Oriente, Centro per le Antichità e la Storia dell'Arte del Vicino Oriente, 1981. (Orientis antiqui collectio, 17.) ▸ Essay on Assyrian annals, their interpretation, and their use for constructing history. Discussion of earlier ideas on and approaches to these royal inscriptions. [EL]

5.101 Hayim Tadmor, Benno Landsberger, and Simo Parpola.

"The sin of Sargon and Sennacherib's last will." *State Archives of Assyria bulletin* 3.1 (1989) 3–51. ISSN 1120-4699. ▸ First-rate study of reigns of kings Sargon, Sennacherib, and Esarhaddon of Assyria, 721–669 BCE, centered on study of important, unique document. Deals with issues of political motivation. [EL]

5.102 D. J. Wiseman. *Nebuchadnezzar and Babylon*. New York: Oxford University Press for the British Academy, 1991. ISBN 0-19-726100-0. ▸ Biography of Nebuchadnezzar II, king of Babylon (605–562 BCE), and description of Babylon at time of Babylonian captivity. [EL]

5.103 Stefan Zawadzki. *The fall of Assyria and Median-Babylonian relations in light of the Nabopolassar chronicle*. Delft: Eburon, 1988. ISBN 90-5166-034-0. ▸ Recent, interpretive history of collapse of Assyrian empire in 612 BCE and Babylonian-Median alliance. Many conclusions debatable. [EL]

5.104 Paul Zimansky. "Urartian geography and Sargon's eighth campaign." *Journal of Near Eastern studies* 49.1 (1990) 1–21. ISSN 0022-2968. ▸ Thorough study of Sargon's eighth campaign against Urartu in 714 BCE. Extensive treatment of historical geography of Urartu. [EL]

Military History

5.105 Alan Buttery. *Armies and enemies of ancient Egypt and Assyria*. London: War Games Research Group, 1974. ISBN 0-10-441704-2. ▸ Concise, superficial history of warfare in ancient Near East, 3200–612 BCE. Useful line drawings of weaponry and armor. [EL]

5.106 Stephanie Dalley. "Foreign chariotry and cavalry in the armies of Tiglath Pilesar III and Sargon II." *Iraq* 47 (1985) 31–48. ISSN 0021-0889. ▸ Discussion of use of foreigners in Assyrian army. [EL]

5.107 Stephanie Dalley and J. N. Postgate. "New light on the composition of Sargon II's army." In *The tablets from Fort Shalmaneser*, pp. 27–47. London: British School of Archaeology in Iraq, 1984. (Cuneiform texts from Nimrud, 3.) ISBN 0-903472-08-2. ▸ Excellent discussion of available evidence on Assyrian military, based on new documentation from Fort Shalmanesar at Nimrud. Assyrian military in need of serious full-length study. [PG]

5.108 Pamela Gerardi. "Declaring war in Mesopotamia." *Archiv für Orientforschung* 33 (1986) 30–38. ISSN 0066-6440. ▸ Translation and discussion of first-millennium BCE declaration of war from Babylonia. [EL]

5.109 Florence Malbran-Labat. *L'armée et l'organisation militaire de l'Assyrie*. Geneva: Droz, 1982. (École Pratique des Hautes Études, Quatrième section: sciences historiques et philologiques, 2, Hautes études orientales, 19.) ▸ Treatment of Assyrian military establishment based on letters from Nineveh. Only source to cover entire topic. Extensive bibliography. [EL]

5.110 Walter Mayer. "Die Finanzierung einer Kampagne (TCL 3, 346–410)." *Ugarit Forschungen* 11 (1979) 571–95. ▸ Only study of its kind. Examines extensive booty-list in composition known as "Sargon's Eighth Campaign" and related narrative reliefs. [PG]

5.111 Jack M. Sasson. *The military establishments at Mari*. Rome: Pontifical Biblical Institute, 1969. (Studia Pohl, Series minora, 3.) ▸ Thorough description of military in second millennium BCE, based on data from city of Mari in northwestern Mesopotamia. [EL]

Social and Cultural History

5.112 John A. Brinkman. "Hurrians in Babylonia in the late second millennium B.C." In *Studies on the civilization and culture of*

Nuzi and the Hurrians in honor of E.R. Lacheman. M. A. Morrison and D. I. Owen, eds., vol. 1, pp. 27–36. Winona Lake, Ind.: Eisenbrauns, 1981. ISBN 0-931464-08-0. ▸ Thorough study of role of Hurrians in Babylonia in second millennium BCE. [EL]

5.113 John A. Brinkman. "The monarchy in the time of the Kassite dynasty." In *Le palais et la royauté: archéologie et civilisation*. Paul Garelli, ed., pp. 395–408. Paris: Geuthner, 1974. (Rencontre assyriologique internationale, 19.) ▸ Discussion of concept of kingship in Babylonia in Kassite period. First treatment of topic in what is usually thought of as dark age. [EL]

5.114 John A. Brinkman. "Notes on Arameans and Chaldeans in southern Babylonia in the early seventh century, B.C." *Orientalia*, n.s., 46.2 (1977) 304–25. ISSN 0030-5367. ▸ Good summary of Babylonians' problems with various West Semitic groups that migrated into region during first millennium BCE. [EL]

5.115 Georges Contenau. *Every-day life in Babylon and Assyria*. 1954 ed. K. R. Maxwell-Hyslop and A. R. Maxwell-Hyslop, trans. New York: Norton, 1966. ▸ Description of culture of Assyria and Babylonia, with emphasis on first millennium BCE. Highly personalized view of Mesopotamian civilization. Dated but still useful. [EL]

5.116 Henri Frankfort. *The birth of civilization in the Near East*. 1951 ed. New York: Barnes & Noble, 1968. ISBN 0-510-26801-3. ▸ Dated but still useful treatment of beginnings of civilization in Mesopotamia and Egypt and interconnections between two areas in third millennium BCE. [EL]

5.117 Ignace J. Gelb. "Household and family in early Mesopotamia." In *State and temple economy in the ancient Near East*. 2 vols. Edward Lipiński, ed., vol. 1, pp. 1–98. Louvain: Département Orientalistiek, 1979. (Orientalia Lovaniensia analecta, 5–6.) ISBN 90-70192-03-9 (set). ▸ Lengthy, thorough study of social structure in third-millennium Mesopotamia. [EL]

5.118 Ignace J. Gelb. "Prisoners of war in early Mesopotamia." *Journal of Near Eastern studies* 32.1–2 (1973) 70–98. ISSN 0022-2968. ▸ Thorough discussion of prisoners of war, slavery, and labor in second half of third millennium BCE in Mesopotamia. Bibliography. [EL]

5.119 Thorkild Jacobsen. "The assumed conflict between the Sumerians and Semites in early Mesopotamian history." In *Towards the image of Tammuz and other essays on Mesopotamian history and culture*. William L. Moran, ed., pp. 187–92. Cambridge, Mass.: Harvard University Press, 1970. (Harvard Semitic series, 21.) ISBN 0-674-89810-9. ▸ Reprint of author's answer to Nazi propaganda about Sumerians and Semites. Shows peaceful coexistence of Sumerians and Akkadians in early Sumer. [EL]

5.120 Jean-Robert Kupper. *Les nomades en Mésopotamie au temps des rois de Mari*. Paris: Société d'Édition "Les Belles Lettres," 1957. (Bibliothèque de la Faculté de Philosophie et Lettres de l'Université de Liège, 117.) ▸ Thorough study of nomadism on Upper Euphrates in second millennium BCE. Based on letters and documents from Mari. [EL]

5.121 Benno Landsberger. *Three essays on the Sumerians*. Maria de J. Ellis, trans. Los Angeles: Undena, 1974. (Monographs on the ancient Near East, 1.2.) ISBN 0-89003-002-2. ▸ Classic discussion of origin and achievements of Sumerians by most prominent Assyriologist of twentieth century. [EL]

5.122 Victor Harold Matthews. *Pastoral nomadism in the Mari kingdom, 1830–1760 B.C.* Cambridge: American Schools of Oriental Research, 1978. (American Schools of Oriental Research dissertation series, 3.) ISBN 0-89757-103-7. ▸ Study of nomadism in northwestern Mesopotamia in second millennium BCE. Treats social structure of countryside based on texts from Mari. [EL]

5.123 Nadav Na'aman and Ran Zadok. "Sargon II's deportations to Israel and Philistia." *Journal of cuneiform studies* 40.1 (1988) 36–46. ISSN 0022-0256. ‣ Analysis of Sargon II's campaigns to Media and to West, with emphasis on deportation of Iranian populace to West. [EL]

5.124 Bustenay Oded. *Mass deportations and deportees in the neo-Assyrian empire*. Wiesbaden: Reichert, 1979. ISBN 3-88226-043-2. ‣ Survey of Assyrian deportation policy. [EL]

5.125 J. N. Postgate. "Some remarks on conditions in the Assyrian countryside." *Journal of the economic and social history of the Orient* 17.3 (1974) 225–43. ISSN 0022-4995. ‣ Discussion of rural Assyria in first millennium BCE. [EL]

5.126 M. B. Rowton. "Autonomy and nomadism in western Asia." *Orientalia*, n.s., 42.1–2 (1973) 247–58. ISSN 0030-5367. ‣ Thoughtful essay on nomadism along Upper Euphrates in second millennium BCE. [EL]

5.127 Klaas R. Veenhof, ed. *Cuneiform archives and libraries: papers read at the 30e Rencontre Assyriologique Internationale, Leiden, 4–8 July 1983*. Leiden: Nederlands Historisch-Archaeologisch Instituut te Istanbul, 1986. (Uitgaven van het Nederlands Historisch-Archaeologisch Instituut te Istanbul, 42.) ISBN 90-6258-057-2. ‣ Conference volume focusing on content and reconstruction of cuneiform libraries and archives. Several important contributions. [PG]

5.128 David B. Weisberg. "Kinship and social organization in Chaldean Uruk." *Journal of the American Oriental Society* 104.4 (1984) 739–44. ISSN 0003-0279. ‣ Review and summary of major work in German on social organization of important Babylonian city of Uruk in late first millennium BCE. [EL]

Economic History

5.129 Erik Aerts and Horst Klengel, eds. *The town as regional economic center in the ancient Near East*. Louvain: Louvain University Press, 1990. (Proceedings: tenth international economic history congress, 5.) ISBN 90-6186-389-9. ‣ Frequently cited collection of essays by various authors on economic organization of Mesopotamia. [EL]

5.130 Alphonso Archi, ed. *Circulation of goods in non-palatial context in the ancient Near East*. Rome: Ateneo, 1984. (Incunabula Graeca, 82.) ‣ Eclectic collection of essays on Mesopotamian trade in several major periods and many areas of Mesopotamia, Syria, and Levant. Attempt to define economic systems functioning in ancient western Asia. [EL]

5.131 Muhammad A. Dandamaev. "State and temple in Babylonia in the first millennium B.C." In *State and temple economy in the ancient Near East*. Edward Lipiński, ed., vol. 2, pp. 589–96. Louvain: Département Orientalistiek, 1979. (Orientalia Lovaniensia analecta, 5–6.) ISBN 90-70192-03-9 (set). ‣ Essay on organization of economy of first-millennium BCE. Babylonia, with emphasis on role of crown and temple. Only article on topic for this period. [EL]

5.132 I. M. Diakonoff, ed. *Ancient Mesopotamia: socio-economic history*. 1969 ed. Liechtenstein: Sundig, 1981. ISBN 3-500-26710-6. ‣ Interesting collection of essays giving Marxist overview of Mesopotamian social and economic history. Contains articles by all leading scholars of ancient Near East from former Soviet Union. Several excellent contributions. [EL]

5.133 Adam Falkenstein. *The Sumerian temple city*. Maria de J. Ellis, trans. Los Angeles: Undena, 1974. (Monographs on the ancient Near East, 1.1.) ISBN 0-89003-002-2. ‣ Dated, now controversial concept of Sumerian economic organization. Used extensively by Marxist historians as model of Sumerian society. [EL]

5.134 Ignace J. Gelb. "On the alleged temple and state econo-

mies in ancient Mesopotamia." In *Studi in onore di Edoardo Volterra*. Vol. 6, pp. 137–54. Milan: Giuffre, 1969. ‣ Rejoinder to popular theory of temple economy in early Sumer (Falkenstein 5.133). Addresses major controversy between Marxist and capitalist scholars over economy of Sumer. [EL]

5.135 Thorkild Jacobsen. "On the textile industry at Ur under Ibbi-Sin." In *Toward the image of Tammuz and other essays on Mesopotamian history and culture*. William L. Moran, ed., pp. 216–29. Cambridge, Mass.: Harvard University Press, 1970. (Harvard Semitic series, 21.) ISBN 0-674-89810-9. ‣ Description of textile industry in Sumer, ca. 2000 BCE, most important industry in ancient Mesopotamia. [EL]

5.136 Géza Komoróczy. "Zu den Eigentumsverhältnissen in der altbabylonischen Zeit: das Problem der Privatwirtschaft." In *State and temple economy in the ancient Near East*. Edward Lipiński, ed., vol. 2, pp. 411–22. Louvain: Département Orientalistiek, 1979. (Orientalia Lovaniensia analecta, 5–6.) ISBN 90-70192-03-9. ‣ Discussion of organization of economy in Mesopotamia in second millennium BCE. [EL]

5.137 W. F. Leemans. "Old Babylonian letters and economic history: a review article with a digression on foreign trade." *Journal of the economic and social history of the Orient* 11.2 (1968) 171–226. ISSN 0022-4995. ‣ Discussion of trade in second-millennium Mesopotamia concentrating on overland trade, its organization, financing, and division of profits. [EL]

5.138 A. Leo Oppenheim. "Essay on overland trade in the first millennium B.C." *Journal of cuneiform studies* 21.1–4 (1967) 236–54. ISSN 0022-0256. ‣ Description of organization of Mesopotamian land trade in first millennium BCE. Discusses goods traded and how. [EL]

5.139 A. Leo Oppenheim. "The seafaring merchants of Ur." *Journal of the American Oriental Society* 74.1 (1954) 6–17. ISSN 0003-0279. ‣ Detailed description of second-millennium sea trade in Persian Gulf, its organization, financing, and division of profits. [EL]

5.140 Johannes Renger. "Interaction of temple, palace, and 'private enterprise' in the Old Babylonian economy." In *State and temple economy in the ancient Near East*. Edward Lipiński, ed., vol. 1, pp. 249–56. Leuven: Departement Orientalistiek, 1979. (Orientalia Lovaniensia analecta, 5–6.) ISBN 90-70192-03-9 (set). ‣ Description of economic organization in cities of second-millennium BCE Mesopotamia. [EL]

5.141 Matthew W. Stolper. *Entrepreneurs and empire: the Murašu archive, the Murašu firm, and Persian rule in Babylonia*. Leiden: Nederlands Historisch-Archaeologisch Instituut te Istanbul, 1985. (Uitgaven van het Nederlands Historisch-Archaeologisch Instituut te Istanbul, 54.) ISBN 90-6258-054-8. ‣ Thorough study of Murashu banking family in fifth-century Babylonia and organization of Babylonian economy. [EL]

5.142 Richard L. Zettler. *The Ur III temple of Inanna at Nippur*. Berlin: Reimer, 1992. ISBN 3-496-00422-3. ‣ Thorough discussion of operation and organization of urban religious institutions in Mesopotamia. [EL]

Agricultural History

5.143 Maria de J. Ellis. *Agriculture and state in ancient Mesopotamia: an introduction to problems of land tenure*. Philadelphia: The University Museum, Babylonian Fund, 1976. (Occasional publications of the Babylonian Fund, 1.) ISBN 0-934718-28-8. ‣ Fine study of organization and practice of agriculture in ancient Mesopotamia. Difficult reading but very useful. [EL]

5.144 Thorkild Jacobsen. *Salinity and irrigation agriculture in antiquity*. Malibu, Calif.: Undena, 1982. (Bibliotheca Mesopotamica, 14.) ISBN 0-89003-093-6 (cl), 0-89003-092-8 (pbk).

‣ Explanation of changing settlement patterns in Mesopotamia due to soil salinization caused by poor irrigation practices. [EL]

Labor History

5.145 John A. Brinkman. "Forced laborers in the Middle Babylonian period." *Journal of cuneiform studies* 32.1 (1980) 17–22. ISSN 0022-0256. ‣ Thorough study of laborers in second-millennium BCE Babylonia. [EL]

5.146 Ignace J. Gelb. "The *arua* institution." *Revue d'assyriologie et d'archéologie orientale* 66.1 (1972) 1–32. ISSN 0373-6032. ‣ Analysis of temple labor in third-millennium BCE Mesopotamia, performed by women and children who were then given to temple. Meticulous study of their family, status, and labor. [EL]

5.147 Ignace J. Gelb. "From freedom to slavery." In *Gesellschaftsklassen im alten Zweistromland und in angrenzenden Gebieten.* Dietz Otto Edzard, ed., pp. 81–92. Munich: Verlag der Bayrischen Akademie der Wissenschaften, 1972. ISBN 3-7696-0070-3. ‣ Extensive discussion of labor in third-millennium BCE Mesopotamia. [EL]

5.148 Marvin A. Powell, ed. *Labor in the ancient Near East.* New Haven: American Oriental Society, 1987. (American Oriental series, 68.) ISBN 0-940490-68-4. ‣ Thirteen essays on use of labor in ancient Mesopotamia, Egypt, Anatolia, and Palestine. Wideranging coverage. [EL]

Slavery

5.149 Muhammad A. Dandamaev. *Slavery in Babylonia.* Marvin A. Powell and David B. Weisberg, eds. Victoria A. Powell, trans. DeKalb: Northern Illinois University Press, 1984. ISBN 0-87580-104-8. ‣ Comprehensive treatment of slavery in first-millennium BCE Babylonia. Latest word on subject. [EL]

5.150 I. M. Diakonov. *Slaves, helots, and peasants in early antiquity.* Budapest: Akademia Kiadó, 1976. ISBN 963-05-1015-4. ‣ Marxist study of underclasses in ancient Mesopotamia, with emphasis on earlier period. [EL]

5.151 Ignace J. Gelb. "Definition and discussion of slavery and serfdom." *Ugarit-Forschungen* 11 (1979) 283–97. ISSN 0342-2356. ‣ Discussion of slavery in Mesopotamia and fine line between slavery and free peasantry. [EL]

5.152 Isaac Mendelsohn. *Slavery in the ancient Near East: a comparative study of slavery in Babylonia, Assyria, Syria, and Palestine from the middle of the third millennium to the end of the first millennium.* 1949 ed. Westport, Conn.: Greenwood, 1978. ISBN 0-313-20499-3. ‣ General but superficial study. Now superseded for first millennium by Dandamaev 5.149. [EL]

5.153 Bernard J. Siegal. *Slavery during the third dynasty of Ur.* 1944 ed. New York: Kraus Reprint, 1947. (Memoir series of the American Anthropology Association, 66.) ISBN 0-527-00565-7 (pbk). ‣ Dated discussion of slavery in third-millennium Mesopotamia. Needs to be restudied. [EL]

Women's History

5.154 Julia M. Ashur-Greve. *Frauen in altsumerischer Zeit.* Malibu: Undena, 1985. (Biblioteca Mesopotamica, 18.) ISBN 0-89003-161-4 (cl), 0-89003-162-2 (pbk). ‣ Discussion of role and function of women in early third millennium BCE. Largely based on pictorial evidence. [EL]

5.155 Bernard Frank Batto. *Studies on women at Mari.* Baltimore: Johns Hopkins University Press, 1974. ISBN 0-8018-1605-x. ‣ Thorough study of status of women in second-millennium BCE Mesopotamia, based on data from city of Mari in northwestern Mesopotamia. [EL]

5.156 I. M. Diakonoff. "Women in Old Babylonia not under patriarchal authority." *Journal of the economic and social history of the Orient* 29.3 (1986) 225–38. ISSN 0022-4995. ‣ Discussion of status of women in second-millennium BCE Mesopotamia, concentrating on groups that could function without male approval. [EL]

5.157 Jean-Marie Durand. *Les dames du palais de Mari à l'époque du royaume de haute-Mesopotamie.* Paris: Éditions Recherche sur les Civilisations, 1985. (Mari: annales de recherches interdisciplinaires, 4.) ISBN 2-86538-134-3. ‣ Discussion of role and status of women in royal household at Mari in Old Babylonian period (ca. 1800 BCE). [EL]

5.158 Jean-Marie Durand, ed. *La femme dans le proche orient antique.* Paris: Éditions Recherche sur les Civilisations, 1987. ISBN 2-86538-177-3. ‣ Collection of conference papers on women in Mesopotamia, mostly in English and French; no common theme. Covers wide range of topics, geographical areas, and time periods. Mixed quality but good sampling of available evidence. [EL]

5.159 Katarzyna Grosz. "Bridewealth and dowry in Nuzi." In *Images of women in antiquity.* Averil Cameron and Amélie Kuhrt, eds., pp. 193–206. Detroit: Wayne State University Press, 1983. ISBN 0-8143-2466-5. ‣ Applies social anthropological theory to bridewealth and dowry in city of Nuzi in fifteenth century BCE. Gives thumbnail history of city. [EL]

5.160 William W. Hallo. "Women of Sumer." In *The legacy of Sumer: invited lectures on the Middle East at the University of Texas at Austin.* Denise Schmandt-Besserat, ed., pp. 23–40. Malibu: Undena, 1976. (Bibliotheca Mesopotamica, 4.) ISBN 0-89003-019-7 (cl), 0-89003-018-9 (pbk). ‣ Third-millennium Sumerian history from standpoint of women. [EL]

5.161 Rivkah Harris. "The *naditu* woman." In *Studies presented to A. Leo Oppenheim, June 7, 1964.* Robert D. Biggs and John A. Brinkman, eds., pp. 106–35. Chicago: University of Chicago, Oriental Institute, 1964. ‣ Discussion of special class of Babylonian women associated with temple (*naditu*) in second millennium BCE. [EL]

5.162 Samuel A. Meier. "Women and communication in the ancient Near East." *Journal of the American Oriental Society* 111.3 (1991) 540–47. ISSN 0003-0279. ‣ Discussion of women's role in communication in Israel and Mesopotamia. [EL]

5.163 Sue Rollin. "Women and witchcraft in ancient Assyria (c. 900–600 B.C.)." In *Images of women in antiquity.* Averil Cameron and Amélie Kuhrt, eds., pp. 34–46. Detroit: Wayne State University Press, 1983. ISBN 0-8143-2466-5. ‣ Study of association of women with witchcraft in first-millennium Assyria. [EL]

5.164 Elizabeth C. Stone. "The social role of the *naditu* women in Old Babylonian Nippur." *Journal of the economic and social history of the Orient* 25.1 (1982) 50–70. ISSN 0022-4995. ‣ Discussion of special class of Babylonian women known as *naditu* in second millennium BCE. [EL]

5.165 Hayim Tadmor. "Assyria and the West: the ninth century and its aftermath." In *Unity and diversity.* Hans Goedicke and J.J.M. Roberts, eds., pp. 36–48. Baltimore: Johns Hopkins University Press, 1975. ISBN 0-8018-1638-6. ‣ Careful study of western, specifically Aramaean, influence on Assyrian culture during Assyrian political-economic expansion in West. [EL]

Religion

5.166 Thorkild Jacobsen. *The treasures of darkness: a history of Mesopotamian religion.* New Haven: Yale University Press, 1976. ISBN 0-300-01844-4 (cl), 0-300-02291-3 (pbk). ‣ Basic, readable history of Mesopotamian religion, with emphasis on literary sources. [EL]

Legal History

5.167 Guillaume Cardascia and Joseph Klíma, comps. *Droits cuneiformes*. Brussels: Éditions de l'Institut de Sociologie, 1966. (Introduction bibliographique à l'histoire du droit et à l'ethnologie juridique, A/2.) ▸ Extensive bibliography of works on Mesopotamian legal system. [EL]

5.168 Barry L. Eichler. "Literary structure in the Laws of Eshnunna." In *Language, literature, and history: philological and historical studies presented to Erica Reiner*. Francesca Rochberg-Halton, ed., pp. 71–84. New Haven: American Oriental Society, 1987. (American Oriental series, 67.) ISBN 0-949490-67-6. ▸ Interesting analysis of one law code, with comparison to others, suggesting code falls within Mesopotamian scholastic tradition, rather than legislated statutory laws or verdicts from legal cases. [PG]

5.169 Thorkild Jacobsen. "An ancient Mesopotamian trial for homicide." In *Toward the image of Tammuz and other essays on Mesopotamian history and culture*. William L. Moran, ed., pp. 193–214. Cambridge, Mass.: Harvard University Press, 1970. (Harvard Semitic series, 21.) ISBN 0-674-89810-9. ▸ Study of school text of Old Babylonian period preserving record of Sumerian murder trial. [EL]

5.170 Raymond Westbrook. "Cuneiform law codes and the origins of legislation." *Zeitschrift für Assyriologie und vorderasiatische Archäologie* 79.2 (1989) 201–22. ISSN 0084-5299. ▸ Arguable interpretation of Mesopotamian law codes. [EL]

Literature

5.171 Tsvi Abusch, John Huehnergard and Piotr Steinkeller, eds. *Lingering over words: studies in ancient Near Eastern literature in honor of William L. Moran*. Atlanta: Scholars Press, 1990. (Harvard Semitic series, 37.) ISBN 1-55540-502-9. ▸ Collection of essays including several fine studies of Sumerian and Akkadian literature by leading scholars. [PG]

5.172 Stephanie Dalley. *Myths from Mesopotamia: Creation, the Flood, and others*. Oxford: Oxford University Press, 1991. ISBN 0-19-281789-2 (pbk). ▸ Good, up-to-date translation of basic myths of Mesopotamian civilizations. Brief introductions to each myth; glossary of names and terms. [PG]

5.173 William W. Hallo. "Toward a history of Sumerian literature." In *Sumerological studies in honor of Thorkild Jacobsen on his seventieth birthday, June 7, 1974*. Stephen J. Lieberman, ed., pp. 181–203. Chicago: University of Chicago, Oriental Institute, 1976. (Assyriological studies, 20.) ISBN 0-226-62282-7. ▸ Brief discussion of Sumerian literary genres, patronage, and transmission. [PG]

5.174 Thorkild Jacobsen. *The harps that once . . . : Sumerian poetry in translation*. New Haven: Yale University Press, 1987. ISBN 0-300-03906-9. ▸ Annotated anthology (thirty-seven compositions) of Sumerian literature in translation by one of foremost Sumerologists. [EL]

5.175 W. G. Lambert. *Babylonian wisdom literature*. 1960 ed. New York: Oxford University Press, 1967. ISBN 0-19-815424-0. ▸ Annotated anthology of Babylonian wisdom literature in Akkadian and English translation. [EL]

5.176 Jeffrey H. Tigay. *The evolution of the Gilgamesh epic*. Philadelphia: University of Pennsylvania Press, 1982. ▸ Comprehensive, detailed, scholarly discussion of cycle of stories of Sumerian hero and king of Uruk, and their development into later Akkadian epic. [PG]

5.177 Marianna E. Vogelsang and Herman L. J. Vanstiphout, eds. *Mesopotamian epic literature: oral or aural?* Lewiston, N.Y.: Mellen, 1972. ISBN 0-7734-9538-X. ▸ Good collection of essays from 1990 conference, exploring relationship between oral literature and Mesopotamian epic origins and tradition. [PG]

Education, Literacy, and Writing

5.178 C. J. Gadd. *Teachers and students in the oldest schools*. London: University of London, School of Oriental and African Studies, 1956. ▸ Description of Mesopotamian scribal schools of second millennium. [EL]

5.179 Samuel Noah Kramer. "Schooldays: a Sumerian composition relating to the education of a scribe." *Journal of the American Oriental Society* 69.4 (1949) 199–215. ISSN 0003-0279. ▸ Describes a day at school for Sumerian scribe. [EL]

5.180 Mogens Trolle Larsen. "The Babylonian lukewarm mind: reflections on science, divination, and literacy." In *Language, literature, and history: philological and historical studies presented to Erica Reiner*. Francesca Rochberg-Halton, ed., pp. 203–25. New Haven: American Oriental Society, 1987. (American Oriental series, 67.) ISBN 0-940490-67-6. ▸ Provocative, controversial discussion of relationship between writing, literacy, and development of science. [PG]

5.181 Åke W. Sjöberg. "The Old Babylonian edubba." In *Sumerological studies in honor of Thorkild Jacobsen on his seventieth birthday, June 7, 1974*. Stephen J. Lieberman, ed., pp. 159–79. Chicago: University of Chicago, Oriental Institute, 1976. (Assyriological studies, 20.) ISBN 0-226-62282-7. ▸ Good discussion of second-millennium BCE schools, including methods of instruction and curriculum content. [PG]

5.182 *Visible language* 15.4 (1981) 321–440. ISSN 0022-2224. ▸ Issue of journal devoted to discussion of cuneiform writing system. Five articles on origins, early development and implementation, scribes, technology of writing, and literacy. Good, up-to-date collection. [PG]

Science, Technology, and Medicine

5.183 Marie-Christine De Graeve. *The ships of the ancient Near East (c. 2000–500 B.C.)* Louvain: Département Orientalistiek, 1981. (Orientalia Lovaniensia analecta, 7.) ISBN 90-70192-07-1. ▸ Thorough study of boats and bridges in Mesopotamia. [EL]

5.184 Thorkild Jacobsen and Seton Lloyd. *Sennacherib's aqueduct at Jerwan*. Chicago: University of Chicago Press, 1935. (Oriental Institute publications, 24.) ISBN 0-226-62120-0. ▸ Building of aqueduct during reign of Sennacherib, king of Assyria (704–681 BCE). [EL]

5.185 Jørgen Laessøe. "Reflexions on modern and ancient Oriental water works." *Journal of cuneiform studies* 7.1 (1953) 5–26. ISSN 0022-0256. ▸ Study of hydrologic engineering in ancient Mesopotamia. [EL]

5.186 A. Leo Oppenheim. "Mesopotamia in the early history of alchemy." *Revue d'assyriologie et d'archéologie orientale* 60.1 (1966) 29–45. ISSN 0373-6032. ▸ Description of early attempts at alchemy and introduction of new scientific methods to Mesopotamia. [EL]

5.187 A. Leo Oppenheim. "Mesopotamian medicine." *Bulletin of the history of medicine* 36.2 (1962) 97–108. ISSN 0007-5140. ▸ Survey of Mesopotamian medicine. [EL]

5.188 A. Leo Oppenheim et al. *Glass and glassmaking in ancient Mesopotamia: an edition of the cuneiform texts which contain instructions for glass makers*. Corning, N.Y.: Corning Museum of Glass Press, 1988. (Corning Museum of Glass monographs, 3.) ISBN 0-87290-058-4. ▸ Thorough study of glassmaking in ancient Mesopotamia. [EL]

5.189 A. Sachs. "Babylonian observational astronomy." *Philosophical Transactions of the Royal Society of London*, Series A, 276

(1974) 43–50. ISSN 0264-3952. ‣ Summary of available evidence of Mesopotamian astronomical observation. [PG]

Art, Archaeology, and Architecture

5.190   Pauline Albenda. *The palace of Sargon, king of Assyria.* Paris: Éditions Recherche sur les Civilisations, 1986. (Éditions sur les civilisations, Synthèse, 22.) ISBN 2-86538-152-8. ‣ Publication of nineteenth-century plans and drawings of Sargon II's palace, Dur-šarru-ken (Khorsabad). Discussion of excavations; reconstruction of placement of reliefs. [PG]

5.191   Pierre Amiet. *Art of the ancient Near East.* 1977 ed. Naomi Noble Richard, ed. John Shepley and Claude Choquet, trans. New York: Abrams, 1980. ISBN 0-8109-0638-4. ‣ Richly illustrated survey of art of Mesopotamia and surrounding areas, based primarily on collections of Louvre. [EL]

5.192   Richard D. Barnett. *Assyrian palace reliefs and their influence on the sculptures of Babylonia and Persia.* 1960 ed. London: British Museum, 1970. ISBN 0-7141-1074-4 (pbk). ‣ Mostly plates of selections of reliefs from various Assyrian palaces, based on collections of British Museum. [EL]

5.193   Dominique Collon. *First impressions: cylinder seals in the ancient Near East.* Chicago: University of Chicago Press, 1987. ISBN 0-226-11388-4. ‣ Introduction to glyptic art (cylinder seals). Large bibliography. [EL]

5.194   Henri Frankfort. *The art and architecture of the ancient Orient.* 1969 4th ed. Baltimore: Pelican, 1977. ISBN 0-14-056007-6 (cl, 1969), 0-14-056107-2 (pbk). ‣ Standard introduction to and survey of art and architecture of Mesopotamia and surrounding areas. [EL]

5.195   H. A. Groenewegen-Frankfort. *Arrest and movement: an essay on space and time in the representational art of the Near East.* 1951 ed. Cambridge, Mass.: Belknap, 1987. ISBN 0-674- 04656-0 (pbk). ‣ Excellent introduction to ancient Near Eastern art. [EL]

5.196   Seton Lloyd. *The archaeology of Mesopotamia.* London: Thames & Hudson, 1978. ISBN 0-500-79007-8 (pbk). ‣ Dated but still usable introduction to archaeology and material culture of Mesopotamia. Nicely illustrated. [EL]

5.197   John Malcolm Russell. *Sennacherib's palace without rival.* Chicago: University of Chicago Press, 1991. ISBN 0-226-73175-8. ‣ Prize-winning study of reliefs and related texts of Southwest palace at Nineveh. Interesting analysis; well illustrated. [PG]

5.198   Irene J. Winter. "Royal rhetoric and the development of historical narrative in neo-Assyrian reliefs." *Studies in visual communication* 7.2 (1981) 2–38. ‣ Interesting discussion of development of historical narrative, relationship to associated texts, and royal ideology. [PG]

SYRIA-PALESTINE

General Studies

5.199   Yohanan Aharoni. *The land of the Bible: a historical geography.* Rev. ed. Anson F. Rainey, ed. and trans. Philadelphia: Westminster, 1980. ISBN 0-664-24266-9 (pbk). ‣ Geographical setting of Bible, sources and toponyms, followed by comprehensive historical study of major periods. [MC]

5.200   Yohanan Aharoni and Michael Avi-Yonah. *Macmillan Bible atlas.* Rev. ed. New York: Macmillan, 1977. ISBN 0-02-500590-1. ‣ Atlas of land of Israel from earliest times until Christianity, with topographical and historical divisions and maps of major events and battles. [MC]

5.201   William Foxwell Albright. "The role of the Canaanites in the history of civilization." In *The Bible and the ancient Near East: essays in honor of William Foxwell Albright.* 1961 ed. G. Ernest

Wright, ed., pp. 438–87. Winona Lake, Ind.: Eisenbrauns, 1979. ISBN 0-931464-03-X. ‣ History of Phoenicians and their contribution to ancient culture. [MC]

5.202   Gedalia Alon. *Jews, Judaism, and the classical world: studies in Jewish history in the times of the Second Temple and Talmud.* Israel Abrahams, trans. Jerusalem: Magnes, 1977. ‣ Collected studies in Jewish history from Second Temple through late Roman periods. [MC]

5.203   John Bright. *A history of Israel.* 3d ed. Philadelphia: Westminster, 1981. ISBN 0-664-21381-2. ‣ Thorough, well-organized survey of Israelite history; conservative on a number of critical issues such as basic reliability of biblical record. [MC]

5.204   Frank Moore Cross, Jr. "The development of the Jewish scripts." In *The Bible and the ancient Near East: essays in Honor of William Foxwell Albright.* 1961 ed. G. Ernest Wright, ed., pp. 170–264. Garden City, N.Y.: Doubleday, 1965. ‣ Paleographical study of Jewish scripts based on manuscript finds, especially Qumran scrolls. [MC]

5.205   Frank Moore Cross, Jr., ed. *Symposia celebrating the seventy-fifth anniversary of the founding of the American Schools of Oriental Research (1900–1975).* Cambridge, Mass.: American Schools of Oriental Research, 1979. (Occasional publications, Zion Research Foundation, 1–2.) ISBN 0-89757-503-2. ‣ Collected essays on archaeology and early Israelite history, sanctuaries in Israel, and chronology of ancient Near East. [MC]

5.206   Israel Eph'al. *The ancient Arabs: nomads on the borders of the Fertile Crescent, ninth to fifth centuries B.C.* Jerusalem: Magnes, 1984. ISBN 965-223-400-1. ‣ Comprehensive survey of nomadic peoples on borders of Bible lands. Thorough analysis of biblical and contemporary sources. [MC]

5.207   David Noel Freedman, ed. *Anchor Bible dictionary.* 6 vols. New York: Doubleday, 1992. ISBN 0-385-19351-3 (v. 1), 0-385-19360-2 (v. 2), 0-385-19361-0 (v. 3), 0-385-19362-9 (v. 4), 0-385-19363-7 (v. 5), 0-385-19261-X (v. 6). ‣ Most up-to-date reference work on all aspects of biblical life and times; many synthetic entries on modern issues, including art and architecture, education, folklore, trade and commerce, and zoology. [MC]

5.208   Moshe Greenberg. *The hab/piru.* New Haven: American Oriental Society, 1955. (American Oriental series, 39.) ‣ Fundamental study of rootless elements in ancient Near East and their relation to Hebrews. Based on analysis of source material. [MC]

5.209   Philip C. Hammond. *The Nabataeans: their history, culture, and archaeology.* Gothenburg: Åström, 1973. (Studies in Mediterranean archaeology and literature, 37.) ISBN 91-8505-857-2. ‣ Readable, informative survey of Israel's Negev desert from late Persian to Byzantine ages, its trading activity and unique culture. [MC]

5.210   Donald B. Harden. *The Phoenicians.* 1962 ed. Harmondsworth: Penguin, 1971. ‣ Archaeological and literary study of Phoenicians and their colonial spread through Mediterranean in first millennium BCE. [MC]

5.211   John H. Hayes and J. Maxwell Miller. *Israelite and Judaean history.* 1977 ed. Philadelphia: Trinity Press, 1990. ISBN 0-334-00742-9 (cl), 0-334-02435-8 (pbk). ‣ Fourteen essays surveying history from patriarchs to Roman age. Critical approach, rich bibliographies. [MC]

5.212   Zechariah Kallai. *Historical geography of the Bible: the tribal territories of Israel.* Jerusalem and Leiden: Magnes and Brill, 1986. ISBN 965-223-631-4. ‣ Comprehensive study of historical map of ancient Israel, reconstructed from all available sources. Critical methodology throughout. [MC]

5.213   H. Jacob Katzenstein. *The history of Tyre: from the beginning of the second millennium B.C.E. until the fall of the neo-Bab-*

ylonian empire in 538 B.C.E. Jerusalem: Shocken Institute for Jewish Research of the Jewish Theological Seminary of America, 1973. ‣ Survey of history of major Phoenician trading city from second millennium through Babylonian conquest. [MC]

5.214 Peter Machinist. "The question of distinctiveness in ancient Israel: an essay." In *Ah, Assyria . . . : studies in Assyrian history and ancient Near Eastern historiography presented to Hayim Tadmor.* Mordechai Cogan and Israel Eph'al, eds., pp. 196–212. Jerusalem: Magnes, 1991. (Scripta Hierosolymitana, 33.) ISSN 0080-8369. ‣ Discussion of Israel's distinctiveness among people of ancient Near East seen through contrasting societal values. [MC]

5.215 Benjamin Mazar. *Biblical Israel: state and people.* Jerusalem: Magnes and Israel Exploration Society, 1992. ISBN 965-223-797-3. ‣ Collected essays on various aspects of Israelite cult, priests and monarchy, and foundation and role of Jerusalem as capital and sanctuary site. [MC]

5.216 Benjamin Mazar. *The early biblical period: historical essays.* Shmuel Ahitav and Baruch A. Levine, eds. Ruth Rigbi and Elisheva Rigbi, trans. Jerusalem: Israel Exploration Society, 1986. ISBN 965-221-005-6. ‣ Collected essays on key issues such as early settlement of Israelite tribes, monarchic administration, and foreign relations. [MC]

5.217 William L. Moran. "The Hebrew language in its Northwest Semitic background." In *The Bible and the ancient Near East: essays in honor of William Foxwell Albright.* 1961 ed. G. Ernest Wright, ed., pp. 59–84. Winona Lake, Ind.: Eisenbrauns, 1979. ISBN 0-931464-03-X. ‣ Summary study of historical development of Hebrew language against background of related Semitic languages. [MC]

5.218 Martin Noth. *The history of Israel: biblical history.* 1960 2d ed. London: SCM Press, 1983. ISBN 0-334-02044-1 (pbk). ‣ Comprehensive reconstruction of history of ancient Israel after critical source analysis. Basic textbook. [MC]

5.219 Martin Noth. *The Old Testament world.* Victor I. Gruhn, trans. Philadelphia: Fortress, 1966. ‣ Popular study of the social and cultural features of ancient Israel, seen as part of ancient Near East. [MC]

5.220 Giovanni Pettinato. *Ebla: a new look at history.* C. Faith Richardson, trans. Baltimore: Johns Hopkins University Press, 1991. ISBN 0-8018-4150-X. ‣ General history of Ebla, important kingdom in Syria during late third millennium BCE. Discovery and identification of Ebla in 1968 has revised history for this period in Middle East. Extensive bibliography. [EL]

5.221 Wayne T. Pitard. *Ancient Damascus: a historical study of the Syrian city-state from earliest times until its fall to the Assyrians in 732 B.C.E.* Winona Lake, Ind.: Eisenbrauns, 1987. ISBN 0-931464-29-3. ‣ Thorough study of history of ancient Damascus, both city and state, from founding to destruction in 732 BCE. [EL]

5.222 Hershel Shanks, ed. *Ancient Israel: a short history from Abraham to the Roman destruction of the temple.* Englewood Cliffs, N.J., and Washington, D.C.: Prentice-Hall and Biblical Archaeological Society, 1988. ISBN 0-9613089-4-X (cl), 0-13-036435-5 (pbk). ‣ Multiauthored introductory survey of major historical and sociological trends in ancient Israel; extensive use of archaeological data. [MC]

5.223 E. Mary Smallwood. *The Jews under Roman rule from Pompey to Diocletian: a study in political relations.* 1976 ed. Leiden: Brill, 1981. ISBN 90-04-06403-6. ‣ Thorough historical survey emphasizing issues surrounding political and religious policies of Roman rule in East. [MC]

5.224 George Adam Smith. *The historical geography of the Holy Land.* 1932 25th ed. Gloucester, Mass.: Smith, 1972. ISBN 0-8446-4006-9 (cl), 0-8446-2956-1 (pbk). ‣ Reprint of classic description of Palestine (1884), with rich detail of life, now lost, culled from personal visits. Highly readable and informative. [MC]

5.225 J. Alberto Soggin. *A history of Israel from the beginnings to the Bar Kochba revolt, AD 135.* Philadelphia: Westminster, 1985. ISBN 0-664-21258-1. ‣ Critical survey of Israelite history, Davidic monarchy to Roman occupation. [MC]

5.226 Roland de Vaux. *The early history of Israel: to the period of the judges.* 1976 ed. Philadelphia: Westminster, 1978. ISBN 0-664-20762-6. ‣ Historical and archaeological study of premonarchic Israel; sober evaluation of scholarly theories. [MC]

5.227 Robert R. Wilson. *Genealogy and history in the biblical world.* New Haven: Yale University Press, 1977. (Yale Near Eastern researches, 7.) ISBN 0-300-02038-4. ‣ Examination of tribal relationships as expressed in genealogies, their analysis and definition. [MC]

5.228 D. J. Wiseman, ed. *Peoples of Old Testament times.* Oxford: Clarendon, 1973. ISBN 0-19-826316-3. ‣ Multiauthored, general historical surveys of thirteen nations bordering on ancient Israel. [MC]

5.229 Gordon D. Young, ed. *Ugarit in retrospect: fifty years of Ugarit and Ugaritic.* Winona Lake, Ind.: Eisenbrauns, 1981. ISBN 0-931464-07-2. ‣ Collection of essays summarizing current knowledge of Ugarit, important city on Syrian coast ca. 1450 BCE. Large archives in seven languages found there. Important for biblical parallels. Extensive bibliography. [EL]

Historiography and Biblical Interpretation

5.230 B. Albrektson. *History and the gods: an essay on the idea of historical events as divine manifestations in the ancient Near East and in Israel.* Lund: Gleerup, 1967. ‣ Discussion of common features of historical thinking between Israel and its neighbors, pointing to Israelite departures from tradition. [MC]

5.231 William Foxwell Albright. *From the Stone Age to Christianity: monotheism and the historical process.* 2d ed. Garden City, N.Y.: Doubleday, 1957. ‣ Classic statement on historical method for study of early Israel, seen against background of ancient Near East. [MC]

5.232 Robert Alter. *The world of biblical literature.* New York: Basic Books, 1992. ISBN 0-465-09255-1. ‣ Stimulating, accessible collection of essays on reading the Bible as literature. Addresses such issues as authorship and narrative technique, literary character of the Bible, and literary criticism. [MC]

5.233 Robert Alter and Frank Kermode, eds. *The literary guide to the Bible.* Cambridge, Mass.: Harvard University Press, 1987. ISBN 0-674-87530-3. ‣ Book-by-book survey of Old Testament, stressing literary and thematic elements. [MC]

5.234 John Bright. *Early Israel in recent history writing.* 1956 ed. Zurich: Zwingli, 1961. (Abhandlungen zur theologie des Alten und Neuen Testaments, 40.) ‣ Evaluation of major twentieth-century schools of historical investigation of Israel's early traditions. [MC]

5.235 Frank Moore Cross, Jr. *The ancient library of Qumran and modern biblical studies.* Garden City, N.Y.: Anchor, 1961. ‣ Basic introduction to Dead Sea Scrolls, their discovery and contents, and historical setting of Qumran community. [MC]

5.236 Frank Moore Cross, Jr. "The epic tradition of early Israel: epic narrative and the reconstruction of early Israelite institutions." In *The poet and the historian: essays in literary and historical biblical criticism.* Richard E. Friedman, ed., pp. 13–40. Chico, Calif.: Scholars Press, 1983. ISBN 0-89130-629-3. ‣ Examination of biblical epics for historical reconstruction. [MC]

5.237 Richard E. Friedman. *Who wrote the Bible?* New York: Prentice-Hall and Harper & Row, 1988. ISBN 0-13-958513-3 (cl), 0-06-097214-9 (pbk). ▸ Critical approach to authorship of Bible, with emphasis on documentary hypothesis in analyses of five books of Moses. Highly readable. [MC]

5.238 A.D.H. Mayes. *Israel in the period of the judges.* Naperville, Ill.: Allenson, 1974. (Studies in biblical theology, Second series, 29.) ISBN 0-8401-3079-1. ▸ Literary study of sources for premonarchic Israel, with discussion of historical implications. [MC]

5.239 Gerhard von Rad. *Old Testament theology.* 1962 ed. 2 vols. D. M. G. Stalker, trans. New York: Harper & Row, 1965. ISBN 0-06-068930-7 (v. 1), 0-06-068931-5 (v. 2). ▸ Fundamental study of ideological and theological trends in Israel's major historical traditions. [MC]

5.240 H. H. Rowley. *From Joseph to Joshua: biblical traditions in the light of archaeology.* London: Oxford University Press for the British Academy, 1950. ▸ Survey of major scholarly approaches to Israel's early traditions. Extensive bibliography up to 1950. [MC]

5.241 E. A. Speiser, ed. *At the dawn of civilization.* Vol. 1 of *The world history of the Jewish people.* New Brunswick, N.J.: Rutgers University Press, 1964. ▸ Valuable collection of essays on ancient Near Eastern background to biblical history. [MC]

5.242 E. A. Speiser. "The biblical idea of history in its common Near Eastern setting." In *The Jewish expression.* 1970 ed. Judah Goldin, ed., pp. 1–17. New Haven: Yale University Press, 1976. ISBN 0-300-01948-3 (cl), 0-300-01975-0 (pbk). ▸ Critical analysis of common themes in biblical and ancient Near Eastern historiographical writing. [MC]

5.243 Menaham Stern, ed. and trans. *Greek and Latin authors on Jews and Judaism.* 3 vols. Jerusalem: The Israel Academy of Sciences and Humanities, 1974–84. ISBN 965-208-035-7 (v. 3), 965-208-063-2 (v. 3). ▸ Comprehensive corpus of all known classical texts relating to Palestine; the land and its people, customs, and religion. [MC]

5.244 Victor Tcherikover. *Hellenistic civilization and the Jews.* 1959 ed. S. Applebaum, trans. New York: Atheneum, 1970. ISBN 0-689-70248-5. ▸ Thorough, provocative study of contacts between Hellenism and ancient civilizations of Near East. [MC]

5.245 Thomas L. Thompson. *The historicity of the patriarchal narratives: the quest for the historical Abraham.* New York: de Gruyter, 1974. (*Zeitschrift für alttestamentliche Wissenschaft,* Beihefte, 133.) ISBN 3-11-004096-4. ▸ Critical review of modern theories of origin and dating of Hebrew patriarchs. [MC]

5.246 Moshe Weinfeld. *Deuteronomy and the Deuteronomic school.* Oxford: Clarendon, 1972. ISBN 0-19-826626-X. ▸ Investigation of emergence of Deuteronomic scribal school responsible for major reform of Israelite life and literature in seventh century BCE. [MC]

Political History

5.247 Albrecht Alt. "The settlement of the Israelites in Palestine." In *Essays on Old Testament history and religion.* 1966 ed. Albrecht Alt, ed. R. A. Wilson, trans., pp. 133–69. Sheffield, England: Journal for the Study of the Old Testament, 1989. (Biblical seminar, 9.) ISBN 1-85075-204-4 (cl), 1-85075-203-6 (pbk). ▸ Seminal study of settlement of Israelite tribes. Replaces biblical conquest tradition with historical-sociological alternative of peaceful advance of semi-nomads. [MC]

5.248 Giorgio Buccellati. *Cities and nations of ancient Syria: an essay on political institutions with special reference to the Israelite kingdoms.* Rome: Istituto di Studi del Vicino Oriente, Università di Roma, 1967. (Studi Semitici, 26.) ▸ Well-written discussion of

governments of Syria-Palestine cities and city-states. Aimed at general public. [MC]

5.249 Morton Cogan. *Imperialism and religion: Assyria, Judah, and Israel in the eighth and seventh centuries B.C.E.* Missoula, Mont.: Society of Biblical Literature and Scholars, 1974. (Society of Biblical Literature monograph series, 19.) ISBN 0-88414-041-5. ▸ Political relations between Israelite states and Assyrian empire and their cultural consequences, based on analysis of Bible and royal inscriptions. [MC]

5.250 Israel Finkelstein. *The archaeology of the Israelite settlement.* D. Saltz, trans. Jerusalem: Israel Exploration Society, 1988. ISBN 965-221-007-2. ▸ New reconstruction of settlement of Israel in Canaan, based on thorough archaeological surveys and site studies. [MC]

5.251 Baruch Halpern. *The constitution of the monarchy in Israel.* Chico, Calif.: Scholars Press, 1981. (Harvard Semitic monographs, 25.) ISBN 0-89130-536-X. ▸ Investigations into theoretical background of monarchy and royal ritual in Israel. [MC]

5.252 Siegfried Hermann. *Israel in Egypt.* Naperville, Ill.: Allenson, 1973. ISBN 0-8401-3077-5. ▸ Judicious analysis of sources for Egyptian sojourn of Israelites in terms of world history. [MC]

5.253 Tomoo Ishida. *The royal dynasties in ancient Israel: a study on the formation and development of royal-dynastic ideology.* New York: de Gruyter, 1977. (*Zeitschrift für alttestamentliche Wissenschaft,* Beihefte, 142.) ISBN 3-11-006519-3. ▸ Study of formation and development of royal-dynastic ideology as realized in kingdom of Judah and house of David. Sees parallel phenomena in ancient Near East. [MC]

5.254 Abraham Malamat. "Aspects of the foreign policies of David and Solomon." *Journal of Near Eastern studies* 22 (1963) 1–17. ISSN 0022-2968. ▸ Development of foreign relations in early Israelite monarchy, through diplomacy and war. [MC]

5.255 Abraham Malamat. "Origins and formative period." In *A history of the Jewish people.* 1976 ed. H. H. Ben-Sasson, ed., pp. 3–87. Cambridge, Mass.: Harvard University Press, 1985. ISBN 0-674-39730-4 (cl, 1976), 0-674-39731-2 (pbk). ▸ Survey of earliest history of Israel through settlement; bibliography. Good introductory text. [MC]

5.256 Abraham Malamat. "The twilight of Judah in the Egyptian-Babylonian maelstrom." *Vetus Testamentum,* Supplement, 28 (1975) 123–45. ▸ Detailed study of final days of Judaean kingdom to Babylonian conquest. [MC]

5.257 Abraham Malamat, ed. *The age of the monarchies: political history.* Vol. 4.1 of *The world history of the Jewish people.* Jerusalem: Massadah, 1979. ISBN 965-257-034-6. ▸ Multiauthored work treating sources and major stages of monarchy from inception to Babylonian exile. Full bibliographies. [MC]

5.258 Benjamin Mazar. "The Aramean empire and its relations with Israel." *Biblical archaeologist* 25 (1962) 97–120. ISSN 0006-0895. ▸ Development of Aramaean states in first millennium BCE. Discusses conflicts with Israel, especially kingdom of Aram-Damascus. [MC]

5.259 Benjamin Mazar, ed. *Judges.* Vol. 3 of *The world history of the Jewish people.* New Brunswick, N.J.: Rutgers University Press, 1971. ISBN 0-8135-0663-8. ▸ Multiauthored surveys of period of crystallization of Israelite nation from settlement in Canaan to monarchy. [MC]

5.260 Benjamin Mazar, ed. *Patriarchs.* Vol. 2.1 of *The world history of the Jewish people.* New Brunswick, N.J.: Rutgers University Press, 1970. ISBN 0-8135-0615-8. ▸ Multiauthored studies of Hebrew origins in second millennium BCE against background of ancient Near East. Some discussions dated. [MC]

5.261 George E. Mendenhall. "The Hebrew conquest of Palestine." *Biblical archaeologist* 25 (1962) 66–87. ISSN 0006-0895. ‣ Presents new theory on origin of Israel: Canaanite peasant population revolted against masters, later galvanized by ideology of Israelites who escaped Egyptian slavery. [MC]

5.262 Trygve N. D. Mettinger. *Solomonic state officials: a study of the civil government officials of the Israelite monarchy.* Lund, Sweden: Gleerup, 1971. ‣ Thorough analysis of monarchic organization through study of Solomon's administrative staff and appointments. Full use of extra-biblical materials. [MC]

5.263 Harry M. Orlinsky. "The tribal system of Israel and related groups in the period of the judges." In *Studies and essays in honor of A. A. Neuman*, pp. 375–85. Philadelphia: Dropsie College, 1962. ‣ Common-sense reevaluation of theory of amphictyonic organization of Israelite tribes. [MC]

5.264 Hanoch Reviv. *The elders in ancient Israel.* 1983 ed. Jerusalem: Magnes, 1989. ISBN 965-223-701-1. ‣ Thorough study of political and social institution in its changing role from tribal society to village life. Comparative discussion of similar functions in neighboring societies. [MC]

5.265 S. Safrai and Menahem Stern, eds. *The Jewish people in the first century: historical geography, political history, social, cultural, and religious life and institutions.* 2 vols. Assen and Philadelphia: Van Gorcum and Fortress, 1974. (Compendia rerum Iudacarum ad Novum Testamentum, 1.) ISBN 90-232-1070-0 (v. 1), 90-232-1436-6 (v. 2). ‣ Multiauthored volumes discussing social and cultural life and institutions of communities in Palestine at crucial stage of political defeat and religious schism. [MC]

5.266 Emil Schürer. *The history of the Jewish people in the age of Jesus Christ (175 B.C.–A.D. 135).* Rev. ed. 3 vols. Geza Vermes and Fergus Millar, eds. T. A. Burkill et al., trans. Edinburgh: Clark, 1973–87. ISBN 0-567-02242-0 (v. 1). ‣ Classic study of Second Temple period of Jewish history. Newly updated with bibliographies. [MC]

5.267 Menahem Stern. "The period of the Second Temple." In *A history of the Jewish people.* 1976 ed. H. H. Ben-Sasson, ed., pp. 183–303. Cambridge, Mass.: Harvard University Press, 1985. ISBN 0-674-39730-4 (cl, 1976), 0-674-39731-2 (pbk). ‣ Basic survey of political and social history of Palestine, Greek conquest to Roman rule. [MC]

5.268 Hayim Tadmor. "'The people' and the kingship in ancient Israel." *Journal of world history* 11 (1968) 1–23. ISSN 0022-5436. ‣ Provocative study of Israelite tribal institutions in transition to urban setting and their effect on nascent monarchy. [MC]

5.269 Hayim Tadmor. "The period of the First Temple, the Babylonian exile, and the restoration." In *A history of the Jewish people.* 1976 ed., pp. 91–182. H. H. Ben-Sasson, ed. Cambridge, Mass.: Harvard University Press, 1985. ISBN 0-674-39730-4 (cl, 1976), 0-674-39731-2 (pbk). ‣ Survey of periods of Israelite monarchy, exile, and restoration emphasizing social as well as political changes. Bibliography. [MC]

5.270 Hayim Tadmor. "Philistia under Assyrian rule." *Biblical archaeologist* 29 (1966) 86–102. ISSN 0006-0895. ‣ Historical analysis of Assyrian imperial policy in coastal towns of southern Palestine. [MC]

5.271 Edwin R. Thiele. *The mysterious numbers of the Hebrew kings.* 3d ed. Grand Rapids: Zondervan, 1983. ISBN 0-310-36010-2. ‣ Classic presentation of chronology of Israelite and Judaean monarchies, its organizing principles and relations to extra-biblical data. [MC]

5.272 Manfred Weippert. *The settlement of the Israelite tribes in Palestine: a critical survey of the recent scholarly debate.* Naperville, Ill.: Allenson, 1971. ISBN 0-8401-3071-7. ‣ Review and examination of various theories involving conquest and settlement. [MC]

Military History

5.273 Israel Eph'al. "On warfare and military control in the ancient Near Eastern empires: a research outline." In *History, historiography, and interpretation: studies in biblical and cuneiform literatures.* Hayim Tadmor and M. Weinfeld, eds., pp. 88–106. Jerusalem and Leiden: Magnes and Brill, 1983. ISBN 965-223-459-1. ‣ Suggestions for new military-historical investigations through comprehensive study of royal inscriptions, correspondence, and reliefs. [MC]

5.274 William W. Hallo. "From Qarqar to Carchemish, Assyria and Israel in the light of new discoveries." *Biblical archaeologist* 23 (1960) 34–61. ISSN 0006-0895. ‣ Discussion of Assyrian conquests in west, emphasizing military encounters with Israel; includes source studies. Basic introductory essay. [MC]

5.275 Yigael Yadin. *The art of warfare in the biblical lands: in the light of archaeological study.* New York: McGraw-Hill, 1963. ‣ Richly documented and illustrated study of weapons, tactics, and strategies of ancient warfare; analyses of several major battles. Fundamental for warfare throughout ancient Near East. [MC]

Society and Culture

5.276 Tikva Frymer-Kensky. *In the wake of the goddess: women, culture, and the biblical transformation of pagan myth.* New York: Free Press, 1992. ISBN 0-02-910800-4. ‣ Provocative study of place of women in ancient society through role of goddesses in pagan religion and their replacement in biblical monotheistic thought by egalitarian humanity. Important scholarly critique of feminist issues. [MC]

5.277 Moshe Greenberg. "Some postulates of biblical criminal law." In *The Jewish expression.* 1970 ed. Judah Goldin, ed., pp. 18–37. New Haven: Yale University Press, 1976. ISBN 0-300-01948-3 (cl), 0-300-01975-0 (pbk). ‣ Contrastive study of Israelite and ancient Near Eastern laws concerning homicide and its punishment. Reveals divergent principles in two cultures. [MC]

5.278 Menahem Haran. "On the diffusion of literacy and schools in ancient Israel." *Vetus Testamentum, Supplement* 40 (1988) 377–83. ISSN 0083-5889, ISBN 90-04-08499-1. ‣ Overview of scribes, schooling, and literacy in biblical period. [MC]

5.279 Abraham Malamat. *Mari and the early Israelite experience.* Oxford: Oxford University Press for British Academy, 1989. ISBN 0-19-726072-1 (cl), 0-19-726117-5 (pbk). ‣ Study of Israel's patriarchs and their social history against background of eighteenth-century Mesopotamian city of Mari, especially its West Semitic population. [MC]

5.280 Abraham Malamat, ed. *The age of the monarchies: culture and society.* Vol. 4.2 of *The world history of the Jewish people.* New Brunswick, N.J.: Rutgers University Press, 1979. ‣ Multiauthored work treating kingship and administration, language and literature, and society and religion. Full bibliographies. [MC]

5.281 Bezalel Porten. *Archives from Elephantine: the life of an ancient Jewish military colony.* Berkeley: University of California Press, 1968. ISBN 0-520-01028-0. ‣ Informative survey of life of Jewish colonists in southern Egypt during Persian period. Evaluates historical and cultural features. [MC]

5.282 R.B.Y. Scott. "Weights and measures of the Bible." *Biblical archaeologist* 22 (1959) 114–25. ISSN 0006-0895. ‣ Basic survey of ancient metrology utilizing textual evidence and archaeological finds. [MC]

5.283 Roland de Vaux. *Ancient Israel: its life and institutions.* John

McHugh, trans. New York: McGraw-Hill, 1961. ‣ Masterly study of society of ancient Israel. Analyzes and reconstructs family, civil, military, and religious institutions. [MC]

Economic History

5.284 Moshe Elat. "The monarchy and the development of trade in ancient Israel." In *State and temple economy in the ancient Near East*. Edward Lipiński, ed., vol. 2, pp. 527–46. Louvain: Département Orientalistiek, 1979. (Series Orientalia Lovaniensia analecta, 5–6.) ISBN 90-9701920-3-9 (set). ‣ Discussion of economic life of Israelite monarchy, international trade and sources of wealth. [MC]

5.285 Isaac Mendelsohn. "On corvée labour in ancient Canaan and Israel." *Bulletin of the American Schools of Oriental Research* 167 (1962) 31–35. ISSN 0003-097X. ‣ Study of state labor in Israel, its extent and enforcement in monarchic period from perspective of Canaanite practice. [MC]

5.286 Ya'akov Meshorer. *Ancient Jewish coinage*. 2 vols. Dix Hills, N.Y.: Amphora, 1982. ISBN 0-89757-006-5. ‣ Earliest numismatic evidence from Persian and Hasmonean periods. Valuable source for study of provincial organization, economics, and cultural contacts. [MC]

5.287 J. Alberto Soggin. "Compulsory labor under David and Solomon." In *Studies in the period of David and Solomon and other essays: papers read at the International Symposium for Biblical Studies, Tokyo, 5–7 December 1979*. Tomoo Ishida, ed., pp. 259–67. Winona Lake, Ind.: Eisenbrauns, 1982. ISBN 0-931464-16-1 (cl), 0-931464-12-9 (pbk). ‣ Study of *corvée* labor system in ancient Israel. [MC]

5.288 Daniel Sperber. *Roman Palestine, 200–400: the land, crisis and change in agrarian society as reflected in rabbinic sources*. Ramat-Gan, Israel: Bar-Ilan University, 1978. ‣ Agrarian history of Palestine surveying transition from small peasant economy to large estate control of farming. Extensive review of classical and rabbinic sources. [MC]

5.289 Ephraim E. Urbach. *The sages: their concepts and beliefs*. 1979 2d ed. Cambridge, Mass.: Harvard University Press, 1987. ISBN 0-674-78523-1 (pbk). ‣ Reconstructs Jewish religious and intellectual thought from sources of Second Temple through Byzantine period; fully documented. [MC]

Religion

5.290 William Foxwell Albright. *Yahweh and the gods of Canaan: a historical analysis of two contrasting faiths*. Winona Lake, Ind.: Eisenbrauns, 1968. ISBN 0-931464-01-3. ‣ Analysis of religions of Canaan and Israel in their historical settings. Discusses nature of cultural influences on Israel's developing monotheistic faith. [MC]

5.291 Elias J. Bickerman. *From Ezra to the last of the Maccabees: foundations of post-biblical Judaism*. New York: Schocken, 1962. ISBN 0-8052-0036-3. ‣ Introductory essay to formative period of early Judaism from return of Babylonian exiles through confrontation with Hellenic culture. [MC]

5.292 Frank Moore Cross, Jr. *Canaanite myth and Hebrew epic: essays in the history of the religion of Israel*. Cambridge, Mass.: Harvard University Press, 1973. ISBN 0-674-09175-2. ‣ Essays in history of Israel's religion from emergence from Canaanite culture to Qumran apocalypse. Valuable discussions on royal ideology and historical writing. [MC]

5.293 Menahem Haran. *Temples and temple-service in ancient Israel: an inquiry into biblical cult phenomena and the historical setting of the priestly school*. 1977 ed. Winona Lake, Ind.: Eisenbrauns, 1985. ISBN 0-931464-18-8. ‣ Phenomenological inquiry

into biblical cult and its historical context. Highlights unique features of priestly ritual. [MC]

5.294 Yehezkel Kaufmann. *The religion of Israel: from its beginnings to the Babylonian exile*. Moshe Greenberg, trans. and abridgement. Chicago: University of Chicago Press, 1960. ISBN 0-226-42728-5. ‣ Important comparative study of pagan and Israelite religious forms. Discusses folk background of monotheism and its biblical expressions. Survey of literature, problematically seen by author as mostly contemporary with events described. [MC]

5.295 Hans-Joachim Kraus. *Worship in Israel*. Geoffrey Buswell, trans. Richmond: John Knox, 1966. ‣ History of Israelite cult, its organization, and underlying principles. [MC]

5.296 Johannes Pedersen. *Israel, its life and culture*. 1964 ed. 2 vols. Atlanta: Scholars Press, 1991. ISBN 1-55540-643-2. ‣ Important study of life and institutions of ancient Israel. Sociological approach to family life, law, and tribal state, and cultic leadership. [MC]

5.297 James D. Purvis. *The Samaritan Pentateuch and the origin of the Samaritan sect*. Cambridge, Mass.: Harvard University Press, 1968. (Harvard Semitic monographs, 2.) ‣ Study of origins of Samaritan sect and their separation from Judaism. Also discusses history of their sacred text. [MC]

5.298 David Rokeah. *Jews, pagans, and Christians in conflict*. Jerusalem: Magnes, 1982. ISBN 90-04-06560-1. ‣ Interreligious conflicts in Roman empire. Study of polemics and propaganda used by competing groups. [MC]

5.299 Jeffrey H. Tigay. *You shall have no other gods: Israelite religion in the light of Hebrew inscriptions*. Atlanta: Scholars Press, 1986. (Harvard Semitic series, 31.) ISBN 1-55540-063-9. ‣ Provocative study of inscriptional evidence for ancient Israelite religion. Challenges claim of rampant polytheism. [MC]

5.300 Max Weber. *Ancient Judaism*. Don Martindale, ed. Hans H. Gerth, trans. New York: Free Press, 1967. ISBN 0-02-934130-2 (pbk). ‣ Classic essay and sociological analysis of biblical culture, forms, and patterns. [MC]

Art and Archaeology

5.301 Yohanan Aharoni. *The archaeology of the land of Israel: from the prehistoric beginnings to the end of the First Temple period*. Miriam Aharoni, ed. Anson F. Rainey, trans. Philadelphia: Westminster, 1982. ISBN 0-664-21384-7 (cl), 0-664-24430-0 (pbk). ‣ Illustrated survey of archaeological research in Holy Land from prehistoric beginnings to fall of Jerusalem in 586 BCE. Useful as textbook. [MC]

5.302 Janet Amitai, ed. *Biblical archaeology today*. Jerusalem: Israel Exploration Society, Israel Academy of Sciences and Humanities, and American Schools of Oriental Research, 1985. ISBN 965-221-004-8. ‣ Proceedings of international congress on biblical archaeology, surveying major achievements of century of archaeological and historical research. [MC]

5.303 Nahman Avigad. *Discovering Jerusalem*. Nashville: Nelson, 1983. ISBN 0-8407-5299-7. ‣ Account of excavations in Jewish quarter of old city of Jerusalem, revealing earliest Israelite settlement in Iron Age through Byzantine period. Important findings for history of city's growth and development. [MC]

5.304 Michael Avi-Yonah and Ephraim Stern, eds. *Encyclopedia of archaeological excavations in the Holy Land*. 4 vols. Jerusalem: Israel Exploration Society, 1978. ‣ Site-by-site description of excavations and finds. Richly illustrated, basic bibliography. [MC]

5.305 William G. Dever. "Monumental architecture in ancient Israel in the period of the United Kingdom." In *Studies in the* *period of David and Solomon and other essays: papers read at the International Symposium for Biblical Studies, 6–7 December 1979.* Tomoo Ishida, ed., pp. 269–306. Winona Lake, Ind.: Eisenbrauns, 1982. ISBN 0-931464-16-1. ▸ Survey and analysis of architecture at major archaeological sites in Israel. [MC]

5.306 Trude Dothan. *The Philistines and their material culture.* New Haven: Yale University Press, 1982. ISBN 0-300-02258-1. ▸ Detailed survey of cultural remains and historical sources of Philistines (Sea Peoples); relation to their Mycenaean roots and ethnic influences absorbed in their migrations. Richly illustrated. [MC]

5.307 Erwin R. Goodenough. *Jewish symbols in the Greco-Roman period.* 13 vols. Princeton: Princeton University Press, 1953–69. ▸ Most comprehensive comparative survey and analysis of all art styles and motifs in Jewish art of classical period. Illustrated. [MC]

5.308 Aharon Kempinski and Ronny Reich, eds. *The architecture of ancient Israel: from the prehistoric to the Persian periods.* Jerusalem: Israel Exploration Society, 1992. ISBN 965-221-013-7. ▸ Multiauthored discussion of ancient architecture in chronological sequence. Treats materials and construction, residential and palatial buildings, tombs and water systems. [MC]

5.309 Kathleen Kenyon. *Royal cities of the Old Testament.* New York: Schocken, 1971. ISBN 0-8052-3412-8. ▸ Archaeological accounts of development of five major cities (Jerusalem, Megiddo, Hazor, Gezer, Samaria) in Israelite kingdoms in attempt to integrate finds into historical picture. Includes site plans and illustrations. [MC]

5.310 Lee I. Levine, ed. *Ancient synagogues revealed.* 1981 ed. Detroit: Wayne State University Press, 1982. ISBN 0-8143-1706-5. ▸ Historical and archaeological researches of ancient synagogues in Israel and Jewish diaspora, their origin, typologies, and epigraphic remains. Richly illustrated. [MC]

5.311 Amihai Mazar. *Archaeology of the land of the Bible, 10,000–586 B.C.E.* New York: Doubleday, 1990. ISBN 0-385-23970-X. ▸ Survey of archaeological research in Israel and Jordan, prehistory to end of Hebrew monarchy. Photographs, maps, and diagrams. Good introductory textbook. [MC]

5.312 Lawrence E. Stager. "The archaeology of the family in ancient Israel." *Bulletin of the American Schools of Oriental Research* 260 (1985) 1–35. ISSN 0003-097X. ▸ Reconstruction of ancient family and life style, based on archaeological evidence, with references to biblical texts. [MC]

5.313 Ephraim Stern. *Material culture of the land of the Bible in the Persian period, 538–332 B.C.* Warminster and Jerusalem: Aris & Phillips and Israel Exploration Society, 1982. ISBN 0-85668-137-7 (pbk). ▸ In-depth study of archaeology of Persian period in Palestine. [MC]

ANATOLIA

General Histories

5.314 Michael C. Astour. *Hittite history and absolute chronology of the Bronze Age.* Partille, Sweden: Åström, 1989. (Studies in Mediterranean archaeology and literature, 73.) ISBN 91-86098-86-1 (pbk), ISSN 0283-8494. ▸ Spirited defense of so-called low chronology that omits virtually all of Middle Kingdom period. Responds to evidence, published while book was in progress, supporting extended list of Hittite kings. [JDM]

5.315 Richard D. Barnett. "Phrygia and the peoples of Anatolia in the Iron Age." In *The Cambridge ancient history.* 3d ed. I.E.S. Edwards et al., eds., vol. 2.2, pp. 417–42. Cambridge: Cambridge University Press, 1981. ISBN 0-521-08691-4 (cl), 0-521-29823-7 (pbk). ▸ Early, not very successful, attempt to deal with history

of Iron Age Anatolia. Speculations no longer taken very seriously. [JDM]

5.316 Kurt Bittel. *Hattuscha, Hauptstadt der Hethiter: Geschichte und Kultur einer altorientalischen Grossmacht.* Cologne: DuMont, 1983. ISBN 3-7701-1456-6. ▸ General account of excavation of Hittite capital city by long-time excavation director. Revised German version of author's 1970 English-language study (5.317). [JDM]

5.317 Kurt Bittel. *Hattusha: the capital of the Hittites.* New York: Oxford University Press, 1970. ▸ General account of excavation by long-time director of those excavations (1931–72). Text of Mary Flexner Lectures, Bryn Mawr College, 1967. Updated in 1983 German edition (5.316). [JDM]

5.318 Trevor R. Bryce. *The Lycians in literary and epigraphic sources.* Copenhagen: Museum Tusculanum Press. (The Lycians: a study of Lycian history and civilisation to the conquest of Alexander the Great, 1.) ISBN 87-7289-023-1 (pbk). ▸ History of southern coast of Turkey between Fethiye and Anatalya, known to Hittites as Lukka and to ancient Greeks as Lycia. Includes discussion of Lycian language and alphabet and selection of Lycian inscriptions. [JDM]

5.319 W.A.P. Childs. "Prolegomena to a Lycian chronology: the Nereid monument from Xanthos." *Opuscula Romana* 9.1 (1973) 105–16. ISSN 0081-993X. ▸ Dates important monument, crucial for chronology of Lycian dynasty reliefs now in British Museum, to 390–380 BCE; monument represents tomb of Lycian ruler Erbbina. Excellent bibliography. [JDM]

5.320 Paolo Desideri and Anna Margherita Jasink. *Cilicia: dall'età di Kizzuwatna alla conquista macedone.* Turin: Casa Editrice le Lettere, 1990. (Università degli Studi di Torino: Fondo di Studi Parini-Chirio, Storia, 1.) ISBN 88-7166-012-9. ▸ Only regional history of Cilicia, Hittite times to conquests of Alexander the Great. Poor proofreading of non-Italian bibliography. [JDM]

5.321 Donald F. Easton. "Towards a chronology for the Anatolian Early Bronze Age." *Anatolian studies* 26.1 (1976) 145–73. ISSN 0066-1546. ▸ Much cited but very wrongheaded attempt to defend ultra-high chronology for Early Bronze Age Anatolia. Author himself no longer believes in this chronology. [JDM]

5.322 John Garstang and Oliver R. Gurney. *The geography of the Hittite empire.* London: British Institute of Archaeology at Ankara, 1959. (Occasional publications of the British Institute of Archaeology at Ankara, 5.) ▸ Dated but still basic work on Hittite geography; badly in need of revision. Presents evidence for identifications generally taken for granted today. [JDM]

5.323 Albrecht Goetze. "State and society of the Hittites." In *Neuere Hethiterforschung.* Gerold Walser, ed., pp. 23–33. Wiesbaden: Steiner, 1964. (*Historia*, Einzelschriften, 7.) ▸ Now somewhat dated but only account by prominent Hittitologist, in English, presenting his basic ideas on organization of Hittite state and nature of Hittite society. [JDM]

5.324 Ronald L. Gorny, ed. "Reflections of a Late Bronze Age empire: the Hittites." *Biblical archaeologist* 52.2–3 (1989) 78–96. ISSN 0006-0895. ▸ Special issue of popular journal devoted to Hittites. For other individual articles see McMahon 5.339 and Beckman 5.396. [JDM]

5.325 Crawford H. Greenewalt. "When a mighty empire was destroyed: the common man at the fall of Sardis, ca. 546 B.C." *Proceedings of the American Philosophical Society* 136.2 (1992) 247–71. ISSN 0003-049X. ▸ Presents recent archaeological evidence for conquest of Lydian kingdom of Croesus by Cyrus of Persia, especially remarkable skeleton of warrior killed during siege of Sardis. [JDM]

5.326 Oliver R. Gurney. "Anatolia, c. 1600–1380 B.C." In *The*

Cambridge ancient history. 3d ed. I.E.S. Edwards et al., eds., vol. 2.1, pp. 659–83. Cambridge: Cambridge University Press, 1973. ISBN 0-521-08230-7. ▸ Survey of Hittite state during latter part of Old Kingdom to creation of empire, from death of Muršili I to accession of Šuppiluliuma I. First account in English to incorporate redating of Middle Hittite texts. [JDM]

5.327   Oliver R. Gurney. "Anatolia, c. 1750–1600 B.C." In *The Cambridge ancient history.* 3d ed. I.E.S. Edwards et al., eds., vol. 2.1, pp. 228–55. Cambridge: Cambridge University Press, 1973. ISBN 0-521-08230-7. ▸ Excellent account of early Hittite history from foundations of Old Kingdom to reign of Muršili I. Takes account of bilingual annals of Hattušili I, discovered in 1957. [JDM]

5.328   Oliver R. Gurney. "The Hittite empire." In *Power and propaganda: a symposium on ancient empires.* Mogens Trolle Larsen, ed., pp. 151–65. Copenhagen: Akademisk Forlag, 1979. (Mesopotamia, 7.) ISBN 87-500-1878-7. ▸ Brief sketch of Hittite history, with emphasis on modern rediscovery of Hittites in late nineteenth century. [JDM]

5.329   Oliver R. Gurney. *The Hittites.* 1954 2d ed. New York: Penguin, 1990. ISBN 0-14-012601-5. ▸ Classic account of Hittite civilization in English. Broad overview of all aspects of Hittite history and culture. Balanced survey with useful bibliography. Most recent revision of work first published in 1952. [JDM]

5.330   Hans Gustav Güterbock. "Hittite historiography: a survey." In *History, historiography, and interpretation: studies in biblical and cuneiform literatures.* Hayim Tadmor and Moshe Weinfeld, eds., pp. 21–35. Jerusalem: Magnes, 1983. ISBN 965-223-459-1. ▸ Examination of Hittite concept of history and how Hittites wrote their own history. See also similar study by Hoffner 5.334. [JDM]

5.331   Hans Gustav Güterbock. "The Hittites and the Aegean world. Part 1: The Ahhiyawa problem reconsidered." *American journal of archaeology* 87.2 (1983) 133–38. ISSN 0002-9114. ▸ New interpretations of key Hittite texts crucial for shift from negative to positive evaluation of Ahhiyawa-Mycenaean equation. [JDM]

5.332   J. D. Hawkins and Anna Morpurgo Davies. "On the problems of Karatepe: the hieroglyphic text." *Anatolian studies* 28.1 (1978) 103–19. ISSN 0066-1546. ▸ Most accessible discussion of this most important of all neo-Hittite (hieroglyphic Luwian) inscriptions. Includes translations of both hieroglyphic and Phoenician inscriptions. [JDM]

5.333   Jim Hicks. *The empire builders.* New York: Time-Life, 1974. ▸ Popular, well-illustrated, good account of Hittite civilization. Consultants were prominent Hittitologists, O. R. Gurney and H. A. Hoffner, Jr. [JDM]

5.334   Harry A. Hoffner, Jr. "Histories and historians of the ancient Near East: the Hittites." *Orientalia,* n.s., 49.4 (1980) 283–332. ISSN 0030-5367. ▸ Good discussion of surviving Hittite historical texts as well as Hittite concept of history. Divides Hittite historical texts into narratives of military campaigns, court histories, and so-called accession narratives or political apologies. [JDM]

5.335   Harry A. Hoffner, Jr. "Propaganda and political justification in Hittite historiography." In *Unity and diversity: essays in the history, literature, and religion of the ancient Near East.* Hans Goedicke and J.J.M. Roberts, eds., pp. 49–62. Baltimore: Johns Hopkins University Press, 1975. ISBN 0-8018-1638-6. ▸ Places so-called Apology of Hattušili III in its Hittite historical and cultural context, going back to time of Telepinu (ca. 1500 BCE). Suggests existence of Hittite tradition of apologies issued by usurpers of throne. [JDM]

5.336   Philo H. J. Houwink ten Cate. *The Luwian population groups of Lycia and Cilicia during the Hellenistic period.* Leiden:

Brill, 1961. ▸ Study of ethnic make-up of Lycia and Cilicia in Hellenistic period, based on linguistic analysis of personal names. Traces sources to their Bronze Age origins; contributes much to discussion of cultural continuity and related matters. [JDM]

5.337   Horst Klengel. *Syria, 3000–300 B.C.: a handbook of political history.* Berlin: Akademie Verlag, 1992. ISBN 3-05-001820-8. ▸ Good, sound survey of history of ancient Syria. Well documented with extensive reference to texts and recent secondary literature. Chapter 3 treats Late Bronze Age and Hittite relations with various Syrian kingdoms; chapter 4, Iron Age and neo-Hittite kingdoms of Syria. [JDM]

5.338   Emmanuel Laroche. *Catalogue des textes hittites.* Paris: Klincksieck, 1971. ▸ Basic catalog of Hittite texts, citing editions and translation of each text. Essential because texts are often cited in literature by CTh numbers assigned here. One supplement published in *Revue Hittite et Asianique* 30 (1972–73) 94–133. [JDM]

5.339   Gregory McMahon. "The history of the Hittites." *Biblical archaeologist* 52.2–3 (1989) 62–77. ISSN 0006-0895. ▸ Excellent, popular survey of Hittite history, including up-to-date chronological table with many new additions to list of Hittite kings. [JDM]

5.340   John Griffiths Pedley. *Sardis in the age of Croesus.* Norman: University of Oklahoma Press, 1968. ▸ Describes golden age of Lydian culture and of Mermnad dynasty with Sardis as its capital city, ca. 650–550 BCE. Excellent introduction to important role played by Lydia in development of archaic Greece. [JDM]

5.341   Jak Yakar. *Prehistoric Anatolia: the Neolithic transformation and the early Chalcolithic period.* Tel Aviv: Tel Aviv University, Sonia and Marco Nadler Institute of Archaeology, 1991. (Monograph series of the Institute of Archaeology, Tel Aviv University, 9.) ISBN 965-440-000-6. ▸ Treats development of village cultures in Anatolia during seventh, sixth, and early fifth millennia BCE. Divides Turkey into seven main geographic areas or ecological zones. [JDM]

Political History

5.342   Gary M. Beckman. "The Hittite assembly." *Journal of the American Oriental Society* 102.3 (1982) 435–42. ISSN 0003-0279. ▸ Argues Hittite assembly (*pankuš*) was primarily judicial body that assembled in *tuliya* (term not designating a political institution). [JDM]

5.343   Gary M. Beckman. "Inheritance and royal succession among the Hittites." In *Kaniššuwar: a tribute to Hans G. Güterbock on his seventy-fifth birthday, May 27, 1983.* Harry A. Hoffner, Jr., and Gary M. Beckman, eds., pp. 13–31. Chicago: University of Chicago, Oriental Institute, 1986. (Assyriological studies, 23.) ISBN 0-918986-44-3 (pbk), ISSN 0066-9903. ▸ Basic discussion of murky matters connected with accessions of most Hittite kings. Contrast drawn between ideal situation set out in Telepinu Proclamation and realities as they can be recovered from surviving texts. [JDM]

5.344   Shoshana R. Bin-Nun. *The tawananna in the Hittite kingdom.* Heidelberg: Winter, 1975. (Texte der Hethiter, 5.) ISBN 3-533-02439-3 (cl), 3-533-02438-5 (pbk). ▸ Investigates role of *tawananna* (queen mother) in Hittite royal family and questions of matriarchal period prior to establishment of Hittite Old Kingdom. Written as Oxford thesis under direction of Oliver Gurney. [JDM]

5.345   Trevor R. Bryce. "Ahhiyawans and Mycenaeans—an Anatolian viewpoint." *Oxford journal of archaeology* 8.3 (1989) 297–310. ISSN 0262-5253. ▸ Discussion of recent scholarship on relations between lands of Hatti and Ahhiyawa. Argues for compelling (if still circumstantial) support for Ahhiyawa-Mycenaean equation. [JDM]

5.346 Trevor R. Bryce. "The death of Niphururiya and its aftermath." *Journal of Egyptian archaeology* 76.1 (1990) 97–105. ISSN 0075-4234. ▸ Discussion of letter from Egyptian widow of Niphururiya who wrote to Hittite king Šuppiluliuma I requesting that one of his sons be sent to Egypt as her husband and pharaoh of Egypt. Demonstrates that Niphururiya must be pharaoh Tutankhamen. [JDM]

5.347 Trevor R. Bryce. "Hattušili I and the problem of the royal succession in the Hittite kingdom." *Anatolian studies* 31.1 (1981) 9–17. ISSN 0066-1546. ▸ Analysis of opening lines of bilingual annals of Hattušili I. Discusses parentage of Hattušili and question of royal succession. [JDM]

5.348 Trevor R. Bryce. "Madduwatta and Hittite policy in western Anatolia." *Historia* 35.1 (1986) 1–12. ISSN 0018-2311. ▸ Argues Hittites tried to stay away from involvement in western affairs. Campaigned in west only when local states formed coalition that presented real threat to Hittite interests. [JDM]

5.349 Trevor R. Bryce. "Some observations on the chronology of Šuppiluliuma's reign." *Anatolian studies* 39.1 (1989) 1930. ISSN 0066-1546. ▸ Summarizes current discussions on chronology and efforts, especially by German scholars, both to shorten length and lower dates of reign of Šuppiluliuma I. [JDM]

5.350 Albrecht Goetze. "Anatolia from Shuppiluliumash to the Egyptian war of Muwatallish." In *The Cambridge ancient history*. 3d ed. I.E.S. Edwards et al., eds., vol. 2.2, pp. 117–29. Cambridge: Cambridge University Press, 1981. ISBN 0-521-08691-4 (cl), 0-521-29823-7 (pbk). ▸ Hittite history during reign of Muršili II, making extensive use of ruler's royal annals edited by the author (in German) in 1933. [JDM]

5.351 Albrecht Goetze. "The Hittites and Syria (1300–1200 B.C.)." In *The Cambridge ancient history*. 3d ed. I.E.S. Edwards et al., eds., vol. 2.2, pp. 252–73. Cambridge: Cambridge University Press, 1981. ISBN 0-521-08691-4 (cl), 0-521-29823-7 (pbk). ▸ History of last century of Hittite empire, from battle of Qadesh in reign of Muwatalli II to destruction of capital city of Hattuša, presumably by Sea Peoples. [JDM]

5.352 Albrecht Goetze. "The struggle for the domination of Syria." In *The Cambridge ancient history*. 3d ed. I.E.S. Edwards et al., eds., vol. 2.2, pp. 1–20. London: Cambridge University Press, 1981. ISBN 0-521-08691-4 (cl), 0-521-29823-7 (pbk). ▸ Detailed account of reign of Šuppiluliuma I, concentrating on campaigns in Syria against Tushratta, king of Mitanni. [JDM]

5.353 Hans Gustav Güterbock. "The deeds of Šuppiluliuma as told by his son Muršili II." *Journal of cuneiform studies* 10.1–2–3 (1956) 41–68, 75–98, 107–30. ISSN 0022-0256. ▸ Basic edition of most important historical text of reign of preeminent Hittite king. Published as three-part journal article, giving Hittite text and English translation. [JDM]

5.354 Hans Gustav Güterbock. "Hittites and Akhaeans: a new look." *Proceedings of the American Philosophical Society* 128.2 (1984) 114–22. ISSN 0003-049X. ▸ Discussion of textual and archaeological evidence for relations between Mycenaeans and Hittites during Late Bronze Age by firm believer in equation of Ahhiyawa with Achaea (Mycenaeans). [JDM]

5.355 J. D. Hawkins. "Assyrians and Hittites." *Iraq* 36.1 (1974) 67–83. ISSN 0021-0889. ▸ Historical background for neo-Hittite kingdoms through reference to those kingdoms and their rulers in neo-Assyrian royal inscriptions. Compares Luwian and Assyrian versions of personal and place names. [JDM]

5.356 J. D. Hawkins. "Kuzi-Tešub and the 'great kings' of Karkamiš." *Anatolian studies* 38.1 (1988) 99–108. ISSN 0066-1546.

▸ New evidence for rulers of Carchemish and Malatya at end of Late Bronze Age, connecting Bronze Age Hittites with Iron Age neo-Hittites. [JDM]

5.357 J. D. Hawkins. "The neo-Hittite states in Syria and Anatolia." In *The Cambridge ancient history*. 2d ed. John Boardman et al., eds., vol. 3.1, pp. 372–441. Cambridge: Cambridge University Press, 1982. ISBN 0-521-22496-9. ▸ Only detailed account of history of neo-Hittite kingdoms available, written by scholar who has played leading role in decipherment of hieroglyphic Luwian inscriptions. [JDM]

5.358 J. D. Hawkins. "The new inscription from the Sudburg of Bogazkoy-Hattuša." *Archäologischer Anzeiger* 3 (1990) 305–13. ISSN 0003-8105. ▸ Discussion of hieroglyphic inscription written boustrophedon on west wall of what seems to be monument commemorating Šuppiluliuma II, last Hittite king. [JDM]

5.359 Harry A. Hoffner, Jr. "The last days of Khattusha." In *The crisis years: the twelfth century B.C. from beyond the Danube to the Tigris*. William A. Ward and Martha Sharp Joukowsky, eds., pp. 46–52. Dubuque, Iowa: Kendall/Hunt, 1992. ISBN 0-8403-7118-9 (cl), 0-8403-7148-9 (pbk). ▸ Hittite history in thirteenth century BCE, making use of bronze tablet giving text of treaty between Tudhaliya IV (III) and Kurunta, ruler of Tarhuntassa. Text has greatly revised our understanding of the final years of the Hittite empire. [JDM]

5.360 Philo H. J. Houwink ten Cate. "The bronze tablet of Tudhaliyas IV and its geographical and historical relations." *Zeitschrift für Assyriologie und vorderasiatische Archäologie* 82.2 (1992) 233–70. ISSN 0084-5299. ▸ Review article of H. Otten's important edition of bronze tablet containing text of treaty with Kurunta of Tarhuntassa (published in 1988). Discusses many important issues of Hittite history raised by this new text. [JDM]

5.361 Philo H. J. Houwink ten Cate. "The early and late phases of Urhi-Tešub's career." In *Anatolian studies presented to Hans Gustav Güterbock on the occasion of his sixty-fifth birthday*. Kurt Bittel, Philo H. J. Houwink ten Cate, and Erica Reiner, eds., pp. 123–50. Istanbul: Nederlands Historisch-Archaeologisch Instituut in het Nabije Oosten, 1974. (Uitgaven van het Nederlands Historisch-Archaeologisch Instituut te Istanbul, 35.) ▸ Historical background for brief career of Urhi-Tešub and his overthrow by Hattušili III (ca. 1287). Documents presence of Urhi-Tešub in Egypt after being deposed by his nephew. [JDM]

5.362 Philo H. J. Houwink ten Cate. *The records of the early Hittite empire (c. 1450–1380 B.C.)* Istanbul: Nederlands Historisch-Archaeologisch Instituut in het Nabije Oosten, 1970. (Uitgaven van het Nederlands Historisch-Archaeologisch Instituut te Instanbul, 26.) ▸ First important discussion of historical implications of redating of Hittite texts and recognition of a Middle Hittite period. Reconstructs important career of Tudhaliya I (II). [JDM]

5.363 Fiorella Imparati. "Aspects de l'organisation de l'état Hittite dans les documents juridiques et administratifs." *Journal of the economic and social history of the Orient* 25.2 (1982) 225–67. ISSN 0022-4995. ▸ Basic discussion of legal and administrative documentation for organization of Hittite state, especially for so-called feudal obligations designated *sahhan* and *luzzi*. [JDM]

5.364 Annelies von Kammenhuber. *Hippolgia Hethitica*. Wiesbaden: Harrassowitz, 1961. ▸ Still only comprehensive edition of famous how-to manual written by Kikkuli, horse trainer from kingdom of Mitanni. Most important text for theory that Indo-Aryan played major role in development of horse and chariot warfare. [JDM]

5.365 Antony G. Keen. "The dynastic tombs of Xanthos—who was buried where." *Anatolian studies* 42 (1992) 53–63. ISSN 0066-1546. ▸ Discussion of dynasts of Xanthos, Lycian capital, and their decorated (and inscribed) tombs, ca. 540–370 BCE. These tombs provide main examples of Lycian stone sculpture. [JDM]

5.366 Kenneth A. Kitchen. *Šuppiluliuma and the Amarna pharaohs: a study in relative chronology.* Liverpool: Liverpool University Press, 1962. ▸ Attempts to establish actual course of events in Egyptian, Syrian, and Hittite political interrelationships during Amarna age. [JDM]

5.367 Mogens Trolle Larsen. *The Old Assyrian city state and its colonies.* Copenhagen: Akademisk Forlag, 1976. (Mesopotamia, 4.) ISBN 87-500-1640-7. ▸ Excellent study and analysis of political structure of Old Assyrian state. Emphasis on internal structure of Assyrian society and of political institutions in Assur and in Anatolian colonies. [JDM]

5.368 J. G. Macqueen. *The Hittites and their contemporaries in Asia Minor.* Rev. ed. London: Thames & Hudson, 1986. ISBN 0-500-021208-2. ▸ Well-illustrated account of civilizations of Bronze Age Anatolia. Should be used with caution; maps are attractive but inaccurate. Originally published 1975. [JDM]

5.369 James Mellaart. *The Chalcolithic and Early Bronze ages in the Near East and Anatolia.* Beirut: Khayats, 1966. ▸ Pioneering discussion of pre-Hittite Anatolia and Anatolian contacts with Egypt and Syria-Palestine. Well illustrated with excellent maps, but difficult to find in most libraries. [JDM]

5.370 James Mellaart. "Western Anatolia, Beyçesultan, and the Hittites." In *Mansel'e armagan/Mélanges Mansel.* Ekrem Akurgal and U. Bahadir Alkim, eds., vol. 1, pp. 493–526. Ankara: Turk Tarih Kurumu Basimevi, 1974. (Turk Tarih Kurumu Yayinlari, 7 dizi, 60.) ▸ Imaginative account of Hittite, Egyptian, and Aegean interests in western Anatolia during Late Bronze Age. Believes various groups of Sea Peoples came from southern Anatolia, Cyprus, and Rhodes. [JDM]

5.371 Machteld J. Mellink. "Anatolia: old and new perspectives." *Proceedings of the American Philosophical Society* 110.2 (1966) 111–29. ISSN 0003-049X. ▸ Discussion of importance of archaeological evidence for Anatolian history in Bronze and Iron ages. Stresses independent developments within Anatolia itself. [JDM]

5.372 Machteld J. Mellink. "A Hittite figurine from Nuzi." In *Vorderasiatische Archaeologie: Festschrift Anton Moortgat.* Kurt Bittel et al., eds., pp. 155–64. Berlin: Mann, 1964. ▸ Rare example of Hittite ivory figurine found in fifteenth-century BCE context at Nuzi in northern Iraq. Important evidence for Hittite contact with Hurrian cultural center. [JDM]

5.373 Machteld J. Mellink. "Midas in Tyana." In *Florilegium Anatolicum: mélanges offerts à Emmanuel Laroche,* pp. 249–57. Paris: de Boccard, 1979. ▸ Shows that famous monument known as black stone of Tyana actually relates to Mita of Mushki, Midas of later Greek legend and king of Phrygia in late eighth century BCE (reign of neo-Assyrian king Sargon II). [JDM]

5.374 Henri Metzger. *Anatolia II: first millennium B.C. to the end of the Roman period.* Geneva: Nagel, 1969. ▸ Well illustrated with rather brief text covering culture of Anatolia, post-Bronze Age to Roman times. Emphasizes impact of native background on development of Greco-Roman culture in Anatolia. [JDM]

5.375 Nadav Na'aman. "The historical introduction of the Aleppo treaty reconsidered." *Journal of cuneiform studies* 32.1 (1980) 34–42. ISSN 0022-0256. ▸ Convincing analysis of important historical prologue to this treaty, which remains our best evidence for existence of Hittite king Hattušili II. [JDM]

5.376 Louis Lawrence Orlin. *Assyrian colonies in Cappadocia.* The Hague: Mouton, 1970. ISBN 0-686-22408-6 (pbk). ▸ Analysis of political relationships between Old Assyrian traders and indigenous administrations of Anatolian cities, ca. 1900–1780 BCE. Attempts to define nature of Old Assyrian colonization. [JDM]

5.377 Tahsin Özgüç. "New observations on the relationship of Kultepe with Southeast Anatolia and North Syria during the third millennium B.C." In *Ancient Anatolia: aspects of change and cultural development, essays in honor of Machteld J. Mellink.* Jeanny Vorys Canby et al., eds., pp. 31–47. Madison: University of Wisconsin Press, 1986. ISBN 0-299-10620-9. ▸ Most detailed account of late third-millennium BCE material (Early Bronze III) from author's excavations at Kultepe. Crucial for historical background of Old Assyrian colonies in Anatolia. One of several important articles in this volume dedicated to world's foremost Anatolian archaeologist. [JDM]

5.378 Itamar Singer. "The battle of Nihriya and the end of the Hittite empire." *Zeitschrift für Assyriologie und vorderasiatische Archäologie* 75.1 (1985) 100–23. ISSN 0084-5299. ▸ Important evaluation of text from Ugarit recording battle between Hittites and Assyria, when Tudhaliya III (IV) was Hittite king and Tukulti-Ninurta I was king of Assyria. Gives procedures involved in Hittite declaration of war. [JDM]

5.379 Itamar Singer. "Hittites and Hattians in Anatolia at the beginning of the second millennium B.C." *Journal of Indo-European studies* 9.1–2 (1981) 119–32. ISSN 0092-2323. ▸ Best discussion of important role played by non-Indo-European Hattian inhabitants of Anatolia who were already present when Hittites arrived in region. [JDM]

5.380 Itamar Singer. "Western Anatolia in the thirteenth century B.C. according to the Hittite sources." *Anatolian studies* 33.1 (1983) 205–17. ISSN 0066-1546. ▸ Discussion of situation in western Anatolia at end of Late Bronze Age in light of new evidence from Bogazköy and Ugarit. [JDM]

5.381 Ferdinand Sommer. *Die Ahhijava-Urkunden.* 1932 ed. Hildesheim: Gerstenberg, 1975. ISBN 3-8067-0515-1. ▸ Basic collection of all Hittite texts that mention Ahhiyawa. All passages given in Hittite with German translation. [JDM]

5.382 Gerd Steiner. "The immigration of the first Indo-Europeans into Anatolia reconsidered." *Journal of Indo-European studies* 18.1–2 (1990) 185–214. ISSN 0093-2323. ▸ Evaluation of new archaeological and textual evidence for origins of Anatolian branch of Indo-Europeans and for beginnings of Hittite history. Believes proto-Hittites came from Balkans. [JDM]

5.383 Theo P. J. Van den Hout. "A chronology of the Tarhuntassa treaties." *Journal of cuneiform studies* 41.1 (1989) 100–14. ISSN 0022-0256. ▸ Discussion of chronology of treaties between Hittites and Tarhuntassa in light of text of recently discovered bronze tablet containing treaty between Tudhaliya III (IV) and Kurunta, ruler of Tarhuntassa. [JDM]

5.384 Gernot Wilhelm and Johannes Boese. "Absolute chronologie und die hethitische Geschichte des fünfzehnten und vierzehnten Jahrhunderts v. Chr." In *High, middle, or low? Acts of an international colloquium on absolute chronology held at the University of Gothenburg, 20th–22nd August 1987.* Paul Åström, ed., vol. 1, pp. 74–117. Gothenburg: Åström, 1987–89. (Studies in Mediterranean archaeology and literature, 56.) ISBN 91-86098-64-0 (pbk). ▸ Argues reign of Šuppiluliuma I was only about twenty years long and can be dated ca. 1343–1322 BCE. Especially valuable for analysis of textual tradition of "Deeds of Šuppiluliuma I." [JDM]

5.385 Irene J. Winter. "Carchemish ša kišad puratti." *Anatolian studies* 33.1 (1983) 177–97. ISSN 0066-1546. ▸ Presents Carchemish as dominant state in northern Syria and southeastern Anatolia prior to Assyrian takeover. [JDM]

5.386 Werner Wouters. "Urhi-Tešub and the Ramses-letters from Boghazköy." *Journal of cuneiform studies* 41.2 (1989) 226–

34. ISSN 0022-0256. ‣ Discussion of evidence for later career of Urhi-Tešub following his overthrow by Hattusili III. Supports argument advanced by W. Helck, in German article published in same journal in 1963, that Urhi-Tešub went to Egypt after being deposed. See also Houwink ten Cate 5.361. [JDM]

5.387 Jak Yakar. *The later prehistory of Anatolia: the late Chalcolithic and Early Bronze Age.* Oxford: British Archaeological Reports, 1985. (British Archaeological Reports international series, 268.) ISBN 0-86054-341-2. ‣ Comprehensive picture of life in fourth and third millennia BCE. Some curious ideas about movements of peoples; discussion of development of metal technology riddled with errors. [JDM]

Military History

5.388 Richard H. Beal. *The organisation of the Hittite military.* Heidelberg: Winter, 1992. (Texte der Hethiter, 20.) ISBN 3-533-04562-5. ‣ First detailed description of Hittite army, including discussions of organization, strategy, tactics, weapons, and armor. Based mainly on evidence from Hittite texts. [JDM]

5.389 Albrecht Goetze. "Warfare in Asia Minor." *Iraq* 25 (1963) 124–30. ISSN 0021-0889. ‣ Short discussion of Hittite warfare, 1800–1200 BCE. [EL]

Social and Cultural History

5.390 Gary M. Beckman. "Mesopotamians and Mesopotamian learning at Hattuša." *Journal of cuneiform studies* 35.1–2 (1983) 97–114. ISSN 0022-0256. ‣ Outline of Mesopotamian origins of Hittite scribal tradition and Hittite use of cuneiform writing system. Argues Hittite scribes, in turn, taught their Egyptian counterparts how to write cuneiform. [JDM]

5.391 Elmar Edel. *Ägyptische Ärtze und ägyptische Medizin am hethitischen Königshof: neue Funde von keilschriftbriefen Ramses' II. aus Bogazkoy.* Opladen: Westdeutscher, 1976. (Rheinisch-Westfalische Akademie der Wissenschaften, G205.) ISBN 3-531-07205-6. ‣ Role of Egyptian medicine and Egyptian doctors at Hittite court in thirteenth century BCE. [JDM]

5.392 Johannes Friedrich. *Die hethitischen Gesetze.* Leiden: Brill, 1959. ‣ Only reliable edition of Hittite law code; transcription, translation, and brief commentary. Wealth of information on Hittite socioeconomic organization. [JDM]

5.393 Albrecht Goetze. *Kleinasien zur Hethiterzeit: eine geographische Untersuchung.* 1924 ed. Nendeln, Liechtenstein: Kraus Reprint, 1975. ‣ Hittite cultural history within context of archaeology of Bronze Age Anatolia. Summarized then present knowledge on all aspects of Hittite civilization. Includes Iron Age kingdoms of Urartu, Phrygia, and Lydia. [JDM]

5.394 Harry A. Hoffner, Jr. *Alimenta Hethaeorum: food production in Hittite Asia Minor.* New Haven: American Oriental Society, 1974. (American Oriental series, 55.) ‣ Lexical study of Hittite cuisine, with emphasis on identification of foodstuffs mentioned in Hittite texts, not on how Hittites cooked these foods. [JDM]

Economic History

5.395 James D. Muhly et al. "Iron in Anatolia and the nature of the Hittite iron industry." *Anatolian studies* 35.1 (1985) 67–84. ISSN 0066-1546. ‣ Presents new analytical evidence for development of iron technology in Bronze Age Anatolia. Reviews earlier literature relating to theory of Hittite iron "monopoly." [JDM]

Religion

5.396 Gary M. Beckman. "The religion of the Hittites." *Biblical archaeologist* 52.2–3 (1989) 98–108. ISSN 0006-0895. ‣ Excellent popular account of basic aspects of Hittite religious beliefs and practices. Argues religious conceptions of Hittites were in accord with their social structure and environment. [JDM]

5.397 Oliver R. Gurney. *Some aspects of Hittite religion.* Oxford: Oxford University Press for British Academy, 1977. ISBN 0-19-725974-X. ‣ Study of Hittite pantheon and cult, both local and official. Discussion of purpose of site of Yazilikaya and nature of Hittite rituals. Emphasizes Canaanite and Hebrew parallels (especially scapegoat ritual) and non-Hittite elements in Hittite religion. [JDM]

Literature

5.398 Harry A. Hoffner, Jr. *Hittite myths.* Gary M. Beckman, ed. Atlanta: Scholars Press, 1990. (Society of Biblical Literature, Writings from the ancient world, 2.) ISBN 1-55540-481-2 (cl), 1-55540-482-0 (pbk). ‣ Translations, with notes and commentary, of Hittite mythological texts. Material divided into Old Anatolian myths, Hurrian myths, tales involving deities and mortals, and Canaanite myth of Elkunirsa and Ashertu. [JDM]

Art and Archaeology

5.399 Ekrem Akurgal. *The art of Greece: its origins in the Mediterranean and Near East.* Wayne Dynes, trans. New York: Crown, 1966. ‣ Practically only discussion in English of various national art styles during first half of first millennium BCE and their impact on development of Greek art. Includes long chapter on neo-Hittite art. [JDM]

5.400 Ekrem Akurgal. *The art of the Hittites.* New York: Abrams, 1962. ‣ Basic work on Hittite art with excellent photographs of sites, monuments, and minor works of art, all taken by Max Hirmer for original German edition. [JDM]

5.401 Robert L. Alexander. "A great queen of the sphinx gate at Alaca Hüyük." *Anatolian studies* 39.1 (1989) 151–58. ISSN 0066-1546. ‣ Discussion of sculptures decorating so-called sphinx gate at Alaça Hüyük. Examines interesting parallels between art of Hittite period Alaça and that at site of Yazilikaya. [JDM]

5.402 Robert L. Alexander. "Šaušga and the Hittite ivory from Megiddo." *Journal of Near Eastern studies* 50.3 (1991) 161–82. ISSN 0022-2968. ‣ Particularly important because very little Hittite material has been found outside Anatolia. Ivory plaque studied here remains something of a mystery, sole Anatolian piece in hoard of some 300 ivories. [JDM]

5.403 Robert L. Alexander. *The sculpture and sculptors of Yazilikaya.* Newark: University of Delaware Press, 1986. ISBN 0-87413-279-7. ‣ Art historical analysis of relief at Yazilikaya, establishing relative chronology of all reliefs. [JDM]

5.404 U. Bahadir Alkim. *Anatolia.* Vol. 1: *From the beginnings to the end of the second millennium B.C.* James Hogarth, trans. Cleveland: World, 1968. ISSN 0570-0116. ‣ Well-illustrated account of archaeological evidence for Anatolian prehistory, from Çatal Hüyük to Miletus. [JDM]

5.405 Kurt Bittel. *Die Hethiter.* Munich: Beck, 1976. ISBN 3-406-03024-6. ‣ Standard discussion of Anatolian art and architecture from end of third millennium to beginning of first millennium BCE. Also treats relief sculpture and some examples of minor arts. First published in French; no English edition exists. Superb illustrations. [JDM]

5.406 Rainer Michael Boehmer and Hans Gustav Güterbock. *Die glyptick von Boğazköy.* Vol. 2: *Glyptik aus dem Stadtgebiet von Boğazköy, Grabungskampagnen 1931–1939, 1952–1978.* Berlin: Mann, 1987. (Boğazköy-Hattuša: Ergebnisse der Ausgrabungen, 14.) ISBN 3-7861-1494-3. ‣ Authoritative discussion of development of Bronze and Iron Age glyptic art in Anatolia from Old Assyrian colonies to Achaemenid empire. Deals both with iconography (Boehmer) and with hieroglyphic and cuneiform inscriptions (Güterbock) on seal impressions. Especially important discussion of transition from Old Assyrian to Old Hittite glyptic style. [JDM]

5.407 Billie Jean Collins. "The representation of wild animals in Hittite texts." Ph.D. dissertation. Ann Arbor: University Microfilms International, 1989. ▸ Discussion of all evidence—textual, artistic, and archaeological—for wild animals known in Hittite Anatolia. Includes evaluation of symbolic, iconographic, and ritual use of wild animals. [JDM]

5.408 Ann C. Gunter. *The Gordion excavations: final reports.* Vol. 3: *The Bronze Age.* Philadelphia: University of Pennsylvania, The University Museum, 1991. (University of Pennsylvania, University Museum monographs, 43.) ISBN 0-934718-95-4 (v. 3), 0-934718-39-3 (set). ▸ Account of Bronze Age remains excavated at Gordion between 1950 and 1973, with complete catalog of all finds. Gordion, capital of later Phrygian kingdom, already important site in Hittite period. [JDM]

5.409 George M. A. Hanfmann et al. *Sardis from prehistoric to Roman times: results of the archaeological exploration of Sardis, 1958–1975.* Cambridge, Mass.: Harvard University Press, 1983. ISBN 0-674-78925-3. ▸ Excavations at site of Sardis, capital of kingdom of Lydia, under general direction of Hanfmann, are being published in series of final reports. This volume, with contributions by most members of senior staff, is best synthesis of results. [JDM]

5.410 C. H. Emilie Haspels. *The highlands of Phrygia: sites and monuments.* Princeton: Princeton University Press, 1971. ISBN 0-691-03863-5. ▸ Description of Phrygian rock monuments in mountainous region of Turkmen Dag, especially remains at site known as Midas City. [JDM]

5.411 James Mellaart. *Çatal Hüyük: a Neolithic town in Anatolia.* New York: McGraw-Hill, 1967. ▸ Basic report on this still unpublished site, most important Neolithic site ever excavated in Turkey. Famous for its shrines and associated wall paintings. New excavations scheduled to begin in 1993, under direction of Ian Hodder. [JDM]

5.412 Machteld J. Mellink. "Archaeology in Anatolia." *American journal of archaeology* 97.1 (1993) 105–33. ISSN 0002-9114. ▸ Latest installment of annual review of archaeological work in Turkey, prehistoric to Roman period; begun in volume 59 (1955, earlier title: "Archaeology in Asia Minor"). Basic survey of year's work in field by world's foremost authority. Beginning 1994, review will be written by Marie-Henriette Gates. [JDM]

5.413 Peter Neve. "Die Ausgrabungen in Boğazköy-Hattuša, 1991." *Archäologischer Anzeiger* 3 (1992) 307–38. ISSN 0003-8105. ▸ Detailed reports on current excavations at site of Hittite capital by present field director. Such reports published almost every year; basic for understanding ongoing work at site. [JDM]

5.414 Peter Neve. *Buyükkale: die Bauwerke, Grabungen, 1954–1966.* Berlin: Mann, 1982. (Boğazköy-Hattuša: Ergebnisse der Ausgrabungen, 12.) ISBN 3-7861-1252-5. ▸ Essential for study of Hittite architecture. Discusses buildings on citadel (Turkish Buyükkale), containing residential and administrative quarters of Hittite capital. Concentrates on work since 1954, but summarizes results of excavations since 1906. [JDM]

5.415 Winfried Orthmann. *Untersuchungen zur späthethitischen Kunst.* Bonn: Habelt, 1971. ▸ Basic publication of monumental art of neo-Hittite kingdoms. Attempts to place all known reliefs in chronological sequence. [JDM]

5.416 Friedhelm von Prayon. *Phrygische Plastik: die fruheisenzeitliche Bildkunst Zentral-Anatoliens und ihre Beziehungen zu Griechenland und zum alten Orient.* Tubingen: Wasmuth, 1987. ISBN 3-8030-1906-0. ▸ Basic study of Phrygian sculpture, ca. 900–

500 BCE, and its relationship to art of Greece and Near East. [JDM]

5.417 Irene J. Winter. "On the problems of Karatepe: the reliefs and their context." *Anatolian studies* 29.1 (1979) 115–51. ISSN 0066-1546. ▸ Best discussion of archaeological and historical background of most important neo-Hittite site. Convincing arguments in favor of late seventh-century BCE dating for site and its orthostat reliefs. [JDM]

5.418 Rodney S. Young. *The Gordion excavations: final reports.* Vol. 1: *Three great early tumuli.* Philadelphia: University of Pennsylvania, The University Museum, 1981. (University of Pennsylvania, University Museum monographs, 43.) ISBN 0-934718-39-3. ▸ Final report on excavation of Tumulus P, Tumulus W, and Tumulus MM, and king's tumulus of Midas mound, presumably burial of Midas, king of Phrygia, known from Greek mythology and from letters of Assyrian king Sargon II. [JDM]

IRAN

General Histories

5.419 Pierre Amiet. *Suse: 6000 ans d'histoire.* Paris: Éditions de la Réunion des Musées Nationaux, 1988. ISBN 2-71182-165-X, ISSN 0297-3995. ▸ Good survey of archaeological exploration at Susa. Chronicles history of Elam, ca. 3000–550 BCE, and Achaemenid empire, 550–330 BCE, as seen from this important city. Select bibliography. [MWW]

5.420 W. Barthold. *An historical geography of Iran.* C. E. Bosworth, ed. Svat Soucek, trans. Princeton: Princeton University Press, 1984. ISBN 0-691-05418-5. ▸ Sound treatment of Iranian geography by region and its role in Iranian history. [MWW]

5.421 Arthur Emanuel Christensen. *L'Iran sous les Sassanides.* 1944 2d ed. Osnabrück: Zeller, 1971. ▸ Fundamental treatment of Sasanian history, 224–651 CE. [MWW]

5.422 Malcolm A. R. Colledge. *The Parthians.* London: Thames & Hudson, 1967. ▸ Historical survey of Parthian period—Arsacid dynasty, 250 BCE–224 CE. Discussions of religion, archaeology, and art. Includes section on relations with Roman empire. [MWW]

5.423 William Culican. *The Medes and the Persians.* New York: Praeger, 1965. ▸ Overview of migrations of Medes and Persians into Iran, rise of Achaemenid empire, and survey of its history, 550–330 BCE. Useful introduction, but several parts outdated. [MWW]

5.424 John Curtis. *Ancient Persia.* Cambridge, Mass.: Harvard University Press, 1990. ISBN 0-674-03415-5. ▸ Brief but good overview of ancient Iran from its prehistoric origins to Islamic conquest (651 CE). Numerous photographs. [MWW]

5.425 I. M. Diakonoff. "Media." In *The Cambridge history of Iran.* Ilya Gershevitch, ed., vol. 2, pp. 36–148. Cambridge: Cambridge University Press, 1985. ISBN 0-521-20091-1. ▸ Extensive overview of Medes from arrival in Iran (ca. early first millennium BCE) to incorporation into Achaemenid empire (550 BCE). Detailed discussions of Indo-Iranian (Mede and Persian) migrations into Iran, chronological problems, relations with Assyria and other neighbors, and society and culture. [MWW]

5.426 Richard N. Frye. *The history of ancient Iran.* Munich: Beck, 1984. (Handbuch der Altertumswissenschaft, 3.7.) ISBN 3-406-09397-3. ▸ Essential source; surveys of geography and demography. Traces migration of Iranians into Iran and their subsequent history through Sasanian period (seventh century CE). Select bibliography at beginning of each chapter. [MWW]

5.427 Ilya Gershevitch and Ehsan Yarshater, eds. *The Cambridge history of Iran.* Vol. 1: *The land of Iran.* Vol. 2: *Median and Achaemenian periods.* Vol. 3: *The Seleucid, Parthian, and Sasanian* *periods.* Cambridge: Cambridge University Press, 1983–85. ISBN 0-521-06035-1 (v. 1), 0-521-20091-1 (v. 2), 0-521-24693-8 (v. 3). ▸ Collection of essays on various aspects of Iranian history before Islamic conquest (651 CE). Also includes survey of Elamite history, ca. 3000–550 BCE, in volume 1. Excellent resource, full bibliography. [MWW]

5.428 Roman Ghirshman. *Iran: from the earliest times to the Islamic conquest.* Baltimore: Penguin, 1954. ▸ Classic survey of Iran and its history from arrival of Iranians through Sasanian period (seventh century CE). Dated; must be used with caution. [MWW]

5.429 Walther Hinz. *The lost world of Elam: re-creation of a vanished civilization.* 1972 ed. Jennifer Barnes, trans. New York: New York University Press, 1973. ISBN 0-8147-3365-4. ▸ Historical and cultural overview of Elamite kingdom in Iran, third through first millennia BCE. Some historical conclusions outdated. Useful survey. Translation of *Das Reich Elam* (1964). [MWW]

5.430 Amélie Kuhrt. "A brief guide to some recent work on the Achaemenid empire." *Liverpool classical monthly* 8.10 (1983) 146–53. ISSN 0309-3700. ▸ Brief but excellent summary of scholarship on Achaemenid empire, 550–330 BCE, and main historical issues. Includes useful overview of published material (to early 1980s) dealing with various aspects of Achaemenid scholarship. [MWW]

5.431 Pierre de Miroschedji. "La fin de l'Elam: essai d'analyse et d'interprétation." *Iranica antiqua* 25 (1990) 47–95. ISSN 0021-0870. ▸ Discussion of downfall of Elamite state, late second to mid-first millennium BCE, based on archaeological record and ancient texts. Good synthesis, but much remains speculative. Complete references to relevant recent work. [MWW]

5.432 Albert T. E. Olmstead. *History of the Persian empire.* 1948 ed. Chicago: University of Chicago Press, 1959. ISBN 0-226-62777-2. ▸ Classic treatment of Achaemenid empire, 550–330 BCE. Several parts outdated but remains useful overview. [MWW]

5.433 Heleen Sancisi-Weerdenburg. "Decadence in the empire or decadence in the sources?" In *Achaemenid history.* Heleen Sancisi-Weerdenburg, ed., vol. 1, pp. 33–46. Leiden: Nederlands Instituut voor het Nabije Oosten, 1987. ISBN 90-6258-401-2. ▸ Excellent discussion and refutation of traditional view of decline (fourth century BCE) of Achaemenid empire, attributed by Greek sources to decadence. Focuses on unreliability of certain aspects of Greek historiography. [MWW]

5.434 Heleen Sancisi-Weerdenburg, Amélie Kuhrt, and Jan Wilhelm Drijvers, eds. *Achaemenid history.* 8 vols. Leiden: Nederlands Instituut voor het Nabije Oosten, 1987–92. ISBN 90-6258-401-2 (v. 1), 90-6258-402-0 (v. 2), 90-6258-403-9 (v. 3), 90-6258-404-7 (v. 4), 90-6258-405-5 (v. 5), 90-6258-406-3 (v. 6), 90-6258-407-1 (v. 7). ▸ Collections of papers covering wide range of topics. Each volume focuses on theme in Achaemenid studies. Foremost resource for latest work and bibliography on Achaemenid empire, 550–330 BCE. Articles in English, German, French, and Italian. Essential for any in-depth work. [MWW]

5.435 Chester G. Starr. "Greeks and Persians in the fourth century BC." *Iranica antiqua* 11, 12 (1975, 1976) 39–99. ISSN 0021-0870. ▸ Analysis of Greek–Achaemenid Persian relations from Persian perspective. Necessary balance to generally Hellenocentric treatments of this period by most modern scholarship. Focuses on Greek views of Persians, political history, and cultural connections, especially in Asia Minor. [MWW]

5.436 Piotr Steinkeller. "On the identity of the toponym LÚ.SU(.A)." *Journal of the American Oriental Society* 108.2 (1988) 197–202. ISSN 0003-0279. ▸ Discussion of location of Elamite people referred to as LÚ.SU in ancient texts, late third

millennium BCE. Identifies them with Shimashkians, an early Elamite dynasty. Specialist study. [MWW]

5.437 Piotr Steinkeller. "The question of Marḫaši: a contribution to the historical geography of Iran in the third millennium BC." *Zeitschrift für Assyriologie und vorderasiatische Archäologie* 72.2 (1982) 237–65. ISSN 0084-5299. ▸ Challenges traditional view of Marhashi (third millennium BCE) as Iranian political entity bordering Mesopotamia. Argues for its location in what is now central Iran. [MWW]

Political History

5.438 Jack Martin Balcer. *Herodotus and Bisitun: problems in ancient Persian historiography.* Stuttgart: Steiner, 1987. (*Historia, Einzelschriften, 49.*) ISBN 3-515-04790-5. ▸ Examination of circumstances surrounding Darius I's accession to throne (522–521 BCE). Compares Herodotus's account with Darius's Bisitun Inscription. Good overview of complex issue. [MWW]

5.439 Hermann Bengtson, ed. *The Greeks and the Persians: from the sixth to the fourth centuries.* John Conway, trans. New York: Delacorte, 1968. ▸ Collection of essays tracing Greek-Persian history and relations from rise of Achaemenid empire (sixth century BCE) to its overthrow by Alexander the Great (fourth century BCE). Includes chapters on Greek democracy, Pericles, Athenian-Spartan relations, and subject lands of Achaemenid empire. [MWW]

5.440 Elias J. Bickerman. "Notes on Seleucid and Parthian chronology." *Berytus: archaeological studies* 8.2 (1944) 73–83. ISSN 0067-6195. ▸ Examination of various chronological problems in ancient reckonings of Seleucid and Parthian eras. [MWW]

5.441 Elias J. Bickerman. "The Seleucids and the Achaemenids." In *La Persia e il mondo greco-romano: Roma, 11–14 aprile 1965.* Rome: Accademia Nazionale dei Lincei, 1966. (*Problemi attuali di scienza e di cultura, 76.*) ▸ Overview of transition of power in Mesopotamia and Iran from downfall of Achaemenid empire to rise of Seleucids, fourth to third century BCE. Discusses various historical problems. [MWW]

5.442 Stuart C. Brown. "The *Mêdikos Logos* of Herodotus and the evolution of the Median state." In *Achaemenid history.* Amélie Kuhrt and Heleen Sancisi-Weerdenburg, eds., vol. 3, pp. 71–86. Leiden: Nederlands Instituut voor het Nabije Oosten, 1988. ISBN 90-6258-403-9 (pbk). ▸ Discussion of Median history (seventh and sixth centuries BCE) based on Herodotus. Treats reliability of this account in comparison with cuneiform sources. Excellent treatment. [MWW]

5.443 Andrew R. Burn. *Persia and the Greeks: the defence of the west, c. 546–478 BC.* 2d ed. Stanford, Calif.: Stanford University Press, 1984. ISBN 0-8047-1235-2. ▸ General survey covering rise of Achaemenid empire (sixth century BCE), Ionian revolt (499–494 BCE), and rise of Athens' Delian League (fifth century BCE). Extensive treatment of Persian invasion of Greece (480–479 BCE). Good source. [MWW]

5.444 George G. Cameron. *History of early Iran.* 1936 ed. New York: Gordon, 1976. ISBN 0-8490-1972-9. ▸ One of first treatments of Elamites and their history, ca. 3000–550 BCE. Classic work; still extremely useful as general survey, but many chronological details superseded by recent discoveries. [MWW]

5.445 George G. Cameron. "The Persian satrapies and related matters." *Journal of Near Eastern studies* 32.1 (1973) 47–56. ISSN 0022-2968. ▸ Excellent discussion of peoples of Achaemenid empire, 550–330 BCE, as enumerated in Achaemenid royal inscriptions. [MWW]

5.446 Elizabeth Carter and Matthew W. Stolper. *Elam: surveys of political history and archaeology.* Berkeley: University of California Press, 1984. ISBN 0-520-09950-8 (pbk). ▸ Most up-to-date survey of earliest periods in Iranian history. Essential reading for any study of Elam, ca. 3000–550 BCE. Complete references. [MWW]

5.447 J. M. Cook. *The Persian empire*. New York: Schocken, 1983. ISBN 0-8052-3846-8. ▸ Historical survey of Achaemenid period, 550–330 BCE. Useful overview. [MWW]

5.448 Muhammad A. Dandamaev. *Persien unter den ersten Achämeniden*. Heinz-Dieter Pohl, trans. Wiesbaden: Reichert, 1976. (Beiträge zur Iranistik, 8.) ISBN 3-920153-25-1. ▸ In-depth exploration of Darius's Bisitun Inscription as historical source, followed by discussion of Achaemenid empire under Cyrus II (d. 530 BCE) through reign of Darius I (522–486 BCE). [MWW]

5.449 Muhammad A. Dandamaev. *A political history of the Achaemenid empire*. W. J. Vogelsang, trans. New York: Brill, 1989. ISBN 90-04-09172-6. ▸ Best, most up-to-date historical survey of Achaemenid empire, 550–330 BCE. Comprehensive bibliography. [MWW]

5.450 Neilson C. Debevoise. *A political history of Parthia*. 1938 ed. New York: Greenwood, 1968. ▸ Classic treatment of Parthian empire from its origins to its collapse, 250 BCE–224 CE. [MWW]

5.451 John R. Gardiner-Garden. "Dareios' Scythian expedition and its aftermath." *Klio* 69.2 (1987) 326–50. ISSN 0075-6334. ▸ In-depth exploration of Darius's expedition into Europe (beyond the Danube), 515–513 BCE, as related by Herodotus, *Histories*, Book IV. Full references. [MWW]

5.452 David F. Graf. "Medism: the origin and significance of the term." *Journal of Hellenic studies* 104 (1984) 15–30. ISSN 0075-4269. ▸ Excellent discussion of Greek-Persian relations. Focuses on Greeks' use of term "Medism" in context of perceptions of Median and Achaemenid empires (seventh to fourth century BCE). Full references. [MWW]

5.453 John Hansman. "Elamites, Achaemenians, and Anshan." *Iran* 10 (1972) 101–25. ISSN 0578-6967. ▸ Overview of Elamite and early Achaemenid history in relation to important city of Anshan, in modern Fars. Identification of Anshan with site Tal-e Malyan. Good discussion, but supposition that ancient Awan is later Anshan (Elamite capital) uncertain. [MWW]

5.454 Peyton R. Helm. "Herodotus' *Mêdikos Logos* and Median history." *Iran* 19 (1981) 85–90. ISSN 0578-6967. ▸ Sound discussion of Greek historian's account of pre-Achaemenid Media (eighth to mid-sixth century BCE) and its usefulness in modern reconstructions of period. Chronological problems not yet settled. [MWW]

5.455 Ernst Herzfeld. *The Persian empire: studies in geography and ethnography of the ancient Near East*. Gerold Walser, ed. Wiesbaden: Steiner, 1968. ISBN 3-515-00091-7 (pbk). ▸ Collection of works edited posthumously. Essays on various topics, including geography of various regions of ancient Near East. See especially chapters 12 and 14–16 for discussions of matriarchy in ancient Elam and satrapies of Achaemenid empire, 550–330 BCE. [MWW]

5.456 Amélie Kuhrt. "The Cyrus cylinder and Achaemenid imperial policy." *Journal for the study of the Old Testament* 25 (1983) 83–97. ISSN 0309-0892. ▸ Excellent discussion of text commemorating Cyrus II's (the Great) conquest of Babylon (539 BCE), emphasizing its role as building inscription and propaganda piece rather than as evidence for Cyrus's magnanimity. [MWW]

5.457 Frank A. Lepper. *Trajan's Parthian War*. 1948 ed. Westport, Conn.: Greenwood, 1979. ISBN 0-313-20845-X. ▸ Chronicles Roman emperor's campaigns against Parthians (113–117 CE). Full discussions of topography, chronology, strategy, and motivation for war. [MWW]

5.458 David M. Lewis. *Sparta and Persia: lectures delivered at the University of Cincinnati, Autumn 1976, in memory of Donald W.*

Bradeen. Leiden: Brill, 1977. ISBN 90-04-05427-8. ▸ Collection of lectures on theme of Greek-Persian relations during and after Peloponnesian War (431–404 BCE). Examines issue from both Persian and Greek viewpoints. Excellent resource. [MWW]

5.459 B. Philip Lozinski. "The Parthian dynasty." *Iranica antiqua* 19 (1984) 119–39. ISSN 0021-0870. ▸ Survey and discussion of Arsacid dynasty (Parthian empire, 250 BCE–224 CE) based on Middle Eastern sources (i.e., those written in Arabic, Armenian, and Iranian as opposed to Greek and Latin sources), from Middle Ages to nineteenth century. [MWW]

5.460 G. Posener. *La première domination Perse en Egypte*. Le Caire: L'Institut Français d'Archéologie Orientale, 1936. (Bibliothèque d'étude, 11.) ▸ In-depth exploration of Achaemenid rule in Egypt, late sixth through fourth centuries BCE. Essential source. [MWW]

5.461 Heleen Sancisi-Weerdenburg. "Was there ever a Median empire?" In *Achaemenid history*. Amélie Kuhrt and Heleen Sancisi-Weerdenburg, eds., vol. 1, pp. 197–212. Leiden: Nederlands Instituut voor het Nabije Oosten, 1988. ISBN 90-6258-403-9 (pbk). ▸ Examination of literary and archaeological sources to determine nature of Median state (seventh to sixth century BCE) and if designation "empire" is warranted. [MWW]

5.462 Matthew W. Stolper. "The death of Artaxerxes I." *Archäologische Mitteilungen aus Iran*, n.F., 16 (1983) 223–36. ISSN 0066-6033. ▸ Essential discussion of Greek and especially Babylonian sources (economic texts) relevant to death of Artaxerxes I (424/23 BCE). [MWW]

5.463 Matthew W. Stolper. "The governor of Babylon and across-the-river in 486 BC." *Journal of Near Eastern studies* 48.4 (1989) 283–307. ISSN 0022-2968. ▸ Examination of administrative structure of Achaemenid empire, 550–330 BCE, focusing on satrapies in Greater Mesopotamia as glimpsed from ancient sources. Includes list and discussion of governors of this region. [MWW]

5.464 Matthew W. Stolper. "On the dynasty of Shimashki and the early *sukkalmahs*." *Zeitschrift für Assyriologie und vorderasiatische Archäologie* 72.1 (1982) 42–67. ISSN 0084-5299. ▸ Explores nation of Elam (third to second millennium BCE) and formation of one of its earliest dynasties. Excellent reference for early historical Iran. [MWW]

5.465 S. H. Taqizadeh. "The early Sasanians." *Bulletin of the School of Oriental and African Studies* 11 (1943–46) 6–51. ISSN 0041-977X. ▸ Detailed discussion of rulers and chronology of early Sasanian period (mid-third century CE). [MWW]

5.466 François Vallat. "Reflexions sur l'époque des *sukkalmah*." In *Contributions à l'histoire de l'Iran: mélanges offerts à Jean Perrot*. François Vallat, ed., pp. 119–28. Paris: Éditions Recherche sur les Civilisations, 1990. ISBN 2-86538-209-1. ▸ Discussion of *sukkalmah* period (ca. 2000–1600 BCE) of ancient Elam. Provides chart of rulers and their filiations. Good overview of complex historical period. [MWW]

5.467 F. Vallat. *Suse et l'Elam*. Paris: Éditions ADPF, 1980. (Études élamites: recherche sur les grandes civilisations, Mémoire, 1.) ISBN 2-86538-001-7. ▸ Brief overview of various problematic aspects of Elamite history, ca. 3000–550 BCE. [MWW]

5.468 W. J. Vogelsang. "Four short notes on the Bisitun text and monument." *Iranica antiqua* 21 (1986) 121–40. ISSN 0021-0870. ▸ Discussion and treatment of four controversial aspects of Darius's Bisitun Inscription (521–519 BCE). Good reference for discussions of this monument and problems involved in its study. [MWW]

5.469 W. J. Vogelsang. *The rise and organization of the Achaemenid empire: the eastern Iranian evidence*. New York: Brill, 1992. ISBN 90-04-09682-5. ▸ Focuses on developments in modern eastern Iran and Afghanistan before and during genesis of Achaemenid empire (mid-sixth century BCE). Role of Central Asian nomads in eastern part of empire. Good resource. [MWW]

5.470 Gerold Walser. *Hellas und Iran: Studien zu den griechisch-persischen Beziehungen vor Alexander.* Darmstadt: Wissenschaftliche Buchgesellschaft, 1984. (Erträge der Forschung, 209.) ISBN 3-534-07272-3, ISSN 0174-0695. ▸ Extensive survey of Greek-Persian relations and interaction, from rise of Achaemenid empire (mid-sixth century BCE) to conquest of Greece by Philip of Macedon (330s BCE). Comprehensive source. [MWW]

5.471 Michael Weiskopf. *The so-called "great-satraps' revolt," 366–360 BC: concerning local instability in the Achaemenid Far West.* Stuttgart: Steiner, 1989. (*Historia,* Einzelschriften, 63.) ISBN 3-515-05387-5, ISSN 0071-7665. ▸ Thorough examination (via relevant Greek and Latin sources) of troubles facing Achaemenid empire in 360s BCE in Anatolia. Downplays traditional belief of concerted rebellion against crown and focuses on localized instability. Good treatment. [MWW]

5.472 Josef Wolski. "The decay of the Iranian empire of the Seleucids and the chronology of the Parthian beginnings." *Berytus* 12.1 (1956–57) 35–52. ISSN 0067-6195. ▸ Good survey, tracing transition of power from Seleucids (305–64 BCE) to Parthian (Arsacid) empire (250 BCE–224 CE) in Iran and Near East. [MWW]

Cultural and Social History

5.473 Pierre Amiet. "Archaeological discontinuity and ethnic duality in Elam." *Antiquity* 53 (1979) 195–204. ISSN 0003-598X. ▸ Focuses on city of Susa in Khuzistan (western Iran) and its alternating orientation toward Mesopotamia and Elam proper (the Iranian highlands) throughout its history, as reflected in archaeological and textual records. [MWW]

5.474 Muhammad A. Dandamaev and Vladimir G. Lukonin. *The culture and social institutions of ancient Iran.* Philip L. Kohl and D. J. Dadson, trans. New York: Cambridge University Press, 1989. ISBN 0-521-32107-7. ▸ Traces Iranian cultural and social history from arrival of Iranians (i.e., Medes and Persians) in early first millennium BCE through Achaemenid period (550–330 BCE). Applies evidence from archaeology, architecture, art, and written sources. Much remains speculative. Extensive bibliography. [MWW]

5.475 Richard N. Frye. *The heritage of Persia.* 2d ed. London: Sphere, 1976. ISBN 0-351-16340-9. ▸ Excellent discussion of social and cultural history of Iran from arrival of Medes and Persians (early first millennium BCE) to Islamic conquest (seventh century CE). [MWW]

5.476 Richard N. Frye. "The institutions." In *Beiträge zur Achämenidengeschichte.* Gerold Walser, ed., pp. 83–93. Wiesbaden: Steiner, 1972. (*Historia,* Einzelschriften, 18.) ▸ Overview of ancient sources for social and cultural traditions in Achaemenid period, 550–330 BCE. [MWW]

5.477 Walther Hinz. *Darius und die Perser: eine Kulturgeschichte der Achämeniden.* 2 vols. Baden-Baden: Holle, 1976–79. ISBN 3-87355-165-9 (v. 1), 3-87355-167-5 (v. 2). ▸ Cultural and social history of early Achaemenid period through Darius I (522–486 BCE). Good resource. [MWW]

Economic History

5.478 Raymond A. Bowman. *Aramaic ritual texts from Persepolis.* Chicago: University of Chicago Press, 1970. (Oriental Institute publications, 91.) ISBN 0-226-62194-4. ▸ Translation and discussion of various Aramaic texts found at Persepolis, capital of Achaemenid empire. Debates significance of texts. Compare Naveh and Shaked 5.481. [MWW]

5.479 George G. Cameron. *Persepolis treasury tablets.* Chicago: University of Chicago Press, 1948. (Oriental Institute publications, 65.) ▸ Translation and excellent discussion of Elamite economic texts (fifth century BCE) discovered in treasury building at Persepolis, capital of Achaemenid empire. Texts help illustrate Achaemenid empire's economy in this period. [MWW]

5.480 R. T. Hallock. "The evidence of the Persepolis tablets." In *The Cambridge history of Iran.* Ilya Gershevitch, ed., vol. 1, pp. 588–609. Cambridge: Cambridge University Press, 1985. ISBN 0-521-20091-1. ▸ Discussion of various tablets found at capital of Achaemenid empire. Provides important information on functioning of economy in and around Persepolis during late sixth to early fifth century BCE. [MWW]

5.481 Joseph Naveh and Shaul Shaked. "Ritual texts or treasury documents?" *Orientalia,* n.s., 42.3 (1973) 445–57. ISSN 0030-5367. ▸ Examination of significance of Aramaic documents discovered at Persepolis (fifth century BCE) and difficult problems in their interpretation. Compare Bowman 5.478. [MWW]

Religion

5.482 Mary Boyce. *A history of Zoroastrianism.* 2 vols. Leiden: Brill, 1975–82. (Handbuch der Orientalistik, 8.1.2.) ISBN 90-04-04319-5 (v. 1), 90-04-06506-7 (v. 2), ISSN 0169-9423. ▸ Extensive introduction to background of prophet Zoroaster, his teachings, and their subsequent development. Overview of Iranian traditions before Zoroaster and their influence on him in volume 1. Volume 2 continues historical survey into Achaemenid period (550–330 BCE). Essential work for early development of Zoroastrianism. [MWW]

5.483 Malcolm A. R. Colledge. *The Parthian period.* Leiden: Brill, 1986. ISBN 90-04-07115-6. ▸ Brief survey of Parthian history. Discussion of religion in Parthian period (250 BCE–224 CE) gleaned primarily from archaeological remains. Good introduction. [MWW]

5.484 Jacques Duchesne-Guillemin. *The religion of ancient Iran.* K. M. Jamaspasa, trans. Bombay: Tata, 1973. ▸ Survey and discussion of early Iranian religion, including Zoroaster and Zoroastrianism, beliefs and practices, and brief history of religion through Sasanian period (224–651 CE). Good overview. Translation of *La religion de l'Iran ancien* (1962). [MWW]

5.485 Richard N. Frye. "Religion in Fars under the Achaemenids." In *Orientalia J. Duchesne-Guillemin Emerito Oblata,* pp. 171–78. Leiden: Brill, 1984. (Acta Iranica, Deuxième série, Hommages et Opra minora, 23.) ISBN 90-6831-002-X. ▸ Examination of religion in homeland of Achaemenid Persians (Fars, Iran) and influence of older Elamite beliefs in that area. [MWW]

5.486 Gherardo Gnoli. *Zoroaster's time and homeland: a study on the origins of Mazdeism and related problems.* Naples: Istituto Universitario Orientale, 1980. (Serie minori: Istituto Universitario Orientale, Seminario di studi asiatici, 7.) ▸ Extensive survey of historical geography of Avesta and its relations to geography of (Indo-)Iranians in Iran, followed by in-depth examination of Zoroaster and religion named for him. Sound treatment of historical problem of prophet Zoroaster. [MWW]

5.487 John R. Hinnells. *Persian mythology.* New York: Bedrick, 1973. ISBN 0-87226-017-8. ▸ Excellent introduction to ancient Iranian religion. Surveys of ancient Persian and Zoroastrian mythologies and development of Zoroastrianism, including its heretical strains, e.g., Zurvanism. Numerous illustrations of antiquities portraying religious themes. [MWW]

5.488 S. Insler. *The Gathas of Zarathustra.* Leiden: Brill, 1975. (Acta Iranica, Troisième série, Textes et mémoires, 1.8.) ISBN 90-04-03902-3. ▸ English translation of original hymns of prophet Zoroaster. Includes introduction and commentary. [MWW]

5.489 William H. Malandra, ed. and trans. *An introduction to ancient Iranian religion: readings from the Avesta and the Achaemenid inscriptions.* Minneapolis: University of Minnesota Press, 1983. ISBN 0-8166-1114-9 (cl), 0-8166-1115-7 (pbk). ▸ Good introduction to material. Provides translations and commentary of selected primary sources dealing with Iranian religion in first millennium BCE. [MWW]

5.490 A. Shapur Shahbazi. "The 'traditional date of Zoroaster' explained." *Bulletin of the School of Oriental and African Studies* 40.1 (1977) 25–35. ISSN 0041-977X. ▸ Excellent treatment of problem regarding date of prophet Zoroaster. Thorough discussion of traditional date (sixth century BCE) and reasons why it must be rejected for earlier date. [MWW]

5.491 Morton Smith. "II Isaiah and the Persians." *Journal of the American Oriental Society* 83 (1963) 415–21. ISSN 0003-0279. ▸ Explores parallels in 2 Isaiah with Iranian religious beliefs. Discusses Zoroastrian notion of creator god and its parallels in Hebrew scriptures. [MWW]

5.492 David Stronach. "Notes on religion in Iran in the seventh and sixth centuries BC." In *Orientalia J. Duchesne-Guillemin Emerito Oblata*, pp. 479–90. Leiden: Brill, 1984. (Acta Iranica, Deuxième série, Hommages et opera minora, 23.) ISBN 90-683-1002-X. ▸ Discussion of Iranian religion in context of archaeological remains at Tepe Nush-i Jan in northwestern Iran, and temples recovered there. Relation of these finds to evidence from time of Darius I (522–486 BCE). [MWW]

Art and Archaeology

5.493 Pierre Amiet. *Elam.* Paris: Centre National de la Recherche Scientifique, 1966. ▸ Examination of various artifacts recovered from all periods of Elamite history, ca. 3000–550 BCE. Many plates; excellent visual guide. [MWW]

5.494 Malcolm A. R. Colledge. *Parthian art.* Ithaca, N.Y.: Cornell University Press, 1977. ISBN 0-8014-1111-4. ▸ Survey of Parthian architecture, sculpture, style, and iconography, 250 BCE–224 CE. Good handbook. [MWW]

5.495 Ann E. Farkas. *Achaemenid sculpture.* Istanbul: Nederlands Historisch-Archaeologisch Instituut in het Nabije Oosten, 1974. (Uitgaven van het Nederlands Historisch-Archaeologisch Instituut te Istanbul, 33.) ▸ Extensive survey of Achaemenid art and architecture, concentrating on reigns of Cyrus through Xerxes (550–465 BCE). Many plates; general bibliography. [MWW]

5.496 R. W. Ferrier, ed. *The arts of Persia.* New Haven: Yale University Press, 1989. ISBN 0-300-03987-5. ▸ Brief historical surveys for each major period of Iran, including Elam (ca. 3000–550 BCE), Achaemenid (550–330 BCE), Parthian (250 BCE–224 CE), and Sasanian empires (224–651 CE). Superb plates. [MWW]

5.497 Percy Gardner. *The coinage of Parthia.* 1877 ed. San Diego, Calif.: Malter-Westerfield, 1968. ▸ Outline of Parthian history, 250 BCE–224 CE, and discussion of monetary standard. Traces development and types of coinage used by each of various Parthian rulers. Good handbook. [MWW]

5.498 Robert Göbl. *Sasanian numismatics.* Paul Severin, trans. Braunschweig: Klinkhardt & Biermann, 1971. ▸ Detailed examination of coin types and denominations used throughout Sasanian period, 224–651 CE. Good resource. [MWW]

5.499 Prudence O. Harper, Joan Aruz, and Françoise Tallon, eds. *The royal city of Susa: ancient Near Eastern treasures in the Louvre.* New York: Abrams for Metropolitan Museum of Art, 1992. ISBN 0-8109-6422-8. ▸ Exhibition catalog; survey of ancient Iranian city of Susa, prehistory to Achaemenid period, as revealed by artifacts uncovered there. Analysis of individual pieces by period. Excellent photographs; comprehensive bibliography. [MWW]

5.500 Ernst Herzfeld. *Iran in the ancient East: archaeological studies presented in the Lowell Lectures at Boston.* 1941 ed. New York: Hacker, 1988. ISBN 0-87817-308-0. ▸ Collection of lectures covering archaeology of Iran, prehistory through Sasanian empire (224–651 CE). Well illustrated. [MWW]

5.501 Frank Hole, ed. *The archaeology of western Iran: settlement and society from prehistory to the Islamic conquest.* Washington, D.C.: Smithsonian Institution Press, 1987. ISBN 0-87474-526-8. ▸ Survey of major archaeological sites. Places individual sites in framework of whole of western Iran. Excellent overview. [MWW]

5.502 Jean-Louis Huot. *Persia.* Vol. 1: *From the origins to the Achaemenids.* H.S.B. Harrison, trans. Cleveland: World, 1965. ▸ Survey of archaeological research in Iran. Traces Iranian art and archaeology from prehistory through Achaemenid empire. Good introduction. [MWW]

5.503 Friedrich Krefter. *Persepolis Rekonstruktionen.* Berlin: Mann, 1971. ISBN 3-7861-2189-3. ▸ Excellent source containing reconstructions of how ancient city of Persepolis (sixth to fourth century BCE) looked in its time. Based on examination of archaeological remains. Good teaching aid. [MWW]

5.504 Vladimir G. Lukonin. *Persia.* Vol. 2: *From the Seleucids to the Sassanids.* 1967 ed. James Hogarth, trans. London: Barnes & Jenkins, 1970. ▸ Contains brief historical survey, fourth century BCE to seventh century CE, with discussions of social history and excursus on archaeology's contribution to modern scholarship. Many plates; general bibliography. [MWW]

5.505 P.R.S. Moorey. "The Iranian contribution to Achaemenid material culture." *Iran* 23 (1985) 21–37. ISSN 0578-6967. ▸ Examination of Iranian tradition, rather than often discussed Western or Greek influences, in Achaemenid art, 550–330 BCE. [MWW]

5.506 Oscar White Muscarella. "Median art and medizing scholarship." *Journal of Near Eastern studies* 46.2 (1987) 109–27. ISSN 0022-2968. ▸ Discussion of attempts to identify various archaeological finds as examples of Median art, eighth to sixth century BCE. Argues designation currently impossible. [MWW]

5.507 Carl Nylander. *Ionians in Pasargadae: studies in Old Persian architecture.* Stockholm: Almqvist & Wiksell, 1970. (Uppsala studies in ancient Mediterranean and Near Eastern civilizations, 1.) ▸ In-depth examination of architectural methods and tools used in Achaemenid period, based primarily on excavations at Cyrus II's capital, Pasargadae (sixth century BCE). Greek influence discussed. Full references. [MWW]

5.508 Arthur Upham Pope. *Persian architecture.* 1965 ed. London: Oxford University Press, 1971. ISBN 0-19-647629-1. ▸ Examination of architecture in Iran and its continuity through various periods of history, ancient to modern. Chapter 1 treats Elam through Achaemenid period, ca. 3000–330 BCE; chapter 2 surveys Seleucid through Sasanian periods, 311 BCE–651 CE. [MWW]

5.509 Edith Porada. *Ancient Iran: the art of pre-Islamic times.* Baden-Baden: Holle, 1962. ▸ Classic, well-illustrated overview of art in ancient Iran up to Islamic conquest (651 CE). [MWW]

5.510 Margaret Cool Root. *The king and kingship in Achaemenid art: essays on the creation of an iconography empire.* Brill: Leiden, 1979. (Acta Iranica, Troisième série: texte et mémoires, 9.) ISBN 90-04-03902-3, 90-04-05836-2. ▸ Traces and interprets development and expression of royal iconography of Achaemenid empire, 550–330 BCE. Includes select bibliography. Good source. [MWW]

5.511 Denise Schmandt-Besserat, ed. *Ancient Persia: the art of an empire.* Malibu: Undena, 1980. ISBN 0-89003-039-1 (cl), 0-89003-040-5 (pbk). ▸ Collection of articles on various aspects of Achaemenid art, 550–330 BCE. Includes discussions on Persepolis, women in Persian art, Achaemenid influence on later periods, and Greek influence on Achaemenid art. [MWW]

5.512 Erich F. Schmidt. *Persepolis.* 3 vols. Chicago: University of Chicago Press, 1953–70. (Oriental Institute publications, 68–70.) ‣ Excavation report on capital of Achaemenid empire, built by Darius I (522–486 BCE). Volume 1 contains summary of expedition and examination of major monuments and finds. Volumes 2 and 3 detail finds and excavations, Achaemenid through Sasanian (seventh century CE) periods. Superb plates. [MWW]

5.513 Aurel Stern. *Old routes of western Iran: narrative of an archaeological journey carried out and recorded.* 1940 ed. New York: Greenwood, 1969. ISBN 0-8371-2256-2. ‣ Classic work tracing author's travels through Iran, chronicling geography, people, and important ancient sites. Traces parts of Alexander the Great's march through region. [MWW]

5.514 David Stronach. *Pasargadae: a report on the excavations conducted by the British Institute of Persian Studies from 1961 to 1963.* New York: Clarendon, 1978. ISBN 0-19-813190-9. ‣ Excavation report of first capital of Achaemenid empire under Cyrus II (d. 530 BCE). Excellent plates. [MWW]

5.515 Donald N. Wilber. *Persepolis: the archaeology of Parsa, seat of the Persian kings.* Rev. ed. Princeton: Darwin, 1989. ISBN 0-87850-062-6. ‣ Good introduction to archaeology of Persepolis, capital of Achaemenid empire, 550–330 BCE. Excellent plates. [MWW]

Indo-Aryan and Indo-Iranian Migrations

5.516 T. Burrow. "The proto-Indo-Aryans." *Journal of the Royal Asiatic Society* (1973) 123–40. ISSN 0035-869x. ‣ Exploration of problem of Indo-Aryan–Iranian migrations into ancient Near East and Iran in second and first millennia BCE. Proposed term "proto–Indo-Aryans" (for Indo-Aryans) not generally followed. [MWW]

5.517 I. M. Diakonoff. "Die Arier im vorderen Orient: Ende eines Mythos." *Orientalia,* n.s., 41.1 (1972) 91–120. ISSN 0030-5367. ‣ Downplays presence and influence of Indo-Aryans (forerunners of Iranians in first millennium BCE) in ancient Near East in second millennium BCE. See Mayrhofer 5.521 for opposing view. [MWW]

5.518 Roman Ghirshman. *L'Iran et la migration des Indo-Aryens et des Iraniens.* Leiden: Brill, 1977. ISBN 90-04-04876-6. ‣ Exploration of complex and still unsettled problem of Indo-Iranian migrations into ancient Near East and Iran, second to first millennium BCE. Focuses on archaeological evidence rather than linguistic sources. [MWW]

5.519 Frederik T. Hiebert and C. C. Lamberg-Karlovsky. "Central Asia and the Indo-Iranian borderlands." *Iran* 30 (1992) 1–15. ISSN 0578-6967. ‣ Discussion of archaeological evidence from Central Asia and its bearing on Indo-Iranian migrations into Iran and India. First step in new branch of this scholarship. Integrates recent Russian work on subject. [MWW]

5.520 J. P. Mallory. *In search of the Indo-Europeans: language, archaeology, and myth.* New York: Thames & Hudson, 1989. ISBN 0-500-05052-X. ‣ Excellent introduction to Indo-European problem, approached from primarily archaeological point of view. See especially chapter 2 for Iranians. [MWW]

5.521 Manfred Mayrhofer. *Die Arier im vorderen Orient—ein Mythos?* Vienna: Der Österreichischen Akademie der Wissenschaften, 1974. (Österreichischen Akademie der Wissenschaften: Philosophisch-historische Klasse 294, Paper, 3.) ISBN 3-7001-0078-7. ‣ Discussion of difficult issue of presence of Indo-Aryans (forerunners of Medes and Persians in Iran) in ancient Near East. Argues for important Indo-Aryan role among Hurrians; see Diakonoff 5.517. Full bibliography. [MWW]

5.522 T. Cuyler Young, Jr. "Early Iron Age Iran revisited." In *De l'Indus aux Balkans: recueil à la mémoire de Jean Deshayes.* Jean-Louis Huot, M. Yon, and Y. Calvet, eds., pp. 361–77. Paris: Éditions Recherche sur les Civilisations, 1985. ISBN 2-86538-136-X. ‣ Archaeological discussion of Iranian (i.e., Mede and Persian) migrations into Iran, late second to early first millennium BCE, and problems involved. Full references. [MWW]

EGYPT

General Studies

5.523 William Yewdale Adams. "Doubts about the 'Lost Pharaohs.'" *Journal of Near Eastern studies* 44 (1985) 185–92. ISSN 0022-2968. ‣ Disputes theory that form and ideology of pharaonic Egyptian kingship is Nubian in origin. Suggests relevant evidence does not antedate documented earliest Egyptian pharaohs as theory requires. [DO'C]

5.524 Cyril Aldred. *The Egyptians.* Rev. ed. New York: Thames & Hudson, 1987. ISBN 0-500-27345-6. ‣ Popular but scholarly outline of history and culture to 500 BCE. Well illustrated, especially sensitive to cultural roles of art. [DO'C]

5.525 John Baines. "Literacy and ancient Egyptian society." *Man* 18 (1983) 572–99. ISSN 0025-1496. ‣ Study of writing as historical phenomenon. Concludes writing crucial for self-definition of culture, but not prime mover of social change or stability. [DO'C]

5.526 Abd el-Mohsen Bakir. *Slavery in pharaonic Egypt.* Cairo: Institut Français d'Archéologie Orientale, 1952. (Annales du Service des Antiquités de l'Égypte, Supplement, 18.) ‣ Comprehensive history and analysis of slavery in Egypt. Debatable and outdated in some regards, but remains useful, unique introduction. [DO'C]

5.527 James Henry Breasted. *A history of Egypt: from the earliest times to the Persian conquest.* 1912 2d ed. New York: Scribner's, 1967. ‣ Classic history; outdated but invaluable as brilliant exposition of early twentieth-century approach to ancient Egypt, characterized by search for moral worth. [DO'C]

5.528 Karl W. Butzer. "Physical conditions in eastern Europe, western Asia, and Egypt before the period of agricultural and urban settlement." In *The Cambridge ancient history.* 3d ed. I.E.S. Edwards et al., eds., vol. 1.1, pp. 35–69. Cambridge: Cambridge University Press, 1981. ISBN 0-521-07051-1 (cl), 0-521-29821-0 (pbk). ‣ Focuses on environmental conditions in Egypt and elsewhere before Neolithic period; much of fundamental data relevant to historic periods as well. [DO'C]

5.529 Karl W. Butzer and Leslie G. Freeman. *Early hydraulic civilization in Egypt: a study in cultural ecology.* Chicago: University of Chicago Press, 1976. ISBN 0-226-08634-8 (cl), 0-226-08635-6 (pbk). ‣ Brilliant overview of interactions of environmental and historical change, including discussions of technology, settlement patterns, and demography. Argues for major impact on society of long-term fluctuations in annual Nile flood levels. [DO'C]

5.530 Wolfgang Decker. *Sports and games of ancient Egypt.* Allen Guttmann, trans. New Haven: Yale University Press, 1992. ISBN 0-300-04463-1. ‣ Well-documented discussion of all known sports in ancient Egypt, with perceptive commentary on symbolic aspects. [DO'C]

5.531 R.A.O. Faulkner. "Egyptian military organization." *Journal of Egyptian archaeology* 39 (1953) 32–47. ISSN 0075-4234. ‣ Best available English-language survey of Egyptian military organization through Bronze Age, 3100–1070 BCE. Based on textual sources rather than pictorial sources or military archaeology. [DO'C]

5.532 Alan Henderson Gardiner. *Egypt of the pharaohs: an introduction.* 1961 ed. Oxford: Clarendon, 1966. ISBN 0-19-500267-9 (pbk). ▸ Traditional but excellent historical treatment, descriptive rather than interpretive, emphasizing political history. Especially valuable for frequent, extensive citations from textual sources. [DO'C]

5.533 Paul Ghalioungui. *The physicians of pharaonic Egypt.* Springfield, Va.: United States Department of Commerce, National Technical Information Service, 1983. (Deutsches Archäologisches Institut, Abteilung Kairo, Sonderschrift, 10.) ISBN 3-8053-0600-8. ▸ Best, recent, descriptive history of Egyptian medicine. Substantial bibliography for access to wider literature. [DO'C]

5.534 Lisa Giddy. *Egyptian oases: Bahariya, Dakhla, Farafra, and Kharga during pharaonic times.* Warminster: Aris & Phillips, 1987. ISBN 0-85668-367-1 (pbk). ▸ Exemplary study of western oases and their role in Egyptian history through Bronze Age, 3100–1070 BCE. Covers environment, history, and local peculiarities in their Egyptian-derived culture. [DO'C]

5.535 Nicolas-Christophe Grimal. *A history of ancient Egypt.* Ian Shaw, trans. Cambridge, Mass.: Blackwell, 1992. ISBN 0-631-17472-9. ▸ Recent, well-written history, prehistory to Alexander the Great. Traditional narrative, emphasizing politics and culture, especially monumental sites, rather than society and economy. [DO'C]

5.536 William C. Hayes. "Chronology, 1: Egypt—to the end of the Twentieth Dynasty." In *The Cambridge ancient history.* 3d ed. I.E.S. Edwards et al., eds., vol. 1.1, pp. 173–93. Cambridge: Cambridge University Press, 1981. ISBN 0-521-07051-1 (cl), 0-521-29821-0 (pbk). ▸ Excellent coverage of fundamental textual evidence on Egyptian absolute chronology to ca. 1070 BCE. Still of great value, despite recent disagreements on Egyptian chronology. [DO'C]

5.537 Barry J. Kemp. *Ancient Egypt: anatomy of a civilization.* New York: Routledge, 1989. ISBN 0-415-01281-3. ▸ Detailed, provocative discussion of all phases of Bronze Age history, 3100–1070 BCE. Special emphasis on interactions between ideology, economy, and social structure, with emphasis on archaeological evidence unprecedented in Egyptological historiography. [DO'C]

5.538 Kenneth Kitchen. "The basics of Egyptian chronology in relation to the Bronze Age" and "Supplementary note." In *High, middle or low? Acts of an international colloquium on absolute chronology held at the University of Gothenberg, 20th–22nd August 1987.* Part 1, pp. 37–55, 152–59. Gothenberg: Åström, 1987. ISBN 91-86098-64-0. ▸ Good general discussion of Egyptian chronology and its associated problems. [DO'C]

5.539 David Lorton. *The juridical terminology of international relations in Egyptian texts through Dynasty XVIII.* Baltimore: Johns Hopkins University Press, 1974. ISBN 0-8018-1535-5. ▸ Important study of historical value of Egyptian terminology in foreign relations. International system with force of law existed, but was unenforceable. Somewhat technical in presentation. [DO'C]

5.540 Mohamed Gamal el-Din Mokhtar, ed. *Ancient civilizations of Africa.* Vol. 2 of *General history of Africa: UNESCO International Scientific Committee for the Drafting of a General History of Africa.* Paris, Berkeley, and Oxford: UNESCO, University of California Press, and Heinemann, 1981. ISBN 92-3-101708-X, 0-520-03913-0, 0-435-94085-9 (cl), 0-435-94806-7 (pbk). ▸ Numerous essays by recognized experts systematically covering Egypt and Nubia, prehistory to Christian period. Valuable introduction. [DO'C]

5.541 William J. Murnane. *Ancient Egyptian coregencies.* Chicago: University of Chicago, Oriental Institute, 1977. (Studies in ancient Oriental civilization, 40.) ISBN 0-918986-03-6, ISSN 0081-7554. ▸ Thorough, critical review of all available evidence on co-regencies (formally shared kingship) from early times to Ptolemaic period. Includes detailed discussion of co-regency's role in limiting factionalism and civil war. [DO'C]

5.542 Donald B. Redford. *Egypt, Canaan, and Israel in ancient times.* Princeton: Princeton University Press, 1992. ISBN 0-691-03606-3. ▸ Broad, sweeping discussion of Egyptian relations with western Asia, prehistory to 586 BCE. Fundamental, important work with strong narrative flow and many valuable if sometimes debatable commentaries on specific events, sources, and processes. Primary emphasis on relations with Palestine and Syria. [DO'C]

5.543 Donald B. Redford. *Pharaonic king-lists, annals, and day-books: a contribution to the study of the Egyptian sense of history.* Mississauga, Ont.: Benben, 1986. (Society for the Study of Egyptian Archaeology publication, 4.) ISBN 0-920168-08-6 (cl), 0-920168-07-8 (pbk). ▸ Fundamental study of sources reflective of historical consciousness in all phases of Egyptian history. Covers Egyptian awareness of historical past and efforts to reinterpret or deny it. Detailed discussion of history of third-century BCE priest, Manetho, a primary chronological source. [DO'C]

5.544 Bruce G. Trigger et al., eds. *Ancient Egypt: a social history.* New York: Cambridge University Press, 1983. ISBN 0-521-24080-8 (cl), 0-521-28427-9 (pbk). ▸ Only available study of Egyptian history as social and economic phenomenon, deemphasizing historical narrative and cultural history. Prehistory to Alexander the Great. [DO'C]

5.545 Lana Troy. *Patterns of queenship in ancient Egyptian myth and history.* Uppsala: Universitetet, 1986. (Acta Universitatis Upsaliensis, Boreas, 14.) ISBN 91-554-1919-4, ISSN 0346-6442. ▸ First full-scale study of queenship in Egypt. Ideology rather than history emphasized, but fundamental for understanding queen's role in society and history. [DO'C]

5.546 L.M.J. Zonhoven, ed. *Annual Egyptological bibliography.* Leiden: International Association of Egyptologists with Nederlands Instituut voor het Nabije Oosten, 1948–. ISBN 90-7214-704-9. ▸ Invaluable, complete annual bibliography of all publications relating to ancient Egypt. Extensive sections specifically on history. [DO'C]

Early Dynastic Period, 5000–3000 BCE

5.547 E. J. Baumgartel. "Predynastic Egypt." In *The Cambridge ancient history.* 3d ed. I.E.S. Edwards et al., eds., vol. 1.1, pp. 463–97. Cambridge: Cambridge University Press, 1981. ISBN 0-521-07051-1 (cl), 0-521-29821-0 (pbk). ▸ Useful introduction to Egyptian prehistory, but now outdated, especially regarding recent discoveries in northern Egypt. [DO'C]

5.548 I.E.S. Edwards. "The Early Dynastic period in Egypt." In *The Cambridge ancient history.* 3d ed. I.E.S. Edwards et al., eds., vol. 1.2, pp. 1–70. Cambridge: Cambridge University Press, 1981. ISBN 0-521-07791-5 (cl), 0-521-29822-9 (pbk). ▸ Detailed coverage of Egypt during First and Second dynasties (2920–2649 BCE), period of fundamental importance in evolution of society and culture. Outdated in part, but remains valuable introduction. [DO'C]

5.549 Walter Bryan Emery. *Archaic Egypt.* 1961 ed. Baltimore: Penguin, 1974. ISBN 0-14-020462-8 (pbk). ▸ Political and cultural history of Egypt's First and Second dynasties (2920–2649 BCE). Straightforward, comprehensive study, with substantial coverage of crucial archaeological evidence. Requires revision but remains valuable introduction. [DO'C]

5.550 Michael A. Hoffman. *Egypt before the pharaohs: the prehistoric foundations of Egyptian civilization.* Rev. ed. Austin: University of Texas Press, 1991. ISBN 0-292-72073-4. ⁃ Exhaustive, accessible introduction to Egyptian prehistory and Egypt's earliest dynasties. Outdated in detail but remains valuable introduction, unusual for its anthropological perspective. [DO'C]

5.551   John A. Wilson. *The culture of ancient Egypt.* 1951 ed. Chicago: University of Chicago Press, 1956. ISBN 0-226-90152-1 (pbk). ⁃ Extraordinary, fascinating analysis of causation for historical stasis and change, especially in Old Kingdom and First Intermediate period (2575–2040 BCE). Of enduring value, although highly debatable in part. [DO'C]

Old Kingdom, 2575–2134 BCE

5.552   Klaus Baer. *Rank and title in the Old Kingdom: the structure of the Egyptian administration in the Fifth and Sixth dynasties.* Chicago: University of Chicago Press, 1960. ISBN 0-226-03412-7. ⁃ Historically useful but technical study of ranking, or variable status of, officials' titles in Old Kingdom. Important observations on royal manipulation of political system by means of ranking adjustments. [DO'C]

5.553   Margaret S. Drower. "Syria before 2200 B.C." In *The Cambridge ancient history.* 3d ed. I.E.S. Edwards et al., eds., vol. 2.1, pp. 328–62. Cambridge: Cambridge University Press, 1981. ISBN 0-521-07791-5 (cl), 0-521-29822-9 (pbk). ⁃ Discussion of Egyptian relations with Byblos and Egyptian activity in Sinai and Palestine, by professional historian. Develops important historical themes in coherent fashion. [DO'C]

5.554   Christopher Eyre. "Work and the organisation of work in the Old Kingdom." In *Labor in the Ancient Near East.* Marvin A. Powell, ed., pp. 5–48. New Haven: American Oriental Society, 1987. (American Oriental series, 68.) ISBN 0-940490-68-4. ⁃ Exhaustive coverage of all relevant aspects of data. Descriptive rather than interpretive but with important observations. Covers organization; royal and private patronage; and wages, trade, and markets. [DO'C]

5.555   Hans Goedicke. "Cult-temple and state during the Old Kingdom in Egypt." In *State and temple economy in the ancient Near East.* Edward Lipiński, ed., vol. 1, pp. 113–31. Louvain: Département Orientalistiek, 1979. (Orientalia Lovaniensia analecta, 5–6.) ISBN 90-70192-03-9 (set). ⁃ Socioeconomic history arguing local temples rarely received royal support in early Old Kingdom, but that priests did so in Fifth Dynasty, and local temples later won economic independence from crown in return for support of individual pharaohs. [DO'C]

5.556   Naguib Kanawati. *The Egyptian administration in the Old Kingdom: evidence on its economic decline.* Warminster: Aris & Phillips, 1977. ISBN 0-85668-102-4. ⁃ Study of Old Kingdom administration and economy based on tomb-size analysis. Provides statistical basis for estimating wealth of different levels of bureaucracy. Individual wealth decreased as bureaucracy increased in size. [DO'C]

5.557   Mark Lehner. "The development of the Giza necropolis: the Khufu project." *Mitteilungen des Deutschen Archäologischen Instituts, Abteilung Kairo* 41 (1985) 109–143. ISSN 0342-1279. ⁃ Original, well-researched analysis of development of Giza pyramid site (Fourth Dynasty, 2575–5465 BCE), with important historical implications for organizational resources of contemporary state. [DO'C]

5.558   William Stevenson Smith. "The Old Kingdom in Egypt and the beginning of the First Intermediate period." In *The Cambridge ancient history.* 3d ed. I.E.S. Edwards et al., eds., vol. 1.2, pp. 145–207. Cambridge: Cambridge University Press, 1981. ISBN 0-521-07791-5 (cl), 0-521-29822-9 (pbk). ⁃ Idiosyncratic treatment of early historic Egypt. Much useful material and valuable insights, but conveys little sense of evolving society. [DO'C]

5.559   Nigel Strudwick. *The administration of Egypt in the Old Kingdom: the highest titles and their holders.* London: Kegan Paul International, 1985. ISBN 0-7103-0107-3. ⁃ Most thorough analysis to date of central government organization in Old Kingdom. Often technical and detailed, but comes to broad and useful historical conclusions. [DO'C]

First Intermediate Period, 2134–2040 BCE

5.560   B. Bell. "The Dark Ages in ancient history. Part 1: The first Dark Age in Egypt." *American journal of archaeology* 75 (1971) 1–26. ISSN 0002-9114. ⁃ Valuable synthesis presenting thesis that environmental change (increased aridity, decreased Nile inundation) caused historical change and social disorder in First Intermediate period. Undue reliance on ancient literary exaggerations and outdated chronology of relevant sources. [DO'C]

5.561   William A. Ward. *Egypt and the East Mediterranean world, 2200–1900 B.C.: studies in Egyptian foreign relations during the First Intermediate period.* Beirut: American University of Beirut, 1971. ISBN 0-86685-031-7. ⁃ Important study of supposed western Asiatic invasion of Egypt after Old Kingdom; concludes contacts limited and Asiatic impact slight in reality. Includes discussion of Egyptian-Aegean relations. [DO'C]

Middle Kingdom, 2040–1640 BCE

5.562   B. Bell. "Climate and the history of Egypt: the Middle Kingdom." *American journal of archaeology* 79 (1975) 223–69. ISSN 0002-9114. ⁃ Drop in annual inundation level increased social instability and caused rapid turnover in pharaohs as each failed as "rain-maker" in late Middle Kingdom. [DO'C]

5.563   A. Rosalie David. *The pyramid builders of ancient Egypt: a modern investigation of pharaoh's workforce.* New York: Routledge & Kegan Paul, 1986. ISBN 0-7100-9909-6. ⁃ Useful introduction to best-documented Middle Kingdom community, "pyramid town" of Kahun (ca. 1640 BCE). Covers town plan, religion, daily life, and foreign elements. [DO'C]

5.564   William G. Dever. "Relations between Syria-Palestine and Egypt in the 'Hyksos' period." In *Palestine in the Bronze and Iron ages: papers in honor of Olga Tufnell.* Jonathan N. Tubb, ed., pp. 69–87. London: University of London, Institute of Archaeology, 1985. (University of London, Institute of Archaeology occasional publication, 11.) ISBN 0-905853-15-6 (pbk), ISSN 0141-8505. ⁃ Important study of Canaanite (Middle Bronze IIA–C) relations with Egypt. Includes significant criticism of Bietak's proposals (5.570) to lower Syro-Palestinian archaeological chronology by reference to Tell el-Dab'a. [DO'C]

5.565   William G. Dever. "Tell el-Dab'a and Levantine Middle Bronze Age chronology: a rejoinder to Manfred Bietak." *Bulletin of the American Schools of Oriental Research* 281 (1991) 73–79. ISSN 0003-097X. ⁃ New criticism of Bietak's arguments (5.570) for using Tell el-Dab'a evidence to lower Middle Bronze Age Syro-Palestinian archaeological chronology. [DO'C]

5.566   William C. Hayes. "The Middle Kingdom in Egypt." In *The Cambridge ancient history.* 3d ed. I.E.S. Edwards et al., eds., vol. 1.2, pp. 464–531. Cambridge: Cambridge University Press, 1981. ISBN 0-521-07791-5 (cl), 0-521-29822-9 (pbk). ⁃ Excellent mix of data and narrative, based on unrivaled knowledge of period. Remains best historical treatment of Middle Kingdom. [DO'C]

5.567   Stephen Quirke. *The administration of Egypt in the late Middle Kingdom: the hieratic documents.* New Malden: SIA, 1990. ISBN 1-872561-01-2. ⁃ Somewhat technical but historically useful study of rarely studied phase of Egyptian governance. Argues for oligarchic system. [DO'C]

5.568   Herbert Eustis Winlock. *The rise and fall of the Middle*

Kingdom in Thebes. New York: Macmillan, 1947. ▸ Old but only in-depth discussion of complex historical circumstances opening and closing Middle Kingdom. Requires revision, but powerful interrelating of archaeological and historical sources. [DO'C]

Second Intermediate Period, 1640–1532 BCE

5.569 Manfred Bietak. *Avaris and Piramesse: archaeological exploration in the eastern Nile Delta*. London: Oxford University Press for British Academy, 1981. (Proceedings of the British Academy, 65.) ISBN 0-85672-201-4. ▸ Overview of results and historical significance of excavation at Tell el-Dab'a, capital of Hyksos (Canaanite) overlords of northern Egypt (ca. 1600–1532 BCE). Outdated by subsequent discoveries, but remains useful introduction. [DO'C]

5.570 Manfred Bietak. "Egypt and Canaan during the Middle Bronze Age." *Bulletin of the American Schools of Oriental Research* 281 (1991) 27–79. ISSN 0003-097X. ▸ Fundamental discussion of stratigraphy and historical implications of Tell el-Dab'a, key site for Hyksos (Canaanite) occupation of northern Egypt. Debatable argument for revisions in archaeological chronology of Middle Bronze Syria-Palestine. [DO'C]

5.571 William C. Hayes. "Egypt: from the death of Ammenemes III to Seqenenre II." In *The Cambridge ancient history*. 3d ed. I.E.S. Edwards et al., eds., vol. 2.1, pp. 42–76. Cambridge: Cambridge University Press, 1973. ISBN 0-521-08230-7. ▸ Good historical treatment of period, with notoriously difficult source material (Second Intermediate period: 1640–1532 BCE). Important new material has appeared since; see Smith and Smith 5.573, Trigger et al., eds. 5.544, and Bietak 5.570. [DO'C]

5.572 T.G.H. James. "Egypt: from the expulsion of the Hyksos to Amenophis I." In *The Cambridge ancient history*. 3d ed. I.E.S. Edwards et al., eds., vol. 2.1, pp. 289–312. Cambridge: Cambridge University Press, 1973. ISBN 0-521-08230-7. ▸ Good coverage of transition from Second Intermediate period to New Kingdom; still remarkably relevant, except for recent discoveries at Tell el-Dab'a in connection with the Hyksos (Canaanite) occupation of northern Egypt. See also Bietak 5.570. [DO'C]

5.573 H. S. Smith and A. Smith. "A reconsideration of the Kamose texts." *Zeitschrift für ägyptische Sprache und Altertumskunde* 103 (1976) 48–76. ISSN 0044-216X. ▸ Best available translation and commentary on key historical text describing in great detail conflict between pharaoh Kamose (ca. 1555–1550 BCE) and Canaanite (Hyksos) occupiers of northern Egypt. [DO'C]

New Kingdom, 1550–1070 BCE

5.574 William Foxwell Albright. "The Amarna letters from Palestine." In *The Cambridge ancient history*. 3d ed. I.E.S. Edwards et al., eds., vol. 2.2, pp. 98–116. Cambridge: Cambridge University Press, 1981. ISBN 0-521-08691-4 (cl), 0-521-29823-7 (pbk). ▸ Outstanding study of diplomatic correspondence between Egypt and Palestine (known as Amarna letters) primarily during reigns of Amenhotep III and Akhenaten, 1391–1335 BCE. Reconstructs political organization of city-states and tribes of Palestine. [DO'C]

5.575 Cyril Aldred. *Akhenaten, king of Egypt*. New York: Thames & Hudson, 1988. ISBN 0-500-05048-1. ▸ Solid, well-researched study of "heretic" pharaoh, who promoted monotheism (or henotheism) in polytheistic Egypt. Argues for much continuity with past, despite recognized innovations and consequent near anarchy. [DO'C]

5.576 Cyril Aldred. "The Amarna period and the end of the Eighteenth Dynasty." In *The Cambridge ancient history*. 3d ed. I.E.S. Edwards et al., eds., vol. 2.2, pp. 49–97. Cambridge: Cambridge University Press, 1981. ISBN 0-521-08691-4 (cl), 0-521-29823-7 (pbk). ▸ Thorough coverage of Akhenaten and remain-

der of Eighteenth Dynasty. Descriptive rather than analytical, but important observations of Akhenaten's heretical (to traditional religion) innovations. [DO'C]

5.577 Morris L. Bierbrier. *The tomb-builders of the pharaohs*. London: British Museum Publications, 1982. ISBN 0-7141-8044-0. ▸ Highly accessible study of Egypt's best-documented community, artisans of royal tombs living at Deir el Medineh (1550–1070 BCE). Discusses labor organization, social life, and religion. [DO'C]

5.578 G.P.F. van den Boorn. *The duties of the vizier: civil administration in the early New Kingdom*. London: Kegan Paul International, 1988. ISBN 0-7103-0330-0. ▸ Dense presentation and often technical exposition of primary source on New Kingdom governance. Invaluable insight into governmental process; reaches important historical conclusions. [DO'C]

5.579 Betsy M. Bryan. *The reign of Thutmose IV*. Baltimore: Johns Hopkins University Press, 1991. ISBN 0-8018-4202-6. ▸ Rare in-depth study of individual Eighteenth Dynasty pharaoh, Thutmosis IV (1401–1391 BCE). Model of its kind; detailed discussion of each category of evidence and its implications. [DO'C]

5.580 Jaroslav Černý. *A community of workmen at Thebes in the Ramesside period*. Cairo: Institut Français d'Archéologie Orientale, 1973. (Bibliothèque d'étude, 50.) ISBN 0255-0962. ▸ Classic though incomplete study of artisans of royal tomb at Deir el Medineh (1550–1070 BCE), best-documented community of Bronze Age Egypt. [DO'C]

5.581 Jaroslav Černý. "Egypt: from the death of Ramesses III to the end of the Twenty-First Dynasty." In *The Cambridge ancient history*. 3d ed. I.E.S. Edwards et al., eds., vol. 2.2, pp. 606–57. Cambridge: Cambridge University Press, 1981. ISBN 0-521-08691-4 (cl), 0-521-29823-7 (pbk). ▸ Excellent treatment of complex, relatively poorly documented period (later Twentieth Dynasty and earlier Third Intermediate period, 1163–712 BCE). Displays sensitivity to social as well as political issues; provides significant insight into several important sources. [DO'C]

5.582 Christiane Desroches-Noblecourt. *Tutankhamen: life and death of a pharaoh*. 1964 ed. Garden City, N.Y.: Doubleday, 1965. ▸ Extensive coverage of Tutankhamen's reign and its cultural and ideological setting. Insightful if sometimes debatable commentary on symbolism of this pharaoh's burial goods. [DO'C]

5.583 Margaret S. Drower. "Syria, c. 1550–1400 B.C." In *The Cambridge ancient history*. 3d ed. I.E.S. Edwards et al., eds., vol. 2.1, pp. 417–525. Cambridge: Cambridge University Press, 1973. ISBN 0-521-08230-7. ▸ Masterly treatment of complex cultural and political picture, including much discussion of Egyptian policies and activities in key region of Syria and its environs for most of Eighteenth Dynasty. [DO'C]

5.584 William F. Edgerton. "The government and the governed in the Egyptian empire." *Journal of Near Eastern studies* 6.3 (1947) 152–60. ISSN 0002-2968. ▸ Classic exposition of governmental structure and political attitudes of populace in New Kingdom Egypt. [DO'C]

5.585 Christopher Eyre. "Work and the organisation of work in the New Kingdom." In *Labor in the ancient Near East*. Marvin A. Powell, ed., pp. 167–222. New Haven: American Oriental Society, 1987. (American Oriental series, 68.) ISBN 0-940490-68-4. ▸ Exhaustive coverage, descriptive rather than interpretive. Includes much discussion of royal artisans (Deir el Medineh) but also others. Discusses slaves and prisoners of war as well as regular labor. [DO'C]

5.586 R.A.O. Faulkner. "Egypt: from the inception of the Nineteenth Dynasty to the death of Ramesses III." In *The Cambridge ancient history*. 3d ed. I.E.S. Edwards et al., eds., vol. 2.2, pp. 217–51. Cambridge: Cambridge University Press, 1981. ISBN

0-521-08691-4 (cl), 0-521-29823-7 (pbk). ▸ Descriptive, well-researched, but disappointingly short treatment of important and richly documented Ramesside period (Nineteenth and earlier Twentieth dynasties, 1307–1163 BCE). See also Kitchen 5.598. [DO'C]

5.587 P. Frandsen. "Egyptian imperialism." In *Power and propaganda: a symposium on ancient empires.* Mogens Trolle Larsen, ed., pp. 167–90. Copenhagen: Akademisk Forlag, 1979. (Mesopotamia, 7.) ISBN 87-500-1878-7. ▸ Comparison of New Kingdom imperialism in Syria-Palestine and Nubia. In former, Egypt built on existing political organization; in latter, sought conscious egyptianization and economic integration. [DO'C]

5.588 Hans Goedicke, ed. *Perspectives on the battle of Kadesh.* Baltimore: Halgo, 1985. ISBN 0-9613805-1-9 (pbk). ▸ Four important studies of Ramesses II's battle against Hittites at Qadesh, one of best-documented battles in Near East. Some find new historical insights, others compare variable reliability of different textual and pictorial sources. [DO'C]

5.589 William C. Hayes. "Egypt: internal affairs from Tuthmosis I to the death of Amenophis III." In *The Cambridge ancient history.* 3d ed. I.E.S. Edwards et al., eds., vol. 2.1, pp. 313–416. Cambridge: Cambridge University Press, 1973. ISBN 0-521-08230-7. ▸ Historical narrative and systemic analysis of enduring value of Eighteenth Dynasty Egypt. Includes consideration of roles of priesthood, army, and civil bureaucracy, as well as economic structure. [DO'C]

5.590 Thomas Garnet Henry James. *Pharaoh's people: scenes from life in imperial Egypt.* Chicago: University of Chicago Press, 1984. ISBN 0-226-39193-0. ▸ Social history of mid-Eighteenth Dynasty. Lively and informative; covers literacy, governance, agriculture, technology, and housing. Notable, lavish use of newly retranslated texts. [DO'C]

5.591 Jac J. Janssen. "Agrarian administration in Egypt during the Twentieth Dynasty." *Bibliotheca Orientalis* 43 (1986) 351–66. ISSN 0006-1913. ▸ Important review article summarizing important Russian work by I. A. Stuchevsky on agrarian administration in New Kingdom, relating it to other studies and theories on Egyptian economy. [DO'C]

5.592 Jac J. Janssen. *Commodity prices from the Ramesside period: an economic study of the village of Necropolis workmen at Thebes.* Leiden: Brill, 1975. ISBN 90-04-04211-3. ▸ Most detailed study to date of economic aspects of exceptionally well-documented community, artisans of Deir el Medineh. Scrupulous scholarship, judicious but rewarding use of economic anthropology. [DO'C]

5.593 Jac J. Janssen. "Prolegomena to the study of Egypt's economic history during the New Kingdom." *Studien zur altägyptischen Kultur* 3 (1975) 127–85. ISSN 0340-2215, ISBN 3-87-118212-5. ▸ Important overview of all aspects of New Kingdom economic history by leading expert. Valuable commentary on limitations of data and suggestions for future research. Argues for primarily redistributive economy with little free-market activity. [DO'C]

5.594 Jac J. Janssen. "The role of the temple in the Egyptian economy during the New Kingdom." In *State and temple economy in the ancient Near East.* Edward Lipiński, ed., vol. 2, pp. 505–16. Louvain: Département Orientalistiek, 1979. (Orientalia Lovaniensia analecta, 5–6.) ISBN 90-70192-03-9 (set). ▸ Important study of New Kingdom temples, suggesting they were state agencies, exempt from taxation, but nevertheless still economically useful to pharaoh, since he had full access to temple resources. [DO'C]

5.595 Ahmed Kadry. "Officers and officials in the New Kingdom." *Studia Aegyptica* 8 (1982). ISSN 0324-4164. ▸ Survey of military's historical role in New Kingdom. Initially, military and civil bureaucracies competed with each other for economic

advantages; later, military elite and ecclesiastical establishment developed close political and ideological relations, to their mutual economic benefit. [DO'C]

5.596 Sally L. D. Katary. *Land tenure in the Ramesside period.* New York: Routledge, Chapman & Hall for Kegan Paul, 1989. ISBN 0-7103-0298-3. ▸ Computerized analysis of Wilbour Papyrus, chief source on land tenure. Provides rich new data on economic system and social structure of New Kingdom Egypt. Dense presentation. [DO'C]

5.597 Barry J. Kemp. "Imperialism and empire in New Kingdom Egypt." In *Imperialism in the ancient world: the Cambridge University research seminar in ancient history.* P.D.A. Garnsey and C. R. Whittaker, eds., pp. 7–57, 284–97, 368–73. Cambridge: Cambridge University Press, 1978. ISBN 0-521-21882-9. ▸ Thoughtful discussion of organization and economy of New Kingdom empire in Palestine and Nubia. Sees Egypt's basic motivations as "glory" and only secondarily economic return. [DO'C]

5.598 Kenneth A. Kitchen. *Pharaoh triumphant: the life and times of Ramesses II, king of Egypt.* Warminster: Aris & Phillips, 1983. ISBN 0-85668-215-2 (pbk). ▸ Lively history, valuable to scholar and public. Superbly researched, covers all aspects of Ramesses' reign and its broader social and religious milieux. [DO'C]

5.599 Anthony Leahy. *Libya and Egypt, c. 1300–750 B.C.* London: School of Oriental and African Studies, Centre of Near and Middle Eastern Studies and the Society for Libyan Studies, 1990. ISBN 0-7286-0174-5. ▸ Diverse essays on historical roles of Libyans in New Kingdom and Third Intermediate period (1550–664 BCE). Includes most comprehensive study available (O'Connor) of Late Bronze Age Libyans. [DO'C]

5.600 Peter der Manuelian. *Studies in the reign of Amenophis II.* Hildesheim: Gerstenberg, 1987. ISBN 3-8067-8105-2. ▸ Rare study of specific pharaoh (1427–1401 BCE). Positive reading of military record and good treatment of internal government. [DO'C]

5.601 Andrea Griet McDowell. *Jurisdiction in the workmen's community of Deir el-Medina.* Leiden: Nederlands Instituut voor het Nabije Oosten, 1990. (Egyptologischen uitgaven, 5.) ISBN 90-625-8205-2. ▸ Study of aspects of legal practices within best-documented New Kingdom community, Deir el Medinah. Sensitive to law as social process, rather than abstract theory. [DO'C]

5.602 R. Morkot. "The empty years of Nubian history: Egypt, the centre of the problem." In *Centuries of darkness: a challenge to the conventional chronology of Old World archaeology.* 1991 ed. Peter James et al., eds., pp. 204–19, 220–60. New Brunswick, N.J.: Rutgers University Press, 1993. ISBN 8135-1950-0. ▸ Revisionist study of Late Bronze Age and post–Bronze Age chronology, arguing for Twentieth Dynasty ending ca. 825 BCE instead of 1070 BCE. Far-ranging implications for chronologies elsewhere, but conclusions highly debatable. [DO'C]

5.603 William J. Murnane. *The road to Kadesh: a historical interpretation of the battle reliefs of King Sety I at Karnak.* 2d ed. Chicago: University of Chicago, Oriental Institute, 1990. (Studies in ancient Oriental civilization, 42.) ISBN 0-918986-43-5 (pbk), ISSN 0081-7554. ▸ Excellent discussion of Egyptian relations with Hittites to peace treaty with Ramesses II (1290–1224 BCE). Focuses on role of pictorial material as historical evidence. [DO'C/JDM]

5.604 Donald B. Redford. *Akhenaten: the heretic king.* Princeton: Princeton University Press, 1984. ISBN 0-691-03567-9. ▸ Lively, well-researched study of pharaoh and his historical and cultural setting by recognized authority. Includes valuable evidence from recent excavations, but attitude toward Akhenaten controversially harsh. [DO'C]

5.605 Donald B. Redford. *History and chronology of the Eighteenth Dynasty of Egypt: seven studies.* Toronto: University of

Toronto Press, 1967. ▸ Essays on important aspects of Eighteenth Dynasty history (1550–1307 BCE). Some highly technical; but distinguished historical treatments of pharaohs Ahmose and Hatshepsut, rare female pharaoh. [DO'C]

5.606 Nicholas Reeves. *The complete Tutankhamun: the king, the tomb, the royal treasure.* New York: Thames & Hudson, 1990. ISBN 0-500-05058-9. ▸ Lavishly illustrated, superbly researched account of Tutankhamen. Discusses tomb and its contents and circumstances of their discovery. [DO'C]

5.607 Alan R. Schulman. *Military rank, title, and organization in the Egyptian New Kingdom.* Berlin: Hessling, 1964. ▸ Most thorough study of New Kingdom army. Covers all ranks; discusses pictorial and textual sources and *comparanda* from Assyrian texts. [DO'C]

5.608 Anthony J. Spalinger. *Aspects of the military documents of the ancient Egyptians.* New Haven: Yale University Press, 1982. (Yale Near Eastern researches, 9.) ISBN 0-300-02381-2. ▸ Substantial introduction to military records of New Kingdom as well as Twenty-Fifth and Twenty-Sixth dynasties (770–525 BCE). Discusses sources and literary implications of genre. [DO'C]

5.609 George Steindorff and Keith C. Seele. *When Egypt ruled the East.* 1957 rev. ed. Chicago: University of Chicago Press, 1966. ISBN 0-226-77199-7 (pbk). ▸ Classic study of Egypt's New Kingdom foreign relations, especially with western Asia. Outdated in detail but rich in insight and illuminating perspectives. [DO'C]

Third Intermediate Period, 1070–712 BCE

5.610 I.E.S. Edwards. "Egypt: from the Twenty-Second to the Twenty-Fourth Dynasty." In *The Cambridge ancient history.* 2d ed. John Boardman et al., eds., vol. 3.1, pp. 534–81. Cambridge: Cambridge University Press, 1982. ISBN 0-521-22496-9 (pbk). ▸ Well-documented study of Third Intermediate period to Twenty-Fifth Dynasty (1070–712 BCE). Descriptive rather than interpretive, but invaluable source of information. [DO'C]

5.611 Kenneth A. Kitchen. *The Third Intermediate period in Egypt, 1100–650 B.C.* 2d ed. Warminster: Aris & Phillips, 1986. ISBN 0-85668-298-5 (pbk). ▸ Magisterial study of very complicated but historically fascinating period. First half highly technical, but second half provides excellent history of fundamental importance. [DO'C]

Late Period, 713–323 BCE

5.612 Edda Bresciani. "The Persian occupation of Egypt." In *Cambridge history of Iran.* Ilya Gershevitch, ed., vol. 2, pp. 502–28. Cambridge: Cambridge University Press, 1985. ISBN 0-521-20091-1. ▸ Comprehensive overview of Egypt under Persian occupation, 525–332 BCE. Historical outline and discussions of administration, economy, art, and religion. Valuable analysis of complex history of Twenty-Eighth through Thirtieth dynasties. [DO'C]

5.613 Mary F. Gyles. *Pharaonic policies and administration, 663 to 323 B.C.* Chapel Hill: University of North Carolina Press, 1959. ▸ Comprehensive study of rarely discussed period, Twenty-Sixth through Thirtieth dynasties (663–323 BCE). Concentrates on administrative policy, which occupying foreign powers were reluctant to change, and royal ideology. [DO'C]

NUBIA

5.614 William Yewdale Adams. *Nubia: corridor to Africa.* Princeton: Princeton University Press, 1977. ISBN 0-691-09370-9. ▸ Invaluable, comprehensive study of Nubian history and relations with Egypt, prehistory to modern times. Although sensitive to Nubian achievement, sees Nubia as peripheral to Egypt. [DO'C]

5.615 David O'Connor. *Ancient Nubia: Egypt's rival in Africa.* Philadelphia: University of Pennsylvania, University Museum, 1993. ISBN 0-924171-28-6. ▸ Revisionist history, stressing Nubian political and military resources and deemphasizing Nubia's supposed cultural and economic dependence on Egypt. [DO'C]

5.616 Bruce G. Trigger. *Nubia under the pharaohs.* Boulder: Westview, 1976. ISBN 0-89158-544-3. ▸ Excellent short history of Nubia and its relations with Egypt in Bronze Age, 3100–1070 BCE, from anthropological perspective. Discusses ancient Nubian cultures and Egypt's impact on them. [DO'C]

5.617 Bruce B. Williams. *The A-group royal cemetery at Qustul: cemetery L.* Chicago: University of Chicago, Oriental Institute, 1986. (Oriental Institute, Nubian expedition, Excavations between Abu Simbel and the Sudan Frontier, 3.1.) ISBN 0-918986-46-x. ▸ Excavation report including detailed exposition of controversial theory on Nubian origins of Egyptian pharaonic kingship, rejected by most specialists in Egyptian and Nubian history. [DO'C]

ARABIA AND THE PERSIAN GULF

5.618 Muhammed Abd al-Qadir Bafaqih. *L'unification du Yemen antique: la lutte entre Saba', Himyar, et le Hadramawt du premier au troisième siècle de l'ère chrétienne.* Paris: Geuthner, 1990. ISBN 2-7053-0494-2. ▸ First monograph-length study devoted to complex political history of first centuries CE in Saudi Arabia. Incorporates enormous amount of new material with many long-known sources. [DTP]

5.619 G. W. Bowersock. *Roman Arabia.* Cambridge, Mass.: Harvard University Press, 1983. ISBN 0-674-77755-7. ▸ Standard work on Roman provinces of Arabia. Provides good overview of Nabataean and other Arabian sources pertaining to period of Roman control. [DTP]

5.620 T. Fahd, ed. *L'Arabie préislamique et son environnement historique et culturel: actes du Colloque de Strasbourg, 24–27 juin 1987.* Leiden: Université de Sciences Humaines de Strasbourg; distributed by Brill, 1989. (Travaux du Centre de Recherche sur le Proche-Orient et la Grèce Antique, 10.) ISBN 90-04-09115-7. ▸ Proceedings of international conference on Arabia held in Strasbourg, 1987. Wide-ranging papers touching on many different aspects of archaeology, history, religion, iconography, etc., in all parts of peninsula. [DTP]

5.621 W. Heimple. "Das untere Meer." *Zeitschrift für Assyriologie und vorderasiatische Archäologie* 77 (1987) 22–91. ISSN 0084-5299. ▸ Convenient compilation and evaluation of cuneiform sources dealing with Dilmun, Magan, and Meluhha. Provides up-to-date, reliable translations of all relevant texts. [DTP]

5.622 Haya Ali Al-Khalifa and M. Rice, eds. *Bahrain through the ages: the archaeology.* London: Kegan Paul International, 1986. ▸ Proceedings of international conference on Gulf archaeology held in Bahrain, 1983. Touches on wide range of issues encompassing area from Oman to Kuwait. [DTP]

5.623 Daniel T. Potts. *Arabian Gulf in antiquity.* 2 vols. New York: Oxford University Press, 1990. ISBN 0-19-814390-7 (v. 1), 0-19-814391-5 (v. 2). ▸ Synthesis of archaeology and early history of Gulf region from beginnings of human settlement to Islamic conquest. Covers much historical background of area's relations with its neighbors. Comprehensive bibliography. [DTP]

5.624 Daniel T. Potts. *The pre-Islamic coinage of eastern Arabia.* Njalsgade, Denmark, and Copenhagen: Museum Tusculanum and Carsten Niebuhr Institute, 1991. (Carsten Niebuhr Institute publications, 14.) ISBN 87-7289-156-4, 0902-5499. ▸ First full study of indigenous, pre-Islamic coinage minted in northeastern and southeastern Arabia before Islam. Presents classification and discusses historical implications of finds. [DTP]

5.625 Daniel T. Potts, ed. *Araby the Blest: studies in Arabian archaeology.* Copenhagen: Museum Tusculanum and Carsten Niebuhr Institute, 1988. (Carsten Niebuhr Institute publications, 7.) ISBN 87-7289-051-7, ISSN 0902-5499. ▸ Collection of essays touching on wide variety of topics in Arabian archaeology. Includes studies on Yemen, the Hijaz, northeastern Arabia, and Oman peninsula. [DTP]

5.626 Daniel T. Potts, ed. *Dilmun: new studies in the archaeology and early history of Bahrain.* Berlin: Reimer, 1983. ISBN 3-496-00744-3. ▸ Collection of essays on Dilmun (Bahrain) from its earliest attestation in archaic texts from Uruk (ca. 3400 BCE) to Sasanian period. Covers archaeological, historical, and philological problems. [DTP]

5.627 C. Robin. "L'Arabie antique de Karib'il à Mahomet: nouvelle donnée sur l'histoire de Arabes grace aux inscriptions." *Revue du monde musulman et de la Méditerranée* 61 (1991) 7–166.

ISSN 0035-1474. ▸ Masterly review of recent epigraphic evidence from all parts of Arabia, focusing primarily on South Arabia. Touches on wide variety of topics on social, political, economic, and religious history of peninsula. [DTP]

5.628 J.-F. Salles. "The Arab-Persian Gulf under the Seleucids." In *Hellenism in the East: interaction of Greek and non-Greek civilizations from Syria to Central Asia after Alexander.* Amélie Kuhrt and S. Sherwin-White, eds., pp. 75–184. London: Duckworth, 1987. ISBN 0-520-06054-7. ▸ Synthesis of what is known about Gulf region during Hellenistic period. Sets eastern Arabia in broader context of Seleucid policy in East. [DTP]

5.629 J.-F Salles. "Découvertes du Golfe arabo-persique aux époques grecque et romaine." *Revue des études anciennes* 94.1–2 (1992) 79–97. ISSN 0035-2004. ▸ Review of recent discoveries of Hellenistic and Parthian periods in Gulf region. Discusses these in context of wider history of Near East in Greco-Roman era. [DTP]

MORTIMER CHAMBERS

Ancient Greece to the End of the Hellenistic Period

Greek history rests primarily on the literary sources handed down from antiquity and selected for us, unwittingly, by scribes, grammarians, teachers, and theologians during the Byzantine period. Guided probably by their wishes for the education of their pupils, they preserved many manuscripts of Homer, Plato, Thucydides, and other edifying authors but neglected those whom they considered authors of the second rank (and, unfortunately, nearly all Greek lyric poetry).

Not a few of those neglected were historians, who must therefore rank as "lost" historians. From them we have only quotations in the works of other writers. Any introduction to Greek historiography must therefore salute the genius, learning, and above all the iron determination of Felix Jacoby (1876–1959), who collected the "fragments" (that is, the quotations in other writers) of over 800 "lost" Greek historians in a multivolume set (6.110). Jacoby and his colossal work survived two world wars and his exile, for racial reasons, from Germany; but even he fell short of completing the task, for the quotations from the works of the geographic writers and the school of Aristotle have yet to be compiled (further volumes are planned). Jacoby's great work includes commentaries, but no translations of the fragments; it would be desirable to publish such versions with brief commentaries on some of the better preserved historians that would bring his pioneering editions up to date. This has been done for the historians of Alexander (C. A. Robinson 6.237), and another such venture has appeared, Phillip Harding, *Androtion and the "Atthis"* (Oxford 1994).

The continuous refining of our knowledge through commentaries on and studies of the major historians (Herodotus, Thucydides, Polybius) and smaller historical works such as Aristotle's *Constitution of the Athenians* (this latter has recently had two long commentaries [M. Chambers 6.100; P. J. Rhodes 6.103], while the flow of papers about it never stops) is the fundamental nourishment of scholarship in Greek history. But the ancient historians rarely discuss such themes as the role of women in Greek life, the nature of the family, homosexuality, and laws regarding marriage and inheritance. Older generations of historians by no means neglected such questions; indeed, they laid the groundwork for their successors. But it is right to notice newer work that has continued to ask questions about the structure and inner character of Greek society.

The Athenian state, for example, has often been studied from the point of view of its legal and constitutional development, and this is of course legitimate (C. Hignett 6.332, among others). The work of M. H. Hansen (6.330, 6.331) has continued this kind of inquiry with microscopic accuracy. But books have now appeared on the infrastructure, on how things actually worked, such as R. K. Sinclair's study of participation in Athenian democracy (6.342) and R. Osborne's work on the relationship between the city and countryside in Attica (6.335). Parallel to these is the work of P. Cartledge (6.402) on the regional history of Laconia, which ranges beyond the military history of the Spartans, the champions in Greek warfare.

Questions about population, food supply, and conditions of labor have, naturally, long been asked. In the field of population studies, the work of K. J. Beloch (6.159) remains unreplaced, indeed unchallenged; but specialists have continued to argue about the fluctuating population of Athens (M. H. Hansen 6.374). A wholly original work was the final contribution of R. Meiggs (6.543) on trees and timber in antiquity. The American excavations in the market place of Athens, the *agora*, have led to a series of volumes (6.277) that have shed much new light on urban history in antiquity; and excavations have provided fresh evidence for debate about how the Greeks built cities and temples (R. E. Wycherley 6.474; A. Burford 6.470). The fertile investigations of M. I. Finley at Cambridge produced a school of younger social and economic historians who continue to study the economic questions already asked in the first half of our century, but now with more evidence (see, for example, a collection of Finley's papers, 6.501). Work continues also on the study of literacy within ancient populations (W. V. Harris 6.555; R. Thomas 6.565).

Concerning the role of women, who probably composed half the population of Greek states, a clear advance over all previous feminist studies was the pioneering book of S. B. Pomeroy (6.571), and others have followed her lead in several modern studies of the legal status of women. We have also made progress into something more elusive, the psychology of the Greek attitude toward women, which ranged from the affectionate to the fearful—the reaction of fear toward women is attested by the women in Greek tragedy, who are often far more powerful and dominating than their men.

Beyond the authors left to us from the Middle Ages, we may hope to recover Greek history from the documentary sources. The richest and most dramatic source is the stone inscriptions on which the Greeks recorded treaties, dedications to both gods and human beings, religious regulations and calendars, financial records, and all manner of other public decisions. Athens, the largest Greek city by far, was also the most addicted to setting up such inscriptions; and, since the classical period of Greek history revolves around Athens, its allies, and its rivals, the Athenian inscriptions are both the most informative and the most intensively studied. The queen of Attic inscriptions is the great block (the first of two) that records the portion given to the goddess Athena of payments of tribute to the Athenian empire, 453–439. This *lapis primus* ("first stone") is the main subject of the edition of the Athenian tribute lists (B. D. Meritt et al. 6.313), which offers the year-by-year account, with its fluctuations, of receipts of tribute by the Athenians and constructs on this basis the history of their empire.

The other Athenian inscriptions from the fifth century BCE have recently had a new edition (D. M. Lewis 6.282). Since the marble slabs have seldom survived complete, the art of restoring the lost letters is crucial, and no less so is arriving at a date for a particular document.

One important issue has been the history of the Delian League (which became the Athenian empire), formed on the morrow after the Second Persian War by the Athenians and many smaller Greek states. Our documents confirm the report of Thucydides (I.99), that the Athenians came to exercise a stringent control over the allies. They required their subjects to pay tribute in carefully controlled ways, they imposed humiliating oaths of allegiance on them, and they forbade them to strike coins and made them use Athenian money exclusively.

But when did the more stringent control of the allies by the Athenians begin? The answer to this question must influence critically our grasp of Greek history during its most important period. According to one interpretation, this movement began about 450 BCE and continued into the Peloponnesian War (431–404). Those who hold to this date point to the presence, in some inscriptions related to the Athenian empire, of the letter "sigma" written with only three bars (rather like an angular modern S); it has long been a canonical view that the three-barred sigma was not written in public inscriptions after 446; if this rule is valid, then the documents with the three-barred sigma showing this repressive attitude on the part of the Athenians would be securely dated to the early 440s.

The English historian Harold Mattingly often challenged this doctrine (see especially 6.311) on historical and prosopographic grounds and tried to lower the beginning of repressive imperialism into the 420s, when Cleon and other Athenian demagogues came to the fore. A recent study (M. Chambers et al. 6.303) has confirmed at least part of Mattingly's case by using modern photographic techniques to redate an inscription with the three-barred sigma to 418, forty years later than the date most often accepted by earlier scholars. Since 418 is markedly later than 446, it can no longer be maintained that the three-barred sigma is automatically sufficient to date Athenian inscriptions, and the whole debate about Athenian imperial policy in the middle and late fifth century can thus be reopened.

Athenian inscriptions are by no means the only ones that stream in to provide evidence. For many years Louis Robert, of the Collège de France, published widely in this field and, with his wife Jeanne, reviewed the progress of Greek epigraphy in the equally austere and learned *Bulletin épigraphique* (6.124). The *Bulletin* is now continued by several scholars who take responsibility for reviewing publications of inscriptions in separate fields.

The standard collection of Greek inscriptions (6.120), the successor to the project conceived by the great August Böckh, plods on slowly, and it is now necessary to collect inscriptions from a given area or period in special volumes rather than wait for *Inscriptiones Graecae* to include them. For example, a large number of epigraphic documents from Greek towns in Asia Minor have been edited in a long series of volumes sponsored by the Austrian Academy of Sciences: *Inschriften griechischer Städte aus Kleinasien* (1972–), by many editors (no translations provided). As for documentary papyri, which concern above all the administration of Egypt under the Roman empire, these appear in multiple journals and collections and form a second class of documents that continues to grow in number. A general work on life and letters in the papyri, to replace the still valuable one of J. G. Winter (6.132), is desirable.

In Greek history after the flowering of Athens and its empire, the major figure is Alexander the Great of Macedon; indeed, he is by far the most famous person in all Greek history and overshadows his father, Philip II, on whom important studies have recently appeared. Alexander's historical image is so huge that there were and are conflicting interpretations of his aims and personality. To change general opinion about him is a formidable task, but the work of E. Badian and his pupils and associates has at least made considerable progress toward a reevaluation of the conqueror (see 6.240 and others). W. W. Tarn, a genuinely outstanding British scholar and an aristocrat, had long sponsored the superficially attractive thesis that Alexander was trying to unite mankind into a brotherhood. This unlikely theory rests ultimately on an innocent rhetorical flight in Plutarch, but Tarn's repeated and dogmatic statements in favor of this hypothesis influenced journalists, popular writers, and even a few scholars. The reaction led by Badian since 1958 has portrayed Alexander as a suspicious despot with little self-control, despite his astounding leadership and utter fearlessness. Badian has called him an almost embarrassingly perfect example of a man who conquered the world only to lose his own soul.

In the last centuries of Greek history before the absorption of Greece by the expanding Roman republic, the era known as the Hellenistic period (323–30 BCE), more unplowed territory lies open to the historian than in the thoroughly worked classical age. The political events are largely a complex series of wars among the various kings who held the fragments of Alexander's empire, and social and cultural history claim as much space in recent work as the more traditional battles and constitutions (e.g., E. S. Gruen 6.261; H. Koester 6.263). On the social and economic history of this age, the historian has long had the colossal final work of the greatest ancient historian of his era, M. Rostovtzeff (6.271). In its wake has come the best recent portrayal of this age, on a large canvass, in the work of P. Green (6.260), which in turn is likely to inspire further probing of the period and its many cultural currents.

Finally, we have begun to look backward systematically at our predecessors and to write the history of scholarship: the works of K. Christ (6.153, 6.154), A. Momigliano (6.146), and W. M. Calder III and A. Demandt, eds. (6.150) must be mentioned among others. We see the contemporary issues that concerned the great scholars of the past (see Calder and Demandt, eds. on Eduard Meyer, 6.150), and thus we understand better their approach to history. Often the publication of letters and other documents brings these somewhat remote figures to life.

Turning to the organization of the present chapter, we begin with reference works and geographic manuals. Literary sources follow, but in severe selection. Then come inscriptions and papyri (these are also literary sources, a fact sometimes overlooked) and studies in numismatics. Next are historiography and historical theory, with general histories of Greece including the vast *Cambridge Ancient History* (6.160). Writings on special periods, including that of Alexander the Great, precede treatments of special regions, including Athens and Attica; this last is especially long given the central importance of Athens in Greek history. Then come topical studies on such fields as social and economic history, political institutions, warfare, philosophy, and art and architecture. Many more suggestions for reading are found in such useful compendia as the *Oxford History of Greece and the Hellenistic World* (6.161).

Entries are arranged under the following headings:

[Contributors: CGT = Carol G. Thomas, CMW = Colin M. Wells, CWH = Charles W. Hedrick, DLB = David L. Blank, EB = E. Badian, EMH = Edward M. Harris, GND = Gregory N. Daugherty, JB = John Buckler, JDM = Jon D. Mikalson, JJD = John J. Dobbins, MC = Mortimer Chambers, RAB = Richard A. Billows, RWW = Robert W. Wallace, SMB = Stanley M. Burstein, THC = Thomas H. Carpenter]

REFERENCE WORKS

Bibliographies

6.1 *Ancient Greek literature: classification schedules, classified listing by call number, chronological listing, author and title listing.* Cambridge, Mass.: Harvard University Library, 1979. (Widener Library shelflist, 58.) ISBN 0-674-03310-8. ▸ Classified listing of Greek literature in Widener Library, Harvard University before July 1976. Unique survey. [MC]

6.2 *Ancient history: classification schedules, classified listing by call number, chronological listing, author and title listing.* Cambridge, Mass.: Harvard University Library, 1975. (Widener Library shelflist, 55.) ISBN 0-674-03312-4. ▸ Classified listing of ancient history in Widener Library, Harvard University. Unique survey. [MC]

6.3 *Archaeology: classification schedules, classified listing by call number, chronological listing, author and title listing.* Cambridge, Mass.: Harvard University Library, 1979. (Widener Library shelflist, 56.) ISBN 0-674-04318-9. ▸ Classified listing of archaeology in Widener Library, Harvard University. Unique survey. [MC]

6.4 Hermann Bengtson. *Einführung in die alte Geschichte.* 7th ed. Munich: Beck, 1975. ISBN 3-406-00443-1. ▸ Succinct but learned chapters on various disciplines within ancient history. Sixth edition translated into English, *Introduction to Ancient History*, R. I. Frank and Frank D. Gilliard, trans. (1970). Bibliography largely German, but revised for English translation. [MC]

6.5 "Bibliotheca philologica classica." In *Jahresbericht über die Fortschritte der klassischen Altertumswissenschaft.* Conrad Bursian, ed. Berlin: Calvary, 1874–1945. ▸ Once standard annual bibliography; now replaced by Marouzeau and Ernst, eds. 6.16 and *Lustrum* (6.14). Under heading "Geschichte," contains surveys of various fields; yearbooks have obituaries of major scholars. Indexes to surveys after volume 91 and in volumes 122, 138, 166, 201. [MC]

6.6 Manfred Clauss. *Einführung in die alte Geschichte.* Munich: Beck, 1993. ISBN 3-406-37329-1. ▸ Replaces Bengtson 6.4 with more recent bibliography. [MC]

6.7 Hans-Joachim Drexhage. *Deutschsprachige Dissertationen zur alten Geschichte, 1844–1978.* Wiesbaden: Steiner, 1980. ISBN 3-515-03297-9. ▸ Lists 2,161 dissertations on ancient history, written in German, in universities in Germany (both East and West after World War II), Austria, and Switzerland. Excellent indexes. [EB]

6.8 Wilhelm Engelmann. *Bibliotheca scriptorum classicorum.* 8th ed. 2 vols. E. Preuss, ed. Leipzig: Engelmann, 1880–82. ▸ Bibliography of writings on ancient authors published 1700–1878; now occasionally obsolete. Continued by Klussmann 6.12. [MC]

6.9 Javier L. Facal and Aníbal González. *Repertorium litterarum Graecarum ex codicibus, papyris, epigraphis.* Madrid: Instituto "Antonio de Nebrija" del C.S.I.C., 1982. ISBN 84-300-8374-X (pbk). ▸ Bibliography to Greek sources. List of widely scattered collections of papyri, ostraca (writings on clay potsherds), and inscriptions. [MC]

6.10 Gustav Fock. *Catalogus dissertationum philologicarum classicarum: zusammengestellt von der Zentralstelle für Dissertationen und Programme der Buchhandlung Gustav Fock.* 1910–37 2d–3d ed. New York: Johnson Reprint, 1963. ‣ Catalog listing thousands of German doctoral dissertations on broad range of specialized subjects concerning antiquity through 1936 compiled by German bookseller. [MC]

6.11 *Gnomon.* Munich: Beck, 1925–. ISSN 0017-1417. ‣ International journal of book reviews in Greco-Roman studies; bibliographical "Beilagen" appear four times a year and list recent books and articles in all fields. See also lists of books received in such journals as *Classical Review, Classical Philology,* and *Journal of Hellenic Studies.* [MC]

6.12 Rudolf Klussmann. *Bibliotheca scriptorum classicorum Graecorum et Latinorum: die Literatur von 1878 bis 1896 umfassend.* 2 vols. in 4. Leipzig: Reisland, 1909–13. ‣ Called *Supplementbände,* actually volumes 146, 151, 156, 165 of Bursian, ed. 6.5. Volume 1, Greek authors, volume 2, Roman authors. Excellent, thorough; continued by Lambrino 6.13. [MC]

6.13 Scarlat Lambrino. *Bibliographie de l'antiquité classique.* Part 1: *1896–1914: auteurs et textes.* Paris: Belles Lettres, 1951. ‣ Closes gap between Klussmann 6.12 and Marouzeau 6.15; second part never published. [MC]

6.14 *Lustrum.* Göttingen: Vandenhoeck & Ruprecht, 1956–. ISSN 0024-7421. ‣ Successor to Bursian, ed. 6.5; surveys work in various fields, but no annual bibliography. [MC]

6.15 Jules Marouzeau. *Dix années de bibliographie classique: bibliographie critique et analytique de l'antiquité gréco-latine pour la période 1914–1924.* 1927–28 ed. 2 vols. New York: Franklin, 1969. ‣ Immediate predecessor of and model for Marouzeau and Ernst, eds. 6.16; covers "Auteurs classiques" and "Matières et disciplines." [MC]

6.16 Jules Marouzeau and Juliette Ernst, eds. *L'année philologique: bibliographie critique et analytique de l'antiquité gréco-latine.* Paris: Belles Lettres, 1928–. ISSN 0184-6949. ‣ Standard annual bibliography for classical studies; sections for work on ancient authors and Greco-Roman history, archaeology, and institutions, with brief summaries of articles and references to book reviews. [MC]

6.17 J. A. Nairn. *Classical hand-list.* 1953 3d ed. Oxford: Blackwell, 1960. ‣ Only bibliography for classical studies as a whole. Despite its age, not wholly obsolete; excellent for quick orientation. Unique list of journals showing date of inception. [MC]

Encyclopedias, Dictionaries, and Handbooks

6.18 Klaus Bartels and Ludwig Huber, eds. *Lexikon der alten Welt.* Zurich: Artemis, 1965. ‣ One-volume lexicon comparable to Hammond and Scullard, eds. 6.21, but much larger. [MC]

6.19 Charles Daremberg and Edmond Saglio, eds. *Dictionnaire des antiquités grecques et romaines d'après les textes et les monuments.* 1873–1919 ed. 5 vols. in 10. Paris: Hachette, 1881–1919. ‣ Encyclopedic dictionary, dated but still useful for political and social institutions. [MC]

6.20 Michael Grant and Rachel Kitzinger, eds. *Civilization of the ancient Mediterranean: Greece and Rome.* 3 vols. New York: Scribner's, 1988. ISBN 0-684-17954-0 (cl). ‣ Comprehensive, topically arranged encyclopedia. [SMB]

6.21 N.G.L. Hammond and H. H. Scullard, eds. *The Oxford classical dictionary.* 2d ed. Oxford: Clarendon, 1970. ‣ Basic English-language encyclopedic dictionary of all classical studies; articles by leading scholars of the day, many added or rewritten for second edition. Third edition, enlarged and entirely revised (Simon Hornblower and Antony Spawforth, eds.), to appear 1996. [MC]

6.22 Iwan von Müller et al., eds. *Handbuch der Altertumswissenschaft.* 10 parts in several vols. Munich: Beck, 1885–. ‣ Excellent, detailed surveys by leading scholars on various disciplines in study of antiquity (history, archaeology, literature, religion, etc.) Volumes constantly updated. [MC]

6.23 August Pauly, ed. *Paulys Realencyclopädie der classischen Altertumswissenschaft.* 2d ed. 2 series (A–Q, R–Z) with 15 supplements. Georg Wissowa et al., eds. Konrat Ziegler, final ed. Waldsee, Stuttgart, and Munich: Metzler and Druckenmüller, 1894–1963 (series A–Q), 1914–72 (series R–Z), 1903–78 (suppl.) ‣ First work to consult on any topic; exhaustive articles, ample bibliographies. Monument to a century of classical scholarship undeterred by two world wars. Articles necessarily uneven, but generally authoritative. Commonly known as Pauly-Wissowa or RE. Consult also 6.24. [MC]

6.24 August Pauly, Konrat Ziegler, and Walther Sontheimer, eds. *Der kleine Pauly: Lexikon der Antike.* 1964–75 abr. ed. 5 vols. Munich: Deutsche Taschenbuch, 1979. ISBN 3-423-05963-x. ‣ Newly written articles based on 6.23, compendium of modern scholarship, giving references to ancient sources and essential bibliography. Standard work, often more up-to-date than 6.23. [MC]

Cartography, Atlases, and Geographies

6.25 Hermann Bengtson and Vladimir Milojčić, eds. *Grosser historischer Weltatlas.* Part 1: *Vorgeschichte und Altertum.* Vol. 1, 1954 5th ed.; vol. 2, 4th ed. 2 vols. Munich: Bayerischer Schulbuch, 1972–76. ISBN 3-7627-6005-5 (v. 1), 3-7627-6061-6 (v. 2). ‣ One hundred maps with accompanying notes, more modern but much less detailed than Kiepert and Kiepert 6.36. Good special maps. [MC]

6.26 Fernand Braudel. *The Mediterranean and the Mediterranean world in the age of Philip II.* 1972–73 ed. 2 vols. New York: Harper & Row, 1976. ‣ Classic portrait of Mediterranean world from leader of French Annales school. Volume 1.1 superb on physical geography of region. [MC]

6.27 Max Cary. *The geographic background of Greek and Roman history.* Oxford: Clarendon, 1949. ‣ Excellent discussion of physical geography, climate, and products of ancient world from Britain to India and their impact on Greek and Roman history. [MC/CMW]

6.28 Max Cary and E. H. Warmington. *The ancient explorers.* Rev. ed. Baltimore: Penguin, 1963. ‣ Discussion of voyages of exploration on frontiers of ancient world. [MC]

6.29 O.A.W. Dilke. *Greek and Roman maps.* Ithaca, N.Y.: Cornell University Press, 1985. ISBN 0-8014-1801-1. ‣ Study of ancient cartography stressing work of Greek scientists and Roman surveyors. Argues for greater use of maps than some commentators would allow. [CMW]

6.30 M. I. Finley, ed. *Atlas of classical archaeology.* New York: McGraw-Hill, 1977. ISBN 0-07-021025-x. ‣ Maps and pictures of special sites (eighteen in Greece). Historical and geographical commentary by experts in each area. [MC]

6.31 Clive Foss. "Classical atlases." *Classical world* 80.5 (1986–87) 337–65. ISSN 0009-8418. ‣ Critical review of twelve generally available atlases to classical world; see Talbert 6.44. [MC]

6.32 N.G.L. Hammond, ed. *Atlas of the Greek and Roman world in antiquity.* Park Ridge, N.J.: Noyes, 1981. ISBN 0-8155-5060-x. ‣ Large modern maps, many more place names, but less detailed than Kiepert and Kiepert 6.36. Sometimes weak in organization. [MC]

6.33 John B. Harley and David Woodward. *Cartography in prehistoric, ancient, and medieval Europe and the Mediterranean.* Chicago: University of Chicago Press, 1987. ISBN 0-226-31633-5. ▸ Covers Europe and Near East from prehistoric times to ca. 1500 CE; discusses everything that could be called a map or plan. Overrates actual use of maps in Greco-Roman times. [MC]

6.34 Richard Hennig. *Terrae incognitae: eine Zusammenstellung und kritische Bewertung der wichtigsten vorcolombischen Entdekkungsreisen an Hand der darüber vorliegenden Originalberichte.* Vol. 1: *Altertum bis Ptolemäus.* Vol. 2: *200–1200 n. Chr.* 2d ed. 4 vols. Leiden: Brill, 1944–50. ▸ Volume 1 and parts of volume 2 relevant to antiquity. Lists and discusses all recorded voyages of exploration. All sources are quoted, largely in full, in German translation. Masterly and basic. [EB]

6.35 Heinrich Kiepert. *Atlas antiquus.* 12th ed. Berlin: Reimer, 1902. ▸ Twelve double-page maps from Persian through Roman empire. Unsurpassed in their detail. See also Kiepert and Kiepert 6.36. [MC]

6.36 Heinrich Kiepert and Richard Kiepert. *Formae orbis antiqui.* Richard J. A. Talbert, Introduction. Berlin: Reimer, 1894–1914. ▸ Twenty-five double-page maps of classical world with both German and English text. Most detailed and admirable of all classical maps (series never completed). Reprint by Quasar in progress. [MC]

6.37 Benjamin Dean Meritt, H. T. Wade-Gery, and Malcolm Francis McGregor, eds. "The gazetteer." In *The Athenian tribute lists.* Vol. 1, pp. 461–566. Cambridge, Mass.: Harvard University Press, 1939. ▸ Exact location of regions and towns within Athenian empire; largely work of Wade-Gery. Many places play roles in historical narratives. Only source of its kind. For other volumes see 6.313. [MC]

6.38 J. Wilson Myers, Eleanor Emlen Myers, and Gerald Cadogan, eds. *The aerial atlas of ancient Crete.* Berkeley: University of California Press, 1992. ISBN 0-520-07382-7. ▸ Innovative atlas of forty-four Cretan sites photographed with cameras suspended from balloon. Offers unique visual perspective and includes drawings with commentaries. [MC]

6.39 Alfred Philippson. *Die griechischen Landschaften: eine Landeskunde.* 4 vols. in 8. Herbert Lehmann and Ernst Kirsten, eds. Frankfurt: Kostermann, 1950–59. ▸ Largest single comprehensive survey of Greek geography; important historical contributions by Kirsten in first volumes. [MC]

6.40 Claudius Ptolemy. *The geography.* 1932 ed. Edward Luther Stevenson, ed. and trans. Joseph Fischer, Introduction. New York: Dover, 1991. ISBN 0-486-26896-9 (pbk). ▸ Only complete English translation of most comprehensive of ancient geographic works (second century CE). [MC]

6.41 W. M. Ramsay. *The historical geography of Asia Minor.* 1890 ed. Amsterdam: Hakkert, 1962. ▸ Despite its age, unsurpassed as survey in English. [MC]

6.42 N.H.H. Sitwell. *The world the Romans knew.* London: Hamish Hamilton, 1984. ISBN 0-241-11318-0. ▸ Survey of ancient geography; contains geographic material relating to diverse persons, places, and events such as Alexander the Great and India. [MC]

6.43 Richard Stillwell, William L. MacDonald, and Marian Holland McAllister, eds. *The Princeton encyclopedia of classical sites.* Princeton: Princeton University Press, 1976. ISBN 0-691-03542-3. ▸ Invaluable work of reference with over 2,800 entries, arranged alphabetically, giving location, brief history, and bibliographic references for each site. [CMW]

6.44 Richard J. A. Talbert. "Mapping the classical world: major atlases and map series, 1872–1990." *Journal of Roman archaeology* 5 (1992) 5–38. ISSN 1047-7594. ▸ Unique history and critique of existing atlases. Major new classical atlas planned for 1999. [MC]

6.45 Richard J. A. Talbert, ed. *Atlas of classical history.* New York: Macmillan, 1985. ISBN 0-02-933110-2. ▸ Maps (no pictures) of areas and special sites. Commentary by various experts. [MC]

Chronology

6.46 E. J. Bickerman. *Chronology of the ancient world.* 2d ed. Ithaca, N.Y.: Cornell University Press, 1980. ISBN 0-8014-1282-X. ▸ Introduction to chronology with many tables (new moons, lists of monarchs and dynasties, and much else) for rapid reference. [MC]

6.47 Wilhelm Kubitschek. *Grundriss der antiken Zeitrechnung.* Munich: Beck, 1928. (Handbuch der Altertumswissenschaft, Erste Abteilung, 7.) ▸ Predecessor of Samuel 6.48 containing much material not treated by Samuel. [EB]

6.48 Alan E. Samuel. *Greek and Roman chronology: calendars and years in classical antiquity.* Munich: Beck, 1972. (Handbuch der Altertumswissenschaft, Erste Abteilung, 7.) ISBN 3-406-03348-2. ▸ Standard survey of ancient chronology with notes on local calendars for many localities. [MC]

Prosopography

6.49 John M. Fossey. *The study of ancient Greek prosopography.* Chicago: Ares, 1990. ISBN 0-89005-449-5. ▸ History and procedures, but above all essential list of main prosopographies throughout Greek world. Appendix on onomastics. [MC]

6.50 Josef Hofstetter. *Die Griechen in Persien: Prosopographie der Griechen im persischen Reich vor Alexander.* Berlin: Reimer, 1978. (Archäologische Mitteilungen aus Iran, Ergänzungsband, 5.) ▸ Lists all Greeks recorded as living in or visiting any part of Persian empire down to Alexander's invasion (334 BCE). Highly useful; indexes. [EB]

6.51 Luigi Moretti. *Olympionikai: I vincitori negli antichi agoni olimpici.* Rome, 1957. (Atti della Accademia Nazionale dei Lincei. Memorie, Classe di scienze morali, storiche, e filologiche, Series 8, 8.2.) ▸ Chronological list of winners in Olympic games with alphabetic and local indexes. See author's "Supplemento" in *Klio* 52 (1970) 295–303. [MC]

6.52 Linda Collins Reilly. *Slaves in ancient Greece: slaves from Greek manumission inscriptions.* Chicago: Ares, 1978. ISBN 0-89005-223-9. ▸ Alphabetic list of manumitted slaves in Greek inscriptions, fifth century BCE to third century CE. Specialized; of limited use. [MC]

LITERARY SOURCES

6.53 Association Guillaume Budé. Collection des Universités de France. Paris: Belles Lettres. ISSN 0184-7155. ▸ Greek (and Latin) texts of all major authors with facing French translation. Informative introductions, often with excellent notes (e.g., Thucydides, Aristotle's *Politics*). Introductions, name indexes, bibliographies shorter than Teubner (6.54). Often more modern than Loeb and Teubner; series continues, older texts seldom revised. [MC]

6.54 Bibliotheca Teubneriana. Leipzig: Teubner. ▸ Largest series of Greek and Latin texts, constantly revised and augmented. Latin prefaces, no translations, often ample bibliographies; indexes of personal and geographical names and important words. [MC]

6.55 Loeb Classical Library. Cambridge, Mass.: Harvard University Press. ▸ Publishes works of virtually all Greek (and Latin) authors with Greek text and English translation on facing pages.

Some older translations (e.g., Homer and Herodotus) now seriously antiquated, but some (e.g., Thucydides) among best available. Introductions often good; texts have only brief selection of variant readings. Series constantly expanded and revised. [MC]

6.56 Oxford classical texts (Scriptorum classicorum bibliotheca Oxoniensis). Oxford: Clarendon. ‣ Mainly reliable texts with selection of variant readings in manuscripts; Latin prefaces, personal and geographical name indexes, no translations or bibliographies. Smaller collection than Loeb (6.55); new titles added regularly, older titles seldom revised. [MC]

6.57 Penguin classics. Harmondsworth: Penguin. ‣ Large selection of Greek and Latin sources in all genres; often most accessible translations. Well suited for college courses. [MC]

Herodotus

Works and commentary

6.58 Herodotus. *Herodotus: erklärt von Heinrich Stein*. 4th–6th ed. 5 vols. Heinrich Stein, ed. Berlin: Weidmann, 1893–1908. ‣ Only complete commentary in German on Herodotus; still useful. [MC]

6.59 Herodotus. *Historiae*. Vol. 1: Books 1–4. 1 vol. to date. Haiim B. Rosén, ed. Leipzig: Teubner, 1987–. ISBN 3-322-00359-0. ‣ Controversial Greek text. Much information on manuscripts. Volume one covers Books I–IV. [EB]

6.60 Herodotus. *The Histories*. Rev. 1954 ed. A. R. Burn, ed. Aubrey de Sélincourt, trans. Harmondsworth: Penguin, 1972. ISBN 0-14-044034-8. ‣ Delightful translation, only one capturing author's personality and wit. [MC]

6.61 W. W. How and J. Wells. *A commentary on Herodotus*. 1912 ed. 2 vols. Oxford: Clarendon, 1967. ‣ Only complete commentary in English; now seriously out of date. [MC]

6.62 Alan B. Lloyd. *Herodotus, Book II*. 3 vols. Leiden: Brill, 1974–88. ISBN 90-04-04179-6 (set). ‣ Introduction (volume 1), with long chapter on sources; most detailed commentary (volumes 2–3) on Herodotus' description of Egypt. [MC]

6.63 J. E. Powell. *A lexicon to Herodotus*. 1938 ed. Hildesheim: Olms, 1977. ISBN 3-487-0036-9. ‣ Lists and classifies every word in Herodotus (except *kai*, "and"). Model for such lexica, essential for studying Herodotus' usage. [MC]

Studies

6.64 Deborah Boedeker and John Peradotto, eds. "Herodotus and the invention of history." *Arethusa* 20.1–2 (1987) 1–282. ISSN 0004-0975. ‣ Ten excellent conference essays, with responses, informed by various contemporary approaches. Includes lengthy survey of Herodotean scholarship. [RWW]

6.65 Charles W. Fornara. *Herodotus: an interpretative essay*. Oxford: Clarendon, 1971. ISBN 0-19-814293-3. ‣ Concise treatment, especially of historian's development; shows that Book II was first to be written. [MC]

6.66 François Hartog. *The mirror of Herodotus: the representation of the other in the writing of history*. Janet Lloyd, trans. Berkeley: University of California Press, 1988. ISBN 0-520-05487-3. ‣ Groundbreaking study of Herodotus' perception of space and attitudes toward non-Greek world (especially Scythia and Egypt) in a cultural geography. Inspired by structuralism and Jacques Lacan. [RWW]

6.67 Henry R. Immerwahr. *Form and thought in Herodotus*. 1966 ed. Atlanta, Ga.: Scholars Press, 1986. (American Philological Association, Monographs, 23.) ISBN 0-89130-478-9. ‣ Systematic analyses of coherent, unified structure in Herodotus' work and patterns of thought, as shown especially by arrangement of structural units and vocabulary. [RWW]

6.68 Felix Jacoby. "Herodotos." In *Paulys Realencyclopädie der classischen Altertumswissenschaft*. 2d ed. Suppl. 2, cols. 205–520. Stuttgart: Metzler, 1913. ‣ Most profound treatment of every aspect of Herodotus. Indispensable for study of historian; starting point for all subsequent analyses. See 6.23. [MC]

6.69 Donald Lateiner. *The historical method of Herodotus*. 1989 ed. Toronto: University of Toronto Press, 1992. (*Phoenix*, Supplementary volume, 23.) ISBN 0-8020-5793-4 (cl, 1989), 0-8020-7684-x (pbk). ‣ Sophisticated but accessible study of Herodotus as creative historian; his selection and organization of material and structure and patterns of interpretation inform whole. [RWW]

6.70 John L. Myres. *Herodotus: father of history*. 1953 ed. Chicago: Regnery, 1971. ‣ Especially valuable for analysis of organization and layout of *Histories* as a whole, showing patterns of repetitions and cross-references. [MC]

Thucydides

Works and commentary

6.71 A. W. Gomme, A. Andrewes, and K. J. Dover. *A historical commentary on Thucydides*. 5 vols. Oxford: Clarendon, 1945–81. ISBN 0-19-814198-x (v. 5). ‣ Indispensable commentary, far outstripping all predecessors. Completed by Andrewes and Dover after death of Gomme. [MC]

6.72 Simon Hornblower. *A commentary on Thucydides*. Vol. 1: *Books I–III*. 1 vol. to date. Oxford: Clarendon, 1991–. ISBN 0-19-814880-1 (v. 1). ‣ Successor to Gomme 6.71, but with more attention to Thucydides' literary procedures and more help for readers who do not know Greek. Two additional volumes forthcoming. [MC]

6.73 Thucydides. *Historiae*. 1898–1901 ed. 2 vols. Carolus Hude, ed. Leipzig: Teubner, 1960. ‣ Most extensive report on readings of manuscripts for complete text with testimonia from later writers. Indispensable for study of text. [MC]

6.74 Thucydides. *Historiae*. Vol. 1: *Libri I–II*. Iohannes Baptista Alberti, ed. Rome: Typis Publicae Officinae Polygraphicae, 1972. ‣ Critical edition of Books I–II; exhaustive report on manuscripts and testimonia for those books only. Long discussion of manuscript genealogy in Latin; for specialists. See review, A. Kleinlogel, *Gnomon* 49 (1977) 754–73. [MC]

6.75 Thucydides. *History II*. P. J. Rhodes, ed. and trans. Warminster: Aris & Phillips, 1988. ISBN 0-85668-396-5 (cl), 0-85668-397-3 (pbk). ‣ Introduction, Greek text taken from Oxford text, translation, and brief but up-to-date commentary. [MC]

6.76 Thucydides. *History of the Peloponnesian War*. Rev. ed. Rex Warner, trans. M. I. Finley, Introduction. Harmondsworth: Penguin, 1972. ISBN 0-14-044039-9. ‣ Elegant translation; important historical appendixes by Finley. [MC]

6.77 Thucydides. *The Peloponnesian War, Book II*. J. S. Rusten, ed. Cambridge: Cambridge University Press, 1989. ISBN 0-521-32665-6 (cl), 0-521-33929-4 (pbk). ‣ Introduction, Greek text, translation, and commentary. Comparable to Rhodes, ed. 6.75. [MC]

Studies

6.78 E.-A. Bétant. *Lexicon Thucydideum*. 1843–47 ed. 2 vols. Hildesheim: Olms, 1969. ‣ Not complete, but useful even in age of computer-assisted searches of author's vocabulary. Context of word usually given; definitions in Latin. [MC]

6.79 W. Robert Connor. *Thucydides*. Princeton: Princeton University Press, 1984. ISBN 0-691-03569-5 (cl), 0-691-10239-2 (pbk). ▸ Clear, book-by-book critique of Thucydides as literary artist. Focuses especially on thematic contrasts, power, and suffering of war. [RWW]

6.80 John H. Finley, Jr. *Three essays on Thucydides.* Cambridge, Mass.: Harvard University Press, 1967. ▸ Reprint of influential, technical essays, two linking Thucydides' thought and style with contemporary world and third favoring unity of his work as opposed to earlier scholars' preoccupation with stages of composition. [RWW]

6.81 Simon Hornblower. *Thucydides.* London: Duckworth, 1987. ISBN 0-7156-2156-4. ▸ Well-informed, well-organized modern biography and discussion of historian. [EB]

6.82 Jacqueline de Romilly. *Histoire et raison chez Thucydide.* 2d ed. Paris: Belles Lettres, 1967. ▸ Closely reasoned analysis of text not as objective reporting but as coherent, artificial construction. Informed by patterns of events as perceived and reinforced by internal echoes of concept and word. [RWW]

6.83 Jacqueline de Romilly. *Thucydides and Athenian imperialism.* 1963 ed. Philip Thody, trans. Salem, N.H.: Ayer, 1988. ISBN 0-88143-072-2. ▸ Study of foreign policy and internal affairs of Athens. Important discussions of individuals in Thucydides such as Pericles and Cleon. [CWH]

Xenophon

6.84 Hartvig Frisch, ed. and trans. *The constitution of the Athenians: a philological-historical analysis of pseudo-Xenophon's treatise "De re Publica Atheniensium."* Copenhagen: Gyldendal, 1942. (*Classica et mediaevalia,* Dissertations, 2.) ISSN 0106-5815. ▸ Thorough discussion of work that, although attributed to Xenophon in manuscripts, is actually pamphlet of ca. 430 BCE, written by critic of Athenian democracy (often called the Old Oligarch). [MC]

6.85 G. E. Underhill. *A commentary with introduction and appendix on the Hellenica of Xenophon.* 1900 ed. New York: Arno, 1979. ISBN 0-405-11452-4. ▸ Greek text and English commentary on ancient historian treating Greek history, 411–362 BCE. [MC]

6.86 Xenophon. *Education of Cyrus.* Henry Graham Dakyns, trans. New York: Dutton, 1914. ▸ Historical novel about Cyrus the Elder of Persia, giving Xenophon's ideas about raising of children, leadership, and family life; important for fourth-century BCE debate about how to train statesmen and leaders. [MC]

6.87 Xenophon. *A history of my times.* 1966 ed. Rex Warner, trans. George Cawkwell, Introduction and Notes. Harmondsworth: Penguin, 1979. ISBN 0-14-044175-1 (pbk). ▸ Translation of *Hellenica.* Continuation of Thucydides' history, covering years 411–362 BCE. Excellent informative notes in this edition. [EB]

Greek Orators

6.88 Aeschines. *The speeches.* Charles Darwin Adams, trans. Cambridge, Mass.: Harvard University Press, 1919. ▸ Greek text and translation of speeches of political opponent of Demosthenes (6.91). [MC]

6.89 Andocides [Andokides]. *On the mysteries.* 1962 ed. Douglas M. MacDowell, ed. Oxford: Clarendon, 1989. ISBN 0-19-814692-2. ▸ Historically important speech: defense by Athenian accused in mutilation of the Herms, 415 BCE. Greek text with commentary. [MC]

6.90 Demosthenes. *Against Midias: oration 21.* Douglas M. MacDowell, ed. and trans. Oxford: Clarendon, 1990. ISBN 0-19-814763-5. ▸ Detailed political and literary commentary on Demosthenes' attack on Athenian politician. [MC]

6.91 Demosthenes. [Works]. 7 vols. J. H. Vince et al., trans.

Cambridge, Mass.: Harvard University Press, 1926–49. ▸ Greek text of speeches, with translations, of Athenian patriot who tried to rally countrymen to resist Macedonian encroachment under Philip II. [MC]

6.92 Isocrates. [Works]. 3 vols. George Norlin and La Rue Van Hook, trans. Cambridge, Mass.: Harvard University Press, 1928–45. ▸ Although called orations, actually written pamphlets by conservative rhetorician and teacher. Important for fourth-century history. [MC]

Hellenica Oxyrhynchia

6.93 I. A. F. Bruce. *An historical commentary on the "Hellenica Oxyrhynchia."* Cambridge: Cambridge University Press, 1967. ▸ Commentary on historian (variously identified as Cratippus or Theopompus) who continued work of Thucydides; portions from 390s BCE preserved in papyri. Most recent fragment from Cairo not included. [MC]

6.94 Mortimer Chambers, ed. *Hellenica Oxyrhynchia.* Leipzig: Teubner, 1993. ISBN 3-8154-1365-6. ▸ Edition of three papyri preserving narrative of war, ca. 395 BCE, involving Sparta, Athens, and Persia by fourth-century military historian, identified with either Cratippus or (less probably) Theopompus. Text in Greek, explanatory matter and introduction in Latin. [MC]

6.95 Paul R. McKechnie and Stephen J. Kern, eds. and trans. *Hellenica Oxyrhynchia.* Warminster: Aris & Phillips, 1988. ISBN 0-85668-357-4 (cl), 0-85668-358-2 (pbk). ▸ Greek text and only English translation of all portions of work, including papyri from London, Florence, Cairo. Succinct historical commentary. [MC]

Aristotle

6.96 Aristotle. *The Athenian Constitution.* P. J. Rhodes, trans. Harmondsworth: Penguin, 1984. ISBN 0-14-044431-9 (pbk). ▸ Most recent English translation with brief commentary based on Rhodes 6.103. [MC]

6.97 Aristotle. *The Politics: translated with an introduction, notes, and appendixes.* 1946 ed. E. Barker, trans. Oxford: Clarendon, 1968. ▸ Translation with running summaries and helpful appendixes. Practically a small commentary on seminal work of political theory in Western civilization. [MC]

6.98 Aristotle. *The Politics of Aristotle.* 1887–1902 ed. 4 vols. W. L. Newman, ed. Salem, N.H.: Ayer, 1985. ▸ Greek text with exhaustive commentary; no translation. Places Books IV–VI after Books VII–VIII. Classic; still valuable. [MC]

6.99 Aristotle. *Politik.* 4 vols. Eckart Schütrumpf, ed. and trans. Berlin: Akademie-Verlag, 1991–. (Aristoteles, Werke in deutscher Übersetzung, 9.) ISBN 3-05-000011-2 (set). ▸ Translation and German commentary on massive scale of Newman, ed. 6.98. [MC]

6.100 Aristotle. *Staat der Athener.* Mortimer Chambers, ed. and trans. Berlin: Akademie-Verlag, 1990. (Aristoteles, Werke in deutscher Übersetzung, 10.1.) ISBN 3-05-000026-0. ▸ German translation of and commentary on Aristotle's, *Constitution of the Athenians.* Accepts Aristotle as author; seeks influence of his philosophical theories in his narrative. Comparable to Rhodes 6.103, but shorter. [MC]

6.101 James Day and Mortimer Chambers. *Aristotle's history of Athenian democracy.* 1962 ed. Millwood, N.Y.: Kraus Reprint, 1980. ▸ Best general treatment of *Athenaion Politeia* in English; discussion of treatise and defense of Aristotle's authorship. Explication of text and its historical and historiographic significance. [JB]

6.102 John J. Keaney. *The composition of Aristotle's "Athenaion Politeia": observation and explanation.* New York: Oxford University Press, 1992. ISBN 0-19-507032-1. ▸ Detailed study of stylistic features and structure of text; highly original and stimulating. [MC]

6.103   P. J. Rhodes. *A commentary on the Aristotelian "Athenaion Politeia."* Oxford: Clarendon, 1981. ISBN 0-19-814004-5. ▸ Extensive introduction to and profound commentary on this seminal text. Denies Aristotelian authorship of work. [MC]

Polybius

6.104   Emilio Gabba, ed. *Polybe: neuf exposés suivis de discussions.* Vandoeuvres-Geneva: Fondation Hardt, 1974. (Entretiens sur l'antiquité classique, 20.) ▸ Nine essays, some specialist, on Polybius, covering such topics as Roman imperialism, Polybius' scientific approach, relations with Greek predecessors, Roman sources, concepts of balance of power, constitutions, Polybius as military historian, Polybius in later antiquity, and Polybius in Renaissance. [RWW]

6.105   Paul Pédech. *La méthode historique de Polybe.* Paris: Belles Lettres, 1964. ▸ Sophisticated evaluations of Polybius' conception of history and techniques of narrative. Discussions of causality (from individual psychology to goddess Fortune) and critical method. Argues in support of intellectual Polybius. For informed reader. [RWW]

6.106   F. W. Walbank. *A historical commentary on Polybius.* Vol. I rev. ed.; vols. 2–3 1957–79 ed. 3 vols. Oxford: Clarendon, 1967–79. ▸ Superb, exhaustive commentary on historian who described Rome's rise to world power. [MC]

6.107   F. W. Walbank. *Polybius.* Berkeley: University of California Press, 1972. ISBN 0-520-02190-8 (cl), 0-520-06981-1 (pbk). ▸ Synthetic treatment by leading Polybius scholar: context and date, predecessors, didactic-moral purposes, methods, structure, and attitude toward Rome. Emphasizes historian's contradictory, sometimes muddled qualities. [RWW]

Diodorus Siculus

6.108   Diodorus Siculus. [Works]. 12 vols. Charles H. Oldfather et al., trans. Cambridge, Mass.: Harvard University Press, 1933–67. ▸ Greek text and translation of works of universal historian of antiquity from Egypt to Julius Caesar. Often uncritical but unique source for many events and eras. See 6.232. [MC]

Plutarch

6.109   Plutarch. *Lives.* 11 vols. Bernadotte Perrin, trans. Cambridge, Mass.: Harvard University Press, 1914–26. ▸ Greek text and translation of Plutarch's *Lives*, biographies of important Greeks and Romans. References to individual *Lives* appear in appropriate locations in following bibliography. [MC]

Lost (Fragmentary) Historians

6.110   Felix Jacoby, ed. *Die Fragmente der griechischen Historiker.* Rev. ed. 3 vols. in 15. Leiden: Brill, 1923–. ▸ Fragments (quotations) of over 700 Greek historians whose work has not survived complete. Two volumes in English, all others in Greek and German. Work of unparalleled scope and learning; no translations of fragments. [MC]

6.111   H. J. Mette. "Die 'kleinen' griechischen Historiker heute." *Lustrum* 21 (1978) 5–43. ISSN 0024-7421. ▸ Supplements Jacoby, ed. 6.110, citing and occasionally reproducing publications of new fragments of lost works of Greek historians. [MC]

6.112   Lionel Pearson. *Early Ionian historians.* 1939 ed. Westport, Conn.: Greenwood, 1975. ISBN 0-8371-5314-X. ▸ Basic information on earliest historians: logographers, Hecataeus, Xanthus, Charon, Hellanicus, whose works are known only from fragments. Chronology, scope, specific works, and commentary on significant fragments. Dated but not yet replaced. [RWW]

Inscriptions

6.113   Friedrich Bechtel et al. *Sammlung der griechischen Dialekt-Inschriften.* 1884–1915 ed. 4 vols. in 5 parts. Hermann Collitz, ed. Nendeln, Liechtenstein: Kraus Reprint, 1973. ▸ Collection of inscriptions from locations other than Attica; volume 4, index. Basic for evidence about various Greek dialects. [MC]

6.114   François Bérard et al. *Guide de l'épigraphiste: bibliographie choisie des épigraphies antiques et médiévales.* Paris: Presses de l'École Normale Supérieure, 1986. (Bibliothèque de l'École Normale Supérieure, Guides et inventaires bibliographiques, 2.) ISBN 2-7288-0116-9. ▸ Extensive bibliography to editions and collections of inscriptions continuing through Roman empire. Includes sections on prosopographies and economics. [MC]

6.115   Wilhelm Dittenberger, ed. *Orientis Graeci inscriptiones selectae: supplementum Sylloges inscriptionum Graecarum.* 1903–05 ed. 2 vols. Hildesheim: Olms, 1986. ISBN 3-487-00028-8 (v. 1), 3-487-00029-6 (v. 2). ▸ Similar to Dittenberger, ed. 6.116, but covers regions brought into Greek orbit by conquests of Alexander the Great. Abbreviated OGIS. [MC]

6.116   Wilhelm Dittenberger, ed. *Sylloge inscriptionum Graecarum.* 1915–24 3d ed. 4 vols. Hiller von Gaertringen, 3d edition ed. Hildesheim: Olms, 1982. ISBN 3-487-00024-5. ▸ Selection of important inscriptions from Greek world (abbreviated SIG or Syll.) with notes in Latin. Volume 4, index. [MC]

6.117   Wilfried Gawantka. *Aktualisierende Konkordanzen zu Dittenbergers "Orientis Graeci Inscriptiones Selectae" (OGIS) und zur dritten Auflage der von ihm begründeten "Sylloge Inscriptionum Graecarum" (Syll.3).* Hildesheim: Olms, 1977. ISBN 3-487-06447-2. ▸ Essential concordance to both earlier and later editions of inscriptions in Dittenberger, ed. 6.115, 6.116, which no longer need to be used in isolation. [MC]

6.118   Margherita Guarducci. *Epigrafia greca.* 4 vols. Rome: Istituto Poligrafico dello Stato, Libreria dello Stato, 1967–78. ▸ Examples of Greek inscriptions, arranged topically, with ample commentary. Similar to Dittenberger, ed. 6.116. [MC]

6.119   George F. Hill, comp. *Sources for Greek history between the Persian and Peloponnesian wars.* Rev. ed. Russell Meiggs and A. Andrewes, eds. Oxford: Clarendon, 1966. ▸ Collection of sources without translations from historians and primary documents for period 479–431 BCE. Essential for its extensive indexes. [MC]

6.120   *Inscriptiones Graecae.* 23 vols. to date. Various editors. Berlin: Reimer & de Gruyter, 1873–. ▸ Basic collection of Greek inscriptions; succeeds *Corpus Inscriptionum Graecarum*, founded by August Böckh (4 volumes published). Originally planned to include inscriptions from entire Hellenic world. [MC]

6.121   Institut Fernand-Courby, ed. *Index du Bulletin épigraphique de J. et L. Robert.* 5 vols. Paris: Belles Lettres, 1972–83. ISBN 2-251-91403-X (v. 4), 2-251-71404-9 (v. 5). ▸ Copious indexes to Robert and Robert 6.124. Includes all inscriptions studied, Greek words, French words. Essential for further study of documents surveyed by Robert and Robert over four decades. [MC]

6.122   Vasilii Latyschev, ed. *Inscriptiones antiquae orae septentrionalis Ponti Euxini Graecae et Latinae.* Vol. I, 2d ed. 3 vols. St. Petersburg: Imperial Russian Archaeological Society, 1885–1901. ▸ Edition of inscriptions found in region of Black Sea; unique collection. Volumes 1, 2, and 4; volume 3 never published. [EB]

6.123   Russell Meiggs and David M. Lewis. *A selection of Greek historical inscriptions to the end of the fifth century B.C.* Rev. ed. Oxford: Clarendon, 1988. ISBN 0-19-814266-8. ▸ Selection of mentary, no translations. Largely replaces Tod, ed. 6.125 for fifth century only. [MC]

6.124 Jeanne Robert and Louis Robert. "Bulletin épigraphique." *Revue des études grecques* (1938–84). ISSN 0035-2039. ▸ Series of articles offering masterly surveys of publications in Greek epigraphy, often with severe criticism. Essential for further research on any inscription mentioned. Collected and reprinted in special volumes. Annual survey now continued by several scholars following model of the Roberts. [MC]

6.125 Marcus N. Tod, ed. *A selection of Greek historical inscriptions from the sixth century B.C. to the death of Alexander the Great in 323 B.C.* Vol. 1, 1946 2d ed.; vol. 2, 1948 ed. 2 vols. in 1. Al. N. Oikonomides, ed. Chicago: Ares, 1985. ISBN 0-89005-541-6. ▸ One-volume edition of author's two-volume selection of historically important inscriptions. Same format as Meiggs and Lewis 6.123 but extends farther chronologically; volume 1 largely replaced by 6.123, volume 2 still indispensable. Reprint adds concordances to other editions; brief commentaries, no translations. [MC]

6.126 A. G. Woodhead. *The study of Greek inscriptions.* 1981 2d ed. Norman: University of Oklahoma Press, 1992. ISBN 0-8061-2431-8 (pbk). ▸ Best introduction with bibliography, lists of collections, and editorial procedures. Discussion of inscriptions in Greek life. [MC]

Papyri and Papyrology

6.127 Martin David and B. A. van Groningen. *The new papyrological primer.* 5th ed. P. W. Pestman, ed. Leiden: Brill, 1990. ISBN 90-04-09348-6. ▸ Brief introduction to papyrology with selected papyri and photographs. Texts in Greek with commentary and some translations. [MC]

6.128 Bernard P. Grenfell and A. S. Hunt, original eds. *The Oxyrhynchus papyri.* London: Egypt Exploration Society, 1898–. ▸ Largest single series of Greek papyri, both literary and documentary. Translations and notes. [MC]

6.129 Ludwig Mitteis and Ulrich Wilcken. *Grundzüge und Chrestomathie der Papyruskunde.* 1912 ed. 2 vols. in 4. Hildesheim: Olms, 1963. ▸ Introduction to documents in papyri. Historical texts with commentary in volume 1 (Wilcken) and juridical texts in volume 2 (Mitteis). [MC]

6.130 John F. Oates et al., eds. *Checklist of editions of Greek and Latin papyri, ostraca, and tablets.* 4th ed. Atlanta: Scholars Press, 1992. (Bulletin of the American Society of Papyrologists, Supplement, 7.) ▸ Most current list of many editions of Greco-Latin papyri and ostraca (writings on clay potsherds). Updates Facal and González 6.9. [MC]

6.131 E. G. Turner. *Greek papyri: an introduction.* 2d ed. Oxford: Clarendon, 1980. ISBN 0-19-814841-0 (pbk). ▸ Excellent introduction to study of papyri by one of Britain's leading papyrologists of last forty years. Includes making of papyrus, editing of texts, and lists of publications. [MC]

6.132 John Garrett Winter. *Life and letters in the papyri.* Ann Arbor: University of Michigan Press, 1933. ▸ Portrait of what papyri offer about literature and society. Despite age not wholly replaced by any other single work. [MC]

Selected Sources in Translation

6.133 Stanley M. Burstein, ed. and trans. *The Hellenistic age from the battle of Ipsos to the death of Kleopatra VII.* Cambridge: Cambridge University Press, 1985. ISBN 0-521-23691-6 (cl), 0-521-28158-x (pbk). ▸ Comparable to Fornara, ed. 6.135. Includes 112 documents, largely inscriptions (including Rosetta Stone) down to end of Hellenistic period. This and following selections especially good for teaching. [MC]

6.134 Michael H. Crawford and David Whitehead, eds. and trans. *Archaic and classical Greece: a selection of ancient sources in translation.* Cambridge: Cambridge University Press, 1983. ISBN 0-521-22775-5 (cl), 0-521-29638-2 (pbk). ▸ Collection of translated literary sources and inscriptions. [MC]

6.135 Charles W. Fornara, ed. and trans. *Archaic times to the end of the Peloponnesian War.* 2d ed. Cambridge: Cambridge University Press, 1983. ISBN 0-521-25019-6 (cl), 0-521-29946-2 (pbk). ▸ Large collection of translated documents including many important inscriptions. Succinct commentary; references to other editions. [MC]

6.136 A. S. Hunt, C. C. Edgar, and D. L. Page, eds. *Select papyri.* Vols. 1–2, 1932–34 ed.; vol. 3, 1942 rev. ed. 3 vols. Cambridge, Mass.: Harvard University Press, 1959–63. ▸ Two volumes of nonliterary papyri and one of poetic selections with translations. [MC]

NUMISMATICS

6.137 Ernest Babelon. *Traité des monnaies grecques et romaines.* 1901–32 ed. 4 vols. Bologna: Forni, 1965. ▸ Most comprehensive single work on ancient coinage; Greek coins treated in volumes 1–2. Work never completed. [MC]

6.138 British Museum. Department of Coins and Metals. *Catalogue of Greek coins in the British Museum.* Various eds. London: British Museum, 1873–1927. ▸ Most extensive publication of ancient Greek coins from all places where they were minted, with full illustrations. Still indispensable. [EB]

6.139 Barclay V. Head et al. *Historia numorum: a manual of Greek numismatics.* Rev. 1911 ed. Chicago: Argonaut, 1967. ▸ Only comprehensive handbook on ancient Greek coinage in English covering every region of Greek world. [MC]

6.140 C. M. Kraay. *Archaic and classical Greek coins.* Berkeley: University of California Press, 1976. ISBN 0-520-03254-3. ▸ Best introduction in English to history and study of Greek coins down to ca. 300 BCE; 1,110 coins photographed. [MC]

6.141 C. M. Kraay. *Greek coins.* New York: Harry N. Abrams, 1966. ▸ Based on geographic areas; 809 superb photographs. Largely English-language edition of Peter R. Franke and Max Hirmer, *Die griechische Münze* (1964). [MC]

HISTORIOGRAPHY

6.142 Charles W. Fornara. *The nature of history in ancient Greece and Rome.* 1983 ed. Berkeley: University of California Press, 1988. ISBN 0-520-04910-1 (cl, 1983), 0-520-06332-5 (pbk). ▸ Concise, general discussions of historiography as genre in antiquity; research, orientation, causality, purpose of history, speeches, historiographic theory, and history's competitors (e.g., biography). [RWW]

6.143 Felix Jacoby. *Abhandlungen zur griechischen Geschichtschreibung von Felix Jacoby: zu seinem achtzigsten Geburtstag am 19. Marz 1956.* Herbert Bloch, ed. Leiden: Brill, 1956. ▸ Reprints of twenty-five articles and reviews, some in English, mostly on Greek historiography by distinguished authority. Includes seminal "Über die Entwicklung der griechischen Historiographie" from *Klio* 9 (1909) 80–123. [RWW]

6.144 Arnaldo Momigliano. *The classical foundations of modern historiography.* Berkeley: University of California Press, 1990. ISBN 0-520-06890-4. ▸ Six lectures on historiography from Persia through Greece and Rome to ecclesiastical history; delivered 1962, no annotation. [MC]

6.145 Arnaldo Momigliano. *Contributi alla storia degli studi classici.* 11 vols. Rome: Storia e Letteratura, 1955–87. ▸ Over 500 articles and reviews (many in English) on Greek and Roman history, historiography (both ancient and modern), and other topics from brilliant, wide-ranging historian. [RWW]

6.146 Arnaldo Momigliano. *Studies in historiography.* New York: Harper & Row, 1966. ▸ Selected, nontechnical, English-language articles from Momigliano 6.145 on conceptions and problems of historical writing, ancient, medieval, and modern. [RWW]

6.147 Lionel Pearson. *Greek historians of the West: Timaeus and his predecessors.* Atlanta: Scholars Press for American Philological Association, 1987. (American Philological Association, Monographs, 35.) ▸ Helpful discussion supplementing fragments collected by Jacoby, ed. 6.110; on Philistus, Timaeus, and others. [MC]

HISTORY OF SCHOLARSHIP

6.148 William M. Calder III. *Studies in the modern history of classical scholarship.* Naples: Jovene, 1984. (Antiqua, 27.) ▸ Nineteen articles reprinted, most on German scholars and scholarly problems, by a leading authority in the history of scholarship. [MC]

6.149 William M. Calder III and Justus Cobet, eds. *Heinrich Schliemann nach hundert Jahren.* Frankfurt: Klostermann, 1990. ISBN 3-465-02266-1. ▸ Twenty-one essays, eight in English, on controversial career of one of founders of archaeology, excavator of Mycenae and Troy. [MC]

6.150 William M. Calder III and Alexander Demandt, eds. *Eduard Meyer: Leben und Leistung eines Universalhistorikers.* Leiden: Brill, 1990. (Mnemosyne, Supplement, 112.) ISBN 90-04-09131-9, ISSN 0169-8958. ▸ Eighteen essays, four in English, on life and work of leading ancient historian of his time. See Meyer 6.166. [MC]

6.151 John Chadwick. *The decipherment of Linear B.* Canto ed. Cambridge: Cambridge University Press, 1990. ISBN 0-521-04599-1 (cl), 0-521-39830-4 (pbk). ▸ Account of decoding of Linear B by M. Ventris, written by his primary associate in task. Describes preliminary steps by others as well as final solution. [CGT]

6.152 Mortimer Chambers. *Georg Busolt: his life in his letters.* Leiden: Brill, 1990. (Mnemosyne, Supplement, 113.) ISBN 90-04-09225-0, ISSN 0169-8958. ▸ Biography, based on letters, of one of Germany's leading Greek historians; much information on other German scholars and university life of nineteenth and twentieth centuries. [MC]

6.153 Karl Christ. *Neue Profile der alten Geschichte.* Darmstadt: Wissenschaftliche Buchgesellschaft, 1990. ISBN 3-534-10289-4. ▸ Seven further essays on ancient historians of twentieth century; see Christ 6.154. [MC]

6.154 Karl Christ. *Von Gibbon zu Rostovtzeff: Leben und Werk führender Althistoriker der Neuzeit.* 3d ed. Darmstadt: Wissenschaftliche Buchgesellschaft, 1989. ISBN 3-534-06070-9. ▸ Twelve masterly essays in German on leading historians of antiquity. See also Christ 6.153 for additional essays. [MC]

6.155 William A. McDonald and Carol G. Thomas. *Progress into the past.* 2d ed. Bloomington: Indiana University Press, 1990. ISBN 0-253-33627-9 (cl), 0-253-20553-0 (pbk). ▸ Beginning with rediscovery of preclassical Greece in 1870, study focuses on contributions of major figures—Schliemann, Evans, Blegen, Ventris—and assesses current state of knowledge. Good introduction for general reader. [CGT]

6.156 Leandro Polverini, ed. *Aspetti della storiografia di Giulio Beloch.* Perugia: Edizioni Scientifiche Italiane, 1990. ISBN 88-7104-571-8. ▸ Eleven essays, in German and Italian, on work of Karl Julius Beloch, highly original Greco-Roman historian who spent most of his career in Italy. [MC]

6.157 Marinus A. Wes. *Michael Rostovtzeff, historian in exile:*

Russian roots in an American context. Stuttgart: Steiner, 1990. (Historia, Einzelschriften, 95.) ISBN 0-515-05664-5, ISSN. ▸ Biographical study of leading ancient historian of 1920s and 1930s, exile from Soviet Union. [MC]

GENERAL STUDIES

6.158 A. Andrewes. *Greek society.* 4th ed. Lexington, Mass.: Heath, 1992. ISBN 0-669-24499-6. ▸ Survey of political history, including Mycenaean and Dark Ages, focusing on social and economic organization, religion, and values of Greek society in archaic to classical periods. Clear and accessible. Original title: *The Greeks.* [RWW]

6.159 Karl Julius Beloch. *Griechische Geschichte.* 1912–27 2d ed. 4 vols. in 8. Berlin: de Gruyter, 1967. ▸ Standard, older German history containing original, though sometimes erratic, judgments. Many innovative treatments, especially of chronology; much attention to population and statistics. Many learned appendixes in part 2 of each volume. [RWW]

6.160 John Boardman et al., eds. *The Cambridge ancient history.* Vol. 1.1: *Prolegomena and prehistory.* Vol. 1.2: *Early history of the Middle East.* Vol. 2.1: *History of the Middle East and the Aegean region, c. 1800–1380 B.C.* Vol. 2.2: *Assyrian and Babylonian empires 8th–6th centuries B.C.* Vol. 3.1: *Assyrian empire.* Vol. 3.2: *The prehistory of the Balkans, and the Middle East, and the Aegean world, 10th–8th centuries B.C.* Vol. 3.3: *The expansion of the Greek world, 8th–6th centuries B.C.* Vol. 4: *Persian empire and the West.* Vol. 5: *Athens, 478–401 B.C.* Vol. 6: *Macedon, 401–301 B.C.* Vol. 7.1: *The Hellenistic world.* Vol. 8: *Rome and the Mediterranean, 218–133 B.C.* Vol. 9: *Roman republic, 133–44 B.C.* Vol. 10: *Augustan empire, 44 B.C.–A.D. 70.* Vol. 11: *Imperial peace, A.D. 70–192.* Vol. 12: *Imperial crisis and recovery, A.D. 193–324.* Vols. 1–2, 3d ed.; vols. 3–8, 2d ed.; plates, 2d ed. 12 vols.; 5 vols. of plates. Cambridge: Cambridge University Press, 1932–91. ISBN 0-521-07051-1 (v. 1.1, cl), 0-521-29821-0 (v. 1.1, pbk), 0-521-07791-5 (v. 1.2, cl), 0-521-29822-9 (v. 1.2, pbk), 0-521-08230-7 (v. 2.1, pbk), 0-521-08691-4 (v. 2.2, cl), 0-521-29823-7 (v. 2.2, pbk), 0-521-20571-9 (v. 1–2, pls.) 0-521-22804-2 (v. 4), 0-521-04487-1 (v. 5), 0-521-04488-X (v. 6), 0-521-04495-2 (v. 5–6, pls.), 0-521-23445-X (v. 7.1), 0-521-04490-1 (v. 8), 0-521-04497-9 (v. 9–10, pls.). ▸ Standard multivolume narrative with long bibliographies and accompanying volumes of plates. Prehistory and ancient Near East treated in volumes 1–3; Greek history in volumes 3–7; Roman history in volumes 8–12; volumes 3.1, 6 and 10–12 still undergoing revision. [RWW]

6.161 John Boardman, Jasper Griffin, and Oswyn Murray, eds. *Oxford history of Greece and the Hellenistic world.* Oxford: Oxford University Press, 1991. ISBN 0-19-285247-7 (pbk). ▸ Sixteen essays by prominent scholars on history, literature, philosophy, and society of Greece. Excellent introductions to all topics; cf. Finley, ed. 6.164. Revision of volume 1 of *The Oxford History of the Classical World.* [MC]

6.162 Georg Busolt. *Griechische Geschichte.* 1893–1904 ed. 3 vols. in 4. Hildesheim: Olms, 1967. (Handbücher der alten Geschichte, Zweite Serie, 2.) ▸ Detailed account of Greek history to 404 BCE. Essential for thorough, penetrating assessment of literary sources and solid if uninspired judgment. [RWW]

6.163 M. I. Finley. *Politics in the ancient world.* Cambridge: Cambridge University Press, 1983. ISBN 0-521-25489-2 (cl), 0-521-27570-9 (pbk). ▸ Six essays in social-conceptual structures of politics, especially in Roman republic and Athenian democracy: wealth, social inequality, media, economic relations of state and subject, and popular participation. Typically good at both material and conceptual level. [RWW/CWH]

6.164 M. I. Finley, ed. *The legacy of Greece: a new appraisal.* 1981 ed. Oxford: Oxford University Press, 1984. ISBN 0-19-285136-5 (pbk). ‣ Essays on various phases of Greek civilization; excellent introductions by experts. [MC]

6.165 N.G.L. Hammond. *A history of Greece to 322 B.C.* 3d ed. Oxford: Clarendon, 1986. ISBN 0-19-873096-9 (cl), 0-19-873095-0 (pbk). ‣ One-volume traditional history. Reflects author's special interests in military history, prehistory, Macedonia, and northern Greece. Idiosyncratic views on certain major and minor issues. [RWW]

6.166 Eduard Meyer. *Geschichte des Altertums.* 1910–58 2d–4th ed. 5 vols. in 8. Hans Erich Stier, ed. Darmstadt: Wissenschaftliche Buchgesellschaft, 1965–69. ISBN 3-534-07464-5. ‣ Multivolume German history based on mastery of sources in all original languages, by towering universal historian of modern German scholarship. Syntheses of Greek and Near Eastern history, ending about 350 BCE. [RWW]

6.167 Raphael Sealey. *A history of the Greek city states, ca. 700–338 BC.* Berkeley: University of California Press, 1976. ISBN 0-520-03177-6 (pbk). ‣ Begins with appearance of polis about 750 BCE. Problem-oriented treatment rather than narrative history. Discovers personal rather than ideological motivations for political figures; see Sealey 6.299. [MC]

BRONZE AGE GREECE, ca. 2000–ca. 1100 BCE

6.168 George Bass. "Oldest known shipwreck reveals Bronze Age splendors." *National geographic* 172.6 (1987) 692–733. ISSN 0027-9358. ‣ Examination of trading ship wrecked at Ulu Burun, off southern coast of Turkey, in fourteenth century BCE. Products of seven cultures show trading pattern joining eastern and central Mediterranean. [CGT]

6.169 Carl W. Blegen. *Troy and the Trojans.* 1963 ed. New York: Praeger, 1966. ‣ Basic description of site regarded as Troy, written by American excavator who systematically investigated strata first uncovered by Schliemann. Includes chronology and phases of site from fourth into first millennium. [CGT]

6.170 Carl W. Blegen and J. B. Haley. "The coming of the Greeks." *American journal of archaeology* 32.2 (1928) 141–54. ISSN 0002-9114. ‣ Reconstruction of geographical distribution of pre-Greek place names that, when corroborated by archaeological evidence, suggests Anatolian migration into Greece. Established chronology and demography of Bronze Age Greece. [CGT]

6.171 Carl W. Blegen, Marion Rawson, and Mabel Lang. *The palace of Nestor at Pylos in western Messenia.* 3 vols. in 4. Princeton: Princeton University Press for the University of Cincinnati, 1966–73. ‣ Official archaeological publication of excavation of Pylos, best preserved Mycenaean palace and source of majority of Linear B tablets; volume 2, by Lang, contains frescoes. [CGT]

6.172 R. J. Buck. "The Minoan thalassocracy re-examined." *Historia* 11.2 (1962) 129–37. ISSN 0018-2311. ‣ Posits historical reality of Minoan naval hegemony dominating Cyclades in middle Bronze Age. Reopens debate over actuality of thalassocracy (sea empire) in light of challenges; current scholarship largely follows this position. See Starr 6.189. [CGT]

6.173 John Chadwick. *Linear B and related scripts.* Berkeley: University of California Press, 1987. ISBN 0-520-06019-9. ‣ Brief, introductory survey of decipherment of Linear B and related Bronze Age scripts by leading expert. Recounts origins of scripts and their uses; related scripts as yet undeciphered. [CGT]

6.174 John Chadwick. *The Mycenaean world.* Cambridge: Cambridge University Press, 1976. ISBN 0-521-21077-1 (cl), 0-521-29037-6 (pbk). ‣ Thoughtful discussion of social, economic, and political nature of life in Mycenaean Greece based on contents of Linear B tablets. [CGT]

6.175 O.T.P.K. Dickinson. *The origins of Mycenaean civilisation.*

Göteborg, Sweden: Åström, 1977. (Studies in Mediterranean archaeology, 49.) ISBN 91-85085-74-2, ISSN 0081-8232. ‣ Detailed presentation of archaeological evidence. [MC]

6.176 Christos G. Doumas. *Thera, Pompeii of the ancient Aegean: excavations at Akrotiri, 1967–79.* London: Thames & Hudson, 1983. ISBN 0-500-39016-9. ‣ Introductory survey of remains of ancient Akrotiri, on Aegean island of Santorini (Thera), buried in massive volcanic eruption ca. 1500 BCE. Discussion of excavation, its finds, and city's role vis-à-vis Minoan and Mycenaean civilizations by excavation director. [CGT]

6.177 Robert Drews. *The end of the Bronze Age: changes in warfare and the catastrophe, ca. 1200 B.C.* Princeton: Princeton University Press, 1993. ISBN 0-691-04811-8. ‣ Adventurous attempt to explain widespread destruction of cities in Mediterranean, ca. 1200 BCE. Conjectures that chariot warfare gave way to massed infantry attacks. [MC]

6.178 Henri van Effenterre. *Mycènes, vie et mort d'une civilisation: la seconde fin du monde.* 1974 ed. Paris: Errance, 1985. ISBN 2-903442-09-6. ‣ Cohesive, readable overview of collapse of Bronze Age civilizations by leading French historian. Treats nature of Bronze Age, evidence of collapse, possible explanations, and continuities before and after collapse. [CGT]

6.179 Arthur Evans. *The Palace of Minos: a comparative account of the successive stages of the early Cretan civilization as illustrated by the discoveries at Knossos.* 1921–36 ed. 4 vols. in 6 plus index. Joan Evans, Index. New York: Biblo & Tannen, 1964. ‣ Discussion of evidence uncovered at palace site named from legendary king Minos. Site's excavator describes material and defines chronological stages from late Neolithic through Bronze Age. Initiated continuing debate. [CGT]

6.180 M. I. Finley et al. "The Trojan War." *Journal of Hellenic studies* 84 (1964) 1–20. ISSN 0075-4269. ‣ Good formulation of major historical problem. Finley challenges reliability of tradition attesting to Trojan War as involving mainland Greece. Caskey responds on archaeological grounds, Kirk through nature of oral tradition, and Page through historical reconstruction. [CGT]

6.181 William A. McDonald and George R. Rapp, Jr., eds. *The Minnesota Messenia expedition: reconstructing a Bronze Age regional environment.* Minneapolis: University of Minnesota Press, 1972. ISBN 0-8166-0636-6. ‣ Technical presentation of finds of multidisciplinary, intensive archaeological exploration of southwest Peloponnese that endeavored to understand relationship between inhabitants and natural environment from prehistoric into Greco-Roman times. [CGT]

6.182 René A. van Noyen and Benjamin Isaac. *The arrival of the Greeks: the evidence from the settlements.* Amsterdam: Grüner, 1979. (Publications of the Henry Frankfort Foundation, 5.) ISBN 90-6032-109-X. ‣ On basis of archaeological evidence, argues for "discontinuity" in invasions by Greeks ca. 2000 and ca. 1600 BCE. [MC]

6.183 D. L. Page. *History and the Homeric "Iliad."* 1959 ed. Berkeley: University of California Press, 1966. ISBN 0-520-03246-2. ‣ Still valuable attempt to settle major historical issues of heroic Greece such as history of Troy, historical background of Trojan War, Homeric description of Mycenaean Greece, and Hittite references to Achaean Greeks. [CGT]

6.184 Colin Renfrew. *Archaeology and language: the puzzle of Indo-European origins.* 1988 ed. Cambridge: Cambridge University Press, 1990. ISBN 0-521-35432-3 (cl), 0-521-38675-6 (pbk). ‣ Controversial challenge to view that Indo-European languages were spread by mounted warriors departing western Russia during early Bronze Age. Language and archaeology reveal spread through peaceful diffusion of agriculture from ca. 7000 BCE. [CGT]

6.185 Colin Renfrew. *The emergence of civilisation: the Cyclades and the Aegean in the third millennium B.C.* London: Methuen, 1972. ISBN 0-416-16480-3. ‣ Employing systems analysis, shows forces transforming Aegean culture into complex civilization, ca. 3000 BCE. Description of evidence and examination of process. [CGT]

6.186 N. K. Sandars. *The Sea Peoples: warriors of the ancient Mediterranean, 1250–1150 BC.* Rev. ed. London: Thames & Hudson, 1985. ISBN 0-500-27387-1 (pbk). ‣ Fullest English-language account of late Bronze Age migrating peoples known as Land and Sea Peoples. Convincingly shows how these disparate groups bear some responsibility for collapse of Bronze Age civilization in eastern Mediterranean. [CGT]

6.187 R. Hope Simpson. *Mycenaean Greece.* Park Ridge, N.J.: Noyes, 1981. ISBN 0-8155-5061-8. ‣ Fullest English-language archaeological gazetteer of Mycenaean sites of mainland, Ionian islands, Aegean islands, and western Asia Minor. Provides basic data, maps, and references to ca. 900 sites. [CGT]

6.188 R. Hope Simpson and J. F. Lazenby. *The catalogue of ships in Homer's "Iliad."* Oxford: Clarendon, 1970. ISBN 0-19-814349-4. ‣ Sensitive use of excavation and topographical research to show how catalog of Greek forces in Book II of *Iliad* survived as poetic reconstruction based on actual Mycenaean sites. [CGT]

6.189 Chester G. Starr. "The myth of the Minoan thalassocracy." *Historia* 3.3 (1954–55) 282–91. ISSN 0018-2311. ‣ Asserts that myth of Minoan thalassocracy (sea empire) originated in fifth-century imperialist Athens. First serious challenge to accepted view of Evans 6.179; see also Buck 6.172. [CGT]

6.190 William Taylour. *The Mycenaeans.* 1983 rev. ed. London: Thames & Hudson, 1990. ISBN 0-500-27586-6 (pbk). ‣ General account of Mycenaean civilization grounded in archaeological evidence. Presents picture of basic features of life along with historical overview. [CGT]

6.191 Carol G. Thomas. "A Mycenaean hegemony? A reconsideration." *Journal of Hellenic studies* 90 (1970) 184–92. ISSN 0075-4269. ‣ Reevaluation of controversial consideration of issue of Mycenaean political unity. Evidence for cultural *koine* (commonality) does not support view of unified political structure linking kingdoms. [CGT]

6.192 Michael Ventris and John Chadwick. *Documents in Mycenaean Greek.* 2d ed. Cambridge: Cambridge University Press, 1973. ISBN 0-521-08558-6. ‣ Translation of selected Linear B texts from Knossos, Pylos, and Mycenae along with introductory chapters on decipherment, writing system, language, and implications for Mycenaean civilization. [CGT]

6.193 Michael Ventris and John Chadwick. "Evidence for Greek dialect in the Mycenaean archives." *Journal of Hellenic studies* 73 (1953) 84–105. ISSN 0075-4269. ‣ Astounding, initially controversial announcement of decipherment of Linear B as script for early form of Greek. States linguistic, historical, and archaeological reasons for claim; prints grid used in decipherment; explains basic orthography. [CGT]

6.194 Emily Vermeule. *Greece in the Bronze Age.* 1964 ed. Chicago: University of Chicago Press, 1972. ISBN 0-226-85353-3. ‣ Survey of evidence and reconstruction of civilization of Bronze Age Greece. Chronological framework provides account of historical development and problematic issues of interpretation. [CGT]

ARCHAIC GREECE, ca. 1100–ca. 500 BCE

6.195 A. Andrewes. *The Greek tyrants.* London: Hutchinson's University Library, 1956. ‣ Origin and role of tyrants in archaic Greek states, ca. 650–510 BCE, illustrating link to hoplite revolu-

tion, economic developments, and changes in social structure. Necessary, valuable phase in Greek political development. [CGT]

6.196 J. N. Coldstream. *Geometric Greece.* New York: St. Martin's, 1977. ISBN 0-312-32365-4. ‣ Description of recovery of Greece from Dark Age isolation and poverty through detailed archaeological evidence of basic regions. Final section offers reconstruction of basic features of daily life. [CGT]

6.197 Robert Drews. *Basileus: the evidence for kingship in geometric Greece.* New Haven: Yale University Press, 1983. ISBN 0-300-02831-8. ‣ Revisionist work arguing that *basileis* (kings) in early Greek history were groups of hereditary nobles who held power through informal regimes; true individual kings probably existed in many fewer states than has been thought. [MC]

6.198 M. I. Finley. *The world of Odysseus.* 1978 2d ed. Harmondsworth: Penguin, 1979. ISBN 0-14-020570-5 (pbk). ‣ Reconstruction of sociopolitical world depicted in *Odyssey* within tenth-ninth century context. Two appendixes, "The World of Odysseus Revisited" and "Schliemann's Troy—One Hundred Years After," reappraise fundamental issues of interpretation. Most widely read account of Dark Age Greece. [CGT]

6.199 W. G. Forrest. *The emergence of Greek democracy, 800–400 B.C.* 1966 ed. New York: McGraw-Hill, 1979. ‣ Brief, lively assessment of key moments in Greek political history: rise of tyranny, colonization, early Sparta, and emergence of Athenian democracy. Progressive exposition, countering conservative bias of many historians. [RWW]

6.200 A. J. Graham. *Colony and mother city in ancient Greece.* 2d ed. Chicago: Ares, 1983. ISBN 0-89005-520-3. ‣ Still best available account of process of foundation of colonies and ensuing relations between colonies and their mother-cities, eighth through fifth centuries BCE. [CGT]

6.201 R. J. Hopper. *The early Greeks.* 1976 ed. New York: Barnes & Noble, 1977. ISBN 0-06-492978-7. ‣ Useful survey ranging from Cretan civilization down to ca. 500 BCE; references and bibliography. [MC]

6.202 L. H. Jeffery. *Archaic Greece: the city-states, c. 700–500 B.C.* New York: St. Martin's, 1976. ‣ Overview of archaic Greece, arranged according to major regions. Political-military orientation. [CGT]

6.203 C. M. Kraay. "Hoards, small change, and the origins of coinage." *Journal of Hellenic studies* 84 (1964) 76–91. ISSN 0075-4269. ‣ General discussion of origin and use of coins of Greece. Absence of small denominations suggests coins initially used for storing surplus wealth rather than for common trade, which developed later. [CGT]

6.204 Ian Morris. "The use and abuse of Homer." *Classical antiquity* 5.1 (1986) 81–138. ISSN 0278-6656. ‣ Rigorous bibliographic analysis of Homeric scholarship directed to dating historical framework of epics. Nature of oral tradition makes context of epics Dark Age, not Mycenaean. [CGT]

6.205 Oswyn Murray. *Early Greece.* 1980 ed. Stanford, Calif.: Stanford University Press, 1983. ISBN 0-8047-1185-2. ‣ Textbook survey of early Greece from end of Dark Age through Persian wars. Based on recent discoveries and new approaches; emphasizes social, economic, and cultural developments. [CGT]

6.206 A. M. Snodgrass. *Archaic Greece: the age of experiment.* Berkeley: University of California Press, 1980. ISBN 0-520-04373-1. ‣ Examination of 200 years when Greece emerged from backward obscurity to conspicuous position in Mediterranean. Draws from archaeological evidence its social, economic, political, and cultural implications. [CGT]

6.207 A. M. Snodgrass. "The hoplite reform and history." *Journal of Hellenic studies* 85 (1965) 110–33. ISSN 0075-4269. ‣ Refutation of traditional seventh-century date of hoplite military reform; minimizes political significance of development. [CGT]

6.208 Chester G. Starr. *The economic and social growth of ancient Greece, 800–500 B.C.* New York: Oxford University Press, 1977. ISBN 0-19-502223-8 (cl), 0-19-502224-6 (pbk). ▸ Interdisciplinary account of social and economic revolution between 800 and 500 BCE, setting base for classical period of Greek history. Brief treatment of basic elements of economic life and social consequences. [CGT]

CLASSICAL GREECE, ca. 500–ca. 323 BCE

6.209 M. Amit. *Great and small poleis: a study in the relations between the great powers and small cities in ancient Greece.* Brussels: Latomus, 1973. ▸ Important study focusing on role of three pairs of states—Sparta and Mantinea, Thebes and Plataea, and Athens and Aegina—in Greek affairs. [CWH]

6.210 P. A. Brunt. "The Hellenic League against Persia." *Historia* 2.2 (1953–54) 135–63. ISSN 0018-2311. ▸ Discussion of defensive alliance against Persians, contrasting it with and distinguishing it from Peloponnesian and Delian leagues. [CWH]

6.211 P. A. Brunt. "Spartan policy and strategy in the Archidamian War." *Phoenix* 19 (1965) 255–80. ISSN 0031-8299. ▸ Classic statement of Spartan strategy in early years of Peloponnesian War. Consideration of annual invasions of Attica and Brasidas' northern campaign; factions in Sparta. [CWH]

6.212 A. R. Burn. *Persia and the Greeks: the defence of the West, c. 546–478 B.C.* 2d ed. David M. Lewis, Postscript. Stanford, Calif.: Stanford University Press, 1984. ISBN 0-8047-1235-2. ▸ Lively military history. Appendix by Lewis brings Burn up to date on Persia and new epigraphic developments. [CWH]

6.213 Victor Ehrenberg. *From Solon to Socrates: Greek history and civilization during the sixth and fifth centuries B.C.* 2d ed. London: Methuen; distributed by Barnes & Noble, 1973. ISBN 0-416-77610-8 (cl), 0-416-77760-0 (pbk). ▸ Exemplary mixture of political, military, social, and intellectual history. Accessible introduction to fifth and fourth centuries. [CWH]

6.214 A. W. Gomme. *Essays in Greek history and literature.* 1937 ed. Freeport, N.Y.: Books for Libraries, 1967. ▸ Collection of Gomme's essays; notable for articles on Thucydides, politics, demography, and society of classical Athens. [CWH]

6.215 A. W. Gomme. *More essays in Greek history and literature.* David A. Campbell, ed. Oxford: Blackwell, 1962. ▸ Essays on Greek history and literature similar to those in Gomme 6.214. [CWH]

6.216 Charles D. Hamilton. *Sparta's bitter victories: politics and diplomacy in the Corinthian War.* Ithaca, N.Y.: Cornell University Press, 1979. ISBN 0-8014-1158-0. ▸ Historical treatment of period between 403 and 386 BCE. Discussion of Spartan diplomatic relations with allies, other Greeks, and Persians and internal Spartan politics. [JB]

6.217 C. Hignett. *Xerxes' invasion of Greece.* Oxford: Clarendon, 1963. ▸ Immensely detailed history of famous battles. At its best on topography. [CWH]

6.218 Louis Robert. *Opera minora selecta: épigraphie et antiquités grecques.* 7 vols. Amsterdam: Hakkert, 1969–90. ISBN 90-256-0526-5 (set). ▸ Collection of articles spanning career of almost sixty years. Showcases incredible range and learning of author particularly known for work on Greco-Roman Asia Minor and Greek inscriptions. Rather technical. [CWH]

6.219 G.E.M. de Ste. Croix. *The origins of the Peloponnesian War.* Ithaca, N.Y.: Cornell University Press, 1972. ISBN 0-8014-0719-2. ▸ Among much else, important discussions of economic factors leading to war, religious and Megarian decrees, and Spartan foreign policy. See Kagan 6.309. [CWH]

6.220 Robin Seager. "The King's Peace and the balance of power in Greece, 386–362 B.C." *Athenaeum: studi periodici di letteratura e storia dell' antichità,* n.s., 52.1–2 (1974) 36–63. ISSN 0004-6574. ▸ Analysis of relations among Athens, Sparta, and Thebes after King's Peace. [CWH]

6.221 Robin Seager and Christopher Tuplin. "The freedom of the Greeks in Asia: on the origins of a concept and the creation of a slogan." *Journal of Hellenic studies* 100 (1980) 141–54. ISSN 0075-4269. ▸ Essay on local formation of specific ideal of freedom in first decade of fourth century. Antidote to general obsession with Athenian political ideology. [CWH]

6.222 H. T. Wade-Gery. *Essays in Greek history.* Oxford: Blackwell, 1958. ▸ Although written mainly in 1930s and 1940s, articles remain worthwhile, full of bold ideas and impressive detail. Note especially essays on Thucydides, son of Melesias, Peace of Callias, and Demotionidai. [CWH]

6.223 Édouard Will. *Le cinquième siècle (510–403).* Vol. 1 of *Le monde grec et l'Orient.* 4th ed. Paris: Presses Universitaires de France, 1991. ISBN 2-13-043990-X (v. 1). ▸ Probably best one-volume history of fifth century; continued by 6.224. [CWH]

6.224 Édouard Will, Claude Mossé, and P. Goukowsky. *Le quatrième siècle et l'époque hellénistique.* Vol. 2 of *Le monde grec et l'Orient.* 3d ed. Paris: Presses Universitaires de France, 1990. ISBN 2-13-042985-8 (v. 2). ▸ Continues 6.223 into Hellenistic age, concentrating on Greek politics and kingdoms of successor states; thorough, well-organized survey. [CWH]

PHILIP II OF MACEDONIA, 359–336 BCE

6.225 John Buckler. *Philip II and the Sacred War.* Leiden: Brill, 1989. (*Mnemosyne,* Supplement, 109.) ISBN 90-04-09095-9, ISSN 0169-8958. ▸ Study of outbreak of Third Sacred War. Topographical discussion of areas of conflict, narrative of course of war, and Philip's entry into Greek politics. [JB]

6.226 George Cawkwell. *Philip of Macedon.* London: Faber & Faber, 1978. ISBN 0-571-10958-6. ▸ Topics include Macedonia before Philip, consolidation of borders, Philip's reorganization of army, royal government, Philip's career, and League of Corinth. [JB]

6.227 J. R. Ellis. *Philip II and Macedonian imperialism.* London: Thames & Hudson, 1976. ISBN 0-500-40028-8. ▸ Chronology of Philip's reign. Discussion of ambitions in northern Aegean, relations with Athens; hypotheses about his peaceful intentions toward Athens, his triumphs and ultimate aims. [JB]

ALEXANDER THE GREAT, 336–323 BCE
Sources and Commentaries

6.228 Arrian. *Anabasis Alexandri, Indica.* Rev. ed. 2 vols. P. A. Brunt, trans. Cambridge, Mass.: Harvard University Press, 1976–83. ISBN 0-674-99260-1 (v. 1), 0-674-99297-0 (v. 2). ▸ Greek text and translation. Introduction and extensive historical-historiographic notes and appendixes. Major scholarly aid. [EB]

6.229 J. E. Atkinson. *A commentary on Q. Curtius Rufus' "Historiae Alexandri Magni," Books 3 and 4.* Amsterdam: Gieben, 1980. ISBN 90-7026-561-3. ▸ Only modern commentary on Latin historian of Alexander; additional volumes forthcoming. [EB]

6.230 A. B. Bosworth. *From Arrian to Alexander: studies in historical interpretation.* Oxford: Clarendon, 1988. ISBN 0-19-814863-1. ▸ Exact discussion of Arrian as source for history of Alexander, in context of other sources. [EB]

6.231 A. B. Bosworth. *A historical commentary on Arrian's "History of Alexander."* Vol. 1: *Commentary on Books 1–3.* 1 vol. to date. Oxford: Clarendon, 1980–. ISBN 0-19-814828-3 (v. 1). ▸ Parallel to other Oxford commentaries; thorough discussion of historical and topographic problems. [MC]

6.232 Diodorus Siculus. *Bibliothèque historique.* Vol. 17. P. Goukowsky, ed. Paris: Belles Lettres, 1976. ▸ Standard edition with French translation and extensive annotation on text and points of historical-historiographic interest. See 6.108. [EB]

6.233 J. R. Hamilton. *Plutarch: Alexander, a commentary.* Oxford: Clarendon, 1969. ISBN 0-19-814177-7. ▸ Commentary on one of Plutarch's most important biographies. See also Hamilton 6.247. [MC]

6.234 A. J. Heisserer. *Alexander the Great and the Greeks: the epigraphical evidence.* Norman: University of Oklahoma Press, 1980. ISBN 0-8061-1612-9. ▸ Epigraphic study of messages Alexander sent to Greek states in response to specific problems. Examination and dating of stones themselves; discussion of their significance. [JB]

6.235 Lionel Pearson. *The lost histories of Alexander the Great.* 1960 ed. Chico, Calif.: Scholars Press, 1983. ISBN 0-89130-641-2. ▸ Valuable discussion, supplementing Jacoby, ed. (6.110), of historians preserved in fragments. [EB]

6.236 Martin Jessop Price. *The coinage in the name of Alexander the Great and Philip Arrhidaeus: a British Museum catalogue.* 2 vols. Zurich: Swiss Numismatic Society, 1991. ISBN 3-908103-00-2 (set). ▸ Huge work, standard annotated collection of contemporary and posthumous Alexander coinage. [EB]

6.237 Charles Alexander Robinson, Jr. *The history of Alexander the Great.* Vol. 1: *An index to the extant historians.* 1953 ed. Millwood, N.Y.: Kraus Reprint, 1977. ISBN 0-527-76000-5. ▸ Translations of Greek fragments of historians of Alexander collected by Jacoby (6.110). [EB]

6.238 Q. Curtius Rufus. *History of Alexander.* H. Yardley, trans. W. Heckel, Introduction and notes. Harmondsworth: Penguin, 1984. ISBN 0-14-044412-2 (pbk). ▸ Useful annotated translation of rhetorical Latin history of Alexander from early Roman empire, based on romanticizing fourth-century BCE source. [EB]

Biography and General Studies

6.239 E. Badian. "Alexander in Iran." In *Cambridge history of Iran.* Ilya Gershevitch, ed., vol. 2, pp. 420–501 (text), 897–903 (notes). Cambridge: Cambridge University Press, 1985. ▸ Outline of Alexander's life and first decade of the Successors, with detailed account of Alexander's movements in Iran and dealings with Iranians. Selective, partly critical bibliography organized by subject. [EB]

6.240 E. Badian. "Alexander the Great and the unity of mankind." *Historia* 7 (1958) 425–44. ISSN 0018-2311. ▸ Refutation of W. W. Tarn's theory, still encountered in some popular works, that Alexander was striving for harmony within whole human race. [MC]

6.241 E. Badian. "The death of Parmenio." *Transactions of the American Philological Association* 91 (1960) 324–38. ▸ One of many studies by author reappraising Alexander. Treats Alexander's elimination of potential rival as evidence of his suspicious, vengeful character. [MC]

6.242 E. Badian. "Harpalus." *Journal of Hellenic studies* 81 (1961) 16–43. ISSN 0075-4269. ▸ Study of Alexander from return from India to death, including purge of commanders, decree ordering return of exiles, desire for deification, and dealings with Athens. [EB]

6.243 E. Badian, ed. *Alexandre le grand, image et réalité: sept exposés suivis de discussions.* Geneva: Fondation Hardt; distributed by Droz, 1976. (Entretiens sur l'antiquité classique, 22.) ▸ Recent interpretations of Alexander's career, discussions of sources, relations with subject nations, Macedonian army, historical impact on Hellenistic and Roman worlds. [JB]

6.244 Helmut Berve. *Das Alexanderreich auf prosopographischer Grundlage.* 1926 ed. 2 vols. New York: Arno, 1973. ISBN 0-405-04779-7. ▸ Volume 2 contains exhaustive prosopography of all persons connected with Alexander the Great; historical notes on each one. Essential. [MC]

6.245 A. B. Bosworth. *Conquest and empire: the reign of Alexander the Great.* Cambridge: Cambridge University Press, 1988. ISBN 0-521-34320-8 (cl), 0-521-34823-4 (pbk). ▸ Now standard treatment; discussion of sources, bibliography of ca. 500 items. [EB]

6.246 Donald W. Engels. *Alexander the Great and the logistics of the Macedonian army.* Berkeley: University of California Press, 1978. ISBN 0-520-04272-7 (cl), 0-520-03433-3 (pbk). ▸ Original study of terrain, climate, and supply requirements of Alexander's campaign. Constraints of logistics in military strategy, numbers of troops, food requirements, rates of march, and routes followed by army. [EMH]

6.247 J. R. Hamilton. *Alexander the Great.* Pittsburgh: University of Pittsburgh Press, 1973. ISBN 0-8229-6084-2. ▸ Perhaps best general treatment of Alexander in English. Evaluation of Alexander's life and career and analysis of sources; not romanticized. [JB]

6.248 N.G.L. Hammond. *Alexander the Great: king, commander, and statesman.* 2d ed. Bristol: Bristol Classical, 1989. ISBN 1-85399-068-X (pbk). ▸ Especially useful for battles and topography, by veteran connoisseur of Macedonia. Many maps and plans. [MC]

6.249 Jakob Seibert. *Alexander der Große.* Darmstadt: Wissenschaftliche Buchgesellschaft, 1972. ISBN 3-534-04492-4. ▸ Almost complete bibliography of nineteenth- and twentieth-century scholarship. Critical surveys of main problems; best on German work. [EB]

6.250 Jakob Seibert, ed. *Die Eroberung des Perserreiches durch Alexander d. Gr. auf kartographischer Grundlage.* Wiesbaden: Reichert, 1985. (Beihefte zum Tübinger Atlas des Vorderen Orients, Reihe B, 68.) ISBN 3-88226-246-X. ▸ Narrative of Alexander's campaign in Persia along with packet of loose-leaf maps tracing military operations and administrative arrangements from Alexander's accession (336 BCE) to his death (323). Basic for study of Alexander. [EB]

6.251 Ulrich Wilcken. *Alexander the Great.* Eugene N. Borza, ed. G. C. Richards, trans. New York: Norton, 1967. ISBN 0-393-00381-7. ▸ Contributions of Philip and transformation of Macedonia. Alexander's youth, invasion of Asia, and effects of Alexander's career on later history. Includes introduction to Alexander studies by editor. [JB]

HELLENISTIC WORLD, 323–30 BCE

6.252 R. E. Allen. *The Attalid kingdom: a constitutional history.* Oxford: Clarendon, 1983. ISBN 0-19-814845-3. ▸ General history of Attalid kingdom in Asia Minor with special emphasis on governing system and administrative institutions and policies. Special studies of Galatians, royal cult, and Pergamum city. [RAB]

6.253 Roger S. Bagnall. *The administration of the Ptolemaic possessions outside Egypt.* Leiden: Brill, 1976. ISBN 90-04-04490-6. ▸ Investigation of Ptolemaic rule in Palestine, Cyrenaica, Cyprus, Asia Minor, and Aegean; based heavily on epigraphic evidence. Fundamental study of institutions of imperial rule. [RAB]

6.254 E. J. Bickerman. *Institutions des Séleucides.* Paris:

Geuthner, 1938. ‣ Dated but still standard work on most aspects of structure and administration of Seleucid empire (late fourth to first century BCE). [RAB]

6.255 Richard A. Billows. *Antigonos the One-Eyed and the creation of the Hellenistic state.* Berkeley: University of California Press, 1990. ISBN 0-520-06378-3. ‣ Biography of Antigonos Monophthalmos and history of period of Alexander's successors and organization of Macedonian conquests in Asia. Shows that Antigonos anticipated much of work of Seleucus in founding Seleucid empire. [RAB]

6.256 Getzel M. Cohen. *The Seleucid colonies.* Wiesbaden: Steiner, 1978. (*Historia*, Einzelschriften, 30.) ISBN 3-515-02581-2, ISSN 0341-0056. ‣ Comprehensive account of process of settling colonies in Seleucid empire with discussion of structure and institutions of colonies. Based heavily on archaeological and epigraphic evidence. [RAB]

6.257 P. M. Fraser. *Ptolemaic Alexandria.* 3 vols. Oxford: Clarendon, 1972. ISBN 0-19-814278-1. ‣ Outstanding study of Alexandria as Hellenistic city, as Ptolemaic capital, as great trading center, and especially as cultural center of Hellenistic civilization; text (volume 1), notes (volume 2), and indexes (volume 3). [RAB]

6.258 Koen Goudriaan. *Ethnicity in Ptolemaic Egypt.* Amsterdam: Gieben, 1988. ISBN 90-5063-022-7. ‣ Technical study of social boundaries between Greeks and Egyptians in Ptolemaic Egypt. Ethnicity a social rather than juridical or political phenomenon. Papyrologically based social history. [SMB]

6.259 John D. Grainger. *The cities of Seleukid Syria.* Oxford: Clarendon, 1990. ISBN 0-19-814694-9. ‣ Excellent account of colonies in Seleucid empire's Syrian heartland, emphasizing process of city foundation under Seleucus I and life of colonists in cities subsequently. [RAB]

6.260 Peter Green. *Alexander to Actium: the historical evolution of the Hellenistic age.* Berkeley: University of California Press, 1990. ISBN 0-520-05611-6. ‣ Emphasizes politics, but includes culture and society. Massive, yet selective and critical bibliography. Surprisingly readable. [CWH]

6.261 Erich S. Gruen. *The Hellenistic world and the coming of Rome.* 2 vols. Berkeley: University of California Press, 1984. ISBN 0-520-04569-6 (set). ‣ Exceptional on Roman diplomacy and Greeks; analysis of Roman notions of *amicitia* (friendship) and *clientela* (patronage), two common types of relations between Rome and other states. [CWH]

6.262 Esther V. Hansen. *The Attalids of Pergamon.* 2d ed. Ithaca, N.Y.: Cornell University Press, 1971. ISBN 0-8014-0615-3. ‣ Excellent general history of Attalid dynasty with special studies of geography and organization of kingdom, city of Pergamum and its buildings, art, culture, and religious cults. [RAB]

6.263 Helmut Koester. *History, culture, and religion of the Hellenistic age.* Vol. 1 of *Introduction to the New Testament.* New York: de Gruyter, 1982. ISBN 0-89925-198-6. ‣ General survey of history, society, economics, education, literature, philosophy, religion, and Judaism in Hellenistic and Roman worlds. Translation of *Einführung in das Neue Testament* (1980). [GND]

6.264 Amélie Kuhrt and Susan M. Sherwin-White. *From Samarkhand to Sardis: a new approach to the Seleucid empire.* Berkeley: University of California Press, 1992. ISBN 0-520-08183-8. ‣ Social and administrative history of Seleucid empire (late fourth to first century BCE). Uses fresh evidence from archaeology and cuneiform sources. Dispels old ideas about ethnic exclusivity and decadence of Seleucid empire. [RAB]

6.265 Naphtali Lewis. *Greeks in Ptolemaic Egypt: case studies in the social history of the Hellenistic world.* Oxford: Clarendon, 1986. ISBN 0-19-814867-4. ‣ Special studies on Greek colonists and

administrators in Ptolemaic Egypt and relations with natives; theorizes that persons with Greek and Egyptian names are products of intermarriage, not hellenization. [RAB]

6.266 Ernst Meyer. *Die Grenzen der hellenistischen Staaten in Kleinasien.* Zurich: Füssli, 1925. ‣ General study of Asia Minor in Hellenistic Age, concentrating on various state structures in region (Seleucid and Ptolemaic empires, Bithynia, Pontus, Cappadocia, Pergamum, Rhodes, and minor dynasts). Substantially out of date but not replaced. [RAB]

6.267 Eckart Olshausen. *Prosopographie der hellenistischen Königsgesandten.* Vol. 1: *Von Triparadeisos bis Pydna.* Louvain: Nauwelaerts, 1974. (Studia Hellenistica, 19.) ‣ Important prosopography of 223 functionaries dispatched on diplomatic missions by Hellenistic kings from 321 BCE to 168 BCE. Succeeds chronologically Berve 6.244. Second volume, to 31 BCE, never published. [MC]

6.268 W. Peremans and E. van't Dack. *Prosopographia Ptolemaica.* 9 vols. Louvain: Bibliotheca Universitatis Lovanii, 1950–81. (Studia Hellenistica, 6, 8, 11–13, 17, 20, 21, 25.) ‣ Immense prosopography of Hellenistic period, especially civil servants. Follows model of Kirchner 6.289. [MC]

6.269 P. W. Pestman, ed. and comp. *A guide to the Zenon archive.* 2 vols. Leiden: Brill, 1981. (Papyrologica Lugduno-Batava, 21 A/B.) ISBN 90-04-06325-0 (v. 21A), 90-04-06326-9 (v. 21B). ‣ Guide to most important collection of papyri for understanding Ptolemaic administration of Egypt and social and economic history of Ptolemaic Egypt. Very technical but indispensable for scholars. Text (volume 1), indexes and maps (volume 2). [RAB]

6.270 Claire Préaux. *Le monde hellénistique: la Grèce et l'Orient de la mort d'Alexandre à la conquête romaine de la Grèce (323–146 av. J.-C.)* 2 vols. Paris: Presses Universitaires de France, 1978. ISBN 2-13-035263-4 (v. 1), 2-13-035264-2 (v. 2). ‣ Monumental, critical survey of problems within Hellenistic history and culture with ample bibliographies. Omits political history, for which see Will 6.276. [MC]

6.271 M. Rostovtzeff. *The social and economic history of the Hellenistic world.* 1941 ed. 3 vols. Oxford: Clarendon, 1986. ISBN 0-19-814230-7. ‣ History of Hellenistic world from 323 BCE to 30 BCE with emphasis on social history; how Greek immigrant bourgeoisie created Hellenistic culture. Nonquantitative social history on monumental scale by leading historian of ancient world in his time. [SMB]

6.272 W. W. Tarn. *Hellenistic civilisation.* 1952 3d ed. G. T. Griffith, ed. New York: New American Library, 1975. ‣ At one time standard textbook in English, by Britain's leading authority on Hellenistic age; still worth consulting. [CWH]

6.273 Dorothy Thompson. *Memphis under the Ptolemies.* Princeton: Princeton University Press, 1988. ISBN 0-691-03593-8. ‣ Investigation of urban, economic, and religious life of Egyptian city down to Roman empire. [MC]

6.274 Giovanni Vitucci. *Il regno di Bitinia.* Rome: Signorelli, 1953. (Studi pubblicati dall'Istituto Italiano per la Storia Antica, 10.) ‣ History of Bithynia in Asia Minor under Zipoitid dynasty, late fourth to first century BCE. Royal institutions and policies emphasized; special study of hellenization in Bithynia. [RAB]

6.275 F. W. Walbank. *The Hellenistic world.* 1981 ed. Cambridge, Mass.: Harvard University Press, 1982. ISBN 0-674-38725-2 (pbk). ‣ Convenient, reliable, and brief college text introducing Hellenistic history. [CWH]

6.276 Édouard Will. *Histoire politique du monde hellénistique, 323–30 av. J.-C.* 2d ed. 2 vols. Nancy: Presses Universitaires de Nancy, 1979–82. (Annales de l'Est, Mémoires, 30, 32.) ISBN 2-86480-028-4 (v. 2). ‣ Political history of successors to Alexander and Hellenistic kingdoms on broadest possible scale; full discussions of controversies. For cultural history see Préaux 6.270. [CWH]

ATHENS AND ATTICA

Physical Setting and Archaeology

6.277 *The Athenian agora.* Princeton: American School of Classical Studies, 1953–. ▸ Series of volumes, by various authors, publishing results of excavations in *agora* (market place) of Athens. Indispensable. [MC]

6.278 John M. Camp. *The Athenian agora: excavations in the heart of classical Athens.* New York: Thames & Hudson, 1986. ISBN 0-500-39021-5. ▸ Archaeologically based introductory history of civic center of Athens from prehistory to beginning of Byzantine period. [SMB]

6.279 Homer A. Thompson and R. E. Wycherley. *The agora of Athens: the history, shape, and uses of an ancient city center.* Princeton: American School of Classical Studies at Athens, 1972. (Athenian agora, 14.) ISBN 0-87661-214-1. ▸ Synthesis of American excavations since 1931 and of earlier findings by Greek and German archaeologists. Covers period from before Solon to after Heruli; material organized by type and function rather than by date. Part of series at 6.277. [JJD]

6.280 John Travlos. *Pictorial dictionary of ancient Athens.* 1971 ed. New York: Hacker, 1980. ISBN 0-87817-267-X. ▸ Topographical dictionary with alphabetically arranged short essays accompanied by plans, photographs, reconstructions, and bibliographies. Fuller treatments of agora, Acropolis, and Kerameikos. [JJD]

Documents and Sources

6.281 Felix Jacoby. *Atthis: the local chronicles of ancient Athens.* Oxford: Clarendon, 1949. ▸ Densely argued and documented study focusing on seven, mostly fourth-century, Atthidographers. Rich source of information and opinion on Greek history and historiography. See also Jacoby, ed. 6.110. [RWW]

6.282 David M. Lewis, ed. *Inscriptiones Atticae Euclidis anno anteriores.* 3d ed. Berlin: de Gruyter, 1981–. (Inscriptiones Graecae, I.) ISBN 3-11-007676-4. ▸ Latest revision of Athenian inscriptions of fifth century BCE; contributions by many editors. Will be standard for decades. [MC]

6.283 Al. N. Oikonomides, ed. *Inscriptiones Atticae: supplementum inscriptionum Atticarum.* 5 vols. Chicago: Ares, 1976–84. ▸ Reprints various collections of Athenian inscriptions as supplements to *Inscriptiones Graecae* (6.120). Some important separate papers, especially on ostracism, included in volume 5. [MC]

6.284 Lionel Pearson. *The local historians of Attica.* Philadelphia: American Philological Association, 1942. (American Philological Association, Monographs, 11.) ▸ Treatment of Athenian local historians from literary rather than historical point of view. Cf. Jacoby 6.281. [MC]

6.285 Rosalind Thomas. *Oral tradition and written record in classical Athens.* 1989 ed. Cambridge: Cambridge University Press, 1992. ISBN 0-521-35025-5 (cl), 0-521-42518-2 (pbk). ▸ Argues that Athens became document-minded in late fifth century, but documents remained in disorder and were seldom consulted even in fourth century. Important for our conception of Greek historiography. Cf. Jacoby 6.281. [MC]

Prosopography

6.286 T. J. Cadoux. "The Athenian archons from Kreon to Hypsichides." *Journal of Hellenic studies* 68 (1948) 70–123. ISSN 0075-4269. ▸ Presentation of ancient evidence and modern infer-

ences for dating Athenian archons, 682–481 BCE; many precise historical observations. Needs updating, but remains essential. [MC]

6.287 J. K. Davies. *Athenian propertied families, 600–300 B.C.* Oxford: Clarendon, 1971. ISBN 0-19-814273-0. ▸ Biographic dictionary of Athenians who performed civic or military service for state; often with long notes on families and their histories. Follows numbering system of Kirchner 6.289. Important contribution to Athenian history. [MC]

6.288 Robert Develin. *Athenian officials, 684–321 B.C.* Cambridge: Cambridge University Press, 1989. ISBN 0-521-32880-2. ▸ Prosopographic catalog of all known office holders in Athens down to Hellenistic age. Important supplement to Kirchner 6.289. [MC]

6.289 Johannes Kirchner. *Prosopographia Attica.* Rev. ed. 2 vols. Siegfried Lauffer, ed. Berlin: de Gruyter, 1966. ▸ Groundbreaking work, listing some 15,000 men with notes in Latin on sources and their careers. Basic who's who of ancient Athens. [MC]

6.290 Paul MacKendrick. *The Athenian aristocracy, 399 to 31 B.C.* Cambridge, Mass.: Harvard University Press for Oberlin College, 1969. ▸ Prosopographic study of Athenian aristocracy from beginning of fourth century BCE to end of Hellenistic period. Specialist study. [SMB]

6.291 M. J. Osborne. *Naturalization in Athens.* 4 vols. in 3. Brussels: Paleis der Academiën, 1981–83. (Koninklijke Academie voor Wetenschappen, Letteren en schone Kunsten van België, klasse der Letteren, Verhandelingen, Jaargang 43.98, 44.101, 45.109.) ISBN 90-6569-304-1 (v. 1, pbk), 90-6569-313-0 (v. 2, pbk), 90-6569-334-3 (v. 3–4, pbk). ▸ Indispensable collection of documents concerning grants of citizenship in Athens. Volume 1, documents; volume 2, commentary; volume 3, testimonia; volume 4, essay on law and working of naturalization. [EB/MC]

6.292 J. Sundwall. *Supplement to J. Kirchner's "Prosopographia Attica".* 1910 ed. Chicago: Ares, 1981. ISBN 0-89005-383-9. ▸ About 3,000 names not found in Kirchner 6.289, chiefly from gravestones. No notes on careers; now dated. [MC]

Athenian History to 479 BCE

6.293 Frank J. Frost. *Plutarch's "Themistocles": a historical commentary.* Princeton: Princeton University Press, 1980. ISBN 0-691-05300-6. ▸ Succinct, useful commentary on life of great Athenian statesman and general. [MC]

6.294 Christian Habicht. "Falsche Urkunden zur Geschichte Athens im Zeitalter der Perserkriege." *Hermes* 89.1 (1961) 1–35. ISSN 0018-0777. ▸ Discussion of Athenian accounts of Persian wars from third and fourth centuries. Important for source criticism of Persian wars. Attacks authenticity of Themistocles Decree. [CWH]

6.295 Robert J. Lenardon. *The saga of Themistocles.* Ithaca, N.Y.: Cornell University Press, 1978. ▸ Well-balanced, thorough treatment of great strategist. [MC]

6.296 David M. Lewis. "Cleisthenes and Attica." *Historia* 12.1 (1963) 22–40. ISSN 0018-2311. ▸ Penetrating study of regional politics of sixth century; *demes* (villages), *trittyes* (thirds), their names and distribution. Examines effects of reform on religious organizations and purpose of *trittyes*. Evaluates significance of Cleisthenes' reforms. [JB]

6.297 Alain Martin. "L'ostracisme athénien." *Revue des études grecques* 102.1 (1989) 124–45. ISSN 0035-2039. ▸ Immensely helpful history of study of ostracism. Bibliography of 265 publications with brief summaries and index of authors. [MC]

6.298 Anthony J. Podlecki. *The life of Themistocles: a critical survey of the literary and archaeological evidence.* Montreal: McGill-

Queen's University Press, 1975. ISBN 0-7735-0185-1. ▸ Discussion of literary and archaeological sources for Themistocles with special attention to Herodotus and Thucydides. Examines attitudes of philosophical and rhetorical schools toward Themistocles. Discussion of Themistocles' decree on Troezen inscription. [JB]

6.299 Raphael Sealey. *Essays in Greek politics.* New York: Manyland Books [1967]. ▸ Political history of archaic and classical Athens; prosopographic inquiries on Roman model. Notable emphasis on personal rather than ideological motivations of politicians. [CWH]

6.300 Rudi Thomsen. *The origin of ostracism: a synthesis.* Copenhagen: Gyldendal, 1972. ISBN 87-00-60712-6. ▸ Basic study of ostracism. Examines nature of sources, ostraca (sherds used to vote), and implementation of procedure. Assigns origin of practice to time of Cleisthenes (508–507 BCE). [JB]

6.301 Franz Willemsen and Stefan Brenne. "Verzeichnis der Kerameikos-Ostraka." *Mitteilungen des Deutschen Archäologischen Instituts,* Athenische Abteilung, 106 (1991) 148–56. ▸ List of some 150 names on 8,653 ostraca (sherds used to vote) found in German excavations of Ceramicus at Athens. Long-awaited preliminary publication. [EB]

Athenian Empire, 479–404 BCE

6.302 E. Badian. *From Plataea to Potidaea: studies in the history and historiography of the Pentecontaetia.* Baltimore: Johns Hopkins University Press, 1993. ISBN 0-8018-4431-2. ▸ Six profound, detailed essays on major issues of fifth century such as Peace of Callias, chronology, Thucydides, and outbreak of Peloponnesian War. [JB]

6.303 Mortimer Chambers, Ralph Gallucci, and Pantelis Spanos. "Athens' alliance with Egesta in the year of Antiphon." *Zeitschrift für Papyrologie und Epigraphik* 83 (1990) 38–63. ISSN 0084-5388. ▸ New use of image enhancement to decipher worn letters of inscription. Important for debate about chronology and letter forms in fifth-century Athens. [CWH]

6.304 W. Robert Connor. *The new politicians of fifth-century Athens.* 1971 ed. Indianapolis: Hackett, 1992. ISBN 0-87220-142-2. ▸ Valuable study of politicians, often called demagogues, who took over political leadership in Athens, especially during Peloponnesian War. [MC]

6.305 Charles W. Fornara and Loren J. Samons II. *Athens from Cleisthenes to Pericles.* Berkeley: University of California Press, 1991. ISBN 0-520-06923-4. ▸ Detailed study on development of Athenian democracy and Athenian empire and internal politics. Appendixes on special points. [MC]

6.306 A. J. Holladay. "Athenian strategy in the Archidamian War." *Historia* 27.3 (1978) 399–427. ISSN 0018-2311. ▸ Evaluation of Athenian strategy in early years of Peloponnesian War. General strategic principles enunciated by Pericles in Thucydides measured against Athenian actions. [CWH]

6.307 Donald Kagan. *The Archidamian War.* Ithaca, N.Y.: Cornell University Press, 1974. ISBN 0-8014-0889-X. ▸ Useful supplement to Thucydides 6.73. Narrative history of Peloponnesian War in combination with author's other works (6.308, 6.309, 6.310). [CWH]

6.308 Donald Kagan. *The fall of the Athenian empire.* Ithaca, N.Y.: Cornell University Press, 1987. ISBN 0-8014-1935-2. ▸ Covers closing years of Peloponnesian War. See also Kagan 6.307, 6.309, 6.310. [CWH]

6.309 Donald Kagan. *The outbreak of the Peloponnesian War.* Ithaca, N.Y.: Cornell University Press, 1969. ISBN 0-8014-0501-7. ▸ Political, not economic, explanations for great war. Critical of Thucydides' theories of causes. See author's related works (6.307, 6.308, 6.310), and de Ste. Croix 6.219. [CWH]

6.310 Donald Kagan. *The Peace of Nicias and the Sicilian expedition.* Ithaca, N.Y.: Cornell University Press, 1981. ISBN 0-8014-1367-2. ▸ Covers middle period of "uneasy peace" in Peloponnesian War. See also Kagan 6.307, 6.308, and 6.309. [CWH]

6.311 Harold B. Mattingly. "The Athenian coinage decree." *Historia* 10.2 (1961) 148–88. ISSN 0018-2311. ▸ Mattingly's most important paper on dating of fifth-century Athenian inscriptions. Contests use of letter forms (especially three-barred sigma) for dating inscriptions. See Chambers et al. 6.303. [CWH]

6.312 Russell Meiggs. *The Athenian empire.* 1972 ed. Oxford: Clarendon, 1979. ISBN 0-19-814843-7. ▸ Particularly useful for discussion of institutions of empire and for analysis of tribute lists. Appendixes contain discussion opposing theories of Mattingly 6.311 as well as detailed discussion of other controversies. [CWH]

6.313 Benjamin Dean Meritt, H. T. Wade-Gery, and Malcolm Francis McGregor, eds. *The Athenian tribute lists.* 4 vols. Cambridge, Mass. and Princeton: Harvard University Press and American School of Classical Studies at Athens, 1939–53. ▸ Athenian inscriptions recording tribute paid to Athens by members of Delian League; most important single set of inscriptions for Athenian history, 453–404 BCE. Volume 3 contains historical discussion of Athenian empire; volume 4, index. See also 6.37. [MC]

6.314 T. J. Quinn. *Athens and Samos, Lesbos and Chios, 478–404 B.C.* Manchester: Manchester University Press, 1981. (Publications of the Faculty of Arts of the University of Manchester, 27.) ISBN 0-7190-1297-X. ▸ Detailed study of Athens' relationships with three major island subject allies. [MC]

6.315 G.E.M. de Ste. Croix. "The character of the Athenian empire." *Historia* 3.1 (1954–55) 1–21. ISSN 0018-2311. ▸ Challenges idea that fifth-century empire was hated by its members; empire protected *demos* from its own oligarchs. [JB]

6.316 Philip A. Stadter. *A commentary on Plutarch's "Pericles."* Chapel Hill: University of North Carolina Press, 1989. ISBN 0-8078-1861-5. ▸ Well-informed, useful commentary on Athens' leading statesman of fifth century. [EB]

6.317 J. B. Wilson. *Pylos, 425 B.C.: a historical and topographical study of Thucydides' account of the campaign.* Warminster: Aris & Phillips, 1979. ISBN 0-85668-145-8. ▸ Microscopically detailed study of Athenian campaign at Pylos. New geographic interpretations; excellent specimen study of single military operation. [MC]

Athenian History after 404 BCE

6.318 Jack Cargill. *The second Athenian League: empire or free alliance?* Berkeley: University of California Press, 1981. ISBN 0-520-04069-4. ▸ Sane, revisionist view of nature of this naval league; careful treatment of epigraphic evidence. Argues league less oppressive than often portrayed. [JB]

6.319 William Scott Ferguson. *Hellenistic Athens: an historical essay.* 1911 ed. New York: Fertig, 1969. ▸ Old-fashioned but still interesting history from Macedonian to Roman conquests. Covers nature of Roman government and relations between Rome and Athens. [JB]

6.320 Alexander Fuks. *The ancestral constitution: four studies in Athenian party politics at the end of the fifth century B.C.* 1953 ed. Westport, Conn.: Greenwood, 1971. ISBN 0-8371-5592-4. ▸ Thesis that Theramenes and other moderates promoted concept of *patrios politeia.* Subtle, detailed study examining moderates' interpretation of Athens' early constitution in the light of contemporary politics. [JB]

6.321 Fordyce W. Mitchel. "Lykourgan Athens, 338–322." In Vol. 2 of *Lectures in memory of Louise Taft Semple*. C. G. Boulter et al., eds., pp. 163–214. Norman: University of Oklahoma Press for University of Cincinnati, 1973. (Classical studies, 2.) ISBN 0-8061-1062-7. ▸ Overview of government after defeat at Chaeronea. Examines nature of Athenian freedom under Macedonian hegemony and Lycurgus' administration with emphasis on his handling of financial matters. [JB]

6.322 Claude Mossé. *Athens in decline, 404–86 B.C.* Jean Stewart, trans. London: Routledge & Kegan Paul, 1973. ISBN 0-7100-7649-5. ▸ Postulates imperialistic democracy after Peloponnesian War. Examines Athenian failure against Philip, relations with Alexander, and final loss of freedom to Successors and Rome. [JB]

6.323 M. J. Osborne. "The chronology of Athens in the mid-third century B.C." *Zeitschrift für Papyrologie und Epigraphik* 78 (1989) 209–42. ISSN 0084-5388. ▸ Review of important and troubled chronology of Hellenistic Athens. Especially critical of mechanical applications of Ferguson's Law of secretarial cycles as basis for chronology of Hellenistic Athens. [CWH]

6.324 Raphael Sealey. *Demosthenes and his time: a study in defeat.* Berkeley: University of California Press, 1993. ISBN 0-19-507928-0. ▸ Detailed analysis of both internal and interstate politics in fourth century. Argues against ideological motivations. More on period than on Demosthenes himself. [MC]

6.325 Barry S. Strauss. *Athens after the Peloponnesian War: class, faction, and policy, 403–386 B.C.* 1986 ed. Ithaca, N.Y.: Cornell University Press, 1987. ISBN 0-8014-1942-5. ▸ Athenian politics in postwar period; covers social and economic composition of Athens; internal political turmoil, 403–395 BCE, and Athens' defeat in Corinthian War. [JB]

Constitution and Political Practices

6.326 E. Badian. "Archons and *strategoi*." *Antichthon* 5 (1971) 1–34. ISSN 0066-4774. ▸ Challenging treatment of political and social status of archons and *strategoi* (generals) in early period after reforms of Cleisthenes. Concludes archons not politically important. [JB]

6.327 Jochen Bleicken. *Die athenische Demokratie.* Paderborn: Schöningh, 1985. ISBN 3-506-71900-9. ▸ Comprehensive account summarizing recent research on political, economic, social, and military institutions. Emphasis primarily on golden age of Pericles. Treats fourth century as period of decline. [EMH]

6.328 Sterling Dow. "Aristotle, the *kleroteria*, and the courts." *Harvard studies in classical philology* 50 (1939) 1–34. ISSN 0073-0688. ▸ Classic article illustrating contribution of archaeology to study of Athenian institutions. Study of allotment machines used to assign citizens to popular courts. [EMH]

6.329 Daniel J. Geagan. *The Athenian constitution after Sulla.* Princeton: American School of Classical Studies at Athens, 1967. (*Hesperia*, Supplement, 12.) ISBN 0018-098-X. ▸ Cautious attempt to reconstruct from slender evidence changes in Athenian institutions under Roman rule. [EMH]

6.330 Mogens Herman Hansen. *The Athenian democracy in the age of Demosthenes: structure, principles, and ideology.* J. A. Crook, trans. Oxford: Blackwell, 1991. ISBN 0-631-13822-6 (cl), 0-631-18017-6 (pbk). ▸ Historical sketch of constitution. Combines careful analysis of procedural details with awareness of broader issues, such as role of people in electing magistrates and making legal decisions and character of government. [JB/CWH]

6.331 Mogens Herman Hansen. *The Athenian ecclesia: a collection of articles.* Vol. 1: *1976–83.* Vol. 2: *1983–89.* Copenhagen: Museum Tusculanum Press, 1983–89. (Opuscula graecolatina, 26, 31.) ISBN 87-88073-54-8 (v. 1, cl), 87-7289-060-6 (v. 2, cl), 87-88073-52-1 (v. 1, pbk), 87-7289-058-4 (v. 2, pbk), ISSN 0107-8089. ▸ Important detailed studies of democratic procedures: size of assembly, frequency of meetings, lawmaking, level of political participation, distinction between decrees and laws, and methods of voting. Excellent use of epigraphical sources to pursue novel paths of inquiry. [EMH]

6.332 C. Hignett. *A history of the Athenian constitution to the end of the fifth century B.C.* 1958 ed. Oxford: Clarendon, 1975. ▸ Historical criticism of Aristotelian *Constitution of the Athenians* (6.96) and other sources for constitutional history. Thorough evaluation of evidence and polemical discussion of views of earlier scholars about Solon, Cleisthenes, Ephialtes, and revolution of 411. Overly skeptical in places. [EMH]

6.333 A.H.M. Jones. *Athenian democracy.* 1957 ed. Baltimore: Johns Hopkins University Press, 1986. ISBN 0-8018-3380-9. ▸ Defense of Athenian democracy against charges of inefficiency and instability. Examines social and economic issues as well as political institutions. [EMH/JB]

6.334 Josiah Ober. *Mass and elite in democratic Athens: rhetoric, ideology, and the power of the people.* Princeton: Princeton University Press, 1989. ISBN 0-691-09443-8. ▸ Analysis of nature of democracy, concentrating on social and political factors such as rhetoric, ideology, and power of people. Draws heavily on sociological theory. [JB]

6.335 Robin Osborne. *Demos: the discovery of classical Attika.* Cambridge: Cambridge University Press, 1985. ISBN 0-521-26776-5. ▸ Provocative study of relationship between city of Athens and countryside of Attica to determine how Athenian polis functioned as a whole. Topographical study of rural basis of Athenian democracy; cf. 6.544. [SMB]

6.336 Martin Ostwald. *From popular sovereignty to the sovereignty of law: law, society, and politics in fifth-century Athens.* Berkeley: University of California Press, 1986. ISBN 0-520-05426-1 (cl), 0-520-06798-3 (pbk). ▸ Discussion of how and why notion of sovereignty of people became institutionalized and challenges to it during fifth century. Combines intellectual history with narrative of political events. [JB/EMH]

6.337 Martin Ostwald. *Nomos and the beginnings of the Athenian democracy.* Oxford: Clarendon, 1969. ISBN 0-19-814277-3. ▸ Discussion of concept of law and its evolution. Focuses on impact of Cleisthenes and his originality in applying to entire polis concept of *isonomia* (equality of political rights), thus paving the way to Athenian concept of democracy. [JB]

6.338 P. J. Rhodes. *The Athenian boule.* Rev. ed. Oxford: Clarendon, 1985. ISBN 0-19-814291-9. ▸ Comprehensive study of Athenian Council based primarily on epigraphy; treats membership and organization, role in legislation and public administration, and general powers of jurisdiction. [JB]

6.339 P. J. Rhodes. "Political activity in classical Athens." *Journal of Hellenic studies* 106 (1986) 132–44. ISSN 0075-4269. ▸ Study of nature of political activity looking at social origins of citizenry and how citizenry functioned. Also examines political functions of *hetaireiai* (political clubs) and changes in fourth century. [JB]

6.340 Jennifer Tolbert Roberts. *Accountability in Athenian government.* Madison: University of Wisconsin Press, 1982. ISBN 0-299-08680-1. ▸ Analysis of procedures employed by democracy to keep magistrates accountable to people. History and analysis of political trials in late fifth and fourth centuries BCE. [EMH]

6.341 Raphael Sealey. *The Athenian republic: democracy or rule of law?* University Park: Pennsylvania State University Press, 1987. ISBN 0-271-00443-6. ▸ Ideal of rule of law most important factor in Athenian history, not aspiration to popular sovereignty. Stress on role of law code and courts at expense of council and assembly. [EMH]

6.342 R. K. Sinclair. *Democracy and participation in Athens.* Cambridge: Cambridge University Press, 1988. ISBN 0-521-33357-1. ‣ Excellent summary of recent scholarship for general reader. Brief sketch of political development to 322 BCE, focusing on opportunities for average citizens to participate in politics and rewards and risks for leaders. [EMH]

6.343 David Stockton. *The classical Athenian democracy.* Oxford: Oxford University Press, 1990. ISBN 0-19-814697-3 (cl), 0-19-872136-6 (pbk). ‣ Several essays forming portrait of city and its life. Good introduction to topic; sympathetically written. [MC]

6.344 John S. Traill. *Demos and trittys: epigraphical and topographical studies in the organization of Attica.* Toronto: Athenians, Victoria College, 1986. ISBN 0-9692685-0-2. ‣ Substantial additions and corrections to Traill 6.345. Major new work for specialists. [MC]

6.345 John S. Traill. *The political organization of Attica: a study of the demes, trittyes, and phylai, and their representation in the Athenian Council.* Princeton: American School of Classical Studies at Athens, 1975. (*Hesperia*, Supplement, 14.) ISBN 0-87661-514-0, ISSN 0018-098X. ‣ Classic study of constituent political units of democracy. Location of *demes* (villages) and composition of *trittyes* (thirds) and *phylai* (tribes). Main conclusions summarized in Jones 6.455. [EMH]

6.346 Michael B. Walbank. *Athenian proxenies of the fifth century B.C.* Toronto: Samuel Stevens, 1978. ISBN 0-88866-598-9. ‣ Collection of inscriptions relating to foreigners who looked after Athenian interests in their native communities and rewards granted to them. Introduction, Greek texts, epigraphical commentary with full bibliography. No English translation of documents. [EMH]

6.347 Robert W. Wallace. *The Areopagos Council to 307 B.C.* Baltimore: Johns Hopkins University Press, 1989. ISBN 0-8018-3646-8. ‣ History and function of one of oldest and most conservative institutions in Athens. Fortunes of Areopagos connected to shifts in ideological struggles of classical period. [EMH]

Law

6.348 Edward E. Cohen. *Ancient Athenian maritime courts.* Princeton: Princeton University Press, 1973. ISBN 0-691-09227-3. ‣ Basic study of basic institution; discussion of "monthly cases." [MC]

6.349 Michael Gagarin. *Drakon and early Athenian homicide law.* New Haven: Yale University Press, 1981. ISBN 0-300-02627-7. ‣ Important, controversial study of archaic law on homicide republished in 409/8. Central for understanding evolution of legal procedure. See Stroud 6.358. [EMH]

6.350 Edward M. Harris. "When is a sale not a sale? The riddle of Athenian terminology for real security revisited." *Classical quarterly,* n.s., 38.2 (1988) 351–81. ISSN 0009-8388. ‣ Critique of previous attempts to use Roman law to explain Athenian law of security. Explains conflicting views of legal status of real security and discusses relationship between Athenian law and economy. [EMH]

6.351 A.R.W. Harrison. *The law of Athens.* 2 vols. Douglas M. MacDowell, ed. vol. 2. Oxford: Clarendon, 1968–71. ISBN 0-19-825172-6 (v. 1), 0-19-825196-3 (v. 2). ‣ Discussion of real security and legal procedure. Standard account in English. Same general categories as Lipsius 6.352. [EMH]

6.352 Justus Hermann Lipsius. *Das attische Recht und Rechtsverfahren: mit Benutzung des attischen Processes von M.H.E. Meier und G. F. Schömann.* 1905–15 ed. 3 vols. in 1. Hildesheim: Olms, 1966. ‣ Exhaustive account of legal procedures with copious references to ancient sources. Stronger on minutiae than on general legal issues. [EMH]

6.353 W. T. Loomis. "The nature of premeditation in Athenian homicide law." *Journal of Hellenic studies* 92 (1972) 257–81. ISSN 0075-4269. ‣ Greeks did not necessarily distinguish premeditated from unpremeditated homicide; basic distinction, accidental and nonaccidental. [MC]

6.354 Douglas M. MacDowell. *Athenian homicide law in the age of the orators.* Manchester: Manchester University Press, 1963. (Publications of the Faculty of Arts of the University of Manchester, 15.) ISBN 0-7190-1212-0. ‣ Astonishingly compact treatment of several courts and institutions responsible for homicide law. Translations of most important passages from Greek sources. [MC]

6.355 Douglas M. MacDowell. *The law in classical Athens.* Ithaca, N.Y.: Cornell University Press, 1978. ISBN 0-8014-1198-X (cl), 0-8014-9365-X (pbk). ‣ Best introductory account in English. Emphasis on aspects of procedure rather than on substantive legal issues and social background. [EMH]

6.356 Harald Meyer-Laurin. *Gesetz und Billigkeit im attischen Prozess.* Weimar: Böhlaus Nachfolger, 1965. ‣ Defense of Athenian legal system against charge that courts paid little attention to letter of law. Careful analysis of legal issues in selected cases to support thesis. [EMH]

6.357 Ronald S. Stroud. *The axones and kyrbeis of Drakon and Solon.* Berkeley: University of California Press, 1979. ISBN 0-520-09590-1. ‣ Convincing analysis of controversy over how Draco and Solon displayed their laws for Athenian public. Important for whole question of how legal documents were preserved in antiquity. [MC]

6.358 Ronald S. Stroud. *Drakon's law on homicide.* Berkeley: University of California Press, 1968. ‣ Definitive text with translation and full commentary of inscription republishing Draco's law on homicide. Starting point for study of Draco; see Gagarin 6.349. [MC]

6.359 Hans Julius Wolff. "Marriage law and family organization in ancient Athens." *Traditio* 2 (1944) 43–95. ISSN 0362-1529. ‣ Influential article about marriage, dowry, and inheritance. Connections between laws about family and structure of polis. Some conclusions debatable. [EMH]

Social and Economic History

6.360 August Böckh. *Die Staatshaushaltung der Athener.* 1886 3d ed. 2 vols. Max Fränkel, ed. Berlin: de Gruyter, 1967. ‣ Pioneering and still valuable study of Athenian public finance based primarily on literary sources. [SMB]

6.361 Patrice Brun. *Eisphora-syntaxis-stratiotika: recherches sur les finances militaires d'Athènes au quatrième siècle av. J.-C.* Paris: Belles Lettres, 1983. (Centre de Recherches d'Histoire Ancienne, 50. Annales littéraires de l'Université de Besançon, 284.) ‣ Collection of studies about how Athenians raised funds from citizens and allies for military campaigns. [EMH]

6.362 L. B. Carter. *The quiet Athenian.* Oxford: Clarendon, 1986. ISBN 0-19-814870-4. ‣ Basic study of phenomenon of political noninvolvement in classical Athens. Quietism, in form of ideal of contemplative life, a product of elite disenchantment with Athenian democracy. [SMB]

6.363 David Cohen. *Law, sexuality, and society: the enforcement of morals in classical Athens.* Cambridge: Cambridge University Press, 1991. ISBN 0-521-37447-2. ‣ Sociological approach to Athenian customs and laws about adultery, homosexuality, and impiety. Valuable comparative material from Mediterranean communities for understanding Athenian society. [EMH]

6.364 Edward E. Cohen. *Athenian economy and society: a banking perspective.* Princeton: Princeton University Press, 1992. ISBN

0-691-03609-8. ▸ Detailed examination of banking practices within Athenian society. [MC]

6.365 J. K. Davies. *Wealth and the power of wealth in classical Athens.* 1981 ed. Salem, N.H.: Ayer, 1984. ISBN 0-88143-019-6. ▸ Pioneering social and economic study of Athenian elite families in fifth and fourth centuries BCE. Economic elite of classical Athens small and political significance of their wealth limited. [SMB]

6.366 Victor Ehrenberg. *The people of Aristophanes: a sociology of old Attic comedy.* 3d ed. New York: Schocken, 1962. ▸ Traditional analysis of socioeconomic life of fifth-century BCE Athens based on stereotypical depictions of characters in Aristophanic comedy. [SMB]

6.367 John V. A. Fine. *Horoi: studies in mortgage, real security, and land tenure in ancient Athens.* 1951 ed. Amsterdam: Swets & Zeitlinger, 1975. (*Hesperia*, Supplement, 9.) ISSN 0018-098X. ▸ Analysis of *horos* stones, markers showing property pledged as debt surety, revealing extent of agrarian distress in archaic Athens. [CGT]

6.368 M. I. Finley. *Studies in land and credit in ancient Athens, 500–200 B.C.: the horos inscriptions.* 1952 ed. New Brunswick, N.J.: Transaction, 1985. ISBN 0-88738-066-2. ▸ Study of landed debt in all its ramifications in Athens on basis of *horos* inscriptions, markers showing property pledged as debt surety. Loans on land result of nonbusiness needs of Athenian elite rather than evidence of economic crisis. [SMB]

6.369 A. French. "The economic background to Solon's reforms." *Classical quarterly,* n.s., 6.1 (1956) 11–25. ISSN 0009-8388. ▸ Penetrating discussion of causes and nature of rural discontent and reasons behind aristocratic readiness to support Solon's reforms. Examines significance of return of land to peasants for social stability. Views Solon as arbitrator by consent. [JB]

6.370 A. French. *The growth of the Athenian economy.* 1964 ed. Westport, Conn.: Greenwood, 1975. ISBN 0-8371-8506-8. ▸ Chronological survey of Athenian economic history from seventh century BCE to 431 BCE. How Athens became most prosperous and powerful Greek state. Narrative economic history. [SMB]

6.371 Louis Gernet. *L'approvisionnement d'Athènes en blé au cinquième et au quatrième siècle.* 1909 ed. New York: Arno, 1979. ISBN 0-405-12363-9. ▸ Classic study of Athens' needs in grain and extent of grain imports in classical period. Large grain imports documented for fourth century BCE not typical of fifth century BCE. [SMB]

6.372 Mark Golden. *Children and childhood in classical Athens.* Baltimore: Johns Hopkins University Press, 1990. ISBN 0-8018-3980-7. ▸ Groundbreaking study spanning 300 years on how children interacted with adults. [MC]

6.373 A. W. Gomme. *The population of Athens in the fifth and fourth centuries B.C.* 1933 ed. Chicago: Argonaut, 1967. ▸ Pioneering attempt to determine demographic profile of classical Athens on basis of literary sources. Concludes population expanded in fifth century BCE and declined in fourth century BCE. [SMB]

6.374 Mogens Herman Hansen. *Demography and democracy: the number of Athenian citizens in the fourth century B.C.* Henning, Denmark: Systime, 1986. ISBN 87-7351-421-7. ▸ Fundamental reconsideration of evidence for Athenian population in fourth century BCE. Population of ca. 30,000 probable; sufficient for proper functioning of democratic institutions. [SMB]

6.375 Signe Isager and Mogens Herman Hansen. *Aspects of Athenian society in the fourth century B.C.: a historical introduction to and commentary on the paragraphe speeches and the speech against Dionysodorus in the corpus Demosthenicum (XXXII–XXXVIII and LVI).* Judith Hsiang Rosenmeier, trans. Odense: Odense University classical studies, 5.) ISBN 87-7492-129-0. ▸ Detailed analysis of Athenian commerce and legal procedure in fourth century BCE in form of commentary on eight private speeches of Demosthenes. [SMB]

6.376 Peter V. Jones, ed. *The world of Athens: an introduction to classical Athenian culture, background book.* Cambridge: Cambridge University Press, 1984. ISBN 0-521-26789-7 (cl), 0-521-27389-7 (pbk). ▸ Companion to textbook *Reading Greek.* Basic outline of Athenian history to 322 BCE with comprehensive chapters on physical environment, religion, values, socioeconomic structures, democracy, warfare, and intellectual life. [GND]

6.377 Roger Just. *Women in Athenian law and life.* New York: Routledge, 1989. ISBN 0-415-00346-6. ▸ Comprehensive analysis of place of women in Athenian society in fifth and fourth centuries BCE to recover Athenian idea of womanhood. Anthropological social history. [SMB]

6.378 Robert J. Littman. *Kinship and politics in Athens, 600–400 B.C.* New York: Lang, 1990. ISBN 0-8204-1159-0. ▸ Controversial study of role of kinship in Athenian social and political life. Finds patrilineal kinship relationships of fundamental importance for formation of social and political groups; anthropologically based social history. [SMB]

6.379 Paul Millett. *Lending and borrowing in ancient Athens.* Cambridge: Cambridge University Press, 1991. ISBN 0-521-37333-6. ▸ Detailed study of role of lending and borrowing in economic life of classical Athens. Use of credit widespread in Athens but usually restricted to social life. Narrative economic history. [SMB]

6.380 Chrysis Pélékidis. *Histoire de l'éphébie attique des origines à 31 av. J.-C.* Paris: de Boccard, 1962. (École Française d'Athènes: travaux et mémoires d'anciens membres étrangers de l'École et de divers savants, 13.) ▸ Study of military training of Athenian youth. History and sharp decline of cadet corps of young citizens. [EMH]

6.381 David Whitehead. *The demes of Attica 508/7–ca. 250 B.C.: a political and social study.* Princeton: Princeton University Press, 1986. ISBN 0-691-09412-8. ▸ Fundamental study of social and political institutions of rural villages (*demoi*) of Attica from late sixth to mid-third century BCE. Significant proportion of Athenians lived in rural villages throughout this period. [SMB]

6.382 David Whitehead. *The ideology of the Athenian metic.* Cambridge: Cambridge Philological Society, 1977. (Cambridge Philological Society, Supplement, 4.) ISBN 0-906014-00-X, ISSN 0068-6735. ▸ Penetrating analysis of Athenian ideas concerning resident aliens and demarcation of statuses of citizens and metics during classical and early Hellenistic periods. [SMB/EMH]

6.383 Ellen Meiksins Wood. *Peasant-citizen and slave: the foundations of Athenian democracy.* Rev. ed. London: Verso, 1989. ISBN 0-86091-911-0. ▸ Controversial historiographic study of nature of Athenian citizen body. Athenian agriculture not based on slavery but free peasants who constituted bulk of Athenian citizenry. [SMB]

Calendars

6.384 Benjamin Dean Meritt. *The Athenian year.* Berkeley: University of California Press, 1961. ▸ Technical presentation of one of two main theories about Athenian calendar, especially of fourth century BCE; see also Pritchett and Neugebauer 6.385. [MC]

6.385 W. Kendrick Pritchett and Otto Neugebauer. *The calendars of Athens.* Cambridge, Mass.: Harvard University Press for American School of Classical Studies at Athens, 1947. ▸ Shows that Athens had three calendars in fourth and later centuries. Accepts Aristotle's statement that duration of *prytanies* (thirty-five- or thirty-six-day periods when councillors from one tribe administered state) within year was fixed; festival calendar could fluctuate. Technical study; see also Meritt 6.384. [MC]

Religion

6.386 Borimir Jordan. *Servants of the gods: a study in the religion, history, and literature of fifth-century Athens.* Göttingen: Vandenhouck & Ruprecht, 1979. (Hypomnemata, 55.) ISBN 3-525-25150-5. ▸ Essays on various priests, officials, and historical incidents connected with Athenian Acropolis. [EB]

6.387 Jon D. Mikalson. *Athenian popular religion.* 1983 ed. Chapel Hill: University of North Carolina Press, 1989. ISBN 0-8078-1563-2 (cl), 0-8078-4194-3 (pbk). ▸ Survey of beliefs concerning gods, justice, oaths, divination, and death that Athenians of classical period treated as conventional in forensic and political oratory, inscriptions, and historical writings. [JDM]

6.388 George E. Mylonas. *Eleusis and the Eleusinian mysteries.* 1961 ed. Princeton: Princeton University Press, 1969. ISBN 0-691-03513-X (cl), 0-691-00205-3 (pbk). ▸ Detailed account of archaeological and literary evidence for site and history of Eleusis and for nature of Eleusinian mysteries with plans and photographs. [JDM]

6.389 H. W. Parke. *Festivals of the Athenians.* Ithaca, N.Y.: Cornell University Press, 1977. ISBN 0-8014-1054-1 (cl), 0-8014-9440-0 (pbk). ▸ Best account in English of whole program of Athenian religious festivals. Valuable especially for inclusion of anecdotal material. [JDM]

6.390 A. W. Pickard-Cambridge. *The dramatic festivals of Athens.* 1968 2d ed. John Gould and David M. Lewis, eds. Oxford: Clarendon, 1988. ISBN 0-19-814258-7. ▸ Detailed descriptions of Anthesteria, Lenaia, Rural and City Dionysia, and of actors, costumes, choruses, and audiences of dithyramb, tragedy, and comedy throughout history of Athens. [JDM]

Military History

6.391 Glenn Richard Bugh. *The horsemen of Athens.* Princeton: Princeton University Press, 1988. ISBN 0-691-05530-0. ▸ Narrative history of Athenian cavalry through Hellenistic Age. Replaces all earlier treatments. [MC]

6.392 J. S. Morrison and J. F. Coates. *The Athenian trireme: the history and reconstruction of an ancient Greek warship.* Cambridge: Cambridge University Press, 1986. ISBN 0-521-32202-2 (cl), 0-521-31100-4 (pbk). ▸ Study of construction of Greek oared warships. Analysis of tactics in naval battles of Persian and Peloponnesian wars. Discusses officers, marines, and crew. Modern reconstruction of trireme. [EMH]

Art and Architecture

6.393 J. D. Beazley. *The development of Attic black-figure.* Rev. ed. Dietrich von Bothmer and Mary B. Moore, revisers. Berkeley: University of California Press, 1986. ISBN 0-520-05593-4. ▸ History of leading style of vase painting, by greatest master ever. Precise observations, poetic style, amply illustrated. [MC]

6.394 John Boardman. *Athenian black figure vases: a handbook.* London: Thames & Hudson, 1974. ISBN 0-500-18144-6 (cl), 0-500-20138-2 (pbk). ▸ Survey of Attic black figure vases from late seventh through early fifth centuries, organized on basis of Beazley's identification of individual painters. Discussion of shapes, chronology, and iconography in addition to style. Extensive bibliography, numerous illustrations. [THC]

6.395 John Boardman. *Athenian red figure vases, the archaic period: a handbook.* 1975 ed. New York: Oxford University Press, 1979. ISBN 0-19-520155-8. ▸ Survey of Attic red figure vases from first appearance ca. 530 through ca. 480 BCE, organized on basis

of Beazley's identification of individual painters. Discussion of shapes, chronology, and iconography in addition to style. Extensive bibliography, many illustrations. [THC]

6.396 John Boardman. *Athenian red figure vases, the classical period: a handbook.* New York: Thames & Hudson, 1989. ISBN 0-500-20244-3 (pbk). ▸ Survey of Attic red figure vases from ca. 480 BCE through end of fifth century, organized on basis of Beazley's identification of individual hands. Discussion of style, shapes, chronology, and iconography. Extensive bibliography, many illustrations. [THC]

PELOPONNESE

6.397 J. K. Anderson. "A topographical and historical study of Achaea." *Annual of the British School at Athens* 49 (1954) 72–92. ISSN 0068-2454. ▸ Study of relationship of regional topography to population patterns with political history of Achaeans from Archaic to Hellenistic period. [JB]

6.398 Raoul Baladié. *Le Péloponnèse de Strabon: étude de géographie historique.* Paris: Belles Lettres, 1980. ISBN 2-251-32507-7. ▸ Lavish, illustrated study of geography and history of regions described by Strabo, including topography, natural resources, roads, and history. [JB]

6.399 Terrence A. Boring. *Literacy in ancient Sparta.* Leiden: Brill, 1979. (Mnemosyne, Supplement, 54.) ISBN 90-04-05971-7, ISSN 0169-8958. ▸ Evidence for writing in Sparta down to second century CE. Concludes that commanders and diplomats had advanced writing skills, while ordinary Spartans' literacy had more breadth than depth prior to Roman period. [EB]

6.400 Alfred S. Bradford. *A prosopography of Lacedaemonians from the death of Alexander the Great, 323 B.C., to the sack of Sparta by Alaric, A.D. 396.* Munich: Beck, 1977. ISBN 3-406-04797-1. ▸ Continuation of Poralla 6.408. [MC]

6.401 Paul Cartledge. *Agesilaos and the crisis of Sparta.* Baltimore: Johns Hopkins University Press, 1987. ISBN 0-8018-3505-4. ▸ Discussion of career of Agesilaos and of political, diplomatic, and social conditions in Sparta during his reign. Liberally illustrated with maps; not an attempt at biography. [JB]

6.402 Paul Cartledge. *Sparta and Lakonia: a regional history, 1300–362 BC.* London: Routledge & Kegan Paul, 1979. ISBN 0-7100-0377-3. ▸ Study of physical features of region and its history from preclassical period to mid-fourth century. Political and institutional developments with analysis of sources. [JB]

6.403 Paul Cartledge and Antony Spawforth. *Hellenistic and Roman Sparta: a tale of two cities.* London: Routledge, 1989. ISBN 0-415-03290-3. ▸ Examines Hellenistic Sparta and its resistance to Macedonia; careers of Agis IV, Cleomenes III, and Nabis; Spartan response to Rome; and civic, social, and religious institutions during Roman period. [JB]

6.404 L. F. Fitzhardinge. *The Spartans.* London: Thames & Hudson, 1980. ISBN 0-500-02096-5. ▸ Well-written, brief history and portrait of Spartans; illlustrated. More accessible than Cartledge 6.402. [MC]

6.405 Audrey Griffin. *Sikyon.* Oxford: Clarendon, 1982. ISBN 0-19-814718-X. ▸ Description of city and analysis of political and social organization of its land. Study of its institutions and agriculture with brief political history. Also treats art, literature, and music. [JB]

6.406 Josef Hejnic. *Pausanias the Perieget and the archaic history of Arcadia.* Prague: Nakladatelství Československé Akademie Věd, 1961. (Rozpravy Československé Akademie Věd: Řada spolecenskych věd; Rocnik 17, Sešit 17.) ▸ Study of Arcadian traditions and Pausanias' treatment of them. Discussion of material culture, including archaeology, topography, and numismatics. Also treats political development. [JB]

6.407 J. F. Lazenby. *The Spartan army.* Warminster: Aris & Phillips, 1985. ISBN 0-85668-142-3 (pbk). ▸ Organization, tactics, size, and strategy of Spartan army in classical period. [EMH]

6.408 Paul Poralla. *A prosopography of Lacedaemonians from the earliest times to the death of Alexander the Great (323 B.C.)* 2d ed. Alfred S. Bradford, ed. Chicago: Ares, 1985. ISBN 0-89005-521-1. ▸ Revision (introduction, addenda, corrigenda) updates German edition (1913); see also Bradford 6.400. Text in German; title and introduction in English. [MC]

6.409 Carl A. Roebuck. *A history of Messenia from 369 to 146 B.C.* Chicago: University of Chicago Press, 1941. ▸ Physical description of Messenia with historical narrative of political institutions, relations with Thebes during its hegemony and later with Macedonians, and social and economic conditions. [JB]

6.410 J. B. Salmon. *Wealthy Corinth: a history of the city to 338 B.C.* Oxford: Clarendon, 1984. ISBN 0-19-814833-X. ▸ Geographical description of land and discussion of origins, economy, and constitution of city; Bacchiadae; Corinthian expansion; and outline of political history. [JB]

6.411 E. N. Tigerstedt. *The legend of Sparta in classical antiquity.* 3 vols. Stockholm: Almqvist & Wiksell, 1965–68. ISBN 91-22-00258-8 (v. 3). ▸ Broad, unique survey of views of Sparta in all eras down through Roman empire in historiography, literature, and philosophy. [MC]

6.412 R. A. Tomlinson. *Argos and the Argolid: from the end of the Bronze Age to the Roman occupation.* London: Routledge & Kegan Paul, 1972. ISBN 0-7100-7254-6. ▸ Physical description of land and discussion of Bronze Age including return of Heracleidae and Dorian settlement. Narrative of events from seventh century to Hellenistic period. [JB]

6.413 Édouard Will. *Korinthiaka: recherches sur l'histoire et la civilisation de Corinthe des origines aux guerres médiques.* Paris: de Boccard, 1955. ▸ Archaeological discoveries and history of seventh century. Extensive study of religion, myth, and examination of literary sources. Chronology of Cypselid rule, Cypselid tyranny, and fall of tyranny. [JB]

CENTRAL AND NORTHERN GREECE

6.414 John Buckler. *The Theban hegemony, 371–362 BC.* Cambridge, Mass.: Harvard University Press, 1980. ISBN 0-674-87645-8. ▸ Study of rise of Thebes after defeat in Corinthian War. Discussion of careers of Epaminondas and Pelopidas, defeat of Sparta, diplomatic relations with Persia, and reasons for ultimate failure. [JB]

6.415 Paul Cloché. *Thèbes de Béotie: des origines à la conquête romaine.* Namur: Secretariat des publications, Facultés universitaires, 1952. (Bibliothèque de la Faculté de Philosophie et Lettres de Namur, 13.) ▸ Geographical discussion of position of Thebes in Boeotia. Political, diplomatic, and military history, focusing on Theban role in development of Boeotian federalism. [JB]

6.416 John M. Fossey. *The ancient topography of eastern Phokis.* Amsterdam: Gieben, 1986. ISBN 90-70265-87-7. ▸ Detailed archaeological-topographic exploration of sites examining development of settlements, fortification, and local cults. [JB]

6.417 John M. Fossey. *The ancient topography of Opountian Lokris.* Amsterdam: Gieben, 1990. ISBN 90-5063-053-7. ▸ Detailed treatment of sites and settlement patterns, fortifications, local cults, and ancient and modern accounts of region. [JB]

6.418 John M. Fossey. *Topography and population of ancient Boiotia.* 2 vols. Chicago: Ares, 1988. ISBN 0-89005-482-7 (pbk).

▸ Detailed archaeological-topographic description of Boeotia, with history and economy of settlements. [JB]

6.419 W. A. Oldfather. "Studies in the history and topography of Locris." *American journal of archaeology* 20.1, 2, 3 (1916) 32–61, 154–72, 346–49. ISSN 0002-9114. ▸ Pioneering work on sites with excellent knowledge of sources and archaeological finds to that date; places Locris within historical context. [JB]

6.420 Georges Roux. *L'Amphictionie, Delphes, et le temple d'Apollon au quatrième siècle.* Lyons: Maison de l'Orient; distributed by de Boccard, 1979. (Collection de la Maison de l'Orient Mediterranéen, 8, Série archéologique, 6.) ISBN 2-02-005004-8, ISSN 0395-8027. ▸ Study of composition of league, its political and cultic relations with Delphi, and sanctuary of Apollo. Focuses on institutions and administration of Amphictyony. [JB]

6.421 Pierre Salmon. *Étude sur la Confédération béotienne (447/6–386): son organisation et son administration.* Brussels: Académie Royale de Belgique, 1976. (Mémoires de la Classe des lettres, Collection in-8°, Deuxième série, 63.3.) ISBN 2-8031-007-fl. ▸ Analysis of organization and functioning of league. Discussion of federal districts and officials and relations between federated cities and central government. [JB]

6.422 Friedrich Schober. *Phokis.* Crossen: Zeidler, 1924. ▸ Survey of Phocian history with overview of geography, climate, vegetation, and population. Location and identification of sites from prehistoric period to Roman conquest. [JB]

6.423 Friedrich Stählin. *Das hellenische Thessalien.* 1924 ed. Amsterdam: Hakkert, 1967. ▸ Topography of all regions and nature of remains. Various historical discussions of events from prehistory to Macedonian hegemony. [JB]

6.424 Aleksandar Stipčević. *The Illyrians: history and culture.* Stojana Čulić Burton, trans. Park Ridge, N.J.: Noyes, 1977. ISBN 0-8155-5052-9. ▸ Examination of modern Illyrian scholarship. Political history from heroic period to arrival of Slavs. Includes discussion of economic and social structure of region. [JB]

6.425 H. D. Westlake. *Thessaly in the fourth century B.C.* 1935 ed. Groningen: Bouma's Boekhuis, 1969. ▸ Study of country and people, with emphasis on regions of Pherai and Larisa. Full treatment of careers of Jason of Pherai, Philip, and Alexander. [JB]

MACEDONIA AND ITS ENVIRONS

6.426 Eugene N. Borza. *In the shadow of Olympus: the emergence of Macedon.* 1990 ed. Princeton: Princeton University Press, 1992. ISBN 0-691-00880-9. ▸ Study covering geography, prehistoric Macedonia, ethnic identification of Macedonians, political history, and prehistory to time of Alexander. Also political institutions of Philip II and Alexander. 1992 edition contains important additions. [JB]

6.427 Stanley Casson. *Macedonia, Thrace, and Illyria: their relations to Greece from the earliest times down to the time of Philip, son of Amyntas.* 1926 ed. Westport, Conn.: Greenwood, 1971. ISBN 0-8371-4727-1. ▸ Pioneering work on northern Greek topography. Archaeological descriptions of regions and reports on sites. Discussion of Thracian and Macedonian kingship. Good maps and many splendid illustrations. [JB]

6.428 R. M. Errington. *A history of Macedonia.* Catherine Errington, trans. Berkeley: University of California Press, 1990. ISBN 0-520-06319-8. ▸ Description of geography and population and Macedonia in Greek history. Discusses careers of Philip, Alexander, Successors, and Antigonids with survey of position of king within state and Macedonian army. [JB]

6.429 R. M. Errington. "The nature of the Macedonian state under the monarchy." *Chiron* 8 (1978) 77–133. ISSN 0069-3715. ▸ Argues for absence of Macedonian constitution and assembly with formal powers. Macedonians ruled by personal monarchy by which kings enjoyed untrammeled power. [EMH]

6.430   N.G.L. Hammond. *Epirus: the geography, the ancient remains, the history, and the topography of Epirus and adjacent areas.* Oxford: Clarendon, 1967. ▸ Definitive work on geography of Epirus and adjacent areas with district-by-district description of ancient remains. Discussion of origin of native tribes and early connections with Greeks. Includes narrative history from 480 to ca. 232 BCE. [JB]

6.431   N.G.L. Hammond, G. T. Griffith, and F. W. Walbank. *A history of Macedonia.* 3 vols. Oxford: Clarendon, 1972–88. ISBN 0-19-814294-3 (v. 1), 0-19-814814-3 (v. 2), 0-19-814815-1 (v. 3). ▸ Detailed political, diplomatic, and military history from prehistory to 167 BCE of Macedonia and Greeks, especially careers of Philip II, Alexander, Successors, and later kings. Includes relations with Rome and fall of Macedonia, as well as discussion of geography and topography. [JB]

6.432   Demetrios K. Kanatsoulis. *Prosopographia Macedonica: from 148 B.C. until the time of Constantine the Great.* 1955 ed. Chicago: Ares, 1984. ISBN 0-89005-316-2. ▸ Prosopography of Macedonia from its conquest by Rome up to Constantine. Includes Romans who served in Macedonia as soldiers or administrators. [MC]

GREEK ISLANDS

6.433   S. C. Bakhuizen and R. Kreulen. *Chalcis-in-Euboea, iron and Chalcidians abroad.* Leiden: Brill, 1976. (Chalcidian studies, 3. Studies of the Dutch Archaeological and Historical Society, 5.) ISBN 90-04-04546-5. ▸ Early history of Euboea. Role of Euboeans and especially Chalcidians in development of early Greek trade and colonization. Stresses importance of trade in metal ores and products, especially iron. [RAB]

6.434   Richard M. Berthold. *Rhodes in the Hellenistic age.* Ithaca, N.Y.: Cornell University Press, 1984. ISBN 0-8014-1640-X. ▸ Political history of Rhodes from Alexander to Roman empire, noting importance of Rhodian trade, naval strength, and tradition of neutrality. [RAB]

6.435   John Boardman and C. E. Vaphopoulou-Richardson, eds. *Chios: a conference at the Homereion in Chios, 1984.* Oxford: Clarendon, 1986. ISBN 0-19-814864-X. ▸ Papers concerning ancient Chios covering literary history, history of Chios in relation to rest of Greek world, and art and archaeology of Chios. Relates island to rest of Greece. [RAB]

6.436   Elizabeth M. Craik. *The Dorian Aegean.* London: Routledge & Kegan Paul, 1980. ISBN 0-7100-0378-1. ▸ Survey of Dorian islands in southeastern Aegean (Rhodes, Cos, Carpathos, Melos, Thera) concentrating on archaic and classical periods with emphasis on geography, cultural history, and religious cults. [RAB]

6.437   Henri van Effenterre. *La Crète et le monde grec de Platon à Polybe.* Paris: de Boccard, 1948. (Bibliothèque des Écoles Françaises d'Athènes et de Rome, 163.) ▸ History of Crete in fourth and third centuries BCE with emphasis on Cretan social and legal systems and their influence on Greek thought. [RAB]

6.438   Thomas J. Figueira. *Aegina: society and politics.* New York: Arno, 1981. ISBN 0-405-14036-3. ▸ Social and economic history of Aegina stressing importance of trade in economy, political developments, and relations with Athens. [RAB]

6.439   P. M. Fraser and G. E. Bean. *The Rhodian Peraea and islands.* London: Oxford University Press, 1954. ▸ Specialized study of Asia Minor coast and islands controlled by Rhodes based on travel in region. Topographical data, epigraphic finds, and analysis of Rhodian administration. [RAB]

6.440   W. A. Laidlaw. *A history of Delos.* Oxford: Blackwell, 1933. ▸ General history of Delos island from archaic Greek times to first century BCE, drawing on results of French excavations and epigraphic finds. Rather dated and in need of replacement. [RAB]

6.441   D. Lazarides. *Thasos and its peraia.* Athens: Athens Center of Ekistics, 1971. (Ancient Greek cities, 5.) ▸ Study of social and economic history of Thasos based on archaeological evidence. Stresses Thasian mines, control of adjacent mainland, and trade. [RAB]

6.442   Karl Lehmann. *Samothrace: a guide to the excavations and the museum.* 5th ed. Phyllis Williams Lehmann, ed. Locust Valley, N.Y.: Augustin for New York University, Institute of Fine Arts, 1983. ▸ Short survey of history of Samothrace, good detailed study of important cult of Great Gods, and general account of archaeological remains and finds. [RAB]

6.443   Colin Renfrew and Malcolm Wagstaff, eds. *An island polity: the archaeology of exploitation in Melos.* Cambridge: Cambridge University Press, 1982. ISBN 0-521-23785-8. ▸ Archaeological history of settlement in and exploitation of Melos from earliest habitation through Roman times. Technical studies by various authors emphasizing relationship between humans and environment and placing Melos in general Aegean-Greek context. [RAB]

6.444   Susan M. Sherwin-White. *Ancient Cos: an historical study from the Dorian settlement to the imperial period.* Göttingen: Vandenhoeck & Ruprecht, 1978. ISBN 3-525-25146-7. ▸ Survey of history of Cos from Dark Ages through Roman empire, drawing heavily on archaeological evidence. Emphasis on social structures, constitution, trade and economic life, and Hippocratic school of medicine. [RAB]

6.445   Graham Shipley. *A history of Samos, 800–188 B.C.* Oxford: Clarendon, 1987. ISBN 0-19-814868-2. ▸ General history of Samos emphasizing archaeological and epigraphic evidence. Tyranny of Polycrates, relations with Athens, and Samian historiography. [RAB]

6.446   R. F. Willetts. *Ancient Crete: a social history from early times until the Roman occupation.* London: Routledge & Kegan Paul, 1965. ▸ Broad social and economic history, studying communal life, Cretan law, serfdom, practice of piracy, and Cretan religion. Emphasis on archaeological and epigraphic source material. [RAB]

TOPICAL STUDIES

City-States, Leagues, and Non-Athenian Law

6.447   André Aymard. *Les assemblées de la confédération achaienne: étude critique d'institutions et d'histoire.* 1938 ed. Rome: Bretschneider, 1967. (Studia historica, 39.) ▸ Decision-making power of assembly of Achaean League. Detailed study of organization, election, and voting procedures. [EMH]

6.448   Helmut Berve. *Die Tyrannis bei den Griechen.* 2 vols. Munich: Beck, 1967. ▸ Exhaustive survey of archaic tyranny, with long bibliographies. Standard work for consultation, not continuous narrative. [MC]

6.449   Felix Bourriot. *Recherches sur l'histoire du "genos."* 2 vols. Lille: Université Lille III, Atelier Reproduction des Thèses; distributed by Champion, 1976. ▸ Iconoclastic study of small kinship groups in Greek society. Challenges traditional views about evolution of Greek society and development of polis. [EMH]

6.450   Georg Busolt. *Griechische Staatskunde.* 1920–26 3d ed. 2 vols. Heinrich Swoboda, ed. Munich: Beck, 1963–72. (Handbuch der Altertumswissenschaft, Vierte Abteilung, 1.1.1–2.) ▸ Monumental handbook, still indispensable, on Greek states. Volume 1 on city-state in general; volume 2 on Sparta and Athens. [MC]

6.451 Victor Ehrenberg. *The Greek state.* 2d ed. London: Methuen, 1969. ISBN 0-416-12820-3. ▸ Influential analysis of common features shared by Greek political communities in archaic and classical periods. [EMH]

6.452 M. I. Finley. *Democracy ancient and modern.* Rev. ed. New Brunswick, N.J.: Rutgers University Press, 1985. ISBN 0-8135-1126-7 (cl), 0-8135-1127-5 (pbk). ▸ Spirited defense of Athenian democracy against ancient and modern detractors. Contains Finley's famous rehabilitation of demagogues. Shrewd comments on realities of politics at Athens, intellectual freedom, and censorship. [EMH]

6.453 Michael Gagarin. *Early Greek law.* Berkeley: University of California Press, 1986. ISBN 0-520-05678-7 (cl), 0-520-06602-2 (pbk). ▸ Good introductory survey covering settlement of disputes, earliest written law, and work of lawgivers. Not restricted to Athens. [MC]

6.454 Louis Gernet. *Droit et société dans la Grèce ancienne.* Rev. ed. Paris: Librairie du Recueil Sirey, 1964. (Publications de l'Institut du Droit Romain de l'Université de Paris, 13.) ▸ Important essays on Athenian legal procedure, arbitrators, inheritance, regulations for slaves, commercial law, and Gortyn law code. [EMH]

6.455 Nicholas F. Jones. *Public organization in ancient Greece: a documentary study.* Philadelphia: American Philosophical Society, 1987. (Memoirs of the American Philosophical Society, 176.) ISBN 0-87169-176-0, ISSN 0065-9738. ▸ Collection of evidence about ways Greek poleis divided citizens into *phylai* (tribes), *trittyes* (thirds), and *demes* (villages). Valuable introduction summarizes main features of organization. [EMH]

6.456 J.A.O. Larsen. *Greek federal states: their institutions and history.* Oxford: Clarendon, 1968. ISBN 0-19-814265-X. ▸ History and organization of leagues of Greek states from classical to Hellenistic periods. [EMH]

6.457 J.A.O. Larsen. *Representative government in Greek and Roman history.* 1955 ed. Berkeley: University of California Press, 1976. ISBN 0-520-03240-3. ▸ Representative institutions in Greek city-states, federal leagues, and Roman provincial assemblies. [EMH]

6.458 Denis Roussel. *Tribu et cité: études sur les groupes sociaux dans les cités grecques aux époques archaïque et classique.* Paris: Belles Lettres, 1976. (Centre de Recherches d'Histoire Ancienne, 23. Annales littéraires de l'Université de Besançon, 193.) ▸ Challenge to traditional evolutionary view of polis. Historical analysis of *genos* (clan), *phratriai* (brotherhoods), and *phylai* (tribes) in archaic and classical Greek cities demonstrating they were not true kinship structures. Important example of French historical sociology. [SMB]

6.459 E. S. Staveley. *Greek and Roman voting and elections.* Ithaca, N.Y.: Cornell University Press, 1972. ISBN 0-8014-0693-5. ▸ Excellent detailed explanations. [EMH]

6.460 R. F. Willetts, ed. and trans. *The law code of Gortyn.* Berlin: de Gruyter, 1967. (Kadmos, Supplement, 1.) ▸ Most recent edition in English of longest legal inscription from classical period. Introductory essays, Greek text, English translation, and detailed commentary. Interpretation of some provisions flawed by outmoded views of social evolution. [EMH]

6.461 Hans Julius Wolff. "The origin of judicial litigation among the Greeks." *Traditio* 4 (1946) 31–87. ISSN 0362-1529. ▸ Classic article about legal procedure in Homer and Hesiod and subsequent development in archaic period. Legal procedure originated as means of regulating revenge and other kinds of self-help. [EMH]

Interstate Relations

6.462 Peter Garnsey and C. R. Whittaker, eds. *Imperialism in the ancient world: the Cambridge University research seminar in ancient history.* Cambridge: Cambridge University Press, 1978. ISBN 0-521-21882-9. ▸ General essays by Finley on fifth-century Athenian empire, Griffith on fourth-century Athenian League, Andrewes on Spartan empire, and Briscoe on Antigonids and Macedonian imperialism. Useful discussion of nature of relations between imperial powers and subject states. [EMH]

6.463 Philippe Gauthier. *Symbola: les étrangers et la justice dans les cités grecques.* Nancy: Université de Nancy II, 1972. (Annales de l'Est, Mémoires, 42.) ▸ Study of commercial treaties between poleis and role in facilitating international relations. Discussion of judicial position of foreigners. [EMH]

6.464 Wilfried Gawantka. *Isopolitie: ein Beitrag zur Geschichte der zwischenstaatlichen Beziehungen in der griechischen Antike.* Munich: Beck, 1975. ISBN 3-406-04792-0. ▸ Survey of literary and epigraphical evidence for individual and collective grants of citizenship during classical and Hellenistic periods. [EMH]

6.465 Alfred Heuss. *Stadt und Herrscher des Hellenismus in ihren staats- und völkerrechtlichen Beziehungen.* Rev. ed. Aalen: Scientia, 1963. (*Klio*, Beiheft, 39.) ▸ Relationship between Hellenistic kings and Greek poleis. Emphasis on *Staatsrecht* somewhat outdated, but still useful for discussion of evidence. With new afterword by author. [EMH]

6.466 Victor Martin. *La vie internationale dans la Grèce des cités, vie–ive siècle avant J.-C.* Paris: Librairie du Recueil Sirey, 1940. (Publications de l'Institut Universitaire de Hautes Études Internationales, Genève, 21.) ▸ General treatment of imperialism, peace treaties, arbitration, and other topics. [EMH]

6.467 D. J. Mosley. *Envoys and diplomacy in ancient Greece.* Wiesbaden: Steiner, 1973. (*Historia*, Einzelschriften, 22.) ISSN 0341-0056. ▸ Detailed study of Greek embassies: size, composition, election of members, diplomatic credentials, payment, powers of negotiation, regulation, etc. Primarily useful as collection of evidence. [EMH]

6.468 T.T.B. Ryder. *Koine eirene: general peace and local independence in ancient Greece.* London: Oxford University Press, 1965. ▸ Standard essay examining diplomatic complexities of Greek states' relations with one another and with Persian king. One of most important political developments of fourth century BCE. [CWH]

6.469 *Die Staatsverträge des Altertums.* Vol. 2: *Die Verträge der griechisch-römischen Welt von 700 bis 338 v. Chr.* Vol. 3: *Die Verträge der griechisch-römischen Welt von 338 bis 200 v. Chr.* Vol. 2, 2d ed. 2 vols. Hermann Bengtson and Robert Werner, v. 2 eds. Hatto H. Schmitt, v. 3 ed. Munich: Beck, 1969–75. ISBN 3-406-04214-7 (v. 2), 3-406-02694-X (v. 3). ▸ Collection of all known treaties, agreements, and negotiations among states to 200 BCE. Includes both inscriptions and references in literary sources. Volume 1 never published. [MC]

Urban History

6.470 Alison Burford. *The Greek temple builders at Epidauros: a social and economic study of building in the Asklepian sanctuary during the fourth and early third centuries B.C.* Toronto: University of Toronto Press, 1969. ISBN 0-8020-1646-4. ▸ Comprehensive reconstruction of social and economic aspects of temple building based on inscribed building accounts of sanctuary of Asclepius at Epidaurus. [SMB]

6.471 Nancy H. Demand. *Urban relocation in archaic and classical Greece: flight and consolidation.* Norman: University of Oklahoma Press, 1990. ISBN 0-8061-2278-1. ▸ Pioneering study of phenomenon of urban relocation in Greece from Homer to 300 BCE.

Urban relocation primarily caused by political rather than economic or environmental factors. Text-based urban history. [SMB]

6.472 A.H.M. Jones. *The Greek city: from Alexander to Justinian.* 1940 ed. Oxford: Clarendon, 1979. ISBN 0-19-814842-9. ▸ Historical survey of spread of Greek city during Hellenistic and Roman periods together with topical analysis of urban institutions. Well-documented, traditional narrative history. [SMB]

6.473 Oswyn Murray and Simon Price, eds. *The Greek city from Homer to Alexander.* Oxford: Clarendon, 1990. ISBN 0-19-814888-7. ▸ Fourteen essays on modern methods of study of ancient Greek city; multidisciplinary in approach. [MC]

6.474 R. E. Wycherley. *How the Greeks built cities.* 1962 2d ed. New York: Norton, 1976. ISBN 0-393-00814-2. ▸ Historical survey of Greek town planning from sixth to fourth century BCE with description of principal types of urban public buildings. [SMB]

Greek Relations with Non-Greeks

6.475 M. M. Austin. *Greece and Egypt in the archaic age.* Cambridge: Cambridge Philological Society, 1970. (Proceedings of the Cambridge Philological Society, Supplement, 2.) ISSN 0068-6743. ▸ Short (seventy-five pages) but excellent monograph on interrelations between Greeks and Egyptians in archaic period based on archaeology and inscriptions. Emphasizes trade, mercenary settlements, and Greek colony at Naukratis. [RAB]

6.476 Eugène Belin de Ballu. *Olbia: cité antique du littoral nord de la mer Noire.* Leiden: Brill, 1972. ISBN 90-04-03464-1. ▸ General history of Olbia (Greek colony in southern Russia) from original colonization through Roman empire. Analyzes civic life, economy, and relations with indigenous Scythian tribes; based on extensive knowledge of Russian excavations on Black Sea coast. [RAB]

6.477 John Boardman. *The Greeks overseas: their early colonies and trade.* Rev. ed. New York: Thames & Hudson, 1980. ISBN 0-500-25069-3. ▸ Eminent archaeologist's history of archaic Greek trade and colonization, covering Near East, Egypt, Italy, Sicily, and Adriatic and Black seas. Outstanding synthesis of crucial archaeological evidence. [RAB]

6.478 Stanley M. Burstein. *Outpost of Hellenism: the emergence of Heraclea on the Black Sea.* Berkeley: University of California Press, 1976. ISBN 0-520-09530-8. ▸ Excellent general history of Heraclea Pontica (Eregli, Turkey) from original Greek colonization to third century BCE. General discussion of Black Sea colonization, study of fourth-century tyranny, and considerations of relations with indigenous people (Mariandynoi). [RAB]

6.479 Jean-Paul Descoeudres, ed. *Greek colonists and native populations.* Oxford: Clarendon, 1990. ISBN 0-19-814869-0. ▸ Forty-five essays on Greeks in Italy, Asia Minor, and elsewhere; much modern archaeological reporting. [MC]

6.480 Robert Drews. "The earliest Greek settlements on the Black Sea." *Journal of Hellenic studies* 96 (1976) 18–31. ISSN 0075-4269. ▸ Argues that literary and scanty archaeological evidence, despite problems, points to eighth century BCE for first Greek penetration and settlement on southern Black Sea coast. Emphasis on importance of trade. [RAB]

6.481 T. J. Dunbabin. *The western Greeks: the history of Sicily and South Italy from the foundation of the Greek colonies to 480 BC.* 1948 ed. Oxford: Clarendon, 1968. ▸ Comprehensive study of Greek cities of Sicily and southern Italy with full treatment of political, social, and economic development. Dated but still useful. [RAB]

6.482 M. I. Finley. *Ancient Sicily.* Rev. ed. Totowa, N.J.: Rowman & Littlefield, 1979. ISBN 0-8476-6190-3. ▸ Comprehensive

history of Sicily from arrival of Greek colonists to end of ancient period (end of Byzantine rule in 878). Emphasis on archaeological evidence; late archaic and classical Greek period most fully covered. [RAB]

6.483 Richard G. Goodchild. *Cyrene and Apollonia: an historical guide.* 2d ed. Tripoli: United Kingdom of Libya, Department of Antiquities, Eastern Region, 1963. ▸ Short history of Greek colonies in Cyrenaica (Libya) from original colonization through Byzantine times with description of key archaeological remains and evidence. Needs updating. [RAB]

6.484 Simon Hornblower. *Mausolus.* Oxford: Clarendon, 1982. ISBN 0-19-814844-5. ▸ Relatively rare discussion of an outsider, a Hellenized potentate who lived on edge of classical Greek world. [CWH]

6.485 Benjamin Isaac. *The Greek settlements in Thrace until the Macedonian conquest.* Leiden: Brill, 1986. (Studies of the Dutch Archaeological and Historical Society, 10.) ISBN 90-04-06921-6. ▸ One of few studies dealing with this part of Greek world. Information on towns and history of several regions. [EB]

6.486 Amélie Kuhrt and Susan M. Sherwin-White, eds. *Hellenism in the East: the interaction of Greek and non-Greek civilizations from Syria to Central Asia after Alexander.* Berkeley: University of California Press, 1987. ISBN 0-520-06054-7. ▸ Six studies by various authors on installation of Greco-Macedonian rule in Seleucid empire and on interaction with indigenous population. Emphasis on new cuneiform and archaeological evidence, downplays old Hellenocentric cultural stereotypes. [RAB]

6.487 David M. Lewis. *Sparta and Persia: lectures delivered at the University of Cincinnati, Autumn 1976, in memory of Donald W. Bradeen.* Leiden: Brill, 1977. ISBN 90-04-05427-8. ▸ Broad examination of Spartan relations with Persia. Treats Persian imperial administration, Spartan government and constitution, warfare between Sparta and Persia in Asia Minor, and King's Peace. [JB]

6.488 A. K. Narain. *The Indo-Greeks.* Rev. ed. Oxford: Clarendon, 1962. ▸ Detailed study of Greek kingdoms in Bactria (Afghanistan) and northern India in Hellenistic period based mostly on numismatic evidence. Places kingdoms in context of contemporary Indian rather than Greek history. [RAB]

6.489 Giuseppe Nenci, ed. *Hérodote et les peuples non-grecs.* Vandoeuvres-Geneva: Fondation Hardt, 1990. (Entretiens sur l'antiquité classique, 35.) ▸ Nine papers (in English, French, German, and Italian), with following discussion, on Herodotus' treatment of various eastern civilizations, of northern and western barbarians, and of non-Greek religions. Useful synthesis of topics often discussed in detail. [EB]

6.490 David Ridgway. *The first western Greeks.* Cambridge: Cambridge University Press, 1992. ISBN 0-521-30882-8, 0-521-42164-0 (pbk.). ▸ English version of *L'alba della Magna Grecia* (1984). Study of early Greek colonization in southern Italy (Magna Graecia); superb knowledge of archaeological evidence, especially excavation at key site of Pithekoussai (Ischia). [RAB]

6.491 M. Rostovtzeff. *Iranians and Greeks in South Russia.* 1922 ed. New York: Russell & Russell, 1969. ▸ Treatment unrivaled in any western language. Especially valuable for archaeological data. [EB]

6.492 Stephen Ruzicka. *Politics of a Persian dynasty: the Hecatomnids in the fourth century B.C.* Norman: University of Oklahoma Press, 1992. ISBN 0-8061-2460-1. ▸ Study of whole history of dynasty with special attention to their attempts to preserve independence of action between nominal Persian suzerains and Greek cities. [EB]

6.493 Erik Sjöqvist. *Sicily and the Greeks: studies in the interrelationship between the indigenous population and the Greek colonists.*

Ann Arbor: University of Michigan Press, 1973. ISBN 0-472-08795-9. ‣ Study of Greek colonization of Sicily and impact on indigenous population, eighth to fourth centuries BCE. Evidence of archaeology stressed, especially from excavation of Sicel town of Morgantina. [RAB]

6.494 A. G. Woodhead. *The Greeks in the West*. New York: Praeger, 1962. ‣ General survey of Greek colonization in Sicily and southern Italy. History of colonies to Roman conquest and cultural achievements of Western Greeks. Fairly popular treatment. [RAB]

Economic History and Slavery

6.495 A. M. Andreades. *A history of Greek public finance*. 1933 rev. ed. Caroll N. Brown, trans. New York: Arno, 1979. ISBN 0-405-12347-7. ‣ Financial history of Greek city-states from Homer to Battle of Chaeronea. [SMB]

6.496 M. M. Austin and Pierre Vidal-Naquet. *Economic and social history of ancient Greece: an introduction*. M. M. Austin, trans. Berkeley: University of California Press, 1977. ISBN 0-520-02658-6. ‣ Introductory survey of economic history of Greece from end of Mycenaean period to beginning of Hellenistic period. Social and institutional focus; includes translated sources. [SMB]

6.497 Raymond Bogaert. *Banques et banquiers dans les cités grecques*. Leiden: Sijthoff, 1968. ‣ Comprehensive study of nature and function of banks in Greek world. Banks facilitated commerce through exchange and payment services but not as sources of credit and finance. [SMB]

6.498 Norbert Brockmeyer. *Antike Sklaverei*. Darmstadt: Wissenschaftliche Buchgesellschaft, 1979. ISBN 3-534-06363-5. ‣ Critical review of scholarship on slavery in Greece and Rome from second millennium BCE to end of antiquity. [SMB]

6.499 M. I. Finley. *The ancient economy*. 2d ed. Berkeley: University of California Press, 1985. ISBN 0-520-05452-0 (pbk). ‣ Controversial attempt to establish nonquantitative model of economy of Greece and Rome; holds that ancient economy was based mainly on land. Important synthetic work. [SMB]

6.500 M. I. Finley. *Ancient slavery and modern ideology*. 1980 ed. Harmondsworth: Penguin, 1983. ISBN 0-14-022500-5 (pbk). ‣ Controversial topical analysis of slave systems of Greece and Rome. Concludes that influence of ideology in formation of historiography of slavery since eighteenth century was decisive. Comparative social history. [SMB]

6.501 M. I. Finley. *Economy and society in ancient Greece*. 1981 ed. Brent D. Shaw and Richard P. Saller, eds. New York: Penguin, 1983. ISBN 0-14-022520-X (pbk). ‣ Representative collection of essays by major scholar dealing with Greek city, ancient slavery, and relationship between Mycenaean and Homeric Greece. Bibliography of Finley's writings. [SMB]

6.502 Alexander Fuks. *Social conflict in ancient Greece*. Jerusalem: Magnes, 1984. ISBN 965-223-466-4. ‣ Important collection of essays dealing with historical and theoretical aspects of social and economic crisis of Greek world between fourth and second centuries BCE. [SMB]

6.503 Yvon Garlan. *Slavery in ancient Greece*. Rev. ed. Janet Lloyd, trans. Ithaca, N.Y.: Cornell University Press, 1988. ISBN 0-8014-1841-0 (cl), 0-8014-9504-0 (pbk). ‣ Basic discussion of origins, character, and practice of slavery in archaic and classical Greece concluding that concept of slave mode of production is not completely applicable to Greece. Revisionist Marxist social history. [SMB]

6.504 Peter Garnsey, ed. *Non-slave labour in the Greco-Roman world*. Rev. ed. Cambridge: Cambridge Philological Society, 1980. (Cambridge Philological Society, Supplement, 6.) ISBN 0-906014-02-6 (pbk), ISSN 0068-6735. ‣ Stimulating collection of essays concerning varieties of nonslave labor in Greco-Roman world. Dependent labor and free peasantries common in both democracies and imperial states. [SMB]

6.505 Peter Garnsey, Keith Hopkins, and C. R. Whittaker, eds. *Trade in the ancient economy*. Berkeley: University of California Press, 1983. ISBN 0-520-04803-2. ‣ Stimulating essays exploring role of trade and traders in economies of Greece and Rome. Essays linked by use of archaeological evidence and emphasis on tie between economic structure and cultural values. [SMB]

6.506 Johannes Hasebroek. *Trade and politics in ancient Greece*. 1933 ed. L. M. Fraser and D. C. Macgregor, trans. Chicago: Ares, 1978. ISBN 0-89005-240-9. ‣ Controversial analysis of relationship between classical Greek state and commerce and description of its trade policy. Greek trade predominantly in noncitizen hands and not capitalistic in character. Antiquated but interesting. [SMB]

6.507 Fritz M. Heichelheim. *An ancient economic history: from the Paleolithic Age to the migration of the Germanic, Slavic, and Arab nations*. Rev. ed. 3 vols. Joyce Stevens, trans. Leiden: Sijthoff, 1957–70. ‣ Comprehensive economic history of ancient world with particular emphasis on Greece and Rome. Sees primitivist interpretations of ancient economy as invalid. [SMB]

6.508 R. J. Hopper. *Trade and industry in classical Greece*. London: Thames & Hudson, 1979. ISBN 0-500-40038-5. ‣ Traditional topical survey of Greek economic activity in archaic and classical periods with emphasis on Athens; particular attention given to influence of politics on conduct of trade. [SMB]

6.509 H. Knorringa. *Emporos: data on trade and trader in Greek literature from Homer to Aristotle*. 1926 ed. Amsterdam: Hakkert, 1961. ‣ Basic philological analysis of Greek terminology dealing with merchants and commerce in archaic and classical Greek literature; Greek economy more primitive than modern in character. [SMB]

6.510 Claire Préaux. *L'économie royale des Lagides*. Brussels: Fondation Égyptologique Reine Élisabeth, 1939. ‣ Detailed study of organization and functioning of state-controlled sectors of economy of Ptolemaic Egypt; planned economy with primarily fiscal goals. Economic history based on papyrological sources. [SMB]

6.511 Rudi Thomsen. *Eisphora: a study of direct taxation in ancient Athens*. Copenhagen: Gyldendal, 1964. ‣ *Eisphora* not Solonian but extraordinary tax levied in fifth and fourth centuries BCE when expenses exceeded normal state revenues. Philologically based economic history. Technical study. [SMB]

6.512 William L. Westermann. *The slave systems of Greek and Roman antiquity*. Philadelphia: American Philosophical Society, 1955. (Memoirs of the American Philosophical Society, 40.) ‣ Encyclopedic analysis of slavery in Greece and Rome with particular emphasis on its juridical rather than its sociological aspects. Nonquantitative social history. English translation of article "Sklaverei" in Pauly, ed. 6.23. [SMB]

Military History

6.513 F. E. Adcock. *The Greek and Macedonian art of war*. 1957 ed. Berkeley: University of California Press, 1962. ISBN 0-520-00005-6. ‣ Introduction to battle tactics and strategy for general reader. Hoplite fighting of classical period; military innovations of Macedonian phalanx. [EMH]

6.514 J. K. Anderson. *Military theory and practice in the age of Xenophon*. Berkeley: University of California Press, 1970. ISBN 0-520-01564-9. ‣ Standard account of warfare in late fifth and fourth centuries BCE. [EMH]

6.515 Jan G. P. Best. *Thracian peltasts and their influence on Greek warfare.* Groningen: Wolters-Noordhoff, 1969. (Studies of the Dutch Archaeological and Historical Society, 1.) ▸ Use of light-armed troops during late fifth and fourth centuries. Peltasts were integral component of hoplite warfare, not new style of fighting. [EMH]

6.516 Yvon Garlan. *War in the ancient world: a social history.* Janet Lloyd, trans. London: Chatto & Windus, 1975. ISBN 0-7011-1888-1. ▸ Sociological approach to Greek and Roman warfare. [EMH]

6.517 P.A.L. Greenhalgh. *Early Greek warfare: horsemen and chariots in the Homeric and archaic ages.* Cambridge: Cambridge University Press, 1973. ISBN 0-521-20056-3. ▸ Chariots in Homeric period used only to transport warriors to battlefield, not for fighting. Stresses importance of infantry. Critique of conventional view of hoplite reform at Sparta. [EMH]

6.518 G. T. Griffith. *The mercenaries of the Hellenistic world.* 1935 ed. Groningen: Bouma, 1968. ▸ Study of role of mercenaries in Hellenistic armies, sources of mercenaries, and their number and payment. [EMH]

6.519 Victor Davis Hanson. *Warfare and agriculture in classical Greece.* Pisa: Giardini, 1983. ▸ Stimulating analysis of effectiveness of ravaging as military tactic in classical Greece. Subsistence character of Greek agriculture and practical difficulty of extensive crop destruction indicate that significant economic impact of tactic is often exaggerated. [SMB]

6.520 Victor Davis Hanson. *The western way of war: infantry battle in classical Greece.* John Keegan, Introduction. New York: Knopf, 1989. ISBN 0-394-57188-6. ▸ Study of hoplite tactics tracing western tradition of decision through decisive battle, rather than through prolonged period of attrition, to influence of Greek military practice. Unusual degree of realism. [EB]

6.521 Johannes Kromayer, ed. *Schlachten-Atlas zur antiken Kriegsgeschichte.* 5 parts in 6 fascicules. Leipzig: Wagner & Debes, 1922–29. ▸ Essentially part of Kromayer and Veith 6.522; 120 maps of battles on thirty-four plates. [MC]

6.522 Johannes Kromayer and Georg Veith. *Antike Schlachtfelder: Bausteine zu einer antiken Kriegsgeschichte.* 4 vols. in 8 parts. Berlin: Weidmann, 1903–31. ▸ Discussion of ancient battle sites; essentially accompaniment to Kromayer and Veith 6.523. [MC]

6.523 Johannes Kromayer and Georg Veith. *Heerwesen und Kriegführung der Griechen und Römer.* 1928 ed. Munich: Beck, 1963. (Handbuch der Altertumswissenschaft, Vierte Abteilung, 3.2.) ▸ Standard handbook for military organization and tactics in Greek and Roman world. [EMH]

6.524 Marcel Launey. *Recherches sur les armées hellénistiques.* Rev. ed. 2 vols. Paris: de Boccard, 1987. (Bibliothèque des Écoles Françaises d'Athènes et de Rome, 169.) ▸ Massive specialized studies on various aspects of Hellenistic armies; see Tarn 6.533. [EMH]

6.525 A. W. Lawrence. *Greek aims in fortification.* Oxford: Clarendon, 1979. ISBN 0-19-814824-0. ▸ Development of Greek fortifications analyzed in light of contemporary military tactics and technology. [EMH]

6.526 Włodzimierz Lengauer. *Greek commanders in the fifth and fourth centuries B.C.: politics and ideology, a study of militarism.* Warsaw: Wydawnictwa Uniwersytetu Warszawskiego, 1979. ▸ Traces development by which military command was transformed from civic duty to professional career; loyalty of commanders and troops turned more toward each other than to the state. [MC]

6.527 E. W. Marsden. *Greek and Roman artillery.* Vol. 1: *Historical development.* Vol. 2: *Technical treatises.* 2 vols. Oxford:

Clarendon, 1967–71. ISBN 0-19-814269-2 (v. 2). ▸ History of construction and use of catapults and missiles. Introductory essays accompanied by Greek texts with English translation and commentary. [EMH]

6.528 J. S. Morrison and R. T. Williams. *Greek oared ships, 900–322 B.C.* London: Cambridge University Press, 1968. ▸ Scholarly study of ancient literary and archaeological evidence for oared ships including penteconters and triremes. Discussion of trireme summarized in Morrison and Coates 6.392. [EMH]

6.529 W. Kendrick Pritchett. *The Greek state at war.* 1971–91 ed. 5 vols. Berkeley: University of California Press, 1974. ISBN 0-520-02758-2 (v. 1), 0-520-02565-2 (v. 2), 0-520-03781-2 (v. 3), 0-520-05379 (v. 4), 0-520-07374-6 (v. 5). ▸ Indispensable series of detailed studies with full references to ancient sources. Prisoners, trials of generals, tactics, soldiers' pay, sacrifices before battle, military training, and much more. Earlier title: *Ancient Greek Military Practices.* [EMH]

6.530 W. Kendrick Pritchett. *Studies in ancient Greek topography.* 8 vols. Berkeley and Amsterdam: University of California Press and Gieben; distributed by Benjamins, 1965–1993. ISBN 0-520-09635-5 (v. 3), 0-520-09660-6 (v. 4), 0-520-09698-3 (v. 5), 0-520-09746-7 (v. 6), 90-5063-071-5 (v. 7), 90-5063-087-1 (v. 8). ▸ Companion volumes to Pritchett 6.529; mainly studies of locations of battles and places enroute to battles (passes, routes). [MC]

6.531 A. M. Snodgrass. *Arms and armour of the Greeks.* Ithaca, N.Y.: Cornell University Press, 1967. ISBN 0-8014-0399-5. ▸ History of Greek arms from beginnings through Macedonian kingdoms. Less technical than Snodgrass 6.532. [MC]

6.532 A. M. Snodgrass. *Early Greek armour and weapons, from the end of the Bronze Age to 600 B.C.* Edinburgh: Edinburgh University Press, 1964. ▸ Thorough study of archaeological evidence for development of armor and weapons in early archaic period. [EMH]

6.533 W. W. Tarn. *Hellenistic military and naval developments.* 1930 ed. New York: Biblo & Tannen, 1966. ▸ Three lectures plus then new material especially on great war horse and great ships. [MC]

6.534 H. T. Wallinga. *Ships and sea-power before the great Persian War: the ancestry of the ancient trireme.* Leiden: Brill, 1993. (*Mnemosyne,* Supplement, 121.) ISBN 90-04-09650-7 (cl), 90-04-09709-0 (pbk), ISSN 0169-8958. ▸ Survey of development of Greek warships; cf. Morrison and Williams 6.528. [MC]

6.535 H. van Wees. "Kings in combat: battles and heroes in the *Iliad.*" *Classical quarterly,* n.s., 38.1 (1988) 1–24. ISSN 0009-8388. ▸ With 6.536, pair of important articles about role of commanders and nature of warfare in Homeric poems. [EMH]

6.536 H. van Wees. "Leaders of men? Military organization in the *Iliad.*" *Classical quarterly,* n.s., 36.2 (1986) 285–303. ISSN 0009-8388. ▸ With 6.535, pair of important articles about role of commanders and nature of warfare in Homeric poems. Difficulty of using *Iliad* as historical source for military tactics. Discusses differences between Homeric warfare and hoplite fighting of classical period. [EMH]

Rural History

6.537 Tjeerd H. van Andel and Curtis Runnels. *Beyond the Acropolis: a rural Greek past.* Stanford, Calif.: Stanford University Press, 1987. ISBN 0-8047-1389-8. ▸ Pioneering, archaeologically based environmental history of southern Argolid from Paleolithic to end of antiquity. [SMB]

6.538 Alison Burford. *Land and labor in the Greek world.* Baltimore: Johns Hopkins University Press, 1993. ISBN 0-8018-

4463-0. ▸ Modern treatment of land tenure, agricultural techniques, and distribution of land. [MC]

6.539 Dorothy J. Crawford. *Kerkeosiris: an Egyptian village in the Ptolemaic period.* Cambridge: Cambridge University Press, 1971. ISBN 0-521-07607-2. ▸ Classic reconstruction of life of agricultural village in Ptolemaic Egypt on basis of papyrological archive. Greek and Egyptian elements intertwined in all aspects of village life. [SMB]

6.540 M. I. Finley, ed. *Problèmes de la terre en Grèce ancienne.* Paris: Mouton, 1973. ISBN 2-7132-0001-6. ▸ Collection of sixteen essays (three in English) concerning land tenure in Greek world and its influence on Greek agriculture, social organization, and religious thought. [SMB]

6.541 Peter Garnsey. *Famine and food supply in the Graeco-Roman world: responses to risk and crisis.* Cambridge: Cambridge University Press, 1988. ISBN 0-521-35198-7. ▸ Revisionist study of extent and severity of famine in classical Athens and republican and early imperial Rome; also survival strategies used. Concludes Athenian agricultural productivity underestimated and Roman economic intervention exaggerated by previous scholars. [SMB]

6.542 Auguste F. V. Jardé. *Les céréales dans l'antiquité grecque: la production.* 1925 ed. Paris: de Boccard, 1979. (Bibliothèque des Écoles Françaises d'Athènes et de Rome, 130.) ▸ Pioneering study of Greek agricultural methods and productivity in classical and Hellenistic periods. Methods remained largely unchanged and productivity consistently low. [SMB]

6.543 Russell Meiggs. *Trees and timber in the ancient Mediterranean world.* Oxford: Clarendon, 1982. ISBN 0-19-814840-2. ▸ Outstanding fundamental study of timber resources of central and eastern Mediterranean, their extent, management, and commercial exploitation, from Bronze Age to end of antiquity. [SMB]

6.544 Robin Osborne. *Classical landscape with figures: the ancient Greek city and its countryside.* Dobbs Ferry, N.Y.: Sheridan House, 1987. ISBN 0-911378-73-1. ▸ Analysis of character of Greek countryside, its settlement patterns and agricultural regime. Shows that these factors fundamentally influenced polis life. Innovative urban history; cf. Osborne 6.335. [SMB]

6.545 M. Rostovtzeff. *A large estate in Egypt in the third century B.C.* 1922 ed. New York: Arno, 1979. ISBN 0-405-12392-2. ▸ Detailed study of organization and functioning of personal estate of high government official in Ptolemaic Egypt. Economic history based on papyrological sources. [SMB]

6.546 P. Walcot. *Greek peasants ancient and modern: a comparison of social and moral values.* New York: Barnes & Noble, 1970. ISBN 0-389-03972-1. ▸ Comparative study of Greek peasants, their values and relations with rest of society in ancient and modern Greece. Historical ethnographic case study. [SMB]

6.547 C. R. Whittaker, ed. *Pastoral economies in classical antiquity.* Cambridge: Cambridge Philological Society, 1988. (Cambridge Philological Society, Supplement, 14.) ISBN 0-906014-13-1 (pbk), ISSN 0068-6735. ▸ Modern essays on animal husbandry, transhumance, animals in sacrifice, and other topics. [EB]

Demography, Population, and Social Life

6.548 Frederick A. G. Beck. *Greek education, 450–350 B.C.* New York: Barnes & Noble, 1964. ▸ Discussion of Athenian practices, theories of individual teachers and philosophers such as Sophists, Socrates, Plato, Xenophon, and Isocrates. Chapter on early Greece outdated. [GND]

6.549 Alison Burford. *Craftsmen in Greek and Roman society.* Ithaca, N.Y.: Cornell University Press, 1972. ISBN 0-8014-0717-6.

▸ Detailed survey of place of craftsmen in Greek and Roman society and thought. [SMB]

6.550 Robert Flacelière. *Daily life in Greece at the time of Pericles.* Peter Green, trans. New York: Macmillan, 1965. ▸ Introductory social history of everyday Greek social life in fifth century BCE. Argument that idealistic reconstructions of Greek life by previous scholars seriously distort reality. [SMB]

6.551 Robert Garland. *The Greek way of life: from conception to old age.* Ithaca, N.Y.: Cornell University Press, 1990. ISBN 0-8014-2335-X. ▸ Reconstruction of normal life cycle of classical and Hellenistic Greek men and women and Greek attitudes concerning various phases of life. Treatment biased toward privileged classes by availability of sources. [SMB]

6.552 Louis Gernet. *The anthropology of ancient Greece.* John D. B. Hamilton and Blaise Nagy, trans. Baltimore: Johns Hopkins University Press, 1981. ISBN 0-8018-2112-6. ▸ Representative selection of essays concerning Greek law, religion, and mythical thought by important French historian of ancient world. Application of Durkheimian sociology to history. [SMB]

6.553 Fritz Gschnitzer. *Griechische Sozialgeschichte von der mykenischen bis zum Ausgang der klassischen Zeit.* Wiesbaden: Steiner, 1981. ISBN 3-515-03552-4. ▸ Introductory survey of social and economic history of Greece from second millennium BCE to end of fourth century BCE. [SMB]

6.554 A. R. Hands. *Charities and social aid in Greece and Rome.* Ithaca, N.Y.: Cornell University Press, 1968. ▸ Stimulating revisionist study of character and extent of organized social welfare institutions in Greece and Rome showing existence of large-scale philanthropy. [SMB]

6.555 William V. Harris. *Ancient literacy.* Cambridge, Mass.: Harvard University Press, 1989. ISBN 0-674-03380-9. ▸ Treats levels and functions of literacy with general survey of literacy from archaic Greece to late antiquity. Puts forth controversial thesis that literacy was restricted to privileged minority. [GND]

6.556 Gabriel Herman. *Ritualised friendship and the Greek city.* Cambridge: Cambridge University Press, 1987. ISBN 0-521-32541-2. ▸ Pioneering anthropological study of role of guest friendship (reciprocal hospitality) in social and political life of elites of Greek cities. Guest friendship instrumental in linking elites across city boundaries. [SMB]

6.557 S. C. Humphreys. *Anthropology and the Greeks.* New York: Routledge & Kegan Paul, 1978. ISBN 0-7100-8785-3 (cl), 0-7102-0016-1 (pbk). ▸ Essays dealing with various aspects of social and economic structure of Athens and other Greek cities between 800 and 300 BCE. Provocative effort to apply anthropological and sociological theory to Greek history. [SMB]

6.558 A. W. Lintott. *Violence, civil strife, and revolution in the classical city, 750–330 B.C.* Baltimore: Johns Hopkins University Press, 1982. ISBN 0-8018-2789-2. ▸ Historical survey of urban violence in cities of Greece, southern Italy, and Sicily, from eighth to fourth century BCE, and its impact on Greek political thought. [SMB]

6.559 H. I. Marrou. *A history of education in antiquity.* 1956 ed. George Lamb, trans. Madison: University of Wisconsin Press, 1982. ISBN 0-299-08814-6 (pbk). ▸ Standard chronological survey treating both theory and practice. Covers classical Greece, Hellenistic Age, and Rome. Dated but still useful. Translation of *Histoire de l'éducation dans l'antiquité*. [GND]

6.560 Paul R. McKechnie. *Outsiders in the Greek cities in the fourth century BC.* New York: Routledge, 1989. ISBN 0-415-00340-7. ▸ Well-focused, nonquantitative social history of place of exiles and occupational wanderers in fourth-century BCE

Greece. Argues their existence essential to origins of Hellenistic kingdoms. [SMB]

6.561 Oswyn Murray, ed. *Sympotica: a symposium on the symposion.* Oxford: Clarendon, 1990. ISBN 0-19-814861-5. ▸ Proceedings of conference concerning character and place in Greek culture of symposium, principal social ritual of Greek aristocracy. Fundamental studies. [SMB]

6.562 G.E.M. de Ste. Croix. *The class struggle in the ancient Greek world from the archaic age to the Arab conquests.* Rev. ed. London: Duckworth, 1983. ISBN 0-7156-0738-3 (pbk). ▸ Social history of Greek world from archaic period to Arab conquest demonstrating value of Marxist analysis. Second half largely relevant to whole Roman empire. Brilliant, idiosyncratic Marxist history on grand scale. Invaluable bibliography. [SMB]

6.563 Robert Sallares. *The ecology of the ancient Greek world.* Ithaca, N.Y.: Cornell University Press, 1991. ISBN 0-8014-2615-4. ▸ Intellectually ambitious interdisciplinary study of relationship between population and land use in ancient Greece. Introduction of Mediterranean multicrop agriculture in first millennium BCE led to larger populations than usually assumed. [SMB]

6.564 Jakob Seibert. *Die politischen Flüchtlinge und Verbannten in der griechischen Geschichte: von den Anfangen bis zur Unterwerfung durch die Römer.* 2 vols. Darmstadt: Wissenschaftliche Buchgesellschaft, 1979. ISBN 3-534-06389-9 (set). ▸ Encyclopedic study of phenomena of political exile and banishment in Greek history and thought up to end of Hellenistic period. Social history reference work. [SMB]

6.565 Rosalind Thomas. *Literacy and orality in ancient Greece.* Cambridge: Cambridge University Press, 1992. ISBN 0-521-37346-8 (cl), 0-521-37742-0 (pbk). ▸ Studies of oral poetry, problem of Homeric texts, arrival of alphabet, and growth of record keeping. Cf. Thomas 6.285. [MC]

6.566 David C. Young. *The Olympic myth of Greek amateur athletics.* 1984 ed. Chicago: Ares, 1985. ISBN 0-89005-523-8 (pbk). ▸ Provocative analysis of how nineteenth-century European aristocrats created myth of Greek amateurism; economic incentives in form of prizes and hope of public glory central to Greek athletics. [SMB]

Family, Women, Children, and Sexuality

6.567 K. J. Dover. *Greek homosexuality.* Rev. ed. Cambridge, Mass.: Harvard University Press, 1989. ISBN 0-674-36261-6 (cl), 0-674-36270-5 (pbk). ▸ Detailed survey and analysis of male and female homosexual behavior and attitudes toward such behavior in Greece from eighth to second century BCE. [SMB]

6.568 Sharon Kelly Heyob. *The cult of Isis among women in the Graeco-Roman world.* Leiden: Brill, 1975. ISBN 90-04-04368-3. ▸ Important study of role of women in cult of Isis outside Egypt during Hellenistic and Roman periods. Argues that theories assigning women major role in organization and spread of cult are unacceptable. [SMB]

6.569 Marc Kleijwegt. *Ancient youth: the ambiguity of youth and the absence of adolescence in Greco-Roman society.* Amsterdam: Gieben, 1991. ISBN 90-5063-063-4. ▸ Pioneering comparative study of social and occupational roles of youths in Greek and Roman society. No specific phase of life comparable to modern adolescence recognized in antiquity. [SMB]

6.570 W. K. Lacey. *The family in classical Greece.* 1968 ed. Ithaca, N.Y.: Cornell University Press, 1984. ISBN 0-8014-9274-2 (pbk). ▸ Topical survey of institution of family in Greek life and thought during archaic and classical periods with emphasis on Athens and Sparta; clear, well-documented reference work. [SMB]

6.571 Sarah B. Pomeroy. *Goddesses, whores, wives, and slaves: women in classical antiquity.* New York: Schocken, 1975. ISBN 0-8052-3562-0 (cl), 0-8052-0530-6 (pbk). ▸ Narrative social history of women in Greece and Rome based on literary and artistic sources. Pioneering analysis of varied roles of women in ancient history. [SMB]

6.572 Sarah B. Pomeroy. *Women in Hellenistic Egypt from Alexander to Cleopatra.* New York: Schocken, 1984. ISBN 0-8052-3911-1. ▸ Stimulating analysis of status of Greek and Macedonian women in Hellenistic Egypt; status higher than in classical Athens because of reduced polarity between sexes. Social history based on papyrological sources. [SMB]

6.573 David M. Schaps. *Economic rights of women in ancient Greece.* Edinburgh: Edinburgh University Press, 1979. ISBN 0-85224-343-X (cl), 0-85224-423-1 (pbk). ▸ Fundamental thematic analysis of economic rights of women in Greece to 146 BCE. Determines scope and character of women's property rights and legal aspects of Greek women's economic role. [SMB]

6.574 Raphael Sealey. *Women and law in classical Greece.* Chapel Hill: University of North Carolina Press, 1990. ISBN 0-8078-1872-0 (cl), 0-8078-4262-1 (pbk). ▸ Controversial case studies of legal position of women in Greece from Homer to Hellenistic period. Sees law as most reliable guide to attitudes of Greek men toward women. [SMB]

Religion

6.575 Walter Burkert. *Ancient mystery cults.* Cambridge, Mass.: Harvard University Press, 1987. ISBN 0-674-03386-8 (cl), 0-674-03387-6 (pbk). ▸ Comprehensive phenomenology of mystery cults of Demeter, Dionysus, Magna Mater, Isis, and Mithras. Basic beliefs, administrative structures, theologies, and mystic experiences. [JDM]

6.576 Walter Burkert. *Greek religion: archaic and classical.* John Raffan, trans. Cambridge, Mass.: Harvard University Press, 1985. ISBN 0-674-36280-2 (cl), 0-674-36281-0 (pbk). ▸ Encyclopedic account of personnel, rituals, deities, beliefs, and social relevance of Greek religion from beginnings to classical period. Summaries of previous scholarship, notes, and bibliography. Translation of *Griechische Religion der archaischen und klassischen Epoche* (1977). [JDM]

6.577 Walter Burkert. *Homo necans: the anthropology of ancient Greek sacrificial ritual and myth.* Peter Bing, trans. Berkeley: University of California Press, 1983. ISBN 0-520-03650-6 (cl), 0-520-05875-5 (pbk). ▸ Bold interpretation of Greek sacrificial ritual, myths, festivals, and Eleusinian mysteries, based on then current anthropological and psychological theories, often stressing prehistorical influences and survivals. [JDM]

6.578 T. H. Carpenter and Christopher A. Faraone, eds. *Masks of Dionysus.* Ithaca, N.Y.: Cornell University Press, 1993. ISBN 0-8014-2779-7 (cl), 0-8014-8062-0 (pbk). ▸ Papers of conference on nature, representation, literary treatment, and cultic (especially mystery) aspects of Dionysus. Very current on method and new evidence; extensive bibliography. [JDM]

6.579 W. Robert Connor. "City Dionysia and Athenian democracy." *Classica et mediaevalia* 40 (1989) 7–32. ISSN 0106-5815. ▸ Probing investigation of date and origin of major dramatic festival dedicated to Dionysus and its relationship to Athenian democratic institutions and ideals. [JDM]

6.580 E. R. Dodds. *The Greeks and the irrational.* 1951 ed. Berkeley: University of California Press, 1973. ISBN 0-520-00327-6 (pbk). ▸ Eight pioneering lectures illustrating elements of irrational and subconscious in Greek life, literature, religion, and philosophy from Homer to Hellenistic period. [JDM]

6.581 E. R. Dodds, ed. *Bacchae.* 1960 2d ed. Oxford: Clarendon,

1986. ISBN 0-19-872125-0 (pbk). ‣ Brief but informative and balanced description of Dionysiac cult and myth as introduction to single most important text for understanding this deity. [JDM]

6.582 P. E. Easterling and J. V. Muir, eds. *Greek religion and society.* Cambridge: Cambridge University Press, 1985. ISBN 0-521-24552-4 (cl), 0-521-28785-5 (pbk). ‣ Eight essays, at intermediate level, by British scholars on general beliefs, eschatology, sanctuaries, festivals, and divination and on relationship of Greek religion to art, poetry, and Sophists. [JDM]

6.583 L. R. Farnell. *The cults of the Greek states.* 1896–1909 ed. 5 vols. New Rochelle, N.Y.: Caratzas Brothers, 1977. ‣ Primarily valuable as well-indexed, useful collection of literary references to cults of Olympian and some minor deities with inscriptions, coins, and art. Available on microfilm from Cambridge, Mass.: General Microfilm Company. [JDM]

6.584 Joseph Fontenrose. *The Delphic oracle: its responses and operations, with a catalogue of responses.* Berkeley: University of California Press, 1978. ISBN 0-520-03360-4 (cl), 0-520-04359-6 (pbk). ‣ Description of workings and personnel of Delphic oracle and detailed typology and catalog of its 535 responses, all divided into categories of historical, quasi-historical, legendary, and fictitious. [JDM]

6.585 Robert Garland. *The Greek way of death.* Ithaca, N.Y.: Cornell University Press, 1985. ISBN 0-8014-1823-2 (cl), 0-8014-9528-8 (pbk). ‣ Survey of Greek popular beliefs and practices concerning death, burial, tombs, and afterlife based on literary, archaeological, and artistic evidence. Emphasis on geometric and classical periods. [JDM]

6.586 W.K.C. Guthrie. *The Greeks and their gods.* 1950 ed. Boston: Beacon, 1985. ISBN 0-8070-5793-2. ‣ Good general introduction though somewhat dated tracing Greek concepts of relations between gods and men through accounts of major deities and of literary and philosophical works. [JDM]

6.587 G. S. Kirk. *Myth: its meaning and functions in ancient and other cultures.* 1970 ed. Cambridge: Cambridge University Press, 1974. ISBN 0-520-01651-3 (cl), 0-520-02389-7 (pbk). ‣ Six lectures offering comparative approach to Greek, Near Eastern, and other myths. Concise surveys of theories and coherent attempts to establish definitions, typologies, and interrelationships. [JDM]

6.588 Martin P. Nilsson. *Geschichte der griechischen Religion.* 3d ed. 2 vols. Munich: Beck, 1967–74. (Handbuch der Altertumswissenschaft, Fünfte Abteilung, 2.) ISBN 3-406-01430-5. ‣ Encyclopedic account of nature and history of archaic and classical Greek religious concepts, rites, cults, and major and minor deities. Exemplary integration of literary and archaeological evidence. [JDM]

6.589 Martin P. Nilsson. *The Minoan-Mycenaean religion and its survival in Greek religion.* 1950 2d rev. ed. New York: Biblo & Tannen, 1971. ISBN 0-8196-0273-6. ‣ Early but enduring description of fundamental characteristics of Minoan and Mycenaean religions, of differences between them, and of survivals of Mycenaean into archaic and classical Greek religion. [JDM]

6.590 Robert Parker. *Miasma: pollution and purification in early Greek religion.* 1983 ed. Oxford: Clarendon, 1990. ISBN 0-19-814742-2 (pbk). ‣ Comprehensive account of archaic and classical Greek beliefs about pollution and purification in matters of birth, death, sex, homicide, sacrilege, curses, and disease. [JDM]

Political Philosophy

6.591 Julia Annas. *An introduction to Plato's "Republic."* Oxford: Clarendon, 1981. ISBN 0-19-827428-9 (cl), 0-19-827429-7 (pbk). ‣ Lively, thorough account of various topics in *Republic*; treated in approximate order in which they occur in text. [DLB]

6.592 Renford Bambrough, ed. *Plato, Popper, and politics: some contributions to a modern controversy.* Cambridge: Cambridge University Press, 1967. ‣ Essays written in response to Popper's influential attack on Plato (6.602). [EMH]

6.593 E. Barker. *The political thought of Plato and Aristotle.* 1906 ed. New York: Dover, 1959. ISBN 0-486-20521-5. ‣ General account of political thought from pre-Socratics to Aristotle; mostly on Aristotle's *Politics* with less on Plato. [EMH]

6.594 Jonathan Barnes, M. Schofield, and Richard Sorabji, eds. *Articles on Aristotle.* Vol. 2: *Ethics and politics.* New York: St. Martin's, 1978. ISBN 0-312-05478-5 (v. 2). ‣ Important articles on Aristotle's political thought by von Fritz and Kapp (political philosophy and concept of nature), Fortenbaugh (slaves and women), Finley (economic analysis), Wheeler (political struggle), Kelsen (Aristotle and contemporary politics), de Fourny (aim of state), and Weil (view of history). [EMH]

6.595 E. B. England, ed. *The "Laws" of Plato.* 1921 ed. 2 vols. New York: Arno, 1976. ISBN 0-405-07327-5. ‣ Scholarly edition of Plato's final thoughts on political philosophy and state. Out of date in many respects but still only commentary in English; see Piérart 6.600, Stalley 6.604, and Morrow 6.598. [EMH]

6.596 Kurt von Fritz. *The theory of the mixed constitution in antiquity: a critical analysis of Polybius' political ideas.* 1954 ed. New York: Arno, 1975. ISBN 0-405-07082-9. ‣ Study of genesis and development of theory of mixed constitution. Discussion of intellectual and historical background of Polybius and relationship of Polybius' ideas to Roman historical development. [EMH]

6.597 Erwin R. Goodenough. "The political philosophy of Hellenistic kingship." *Yale classical studies* 1 (1928) 55–102. ISSN 0084-330X. ‣ Criticism of work by earlier scholars, especially Julius Kaerst (*Studien zur Entwicklung und theoretischen Begründung der Monarchie im Altertum*), on Hellenistic kingship. [EMH]

6.598 Glenn R. Morrow. *Plato's Cretan city: a historical interpretation of the "Laws."* Princeton: Princeton University Press, 1960. ‣ Comparison of legislation in Plato's *Laws* with statutes of contemporary Greek states. Discussion of political institutions in utopian community of Magnesia; see England, ed. 6.595, Piérart 6.600, and Stalley 6.604. [EMH]

6.599 Wilfried Nippel. *Mischverfassungstheorie und Verfassungsrealität in Antike und früher Neuzeit.* Stuttgart: Klett-Cotta, 1980. ISBN 3-12-913160-4. ‣ Development of theory of mixed constitution from fifth-century Athens to Polybius. Comparison with ideas about mixed constitution in seventeenth-century England and eighteenth-century America. [EMH]

6.600 Marcel Piérart. *Platon et la cité grecque: théorie et réalité dans la constitution des "Lois."* Brussels: Académie Royale de Belgique, 1974. (Mémoires de la classe des lettres, Collection in-8°, Deuxième série, 62.3.) ‣ General study of all aspects of Plato's final work of political philosophy, usually ignored in favor of his *Republic*; see England, ed. 6.595, Stalley 6.604, and Morrow 6.598. [EMH]

6.601 Plato. *The Republic.* 1963 2d ed. 2 vols. James Adam, ed. D. A. Rees, Introduction. Cambridge: Cambridge University Press, 1979–80. ISBN 0-521-05963-1. ‣ Scholarly edition of Greek text with critical apparatus and detailed commentary on philological matters. No English translation provided. Old but unchallenged. [EMH]

6.602 Karl R. Popper. *The open society and its enemies.* Vol. 1: *The spell of Plato.* 1966 5th ed. Princeton: Princeton University Press, 1971. ISBN 0-691-01968-1 (v. 1). ‣ Stimulating but overdone attack on Plato as spiritual father of modern totalitarianism; see Bambrough, ed. 6.592. [MC]

6.603 T. A. Sinclair. *A history of Greek political thought.* 1967 2d ed. Cleveland: World, 1968. ‣ Succinct, clear sketch of development of Greek political thought, meant to be read with original sources at hand. [EMH]

6.604 R. F. Stalley. *An introduction to Plato's "Laws."* Indianapolis: Hackett, 1983. ISBN 0-915145-84-7. ‣ General discussion of Plato's political philosophy. Role of education, function of punishment, moral responsibility, religious views, political institutions, and sovereignty of law. Good introduction for general reader; see England, ed. 6.595, Morrow 6.598, and Piérart 6.600. [EMH]

6.605 Ellen Meiksins Wood and Neal Wood. *Class ideology and ancient political theory: Socrates, Plato, and Aristotle in social context.* New York: Oxford University Press, 1978. ISBN 0-19-520100-0. ‣ Marxist analysis of aristocratic bias and hostility toward democracy in thought of Socrates, Plato, and Aristotle. [EMH]

Speculative Philosophy

6.606 A. H. Armstrong, ed. *The Cambridge history of later Greek and early medieval philosophy.* Rev. ed. Cambridge: Cambridge University Press, 1970. ‣ Essays giving good account of vast field beginning about where Guthrie 6.609 ends. Merlan's chapters represent Continental more than Anglo-American tradition. [DLB]

6.607 Walter Burkert. *Lore and science in ancient Pythagoreanism.* Edwin L. Minar, Jr., trans. Cambridge, Mass.: Harvard University Press, 1972. ISBN 0-674-53918-4. ‣ Best introduction to study of Pythagorean community and its philosophy, topics in which historiographic problems are particularly vexatious. [DLB]

6.608 John M. Dillon. *The middle Platonists: a study of Platonism, 80 B.C. to A.D. 220.* Ithaca, N.Y.: Cornell University Press, 1977. ISBN 0-8014-1083-5. ‣ Survey of difficult area that influenced church fathers and prepared way for neo-Platonism. Chapters on figures such as Plutarch and Philo Judaeus and on Old Academy, school of Gaius, and Gnostics. [DLB]

6.609 W.K.C. Guthrie. *A history of Greek philosophy.* 6 vols. Cambridge: Cambridge University Press, 1962–81. ISBN 0-521-20002-4 (v. 4), 0-521-20003-2 (v. 5), 0-521-23573-1 (v. 6). ‣ Comprehensive, often detailed survey of field. In general, represents state of subject in Anglo-American world of 1960s. [DLB]

6.610 Terence Irwin. *Plato's moral theory: the early and middle dialogues.* 1977 ed. Oxford: Clarendon, 1979. ISBN 0-19-824614-5 (pbk). ‣ Monumental study of Plato's dialogues down through *Republic.* Aims to show logical structure, development, and coherence of arguments. Highly philosophical book, perhaps difficult for beginners. [DLB]

6.611 G. B. Kerferd. *The Sophistic movement.* Cambridge: Cambridge University Press, 1981. ISBN 0-521-23936-2 (cl), 0-521-28357-4 (pbk). ‣ Brief, readable book; best introduction to history, philosophy, politics, and significance of Sophists. Chapters on dialectic, linguistics, relativism, *nomos-physis* controversy, sociology, and religious theory. [DLB]

6.612 G. S. Kirk, J. E. Raven, and M. Schofield. *The Presocratic philosophers.* 2d ed. Cambridge: Cambridge University Press, 1983. ISBN 0-521-25444-2 (cl), 0-521-27455-9 (pbk). ‣ Effective updating of old standby. Introduction and collection of texts with translation for major figures of early Greek philosophy, from Hesiod and mythical background to Atomists. [DLB]

6.613 G.E.R. Lloyd. *Aristotle: the growth and structure of his thought.* London: Cambridge University Press, 1968. ISBN 0-521-07049-X (cl), 0-521-09456-9 (pbk). ‣ Good introductory account of Aristotle including at least some coverage of each area of his philosophy. [DLB]

6.614 G.E.R. Lloyd. "Science and mathematics." In *The legacy of Greece: a new appraisal.* 1981 ed. M. I. Finley, ed., pp. 256–300. Oxford: Oxford University Press, 1984. ISBN 0-19-285136-5 (pbk). ‣ Concise introduction to Greek contribution to birth and development of scientific-mathematical thought. [DLB]

6.615 A. A. Long. *Hellenistic philosophy: Stoics, Epicureans, Sceptics.* 2d ed. Berkeley: University of California Press, 1986. ISBN 0-520-05807-0 (cl), 0-520-05808-9 (pbk). ‣ Excellent introduction to field that has been expanding since 1960s. Extended essay on each major school. [DLB]

6.616 A. A. Long and D. N. Sedley. *The Hellenistic philosophers.* 2 vols. Cambridge: Cambridge University Press, 1987. ISBN 0-521-25561-9 (v. 1, cl), 0-521-25562-7 (v. 2), 0-521-27556-3 (v. 1, pbk). ‣ Translations of principal sources (volume 1) and Greek and Latin texts with notes and bibliography (volume 2). General accounts of major schools (early Pyrrhonism, Epicureanism, Academics, Pyrrhonist revival) with detailed philological commentary. [DLB]

6.617 C. J. Rowe. *Plato.* New York: St. Martin's, 1984. ISBN 0-312-61502-7. ‣ One of number of good, recent introductions. Up-to-date with good bibliography. [DLB]

6.618 Gregory Vlastos. *Socrates: ironist and moral philosopher.* Ithaca, N.Y.: Cornell University Press, 1991. ISBN 0-8014-2551-4 (cl), 0-8014-9787-6 (pbk). ‣ Riveting study of Socrates' style and moral philosophy and significance of both. Result of labors of more than a quarter century. Revises style and conclusions of author's work before mid-1970s. [DLB]

6.619 Bernard Williams. "Philosophy." In *The legacy of Greece: a new appraisal.* 1981 ed. M. I. Finley, ed., pp. 202–55. Oxford: Oxford University Press, 1984. ISBN 0-19-285136-5 (pbk). ‣ Introduction to Greek philosophy for student and general reader. [DLB]

Art and Architecture

6.620 P. E. Arias and Max Hirmer. *A history of 1000 years of Greek vase painting.* B. B. Shefton, ed. and trans. New York: Abrams, 1962. ‣ Detailed examinations of selected Greek vases illustrating major developments in vase painting from tenth to third century. Photographs by Hirmer. [THC]

6.621 Ranuccio Bianchi Bandinelli, ed. *Enciclopedia dell'arte antica classica e orientale.* 7 vols. Rome: Istituto della Enciclopedia Italiana, 1958–66. ‣ Standard reference work with articles on all aspects of artistic production in ancient world, including individual artists, works, genres, places, technical terms, etc. [CMW]

6.622 John Boardman. *Greek gems and finger rings: early Bronze Age to late classical.* London: Thames & Hudson, 1970. ISBN 0-500-16015-5. ‣ Comprehensive study of Greek gem engraving from Bronze Age to Hellenistic period. Techniques discussed and system of classification established. Illustrated with more than 1,000 photographs and line drawings. [THC]

6.623 John Boardman. *Greek sculpture, the archaic period: a handbook.* New York: Oxford University Press, 1978. ISBN 0-19-520047-0 (pbk). ‣ Survey of Greek free-standing and relief sculpture from eighth century to ca. 480 BCE. Focuses on development of forms for male and female figures. Extensive bibliography, well illustrated. [THC]

6.624 John Boardman. *Greek sculpture, the classical period: a handbook.* London: Thames & Hudson, 1985. ISBN 0-500-23419-1 (cl), 0-500-20198-6 (pbk). ‣ Survey of Greek free-standing and relief sculpture from ca. 480 BCE through end of fifth century. Particular attention paid to sculpture from temple of Zeus at Olympia and Parthenon. Extensive bibliography, well illustrated. [THC]

6.625 T. H. Carpenter. *Art and myth in ancient Greece: a handbook.* London: Thames & Hudson, 1991. ISBN 0-500-20236-2. ▸ Survey of Greek myth as depicted in vase painting, sculpture, coins, and bronze reliefs from beginning of sixth century to death of Alexander. Discussion of types of sources and of method. Extensive bibliography, numerous illustrations. [THC]

6.626 R. M. Cook. *Greek painted pottery.* 2d ed. London: Methuen; distributed by Harper & Row, 1972. ISBN 0-416-76170-4. ▸ Concise descriptions and analyses of major fabrics of Greek pottery. Extensive bibliographies. [THC]

6.627 J. J. Coulton. *Ancient Greek architects at work: problems of structure and design.* Ithaca, N.Y.: Cornell University Press, 1977. ISBN 0-8014-1077-0. ▸ Focuses particularly on temple; treats technical and design aspects of Greek architecture, role of architect, beginnings of monumental architecture, design and scale, and orders of columns. [JJD]

6.628 William Bell Dinsmoor. *The architecture of ancient Greece.* 1950 3d ed. New York: Norton, 1975. ISBN 0-393-04412-2 (cl), 0-393-00781-2 (pbk). ▸ Survey of Greek architecture from Bronze Age to Hellenistic period, treating origins, rise of Doric and Ionic orders, achievements of fifth century, and later developments. [JJD]

6.629 Werner Fuchs. *Die Skulptur der Griechen.* 3d ed. Munich: Hirmer, 1983. ISBN 3-7774-3460-4. ▸ Greek sculpture from Geometric to Hellenistic period, presented thematically and arranged chronologically in each category. Treats statuary in various positions, pedimental sculpture, metopes, friezes, grave reliefs, and heads. Numerous illustrations. [JJD]

6.630 A. W. Lawrence. *Greek architecture.* 1983 4th ed. R. A. Tomlinson, ed. Harmondsworth: Penguin, 1987. ISBN 0-14-056011-4 (cl), 0-14-056111-0 (pbk). ▸ Greek architecture from Neolithic through Hellenistic period. Treats early periods, developments (mainly of temples) to late fourth century, and Hellenistic architecture including town planning, residential buildings, and building techniques. [JJD]

6.631 Friedrich Matz. *Crete and early Greece: the prelude to Greek art.* Ann E. Keep, trans. London: Methuen, 1962. ▸ Basic nature and historical development of Bronze Age cultures of Crete and mainland Greece discussed through their art and architecture. [CGT]

6.632 J. J. Pollitt. *Art in the Hellenistic Age.* Cambridge: Cambridge University Press, 1986. ISBN 0-521-25712-3 (cl), 0-521-27672-1 (pbk). ▸ Exploration of Hellenistic art as expression of cultural experience: genres, schools, and styles. Rich treatment of sculpture, painting, and architecture in historical, cultural, and artistic context. [JJD]

6.633 Gisela M. A. Richter. *The sculpture and sculptors of the Greeks.* 4th ed. New Haven: Yale University Press, 1970. ISBN 0-300-01281-0. ▸ Comprehensive survey of Greek sculpture from Geometric through Hellenistic period. Historical background, discussion of human figure, drapery, composition, style, and technique with chronological treatment of works of known sculptors. [JJD]

6.634 Martin A. Robertson. *A history of Greek art.* 2 vols. London: Cambridge University Press, 1975. ISBN 0-521-20277-9. ▸ Detailed history of Greek sculpture and painting. Brief discussion of pre–Iron Age art, evolution of Greek art from Geometric through Hellenistic period. Concentrates on major figures and developments. [JJD]

6.635 R.R.R. Smith. *Hellenistic sculpture: a handbook.* New York: Thames & Hudson, 1991. ISBN 0-500-20249-4. ▸ Introduction to historical context and nature of evidence, grouped by major types of statues (kings, philosophers, etc.) and sculpture from major centers and royal capitals. Stresses innovative quality of Hellenistic sculpture. [JJD]

6.636 A. D. Trendall. *Red figure vases of South Italy and Sicily: a handbook.* New York: Thames & Hudson, 1989. ISBN 0-500-20225-7 (cl), 0-500-23512-0 (pbk). ▸ Development of Lucanian, Apulian, Campanian, Paestan, and Sicilian styles of red figure vase painting, ca. 425–300 BCE. Brief discussion of iconography. Extensive bibliography, numerous illustrations. [THC]

Section 7

C O L I N   M .   W E L L S

Early Western Europe, Pre-Roman North Africa, and Rome

For the 1961 edition of the *Guide*, T.R.S. Broughton wrote the following in his intro-duction to the section on Rome: "The space devoted to political, constitutional, and legal history in this section may seem disproportionately large, but it reflects fairly the nature of material available and the fields in which Roman contribution was greatest." Up to 1961, this was basically true, although Broughton may have somewhat overstated the case; after all, political and constitutional history was his field, and it was his own great prosopographical dictionary (7.41) that revolutionized the study of Roman repub-lican politics. Certainly one could list twenty or thirty works of lasting value in English alone from the 1920s and 1930s that do not deal primarily with "political, constitutional, and legal history." What is clear, however, is that the balance has so shifted that nobody today could write as Broughton did. Political and constitutional history still has its practitioners, and always will, but the main emphasis over the last two decades has been on social and economic history. Even legal history, which Broughton linked with political and constitutional, has come to have a predominantly social orientation, con-cerned not only with what the law was and how lawyers regarded it, but with the social conditions that gave rise to it and with the impact that the law itself had on society.

Of course the great historians of antiquity were themselves primarily interested in politics, or in war as an extension of politics—this is as true of the Latin writers of the late republic and early empire, like Sallust, Livy, and Tacitus, as of the Greek historians of Rome, like Polybius and Dio, or of Ammianus and other historians of late antiquity. But modern scholarship has learned to look more closely at objectives and motives, to see how a writer is influenced by the interests of the age in which he writes, to exercise a salutary scepticism. No one today would dare to write the history of the Julio-Claudian dynasty as a mere commentary on Tacitus, and sentiment and language are equally offensive to our ears when Kipling's schoolmaster of the 1890s is made to damn Car-thage as "a sort of godforsaken nigger Manchester," totally unaware that Polybius, on whom this judgment is based, was scarcely impartial. Political history has thus become more sophisticated, and other forms of history more widely practiced. Not that we can write the social or economic history of the second century CE as if it were the nineteenth. A leading Roman historian on the verge of retirement once said to me, regretfully, that for most of the questions he wanted to ask, the evidence simply was not there. We do our best to extract historical nuggets from such literary genres, not primarily concerned with transmitting historical data, as elegiac poetry, satire, novels, or technical hand-books, but they cannot replace either the census returns and financial reports on the one hand, or the personal diaries and intimate letters on the other, that illuminate more recent periods. Imagine having Vespasian's letters to Caenis or Hadrian's to Antinous, as we have Asquith's to Venetia Stanley! So we supplement the written sources with archaeology, and we turn to epigraphy, papyrology, and numismatics, fortunate to possess the great corpora assembled by earlier generations, "dwarfs on the shoulders of giants" indeed. But more and more over the last twenty or thirty years Roman historians, wanting to ask new questions, have tended to look outside the traditional historiographical canon for evidence with which to answer them, and the works listed in the *Guide* attest to a striking expansion in the scope of the historian's interests and the range of evidence cited.

Particularly striking is the integration of literary and nonliterary evidence. When M. Rostovtzeff brought the two together in his *Social and Economic History of the Roman Empire* (7.357), first published in 1926, and asserted that the objects themselves were as much primary sources as the literary and documentary evidence, he was regarded as very daring, but the lesson has now been learned. Moreover, the number and sophistication of excavations and archaeological surveys increased enormously in the 1970s and 1980s, much of the work being directed towards economic questions or to the elucidation of life at a social level below that treated by most surviving ancient authors. It is no longer respectable to make the clearing of monumental buildings or the search for treasures and museum pieces an end in itself. Art historians too have stressed more forcibly the social context that produced works of art; "patronage" is the key word, "who paid for it?" the question. On the other hand, the geographical distribution of archaeological knowledge is still very uneven. Although excavation in Rome restarted in the 1980s on a scale unmatched since Mussolini's day, the other great cities of the empire are still very imperfectly understood. What we now know of Carthage, even after the international "Save Carthage" campaign of the last twenty years, is tantalizingly incomplete, with relatively little on the early empire, for instance, but still enough to make us realize that in comparison we know virtually nothing of the archaeology of Alexandria or Antioch. So too archaeology casts light on agriculture and acculturation in northwest Europe to an extent totally impossible on the lower Danube, and even the smallest military installation in Britain and Germany is meticulously excavated, when not even a single legionary fortress has ever been excavated on the Euphrates. For the whole Roman period, the weight of archaeological evidence is skewed toward the West, to a degree that is not always recognized.

On the other hand, the trawl for new literary evidence has favored the East. We have already referred to the use of Greek and Latin writers outside the traditional canon and especially those not usually thought of as historical sources. Greek literature of the Roman period has been reevaluated and used as evidence for the eastern provinces and for Greek attitudes toward Rome. The value of early Christian writings and of Jewish sources for social history has been recognized, as have texts in languages other than Greek and Latin. The Syriac and still more the Hebrew documents provide a mine of information on the workings of the empire and on relationships between the rulers and the ruled. The value of this material can scarcely be exaggerated. No one now can presume to write about the social and economic life of the eastern provinces without reference to it, and older scholars who do not read Hebrew can only be grateful to colleagues who do and who have made this material accessible to them, while younger scholars intending to devote their careers to the Roman Near East would be well advised to include Hebrew among their languages. F. Millar's newest work (7.462), in which he expresses the hope that it may encourage other Graeco-Roman historians to gain "a wider linguistic base," is surely a landmark in studies of the eastern provinces, as are in different ways the works of S. Mitchell (7.463) and G. Tate (7.468).

Along with this acceptance of material from other languages we have seen the breaking down of disciplinary boundaries. Roman historians have come to recognize, for instance, that the history of the early Christian church is part of the history of the Roman empire, though whether New Testament scholars have come to the same conclusion is less clear. This is exciting. Having myself been brought up at high school and even as an undergraduate on a strict separation between history and "divinity," I well remember first reading A. N. Sherwin-White's *Roman Society and Roman Law in the New Testament* (7.392) with the emotions that Keats so unhistorically ascribes to "stout Cortes" on his peak in Darien. Methodologies from the social sciences have also been applied to Roman history and parallels from other cultures adduced to suggest how gaps in our direct evidence from antiquity may be filled. Rome's relationship to non-Roman cultures has been examined anew from a non-Roman standpoint, to a degree that is especially evident in the treatment of early Italic history and in studies of western Europe and North Africa before Rome. There has been an interest in mentalities (*mentalités*) and in the approach of the Annales school, while the retreat from political history has brought about a greater appreciation of the Braudelian *longue durée*, which perhaps lies behind the reevaluation of late antiquity. In this area, although works continue to be produced that speak in traditional terms of "decline and fall," the liveliest scholarship concentrates on continuity.

Social groups and issues that were marginal in the picture drawn by ancient writers have come more into focus. Slavery, though never totally neglected in the past, has been studied from different perspectives, and there has been a vast outpouring of research on the Roman family and the status of women. Agriculture, peasants and tenant farmers, nomads, and migrant labor have all attracted attention. A major controversy has grown up over the nature and the scale of the Roman economy. The attempt to integrate the rise of Christianity into the social history of the Roman empire has also led to the realization, articulated most compellingly by S.R.F. Price (7.104), that it is necessary to look at "pagan" religion without christianizing assumptions. The attention paid to the eastern half of the empire has led to a better understanding of its cultural and economic importance and an appreciation of the continuity of Greek culture, which accords well with the emphasis in the later period on continuity rather than on concepts of "decline and fall." There has also been a revulsion against conventional moralizing interpretations of Rome's "decadence," which go back to the ancient writers themselves. Rome was not all orgies, and Juvenal and Tertullian must be seen in perspective. There has been in general an attempt to place writers in their own social context and to understand their objectives. One result of this, crucial for the understanding of the later empire, has been the debunking of the *Historia Augusta*, now recognized as a historical novel à la Robert Graves, even though it contains much valuable information for the early second century, for instance the reign of Hadrian.

Where did this interest in social and economic matters come from? In part, it arose because research on Roman political history seemed to have worked itself out. The prosopographical method, as pioneered in English history by Namier, was slow to catch on in the study of the ancient world, and some of the works that would later be seen as fundamental were largely ignored when they first appeared. Prosopography applied to Rome, however, burst into luxuriant bloom in the most influential single work written in English on Roman history during this century, Sir Ronald Syme's *The Roman Revolution* (7.294), published in 1939 but because of World War II little noticed until 1951–1952. It revolutionized the approach to the late republic and the Augustan age, refusing to take Augustus at the estimate of his own propaganda and tracing a brilliant and complex picture of upper-class society and politics from 60 BCE to Augustus's death. The fiftieth anniversary of its publication was marked by collections of essays (7.292, 7.293, 7.297) that testify to its lasting influence. Syme, however, building on the foundations laid by M. Gelzer, *Die Nobilität der römischen Republik* (cf. 7.188), F. Münzer,

Römische Adelsparteien und Adelsfamilien, and the work of E. Groag and E. Stein (cf. 7.44), was the consummate practitioner of an established method, rather than the founder of a new one. His *Tacitus* (7.417), in some ways a greater work even than *The Roman Revolution,* pioneered an approach applied by his pupils to other authors, such as Dio (7.413) and Tertullian (7.407); he then turned to the *Historia Augusta.* But apart from that, Syme's main concern in the last twenty years of his life remained the Roman elite. He was not responsible for the impulse toward social and economic questions.

In fact, the simultaneous recognition of *The Roman Revolution* and the publication of the first two volumes of T.R.S. Broughton's *Magistrates* (7.41) gave a new impetus to the study of republican and Augustan politics. Ernst Badian, combining erudition with acuity, never more valuable than where the evidence is tangled and incomplete (7.221, 7.222) and always marvellously lucid (7.178, 7.289), firmly placed the nature of Roman imperialism in the center of historical debate, just as he set the tangled history of the period from the Gracchi to Sulla on a wholly new footing. Other topics that have exercised historians of the republic are the working of the constitution and especially of the assemblies, and the relationship between politics and religion. Some have asked how much we really know of Rome before the Second Punic War. Others, such as E. S. Gruen (6.261, 7.251, 7.252), have tried to integrate Roman history with that of the Hellenistic world. Prosopography still has its practitioners, but gleaning where Syme and Badian have reaped brings increasingly sparse returns, and the most influential recent research on politics and administration and their relationship to social history takes a broader view. This is particularly apparent in the contribution of P. A. Brunt (7.184, 7.182, 7.299, etc.), whose books and magisterial articles on both the republic and the early empire have cleared away much dead wood and established just what we can know from the evidence available on numerous questions of fundamental importance, so settling the matter in dispute that the question need not be reexamined for twenty years unless new evidence comes to light.

It was however from other periods and fields of history that the main impulse toward the study of social and economic questions came, and from events and attitudes in the contemporary world outside, where economic questions dominated politics, and social certainties were so challenged that nothing could any longer be considered certain. There were indeed great works in this area in the first half of the century, such as Rostovtzeff's aforementioned *Social and Economic History of the Roman Empire* (7.357), T. Frank's *Economic Survey of Ancient Rome* (7.62), and A.H.M. Jones's *The Greek City: from Alexander to Justinian* (6.472), but in the last twenty years the book that lit the fuse for the explosion of controversy over the nature of the Roman economy was M. I. Finley, *The Ancient Economy* (7.340). The book itself is relatively short, little more than two hundred pages in the first edition, and not overburdened with evidence, but no recent work in ancient history has stimulated such controversy. While *The Roman Revolution,* closely argued, its thesis dug in behind serried ranks of data, still holds its ground as the new orthodoxy, *The Ancient Economy* darted in like a cavalry force to deliver its attack, and then left it to others on both sides to bring up their heavy guns and exchange barrages in the fight between minimalist and maximalist views of the ancient economy, between those who see the ancient city as parasitical and those who see it as a vital economic link (e.g., P. Garnsey and R. P. Saller 7.343, W. Jongman 7.347 versus F. Vittinghoff, ed. 7.361, D. Rathbone 7.372). At the moment, the maximalists seem to be having the better of it. M. I. Finley's work on slavery was also important, and his influence is still felt through his pupils and his Cambridge colleagues who tend to share an interest in the same fundamental questions.

The study of slavery, of the lower classes, of peasants, and of women and the family requires the use of epigraphic, papyrological, and archaeological sources. The epigraphic record, for instance, which an earlier generation exploited largely for elite prosopography or for special studies like that of the Roman army (e.g., E. Birley 7.310), is now especially valued for the access that it gives to marginal groups poorly represented in the literary sources. There has been an explosion of publications in these areas. A work published as recently as 1986 (B. Rawson, ed. 7.139) could lament that so little material was readily available on the Roman family; five years later, at least six books related to the family were published in English in a single year (1991). Social and legal history now intersect; J. A. Crook's *Law and Life of Rome* (7.71) showed the way, and a work such as S. Treggiari's *Roman Marriage* (7.143), setting legal theory beside social reality, exemplified the new approach. Sociology and anthropology have made their contribution, for instance in K. Hopkins's *Death and Renewal* (7.191) and S.R.F. Price's *Rituals and Power* (7.104). Nor has anyone raised more questions or done more to stimulate new ways of thinking about Roman society than R. MacMullen (7.385, 7.386, etc.), whose many books and articles blaze new trails for others to explore further.

Others have left the broad highways to explore more specialized topics. So we have the works of K. D. White on farming (7.237) and technology (4.378); studies of cities and building types, such as circuses and amphitheaters, and of the social rituals that they housed; and monographs on such esoteric subjects as fish sauce, sheep rearing, and textile manufacture. It might perhaps be said that a common thread linking the scholarship of the last thirty years has been a concern with how things actually worked. How, for instance, did the administration of the empire work, and what was the emperor's actual job? How did the Roman family function? How did the Roman house work, or baths, or aqueducts? The range of questions studied, compared with those of thirty years ago, is enormous. Broughton seemed to fear that historians in other fields might consider Roman historians narrow in their approach; this is no longer the case!

The trends we have been discussing have affected most significantly the interpretation of the late republic and early empire. Students of the later empire have had other preoccupations, with the rise of Christianity, with the evaluation of sources, and with the evolution of mentalities. No one has had a greater impact on our understanding of this period than P. Brown (7.553, 7.579, etc.), whose brilliant insights into how people of late antiquity really felt and thought have profoundly and permanently altered our perceptions. His insistence on the interpenetration of the pagan and Christian worlds and on concepts of continuity and change, rather than of "decline and fall," is seminal, and his influence is unmistakeable in the work of his pupils and in his editing of the University of California Press series, The Transformation of the Classical Heritage.

What next? For new material, as opposed to new methodologies, we must pin our hopes on archaeology. Political conditions, however, so much affect the opportunities for archaeological research that it is hard to know what countries will be open to Roman archaeologists five or ten years from now. At the moment Jordan and Syria welcome foreign teams, and we can hope for more evidence to emerge from work in those countries. So does Egypt, and even if the Roman period has scarcely been a priority there in the past, the excavations at Mons Claudianus in the Eastern Desert are not the only sign that this is changing. Israel has adopted archaeology as a national sport and is also notably hospitable to foreign teams, especially American. Years ago, the standard of archaeology in "the Holy Land" was notoriously low, the desire to find evidence in support of a preconceived position taking precedence over sober evaluation of the evidence, but things have now improved. Turkey also has a long archaeological tradition, with spectacular long-term excavations along the Aegean seaboard and in its hinterland, as at Ephesus, Aphrodisias, and Sardis, even if in eastern Anatolia today the building of dams on the Euphrates and disturbances in Kurdish areas are not wholly conducive to the recovery of knowledge.

In Europe, as has long been the case, archaeology is stronger in the West than in the East. The sheer quantity of excavation in Britain and Germany, for instance, is hard to keep up with, and even the Iberian peninsula, which long lagged behind, is coming into its own. In the former Communist block, Slovenia and Hungary are important players, but conditions for work in the rest of what used to be Yugoslavia and in Bulgaria and Romania, despite the efforts of devoted and talented individuals, are not currently promising. In North Africa, neither Libya nor Algeria is very hospitable to would-be excavators, unlike Tunisia, where the "Save Carthage" campaign has been a model of international cooperation, and where the Tunisian archaeologists themselves have done excellent work. Over the next ten years, therefore, we may find ourselves still heavily dependent on western Europe and Italy, increasingly supplemented by work in the Iberian peninsula and on the middle Danube, with excavation and survey in Jordan, Syria, and Tunisia yielding data, not only on the Roman cities that have traditionally been the focus of archaeological activity in those countries, but also on agriculture and the countryside and on the pre- and post-Roman periods east and south of the Mediterranean.

Archaeology apart, it seems likely that the current preoccupation with social and economic issues will continue. There is more to be done on women and the family, but perhaps the current intensity cannot be maintained, and it is likely that ten years from now family history will to a large extent be subsumed into social history at large, as slavery has long since been. We can no doubt also expect more publications on aspects of sexuality, since the Foucauldian revolution has so far had more impact on the study of the Greek world than on the Roman, but much work so far in this area merits the same reservations as were expressed above about earlier phases of archaeology in the Holy Land. We can hope for more work on the eastern provinces and on Rome's relations with its subjects and neighbors in the Near East, drawing largely on sources in languages other than Greek and Latin. Crossfertilization from the social sciences still has more to teach us, along with parallels from other cultures. An area crying out for more work is Roman religion, both in its relationship to politics and in trying to understand religious attitudes without the unconscious, patronizing, christianizing assumption that the Romans could not possibly have taken their beliefs seriously.

A further word remains to be said about sources. Roman historians are fortunate that the privileged position so long accorded to the classics in European and North American education means that the source material has long since been inventoried and compiled into dictionaries, corpora of inscriptions, and collections of texts. A wide range of literary sources will be found in the Loeb Classical Library, published by Harvard University Press, with the Greek or Latin text on one page and an English translation facing. The series goes back to the last century, and many volumes are outdated, both in the editing of the text and in the stilted English of the translation, which sometimes gives the impression that many Latin and Greek authors modeled their style on Victorian sermons. Livelier translations may be found in the Penguin translations and elsewhere, but the Loeb series is invaluable, and would be still more valuable if it extended its choice of authors. So strong is its hold on English-speaking classicists that it constitutes virtually a canon. The French equivalent, also with translation, is the Budé series, published in Paris by Les Belles Lettres, and containing some works that the Loeb series omits. The standard critical editions of the major authors are those published by Oxford University Press in the Oxford Classical Text series, and the more extensive Teubner series, published in Stuttgart. A list of standard or recent editions, translations, and commentaries on individual authors is to be found in the *Cambridge History of Classical Literature* (7.63), and for that reason it does not seem necessary to repeat it here. A useful guide to the sources will also be found in K. Christ, *Römische Geschichte* (7.39).

The list of works that follows is arranged partly by topic, partly by period. Works that span more than one period will usually be found listed under the period they start in, but sometimes under a later period, if they devote more space to it or have more to say about it. Topics overlap, and any topical classification inevitably contains anomalies, a fact that surely needs no long demonstration. For instance, although it proved possible and seemed desirable to create a special topical category for women and family, not divided by period, an attempt to do the same for slavery was abandoned because slavery overlapped almost imperceptibly but ever more inextricably with other topics, like patronage and economic life. Similarly, the discussion of religion in late antiquity is so pervasive that, although religion is recognized as a special topic, works relating to religion are to be found in other sections of the late empire, for instance under intellectual life (A. M. Palmer 7.563; F. M. Young 7.565), biography and hagiography (S. P. Brock and S. A. Harvey 7.599; P. Rousseau 7.602; C. Stancliffe 7.603), and literary sources. Agriculture was so fundamental to the economy that the division between these two topics in the early empire may sometimes appear arbitrary. Architecture and engineering overlap, works on the Jews appear under politics as well as under religion, and so on. I cannot hope that all users of the *Guide* will approve of my decision to place a given work here rather than there. I can only hope that the index terms will palliate the more egregious errors that I may have made.

ACKNOWLEDGMENTS   *The following persons gave invaluable assistance in the early stages of this project by agreeing to comment on the initial list of works selected; they bear no responsibility for subsequent errors and omissions: Timothy Barnes, Anthony Barrett, Roger Blockley, Mary Taliaferro Boatwright, Glen Bowersock, Keith Bradley, Kai Brodersen, Peter Brunt, Richard Burgess, Edward Champlin, Frank Clover, Brian Dobson, Garth Fowden, Joann Freed, Sheppard Frere, James Gallagher, Peter Garnsey, Mark Garrison, Miriam Griffin, Erich Gruen, Kenneth Harl, Bruce Hitchner, Dennis Kehoe, Fred Kleiner, Barbara Levick, Ramsay MacMullen, John Matthews, Valerie Maxfield, Fergus Millar, John Oleson, Tom Parker, Tim Potter, Simon Price, John Rist, Richard Talbert, Susan Treggiari, Ray Van Dam, and Roger Wilson. I owe a great debt to Diana Murin, who compiled or verified all of the bibliographic information. Ernst Badian read the whole text, as well as this introduction, and made numerous suggestions. Those that I accepted improved the work enormously, and those that I rejected, I rejected with the consciousness that I might be wrong to do so.*

Entries are arranged under the following headings:

Early Western Europe

North Africa Before the Roman Conquest

Rome
Reference Works
Prosopographical Dictionaries
Inscriptions and Papyri
Numismatics
General Studies
Law
Religion
Women and Family

Rome and Italy to 31 BCE
General Studies
Pre-Roman Italy and Etruscans
Early Rome to ca. 300 BCE
Roman Conquest and Settlement of Italy
Politics and Government
The Army, War, and Imperialism
Foreign Policy and External Relations
Economy, Demography, and Material Conditions
Society
Intellectual Life: Literature, Philosophy, Education
Historians and Historiography
Biography

Early Empire
General Studies
The Work of Augustus
Politics and Government
The Army and the Frontiers
Economy, Production, and Trade
Agriculture and the Countryside
Society
Intellectual Life: Literature, Philosophy, and Education
Historians and Historiography
Biography
Regional Studies

Art and Technology of the Republic and Early Empire
General Studies
Architecture and Urbanism
Engineering and Technology
Sculpture
Painting, Stucco, and Mosaics
Ceramics, Glass, and Other Crafts

Later Roman Empire
Politics and Government
The Army, War, and External Relations
Economy, Trade, and Agriculture
Society
Intellectual Life: Literature, Philosophy, Education
Art and Architecture
"Decline and Fall": Concept and Causes
Late Antiquity: Continuity and Change
Historians and Historiography
Biography and Hagiography
Regional Studies and Individual Cities

[Contributors: CMW = Colin M. Wells, DAC = David Cherry, FLC = Fredric L. Cheyette, PSW = Peter S. Wells, SSB = Shelby Brown]

EARLY WESTERN EUROPE

7.1 D. F. Allen. *The coins of the ancient Celts.* Daphne Nash, ed. Edinburgh: Edinburgh University Press, 1980. ISBN 0-85224-371-5. ▸ Description and interpretation of coinages from Iron Age Europe. Discusses variation over time and space in character and function of coins. Best survey of subject available in English. [PSW]

7.2 Françoise Audouze and Olivier Büchsenschütz. *Towns, villages, and countryside of Celtic Europe: from the beginning of the second millennium to the end of the first century BC.* Henry Cleere, trans. Bloomington: Indiana University Press, 1991. ISBN 0-253-31082-2. ▸ Settlement patterns, structures, and economy of Bronze and Iron ages; treats organization of space and evolution of commercial complexity through end of prehistoric times. Valuable for information about settlements; illustrated with numerous plans. [PSW]

7.3 José María Blázquez and Arcadio del Castillo. *Manual de historia de España I: prehistoria y edad antigua.* Madrid: Espasa-Calpe, 1988 (set), 1991 (v. 1). ISBN 84-239-5090-5 (set), 84-239-5091-3 (vol. 1). ▸ Authoritative survey, primarily diachronic, by leading scholars of prehistoric, Punic, Roman, and Visigothic Spain to end of seventh century CE. Useful bibliography. [CMW]

7.4 John Collis. *The European Iron Age.* New York: Schocken, 1984. ISBN 0-8052-3941-3. ▸ Survey of seventh through first centuries BCE in temperate Europe, with emphasis on interactions with Mediterranean societies, trade, and settlement development. One of few English-language syntheses. [PSW]

7.5 John Collis. *Oppida: earliest towns north of the Alps.* Sheffield: University of Sheffield, Department of Prehistory and Archaeology, 1984. ISBN 0-906090-23-7 (cl), 0-906090-19-9 (pbk). ▸ Study of large urban settlements of late Iron Age; catalog and synthesis of topography and organization, industry, and trade. Excellent compilation of data, including numerous informative illustrations. [PSW]

7.6 Carole L. Crumley. *Celtic social structure: the generation of archaeologically testable hypotheses from literary evidence.* Ann Arbor: University of Michigan, Museum of Anthropology, 1974. (Museum of Anthropology, Anthropological papers, 54.) ▸ Descriptions of peoples north of Alps, based on classical writers and archaeological evidence. Critical discussion of potential for bringing different sources of information together. Pioneering and influential. [PSW]

7.7 Barry Cunliffe. *Iron Age communities in Britain: an account of England, Scotland, and Wales from the seventh century BC until the Roman conquest.* 3d ed. London: Routledge, 1991. ISBN 0-415-05416-8. ▸ Discussion of regional groups of late prehistoric cultures; treats settlements, hillforts, subsistence, trade, industry, and religion. Provides models for understanding change. Excellent overview, standard work on subject. [PSW]

7.8 H. R. Ellis Davidson. *Myths and symbols in pagan Europe: early Scandinavian and Celtic religions.* Syracuse, N.Y.: Syracuse University Press, 1988. ISBN 0-8156-2438-7 (cl), 0-8156-2441-7 (pbk). ▸ Excellent synthesis by leading scholar on ancient traditions regarding sacred places, feasts and sacrifice, battle, spirits, and deities. Combines literary evidence with archaeological data. [PSW]

7.9 Miranda J. Green. *Dictionary of Celtic myth and legend.* London: Thames & Hudson, 1992. ISBN 0-500-01516-3. ▸ Articles on names of deities, heroes, sites, objects, and various other topics. Extensive bibliography, excellent up-to-date resource. [PSW]

7.10 Rolf Hachmann. *The Germanic peoples.* James Hogarth, trans. London: Barrie & Jenkins, 1971. ISBN 0-214-65218-1. ▸ Clearest analysis in English of different usages of term "Germani" (see also 7.11), concluding that Germanic heartland was Elbe-Oder-Vistula region and Scandinavia. Discussion of Germanic religion. Excellent illustrations. [CMW]

7.11 Rolf Hachmann, Georg Kossack, and Hans Kühn. *Völker zwischen Germanen und Kelten: Schriftquellen, Bodenfunde, und Namengut zur Geschichte des nördlichen Westdeutschlands um*

Christi Geburt. Neumünster: Wachholtz, 1962. ▸ Interdisciplinary approach to identifying "Celts" and "Germans" in late Iron Age. Emphasizes ancient texts, archaeology, and place names as sources of data. Very important study on subject of current interest. [PSW]

7.12 Richard J. Harrison. *Spain at the dawn of history: Iberians, Phoenicians, and Greeks.* New York: Thames & Hudson, 1988. ISBN 0-500-02111-2. ▸ Synthesis of development of Iberian culture, 1000–200 BCE, with emphasis on change brought by incoming peoples, including Phoenicians and Greeks. Many fine illustrations; succinct, up-to-date survey, best available in English. [PSW]

7.13 Paul Jacobsthal. *Early Celtic art.* 1944 ed. 2 vols. Oxford: Clarendon, 1970. ▸ Classic synthesis of European Iron Age art, emphasizing links with Mediterranean traditions and development of northern ornament. Pioneering work, very influential for all subsequent research on subject. [PSW]

7.14 Ruth Megaw and Vincent Megaw. *Celtic art: from its beginnings to the Book of Kells.* New York: Thames & Hudson, 1989. ISBN 0-500-05050-3. ▸ New synthesis with abundant illustrations and discussion both of specific objects and of trends. Emphasizes interaction between groups and social context of art. Supplements Jacobsthal 7.13, new standard work. [PSW]

7.15 Sabatino Moscati et al., eds. *The Celts.* New York: Rizzoli, 1991. ISBN 0-8478-1407-6. ▸ Encyclopedic survey of Iron Age archaeology; synthetic essays and specific reports on major sites and special objects. Valuable source of information on wide range of topics, excellent illustrations. [PSW]

7.16 Ludwig Pauli. *The Alps: archaeology and early history.* Eric Peters, trans. London: Thames & Hudson, 1984. ISBN 0-500-05041-4. ▸ Archaeology of circum–Alpine Europe organized around topics including settlement, burial, religion, travel, and economy. Pioneering synthesis with wealth of important ideas and information. [PSW]

7.17 T.G.E. Powell. *The Celts.* 1958 ed. New York: Thames & Hudson, 1983. ISBN 0-500-02094-9 (cl), 0-500-27275-1 (pbk). ▸ Standard synthesis of classical descriptions of Iron Age peoples north of Alps and of their archaeology; emphasis on Britain. Very readable but dated; good starting point. [PSW]

7.18 Anne Ross. *Pagan Celtic Britain: studies in iconography and tradition.* 1967 ed. London: Constable, 1992. ISBN 0-09-471780-X. ▸ Standard work on Iron Age ritual and archaeology, with discussion of sacred sites, cults, and deities; myths considered in concert with archaeological evidence, mostly from Britain, but continental examples as well. [PSW]

7.19 N. Roymans. *Tribal societies in northern Gaul: an anthropological perspective.* Amsterdam: Universiteit van Amsterdam, Albert Egges van Giffen Instituut voor Prae- en Protohistorie, 1990. (Cingula, 12.) ISBN 90-70319-13-6. ▸ Detailed synthesis of late Iron Age evidence with comparative material from other cultures; anthropological perspective stressing sociocultural interaction with increasing differentiation in late La Tène period. New approach, useful bibliography. [CMW]

7.20 I. M. Stead, J. B. Bourke, and Don Brothwell, eds. *Lindow man: the body in the bog.* London and Ithaca, N.Y.: British Museum Publications and Cornell University Press, 1986. ISBN 0-8014-1998-0. ▸ Scientific reports on Lindow corpse and its environment. Case study as well as overview of all bog bodies. Discussion of bog burials and tradition in northern Europe. Pioneering interdisciplinary study. [PSW]

7.21 E. A. Thompson. *The early Germans.* 1965 ed. Oxford: Clarendon, 1968. ▸ Survey of German culture and society, based on Caesar, Tacitus, and other ancient writers; some archaeological data cited. Valuable synthesis, dated by absence of recent text criticism and archaeological results. [PSW]

7.22 Malcolm Todd. *The northern barbarians, 100 BC–AD 300.* Rev. ed. New York: Blackwell, 1987. ISBN 0-631-15159-1 (cl), 0-631-15161-3 (pbk). ▸ Archaeological and literary sources pertaining to early Germans. Discusses regional groups and their settlements, cemeteries, crafts, and religions. Best synthesis of subject available in English. [PSW]

7.23 Peter S. Wells. *Culture contact and culture change: early Iron Age Central Europe and the Mediterranean world.* Cambridge: Cambridge University Press, 1980. ISBN 0-521-22808-5. ▸ Interactions between Celtic groups and Mediterranean peoples (Greeks, Etruscans), 600–450 BCE; change viewed in context of trade and other forms of interaction. Methodologically important for study of contacts between peoples. [PSW]

SEE ALSO
2.92 Peter S. Wells. *Farms, villages, and cities.*

NORTH AFRICA BEFORE THE ROMAN CONQUEST

7.24 *Atti del I Congresso Internazionale di Studi Fenici e Punici, Roma, 5–10 novembre 1979.* 3 vols. Piero Bartoloni et al., eds. Rome: Consiglio Nazionale delle Ricerche, 1983. (Collezione di studi fenici, 16.) ▸ International collection of essays covering variety of topics in Punic-Phoenician material culture, history, and language. Useful resource on recent scholarly interests and controversies and primary and secondary sources; state-of-field summaries. [SSB]

7.25 Shelby Brown. *Late Carthaginian child sacrifice and sacrificial monuments in their Mediterranean context.* Sheffield, England: Journal for the Study of the Old Testament for American Schools of Oriental Research, 1991. (*JSOT/ASOR* monograph series, 3.) ISBN 1-85075-240-0. ▸ Summary of literary, epigraphic, and archaeological evidence from known Phoenician sacrificial cemeteries, seventh century BCE to second century CE, with focus on twentieth-century excavations at Carthage. Discusses dating and interpretations of iconography and rituals. [SSB]

7.26 Pierre Cintas. *Manuel d'archéologie punique.* Vol. 1: *Histoire et archéologie comparées: chronologie des temps archaïques de Carthage et des villes phéniciennes de l'ouest.* Vol. 2: *La civilisation carthaginoise: les réalisations matérielles.* Paris: Picard, 1970–76. ISBN 2-7084-0003-7 (v. 2). ▸ Historical and archaeological evidence for western Phoenician, especially Carthaginian, civilization. Volume 1 contains useful overview of classical and Christian sources. Focuses on foundation of Carthage and other sites, sometimes taking ancient sources too literally; archaeological evidence partly superseded. Volume 2 on archaeology of Carthage; now largely out of date and proved wrong about ports. Illustrations, good bibliography through 1975. [SSB]

7.27 J. D. Fage, ed. *The Cambridge history of Africa.* Vol. 2: *From c. 500 B.C. to A.D. 1050.* J. D. Fage and Roland Oliver, eds. London: Cambridge University Press, 1979. ISBN 0-521-21592-7. ▸ Chapters by Law on Phoenician and Greek colonization and Hellenistic and Roman periods cover Phoenician, especially Carthaginian, expansion and influence in North Africa, Punic maritime exploration of west coast, and evidence for indigenous tribes, ca. 500 BCE to 40 CE. [SSB]

7.28 Mhamed Fantar. *Kerkouane: cité punique du Cap Bon, Tunisie.* Vol. 1: [without special title]. Vol. 2: *Architecture domestique.* Vol. 3: *Sanctuaires et cultes: société-économie.* Tunis: Institut National d'Archéologie et d'Art, 1984–86. ▸ Extensive excavation report on fortified Punic town, sixth to third century BCE, not overbuilt by Romans. Important information on domestic, military, and sacred architecture, including materials, construction techniques, water supply, and decoration. Surveys other Punic evidence and Phoenician parallels outside North Africa. Summarizes classical sources. Illustrations, useful bibliography. [SSB]

7.29 Stéphane Gsell. *Histoire ancienne de l'Afrique du Nord.* Vol. 1: *Les conditions du développement historique, les temps primitifs: la colonisation phénicienne et l'empire de Carthage.* Vol. 2: *L'état carthaginois.* Vol. 3: *Histoire militaire des Carthaginois.* Vol. 4: *La civilisation carthaginoise.* Vol. 5: *Les royaumes indigènes: organisation sociale, politique et économique.* Vol. 6: *Les royaumes indigènes: vie matérielle, intellectuelle, et morale.* Vol. 7: *La République romaine et les rois indigènes.* Vol. 8: *Jules César et l'Afrique: fin des royaumes indigènes.* Vol. 1, 4th ed.; vols. 2–4, 3d ed.; vol. 5–6, 2d ed. Paris: Hachette, 1921–29. ‣ Seminal survey of evidence for Phoenicians and natives, Stone Age to Roman conquest. Useful resource for social, political, and military history. Often methodologically and archaeologically out of date, but never superseded by equally comprehensive work. Too often assumes Phoenician culture monolithic or chronologically undifferentiated. [SSB]

7.30 Donald B. Harden. *The Phoenicians.* 3d rev. ed. New York: Penguin, 1980. ISBN 0-14-021375-9. ‣ Generalizing but useful introduction to evidence for Phoenicians throughout Mediterranean, with focus on Carthage. Overview of Phoenician history, social and political organization, religion, art, trade, and expansion. Illustrations; text only minimally revised since 1962, bibliography expanded 1980. [SSB]

7.31 Heinz Günter Horn and Christoph B. Rüger, eds. *Die Numider: Reiter und Könige nördlich der Sahara.* Cologne and Bonn: Rheinland und Habelt, 1979. ISBN 3-7927-0498-6. ‣ Historical and archaeological survey focusing on Numidians and Phoenicians in late first millennium. Includes reports on specific monuments, tombs, artifacts, and sites. Good illustrations, useful references; exhibition catalog. [SSB]

7.32 Serge Lancel. "Fouilles françaises à Carthage: la colline de Byrsa et l'occupation punique (VIIe siècle–146 av. J.C.), bilan de sept années de fouilles." *Comptes rendus des séances de l'année, Académie des Inscriptions et Belles-Lettres* (1981) 156–93. ISSN 0065-0536. ‣ Report on 1974–80 excavations of probable acropolis of Carthage. Chronological survey of tombs, metallurgical activity, and important second-century domestic architecture. Illustrations, useful references to other primary sources. [SSB]

7.33 Mohamed Gamal el-Din Mokhtar, ed. *Ancient civilizations of Africa.* Vol. 2 of *General history of Africa;* UNESCO International Scientific Committee for the Drafting of a General History of Africa. Paris, Berkeley, and Oxford: UNESCO, University of California Press, and Heinemann, 1981. ISBN 92-3-101-708-X, 0-520-03913-0, 0-435-94085-9 (cl), 0-435-94806-7 (pbk). ‣ Articles on proto-Berbers and Carthaginian period: origins and physical anthropology of pre-Carthaginian peoples; simplified summary of relations with Egypt; agricultural and religious practices; historical overview of Carthage, its foundation, trade, treaties, and conflicts; and discussion of post-Carthaginian successor states. [SSB]

7.34 Sabatino Moscati, ed. *The Phoenicians.* New York: Abbeville, 1988. ISBN 0-89659-892-6. ‣ Collaborative survey of historical and archaeological evidence, covering all major areas of Phoenician expansion, including Spain. Good resource, sometimes oversimplifies complex or disputed issues. Excellent illustrations, useful bibliography; exhibition catalog. [SSB]

7.35 John Griffiths Pedley, ed. *New light on ancient Carthage: papers of a symposium sponsored by the Kelsey Museum of Archaeology, University of Michigan, marking the fiftieth anniversary of the museum.* Ann Arbor: University of Michigan Press, 1980. ISBN 0-472-10003-3. ‣ Collection of papers from 1979 symposium on Punic-Byzantine Carthage. Punic chapters include recent archaeological evidence for seventh- to second-century BCE sacrificial cemetery (Stager), already partly outdated, and second-

century BCE domestic architecture from acropolis (Lancel). Illustrations, useful bibliography. [SSB]

7.36 Gilbert Charles Picard and Colette Picard. *Carthage: a survey of Punic history and culture from its birth to the final tragedy.* 1964 ed. Dominique Collon, trans. London: Sidgwick & Jackson, 1987. ISBN 0-283-99532-7. ‣ General historical overview including social and political topics; archaeological evidence sometimes outdated or too dogmatically identified or explained. Illustrations, bibliography updated to 1980. Translation of *Le monde de Carthage*, rev. ed. (1956). [SSB]

7.37 F. Rakob, ed. *Karthago.* Vol. 1: *Die deutschen Ausgrabungen in Karthago.* Mainz: von Zabern, 1991. ISBN 3-8053-0985-6. ‣ Detailed excavation report, mostly Punic period. Important discussions of building techniques and Punic floors. Summary of recent archaeological evidence for eighth-century Punic settlement of site. Illustrations, useful bibliography. [SSB]

7.38 M. Sznycer. "Carthage et la civilisation punique." In *Rome et la conquête du monde méditerranéen, 264–27 av. J.C.* 1987 3d ed. Claude Nicolet, ed., vol. 2, pp. 545–93. Paris: Presses Universitaires de France, 1991. ISBN 2-13-035850-0 (v. 2). ‣ Survey of sources, mostly classical, on Carthaginian topography, social and political organization, religion, and language, with valuable reviews of recent scholarship. Upholds reality of child sacrifice, contested by some recent publications. [SSB/CMW]

ROME

Reference Works

7.39 Karl Christ. *Römische Geschichte: Einführung, Quellenkunde, Bibliographie.* 1980 3d ed. Darmstadt: Wissenschaftliche Buchgesellschaft, 1990. ISBN 3-534-04908-X. ‣ Handbook of sources, main problems, and modern bibliography, from beginnings of Rome to late antiquity and transition to early Middle Ages. [CMW]

7.40 Ettore de Ruggiero. *Dizionario epigrafico di antichità romane.* 1895– ed. Rome: Bretschneider, 1961. ‣ Standard reference work with articles on topics and terminology to be found in or capable of illustration from epigraphic record. [CMW]

SEE ALSO

6.19 Charles Daremberg and Edmond Saglio, eds. *Dictionnaire des antiquités grecques et romaines d'après les textes et les monuments.*
6.21 N.G.L. Hammond and H. H. Scullard, eds. *The Oxford classical dictionary.*
6.23 August Pauly and Georg Wissowa, eds. *Pauly's Realencyclopädie der classischen Altertumswissenschaft.*
6.24 August Pauly, Konrat Ziegler, and Walther Sontheimer, eds. *Der kleine Pauly.*
6.27 Max Cary. *The geographic background of Greek and Roman history.*
6.29 O.A.W. Dilke. *Greek and Roman maps.*
6.32 N.G.L. Hammond, ed. *Atlas of the Greek and Roman world in antiquity.*
6.33 John B. Harley and David Woodward. *Cartography in prehistoric, ancient, and medieval Europe and the Mediterranean.*
6.43 Richard Stillwell, William L. MacDonald, and Marian Holland McAllister, eds. *The Princeton encyclopedia of classical sites.*
6.44 Richard J. A. Talbert. "Mapping the classical world."
6.46 E. J. Bickerman. *Chronology of the ancient world.*
6.48 Alan E. Samuel. *Greek and Roman chronology.*
6.160 *Cambridge ancient history.*
6.621 Ranuccio Bianchi Bandinelli, ed. *Enciclopedia dell'arte antica classica e orientale.*

Prosopographical Dictionaries

7.41 T. Robert S. Broughton. *The magistrates of the Roman republic.* 1951–52 ed.; vol. 3, rev. ed. 3 vols. Chico, Calif.: Scholars Press, 1984–86. (American Philological Association, Monographs, 15.) ISBN 0-89130-706-0 (v. 1), 0-89130-812-1 (v. 2), 0-89130-811-3 (v. 3). ‣ Standard reference work listing all known or conjectural magistrates annually from 509 to 31 BCE. Volume 1, published 1951, covers to 100 BCE; volume 2, published 1952, thereafter; volume 3 contains additions and corrections. Fundamental for study of republican politics and society. [CMW]

7.42 A.H.M. Jones, John R. Martindale, and John Morris. *The prosopography of the later Roman empire.* Vol. 1: *AD 260–395.* Cambridge: Cambridge University Press, 1971. ISBN 0-521-07233-6. ‣ Standard reference work, though with some omissions, continues 7.44 down to end of fourth century. [CMW]

7.43 H. G. Pflaum. *Les carrières procuratoriennes équestres sous le haut-empire romain* and *Supplement.* 4 vols. with supplement. Paris: Geuthner, 1960–61, 1982. ‣ Standard reference work for equestrian order. Complements 7.44. [CMW]

7.44 *Prosopographia imperii Romani saec. I, II, III.* Rev. ed. 5 vols. in 8. Edmund Groag and Arturus Stein, vols. 1–2, 4.1–2 eds. Leiva Peterson, vol. 4.3 ed. Berlin: de Gruyter, 1933–. ‣ Standard reference work; "Who's Who" for elite of Roman empire down to third century. [CMW]

7.45 M. T. Raepsaet-Charlier. *Prosopographie des femmes de l'ordre sénatorial (Ier–IIe siècles).* 2 vols. Louvain: Peeters, 1987. ISBN 90-6831-086-0. ‣ Reference work listing women of senatorial families for first two centuries of empire. Some overlap with 7.44, but extremely useful. [CMW]

Inscriptions and Papyri

7.46 R. Cagnat et al., eds. *Inscriptiones graecae ad res romanas pertinentes.* 1906–27 ed. 4 vols. in 3. Chicago: Ares, 1975. ISBN 0-89005-072-4 (set), 0-89005-073-2 (v. 1–2), 0-89005-074-0 (v. 3), 0-89005-075-9 (v. 4). ‣ Although out of date and therefore incomplete, still valuable reference work for inscriptions in Greek from Roman period. [CMW]

7.47 *Corpus inscriptionum latinarum: consilio et auctoritate Academiae Litterarum Regiae Borussicae editum.* Berlin: de Gruyter, 1862–. ‣ Multivolume collection of inscriptions from whole empire, geographically arranged. No longer complete but still standard reference. Useful computer index to volume 6 on city of Rome. Individual volumes supplemented or replaced by national and regional collections (see Keppie 7.51). [CMW]

7.48 Hermann Dessau. *Inscriptiones latinae selectae.* 1892–1916 ed. 3 vols. in 5. Chicago: Ares, 1979. ISBN 0-89005-274-3 (set, pbk). ‣ Invaluable collection of significant inscriptions touching on all aspects of Roman life, including some too recent to appear in 7.47, topically arranged with comprehensive indexes. [CMW]

7.49 Arthur E. Gordon. *Illustrated introduction to Latin epigraphy.* Berkeley: University of California Press, 1983. ISBN 0-520-03898-3. ‣ Introductory manual, notable for photographs of 100 datable inscriptions ranging from sixth century BCE to 525 CE, each translated with commentary; general introduction covering main facets of Latin epigraphy. [CMW]

7.50 Arthur E. Gordon and Joyce S. Gordon. *Album of dated Latin inscriptions.* 4 vols. and 3 portfolios. Berkeley: University of California Press, 1958–65. ‣ Collection with photographs of inscriptions from Rome and environs, designed to illustrate chronological development of epigraphic style and technique. [CMW]

7.51 Lawrence Keppie. *Understanding Roman inscriptions.* Baltimore: Johns Hopkins University Press, 1991. ISBN 0-8018-4322-7. ‣ Best introduction to Roman epigraphy available in English. Stresses function and context of Roman inscriptions and explains epigraphic conventions. Bibliography lists national and regional collections supplementing or replacing 7.47. [CMW]

7.52 Naphtali Lewis and Meyer Reinhold, eds. *Roman civilization: selected readings.* 3d ed. 2 vols. New York: Columbia University Press, 1990. ISBN 0-231-07054-3 (cl, set), 0-231-07130-2 (v. 1, cl), 0-231-07132-9 (v. 2, cl), 0-231-07055-1 (set, pbk), 0-231-07131-0 (v. 1, pbk), 0-231-07133-7 (v. 2, pbk). ‣ Still most comprehensive selection of documents in translation, especially inscriptions and papyri; latest edition less useful than predecessor, awkwardly including Augustan age with republic in volume 1 and omitting or abbreviating some major texts that previously appeared in full. [CMW]

SEE ALSO
6.127 Martin David and B. A. van Groningen, eds. *The new papyrological primer.*
6.129 Ludwig Mitteis and Ulrich Wilcken. *Grundzüge und Chrestomathie der Papyruskunde.*
6.130 John F. Oates et al., eds. *Checklist of editions of Greek and Latin papyri, ostraca, and tablets.*
6.131 E. G. Turner. *Greek papyri.*

Numismatics

7.53 British Museum, Department of Coins and Metals. *Coins of the Roman empire in the British Museum.* Rev. ed. 6 vols. in 8. H. Mattingly (v. 1–2), R.A.G. Carson (v. 5–6), and P. V. Hill (v. 5). London: British Museum Publications for the Trustees of the British Museum, 1968–76. ISBN 0-7141-0831-6 (v. 1), 0-7141-0832-4 (v. 2), 0-7141-0833-2 (v. 3), 0-7141-0806-5 (v. 4.1), 0-7141-0805-7 (v. 4.2), 0-7141-0828-6 (v. 4, set), 0-7141-0836-7 (v. 5.1), 0-7141-0835-9 (v. 5.2), 0-7141-0834-0 (v. 5, set), 0-7141-0809-X (v. 6). ‣ Standard reference work for Roman coinage from Augustus to Balbinus and Pupienus; collection of specimens. Complements Sutherland and Carson, eds. 7.59; particularly valuable for first half of third century. [CMW]

7.54 Andrew Burnett, Michel Amandry, and Pau Ripollès. *Roman provincial coinage.* Vol. 1: *From the death of Caesar to the death of Vitellius (44 BC–AD 69).* 1 vol. to date. London: British Museum Publications with Bibliothèque Nationale Paris, 1991–. ISBN 0-7141-0871-5 (set). ‣ First volume of new series of publications of civic and provincial coins in British Museum and Bibliothèque Nationale. Destined to become standard work on Roman provincial issues; good bibliography and discussion. [CMW]

7.55 R.A.G. Carson. *Principal coins of the Romans.* 3 vols. London: British Museum Publications, 1978–81. ISBN 0-7141-0839-1 (set), 0-7141-0844-8 (v. 1), 0-7141-0852-9 (v. 2), 0-7141-0853-7 (v. 3). ‣ Illustrated introductory catalog of Roman coins, showing main issues at various periods and explaining successive monetary systems. See also Burnett et al. 7.54 and Sutherland and Carson, eds. 7.59. [CMW]

7.56 Michael H. Crawford. *Roman republican coinage.* 1974 ed. 2 vols. Cambridge: Cambridge University Press, 1987. ISBN 0-521-07492-4 (set). ‣ Standard reference work, superseding all earlier classifications of republican coinage, though sometimes outdated by more recent finds. Introductory survey of history and economic implications of republican coinage considered controversial. Supplemented by Crawford 7.232. [CMW]

7.57 Clive Foss. *Roman historical coins.* 1987 ed. London: Seaby; distributed by Batsford, 1990. ISBN 0-900652-97-7. ‣ Study of coins, 121 BCE–476 CE, that can be related to specific historical data. Useful numismatic sourcebook for historians. [CMW]

7.58 Philip Grierson and Melinda Mays. *Catalogue of late Roman coins in the Dumbarton Oaks collection and in the Whittemore collection: from Arcadius and Honorius to the accession of Anastasius.* Washington, D.C.: Dumbarton Oaks Research Library and Collection, 1992. ISBN 0-88402-193-9. ‣ Authoritative account of representative collection. Only comprehensive study of coinage in fifth century CE; will become standard reference for period. Completes Sutherland and Carson, eds. 7.59. [CMW]

7.59 C.H.V. Sutherland and R.A.G. Carson, eds. *The Roman imperial coinage.* Rev. ed. 9 vols. London: Spink, 1984. ISBN 0-907605-09-5 (v. 1). ‣ Standard reference work; comprehensive chronological framework by reigns and, within reigns, by mints and dates. Unsatisfactory on third century; later volumes excellent. [CMW]

General Studies

7.60 John Boardman, Jasper Griffin, and Oswyn Murray, eds. *The Oxford history of the Roman world.* Oxford: Oxford University Press, 1991. ISBN 0-19-285248-5. ‣ Seventeen introductory essays on historical and literary topics, representative of contemporary scholarship. Annotated suggestions for further reading. [CMW]

7.61 M. Cary and H. H. Scullard. *A history of Rome down to the reign of Constantine.* 1975 3d ed. New York: St. Martin's, 1976. ISBN 0-312-38395-9. ‣ Standard history of Rome, first published 1935; convenient for reference, useful notes, and glossary. Conventional approach stressing political and military events. [CMW]

7.62 Tenney Frank et al., eds. *An economic survey of ancient Rome.* 1933–40 ed. 6 vols. New York: Octagon Books, 1975. ISBN 0-374-92848-7 (set). ‣ Surveys of evidence for agriculture, manufacture, and trade in Rome and Italy and in provinces of Egypt, Britain, Spain, Sicily, Gaul, Africa, Syria, Greece, and Asia. Uneven and out of date archaeologically but invaluable for literary references. [CMW]

7.63 E. J. Kenney, ed. *Latin literature.* Vol. 2 of *The Cambridge history of classical literature.* W. V. Clausen, Advisory ed. Cambridge: Cambridge University Press, 1982. ISBN 0-521-27375-7 (pbk). ‣ Survey of Latin literature from Ennius to Apuleius, by leading authorities. Chapters uneven in quality and balance, but invaluable appendix gives ancient evidence for each author's life, list of works, and bibliography. [CMW]

7.64 A. N. Sherwin-White. *The Roman citizenship.* 1973 2d ed. Oxford: Clarendon, 1980. ISBN 0-19-814813-5 (cl), 0-19-814847-x (pbk). ‣ Standard work on development of citizenship, ca. 700 BCE–400 CE. Close analysis of Roman-Latin relations, limited franchise, nature and purpose of colonization, and political organization of conquered Italy. [DAC]

7.65 Hildegard Temporini and Wolfgang Haase, eds. *Aufstieg und Niedergang der römischen Welt: Geschichte und Kultur Roms im Spiegel der neueren Forschung.* 37 vols. in 60 parts to date. Berlin: de Gruyter, 1972–. ‣ Encyclopedic study of almost all aspects of Roman world, with articles in five languages, many by leading scholars. Political history, provinces, and religion (including Christianity) predominate. Many articles comprise invaluable bibliographical surveys or surveys of recent scholarship. [CMW]

7.66 John Wacher, ed. *The Roman world.* 2 vols. London: Routledge & Kegan Paul, 1987. ISBN 0-7100-9975-4 (set), 0-7102-0894-4 (v. 1), 0-7102-0895-2 (v. 2). ‣ Thirty-five articles on wide range of topics, each by leading authority. Sparse on republic but most authoritative general survey of empire currently available. [CMW]

Law

7.67 Richard A. Bauman. *Lawyers in Roman republican politics: a study of the Roman jurists in their political setting, 316–82 BC.* Munich: Beck, 1983. (Münchner Beiträge zur Papyrusforschung und antiken Rechtsgeschichte, 75.) ISBN 3-406-09114-8 (pbk). ‣ Vigorously argued analytical survey of political careers and activities of twelve jurisconsults, emphasizing sociopolitical consequences of legal expertise. Views on political appeal of legal knowledge not widely accepted. [DAC]

7.68 P. A. Brunt. "Judiciary rights in the republic." In *The fall of the Roman republic and related essays,* pp. 194–239. New York: Oxford University Press, 1988. ISBN 0-19-814849-6. ‣ Exact, persuasive discussion of composition of juries in civil and criminal courts from Gaius Gracchus (123 BCE) to 70 BCE, discussing nature and inadequacies of sources and varying roles of senators and *equites* (nonsenatorial elite). [DAC]

7.69 W. W. Buckland. *A text-book of Roman law from Augustus to Justinian.* 1963 3d ed. Peter Stein, ed. Cambridge: Cambridge University Press, 1975. ISBN 0-521-04360-3. ‣ First published 1921, much revised, still standard reference work on Roman private law from Augustus to Justinian. [CMW]

7.70 Percy Ellwood Corbett. *The Roman law of marriage.* 1930 ed. Aalen: Scientia, 1979. ISBN 3-511-09102-0. ‣ Still standard handbook on legal aspects of Roman marriage, tracing development of law from jurisprudential standpoint. Now complemented by Treggiari 7.143. [CMW]

7.71 J. A. Crook. *Law and life of Rome, 90 BC to AD 212.* 1967 ed. Ithaca, N.Y.: Cornell University Press, 1984. ISBN 0-8014-0096-1 (cl), 0-8014-9273-4 (pbk). ‣ Pioneering, highly influential study of Roman law in its social context, using legal institutions to illuminate social practice and vice versa. [CMW]

7.72 Pál Csillag. *The Augustan laws on family relations.* József Decsényi, trans. Imre Gombos, ed. Budapest: Akadémiai Kiadó, 1976. ISBN 963-05-0941-5. ‣ Most comprehensive treatment of Augustan legislation, in detail sometimes disputable, but useful work of reference. Translation often clumsy but understandable. [CMW]

7.73 David Daube. *Forms of Roman legislation.* 1956 ed. Westport, Conn.: Greenwood, 1979. ‣ Lively, learned discussion of forms and usage of legal language, relation between literary forms and legislators' intentions, and practical implications of different usages. Application of "form criticism" to law. [DAC]

7.74 David Daube. *Roman law: linguistic, social, and philosophical aspects.* Edinburgh and Chicago: Edinburgh University Press and Aldine, 1969. ISBN 0-85224-051-1. ‣ Immensely readable study of relationship between language and development of legal concepts. Includes discussion of place of poor in juristic interpretation and origins of Roman understanding of degrees of liability, derived from Aristotle. [DAC]

7.75 Bruce W. Frier. *Landlords and tenants in imperial Rome.* 1980 ed. Princeton: Princeton University Press, 1985. ISBN 0-691-05299-9. ‣ Study of Roman lease law in theory and in practice, showing it was overwhelmingly concerned with upper-class apartments. Important contribution to study of relationship between law and society. [CMW]

7.76 Bruce W. Frier. *The rise of the Roman jurists: studies in Cicero's "Pro Caecina."* Princeton: Princeton University Press, 1985. ISBN 0-691-03578-4. ‣ Shrewd elucidation of Cicero's defense of Caecina provides explanation of causes and shape of professionalization of legal discipline and jurists' dominant influence in law from late republic. Effective interdisciplinary study. [DAC]

7.77 Tony Honoré. *Ulpian.* New York: Oxford University Press, 1982. ISBN 0-19-825358-3. ‣ Study of Ulpian's career, working methods, and writings. Avowedly controversial, based on assumptions not universally accepted, but vindicates Ulpian's importance in transmission of Roman law. [CMW]

7.78 H. F. Jolowicz and Barry Nicholas. *Historical introduction to the study of Roman law.* 3d ed. Cambridge: Cambridge University Press, 1972. ISBN 0-521-08253-6. ‣ History of development of Roman public and private law, originally conceived as supplement to Buckland 7.69. [CMW]

7.79 A.H.M. Jones. *The criminal courts of the Roman republic and* *principate*. Totowa, N.J.: Rowman & Littlefield, 1972. ISBN 0-87471-064-2. ▸ Erudite, closely argued analysis of structure, character, procedure, and functions of popular and public courts (*iudicia populi, iudicia publica*). Judiciary laws, composition of juries, administration of justice, and developments during empire. [DAC]

7.80 J. M. Kelly. *Roman litigation*. Oxford: Clarendon, 1966. ▸ Cogent, challenging study of place of poor and humble in civil procedure, including access to courts, methods of executing judgments, bribery and undue influence, and cash and other penalties. [DAC]

7.81 J. M. Kelly. *Studies in the civil judicature of the Roman republic*. Oxford: Clarendon, 1976. ISBN 0-19-825337-0. ▸ Study of distribution of jurisdiction among types of republican courts. Discussion of kinds and number of cases assigned and nature and causes of state's intervention in civil cases. Learned and careful; now generally accepted. [DAC]

7.82 Wolfgang Kunkel. *An introduction to Roman legal and constitutional history*. 2d ed. J. M. Kelly, trans. Oxford: Clarendon, 1973. ISBN 0-19-825317-6. ▸ Lucid, accessible overview of early republican economy, society, and demography. Discusses development of governmental and constitutional organs, assemblies, magistracies, Senate, and origins and development of civil law. Later chapters continue into late empire. [DAC]

7.83 Barry Nicholas. *An introduction to Roman law*. 1962 ed. Oxford: Clarendon, 1988. ISBN 0-19-876063-9 (cl), 0-19-876003-5 (pbk). ▸ Study of fundamental assumptions and distinctions underlying Roman law, with some account of its survival into medieval and modern legal systems. [CMW]

7.84 Alan Watson. *Law making in the later Roman republic*. Oxford: Clarendon, 1974. ISBN 0-19-825326-5. ▸ Thorough study of sources of law, their characteristics and force. Discusses legislation, senatorial decrees, praetors' and other magistrates' edicts, and jurists' writings. Concluding chapter on Greek influences. [DAC]

7.85 Alan Watson. *The law of obligations in the later Roman republic*. Oxford: Clarendon, 1965. ▸ Lucid, comprehensive survey of rules and principles of contracts and delicts (e.g., duress) in historical setting, discussing state of law and legal opinion. [DAC]

7.86 Alan Watson. *The law of persons in the later Roman republic*. 1967 ed. Aalen: Scientia, 1984. ISBN 3-511-09178-0. ▸ Rules and theory of law of marriage (including concubinage, dowry), fathers' powers (adoption, guardianship), slavery, and rights and disabilities of ex-slaves. Sensible, sometimes difficult analysis of key texts. [DAC]

7.87 Alan Watson. *The law of property in the later Roman republic*. Oxford: Clarendon, 1968. ISBN 0-19-825185-8. ▸ Dense, systematic survey of rules and underlying principles: classifications of property, sale and delivery, possession, ownership and usufruct, and relations between neighboring properties (servitudes). [DAC]

7.88 Alan Watson. *The law of succession in the later Roman republic*. Oxford: Clarendon, 1971. ISBN 0-19-825195-5. ▸ Comprehensive introduction to developed rules governing wills (form and effects), heirship, legacies, trusts, probate, and intestate succession (rights of children, relations, wives, husbands). [DAC]

7.89 Alan Watson. *The law of the ancient Romans*. Dallas: Southern Methodist University Press, 1970. ▸ Basic introduction to history and main precepts of Roman private law and its legacy. Model of lucidity. [CMW]

7.90 Alan Watson. *Rome of the Twelve Tables: persons and property*. Princeton: Princeton University Press, 1976. ISBN 0-691-03548-2. ▸ Lucid, careful reconstruction of rules and their oper-

ation, often from late republican material, giving description, explanation, and social context. [DAC]

7.91 Alan Watson. *Roman private law around 200 BC*. Edinburgh: Edinburgh University Press, 1971. ISBN 0-85224-189-5. ▸ Compact survey of evidence from comedy and elsewhere for sources of law and rules governing personal status, property, succession, obligations (contracts), and legal procedure (actions). [DAC]

7.92 Alan Watson. *Roman slave law*. Baltimore: Johns Hopkins University Press, 1987. ISBN 0-8018-3439-2. ▸ Account of Roman law of slavery; valuable both for itself and for explicit contrast between "color-blind" Roman slavery and New World slavery. [CMW]

Religion

Pagan Religion

7.93 R. Beck. "Mithraism since Franz Cumont." *Aufstieg und Niedergang der römischen Welt*, Series 2: *Principat*, 17.4 (1984) 2002–2115. ISBN 3-11-010213-7. ▸ Valuable common-sense survey of recent work on Mithraism, a central topic on which much nonsense has been written; complements Hinnells, ed. 7.99. [CMW]

7.94 Pierre Chuvin. *A chronicle of the last pagans*. B. A. Archer, trans. Cambridge, Mass.: Harvard University Press, 1990. ISBN 0-674-12970-9. ▸ Brief account of pagan practice and belief, especially in East, after establishment of Christianity as state religion. [CMW]

7.95 Georges Dumézil. *Archaic Roman religion: with an appendix on the religion of the Etruscans*. 2 vols. Philip Krapp, trans. Chicago: University of Chicago Press, 1970. ISBN 0-226-16968-5. ▸ Classic interpretation of Roman cult and ritual that aims at revealing original myths and interpreting them in socioreligious, ideological context, using Indo-European tripartite social-ideological framework and arguing against primitivist interpretation of early religion. Traces developments to end of republic. Original and controversial. [DAC]

7.96 Duncan Fishwick. *The imperial cult in the Latin West: studies in the ruler cult of the western provinces of the Roman empire*. 2 vols. to date. Leiden: Brill, 1987–91. (Études préliminaires aux religions orientales dans l'empire romain, 108.) ISBN 90-04-07105-6 (v. 1, cl), 90-04-09144-0 (v. 2, cl), 90-04-07179-2 (set, pbk), 90-04-07180-6 (v. 1, pbk), 90-04-09495-4 (v. 2, pbk). ▸ Massive history of imperial cult; antecedents and studies of individual provinces in volume 1; concepts, liturgy, and ceremonial in volume 2. Two more volumes are promised. [CMW]

7.97 Garth Fowden. *The Egyptian Hermes: a historical approach to the late pagan mind*. Cambridge: Cambridge University Press, 1986. ISBN 0-521-32583-8. ▸ Intellectual basis of Hermetism in relation to traditional Egyptian thought and to gnosticism. Discusses Hermetism as spiritual way and also social milieu of its followers. [CMW]

7.98 Gaston H. Halsberghe. *The cult of Sol Invictus*. Leiden: Brill, 1972. ▸ Argues importance of Syrian cult of Sol Invictus throughout empire in third century has been underestimated. Stresses influence of Aurelian and rivalry with Mithraism and Christianity. [CMW]

7.99 John R. Hinnells, ed. *Mithraic studies: proceedings of the First International Congress of Mithraic Studies*. 2 vols. Totowa, N.J.: Rowman & Littlefield, 1975. ISBN 0-87471-557-1. ▸ Twenty-eight papers and summaries of two discussions covering all approaches to Mithraism. Still best introduction to wide range of interpretations and some of archaeological evidence. [CMW]

7.100 J.H.W.G. Liebeschuetz. *Continuity and change in Roman* *religion.* New York: Oxford University Press, 1979. ISBN 0-19-814822-4. ▸ Survey of religious attitudes and relation between religion, morality, and politics in Latin literature down to Constantine. [CMW]

7.101 Samuel N. C. Lieu. *Manichaeism in the later Roman empire and medieval China: a historical survey.* 2d ed. Tübingen: Mohr, 1992. ISBN 3-16-145820-6. ▸ History of Manichaeism in Roman empire and its survival in China to sixteenth century, based primarily on Greek, Latin, Syriac, and Chinese sources (with some Sogdian, Uighur, and Arabic). [CMW]

7.102 Ramsay MacMullen. *Paganism in the Roman empire.* New Haven: Yale University Press, 1981. ISBN 0-300-02655-2 (cl), 0-300-02984-5 (pbk). ▸ Study of pagan practices and pagan mentalities, seeking to establish who worshipers were, how important religion was, how the divine was envisioned, how cults were propagated, etc. [CMW]

7.103 Agnes Kirsopp Michels. *The calendar of the Roman republic.* 1967 ed. Westport, Conn.: Greenwood, 1978. ISBN 0-313-20226-5. ▸ Analysis of pre-Julian, lunisolar calendar, its contents, meaning of symbols, origins and functions, and popular and religious motives. Short, clear account of confusing subject. [DAC]

7.104 S.R.F. Price. *Rituals and power: the Roman imperial cult in Asia Minor.* 1984 ed. Cambridge: Cambridge University Press, 1986. ISBN 0-521-25903-7 (cl), 0-521-31268-x (pbk). ▸ Original, influential study arguing imperial cult was deeply rooted in Greek cities, not just form of political honors. Discusses anthropological parallels; warns against christianizing assumption that emotion is test of religious authenticity. [CMW]

7.105 John Scheid. *Religion et piété à Rome.* Paris: Découverte, 1985. ISBN 2-7071-1530-4. ▸ Lively examination of role of priests and their relation to community in late republic and interaction of religion and politics. Unorthodox idea of priests' autonomy and separation of priestly and magisterial powers. [DAC]

7.106 H. H. Scullard. *Festivals and ceremonies of the Roman republic.* 1981 ed. Ithaca, N.Y.: Cornell University Press, 1987. ISBN 0-8014-1402-4. ▸ Readable account of nature of state religion, cult, belief, games, and calendar, followed by descriptive accounts of major annual festivals and occasional ceremonies (triumphs, funerals, census). [DAC]

7.107 Robert Turcan. *Les cultes orientaux dans le monde romain.* Paris: Belles Lettres, 1989. ISBN 2-251-38001-9. ▸ More comprehensive study than any available in English of imported cults, including those of Great Mother, Isis, Mithras, Dionysus and Sabazius, and other Oriental divinities. Complements Burkert 6.575. [CMW]

7.108 Maarten J. Vermaseren. *Cybele and Attis: the myth and cult.* A.M.H. Lemmers, trans. London: Thames & Hudson, 1977. ISBN 0-500-25054-5. ▸ First study in over sixty years of cult of Cybele and Attis and its evolution through time. [CMW]

7.109 H. S. Versnel. *Triumphus: an inquiry into the origin, development, and meaning of the Roman triumph.* Leiden: Brill, 1970. ▸ Careful analysis of terminology, religious, political and legal associations, and function of triumphal gate, underpinning attempt to link triumph to New Year ceremony. [DAC]

7.110 Alan Wardman. *Religion and statecraft among the Romans.* London: Granada, 1982. ISBN 0-246-11743-5. ▸ Fresh, generally sound study of interaction of cult, religion, and political conduct of rulers, 200 BCE–400 CE. Opening chapters describe gods, temples, priesthoods, and changes in late republican religious system. [DAC]

7.111 Stefan Weinstock. *Divus Julius.* Oxford: Clarendon, 1971. ISBN 0-19-814287-0. ▸ Learned, mostly diachronic treatment of Caesar's religious reforms and personal honors, interpreted in context of cult practice and ancestral tradition, with discussion of origins of Roman ruler cult. [DAC]

SEE ALSO
  6.568 Sharon Kelly Heyob. *The cult of Isis among women in the Graeco-Roman world.*
  6.575 Walter Burkert. *Ancient mystery cults.*

Judaism and Christianity

7.112 Stephen Benko. *Pagan Rome and the early Christians.* Bloomington: Indiana University Press, 1984. ISBN 0-253-34286-4. ▸ Study of pagan attitudes toward and charges against Christians, giving pagans credit for actually believing what they said. Discusses Christian practice and Christian reply. [CMW]

7.113 H.J.W. Drijvers. *East of Antioch: studies in early Syriac Christianity.* London: Variorum, 1984. ISBN 0-86078-146-1. ▸ Papers by leading Syriac scholar on origins and development of Syriac Christianity, with special discussions of "Odes of Solomon," Bardaisan of Edessa, and gnosticism. [CMW]

7.114 W.H.C. Frend. *The Donatist church: a movement of protest in Roman North Africa.* 1952 ed. New York: Oxford University Press, 1985. ISBN 0-19-826408-9. ▸ Standard account of rise and fall of Donatism in Numidia seeking to combine archaeological and literary evidence. New bibliography and brief survey of recent scholarship to 1984. [CMW]

7.115 W.H.C. Frend. *Martyrdom and persecution in the early church: a study of a conflict from the Maccabees to Donatus.* 1965 ed. Grand Rapids: Baker Book House, 1981. ISBN 0-8010-3502-3 (pbk). ▸ History of early persecutions and Christian attitudes toward martyrdom, stressing Christian inheritance from Judaism and how eastern and western attitudes came to diverge. [CMW]

7.116 C. Wilfred Griggs. *Early Egyptian Christianity: from its origins to 451 CE.* 2d ed. Leiden: Brill, 1990. ISBN 90-04-09159-9. ▸ Shows development of features unique to Egyptian Christianity eventually led to establishment of Coptic church as national religion. [CMW]

7.117 Robin Lane Fox. *Pagans and Christians.* 1986 ed. San Francisco: Harper & Row, 1988. ISBN 0-06-062852-9 (pbk). ▸ Brilliant study of Christian and non-Christian mentalities and their interaction in urban settings. Discusses historicity of Acts, pagan oracles, martyrdom, virginity, visions, and Constantine's conversion. [CMW]

7.118 Judith Lieu, John A. North, and Tessa Rajak, eds. *The Jews among pagans and Christians in the Roman empire.* London: Routledge, 1992. ISBN 0-415-04972-5. ▸ Eight essays emphasizing Jewish role in Roman world: Jewish proselytizing, Christian views of Judaism, diaspora, Syriac Christianity and Syriac sources, etc. [CMW]

7.119 Ramsay MacMullen. *Christianizing the Roman empire (A.D. 100–400).* 1984 ed. New Haven: Yale University Press, 1986. ISBN 0-300-03216-1 (cl), 0-300-03642-6 (pbk). ▸ History of spread of Christianity to fourth century, with emphasis on mentality of converted and changes brought about by Constantine's conversion. [CMW]

7.120 Wayne A. Meeks. *The first urban Christians: the social world of the apostle Paul.* New Haven: Yale University Press, 1983. ISBN 0-300-02876-8 (cl), 0-300-03244-7 (pbk). ▸ Study of composition, life style, and mentalities of early urban Christian communities founded by Paul. [CMW]

7.121 Herbert Musurillo, ed. *The acts of the Christian martyrs.* 1972 ed. Oxford: Clarendon, 1979. ISBN 0-19-826806-8. ▸ Text and translations of early Christian accounts of torture and execution, with introduction. Vivid picture of Christian communities in relationship with Roman authorities and in communication with one another. [CMW]

7.122 Alan F. Segal. *Rebecca's children: Judaism and Christianity in the Roman world.* Cambridge, Mass.: Harvard University Press, 1986. ISBN 0-674-75075-6. ‣ Controversial study of common origins of rabbinic Judaism and Christianity, seeing in their divergence reflections of class conflict and competition for possession of old national symbols. [CMW]

7.123 Graydon F. Snyder. *Ante pacem: archaeological evidence of church life before Constantine.* 1985 ed. Macon, Ga.: Mercer University Press, 1991. ISBN 0-86554-147-7. ‣ Useful collection of evidence, some not widely known, including pictorial representations of early church buildings, inscriptions, and graffiti. [CMW]

7.124 Paul R. Trebilco. *Jewish communities in Asia Minor.* Cambridge: Cambridge University Press, 1991. (Society for New Testament Studies, Monograph series, 69.) ISBN 0-521-40120-8. ‣ Studies of Jewish communities in Sardis, Priene, Acmonia, and Apamea, and of role of Jewish women, syncretism, and Jewish participation in city life. [CMW]

7.125 L. Michael White. *Building God's house in the Roman world: architectural adaptation among pagans, Jews, and Christians.* Baltimore: Johns Hopkins University Press for American Schools for Oriental Research, 1990. ISBN 0-8018-3906-8. ‣ Account, both historical and architectural, of how Christian church architecture evolved from meeting places in private homes to Constantinian basilicas; attention also to Judaism and Mithraic worship centers. [CMW]

7.126 Robert L. Wilken. *The Christians as the Romans saw them.* New Haven: Yale University Press, 1984. ISBN 0-300-03066-5 (cl), 0-300-03627-2 (pbk). ‣ Study of pagan attitudes toward Christianity concentrating on five major figures: Pliny, Galen, Celsus, Porphyry, and Julian. Shows how Christian theology evolved in response to hostile critics. [CMW]

7.127 Robert L. Wilken. *John Chrysostom and the Jews: rhetoric and reality in the late fourth century.* Berkeley: University of California Press, 1983. ISBN 0-520-04757-5. ‣ Study of background to Chrysostom's violent sermons against Jews and Judaizers, especially strength and attraction of Judaism in cities like Antioch and alarm at Julian's proposal to rebuild Temple. [CMW]

SEE ALSO
8.15 E. D. Hunt. *Holy Land pilgrimage in the later Roman empire, AD 312–460.*
20.1002 W.H.C. Frend. *The rise of Christianity.*
20.1007 Robert A. Markus. *The end of ancient Christianity.*
20.1025 Peter Brown. *The body and society.*
20.1026 Peter Brown. *The cult of the saints.*

Women and Family

7.128 J.P.V.D. Balsdon. *Roman women: their history and habits.* 1962 ed. New York: Barnes & Noble, 1983. ISBN 0-06-464062-0 (pbk). ‣ Lively survey of women in legend and sketches of prominent women of late republic and early empire, followed by description of marriage, prostitution, religion, and daily life, with emphasis on elite women. [DAC]

7.129 Keith R. Bradley. *Discovering the Roman family: studies in Roman social history.* New York: Oxford University Press, 1991. ISBN 0-19-505857-7 (cl), 0-19-505858-5 (pbk). ‣ Important collected papers on wet-nursing, male child-tenders, apprentices and child workers, dislocation and remarriage in elite families, and relationships in Cicero's family, concluding childrearing collaborative. [DAC]

7.130 Edward Champlin. *Final judgments: duty and emotion in Roman wills, 200 BC–AD 250.* Berkeley: University of California Press, 1991. ISBN 0-520-07103-4. ‣ Study of who made wills and

how. Finds more men than women, main concern immediate family, especially children; thereafter legacies to close friends, sometimes the emperor, and freedmen. Conclusions unsurprising but well documented. [CMW]

7.131 Suzanne Dixon. *The Roman family.* Baltimore: Johns Hopkins University Press, 1992. ISBN 0-8018-4199-2 (cl), 0-8018-4200-X (pbk). ‣ Excellent introduction to Roman concept of family, legal status, and social reality. Discusses marriage as institution, evidence for feelings between spouses, and children and life cycle. [CMW]

7.132 Suzanne Dixon. *The Roman mother.* Norman: University of Oklahoma Press, 1988. ISBN 0-8061-2125-4. ‣ Readable and methodologically disciplined study assembling evidence for attitudes toward and stereotypes of maternal role, ca. 200 BCE–200 CE. Contrasts Roman and modern Western images of motherhood. [DAC]

7.133 John K. Evans. *War, women, and children in ancient Rome.* London: Routledge, 1991. ISBN 0-415-05723-X. ‣ Survey of republican women's legal status followed by analysis of imperialism's effects on propertied women, working women in town and country, and ties between parents and children. Lively, unconventional interpretation. [DAC]

7.134 Jane F. Gardner. *Women in Roman law and society.* 1986 ed. Bloomington: Indiana University Press, 1991. ISBN 0-253-36609-7 (cl, 1986), 0-253-20635-9 (pbk). ‣ Sensible, accessible, analytical survey of evidence for main issues from early republic to ca. 200 CE. Treats guardianship, marriage, divorce, dowry, sexuality, children, inheritance, slavery, ex-slaves, work, and emancipation. [DAC]

7.135 Jane F. Gardner and Thomas Wiedemann, eds. *The Roman household: a sourcebook.* London: Routledge, 1991. ISBN 0-415-04421-9 (cl), 0-415-04422-7 (pbk). ‣ Judicious selection of approximately 200 translated, annotated excerpts from literary, legal, and inscriptional sources, illustrating major themes such as marriage, powers of head of household, mortality, inheritance, and relations between patrons and ex-slaves. [DAC]

7.136 Judith P. Hallett. *Fathers and daughters in Roman society: women and the elite family.* Princeton: Princeton University Press, 1984. ISBN 0-691-03570-9 (cl), 0-691-10160-4 (pbk). ‣ Sketches of elite women followed by sustained argument for cultural prominence of daughters; particular emphasis on Cicero and his daughter Tullia. Anecdotal, controversial, often unconvincing. [DAC]

7.137 Keith Hopkins. "Brother-sister marriage in Roman Egypt." *Comparative studies in society and history* 22 (1980) 303–354. ISSN 0010-4175. ‣ Study of brother-sister marriage in first three centuries CE, arguing such marriages considered normal and based on mutual attraction until made illegal under Roman law when citizenship extended by Caracalla (212/3 CE). [CMW]

7.138 Natalie Kampen. *Image and status: Roman working women in Ostia.* Berlin: Mann, 1981. ISBN 3-7861-1150-2. ‣ Scholarly, original study of reliefs and inscriptions from Ostia depicting working women, primarily in food, fabrics, health, and personal service, and discussing iconography, patronage, and status of women. [CMW]

7.139 Beryl Rawson, ed. *The family in ancient Rome: new perspectives.* Ithaca, N.Y.: Cornell University Press, 1986. ISBN 0-8014-1873-9 (cl), 0-8014-9460-5 (pbk). ‣ Excellent introductory essay by Rawson; eight other papers include women's property and succession rights (Crook), finances of women of Cicero's family (Dixon), slave children (Rawson), wet-nursing (Bradley), and theories of conception (Blayney). [DAC]

7.140 Beryl Rawson, ed. *Marriage, divorce, and children in ancient Rome.* New York: Oxford University Press, 1991. ISBN

0-19-814918-2. ▸ Brief survey of recent work with nine papers by leading authorities on adult-child relationships, parental discipline, divorce and remarriage, ex-slaves' families, and housing at Pompeii and Herculaneum as evidence for family life. [CMW]

7.141 Brent D. Shaw. "The family in late antiquity: the experience of Augustine." *Past and present* 115 (1987) 3–51. ISSN 0031-2746. ▸ Study of family as revealed in Augustine's writings; very patriarchal, harsh discipline normal, sons dependent, and problems of drinking and of husband's access to slave women, etc. [CMW]

7.142 Brent D. Shaw. "Latin funerary epigraphy and family life in the later Roman empire." *Historia: Zeitschrift für alte Geschichte* 33.4 (1984) 457–97. ISSN 0018-2311. ▸ Article suggesting that nuclear family is and remains dominant Roman family type, late republic to seventh century, contrary to views of scholars who claim to see evolutionary change. [CMW]

7.143 Susan Treggiari. *Roman marriage: iusti coniuges from the time of Cicero to the time of Ulpian.* 1991 ed. Oxford: Clarendon, 1993. ISBN 0-19-814890-9 (cl, 1991), 0-19-814939-5 (pbk). ▸ Comprehensive discussion of law, theory, and practice of betrothal, marriage, dowry and other property, divorce, widowhood, relations between husbands and wives, and legislation and governmental intervention. [DAC]

7.144 Thomas Wiedemann. *Adults and children in the Roman empire.* New Haven: Yale University Press, 1989. ISBN 0-300-04380-5. ▸ Wide-ranging, controversial survey of changes in adult attitudes toward childhood (to ca. 400 CE). Treats demography, education, and impact of Christianity. Concludes children in classical Roman world were marginalized. [DAC]

SEE ALSO
6.571 Sarah B. Pomeroy. *Goddesses, whores, wives, and slaves.*

ROME AND ITALY TO 31 BCE
General Studies

7.145 Jacques Heurgon. *The rise of Rome to 264 B.C.* James Willis, trans. Berkeley: University of California Press, 1973. ISBN 0-520-01795-1. ▸ Analytical survey of early social and political institutions set against wider background of Mediterranean culture. Firm control of textual and archaeological evidence; balanced and sensible. [DAC]

7.146 Arnaldo Momigliano and A. Schiavone, eds. *Roma in Italia.* Vol. 1 of *Storia di Roma.* Turin: Einaudi, 1988. ISBN 88-06-11396-8 (v. 1). ▸ Excellent collaborative survey of Italy from Bronze Age to ca. 450 BCE. Treats topography and early community, Roman origins (legends), land, economy, demography, government, society, war, and imperialism. [DAC]

7.147 Claude Nicolet. *Rome et la conquête du monde méditerranéen, 264–27 avant J.-C.* Vol. 1: *Les structures de l'Italie romaine.* Vol. 2: *Genèse d'un empire.* Vol. 1, 5th ed.; vol. 2, 3d ed. 2 vols. Claude Nicolet, Vol. 2 ed. Paris: Presses Universitaires de France, 1991–93. ISBN 2-13-042465-1 (set), 2-13-035950-7 (v. 1), 2-13-035850-0 (v. 2). ▸ Volume 1 comprises lucid analysis of institutions of Roman Italy, treating demography, agriculture, industry and commerce, social relations, state finances, Italians, army, governmental organs, and political life; volume 2 discusses Africa, Iberia, Gaul, East, Jews, and nature of Roman imperialism. [DAC/CMW]

7.148 H. H. Scullard. *From the Gracchi to Nero: a history of Rome from 133 BC to AD 68.* 1982 5th ed. London: Methuen, 1984. ISBN 0-416-32890-3 (cl), 0-416-32900-4 (pbk). ▸ Diachronic narrative combined with synoptic account of economy, society, art, literature, and thought. Comprehensive, balanced, readable introduction. Controversial issues and approaches identified in notes. [DAC]

7.149 H. H. Scullard. *A history of the Roman world, 753–146 BC.* 4th ed. London: Methuen, 1980. ISBN 0-416-71480-3 (cl), 0-416-71490-0 (pbk). ▸ Diachronic survey of main developments and personalities. Readable, balanced introduction with traditional emphasis on politics and government (first published 1935); controversial ideas and approaches identified in notes. [DAC]

SEE ALSO
6.160 *The Cambridge ancient history.* Vol. 7.2, Vols. 8–9.

Pre-Roman Italy and Etruscans

7.150 Graeme Barker. *Landscape and society: prehistoric central Italy.* London: Academic Press, 1981. ISBN 0-12-078650-8. ▸ Narrative framework for Italian history from Palaeolithic to ca. 1000 BCE, followed by analysis of technology, subsistence patterns, communications, society and change or stability. Highly readable reinterpretation from British "ideas archaeology." [DAC]

7.151 Larissa Bonfante. *Out of Etruria: Etruscan influence north and south.* Oxford: British Archaeological Reports, 1981. (British Archaeological Reports international series, 103.) ISBN 0-86054-121-5. ▸ Readable, well-illustrated study of Etruscan influence on situla art (decorated bronze vessels) of seventh and sixth centuries BCE in Northeast Italy, and regional impact of Etruscan language. [DAC]

7.152 Larissa Bonfante, ed. *Etruscan life and afterlife: a handbook of Etruscan studies.* Detroit: Wayne State University Press, 1986. ISBN 0-8143-1772-3 (cl), 0-8143-1813-4 (pbk). ▸ Collaborative introduction to Etruscan culture treating history, art, architecture, coinage, daily life, and language. Several contributions of high quality; richly illustrated, accessible to nonspecialist. [DAC]

7.153 Hugh Hencken. *Tarquinia and Etruscan origins.* New York: Praeger, 1968. ▸ Survey and interpretation of archaeological evidence for Villanovan culture and art (1000–700 BCE), followed by balanced discussion of problem of Etruscan roots. Lucid, richly illustrated; accessible to nonspecialists. [DAC]

7.154 Massimo Pallottino. *The Etruscans.* Rev. ed. J. Cremona, trans. David Ridgway, ed. Bloomington: Indiana University Press, 1975. ISBN 0-253-32080-1. ▸ Classic discussion of Etruscan society and culture treating burial, art, literature, religion, and customs against wider Italian and western Mediterranean background. [DAC]

7.155 Massimo Pallottino. *A history of earliest Italy.* Martin Ryle and Kate Soper, trans. Ann Arbor: University of Michigan Press, 1991. ISBN 0-472-10097-1. ▸ Synoptic, narrative account of Italian peoples, cultures, institutions, languages, and trade, Bronze Age to first century BCE. Authoritative on pre-Roman Italy; generally incisive, highly readable. [DAC]

7.156 Massimo Pallottino et al., eds. *Popoli e civiltà dell'Italia antica.* 7 vols. Rome: Ente per la Diffusione e l'Educazione Storica, 1974–78. ▸ Collective, scholarly, generally reliable synthesis on Italy, Palaeolithic to Villanovans and Etruscans, Italo-Siciliote, Punic and Nuragic (Sardinian) civilizations. Especially valuable on Iron Age southern Italy and Sicily (Greek colonies), pre- and proto-historical Rome and Latium, early Middle Adriatic Italy, Villanovans, and Etruscans. [DAC]

7.157 David Ridgway and Francesca R. Ridgway, eds. *Italy before the Romans: the Iron Age, orientalizing, and Etruscan periods.* London: Academic Press, 1979. ISBN 0-12-588020-0. ▸ Collected and thematically arranged papers by Bronze and Early Iron Age specialists. Accessible, generally reliable; especially important for interpretations of Etruscan and early Roman culture. [DAC]

7.158 H. H. Scullard. *The Etruscan cities and Rome.* Ithaca, N.Y.: Cornell University Press, 1967. ▸ Survey of Etruscan prehistory, developed culture, principal cities, influence north and south, and relations with early Rome. Densely textured, but clearly written and well illustrated. [DAC]

7.159 Maja Sprenger and Gilda Bartoloni. *The Etruscans: their history, art, and architecture.* Robert Erich Wolf, trans. New York: Abrams, 1983. ISBN 0-8109-0867-0. ▸ Outline of Etruscan history and history of Etruscan art, chronologically arranged, followed by study of different genres. Magnificent photographs with commentary. [DAC/CMW]

SEE ALSO
6.477 John Boardman. *The Greeks overseas.*

Early Rome to ca. 300 BCE

7.160 Andreas Alföldi. *Early Rome and the Latins.* Ann Arbor: University of Michigan Press, 1965. ▸ Study of relations among monarchical Rome, Etruscans, and Latin League. Discusses Rome's political subordination and mendacity in Roman historical writing (e.g., Fabius Pictor). Bold, unconventional interpretation that has found little support. [DAC]

7.161 Raymond Bloch. *The origins of Rome.* New York: Praeger, 1960. ▸ Pre- and early republican history treating ethnography of Iron Age Italy, Roman relations with Latin, Osco-Umbrian, and Etrusco-Greek civilizations, and foundation legends. Supports archaeological evidence against Roman tradition. Judicious and readable. [DAC]

7.162 J. N. Bremmer and N. M. Horsfall. *Roman myth and mythography.* London: University of London, Institute of Classical Studies, 1987. (Bulletin of the Institute of Classical Studies, Supplements, 52.) ISBN 0-900587-53-9. ▸ Methodological discussion of Roman attitudes, Greek influences, and methods of transmission, followed by analysis of selected legends (Aeneas, Romulus and Remus, etc.) Learned and judicious. [DAC]

7.163 W. Eder, ed. *Staat und Staatlichkeit in der frühen römischen Republik.* Stuttgart: Steiner, 1990. ISBN 3-515-05539-8. ▸ Collected conference papers (Berlin, 1988) analyzing politics, government, constitutional developments, religion, law, war, and imperialism, ca. 500–300 BCE. Valuable sections on sources, source criticism, and methodologies. [DAC]

7.164 Endre Ferenczy. *From the patrician state to the patricio-plebeian state.* G. Dedinszky, trans. Amsterdam: Hakkert, 1976. ISBN 90-256-0778-0. ▸ Career of censor Appius Claudius Caecus against background of conflict between patricians and plebeians. Controversial interpretation of Claudius as social reformer. Ideologically informed, difficult reading. [DAC]

7.165 Ernst Meyer. *Römischer Staat und Staatsgedanke.* 4th ed. Zurich: Artemis, 1975. ISBN 3-7608-3215-6. ▸ Development of governmental and constitutional organs (magistracies, coinage, census) and circumstances and attitudes that shaped them. Valuable reference work; learned and dense. [DAC]

7.166 Richard E. Mitchell. *Patricians and plebeians: the origin of the Roman state.* Ithaca, N.Y.: Cornell University Press, 1990. ISBN 0-8014-2496-8. ▸ Highly controversial account of early republican political and social development, discussing origins of patricians, plebeians, governmental institutions, and plebeian participation. Redefines patricians as hereditary religious elite; depreciates patricio-plebeian struggle. [DAC]

7.167 R. M. Ogilvie. *A commentary on Livy, Books 1–5.* Oxford: Clarendon, 1965. ISBN 0-19-814432-6. ▸ Historical, textual, and literary analysis of Livy's narrative. Amounts to history of Rome from its foundation to 390 BCE. All major issues and problems handled with clarity and sound judgment. [DAC]

7.168 Jacques Poucet. *Les origines de Rome: tradition et histoire.* Brussels: Facultés Universitaires Saint Louis, 1985. (Publications des Facultés Universitaires Saint Louis, 38.) ISBN 2-8028-0043-

4. ▸ Study of premonarchical Rome comparing Roman historical tradition with archaeological evidence. Discusses ethnology, mythology, and religious, political, and social institutions. Readable introduction to current research. [DAC]

7.169 Kurt A. Raaflaub, ed. *Social struggles in archaic Rome: new perspectives on the conflict of the orders.* Berkeley: University of California Press, 1986. ISBN 0-520-05528-4. ▸ Important papers by distinguished specialists on literary tradition about early Rome, methodology (comparative approaches), origins of patriciate, and codification of law (Twelve Tables). [DAC]

7.170 C. Saulnier. *L'armée et la guerre dans le monde étrusco-romain (VIIIe–IVe siècle).* Paris: de Boccard, 1980. ▸ Wordy account of archaeological and iconographical evidence (grave goods, painting, sculpture) for pre- and early republican weapons and tactics, set against broader historical background of Etruscan expansion, eastern chariot warfare, etc. [DAC]

Roman Conquest and Settlement of Italy

7.171 William V. Harris. *Rome in Etruria and Umbria.* Oxford: Clarendon, 1971. ISBN 0-19-814297-8. ▸ Comprehensive discussion of region's history and romanization. Treats Roman imperialism to 264 BCE, political settlement of conquered Italy, Rome's relations with upper class, and Etruscans and Umbrians in Social War (91–88 BCE). [DAC]

7.172 M. Humbert. *Municipium et civitas sine suffragio: l'organisation de la conquête jusqu'à la guerre sociale.* Rome: École Française de Rome, 1978. (Collection de l'École Française de Rome, 36.) ▸ Lucid, sensible narrative of Roman expansion and Roman-Italian relations. Describes and explains juridical and institutional framework for political organization of conquered Italy. [DAC]

7.173 Edward Togo Salmon. *The making of Roman Italy.* Ithaca, N.Y.: Cornell University Press, 1982. ISBN 0-8014-1438-5. ▸ Analysis of romanization and latinization of Italy, ca. 350–30 BCE, from non-Roman standpoint. Discusses pre-Roman Italic cultures, military conquest, political reorganization, and assimilation. Accessible, nicely illustrated. [DAC]

7.174 Edward Togo Salmon. *Roman colonization under the republic.* 1969 ed. Ithaca, N.Y.: Cornell University Press, 1970. ISBN 0-8014-0547-5. ▸ Diachronic analysis of purpose and nature of Latin and Roman colonies, ca. 500 BCE–200 CE, their military, social, and economic functions, and role in romanization. Lucid, well illustrated. [DAC]

7.175 Edward Togo Salmon. *Samnium and the Samnites.* Cambridge: Cambridge University Press, 1967. ▸ Study of Samnite topography, culture, religion, economy, government, and relations and wars with Rome; character of romanization of Samnium; Social War from Italian viewpoint. Evocative, authoritative, non-Romanocentric. [DAC]

7.176 Arnold J. Toynbee. *Hannibal's legacy: the Hannibalic War's effects on Roman life.* Vol. 1: *Rome and her neighbours before Hannibal's entry.* Vol. 2: *Rome and her neighbours after Hannibal's exit.* 2 vols. London: Oxford University Press, 1965. ▸ Sweeping survey of Rome's expansion. Volume 1 analyzes state of Roman Italy to 266 BCE; volume 2 argues disastrous consequences of Hannibalic War, agriculturally, demographically, and morally. Immensely learned, stimulating, moralistic, and unreliable. [DAC/CMW]

Politics and Government

7.177 E. Badian. "The consuls, 179–49 B.C." *Chiron* 20 (1990) 371–413. ISSN 0069-3715. ▸ Magisterial study establishes list of consuls and their descent. Supplements or supersedes all earlier lists and reaffirms overwhelming domination of consulship by men of consular background. [CMW]

7.178 E. Badian. *Publicans and sinners: private enterprise in the service of the Roman republic.* Rev. ed. Ithaca, N.Y.: Cornell University Press, 1983. ISBN 0-8014-9241-6. ‣ Important study of structure and operation of public contracts, provincial government, and tax collection, ca. 200–44 BCE, including identity, activities, and political involvement of contractors (publicans). Cogent narrative, good bibliography. [DAC]

7.179 E. Badian. "Tiberius Gracchus and the beginning of the Roman revolution." *Aufstieg und Niedergang der römischen Welt,* Series 1: *Republik,* 1 (1972) 668–731. ISBN 3-11-001885-3. ‣ Magisterial overview of 1950s and 1960s scholarship. Still valuable, stressing social and economic crisis leading to military weakness that Gracchus tried to relieve, with unforeseen consequences. [CMW]

7.180 D. R. Shackleton Bailey. "*Nobiles* and *novi* reconsidered." *American journal of philology* 107 (1986) 255–260. ISSN 0002-9475. ‣ Adduces strong arguments against view that *nobilis* means someone descended from any curule magistrate and not only from a consul, in opposition to Brunt 7.183. [CMW]

7.181 Mary Beard and Michael H. Crawford. *Rome in the late republic.* Ithaca, N.Y.: Cornell University Press, 1985. ISBN 0-8014-1824-0 (cl), 0-8014-9333-1 (pbk). ‣ Studies in collapse of republican government stressing aristocratic culture, approaches to religion, working of politics, and imperialism. Assumes knowledge of narrative and geography; identifies methodologies and controversial issues. [DAC]

7.182 P. A. Brunt. *The fall of the Roman republic and related essays.* Oxford: Clarendon, 1988. ISBN 0-19-814849-6. ‣ Nine papers, some previously published, interpreting late republican sociopolitical conflicts largely as divergencies of interest between nobility and Italians, *equites* (nonsenatorial elite), urban poor, soldiers, and peasantry. Rigorous, dense, sometimes controversial. [DAC]

7.183 P. A. Brunt. "*Nobilitas* and *novitas.*" *Journal of Roman studies* 72 (1982) 1–17. ISSN 0075-4358. ‣ Controversial discussion of concept of nobility and penetrability of Senate and governing class, arguing against traditional view of Roman aristocratic exclusivity. [DAC]

7.184 P. A. Brunt. *Social conflicts in the Roman republic.* 1971 ed. New York: Norton, 1974. ISBN 0-393-04335-5 (cl), 0-393-00586-0 (pbk). ‣ Sketch of citizen body and economy, followed by essay on social inequalities and their effect on political life. Balanced, highly readable account eschewing traditional approaches and subordinating politics to material conditions. [DAC]

7.185 Werner Dahlheim. *Gewalt und Herrschaft: das provinziale Herrschaftssystem der römischen Republik.* Berlin: de Gruyter, 1977. ISBN 3-11-006973-3. ‣ Wide-ranging analysis of attitudes toward empire and system and policy of provincial government, ca. 240–30 BCE, methodologically informed by Weberian social analysis. [DAC]

7.186 Donald Earl. *The moral and political tradition of Rome.* Ithaca, N.Y.: Cornell University Press, 1967. ISBN 0-8014-0110-0. ‣ Traces continuity in key moral-political concepts (e.g., glory) that shaped political thought and action from about 200 BCE. Standard in its field; clearly written, vigorously argued. [DAC]

7.187 David F. Epstein. *Personal enmity in Roman politics, 218–43 BC.* London: Croom Helm, 1987. ISBN 0-7099-5304-6. ‣ Study of personal enmity, its causes, effect on political life, and place in criminal trials. Also discusses public and political behavior of personal enemies. Interprets politics as nonideological competition of factions. [DAC]

7.188 Matthias Gelzer. *The Roman nobility.* Robin Seager, trans. New York: Barnes & Noble, 1969. ‣ Study of composition of republican nobility and basis for its predominance, analyzing role of political and personal relationships in distributing political power, with appendix on nobility during empire. First published in German in 1912, shaped subsequent research on republican politics and society. [DAC]

7.189 Erich S. Gruen. *The last generation of the Roman republic.* Berkeley: University of California Press, 1974. ISBN 0-520-02238-6. ‣ Readable survey of politics and society, 78–49 BCE, treating prosopography of governing class, legislation and political trials, popular grievances and violence, and causes of civil war. Controversial emphasis on continuity and nonideological politics. [DAC]

7.190 Erich S. Gruen. *Roman politics and the criminal courts, 149–78 BC.* Cambridge, Mass.: Harvard University Press, 1968. ‣ Diachronic, prosopographical survey and analysis of criminal trials and their place in political life. Emphasis on shifting political and personal motives. Judicious treatment of complicated subject. [DAC]

7.191 Keith Hopkins. *Death and renewal.* 1983 ed. Cambridge: Cambridge University Press, 1985. ISBN 0-521-24991-0 (cl), 0-521-27117-7 (pbk). ‣ Intensive statistical analysis of patterns in senatorial officeholding and heritability of consulship, documenting fluidity and permeability of governing class. Other chapters comprise descriptive accounts of gladiatorial games and funerary customs. [DAC]

7.192 Christian Meier. *Res publica amissa: eine Studie zur Verfassung und Geschichte der späten römischen Republik.* 1966 ed. Frankfurt: Suhrkamp, 1980. ISBN 3-518-07506-3. ‣ Weighty study of structure and working of political and governmental system, treating political concepts, language, relationships, class solidarities and divergencies, and continuity and change. Morphological, explicitly antiprosopographical approach. [DAC]

7.193 Fergus Millar. "The political character of the classical Roman republic, 200–151 BC." *Journal of Roman studies* 74 (1984) 1–19. ISSN 0075-4358. ‣ Closely argued discussion of social and institutional framework of political and governmental system and of popular participation in political decision making. Unorthodox in its approval of Polybius's views of popular political power. [DAC]

7.194 Claude Nicolet. *The world of the citizen in republican Rome.* P. S. Falla, trans. Berkeley: University of California Press, 1980. ISBN 0-520-03545-3 (cl), 0-520-06342-2 (pbk). ‣ Comprehensive, readable examination of legal and *de facto* relationship between ordinary citizens and political and governmental system. Treats citizenship, census, military service, taxation, popular assemblies, and popular culture, translating important ancient texts. [DAC]

7.195 Nathan S. Rosenstein. *Imperatores victi: military defeat and aristocratic competition in the middle and late republic.* Berkeley: University of California Press, 1990. ISBN 0-520-06939-0. ‣ Systematic, original study of ruling elite's stability and coherence, stressing psychology and strategies for limiting political consequences of defeat. Discusses religious beliefs, common soldiers' duties, and definitions of honorable aristocratic behavior. [DAC]

7.196 H. H. Scullard. *Roman politics, 220–150 BC.* 1973 2d ed. Westport, Conn.: Greenwood, 1981. ISBN 0-313-23296-2. ‣ Analysis of nature and techniques of aristocratic monopoly of political power, with narrative survey of Roman politics and politicians. First published 1951, now old fashioned in emphasis on political functions. [DAC]

7.197 Robin Seager, ed. *The crisis of the Roman republic: studies in political and social history.* Cambridge: Heffer, 1969. ISBN 0-85270-024-5. ‣ Reprinted articles on topics linked loosely to theme of republic's fall. Especially valuable on period from Gracchi to Sulla (Badian), *equites* (nonsenatorial elite) and friendship

(Brunt), political violence (Sherwin-White), and living conditions of poor (Yavetz). [DAC]

7.198 Israel Shatzman. *Senatorial wealth and Roman politics.* Brussels: Latomus, 1975. ‣ Largely compilatory and statistical treatment of sources of income, modes of expenditure, and real estate of republican senators. Explicitly noneconomic interpretation of senatorial policy on imperialism. [DAC]

7.199 David Stockton. *The Gracchi.* Oxford: Clarendon, 1979. ISBN 0-19-872104-8 (cl), 0-19-872105-6 (pbk). ‣ Account of two brothers' political careers and legislation from their point of view and that of their opponents. Lucid, accessible exposition of main themes and controversies. [DAC]

7.200 Lily Ross Taylor. *Party politics in the age of Caesar.* 1949 ed. Berkeley: University of California Press, 1971. ISBN 0-520-01257-7 (pbk). ‣ Learned, lively study of mechanics of political life, 70–50 BCE. Discusses patronage and dependency; elections and legislation; political manipulation of state religion; and nature, composition, and role of factions, conservative and populist. [DAC]

7.201 Lily Ross Taylor. *Roman voting assemblies: from the Hannibalic War to the dictatorship of Caesar.* Ann Arbor: University of Michigan Press, 1966. ISBN 0-472-08125-X. ‣ Standard guide to methods, procedure, and topography of assemblies and balloting. Concise exposition of literary, inscriptional, and numismatic evidence. [DAC]

7.202 Chaim Wirszubski. *Libertas as a political idea at Rome during the late republic and early principate.* 1950 ed. Cambridge: Cambridge University Press, 1968. ‣ Fundamental study of political terminology. Finds "liberty" identified with republican constitution, used as slogan and not always defined. In principate, personal freedom dependent on emperor's good will and without constitutional safeguards. [CMW]

7.203 T. P. Wiseman. *New men in the Roman Senate, 139 BC–AD 14.* London: Oxford University Press, 1971. ISBN 0-19-814713-9. ‣ Careful analysis of penetrability of Senate and ruling class, followed by prosopographical study of careers of political parvenus and analysis of mechanics of their success. [DAC]

SEE ALSO
6.596 Kurt von Fritz. *The theory of the mixed constitution in antiquity.*

The Army, War, and Imperialism

7.204 E. Badian. *Roman imperialism in the late republic.* 1968 2d ed. Ithaca, N.Y.: Cornell University Press, 1971. ISBN 0-8014-9109-6. ‣ Interpretive survey of nature, forms, and causes of imperialism, treating interplay of politics and foreign policy, morality of ruling class, and differences east and west. Finds explanation in nature, values, and psychology of Roman aristocratic society. [DAC]

7.205 P. A. Brunt. "The army and the land in the Roman revolution." In *The fall of the Roman republic and related essays,* pp. 240–80. Oxford: Clarendon, 1988. ISBN 0-19-814849-6. ‣ Wide-ranging study of veterans' demands for land allotments in first century BCE and their political consequences. Discusses rural social structure and conditions, effects of conscription and service, and soldiers' discipline and loyalties. [DAC]

7.206 P. A. Brunt. "Italian aims at the time of the Social War." In *The fall of the Roman republic and related essays,* pp. 93–143. Oxford: Clarendon, 1988. ISBN 0-19-814849-6. ‣ Cogent study of Roman-Italian conflict culminating in Social War (91–88 BCE). Discusses romanization and Italian unity. Sees origins of conflict in demand for Roman citizenship and allies' objectives as political rights. [DAC]

7.207 P. A. Brunt. "Laus imperii." In *Roman imperial themes,* pp. 288–323. Oxford: Clarendon, 1990. ISBN 0-19-814476-8. ‣ Balanced, cogent discussion of late republican concepts of empire. Discusses nature of evidence, especially Cicero and Caesar, conceptions of glory, virtue, fortune, and unlimited expansion; theory of justified war; and attitudes toward subjects. [DAC]

7.208 Brian Caven. *The Punic wars.* New York: St. Martin's, 1980. ISBN 0-312-65580-0. ‣ Military narrative of conflict between Rome and Carthage, 280–146 BCE. Readable analysis of causes, description of events, and sketch of social and political background. [DAC]

7.209 Stephen L. Dyson. *The creation of the Roman frontier.* 1985 ed. Princeton: Princeton University Press, 1987. ISBN 0-691-10232-5 (cl), 0-691-03577-6 (pbk). ‣ Lucid, readable survey of Roman expansion and its effects on indigenous cultures (trade patterns, acculturation) from about 390–50 BCE, covering northern Italy, southern Gaul, Spain, Sardinia, and Corsica. [DAC]

7.210 Emilio Gabba. *Republican Rome: the army and the allies.* P. J. Cuff, trans. Berkeley: University of California Press, 1976. ISBN 0-520-03259-4. ‣ Reprint of selected articles and reviews. Especially valuable on professionalization and political impact of late republican army. Argument for commercial motives underlying Roman-Italian conflict (Social War, 91–88 BCE); not widely accepted. [DAC]

7.211 William V. Harris. *War and imperialism in republican Rome, 327–70 BC.* 1979 ed. New York: Oxford University Press, 1985. ISBN 0-19-814827-5 (cl, 1979), 0-19-814866-6 (pbk). ‣ Analysis of foreign policy and attitudes toward war and territorial expansion, arguing that Rome was consistently aggressive and imperialistic, a view revisionist at the time (cf. Badian 7.204), now generally accepted. [DAC]

7.212 William V. Harris, ed. *The imperialism of mid-republican Rome.* Rome: American Academy in Rome, 1984. (American Academy in Rome, Papers and monographs, 29.) ‣ Collected papers by leading historians from 1982 colloquium on character and causes of Roman policy, invoking economic, political, and popular motives, with valuable discussion by editor of approaches and methodologies. [DAC]

7.213 Keith Hopkins. *Conquerors and slaves.* 1978 ed. Cambridge: Cambridge University Press, 1981. ISBN 0-521-21945-0 (cl, 1978), 0-521-28181-4 (pbk). ‣ Highly readable, partly quantitative analysis of processes affecting growth and characteristics of slave society of republican Italy, with criticism of traditional approaches and methodologies. Bold and imaginative. [DAC]

7.214 Lawrence Keppie. *Colonisation and veteran settlement in Italy, 47–14 BC.* London: British School at Rome, 1983. ISBN 0-904152-06-5. ‣ Unfashionable argument that veterans settled by Caesar and Augustus generally persevered on their farms, based on survey of over fifty communities affected. Strong on epigraphic and archaeological evidence. [CMW]

7.215 Lawrence Keppie. *The making of the Roman army: from republic to empire.* Totowa, N.J.: Barnes & Noble, 1984. ISBN 0-389-20447-1. ‣ Lively, readable diachronic account of growth and development of military institutions and traditions, ca. 600 BCE–50 CE, treating campaigns, tactics, and professionalization of citizen militia. [DAC]

7.216 J. F. Lazenby. *Hannibal's war: a military history of the Second Punic War.* Warminster: Aris & Phillips, 1978. ISBN 0-85668-080-X. ‣ Comprehensive narrative survey and analysis treating campaigns, generalship, strategic issues, and causes of Roman victory. Traditional military history firmly grounded in ancient sources. [DAC]

7.217 J. S. Richardson. *Hispaniae: Spain and the development of Roman imperialism, 218–82 B.C.* Cambridge: Cambridge University Press, 1986. ISBN 0-521-32183-2. ▸ Survey of Spanish geography and ethnography followed by diachronic account of campaigns, analysis of development of concept of province and provincial government, and of relations between Senate and commanders. [DAC]

7.218 Jakob Seibert. *Forschungen zu Hannibal*. Darmstadt: Wissenschaftliche Buchgesellschaft, 1993. ISBN 3-534-12091-4. ▸ Comprehensive bibliography and analysis of scholarship on Hannibal's campaigns and related topics, including Roman politics, economy, religion, and leaders in Second Punic War period. [CMW]

7.219 Jakob Seibert. *Hannibal*. Darmstadt: Wissenschaftliche Buchgesellschaft, 1993. ISBN 3-534-12029-9. ▸ Narrative of Hannibal's career and campaigns, presenting conclusions for which detailed argument must be sought in Seibert 7.218. [CMW]

7.220 R. E. Smith. *Service in the post-Marian Roman army*. Manchester: Manchester University Press, 1958. ▸ Careful study of recruitment and conditions of service, ca. 100 BCE (Marius) to 14 CE (Augustus). Treats Marius's reforms, provinces and provincial armies, terms of service, conscription and volunteering, officers, and Augustus's reforms. [DAC]

SEE ALSO
6.462 Peter Garnsey and C. R. Whittaker, eds. *Imperialism in the ancient world*.
6.527 E. W. Marsden. *Greek and Roman artillery*.

Foreign Policy and External Relations

7.221 E. Badian. *Foreign clientelae (264–70 B.C.)*. Corr. 1958 ed. Oxford: Oxford University Press, 1985. ISBN 0-19-814204-8. ▸ Lucid, cogent, influential survey of development of client relationships in foreign policy to 146/133 BCE and of personal and political dependent relationships of individual families and leaders within Italy, 133–70 BCE. [DAC]

7.222 E. Badian. "Notes on Roman policy in Illyria (230–201 BC)." In *Studies in Greek and Roman history*, pp. 1–33. Oxford: Blackwell, 1964. ISBN 0-631-08140-2. ▸ Meticulous essay on relations with kings, tribes, and cities of Illyria; their role in formative period of Roman expansion, development of foreign policy, and early imperial organization. [DAC]

7.223 David C. Braund. *Rome and the friendly king: the character of client kingship*. New York: St. Martin's, 1984. ISBN 0-312-69210-2. ▸ Analysis of relations between Rome and dependent rulers in late republic and early empire, treating objectives, mutual benefits, and personal relationships. Clears away some traditional misconceptions. [CMW]

7.224 Michael H. Crawford. "Rome and the Greek world: economic relationships." *Economic history review* 30 (1977) 42–52. ISSN 0013-0117. ▸ Examination from non-Romanocentric perspective of Roman exploitation of eastern Mediterranean from second century BCE, discussing motives for imperialism and economic consequences. Unromantic assessment of slave trade. [DAC]

7.225 Jürgen Deininger. *Der politische Widerstand gegen Rom in Griechenland, 217–86 v. Chr.* Berlin: de Gruyter, 1971. ISBN 3-11-001605-2. ▸ Controversial, anti-Marxist analysis of origins and nature of Greek resistance to Roman conquest and rule, denying existence of internal Greek political disputes arising from class differences. [DAC]

7.226 Arthur M. Eckstein. *Senate and general: individual decision-making and Roman foreign relations, 264–194 B.C.* Berkeley: University of California Press, 1987. ISBN 0-520-05582-9. ▸ Documents role of field commanders in determining foreign policy and military strategy; regional account and analysis including northern Italy (Celts), Sicily, Spain, Africa, and Greece. [DAC]

7.227 David Magie. *Roman rule in Asia Minor: to the end of the third century after Christ*. 1950 ed. 2 vols. Salem, Mass.: Ayer, 1975. ISBN 0-405-07099-3. ▸ Beginning essentially with Hellenistic kingdoms, volume 1 offers conventional chronicle of events; volume 2, 1,000 pages of learned notes identifying and discussing ancient sources and interpretive problems. Valuable as collection of source materials and regarded as classic, but partly outdated; see Mitchell 7.463. [DAC/CMW]

7.228 Elizabeth Rawson. "Caesar's heritage: Hellenistic kings and their Roman equals." In *Roman culture and society: collected papers*, pp. 169–88. Oxford: Clarendon, 1991. ISBN 0-19-814752-x. ▸ Important study of Hellenistic attitudes toward kingship and history of Roman equivalents (e.g., triumphant generals) to explore whether Caesar's political ambitions included kingship. [DAC]

7.229 A. N. Sherwin-White. *Roman foreign policy in the East, 168 B.C.–A.D. 1*. Norman: University of Oklahoma Press, 1984. ISBN 0-8061-1878-4. ▸ Analytical narrative of origins, course, and aftermath of Roman wars against Mithridates of Pontus, discussing senatorial decision making, motives, dynastic issues, and logistical and topographical factors. [DAC]

7.230 Richard D. Sullivan. *Near Eastern royalty and Rome, 100–30 BC*. Toronto: University of Toronto Press, 1990. ISBN 0-8020-2682-6. ▸ Wide-ranging study of Hellenistic kings and their relations with Rome, covering rulers and dynasties from Asia Minor to Egypt, including Armenia and Parthia. Detailed scholarship, with extensive notes and bibliography, in neglected field. [CMW]

SEE ALSO
6.261 Erich S. Gruen. *The Hellenistic world and the coming of Rome*.

Economy, Demography, and Material Conditions

7.231 P. A. Brunt. *Italian manpower, 225 B.C.–A.D. 14, with a new postscript*. 1971 ed. Oxford: Clarendon, 1987. ISBN 0-19-814283-8. ▸ Detailed study of Italian population linked with consequences of war (cf. Toynbee 7.176): census figures, mortality and fertility rates, emigration, population of Rome, conscription, and size of army. Estimates generally conservative. [DAC]

7.232 Michael H. Crawford. *Coinage and money under the Roman republic: Italy and the Mediterranean economy*. Berkeley: University of California Press, 1985. ISBN 0-520-05506-3. ▸ Regional, partly diachronic analysis of local coinage and effects of Roman conquest on monetary system and circulation patterns, covering Sicily and Africa, Spain, and eastern Mediterranean. Considerably modifies Crawford 7.56. [DAC]

7.233 Joan M. Frayn. *Subsistence farming in Roman Italy*. Fontwell: Centaur, 1979. ISBN 0-900000-92-9. ▸ Illuminating study of economy of small farms in Italy during republic and early empire from literary, archaeological, and comparative evidence, discussing pastoralism, transhumance, communications, marketing, the year's work, and buildings and equipment. [CMW]

7.234 Emilio Gabba and M. Pasquinucci. *Strutture agrarie e allevamento transumante nell'Italia romana (III–I sec. a.c.)* Pisa: Giardini, 1979. ▸ Important synthesis of changes in land use, discussing decline of small farmer, growth of public land and large estates, relationship between arable and pastoral land (Gabba) and nature and extent of long-distance transhumant pastoralism (Pasquinucci). [DAC]

7.235 A. Giardina and A. Schiavone, eds. *Società romana e produzione schiavistica*. 3 vols. Bari: Laterza, 1981. ▸ Collected conference papers from primarily Marxist viewpoint on nature and effects of exploitation of slave labor: landownership and use in central and southern Italy, 200 BCE–200 CE, raising all main issues and discussing agriculturally and industrially produced artifacts such as amphoras, their trade, and contemporary views of economic changes. [DAC]

7.236 M. S. Spurr. *Arable cultivation in Roman Italy, c. 200 B.C.–A.D. 100.* London: Society for the Promotion of Roman Studies, 1986. (*Journal of Roman studies*, Monographs, 3.) ISBN 0-907764-06-1. ▸ Study of techniques of cereal cultivation (wheat, barley, millet, legumes), role of animals, labor, and marketing. Identifies regional variations in farming practices and challenges many traditional views, e.g., extent of cereal production. [DAC]

7.237 K. D. White. *Roman farming.* Ithaca, N.Y.: Cornell University Press, 1970. ISBN 0-8014-0575-0. ▸ Comprehensive survey of literary and archaeological evidence for soils and crops, soil fertility, crop rotation and fertilization, crop husbandry, arboriculture, horticulture, animal husbandry, labor, and technology. Nicely illustrated, accessible to nonspecialists. [DAC]

7.238 A.J.N. Wilson. *Emigration from Italy in the republican age of Rome.* New York: Barnes & Noble, 1966. ▸ Regionally organized account of movement of groups and individuals to provinces, discussing settlers' origins, distribution, occupations, relations with natives, and influence on Roman politics. Epigraphic evidence outdated but still useful. [DAC]

SEE ALSO
6.541 Peter Garnsey. *Famine and food supply in the Graeco-Roman world.*

Society

7.239 Keith R. Bradley. *Slavery and rebellion in the Roman world, 140 BC–70 BC.* Bloomington: Indiana University Press, 1989. ISBN 0-253-31259-0. ▸ Lucid description and interpretation of three slave rebellions in Sicily and Italy, including that of Spartacus, with parallels from New World. Discusses material conditions underlying rebellion and techniques of maintaining resistance. [DAC]

7.240 P. A. Brunt. "The *equites* in the late Republic." In *The fall of the Roman republic and related essays*, pp. 144–93. Oxford: Clarendon, 1988. ISBN 0-19-814849-6. ▸ Definition of *equites* (nonsenatorial elite) and their relations with senators, treating noneconomic causes of conflict, incomes from landownership and trade, place of publicans, and role in imperialism. [DAC]

7.241 P. A. Brunt. "The Roman mob." In *Studies in ancient society*. M. I. Finley, ed., pp. 74–102. London: Routledge & Kegan Paul, 1974. ISBN 0-7100-7781-5. ▸ Study of violence in public and political life in last century BCE, treating causes and development, mob composition, and aims and achievements, with pioneering emphasis on material conditions. [DAC]

7.242 John H. D'Arms. *Commerce and social standing in ancient Rome.* Cambridge, Mass.: Harvard University Press, 1981. ISBN 0-674-14475-9. ▸ Lively, judicious analysis of literary, archaeological, and inscriptional evidence for role of senatorial class in trade. Case studies of senators and senatorial families. [DAC]

7.243 John H. D'Arms. *Romans on the bay of Naples: a social and cultural study of the villas and their owners from 150 BC to AD 400.* Cambridge, Mass.: Harvard University Press, 1970. ISBN 0-674-77925-8. ▸ Study of villa owners and their activities in historical context, including catalog of owners. Discusses types of villas and their impact on local society and economy. Nicely illustrated. [DAC]

7.244 A. W. Lintott. *Violence in republican Rome.* London: Clarendon, 1968. ISBN 0-19-814267-6. ▸ Careful diachronic study of violence in public and political life and its underlying causes. Treats early forms of private self-help, popular vigilante justice, and their accommodation in law. [DAC]

7.245 Claude Nicolet. *L'ordre équestre à l'époque républicaine*

(312–43 av. J.-C.) 2 vols. Paris: de Boccard, 1966–74. ▸ Thorough analysis of origins and definition of equestrian class followed by prosopographical study of about 375 late republican *equites* (nonsenatorial elite). Discusses role in juries, terms of judiciary laws to 46 BCE, and relations with Senate. [DAC]

7.246 Wilfried Nippel. *Aufruhr und "Polizei" in der römischen Republik.* Stuttgart: Klett-Cotta, 1988. ISBN 3-608-91434-X. ▸ Subtle, dense examination of maintenance of public order in Rome in first century BCE. Diachronic analysis of political and popular violence, its causes, and government's response. [DAC]

7.247 Susan Treggiari. *Roman freedmen during the late republic.* Oxford: Clarendon, 1969. ▸ Definitive, systematic treatment of main issues, including origins and numbers of ex-slaves, social status and economic roles, and methods and causes of emancipation and its legal and customary effects. [DAC]

7.248 Andrew Wallace-Hadrill. "Patronage in Roman society: from republic to empire." In *Patronage in ancient society.* 1989 ed. Andrew Wallace-Hadrill, ed., pp. 63–87. London: Routledge, 1990. ISBN 0-415-00341-5 (cl), 0-415-04892-3 (pbk). ▸ Study of patronage in theory and practice. Discusses definition and nature, legal status, cultural and ideological functions, role in late republican politics and social control, and application to slaves and ex-slaves. [DAC]

SEE ALSO
6.500 M. I. Finley. *Ancient slavery and modern ideology.*
6.512 William L. Westermann. *The slave systems of Greek and Roman antiquity.*
6.549 Alison Burford. *Craftsmen in Greek and Roman society.*
6.562 G.E.M. de Ste. Croix. *The class struggle in the ancient Greek world from the archaic age to the Arab conquests.*
6.569 Marc Kleijwegt. *Ancient youth.*

Intellectual Life: Literature, Philosophy, Education

7.249 Mary Beard et al. *Literacy in the Roman world.* J. H. Humphrey, ed. Ann Arbor: Journal of Roman Archaeology, 1991. (*Journal of Roman archaeology*, Supplementary series, 3.) ▸ Major contribution to debate on extent of literacy. Eight papers, generally more optimistic about extent of literacy than Harris 6.555. Readable, scholarly, exciting. [CMW]

7.250 Stanley F. Bonner. *Education in ancient Rome: from the elder Cato to the younger Pliny.* Berkeley: University of California Press, 1977. ISBN 0-520-03439-2 (cl), 0-520-03501-1 (pbk). ▸ Historical sketch of development of public education followed by authoritative account of teaching conditions (schools, equipment, teachers' pay) and detailed analysis of program of instruction. [DAC]

7.251 Erich S. Gruen. *Culture and national identity in republican Rome.* Ithaca, N.Y.: Cornell University Press, 1992. ISBN 0-8014-2759-2. ▸ Survey of response of Roman elites to Greek culture showing how this paradoxically highlighted Roman values and produced distinctively Roman forms of artistic expression in Hellenistic context. [CMW]

7.252 Erich S. Gruen. *Studies in Greek culture and Roman policy.* Leiden: Brill, 1990. ISBN 90-04-09051-7. ▸ Five lively, unconventional essays explore particular episodes and developments in history of ambivalent Roman attitudes toward Greek culture, ca. 200–100 BCE. [DAC]

7.253 George Kennedy. *The art of rhetoric in the Roman world, 300 B.C.–A.D. 300.* 1973 ed. 3 vols. Princeton: Princeton University Press, 1982. (*A history of rhetoric*, 2.) ISBN 0-691-03505-9 (set). ▸ Comprehensive survey of origins and development of Latin oratory and rhetorical theory, treating types of oratory, style, technique, and art of individual authors, including Cato the

Elder and Cicero. Also available from Ann Arbor: University Microfilms International. [DAC]

7.254 Arnaldo Momigliano. *Alien wisdom: the limits of hellenization.* Cambridge: Cambridge University Press, 1975. ISBN 0-521-20876-9 (cl), 0-521-38761-2 (pbk). ▸ Sweeping, illuminating study of cultural and intellectual interrelations between Greeks and Romans, Celts, Jews, and Iranians from fourth to first century BCE, discussing Greek views of Roman life, including Polybius and Posidonius. [DAC]

7.255 Elizabeth Rawson. *Intellectual life in the late Roman republic.* Baltimore: Johns Hopkins University Press, 1985. ISBN 0-8018-2899-6. ▸ Erudite historical survey of intellectual climate treating Greek writers and their audience, the arts, language and rhetoric, mathematics, medicine, architecture, law, historiography, geography and ethnography, philosophy, and theology. [DAC]

7.256 Erich Segal. *Roman laughter: the comedy of Plautus.* 2d ed. New York: Oxford University Press, 1987. ISBN 0-19-504166-6. ▸ Relates Plautus's plays and values to contemporary culture and comedic tradition. Discusses Greek "festive" and Roman "unfestive" morality. Lively, readable; texts translated, accessible to nonspecialists. [DAC]

7.257 Alan Wardman. *Rome's debt to Greece.* London: Elek, 1976. ISBN 0-236-40038-X. ▸ Readable, introductory survey of Romans' conscious attitudes toward Greek cultural heritage, examining bilingualism, rhetoric and rhetorical theory, views of Greek history, and attitudes to philosophy and perceptions of its value. [DAC]

7.258 T. P. Wiseman. *Roman studies: literary and historical.* Liverpool: Cairns, 1987. ISBN 0-905205-62-6. ▸ Twenty-nine articles, mostly reprinted, on historical themes, historiography, prosopography, topography, and literature; includes papers on late republican poets and patrons and on Greek cultural and intellectual influences. Vivid, imaginative, exacting. [DAC]

SEE ALSO
6.555 William V. Harris. *Ancient literacy.*
6.559 H.-I. Marrou. *A history of education in antiquity.*

Historians and Historiography

7.259 E. Badian. "The early historians." In *Latin historians.* T. A. Dorey, ed., pp. 1–38. New York: Basic Books, 1966. ▸ Thorough, incisive discussion of development of Roman historical writing including Fabius Pictor writing in Greek, origins of history in Latin (Cato the Elder), Latin annalists before Livy, and autobiography and contemporary history. [DAC]

7.260 Averil Cameron, ed. *History as text: the writing of ancient history.* Chapel Hill: University of North Carolina Press, 1990. ISBN 0-8078-1889-5. ▸ Lively, unorthodox collection of eight essays offering poststructuralist interpretations, some deconstructionist, of Greek and Latin writers, including Livy, narrative emplotment, and positivistic realism. Editorial introductions and postscripts. [DAC]

7.261 Donald Earl. *The political thought of Sallust.* Cambridge: Cambridge University Press, 1961. ▸ Sensible, balanced examination of Sallust's politico-moral ideals and their influence on his historical interpretations and analysis of causation and development of alleged late republican moral degeneration. [DAC]

7.262 Kenneth S. Sacks. *Diodorus Siculus and the first century.* Princeton: Princeton University Press, 1990. ISBN 0-691-03600-4. ▸ Careful reinterpretation of historian's organizational methods, techniques, writing style, themes, and political sentiments. Aims at revealing and interpreting Diodorus's own views in social context of mid-first-century BCE Rome. [DAC]

7.263 Ronald Syme. *Sallust.* Berkeley: University of California Press, 1964. ▸ Sketch of early life, career, contemporary political life, and retirement, followed by closely argued analysis of surviving monographs and fragments and of Sallust's place in historiographical tradition. [DAC]

7.264 P. G. Walsh. *Livy: his historical aims and methods.* 1961 ed. Bristol: Bristol Classical, 1989. ISBN 1-85399-130-9 (pbk). ▸ Biographical sketch and survey of historiographical tradition followed by sensible analysis of Livy's religious, moral, and philosophical views, sources and methods, literary techniques, and style. Dated but still excellent introduction. [DAC]

7.265 T. P. Wiseman. "Practice and theory in Roman historiography." In *Roman studies: literary and historical,* pp. 244–62. Liverpool: Cairns, 1987. ISBN 0-905205-62-6. ▸ Imaginative exploration of views and techniques of historical writing in first century BCE, including types of historiography (e.g., contemporary) and analysis of main authors (e.g., Sallust). [DAC]

7.266 A. J. Woodman. *Rhetoric in classical historiography: four studies.* Portland, Ore.: Areopagitica, 1988. ISBN 0-918400-07-4. ▸ Lively, unorthodox exploration of nature and place of truth in historical writing, starting with Thucydides, discussing Cicero's views of historiography, style and its relation to subject in Sallust and Livy, and Tacitus and "alternative history." [DAC]

SEE ALSO
6.107 F. W. Walbank. *Polybius.*

Biography

7.267 A. E. Astin. *Cato the Censor.* Oxford: Clarendon, 1978. ISBN 0-19-814809-7. ▸ Comprehensive diachronic account of Marcus Porcius Cato's political career and policies, ca. 200–150 BCE. Describes his oratory, writing, and attitudes toward Greeks. [DAC]

7.268 A. E. Astin. *Scipio Aemilianus.* Oxford: Clarendon, 1967. ▸ Critical evaluation of source material (Polybius, Appian, Cicero) with largely diachronic survey of military and political career, policies, and literary and philosophical interests (ca. 160–130 BCE). [DAC]

7.269 D. R. Shackleton Bailey. *Cicero.* New York: Scribner's, 1972. ISBN 0-684-12683-4. ▸ Trenchant diachronic account of life (100–43 BCE), literary and philosophical interests, and activities, with particular emphasis on his letters and many quotations from Cicero's own words. [DAC]

7.270 T. F. Carney. *A biography of C. Marius.* 2d ed. Chicago: Argonaut, 1970. ISBN 0-8244-0023-2. ▸ Analytical survey of military and political career, activities, and policies set against wider background of political life and foreign affairs (ca. 120–86 BCE). Useful evaluation of source materials; conclusions often controversial. [DAC]

7.271 M. L. Clarke. *The noblest Roman: Marcus Brutus and his reputation.* Ithaca, N.Y.: Cornell University Press, 1981. ISBN 0-8014-1393-1. ▸ Brief diachronic biography emphasizing assassination of Caesar and its effects, followed by survey of Brutus's treatment by later writers, especially Shakespeare. [DAC]

7.272 Matthias Gelzer. *Caesar: politician and statesman.* Peter Needham, trans. Cambridge, Mass.: Harvard University Press, 1968. ▸ Best available biography of Caesar, combining sketch of nature of late republican political life with diachronic survey of military and political career and policies (ca. 65–44 BCE). Translated from sixth edition of book first published 1921. [DAC]

7.273 P.A.L. Greenhalgh. *Pompey.* Vol. 1: *Pompey: the Roman Alexander.* Vol. 2: *Pompey: the republican prince.* 2 vols. Columbia: University of Missouri Press, 1981–82. ISBN 0-8262-0335-3 (v. 1), 0-8262-0356-6 (v. 2). ▸ Highly readable, diachronic survey of general and statesman's career and Roman politics, ca. 80–48 BCE. Sound on military campaigns, collects important source materials, but analysis of political life sometimes unsophisticated. [DAC]

7.274 Erich S. Gruen. "M. Licinius Crassus: a review article." *American journal of ancient history* 2.2 (1977) 117–28. ▸ Review of recent biographies, including Ward 7.284, arguing against conventional view that sees Crassus as subordinate figure and understates his importance and independent role in late republican politics. [CMW]

7.275 Eleanor Goltz Huzar. *Mark Antony: a biography.* 1978 ed. London: Croom Helm, 1986. ISBN 0-7099-4719-4. ▸ Conventional biography with good bibliography and full references to sources. Favorable appreciation of Antony's career, crediting him with policy of reconciling Hellenistic and Roman ideals. [CMW]

7.276 Arthur Keaveney. *Sulla: the last republican.* London: Croom Helm, 1982. ISBN 0-7099-1507-1 (cl), 0-7099-3104-2 (pbk). ▸ Diachronic account of Sulla's military and political career and policies (ca. 107–78 BCE), with particular emphasis on personality. Only English-language biography, but excessively favorable to Sulla. [DAC]

7.277 John Leach. *Pompey the Great.* 1978 ed. London: Croom Helm, 1986. ISBN 0-8476-6035-4 (cl, 1978), 0-7099-4127-7 (pbk). ▸ Sober, diachronic account of Pompey's military and political career and activities (ca. 85–48 BCE), followed by review of source materials and selection of translated sources. Also available from Ann Arbor: University Microfilms International. [DAC]

7.278 Thomas N. Mitchell. *Cicero.* Vol. 1: *The ascending years.* Vol. 2: *The senior statesman.* 2 vols. New Haven: Yale University Press, 1979–91. ISBN 0-300-02277-8 (v. 1), 0-300-04779-7 (v. 2). ▸ Thorough, diachronic, analytical survey of career and thought of Roman statesman and orator set against historical background, discussing moral and political ideas and writing (influences and development) and place in political life. Volume 1 covers to 63 BCE, volume 2 thereafter. Also examines causes of collapse of republican government. [DAC]

7.279 Elizabeth Rawson. *Cicero: a portrait.* 1975 ed. Ithaca, N.Y.: Cornell University Press, 1983. ISBN 0-8014-1628-0 (cl), 0-8014-9256-4 (pbk). ▸ Balanced, immensely readable, diachronic account of political career and policies, integrating literary and philosophical interests and setting activities against historical background (ca. 80–43 BCE). Full references to sources. [DAC]

7.280 H. H. Scullard. *Scipio Africanus: soldier and politician.* Ithaca, N.Y.: Cornell University Press, 1970. ISBN 0-8014-0549-1. ▸ Analytical survey of military career and activities and later political career and policies (ca. 210–184 BCE). Especially valuable on strategy and tactics, controversial on political matters. [DAC]

7.281 Robin Seager. *Pompey: a political biography.* Berkeley: University of California Press, 1979. ISBN 0-520-03909-2. ▸ Lucid, readable, diachronic account of political career and activities (ca. 85–48 BCE) set against sociopolitical and strategic background. Eschews systematic treatment of military activities and policies. [DAC]

7.282 Philip O. Spann. *Quintus Sertorius and the legacy of Sulla.* Fayetteville: University of Arkansas Press, 1987. ISBN 0-938626-64-7. ▸ First biography of Sertorius in sixty years; sees him as tactician of genius, less of a strategist. Notes ancient sources generally hostile, questions nature of treason, and emphasizes importance of Spain in Roman political and military affairs. [CMW]

7.283 David Stockton. *Cicero: a political biography.* London: Oxford University Press, 1971. ISBN 0-19-872032-7 (cl), 0-19-872033-5 (pbk). ▸ Brief sketch of early life with balanced diachronic account of political career, activities, and policies (ca. 70–43 BCE), set against political and legislative background. [DAC]

7.284 Allen M. Ward. *Marcus Crassus and the late Roman republic.* Columbia: University of Missouri Press, 1977. ISBN 0-8262-0216-0. ▸ Readable account of historical setting and early life followed by military and political career and activities (ca. 85–53 BCE). Probably best biography available, but conventional in interpretation; see Gruen 7.274. [DAC]

EARLY EMPIRE

General Studies

7.285 Albino Garzetti. *From Tiberius to the Antonines: a history of the Roman empire, AD 14–192.* 1974 ed. J. R. Foster, trans. London: Methuen, 1976. ISBN 0-416-16800-0 (cl), 0-416-70480-8 (pbk). ▸ History of period, invaluable for its extensive bibliographic excursus; beware of English translation, particularly unreliable on proper names, family relationships, and technical terminology. [CMW]

7.286 Fergus Millar et al. *The Roman empire and its neighbours.* 2d ed. New York: Holmes & Meier, 1981. ISBN 0-8419-0711-0. ▸ Excellent introduction to empire in all aspects—social, political, and cultural—with chapters on Parthians and Persians, Dacians, Scythians and Sarmatians, and Germans. [CMW]

7.287 Theodor Mommsen. *Römische Kaisergeschichte: nach den Vorlesungs-Mitschriften von Sebastian und Paul Hensel, 1882/86.* Barbara Demandt and Alexander Demandt, eds. Munich: Beck, 1992. ISBN 3-406-36078-5. ▸ Reconstruction of unpublished fourth volume of Mommsen's famous and influential history of Rome, reconstructed from students' lecture notes. [CMW]

7.288 Colin M. Wells. *The Roman empire.* 2d ed. London: Fontana, 1992. ISBN 0-00-686252-7. ▸ Account of Roman empire to 235 CE, stressing social and economic as well as political developments and drawing on archaeological, literary, and epigraphic evidence. Extensive forty-two-page annotated bibliography; U.S. 2d ed. forthcoming, Harvard University Press, 1994. [CMW]

SEE ALSO

6.160 *The Cambridge ancient history.* Vols. 10–11.

The Work of Augustus

7.289 E. Badian. "'Crisis theories' and the beginning of the principate." In *Romanitas, Christianitas: Untersuchungen zur Geschichte und Literatur der römischen Kaiserzeit; Johannes Straub zum siebzehnten Geburtstag am 18. Oktober 1982 gewidmet.* Gerhard Wirth, ed., pp. 18–41. Berlin: de Gruyter, 1982. ISBN 3-11-008551-8. ▸ Definitive discussion laying to rest once fashionable theory that dated conspiracy of Murena to 23 rather than 22 BCE. Argues changes in Augustus's status not improvised but carefully planned. [CMW]

7.290 Glen W. Bowersock. *Augustus and the Greek world.* 1965 ed. Westport, Conn.: Greenwood, 1981. ISBN 0-313-23298-9. ▸ Succinct reminder of how Augustus conciliated leaders of Greek-speaking half of empire. Discusses Roman connections, client rulers, imperial cult, and Greek literature under Augustus. [CMW]

7.291 Donald Earl. *The age of Augustus.* 1968 ed. New York: Exeter; distributed by Bookthrift, 1980. ISBN 0-89673-044-1. ▸ Easily the best general survey in English of political and social life in Augustan age. Excellent illustrations. [CMW]

7.292 Fergus Millar and Erich Segal, eds. *Caesar Augustus: seven aspects.* 1984 ed. New York: Oxford University Press, 1990. ISBN 0-19-814851-8 (cl), 0-19-814858-5 (pbk). ▸ Papers for Sir Ronald Syme's eightieth birthday, building on *The Roman Revolution* (7.294). Topics include Augustus's image, monarchical power, the historians, consent of propertied classes, Senate, East, and poets. [CMW]

7.293 Kurt A. Raaflaub and Mark Toher, eds. *Between republic* *and empire: interpretations of Augustus and his principate.* Berkeley: University of California Press, 1990. ISBN 0-520-06676-6. ▸ Nineteen papers summing up current thinking; good reassessment of *The Roman Revolution* (7.294), comparison of Mommsen and Syme, papers on Augustus as link between republic and principate, and Augustus's pontificate. [CMW]

7.294 Ronald Syme. *The Roman revolution.* 1939 ed. Oxford: Oxford University Press, 1987. ISBN 0-19-881001-6 (pbk). ▸ Prosopographical analysis of politics and power struggle, 60 BCE–14 CE, with Octavian/Augustus as party boss prefiguring Mussolini. Intellectual *tour de force*, hugely influential interpretation defining all subsequent research in field. [DAC/CMW]

7.295 Andrew Wallace-Hadrill. "Image and authority in the coinage of Augustus." *Journal of Roman studies* 76 (1986) 66–87. ISSN 0075-4358. ▸ After initial hesitation, Augustan coinage finally conveyed monarchical autocracy with images of power and glory; coins issued through Senate show this body as vehicle for, not rival to, Augustus's authority. [CMW]

7.296 Colin M. Wells. *The German policy of Augustus: an examination of the archaeological evidence.* Oxford: Clarendon, 1972. ISBN 0-19-813162-3. ▸ Concludes Augustus's policy not basically defensive, but expansionist in republican tradition; would have continued conquests but for military reverses late in reign. Summary of archaeological evidence still valuable, though now incomplete. [CMW]

7.297 Rolf Winkes, ed. *The age of Augustus: interdisciplinary conference held at Brown University, April 30–May 2, 1982.* Louvain and Providence: Institut Supérieur d'Archéologie et d'Histoire de l'Art, College Érasme and Brown University, Center for Old World Archaeology and Art, 1985. (Publications d'histoire d'art et d'archéologie de l'Université Catholique de Louvain, 44. Archaeologia transatlantica, 5.) ▸ Thirteen papers, uneven in value, strong on iconography in historical reliefs, private portraits, Temple of Apollo, Prima Porta statue, painting, and literature. [CMW]

7.298 Paul Zanker. *The power of images in the age of Augustus.* Alan Shapiro, trans. Ann Arbor: University of Michigan Press, 1988. ISBN 0-472-10101-3. ▸ Pervasive visual imagery orchestrated to create new idea of Rome and transform society: the world at peace under great and benevolent ruler. Most important book on Augustus since Syme 7.294. [CMW]

Politics and Government

7.299 P. A. Brunt. *Roman imperial themes.* New York: Oxford University Press, 1990. ISBN 0-19-814476-8. ▸ Eighteen papers, all but two reprinted from periodicals, mostly with substantial addenda. Magisterial discussions of imperialism, administration, fiscal affairs, and assimilation of provincial elites. [CMW]

7.300 Niels Hannestad. *Roman art and imperial policy.* 1986 ed. P. J. Crabb, trans. Århus, Denmark: Århus University Press, 1988. ISBN 87-7288-043-0 (cl, 1985), 87-7288-166-6 (pbk). ▸ Study of imperial propaganda as expressed in art, especially coins and sculpture, from Augustus to fourth century. [CMW]

7.301 Ramsay MacMullen. *Enemies of the Roman order: treason, unrest, and alienation in the empire.* 1966 ed. London: Routledge, 1992. ISBN 0-415-08621-3. ▸ Discussion of senatorial opposition, philosophers, magicians, astrologers, urban unrest, brigandage, barbarian and eastern influences, native cultural survivals, and dilution of "Roman," i.e., senatorial, ideals between first and fourth centuries. [CMW]

7.302 Fergus Millar. *The emperor in the Roman world, 31 BC–AD 337.* 2d ed. London: Duckworth, 1992. ISBN 0-7156-1722-2. ▸ Massive account of emperor's nonmilitary functions, stressing personal nature of his activity, general acceptance of his author-

ity, and role of subjects in initiating petitions to which he responded. [CMW]

7.303 Geoffrey Rickman. *The corn supply of ancient Rome.* New York: Oxford University Press, 1980. ISBN 0-19-814838-0. ▸ Standard, indispensable account of how system supplying Rome with grain developed and how it operated; includes eleven specialized appendixes. [CMW]

7.304 E. Mary Smallwood. *The Jews under Roman rule from Pompey to Diocletian: a study in political relations.* 1976 ed. Leiden: Brill, 1981. ISBN 90-04-06403-6. ▸ Scholarly study of policy toward Jews throughout empire. Finds general Roman tolerance for Judaism, dislike of proselytism, and fear of Jewish nationalism in Judaea. [CMW]

7.305 Ronald Syme. *Roman papers.* 7 vols. E. Badian (vols. 1–2) and Anthony R. Birley (vols. 3–7), eds. New York: Oxford University Press, 1979–91. ISBN 0-19-814367-2 (set), 0-19-814839-9 (v. 3), 0-19-814873-9 (v. 4), 0-19-814885-2 (v. 5), 0-19-814494-6 (v. 6), 0-19-814490-3 (v. 7). ▸ Over two hundred collected papers, largely prosopographical, discussing Pliny, Tacitus, and their contemporaries; Augustan aristocracy; Antonine age; major Latin authors; Spain, Balkans and East, and much more. Small part of life's work of one of most influential Roman historians of this century. [CMW]

7.306 Richard J. A. Talbert. *The Senate of imperial Rome.* Princeton: Princeton University Press, 1984. ISBN 0-691-05400-2. ▸ Discusses composition, procedure, functions of Senate, arguing senators were conscientious and hardworking and that Senate handled much complex business in partnership with emperor. Essential work of reference. [CMW]

7.307 Kenneth Wellesley. *The long year, AD 69.* 2d ed. Bristol: Bristol Classical, 1989. ISBN 1-85399-049-3 (cl), 1-85399-050-7 (pbk). ▸ Straightforward narrative of political and military events, largely but not uncritically based on Tacitus. Good grasp of geographical factors. [CMW]

7.308 Zvi Yavetz. *Plebs and princeps.* 1969 ed. New Brunswick, N.J.: Transaction, 1988. ISBN 0-88738-154-5. ▸ Study of how Julio-Claudian emperors sought support of urban plebs by economic measures, such as grain supply, entertainments, largesse, and well-advertised clemency. [CMW]

The Army and the Frontiers

7.309 John C. Barrett, Andrew P. Fitzpatrick, and Lesley Macinnes, eds. *Barbarians and Romans in North-West Europe from the later republic to late antiquity.* Oxford: British Archaeological Reports, 1989. (British Archaeological Reports international series, 471.) ISBN 0-86054-603-9. ▸ Thirteen papers seeking to establish common ground between prehistorians and Romanists. Treats concepts of acculturation, romanization, etc., and argues "barbarism" found inside as well as outside empire. [CMW]

7.310 Eric Birley. *The Roman army: papers, 1929–1986.* Amsterdam: Gieben, 1988. ISBN 90-5063-007-3. ▸ Forty-five papers by doyen of Roman army and frontier studies; major contributions on senatorial, equestrian, and centurions' careers. [CMW]

7.311 Alan K. Bowman and J. David Thomas. *Vindolanda: the Latin writing tablets.* 1983 ed. Gloucester, Mass.: Sutton, 1984. ISBN 0-86299-118-8 (pbk). ▸ Definitive publication of first lot of writing tablets from important deposit in pre-Hadrianic fort at Vindolanda, including official documents and private letters; more to follow. [CMW]

7.312 J. B. Campbell. *The emperor and the Roman army, 31 BC–AD 235.* New York: Oxford University Press, 1984. ISBN 0-19-814834-8. ▸ Discussion of means by which emperor kept all-important support of army. Treats military career, soldiers' legal status, military law, military commands, and role of army in politics. [CMW]

7.313 Roy W. Davies. *Service in the Roman army*. David J. Breeze and Valerie A. Maxfield, eds. New York: Columbia University Press, 1989. ISBN 0-231-06992-8. ‣ Ten valuable papers on disparate topics, including soldier's daily life, training grounds and practice camps, remounts, diet, and medical service. [CMW]

7.314 Karen R. Dixon and Pat Southern. *The Roman cavalry: from the first to the third century A.D.* London: Batsford, 1992. ISBN 0-7134-6396-1. ‣ Intelligent study of organization, training, employment, and daily routine of Roman cavalry units. [CMW]

7.315 Brian Dobson and David J. Breeze. *Roman officers and frontiers*. Stuttgart: Steiner, 1993. ISBN 3-515-06181-9. ‣ Thirteen essential papers on legionary organization and career structures, especially of centurionate, stressing pay, prospects, and social mobility, followed by twenty-five papers on northern frontiers of Britain. [CMW]

7.316 Robert O. Fink. *Roman military records on papyrus*. Cleveland: Press of Case Western Reserve University for American Philological Association, 1971. (American Philological Association, Monographs, 26.) ISBN 0-8295-0174-6. ‣ Definitive publication of military records on papyri from Dura-Europus and other sites, giving unrivaled insight into Roman military organization at unit level. [CMW]

7.317 Ann Hyland. *Equus: the horse in the Roman world*. New Haven: Yale University Press, 1990. ISBN 0-300-04770-3. ‣ Study by professional horsewoman of Roman horse breeding and management, veterinary medicine, cavalry horses and their care, training, and equipment. Additional chapters on circus, daily life, and transport animals. [CMW]

7.318 Benjamin Isaac. *The limits of empire: the Roman army in the East*. 2d ed. New York: Oxford University Press, 1992. ISBN 0-19-814926-3 (pbk). ‣ Concludes Roman policy in East generally expansionist; army's prime function internal security rather than frontier defense. Finds no "grand strategy" (cf. Luttwak 7.322), just ad hoc decisions based on short-term interests. [CMW]

7.319 Anne Johnson. *Römische Kastelle des ersten und zweiten Jahrhunderts n. Chr. in Britannien und in den germanischen Provinzen des Römerreiches*. Dietwulf Baatz, ed. Gabriele Schulte-Holtey, trans. Mainz: von Zabern, 1987. ISBN 3-8053-0868-X. ‣ Compendium of archaeological evidence for Roman forts in early empire in Britain and Germany. Considerably updated and enlarged from original English edition, *Roman Forts* (1983). [CMW]

7.320 David L. Kennedy and Derrick Riley. *Rome's desert frontier from the air*. Austin: University of Texas Press, 1990. ISBN 0-292-77045-6. ‣ Spectacular air photographs, largely from the 1920s and 1930s, showing frontier installations. Commentary, history of research, and sketch of frontier history. [CMW]

7.321 Frank A. Lepper and Sheppard S. Frere, eds. *Trajan's Column: a new edition of the Cichorius plates*. Wolfboro, N.H.: Sutton, 1988. ISBN 0-86299-467-5. ‣ Comprehensive, commonsense analysis, scene by scene, of reliefs, with detailed notes on controversial points. Indispensable for understanding column and its contribution to Roman history and Roman army studies. [CMW]

7.322 Edward N. Luttwak. *The grand strategy of the Roman empire: from the first century AD to the third*. 1976 ed. Baltimore: Johns Hopkins University Press, 1977. ISBN 0-8018-1863-X (cl), 0-8018-2158-4 (pbk). ‣ Stimulating reappraisal of Roman strategy at different periods by contemporary strategic analyst in light of NATO doctrine. Based on secondary sources; some factual errors but cannot be ignored. [CMW]

7.323 J. C. Mann. *Legionary recruitment and veteran settlement during the principate*. M. M. Roxan, ed. London: University of London, Institute of Archaeology, 1983. (Institute of Archaeology, Occasional publications, 7.) ISBN 0-905853-11-3. ‣ Epigraphic evidence for geographical origin of recruits from late republic to Diocletian, presented in tabular form with competent analyses by province and period. [CMW]

7.324 Valerie A. Maxfield et al. "The frontiers." In *The Roman world*. John Wacher, ed., vol. 1, pp. 139–325. London: Routledge & Kegan Paul, 1987. ISBN 0-7102-0894-4. ‣ Best general account in English of Roman frontier systems; four chapters on mainland Europe, Britain, Africa, and East. Extensive bibliography including complete list of frontier congresses (see Maxfield and Dobson, eds. 7.325). [CMW]

7.325 Valerie A. Maxfield and Michael J. Dobson, eds. *Roman frontier studies, 1989: proceedings of the twenty-fifth International Congress of Roman Frontier Studies*. Exeter: University of Exeter Press, 1991. ISBN 0-85989-364-2. ‣ One hundred papers from most recent Roman frontier congress covering entire empire and bearing witness to range and vitality of current research topics in frontier studies. [CMW]

7.326 T. B. Mitford. "Cappadocia and Armenia Minor: the historical setting of the *limes*." *Aufstieg und Niedergang der römischen Welt*, Series 2: *Principat*, 7.2 (1980) 1169–1228. ISBN 3-11-008015-X. ‣ Results of personal exploration and field survey in Roman frontier zone. Invaluable contribution in area still so little known. [CMW]

7.327 S. Thomas Parker. *Romans and Saracens: a history of the Arabian frontier*. Philadephia: American Schools of Oriental Research; distributed by Eisenbrauns, 1986. (American Schools of Oriental Research dissertation series, 6.) ISBN 0-89757-106-1. ‣ Convenient survey of earlier scholarship and visible remains along Arabian sector of Roman frontier. [CMW]

7.328 H. Russell Robinson. *The armour of imperial Rome*. New York: Scribner's, 1975. ISBN 0-684-13956-1. ‣ Evolution and typology of helmets to third century CE; evidence for body armor, greaves, and horse armor. Reconstructions by author; excellent photographs. [CMW]

7.329 D. B. Saddington. *The development of the Roman auxiliary forces from Caesar to Vespasian (49 BC–AD 79)*. Harare: University of Zimbabwe, 1982. ISBN 0-86924-078-1 (pbk). ‣ History of evolution of auxiliary regiments into permanent units of Roman army, based largely on literary sources, supplemented by epigraphy. [CMW]

7.330 G. R. Watson. *The Roman soldier*. 1969 ed. Ithaca, N.Y.: Cornell University Press, 1985. ISBN 0-8014-0519-X (cl), 0-8014-9312-9 (pbk). ‣ Well-documented account of recruitment, training, and conditions of service, covering all military units, *vigiles* (police force), urban cohorts, and fleet. [CMW]

7.331 Graham Webster. *The Roman imperial army of the first and second centuries AD*. 3d ed. Totowa, N.J.: Barnes & Noble, 1985. ISBN 0-389-20590-7. ‣ Still best general account of imperial army in English; covers composition, installations, mode of operation, and peacetime activities. Heavily dependent on evidence from Britain and other western provinces. [CMW]

Economy, Production, and Trade

7.332 *Amphores romaines et histoire économique, dix ans de recherches: actes du colloque de Sienne (22–24 mai 1986)/organisé par l'Università degli Studi di Siena*. Rome: École Française de Rome, 1989. (Collection de l'École Française de Rome, 114.) ISBN 2-7283-0180-8, ISSN 0223-5099. ‣ Indispensable collection of roughly twenty papers, plus shorter communications, covering virtually all topics in expanding field of Roman amphora studies, especially informative on production and trade. [CMW]

7.333 P. A. Brunt. "Free labour and public works." *Journal of Roman studies* 70 (1980) 81–100. ISSN 0075-4358. ▸ Demonstrates that casual free labor was important in building and other unskilled employments at Rome and that such work was not usually done by slaves. [CMW]

7.334 A. Carandini. "Columella's vineyard and the rationality of the Roman economy." *Opus* 2.1 (1983) 177–204. ISSN 0392-4645. ▸ Argues Columella's calculations of income obtainable from vineyard show concern to maximize profit and disprove Finley's view (7.340) that considerations of efficiency, productivity, and profitability were unimportant. [CMW]

7.335 Robert I. Curtis. *Garum and salsamenta: production and commerce in materia medica.* Leiden: Brill, 1991. ISBN 90-04-09423-7. ▸ Fascinating account of production and commerce in fish sauces and salt fish products, medicinal and dietary uses, and modern parallels. Based largely on archaeological and epigraphic evidence. [CMW]

7.336 John H. D'Arms and E. C. Kopff, eds. *The seaborne commerce of ancient Rome: studies in archaeology and history.* Rome: American Academy in Rome, 1980. (Memoirs of the American Academy in Rome, 36.) ▸ Twenty-four articles in English, French, and Italian on aspects of trade by sea, including slave trade, grain, wine, oil, marble, and timber. Also discusses dock facilities and administration, customs, loans, etc. [CMW]

7.337 Richard Duncan-Jones. *The economy of the Roman empire: quantitative studies.* 2d ed. Cambridge: Cambridge University Press, 1982. ISBN 0-521-24970-8 (cl), 0-521-28793-6 (pbk). ▸ Study of prices, wages, and population in Roman empire. Particularly valuable for collation of epigraphic and other data from Italy and Africa. [CMW]

7.338 Richard Duncan-Jones. *Structure and scale in the Roman economy.* Cambridge: Cambridge University Press, 1990. ISBN 0-521-35477-3. ▸ Papers on speed of communications in Roman world, demography and life expectancy, commodity prices, and changes in economy. Imperial taxation not to be seen as positive commercial stimulus. [CMW]

7.339 Donald W. Engels. *Roman Corinth: an alternative model for the classical city.* Chicago: University of Chicago Press, 1990. ISBN 0-226-20870-2. ▸ Rejects Finley's consumer-city theory (7.340), arguing that Corinth, far from being parasitical, offered wide range of goods and services in exchange for agricultural surpluses. [CMW]

7.340 M. I. Finley. *The ancient economy.* 2d ed. Berkeley: University of California Press, 1985. ISBN 0-520-05452-0 (pbk). ▸ Enormously provocative account postulating minimalist view of ancient economy: small self-sufficient units, little interregional trade, cities parasitical, and taxation regressive. Less important in itself than as trigger for discussion. [CMW]

7.341 M. I. Finley, ed. *Studies in Roman property by the Cambridge University Research Seminar in Ancient History.* Cambridge: Cambridge University Press, 1976. ISBN 0-521-21115-8. ▸ Eight papers on size of holdings, imperial estates, sale and tenancy law, property in Cicero, urban property investment, and depopulation of countryside. [CMW]

7.342 Peter Garnsey, Keith Hopkins, and C. R. Whittaker, eds. *Trade in the ancient economy.* Berkeley: University of California Press, 1983. ISBN 0-520-04803-2. ▸ Excellent introduction setting out conflicting views of ancient economy (Hopkins), plus twelve further articles. Valuable discussion of urban elites' role in business (Pleket). [CMW]

7.343 Peter Garnsey and Richard P. Saller. *The Roman empire:* *economy, society, and culture.* Berkeley: University of California Press, 1987. ISBN 0-520-06066-0 (cl), 0-520-06067-9 (pbk). ▸ Excellent summary of main preoccupations of recent research in social and economic history. Argues for underdeveloped economy, primacy of agriculture, and society based on status hierarchy. [CMW]

7.344 Kevin Greene. *The archaeology of the Roman economy.* 1986 ed. Berkeley: University of California Press, 1990. ISBN 0-520-05915-8 (cl, 1986), 0-520-07401-7 (pbk). ▸ Discussion of importance of archaeology in illustrating means of transport, role of money, agricultural production, and production and marketing in metal, stone, and pottery. [CMW]

7.345 Heinz Heinen, ed. *Die Geschichte des Altertums im Spiegel der sowjetischen Forschung.* Darmstadt: Wissenschaftliche Buchgesellschaft, 1980. ISBN 3-534-07314-2. ▸ Particularly important articles by Shtaerman on late republic and early empire, and by Heinen on late antiquity. Valuable for understanding Marxist interpretation of history and economy, especially emphasis on slavery. [CMW]

7.346 Keith Hopkins. "Taxes and trade in the Roman empire (200 BC–AD 400)." *Journal of Roman studies* 70 (1980) 101–25. ISSN 0075-4358. ▸ Controversial article asserting that need to pay taxes in money stimulated trade (see countervailing arguments in Duncan-Jones 7.338). Interregional trade increased considerably between 200 BCE and 200 CE, becoming integrated into single empire-wide system. [CMW]

7.347 Willem Jongman. *The economy and society of Pompeii.* 1988 ed. Amsterdam: Gieben, 1991. ISBN 90-70265-24-9. ▸ Extreme minimalizing account of economy of Pompeii and surrounding area, starting *a priori* from Finley's consumer-city hypothesis (7.340); virtually denies existence of wine and wool trade. Highly controversial. [CMW]

7.348 A. Kirschenbaum. *Sons, slaves, and freedmen in Roman commerce.* Washington, D.C.: Catholic University of America Press, 1987. ISBN 0-8132-0644-8. ▸ Study of role in law and society of subordinate members of Roman *familia* in facilitating legal and commercial transactions. [CMW]

7.349 D. J. Mattingly. "Oil for export? A comparison of Libyan, Spanish, and Tunisian olive oil production in the Roman empire." *Journal of Roman archaeology* 1 (1988) 33–56. ISSN 1047-7594. ▸ Important study of oil production and oil trade in Roman period, arguing for intensive, organized production of oil for export and evidence for considerable long-distance trade. [CMW]

7.350 Anna Marguerite McCann et al., eds. *The Roman port and fishery of Cosa: a center of ancient trade.* Princeton: Princeton University Press, 1987. ISBN 0-691-03581-4. ▸ Archaeological report, important for ancient ports and fishing. Introduction with useful bibliography of port studies; catalog of amphoras and their evidence for trade. [CMW]

7.351 Peter Ørsted. *Roman imperial economy and romanization: a study in Roman imperial administration and the public-lease system in the Danubian provinces from the first to the third century AD.* David Gress-Wright, trans. Copenhagen: Museum Tusculanum Press, 1985. ISBN 87-88073-81-5 (cl), 87-88073-97-1 (pbk). ▸ Ambitious, controversial study of public-lease system in provinces, especially for mining and customs duties, and of use of profits for benefactions to cities (euergetism). [CMW]

7.352 A. J. Parker. *Ancient shipwrecks of the Mediterranean and the Roman provinces.* Oxford: British Archaeological Reports, 1992. (British Archaeological Reports international series, 580.) ISBN 0-86054-736-1. ▸ Introduction and catalog of shipwrecks from ca. 1500 BCE to ca. 1500 CE. Extremely useful work of reference for those interested in evidence provided by underwater archaeology, especially for trade and exports. [CMW]

7.353 D.P.S. Peacock and D. F. Williams. *Amphorae and the Roman economy: an introductory guide.* 1986 ed. London: Longman, 1991. ISBN 0-582-49304-8 (cl, 1986), 0-582-06555-0 (pbk). ▸ Part 1 discusses role of amphoras in Roman trade and knowledge to be derived from amphora studies (7.332); part 2 offers classification of more common amphora types. [CMW]

7.354 Avner Raban, ed. *Harbour archaeology: proceedings of the first international workshop on ancient Mediterranean harbours, Caesarea Maritima, 24–28.6.83.* Oxford: British Archaeological Reports, 1985. (British Archaeological Reports international series, 257.) ISBN 0-86054-328-5 (pbk). ▸ Papers on various harbor sites, with especially valuable survey by Rickman, stressing need for research to relate harbors to supply routes, hinterland, etc. [CMW]

7.355 Manfred G. Raschke. "New studies in Roman commerce with the East." *Aufstieg und Niedergang der römischen Welt,* Series 2: *Principat,* 9.2 (1978) 604–1378. ISBN 3-11-007175-4. ▸ Account of Roman trade with India and China, especially in silk and spices. Invaluable for massive documentation (77 pages of text; 563 pages of notes and bibliography). [CMW]

7.356 John Rich and Andrew Wallace-Hadrill, eds. *City and country in the ancient world.* London: Routledge, 1991. ISBN 0-415-01974-5. ▸ Important collection; twelve papers for and against concept of consumer-city (Finley 7.340); case against most strongly argued by Wallace-Hadrill, "Elites and Trade in the Roman Town." [CMW]

7.357 M. Rostovtzeff. *The social and economic history of the Roman empire.* Corr. 1957 2d ed. 2 vols. P. M. Fraser, ed. Oxford: Clarendon, 1979. ISBN 0-19-814231-5. ▸ Classic work (first published 1926) which launched modern study of Roman economy and society and pioneered integration of evidence from different disciplines. Views on class conflict and ancient bourgeoisie outmoded. [CMW]

7.358 Daniel Sperber. *Roman Palestine, 200–400: money and prices.* 2d ed. Ramat-Gan, Israel: Bar-Ilan University Press, 1991. ISBN 965-226-147-5. ▸ Study of prices and wages in Roman Palestine, based on rabbinic literature; valuable supplement to Duncan-Jones 7.337. [CMW]

7.359 André Tchernia. *Le vin de l'Italie romaine: essai d'histoire économique d'après les amphores.* Rome: École Française de Rome, 1986. (Bibliothèque des Écoles Françaises d'Athènes et de Rome, 261.) ISBN 2-7283-0106-9. ▸ Best account in any language of Italian wine production and wine trade. [CMW]

7.360 Paul Veyne. *Bread and circuses: historical sociology and political pluralism.* 1990 ed. Brian Pearce, trans. London: Penguin, 1992. ISBN 0-14-012485-3. ▸ History of social and economic pressures in ancient city that led rich to spend their money on public benefactions (euergetism) in return for honor and prestige. Abridged translation of *Le pain et le cirque* (1976). [CMW]

7.361 Friedrich Vittinghoff, ed. *Europäische Wirtschafts- und Sozialgeschichte in der römischen Kaiserzeit.* Vol. 1 of *Handbuch der europäischen Wirtschafts- und Sozialgeschichte.* Wolfram Fischer et al., eds. Stuttgart: Klett-Cotta, 1990. ISBN 3-12-904730-1. ▸ Important studies of Roman economy (Pleket) and society (Vittinghoff), followed by studies of individual provinces and regions by leading specialists. Especially important contribution by Pleket arguing for maximalist view of economy. [CMW]

SEE ALSO
6.504 Peter Garnsey, ed. *Non-slave labour in the Greco-Roman world.*

Agriculture and the Countryside

7.362 Shimon Applebaum. "Roman Britain." In *The agrarian history of England and Wales.* H.P.R. Finberg, ed., vol. 1.2, pp.

3–277. London: Cambridge University Press, 1972. ISBN 0-521-08423-7. ▸ Account of Romano-British agriculture covering soils, implements, crops, animals, and buildings and tracing change through time. Model of lucidity; still invaluable, although archaeological evidence dated. [CMW]

7.363 Graeme Barker and John Lloyd, eds. *Roman landscapes: archaeological survey in the Mediterranean region.* London: British School at Rome, 1991. (Archaeological monographs of the British School at Rome, 2.) ISBN 0-904152-16-2. ▸ Twenty-four papers, beginning with one on methodologies, that exemplify enormous contribution in recent years of archaeological survey to our knowledge of Mediterranean world. [CMW]

7.364 Joan M. Frayn. *Sheep-rearing and the wool trade in Italy during the Roman period.* Liverpool: Cairns, 1984. (ARCA, Classical and medieval texts, Papers and monographs, 15.) ISBN 0-905205-22-7. ▸ Story of sheep and shepherds from wide range of ancient evidence and much comparative material. Discusses transhumance, ranching, and wool trade. [CMW]

7.365 Peter Garnsey and C. R. Whittaker, eds. *Trade and famine in classical antiquity.* Cambridge: Cambridge Philological Society, 1983. (Cambridge Philological Society, Supplementary, 8.) ISBN 0-906014-04-2. ▸ Eleven papers including discussions of famine in Rome, pottery as index of trade, role of army, maritime trade in staple commodities, and trade in frontier zones. [CMW]

7.366 Dennis P. Kehoe. *The economics of agriculture on Roman imperial estates in North Africa.* Göttingen: Vandenhoeck & Ruprecht, 1988. (Hypomnemata, 89.) ISBN 3-525-25188-2. ▸ Detailed study of conditions on imperial estates in Bagradas valley, utilizing six famous inscriptions from that area referring to *coloni* ("tenant farmers"); includes translation of and commentary on each inscription. [CMW]

7.367 Dennis P. Kehoe. *Management and investment on estates in Roman Egypt during the early empire.* Bonn: Habelt, 1992. ISBN 3-7749-2532-1. ▸ Analysis of papyrological evidence for estates in Egypt, concluding owners sought financial security with minimum outlay. [CMW]

7.368 Tamara Lewit. *Agricultural production in the Roman economy, AD 200–400.* Oxford: British Archaeological Reports, 1991. (British Archaeological Reports international series, 568.) ISBN 0-86054-717-5. ▸ Survey, primarily of archaeological evidence from western provinces, discounting theory of agricultural crisis in third and fourth centuries. No evidence for economic decline, abandonment of land, or end of long-distance trade. [CMW]

7.369 P. W. de Neeve. *Colonus: private farm-tenancy in Roman Italy during the republic and the early principate.* Amsterdam: Gieben, 1984. ISBN 90-70265-15-X. ▸ Valuable contribution to discussion on meaning of *colonus,* more ambiguous than some scholars admit. Need not mean "tenant"; but author's own conclusions excessively schematic. [CMW]

7.370 John Percival. *The Roman villa: an historical introduction.* Berkeley: University of California Press, 1976. ISBN 0-520-03233-0. ▸ Pioneering study of architecture and role of villas in western provinces of empire. [CMW]

7.371 T. W. Potter. *The changing landscape of South Etruria.* New York: St. Martin's, 1979. ISBN 0-312-12953-X. ▸ Study of changing settlement patterns north of Rome, prehistory to 1300 CE, based largely on survey and excavation since 1950s. Shows settlement in early empire more dense than previously supposed. Rare study of transition from antique to medieval landscape. [CMW/FLC]

7.372 Dominic Rathbone. *Economic rationalism and rural society in third-century AD Egypt: the Heroninos archive and the Appianus estate.* Cambridge: Cambridge University Press, 1991. ISBN 0-521-40149-6. ▸ Extensive archive of accounts and letters from large estate. Discusses questions of status, production, marketing, and accounting systems, revealing sophisticated organization that challenges "primitive" ideas of ancient economic practice. [CMW]

7.373 Brent D. Shaw. "Fear and loathing: the nomad menace and Roman Africa." In *L'Afrique romaine: les conférences Vanier, 1980/Roman Africa: the Vanier lectures, 1980.* Colin M. Wells, ed., pp. 29–50. Ottawa: University of Ottawa Press, 1982. ISBN 2-7603-4690-0. ‣ Study suggesting that traditional view of nomads and settled cultivators as natural enemies is false; symbiotic relationship exists in which nomadic labor is essential. [CMW]

7.374 Brent D. Shaw. "Rural markets in North Africa and the political economy of the Roman empire." *Antiquités africaines* 17 (1981) 37–84. ISSN 0066-4871. ‣ Study of periodic markets in North Africa, their pre-Roman antecedents, and Roman control and taxation mechanisms. Rural and urban markets not integrated to form simple market system. [CMW]

7.375 K. D. White. "Food requirements and food supplies in classical times in relation to the diet of the various classes." *Progress in food and nutrition science* 2.4 (1976) 143–91. ISSN 0306-0632. ‣ Study of ancient diet, especially for poorer classes. Emphasizes importance of bread as basic foodstuff. [CMW]

7.376 C. R. Whittaker. "Land and labour in North Africa." *Klio* 60.2 (1978) 331–62. ISSN 0075-6334. ‣ Influential article on importance of nomads and semi-nomads as source of seasonal labor. [CMW]

7.377 C. R. Whittaker, ed. *Pastoral economies in classical antiquity.* Cambridge: Cambridge Philological Society, 1988. (Proceedings of the Cambridge Philological Society, Supplementary, 14.) ISBN 0-906014-13-1 (pbk), ISSN 0068-6735. ‣ Eleven papers and three additional communications on pastoralism, animal husbandry, transhumance, etc., agreeing on their importance but revealing notable differences of definition and interpretation. [CMW]

SEE ALSO
    6.543 Russell Meiggs. *Trees and timber in the ancient Mediterranean world.*

Society

7.378 J.P.V.D. Balsdon. *Life and leisure in ancient Rome.* Rev. ed. London: Bodley Head, 1974. ‣ Best account of everyday life in Rome. Highly readable and sadly underestimated; avoids excessive and sensational dependence on Juvenal and Martial. [CMW]

7.379 Keith R. Bradley. *Slaves and masters in the Roman empire: a study in social control.* 1984 ed. New York: Oxford University Press, 1987. ISBN 0-19-520607-X. ‣ Excellent, up-to-date introduction to system of slavery during empire. Treats slave family, manumission, and rewards and punishments. Important appendixes on details of interpretation. [CMW]

7.380 Stephen L. Dyson. *Community and society in Roman Italy.* Baltimore: Johns Hopkins University Press, 1992. ISBN 0-8018-4175-5. ‣ History of small rural communities and their place in local economies. Small-town life and Italian countryside. Extensive bibliography. [CMW]

7.381 M. I. Finley, ed. *Classical slavery.* Totowa, N.J.: Cass, 1987. ISBN 0-7146-3320-8. ‣ Contains important papers on slave breeding (Bradley), impact of slavery on Roman family (Saller), and slaves, *coloni*, and serfdom in late antiquity (Whittaker). [CMW]

7.382 Peter Garnsey. *Social status and legal privilege in the Roman empire.* Oxford: Clarendon, 1970. ISBN 0-19-825194-7. ‣ Com-

prehensive study of forms of legal privilege and inequality before the law, set in both juridical and social context. [CMW]

7.383 Gustav Hermansen. *Ostia: aspects of Roman city life.* Edmonton: University of Alberta Press, 1982. ISBN 0-88864-066-8 (cl), 0-88864-072-2 (pbk). ‣ Important study of layout of Roman apartment buildings, with chapters on taverns and their social role, guilds, fires and fire protection, and grain storage in Ostian warehouses. [CMW]

7.384 Sandra R. Joshel. *Work, identity, and legal status at Rome: a study of the occupational inscriptions.* Norman: University of Oklahoma Press, 1992. ISBN 0-8061-2413-X (cl), 0-8061-2444-X (pbk). ‣ Study of nearly 1,500 inscriptions in which people mention their work; seeks to use feminist and ethnographic methodologies. Argues work important to slaves and ex-slaves in defining their identity. [CMW]

7.385 Ramsay MacMullen. *Changes in the Roman empire: essays in the ordinary.* Princeton: Princeton University Press, 1990. ISBN 0-691-03601-2. ‣ Twenty-four wide-ranging, original papers, full of insight, provocative and often controversial, on ancient mentalities and other topics. Major contribution to Roman social history. [CMW]

7.386 Ramsay MacMullen. *Roman social relations, 50 BC to AD 284.* New Haven: Yale University Press, 1974. ISBN 0-300-01697-2. ‣ Essay on relationships between individuals and social groups, focusing on lower classes and stressing importance of status and patronage. [CMW]

7.387 Russell Meiggs. *Roman Ostia.* 1973 2d ed. Oxford: Clarendon, 1985. ISBN 0-19-814810-0. ‣ Magisterial study of history, buildings, economy, and life of Ostia; perhaps no other city in Roman world so comprehensively covered in single volume. [CMW]

7.388 Günter Neumann and Jürgen Untermann, eds. *Die Sprachen im römischen Reich der Kaiserzeit: Kolloquium vom 8. bis 10. April 1974.* Cologne and Bonn: Rheinland and Habelt, 1980. (*Bonner Jahrbücher*, Beiheft, 40.) ISBN 3-7927-0431-5. ‣ Seventeen invaluable articles, arranged by geographic region, on survival of languages other than Greek or Latin and on provincial dialects of Latin. [CMW]

7.389 Richard P. Saller. *Personal patronage under the early empire.* Cambridge: Cambridge University Press, 1982. ISBN 0-521-23300-3. ‣ Study of overwhelming importance of patronage in Roman politics and society to third century, with special study of North Africa and comparative material from China. [CMW]

7.390 A. Scobie. "Slums, sanitation, and mortality in the Roman world." *Klio* 68.2 (1986) 399–433. ISSN 0075-6334. ‣ Important contribution to understanding life of urban poor, living at or below subsistence level, with parallels from Third World conditions today. [CMW]

7.391 A. N. Sherwin-White. *Racial prejudice in imperial Rome.* Cambridge: Cambridge University Press, 1970. ISBN 0-521-06438-4. ‣ Brief account documenting "racial" prejudice against Celts and Germans and cultural hostility toward Greeks and Jews; "blacks," "Africans," "Ethiopians" do not even appear in index. [CMW]

7.392 A. N. Sherwin-White. *Roman society and Roman law in the New Testament.* 1963 ed. Grand Rapids: Baker Book House, 1978. ISBN 0-8010-8148-3. ‣ Study of Roman legal and administrative practice and relevance to narrative of Gospels and Acts. Value of latter for insight into how empire appeared to underprivileged provincials. [CMW]

7.393 Frank M. Snowden, Jr. *Before color prejudice: the ancient view of blacks.* 1983 ed. Cambridge, Mass.: Harvard University Press, 1991. ISBN 0-674-06380-5 (cl, 1983), 0-674-06381-3 (pbk).

▸ History of blacks in Mediterranean society. Argues blacks were physically and culturally assimilated; there was no theory of black inferiority, and color prejudice as in contemporary world was unknown. [CMW]

7.394 John E. Stambaugh. *The ancient Roman city.* Baltimore: Johns Hopkins University Press, 1988. ISBN 0-8018-3574-7 (cl), 0-8018-3692-1 (pbk). ▸ Chronological study of Rome's development to third century. Study of specific topics such as population, services, housing, commerce, religion, and daily life. Comparisons with Cosa, Pompeii, Ostia, Arles, and Timgad. [CMW]

7.395 Lloyd A. Thompson. *Romans and blacks.* Norman: University of Oklahoma Press, 1989. ISBN 0-8061-2201-3. ▸ Study of Roman attitudes to blacks arguing that reaction to physical characteristics was primarily aesthetic; people of black or partially black descent were not socially defined as inferior. [CMW]

7.396 Susan Treggiari. "Jobs in the household of Livia." *Papers of the British School at Rome* 43 (1975) 48–77. ISSN 0068-2462. ▸ Analysis of jobs of slaves and ex-slaves in imperial household as recorded on inscriptions in *columbarium* (burial-place), with suggestive eighteenth- and nineteenth-century parallels. [CMW]

7.397 Paul Veyne, ed. *From pagan Rome to Byzantium.* Vol. 1 of *A history of private life.* Philippe Ariès and Georges Duby, eds. Arthur Goldhammer, trans. Cambridge, Mass.: Belknap, 1987. ISBN 0-674-39975-7 (v. 1). ▸ Valuable discussions of family structures and daily life (Veyne); of changed mentalities of late antiquity (Brown); and of private life and domestic architecture in Roman Africa (Thébert). [CMW]

7.398 Georges Ville. *La gladiature en occident des origines à la mort de Domitien.* Rome: École Française de Rome, 1981. (Bibliothèque des Écoles Françaises d'Athènes et de Rome, 245.) ISBN 2-7283-0010-0. ▸ Comprehensive account; controversial but convincing argument for Oscan-Samnite origin of gladiatorial games. Detailed description of performances. [CMW]

7.399 Andrew Wallace-Hadrill. "The social structure of the Roman house." *Papers of the British School at Rome* 56 (1988) 43–97. ISSN 0068-2462. ▸ Pioneering study of Roman houses showing layout and decoration determined by public nature of domestic life and by absence of separate quarters for women. [CMW]

7.400 P.R.C. Weaver. *Familia Caesaris: a social study of the emperor's freedmen and slaves.* Cambridge: Cambridge University Press, 1972. ISBN 0-521-08340-0. ▸ Fundamental study of imperial household, based on over 4,000 inscriptions, discussing status differentiation, slave families, employment patterns, and social mobility. [CMW]

SEE ALSO
    4.669 Ralph Jackson. *Doctors and diseases in the Roman empire.*
    4.675 John Scarborough. *Roman medicine.*

Intellectual Life: Literature, Philosophy, and Education

7.401 Glen W. Bowersock. *Greek sophists in the Roman empire.* Oxford: Clarendon, 1969. ISBN 0-19-814279-X. ▸ Analysis of Greek culture in second and third centuries and so-called Second Sophistic; wealth, influence, and political role of Sophists and their relations with imperial court and Roman aristocracy. [CMW]

7.402 P. A. Brunt. "Stoicism and the principate." *Papers of the British School at Rome* 43 (1975) 7–35. ISSN 0068-2462. ▸ Fundamental discussion of Stoicism and public life at Rome; Stoics' principles did not favor any particular form of government, but encouraged individuals to fulfill their duty, whatever their station. [CMW]

7.403 Jasper Griffin. *Latin poets and Roman life.* 1985 ed. Chapel Hill: University of North Carolina Press, 1986. ISBN 0-8078-

1682-5. ▸ Ten papers on Augustan poetry and relationship between artistic convention and real life. Important contribution to understanding intellectual and social history of period. [CMW]

7.404 F. H. Sandbach. *The Stoics.* 2d ed. Bristol: Bristol Classical, 1989. ISBN 1-85399-143-0 (cl), 1-85399-106-6 (pbk). ▸ Standard account of Stoic theory and practice. Brief chapter on Stoics and politics. [CMW]

7.405 J. P. Sullivan. *Literature and politics in the age of Nero.* Ithaca, N.Y.: Cornell University Press, 1985. ISBN 0-8014-1740-6. ▸ Study of influence of patronage and politics on literature of Nero's reign, situating that literature firmly in its historical and intellectual context. [CMW]

7.406 A. J. Woodman and David West, eds. *Poetry and politics in the age of Augustus.* Cambridge: Cambridge University Press, 1984. ISBN 0-521-24553-2. ▸ Eight papers and epilogue analyzing different poems and passages in light of their political commitment. Demonstrates relationship between poetry and politics and between poetic convention and life. [CMW]

Historians and Historiography

7.407 Timothy David Barnes. *Tertullian: a historical and literary study.* 1971 ed. New York: Oxford University Press, 1985. ISBN 0-19-814362-1. ▸ Incisive, now standard account of Tertullian's writings and ideas in historical context, especially that of Christian society in Africa and of rhetorical education and the Christian Sophist. [CMW]

7.408 Edward Champlin. *Fronto and Antonine Rome.* Cambridge, Mass.: Harvard University Press, 1980. ISBN 0-674-32668-7. ▸ Account of family, education, and career of consul and tutor to Emperor Marcus Aurelius, and of Antonine society as revealed in his letters. [CMW]

7.409 Louis H. Feldman. *Josephus and modern scholarship (1937–1980).* Berlin: de Gruyter, 1984. ISBN 3-11-008138-5. ▸ Mammoth survey, over 1,000 pages, of work on Josephus and on topics and events covered by him. Discusses Jewish sects, early Christianity, relevant archaeological sites, and Josephus's influence. [CMW]

7.410 C. P. Jones. *Plutarch and Rome.* Corr. 1971 ed. Oxford: Clarendon, 1972. ISBN 0-19-814363-X. ▸ Study of Plutarch's career, circle in which he moved, and attitude toward Rome revealed in his writings. [CMW]

7.411 C. P. Jones. *The Roman world of Dio Chrysostom.* Cambridge, Mass.: Harvard University Press, 1978. ISBN 0-674-77915-0. ▸ Study of Dio's oratory and career and light they throw on Greek cities of period. Argues Dio accepted Rome's preeminence but without enthusiasm. [CMW]

7.412 Ronald Martin. *Tacitus.* Berkeley: University of California Press, 1981. ISBN 0-520-04427-4. ▸ Best general introduction to Tacitus's career and writings, with emphasis on what constitutes his greatness as historian. [CMW]

7.413 Fergus Millar. *A study of Cassius Dio.* Oxford: Clarendon, 1964. ▸ Study of career, personality, and opinions of Cassius Dio and their impact on his history, with particular stress on history of his own time. [CMW]

7.414 Tessa Rajak. *Josephus: the historian and his society.* 1983 ed. Philadelphia: Fortress, 1984. ISBN 0-8006-0717-1. ▸ Study of Josephus and his work, in context of his own career and of his awareness both of Jewish values and of Greek historiographical tradition. [CMW]

7.415 A. N. Sherwin-White. *The letters of Pliny: a historical and social commentary.* 1966 ed. New York: Oxford University Press, 1985. ISBN 0-19-814435-0. ▸ Commentary more political and prosopographical than social, with special emphasis on what we can learn about political life and Roman administration. Indispensable despite some ommissions. [CMW]

7.416 Ronald Syme. *History in Ovid.* New York: Oxford University Press, 1979. ISBN 0-19-814825-9. ‣ Study of Ovid and his milieu, seeking lost historical detail (e.g., "forgotten campaigns"), investigating prosopographical detail, and examining Ovid's attitude toward regime. [CMW]

7.417 Ronald Syme. *Tacitus.* 1958 ed. 2 vols. Oxford: Clarendon, 1979. ISBN 0-19-814327-3 (set). ‣ Magisterial investigation of Tacitus and his writings in their social and political context, casting light on Tacitus's methods and on history of his own time. Enormously influential. [CMW]

7.418 Andrew Wallace-Hadrill. *Suetonius: the scholar and his caesars.* 1983 ed. New Haven: Yale University Press, 1984. ISBN 0-300-03000-2. ‣ Study of Suetonius in his social and cultural context, considering genre of ancient biography and examining how Suetonius's moral and cultural preoccupations influenced his choice of material. [CMW]

Biography

7.419 Anthony A. Barrett. *Caligula: the corruption of power.* 1989 ed. New Haven: Yale University Press, 1990. ISBN 0-300-04653-7. ‣ Best recent biography; based on judicious reappraisal of literary sources, supplemented with archaeological and numismatic evidence. [CMW]

7.420 Anthony R. Birley. *Marcus Aurelius: a biography.* Rev. ed. New Haven: Yale University Press, 1987. ISBN 0-300-03844-5. ‣ Standard account of Marcus Aurelius's life and reign, based on archaeology and epigraphy as well as literary sources, with detailed study of his military activities. [CMW]

7.421 Anthony R. Birley. *Septimius Severus: the African emperor.* Rev. ed. New Haven: Yale University Press, 1989. ISBN 0-300-04467-4. ‣ Standard account of Septimius Severus's life and reign using recent archaeological evidence. Excellent on his travels and military campaigns. [CMW]

7.422 Miriam T. Griffin. *Nero: the end of a dynasty.* 1984 ed. New Haven: Yale University Press, 1985. ISBN 0-300-03285-4. ‣ Study of Nero's reign in light of Nero's personality and analysis of reasons for his fall. Judicious, scholarly, indispensable; good account of artistic and architectural interests. [CMW]

7.423 Miriam T. Griffin. *Seneca: a philosopher in politics.* 1976 ed. Oxford: Clarendon, 1992. ISBN 0-19-814365-6 (cl, 1976), 0-19-814774-0 (pbk). ‣ Study of Seneca's career, set beside analysis of his published views on government, slavery, wealth, suicide, and morality in general. Reveals considerable discrepancies. [CMW]

7.424 A.H.M. Jones. *The Herods of Judaea.* 1938 ed. Oxford: Clarendon, 1967. ISBN 0-19-814263-3. ‣ Still best short introduction to life of Herod the Great and to his successors and problems of Palestine in first century CE. [CMW]

7.425 Brian W. Jones. *The emperor Domitian.* London: Routledge, 1992. ISBN 0-415-04229-1. ‣ Biography of Domitian, arguing that epigraphic and archaeological evidence proves him efficient administrator, reformer, and good judge of foreign affairs, whose notorious harshness affected only those close to him. [CMW]

7.426 Brian W. Jones. *The emperor Titus.* New York: St. Martin's, 1984. ISBN 0-312-24443-6. ‣ Conventional biography stressing epigraphic and numismatic evidence to supplement scant literary sources. [CMW]

7.427 Dietmar Kienast. *Augustus: Prinzeps und Monarch.* Darmstadt: Wissenschaftliche Buchgesellschaft, 1982. ISBN 3-534-

07058-5. ‣ Best modern biography of Augustus; nothing comparable in English. [CMW]

7.428 Barbara Levick. *Claudius.* New Haven: Yale University Press, 1990. ISBN 0-300-04734-7. ‣ Best available account of Claudius's reign, stressing many excellent administrative measures and denying Claudius was reluctant emperor, although denying him excessive credit for his personal contribution. [CMW]

7.429 Barbara Levick. *Tiberius the politician.* 1976 ed. London: Croom Helm, 1986. ISBN 0-7099-4132-3 (pbk). ‣ Study of Tiberius's career and events of his reign, deducing from sources hushed-up intrigues that permeated imperial family in succession struggle. [CMW]

7.430 Jean-Michel Roddaz. *Marcus Agrippa.* Rome: École Française de Rome, 1984. (Bibliothèque des Écoles Françaises d'Athènes et de Rome, 253.) ISBN 2-7283-0000-0, ISSN 0223-5099. ‣ Only recent biography of Augustus's chief lieutenant Agrippa, discussing also his image, coinage, and iconography. Conventional approach, no startling conclusions, extensive bibliography. [CMW]

7.431 Robin Seager. *Tiberius.* Berkeley: University of California Press, 1972. ISBN 0-520-02212-2. ‣ Study of Tiberius's career and character as man genuinely reluctant to assume supreme power, but subsequently warped by it and driven to autocracy and reign of terror. [CMW]

Regional Studies

Italy and the West

7.432 Géza Alföldy. *Noricum.* Anthony R. Birley, trans. London: Routledge & Kegan Paul, 1974. ISBN 0-7100-7372-0. ‣ History of Noricum with particular emphasis on social and economic matters in first and second centuries CE and more attention to military affairs from late second century onward. [CMW]

7.433 Thomas Blagg and Martin Millett, eds. *The early Roman empire in the West.* Oxford: Oxbow, 1990. ISBN 0-946897-22-0. ‣ Fifteen papers on romanization and urban development in Britain, Gaul, Germany, and Spain. Important contribution to discussion and interpretation of archaeological evidence. [CMW]

7.434 R. G. Collingwood and Ian A. Richmond. *The archaeology of Roman Britain.* Rev. ed. London: Methuen, 1969. ISBN 0-416-27580-X. ‣ Still invaluable reference work on Roman remains and artifacts; detailed bibliographies. New edition urgently required. [CMW]

7.435 Leonard A. Curchin. *Roman Spain: conquest and assimilation.* New York: Routledge, 1991. ISBN 0-415-06451-1. ‣ Chronicle of conquest and study of development of Hispano-Roman cults, economic integration, and indigenous resistance to romanization and christianization. Surveys chief cities and rural and social conditions. [DAC]

7.436 John F. Drinkwater. *Roman Gaul: the three provinces, 58 BC–AD 260.* Ithaca, N.Y.: Cornell University Press, 1983. ISBN 0-8014-1642-6. ‣ Useful introduction to history of Gaul, primarily based on archaeological evidence. Emphasizes changes caused by Rome, stressing absence of Gaulish nationalism, and assessing state of economy and society in third century. [CMW]

7.437 Elizabeth W. B. Fentress. *Numidia and the Roman army: social, military, and economic aspects of the frontier zone.* Oxford: British Archaeological Reports, 1979. (British Archaeological Reports international series, 53.) ISBN 0-86054-044-8. ‣ Study of role of army in Numidia and its social and economic impact on local population. Importance of olive cultivation and of pastoralism in Roman period. [CMW]

7.438 Paul-Albert Février. *Approches du Maghreb romain: pou-*

voirs, différences, et conflits. 2 vols. Aix-en-Provence: Edisud, 1989–90. ISBN 2-85744-403-6 (v. 1), 2-85744-404-4 (v. 2). ▸ Account of Roman North Africa tracing progress of archaeological and historical research in Maghreb by French scholars. Shows how contemporary preoccupations influence interpretation of past. Useful bibliographies. [CMW]

7.439 Sheppard S. Frere. *Britannia: a history of Roman Britain.* 3d ed. London: Routledge & Kegan Paul, 1987. ISBN 0-7102-1215-1. ▸ Authoritative synthesis of archaeological evidence for Roman Britain and its bearing on history of province to fifth century. First published 1967; third edition extensively updated, supersedes earlier ones. [CMW]

7.440 Sheppard S. Frere and J.K.S. St Joseph. *Roman Britain from the air.* Cambridge: Cambridge University Press, 1983. ISBN 0-521-25088-9. ▸ Excellent photographs with detailed commentary on each and discussion of significance of individual sites for knowledge of Roman Britain. [CMW]

7.441 S. J. Keay. *Roman Spain.* Berkeley: University of California Press, 1988. ISBN 0-520-06380-5. ▸ Best available account in English of history and archaeology of Iberian peninsula to end of Roman period. [CMW]

7.442 Anthony King. *Roman Gaul and Germany.* Berkeley: University of California Press, 1990. ISBN 0-520-06989-7. ▸ Useful summary, stressing main archaeological sites. [CMW]

7.443 Martin Millett. *The romanization of Britain: an essay in archaeological interpretation.* Cambridge: Cambridge University Press, 1990. ISBN 0-521-36084-6. ▸ Important study of nature of "romanization" and evidence, primarily archaeological, for social and economic change in Roman Britain. Uses social science models and concepts. [CMW]

7.444 András Mócsy. *Pannonia and Upper Moesia: a history of the middle Danube provinces of the Roman empire.* Sheppard S. Frere, trans. Boston: Routledge & Kegan Paul, 1974. ISBN 0-7100-7714-9. ▸ Only comprehensive account in English of central Danubian provinces. Irreplaceable even if now outdated in detail. [CMW]

7.445 T. W. Potter. *Roman Italy.* Berkeley: University of California Press, 1987. ISBN 0-520-06065-2. ▸ Excellent survey of current state of archaeological knowledge in Italy, arranged by topics and set in historical framework. [CMW]

7.446 Susan Raven. *Rome in Africa.* 3d ed. New York: Routledge, 1993. ISBN 0-415-08261-7 (cl), 0-415-08150-5 (pbk). ▸ Only reliable and readable introductory account in English of North African history and archaeology. First published 1969, approach sometimes dated, but third edition extensively revised. Well illustrated. [CMW]

7.447 A.L.F. Rivet. *Gallia Narbonensis, with a chapter on Alpes Maritimae: southern France in Roman times.* London: Batsford, 1988. ISBN 0-7134-5860-7. ▸ Brief historical survey followed by account, geographically arranged, of evidence for each of main towns, and chapter on Alpes Maritimae. [CMW]

7.448 Peter Salway. *Roman Britain.* 1981 ed. Oxford: Oxford University Press, 1989. ISBN 0-19-821717-X (cl), 0-19-285143-8 (pbk). ▸ Standard history of Roman Britain to 500 CE. Highly readable, judiciously reexamining many familiar controversies in light of new archaeological evidence, historical parallels, and good common sense. [CMW]

7.449 Malcolm Todd, ed. *Research on Roman Britain, 1960–89.* London: Society for the Promotion of Roman Studies, 1989. (*Britannia* monograph, 11.) ISBN 0-907764-13-4. ▸ Sixteen papers on conquest and frontiers, towns, agriculture, economy, art and architecture, religion, Roman fenland, and fourth century. Brief survey of research; useful bibliography. [CMW]

7.450 Edith Mary Wightman. *Gallia Belgica.* Berkeley: University of California Press, 1985. ISBN 0-520-05297-8. ▸ Exemplary, influential provincial history combining evidence from all sources and asking basic questions about historical process. Published posthumously. [CMW]

7.451 J. J. Wilkes. *Dalmatia.* Cambridge, Mass.: Harvard University Press, 1969. ▸ Only survey in English of history and archaeology of Dalmatia. Indispensable and not greatly overtaken by more recent research. [CMW]

7.452 R.J.A. Wilson. *Sicily under the Roman empire: the archaeology of a Roman province, 36 BC–AD 535.* Warminster: Aris & Phillips, 1990. ISBN 0-85668-552-6 (cl), 0-85668-160-1 (pbk). ▸ Magisterial study of previously neglected topic, based primarily on archaeological evidence. Treats urbanization, countryside, economy and trade, and religion. Detailed account of surviving buildings. [CMW]

Greece, Egypt, and the East

7.453 Gedalia Alon. *The Jews in their land in the Talmudic age.* 1980 ed. Gershon Levi, ed. and trans. Cambridge, Mass.: Harvard University Press, 1989. ISBN 0-674-47495-3 (pbk). ▸ Jewish life under Roman and Byzantine rule after destruction of Second Temple, largely from Jewish sources. Covers economic conditions, Jewish and Roman law, resistance, and decline of Jewish population. [CMW]

7.454 Glen W. Bowersock. *Roman Arabia.* Cambridge, Mass.: Harvard University Press, 1983. ISBN 0-674-77755-7. ▸ History of Nabataeans based on Petra, Roman conquest, and creation of province of Arabia. Stresses relationship between native Arabs and Roman culture and power. [CMW]

7.455 Alan K. Bowman. *Egypt after the pharaohs, 332 BC–AD 642: from Alexander to the Arab conquest.* Corr. 1986 ed. Berkeley: University of California, 1989. ISBN 0-520-06665-0 (pbk). ▸ Well-balanced synthesis of history of Hellenistic, Roman, and Byzantine Egypt, with emphasis on archaeological and papyrological evidence. New appendix. [CMW]

7.456 Glanville Downey. *A history of Antioch in Syria: from Seleucus to the Arab conquest.* Princeton: Princeton University Press, 1961. ▸ Fullest account, historical and topographical, of one of major cities of Roman empire that was also important for development of Christianity. Based on literary evidence and 1930s excavations. [CMW]

7.457 Martin Goodman. *State and society in Roman Galilee, AD 132–212.* Totowa, N.J.: Rowman & Allanheld, 1983. ISBN 0-86598-089-6. ▸ Detailed study of village society in Galilee after Bar Kokhba revolt, based primarily on rabbinic texts. [CMW]

7.458 Kenneth W. Harl. *Civic coins and civic politics in the Roman East, AD 180–275.* Berkeley: University of California Press, 1987. ISBN 0-520-05552-7. ▸ Discussion of coinage of Greek cities revealing persistence of traditional city-state values or institutions, including pagan cult, but also notables' growing consciousness of Roman identity. [CMW]

7.459 Hans-Peter Kuhnen, Leo Mildenberg, and Robert Wenning. *Palästina im griechisch-römischer Zeit.* Munich: Beck, 1990. (Handbuch der Archäologie, Vorderasien, 2.2.) ISBN 3-406-32876-8. ▸ Comprehensive survey of archaeological evidence from Palestine in Hellenistic and Roman times. Valuable complement to Schürer 7.466. [CMW]

7.460 Naphtali Lewis. *Life in Egypt under Roman rule.* New York: Oxford University Press, 1983. ISBN 0-19-814848-8. ▸ Concentrates on small towns and village life. Topics include religion, agriculture, trades and professions, taxes, law, and resistance. [CMW]

7.461 Fergus Millar. "The Roman *coloniae* of the Near East: a study of cultural relations." In *Roman Eastern policy and other studies in Roman history: proceedings of a colloquium at Tvärminne, 2–3 October 1987.* Heikki Solin and Mika Kajava, eds., pp. 7–58. Helsinki: Societas Scientiarum Fennica, 1990. (Commentationes humanarum litterarum, 91.) ISBN 951-653-208-X, ISSN 0069-6587. ▸ Study of Beirut, earliest Roman colony in area, and later colonies, as melting pots for Roman and other cultures. [CMW]

7.462 Fergus Millar. *The Roman Near East, 31 BC–AD 337.* Cambridge, Mass.: Harvard University Press, 1993. ISBN 0-674-77885-5. ▸ Diachronic account of Roman expansion followed by regional survey stressing cultural and religious interactions, ethnicity, and survival of languages and traditions other than Greek and Latin. Use of Semitic-language sources, sets agenda for future research. [CMW]

7.463 Stephen Mitchell. *Anatolia: land, men, and gods in Asia Minor.* Vol. 1: *The Celts in Anatolia and the impact of Roman rule.* Vol. 2: *The rise of the Church.* Oxford: Clarendon Press, 1993. ISBN 0-19-814080-0 (v. 1), 0-19-814933-6 (v. 2). ▸ Magisterial account of pre-Roman and Roman Anatolia, supplementing and updating Magie 7.227, stresses Celtic settlement, Roman conquest and impact of army, urban development, agriculture, and religion. Volume 2 stresses rise of Christianity from first century (Paul's journeys), pagan-Christian interactions, and Christian impact on society. [CMW]

7.464 Herbert A. Musurillo. *The acts of the pagan martyrs: acta Alexandrinorum.* 1954 ed. Salem, Mass.: Ayer, 1988. ISBN 0-405-11430-3. ▸ Edition and discussion of various anti-Roman and antisemitic texts reflecting Alexandria's struggle for political autonomy in early empire, culminating in grant of Alexandrian senate by Septimius Severus (199/200 CE). [CMW]

7.465 Maurice Sartre. *L'Orient romain: provinces et sociétés provinciales en Méditerranée orientale d'Auguste aux Sévères (31 avant J.-C.–235 après J.-C.)* Paris: Seuil, 1991. ISBN 2-02-012705-9. ▸ Valuable treatment of eastern provinces, including Greece and Balkans, stressing importance of cities. Special chapter on Jews. Complements Millar 7.462. [CMW]

7.466 E. Schürer. *The history of the Jewish people in the age of Jesus Christ (175 B.C.–A.D. 135).* Rev. ed. 3 vols. in 4. Geza Vermes et al., eds. and Revisions. T. A. Burkill et al., trans. Edinburgh: Clark, 1973–87. ISBN 0-567-02242-0 (v. 1), 0-567-02243-9 (v. 2), 0-567-02244-7 (v. 3.1), 0-567-09373-5 (v. 3.2). ▸ Authoritative, comprehensive revision of standard work of reference, bringing together material from all possible sources. Indispensable. [CMW]

7.467 Irfan Shahîd. *Rome and the Arabs: a prolegomenon to the study of Byzantium and the Arabs.* Washington, D.C.: Dumbarton Oaks, Center for Byzantine Studies, 1984. ISBN 0-88402-115-7. ▸ Often controversial study of political and military relationships down to Diocletian and of Arab contribution to culture and religion. Image of Arabs in Greco-Roman historiography. [CMW]

7.468 Georges Tate. *Les campagnes de la Syrie du nord du deuxième au septième siècle.* Vol. 1: *Un exemple d'expansion démographique et économique à la fin de l'antiquité.* Paris: Geuthner, 1992. ISBN 2-7053-0670-6. ▸ Study of North Syrian massif, where remains of 700 ancient villages are identified. Argues for sustained demographic and economic growth until mid-sixth century without major social or cultural change. [CMW]

SEE ALSO

6.403 Paul Cartledge and Antony Spawforth. *Hellenistic and Roman Sparta.*

6.472 A.H.M. Jones. *The Greek city.*

ART AND TECHNOLOGY OF THE REPUBLIC AND EARLY EMPIRE

General Studies

7.469 Bernard Andreae. *The art of Rome.* Robert Erich Wolf, trans. New York: Abrams, 1977. ISBN 0-8109-0626-0. ▸ History of Roman art, chronologically arranged, in social and political context. Comprehensively illustrated; valuable documentation on individual sites. [CMW]

7.470 Ranuccio Bianchi Bandinelli. *Rome, the centre of power: Roman art to AD 200.* Peter Green, trans. New York: Braziller, 1970. ISBN 0-8076-0559-X. ▸ History of Roman art and architecture, especially of city of Rome, in its social and political context, seen from Marxist perspective. Stimulating and controversial; splendid illustrations. [CMW]

7.471 Martin Henig, ed. *A handbook of Roman art: a comprehensive survey of all the arts of the Roman world.* Ithaca, N.Y.: Cornell University Press, 1983. ISBN 0-8014-1539-X (cl), 0-8014-9242-4 (pbk). ▸ Twelve disparate chapters, each on a different art form; particularly valuable introduction to minor arts. Useful bibliography. [CMW]

7.472 Nancy H. Ramage and Andrew Ramage. *Roman art: Romulus to Constantine.* Englewood Cliffs, N.J.: Prentice-Hall, 1991. ISBN 0-13-782947-7. ▸ Introductory survey, chronologically ordered; strongest on sculpture and architecture, but also covers painting, mosaics, colored plates, etc. Probably best basic text currently available. [CMW]

7.473 Donald E. Strong. *Roman art.* 2d ed. Roger Ling, ed. New York: Penguin, 1988. ISBN 0-14-056139-0 (pbk). ▸ Comprehensive account, arranged by period, surveying all arts except architecture and covering entire empire. Relates art to social and political context. Good black-and-white plates. [CMW]

7.474 Cornelius C. Vermeule III. *Roman imperial art in Greece and Asia Minor.* Cambridge, Mass.: Harvard University Press, 1968. ISBN 0-674-77775-1. ▸ Roman official art, including architecture, in Greek provinces to Justinian. Strong on portraiture, including numismatic; private patronage not considered. [CMW]

Architecture and Urbanism

7.475 Jean-Pierre Adam. *La construction romaine: matériaux et techniques.* 2d ed. Paris: Picard, 1989. ISBN 2-7084-0381-8. ▸ Roman building materials and techniques, with excellent photographs and drawings, based on examples from throughout empire, but especially Pompeii and Herculaneum. Nothing comparable in English. Bibliography. [CMW]

7.476 Mary Taliaferro Boatwright. *Hadrian and the city of Rome.* Princeton: Princeton University Press, 1987. ISBN 0-691-03588-1. ▸ Hadrian's building program and administrative reforms and their impact on life at Rome; arrangement geographical and roughly chronological. Invaluable for understanding both Roman topography and Hadrian's policies. [CMW]

7.477 Axel Boëthius. *Etruscan and early Roman architecture.* 2d ed. Roger Ling and Tom Rasmussen, Revisions. New York: Penguin, 1978. ISBN 0-14-056144-7. ▸ Architecture in Italy from prehistoric times, tracing development of republican Rome from Etruscan and Greek models. Standard account. First published as part 1 of *Etruscan and Roman Architecture* (1970), considerably revised. [CMW]

7.478 John R. Clarke. *The houses of Roman Italy, 100 BC–AD 250: ritual, space, and decoration.* Berkeley: University of California Press, 1991. ISBN 0-520-07267-7 (cl), 0-520-08429-2 (pbk). ▸ Important study of architecture and decorative schemes, especially painting, in overall context. Discusses function of rooms, use of space, patterns of living, and patrons and craftsmen. Clear, well-chosen illustrations. [CMW]

7.479 Jean-Claude Golvin. *L'amphithéâtre romain: essai sur la théorisation de sa forme et de ses fonctions.* 2 vols. Paris: de Boccard, 1988. ISSN 0339-1736. ▸ Detailed study of origins of amphitheater, with typological and chronological classification of all known examples and analysis of form and function. Valuable bibliography. [CMW]

7.480 Michael Grant. *Cities of Vesuvius: Pompeii and Herculaneum.* 1971 ed. New York: Penguin, 1976. ISBN 0-14-004394-2. ▸ Best general introductory account in English of architecture, art, and life of these two cities. [CMW]

7.481 John H. Humphrey. *Roman circuses: arenas for chariot racing.* Berkeley: University of California Press, 1986. ISBN 0-520-04921-7. ▸ Massive, magisterial account of evidence from whole empire for Roman circuses and chariot racing. Corrects many previous misconceptions; invaluable work of reference. [CMW]

7.482 Wilhelmina F. Jashemski. *The gardens of Pompeii, Herculaneum, and the villas destroyed by Vesuvius.* New Rochelle, N.Y.: Caratzas, 1979. ISBN 0-89241-096-5. ▸ Brilliant, pioneering palaeobotanical study based on meticulous excavation. Domestic gardens, vineyards, and orchards within city walls reveal new aspect of urban life; excellent photographs. [CMW]

7.483 Theodor Kraus. *Pompeii and Herculaneum: the living cities of the dead.* 1973 ed. Robert Erich Wolf, trans. Leonard von Matt, Photographs. New York: Abrams, 1975. ISBN 0-8109-0418-7. ▸ History of excavations, topography, buildings, art, and life of these two cities. Excellent photographs. [CMW]

7.484 Heinz-Otto Lamprecht. *Opus Caementitium: Bautechnik der Römer.* 3d ed. Düsseldorf: Beton, 1987. ISBN 3-7640-0229-8. ▸ Study of Roman concrete and its uses, mostly in Italy and western provinces. Color plates of different mortars with technical analyses. [CMW]

7.485 Margaret Lyttelton. *Baroque architecture in classical antiquity.* Ithaca, N.Y.: Cornell University Press, 1974. ISBN 0-8014-0784-2. ▸ Nature of "baroque" art and its appearance in Roman empire, especially in East (Petra, Baalbek, Palmyra, etc.), with some seventeenth-century parallels. [CMW]

7.486 William L. MacDonald. *The architecture of the Roman empire.* Vol. 1, rev. ed. 2 vols. New Haven: Yale University Press, 1982–86. ISBN 0-300-02818-0 (cl, v. 1), 0-300-02819-9 (pbk, v. 1), 0-300-03456-3 (cl, v. 2), 0-300-03470-9 (pbk, v. 2). ▸ Standard work: volume 1 analyzes four major imperial buildings at Rome (Nero's palaces, Domitian's palace, Trajan's markets, Pantheon); volume 2 discusses architecture and urban planning throughout empire. [CMW]

7.487 William L. MacDonald. *The Pantheon: design, meaning, and progeny.* Cambridge, Mass.: Harvard University Press, 1976. ISBN 0-674-65345-9. ▸ Analysis of Hadrian's building and its influence, to middle of twentieth century. [CMW]

7.488 Elisabeth Blair MacDougall, ed. *Ancient Roman villa gardens (Dumbarton Oaks colloquium on the history of landscape architecture, 10).* Washington, D.C.: Dumbarton Oaks Research Library and Collection, 1987. ISBN 0-88402-162-9. ▸ Several important papers on literary evidence for villa gardens, garden excavations at Boscoreale and Oplontis, Oplontis sculptures, water triclinia, town and country, villas at Montmaurin, and Via Galina. [CMW]

7.489 Ernest Nash. *Pictorial dictionary of ancient Rome.* 1968 rev. ed. 2 vols. New York: Hacker, 1981. ISBN 0-87817-265-3. ▸ Description of all surviving monuments and buildings of Rome, beautifully photographed, with bibliography. Comprehensive,

authoritative, and indispensable, although in part becoming outdated. [CMW]

7.490 Inge Nielsen. *Thermae et balnea: the architecture and cultural history of Roman public baths.* 2 vols. Århus, Denmark: Århus University Press, 1990. ISBN 87-7288-212-3 (set). ▸ History, architecture, and social function of Roman baths; volume 2 contains catalog of sites and invaluable plans. Fundamental for all future research. [CMW]

7.491 L. Richardson, Jr. *A new topographical dictionary of ancient Rome.* Baltimore: Johns Hopkins University Press, 1992. ISBN 0-8018-4300-6. ▸ Invaluable survey listing known buildings and topographical features, with basic references to ancient and modern accounts. Fundamental, complementing Nash 7.489, but beware some controversial and idiosyncratic opinions included without warning. [CMW]

7.492 L. Richardson, Jr. *Pompeii: an architectural history.* Baltimore: Johns Hopkins University Press, 1988. ISBN 0-8018-3533-x. ▸ History of Pompeii and chronological account of development of public and domestic architecture. Interesting, highly selective, idiosyncratic, inadequately illustrated, and controversial. [CMW]

7.493 John B. Ward-Perkins. *Cities of ancient Greece and Italy: planning in classical antiquity.* New York: Braziller, 1974. ISBN 0-8076-0679-0 (cl), 0-8076-0678-2 (pbk). ▸ Brief introductory account of particular value for excellent air photographs. [CMW]

7.494 John B. Ward-Perkins. *Roman architecture.* 1977 ed. New York: Electa/Rizzoli, 1988. ISBN 0-8478-0972-2. ▸ General history of Roman architecture, stressing importance of concrete construction and variations of regional style in provinces. Excellent photographs. [CMW]

7.495 John B. Ward-Perkins. *Roman imperial architecture.* 1981 2d ed. Harmondsworth: Penguin, 1989. ISBN 0-14-056045-9 (cl), 0-14-056145-5 (pbk). ▸ Standard history linking Rome and provinces; excellent plans and drawings; invaluable reference work. First published as parts 2–4 of *Etruscan and Roman Architecture* (1970). [CMW]

7.496 Fikret K. Yegül. *Baths and bathing in classical antiquity.* Cambridge, Mass.: MIT Press, 1992. ISBN 0-262-24035-1. ▸ Architecture and cultural importance of baths; their role in development of building technology, especially in concrete. Valuable chapter on heating and water supply. [CMW]

Engineering and Technology

7.497 Christer Bruun. *The water supply of ancient Rome: a study of Roman imperial administration.* Helsinki: Societas Scientiarum Fennica, 1991. (Commentationes humanarum litterarum, 93.) ISBN 951-653-223-3. ▸ Study of organization of water supply at Rome examining who benefited, who was in charge, capacity and distribution, and use of lead pipes and inscriptions thereon. Fundamental for all future research. [CMW]

7.498 Raymond Chevallier. *Roman roads.* Rev. ed. N. H. Field, trans. London: Batsford, 1989. ISBN 0-7134-3039-7. ▸ Examination of Roman road construction, engineering works, and road stations, with particular stress on Gaul and Italy. Useful bibliography. [CMW]

7.499 J. Clayton Fant. *Cavum antrum Phrygiae: the organization and operations of the Roman imperial marble quarries in Phrygia.* Oxford: British Archaeological Reports, 1989. (British Archaeological Reports international series, 482.) ISBN 0-86054-619-5. ▸ Important contribution to study of Roman marble trade, based on some 360 inscriptions from quarries at Docimium, showing closer imperial oversight developing under Hadrian. [CMW]

7.500 John F. Healy. *Mining and metallurgy in the Greek and*

Roman world. London: Thames & Hudson, 1978. ISBN 0-500-40035-0. ▸ Best available, but not wholly adequate, study of mining and metalworking. Useful lists and references. [CMW]

7.501 A. Trevor Hodge. *Roman aqueducts and water supply.* London: Duckworth, 1992. ISBN 0-7156-2194-7. ▸ Comprehensive study of Roman aqueducts, together with wells, cisterns, dams, and drains, stressing technical aspects of hydraulic engineering as well as social implications. Fundamental work with extensive bibliography and notes. [CMW]

7.502 A. Trevor Hodge, ed. *Future currents in aqueduct studies.* Leeds: Cairns, 1991. ISBN 0-905205-80-4. ▸ Fourteen articles on aspects of Roman aqueducts, including maintenance, distribution, mills, specific sites (Lugdunum, Auara), regions (Africa, Greece, Israel), and recent research. [CMW]

7.503 Colin O'Connor. *Roman bridges.* Cambridge: Cambridge University Press, 1993. ISBN 0-521-39326-4. ▸ Study by civil engineer of all known Roman bridges and bridge-aqueducts, elucidating principles of design and subjecting Roman arch construction to modern analysis. Well-illustrated, useful catalog of surviving structures. [CMW]

7.504 John B. Ward-Perkins. *Marble in antiquity: collected papers of J. B. Ward-Perkins.* Hazel Dodge and Bryan Ward-Perkins, eds. London: British School at Rome, 1992. (Archaeological monographs of the British School at Rome, 6.) ISBN 0-904152-20-0. ▸ Ten papers on quarrying techniques, transportation, and especially organization of marble trade under empire. List of main quarries; useful bibliography. [CMW]

SEE ALSO
4.375 John G. Landels. *Engineering in the ancient world.*
4.377 John Peter Oleson. *Greek and Roman mechanical water-lifting devices.*
4.378 K. D. White. *Greek and Roman technology.*
4.499 Lionel Casson. *Ships and seamanship in the ancient world.*

Sculpture

7.505 Richard Brilliant. *Gesture and rank in Roman art: the use of gestures to denote status in Roman sculpture and coinage.* New Haven: Connecticut Academy of Arts and Sciences, 1963. (Connecticut Academy of Arts and Sciences, Memoirs, 14.) ▸ Study of gesture in iconography of status, developing out of Greek sculptural tradition and reaching its apogee in late empire. [CMW]

7.506 Kenan T. Erim. *Aphrodisias: city of Venus Aphrodite.* New York: Facts on File, 1986. ISBN 0-8160-1541-4. ▸ Account of excavation of city and important school of sculptors that worked there. Magnificent illustrations. [CMW]

7.507 Diana E. E. Kleiner. *Roman group portraiture: the funerary reliefs of the late republic and early empire.* New York: Garland, 1977. ISBN 0-8240-2703-5. ▸ Study of funerary reliefs of republican and Augustan freedmen and their families from Rome and its environs. [CMW]

7.508 Diana E. E. Kleiner. *Roman sculpture.* New Haven: Yale University Press, 1992. ISBN 0-300-04631-6. ▸ Magisterial history of Roman sculpture, public and private, chronologically arranged, to CE 330, covering both Italy and provinces. Emphasis on patronage and on social and stylistic diversity. [CMW]

7.509 Guntram Koch, Hellmut Sichtermann, and Friederike Sinn-Henninger. *Römische Sarkophage.* Munich: Beck, 1982. ISBN 3-406-08709-4. ▸ Comprehensive account, geographically arranged, of relief sculpture found on sarcophagi throughout empire. [CMW]

7.510 Erika Simon. *Ara Pacis Augustae.* 1967 ed. Greenwich, Conn.: New York Graphic Society, 1968. ▸ Brief, standard account of reliefs of Ara Pacis with excellent photographs. Attempts to identify persons depicted; identifications generally accepted, though subsequent rectifications on some points. Translation of 1967 German edition. [CMW]

7.511 Mario Torelli. *Typology and structure of Roman historical reliefs.* Ann Arbor: University of Michigan Press, 1982. ISBN 0-472-10014-9. ▸ Controversial discussion of content and function of narrative reliefs in cultural and historical context, with Augustan and Tiberian periods seen as central to their development. [CMW]

7.512 Cornelius C. Vermeule III. *Greek sculpture and Roman taste: the purpose and setting of Graeco-Roman art in Italy and the Greek imperial East.* Ann Arbor: University of Michigan Press, 1977. ISBN 0-472-08940-4. ▸ Important study of use made in Roman architectural settings of copies, adaptations, and mirror images of Greek sculpture. [CMW]

Painting, Stucco, and Mosaics

7.513 Peter H. von Blanckenhagen and Christine Alexander. *The Augustan villa at Boscotrecase.* Rev. ed. Mainz: von Zabern, 1990. (Deutsches Archäologisches Institut Rom, Sonderschriften, 8.) ISBN 3-8053-1127-3. ▸ Magnificent new photographs of newly restored frescoes from Boscotrecase near Pompeii, masterpieces of Roman painting; text from original 1962 publication, modestly revised, concentrates on art historical questions. [CMW]

7.514 John R. Clarke. *Roman black-and-white figural mosaics.* 1979 ed. University Park: Pennsylvania State University Press, 1985. ISBN 0-271-00401-0. ▸ Analysis of composition and style of Italian black-and-white mosaics. Useful photographs include many monopod views. [CMW]

7.515 Katherine M. D. Dunbabin. *The mosaics of Roman North Africa: studies in iconography and patronage.* New York: Oxford University Press, 1978. ISBN 0-19-813217-4. ▸ Fundamental study concentrating on patronage and subject matter. Examines hunting scenes, amphitheater, circus, rural and everyday life, and religious subjects. Notes influence of African school in Italy and elsewhere. Catalog and bibliography. [CMW]

7.516 Elaine K. Gazda and Anne E. Haeckl, eds. *Roman art in the private sphere: new perspectives on the architecture and decor of the domus, villa, and insula.* Ann Arbor: University of Michigan Press, 1991. ISBN 0-472-10196-X. ▸ Six papers on private houses and private art as expression of Roman social and cultural values. Important and original contribution. [CMW]

7.517 Hetty Joyce. *The decoration of walls, ceilings, and floors in Italy in the second and third centuries AD.* Rome: Bretschneider, 1981. ISBN 88-85007-45-7 (pbk). ▸ Study of interior decoration of houses arguing walls and ceilings were treated as single unit, but floor mosaics not integrated into decorative scheme. [CMW]

7.518 Roger Ling. *Roman painting.* New York: Cambridge University Press, 1991. ISBN 0-521-30614-0 (cl), 0-521-31595-6 (pbk). ▸ Excellent historical survey essentially of wall painting, based on four traditional Pompeian "styles." Discusses wall painting as part of overall decorative scheme, patronage, and subject matter. [CMW]

Ceramics, Glass, and Other Crafts

7.519 D. M. Bailey. *A catalogue of the lamps in the British Museum.* Vol. 1: *Greek, Hellenistic, and early Roman pottery lamps.* Vol. 2: *Roman lamps made in Italy.* Vol. 3: *Roman provincial lamps.* 3 vols. London: British Museum, 1975–88. ISBN 0-7141-1243-7 (v. 1), 0-7141-1259-3 (v. 2), 0-7141-1278-X (v. 3). ▸ Fundamental study of Roman lamps, whose importance in Roman domestic life and as source for study of popular taste should be emphasized. [CMW]

7.520 Gerald Brodribb. *Roman brick and tile.* Wolfboro, N.H.: Sutton, 1987. ISBN 0-86299-363-6. ‣ Pioneering study of types of ceramic building materials and their use, primarily concentrating on Britain. Very useful, if not comprehensive, and only study available. [CMW]

7.521 Elisabeth Ettlinger et al. *Conspectus formarum terrae sigillatae italico modo confectae.* Bonn: Habelt, 1990. (Materialien zur römisch-germanischen Keramik, 11.) ISBN 3-7749-2456-2. ‣ Collaborative study of Italian-type sigillata pottery (red-gloss tableware) as made at Arezzo and many sites in Italy and elsewhere. Current state of knowledge and proposed new typology; should become standard work. [CMW]

7.522 Donald B. Harden et al. *Glass of the caesars.* Milan: Olivetti, 1987. ‣ Catalog of major exhibition with six invaluable introductory historical chapters by Harden and one by Kenneth Painter. Virtually a history of Roman luxury glass under empire. [CMW]

7.523 Reynold Higgins. *Greek and Roman jewellery.* 2d ed. Berkeley: University of California Press, 1980. ISBN 0-520-03601-8. ‣ Essential introduction to ancient jewelry and manufacturing techniques from Bronze Age onward, followed by historical and typological survey to ca. 400 CE. Bibliography and list of sites. [CMW]

7.524 J.P.C. Kent. *Roman coins.* Rev. ed. New York: Abrams, 1978. ISBN 0-8109-1584-7. ‣ Study of coin as work of art. Particularly valuable for historian or art historian searching for motif or date. Magnificent illustrations. [CMW]

7.525 Martine Newby and Kenneth Painter, eds. *Roman glass: two centuries of art and invention.* London: Society of Antiquaries, 1991. (Occasional papers, 13.) ISBN 0-85431-255-2 (pbk). ‣ Twelve papers on production and distribution of glass tableware and on specific objects, from first centuries BCE and CE. Virtual history of glass in period; bibliography. [CMW]

7.526 D.P.S. Peacock. *Pottery in the Roman world: an ethnoarchaeological approach.* London: Longman, 1982. ISBN 0-582-49127-4. ‣ Important study of modes of pottery production and underlying social and economic factors, combining archaeological evidence with modern parallels. [CMW]

7.527 D. E. Strong. *Greek and Roman gold and silver plate.* 1966 ed. London: Methuen, 1979. ISBN 0-416-72510-4. ‣ Chronological survey of ritual and domestic plate from Bronze Age to late antiquity, with discussion of function of silver plate in Roman society. Emphasizes fourth- and fifth-century hoards. Good illustrations; standard work. [CMW]

7.528 D. E. Strong and David Brown, eds. *Roman crafts.* New York: New York University Press, 1976. ‣ Nineteen articles on ancient crafts, devoted to how things were made. Analyzes manufacturing processes and techniques and discusses organization of production, giving modern parallels. Excellent illustrations. [CMW]

7.529 J. P. Wild. *Textile manufacture in the northern Roman provinces.* Cambridge: Cambridge University Press, 1970. ISBN 0-521-07491-6. ‣ Study of textile fibers, their preparation and spinning; preserved textiles; types of looms; and dyeing and finishing. List of preserved textiles from Britain, Gaul, and Germany, and of textile implements. [CMW]

LATER ROMAN EMPIRE

Politics and Government

7.530 Timothy David Barnes. *Constantine and Eusebius.* Cambridge, Mass.: Harvard University Press, 1981. ISBN 0-674-16530-6. ‣ Stresses value, often neglected, of Eusebius's voluminous works, set in historical context. Argues Constantine was sincere Christian from his conversion in 312. [CMW]

7.531 Timothy David Barnes. *The new empire of Diocletian and Constantine.* Cambridge, Mass.: Harvard University Press, 1982. ISBN 0-674-61126-8. ‣ Detailed analysis of disputed facts and dates; seeks to establish basic framework for imperial chronology, careers of high officials, and imperial administration. Companion volume to Barnes 7.530. [CMW]

7.532 Lukas de Blois. *The policy of the emperor Gallienus.* Leiden: Brill, 1976. (Studies of the Dutch Archaeological and Historical Society, 7.) ISBN 90-04-04508-2. ‣ Study of career and policies of Gallienus, crediting him with giving undue power and influence to army and weakening Senate. Lacked broad vision, but better emperor than tradition suggests. [CMW]

7.533 Averil Cameron. *The later Roman empire, AD 284–430.* Cambridge, Mass.: Harvard University Press, 1993. ISBN 0-674-51194-8. ‣ Excellent introduction to history of fourth century, reflecting insights of best contemporary scholarship. Annotated bibliography and useful survey of primary sources. [CMW]

7.534 Alexander Demandt. *Die Spätantike: römische Geschichte von Diocletian bis Justinian 284–565 n. Chr.* Munich: Beck, 1989. (Handbuch der Altertumswissenschaft, 3.) ISBN 3-406-07992-X. ‣ Magisterial account of late Roman and early Byzantine empires, with long and valuable bibliography. [CMW]

7.535 Ramsay MacMullen. *Roman government's response to crisis, AD 235–237.* New Haven: Yale University Press, 1976. ISBN 0-300-02008-2. ‣ After military anarchy of third century, administrative reforms of Diocletian and Constantine restored order but led to progressive alienation of citizen from state. [CMW]

7.536 John Matthews. *Western aristocracies and imperial court, AD 364–425.* 1975 ed. New York: Oxford University Press, 1990. ISBN 0-19-814499-7. ‣ Public and private worlds of late Roman governing class, especially in Italy and Gaul, with forms of Roman life maintained even after collapse of imperial government. Influential work with 1990 postscript. [CMW]

7.537 John Michael O'Flynn. *Generalissimos of the western Roman empire.* Edmonton: University of Alberta Press, 1983. ISBN 0-88864-031-5. ‣ Covers period from death of Valentinian I to reign of Odoacer: how Stilicho, Aëtius, Ricimer, and others gained power in West in absence of effective emperors. [CMW]

SEE ALSO

6.160 *The Cambridge ancient history.* Vol. 12.

8.129 John B. Bury. *History of the later Roman empire from the death of Theodosius I to the death of Justinian (A.D. 395 to A.D. 565).*

8.137 Kenneth G. Holum. *Theodosian empresses.*

8.138 Arnold H. M. Jones. *The later Roman empire, 284–602.*

8.261 Roger Goodburn and Philip Bartholomew, eds. *Aspects of the "Notitia Dignitatum."*

The Army, War, and External Relations

7.538 Michael H. Dodgeon and Samuel N. C. Lieu, eds. *The Roman eastern frontier and the Persian wars (AD 226–363): a documentary history.* London: Routledge, 1990. ISBN 0-415-00342-3. ‣ Collection of source material with some commentary. Particularly useful translations from Armenian, Arabic, and Persian documents. [CMW]

7.539 Stephen Johnson. *Late Roman fortifications.* Totowa, N.J.: Barnes & Noble, 1983. ISBN 0-389-20404-8. ‣ Town walls and new designs of frontier forts in third and fourth centuries; western provinces only, especially Britain, Gaul, and the Rhine. Useful compendium. [CMW]

7.540 Ramsay MacMullen. *Soldier and civilian in the later Roman* *empire.* 1963 ed. Cambridge, Mass.: Harvard University Press, 1967. ISBN 0-674-81690-0. ▸ Brief but fundamental account of army in its nonmilitary aspects: soldiers as farmers, builders, and administrators; career structure and economic impact. Mostly third and fourth centuries, but some earlier material. [CMW]

7.541 J. R. Moss. "The effects of the policies of Aëtius on the history of western Europe." *Historia: Zeitschrift für alte Geschichte* 22.4 (1973) 711–31. ISSN 0018-2311. ▸ Concludes Aëtius's preoccupation with Gaul led to weakening of Roman position elsewhere, including loss of Africa and further encroachments of Huns. [CMW]

7.542 Irfan Shahîd. *Byzantium and the Arabs in the fourth century.* Washington, D.C.: Dumbarton Oaks Research Library and Collection, 1984. ISBN 0-88402-116-5. ▸ Study of role of Arab *foederati* (foreign troops in service of Roman army) in Byzantine service and their contribution to the Christian church. Much attention to evaluation of sources. Invaluable, though some conclusions controversial. [CMW]

7.543 E. A. Thompson. *Romans and barbarians: the decline of the western empire.* Madison: University of Wisconsin Press, 1982. ISBN 0-299-08700-X. ▸ Twelve essays on West in fifth and sixth centuries, primarily from point of view of Germanic invaders. [CMW]

SEE ALSO

8.142 J.H.W.G. Liebeschuetz. *Barbarians and bishops.*
20.145 Thomas S. Burns. *A history of the Ostrogoths.*
20.146 Walter Goffart. *Barbarians and Romans, A.D. 418–584.*
20.147 Peter Heather. *Goths and Romans, 332–489.*
20.153 Herwig Wolfram. *History of the Goths.*
20.175 Edward James, ed. *Visigothic Spain.*
20.180 E. A. Thompson. *The Goths in Spain.*

Economy, Trade, and Agriculture

7.544 J. M. Carrié. "Un roman des origines: les généalogies du 'colonat du Bas-empire.'" *Opus* 2.1 (1983) 205–51. ISSN 0392-4645. ▸ Revisionist study arguing that colonate not halfway to slavery, and that term covers more diversity than many modern authors assume. [CMW]

7.545 Christian Courtois et al., eds. *Tablettes Albertini: actes privés de l'époque vandale, fin du cinquième siècle.* Paris: Arts et Métiers Graphiques, 1952. ▸ Unique series of documents from Africa, mostly relating to sale of land. Demonstrates persistence of Mancian tenancy into Vandal period and social and economic resurgence of old landowning family. [CMW]

7.546 Michael H. Crawford. "Finance, coinage, and money from the Severans to Constantine." *Aufstieg und Niedergang der römischen Welt,* Series 2: *Principat,* 2 (1975) 560–93. ISBN 3-11-004971-6. ▸ Attempts to trace process whereby coinage of Commodus, still basically on Augustan model, evolved into that of Constantine. [CMW]

7.547 Siegfried Lauffer, ed. *Diokletians Preisedikt.* Berlin: de Gruyter, 1971. ▸ Definitive edition of all fragments known to that date of Diocletian's edict on prices, with brief introduction, notes, and extensive bibliography. [CMW]

7.548 Boudewijn Sirks. *Food for Rome: the legal structure of the transportation and processing of supplies for the imperial distributions in Rome and Constantinople.* Amsterdam: Gieben, 1991. ISBN 90-5063-069-3. ▸ Study of legal, epigraphic, and papyrological texts, primarily focusing on legal history and changes through time in juridical framework of system. [CMW]

7.549 Courtenay Edward Stevens. "Agriculture and rural life in the later Roman empire." In *The Cambridge economic history of Europe.* 2d ed. M. M. Postan, ed., vol. 1, pp. 92–124. Cambridge: Cambridge University Press, 1971. ISBN 0-521-04505-3. ▸ Survey of agriculture and rural conditions in later empire. In certain points outdated, but still useful; stresses theme of continuity and sees excessive exploitation driving people off land. [CMW]

7.550 F. W. Walbank. "Trade and industry under the later Roman empire in the West." In *The Cambridge economic history of Europe.* 2d ed. M. M. Postan and Edward Miller, eds., vol. 2, pp. 71–131. Cambridge: Cambridge University Press, 1987. ISBN 0-521-08709-0. ▸ Survey of trade and industry in West from early empire onward, arguing that imperial interference and excessive taxation eventually destroyed independent enterprises and diminished long-distance trade. [CMW]

7.551 Chris Wickham. "Marx, Sherlock Holmes, and late Roman commerce." *Journal of Roman studies* 78 (1988) 183–93. ISSN 0075-4358. ▸ Important review article interpreting Italian Marxist historical arguments of A. Carandini and others for English-speaking readers. Includes argument for considerable long-distance trade, in opposition to Finley 7.340 and others. [CMW]

Society

7.552 H. Idris Bell et al. *The Abinnaeus archive: papers of a Roman officer in the reign of Constantius II.* 1962 ed. Milan: Cisalpino-Goliardica, 1975. ▸ Important documents and correspondence of retired Roman officer and wife from Philadelphia in Egypt, mid-fourth century. Documents cover property transactions, petitions, money matters, and soldier-civilian relationships. Text, translation, commentary. [CMW]

7.553 Peter Brown. *The making of late antiquity.* Cambridge, Mass.: Harvard University Press, 1978. ISBN 0-674-54320-3. ▸ Influential study of social and intellectual changes, second to fourth century. Omnipresence of supernatural, new ceremonies of power, decline of public buildings, and spread of monastic asceticism. [CMW]

7.554 Peter Brown. *Power and persuasion in late antiquity: towards a Christian empire.* Madison: University of Wisconsin Press, 1992. ISBN 0-299-13340-0 (cl), 0-299-13344-3 (pbk). ▸ Study of upper-class culture, 300–450 CE, discussing religious and cultural expectations of educated people and emergence of Christian leaders in face of imperial power. Attempts synthesis of recent scholarship. [CMW]

7.555 Peter Brown. *Religion and society in the age of Saint Augustine.* New York: Harper & Row, 1972. ISBN 0-06-010554-2. ▸ Collected articles and reviews illuminating intellectual world of late fourth century, especially in Italy and North Africa, with Augustine as central figure. [CMW]

7.556 Sabine G. MacCormack. *Art and ceremony in late antiquity.* 1981 ed. Berkeley: University of California Press, 1990. ISBN 0-520-03779-0 (cl), 0-520-06966-8 (pbk). ▸ Imperial iconography and ceremonial from late third to late sixth century as reflecting nature and exercise of power and influence of Christianity. [CMW]

7.557 Michele Renee Salzman. *On Roman time: the codex-calendar of 354 and the rhythms of urban life in late antiquity.* Berkeley: University of California Press, 1990. ISBN 0-520-06566-2. ▸ Analysis of contents of illustrated calendar, prepared for Christian aristocrat, suggesting conflict between Christian rigor and social obligations and attempts of Christian church to integrate itself into Roman life. [CMW]

SEE ALSO

8.247 Alan Cameron. *Circus factions.*
8.453 Alan Cameron. *Porphyrius the charioteer.*
20.1027 Peter Brown. *Society and the holy in late antiquity.*

Intellectual Life: Literature, Philosophy, Education

7.558 J. W. Binns, ed. *Latin literature of the fourth century.* London: Routledge & Kegan Paul, 1974. ISBN 0-7100-7796-3. ▸ Six studies of fourth-century writers: Augustine, Ausonius, Symmachus, Paulinus, Claudian, and Prudentius. [CMW]

7.559 Glen W. Bowersock. *Hellenism in late antiquity.* Ann Arbor: University of Michigan Press, 1990. ISBN 0-472-09418-1. ▸ Argues persistence of Greek culture provided shared repertoire of customs, language, and iconography that both kept paganism alive and facilitated development of Christianity and, later, Islam. [CMW]

7.560 Alan Cameron. *Claudian: poetry and propaganda at the court of Honorius.* Oxford: Clarendon, 1970. ISBN 0-19-814351-6. ▸ Study of life and work of Claudian, stressing his relationship with Stilicho and other leading men of day. Brief sketch of his influence on later writers. [CMW]

7.561 Patricia Cox. *Biography in late antiquity: a quest for the holy man.* Berkeley: University of California Press, 1983. ISBN 0-520-04612-9. ▸ In general context of ancient biographical tradition, shows how Eusebius's life of Origen and Porphyry's of Plotinus depict their subjects as inspired exemplars. [CMW]

7.562 Robert A. Kaster. *Guardians of language: the grammarian and society in late antiquity.* Berkeley: University of California Press, 1988. ISBN 0-520-05535-7. ▸ Study of grammarian's profession, social status, and role as guarantor of social and cultural continuity; part 2, prosopography of grammarians and the like. [CMW]

7.563 Anne-Marie Palmer. *Prudentius on the martyrs.* New York: Oxford University Press, 1989. ISBN 0-19-814721-X. ▸ Study of perhaps greatest of early Christian poets in intellectual context of his day. Discusses his audience's knowledge of both classical literature and Christian tradition. [CMW]

7.564 J. M. Rist. *Plotinus: the road to reality.* 1967 ed. Cambridge: Cambridge University Press, 1977. ISBN 0-521-29202-6. ▸ Account of Plotinus's life and teachings, leading to discussion of Neoplatonic faith and Plotinus's influence on both pagan and Christian successors. [CMW]

7.565 Frances M. Young. *From Nicaea to Chalcedon: a guide to the literature and its background.* Philadelphia: Fortress, 1983. ISBN 0-8006-1754-1 (cl), 0-8006-0711-2 (pbk). ▸ Study of Christian writers and controversialists of fourth century in context of intellectual life and influence of period. [CMW]

SEE ALSO
    6.606 A. H. Armstrong, ed. *The Cambridge history of later Greek and early medieval philosophy.*

Art and Architecture

7.566 Ranuccio Bianchi Bandinelli. *Rome, the late empire: Roman art, AD 200–400.* Peter Green, trans. New York: Braziller, 1971. ISBN 0-8076-0593-X. ▸ Study of Roman art, especially sculpture, stressing importance of provinces as well as Rome, and of popular art, especially in West. [CMW]

7.567 Wladimiro Dorigo. *Late Roman painting.* 1970 ed. James Cleugh and John Warrington, trans. New York: Praeger, 1971. ▸ Controversial study of painting and mosaic in third and fourth centuries, tracing influence of "ideological crisis" on artistic development. Attempts to identify individual artists. [CMW]

7.568 Hans Peter L'Orange. *The Roman empire: art forms and civic life.* 1965 ed. Dr. and Mrs. Knut Berg, trans. New York: Rizzoli, 1985. ISBN 0-8478-0663-4. ▸ Study of late third- and fourth-century art whose block forms and static conceptions model changes in structure of society. Followed by essay on Ara

Pacis. Earlier title: *Art Forms and Civic Life in the Late Roman Empire.* [CMW]

7.569 Robert Milburn. *Early Christian art and architecture.* Berkeley: University of California Press, 1988. ISBN 0-520-06326-0. ▸ History of art from beginnings of Christianity to Justinian, emphasizing architecture and sculpture but embracing other arts and crafts. [CMW]

7.570 J. J. Wilkes. *Diocletian's palace, Split: residence of a retired Roman emperor.* Sheffield, England: University of Sheffield Press, Department of Ancient History and Classical Archaeology, 1986. (University of Sheffield, Department of Ancient History and Classical Archaeology, Occasional publications, 2.) ISBN 0-9511263-0-X. ▸ Fullest account in English of architecture and history of Diocletian's palace, with report on its condition as of 1982. [CMW]

7.571 R.J.A. Wilson. *Piazza Armerina.* London: Granada, 1983. ISBN 0-246-11396-0 (pbk). ▸ Account of Piazza Armerina villa in geographical and historical context, with convincing arguments disassociating it from Emperor Maximian or his son Maxentius and assigning it to unknown wealthy senator. [CMW]

SEE ALSO
    8.439 Ernst Kitzinger. *Byzantine art in the making.*

"Decline and Fall": Concept and Causes

7.572 Norman H. Baynes. "The decline of Roman power in western Europe: some modern explanations." *Journal of Roman studies* 33 (1943) 29–35. ISSN 0075-4358. ▸ Dismisses fashionable explanations; concludes West suffered severer military pressure than East, and each incursion cut revenues and weakened resistance, whereas Asia Minor was reservoir of men and money. Still fundamental. [CMW]

7.573 Alexander Demandt. *Der Fall Roms: die Auflösung des römischen Reiches im Urteil der Nachwelt.* Munich: Beck, 1984. ISBN 3-406-09598-4. ▸ History of research into causes of Rome's fall shows perennial fascination with topic; lists 210 suggested factors, from *Aberglaube* (superstition) to *Zölibat* (celibacy) and *Zweifrontenkrieg* (war on two fronts). [CMW]

7.574 Arther Ferrill. *The fall of the Roman empire: the military explanation.* 1986 ed. London: Thames & Hudson, 1988. ISBN 0-500-25095-2 (cl, 1986), 0-500-27495-9 (pbk). ▸ Study of late Roman army and campaigns, arguing emphasis on cavalry and introduction of barbarian allies fatally weakened Roman infantry, which lost decisive battles. [CMW]

7.575 Ramsay MacMullen. *Corruption and the decline of Rome.* New Haven: Yale University Press, 1988. ISBN 0-300-04313-9. ▸ Study of collapse of empire in North and West due to decline in traditional values and growth in number of persons in authority who used authority solely for private profit. [CMW]

7.576 Jaroslav Pelikan. *The excellent empire: the fall of Rome and the triumph of the church.* 1987 ed. San Francisco: Harper & Row, 1990. ISBN 0-06-254867-0 (pbk). ▸ Study of Christian responses to fall of Rome, replacing Gibbon's "triumph of barbarism and religion" with "social triumph of the ancient church." [CMW]

7.577 Frank W. Walbank. *The awful revolution: the decline of the Roman empire in the West.* Liverpool: Liverpool University Press, 1978. ISBN 0-85323-030-7 (cl), 0-85323-040-4 (pbk). ▸ Study of Rome's decline, attributing it primarily to lack of technological advance, associated with prevalence of slavery; classic statement of position once widely held. Revised edition of *The Decline of the Roman Empire in the West* (1946). [CMW]

Late Antiquity: Continuity and Change

7.578 S.J.B. Barnish. "Transformation and survival in the western senatorial aristocracy, c. AD 400–700." *Papers of the British*

School at Rome 56 (1988) 120–55. ISSN 0068-2462. ▸ Study of great senatorial families and their strength in fifth century. Changing marriage patterns, ideals of celibacy, and other pressures caused subsequent decline. Individual families survived into eighth century. [CMW]

7.579 Peter Brown. *The world of late antiquity, AD 150–750.* New York: Harcourt Brace Jovanovich, 1971. ISBN 0-15-597633-8. ▸ Brilliant introductory essay on changing mentalities, with emphasis on new beginnings rather than on concepts of decline. [CMW]

7.580 Frank M. Clover and R. Stephen Humphreys, eds. *Tradition and innovation in late antiquity.* Madison: University of Wisconsin Press, 1989. ISBN 0-299-12000-7. ▸ Thirteen papers on cultural interaction, persistent concepts of *Romanitas*, and coming of Islam; see especially editors' "Toward a Definition of Late Antiquity." [CMW]

SEE ALSO
 8.135 Judith Herrin. *The formation of Christendom.*
 20.166 Bryan Ward-Perkins. *From classical antiquity to the Middle Ages.*
 20.167 Chris Wickham. *Early medieval Italy.*

Historians and Historiography

Ammianus Marcellinus

7.581 N.J.E. Austin. *Ammianus on warfare: an investigation into Ammianus' military knowledge.* Brussels: Latomus, 1979. ISBN 2-87031-105-2. ▸ Study of Ammianus's treatment of military operations, vindicating his understanding of both strategy and tactics, and particularly of intelligence work. Viewpoint of staff officer rather than field commander. [CMW]

7.582 R. C. Blockley. *Ammianus Marcellinus: a study of his historiography and political thought.* Brussels: Latomus, 1975. ▸ Study of Ammianus's career and aspects of his narrative: conservative values, sense of moral decline, reverence for Julian, etc. [CMW]

7.583 John Matthews. *The Roman empire of Ammianus.* Baltimore: Johns Hopkins University Press, 1989. ISBN 0-8018-3965-3. ▸ Magisterial study of Ammianus's career and history. Extraordinarily vivid sense of place, analysis of main topics discussed in his work, and extensive notes. [CMW]

7.584 R. L. Rike. *Apex omnium: religion in the "Res Gestae" of Ammianus.* Berkeley: University of California Press, 1987. ISBN 0-520-05858-5. ▸ Study of Ammianus's religious belief arguing he was thoughtful, aggressive pagan whose religious commitment is commonly underestimated. [CMW]

The *Historia Augusta*

7.585 Timothy David Barnes. *The sources of the "Historia Augusta."* Brussels: Latomus, 1978. ISBN 2-87031-005-6. ▸ Study of sources of *Historia Augusta*, accepting single authorship and arguing that six, and only six, main sources can be identified. [CMW]

7.586 Tony Honoré. "Scriptor *Historiae Augustae*." *Journal of Roman studies* 77 (1987) 156–76. ISSN 0075-4358. ▸ Article accepting attribution of *Historia Augusta* to single author in last decade of fourth century. Suggests its objective was veiled contemporary political satire. [CMW]

7.587 Arnaldo Momigliano. "Ammiano Marcellino e la *Historia Augusta* (a proposito del libro di Ronald Syme)." In *Quinto contributo alla storia degli studi classici e del mondo antico.* Vol. 1, pp. 93–108. Rome: Edizioni di Storia e Letteratura, 1975. ▸ Two reviews of Syme 7.588, republished in author's collected papers. Regards arguments for single authorship of *Historia Augusta* as

not proven; most explicit statement of conservative position, provoking rejoinder from Syme 7.590. [CMW]

7.588 Ronald Syme. *Ammianus and the "Historia Augusta."* Oxford: Clarendon, 1968. ISBN 0-19-814344-3. ▸ Study of *Historia Augusta*, arguing for date of composition in 395 or 396. Specifically notes certain passages apparently based on Ammianus, Book 15, published 392. [CMW]

7.589 Ronald Syme. *Emperors and biography: studies in the "Historia Augusta."* Oxford: Clarendon, 1971. ISBN 0-19-814357-5. ▸ Eighteen studies, reaffirming conclusions of 7.588, stressing author's "bent and delight" for historical fiction, discussing his sources, and offering solutions to a number of third-century conundrums. [CMW]

7.590 Ronald Syme. *The "Historia Augusta": a call of clarity.* Bonn: Habelt, 1971. ISBN 3-7749-1160-6. ▸ Brief polemical reply to Momigliano 7.587, again identifying work as "erudite imposture" written toward end of fourth century. Useful summary of author's arguments, less convoluted than 7.588 or 7.589. [CMW]

7.591 Ronald Syme. *"Historia Augusta" papers.* New York: Oxford University Press, 1983. ISBN 0-19-814853-4. ▸ Fifteen papers on aspects of *Historia Augusta*, brilliantly demonstrating bogus nature of these purported biographies. [CMW]

Other Topics

7.592 H. W. Bird. *Sextus Aurelius Victor: a historiographical study.* Liverpool: Cairns, 1984. (ARCA, Classical and medieval texts, Papers and monographs, 14.) ISBN 0-905205-21-9. ▸ Study of work of Sextus Aurelius Victor, described as "sober, honest, well-intentioned bureaucrat." [CMW]

7.593 W. den Boer. *Some minor Roman historians.* Leiden: Brill, 1972. ISBN 90-04-03545-1. ▸ Studies place of Aurelius Victor, Eutropius, and Festus in historiographical tradition. [CMW]

7.594 Brian Croke and Alanna M. Emmett, eds. *History and historians in late antiquity.* Sydney: Pergamon, 1983. ISBN 0-08-029840-0. ▸ Papers from conference in 1981 on Ammianus Marcellinus and other writers and on historiographical tradition in late antiquity. Useful collection. [CMW]

7.595 Steven Muhlberger. *The fifth-century chroniclers: Prosper, Hydatius, and the Gallic chronicler of 452.* Leeds: Cairns, 1990. (ARCA, Classical and medieval texts, Papers and monographs, 27.) ISBN 0-905205-76-6. ▸ Study of historical background and works of writers mentioned; especially strong on Hydatius. [CMW]

Biography and Hagiography

7.596 Polymnia Athanassiadi. *Julian: an intellectual biography.* 1981 ed. London: Routledge, 1992. ISBN 0-415-07763-X. ▸ Scholarly account of Julian's emotional, spiritual, and intellectual life, against background of his career. Written from overtly sympathetic viewpoint. Useful new introduction in 1992 edition. Earlier title: *Julian and Hellenism: An Intellectual Biography.* [CMW]

7.597 Glen W. Bowersock. *Julian the apostate.* Cambridge, Mass.: Harvard University Press, 1978. ISBN 0-674-48881-4. ▸ Brief account of Julian's life and career, with particular attention to analysis of sources. [CMW]

7.598 Jay Bregman. *Synesius of Cyrene: philosopher-bishop.* Berkeley: University of California Press, 1982. ISBN 0-520-04192-5. ▸ Study of ruling-class attitudes as exemplified in career of Synesius, bishop of Ptolemaïs, brilliant philosopher with little grounding in scriptures, primarily concerned with preserving Hellenic values and ideas. [CMW]

7.599 Sebastian P. Brock and Susan Ashbrook Harvey. *Holy women of the Syrian Orient.* Berkeley: University of California

Press, 1987. ISBN 0-520-05705-8. ‣ Collection of saints' lives, translated from Syriac, with introduction and commentaries stressing Syriac emphasis on asceticism. [CMW]

7.600 Ramsay MacMullen. *Constantine.* 1969 ed. London: Croom Helm, 1987. ISBN 0-7099-4685-6. ‣ Readable biography of Constantine, conventional in approach and interpretation. Useful introduction to his reign. [CMW]

7.601 Stewart Irvin Oost. *Galla Placidia Augusta: a biographical essay.* Chicago: Chicago University Press, 1968. ‣ Biography of Galla Placidia, daughter of Theodosius I. Useful introduction to politics of early fifth century. [CMW]

7.602 Philip Rousseau. *Pachomius: the making of a community in fourth-century Egypt.* Berkeley: University of California Press, 1985. ISBN 0-520-05048-7. ‣ Life of Pachomius with stress on his achievements in founding monasteries, on monastic life, and on relationship between monastery and society. [CMW]

7.603 Clare Stancliffe. *St. Martin and his hagiographer: history and miracle in Sulpicius Severus.* Oxford: Oxford University Press, 1983. ISBN 0-19-821895-8. ‣ Study of Sulpicius's biography of Martin, attempting to reconstruct Martin's life and mentality in context of state of Gaul and intellectual and ecclesiastical context of period. [CMW]

7.604 Stephen Williams. *Diocletian and the Roman recovery.* New York: Methuen, 1985. ISBN 0-416-01151-9. ‣ Conventional biography, only one in English. Stresses Diocletian's administrative reforms and their failure to achieve permanent solution. [CMW]

SEE ALSO
20.1004 Peter Brown. *Augustine of Hippo.*
20.1006 J.N.D. Kelly. *Jerome.*
20.1055 James J. O'Donnell. *Cassiodorus.*

Regional Studies and Individual Cities

7.605 Roger S. Bagnall. *Egypt in late antiquity.* Princeton: Princeton University Press, 1993. ISBN 0-691-06986-7. ‣ Authoritative study of Egypt in fourth and early fifth century, based primarily on papyri, concentrating on countryside, relations between towns and villages, development of Christianity, power and dependence, language, and ethnicity. [CMW]

7.606 Christian Courtois. *Les Vandales et l'Afrique.* 1955 ed. Aalen: Scientia, 1964. ‣ Standard history of Vandal kingdom in Africa. Well documented, sound judgment, correcting many earlier preconceptions. [CMW]

7.607 John F. Drinkwater. *The Gallic empire: separatism and continuity in the northwestern provinces of the Roman empire, AD 260–274.* Stuttgart: Steiner, 1987. (*Historia,* Einzelschriften, 52.) ISBN 3-515-04806-5. ‣ Study of briefly independent so-called Impe-

rium Galliarum. Heavily dependent on numismatic evidence; sequel to Drinkwater and Elton 7.608. [CMW]

7.608 John F. Drinkwater and Hugh Elton, eds. *Fifth-century Gaul: a crisis of identity?* Cambridge: Cambridge University Press, 1992. ISBN 0-521-41485-7. ‣ Twenty-eight papers from various disciplinary perspectives discussing reactions of inhabitants of Gaul to establishment of barbarian kingdoms and to Gaul's excision from empire. [CMW]

7.609 A. S. Esmonde Cleary. *The ending of Roman Britain.* 1989 ed. Savage, Md.: Barnes & Noble, 1990. ISBN 0-389-20893-0. ‣ History of Britain in late fourth and fifth centuries, based primarily on archaeological evidence. Ends with discussion of degree of continuity into Anglo-Saxon period. [CMW]

7.610 Anthony King and Martin Henig, eds. *The Roman West in the third century: contributions from archaeology and history.* Oxford: British Archaeological Reports, 1981. (British Archaeological Reports international series, 109.) ISBN 0-86054-127-4. ‣ Thirty-three papers touching on all western provinces. Especially useful in summarizing and interpreting archaeological data. Topics discussed include pottery evidence, coinage, and burial customs. [CMW]

7.611 Claude Lepelley. *Les cités de l'Afrique romaine au Bas-empire.* Vol. 1: *La permanence d'une civilisation municipale.* Vol. 2: *Notices d'histoire municipale.* 2 vols. Paris: Études Augustiniennes, 1979–81. ISBN 2-85121-029-7 (v. 1), 2-85121-032-7 (v. 2). ‣ Detailed study comprising chronological account of history of African cities in later empire (volume 1), followed by summary of evidence, arranged city by city (volume 2). [CMW]

7.612 J.H.W.G. Liebeschuetz. *Antioch: city and imperial administration in the later Roman empire.* Oxford: Clarendon, 1972. ISBN 0-19-814295-1. ‣ Social history and civic institutions of Antioch in fourth century, based primarily on writings of Libanius with epilogue looking forward to Muslim city. [CMW]

7.613 J. B. Segal. *Edessa, "the blessed city."* Oxford: Clarendon, 1970. ISBN 0-19-821545-2. ‣ Stresses city's strategic position and importance in frontier wars as well as its role in development of early Christianity. [CMW]

7.614 B. H. Warmington. *The North African provinces from Diocletian to the Vandal conquest.* 1954 ed. Westport, Conn.: Greenwood, 1971. ISBN 0-8371-5202-X. ‣ Outline history of North Africa in fourth and early fifth centuries, primarily based on epigraphic evidence. Dated, but still best account available in English. [CMW]

SEE ALSO
8.236 Clive Foss. *Ephesus after antiquity.*
20.143 Raymond Van Dam. *Leadership and community in late antique Gaul.*

ALEXANDER P. KAZHDAN

Byzantium

Serious study of Byzantium began in the seventeenth century, primarily in France. It was the period of the "erudite" approach, when major texts were published and translated into Latin, commentaries made, a dictionary of medieval Greek compiled, and the first studies of Byzantine topography, prosopography, and diplomatics appeared. The most all-embracing figure of this period was Charles Du Cange (1610–1688), some of whose pioneering works, though obsolete, have not yet been replaced.

The second period of Byzantine studies, inaugurated by E. Gibbon (1737–1794) (8.111), was a period of scornful rejection: Byzantium was proclaimed the worst of states because it was a Christian monarchy that destroyed the values of ancient civilization. Not only was it a Christian state, but an Orthodox one, and according to Catholic scholars of the nineteenth century (e.g., Cardinal Joseph Hergenröther, 1824–1890 [8.155]), Orthodoxy was a vicious religion that contributed to the enslavement of man by a powerful state apparatus. The theory of the slavization of Greece was suggested to "explain" the drastic decline of the Greek nation. One of its primary adherents, J. P. Fallmerayer (1797–1861) (8.90), argued that the Slavic invasions of the seventh century exterminated the Hellenic population along with its institutions and virtues.

Naturally, this negative evalution of Byzantium by Gibbon and Fallmerayer met with resistance from Russian and Greek scholars, but the latter's views had little effect until the end of the nineteenth century, when a trend toward the rehabilitation of Byzantium slowly developed. At that time many great scholars in various countries began a thorough and critical study of the sources for the history (at first political history) of Byzantium. But instead of presenting events in a narrative manner, these scholars, armed with positivist philosophy, tried to penetrate beyond the surface of chronography to establish the "true facts." K. E. Zachariä von Lingenthal (1812–1894), K. Krumbacher (1856–1909) (8.386), C. Diehl (1859–1944) (8.110), and J. B. Bury (1816–1927) (8.129) produced remarkable works that formed the basis of modern Byzantine studies. Even though some elements of the negative approach lingered (the emphasis on state monopolies, the lack of creativity, etc.), certain positive features of the Eastern Roman empire began to emerge; Byzantine art and architecture, for example, acquired a certain respect. Russian scholars, the greatest of whom was V. Vasil'evskij (1838–1899) (8.91), were particularly eager to rehabilitate Byzantium; ironically, in their positive assessment, they made use of exactly those observations that had led Gibbon and Fallmerayer to the censure of Eastern Rome. Developing the ideas expressed by von Lingenthal, Vasil'evskij launched a theory that, with some modifications, remained dominant in Slavic countries until recently and was widely accepted in the West: the later Roman empire degenerated but was saved by the influx of new peoples—in the West, the Germanic peoples; in the East, the Slavs. The Slavic rural community obtained the support of the Orthodox monarchy and secured the flourishing of Byzantium under the rule of the Macedonian dynasty that, in turn, focused more attention on the needs of the peasantry and soldiers. It was only with the penetration of Western influence and feudal institutions that the natural alliance of the emperors, Orthodox clergy, and rural community was shattered.

In the West, the trend toward the rehabilitation of Byzantium took a different path (although the idea that the feudal "disease" had destroyed the sound and strong Macedonian state was propagated by many a scholar). Here the focus lay on the role of Byzantium as the guardian and transmitter of Hellenic civilization. Byzantine immobility, cultural imitation (*mimesis*), and state control over trade began to acquire a positive appreciation. Byzantium was treated as a state based on law (it accepted Roman law), with an effective administrative and military system, a continually functioning urban life, and a brilliant Renaissance art. Even the conflict between the Catholic and Orthodox churches was played down, and at least part of the responsibility for their earlier struggle was laid on the West.

Developments in recent decades have been determined, in substantial part, by two factors. First, the application of new sources of different character from the narrative materials that dominated the scholarship of the early twentieth century: data from archaeology, numismatics, sigillography, and documents helped to reshape the earlier perception of Byzantium. And second, the position of Byzantium was slowly shifted from the outskirts of "distorted" antiquity to the medieval world to which it properly belonged, at least chronologically. Modern scholars began to apply to it the methodology of medieval studies. As the veil of subjective opinion expressed in the storytelling of Byzantine historians and rhetoricians was gradually removed, and the substantial similarity of Western medieval and Byzantine development became evident, Byzantium began to lose its traditional image of immutability. Not only did the administration, the army, and agrarian relations turn out to have been changing, but even the view that Byzantium did not experience an urban crisis (the decline of the ancient polis) is now challenged. Scholars noticed that from the tenth to the twelfth century, Byzantium, like the West, experienced economic expansion. Byzantine science, literature, and even law have been gradually liberated from the theory that they were pure imitations of ancient models. The Byzantines, it turns out, not only copied old manuscripts but also coped with their own economic, political, and cultural problems. Even though Byzantine continuity with its ancient past is given its due respect, discontinuity, novelty, and change are attracting more and more scholarly attention.

This does not mean, however, that Byzantium and the West were identical: recent works have emphasized the need for caution in the application to Byzantium of such Western concepts as feudalism or Renaissance. While the Byzantine dependent peasant paid rents similar to those in the Occident, the ruling class in Byzantium had its own distinct features, and the Byzantine centralized government was a unique institution in medieval Europe.

Recent studies also have led to the reconsideration of the role of Byzantine clergy and intelligentsia. On the one hand, the nineteenth-century thesis of Byzantine caesaropapism has been rejected; on the other hand, the role of Byzantine intellectuals has begun to be more appreciated. Byzantium was not only the land of hermits and pious nuns but also a world in which generations of literati, operating under the strict control of the state machine, nevertheless found the means to protect their ideological and cultural independence.

The study of Byzantium is truly an international discipline; the major centers are found in Washington, D.C., Cambridge, Mass., London, Oxford, Cambridge, Birmingham, Paris, Brussels, Munich, Frankfurt, Naples, Uppsala, Athens, Thessalonica, Ioannina (Greece), Prague, Moscow, St. Petersburg, Sofia, and Belgrade. Important works on Byzantine history and culture are written not only in leading Western languages but also in modern Greek, Russian, Serbo-Croatian, and Bulgarian, and these are rarely (if ever) translated into English. While the major narrative texts are available in English translation, the documents are not, and the serious study of Byzantine economy, social relations, the administrative system, and law (let alone literature and theology) presumes the ability to use the Greek originals, as well as knowledge of the foreign languages in which many modern works have been published.

[Contributors: APK = Alexander P. Kazhdan, PFG = Paul F. Grendler, RJC = Richard J. Crampton, SBV = Steven Béla Várdy]

REFERENCE WORKS

Bibliographies and Dictionaries

8.1 Franz Dölger and Alfons Maria Schneider. *Byzanz.* Bern: Francke, 1952. (Wissenschaftliche Forschungsberichte, Geisteswissenchaftenliche Reihe, 5.) ▸ Bibliographic handbook organized according to subject: sources, history, literature, language, palaeography; and architecture, painting, and minor arts. First section includes works published 1938–50; second, works published 1939–49. Works categorized and discussed. [APK]

8.2 Alexander P. Kazhdan et al., eds. *The Oxford dictionary of Byzantium.* 3 vols. New York: Oxford University Press, 1991. ISBN 0-19-504652-8. ▸ 5,200 entries on all spheres of Byzantine life: political history, economy, administration, religion, science, law, art, music, literature, everyday life, etc. Maps, illustrations, chronological and genealogical tables; selected bibliography. [APK]

8.3 Donald Nicol. *A biographical dictionary of the Byzantine empire.* London: Seaby, 1991. ISBN 1-85264-048-0. ▸ Alphabetical list of Byzantine politicians, church leaders, and writers; short biographies and elementary bibliography. Chronological table of

main events 324–1461 and partial genealogical tables of imperial families. [APK]

8.4 Peter Wirth. *Reallexikon der Byzantinistik* (Dictionary of Byzantium). Amsterdam: Hakkert, 1968–76. ▸ Only six fascicles appeared; publication ceased in middle of article "Abendland und Byzanz." [APK]

Geography and Demography

8.5 *Actes de l'Athos.* Paris: Lethielleux, 1937–. ISSN 0768-1291. ▸ Ongoing series. Excellent, critical, and diplomatic edition of documents from archives of Mount Athos. Greek text with French summary and extensive commentary; each volume provided with album containing photographs of major documents. Organized by individual monasteries and, within each collection, in chronological order. Most important source material for geography, social history, and prosopography of southern Macedonia. Two earliest volumes (Lavra I and Koutloumousiou) have been revised. [APK]

8.6 Hélène Ahrweiler. *Byzance: les pays et les territoires.* London: Variorum, 1976. ISBN 0-902089-85-4. ▸ Articles on Byzantine geography previously published 1967–74. General problems of Byzantine geography, historical geography of particular areas (Smyrna and its region), and particular themes (e.g., the frontier). [APK]

8.7 Hélène Ahrweiler, ed. *Byzantina Sorbonensia.* Vol. 3: *Geographica Byzantiana.* Vol. 4: *Philadelphie et autres études.* Vol. 7: *Géographie historique du monde Méditerranéen.* Vol. 8: *Les îles de l'empire byzantin, VIIIe–XIIe siècles.* Paris: Publications de la Sorbonne, 1975–. ISBN 2-85944-041-0 (v. 3), 2-85944-079-8 (v. 4), 2-85944-152-2 (v. 7), 2-85944-164-6 (v. 8), ISSN 0398-7965. ▸ Ongoing publication including several collections of articles on Byzantine geography. [APK]

8.8 Michael Avi-Yonah. *The Madaba mosaic map.* Jerusalem: Israel Exploration Society, 1954. ▸ Topographical pavement of late sixth century from church at Madaba or Madeba (Jordan); major fragment presents region from Jordan River to Nile delta. [APK]

8.9 Peter Charanis. *The Armenians in the Byzantine empire.* Lisbon: Fundacao Calouste Gulbenkian, 1963. ▸ Armenians on throne of Constantinople, within aristocracy, in army, in commerce, and in intellectual life of empire. [APK]

8.10 Peter Charanis. *Studies on the demography of the Byzantine empire.* London: Variorum, 1972. ISBN 0-902089-25-0. ▸ Collection of studies (1946–71) on ethnic composition of Byzantium, mostly on Slavic settlements in Greece. In multinational Byzantium, Greek-speaking element more numerous than any other group, but not majority. [APK]

8.11 Karl Dieterich. *Byzantinische Quellen zur Länder- und Völkerkunde (5.–15. Jahrhundert).* 1912 ed. Hildesheim: Olms, 1973. ▸ German translation of fragments from sixty Byzantine writers on geography. First fascicle on general principles of geography and on ancient civilized peoples of Asia, Africa, and Europe. Second on "new" tribes within purview of Byzantines, such as Huns, Slavs, Germanic peoples (from Goths to Varangians). [APK]

8.12 Ernst Honigmann. *Die Ostgrenze des byzantinischen Reiches von 363 bis 1071 nach griechischen, arabischen, syrischen, und armenischen Quellen.* Brussels: Institut de Philologie et d'Histoire Orientales et Slaves, 1935. (Byzance et les Arabes, 3. Corpus Bruxellense historiae Byzantinae, 3.) ▸ Best description of the Byzantine territory on frontier with Persia through 603 and with Arab caliphate in seventh through eleventh centuries. Unlike Ramsay 8.22, territory is not divided into small units but investigated as whole. See also Makk 8.336. [APK]

8.13 Ernst Honigmann, ed. *Le Synekdèmos d'Hiéroklès et l'opus-*

cule géographique de Georges de Chypre. Brussels: Institut de Philologie et d'Histoire Orientales et Slaves, 1939. (Corpus Bruxellense historiae Byzantinae, forma imperii Byzantini, 1.) ▸ Publication of manuscript (composed before 535), with commentary and maps, of list of cities of Eastern Roman empire. List organized according to province. *Synekdemos* followed by related text, the *Description* (so-called "Iconoclast notitia"), by one George of Cyprus. [APK]

8.14 Herbert Hunger, ed. *Tabula imperii Byzantini.* 7 vols. to date. Vienna: Verlag der Österreichischen Akademie der Wissenschaften, 1976–. (Veröffentlichungen der Kommission für die *Tabula imperii Byzantini,* 1–.) ISBN 3-7001-0182-1 (v. 1), 3-7001-0401-4 (v. 2), 3-7001-0399-9 (v. 3), 3-7001-0634-3 (v. 4), 3-7001-1811-2 (v. 5), 3-7001-1898-8 (v. 6), 3-7001-1698-5 (v. 7). ▸ Important, ongoing publication. Each volume contains survey of particular region. General description followed by alphabetical list of towns, villages, castles, etc., known from literary and archaeological sources; in each case, comprehensive data on history, economy, and architecture of site. [APK]

8.15 E. D. Hunt. *Holy Land pilgrimage in the later Roman empire, AD 312–460.* Oxford: Clarendon, 1982. ISBN 0-19-826438-0. ▸ Pilgrims' routes and social and political role of pilgrimage. Important for study of Byzantine geography as well as economy and culture. [APK]

8.16 David Jacoby. *Société et démographie à Byzance et en Romanie latine.* London: Variorum, 1975. ISBN 0-902089-74-9. ▸ Articles published 1961–71 on population of Constantinople, rural demography, and Jews and Catalans in Byzantium; also composition and prosopography of ruling elite. [APK]

8.17 Raymond Janin and Jean Darrouzès. *La géographie ecclésiastique de l'empire byzantin.* Vol. 1: *Notitiae episcopatuum ecclesiae Constantinopolitanae.* Vol. 2: *Les églises et les monastères des grands centres byzantins.* Vol. 3: *Les églises et les monastères (de Constantinople).* 3 vols. Paris: Institut Français d'Études Byzantines, 1953–81. (Publications de l'Institut Français d'Études Byzantines, 3.) ▸ Volume 1, by Darrouzès, contains lists (from seventh century on) of bishoprics of patriarchate of Constantinople; volumes 2 and 3, by Janin, history of individual churches and monasteries in Bithynia (including Olympos), Hellespont, Latros, Galesios, Trebizond, Athens, Thessalonike, and Constantinople. [APK]

8.18 Johannes Koder. *Der Lebensraum der Byzantiner: historisch-geographischer Abriss ihres mittelalterlichen Staates im östlichen Mittelmeerraum.* Graz: Styria, 1984. (Byzantinische Geschichtsschreiber, Ergänzungsband, 1.) ISBN 3-222-10294-5. ▸ New approach to Byzantine geography. Examines routes, frontier, climate, and environmental changes (erosion, deforestation) of Balkans, Aegean Sea, and Asia Minor, as well as social problems: use of environment, settlement patterns, state and church administrative organization of territory, and ethnic and linguistic structure of empire. [APK]

8.19 George P. Majeska. *Russian travelers to Constantinople in the fourteenth and fifteenth centuries.* Washington, D.C.: Dumbarton Oaks Center for Byzantine Studies, 1984. (Dumbarton Oaks studies, 19.) ISBN 0-88402-101-7. ▸ Edition and translation, with detailed commentary, of five Russian descriptions of journeys (Stephen of Novgorod, Ignatij of Smolensk, Alexander the Clerk, Zosima the Deacon, and Anonymous). [APK]

8.20 John Watson McCrindle, ed. and trans. *The Christian topography of Cosmas, an Egyptian monk.* London: Hakluyt Society, 1897. (Works issued by the Hakluyt Society, 98.) ▸ Translation from Greek of sixth-century book describing region between Egypt and India. [APK]

8.21 Alfred Philippson. *Das byzantinische Reich als geographische Erscheinung.* Leiden: Brill, 1939. ▸ Classic, general survey and discussion of regions divided into two parts: the West (Italy, Sicily, North Africa, Spain) and East (Balkans, Crimea, Greece, Asia Minor, Cyprus, Armenia, northern Mesopotamia, Syria, Egypt, and Cyrenaica). Shrinking of territory connected with political ideology and geographical factors. [APK]

8.22 William Mitchell Ramsay. *The historical geography of Asia Minor.* 1890 ed. Amsterdam: Hakkert, 1962. ▸ Classic, general survey. Discussions of particular provinces with special attention to roads and bishoprics. [APK]

8.23 Aubrey Stewart, trans. *The pilgrimage of Joannes Phocas in the Holy Land (in the year 1185 A.D.).* London: Palestine Pilgrims' Text Society, 1896. (Palestine Pilgrims' Text Society, Library, 5.3.) ▸ English translation of description of Palestine by Greek traveler in 1185. Another translation at 8.11. [APK]

8.24 J.P.A. Van der Vin. *Travellers to Greece and Constantinople: ancient monuments and old traditions in medieval travellers' tales.* 2 vols. Leiden: Nederlands Historisch-Archaelogisch Instituut te Istanbul, 1980. (Publications de l'Institut Historique et Archéologique Néerlandais de Stamboul, 49.) ISBN 90-6258-049-1 (pbk, set). ▸ Discussion of travelers of seventh through fifteenth centuries and their categorization (pilgrims, Crusaders, envoys, merchants, mercenaries, prisoners of war, missionaries, geographers, scholars, tourists); description of monuments as seen by travelers. First volume contains text; second, notes and appendixes. [APK]

8.25 Ekkehard Weber. *Tabula Peutingeriana: Codex Vindobonensis 324.* Graz: Akademische Druck- und Verlagsanstalt, 1976. ISBN 3-201-00975-X. ▸ Facsimile edition of medieval copy of late Roman tourist map (probably of fifth century). [APK]

8.26 John Wilkinson, Joyce Hill, and W. F. Ryan. *Jerusalem pilgrimage, 1099–1185.* London: Hakluyt Society, 1988. (Works issued by the Hakluyt Society, Second series, 167.) ISBN 0-904180-21-2. ▸ General discussion of pilgrimage in twelfth century and translation of texts (mostly Western, including Icelandic, but also Slavic, Oriental, and Byzantine). [APK]

SEE ALSO
21.54 Steven B. Bowman. *The Jews of Byzantium, 1204–1453.*
21.77 Andrew Sharf. *Byzantine Jewry from Justinian to the Fourth Crusade.*

Serial Editions and Collections of Documents

8.27 *Corpus fontium historiae Byzantinae.* 1949–. ISSN 0589-8048. ▸ Internationally coordinated series of publications issued in Washington, Berlin, Brussels, Rome, Vienna, Thessalonike, and Paris. Primarily histories (among others, first edition of "Short Chronicle" by Michael Psellos) but also treatises, letters, patriarchal documents, *Book of the Eparch* (see 8.260 and 8.302) etc. Greek originals usually (not always) accompanied by English, German, or French translations and sometimes by extensive commentary (Constantine VII Porphyrogennetos, "On the Administration of the Empire") or notes. [APK]

8.28 *Corpus scriptorum historiae Byzantinae.* 50 vols. Bonn: Weber, 1828–97. ▸ Works of Byzantine authors, primarily historians, with Latin translations and in some cases commentary. Most have been replaced by modern critical editions, but for others this still best edition available. [APK]

8.29 Jacques-Paul Migne. *Patrologiae cursus completus, Series graeca.* Paris: Migne, 1857–66. ▸ Collection of Greek authors allegedly from first century CE (Pseudo-Dionysios Areopagite) through fifteenth century, mostly theologians. Texts, with rare exceptions, reproduced from previous editions and provided with Latin translation. [APK]

8.30 Franz Miklosich and Joseph Müller. *Acta et diplomata Graeca medii aevi sacra et profana.* 1860–90 ed. 6 vols. Aalen:

Scientia, 1960. ▸ Collection of imperial, ecclesiastical, and private acts, primarily of thirteenth through fifteenth centuries. Greek text only. Some sections available in modern critical editions (e.g., documents of monastery of Patmos and those of Menoikeion). [APK]

8.31 *Sources chrétiennes.* Paris: Cerf, 1941–. ISBN 0750-1978. ▸ Important, ongoing publication. Includes western as well as Greek and Oriental texts, mostly patristic but also Byzantine, e.g., Romanos the Hymnographer, Kosmas Indikopleustes, Symeon the Theologian, Manuel II. Most texts in original with French translation and thorough commentary. Certain texts (e.g., John Moschos) only in translation. [APK]

Epigraphy

8.32 Jelisaveta Stanojevich Allen and Ihor Ševčenko, eds. *Epigraphy.* Vol. 1 of *Literature in various Byzantine disciplines, 1892–1977.* Washington, D.C.: Mansell for Dumbarton Oaks, 1981. (Dumbarton Oaks bibliographies based on *Byzantinische Zeitschrift,* Series 2: Literature in various Byzantine disciplines, 1892–1977). ISBN 0-7201-0216-2 (set), 0-7201-1586-8 (v. 1). ▸ Material classified first by language (Greek, Armenian, Coptic inscriptions, etc.), then by location (Africa, Asia, Europe with subsections). Special topics (brick stamps, milestones, weights, etc.) treated separately. Within subsections material in chronological order. [APK]

8.33 Denis Feissel et al. "Inventaires en vue d'un recueil des inscriptions historiques de Byzance." *Travaux et mémoires* 5, 7, 9, and 10 (1973, 1979, 1985, and 1987) 145–80, 303–48, 267–395, and 357–98. ISSN 0577-1471. ▸ Ongoing publication. Greek inscriptions with French translation and commentary from Thessalonike, the Peloponnesos (Mistra excluded), and Thessaly (except Meteora). [APK]

8.34 Henri Grégoire. *Recueil des inscriptions grecques chrétiennes d'Asie Mineure.* 1922 ed. Amsterdam: Hakkert, 1968. ▸ Inscriptions, mostly of fourth through sixth centuries, from provinces of Asia, Caria, Lycia, Pamphylia, Lydia, and some Aegean islands; only a few of later period, including some post-Byzantine. Organized geographically. Greek with French commentary. [APK]

8.35 Anastasios K. Orlandos and Leandros I. Vranoussis. *Les graffiti du Parthénon: inscriptions gravées sur les colonnes du Parthénon à l'époque paléochrétienne et byzantine.* Athens: Academy of Sciences, 1973. ▸ Inscriptions carved on columns of Parthenon in Athens during proto-Christian and Byzantine periods. Modern Greek with French title. [APK]

Numismatics and Sigillography

8.36 Alfred R. Bellinger and Philip Grierson. *Catalogue of the Byzantine coins in the Dumbarton Oaks collection and in the Whittemore collection.* 1966 ed. Washington, D.C.: Dumbarton Oaks Research Library and Collection, 1992. ISBN 0-88402-012-6. ▸ Publication of coins from Anastasios I (491–518) through Nikephoros III Botaneiates (1078–81) with extensive commentary describing development of monetary system, activity of mints, and coin types and inscriptions. Continued by Hendy 8.40. [APK]

8.37 Simon Bendall and P. J. Donald. *The later Palaeologan coinage, 1282–1453.* London: Baldwin, 1979. ▸ Catalog of coins. [APK]

8.38 Philip Grierson. *Byzantine coins.* Berkeley: University of California Press, 1982. ISBN 0-520-04897-0. ▸ Convenient handbook; one-volume general history of Byzantine coins (491–1453). [APK]

8.39 Wolfgang R. O. Hahn. *Moneta imperii Byzantini: Rekonstruktion des Prägeaufbaues auf synoptisch-tabellarischer Grundlage.* 3 vols. to date. Vienna: Verlag der Österreichischen Akademie der Wissenschaften, 1973–. ISBN 3-7001-0005-1 (v. 1), 3-7001-0096-5 (v. 2), 3-7001-0400-6 (v. 3). ▸ Ongoing publication. First three volumes cover period 491–720. Survey of Byzantine coinage in form of systematic tables rather than catalog. [APK]

8.40 Michael F. Hendy. *Coinage and money in the Byzantine empire, 1081–1261.* Washington, D.C.: Dumbarton Oaks Center for Byzantine Studies, 1969. (Dumbarton Oaks studies, 12.) ▸ Coins from Alexios I Komnenos to reconquest of Constantinople by Michael VIII Palaiologos. To some extent, continuation of catalog by Bellinger and Grierson (8.36) with more emphasis on economic changes (monetary crisis and monetary recovery). [APK]

8.41 Vitalien Laurent. *Le corpus des sceaux de l'empire byzantin.* 2 vols. Paris: Éditions du Centre National de la Recherche Scientifique, 1963–81. ISBN 2-222-02505-2 (v. 2). ▸ Planned as comprehensive annotated catalog of Byzantine seals organized by subject. Only two volumes available: volume 2 on central administration, and volumes 5.1–3 (with separate album) on ecclesiastical structure. [APK]

8.42 Cécile Morrisson. *Catalogue des monnaies byzantines de la Bibliothèque Nationale.* 2 vols. Paris: Bibliothèque Nationale, 1970. ▸ Coins from Anastasios I (491–518) through Alexios III Angelus (1195–1203). Emphasis on catalog itself rather than on characterization of coinage, as in Bellinger and Grierson 8.36 and Hendy 8.40. [APK]

8.43 John Nesbitt and Nicolas Oikonomides, eds. *Catalogue of Byzantine seals at Dumbarton Oaks and in the Fogg Museum of Art,* Vol. 1. Washington, D.C.: Dumbarton Oaks Research Library and Collection, 1991. ISBN 0-88402-194-7. ▸ Catalogs one of largest collections in the world; includes seals of western and northern regions of empire, from Africa and Italy to Crimea and Rus'. Includes detailed commentary. [APK]

8.44 Nicolas Oikonomides. *A collection of dated Byzantine lead seals.* Washington, D.C.: Dumbarton Oaks Research Library and Collection, 1986. ISBN 0-88402-150-5 (pbk). ▸ Number of seals that bear date or can be dated insignificant but particularly important since they create basis for dating of other specimens by palaeographic, iconographic, and various other formal characteristics. [APK]

8.45 Nicolas Oikonomides, ed. *Studies in Byzantine sigillography.* 2 vols. Washington, D.C.: Dumbarton Oaks Research Library and Collection, 1987–90. ISBN 0-88402-171-8 (v. 1), 0-88402-188-2 (v. 2). ▸ Papers (in English and other languages) presented to international colloquia on Byzantine sigillography. Seals are important source for study of prosopography, administrative systems, and even art. [APK]

8.46 George Zacos and Alexander Veglery. *Byzantine lead seals.* 2 vols. John Nesbitt, ed. and comp., vol. 2. Basel and Bern: Augustin and Benteli, 1972–85. (Tetradia archaiologias kai technes, 3.) ISBN 3-7165-0477-7 (v. 2). ▸ Seals from Zacos's private collection. Organized by groups distinguished by formal characteristics, such as dated, iconographic, or bilateral seals. Other groups such as imperial or patriarchal seals treated separately. [APK]

Archaeology

8.47 Anthony A. M. Bryer. "Byzantine agricultural implements: the evidence of medieval illustrations of Hesiod's *Works and Days.*" *Annual of the British School at Athens* 81 (1986) 45–80. ISSN 0068-2454. ▸ List of agricultural tools compiled on basis of Byzantine miniatures and archaeological discoveries. Most important source of improvement not development of new kind of implement, but more efficient use of metal to shoe wooden tools. [APK]

8.48   Gladys R. Davidson. *Corinth XII: the minor objects*. Princeton: American School of Classical Studies at Athens, 1952. (Corinth, 12.) ▸ Catalog of finds in medieval Corinth: figurines, vessels (metal, glass, stone), furniture, boxes, keys, implements and instruments, jewelry, and seals. [APK]

8.49   V. Déroche and J. M. Spieser, eds. *Recherches sur la céramique byzantine*. Athens: École Française d'Athènes, 1989. (Bulletin de correspondance hellénique, Supplément, 18.) ISBN 2-86958-025-8, ISSN 0304-2465. ▸ Papers (in Greek, French, English, and Italian) delivered at colloquium organized by École Française d'Athènes and University of Strasbourg in Athens in 1987, treating various aspects of Byzantine ceramics. [APK]

8.50   Clive Foss. *History and archaeology of Byzantine Asia Minor*. Aldershot, England: Variorum, 1990. ISBN 0-86078-263-8. ▸ Collected essays published 1975–88 based primarily on archaeological and epigraphical materials. Particularly important, "Archaeology and the 'Twenty Cities' of Byzantine Asia" and studies of individual cities: Ankara, the city on Mount Tmolus, and Strobilos. See also Foss 8.235 and 8.236. [APK]

8.51   Joachim Henning. *Südosteuropa zwischen Antike und Mittelalter: archäologische Beiträge zur Landwirtschaft des ersten Jahrtausends u.Z.* Berlin: Akademie, 1987. (Schriften zur Ur- und Frühgeschichte, 42.) ISBN 3-05-000121-6, ISSN 0138-3361. ▸ Catalog of archaeological finds of agrarian implements in Danube basin. Marxist analysis. Presents paradox: development (not stagnation!) of agrarian technology did not lead to increase in productivity. [APK]

8.52   Charles Hill Morgan. *The Byzantine pottery*. 1942 ed. Ann Arbor: University Microfilms International, 1990. (Corinth: results of excavations, 11.) ▸ Typology of Byzantine ceramics found in Corinth; flourishing industry in eleventh and twelfth centuries. [APK]

8.53   Joseph Philippe. *Le monde byzantin dans l'histoire de la verrerie (cinquième–seizième siècles)*. Bologna: Pàtron, 1970. ▸ General and popular survey of glass objects produced in Byzantium and adjacent countries. [APK]

8.54   James Russell. "Transformations of early Byzantine urban life: the contributions and limitations of archaeological evidence." In *The Seventeenth International Byzantine Congress, Major papers*, pp. 137–54. New Rochelle, N.Y.: Caratzas, 1986. ISBN 0-89241-443-X (cl), 0-89241-444-8 (pbk). ▸ Eastern Roman cities underwent decline in sixth and seventh centuries, but urban crisis not all encompassing. Discussion of need to interpret archaeological and numismatic evidence with caution (limited size of excavated cities, complexity of stratigraphy, contradiction with written sources). [APK]

8.55   Axel von Saldern. *Ancient and Byzantine glass from Sardis*. Cambridge, Mass.: Harvard University Press, 1980. ISBN 0-674-03303-5. ▸ Catalog and typology of hollow glass objects (lamps, vessels, etc.) and bracelets found mostly in fragments. Divided into four chronological periods: pre-Roman, Roman, and early and middle Byzantine. Last chapter concerns rings and beads. [APK]

8.56   Jane C. Waldbaum. *Metalwork from Sardis: the finds through 1974*. Cambridge, Mass.: Harvard University Press, 1983. (Archaeological exploration of Sardis, Monographs, 8.) ISBN 0-674-57070-7. ▸ Catalog of gold, silver, copper and bronze, iron, and zinc objects categorized by function (weapons, horsetrappings, bells, tools, etc.). Byzantine objects described at end of each chapter. [APK]

8.57   Caroline Williams. *Anemurium: the Roman and early Byzantine pottery*. Toronto: Pontifical Institute of Mediaeval Studies, 1989. (Studia mediaevalia, 16.) ISBN 0-88844-365-X (pbk), ISSN 0316-0769. ▸ Catalog of vessels and fragments from Anemourion,

Cilicia, categorized by ware and by type within ware. Three groups of late Roman fineware: African, Cypriot, and Phokaian origin. Cessation of imports from western Asia Minor in late sixth century and decline of imports of African pottery in seventh century. Only coarse pottery produced in Anemourion itself. [APK]

Palaeography and Codicology

8.58   Ruth Barbour. *Greek literary hands, A.D. 400–1600*. Oxford: Clarendon, 1981. ISBN 0-19-818229-5. ▸ Album of specimens from dated Greek manuscripts (mostly minuscule) from early sixth century through 1610, prefaced by short and clear characterization of evolution of medieval Greek handwriting from fifth century onward. [APK]

8.59   Guglielmo Cavallo. *Ricerche sulla maiuscola biblica*. Florence: Le Monnier, 1967. (Studi e testi di papirologia editi dall'Istituto Papirologico G. Vitelli di Firenze, 2.) ▸ Classic analysis of development of so-called biblical uncial from second through early ninth centuries: perfected in fourth century and fell into decline in sixth. Influence of biblical uncial on other Greek and Latin calligraphic handwritings. [APK]

8.60   Guglielmo Cavallo and H. Maehler. *Greek bookhands of the early Byzantine period, A.D. 300–800*. London: University of London, Institute of Classical Studies, 1987. (Bulletin, Supplement, 47.) ISBN 0-900587-51-2, ISSN 0076-0749. ▸ Album of specimens of Greek script from papyri of early fourth century through codex of 800, with short introduction. Categorization of early Byzantine scripts: majuscule (uncial) and documentary cursive. [APK]

8.61   Colloque International sur la Paléographie Grecque et Byzantine. *La paléographie grecque et byzantine*. Paris: Centre National de la Recherche Scientifique, 1977. (Colloques internationaux du Centre National de la Recherche Scientifique, 559.) ISBN 2-222-01900-1. ▸ Papers presented at colloquium (Paris, 1974) treat problems of codicology, palaeography, and diplomatics. [APK]

8.62   Viktor Emil Gardthausen. *Griechische Palaeographie*. 1911–13 ed. 2 vols. Leipzig: Zentralantiquariat der Deutschen Demokratischen Republik, 1978. ▸ Best detailed description of Greek manuscript book (materials, form, writing implements, ink, binding) and script (uncial, cursive, miniscule, local scripts); also artificial scripts (tachygraphy, cryptography), abbreviations, numbers, scribes' signatures, chronology. [APK]

8.63   Marcel Richard. *Répertoire des bibliothèques et des catalogues de manuscrits grecs (avec supplément)*. 2d ed. Paris: Centre National de la Recherche Scientifique, 1958–64. (Publication de l'Institut de Recherche et d'Histoire des Textes, 1.) ▸ Alphabetical list of locations of collections of Greek manuscripts with bibliography. [APK]

8.64   Colin Henderson Roberts and T. C. Skeats. *The birth of the codex*. London: Oxford University Press, 1983. ISBN 0-19-726024-1. ▸ Discussion of replacement of roll by codex by sixth century when roll vanished as vehicle of literature. [APK]

8.65   Edward Maunde Thompson. *An introduction to Greek and Latin palaeography*. 1912 ed. New York: Franklin, 1965. ▸ General survey. [APK]

Auxiliary Disciplines

8.66   Roger S. Bagnall and Klaas A. Worp. *The chronological systems of Byzantine Egypt*. Zutphen, Holland: Terra, 1978. (Studia Amstelodamensia ad epigraphicam, ius antiquum et papyrologicam pertinentia, 8.) ISBN 90-6255-206-4 (cl), 90-6255-200-5 (series). ▸ Synoptic chronological chart for 284–641 that takes into consideration indictions, regnal years, consulates, as well as local eras (Oxyrhynchite and Diocletianic); origin and development of indiction system of dating documents. [APK]

8.67 Konstantinos Barzos. *He genealogia ton Komnenon.* 2 vols. Thessalonike: Kentron Byzantinon Ereunon, 1984. (Byzantina keimena kai meletai, 20AB.) ‣ Prosopography of most important Byzantine lineage of eleventh and twelfth centuries, imperial dynasty of Komnenoi and related families; detailed biographies of individual members of lineage. [APK]

8.68 Jean-Claude Cheynet and Jean-François Vannier. *Études prosopographiques.* Paris: Publications de la Sorbonne, 1986. (Bibliotheca Sorbonensia, 5.) ‣ Four aristocratic lineages of tenth through twelfth centuries: Bourtzes, Brachamioi, Dalassenoi, and Palaiologoi. [APK]

8.69 Franz Dölger and Johannes Karayannopulos. *Byzantinische Urkundenlehre.* Munich: Beck, 1968. (Handbuch der Altertumswissenschaft, 12.3.1.1.) ‣ General description of imperial chancellery and categorization of imperial documents (*edictum*, letters to foreign rulers, treaties, chrysobulls) as well as their official copies. [APK]

8.70 Franz Dölger and Peter Wirth, eds. *Regesten der Kaiserurkunden des oströmischen Reiches von 565–1453.* Vol. 3, 2d rev. ed. 5 vols. Munich and Berlin: Oldenbourg and Beck, 1924–65, 1977 (v. 3). (Corpus der griechischen Urkunden des Mittelalters und der neueren Zeit, Reihe A, Regesten, Erste Abteilung, 3.) ISBN 3-406-00738-4 (v. 3). ‣ Chronologically (by reign) arranged list of imperial documents, letters, and embassies (565–1453) indicating date, type of missive, content, source, publication, secondary sources, and when necessary, critical analysis of document. Excellent reference work. [APK]

8.71 Venance Grumel. *La chronologie.* Paris: Presses Universitaires de France, 1958. (Traité d'études byzantines, 1.) ‣ General introduction (Christian world eras, calendars, cycles of time); chronological and genealogical tables. [APK]

8.72 Venance Grumel, Vitalien Laurent, and Jean Darrouzès. *Les actes des patriarches.* Vol. 1 (=7 fasc.) of *Les regestes des actes du patriarcat de Constantinople.* Paris: Socii Assumptionistae Chalcedonenses, 1932–91. (Le patriarcat byzantin, 1.) ISBN 2-901049-27-3 (fasc. 7). ‣ Chronologically (by pontificates) arranged list of patriarchal documents and letters, as well as synodal decisions (381–1453) indicating chronology, content, source with critical analysis of text (with references to scholarly works). Excellent reference work. [APK]

8.73 Arnold H. M. Jones, John R. Martindale, and J. Morris. *The prosopography of the later Roman empire.* 3 vols. in 4. Cambridge: Cambridge University Press, 1971–92. ISBN 0-521-07233-6 (v. 1), 0-521-20159-4 (v. 2), 0-521-20160-8 (v. 3.a–b). ‣ Biographies (in alphabetical order in each volume) of Roman politicians (primarily secular) and members of noble families 260–647: local personalities usually omitted. Mostly a comprehensive list of offices and titles with references to primary sources. [APK]

8.74 Angeliki E. Laiou-Thomadakis. "Peasant names in fourteenth-century Macedonia." *Byzantine and modern Greek studies* 1 (1975) 71–96. ISSN 0307-0131. ‣ Names as means of social identification originating from crafts or professions and from toponyms (in part, Slavic); others identified through family ties or sobriquets. [APK]

8.75 Igor' P. Medvedev. *Očerki vizantijskoj diplomatiki* (Essays on Byzantine diplomatics). Leningrad: Nauka, 1988. ISBN 5-02-027225-6. ‣ Only general study of Byzantine private document of ninth through fifteenth centuries. Analysis of its formulary, structure of notarial office, and role of private act in judicial process. [APK]

8.76 Donald M. Nicol. *The Byzantine family of Kantakouzenos (Cantacuzenus), ca. 1100–1460: a genealogical and prosopographical study.* Washington, D.C.: Dumbarton Oaks Center for Byzantine Studies, 1968. (Dumbarton Oaks studies, 11.) ‣ Biographies of individual members of important lineage that contested right of Palaiologoi to throne of Constantinople in fourteenth century. [APK]

8.77 Donald M. Nicol. *Studies in late Byzantine history and prosopography.* London: Variorum, 1986. ISBN 0-86078-190-9. ‣ Collection of articles published 1965–84, one a general survey (prosopography of Byzantine aristocracy) and others on individual families (Akropolites, Tagaris, Dermokaites). [APK]

8.78 Aberkios T. Papadopulos. *Versuch einer Genealogie der Palaiologen, 1259–1453.* 1938 ed. Amsterdam: Hakkert, 1962. ‣ Biographies of members of last Byzantine imperial dynasty and their relatives. [APK]

8.79 Demetrios I. Polemis. *The Doukai: a contribution to Byzantine prosopography.* London: Athlone, 1968. ISBN 0-485-13122-6. ‣ Biographies of individual members of aristocratic family of Doukai from mid-ninth through early twelfth centuries, as well as other lineages that assumed name of Doukai. [APK]

8.80 Erich Schilbach. *Byzantinische Metrologie.* Munich: Beck, 1970. (Handbuch der Altertumswissenschaft, 19.4.) ISBN 3-406-01424-0. ‣ Only general work of Byzantine metrology available. Measures of length, surface, volume, and weight both official and local. [APK]

8.81 Werner Seibt. *Die Skleroi: eine prosopographisch-sigillographische Studie.* Vienna: Österreichische Akademie der Wissenschaften, 1976. (Byzantinal Vindobonensia, 9.) ISBN 3-7001-0180-5. ‣ Study of aristocratic lineage of Skleroi active in ninth to eleventh centuries and surviving until fourteenth. [APK]

8.82 Erich Trapp, ed. *Prosopographisches Lexikon der Palaiologenzeit.* Vienna: Österreichische Akademie der Wissenschaften, 1976–. (Veröffentlichungen der Kommission Byzantinistik, 1.) ISBN 3-7001-0169-4 (fasc. 1). ‣ Alphabetical list of persons (Greek and foreign) mentioned in Byzantine sources of late thirteenth through fifteenth centuries with short biographical data and bibliography. Excellent ongoing publication. [APK]

GENERAL STUDIES

Festschriften and Collections of Articles

8.83 Paul J. Alexander. *Religious and political history and thought in the Byzantine empire.* London: Variorum, 1978. ISBN 0-86078-016-3. ‣ Articles published 1940–77 on ideology of imperial power, iconoclasm, and apocalyptic literature. [APK]

8.84 Hans-Georg Beck. *Ideen und Realitaeten in Byzanz: gesammelte Aufsaetze.* London: Variorum, 1972. ISBN 0-902089-41-2. ‣ Articles published 1952–71 on Byzantine studies in Germany. Other topics include theology, relations between Byzantium and the West, administration, and history of literature. [APK]

8.85 Robert Browning. *History, language, and literacy in the Byzantine world.* Northampton, England: Variorum, 1989. ISBN 0-86078-247-6. ‣ Collected studies published 1977–87 on Byzantine history. See especially "Athens in the 'Dark Age'" and studies on culture (literacy, medicine, etc.). First publication of "Greeks and Others from Antiquity to Renaissance." [APK]

8.86 Robert Browning. *Studies on Byzantine history, literature, and education.* London: Variorum, 1977. ISBN 0-86078-003-1. ‣ Articles published 1952–76; "The Patriarchal School at Constantinople in the Twelfth Century" and "Correspondence of a Tenth-Century Byzantine Scholar" especially important. [APK]

8.87 J. Chrysostomides, ed. *Kathegetria: essays presented to Joan Hussey on her eightieth birthday.* Camberley, England: Porphyrogenitus, 1988. ISBN 1-871328-00-4. ▸ Articles on Byzantine history, literature, and church history. [APK]

8.88 Gilbert Dagron. *La romanité chrétienne en Orient: héritages et mutations.* London: Variorum, 1984. ISBN 0-86078-141-0. ▸ Articles published 1969–82 on Byzantine society, ideology, culture, religion, and religious art (e.g., "The Cult of Images in the Byzantine World"). [APK]

8.89 John Duffy and John Peradotto, eds. *Gonimos: Neoplatonic and Byzantine studies presented to Leendert G. Westerink at 75.* Buffalo, N.Y.: Arethusa, 1988. ▸ Articles primarily on late Roman and Byzantine literati (especially Michael Psellos), also on Byzantine epistolography and military administration. Includes Westerink's bibliography. [APK]

8.90 Jakob Philipp Fallmerayer. *Fragmente aus dem Orient.* 2d ed. Georg Martin Thomas, ed. Stuttgart: Cotta, 1877. ▸ Collection of Fallmerayer's articles published in periodicals. On Fallmerayer, see Section 8, introductory essay. [APK]

8.91 Vasilij Grigor'evic Vasil'evskij. *Trudy* [Works]. 4 vols. St. Petersburg: Akademija Nauk, 1914–30. ▸ Articles of Russian Byzantinist published 1870s and 1880s primarily on Byzantine relations with Rus' and their neighbors. Also articles on legislation of iconoclast emperors and on protection of peasantry by Macedonian dynasty. On Vasil'evskij, see Section 8, introductory essay. Publication is incomplete. [APK]

8.92 Wolfram Hörandner et al., eds. *Byzantios: Festschrift für Herbert Hunger zum 70. Geburtstag.* Vienna: Becvar, 1984. ISBN 3-900538-04-2. ▸ Collection of articles by friends and pupils of Hunger; many articles on Byzantine geography. Bibliography of his works (1936–84). [APK]

8.93 Angeliki E. Laiou. *Gender, society, and economic life in Byzantium.* Brookfield, Vt.: Variorum, 1992. ISBN 0-86078-322-7. ▸ Collection of author's articles, published 1973–90, on role of women and on Byzantine trade (especially in late period). Includes article on late Byzantine aristocracy. [APK]

8.94 Angeliki E. Laiou, ed. *Charanis studies: essays in honor of Peter Charanis.* New Brunswick, N.J.: Rutgers University Press, 1980. ISBN 0-8135-0875-4. ▸ Collection of articles on various themes of Byzantine history. [APK]

8.95 Robert S. Lopez. *Byzantium and the world around it: economic and institutional relations.* London: Variorum, 1978. ISBN 0-86078-030-9. ▸ Articles published 1944–76 on Byzantine economy, law, coinage (mostly seventh through tenth centuries), and on relations of Byzantium with English, Muslims, and other foreigners. [APK]

8.96 Cyril Mango. *Byzantium and its image: history and culture of the Byzantine empire and its heritage.* London: Variorum, 1984. ISBN 0-86078-139-9. ▸ Collection of articles 1960–82 mostly on cultural tradition and literature (including hagiography), but also on everyday life. Emphasis on seventh to ninth centuries. [APK]

8.97 Cyril Mango and Omeljan Pritsak, eds. *Okeanos: essays presented to Ihor Ševčenko on his sixtieth birthday by his colleagues and students.* Cambridge, Mass.: Harvard Ukrainian Research Institute, 1983. (Harvard Ukrainian studies, 7.). ISSN 0363-5570. ▸ Collection of articles on Byzantine history and Greek medieval literature. [APK]

8.98 Ann Moffatt, ed. *Maïstor: classical, Byzantine, and Rennaisance studies for Robert Browning.* Canberra: Australian Association for Byzantine Studies, 1984. (Byzantina Australiensia, 5.) ISBN 0-9593626-1-4, ISSN 0725-3079. ▸ Articles on Byzantine culture; publications of Greek texts (e.g., *Vita of St. Athanasia of Aegina*). Includes bibliography of Browning's works (1936–83). [APK]

8.99 Nicolas Oikonomides. *Byzantium from the ninth century to the Fourth Crusade: studies, texts, monuments.* Brookfield, Vt.: Variorum, 1992. ISBN 0-86078-321-9. ▸ Collection of author's articles, published 1967–86, primarily on economic and administrative history of Byzantium; also on history of individual towns. Political interpretation of several Byzantine monuments of art. [APK]

8.100 Günter Prinzing and Dieter Simon, eds. *Fest und Alltag in Byzanz.* Munich: Beck, 1990. ISBN 3-406-343260. ▸ Articles, mostly on Byzantine culture and economy, presented to Hans-Georg Beck on his birthday. [APK]

8.101 Speros Vryonis, Jr. *Studies on Byzantium, Seljuks, and Ottomans.* Malibu, Calif.: Undena, 1981. (Byzantina kai Metabyzantina, 2.) ISBN 0-89003-072-3 (cl), 0-89003-071-5 (pbk). ▸ Comparative study of two civilizations and their interrelations using Islamic sources for Byzantium, Greek and Western sources for Turks. [APK]

8.102 Peter Wirth, ed. *Polychronion: Festschrift Franz Dölger zum fünfundsiebzigen Geburtstag.* Heidelberg: Carl Winter Universitätsverlag, 1966. ▸ Collection of articles on diverse subjects of Byzantine history. Includes Dölger's bibliography (1919–66). [APK]

Overviews

8.103 Norman H. Baynes and Henry St. L. B. Moss, eds. *Byzantium: an introduction to East Roman civilization.* Oxford: Clarendon, 1948. ▸ Separate discussions of each branch of Byzantine culture; also relationship of Byzantium to Islam, Slavs, and Russia. Written by leading scholars of prewar period. [APK]

8.104 Hans-Georg Beck. *Das byzantinische Jahrtausend.* Munich: Beck, 1978. ISBN 3-406-05997-X. ▸ Thorough presentation of Byzantine culture as living, complex phenomenon, full of contradictions and ambivalence; limits of imperial power, political orthodoxy and attempts to overcome it, mystical systems within official dogmatics, vertical social mobility. [APK]

8.105 Hans-Georg Beck. *Byzantinistik heute.* Berlin: de Gruyter, 1977. ISBN 3-11-007220-3. ▸ Critique of contemporary Byzantine studies emphasizing that industrious search for new sources often obscures and curtails understanding of historical processes. [APK]

8.106 Robert Browning. *The Byzantine empire.* Rev. ed. Washington, D.C.: Catholic University of America Press, 1992. ISBN 0-8132-0754-1. ▸ Short survey of history of Byzantium (500–1453); political and cultural history. Good introductory book. [APK]

8.107 Robert Browning. "The continuity of Hellenism in the Byzantine world: appearance or reality?" In *Greece old and new.* Tom Winnifrith and Penelope Murray, eds., pp. 111–28. New York: St. Martin's, 1983. ISBN 0-312-34716-2. ▸ Byzantine world inherited not classical Greek culture of city-state but rich culture of Hellenistic age and Roman empire. Romanity of Byzantium exaggerated in historiography; Byzantium not "barbarized" in wake of Slavic invasions. Byzantine Christianity permeated by Hellenic influences. [APK]

8.108 Guglielmo Cavallo, ed. *L'uomo bizantino.* Bari: Laterza, 1992. ISBN 88-420-3979-9. ▸ Collection of essays by leading Byzantinists (Patlagean, Schreiner, Browning, and others) on different representatives of Byzantine society: poor, peasant, soldiers, scholars, women, merchants, bishops, officials, emperors, and saints. [APK]

8.109 Charles Diehl. *Byzantine portraits.* Harold Bell, trans. New York: Knopf, 1927. ▸ Beautifully written essays primarily on Byzantine empresses and related questions (i.e., four marriages of Leo VI). Also portraits of nonroyal women: Theoktiste, mother of Theodore of Stoudios, and Theodote, mother of

Michael Psellos. Two chapters on men (Basil I and Kekaumenos). [APK]

8.110 Charles Diehl. *Byzantium: greatness and decline.* Naomi Walford, trans. New Brunswick, N.J.: Rutgers University Press, 1957. ▸ Basic survey of political history and institutions of power (government, army, and economy); elements of weakness (political and social demoralization, feudal peril, imperialism, etc.); and Byzantine contribution to world civilization. [APK]

8.111 Edward Gibbon. *The history of the decline and fall of the Roman empire.* 7 vols. London: Methuen, 1897–1902. ▸ Established foundation for perception of Byzantium as Roman empire in continuous decline caused by acceptance of Christianity. First published in 1776–88. On Gibbon, see Section 8, introductory essay. [APK]

8.112 André Guillou. *La civilisation byzantine.* Paris: Arthaud, 1974. ISBN 2-7003-0020-3. ▸ Geographical survey of Byzantine territory, sixth to fifteenth century; state machine, society and its conceptual world (law, time, labor, family, etc.), economy, intellectual life, and religion. Convenient, well-illustrated, introductory work. [APK]

8.113 Judith Herrin. "A Christian millennium: Greece in Byzantium." In *The Greek world.* Robert Browning, ed., pp. 233–50. London: Thames & Hudson, 1985. ISBN 0-500-25092-8. ▸ As heir to both ancient Greece and Rome, Byzantium preserved Hellenic culture of former and imperial organization of latter. By promoting Christian faith to position of absolute dominance, became medieval theocracy. [APK]

8.114 Herbert Hunger. *Reich der neuen Mitte: der christliche Geist der byzantinischen Kultur.* Graz: Styria, 1965. ▸ First attempt to see Byzantine civilization as unified whole, all elements of which developed from pagan to Christian worldview: notion of imperial power, dogmatics, legislation, social system, and everyday life. Byzantine legacy primarily in Eastern Europe. [APK]

8.115 Romilly J. H. Jenkins. *Byzantium and Byzantinism: lectures in memory of Louise Taft Semple.* Cincinnati: University of Cincinnati, 1963. ▸ Makes radical distinction between Byzantium and ancient civilization. Byzantine concept of empire as divinely ordained and achieved perfection and their conviction in innate superiority to all others prepared their political and cultural decline, despite period of recovery and glory from ninth to eleventh century. [APK]

8.116 Romilly J. H. Jenkins. *Byzantium: the imperial centuries, A.D. 610–1071.* 1966 ed. Toronto: University of Toronto Press, 1987. (Mediaeval Academy reprints for teaching, 18.) ISBN 0-8020-6667-4. ▸ Excellently written political history from Herakleios to battle of Mantzikert. [APK]

8.117 Alexander P. Kazhdan and Anthony Cutler. "Continuity and discontinuity in Byzantine history." *Byzantion* 52 (1982) 429–78. ISSN 0378-2506. ▸ Despite preservation of ancient traditions (ethnos, language, technical equipment, unique role of capital, state apparatus, imperial power, law), Byzantium underwent substantial structural change (crisis of late antique polis, change type of ownership and class domination, transformation of social structure, microstructures, everyday life, intellectual life, and visual art). [APK]

8.118 Alexander P. Kazhdan and Giles Constable. *People and power in Byzantium: an introduction to modern Byzantine studies.* 1982 ed. Washington, D.C.: Dumbarton Oaks Center for Byzantine Studies, 1991. ISBN 0-88402-103-3. ▸ Problems and methodology of modern Byzantine studies: economy, society, behavior, religion, literature. [APK]

8.119 Cyril Mango. *Byzantium: the empire of New Rome.* London: Weidenfeld & Nicolson, 1980. ISBN 0-297-77747-5. ▸ New approach to Byzantine culture as unified entity rather than

mechanical conglomerate of independent parts. Important discussion of Byzantine life (with focus on disappearance and revival of cities) and Byzantine conceptual world. Chapters on Byzantine legacy in spheres of literature, art, and architecture. Emphasis on period of fourth to twelfth century. [APK]

8.120 Cyril Mango. "Discontinuity with the classical past in Byzantium." In *Byzantium and the classical tradition.* Margaret Mullet and Robert Scott, eds., pp. 48–57. Birmingham: University of Birmingham, Centre for Byzantine Studies, 1981. ISBN 0-7044-0420-6. ▸ True culture of Byzantium dominated not by classical antiquity, but by construct built by Christian and Jewish apologists in first five or six centuries CE. [APK]

8.121 Georgij A. Ostrogorsky. *History of the Byzantine state.* Rev. ed. Joan M. Hussey, trans. New Brunswick, N.J.: Rutgers University Press, 1969. ISBN 0-8135-0599-2. ▸ Comprehensive political history of Byzantium (324–1453) with excurses into economic and administrative (but not cultural) history. [APK]

8.122 Ihor Ševčenko. "Two varieties of historical writing." *History and theory* 8 (1969) 332–45. ISSN 0018-2656. ▸ Identification of different approaches to Byzantine studies: "caterpillar" investigates details and publishes sources; "butterfly" produces sweeping generalizations. Attempt to reconcile conflict between facts without theory and theory of civilization without facts. [APK]

8.123 Alexander Aleksandrovich Vasiliev. *History of the Byzantine empire, 324–1453.* 2d English ed. Madison: University of Wisconsin Press, 1952. ▸ Primarily political history from Constantine the Great to fall of Constantinople. Sections on literature, learning, education, and art. Chapter on Byzantine feudalism (563–79) revolutionary in its time. Survey of development of Byzantine studies. Translation and revision of Russian original (1917–25, 4 vols.). [APK]

8.124 Speros Vryonis, Jr. "Recent scholarship on continuity and discontinuity of culture: classical Greeks, Byzantines, modern Greeks." In *The "past" in medieval and modern Greek culture.* Speros Vryonis, Jr., ed., pp. 237–56. Malibu, Calif.: Undena, 1978. (Byzantina kai Metabyzantina, 1.) ▸ Polemic against so-called static schools which deny continuity of Greek culture on basis of such arguments as existence of late antique stratum between classical polis and Byzantium, or extinction of Greek racial element, or degradation of pure classical culture. [APK]

8.125 Günter Weiss. "Antike und Byzanz: die Kontinuität der Gesellschaftsstruktur." *Historische Zeitschrift* 224 (1977) 529–60. ISSN 0933-5420. ▸ Substantial structures of late Roman society incorporated into Christianity and continued to exist to very fall of Byzantium. First attempt to prove thesis of Byzantine continuity not by use of metaphysical categories (race, faith, power) but by analysis of concrete elements of economic, social, administrative, and cultural life. [APK]

PROTO-BYZANTINE OR LATE ROMAN PERIOD, ca. 400–ca. 650

8.126 John W. Barker. *Justinian and the later Roman empire.* 2d ed. Madison: University of Wisconsin Press, 1977. ISBN 0-299-03944-7. ▸ General survey with few notes. Despite collapse of empire after Justinian I's reign (527–565), his outlook consistent and correct; if he was wrong in hindsight, not entirely his fault. [APK]

8.127 Ernest W. Brooks. "The emperor Zenon and the Isaurians." *English historical review* 8 (1893) 209–38. ISSN 0013-8266. ▸ During reign of Zenon (474–491), power of barbarian generals overthrown by mountaineers of Isauria (in Asia Minor); their chief reigned over Eastern empire. Isaurians remained useful servants of emperor of Constantinople after Zenon's death, warring against rebels and barbarians of Danube. [APK]

8.128 Robert Browning. *Justinian and Theodora*. Rev. ed. London: Thames & Hudson, 1987. ISBN 0-500-25099-5. ‣ General survey without footnotes. Justinian I's reign not inauguration of new era, rather end of great age; his restoration of ancient grandeur of Roman empire a failure. For broad audience. [APK]

8.129 John B. Bury. *History of the later Roman empire from the death of Theodosius I to the death of Justinian (A.D. 395 to A.D. 565)*. 1923 ed. 2 vols. New York: Dover, 1958. ‣ Classic, detailed study of political history of period, primarily on barbarian conquest of western Europe and reign of Justin I. [APK]

8.130 Averil Cameron. *Continuity and change in sixth-century Byzantium*. London: Variorum, 1981. ISBN 0-86078-090-2. ‣ Collection of works published 1964–80 on Greek and Latin sixth-century writers (Prokopios, Agathias, Corippus, Gregory of Tours), on late sixth-century history (Sophia, Justin II), and on some cult objects (Shroud of Turin, Virgin's robe, icons). [APK]

8.131 Carmelo Capizzi. *L'imperatore Anastasio I (491–518): studio sulla sua vita, la sua opera e la sua personalità*. Rome: Pontificale Institutum Orientalium Studiorum, 1969. (Orientalia Christiana analecta, 184.) ‣ Comprehensive biography of emperor; his ascent to throne, internal and external policy, construction works, and posthumous fate. Attempt to liberate Anastasios from lopsided characterization of sources hostile toward his non-Orthodox religious policy. [APK]

8.132 Peter Charanis. *Church and state in the later Roman empire: the religious policy of Anastasius the First, 491–518*. 2d ed. Thessalonike: Kentron Byzantinon Ereunon, 1974. ‣ Anastasios's non-Orthodox (monophysite) policy resulted from his perception of the eastern provinces of empire (where monophysitism flourished) as most vital centers of his state. [APK]

8.133 Glanville Downey. *The late Roman empire*. New York: Holt, Rinehart & Winston, 1969. ISBN 0-03-080970-3. ‣ Historical survey from third century to 565. Discusses intricacy of problem of decline and fall of Rome; not explained by isolated causes, such as barbarian invasions or soil exhaustion. Decline of West and brilliant epoch of Justin I in East contrasted. [APK]

8.134 Paul Goubert. *Byzance avant l'Islam*. 2 vols. Paris: Picard, 1951–65. ‣ Thorough analysis of external policy of Emperor Maurice (582–602) in Orient, in relations with Franks, with Rome, and with Carthage. [APK]

8.135 Judith Herrin. *The formation of Christendom*. Princeton: Princeton University Press, 1987. ISBN 0-691-05482-7. ‣ History of Mediterranean from sixth to early ninth century. Focus on division of Christian world; roots of disunity prepared in second half of seventh century and strengthened during Iconoclasm. Iconoclasm both political and theological. [APK]

8.136 Robert L. Hohlfelder. "Marcian's gamble: a reassessment of Eastern imperial policy toward Attila, A.D. 450–453." *American journal of ancient history* 9 (1984) 54–69. ISSN 0362-8914. ‣ Marcian's imperial tenure considered golden age by later Byzantine chroniclers, not only because of his religious orthodoxy but also because of his daring and risky initiative to stop paying humiliating tribute to Huns. [APK]

8.137 Kenneth G. Holum. *Theodosian empresses: women and imperial dominion in late antiquity*. Berkeley: University of California Press, 1982. ISBN 0-520-04162-3. ‣ Role of empresses in political life ca. 376–451, and in controversy over Virgin Mary's title, Mother of God. Shift from political aspirations to promotion of religious piety. [APK]

8.138 Arnold H. M. Jones. *The later Roman empire, 284–602*. 1964 ed. 2 vols. Baltimore: Johns Hopkins University Press, 1986. ISBN 0-8018-3284-5 (set, cl), 0-8018-3348-5 (v. 1, cl), 0-8018-3349-3 (v. 2, cl), 0-8018-3285-3 (set, pbk), 0-8018-3353-1 (v. 1, pbk), 0-8018-3354-X (v. 2, pbk). ‣ Excellent survey of political history from Diocletian to collapse of Maurice. Descriptions of government, city and countryside, religion, and culture. Analysis of decline of empire due to multiple causes: barbarian attacks, political weakness, military defeats, economic decline, depopulation, social weaknesses, administrative abuses, decline of morality. [APK]

8.139 Walter Emil Kaegi. *Byzantine military unrest, 471–843: an interpretation*. Amsterdam: Hakkert, 1981. ISBN 90-256-0902-3. ‣ Chronological survey of military revolts. Occurred during great crises, either external or internal, at moments of uncertainty when normal institutional safeguards most vulnerable. [APK]

8.140 Walter Emil Kaegi. *Byzantium and the decline of Rome*. Princeton: Princeton University Press, 1968. ISBN 0-691-035103-5. ‣ History of the Mediterranean (400–475); focuses on attitude of Eastern emperors toward the crisis in West and on Eastern interpretation of decline of Rome by both pagan (Zosimos) and Christian ideologists. [APK]

8.141 Walter Emil Kaegi. "Heraklius and the Arabs." *Greek Orthodox theological review* 27 (1982) 109–33. ISSN 0017-3894. ‣ Effective Byzantine resistance to Arab invasion after debacle at Yarmuk in 636. Emperor Herakleios's efforts to create viable defense in northern Syria. Based primarily on Arabic sources. [APK]

8.142 J.H.W.G. Liebeschuetz. *Barbarians and bishops: army, church, and state in the age of Arcadius and Chrysostom*. Oxford: Clarendon, 1990. ISBN 0-19-814886-0. ‣ Barbarization of Roman army by ca. 400 and conflict between Germanic generals (Gainas and others) and civilian government (Rufinus, Eutropios). Chrysostomrole in Gainas crisis and in formation of Christian ideal of charity. [APK]

8.143 Irfan Shahîd. *Byzantium and the Semitic Orient before the rise of Islam*. London: Variorum, 1988. ISBN 0-86078-218-2. ‣ Articles published 1956–82 primarily on Byzantine relations with Arabs, Himyarites, and Ethiopians (mainly in sixth century). Analyzes act of first importance, Herakleios's claim to be *pistos en Christo basileus* of 629, which marked formal assumption of imperial title *basileus* (king) by Roman ruler. [APK]

8.144 Andreas N. Stratos. *Byzantium in the seventh century*. 5 vols. Amsterdam: Hakkert, 1968–80. ISBN 90-256-0852-3. ‣ Systematic survey of history (602–711) with emphasis on military and ecclesiastical policy. Original Greek edition in six volumes. [APK]

8.145 Vladimír Vařínek, ed. *From late antiquity to early Byzantium: proceedings of the Byzantinological symposium in the sixteenth International Eirene conference*. Prague: Academia, 1985. ‣ Collection of papers on Roman society in transition (fourth to seventh centuries). General problems, relations with neighbors, church, agrarian and urban conditions, spiritual culture. [APK]

8.146 Alexander Aleksandrovich Vasiliev. *Justin the First: an introduction to the epoch of Justinian the Great*. Cambridge, Mass: Harvard University Press, 1950. ‣ Comprehensive biography of Justin (518–527), former swineherd; his religious policy, external policy, legislation, as well as fiscal policy. Justin's expenditures unavoidable and accusations of senseless prodigality (by Prokopios) biased. [APK]

8.147 Michael Whitby. *The emperor Maurice and his historian: Theophylact Simocatta on Persian and Balkan warfare*. Oxford: Clarendon, 1988. ISBN 0-19-822945-3. ‣ Balkan and Persian wars and their aftermath as presented by Theophylaktos Simokattes and other sources and in archaeological evidence. Theophylaktos as last representative of classical Greek literature, making Maurice's reign turning-point in history of Eastern Roman empire. [APK]

DARK AGES

8.148   Paul J. Alexander. *The patriarch Nicephorus of Constantinople.* Oxford: Clarendon, 1958. ▸ Ecclesiastical controversies in Byzantine empire ca. 780–815 viewed through biography and literary activity of patriarch Nikephoros I (r. 806–815, d. 828). Positive aspects of personality offset by weakness of character; maneuvered between court and uncompromising monastic party. [APK]

8.149   Peter R. L. Brown. *Society and the holy in late antiquity.* Berkeley: University of California Press, 1982. ISBN 0-520-04305-7. ▸ Profound analysis of conflict between political authority and charismatic authority of saints. Especially important: "A Dark Age Crisis: Aspects of the Iconoclastic Controversy." [APK]

8.150   Anthony A. M. Bryer and Judith Herrin, eds. *Iconoclasm.* Birmingham: University of Birmingham, Centre for Byzantine Studies, 1977. ISBN 0-7044-0226-2. ▸ Papers delivered at Ninth Spring Symposium of Byzantine Studies in 1975 on history, theology, geography, literature, and art in Byzantium in eighth through mid-ninth centuries. [APK]

8.151   Francis Dvornik. *The Photian schism: history and legend.* Cambridge: Cambridge University Press, 1948. ▸ Byzantium's religious and foreign policy in second half of ninth century. Photian rupture with West of short duration and second Photian schism a fabrication. Revision of negative judgment on Photios in Hergenröther 8.155. [APK]

8.152   Stephen Gero. *Byzantine Iconoclasm during the reign of Constantine V.* Louvain: Secretariat du Corpus, 1977. (Corpus scriptorum Christianorum Orientalium, Subsidia, 52.) ▸ Discussion of theological controversy during reign of Constantine V (741–775). Constantine not consistent Iconoclast, position limited to scriptural ban on idolatry at beginning of reign. By council of 754, discussion transposed to level of christological doctrine, and material image of Christ proclaimed violation of Orthodox dyophysite theology. [APK]

8.153   Stephen Gero. *Byzantine Iconoclasm during the reign of Leo III.* Louvain: Secretariat du Corpus, 1973. (Corpus scriptorum Christianorum Orientalium, Subsidia, 41.) ▸ Though Iconoclastic sentiments present in eastern Mediterranean before Leo III (717–741), emperor's commitment to Iconoclastic cause not incited by Jewish, Muslim, or Anatolian influence but emerged as personal reaction to intensified, expanded cult of images. Based on Greek, Syriac, Arabic, and Armenian sources. [APK]

8.154   Constance Head. *Justinian II of Byzantium.* Madison: University of Wisconsin Press, 1972. ISBN 0-299-06030-6. ▸ Attempt to defend Justinian II (685–695 and 705–711) from hostility of Byzantine writers, as man of energy and determination with substantial accomplishments in administrative, military, diplomatic, and religious spheres. [APK]

8.155   Joseph A. G. Hergenröther. *Photius, Patriarch von Constantinopel: sein Leben, seine Schriften und das griechische Schisma.* 4 vols. Regensburg: Manz, 1867–69. ▸ Classic, although obsolete, study of biography of Photios (858–867, 877–886) depicting patriarch as instigator of rupture with West. For revised view of Photios, see Dvornik 8.151. [APK]

8.156   Patricia Karlin-Hayter. "Imperial charioteers seen by the Senate or by the plebs." *Byzantion* 57 (1987) 326–35. ISSN 0378-2506. ▸ On Michael III (842–867), one of most controversial figures on Byzantine throne. Discussion of political implications of Michael's passion for chariotry; search for popularity with populace and ritual character. [APK]

8.157   Helga Köpstein. *Thomas, Rebell und Gegenkaiser in Byzanz.* Berlin: VEB Deutscher Verlag der Wissenschaften, 1986. (Illustrierte historische Hefte, 39.) ▸ Popular exposé of rebellion of 821–824 from viewpoint of class struggle. [APK]

8.158   Ralph-Johannes Lilie. *Die byzantinische Reaktion auf die Ausbreitung der Araber: Studien zur Strukturwandel des byzantinischen Staates im siebten und achten Jahrhundert.* Munich: Institut für Byzantinistik und neugriechische Philologie der Universität, 1976. (Miscellanea Byzantina Monacensia, 22.) ▸ Analysis of Arabo-Byzantine Wars, 640–800, and restructuring of Byzantine economy and defense system: economic center relocated to Northwest Asia Minor (concentrated around Constantinople) and was supplemented in eighth century by western litoral. Anatolia and eastern parts of Asia Minor were viewed as buffer zones for defense of new economic centers. [APK]

8.159   Edward James Martin. *A history of the Iconoclastic controversy.* 1930 ed. New York: AMS Press, 1978. ISBN 0-404-16117-0. ▸ Ecclesiastical history of Byzantium from end of seventh to mid-ninth century. During second Iconoclastic period theological problem of icon veneration was simplified. Last two chapters on Iconoclastic controversy in Frankish kingdom. [APK]

8.160   Pavlos E. Niaves. *The reign of the Byzantine emperor Nicephorus I (AD 802–811).* Athens: Historical Publications St. D. Basilopoulos, 1987. ▸ Analysis of three major aspects of Nikephoros's reign: domestic, religious, and foreign policies. Although reign ended in disaster (defeat by Bulgarians), set foundations of Byzantine fiscal and economic systems and established principles of relations with West and with monastic party. [APK]

8.161   John H. Rosser. "Theophilus' Khurramite policy and its finale: the revolt of Theophobus' Persian troops in 838." *Byzantina* 6 (1974) 263–71. ▸ Theophilos's support of revolt of Khurramites (Persians) against caliphate a failure; led to last successful raid of Arabs in Asia Minor (sack of Amorion in 838). Excerpt from unpublished dissertation "Theophilos 'The Unlucky' (829 to 842)." [APK]

8.162   Steven Runciman. "The empress Irene the Athenian." In *Medieval women: dedicated and presented to professor Rosalind M. T. Hill on the occasion of her seventieth birthday.* Derek Baker, ed., pp. 101–18. Oxford: Blackwell, 1978. ISBN 0-631-19260-3. ▸ Rehabilitation of Irene (797–802). First years of her regency (before she blinded her son Constantine VI) a prudent ruler: abolished Iconoclasm and reduced taxes and tolls, fiscal policy far from disastrous. Only foreign policy met with failure. [APK]

8.163   Paul Speck. *Kaiser Konstantin VI: die Legitimation einer Fremden und der Versuch einer eigenen Herrschaft.* 2 vols. Munich: Fink, 1978. ISBN 3-7705-1726-1. ▸ Political history of Byzantium from 775 (enthronization of Leo IV) to 797 (blinding of Constantine VI by his mother Irene) with emphasis on critical analysis of *Chronographia* of Theophanes and his multiple sources. [APK]

8.164   Warren Treadgold. *The Byzantine revival, 780–842.* Stanford, Calif.: Stanford University Press, 1988. ISBN 0-8047-1462-2. ▸ Comprehensive survey of political history from regency of Irene to death of Theophilos. Discussion of economy, society, administration, and culture of empire, ca. 780 and 842. [APK]

AGE OF RECOVERY

8.165   W. A. Farag. "Some remarks on Leo of Tripoli's attack on Thessaloniki in 904 A.D." *Byzantinische Zeitschrift* 82 (1989) 133–39. ISSN 0007-7704. ▸ Discussion of successful Arab naval expedition against second largest city of Byzantium as described in Greek and Oriental sources. Many problems remain. [APK]

8.166   Romilly J. H. Jenkins. *Studies on Byzantine history of the ninth and tenth centuries.* London: Variorum, 1970. ISBN 0-902089-07-2. ▸ Articles published 1948–66 on political conflicts, relations with Rus', Slavs, and Arabs, and on literature (chronicles and homily of Photios); some Greek texts included (primarily letters of Arethas, archbishop of Caesarea, early tenth century). [APK]

8.167 Patricia Karlin-Hayter. *Studies in Byzantine political history: sources and controversies.* London: Variorum, 1981. ISBN 0-86078-088-0. ▸ Collection of articles published 1962–81, mostly on political conflicts at end of ninth and beginning of tenth century. Part 18 on administrative history: function of *hetaireiarches*. [APK]

8.168 Karl J. Leyser. "The tenth century in Byzantine-Western relationships." In *Relations between East and West in the Middle Ages.* Derek Baker, ed., pp. 29–63. Edinburgh: Edinburgh University Press, 1973. ISBN 0-85224-237-9. ▸ Characterization of Byzantium's relationship with West as inward-looking: rather than come to terms with changing situations, more concerned with preserving ideal status of empire against foreign contamination. [APK]

8.169 Rosemary Morris. "The two faces of Nikephoros Phokas." *Byzantine and modern Greek studies* 12 (1988) 83–115. ISSN 0307-0131. ▸ The contradictory character of Nikephoros II Phokas (963–969), hermit and general, explains his contradictory characterization in available sources both Greek and foreign. [APK]

8.170 Nicolas Oikonomides. "Leo VI and the narthex mosaic of Saint Sophia." *Dumbarton Oaks papers* 30 (1976) 151–72. ▸ Discussion of conflict between imperial power and patriarchate of Constantinople in connection with fourth marriage of Leo VI (886–912). Mosaic, a monument of triumph of patriarch Nicholas I Mystikos over emperor. [APK]

8.171 Steven Runciman. *The emperor Romanus Lecapenus and his reign.* 1929 ed. Cambridge: Cambridge University Press, 1988. ISBN 0-521-35722-5 (pbk). ▸ Obsolete but only monograph on history of Byzantium from death of Leo VI (912) to dethronement of sons of Romanos I Lekapenos in 945. Focusing primarily on Romanos's wars and diplomacy; relations with each region (Bulgaria, the Steppes, Armenia, etc.) described separately. [APK]

8.172 Arnold Toynbee. *Constantine Porphyrogenitus and his world.* London: Oxford University Press, 1973. ISBN 0-19-215253-X. ▸ Characterizes Constantine VII (913–959) as industrious scholar and weak politician. Gives broad picture of Byzantine economy, administration, diplomacy, and civilization in seventh through tenth centuries, emphasizing differences from antiquity. [APK]

8.173 Albert Vogt. *Basile Ier, empereur de Byzance (867–886), et la civilisation byzantine à la fin du neuvième siècle.* Paris: Picard, 1908. ▸ Only monograph on this emperor. Career and character of Basil—fine, intelligent, and energetic ruler; his legislation, administration, religious, and military policies. Summary of economic and cultural state of empire. [APK]

8.174 Paul E. Walker. "The 'crusade' of John Tzimisces in the light of new Arabic evidence." *Byzantion* 47 (1977) 301–27. ISSN 0378-2506. ▸ Results of campaign of John I (969–976) in Syria insignificant and temporary, posing no threat to Jerusalem; formed buffer centered in Damascus between empire and Fatimids. Boastful letter to Armenian king Ašot III exaggerated Byzantine successes. [APK]

PERIOD OF "WESTERNIZATION"

8.175 Michael Angold. *The Byzantine empire, 1025–1204: a political history.* London: Longman, 1984. ISBN 0-582-49060-X (cl), 0-582-49061-8 (pbk). ▸ Political history with essays on economy, society, and culture. Great prosperity for Byzantium in

twelfth century until failure of system created by Komnenoi. Good introductory study. [APK]

8.176 Charles M. Brand. *Byzantium confronts the West, 1180–1204.* Cambridge, Mass: Harvard University Press, 1968. ▸ Best analysis of political situation of empire after death of Manuel I. Byzantium's diplomacy confused, and attitude of different classes to "Latins" differed, accounting for failure of Byzantine policy and fall of Constantinople in 1204. [APK]

8.177 Ferdinand Chalandon. *Les Comnène: études sur l'empire byzantin au onzième et au douzième siècles.* 1900–12 ed. 2 vols. New York: Franklin, 1912. ▸ Best political history of three reigns of Komnenoi: Alexios I (1081–1118), John II (1118–43), and Manuel I (1143–80) with chapters on specific topics (Turks, Hungary, Crusaders, etc.). Brief characterization of court and administration. [APK]

8.178 Jean-Claude Cheynet. *Pouvoir et contestations à Byzance (963–1210).* Paris: Publications de la Sorbonne, 1990. (Byzantina Sorbonensia, 9.) ▸ List of revolts, technique of rebellion, social and geographic basis. Predominant number of attempts came from ranks of aristocracy; stratification of aristocracy based on geographical rather than social (military versus civil) principles. [APK]

8.179 Alfred Friendly. *The dreadful day: the battle of Manzikert, 1071.* London: Hutchinson, 1981. ISBN 0-09-143570-6. ▸ Popular presentation of first major battle between Turks and Byzantium. [APK]

8.180 Benjamin Hendrickx and Corinna Matzukis. "Alexios V Doukas Mourtzouphlos: his life, reign, and death (?–1204)." *Hellenika* 31 (1979) 108–32. ISSN 0024-8215. ▸ Ephemeral Byzantine emperor on eve of fall of Constantinople: man of rather humble origin; courageous, intelligent, and cautious leader who took advantage of nationalistic feelings of masses. [APK]

8.181 Paolo Lamma. *Comneni e Staufer: ricerche sui rapporti fra Bisanzio e l'Occidente nel secolo 12.* Rome: Istituto Storico Italiano per il Medioevo, 1955–57. ▸ Excellent analysis of relations between Byzantium, Germany, and Italy during reign of Manuel I: emperor saw in "Latins" catalyst for renovation of Byzantium, but his policy contributed to strengthening of Frederick Barbarossa. [APK]

8.182 Paul Lemerle. *Cinq études sur le onzième siècle byzantin.* Paris: Centre National de la Recherche Scientifique, 1977. ISBN 2-222-02053-0. ▸ Detailed analysis of three documents: will of Eustathios Boilas, 1059; monastic rules of Michael Attaleiates, 1077; and monastic rules of Gregory Pakourianos, 1083. Rehabilitation of eleventh-century government based on new economic structures and new society. This healthy system destroyed by Komnenian dynasty in twelfth century. [APK]

8.183 Ralph-Johannes Lilie. *Byzanz und die Kreuzfahrerstaaten: Studien zur Politik des byzantinischen Reiches gegenüber den Staaten der Kreuzfahrer in Syrien und Palästina bis zum Vierten Kreuzzug (1096–1204).* Munich: Fink, 1981. ISBN 3-7705-2042-4. ▸ Concludes Byzantium had no substantial impact on states of Crusaders, except for short period (1156–80). Byzantine government misunderstood and underestimated First Crusade, did not consider states as threat to empire and rarely interfered in their existence. [APK]

8.184 Paul Magdalino. *Tradition and transformation in medieval Byzantium.* London: Variorum, 1991. ISBN 0-86078-295-6. ▸ Collected studies published 1978–89 mostly on culture and ideology of twelfth century, but also on jurisprudence, prosopography, historical geography, administration, literature. Especially important: "The Phenomenon of Manuel I Komnenos"; however admirable, Manuel's policies hastened catastrophe they were intended to avert. [APK]

8.185 Mahlon H. Smith III. *And taking bread . . . : Cerularius and the azyme controversy of 1054.* Paris: Beauchesne, 1978. ▸ Reconstruction of political and ecclesiastical controversy between Rome and Constantinople over use of unleavened host for liturgy. Neither party able to compromise its own normative traditions. [APK]

8.186 Speros Vryonis, Jr. *Byzantium: its internal history and relations with the Muslim world.* London: Variorum, 1971. ISBN 0-902089-16-1. ▸ Collected papers published 1956–70 on Byzantine economic, social, and political relations. Especially important: "Byzantine *Demokratia* and the Guilds in the Eleventh Century" on urban political activity in Constantinople, 1042–81. Sees emergence of guilds as political factor. [APK]

LATE BYZANTIUM

8.187 Michael Angold. *A Byzantine government in exile: government and society under the Laskarids of Nicaea (1204–1261).* London: Oxford University Press, 1975. ISBN 0-19-821854-0. ▸ Economic and administrative structure of empire of Nicaea established after fall of Constantinople to Crusaders: essentials of Byzantium preserved in exile and Laskarids continued domestic policies of Komnenoi. [APK]

8.188 John W. Barker. *Manuel II Palaeologus (1391–1425): a study in late Byzantine statesmanship.* New Brunswick, N.J.: Rutgers University Press, 1969. ISBN 0-8135-0582-8. ▸ Manuel had potential to become one of greatest Byzantine emperors, but ruled country during period of agonizing crisis, undergoing territorial constriction and diminishing resources. [APK]

8.189 Ursula V. Bosch. *Kaiser Andronikos III. Palaiologos: Versuch einer Darstellung der byzantinischen Geschichte in den Jahren 1321–1341.* Amsterdam: Hakkert, 1965. ▸ Reign of Andronikos III as last revival of Byzantine state. After civil war of 1321–28, Andronikos raised again international prestige of empire and curbed destructive tendency of John Kantakouzenos. [APK]

8.190 Slobodan Ćurčić and Doula Mouriki, eds. *The twilight of Byzantium: aspects of cultural and religious history in the late Byzantine empire; papers from the colloquium held at Princeton University, 8–9 May 1989.* Princeton: Princeton University, Program in Hellenic Studies, 1991. ISBN 0-691-04091-5. ▸ Collection of articles, mostly on art and architecture, but also on Byzantine cultural self-consciousness in fifteenth century (by Vryonis) and on some features of literary development. [APK]

8.191 George T. Dennis. *The reign of Manuel II Palaeologus in Thessalonica, 1382–1387.* Rome: Pontificale Institutum Orientalium Studiorum, 1960. (Orientalia Christiana analecta, 159.) ▸ While Turkish policy of John V (1341–91) was one of appeasement, his son Manuel, during his short reign in Thessaly, took up arms and gained some victories. In final account, his subjects surrendered city to Turks. [APK]

8.192 Alice Gardner. *The Lascarids of Nicaea: the story of an empire in exile.* London: Methuen, 1912. ▸ Standard political history of Nicaean empire, 1204–61, with final chapter on literature and art. Laskarids of Nicaea established state which upheld old imperial prestige and recovered ancient capital. [APK]

8.193 Deno John Geanakoplos. *Emperor Michael Palaeologus and the West, 1258–1282: a study in Byzantine-Latin relations.* 1959 ed. Hamden, Conn.: Archon, 1973. ISBN 0-208-01310-5. ▸ Survey of history of empire of Nicaea, followed by discussion of international and religious policy of Michael VIII; conflict with Angevins of Naples and Union of Lyons; Michael's undeniable successes dearly bought. [APK]

8.194 Apostolos D. Karpozilos. *The ecclesiastical controversy between the kingdom of Nicaea and the principality of Epiros (1217–1233).* Thessalonike: Kentron Byzantinon Ereunon, 1973.

(Byzantina keimena kai meletai, 7.) ▸ Clergy of Epiros risked schism with patriarchate of Constantinople (relocated to Nicaea after 1204) since they supported claims of their ruler Theodore (ca. 1215–30) to Constantinople and to title of emperor. [APK]

8.195 Angeliki E. Laiou. *Constantinople and the Latins: the foreign policy of Andronicus II, 1282–1328.* Cambridge, Mass.: Harvard University Press, 1972. ISBN 0-674-16535-7. ▸ Best monograph on subject. Depiction of Andronikos as pious, honorable, and generous man who faced dangerous situation and prevented Constantinople from becoming capital of second Latin empire. Relations with West influenced by question of Union and by domestic pressures. [APK]

8.196 Klaus-Peter Matschke. *Fortschritt und Reaktion in Byzanzim 14. Jahrhundert: Konstantinopel in der Bürgerkriegsperiode von 1341 bis 1354.* Berlin: Akademie, 1971. (Berliner byzantinistische Arbeiten, 42.) ▸ Social analysis of crisis (civil war) of mid-fourteenth century: whereas feudal aristocracy core of both contesting groups, Kantakouzenos found support among lower layer of nobility (*stratiotai-proniars*) while regency promoted by Constantinopolitan real estate owners involved in trade and industrial activity. [APK]

8.197 Klaus-Peter Matschke. *Die Schlacht bei Ankara und das Schicksal von Byzanz: Studien zur spätbyzantinischen Geschichte zwischen 1402 und 1422.* Weimar: Böhlau, 1981. ▸ Timur's victory over Ottomans (1402) postponed Ottoman conquest of Constantinople and created relative equilibrium of power. But despite limited success, Byzantine economy and social and political organization unable to restructure and produce forces that could respond to double pressure from both east and west. [APK]

8.198 Donald M. Nicol. *The despotate of Epiros.* Oxford: Blackwell, 1957. ▸ Foundation of Greek independent state in Epiros and later of empire of Thessaly; political history until battle of Pelagonia in 1259 after which Epiros ceased to rival empire of Nicaea. See also Gardner 8.192 and Angold 8.187. Continued in Nicol 8.199. [APK]

8.199 Donald M. Nicol. *The despotate of Epiros, 1267–1479.* Cambridge: Cambridge University Press, 1984. ISBN 0-521-26190-2. ▸ Continuation of Nicol 8.198. Restoration of despotate and its desperate struggle against Constantinople, Italians, Serbs, and Turks. Two short chapters on economy, administration, church, and culture. Standard work. [APK]

8.200 Donald M. Nicol. *The immortal emperor: the life and legend of Constantine Palaeologus, last emperor of the Romans.* Cambridge: Cambridge University Press, 1992. ISBN 0-521-41456-3. ▸ Study of Constantine XI (1448–53) as despot of Mistra and emperor of Constantinople and his place in folklore as embodiment of Great Idea, restoration of Byzantine empire. [APK]

8.201 Donald M. Nicol. *The last centuries of Byzantium, 1261–1453.* London: Rupert-Hart-Davis, 1972. ISBN 0-246-10559-3. ▸ General survey of Palaiologan period. Fall of Byzantium primarily explained by outlining its place in history and resistance to innovation. [APK]

8.202 Steven Runciman. *The fall of Constantinople, 1453.* Canto ed. Cambridge: Cambridge University Press, 1990. ISBN 0-521-09573-5 (cl), 0-521-39832-0 (pbk). ▸ Detailed description of Turkish siege and conquest of Constantinople. Standard work. [APK]

8.203 Apostolos E. Vacalopoulos. *Origins of the Greek nation: the Byzantine period, 1204–1461.* New Brunswick, N.J.: Rutgers University Press, 1970. ISBN 0-8135-0659-X. ▸ Survey of political and cultural history of primarily Palaiologan period. Unlike Nicol 8.201, focuses not on fall of empire but on survival of Greek ethnos and classical civilization. [APK]

8.204 Günter Weiss. *Joannes Kantakuzenos—Aristokrat, Staatsmann, Kaiser, und Mönch—in der Gesellschaftsentwicklung von Byzanz im 14. Jahrhundert.* Wiesbaden: Harrassowitz, 1969. ‣ Composition of ruling class in late Byzantium (especially character of *hetaireia* [retinue]); Kantakouzenos's attitude toward common people, particularly during civil war of 1341–47, and Palamites. Kantakouzenos representative of Byzantine aristocracy. [APK]

REGIONAL STUDIES

Greece and the Islands

8.205 Catherine Asdracha. *La région des Rhodopes aux XIIIe et XIVe siècles: étude de géographie historique.* Athens: Verlag der "Byzantinisch-neugriechischen Jahrbücher," 1976. (Texte und Forschungen zur byzantinisch-neugriechischen Philologie, 49.) ‣ Geography and climate, routes, population, economy, and society. Survey of political events, 1185–1354. [APK]

8.206 Charalampos N. Bakirtzis, ed. *First international symposium for Thracian studies: "Byzantine Thrace," image and character.* 2 vols. Amsterdam: Hakkert, 1989. (Byzantinische Forschungen, 14.1–2.) ISBN 90-256-0978-3. ‣ Collection of papers, mostly on archaeology and art; general survey of recent excavations by Charalampos Bakirtzis, "Western Thrace in the Early Christian and Byzantine Periods." [APK]

8.207 Antoine Bon. *Le Péloponnèse byzantin jusqu'en 1204.* Paris: Presses Universitaires de France, 1951. ‣ Best general survey; ethnic composition, administration, economy, and intellectual life in sixth through twelfth centuries. Discussion of symptoms of decline on eve of Fourth Crusade. [APK]

8.208 Anthony A. M. Bryer. *The empire of Trebizond and the Pontos.* London: Variorum, 1980. ISBN 0-86078-062-7. ‣ Collected articles on geography, prosopography, and economy of Trebizond and adjacent area. Especially important: "The Estates of the Empire of Trebizond." [APK]

8.209 Nicolas Cheetham. *Mediaeval Greece.* New Haven: Yale University Press, 1981. ISBN 0-300-02421-5. ‣ Brief description of decline of ancient Greece and its rehellenization from ninth century onward. Focuses on struggle for Western domination in area. [APK]

8.210 Vassilios Christides. *The conquest of Crete by the Arabs (ca. 824): a turning point in the struggle between Byzantium and Islam.* Athens: Akademia Athenon, 1984. ‣ Crete under Arab rule (ca. 824–961) not nest of pirates, rather center of intermingling of Greek and Arab civilization with prosperous economy (even though these phenomena hardly reflected in available sources). [APK]

8.211 John H. Finley, Jr. "Corinth in the Middle Ages." *Speculum* 7 (1932) 477–99. ISSN 0038-7143. ‣ General survey of political events primarily based on narrative sources, especially of thirteenth through fifteenth centuries. Written before major excavations, results published by Morgan 8.52 Davidson 8.48, and Scranton 8.224. [APK]

8.212 Alison Frantz. *Late antiquity, A.D. 267–700.* Princeton: American School of Classical Studies at Athens, 1988. (Athenian agora, 24.) ISBN 0-87661-224-9. ‣ One of best excavated areas in Greece reveals private houses, churches, bronze foundries, water mills, and governor's palace. Period of prosperity (396–450) followed by decline (450–529), disintegration (529–582), and Dark Ages (582–700) interrupted by short recovery under Constans II. [APK]

8.213 Frederick William Hasluck. "Depopulation of the Aegean Islands and the Turkish conquest." *Annual of the British School at Athens* 17 (1910–11) 151–75. ISSN 0068-2454. ‣ Survey of individual islands; better populated and more prosperous after final establishment of Turks than in previous years; even smaller islands beginning to be occupied. [APK]

8.214 George F. Hill. *A history of Cyprus.* 4 vols. Cambridge: Cambridge University Press, 1940–52. ‣ General survey, Stone Age to 1948. Chapter 12 of volume 1 deals with island under Byzantine and Islamic rule: predominantly political history. [APK]

8.215 Costas P. Kyrris. "The nature of the Arab-Byzantine relations in Cyprus from the middle of the seventh to the middle of the tenth century A.D." *Graeco-arabica* 3 (1984) 149–75. ‣ Description of neutral regime of condominium of two powers over island. See also Jenkins 8.166. [APK]

8.216 Paul Lemerle. *Philippes et la Macédoine orientale à l'époque chrétienne et byzantine: recherches d'histoire et d'archéologie.* 2 vols. Paris: de Boccard, 1945. (Bibliothèque des Écoles Françaises d'Athènes et de Rome, 158.) ‣ Excellent political and administrative history from days of St. Paul to Turkish conquest. Metropolitan see of Philippi, stronghold of Hellenism and bridge between Constantinople and Thessaly. Description of two basilicas in Philippi. [APK]

8.217 Anthony Luttrell. "Greeks, Latins, and Turks on late-medieval Rhodes." In *Symposium Byzantinon.* Freddy E. Thiriet, ed., pp. 357–74. Amsterdam: Hakkert, 1987. (Byzantinische Forschungen, 11.) ISBN 90-256-0619-9 (series), 90-256-0927-9. ‣ Discussion of cultural contacts in period 1306–1522; introduction by Latins of modern fortifications, Gothic palaces and churches, illuminated missals, and numerous domestic items. Includes five Latin documents (1366–83) on subject. [APK]

8.218 Anthony Luttrell. "Rhodes and Jerusalem: 1291–1411." In *Symposium Byzantinon.* Freddy E. Thiriet, ed., pp. 187–207. Amsterdam: Hakkert, 1987. (Byzantinische Forschungen, 12.) ISBN 90-256-0619-9 (series), 90-256-0927-9. ‣ After evacuation of Hospitallers from Palestine in 1291, Order maintained continuous contact with Jerusalem. One Italian and one Latin document, each from 1403, concerning negotiations between Order and Mamlūks. [APK]

8.219 Elisabeth Malamut. *Les îles de l'empire byzantin, VIIIe–XIIe siècles.* 2 vols. Paris: Publications de la Sorbonne, 1988. (Byzantina Sorbonensia, 8.) ISBN 2-85944-164-6. ‣ Intellectually ambitious portrait of insular world (Aegean and Ionian seas, Crete, and Cyprus) as an entity and not as sum of individual islands; population, administration, economy, and society. Integration of islands into outer world. [APK]

8.220 Arthur H. S. Megaw. "Progress in early Christian and medieval archaeology, 1960–85." In *Archaeology in Cyprus.* Vassos Karageorghis, ed., pp. 292–98. Nicosia, Cyprus: Leventis Foundation, 1985. ISBN 9963-560-00-4. ‣ Excavations of episcopal basilica at Kourion and Saranda Kolonnes castle at Paphos. Artifacts of datable context reveal beginning of Dark Ages in seventh century. Important supplement to purely political history. See Hill 8.214. [APK]

8.221 Emmanuel Amand de Mendieta. *Mount Athos: the garden of the Panaghia.* Michael R. Bruce, trans. Berlin and Amsterdam: Akademie and Hakkert, 1972. (Berliner byzantinistische Arbeiten, 41.) ‣ Landscape, history of monastic confederation, administration (twenty ruling monasteries and their dependencies), monks' life, art, and liturgy. [APK]

8.222 Donald M. Nicol. *Meteora: the rock monasteries of Thessaly.* Rev. ed. London: Variorum, 1975. ISBN 0-902089-73-0. ‣ General discussion of Byzantine monasticism and medieval Thessaly. Foundation and history of Great Meteoron and other monasteries in area. [APK]

8.223 Steven Runciman. *Mistra, Byzantine capital of the Peloponnese.* London: Thames & Hudson, 1980. ISBN 0-500-25071-5.

▸ Foundation and political history of city through period of Turkish rule. Architecture and intellectual life in Mistra. [APK]

8.224 Robert L. Scranton. *Mediaeval architecture in the central area of Corinth.* Princeton: American School of Classical Studies at Athens, 1957. (Corinth, 16.) ▸ Excavations in central area of Corinth reveal history of Byzantine provincial city and show period of decay in seventh and eighth centuries, recovery in ninth to eleventh centuries; pattern of development in twelfth century debatable. Impression of opulent design possibly false historically; shows Latin conquest of 1204 not catastrophic. [APK]

8.225 Kenneth M. Setton. *Athens in the Middle Ages.* London: Variorum, 1975. ISBN 0-902089-84-6. ▸ Six articles written 1944–75 mostly on Catalans in Greece and on dismal situation in Athens in ninth through twelfth centuries. Pioneering work based on archaeological evidence. Despite enormous increase of archaeological data since publication, no updated general survey available. See Setton 8.347. [APK]

8.226 Cecil Torr. *Rhodes under the Byzantines.* Cambridge: Clay & Sons, 1886. ▸ Out of date but only general survey available. Must be supplemented by works of Luttrell (8.217, 8.218). [APK]

8.227 Dimitris Tsougarakis. *Byzantine Crete: from the fifth century to the Venetian conquest.* Athens: Basilopoulos, 1988. ISBN 960-7100-04-2. ▸ Political, economic, social, administrative, and ecclesiastical history. Reduced economic activity from seventh century on (due, in part, to Arab conquest) and monetized economic transactions, especially during reign of Manuel I. Based on written, archaeological, and numismatic sources. [APK]

8.228 Apostolos E. Vacalopoulos. *A history of Thessaloniki.* Thomas F. Carney, trans. Thessalonike: Institute for Balkan Studies, 1984. (Hetaireia Makedonikon Spoudon, Hidryma Meleton Chersonesou tou Haimou, Ekdoseis, 63.) ▸ Political history of ancient, medieval, and modern eras with short chapter on administration and intellectual life in fourteenth century. [APK]

8.229 *Villes et peuplement dans l'Illyricum protobyzantin: actes du colloque organisé par l'École Française de Rome.* Rome: École Française de Rome, 1984. (Collection de l'École Française de Rome, 77.) ISBN 2-7283-0067-4, ISSN 0223-5099. ▸ Papers presented to 1982 colloquium. Balkan city of fourth through seventh centuries and Slavic invasions, based primarily on new archaeological and numismatic materials. Decline of city evident; what replaced ancient municipal system less clear. [APK]

8.230 Dionysios A. Zakythenos. *Le despotat grec de Morée.* 2d rev. ed. 2 vols. Chryssa Maltézou, ed. London: Variorum, 1975. ISBN 0-902089-81-1 (v. 1), 0-902089-82-X (v. 2). ▸ Foundation of Kantakouzenoi and Palaiologoi. Essays on population, economy, society, institutions, church, and intellectual life. [APK]

Asia Minor

8.231 Anthony A. M. Bryer. *Peoples and settlement in Anatolia and the Caucasus, 800–1900.* London: Variorum, 1988. ISBN 0-86078-222-0. ▸ Collection of articles published 1960–87 on geography, economy, and ethnic composition of Asia Minor and Lazika predominantly during Byzantine period. [APK]

8.232 Anthony A. M. Bryer and David Winfield. *The Byzantine monuments and topography of the Pontos.* 2 vols. Washington, D.C.: Dumbarton Oaks Research Library and Collection, 1985. (Dumbarton Oaks studies, 20.) ISBN 0-88402-122-X. ▸ Best available guide to geography (coastal and inland towns, routes, and individual sites) from Cape Karambis (westernmost outpost of empire of Trebizond) to marchlands of Georgia. History of each site and description of its monuments. [APK]

8.233 J. Stephens Crawford. *The Byzantine shops at Sardis.* Cambridge, Mass.: Harvard University Press, 1990. (Archaeo-

logical exploration of Sardis, Monographs, 9.) ISBN 0-674-08968-5. ▸ Line of shops on north side of marble-paved main avenue, their structural elements, and locally produced objects; traces of dye shops. Parallel material from Asia Minor, Constantinople, Greece, and other places. [APK]

8.234 Robert W. Edwards. "The garrison forts of the Pontos: a case for the diffusion of the Armenian paradigm." *Revue des études arméniennes* 19 (1985) 181–284. ▸ Catalog of fortresses in territory of empire of Trebizond. Influence of Armenian architecture with exception of Akça Kalesi, which preserved anachronistic Byzantine traditions. [APK]

8.235 Clive Foss. *Byzantine and Turkish Sardis.* Cambridge, Mass: Harvard University Press, 1976. (Archaeological exploration of Sardis, Monographs, 4.) ISBN 0-674-08969-3. ▸ City flourished in late antiqity, became ruralized in seventh century, and recovered after ca. 850. Based mainly on archaeological remains, few written records. [APK]

8.236 Clive Foss. *Ephesus after antiquity: a late antique Byzantine and Turkish city.* Cambridge: Cambridge University Press, 1979. ISBN 0-521-22086-6. ▸ Prosperity during late antiquity, notable decline in seventh century, recovery from mid-ninth century onward; based on literary and archaeological sources. [APK]

8.237 Mary Gough, ed. *Alahan, an early Christian monastery in southern Turkey, based on the work of Michael Gough.* Toronto: Pontifical Institute of Mediaeval Studies, 1985. (Studies and texts, 73.) ISBN 0-88844-073-1 (pbk), ISSN 0082-5328. ▸ Chapters deal with inscriptions, objects, coins, and buildings. Coins testify to occupation of site to at least 586. Discussion of religious life and monastic organization in monastery. [APK]

8.238 Sergej Pavlovich Karpov. *L'impero di Trebizonda, Venezia, Genova, e Roma, 1204–1461.* Eleonora Zambelli, trans. Rome: Il Veltro Editrice, 1986. ISBN 88-85015-26-3. ▸ Based on narrative and documentary sources (from Italian archives); political, economic, and diplomatic relations with Venice, Genoa, and some countries of western Europe. Translated from Russian. [APK]

8.239 Barnardin A. A. Menthon. *Une terre de légende: l'Olympe de Bithynie, ses saints, ses couvents, ses sites.* Paris: Bonne Press, 1935. ▸ Topography and history of one of most important monastic centers, especially during Iconoclasm. Material organized by monasteries; also biographies of saints active in area. Partially replaced by Janin and Darrouzès 8.17, vol. 2. [APK]

8.240 William Miller. *Trebizond: the last Greek empire.* 1926 ed. Amsterdam: Hakkert, 1968. ▸ Standard though in part obsolete political history divided into five periods: foundation of empire of Trebizond, prosperity during period 1222–1330, civil wars, decline, and fall in 1461. [APK]

8.241 Lyn Rodley. *Cave monasteries of Byzantine Cappadocia.* Cambridge: Cambridge University Press, 1985. ISBN 0-521-26798-6. ▸ Rock-cut monasteries and churches in area of ancient cities of Caesarea, Koloneia, and Nakida. Hermitages known from ninth century, monasteries from late tenth century on, description of remains, and categorization and characterization of functions and architecture. [APK]

8.242 Charlotte Roueché. *L'histoire d'Aphrodisias après 250, d'après les inscriptions.* In *Aphrodisias de Carie.* Juliette de la Genière and Kenan T. Erim, eds. Paris: Recherche sur les Civilisations, 1987. ISBN 2-86538-173-0. ▸ Sharp decrease in inscriptions after 250 and disappearance after mid-sixth century; evidence of continued urban administration through beginning of sixth century. [APK]

8.243 Speros Vryonis, Jr. *The decline of medieval Hellenism in Asia Minor and the process of islamization from the eleventh through the fifteenth century.* 1971 ed. Berkeley: University of California

Press, 1986. (Publications of the Center for Medieval and Renaissance Studies, 4.) ISBN 0-520-01597-5 (cl), 0-520-05753-8 (pbk). ▸ Discussion of restructuring of Hellenic administration, urban life, and civilization following eleventh-century conquest by Turks of significant part of Asia Minor. [APK]

8.244 Speros Vryonis, Jr. "The decline of medieval Hellenism in Asia Minor and the process of islamization from the eleventh through the fifteenth century." *Greek Orthodox theological review* 27 (1982) 225–85. ISSN 0017-3894. ▸ Defense of thesis concerning destructive role of Turkish invasion; author's response to critics of 8.243. [APK]

Constantinople

8.245 Hélène Ahrweiler. *L'idéologie politique de l'Empire byzantin.* Paris: Presses Universitaires de France, 1975. (L'historien: section dirigée par Roland Mousnier, 20.) ▸ Analysis of two major concepts of Byzantine political thought: order (*taxis*) and dispensation/prudence (*oikonomia*), latter allowing slight deviation from rigid state and legal norms. [APK]

8.246 Hans-Georg Beck, ed. *Studien zur Frühgeschichte Konstantinopels.* Munich: Institut für Byzantinistik und neugriechische Philologie der Universität, 1973. (Miscellanea byzantina monacensia, 14.) ▸ Collection of articles including general characterization of Constantinople in fourth to sixth centuries, and territorial distribution of parties of Greens and Blues. See Cameron 8.247. [APK]

8.247 Alan Cameron. *Circus factions: Blues and Greens at Rome and Byzantium.* Oxford: Clarendon, 1976. ISBN 0-19-814804-6. ▸ Critical reconsideration of traditional view of factions in Constantinople: they did not champion popular causes or resist demands of central government. By seventh century, part of court. See also Cameron 8.453. [APK]

8.248 Gilbert Dagron. *Naissance d'une capitale: Constantinople et ses institutions de 330 à 451.* 2d ed. Paris: Presses Universitaires de France, 1984. (Bibliothèque byzantine, 7.) ISBN 2-13-038902-3. ▸ Excellent study of transformation of Constantinople from imperial residence into capital of empire and ecclesiastical center of East. [APK]

8.249 Raymond Janin. *Constantinople byzantine: développement urbain et répertoire topographique.* 2d ed. Paris: Institut Français d'Études Byzantines, 1964. (Archives de l'Orient chrétien, 4A.) ▸ Topography of Constantinople. Introductory section on city's development in fourth and fifth centuries, followed by description of various buildings, monuments, and other urban features (squares, porticoes, palaces, ports, etc.). Individual areas in alphabetical order in second part. [APK]

8.250 Michael Maclagan. *The city of Constantinople.* New York: Praeger, 1968. ▸ Popular history of city from antiquity to Turkish period with focus on its monuments. [APK]

8.251 Cyril Mango. *Le développement urbain de Constantinople (quatrième–huitième siècles).* Rev. ed. Paris: de Boccard, 1990. (Travaux et mémoires du Centre de Recherche d'Histoire et Civilisation de Byzance, Monographies, 2.) ISBN 2-7018-0059-5. ▸ Excellent work on discontinuity in history of Byzantine capital. City remained late antique up to mid-fifth century. Justinian I's activity heralded transition to Middle Ages; in seventh century, city declined (grain supply decreased, capacity of ports contracted, public monuments abandoned, and city ruralized). [APK]

8.252 Dean A. Miller. *Imperial Constantinople.* New York: Wiley, 1969. ISBN 0-471-60370-8 (cl), 0-471-60371-6 (pbk). ▸ Economy, administration, everyday life, and position of aristocracy in Byzantine capital. Good introduction. [APK]

ADMINISTRATION AND LAW

8.253 Walter Ashburner. "The Farmer's Law." *Journal of Hellenic studies* 30, 32 (1910, 1912) 85–108, 68–95. ISSN 0075-4269. ▸ Greek original and English translation of legal code (probably of seventh or eighth century) that regulated relations in Byzantine countryside. [APK]

8.254 Roger S. Bagnall et al. *Consuls of the later Roman empire.* Atlanta: American Philological Association, 1987. (Philological monographs, 36.) ISBN 1-55540-099-X. ▸ Lists of consuls 284–541; introduction contains history of consulate, form of proclamation, nomenclature, and sources mentioning consuls. [APK]

8.255 Mark C. Bartusis. "The rhythm of the chancery: seasonality in the issuance of the Byzantine imperial documents." *Byzantine and modern Greek studies* 13 (1989) 1–21. ISSN 0307-0131. ▸ March through June busiest period of activity for imperial chancery in eleventh through thirteenth centuries. [APK]

8.256 John B. Bury. *The imperial administrative system in the ninth century.* 1911 ed. New York: Franklin, 1958. ▸ Classic survey of Byzantine dignities (titles) and offices of sixth through tenth centuries. Appendix contains Greek text of *Kletorologion* by Philotheos (ca. 899), treatise on position of individual functionaries in court ceremonial. [APK]

8.257 Averil Cameron. "The construction of court ritual: the Byzantine *Book of Ceremonies.*" In *Rituals of royalty.* 2d ed. David Cannadine and Simon Price, eds., pp. 106–36. Cambridge: Cambridge University Press, 1992. ISBN 0-521-33513-2. ▸ Traditional roots and new aspects in Byzantine imperial ceremonial of tenth century. *Book of Ceremonies* an attempt to restore sense of order in society after centuries of dislocation and to reinforce position of ruling dynasty. [APK]

8.258 Franz Dölger. *Beiträge zur Geschichte der byzantinischen Finanzverwaltung besonders des 10. und 11. Jahrhunderts.* Rev. ed. Hildesheim: Olms, 1960. ▸ Excellent analysis of Byzantine tax system, fiscal administration, and cadastre. "Treatise on Taxation," anonymous handbook for tax collector, in appendix. [APK]

8.259 Edwin Hanson Freshfield. *A manual of Roman law: the Ecloga ad procheiron mutata.* Cambridge: Cambridge University Press, 1927. ▸ English translation of Byzantine lawbook, issued probably in 741. [APK]

8.260 Edwin Hanson Freshfield. *Roman law in the later Roman empire: Byzantine guilds, professional and commercial.* Cambridge: Cambridge University Press, 1938. ▸ English translation of tenth-century *Book of the Eparch*—collection of statutes of Constantinopolitan guilds. [APK]

8.261 Roger Goodburn and Philip Bartholomew, eds. *Aspects of the Notitia dignitatum.* Oxford: British Archaeological Reports, 1978. (British archaeological reports, Supplementary series, 15.) ISBN 0-904531-58-9. ▸ Papers presented to conference in Oxford on late Roman list of offices produced ca. 395–408. Specific institutions (*gynaecea*, etc.) and specific areas (Britain, Lower Egypt, etc.). [APK]

8.262 André Grabar. *L'empereur dans l'art byzantin: recherches sur l'art officiel de l'empire d'Orient.* 1936 ed. London: Variorum, 1971. ▸ Byzantium developed art that served needs of monarchy as did official art of Oriental, Hellenistic, and Roman empires. Classic survey of monuments (portraits, symbols of power) and evolution of imperial art under influence of Christianity. [APK]

8.263 Rodolphe Guilland. "L'éparque de la ville." *Byzantinoslavica* 41 (1980) 17–32. ISSN 0007-7712. ▸ Supreme judge over population of Constantinople, his functions, staff, and prosopography. For so-called *Book of the Eparch*, see Freshfield 8.260. [APK]

8.264 Rodolphe Guilland. "Les logothètes: étude sur l'histoire administrative de l'empire byzantin." *Revue des études byzantines* 29 (1971) 5–115. ISSN 0373-5729. ‣ Comprehensive survey of various offices (*logothesia*) that administered taxation, postal service, diplomacy, etc.; functions of *logothetes* and their staff and prosopography. [APK]

8.265 Rodolphe Guilland. *Recherches sur les institutions byzantines.* 2 vols. Amsterdam: Hakkert, 1967. (Berliner byzantinistische Arbeiten, 35.) ‣ Collection of articles on Byzantine administrative system: nobility, eunuchs, military commanders, court titles, etc. [APK]

8.266 Rodolphe Guilland. *Titres et fonctions de l'empire byzantin.* London: Variorum, 1976. ISBN 0-902089-94-3. ‣ Collection of articles (1963–73) on Byzantine dignities (especially *patrikioi* of fourth through eleventh centuries) and offices. Continuation of 8.265. [APK]

8.267 Armin Hohlweg. *Beiträge zur Verwaltungsgeschichte des oströmischen Reiches unter den Komnenen.* Munich: Institut für Byzantinistik und neugriechische Philologie der Universität, 1965. (Miscellanea byzantina monacensia, 1.) ‣ New system of titles, organization of army and navy. Administrative system of twelfth century based on network of lineages related to Komnenian dynasty. [APK]

8.268 Walter Emil Kaegi. "Some perspectives on Byzantine bureaucracy." In *The organization of power: aspects of bureaucracy in the ancient Near East.* McGuire Gibson and Robert D. Biggs, eds., pp. 151–59. Chicago: Oriental Institute of the University of Chicago, 1987. (Studies in ancient Oriental civilization, 46.) ISBN 0-918986-72-9 (cl), 0-918986-51-6 (pbk), ISSN 0081-7554. ‣ Discussion of twenty-eight topics for future investigation in study of Byzantine administrative system, including Byzantine bureaucracy's responsibility for lengthy survival of empire. [APK]

8.269 Walter Emil Kaegi. "Some reconsiderations on the *themes* (seventh–ninth centuries)." *Jahrbuch der Österreichischen Byzantinischen Gesellschaft* 16 (1967) 39–53. ISSN 0075-2355. ‣ Themes not conscious creation of Emperor Herakleios; critical reassessment of nature of thematic soldiers (so-called farmer-soldiers) and of military efficiency of *themes*. [APK]

8.270 Alexander P. Kazhdan. "Do we need a new history of Byzantine law?" *Jahrbuch der österreichischen Byzantinistik* 39 (1989) 1–28. ISSN 0378-8660. ‣ Byzantine legal practice, known primarily from documentary and narrative sources, differs from legal theory as reflected in legislation and juridical treatises. [APK]

8.271 Ralph-Johannes Lilie. "Die byzantinischen Staatsfinanzen und die stratiotika ktemata." *Byzantinoslavica* 48 (1987) 49–55. ISSN 0007-7712. ‣ Critical evaluation of Treadgold 8.282. [APK]

8.272 Karl Eduard Zachariä von Lingenthal. *Geschichte des griechisch-römischen Rechts.* 1892 3d ed. Aalen: Scientia, 1955. ‣ Classic and only survey of system of Byzantine law from sixth century onward: law of persons, succession, things, and obligations; penalty and procedure. [APK]

8.273 Ruth J. Macrides. "Justice under Manuel I Komnenos: four novels on court business and murder." *Fontes minores* 6 (1984) 99–204. ‣ English translation of and commentary on several twelfth-century legislative acts and court procedure in Byzantium. [APK]

8.274 Ruth J. Macrides. "Killing, asylum, and the law in Byzantium." *Speculum* 63.3 (1988) 509–38. ISSN 0038-7134. ‣ Seemingly monolithic structure of Roman law changed in Byzantine era under influence of church; state not always in full control of jurisdiction. [APK]

8.275 Ljubomir Maksimović. *The Byzantine provincial admin-*

istration under the Palaiologoi. Rev. ed. Amsterdam: Hakkert, 1988. ISBN 90-256-0968-6. ‣ Revised translation of his Serbian book (1972). Emphasizes feudal character of provincial administration; final chapter on privileges of towns (Thessaly, Ioannina, Monembasia, etc.). [APK]

8.276 Michael McCormick. *Eternal victory: triumphal rulership in late antiquity, Byzantium, and the early medieval West.* 1987 ed. Cambridge and Paris: Cambridge University Press and Éditions de la Maison des Sciences de l'Homme, 1990. ISBN 0-521-26180-5 (cl), 0-521-38659-4 (pbk). ‣ Pioneering work. Imperial victory celebrations from Constantine I to 1043. Change in content, structure, setting, and participants; emergence of nonimperial participants as central focus of ceremony. [APK]

8.277 Dean A. Miller. "The logothete of the drome in the middle Byzantine period." *Byzantion* 36 (1966) 438–70. ISSN 0378-2506. ‣ Rank and duties of one of highest officials in eighth through tenth centuries: postmaster, supreme diplomat, and one of masters of ceremonial. [APK]

8.278 Nicolas Oikonomides. "L'évolution de l'organisation administrative de l'empire byzantin (1025–1118)." *Travaux et mémoires* 6 (1976) 125–52. ISSN 0577-1471. ‣ Concludes transformation of Byzantine administrative system began before 1025, during reign of Basil II. Changes of 1040s did not constitute proper reform—restructuring started again after debacle of Manzikert (1071). Analysis of individual branches of state machine. [APK]

8.279 Nicolas Oikonomides. *Les listes de préséance byzantines du IXe et Xe siècles.* Paris: Éditions du Centre National de la Recherche Scientifique, 1972. ‣ Publication (with French translation) of four treatises on position of functionaries in court ceremonial; in commentary, system of dignities and offices in Byzantium of ninth and tenth centuries. [APK]

8.280 Irfan Shahîd. "Heraclius and the *theme* system: new light from the Arabic" and "Herakleios and the *theme* system: further observations." *Byzantion* 57, 59 (1987, 1989) 391–406, 208–43. ISSN 0378-2506. ‣ New hypothesis concerning origin of *themes*. After his victory over Persians Herakleios created four *themes* in Syria, replacing former eleven provinces and establishing foundation for system. [APK]

8.281 Jonathon Shepard and Simon Franklin, eds. *Byzantine diplomacy: papers from the twenty-fourth spring symposium of Byzantine studies, March 1990.* London: Variorum, 1992. ‣ Collection of articles on notion of Byzantine diplomacy, its means and ends, during three periods (300–800, 800–1204, and 1204–1453). Covers Byzantium's relations with neighbors (Rome, Khazars, Arabs, Rus' and Turks), including dynastic marriages, and particular sources and methods. [APK]

8.282 Warren Treadgold. *The Byzantine state finances in the eighth and ninth centuries.* Boulder and New York: East European Monographs; distributed by Columbia University Press, 1982. (East European monographs, Byzantine series, 2.) ISBN 0-88033-014-7. ‣ Attempt to express budget of empire (for period of scarce sources) in relatively precise numbers. [APK]

8.283 Otto Treitinger. *Die oströmische Kaiser- und Reichsidee nach ihrer Gestaltung im höfischen Zeremoniell.* 1956 2d ed. Darmstadt: Wissenschaftliche Buchgesellschaft, 1956. ‣ Only monograph on subject. Ritual of Byzantine court expressed concept of emperor as divinely chosen. Detailed study of ceremonies and regalia; emperor as priest and as embodiment of law. [APK]

8.284 Friedhelm Winkelmann. *Byzantinische Rang- und Ämterstruktur im achten und neunten Jahrhundert: Faktoren und Tendenzen ihrer Entwicklung.* Berlin: Akademie, 1985. (Berliner byzantinistische Arbeiten, 53.) ‣ Critical analysis of literary texts and lead seals. Neither system of ranks nor provincial administration arranged on basis of consistent principle (imperial law) but fluctuated under pressure of various factors. [APK]

ECONOMY

8.285 Charlampos Bouras. "City and village: urban design and architecture." *Jahrbuch der österreichischen Byzantinistik* 31.2 (1981) 611–53. ISSN 0378-8660. ▸ After seventh century, ancient urbanism collapsed and medieval provincial city assumed different character. Significance of public places declined in favor of organic growth of private dwelling. [APK]

8.286 Alan Harvey. *Economic expansion in the Byzantine empire, 900–1200.* Cambridge: Cambridge University Press, 1989. ISBN 0-521-37151-1. ▸ Upsurge in economic activity in eleventh and twelfth centuries: demographic growth, extension of cultivated area, growth in monetary circulation, and development of towns. See Hendy 8.287 and Kazhdan 8.291. [APK]

8.287 Michael F. Hendy. *The economy, fiscal administration, and coinage of Byzantium.* Northampton, England: Variorum, 1989. ISBN 0-86078-253-0. ▸ Collected papers, most published 1970–83, three for first time. Especially important, "Byzantium, 1081–1204: An Economic Reappraisal" (1970), critical reconsideration of traditional view of Byzantium in decline in eleventh and twelfth centuries; concept of economic expansion further developed in following article. See also Harvey 8.286. [APK]

8.288 Michael F. Hendy. *Studies in the Byzantine monetary economy, c. 300–1450.* Cambridge: Cambridge University Press, 1985. ISBN 0-521-24715-2. ▸ State's need to provide for itself standard medium for taxation and expenditure fundamental dynamic behind production of coins. Needs of private sector of secondary consideration. [APK]

8.289 *Hommes et richesses dans l'Empire byzantin.* 2 vols. Vassiliki Kravari, Jacques Lefort, and Cécile Morrisson. Paris: Lethielleux, 1989–91. ISBN 2-283-60451-6 (v. 1), 2-283-60453-2 (v. 2), ISSN 1147-4963. ▸ Collection of articles divided chronologically: volume 1: fourth to seventh century, volume 2: ninth to fifteenth century (with exception of Dagron: Constantinople fourth to tenth century). Topics include population and organization of space (habitat), society (family and fortune), trade and exchange, and coins and taxation. [APK]

8.290 Michel Kaplan. *Les hommes et la terre à Byzance du sixième au onzième siècle.* Paris: Publications de la Sorbonne, 1992. (Byzantina Sorbonnensia, 10.) ISBN 2-85944-170-0. ▸ Study of agriculture in Syria, Asia Minor, and Balkans. Lack of technological progress in countryside, as both large estates and state taxes increased, created situation of "blocked economy" with peasants unable to support themselves. [APK]

8.291 Alexander P. Kazhdan. "Vizantijskie goroda v VII–XI vv (The Byzantine city of the seventh to eleventh centuries)." *Sovetskaja archeologija* (Soviet archaeological studies) 21 (1954) 164–88. ▸ First attempt to postulate thesis of urban crisis in seventh century and formation of new medieval urbanism in tenth to twelfth centuries. [APK]

8.292 Johannes Koder. "The urban character of the early Byzantine empire: some reflections on a settlement geographical approach to the topic." In *The seventeenth international Byzantine congress, major papers.* , pp. 155–87. New Rochelle, N.Y.: Caratzas, 1986. ISBN 0-89241-443-X (cl), 0-89241-444-8 (pbk). ▸ Attempt to apply central place theory to structure of Byzantine urban network, especially in Illyricum, ca. sixth century. In some areas city network adequate from administration's viewpoint; in others, overdense and explained only by historical reasons. In Asia Minor cities oriented more toward Rome than Constantinople. [APK]

8.293 Angeliki E. Laiou-Thomadakis. *Peasant society in the late*

Byzantine empire: a social and demographic study. Princeton: Princeton University Press, 1977. ISBN 0-691-05252-2. ▸ Excellent social and demographic study of *praktika* of fourteenth century: economy, structure of village and family; status of dependent peasant and his holdings; and population movements. Devastation of Macedonia by mid-fourteenth century. [APK]

8.294 Paul Lemerle. *The agrarian history of Byzantium from the origins to the twelfth century: the sources and problems.* Galway, Ireland: Galway University Press, 1979. ▸ Comprehensive analysis of sources, primarily legislation of tenth century. More continuity of late Roman agrarian relations than transformation. [APK]

8.295 Klaus-Peter Matschke. "Tuchproduxtion und Tuchproduzenten in Thessalonike und in anderen Städten und Regionen des späten Byzanz." *Byzantiaka* 9 (1989) 47–87. ▸ Concludes production of woolen textiles, although more developed in Thessalonike than in other centers (including Constantinople), never reached level of capitalist organization. [APK]

8.296 Gunnar Mickwitz. *Die Kartellfunktionen der Zünfte und ihre Bedeutung bei der Entstehung des Zunftwesens: eine Studie in spätantiker und mittelalterlicher Wirtschaftsgeschichte.* 1936 ed. Amsterdam: Hakkert, 1968. (Societas scientarum Fennica, Commentationes humanarum litterarum, 8.3.) ▸ Chapter 8 on Byzantine guilds of tenth century. Byzantine trade system had beneficial role similar to that of modern cartels. Criticizes previous scholars who advocate theory that Byzantine state restricted economic activity by creating paradise of monopolies. [APK]

8.297 Nicolas Oikonomides. *Hommes d'affaires: grecs et latins à Constantinople (XIIIe–XIVe siècles).* Montreal: Institut d'Études Médiévales Albert-le-Grand, 1979. ▸ Good introductory book. Treats handicraft, trade, and credit in Constantinople, and interactions between local artisans and merchants and Western businessmen. [APK]

8.298 Georgij A. Ostrogorsky. *Pour l'histoire de la féodalité byzantine.* Henri Gregoire, trans. Brussels: Institut de Philologie et d'Histoire Orientales et Slaves, 1954. (Corpus Bruxellense historiae Byzantinae, Subsidia, 1.) ▸ Translation of two works on *pronoia* (fief) and on tax registers (*praktika*) published in Serbian (1951) and Russian (1948). Feudal nature of late Byzantine property holdings and of peasants' obligations. [APK]

8.299 Georgij A. Ostrogorsky. *Quelques problèmes d'histoire de la paysannerie byzantine.* Brussels: Éditions de Byzantion, 1956. (Corpus Bruxellense historiae Byzantinae, Subsidia, 2.) ▸ Discussion of transition from state exploitation of peasantry to private exploitation. Ambivalent status of late Byzantine dependent peasants (*paroikoi*). [APK]

8.300 Georgij A. Ostrogorsky, ed. *Zur byzantinischen Geschichte: ausgewählte kleine Schriften.* Darmstadt: Wissenschaftliche Buchgesellschaft, 1973. ISBN 3-534-04456-8. ▸ Collected articles on Byzantine administration and economy. Two papers on Byzantine relations with Turks. Especially important, "Byzantine Cities in the Early Middle Ages," critical analysis of Kazhdan's thesis (8.291) on urban crisis in seventh century. Defends traditional idea of uninterrupted existence of ancient polis. [APK]

8.301 Helen Saradi-Mendelovici. "The demise of the ancient city and the emergence of the medieval city in the eastern Roman empire." *Echos du monde classique/Classical views* 32.7 (1988) 365–401. ISSN 0012-9356. ▸ Eastern Roman city showed signs of decline in sixth century. Disintegration complete by seventh century. Cannot be explained by external factors (enemy attacks, natural disasters). Prokopios speaks of "neglect"; accounted for by economic and administrative factors as well as cultural change. [APK]

8.302 Albert Stöckle. *Spätrömische und byzantinische Zünfte: Untersuchungen zum sogenannten Eparchikon biblion Leos des Wei-*

sen. 1911 ed. Aalen: Scientia, 1963. (Klio: Beiträge zur alten Geschichte, 9.) ▸ Comprehensive analysis of *Book of the Eparch* (English translation, see Freshfield 8.260). Tenth-century Constantinopolitan guilds continuation of Roman collegia, although some changes took place. [APK]

8.303 John P. Thomas. *Private religious foundations in the Byzantine empire.* Washington, D.C.: Dumbarton Oaks Research Library and Collection, 1987. (Dumbarton Oaks studies, 24.) ISBN 0-88402-164-5. ▸ Chronological survey from fifth century on, with special attention to papyri evidence and system of *charistikion*, grants from monasteries to secular individuals or ecclesiastical institutions. Shows considerable variation in legal relationship of private patron with his foundation. [APK]

SOCIETY AND FAMILY

8.304 John F. Haldon. *Byzantium in the seventh century: the transformation of the culture.* Cambridge: Cambridge University Press, 1990. ISBN 0-521-26492-8. ▸ Comprehensive survey of economy and social relations, state apparatus, religion, infrastructures and hierarchies, and forms of representation. Two dominant tendencies: increasing introversion of Orthodox culture (primarily stress on personal relationship of individuals to God) and quest for security (search for an imagined ancient order of security and confidence). [APK]

8.305 Alexander P. Kazhdan. *Socsial'nyi sostav gospodstvujuščego klassa Vizantii XI–XII vv.* (Social composition of the ruling class in eleventh- and twelfth-century Byzantium). Moscow: Nauka, 1974. ▸ Byzantine definitions of social composition of ruling class and statistical data. Major groups—military (of which imperial lineage was upper crust) and civil nobility—differed in origin, stability, economic position, and attitude toward church and culture. French summary by Irène Sorlin, "Publications soviétiques sur le onzième siècle" *Travaux et mémoires* 6 (1976) 367–80. [APK]

8.306 Angeliki E. Laiou. *Mariage, amour, et parenté à Byzance aux XIe–XIIIe siècles.* Paris: de Boccard, 1992. (Travaux et mémoires du Centre de Recherche d'Histoire et Civilisation de Byzance, Monographies, 7.) ISBN 2-7018-0074-9. ▸ Study of legal, psychological, and economic aspects of Byzantine marriage including sexual passion, control over marriage, divorce, and attempts of state to restrict marriages between cousins, uncles and nieces, etc., to prevent growth of aristocratic properties. [APK]

8.307 Angeliki E. Laiou. "The role of women in Byzantine society." *Jahrbuch der österreichischen Byzantinistik* 31.1 (1981) 233–60. ISSN 0378-8660. ▸ Discussion of increasing role of women in economic and political activities. Abolition of certain legal limitations and discrepancy between legal theory and court practice in cases concerning women. [APK]

8.308 Ann Moffatt. "The Byzantine child." *Social research* 53 (1986) 705–23. ISSN 0037-783X. ▸ Argument that much of Roman civil law affecting children continued into Byzantine period. Canon law dealt less harshly with sexual offenses and sanctioned betrothals of young children. Decline in infanticide and abortion; castration most significant abuse of children. [APK]

8.309 Evelyne Patlagean. *Pauvreté économique et pauvreté sociale à Byzance, 4e–7e siècles.* Paris: Mouton, 1977. ISBN 2-7193-0835-8. ▸ Important monograph treating terminology of poverty and wealth and seminal economic and social categories: land, city, and family. Mortality of different social and gender groups. [APK]

8.310 Evelyne Patlagean. *Structure sociale, famille, chrétienté à Byzance, IVe–XIe siècle.* London: Variorum, 1981. ISBN 0-86078-080-5. ▸ Collected studies published 1964–79 on Byzantine economy and social composition (especially significant, "Economie Paysanne" and "Féodalité Byzantine"), situation of women and children, christianization, and attitude toward Jews and barbarians. Attempt to use hagiography as source for social relationships. [APK]

8.311 "Symposium on the Byzantine family and household." Angeliki E. Laiou, Introduction. *Dumbarton Oaks papers* 44 (1990) 97–226. ISSN 0070-7546, ISBN 0-88402-189-0. ▸ Collection of articles on marriage, kinship, family versus monastery, sexuality, household, and family as reflected in art. [APK]

8.312 Victor Tiftixoglu. "Gruppenbildungen innerhalb des konstantinopolitanischen Klerus während der Komnenenzeit." *Byzantinische Zeitschrift* 62 (1969) 25–72. ISSN 0007-7704. ▸ Study of upper echelon of Constantinopolitan clergy of twelfth century which consisted of two rival groups of different status and political ideology: representatives of episcopate and officials of patriarchal administrative departments. [APK]

8.313 P. A. Yannopoulos. *La société profane dans l'empire byzantin des septième, huitième, et neuvième siècles.* Louvain: Bureau du Recueil, Bibliothèque de l'Université, 1975. (Recueil de travaux d'histoire et de philologie, 6 série, fasc. 6.) ▸ "Law of the Ecloga" (English translation, see Freshfield 8.259) proclaims all citizens equal. In reality, however, there were layers which however cannot be termed classes since there was no social equilibrium. [APK]

ARMY

8.314 Hélène Ahrweiler. *Byzance et la mer: la marine de guerre, la politique et les institutions maritimes de Byzance aux VIIe–XVe siècles.* Paris: Presses Universitaires de France, 1966. (Bibliothèque byzantine, Études, 5.) ▸ Historical development of Byzantine navy and maritime bases (from seventh to fifteenth century) with emphasis on administrative organization and reform until period of decline of fleet under Palaiologan dynasty. [APK]

8.315 Mark C. Bartusis. "The cost of late Byzantine warfare and defense." *Byzantinische Forschungen* 16 (1991) 75–89. ▸ First half of fourteenth century, military consumed approximately 5 percent of empire's total resources. Social and economic costs of warfare determined by two factors: localization of warfare within empire and state's inability to recruit enough soldiers from local population. [APK]

8.316 Mark C. Bartusis. *The late Byzantine army: arms and society, 1204–1453.* Philadelphia: University of Pennsylvania Press, 1992. ISBN 0-8122-3179-1. ▸ Only monograph on late Byzantine army. Two sections: army as instrument of policy and army as institution. Treats social composition of army, guard service, and weapons and equipment. [APK]

8.317 Clive Foss and David Winfield. *Byzantine fortifications: an introduction.* Pretoria: University of South Africa, 1986. ISBN 0-86981-321-8. ▸ General characterization, atypical ramparts of Constantinople and Nicaea, and fortresses of Asia Minor. Types of masonry and functions of fortifications in historical perspective and in comparison with West. [APK]

8.318 John F. Haldon. *Byzantine praetorians: an administrative, institutional, and social survey of the Opsikion and Tagmata, c. 580–900.* Bonn: Habelt, 1984. (Poikila Byzantina, 3.) ISBN 3-7749-2004-4. ▸ Social vacuum following decline of provincial cities tended to strengthen local administrative units in which most senior military commanders expanded power by assuming responsibility for providing for troops. [APK]

8.319 John F. Haldon. *Recruitment and conscription in the Byzantine army, c. 550–950: a study on the origins of the stratiotika ktemata.* Vienna: Verlag der Österreichischen Akademie der Wissenschaften, 1979. (Sitzungsberichte der philosophisch-historischen Klasse, 357.) ISBN 3-7001-0314-X. ▸ Drafting of volunteers replaced in seventh century by hereditary system. Soldiers gradually granted holdings in various provinces. By tenth century, soldier's duty transferred from person to holding, thus becoming alienable. [APK]

8.320 Ian Heath. *Byzantine armies, 886–1118*. London: Osprey, 1979. ISBN 0-85045-306-2. ▸ Popular survey; Byzantine army in tenth and early eleventh centuries best organized, best trained, best equipped, and highest paid in Europe. [APK]

8.321 Walter Emil Kaegi. *Some thoughts on Byzantine military strategy*. Brookline, Mass.: Hellenic College Press, 1983. ISBN 0-916586-95-2 (pbk). ▸ Clear introductory study attributing longevity of Byzantium to adoption of cautious military strategy: avoidance of decisive battles, warfare of slow attrition, and initial passive resistance to invaders, followed by tactic of cutting them off. [APK]

8.322 Taxiarchis G. Kolias. *Byzantinische Waffen: ein Beitrag zur byzantinischen Waffenkunde von den Anfängen bis zur lateinischen Eroberung*. Vienna: Verlag der Österreichischen Akademie der Wissenschaften, 1988. (Byzantina Vindobonensia, 17.) ISBN 3-7001-1471-0. ▸ Categorization and description of weaponry (defensive and offensive weapons, crossbow, and sling). Ancient traditions and development under influence of neighbors and in response to changes in tactics and technology. [APK]

8.323 John L. Teall. "The barbarians in Justinian's army." *Speculum* 40 (1965) 294–322. ISSN 0038-7134. ▸ Discussion of barbarian character of army, which both resulted from and accounted for success in time of war and made discipline difficult. [APK]

BYZANTIUM AND ITS NEIGHBORS

8.324 Benjamin Arbel, Bernard Hamilton, and David Jacoby. *Latins and Greeks in the eastern Mediterranean*. London: Cass, 1989. ISBN 0-7146-3372-0. ▸ Collection of articles by several scholars on relations between Byzantium and Latin conquerors, individual regions, two churches, and Mongols and Turks in eastern Mediterranean. [APK]

8.325 Thomas S. Brown. *Gentlemen and officers: imperial administration and aristocratic power in Byzantine Italy, A.D. 554–800*. London: British School at Rome, 1984. ISBN 0-904152-09-X. ▸ Concludes army commanders of imperial Italy developed into powerful aristocracy, while traditions of Roman gentleman remained alive among soldiers and clerics. [APK]

8.326 Robert Browning. *Byzantium and Bulgaria: a comparative study across the early medieval frontier*. Berkeley: University of California Press, 1975. ISBN 0-520-02670-5. ▸ Despite seminal Byzantine influence on medieval Bulgaria several factors determined different course of events in Bulgaria: lower level of agricultural and industrial production, division into infinite number of tiny political units, relative inalienability of land, and less social mobility. Valuable social and economic data. [APK/RJC]

8.327 Anthony A. M. Bryer and Michael Ursinus, eds. *Manzikert to Lepanto: the Byzantine world and the Turks, 1071–1571; papers given at the nineteenth spring symposium of Byzantine studies, March 1985*. Amsterdam: Hakkert, 1991. (Byzantinische Forschungen, 16.) ISBN 90-256-0619-9, 90-256-1005-6. ▸ Collection of articles (by Angold, Lilie, Bartusis, and others) treating political framework, warfare, contacts, economy, literature, and foreign relations "beyond Byzantines and Ottomans" including Arabs, Jews, Romanians, Great Horde, and Angevins. [APK]

8.328 Ivan Dujčev. *Medioevo bizantino-slavo*. 3 vols. Rome: Edizioni di Storia e Letteratura, 1965–71. (Storia e letteratura, 102, 113, 119.) ▸ Collection of articles (Italian, French, and German) on political and cultural relations between Slavs and Byzantium, supplemented by addenda and Dujčev's bibliography compiled by Enrica Follieri. [APK]

8.329 Francis Dvornik. *Les Slaves, Byzance, et Rome au neuvième siècle*. 1926 ed. Hattiesburg, Miss.: Academic International, 1970. (Travaux publiés par l'Institut d'Études Slaves, Russian series, 4.) ISBN 0-87569-016-5. ▸ Once standard monograph, now obsolete. Struggle between Byzantium, papacy, and Germany over impact on newly baptized Slavic countries: Bulgaria, Moravia, and Pannonia. [APK]

8.330 Vera von Falkenhausen. *Untersuchungen über die byzantinische Herrschaft in Süditalien vom neunten bis ins elfte Jahrhundert*. Wiesbaden: Harrassowitz, 1967. (Schriften zur Geistesgeschichte des östlichen Europa, 1.) ▸ Study of Byzantine administration in southern Italy; thematic organization and new administrative unit: katepanate/ducate; army, justice, and finances; the town; Greek and Latin bishoprics. Revised Italian translation: *La dominazione bizantina nell'Italia meridionale dal IX all'XI secolo* (Bari: Ecumenica Editrice, 1978). [APK]

8.331 Jules Gay. *L'Italie méridionale et l'empire byzantin depuis l'avènement de Basile Ier jusqu'à la prise de Bari par les Normands (867–1071)*. 1904 ed. 2 vols. New York: Franklin, 1960. ▸ Classic, systematic survey of political history. [APK]

8.332 Deno John Geanakoplos. *Interaction of the "sibling": Byzantine and Western cultures in the Middle Ages and Italian Renaissance (330–1600)*. New Haven: Yale University Press, 1976. ISBN 0-300-01831-2. ▸ Sociological analysis. Four periods of cultural interconnection: 330–1096, 1096–1261, 1261–1453, 1453–1600 (after the fall of Byzantium); and three modes of acculturation: dominance, amalgamation, and confrontation. Discusses attitudes of different social classes to sibling culture and Greek influences on Italian learning in fifteenth century. Despite limitations, unique English-language study. [APK/PFG]

8.333 Michael Graebner. "The Slavs in Byzantine population: transfers of the seventh and eighth centuries." *Études balkaniques* 11 (1975) 40–52. ISSN 0014-1976. ▸ Results of relocation of Slavs in Byzantine territory by Constans II, Justinian II, and Constantine V positive. [APK]

8.334 André Guillou and Filippo Burgarella. *L'Italia bizantina: dall'esarcato di Ravenna al tema di Sicilia*. Turin: UTET, 1988. ISBN 88-7750-126-X. ▸ Chronological framework broader than title, from Justinianic conquest to Norman invasion (sixth to eleventh century). Treats economy, administration, and society in first two sections, relations with Byzantium in third. [APK]

8.335 Angeliki E. Laiou and Henry Maguire, eds. *Byzantium: a world civilization*. Washington, D.C.: Dumbarton Oaks, 1992. ISBN 0-88402-200-5. ▸ Collection of heterogeneous articles, most on place of Byzantium in world civilization and relations with Slavs, Muslims, and West, but also on art. One paper (by Anastos) on development of Byzantine studies at Dumbarton Oaks. [APK]

8.336 Ferenc Makk. *The Árpáds and the Comneni: political relations between Hungary and Byzantium in the twelfth century*. Rev. ed. Maurice F. Cassidy and Istvan Petrovics, eds. György Gy Novak, trans. Budapest: Akadémiai Kiadó, 1989. ISBN 963-05-5268-X. ▸ Analysis of military, dynastic, and diplomatic relations between two countries within general framework of East European policy. Also discusses shifts in social structure in Hungary. [APK/SBV]

8.337 Otto Mazal. *Byzanz und das Abendland: Ausstellung der Handschriften- und Inkunabelsammlung der Österreichen Nationalbibliotek: Handbuch und Katalog*. Graz: Akademische Druck- & Verlaganstalt, 1981. ISBN 3-201-01158-4. ▸ Catalog of exhibition of manuscripts of Austrian National Library with introductory notes both general and on particular topics such as theology, music, medicine, geography. West used Byzantine legacy while confronting East and emancipating itself from it. [APK]

8.338 Michael McCormick. "Byzantium's role in the formation of early medieval civilization: approaches and problems." *Illinois classical studies* 12.2 (1987) 207–20. ISSN 0363-1923. ▸ Positive appraisal of Byzantium's creative role in formation of early medieval culture. Necessary to differentiate Byzantine contribution in time, space, social strata, and content. [APK]

8.339 John Meyendorff. *Byzantium and the rise of Russia: a study of Byzantino-Russian relations in the fourteenth century.* Cambridge: Cambridge University Press, 1981. ISBN 0-521-23183-3. ▸ Analysis of transmission of complex political theories and ideas from Byzantium to Russia. Fourteenth-century Russia belonged to supranational community, conventionally named Commonwealth of Orthodox Nations. See also Obolensky 8.343. [APK]

8.340 Gyula Moravcsik. *Byzantinoturcica.* 2d rev. ed. 2 vols. Berlin: Akademie, 1958. (Berliner byzantinistische Arbeiten, 10–11.) ▸ Comprehensive list of Turkish and related names and words preserved in Byzantine texts (narrative, documentry, epigraphic). First volume contains discussion of Turkish peoples (including Huns, Bulgarians, Pechenegs, etc.) and of sources used to develop the list. Enormous bibliography of early scholarship. [APK]

8.341 Gyula Moravcsik. *Byzantium and the Magyars.* Samuel R. Rosenbaum, trans. Amsterdam: Hakkert, 1970. ▸ Standard introductory work. Byzantium's political and military relations with Hungary and role of Byzantine church and culture in Hungary. [APK/SBV]

8.342 Donald M. Nicol. *Byzantium and Venice: a study in diplomatic and cultural relations.* Cambridge: Cambridge University Press, 1988. ISBN 0-521-34157-4. ▸ General survey of political and economic relations. Minimal cultural exchange between Byzantines and Venetians; peoples kept their distance from one another. [APK]

8.343 Dimitri Obolensky. *The Byzantine commonwealth: eastern Europe, 500–1453.* 1971 ed. Crestwood, N.Y.: St. Vladimir's Seminary Press, 1982. ISBN 0-913836-98-2 (pbk). ▸ Discussion of diffusion of Byzantine civilization, religion, law, literature, and art in Balkans and Eurasian Steppe; and of bonds of commonwealth. [APK]

8.344 Omeljan Pritsak and Ihor Ševčenko, eds. *Proceedings of the international congress commemorating the millennium of Christianity in Rus'-Ukraine.* Cambridge, Mass.: Harvard Ukrainian Research Institute, 1990. (Harvard Ukrainian studies, 12–13.). ISSN 0363-5570. ▸ Collection of papers, many on Russo-Byzantine political and ecclesiastical relations. [APK]

8.345 Steven Runciman. *The Sicilian Vespers: a history of the Mediterranean world in the later thirteenth century.* 1958 ed. New York: Cambridge University Press, 1982. ISBN 0-521-28652-2. ▸ Standard monograph. Conflict between Byzantium and Angevin dynasty in Sicily culminated in revolt of 1282 against Charles I of Anjou, ruining his plan to attack Constantinople. [APK]

8.346 Peter Schreiner. *Studia Byzantino-Bulgarica.* Vienna: Verein "Freunde des Hauses Wittgenstein," 1986. (Miscellanea bulgarica, 2.) ▸ Collection of articles published 1978–86 on sources for Bulgarian medieval history and on Byzantino-Bulgarian (primarily economic) relations. [APK]

8.347 Kenneth M. Setton. *Catalan domination of Athens, 1311–1388.* Rev. ed. London: Variorum, 1975. ISBN 0-902089-77-3. ▸ Predominantly political history of relations of Catalan Company, Greeks, and Crusader states in Greece, with concluding chapter on social conditions and culture in Athens. See Setton 8.225. [APK]

8.348 Ihor Ševčenko. *Byzantium and the Slavs in letters and culture.* Cambridge, Mass.: Harvard Ukrainian Research Institute, 1991. (Renovatio, 1.) ISBN 0-916458-12-1. ▸ Collected articles,

reviews, and obituaries on problems of Byzantine relations with Kievan and Muscovite Rus' and their study by modern historians. Especially important: general survey, "Byzantium and the Slavs," and "The Date and the Author of the So-Called Fragments of Toparcha Gothicus"; contains addenda. [APK]

8.349 Irfan Shahîd. *Byzantium and the Arabs in the fifth century.* Washington, D.C.: Dumbarton Oaks Research Library and Collection, 1989. ISBN 0-88402-152-1. ▸ Survey of Greek, Latin, and Arabic sources. Relations between empire and federates and discussion of Arabs in service of empire. [APK]

8.350 Jonathan Shepard. "Aspects of Byzantine attitudes and policy towards the West in the tenth and eleventh centuries." *Byzantinische Forschungen* 13 (1988) 67–118. ▸ Byzantine propaganda stressed affinity and religious community of Byzantium and the West, accepted by many Westerners. Government of Alexios I doubted their acceptance and behaved accordingly. [APK]

8.351 Jonathan Shepard. "The English and Byzantium: a study of their role in the Byzantine army in the later eleventh century." *Traditio* 29 (1973) 53–92. ISSN 0362-1529. ▸ Discussion of arrival of Anglo-Saxons in Constantinople soon after disaster of 1066; their important role in army and at court of Alexios I Komnenos. [APK]

8.352 Jonathan Shepard. "Some problems of Russo-Byzantine relations, c. 860–c. 1050." *Slavonic and East European review* 52 (1974) 10–33. ISSN 0037-6795. ▸ Discussion of radical change in political and cultural situation of Kievan Rus' by 1050; thesis that building of St. Sophia in Kiev put "Russia" on map of Europe far more surely than Svjatoslav's wars. [APK]

8.353 Alexander Aleksandrovich Vasiliev. *Byzance et les Arabes.* 3 vols. Henri Grégoire and Marius Canard, eds. Brussels: Institut de Philologie et d'Histoire Orientales et Slaves, 1935–59. (Corpus Bruxellense historiae Byzantinae, 1–3.) ▸ Excellent presentation of military and diplomatic relations (820–959), subdivided by region. French translations by Canard of extracts from Arabic sources in appendix. Translated from Russian 1900–1902 revised edition. [APK]

8.354 Alexander Aleksandrovich Vasiliev. *The Russian attack on Constantinople in 860.* Cambridge, Mass.: Mediaeval Academy of America, 1946. ▸ Survey of sources and literature. Addresses controversial issues, including alleged Russian attack on Amastris and name of Rus'. Focuses on attack of 860 and on commercial relations after 860. [APK]

8.355 Speros Vryonis, Jr., ed. *Byzantine studies: essays on the Slavic world and the eleventh century.* New Rochelle, N.Y.: Caratzas, 1992. ISBN 0-89241-517-7. ▸ Collection of articles on Slavic settlements in Balkans, Serbo-Byzantine relations, Byzantine traditions under Ottomans and in Muscovy, battle of Manzikert (1071), and intellectual and religious life in eleventh-century Byzantium. [APK]

SEE ALSO
28.155 Joseph Gill. *The Council of Florence.*

RELIGION

8.356 Milton V. Anastos. *Studies on Byzantine intellectual history.* London: Variorum, 1979. ISBN 0-86078-031-7. ▸ Collected papers published 1946–79 on Byzantine political thought, theology, and science. Among others see especially "Nestorius Was Orthodox" and articles on Iconoclasm. [APK]

8.357 Hans U. von Balthasar. *Kosmische Liturgie: das Weltbild Maximus' des Bekenners.* Einsiedeln: Johannes-Verlag, 1988. ISBN 3-265-10009-X. ▸ Classic, doctrinal analysis of Maximos the Confessor's theology with focus on God-Man synthesis in person of

Christ. Includes German translation of some works of Maximos the Confessor (d. 662). [APK]

8.358 John Lawrence Boojamra. *Church reform in the late Byzantine empire: a study for the patriarchate of Athanasios of Constantinople.* Thessalonike: Patriarchikon Hidryma Paterikon Meleton, 1983. (Analekta Blatadon, 35.) ISBN 0-916586-76-6. ‣ Study of Patriarch Athanasios's relationship to government of Andronikos II (1282–1328), attempts to reorganize church hierarchy, problem of refugees in Constantinople, ecclesiastical philanthropy during famine of 1306/7, and conflict of rigorous patriarch with court and society. [APK]

8.359 Demetrios J. Constantelos. *Byzantine philanthropy and social welfare.* 2d ed. New Rochelle, N.Y.: Caratzas, 1991. ISBN 0-89241-402-2. ‣ Study of concept of philanthropy and philanthropic institutions of Byzantium, medieval state which excelled in philanthropy above all other nations. Topics include hospitals, hospices, homes for aged, orphanages, and poor houses. First published 1968. [APK]

8.360 Leo D. Davis. *The first seven ecumenical councils (325–787): their history and theology.* 1987 ed. Collegeville, Minn.: Liturgical Press, 1990. ISBN 0-8146-5616-1. ‣ Popular survey. Each council described separately: gist of theological controversies, development of events, aftermath, and chronology. [APK]

8.361 George Every. *The Byzantine patriarchate, 451–1204.* 2d rev. ed. London: Society for Promoting Christian Knowledge, 1962. ‣ Short survey of Byzantine church from Council of Chalcedon to conquest of Constantinople by Crusaders. Good for beginner. [APK]

8.362 William H. C. Frend. *The rise of the monophysite movement: chapters in the history of the church in the fifth and sixth centuries.* Cambridge: Cambridge University Press, 1974. ISBN 0-521-08130-0. ‣ Integrated study combining factors of secular history with outlines of doctrinal development in fifth and sixth centuries. Justinian's Western-oriented policy, although doomed, led to neglect of vital interests of East and prepared way for Arab conquest of eastern provinces. [APK]

8.363 Joseph Gill. "The church union of the Council of Lyons (1274) portrayed in Greek documents." *Orientalia Christiana periodica* 40 (1974) 5–45. ISSN 0030-5375. ‣ Greek original and English translation of eight texts. Shows Greek ecclesiasticals bothered by canonical position of pope (primacy, appeal, and commemoration), not procession of Holy Spirit. [APK]

8.364 Joan M. Hussey. *The Orthodox church in the Byzantine empire.* New York: Oxford University Press, 1986. ISBN 0-19-826901-3. ‣ History (seventh to fifteenth century) with emphasis on major controversies (monotheletism, Iconoclasm, conflict with West). Discussion of administration and spiritual life. Good introductory study. [APK]

8.365 John Meyendorff. *Byzantine theology: historical trends and doctrinal themes.* 2d ed. New York: Fordham University Press, 1987. ISBN 0-8232-0967-9. ‣ Clear, concise presentation of major theological controversies after Council of Chalcedon (451): christological issue, Iconoclasm, monastic theology, and schism. Concepts of God, man, creation, and sacrament. [APK]

8.366 John Meyendorff. *Imperial unity and Christian divisions: the church, 450–680 A.D.* Crestwood, N.Y.: St. Vladimir's Seminary Press, 1989. ISBN 0-88141-056-X (cl), 0-88141-055-1 (pbk). ‣ Organization and history of church beginning with Council of Chalcedon. Tendency to free church from oversimplified characterization of caesaro-papism, period of extraordinary expansion west and east; monophysitism does not imply christological heresy. [APK]

8.367 John Meyendorff. *St. Gregory Palamas and Orthodox spir-*

ituality. Adele Fiske, trans. Crestwood, N.Y.: St. Vladimir's Seminary Press, 1974. ISBN 0-913836-11-7. ‣ Theology of hesychasm in fourteenth century within framework of patristic tradition and in opposition to nominalism of Barlaam of Calabria. Translated from French edition: *St. Grégoire Palamas et la mystique orthodoxe.* [APK]

8.368 Luigi I. Scipioni. *Nestorio e il concilio di Efeso: storia, dogma, critica.* Milan: Vita e Pensiero, 1974. (Pubblicazioni della Università Cattolica del Sacro Cuore. Studia patristica mediolanensia, 1.) ‣ Biography and theology of Nestorios who anticipated the formula of Chalcedon and stressed Christ's human nature soteriologically rather than ontologically. Attempt to exonerate him from accusation of heresy. English summary (pp. 425–32). [APK]

8.369 Philip Sherrard. *Church, papacy, and schism: a theological enquiry.* London: Society for Promoting Christian Knowledge, 1978. ISBN 0-281-03620-9. ‣ Critique of two traditional viewpoints; one placing responsibility for schism with Eastern church, other on political question of papal primacy. Argues that even political divergency originated in theological diversity. [APK]

8.370 Robert F. Taft. *The Byzantine rite.* Collegeville, Minn.: Liturgical Press, 1992. ISBN 0-8146-2163-6. ‣ Brief, excellent introduction to topic: origins and development of Byzantine liturgy (imperial rite, Dark Ages, "Studite era," synthesis of tenth to twelfth century, neo-Sabaitic period). Discusses iconography, church architecture, and symbolism of liturgy. [APK]

8.371 Alice-Mary M. Talbot. "An introduction to Byzantine monasticism." *Illinois classical studies* 12.2 (1987) 229–41. ISSN 0363-1923. ‣ Short survey of history, activities, and economic role of monasteries; major monastic centers (Constantinople, Sinai, Athos, Meteora). [APK]

8.372 Alice-Mary M. Talbot, ed. *The correspondence of Athanasius I patriarch of Constantinople.* Washington, D.C.: Dumbarton Oaks Center for Byzantine Studies, 1975. (Corpus Fontium historiae Byzantinae, 7. Dumbarton Oaks texts, 3.) ISBN 0-88402-040-1. ‣ Greek original, English translation of, and commentary on letters of Athanasios (1289–93, 1303–09)—important source for political and ecclesiastical history of period. [APK]

8.373 Franz Tinnefeld. "Michael I. Kerullarios, Patriarch von Konstantinopel (1043–1058): kritische Überlegungen zu einer Biographie." *Jahrbuch der österreichischen Byzantinistik* 39 (1989) 95–127. ISSN 0378-8660. ‣ Critical revision of Michael Keroularios's biography and of his authorship of so-called *Panoplia*. Includes brief personality profile. [APK]

8.374 Friedhelm Winkelmann. "Die Quellen zur Erforschung der monoenergetisch-monotheletischen Streites." *Klio* 69 (1987) 515–59. ‣ Comprehensive list of Greek, Latin, and Oriental sources citing edition, literature, content, and dating. [APK]

LITERATURE

General Works and Genres

8.375 Roderick Beaton. *The medieval Greek romance.* Cambridge: Cambridge University Press, 1989. ISBN 0-521-33335-0. ‣ Development of romance in twelfth to fifteenth centuries as single genre (those written in pure language as well as vernacular) whose aesthetic values can be understood in connection with works of other genres of same period. Goal of twelfth century Romans was quest for redemption on level of traditional story; purpose of later writers was creation of fictional world in which western achievements merged with Greek tradition. [APK]

8.376 Hans-Georg Beck. *Geschichte der byzantinischen Volksliteratur.* Munich: Beck, 1971. (Handbuch der Altertumswissenschaft, Abteilung 12. Byzantinisches Handbuch, 2.3.) ISBN 3-406-

01420-8. ‣ Best survey of Byzantine literature in vernacular, including epic of Digenes Akritas (8.374), and poems of so-called "Ptochoprodromos" (The Poor Prodromos), late Byzantine romance. [APK]

8.377 Hans-Georg Beck. *Kirche und theologische Literatur im byzantinischen Reich.* 1959 ed. Munich: Beck, 1977. (Handbuch der Altertumswissenschaft, Abteilung 12. Byzantinisches Handbuch, 2.1.) ISBN 3-406-01416-X. ‣ Survey of church structure, liturgy, and main tendencies of theological development (sixth to fifteenth century); comprehensive survey of theological literature in chronological order, each period divided into genres (dogmatic literature, hagiography, exegesis, canon law, etc.). [APK]

8.378 Hippolyte Delehaye. *The legends of the saints.* Donald Attwater, trans. New York: Fordham University Press, 1962. ‣ Saints' vitae as literary genre; work of hagiographer, classification of hagiographical texts, and pagan survivals. Concludes with memoire by Paul Peeters on Delehaye and Delehaye's bibliography. Translated from French, *Les légendes hagiographique* (1955). [APK]

8.379 George T. Dennis. "The Byzantines as revealed in their letters." In *Gonimos: Neoplatonic and Byzantine studies presented to Leendert G. Westerink at 75.* John Duffy and John Peradotto, eds., pp. 155–66. Buffalo: Arethusa, 1988. ‣ Attempt to judge literary quality of Byzantine epistolography on its own merits; letters add new dimension to authors' personalities. [APK]

8.380 Albert Ehrhard. *Überlieferung und Bestand der hagiographischen und homiletischen Literatur der griechischen Kirche von den Anfängen bis zum Ende des sechzehnten Jahrhunderts.* Vol. 1: *Die Überlieferung.* 3 vols. Leipzig: Hinrichs, 1937–52. (Texte und Untersuchungen zur Geschichte der altchristlichen Literatur, 50-52.) ‣ General discussion of Byzantine collections of saints' lives. Description and categorization of individual manuscripts containing vitae. Supplemented by index: Lidia Perria, *I manoscritti citati da Albert Ehrhard* (1979). [APK]

8.381 Enrica Follieri. *Initia hymnorum ecclesiae Graecae.* 5 vols. in 6. Vatican City: Biblioteca Apostolica Vaticana, 1960–66. (Studie e testi, 211–215.) ‣ Important reference book on Byzantine hymnography: alphabetical list of first lines of all hymns available, list of saints praised in hymns, and list of hymnographers with index of hymns attributed to each of them. Bibliography. [APK]

8.382 François Halkin, ed. *Bibliotheca hagiographica graeca.* 3d rev. ed. 3 vols. Brussels: Société des Bollandistes, 1957. (Subsidia hagiographica, 8a.) ‣ Catalog of hagiographical texts both published and unpublished. Contains vitae, martyrdoms, miracles of saints (arranged by saint). Appendixes give several specific groups of texts: on Christ, on St. Mary, on festivals, etc.; supplemented by *Auctarium* (1969) and *Novum auctarium* (1984). [APK]

8.383 Herbert Hunger. *Die hochsprachliche profane Literatur der Byzantiner.* 2 vols. Munich: Beck, 1978. (Handbuch der Altertumswissenschaft, Abteilung 12.5. Byzantinisches Handbuch, 5.) ISBN 3-406-01427-5 (v. 1). ‣ Excellent reference book; survey of Byzantine philosophical, oratorial, epistolographic, historical, geographic, and other works by genre and subgenre. Chapter on music (Hannick) and on legal literature (Peeler). [APK]

8.384 Elizabeth M. Jeffreys and Michael J. Jeffreys. "The style of Byzantine popular poetry: recent work." *Harvard Ukrainian studies* 7 (1983) 309–43. ISSN 0363-5570. ‣ Survey of recent publications and goals for future investigation. Treats problems in texts with constant variation in copying, repetition, and grammar. [APK]

8.385 Johannes Karayannopulos and Günter Weiss. *Quellenkunde zur Geschichte von Byzanz (324–1453).* 2 vols. Wiesbaden: Harrassowitz, 1982. (Schriften zur Geistesgeschichte des östlichen Europa, 14.) ISBN 3-447-02244-2 (set). ‣ Seminal reference work. Methodology, typology of sources (material and written), list of non-Byzantine sources (Latin, Slavic, Oriental), and list of Greek and Latin texts from territory of empire. Entries contain short description and bibliography. [APK]

8.386 Karl Krumbacher. *Geschichte der byzantinischen Literatur von Justinian bis zum Ende des oströmischen Reiches (527–1453).* 2d rev. ed. Munich: Beck, 1897. (Handbuch der klassischen Altertumswissenschaft, 9.1.) ISBN 0-7905-8040-3 (microfiche, Evanston, Ill.: American Theological Library). ‣ Classic survey of Byzantine literature by genre and subgenre. Chapters on theological and hagiographical literature (Ehrhard) and survey of political history (Gelzer). [APK]

8.387 George L. Kustas. *Studies in Byzantine rhetoric.* Thessalonike: Patriarchal Institute for Patristic Studies, 1973. (Analekta Blatadon, 17.) ‣ Study of Byzantine rhetoric as part of broad stream of cultural development and change (mostly on basis of Byzantine commentaries on Hermogenes). Explores such concepts as obscurity, dignity, and emphasis. [APK]

8.388 Henry Maguire. *Art and eloquence in Byzantium.* Princeton: Princeton University Press, 1981. ISBN 0-691-03972-0. ‣ Affinity of Byzantine rhetoric with visual arts: rhetoric helped add vividness to works of art, structure composition through antithetic parallel scenes, and enrich work with supplementary images. [APK]

8.389 Cyril Mango. *Byzantine literature as a distorting mirror: an inaugural lecture delivered before the University of Oxford on 21 May 1974.* Oxford: Clarendon, 1975. ISBN 0-19-951501-8. ‣ Dichotomy between literature and changing reality as one of salient features of Byzantine culture. [APK]

8.390 Ihor Ševčenko. "Levels of style in Byzantine prose." *Jahrbuch der österreichischen Byzantinistik* 31.1 (1981) 289–312. ISSN 0378-8660. ‣ Analysis of relationship of style and audience: high style of educated writing for small circle of peers, middle style of more numerous group producing for larger audience, and low style of less educated whose audience could not have been substantial. [APK]

Individual Periods, Authors, and Works

8.391 Alan Cameron. *Literature and society in the early Byzantine world.* London: Variorum, 1985. ISBN 0-86078-157-7. ‣ Collected papers (1965–83) on politicians, philosophers, and writers, mostly Greek, of late third through seventh centuries, both pagan and Christian. [APK]

8.392 Averil Cameron. *Procopius and the sixth century.* Berkeley: University of California Press, 1985. ISBN 0-520-05517-9. ‣ Study of Prokopios as conventional thinker grappling with difficult set of changing circumstances. Finds works have certain unity, whereas differences may be explained by development of author's thinking. [APK]

8.393 Nicetas Choniates. *O city of Byzantium, annals of Niketas Choniates.* Harry J. Magoulias, trans. Detroit: Wayne State University Press, 1984. ISBN 0-8143-1764-2. ‣ English translation of history of Byzantium from 1118 to 1206. Masterpiece of Greek literature. [APK]

8.394 Anna Comnena. *The Alexiad of Anna Comnena.* Edgar R. A. Sewter, trans. Baltimore: Penguin, 1969. ISBN 0-14-044215-4. ‣ English translation of Anna Komnena's history of reign of her father, Emperor Alexios I Komnenos (1081–1118). [APK]

8.395 Constantine VII Porphyrogenitus. *De administrando imperio.* Vol. 1, rev. ed. 2 vols. Gyula Moravcsik, ed. Romilly J. H. Jenkins, trans. Washington, D.C.: Dumbarton Oaks Center for Byzantine Studies, 1962, 1967. (Corpus Fontium historiae

Byzantinae, 1. Dumbarton Oaks texts, 1.) ▸ Translation of treatise by emperor Constantine VII (913–959), *On the Administration of the Empire*; description of neighboring peoples and of Byzantine diplomacy. Commentary by Romilly J. H. Jenkins and others. Volume 1 originally published 1949. [APK]

8.396 *Crusaders as conquerors: the Chronicle of Morea.* Harold E. Lurier, trans. New York: Columbia University Press, 1964. ▸ Translation of fourteenth-century vernacular Greek chronicle in verse depicting Frankish conquest of the Peloponnesos. [APK]

8.397 Doukas. *Decline and fall of Byzantium to the Ottoman Turks.* Harry J. Magoulias, trans. Detroit: Wayne State University Press, 1975. ISBN 0-8143-1540-2. ▸ English translation of Byzantine chronicle of Ottoman conquest of Constantinople and Greece (especially detailed from end of fourteenth century to 1462). Nostalgic for heroic past of Hellenes: author expects fall of Ottomans and restoration of Hellenic nation. [APK]

8.398 Patricia Karlin-Hayter, ed. *Vita Euthymii patriarchae Cp: text, translation, introduction, and commentary.* Brussels: Éditions de Byzantion, 1970. (Bibliothèque de Byzantion, 3.) ▸ Greek original and English translation (with introduction and commentary) of anonymous *Life of Euthymios*, patriarch of Constantinople (907–912). One of most interesting hagiographical texts and important source for history of Byzantium at end of ninth and beginning of tenth century. [APK]

8.399 Alexander P. Kazhdan. *Studies on Byzantine literature of the eleventh and twelfth centuries.* Simon Franklin, collaborator. Cambridge and Paris: Cambridge University Press and Éditions de la Maison des Sciences de l'Homme, 1984. ISBN 0-521-24656-3. ▸ Essays on individual authors; biographies, social and political views, and literary technique. [APK]

8.400 John Kinnamos. *Deeds of John and Manuel Comnenus.* Charles M. Brand, trans. New York: Columbia University Press, 1976. ISBN 0-231-04080-6. ▸ English translation of book written by secretary of Manuel I Komnenos and encompassing period 1118–76, including such events as Second Crusade. Manuel praised as ideal warrior. [APK]

8.401 John Mavrogordato, ed. and trans. *Digenes Akrites.* Oxford: Clarendon, 1956. ▸ Byzantine epic written probably in eleventh century and edited on basis of so-called Grotta-Ferrata manuscript of fourteenth century. Greek original and English translation. [APK]

8.402 Maximus Confessor, Saint. *Maximus Confessor: selected writings.* George C. Berthold, ed. and trans. New York: Paulist Press, 1985. ISBN 0-8091-353-2 (cl), 0-8091-2659-1 (pbk). ▸ Works of greatest theologian of seventh century, best known for his stand in controversy about two wills of Christ. [APK]

8.403 Photius I. *The library of Photius I, saint patriarch of Constantinople.* John H. Freese, trans. London: Society for Promoting Christian Knowledge, 1920. (Translations of Christian literature, Series 1: Greek texts, 2.) ▸ English translation of 165 bibliographical notes by Patriarch Photios (d. after 893). [APK]

8.404 Procopius. *Procopius.* 7 vols. Henry B. Dewing, trans. Cambridge, Mass.: Harvard University Press, 1914–40. ▸ Translation of Greek historian of sixth century whose works (*Wars*, *Secret History*, and *Buildings*) were major source for reign of Justinian I. [APK]

8.405 Michael Psellus. *The Chronographia.* Edgar R. A. Sewter, trans. New Haven: Yale University Press, 1953. ▸ English translation of memoirs of Psellos, one of most important sources for history of Byzantium, 976–1078. [APK]

8.406 Pseudo-Dionysius the Areopagite. *Pseudo-Dionysius: the complete works.* Colm Luibheid, trans. Jaroslav Pelikan, Jean

Leclercq, and Karlfried Froelich, Introductions. New York: Paulist Press, 1987. ISBN 0-8091-0383-4 (cl), 0-8091-2838-1 (pbk). ▸ Theologian and writer, ca. 500, who had enormous impact on Western thought. [APK]

8.407 Romanus Melodos, Saint. *Kontakia of Romanos: Byzantine melodist.* 2 vols. Marjorie Carpenter, trans. and annotator. Columbia: University of Missouri Press, 1970–72. ISBN 0-8262-0073-7. ▸ Translation and annotation of works of greatest Byzantine poet of sixth century who wrote hymns on person of Christ and on Christian life. [APK]

8.408 George Sphrantzes. *The fall of the Byzantine empire: a chronicle, 1401–1477.* Marios Philippides, trans. Amherst: University of Massachusetts Press, 1980. ISBN 0-87023-290-8. ▸ English translation of history of Ottoman conquest of Byzantium, by eyewitness and active participant in events, courtier and diplomat. [APK]

8.409 Theophanes the Confessor. *The Chronicle of Theophanes: an English translation of anni mundi 6095–6305 (A.D. 602–813).* Harry Turtledove, trans. Philadelphia: University of Pennsylvania Press, 1982. ISBN 0-8122-7842-9 (cl), 0-8122-1128-6 (pbk). ▸ Partial translation (years 602–813) of *Chronographia* of Theophanes the Confessor, major source for seventh and eighth centuries of Byzantine history. [APK]

8.410 *Three Byzantine saints.* 1948 ed. Elizabeth Dawes and Norman H. Baynes, trans. Crestwood, N.Y.: St. Vladimir's Seminary Press, 1977. ISBN 0-913836-44-3. ▸ English translation, with introductions and notes, of three hagiographical texts: vita of St. Daniel the Stylite (d. 493), of St. Theodore of Sykeon (d. 613), and of St. John the Almsgiver (or Merciful), patriarch of Alexandria (610–619). Not only important sources but beautifully written biographies. [APK]

SCIENCE

8.411 Lawrence J. Bliquez and Alexander P. Kazhdan. "Four testimonia to human dissection in Byzantine times." *Bulletin of the history of medicine* 58 (1984) 554–57. ISSN 0007-5140. ▸ Cases of autopsy in late Roman empire and in Byzantium (eighth to twelfth century). [APK]

8.412 Timothy S. Miller. *The birth of the hospital in the Byzantine empire.* Baltimore: Johns Hopkins University Press, 1985. (Henry E. Sigerist supplements to the *Bulletin of the History of Medicine*, n.s., 10.) ISBN 0-8018-2676-4. ▸ Discussion of organization of hospital services, especially in Pantokrator monastery in twelfth-century Constantinople and impact of Christianity, role of philanthropy. [APK]

8.413 Otto Neugebauer. "Studies in Byzantine astronomical terminology." *Transactions of the American Philosophical Society* 50.2 (1960) 3–45. ISSN 0065-9746. ▸ Glossary of technical terms; meaning determined by their usage in *Codex Vaticanus graecus* (text number 1058) written in fifteenth century and by parallels in Persian and Arabic astronomical treatises. [APK]

8.414 David Pingree. "The astrological school of John Abramius." *Dumbarton Oaks papers* 25 (1971) 118–215. ISSN 0070-7546. ▸ Unsuccessful attempt by Abramios, astrological adviser of Emperor Andronikos IV (1376–79), to revise Ptolemaic astronomical parameters based on own observations and knowledge of Islamic material. Pupils carried on work of school into fifteenth century. [APK]

8.415 Utto Riedinger. *Die heilige Schrift im Kampf der griechischen Kirche gegen die Astrologie, von Origenes bis Johannes von Damaskos: Studien zur Dogmengeschichte und zur Geschichte der Astrologie.* Innsbruck: Universitätsverlag Wagner, 1956. ▸ List of church fathers (from Origen to John of Damascus) who dealt with astrology. Patristic interpretation of biblical astrological evidence (especially the star of Magi) and principles of refutation of astrology. [APK]

8.416 John Scarborough, ed. "Symposium on Byzantine medicine." *Dumbarton Oaks papers* 38 (1984). ISSN 0070-7546. ▸ Papers given at 1983 symposium; Byzantine doctors and hospitals, medical treatises and commentaries, veterinary medicine, ophthalmology, pharmacology, and interactions with Islamic and Hebrew medicine. [APK]

8.417 Paul Tannery. "Sciences exactes chez les Byzantins." In *Mémoires scientifiques 4.* 1912 ed. Pierre Louis, ed. Toulouse: Privat, 1950. ▸ Collected papers published 1884–1919, primarily on Byzantine mathematics. Available in microform from New York: National Cash Register Company. [APK]

8.418 Owsei Temkin. "Byzantine medicine: tradition and empiricism." *Dumbarton Oaks papers* 16 (1962) 92–115. ISSN 0070-7546. ▸ Study of medicine in formative period, Alexandrian period to 642. Includes commentaries on ancient authors and discusses some traces of everyday practice (especially pharmacology) from later period. [APK]

8.419 Anne Tihon. "L'astronomie byzantine (du cinquième au quinzième siècle)." *Byzantion* 51 (1981) 603–24. ISSN 0378-2506. ▸ Islamic influence and Ptolemaic tradition. Chronological survey of treatises on astronomy. [APK]

8.420 Nigel G. Wilson. *Scholars of Byzantium.* Baltimore: Johns Hopkins University Press, 1983. ISBN 0-8018-3052-4. ▸ Study of Byzantine attitude toward classical heritage. Byzantine scholarship as product of educational system in which poetry met challenges of rhetoric and philosophy. Chronological survey based on published texts and manuscripts. [APK]

PHILOSOPHY AND LEARNING

8.421 *Byzantine books and bookmen.* Washington, D.C.: Dumbarton Oaks Center for Byzantine Studies, 1975. (Dumbarton Oaks colloquium, 1971.) ISBN 0-88402-065-7. ▸ Papers on centers of book production, illustrations, book trade, and book readers by Nigel G. Wilson, Jean Irigoin, Cyril Mango, Hans-Georg Beck, and Kurt Weitzmann. [APK]

8.422 Ilsetraut Hadot, ed. *Simplicius: sa vie, son oeuvre, sa survie.* Berlin: de Gruyter, 1987. (Peripatoi, 15.) ISBN 3-11-010924-7. ▸ Papers in French and English presented at 1985 international colloquium in Paris. Survey of Simplikios's biography and work, several articles on his Aristotelian philosophy (including his polemics against Philoponos) and on how he was perceived by later generations. [APK]

8.423 Joan M. Hussey. *Church and learning in the Byzantine empire, 867–1185.* 1937 ed. New York: Russell & Russell, 1963. ▸ Revival of learning in eleventh century; reopening of university in Constantinople and activity of individual literati both secular (Psellos, Italikos) and ecclesiastical (especially mystical writer Symeon the Theologian). [APK]

8.424 Paul Lemerle. *Byzantine humanism, the first phase: notes and remarks on education and culture in Byzantium from its origins to the tenth century.* Helen Lindsay and Ann Moffatt, trans. Canberra: Australian Association for Byzantine Studies, 1986. (Byzantina Australiensia, 3.) ISBN 0-9593626-3-0 (pbk). ▸ Translation of his excellent study *Le premier humanisme byzantin* (1971), critical analysis of sources and of scholarly hypotheses. Discusses ambivalence of Byzantine education and culture in general and traditions of ancient *paideia* and continuous (though slow) changes. [APK]

8.425 Ann Moffatt. "Science teachers in the early Byzantine

empire: some statistics." In *Actes du quinzième Congrès International des Études Byzantines,* pp. 659–61. Bucharest: Editura Academiei Repuglicii Socialiste Romania, 1976. ▸ Statistical study of 303 known teachers: 131 from fourth century, 108 from fifth, and 62 from sixth. Numbers of science teachers respectively 22, 26, 14. [APK]

8.426 Gerhardt Podskalsky. *Theologie und Philosophie in Byzanz.* Munich: Beck, 1977. (Byzantinisches Archiv, 15.) ISBN 3-406-00415-6. ▸ Study of relationship between philosophy and theology, primarily in fourteenth and fifteenth centuries. Finds no systematic methodology and no clearly established, institutionalized teaching chair; theology in images dominated over conceptual theology. [APK]

8.427 Proclus. *The elements of theology.* 2d ed. Eric R. Dodds, ed. and trans. Oxford: Clarendon, 1963. ▸ Study of work of fifth-century Neoplatonist and last pagan philosopher includes Greek original, English translation, and commentary. [APK]

8.428 Richard Sorabji, ed. *Philoponus and the rejection of Aristotelian science.* Ithaca, N.Y.: Cornell University Press, 1987. ISBN 0-8014-2049-0. ▸ Anthology of articles discussing John Philoponos and his place in history of theology with essays on particular questions (creation, impetus, space) and attitudes of Greek, Arab, and Renaissance philosophers toward him. [APK]

8.429 Paul Speck. *Die kaiserliche Universität von Konstantinopel: Prazisierungen zur Frage des hoheren Schulwesens in Byzanz im neunten und zehnten Jahrhundert.* Munich: Beck, 1974. (Byzantinisches Archiv, 14.) ISBN 3-406-00414-8. ▸ Critical revision of theory that Byzantium retained or organized new university style of education in ninth and tenth centuries. Discusses guildlike and private organization of teaching. [APK]

8.430 Basile Tatakis. *La philosophie byzantine.* Paris: Presses Universitaires de France, 1949. (Histoire de la philosophie, fasc. supplémentaire, 2.) ▸ Introductory study on Christian attitude toward ancient legacy. General survey in chronological order (from sixth to fifteenth century) with individual characterizations of single authors, both secular writers and theologians. [APK]

8.431 Christian Wildberg. *John Philoponus' criticism of Aristotle's theory of aether.* New York: de Gruyter, 1988. (Peripatoi, 16.) ISBN 0-11-010446-6. ▸ Despite certain theoretical continuity, Philoponos, sixth-century Neoplatonist and Christian theologian, unlike Aristotle, postulated world as temporally finite, created by God out of nothing, and materially uniform. [APK]

8.432 Nigel G. Wilson. "The libraries of the Byzantine world." In *Griechische Kodikologie und Textüberlieferung.* 1967 ed. Dieter Harlfinger, ed., pp. 276–309. Darmstadt: Wissenschaftliche Buchgesellschaft, 1980. ISBN 3-534-05682-5. ▸ Survey of libraries in Constantinople, in some monasteries, in provinces, and separately in South Italy. Special attention to survival of classical texts in Byzantine libraries. [APK]

8.433 Christopher M. Woodhouse. *George Gemistos Plethon: the last of the Hellenes.* Oxford: Clarendon, 1986. ISBN 0-19-824767-2. ▸ Monograph on life and views of Byzantine humanist of fifteenth century. [APK]

ART, ARCHITECTURE, MUSIC, THEATER

8.434 John Beckwith. *Early Christian and Byzantine art.* 2d ed. Harmondsworth: Penguin, 1979. ISBN 0-14-0561-33-1. ▸ General introduction to subject. [APK]

8.435 Robin Cormack. *Writing in gold: Byzantine society and its icons.* London: Philip, 1985. ISBN 0-540-01085-5. ▸ Study of functions of icons in Byzantine society from seventh through twelfth centuries. Sees works of art and literature as evidence and, conversely, instigators of attitudes and beliefs and also sees differences between art and literature in expression of ideas. [APK]

8.436 Ormande M. Dalton. *Byzantine art and archaeology.* Oxford: Clarendon, 1911. ‣ Comprehensive (to date of publication) survey of arts (sculpture, painting, minor arts, textile, ceramics, glass, etc.) with special chapters on iconography and ornamental motives. [APK]

8.437 Otto Demus. *Byzantine mosaic decoration: aspects of monumental art in Byzantium.* New Rochelle, N.Y.: Caratzas, 1976. ISBN 0-89241-018-3. ‣ "Middle" Byzantine monuments analyzed as works of art, not archaeologically or iconographically, in relation to each other, their architectural framework, and viewer. Sees single images in church decoration as parts of organic entity governed by certain fixed principles. [APK]

8.438 André Grabar. *Byzantium from the death of Theodosius to the rise of Islam.* Stuart Gilbert and James Emmons, trans. London: Thames & Hudson, 1966. ‣ Survey of architecture, painting, sculpture, and sumptuary art in fifth and sixth centuries. Flourishing Christian art of late antiquity left strong imprint, despite artistic stagnation of Dark Ages, on medieval development. [APK]

8.439 Ernst Kitzinger. *Byzantine art in the making: main lines of stylistic development in Mediterranean art, third-seventh century.* Cambridge, Mass.: Harvard University Press, 1977. ISBN 0-674-08955-3. ‣ Analysis of stylistic development in pictorial arts. Sees sequence of stylistic trends as dialectical relationship between exploration of new nonclassical forms on one hand and retrospective movements and revivals on other. [APK]

8.440 Richard Krautheimer. *Early Christian and Byzantine architecture.* 4th rev. ed. New York: Penguin, 1986. ISBN 0-14-056168-4 (pbk). ‣ Survey of buildings from early Christian period through fifteenth century, including Byzantine-influenced areas (Italy, Africa, Egypt, Mesopotamia, Serbia, and Bulgaria), with special attention to monuments of age of Justinian I. [APK]

8.441 George La Piana. "The Byzantine theater." *Speculum* 11 (1936) 171–211. ISSN 0038-7134. ‣ Historiographical survey of then recent publications concluding that both secular and religious theater existed in Byzantium throughout its history. [APK]

8.442 Viktor Nikitich Lazarev. *Storia della pittura bizantina.* Turin: Einaudi, 1967. (Biblioteca di storia dell'arte, 7.) ‣ Revised Italian translation of Russian original published 1947–48 (reprinted 1986 with an epilogue by Gerold I. Vzdornov). Chapters on principles of Byzantine art and aesthetics. Chronological survey of Byzantine and Byzantine-influenced painting. [APK]

8.443 Henry Maguire. *Earth and ocean: the terrestrial world in early Byzantine art.* University Park: Pennsylvania State University Press for the College Art Association of America, 1987. ISBN 0-271-00477-0. ‣ Study of different representational approaches to physical world in fifth- and sixth-century art: literal, symbolic, combination of literal and symbolic, and moralizing. [APK]

8.444 Cyril Mango. *The art of the Byzantine empire, 312–1453.* 2d ed. Toronto: University of Toronto Press and Mediaeval Academy of America, 1986. (Mediaeval Academy reprints for teaching, 16.) ISBN 0-8020-6627-5 (pbk). ‣ Anthology of passages from Byzantine authors (in English translation) on works of art, organized by period. [APK]

8.445 Cyril Mango. *Byzantine architecture.* 1976 ed. New York: Rizzoli International, 1985. ISBN 0-8478-0615-4 (pbk). ‣ Byzantine architecture within framework of historical, geographical, social, and economic realities of Middle Ages. Late Roman and Byzantine periods divided by "Dark Ages" characterized by decline of ancient polis. Historical rather than typological and functional approach. [APK]

8.446 David T. Rice. *Art of the Byzantine era.* New York: Praeger, 1963. ‣ Accurate and concise survey. [APK]

8.447 William O. Strunk. *Essays on music in the Byzantine world.* New York: Norton, 1977. ISBN 0-393-02183-1. ‣ Collected papers (1942–73). Last chapter on the chant of Byzantine-Greek liturgy gives general survey of Byzantine music. [APK]

8.448 Miloš M. Velimirovic. "Liturgical drama in Byzantium and Russia." *Dumbarton Oaks papers* 16 (1962) 349–85. ISSN 0070-7546. ‣ Discussion of performances of religious plays inside churches in Byzantium (at least in fifteenth century) and in medieval Russia primarily ("Three Young Hebrews in the Furnace"). Also includes Greek text of *Akolouthia* and music of the play. [APK]

8.449 Kurt Weitzmann. *Illustrations in roll and codex: a study of the origin and method of text illustration.* 1947 ed. Princeton: Princeton University Press, 1970. ISBN 0-691-03865-1. ‣ Relationship between text and illustration in medieval Greek manuscripts (reflecting ancient models). Basic unit in illustrated manuscripts neither single miniature nor sum of all miniatures in single codex, but monocycle of scenes corresponding to textual unit. [APK]

8.450 Kurt Weitzmann et al. *The icon.* New York: Dorset, 1987. ‣ Origins and significance of icon with essays on icons from different geographical areas (Constantinople, the Balkans, Georgia, Russia, Wallachia/Moldavia, and Crusader states). [APK]

8.451 Egon Wellesz. *A history of Byzantine music and hymnography.* 2d rev. ed. Oxford: Clarendon, 1961. ‣ Standard survey on origins of Byzantine music, its pagan and Jewish background, function in ceremonies and liturgy, deciphering of Byzantine notation and melodic composition, and relationship between words and music. [APK]

EVERYDAY LIFE AND POPULAR CULTURE

8.452 Albrecht Berger. *Das Bad in der Byzantinischen Zeit.* Munich: Institut für Byzantinistik und neugriechische Philologie der Universität, 1982. (Miscellanea byzantina monacensia, 27.) ‣ Comprehensive description of bath culture: bathhouse building; customs connected with its use; and treatment of bath in literature, popular belief, and proverb. [APK]

8.453 Alan Cameron. *Porphyrius the charioteer.* Oxford: Clarendon, 1973. ISBN 0-19-814803-4. ‣ Hippodrome of Constantinople: organization of races, charioteer's career, factional violence. Refutation of traditional view on factions of hippodrome as political parties. See also Cameron 8.247. [APK]

8.454 Angeliki E. Laiou. "The festival of Agathe: comments on the life of Constantinopolitan women." *Byzantion: aphieroma ston Andrea N. Strato* 1 (1986) 111–22. ‣ Discussion of Michael Psellos's description of annual festivities in Constantinople (May 12) celebrated by women—spinners, weavers, and wool carders (eleventh century). [APK]

8.455 Paul Magdalino. "The literary perception of everyday life in Byzantium." *Byzantinoslavica* 48 (1987) 28–38. ISSN 0007-7712. ‣ Tight, conformist culture, imitation of antique models, and archaizing literary language created nonproductive atmosphere for describing everyday life; some late twelfth-century authors (e.g., John Apokaukos), confident in value of personal experience, overcame traditional restrictions. [APK]

8.456 Harry J. Magoulias. "The lives of Byzantine saints as sources of data for the history of magic in the sixth and seventh centuries A.D.: sorcery, relics, and icons." *Byzantion* 37 (1967) 228–69. ISSN 0378-2506. ‣ Discussion of sorcery's interrelationship with cult of relics and icons despite church condemnation. [APK]

8.457 Cyril Mango. "Daily life in Byzantium." *Jahrbuch der* *österreichischen Byzantinistik* 31.1, 32.1 (1981, 1982) 337–53, 252–57. ISSN 0378-8660. ▸ Emphasis on change; great public baths of late Roman period lost their social importance, pantomime lingered until end of seventh century, and chariot races declined. [APK]

8.458 Tamara Talbot Rice. *Everyday life in Byzantium.* New York: Putnam, 1967. ▸ Only general survey available in English (without references). Topics include imperial court, church, army, etc. Best books on subject are in Greek (Phaidon Koukoules, *Byzantinon bios kai politismos* [Byzantine Everyday Life and Civilization], 1948–55) and in Russian (Alexander P. Rudakov, *Vizantijskaja kul'tura po dannym grečeskoj agiografii* [Byzantine Culture According to the Greek Hagiographical Sources], 1917). [APK]

8.459 Frank R. Trombley. "Paganism in the Greek world at the end of antiquity: the case of rural Anatolia and Greece." *Harvard theological review* 78 (1985) 327–52. ISSN 0017-8160. ▸ Analysis of survival of rural paganism in fifth and sixth centuries. Monks founding monasteries met intractable ethos based on cultural, linguistic, and economic barriers. [APK]

PETER B. GOLDEN

Central Asia

The geographical contours of this field are not as closely defined or as unanimously agreed upon as is true of many other regions. Politically, the borders of Central Asia have often expanded to encompass substantial portions if not all of the major neighboring states. China, Iran, and Russia, for example, have been part of Central Asia–based empires. In general, we may say that Central Asia, sometimes also termed Inner Asia, covers the Eurasian landmass from Manchuria to the Ukrainian steppes. Indeed, some scholars would include the Hungarian plains, the westernmost outpost of nomadic steppe society in the Middle Ages. The southern boundaries are more clearly defined: the Black Sea and the Sea of Azov in the southwest, the Caucasus mountains and North Caucasian steppelands, the Caspian Sea and the mountainous terrain, interspersed with fortifications culminating in the Great Wall of China. The westernmost zones we may term "Western Eurasia," extending to the Volga-Ural lands. The adjoining territory, the central zone, until recently termed Soviet and Chinese Central Asia or historically western and eastern Turkistan, is today refashioning its politico-geographical contours once again. The eastern zone, Tibet, Mongolia, and Manchuria, constitutes Inner Asia proper.

The whole of this region has also been called the Empire of the Steppes, implying that its dominant political and economic culture was that of the pastoral nomadic peoples and polities. To some extent, this is true. But, it would be a mistake to neglect the extraordinary sedentary oasis cultures that flourished on the periphery of and in symbiosis with the steppe. These were the important links to the great civilizations (Chinese, Iranian, Islamic, and Romano-Byzantine) that hemmed the steppe and with whom the nomads intensely interacted. The Soghdians, Khwârazmians, and Tokharian city-states of Turkistan were an integral and vital part of Central Asian civilization. Representatives from these groups often fulfilled the role of culture bearers, bringing the ideas, religions, and goods of the Mediterranean and Chinese cultural orbits to Central Asia and serving as a clearinghouse for the movement of culture and technology between East and West.

A more free-ranging definition would also include the peoples and cultures of the forest-steppe, forest, taiga, and tundra belts of the North. The steppe also interacted with this region, in particular because of the nomads' interest in the lucrative fur trade. The Caucasus region, divided into Transcaucasia (today Armenia, Georgia, and Azerbaijan) and the North Caucasus, with its bewildering array of languages (the "mountain of tongues" of the Medieval Islamic geographers), constitutes a unique cultural zone, influenced by the Middle East to the south and the steppe cultures to the north. Some scholars would place this region, too, into the catchall category of Central Asia, although strictly speaking, the Caucasus is distinct.

The study of Central Asia has often been the stepchild of other areas of research: Chinese, Islamic, Iranian, Russian, Byzantine, and proto-Hungarian studies. It attracted few real practitioners because of the very considerable investment in languages required of the scholar. People wandered in from Chinese frontier studies, Islamics, or Russian history, bringing with them the language preparation required for those fields and hence predisposed toward reliance on limited groups of sources. Very few were or are able to cover the whole range of sources. Ideally, one should be prepared to read materials in Chinese, Persian (Farsi, and perhaps other Iranian languages: Soghdian, Khwârazmian, Khotanese), a number of Turkic languages (Orkhon, Uighur, Qarakhanid, etc.), Mongol, Arabic, Syriac, Hebrew, Armenian, Georgian, Greek, Latin, medieval eastern Slavic (the Rus' chronicles), as well as a rich array of scholarly literature in western and eastern European languages—in particular, Russian and Hungarian—and the often neglected studies in Japanese. In addition, the linguistic data of the indigenous Altaic languages, the lesser-known Uralic tongues of the forest zone, and the palaeo-Siberian languages (e.g., Kettic) also contain important clues to ethnogenetic processes. Regrettably, this is an area that has been little explored.

Southern Siberia, where the last remnants of the palaeo-Siberian peoples are in the process of being assimilated (largely by Turkic peoples), has played a key role in the formation of Inner Asian peoples. It is an area that merits deeper investigation. Some of the keys to the earliest patterns of Central Asian ethnogenesis and state formation undoubtedly lie here.

In addition to the very formidable linguistic hurdles that the researcher faces, there is the problem of the sources themselves. The nomads, although not unacquainted with a great variety of scripts, often did not leave behind much in the way of written evidence. We are forced to rely largely on the unsympathetic testimony of neighboring sedentary peoples who viewed the steppe horsemen as predatory "barbarians." These prejudices are clearly visible in our sources. Thus, the researcher faces the double problem of trying to understand a society that is remote in time and space from our own through the distorting refractions of sources penned by its enemies. The growing body of anthropological literature dealing with nomadic society (see in particular the work of Anatoly Khazanov, with its strong historical interests) has been of great help, enriching and nuancing our understanding of the internal dynamics of nomadic society.

The problems within each source group vary. The Chinese, with ancient and well-established historical traditions, have good editions of the surviving sources. Many of these, however, should be translated to make them available to those approaching the field from the Islamic or western Eurasian perspective. The Chinese dynastic histories and other compilations often have much important data for the westernmost regions as well. A collection of all the Chinese data on the steppe peoples, a huge but worthwhile project, is the sort of enterprise that should be undertaken by an international team of scholars. The Russian scholar V. S. Taskin, who has put together a valuable collection of translations on the Tung-hu (eastern barbarians), has begun a series, *Materialy po istorii kochevykh narodov v Kitae III–V vv.* (Materials on the History of the Nomadic Peoples in China, Third–Fifth Centuries), the first volume of which deals with the Hsiung-nu. These editions, however, lack the Chinese texts. Eastern European Orientalists (Russian, Polish, and Hungarian), at least with regard to sources in Semitic (Arabic, Hebrew, Syriac) and Iranian languages, have long viewed these sources as an integral part of their protohistorical historiographical tradition. Such collections (the oft-quoted but outdated editions of Harkavy and Kuun and the more recent, excellent work of Lewicki), focusing mainly on their own national or linguistic grouping, but touching, often in great detail, on the steppe peoples as well, have served as the gateway from eastern European to Central Asian studies. The sources for the pre-Chinggisid era, especially the Muslim geographers, although known for well over a century, could be reedited with profit, on the basis of additional manuscripts that have come to light. The great compilation by the Russian scholar Tizengauzen (Tiesenhausen) of materials relating to the history of the Golden Horde (*Sbornik materialov otnosiashchikhsia k istorii Zolotoi Ordy* [Collection of materials pertaining to the history of the Golden Horde]), now over a century old (although the second part was published only in 1941), should be redone, expanding the base to include the whole of the Chinggisid realm. The sources for the late Chinggisid period, in particular those in various Turkic languages and Persian, have been largely neglected. Scholars in the former Soviet Union appear to have been alone in producing critical editions of these sources. Regrettably, these volumes have appeared only irregularly.

The field of Soghdian and Khwârazmian studies remains in its infancy. Similarly, work on the indigenous pre-Turkic sources (Iranian and Tokharian) of eastern (Chinese) Turkistan, a very special field requiring more than a nodding acquaintance with the Indic world as well as China, has been carried on by very few. Fortunately, we have the superb editions and erudite commentaries of Sir Harold Bailey, the pioneer of Khotanese studies. Nonetheless, there are many unresolved questions here as well.

On the whole, a better integration of the Chinese and Tibetan data with those of the Islamic sources is very much to be desired.

The historical problems awaiting resolution are numerous and often quite basic. For example, we still lack a well-grounded theory regarding the origins and earliest habitat of the Altaic peoples. Indeed, the linguists have split into two hostile camps: those who accept the notion of a genetic relationship between the Altaic languages (Turkic, Mongolic, Manchu-Tungusic, perhaps Korean, and at least some of the elements of what became Japanese) and those who reject such a relationship, explaining the similarities on the basis of borrowing and areal contact over centuries. As a consequence of the uncertainty here, there are widely diverging views placing the origins of the Turkic peoples in either western Eurasia or east of Lake Baikal. The earliest contacts between the Iranian and Altaic peoples, including the process by which pastoral nomadism was adopted by the latter, require illumination. The early history of the Soghdians, Khwârazmians, and other Iranian and Indo-European peoples (the Tokharians) has been discussed in only the vaguest terms. The Yüeh-chih–Tokharian–Kushan relationship demands further exploration. Kushan chronology remains unclear. The ethnicity of the Hsiung-nu and their relationship to the peoples called "Huns" in western Eurasia remains a perennial problem and one no nearer to a solution. The early history of the Turks and their relationship to the A-shih-na and various Indo-European peoples resident in eastern Turkistan remain unclear. Indeed, one of the greatest desiderata of Central Asian studies is a good history of the First and Second Türk Qaghanates. Gumilev's work, available only in Russian, while always interesting, is too idiosyncratic and controversial. The Uighurs, in some respects, have been better served (by the work of Hamilton, Mackerras, and Maliavkin), but like most of the medieval Turkic peoples, they still await a comprehensive study. The many questions of the ethnogenesis and history of the Qïpchaqs, the most important element in the composition of the modern Turkic peoples of Central Asia, seem no closer to resolution than when Marquart first posed the problem in 1914. The impact of Chinggisid Mongol empire-building on the political structure of the Turkic tribes of Eurasia is another area that wants detailed examination. While it is clear that the Chinggisids broke up the old tribal confederations and even tribes, scattering them throughout their realm and giving rise to the configurations in which we more or less find them today, the history of the Chaghatai khanate, crucial to any understanding of this process, remains murky. The role of outside powers, especially the Russian and Soviet states, in the shaping of the present-day Turkic peoples, noted but not sufficiently researched, is another area of potentially fruitful inquiry. The role of women (often prominent in political affairs) and gender issues remain largely unexplored.

Among the encouraging signs, we may note the increasing integration of the results of anthropological and other social science research, both theoretical and empirical, into the array of tools, heretofore largely philological, at the disposal of the Central Asianist. There is a growing interest in a more concrete understanding of commercial relations and technology transfer. Larger questions regarding the relationship of Central Asia to the various world systems of medieval and modern times are now being posed. It has long been axiomatic to note that Central Asia often served as a conduit for the movement of goods, technologies, and ideas between East and West. These generalities must now be detailed. The impact of the opening by the Europeans of new routes to the East, its consequences for the Central Asian trade, and its role in the political and cultural decline of the region is now beginning to be explored with greater vigor.

The remarkable religious history of the region, which in various places and at various times embraced Christian sects (Nestorianism), Judaism, Manichaeism, Buddhism, Islam, and a variety of syncretistic cults (in addition to the indigenous shamanism and Tengri/sky-god cult), would profit enormously from a comparative study of conversion processes.

In many respects, the field is in its infancy. There is much of a fundamental nature that remains to be done.

ACKNOWLEDGMENTS   *I would like to acknowledge here the technical assistance of Tammy Proctor whose many labors helped to bring this project to fruition.*

[Contributors: DAD = Devin A. DeWeese, EEW = Elizabeth Endicott-West, EJ = Esther Jacobson, ES = Elliot Sperling, JG = Jo-Ann Gross, JHC = James H. Cole, KRS = Kenneth R. Stow, MR = Morris Rossabi, MRD = Michael Robert Drompp, NSK = Nancy Shields Kollmann, PBG = Peter B. Golden, RPH = Robert P. Hymes, RWD = Ruth W. Dunnell, SBV = Steven Belá Várdy, SCF = Simon C. Franklin, TTA = Thomas T. Allsen, US = Uli Schamiloglu]

REFERENCE WORKS

9.1 Shirin Akiner. *The Islamic peoples of the Soviet Union, with an appendix on the non-Muslim Turkic peoples of the Soviet Union: an historical and statistical handbook.* 2d ed. London: Kegan Paul, 1986. ISBN 0-7103-0188-X. ▸ Ethnolinguistic survey of Muslim populations with particular emphasis on statistical data (census reports of 1926, 1959, 1970, 1979) relating to language maintenance, scripts, education, religious institutions, and economy. Brief ethnogenetic and historical sketches. Dispassionate and informative. [PBG]

9.2 Alexandre A. Bennigsen and S. Enders Wimbush. *Muslims of the Soviet empire: a guide.* Bloomington: Indiana University Press, 1986. ISBN 0-253-33958-8. ▸ Useful survey of status of Islam, questions of national identity, and political, cultural, demographic, and economic trends. Statistical survey of Soviet Muslim populations. Underscores importance of Islam as cultural, psychological force. [PBG]

9.3 Helmut Hoffman et al. *Tibet: a handbook.* Bloomington: Research Center for the Language Sciences for Asian Studies Research Institute, 1975. (Indiana University Asian Studies Research Institute, Oriental series, 5.) ISBN 0-87750-180-7. ▸ Basic guide to Tibetan studies. Chronological surveys of Tibetan history and discussion of various categories of sources (Chinese, Western, etc.) Somewhat dated and lacking index, but includes useful bibliographic information. [ES]

9.4 Luciano Petech. "The Dalai-Lamas and regents of Tibet: a chronological study." In *Selected papers on Asian history*, pp. 125–47. Rome: Istituto Italiano per il Medio ed Estremo Oriente, 1988. (Istituto Italiano per il Medio ed Estremo Orient, 60.) ▸ Concise and convenient guide to basic biographical data on Dalai Lamas, Tibet's rulers under traditional government dominated by Dge-lugs-pa sect and regents who at times ruled in their place. [ES]

9.5 Denis Sinor. *Introduction à l'étude de l'Eurasie Centrale.* Wiesbaden: Harrassowitz, 1963. ▸ Extensive bibliographical essay divided into three categories: language and peoples, history, and ethnography (very brief); over 4,000 entries. Although dated, in some respects remains fundamental introduction to field. [PBG]

9.6 Ronald Wixman. *The peoples of the USSR: an ethnographic handbook.* Armonk, N.Y.: Sharpe, 1984. ISBN 0-87332-203-7 (cl), 0-87332-506-0 (pbk). ▸ Alphabetically arranged (by peoples) guide with data on ethnonyms, population-demographic trends, religion, and linguistic affiliations; brief historical sketches. Extremely useful. [PBG]

REGIONAL STUDIES

General Studies

9.7 Annemarie von Gabain. *Einführung in die Zentralasienkunde.* Darmstadt: Wissenschaftliche Buchgesellschaft, 1979. ISBN 3-537-07136-0. ▸ Brief but informative introductory work. Topics include geography, historical sketches (ancient to modern), literary sources, ethnography, religions, philology, archaeology (extensive), and arts and architecture. Relative absence of illustrative material detracts from otherwise masterful summation. [PBG]

9.8 Peter Hajdú. *Finno-Ugrian languages and peoples.* G. F. Cushing, trans. London: Deutsch, 1975. ISBN 0-233-96552-1. ▸ Masterful synthesis of historical, ethnogenetic, ethnological, and linguistic data. Excellent introduction to field. [PBG]

9.9 Sechin Jagchid and Paul Hyer. *Mongolia's culture and society.* Boulder: Westview, 1979. ISBN 0-89158-390-4. ▸ Somewhat rambling but invaluable information on religion, lifestyle, culture, and economy of Mongols and by extension other steppe peoples of Inner Asia. [MR]

9.10 Lawrence Krader. *Peoples of Central Asia.* 3d ed. Bloomington: Indiana University Press, 1971. (Uralic and Altaic series, 26.) ISBN 0-87750-085-1. ▸ Introductory survey to ecology, economy, languages, history, religions, social structure, and demography. Statistical data up to 1960. [PBG]

9.11 Owen Lattimore. *Studies in frontier history: collected papers, 1928–1958.* London: Oxford University Press, 1962. ▸ Insightful and stimulating collection of Lattimore's essays dealing with questions of social organization (e.g., frontier feudalism), historical geography, and role of frontier. [PBG]

263

9.12 Richard H. Rowland et al. "Central Asia." In *Encyclopaedia Iranica*. Ehsan Yarshater, ed., vol. 5.2, pp. 159–244. Costa Mesa, Calif.: Mazda, 1990. ISBN 0-939214-69-5. ▸ Entries dealing with geography, demography, history, economy, languages, literature, and music. Convenient for reference, helpful introduction. [PBG]

9.13 Denis Sinor. "Central Eurasia." In *Orientalism and history*. 2d ed. Denis Sinor, ed., pp. 82–103. Bloomington: Indiana University Press, 1970. ISBN 0-253-34261-9. ▸ Defines Eurasian history as that of "barbarian" other of civilized, sedentary society. Climate and geography determined pastoral-nomadic and hunting-gathering economies; scarcity of goods and resources produced predatory societies. Eurasia, however, also served as intermediary between East and West. Thoughtful and stimulating. [PBG]

9.14 Denis Sinor. *Inner Asia, history-civilization-languages: a syllabus*. 1969 ed. The Hague: Mouton, 1987. ISBN 0-87750-081-9. ▸ Useful volume aimed at instructors in undergraduate introductory courses (but can be used as textbook). Brief chapters covering basic outlines of Central Asian history and culture, concluding with bibliographic information. Clearly written. [PBG]

Geography and Travel Accounts

9.15 Ippolito Desideri. *An account of Tibet: the travels of Ippolito Desideri of Pistoria S.J., 1712–1727*. 1932 ed. Filippo de Filippi, ed. Janet Ross, trans. Taipei: Ch'eng Wen, 1971. (Broadway travellers. Ch'eng Wen reprint series, 205.) ▸ One of most extensive of pre-nineteenth-century Western accounts of Tibet. Includes details on early Catholic missionary effort and important eyewitness record of events leading to beginning of Ch'ing domination. [ES]

9.16 Peter Hopkirk. *Foreign devils on the Silk Road: the search for the lost cities and treasures of Chinese Central Asia*. 1980 ed. Amherst: University of Massachusetts Press, 1984. ISBN 0-87023-435-8 (pbk). ▸ Lively popular account of expeditions of Hedin, Stein, von le Coq, Pelliot, and other notable travelers, treasure-seekers, and scholars to Turkistan. Excellent introduction to their writings; contains bibliography of principal works. [PBG]

9.17 Albert von Le Coq. *Buried treasures of Chinese Turkistan*. 1928 ed. Anna Barwell, trans. Hong Kong: Oxford University Press, 1985. ISBN 0-19-583878-5 (pbk). ▸ Account of second (1904) and third (1905–1906) German expeditions to Chinese Turkistan (Turfan–Qara Khoja). Includes discoveries of Bezeklik and author's missed opportunity to discover Tunhuang library. Lively, personal account. [PBG]

9.18 Wilhelm Radloff. *Iz Sibiri: stranitsy dnevnika* (Aus Sibirien). 1893 ed. Moscow: Nauka, Glavnaia Redaktsiia Vostochnoi Literatury, 1989. ISBN 5-02-017025-9. ▸ Travel notes and observations by one of founders of modern Turkic studies of his journeys (1860–1870) to Siberia, the Kazakh steppe, and Turkistan. Rich in ethnographic detail. Essential for study of steppe society. Russian translation and abridgment of 1893 work *Aus Sibirien: lose Blätter aus dem Tagebuches eines reisenden Linguisten*. [PBG]

9.19 Aurel Stein. *On ancient Central Asian tracks: brief narrative of three expeditions in innermost Asia and north-western China*. 1933 ed. Jeannette Mirsky, ed. New York: Pantheon, 1964. ▸ Brief account by pioneer of Inner Asian archaeology of three expeditions (1900–1901, 1906–1908, 1913–16) to Turkistan. Excellent, semipopular introduction to his more detailed, scholarly works. Excellent descriptions of region with discussions of historical significance of discoveries. [PBG]

Archaeology

9.20 Csanád Bálint. *Die Archäologie der Steppe: Steppenvölker zwischen Volga und Donau vom sechsten bis zum zehnten Jahrhundert*. Vienna: Böhlau, 1989. ISBN 3-205-07242-1. ▸ Detailed survey of the archaeological remains of steppe peoples (Türks, Avars, and Hungarians) from sixth to tenth century in western Eurasia. [PBG]

9.21 Vladimir Nikolaevich Basilov, ed. *Nomads of Eurasia*. Mary Fleming Zirin, trans. Los Angeles: Natural History Museum of Los Angeles County; distributed by University of Washington Press, 1989. ISBN 0-295-96815-X (cl), 0-295-96816-8 (pbk). ▸ Collection of essays by Soviet scholars to accompany and explicate exhibition of nomadic art that toured United States in 1989–90. Essays address political history, folk culture, material culture, social life, musical instruments, and religion. Excellent illustrations. [PBG]

9.22 Gregoire Frumkin. *Archaeology in Soviet Central Asia*. Leiden: Brill, 1970. (Handbuch der Orientalistik, Siebente Abteilung, Kunst und Archäologie, 3.1.) ▸ Soviet archaeology in Kazakhstan, Kirghizia and the Ferghana valley, Tadzhikistan, Uzbekistan, and Turkmenistan. Emphasis on archaeology and material culture of Kushan period and of contemporary nomadic groups and city-states. [EJ]

9.23 Karl Jettmar. *Art of the steppes*. Rev. ed. Ann E. Keep, trans. New York: Greystone, 1967. ▸ Art of Scytho-Siberians and historical background, first millennium BCE. Dated, but remains most useful overview of Scytho-Siberian traditions. [EJ]

9.24 Edgar Knobloch. *Beyond the Oxus: archaeology, art, and architecture of Central Asia*. Totowa, N.J.: Rowman & Littlefield, 1972. ISBN 0-87971-060-X. ▸ Semipopular introductory work. Brief overview of land, peoples, and history followed by survey of archaeological sites and points of art historical interest in Western and Eastern Turkistan. [PBG]

Ethnography

9.25 Elizabeth E. Bacon. *Central Asians under Russian rule: a study in culture change*. 1966 ed. Ithaca, N.Y.: Cornell University Press, 1980. ISBN 0-8014-9211-4 (pbk). ▸ Historical-anthropological survey of pastoral nomadic peoples (especially Kazakhs), focusing on cultural change during centuries of Russian domination. Occasionally dated, but still useful. [PBG]

9.26 Lawrence Krader. *Social organization of the Mongol-Turkic pastoral nomads*. The Hague: Mouton, 1963. (Uralic and Altaic series, 20.) ▸ Detailed analysis of social structure of Turkic Kazakhs and Ordos, Buryat, Volga Kalmuk, and Monguor Mongols. [PBG]

9.27 M. G. Levin and L. P. Potapov, eds. *The peoples of Siberia*. Stephen P. Dunn, ed. and trans. Chicago: University of Chicago Press, 1964. ▸ Very useful ethnographic survey containing information on ethnogenesis, history, and contemporary culture (material and social) of Turkic peoples of Siberia. Comments on modern period colored by official Soviet doctrines. [PBG]

9.28 S. M. Shirokogoroff. *Social organization of the Manchus: a study of the Manchu clan organization*. 1924 ed. New York: AMS Press, 1973. (North China Branch of the Royal Asiatic Society, Publications, 3.) ISBN 0-404-56946-3. ▸ Classic study, based on author's observations, ca. 1915, of Manchus living in Aigun region of Russo-Chinese border. [RWD]

Linguistics

9.29 Harold W. Bailey. "The languages of the Saka." In *Iranistik*. Vol. 1, pp. 131–54. Leiden: Brill, 1958. (Handbuch der Orientalistik, Erste Abteilung, Der nahe und der mittlere Osten, 4.) ▸ Brief survey of principal features of Khotanese "Saka," Iranian language spoken in ancient and early medieval Eastern Turkistan. [PBG]

9.30 Jean Deny et al., eds. *Philologiae Turcicae Fundamenta*. Wiesbaden: Steiner, 1959. ▸ Brief sketches of Turkic languages, living and dead, by leading European Turkologists, with historical introductions. Articles largely in German and French. [PBG]

9.31 Tomas V. Gamkrelidze and Viascheslav V. Ivanov. *Indoevropeiskii iazyk i indoevropeitsy* (The Indo-European language and the Indo-Europeans). 2 vols. Tblisi, 1984. ▸ Detailed analysis of Indo-European origins, linguistic history, myths and contacts with other language groups of Eurasia and Near East. Revises older hypothesis of Central Asian primary habitat of Indo-Europeans, placing it in eastern Anatolia–southern Transcaucasia–northwestern Mesopotamia. [PBG]

9.32 J. P. Mallory. *In search of the Indo-Europeans: language, archaeology, and myth.* London: Thames & Hudson, 1989. ISBN 0-500-05052-X. ▸ Excellent introduction to Indo-European historical studies. Synthesis of most recent research into questions of Indo-European homeland and migrations. Defends older concept of Indo-European homeland in Eurasia (contra Gamkrelidze and Ivanov 9.31). Essential reading. [PBG]

9.33 Karl Heinrich Menges. *The Turkic languages and peoples: an introduction to Turkic studies.* Wiesbaden: Harrassowitz, 1968. (Ural-altaische Bibliothek, 15.) ▸ Brief historical introduction dealing with ethnogenesis and migrations, followed by close analysis of Turkic languages and their interaction with surrounding peoples. Not for beginners. [PBG]

9.34 Nikolai Nikolaevich Poppe. *Introduction to Altaic linguistics.* Wiesbaden: Harrassowitz, 1965. (Ural-altaische Bibliothek, 14.) ▸ Survey of Altaic languages and brief history of their study. Author is partisan of now much-disputed theory of genetic relationship between Altaic languages. [PBG]

9.35 Denis Sinor, ed. *The Uralic languages: description, history, and foreign influences.* Leiden: Brill, 1988. (Handbuch der Orientalistik, Achte Abteilung, Handbook of Uralic studies, 1.) ISBN 90-04-07741-3. ▸ Authoritative diachronic and synchronic survey with separate chapters devoted to comparative questions and linguistic contacts with other language groupings, especially Indo-European and Altaic. [PBG]

Economy and Economic Organization

9.36 Anatoli Mikhailovich Khazanov. "Nomads and oases in Central Asia." In *Transition to modernity: essays on power, wealth, and belief.* John A. Hall and Ian C. Jarvie, eds., pp. 69–89. Cambridge: Cambridge University Press, 1992. ISBN 0-521-38202-5. ▸ Brief characterization of economy, ethnic and social changes of oases, focal points of nomadic-sedentary interaction. [PBG]

9.37 Anatoli Mikhailovich Khazanov. *Nomads and the outside world.* Julia Crookenden, trans. Cambridge: Cambridge University Press, 1984. ISBN 0-521-23813-7. ▸ Seminal work on nomadic pastoral economy and its need to interact with sedentary world. Essential reading. [PBG]

9.38 Sev'ian Izrailevich Vainshtein. *Nomads of South Siberia: the pastoral economies of Tuva.* Caroline Humphrey, ed. Michael Colenso, trans. Cambridge: Cambridge University Press, 1980. ISBN 0-521-22089-0. ▸ Important introductory chapter on livestock and forms of nomadism. Particularly interesting analysis of historical evolution and adaptation of Central Asian forms of pastoral nomadism to conditions of the north. Soviet Marxist perspective. [PBG]

Sociopolitical Organization

9.39 Károly Czeglédy. "Das sakrale Königtum bei den Steppenvölkern." *Numen* 13 (1966) 14–26. ISSN 0029-5973. ▸ Discussion of textual sources on religious roles of Inner Asian rulers and religious sanction of political legitimacy. [DAD]

9.40 Wolfram Eberhard. *Conquerors and rulers: social forces in medieval China.* 2d rev. ed. Leiden: Brill, 1965. ▸ Contains impor-

tant sections on organization and structure of steppe empires. [PBG]

9.41 Peter B. Golden. "Imperial ideology and the sources of political unity amongst the pre-Činggisid nomads of western Eurasia." *Archivum Eurasiae medii aevi* 2 (1982) 37–76. ISSN 0724-8822. ▸ Political traditions, ideologies, and structures of Türk qaghanate and its successors in Central Asia and western Eurasia to thirteenth century: imperial forms and institutions and religious foundations of political legitimacy in pre-Mongol Inner Asia. [DAD]

9.42 Anatoli Mikhailovich Khazanov. "The early state among the Eurasian nomads." In *Oikumene: studia ad historiam antiquam classicam et orientalem spectantia.* I. Hahn et al., eds., vol. 4, pp. 269–83. Budapest: Akadémiai Kiadó, 1983. ISBN 963-05-1589-X (series). ▸ Higher levels of nomadic political organization predicated on internal (distribution of pasturages, conflict resolution, social stratification) and external (relations with nonnomadic world) factors. Conflict with or expansion against sedentary states contributed to nomadic state-formation. Useful theoretical models. [PBG]

9.43 Lawrence Krader. "Feudalism and the Tatar polity." *Comparative studies in society and history* 1 (1958) 76–99. ISSN 0010-4175. ▸ Compares common features of Eurasian nomadic and European feudal systems (patrilineal-agnatic kinship system, aristocracy of birth, elite retinue of ruler, weak civil organization). Close analysis of Vladimirtsov 9.46, Radloff 9.18, and Bartol'd 9.71, 9.72, 9.152, 9.250, 17.166. Finds difficulty, however, in applying term "feudal" to Chinggisid Mongol system. [PBG]

9.44 Lawrence Krader. "The origins of the state among the nomads of Asia." In *Die Nomaden in Geschichte und Gegenwart.* Rolf Krusche, ed., pp. 71–82. Berlin: Akademieverlag, 1981. (Veröffentlichungen des Museums für Völkerkunde zu Leipzig, 33.) ▸ Nomads develop state in interaction with and in response to state-formation of neighboring sedentary societies. Mongol conquest-state product of internal class contradictions. Chinggisids developed feudal society, but different in character from that of western Europe. Thoughtful analysis, but occasionally dogmatic in tone. [PBG]

9.45 Rudi Paul Lindner. "What was a nomadic tribe?" *Comparative studies in society and history* 24.4 (1982) 689–711. ISSN 0010-4175. ▸ Dissents from segmentary lineage concept, underscoring, rather, fluidity of Eurasian nomadic political structure. Stresses use of traditional kinship terminology to mask political ties. Cites Huns and Ottomans as examples. [PBG]

9.46 Boris Iakovlevich Vladimirtsov. *La régime sociale des Mongols: le féodalisme nomade.* Michel Carsow, trans. Paris: Adrien-Maisonneuve, 1948. (Annales du Musée Guimet, Bibliothèque d'études, 52.) ▸ Classic analysis of medieval kinship and social system from Marxist perspective. Central and subsidiary theses challenged by recent scholarship but still valuable. [TTA]

Religions

9.47 N. A. Alekseev. "Shamanism among the Turkic peoples of Siberia." *Soviet anthropology and archeology* 28.1 (1989) 56–107. ISSN 0038-528X. ▸ Partial translation of author's Russian study, important ethnographically based treatment of religion among non-Islamic, non-Buddhist, and non-Christian Turkic peoples. More useful for wealth of descriptive material than for analytical or theoretical approach. [DAD]

9.48 C. E. Bosworth. "Islamic frontiers in Africa and Asia: (B) Central Asia." In *The legacy of Islam.* 2d ed. Joseph Schacht and C. E. Bosworth, eds., pp. 116–30. Oxford: Clarendon, 1974. ISBN 0-19-821913-X. ▸ Concise survey of spread of Islam into Central and Inner Asia. One of few reliable overviews in English. [DAD]

9.49 John Andrew Boyle. "Turkish and Mongol shamanism in the Middle Ages." *Folklore* 83 (1972) 177–93. ISSN 0015-587X. ▸ Fine discussion of textual sources (primarily Islamic) on shamanism among various medieval Turkic peoples and thirteenth-century Mongols. [DAD]

9.50 Robert Dankoff. "Kašgari on the beliefs and superstitions of the Turks." *Journal of the American Oriental Society* 95 (1975) 68–80. ISSN 0003-0279. ▸ Study of evidence on pre-Islamic Turkic religion in late eleventh-century dictionary of Turkic languages. Useful summary of material. [DAD]

9.51 Mircea Eliade. *Shamanism: archaic techniques of ecstasy.* 1964 ed. Willard R. Trask, trans. London: Arkana, 1989. ISBN 0-14-019155-0. ▸ Often factually unreliable for Inner Asian shamanism, but still standard work for its analytical approach. Indispensible, remains the signal reference point from which other studies (by supporters or, now more commonly, critics of Eliade's approach) begin. [DAD]

9.52 R. E. Emmerick. "Buddhism among the Iranian peoples." In *The Cambridge history of Iran.* Ehsan Yarshater, ed., vol. 3.2, pp. 949–64. Cambridge: Cambridge University Press, 1983. ISBN 0-521-24693-8 (v. 3.2), 0-521-24699-7 (v. 3). ▸ Concise review of Buddhism's history in Central Asia from Kushan times to disappearance of Buddhist Khotanese kingdom in eleventh century. [DAD]

9.53 Annemarie von Gabain. "Inhalt und magische Bedeutung der alttürkischen Inschriften." *Anthropos* 48 (1953) 537–56. ISSN 0257-9774. ▸ Philological and historical examination of native Turkic religious conceptions and practices on basis of Old Turkic inscriptions of Mongolia, dating from Second Türk qaghanate (seventh to eighth century). Essential reading. [DAD]

9.54 Peter B. Golden. "Khazaria and Judaism." *Archivum Eurasiae medii aevi* 3 (1983) 127–56. ISSN 0724-8822. ▸ Excellent survey of question of Khazar Judaism. [DAD]

9.55 Jo-Ann Gross, ed. *Muslims in Central Asia: expressions of identity and change.* Durham, N.C.: Duke University Press, 1992. ISBN 0-8223-1187-9 (cl), 0-8223-1190-9 (pbk). ▸ Collection of nine essays (all of high quality) on role of Islam in shaping national identity in Central Asia. Emphasis on nineteenth- and twentieth-century developments. [PBG]

9.56 Uno Harva. *Die religiösen Vorstellungen der altaischen Völker.* Helsinki: Suomalainen Tiedeakatemia, 1938. (Folklore fellows communications, 125.) ▸ Detailed survey of concepts of structure and origin of world, souls and death, hunting rites, shamanism, etc. Still essential work, more complete than English version (which presents only small portion of material in this volume) and two other works (on Cheremis and Mordvin religion) in same series, and other studies by Harva. Conceptually and bibliographically dated, but still useful for mass of detail. [DAD]

9.57 Walther Heissig. *The religions of Mongolia.* Geoffrey Samuel, trans. Berkeley: University of California Press, 1980. ISBN 0-520-03857-6. ▸ Descriptive survey of Mongol Buddhism and pre- and non-Buddhist Mongol "folk religion." Best brief introduction, with extensive bibliography; historically and philologically oriented, factually unassailable, yet lacking analytical and theoretical framework of religious studies. [DAD]

9.58 Uno Holmberg. *Finno-Ugric, Siberian.* 1927 ed. New York: Cooper Square, 1964. ▸ Marred by organizational scheme assuming first linguistic then geographic commonalities and presenting material from several groups, respectively, in thematic arrangement. Remains best English introduction to worldview and religious conceptions of peoples of northern Inner Asia. [DAD]

9.59 Samten G. Karmay. "A general introduction to the history and doctrines of Bon." *Memoirs of the Research Department of the*

Toyo Bunko 33 (1975) 171–218. ISSN 0082-562X. ▸ Concise but useful historical survey of Tibetan Bon religion, placed within context of doctrinal developments. [ES]

9.60 Bernard Lewis. "The Mongols, the Turks, and the Muslim polity." *Transactions of the Royal Historical Society* 18 (1968) 49–68. ISSN 0080-4401. ▸ Insightful survey of mutual effects of meeting of Inner Asian and Islamic peoples and traditions down to fourteenth century. [DAD]

9.61 Samuel N. C. Lieu. *Manichaeism in the later Roman empire and medieval China: a historical survey.* Manchester: Manchester University Press, 1985. ISBN 0-7190-1088-8. ▸ Includes fine, readable survey of Uighur Manichaeism and contribution of Central Asian Turkic and Soghdian literary remains for Manichaean studies. [DAD]

9.62 Wilferd Madelung. "The spread of Mâturidism and the Turks." In *Actas do quarto Congresso dos Estudos Arabes e Islamicos, Coimbra-Lisboa,* pp. 109–68. Leiden: Brill, 1971. ▸ Essential work with prosopographical approach to problem of early Islam in Central Asia and among Türks. Contains best survey of islamization of Türks in pre-Mongol Inner Asia with useful correctives to earlier scholarship. [DAD]

9.63 Robert D. McChesney. *Waqf in Central Asia: four hundred years in the history of a Muslim shrine, 1480–1889.* Princeton: Princeton University Press, 1991. ISBN 0-691-05584-X. ▸ Pioneering study of economic, social, religious, and political roles of major shrine in Balkh in present-day Afghanistan. Best available political history of this part of Central Asia during obscure period (seventeenth and eighteenth centuries) in Western scholarship. Outstanding contribution to Central Asian socioeconomic, religious history. [DAD/US]

9.64 Theodor Menzel. "Köprülüzade Mehmed Fuad's Werk über die ersten Mystiker in der türkishen Literatur." *Körösi csoma archivum* 2 (1926–32) 281–310, 345–57, 406–22. ▸ Summary of M. F. Köprülü's Turkish work *Turk edebiyatinda ilk mutasavvi-flar,* originally published in 1919 and still only extended treatment of Yasaviya, the major Turkic Ṣūfī order of Central Asia. [DAD]

9.65 Omeljan Pritsak. "The Khazar kingdom's conversion to Judaism." In *Studies in medieval Eurasian history,* pp. [261–81]. London: Variorum, 1981. ISBN 0-86078-078-3. ▸ Reexamination of accounts of and evidence for conversion to and role and development of Khazar Judaism. Overview of Khazar origins and history with survey of sources arguing conversion to Judaism was influenced by long-distance merchants. [DAD/US]

9.66 Jean-Paul Roux. *La religion des Turcs et des Mongols.* Paris: Payot, 1984. ISBN 2-228-13430-9. ▸ Survey based primarily on textual sources; valuable as rare attempt at comprehensive survey of religion in Inner Asia in historical perspective. Helpful bibliography. Good introduction to author's views. Idiosyncratic theoretical and analytical approach and questionable philological assumptions and conclusions require that volume be used with caution. [DAD]

9.67 J. J. Saunders. "The decline and fall of Christianity in medieval Asia." *Journal of religious history* 5 (1968) 93–104. ISSN 0022-4227. ▸ Concise survey of Christianity's history in Inner Asia down to Timurid times with particular attention to Nestorianism in the steppe and Catholic missions of Mongol era. [DAD]

9.68 Wilhelm Schmidt. *Der Ursprung der Gottesidee: eine historische-kritische und positive Studie.* 12 vols. Münster: Aschendorff, 1912–55. ▸ Volumes 9–12 of author's monumental work cover indigenous religious traditions of Inner Asian peoples, providing single most substantial work on subject as well as decisive, albeit now discredited, interpretive framework (with his assumptions of "original monotheism"). Despite this drawback, remains indispensable for wealth of information and insights. [DAD]

9.69 Manabu Waida. "Notes on sacred kingship in Central Asia." *Numen* 23 (1976) 179–90. ISSN 0029-5973. ▸ Survey of textual sources on religious foundations of political legitimacy and on religious roles of rulers in medieval Inner Asia. [DAD]

9.70 Yusuf Khass Hajib of Balasaghun. *Wisdom of Royal Glory (Kutadgu Bilig): a Turko-Islamic mirror for princes.* Robert Dankoff, trans. Chicago: University of Chicago Press, 1983. (Publications of the Center for Middle Eastern Studies, 16.) ISBN 0-226-97179-1. ▸ Translation of earliest (eleventh century) example of Islamic Turkic literature from Central Asia, the *Qutadghu Bilig*, with introduction on islamization and currents of political and religious thought reflected in work. Essential native text for islamization of Turks. [DAD]

HISTORICAL STUDIES

General Studies

9.71 Vasilii Vladimirovich Bartol'd. "Dvenadtsadt'lektsii po istorii turetskikh narodov Srednei Azii (Twelve lectures on the history of the Turkish peoples of Central Asia)." In *Raboty po istorii i filologii tiurkskikh i mongolskikh narodov*, pp. 17–192. Moscow: Nauka, 1968. (Sochineniia [works], 5.) ▸ Simple but sound description of influence of Turkic peoples on Central Asia with emphasis on period through Timurids. Lectures first read in Istanbul in 1926. Translated into Turkish (1927), German (1932–35), and French (1945). [MR]

9.72 Vasilii Vladimirovich Bartol'd. *Four studies on Central Asia.* Vol. 1: *A short history of Turkestan* and *History of the Semirechye.* Vol. 3: *Mir ᶜAli-Shir* and *A history of the Turkman people.* Leiden: Brill, 1962. ▸ First part of volume 1 provides brief historical account of region to nineteenth century; second part, succinct sketch of Kirghiz-Kazakh region to 1758. Excellent account of history of this Oghuz grouping to nineteenth century and brief account of life and times of Timurid literary figure in volume 3. Masterly, classic studies. [PBG]

9.73 Dung-dkar blo-bzang'phrin-las. *The merging of religious and secular rule in Tibet.* Chen Guansheng, trans. Beijing: Foreign Languages Press, 1991. ISBN 0-8351-2217-4, 7-119-00672-X. ▸ Translation (from Tibetan to Chinese to English) of general survey of Tibetan history up to Tibet's incorporation into People's Republic of China. Written from Chinese-Marxist perspective; includes interesting information not found in other English-language works on Tibet. [ES]

9.74 Peter B. Golden. *An introduction to the history of the Turkic peoples.* Wiesbaden: Harrassowitz, 1992. ISBN 3-447-03274-X. ▸ Survey focusing on process of ethnogenesis and state-formation (or lack thereof). Includes both Turkic populations of Central Asia and Near and Middle East. [PBG]

9.75 René Grousset. *The empire of the steppes.* Naomi Walford, trans. New Brunswick, N.J.: Rutgers University Press, 1970. ISBN 0-8135-0627-1. ▸ Engrossing, highly readable account of major steppe confederations and their influences on sedentary civilizations. Based largely on secondary literature and sources consulted in translation. [MR]

9.76 Gavin Hambly, ed. *Central Asia.* New York: Delacorte, 1969. ▸ Best general history of Central Asia in one volume. Emphasis on early history of Central Asia, slights East Asian elements and sources on Central Asia. Authors give authoritative summaries of various periods and peoples. [MR/US]

9.77 Karl Jettmar et al., eds. *Geschichte Mittelasiens.* Leiden-Köln: Brill, 1966. (Handbuch der Orientalistik, Erste Abteilung, Der nahe und der mittlere Osten, 5, Fünfte Abschnitt.) ▸ Author-

itative, clear, and nontechnical accounts, focusing on premodern times. [MR]

9.78 Hugh E. Richardson. *Tibet and its history.* 2d rev. ed. Boulder: Shambhala, 1984. ISBN 0-87773-292-2 (cl), 0-87773-376-7 (pbk). ▸ Survey written by last representative of British India in Lhasa. Emphasis on twentieth century (up to 1960) and Tibet's external relations during that time. Brief epilogue updates events from time of book's first publication (1962) to early 1980s. [ES]

9.79 Jean-Paul Roux. *Histoire des Turcs: deux mille ans du Pacifique à la Mediterranée.* Paris: Fayard, 1984. ISBN 2-213-01491-4. ▸ Survey of history of Turkic peoples in Central Asia and Middle East by leading French specialist in cultural history of Inner Asia. Main emphasis on period prior to 1700. [PBG]

9.80 Tsepon W. D. Shakabpa. *Tibet: a political history.* 1967 ed. New York: Potala, 1984. ISBN 0-9611474-1-5. ▸ Although somewhat dated by appearance of other detailed and specialized studies of specific topics, remains best one-volume general survey of Tibetan political history available in English. Contents weighted to emphasize last 150 years of Tibetan history and case for Tibetan independence. [ES]

9.81 Denis Sinor, ed. *The Cambridge history of early Inner Asia.* Cambridge: Cambridge University Press, 1990. ISBN 0-521-24304-1. ▸ Collection of essays by leading specialists on major political developments from prehistory, early Iranians, Xiongnu, Türks, Uighurs, peoples of western Eurasia (Huns, Avars, Western Turkus, Khazars, Bulghars, Pechenegs, Cuman-Qïpchaqs), Qarakhanid realm, Qitans and Jürchens, Islam to early thirteenth-century (pre-Chinggisid) era. [PBG]

9.82 David Snellgrove and Hugh E. Richardson. *A cultural history of Tibet.* 1980 rev. ed. Boston: Shambhala; distributed by Random House, 1986. ISBN 0-394-74380-6 (pbk). ▸ General historical survey with reference to diverse aspects of Tibetan literature, religion, etc; organized chronologically. Somewhat dated but includes new epilogue on Tibet's recent history and addenda to original bibliography listing selected recent works on Tibet. [ES]

9.83 Rolf A. Stein. *Tibetan civilization.* 1962 ed. J. E. Stapleton Driver, trans. Stanford, Calif.: Stanford University Press, 1972. ISBN 0-8047-0806-1. ▸ Translation with minor revisions of major introductory text for study of diverse aspects of Tibet's civilization, including Tibetan history, society, religion, art, etc. Second edition available in French: *La civilization tibétane.* 2d ed. Paris: Le Sycomore, l'Asiatique, 1981. ISBN 2-901795-06-4. [ES]

9.84 G. E. Wheeler. *The modern history of Soviet Central Asia.* New York: Praeger, 1964. ▸ Well-written, clear description of Russian conquest and Soviet rule. Needs to be supplemented with specialized works of Edward A. Allworth (9.285, 9.309, 9.310), Alexandre Bennigsen (9.2, 9.274, 9.275, 9.322, 9.344, 9.345), Hélène Carrère d'Encausse (9.313), and others. [MR]

China and the Nomads

9.85 Thomas Barfield. *The perilous frontier.* Cambridge, Mass.: Blackwell, 1989. ISBN 1-57786-043-2. ▸ Anthropological perspective on causes for rise and decline of nomadic confederations in Inner Asia. Argues that nomadic states arose to exploit strong China. [MR]

9.86 Paul D. Buell. "Steppe perspectives on the medieval history of China: modern Mongol scholarship on the Liao, Chin, and Yuan periods." *Zentralasiatische Studien* 15 (1981) 129–49. ISSN 0514-857X. ▸ Rare window on modern Mongolian views of their own history; notes Mongols' affinity with Qitans, coolness toward Jürchens. [RWD]

9.87 Sechin Jagchid and Van Jay Symons. *Peace, war, and trade along the Great Wall: nomadic-Chinese interaction through two mil-*

lennia. Bloomington: Indiana University Press, 1989. ISBN 0-253-33187-0. ▸ Essays by leading Mongolist on historical interactions between China and Inner Asian neighbors, focusing on institutions developed by Chinese to deal with nomadic pastoral peoples. Marred by poor editing. Argues varying commerce was primary determinant of friendly or hostile relations. [MR/RPH]

9.88 Owen Lattimore. *The Inner Asian frontiers of China.* 1940 ed. Hong Kong: Oxford University Press, 1988. ISBN 0-19-582781-3. ▸ Interpretive, influential, and occasionally highly speculative analysis of historical relationships between China and Inner Asian neighbors. [MR]

9.89 Morris Rossabi. *China and Inner Asia from 1368 to the present day.* New York: Pica; distributed by Universe Books, 1975. ISBN 0-87663-716-0. ▸ Survey of China's relations with Mongols, Manchus, and Central Asian Turks from fourteenth century, emphasizing Ming period and political and trade relations. Finds continuity in Ming, Ch'ing, and Communist policies on border defense, economic profit, and sinicization (except during early Ch'ing dynasty). [PBG/JHC]

SEE ALSO
10.348 Arthur Waldron. *The Great Wall.*

ANCIENT CENTRAL ASIA TO ca. 550 CE

Prehistory and Indo-Europeans in Inner Asia

9.90 R. Ghirshman. *L'Iran et la migration des Indo-Aryans et des Iraniens.* Leiden: Brill, 1977. ISBN 90-04-04876-6. ▸ Indo-Aryans and Iranians in Iran and Central Asia. Dated, but useful. [EJ]

9.91 M. P. Gryaznov. *The ancient civilization of southern Siberia.* James Hogarth, trans. New York: Cowles, 1969. ISBN 0-402-10181-2. ▸ Archaeology and culture of South Siberia, Neolithic to Early Iron Age. Marred by ideological considerations, but still useful. [EJ]

9.92 A. P. Okladnikov. *Ancient population of Siberia and its cultures.* 1959 ed. New York: AMS Press, 1971. (Harvard Peabody Museum of Archaeology and Ethnology, Russian translation series, 1.) ▸ Exemplary study of prevailing view in Soviet scholarship on Siberian populations, first millennium BCE to first millennium CE. Ethnic origins and material culture. [EJ]

9.93 A. P. Okladnikov. "Inner Asia at the dawn of history." In *The Cambridge history of early Inner Asia.* Denis Sinor, ed., pp. 41–96. Cambridge: Cambridge University Press, 1990. ISBN 0-521-24304-1. ▸ Geography of Inner Asia and its relationship to human cultural development from Palaeolithic through Bronze Age cultures (Andronovo, Karasuk), with references to sites in Mongolia and throughout Siberia. Best introduction in English. [EJ]

9.94 Konstantin Fedorovich Smirnov and Elena Efimovna Kuz'mina. *Proiskhozhdenie indoirantsev v svete noveishikh arkheologicheskikh otkrytii* (The origins of the Indo-Europeans in light of the most recent archaeological discoveries). Moscow: Nauka, 1977. ▸ Indo-European origins of early stockbreeders of Central Asia. Useful as example of prevailing view in Soviet scholarship. [EJ]

The Yüeh-chih and Tokharian Problem

9.95 A. K. Narain. "Indo-Europeans in Inner Asia." In *The Cambridge history of early Inner Asia.* Denis Sinor, ed., pp. 151–76. Cambridge: Cambridge University Press, 1990. ISBN 0-521-24304-1. ▸ Review of Yüeh-chih political history from appearance in Chinese annals (ca. 1000 BCE) through conquest of northern India, mixing of Yüeh-chih and Indo-Greeks; Kidarite succession and subsequent defeat of Sāsānids in fourth and fifth centuries CE. [EJ]

9.96 A. K. Narain. *On the "first" Indo-Europeans: the Tokharian–Yüeh-chih and their Chinese homeland.* Bloomington: Indiana University, Research Institute for Inner Asian Studies, 1987. (Ancient Inner Asia. Papers on Inner Asia, 2.) ISSN: 0893-1860. ▸ Review of questions regarding Tokharian problem including identity of Yüeh-chih and Tokharians, possible origins of Indo-Europeans in Inner Asia. Good overview of problem and scholarship. [EJ]

Iranian Nomads, Scytho-Sakas, and Sarmatians

9.97 Anatoli Mikhailovich Khazanov. *Sotsial'naya istoriya skifov: osnovnye problemy razvitiia drevnikh kochevnikov evraziiskikh stepei* (Social history of the Scythians: fundamental problems of the development of the ancient nomads of the Eurasian steppes). Moscow: Nauka, 1975. ▸ Interpretation of mythic traditions regarding origins of Scythians. Covers origins and development of Scythian social organization, relationship of Scythian state with contemporary nomadic states of Near East, and interrelationships of nomadic and settled communities. English summary. Comparative in approach, masterful synthesis. Essential resource. [EJ]

9.98 Sergei Vladimirovich Kiselev. *Drevniaia istoriia iuzhnoi Sibiri* (Ancient history of South Siberia). Moscow: Academy of Sciences of USSR, 1951. ▸ Archaeology and material culture of Neolithic, Bronze, and early Iron Ages in Altai and in Minusinsk-Yenisei basin. Classic, pioneering work. [EJ]

9.99 A. I. Melyukova. "The Scythians and the Sarmatians." In *The Cambridge history of early Inner Asia.* Denis Sinor, ed., pp. 97–117. Cambridge: Cambridge University Press, 1990. ISBN 0-521-24304-1. ▸ Overview of nomadic cultures of South Russia and Caucasus of later first millennium BCE. [EJ]

9.100 Ellis H. Minns. *Scythians and Greeks: a survey of ancient history and archaeology on the north coast of the Euxine from the Danube to the Caucasus.* 1913 ed. 2 vols. in 1. New York: Biblo & Tannen, 1971. ▸ Ancient history and archaeology in former Scythian steppes of Black Sea from Danube to Caucasus, and Crimea. Scythian and Hellenic antiquities. Dated, but remains best overview in English of Scythian antiquities. [EJ]

9.101 Renata Rolle. *The world of the Scythians.* F. Gayna Walls, trans. Berkeley: University of California Press, 1989. ISBN 0-520-06864-5. ▸ Art, culture, and society of Scythians. Useful introduction to Scythian studies. [EJ]

9.102 Michael Ivanovich Rostovzeff. *Iranians and Greeks in South Russia.* 1922 ed. New York: Russell & Russell, 1969. ▸ Antiquities of Scythians and Greeks in South Russia. Political interrelationships. Classic study. [EJ]

9.103 Sergei I. Rudenko. *Frozen tombs of Siberia: the Pazyryk burials of Iron Age horsemen.* M. W. Thompson, trans. Berkeley: University of California Press, 1970. ISBN 0-520-01395-6. ▸ Major frozen burials of early Iron Age nomads at Pazyryk, Gorno-Altai; major source for early nomadic material culture. [EJ]

9.104 Tadeusz Sulimirski. *The Sarmatians.* New York: Praeger, 1970. ▸ Substantial survey of Sarmatian history and culture from first millennium BCE to Alans of fourth century CE. [EJ]

9.105 Tadeusz Sulimirski. "The Scyths." In *The Cambridge history of Iran.* Ilya Gershevitch, ed., vol. 2, pp. 149–99. Cambridge: Cambridge University Press, 1985. ISBN 0-521-20091-1. ▸ Succinct survey of history and culture of Scythian and Sarmatian peoples. [EJ]

Graeco-Bactria

9.106 Frank L. Holt. *Alexander the Great and Bactria: the formation of a Greek frontier in Central Asia.* Leiden: Brill, 1988.

(Mnemosyne bibliotheca classica Batava, Supplementum, 104.) ISBN 90-04-08612-9 (pbk), ISSN 0169-8958. ▸ Political and ethnic situation in Bactria on eve of Greco-Macedonian invasion. Detailed analysis of Alexander's activities in Central Asia. [PBG]

9.107 A. K. Narain. *The Indo-Greeks.* Delhi: Oxford University Press, 1980. ISBN 0-19-561046-6. ▸ Political history of Indo-Greek kingdoms, third to first century BCE, considered within orbit of Indian culture. Useful resource for relevant scholarship. [EJ]

9.108 William W. Tarn. *The Greeks in Bactria and India.* 3d rev. ed. Frank L. Holt, ed. Chicago: Ares, 1984. ISBN 0-89005-524-6. ▸ Consideration of Indo-Greek kingdoms within orbit of Hellenistic rather than Indian culture. Seleucid period, Yüeh-chih conquest of Bactria, cultural relations to other nomadic groups of Central Asia, and Greeks and nomads in India. Dated, but best statement of this point of view. [EJ]

Kushans

9.109 A. L. Basham, ed. *Papers on the date of Kanishka: submitted to the Conference on the Date of Kanishka, London, April 20–22, 1960.* Leiden: Brill, 1969. (Australian National University, Centre of Oriental Studies, Oriental monograph series, 4.) ▸ Chronology of Yüeh-chih–Kushans and disputed dating of Kaniṭka. [EJ]

9.110 B. G. Gafurov et al., eds. *Tsentral'naia Aziia v Kushanskuiu epokhu: trudy Mezhudnar. konf. po istorii, arkheologii, i kulture Tsentral'noi Azii v kushanskuiu epokhu, Dushanbe, 27 sent.–6 okt. 1968* (Central Asia in the Kushan period: proceedings of the International Conference on the History, Archaeology, and Culture of Central Asia in the Kushan Period, Dushanbe, September 27–October 6, 1968). 2 vols. Moscow: Nauka, 1974. ▸ Topics include general problems of Kushan studies, historical origins and ethnicity of Kushans, Kushan chronology, language and writing, history, foreign relations, ideology, religion, art and archaeology. Useful, uneven papers, many in English. [EJ]

9.111 John Rosenfield. *The dynastic arts of the Kushans.* Berkeley: University of California Press, 1967. ▸ Art, history, and culture of Kushans, texts, numismatics, sculpture. Dated, but remains outstanding resource for Kushans. [EJ]

Khwârazamians, Soghdians, and Khotanese

9.112 Harold W. Bailey. *The culture of the Sakas in ancient Iranian Khotan.* Delmar, N.Y.: Caravan, 1982. (Bibliotheca Persica. Columbia lectures on Iranian studies, 1.) ISBN 0-88206-053-8. ▸ Five lectures (1979) on Iranian culture of ancient Khotan, based largely on linguistic analysis of scattered written fragments. Reconstructs society and culture and reviews main literary documents. Attention to Buddhist history and literature down to early eleventh century. Excellent overview of scholarship with extensive references. [DAD/EJ]

9.113 R. E. Emmerick. "Iranian settlements east of the Pamirs." In *The Cambridge history of Iran.* Ehsan Yarshater, ed., vol. 3.1, pp. 263–75. Cambridge: Cambridge University Press, 1983. ISBN 0-521-20092-X (v. 3.1), 0-521-24693-8 (v. 3.2), 0-521-24699-7 (v. 3.1–2). ▸ Brief sketch of political history of Khotan from its founding (ca. third century BCE) to tenth century CE. Some data on eastern Soghdian settlements. Useful synthesis of available information. [PBG]

9.114 E. V. Zeimal. "The political history of Transoxiana." In *The Cambridge history of Iran.* Ehsan Yarshater, ed., vol. 3.1, pp. 232–62. Cambridge: Cambridge University Press, 1983. ISBN 0-521-20092-X (v. 3.1), 0-521-24693-8 (v. 3.2), 0-521-24699-7 (v. 3.1–2). ▸ Survey of history of Central Asian Iranian peoples from fourth century BCE to seventh century CE. Useful introduction to political history by Soviet specialist. Good integration of literary sources with archaeological and numismatic evidence. [PBG]

EARLY MEDIEVAL CENTRAL ASIA, ca. 550–1200

Eastern Steppe

Sources and Collections

9.115 Anthony F. P. Hulsewé. *China in Central Asia: the early stage, 125 BC–AD 23.* M.A.N. Loewe, Introduction. Leiden: Brill, 1979. (Sinica Leidensia, 14.) ISBN 90-04-05884-2 (pbk). ▸ Annotated translation of early standard dynastic accounts of far West (modern Sinkiang and environs), including such peoples as Wu-sun, (Ta) Yüeh-chih. Also important for Hsiung-nu history. [MRD]

9.116 Liu Mau-tsai. *Die chinesischen Nachrichten zur Geschichte der Ost-Türken (T'u-küe).* 2 vols. Wiesbaden: Harrassowitz, 1958. (Göttinger asiatische Forschungen, 10.) ▸ Copiously annotated translations of many important sources, primarily (but not exclusively) standard dynastic histories. Notes are useful, but very little historical analysis. [MRD]

9.117 Talât Tekin. *A grammar of Orkhon Turkic.* Bloomington: Indiana University Press, 1968. (Uralic and Altaic series, 69.) ▸ The most convenient collection of important primary sources in English translation written by early (eighth-century) Turkic peoples on Mongolian plateau. Essentially work of linguistics; important for Central Asian history from Central Asian perspective. [MRD]

SEE ALSO
10.198 Ssu-ma Ch'ien. *Records of the Grand Historian of China.*

Hsiung-nu, Hsien-pi, and Tabghach (T'o-pa Wei)

9.118 Thomas Barfield. "The Hsiung-nu imperial confederacy: organization and foreign policy." *Journal of Asian studies* 4.1 (1981) 45–61. ISSN 0021-9118. ▸ Theoretical investigation of founding of Hsiung-nu empire as model for emergence of other nomadic confederations in eastern steppe zone. Particular emphasis placed on relations with China to explain this model. [MRD]

9.119 Peter A. Boodberg. *Selected works of Peter A. Boodberg.* Alvin P. Cohen, comp. Berkeley: University of California Press, 1979. ISBN 0-520-03314-0. ▸ Collection of articles, many concerned with medieval history of Central Asia, particularly in regard to information culled from Chinese sources on peoples such as Hsiung-nu, Tabghach (T'o-pa), and Türks. [MRD]

9.120 Rafe de Crespigny. *Northern frontier: the policies and strategy of the Later Han empire.* Canberra: Australian National University Press for the Faculty of Asian Studies, 1984. (Faculty of East Asian studies monographs, n.s., 4.) ISBN 0-86784-410-8. ▸ Lengthy diplomatic, political, and military history focusing on relations between China and neighbors, particularly Ch'iang, Hsiung-nu, and Hsien-pi during the later Han period. [MRD]

9.121 Wolfram Eberhard. *Das Toba-Reich Nordchinas: eine soziologische Untersuchung.* Leiden: Brill, 1949. ▸ Detailed study of structure of T'o-pa Wei state through examination of various social, anthropological, political, and economic topics. Provides important data from Northern Wei sources. [MRD]

9.122 Karl Jettmar. *The Altai before the Turks.* Stockholm: Reprinted from the *Museum of Far Eastern Antiquities, Bulletin,* no. 23 (1951). ▸ Survey of pre-Turkic archaeological sites, concluding, hesitantly, that Türks were relative newcomers to region (early Middle Ages). Index and table of contents lacking; thirty-six pages of plates. [PBG]

9.123 Gabriella Molé. *The T'u-yü Hun from the Northern Wei to the time of the Five Dynasties.* Rome: Istituto Italiano per il Medio ed Estremo Oriente, 1970. (Serie Orientale Roma, 41.) ▸ Primarily compilation of translations of accounts from Chinese standard histories (excluding *Chin Shu*) of this people, including copious annotations. Also brief historical and cultural overview. [MRD]

9.124 Gerhard Schreiber. "Das Volk der Hsien-pi zur Han-Zeit." *Monumenta serica* 12 (1947) 145–203. ISSN 0077-149X. ▸ Study of oldest Chinese sources on this people, translated (and including Chinese text) with commentary. Only sizeable study devoted to this rather obscure group. [MRD]

SEE ALSO
10.219 Jennifer Holmgren. *Annals of Tai.*
10.227 Ying-shih Yü. *Trade and expansion in Han China.*

First and Second Türk qaghanates in the East

9.125 Louis Bazin. *Les systèmes chronologiques dans le monde turc ancien.* Budapest and Paris: Akadémiai Kiadó and Centre National de la Recherche Scientifique, 1991. (Bibliotheca orientalis Hungarica, 34.) ISBN 963-05-5614-6, 2-222-04-217-8. ▸ Considers subject from time of earliest known Turkic peoples (sixth to fourteenth century). Of great importance in dating of events mentioned in many Turkic inscriptions as well as of interest for Turkic cultural history. [MRD]

9.126 Wolfram Eberhard. *Conquerors and rulers: social forces in medieval China.* 1965 ed. Leiden: Brill, 1970. ▸ Sociological approach to history of Sha-t'o Türks with broader implications for other nomadic states. Contains particularly interesting chapter on patterns of nomadic rule. [MRD]

9.127 Hilda Ecsedy. "Trade-and-war relations between the Turks and China in the second half of the sixth century." *Acta orientalia academiae scientiarum Hungaricae* 21 (1968) 131–80. ISSN 0001-6446. ▸ Informative study of nature and purpose of nomadic contacts with China, using this period to explore broader implications. Much data provided in both text and extensive notes. [MRD]

9.128 René Giraud. *L'empire des turcs célestes, les regnes d'Elterich, Qapghan, et Bilge (680–734): contribution à l'histoire des Turcs d'Asie Centrale.* Paris: Librairie d'Amérique et d'Orient, 1960. ▸ Careful analysis of Orkhon Türk inscriptions, shedding light on political, social, and cultural life of Second Türk qaghanate. [PBG]

9.129 Sergei Grigor'evich Kliashtornyi. *Drevnetiurkskie runicheskie pamiatniki kak istochnik po istorii Srednei Azii* (The ancient Turkic runic monuments as a source for the history of Central Asia). Moscow: Nauka, 1964. ▸ Series of interrelated essays, by one of leading specialists, on Türk Orkhon inscriptions and on data they contain on Soghdian-Türk relations and eastern qaghanate's relations with Central Asia. Filled with important insights. [PBG]

9.130 Denis Sinor. "The establishment and dissolution of the Türk empire." In *The Cambridge history of early Inner Asia.* Denis Sinor, ed., pp. 285–316. Cambridge: Cambridge University Press, 1990. ISBN 0-521-24304-1. ▸ Useful if brief sketch of history of early Türks. Primarily recounting of political events, some cultural material as well. [MRD]

9.131 Denis Sinor. "The legendary origin of the Turks." In *Folklorica: Festschrift for Felix J. Oinas.* Egle Victoria Žygas and Peter Voorheis, eds., pp. 223–57. Bloomington: Indiana University, Research Institute for Inner Asian Studies, 1982. (Uralic and Altaic series, 141.) ISBN 0-933070-09-8. ▸ Comparative study, with translations, of divergent Türk origin myths as presented in Chinese sources; some reference to later Mongol myths. Information on culture of early Türks. [MRD]

Uighur Empire

9.132 Annemarie von Gabain. *Das Leben im uigurischen Königreich von Qočo (850–1250).* 2 vols. Wiesbaden: Harrassowitz, 1973. (Societas Uralo-Altaica, Veröffentlichungen, 6.) ISBN 3-447-02196-X (cl, v. 1), 3-447-01297-8 (pbk). ▸ Detailed study of culture of later Uighur state of Qocho. Topics discussed include transport, economy, administration, titulature, architecture, clothing, music, decorative arts, and weapons. [MRD]

9.133 James Russell Hamilton. *Les Ouïghours à l'époque des Cinq Dynasties d'après les documents chinois.* Paris: Imprimerie Nationale, 1955. (Bibliothèque de l'Institut des Hautes Études Chinoises, 10.) ▸ Study of Chinese sources on Uighurs (and their neighbors) in Sinkiang after collapse of steppe empire. Sources are translated with copious annotations. [MRD]

9.134 Colin Mackerras, ed. and trans. *The Uighur empire according to the T'ang dynastic histories: a study in Sino-Uighur relations, 744–840.* 2d ed. Columbia: University of South Carolina Press, 1972. ISBN 0-87249-279-6. ▸ Annotated translation of basic standard history accounts, including useful introduction. Largely devoted to Uighur political history and relations with T'ang China. [MRD]

9.135 Vladimir Minorsky. "Tamîm ibn Baḥr's journey to the Uyghurs." *Bulletin of the School of Oriental and African Studies* 12 (1948) 275–305. ISSN 0041-977X. ▸ Translation and study of important Arabic text describing Central Asia, particularly Uighur steppe empire in ninth century. Provides important data on cultural, economic, and political history. [MRD]

9.136 Elisabeth Pinks. *Die Uiguren von Kan-chou in der frühen Sung-Zeit.* Wiesbaden: Harrassowitz, 1968. (Asiatische Forschungen, 24.) ▸ Study of Chinese sources, including translations (primarily excerpts in chronological order), followed by historical study that focuses on political and economic relations with China. [MRD]

Tibetan Empire

9.137 Christopher I. Beckwith. "Tibet and the early medieval florissance in Eurasia: a preliminary note on the economic history of the Tibetan empire." *Central Asiatic journal* 21.2 (1977) 89–104. ISSN 0008-9192. ▸ Preliminary survey of information derived from number of secondary sources attesting to major role of Tibetan empire in international economy of medieval Eurasia. Important article on otherwise largely ignored subject. [ES]

9.138 Christopher I. Beckwith. *The Tibetan empire in Central Asia: a history of the struggle for great power among Tibetans, Turks, Arabs, and Chinese during the early Middle Ages.* Princeton: Princeton University Press, 1987. ISBN 0-691-05494-0. ▸ Major study of poorly understood facet of history of Tibetan empire (seventh to ninth century). Densely packed with information drawn from primary sources. Epilogue on learning and literary activity, architecture, technology, economy, and political activity in comparative perspective. [ES/US]

9.139 Paul Pelliot. *Histoire ancienne du Tibet.* Paris: Librairie d'Amérique et d'Orient, 1961. ▸ Translation of chapters describing Tibet in official histories of T'ang dynasty (618–907), *Chiu T'angshu* and *Hsin T'angshu.* Important sources for history of Tibetan empire and its relations with China. [ES]

9.140 Rolf A. Stein. *Les tribus anciennes des marches sino-tibétaines: légendes, classifications, et histoire.* Paris: Presses Universitaires de France, 1961. (Bibliothèque de l'Institut des Hautes Études Chinoises, 15.) ▸ Important treatise on history of earliest known clans and tribes in eastern part of Tibetan plateau. Grouped by name with analysis of information found in Chinese and Tibetan sources. [ES]

9.141 Geza Uray. "The four horns of Tibet according to the Royal Annals." *Acta orientalia academiae scientiarum Hungaricae* 10.1 (1960) 31–57. ISSN 0001-6446. ▸ Important article elucidating military-administrative organization of Tibetan empire, based on Old Tibetan documents. [ES]

Qitan (Khitan, Liao Dynasty)

9.142 Herbert Franke. "The forest peoples of Manchuria: Kitans and Jürchens." In *The Cambridge history of early Inner Asia*. Denis Sinor, ed., pp. 400–23. Cambridge: Cambridge University Press, 1990. ISBN 0-521-24304-1. ▸ General overview of origins, history, and cultures of these people based on scholarship through early 1980s, with bibliography. [RWD]

9.143 Sechin Jagchid. "Kitan struggles against Jürchen oppression—nomadism versus sinicization." In *Essays in Mongolian studies*, pp. 34–48. Provo, Utah: Brigham Young University, 1988. (David M. Kennedy Center for International Studies, Monograph series, 3.) ISBN 0-912575-06-9 (pbk). ▸ Detailed analysis of Qitan nomads' resistance to Jürchen Ch'in efforts to control them and their subsequent assimilation to Mongols. [RWD]

9.144 Sechin Jagchid. "The Kitans and their cities." In *Essays in Mongolian studies*, pp. 21–33. Provo, Utah: Brigham Young University, 1988. (David M. Kennedy Center for International Studies, Monograph series, 3.) ISBN 0-912575-06-9. ▸ Survey of Qitan-sponsored urbanization, suggesting that city-building was historical loss, not gain, for Qitans, and set precedent for Chinese urbanization among twentieth-century Inner Mongols. [RWD]

Jürchens (Ch'in Dynasty)

9.145 V. E. Medvedev. *Kul'tura amurskikh chzhurchzhenei, konets X–XI veka* (The culture of the Jürchens of the Amur, end of the tenth to the eleventh century). Novosibirsk: Nauka, 1977. ▸ Nicely produced work based on Soviet archaeological finds in Amur basin in 1960s and 1970s; plentiful illustrations of four tomb complexes analyzed. [RWD]

9.146 Ernst Vladimirovich Shavkunov. *Kul'tura chzhurchzhenei-udige XII–XIII vv. i problema proiskhozhdeniia tungusskikh narodov Dal'nego Vostoka* (The culture of the Jürchen-Udehe of the twelfth to thirteenth centuries and the problem of the origin of the Tunguz peoples of the Far East). Moscow: Nauka, 1990. ISBN 5-02-016485-2. ▸ Based largely on archaeological materials, author attempts to reconstruct history and culture of Jürchen tribes, especially Udehe. Underscores syncretistic elements of Jürchen culture. [PBG]

9.147 M. V. Vorob'ev. *Chzhurchzheni i gosudarstvo Tszin' (X v.–1234g.)* (The Jürchens and the Ch'in state, tenth century to 1234). Moscow: Nauka, 1975. ▸ Includes thorough discussion of predynastic Jürchens; English table of contents, charts, and indexes. [RWD]

Tangut (Hsi-hsia)

9.148 Ruth Dunnell. "The fall of Xia: Sino-steppe relations in the late twelfth and early thirteenth centuries." In *Rulers from the steppe: state formation on the Eurasian periphery*. Gary Seaman and Daniel Marks, eds., pp. 158–85. Los Angeles: University of Southern California, Center for Visual Anthropology, Ethnographics Press, 1991. (Proceedings of the Soviet-American Academic Symposia in conjunction with the museum exhibition, "Nomads: Masters of the Eurasian Steppe," 2. Ethnographics monograph series, 2.) ISBN 1-878986-01-5. ▸ Detailed reconstruction of Mongolian conquest of Hsia and its Inner Asian background. [RWD]

9.149 Ruth Dunnell. "Who are the Tanguts? Remarks on Tangut ethnogenesis and the ethnonym Tangut." *Journal of Asian history* 18.1 (1984) 78–89. ISSN 0021-910X. ▸ Maps out history of term "Tangut" and its use. Very helpful summary of data. [RWD]

9.150 Luc Kwanten and Susan Hesse. *Tangut (Hsi hsia) studies:*

a bibliography. Bloomington: Indiana University, Research Institute for Inner Asian Studies, 1980. (Uralic and Altaic series, 137.) ISBN 0-933070-05-5 (pbk). ▸ Flawed but useful reference for early scholarship in field. [RWD]

9.151 E. I. Kychanov. *Ocherk istorii tangutskogo gosudarstva* (Sketch of the history of the Tangut state). Moscow: Nauka, 1968. ▸ Basic reference text for Tangut studies and history. [RWD]

SEE ALSO

  10.330 Ruth Dunnell. *The 1094 Sino-Tangut Gantong stupa stele inscription of Wuwei.*

Central Lands

General Studies

9.152 Vasilii Vladimirovich Bartol'd. *Turkestan down to the Mongol invasion*. 4th ed. C. E. Bosworth, ed. Tatiana Minorsky, trans. Philadelphia: E.J.W. Gibb Memorial Trust; distributed by Porcupine, 1977. ISBN 0-87991453-fl. ▸ Classic work on historical geography, primary sources, and political history of Central Asia from Arab conquests to end of twelfth century with additional chapter on Mongol rulers of Turkistan in thirteenth century. [US]

9.153 Károly Czeglédy. "From East to West: the age of nomadic migrations in Eurasia." Peter B. Golden, trans. *Archivum Eurasiae medii aevi* 3 (1983) 25–125. ISSN 0724-8822. ▸ Magisterial survey of antecedents to western migrations of Asiatic Huns, hegemony of Asi, history of K'ang-chü, Avars (Uar-Huns) from east to west, names of Hepthalites, later migrations in steppe, and letter of Türk qaghan to Emperor Maurice. [US]

9.154 Guy Le Strange. *The lands of the eastern caliphate: Mesopotamia, Persia, and Central Asia from the Moslem conquest to the time of Timur*. 1905 ed. New York: AMS Press, 1976. ISBN 0-404-56287-6. ▸ Outstanding compilation of information from Islamic geographical and historical literature on Central Asia and other territories from Arab conquests to fifteenth century. [US]

9.155 Arsenio Peter Martinez. "Gardizi's two chapters on the Turks." *Archivum Eurasiae medii aevi* 2 (1982) 109–217. ISSN 0724-8822. ▸ Outstanding source by Gardizi describing land and peoples of Central Asia in eighth to eleventh centuries with extensive historical and philological commentary. [US]

9.156 Vladimir Minorsky and C. E. Bosworth, eds. *Ḥudud al-ᶜĀlam, the regions of the world: a Persian geography, 372 A.H.–982 A.D.* 2d ed. Vladimir Minorsky, trans. London: Luzac, 1970. (E.J.W. Gibb memorial series, n.s., 11.) ISBN 0-7189-0201-7. ▸ Outstanding geographical work on lands and peoples of Central Asia in tenth century, derived from earlier sources; commentary by Minorsky. [US]

9.157 William Samolin. *East Turkestan to the twelfth century: a brief political survey*. The Hague: Mouton, 1964. ▸ Brief but thorough survey, based largely on Chinese sources, beginning with Hsiung-nu and Yüeh-chih migrations and ending with Qarakhanids and islamization of region. [PBG]

SEE ALSO

  17.166 Vasili Vladimirovich Bartol'd. *An historical geography of Iran.*

First and Second Türk Qaghanates in the West

9.158 Edouard Chavannes. *Documents sur les Tou-kioue (Turcs) occidentaux: recueillis et commentés, suivi des notes additionelles*. 1903 ed. Taipei: Ch'eng Wen, 1969. ▸ Classic study based on Chinese sources supplemented by Byzantine, Arabic, and Persian data. Provides translations of principal Chinese accounts and reconstructs history of Western Türk qaghanate. Essential reading. [PBG]

9.159 Hamilton A. R. Gibb. *The Arab conquests in Central Asia.* 1923 ed. New York: AMS Press, 1970. ISBN 0-404-02718-0. ‣ Nicely complements Chavannes's work (9.158) from the perspective of close reading of Arab sources. Main focus on Arab takeover, but much data on western Türks and local Iranian peoples. Concentrates on first half of eighth century. [PBG]

Irano-Islamic Central Asia

9.160 C. E. Bosworth. *The Ghaznavids: their empire in Afghanistan and eastern Iran, 994–1040.* 2d ed. Beirut: Librairie du Liban, 1973. ISBN 0-86685-005-8. ‣ Standard treatment of this Turkic dynasty in eastern Iran and Afghanistan, including arrival of Oghuz (Seljuk) Türks into Islamic world. [US]

9.161 C. E. Bosworth. "The political and dynastic history of the Iranian world (AD 1000–1217)." In *The Cambridge history of Iran.* John Andrew Boyle, ed., vol. 5, pp. 1–202. Cambridge: Cambridge University Press, 1968. ISBN 0-521-06936-X (v. 5). ‣ Authoritative survey of Turkic dynasties of Central Asia in eleventh to twelfth centuries, including Seljuqs, Qarakhitays, and Khwârazmshâhs. [US]

9.162 Richard N. Frye. *Bukhara: the medieval achievement.* Norman: University of Oklahoma Press, 1965. ‣ Survey of Bukhara from Arab conquests through twelfth century covering many topics in political, social, economic, and cultural history. [US]

9.163 Abu Bakr Muhammad ibn Ja'far Narshakhî. *The history of Bukhara.* Richard N. Frye, ed. and trans. Cambridge, Mass.: Mediaeval Academy of America, 1954. (Mediaeval Academy of America, Publications, 61.) ISBN 0-910956-35-9. ‣ Translation of Narshakhî's *Ta'rikh-i Bukhârâ,* a standard source on history of Bukhara from Arab conquests to tenth century. [US]

SEE ALSO
    5.475 Richard N. Frye. *The heritage of Persia.*
    17.176 C. E. Bosworth. "The Tahirids and Saffarids."
    17.182 Richard N. Frye. *The golden age of Persia.*
    17.183 Richard N. Frye. "The Samanids."

Qarakhanids, Oghuz-Seljuks, and Khwârazmshâhs

9.164 Peter B. Golden. "The Karakhanids and early Islam." In *The Cambridge history of early Inner Asia.* Denis Sinor, ed., pp. 343–70. Cambridge: Cambridge University Press, 1990. ISBN 0-521-24304-1. ‣ Authoritative survey of first Central Asian Turkic royal dynasty to adopt Islam, of Arab conquest and early administration of Central Asia, and of Turkic steppe. Based on Islamic sources. [DAD/US]

9.165 Peter B. Golden. "The migrations of the Oğuz." *Archivum Ottomanicum* 4 (1972) 45–84. ISSN 0378-2808. ‣ Clear outline of Oghuz history from participation in Second Türk qaghanate to rise of Seljuks and their migrations west to Europe and Middle East. [US]

9.166 Omeljan Pritsak. "The decline of the empire of the Oghuz *yabghu.*" In *Studies in medieval Eurasian history,* pp. 279–92. London: Variorum, 1981. ISBN 0-86078-078-3. ‣ Important study tracing origin of Oghuz *yabghus* (leaders) to time of Uighur empire in eighth century and their subsequent rise and fall in connection with Cumans and Seljuks. [US]

9.167 Omeljan Pritsak. "Die Karachaniden." In *Studies in medieval Eurasian history,* pp. 17–68. London: Variorum, 1981. ISBN 0-86078-078-3. ‣ Standard treatment of modern name, origins, and history of this Turkic Muslim dynasty and its later divisions. [US]

9.168 Omeljan Pritsak. "Von den Karluk zu den Karachaniden." In *Studies in medieval Eurasian history,* pp. 270–300. London: Variorum, 1981. ISBN 0-86078-078-3. ‣ Argues that so-called

Qarakhanid dynasty originates from the Qarluq. Important study presenting idea of *translatio imperii* among Turkic peoples. [US]

Western Eurasia
General Studies

9.169 Peter B. Golden. "The peoples of the Russian forest belt." In *The Cambridge history of early Inner Asia.* Denis Sinor, ed., pp. 229–55. Cambridge: Cambridge University Press, 1990. ISBN 0-521-24304-1. ‣ Authoritative survey of Finno-Ugrians, Oghur, Volga Bulgaria, Hungarians, extinct Uralic peoples, Volga-Finnic peoples, Permians, Ob-Ugrians down to Mongol conquests. [US]

9.170 Peter B. Golden. "The peoples of the South-Russian steppes." In *The Cambridge history of early Inner Asia.* Denis Sinor, ed., pp. 256–84. Cambridge: Cambridge University Press, 1990. ISBN 0-521-24304-1. ‣ Authoritative survey of Oghur, Sabirs, Avars, Türks, Magna Bulgaria, Khazars, Pechenegs, Oghuz (Torki), Cumans down to Mongol conquests. [US]

9.171 Josef Markwart. *Osteuropäische und ostasiatische Streifzüge: ethnologische und historisch-topographische Studien zur Geschichte des neunten und zehnten Jahrhunderts (ca. 840–940).* 1903 2d ed. Hildesheim: Olms, 1961. ‣ Classic, dense philological treatment of selected problems in study of Byzantine, Islamic, Syriac, Iranian, and Slavic sources for steppe north of Black Sea in eighth and ninth centuries. [US]

9.172 Gyula Moravcsik. *Byzantino-Turcica.* 3d ed. 2 vols. Leiden: Brill, 1983. (Berliner byzantinistische Arbeiten, 10–11.) ‣ Complete references to notices on Turkic peoples of Black Sea, Caucasus, and Volga region in Byzantine sources. Volume 1 contains extensive historiographical data; volume 2 alphabetically arranged entries (in Greek script). Essential research tool. [US]

9.173 Alexander A. Vasiliev. *The Goths in the Crimea.* Cambridge, Mass.: Mediaeval Academy of America, 1936. (Monographs of the Mediaeval Academy of America, 11.) ISBN 0-8490-1897-8. ‣ Standard early work focusing on Goths in Crimea but also serving as general history of Crimea from third to eighteenth century based on wide range of sources in many languages. [US]

9.174 Boris Nikolaevich Zakhoder. *Kaspiiskii svod svedenii o Vostochnoi Evrope* (The Caspian corpus of information on eastern Europe). 2 vols. Moscow: Nauka, Izdatel'stvo Vostochnoi Literatury, 1962–67. ‣ Detailed analysis of evidence in Arabic and Persian geographical and historical works on peoples of eastern Europe and Volga region, including Slavs, Hungarians, Khazars, and Volga Bulgarians. [US]

Huns

9.175 Otto Maenchen-Helfen. *The world of the Huns: studies in their history and culture.* M. Knight, ed. Berkeley: University of California Press, 1973. ISBN 0-520-01596-7. ‣ Authoritative study of history, economy, society, warfare, religion, art, race, and language of Huns based on extensive research in primary sources and archaeology. Posthumously published, incomplete work. [US]

9.176 Denis Sinor. "The Hun period." In *The Cambridge history of early Inner Asia.* Denis Sinor, ed., pp. 177–205. Cambridge: Cambridge University Press, 1990. ISBN 0-521-24304-1. ‣ Readable summary of wide range of scholarship on migrations and ethnic composition of Huns from obscure origins to migrations to Europe and later successor states such as Sabirs. [US]

9.177 E. A. Thompson. *A history of Attila and the Huns.* 1948 London ed. Westport, Conn.: Greenwood, 1975. ISBN 0-8371-7640-9. ‣ Standard early work on political history, society, and economy of Huns based on wide range of classical sources. [US]

Oghurs and Bulghars

9.178 Veselin Beševliev. *Die protobulgarische Periode der bulgarischen Geschichte.* Amsterdam: Hakkert, 1981. ISBN 90-256-0882-5. ▸ Exhaustive compilation by Bulgarian specialist of data on political, social, economic, and cultural history of Turkic Bulghars in their western Eurasian and Balkan homelands prior to conversion to Orthodox Christianity (864). Considerable controversy regarding interpretation of data. [PBG]

9.179 Imre Boba. *Nomads, Northmen, and Slavs: eastern Europe in the ninth century.* Wiesbaden: Harrassowitz, 1967. (Slavo-Orientalia, 2.) ▸ Controversial reinterpretation of Hungarians, Slavs, and Türks in steppe north of Black Sea in ninth century. [US]

9.180 Gyula Moravcsik. "Zur Geschichte der Onoguren." In *Studia Byzantina.* Gyula Moravcsik, ed., pp. 84–118. Budapest: Akadémiai Kiadó, 1967. ▸ Standard treatment of history of Onoghurs in Caucasus and north of Black Sea in fifth to ninth centuries based on Byzantine sources. [US]

9.181 Omeljan Pritsak. *Die bulgarische Fürstenliste und die Sprache der Protobulgaren.* Wiesbaden: Harrassowitz, 1955. (Uralaltaische Bibliothek, 1.) ▸ Examination of Turkic Bulgharic linguistic remnants in Bulgharian *Prince-list.* Important data on continuity of Inner Asian culture (e.g., twelve-year animal cycle calendar) among the proto-Bulghars. [PBG]

Avars

9.182 Arnulf Kollautz and Hisayuki Miyakawa. *Geschichte und Kultur eines völkerwanderungszeitlichen Nomadenvolkes: Die Jou-jan der Mongolei und die Awaren in Mitteleuropa.* 2 vols. Klagenfurt: Habelt, 1970. (Aus Forschung und Kunst, Geschichtsverein für Kärnten, 10.) ▸ Links Asiatic Jou-jan of Mongolia with European Avars, tracing their migrations to Carpathian basin. Detailed treatment of political history, settlements, and archaeology. [US]

9.183 S. Szádeczky-Kardoss. "The Avars." In *The Cambridge history of early Inner Asia.* Denis Sinor, ed., pp. 206–28. Cambridge: Cambridge University Press, 1990. ISBN 0-521-24304-1. ▸ Best survey in English of written sources on history of Avars: ethnicity and language, migrations and settlement in eastern Europe, and archaeological record. [US]

Khazars

9.184 Mikhail Illarionovich Artamonov. *Istoriia Khazar* (The history of the Khazars). Leningrad: Izdatel'stvo Gosudarstvennogo Ermitazha, 1962. ▸ Sweeping survey of Khazar history and immediate antecedents in western Eurasian steppes. Excellent coverage of archaeological material. Based almost entirely on (often outdated) translations. Marred by numerous errors of interpretation and anti-Judaic bias. English summary. [PBG]

9.185 Douglas Morton Dunlop. *The history of the Jewish Khazars.* Princeton: Princeton University Press, 1954. (Princeton Oriental studies, 16.) ▸ Analysis of primary sources (Islamic and Hebrew) on Judaism among Khazars, seventh to tenth centuries. Standard work; most complete one-volume assemblage of translated primary accounts. Misleading theories on Uighur origins of Khazars. Solid coverage of Arab-Khazar wars in sixth to eighth centuries, conversion to Judaism, and defeat in tenth century. [DAD/US/KRS]

9.186 Norman Golb and Omeljan Pritsak. *Khazarian Hebrew documents of the tenth century.* Ithaca, N.Y.: Cornell University Press, 1982. ISBN 0-8014-1221-8. ▸ Text and translation of recently discovered and hitherto unpublished tenth-century document, new edition and translation of important text, and historical survey of Khazar Judaism with new interpretation of its periodization. [DAD]

9.187 Peter B. Golden. *Khazar studies: an historico-philological inquiry into the origins of the Khazars.* 2 vols. Budapest: Akadémiai Kiadó, 1980. (Bibliotheca orientalis Hungarica, 25.1–2.) ISBN 963-05-1548-2 (set), 963-05-1549-0 (v. I), 963-05-1550-4 (v. 2). ▸ Overview of Khazar history, society, institutions with study of remnants of Khazar language from sources in various languages showing it was Standard Turkic language. Includes facsimiles of relevant passages from many sources. [US]

9.188 Thomas S. Noonan. "What does historical numismatics suggest about the history of Khazaria in the ninth century?" *Archivum Eurasiae medii aevi* 3 (1983) 265–81. ISSN 0724-8822. ▸ Examines role of Khazars in international trade beginning 800 and explores causes for development of monetary systems at sources of Khazar exports but not in Khazaria itself. Preliminary research report raising many fundamental questions. Essential work. [US]

9.189 Thomas S. Noonan. "Why dirhams reached Russia: the role of Arab-Khazar relations in the development of the earliest Islamic trade with eastern Europe." *Archivum Eurasiae medii aevi* 4 (1984) 151–282. ISSN 0724-8822. ▸ Argues that easing of Arab-Khazar hostilities in eighth century allowed development of Arab-Khazar trade leading to later Khazar expansion into north to sources of exports. Includes detailed description of Arab-Khazar relations. Offers fundamental insights into political, socioeconomic, and cultural history of Khazars. [US]

9.190 Anatolii Petrovich Novosel'tsev. *Khazarskoe gosudarstvo i ego rol' v istorii Vostochnoi Evropy i Kavkaza* (The Khazar state and its role in the history of eastern Europe and the Caucasus). Moscow: Nauka, 1990. ISBN 5-02-009552-4. ▸ Attempt at summation of Khazar studies. Thorough discussion of sources (consulted in original languages), historiography, predecessors of Khazar state, socioeconomic and religious history, political structure, and relations with neighbors. [PBG]

Volga Bulgaria

9.191 Ravil' Gabdrakhmanovich Fakhrutdinov. *Ocherki po istorii Volzhskoi Bulgarii* (Sketches of the history of Volga Bulgaria). S. A. Pletneva, ed. Moscow: Nauka, 1984. ▸ General survey of history, society, economy, and archaeology of Volga Bulgaria from pre-Mongol period to sixteenth century with extensive references to sources and literature. [US]

9.192 German Alekseevich Fedorov-Davydov, ed. *Gorod Bolgar: Ocherki istorii i kul'tury* (The city Bulgar: sketches of its history and culture). Moscow: Nauka, 1987. ▸ Important contributions on history, archaeology, epigraphy, coinage, and agriculture in Volga Bulgaria. [US]

9.193 Ahmad Ibn Fadlan. *The "Risalah" of Ibn Fadlan: an annotated translation with introduction.* James E. McKeithan, trans. Bloomington: Indiana University Press, 1979. ▸ Most important source on Khazars, Volga Bulgarians, and other peoples of Volga region in early ninth century, written by caliphal envoy to Volga Bulgaria. [US]

9.194 Thomas S. Noonan. "Russia's eastern trade, 1150–1350: the archaeological evidence." *Archivum Eurasiae medii aevi* 3 (1983) 201–64. ISSN 0724-8822. ▸ Describes wide range of goods traded by Russia with Volga Bulgaria and Golden Horde (1150–1350) based on archaeological and numismatic evidence. Sees no decline of eastern trade after tenth century, and no cessation of eastern trade after Mongol conquest. Important study. [US/SCF]

9.195 Istvan Zimonyi. *The origins of the Volga Bulghars.* Szeged: Universitas Szegediensis de Attila Josef Nominata, 1990. (Studia Uralo-Altaica, 32.) ISSN 0133-4239. ▸ Argues for two Turkic migrations north to Volga-Kama confluence (eighth to ninth and ninth to tenth centuries) with extensive analysis of different Arabic and Persian source traditions. Excellent introduction to sources for this period. [US]

SEE ALSO
34.202 Janet Martin. *Treasure of the land of darkness.*

Pechenegs and Cuman-Qïpchaqs

9.196 Serzhan Musataevich Akhinzhanov. *Kypchaki v istorii srednevekovogo Kazakhstana* (The Qïpchaqs in the history of medieval Kazakhstan). Alma-Ata: Nauka, 1989. ISBN 5-628-00146-5. ▸ Focuses on eastern Qïpchaq-Qanglï union and its relations with Khwârazm from late eleventh to early thirteenth century. Discussion of Qïpchaq origins should be treated with caution. One of few works dealing with this important but neglected subject. [PBG]

9.197 Peter B. Golden. "Cumanica I: the Qïpčaqs in Georgia." *Archivum Eurasiae medii aevi* 4 (1984) 45–87. ISSN 0724-8822. ▸ Study of Cuman relations with Georgian kingdom and Cuman resettlement in Georgia in twelfth to early thirteenth centuries, based on Georgian and other sources. Exceptionally important for lengthy extracts and citations from Georgian chronicles not otherwise available in English. [US]

9.198 Peter B. Golden. "Cumanica II: the Ölberli (Ölperli), the fortunes and misfortunes of an Inner Asian nomadic clan." *Archivum Eurasiae medii aevi* 6 (1986) 5–29. ISSN 0724-8822. ▸ Detailed examination of origins and westward migrations of Ölberli clan in wake of rise of Qitans and later role in ruling stratum of eastern Qïpchaqs. Unique case study examining single group. [US]

9.199 Peter B. Golden. "The Polovci Dikii." *Harvard Ukrainian studies* 3–4.1 (1979–80) 296–309. ISSN 0363-5570. ▸ Study of "Wild Cuman" subconfederation and its relations with various Rus' rulers in twelfth to thirteenth centuries. Reexamines subconfederation from perspective of steppe politics, revising earlier Kiev-centered interpretations. [US]

9.200 Bulat Eshmukhambetovich Kumekov. *Gosudarstvo Kimakov IX–XI vv. po arabskim istochnikam* (The Kimak state of the ninth to tenth centuries according to Arab sources). Alma-Ata: Nauka, 1972. ▸ Only monograph-length work dealing with Kimeks, parent tribal confederation from which Qïpchaqs evolved. Based on archaeological data and Arab sources, especially al-Idrisi. [PBG]

9.201 Josef Markwart. "Über das Volkstum der Komanen." In *Osttürkische Dialektstudien.* Willy Bang and Josef Markwart, pp. 25–238. Göttingen: Vandenhoeck & Ruprecht, 1970. (Akademie der Wissenschaften, Göttingen, Philosophisch-historische Klasse, Abhandlungen, n.F., 13.1.) ▸ Classic study of origins of Cumans, their various names, and relations with surrounding states based on detailed study of Islamic, Slavic, Byzantine, and other sources. [US]

9.202 András Palóczi Horváth. *Pechenegs, Cumans, Iasians: steppe peoples in medieval Hungary.* Timothy Wilkinson, trans. Budapest: Corvina Kiadó; distributed by Kultura, 1989. ISBN 963-13-2740-X. ▸ Important study of Pecheneg, Cuman, and Jasz migrations to and settlement in medieval Hungary based largely on archaeological materials. [PBG]

9.203 Omeljan Pritsak. "The Pečenegs: a case of social and economic transformation." *Archivum Eurasiae medii aevi* 2 (1982) 211–35. ISSN 0724-8822. ▸ Detailed survey of history, institutions, military, and social organization of Pechenegs based on written and toponymic sources. [US]

9.204 Omeljan Pritsak. "The Polovcians and Rus." *Archivum Eurasiae medii aevi* 2 (1982) 321–80. ISSN 0724-8822. ▸ Detailed study of names, origins, migrations, and history of Polovcians

(Cumans), including attempt to reconstruct their settlements based on archaeological records. [US]

Uralic Peoples of the Forest Belt

9.205 István Dienes. *The Hungarians cross the Carpathians.* Barna Balogh, trans. Budapest: Corvina Kiadó, 1972. ▸ Very brief account, with strong archaeological emphasis, of proto-Hungarian tribal migrations from Bashkiria to Hungary. Useful chapters on social and economic history. Beautifully illustrated. [PBG/SBV]

9.206 István Fodor. *In search of a new homeland: the prehistory of the Hungarian people and the conquest.* 1975 ed. Helen Tarnoy, trans. Budapest: Corvina Kiadó, 1982. ISBN 963-13-1126-0, ISSN 0139-3014. ▸ Survey of history and culture of early Finno-Ugrians, formation of Hungarians in their Uralic homeland, and migration to Central Europe. Makes good use of archaeological data. [PBG/SBV]

9.207 C. A. Macartney. *The Magyars in the ninth century.* 1930 ed. Cambridge: Cambridge University Press, 1968. ISBN 0-521-07391-X. ▸ Somewhat dated but still useful analysis of Arabo-Persian geographical data (used in translation) and Greek, Latin, and Slavic sources for Hungarian preconquest period. One of few works on subject in English. [PBG]

9.208 István Vásáry. "The Hungarians or Možars and the Meščers/Mišers of the Middle Volga region." *Archivum Eurasiae medii aevi* 1 (1975) 237–75. ISSN 0724-8822. ▸ Elaborate history of Mishar subgrouping of Kazan Tatars through historical, toponymic, and linguistic evidence, arguing that no connection exists with Hungarians (i.e., Magyars). [US]

LATE MEDIEVAL CENTRAL ASIA, 1200–1450

General Studies

9.209 Thomas T. Allsen. "Mongolian princes and their merchant partners." *Asia major* 2.2 (1989) 83–126. ISSN 0004-4482. ▸ Influence of trading interests on policies and institutions of early empire. Sheds new light on economy of Mongol empire. [TTA]

9.210 Joseph F. Fletcher, Jr. "The Mongols: ecological and social perspectives." *Harvard journal of Asiatic studies* 46.1 (1986) 11–50. ISSN 0073-0548. ▸ Motivations and institutions underlying imperial expansion. Summarizes earlier views and sets stage for new debate. [TTA]

9.211 Lev Nikolaevich Gumilev. *Searches for an imaginary kingdom: the legend of the kingdom of Prester John.* R.E.F. Smith, trans. Cambridge: Cambridge University Press, 1987. ISBN 0-521-32214-6. ▸ Argues pivotal role for Eastern Christians in expansion of empire. Eccentric and provocative panorama of steppe history. [TTA]

9.212 Charles J. Halperin. "Russia in the Mongol empire in comparative perspective." *Harvard journal of Asiatic studies* 43.1 (1983) 239–61. ISSN 0073-0548. ▸ Places history of Golden Horde in context of empire at large. Fine analysis of cultural underpinnings of four regional khanates. [TTA]

9.213 Peter Jackson. "The dissolution of the Mongol empire." *Central Asiatic journal* 22.3–4 (1978) 186–244. ISSN 0008-9192. ▸ Role of territorial disputes in formation of regional khanates. Focus on western Asia but with implications for empire as whole. Influential and productive revision. [TTA]

9.214 David O. Morgan. *The Mongols.* Oxford: Blackwell, 1986. ISBN 0-631-13556-1 (cl), 0-631-17563-6 (pbk). ▸ Survey of imperial expansion and rise of successor states. Best modern synthesis; entry point to field. [TTA]

9.215 Constantin d'Ohsson. *Histoire des Mongols depuis Tchinguiz-Khan jusqu'a Timour Bey ou Tamerlan.* 1834–35 ed. 4 vols. Tientsin, China: La Haye at Amsterdam, Les Frères Van Cleef,

1940. ▸ Detailed narrative of rise and decline of empire based mainly on Muslim sources. Dated but still useful in absence of modern synthesis of similar scope. [TTA]

9.216 Igor de Rachewiltz. *Papal envoys to the great khans.* Stanford, Calif.: Stanford University Press, 1971. ISBN 0-8047-0770-7. ▸ Surveys diplomatic relations between Mongols and Latin West. Popular format but grounded in thorough knowledge of sources. [TTA]

9.217 Igor de Rachewiltz. "Some remarks on the ideological foundations of Chingis Khan's empire." *Papers on Far Eastern history* 7 (1973) 21–36. ISSN 0048-2870. ▸ Exposition of nomadic political notions revealing interplay of indigenous, Chinese, and West Asian influences. Starting point for research on topic. [TTA]

9.218 J. J. Saunders. *The history of the Mongol conquests.* New York: Barnes & Noble, 1971. ISBN 0-389-04451-2. ▸ Overview of expansion and emergence of regional khanates. Useful introduction by thoughtful, well-informed nonspecialist. [TTA]

9.219 John Masson Smith. "Mongol and nomadic taxation." *Harvard journal of Asiatic studies* 30 (1970) 48–85. ISSN 0073-0548. ▸ Revises earlier efforts to sort out tax categories and terminology found in diverse sources. Insightful analysis of pastoralists' attitudes toward governmental imposts of all types. [TTA]

Sources and Collections

9.220 Robert P. Blake and Richard N. Frye. "The 'History of the Nation of Archers (the Mongols)' by Grigor of Akanc'." *Harvard journal of Asiatic studies* 12.3–4 (1949) 269–399. ISSN 0073-0548. ▸ Account of early attacks and subsequent conquest of West Asia. Informative on invader's policies and local response. [TTA]

9.221 Emilii V. Bretschneider. *Medieval researches from eastern Asiatic sources: fragments towards the knowledge of the geography and history of central and western Asia from the thirteenth to the seventeenth century.* Rev. 1910 ed. 2 vols. in 1. Osnabrück: Biblio, 1987. ISBN 3-7648-0191-3. ▸ Collects and translates Chinese sources on Mongols in West. Now dated but translations serviceable and geographical commentary sound. [TTA]

9.222 Francis Woodman Cleaves, trans. *The secret history of the Mongols.* Vol. 1: *Translation.* Cambridge, Mass.: Harvard University Press, 1982. ISBN 0-674-79670-5 (v. 1). ▸ Only extant native account of rise of empire. Full of obscurities, contradictions, and chronological confusion. Nevertheless, invaluable guide to Mongols' own motives, goals, and institutions. [TTA]

9.223 Christopher Dawson, ed. *The Mongol mission: narratives and letters of the Franciscan missionaries in Mongolia and China in the thirteenth and fourteenth centuries, translated by a nun of Stanbrook Abbey.* New York: Sheed & Ward, 1955. ▸ Convenient selection of Latin sources, including travels of Carpini and Rubruck which provide vital data on institutions, policies, and personalities of empire in 1240s and 1250s. [TTA]

9.224 Ala al-Din ᶜAta-Malik ibn Muhammad Juvaini. *The history of the world conqueror.* 2 vols. John Andrew Boyle, trans. Cambridge, Mass.: Harvard University Press, 1958. ▸ Personal narrative of reigns of first four khans by midlevel Persian official who traveled widely in empire. Particularly informative on military, political, and economic institutions. Excellent translation and commentary. [TTA]

9.225 Paul Pelliot. *Notes on Marco Polo.* 1959 ed. 3 vols. Paris: Imprimerie Nationale, 1973. ▸ Indispensable companion to Polo's account of empire. Entries range from brief philological comments to extended monographs on specific places, peoples, and events. Incomplete at author's death. [TTA]

9.226 Paul Pelliot and Louis Hambis, trans. *Histoire des campagnes de Gengis Khan,* Vol. 1. Leiden: Brill, 1951. ▸ Anonymous Chinese account of rise of Chinggis Khan based on lost Mongolian chronicle. Extensive philological and historical commentary. Essential source. [TTA]

9.227 Marco Polo. *The description of the world.* 1938 ed. A. C. Moule and Paul Pelliot, trans. New York: AMS Press, 1976. 2 vols. ISBN 0-404-11525-X. ▸ Definitive translation. Account is weak on chronology and vague on events but highly informative on cultural and social conditions. [TTA]

9.228 Rashid al-Din Tabib. *The successors of Genghis Khan.* John Andrew Boyle, trans. New York: Columbia University Press, 1971. ISBN 0-231-03351-6. ▸ Official account of dynasty's expansion and rule throughout Eurasia by Persian official in Mongol employ. Based on direct observation, interviews with participants, and lost records. Essential source. [TTA]

9.229 Bertold Spuler, comp. *History of the Mongols, based on Eastern and Western accounts of the thirteenth and fourteenth centuries.* Helga Drummond and Stuart Drummond, trans. Berkeley: University of California Press, 1972. ISBN 0-520-01960-1. ▸ Handy selection of contemporary Muslim and European sources with commentary. Lacks East Asian component. [TTA]

Chinggisid East Asia

9.230 Thomas T. Allsen. *Mongol imperialism: the policies of the Grand Qan Möngke in China, Russia, and the Islamic lands, 1251–1259.* Berkeley: University of California Press, 1987. ISBN 0-520-05527-6. ▸ Detailed, authoritative study of means by which human and material resources were identified, mobilized, and deployed during apogee of empire. Focuses on Mongols' motives, priorities, and goals. [TTA]

9.231 Chuluuny Dalai. *Mongoliia v xiii–xiv vekakh* (Mongolia in the thirteenth to fourteenth centuries). Moscow: Nauka, 1983. ▸ Detailed study of Mongolian homeland during imperial era presented from native point of view. Successfully integrates literary and archaeological data. [TTA]

9.232 H. Desmond Martin. *The rise of Chingis Khan and his conquest of North China.* 1950 ed. Eleanor Lattimore, ed. New York: Octagon Books, 1971. ▸ Well-organized account of early campaigns in East and Central Asia. Useful in absence of alternative but must be treated with caution. [TTA]

9.233 Igor de Rachewiltz. "Turks in China under the Mongols: a preliminary investigation of Turco-Mongolian relations in the thirteenth and fourteenth centuries." In *China among equals: the Middle Kingdom and its neighbors, tenth to fourteenth centuries.* Morris Rossabi, ed., pp. 281–310. Berkeley: University of California Press, 1982. ISBN 0-520-04383-9 (cl), 0-520-04562-9 (pbk). ▸ One of most influential ethnolinguistic groups among numerous foreigners serving Yüan court. Excellent guide to Chinese sources on medieval Turkic history. [TTA]

9.234 Igor de Rachewiltz. "Yeh-lu Ch'u-ts'ai: Buddhist idealist and Confucian stateman." In *Confucian personalities.* Arthur F. Wright and Denis Twitchett, eds., pp. 189–216. Stanford, Calif.: Stanford University Press, 1962. ▸ Biographical sketch of central figure in clash between Chinese and Mongolian political culture during formative stages of empire. [TTA]

9.235 Paul Ratchnevsky. *Genghis Khan: his life and legacy.* Thomas N. Haining, ed. and trans. Oxford: Blackwell, 1992. ISBN 0-631-16785-4. ▸ First extended biography based on primary sources. Clearly organized and reliable; entry point for study of early Mongolian history. [TTA]

9.236 Morris Rossabi. *The Jürchens in the Yuan and Ming.* Ithaca, N.Y.: Cornell University Press, 1982. (Cornell University East Asia papers, 27.) ▸ Useful sketch of postdynastic Jurchen history; map and chronological table. [RWD]

SEE ALSO
10.332 Ch'en Yuan. *Western and Central Asians in China under the Mongols.*
10.335 Elizabeth Endicott-West. *Mongolian rule in China.*

Chinggisid Iran and Transcaucasia

9.237 John Andrew Boyle. "Dynastic and political history of the Il-khans." In *The Cambridge history of Iran.* John Andrew Boyle, ed., vol. 5, pp. 303–421. Cambridge: Cambridge University Press, 1968. ISBN 0-521-06936-X. ‣ Summary of major events based on close scrutiny of Persian sources. Clearly presented and accurate; entry point into field. [TTA]

9.238 Bertold Spuler. *Die Mongolen in Iran: Politik, Verwaltung, und Kultur der Ilchanzeit 1220–1350.* 4th rev. ed. Leiden: Brill, 1985. ISBN 90-04-07099-0. ‣ Narrative of dynastic history followed by thematic chapters on religion, government, trade, etc. Detailed, reliable, with massive bibliography. [TTA]

Chinggisid Central Asia

9.239 Thomas T. Allsen. "The Yuan dynasty and the Uighurs of Turfan in the thirteenth century." In *China among equals: the Middle Kingdom and its neighbors, tenth to fourteenth centuries.* Morris Rossabi, ed., pp. 243–80. Berkeley: University of California Press, 1983. ISBN 0-520-04383-9 (cl), 0-520-04562-9 (pbk). ‣ Detailed case study of subordinate state. How Mongols controlled and utilized resources of allies. [TTA]

9.240 Jean Aubin. "Le khanat de Čagatai et le Khorasan, 1334–1380." *Turcica* 9.2 (1976) 16–60. ISSN 0082-6847. ‣ Expansion into northern Iran in context of internal political struggles. Fine analysis of disintegration of khanate and rise of Timur. [TTA]

9.241 Paul D. Buell. "Sino-Khitan administration in Mongol Bukhara." *Journal of Asian history* 13 (1979) 121–51. ISSN 0021-910X. ‣ Case study of personnel policies and governmental style founded on solid textual scholarship. Major contribution to emergence of regional khanates. [TTA]

Golden Horde

9.242 Thomas T. Allsen. "The princes of the left hand: an introduction to the history of the Ulus of Orda in the thirteenth and fourteenth centuries." *Archivum Eurasiae medii aevi* 5 (1985) 5–40. ISSN 0724-8822. ‣ Role of eastern wing of Golden Horde in evolution of empire. Brief characterization of economy, culture, and ethnic composition. Pioneering effort in much neglected area. [TTA]

9.243 German Alekseevich Fedorov-Davydov. *The culture of the Golden Horde cities.* H. Bartlett Wells, trans. Oxford: British Archaeological Reports, 1984. (BAR international series, 198.) ISBN 0-86054-256-4. ‣ Systematic treatment of material culture and economy of urban life in steppe. Masterful synthesis of extensive archaeological data. [TTA]

9.244 German Alekseevich Fedorov-Davydov. *Obshchestvennyi stroi zolotoi Ordy* (The social structure of the Golden Horde). Moscow: Izdatel'stvo Moskovskogo Gosudarstvennogo Universiteta, 1973. ‣ Transformation of nomadic political system over three centuries. Sophisticated Marxist social history. [TTA]

9.245 Boris D. Grekov and A. Iu. Iakubovskii. *La Horde d'Or et la Russie.* François Thuret, trans. Paris: Payot, 1961. ‣ Valuable and enduring characterization of urban life and material culture by Iakoubovski in part 1. Analyzes Mongol invasion; Horde's economic, social, and political organization; cities; and civilization. Grekov examines conquest of Northeast Rus' and fourteenth-century political relations, summarizing Mongol impact on Russia in part 2. [TTA/NSK]

9.246 Mark G. Kramarovsky. "The culture of the Golden Horde and the problem of the 'Mongol legacy.' " In *Rulers from the steppe: state formation on the Eurasian periphery.* Gary Seaman and Daniel Marks, eds., pp. 255–73. Los Angeles: University of Southern California, Center for Visual Anthropology, Ethnographics Press, 1991. (Proceedings of the Soviet-American Academic Symposia in conjunction with the museum exhibition, "Nomads: Masters of the Eurasian Steppe," 2. Ethnographics monograph series, 2.) ISBN 1-878986-01-5. ‣ Formation of state-bound culture in western steppe combining local and East Asian elements. Effectively integrates literary and archaeological data. [TTA]

9.247 Uli Schamiloglu. "The *qaraçi* beys of the later Golden Horde: notes on the organization of the Mongol world-empire." *Archivum Eurasiae medii aevi* 4 (1984) 283–98. ISSN 0724-8822. ‣ Role of clan leaders as councils of state and as principal power brokers in Chinggisid states. Important revision of earlier views. [TTA]

9.248 Bertold Spuler. *Die Goldene Horde: die Mongolen in Russland, 1223–1502.* 2d rev. ed. Wiesbaden: Harrassowitz, 1965. ‣ Narrative of Jochid dynasty followed by thematic chapters on economy, religion, administration, etc. Descriptive, reliable, with massive bibliography. [TTA]

Timur (Temür) and the Timurids

9.249 Zahiruddin Muhammad Babur. *The Babar-Nama: being the autobiography of the emperor Babar, the founder of the Moghul dynasty in India.* 1922 ed. Annette Susannah Beveridge, ed. and trans. New Delhi: Oriental Books Reprint, 1979. (E.J.W. Gibb memorial series, 1.) ‣ Memoirs of founder of Mughul empire in India, a descendant of both Timur and Chinggis Khan. Rich source for key persons and events, cultural and social life, and towns and environs. [JG]

9.250 Vasilii Vladimirovich Bartol'd. *Ulugh-Beg.* Vol. 2 of *Four studies on the history of Central Asia.* 1958 2d ed. Vladimir Minorsky and Tatiana Minorsky, trans. Leiden: Brill, 1963. 4 parts. ‣ Study of Ulugh Beg's reign (r. 1409–46) and his struggle to maintain power by preeminent Russian historian. Classic treatment of political and religious aspects, although dated for certain aspects of Timurid social history. [JG]

9.251 Ruy Gonzalez de Clavijo. *Embassy to Tamerlane, 1403–1406.* Guy Le Strange, trans. New York: Harper & Brothers, 1928. ‣ Travel account of Spanish envoy to Timur's court. Valuable for European perspective of Timur, court etiquette, and cultural commentary. [JG]

9.252 Lisa Golombek and Donald Wilber. *The Timurid architecture of Iran and Turan.* 2 vols. Princeton: Princeton University Press, 1988. ISBN 0-691-03587-3 (set). ‣ Comprehensive study of building activity sponsored by Timurids in fifteenth-century Iran and Central Asia. Interpretive essays, catalog of 257 monuments. Rich source of information. [JG]

9.253 Jo-Ann Gross. "The economic status of a Timurid Sufi Shaykh: a matter of conflict or perception?" *Iranian studies* 21.1–2 (1988) 84–104. ISSN 0021-0862. ‣ Study of prominent Timurid Ṣūfī shaikh, Khwaja Ahrar. Useful for exploring contrasts between asceticism and material wealth attained by some Ṣūfīs as well as economic role of Ṣūfīs. [JG]

9.254 Jo-Ann Gross. "Multiple roles and perceptions of a Sufi shaikh: symbolic statements of political and religious authority." In *Naqshbandis: cheminements et situations actuelle d'un ordre mystique musulman: actes de la table ronde de Sevres.* Marc Gaborieau, Alexandre Popovic, and Thierry Zarcone, eds., pp. 109–21. Istanbul: Isis, 1990. (Varia Turcica, 18.) ISBN 2-906053-12-0. ‣ Study of basis of power, authority, and popular perceptions of role of Khwaja Ahrar, leader of Naqshbandī order in late fifteenth-century Central Asia. Comparative analysis of hagiographical and chronicle sources. [JG]

9.255 Mirza Muhammad Haydar. *A history of the Moghuls of Central Asia, being the "Tarikh-i Rashidi" of Mirza Muhammad Haidar, Dughlat: an English version.* 2d ed. N. Elias, ed. E. Denison Ross, trans. New York: Barnes & Noble, 1972. ISBN 0-389-04664-7. ▸ Chronicle (sixteenth century) written by cousin of Babur. Valuable source for history of eastern branch of Chaghatayids (Mughal Khans); parts of editor's introduction outdated. [JG]

9.256 Ibn Arabshah. *Tamerlane, or, Timur the great amir, from the Arabic life of Ahmed ibn Arabshah.* 1936 ed. J. J. Saunders, trans. Lahore: Progressive Books, 1976. ▸ Biography of Timur written by a Damascene Arab. Remains important source for personal view, wealth of detail on campaigns, and daily life and customs despite negative bias toward Timur. [JG]

9.257 Ibn Khaldûn. *Ibn Khaldun and Tamerlane.* Walter Fischel, ed. and trans. Berkeley: University of California Press, 1952. ▸ Ibn Khaldûn's account of his meeting with Timur in Damascus in 1401. Valuable as personal, contemporary, non-Timurid source. [JG]

9.258 Thomas W. Lentz and Glenn D. Lowry. *Timur and the princely vision: Persian art and culture in the fifteenth century.* Washington, D.C.: Smithsonian Institution for Arthur M. Sackler Gallery, 1989. ISBN 0-87474-706-6. ▸ Catalog accompanying exhibition of Timurid art at Los Angeles County Museum and Arthur M. Sackler Gallery (Washington D.C.) in 1989. Wonderfully illustrated examination of artistic production from perspective of Timurid patronage, political power, and legitimacy. [JG]

9.259 Beatrice Forbes Manz. *The rise and rule of Tamerlane.* Cambridge: Cambridge University Press, 1989. ISBN 0-521-34595-2. ▸ Timur's rise to power as founder of nomadic conquest dynasty. Excellent study of tribal politics, state formation, and political culture in Turko-Mongol society in general and the Ulus Chaghatai in particular. [JG]

9.260 Hans R. Roemer. "The successors of Timur." In *The Cambridge history of Iran.* Peter Jackson and Laurence Lockhart, eds., vol. 6, pp. 98–146. Cambridge: Cambridge University Press, 1986. ISBN 0-521-20094-6 (v. 6). ▸ Authoritative study of Timurid throne-struggles and administration in Iran and Transoxiana. Special attention paid to cultural patronage, historiography, and religious trends in late Timurid period. [JG]

9.261 Hans R. Roemer. "Timur in Iran." In *The Cambridge history of Iran.* Peter Jackson and Laurence Lockhart, eds., vol. 6, pp. 42–97. Cambridge: Cambridge University Press, 1986. ISBN 0-521-20094-6 (v. 6). ▸ Timur's early career and military campaigns. Appraisal of his personality, reasons for success, and attitudes toward rulership, religion, and culture. Useful overview within context of Iranian history. [JG]

9.262 Maria Subtelny. "Ali Shir Nava-i: *bakhshi* and *beg.*" In *Eucharisterion: essays presented to Omeljan Pritsak on his sixtieth birthday by his colleagues and students.* 2 vols. Ihor Ševčenko and Frank E. Sysyn, eds., pp. 797–807. Cambridge, Mass.: Harvard Ukrainian Research Institute, 1980. (Harvard Ukrainian studies, 3–4.) ISSN 0363-5570. ▸ Examination of Navâi's (1441–1501) prominent position at Timurid court of Sultan Ḥusayn Bayqara (r. 1469–1506). Excellent study of power and authority based on concepts of rank, status, closeness, and relationship to dual Turko-Mongol–Perso-Islamic Timurid system of government. [JG]

9.263 Maria Subtelny. "Art and politics in early sixteenth-century Central Asia." *Central Asiatic journal* 27.1–2 (1983) 121–48. ISSN 0008-9192. ▸ Valuable study of Uzbek assimilation of Timu-

rid cultural traditions, court patronage, and cultural activities as legitimizing principle. [JG]

9.264 Maria Subtelny. "Socio-economic bases of cultural patronage under the later Timurids." *International journal of Middle East studies* 20 (1988) 479–505. ISSN 0020-7438. ▸ Explains paradox between political decline/decentralization and cultural efflorescence in late fifteenth-century Timurid realm. Meticulous investigation of landholding and tax-immunity systems. Reveals connection between base of patronage and socioeconomic institutions. [JG]

9.265 W. M. Thackston, trans. *A century of princes: sources on Timurid history and art.* Cambridge, Mass.: Aga Khan Program for Islamic Architecture, 1989. ISBN 0-922673-11-X (pbk). ▸ Translations of excerpted Persian texts to accompany exhibition of Timurid art. Useful sampling, but little background information on sources and no apparent overall focus. [JG]

9.266 John E. Woods. "The rise of Timurid historiography." *Journal of Near Eastern studies* 46.12 (1987) 81–108. ISSN 0022-2968. ▸ Detailed study of formation of Timur's biography. Best and most thorough study of primary sources in development of Timurid tradition. Includes relevance of patronage networks, political succession struggles, and relationships between nomadic and sedentary lifestyles in Iran and Central Asia. [JG]

9.267 John E. Woods. *The Timurid dynasty.* Bloomington: Indiana University, Research Institute for Inner Asian Studies, 1990. (Papers on Inner Asia, 14.) ISSN 0893-1860. ▸ Largely based on manuscript, the *Muʿizz al-Ansâb (Glorifier of Genealogies)*. List of Timur's immediate family, wives, and concubines. Major contribution to understanding Timurid family and sociopolitical culture. [JG]

9.268 John E. Woods. "Timur's genealogy." In *Intellectual studies on Islam: essays written in honor of Martin B. Dickson.* Michel M. Mazzaoui and Vera B. Moreen, eds., pp. 85–125. Salt Lake City: University of Utah Press, 1990. ISBN 0-87480-342-X. ▸ Discussion of legendary background and authenticity of sources, making use of many rare and unpublished materials. Indispensible source for rise of Timur, ideology of Timurid family tradition, and significance of Chinggisid custom and law. [JG]

Tibet and the Mongols

9.269 Herbert Franke. "Tibetans in Yuan China." In *China under Mongol rule.* John D. Langlois, ed., pp. 296–328. Princeton: Princeton University Press, 1981. ISBN 0-691-03127-4 (cl), 0-691-10110-8 (pbk). ▸ Interesting study of varied roles of certain Tibetans at Yüan court. Based largely on Chinese sources and contains useful information and details not adduced elsewhere. [ES]

9.270 Leonard W. J. van der Kuijp. "On the life and career of Ta'i-si-tu Byang-chub rgyal-mtshan (1302–?1364)." In *Tibetan history and language: studies dedicated to Uray Geza on his seventieth birthday.* Ernst Steinkellner, ed., pp. 277–327. Vienna: Universität Wien, Arbeitskreis für tibetische und buddhistische Studien, 1991. (Wiener Studien zur Tibetologie und Buddhismuskunde, 26.) ▸ Important biographical study of major Tibetan figure who ousted Mongol-allied Sa-skya-pa sect from position of dominance in Tibet in mid-fourteenth century. Main source is Byang-chub-rgyal-mtshan's autobiographical account of his times; difficult but very valuable work. [ES]

9.271 Ariane Macdonald. "Préambule à la lecture d'un *Rgya-Bod Yig-chan.*" *Journal asiatique* 251 (1963) 53–159. ISSN 0021-762X. ▸ Important, detailed study of fifteenth-century *Rgya-Bod yig-tshang* (A Storehouse of Documents of China and Tibet). Deals with a variety of topics, including sects-administration, history of religious lineages, Mongol-Tibetan relations, and Sino-Tibetan relations. [ES]

9.272 Luciano Petech. *Central Tibet and the Mongols: the Yuan*

Sa-skya period of Tibetan history. Rome: Istituto Italiano per il Medio ed Estremo Oriente, 1990. (Serie Orientale Roma, 65.) ‣ Succinct and comprehensive survey of thirteenth- and four- teenth-century Tibetan-Mongol relations drawn from studies of major Tibetan and Chinese sources on subject. [ES]

9.273 Luciano Petech. "Sang-ko, a Tibetan statesman in Yuan China." In *Selected papers on Asian History*, pp. 395–412. Rome: Istituto Italiano per il Medio ed Estremo Oriente, 1988. (Serie Orientale Roma, 60.) ‣ Important study of prominent political figure in Yüan China who served at court of Qubilai (first iden- tified as Tibetan by Petech in this 1980 paper) with major respon- sibility for realm's financial administration. In addition to bio- graphical information, important information about Tibet under Mongol domination. [ES]

EARLY MODERN CENTRAL ASIA, 1450–1850

Volga and Crimean Khanates

9.274 Alexandre A. Bennigsen et al. *Le khanat de Crimée dans les Archives du Musée du Palais de Topkapi.* Paris: Mouton, 1978. ‣ Essential collection of documents dated 1435–1790 in Crimean Tatar and Ottoman Turkish concerning Crimean khanate. Authoritative biographies of Crimean khans and notables, tables of rulers, glossary, and annotated bibliography of sources. [US]

9.275 Alexandre A. Bennigsen and Chantal Lemercier- Quelquejay. "La Grande Horde Nogay et le problème des com- munications entre l'empire Ottoman et l'Asie Centrale en 1552– 1556." *Turcica* 8.2 (1976) 203–36. ISSN 0082-6847. ‣ Ottoman documents on Nogay Horde with authoritative sketch of Nogay history in sixteenth century. [US]

9.276 Alton S. Donnelly. *The Russian conquest of Bashkiria, 1552–1740: a case study in imperialism.* New Haven: Yale Uni- versity Press, 1968. ‣ Russian expansion into Bashkiria, Kazakh territory; colonial administration of southeastern frontier. [US]

9.277 Alan W. Fisher. *The Russian annexation of the Crimea, 1722–1783.* Cambridge: Cambridge University Press, 1970. ‣ Standard treatment of Russian conquest of Crimean khanate and treaties of annexation based on Russian and Ottoman sources. [US]

9.278 J. Hammer-Purgstall. *Geschichte der Chane der Krim unter osmanischer Herrschaft, vom fünfzehnten Jahrhundert bis zum Ende des achtzehnten Jahrhundert als Anhang zur Geschichte des osma- nischen Reichs zusammengetragen aus turkischen Quellen.* 1856 ed. Amsterdam: Philo, 1970. ISBN 90-6022-100-1. ‣ Political history of Crimean khans based on Crimean and Ottoman sources. Dated but still useful. [US]

9.279 Halil Inalcik. "The khan and the tribal aristocracy: the Crimean khanate under Sahib Giray I." In *Eucharisterion: essays presented to Omeljan Pritsak on his sixtieth birthday by his colleagues and students.* 2 vols. Ihor Ševčenko and Frank E. Sysyn, eds., pp. 445–66. Cambridge, Mass.: Harvard Ukrainian Research Insti- tute, 1980. (Harvard Ukrainian studies, 3–4.) ISSN 0363-5570. ‣ Description of relationship between khan and four tribal leaders under Ṣâḥib Giray I on basis of *Ta'rîḥ-i Ṣâḥib Giray Khan.* Useful study. [US]

9.280 Josef Matuz. "Qalġa." *Turcica* 2 (1970) 101–129. ISSN 0082-6847. ‣ Detailed study of the institution of *qalgha* referring to designated successor to Crimean khan, including etymology and list of holders of office from end of sixteenth to late seven- teenth century. [US]

9.281 Mirkasyn Abdulakhatovich Usmanov. *Tatarskie istoriche- skie istochniki XVII–XVIII vv.* (Tatar historical sources of the seventeenth to eighteenth centuries). Kazan: Izdatel'stvo Kazan- skogo Universiteta, 1972. ‣ Standard survey of Kazan Tatar his-

torical sources written in seventeenth and eighteenth centuries, often including valuable data on earlier periods. [US]

9.282 V. V. Vel'iaminov-Zernov. *Izsledovanie o kasimovskikh tsariakh i tsarevichakh, i-iv* (A study of the Kasimov kings and crown princes). 4 vols. St. Petersburg, 1863–87. (Trudy vostoch- nogo otedeleniia imperatorskogo russkogo arkheologicheskogo obshchestva, 9–12.) ‣ Classic study and only work on Kasimov khanate; khanate linked with rulers of Kazan khanate, but in Muscovite service in fifteenth to seventeenth centuries. Based on wide range of Slavic, Turkic, and other sources. [US]

SEE ALSO
    34.176 Jaroslaw Pelenski. *Russia and Kazan.*
    34.318 Andreas Kappeler. *Russlands erste Nationalitäten.*

The Uzbek Khanates

9.283 Abul-Ghazi Bahadur Khan [Khan of Khiva]. *Histoire des Mongols et des Tatares par Aboul-Ghazi Behadour Khan.* 1871–74 ed. Petr I. Desmaisons, ed. and trans. Amsterdam: Philo, 1970. ISBN 90-6022-093-5. ‣ Important indigenous source written by khan of Khiva covering history of Khiva from rise of Mongol world empire to mid-seventeenth century. [US]

9.284 Buri Akhmedov. *Istoriko-geograficheskaia literatura Srednei Azii, XVI–XVIII vv. (pis'mennye pamiatniki)* (The historico-geo- graphical literature of Central Asia, sixteenth to eighteenth cen- turies [written monuments]). Tashkent: Fan, 1985. ‣ Survey of sources describing authors, manuscripts, and contents of pub- lished and unpublished works in Persian and Turkic. [US]

9.285 Edward A. Allworth. *The modern Uzbeks: from the four- teenth century to the present, a cultural history.* Stanford, Calif.: Hoover Institution Press, 1990. ISBN 0-8179-8731-2 (cl), 0-8179- 8732-0 (pbk). ‣ Useful but uneven description of formation of modern Uzbek nation and political and cultural history in nine- teenth and twentieth centuries. [US]

9.286 Yuri Bregel. "Introduction." In *Firdaws al-Iqbal: history of Khorezm.* Yuri Bregel, ed., pp. 1–58. Leiden: Brill, 1988. ISBN 90- 04-08314-6. ‣ Introduction to Turkic historical sources relating to Khwârazm from 1550 to nineteenth century focusing on careers of Munis and Agahi and historical work *Firdaws al-iqbâl.* [US]

9.287 Yuri Bregel. "Tribal tradition and dynastic history: the early rulers of the Qongrats according to Munis." *Asian and Afri- can studies* 16 (1982) 357–98. ISSN 0571-2472. ‣ Translation and commentary of history of ancestors of Qongrat rulers in thir- teenth to seventeenth centuries excerpted from nineteenth cen- tury *Firdaws al-iqbâl* of Munis and Agahi. [US]

9.288 M. B. Dickson. "Shah Tahmasb and the Uzbeks: the duel for Khurasan with Ubayd Khan, 930–46/1524–40." Ph.D. dis- sertation. Princeton: Princeton University, 1958. ‣ Standard work on Uzbeks and Safavids, 1524–40. Available on microfilm from Ann Arbor: University Microfilms International, 1983. [US]

9.289 Mansura Haider. "Agrarian system in the Uzbek khanates of Central Asia, sixteenth–seventeenth centuries." *Turcica* 7 (1975) 157–78. ISSN 0082-6847. ‣ Concise summary of Uzbek sedentarization, various categories of land use, land grants, rev- enues, irrigation, and conditions of peasants. [US]

9.290 S. K. Ibragimov et al., eds. and trans. *Materialy po istorii kazakhskikh xanstv XV–XVII vekov* (Materials on the history of the Kazakh khanates of the fifteenth to seventeenth centuries). Alma-Ata: Nauka, 1969. ‣ Valuable collection of translated excerpts from Persian and Turkic sources related to Kazakh and Uzbek khanates of fifteenth to eighteenth centuries. [US]

9.291 P. P. Ivanov. *Ocherki po istorii Srednei Azii (XVI–seredina XIX v.)* (Sketches of the history of Central Asia [sixteenth to mid- nineteenth centuries]). Moscow, 1958. ‣ Authoritative outline of

Central Asian history from sixteenth to mid-nineteenth century. [US]

9.292 Beatrice Forbes Manz. "Central Asian uprisings in the nineteenth century: Ferghana under the Russians." *Russian review* 46 (1987) 267–81. ISSN 0036-0341. ▸ Argues that nomadic elements in Kokand khanate turned to Ṣūfī shaikhs for political leadership following Russian conquest and that violence was not a result of Russian occupation but of structure and politics of former Kokand khanate. Useful study. [US]

9.293 Robert D. McChesney. "The amirs of Muslim Central Asia in the seventeenth century." *Journal of the economic and social history of the Orient* 26.1 (1983) 33–70. ISSN 0022-4995. ▸ Important study of source of authority, education, career, personal wealth, and relations with other classes of Muslim emirs of Tuqay-Timurid (Ashtarkhanid, Janid) house. [US]

9.294 Vladimir Petrovich Nalivkine. *Histoire du khanat de Khokand.* Auguste Dozon, trans. Paris: Ledoux, 1889. (Publications de l'École des Langues Orientales Vivantes, Troisième série, 4.) ▸ Survey of rulers of Kokand khanate focusing on nineteenth century; based on indigenous narrative histories, early Western scholarship, and official acts from local archives. [US]

9.295 Martha Brill Olcott. *The Kazakhs.* Stanford, Calif.: Hoover Institution Press, 1987. ISBN 0-8179-8381-3 (cl), 0-8179-8382-1 (pbk). ▸ Standard survey of Kazakh history from origins to rise of a modern nation based on Russian sources. [US]

9.296 Bertold Spuler. "Central Asia: the last centuries of independence." In *The Muslim World: a historical survey.* Bertold Spuler. F.R.C. Bagley, trans., vol. 3, pp. 219–59. Leiden: Brill, 1969. ▸ Concise political history of Central Asia in fifteenth to nineteenth centuries. [US]

Mongol Successor States, Early Manchus

9.297 David Farquhar. "Mongolian versus Chinese elements in the early Manchu state." *Ch'ing-shih wen-t'i* (Bulletin for the society of Ch'ing studies) 2.6 (1971) 11–23. ISSN 0884-3236. ▸ Carefully details importance of Mongolian influence on Manchu military organization. [RWD]

9.298 Joseph F. Fletcher, Jr. "Ch'ing Inner Asia c. 1800." In *The Cambridge history of China.* Denis Twitchett and John K. Fairbank, eds., vol. 10.1, pp. 35–106. New York: Cambridge University Press, 1978. ISBN 0-521-21447-5 (set). ▸ Discusses Ch'ing incorporation and administration of Manchuria, Mongolia, Sinkiang, and Tibet. General social, political, and economic outline with emphasis on Ch'ing goals and policies. [EEW]

9.299 Joseph F. Fletcher, Jr. "The heyday of the Ch'ing order in Mongolia, Sinkiang, and Tibet." In *The Cambridge history of China.* Denis Twitchett and John K. Fairbank, eds., vol. 10.1, pp. 351–408. New York: Cambridge University Press, 1978. ISBN 0-521-21447-5 (set). ▸ Describes expansion of Chinese empire into Inner Asia to detriment of economic and political fortunes of Mongols, Muslims, and Tibetans. Stresses different Manchu policies and results in each of three regions. [EEW]

9.300 Junko Miyawaki. "The Qalqa Mongols and the Oyirad in the seventeenth century." *Journal of Asian history* 18.2 (1984) 136–73. ISSN 0021-910X. ▸ Discussion of internal organization of Khalkha and Oyirad Mongols before their final conquest by and incorporation into Ch'ing empire. Five useful genealogical tables appended. [EEW]

9.301 Dmitri Dmitrievich Pokotilov. *History of the eastern Mongols during the Ming dynasty from 1368 to 1364.* 1947–49 ed. Wolfgang Franke, ed. Rudolf Lowenthal, trans. Philadelphia: Porcupine, 1976. ISBN 0-87991-602-8. ▸ Uses Chinese sources, mainly Ming dynastic history, to trace Mongolian-Chinese relations and

internal events among Mongols. Essential addenda and corrigenda supplied by Franke. [EEW]

9.302 M. Sandorj. *Manchu Chinese colonial rule in northern Mongolia.* Urgungge Onon, trans. New York: St. Martin's, 1980. ISBN 0-312-51249-X. ▸ Detailed economic history of Chinese trade in Mongolia from seventeenth to early twentieth century. Concentrates on negative effects of such trade on Mongols' pastoral economy. [EEW]

9.303 Henry Serruys. *The Mongols and Ming China: customs and history.* Françoise Aubin, ed. London: Variorum, 1987. ISBN 0-86078-210-7. ▸ Collection of eight valuable articles published 1945–75. Article on surviving Mongolian customs in Ming China discusses Mongolian influences on government institutions, material life, and marriage customs. [EEW]

9.304 Henry Serruys. *The tribute system and diplomatic missions (1400–1600).* Vol. 2 of *Sino-Mongol relations during the Ming.* Brussels: Institut Belge des Hautes Études Chinoises, 1967. ▸ Highly detailed discussion of protocol and substance of trade, emphasizing Mongols' motives, needs, and points of view. [EEW]

9.305 Il'ia Iakovlevich Zlatkin. *Istoriia Dzhungarskogo khanstva (1635–1758)* (History of the Jungarian khanate [1635–1758]). 2d ed. Moscow: Nauka, 1983. ▸ Detailed study of western Mongols, formation of Jungar khanate, Jungar wars, and final annihilation by Ch'ing dynasty. Only such book-length treatment of Ch'ing period western Mongols. [EEW]

Early Modern Tibet

9.306 Zahiruddin Ahmad. *Sino-Tibetan relations in the seventeenth century.* Rome: Istituto Italiano per il Medio ed Estremo Oriente, 1970. (Serie Orientale Roma, 40.) ▸ Major study of Tibet's international relations in seventeenth century and establishment of Dge-lugs-pa political dominance. [ES]

9.307 Gos Lo-tsa-ba Gzon-nu dpal. *The Blue Annals.* 1976 2d ed. George N. Roerich, ed. and trans. Delhi: Motilal Banarsidass, 1979. ▸ Full translation of fifteenth-century *Deb-ther sngon-po* by Gos Lo-tsa-ba Gzon-nu dpal, important Tibetan example of Tibetan Buddhist historiography. Indexes clarify or identify personages, teaching lineages, and geographical names. [ES]

9.308 Luciano Petech. *China and Tibet in the early eighteenth century.* 2d rev. ed. Leiden: Brill, 1972. (*T'oung Pao*, Monographie, 1.) ▸ Thoroughly revised version of author's 1950 monograph of same title. Classic study of Tibet's incorporation into Ch'ing empire. [ES]

MODERN CENTRAL ASIA SINCE 1850

Tsarist Conquest and Rule

9.309 Edward A. Allworth, ed. *Central Asia: one hundred and twenty years of Russian rule.* Rev. ed. Durham, N.C.: Duke University Press, 1989. ISBN 0-8223-0912-2 (cl), 0-8223-0930-0 (pbk). ▸ Authoritative survey by different authors of geography, ethnography, economy, culture, and modern history. Original title: *Central Asia: A Century of Russian Rule.* [US]

9.310 Edward A. Allworth, ed. *Tatars of the Crimea, their struggle for survival: original studies from North America, unofficial and official documents from czarist and Soviet sources.* Durham, N.C.: Duke University Press, 1988. ISBN 0-8223-0758-8. ▸ Includes studies of Ismail Bey Gaspirali and modernism, translations of essays from early twentieth century, additional sources on modern national leaders, relations with Russia, and family relations. Useful collection. [US]

9.311 Audrey L. Altstadt. *The Azerbaijani Turks: power and identity under Russian rule.* Stanford, Calif.: Hoover Institution Press, 1992. ISBN 0-8179-9181-6 (cl), 0-8179-9182-4 (pbk). ▸ Standard survey of Azeri history from earliest times but focusing on nineteenth and twentieth centuries based on extensive use of Azeri and Russian sources. [US]

9.312 Seymour Becker. *Russia's protectorates in Central Asia: Bukhara and Khiva, 1865–1925.* Cambridge, Mass.: Harvard University Press, 1968. (Russian Research Center studies, 54.) ▸ Detailed study of Russian conquest and colonial administration of Bukhara and Khiva from perspective of history of Russian expansion and its sources. [US]

9.313 Hélène Carrere d'Encausse. *Islam and the Russian empire: reform and revolution in Central Asia.* Quintin Hoare, trans. Berkeley: University of California Press, 1988. ISBN 0-520-06504-2. ▸ Authoritative study of Bukhara from nineteenth century to early Soviet period including reform and national movements based on Western, Russian, and indigenous sources. [US]

9.314 Baymirza Hayit. *Turkestan zwischen Russland und China: eine ethnographische, kulturelle, und politische Darstellung zur Geschichte der nationalen Staaten und des nationalen Kampfes Turkestans im Zeitalter der russischen und chinesischen Expansion vom achtzenten bis ins zwanzigsten Jahrhundert.* Amsterdam: Philo, 1971. (Türk Kültürünü Araştırma Enstitüsü yayınları, 37.) ISBN 90-6022-347-0. ▸ Russian and Chinese expansion into Central Asia, Russian colonial administration, rise of national movement under Russian and Soviet domination. Invaluable for use of Western, Russian, and indigenous sources. [US]

9.315 Sirri Hakan Kirimli. "National movements and national identity among the Crimean Tatars (1905–1916)." Ph.D. dissertation. Madison: University of Wisconsin, 1990. ▸ Detailed study of stages of identity formation in Crimea, from broader Turkic Muslim approach of Ismail Bey Gaspirali to narrower territorial nationalism of Young Tatars. [US]

9.316 Chantal Lemercier-Quelquejay. "Les missions orthodoxes en pays musulmans de moyenne-et-basse-Volga, 1552–1865." *Cahiers du monde russe et soviétique* 8.3 (1967) 369–403. ISSN 0008-0160. ▸ Fundamental survey of Russian administration and religious policies toward Muslims of Volga region, establishment of Orthodox institutions, policies toward converted Tatars (Krashens), and final reaction of Muslims. [US]

9.317 Ole Olufsen. *The emir of Bokhara and his country: journeys and studies in Bokhara (with a chapter on my voyage on the Amu Darya to Khiva).* Copenhagen: Nordisk, 1911. ▸ Excellent survey of geography, climate, vegetation, animals, peoples, housing, communication, transportation, religion, religious establishments, tombs, games, disease, medicine, food, narcotics, dress, agriculture, towns, and emir and officials in his government. [US]

9.318 Richard A. Pierce. *Russian Central Asia, 1867–1917: a study in colonial rule.* Berkeley: University of California Press, 1960. ▸ Highly recommended study of conquest and colonial administration of Central Asia featuring systematic treatment of wide range of topics in economic development of territory (land tenure, taxation, water law), and other subjects. Based on Russian sources reflecting perspective of center. [US]

9.319 Azade-Ayşe Rorlich. *The Volga Tatars: a profile in national resilience.* Stanford, Calif.: Hoover Institution Press, 1986. ISBN 0-8179-8391-0 (cl), 0-8179-8392-9 (pbk). ▸ Standard survey of Volga Tatars (or Kazan Tatars) including Volga Bulgarian, Golden Horde, and Kazan khanate periods but focusing on Russian conquest (1552) and later, especially nineteenth and twentieth centuries, based on extensive use of Tatar and Russian sources. [US]

9.320 Michael Rywkin, ed. *Russian colonial expansion to 1917.* 3 vols. London: Mansell, 1988. (ASN series in issue studies [USSR and Eastern Europe], 4. Institute of Muslim Minority Affairs,

Monograph series, 1.) ISBN 0-7201-1867-0. ▸ Collective work offering succinct authoritative surveys of Russian conquest and administration of Far North, Volga region, Crimea, Caucasus, Kazakh steppe, and Turkistan. [US]

9.321 Eugene Schuyler. *Turkistan: notes of a journey in Russian Turkistan, Khokand, Bukhara, and Kuldja.* New York: Scribner, Armstrong, 1876. ▸ Travels of American diplomat to Central Asia in nineteenth century; important source. Available in abridged edition (New York: Praeger, 1966). Original available on microfilm from Cambridge, Mass.: Harvard University Library Microreproduction Service, 1 reel. [US]

Modernization Movements

9.322 Alexandre A. Bennigsen and Chantal Lemercier-Quelquejay. *La presse et les mouvements nationaux chez les musulmans de Russie avant 1920.* Paris: Mouton, 1964. (Les mouvements nationaux chez les musulmans de la Russie, 2.) ▸ Useful study of rise of publishing and journalism among Muslims of Russia to 1920 with bibliography of indigenous publications. [US]

9.323 Cyril Edwin Black et al. *The modernization of Inner Asia.* Armonk, N.Y.: Sharpe, 1991. ISBN 0-87332-778-0. ▸ Discussion of premodern heritage, political, social, economic, and educational institutions within regional and international context. Highlights patterns of adaptation to modern world and its values. Useful synthesis. [PBG]

9.324 Edward J. Lazzerini. "Beyond renewal: the jadid response to pressure for change in the modern age." In *Muslims in Central Asia: expressions of identity and change.* Jo-Ann Gross, ed., pp. 151–66. Durham, N.C.: Duke University Press, 1992. ISBN 0-8223-1187-9 (cl), 0-8223-1190-9 (pbk). ▸ Clearest summary of Islamic modernism movement known among Muslim Turks of Russia as jadidism focusing on careers of Abu Nasir Kursavi (b. 1783) and Ismail Bey Gasprinskii (Gaspirali, 1851–1914). [US]

9.325 Edward J. Lazzerini. "Ethnicity and the uses of history: the case of the Volga Tatars and jadidism." *Central Asian survey* 1.2–3 (1982) 61–69. ISSN 0263-4937. ▸ Useful study treating response of Soviet historiography to Islamic modernist movement known as jadidism focusing on early favorable view later superceded by hostility in Stalinist period. [US]

9.326 Edward J. Lazzerini. "Ğadidism at the turn of the twentieth century: a view from within." *Cahiers du monde russe et soviétique* 16.2 (1975) 245–77. ISSN 0008-0160. ▸ Translates 1901 essay by Ismail Bey Gasprinskii (Gaspirali), "First Steps toward Civilizing the Russian Muslim," including discussions of books, schools, students, women, treaters, charitable trusts, publishing houses, and lists of books, with introduction and extensive notes on reformist leaders. Useful study. [US]

9.327 Chantal Lemercier-Quelquejay. "Abdul Kayum al-Nasyri: a Tatar reformer of the nineteenth century." *Central Asian survey* 1.4 (1983) 109–32. ISSN 0263-4937. ▸ Examines legacy of Abdul Kayum al-Nasyri as first great Kazan Tatar *Kulturträger* responsible for developing modern literary language, translating numerous scientific works, studying Tatar customs, and continuing historical research of Shihabeddin Merjani. [US]

9.328 Uli Schamiloglu. "The formation of a Tatar historical consciousness: Şihabaddin Marcani and the image of the Golden Horde." *Central Asian survey* 9.2 (1990) 39–49. ISSN 0263-4937. ▸ Argument that Shihabeddin Merjani created modern Tatar national identity in formative work of national history arguing for territorial nation, inventing continuity with past on basis of name "Tatar" where there actually has been discontinuity. Useful study. [US]

9.329 Tadeusz Swietochowski. *Russian Azerbaijan, 1905–1920:*

the shaping of national identity in a Muslim community. Cambridge: Cambridge University Press, 1985. ISBN 0-521-26310-7. ▸ Transformation from Muslim identity to modern Azeri nation studied through extensive use of indigenous sources in Azeri and Turkish as well as Russian and other sources. Important work. [US]

9.330 Serge Zenkovsky. *Pan-Turkism and Islam in Russia.* Cambridge, Mass.: Harvard University Press, 1960. (Russian Research Center studies, 36.) ▸ Systematic survey of various national movements among Tatars, Azeris, and others. Covers Islamic identities, pan-Turkism, and smaller territorial nationalisms. Some use of indigenous sources. [US]

Modern Tibet

9.331 Melvyn C. A. Goldstein. *A history of modern Tibet, 1913–1951: the demise of the Lamaist state.* Berkeley: University of California Press, 1989. ISBN 0-520-06140-3. ▸ Most detailed history of Tibet available; details political and systemic factors leading to loss of independence. Particularly significant for use of extensive oral data (interviews with many participants in and eyewitnesses to events described). [ES]

9.332 Alastair Lamb. *Tibet, China, and India, 1914–1950: a history of imperial diplomacy.* Hertingfordbury, England: Roxford Books, 1989. ISBN 0-907129-03-X. ▸ Although based exclusively on English-language materials, presents useful account of diplomatic activity concerning Tibet during last period of independence. Extensive use of official British archival records. [ES]

9.333 Nai-min Ling, comp. *Tibet, 1950–1967.* 1964 ed. Hong Kong: Union Research Institute, 1968. ▸ Compilation of Chinese documents and news reports issued 1950–67, dealing with various aspects of situation in Tibet. Documents are all in English translation and classified by period and subject. Earlier title: *Tibetan Sourcebook.* [ES]

9.334 Luciano Petech. *Aristocracy and government in Tibet, 1728–1959.* Rome: Istituto Italiano per il Medio ed Estremo Oriente, 1973. (Serie Orientale Roma, 45.) ▸ Important, highly detailed study of genealogies of major aristocratic families of central Tibet, based on literary and oral sources. [ES]

9.335 Heather Stoddard. *Le mendiant de l'Amdo.* Paris: Société d'Ethnographie, 1985. (Recherches sur la Haute Asie, 9.) ISBN 2-901161-28-6 (pbk). ▸ Biography of Dge-'dun chos-'phel, one of leading Tibetan intellectuals in pre-1950 Tibet. Although somewhat subjective in parts, contains much information about intellectual environment in Tibet during lifetime of its subject. Largely based on Tibetan literary and oral sources. [ES]

Modern Mongolia

9.336 Charles R. Bawden. *The modern history of Mongolia.* 2d rev. ed. New York: Kegan Paul, 1989. ISBN 0-7103-0326-2 (pbk). ▸ Chronological survey covering period from seventeenth century to mid-1960s with Afterword by Alan J. K. Sanders as update to 1968. Concentrates on Khalkha and Mongolian People's Republic. [EEW]

9.337 Walther Heissig. *A lost civilization: the Mongols rediscovered.* D.J.S. Thomson, trans. New York: Basic Books, 1966. ▸ Intended for wide readership; impressionistic survey concentrating on cultural history. Much based on author's eyewitness observations and extensive readings in Mongolian literature. [EEW]

9.338 Owen Lattimore and Urgungge Onon. *Nationalism and revolution in Mongolia.* New York: Oxford University Press, 1955. ▸ Part 1, by Lattimore, surveys Mongolian history from seventeenth century to death of Choibalsang in 1952. Part 2, by Lat-timore and Urgungge Onon, translation of dated but still useful *The Life of Sukhebatur* by Sh. Nachukdorji. [EEW]

9.339 Robert James Miller. *Monasteries and culture change in Inner Mongolia.* Wiesbaden: Harrassowitz, 1959. (Asiatische Forschungen, 2.) ▸ Unsurpassed study of internal dynamics of monastery life and of role of monastery in Manchu-Chinese-Mongolian politics in eighteenth to early twentieth centuries. Views Lamaism and its institutions as beneficial to Mongols. [EEW]

9.340 S. Rasidondug and Veronica Veit, trans. *Petitions of grievances submitted by the people (eighteenth to beginning of twentieth century).* Wiesbaden: Harrassowitz, 1975. (Asiatische Forschungen, 45.) ISBN 3-447-01650-7. ▸ Translation of *Ardyn zargyn bicig*, compiled by Ts. Nasanbalzir and S. Natsagdorz, selection of documents published in Ulan Bator in 1966. Rich in legal and social history, particularly disputes between Khalkha Mongolian banner princes and their subjects. Documents date from 1739 to 1919. [EEW]

9.341 Robert A. Rupen. *How Mongolia is really ruled: a political history of the Mongolian People's Republic, 1900–1978.* Stanford, Calif.: Hoover Institution Press, 1979. ISBN 0-8179-7122-X. ▸ Views Mongolian People's Republic in context of Soviet influence, ideological issues, and Sino-Soviet relations. Useful appendixes contain biographical notices on political figures. [EEW]

9.342 Alan J. K. Sanders. *Mongolia: politics, economics, and society.* Boulder: Rienner, 1987. ISBN 0-931477-37-9 (cl), 0-931477-38-7 (pbk). ▸ Concentrates on period 1921 to 1986 with emphasis on politics and ideological motivation behind domestic and foreign policies. Organized in straightforward, handbooklike style and accompanied by fourteen useful tables. [EEW]

9.343 Bagaryn Shirendyb et al., eds. *History of the Mongolian People's Republic.* William A. Brown and Urgungge Onon, trans. and annotators. Cambridge, Mass.: Harvard University, East Asian Research Center, 1976. (Harvard East Asian monographs, 65.) ISBN 0-674-39862-9. ▸ Official version compiled by Mongol historians using Marxist historical analysis for period 1921 to 1966. One hundred pages of indispensible notes provided by translators. [EEW]

Under Communist Rule

9.344 Alexandre A. Bennigsen and Chantal Lemercier-Quelquejay. *Le "sultangalievisme" au Tatarstan.* Paris: Mouton, 1960. (Société et ideologies, 2. Documents et temoignages, 3. Les Mouvements nationaux chez les musulmans de la Russie, 1.) ISBN 0-686-22176-1. ▸ Rise of Kazan Tatar nationalism and career of Mir-Said Sultan Galiev, member of Central Muslim Commissariat dismissed in 1923 for Muslim national communist activities; translations of his essays. Useful work. [US]

9.345 Alexandre A. Bennigsen and S. Enders Wimbush. *Muslim National Communism in the Soviet Union: a revolutionary strategy for the colonial world.* Chicago: University of Chicago Press, 1979. ISBN 0-226-04235-9 (cl). ▸ Reconciliation of Marxist nationalism and Islam by Mir-Said Sultan Galiev and contemporaries. Detailed appendixes include essays by leading figures, their biographies, and party platforms. [US]

9.346 Olaf K. Caroe. *The Soviet empire: the Turks of Central Asia and Stalinism.* 2d ed. New York: St. Martin's, 1967. ▸ Russian expansion into and Soviet domination of Central Asia with focus on native culture and opposition to colonial rule based on Western and Russian sources. Dated but still useful. [US]

9.347 Alan W. Fisher. *The Crimean Tatars.* Stanford, Calif.: Hoover Institution Press, 1978. ISBN 0-8179-6661-7 (cl), 0-8179-6662-5 (pbk). ▸ Standard survey of history of Crimean khanate, rise of modern Crimean Tatar nation, and Crimean national movement in Soviet period based on Crimean and Russian sources. [US]

9.348 Gregory J. Massell. *The surrogate proletariat: Muslim women and revolutionary strategies in Soviet Central Asia, 1919–1929*. Princeton: Princeton University Press, 1974. ISBN 0-691-07562-X. ‣ Fundamental work on role of women in modern Central Asia from their role in society at time of conquest to their exploitation as tool of revolutionary change in Central Asia and their response to this based on Russian sources. [US]

9.349 Hasan B. Paksoy. *Alpamysh: Central Asian identity under Russian rule*. Hartford, Conn.: Association for the Advancement of Central Asian Research, 1989. ISBN 0-9621379-9-5 (cl), 0-9621379-0-1 (pbk). ‣ Useful case study of Central Asian epic, *Alpamysh*, and its manipulation in process of identity formation in Russian and Soviet periods. [US]

9.350 Michael Rywkin. *Moscow's Muslim challenge: Soviet Central Asia*. Rev. ed. Armonk, N.Y.: Sharpe, 1990. ISBN 0-87332-613-X (cl), 0-87332-614-8 (pbk). ‣ Concise overview of Central Asia under Russian and Soviet domination with emphasis on political, social, and economic aspects contributing to national resistance. [US]

SEE ALSO

35.80 Richard Pipes. *The formation of the Soviet Union.*

PATRICIA BUCKLEY EBREY

China to 1644

English-language scholarship on Chinese history has grown enormously in the last thirty years. Of the nearly four hundred items listed below, only about 10 percent were published before 1960. The explosion in scholarship on Chinese history in part reflects the general expansion of graduate education and scholarly publishing. Nevertheless, the rhythms of the growth of the field are also a product of the changing relations between the United States and China; the directions of the growth of the field, similarly, reflect trends in scholarship in East Asia as well as in the West.

Before World War II, Western study of premodern Chinese history was dominated by Sinologists, scholars who immersed themselves in Chinese culture, often living in China for long periods. They often worked closely with Chinese scholars and shared their interests in ancient history and the great figures of the past. The translations of key religious, philosophical, and historical texts that they prepared remain an important and lasting contribution. Europeans were more dominant than Americans, even when looking only at English-language works. Key figures include James Legge, J.J.L. Duyvendak, Helmut Wilhelm, Arthur Waley, and Bernhard Karlgren. After World War II, scholars able to write about China in English were as likely as not to be Chinese intellectuals who had immigrated to the United States. This generation included not only traditional humanistic scholars but also intellectuals deeply engaged by China's current problems who turned to Western theories and concepts for approaches to the study of China's past. Particularly notable works of this postwar generation are studies of China's political and economic institutions and class structure by scholars such as Lien-sheng Yang, T'ung-tsu Ch'ü, Ping-ti Ho, Cho-yun Hsu, and James T. C. Liu.

In the 1960s, when the American government and the Ford Foundation funded a major expansion of language training and graduate programs, Americans who had no prior connection to China began to study Chinese history in large numbers. They, too, often became absorbed in issues important to East Asian scholars, for they usually went to Taiwan or Japan for language study and began their dissertation research by working their way through the voluminous secondary literature in the Chinese and Japanese languages. Nevertheless, the expansion of China studies from the early 1960s on was coupled with a trend toward closer links to the larger discipline of history. As social and cultural history gained popularity, scholars of Chinese history wrote on class structure and social stratification, family and kinship, popular culture, and folk religion. Since discovering adequate sources is a major challenge for these sorts of studies, interest in these topics has reinforced the tendency for historians to research the later, better-documented periods, particularly the Sung (960–1279) and Ming (1368–1644) dynasties. By contrast, many of the most useful books on the Han period (202 BCE–220) are still those written decades ago.

Once relations between the United States and China improved after the end of the war in Vietnam and the waning of the Cultural Revolution in China, American citizens gained access to new research opportunities in China. Doctoral students were less likely to spend much time in Japan, and the general influence of Japanese scholarship declined as the influence of Chinese scholarship increased. Scholars could more easily tackle topics that required access to archives, rare books, or archaeological evidence. Greater access to China coincided with another wave of migration of Chinese (from Taiwan, Hong Kong, and mainland China), this time largely for graduate training. The prominence of these scholars in graduate programs and on university faculties is again shifting the agenda toward questions of particular importance to Chinese intellectuals.

Much that has been said above applies as much to the study of modern as premodern China. What distinguishes premodern China as a field of historical inquiry is the very strong, continuing interest in intellectual history broadly conceived (including what could be labeled history of philosophy and history of religion). One-third of the items listed below fall into this category, reflecting the leadership and lasting impact of such scholars as Herlee Creel, Derk Bodde, Wing-Tsit Chan, Arthur Wright, Benjamin Schwartz, W. Theodore De Bary, and Angus Graham. The number of important philosophical and religious texts available in English continues to increase steadily, but translations make up a smaller and smaller proportion of the works being published. As the field has grown, so too has specialization, and most scholars would identify themselves with a particular segment of the field (such as Buddhism, Taoism, Neo-Confucianism, or even narrower specialties such as Ming Neo-Confucianism or T'ang Buddhism). Numerous studies of the writings of individual teachers and thinkers, many based on Ph.D. dissertations, have greatly added to the level of detail now available in English-language works. Among the more groundbreaking studies published in recent years are those that characterize and analyze an entire school of thinkers or trace a theme through a long time span. On the whole, studies of religion and philosophy tend to focus narrowly on ideas, but there are exceptions that analyze the links between ideas and society. A few works that could be classed as cultural history have recently appeared.

Given the profusion of specialist's monographs, there is now clearly a need for new synthetic histories that will retell Chinese history in the light of recent monographic research. This need is being met in part by the large collaborative effort to produce a multivolume *Cambridge History of China*. For the first time, a detailed political history of the whole span of imperial China is gradually appearing in print. When complete, the *Cambridge History* will also include interpretive summaries of current knowledge in social, intellectual, and economic history.

A few comments on the organization of the entries that follow are warranted. First come works that defy chronological classification, mostly reference books, broad interpretive histories, and studies of special topics over time. Most scholarly works, however, cover shorter periods and are arranged according to the conventional periodization by dynasties. Because of limitations of space, only a small proportion of useful works could be listed. Preference was given to books over articles and works easily accessible to nonspecialists over scholarly monographs. Biographies, for instance, were often favored over studies of institutional history not easily penetrated by readers with no background. Even greater selectivity had to be used for books on cognate fields (art, literature, language, and philosophy). Thus readers with more specialized interests should consult the annual *Bibliography of Asian Studies* (11.1) and other listed reference works.

Finally, it should be noted that the English-language literature on Chinese history is only a small fraction of the literature published. Not only are important works published in other European languages (French, German, and Russian especially), but there is a vast and continually growing scholarly literature in Chinese and Japanese. Chinese scholars publish thousands of articles and hundreds of books on Chinese history and related topics every year. In the United States, excellent Chinese-language research libraries are to be found at the Library of Congress, Harvard, Princeton, the University of California at Berkeley, the University of Michigan, Columbia, and the University of Chicago. Some sense of the richness of publications in Chinese and Japanese can be discerned from the abstracts of scholarly publications found in the periodical, *Revue Bibliographique de Sinologie.* For those able to read Chinese and Japanese, there are numerous subject and period bibliographies and a convenient annual bibliography published in Kyoto, *Kyoto daigaku jinbun kagaku kenkyūjo kanseki bunrui mokuroku.*

Entries are arranged under the following headings:

Reference Works
  Bibliographies
  Guides, Encyclopedias, and Atlases
  Dictionaries
  Historiography

General Studies
  Surveys
  Collections of Essays
  Institutional, Military, and Diplomatic History
  Economic History
  Social History
  Literature, Art, and Language

Religion, Philosophy, and Thought
  General Studies
  Pre-Han Thought
  Han-T'ang Thought
  Buddhism
  Taoist and Folk Religion
  Sung Neo-Confucianism
  Yüan-Ming Neo-Confucianism
  Science

Ancient Period
  General Studies
  Neolithic and Shang Dynasty
  Chou Dynasty
  The Classics

Ch'in-Han to Sui Dynasties
  General Studies
  Political and Institutional History
  Economic History
  Social and Cultural History
  Historiography
  Biographies of Literary Figures

T'ang Dynasty
  General Studies
  Political History
  Institutional History
  Cultural History
  Biographies of Literary Figures

Sung Dynasty
  General Studies
  Political History and Law
  Diplomatic and Military History
  Economic History
  Social History
  Education, Examinations, and Literati Lives
  Biographies of Literary Figures

Conquest Dynasties
  General Studies
  Liao Dynasty
  Chin Dynasty
  Hsia Dynasty
  Yüan Dynasty

Ming Dynasty
  Historiography
  Economic History
  Political and Institutional History
  Social and Cultural History
  Foreign Relations

[Contributors: CH = Charles Hartman, DG = Dennis Grafflin, DKW = David K. Wyatt, DNK = David N. Keightley, HCT = Hoyt Cleveland Tillman, JWC = John W. Chaffee, MR = Morris Rossabi, MRD = Michael Robert Drompp, PBE = Patricia Buckley Ebrey, PNG = Peter N. Gregory,

RPH = Robert P. Hymes, RWD = Ruth W. Dunnell, TTA = Thomas T. Allsen, WSA = William S. Atwell]

REFERENCE WORKS

Bibliographies

10.1 Leonard H. D. Gordon and Frank Joseph Shulman, eds. and comps. *Doctoral dissertations on China: a bibliography of studies in Western languages, 1945–1970.* Seattle: University of Washington Press, 1972. (Association for Asian Studies, Reference series, 1.) ISBN 0-295-95176-1 (cl), 0-295-95193-1 (pbk). ‣ Topically arranged list of 2,271 dissertations written primarily in United States, Soviet Union, France, Germany, and other European countries. Includes translations of non-English titles and indexes. [PBE]

10.2 Charles O. Hucker. *China: a critical bibliography.* Tucson: University of Arizona Press, 1962. ‣ Annotated bibliography of over 2,000 books and articles on China, primarily in English, written between 1940 and 1960, but with important works of earlier date or written in French or German. [PBE]

10.3 Gilbert Rozman, ed. *Soviet studies of premodern China: assessments of recent scholarship.* Ann Arbor: University of Michigan, Center for Chinese Studies, 1984. (Michigan monographs in Chinese studies, 50.) ISBN 0-89264-052-9 (cl), 0-89264-053-7 (pbk). ‣ Assessments of contributions of Soviet scholars from 1960 to 1982 to study of history and literature of China to 1911, written by nine American specialists. [PBE]

10.4 Frank Joseph Shulman, ed. and comp. *Doctoral dissertations on China, 1971–1975: a bibliography of studies in Western languages.* Seattle: University of Washington Press, 1978. ISBN 0-295-95592-9 (cl), 0-295-95593-7 (pbk). ‣ Supplement to Gordon and Shulman 10.1; 1,800 listings. [PBE]

10.5 Ssu-yü Teng and Knight Biggerstaff, comps. *An annotated bibliography of selected Chinese reference works.* 3d ed. Cambridge, Mass.: Harvard University Press, 1971. (Harvard-Yenching Institute studies, 2.) ISBN 0-674-03851-7. ‣ Best available guide to Chinese-language reference works, including bibliographies, library catalogs, encyclopedias, dictionaries, atlases, biographical dictionaries, and Sinological indexes. [PBE]

Guides, Encyclopedias, and Atlases

10.6 Caroline Blunden and Mark Elvin. *Cultural atlas of China.* New York: Facts on File, 1983. ISBN 0-87196-132-6. ‣ Not so much atlas of contemporary China as lavishly illustrated survey of Chinese history and culture with generous supply of maps. [PBE]

10.7 Michael Dillon. *Dictionary of Chinese history.* London: Cass, 1979. ISBN 0-7146-3107-8. ‣ Not as complete as O'Neill 10.12, but contains many entries not in it. No references given. [PBE]

10.8 P.J.M. Geelan and Denis C. Twitchett, eds. *The Times atlas of China.* New York: Quadrangle and New York Times Book Co., 1974. ISBN 0-7230-0118-9. ‣ Large, well-prepared atlas with maps of provinces and cities, physical geography, peoples, climates, and economic conditions. Includes extensive text, Chinese characters, and indexes. [PBE]

10.9 Albert Herrmann. *An historical atlas of China.* New ed. Norton Ginsburg, ed. Chicago: Aldine, 1966. ‣ Only historical atlas giving place names in romanization, but of little use to those who read Chinese. Good indexes. [PBE]

10.10 Charles O. Hucker. *A dictionary of official titles in imperial China.* Stanford, Calif.: Stanford University Press, 1985. ISBN 0-8047-1193-3. ‣ Useful overview of evolution of Chinese government institutions. Identifies over 8,000 offices, giving English translation for each. Extensive cross-indexing. [PBE]

10.11 William H. Nienhauser, Jr., ed. and comp. *The Indiana companion to traditional Chinese literature.* Bloomington: Indiana University Press, 1986. ISBN 0-253-32983-3. ‣ Large, scholarly book with ten introductory essays followed by 500 substantial entries on famous writers, books, genres, and movements; each entry gives references to editions, studies, and translations. [PBE/RPH]

10.12 Hugh B. O'Neill. *Companion to Chinese history.* New York: Facts on File, 1987. ISBN 0-87196-841-X (cl), 0-8160-1825-1 (pbk). ‣ Handy, encyclopedialike entries on people, places, events, and institutions, with references to reliable works in English. Strongest for last two centuries but useful even for early history. [PBE]

SEE ALSO
11.31 Brian Hook and Denis Twitchett, eds. *Cambridge encyclopedia of China.*
13.1 Ainslee T. Embree, ed. *Encyclopedia of Asian history.*

Dictionaries

10.13 A. P. Cowie et al. *Concise English-Chinese Chinese-English dictionary.* Beijing and Hong Kong: Commercial Press and Oxford University Press, 1986. ISBN 0-19-584097-6 (pbk), 0-19-584048-8 (flexicover). ‣ Most convenient of compact dictionaries. First half has about 20, 000 English words, second half has about as many Chinese words arranged by *pinyin* pronunciation. [PBE]

10.14 R. H. Mathews. *Mathews' Chinese-English dictionary.* 1943 rev. ed. Cambridge, Mass.: Harvard University Press, 1979. ISBN 0-674-12350-6. ‣ Contains 7,785 characters and over 104,000 combinations. Arranged by Wade-Giles pronunciation with index by radical. Based on 1931 Shanghai edition. [PBE]

10.15 Wu Jingrong, ed. *The pinyin Chinese-English dictionary.* New York: Wiley, 1979. ISBN 0-471-86796-9. ‣ Best Chinese-English dictionary for contemporary mainland China. Over 6,000 characters and over 50,000 compound words arranged by *pinyin* pronunciation with index by nonstandard radicals. Also sold under title: *The Chinese-English Dictionary.* [PBE]

Historiography

10.16 William G. Beasley and Edwin G. Pulleyblank, eds. *Historians of China and Japan.* Vol. 3 of *Historical writing on the peoples of Asia.* London: Oxford University Press, 1961–62. 4 vols. ‣ Collected studies on periods and types of Chinese and Japanese history writing from first beginnings to this century. Final essays touch on Western historiography of "the East." [RPH]

10.17 Han Yu-shan. *Elements of Chinese historiography.* Hollywood, Calif.: Hawley, 1955. ‣ Broad survey of traditional Chinese historiography with listings of key books, glossaries of terms, and descriptions of various genres and their limitations. [PBE]

10.18 Donald D. Leslie, Colin Mackerras, and Wang Gungwu, eds. *Essays on the sources for Chinese history.* Canberra: Australian National University Press, 1973. ISBN 0-7081-0398-7. ‣ Twenty-six brief essays on uses of such sources as histories, archaeological evidence, and newspapers. Includes discussion of sources in Tibetan, Manchu, Arabic, and other languages. [PBE]

10.19 Endymion Wilkinson. *The history of imperial China: a research guide.* Cambridge, Mass.: Harvard University, East Asian Research Center, 1973. (Harvard East Asian monographs, 49.) ISBN 0-674-39680-4. ‣ Excellent introduction to materials in Chinese and Japanese for study of imperial China. How-to manual with numerous bibliographical references. [PBE]

10.20 Ernst Wolff. *Chinese studies: a bibliographic manual.* San Francisco, Calif.: Chinese Materials Center, 1981. (Chinese Materials Center, Bibliographic series, 1.) ISBN 0-89644-627-1. ‣ Listing of reference tools available to aid research in Chinese studies, usually with brief annotation. [PBE]

SEE ALSO
11.1 *Bibliography of Asian studies.*
11.17 Frank Joseph Shulman, ed. *Doctoral dissertations on Asia.*

GENERAL STUDIES

Surveys

10.21 Patricia Buckley Ebrey, ed. *Chinese civilization: a sourcebook.* Rev. ed. New York: Free Press, 1983. ISBN 0-02-908752-X. ‣ Original documents of Chinese social and cultural history in translation, arranged chronologically with editor's commentary. Usefully complements De Bary et al. 10.50 with only occasional overlap. [RPH]

10.22 John K. Fairbank and Edwin O. Reischauer. *China: tradition and transformation.* Rev. ed. Boston: Houghton-Mifflin, 1989. ISBN 0-395-49692-6. ‣ Rich textbook drawing on American scholarship on China, many illustrations. Suited to one-year courses on Chinese history. [PBE]

10.23 Jacques Gernet. *A history of Chinese civilization.* J. R. Foster, trans. Cambridge: Cambridge University Press, 1982. ISBN 0-521-24130-8 (cl), 0-521-31647-2 (pbk). ‣ Intellectually ambitious general history informed by recent developments. Basic text but with definite personal flavor. [RPH]

10.24 Charles O. Hucker. *China's imperial past: an introduction to Chinese history and culture.* Stanford, Calif.: Stanford University Press, 1975. ISBN 0-8047-0887-8. ‣ Basic, comprehensive introduction by leading scholar. Standard text. [RPH]

10.25 Michael Loewe. *The pride that was China.* New York: St. Martin's, 1990. ISBN 0-312-03739-2. ‣ Topically organized presentation of Chinese civilization by leading British Sinologist. Draws extensively on archaeological evidence. Numerous useful tables. [PBE]

10.26 Denis C. Twitchett and John K. Fairbank, eds. *The Cambridge history of China.* Cambridge: Cambridge University Press, 1978–. ISBN 0-521-21447-5 (set). ‣ Multivolume, ongoing series covering Chinese history dynasty-by-dynasty in detailed essays by period specialists. Most periods span two volumes: first offers narrative history in reign-by-reign essays, second provides overview articles on such topics as government, economy, and intellectual life. Far from introductory text, often best resort for deeper but still comprehensive treatment of individual dynasties. [RPH]

Collections of Essays

10.27 Raymond S. Dawson, ed. *The legacy of China.* Boston: Chen and Tsui, 1990. ‣ Synthesizing essays by specialists on Chinese philosophy, religion, literature, historiography, art, science, and government, examining contributions of each to present-day Western and world civilization. Ropp 10.29 is comparable, more recent effort, but Dawson collection still useful. [RPH]

10.28 John A. Harrison, ed. *China.* Vol. 1 of *Thirtieth anniversary commemorative series: enduring scholarship selected from the "Far Eastern Quarterly" and the "Journal of Asian Studies," 1941–1971.* Tucson: University of Arizona Press, 1971–72. ISBN 0-8165-0352-4. ‣ Selection of especially notable or influential essays from past issues of journal, ranging across institutional, economic, diplomatic, intellectual, and naval history, and across time from Chou dynasty to Communist period. [RPH]

10.29 Paul S. Ropp, ed. *Heritage of China: contemporary per-*

spectives on Chinese civilization. Berkeley: University of California Press, 1990. ISBN 0-520-06440-2 (cl), 0-520-06441-0 (pbk). ▸ First-rate synthesizing essays on Chinese government, thought, religion, science, family, economy, art, and literature. In some respects updates Dawson, ed. 10.27 but with more emphasis on Chinese-Western comparisons than on China's "contributions." [RPH]

Institutional, Military, and Diplomatic History

10.30 T'ung-tsu Ch'ü. *Law and society in traditional China.* Paris: Mouton, 1961. (Le Monde d'outre-mer, passé et present, Première série, Études, 4.) ▸ Useful introduction to legal structure of Chinese society, drawn from successive legal codes. Describes legal basis of family, kinship, marriage, and privileges. [PBE]

10.31 Frank A. Kierman, Jr. and John K. Fairbank, eds. *Chinese ways in warfare.* Cambridge, Mass.: Harvard University Press, 1974. ISBN 0-674-12575-4. ▸ Essays on military history and technique from Chou through Ming dynasties, usually focusing on specific campaigns or battles. Best route of entry to understudied topic. [RPH]

10.32 Taisuke Mitamura. *Chinese eunuchs: the structure of intimate politics.* Charles A. Pomeroy, trans. Rutland, Vt.: Tuttle, 1970. ISBN 0-8048-0653-5. ▸ Basic work in English on social group that constituted both recurring factor in Chinese court politics and basic theme in traditional explanations of dynastic misfortunes and falls. [RPH]

10.33 Ichisada Miyazaki. *China's examination hell: the civil service examinations of imperial China.* 1976 ed. Conrad Schirokauer, trans. New Haven: Yale University Press, 1981. ISBN 0-300-02639-0. ▸ Only general work in English on topic, useful introduction. For more specific treatment of individual periods, see Chaffee 10.307 and Ho 10.373. [RPH]

SEE ALSO
9.87 Sechin Jagchid and Van Jay Symons. *Peace, war, and trade along the Great Wall.*

Economic History

10.34 E. N. Anderson. *The food of China.* New Haven: Yale University Press, 1988. ISBN 0-300-03955-7 (cl), 0-300-04739-8 (pbk). ▸ Broad-ranging, historically organized account of development of Chinese agriculture and Chinese diet by an anthropologist. [PBE]

10.35 Kwang-chih Chang, ed. *Food in Chinese culture: anthropological and historical perspectives.* New Haven: Yale University Press, 1977. ISBN 0-300-01938-6 (cl), 0-300-02759-1 (pbk). ▸ Pioneering essays by period specialists on cuisine and eating habits of Chinese in successive dynasties and at present, with unifying introduction by editor. Emphasis on social, economic, and cultural settings. [RPH]

10.36 Kang Chao. *Man and land in Chinese history: an economic analysis.* Stanford, Calif.: Stanford University Press, 1986. ISBN 0-8047-1271-9. ▸ Provocative examination of Chinese history from demographic and economic points of view, arguing continuous existence of market economy for two thousand years and constructing labor-supply explanation for failure to develop. [RPH]

10.37 Mark Elvin. *The pattern of the Chinese past.* Stanford, Calif.: Stanford University Press, 1973. ISBN 0-8047-0826-6. ▸ Provocative and influential study of major issues in political economy from Han through Ming dynasties, seeking explanation for China's failure to maintain economic-technological lead. Draws heavily on research of Japanese Sinologists. [RPH]

SEE ALSO
11.275 W. E. Willmott, ed. *Economic organization in Chinese society.*

Social History

10.38 Patricia Buckley Ebrey and James L. Watson, eds. *Kinship organization in late imperial China, 1000–1940.* Berkeley: University of California Press, 1986. ISBN 0-520-05416-4. ▸ Collection of studies in family and kin-group history ranging from Sung dynasty through Republic; synthesizing introduction and conclusion by editors. New perspectives on origins and functions of Chinese lineages. [RPH]

10.39 Richard W. L. Guisso and Stanley Johannesen, eds. *Women in China: current directions in historical scholarship.* Youngstown, N.Y.: Philo, 1981. (Historical reflections/Réflexions historiques: directions, 3.) ISBN 0-941650-00-6. ▸ Studies of women and gender in religion, literature, and everyday life from classical period to twentieth century, with general emphasis on *mentalités.* Essays by Ames, Guisso, Ebrey, and Waltner especially strong. See also Wolf and Witke, eds. 11.229, which focuses largely on more recent period. [RPH]

10.40 Robert H. van Gulik. *Sexual life in ancient China: a preliminary survey of Chinese sex and society from ca. 1500 B.C. till 1644 A.D.* 1961 ed. Leiden: Brill, 1974. ISBN 90-04-03917-1. ▸ Founding, even precocious, work on sexuality in China, arranged chronologically with abundant literary and artistic examples and illustrations. [RPH]

10.41 Bret Hinsch. *Passions of the cut sleeve: the male homosexual tradition in China.* Berkeley: University of California Press, 1990. ISBN 0-520-06720-7. ▸ At present only book in English on homosexuality in China. Mines poetry, fiction, and historiography for material from classical times through Ch'ing dynasty. [RPH]

SEE ALSO
11.192 Maurice Freedman, ed. *Family and kinship in Chinese society.*
11.218 G. William Skinner, ed. *The city in late imperial China.*
11.229 Margery Wolf and Roxane Witke, eds. *Women in Chinese society.*

Literature, Art, and Language

10.42 Cyril Birch, ed. and comp. *Anthology of Chinese literature.* Vol. 1: *From early times to the fourteenth century.* Vol. 2: *From the fourteenth century to the present day.* New York: Grove, 1965–72. ISBN 0-394-1766-5 (v. 2). ▸ Basic, comprehensive collection of Chinese poetry, literary prose, and drama in translation, from beginnings to twentieth century. Arranged chronologically with brief but informative introductions to each section. [RPH]

10.43 James Francis Cahill. *Chinese painting.* Geneva and New York: Skira and Rizzoli International, 1985. ISBN 0-8478-0079-2. ▸ Introduction by leading scholar in field, covering Han dynasty through eighteenth century; abundant color illustrations. [RPH]

10.44 Weldon South Coblin. *A Sinologist's handlist of Sino-Tibetan lexical comparisons.* Nettetal, Germany: Steyler, 1986. (Monumenta serica, Monographs, 18.) ISBN 3-87787-208-5. ▸ Lexical correspondences between Chinese and Tibeto-Burman words here presented (ordered by English equivalents; indexes to Tibetan and Chinese forms) suggest possible reconstruction of Sino-Tibetan protoforms. Useful reference. [DNK]

10.45 Wu-chi Liu. *An introduction to Chinese literature.* 1966 ed. New York: Greenwood, 1991. ISBN 0-313-26703-0. ▸ Basic but thorough introduction to development of literary genres from earliest poetry to modern fiction and drama. Arrangement of topics and genres in relation to periods largely echoes indigenous critical traditions. [RPH]

10.46 S. Robert Ramsey. *The languages of China.* Princeton: Princeton University Press, 1987. ISBN 0-691-06694-9. ‣ General introduction to languages of China treating non-Chinese languages as well as Chinese dialects, with strong attention to social setting. Includes chapter on history of Chinese. [RPH]

10.47 Laurence C. S. Sickman and Alexander Coburn Soper. *The art and architecture of China.* 1968 3d ed. Harmondsworth: Penguin, 1978. ISBN 0-14-056010-6 (h, 1968), 0-14-056110-2 (pbk). ‣ Basic single-volume introduction. Treats art (painting and sculpture) and architecture in separate sections, each chronologically by dynasty or school. Abundant black-and-white photographic reproductions and illustrations. [RPH]

RELIGION, PHILOSOPHY, AND THOUGHT

General Studies

10.48 Derk Bodde. *Chinese thought, society, and science: the intellectual and social background of science and technology in pre-modern China.* Honolulu: University of Hawaii Press, 1991. ISBN 0-8248-1334-0. ‣ Wide-ranging, thought-provoking essay on those aspects of Chinese culture and thought that have bearing on development of science. Examines language, philosophical concepts, and approaches to nature. [PBE]

10.49 Wing-tsit Chan, trans. and comp. *A source book in Chinese philosophy.* Princeton: Princeton University Press, 1969. ISBN 0-691-01964-9. ‣ Selected important philosophical writings in translation, arranged chronologically from classical period to Communist regime, with introductions and comments by compiler. Emphasis on Confucian and Neo-Confucian traditions. Remains an indispensable source. [RPH]

10.50 Wm. Theodore De Bary, Wing-tsit Chan, and Burton Watson, eds. *Sources of Chinese tradition.* 2 vols. New York: Columbia University Press, 1960. ISBN 0-231-08602-4 (v. 1), 0-231-08603-2 (v. 2). ‣ Translated source readings in thought and culture, arranged chronologically with introductions and comments, by compilers. Founding work but still basic resource. [RPH]

10.51 Patricia Buckley Ebrey. *Confucianism and family rituals in imperial China: a social history of writing about rites.* Princeton: Princeton University Press, 1991. ISBN 0-691-03150-9. ‣ Wide-ranging examination of social and cultural process through which Confucian texts on family rituals were written, circulated, interpreted, and used as guides to action; emphasis on Chu Hsi's *Family Rituals.* [PBE]

10.52 Fung [Feng] Yu-lan. *A history of Chinese philosophy.* Vol. 1: *The period of the philosophers: from the beginnings to circa 100 B.C.* Vol. 2: *The period of classical learning: from the second century B.C. to the twentieth century A.D.* 1952 2d ed. Derk Bodde, trans. Princeton: Princeton University Press, 1983. ISBN 0-691-07114-4 (v. 1, cl), 0-691-07115-2 (v. 2, cl), 0-691-02021-3 (v. 1, pbk), 0-691-02022-1 (v. 2, pbk). ‣ Comprehensive examination of development of speculative and ethical thinking from beginnings to recent times by leading Chinese intellectual of this century. [RPH]

10.53 John B. Henderson. *The development and decline of Chinese cosmology.* New York: Columbia University Press, 1984. ISBN 0-231-05772-5 (cl), 0-231-05773-3 (pbk). ‣ Lucid analysis of Chinese correlative thinking and its development from early times with particular attention to critics of this mode of thought. [PBE]

10.54 Kung-chuan Hsiao. *A history of Chinese political thought.* Vol. 1: *From the beginnings to the sixth century A.D.* Frederick W. Mote, trans. Princeton: Princeton University Press, 1979. ISBN 0-691-03116-9 (cl), 0-691-10061-6 (pbk). ‣ Comprehensive survey (published in Chinese 1945–46) of political philosophy from

Chou through Wei-Chin dynasties; detailed anecdotal and analytical accounts of major schools and thinkers. [DNK]

10.55 Donald D. Leslie. *The survival of the Chinese Jews: the Jewish community of Kaifeng.* Leiden: Brill, 1972. (*T'oung Pao,* Monographie, 10.) ISBN 90-04-03413-7. ‣ Basic study of origins and history of largest Jewish community in China from tenth century through arrival of West. [RPH]

10.56 Thomas A. Metzger. *Escape from predicament: Neo-Confucianism and China's evolving political culture.* New York: Columbia University Press, 1977. ISBN 0-231-03979-4 (cl), 0-231-03980-8 (pbk). ‣ Contribution of Confucian goals to Chinese modernization. Stimulating but controversial interpretation. [HCT]

10.57 Kiyohiko Munakata. *Sacred mountains in Chinese art.* Urbana and Champaign: University of Illinois Press and Krannert Art Museum, 1991. ISBN 0-252-06188-8. ‣ Catalog of major exhibition exploring religious significance of sacred mountains in Chinese art from Chou dynasty to modern times; over 100 plates. [PNG]

10.58 David S. Nivison and Arthur F. Wright, eds. *Confucianism in action.* 1959 ed. Stanford, Calif.: Stanford University Press, 1961. ‣ Solid collection of studies from early days of field ranging across dynasties. Chapters examine varying expressions and uses of Confucianism in design of institutions, practical politics, kinship organization, and education. [RPH]

10.59 Laurence A. Schneider. *A madman of Ch'u: the Chinese myth of loyalty and dissent.* Berkeley: University of California Press, 1980. ISBN 0-520-03685-9. ‣ Study of transformations of Ch'ü Yüan myth from its origins to modern times. Basic for study of Chinese forms and traditions of political dissent and antigovernment expression. [CH]

10.60 Rolf A. Stein. *The world in miniature: container gardens and dwellings in Far Eastern religious thought.* Phyllis Brooks, trans. Stanford, Calif.: Stanford University Press, 1990. ISBN 0-8047-1674-9. ‣ Explores microcosm/macrocosm theme in Chinese and Tibetan religious thought as reflected in architecture, gardens, and mythology. Erudite and intellectually stimulating. [PNG]

10.61 Rodney Taylor, ed. *Current perspectives in the study of Chinese religions.* Chicago: University of Chicago Press, 1978. ISSN 0018-2710. ‣ Collection of ten essays on Chinese religion and Taoism; important contributions by Schipper, Sivin, and Strickmann. [PNG]

10.62 Laurence G. Thompson. *Chinese religion in Western languages: a comprehensive and classified bibliography of publications in English, French, and German through 1980.* Tucson: University of Arizona Press for the Association for Asian Studies, 1985. (Association for Asian Studies monographs, 41.) ISBN 0-8165-0926-3. ‣ Bibliography of Western sources spanning entirety of Chinese history. [PNG]

10.63 Laurence G. Thompson, comp. *The Chinese way in religion.* Encino, Calif.: Dickenson, 1973. ISBN 0-8221-0109-2. ‣ Well-chosen source readings spanning full range and variety of Chinese religious practices and ideas chronologically and topically arranged. [RPH]

10.64 Tu Wei-ming. *Confucian thought: selfhood as creative transformation.* Albany: State University of New York Press, 1985. ISBN 0-88706-005-6 (cl), 0-88706-006-4 (pbk). ‣ Thought-provoking collection of essays by leading interpreter of Confucianism with emphasis on philosophical issues. [PBE]

10.65 Aat Vervoorn. *Men of the cliffs and caves: the development of the Chinese eremitic tradition to the end of the Han dynasty.* Hong Kong: Chinese University Press, 1990. ISBN 962-201-415-1. ‣ Inquiry into origins of type of monasticism as characteristic feature of elite culture. Examines Confucius's role and development of three eremetic styles (eremetic advisers, unconditional eremetism, imposters) in Han power struggles. [DNK]

10.66 Max Weber. *The religion of China: Confucianism and Taoism.* Hans H. Gerth, ed. and trans. New York: Free Press, 1968. ▸ Early statement by founding figure in historical sociology without specific expertise as student of China. Part of Weber's larger project to identify contribution of religious ideas (here, Puritanism versus Confucianism) to development or nondevelopment of capitalism. Still influential, perhaps especially as work for scholars of Chinese religion to react to. [RPH]

10.67 Arthur F. Wright, ed. *The Confucian persuasion.* Stanford, Calif.: Stanford University Press, 1960. ▸ Classic collection of essays on diverse manifestations (mainly intellectual, literary, or artistic) of Confucianism across time. Articles by Pulleyblank, Cahill, and Nivison particularly important. [RPH]

10.68 Arthur F. Wright and Denis C. Twitchett, eds. *Confucian personalities.* Stanford, Calif.: Stanford University Press, 1962. ▸ Essays on manifestations of Confucianism in lives and careers of selected major political, intellectual, and literary figures in Chinese history. Approach somewhat dated, but contains strong chapters. [RPH]

SEE ALSO

11.315 J.J.M. de Groot. *The religious system of China.*

11.733 Arthur P. Wolf, ed. *Religion and ritual in Chinese society.*

Pre-Han Thought

10.69 Peter A. Boodberg. "The semasiology of some primary Confucian concepts." *Philosophy East and West* 2 (1952–53) 317–32. ISSN 0031-8221. ▸ Graphic and phonetic analyses suggest retranslation of key terms like *chün-tzu* (lordson, lordling not gentleman), *te* (enrectitude not virtue), *jen* (cohumanity not benevolence); raises important glosso-philosophical issues. [DNK]

10.70 Chuang-tzu. *Chuang Tzu: the seven inner chapters and other writings from the book "Chuang-Tzu."* Angus C. Graham, trans. London: Allen & Unwin, 1981. ISBN 0-04-299010-6. ▸ Major retranslation and reinterpretation of important Taoist text. Identification of various traditions—primitivist, syncretist, school of Chuang-tzu, and Yang Chu miscellany—written at different times, some as late as Han dynasty. [DNK]

10.71 Chuang-tzu. *The complete works of "Chuang Tzu."* Burton Watson, trans. New York: Columbia University Press, 1968. ISBN 0-231-03147-5. ▸ Accessible, unannotated translation of seminal work of contemplative Taoism (compiled late Chou to early Han dynasty) that wittily rejects social and political conventions (usually Confucian) in favor of pantheistic mysticism. [DNK]

10.72 Confucius. *The Analects.* D. C. Lau, trans. New York: Dorset, 1988. ISBN 0-88029-102-8. ▸ Scholarly introduction to Confucius's life (551–479 BCE). Contributions include analysis of key concepts like virtue, benevolence, the sage, wisdom, courage, and moral purpose of government. Accessible translation of *Lun-yü* (The Analects). [DNK]

10.73 Herrlee Glessner Creel. *Shen Pu-hai: a Chinese political philosopher of the fourth century B.C.* Chicago: University of Chicago Press, 1974. ISBN 0-226-12027-9. ▸ Attempt at reconstruction of fourth-century BCE chancellor's thought from fragmentary citations. Finds Shen surprisingly modern theorist of administrative and psychological techniques who (though generally unacknowledged) influenced Western Han practice. [DNK]

10.74 Herrlee Glessner Creel. *What is Taoism? And other studies in Chinese cultural history.* 1970 ed. Chicago: University of Chicago Press, 1982. ISBN 0-226-12041-4 (cl, 1970), 0-226-12047-3 (pbk). ▸ Seminal introductions, partly dated, on early Taoism (classified as contemplative or purposive) and legalism, their key

terms and philosophic interactions. Origins of bureaucracy and *hsien* (prefecture). The horse in China. [DNK]

10.75 Robert Eno. *The Confucian creation of heaven: philosophy and the defense of ritual mastery.* Albany: State University of New York Press, 1990. ISBN 0-7914-0190-1 (cl), 0-7914-0191-X (pbk). ▸ Revisionist view of early Confucians as communities of ritual experts and of their evolving theories of heaven and ritual skills (including dance). Sagehood of "Ruism" based on concentration, integration, control, and joy. [DNK]

10.76 N. J. Girardot. *Myth and meaning in early Taoism: the theme of chaos.* Berkeley: University of California Press, 1983. (*Hermeneutics*, 11.) ISBN 0-520-04330-8 (cl), 0-520-06460-7 (pbk). ▸ Discerns exotic chaos of order in multivalent symbolic images of creation, fall, and salvational return in early Taoist texts. Stimulating use of cross-cultural analogies to demonstrate significance of Taoist vision. [DNK]

10.77 Angus C. Graham. *Disputers of the Tao: philosophical argument in ancient China.* La Salle, Ind.: Open Court, 1989. ISBN 0-8126-9087-7 (cl), 0-8126-9088-5 (pbk). ▸ Lucid, nontechnical analyses of Confucians, Mohists, Taoists, and logicians organized under such rubrics as breakdown of order, social and metaphysical crisis, and reunification of empire. Focuses on heaven-man relations. [DNK]

10.78 Angus C. Graham. *Studies in Chinese philosophy and philosophical literature.* Albany: State University of New York Press, 1990. ISBN 0-7914-0449-8 (cl), 0-7914-0450-1 (pbk). ▸ Important essays on Mencius's theory of human nature, peasant utopianism, legend of Lao Tan, logical discourses of Kung-sun Lung, and date and composition of *Lieh-tzu*. [DNK]

10.79 David L. Hall and Roger T. Ames. *Thinking through Confucius.* Albany: State University of New York Press, 1987. ISBN 0-88706-376-4 (cl), 0-88706-377-2 (pbk). ▸ Cross-culturally anachronistic meditations on key terms and conceptual structure of Confucius's thinking set against background of Western philosophy. *Analects* as relevant to present philosophic concerns. [DNK]

10.80 Chad Hansen. *Language and logic in ancient China.* Ann Arbor: University of Michigan Press, 1983. ISBN 0-472-10020-3. ▸ Controversial analysis, linguistic and philosophical, of abstraction, mind, meaning, concept, and thought. Preference for mass noun syntax suggests stuff ontology; grammar illuminates absence of Platonic realism and nature of conceptualist philosophies of mind. [DNK]

10.81 John Knoblock, trans. *Xunzi: a translation and study of the complete works.* Vol. 1: *Books 1–6. ff* 2: *Books 7–16.* 2 vols. to date. Stanford, Calif.: Stanford University Press, 1988–90. ISBN 0-8047-1451-7 (v. 1), 0-8047-1771-0 (v. 2). ▸ Biography, influence, philosophical and social categories, and text history of systematic early Confucian thinker, Hsün-tzu. Volume 1: self-cultivation, learning; volume 2: political theory, ethics; volume 3 (in press): knowledge, language, human nature, etc. [DNK]

10.82 Kuan Chung. *Guanzi: political, economic, and philosophic essays from early China.* Vol. 1: *A study and translation.* W. Allyn Rickett, trans. Princeton: Princeton University Press, 1985–. 1 vol. to date. ISBN 0-691-06605-1. ▸ Extensive textual study and translation of large repository of miscellaneous essays (fifth to first centuries BCE) embracing socioeconomic theory, military organization, Huang-lao Taoism, naturalist theories, etc. [DNK]

10.83 Lao-tzu. *Tao Te Ching.* Rev. ed. D. C. Lau, trans. Hong Kong: Chinese University Press, 1982. ISBN 962-201-252-3. ▸ Revision of Lau's 1963 Penguin translation plus translation of recently excavated Ma-wang-tui *Lao-tzu* text; both texts in bilingual format with extensive and useful critical apparatus. [DNK]

10.84 Lao-tzu. *Tao Te Ching: the classic "Book of Integrity and* *the Way," Lao Tzu.* Victor H. Mair, trans. New York: Bantam, 1990. ISBN 0-553-07005-3 (cl), 0-553-34935-X (pbk). ‣ Translation of recently excavated Ma-wang-tui text. Seeks to avoid distortions of traditional commentaries and views (reordered) text as transmitted sayings rather than single author's work; posits relationship with yogic *Bhagavadgītā*, a controversial view. [DNK]

10.85 D. C. Lau, trans. *Mencius.* 2 vols. Hong Kong: Chinese University Press, 1984. ISBN 962-201-301-5 (v. 1), 962-201-313-9 (v. 2). ‣ Introduction to life and characteristic ideas (moral psychology, human nature, compassion, cosmology, etc.) of second major Confucian thinker (late fourth century BCE). Appendixes on dates, text history, argumentation, etc., follow translation. [DNK]

10.86 Mo Tzu, Hsun Tzu, and Han Fei Tzu. *Basic writings of Mo Tzu, Hsun Tzu, and Han Fei Tzu.* Burton Watson, trans. New York: Columbia University Press, 1967. ‣ Selected chapters, with basic introductions, from three major Chou social and political thinkers who, although excluded from subsequent Confucian canon, exerted great influence during Chou and Han dynasties. Fluent, accessible translation. [DNK]

10.87 Donald J. Munro. *The concept of man in early China.* Stanford, Calif.: Stanford University Press, 1969. ISBN 0-8047-0829-0 (cl), 0-8047-0682-4 (pbk). ‣ Classic study of Confucian and Taoist conceptions of human nature; stress on education and opposition to hereditary privilege. Discerns doctrine of natural equality and self-cultivation (involving emulation of virtuous exemplars) that permits rise in social hierarchy. [DNK]

10.88 Benjamin I. Schwartz. *The world of thought in ancient China.* Cambridge, Mass.: Harvard University Press, 1985. ISBN 0-674-96190-0 (cl), 0-674-96191-9 (text ed.) ‣ Mature, extensive, probing reflections, elegantly informed by comparative philosophical perspective, on early orientations and evolving thought of Confucians, Mohists, Taoists, legalists, and cosmologists; emergence of common discourse; development of five classics. [DNK]

10.89 Shang Yang. *The book of Lord Shang: a classic of the Chinese school of law.* J.J.L. Duyvendak, trans. Chicago: University of Chicago Press, 1963. ‣ Translation (1928) of text attributed to Shang Yang, minister (fourth century BCE) of preunification Ch'in dynasty. Copious introduction to life, administrative philosophy, social reforms, school of law, and historiographical issues. Remains standard work. [DNK]

10.90 Iulian K. Shchutskii. *Researches on the I Ching.* William L. MacDonald, Tsuyoshi Hasegawa, and Hellmut Wilhelm, trans. Gerald W. Swanson, Introduction. Princeton: Princeton University Press, 1979. ISBN 0-691-09939-1. ‣ Shchutskii's 1920s dissertation summarized Western and some Chinese scholarship about *Book of Changes.* Pioneering in its focus on original rather than received meaning of text. Swanson's introduction valuable on scholarship. [DNK]

10.91 Kidder Smith, Jr. "*Zhouyi* interpretation from accounts in the *Zuozhuan.*" *Harvard journal of Asiatic studies* 49 (1989) 421–63. ISSN 0073-0548. ‣ Argues that meanings of Eastern Chou *Book of Changes* often shaped by *Tso chuan*'s moral-retributive vision and that diviners were generally political advisers and officeholders. Concludes today's *Book of Changes* hardly differs from Chou text. [DNK]

10.92 Hellmut Wilhelm. *Change: eight lectures on the I Ching.* 1960 ed. Cary F. Baines, trans. Princeton: Princeton University Press, 1973. ISBN 0-691-09714-3, 0-691-01787-5. ‣ Systematic introduction to meaning of *Book of Changes*, yin-yang antithesis, trigrams and hexagrams, ten wings, and classic's later history. [DNK]

Han-T'ang Thought

10.93 Roger T. Ames. *The art of rulership: a study in ancient Chinese political thought.* Honolulu: University of Hawaii Press, 1983. ISBN 0-8248-0825-8. ‣ Valuable study of chapter in Han period *Huai-nan-tzu* to show growth of key concepts in Chinese political thought: nonaction, strategic advantage, penal law, utilizing the people, and benefiting the people. [PBE]

10.94 Timothy Hugh Barrett. *Li Ao: Buddhist, Taoist, or Neo-Confucian?* Oxford: Oxford University Press, 1992. ISBN 0-19-713609-5. ‣ Monumental study of important forerunner of Neo-Confucianism, with major implications for study of Chinese religious syncretism. A must for serious student of Chinese thought. [CH]

10.95 Ch'i-yün Ch'en, trans. *Hsün Yüeh and the mind of late Han China: a translation of the "Shen-chien" with introduction and annotations.* Princeton: Princeton University Press, 1980. ISBN 0-691-05292-6. ‣ Study of writings of Confucian scholar who raised basic questions about moral and political philosophy in turbulent age. [PBE]

10.96 Alfred Forke, trans. and annotator. *Lun-heng, philosophical essays of Wang Ch'ung.* 2d ed. 2 vols. New York: Paragon Book Gallery, 1962. ‣ Translation (1907, 1911), often unreliable, of original and spirited thinker, often skeptical of more superstitious side of his contemporaries' ideas. [PBE]

10.97 Charles Hartman. *Han Yü and the T'ang search for unity.* Princeton: Princeton University Press, 1986. ISBN 0-691-06665-5. ‣ Only available analysis of this major Confucian thinker. Details his efforts to promote both political unity and cultural orthodoxy in multiethnic empire. Strong use of Han's literary works, including poetry, to examine his life, ideas, and goals. [MRD]

10.98 Donald Holzman. *Poetry and politics: the life and works of Juan Chi (210–263).* Cambridge: Cambridge University Press, 1976. ISBN 0-521-20855-6. ‣ Among best and most complete studies of any Chinese poet. Good introduction to history and culture of period. Meticulous translations and commentaries of eighty-two–poem series, "Poems from My Heart." Substantial book for serious students. [CH]

10.99 Huan K'uan. *Discourse on salt and iron: a debate on state control of commerce and industry in ancient China, chapters 1–28.* Esson M. Gale, trans. and Introduction. New York: Paragon Book Gallery, 1967. (Sinica Leidensia, 2.) ISSN 0169-9562. ‣ Chapters 1–19 of an 81 BCE court debate on proper role of government in economy, also of interest for light it sheds on status of Confucian ideas at time. [DG]

10.100 Ko Hung. *Alchemy, medicine, and religion in the China of A.D. 320: the "Nei P'ien" of Ko Hung.* 1966 ed. James R. Ware, ed. and trans. New York: Dover, 1981. ISBN 0-486-24088-6 (pbk). ‣ Pioneering, if idiosyncratic, translation of crucial text for study of intersection of science, medicine, and religion in esoteric practices of early medieval China. Author's autobiographical essay, rarity for this period, is included. [DG]

10.101 Michael Loewe. *Chinese ideas of life and death: faith, myth, and reason in the Han period (202 BC–AD 220).* London: Allen & Unwin, 1982. ISBN 0-04-180001-X. ‣ Broad, nontechnical introduction to ideas concerning gods, afterlife, religious rites, the heavens, oracles, rulers, government, and scriptures. [PBE]

10.102 David McMullen. *State and scholars in T'ang China.* Cambridge: Cambridge University Press, 1988. ISBN 0-521-32991-4. ‣ Thorough examination of relationship between literary scholarship and central government, particularly in realms of education, Confucian ritual, historiography, and literary composition. Organized chronologically and topically. [MRD]

10.103 Pan Ku et al. *Po-hu t'ung: the comprehensive discussions in the White Tiger Hall.* 2 vols. Tjan Tjoe Som, trans. Leiden: Brill, 1949–52. (Sinica Leidensia, 6.) ISSN 0169-9562. ‣ Translation of influential report of government-sponsored conference on classics held in 79 CE. Includes extensive and useful introduction. [PBE]

10.104 Yen Chih-t'ui. *Family instructions for the Yen clan: Yen-shih Chia-hsün.* Ssu-yü Teng, trans. Leiden: Brill, 1968. (*T'oung Pao*, Monographie, 4.) ISBN 90-04-02281-3. ‣ Earliest handbook of family advice to survive intact. Vital source for explicit value structure of stern patriarch and official. Revealing of social, intellectual, and religious tensions of sixth-century North China. [DG]

Buddhism

10.105 Robert E. Buswell, Jr. *The formation of Ch'an ideology in China and Korea: the "Vajrasamadhi-Sutra," a Buddhist apocryphon.* Princeton: Princeton University Press, 1989. ISBN 0-691-07336-8. ‣ Part 1 a valuable study of role of apocryphal texts in formation of Ch'an Buddhist ideology during seventh and eighth centuries and importance of Korean contribution. Annotated translation of *Vajrasamadhi-Sutra* in part 2. [PNG]

10.106 Kenneth K. S. Ch'en. *Buddhism in China: a historical survey.* 1964 ed. Princeton: Princeton University Press, 1972. ISBN 0-691-03005-7 (cl, 1964), 0-691-00015-8 (pbk). ‣ Although out of date in many places, still useful reference if used cautiously. Discussions of doctrine overly simplistic; historical sources often used uncritically. Best when discussing economic and political aspects of Buddhism. Useful annotated bibliography for scholarship before 1964. [PNG]

10.107 Kenneth K. S. Ch'en. *The Chinese transformation of Buddhism.* Princeton: Princeton University Press, 1973. ISBN 0-691-07187-X (pbk). ‣ Accessible examination of Chinese transformation of Buddhism in terms of ethical, political, economic, literary, educational, and social life. [PNG]

10.108 Bernard Faure. *The rhetoric of immediacy: a cultural critique of Chan/Zen Buddhism.* Princeton: Princeton University Press, 1991. ISBN 0-691-07374-0. ‣ Provocative and occasionally exasperating exploration of key metaphors and paradigms of Ch'an-Zen Buddhist tradition from perspective of Western social-scientific methodology and literary criticism. [PNG]

10.109 Jacques Gernet. *Les aspects économiques du bouddhisme dans la société chinoise du cinquième au dixième siècle.* Saigon: École Française d'Extrême-Orient, 1956. ‣ Documents economic activities of Chinese monasteries from fifth through tenth centuries, discusses their interaction with other economic developments in Chinese society, and speculates on their contribution to nascent ideas of capitalism. Remains best treatment in a Western language. [PNG]

10.110 Peter N. Gregory. *Tsung-mi and the sinification of Buddhism.* Princeton: Princeton University Press, 1991. ISBN 0-691-07373-2. ‣ Intellectual history of Buddhism during T'ang dynasty focused around life and thought of Ch'an and Hua-yen Buddhist patriarch Tsung-mi. Most thorough available account of medieval Chinese Buddhist thought. [PBE]

10.111 Victor H. Mair. *T'ang transformation texts: a study of the Buddhist contribution to the rise of vernacular fiction and drama in China.* Cambridge, Mass.: Harvard University, Council on East Asian Studies, 1989. (Harvard-Yenching Institute monograph series, 28.) ISBN 0-674-86815-3. ‣ Defines nature and scope of Tun-huang transformation texts (*pien-wen*), discusses their social origins, and traces their influence on development of vernacular literature and drama in China. Extensively researched and carefully argued. [PNG]

10.112 John R. McRae. *The Northern School and the formation of*

early Ch'an Buddhism. Honolulu: University of Hawaii Press, 1986. (Kuroda Institute studies in East Asian Buddhism, 3.) ISBN 0-8248-1056-2. ‣ Definitive reconstruction of early history of Ch'an Buddhism in China from sixth through eighth centuries by examining history and teachings of what came to be called Northern School. [PNG]

10.113 Edwin O. Reischauer, trans. *Ennin's diary: the record of a pilgrimage to China in search of the law.* New York: Ronald, 1955. ‣ Annotated translation of Japanese Buddhist's eyewitness account of pilgrimage to China from 838 to 847. Wealth of detail on medieval Chinese Buddhist practices, beliefs, and political situation. [PNG]

10.114 Stanley Weinstein. *Buddhism under the T'ang.* Cambridge: Cambridge University Press, 1987. ISBN 0-521-25585-6. ‣ Detailed examination of Buddhism and its interaction with court during T'ang dynasty with much new and valuable research. Not for readers interested in social or doctrinal questions. [PNG]

10.115 Arthur F. Wright. *Buddhism in Chinese history.* 1959 ed. Stanford, Calif.: Stanford University Press, 1971. ISBN 0-8047-0546-1 (cl), 0-8047-0548-8 (pbk). ‣ Succinctly sketches Chinese historical context in which Buddhism was introduced and developed from Han dynasty to twentieth century. [PNG]

10.116 Philip B. Yampolsky. *The Platform Sutra of the sixth patriarch: the text of the Tun-huang manuscript with translation, introduction, and notes.* New York: Columbia University Press, 1967. ISBN 0-231-08361-0 (pbk). ‣ Although translation not entirely reliable, introduction presents excellent reconstruction of Ch'an Buddhism during seventh and eighth centuries through examination of early Ch'an histories recovered from Tun-huang. [PNG]

10.117 Chün-fang Yü. *The renewal of Buddhism in China: Chu-hung and the late Ming synthesis.* New York: Columbia University Press, 1981. ISBN 0-231-04972-2. ‣ Chu-hung (1535–1615), charismatic preacher and advocate of monastic reform who led revival of Buddhism; puts into context of Buddhism during the Ming dynasty. Best available study of Ming Buddhism. [PBE]

10.118 Erik Zürcher. *The Buddhist conquest of China: the spread and adaptation of Buddhism in early medieval China.* 1959 rev. ed. 2 vols. Leiden: Brill, 1972. (Sinica Leidensia, 11.) ISSN 0169-9562. ‣ Examination of Buddhist penetration into elite culture of gentry class in southern China from end of Han dynasty through fourth century. Superb work, although level of detail may be daunting for beginners. Chapter 4 on Tao-yüan and Hui-yüan particularly outstanding. [PNG]

Taoist and Folk Religion

10.119 Charles Benn. *The cavern-mystery transmission: a Taoist ordination rite of A.D. 711.* Honolulu: University of Hawaii Press, 1991. ISBN 0-8248-1359-6. ‣ Description and analysis of two elaborate T'ang dynasty Taoist rituals performed in palace for imperial family. Carefully researched but narrowly focused. [PNG]

10.120 Judith A. Berling. *The syncretic religion of Lin Chao-en.* New York: Columbia University Press, 1980. ISBN 0-231-04870-X. ‣ Important study of sixteenth-century religious teacher who developed synthesis of Confucianism, Taoism, and Buddhism. Includes long discussion of syncretism in China. [PBE]

10.121 Judith M. Boltz. *A survey of Taoist literature: tenth to seventeenth centuries.* Berkeley: University of California, Institute of East Asian Studies, and Center for Chinese Studies, 1987. (Chinese research monographs, 32.) ISBN 0-912966-88-2 (pbk). ‣ Comprehensive survey of Taoist literature from tenth to seventeenth century providing important historical background on various figures and schools. Organized by genre; good bibliography, useful index. [PNG]

10.122 Valerie Hansen. *Changing gods in medieval China, 1127–1276.* Princeton: Princeton University Press, 1990. ISBN 0-691-05559-9. ▸ Important contribution to social history of popular religion. Explores how changing pantheon in Chinese popular religion related to broader social and economic changes during Southern Sung dynasty. [PNG]

10.123 David G. Johnson. "The city-god cults of T'ang and Sung China." *Harvard journal of Asiatic studies* 45.2 (1985) 363–457. ISSN 0073-0548. ▸ Groundbreaking article connects development of idea of city-god with urbanization, commercialization, and political centralization of Sung period, arguing that merchant class played central role in process. [PNG]

10.124 Livia Kohn. *Early Chinese mysticism: philosophy and soteriology in the Taoist tradition.* Princeton: Princeton University Press, 1991. ISBN 0-691-07381-3 (cl), 0-691-02065-5 (pbk). ▸ Pioneering discussion of mystical tradition within Taoism from *Lao-tzu* to end of T'ang dynasty, relationship between philosophical and religious Taoism, and influence of Buddhism. Occasionally more enthusiastic than critical. [PNG]

10.125 Livia Kohn. *Taoist mystical philosophy: the "Scripture of Western Ascension."* Albany: State University of New York Press, 1991. ISBN 0-7914-0542-7 (cl), 0-7914-0543-5 (pbk). ▸ Discussion of Taoist mysticism in light of "Scripture of Western Ascension," important text for Buddhist-Taoist controversies. Annotated translation of scripture and Chinese text included as appendixes. [PNG]

10.126 John Lagerwey. *Taoist ritual in Chinese society and history.* New York: Macmillan, 1987. ISBN 0-02-896480-2. ▸ Best available account of Taoist liturgy for the living and the dead, although author's speculations in introduction and conclusion are bizarre. [PNG]

10.127 Henri Maspero. *Taoism and Chinese religion.* Frank A. Kierman, Jr., trans. Amherst: University of Massachusetts Press, 1981. ISBN 0-87023-308-4. ▸ Translation of works on Taoism and Chinese religion by great French Sinologist. Research dated, but still valuable. [PNG]

10.128 Anna Seidel. "Chronicle of Taoist studies in the West, 1950–1990." *Cahiers d'Extrême-Asie: revue de l'École Française d'Extrême-Orient, Section de Kyoto* 5 (1989–90) 223–347. ISSN 0766-1177. ▸ Comprehensive discussion of Western scholarship from 1950 on and related to Taoism with extensive bibliography of over 550 listings; excellent place to begin any research on Taoism. [PNG]

10.129 Michel Strickmann, ed. *Tantric and Taoist studies in honour of R. A. Stein.* 2 vols. Brussels: Institut Belge des Hautes Études Chinoises, 1981–83. (Mélanges chinois et bouddhiques, 21–22.) ISBN 2-8017-0190-4 (set). ▸ Important contributions on Taoism by Schafer, Robinet, Bokenkamp, Boltz, and Schipper; Anna Seidel's "Imperial Treasures and Taoist Sacraments" in series volume 21 especially outstanding. [PNG]

10.130 Stephen F. Teiser. *The ghost festival in medieval China.* Princeton: Princeton University Press, 1988. ISBN 0-691-05525-4. ▸ Important discussion of development of ghost festival in terms of Buddhist canonical sources, Mu-lien legend, and Tunhuang transformation texts against backdrop of Chinese cosmology, mythology, shamanism, and ancestral cult. [PNG]

10.131 Holmes Welch and Anna Seidel, eds. *Facets of Taoism: essays in Chinese religion.* New Haven: Yale University Press, 1979. ISBN 0-300-01695-6. ▸ Nine important contributions on Taoism and Chinese religion from second international conference on Taoism. [PNG]

Sung Neo-Confucianism

10.132 Anne D. Birdwhistell. *Transition to Neo-Confucianism: Shao Yung on knowledge and symbols of reality.* Stanford, Calif.: Stanford University Press, 1989. ISBN 0-8047-1550-5. ▸ Basic introduction to thought of, and survey of scholarship on, seminal eleventh-century philosopher who was later included in Confucian orthodoxy despite his borrowings from Buddhism and Taoism. Emphasis on philosophical idealism and broad synthesis. [HCT]

10.133 Peter K. Bol. *"This culture of ours": intellectual transitions in T'ang and Sung China.* Stanford, Calif.: Stanford University Press, 1992. ISBN 0-8047-1920-9. ▸ Traces transformation of elite culture between eighth and twelfth centuries with particular attention to literary and social contexts for redefinitions of elite values. Stimulating interpretation of intellectual foundations. [HCT]

10.134 Wing-tsit Chan. *Chu Hsi: new studies.* Honolulu: University of Hawaii Press, 1989. ISBN 0-8248-1201-8. ▸ Thirty-three essays with copious translations detailing aspects of personal life, relationships, and ideas of this architect of Confucian orthodoxy. Mature reflections by senior twentieth-century champion of this philosophy. [HCT]

10.135 Wing-tsit Chan, ed. *Chu Hsi and Neo-Confucianism.* Honolulu: University of Hawaii Press, 1986. ISBN 0-8248-0961-0. ▸ Thirty-one essays on philosophical topics. Some attention to later influence in China, Korea, and Japan. Monument to classical statements by important senior authorities from United States and East Asia. [HCT]

10.136 Ch'en Ch'un. *Neo-Confucian terms explained (the "Pei-hsi Tzu-i").* Wing-tsit Chan, ed. and trans. New York: Columbia University Press, 1986. ISBN 0-231-06384-9. ▸ Text written by Chu Hsi's student to set forth systematically major concepts in master's version of Confucian philosophy. Supplements show Ch'en's interpretations and history of text. Ably introduced and translated. [HCT]

10.137 Chu Hsi. *Chu-tzu yü lei, "Learning to be a sage": selections from the conversations of Master Chu, arranged topically.* Daniel K. Gardner, trans. Berkeley: University of California Press, 1990. ISBN 0-520-06524-7 (cl), 0-520-06525-5 (pbk). ▸ Introduces his educational activities, pedagogy, and transformation of Confucian tradition. Readable and reliable translation of chapters 8 through 10 of major text recording Chu's conversations with his students. [HCT]

10.138 Chu Hsi and Lü Tsu-ch'ien, comps. *Reflections on things at hand: the Neo-Confucian anthology.* Wing-tsit Chan, trans. New York: Columbia University Press, 1967. ISBN 0-231-06037-8 (cl), 0-231-05884-5 (pbk). ▸ Works of four major eleventh-century masters: Ch'eng Hao, Ch'eng I, Chang Tsai, and Chou Tun-i. Topics include philosophy and self-cultivation, and how to teach and serve in government. Important translation. [HCT]

10.139 Wm. Theodore De Bary. *The message of the mind in Neo-Confucianism.* New York: Columbia University Press, 1989. ISBN 0-231-06808-5. ▸ Traces teachings regarding mind/heart within Chu Hsi's school from his disciples into mid-nineteenth century. May go too far in correcting evaluation of Wang Yang-ming's role. [HCT]

10.140 Wm. Theodore De Bary and John W. Chaffee, eds. *Neo-Confucian education: the formative stage.* Berkeley: University of California Press, 1989. ISBN 0-520-06393-7. ▸ Most of eighteen essays on Chu Hsi's contributions to pedagogy and practice and only few deal with roots. Little attention to critics; pushes theme of progressive contributions to modernization. [HCT]

10.141 Daniel K. Gardner. *Chu Hsi and the "Ta-hsueh": Neo-Confucian reflection of the Confucian canon.* Cambridge, Mass.: Harvard University, Council on East Asian Studies, 1986. (Harvard East Asian monographs, 118.) ISBN 0-674-13065-0. ▸ Study of classic *Great Learning* prior to twelfth century and philosophical reasons for its new prominence then. Later, core curriculum in governmental examinations. Includes well-annotated translation following Chu's pivotal reading. [HCT]

10.142 Angus C. Graham. *Two Chinese philosophers: Ch'eng Ming-tao and Ch'eng Yi-ch'uan.* London: Lund Humphries, 1958. ISBN 0-85331-417-9. ▸ Classic exposition of major concepts of two eleventh-century founding masters (usually called Ch'eng Hao and Ch'eng I) of later orthodoxy. Illustrated with copious translations. Erudite appendixes on intellectual issues. [HCT]

10.143 Ira E. Kasoff. *The thought of Chang Tsai (1020–1077).* Cambridge: Cambridge University Press, 1984. ISBN 0-521-25549-X. ▸ Analysis of key concepts (heaven-and-earth, *ch'i* [vital energy], sagehood) in Chang Tsai's thought. Attempts to place Chang Tsai in historical context and examines his relationship to Ch'eng brothers. [PBE]

10.144 James T. C. Liu. *China turning inward: intellectual-political changes in the early twelfth century.* Cambridge, Mass.: Harvard University, Council on East Asian Studies, 1988. (Harvard East Asian monographs, 132.) ISBN 0-674-11725-5. ▸ Explores military crises and political struggles during Kao-tsung's reign (1127–63) as factors in decline of Confucian activism. Senior scholar's personal reflections on pivotal changes. [HCT]

10.145 Winston W. Lo. *The life and thought of Yeh Shih.* Hong Kong: Chinese University of Hong Kong; distributed by University Presses of Florida, 1974. ISBN 0-8130-0517-5. ▸ Pioneering study of practical statesman (1150–1223) who advocated war to restore North to dynasty's control and criticized his contemporaries for slighting historical, practical, and literary scholarship in their version of Confucianism. [HCT]

10.146 Donald J. Munro. *Images of human nature: a Sung portrait.* Princeton: Princeton University Press, 1988. ISBN 0-691-07330-9. ▸ Extensive philosophical expositions of structural images (like body and mirror) that reveal polarities between family preference and social altruism and between obedience to external authority and self-discovery of moral truth in Chu Hsi's writings. [HCT]

10.147 Kidder Smith, Jr., et al. *Sung dynasty uses of the I Ching.* Princeton: Princeton University Press, 1990. ISBN 0-691-05590-4. ▸ Su Shih, Shao Yung, Ch'eng I, and Chu Hsi used classic *Book of Changes* differently in distinct philosophical systems, but each saw in it a foundation for human values. Essay on Chu particularly good. [HCT]

10.148 Hoyt Cleveland Tillman. *Confucian discourse and Chu Hsi's ascendancy.* Honolulu: University of Hawaii Press, 1992. ISBN 0-8248-1416-9. ▸ New approach places ultimate philosophical synthesizer within context of contemporaries and historical issues. Shows how interactions within a fellowship defined tradition and philosophy that became intellectual and state orthodoxy. [HCT]

10.149 Hoyt Cleveland Tillman. *Utilitarian Confucianism: Ch'en Liang's challenge to Chu Hsi.* Cambridge, Mass.: Harvard University, Council on East Asian Studies, 1982. (Harvard East Asian monographs, 101.) ISBN 0-674-93176-9. ▸ Provocative reinterpretation of debates over history, values, and politics between radical statecraft thinker and architect of emerging intellectual orthodoxy. Issue is whether focus on utility and results confirm or subvert tradition's ethics. [HCT]

Yüan-Ming Neo-Confucianism

10.150 Chan Hok-lam and Wm. Theodore De Bary, eds. *Yüan thought: Chinese thought and religion under the Mongols.* New York: Columbia University Press, 1982. ISBN 0-231-05324-X. ▸ Ten essays emphasizing cultural continuity from Sung era despite foreign influences under Mongol rule. Essays on historical studies, law, and government particularly outstanding. [HCT]

10.151 Edward T. Ch'ien. *Chiao Hung and the restructuring of Neo-Confucianism in the late Ming.* New York: Columbia University Press, 1986. ISBN 0-231-06022-X. ▸ Besides presenting Chiao Hung's (1540?–1620) thought, this book examines incorporation of Buddhist and Taoist currents into Neo-Confucianism and disputes within Neo-Confucianism. Controversial. [PBE]

10.152 Julia Ching. *To acquire wisdom: the way of Wang Yang-ming.* New York: Columbia University Press, 1976. ISBN 0-231-03938-7. ▸ Study of life and philosophy of this statesman and teacher (1472–1529). Examines divergence from Chu Hsi's orthodox philosophy of mind, knowledge, and metaphysics. Useful translations of seven essays and twenty-five poems appended. [HCT]

10.153 Wm. Theodore De Bary and Conference on Ming Thought. *Self and society in Ming thought.* New York: Columbia University Press, 1970. ISBN 0-231-03271-4. ▸ Twelve scholarly essays ranging broadly over Ming Confucianism, Buddhism, Taoism, and literature. Influential collection. [PBE]

10.154 Joanna F. Handlin. *Action in late Ming thought: reorientation of Lü K'un and other scholar-officials.* Berkeley: University of California Press, 1983. ISBN 0-520-04380-4. ▸ Social history approach to thinker (1536–1618) who used didactic works to reach women and illiterates and to free education from traditional relationships. Sought order and meaning directly from personal experiences instead of relying on earlier texts. [HCT]

10.155 Huang Tsung-hsi. *The records of Ming scholars.* Julia Ching, ed. Honolulu: University of Hawaii Press, 1987. ISBN 0-8248-1028-7. ▸ Good selected translations from *Ming-ju hsüeh-an*, major seventeenth-century history of Ming schools of thought. Emphasis on men in difficult times committed to quest for wisdom, virtue, and Tao. [HCT]

10.156 Lo Ch'in-shu. *Knowledge painfully acquired: the "K'un-chih chi" by Lo Ch'in-shu.* Irene Bloom, ed. and trans. New York: Columbia University Press, 1987. ISBN 0-231-06408-X. ▸ Masterfully translates and introduces most of this orthodox philosophical treatise and twenty letters to Wang Yang-ming. Gives context of Ming period intellectual debates and philosophical reflections on history and investigation of things. [HCT]

10.157 Tu Wei-ming. *Neo-Confucian thought and action: Wang Yang-ming's youth (1472–1509).* Berkeley: University of California Press, 1976. ISBN 0-520-02968-2. ▸ Survey of search for sagehood, existential choice, enlightenment experience, and philosophical meaning of unity of knowledge and action. Pioneering effort to apply Erik Erikson's methodology to major reformer of Confucian tradition. [HCT]

10.158 Wang Yang-ming. *"Instructions for Practical Living" and other Neo-Confucian writings.* Wing-tsit Chan, trans. New York: Columbia University Press, 1963. (Records of civilization: sources and studies.) ISBN 0-231-02484-3 (cl), 0-231-06039-4 (pbk). ▸ Important translation of *Ch'uan-hsi lu*, along with *Inquiry on Great Learning* and documents illustrating doctrines' daily applications. Overly conventional identification of early sixteenth-century thinker with idealism in reaction to Chu Hsi's rationalism. [HCT]

Science

10.159 Joseph Needham. *Science and civilisation in China.* 6 vols. to date. Cambridge: Cambridge University Press, 1954–. ▸ Monumental, multivolume, multidecade, ongoing work on history of science, technology, and ideas about natural world. Separate, specialist authors for some volumes. Animated throughout by concern for comparison with history of science in West and for assessing Chinese contribution to development of world science. [RPH]

10.160 Edward H. Schafer. *Pacing the void: T'ang approaches to the stars.* Berkeley: University of California Press, 1977. ISBN 0-520-03344-2. ▸ Explores Chinese conceptions of celestial bodies (including sun, moon, planets) through science, literature, and religion. Thoughtful study of medieval Chinese imagination. [MRD]

10.161 Nathan Sivin. "Science and medicine in imperial China—the state of the field." *Journal of Asian studies* 47.1 (1988) 41–90. ISSN 0021-9118. ▸ Wide-ranging overview of accomplishments, directions, and difficulties of scholarship on Chinese science and medicine. [PBE]

10.162 Sung Tz'u. *The washing away of wrongs: forensic medicine in thirteenth-century China.* Brian McKnight, trans. Ann Arbor: University of Michigan, Center for Chinese Studies, 1981. (Science, medicine, and technology in East Asia, 1.) ISBN 0-89264-801-5 (cl), 0-89264-800-7 (pbk). ▸ Translation of this thirteenth-century classic, revealing both of criminal law and medical theory and practice. Includes useful introduction on forensic practice. [JWC]

10.163 Sung Ying-hsing. *"T'ien-kung k'ai-wu": Chinese technology in the seventeenth century.* E-tu Zen Sun and Shiou-chuan Sun, trans. University Park: Pennsylvania State University Press, 1966. ▸ Valuable annotated translation of famous 1637 compendium on food production, handicraft industries, boat and vehicle construction, mining, metallurgy, and engineering. Contains information on late Ming economic conditions. Reproductions of seventeenth-century illustrations. [WSA]

10.164 Paul U. Unschuld. *Medicine in China: a history of ideas.* Berkeley: University of California Press, 1985. ISBN 0-520-05023-1. ▸ Comprehensive introduction, from intellectual-historical more than social-historical point of view. [RPH]

ANCIENT PERIOD

General Studies

10.165 Sarah Allan. *The heir and the sage: myth, art, dynastic legend in early China.* San Francisco, Calif.: Chinese Materials Center, 1981. ISBN 0-89644-636-0. ▸ Lévi-Straussian analysis reveals sets of dynastic succession legends that consistently mediated conflict between heredity and virtue; late Chou philosophers shaped those legends to suit own teachings. [DNK]

10.166 Sarah Allan. *The shape of the turtle: myth, art, and cosmos in early China.* Albany: State University of New York Press, 1991. ISBN 0-7914-0459-5 (cl), 0-7914-0460-9 (pbk). ▸ Imaginative reconstruction of Shang religious cosmology from divination inscriptions and Chou myths; further addresses sun cult, relation of myth to divination and sacrifice, and meaning of art motifs. [DNK]

10.167 Kwang-chih Chang. *The archaeology of ancient China.* 4th rev. ed. New Haven: Yale University Press, 1986. ISBN 0-300-03782-1 (cl), 0-300-03784-8 (pbk). ▸ Comprehensive synthesis of data bearing on origins of civilization in China from Paleolithic through Neolithic, to Hsia, Shang, and Chou dynasties; emphasis on agricultural origins, regional developments, and interaction spheres. [DNK]

10.168 Kwang-chih Chang. *Art, myth, and ritual: the path to political authority in ancient China.* Cambridge, Mass.: Harvard University Press, 1983. ISBN 0-674-04807-5 (cl), 0-674-04808-3 (pbk). ▸ Senior scholar's synthesis of religious, social, and artistic evidence concerning kinship, ancestral status and merit, shamanistic elements in kingship and iconography, and emblematic origins of writing. Argues primacy of political considerations. [DNK]

10.169 Kwang-chih Chang. *Early Chinese civilization: anthropological perspectives.* Cambridge, Mass.: Harvard University Press, 1976. (Harvard-Yenching Institute monograph series, 23.) ISBN 0-674-21999-6. ▸ Stimulating interpretations of early political culture, agricultural origins, urbanization, lineages, dualisms in art and social organization, food codes, and evolving relations of man and animal in myth and art. [DNK]

10.170 Herrlee Glessner Creel. *The birth of China: a study of the formative period of Chinese civilization.* 1937 ed. New York: Ungar, 1954. ▸ Dated but basic, accessible introduction to Shang and Western Chou culture, and early classical texts; covers economy, religion, warfare, writing, political history, ideology, family, and daily life. [DNK]

10.171 Wen Fong, ed. *The great Bronze Age of China: an exhibition from the People's Republic of China.* New York: Metropolitan Museum of Art, 1980. ISBN 0-87099-226-0. ▸ Extensively annotated, illustrated catalog of 105 objects, mainly recently excavated bronzes (some jades, sculptures), from pre-Shang ritual vessels to Ch'in terracotta tomb figures. Introductions to each chronological section. [DNK]

10.172 Cho-yun Hsu. *Bibliographic notes on studies of early China.* Hong Kong: Chinese Materials Center, 1982. ISBN 0-89644-637-9. ▸ Bibliographic essays on major Chinese, Japanese, and Western scholarship on Shang through Han dynasties arranged by country of origin. Author-title index leads readers to capsule summaries of works cited. [DNK]

10.173 David N. Keightley. "Early civilization in China: reflections on how it became Chinese." In *Heritage of China: contemporary perspectives on Chinese civilization.* Paul S. Ropp, ed., pp. 15–54. Berkeley: University of California Press, 1990. ISBN 0-520-06440-2 (cl), 0-520-06441-0 (pbk). ▸ Broad-ranging interpretation of hero (clean- or dirty-handed) as rubric for comparing aesthetics, worldviews (optimistic and tragic), death, origins and eschatology, and urbanism in classical China and Greece. Ancestor worship the strategic custom. [DNK]

10.174 David N. Keightley, ed. *The origins of Chinese civilization.* Berkeley: University of California Press, 1983. ISBN 0-520-04229-8 (cl), 0-520-04230-1 (pbk). ▸ Seventeen exploratory analyses (dated by new excavations) of paleoenvironment, paleobotany, cultural and physical anthropology, linguistics, cultural interaction, and origins of agriculture, metallurgy, writing, and the state. [DNK]

10.175 Ladislav Kesner. "The *Taotie* reconsidered: meanings and functions of Shang theriomorphic imagery." *Artibus Asiae* 51.1–2 (1991) 29–53. ISSN 0004-3648. ▸ Reviews interpretations of monster masks as shamanistic familiars or ornamental patterns; discerns origins in Neolithic designs. Argues that mask's functions and meanings, seen in context, evolved with Shang political culture. [DNK]

10.176 Jessica Rawson. *Ancient China: art and archaeology.* London: British Museum, 1980. ISBN 0-7141-1415-4 (cl), 0-7141-1414-6 (pbk). ▸ Ceramics and jades demonstrate independent Neolithic cultures; interaction in Honan stimulated Bronze Age cultures; bronzes and other art forms through Han dynasty described (using British Museum holdings) in cultural context. [DNK]

10.177   Tsuen-hsuin Tsien. *Written on bamboo and silk: the beginnings of Chinese books and inscriptions.* Chicago: University of Chicago Press, 1962. ▸ Dated but useful introduction to early writing on bone, metal, clay, stone, wood, cloth, and paper; implements and technologies involved; and evolution of Chinese script and vocabulary. [DNK]

SEE ALSO
2.52 Paul Wheatley. *The pivot of the four quarters.*

Neolithic and Shang Dynasty

10.178   Robert W. Bagley. *Shang ritual bronzes in the Arthur M. Sackler collections.* Washington, D.C. and Cambridge, Mass.: Arthur M. Sackler Foundation and Arthur M. Sackler Museum, 1987. (Ancient Chinese bronzes in the Arthur M. Sackler collections, 1.) ISBN 0-674-80525-9. ▸ Lavishly illustrated, annotated catalog of 104 privately collected bronzes. Comprehensive preface analyzes development of Shang bronze-casting technology, section molds, and influence on decor (masks, dragons, etc.). [DNK]

10.179   Kwang-chih Chang. *Shang civilization.* New Haven: Yale University Press, 1980. ISBN 0-300-02428-2 (cl), 0-300-02885-7 (pbk). ▸ Wide-ranging survey of historiography, economy, ruling elites, religious and kinship organization, and state. Focuses on Anyang core, but considers archaeology of predynastic Erligang sites and nature of Hsia dynasty. [DNK]

10.180   Herrlee Glessner Creel. *Studies in early Chinese culture, first series.* Philadelphia: Porcupine Press, 1978. (Perspectives in Asian history, 3. American Council of Learned Societies, Studies in Chinese and related civilizations, 3.) ISBN 0-87991-601-X. ▸ Dated but valuable for examination of historicity of Hsia and Shang dynasties, based on oracle-bone inscriptions, relevant chapters in *Book of Documents,* and archaeological evidence. [DNK]

10.181   Ping-ti Ho. *The cradle of the East: an inquiry into the indigenous origins of techniques and ideas of Neolithic and early historic China, 5000–1000 B.C.* Hong Kong and Chicago: Chinese University Press and University of Chicago Press, 1975. ISBN 0-226-34524-6. ▸ Controversial interpretations of paleoenvironment, origins of agriculture, ceramics, metallurgy, and writing; argues for emergence of unique and indigenous Sinitic culture. [DNK]

10.182   David N. Keightley. "Archaeology and mentality: the making of China." *Representations* 18 (Spring 1987) 91–128. ISSN 0734-6018. ▸ Symbolic-structuralist hypothesis that ceramic and jade technologies of East Coast Neolithic (which involved model-use, airborne aesthetic, componential construction, mensuration, and constrained usage) contributed to rise of Shang culture. [DNK]

10.183   David N. Keightley. "The religious commitment: Shang theology and the genesis of Chinese political culture." *History of religions* 17.3–4 (1978) 211–25. ISSN 0018-2710. ▸ Speculates how early political culture influenced, and was influenced by, proto-bureaucratic features of Shang religious logic involving generational hierarchy, impersonal administration, contractual sacrifices, and love of order. [DNK]

10.184   David N. Keightley. *Sources of Shang history: the oracle-bone inscriptions of Bronze Age China.* Berkeley: University of California Press, 1978. ISBN 0-520-02969-0 (cl), 0-520-05455-5 (pbk). ▸ Introduction to Shang pyromantic procedures and divination inscriptions; their decipherment and periodization, introduction to reference books and rubbing collections, nature of inscription sample, and historiographical cautions to observe in its use. [DNK]

10.185   Edward L. Shaughnessy. "Historical perspectives on the introduction of the chariot into China." *Harvard journal of Asiatic studies* 48.1 (1988) 189–237. ISSN 0073-0548. ▸ Chariot entered China from Central Asia ca. 1200 BCE; decisive in Chou conquest of Shang; increasingly numerous in Eastern Chou warfare until displaced by cavalry, ca. 200 BCE. [DNK]

10.186   Robert L. Thorp. "The growth of early Shang civilization: new data from ritual vessels." *Harvard journal of Asiatic studies* 45.1 (1985) 5–75. ISSN 0073-0548. ▸ Typology, frequency, and distribution of 325 vessels from 67 finds (1948–83), syntax of their assemblages, and evolution of their decor reveals relatively uniform, widespread early Shang bronze production. [DNK]

Chou Dynasty

10.187   Herrlee Glessner Creel. *The Western Chou empire.* Vol. 1 of *The origins of statecraft in China.* Chicago: University of Chicago Press, 1970. ISBN 0-226-12043-0. ▸ Detailed introduction, based on texts and bronze inscriptions, to political ideology, government organization and finance, administration of justice, military power, and nature of feudalism in early Chou period. [DNK]

10.188   James I. Crump, Jr. *Intrigues: studies of the "Chan-kuo ts'e."* Ann Arbor: University of Michigan Press, 1964. ▸ Well-documented account of traveling persuaders in *Intrigues of the Warring States,* their appeals to inevitable change and rhetorical use of allegories and fables. Historicity of text; development of persuader's tradition. [DNK]

10.189   James I. Crump, Jr., trans. *Chan-kuo ts'e* (Intrigues of the Warring States). 2d rev. ed. San Francisco, Calif.: Chinese Materials Center, 1979. (Chinese Materials and Research Aids Service Center, Occasional series, 41.) ISBN 0-89644-583-6. ▸ Scholarly text history of *Intrigues of the Warring States,* its unorthodox reputation, fictional character, and dominance of persuasion rhetoric. Translation of text containing numerous anecdotes and fables about famous pre-Han figures, divided by states. [DNK]

10.190   Cho-yun Hsu. *Ancient China in transition: an analysis of social mobility, 722–222 B.C.* 1965 ed. Stanford, Calif.: Stanford University Press, 1977. ISBN 0-8047-0224-1. ▸ Classic study of social mobility as related to official career patterns, intensified warfare, new political institutions, agricultural and urban developments, shift from familial to contractual relationships, and revolutionary impact of Confucius's teachings. [DNK]

10.191   Cho-yun Hsu and Katheryn M. Linduff. *Western Chou civilization.* New Haven: Yale University Press, 1988. ISBN 0-300-03772-4. ▸ Historical survey, based on archaeological, inscriptional, and textual evidence, of Chou culture and ideology (pre- and postconquest), nationbuilding, feudalism, government, material culture, and daily life. [DNK]

10.192   David G. Johnson. "Epic and history in early China: the matter of Wu Tzu-hsu." *Journal of Asian studies* 40.2 (1981) 255–71. ISSN 0021-9118. ▸ Detailed analysis of five versions of Wu's story in texts like *Tso chuan,* commentary to chronicle, suggest loss of earlier, more complex epic during Han dynasty as narrative drive was subordinated to generic, moral classification. [DNK]

10.193   Frank A. Kierman, Jr. "Phases and modes of combat in early China." In *Chinese ways in warfare.* Frank A. Kierman, Jr., and John K. Fairbank, eds., pp. 26–66. Cambridge, Mass.: Harvard University Press, 1974. ISBN 0-674-12575-4. ▸ Argues that Chou set-piece accounts, colored by moral fictionalizing, portray warfare as part of ritual system that grew more rationalized as society did. Describes shift from chariotry to cavalry and infantry. [DNK]

10.194 Li Xueqin. *Eastern Zhou and Qin civilizations.* K. C. Chang, trans. New Haven: Yale University Press, 1985. ISBN 0-300-03286-2. ‣ Recently excavated artifacts, presented in detail by state and object type, demonstrate shift from bronze to iron, complex cultural development of strictly ranked society, and unification of Chinese state. [DNK]

10.195 Henri Maspero. *China in antiquity.* Frank A. Kierman, Jr., trans. Amherst: University of Massachusetts Press, 1978. ISBN 0-87023-193-6. ‣ Dated, idealizing, richly documented synthesis of Chou culture; peasant and patrician society, royal religious authority, ancestral and other cults, secularization rooted in religious sentiments, agricultural cycle, and individual states' political histories. [DNK]

10.196 David S. Nivison. "The dates of Western Chou." *Harvard journal of Asiatic studies* 43 (1983) 481–580. ISSN 0073-0548. ‣ Technical reconstruction of dates of Chou conquest (1045 BCE) and reigns based on bronze inscriptions, literary sources, and decoding systematic distortions in *Bamboo Annals.* Valuable for method and conclusions. [DNK]

10.197 Edward L. Shaughnessy. *Sources of Western Zhou history: inscribed bronze vessels.* Berkeley: University of California Press, 1991. ISBN 0-520-07028-3. ‣ Introduction to decipherment of inscriptions on Western Chou ritual bronzes. Addresses periodization, authenticity, and vessel decor. Grapples directly with major inscriptions, their historical importance, and context. [DNK]

10.198 Ssu-ma Ch'ien. *Records of the Grand Historian of China: translated from the "Shi chi" of Ssu-ma Ch'ien.* 2 vols. Burton Watson, trans. New York: Columbia University Press, 1961. (Translations from Oriental classics. UNESCO collection of representative works, Chinese series. Records of civilization: sources and studies, 65.) ‣ Fluent translation of chapters from first and model history (ca. 90 BCE) includes biographies of statesmen, philosophers, soldiers, adventurers, etc., of late Chou and Han dynasties; treatises on sacrifices, water conservancy, and economics. [DNK]

10.199 C. H. Wang. "Towards defining a Chinese heroism." *Journal of the American Oriental Society* 95.1 (1975) 25–35. ISSN 0003-0279. ‣ Inquiry into lack of epic narrative form in Chinese literature. Defines early heroism in terms of civilian cultural style that repudiates martial spirit and deemphasizes battle accounts. [DNK]

10.200 Burton Watson. *Early Chinese literature.* 1962 ed. New York: Columbia University Press, 1971. ISBN 0-231-02579-3 (cl), 0-231-08671-7 (pbk). ‣ Basic introduction to early works in history (comparisons with Greek and Roman historiography), philosophy (including ritual texts), and poetry; their historical context, key features, representative passages, and classical Chinese language. [DNK]

The Classics

10.201 Ronald C. Egan. "Narratives in *Tso chuan.*" *Harvard journal of Asiatic studies* 37.2 (1977) 323–52. ISSN 0073-0548. ‣ Detailed demonstration of how *Tso chuan,* assuming rather than articulating its consistent moral values, may have largely developed from tradition of didactic historical anecdotes rather than corpus of historical romances. [DNK]

10.202 Bernhard Karlgren, trans. *The Book of Documents.* Goteborg: Elanders Boktryckeri Aktiebolag, 1950. ‣ Scholarly translation (glosses published separately) of twenty-eight policy pronouncements and moral-political admonishments purportedly associated with major historical figures and events, most notably Chou conquest. One of the classics. [DNK]

10.203 Bernhard Karlgren, trans. *The "Book of Odes": Chinese text, transcription, and translation.* Stockholm: Museum of Far Eastern Antiquities, 1950. ‣ Scholarly translation (glosses published separately) of 305 songs compiled ca. 600 BCE, many of folk origin but reworked, about nature, love, war, family, officials, etc.; often read allegorically. One of the classics. [DNK]

10.204 James Legge, trans. *The Chinese classics, with a translation, critical and exegetical notes, prolegomena, and copious indexes.* Vol. 1: *Confucian Analects, the Great Learning, the Doctrine of the Mean.* Vol. 2: *The works of Mencius.* Vol. 3: *The Shoo King or the Book of Historical Documents.* Vol. 4: *The She King or the Book of Poetry.* Vol. 5: *The Ch'un Ts'ew with the Tso Chuen.* 1893–95 rev. ed. Hong Kong: Chinese University Press, 1960. ‣ Standard translation of fundamental classics, philosophical and historical, with original Chinese text and extensive annotation based on orthodox Confucian views. Monument to nineteenth-century missionary scholarship. [DNK]

10.205 James Legge, trans. *Li chi, Book of Rites: an encyclopedia of ancient usages, religious creeds, and social institutions.* 2 vols. Ch'u Chai and Winberg Chai, eds. New Hyde Park, N.Y.: University Books, 1967. ‣ 1885 translation of important compendium of late Chou and early Han Confucian writing, mostly dealing in some way with ritual, but also rich for moral and political philosophy. [PBE]

10.206 John Steele, trans. *The I-li or Book of Etiquette and Ceremonial.* 2 vols. London: Probsthain, 1917. ‣ Reliable translation of classic manual for steps gentlemen (*shih*) should follow in weddings, ancestral rites, funerals, visits, and official business. [PBE]

10.207 Burton Watson, trans. *The Tso chuan: selections from China's oldest narrative history.* New York: Columbia University Press, 1989. ISBN 0-231-06714-3. ‣ Selections from massive prose repository of quasi-historical anecdotes about political and military leaders and struggles, 722–468 BCE; subsequently a Confucian classic, of fundamental historiographical and cultural importance. [DNK]

10.208 Richard Wilhelm, trans. *The I Ching or "Book of Changes."* 1967 3d ed. Cary F. Baynes, English trans.: Arkana, 1989. ISBN 0-14-019408-8 (cl), 0-14-019207-7 (pbk). ‣ Translation and extensive discussion of sixty-four hexagram texts (judgment, image, lines) composing China's first classic, a work of divination and philosophy. Introduction covers use and history of *Changes.* [DNK]

CH'IN-HAN TO SUI DYNASTIES

General Studies

10.209 Étienne Balazs. *Chinese civilization and bureaucracy: variations on a theme.* Arthur F. Wright, ed. H. M. Wright, trans. New Haven: Yale University Press, 1964. ‣ Selected essays of great European pioneer in the study of medieval thought and institutions. Still invigorating for its challenge to traditional Sinology and its humane penetration. [DG]

10.210 Albert E. Dien, ed. *State and society in early medieval China.* Stanford, Calif.: Stanford University Press, 1990. ISBN 0-8047-1745-1. ‣ Pioneering collection of studies attempting to reinterpret key aspects of least understood period of Chinese history. Editor's introduction relates essays to each other, but book contains no general overview for reader lacking grounding in premodern China. [DG]

10.211 Michael Loewe. *Everyday life in early imperial China during the Han period, 202 B.C.–A.D. 220.* New York: Dorset, 1988. ISBN 0-88029-177-X. ‣ Survey of Han life aimed at general audience. Addresses history, geography, government, army, society, writing, literature, religion, cities, trade, countryside, industry, technology, craftsmanship, etc. Almost 100 line drawings and photographs. [DG]

10.212 Michele Pirazzoli-t'Serstevens. *The Han dynasty.* Janet Seligman, trans. New York: Rizzoli, 1982. ISBN 0-8478-0438-0. ‣ Large-format, richly illustrated overview of Han culture and history. [PBE]

10.213 Denis C. Twitchett and Michael Loewe, eds. *The Ch'in and Han empires, 221 B.C.–A.D. 220.* Vol. 1 of *The Cambridge history of China.* Denis C. Twitchett and John K. Fairbank, eds. New York: Cambridge University Press, 1986. ISBN 0-521-21447-5 (set), 0-521-24327-0 (v. 1). ‣ Comprehensive survey of political, institutional, intellectual, economic, social, and religious history by major scholars. Good introduction to primary sources and secondary scholarship. [PBE]

10.214 Wang Zhongshu. *Han civilization.* Kwang-chih Chang et al., trans. New Haven: Yale University Press, 1982. ISBN 0-300-02723-0. ‣ Magisterial survey of two Han capitals, agriculture, lacquerware, bronzes, ironware, ceramics, and tombs based on archaeological discoveries. More than 300 photographs and drawings illustrate this translation of series of nine lectures by leading Chinese archaeologist. [DG]

Political and Institutional History

10.215 Hans Bielenstein. *The bureaucracy of Han times.* Cambridge: Cambridge University Press, 1980. ISBN 0-521-22510-8. ‣ Premier description of government structure. Argues extreme position that our sources depict rationalized, Weberian bureaucracy that actually functioned, rather than being mythologized recasting of much more diverse elements. [DG]

10.216 Hans Bielenstein. "The restoration of the Han dynasty (Parts 1–4 and supplement)." *Bulletin of the Museum of Far Eastern Antiquities (Bulletin-Museum of Far Eastern Antiquities)* 26, 31, 39, 51, 48 (1954, 1959, 1967, 1979, 1976) 1–209, 1–287, 1–198, 1–300, 1–142. ISSN 0081-5691. ‣ Most important English-language study of Later Han dynasty. Part 1 (1954) deals with fall of Wang Mang and nature of *Hou Han shu* (History of the Later Han) as a source; part 2 (1959), with civil strife as Later Han emerged; part 3 (1967), with lives of people; part 4 (1979), with nature of government; and supplement to part 4 (1976), with capital city of Lo-yang. [DG]

10.217 Derk Bodde. *China's first unifier: a study of the Ch'in dynasty as seen in the life of Li Ssu.* 1938 ed. Hong Kong: Chinese University Press, 1967. (Sinica Leidensia, 3.) ISSN: 0169-9562. ‣ Overview of creation of first Chinese imperial system. Exploits traditional sources for policies of crucial functionary. [DG]

10.218 Fang Hsüan-ling. *The "Chronicle of Fu Chien": a case of exemplar history.* Michael C. Rogers, trans. Berkeley: University of California Press, 1968. ‣ Massively annotated translation of chapters from chronicle of non-Chinese state. Argues that Chinese historiographers were shaping narrative to influence contemporary governmental policies. [DG]

10.219 Jennifer Holmgren. *Annals of Tai: early T'o-pa history according to the first chapter of the Wei-shu.* Canberra: Faculty of Asian Studies with Australian National University Press, 1982. (Australian National University, Faculty of Asian Studies monographs, n.s., 1.) ISBN 0-909879-16-8. ‣ Studies origins of most significant of non-Chinese conquest regimes in North China during early medieval period. Analysis of unusually revealing traditional source material by most energetic student of period. [DG]

10.220 Michael Loewe. *Crisis and conflict in Han China, 104 B.C. to A.D. 9.* London: Allen & Unwin, 1974. ISBN 0-04-951021-5. ‣ Traces official attitudes through nine crises during latter half (104 BCE–9 CE) of Former Han dynasty. Argues for ongoing tension between legalist-pragmatic orientation and Confucian-ide-

alistic stance that after initial triumph faced disappointments of real-world politics. [DG]

10.221 Michael Loewe. *Records of Han administration.* Vol. 1: *Historical assessment.* Vol. 2: *Documents.* 2 vols. London: Cambridge University Press, 1967. ‣ Revealing study of low-level administrative records on bamboo strips recovered by archaeologists. Offers fascinating insights but relevance of material to Han government generally limited by its origins in military garrisons of northwest. [DG]

10.222 Arthur F. Wright. *The Sui dynasty.* New York: Knopf, 1978. ISBN 0-394-49276-5. ‣ History of short-lived regime whose extraordinary achievements set stage for subsequent T'ang dynasty. Author is alert to political, religious, economic, and social dimensions of two Sui rulers' violent reintegration of empire after centuries of disunion. [DG]

Economic History

10.223 Hans Bielenstein. "The census of China during the period 2–742 A.D." *Bulletin of the Museum of Far Eastern Antiquities* 19 (1947) 125–163, 10 pls. ‣ Pioneering quantitative study of traditional population registration records for evidence on household size, expansion of territorial control, movement of Chinese people, etc. [DG]

10.224 Cho-yun Hsu. *Han agriculture: the formation of early Chinese agrarian economy (206 B.C.–A.D. 220).* Jack L. Dull, ed. Seattle: University of Washington Press, 1980. ISBN 0-295-95676-3. ‣ Topical overview, supported by translated passages (mostly from standard histories). Makes controversial argument that Warring States protocommercialism was crushed by imperial bias toward agrarian economy. [DG]

10.225 Pan Ku. *Food and money in ancient China: the earliest economic history of China to A.D. 25.* 1950 ed. Nancy Lee Swann, trans. New York: Octagon Books, 1974. ‣ Careful study of treatises on economics from first two standard histories. Presents information on first millennium BCE within context of traditional Chinese historiography. [DG]

10.226 C. Martin Wilbur. *Slavery in China during the Former Han dynasty, 206 B.C.–A.D. 25.* 1943 ed. New York: Russell & Russell, 1967. ‣ Somewhat dated survey of society and economy of ancient China, with focus on slavery. Overall, slavery is shown not to have played significant role in Chinese history. [DG]

10.227 Ying-shih Yü. *Trade and expansion in Han China: a study in the structure of Sino-barbarian economic relations.* Berkeley: University of California Press, 1967. ‣ Survey of early foreign trade and diplomacy within paradigm of tributary system. Takes relatively traditional, Sinocentric approach to China's neighbors. [DG]

Social and Cultural History

10.228 Derk Bodde. *Festivals in classical China: New Year and other annual observances during the Han dynasty, 206 B.C.–A.D. 220.* Princeton: Princeton University Press, 1975. ISBN 0-691-03098-7. ‣ Chinese annual festivals described for "earliest period for which the data permit a fairly detailed and systematic description to be written." First half deals with multiple New Year festivals, both vernacular and official; second half covers other annual rituals, arranged by season, the whole offering rich window into popular religion and belief. [DG]

10.229 T'ung-tsu Ch'ü. *Han social structure.* Jack L. Dull, ed. Seattle: University of Washington Press, 1972. ISBN 0-295-95068-4. ‣ First half an analysis by great scholar of kinship, marriage, position of women, social classes, and powerful families during Han dynasty. Second half consists of translations of more than 200 supporting passages from *Shih chi* (Records of the History),

Han shu (History of the Han), and *Hou Han shu* (History of the Later Han), arranged under headings of kinship and marriage, social classes, and powerful families. [DG]

10.230   Kenneth J. DeWoskin, trans. *Doctors, diviners, and magicians of ancient China: biographies of Fang-shih.* New York: Columbia University Press, 1983. ISBN 0-231-05596-X (cl), 0-231-05597-8 (pbk). ▸ Preliminary translations of biographies of heterodox practitioners of early first millenium CE. Our poor understanding of parascientific disciplines represented makes technical detail unreliable. [DG]

10.231   Patricia Buckley Ebrey. *The aristocratic families of early imperial China: a case study of the Po-ling Ts'ui family.* Cambridge: Cambridge University Press, 1978. ISBN 0-521-21484-X. ▸ Painstaking reconstruction of history of powerful Chinese family throughout first millennium CE from diverse sources. Argues for complex evolution of sources of power of such enduring elite kin groups. [DG]

10.232   David G. Johnson. *The medieval Chinese oligarchy.* Boulder: Westview, 1977. ISBN 0-89158-140-5. ▸ Highly interpretative analysis of medieval Chinese elite, arguing against aristocratic models of great families, and for view that enduring power was rooted solely in holding of high civil office. [DG]

10.233   Liu I-ch'ing. *Shih-shuo hsin-yü: a new account of tales of the world.* Richard B. Mather, trans. Minneapolis: University of Minnesota Press, 1976. ISBN 0-8166-0760-5. ▸ Fifth-century CE Chinese collection of anecdotes on distinguished persons of second, third, and fourth centuries CE, with sixth-century commentary. Translation is extraordinary labor of love on extremely recalcitrant text that is crucial, if bewildering, window on early medieval Chinese elite. [DG]

10.234   Nancy Lee Swann. *Pan Chao, foremost woman scholar of China, first century A.D.: background, ancestry, life, and writings of the most celebrated Chinese woman of letters.* 1932 ed. New York: Russell & Russell, 1968. ▸ Pioneering study of most famous Chinese woman historian, placed carefully within context of her time and of her scholarly family, head of which was historian Pan Ku. [DG]

10.235   Wu Hung. *The Wu Liang shrine: the ideology of early Chinese pictorial art.* Stanford, Calif.: Stanford University Press, 1989. ISBN 0-8047-1529-7. ▸ Lavishly illustrated analysis of decoration of carved-stone ancestral shrine and historical and mythological stories depicted on it. [PBE]

10.236   Hsüan-chih Yang. *Memories of Loyang: Yang Hsüan-chih and the lost capital (493–534).* W.J.F. Jenner, trans. Oxford: Oxford University Press, 1981. ISBN 0-19-821568-1. ▸ Annotated translation of earliest substantial account of Chinese city, Yang Hsüan-chih's *Lo-yang Ch'ieh-lan Chi* (Record of the Monasteries of Lo-yang), description of Northern Wei capital of Lo-yang. Yang's memoir also political tract on crisis of legitimacy in succeeding Eastern Wei regime. [DG]

Historiography

10.237   Pan Ku. *Courtier and commoner in ancient China: selections from the "History of the Former Han" by Pan Ku.* Burton Watson, trans. New York: Columbia University Press, 1974. ISBN 0-231-03765-1, 0-231-08354-8. ▸ Accessible translation of biographical material, some of it on women, selected from ten chapters of *Han shu* (History of the Han). Passages were chosen for intrinsic literary merit and for their subsequent impact on Chinese literature and culture. [DG]

10.238   Pan Ku. *The history of the Former Han dynasty.* 3 vols. Homer H. Dubs, trans. Baltimore: Waverly, 1938. ▸ Heavily annotated translation of basic annals of *Han shu* (History of the Han). Traditional political history of Former Han dynasty. [DG]

10.239   Ssu-ma Kuang. *The chronicle of the Three Kingdoms (220–265).* 2 vols. to date (vols. 1 and 3). Glen W. Baxter (v. 1) and Bernard S. Solomon (v. 3), eds. Achilles Fang, trans. Cambridge, Mass.: Harvard University Press, 1952–. (Harvard-Yenching Institute studies, 6.) ▸ Authoritative translation of chapters 69–78 of *Tzu-chih T'ung-chien* (Comprehensive Mirror for Aid in Government). Deals with political history of states of Wei, Wu, and Shu Han that emerged from collapse of Later Han dynasty. [DG]

10.240   Ssu-ma Kuang. *The last of the Han: being the chronicle of the years 181–220 A.D. as recorded in chapters 58–68 of the "Tzu-chih T'ung-chien" of Ssu-ma Kuang.* Rafe de Crespigny, trans. Canberra: Australian National University, Centre of Oriental Studies, 1969. (Australian National University, Centre of Oriental Studies, Oriental monograph series, 9.) ISBN 0-7081-0163-1. ▸ Careful translation of chief traditional compilation of standard sources for political history of end of Later Han dynasty by leading scholar of period. Covers period from Yellow Turban Rebellion through defeat of metropolitan eunuchs to emergence of regional military commanders prefiguring regimes of following Three Kingdoms. [DG]

Biographies of Literary Figures

10.241   A. R. Davis. *Tao Yüan-ming (AD 365–427): his works and their meaning.* 2 vols. Cambridge: Cambridge University Press, 1983. ISBN 0-521-25347-0 (set). ▸ Complete, annotated translation of all poems. Although Davis eschews biographical approach to Tao's verse, his book contains careful research into details of poet's life. [CH]

10.242   Hugh Dunn. *Cao Zhi: the life of a princely Chinese poet.* Beijing: New World Press; distributed by China Publications Centre, 1983. ▸ Short, readable biography of major poet and political figure of early third century. Good translations of poems. [CH]

10.243   John D. Frodsham. *The murmuring stream: the life and works of the Chinese poet Hsieh Ling-yün (385–433), Duke of K'ang-lo.* Kuala Lumpur: University of Malaya Press, 1967. ▸ Complete translation with Sinological annotation of all Hsieh's poetry. Much research on his biography. Important for understanding religious development of period. [CH]

10.244   William T. Graham. *The Lament for the South: Yü Hsin's "Ai Chiang-nan Fu."* Cambridge: Cambridge University Press, 1980. ISBN 0-521-22713-5. ▸ Complete, annotated translation of Yü Hsin's best-known work. Introductory material contains succinct history of period and good account of author's life. Important book for serious student of medieval Chinese history and literature. [CH]

10.245   Richard B. Mather. *The poet Shen Yüeh (441–513): the reticent marquis.* Princeton: Princeton University Press, 1988. ISBN 0-691-06734-1. ▸ Intellectual biography of great Southern Dynasties polymath by leading student of that intricately Buddho-Taoist, yet still Confucian, milieu. Cultural and social tensions of period are mirrored in Shen Yüeh's life as poet, critic, historian, official, and frustrated recluse. [DG/CH]

10.246   Ronald C. Miao. *Early medieval Chinese poetry: the life and verse of Wang Ts'an (A.D. 177–217).* Wiesbaden: Steiner, 1982. (Münchener ostasiatische Studien, 30.) ISBN 3-515-03718-7. ▸ Careful study of late Han dynasty poet. Contains translations and detailed commentary on virtually all of Wang's major poems. Can serve as good introduction to poetry of this period. [CH]

10.247   Burton Watson. *Ssu-ma Ch'ien: grand historian of China.* New York: Columbia University Press, 1958. ▸ Comprehensive study of life and works of Ssu-ma Ch'ien, great Han dynasty historian. Focus on early development of Chinese historiography and on value of Ssu-ma Ch'ien's writings as literature. An important book. [CH]

T'ANG DYNASTY
General Studies

10.248 John Curtis Perry and Bardwell L. Smith, eds. *Essays on T'ang society: the interplay of social, political, and economic forces.* Leiden: Brill, 1976. ISBN 90-04-04761-1. ‣ Seven articles on important topics, including career of emperor T'ang T'ai-tsung, An Lu-shan Rebellion, foreign relations, and problem of late T'ang provincial autonomy. Concludes with useful bibliographic essay. [MRD]

10.249 Denis C. Twitchett and John K. Fairbank, eds. *Sui and T'ang China, 589–906.* Vol. 3.1 of *The Cambridge history of China.* Cambridge: Cambridge University Press, 1979. ISBN 0-521-21447-5 (set). ‣ Large-scale political history with ten chapters by various authors. Detailed approach to domestic and foreign affairs that concentrates on dynasty's early and middle periods. [MRD]

10.250 Arthur F. Wright and Denis C. Twitchett, eds. *Perspectives on the T'ang.* New Haven: Yale University Press, 1973. ISBN 0-300-01522-4 (cl), 0-300-02674-9 (pbk). ‣ Twelve articles of generally high quality on political-institutional history as well as thought, religion, and literature (poetry), written by various authors. Deals with many of era's most important issues. [MRD]

Political History

10.251 Charles Backus. *The Nan-chao kingdom and T'ang China's southwestern frontier.* Cambridge: Cambridge University Press, 1981. ISBN 0-521-22733-X. ‣ Examines Chinese relations, often hostile, with dynamic state that challenged T'ang power in region, including Vietnam, during dynasty's last century. Straightforward diplomatic/military history. [MRD]

10.252 Woodbridge Bingham. *The founding of the T'ang dynasty: the fall of Sui and rise of T'ang, a preliminary survey.* 1941 ed. New York: Octagon Books, 1975. (American Council of Learned Societies, Studies in Chinese and related civilizations, 4.) ISBN 0-374-90635-1. ‣ Analysis of causes for Sui decline and numerous rebellions that ended in founding of T'ang dynasty. Straightforward political history that highlights both domestic factors as well as foreign (especially Türk) involvement. [MRD]

10.253 Richard W. L. Guisso. *Wu Tse-t'ien and the politics of legitimation in T'ang China.* Bellingham: Western Washington University Press, 1978. (Western Washington University, Program in East Asian Studies occasional papers, 11.) ISBN 0-914584-11-1. ‣ Thorough analysis of imperial China's only instance of female rule. Examines social as well as political factors involved in her rise to power, important aspects of her reign, and historiography of her career. [MRD]

10.254 Ou-yang Hsiu and Sung Ch'i. *Biography of An Lu-shan.* Howard S. Levy, ed. and trans. Berkeley: University of California Press, 1961. ‣ Annotated translation of primary source describing career of military leader of mid-T'ang rebellion which profoundly altered and nearly toppled dynasty. Useful only as supplement to other synthetic works. [MRD]

10.255 Ou-yang Hsiu and Sung Ch'i. *Biography of Huang Ch'ao.* 2d rev. ed. Howard S. Levy, ed. and trans. Berkeley: University of California Press, 1961. ‣ Translation of primary source concerning leader of great popular uprising in China that led to T'ang collapse. Copious annotations with some analysis; includes translations of Arabic accounts. Use to supplement other material. [MRD]

10.256 Edwin G. Pulleyblank. *The background of the rebellion of An Lu-shan.* 1955 ed. Westport, Conn.: Greenwood, 1982. ISBN 0-313-23549-X. ‣ Thorough study of economic, political, and military institutions in China prior to cataclysmic revolt that pro-

foundly altered them. Also examines personal factors in setting stage for rebellion. [MRD]

10.257 Howard J. Wechsler. *Mirror to the son of heaven: Wei Cheng at the court of T'ang T'ai-tsung.* New Haven: Yale University Press, 1974. ISBN 0-300-01715-4. ‣ Fine biography of model minister who served one of China's greatest emperors. Examines not only Wei's life, but also early T'ang bureaucracy, particularly relations between monarchs and officials and historiography of this subject. [MRD]

SEE ALSO
  9.138 Christopher I. Beckwith. *The Tibetan empire in Central Asia.*

Institutional History

10.258 Wallace Johnson, ed. and trans. *The T'ang code.* Vol. 1: *General principles.* 1 vol. to date. Princeton: Princeton University Press, 1979. ISBN 0-691-09239-7. ‣ Translation of first section of legal code that had powerful influence on Japanese, Korean, and Vietnamese as well as later Chinese codes. Author's introduction effectively examines history, principles, organization of legal code. [MRD]

10.259 Ou-yang Hsiu and Sung Ch'i. *Traité des fonctionnaires et traité de l'armée: traduits de la nouvelle histoire des T'ang (chap. 26–50).* 2d rev. ed. Robert Des Rotours, trans. San Francisco, Calif.: Chinese Materials Center, 1974. (Chinese Materials Center, Reprint series, 11.) ‣ Detailed study of T'ang bureaucratic and military establishments, with discussion of each office and its functions. Focus on translations of T'ang sources. [MRD]

10.260 Denis C. Twitchett. *Financial administration under the T'ang dynasty.* 2d ed. Cambridge: Cambridge University Press, 1970. ISBN 0-521-07823-7. ‣ Detailed description of T'ang state fiscal policy and its history. Focus on land tenure, taxation and tax reform, currency and monetary policy, canal system, and structure of state's financial administration. [MRD]

10.261 Howard J. Wechsler. *Offerings of jade and silk: ritual and symbol in the legitimation of the T'ang dynasty.* New Haven: Yale University Press, 1985. ISBN 0-300-03191-2. ‣ Detailed bureaucratic history of dynasty's early period. Revealing of elite culture and beliefs, particularly those surrounding functions of emperor. Includes discussion of important ceremonies, sacrifices, other imperial activities. [MRD]

Cultural History

10.262 Ryoichi Hayashi. *The Silk Road and the Shoso-in.* Robert Ricketts, trans. New York: Weatherhill, 1975. ISBN 0-8348-1022-0. ‣ Well-illustrated and coherent study of objects brought to eighth-century Japan from various parts of Eurasia through T'ang China. Reveals not only extent of luxury trade but also important examples of cultural and artistic borrowing. [MRD]

10.263 Stephen Owen. *The great age of Chinese poetry: the High T'ang.* New Haven: Yale University Press, 1981. ISBN 0-300-02367-7. ‣ Comprehensive study of eighth-century apogee of China's poetic output. Close attention to social and political context illuminates the period through its poets, including several of China's greatest. [MRD]

10.264 Stephen Owen. *The poetry of the early T'ang.* New Haven: Yale University Press, 1977. ISBN 0-300-02103-8. ‣ Best available study of tradition and innovation in court poetry that paved way for brilliant High T'ang poetry. Reveals many aspects of period's culture and political history. [MRD]

10.265 Edwin O. Reischauer. *Ennin's travels in T'ang China.* New York: Ronald, 1955. ‣ Skillful narrative examination of information found in monk's diary, with significant additions from other sources to complete story of this remarkable source.

Describes journey as well as late T'ang political and social conditions. [MRD]

10.266 Edward H. Schafer. *The golden peaches of Samarkand: a study of T'ang exotics.* Berkeley: University of California Press, 1963. ISBN 0-520-01144-9 (cl), 0-520-05462-8 (pbk). ‣ Exhaustive catalog of exotica that proves highly revealing of T'ang elite culture and attitudes toward foreign cultures, primarily those to west. Implications for economic history, particularly trade. Innovative work, perhaps Schafer's finest. [MRD]

10.267 Edward H. Schafer. *The vermilion bird: T'ang images of the South.* 1967 ed. Berkeley: University of California Press, 1985. ISBN 0-520-05463-6 (pbk). ‣ Imaginative study of empire's tropical southern regions (including northern Vietnam) and Chinese conceptions of those regions. Effective use of poetic and other descriptions to invoke medieval attitudes. [MRD]

Biographies of Literary Figures

10.268 William Hung. *Tu Fu: China's greatest poet (with notes).* Cambridge, Mass.: Harvard University Press, 1952. ‣ Painstaking, thoroughly researched biography of China's greatest poet by one of greatest Sinologists of twentieth century. Still unsurpassed. Contains translations of almost 400 poems. A must read for any student of traditional China. [CH]

10.269 Paul W. Kroll. *Meng Hao-jan.* Boston: Twayne, 1981. ISBN 0-8057-6470-4. ‣ Meticulous study of renowned eighth-century poet with focus on religious influences on his verse. Many careful translations. One of best books in Twayne series. [CH]

10.270 Thomas P. Nielson. *The T'ang poet-monk Chiao-jan.* Tempe: Arizona State University, Center for Asian Studies, 1972. (Arizona State University, Center for Asian Studies, Occasional paper, 3.) ‣ Detailed study of life of Chiao-jan, central figure in development of Chinese poetics; careful translations of primary sources. Much useful information on Buddhism and Chinese poetry in eighth century. [CH]

10.271 William H. Nienhauser, Jr. *P'i Jih-hsiu.* Boston: Twayne, 1979. ISBN 0-8057-6372-4. ‣ Wide-ranging study of little-known but fascinating literary figure of ninth century. Excellent chapters on his life and times and on literary criticism of period. Good bibliography. [CH]

10.272 William H. Nienhauser, Jr., et al. *Liu Tsung-yüan.* New York: Twayne, 1973. ‣ Brief, yet comprehensive, treatment of Liu Tsung-yüan (773–819), important literatus of mid-T'ang period. Chapters on historical and literary background, philosophical and intellectual thought as well as studies of Liu's major writings. [CH]

10.273 Marsha L. Wagner. *Wang Wei.* Boston: Twayne, 1981. ISBN 0-8057-6448-8. ‣ Comprehensive study of important eighth-century poet. Particularly good material on symbolism and imagery in his Buddhist inspired verse. [CH]

10.274 Arthur Waley. *The life and times of Po Chü-i, 772–846 A.D.* 1949 ed. London: Allen & Unwin, 1970. ‣ Reliable and informative biography of late T'ang dynasty's most important poet and important government official. Contains information pertinent to cultural and social history of period. [MRD]

10.275 Arthur Waley. *The poetry and career of Li Po, 701–762 A.D.* 1950 ed. London: Allen & Unwin, 1979. ISBN 0-04-895012-2. ‣ Although not one of author's better efforts, still best introduction to Li Po in English; also contains much of general interest on mid-eighth-century China. [CH]

10.276 Arthur Waley. *The real "Tripitaka" and other pieces.* New York: Macmillan, 1952. ‣ Well-researched, yet highly readable, account of life of Chinese monk Hsüan-tsang (596–664), whose journey to India in search of Buddhist scriptures formed base of sixteenth-century Chinese novel *Journey to the West.* Useful for history of Chinese Buddhism and religious life of seventh century. [CH]

10.277 Wong Yoon Wah. *Ssu-K'ung T'u: a poet-critic of the T'ang.* Hong Kong: Chinese University Press, 1976. ‣ One of few biographies in English of late T'ang literary figure; does not discuss subject's poetry or critical theories. [CH]

SUNG DYNASTY

General Studies

10.278 Herbert Franke, ed. *Sung biographies.* 3 vols. Wiesbaden: Steiner, 1976. (Münchener ostasiatische Studien, 16–17.) ISBN 3-515-02412-3. ‣ Uneven but useful biographies in English and German of important Sung individuals: officials, generals, writers, and thinkers. Best offer detailed and definitive treatments of their subjects. [JWC]

10.279 John W. Haeger, ed. *Crisis and prosperity in Sung China.* Tucson: University of Arizona Press, 1975. ISBN 0-8165-0494-6 (pbk). ‣ Broad-ranging collection of essays dealing with varied aspects of Sung history. Those by Shiba on urbanization and Schirokauer on Neo-Confucianism outstanding and widely cited. [JWC]

10.280 Tsuyoshi Kinugawa, ed. *Liu Tzu-chien po shih sung shou chi nien Sung shih yen chiu lun chi.* [Collected studies on Sung history dedicated to Professor James T. C. Liu in celebration of his seventieth birthday]. Kyoto: Dohosha, 1989. ISBN 4-8104-0805-1. ‣ Voluminous work containing forty-five essays (fifteen in English) on all aspects of Sung history, intended for scholars. English essays center on political history, but important contributions to cultural, economic, and institutional history as well. [JWC]

10.281 James T. C. Liu and Peter Golas, eds. *Change in Sung China: innovation or renovation?* Lexington, Mass.: Heath, 1969. ‣ Provocative but dated selections from wide range of scholarship dealing with socioeconomic changes during Sung dynasty. Intended for college classroom use. [JWC]

10.282 Ting Ch'uan-ching. *A compilation of anecdotes of Sung personalities.* Chu Djang and Jane C. Djang, trans. Jamaica, N.Y.: Taipei Paper Manufactory Press; distributed by St. John's University Press, 1990. ‣ Translation of early twentieth-century scholar Ting Ch'uan-ching's collection of anecdotes about famous Sung individuals, drawn mainly from Sung anecdotal literature, some of questionable reliability. Valuable repository of informal historical information. [JWC]

Political History and Law

10.283 Richard L. Davis. *Court and family in Sung China, 960–1279: bureaucratic success and kinship fortunes for the Shih of Ming-chou.* Durham, N.C.: Duke University Press, 1986. ISBN 0-8223-0512-7. ‣ Account of spectacularly successful Shih family, which produced two chief councilors and many lesser officials in the Sung. Includes general discussion of bureaucratic achievement and social standing. [JWC]

10.284 Robert M. Hartwell. "Financial expertise, examinations, and the formulation of economic policy in Northern Sung China." In *Thirtieth anniversary commemorative series: enduring scholarship selected from the "Far Eastern Quarterly"—the "Journal of Asian Studies," 1941–1971.* 3 vols. John A. Harrison, ed., pp. 103–59. Tucson: University of Arizona Press, 1972. ISBN 0-8165-0362-1. ‣ Brilliant study of recruitment, composition, and career patterns of Northern Sung fiscal bureaucracy. Contrary to Weber, argues that Sung economic policies were products of professional financial service. [JWC]

10.285 Edward A. Kracke, Jr. *Civil service in Sung China, 960–1067.* Cambridge, Mass.: Harvard University Press, 1968. (Harvard-Yenching Institute monograph series, 13.) ▸ Older but masterly overview of civil service organization and recruitment during Northern Sung dynasty; special emphasis on role of formal sponsorship in bureaucracy. [JWC]

10.286 James T. C. Liu. *Reform in Sung China: Wang An-shih (1021–1086) and his new policies.* Cambridge, Mass.: Harvard University Press, 1959. ▸ Brief historical account and analysis of far-reaching reform program of Wang An-shih. Only general treatment in English. [JWC]

10.287 Winston W. Lo. *An introduction to the civil service of Sung China, with an emphasis on its personnel administration.* Honolulu: University of Hawaii Press, 1987. ISBN 0-8248-1108-9. ▸ Detailed and authoritative study of recruitment, evaluation, and promotion practices of Sung bureaucracy in light of contemporary management theories. Special attention is paid to case of Szechuan. [JWC]

10.288 Brian McKnight. *Village bureaucracy in Southern Sung China.* Chicago: University of Chicago Press, 1971. ISBN 0-226-56059-7. ▸ Pathbreaking analysis of Sung government's village level administration, especially personnel regulations and policies designed to deal with rural society transformed by commercialization. Highlights role of rural landholding class. [JWC]

10.289 John Meskill, ed. *Wang An-shih: practical reformer?* Boston: Heath, 1963. ▸ Collection of judgments and appraisals of Wang and his reforms with critics and apologists ranging from his contemporaries to modern scholars. Intended for use in college classrooms. [JWC]

10.290 Henry Raymond Williamson. *Wang An-shih: a Chinese statesman and educationalist of the Sung dynasty.* 1935–37 ed. 2 vols. Westport, Conn.: Hyperion, 1973. ISBN 0-88355-096-2 (v. 1). ▸ Biography of Wang An-shih with numerous translations from his writings. Outdated in its political analysis, but still useful for biographical purposes. [JWC]

Diplomatic and Military History

10.291 Herbert Franke. "Siege and defense of towns in medieval China." In *Chinese ways in warfare.* Frank A. Kierman, Jr., and John K. Fairbank, eds., pp. 151–201. Cambridge, Mass.: Harvard University Press, 1974. ISBN 0-674-12575-4. ▸ Pioneering study of technology, logistics, theory, and practice of defensive warfare in Sung and Yüan China. Includes analyses of three famous sieges in twelfth and thirteenth centuries. [JWC]

10.292 Gungwu Wang. *The structure of power in North China during the Five Dynasties.* 1963 ed. Stanford, Calif.: Stanford University Press, 1967. ▸ Masterly treatment of military and political policies of five Northern Dynasties of tenth-century China, with emphasis on strengthening of palace armies to curb power of provincial military governors. [JWC]

Economic History

10.293 Chao Ju-kua. *Chau Ju-kua: his work on the Chinese and Arab trade in the twelfth and thirteenth centuries, entitled "Chu-fan-chi."* Friedrich Hirth and W. W. Rockhill, trans. Taipei: Ch'eng-wen, 1970. ▸ Important source for our knowledge of Sung maritime trade and relations with Arabs and other Asians. [JWC]

10.294 Richard von Glahn. *The country of streams and grottoes: expansion, settlement, and the civilizing of the Sichuan frontier in Song times.* Cambridge, Mass.: Harvard University, Council on East Asian Studies, 1987. (Harvard East Asian monographs, 123.) ISBN 0-674-17543-3. ▸ Pioneering Annales-style study of Szechuan frontier during Sung and of processes of agrarian settlement, industrial development (of salt mines), and political incorporation into empire. [JWC]

10.295 Peter Golas. "Rural China in the Song." *Journal of Asian studies* 39.2 (1980) 291–325. ISSN 0021-9118. ▸ Succinct, lucid review of prolific and largely Japanese literature on Sung rural economy and society with particular attention to issues of manors and serfs that have long vexed Sung scholarship. [JWC]

10.296 Robert M. Hartwell. "Markets, technology, and the structure of enterprise in the development of the eleventh-century Chinese iron and steel industry." *Journal of economic history* 26 (1966) 29–58. ISSN 0022-0507. ▸ Pathbreaking treatment of remarkable iron and steel industry of Northern Sung. Examines question of what kept these developments from leading to industrial revolution. [JWC]

10.297 Lawrence J. C. Ma. *Commercial development and urban change in Sung China (960–1279).* Ann Arbor: University of Michigan, Department of Geography, 1971. (Michigan geographical publication, 6.) ▸ Historical geographer's analysis of how domestic and overseas commerce affected Sung urbanization with case study of Northern Sung capital of K'ai-feng. Most interesting for its attention to spatial dimensions. [JWC]

10.298 Shiba Yoshinobu. *Commerce and society in Sung China.* Mark Elvin, trans. Ann Arbor: University of Michigan, Center for Chinese Studies, 1970. (Michigan abstracts of Chinese and Japanese works on Chinese history, 2.) ISBN 0-89264-902-X. ▸ Abstracted translation of Shiba's classic study of Sung commerce with sections on communications, marketing, urbanization, commercial organization and capital, and commerce and society. Remains best treatment in English. [JWC]

10.299 Paul J. Smith. *Taxing heaven's storehouse: horses, bureaucrats, and the destruction of the Sichuan tea industry, 1074–1224.* Cambridge, Mass.: Harvard University, Council on East Asian Studies, 1991. (Harvard-Yenching Institute monograph series, 32.) ISBN 0-674-40641-9. ▸ Masterly study of state capitalist enterprise that managed tea and horse markets in Szechuan during new policies of Wang An-shih. Key work for understanding state's economic role. [JWC]

Social History

10.300 Chu Hsi. *Chu Hsi's "Family Rituals": a twelfth-century Chinese manual for the performance of cappings, weddings, funerals, and ancestral rites.* Patricia Buckley Ebrey, trans. Princeton: Princeton University Press, 1991. ISBN 0-691-03149-5. ▸ Translation and study of Neo-Confucian master Chu Hsi's influential treatise on family ritual. Treats not only Confucian kinship values but also role of ritual in Sung daily life. [JWC]

10.301 Priscilla Ching Chung. *Palace women in the Northern Sung.* Leiden: Brill, 1981. (T'oung Pao, Monographie, 12.) ISBN 90-04-06507-5 (pbk). ▸ Pioneering study of women of Northern Sung imperial harem, with emphasis on their social origins, hierarchical organization, and palace institutions. [JWC]

10.302 Fan Chengda. *On the road in twelfth-century China: the travel diaries of Fan Chengda (1126–1193).* James M. Hargett, trans. Wiesbaden: Steiner, 1989. (Münchener ostasiatische Studien, 52.) ISBN 3-515-05375-1, ISSN 0170-3668. ▸ Painstaking translation of scholar-official Fan Ch'eng-ta's travels north to Chin capital and west to Szechuan. Provides interesting vignettes of Sung life and numerous details of historical geography. [JWC]

10.303 Jacques Gernet. *Daily life in China on the eve of the Mongol invasion, 1250–1276.* H. M. Wright, trans. Stanford, Calif.: Stanford University Press, 1962. ISBN 0-8047-0720-0. ▸ Readable and learned introduction to Sung society. Emphasis on urban life of Southern Sung capital, Hang-chou, and on annual cycles and life cycles of urban population. [JWC]

10.304 Lu Yu. *South China in the twelfth century: a translation of Lu Yu's travel diaries July 3–December 6, 1170.* Chun-shu Chang and Joan Smythe, trans. Hong Kong: Chinese University Press, 1981. ISBN 962-201-221-3. ▸ Careful translation of poet Lu Yu's richly textured account of his travel to Szechuan, with profuse annotations. [JWC]

10.305 Yüan Ts'ai. *Family and property in Sung China: Yüan Ts'ai's "Precepts for Social Life."* Patricia Buckley Ebrey, trans. Princeton: Princeton University Press, 1984. ISBN 0-691-05426-6. ▸ Translation of Yüan Ts'ai's famous work on family management, revealing for its non-literati values, with book-length introduction. Best work available in English on Sung family life. [JWC]

Education, Examinations, and Literati Lives

10.306 Susan Bush. *The Chinese literati on painting: Su Shih (1037–1101) to Tung Ch'i-ch'ang (1555–1636).* Cambridge, Mass.: Harvard University Press, 1971. (Harvard-Yenching Institute studies, 27.) ISBN 0-674-12425-1. ▸ Study of theory of *wen-jen hua,* or literati painting, from its Sung origins to Ming dynasty, and of its relationship to literati culture. [JWC]

10.307 John W. Chaffee. *The thorny gates of learning in Sung China: a social history of examinations.* Cambridge: Cambridge University Press, 1985. ISBN 0-521-30207-2. ▸ Pathbreaking treatment of Sung schools and examinations and analysis of their geographical character and cultural impact. Argues that meritocratic ideals of early Sung emperors were frustrated by formal and informal systems of privilege. [JWC]

10.308 Robert P. Hymes. *Statesmen and gentlemen: the elite of Fu-chou, Chiang-hsi in Northern and Southern Sung.* Cambridge: Cambridge University Press, 1986. ISBN 0-521-30631-0. ▸ Exhaustively researched social history of prosperous prefecture in southeastern China. Revisionist analysis of Sung local society stressing importance of marriage and social ties in determining elite status and arguing that growing localism permeated Southern Sung elite society. [JWC]

10.309 Thomas H. C. Lee. *Government education and examinations in Sung China.* New York and Hong Kong: St. Martin's and Chinese University Press, 1985. ISBN 0-312-34131-8. ▸ Detailed treatment of Sung government's involvement in education and examinations with emphasis on institutional evolution, educational policy discussions, special schools at capital, and social impact of education. [JWC]

Biographies of Literary Figures

10.310 Jonathan Chaves. *Mei Yao-ch'en and the development of early Sung poetry.* New York: Columbia University Press, 1976. ISBN 0-231-03965-4. ▸ Full critical study of major eleventh-century poet; one of best such books on any Chinese author. [CH]

10.311 Michael Duke. *Lu Yu.* Boston: Twayne, 1977. ISBN 0-8057-6267-1. ▸ Good study of important Southern Sung literary figure. Chapters on his poetic style, his patriotic verse, and his involvement with Taoist alchemy. [CH]

10.312 Ronald C. Egan. *The literary works of Ou-yang Hsiu (1007–72).* Cambridge: Cambridge University Press, 1984. ISBN 0-521-25888-x. ▸ Thoughtful and well-researched study of Ou-yang Hsiu's prose, poetry, rhapsody (*fu*), and song-poetry (*tz'u*). Good companion volume to Liu's earlier study of Ou-yang Hsiu's political life (10.317). [CH]

10.313 Grace S. Fong. *Wu Wenying and the art of Southern Sung ci poetry.* Princeton: Princeton University Press, 1987. ISBN 0-691-06703-1. ▸ Best book on difficult subject of late Southern Sung lyric poetry (*tz'u*). Chapters on Wu Wen-ying's biography, on late Southern Sung poetics, and examination of Wu's poetry by theme. [CH]

10.314 Michael Anthony Fuller. *The road to east slope: the development of Su Shi's poetic voice.* Stanford, Calif.: Stanford University Press, 1990. ISBN 0-8047-1587-4. ▸ Good study of development of Su Shih as poet through 1084. Some mention of poet's biography, but major focus on aesthetic and formal issues. Many careful translations. [CH]

10.315 Shuen-fu Lin. *The transformation of the Chinese lyrical tradition: Chiang K'uei and Southern Sung tz'u poetry.* Princeton: Princeton University Press, 1978. ISBN 0-691-06351-6. ▸ Critical study of Chiang K'uei (ca. 1155–ca. 1235). Excellent material on cultural and artistic life of this important period of Chinese history in first chapter. [CH]

10.316 Lin Yutang. *The gay genius: the life and times of Su Tungpo.* New York: Day, 1947. ▸ Despite its popular orientation and unabashed enthusiasm for its subject, this book remains essential for student of eleventh-century cultural history. A pleasure to read, and still only complete biography of Su Shih (Su Tungpo) in European language. [CH]

10.317 James T. C. Liu. *Ou-yang Hsiu: an eleventh-century Neo-Confucianist.* Stanford, Calif.: Stanford University Press, 1967. ▸ Important biography that highlights political life of Ou-yang Hsiu (1007–72). Basic for study of Northern Sung China. Revision of author's 1963 book in Chinese on same subject. If possible, readers should also consult Chinese version. [CH]

10.318 Irving Yucheng Lo. *Hsin Ch'i-chi.* New York: Twayne, 1971. ▸ Biographical and critical study of Hsin Ch'i-chi (1140–1207), major lyric (*tz'u*) writer of Southern Sung period whose verse constitutes important expression of Chinese patriotism and early nationalism. Many translations of his poems. [CH]

10.319 Jerry Schmidt. *Yang Wan-li.* Boston: Twayne, 1976. ISBN 0-8057-6255-8. ▸ Detailed study of life and works of major Southern Sung poet and literary theorist. One of best explications in English of relationship between Ch'an Buddhism and Chinese poetics. [CH]

CONQUEST DYNASTIES
General Studies

10.320 Morris Rossabi, ed. *China among equals: the middle kingdom and its neighbors, X–XIV centuries.* Berkeley: University of California Press, 1983. ISBN 0-520-04383-9 (cl), 0-520-04562-9 (pbk). ▸ Wide-ranging and interesting essays on diplomacy, ideology, trade, politics, Korea, foreigners in Yüan China, etc. [RWD]

Liao Dynasty

10.321 Jennifer Holmgren. "Marriage, kinship, and seccession under the Ch'i-tan rulers of the Liao dynasty (907–1125)." *T'oung Pao* 72.1–3 (1986) 44–91. ISSN 0082-5433. ▸ First English-language analysis of social and political history of Liao ruling elite. Confirms link between aristocratic influence and power of women at imperial court. [RWD]

10.322 Masao Shimada. "The characteristic of northern region Liao bureaucracy and the significance of the hereditary official system." *Memoirs of the research department of the Toyo bunko* 41 (1983) 33–62. ISSN 0082-562X. ▸ English summary of studies by Japanese Liao specialist, who concludes that Liao was not conquest dynasty for its government emerged as compromise between old and new tribal power holders. Best available recent discussion in English on Liao government. [RWD]

10.323 Jing-shen Tao. *Two sons of heaven: studies in Sung-Liao relations.* Tucson: University of Arizona Press, 1988. ISBN 0-8165-1051-2. ▸ Collected essays of Taiwan-trained historian based largely on work previously published in Chinese; useful references to original and secondary sources. [RWD]

10.324 Karl A. Wittfogel and Feng Chia-sheng. *History of Chinese society, Liao (907–1125)*. Philadelphia: American Philosophical Society; distributed by Macmillan, 1949. (Transactions of the American Philosophical Society, 36.) ▸ Essays on institutional history and accompanying translations from Liao dynastic history remain unsurpassed and invaluable; bibliography is starting point for any student of Liao history. [RWD]

Chin Dynasty

10.325 Chan Hok-lam. *The historiography of the Chin dynasty: three studies*. Wiesbaden: Steiner, 1970. (Münchener ostasiatische Studien, 4.) ISBN 3-515-00728-8. ▸ Critical essays on sources for and writing of Chin history. Essential reference for students and scholars of Chin history. [RWD]

10.326 Chan Hok-lam. *Legitimation in imperial China: discussion under the Jurchen-Chin dynasty (1115–1234)*. Seattle: University of Washington Press, 1984. (University of Washington, Publications on Asia of the Henry M. Jackson School of International Studies, 38.) ISBN 0-295-96149-x. ▸ Comparative analysis of political ideology thoroughly grounded in primary sources and secondary scholarship. Reviewed in *Bulletin of Sung Yüan Studies* 20 (1988). [RWD]

10.327 Herbert Franke. "Jurchen customary law and the Chinese law of the Chin dynasty." In *State and law in East Asia: Festschrift Karl Bünger*. Eikemeier Dieter and Herbert Franke, eds., pp. 215–33. Wiesbaden: Harrassowitz, 1981. ▸ Traces evolution of Jürchen legal practice (penal, family, and inheritance) with copious translations from the scanty sources. Best available treatment in English. [RWD]

10.328 Igor de Rachewiltz. "Personnnel and personalities in North China in the early Mongol period." *Journal of the economic and social history of the Orient* 9.1–2 (1966) 88–144. ISSN 0022-4995. ▸ Detailed, useful survey of the confused early decades of thirteenth century. [RWD]

10.329 Jing-shen Tao. *The Jurchen in twelfth-century China: a study of sinicization*. Seattle: University of Washington Press, 1976. (Publications on Asia of the Institute for Comparative and Foreign Area Studies, 29.) ISBN 0-295-95514-7. ▸ The only English-language monographic survey of Chin history. [RWD]

Hsia Dynasty

10.330 Ruth Dunnell. "The 1094 Sino-Tangut Gantong stupa stele inscription of Wuwei: introduction, translation of Chinese text, and source study." In *Languages and history in East Asia: a Festschrift for Professor Tatsuo Nishida in honour of his sixtieth birthday*. Paul Kazuhisa Eguchi et al., eds. Kyoto: Shokado, 1988. ISBN 4-87974-882-x. ▸ Text and translation of important internal source for eleventh-century Hsia history and Sung-Hsia relations. Provides valuable material for comparative study of Buddhist state relations in East Asia. [RWD]

SEE ALSO
9.150 Luc Kwanten and Susan Hesse. *Tangut (Hsi hsia) studies.*

Yüan Dynasty

10.331 Paul Heng-chao Ch'en. *Chinese legal tradition under the Mongols: the code of 1291 as reconstructed*. 1966 ed. Princeton: Princeton University Press, 1979. ISBN 0-691-09238-9. ▸ Survey of Yüan legal institutions and translation of *Chih-yüan Hsin-ko* (New Code of the Chih-yüan Period). Argues that Yüan contribution to Chinese legal system far more significant than previously assumed. [RWD]

10.332 Ch'en Yuan. *Western and Central Asians in China under the Mongols: their transformation into Chinese*. 1966 ed. Ch'ien Hsing-hai and L. Carrington Goodrich, trans. Nettetal: Steyler Verlag–Wort und Werk, 1989. ISBN 3-8050-0243-2. ▸ Biographical gold mine for exploring the ethnic range of Yüan social and cultural history. Accounts of numerous foreigners in Mongol service and their cultural contributions. Despite subtitle, little analysis of acculturation process. [RWD/TTA]

10.333 James I. Crump, Jr. *Chinese theater in the days of Kublai Khan*. 1980 ed. Ann Arbor: University of Michigan, Center for Chinese Studies, 1990. (Michigan monographs in Chinese studies, 62.) ISBN 0-89264-101-0 (cl), 0-89264-093-6 (pbk). ▸ Fun book, constructed as Yüan play, that explores emergence of Chinese theater under Mongols and gives translations of three plays with helpful program notes. [RWD]

10.334 John W. Dardess. *Conquerors and Confucians: aspects of political change in late Yuan China*. New York: Columbia University Press, 1973. ISBN 0-231-03689-2. ▸ Interpretation of Mongolian accommodation to Chinese politics (or was it the other way around?). First in-depth, English-language study of Yüan politics. An important and controversial study. [RWD]

10.335 Elizabeth Endicott-West. *Mongolian rule in China: local administration in the Yüan dynasty*. Cambridge, Mass.: Council on East Asian Studies, Harvard University Press and Harvard-Yenching Institute, 1989. (Harvard-Yenching Institute monograph series, 29.) ISBN 0-674-58525-9. ▸ Pathbreaking analysis of Yüan government at level where it counted for most people. Emergence of hybrid style of governance in sedentary zone revealing persistence of Mongolian traditions. Suggestive for comparison with other parts of empire. [RWD/TTA]

10.336 Ch'i-ch'ing Hsiao. *The military establishment of the Yüan dynasty*. Cambridge, Mass.: Harvard University, Council on East Asian Studies, 1978. (Harvard East Asian monographs, 77.) ISBN 0-674-57461-3. ▸ Annotated translation of treatise on military in Yüan dynastic history. Valuable primary source on key Mongolian institution and its adaptation to China. [RWD]

10.337 John D. Langlois, ed. *China under Mongol rule*. Princeton: Princeton University Press, 1981. ISBN 0-691-10110-8. ▸ Contributions deal with government, politics, religion, education, art and literature, and society. Advances level of discourse on Yüan period. [RWD]

10.338 Li Chih-Chang. *The travels of an alchemist: the journey of the Taoist Chang-chun from China to the Hindukush at the summons of Chingiz khan*. 1931 ed. Arthur Waley, trans. New York: AMS Press, 1979. ISBN 0-404-14481-0. ▸ Translation of diary of Ch'ang-ch'un's journey to Chinggis Khan's camp in Hindukush, as kept by Taoist's adept disciple. Fascinating primary source for history and geography of early Mongol period. [RWD]

10.339 Richard John Lynn. *Kuan Yün-shih*. Boston: Twayne, 1980. ISBN 0-8057-6404-6. ▸ One of few in-depth studies of Yüan dynasty and non-Han Chinese poet. Translations of all Kuan's extant verse and extensive biographical and critical studies. Among best volumes in Twayne series. [CH]

10.340 Frederick W. Mote. *The poet Kao Ch'i, 1336–1374*. Princeton: Princeton University Press, 1962. ▸ Full study of the life and works of this late Yüan, early Ming dynasty poet and official; focus is on historical background and biography. One of few book-length studies on literary figure from this period. [CH]

10.341 Paul Ratchnevsky. *Un code des Yuan, vol. 1*. 1937 ed. Paris: Collège de France, Institut des Hautes Études Chinoises, 1985. (Bibliothèque de l'Institut des Hautes Études Chinoises, 4.) ISBN 2-85557-034-1. ▸ Translation and annotation of "Treatise on Punishment and Law" and "Treatise on the Exercise of Public Functions" from Yüan dynastic history. More survey of legal institutions than law code per se. Essential for comparative study of Chinese legal institutions. [RWD]

10.342 Morris Rossabi. *Khubilai Khan: his life and times.* Berkeley: University of California Press, 1988. ISBN 0-520-05913-1. ‣ First English-language biography of major historical figure. Reviewed in *Bulletin of Sung Yüan Studies* 21 (1989) and *Journal of Asian Studies* 48.2 (1989). [RWD]

10.343 Sung Lien. *Economic structure of the Yüan dynasty: translation of chapters 93 and 94 of the "Yüan Shih."* Herbert Franz Schurmann, ed. and trans. Cambridge, Mass.: Harvard University Press, 1967. (Harvard-Yenching Institute studies, 16.) ISBN 0-674-23050-7. ‣ Pioneering effort to unravel Yüan economic practices and institutions. [RWD]

SEE ALSO
9.222 Francis Woodman Cleaves, trans. *The secret history of the Mongols.*
9.230 Thomas T. Allsen. *Mongol imperialism.*

MING DYNASTY

Historiography

10.344 Timothy Brook. *Geographical sources of Ming-Qing history.* Ann Arbor: University of Michigan, Center for Chinese Studies, 1988. (Michigan monographs in Chinese studies, 58.) ISBN 0-89264-075-8 (cl), 0-89264-076-6 (pbk). ‣ Introductions to and annotated bibliographies of two genres of primary sources: route books or handbooks for travelers and topographical and institutional gazetteers. Possible use for these sources in historical research. [WSA]

10.345 Wolfgang Franke. *An introduction to the sources of Ming history.* Tai-pei shih: Tsung ching tu shu chu pan kung ssu, 1978. ‣ Valuable introduction to Ming history and historiography followed by extensive annotations on more than 800 primary sources. Includes information on libraries, availability of editions. Indispensable reference work for serious student. [WSA]

10.346 L. Carrington Goodrich, ed. *Dictionary of Ming biography, 1368–1644.* 2 vols. New York: Columbia University Press, 1976. ISBN 0-231-03801-1 (v. 1), 0-231-03833-X (v. 2). ‣ Biographies of 650 people prominent in Ming history, foreigners as well as Chinese. Each biography includes select bibliography. Excellent maps, tables, illustrations, and indexes. Standard reference work. [WSA]

10.347 Frederic E. Wakeman, Jr., ed. *Ming and Qing historical studies in the People's Republic of China.* Berkeley: University of California, Institute of East Asian Studies, 1980. (Chinese research monographs, 17.) ISBN 0-912966-27-0. ‣ Report by United States academic delegation to China in 1979. Discusses most important academic centers, libraries, and archives for Ming-Ch'ing studies. Describes current research, intellectual concerns of leading Chinese scholars. [WSA]

10.348 Arthur Waldron. *The Great Wall: from history to myth.* Cambridge: Cambridge University Press, 1990. ISBN 0-521-36518-X. ‣ Wall-building in Chinese history with emphasis on Great Wall in Ming times. Examines geographical, military, political, and economic factors; places construction of Wall in historical perspective. Dispels many myths. [WSA/MR]

Economic History

10.349 Linda Grove and Christian Daniels, eds. *State and society in China: Japanese perspectives on Ming-Qing social and economic history.* Tokyo: Tokyo University Press and Columbia University Press, 1984. ISBN 4-13-026042-1, 0-86008-356-X. ‣ Articles by leading Japanese scholars on handicraft industries, problems of landownership, popular uprisings, nature of rural society, foreign trade. Most articles date from 1950s and 1960s and have strong Marxist flavor. [WSA]

10.350 Ayao Hoshi. *The Ming tribute grain system.* Mark Elvin, ed. and trans. Ann Arbor: University of Michigan, Center for Chinese Studies, 1969. (Michigan abstracts on Chinese and Japanese works on Chinese history, 1.) ISBN 0-89264-901-1. ‣ System for moving grain, other goods to and from capital via Grand Canal and other waterways. Examines system's administration, structure of transport, role of granaries. Contains useful maps, glossaries. [WSA]

10.351 Ray Huang. *Taxation and governmental finance in sixteenth-century Ming China.* Cambridge: Cambridge University Press, 1974. ISBN 0-521-20283-2, 0-521-20283-3. ‣ Detailed, invaluable study of dynasty's administration of land taxes and salt monopoly, its management of revenues from commerce and industry, and nature of government's overall financial management. Includes numerous charts and tables. [WSA]

10.352 Liang Fang-chung. *The single-whip method of taxation in China.* 1950 ed. Yu-ch'uan Wang, trans. Cambridge, Mass.: Harvard University, East Asian Research Center, 1970. (Harvard East Asian monographs, 1.) ‣ Pioneering study of Ming government's attempts to simplify most tax collections into payments in silver. Examines dynasty's fiscal system and relationship between central and local government. [WSA]

SEE ALSO
11.197 Ping-ti Ho. *Studies on the population of China, 1368–1953.*
11.263 Dwight H. Perkins. *Agricultural development in China, 1368–1968.*
11.264 Evelyn Sakakida Rawski. *Agricultural change and the peasant economy of South China.*

Political and Institutional History

10.353 Étienne Balazs. *Political theory and administrative reality in traditional China.* London: University of London, School of Oriental and African Studies, 1965. ‣ Two pathbreaking lectures on three famous seventeenth-century scholars whose ideas are sometimes linked to modern notions of science, democracy, and nationalism. Third lecture analyzes eighteenth-century handbook for local administration. [WSA]

10.354 Albert Chan. *The glory and fall of the Ming dynasty.* Norman: University of Oklahoma Press, 1982. ISBN 0-8061-1741-9. ‣ Informative but rambling account of empire in ascendancy and in decline. Covers government, army, social structure, economics, religion. Emphasis on dynastic founding and circumstances surrounding its collapse in 1640s. [WSA]

10.355 David B. Chan. *The usurpation of the prince of Yen, 1398–1402.* San Francisco: Chinese Materials Center, 1976. (Chinese Materials and Research Aids Service Center, Occasional series, 7.) ‣ Best available study of usurpation of throne by dynastic founder's fourth son. Regarded as major turning point in Ming history as entire tone and policy orientation of government changed. [WSA]

10.356 Edward L. Dreyer. *Early Ming China: a political history.* Stanford, Calif.: Stanford University Press, 1982. ISBN 0-8047-1105-4. ‣ Best available account of dynastic founding and governmental policies of first five Ming emperors. Especially concerned with gradual decline of early Ming military and rise of civilian, Confucian-oriented bureaucracy. [WSA]

10.357 Edward L. Farmer. *Early Ming government: the evolution of dual capitals.* Cambridge, Mass.: Harvard University, East Asian Research Center, 1976. (Harvard East Asian monographs, 66.) ISBN 0-674-22175-3. ‣ Pathbreaking institutional study emphasizing military and national defense. Analyzes placement of capital at Nanking, its subsequent removal to Peking, and logistical problems involved in supplying capital in north of country. [WSA]

10.358 Carney T. Fisher. *The chosen one: succession and adoption in the court of Ming shizong.* Sydney: Allen & Unwin, 1990. ISBN 0-04-442113-3. ▸ Important study of sixteenth-century controversy over imperial succession. Emperor died without heir, throne passed to nephew. Conflict then erupted over Confucian concepts of filial piety, imperial perogatives, and limits of bureaucratic power. [WSA]

10.359 Ray Huang. *1587, a year of no significance: the Ming dynasty in decline.* New Haven: Yale University Press, 1981. ISBN 0-300-02518-1 (cl), 0-300-02884-9 (pbk). ▸ Critical examination of Ming bureaucratic system through biographical studies of prominent figures. Noteworthy for accounts of life inside imperial palace and at court. Wealth of information on central government institutions. [WSA]

10.360 Charles O. Hucker. *The censorial system of Ming China.* Stanford, Calif.: Stanford University Press, 1966. ISBN 0-8047-0289-6. ▸ Solid study of censorial institution in imperial China with detailed examination of Censorate's operations from 1424 to 1434 and 1620 to 1627. Concluding chapter on censorship and traditional Chinese state. [WSA]

10.361 Charles O. Hucker. *The Ming dynasty: its origins and evolving institutions.* Ann Arbor: University of Michigan, Center for Chinese Studies, 1978. (Michigan papers in Chinese studies, 34.) ISBN 0-89264-034-0. ▸ Succinct, nontechnical account of Mongol collapse and Ming founding followed by examination of Ming governmental institutions and first emperor's administrative policies. Analyzes nature of early Ming autocracy and its legacy. [WSA]

10.362 Charles O. Hucker. *Two studies on Ming history.* Ann Arbor: University of Michigan, Center for Chinese Studies, 1971. (Michigan papers in Chinese studies, 12.) ▸ General account of government attempts to control piracy in sixteenth century and pathbreaking study of famous urban uprising to protest power of imperial eunuchs. Latter article contains lengthy translation of primary materials. [WSA]

10.363 Charles O. Hucker, ed. *Chinese government in Ming times: seven studies.* New York: Columbia University Press, 1969. ▸ Articles by leading specialists on local administration, military and local defense, policy formulation and decisionmaking, fiscal administration, educational institutions, and civil service examination system. Articles by Yang, Lo, and Huang especially recommended. [WSA]

10.364 Leif Littrup. *Sub-bureaucratic government in China in Ming times: a study of Shandong province in the sixteenth century.* Oslo and Irvington-on-Hudson, N.Y.: Universitets Forlaget; distributed by Columbia University Press, 1981. ISBN 82-00-09531-2, ISSN 0332-6217. ▸ Important study of local government below district level. Focusing on Shantung province, examines impact of monetization, economic expansion, and tax reform on local society during late sixteenth century. [WSA]

10.365 Frederick W. Mote and Denis C. Twitchett, eds. *The Ming dynasty, 1368–1644.* Vol. 7.1 of *The Cambridge history of China.* Cambridge: Cambridge University Press, 1988. ISBN 0-521-24332-7 (v. 7.1). ▸ Chronological political history, ca. 1330–1652. Contains numerous maps, an extensive bibliography, bibliographical notes to each chapter, and concluding chapter on historical writing during dynasty. Standard reference work. [WSA]

10.366 James Bunyan Parsons. *The peasant rebellions of the late Ming dynasty.* Tucson: University of Arizona Press for the Association for Asian Studies, 1970. (Association for Asian Studies, Monographs and papers, 26.) ISBN 0-8165-0155-6. ▸ Detailed chronological study of domestic uprisings that helped cause Ming collapse in 1644. Emphasis on military and political history

surrounding rebellions of Li Tzu-ch'eng and Chang Hsien-chung. [WSA]

10.367 Romeyn Taylor, trans. *The basic annals of Ming T'ai-tsu.* San Francisco, Calif.: Chinese Materials Center, 1975. (Chinese Materials and Research Aids Service Center, Occasional series, 24.) ▸ Translations of three chapters from official Ming history dealing with reign of founding emperor. Includes important introductory essay on primary sources, historiographical problems surrounding study of early Ming political history. [WSA]

10.368 Frederic E. Wakeman, Jr. *The great enterprise: the Manchu reconstruction of imperial order in seventeenth-century China.* 2 vols. Berkeley: University of California Press, 1985. ISBN 0-520-04804-0 (set). ▸ Detailed account of Ming collapse, beginnings of Manchu rule. Emphasizes political and intellectual history but with important discussions of economic and cultural issues as well. Extensive bibliography, numerous illustrations. [WSA]

SEE ALSO
11.151 Jonathan D. Spence and John E. Wills, Jr., eds. *From Ming to Ch'ing.*
11.152 Lynn A. Struve. *The Southern Ming, 1644–1662.*

Social and Cultural History

10.369 Hilary J. Beattie. *Land and lineage in China: a study of T'ung-ch'eng county in the Ming and Ch'ing dynasties.* Cambridge: Cambridge University Press, 1979. ISBN 0-521-21974-4. ▸ Pathbreaking study of landholding, taxation, and social structure in one local area. Examines composition and organization of local elite; especially concerned with large kinship groups. Includes translation of important seventeenth-century treatise on landholding. [WSA]

10.370 K'ang-i Sun Chang. *The late-Ming poet Ch'en Tzu-lung: the crises of love and loyalism.* New Haven: Yale University Press, 1991. ISBN 0-300-04872-6. ▸ Brilliant study of the use of allegory and erotic symbolism for purposes of political protest in seventeenth century. Important book on important period. [CH]

10.371 John W. Dardess. *Confucianism and autocracy: professional elites in the founding of the Ming dynasty.* 1962 ed. Berkeley: University of California Press, 1983. ISBN 0-520-04659-5 (cl), 0-520-04733-8 (pbk). ▸ Stimulating, controversial study arguing that autocracy in early Ming can be fully understood only if Confucianists are seen as professional collegial body intent on national sociomoral regeneration. [WSA]

10.372 Jerry Dennerline. *The Chia-ting loyalists: Confucian leadership and social change in seventeenth-century China.* New Haven: Yale University Press, 1981. ISBN 0-300-02548-3. ▸ Ideological, social underpinnings of Chinese resistence to Manchu conquest. Detailed analysis of local social and political networks. Important discussion of relationship between Confucian education and concepts of dynastic loyalty. [WSA]

10.373 Ping-ti Ho. *The ladder of success in imperial China.* New York: Columbia University Press, 1980. ISBN 0-231-05161-1 (pbk). ▸ Pioneering analysis of elite mobility, 1368–1911. Examines social stratification, fluidity of status system, factors affecting upward and downward mobility, and regional differences. Twenty-seven case studies draw on wide range of primary sources. [WSA]

10.374 John Meskill. *Academies in Ming China: a historical essay.* Tucson: University of Arizona Press for the Association for Asian Studies, 1982. (Association for Asian studies, Monographs, 39.) ISBN 0-8165-0771-6. ▸ Best available study of private academies as educational institutions and centers of political activity. Examines role of academies in promoting Neo-Confucian political and philosophical ideals, relationship between academies and civil service examination system. [WSA]

10.375 Ann Paluden. *The imperial Ming tombs.* New Haven: Yale University Press, 1981. ISBN 0-300-02511-4. ▸ History, topography, and architecture of imperial tombs in China followed by detailed discussions of Ming tombs in Peking and Nanking. Information on tomb administration, ritual sacrifices, and iconography. Numerous maps, charts, and photographs. [WSA]

10.376 Jonathan D. Spence. *The memory palace of Matteo Ricci.* New York: Viking, 1984. ISBN 0-670-46430-4. ▸ Highly original study of cultural interaction between China and West in late sixteenth century. Explores eminent Jesuit priest's attempts to influence Chinese elite through introduction of European mnemonic techniques. [WSA]

SEE ALSO
11.161 Frederic E. Wakeman, Jr., and Carolyn Grant, eds. *Conflict and control in late imperial China.*
11.339 Willard J. Peterson. *Bitter gourd.*

Foreign Relations

10.377 C. R. Boxer, ed. and trans. *South China in the sixteenth century, being the narratives of Galeote Pereira, Fr. Gaspar da Cruz, O.P, [and] Fr. Martin de Rada. O.E.S.A.* London: Hakluyt Society, 1953. (Works issued by the Hakluyt Society, Second series, 106.) ▸ Translations of three European accounts of life in sixteenth-century China. Annotations provide valuable information on economic and political background of European expansion, nature of early Sino-Western relations. [WSA]

10.378 Ma Huan. *Ying-yai sheng-lan: the overall survey of the ocean's shores [1433].* J.V.G. Mills, ed. and trans. Cambridge: Cambridge University Press for the Hakluyt Society, 1970. (Works issued by the Hakluyt Society, Extra series, 42.) ISBN 0-521-01042-2. ▸ Annotated translation of travelog by Chinese Muslim who sailed with government fleets to South and Southeast Asia, and Middle East. Introduction and translation contain valuable information on medieval trade and Chinese attitudes toward foreign cultures. [WSA/DKW]

10.379 Kwan-wai So. *Japanese piracy in Ming China during the sixteenth century.* East Lansing: Michigan State University Press, 1975. ISBN 0-87013-179-6. ▸ Smuggling, piracy along Chinese coast. Argues Japanese are often blamed for acts committed by native Chinese in conflicts with Ming government over trade and taxation. Includes extensive translations from primary materials. [WSA]

10.380 Wang Yi-t'ung. *Official relations between China and Japan, 1368–1549.* Cambridge, Mass.: Harvard University Press, 1953. (Harvard-Yenching Institute series, 9.) ▸ Pioneering study of Chinese and Japanese attitudes toward foreign relations, Ming attempts to control piracy and smuggling, and Japan's desire for expanded trade. Collapse of official relations and violent consequences in sixteenth century. [WSA]

SEE ALSO
9.89 Morris Rossabi. *China and Inner Asia from 1368 to the present day.*

JAMES H. COLE

China since 1644

Since the early 1950s there have been several clear historiographical trends in the study of China since 1644, that is, modern China. It should be noted at the outset, however, that there is still no international consensus as to when "modern China" began. Answers range from the Sung dynasty to "not yet." Many socioeconomic historians point to the sixteenth century, diplomatic historians to the Opium War (1840–1842), intellectual historians to the 1890s. Others have come to reject the "traditional versus modern" dichotomy entirely and are searching for a new paradigm. In the 1950s diplomatic history was still in vogue, as exemplified by J. K. Fairbank's *Trade and Diplomacy on the China Coast* (11.96), published in 1953. Fairbank's dominant influence on the study of modern Chinese history in the United States began in the mid-1940s and remained largely unchallenged intellectually or institutionally until the mid-1960s. His emphasis on nineteenth-century Sino-Western relations followed in the tradition of his mentor H. B. Morse, whose three-volume *International Relations of the Chinese Empire* (11.133) was published 1910–1918. But in a more important sense, Fairbank was reacting against Morse's kind of diplomatic history, which was written from the perspective of Western activity in China, with little regard to the Chinese response, and was based solely on Western sources. Eventually, Fairbank was in turn criticized by the next generation of scholars, exemplified by his student P. Cohen (11.35), for portraying the Chinese as responders rather than as prime movers. There have been, in short, three intellectual generations: Morse's presentation of Western actors on a Chinese stage, Fairbank's Chinese audience responding to the Western actors, and Cohen's Chinese actors on a Chinese stage.

The 1960s was a golden age of modern China studies in the United States. The East Asian Research Center at Harvard became the hub of an unprecedented boom in scholarly publications (virtually all revised Ph.D. dissertations), spurred by what might facetiously be termed Fairbank's dental approach: his preoccupation with filling the gaps. In those days the federal government and private foundations (led by Ford) provided plentiful funding for language study and dissertation research at a growing number of interdisciplinary China centers at major American universities. A large percentage of Fairbank's graduate students, who at first dominated the field, was drawn to modern Chinese intellectual history, both for its inherent fascination and also, I suspect, because an intellectual biography was a manageable dissertation topic: you knew when you were done. Thus in the late 1950s and early 1960s the trend toward intellectual history ran strong, exemplified most brilliantly by J. R. Levenson (11.326).

But starting in the mid-1960s the tide began to turn toward social history. The major influences were not only the French Annales school but also the Berkeley historian F. Wakeman (11.225), himself the student of Fairbank's student Levenson, and especially the anthropologist G. W. Skinner (then at Cornell but soon at Stanford). Skinner's series of articles—"Marketing and Social Structure in Rural China" (11.218, 11.644), published 1964–1965—was a revelation, reshaping patterns of intellectual and institutional influence within the modern China field.

On a personal note, when I was an undergraduate in history at Fairbank's Harvard in the mid-1960s, Chinese history was conceived from the top down, starting with the central government in Peking and reaching down to the county-magistrate level but not below. At a senior oral exam I was asked a question on Chinese local society (by a Japan specialist) and clearly remember feeling that the question was rather out of bounds. Subsequently China historians' increased sensitivity to variation through space as well as time prompted the realization that China was too big to generalize about: what was needed was research in local history, especially local social history. Given this new inclination, anthropological influence was to be expected, for who knew more about local society than anthropologists? Anthropology has indeed revolutionalized the China historian's conception of the scope and content of social history; its cross-disciplinary influence is clearly evident in many of the entries below.

The next major trend to emerge was an increased attention to economic history, sparked by controversy over R. Myers's *The Chinese Peasant Economy* (11.259), published in 1970. This new focus on economic history complemented the emerging interest in local society. Economic history remains the most underresearched branch of modern China studies and, in terms of interpretation, the most confused. This confusion or, rather, lack of consensus, since the disputants know very well where they stand, stems primarily from two sources: first, from at least the Vietnam War period onward, economic history has borne the brunt of heated ideological controversies within the modern China field, especially over the impact of Western imperialism; second, and more basic, is that for many topics in Chinese economic history, reliable hard data are relatively (or even absolutely) lacking—an obvious impediment to definitive research. One exception is the subfield of Taiwan studies, which has benefited from the reliable statistics compiled by the 1895–1945 Japanese colonial administration.

The most recent historiographical development, too new yet to constitute a trend, has been the first sprouting of an approach that might be termed sociointellectual history. This approach seeks to place specific developments in intellectual history in their social contexts without, however, making deterministic assumptions about causation. The best example of sociointellectual history to date is *Classicism, Politics, and Kinship*, by UCLA's B. Elman (11.310), published in 1990. Elman, who prefers the term cultural history, explores how a major development in Chinese philosophy (reformist New Text Confucianism) originated among the members of specific lineages in one region of Kiangsu province during the seventeenth century.

Finally, the omission of political and institutional history from the above *tour d'horizon* should not leave the impression that these approaches have been neglected by Western scholars of modern China. On the contrary, in purely quantitative terms, political and institutional studies probably predominate. Indeed, Western historians' fascination with the fluctuating fortunes of the Chinese Communist party has resulted in a decided emphasis on political history among studies of the republican period (1912–1949), not to mention the People's Republic. And access to the massive Ch'ing dynasty archives, held in Peking and Taipei, has already resulted in institutional analyses of unprecedented sophistication (e.g., B. S. Bartlett 11.79; P. E. Will and R. B. Wong 11.165; and J. M. Polachek 11.139). In short, while China's future is murky at present (summer 1992), prospects for the study of modern Chinese history are bright.

Section 11 contains some 760 annotated entries on published works in English and French treating China since 1644, plus cross-references to other sections. With a few notable exceptions, virtually all entries are books rather than articles. Unpublished dissertations are excluded. Since space is limited, works published in more than one format are included only once (e.g., chapters in *The Cambridge History of China* that have also been published separately are not included as separate publications). Although, like the entire *Guide*, this section is selective rather than comprehensive, apologies are offered in advance for worthy works that may have been inadvertently omitted.

The section is organized as follows. The first subsection, Reference Works, is divided into seven categories: bibliographical, biographical, chronological, encyclopedic, general histories (including textbooks), geographical, and research guides. The remaining subsections are Ch'ing Dynasty (1644–1911), Republic of China (1912–1949), People's Republic of China (1949–), Taiwan, and Hong Kong and Macao. Each of these subsections is divided into four categories: political history (including foreign relations, legal, and military history), social history, economic history, and intellectual-cultural history (including biography). Since assigning an entry to one of these categories is sometimes arbitrary—works on socioeconomic history and on the political economy of the People's Republic come immediately to mind—users should be flexible in their search strategies. A few entries defying subject categories may be found in Reference Works: General Histories. Entries within each category (with a very few exceptions) are listed alphabetically, either by author or (in a few cases) by title.

Items covering more than one time period are listed under the first period that they cover extensively. Thus, for example, biographies of Mao Tse-tung are included under Republic of China (1912–1949): Intellectual History, not under People's Republic: Intellectual History. For the same reason, the Ch'ing Dynasty (1644–1911) subsection contains not only works solely on the Ch'ing, but also works on both the Ch'ing and republican periods, and on the Ch'ing, republic, and People's Republic.

Rather than include only the single "best" work on a given topic, I have, as far as space permits, tried to provide a variety of interpretations, so the user can, by comparing and contrasting them, draw his or her own conclusions. Since users, however, are presumed to be looking for guidance as well as information, I have not included interpretations that are clearly outdated or discredited unless, as happens once or twice, they are referred to so centrally by cited works that omitting them would leave the user at a loss.

At what point approaching the present does history transmogrify into political science and journalism? Although I do not necessarily agree with Chou En-lai that it is still too early to evaluate the significance of the French Revolution, historical judgment does require a modicum of temporal elbow room. Consequently, the cut-off date for coverage of the People's Republic is 1976 (the death of Mao Tse-tung and, with the arrest of the Gang of Four, the termination of the Cultural Revolution), clearly the end of an era, if not yet the beginning of a new one. The Taiwan subsection covers, in principle, from 1644 through 1975 (the death of Chiang Kai-shek). The Hong Kong and Macao subsection covers, in principle, Hong Kong, including the New Territories, from the 1840s to 1984 (the Sino-British Agreement on the 1997 retrocession), plus Macao since its sixteenth-century origins. The overseas Chinese are not covered here in Section 11 but rather in the *Guide*'s other relevant geographical sections, for example, Southeast Asia.

In accordance with specified guidelines, the personal and family names of a Chinese, Japanese, or Korean author are given in the order used by that author in the West, for example, Noriko Kamachi but Ono Kazuko, Chong-sik Lee but Chow Tse-tsung.

All annotations and their relevant index entries are in Wade-Giles romanization, since virtually all American library catalogs (both computerized and card) use only Wade-Giles. If an entry's title uses pinyin romanization, the annotation includes the Wade-Giles version for key terms.

Some users will wish to go beyond Western-language studies and dive into the even vaster sea of research on China in Asian languages (especially Chinese, Japanese, and Korean). The single most important guide is the bibliography published annually since 1935 by Kyoto University's Jinbun Kagaku Kenkyūjo (Institute of Humanistic Sciences) titled *Tōyōgaku bunken ruimoku* (Classified Bibliography of Oriental Studies).

ACKNOWLEDGMENTS   *I wish to offer thanks to the Chinese Information and Culture Center Library (New York), Columbia University Libraries (including the Interlibrary Loan Department), Harvard University Libraries, the Library of Congress, and the New York Public Library.*

Entries are arranged under the following headings:

Reference Works
Bibliographies
Biographies
Chronologies
Encyclopedias
General Histories and Textbooks
Geographies
Research Guides

Ch'ing Dynasty, 1644–1911
Political History
Social History
Economic History
Intellectual and Cultural History

Republic of China, 1912–1949
Political History
Social History
Economic History
Intellectual and Cultural History

People's Republic of China, since 1949
Political History
Social History
Economic History
Intellectual and Cultural History

Taiwan
Political History
Social History
Economic History
Intellectual and Cultural History

Hong Kong and Macao
Political History
Social History
Economic History
Intellectual and Cultural History

[Contributors: AJR = Alan J. Rocke, DHK = David H. Kaiser, FN = F. G. Notehelfer, JHC = James H. Cole, PBE = Patricia Buckley Ebrey, WSA = William S. Atwell]

REFERENCE WORKS

Bibliographies

11.1 *Bibliography of Asian studies.* Ann Arbor: Association for Asian Studies, 1956–. ISSN 0067-7159. ▸ Invaluable annual listing of Western-language publications (books, articles) on any Asian (not just Chinese) topic. Arranged by subject-country, then by topic. Includes author index. Originally (1936–40) titled *Bulletin of Far Eastern Bibliography.* [JHC]

11.2 Lucie Cheng, Charlotte Furth, and Hon-ming Yip, comps. *Women in China: bibliography of available English-language materials.* Berkeley: University of California, Center for Chinese Studies and Institute of East Asian Studies, 1984. ISBN 0-912966-72-6 (pbk). ▸ Contains 4,107 entries, arranged by subject, covering both pre- and post-1911 (including post-1949). Separate name indexes for authors and Chinese women who appear as subjects in bibliography. [JHC]

11.3 Peter P. Cheng. *China.* Oxford: Clio, 1983. ISBN 0-903450-81-x. ▸ Annotated bibliography of 1,460 books (no articles), arranged by topic. Covers antiquity to present. Includes combined author-title-subject index. [JHC]

11.4 James H. Cole. *Updating Wilkinson: an annotated bibliography of reference works on imperial China published since 1973.* New York: Cole, 1991. ISBN 0-9629122-0-4. ▸ Supplements Wilkinson 10.19. Contains Western-, Chinese-, and Japanese-lan-

guage works. Includes special sections on biography and local history. [JHC]

11.5 Richard Louis Edmonds, comp. *Macau.* Oxford: Clio, 1989. ISBN 1-85109-090-8. ▸ Annotated bibliography of 381 books and articles on Macao arranged by topic. Includes thirty-eight-page introductory essay and combined author-title-subject index. [JHC]

11.6 Joshua A. Fogel, ed. and trans. *Recent Japanese studies of modern Chinese history.* 2 vols. Armonk, N.Y.: Sharpe, 1984–89. ISBN 0-87332-308-4 (v. 1, pbk), 0-87332-564-8 (v. 2, pbk). ▸ Two collections of bibliographical essays (covering publications 1979–82 [v. 1], 1983–86 [v. 2]) translated from annual May issues of *Shigaku zasshi* (Journal of Historical Studies). Convenient entry into recent Japanese scholarship on China, 1368–1919. Volume 2 subtitled *Translations from Shigaku zasshi for 1983–86.* [JHC]

11.7 Donald A. Gibbs and Yun-chen Li. *A bibliography of studies and translations of modern Chinese literature, 1918–1942.* Cambridge, Mass.: Harvard University, East Asian Research Center, 1975. (Harvard East Asian monographs, 61.) ISBN 0-674-07111-5. ▸ Careful listing of Western-language studies and English translations of literary works (broadly defined) from appearance of Lu Hsun's first short stories to eve of Mao Tse-tung's 1942 Yenan Talks. [JHC]

11.8 Rainer Hoffmann. *Bücherkunde zur chinesischen Geschichte, Kultur, und Gesellschaft.* Munich: Weltforum, 1973. ISBN 3-8039-0074-3. ▸ Annotated bibliography of Western-language books and articles on history, culture, and society from high antiquity through 1911 plus reference works. Useful citations of book reviews and author and subject indexes. [JHC]

11.9 David Fu-keung Ip, Leung Chi-keung, and Wu Chung-tong. *Hong Kong: a social sciences bibliography.* Hong Kong: University of Hong Kong, Centre of Asian Studies, 1974. (Centre of Asian Studies bibliographies and research guides, 7.) ▸ Annotated listing of English- and Chinese-language items (published and unpublished), arranged in thirty-four categories covering social, economic, political, and cultural topics. Emphasizes post-1945 materials. Includes cross-reference and author indexes. [JHC]

11.10 J. Bruce Jacobs, Jean Hagger, and Anne Sedgley, comps. *Taiwan: a comprehensive bibliography of English-language publications.* New York: Columbia University, East Asian Institute, 1984. ISBN 0-913418-09-9. ▸ Emphasizes works published 1945–80. Arranged by social science and humanities subjects. Includes author-title index. [JHC]

11.11 Lee Wei-chin. *Taiwan.* Oxford: Clio, 1990. ISBN 1-85109-091-6. ▸ Annotated bibliography of 825 books, articles, and dissertations arranged by topic. Includes author, title, and subject indexes. [JHC]

11.12 Lin Fu-shun, ed. and comp. *Chinese law, past and present: a bibliography of enactments and commentaries in English text.* New York: Columbia University, East Asian Institute, 1966. ▸ Seventy percent of 3,500 entries on People's Republic; also covers pre-1911 period and Republic of China (pre- and post-1949). Arranged by subject with author index. Useful but needs updating. [JHC]

11.13 John Lust. *Western books on China published up to 1850 in the Library of the School of Oriental and African Studies, University of London: a descriptive catalogue.* London: Bamboo Publishing, 1987. ISBN 1-870076-02-8. ▸ Annotated subject catalog of 1,293 items printed 1550–1850. Delight for bibliophiles. Includes title, name, and supplementary subject indexes. [JHC]

11.14 "Republican China studies in Asia and Europe: bibliographic reports." *Republican China* 16.2 (1991) 69–112. ISSN 0884-4496. ▸ Six contributions on recent research in Australia,

France, Germany, Japan, Taiwan, and Soviet Union, all on period 1912–49. [JHC]

11.15 Edward J. M. Rhoads et al. *The Chinese Red Army, 1927–1963: an annotated bibliography.* Cambridge, Mass.: Harvard University, East Asian Research Center, 1964. (Harvard East Asian monographs, 16.) ▸ Cites some 600 books and articles in six languages. Arranged by subject; author index. [JHC]

11.16 Ian Scott. *Hong Kong.* Oxford: Clio, 1990. ISBN 1-85109-089-4. ▸ Annotated bibliography of 838 books and articles arranged by topic. Includes author-title-subject index. [JHC]

11.17 Frank Joseph Shulman, ed. and comp. *Doctoral dissertations on Asia.* Ann Arbor: Association for Asian Studies, 1975–. ISSN 0098-4485. ▸ Invaluable guide to new North American and European dissertations on all Asian (not just Chinese) topics. Arranged by subject-country and then chronologically. Includes author index. Published semiannually 1975–80, annually since 1981. [JHC]

11.18 *Sino-Soviet conflict: a historical bibliography.* Santa Barbara, Calif.: ABC-Clio, 1985. ISBN 0-317-69754-4. ▸ Abstracts of 842 journal articles published 1965–82 in Western languages (including Russian) on Sino-Soviet relations since 1914 with full citations. Arranged alphabetically by author. Includes author and detailed subject indexes. [JHC]

11.19 G. William Skinner, ed. *Publications in Western languages, 1644–1972.* Vol. 1 of *Modern Chinese society: an analytical bibliography.* Stanford, Calif.: Stanford University Press, 1973. ISBN 0-8047-0751-0 (v. 1). ▸ Monumental listing covers works on post-1644 society, economy, polity, and culture. Arranged by subject; sophisticated indexes provide access by historical period, geographical region, urban-rural hierarchy (by province), author, and specific topic. [JHC]

11.20 Ssu-yu Teng. *Protest and crime in China: a bibliography of secret associations, popular uprisings, peasant rebellions.* New York: Garland, 1981. ISBN 0-8240-9354-2. ▸ Covers from high antiquity through Communists. Contains 3,854 items (35 percent in Western-languages) arranged by author and cross-listed by title with subject index. [JHC]

11.21 Meishi Tsai. *Contemporary Chinese novels and short stories, 1949–1974: an annotated bibliography.* Cambridge, Mass.: Harvard University, Council on East Asian Studies, 1979. (Harvard East Asian monographs, 78.) ISBN 0-674-16681-7. ▸ Biographical sketches and plot summaries for works of 455 writers. Arranged by author; author, title, and subject indexes. [JHC]

11.22 Tsuen-hsuin Tsien, comp. *China: an annotated bibliography of bibliographies.* Boston: Hall, 1978. ISBN 0-8161-8086-5. ▸ Describes 2,616 bibliographies in all languages on all fields of China studies. Exhaustive and invaluable. Author, title, and subject indexes. [JHC]

11.23 James C. F. Wang. *The Cultural Revolution in China: an annotated bibliography.* New York: Garland, 1976. ISBN 0-8240-9973-7. ▸ Abstracts of 364 English-language books and articles, arranged first by subtopic, then by author. Includes brief analytical introductions to each subtopic; author and subject indexes. [JHC]

11.24 Karen T. Wei. *Women in China: a selected and annotated bibliography.* Westport, Conn.: Greenwood, 1984. ISBN 0-313-24234-8. ▸ Covers 1,102 Western-language books, articles, theses, and conference papers arranged by subject. Emphasizes nineteenth and twentieth centuries, but includes earlier periods and Taiwan. Author and title indexes. [JHC]

SEE ALSO
10.1 Leonard H. D. Gordon and Frank Joseph Shulman, eds. *Doctoral dissertations on China.*

10.4 Frank Joseph Shulman, ed. *Doctoral dissertations on China, 1971–1975.*

10.62 Laurence G. Thompson. *Chinese religion in Western languages.*

Biographies

11.25 Howard L. Boorman and Richard C. Howard, eds. *Biographical dictionary of Republican China.* 5 vols. J.K.H. Cheng, Bibliography (v. 4). Janet Krompart, Index (v. 5). New York: Columbia University Press, 1967–79. ISBN 0-231-08957-0 (v. 3), 0-231-08958-9 (v. 4). ▸ First place to look for information on prominent persons, 1912–49. Contains some 600 unsigned entries. Includes bibliographies of primary and secondary sources and list of major biographical reference works. Volume 5 a personal-name index. [JHC]

11.26 Arthur W. Hummel, ed. *Eminent Chinese of the Ch'ing period (1644–1912).* 1943–44 ed. Taipei: Ch'eng Wen, 1975. ▸ Invaluable classic, containing over 800 signed entries. First place to look for information on any prominent Ch'ing-dynasty person. Includes indexes for personal names, book titles, and subjects. [JHC]

11.27 Donald W. Klein and Anne B. Clark. *Biographic dictionary of Chinese communism, 1921–1965.* 2 vols. Cambridge, Mass.: Harvard University Press, 1971. ISBN 0-674-07410-6. ▸ Invaluable collection of 433 annotated biographical articles covering Communist party's founding to eve of Cultural Revolution. Includes appendixes sorting biographies by myriad criteria (participants in 1927 Canton Commune, Long March, etc.). [JHC]

SEE ALSO
10.346 L. Carrington Goodrich and Chao-ying Fang. *Dictionary of Ming biography, 1368–1644.*

Chronologies

11.28 Peter P. Cheng. *A chronology of the People's Republic of China.* Vol. 1: *From October 1, 1949.* Vol. 2: *1970–1979.* 2 vols. Totowa, N.J. and Metuchen, N.J.: Rowman & Littlefield and Scarecrow, 1972–86. ISBN 0-87471-099-5 (v. 1), 0-8108-1751-9 (v. 2). ▸ Day-to-day chronicle, each year preceded by multipage introduction. Includes list of sources and name and subject indexes. [JHC]

11.29 Colin Mackerras. *Modern China: a chronology from 1842 to the present.* San Francisco: Freeman, 1982. ISBN 0-7167-1411-6. ▸ Covers political, economic, and cultural-social events; official appointments and dismissals; natural disasters; births and deaths; and publishing through January 1981. Includes fourteen-page bibliographical essay, indexes. [JHC]

Encyclopedias

11.30 H. S. Brunnert and V. V. Hagelstrom. *Present day political organization of China.* 1912 rev. ed. N. Th. Kolessoff, ed. A. Beltchenko and E. E. Moran, trans. Taipei: Ch'eng Wen, 1971. ▸ Exhaustive, still-standard guide to late Ch'ing bureaucracy on eve of 1911 Revolution. Invaluable for tracking down references to obscure governmental organs and posts. [JHC]

11.31 Brian Hook and Denis Twitchett, eds. *The Cambridge encyclopedia of China.* 2d ed. New York: Cambridge University Press, 1991. ISBN 0-521-35594-X. ▸ High antiquity to present. Organized topically: land and resources, peoples, society, continuity (i.e., history by dynasties), mind and senses, art and architecture, and science and technology. Includes bibliography, many illustrations, and maps. [JHC]

11.32 Edwin Pak-wah Leung, ed. *Historical dictionary of revolutionary China, 1839–1976.* New York: Greenwood, 1992. ISBN 0-313-26457-0. ▸ Valuable guide to persons, events, organizations, terminology, etc., by over seventy specialists. Multipage, signed entries, each with brief list of references. Includes bibliography, chronology, glossary, and general index. [JHC]

SEE ALSO

10.10 Charles O. Hucker. *A dictionary of offical titles in imperial China.*

10.12 Hugh B. O'Neill. *Companion to Chinese history.*

General Histories and Textbooks

11.33 Marie-Claire Bergère, Lucien Bianco, and Jürgen Domes, eds. *La Chine au vingtième siècle.* Vol. 1: *D'une révolution à l'autre (1895–1949).* Vol. 2: *De 1949 à aujourd'hui.* Paris: Fayard, 1989–90. ISBN 2-213-02363-8 (pbk, set). ▸ Impressive two-volume textbook by eleven French and five German scholars, each contributing signed chapters. Volume 2 includes coverage of Taiwan and Hong Kong. Both volumes include substantive bibliographies but inadequate indexes (personal names only). [JHC]

11.34 Hungdah Chiu and Shao-chuan Leng, eds. *China seventy years after the 1911 Hsin-hai Revolution.* Charlottesville: University Press of Virginia, 1984. ISBN 0-8139-1027-7. ▸ Contributions systematically compare and contrast developmental experiences of Republic of China (Taiwan) and People's Republic for period 1949–81 in politics, economics, law, culture, education, society, and foreign relations. [JHC]

11.35 Paul A. Cohen. *Discovering history in China: American historical writing on the recent Chinese past.* New York: Columbia University Press, 1984. ISBN 0-231-05810-1. ▸ Influential historiographical critique focusing on three major interpretive frameworks, all seen as Eurocentric: Teng and Fairbank's *China's Response to the West* (11.357), modernization theory, and imperialism. Argues for China-centered history of China. [JHC]

11.36 John F. Copper. *Taiwan: nation-state or province?* Boulder: Westview, 1990. ISBN 0-8133-0444-X. ▸ Succinct overview of land, people, history, society, culture, political system, economy, and foreign and military policies. Includes selected bibliography and illustrations. [JHC]

11.37 Lloyd E. Eastman. *Family, fields, and ancestors: constancy and change in China's social and economic history, 1550–1949.* New York: Oxford University Press, 1988. ISBN 0-19-505269-2 (cl), 0-19-505270-6 (pbk). ▸ Stimulating textbook (including reading lists) synthesizing recent Western research on population trends, family life, popular religion, agriculture, commerce, manufacturing, new social classes in early modern period, secret societies, and bandits. Inadequately indexed. [JHC]

11.38 John K. Fairbank. *China: a new history.* Cambridge, Mass.: Belknap, 1992. ISBN 0-674-11670-4. ▸ Masterful, eminently readable synthesis of recent Western research, peppered with insights; emphasis on period 1600–1989. Includes fifty-one-page bibliographical essay on books published since 1970, complementing but not replacing bibliography in Fairbank 11.40. [JHC]

11.39 John K. Fairbank. *The great Chinese revolution, 1800–1985.* 1986 ed. New York: Harper Perennial, 1987. ISBN 0-06-039076-X (pbk). ▸ Highly readable synthesis of insights from volumes 10–15 of *The Cambridge History of China* (11.41, 11.42, 11.43, 11.44, 11.54, 11.55), blended with author's predelection for emphasizing historical continuities and drawing megacomparisons. [JHC]

11.40 John K. Fairbank. *The United States and China.* Rev. 4th ed. Cambridge, Mass.: Harvard University Press, 1983. ISBN 0-674-92437-1 (cl), 0-674-92438-X (pbk). ▸ Classic example of successful popularization by leading expert. Despite title, treats Old Regime, modern, and contemporary China in addition to Sino-American relations. Includes excellent ninety-three-page bibliographical essay. [JHC]

11.41 John K. Fairbank, ed. *Late Ch'ing: 1800–1911,* Part 1. Vol. 10 of *The Cambridge history of China.* Denis Twitchett and John K. Fairbank, eds. Cambridge: Cambridge University Press, 1978. ISBN 0-521-21447-5 (set). ▸ Mainstream interpretations by leading specialists. Treats Inner Asia, dynastic decline, Opium War, treaty system, Taiping Rebellion, Sino-Russian relations, T'ung-chih Restoration, self-strengthening movement, and Christian missionaries. Includes detailed bibliographies. [JHC]

11.42 John K. Fairbank, ed. *Republican China: 1912–1949,* Part 1. Vol. 12 of *The Cambridge history of China.* Denis Twitchett and John K. Fairbank, eds. Cambridge: Cambridge University Press, 1983. ISBN 0-521-23541-3 (v. 12). ▸ Mainstream interpretations by leading specialists. Treats economic trends, foreign presence, Yuan Shih-k'ai, Peking government 1916–28, warlordism, intellectual change, literary trends, Communists to 1927, "Nationalist revolution" 1923–28, and bourgeoisie. Includes detailed bibliographies. [JHC]

11.43 John K. Fairbank and Albert Feuerwerker, eds. *Republican China: 1912–1949,* Part 2. Vol. 13 of *The Cambridge history of China.* Denis Twitchett and John K. Fairbank, eds. Cambridge: Cambridge University Press, 1986. ISBN 0-521-24338-6 (v. 13). ▸ Mainstream interpretations by leading specialists. Treats foreign relations 1911–31, Nationalist China 1927–45, Communists 1927–45, agriculture, peasants, local government, academics, literary trends, Japanese aggression, Civil War, and Maoism to 1949. Includes detailed bibliographies. [JHC]

11.44 John K. Fairbank and Kwang-Ching Liu, eds. *Late Ch'ing: 1800–1911,* Part 2. Vol. 11 of *The Cambridge history of China.* Denis Twitchett and John K. Fairbank, eds. Cambridge: Cambridge University Press, 1980. ISBN 0-521-22029-7 (v. 11). ▸ Mainstream interpretations by leading specialists. Treats economic trends, foreign relations, views of West, military, reform movement, Japan and 1911 Revolution, constitutional reform, government-merchant relations, revolutionary movement, and social change. Includes detailed bibliographies. [JHC]

11.45 Feng Han-yi. *The Chinese kinship system.* 1937 ed. Cambridge, Mass.: Harvard University Press, 1967. (Harvard-Yenching Institute studies, 22.) ▸ Classic guide to intricacies of extended-family kinship terminology, covering the last twenty-five centuries. [JHC]

11.46 James C. Hsiung et al., eds. *The Taiwan experience, 1950–1980: contemporary Republic of China.* New York: Praeger, 1981. ISBN 0-03-060298-X. ▸ Valuable collection of reprinted essays with editors' introductions. Treats culture, education, economy, society, law, politics, foreign relations, and military. Includes substantive introduction by Chalmers Johnson on Taiwan model; bibliographies. [JHC]

11.47 Immanuel C. Y. Hsu. *The rise of modern China.* 4th ed. New York: Oxford University Press, 1990. ISBN 0-19-505867-4. ▸ Excellent textbook covering late sixteenth-century rise of Manchus through June 1989 massacres. Close attention to detail makes for superb reference work. Each chapter includes extensive list of further reading. [JHC]

11.48 Philip C. C. Huang. "The paradigmatic crisis in Chinese studies: paradoxes in social and economic history." *Modern China* 17.3 (1991) 299–341. ISSN 0097-7004. ▸ Important critique of basic historiographical assumptions concerning economic, social, and political (including legal) history. For example, uses Chinese evidence to question widespread capitalist-Marxist tenet that commercialization necessarily leads to modernization. [JHC]

11.49 Arthur Kleinman et al., eds. *Medicine in Chinese cultures, comparative studies of health care in Chinese and other societies: papers and discussions from a conference held in Seattle, Washington, U.S.A.* Washington, D.C.: United States Department of Health, Education, and Welfare, National Institutes of Health, Public

Health Service, 1975. (Department of Health, Education, and Welfare publication, (NIH) 75–653.) ‣ Wide-ranging collection of forty-nine papers treating Taiwan, Hong Kong, overseas Chinese (in Southeast Asia, United States), Ch'ing dynasty, and People's Republic. Topics include psychiatry and epidemiology. [JHC]

11.50 Arthur Kleinman and Tsung-yi Lin, eds. *Normal and abnormal behavior in Chinese culture*. Dordrecht: Reidel; distributed by Kluwer Boston, 1981. ISBN 90-277-1104-6. ‣ Twenty contributions on historical and cultural background of beliefs and norms governing behavior, child development and psychopathology, family studies, and both epidemiological and clinical psychiatric studies. [JHC]

11.51 Tai-chun Kuo and Ramon H. Myers. *Understanding communist China: communist China studies in the United States and the Republic of China, 1949–1978*. Stanford, Calif.: Hoover Institution Press, 1986. (Hoover Press publication, 334.) ISBN 0-8179-8341-4 (cl), 0-8179-8331-7 (cl), 0-8179-8332-5 (pbk), 0-8179-8342-2 (pbk). ‣ Historiographical critique of strengths and weaknesses of scholarship done in United States and Taiwan. Faults many American scholars for ignoring insightful research from Taiwan until mid-1970s because of ideological bias. [JHC]

11.52 Kenneth G. Lieberthal et al., eds. *Perspectives on modern China: four anniversaries*. Armonk, N.Y.: Sharpe, 1991. ISBN 0-87332-814-0 (cl), 0-87332-890-6 (pbk). ‣ Sixteen interpretive essays presented at symposium offering *longue durée* assessments of politics, economy, society, and culture in high Ch'ing period (pre-1839), May Fourth era (ca. 1915–23), and People's Republic (Maoist and post-Maoist). [JHC]

11.53 Tzong-biau Lin, Rance P. L. Lee, and Udo-Ernst Simonis, eds. *Hong Kong: economic, social, and political studies in development with a comprehensive bibliography*. White Plains, N.Y.: Sharpe, 1979. ISBN 0-87332-151-0. ‣ Treats small factories, employment relations, family structure, students, government-industry relations, housing, public finance, exports, foreign investment, etc. Includes valuable fifty-two-page bibliography of English- and German-language works on Hong Kong. [JHC]

11.54 Roderick MacFarquhar and John K. Fairbank, eds. *The People's Republic*, Part 1: *The emergence of revolutionary China, 1949–1965*. Vol. 14 of *The Cambridge history of China*. Denis Twitchett and John K. Fairbank, eds. Cambridge: Cambridge University Press, 1987. ISBN 0-521-24336-X (v. 14). ‣ Mainstream interpretations by leading specialists. Treats "China's reunification," new regime's consolidation, first Five-Year Plan, education, Communist party and intellectuals, foreign relations, Great Leap Forward, economy 1958–65, and Sino-Soviet split. Includes detailed bibiliographies. [JHC]

11.55 Roderick MacFarquhar and John K. Fairbank, eds. *The People's Republic*, Part 2: *Revolutions within the Chinese revolution, 1966–1982*. Vol. 15 of *The Cambridge history of China*. Denis Twitchett and John K. Fairbank, eds. Cambridge: Cambridge University Press, 1991. ISBN 0-521-21447-5 (v. 15). ‣ Mainstream interpretations by leading specialists. Treats Mao Tse-tung's thought 1949–76, Cultural Revolution, Sino-Soviet relations, succession to Mao, opening to America, economy, education, literature, rural and urban life, and Taiwan 1949–82. Includes detailed bibliographies. [JHC]

11.56 Maurice Meisner. *Mao's China and after: a history of the People's Republic*. New York: Free Press, 1986. ISBN 0-02-920870-X (cl), 0-02-920880-7 (pbk). ‣ Excellent overview and analysis, judging Maoist and post-Maoist leaders by their own socialist aims, rather than using conventional Western modernization theory as yardstick. Earlier edition titled *Mao's China* (1977). [JHC]

11.57 Susan Naquin and Evelyn Sakakida Rawski. *Chinese society in the eighteenth century*. New Haven: Yale University Press,

1987. ISBN 0-300-03848-8. ‣ Innovative textbook treating government policies, social relations, cultural life, social change, regional societies (using Skinner's approach [11.219] to characterize ten distinct regions), and eighteenth-century legacy. Includes extensive bibliographical essay. [JHC]

11.58 Julian F. Pas, ed. *The turning of the tide: religion in China today*. Hong Kong: Oxford University Press, 1989. ISBN 0-19-584101-8 (cl), 0-19-585117-X (pbk). ‣ Topics include popular religion, Taoist festival, Buddhism (in Hong Kong), aspects of popular religious revivalism, monasteries, and Christianity (in People's Republic). Includes detailed bibliographies of Western- and Chinese-language publications. [JHC]

11.59 Gilbert Rozman, ed. *The modernization of China*. New York: Free Press, 1981. ISBN 0-02-927480-X (cl), 0-02-927360-9 (pbk). ‣ Nine contributors apply Princeton school of modernization theory developed by Cyril Black and others (1.214) to perpetuate dichotomy between tradition and modernity. Covers eighteenth- to twentieth-century international context, polity, economy, society, knowledge, and education. [JHC]

11.60 Robert A. Scalapino and George T. Yu. *Modern China and its revolutionary process: recurrent challenges to the traditional order, 1850–1920*. Berkeley: University of California Press, 1985. ISBN 0-520-05030-4. ‣ Massive survey—virtual textbook—of political thinkers in their institutional and socioeconomic milieux from rise of Taiping Rebellion to eve of Communist party's founding. Includes many portrait photos. [JHC]

11.61 James E. Sheridan. *China in disintegration: the Republican era in Chinese history, 1912–1949*. 1975 ed. New York: Collier Macmillan, 1977. ISBN 0-02-928610-7 (cl), 0-02-928650-6 (pbk). ‣ Well-written overview, especially good on warlordism and Nationalist-communist First United Front (1924–27). Includes substantial bibliographical essay organized by subject, mostly political, but also including intellectual revolution, society, economy, and literature. [JHC]

11.62 Jonathan D. Spence. *The search for modern China*. New York: Norton, 1990. ISBN 0-393-02708-2. ‣ Excellent, well-written textbook covering ca. 1600–1989. Sees search for modernity as unfulfilled process with strongly persisting continuities. Includes 225 choice photographs, forty-nine maps, glossary, and substantial bibliography keyed to chapters. [JHC]

SEE ALSO
10.11 William H. Nienhauser, Jr., ed. *The Indiana companion to traditional Chinese literature*.
10.23 Jacques Gernet. *A history of Chinese civilization*.
10.24 Charles O. Hucker. *China's imperial past*.

Geographies

11.63 China. Population Census Office of the State Council and Chinese Academy of Sciences, Institute of Geography, comps. *The population atlas of China*. Hong Kong: Oxford University Press, 1987. ISBN 0-19-584092-5. ‣ Contains 137 maps (most based on 1982 census) showing population distribution, ethnicity, sex, age, population change (including eight historical maps on Han dynasty through Republic), education, employment, family, marriage, fertility, etc. [JHC]

11.64 P.J.M. Geelan and Denis C. Twitchett, eds. *The Times atlas of China*. New York: Quadrangle and Times Books, 1974. ISBN 0-7230-0118-9. ‣ Large, well-prepared atlas with maps of provinces and cities, physical geography, peoples, climates, and economic conditions. Includes extensive text, Chinese characters, and indexes. [PBE]

11.65 George M. H. Playfair. *The cities and towns of China: a geographical dictionary*. 1910 2d ed. Taipei: Ch'eng Wen, 1971. ‣ Still standard reference for Ch'ing dynasty place names including Taiwan. Gives location by longitude-latitude. Appendixes include principal rivers and lakes and handy list (by province) of prefectures (*fu*) and counties (*hsien*). [JHC]

SEE ALSO

10.6 Caroline Blunden and Mark Elvin. *Cultural atlas of China.*
10.344 Timothy Brook. *Geographical sources of Ming-Qing history.*

Research Guides

11.66 Peter Berton and Eugene Wu. *Contemporary China: a research guide.* Howard Koch, Jr., ed. Stanford, Calif.: Hoover Institution Press, 1967. (Hoover Institution bibliographical series, 31.) ‣ Authoritative survey of primary and secondary sources in all languages on pre-Cultural Revolution People's Republic and post-1945 Taiwan. Essential reference for period covered, but would benefit from updating. [JHC]

11.67 Alan Birch, Y. C. Jao, and Elizabeth Sinn, eds. *Research material for Hong Kong studies.* Hong Kong: University of Hong Kong, Centre of Asian Studies, 1984. (Centre of Asian Studies bibliographies and research guides, 23.) ISSN 0441-1900. ‣ Sixteen contributions treating archaeology, maps, village studies, Chinese business documents, socioeconomic statistics, institutions (bank, government agency and archive, library, hospital), social research, remote sensing data, communications, and legal studies. [JHC]

11.68 Frank H. H. King, ed. *A research guide to China-coast newspapers, 1822–1911.* Frank H. H. King and Prescott Clarke, comps. Cambridge, Mass.: Harvard University, East Asian Research Center, 1965. (Harvard East Asian monographs, 18.) ‣ Valuable descriptions of Western-language journalism, mostly in treaty ports (including Hong Kong and Macao), with appendix on Japanese newspapers. Includes biographies of editors and publishers and information on library-holdings. [JHC]

11.69 Donald D. Leslie, Colin Mackerras, and Wang Gungwu, eds. *Essays on the sources for Chinese history.* Canberra: Australian National University Press, 1973. ISBN 0-7081-0398-7. ‣ Twenty-six brief essays on uses of such sources as histories, archaeological evidence, and newspapers. Includes discussion of sources in Tibetan, Manchu, Arabic, and other languages. [PBE]

11.70 Kenneth G. Lieberthal and Bruce J. Dickson. *A research guide to central party and government meetings in China, 1949–1986.* Rev. ed. Armonk, N.Y.: Sharpe, 1989. ISBN 0-87332-492-7. ‣ Information on date, type, place, attendance, major agenda items, speeches, reports, documents passed, other decisions, remarks, and major secondary sources for 511 meetings. Includes name-subject index. [JHC]

11.71 Andrew J. Nathan. *Modern China, 1840–1972: an introduction to sources and research aids.* Ann Arbor: University of Michigan, Center for Chinese Studies, 1973. (Michigan papers in Chinese studies, 14.) ‣ Covers items in Western and Asian languages. Organized by type of reference work (bibliographies, biographical dictionaries, etc.) and primary source (periodicals, archives, etc.). Successfully bridges 1949 divide, but needs updating. [JHC]

11.72 Endymion Wilkinson. *The history of imperial China: a research guide.* Cambridge, Mass.: Harvard University, East Asian Research Center, 1973. (Harvard East Asian monographs, 49.) ISBN 0-674-39680-4. ‣ Excellent introduction to materials in Chinese and Japanese for study of imperial China. How-to manual with numerous bibliographical references. [PBE]

11.73 Winston L. Y. Yang, Peter Li, and Nathan K. Mao. *Classical Chinese fiction: a guide to its study and appreciation: essays and bibliographies.* Boston: Hall, 1978. ISBN 0-8161-7809-9. ‣ Essays on major genres and novels (e.g., colloquial story, *Romance of*

Three Kingdoms, Water Margin, Golden Lotus, Journey to West, Scholars, Dream of Red Chamber). Annotated bibliographies of translations and studies. [JHC]

11.74 Winston L. Y. Yang and Nathan K. Mao, eds. *Modern Chinese fiction: a guide to its study and appreciation: essays and bibliographies.* Boston: Hall, 1981. ISBN 0-8161-8113-6. ‣ Essays treating 1917–49, post-1949 People's Republic, and Taiwan. Annotated bibliographies of reference works, journals, general works, anthologies, studies, and translations of individual writers. [JHC]

CH'ING DYNASTY, 1644–1911
Political History

11.75 Samuel A. M. Adshead. *The modernization of the Chinese salt administration, 1900–1920.* Cambridge, Mass.: Harvard University Press, 1970. ISBN 0-674-58060-5. ‣ Explores salt administration in late Ch'ing and early Republic with emphasis on Sir Richard Dane's reforms (1913–18). Argues that this example of Sino-Western joint administration successful. [JHC]

11.76 Samuel A. M. Adshead. *Province and politics in late imperial China: viceregal government in Szechwan, 1898–1911.* London: Curzon, 1984. (Scandinavian Institute of Asian Studies, Monograph series, 50.) ISBN 0-7007-0165-6 ISSN 0069-1712. ‣ Case study of abortive attempt, by governors-general of key province in late Ch'ing, to achieve modernization using traditional means. [JHC]

11.77 Pamela Atwell. *British mandarins and Chinese reformers: the British administration of Weihaiwei (1898–1930) and the Territory's return to Chinese rule.* Hong Kong: Oxford University Press, 1985. ISBN 0-19-583798-3. ‣ Study of Leased Territory in Shantung province. Contrasts British policy of minimal interference in existing local sociopolitical institutions with unsuccessful Kuomingtang (Nationalist party) policy of reformist state building after 1930 retrocession. [JHC]

11.78 Masataka Banno. *China and the West, 1858–1861: the origins of the Tsungli yamen.* Cambridge, Mass.: Harvard University Press, 1964. ‣ Combines diplomatic and institutional history to examine circumstances surrounding establishment of China's first foreign office, the Tsungli yamen, to deal with Western threat in aftermath of Arrow War (1856–58). [JHC]

11.79 Beatrice S. Bartlett. *Monarchs and ministers: the Grand Council in mid-Ch'ing China, 1723–1820.* Berkeley: University of California Press, 1991. ISBN 0-520-06591-3. ‣ Very important revisionist analysis of emperors' inner-court high privy council (*chun-chi ch'u*), emerging early in Ch'ien-lung period. Finds trend toward checks and balances imposed on emperors by Grand Council officials. Expertly plumbs Taipei and Peking Ch'ing archives. [JHC]

11.80 Derk Bodde and Clarence Morris. *Law in imperial China: exemplified by 190 Ch'ing dynasty cases, translated from the "Hsing-an hui-lan" with historical, social, and juridical commentaries.* 1967 ed. Philadelphia: University of Pennsylvania Press, 1973. ISBN 0-8122-1060-3. ‣ Pioneering overview of Ch'ing dynasty's legal system. Covers basic concepts of Chinese law, Ch'ing code, penal system, judiciary, *Hsing-an hui-lan* (Conspectus of Penal Cases). Extensive translations with commentaries. [JHC]

11.81 David D. Buck. *Urban change in China: politics and development in Tsinan, Shantung, 1890–1949.* Madison: University of Wisconsin Press, 1978. ISBN 0-299-07110-3. ‣ Political, economic, cultural-social developments in Shantung's provincial capital. Concludes that city's modernization succeeded culturally and socially but failed politically and economically. Includes brief post-1949 account. [JHC]

11.82 Meribeth E. Cameron. *The reform movement in China,*

1898–1912. 1931 ed. New York: AMS Press, 1974. ISBN 0-404-50959-2. ‣ Still useful as basic overview. Some specific sections more outdated than others; best on anti-opium campaign and constitutional reform. Relies solely on Western sources. [JHC]

11.83 Hsin-pao Chang. *Commissioner Lin and the Opium War.* Cambridge, Mass.: Harvard University Press, 1964. ‣ Formerly standard work on Lin Tse-hsu and war's origins, now revised by Polachek 11.139. No treatment of actual fighting or resulting treaties. Concludes postponement of hostilities increased price paid by Chinese. [JHC]

11.84 Jerome Ch'en. *Yuan Shih-k'ai.* 2d ed. Stanford, Calif.: Stanford University Press, 1972. ISBN 0-8047-0789-8. ‣ Standard work on general turned president turned unsuccessful emperor. Concludes that Yuan failed even in self-selected role of strongman. Appendix includes descriptions of Yuan's military officers. [JHC]

11.85 Raymond W. Chu and William G. Saywell. *Career patterns in the Ch'ing dynasty: the office of governor-general.* Ann Arbor: University of Michigan, Center for Chinese Studies, 1984. (Michigan monographs in Chinese studies, 51.) ISBN 0-89264-055-3. ‣ Statistical analysis of 504 officeholders. From early nineteenth century on, majority were Han Chinese (not Manchu or Chinese Bannermen) with typical background of long provincial service. Over one-quarter suffered demotion or dismissal. [JHC]

11.86 T'ung-tsu Ch'u. *Local government in China under the Ch'ing.* 1962 ed. Cambridge, Mass.: Harvard University, Council on East Asian Studies, 1988. (Harvard East Asian monographs, 143.) ISBN 0-674-53678-9. ‣ Classic, monumental, and authoritative. Topics include county-level (*chou/hsien*) administration; magistrate with his private secretaries (*mu-yu*), clerks, runners, and servants; administration of justice; tax collection; and local gentry. [JHC]

11.87 Wen-djang Chu. *The Moslem rebellion in Northwest China, 1862–1878: a study of government minority policy.* The Hague: Mouton, 1966. ‣ Ascribes rebellion's origins in Shensi province to decline in Ch'ing dynasty's military power and increased anti-Muslim prejudice. Focuses on Tso Tsung-t'ang's successful suppression campaigns in Shensi, Kansu, and Sinkiang against both Muslims and Nien. [JHC]

11.88 Jerome Alan Cohen, R. Randle Edwards, and Fu-mei Chang Chen, eds. *Essays on China's legal tradition.* Princeton: Princeton University Press, 1980. ISBN 0-691-09238-9. ‣ Topics include late nineteenth-century commercial contract law; age, youth, and infirmity in Ch'ing law; Ch'ing judicial decisions; Ch'ing legal jurisdiction over foreigners; and slavery at end of Ch'ing dynasty. [JHC]

11.89 Paul A. Cohen and John E. Schrecker, eds. *Reform in nineteenth-century China.* Cambridge, Mass.: Harvard University, East Asian Research Center, 1976. (Harvard East Asian monographs, 72.) ISBN 0-674-75281-3 (pbk). ‣ Thirty-one overly brief contributions treat aspects of reform: its traditions, economics, politics, social and intellectual contexts, implementation at local-provincial level, women's role, new coastal reformers, and 1898 Reform Movement. [JHC]

11.90 Prasenjit Duara. *Culture, power, and the state: rural North China, 1900–1942.* Stanford, Calif.: Stanford University Press, 1988. ISBN 0-8047-1445-2. ‣ Difficult but stimulating analysis of local elites' delegitimization from late Ch'ing period on, resulting ultimately in modernizing state's loss of "cultural nexus of power" (legitimacy). Based empirically on Japanese fieldwork, 1940–42. [JHC]

11.91 Pierre-Henri Durand. *Lettrés et pouvoirs: un procès littéraire dans la Chine impériale.* Paris: Éditions de l'École des Hautes Études en Sciences Sociales, 1992. (Civilisations et sociétés, 84.)

ISBN 2-7132-0951-X. ‣ Sophisticated, comprehensive analysis of 1711–13 sedition case centering on Tai Ming-shih, Han-lin literatus from T'ung-ch'eng (Anhui province) beheaded by emperor K'ang-hsi for loyalty to Ming dynasty. [JHC]

11.92 Michael R. Dutton. *Policing and punishment in China: from patriarchy to "the People."* New York: Cambridge University Press, 1992. ISBN 0-521-40097-X. ‣ Overly ambitious treatment (influenced by Foucault) of understudied topic. Ranging from high antiquity through People's Republic, explores how "traditional collectivist power of patriarchalist state has been rearticulated to empower socialist discourse." [JHC]

11.93 Lloyd E. Eastman. *Throne and mandarins: China's search for a policy during the Sino-French controversy, 1880–1885.* Cambridge, Mass.: Harvard University Press, 1967. ‣ Diplomatic narrative (e.g., of Tricou, Li-Fournier, and Tseng-Paténôtre negotiations) and analysis of role of *ch'ing-i* (righteous literati opinion) in influencing Empress Dowager Tz'u-hsi's policy decisions. [JHC]

11.94 Joseph W. Esherick. *Reform and revolution in China: the 1911 Revolution in Hunan and Hubei.* Berkeley: University of California Press, 1976. ISBN 0-520-03084-2. ‣ Fine regional history assigns leading role to liberal urban elite reformers (neither old gentry nor bourgeoisie), who dominated late Ch'ing provincial assemblies, then leapt on revolutionary bandwagon after October 1911 Wuchang Uprising. [JHC]

11.95 Etō Shinkichi and Harold Z. Schiffrin, eds. *The 1911 Revolution in China: interpretive essays, International Conference in Commemoration of the Seventieth Anniversary of the 1911 Revolution, Tokyo, October 21–23, 1981.* Tokyo: University of Tokyo Press, 1984. ISBN 0-86008-349-7. ‣ Nineteen contributions in five categories: ideological, political, and social currents; Japanese influences; impact upon periphery (i.e., Vietnam, Mongols); revolutionaries in action; and role of foreign governments. [JHC]

11.96 John K. Fairbank. *Trade and diplomacy on the China coast: the opening of the treaty ports, 1842–1854.* 1953 ed. 2 vols. Stanford, Calif.: Stanford University Press, 1969. ‣ Despite later criticism for interpreting China as passively responding to Western impact, Fairbank concludes here that treaty system supplanted tribute system as Chinese means of incorporating foreigners into Confucian universal state. [JHC]

11.97 John K. Fairbank, ed. *The Chinese world order: traditional China's foreign relations.* Cambridge, Mass.: Harvard University Press, 1968. ‣ Emphasizes Ming-Ch'ing period (1368–1911). Best contributions cover interpretive framework, Ming Southeast Asia, Ch'ing tribute system, Hsiung-nu/Tibet, Central Asia 1368–1884, and perception of world order. [JHC]

11.98 Peter Ward Fay. *The Opium War, 1840–1842: barbarians in the Celestial Empire in the early part of the nineteenth century and the war by which they forced her gates ajar.* 1975 ed. New York: Norton, 1976. ISBN 0-393-00823-1. ‣ Excellent overview, although based solely on Western sources. Covers opium trade with India, role of Protestant and Catholic missionaries, detailed account of military campaigns, and peace negotiations. [JHC]

11.99 Albert Feuerwerker. *State and society in eighteenth-century China: the Ch'ing empire in its glory.* Ann Arbor: University of Michigan, Center for Chinese Studies, 1976. (Michigan papers in Chinese studies, 27.) ISBN 0-89264-027-8. ‣ Succinct overview of Manchu conquest, Confucian ideology, emperor and bureaucracy, economy and society, focusing on Ch'ien-lung period (1736–95). Especially good on corruption. [JHC]

11.100 Lanny B. Fields. *Tso Tsung-t'ang and the Muslims: statecraft in Northwest China, 1868–1880.* Kingston, Ont.: Limestone, 1978. ISBN 0-919642-85-3. ‣ Underappreciated analysis of Tso's participation in Hunan Statecraft group and his successful reconquest of Shensi, Kansu, and Sinkiang. Supports Wright's argument (11.168) for a T'ung-chih Restoration. Includes chronology, maps, illustrations. [JHC]

11.101 John H. Fincher. *Chinese democracy: the self-government movement in local, provincial, and national politics, 1905–1914.* New York: St. Martin's, 1981. ISBN 0-312-13384-7. ‣ Finds electorate expanded from 1.7 million adult males in 1909 to approximately 40 million (25 percent of adult male population) in 1912. Stylistically opaque but useful. Boosterish preface goes beyond evidence presented. [JHC]

11.102 Kenneth E. Folsom. *Friends, guests, and colleagues: the mu-fu system in the late Ch'ing period.* Berkeley: University of California Press, 1968. ‣ Useful description of system of provincial officials' privately paid advisers (*mu-yu*), with focus on staffs of leading nineteenth-century statesmen Tseng Kuo-fan and especially Li Hung-chang. [JHC]

11.103 Wolfgang Franke. *The reform and abolition of the traditional Chinese examination system.* Cambridge, Mass.: Harvard University, Center for East Asian Studies, 1960. (Harvard East Asian monographs, 10.) ‣ Still standard work. Traces reform efforts beginning in seventeenth century with focus on late nineteenth- and early twentieth-century measures resulting in eventual 1905 abolition. Includes list of suggested research topics. [JHC]

11.104 Lo-shu Fu, comp. and trans. *A documentary chronicle of Sino-Western relations (1644–1820).* 2 vols. Tucson: University of Arizona Press, 1966. (Association for Asian Studies, Monographs and papers, 22.) ‣ Monumental compendium of meticulously annotated translations from seven varieties of Chinese primary sources: *Shih-lu* (Veritable Record), published archival materials, etc. Arranged chronologically with subject headings added. Includes index. [JHC]

11.105 Edmund S. K. Fung. *The military dimension of the Chinese revolution: the New Army and its role in the Revolution of 1911.* Vancouver: University of British Columbia Press, 1980. ISBN 0-7748-0129-8. ‣ Solid treatment of late Ch'ing military reforms, culminating ironically in October 1911 Wuchang Uprising and New Army's crucial role in overthrowing dynasty. Also examines condition of military through 1913. [JHC]

11.106 Hsiao Kung-chuan. *Rural China: imperial control in the nineteenth century.* 1960 ed. Seattle: University of Washington Press, 1967. (Far Eastern and Russian Institute publications on Asia, 8.) ‣ Early treatment of entire rural sociopolitical order. Useful as mine of translated source materials and storehouse of description, to be tapped via unfortunately marginal index; not to be read cover to cover. [JHC]

11.107 Immanuel C. Y. Hsu. *China's entrance into the family of nations: the diplomatic phase, 1858–1880.* Cambridge, Mass.: Harvard University Press, 1960. ‣ Standard work on establishment of diplomatic relations (on basis of international law) between Ch'ing dynasty and foreign governments. Appendix includes charts of major diplomats to and from China, 1861–1900. [JHC]

11.108 Chun-tu Hsueh, ed. *The Chinese Revolution of 1911: new perspectives.* Hong Kong: Joint Publishing, 1986. ISBN 962-04-0341-X. ‣ Topics include revolutionary leader Huang Hsing, the bourgeoisie, capitalist industry, and women's movement; bibliographic essay on primary sources published post-1949. Contributors mostly academics in People's Republic. [JHC]

11.109 Huang Pei. *Autocracy at work: a study of the Yung-cheng period, 1723–1735.* Bloomington: Indiana University Press for the International Affairs Center, 1974. ISBN 0-253-39103-2. ‣ Detailed examination of Yung-cheng emperor's record covering personality; succession struggle; opposition to factionalism; Censorate's weakening; Manchu banner system's bureaucrati-

zation; and effects of imperial policies on literati, commoners, and ethnic minorities. [JHC]

11.110 Jen Yu-wen. *The Taiping revolutionary movement.* Adrienne Suddard, ed. New Haven: Yale University Press, 1973. ISBN 0-300-01542-9. ‣ Detailed military narrative (especially fascinating on origins and rise) traces Taiping Rebellion (1850–64) through expansion and fall. Includes unusually specific table of contents, chronology, campaign maps, and excellent index. [JHC]

11.111 Noriko Kamachi. "Feudalism or absolute monarchism? Japanese discourse on the nature of state and society in late imperial China." *Modern China* 16.3 (1990) 330–70. ISSN 0097-7004. ‣ Excellent overview of post-1945 Japanese historiography on Ming-Ch'ing dynasties (1368–1911). Treats Marxism, definition of feudalism, social classes, gentry rule, and studies of local society. Includes substantive bibliography. [JHC]

11.112 Lawrence D. Kessler. *K'ang-hsi and the consolidation of Ch'ing rule, 1661–1684.* Chicago: University of Chicago Press, 1976. ISBN 0-226-43203-3. ‣ Important analysis of how and why K'ang-hsi emperor reversed regent Oboi's policy of Manchu reaction, cultivated and coopted Chinese elite, and suppressed Wu San-kuei's Three Feudatories Rebellion. [JHC]

11.113 Philip A. Kuhn. *Rebellion and its enemies in late imperial China: militarization and social structure, 1796–1864.* 1970 ed. Cambridge, Mass.: Harvard University Press, 1980. ISBN 0-674-74954-5 (pbk). ‣ Influential analysis of organizational structures used by elite-led militias in Hunan and Kiangsi to defeat Taiping Rebellion. Includes flawed but important model of orthodox and heterodox hierarchies. Includes new, substantive author's preface. [JHC]

11.114 Philip A. Kuhn. *Soulstealers: the Chinese sorcery scare of 1768.* Cambridge, Mass.: Harvard University Press, 1990. ISBN 0-674-82151-3. ‣ Highly interesting, archive-based account of how popular fears that sorcerers in Kiangsu and Chekiang provinces were using queue-hair cuttings for witchcraft provoked Ch'ien-lung emperor to crack down on bureaucracy. [JHC]

11.115 Luke S. K. Kwong. *A mosaic of the Hundred Days: personalities, politics, and ideas of 1898.* Cambridge, Mass.: Harvard University, Council on East Asian Studies, 1984. (Harvard East Asian monographs, 112.) ISBN 0-674-58742-1. ‣ Controversial, stimulating but not wholly convincing revisionist interpretation of 1898 Reform Movement. Downplays K'ang Yu-wei's influence on Kuang-hsu emperor. Attempts to discredit widely accepted accounts by Liang Ch'i-ch'ao and K'ang. [JHC]

11.116 Lee En-han. *China's quest for railway autonomy, 1904–1911: a study of the Chinese railway-rights recovery movement.* Singapore: Singapore University Press, 1977. ‣ Standard work on how widespread but uncoordinated nationalistic efforts by provincial gentry-merchant-student groups, increasingly alienated from central government's appeasement policy toward foreign interests, became antidynastic, anti-Manchu movement. [JHC]

11.117 Robert H. G. Lee. *The Manchurian frontier in Ch'ing history.* Cambridge, Mass.: Harvard University Press, 1970. ISBN 0-674-54775-6. ‣ Standard work on how Ch'ing dynasty was forced to modify policy of cultural isolation designed to maintain purity of Manchurian homeland, as result of Chinese immigration and foreign governments' pressure. [JHC]

11.118 Leung Yuen-sang. *The Shanghai taotai: linkage man in a changing society, 1843–1890.* Honolulu: University of Hawaii Press, 1990. ISBN 0-8248-1355-3. ‣ Study of circuit intendant (*tao-t'ai*) stationed in Shanghai, who oversaw relations with foreigners among other duties. Especially good on Cantonese-Ningpoese rivalry and emergence of hybrid elites (e.g., gentry-merchants) after Taiping Rebellion. [JHC]

11.119 Charlton M. Lewis. *Prologue to the Chinese revolution: the* *transformation of ideas and institutions in Hunan province, 1891–1907.* Cambridge, Mass.: Harvard University, East Asian Research Center, 1976. (Harvard East Asian monographs, 70.) ISBN 0-674-71441-5. ▸ Finds Hunanese literati dissidents turned quickly from xenophobia and Confucian orthodoxy to radical reform to revolution. Especially good on 1890s reform movement, secret societies, and literati's Independence Society (*Tzu-li hui*). [JHC]

11.120 Liao Kuang-sheng. *Antiforeignism and modernization in China.* 3d ed. Hong Kong: Chinese University Press, 1990. ISBN 962-201-490-9. ▸ Sophisticated analysis, 60 percent on People's Republic. Concludes antiforeignism was political reaction to foreign threat rather than endemic to Chinese political culture. Includes substantive preface by Allen S. Whiting. [JHC]

11.121 K. S. Liew. *Struggle for democracy: Sung Chiao-jen and the 1911 Chinese Revolution.* Berkeley: University of California Press, 1971. ISBN 0-520-01760-9. ▸ Standard work on founder of early Kuomintang (Nationalist party), assassinated in 1913, concluding Sung's goal was Western-style democracy. Includes useful charts of revolutionary societies (1895–1912) and political parties (1912–13). [JHC]

11.122 Adam Yuen-Chung Lui. *Chinese censors and the alien emperor, 1644–1660.* Hong Kong: University of Hong Kong, Centre of Asian Studies, 1978. (Centre of Asian Studies occasional papers and monographs, 26.) ISSN 0378-2689. ▸ Active functioning of censorate as remonstrators, impeachers, political informers, and advisers to Shun-chih emperor, contrasted with previous inactivity during Dorgon's regency. Appendixes include details of impeachment cases against high officials. [JHC]

11.123 Adam Yuen-Chung Lui. *Corruption in China during the early Ch'ing period, 1644–1660.* Hong Kong: University of Hong Kong, Centre of Asian Studies, 1979. (Centre of Asian Studies occasional papers and monographs, 39.) ISSN 0378-2689. ▸ Brief analysis of Shun-chih emperor's anticorruption policies and reasons for their failure at both local and central government levels. Concludes Shun-chih more enthusiastic fighter against corruption than K'ang-hsi. [JHC]

11.124 Adam Yuen-chung Lui. *The Hanlin Academy: training ground for the ambitious, 1644–1850.* Hamden, Conn.: Archon, 1981. ISBN 0-208-01833-6. ▸ Institutional, statistical analysis of emperors' brain trust, staffed by top-ranking examination passers, and producing disproportionate number of high officials. Finds seniority key to promotion. [JHC]

11.125 Stephen R. MacKinnon. *Power and politics in late imperial China: Yuan Shi-kai in Beijing and Tianjin, 1901–1908.* Berkeley: University of California Press, 1980. ISBN 0-520-04025-2. ▸ Yuan Shih-k'ai's rise and career as high-ranking official in Peking, Tientsin. Controversial argument that late Ch'ing central government remained strong vis-à-vis locales, with conservative-reformer Yuan dependent on empress dowager. [JHC]

11.126 Mark Mancall. *China at the center: 300 years of foreign policy.* New York: Free Press, 1984. ISBN 0-02-919810-0. ▸ Ambitious, lightly annotated interpretive overview of early Ch'ing through 1970s. Controversial on recent history. By former specialist on early Sino-Russian relations. Includes thirteen-page bibliographical essay. [JHC]

11.127 Mark Mancall. *Russia and China: their diplomatic relations to 1728.* Cambridge, Mass.: Harvard University Press, 1971. ISBN 0-674-78115-5. ▸ Best available study of military and economic relations along Amur. Special attention to Treaties of Nerchinsk (1689) and Kyakhta (1727) that established diplomatic regime in Sino-Russian relations. [DHK]

11.128 M. J. Meijer. *The introduction of modern criminal law in China.* 1949 2d ed. Hong Kong: Lung Men Bookstore, 1967.

▸ Still valuable description of revision of Ch'ing dynasty's criminal code in pre-1911 decade by jurist Shen Chia-pen et al. Appendixes contain translations of eleven primary sources. [JHC]

11.129 S. M. Meng. *The Tsungli yamen: its organization and functions.* 1962 ed. Cambridge, Mass.: Harvard University, East Asian Research Center, 1970. (Harvard East Asian monographs, 13.) ▸ China's first foreign office, established 1861 under Western governments' pressure. Treats pre-1861 conduct of foreign policy and office's establishment, organization, procedures, "constitutional position," actual role, modernizing function, inefficiency, and transformation. [JHC]

11.130 Thomas A. Metzger. *The internal organization of Ch'ing bureaucracy: legal, normative, and communication aspects.* Cambridge, Mass.: Harvard University Press, 1973. ISBN 0-674-45825-7. ▸ Ambitious attempt to combine technical discussion of legal and bureaucratic procedures with high-level theorizing. Best on bureaucratic specialization and system of administrative punishments for wayward officials. Inadequate index. [JHC]

11.131 Franz Michael. *The Taiping Rebellion: history and documents.* 3 vols. Margery Anneburg et al., trans. Seattle: University of Washington Press, 1966–71. ▸ Good but rather brief general history (with detailed campaign maps) in volume 1, concluding that revolutionary, totalitarian Taiping program failed for lack of widespread peasant support. Volumes 2 and 3 contain massive translation of all 405 extant Taiping documents with commentaries. Volume 3 includes detailed annotated bibliography of primary and secondary sources in six languages. [JHC]

11.132 Min Tu-ki. *National polity and local power: the transformation of late imperial China.* Philip A. Kuhn and Timothy Brook, eds. Choe Hei-je et al., trans. Cambridge, Mass.: Harvard University, Council on East Asian Studies and Harvard-Yenching Institute, 1989. (Harvard-Yenching Institute monograph series, 27.) ISBN 0-674-60225-0. ▸ Essays by leading Korean expert on late Ch'ing period treat character of Ch'ing rule, lower elites (*sheng-yuan, chien-sheng*), principle-utility (*t'i-yung*) theory, political feudalism (*feng-chien*), provincial assemblies, and Chekiang railroad dispute. [JHC]

11.133 Hosea Ballou Morse. *The international relations of the Chinese empire.* 1910 ed. 3 vols. Taipei: Ch'eng Wen, 1978. ▸ Monument to diplomatic history. Despite its obsolete approach (Western actors on passive Chinese stage), useful as most comprehensive narrative overview of Ch'ing dynasty's foreign relations with Western powers and Japan, 1834–1911. Based largely on British sources. Appendixes include texts of documents; well indexed. [JHC]

11.134 David S. Nivison. "Ho-shen and his accusers: ideology and political behavior in the eighteenth century." In *Confucianism in action.* 1959 ed. David S. Nivison and Arthur F. Wright, eds., pp. 209–43. Stanford, Calif.: Stanford University Press, 1966. ▸ Classic analysis of why Ch'ien-lung emperor's favorite official went long unpunished despite gross venality. Finds ideological antipathy to factionalism precluded organized bureaucratic opposition; guiltily defensive emperor reacted by increasing Ho-shen's honors. [JHC]

11.135 Jonathan K. Ocko. *Bureaucratic reform in provincial China: Ting Jih-ch'ang in Restoration Kiangsu, 1867–1870.* Cambridge, Mass.: Harvard University, Council on East Asian Studies, 1983. (Harvard East Asian monographs, 103.) ISBN 0-674-08617-1. ▸ Case study of attempted conservative reform in provinces after Taiping Rebellion's suppression. Concludes, contra Wright 11.168, that judged by its own goals, there was no T'ung-chih Restoration. [JHC]

11.136 Robert B. Oxnam. *Ruling from horseback: Manchu politics in the Oboi regency, 1661–1669.* Chicago: University of Chicago Press, 1975. ISBN 0-226-64244-5. ▸ Emphasizes Manchus' un-

Chinese political behavior, at court and in provinces, before K'ang-hsi emperor took power. Concludes regents made final attempt at exclusive Manchu dominance. [JHC]

11.137 Elizabeth J. Perry. *Rebels and revolutionaries in North China, 1845–1945.* Stanford, Calif.: Stanford University Press, 1980. ISBN 0-8047-1055-4 (cl), 0-8047-1175-5 (pbk). ▸ Influential analysis of two survival strategies resulting in rebellion: predatory (e.g., Nien rebels) and protective (e.g., Red Spear Society). Uses 1930s to 1940s communist movement in same region to stress discontinuity between rebellion and revolution. [JHC]

11.138 Elizabeth J. Perry, ed. *Chinese perspectives on the Nien Rebellion.* Armonk, N.Y.: Sharpe, 1981. ISBN 0-87332-191-X. ▸ Abridged translations of eight scholarly articles by historians in People's Republic (originally published 1955–63) plus eight primary sources (all oral-history stories, originally published 1962). Includes Perry's analytical introduction. [JHC]

11.139 James M. Polachek. *The inner Opium War.* Cambridge, Mass.: Harvard University, Council on East Asian Studies, 1992. (Harvard East Asian monographs, 151.) ISBN 0-674-45446-4. ▸ Brilliant, pathbreaking narrative of factional court politics of foreign policy, 1835–50. Emphasizing primacy of domestic agendas (e.g., patronage struggles), analyzes antipathy of moralistic literati War party (allied with Lin Tse-hsu) toward pragmatic Manchu bureaucrats. [JHC]

11.140 Jonathan Porter. *Tseng Kuo-fan's private bureaucracy.* Berkeley: University of California, Center for Chinese Studies, 1972. (China research monographs, 9.) ISBN 0-912966-10-6. ▸ System of specialist advisers (*mu-yu*) privately hired by nineteenth-century provincial official who spearheaded dynasty's suppression of Taiping Rebellion. Stresses increasing emphasis on advisers' professional expertise over traditional generalist orientation. [JHC]

11.141 Ralph L. Powell. *The rise of Chinese military power, 1895–1912.* 1955 ed. Port Washington, N.Y.: Kennikat, 1972. ISBN 0-8046-1645-0. ▸ Still useful descriptive overview, covering pre-1895 military, creation of new-style armies, military modernization under empress dowager, Yuan Shih-k'ai's Pei-yang (Northern) Army, and army and 1911 Revolution. [JHC]

11.142 Don C. Price. *Russia and the roots of the Chinese revolution, 1896–1911.* Cambridge, Mass.: Harvard University Press, 1974. ISBN 0-674-78320-4. ▸ Revisionist interpretation emphasizing universalism over nationalism in thought of late Ch'ing revolutionaries and radical reformers, notably Liang Ch'i-ch'ao. Stresses Chinese image of Russia as paradigm of universal revolutionary progress before 1911. [JHC]

11.143 Mary Backus Rankin. *Early Chinese revolutionaries: radical intellectuals in Shanghai and Chekiang, 1902–1911.* Cambridge, Mass.: Harvard University Press, 1971. ISBN 0-674-22001-3. ▸ Focuses on self-proclaimed vanguard of "foreknowers": Restoration Society (Kuang-fu hui), especially feminist Ch'iu Chin, nonpopulist and organizationally inept, but merged nationalism with early social radicalism and cultural iconoclasm. [JHC]

11.144 Mary Backus Rankin. *Elite activism and political transformation in China: Zhejiang province, 1865–1911.* Stanford, Calif.: Stanford University Press, 1986. ISBN 0-8047-1321-9. ▸ Traces role of Chekiang province's local elites in precipitating 1911 Revolution back to reconstruction efforts following Taiping Rebellion. Emphasizes changes in balance of power between social leaders and state. [JHC]

11.145 John L. Rawlinson. *China's struggle for naval development, 1839–1895.* Cambridge, Mass.: Harvard University Press, 1967. ▸ Finds post–Opium War response to Western naval impact was tardy (beginning only in 1860s) and inadequate (culminating in

1895 defeat by successfully modernized Japanese navy). Blames Confucian values and institutions. [JHC]

11.146 Edward J. M. Rhoads. *China's Republican revolution: the case of Kwangtung, 1895–1913.* Cambridge, Mass.: Harvard University Press, 1975. ISBN 0-674-11980-0. ▸ Emphasizes post-1895 politicization of large segment of Chinese population, resulting in urban (but not yet rural) mass nationalism. Concludes that 1895–1913 cultural revolution destroyed Confucian value system. [JHC]

11.147 R. Keith Schoppa. *Chinese elites and political change: Zhejiang province in the early twentieth century.* Cambridge, Mass.: Harvard University Press, 1982. ISBN 0-674-12325-5. ▸ Schematically analyzes Chekiang through 1920s as four zones: inner core, outer core, inner periphery, outer periphery. Finds political development proceeding from inner core to outer zones and from elite to nonelite. [JHC]

11.148 John E. Schrecker. *Imperialism and Chinese nationalism: Germany in Shantung.* Cambridge, Mass.: Harvard University Press, 1971. ISBN 0-674-44520-1. ▸ Standard work on German sphere-of-influence, late nineteenth century to 1914. Concludes that China's increasingly nationalistic post-1900 foreign policy successfully contained German threat and that Western presence had favorable impact on economic growth. [JHC]

11.149 Stanley Spector. *Li Hung-chang and the Huai army: a study in nineteenth-century Chinese regionalism.* Franz Michael, Introduction. Seattle: University of Washington Press, 1964. ▸ Standard work on key official finds Li's policies undermined Ch'ing dynasty. Includes important introduction by Michael arguing, contra Wright 11.168, that T'ung-chih Restoration never occurred. Ocko 11.135 agrees. [JHC]

11.150 Jonathan D. Spence. *Ts'ao Yin and the K'ang-hsi emperor, bondservant and master.* 2d ed. New Haven: Yale University Press, 1988. ISBN 0-300-04277-9 (cl), 0-300-04278-7 (pbk). ▸ Chinese hereditary bondservant (*pao-i*) to Manchu royal family (1658–1712), member of Imperial Household Department (Nei-wu fu) serving as textile commissioner, salt administrator, and emperor's secret informant. Includes author's new bibliographical preface. [JHC]

11.151 Jonathan D. Spence and John E. Wills, Jr., eds. *From Ming to Ch'ing: conquest, region, and continuity in seventeenth-century China.* New Haven: Yale University Press, 1979. ISBN 0-300-02218-2 (cl), 0-300-02672-2 (pbk). ▸ Best contributions on urban riots (Yuan) and 1644 Shun Interregnum (Wakeman). Other topics include 1618–36 Manchu-Chinese relations, Nanking politics, Wang Fu-chih, Muslim revolts, and 1550s to 1700s maritime China. [JHC]

11.152 Lynn A. Struve. *The Southern Ming, 1644–1662.* New Haven: Yale University Press, 1984. ISBN 0-300-03057-6. ▸ Solid political and military narrative through death of Ming dynasty's last pretender. Introduction, analyzing dynasty as whole, emphasizes denigration of military and unresolved conflicts between emperors and bureaucracy as fatal weaknesses. Includes campaign maps. [JHC]

11.153 Donald S. Sutton. *Provincial militarism and the Chinese Republic: the Yunnan Army, 1905–25.* Ann Arbor: University of Michigan Press, 1980. ISBN 0-472-08813-0. ▸ Standard work on unusually strong provincial army created by late Ch'ing reforms, its role in 1911 Revolution and against Yuan Shih-k'ai, intervention in seven other provinces, and disintegration after 1920 into discrete warlord armies. [JHC]

11.154 Bruce Swanson. *Eighth voyage of the dragon: a history of China's quest for seapower.* Annapolis, Md.: Naval Institute Press, 1982. ISBN 0-87021-177-3. ▸ Naval history of maritime China from Ming dynasty through 1980. Coverage includes nineteenth-century modernization, 1894–95 Sino-Japanese War, and Nationalist and People's Republic's navies. Two-thirds of text on pre-1949 period. Includes illustrations. [JHC]

11.155 Ssu-Yu Teng. *The Nien Army and their guerrilla warfare, 1851–1868.* 1961 ed. Westport, Conn.: Greenwood, 1984. ► Study of major rebellion in North China, spreading from Anhui province. Concludes that by frustrating central government's attempt to quickly regain authority lost to anti-Taiping regional commanders, Niens hastened dynasty's demise. [JHC]

11.156 Ssu-yu Teng. *The Taiping Rebellion and the Western powers: a comprehensive survey.* Oxford: Clarendon, 1971. ISBN 0-19-821548-7. ► Covers more than foreign relations; finds Taipings' abortive revolution began with radical, totalistic program that degenerated into traditional Chinese peasant insurrection ironically alienating peasants. Westerners mostly anti-Taiping despite vaunted neutrality. [JHC]

11.157 S. L. Tikhvinsky, ed. *Manzhou rule in China.* David Skvirsky, trans. Moscow: Progress, 1983. ► Eighteen essays on Manchu (i.e., Ch'ing) dynasty, including Manchu tribes pre-1644; policies toward Tibet, Central Asia, and Vietnam; popular uprisings; and 1911 Revolution. Includes twenty-page bibliography of post-1957 Soviet research on Ch'ing. Translation of *Man'chzhurskoe vladychestvo v Kitae* (1966). [JHC]

11.158 Preston M. Torbert. *The Ch'ing Imperial Household Department: a study of its organization and principal functions, 1662–1796.* Cambridge, Mass.: Harvard University, Council on East Asian Studies, 1977. (Harvard East Asian monographs, 71.) ISBN 0-674-12761-7. ► Standard work on Nei-wu fu, government department handling emperors' personal finances and affairs. Concludes that misuse of imperial authority by department's bondservants (*pao-i*) was comparable to that of Ming dynasty eunuchs. [JHC]

11.159 Frederic E. Wakeman, Jr. *The great enterprise: the Manchu reconstruction of imperial order in seventeenth-century China.* 2 vols. Berkeley: University of California Press, 1985. ISBN 0-520-04804-0 (set). ► Detailed account of Ming collapse, beginnings of Manchu rule. Emphasizes political and intellectual history but with important discussions of economic and cultural issues as well. Extensive bibliography, numerous illustrations. [WSA]

11.160 Frederic E. Wakeman, Jr. "Rebellion and revolution: the study of popular movements in Chinese history." *Journal of Asian studies* 36.2 (1977) 210–37. ISSN 0021-9118. ► State-of-field article treating Western, Chinese, and Japanese research on peasant subordination, sectarian-millenarian movements, free farmers, market relationships, imperialism, nineteenth-century rebellion, new elites, mass mobilization, peasant nationalism, and other topics. Includes substantial bibliography. [JHC]

11.161 Frederic E. Wakeman, Jr. and Carolyn Grant, eds. *Conflict and control in late imperial China.* Berkeley: University of California Press, 1975. ISBN 0-520-02597-0. ► Treats period ca. 1600–1930. Best contributions: introduction, Ch'ing conquest of Kiangnan (Wakeman), convicted thieves (F. Chang Chen), opium smoking (Spence), Soochow gentry in T'ung-chih Restoration (Polachek), and local self-government during Republic (Kuhn). [JHC]

11.162 Joanna Waley-Cohen. *Exile in mid-Qing China: banishment to Xinjiang, 1758–1820.* New Haven: Yale University Press, 1991. ISBN 0-300-04827-0. ► Theory and practice of frontier colonization via penal colonies for both political and common criminals. Case study of Sinkiang region and its involuntary inhabitants (including literati Hung Liang-chi and Chi Yun). [JHC]

11.163 John R. Watt. *The district magistrate in late imperial China.* New York: Columbia University Press, 1972. ISBN 0-231-03535-7. ► Concludes that eighteenth- and nineteenth-century

district (i.e., county) magistrates, presiding over crucial interface between state and society, were torn between Confucian theory (emphasizing society's welfare) and Legalist practice (emphasizing state's interests). [JHC]

11.164 Pierre-Étienne Will. *Bureaucracy and famine in eighteenth-century China.* Elborg Forster, trans. Stanford, Calif.: Stanford University Press, 1990. ISBN 0-8047-1733-8. ► Excellent, rare account of Ch'ing dynasty bureaucracy functioning well. Focuses on government's effective response to drought-caused famine in Chihli province, 1743–44. Contrasts nineteenth century's increased reliance on gentry's relief efforts. Translation with revisions of *Bureaucratie et famine en Chine au dix-huitième siècle* (1980). [JHC]

11.165 Pierre-Étienne Will and R. Bin Wong. *Nourish the people: the state civilian granary system in China, 1650–1850.* Ann Arbor: University of Michigan, Center for Chinese Studies, 1991. (Michigan monographs in Chinese studies, 60.) ISBN 0-89264-090-1. ► Massive institutional analysis, emphasizing importance of state's role (quite successful ca. 1730–80, collapsing after 1850). Topics include development and decline, structural problems, and spatial patterns (especially in Shantung, Hunan, Yunnan, Kweichow provinces). [JHC]

11.166 John E. Wills, Jr. *Embassies and illusions: Dutch and Portuguese envoys to K'ang-hsi, 1666–1687.* Cambridge, Mass.: Harvard University, Council on East Asian Studies, 1984. (Harvard East Asian monographs, 113.) ISBN 0-674-24776-0. ► Finds seventeenth-century European envoys unwittingly strengthened Ch'ing presumptions as to tribute system's relevance. Emphasizes influence of domestic politics on Ch'ing foreign policy (e.g., toward Macao). Based primarily on European archives. [JHC]

11.167 John E. Wills, Jr. *Pepper, guns, and parleys: the Dutch East India Company and China 1622 [i.e., 1662]–1681.* Cambridge, Mass.: Harvard University Press, 1974. ISBN 0-674-66181-8. ► Analyzes relations among K'ang-hsi emperor's China, Dutch, and Portuguese as case study in early Sino-Western interaction. Finds much more involved than simply tribute system. Based partly on Dutch and Portuguese archives. [JHC]

11.168 Mary Clabaugh Wright. *The last stand of Chinese conservatism: the T'ung-chih Restoration, 1862–1874.* Rev. ed. Stanford, Calif.: Stanford University Press, 1962. ► Central government's attempt to reconstruct status quo ante after Taiping Rebellion. Overly optimistic, relying heavily on *Shih-lu* (Veritable Record), that is, what officials in provinces chose to tell Peking. See Ocko 11.135. [JHC]

11.169 Mary Clabaugh Wright, ed. *China in revolution, the first phase, 1900–1913.* New Haven: Yale University Press, 1968. ► Superb collection on 1911 Revolution, in effect debating Wright's controversial thesis (new China born 1900) outlined in book's introduction. Treats politics, ideology, society, military, revolutionary leadership. Best essays on constitutionalists (Chang Peng-yuan), bourgeoisie (Bergère), and gentry (Ichiko). [JHC]

11.170 Stanley F. Wright. *Hart and the Chinese Customs.* Belfast: Mullan for Queen's University, 1950. ► Massive and still-standard work on Sir Robert Hart: inspector-general (1863–1911) of Western-staffed Maritime Customs Service. Highly esteemed servant of Ch'ing dynasty, which his tax-collecting operation helped keep fiscally afloat. [JHC]

11.171 Silas H. L. Wu. *Communication and imperial control in China: evolution of the palace memorial system, 1693–1735.* Cambridge, Mass.: Harvard University Press, 1970. ISBN 0-674-14801-0. ► Origins and development of secret back-channel system speeding high-priority reports (palace memorials [*tsou-che*]) from provincial officials directly to personal attention of K'ang-hsi and Yung-cheng emperors. [JHC]

11.172 Silas H. L. Wu. *Passage to power: K'ang-hsi and his heir apparent, 1661–1722.* Cambridge, Mass.: Harvard University Press, 1979. ISBN 0-674-65625-3. ‣ Study of court politics with modicum of psychohistory. Argues that K'ang-hsi emperor's fourth son, Yin-chen (future Yung-cheng emperor), was actually father's deathbed choice, not usurper as long suspected. [JHC]

11.173 Yen Ching-hwang. *Coolies and mandarins: China's protection of overseas Chinese during the late Ch'ing period (1851–1911).* Singapore: Singapore University Press, 1985. ISBN 9971-69-087-X (pbk). ‣ Revisionist argument that Ch'ing dynasty tried to protect Chinese laborers working overseas, but was thwarted by its own ineptitude, declining power, and especially Western governments' racist imperialism. [JHC]

SEE ALSO

9.89 Morris Rossabi. *China and Inner Asia from 1368 to the present day.*

10.33 Ichisada Miyazaki. *China's examination hell.*

Social History

11.174 Hugh D. R. Baker. *Chinese family and kinship.* New York: Columbia University Press, 1979. ISBN 0-231-04768-1. ‣ Introduction to family composition, functions of individual (including marriage), lineage and clan, ancestor worship, fictive kinship, and twentieth-century changes (including post-1949). [JHC]

11.175 Marie-Claire Bergère. *La bourgeoisie chinoise et la Révolution de 1911.* The Hague: Mouton, 1968. ‣ Extremely influential, anti-Marxist analysis finds no bourgeois revolution in 1911; middle class played only secondary role, opting by 1913 for law and order. Denies Maoist distinction between nationalist and comprador bourgeoisie. [JHC]

11.176 Kathryn Bernhardt. *Rents, taxes, and peasant resistance: the lower Yangzi region, 1840–1950.* Stanford, Calif.: Stanford University Press, 1992. ISBN 0-8047-1880-6. ‣ Analyzes changing relations among landlords (increasingly absentee), tenants, and state. Concludes that after Taiping Rebellion, decline in rents, increase in taxes (especially after 1927) severely weakened landlordism in Kiangsu-Chekiang region. [JHC]

11.177 David D. Buck, ed. *Recent Chinese studies of the Boxer movement.* Armonk, N.Y.: Sharpe, 1987. ISBN 0-87332-441-2 (pbk). ‣ Following editor's analytical introduction, presents translations of nine contributions by mainland scholars (most written for 1980 conference). Includes four regional maps of North China. [JHC]

11.178 Ming K. Chan. *Historiography of the Chinese labor movement, 1895–1949: a critical survey and bibliography of selected Chinese source materials at the Hoover Institution.* Stanford, Calif.: Hoover Institution Press, 1981. (Hoover Press bibliographical series, 60.) ISBN 0-8179-2601-1. ‣ Valuable analysis (keyed to appended bibliography) considers labor movement on its own terms, not merely as epiphenomenon of Communist party activism. Notes that Nationalist and communist publications both strongly anti-imperialist. [JHC]

11.179 Chang Chung-li. *The Chinese gentry: studies on their role in nineteenth-century Chinese society.* 1955 ed. Seattle: University of Washington Press, 1967. (Institute for Comparative and Foreign Area Studies, Publications on Asia, 3.) ‣ Important, controversial taxonomy of upper gentry (*chin-shih* and *chü-jen* degree holders) and lower gentry (*sheng-yuan* and *chien-sheng* degree holders). Includes authoritative description of gentry's examination life. [JHC]

11.180 Jerome Ch'en. *China and the West: society and culture, 1815–1937.* Bloomington: Indiana University Press, 1979. ISBN 0-253-12032-2. ‣ Underappreciated study of mutual Sino-West-ern images, missionaries, converts, students, scholars, residents, immigrants, politics, law, economy, society, and culture. Strongest on society. Weakened by publisher's elimination of virtually all notes. [JHC]

11.181 Jean Chesneaux. *Secret societies in China in the nineteenth and twentieth centuries.* Gillian Nettle, trans. Ann Arbor: University of Michigan Press, 1971. ISBN 0-472-08207-8. ‣ Useful for extensive translations from primary sources, integrated with Chesneaux's analysis. Most detailed on Triads, but also brief treatment of sixteen other groups. Includes photographs and illustrations of material counterculture. [JHC]

11.182 Jean Chesneaux, ed. and trans. *Popular movements and secret societies in China, 1840–1950.* Stanford, Calif.: Stanford University Press, 1972. ISBN 0-8047-0790-1. ‣ Best contributions: introduction (Chesneaux), peasant self-defense (Bianco), Taiping secret society relations (Curwen), 1911 Revolution (Hsieh). Includes glossaries of secret society names, leaders, terminology. Partial translation of Jean Chesneaux et al., eds., *Mouvements populaires et sociétés secrètes en Chine au dix-neuvième et vingtième siècles* (1970). [JHC]

11.183 James H. Cole. *The people versus the Taipings: Bao Li-sheng's "Righteous Army of Dongan."* Berkeley: University of California, Center for Chinese Studies and Institute of East Asian Studies, 1981. (Chinese research monographs, 21.) ISBN 0-912966-39-4 (pbk). ‣ Examines peasant-led opposition against Taiping Rebellion by heterodox religious leader from Shao-hsing prefecture (Chekiang province). Debunks conventional wisdom on local elite leadership. Finds native-place (*t'ung-hsiang*) stronger bond than class. [JHC]

11.184 James H. Cole. *Shaohsing: competition and cooperation in nineteenth-century China.* Tucson: University of Arizona Press, 1986. (Monographs of the Association for Asian Studies, 44.) ISBN 0-8165-0994-8. ‣ Combines local history of Shao-hsing prefecture (Chekiang) with examination of its native-place (*t'ung-hsiang*) ties at all levels of Ch'ing bureaucracy. Analyzes complementary use of competition and cooperation as survival strategies. [JHC]

11.185 Pamela Kyle Crossley. *Orphan warriors: three Manchu generations and the end of the Qing world.* Princeton: Princeton University Press, 1990. ISBN 0-691-05583-1. ‣ Pathbreaking analysis of Manchu ethnicity as artificial construct. Traces Manchus' decline from Ch'ien-lung emperor's glorification of traditional martial ethnic culture to attempted genocide by Taiping rebels, increasing impoverishment, and abandonment by court. [JHC]

11.186 Mark Elvin and G. William Skinner, eds. *The Chinese city between two worlds.* Stanford, Calif.: Stanford University Press, 1974. ISBN 0-8047-0853-3. ‣ Essays (most covering period 1842–1949) on treaty ports, Shanghai financial institutions, Canton merchant associations, Kwangtung 1911 revolutionary mobilization, Chungking warlord control, Tsinan educational modernization, YMCA social reform, Shanghai administration, Taipei temples, and migration. [JHC]

11.187 Joseph W. Esherick. *The origins of the Boxer Uprising.* Berkeley: University of California Press, 1987. ISBN 0-520-05828-3. ‣ Superb, widely-researched analysis demonstrating why and how *I-ho ch'uan* (Boxers United in Righteousness), never anti-dynastic, rose in Shantung province against Christian converts backed by foreign imperialism. Marvelous on sociocultural roots. [JHC]

11.188 Joseph W. Esherick and Mary Backus Rankin, eds. *Chinese local elites and patterns of dominance.* Berkeley: University of California Press, 1990. ISBN 0-520-06763-0. ‣ Editors' stimulating conclusion follows contributions treating Ning-Shao (Chekiang) gentry, Hupei lineages, Szechwan salt merchants, Kiangsu silk industry, Kweichow militarists, republican politics in Kiangsu,

1920s Peking, Kwangtung lineage estates, North China villages, and Kiangsi periphery. [JHC]

11.189 Albert Feuerwerker. *Rebellion in nineteenth-century China.* 1975 ed. Ann Arbor: University of Michigan, Center for Chinese Studies, 1977. ISBN 0-89264-021-9. ‣ Succinct overview, focusing on Taipings (but fudging rebel-or-revolutionary categorization). Also considers White Lotus, Nien, Miao, and Muslim rebellions. Analyzes sources of social dissidence; proposes hierarchy of dissidence. [JHC]

11.190 Maurice Freedman. *Chinese lineage and society: Fukien and Kwangtung.* London: Athlone, 1966. (London School of Economics, Monographs on social anthropology, 33.) ‣ Continues 11.192. Enormously stimulating analysis, based largely on fieldwork in Hong Kong's New Territories. Topics covered include *feng-shui* (geomancy) and ancestor worship. [JHC]

11.191 Maurice Freedman. *Lineage organization in southeastern China.* 1965 ed. New York: Humanities Press, 1970. ISBN 0-391-00199-X. ‣ Seminal analysis of lineages in Fukien and Kwangtung provinces since ca. 1800. So influential that scholars (e.g., Ebrey 10.38) have only recently begun questioning whether conclusions are valid for other regions' lineages. [JHC]

11.192 Maurice Freedman, ed. *Family and kinship in Chinese society.* Stanford, Calif.: Stanford University Press, 1970. ISBN 0-8047-0713-8. ‣ Essays covering period since mid-1800s treat nature of family (*jia*), child training, farm families, modern fictional accounts, land and lineage, genealogies, rituals of marriage and mourning, and kinship terminology. Comparisons with Japan. [JHC]

11.193 Sue Gronewold. *Beautiful merchandise: prostitution in China, 1860–1936.* 1982 ed. New York: Harrington Park Press, 1985. ISBN 0-918393-15-9 (pbk). ‣ Finds twentieth-century shifts in procurement (from purchase to pawning, thus increasing natal family's profit) and in mentality (semi-westernized urbanites' increased ambivalence toward prostitution as no longer completely disreputable). [JHC]

11.194 Linda Grove and Christian Daniels, eds. *State and society in China: Japanese perspectives on Ming-Qing social and economic history.* Tokyo: Tokyo University Press and Columbia University Press, 1984. ISBN 4-13-026042-1, 0-86008-356-X. ‣ Articles by leading Japanese scholars on handicraft industries, problems of landownership, popular uprisings, nature of rural society, and foreign trade. Most articles date from 1950s and 1960s and have strong Marxist flavor. [WSA]

11.195 Ping-ti Ho. *The ladder of success in imperial China.* New York: Columbia University Press, 1980. ISBN 0-231-05161-1 (pbk). ‣ Pioneering analysis of elite mobility, 1368–1911. Examines social stratification, fluidity of status system, factors affecting upward and downward mobility, and regional differences. Twenty-seven case studies draw on wide range of primary sources. [WSA]

11.196 Ping-ti Ho. "The salt merchants of Yang-chou: a study of commercial capitalism in eighteenth-century China." *Harvard journal of Asiatic studies* 17.1, 2 (1954) 130–68. ISSN 0073-0548. ‣ Fascinating, classic exposition of unchallenged merchant princes, nouveau-riche heirs of government-granted salt monopolies, who spent their immense wealth on everything from scholarly and artistic patronage to very conspicuous consumption. [JHC]

11.197 Ping-ti Ho. *Studies on the population of China, 1368–1953.* Cambridge, Mass.: Harvard University Press, 1959. ‣ Valuable pioneering analysis, based largely on local gazetteers. Finds relatively reliable data for years 1368–98, 1776–1850, 1953, with 1851–1949 as virtual demographer's vacuum. Topics include taxation, migration, food production, and natural disasters. [JHC]

11.198 Jane Hunter. *The gospel of gentility: American women missionaries in turn-of-the-century China.* New Haven: Yale University Press, 1984. ISBN 0-300-02878-4 (cl), 0-300-04603-0 (pbk). ‣ Finds missionaries' secular and social impact outweighed religious. Chinese female converts' unprecedented peer solidarity served as basis for nationalistic student activism; mission institutions served as oases for both Chinese and foreign women. [JHC]

11.199 Maria Jaschok. *Concubines and bondservants: a social history.* London: Zed, 1988. ISBN 0-86232-782-2 (cl), 0-86232-783-0 (pbk). ‣ Discussion of Cantonese practice (formally abolished 1923) of selling young daughters into servitude, usually as prostitutes, concubines, or contract laborers. Based partly on interviews in Hong Kong. [JHC]

11.200 William Lavely, James Lee, and Wang Feng. "Chinese demography: the state of the field." *Journal of Asian studies* 49.4 (1990) 807–34. ISSN 0021-9118. ‣ Review of Western and Chinese research on contemporary and historical demography, Skinner's spatial patterns of population behavior (11.219), marriage and kinship, urban-rural dichotomy, and state and society. Includes substantial bibliography. [JHC]

11.201 Jonathan N. Lipman and Stevan Harrell, eds. *Violence in China: essays in culture and counterculture.* Albany: State University of New York Press, 1990. ISBN 0-7914-0113-8 (cl), 0-7914-0115-4 (pbk). ‣ Topics include southeastern lineage feuding during Ch'ing, Han-Muslim conflict in Kansu province, sectarian eschatology (e.g., White Lotus Rebellion), Cultural Revolution's urban and rural violence, and violence against women in People's Republic. [JHC]

11.202 Daniel Little. *Understanding peasant China: case studies in the philosophy of social science.* New Haven: Yale University Press, 1989. ISBN 0-300-04399-6. ‣ Rigorous analysis of influential Western interpretations: Scott 16.134 and Popkin 16.222 on moral economy; Skinner 11.219 on regional systems; Chao 10.36 and Lippit on agrarian development; and Perry 11.137, Marks 11.205, and Naquin 11.207 on peasant rebellion. [JHC]

11.203 Hui-chen Wang Liu. *The traditional Chinese clan rules.* Locust Valley, N.Y.: Augustin, 1959. (Monographs of the Association for Asian Studies, 7.) ‣ Pioneering description of regulations governing lineage members, based on 151 Columbia University–held genealogies, mostly from Kiangsu, Chekiang, Anhui, Hupei provinces. Appendix contains forty-nine statistical tables. [JHC]

11.204 Colin Mackerras. *The rise of the Peking opera, 1770–1870: social aspects of the theatre in Manchu China.* Oxford: Clarendon, 1972. ISBN 0-19-815137-3. ‣ Traces origins to drama troupes sponsored by rich salt merchants in Yang-chou (Kiangsu province). Details imperial patronage in Peking and roles of actors both on and off stage (including male prostitution). [JHC]

11.205 Robert Marks. *Rural revolution in South China: peasants and the making of history in Haifeng County, 1570–1930.* Madison: University of Wisconsin Press, 1984. ISBN 0-299-09530-4. ‣ Controversial moral economy analysis of *longue durée* causes of China's first rural soviet (1927–28). Rejecting Hofheinz 11.408, concludes capitalist imperialism transformed local social relations in ways conducive to revolution. Devalues role of P'eng P'ai. [JHC]

11.206 Dian H. Murray. *Pirates of the South China coast, 1790–1810.* Stanford, Calif.: Stanford University Press, 1987. ISBN 0-8047-1376-6. ‣ Fascinating examination of Cantonese maritime world. Concludes that pirates—motivated by profit, not politics—were something less than rebels. Documents significant role of women, including leader Cheng I Sao. [JHC]

11.207 Susan Naquin. *Millenarian rebellion in China: the Eight*

Trigrams Uprising of 1813. New Haven: Yale University Press, 1976. ISBN 0-300-01893-2. ‣ Fascinating, detailed narrative of religious sects' sedition, culminating in attempt to seize Peking's Forbidden City. Based on pathbreaking use of Ch'ing archives, including hundreds of confessions by captured rebels. Superb classic. [JHC]

11.208 Susan Naquin. *Shantung rebellion: the Wang Lun Uprising of 1774.* New Haven: Yale University Press, 1981. ISBN 0-300-02638-2. ‣ Narrative account of White Lotus religious sect's rising. Along lines of Naquin 11.207, but less compelling, due to scantier archival sources. Most vivid on rebel community-in-arms on the road. [JHC]

11.209 Vivien W. Ng. *Madness in late imperial China: from illness to deviance.* Norman: University of Oklahoma Press, 1990. ISBN 0-8061-2297-8. ‣ Pathbreaking exploration of how (beginning 1731) government's concern for public safety led to criminalization of mental illness with mandatory registration-and-confinement program; but local implementation proved largely illusory. [JHC]

11.210 Ono Kazuko. *Chinese women in a century of revolution, 1850–1950.* Joshua A. Fogel, ed. Kathryn Bernhardt et al., trans. Stanford, Calif.: Stanford University Press, 1989. ISBN 0-8047-1496-7. ‣ Pioneering overview of women's role in Taiping Rebellion, 1898 Reform Movement, Boxer Rebellion, 1911 Revolution, May Fourth Movement, 1920s factories, and Chinese communist movement. Impact of 1950 Marriage Law. Revised translation of *Chūgoku joseishi* (History of Chinese Women) (1978). [JHC]

11.211 Ida Pruitt and Ning Lao T'ai-t'ai. *A daughter of Han: the autobiography of a Chinese working woman: as told by Ning Lao T'ai-t'ai.* 1945 ed. Stanford, Calif.: Stanford University Press, 1967. ISBN 0-8047-0605-0 (cl), 0-8047-0606-9 (pbk). ‣ Classic of women's history. Full of insight into popular culture and working-class family life (1867–1938), recounted by urban commoner from Shantung province. Fascinating, unadorned, microcosmic self-revelation. [JHC]

11.212 Evelyn Sakakida Rawski. *Education and popular literacy in Ch'ing China.* Ann Arbor: University of Michigan Press, 1979. ISBN 0-472-08753-3. ‣ Pathbreaking, necessarily undefinitive analysis concluding that in nineteenth century as many as 30-45 percent of men and 2-10 percent of women could read and write at least several hundred characters. [JHC]

11.213 Evelyn Sakakida Rawski. "Research themes in Ming-Qing socioeconomic history: the state of the field." *Journal of Asian studies* 50.1 (1991) 84–111. ISSN 0021-9118. ‣ Review of English-, French-, Chinese-, and Japanese-language works on mid-Ming to mid-Ch'ing dynasties (ca. 1500–1840) under categories of economic growth and development, social organization, population, disease, ethnicity, popular culture, and problems and prospects. [JHC]

11.214 William T. Rowe. "Approaches to modern Chinese social history." In *Reliving the past: the worlds of social history.* Olivier Zunz, ed., pp. 236–96. Chapel Hill: University of North Carolina Press, 1985. ISBN 0-8078-1658-2 (cl), 0-8078-4137-4 (pbk). ‣ Valuable, analytical historiographical review of Western, Chinese, and Japanese scholarship on post-sixteenth-century period. Treats stagnation, periodization, impact of West, agrarian regime, local community, state and society, and commerce and capitalism. [JHC]

11.215 William T. Rowe. *Hankow: commerce and society in a Chinese city, 1796–1889.* Stanford, Calif.: Stanford University Press, 1984. ISBN 0-8047-1204-2. ‣ Controversial revisionist analysis. Finds substantial urban autonomy achieved in nineteenth-century Hankow through *de facto* municipal government by guilds, organized by native-place or trade and headed by commercial elites. [JHC]

11.216 William T. Rowe. *Hankow: conflict and community in a Chinese city, 1796–1895.* Stanford, Calif.: Stanford University Press, 1989. ISBN 0-8047-1541-6. ‣ Complementing earlier emphasis on urban administration by commercial elites (11.215), focuses on working class, and social conflict and control. Finds comparative social calm via broad-based, managed consensus. [JHC]

11.217 Gilbert Rozman. *Population and marketing settlements in Ch'ing China.* Cambridge: Cambridge University Press, 1982. ISBN 0-521-23556-1. ‣ Technical analysis of nineteenth-century demographic data, largely from two counties in Chihli province (including Tientsin city). Includes critique of Skinner's analyses of marketing and regional systems (11.218, 11.219). [JHC]

11.218 G. William Skinner. "Marketing and social structure in rural China, Parts 1, 2." *Journal of Asian studies* 24.1, 2 (1964, 1965) 3–43, 195–228. ISSN 0021-9118. ‣ Classic, seminal analysis revolutionizing understanding of late imperial and twentieth-century local social structure. Shifts emphasis from villages to nested hierarchy of marketing systems (standard, intermediate, central) as key units. [JHC]

11.219 G. William Skinner, ed. *The city in late imperial China.* Stanford, Calif.: Stanford University Press, 1977. ISBN 0-8047-0892-4. ‣ Important for Skinner's five contributions (out of nineteen), including his highly influential analysis of macroregions. Also good on Nanking 1350–1400 (Mote), Kwangtung academies (Grimm), urban extended kinship (Baker), and Ch'ing guilds (Golas). Includes three essay on Taiwan. [JHC]

11.220 Arthur H. Smith. *Village life in China: a study in sociology.* 1899 4th ed. Myron L. Cohen, Introduction. Boston: Little, Brown, 1970. ‣ Valuable description of rural society (especially family, local institutions) and material culture in late nineteenth-century Shantung province by rather unsympathetic missionary. Includes rare photographs and new analytical introduction. Also available on microfilm from Ann Arbor: University Microfilms International, 1980. [JHC]

11.221 Jonathan D. Spence. *The death of woman Wang.* 1978 ed. New York: Penguin, 1979. ISBN 0-14-005121-x (pbk). ‣ Fascinating portrait of local society in seventeenth-century Shantung province. By imagining what might have been in mind of abused peasant wife, controversially demolishes boundary between history and creative literature. [JHC]

11.222 Janice E. Stockard. *Daughters of the Canton delta: marriage patterns and economic strategies in South China, 1860–1930.* Stanford, Calif.: Stanford University Press, 1989. ISBN 0-8047-1392-8. ‣ Analysis of delayed transfer marriage, dominant in silk-producing regions of Kwangtung province, whereby married daughters remained at natal home for years to continue providing silk-reeling labor. Precursor of widespread spinsterhood. [JHC]

11.223 Lyman P. Van Slyke. *Yangtze: nature, history, and the river.* Reading, Mass.: Addison-Wesley, 1988. ISBN 0-201-08894-0. ‣ Braudelian exploration of China's greatest river, viewed through three kinds of time: natural (geography), social (migration, settlement, Grand Canal, river's mercantile activity, junk traffic), and eventful (river's symbolism, Westerners' travel accounts, modern dams). [JHC]

11.224 Frederic E. Wakeman, Jr. *The fall of imperial China.* 1975 ed. New York: Free Press, 1977. ISBN 0-02-933680-5. ‣ Often stimulating but unevenly documented social history from Ming dynasty through Yuan Shih-k'ai's death (1916). Best chapters analyze peasants, gentry, merchants, dynastic cycle, and 1911 Revolution and its aftermath. Includes annotated reading list. [JHC]

11.225 Frederic E. Wakeman, Jr. *Strangers at the gate: social disorder in South China, 1839–1861.* Berkeley: University of California Press, 1966. ▸ Pathbreaking local history. Controversial argument that militias in Canton region after Opium War became instruments of class oppression by gentry, provoking peasants' shift of allegiance from clans to secret societies. [JHC]

11.226 Ann B. Waltner. *Getting an heir: adoption and the construction of kinship in late imperial China.* Honolulu: University of Hawaii Press, 1990. ISBN 0-8248-1280-8. ▸ Innovative analysis emphasizing discrepancies between statutory ideology and actual behavior in Ming-Ch'ing dynasties. Covers intersurname adoption (nominally illegal, but common), concubinage, intrasurname marriage, and household division by brothers. [JHC]

11.227 Rubie S. Watson and Patricia Buckley Ebrey, eds. *Marriage and inequality in Chinese society.* Berkeley: University of California Press, 1991. ISBN 0-520-06930-7 (cl), 0-520-07124-7 (pbk). ▸ Treats Ch'ing emperors' marriage patterns, eighteenth-century brides and wives, Hong Kong (wives, concubines, maids), Shanghai (prostitutes), People's Republic (marriage and rural mobility, law and women's property), and marriage from eighth century BCE to seventeenth century CE. [JHC]

11.228 Betty Peh-t'i Wei. *Shanghai: crucible of modern China.* Hong Kong: Oxford University Press, 1987. ISBN 0-19-583831-1 (pbk). ▸ Popularly written urban history, without footnotes but solid, covering pre-nineteenth century to 1949. Mainly on pre-1912 period. Includes illustrations and substantial bibliography of Western- and Chinese-language works. [JHC]

11.229 Margery Wolf and Roxane Witke, eds. *Women in Chinese society.* Stanford, Calif.: Stanford University Press, 1975. ISBN 0-8047-0874-6. ▸ Pioneering collection of essays treating Lu K'un, Ch'iu Chin, Kwangtung marriage resistance, Taiwanese demography, suicide, 1920s to 1930s writers, Chiang Ch'ing, ritual pollution, Hong Kong childbearing, and Communists and rural women. [JHC]

11.230 Harriet T. Zurndorfer. *Change and continuity in Chinese local history: the development of Hui-chou prefecture, 800 to 1800.* Leiden: Brill, 1989. (Sinica Leidensia, Institutum Sinologicum Lugduno Batavium, 20.) ISBN 90-04-08842-3 (pbk), ISSN 0169-9563. ▸ Emphasizes long-term continuities in famous locale in Anhui province (until eighteenth-century overpopulation). Finds key factors were agriculture's ability to absorb steady demographic growth, lineages' control of landholding and commercial networks, and shared elite-popular local culture. [JHC]

11.231 Harriet T. Zurndorfer. "A guide to the 'new' Chinese history: recent publications concerning Chinese social and economic development before 1800." *International review of social history* 33.2 (1988) 148–201. ISSN 0020-8590. ▸ Review of Western-language books and articles published 1970–86 on period 1000–1800. Topics include commoners, women, outsiders, structural approach, state and society, China and world history, nondevelopment of capitalism. Includes sixteen-page bibliography. [JHC]

SEE ALSO
   10.32 Taisuke Mitamura. *Chinese eunuchs.*
   10.38 Patricia Buckley Ebrey and James L. Watson, eds. *Kinship organization in late imperial China, 1000–1940.*
   10.41 Bret Hinsch. *Passions of the cut sleeve.*
   10.369 Hilary J. Beattie. *Land and lineage in China.*

Economic History

11.232 Edwin George Beal, Jr. *The origin of likin, 1853–1864.* Cambridge, Mass.: Harvard University, East Asian Research Center, 1958. (Harvard East Asian monographs, 6.) ▸ Study of new tax levied on goods in transit to help finance suppression of Taiping Rebellion, providing fiscal basis for increased regionalism. Includes translations of fifteen primary sources. [JHC]

11.233 Loren Brandt. *Commercialization and agricultural development: central and eastern China, 1870–1937.* New York: Cambridge University Press, 1989. ISBN 0-521-37196-1. ▸ Concludes that agricultural output increased more than twice the estimated rate of population growth, with benefits rather evenly distributed throughout society. Finds commercialization probably helped to narrow income differentials. [JHC]

11.234 Wellington K. K. Chan. *Merchants, mandarins, and modern enterprise in late Ch'ing China.* Cambridge, Mass.: Harvard University, East Asian Research Center, 1977. (Harvard East Asian monographs, 79.) ISBN 0-674-56915-6. ▸ While debunking thesis of Confucian antimerchant bias, analyzes triangular power struggle among merchant-entrepreneurs, provincial officials, and central government. Finds efforts to establish modern enterprise abortive despite significant private and official innovations. [JHC]

11.235 Chang Chung-li. *The income of the Chinese gentry.* Franz Michael, Introduction. Seattle: University of Washington Press, 1962. ▸ Pioneering analysis of income from public services and teaching, plus income from landownership and mercantile activities. Supplements contain estimates of annual gross national product in 1880s, and gentry's share of national product. [JHC]

11.236 Chao Kang. *The development of cotton textile production in China.* Cambridge, Mass.: Harvard University, East Asian Research Center, 1977. (Harvard East Asian monographs, 74.) ISBN 0-674-20021-7. ▸ Treats introduction of cotton, institutions for production and distribution, technology, external trade, comparative analyses of modern mills, handicraft textiles, and estimates of pre-1949 output and consumption, post-1949 production, exports, and consumption. [JHC]

11.237 Chao Kang. *The economic development of Manchuria: the rise of a frontier economy.* Ann Arbor: University of Michigan, Center for Chinese Studies, 1982. (Michigan papers in Chinese studies, 43.) ISBN 0-89264-043-X (pbk). ▸ Mainly statistical analysis covering 1860–1941, arranged by economic sector. Finds Manchuria's economy less agricultural, more industrial and service-oriented than China's by 1930s. [JHC]

11.238 Chuan Han-sheng and Richard A. Kraus. *Mid-Ch'ing rice markets and trade: an essay in price history.* Cambridge, Mass.: Harvard University, East Asian Research Center, 1975. (Harvard East Asian monographs, 54.) ISBN 0-674-57340-4. ▸ Technical quantitative analysis reveals that due to large-scale, long-distance rice trade, early eighteenth-century Soochow's rice market had no more seasonal price variation than early twentieth-century Shanghai's. [JHC]

11.239 Sherman Cochran. *Big business in China: Sino-foreign rivalry in the cigarette industry, 1890–1930.* Cambridge, Mass.: Harvard University Press, 1980. ISBN 0-674-07262-6. ▸ Pioneering business history, using company records. Explores entrepreneurial marketing competition between British-American Tobacco Company and Nanyang Brothers. Especially fascinating on advertising techniques. Includes statistical appendix. [JHC]

11.240 Louis Dermigny. *La Chine et l'Occident: le commerce à Canton au dix-huitième siècle, 1719–1833.* 4 vols. Paris: Imprimerie Nationale, 1964. (École Pratique des Hautes Études, Sixième section, Centre des Recherches Historiques: Ports, routes, trafics, 18.) ▸ Truly monumental exposition, ending with abolition of East India Companies' trade monopoly. Topics covered include companies, country trade, ships and voyages, conditions at Canton, traded commodities (tea, drugs, porcelain, silk, metals), smuggling, fiscal developments, trade balance, and diplomacy. Extensive use of British and French archives and private papers. Includes bibliography, illustrations, maps, and charts. [JHC]

11.241 Jean-Pierre Drège. *Le Commercial Press de Shanghai, 1897–1949.* Paris: Collège de France, 1978. (Memoires de l'Institut des Hautes Études Chinoises, 7.) ISBN 2-85757-010-4. ▸ Standard work on pre-1949 China's most important publishing house. Includes statistics and biographical sketches of twenty-six key personnel (e.g., director Wang Yun-wu). [JHC]

11.242 Robert Y. Eng. *Economic imperialism in China: silk production and exports, 1861–1932.* Berkeley: University of California, Institute of East Asian Studies, 1986. (China research monographs, 31.) ISBN 0-912966-85-8. ▸ Concludes, contra Li 11.254, Chinese silk industry strongly affected by economic imperialism, despite absence of direct foreign investment. But acknowledges neo-Marxist overemphasis on peasant immiseration. [JHC]

11.243 David Faure. *The rural economy of pre-liberation China: trade expansion and peasant livelihood in Jiangsu and Guangdong, 1870 to 1937.* Hong Kong: Oxford University Press, 1989. ISBN 0-19-582707-4. ▸ Finds success of world trade in raising farm income and continuous prosperity for both landlords and tenants in Kiangsu and Kwangtung provinces until 1930s world depression. Supports Myers 11.259 versus Huang 11.250. [JHC]

11.244 Albert Feuerwerker. *China's early industrialization: Sheng Hsuan-huai (1844–1916) and mandarin enterprise.* 1958 ed. New York: Atheneum, 1970. ▸ Excellent, pioneering study of "official supervision and merchant management" (*kuan-tu shang-pan*) industrial system in late Ch'ing period. Emphasizes weaknesses, concludes system fostered protection of bureaucratic capital, not entrepreneurial spirit. [JHC]

11.245 Yen-p'ing Hao. *The commercial revolution in nineteenth-century China: the rise of Sino-Western mercantile capitalism.* Berkeley: University of California Press, 1986. ISBN 0-520-05344-3. ▸ Stimulating argument for 1820s to 1880s as crucial in revolutionary development of commercial capitalism (Western sparked but Chinese implemented) in coastal regions. Interpretation controversial for downplaying earlier commercial revolution from sixteenth century onward. [JHC]

11.246 Yen-p'ing Hao. *The comprador in nineteenth-century China: bridge between East and West.* Cambridge, Mass.: Harvard University Press, 1970. ISBN 0-674-15525-4. ▸ Standard work on entrepreneurial bicultural middlemen hired by Western merchants to facilitate commercial transactions. Unmoved by lure of traditional gentry-official life, comprador was new type of merchant. [JHC]

11.247 Harold C. Hinton. *The grain tribute system of China (1845–1911).* 1956 ed. Cambridge, Mass.: Harvard University, East Asian Research Center, 1970. (Harvard East Asian monographs, 2.) ▸ Study of shift from use of Grand Canal to sea transport of grain (tax-in-kind) from lower Yangtze Valley to Peking due to neglected hydraulic repairs, Yellow River's flooding and shifted course, and Taiping Rebellion. [JHC]

11.248 Hou Chi-ming. *Foreign investment and economic development in China, 1840–1937.* Cambridge, Mass.: Harvard University Press, 1965. ISBN 0-674-30850-6. ▸ Controversial interpretation, supported by Schrecker 11.148, arguing against equating foreign investment with imperialism. Finds foreign trade and investment important in increasing economic modernization before 1937. [JHC]

11.249 Hsiao Liang-lin. *China's foreign trade statistics, 1864–1949.* Cambridge, Mass.: Harvard University, East Asian Research Center, 1974. (Harvard East Asian monographs, 56.) ISBN 0-674-11960-6. ▸ Detailed statistical tables compiled from Maritime Customs Service publications. Topics include imports and exports (by total value, commodity, country, and Chinese port), foreign exchange rates, domestic interport trade, and balance of payments estimates. [JHC]

11.250 Philip C. C. Huang. *The peasant economy and social change in North China.* Stanford, Calif.: Stanford University Press, 1985. ISBN 0-8047-1220-4. ▸ Sophisticated, controversial analysis of commercialization and population growth from eighteenth century through 1940s, resulting in quantitative growth but without qualitative breakthrough to greater per-capita agricultural productivity. Peasant livelihood in crisis from 1920s onward. [JHC]

11.251 Philip C. C. Huang. *The peasant family and rural development in the Yangzi delta, 1350–1988.* Stanford, Calif.: Stanford University Press, 1990. ISBN 0-8047-1787-7 (cl), 0-8047-1788-5 (pbk). ▸ Important analysis of long-term mutual influences among population growth, increased commercialization, and post-1949 collectivization, all without increased productivity per capita. Focuses on eight villages in Kiangsu province. Includes North China comparisons. [JHC]

11.252 Ralph William Huenemann. *The dragon and the iron horse: the economics of railroads in China, 1876–1937.* Cambridge, Mass.: Harvard University, Council on East Asian Studies, 1984. (Harvard East Asian monographs, 109.) ISBN 0-674-21535-4. ▸ Scrupulous, systematic cost-benefit analysis concluding that, on balance, railways benefited China economically, despite their imperialistic origins. [JHC]

11.253 Frank H. H. King. *Money and monetary policy in China, 1845–1895.* Cambridge, Mass.: Harvard University Press, 1965. ▸ Valuable explication of complex, understudied topic. Topics include cash, silver, banks, mints, case study of Hsien-feng period (1851–61), treaty ports, and reforms. Includes suggestions for standardization of fiscal terminology. [JHC]

11.254 Lillian M. Li. *China's silk trade: traditional industry in the modern world, 1842–1937.* Cambridge, Mass.: Harvard University, Council on East Asian Studies, 1981. (Harvard East Asian monographs, 97.) ISBN 0-674-11962-1. ▸ Study of rise and fall of China's leading export. Concludes that imperialism cannot be blamed for silk industry's failure to compete successfully with Japan on international market. Contrast Eng 11.242. [JHC]

11.255 Susan Mann. *Local merchants and the Chinese bureaucracy, 1750–1950.* Stanford, Calif.: Stanford University Press, 1987. ISBN 0-8047-1341-3. ▸ Wide-ranging analysis emphasizing nineteenth- and twentieth-century governments' use of tax farming to collect trade taxes. Presents revisionist view of *likin* (transit) tax as serving needs of center. Also strong on licensed and unlicensed brokers. [JHC]

11.256 Ernest R. May and John K. Fairbank, eds. *America's China trade in historical perspective: the Chinese and American performance.* Cambridge, Mass.: Harvard University, Department of History, Committee on American–East Asian Relations and Council on East Asian Studies, 1986. (Harvard studies in American–East Asian relations, 11.) ISBN 0-674-03075-3. ▸ On Chinese exportation of tea and silk and importation of textiles, cigarettes, and petroleum. Also overviews of Sino-American commercial relations. [JHC]

11.257 Andrea Lee McElderry. *Shanghai old-style banks (ch'ien-chuang), 1800–1935: a traditional institution in a changing society.* Ann Arbor: University of Michigan, Center for Chinese Studies, 1976. (Michigan papers in Chinese studies, 25.) ISBN 0-89264-025-1 (pbk). ▸ Standard work on traditional commercial banks, distinguishing them from other financial and commercial institutions. Also treats financial crises in late Ch'ing and republican periods (e.g., 1883–84, 1897, 1910–12, 1935). [JHC]

11.258 Rhoads Murphey. *The treaty ports and China's modernization: what went wrong?* Ann Arbor: University of Michigan, Center for Chinese Studies, 1970. (Michigan papers in Chinese studies, 7.) ▸ Controversial argument finding treaty ports largely irrelevant to domestic Chinese economy—not particularly beneficial, but certainly not imperialistically harmful. Concludes their greatest impact was as psychological spur to nationalism. [JHC]

11.259 Ramon H. Myers. *The Chinese peasant economy: agricultural development in Hopei and Shantung, 1890–1949.* Cambridge, Mass.: Harvard University Press, 1970. ISBN 0-674-12451-0. ▸ Controversial interpretation, rejecting socioeconomic exploitation as cause of increased peasant misery. Identifies lack of systematic introduction of new technology (e.g., chemical fertilizers, seeds) as key problem. Pioneering use of 1930s to 1940s Japanese fieldwork. [JHC]

11.260 Ramon H. Myers. "How did the modern Chinese economy develop?—A review article." *Journal of Asian studies* 50.3 (1991) 604–28. ISSN 0021-9118. ▸ Convenient summary of major unresolved controversies concerning Chinese economy, ca. 1870–1937. Includes substantive bibliography. Should be read together with Philip Huang's "Reply to Ramon Myers" in same issue, pp. 629–33. [JHC]

11.261 Ng Chin-keong. *Trade and society: the Amoy network on the China coast, 1683–1735.* Singapore: Singapore University Press, 1983. ISBN 9971-69-068-3 (cl), 9971-69-069-1 (pbk). ▸ Excellent on rise of Amoy (Hsia-men) region in southern Fukien province as maritime center. Finds causation in push of limited land and political turmoil and in pull of rice and sugar trade with Taiwan. [JHC]

11.262 Peter C. Perdue. *Exhausting the earth: state and peasant in Hunan, 1500–1850.* Cambridge, Mass.: Harvard University, Council on East Asian Studies, 1987. (Harvard East Asian monographs, 130.) ISBN 0-674-27504-7. ▸ Analyzes governmental policies (e.g., on resettlement, property rights, water control) attempting to deal with Hunan province's population growth and agrarian commercialization. Finds declining intervention by state in processes of production over long term. [JHC]

11.263 Dwight H. Perkins. *Agricultural development in China, 1368–1968.* Chicago: Aldine, 1969. ISBN 0-202-31005. ▸ Concludes rise in grain output ca. 1400–1950 partially explained by quadrupling of cultivated acreage and partially by rise in yields per acre, despite stagnant technology. Includes detailed statistical appendixes. [JHC]

11.264 Evelyn Sakakida Rawski. *Agricultural change and the peasant economy of South China.* Cambridge, Mass.: Harvard University Press, 1972. ISBN 0-674-01210-0. ▸ Comparative study of agrarian commercialization in two regional economies: coastal sixteenth-century Fukien province and inland eighteenth-century Hunan. Points to availability of cheap, efficient water transport as key to prosperous market economy. [JHC]

11.265 Thomas G. Rawski and Lillian M. Li, eds. *Chinese history in economic perspective.* Berkeley: University of California Press, 1992. ISBN 0-520-07068-2. ▸ Topics include Ch'ing grain prices and markets in Yangtze Delta, Chihli, Kansu, and Hunan provinces; infanticide; republican period income distribution; Kiangsu sericulture; Chekiang women's work; and native-place ties in labor markets. [JHC]

11.266 John Shepherd. "Rethinking tenancy: explaining spatial and temporal variation in late imperial and republican China." *Comparative studies in society and history* 30.3 (1988) 403–31. ISSN 0010-4175. ▸ Important revisionist analysis attacking equation of tenant status with poverty. Finds high tenancy rates caused by multiple factors (managerial landlordism, immigration, reclamation), not merely by debt-sale of land. Includes substantial bibliography. [JHC]

11.267 Shih Min-hsiung. *The silk industry in Ch'ing China.* E-tu Zen Sun, trans. Ann Arbor: University of Michigan, Center for Chinese Studies, 1976. (Michigan abstracts of Chinese and Japanese works on Chinese history, 5.) ▸ Treats production and distribution, business methods in reeling and weaving, three southern imperial silkworks (Nanking, Soochow, Hangchou), modernization, foreign trade, and factors inhibiting growth. Finds deteriorating quality led to export decline. [JHC]

11.268 Alvin Y. So. *The South China silk district: local historical transformation and world-system theory.* Albany: State University of New York Press, 1986. ISBN 0-88706-322-5 (cl), 0-88706-321-7 (pbk). ▸ Pioneering application of Wallerstein's formulations (22.256) to case study of Kwangtung province's silk industry from nineteenth century to 1930s. Treats precapitalist social formations, incorporation, agrarian commercialization, industrialization, proletarianization, and cyclical development. [JHC]

11.269 C. John Stanley. *Late Ch'ing finance: Hu Kuang-yung as an innovator.* 1961 ed. Cambridge, Mass.: Harvard University, East Asian Research Center, 1970. (Harvard East Asian monographs, 12.) ▸ Underappreciated study of semi-official merchant-banker, Tso Tsung-t'ang's purchasing agent, pioneer in arranging interest-bearing loans from foreign merchants (1867–82) to finance Tso's suppression of Muslim rebellions. [JHC]

11.270 Van Jay Symons. *Ch'ing ginseng management: Ch'ing monopolies in microcosm.* Tempe: Arizona State University, Center for Asian Studies, 1981. (Center for Asian Studies, Occasional papers, 13.) ISBN 0-939252-09-0. ▸ Standard work on immensely profitable Manchurian medicinal root and cornerstone of Ming-Manchu trade. Monopoly established very early in Ch'ing (1644–48) by Nei-wu fu (Imperial Household Department); more tightly controlled than salt monopoly. [JHC]

11.271 Eduard B. Vermeer, ed. *Development and decline of Fukien province in the seventeenth and eighteenth centuries.* Leiden: Brill, 1990. (Sinica Leidensia, 22.) ISBN 90-04-09171-8, ISSN 0169-9563. ▸ Topics include settlement through Sung dynasty, maritime trade (including tea, smuggling, Amoy-based junks [Chinese-style ships]), early Ch'ing Hsing-hua prefecture, Coxinga, pirates, 1652 Taiwan Rebellion, temples and cults, Jesuits, and early Ch'ing novels. [JHC]

11.272 Wang Yeh-chien. *Land taxation in imperial China, 1750–1911.* Cambridge, Mass.: Harvard University Press, 1973. ISBN 0-674-50860-2. ▸ Standard work, concluding that total taxes declined as percentage of household income from eighteenth century to 1911. Greatest defect in land tax was its failure to increase revenue from growing economy. [JHC]

11.273 T. S. Whelan. *The pawnshop in China: based on Yang Chao-yu, "Chung-kuo tien-tang yeh" (The Chinese pawnbroking industry) with a historical introduction and critical annotations.* Ann Arbor: University of Michigan, Center for Chinese Studies, 1979. (Michigan abstracts of Chinese and Japanese works on Chinese history, 6.) ▸ Brief but standard work on key moneylending and investment institution, focusing on nineteenth and early twentieth centuries. Notes widespread investment of government funds in pawnshops from eighteenth century to ca. 1911. [JHC]

11.274 Endymion Wilkinson. *Studies in Chinese price history.* New York: Garland, 1980. ISBN 0-8240-4257-3. ▸ Pioneering explication of some 5,000 grain market-price reports produced by county magistrates' staffs in Shensi province, 1900–10. Includes technical analysis of Ch'ing exchange rates (varying widely even within province) between copper cash and silver ingots. [JHC]

11.275 W. E. Willmott, ed. *Economic organization in Chinese society.* Stanford, Calif.: Stanford University Press, 1972. ISBN 0-8047-0794-4. ▸ Topics include Ch'ing salt monopoly, Ningpo traditional banks, silk, cotton, high-level equilibrium trap, commercialized agriculture, Taiwan, Hong Kong, and People's Republic. [JHC]

11.276 Tim Wright. *Coal mining in China's economy and society,*

1895–1937. Cambridge: Cambridge University Press, 1984. ISBN 0-521-25878-2. ‣ Examination of successful growth from virtual nonexistence in 1895 to very respectable proportions in 1930s. Finds Chinese-owned sector grew slightly faster than foreign-owned. Miners' existence hazardous and miserable throughout. [JHC]

11.277 Madeleine Zelin. *The magistrate's tale: rationalizing fiscal reform in eighteenth-century Ch'ing China.* Berkeley: University of California Press, 1984. ISBN 0-520-04930-6. ‣ Standard work on Yung-cheng emperor's failed attempt to eliminate bureaucratic corruption by legalizing (thus controlling) local functionaries' previously unregulated collection of administrative fees. Finds center's penetration of local society inadequate for successful reform. [JHC]

SEE ALSO
10.36 Kang Chao. *Man and land in Chinese history.*

Intellectual and Cultural History

11.278 William Ayers. *Chang Chih-tung and educational reform in China.* Cambridge, Mass.: Harvard University Press, 1971. ISBN 0-674-10762-4. ‣ Prominent late Ch'ing reformist official famous for his failed attempt to preserve Confucian system (*t'i*) by adopting Western techniques (*yung*). Advocated 1905 abolition of traditional examination system. [JHC]

11.279 Paul J. Bailey. *Reform the people: changing attitudes towards popular education in early twentieth-century China.* Vancouver: University of British Columbia Press, 1990. ISBN 0-7748-0383-5. ‣ Analysis of educational thought (1890s–1921), emphasizing continuities. Covers late Ch'ing reorientation of official thinking, public debate 1900–11, popular education during 1904–11 and early republic, 1912 school system, and work-study movement in France (1916–21). [JHC]

11.280 Wm. Theodore De Bary. "Chinese despotism and the Confucian ideal: a seventeenth-century view." In *Chinese thought and institutions.* 1957 ed. John K. Fairbank, ed., pp. 163–203. Chicago: University of Chicago Press, 1967. ‣ Classic exposition of Huang Tsung-hsi's antidespotic, quasi-constitutional political philosophy as expressed in his *Ming-i tai-fang lu* (Plan for the Prince), rejecting standard Confucian antipathy to codified law. [JHC]

11.281 Marianne Bastid. *Educational reform in early twentieth-century China.* Paul J. Bailey, trans. Ann Arbor: University of Michigan, Center for Chinese Studies, 1988. (Michigan monographs in Chinese studies, 53.) ISBN 0-89264-061-8 (cl), 0-89264-062-6 (pbk). ‣ Examination of wide ramifications of late Ch'ing educational reforms. Focuses on educational writings of Chang Chien, outstanding literatus turned modernizer, during period 1901–12. Translation of *Aspects de la réforme de l'enseignement en Chine au debut du vingtième siècle, d'après des écrits de Zhang Jian* (1971). [JHC]

11.282 Daniel H. Bays. *China enters the twentieth century: Chang Chih-tung and the issues of a new age, 1895–1909.* Ann Arbor: University of Michigan Press, 1978. ISBN 0-472-08105-5. ‣ Standard work on leading late Ch'ing official, reformist yet loyalist. Focusing on political-diplomatic narrative, emphasizes Chang's distrust of provincial and local gentry as disruptive force from central government's perspective. [JHC]

11.283 Martin Bernal. *Chinese socialism to 1907.* Ithaca, N.Y.: Cornell University Press, 1976. ISBN 0-8014-0915-2. ‣ Strong on 1906–07 debate between Liang Ch'i-ch'ao and Sun Yat-sen. Excellent on Japanese influence. Conclusion points to irrelevance of pre-Leninist Marxist social democracy to China. [JHC]

11.284 Knight Biggerstaff. *The earliest modern government schools in China.* 1961 ed. Port Washington, N.Y.: Kennikat, 1972. ISBN

0-8046-1512-8. ‣ Standard work on initial nineteenth-century educational innovation from above, focusing on T'ung-wen Kuan (School of Combined Learning), Kiangnan Arsenal, and Fu-chou Navy Yard School. [JHC]

11.285 Alison Harley Black. *Man and nature in the philosophical thought of Wang Fu-chih.* Seattle: University of Washington Press, 1989. (University of Washington, Publications on Asia of the Henry M. Jackson School of International Studies, 41.) ISBN 0-295-96338-7. ‣ Examines both what influential seventeenth-century thinker thought (political philosophy excepted) and how he thought it. Finds Wang had skeptical mentality, unusually analytical for Confucian philosopher. [JHC]

11.286 Joey Bonner. *Wang Kuo-wei: an intellectual biography.* Cambridge, Mass.: Harvard University Press, 1986. ISBN 0-674-94594-8. ‣ Study of polymath of late Ch'ing and early republican periods whose interests ranged from Schopenhauer and Kant to literary aesthetics to Shang dynasty archaeology. Explores his intense loyalty to defunct Ch'ing dynasty, resulting in suicide. [JHC]

11.287 Sally Borthwick. *Education and social change in China: the beginnings of the modern era.* Stanford, Calif.: Hoover Institution Press, 1983. (Education and society series, Hoover Press publication, 268.) ISBN 0-8179-7681-7. ‣ Examination of transition to modern-style schools during period 1890–1911. Concludes that educational reforms proved to be Trojan horse undermining old order. Includes contemporary illustrations. [JHC]

11.288 O. Brière. *Fifty years of Chinese philosophy, 1898–1948.* Rev. ed. Dennis J. Doolin, ed. Laurence G. Thompson, trans. New York: Praeger, 1965. ‣ Still useful as introductory guide, especially for lesser-known thinkers. Includes annotated bibliography of primary sources arranged by topic (Buddhist philosophy, German rationalism, etc.), and detailed name index. Translation of "Les courants philosophiques en Chine depuis 50 ans (1898–1950)." *Bulletin de l'Université l'Aurore* 10.40 (1949) 561–650. [JHC]

11.289 Roswell S. Britton. *The Chinese periodical press, 1800–1912.* 1933 ed. New York: Paragon Book Gallery, 1966. ‣ Still valuable history of both Chinese and Western (treaty port) journalism from *Ching-pao* (Peking Gazette) on, including late Ch'ing reformist and revolutionary press. Includes twenty-four illustrations of rare newspapers. [JHC]

11.290 Cynthia J. Brokaw. *The ledgers of merit and demerit: social change and moral order in late imperial China.* Princeton: Princeton University Press, 1991. ISBN 0-691-05543-2. ‣ Discussion of ethical handbooks (popular during late Ming and early Ch'ing dynasties) for calculating personal morality via numerical values assigned to specific good and bad deeds. Analyzes changing emphasis from social mobility to stability. [JHC]

11.291 Chan Sin-wai. *Buddhism in late Ch'ing political thought.* Boulder: Westview, 1985. (Institute of Chinese Studies, Monograph series, 8.) ISBN 0-8133-0256-0. ‣ Focuses on thought of T'an Ssu-t'ung, martyr of 1898 Reform Movement. Finds Buddhism served as romantic, psychological salve to late Ch'ing thinkers. [JHC]

11.292 Chang Hao. *Chinese intellectuals in crisis: search for order and meaning (1890–1911).* Berkeley: University of California Press, 1987. ISBN 0-520-05378-8. ‣ Examines K'ang Yu-wei, T'an Ssu-t'ung, Chang Ping-lin, Liu Shih-p'ei. Finds striking continuities with tradition in thought of all four, despite indirect, catalytic role of West (strongest in K'ang, Liu). [JHC]

11.293 Chang Hao. *Liang Ch'i-ch'ao and intellectual transition in China, 1890–1907.* Cambridge, Mass.: Harvard University Press, 1971. ISBN 0-674-53009-8. ‣ Demonstrates Liang chose to remain committed to certain aspects of traditional thought, even while rejecting others. Convincingly refutes Levenson's overly schematic formulation of intellectual alienation, emotional attachment. [JHC]

11.294 Sidney H. Chang and Leonard H. D. Gordon. *All under heaven . . . : Sun Yat-sen and his revolutionary thought.* Stanford, Calif.: Hoover Institution Press, 1991. ISBN 0-8179-9081-X (cl), 0-8179-9082-8 (pbk). ▸ Short, not overly critical biography, followed by sympathetic analysis of Sun's ideology, emphasizing *San Min Chu I* (Three People's Principles): nationalism, democracy, and livelihood. Takes Sun seriously as thinker. [JHC]

11.295 Chung-ying Cheng. *Tai Chen's "Inquiry into Goodness": a translation of the "Yuan shan," with an introductory essay.* Honolulu: East-West Center Press, 1971. ISBN 0-8248-0093-1. ▸ Cheng's long, analytical introduction on leading eighteenth-century thinker notes that, quite unlike his later writings, Tai's *Yuan shan* (Inquiry into Goodness) does not explicitly criticize neo-Confucian orthodoxy. [JHC]

11.296 Ann-ping Chin and Mansfield Freeman. *Tai Chen on Mencius: explorations in words and meaning: a translation of "Meng Tzu tzu-i shu-cheng" with a critical introduction.* New Haven: Yale University Press, 1990. ISBN 0-300-04654-5. ▸ Useful preface on major eighteenth-century empirical philosopher's life, times, and thought, followed by translation of "Evidential Study of Meaning of Terms in Mencius." [JHC]

11.297 Ju-hsi Chou and Claudia Brown, eds. *The elegant brush: Chinese painting under the Qianlong emperor, 1735–1795.* Phoenix, Ariz.: Phoenix Art Museum, 1985. ISBN 0-910407-15-0 (pbk). ▸ Exhibition catalog on Ch'ien-lung period, including essays on Ch'ien-lung emperor's taste, court painting under Yung-cheng and Ch'ien-lung emperors, imperial painting academy; information on individual artists. Profusely illustrated. [JHC]

11.298 Samuel C. Chu. *Reformer in modern China: Chang Chien, 1853–1926.* New York: Columbia University Press, 1965. ▸ Standard work on ultimate transitional figure, outstanding literatus turned local modernizer in Nan-t'ung county (Kiangsu province), promoting industrialization (cotton mills) and universal education for both sexes without foresaking Confucian roots. [JHC]

11.299 Paul A. Cohen. *Between tradition and modernity: Wang T'ao and reform in late Ch'ing China.* 1974 ed. Cambridge, Mass.: Harvard University, East Asian Research Center, 1987. (Harvard East Asian monographs, 133.) ISBN 0-674-06876-9 (pbk). ▸ Solid biography proves Wang advocated institutional reform early, from 1870s onward. Conclusion, using littoral-hinterland formulation to examine other reformers, reconfirms westernizing influences spread from coast to interior. [JHC]

11.300 Paul A. Cohen. *China and Christianity: the missionary movement and the growth of Chinese antiforeignism, 1860–1870.* Cambridge, Mass.: Harvard University Press, 1963. ▸ Excellent study of gentry-inspired reaction against Christian missionary presence, threatening local power relations. Contains graphic illustrations of xenophobic propaganda. Coverage includes Tientsin Massacre (1870). [JHC]

11.301 Don J. Cohn, ed. and trans. *Vignettes from the Chinese: lithographs from Shanghai in the late nineteenth century.* Hong Kong: Chinese University, Research Centre for Translation, 1987. ISBN 962-7255-01-7 (pbk). ▸ Sample of fifty illustrations, with translated commentaries, from *Tien-shih-chai hua-pao* (Touchstone Studio Pictorial), published 1884–1898 as supplement to Shanghai newspaper *Shen Pao.* Fascinating on urban elite's mentality. Includes editor's substantive preface. [JHC]

11.302 Ralph C. Croizier. *Koxinga and Chinese nationalism: history, myth, and the hero.* Cambridge, Mass.: Harvard University, East Asian Research Center, 1977. (Harvard East Asian monographs, 67.) ISBN 0-674-50566-2. ▸ Standard work on Cheng Ch'eng-kung (a.k.a. Coxinga), seventeenth-century general loyal to Ming dynasty who seized Taiwan for use as anti-Ch'ing base. Focuses on his heroic image and symbolism in contemporary and later historiography. [JHC]

11.303 Ralph C. Croizier. *Traditional medicine in modern China: science, nationalism, and the tensions of cultural change.* Cambridge, Mass.: Harvard University Press, 1968. ▸ Useful description of uneasy relationship between traditional Chinese and Western medicine since nineteenth century (including People's Republic and Taiwan) as aspect of broader intercultural relations. [JHC]

11.304 Jerry Dennerline. *Qian Mu and the world of seven mansions.* New Haven: Yale University Press, 1988. ISBN 0-300-04296-5. ▸ Sensitive biographical study of culturally conservative historian Ch'ien Mu with much on family life in late Ch'ing and early republican Wu-hsi county (Kiangsu province). Includes partial translation of Ch'ien's memoirs. [JHC]

11.305 Gary Dickinson and Linda Wrigglesworth. *Imperial wardrobe.* London: Bamboo Publishing, 1990. ISBN 1-870076-07-9. ▸ Study of Ch'ing imperial garments, ritual use of court dress (e.g., for various ceremonies), symbolism, insignia on coats and hats reserved for specific official ranks, and male and female court attire. Profusely illustrated in color. [JHC]

11.306 Frank Dikötter. *The discourse of race in modern China.* Stanford, Calif.: Stanford University Press, 1992. ISBN 0-8047-1994-2. ▸ Pioneering analysis of indigenous, strongly rooted racism among educated Chinese toward Westerners and Africans, focusing on late Ch'ing and republican periods (including eugenics, popularized by P'an Kuang-tan). [JHC]

11.307 Henry Doré. *Researches into Chinese superstitions.* 1914–38 ed. 11 vols. M. Kennelly, D. J. Finn, and L. F. McGreal, trans. Taipei: Ch'eng Wen, 1966–67. ▸ Encyclopedic, copiously illustrated description of popular religion by longtime Jesuit missionary in Kiangsu and Anhui provinces. Includes life-cycle beliefs, charms, divination, festivals, deities and worthies (Buddhist, Taoist, Confucian). Partial translation of *Récherches sur les superstitions en Chine,* 18 vols. (1911–38). [JHC]

11.308 Fred W. Drake. *China charts the world: Hsu Chi-yü and his "Geography" of 1848.* Cambridge, Mass.: Harvard University, East Asian Research Center, 1975. (Harvard East Asian monographs, 64.) ISBN 0-674-11643-7. ▸ Standard work on Confucian realist, one of first nineteenth-century Chinese to borrow knowledge from West, emphasizing his *Ying-huan chih-lueh* (Short Account of Maritime Circuit), widely influential in 1850s–60s. [JHC]

11.309 Wolfram Eberhard. *Guilt and sin in traditional China.* Berkeley: University of California Press, 1967. ▸ Stimulating analysis of moral values which upper class thought desirable for lower classes, as expressed in *shan-shu* (morality books). Finds elite lost its sense of shame in nineteenth century. [JHC]

11.310 Benjamin A. Elman. *Classicism, politics, and kinship: the Ch'ang-chou school of New Text Confucianism in late imperial China.* Berkeley: University of California Press, 1990. ISBN 0-520-06673-1. ▸ By demonstrating that lineages in Ch'ang-chou prefecture (Kiangsu province) served from seventeenth century as vehicles for philosophical innovation—New Text (*chin-wen*) Confucianism—Elman succeeds in inaugurating a new field: sociointellectual history. [JHC]

11.311 Benjamin A. Elman. *From philosophy to philology: intellectual and social aspects of change in late imperial China.* Cambridge, Mass.: Harvard University, Council on East Asian Studies, 1984. (Harvard East Asian monographs, 110.) ISBN 0-674-32525-7. ▸ Solid examination of eighteenth-century Kiangnan (lower Yangtze) literati's intellectual shift from deductive neo-Confucianism to inductive evidential research, especially textual philology. Result was specialization and professionalization of scholarship. [JHC]

11.312 Michael Gasster. *Chinese intellectuals and the Revolution of 1911: the birth of modern Chinese radicalism.* Seattle: University of Washington Press, 1969. (Far Eastern and Russian Institute publications on Asia, 19.) ▸ Analysis of diversity among radicals Wang Ching-wei, Chang Ping-lin, Wu Chih-hui, Hu Han-min, Sun Yat-sen, and Liang Ch'i-ch'ao, focusing on 1903–08. Credits T'ung Meng Hui (Alliance Society) with successfully proselytizing republicanism. [JHC]

11.313 Jacques Gernet. *China and the Christian impact: a conflict of cultures.* Janet Lloyd, trans. Cambridge and Paris: Cambridge University Press and Éditions de la Maison des Sciences de l'Homme, 1985. ISBN 0-521-26681-5 (cl), 0-521-31319-8 (pbk). ▸ Highly stimulating analysis of Chinese reactions to (and especially against) Jesuit-introduced Christianity in seventeenth and eighteenth centuries. Interpretation controversial for emphasizing Sino-Western cultural irreconcilability, rooted in incompatible, language-determined thought processes. Translation of *Chine et christianisme: action et réaction* (1982). [JHC]

11.314 Jerome B. Grieder. *Intellectuals and the state in modern China: a narrative history.* New York: Free Press, 1981. ISBN 0-02-912810-2. ▸ Exemplary panorama of intellectual life from seventeenth-century's Huang Tsung-hsi to 1949. Focuses on engagé thinkers, those seeking to influence public opinion. Includes annotated bibliography. [JHC]

11.315 J.J.M. de Groot. *The religious system of China, its ancient forms, evolution, history and present aspect, manners, customs, and social institutions connected therewith.* 1892–1910 ed. 6 vols. Taipei: Southern Materials Center, 1989. ▸ Monumental fieldwork centered on, but not limited to, Amoy (Hsia-men) county (Fukien province). Mostly on death ritual and practices, but also covers soul, ancestor worship, demonology, sorcery, and animism. Illustrated. [JHC]

11.316 R. Kent Guy. *The emperor's four treasuries: scholars and the state in the late Ch'ien-lung era.* Cambridge, Mass.: Harvard University, Council on East Asian Studies, 1987. (Harvard East Asian monographs, 129.) ISBN 0-674-25115-6. ▸ Standard work on imperially-sponsored *Ssu-k'u ch'uan-shu* (Complete Library of Four Treasuries) compilation project, demonstrating that attendant censorship not all emperor's handiwork. Fascinating case study of eighteenth-century academic politics. [JHC]

11.317 Hsiao Kung-chuan. *A modern China and a new world: K'ang Yu-wei, reformer and utopian, 1858–1927.* Seattle: University of Washington Press, 1975. (Publications on Asia of the Institute for Comparative and Foreign Area Studies, 25.) ISBN 0-295-95385-3. ▸ Comprehensive, indeed monumental, study of radical Confucian philosopher, intellectual spark of 1898 Reform Movement. In four parts: family and man, philosophical commitments, reform proposals, and utopian ideas. [JHC]

11.318 Chun-tu Hsueh. *Huang Hsing and the Chinese Revolution.* Stanford, Calif.: Stanford University Press, 1961. ▸ Study of Sun Yat-sen's anti-Ch'ing revolutionary colleague, leader of military operations for T'ung Meng Hui (Alliance Society) who split with Sun in 1914. [JHC]

11.319 Chun-tu Hsueh, ed. *Revolutionary leaders of modern China.* New York: Oxford University Press, 1971. ▸ Useful collection of nineteen biographical articles (both original and reprinted) on nineteenth- and twentieth-century leaders, divided into sections on Taiping Rebellion, republican revolution, and communist movement. [JHC]

11.320 David G. Johnson, Andrew J. Nathan, and Evelyn Sakakida Rawski, eds. *Popular culture in late imperial China.* Berkeley: University of California Press, 1985. ISBN 0-520-05120-3 (cl), 0-520-06172-1 (pbk). ▸ After Johnson's especially stimulating introduction, treats vernacular and sectarian literature, local drama and regional opera, aspects of religion, popularizations of imperial Sacred Edict, and late Ch'ing journalism and fiction. [JHC]

11.321 Harold L. Kahn. *Monarchy in the emperor's eyes: image and reality in the Ch'ien-lung reign.* Cambridge, Mass.: Harvard University Press, 1971. ISBN 0-674-58230-6. ▸ Brilliant, sensitive appreciation of eighteenth-century emperor's historiographical image and personal self-image, focusing on upbringing and education as prince and on abdication in old age (under influence of Ho-shen as untitled regent). [JHC]

11.322 Noriko Kamachi. *Reform in China: Huang Tsun-hsien and the Japanese model.* Cambridge, Mass.: Harvard University, Council on East Asian Studies, 1981. (Harvard East Asian monographs, 95.) ISBN 0-674-75278-3. ▸ Standard work on late Ch'ing reformer comparable to Yen Fu who, looking to Meiji Japan rather than Victorian England for inspiration, called for powerful central government as reform's first priority. [JHC]

11.323 Ronald G. Knapp. *China's traditional rural architecture: a cultural geography of the common house.* Honolulu: University of Hawaii Press, 1986. ISBN 0-8248-1053-8. ▸ Study of historical development since Neolithic period (with post-seventeenth-century focus), variation through space, construction techniques, influence of folk beliefs such as geomancy, and dwellings in Taiwan and People's Republic. [JHC]

11.324 Kauko Laitinen. *Chinese nationalism in the late Qing dynasty: Zhang Binglin as an anti-Manchu propagandist.* London: Curzon, 1990. (Scandinavian Institute of Asian Studies, Monograph series, 57.) ISBN 0-7007-0193-1 (pbk), ISSN 0069-1712. ▸ Finds Chang Ping-lin unrivaled as propagandist among participants in 1911 Revolution. His anti-Manchuism stemmed from nationalistic fear of foreign threat to Chinese culture. Also treats early Ch'ing anti-Manchuism. [JHC]

11.325 Jane Kate Leonard. *Wei Yuan and China's rediscovery of the maritime world.* Wang Gungwu, Introduction. Cambridge, Mass.: Harvard University, Council on East Asian Studies, 1984. (Harvard East Asian monographs, 111.) ISBN 0-674-94855-6. ▸ Standard work on influential Statecraft-school geographer whose 1840s *Treatise on Sea Kingdoms* redirected strategic attention from Inner Asia to maritime frontier and Southeast Asia. Includes substantive introduction. [JHC]

11.326 Joseph R. Levenson. *Confucian China and its modern fate: a trilogy.* Berkeley: University of California Press, 1968. ISBN 0-520-00737-9 (pbk). ▸ Three previously published volumes bound as one, with original pagination. Volume 1: *The Problem of Intellectual Significance* (1958); volume 2: *The Problem of Monarchical Decay* (1964); volume 3: *The Problem of Historical Significance* (1965). Classic of intellectual virtuosity, immensely stimulating, especially volume 1. Essential reading, but some skepticism desirable. [JHC]

11.327 Li Chu-tsing, James Cahill, and Wai-kam Ho, eds. *Artists and patrons: some social and economic aspects of Chinese painting.* Lawrence: University of Kansas, Kress Foundation; Nelson-Atkins Museum of Art; and University of Washington Press, 1989. ISBN 1-878568-00-0, 0-295-97147-9. ▸ Seventeen contributions treat patronage from Sung through Ch'ing dynasties: at court, in Soochow, and elsewhere in Kiangnan (e.g., by Hui-chou and Yang-chou merchants in seventeenth-century Nanking, nineteenth-century Shanghai). [JHC]

11.328 Li Yu-ning. *The introduction of socialism into China.* New York: Columbia University Press, 1971. ISBN 0-231-03541-1. ▸ Succinct overview, emphasizing Japanese influence and 1905–1907 debate between Sun Yat-sen's newspaper *Min pao* (The People) and Liang Ch'i-ch'ao's *Hsin-min ts'ung-pao* (Renewing the People). Includes glossary of Japanese-derived political terminology. [JHC]

11.329 Liang Ch'i-ch'ao. *Intellectual trends in the Ch'ing period.* Immanuel C. Y. Hsu, trans. Cambridge, Mass.: Harvard University Press, 1959. ▸ Still useful for overall trends and treatment of lesser-known thinkers understudied in West. Covers Ku Yen-wu through Chang Ping-lin (including Liang himself). Includes substantive foreward by Benjamin Schwartz. Translation of *Ch'ing-tai hsueh-shu kai-lun* (1927). [JHC]

11.330 Kwang-Ching Liu, ed. *Orthodoxy in late imperial China.* Berkeley: University of California Press, 1989. ISBN 0-520-06542-5. ▸ Collection of essays on Ming-Ch'ing period. Topics include academies (*shu-yuan*), household instructions, lineage feuds in Kwangtung and Fukien provinces, ritual, and twentieth-century peasant proverbs. [JHC]

11.331 Jung-pang Lo, ed. *K'ang Yu-wei: a biography and a symposium.* Tucson: University of Arizona Press, 1967. (Association for Asian Studies, Monographs and papers, 23.) ISBN 0-8165-0152-1. ▸ Combines translation of K'ang's autobiography, sequel by Lo covering 1898–1927, and six articles on aspects of Kang's thought and 1898 Reform Movement. Includes substantial bibliography of K'ang's writings and secondary sources. [JHC]

11.332 Pichon P. Y. Loh. *The early Chiang Kai-shek: a study of his personality and politics, 1887–1924.* New York: Columbia University Press, 1971. ISBN 0-231-03596-9. ▸ Useful biography ending with Chiang's appointment as Whampoa Military Academy commandant. Psychohistorical conclusion: Chiang from childhood constructed a number of strong ego defense mechanisms against experientially hostile world. [JHC]

11.333 Jessie G. Lutz. *China and the Christian colleges, 1850–1950.* Ithaca, N.Y.: Cornell University Press, 1971. ISBN 0-8014-0626-9. ▸ Standard work on Protestant educational missionaries, their Chinese students, and how they interacted. Concludes that Christian colleges stimulated growth of Chinese nationalism, which, ironically, was anti-Western. [JHC]

11.334 Jessie G. Lutz, ed. *Christian missions in China: evangelists of what?* 1965 ed. Boston: Heath, 1966. ▸ Eighteen reprinted excerpts presenting missionaries' goals and methods, Chinese responses (e.g., by local gentry, Taipings, Boxers, and Ch'en Tu-hsiu), and Western scholars' interpretations. Includes detailed bibliographical essay. [JHC]

11.335 Colin Mackerras. *The Chinese theatre in modern times: from 1840 to the present day.* Amherst: University of Massachusetts Press, 1975. ISBN 0-87023-196-0. ▸ Development of Peking opera, famous actors, acting profession in late Ch'ing period and republic, modern spoken plays, pre-1949 regional opera (of Shanghai, Shao-hsing, Fukien, Kwangtung, Hupei, Szechwan), and post-1949 theater. Includes illustrations. [JHC]

11.336 Andrew J. Nathan. *Chinese democracy.* New York: Knopf; distributed by Random House, 1985. ISBN 0-394-51386-X. ▸ Fine analysis of Chinese concepts of democracy since late nineteenth century. Examines, especially, broad influence of Liang Ch'i-ch'ao, provisions for specific political rights in eleven Chinese constitutions dating from 1908 to 1982. [JHC]

11.337 David S. Nivison. *The life and thought of Chang Hsueh-ch'eng (1738–1801).* Stanford, Calif.: Stanford University Press, 1966. ISBN 0-8047-0230-6. ▸ Standard work on unconventional philosopher-historian, famous for his identification of Confucian classics as "history," enthusiasm for local gazetteers, and innovative concept of intellectual as technical specialist (i.e., professional). [JHC]

11.338 Daniel L. Overmyer. *Folk Buddhist religion: dissenting sects in late traditional China.* Cambridge, Mass.: Harvard University Press, 1976. ISBN 0-674-30705-4. ▸ Sophisticated, wide-ranging (Han dynasty to twentieth century) investigation of Buddhist sectarianism with emphasis on White Lotus religion. Clearly distinguishes between sects and secret societies, which differed in intent. [JHC]

11.339 Willard J. Peterson. *Bitter gourd: Fang I-chih and the impetus for intellectual change.* New Haven: Yale University Press, 1979. ISBN 0-300-02208-5. ▸ Sensitive analysis of literatus turned monk, member of *Fu-she* (Restoration Society), leading participant in seventeenth century's first generation of scholars committed to socially relevant empirical research. [JHC]

11.340 Willard J. Peterson. "The life of Ku Yen-wu (1613–1682)." *Harvard journal of Asiatic studies* 28–29 (1968–69) 114–56, 201–47. ISSN 0073-0548. ▸ Brief but solid biography of highly influential scholar and Ming loyalist; advocate of empirical research to counter vapid philosophical speculation characteristic of late Ming thinkers. [JHC]

11.341 Karl-Heinz Pohl. *Cheng Pan-ch'iao: poet, painter, and calligrapher.* Nettetal, Germany: Steyler, 1990. ISBN 3-8050-0261-0 (pbk), ISSN 0179-261X. ▸ Combines biography of famous eighteenth-century Yang-chou eccentric literatus with analysis of his views on literature, calligraphy, and painting. Includes illustrations and translations from his inscriptions, songs, and poems. [JHC]

11.342 James R. Pusey. *China and Charles Darwin.* Cambridge, Mass.: Harvard University, Council on East Asian Studies, 1983. (Harvard East Asian monographs, 100.) ISBN 0-674-11735-2. ▸ Standard work on Social Darwinism's tremendous impact with emphasis on Yen Fu, Liang Ch'i-ch'ao, and Mao Tse-tung. Confirms that breakthrough intellectual revolution occurred ca. 1900, not later during May Fourth Movement. [JHC]

11.343 James Reardon-Anderson. *The study of change: chemistry in China, 1840–1949.* Cambridge: Cambridge University Press, 1991. ISBN 0-521-39150-4. ▸ Explores relationship between science, state, and society. Chinese science's relative golden age of 1930s (when political authority more or less constructive and society more or less autonomous) destroyed by Sino-Japanese War. [JHC/AJR]

11.344 Paul S. Ropp. *Dissent in early modern China: "Ju-lin Wai-shih" and Ch'ing social criticism.* Ann Arbor: University of Michigan Press, 1981. ISBN 0-472-10006-8. ▸ Examines Wu Ching-tzu's eighteenth-century novel *Ju-lin wai-shih* (The Scholars) as satirical critique of civil-service examination system, feminist attack on women's subordination, and debunking of popular religion. [JHC]

11.345 Jon L. Saari. *Legacies of childhood: growing up Chinese in a time of crisis, 1890–1920.* Cambridge, Mass.: Harvard University, Council on East Asian Studies, 1990. (Harvard East Asian monographs, 136.) ISBN 0-674-52160-9. ▸ Ambitious, uneven psychohistorical attempt to plumb sense-of-self and psyches of transitional May Fourth generation (born 1890s) through analysis of childhood experiences and milieu. Based largely on autobiographies and interviews. [JHC]

11.346 Harold Z. Schiffrin. *Sun Yat-sen and the origins of the Chinese revolution.* Berkeley: University of California Press, 1968. ▸ Standard work on Sun's career to 1905 as revolutionary seeking to overthrow Ch'ing dynasty and discredit reformers. Ends with founding of T'ung Meng Hui (Alliance Society). Includes substantive foreward by John Fairbank. [JHC]

11.347 Harold Z. Schiffrin. *Sun Yat-sen: reluctant revolutionary.* Boston: Little, Brown, 1980. ISBN 0-316-77339-5. ▸ Best overall biography. Unlike earlier work (11.346), covers entire life, but in less detail. Concludes Sun was quixotic, lacked expected ferocity, and preferred negotiating to killing. Includes substantial bibliographical essay. [JHC]

11.348 Benjamin I. Schwartz. *In search of wealth and power: Yen Fu and the West.* Cambridge, Mass.: Belknap, 1964. ▸ Superb classic, analyzing highly influential translator-commentator on eighteenth- and nineteenth-century Western liberal philosophy. Emphasizes Yen's attraction to West's Faustian energy, especially Social Darwinism via Herbert Spencer, to strengthen and enrich Chinese state. [JHC]

11.349 Vincent Y. C. Shih. *The Taiping ideology: its sources, interpretations, and influences.* 1967 ed. Seattle: University of Washington Press, 1972. ISBN 0-295-95243-1. ▸ In addition to exhaustive coverage of main topic, includes valuable historiographical survey of previous interpretations and valuable descriptions of pre-Taiping rebel ideologies from Ch'in through Ming dynasties. [JHC]

11.350 Shimada Kenji. *Pioneer of the Chinese Revolution: Zhang Binglin and Confucianism.* Joshua A. Fogel, trans. Stanford, Calif.: Stanford University Press, 1990. ISBN 0-8047-1581-5. ▸ Discussion of Chang Ping-lin as both traditional Chinese scholar and anti-Ch'ing revolutionary in part one. Part two discusses rapid decline in authority of Confucianism, 1895–1919. Translation of *Chūgoku kakumei no senkushatachi* (Pioneers of the Chinese Revolution) (1970) pp. 167–271, and Onogawa Hidemi and Shimada Kenji, eds., *Shingai kakumei no kenkyū* (Studies on the 1911 Revolution) (1978) pp. 3–35. [JHC]

11.351 Jerome Silbergeld. "Chinese painting studies in the West: a state-of-the-field article." *Journal of Asian studies* 46.4 (1987) 849–97. ISSN 0021-9118. ▸ Covers from pre-Sung through mid-Ch'ing dynasties. Includes bibliography of published and unpublished English-language works with over a dozen items on modern (nineteenth- and twentieth-century) painting. [JHC]

11.352 Richard J. Smith. *China's cultural heritage: the Ch'ing dynasty, 1644–1912.* Boulder: Westview, 1983. ISBN 0-86531-627-9 (cl), 0-86531-628-7 (pbk). ▸ Unique survey of elite (especially gentry) culture. Topics include political order, socioeconomic institutions, language and symbolic reference, thought, religion, art, literature, social activities, and tradition and modernity (1860–1982). Well illustrated. [JHC]

11.353 Richard J. Smith. *Fortune-tellers and philosophers: divination in traditional Chinese society.* Boulder: Westview, 1991. ISBN 0-8133-7753-6. ▸ Valuable, detailed description of fortune-telling techniques and practices, ubiquitous among all classes, serving to maintain Ch'ing dynasty's prevailing social order. Focuses on *I-ching* (Book of Changes), geomancy, spirit mediums, and shamans. [JHC]

11.354 Jonathan D. Spence. *Emperor of China: self-portrait of K'ang-hsi.* 1974 ed. New York: Vintage, 1975. ISBN 0-394-71411-3. ▸ Author's brilliant first nudge at boundary between history and creative literature. Recreates mentality and personality of great Ch'ing emperor (r. 1662–1722) by weaving documentary threads into more or less authentic tapestry. [JHC]

11.355 Jonathan D. Spence. *The gate of heavenly peace: the Chinese and their revolution, 1895–1980.* 1981 ed. New York: Penguin, 1982. ISBN 0-14-006279-3 (pbk). ▸ Skillfully uses leading intellectuals' lives and writings as narrative vehicle. Focuses on K'ang Yu-wei, Lu Hsun, and Ting Ling, but also includes Liang Ch'i-ch'ao, Ch'ü Ch'iu-pai, Wen I-to, Hsu Chih-mo, Sun Yat-sen, and Mao Tse-tung. [JHC]

11.356 Jonathan D. Spence. *To change China: Western advisers in China, 1620–1960.* 1969 ed. Harmondsworth: Penguin, 1980. ISBN 0-14-005528-2. ▸ Highly readable biographical essays on Schall, Verbiest, Parker, Ward, Gordon, Lay, Hart, Martin, Freyer, Hume, Borodin, Todd, Bethune, Chennault, Stilwell,

and Wedemeyer. Finds their experiences more a cautionary tale than inspirational tract. [JHC]

11.357 Ssu-yu Teng and John K. Fairbank. *China's response to the West: a documentary survey, 1839–1923.* 1954 ed. Cambridge, Mass.: Harvard University Press, 1979. ISBN 0-674-12000-0 (cl), 0-674-12025-6 (pbk). ▸ Extremely influential collection of key sources with extensive commentaries. Title gave name to once orthodox Fairbank school of interpretation, now criticized for overemphasizing external Western (rather than domestic Chinese) causative factors. [JHC]

11.358 T'ien Ju-k'ang. *Male anxiety and female chastity: a comparative study of Chinese ethical values in Ming-Ch'ing times.* Leiden: Brill, 1988. (*T'oung Pao* monographie, 14.) ISBN 90-04-08361-8 (pbk), ISSN 0169-832x. ▸ Analysis of cult of female marital fidelity, which intensified from late Ming through Ch'ing dynasties. Focuses on suicides of widows and "widowed" fiancées. Finds psychological, vicarious identification between chaste females and their chief advocates: male examination-failers. [JHC]

11.359 Jean-François Vergnaud. *La pensée de Gu Yanwu (1613–1682): essai de synthèse.* Paris: École Française d'Extrême-Orient; distributed by Adrien Maisonneuve, 1990. (Publications de l'École Française d'Extrême-Orient, 159.) ISBN 2-85539-759-6. ▸ Standard work on highly influential empiricist scholar Ku Yen-wu. After introductory life-and-times (including detailed chronology), systematically examines Ku's philosophical, sociopolitical, and economic thought. Includes detailed annotated bibliography of Ku's writings. [JHC]

11.360 Arthur Waley. *Yuan Mei: eighteenth-century Chinese poet.* 1956 ed. Stanford, Calif.: Stanford University Press, 1970. ISBN 0-8047-0718-9. ▸ For general reader but remains standard work on freethinking literatus-aesthete who enjoyed shocking people by publishing on improper topics and mentoring talented female writers. Includes expert translations. [JHC]

11.361 Wang Fang-yu and Richard M. Barnhart. *Master of the lotus garden: the life and art of Bada Shanren (1626–1705).* Judith G. Smith, ed. New Haven: Yale University Press and Yale University Art Gallery, 1990. ISBN 0-300-04933-1 (cl), 0-89467-054-9 (pbk). ▸ Standard work on Ming dynasty prince who (after Manchu conquest) turned Buddhist priest, then idiosyncratic painter-poet (renamed Pa-ta Shan-jen), feigning madness for self-protection. Profusely illustrated. [JHC]

11.362 Marina Warner. *The dragon empress: the life and times of Tz'u-hsi, 1835–1908, empress-dowager of China.* 1972 ed. London: Hamish Hamilton, 1984. ISBN 0-241-11279-6 (pbk). ▸ For general reader, based solely on not consistently reliable Western sources. But remains best published Western-language biography of Ch'ing dynasty's *de facto* ruler during its final decades. [JHC]

11.363 James L. Watson and Evelyn Sakakida Rawski, eds. *Death ritual in late imperial and modern China.* Berkeley: University of California Press, 1988. ISBN 0-520-06081-4. ▸ Topics include North China funerals, Cantonese funeral specialists, Hakka laments, gender-induced ideologies, popular religion, Ming-Ch'ing imperial death ritual, funerals of Mao Tse-tung and Chiang Kai-shek, and death in People's Republic. [JHC]

11.364 J. Y. Wong. *Yeh Ming-ch'en: viceroy of Liang Kuang, 1852–58.* G. F. Hudson, Introduction. Cambridge: Cambridge University Press, 1976. ISBN 0-521-21023-2. ▸ Standard work on governor general of Kwangtung-Kwangsi provinces during Arrow War (1856–60), exiled by British to Calcutta. Concludes Yeh's overall reputation has been unfairly tarnished. Includes substantive introduction. [JHC]

11.365 Young-tsu Wong. *Search for modern nationalism: Zhang Binglin and revolutionary China, 1869–1936.* Hong Kong: Oxford University Press, 1989. ISBN 0-19-582740-6. ▸ Revisionist interpetation of Chang Ping-lin. Neither cultural reactionary nor anti-Manchu racist but advocate of change with continuity, committed to republicanism but opposed to cultural cosmopolitanism. Insisted on each nation's unique quintessence. [JHC]

11.366 Peter Zarrow. *Anarchism and Chinese political culture.* New York: Columbia University Press, 1990. ISBN 0-231-07138-8. ‣ Sophisticated analysis of anarchists (especially Liu Shih-p'ei, Wu Chih-hui), ca. 1900–30, as radical, populist, utopian, iconoclastic, and feminist. Pioneered against Confucian hierarchy and inequality, introduced Marx to China, but fatally antinationalistic. [JHC]

11.367 Etienne Zi. *Pratique des examens littéraires en Chine.* 1894 ed. Nendeln, Lichtenstein: Kraus Reprint, 1975. ‣ Classic exposition of civil service examination system as of late nineteenth century. Covers all three major levels: *sheng-yuan* ("bachelor's" degree), *chü-jen* ("master's" degree), and *chin-shih* ("doctorate"). [JHC]

SEE ALSO
10.50 Wm. Theodore De Bary, Wing-tsit Chan, and Burton Watson, eds. *Sources of Chinese tradition.*
10.53 John B. Henderson. *The development and decline of Chinese cosmology.*
10.55 Donald D. Leslie. *The survival of the Chinese Jews.*
10.56 Thomas A. Metzger. *Escape from predicament.*
10.161 Nathan Sivin. "Science and medicine in imperial China—the state of the field."

REPUBLIC OF CHINA, 1912–1949

Political History

11.368 A. Doak Barnett. *China on the eve of the communist takeover.* New York: Praeger, 1963. ‣ Based on reports researched in various Nationalist-held regions, 1947–49. Covers disintegration of government support in cities, stagnation in countryside, political fragmentation in peripheries, and communist capture of Peiping (Peking). [JHC]

11.369 Robert E. Bedeski. *State-building in modern China: the Kuomintang in the prewar period.* Berkeley: University of California, Center for Chinese Studies and Institute of East Asian Studies, 1981. (China research monographs, 18.) ISBN 0-912966-28-9 (pbk). ‣ Finds Nationalist government in Nanking, 1928–37, partially successful in overcoming warlord fragmentation, building a Chinese state. Full success thwarted by inability to monopolize force completely. [JHC]

11.370 Jack Belden. *China shakes the world.* 1949 ed. Owen Lattimore, Introduction. New York: Monthly Review Press, 1970. ISBN 0-85345-159-1. ‣ Classic of gripping, firsthand reporting from both communist- and Nationalist-controlled areas during period 1947–49. Has aged well. Includes new, substantive introduction. [JHC]

11.371 Lucien Bianco. *Origins of the Chinese Revolution, 1915–1949.* Muriel Bell, trans. Stanford, Calif.: Stanford University Press, 1971. ISBN 0-8047-0746-4. ‣ Fine introduction to rise of Chinese Communists, synthesizing previous monographic research. Emphasizes Communists' role as social revolutionaries. Includes bibliographical essay on suggested readings. Translation of revised *Les origines de la révolution chinoise, 1915–1949* (1967). [JHC]

11.372 John Hunter Boyle. *China and Japan at war, 1937–1945: the politics of collaboration.* Stanford, Calif.: Stanford University Press, 1972. ISBN 0-8047-0800-2. ‣ Focuses on prominent Nationalist leader Wang Ching-wei as Chinese patriot turned Japanese collaborator-puppet. Sensitive to motivational subtleties. Argues for need for healthy ambivalence in judging Wang's actions. [JHC]

11.373 John Byron and Robert Pack. *The claws of the dragon: Kang Sheng, the evil genius behind Mao and his legacy of terror in People's China.* New York: Simon & Schuster, 1992. ISBN 0-671-69537-1. ‣ Despite lurid title and interpretive overstatement of K'ang's importance, best available narrative on communist security chief (in 1931–33 Shanghai, 1938–45 Yenan, and 1967–75 People's Republic of China) and Chiang Ch'ing's patron. Controversially credits K'ang for 1942–43 rectification movement and Cultural Revolution. [JHC]

11.374 F. Gilbert Chan and Thomas H. Etzold, eds. *China in the 1920s: nationalism and revolution.* New York: New Viewpoints, 1976. ISBN 0-531-05383-0 (cl), 0-531-05589-2 (pbk). ‣ Collection of essays treating Sun Yat-sen's reorganization of Kuomintang (Nationalist party), nationalism, Ch'en Tu-hsiu, Whampoa Military Academy, student activism, Wu P'ei-fu, Chekiang province, Chiang Kai-shek's 1927 Shanghai Massacre, Naito Kōnan, and Unequal Treaties. [JHC]

11.375 Maria Hsia Chang. *The Chinese Blue Shirt Society: fascism and developmental nationalism.* Berkeley: University of California, Center for Chinese Studies and Institute of East Asian Studies, 1985. (China research monographs, 30.) ISBN 0-912966-81-5 (pbk). ‣ Sympathetic revisionist interpretation of Blue Shirts (Lan-i she) and Renaissance Society (Fu-hsing she), rejecting Eastman's (11.390) characterization of them as fascist. Rather, argues they are better understood as promoting political development. [JHC]

11.376 Lionel Max Chassin. *The communist conquest of China: a history of the Civil War, 1945–49.* Timothy Osato and Louis Gelas, trans. Cambridge, Mass.: Harvard University Press, 1965. ‣ Military history by former French vice-chief of staff for national defense (1946–49), based largely on secret intelligence reports from Deuxième Bureau. Translation of *La conquête de la Chine par Mao Tse-Tung, 1945–1949* (1952). [JHC]

11.377 Jerome Ch'en. *The military-gentry coalition: China under the warlords.* Toronto: University of Toronto–York University, Joint Centre on Modern East Asia, 1979. (Joint Centre on Modern East Asia, Publications series, 1.4.) ‣ In addition to politics, treats finance, society, and culture. Concludes alliance between military and gentry retarded China's modernization for almost a century. [JHC]

11.378 Chen Yung-fa. *Making revolution: the communist movement in Eastern and Central China, 1937–1945.* Berkeley: University of California Press, 1986. ISBN 0-520-05002-9. ‣ Superbly researched, making full use of confidential Communist party documents from Anhui and Kiangsu base areas. Reveals complexity and messiness of grassroots cadre activity. Includes substantive preface by Lyman P. Van Slyke. [JHC]

11.379 Ch'i Hsi-sheng. *Nationalist China at war: military defeats and political collapse, 1937–45.* Ann Arbor: University of Michigan Press, 1982. ISBN 0-472-10018-1. ‣ Explores Kuomintang (Nationalist party) government's increasing militarization, alienation from population, demoralization, and fragmentation during Sino-Japanese War. Contends Kuomintang fated to lose even before Civil War began. [JHC]

11.380 Ch'i Hsi-sheng. *Warlord politics in China, 1916–1928.* Stanford, Calif.: Stanford University Press, 1976. ISBN 0-8047-0894-0. ‣ Analyzes warlords' behavior in terms of balance of power. Finds qualitative difference between pre- and post-1928 militarist politics. Appendixes include useful chart of military leaders by province, 1916–27. [JHC]

11.381 Ch'ien Tuan-sheng. *The government and politics of China.* Cambridge, Mass.: Harvard University Press, 1950. ‣ Still useful as overview of central government, 1912–49, focusing on Kuomintang (Nationalist party), Nanking government's organizational structure, and military. Written from anti–Chiang Kai-shek perspective. [JHC]

11.382 Nicholas R. Clifford. *Spoilt children of empire: Westerners in Shanghai and the Chinese revolution of the 1920s.* Hanover, N.H.: Middlebury College Press, 1991. ISBN 0-87451-548-3. ‣ Responses of Western businessmen, missionaries, educators in Shanghai's colonial community to challenge posed by rising tide of Chinese nationalism (especially 1925 May 30th Movement and Northern Expedition). [JHC]

11.383 Parks M. Coble. *Facing Japan: Chinese politics and Japanese imperialism, 1931–1937.* Cambridge, Mass.: Harvard University, Council on East Asian Studies, 1991. (Harvard East Asian monographs, 135.) ISBN 0-674-29011-9. ‣ Study of interplay among Japanese expansionism in Manchuria and Hopei province, fluctuating relations between regional leaders (warlords) and Chiang Kai-shek's factionalized Nanking government, and rising forces of nationalistic public opinion. [JHC]

11.384 Parks M. Coble. *The Shanghai capitalists and the Nationalist government, 1927–1937.* 2d ed. Cambridge, Mass.: Harvard University, Council on East Asian Studies, 1986. (Harvard East Asian monographs, 94.) ISBN 0-674-80536-4 (pbk). ‣ Discussion of uneasy relationship between business community and Chiang Kai-shek's regime, finding capitalists were denied political role in Nanking government. Author's new introduction rejects alternative interpretations by Fewsmith (11.392) and Bush (11.489). [JHC]

11.385 Brian Crozier. *The man who lost China: the first full biography of Chiang Kai-shek.* New York: Scribner's, 1976. ISBN 0-684-14686-X. ‣ Useful; best available in absence of full-scale scholarly study of Chiang in English. Good on Nanking politics and Chiang's loss of mainland to Chinese Communists. Includes interesting anecdotes. Not well documented. [JHC]

11.386 Arif Dirlik. *Anarchism in the Chinese Revolution.* Berkeley: University of California Press, 1991. ISBN 0-520-07297-9. ‣ Continues analysis begun in Dirlik 11.387. Finds anarchist heyday 1905–30, including flourishing during May Fourth Movement. Many types of radicals receptive to anarchist ideas, especially in Canton. [JHC]

11.387 Arif Dirlik. *The origins of Chinese communism.* New York: Oxford University Press, 1989. ISBN 0-19-505453-9 (cl), 0-19-505454-7 (pbk). ‣ Revisionist analysis of 1917–21, emphasizing radicals' initial attraction to socialism in general—especially anarchism—not bolshevism or even Marxism. Communist party's formation was direct product of Comintern intervention, not of informed ideological conviction. [JHC]

11.388 Peter Williams Donovan. *The Red Army in Kiangsi, 1931–1934.* Ithaca, N.Y.: Cornell University, China-Japan Program, 1976. (Cornell University East Asia papers, 10.) ‣ Emphasizes unity of military and political work among Kiangsi Soviet's forces under Chu Te and Mao Tse-tung. Finds Communists uniquely successful in fostering soldiers' sense of involvement. Includes thirteen organizational charts. [JHC]

11.389 Peter Duus, Ramon H. Myers, and Mark R. Peattie, eds. *The Japanese informal empire in China, 1895–1937.* Princeton: Princeton University Press, 1989. ISBN 0-691-005561-0. ‣ Standard work on expansion of Japanese economic, social, political, and military influence during prewar period. Topics include trade and investment, cotton mills, South Manchurian Railway Company, Manchukuo, treaty port settlements, cultural associations (especially Tōa Dōbunkai), anti-Japanese boycotts, Japanese China experts, and Kwantung Army. [JHC/FN]

11.390 Lloyd E. Eastman. *The abortive revolution: China under Nationalist rule, 1927–1937.* Rev. ed. Cambridge, Mass.: Harvard University, Council on East Asian Studies, 1990. (Harvard East

Asian monographs, 153.) ISBN 0-674-00176-1 (pbk). ‣ Influential analysis of multifaceted failure—political, intellectual, and economic—of Kuomintang (Nationalist party) regime during Nanking decade. Includes author's new preface and new appendix on origins of fascist Blue Shirt Society. [JHC]

11.391 Lloyd E. Eastman. *Seeds of destruction: Nationalist China in war and revolution, 1937–1949.* Stanford, Calif.: Stanford University Press, 1984. ISBN 0-8047-1191-7. ‣ Continues Kuomintang's tale of woe (11.390) through Sino-Japanese and Civil War periods. Finds 1949 collapse caused by inherent structural infirmities of military-authoritarian regime and enervating effects of anti-Japanese war. [JHC]

11.392 Joseph Fewsmith. *Party, state, and local elites in republican China: merchant organizations and politics in Shanghai, 1890–1930.* Honolulu: University of Hawaii Press, 1985. ISBN 0-8248-0913-0. ‣ Revisionist interpretation of state-society relations under Chiang Kai-shek, challenging Coble's thesis (11.384) of exploited capitalists. Argues provocatively that merchant elite's surest ally against Kuomintang (Nationalist party) was Chiang himself. [JHC]

11.393 Wesley R. Fishel. *The end of extraterritoriality in China.* 1952 ed. New York: Octagon Books, 1974. ISBN 0-374-92749-9. ‣ Standard work on abolition of system (established in 1840s) exempting foreigners from Chinese legal jurisdiction. Focuses on 1919–43; based largely on U.S. State Department archives. Appendixes include relevant treaty texts. [JHC]

11.394 Andrew D. W. Forbes. *Warlords and Muslims in Chinese Central Asia: a political history of republican Sinkiang, 1911–1949.* Cambridge: Cambridge University Press, 1986. ISBN 0-521-25514-7. ‣ Details warlord venality, continuous Muslim rebellions and invasions (not, however, successionist), and periodic Soviet intervention. Finds Sinkiang province best analyzed as three discrete regions. Appendix includes biographical "who was who." [JHC]

11.395 Edward Friedman, Paul G. Pickowicz, and Mark Selden. *Chinese village, socialist state.* New Haven: Yale University Press, 1991. ISBN 0-300-04655-3. ‣ Eye-opening exposé of village in Hopei province from 1930s through Great Leap Forward (1958–60), based on ten years' fieldwork. Documents failure of entrenched socialist agrarian system, which fostered least progressive outcomes. [JHC]

11.396 Keiji Furuya. *Chiang Kai-shek: his life and times.* Chang Chun-ming, ed. New York: St. John's University Press, 1981. ISBN 0-87075-259-4. ‣ Distillation of massive, sympathetic account authorized by Kuomintang (Nationalist party). Emphasizes Sino-Japanese relations. Based on Nationalist government archives held on Taiwan (including Chiang's personal papers, diaries), interviews, and Japanese archives. Abridged translation of *Shō Kaiseki hiroku* (From the Private Files of Chiang Kai-shek), 15 vols. (1975–77). [JHC]

11.397 Fernando Galbiati. *P'eng P'ai and the Hai-Lu-feng Soviet.* Stanford, Calif.: Stanford University Press, 1985. ISBN 0-8047-1219-0. ‣ Standard work on Marxist peasant organization and mobilization during 1920s in Kwangtung province—Maoism before Mao. Culminated in first communist government on Chinese soil, led by P'eng, son of large landlord. [JHC]

11.398 Donald G. Gillin. *Warlord: Yen Hsi-shan in Shansi province, 1911–1949.* Princeton: Princeton University Press, 1967. ‣ Insightful on Yen's failed attempts as transitional, conservative reformer trying to implement ten-year plan of controlled modernization and reduce gentry's power without social revolution. [JHC]

11.399 John Gittings. *The role of the Chinese army.* 1967 ed. Westport, Conn.: Greenwood, 1981. ISBN 0-313-22879-5. ‣ Solid analysis of communist military from Civil War (1946–49) through Korean War to eve of Cultural Revolution (1965), including army's political and social roles, modernization, and leadership. [JHC]

11.400 John Gittings. *The world and China, 1922–1972.* New York: Harper & Row, 1974. ISBN 0-06-011576-9. ‣ Sympathetic yet original account of Chinese Communists' (and especially Mao Tse-tung's) worldview as expressed in foreign policy until President Nixon's 1972 visit. [JHC]

11.401 Jack Gray, ed. *Modern China's search for a political form.* London: Oxford University Press for the Royal Institute of International Affairs, 1969. ‣ Most useful contributions are on 1905–14 Shanghai gentry democracy (Elvin), 1920–23 movement for federation of autonomous provinces (Chesneaux), 1924–29 Kuomintang (Nationalist party) (Cavendish), and 1949–65 legal system (van der Sprenkel). [JHC]

11.402 Samuel B. Griffith II. *The Chinese People's Liberation Army.* New York: McGraw-Hill for the Council on Foreign Relations, 1967. ‣ Usefully combines history of communist military (1927–49) with description of army (1949–66, including Korean War). Includes detailed fold-out chart of national defense organization and personnel as of August 1966. [JHC]

11.403 Jacques Guillermaz. *A history of the Chinese Communist party, 1921–1949.* Anne Destenay, trans. New York: Random House, 1972. ISBN 0-416-14710-0 (v. 1). ‣ By French diplomat and military officer in China during 1930s and 1940s. Very good on 1937–49 period, especially military history. Includes detailed campaign maps, significant photographs. Translation of *Histoire du parti communiste chinois (1921–1949)* (1968). [JHC]

11.404 James P. Harrison. *The long march to power: a history of the Chinese Communist party, 1921–1972.* New York: Praeger, 1972. ‣ Valuable, well-documented synthesis of monographic studies plus author's original research in primary sources. Focuses on pre-1949 period. Includes substantial bibliography. [JHC]

11.405 Kathleen Hartford and Steven M. Goldstein, eds. *Single sparks: China's rural revolutions.* Armonk, N.Y.: Sharpe, 1989. ISBN 0-87332-427-7. ‣ Extensive state-of-field introduction precedes essays on communist base areas, 1928–49: Jiangsi, post-Long March southeastern provinces, Chin-Ch'a-Chi (i.e., Shansi-Chahar-Hopei), Shantung, and Manchuria. [JHC]

11.406 Christian Henriot. *Shanghai 1927–1937: élites locales et modernisation dans la Chine nationaliste.* Paris: Éditions de l'École des Hautes Études en Sciences Sociales, 1991. (Materiaux pour l'étude de l'Asie orientale, moderne, et contemporaine. Cahiers du Centre Chine, 7.) ISBN 2-7132-0962-5, ISSN 0181-1991. ‣ Stimulating analysis of Shanghai's municipal government, its modernization programs, and its relations with Kuomintang (Nationalist party), central government, and local elites. Finds municipal government's record, on balance, rather positive. [JHC]

11.407 William Hinton. *Fanshen: a documentary of revolution in a Chinese village.* New York: Monthly Review Press, 1966. ‣ Classic, sympathetic account of Communists' anti-imperialist, anti-feudal revolution as experienced by one village in Shansi province, 1948. Well-written, reads like Russian novel. Based on 1948 personal observation and interviews. [JHC]

11.408 Roy Hofheinz, Jr. *The broken wave: the Chinese communist peasant movement, 1922–1928.* Cambridge, Mass.: Harvard University Press, 1977. ISBN 0-674-08391-1. ‣ Controversial interpretation, arguing for preeminence of politics (human effort) over social structure, economics, or demography as key factor determining revolutionary potential. Best section: P'eng P'ai and Kwangtung province's Hai-Lu-feng Soviet. [JHC]

11.409 James C. Hsiung and Steven I. Levine, eds. *China's bitter*

victory: the war with Japan, 1937–1945. Armonk, N.Y.: Sharpe, 1992. ISBN 0-87332-708-X. ‣ Twelve contributions treat wartime diplomacy, wartime state, contending political forces, Chinese communist movement, communist foreign policy, the military dimension, war economy, science, literature, art, wartime judicial reform, and world politics. [JHC]

11.410 John Israel. *Student nationalism in China, 1927–1937.* Stanford, Calif.: Stanford University Press for the Hoover Institution on War, Revolution, and Peace, 1966. ‣ Standard work on how ruling Kuomintang (Nationalist party) under Chiang Kai-shek, ambivalent toward increased Japanese aggression, gradually lost nationalistic students' support to Communists. [JHC]

11.411 John Israel and Donald W. Klein. *Rebels and bureaucrats: China's December 9ers.* Berkeley: University of California Press, 1976. ISBN 0-520-02861-9. ‣ Traces "December 9th generation" from 1935 origins as students opposing Chiang Kai-shek's appeasement of Japanese aggression, to leadership role in People's Republic, to downfall as bureaucratic elite during Cultural Revolution. [JHC]

11.412 Chalmers A. Johnson. *Peasant nationalism and communist power: the emergence of revolutionary China, 1937–1945.* 1962 ed. Stanford, Calif.: Stanford University Press, 1967. ‣ Controversial but influential interpretation of how Communists rose to power during Sino-Japanese War by mobilizing peasant anti-Japanese nationalism (undifferentiated by Johnson from localist xenophobia), rather than by implementing Marxist socioeconomic program. [JHC]

11.413 Susan Mann Jones, ed. *Proceedings of the NEH modern China project, 1977–78: political leadership and social change at the local level in China from 1850 to the present.* Chicago: University of Chicago Press, 1979. (Select papers from the Center for Far Eastern Studies, 3, 1978–79.) ‣ Collection of essays with analytical introduction by Jones and P. Kuhn. Collection valuable for "Local Taxation and Finance in Republican China" (Kuhn), which also treats Ming-Ch'ing background, and "Rural Elites in Transition" (Alitto), emphasizing Honan province. [JHC]

11.414 Donald A. Jordan. *Chinese boycotts versus Japanese bombs: the failure of China's "revolutionary diplomacy," 1931–32.* Ann Arbor: University of Michigan Press, 1991. ISBN 0-472-10172-2. ‣ Argues that Nationalist government's support for anti-Japanese boycott (backed by Chinese businessmen and students to promote China's economic autonomy) backfired by forcing Japanese civilian business interests to support Japanese military's aggression. [JHC]

11.415 Donald A. Jordan. *The Northern Expedition: China's national revolution of 1926–1928.* Honolulu: University of Hawaii Press, 1976. ISBN 0-8248-0352-3. ‣ Standard work on how National Revolutionary Army of Kuomintang–communist First United Front marched north from Canton to defeat warlords and militarily unite—but not politically centralize—China. [JHC]

11.416 Robert A. Kapp. *Szechwan and the Chinese Republic: provincial militarism and central power, 1911–1938.* New Haven: Yale University Press, 1973. ISBN 0-300-01604-2. ‣ Useful study of warlordism in Szechwan province from 1911 Revolution through 1938 establishment of Nationalists' capital in Chungking. Emphasizes Szechwan's autonomy under Liu Hsiang even after 1927. [JHC]

11.417 Tetsuya Kataoka. *Resistance and revolution in China: the Communists and the Second United Front.* Berkeley: University of California Press, 1974. ISBN 0-520-02553-9. ‣ Argues that after Long March, Communists successfully deflected Nationalists' military pressure by promoting Second United Front (1937–45) against Japanese aggression, thereby gaining cover for social revolution through land redistribution. [JHC]

11.418 Ilpyong J. Kim. *The politics of Chinese communism: Kiangsi under the Soviets.* Berkeley: University of California Press, 1973. ISBN 0-520-02438-9. ▸ Controversial interpretation blaming Communists' 1934 evacuation of Kiangsi Soviet solely on military failure rather than lack of mass support or differences among top policy makers. Unlike Lotveit 11.428, finds peasant mobilization policy successful. [JHC]

11.419 William C. Kirby. *Germany and republican China.* Stanford, Calif.: Stanford University Press, 1984. ISBN 0-8047-1209-3. ▸ Focuses on Chiang Kai-shek's 1928–38 espousal of German model of state-building and modernization (given Germany's rapid nineteenth-century unification and rise to power), with consequent influence of fascist ideology. [JHC]

11.420 Laszlo Ladany. *The Communist party of China and Marxism, 1921–1985: a self-portrait.* Stanford, Calif.: Hoover Institution Press, 1988. (Hoover Press publication, 362.) ISBN 0-8179-8621-9. ▸ Unsympathetic but highly valuable account by expert China-watcher (1953–82 editor of *China News Analysis*). Based entirely on self-revealing Communist party primary sources. [JHC]

11.421 Diana Lary. *Region and nation: the Kwangsi clique in Chinese politics, 1925–1937.* Cambridge: Cambridge University Press, 1974. ISBN 0-521-20204-3. ▸ Examines nationally influential coterie of warlords from Kwangsi province (including Li Tsung-jen and Pai Ch'ung-hsi). Concludes it was simultaneously regionalist and nationalist. [JHC]

11.422 Diana Lary. *Warlord soldiers: Chinese common soldiers, 1911–1937.* Cambridge: Cambridge University Press, 1985. ISBN 0-521-30270-6. ▸ Brief but useful exploration of understudied topic, covering personnel pools, recruitment, army life, officers and men, bandit-soldier relations, violence and brutalization, and methods of leaving service. [JHC]

11.423 Chong-sik Lee. *Revolutionary struggle in Manchuria: Chinese communism and Soviet interest, 1922–1945.* Berkeley: University of California Press, 1983. ISBN 0-520-04375-8. ▸ Finds key to successful Chinese communist peasant mobilization in anti-Japanese theme based on devastation wrought by Japanese army, not socioeconomic appeals. Thus supports Johnson 11.412. [JHC]

11.424 Steven I. Levine. *Anvil of victory: the communist revolution in Manchuria, 1945–1948.* New York: Columbia University Press, 1987. ISBN 0-231-06436-5. ▸ Finds Manchurian case not triumph of revolutionary countryside over counterrevolutionary city. Rather, points to Communists' strong urban base and organization as key to victory. Moscow's substantial contribution of captured arms helped. [JHC]

11.425 Lincoln Li. *The Japanese army in North China, 1937–1941: problems of political and economic control.* Tokyo: Oxford University Press, 1975. ▸ Study of Japanese efforts at administrative, ideological, and economic control of occupied areas. Finds chronic shortage of manpower and inveterate distrust of Chinese collaborators precluded local control by other than direct occupation. [JHC]

11.426 Frederick F. Liu. *A military history of modern China, 1924–1949.* Princeton: Princeton University Press, 1956. ▸ Still useful overview of understudied field, although superseded on some specific topics. Includes discussion of German advisers' influence on Chiang Kai-shek. By former Nationalist officer. [JHC]

11.427 Pichon P. Y. Loh, ed. *The Kuomintang debacle of 1949: collapse or conquest?* Boston: Heath, 1965. ▸ Still useful collection of reprinted essays by both participants and observers attempting to analyze Nationalists' downfall at hands of Communists. Includes detailed annotated bibliography. [JHC]

11.428 Trygve Lotveit. *Chinese communism, 1931–1934: experi-*

ence in civil government. 2d ed. London: Curzon, 1978. (Scandinavian Institute of Asian Studies, Monograph series, 16.) ISBN 0-7007-0065-x (pbk), ISSN 0069-1712. ▸ Study of Kiangsi Soviet: organization, counterrevolution and corruption, administration of justice, rural class policy, finances. Concludes leftist party line of leadership undermined its very base, mass support. Contrast Kim 11.418. [JHC]

11.429 Michael Y. L. Luk. *The origins of Chinese bolshevism: an ideology in the making, 1920–1928.* Hong Kong: Oxford University Press, 1990. ISBN 0-19-584209-x. ▸ Focusing on evolving and changing patterns of political ideology, Communists' attempts to become fully qualified Bolshevik party. Finds process of sinification of Marxism-Leninism began even before Mao Tse-tung. [JHC]

11.430 Jessie G. Lutz. *Chinese politics and Christian missions: the anti-Christian movements of 1920–28.* Notre Dame, Ind.: Cross Cultural and Crossroad Books, 1988. ISBN 0-940121-05-0. ▸ Finds marked increase in symbiotic interplay between political parties and anti-Christian movements during 1920s, as May Fourth Movement's cosmopolitanism gave way to nationalism of May Thirtieth Movement (1925) and Northern Expedition. Compare Yip 11.574. [JHC]

11.431 Gavan McCormack. *Chang Tso-lin in Northeast China, 1911–1928: China, Japan, and the Manchurian idea.* Stanford, Calif.: Stanford University Press, 1977. ISBN 0-8047-0945-9. ▸ Standard work on bandit turned warlord of all Three Eastern Provinces. Detailed political narrative, with fascinating conclusion. Excellent on Japanese imperialism, which promoted fiction of Manchuria's separateness. [JHC]

11.432 Angus W. McDonald, Jr. *The urban origins of rural revolution: elites and the masses in Hunan province, China, 1911–1927.* Berkeley: University of California Press, 1978. ISBN 0-520-03228-4. ▸ Study of Communists' failure at urban revolution. Focusing on 1920s Changsha, finds mass mobilization followed—rather than preceded—Northern Expedition's arrival (July 1926). Slaughter of Communists began less than year later. [JHC]

11.433 Andrew J. Nathan. *Peking politics, 1918–1923: factionalism and the failure of constitutionalism.* Berkeley: University of California Press, 1976. ISBN 0-520-02784-1. ▸ Presents theoretical model of factionalism, followed by empirically grounded case studies of Peking warlord politics, focusing on Li Yuan-hung, Ts'ao K'un, and Hsu Shih-ch'ang. Appendix profiles seven major factions. [JHC]

11.434 Suzanne Pepper. *Civil war in China: the political struggle, 1945–1949.* Berkeley: University of California Press, 1978. ISBN 0-520-02440-0. ▸ Standard work, covering both urban and rural developments. Concludes that land reform in communist-held areas ended domination by ruling class: Communists' victory over Nationalists was not by default. [JHC]

11.435 Jane L. Price. *Cadres, commanders, and commissars: the training of the Chinese communist leadership, 1920–1945.* Boulder: Westview, 1976. ISBN 0-89158-001-8. ▸ Study of education and indoctrination of higher level cadres in, for example, First United Front's Peasant Movement Training Institute, Whampoa Military Academy, Kiangsi Soviet's Red Army Academy, and Yenan period's Cheng-feng (rectification) movement. [JHC]

11.436 Richard W. Rigby. *The May 30th Movement: events and themes.* Canberra: Australian National University Press, 1980. ISBN 0-7081-1758-9. ▸ Underappreciated analysis of 1925 anti-imperialist movement sparked by foreign police's killing of Shanghai demonstrators protesting factory conditions. Appendixes include chronology, essay on child labor, and text of ten primary sources. [JHC]

11.437 John E. Rue. *Mao Tse-tung in opposition, 1927–1935.*

Stanford, Calif.: Stanford University Press for the Hoover Institution on War, Revolution, and Peace, 1966. ▸ Portrait of Mao as underdog in Communist party during Kiangsi period. Details his opposition to Li Li-san and setbacks at hands of Central Committee dominated by Twenty-eight Bolsheviks (Russian-trained Stalinist theoreticians) and Chou En-lai. [JHC]

11.438 Tony Saich. *The origins of the First United Front in China: the role of Sneevliet (alias Maring).* 2 vols. Leiden: Brill, 1991. ISBN 90-04-09173-4 (set). ▸ Standard work on Comintern's first representative in China (1921–23). Contains detailed analysis of Maring's career plus texts and translation of 174 primary sources. [JHC]

11.439 Harrison E. Salisbury. *The Long March: the untold story.* New York: Harper & Row, 1985. ISBN 0-06-039044-1. ▸ Narrative of Communists' 6,000-mile trek from Kiangsi to Shensi province, 1934–35. Most accurate account available, based on 1984 guided tour of route and furnished interviews and archives (not always provided disinterestedly). [JHC]

11.440 Mark Selden. *The Yenan way in revolutionary China.* Cambridge, Mass.: Harvard University Press, 1971. ISBN 0-674-96560-4. ▸ Prematurely aging but important work on Yenan period (ca. 1936–45), named for capital of Shen-Kan-Ning base area (Mao Tse-tung's locus during Sino-Japanese War). Sympathetic emphasis on attractiveness of Communists' socioeconomic policies. [JHC]

11.441 Kamal Sheel. *Peasant society and Marxist intellectuals in China: Fang Zhimin and the origin of a revolutionary movement in the Xinjiang region.* Princeton: Princeton University Press, 1989. ISBN 0-691-05571-8. ▸ Controversial moral economy interpretation of how peasants utilized Marxist intellectuals for their own purposes in region of Kiangsi province. Focuses on peasant movement leader-intellectual Fang Chih-min (comparable to P'eng P'ai). [JHC]

11.442 James E. Sheridan. *Chinese warlord: the career of Feng Yu-hsiang.* Stanford, Calif.: Stanford University Press, 1966. ▸ Standard work on populist but nonrevolutionary Christian general, fond of mass baptism by fire hose, dominant in Honan, Kansu, and Shensi provinces until 1930 defeat by Chiang Kai-shek. [JHC]

11.443 Milton J. T. Shieh. *The Kuomintang: selected historical documents, 1894–1969.* New York: St. John's University Press, 1970. ▸ Translations of fifty-four major Nationalist party manifestos, platforms, and declarations. Includes items from predecessor parties (Hsing Chung Hui, T'ung Meng Hui). Appendixes include chronology, committee rosters, etc. [JHC]

11.444 Shum Kui-Kwong. *The Chinese Communists' road to power: the anti-Japanese National United Front, 1935–1945.* Hong Kong: Oxford University Press, 1988. ISBN 0-19-584169-7. ▸ Controversial argument against peasant mobilization as key to 1949 communist victory. Instead, emphasizes importance of United Front with majority of both rural and urban elites, initiated by Wang Ming and adopted by Mao Tse-tung. [JHC]

11.445 Paul K. T. Sih, ed. *The strenuous decade: China's nation-building efforts, 1927–1937.* 1970 2d ed. New York: St. John's University Press, 1976. ▸ Sympathetic appraisals of Kuomintang (Nationalist party) achievements during Nanking decade. Treats foreign relations, political reconstruction, fiscal reform, agrarian economy, industrialization, railroads, and education. Sih's prologue blames 1949 communist victory on Sino-Japanese War. [JHC]

11.446 Edgar Snow. *Red star over China.* 1968 rev. ed. New York: Grove, 1973. ISBN 0-394-17797-5. ▸ Classic; first account (1938) in any language of Mao Tse-tung's life, Chinese Communists' history, post–Long March situation. Based on interviews with Mao and others in Pao-an (Shensi province), July–September 1936. [JHC]

11.447 David Strand. *Rickshaw Beijing: city people and politics in the 1920s.* Berkeley: University of California Press, 1989. ISBN 0-520-06311-2. ▸ Focuses mainly on Peking workers' relations with authority in various guises, e.g., police, guilds, unions. Emphasizes rickshaw pullers, culminating in 1929 antistreetcar riot. Also covers power struggles within chamber of commerce. [JHC]

11.448 S. Bernard Thomas. *Labor and the Chinese revolution: class strategies and contradictions of Chinese communism, 1928–48.* Ann Arbor: University of Michigan, Center for Chinese Studies, 1983. (Michigan monographs in Chinese studies, 49.) ISBN 0-89264-049-9. ▸ Primarily on Communists' labor policies during Kiangsi Soviet, Second United Front, Yenan, and Civil War periods. Concludes proletariat's small size precluded leading role. [JHC]

11.449 Tien Hung-mao. *Government and politics in Kuomintang China, 1927–1937.* Stanford, Calif.: Stanford University Press, 1972. ISBN 0-8047-0812-6. ▸ Points up Nationalist government's ineffectiveness and failure (both at center and in provinces) during Nanking decade. Concludes Chiang Kai-shek's regime was militarized, dominated by informal client groups, and moving toward fascism. [JHC]

11.450 Lyman P. Van Slyke. *Enemies and friends: the United Front in Chinese communist history.* Stanford, Calif.: Stanford University Press, 1967. ▸ Standard work on communist theory and practice of strategic alliances to isolate foes. Emphasizes First and Second United Fronts between Communists and Nationalists (1924–27 and 1937–45 respectively), plus post-1949 relations with domestic sympathizers. [JHC]

11.451 Lyman P. Van Slyke, ed. *The Chinese communist movement: a report of the United States War Department, July 1945.* Stanford, Calif.: Stanford University Press, 1968. ▸ Produced by Military Intelligence Division, summarizing Communists' activities during Sino-Japanese War (1937–45), especially in North and Central China base areas. Has aged well. Includes new substantive preface by editor. [JHC]

11.452 Hans J. van de Ven. *From friend to comrade: the founding of the Chinese Communist party, 1920–1927.* Berkeley: University of California Press, 1991. ISBN 0-520-07271-5. ▸ Latest revisionist interpretation of party's origins; critical of Dirlik 11.387. Citing new evidence, finds party evolved in four stages from loose confederation of study societies (1920–21) to centralized mass organization (1925–27). [JHC]

11.453 Derek J. Waller. *The Kiangsi Soviet Republic: Mao and the national congresses of 1931 and 1934.* Berkeley: University of California, Center for Chinese Studies, 1973. (China research monographs, 10.) ISBN 0-912966-11-4 (pbk). ▸ Study of pre-1931 Li Li-san position (postulating rural attack on cities) and Mao Tse-tung's temporary eclipse by Russian-trained "returned students" (i.e., Twenty-eight Bolsheviks). Includes tables of congresses' elected members. [JHC]

11.454 Jeffrey N. Wasserstrom. *Student protests in twentieth-century China: the view from Shanghai.* Stanford, Calif.: Stanford University Press, 1991. ISBN 0-8047-1881-4. ▸ Combines case studies of Shanghai's student demonstrations (May 4, 1919; May 30, 1925; 1931 anti-Japanese; Civil War period; 1989) with political culture analysis of their effectiveness as propaganda and subversive theater. Includes photographs. [JHC]

11.455 William Wei. *Counterrevolution in China: the Nationalists in Jiangxi during the Soviet period.* Ann Arbor: University of Michigan Press, 1985. ISBN 0-472-10057-2. ▸ Discussion of Chiang Kai-shek's suppression of Communists' 1930–34 Kiangsi

Soviet. Concludes relationship between Kuomintang (Nationalist party) and local elite was uneasy marriage of convenience and Chiang's Kiangsi success was Pyrrhic victory of militarism. [JHC]

11.456 William W. Whitson. *The Chinese high command: a history of communist military politics, 1927–71*. New York: Praeger, 1973. ▸ Monumental biographical analysis of military elite. Finds three military models (warlord, Russian, peasant) competing throughout 1924–69 period with high degree of personnel continuity during 1937–67. Includes campaign maps and charts. [JHC]

11.457 C. Martin Wilbur. *Sun Yat-sen: frustrated patriot*. New York: Columbia University Press, 1976. ISBN 0-231-04036-9. ▸ Not overall biography, but well-written standard work on Sun's attempts to raise financial and political support from overseas Chinese and foreign individuals and governments. Most detailed on post-1918 dealings with Soviet Russia. [JHC]

11.458 C. Martin Wilbur and Julie Lien-ying How. *Missionaries of revolution: Soviet advisers and Nationalist China, 1920–1927*. Cambridge, Mass.: Harvard University Press, 1989. ISBN 0-674-57652-7. ▸ Massive account of Soviet Leninist influence on Kuomintang (Nationalist party) and Chinese Communists during First United Front. Includes translations of eighty-one documents seized from Soviet embassy in Peking (April 1927); rare photographs. [JHC]

11.459 Dick Wilson. *When tigers fight: the story of the Sino-Japanese War, 1937–1945*. New York: Viking, 1982. ISBN 0-670-76003-X. ▸ Popularly written military narrative from Marco Polo Bridge Incident to Japanese surrender, based on Western-, Japanese-, and Chinese-language sources. Includes campaign maps and rare photographs. [JHC]

11.460 Odoric Y. K. Wou. *Militarism in modern China: the career of Wu P'ei-fu, 1916–39*. Folkstone: Dawson, 1978. ISBN 0-7129-0766-1. ▸ Standard work on leading warlord (1910s to 1920s), head of Chihli clique, who dominated Honan, Hupei, and Shensi provinces until 1927 defeat by Chiang Kai-shek. Argues that Wu modeled clique on pseudo-clan structure based on fictive kinship. [JHC]

11.461 Tien-wei Wu. *The Sian Incident: a pivotal point in modern Chinese history*. Ann Arbor: University of Michigan, Center for Chinese Studies, 1976. (Michigan papers in Chinese studies, 26.) ISBN 0-89264-026-X (pbk). ▸ Standard work on dramatic December 1936 kidnapping of Chiang Kai-shek by Manchurian warlord Chang Hsueh-liang and subsequent intensive Nationalist-communist negotiations, leading eventually to Second United Front against Japan. [JHC]

11.462 Benjamin Yang. *From revolution to politics: Chinese Communists on the Long March*. Boulder: Westview, 1990. ISBN 0-8133-7672-6 (pbk). ▸ Analyzes 1934–35 Long March as historical period in its own right, characterized by Mao Tse-tung's ascent to power beginning at Tsunyi Conference and Communist party's transformation from revolutionary idealism to political realism. [JHC]

11.463 Ernest P. Young. *The presidency of Yuan Shih-k'ai: liberalism and dictatorship in early republican China*. Ann Arbor: University of Michigan Press, 1977. ISBN 0-472-08995-1. ▸ Examines how, faced with Western imperialism, Yuan attempted to recentralize power but was thwarted by local elites' preference for continued decentralization after 1911 Revolution. Compares Yuan with Chiang Kai-shek as failed centralizer. [JHC]

11.464 George T. Yu. *Party politics in republican China: the Kuomintang, 1912–1924*. Berkeley: University of California Press, 1966. ▸ Describes rejection of Western model of open, democratic political parties. Covers Hsing Chung Hui (Revive China Society), T'ung Meng Hui (Alliance Society), Chung-hua Koming-

tang (Chinese Revolutionary party), and Kuomintang (Nationalist party). [JHC]

SEE ALSO

48.226 John W. Garver. *Chinese-Soviet relations, 1937–1945*.

Social History

11.465 Marie-Claire Bergère. *The golden age of the Chinese bourgeoisie, 1911–1937*. Janet Lloyd, trans. Cambridge and Paris: Cambridge University Press and Éditions de la Maison des Sciences de l'Homme, 1989. ISBN 0-521-32054-2. ▸ Standard work, focusing on Shanghai. Despite title, finds golden age—window of opportunity provided by World War I—lasted only from mid-1910s to mid-1920s, then after 1927 was closed by Chiang Kai-shek. Translation of *L'âge d'or de la bourgeoisie chinoise, 1911–1937* (1986). [JHC]

11.466 Phil Billingsley. *Bandits in republican China*. Stanford, Calif.: Stanford University Press, 1988. ISBN 0-8047-1406-1. ▸ Well-researched, multidimensional study of banditry's spread after 1911 Revolution. Appendixes include glossary of bandit slang, list of bandits turned militarists, and text of proclamation by Pai Lang (White Wolf). [JHC]

11.467 Joseph T. Chen. *The May Fourth Movement in Shanghai: the making of a social movement in modern China*. Leiden: Brill, 1971. (*T'oung Pao* monographie, 9.) ▸ Argues that Shanghai's May Fourth Movement (April–July 1919) was anti-imperialist, popular, patriotic protest movement involving participation of all classes, unlike Peking's movement, which was dominated by intellectuals focusing on New Culture issues. [JHC]

11.468 Jean Chesneaux. *The Chinese labor movement, 1919–1927*. H. M. Wright, trans. Stanford, Calif.: Stanford University Press, 1968. ▸ Conceptually controversial Marxist analysis, tying fate of labor movement to Communist party (thus slighting precommunist labor history). Highly detailed but not entirely reliable. Translation of *Le mouvement ouvrier chinois de 1919 à 1927* (1962). [JHC]

11.469 Jean Chesneaux. *Les syndicats chinois, 1919–1927: répertoire, textes, presse*. The Hague: Mouton, 1965. (Matériaux pour l'étude de l'Extrême-Orient moderne et contemporain, Textes, 2.) ▸ Contains guide to trade unions by province, translated primary sources (with original Chinese texts), and labor periodicals by locale. Companion volume to 11.468. [JHC]

11.470 Sherman Cochran and Andrew C. K. Hsieh, eds. and trans. *One day in China: May 21, 1936*. New Haven: Yale University Press, 1983. ISBN 0-300-02834-2. ▸ Composite national snapshot via rare, primary-source life descriptions written by urban and rural common people. Grouped into following categories: women, political authority, popular religion, and Japanese enemy. Partial translation and reorganization of Mao Tun et al., eds., *Chung-kuo ti i jih* (1936). [JHC]

11.471 Elisabeth J. Croll. *Feminism and socialism in China*. London: Routledge & Kegan Paul, 1978. ISBN 0-7100-8816-7. ▸ On women's movement and feminism from 1890s through mid-1970s. Finds uneasy alliance between women's and communist movements both pre- and post-1949. Based partly on interviews with feminist leaders (1973). [JHC]

11.472 Hsiao-tung Fei. *Peasant life in China: a field study of country life in the Yangtze Valley*. 1939 ed. London: Routledge & Kegan Paul, 1980. ISBN 0-7100-0590-3. ▸ Influential ethnography of highly commercialized village near Soochow (Kiangsu province). Topics include family, kinship, household, village, land tenure, silk industry, marketing, finance. Based on 1936 fieldwork in author's native county. [JHC]

11.473 John Fitzgerald, ed. *The Nationalists and Chinese society 1923–1937: a symposium*. Parkville, Australia: University of Melbourne, History Department, 1989. (Melbourne University history monographs, 4.) ISBN 0-86839-844-6. ‣ Topics include Shanghai Green Gang's opium dealing, Shanghai chamber of commerce's ideology 1925–27, overseas Chinese nationalism in 1927 Vietnam, liberal newspaper *Shen Pao*, and Nanking government's relations with industry and commerce 1932–36. [JHC]

11.474 Sidney D. Gamble. *Peking: a social survey conducted under the auspices of the Princeton University Center in China and the Peking Young Men's Christian Association.* New York: Doran, 1921. ‣ Truly pathbreaking fieldwork conducted 1918–19. Covers government, population, health, education, recreation, prostitution, poverty and philanthropy, prisons, and religion. Thirteen appendixes contain detailed statistics, primary sources, and texts of questionnaires used. [JHC]

11.475 Sidney D. Gamble. *Ting hsien: a North China rural community.* 1954 ed. Stanford, Calif.: Stanford University Press, 1968. ‣ Classic investigation of county in Hopei province based on 1926–33 statistical and qualitative fieldwork. Covers population, families, government, education, agriculture, finance, business, industry, and social and religious activities. [JHC]

11.476 Shirley S. Garrett. *Social reformers in urban China: the Chinese Y.M.C.A., 1895–1926.* Cambridge, Mass.: Harvard University Press, 1970. ISBN 0-674-81220-4. ‣ Well-written examination of how successfully launched reformist social agency with missionary origins foundered in mid-1920s revolutionary China on reefs of student-led anti-Christian and labor movements. [JHC]

11.477 Gail Hershatter. *Workers of Tianjin, 1900–1949.* Stanford, Calif.: Stanford University Press, 1986. ISBN 0-8047-1318-9. ‣ Standard work on Tientsin's proletariat with special attention to female and child labor. Includes case studies of ironworkers, transport industry, and cotton mills. Emphasizes workers' cross-class alliances rather than class consciousness. [JHC]

11.478 Emily Honig. *Sisters and strangers: women in the Shanghai cotton mills, 1919–1949.* Stanford, Calif.: Stanford University Press, 1986. ISBN 0-8047-1274-3. ‣ Fine description, especially interesting on native-place ties. Concludes that for female cotton mill workers in Shanghai, working-class consciousness was rare and alien concept. [JHC]

11.479 Kay Ann Johnson. *Women, the family, and peasant revolution in China.* Chicago: University of Chicago Press, 1983. ISBN 0-226-40187-1 (cl), 0-226-40189-8 (pbk). ‣ Communist policies toward women, family, and marriage, 1921–80. Concludes government policies directly and indirectly supported traditional values, behavior, and family structure. Includes text of 1950 marriage law. [JHC]

11.480 Herbert Day Lamson. *Social pathology in China: a source book for the study of problems of livelihood, health, and the family.* 1935 ed. Taipei: Ch'eng Wen, 1974. ‣ Classic textbook by University of Shanghai professor treating poverty, living standards, wages, various rural and urban problems, housing, illiteracy, demography, physical and mental illnesses, public health, marriage, family, divorce, and desertion. [JHC]

11.481 H. Y. Lowe. *The adventures of Wu: the life cycle of a Peking man.* 1940–41 ed. Derk Bodde, Introduction. Princeton: Princeton University Press, 1983. ISBN 0-691-06552-7 (cl), 0-691-01400-0 (pbk). ‣ Underappreciated gem; fictionalized but realistic semi-autobiographical account of daily life in traditional lower-middle-class Peking family, ca. 1915–1936. Includes substantive new introduction, plus added index. [JHC]

11.482 Ida Pruitt. *Old Madam Yin: a memoir of Peking life, 1926–1938.* Stanford, Calif.: Stanford University Press, 1979. ISBN 0-8047-1038-4. ‣ Marvelous, immensely sensitive portrait of upper-class Peking lady in her milieu. Classic of women's history. Includes substantive preface by Margery Wolf. [JHC]

11.483 Mary Sheridan and Janet W. Salaff, eds. *Lives: Chinese working women.* Bloomington: Indiana University Press, 1984. ISBN 0-253-33604-X (cl), 0-253-20319-8 (pbk). ‣ Collected life stories (mostly autobiographical) of female workers, plus introductions. Covers Republic of China (pre-1949), Taiwan, Hong Kong (all based on fieldwork interviews), Communist's Yenan base area, and People's Republic (translated model biographies). [JHC]

11.484 Tai Hsuan-chih. *The Red Spears, 1916–1949.* Ronald Suleski, trans. Ronald Suleski and Elizabeth Perry, Introductions. Ann Arbor: University of Michigan, Center for Chinese Studies, 1985. (Michigan monographs in Chinese studies, 54.) ISBN 0-89264-060-X (cl), 0-89264-059-6 (pbk). ‣ Standard work on popularly supported self-defense organization trying to protect peasant landowners against bandits, warlords, and Japanese invaders; object of attempted communist infiltration. Includes substantive introductions. Translation of *Hung-chiang hui* [Red Spear Society], *1916–1949* (1973). [JHC]

11.485 G.R.G. Worcester. *The junks and sampans of the Yangtze.* Rev. ed. Annapolis, Md.: Naval Institute Press, 1971. ISBN 0-87021-335-0. ‣ Definitive work by longtime Maritime Customs Service river inspector. Focuses on material culture but also treats sailors (including beliefs and superstitions). Profusely illustrated. Arranged first by locale, then by type of ship. [JHC]

11.486 C. K. Yang. *A Chinese village in early communist transition.* 1959 ed. Cambridge, Mass.: MIT Press, 1965. ‣ Valuable as ethnography of suburban village near Canton, 1948–51. Topics include precommunist land ownership, production, consumption, kinship and power structure, then class struggle and land reform, 1949–51. [JHC]

11.487 Martin C. Yang. *A Chinese village: Taitou, Shantung province.* New York: Columbia University Press, 1945. ‣ Ethnography of author's native locale pre-1937. Topics include agriculture, standard of living, family, marriage, child rearing, village organization, conflicts, leaders, and intervillage relations. Appendixes on farm implements and kinship terminology. [JHC]

Economic History

11.488 John Lossing Buck. *Land utilization in China: a study of 16,786 farms in 186 localities, and 38,256 farm families in twenty-two provinces in China, 1929–1933.* 1937 ed. 3 vols. Taipei: Southern Materials Center, 1986. ‣ Monumental resource, based on data collected by author's University of Nanking students in their home locales. Topics include crops, population, climate, livestock, farm labor, prices, taxation, nutrition, and living standards. Well-to-do regions overrepresented. Consists of text, statistical, and atlas volumes. [JHC]

11.489 Richard C. Bush. *The politics of cotton textiles in Kuomintang China, 1927–1937.* New York: Garland, 1982. ISBN 0-8240-4691-9. ‣ Disputes Coble's thesis (11.384) that Nationalist government exploited Shanghai bourgeoisie. Finds mill owners utilized high-level allies within government to successfully defend their interests (e.g., against proposed initiatives on taxes and labor relations). [JHC]

11.490 Chou Shou-hsin. *The Chinese inflation, 1937–1949.* New York: Columbia University Press, 1963. (Columbia University, Studies of the East Asian Institute.) ‣ Economic analysis of major factor in Nationalist government's 1949 collapse. Finds inflation resulted from inequitable distribution of war costs, devastating all on fixed incomes (especially teachers and public employees). [JHC]

11.491 Hsiao-tung Fei and Chih-i Chang. *Earthbound China: a* *study of rural economy in Yunnan.* 1945 ed. Chicago: University of Chicago Press, 1975. ISBN 0-226-23955-1. ▸ Topics include family income and budgets, land tenure, farm labor, living standards, handicrafts (especially papermaking), and commercialization. Based on fieldwork 1939–43 in three villages west of Kunming. Includes photographs. [JHC]

11.492 Rudolf P. Hommel. *China at work: an illustrated record of the primitive industries of China's masses, whose life is toil, and thus an account of Chinese civilization.* 1937 ed. Cambridge, Mass.: MIT Press, 1969. ISBN 0-262-08035-4. ▸ Invaluable photographic and textual record of material culture (especially handicraft utensils), based on 1920s fieldwork in Central and North China. Covers tools for toolmaking, food, clothing, shelter, and transport. [JHC]

11.493 Thomas G. Rawski. *Economic growth in prewar China.* Berkeley: University of California Press, 1989. ISBN 0-520-06372-4. ▸ Controversial, revisionist analysis concluding sustained expansion of per-capita output became commonplace during period 1912–37. Covers manufacturing, banking, monetary system, transport, communications, and investment. [JHC]

11.494 Charles F. Remer. *A study of Chinese boycotts with special reference to their economic effectiveness.* 1933 ed. Taipei: Ch'eng Wen, 1966. ▸ Still valuable study of nine increasingly effective nationalistic boycotts (1905–31) against Japan, United States, and Great Britain. Focuses on massive 1931 anti-Japanese boycott. Includes statistical appendixes. [JHC]

11.495 Peter Schran. *Guerrilla economy: the development of the Shensi-Kansu-Ninghsia border region, 1937–1945.* Albany: State University of New York Press, 1976. ISBN 0-87395-344-4. ▸ Analysis of Communists' economic strategy to cope with Nationalists' blockade of Yenan (i.e., Shen-Kan-Ning) base area. Finds success in achieving economic self-sufficiency under extremely difficult conditions. [JHC]

11.496 Kungtu C. Sun. *The economic development of Manchuria in the first half of the twentieth century.* Cambridge, Mass.: Harvard University, East Asian Research Center, 1969. (Harvard East Asian monographs, 28.) ▸ Treats agricultural and industrial development both pre-1931 and during 1932–45 Manchukuo period of Japanese occupation. Includes statistical aggregate index of industrial production, 1911–42. [JHC]

11.497 Eduard B. Vermeer. *Economic development in provincial China: the central Shaanxi since 1930.* Cambridge: Cambridge University Press, 1988. ISBN 0-521-34392-5. ▸ Standard work on Shensi province's core (Wei River Valley, including Sian city), 1928–84. Treats famine (1928–31), communications, transport, growth of Sian, industrial development, irrigation, cultivation, cooperatives, collectivization, cotton, and regional inequality. [JHC]

11.498 Andrew Watson, trans. *Transport in transition: the evolution of traditional shipping in China.* Ann Arbor: University of Michigan, Center for Chinese Studies, 1972. (Michigan abstracts of Chinese and Japanese works on Chinese history, 3.) ▸ Partial translations of five 1940s Japanese works (by Nakamura Yoshio et al.) on junks (operations, owners, crews), shipping brokers, and transport companies, all in North China and Soochow (Kiangsu province), mostly twentieth century. [JHC]

11.499 Arthur N. Young. *China and the helping hand, 1937–1945.* Cambridge, Mass.: Harvard University Press, 1963. ▸ Finds Chiang Kai-shek's corrupted government came to view American foreign aid during disastrous Sino-Japanese War as substitute for crucial domestic reforms. Includes statistical appendixes. [JHC]

11.500 Arthur N. Young. *China's nation-building effort, 1927–1937: the financial and economic record.* Stanford, Calif.: Hoover Institution Press, 1971. (Hoover Institution publications, 104.) ISBN 0-8179-1041-7. ▸ Discussion of fiscal and monetary policy, modernization, and development programs by Chiang Kai-shek's financial adviser, 1929–47. Concludes republic was progressing on broad front as of mid-1937. Includes statistical appendixes and detailed bibliographical essay. [JHC]

11.501 Arthur N. Young. *China's wartime finance and inflation.* Cambridge, Mass.: Harvard University Press, 1965. ▸ Treats receipts, expenditure, fiscal policy, debt, foreign aid, currency, monetary management, and inflation for period 1937–45. Finds 1937 prices rose more than 2,500 times by 1945, then rose even faster. Includes statistical appendixes. [JHC]

Intellectual and Cultural History

11.502 Guy S. Alitto. *The last Confucian: Liang Shu-ming and the Chinese dilemma of modernity.* 2d ed. Berkeley: University of California Press, 1986. ISBN 0-520-05318-4 (pbk). ▸ Excellent biography of philosopher-sage and conservative social activist who attempted to reconcile Confucianism with twentieth-century China's needs by promoting rural reconstruction programs. Includes substantive preface by Frederic Wakeman, Jr. [JHC]

11.503 R. David Arkush. *Fei Xiaotong and sociology in revolutionary China.* Cambridge, Mass.: Harvard University, Council on East Asian Studies, 1981. (Harvard East Asian monographs, 98.) ISBN 0-674-29815-2. ▸ Well-researched biography of social anthropologist Fei Hsiao-t'ung with due attention to his additional roles as political journalist and cultural intermediary. Includes annotated chronological bibliography of Fei's writings. [JHC]

11.504 John Z. Bowers, J. William Hess, and Nathan Sivin, eds. *Science and medicine in twentieth-century China: research and education.* Ann Arbor: University of Michigan, Center for Chinese Studies, 1988. (Science, medicine, and technology in East Asia, 3.) ISBN 0-89264-077-4 (cl), 0-89264-078-2 (pbk). ▸ Twelve contributions on republican period genetics, botany, geology; plus biomedical research, schistosomiasis, viral vaccines, genetics, agriculture, plant protection, food policy, nutrition, and education (including medical) in People's Republic. [JHC]

11.505 Arnold C. Brackman. *The last emperor.* New York: Scribner's, 1975. ISBN 0-684-14233-3. ▸ Popularly written biography of P'u-yi, Manchu figurehead emperor of both China, 1909–11, and Manchukuo (Japanese-occupied Manchuria), 1934–45; extradited to People's Republic, 1950. Unannotated but includes twelve-page bibliographical essay; rare illustrations. [JHC]

11.506 Ming K. Chan and Arif Dirlik. *Schools into fields and factories: anarchists, the Guomindang, and the National Labor University in Shanghai, 1927–1932.* Durham, N.C.: Duke University Press, 1991. ISBN 0-8223-1154-2. ▸ Study of anarchists' shortlived revolutionary attempt at social transformation by combining manual labor with education; its complex relationship with ruling Kuomintang (Nationalist party). Draws comparisons with Mao Tse-tung's Cultural Revolution. [JHC]

11.507 Min-chih Chou. *Hu Shih and intellectual choice in modern China.* Ann Arbor: University of Michigan Press, 1984. ISBN 0-472-10039-4. ▸ Deals extensively with leading intellectual's aspirations, fears, and desires. Contrasts Hu's May Fourth generation with late Ch'ing reformers over extent of disillusionment with (and alienation from) traditional culture. Organized thematically, not chronologically. [JHC]

11.508 Chow Tse-tsung. *The May Fourth Movement: intellectual revolution in modern China.* 1960 ed. Stanford, Calif.: Stanford University Press, 1967. ▸ Splendid classic, encyclopedic and invaluable. But tends to portray antitraditional movement as rising precipitously out of nowhere beginning in 1915. More recent interpretations (e.g., Schwartz 11.554) note earlier, turn-of-century precursors. [JHC]

11.509 Chu Pao-chin. *V. K. Wellington Koo: a case study of China's diplomat and diplomacy of nationalism, 1912–1966.* Hong Kong: Chinese University Press, 1981. ISBN 962-201-236-1. ▸ Leading exemplar of Anglo-American group of professional diplomats controlling foreign policy in Republic of China. Emphasizes pre-1938 period. Includes substantive foreward by C. Martin Wilbur. [JHC]

11.510 James H. Cole. "'Total westernization' in Kuomintang China: the case of Ch'en Hsu-ching." *Monumenta serica* 34 (1979–80) 77–143. ISSN 0077-149X. ▸ Examines foremost advocate of total westernization (*ch'uan-p'an hsi-hua*), including his debates with Hu Shih and Wu Ching-ch'ao in *Tu-li p'ing-lun* (Independent Critic) magazine. Finds Ch'en westernistic nationalist. Includes annotated chronological bibliography. [JHC]

11.511 Ralph C. Croizier. *Art and revolution in modern China: the Lingnan (Cantonese) school of painting, 1906–1951.* Berkeley: University of California Press, 1988. ISBN 0-520-05909-3. ▸ Study of attempts by politically engaged artists Kao Chien-fu, Kao Ch'i-feng, and Ch'en Shu-jen to combine modern Western and traditional Chinese painting into school of New National Painting. [JHC]

11.512 Arif Dirlik. *Revolution and history: the origins of Marxist historiography in China, 1919–1937.* Berkeley: University of California Press, 1978. ISBN 0-520-03541-0. ▸ Fruitful study of intellectual sterility. Marxist historians' failure to explain change in Chinese history demonstrated by chart of thirty-five periodization schemes. Only T'ao Hsi-sheng's revised formulation posits any change during eighteen centuries from Ch'in to Ch'ing dynasties. [JHC]

11.513 William J. Duiker. *Ts'ai Yuan-p'ei: educator of modern China.* University Park: Pennsylvania State University Press, 1977. ISBN 0-271-00504-1. ▸ Brief but useful biography of leading educational reformer, chancellor of Peking University (1917–23), who rejected Social Darwinism for Kropotkin's theory of Mutual Aid. Lacks index. [JHC]

11.514 Lee Feigon. *Chen Duxiu: founder of the Chinese Communist party.* Princeton: Princeton University Press, 1983. ISBN 0-691-05393-6. ▸ Revisionist interpretation of Ch'en Tu-hsiu, emphasizing traditional literati roots (not simply a westernized intellectual). Finds Ch'en attracted initially to Chinese, then Western, iconoclasms; spiritual leader who created coherent movement out of rebellious youth. [JHC]

11.515 Yi-tsi Mei Feuerwerker. *Ding Ling's fiction: ideology and narrative in modern Chinese literature.* Cambridge, Mass.: Harvard University Press, 1982. ISBN 0-674-20765-3. ▸ Standard work on life and narrative writings of Communist-feminist Ting Ling, criticized in 1942 Yenan for opposing party's male chauvinism, then rehabilitated and honored, then imprisoned as rightist (1958–70) and again rehabilitated. [JHC]

11.516 Shen C. Y. Fu. *Challenging the past: the paintings of Chang Dai-chien.* Jan Stuart, trans. Washington, D.C.: Smithsonian Institution Press, Arthur M. Sackler Foundation, and University of Washington Press, 1991. ISBN 0-295-97124-X (cl), 0-295-97125-8 (pbk). ▸ Standard work on famous painter Chang Tai-ch'ien, fluent in wide variety of styles, also known as expert forger (e.g., of painter Pa-ta Shan-jen). Profusely illustrated exhibition catalog includes Chang's biography. [JHC]

11.517 Charlotte Furth. *Ting Wen-chiang: science and China's New Culture.* Cambridge, Mass.: Harvard University Press, 1970. ISBN 0-674-89270-4. ▸ Standard work on leading Western-, Japanese-educated geologist, proponent of New Culture movement, active in establishing *Nu-li chou-pao* (Endeavor) and *Tu-li p'ing-*

lun (Independent Critic) magazines, and 1926 mayor of Greater Shanghai. [JHC]

11.518 Charlotte Furth, ed. *The limits of change: essays on conservative alternatives in republican China.* Cambridge, Mass.: Harvard University Press, 1976. ISBN 0-674-53423-9. ▸ Important corrective to infatuation with republic's progressivist movements. Best contributions include overview of conservatism and studies of Liu Shih-p'ei, Yuan Shih-k'ai, 1930s Kuomintang (Nationalist party), Liang Shu-ming, and New Confucianists (Hsin ju-chia). [JHC]

11.519 Merle Goldman, ed. *Modern Chinese literature in the May Fourth era.* Cambridge, Mass.: Harvard University Press, 1977. ISBN 0-674-57910-0. ▸ Defines May Fourth era very broadly (1911–42); 1920s and 1930s focus. Topics include Lu Hsun, Ch'ü Ch'iu-pai, Mao Tun, Ting Ling, Yü Ta-fu, Western-Japanese literary impact, and popular urban fiction, 1910–30. [JHC]

11.520 Jerome B. Grieder. *Hu Shih and the Chinese renaissance: liberalism in the Chinese revolution, 1917–1937.* Cambridge, Mass.: Harvard University Press, 1970. ISBN 0-674-41250-8. ▸ Superb classic of intellectual history. On preeminent American-trained reformist intellectual, leader of vernacular literature movement, advocate of John Dewey's philosophy of pragmatism. [JHC]

11.521 Edward M. Gunn, Jr. *Unwelcome muse: Chinese literature in Shanghai and Peking, 1937–1945.* New York: Columbia University Press, 1980. ISBN 0-231-04730-4. ▸ Fine study of decline of May Fourth romanticism, resurgence of tradition among writers and impact of Japanese occupation's censorship during Sino-Japanese War. Evaluates period as one of considerable literary achievement. [JHC]

11.522 Christoph Harbsmeier. *The cartoonist Feng Zikai: social realism with a Buddhist face.* Oslo: Universitets Forlaget, 1984. (Instituttet for Sammenlignende Kulturforskning, Serie B, Skriften, 67.) ISBN 82-00-06650-9, ISSN 0032-6217. ▸ Sensitive, well-illustrated biographical appreciation of Feng Tzu-k'ai as humanist, populist master of lyric cartoon and informal essay, and illustrator of Lu Hsun's stories; severely criticized during Cultural Revolution. [JHC]

11.523 Charles W. Hayford. *To the people: James Yen and village China.* New York: Columbia University Press, 1990. ISBN 0-231-07204-X. ▸ Standard work on reformer who rejected both Nationalist status quo and communist revolution. Yale-educated transpacific liberal populist and leader of rural reconstruction movement in Ting-hsien (Hopei province), 1926–37. [JHC]

11.524 David Holm. *Art and ideology in revolutionary China.* New York: Oxford University Press, 1991. ISBN 0-19-828716-X. ▸ Detailed analysis of pre-1949 communist cultural policy, focusing on transformation of *yang-ko* (folk dance-drama) in Shen-Kan-Ning (i.e., Yenan) base area into model genre and example of ideology in action. [JHC]

11.525 C. T. Hsia. *A history of modern Chinese fiction.* 2d ed. New Haven: Yale University Press, 1971. ISBN 0-300-01462-7 (cl), 0-300-01461-9 (pbk). ▸ Still best overview of 1917–66 with chapters on virtually all major writers. Chastises Mao for crippling communist literature since 1940s. Includes extensive bibliography. First edition (1966) included appendix on Taiwan by Tsi-an Hsia. [JHC]

11.526 Tsi-an Hsia. *The gate of darkness: studies on the leftist literary movement in China.* Seattle: University of Washington Press, 1968. (Far Eastern and Russian Institute publications on Asia, 17.) ▸ Focuses on clashes between idealistic left-wing writers (e.g., Ch'ü Ch'iu-pai, Lu Hsun, Chiang Kuang-tzu, the Five Martyrs) and Communist party in 1930s Shanghai. Also treats Mao Tse-tung's 1942 Yenan Talks. [JHC]

11.527 Winston Hsieh. *Chinese historiography on the Revolution* *of 1911: a critical survey and a selected bibliography.* Stanford, Calif.: Hoover Institution Press, 1975. ISBN 0-8179-3341-7. ‣ Astute analysis of orthodox (Nationalist) and neo-orthodox (communist) interpretations, pointing up many similarities between them. Bibliography limited to Chinese works. [JHC]

11.528 Hung Chang-tai. *Going to the people: Chinese intellectuals and folk literature, 1918–1937.* Cambridge, Mass.: Harvard University, Council on East Asian Studies, 1985. (Harvard East Asian monographs, 121.) ISBN 0-674-35626-8. ‣ Fascinating account of populist movement by anti-Confucian, New Culture intellectuals (e.g., Lu Fu, Chou Tso-jen, Ku Chieh-kang) who emphasized importance of folk literature and study of folk history. [JHC]

11.529 Dan N. Jacobs. *Borodin: Stalin's man in China.* Cambridge, Mass.: Harvard University Press, 1981. ISBN 0-674-07910-8. ‣ Well-written biography of top Soviet adviser to Sun Yat-sen during First United Front (1924–27) between Kuomintang (Nationalist party) and fledgling Chinese Communists. Includes Borodin's pre- and post-China careers. [JHC]

11.530 Mayching Kao, ed. *Twentieth-century Chinese painting.* Hong Kong: Oxford University Press, 1988. ISBN 0-19-584278-2. ‣ Treats tradition in modern period; Shanghai and Lingnan (Kwangtung) schools; Western-influenced New Art; art and politics in People's Republic; post-1949 painting in Taiwan, Hong Kong, and overseas. Profusely illustrated. [JHC]

11.531 Barry Keenan. *The Dewey experiment in China: educational reform and political power in the early Republic.* Cambridge, Mass.: Harvard University, Council on East Asian Studies, 1977. (Harvard East Asian monographs, 81.) ISBN 0-674-20277-5. ‣ Standard work on American educational philosopher John Dewey's 1919–21 lecture tour and its considerable impact. But concludes Dewey had no strategy to offer that would be politically effective in Chinese context. [JHC]

11.532 Jeffrey C. Kinkley. *The odyssey of Shen Congwen.* Stanford, Calif.: Stanford University Press, 1987. ISBN 0-8047-1372-3. ‣ Standard work on twentieth-century regionalist writer Shen Ts'ung-wen, China's Faulkner, famous for describing life in his native locale of western Hunan province—cultural frontier between Han Chinese and Miao ethnic groups. [JHC]

11.533 Thomas C. Kuo. *Ch'en Tu-hsiu (1879–1942) and the Chinese communist movement.* South Orange, N.J.: Seton Hall University Press, 1975. ‣ Study of lifelong oppositionist, iconoclast, leading New Culture intellectual, promoter of "science" and "democracy," and early leader of Communist party, expelled after 1927 disasters, thereafter leader of Trotskyite leftist opposition. Includes chronology. [JHC]

11.534 Danny W. Y. Kwok. *Scientism in Chinese thought, 1900–1950.* New Haven: Yale University Press, 1965. ‣ Analysis of science as ideology. Best on 1923 science versus metaphysics debate between Ting Wen-chiang and Chang Chun-mai. Also treats thinkers Wu Chih-hui, Ch'en Tu-hsiu, Hu Shih, Jen Hung-chun, and T'ang Yueh. [JHC]

11.535 Olga Lang. *Pa Chin and his writings: Chinese youth between the two revolutions.* Cambridge, Mass.: Harvard University Press, 1967. ‣ Standard work on anarchist novelist extremely popular among 1930s to 1940s students, best known for 1931 semi-autographical novel (*Family*) describing May Fourth generation's rebellion against traditional social system. [JHC]

11.536 Leo Ou-fan Lee. *The romantic generation of modern Chinese writers.* Cambridge, Mass.: Harvard University Press, 1973. ISBN 0-674-77930-4. ‣ Finds equivalent of nineteenth-century European romantic movement in May Fourth generation (fl. 1920s to 1930s). Covers Yü Ta-fu, Hsu Chih-mo, Kuo Mo-jo, Chiang Kuang-tz'u, Hsiao Chun, plus precursors Lin Shu, Su Man-shu. [JHC]

11.537 Leo Ou-fan Lee. *Voices from the iron house: a study of Lu Xun.* Bloomington: Indiana University Press, 1987. ISBN 0-253-36263-6. ‣ Examination of Lu Hsun's genesis, creative writings (stories, prose-poetry, essays), and political context in 1930s Shanghai. Seeks to de-deify him, given official manipulation of his image for ideological purposes. [JHC]

11.538 Leo Ou-fan Lee, ed. *Lu Xun and his legacy.* Berkeley: University of California Press, 1985. ISBN 0-520-05158-0. ‣ Study of great twentieth-century engagé writer Lu Hsun. Eleven contributions in three sections: literature; thought and politics; and impact and reception. Coverage includes disciple Hu Feng and political use of Lu Hsun in Cultural Revolution. [JHC]

11.539 Jay Leyda. *Dianying: an account of films and film audiences in China.* Cambridge, Mass.: MIT Press, 1972. ISBN 0-262-12046-1. ‣ Comprehensive overview (1896–1967) by veteran film historian. Combines historical exposition with firsthand account of early 1960s changes in cultural policy. Appendixes include capsule biographies, chronological filmography, and numerous photographs. [JHC]

11.540 Lin Yü-sheng. *The crisis of Chinese consciousness: radical antitraditionalism in the May Fourth era.* Madison: University of Wisconsin Press, 1979. ISBN 0-299-07410-2. ‣ Sophisticated explication of leading intellectuals' mentalities in terms of totalistic cultural iconoclasm. Covers Ch'en Tu-hsiu, Hu Shih, Lu Hsun, all ca. 1915–27. Includes substantive forward by Benjamin Schwartz. [JHC]

11.541 E. Perry Link, Jr. *Mandarin ducks and butterflies: popular fiction in early twentieth-century Chinese cities.* Berkeley: University of California Press, 1981. ISBN 0-520-04111-9. ‣ Cultural history of love stories, martial arts tales, and scandal fiction plus their authors, publishers, and audiences, focusing on Shanghai, 1910–30. Includes comparisons with popular fiction in People's Republic as of 1979. [JHC]

11.542 Eugene Lubot. *Liberalism in an illiberal age: New Culture liberals in republican China, 1919–1937.* Westport, Conn.: Greenwood, 1982. ISBN 0-313-23256-3. ‣ Useful survey of leading figures: Ts'ai Yuan-p'ei, Hu Shih, T'ao Meng-ho, Fu Ssu-nien, Soong Ch'ing-ling, Chiang T'ing-fu, Chiang Meng-lin, Lo Chia-lun, and Liang Shih-ch'iu plus *Crescent Moon, Independent Critic,* and *China Critic* magazines. [JHC]

11.543 William A. Lyell, Jr. *Lu Hsun's vision of reality.* Berkeley: University of California Press, 1976. ISBN 0-520-02940-2. ‣ Very readable biography and appreciation of great twentieth-century *engagé* writer, inventor of vernacular short story. Emphasizes relationship between his fiction and social reality. [JHC]

11.544 Maurice Meisner. *Li Tao-chao and the origins of Chinese Marxism.* 1967 ed. New York: Atheneum, 1973. ‣ Formerly standard work, now challenged by Dirlik 11.387, on China's first Marxist, first important Chinese intellectual to declare support for Russian October Revolution, and early advocate of populist peasant revolution. [JHC]

11.545 Werner Meissner. *Philosophy and politics in China: the controversy over dialectical materialism in the 1930s.* Richard Mann, trans. Stanford, Calif.: Stanford University Press, 1990. ISBN 0-8047-1772-9. ‣ Controversial deconstruction (indeed, demolition) of Chinese Marxist discourse, demonstrating how theoretical philosophical terminology was used as Aesopian code-words to debate practical political strategy. Also analyzes intellectual poverty of Mao Tse-tung's philosophizing. Translation of *Philosophie und Politik in China: die Kontroverse über den dialektischen Materialismus in den dreissiger Jahren* (1986). [JHC]

11.546 Paul G. Pickowicz. *Marxist literary thought in China: the influence of Ch'ü Ch'iu-pai.* Berkeley: University of California

Press, 1981. ISBN 0-520-04030-9. ▸ Standard work on China's first important Marxist literary thinker, leader of League of Left-Wing Writers in 1930s Shanghai, troubled by cultural Europeanization of fellow progressives from May Fourth generation. [JHC]

11.547 David Tod Roy. *Kuo Mo-jo: the early years.* Cambridge, Mass.: Harvard University Press, 1971. ISBN 0-674-50570-0. ▸ Useful but unanalytical biography of facile Japanese-educated polymath, founder of Creation Society, through his 1924 conversion from romanticism to Marxism-Leninism. No treatment of controversial post-1949 career. [JHC]

11.548 Laurence A. Schneider. *Ku Chieh-kang and China's new history: nationalism and the quest for alternative traditions.* Berkeley: University of California Press, 1971. ISBN 0-520-01804-4. ▸ Standard work on leading twentieth-century historian who, atypical of May Fourth generation, sought value in populist indigenous alternatives to (and revisionist criticism of) Confucian heritage, rather than in westernization. [JHC]

11.549 Stuart R. Schram. "Mao studies: retrospect and prospect." *China quarterly* 97 (1984) 95–125. ISSN 0009-4439. ▸ Masterly state-of-field article, based on critique of sixteen primary and secondary sources on Mao Tse-tung published since his death in 1976. [JHC]

11.550 Stuart R. Schram. *Mao Tse-tung.* New York: Simon & Schuster, 1967. ▸ Fine biography by leading expert. Focuses on pre-1949 period; but, having gone to press early in Cultural Revolution (January 1967), needs updating. Includes photographs and maps. [JHC]

11.551 Stuart R. Schram. *The political thought of Mao Tse-tung.* 1969 rev. ed. New York: Praeger, 1976. ▸ Contains extensive and excellent analytical introduction plus original (unrevised) texts of Mao's major writings in reliable translation, arranged by subject. Includes chronology through 1968 and substantial bibliographical essay. [JHC]

11.552 Vera Schwarcz. *The Chinese enlightenment: intellectuals and the legacy of the May Fourth Movement of 1919.* Berkeley: University of California Press, 1986. ISBN 0-520-05027-4. ▸ Examines May Fourth's still unfulfilled goal of cosmopolitan intellectual emancipation through experiences of Peking University participants during subsequent decades. Based partially on interviews with eight survivors of 1919 generation. [JHC]

11.553 Vera Schwarcz. *Time for telling truth is running out: conversations with Zhang Shenfu.* New Haven: Yale University Press, 1992. ISBN 0-300-05009-7. ▸ Sensitive biography of Chang Shenfu, *engagé* May Fourth generation philosopher, fervent admirer of Bertrand Russell, close friend of Chou En-lai in Europe, and founding member of Communist party (in 1920). Includes many rare photographs. [JHC]

11.554 Benjamin I. Schwartz, ed. *Reflections on the May Fourth Movement: a symposium.* Cambridge, Mass.: Harvard University, East Asian Research Center, 1972. (Harvard East Asian monographs, 44.) ISBN 0-674-75230-9. ▸ Modifies Chow Tse-tsung's conclusions (11.508) by suggesting May Fourth Movement was one of several crucial intellectual turning points. Coverage includes iconoclasm (Meisner, Lin Yü-sheng) and left-wing criticism of vernacular movement (Goldman). [JHC]

11.555 Adolphe C. Scott. *Literature and the arts in twentieth-century China.* 1963 ed. Gloucester, Mass.: Smith, 1968. ▸ Overview of literature, theater, dance, cinema, painting, graphic arts, architecture, sculpture, and music. Also treats Taiwan and Hong Kong, and overseas Chinese in England and in United States. Includes illustrations. [JHC]

11.556 Adolphe C. Scott. *Mei Lan-fang: leader of the pear garden.* Hong Kong: Hong Kong University Press, 1959. ▸ Standard work on Peking opera's leading twentieth-century virtuoso, whose

world-famous career stretched from 1910s to 1960s. Also treats his theatrically long-prominent family. Includes rare photographs. [JHC]

11.557 Agnes Smedley. *The great road: the life and times of Chu Teh.* 1956 ed. New York: Monthly Review Press, 1972. ISBN 0-85345-206-7. ▸ Still standard biography of communist general Chu Te, Mao Tse-tung's comrade-in-arms beginning 1928. Based on interviews with Chu in Yenan (March–July 1937). Incomplete coverage intriguingly omits period 1932–34. [JHC]

11.558 John Bryan Starr. *Continuing the revolution: the political thought of Mao.* Princeton: Princeton University Press, 1979. ISBN 0-691-07596-4. ▸ Topically arranged analysis of Mao Tse-tung. Best on organization, political education, and political history. Also covers conflict, "knowing and doing" (categories of traditional Chinese thought), authority, class, participation, representation, and political development. Understates intellectual change through time. [JHC]

11.559 Ross Terrill. *Madame Mao, the white-boned demon: a biography of Madame Mao Zedong.* Rev. ed. New York: Simon & Schuster, 1992. ISBN 0-671-74484-4 (pbk). ▸ Best available account of Chiang Ch'ing (Mao Tse-tung's wife and Cultural Revolution luminary). Popularized but well researched, using previously untapped sources (e.g., Japanese). Includes new material on final years and 1991 suicide. [JHC]

11.560 Ross Terrill. *Mao: a biography.* New York: Harper & Row, 1980. ISBN 0-06-014243-X. ▸ Narrative life of Mao Tse-tung, popularly written but well grounded in both primary and secondary sources. Gives equal coverage to pre- and post-1949. Unlike Schram 11.550, covers Mao's entire career. [JHC]

11.561 Lee-hsia Hsu Ting. *Government control of the press in modern China, 1900–1949.* Cambridge, Mass.: Harvard University, East Asian Research Center, 1974. (Harvard East Asian monographs, 57.) ISBN 0-674-35820-1. ▸ Concludes Nationalist government's censorship much more effective against constructive criticism and liberal thought than against communist propaganda. Also treats late Ch'ing dynasty, President Yuan Shih-k'ai, and warlords. [JHC]

11.562 Ranbir Vohra. *Lao She and the Chinese revolution.* Cambridge, Mass.: Harvard University, East Asian Research Center, 1974. (Harvard East Asian monographs, 55.) ISBN 0-674-51075-5. ▸ Useful but uninspired descriptive account of leading republican period novelist (of Manchu heritage) best known for works set in Peking. Includes copious plot summaries of his fiction. [JHC]

11.563 Frederic E. Wakeman, Jr. *History and will: philosophical perspectives of Mao Tse-tung's thought.* Berkeley: University of California Press, 1973. ISBN 0-520-02104-5. ▸ Analysis of Mao's debt to various philosophers, writers, and intellectuals (Chu Hsi, Confucius, Darwin, Engels, Fichte, Hegel, K'ang Yu-wei, Kant, Liang Ch'i-ch'ao, Marx, Mencius, Paulsen, Rousseau, Spencer, T'an Ssu-tung, Tung Chung-shu, Wang Fu-chih, Wang Yang-ming, Yen Fu et al.). [JHC]

11.564 Y. C. Wang. *Chinese intellectuals and the West, 1872–1949.* Chapel Hill: University of North Carolina Press, 1966. ▸ Examines deleterious impact of Western- and Japanese-educated returned students. Argues that unlike traditional Confucian rural literati, westernized urban intelligentsia became increasingly amoral and detached from society, 1902–49. Includes useful statistical tables. [JHC]

11.565 Holmes Welch. *The Buddhist revival in China.* Cambridge, Mass.: Harvard University Press, 1968. ▸ Interprets revival, ca. 1850–1950, as series of secularizing innovations and assertion of cultural loyalism versus Western-Christian challenge, not as religious restoration. Covers leader T'ai-hsu, lay Buddhism, education, and relations with state. [JHC]

11.566 Holmes Welch. *The practice of Chinese Buddhism, 1900–1950.* Cambridge, Mass.: Harvard University Press, 1967. ISBN 0-674-69701-4 (pbk). ▸ Standard work, focusing on practices (rather than doctrines) of both monastic institutions and individual Buddhists. Based on extensive interviews, plus documents. Includes numerous photographs. [JHC]

11.567 Philip West. *Yenching University and Sino-Western relations, 1916–1952.* Cambridge, Mass.: Harvard University Press, 1976. ISBN 0-674-96569-8. ▸ Standard work on prominent Protestant missionary–founded university in Peking, alma mater to both communist and Nationalist notables and victim of Korean War xenophobia. Based partly on interviews with alumni and former teachers. [JHC]

11.568 Dick Wilson. *Chou, the story of Zhou Enlai, 1898–1976.* New York: Viking, 1984. ISBN 0-670-22011-6. ▸ Concludes intriguingly that veteran communist leader Chou En-lai was not moderate in Western political terms; was better Communist than Mao Tse-tung. Includes photographs and useful bibliographical essay. [JHC]

11.569 Dick Wilson, ed. *Mao Tse-tung in the scales of history: a preliminary assessment.* Cambridge: Cambridge University Press, 1977. ISBN 0-521-21583-8 (cl), 0-521-29290-9 (pbk). ▸ Premature but stimulating symposium: treats Mao as philosopher, Marxist, political leader, soldier, teacher, economist, patriot, statesman, Chinese, and innovator. [JHC]

11.570 Ernst Wolff. *Chou Tso-jen.* New York: Twayne, 1971. ▸ Succinct examination of life and writings of prominent republican period essayist, Lu Hsun's brother, convicted in 1945 as Japanese collaborator. Appendix contains sample essays. [JHC]

11.571 Wang-chi Wong. *Politics and literature in Shanghai: the Chinese League of Left-Wing Writers, 1930–1936.* Manchester: Manchester University Press; distributed by St. Martin's, 1991. ISBN 0-7190-2924-4. ▸ Contrasts communist organization's 1930–33 successes under Ch'ü Ch'iu-pai's leadership with 1934–36 decline under Chou Yang, caused by internal dissension and alienation of Lu Hsun. Acknowledges league produced more politics than literature. [JHC]

11.572 Raymond F. Wylie. *The emergence of Maoism: Mao Tse-tung, Ch'en Po-ta, and the search for Chinese theory.* Stanford, Calif.: Stanford University Press, 1980. ISBN 0-8047-1051-1. ▸ Well-written standard work on communist ideologue Ch'en's career through 1945, emphasizing his previously underappreciated role helping Mao create Maoism. Epilogue sketches 1945–70 activities, especially during Cultural Revolution. [JHC]

11.573 Wen-hsin Yeh. *The alienated academy: culture and politics in republican China, 1919–1937.* Cambridge, Mass.: Harvard University, Council on East Asian Studies, 1990. (Harvard East Asian monographs, 148.) ISBN 0-674-01585-1. ▸ Study of academic life (campus culture) at college and university level in Shanghai, Peking, and Nanking, focusing on bourgeois St. John's and radical Shanghai University. Emphasizes 1930s students' confusion, despondency, political disenchantment, and disillusionment. [JHC]

11.574 Ka-che Yip. *Religion, nationalism, and Chinese students: the anti-Christian movement of 1922–1927.* Bellingham: Western Washington University Press, Center for Chinese Studies, 1980. (Studies on East Asia, 15.) ISBN 0-914584-15-4. ▸ Ascribes disillusionment with Christianity to missionaries' involvement in cultural imperialism and May Fourth Movement's rejection of religion as outdated. Finds students subordinating goal of personal liberty to national solidarity through revolutionary political parties. Compare Lutz 11.430. [JHC]

PEOPLE'S REPUBLIC OF CHINA, SINCE 1949

Political History

11.575 J. D. Armstrong. *Revolutionary diplomacy: Chinese foreign policy and the United Front doctrine.* Berkeley: University of California Press, 1977. ISBN 0-520-03251-9 (cl), 0-520-04273-5 (pbk). ▸ Concludes that Sino-Soviet ties inhibited United Front from developing as Chinese foreign policy strategy before 1960. Specifically treats relations with Indonesia, Pakistan, Cambodia, and Tanzania. [JHC]

11.576 David M. Bachman. *Bureaucracy, economy, and leadership in China: the institutional origins of the Great Leap Forward.* Cambridge: Cambridge University Press, 1991. ISBN 0-521-40275-1. ▸ Revisionist analysis, arguing Great Leap policies were first prepared by coalition of planning and heavy-industry proponents, especially Li Fu-ch'un and Po I-po, in spring-summer 1957 and only later adopted by Mao Tse-tung. [JHC]

11.577 A. Doak Barnett. *Communist China: the early years, 1949–55.* New York: Praeger, 1964. ▸ Overview of establishment of new regime, political-social control, propaganda, indoctrination, mass mobilization, economic development, and political consolidation. Based primarily on reports researched in Hong Kong during early 1950s. [JHC]

11.578 Richard Baum. *Prelude to revolution: Mao, the party, and the peasant question, 1962–66.* New York: Columbia University Press, 1975. ISBN 0-231-03900-X. ▸ Study of failure of Mao Tse-tung's socialist education movement (1962–66) and split among Mao, Liu Shao-ch'i, and Teng Hsiao-p'ing over future course of Communist party, leading to Cultural Revolution. [JHC]

11.579 John P. Burns. *Political participation in rural China.* Berkeley: University of California Press, 1988. ISBN 0-520-06005-9. ▸ Analysis of village politics in People's Republic, 1962–84. Concludes peasants effectively opposed policies by mobilizing kinship, community, or village loyalties to achieve group solidarity. [JHC]

11.580 Joseph Camilleri. *Chinese foreign policy: the Maoist era and its aftermath.* Seattle: University of Washington Press, 1980. ISBN 0-295-95776-X. ▸ Focuses on China's relations with superpowers, but also treats relations with Japan, Southeast Asia, and Third World. Finds three phases: revolutionary (1949–68), transitional (1969–73), and postrevolutionary (1973–). [JHC]

11.581 Golem W. Choudhury. *China in world affairs: the foreign policy of the PRC since 1970.* Boulder: Westview, 1982. ISBN 0-89158-937-6 (cl), 0-86531-329-6 (pbk). ▸ Analysis by former Pakistani official intimately involved in proceedings leading to Nixon's 1972 breakthrough visit to People's Republic. Treats (through mid-1981) Sino-American relations, Sino-Soviet conflict, and relations with Japan, Korea, South and Southeast Asia, and Third World. [JHC]

11.582 Lowell Dittmer. *China's continuous revolution: the post-liberation epoch, 1949–1981.* Berkeley: University of California Press, 1987. ISBN 0-520-05656-6. ▸ Argues charismatic leadership, effective mass mobilization, and opposition against which to struggle are all prerequisites for continuing revolution after seizure of sovereignty. [JHC]

11.583 Lowell Dittmer. *Liu Shao-ch'i and the Chinese Cultural Revolution: the politics of mass criticism.* Berkeley: University of California Press, 1974. ISBN 0-520-02574-1. ▸ Biographical examination of Liu's rise, then fall during Cultural Revolution in part 1. Part 2 compares Mao Tse-tung and Liu, analyzing Liu's capitalist road. Part 3 presents theory of anti-Liu mass criticism. [JHC]

11.584 Jürgen Domes. *The internal politics of China, 1949–1972.*

Rudiger Machetzki, trans. New York: Praeger, 1973. ‣ Well-researched, hardheaded analysis focusing unfashionably on political reality rather than theoretical claims of Chinese Communists to have created a new society. Has aged well. Translation of *Die Àra Mao Tse-tung* (1971). [JHC]

11.585 Jürgen Domes. *Peng Te-huai: the man and the image.* Stanford, Calif.: Stanford University Press, 1985. ISBN 0-8047-1303-0. ‣ Standard work on leading communist general during Korean War, famous for opposing Mao's Great Leap Forward policies; dismissed 1959 but reputation posthumously rehabilitated. Includes analysis of how his heroic and villainous images were manipulated. [JHC]

11.586 Dennis J. Doolin, ed. and trans. *Communist China: the politics of student opposition.* Stanford, Calif.: Hoover Institution on War, Revolution, and Peace, 1964. ‣ Twelve brief but fascinating student protest documents from 1957 Hundred Flowers period, including two speeches by leader Lin Hsi-ling. Includes substantive introduction by editor. Translation of *Kan! Che shih shen-me yen-lun?* (Look! What Kind of Talk Is This?) (1957). [JHC]

11.587 Jean Esmein. *The Chinese Cultural Revolution.* 1973 ed. W.J.F. Jenner, trans. London: Deutsch, 1975. ISBN 0-233-96361-8. ‣ Thematic rather than chronological discussion of 1966–69 developments, treating Mao Tse-tung's thought, Communist party, army, students, Red Guards, workers, peasants, revolutionary committees, ultra-leftists, and moderates. Based partially on on-site observation. Translation of *La révolution culturelle chinoise* (1970). [JHC]

11.588 Stephen Fitzgerald. *China and the overseas Chinese: a study of Peking's changing policy, 1949–1970.* Cambridge: Cambridge University Press, 1972. ISBN 0-521-08410-5. ‣ Focuses on policy toward ethnic Chinese in Southeast Asia. Debunks myth of overseas Chinese as fifth column. Concludes Communist party discounted them as effective revolutionary vanguard for China. [JHC]

11.589 Keith Forster. *Rebellion and factionalism in a Chinese province: Zhejiang, 1966–1976.* Armonk, N.Y.: Sharpe, 1990. ISBN 0-87332-535-4. ‣ Pioneering analysis of Cultural Revolution at provincial level, focusing on Chekiang (especially capital city Hangchou). Also treats previous interpretations of Cultural Revolution. Based largely on provincial newspapers. [JHC]

11.590 Gao Yuan. *Born red: a chronicle of the Cultural Revolution.* Stanford, Calif.: Stanford University Press, 1987. ISBN 0-8047-1368-5 (cl), 0-8047-1369-3 (pbk). ‣ Gripping, firsthand account of early Cultural Revolution (1966–69) in Hopei province as lived by middle-school student turned Red Guard. Includes substantive foreword by William Joseph. [JHC]

11.591 Jacques Guillermaz. *The Chinese Communist party in power, 1949–1976.* Rev. ed. Anne Destenay, trans. Boulder: Westview, 1976. ISBN 0-89158-041-7. ‣ Comprehensive history of People's Republic to Mao's death, foreign policy as well as domestic politics. Includes substantial bibliography. Translation of *Le parti communiste chinois au pouvoir* (1972), revised and updated by author to include 1972–76. [JHC]

11.592 Harry Harding. *Organizing China: the problem of bureaucracy, 1949–1976.* Stanford, Calif.: Stanford University Press, 1981. ISBN 0-8047-1080-5. ‣ Reliable overview, arguing that like untippable doll, organizational policy stabilized after each experiment. Best on Hundred Flowers period (1956–57) and early Cultural Revolution (1966–68). [JHC]

11.593 Harold C. Hinton. *China's turbulent quest: an analysis of China's foreign relations since 1949.* Rev. ed. Bloomington: Indiana University Press, 1972. ISBN 0-253-20157-8 (pbk). ‣ Discussion in three parts: chronological narrative, 1950–1968; analytical

essays on making of foreign policy and relations with world communism, Asia, Third World, and West; and post–Cultural Revolution. Includes detailed bibliographical essays. [JHC]

11.594 Harold C. Hinton, ed. *The People's Republic of China, 1949–1979: a documentary survey.* Vol. 1: *1949–1957, from liberation to crisis.* Vol. 2: *1957–1965, Great Leap Forward and its aftermath.* Vol. 3: *1965–1967, Cultural Revolution, part I.* Vol. 4: *1967–1970, Cultural Revolution, part II.* Vol. 5: *1971–1979, after the Cultural Revolution.* 5 vols. Wilmington, Del.: Scholarly Resources, 1980. ISBN 0-8420-2253-8. ‣ Full texts of 680 primary sources in reliable translations, each preceded by editor's brief introduction. [JHC]

11.595 Christopher Howe, ed. *Shanghai: revolution and development in an Asian metropolis.* Cambridge: Cambridge University Press, 1981. ISBN 0-521-23198-1. ‣ After 1919–49 overview, treats post-1949 political life (especially aspects of Cultural Revolution), industrialization, food supply, workers' living standard (1930–73), urban spatial development, suburbs, worker-writers, and 1970s radicalism. Includes detailed chronology (1842–1979). [JHC]

11.596 Huang Shu-min. *The spiral road: change in a Chinese village through the eyes of a Communist party leader.* Boulder: Westview, 1989. ISBN 0-8133-7637-8 (cl), 0-8133-0938-7 (pbk). ‣ Well-written life history of Communist party secretary (born 1944) in his native village near Fukien province's Amoy (Hsiamen) city. Based on fieldwork 1984–85. Includes substantive foreword by Bernard Gallin. [JHC]

11.597 Harlan W. Jencks. *From muskets to missiles: politics and professionalism in the Chinese army, 1945–1981.* Boulder: Westview, 1982. ISBN 0-86531-301-6. ‣ Comprehensive analysis of civil-military relations, concluding Chinese officers, especially below corps level, have tried to avoid political involvement, especially during Cultural Revolution. Includes appendixes on military organization and equipment. [JHC]

11.598 Ellis Joffe. *Party and army: professionalism and political control in the Chinese officer corps, 1949–1964.* 1965 ed. Cambridge, Mass.: Harvard University, East Asian Research Center, 1971. (Harvard East Asian monographs, 19.) ISBN 0-674-65500-1. ‣ Analyzes relations between Communist party and People's Liberation Army officers prior to Cultural Revolution. Focuses on clash between emerging military professionalism and need for political control. [JHC]

11.599 William A. Joseph. *The critique of ultra-leftism in China, 1958–1981.* Stanford, Calif.: Stanford University Press, 1984. ISBN 0-8047-1208-5. ‣ Sophisticated analysis of internal Chinese communist criticisms (both before and after Mao's 1976 death) of ultra-left line as exemplified by Great Leap Forward, Lin Piao, and Gang of Four. [JHC]

11.600 William A. Joseph, Christine P. W. Wong, and David Zweig, eds. *New perspectives on the Cultural Revolution.* Cambridge, Mass.: Harvard University, Council on East Asian Studies, 1991. (Harvard contemporary China series, 8.) ISBN 0-674-61757-6 (cl), 0-674-61758-4 (pbk). ‣ Collection of essays on politics (e.g., radicalism, administrative policies, factionalism in Chekiang province), economics (Mao Tse-tung's political economy, strategy of industrial decentralization, rural industrialization, case study of Kiangsu province), and culture (artistic policies, novels, model operas). [JHC]

11.601 Ronald C. Keith. *The diplomacy of Zhou Enlai.* New York: St. Martin's, 1989. ISBN 0-312-03100-9. ‣ Analysis of Chou En-lai, People's Republic's foreign minister, 1949–58, and premier, 1949–76. Notes Chou's brilliance at pragmatic compromise, seeming ability to be all things to all people, and triumph over American containment policy. [JHC]

11.602 Samuel S. Kim. *China, the United Nations, and world order.* Princeton: Princeton University Press, 1979. ISBN 0-691-07599-9 (cl), 0-691-10076-4 (pbk). ▸ Standard work on People's Republic's participation in United Nations since 1971 admittance. Finds effects of its entry have been positive for both U.N. and China. [JHC]

11.603 Richard Curt Kraus. *Class conflict in Chinese socialism.* New York: Columbia University Press, 1981. ISBN 0-231-05182-4. ▸ Tightly written analysis of relationship between Mao Tse-tung's sinification of Marx's class analysis to emphasize political behavior (not property) and reality of social stratification (virtual caste system) in People's Republic. [JHC]

11.604 Hong Yung Lee. *From revolutionary cadres to party technocrats in socialist China.* Berkeley: University of California Press, 1991. ISBN 0-520-06679-0. ▸ Study of structure, personnel, and historical formation of cadre system. As title suggests, argues that transition from emphasis on ideology to expertise is ongoing and inevitable. Also treats pre-1949 communist cadres. [JHC]

11.605 Hong Yung Lee. *The politics of the Chinese Cultural Revolution: a case study.* Berkeley: University of California Press, 1978. ISBN 0-520-03297-7 (cl), 0-520-04065-1 (pbk). ▸ Compelling analysis of 1966–69 period, concluding that radicalism of Red Guard (and other participant) factions correlated inversely with members' social status. The most radical had been lowest on pre–Cultural Revolution totem pole. [JHC]

11.606 John Wilson Lewis and Xue Litai. *China builds the bomb.* Stanford, Calif.: Stanford University Press, 1988. ISBN 0-8047-1452-5. ▸ Standard work on People's Republic's version of Manhattan Project, covering 1955 decision to develop nuclear weapons to October 1964 A-bomb to June 1967 H-bomb. Based largely on declassified Chinese documents. [JHC]

11.607 Victor H. Li. *Law without lawyers.* 1977 ed. Boulder: Westview, 1978. ISBN 0-89158-160-X (cl), 0-89158-161-8 (pbk). ▸ Concise, highly readable overview of legal system in People's Republic, emphasizing relationship between law and cultural values. Contrasts Chinese and American systems. Includes annotated bibliography. [JHC]

11.608 Kenneth G. Lieberthal. *Revolution and tradition in Tientsin, 1949–1952.* Stanford, Calif.: Stanford University Press, 1980. ISBN 0-8047-1044-9. ▸ Focuses on how economic development, organizational control, and mass manipulation interacted in shaping political consciousness of urbanites. Includes Communists' use of focused campaigns and unsuccessful attack on particularistic personal relationships. [JHC]

11.609 Alan P. L. Liu. *Communications and national integration in communist China.* 1971 ed. Berkeley: University of California Press, 1975. ISBN 0-520-02901-1 (pbk). ▸ Useful overview of formal organization of propaganda, mass campaigns, radio broadcasting, and publishing and film industries. Includes new, extensive author's preface. [JHC]

11.610 Roderick MacFarquhar. *Contradictions among the people, 1956–1957.* Vol. 1 of *The origins of the Cultural Revolution.* New York: Columbia University Press for Columbia University, East Asian Institute and Research Institute on Communist Affairs and Royal Institute of International Affairs, 1974. 2 vols. ISBN 0-231-03841-0 (set). ▸ Standard work on Hundred Flowers period of liberalization and (when Chairman Mao realized his mistake) subsequent antirightist campaign targeting intellectuals who had criticized party policies. Meticulous narrative with analysis. [JHC]

11.611 Roderick MacFarquhar. *The Great Leap Forward, 1958–1960.* Vol. 2 of *The origins of the Cultural Revolution.* New York: Columbia University Press for Columbia University, East Asian Institute and Research Institute on Communist Affairs and Royal Institute of International Affairs, 1983. 2 vols. ISBN 0-231-05716-

4 (v. 2). ▸ Formerly standard work, now challenged by Bachman 11.576, on Chairman Mao's utopian commune efforts. In four parts: charge, retreat, clash, and defeat. Finds Great Leap Forward party's greatest trauma before Cultural Revolution. [JHC]

11.612 David G. Muller, Jr. *China as a maritime power.* Boulder: Westview, 1983. ISBN 0-86531-098-X. ▸ Covers 1945–83, focusing on People's Republic's navy. But also treats merchant marine, fishing industry, offshore oil, maritime territorial disputes, and Republic of China's navy pre- and post-1949. [JHC]

11.613 Harvey W. Nelsen. *The Chinese military system: an organizational study of the Chinese People's Liberation Army.* 2d ed. Boulder: Westview, 1981. ISBN 0-86531-069-6. ▸ Topics include provincial and regional military administration, high command, military life, army, navy, air force, militia, production and construction corps, and concept of people's wars of national liberation. Epilogue covering 1977–80. [JHC]

11.614 Kevin J. O'Brien. *Reform without liberalization: China's National People's Congress and the politics of institutional change.* New York: Cambridge University Press, 1990. ISBN 0-521-38086-3. ▸ Analysis of so-called nation's lawmaker under Mao Tse-tung and Teng Hsiao-p'ing, 1954–89; ineffective by time of Mao's death (1976). Also traces pre-1949 origins to republican period legislatures and late Ch'ing constitutionalism. [JHC]

11.615 Jean C. Oi. *State and peasant in contemporary China: the political economy of village government.* Berkeley: University of California Press, 1989. ISBN 0-520-06105-5. ▸ Discussion of politics of surplus-grain allocation (dividing the harvest) at village-level interface between state and society, 1956–86. Emphasizes importance of personalized patron-client relationships and attendant patterns of corruption. [JHC]

11.616 Herbert Franz Schurmann. *Ideology and organization in communist China.* 2d ed. Berkeley: University of California Press, 1968. ISBN 0-520-01553-8 (pbk). ▸ Sympathetic analysis, focusing on 1950s, treating ideology, party, government, management, control, cities, and villages. Supplementary section treats 1961–67: ideology, organization, and society. Readers should avoid error-laden 1966 first edition. [JHC]

11.617 Gerald Segal. *Defending China.* Oxford: Oxford University Press, 1985. ISBN 0-19-827470-X. ▸ Analysis of defense policy and practice in eight case studies of force projection: Tibet 1950–51, Korea 1950–53, Taiwan 1954–55 and 1958, India 1962, Vietnam 1964–65, Soviet Union 1969, Paracel Islands 1974, and Vietnam 1979. [JHC]

11.618 James D. Seymour. *China's satellite parties.* Armonk, N.Y.: Sharpe, 1987. ISBN 0-87332-412-9. ▸ Standard work on minor political parties founded pre-1949, perpetuated by People's Republic under United Front umbrella, briefly flourishing during 1957 Hundred Flowers period, suppressed during 1966–76 Cultural Revolution, and resuscitated around 1980. [JHC]

11.619 Vivienne Shue. *Peasant China in transition: the dynamics of development toward socialism, 1949–1956.* Berkeley: University of California Press, 1980. ISBN 0-520-03734-0. ▸ Analysis of stages of transition from postliberation land reform to cooperatives to collectivization. Finds overall success in management of rural change prior to ill-fated Great Leap Forward. [JHC]

11.620 Frederick C. Teiwes. *Politics and purges in China: rectification and the decline of party norms, 1950–1965.* White Plains, N.Y.: Sharpe, 1979. ISBN 0-87332-132-4. ▸ Analysis of Communist party's changing behavior in dealing with dissidence and heterodoxy, from redemptive rectification according to norms (1950–57) to combination of rectification and purging (1957–65). [JHC]

11.621 Frederick C. Teiwes. *Politics at Mao's court: Gao Gang and party factionalism in the early 1950s.* Armonk, N.Y.: Sharpe,

1990. ISBN 0-87332-590-7 (cl), 0-87332-709-8 (pbk). ‣ Study of Kao Kang Jao-Shu-shih episode (1953–54), first major case of intraparty factionalism since 1949. Finds high-level politics became court politics, revolving around satisfying Chairman Mao's desires. [JHC]

11.622 James R. Townsend. *Political participation in communist China.* 1967 ed. Berkeley: University of California Press, 1969. ‣ Discussion focusing on political life of masses (workers, peasants, housewives), in theory and practice, before Cultural Revolution. Notes Communist party's emphasis on mass mobilization and lack of emphasis on institutions; no freedom to abstain. [JHC]

11.623 James R. Townsend and Brantly Womack. *Politics in China.* 3d ed. Boston: Little, Brown, 1986. ISBN 0-316-85132-9 (pbk). ‣ Discussion of period 1949–85: origins, institutions, evolution of policy, ideology and change, political socialization, communications, political interests, recruitment, conflict, governmental process, and post-Mao modernization. Statistical appendixes (mostly economic). [JHC]

11.624 Ezra F. Vogel. *Canton under communism: programs and politics in a provincial capital, 1949–1968.* 1969 ed. Cambridge, Mass.: Harvard University Press, 1980. ISBN 0-674-09476-1 (pbk). ‣ Pioneering, descriptive case study of developments previously known at national level. Focus fluctuates between Canton city and entire Kwangtung province. Based largely on local newspapers, interviews. Includes author's new preface. [JHC]

11.625 Lynn T. White III. *Policies of chaos: the organizational causes of violence in China's Cultural Revolution.* Princeton: Princeton University Press, 1989. ISBN 0-691-05546-7. ‣ Argument that Cultural Revolution as mass movement was caused by three preexisting policies: using value-laden labels to create status groups, making individuals dependent on boss's patronage, and legitimizing violence in official campaigns. [JHC]

11.626 Hongda Harry Wu. *Laogai—the Chinese gulag.* Ted Slingerland, trans. Boulder: Westview, 1992. ISBN 0-8133-8154-1. ‣ Valuable exposé of labor reform–camp prison system, including its economic role, by former inmate at seven camps (1960–79). Includes photographs and appendixes with maps and charts on known camps (arranged by province). [JHC]

11.627 Tien-wei Wu. *Lin Biao and the Gang of Four: contra-Confucianism in historical and intellectual perspective.* Carbondale: Southern Illinois University Press, 1983. ISBN 0-8093-1022-8. ‣ Study of politically charged, factionally driven historiographical debates sparked by Mao Tse-tung's Criticize Lin Piao, Criticize Confucius campaign (1973–76). Case study of making past serve present. Also covers post-Mao criticism of Gang of Four. [JHC]

11.628 Michael B. Yahuda. *China's role in world affairs.* New York: St. Martin's, 1978. ISBN 0-312-13358-8. ‣ Focuses on intellectual themes (especially nationalism and revolution) dominating Chinese foreign policy. In two parts: Sino-Soviet alliance 1949–63 and post-1963 autonomy. [JHC]

Social History

11.629 Phyllis Andors. *The unfinished liberation of Chinese women, 1949–1980.* Bloomington: Indiana University Press, 1983. ISBN 0-253-36022-6. ‣ Study of both urban and rural women during post-1949 reconstruction, first Five-Year Plan (1953–57), Great Leap Forward, Cultural Revolution, and post-Mao period. Finds greatest progress toward sexual equality during Great Leap Forward and Cultural Revolution. [JHC]

11.630 Judith Banister. *China's changing population.* Stanford, Calif.: Stanford University Press, 1987. ISBN 0-8047-1155-0. ‣ Standard work covering 1949–84. Finds People's Republic in midst of rapid demographic transition from high to low fertility and mortality. Topics include morbidity, mortality, fertility, family planning, internal migration, and ethnic groups. [JHC]

11.631 Gordon A. Bennett. *Huadong: the story of a Chinese people's commune.* Boulder: Westview, 1978. ISBN 0-89158-094-8 (cl), 0-89158-095-6 (pbk). ‣ Introductory ethnography of model commune in Kwangtung province patronized, 1961–65, by high official T'ao Chu. Topics include local government, politics, economy, society, and culture. Includes photographs and lists of suggested readings. [JHC]

11.632 Thomas P. Bernstein. *Up to the mountains and down to the villages: the transfer of youth from urban to rural China.* New Haven: Yale University Press, 1977. ISBN 0-300-02135-6. ‣ Excellent insights into psychology and interest-calculus of educated urban youths vis-à-vis Maoist transfer policy, 1968–77. Points up waste of urban talent in countryside and localist suspicion of outsiders. [JHC]

11.633 Anita Chan, Richard Madsen, and Jonathan Unger. *Chen village: the recent history of a peasant community in Mao's China.* Berkeley: University of California Press, 1984. ISBN 0-520-04720-6. ‣ Well-written local history of village in Kwangtung province from mid-1960s to early 1980s, based largely on Hong Kong interviews with twenty-six emigrés. Story of revolution gone sour. [JHC]

11.634 Elisabeth J. Croll. *The politics of marriage in contemporary China.* Cambridge: Cambridge University Press, 1981. ISBN 0-521-23345-3. ‣ Focuses on early 1960s. Concludes older generation successfully defied new ideology favoring free-choice marriages and maintained control of marriage procedures due to rural household's structure and function. [JHC]

11.635 Delia Davin. *Women-work: women and the party in revolutionary China.* Oxford: Clarendon, 1976. ISBN 0-19-827231-6. ‣ Discussion of women's organizations, marriage, family, and rural-urban situation, focusing on 1950s. Also treats pre-1949 communist policy. Presents mixed but, on balance, upbeat picture of progress toward sexual equality. [JHC]

11.636 Deborah Davis-Friedmann. *Long lives: Chinese elderly and the communist revolution.* Rev. ed. Stanford, Calif.: Stanford University Press, 1991. ISBN 0-8047-1806-7 (cl), 0-8047-1808-3 (pbk). ‣ Analysis of reality of aging and relevant government policies, 1949–88. Points out contradiction between party's ideological opposition to particularistic loyalties and welfare policies' dependence on strength of these same loyalties. [JHC]

11.637 June Teufel Dreyer. *China's forty millions: minority nationalities and national integration in the People's Republic of China.* Cambridge, Mass.: Harvard University Press, 1976. ISBN 0-674-11964-9. ‣ Discussion of successes and failures of Communist party's minorities policy from pre-1949 through 1975. Finds most conspicuous failures in Sinkiang and Tibet. Also treats pre-1949 Kuomintang (Nationalist party) policy. [JHC]

11.638 B. Michael Frolic. *Mao's people: sixteen portraits of life in revolutionary China.* Cambridge, Mass.: Harvard University Press, 1980. ISBN 0-674-54846-9. ‣ Highly readable accounts of daily life from mid-1950s through 1976 with focus on 1966–74 (i.e., Cultural Revolution). Based on Hong Kong interviews of emigrés from all over China. [JHC]

11.639 Lee Lai To. *Trade unions in China, 1949 to the present: the organization and leadership of the All-China Federation of Trade Unions.* Singapore: Singapore University Press, 1986. ISBN 9971-69-093-4 (pbk). ‣ Emphasizes unions' subordination to Communist party with no autonomy or collective-bargaining power. Also treats pre-1949 communist labor-unionizing activities. [JHC]

11.640 John Wilson Lewis, ed. *The city in communist China.* Stanford, Calif.: Stanford University Press, 1971. ISBN 0-8047-0748-0. ‣ Topics include urban law and order, cadre recruitment and mobility, trade unions, T'ang-shan city 1956–69, manpower training 1949–68, Shanghai employment 1949–57, urban-rural inequalities 1958–66, and urban neighborhoods. [JHC]

11.641   William L. Parish and Martin K. Whyte. *Village and family in contemporary China.* Chicago: University of Chicago Press, 1978. ISBN 0-226-64590-8. ▸ Superb analysis of Kwangtung province's rural society to early 1970s, based largely on methodologically sophisticated emigré interviews. Concludes that peasants, rejecting ideological exhortations, continued to evaluate innovations according to family self-interest. [JHC]

11.642   Peng Xizhe. *Demographic transition in China: fertility trends since the 1950s.* New York: Oxford University Press, 1991. ISBN 0-19-828715-1. ▸ Detailed analysis finds fertility rising initially after 1949, leveling off from mid-1950s to 1970 (except for 1959–63 decline), and decreasing by more than 50 percent during 1970s with slightly upward trend since mid-1980s. [JHC]

11.643   Helen F. Siu. *Agents and victims in South China: accomplices in rural revolution.* New Haven: Yale University Press, 1989. ISBN 0-300-04465-8. ▸ Ethnography of commune in Kwangtung province through 1983, including pre-1949. Finds peasants increasingly confined while cadres entrenched themselves further. During fieldwork, author exchanged Marxist idealism for recognition of bureaucratic reality. [JHC]

11.644   G. William Skinner. "Marketing and social structure in rural China, Part 3." *Journal of Asian studies* 24.3 (1965) 363–99. ISSN 0021-9118. ▸ Extends analysis in 11.218 to People's Republic. Analysis includes dire consequences of Great Leap Forward's arbitrary severing of traditional trading relations by ignoring standard marketing community as natural unit. [JHC]

11.645   Andrew G. Walder. *Communist neo-traditionalism: work and authority in Chinese industry.* Berkeley: University of California Press, 1986. ISBN 0-520-05439-3 (cl), 0-520-06470-4 (pbk). ▸ Analysis of how compliance is achieved in workplace. Rejecting totalitarian and group theory models of authority, emphasizes structured incentives and network of patron-client relations maintained by Communist party. Based largely on interviews. [JHC]

11.646   James L. Watson, ed. *Class and social stratification in post-revolution China.* Cambridge: Cambridge University Press, 1984. (Contemporary China Institute publications. Studies on China, 3.) ISBN 0-521-26062-0. ▸ Eight contributions treating traditional Chinese views of social classification, Mao Tse-tung on classes, rise and fall of "virtuocracy," egalitarianism and destratification, class in rural Kwangtung, Shanghai bourgeois radicalism, marriage choice, and socialist sexism. [JHC]

11.647   Lynn T. White III. *Careers in Shanghai: the social guidance of personal energies in a developing Chinese city, 1949–1966.* Berkeley: University of California Press, 1978. ISBN 0-520-00361-2. ▸ Concludes government policies such as educational programs, patriotic rustication plans involving transfer to rural areas, employment procedures, and residence registration all had effects on individuals' career motivations. [JHC]

11.648   Martin K. Whyte and William L. Parish. *Urban life in contemporary China.* Chicago: University of Chicago Press, 1984. ISBN 0-226-89546-7 (cl), 0-226-89547-5 (pbk). ▸ Standard work. Examines changes, continuities, and pros and cons of Chinese model of urbanism as practiced 1970–76. Treats urban political economy, family behavior, and quality of life. Based on interviews with former residents of fifty cities. [JHC]

11.649   Margery Wolf. *Revolution postponed: women in contemporary China.* Stanford, Calif.: Stanford University Press, 1985. ISBN 0-8047-1243-3. ▸ Study based on interviews in six rural and urban locales in 1980. Concludes that for women equality

remains unfulfilled; rhetorical promises belied by rampant sexism. [JHC]

Economic History

11.650   Robert F. Dernberger, ed. *China's development experience in comparative perspective.* Cambridge, Mass.: Harvard University Press, 1980. ISBN 0-674-11890-1. ▸ Topics include central features of China's economic development (Perkins), regional growth and income distribution (Lardy), technology (Rawski), health care (Hu), and characteristics of nation's economic model specific to China (Feuerwerker). [JHC]

11.651   Christopher Howe. *China's economy: a basic guide.* New York: Basic Books, 1978. ISBN 0-465-01099-7. ▸ Reliable, nontechnical survey of People's Republic's economy, 1949–77, covering population, human resources, organization, planning, agriculture, industry, foreign trade, money, prices, and standard of living. [JHC]

11.652   Nicholas R. Lardy. *Economic growth and distribution in China.* Cambridge: Cambridge University Press, 1978. ISBN 0-521-21904-3. ▸ Analysis focuses on attempt to pursue somewhat contradictory goals of decentralized economic administration and centralized economic planning in nonagricultural sectors, particularly industry and government services. Covers through fourth Five Year Plan (1971–75). [JHC]

11.653   Dwight H. Perkins. "Research on the economy of the People's Republic of China: a survey of the field." *Journal of Asian studies* 42.2 (1983) 345–72. ISSN 0021-9118. ▸ Treats Western studies in following categories: quantification, macroanalysis, planning and management, incentives and income distribution, agriculture, industry, foreign trade, and historical heritage. Includes substantial bibliography. [JHC]

11.654   Carl Riskin. *China's political economy: the quest for development since 1949.* 1987 ed. Oxford: Oxford University Press, 1988. ISBN 0-19-877089-8 (cl), 0-19-877090-1 (pbk). ▸ Excellent exposition of economic development and its intersections with social and political dynamics through 1984. Finds Mao alternated between unsatisfactory alternatives of rigid centralism and chaotic decentralization. [JHC]

11.655   Dorothy J. Solinger. *Chinese business under socialism: the politics of domestic commerce, 1949–1980.* Berkeley: University of California Press, 1984. ISBN 0-520-04975-6. ▸ Discussion of recurring cycle of three incompatible policies: from orderly bureaucratic (exemplified by high official Yao I-lin) to productive marketeer (Ch'en Yun) to egalitarian radical (Li Hsien-nien), then to bureaucratic again. [JHC]

11.656   Eduard B. Vermeer. *Water conservancy and irrigation in China: social, economic, and agrotechnical aspects.* The Hague: Leiden University Press, 1977. ISBN 90-6021-410-2. ▸ Topics include natural disasters, state relief, labor organization and mobilization, hydraulic education and research, flood prevention, irrigation, salinization, state allocations for construction, and major river basins (Yellow, Huai, Yangtze). [JHC]

11.657   John Wong. *Land reform in the People's Republic of China: institutional transformation in agriculture.* New York: Praeger, 1973. ▸ Focuses on 1945–52. Finds land reform was very restricted in terms of expropriation and redistribution; built on traditional patterns of rural cooperation. Lacks index. [JHC]

Intellectual and Cultural History

11.658   Clive M. Ansley. *The heresy of Wu Han: his play "Hai Jui's Dismissal" and its role in China's Cultural Revolution.* Toronto: University of Toronto Press, 1971. ISBN 0-8020-1665-0. ▸ English translation of important play with keen analysis of its significance as veiled attack on Mao Tse-tung, prompting Yao

Wen-yuan's counterattack which launched Cultural Revolution. Compare Pusey 11.684. [JHC]

11.659 David M. Bachman. *Chen Yun and the Chinese political system.* Berkeley: University of California, Center for Chinese Studies and Institute of East Asian Studies, 1985. (China research monographs, 29.) ISBN 0-912966-80-7 (pbk). ▸ Study of life and thought of Ch'en Yun, overseer of economic policy making, longest serving member of Communist party's Central Committee (since 1931). Includes chronological bibliography of Ch'en's writings, 1926–84. [JHC]

11.660 Richard C. Bush, Jr. *Religion in communist China.* Nashville, Tenn.: Abington, 1970. ISBN 0-687-36015-3. ▸ Focuses on Christianity (both Catholic and Protestant), including anti-imperialistic Three Self movement in 1950s promoting self-governed, self-financed, and self-propagated churches. Also treats Islam, Buddhism, Confucianism, Taoism, and popular religion. [JHC]

11.661 Arnold Chang. *Painting in the People's Republic of China: the politics of style.* Boulder: Westview, 1980. ISBN 0-89158-676-8. ▸ Well-illustrated study of politics of art. Finds arts policy cycled between periods of popularization (1949–56, 1966–71, 1974–76) and elevation (1958–65, 1971–74, 1977–) with 1957 as year of uncertainty and confusion. Also covers Mao Tse-tung's prescriptive Yenan Talks (1942). [JHC]

11.662 Theodore Hsi-en Chen. *Chinese education since 1949: academic and revolutionary models.* New York: Pergamon, 1981. ISBN 0-08-023861-0. ▸ As title indicates, educational policy since 1949 found to cycle between two models due to complementary vacillation between goals of development and revolution. [JHC]

11.663 Theodore Hsi-en Chen. *Thought reform of the Chinese intellectuals.* 1960 ed. Westport, Conn.: Hyperion, 1981. ISBN 0-8305-0001-4. ▸ Well-documented overview of campaigns, policies, and victims. Appendix includes "Titles of Published Confessions." [JHC]

11.664 Robert Chin and Ai-li S. Chin. *Psychological research in communist China: 1949–1966.* Cambridge, Mass.: MIT Press, 1969. ISBN 0-262-03032-2. ▸ Useful pioneering effort. Most interesting on moral character and individuality. Traces changes from Soviet phase to Great Leap Forward to incipient Cultural Revolution. Includes detailed list of Chinese psychological terminology. [JHC]

11.665 Paul Clark. *Chinese cinema: culture and politics since 1949.* Cambridge: Cambridge University Press, 1987. ISBN 0-521-32638-9. ▸ Focuses on expansion of mass national culture, relations among Communist party, artists, and audiences, and tensions between Yenan and Shanghai. Also treats pre-1949 cinema. Includes 1926–84 filmography. [JHC]

11.666 Ralph C. Croizier, ed. *China's cultural legacy and communism.* New York: Praeger, 1970. ▸ Anthology of primary and secondary sources treating communist policy toward cultural legacy, museums, monuments, history, archaeology, philosophy, religion, language, literature, opera, performing arts, painting, handicrafts, architecture, and science; also Cultural Revolution. [JHC]

11.667 Albert Feuerwerker, ed. *History in communist China.* Cambridge, Mass.: MIT Press, 1968. ▸ Seventeen contributions presenting wide-ranging survey of pre–Cultural Revolution Marxist historiography. Topics include archaeology, Confucianism, Buddhism, Ch'in-Han empire, Yuan dynasty, modern economic history, and Mao Tse-tung as historian. [JHC]

11.668 Albert Feuerwerker and S. Cheng. *Chinese communist studies of modern Chinese history.* 1961 ed. Cambridge, Mass.: Harvard University, East Asian Research Center, 1970. (Harvard East Asian monographs, 11.) ▸ Critical survey of over five hundred titles published 1949–59, mainly on period 1368–1949 (but

including some pre-1368). Useful for insights into 1950s historiographical debates, including attacks on historian Shang Yueh. [JHC]

11.669 Merle Goldman. *China's intellectuals: advise and dissent.* Cambridge, Mass.: Harvard University Press, 1981. ISBN 0-674-11970-3. ▸ Focuses on "liberal" and "radical" intellectuals and their political patrons (e.g., Chou En-lai and Mao Tse-tung respectively), 1959–76. Concludes that alternations in power between each group weakened effectiveness of monolithic ideology. [JHC]

11.670 Merle Goldman. *Literary dissent in communist China.* 1967 ed. New York: Atheneum, 1971. ▸ Excellent account of how nonconforming writers in 1940s and 1950s (e.g., Wang Shih-wei, Feng Hsueh-feng, Hu Feng, Ting Ling, Ho Ch'i-fang, Hsiao Chun) protested Communist party's thought control and were silenced. [JHC]

11.671 Merle Goldman, ed. *China's intellectuals and the state: in search of a new relationship.* Cambridge, Mass.: Harvard University, Council on East Asian Studies, 1987. (Harvard contemporary China series, 3.) ISBN 0-674-11972-X (pbk). ▸ Despite post-1976 focus, contributions also treat Marxist ideologue Ai Ssu-ch'i (Fogel), economists in 1960s (Halpern), historian Chien Po-tsan (Edmunds), self-perception of writers (Wagner), and moral critic Wang Jo-wang (Rubin). [JHC]

11.672 Carol Lee Hamrin and Timothy Cheek, eds. *China's establishment intellectuals.* Armonk, N.Y.: Sharpe, 1986. ISBN 0-87332-336-1 (cl), 0-87332-367-X (pbk). ▸ Studies of P'eng Chen, Yang Hsien-chen, Teng T'o, Sun Yeh-fang, and Wu Han as members of moral-intellectual-political priesthood. Also treats political-intellectual semi-outsider Pai Hua and alienation of youth in People's Republic. [JHC]

11.673 James P. Harrison. *The Communists and Chinese peasant rebellions: a study in the rewriting of Chinese history.* New York: Atheneum, 1969. ▸ Useful description, pointing up relative diversity of interpretations among historians in People's Republic. Also treats pre-1949 historiography (both communist, noncommunist). Appendix describes major peasant rebellions from pre-Ch'in period through Boxer Rebellion. [JHC]

11.674 Joe C. Huang. *Heroes and villains in communist China: the contemporary Chinese novel as a reflection of life.* New York: Pica, 1973. ISBN 0-87663-710-1. ▸ Analysis of how post-1949 novels portray major themes in Chinese communist history: underground operations against Nationalists and Japanese, guerrilla warfare, Civil War (1945–49), land reform, urban workers, agricultural collectivization, and People's Liberation Army. [JHC]

11.675 Richard Curt Kraus. *Pianos and politics in China: middle-class ambitions and the struggle over Western music.* New York: Oxford University Press, 1989. ISBN 0-19-505836-4. ▸ Analysis of controversies surrounding perception of Western and westernized music as elitist, cosmopolitan, and bourgeois. Treats composer Hsien Hsing-hai, pianists Fou Ts'ong, Yin Ch'eng-tsung, and Liu Shih-k'un, and Cultural Revolution's musical czarina Chiang Ch'ing. [JHC]

11.676 Ellen Johnston Laing. *The winking owl: art in the People's Republic of China.* Berkeley: University of California Press, 1988. ISBN 0-520-06097-0. ▸ Profusely illustrated study with focus on painting, especially 1960–76 (including Cultural Revolution), but also treats 1950s and woodcuts from 1930s onward. Ends with Mao Tse-tung's Memorial Hall (completed 1977). [JHC]

11.677 Robert Jay Lifton. *Thought reform and the psychology of totalism: a study of "brainwashing" in China.* 1961 ed. Chapel Hill: University of North Carolina Press, 1989. ISBN 0-8078-4253-2 (pbk). ▸ Classic analysis of communist techniques of psychological manipulation used on foreign prisoners and Chinese intellectuals (e.g., inducing guilt by compulsory rejection of filial piety). Based on Hong Kong emigré interviews. New preface by author. [JHC]

11.678 Kam Louie. *Critiques of Confucius in contemporary China.* New York: St. Martin's, 1980. ISBN 0-312-17645-7. ‣ Traces People's Republic's shifting ideological tides in appraising Confucian tradition, ranging from positive (early 1960s, post-1976) to highly negative (Cultural Revolution, including anti-Confucian campaign, 1973–74). [JHC]

11.679 Richard Madsen. *Morality and power in a Chinese village.* Berkeley: University of California Press, 1984. ISBN 0-520-04797-4. ‣ Political culture analysis finds fourfold typology of local leadership: communist gentry (Confucian-style patron), communist rebel (champion of disadvantaged), moralistic revolutionary (Maoist true-believer), and pragmatic technocrat (Liu Shao-ch'i loyalist). Based on Chan et al. 11.633. [JHC]

11.680 Helmut Martin. *Cult and canon: the origins and development of state Maoism.* Michel Vale, trans. Armonk, N.Y.: Sharpe, 1982. ISBN 0-87332-150-2. ‣ Although most detailed on post-1976 de-Maoization, also traces Maoism's earlier developmental stages as ideological orthodoxy, e.g., proto-Maoism (1935–49), canonization (early 1950s), editorial revisions (1960s), and Little Red Book (Cultural Revolution). Translation, with revisions, of *China ohne Maoismus? Wandlungen einer Staatsideologie* (1980). [JHC]

11.681 Bonnie S. McDougall, ed. *Popular Chinese literature and performing arts in the People's Republic of China, 1949–1979.* Berkeley: University of California Press, 1984. ISBN 0-520-04852-0. ‣ Contributions treat comedy routines, revolutionary songs, model opera, film, fiction and drama, novelist Hao Jan, poetry includes 1949–79 and pre-1949 overviews. [JHC]

11.682 Donald J. Munro. *The concept of man in contemporary China.* Ann Arbor: University of Michigan Press, 1977. ISBN 0-472-08677-4 (cl), 0-472-08678-2 (pbk). ‣ Excellent analysis of Maoism as theory of human nature. Examines both continuities and discontinuities with Confucianism. Stresses Maoism's nondistinction between public and private, and commitment to plasticity of human mind. [JHC]

11.683 Leo A. Orleans, ed. *Science in contemporary China.* Stanford, Calif.: Stanford University Press, 1980. ISBN 0-8047-1078-3. ‣ General overview treating science policy and organization, mathematics, physics, chemistry, astronomy, geography, earth sciences, meteorology, aquaculture, biomedicine, plant breeding, mineral sciences, engineering, energy, electronics, environmental science, and social sciences. [JHC]

11.684 James R. Pusey. *Wu Han: attacking the present through the past.* Cambridge, Mass.: Harvard University, East Asian Research Center, 1969. (Harvard East Asian monographs, 33.) ISBN 0-674-96275-3. ‣ Succinct account of momentous covert attack on Mao Tse-tung by Wu Han (symbol of failure of thought reform) via historical double-entendre. Resulting scholarly-literary controversy became flashpoint for Cultural Revolution (1966–76). [JHC]

11.685 Lucian W. Pye. *The mandarin and the cadre: China's political cultures.* Ann Arbor: University of Michigan, Center for Chinese Studies, 1988. (Michigan monographs in Chinese studies, 59.) ISBN 0-89264-082-0 (cl), 0-89264-083-9 (pbk). ‣ Often stimulating theoretical essay on Confucian Leninism, treating both Maoist and post-Maoist periods. By leading practitioner of psychohistory. [JHC]

11.686 Susan L. Shirk. *Competitive comrades: career incentives and student strategies in China.* Berkeley: University of California Press, 1982. ISBN 0-520-04299-9. ‣ Analysis of student behavior in urban high schools, mostly in 1970s Canton. Finds intense individual competition, privatism (emphasis on personal friend-

ships), suspicion of political activists, and emphasis on careerism via academic achievement. [JHC]

11.687 Anne F. Thurston. *Enemies of the people.* New York: Knopf, 1987. ISBN 0-394-55581-3. ‣ Sensitive, well-written case studies of intellectuals' victimization during Cultural Revolution (1966–76), characterized as failure of morality. Based on intensive psychologically oriented interviews with survivors, 1981–82. [JHC]

11.688 Constantine Tung and Colin Mackerras, eds. *Drama in the People's Republic of China.* Albany: State University of New York Press, 1987. ISBN 0-88706-389-6 (cl), 0-88706-390-X (pbk). ‣ Topics include historical dramas by Wu Han and Kuo Mo-jo, dramatic theory in Cultural Revolution, Mei Lan-fang, post–Cultural Revolution theater, and post-1949 performances of Ibsen. [JHC]

11.689 Jonathan Unger. *Education under Mao: class and competition in Canton schools, 1960–1980.* New York: Columbia University Press, 1982. ISBN 0-231-05298-7. ‣ Finds children of cadres, workers and peasants, "middle class," and "bad class" (former landlords) to constitute four increasingly self-aware student factions by 1965. Educational standards plummeted in 1970s due to Cultural Revolution. [JHC]

11.690 Rudolf G. Wagner. *The contemporary Chinese historical drama: four studies.* Berkeley: University of California Press, 1990. ISBN 0-520-05954-9. ‣ Brilliant analysis of subtexts: covert remonstrance via historical analogies (especially by playwright T'ien Han) and Maoist use of Monkey King, hero of famous novel *Journey to the West.* Includes numerous illustrations. [JHC]

11.691 Holmes Welch. *Buddhism under Mao.* Cambridge, Mass.: Harvard University Press, 1972. ISBN 0-674-08565-5. ‣ Contrasts pre–Cultural Revolution nominal policy of protecting, controlling, and utilizing Buddhism with actual destruction of monastaries, decimation of Sangha (congregations of monks, nuns), and suppression of Buddhist opposition. Then, under Cultural Revolution, conditions deteriorated further: includes discussion of Cultural Revolution's horrors. [JHC]

11.692 Siu-lun Wong. *Sociology and socialism in contemporary China.* London: Routledge & Kegan Paul, 1979. ISBN 0-7100-0089-8. ‣ Theory and practice of sociological and anthropological research in People's Republic. Topics include study of minority nationalities and compilation of local histories (of families, villages, communes, factories). Also treats pre-1949 period. [JHC]

SEE ALSO
10.347 Frederic E. Wakeman, Jr., ed. *Ming and Qing historical studies in the People's Republic of China.*

TAIWAN

Political History

11.693 Ralph N. Clough. *Island China.* Cambridge, Mass.: Harvard University Press, 1978. ISBN 0-674-46875-9. ‣ Treats Taiwan's relations with United States, People's Republic, and Japan; and Taiwan's political system, economy, and effect on United States–China relations. Appendix contains text of 1972 Shanghai Joint Communiqué. [JHC]

11.694 James West Davidson. *The island of Formosa, past and present: history, people, resources, and commercial prospects; tea, camphor, sugar, gold, coal, sulphur, economical plants, and other productions.* 1903 ed. Oxford: Oxford University Press, 1988. ISBN 0-19-584951-5. ‣ Pioneering compendium by United States consul. Still valuable on nineteenth-century political history and foreign relations, culminating in 1895 Japanese occupation and colonization. Also treats natural resources. Includes many rare photographs. [JHC]

11.695 Leonard H. D. Gordon, ed. *Taiwan: studies in Chinese local history.* New York: Columbia University Press, 1970. ISBN 0-231-03376-1. ‣ More than political history, contains useful contributions on gentry family (Meskill), 1895 anti-Japanese resistance (Lamley), nineteenth-century land tenure (Wickberg), and foreign relations, 1840–95 (Gordon). [JHC]

11.696 Mab Huang. *Intellectual ferment for political reforms in Taiwan, 1971–1973.* Ann Arbor: University of Michigan, Center for Chinese Studies, 1976. (Michigan papers in Chinese studies, 28.) ISBN 0-89264-028-6. ‣ Concludes young intellectuals, severely critical of tradition, paradoxically operated in traditional manner by failing to organize opposition party or seek support of peasants or workers. [JHC]

11.697 J. Bruce Jacobs. *Local politics in a rural Chinese cultural setting: a field study of Mazu township, Taiwan.* Canberra: Australian National University, Research School of Pacific Studies, Contemporary China Centre, 1980. ISBN 0-909590-3-4 (pbk). ‣ Emphasizes factionalism and importance of personal, particularistic ties in local electoral politics. Based on 1970s fieldwork in purely Hokkien region. [JHC]

11.698 George H. Kerr. *Formosa betrayed.* 1965 ed. New York: De Capo, 1976. ISBN 0-306-70762-4. ‣ Largely eyewitness description of Taiwanese victimization by newly-arrived Kuomintang (Nationalist party) mainlanders after 1945 Japanese surrender. Includes vivid account of February 28 Incident (1947), ensuing massacre, and United States government's acquiescence. [JHC]

11.699 George H. Kerr. *Formosa: licensed revolution and the home rule movement, 1895–1945.* Honolulu: University of Hawaii Press, 1974. ISBN 0-8248-0323-X. ‣ Study of Japanese colonization of Taiwan, their administrative and economic reforms, Taiwanese movement to mitigate discriminatory Japanese policies and increase island's autonomy, anti-Japanese rebellions, and Taiwan's role in World War II. [JHC]

11.700 Lai Tse-han, Ramon H. Myers, and Wei Wou. *A tragic beginning: the Taiwan Uprising of February 28, 1947.* Stanford, Calif.: Stanford University Press, 1991. ISBN 0-8047-1829-1. ‣ Finds multiple causes for violent clash between Taiwanese and mainlanders: deteriorating economy post-1945; incompetent leadership of corrupt governor Ch'en I; undermanned Nationalist garrison; and collision between radicalized Taiwanese expectations and Nationalists' shift from conciliation to repression. [JHC]

11.701 Mark Mancall, ed. *Formosa today.* New York: Praeger, 1964. ‣ Obviously dated but still useful essays on politics, economic growth, armed forces, foreign policy, intellectuals, literature, Formosan nationalism, independence movement, and outline of Taiwan's history; long introduction by editor. [JHC]

11.702 Douglas Mendel. *The politics of Formosan nationalism.* Berkeley: University of California Press, 1970. ISBN 0-520-01557-6. ‣ Description of Taiwanese attitudes toward ruling Kuomintang (Nationalist party), relations with mainlanders, and Taiwan independence movement through 1968. Appendix contains text of Peng Ming-min's 1966 Declaration of Formosans. Based largely on interviews 1957–68. [JHC]

11.703 Paul K. T. Sih, ed. *Taiwan in modern times.* New York: St. John's University Press, 1973. ISBN 0-87075-067-4. ‣ Topics include early sinicization to 1683, Dutch and Spanish rule, Coxinga, Taiwan in China's foreign relations 1683–1874, internal development 1683–1891, Taiwan republic 1895, Japanese colonial period 1895–1945, and post-1945 development. [JHC]

11.704 Christine Vertente, Hsu Hsueh-chi, and Wu Mi-cha. *The authentic story of Taiwan: an illustrated history, based on ancient maps, manuscripts, and prints.* Marc Hutsebaut, ed. Knokke, Belgium: Mappamundi, 1991. ISBN 90-6958-010-1. ‣ General discussion from earliest times through 1945 with emphasis on ca. 1500–1895. Includes many lavish color illustrations, mainly from European sources since sixteenth century. Text in both English and Chinese. [JHC]

11.705 Yu San Wang, ed. *Foreign policy of the Republic of China on Taiwan: an unorthodox approach.* New York: Praeger, 1990. ISBN 0-275-93471-3. ‣ Treats post-1945 relations with United States, Japan, South Korea, Southeast Asia, Middle East, Western Europe, Africa, Latin America, Canada, and People's Republic. Almost all contributors are Taiwan-based academics. [JHC]

Social History

11.706 Emily M. Ahern and Hill Gates, eds. *The anthropology of Taiwanese society.* Stanford, Calif.: Stanford University Press, 1981. ISBN 0-8047-1043-0. ‣ Topics include local politics, state-society relations, local and regional systems, social organization, ecology, factory women, land tenure, subethnic rivalry, ethnicity and social class, voluntary associations, family organization and division, and sexual politics. [JHC]

11.707 George W. Barclay. *Colonial development and population in Taiwan.* 1954 ed. Port Washington, N.Y.: Kennikat, 1972. ISBN 0-8046-1623-X. ‣ Covers Japanese colonial period (1895–1945). Still useful discussion of population growth, economic development, manpower, migration, urbanization, public health, family, marriage, and divorce. Finds traditionally high fertility and drastically reduced morbidity. Based on Japanese-compiled census records 1905–35. [JHC]

11.708 Myron L. Cohen. *House united, house divided: the Chinese family in Taiwan.* New York: Columbia University Press, 1976. ISBN 0-231-03849-6. ‣ Finds advantage of pooling resources in diversified local economy as reason why large, extended families, uncommon elsewhere in Taiwan, predominate in nonelite village of Hakka tobacco growers. Based on 1964–65 fieldwork. [JHC]

11.709 Norma Diamond. *K'un Shen: a Taiwanese village.* New York: Holt, Reinhart & Winston, 1969. ISBN 0-03-080960-6. ‣ Ethnography of fishing village near Tainan, treating economic relations, life cycle, family, household and lineage, village and community, and religion. Finds life not yet disrupted by process of modernization as of mid-1960s. [JHC]

11.710 Bernard Gallin. *Hsin Hsing, Taiwan: a Chinese village in change.* Berkeley: University of California Press, 1966. ‣ Ethnography finds urbanization-induced decline of village as community with increased independence (both of family from village and lineage and of individual from family). Based on 1957–58 fieldwork near Taichung. [JHC]

11.711 Hill Gates. *Chinese working-class lives: getting by in Taiwan.* Ithaca, N.Y.: Cornell University Press, 1987. ISBN 0-8014-2056-3 (cl), 0-8014-9461-3 (pbk). ‣ Combines analysis with life histories of nine urban workers (both Taiwanese and mainlander) in their own words. Based largely on 1980 fieldwork. Includes useful bibliographical essay. [JHC]

11.712 Stevan Harrell. *Ploughshare village: culture and context in Taiwan.* Seattle: University of Washington Press, 1982. (Publications on Asia of the School of International Studies, University of Washington, 35.) ISBN 0-295-95946-0. ‣ Stimulating ethnography of nonagrarian coal-mining and knitting village analyzed in larger context. Concludes social organization remained largely stable, despite major changes in political economy. Based on fieldwork 1972–73, 1978. [JHC]

11.713 Ronald G. Knapp, ed. *China's island frontier: studies in the historical geography of Taiwan.* Honolulu: University of Hawaii Press and the Research Corporation of the University of Hawaii,

1980. ISBN 0-8248-0743-X. ▸ Topics include pre-1683 development, aboriginal migration, frontier land tenure and social organization, settlement of I-lan plain, walled cities and towns, Lukang city, transport networks 1600–1972, railroads, and sugar industry. [JHC]

11.714 Lydia Kung. *Factory women in Taiwan.* Ann Arbor: UMI Research Press, 1983. ISBN 0-8357-1497-7. ▸ Finds old wine in new bottles: young female factory workers remain bound by role expectations determined by their families. Women workers still lack discretionary control over income. [JHC]

11.715 Johanna Menzel Meskill. *A Chinese pioneer family: the Lins of Wu-feng, Taiwan, 1729–1895.* Princeton: Princeton University Press, 1979. ISBN 0-691-03124-X. ▸ Outstanding study of clan's transformation from strongmen to gentlemen. Finds indigenous common-surname clans typified Taiwan's frontier society, rather than demonstrated-descent lineages typical of mainland. Concludes that clan or communal ties prevailed over class. [JHC]

11.716 Burton Pasternak. *Guests in the dragon: social demography of a Chinese district, 1895–1946.* New York: Columbia University Press, 1983. ISBN 0-231-05610-9. ▸ Analysis of Taiwanese Hakka village survival strategies as expressed via social organization (e.g., nonlocalized descent groups) and marriage (designed to maximize extra-village alliances). Based on computer analysis of household registers. [JHC]

11.717 Burton Pasternak. *Kinship and community in two Chinese villages.* Stanford, Calif.: Stanford University Press, 1972. ISBN 0-8047-0823-1. ▸ Revisionist analysis of differences in social organization between 1960s Hakka and Hokkien villages. Finds key variable is not urbanization or ethnicity but frontier, which required extensive cooperation among unrelated family and lineage units. [JHC]

11.718 Arthur P. Wolf and Huang Chieh-shan. *Marriage and adoption in China, 1854–1945.* Stanford, Calif.: Stanford University Press, 1980. ISBN 0-8047-1027-9. ▸ Study focusing on Taipei region's high prevalence of sexually dysfunctional marriages (girl adopted young, raised with family's son, whom she eventually weds). Emphasizes regional variation. Based on Japanese-compiled household registers. [JHC]

11.719 Margery Wolf. *The house of Lim: a study of a Chinese farm family.* New York: Appleton-Century-Crofts, 1968. ▸ Classic, beautifully written revelation of rural Taiwanese extended family spanning four generations, trying to withstand divisive forces. Based on 1959–61 fieldwork. Includes substantive foreword by Maurice Freedman. [JHC]

11.720 Margery Wolf. *Women and the family in rural Taiwan.* Stanford, Calif.: Stanford University Press, 1972. ISBN 0-8047-0808-8 (cl), 0-8047-0849-5 (pbk). ▸ Absorbing analysis of how women view life cycle and family dynamics. Emphasizes importance of uterine family (mother and her children) as alternative to orthodox male ideology of patrilineal kinship. [JHC]

Economic History

11.721 Walter Galenson, ed. *Economic growth and structural change in Taiwan: the post-war experience of the Republic of China.* Ithaca, N.Y.: Cornell University Press, 1979. ISBN 0-8014-1157-2. ▸ Contributions treat growth and structural shifts (Kuznets), agricultural and industrial development (Thorbecke, Ranis), fiscal and monetary policies (Lundberg), foreign trade (Scott), labor force, wages, living standards (Galenson), and overview (Little). [JHC]

11.722 Thomas B. Gold. *State and society in the Taiwan miracle.* Armonk, N.Y.: Sharpe, 1986. ISBN 0-87332-349-1 (cl), 0-87332-350-5 (pbk). ▸ Fine analysis of reasons for Taiwan's successful development under authoritarian Kuomintang (Nationalist

party), including *de facto* American support for Taiwanese-dominated private sector, and intraparty triumph of technocrats over ideologues. Also treats pre-1945 period. [JHC]

11.723 Samuel P. S. Ho. *Economic development of Taiwan, 1860–1970.* New Haven: Yale University Press, 1978. ISBN 0-300-02087-2. ▸ Concludes agricultural changes occurring early in twentieth century were as significant to development as spectacular post-1960 industrial growth. Includes 165-page statistical appendix. [JHC]

11.724 K. T. Li. *The evolution of policy behind Taiwan's development success.* Gustave Ranis, Introduction. John Fei, Introduction. New Haven: Yale University Press, 1988. ISBN 0-300-04080-6. ▸ Discussion of population policy, manpower policy, and export processing zones; emphasizes importance of pragmatism. By former minister of economic affairs and finance (1965–76). Includes substantive introductory essays. [JHC]

11.725 Edwin A. Winckler and Susan Greenhalgh, eds. *Contending approaches to the political economy of Taiwan.* Armonk, N.Y.: Sharpe, 1988. ISBN 0-87332-440-4 (cl), 0-87332-771-3 (pbk). ▸ Topics include world-system patterns and elite-mass relations 1500–1980, income distribution, colonial origins of Taiwanese capitalism, elite political struggles 1945–85, internal reform, American influence, entrepreneurs, technology transfer, and families and networks. [JHC]

Intellectual and Cultural History

11.726 Emily M. Ahern. *The cult of the dead in a Chinese village.* Stanford, Calif.: Stanford University Press, 1973. ISBN 0-8047-0835-5. ▸ Analysis of ancestor worship, practice of reburial, geomancy, and influence of community type on popular religion. Based on fieldwork 1969–70. Includes striking photographs of filial bone-cleaning preceding reburial. [JHC]

11.727 David K. Jordan. *Gods, ghosts, and ancestors: the folk religion of a Taiwanese village.* Berkeley: University of California Press, 1972. ISBN 0-520-01962-8. ▸ Focuses on belief in ghosts and manipulation of gods via spirit mediums' divination. Finds ongoing dialogue with supernatural, permitting flexible updating of revelation. Based on 1966–68 fieldwork. Includes dramatic photographs. [JHC]

11.728 David K. Jordan and Daniel L. Overmyer. *The flying phoenix: aspects of Chinese sectarianism in Taiwan.* Princeton: Princeton University Press, 1986. ISBN 0-691-07304-X. ▸ Successfully combines anthropologist Jordan's fieldwork and historian Overmyer's textual analysis to study longstanding form of popular religion based on spirit-writing seances, wherein possessed adepts produce divinely inspired texts. [JHC]

11.729 P. Steven Sangren. *History and magical power in a Chinese community.* Stanford, Calif.: Stanford University Press, 1987. ISBN 0-8047-1344-8. ▸ Uses 1976–77 fieldwork in Taiwanese standard marketing community (town plus subordinate villages) to launch sophisticated theoretical analysis emphasizing close relationship between society and cosmology, distinctive cultural logic structuring historical events. [JHC]

11.730 E. Patricia Tsurumi. *Japanese colonial education in Taiwan, 1895–1945.* Cambridge, Mass.: Harvard University Press, 1977. ISBN 0-674-47187-3. ▸ Standard work on enthusiastic, fairly successful Japanese effort to universalize elementary education among Taiwanese population and reluctant establishment of higher education. Includes impact of unprecedented public education for women. Shows importance of education to Japanese development policies. [JHC/FN]

11.731 Robert P. Weller. *Unities and diversities in Chinese religion.* Seattle: University of Washington Press, 1987. ISBN 0-295-96397-2. ▸ Analysis of diversity of beliefs both between and within popular and elite religion through case study of annual Buddhist-Taoist ghost-feeding ritual. Finds no correlation between social class and belief. Based on fieldwork 1976–79. [JHC]

11.732 Richard W. Wilson. *Learning to be Chinese: the political socialization of children in Taiwan.* Cambridge, Mass.: MIT Press, 1970. ISBN 0-262-23041-0. ▸ Analysis of formidable psychological pressures for conformity to authority (e.g., shaming, loss of face) brought to bear on elementary-school children. Based on in-class observation, questionnaires, interviews, and examination of educational materials 1965–66. [JHC]

11.733 Arthur P. Wolf, ed. *Religion and ritual in Chinese society.* Stanford, Calif.: Stanford University Press, 1974. ISBN 0-8047-0858-4. ▸ After Maurice Freedman's overview, topics include village temples, architecture, shamanism, ancestor worship, and Taoist ritual. Virtually all based on Taiwan or Hong Kong fieldwork. Best contribution: Wolf's "Gods, Ghosts, Ancestors." [JHC]

HONG KONG AND MACAO

Political History

11.734 C. R. Boxer. *Fidalgos in the Far East, 1550–1770: fact and fancy in the history of Macao.* 2d ed. Hong Kong: Oxford University Press, 1968. ISBN 0-19-638074-X. ▸ Well-written narrative by expert on Portuguese colonial history. Study of key episodes and periods based on Portuguese, Dutch, and Japanese sources. Appendix includes list of governors- and captains-general. [JHC]

11.735 Nigel Cameron. *An illustrated history of Hong Kong.* Hong Kong: Oxford University Press, 1991. ISBN 0-19-584997-3. ▸ Lightly annotated overview through 1984, treating socioeconomics as well as politics and administration. Includes maps and statistical appendixes. [JHC]

11.736 Chan Lau Kit-ching. *China, Britain, and Hong Kong, 1895–1945.* Hong Kong: Chinese University Press, 1990. ISBN 962-201-409-7. ▸ Solid account of how political developments in China (especially Kwangtung province) and Hong Kong affected each other, e.g., 1911 Revolution, 1920s strikes, Kuomintang (Nationalist party) politics, and Sino-Japanese War. Includes rare photographs. [JHC]

11.737 Austin Coates. *A Macao narrative.* 1978 ed. Hong Kong: Oxford University Press, 1987. ISBN 0-19-584201-4 (pbk). ▸ Succinct, well-written (albeit episodic) overview for general reader, from sixteenth century to 1945. Not footnoted but includes useful bibliography, illustrations, and rare maps. [JHC]

11.738 G. B. Endacott. *A history of Hong Kong.* Rev. ed. London: Oxford University Press, 1973. ▸ Standard work, focusing on politics and administration as seen through eyes of governors and Colonial Office. Based on Colonial Office archives. Appendixes list tenures of governors and colonial secretaries. [JHC]

11.739 G. B. Endacott. *Hong Kong eclipse.* Alan Birch, ed. Hong Kong: Oxford University Press, 1978. ISBN 0-19-580374-4 (cl), 0-19-580375-2 (pbk). ▸ Narrative of 1938–48 period, especially Hong Kong's capture and occupation by Japanese (1941–45) and wartime conditions. Includes illustrations and obituary of Endacott. [JHC]

11.740 C. A. Montalto de Jesus. *Historic Macao: international traits in China old and new.* 1926 2d ed. Hong Kong: Oxford University Press, 1984. ISBN 0-19-581582-3. ▸ Still the only full-scale general history of Macao in English, covering sixteenth century to mid-1920s. Based on Western (especially Portuguese, but not British) sources. Includes illustrations, maps, and valuable new introduction. [JHC]

11.741 Kevin Lane. *Sovereignty and the status quo: the historical roots of China's Hong Kong policy.* Boulder: Westview, 1990. ISBN 0-8133-7681-5 (pbk). ▸ Analyzes Chinese rhetoric and actions concerning Hong Kong since 1912. Contrasts unyielding insistence on China's sovereignty by both Nationalists and Communists with their *de facto* acceptance, even support, of colonial status quo. [JHC]

11.742 Rance P. L. Lee, ed. *Corruption and its control in Hong Kong: situations up to the late seventies.* Hong Kong: Chinese University Press, 1981. ISBN 962-201-251-5. ▸ Contributions treat history of anticorruption legislation, Independent Commission Against Corruption (established 1974), incompatibility of legal codes and folk norms, nineteenth-century bureaucratic corruption and political instability, bribery of officials, and police corruption. [JHC]

11.743 Norman Miners. *The government and politics of Hong Kong.* 5th ed. Hong Kong: Oxford University Press, 1991. ISBN 0-19-585424-1 (cl), 0-19-585425-X (pbk). ▸ Standard work describing social and economic context, institutions of government, and pressures and influences. Appendix contains five constitutional documents from 1898 Peking Convention to 1988 Basic Law (as approved 1990). [JHC]

11.744 Norman Miners. *Hong Kong under imperial rule, 1912–1941.* Hong Kong: Oxford University Press, 1987. ISBN 0-19-584171-9. ▸ Topics include Colonial Office, governors, executive council, legislative council, civil service, finance, abolition of sale of daughters, state regulation of prostitution, and control of opium. Based on British Public Records Office archives. [JHC]

11.745 Ian Scott. *Political change and the crisis of legitimacy in Hong Kong.* Honolulu: University of Hawaii Press, 1989. ISBN 0-8248-1269-7. ▸ Analysis of 1842–1966 unreformed colonial state, 1966–67 riots, subsequent reforms, autonomy 1972–82, Sino-British negotiations 1982–84, changing economic and social structure, and post-Agreement politics. Includes texts of 1984 Sino-British Agreement and 1988 Basic Law. [JHC]

11.746 Peter Wesley-Smith. *Unequal treaty, 1898–1997: China, Great Britain, and Hong Kong's New Territories.* 1980 ed. Hong Kong: Oxford University Press, 1983. ISBN 0-19-583727-4 (pbk). ▸ Standard work on 1898 Peking Convention leasing New Territories to Britain. Treats negotiations, implementation, local armed resistance, later Chinese diplomacy for revision, and differing treaty interpretations. Includes textual appendixes and illustrations. [JHC]

Social History

11.747 Hugh D. R. Baker. *A Chinese lineage village: Sheung Shui.* Stanford, Calif.: Stanford University Press, 1968. ▸ Local history set in Hong Kong's New Territories describes single-surname village, common in South China. Concludes with discussion of increasing changes since 1898. [JHC]

11.748 Chan Wai Kwan. *The making of Hong Kong society: three studies of class formation in early Hong Kong.* New York: Oxford University Press, 1991. ISBN 0-19-827320-7. ▸ Discussion of Jardine, Matheson & Company and British merchant class, emergence of Chinese leadership (case study of Tung Wah Hospital), Chinese merchant class, and laboring class and 1922 Seaman's Strike. [JHC]

11.749 David Faure. *The structure of Chinese rural society: lineage and village in the eastern New Territories, Hong Kong.* Hong Kong: Oxford University Press, 1986. ISBN 0-19-583970-6. ▸ Covers ca. 1400–1900, rejecting elite-centered interpretation of lineages. For most lineage members, right of settlement inherited from founding ancestor was far more valuable than association with officialdom. [JHC]

11.750 David Faure, James Hayes, and Alan Birch, eds. *From village to city: studies in the traditional roots of Hong Kong society.*

Hong Kong: University of Hong Kong, Centre of Asian Studies, 1984. (Centre of Asian Studies occasional papers and monographs, 60.) ISSN 0378-2689. ▸ Topics include early Ch'ing coastal evacuation, gentry family, village life, rural and urban education, funerals, rural voluntary associations, charity during Japanese occupation (1941–45), and landlord-tenant relations. Includes illustrations and maps. [JHC]

11.751 James Hayes. *The Hong Kong region, 1850–1911: institutions and leadership in town and countryside.* Hamden, Conn.: Archon, 1977. ISBN 0-208-01626-0. ▸ Case studies emphasizing successful leadership by commoners (peasants, shopkeepers) in New Territories' villages, due partially to paucity of resident gentry landlords. Also covers Kowloon City. [JHC]

11.752 Ian C. Jarvie and Joseph Agassi, eds. *Hong Kong: a society in transition.* New York: Praeger, 1969. ▸ Topics include rural society, social stratification, Japanese occupation (1941–45), Hakka community, westernization, role of savings and wealth, economic development, urban housing, narcotics, tuberculosis, bilingualism, and university students. [JHC]

11.753 Ambrose Y. C. King and Rance P. L. Lee, eds. *Social life and development in Hong Kong.* Hong Kong: Chinese University Press, 1981. ISBN 962-201-239-6. ▸ Topics include new towns, public housing, small factories, population mobility, grassroots politics, political culture, utilitarian familism, fertility decline, health care, urban religion, and face saving. Includes extensive English-language bibliography. [JHC]

11.754 Almerindo Lessa. *L'histoire et les hommes de la première république démocratique de l'Orient: anthropobiologie et anthroposociologie de Macao.* Paris: Centre National de la Recherche Scientifique, 1974. ▸ Interdisciplinary analysis of history of ethnic variety and convergence within Macao's population (Chinese, Portuguese, Sino-Portuguese), from sixteenth to twentieth century. Based partly on 1960 survey of 7,243 residents. Includes statistical analyses of blood samples. Also available in Portuguese, *A historia e os homens da primeira republica democratica do Oriente: biologia e sociologia de uma ilha civica* (1974). [JHC]

11.755 Jack M. Potter. *Capitalism and the Chinese peasant: social and economic change in a Hong Kong village.* Berkeley: University of California Press, 1968. ▸ Rejects Marxist-Leninist characterization of treaty ports (e.g., Hong Kong) as deleterious to their hinterlands. Concludes rise of Western-type capitalist economy has improved economic conditions of rural villages. [JHC]

11.756 Janet W. Salaff. *Working daughters of Hong Kong: filial piety or power in the family?* Cambridge: Cambridge University Press, 1981. ISBN 0-521-23679-7 (cl), 0-521-28148-2 (pbk). ▸ Examination of family relations of twenty-eight unmarried female workers in various sectors (factory, service, white-collar, semi-professional). Finds increasing rejection of unrewarded familial duty. Based on 1971–76 fieldwork. [JHC]

11.757 James L. Watson. *Emigration and the Chinese lineage: the Mans in Hong Kong and London.* Berkeley: University of California Press, 1975. ISBN 0-520-02647-0. ▸ Study of single-lineage village specializing since early 1960s in exporting restaurant workers for London's Chinatown. Finds emigration helped preserve village's traditional culture. Based on 1969–71 fieldwork. [JHC]

11.758 Rubie S. Watson. *Inequality among brothers: class and kinship in South China.* Cambridge: Cambridge University Press, 1985. ISBN 0-521-26770-6. ▸ Analysis of single-lineage village of rich landlord-merchants and subservient smallholder-tenants since seventeenth century. Finds pre-1960s lineage played important role in maintaining system of class privilege. Based partly on 1977–78 fieldwork. [JHC]

Economic History

11.759 Joseph Y. S. Cheng, ed. *Hong Kong in transition.* Hong Kong: Oxford University Press, 1986. ISBN 0-19-584061-5 (pbk). ▸ Topics include changing political culture, political system, law, banking, economic policy, trade, industry, land tenure, economic relations with China, labor, education, public housing, transport, social welfare, and news media. [JHC]

11.760 Colin N. Crisswell. *The taipans, Hong Kong's merchant princes.* Hong Kong: Oxford University Press, 1981. ISBN 0-19-580495-3. ▸ Popularly written narrative on prominent non-Chinese (e.g., Jardine, Matheson & Company; Sassoon family) trading in opium, etc., in Hong Kong, Macao, and Canton through 1914. Includes rare illustrations. [JHC]

11.761 Frank H. H. King. *The history of the Hongkong and Shanghai Banking Corporation.* 4 vols. Cambridge: Cambridge University Press, 1987–91. ISBN 0-521-32706-7 (v. 1), 0-521-32707-5 (v. 2), 0-521-32708-3 (v. 3), 0-521-32709-1 (v. 4). ▸ Monumental, commissioned company history of Hong Kong's leading private (albeit quasi semi-official) financial institution, 1864–1984, by outstanding specialist committed to unvarnished truth. Based on bank's archives, other collected private papers (especially of Sir Charles Addis), and oral histories. [JHC]

11.762 Ng Sek-Hong and Victor Fung-Shuen Sit. *Labour relations and labour conditions in Hong Kong: a study prepared for the International Labour Office.* Basingstoke: Macmillan, 1989. ISBN 0-333-49123-8. ▸ Analysis of institutional framework, trade union organizations, collective bargaining, industrial conflict, working conditions, wages, women and young workers, subcontract labor, and foreign investment, all with attention to historical perspective. Includes numerous statistical tables. [JHC]

11.763 Siu-lun Wong. *Emigrant entrepreneurs: Shanghai industrialists in Hong Kong.* Hong Kong: Oxford University Press, 1988. ISBN 0-19-584213-8. ▸ Focuses on post-1949 emigrants' use of regional and familistic ties to dominate Hong Kong's cotton spinning industry. Analyzes characteristics of their entrepreneurship. Based on interviews (1978) and company records. [JHC]

Intellectual and Cultural History

11.764 Morris I. Berkowitz, Frederick P. Brandauer, and John H. Reed. *Folk religion in an urban setting: a study of Hakka villagers in transition.* Hong Kong: Christian Study Centre on Chinese Religion and Culture, 1969. ▸ Study of members of distinct Chinese ethnic group resettled in 1966 from village of 600 to market town of 10,000. Treats life environments, celebration of festivals, worship of supernatural beings, rites of passage, and ancestor worship. [JHC]

Section 12

MARTIN COLLCUTT

Premodern Japan

With the proliferation of books and articles now being published about premodern Japanese history, it is virtually impossible for any one person to keep abreast about research for the whole premodern area. As in other areas of historical research, there has been a considerable sharpening of focus and narrowing of specialization in the past few decades. There has also been a proliferation of approaches.

This section presents a selection of the more recent work dealing with the very broad sweep of Japanese history from earliest times to the nineteenth century. Most references are to research in English. It should be remembered that there is a vast, ever growing body of material in Japanese and a substantial amount in French, German, Russian, Korean, Chinese, and other languages. Some basic references are provided to afford access to research on Japanese history in Japanese and European languages, but the main emphasis here is on materials readily available in English.

Periodization of Japanese history is intricate and not all scholars agree on precise dividing lines. This section adopts a periodization corresponding to the Japanese categorization *genshi* (pre- and protohistoric), *kodai* (ancient), *chūsei* (medieval), and *kinsei* (early modern). Each of these broad periods is further subdivided into commonly accepted subperiods.

Prehistoric Japan covers the preceramic paleolithic (pre-10,000 BCE), Jōmon (10,000–300) and Yayoi (300 BCE–300 CE) periods. The protohistoric phase includes the Tumulus period (ca. 300–600), the latter part of which is sometimes referred to as the Yamato period, after the name of first recognizably powerful dynasty that extended its influence outward from the Yamato region during these centuries.

Ancient Japan embraces the Asuka (593–ca. 710), Nara (710–784), and Heian (794–1185) periods. This phase is characterized by the introduction and diffusion of Buddhism, the elaboration of Chinese-style institutions of centralized imperial bureaucratic rule known as the *ritsuryō* state, and the appearance of settled capital cities at Fujiwara, Heijō (Nara), and Heian. The centralized imperial state was at its peak in the Nara period (710–784) and the first century of the Heian period (794–1185); but, from the tenth century, it was eroded by the development of privatized land holdings (*shōen*) and private local military power in the form of provincial warrior bands (*bushidan*) whose influence eventually intruded into politics at the capital.

The Japanese term *chūsei*, middle centuries, is commonly applied to the period from the mid-twelfth to the sixteenth century, embracing the late Heian, Kamakura, and Muromachi eras. Among the distinguishing features of the Japanese "medieval" age are the steady displacement of the imperial court from the center of the political arena, increasing warrior domination of society, warrior government in the form of shogunates (*bakufu*) or provincial warrior domains (*daimyō*), the militarization of society, tightening of vertical ties between warriors and their leaders, weakness at the political center, and growing decentralization of rule and civil war. The tide of war and political fragmentation reached its peak in the age of wars (*sengoku*) of the late fifteenth and early sixteenth centuries.

The categorization of medieval Japan simply as a dark and war-torn age, however, is misleading. Scholars have shown the cohesive and creative features of the age. In the realm of culture and religion the medieval period witnessed the flourishing of warrior-sponsored arts, crafts, and culture. It saw the population and diffusion of Pure Land, Zen, and Nichiren Buddhism as new, and more accessible, paths to salvation. These centuries also witnessed the erosion of private estates (*shōen*), an agricultural surplus and double cropping, market development, urbanization, and commercial and foreign contacts. In commerce it saw the growth of central guilds (*za*) and their challenge by *daimyō* and local merchants. At the village level, self-governing communities appeared and there were rural protests (*ikki*) and religious uprisings (Ikkō *ikki*).

The concept and term medieval (*chūsei*) is borrowed from European history. It is widely used, often in conjunction with the notion of feudal, but neither term is a perfect fit. Some Japanese scholars still think of these centuries of growing warrior domination and periodic shogunates, including the Kamakura and Muromachi eras, as an early phase of feudalism, continuing until 1867. Others question the applicability of the essentially European concept of feudalism to Japanese society or restrict it to the age of wars in the late fifteenth and sixteenth centuries when vertical ties between individuals reached deepest into the warrior society.

While a few scholars may still think of the period of warrior domination of Japanese society between the twelfth and the nineteenth century as one long military or feudal age, most Japanese and Western scholars make a distinction between Japanese society before and after 1600. Tokugawa Japan (1600–1867) is marked by two centuries of peace, relative isolation from the Western world, stable political authority exercized through the shared shogunal-domain (*baku-han*) system of rule, growth in population and agricultural output, urbanization, commerce, mass culture, and a well-defined status system. The term *kinsei* (proximate age) is widely used to describe this period. Neutral in Japanese, this word has been translated into English as "early modern" in order to point to developmental comparisons with early modern Europe and to stress its role as a prelude to modern Japanese political and economic development.

There is fairly general agreement that the basis for these political and social changes, and for the long Pax Tokugawa, lay in the reunification of the country by Oda Nobunaga and Toyotomi Hideyoshi in the late sixteenth century. Historians therefore usually date the early modern period from the second half of the sixteenth century. It thus generally includes the Azuchi-Momoyama as well as Tokugawa periods.

Within each of the major periods outlined above, entries are grouped, when the amount of research justifies it, under the headings of political, economic, cultural, intellectual, and foreign relations. For the Tokugawa period, where most premodern research tends to cluster, the subsections and entries are more numerous.

Since the last *Guide* was published, there have been striking achievements in the range, quantity, and quality of research on Japanese history in English and other European languages. This research derives from the commitment and scholarly productivity of older historians and the burgeoning of a well-trained cohort of younger scholars who have benefitted from the building of strong graduate programs in East Asian history in the United States and more recently in European universities, ready access to graduate training and research in Japan, and the cooperation and collegiality of

Japanese historians in discussing research and participating in conferences. It has been spurred by debates, differences of interpretation, and experimentation with different theoretical approaches, and encouraged by a widespread interest in Japan, sharpened by the growing visibility of Japan on the international stage. In fact, this effort to understand or explain modern Japan may be seen as one of the driving forces in the development of premodern Japanese history. Interpretations of the meaning of Japan's development since the Meiji Restoration of 1867 have inevitably affected the approach and tone of research about earlier periods, especially the Tokugawa period, and sharpened the interpretive debates among scholars.

There have been several broad currents in the post–World War II study of Japan. The major revision of premodern Japanese history in the West was the reaction against the view of the Tokugawa period as an oppressive feudal society, advocated in Japan by predominately Marxist-influenced historians and by E. H. Norman in the West. Revisionists, led by J. W. Hall and M. B. Jansen, favored a positive, institutional, bureaucratic assessment of Tokugawa society. Their ideas were detailed in the still authoritative studies of the Tokugawa *bakufu* and domains, produced in the 1960s and 1970s by C. Totman, A. Craig, and H. Bolitho, and deepened through the steady exposure within Tokugawa society of elements conducive to Japan's post-Tokugawa development. Ronald Dore's research on education, T. Smith's studies of village society, agriculture, and taxation, D. F. Henderson's work on legal history, G. Rozman's comparative work on Tokugawa and Ch'ing cities, and S. Hanley and Kōzō Yamamura's research on the samurai and demographic change were all important contributions to this revisionist movement. This institutional, predominantly "top-down" view was important in establishing a basic framework of postwar scholarship, in deepening our understanding of the Tokugawa political and social structure, and in defining much of the research terrain and terms of debate. Its influence is still felt; but it is no longer the only point of view.

There have been a number of reactions against what some historians have viewed as an overly institutional, proto-modernizing, consensual view of premodern Japan. Some of these differences have been explicitly confrontational, others have been more indirect challenges to the hegemony of the institutional model or its outgrowths. An early challenge was a critique of benign Japanese modern development offered by the Committee of Concerned Asian Scholars during the Vietnam War era and the subsequent effort by J. Dower to reinstate E. H. Norman as a major interpreter of Japan's modern history.

Another challenge arose as part of the larger reaction against modernization theory both in Japan and in the West. A third has been the growing emphasis on conflict rather than consensus as a key factor in premodern as well as modern Japanese history. This in turn has encouraged work on rural and urban protest movements by H. Bix, A. Walthal, and S. Vlastos, among others. A fourth counter-current, or set of currents, may perhaps be seen in the application of theoretical and critical models derived from the study of European history, anthropology, and literary criticism to Japanese historical study. A fifth challenge has been an increasing interest in marginal and victimized groups, gender, protest movements, and "bottom-up" history. A sixth has been the questioning of views, coming especially from Japan, that seem to advocate "Japanism" (*nihonjin-ron*) or to present Japanese culture as unique. A seventh has been a tendency to question the nature of seclusion, at least with regard to China and Korea, and to see Japan in a broader Asian context. This has found expression in the work of R. Toby and Kazui Tashiro on foreign relations and *bakufu* policy and Toby's consideration of Japanese identity as expressed in attitudes toward Korean embassies to Japan. Three recent and very promising developments have been the strong interest in quantitative history and demography led by Hayami Akira, S. Hanley, K. Yamamura, and

L. Cornell; work in the history of medicine and disease by A. Janetta and others; and regional economic and social studies pursued by W. Skinner, W. Kelly, K. Wigen, C. Vaporis, D. Howell, and L. Roberts.

Tokugawa intellectual history has been perhaps the most active and contentious area of research. As a glance at the list of entries will quickly indicate, it deserves a much fuller discussion than can be given here. While excellent studies of individual Confucian scholars and statesment—K. W. Nakai's book on Arai Hakuseki (12.198) is a striking example—continue to be produced, there has been a move away from discrete studies of Neo-Confucian thinkers to consideration of the complex interaction of Confucian, Shintō, and Buddhist thought. This is evident in H. Ooms's *Tokugawa Ideology* (12.325) and the essays in the volume on Tokugawa thought and religion edited by P. Nosco (12.324). The meaning of Japan's intellectual relationship with China has been examined in excellent studies by K. W. Nakai, H. Harootunian, M. Jansen, B. T. Wakabayashi, and others. Dutch learning and Western and Chinese scientific ideas have also received renewed attention. National Learning or nativism (*kokugaku*), however, has received the most attention and has been studied from many views by P. Nosco, N. Sakai, B. T. Wakabayashi, T. Najita, H. Harootunian, and others. Najita has written revealing studies of Tokugawa merchant ethics, and V. Koschman, I. Scheiner, and A. Walthall have examined the intellectual bases for Tokugawa protest movements. Not surprisingly, some scholars have been more receptive to Western critical theories than others. There have been tart exchanges over issues of methodology, critical stance, and the reading (or misreading) of texts.

The Annales school, Foucauldian, poststructuralist, deconstructionist, and postmodernist approaches have all contributed in varying degrees to the study of the Tokugawa period, and to a lesser extent, to the study of ancient and medieval Japan. Theoretical approaches have been most prolific and stimulating in the field of intellectual history. In some cases, however, the bloom is already fading on some European-derived theories even as they are being applied to Japan. Some offer sharper insights and will wear well; many will fade as quickly as they have withered in other areas of the American academy. But, these counter-currents should not be dismissed. They have attracted some of the best minds of the middle and younger generations; they have brought diversity and dialogue to the enterprise; they have swung the focus away from elite, political, top-down history to studies of intellectual and bottom-up social history; they have served as a warning on the subjectivity of all texts; they have brought "process" to the fore; and they are still running.

The surge in Tokugawa studies has been accompanied by a growing interest in earlier periods. Several aspects of the sixteenth century have attracted attention: first has been Western contacts in general and the Iberian Catholic mission effort in particular. This interest is reflected in the work of C. R. Boxer, G. Elison, D. Massarella, and others. The second approach, reflected in studies of Oda Nobunaga and Toyotomi Hideyoshi by G. Elison (12.156) and M. E. Berry (12.152), has viewed the age of reunification both as a prelude to the Tokugawa political system and as a transition from the medieval to the early modern period. Some scholars have even gone so far as to talk of a sixteenth-century revolution. A third approach has looked more closely at Japan's relations with its Asian neighbors, including commercial relations and Hideyoshi's Korean invasions.

Research on the medieval period has been conducted in the United States by a small but devoted group of scholars. They have been encouraged by the boom in medieval studies in Japan, inspired by the work of Amino Yoshihiko and other medievalists and by bi-national conferences with Japanese scholars. Monographic studies on the Kamakura and Muromachi shogunates have been amplified by the collected essays arising from several such conferences. American study of medieval Japanese history has focused on political, institutional, and legal developments. This is reflected in the work of J. Mass, C. Steenstrup in Munich, and H. P. Varley, and in the volumes on *Medieval Japan: Essays in Institutional History* (12.52), *Court and Bakufu in Japan* (12.86), and *Japan in the Muromachi Age* (12.104). The recent *Cambridge History of Japan*, volume three; *Medieval Japan* (12.118), builds on the work of the past several decades and breaks new ground in the area of popular culture in an excellent essay by B. Ruch. Cultural history, especially at the elite level, has been explored by P. Varley. Joan Piggot, A. Grappard, S. Tyler, N. McMullin, and M. Collcutt have begun to examine the history of Buddhist temples and Shintō shrine complexes. There are clear indications, in the work of B. Ruch, Hitomi Tonomura, S. Gaye, A. Goble, and several European scholars, of a widening interest in social history, village history, popular religious institutions, popular resistance, commerce, technology, history of women, medicine, popular performing arts, and urban development. William LaFleur in *Karma of Words: Buddhism and the Literary Arts in Medieval Japan* and T. Keirstead in *The Geography of Power in Medieval Japan* (12.77) have been in the forefront of those who have sought to apply Foucauldian insights to the medieval field. Important work, with significance for historians, is also being produced by scholars of medieval literature, art history, and religion.

The study of ancient Japan, the Nara and Heian periods, has lagged somewhat. Cornelius J. Kiley, C. Hurst, and W. McCullough produced some pathbreaking work on Nara and Heian political institutions. Elizabeth Satō has detailed studies of some important Heian period, as well as medieval, estates (*shōen*). Dana Morris has written thoughtfully on villages, and W. Farris has made a major contribution with studies about population, plague, and land use, and recently, has focused on the rise of warriors and Japan's early military development. A new book by K. F. Friday (12.48) is devoted to the rise of the samurai. Wang Zhen-Ping (12.61) has written on contacts with China. Joan Piggot (12.38) is one of very few Western scholars working on *mokkan*, handwritten wooden tally slips that reveal much about the daily life of the Nara and Heian periods. Translations and studies of Helen and William McCullough, Cameron Hurst, and Francine Herail have provided a better understanding of the Fujiwara family and Heian political institutions. Many areas remain unexplored or call for deeper attention, however, and it will be interesting to see what the first two volumes of the *Cambridge History of Japan*, dealing with the Nara and Heian periods, offer when they appear in the very near future.

Archaeology, a very active field in Japan, has contributed to an understanding of the formation of the earliest Japanese political units. In the past few decades the origins of human settlement on the Japanese islands and the beginnings of settled agriculture have been pushed back in time. Much more is now known about the earliest relations with China, Korea, and North Asia. Scholars such as J. E. Kidder, R. Pearson, and G. Barnes combine professional archaeological expertise and knowledge of the sites with a historical interest in the place of pre- and protohistoric Japanese culture in Asia and in the overall development of Japanese history. Their writings and the exhibits they have organized in the West have helped bring archaeological findings into the orbit of early Japanese history. The recently excavated Yoshinogari site has become, and will continue to be, an important reference point. Excavations there may not radically change our current understanding of early Japanese society, but they will add fuel to the debate over the location of Yamatai and the origins of political organization in Japan.

What lies on the horizon? Recently published volumes three and four, *Medieval Japan* (12.118) and *Early Modern Japan* (12.161), of the *Cambridge History of Japan* provide a summation of the trends and research of the past two decades, and give some indication of what is just beginning and what remains to be done. Reflecting as they do the research interests of the 1970s and early 1980s, they pay relatively little attention to demography, family history, women, outcast and disadvantaged groups, gender, homosexuality, childhood, old age, or climate and the environment. But research is already advancing in most of these fields and is likely to continue.

There is now no single paradigm, if there ever was one, for the study of premodern Japanese history. Marxist historiography is virtually defunct in Japan and the West, where it never had a very strong presence anyway. Modernization theory is either taken for granted or disregarded. Poststructuralist, deconstructionist, and postmodernist analysis is likely to wane as it has waned elsewhere in the American academy since the mid-1980s.

The shift from political and institutional to social and intellectual history, and from a top-down to a bottom-up approach, is likely to continue. There is likely to be increasing fragmentation, and broad studies on the general features of ancient, medieval, or early modern society will be replaced or obscured by deeper but narrower studies. Scholars will talk about the need for overarching holistic studies, but will find it harder and harder to achieve them. Researchers in the field of premodern Japanese history in coming decades face serious tasks in defining a larger meaning for their enterprise. One will be to define, or at least to find and apply, fresh theories and paradigms to succeed feudal, modernization, conflict, and postmodernist paradigms in giving distinctiveness to the Western study of premodern Japan. A second task will be to maintain some balance between evernarrowing research and reflection on what that research adds to the larger understanding of Japanese history and culture. A third task will be to encourage more cooperative effort with scholars in the related fields of anthropology, art history, literature, and religion. Fourth, researchers will need to communicate more effectively with scholars in other areas of historical research. Most directly, this means greater cooperation with students of Korean and Chinese history. It also calls for greater communication with specialists in the history of other societies at comparable phases of development.

Entries are arranged under the following headings:

Reference Works

General Studies

Prehistory and Protohistory: Paleolithic, Jōmon, Yayoi, and Tumulus Eras

Asuka and Nara Periods, Sixth to Eighth Century

Heian Period, 794–1185

Kamakura Period, 1185–1333

Muromachi Period, 1333–1660
  Political History
  Economy and Society
  Culture and Religion
  Foreign Relations and Overseas Trade

Sixteenth Century
  Political and Military Unification
  Economy and Society
  Christianity

Tokugawa Period, 1600–1868
  Political History
  Law and Legal Institutions
  Status System
  Social History and Demographic Change
  Economic History
  Education
  Religion
  Cultural History
  Intellectual History
  Foreign Relations

[Contributors: HW = Haruko Wakabayashi, MC = Martin Collcutt]

REFERENCE WORKS

12.1 Association for Asian Studies. *Bibliography of Asian Studies, 1986.* Ann Arbor: Association for Asian Studies, 1991. ISSN 0067-7159. ‣ Annual series. Comprehensive list of articles and books about Asia written in Western languages. [MC]

12.2 John W. Dower. *Japanese history and culture from ancient to modern times: seven basic bibliographies.* New York: Weiner, 1986. ISBN 0-910129-20-7 (cl), 0-910129-36-3 (pbk). ‣ Excellent guide to materials up to ca. 1984. Topically arranged, some with brief comments. Omits some older works listed in Silberman 13.19. Most thorough bibliographic guide to English-language materials on Japanese history. [MC]

12.3 National Committee of Japanese Historians, eds. *Historical studies in Japan, 1978–82: a bibliography.* Tokyo: Yamakawa Shuppansha, 1985. ‣ Provides access to selection of most important historical research in Japanese published during this period. [MC]

12.4 Nihon Shi Gakkai (Historical Society of Japan). "Kaikō to tenbō" (Retrospect and prospect: historical studies in Japan, 1991). *Shigaku zasshi* (Journal of history) 5 (1992) 1–416. ISSN 0018-3478. ‣ Special bibliographical edition of journal published annually in May. Entire issue devoted to survey of historical publications during past year, with succinct reports on publications and research trends. Crucial for vast research by Japanese scholars in all fields of history. [MC]

12.5 Richard Perren, comp. *Japanese studies from prehistory to 1990: a bibliographic guide.* Manchester: Manchester University Press, 1992. ISBN 0-7190-2458-7. ‣ Up-to-date, comprehensive listing of English-language materials on Japanese history, with 4,000 entries. Some confusion and duplication caused by com-

piler's mistakes in distinguishing between family names and personal names of many of the Japanese authors cited. [MC]

12.6 Frank Joseph Shulman, ed. and comp. *Doctoral dissertations on Asia.* 1991 ed. Ann Arbor: Association for Asian Studies, 1975–. ISSN 0098-4485. ‣ Published annually by Association for Asian Studies, University of Michigan. Includes section on Japan from ancient times to 1800. This, and earlier versions, provide access to Ph.D. dissertations on earlier Japanese history published in English. [MC]

12.7 Herschel Webb. *Research in Japanese sources: a guide.* New York: Columbia University Press for the East Asian Institute, 1965. ‣ Now out of print and somewhat out of date but remains extremely useful research guide. Contains many hints on finding basic historical information in Japanese sources. [MC]

SEE ALSO
  13.18 Frank Joseph Shulman, ed. *Japan and Korea.*

GENERAL STUDIES

12.8 Martin Collcutt, Marius B. Jansen, and Isao Kumakura. *A cultural atlas of Japan.* New York: Facts on File, 1988. ISBN 0-8160-1927-4. ‣ Only historical atlas of Japan in English. Blend of historical atlas and narrative cultural history, prehistory to present. Forty-seven geographical and historical maps. Lavishly illustrated. Brief chronology and glossary, table of Japanese rulers, and bibliography of suggested readings. [MC]

12.9 Wm. Theodore De Bary, Ryūsaku Tsunoda, and Donald Keene, eds. *Sources of Japanese tradition.* 1958 ed. 2 vols. New York: Columbia University Press, 1969. ISBN 0-231-08604-0 (v. 1, pbk), 0-231-08605-9 (v. 2, pbk). ‣ Translations of selected critical documents, most relating to religious, intellectual, and cultural history. Selections also treat political, economic, and aesthetic issues. Brief but pointed commentaries introduce and link sections. Two-volume paperback edition also available. [MC]

12.10 H. Byron Earhart. *Japanese religion: unity and diversity.* 3d ed. Belmont, Calif.: Wadsworth, 1982. ISBN 0-534-01028-8 (pbk). ‣ General survey history of Shintō, Buddhism, Confucianism, and Christianity in Japan and their interactions. Good bibliography. [MC]

12.11 John Whitney Hall. *Government and local power in Japan, 500 to 1700: a study based on Bizen Province.* Princeton: Princeton University Press, 1966. ISBN 0-691-03019-7 (cl), 0-691-00780-2 (pbk). ‣ Still best regional study of premodern political and institutional development. Skillfully blends local developments in Bizen (modern Okayama prefecture) with events at center. Finds Okayama and its regional history contains most of institutional ingredients of larger national community. [MC]

12.12 John Whitney Hall. *Japan: from prehistory to modern times.* 1970 ed. Ann Arbor: Center for Japanese Studies, University of Michigan, 1991. ISBN 0-939512-54-8. ‣ Good, tightly written, single-volume survey history with particular emphasis on pre-Meiji Japan. Strong on premodern political and institutional developments. Concerned with how Japan's political and social institutions have changed and diversified and how this fundamentally Eastern culture grew to modern world power. [MC]

12.13 Mikiso Hane. *Premodern Japan: a historical survey.* Boulder: Westview, 1991. ISBN 0-8133-8066-9 (cl), 0-8133-8065-0 (pbk). ‣ One of better single-volume surveys of premodern Japanese history. Tries to keep focus on history of Japanese common people and on change "from below." [MC]

12.14 Joseph M. Kitagawa. *Religion in Japanese history.* New York: Columbia University Press, 1966. ‣ Good topical survey of history of Japanese religions. [MC]

12.15 David John Lu, comp. *Sources of Japanese history.* Vol. 1.

New York: McGraw-Hill, 1974. ISBN 0-07-038902-0 (v. 1, cl), 0-07-038904-7 (v. 1, pbk). ▸ Well-balanced collection of primary source material, some only excerpts, about Japan with short but informative commentaries. Emphasizes development of Japan's social, economic, and political institutions. First volume covers Japanese history from its mythical beginnings to 1800. See 13.48 for volume 2. [MC]

12.16 Sakamoto Tarō. *The six national histories of Japan.* John S. Brownlee, trans. Vancouver: University of British Columbia, 1991. ISBN 0-7748-0379-7. ▸ Translation of author's critical, scholarly analysis of six first document-based histories of Japan produced at imperial order of court during eighth and ninth centuries. Earlier title: *Rikkokushi* (1970). [MC]

12.17 G. B. Sansom. *A history of Japan.* Vol. 1. Stanford, Calif.: Stanford University Press, 1958. ISBN 0-8047-0523-2 (cl), 0-8047-0522-4 (pbk). ▸ First of three-volume set (with 12.18 and 12.19). Older style narrative history of Japan; elegant, lucid prose. Provides historical details often neglected in more recent monographs. Covers origins of Japanese people, emergence of organized state in Japan based on imported Chinese model, evolution of efficient system of feudal government, and collapse of Kamakura shogunate. [MC]

12.18 G. B. Sansom. *A history of Japan.* Vol. 2. Stanford, Calif.: Stanford University Press, 1961. ISBN 0-8047-0524-0 (cl), 0-8047-0525-9 (pbk). ▸ Second of three-volume set (with 12.17 and 12.19). Chronological narrative of Muromachi and Momoyama eras. Focuses on growth of new feudal hierarchy, events of century-long Warring States period, and rise of Tokugawa Ieyasu, who unified Japan under Tokugawa shogunate. Stronger on narrative than analysis. [MC]

12.19 G. B. Sansom. *A history of Japan.* Vol. 3. Stanford, Calif.: Stanford University Press, 1963. ISBN 0-8047-0526-7 (cl), 0-8047-0527-5 (pbk). ▸ Third of three-volume set (with 12.17 and 12.18). Emphasis on political developments to Meiji Restoration. Less satisfying than earlier volumes. Account of political and social development of Japan under Tokugawa shoguns, Japan's relations with West, and beginnings of modern Japan up to Meiji Restoration. Outdated by recent research, but presents larger sweep of Japanese history as unfolding narrative. [MC]

12.20 G. B. Sansom. *Japan: a short cultural history.* 1931 ed. London: Century Hutchinson, 1987. ISBN 0-09-170431-6 (pbk). ▸ Widely acclaimed as classic of Western writing about Japan. Study of premodern Japanese culture with special attention to evolution of Japanese religion, art, and letters. Offers overview of effects of economic, social, and political conditions on country's cultural development. Still fine introduction. [MC]

12.21 G. B. Sansom. *The Western world and Japan: a study in the interaction of European and Asiatic cultures.* 1950 ed. Rutland, Vt.: Tuttle, 1977. ISBN 0-8048-1510-0 (pbk). ▸ Elegantly written overview of Japan's contacts with West since sixteenth century. One of most readable short histories. Good discussion of complex trading relations among Japan, China, Macao, Philippines, and various European trading countries. [MC]

12.22 Carl Steenstrup. *A history of law in Japan until 1868.* Leiden: Brill, 1991. ISBN 90-04-09405-9. ▸ Lively, opinionated survey of development of Japanese law. Invaluable bibliography of materials in European languages as well as English. [MC]

12.23 Masayoshi Sugimoto and David L. Swain. *Science and culture in traditional Japan, A.D. 600–1854.* 1978 ed. Rutland, Vt.: Tuttle, 1989. ISBN 0-8048-1614-X. ▸ Best overview of history of science and technology examining such issues as development and social role of bronze and iron technologies imported from China in Yayoi period, indigenous development of samurai sword, influence of Iberian and Dutch knowledge, and progress

in astronomy, mathematics, botany, medicine, and other fields during Edo period. [MC]

12.24 Conrad Totman. *The green archipelago: forestry in preindustrial Japan.* Berkeley: University of California Press, 1989. ISBN 0-520-06313-9. ▸ Pioneering venture in growing field of environmental history of Japan. Part 1 traces millennium of forestry exploitation, 600–1600, which carried Japan to brink of ecological disaster. Part 2 shows how trend was reversed by systematic regenerative forestry practiced by many feudal lords (*daimyō*). [MC]

12.25 Conrad Totman. *Japan before Perry: a short history.* Berkeley: University of California Press, 1981. ISBN 0-520-04132-1 (cl), 0-520-04134-8 (pbk). ▸ Overview of Japanese history prior to 1853 within interpretive framework using three major chronological divisions: classical, seventh to twelfth century; medieval Japan, twelfth to sixteenth century; and early modern, sixteenth to nineteenth century. Stresses unifying characteristics and developments central to each era. [MC]

SEE ALSO
13.1 Ainslee T. Embree, ed. *Encyclopedia of Asian history.*
13.53 Edwin O. Reischauer and Albert M. Craig. *Japan.*

PREHISTORY AND PROTOHISTORY: PALEOLITHIC, JŌMON, YAYOI, AND TUMULUS ERAS

12.26 Akazawa Takeru and C. Melvin Aikens, eds. *Prehistoric hunter-gatherers in Japan: new research methods.* Tokyo: University of Tokyo Press, 1986. ISBN 0-86008-395-0. ▸ Edited collection of conference papers addressing two problems in Japanese prehistory: hunter-gatherer subsistence and settlement in Jōmon period, and physical anthropology of Japanese population. Contributors apply scientific-quantitative methods to problems in Japanese prehistory, using continuous record of human occupation of Japanese islands since Pleistocene era. [MC]

12.27 Walter Edwards. "Event and process in the founding of Japan." *Journal of Japanese studies* 9.2 (1983) 265–95. ISSN 0095-6848. ▸ Tests and revises Egami's fifth-century horserider invasion thesis by relating it closely to archaeological finds during Tumulus period. Shifts timing and views it as process rather than event. [MC]

12.28 Mark Hudson and Gina L. Barnes. "Yoshinogari: a Yayoi settlement in northern Kyushu." *Monumenta Nipponica* 46.2 (1991) 211–35. ISSN 0027-0741. ▸ Introduction, based on Saga Prefectual Board of Education report (February 1990), to very important Yayoi period site. [MC]

12.29 Gari K. Ledyard. "Galloping along with the horseriders: looking for the founders of Japan." *Journal of Japanese studies* 1.2 (1975) 217–54. ISSN 0095-6848. ▸ Lively, challenging essay summarizing, amplifying, and qualifying Egami's horserider thesis (see also Edwards 12.27). Welcome Korea-focused perspective on Japanese protohistory. [MC]

12.30 Richard J. Pearson. "The contribution of archaeology to Japanese studies." *Journal of Japanese studies* 2.2 (1976) 305–27. ISSN 0095-6848. ▸ Important general essay by leading Western archaeologist of Japan, pointing out relevance of wealth of archaeological finds in postwar Japan to study of early Japanese history and culture and relationship of Japan to its continental neighbors. [MC]

12.31 John Young. *The location of Yamatai: a case study in Japanese historiography, 720–1945.* Baltimore: Johns Hopkins University Press, 1958. ▸ Early English-language account of one of longest running debates in Japanese historiography: where was

Japanese kingdom of Yamatai mentioned in Chinese records and what, if any, connection did it have with Yamato? [MC]

ASUKA AND NARA PERIODS, SIXTH TO EIGHTH CENTURY

12.32   William G. Aston, trans. *Nihongi: chronicles of Japan from earliest times to A.D. 697*. 1896 ed. Rutland, Vt.: Tuttle, 1990. ISBN 0-8048-0984-4 (pbk). ▸ Only English-language translation of earliest historical chronicle, dated 720. Mythological account of origins of imperial line; becomes increasingly historical as it moves into sixth and seventh centuries CE. [MC]

12.33   Gary L. Ebersole. *Ritual poetry and the politics of death in early Japan*. Princeton: Princeton University press, 1989. ISBN 0-691-07338-4. ▸ Uses ancient poetry to analyze ritual mourning and burial practices of imperial clan. [MC]

12.34   William Wayne Farris. *Population, disease, and land in early Japan, 645–900*. Cambridge, Mass.: Council on East Asian Studies and Harvard-Yenching Institute; distributed by Harvard University Press, 1985. (Harvard-Yenching Institute monograph series, 24.) ISBN 0-674-69031-3. ▸ Makes full use of surviving land, tax, and census records and links periodic epidemics with population decline and sporadic land use to present picture of dwindling economic activity in ninth and tenth centuries. Sophisticated, analytical study. [MC]

12.35   Richard J. Miller. *Japan's first bureaucracy: a study of eighth-century government*. Ithaca, N.Y.: Cornell University, China Japan Program, 1978. (Cornell University, East Asia papers, 19.) ▸ Descriptive account of Nara administrative system. [MC]

12.36   Dana R. Morris. "Peasant economy in early Japan, 650–950." Ph.D dissertation. Berkeley: University of California, 1980. ▸ Careful study of changes in social and economic organization affecting peasantry with development and dissolution of centralized imperial bureaucratic rule (*ritsuryō* system). Available from Ann Arbor: University Microfilms International, 1986. [MC]

12.37   Donald L. Philippi, trans. *Kojiki*. Princeton: Princeton University Press, 1968. ▸ Recent, careful translation of earliest Japanese mythology (712 CE). Supersedes expurgated 1932 translation by Basil Hall Chamberlain. [MC]

12.38   Joan R. Piggot. "*Mokkan*: wooden documents from the Nara period." *Monumenta Nipponica* 45.4 (1990) 449–70. ISSN 0027-0741. ▸ Best introduction in any Western language to important documentary sources for Nara social history. [MC]

12.39   Ronald Toby. "Why leave Nara? Kammu and the transfer of the capital." *Monumenta Nipponica* 40.3 (1985) 331–47. ISSN 0027-0741. ▸ Analysis of factional politics, religious taboos, and other factors that led Emperor Kammu to decide suddenly to find new location for his capital and abandon Nara. [MC]

12.40   Ryūsaku Tsunoda. *Japan in the Chinese dynastic histories: later Han through Ming dynasties*. L. Carrington-Goodrich, ed. South Pasadena, Calif.: Perkins, 1951. ▸ Useful translations of accounts of ancient Japan found in early Chinese chronicles. Earliest accounts of Japan based on hearsay rather than direct observation, but still give valuable impressions of Japanese society in prehistoric era. [MC]

HEIAN PERIOD, 794–1185

12.41   Anonymous. *A tale of flowering fortunes: annals of Japanese aristocratic life in the Heian period*. 2 vols. Helen Craig McCullough and William McCullough, trans. Stanford, Calif.: Stanford University Press, 1980. ISBN 0-8047-1039-2. ▸ Reliable translation of *Eiga monogatari* (Tales of Glory), historical tale compiled in eleventh century purporting to be history of ninth

and tenth centuries. Culminates in illustrious career of great Fujiwara leader, Michinaga (966–1027). [MC]

12.42   Kan'ichi Asakawa. *Land and society in medieval Japan: studies by Kan'ichi Asakawa*. Yale University Committee for the Publication of Dr. K. Asakawa's Works with Council on East Asian Studies, comp. and ed. Tokyo: Japan Society for the Promotion of Science, 1965. ▸ Seven essays by author on various aspects of medieval feudal political and economic development. Essays by Hall and Rizō place author's work in context of more recent Western and Japanese research. [MC]

12.43   Felicia G. Bock, trans. *Engi-shiki: procedures of the Engi era*. Books 1–5. Tokyo: Sophia University Press, 1970. ▸ Careful translations of basic administrative precedents and court procedure of Heian period. Compiled by imperial order in 927, but not enforced until 967; then became basic compendium of court regulations. Book 4, for instance, deals with rebuilding of shrines in Ise province. [MC]

12.44   Felicia G. Bock, trans. *Engi-shiki: procedures of the Engi era*. Books 6–10. Tokyo: Sophia University Press, 1972. ▸ Useful translation of this important compendium of court ritual and administration. [MC]

12.45   Robert Borgen. "The Japanese mission to China, 801–806." *Monumenta Nipponica* 37.1 (1982) 1–28. ISSN 0027-0741. ▸ Discussion of particularly distinguished Japanese official embassy to T'ang China. [MC]

12.46   Robert Borgen. *Sugawara no Michizane and the early Heian court*. Cambridge Mass.: Council on East Asian Studies; distributed by Harvard University Press, 1986. (Harvard East Asian monographs, 120.) ISBN 0-674-85415-2. ▸ One of best studies of early Heian court in English, presented through life of Sugawara no Michizane, poet and scholar, provincial governor of Sanuki, and high court official who was slandered by Fujiwara rivals, died in exile, and was eventually deified as Tenjin, god of poetry and letters. Translation of his poetry and reconstruction of career at court and as governor. [MC]

12.47   William Wayne Farris. *Heavenly warriors, the evolution of Japan's military, 500–1300*. Cambridge, Mass.: Council on East Asian Studies; distributed by Harvard University Press, 1992. (Harvard East Asian monographs, 157.) ISBN 0-674-38703-1. ▸ Excellent study of early military development. Challenges so-called Western-analogy model for emergence of samurai; proposes instead eight-stage developmental model. [MC]

12.48   Karl F. Friday. *Hired swords: the rise of private warrior power in early Japan*. Stanford Calif.: Stanford University Press, 1992. ISBN 0-8047-1978-0. ▸ Evolution of state military institutions, seventh through twelfth centuries—prelude to rise of samurai. [MC]

12.49   Paul Groner. *Saichō: the establishment of the Japanese Tendai school*. Berkeley: University of California, Center for South and South-East Asian Studies, Institute of Buddhist Studies, 1984. ▸ Careful study of religious life and writings of Saichō, founder of Japanese Tendai Buddhism, and of rapid development of Tendai into major current of Japanese religion. [MC]

12.50   Yoshito S. Hakeda. *Kūkai, major works, translated, with an account of his life and a study of his thought*. New York: Columbia University, 1972. ISBN 0-231-03627-2 (cl), 0-231-05933-7 (pbk). ▸ Good introduction to life and thought of most influential Japanese Buddhist, founder of Japanese tantric Shingon tradition. [MC]

12.51   John Whitney Hall. "Kyoto as historical background." In *Medieval Japan: essays in institutional history*. 1974 ed. John Whitney Hall and Jeffrey P. Mass, eds., pp. 3–38. Stanford, Calif.: Stanford University Press, 1988. ISBN 0-8047-1510-6 (cl),

0-8047-1511-4 (pbk). ▸ Discussion of urban history of Kyoto in ancient and medieval periods. [MC]

12.52 John Whitney Hall and Jeffrey P. Mass, eds. *Medieval Japan: essays in institutional history.* 1974 ed. Stanford, Calif.: Stanford University Press, 1988. ISBN 0-8047-1510-6 (cl), 0-8047-1511-4 (pbk). ▸ Basic collection of essays on institutional history of Heian, Kamakura, and Muromachi periods. Presents more diverse and energetic view of Japan than historians have previously portrayed. See especially five essays on court and *shōen* (private landholdings) in Heian Japan. [MC]

12.53 G. Cameron Hurst III. "The development of *insei*: a problem in Japanese history and historiography." In *Medieval Japan: essays in institutional history.* 1974 ed. John Whitney Hall and Jeffrey P. Mass, eds., pp. 60–90. Stanford, Calif.: Stanford University Press, 1988. ISBN 0-8047-1510-6 (cl), 0-8047-1511-4 (pbk). ▸ Survey of system of rule known as cloister government (*insei*) whereby emperors, in effort to resist influence of Fujiwara regents, abdicated but continued to exercise power. [MC]

12.54 G. Cameron Hurst III. *Insei: abdicated sovereigns in the politics of late Heian Japan, 1086–1185.* New York: Columbia University Press, 1976. ISBN 0-231-03932-8. ▸ Thorough examination of system of rule by retired emperors (*insei*). Part 1 discusses origins and development of abdication and explores how and why abdicated sovereigns emerged as important political forces in imperial court. Part 2 analyzes structure and function of *in-no-chō*, ex-sovereign's administrative office, which functioned essentially as government separate from that maintained by reigning emperor. [MC]

12.55 G. Cameron Hurst III. "The structure of the Heian court: some thoughts on the nature of 'familial authority' in Heian Japan." In *Medieval Japan: essays in institutional history.* 1974 ed. John Whitney Hall and Jeffrey P. Mass, eds., pp. 39–59. Stanford, Calif.: Stanford University Press, 1988. ISBN 0-8047-1510-6 (cl), 0-8047-1511-4 (pbk). ▸ Applies suggestion of return to familial authority in provinces with breakdown of *ritsuryō* system (centralized imperial bureaucratic rule) to clarify structural dynamics of imperial court. [MC]

12.56 Cornelius J. Kiley. "Estate and property in the late Heian period." In *Medieval Japan: essays in institutional history.* 1974 ed. John Whitney Hall and Jeffrey P. Mass, eds., pp. 109–24. Stanford, Calif.: Stanford University Press, 1988. ISBN 0-8047-1510-6 (cl), 0-8047-1511-4 (pbk). ▸ Analytical approach to Heian period *shōen* holdings in terms of legal history and distinction between estate and property. [MC]

12.57 William McCullough. "Japanese marriage institutions in the Heian period." *Harvard journal of Asiatic studies* 27 (1967) 103–67. ISSN 0073-0548. ▸ Pathbreaking study of uxorilocal visiting marriage style of Heian nobility. Challenges Morris 12.58, as presented in "Women of Ancient Japan." [MC]

12.58 Ivan J. Morris. *The world of the shining prince: court life in ancient Japan.* 1964 ed. New York: Penguin, 1985. ISBN 0-14-055083-6 (pbk). ▸ Lively literary portrayal of Heian court life and society between mid-tenth and mid-eleventh centuries, age of Murasaki Shikibu, author of "Tale of Genji." Can serve as companion volume to "Tale of Genji" and as introduction to era that witnessed flowering of Heian civilization. [MC]

12.59 Judith Rabinovitch, trans. and ed. *Shōmon-ki: the story of Masakado's rebellion.* Tokyo: Sophia University Press, 1986. ▸ Reliable translation of and commentary on Japan's earliest war chronicle, *Gunkimono*, describing course of Taira no Masakado's rebellion which was crushed in 940. First chapter devoted to historical events; following chapters, textual commentary and translation. [MC]

12.60 Elizabeth S. Satō. "The early development of *shōen*." In *Medieval Japan: essays in institutional history.* 1974 ed. John Whit-

ney Hall and Jeffrey P. Mass, eds., pp. 91–108. Stanford, Calif.: Stanford University Press, 1988. ISBN 0-8047-1510-6 (cl), 0-8047-1511-4 (pbk). ▸ Descriptive account of development of private landholdings (*shōen*) in Nara and Heian periods. [MC]

12.61 Wang Zhen-Ping. "Sino-Japanese relations before the eleventh century: modes of diplomatic communication re-examined in terms of the concept of reciprocity." Ph.D. dissertation. Princeton: Princeton University, 1989. ▸ Good study using Chinese and Japanese documentary sources that explores language of Sino-Japanese diplomacy in Heian period and offers reciprocity as alternative to accepted notion of tributary system. [MC]

12.62 Kōzō Yamamura. "The decline of the *ritsuryō* system: hypotheses on economic and institutional change." *Journal of Japanese studies* 1.1 (1974) 3–37. ISSN 0095-6848. ▸ Argues that erosion of *ritsuryō* system of centralized imperial bureaucratic rule in Heian period was rapid and brought about by market forces expressed in competition from nobles, temples, and shrines as they privatized land and attracted labor from public domain by relatively lighter tax burdens. [MC]

KAMAKURA PERIOD, 1185–1333

12.63 Peter J. Arnesen. "Suō province in the age of Kamakura." In *Court and bakufu in Japan: essays in Kamakura history.* Jeffrey P. Mass, ed., pp. 92–120. New Haven: Yale University Press, 1982. ISBN 0-300-02653-6. ▸ Argues that old central institutions (court and especially Tōdaiji temple) retained influence in Suō throughout Kamakura period and were only seriously challenged in early fourteenth century. [MC]

12.64 Kan'ichi Asakawa. *The documents of Iriki, illustrative of the development of the feudal institutions of Japan.* 1929 ed. Westport, Conn.: Greenwood, 1974. ISBN 0-8371-5432-4. ▸ Documents and study of Kyushu warrior family, Kamakura period (1185–1333) to Meiji Restoration. [MC]

12.65 Delmer M. Brown and Ishida Ichirō, trans. *The future and the past: a translation and study of the "Gukansho," an interpretative history of Japan written in 1219.* Berkeley: University of California Press, 1979. ISBN 0-520-03460-0. ▸ Reliable translation of important history of Japan, written by monk Jien and incorporating Buddhist and Shintō views of historical change and imperial legitimation. Useful commentary by both translators. [MC]

12.66 Martin Collcutt. *Five Mountains, the Rinzai Zen monastic institution in medieval Japan.* Cambridge, Mass.: Council on East Asian Studies, Harvard University; distributed by Harvard University Press, 1981. (Harvard East Asian monographs, 85.) ISBN 0-674-30497-7. ▸ Survey of institutional development of Rinzai Zen from Kamakura period. Chapters on Zen practice, monastic organization and codes, architecture, political patronage, and landholdings. [MC]

12.67 Martin Collcutt. "The Zen monastery in Kamakura society." In *Court and bakufu in Japan: essays in Kamakura history.* Jeffrey P. Mass, ed., pp. 191–220. New Haven: Yale University Press, 1982. ISBN 0-300-02653-6. ▸ Focuses on religious and economic development of Kamakura Rinzai Zen monasteries of Kenchōji and Engakuji under sponsorship of Hōjō regents and other powerful *bushi* (warrior class). [MC]

12.68 James C. Dobbins. *Jōdo Shinshū: Shin Buddhism in medieval Japan.* Bloomington: Indiana University Press, 1989. ISBN 0-253-33186-2. ▸ Best monograph on history and teachings of True Pure Land (Jōdo Shinshū) school of Buddhism in medieval Japan. Thoughtful scholarly chapters on Hōnen, Shinran, Licensed Evil, Kakunyo and Honganji, Shinshū and rival schools, Shinshū factions, and Rennyo and consolidation of Shinshū. [MC]

12.69 Louis Frédéric. *Daily life in Japan at the time of the samurai, 1185–1603.* 1972 ed. Eileen M. Lowe, trans. Rutland, Vt.: Tuttle, 1973. ISBN 0-8048-1546-1. ‣ Lively introduction to medieval Japanese society. [MC]

12.70 Andrew Goble. "The Hōjō and consultative government." In *Court and bakufu in Japan: essays in Kamakura history.* Jeffrey P. Mass, ed., pp. 168–90. New Haven: Yale University Press, 1982. ISBN 0-300-02653-6. ‣ Challenges prevailing notion that early Kamakura shogunate was era of consultation, effectively destroyed by Hōjō after 1247. [MC]

12.71 Allan G. Grapard. *The protocol of the gods: a study of the Kasuga cult in Japanese history.* Berkeley: University of California Press, 1992. ISBN 0-520-07097-6. ‣ Challenging study of history of relations between Japanese native institutions and ideas (Shintō) and imported religion (Buddhism). Using Kasuga Shintō shrine and related Kōfukuji Buddhist temple, exposes combinatory character of premodern Japanese religiosity. [MC]

12.72 Lorraine F. Harrington. "Social control and the significance of the *akutō.*" In *Court and bakufu in Japan: essays in Kamakura history.* Jeffrey P. Mass, ed., pp. 221–50. New Haven: Yale University Press, 1982. ISBN 0-300-02653-6. ‣ Study of regional bands, *akutō* (literally "evil bands"), that defied warrior government in late Kamakura period. [MC]

12.73 Kyotsu Hori. "The economic and political effects of the Mongol wars." In *Medieval Japan: essays in institutional history.* 1974 ed. John Whitney Hall and Jeffrey P. Mass, eds., pp. 184–98. Stanford, Calif.: Stanford University Press, 1988. ISBN 0-8047-1510-6 (cl), 0-8047-1511-4 (pbk). ‣ Argues that burdens of indebtedness caused by struggle against Mongols led to frustration in samurai society and helped undermine authority of Kamakura shogunate. [MC]

12.74 G. Cameron Hurst III. "The kōbu polity: court-*bakufu* relations in Kamakura Japan." In *Court and bakufu in Japan: essays in Kamakura history.* Jeffrey P. Mass, ed., pp. 3–28. New Haven: Yale University Press, 1982. ISBN 0-300-02653-6. ‣ Sketch of historical relationship between court and *bakufu* (shogunate) from point of view of imperial court. Suggests crucial period in development of *bakufu* came in post-1246 era when Kamakura extended its control over imperial succession and reorganized Go-Saga's cloister government (*insei*). [MC]

12.75 Susumu Ishii. "The decline of the Kamakura *bakufu.*" In *The Cambridge history of Japan.* Kōzō Yamamura, ed., vol. 3, pp. 128–74. Cambridge: Cambridge University Press, 1989. ISBN 0-521-22354-7. ‣ Starts from premise that 1260s represented new period for Kamakura shogunate as it faced increasingly complex problems. Highlights impact of Mongol invasions. [MC]

12.76 Frédéric Jouon des Longrais. *Age de Kamakura: sources (1150–1333), archives, chartes, japonaises (monjo).* Paris and Tokyo: L'auteur and Maison Franco-Japonaise, 1950. ‣ Classification of and commentary on major documentary sources of this period. [MC]

12.77 Thomas Keirstead. *The geography of power in medieval Japan.* Princeton: Princeton University Press, 1992. ISBN 0-691-03183-5. ‣ Applies Foucauldian concepts and methods to study of medieval private estate (*shōen*) system, central economic institution of medieval Japan. Not very helpful for information on individual *shōen* but challenging in its effort to provide cultural framework for *shōen* phenomenon as whole. [MC]

12.78 Cornelius J. Kiley. "The imperial court as a legal authority in the Kamakura age." In *Court and bakufu in Japan: essays in Kamakura history.* Jeffrey P. Mass, ed., pp. 29–44. New Haven: Yale University Press, 1982. ISBN 0-300-02653-6. ‣ Thoughtful analysis of Kamakura legal codes and cases to show continuing

legal influence of imperial court and interaction of legal theory and practice of court and warrior regimes in Kamakura. [MC]

12.79 Jeffrey P. Mass. *Antiquity and anachronism in Japanese history.* Stanford, Calif.: Stanford University Press, 1992. ISBN 0-8047-1974-8. ‣ Thoughtful essays spanning first 1,000 years of Japanese history, built around theme that exaggeration of antiquity has distorted historical understanding of Japanese past. [MC]

12.80 Jeffrey P. Mass. *The development of Kamakura rule, 1180–1250: a history with documents.* Stanford, Calif.: Stanford University Press, 1979. ISBN 0-8047-1003-1. ‣ Examines system of justice developed by Kamakura *bakufu* (shogunate), especially after its victory over imperial court in Jōkyū War. Includes annotated translations of 144 documents that illuminate changing power relationships and developing stages of judicial process. [MC]

12.81 Jeffrey P. Mass. "The emergence of the Kamakura *bakufu.*" In *Medieval Japan: essays in institutional history.* 1974 ed. John Whitney Hall and Jeffrey P. Mass, eds., pp. 127–56. Stanford, Calif.: Stanford University Press, 1988. ISBN 0-8047-1510-6 (cl), 0-8047-1511-4 (pbk). ‣ Traces development of early Kamakura shogunate and contrasts its growing power with that of defeated preceding Taira warrior regime. [MC]

12.82 Jeffrey P. Mass. "The Kamakura *bakufu.*" In *The Cambridge history of Japan.* Kōzō Yamamura, ed., vol. 3, pp. 46–88. Cambridge: Cambridge University Press, 1989. ISBN 0-521-22354-7. ‣ Formation and development of Kamakura shogunate from struggle between Taira and Minamoto bands in 1160s to its maturation under Hōjō leadership in mid-thirteenth century. [MC]

12.83 Jeffrey P. Mass. *The Kamakura bakufu: a study in documents.* Stanford, Calif.: Stanford University Press, 1976. ISBN 0-8047-0907-6. ‣ Essential guide for research in ancient or medieval Japanese documents. Part 1 includes translations of and commentaries on 177 edicts and land records; part 2, annotated and geographically classified bibliography of nearly 600 books and articles in Japanese that provide text of official documents. Discusses basic issues in Kamakura political and economic history through translations of important documents. [MC]

12.84 Jeffrey P. Mass. *Lordship and inheritance in early medieval Japan: a study of the Kamakura sōryō system.* Stanford, Calif.: Stanford University Press, 1989. ISBN 0-8047-1540-8. ‣ Document-based study of inheritance practices in Kamakura warrior society, concentrating on rank-and-file warrior houses that made up *bakufu*'s (shogunate) constituency. Examines social and economic milieu in which provincial warrior families operated. [MC]

12.85 Jeffrey P. Mass. *Warrior government in early medieval Japan: a study of the Kamakura bakufu, shugo, and jito.* New Haven: Yale University Press, 1974. ISBN 0-300-01756-1. ‣ Stresses novelty of Kamakura *bakufu* (shogunate) and focuses particularly on warriors appointed *shugo* (provincial constable) and *jitō* (estate steward) as agents of extension of Kamakura authority. [MC]

12.86 Jeffrey P. Mass, ed. *Court and bakufu in Japan: essays in Kamakura history.* New Haven: Yale University Press, 1982. ISBN 0-300-02653-6. ‣ Eleven essays on aspects of political, social, and institutional history of Kamakura period. Kamakura age (1180–1333) commonly known as era of Japan's first warrior government, but actually distinguished by coexistence of two authority centers—*bakufu* (shogunate) military government at Kamakura, and imperial court at Kyoto—and by gradual ascendancy of newer warrior regime over courtier system. [MC]

12.87 Jeffrey P. Mass and William B. Hauser, eds. *The bakufu in Japanese history.* Stanford, Calif.: Stanford University Press, 1985. ISBN 0-8047-1278-6. ‣ Studies of major warrior regimes from Kamakura through Edo shogunates. Only attempt thus far in English at synoptic overview of *bakufu* (shogunate) as political phenomenon, but would have been stronger if essays attempted more comparison among various *bakufu*. [MC]

12.88 William McCullough. "The *Azuma kagami* account of the Shōkyū War." *Monumenta Nipponica* 32 (1968) 102–55. ISSN 0027-0741. ▸ Discussion of brief but critical struggle between Kamakura *bakufu* (shogunate) and imperial court in 1221. [MC]

12.89 Ōyama Kyōhei. "Medieval *shōen*." In *The Cambridge history of Japan*. Kōzō Yamamura, ed., vol. 3, pp. 89–123. Cambridge: Cambridge University Press, 1989. ISBN 0-521-22354-7. ▸ Discussion of internal structure of medieval provinces, overlapping systems of *shōen* (private estates) and *kokuga* (public domain). [MC]

12.90 Joan R. Piggot. "Hierarchy and economics in early medieval Tōdaiji." In *Court and bakufu in Japan: essays in Kamakura history*. Jeffrey P. Mass, ed., pp. 45–91. New Haven: Yale University Press, 1982. ISBN 0-300-02653-6. ▸ Examination of administrative and fiscal organization of Tōdaiji temple in Kamakura period. Argues temple recovered quickly from great fire of 1180 and enjoyed relative prosperity through first decades of thirteenth century. After 1250, however, community faced increasing instability and loss of income from estates. [MC]

12.91 Wilhelm Röhl. "Das *Goseibaishikimoku*: eine Rechtsquelle der Kamakura Zeit." *Oriens extremus* 5 (1958) 228–45. ISSN 0030-5197. ▸ Careful German translation of important Kamakura period warrior code. [MC]

12.92 Minoru Shinoda. *The founding of the Kamakura shogunate, 1180–1185, with selected translations from the "Azuma kagami."* New York: Columbia University Press, 1960. ▸ Detailed narrative account of formation of first shogunate (*bakufu*) drawing heavily on *Azuma kagami*, partial document, compiled after events, by Hōjō family who gained control within *bakufu*. [MC]

12.93 Carl Steenstrup. *Hōjō Shigetoki (1198–1261) and his role in the history of political and ethical ideas in Japan*. London: Curzon, 1979. (Scandinavian Institute of Asian Studies monograph series, 41.) ISBN 0-7007-0132-X (pbk), ISSN 0069-1712. ▸ Discussion of well-connected, high *bakufu* (shogunate) official. Treats Shigetoki as philosopher and rationalist, "who seriously tried to combine various creeds of his age and relate their sum to the actual world." Valuable on Hōjō family, their rise to and exercise of power. [MC]

12.94 H. Paul Varley. "The Hōjō family and succession to power." In *Court and bakufu in Japan: essays in Kamakura history*. Jeffrey P. Mass, ed., pp. 143–67. New Haven: Yale University Press, 1982. ISBN 0-300-02653-6. ▸ Shows how Hōjō, through skillful mixture of political maneuvering and military force, prevailed over rivals and military challenges to assert unassailable control over Kamakura *bakufu* (shogunate) by 1247. [MC]

12.95 Kōzō Yamamura. "Tara in transition: a study of a Kamakura *shōen*." *Journal of Japanese studies* 7 (1981) 349–91. ISSN 0095-6848. ▸ Introduction to history of one of best documented and most fully studied medieval *shōen* (private estates). [MC]

MUROMACHI PERIOD, 1333–1660

Political History

12.96 Peter Judd Arnesen. *The medieval Japanese daimyo: the Ouchi family's rule of Suō and Nagato*. New Haven: Yale University Press, 1979. ISBN 0-300-02341-3. ▸ Argues that Ouchi warrior family represents enduring type of local warrior chieftain referred to as medieval *daimyō* (feudal lord) type, successful in changing military circumstances of late Muromachi period. Covers period 1333–1573. [MC]

12.97 Mary Elizabeth Berry. *The culture of civil war in Kyoto*. Berkeley: University of California Press, 1994. ISBN 0-520-08170-6. ▸ Investigates politics and culture associated with upheavals in Kyoto during age of wars between 1467 and 1568. [MC]

12.98 Peter Duus. *Feudalism in Japan*. 3d ed. New York: Knopf; distributed by Random House, 1993. ISBN 0-07-018412-7. ▸ Nicely written survey of medieval and early modern Japan as feudal society. [MC]

12.99 Suzanne Gaye. "Muromachi *bakufu* rule in Kyoto: administrative and judicial aspects." In *The bakufu in Japanese history*. Jeffrey P. Mass and William B. Hauser, eds., pp. 49–65. Stanford, Calif.: Stanford University Press, 1985. ISBN 0-8047-1278-6. ▸ Best brief discussion of Ashikaga shogunal administration. [MC]

12.100 Andrew Goble. "Go-Daigo and the Kemmu Restoration." Ph.D. dissertation. Stanford, Calif.: Stanford University, 1987. ▸ Positive assessment of Go-Daigo's brief restoration of imperial rule. Contra Varley 12.115. [MC]

12.101 Kenneth A. Grossberg. *Japan's renaissance: the politics of the Muromachi bakufu*. Cambridge, Mass.: Council on East Asian Studies, Harvard University; distributed by Harvard University Press, 1981. (Harvard East Asian monographs, 99.) ISBN 0-674-47251-9. ▸ Attempts to redefine Ashikaga shoguns as innovative European-style Renaissance rulers who based their regime less on land and feudal ties than on commerce, foreign trade, and personal bureaucracy. Suggests Muromachi shogunate first introduced most of major political innovations of following three centuries. [MC]

12.102 Kenneth A. Grossberg and Kanamoto Nobuhisa, trans. *The laws of the Muromachi bakufu: Kemmu Shikimoku (1336) and Muromachi bakufu Tsuikaho*. Tokyo: Monumenta Nipponica, Sophia University Press, 1981. ▸ Only full translation of Ashikaga legal codes, *Kemmu shikimoku* and *Tsuika-hō*. [MC]

12.103 John Whitney Hall. "The Muromachi *bakufu*." In *The Cambridge history of Japan*. Kōzō Yamamura, ed., vol. 3, pp. 175–230. Cambridge: Cambridge University Press, 1989. ISBN 0-521-22354-7. ▸ Good overall view of Muromachi *bakufu* (shogunate), Ashikaga shogunal power, central government institutions, and historiography of Muromachi *bakufu* in Japanese and English works. [MC]

12.104 John Whitney Hall and Toyoda Takeshi, eds. *Japan in the Muromachi age*. Berkeley: University of California Press, 1977. ISBN 0-520-02888-0 (cl), 0-520-03214-4 (pbk). ▸ Eighteen papers on Muromachi period covering political organizaton, lordship and village, commercial economy, foreign trade, social change, and cultural and religious life. [MC]

12.105 Akira Imatani. "Muromachi local government: *shugo* and *kokujin*." In *The Cambridge history of Japan*. Kōzō Yamamura, ed., vol. 3, pp. 231–59. Cambridge: Cambridge University Press, 1989. ISBN 0-521-22354-7. ▸ Examination of shifting power relationship in provinces between military governors (*shugo*) appointed by Muromachi *bakufu* (shogunate) and entrenched local warrior powerholders (*kokujin*). [MC]

12.106 Ryōsuke Ishii. "Japanese feudalism." *Acta Asiatica* 35 (1978) 1–29. ISSN 0567-7254. ▸ Introduction to Japanese discussion of feudal institutions. [MC]

12.107 Masaharu Kawaii. "Shogun and *shugo*: the provincial aspects of Muromachi politics." In *Japan in the Muromachi age*. John Whitney Hall and Toyoda Takeshi, eds., pp. 65–88. Berkeley: University of California Press, 1977. ISBN 0-520-02888-0 (cl), 0-520-03214-4 (pbk). ▸ Examines important and often brittle relationship between Ashikaga shoguns and their principle vassals, the *shugo* (military governors), especially those of western Japan. [MC]

12.108 Kitabatake Chikafusa. *A chronicle of gods and sovereigns: Jinnō Shōtōki of Kitabatake Chikafusa.* H. Paul Varley, trans. New York: Columbia University Press, 1980. ISBN 0-231-04940-4. ▸ Translation of important fourteenth-century loyalist text written during struggle between rival branches of imperial court to assert legitimacy of Go-Daigo and his southern court (or line) by tracing his lineage from sun goddess. [MC]

12.109 Kōnen Kuwayama. "The *bugyōnin* system: a closer look." In *Japan in the Muromachi age.* John Whitney Hall and Toyoda Takeshi, eds., pp. 53–63. Berkeley: University of California Press, 1977. ISBN 0-520-02888-0 (cl), 0-520-03214-4 (pbk). ▸ Essay on roles and power of warrior bureaucrats (*bugyōnin*) who made up Ashikaga shoguns' personal government. [MC]

12.110 Miyagawa Mitsuru. "*Shōen* to *chigyō*: proprietory lordship and the structure of local power." In *Japan in the Muromachi age.* John Whitney Hall and Toyoda Takeshi, eds., pp. 89–105. Berkeley: University of California Press, 1977. ISBN 0-520-02888-0 (cl), 0-520-03214-4 (pbk). ▸ Traces erosion of private estate holdings (*shōen*) in Muromachi period and efforts made by local lords to increase their feudal control by replacing *shōen* rights with titles to fiefs (*chigyō*). [MC]

12.111 Edwin O. Reischauer. "Japanese feudalism." In *Feudalism in history.* 1956 ed. Rushton Coulborn, ed., pp. 26–48. Hamden, Conn.: Archon, 1965. ▸ Argues "feudal" system contributed to Japanese modernization in nineteenth century. [MC]

12.112 Shin'ichi Satō. "The Ashikaga shogun and the Muromachi *bakufu* administration." In *Japan in the Muromachi age.* John Whitney Hall and Toyoda Takeshi, eds., pp. 45–52. Berkeley: University of California Press, 1977. ISBN 0-520-02888-0 (cl), 0-520-03214-4 (pbk). ▸ Brief introduction to bureaucracy serving Ashikaga shoguns. [MC]

12.113 Stephen Turnbull. *The samurai: a military history.* 1977 ed. London: Philip, 1987. ISBN 0-540-01171-1. ▸ Positive view of samurai, but considers military issues generally ignored by institutional historians. Heavy reliance on Japanese- and English-language secondary sources; should be used with caution. [MC]

12.114 H. Paul Varley. "Ashikaga Yoshimitsu and the world of Kitayama: social change and shogunal patronage in early Muromachi Japan." In *Japan in the Muromachi age.* John Whitney Hall and Toyoda Takeshi, eds., pp. 183–204. Berkeley: University of California Press, 1977. ISBN 0-520-02888-0 (cl), 0-520-03214-4 (pbk). ▸ Elegant assessment of political and cultural activities of Yoshimitsu, most vigorous and influential Ashikaga shogun. [MC]

12.115 H. Paul Varley. *Imperial restoration in medieval Japan.* New York: Columbia University Press, 1971. ISBN 0-231-03502-0. ▸ Analysis of Emperor Go-Daigo's Kemmu Restoration (1333–36) and its political aftermath to 1392. Draws on Kuroda Toshio's ideas of power competition among familylike entities (*kenmon*); stresses their anachronistic character. Interesting concluding chapter on rival-courts issue in subsequent Japanese history. [MC]

12.116 H. Paul Varley. *The Ōnin War: history of its origins and background with a selective translation of the "Chronicle of Ōnin."* New York: Columbia University Press, 1967. ISBN 0-231-02943-8. ▸ Study of origins, progress, and effects of civil war of 1467–77, which ushered in age of wars and extreme feudal decentralization in Japan. Includes valuable translation of *Chronicle of Ōnin.* [MC]

12.117 H. Paul Varley. *Samurai.* New York: Delacorte, 1970. ▸ One of the better introductions to samurai traditions. [MC]

12.118 Kōzō Yamamura, ed. *The Cambridge history of Japan,* Vol. 3: *Medieval Japan.* Cambridge: Cambridge University Press, 1989. ISBN 0-521-22354-7 (v. 3). ▸ Solid collection of essays, most summing up research of 1970s and early 1980s. One or two essays break new ground in the areas of popular culture, religion, and women's lives. [MC]

Economy and Society

12.119 Delmer M. Brown. *Money economy in medieval Japan: a study in the use of coins.* New Haven: Yale University, Institute of Far Eastern Languages, 1951. ▸ Still only English-language monograph on medieval coinage and its diffusion through commerce and markets. Traces in detail growth of very complex money economy, including increased transactions in coins, expansion of credit system, and rapid growth in volume of trade. [MC]

12.120 David L. Davis. "*Ikki* in late medieval Japan." In *Medieval Japan: essays in institutional history.* 1974 ed. John Whitney Hall and Jeffrey P. Mass, eds., pp. 221–47. Stanford, Calif.: Stanford University Press, 1988. ISBN 0-8047-1510-6 (cl), 0-8047-1511-4 (pbk). ▸ Study of peasant protest and religious uprisings (*ikki*) in fifteenth and sixteenth centuries. Focuses especially on uprisings of True Pure Land followers (Ikkō *ikki*) and their control of Kaga province. [MC]

12.121 Tatsusaburo Hayashiya. "Kyoto in the Muromachi age." In *Japan in the Muromachi age.* John Whitney Hall and Toyoda Takeshi, eds., pp. 15–37. Berkeley: University of California Press, 1977. ISBN 0-520-02888-0 (cl), 0-520-03214-4 (pbk). ▸ Description of capital and its residents before, during, and after destruction of Ōnin War (1467–77). Emphasis on commoner townspeople (*machishū*). [MC]

12.122 James Kanda. "Methods of land transfer in medieval Japan." *Monumenta Nipponica* 33.4 (1978) 375–405. ISSN 0027-0741. ▸ Focusing on single tract of land, author shows land was bought and sold and how such transfers took place. [MC]

12.123 Nagahara Keiji. "The decline of the *shōen* system." In *The Cambridge history of Japan.* Kōzō Yamamura, ed., vol. 3, pp. 260–300. Cambridge: Cambridge University Press, 1989. ISBN 0-521-22354-7. ▸ Traces waning of *shōen* system of absentee estate holdings between fourteenth and sixteenth centuries. Focuses especially on events of fourteenth century that exacerbated erosion of *shōen.* Process hastened by incursions of *shugo,* weakening of control by central proprietors, and assertion of total domainal control by the *sengoku* period *daimyō* (feudal lords). [MC]

12.124 Nagahara Keiji. "Landownership under the *shōen koku-garyō* system." *Journal of Japanese studies* 1.2 (1975) 269–96. ISSN 0095-6848. ▸ Analysis of shifting interrelationship of provincial public domain (*kokugaryō*) and private landholdings (*shōen*) in medieval period. [MC]

12.125 Nagahara Keiji. "The medieval origins of the *eta-hinin.*" *Journal of Japanese studies* 5.2 (1979) 385–403. ISSN 0095-6848. ▸ Traces origins of Japan's outcast groups (*eta-hinin*) and their role in medieval society. [MC]

12.126 Nagahara Keiji. "The medieval peasant." In *The Cambridge history of Japan.* Kōzō Yamamura, ed., vol. 3, pp. 301–43. Cambridge: Cambridge University Press, 1989. ISBN 0-521-22354-7. ▸ Survey of peasant life and village organization in medieval period. [MC]

12.127 Nagahara Keiji. "The *sengoku daimyo* and the *kandaka* system." In *Japan before Tokugawa: political consolidation and economic growth, 1500–1650.* John Whitney Hall, Nagahara Keiji, and Kōzō Yamamura, eds., pp. 27–63. Princeton: Princeton University Press, 1981. ISBN 0-691-05308-1 (cl), 0-691-10216-3 (pbk). ▸ Assessment of impact of attempts by *daimyō* (feudal lords) of age of wars (*sengoku*) in early sixteenth century to register all land within their domains in terms of its *kandaka,* cash equivalent of yield in goods and services to vassal from his holdings. [MC]

12.128 Nagahara Keiji and Kōzō Yamamura. "Village communities and *daimyo* power." In *Japan in the Muromachi age.* John Whitney Hall and Toyoda Takeshi, eds., pp. 107–24. Berkeley: University of California Press, 1977. ISBN 0-520-02888-0 (cl), 0-520-03214-4 (pbk). ▸ Emphasizes role of organized village communities as participants in economic and political power struggles of fifteenth and sixteenth centuries. [MC]

12.129 Chieko Irie Mulhern, ed. *Heroic with grace: legendary women of Japan.* Armonk, N.Y.: Sharpe, 1991. ISBN 0-87332-527-3 (cl), 0-87332-552-4 (pbk). ▸ Important for studies of three premodern women: Empress Jingū (shamaness ruler), Tomoe (woman warrior), and Hōjō Masako (dowager shogun whose legendary jealousy is placed in sociohistorical context). [MC]

12.130 Karl Ulrich Wolfgang Pauly. *Ikkō-ikki: die Ikkō-Aufstände und ihre Entwicklung aus den Aufstanden der bündischen Bauern und Provinzialen des japanischen Mittelalters.* Bonn: Bonn University Press, 1985. ▸ Detailed study of Ikkō *ikki* as continuation of kokujin rebellions. [MC]

12.131 Ginya Sasaki. "*Sengoku daimyō* rule and commerce." In *Japan before Tokugawa: political consolidation and economic growth, 1500–1650.* John Whitney Hall, Nagahara Keiji, and Kōzō Yamamura, eds., pp. 125–48. Princeton: Princeton University Press, 1981. ISBN 0-691-05308-1 (cl), 0-691-10216-3 (pbk). ▸ Stresses *daimyō* (feudal lords) struggle for economic expoitation of and security within their domains and regulation and control of trade as means of undergirding their political control. Argues control of trade became economic and military necessity for *sengoku daimyō* struggling to establish firm hold over their domains. [MC]

12.132 Toyoda Takeshi. *A history of pre-Meiji commerce in Japan.* Tokyo: Kokusai Bunka Shinkokai; distributed by Japan Publications Trading Co., 1969. ▸ Descriptive account of commercial development from medieval period. [HW]

12.133 Toyoda Takeshi, Sugiyama Hiroshi, and V. Dixon Morris. "The growth of commerce and the trades." In *Japan in the Muromachi age.* John Whitney Hall and Toyoda Takeshi, eds., pp. 129–44. Berkeley: University of California Press, 1977. ISBN 0-520-02888-0 (cl), 0-520-03214-4 (pbk). ▸ Introduction to role of commerce, guilds, and commercial houses in growing economy of fifteenth and sixteenth centuries. Mentions role of nobles and warriors as consumers and argues that merchants in this period moved from subordination to freedom. [MC]

12.134 Hitomi Tonomura. *Community and commerce in late medieval Japan: the corporate villages of Tokuchin-ho.* Stanford, Calif.: Stanford University Press, 1992. ISBN 0-8047-1941-1. ▸ Uses collection of documents, *Imabori Hiyoshi Jinja Monjo Shūsei* edited by Nakamura Ken, to produce fine, comprehensive study of late medieval village. Stresses relative vitality and independence of late medieval village compared with its Tokugawa period successor. [MC]

12.135 Wakita Haruko. "Dimensions of development: cities in fifteenth- and sixteenth-century Japan." In *Japan before Tokugawa: political consolidation and economic growth, 1500–1650.* John Whitney Hall, Nagahara Keiji, and Kōzō Yamamura, eds., pp. 295–326. Princeton: Princeton University Press, 1981. ISBN 0-691-05308-1 (cl), 0-691-10216-3 (pbk). ▸ Good essay on urban development of age of wars (*sengoku*). Considers definitions of city, urban self-government, rights to administer justice and degrees of freedom, economic base and taxation, property rights, and relations with feudal lords (*daimyō*). [MC]

12.136 Wakita Haruko. "Marriage and property in premodern Japan from the perspective of women's history." *Journal of Japanese studies* 10.1 (1984) 73–99. ISSN 0095-6848. ▸ Informative

essay on women's marital status and property rights in medieval society by leading scholar in field. [MC]

12.137 Wakita Haruko. "Towards a wider perspective on medieval commerce." *Journal of Japanese studies* 1.2 (1975) 321–45. ISSN 0095-6848. ▸ Stresses growing importance of commerce in medieval economy. [MC]

12.138 Kōzō Yamamura. "The development of *za* in medieval Japan." *Business history review* 47.4 (1972) 438–65. ISSN 0007-6805. ▸ Introduction to activities of medieval guilds (*za*). [MC]

12.139 Kōzō Yamamura. "The growth of commerce in medieval Japan." In *The Cambridge history of Japan.* Kōzō Yamamura, ed., vol. 3, pp. 344–95. Cambridge: Cambridge University Press, 1989. ISBN 0-521-22354-7. ▸ Outline of initial conditions followed by discussion of acceleration of commerce, transportation, and monetization. Treats growth of guilds, cities, ports, and markets between twelfth and sixteenth centuries. Concludes with discussion of effects of changes on politics and society. [MC]

Culture and Religion

12.140 William M. Bodiford. *Sōtō Zen in medieval Japan.* Honolulu: University of Hawaii Press, 1993. ISBN 0-8248-1482-7. ▸ Excellent study of development of Sōtō tradition of Zen in medieval Japan. Looks at early communities and their leaders, regional expansion, and Sōtō Zen's reach into lives of ordinary people through conduct of funerals and simplification of Zen training and ordination. [MC]

12.141 Martin Collcutt. "*Daimyo* and *daimyo* culture." In *Japan: the shaping of daimyo culture, 1185–1868.* 1988 ed. Yoshiaki Shimizu, ed., pp. 1–46. New York: Braziller, 1989. ISBN 0-8076-1214-6 (cl), 0-89468-122-2 (pbk). ▸ Essay on cultural interests of Japan's warrior leaders in medieval and early modern periods. Stresses importance of civilian culture (*bun*) as well as military arts (*bu*). [MC]

12.142 Martin Collcutt. "Zen and the *gozan*." In *The Cambridge history of Japan.* Kōzō Yamamura, ed., vol. 3, pp. 583–652. Cambridge: Cambridge University Press, 1989. ISBN 0-521-22354-7. ▸ Examination of development of Rinzai Zen in medieval Japan, economy and administration, and changes in Zen practice, culture, and monastic life. [MC]

12.143 Barbara Ruch. "The other side of culture in medieval Japan." In *The Cambridge history of Japan.* Kōzō Yamamura, ed., vol. 3, pp. 500–43. Cambridge: Cambridge University Press, 1989. ISBN 0-521-22354-7. ▸ Fascinating essay on popular culture in medieval Japan; one of the more original essays in volume. Pathbreaking study of medieval popular culture, arts of painting, sculpture, song, dance, and musical epic among common people, and lives of nuns, shamans, singers, dancers, and blind balladiers. [MC]

12.144 H. Paul Varley. "Cultural life in medieval Japan." In *The Cambridge history of Japan.* Kōzō Yamamura, ed., vol. 3, pp. 447–99. Cambridge: Cambridge University Press, 1989. ISBN 0-521-22354-7. ▸ Useful introduction to elite culture and some aspects of popular culture of medieval Japan. Starts with warrior and courtly culture of Kamakura period, treating literary, poetic, and dramatic culture of medieval poetry and Noh plays. Ends with culture of tea and decorative and genre painting of sixteenth century. [MC]

12.145 Stanley Weinstein. "Rennyo and the *shinshū* revival." In *Japan in the Muromachi age.* John Whitney Hall and Toyoda Takeshi, eds., pp. 331–59. Berkeley: University of California Press, 1977. ISBN 0-520-02888-0 (cl), 0-520-03214-4 (pbk). ▸ Examination of role of priest Rennyo in reinvigorating True Pure Land Buddhism (Jōdo Shinshū) by reviving and making accessible, through pastoral letters (*ofumi*), teachings of Shinran and by unifying various groups of believers under leadership of Honganji. [MC]

Foreign Relations and Overseas Trade

12.146 Shōji Kawazoe. "Japan and East Asia." In *The Cambridge history of Japan*. Kōzō Yamamura, ed., vol. 3, pp. 396–446. Cambridge: Cambridge University Press, 1989. ISBN 0-521-22354-7. ‣ Discussion of Mongol invasions, tribute system, Ashikaga Yoshimitsu's use of title king of Japan, official tally trade with China, and piracy under Muromachi *bakufu* (shogunate). Rare discussions in English of East Asian trading sphere including Korean and Ryūkyūan as well as Chinese trade with Japan. [MC]

12.147 Takeo Tanaka. "Japan's relations with overseas countries." In *Japan in the Muromachi age*. John Whitney Hall and Toyoda Takeshi, eds., pp. 159–78. Berkeley: University of California Press, 1977. ISBN 0-520-02888-0 (cl), 0-520-03214-4 (pbk). ‣ Overview of official tally trade with China during Muromachi period and freebooting and marauding activities of Japanese pirates. [MC]

12.148 Charlotte von Verschuer. *Le commerce extérieur du Japon des origines au dix-sixième siècle*. Paris: Maisonneuve & Larose, 1988. ISBN 2-7068-0976-0. ‣ Useful survey of Japanese foreign trade. [MC]

12.149 Wang Yi-t'ung. *Official relations between China and Japan, 1368–1549*. Cambridge Mass.: Harvard University Press, 1953. (Harvard-Yenching Institute studies, 9.) ‣ Study of revival of official relations and tally trade in Muromachi period. [MC]

SIXTEENTH CENTURY

Political and Military Unification

12.150 Galen Dean Amstutz. "The Honganji institution, 1500–1570: the politics of Pure Land Buddhism in late medieval Japan." Ph.D. dissertation. Princeton: Princeton University, 1992. ‣ Study of Honganji-led True Pure Land movement based on Honganji documents. [MC]

12.151 Naohiro Asao. "The sixteenth-century unification." In *The Cambridge history of Japan*. John Whitney Hall and James L. McClain, eds., vol. 4, pp. 40–95. Cambridge: Cambridge University Press, 1991. ISBN 0-521-22355-5. ‣ Discussion of process of unification in terms of politics, military and economic forces, changes in international relations, and power structure of unified state. [HW]

12.152 Mary Elizabeth Berry. *Hideyoshi*. 1982 ed. Cambridge, Mass.: Council on East Asian Studies, Harvard University; distributed by Harvard University Press, 1989. (Harvard East Asian monographs, 146.) ISBN 0-674-39025-3 (cl), 0-674-39026-1 (pbk). ‣ Readable study of Toyotomi Hideyoshi, general and *daimyō* (feudal lord). Goes beyond biography to deal with political, economic, and international issues of period. Stresses durability of Hideyoshi legacy of federal rule, separation of classes, regulation of movement, monopolization of political power by military, restriction on arms, and redistribution of land. Slight attention to Korean invasions and to complex land policies. [MC]

12.153 Michael P. Birt. "Samurai in passage: transformation of the sixteenth-century Kanto." *Journal of Japanese studies* 11 (1985) 369–89. ISSN 0095-6848. ‣ Argues sengoku *daimyō* (feudal lords), long prior to Hideyoshi, began process of withdrawing samurai from scattered fiefs in countryside to residence in or near *daimyō*'s garrison. [MC]

12.154 Delmer M. Brown. "The impact of firearms on Japanese warfare, 1543–98." *Far Eastern quarterly* 7.3 (1948) 236–53. ISSN 0363-6917. ‣ Discussion of important role of firearms by Nobunaga and other *daimyō* (feudal lords) in campaigns that brought reunification of country. More reliable than Perrin 12.166. [MC]

12.155 George Elison. "The cross and the sword: patterns of Momoyama history." In *Warlords, artists, and commoners: Japan in the sixteenth century*. George Elison and Bardwell L. Smith, eds., pp. 56–85. Honolulu: University of Hawaii Press, 1981. ISBN 0-8248-0692-1 (cl), 0-8248-1109-7 (pbk). ‣ Outlines several important themes in history of late sixteenth century. Interesting vignettes of Oda Nobunaga and Toyotomi Hideyoshi. Examines effects of Japan's encounter with Christianity. Argues effort to reduce threat Japanese perceived in all uncompromising religious organizations eventually led to elimination of Christian faith from country; result of conviction that Christian ideology perverted society. [MC]

12.156 George Elison. "Hideyoshi, the bountiful minister." In *Warlords, artists, and commoners: Japan in the sixteenth century*. George Elison and Bardwell L. Smith, pp. 223–44. Honolulu: University of Hawaii Press, 1981. ISBN 0-8248-0692-1 (cl), 0-8248-1109-7 (pbk). ‣ Lively, irreverent, insightful essay on aristocratization of feudal lord Toyotomi Hideyoshi, spectacular *parvenu* who cloaked his raw political power in mantle of bountiful patronage. [MC]

12.157 George Elison and Bardwell L. Smith. *Warlords, artists, and commoners: Japan in the sixteenth century*. Honolulu: University of Hawaii Press, 1981. ISBN 0-8248-0692-1 (cl), 0-8248-1109-7 (pbk). ‣ Excellent essays on culture and politics of sixteenth century. [MC]

12.158 Hisashi Fujiki. "The political posture of Oda Nobunaga." In *Japan before Tokugawa: political consolidation and economic growth, 1500–1650*. John Whitney Hall, Nagahara Keiji, and Kōzō Yamamura, eds., pp. 149–93. Princeton: Princeton University Press, 1981. ISBN 0-691-05308-1 (cl), 0-691-10216-3 (pbk). ‣ Analysis of political aspect of feudal lord's rule, 1568–82, emphasizing problems of legitimacy. Introduces concepts of *kōgi* (public authority) and *tenka* (realm) in reference to legitimation of hegemonic authority. Raises issue of whether Nobunaga aspired to replace emperor and whether he could have done so. Also considers Nobunaga's interest in office of shogun. [MC]

12.159 John Whitney Hall. "Hideyoshi's domestic policies." In *Japan before Tokugawa: political consolidation and economic growth, 1500–1650*. John Whitney Hall, Nagahara Keiji, and Kōzō Yamamura, eds., pp. 194–223. Princeton: Princeton University Press, 1981. ISBN 0-691-05308-1 (cl), 0-691-10216-3 (pbk). ‣ Survey of feudal lord's domestic policies in five levels of activity: national governance, local administration, samurai class, land-cultivating class, and land-tax system. Concludes Toyotomi Hideyoshi neither originator of nor fully responsible for changes that occurred in his time, but was prime mover in establishment of new national order, so-called early modern *baku-han* (combined shogunal-domainal) state. [MC]

12.160 John Whitney Hall. "Japan's sixteenth-century revolution." In *Warlords, artists, and commoners: Japan in the sixteenth century*. George Elison and Bardwell L. Smith, eds., pp. 7–21. Honolulu: University of Hawaii Press, 1981. ISBN 0-8248-0692-1 (cl), 0-8248-1109-7 (pbk). ‣ Advances idea that Japan experienced revolutionary changes of pace and direction in political and economic life during sixteenth and early seventeenth centuries. [MC]

12.161 John Whitney Hall, ed. *Early modern Japan*. Vol. 4 of *The Cambridge history of Japan*. Cambridge: Cambridge University Press, 1991. ISBN 0-521-22355-5. ‣ Chapters by leading Western and Japanese specialists on political, economic, cultural, and intellectual development of Japan in its transition from warring provinces, through unification, to Pax Tokugawa. [MC]

12.162 Marius B. Jansen. "Tosa in the sixteenth century: the 100-article code of Chosokabe Motochika." In *Studies in the institutional history of early modern Japan*. John Whitney Hall and

Marius B. Jansen, eds., pp. 89–114. Princeton: Princeton University Press, 1968. ISBN 0-691-03071-5 (cl), 0-691-00013-1 (pbk). ‣ Translation and detailed commentary on one of the major *daimyō* (feudal lord) house codes of sixteenth century. Insights into life in Tosa seen from perspective of warrior rulers. [HW]

12.163 James Kanda. "Japanese feudal society in the sixteenth century as seen through the Jinkaishū and other legal codes." Ph.D. dissertation. Cambridge, Mass.: Harvard University, 1974. ‣ Study of comprehensive Date warrior-family code. [MC]

12.164 Shizuo Katsumata. "The development of *sengoku* law." In *Japan before Tokugawa: political consolidation and economic growth 1500–1650*. John Whitney Hall, Nagahara Keiji, and Kōzō Yamamura, eds., pp. 101–24. Princeton: Princeton University Press, 1981. ISBN 0-691-05308-1 (cl), 0-691-10216-3 (pbk). ‣ Analysis of laws issued by *daimyō* (feudal lords) of age of wars (*sengoku*) to reveal their concept of ruling authority. Stresses *daimyō* conviction that their territories constituted nation or state (*kokka*), as basis for their right to rule and to issue law. Compares notion of *kokka* with Oda Nobunaga's assertion of *tenka* (realm). [MC]

12.165 Neil McMullin. *Buddhism and the state in sixteenth-century Japan*. Princeton: Princeton University Press, 1984. ISBN 0-691-07291-4. ‣ Lively study of Oda Nobunaga's harsh treatment of Buddhism and curtailing of monastic military power. [MC]

12.166 Noel Perrin. *Giving up the gun: Japan's reversion to the sword, 1543–1879*. Boston: Godine, 1979. ISBN 0-87923-278-1. ‣ Provocative but unreliable; based almost entirely on Western sources. Presses evidence to create utopian vision of Tokugawa disarmament. Brown 12.154 more reliable. [MC]

12.167 Bardwell L. Smith. "Japanese society and culture in the Momoyama era: a bibliographic essay." In *Warlords, artists, and commoners: Japan in the sixteenth century*. George Elison and Bardwell L. Smith, eds., pp. 245–79. Honolulu: University of Hawaii Press, 1981. ISBN 0-8248-0692-1 (cl), 0-8248-1109-7 (pbk). ‣ Essential starting point in establishing bibliography of Western-language works on late sixteenth and early seventeenth centuries. Annotated bibliography and survey of main areas of research. [MC]

12.168 Bernard Susser. "The Toyotomi regime and the *daimyō*." In *The bakufu in Japanese history*. Jeffrey P. Mass and William B. Hauser, eds., pp. 129–52. Stanford, Calif.: Stanford University Press, 1985. ISBN 0-8047-1278-6. ‣ Useful account of policies and military campaigns of Hideyoshi as they affected *daimyō* (feudal lords). Also discusses armies commanded by Hideyoshi, which reached total strength of 280,000 for invasion of Korea in 1593. [MC]

12.169 Wakita Osamu. "The emergence of the state in sixteenth-century Japan, from Oda to Tokugawa." *Journal of Japanese studies* 8 (Summer 1982) 343–67. ISSN 0095-6848. ‣ Study of state formation stressing critical role of Toyotomi Hideyoshi. [HW]

Economy and Society

12.170 Michael Cooper. *They came of Japan: an anthology of European reports on Japan, 1543–1640*. Berkeley: University of California Press, 1965. ISBN 0-520-04509-2 (pbk). ‣ Fascinating firsthand accounts of sixteenth-century Japanese society by European missionaries and merchants. Selections from letters, diaries, and other writings of more than thirty Europeans who came to Japan during so-called Christian century. Brief reports offer composite glimpse of Japanese life. [MC]

12.171 Michael Cooper, trans. and ed. *This island of Japon: João Rodrigues' account of sixteenth-century Japan*. Tokyo: Kodansha

International, 1973. ISBN 0-87011-194-9. ‣ Translation of that part of Rodrigues's (1561–1634) *Historia da Igreja do Japão* (1620–21), that treats customs, history, and daily life of Japan. Astute, culturally sensitive, and influential Jesuit who frequently served as interpreter to both Toyotomi Hideyoshi and Tokugawa Ieyasu. Includes excellent abridged translation of first two-thirds of this work. [MC]

12.172 Seichi Iwao. "Japanese foreign trade in the sixteenth and seventeenth centuries." *Acta Asiatica* 30 (1976) 1–18. ISSN 0567-7254. ‣ Useful introduction by leading Japanese specialist. [MC]

12.173 Atsushi Kobata. "The production and uses of gold and silver in sixteenth- and seventeenth-century Japan." *Economic history review*, Second series, 18.1–3 (1965) 245–66. ISSN 0013-0117. ‣ Discussion of progress of mining industry, development of foreign trade in gold and silver, and increased use of gold and silver as currency. [MC]

12.174 V. Dixon Morris. "The city of Sakai and urban autonomy." *Warlords, artists, and commoners: Japan in the sixteenth century*. George Elison and Bardwell L. Smith, eds., pp. 23–54. Honolulu: University of Hawaii Press, 1981. ISBN 0-8248-0692-1 (cl), 0-8248-1109-7 (pbk). ‣ Explores nature of urban autonomy in Sakai, next to Kyoto most important town of period. Although idea of creative force of people's energy is commonplace in Japanese historiography, author finds in Sakai little trace of spirit of popular resistance against feudal forces. Instead, finds collaboration was citizen's customary mode of political action. [MC]

12.175 Giuliana Stramigioli. "Hideyoshi's expansionist policy on the Asiatic mainland." *Transactions of the Asiatic Society of Japan*, Second series, 3.1 (1954) 74–116. ‣ Introduction to invasions drawing principally on Japanese materials. [MC]

12.176 Wakita Osamu. "The commercial and urban policies of Oda Nobunaga and Toyotomi Hideyoshi." In *Japan before Tokugawa: political consolidation and economic growth, 1500–1650*. John Whitney Hall, Nagahara Keiji, and Kōzō Yamamura, eds., pp. 224–47. Princeton: Princeton University Press, 1981. ISBN 0-691-05308-1 (cl), 0-691-10216-3 (pbk). ‣ Outline of common features in commercial policies of two unifiers. Demonstrates that while, during era of Oda Nobunaga, court families and religious institutions still exercised considerable power, Toyotomi Hideyoshi with stronger power base was able to dissolve guilds and stop development of temple towns. [MC]

12.177 Wakita Osamu. "The social and economic consequences of unification." In *The Cambridge history of Japan*. John Whitney Hall and James L. McClain, eds., vol. 4, pp. 96–127. Cambridge: Cambridge University Press, 1991. ISBN 0-521-22355-5. ‣ Analysis of economic impact of military and political unification achieved in late sixteenth and early seventeenth centuries. [HW]

12.178 Kōzō Yamamura. "From coins to rice: hypotheses on the *kandaka* and *kokudaka* systems." *Journal of Japanese studies* 14 (1988) 348–67. ISSN 0095-6848. ‣ Study of coexistence of cash-based and rice-based economies. [MC]

12.179 Kōzō Yamamura. "Returns on unification: economic growth in Japan, 1550–1650." In *Japan before Tokugawa: political consolidation and economic growth, 1500–1650*. John Whitney Hall, Nagahara Keiji, and Kōzō Yamamura, eds., pp. 327–72. Princeton: Princeton University Press, 1981. ISBN 0-691-05308-1 (cl), 0-691-10216-3 (pbk). ‣ Argues for agricultural revolution in sixteenth and early seventeenth centuries brought about by political unification and increased number of new class of independent peasants. Agricultural spurt, in turn, fed acceleration in commerce. [HW]

Christianity

12.180 Charles R. Boxer. *The Christian century in Japan, 1549–1650*. 1951 ed. Berkeley: University of California Press, 1967.

▸ Standard account of Catholic mission effort stressing great gains in sixteenth century and cruel persecution in seventeenth. Deals with Christian presence within larger social and political framework. Written generally from Western perspective drawing heavily on Western sources. One of best introductions to Christian culture and missionary life during period. [MC]

12.181 Michael Cooper. *Rodrigues the interpreter: an early Jesuit in Japan and China.* New York: Weatherhill, 1974. ISBN 0-8348-0094-2. ▸ Biography of João Rodrigues drawing from his *História da Igreja do Japão.* Less effective than *This Island of Japon* (12.171) but still interesting reading. [MC]

12.182 George Elison. "Christianity and the *daimyo.*" In *The Cambridge history of Japan.* John Whitney Hall and James L. McClain, eds., vol. 4, pp. 301–72. Cambridge: Cambridge University Press, 1991. ISBN 0-521-22355-5. ▸ Thorough survey of Catholic missionary effort in terms of missionary attempts to convert *daimyō* (feudal lords), who were later subjected to intense political pressure under anti-Christian policies of Toyotomi Hideyoshi and Tokugawa Ieyasu. Excellent survey of spread of Christianity, political calculations of missionary leaders, and political concerns of *daimyō* and unifiers. [MC]

12.183 George Elison. *Deus destroyed: the image of Christianity in early modern Japan.* 1973 ed. Cambridge, Mass.: Council on East Asian Studies, Harvard University; distributed by Harvard University Press, 1988. (Harvard East Asian series, 72.) ISBN 0-674-19962-6. ▸ Discussion of intrusion of Christianity from Japanese perspective based primarily on Japanese sources. Complements Boxer 12.180. Particularly valuable for treatment of problems that Christianity faced in Japan, how Catholic church sought to accommodate itself to Japanese culture, and for its account of polemics and counterpolemics engaged in by Christians and Buddhists alike. Includes translations of four anti-Christian tracts published 1620 and 1662. [MC]

12.184 John Laures. *The Catholic church in Japan: a short history.* 1954 ed. Westport, Conn.: Greenwood, 1970. ▸ Survey of Catholic mission effort. [MC]

TOKUGAWA PERIOD, 1600–1868

Political History

12.185 Naohiro Asao. "Shogun and *tennō.*" In *Japan before Tokugawa: political consolidation and economic growth, 1500–1650.* John Whitney Hall, Nagahara Keiji, and Kōzō Yamamura, eds., pp. 248–94. Princeton: Princeton University Press, 1981. ISBN 0-691-05308-1 (cl), 0-691-10216-3 (pbk). ▸ Treatment of problem of legitimacy still encountered by Tokugawa shoguns following Ieyasu's death. Control of imperial symbol was critical, as was image of shogun as national protector; gained through suppression of Christianity and enforcement of National Closure policy. [HW]

12.186 Beatrice Bodart Bailey. "The laws of compassion." *Monumenta Nipponica* 40 (1985) 163–89. ISSN 0027-0741. ▸ Study of Tokugawa Tsunayoshi's laws prohibiting cruelty to animals. [MC]

12.187 Mary Elizabeth Berry. "Public peace and private attachment: the goals and conduct of power in early modern Japan." *Journal of Japanese studies* 12 (1986) 237–71. ISSN 0095-6848. ▸ Thoughtful discussion of power bases and problems of political legitimation in late sixteenth- and early seventeenth-century Japan. [MC]

12.188 Harold Bolitho. "The *han.*" In *The Cambridge history of Japan.* John Whitney Hall and James L. McClain, eds., vol. 4, pp. 183–234. Cambridge: Cambridge University Press, 1991. ISBN 0-521-22355-5. ▸ Looks at the *baku-han* (combined shogunal-domainal) power structure from point of view of domains

(*han*), with emphasis on domain governance, finances, and politics. [HW]

12.189 Harold Bolitho. *Treasures among men: the fudai daimyō in Tokugawa Japan.* New Haven: Yale University Press, 1974. ISBN 0-300-01655-7. ▸ Intrepretive study of Tokugawa political system focusing on role of *fudai daimyō* ("house" feudal lords), group of hereditary feudal lords who owed personal allegiance to Tokugawa shogun and served as powerful bureaucratic administrators in *bakufu* (shogunal) government. [HW]

12.190 Lee A. Butler. "Court and *bakufu* in early seventeenth-century Japan." Ph.D. dissertation. Princeton: Princeton University, 1991. ▸ Only study of court-*bakufu* (shogunate) relations in formative phase of Tokugawa rule. [MC]

12.191 John Whitney Hall. "The *bakuhan* system." In *The Cambridge history of Japan.* John Whitney Hall and James L. McClain, eds., vol. 4, pp. 128–82. Cambridge: Cambridge University Press, 1991. ISBN 0-521-22355-5. ▸ Deals with rise to power of Tokugawa Ieyasu, formation of Edo *bakufu* (shogunate), and entrenchment of Tokugawa power. Describes central power structure and organization of *bakufu* as government. [HW]

12.192 John Whitney Hall. "Feudalism in Japan—a reassessment." In *Studies in the institutional history of early modern Japan.* John Whitney Hall and Marius B. Jansen, eds., pp. 15–54. Princeton: Princeton University Press, 1968. ISBN 0-691-03071-5 (cl), 0-691-00013-1 (pbk). ▸ Considers, and questions, usefulness of feudalism as concept in explaining Tokugawa history. Rejects Marxist view of "feudalism" as central feature of premodern Japanese development in favor of familial organization. [HW]

12.193 John Whitney Hall. "Foundations of the modern Japanese *daimyō.*" In *Studies in the institutional history of early modern Japan.* John Whitney Hall and Marius B. Jansen, eds., pp. 65–77. Princeton: Princeton University Press, 1968. ISBN 0-691-03071-5 (cl), 0-691-00013-1 (pbk). ▸ Distinguishes four main types of *daimyō* (feudal lords) from *sengoku* (age of wars) *daimyō* through sixteenth century to vassal and allied *daimyō* of Tokugawa *baku-han* (shogunal-domainal) system. [HW]

12.194 John Whitney Hall. *Tanuma Okitsugu, 1719–1788: forerunner of modern Japan.* Cambridge, Mass.: Harvard University Press, 1955. ▸ Argues that in spite of his reputation for corruption, Tanuma, as shogunal favorite and chief *bakufu* (shogunate) official, explored novel mercantile solutions to *bakufu*'s chronic indebtedness. [HW]

12.195 John Whitney Hall and Marius B. Jansen, eds. *Studies in the institutional history of early modern Japan.* Princeton: Princeton University Press, 1968. ISBN 0-691-03071-5 (cl), 0-691-00013-19 (pbk). ▸ One of most influential collections of essays on premodern Japan. Twenty-one studies of Tokugawa institutional development analyzing responsiveness of political, social, and economic institutions to changes of that era. [HW]

12.196 William B. Hauser. "Osaka castle and Tokugawa authority in western Japan." In *The bakufu in Japanese history.* Jeffrey P. Mass and William B. Hauser, eds., pp. 153–72. Stanford, Calif.: Stanford University Press, 1985. ISBN 0-8047-1278-6. ▸ Discussion of role of Ōsaka castle as outpost for Tokugawa surveillance and control of western Japan. [HW]

12.197 Marius B. Jansen. "Japan in the early nineteenth century." In *The Cambridge history of Japan.* Marius B. Jansen, ed., vol. 5, pp. 50–115. Cambridge: Cambridge University Press, 1989. ISBN 0-521-22356-3. ▸ Examination of changes in political and social scene in Japan in late eighteenth and early nineteenth centuries. [MC]

12.198 Kate Wildman Nakai. *Shogunal politics: Arai Hakuseki and the premises of Tokugawa rule.* Cambridge, Mass.: Council on East Asian Studies, Harvard University; distributed by Harvard

University Press, 1988. (Harvard East Asian Monographs, 134.) ISBN 0-674-80653-0. ‣ Political and intellectual biography of *bakufu* (shogunate) reformer Arai Hakuseki (1657–1725). Suggests his failures in trying to transform shogun into ruling monarch are as revealing as his successes in reform of currency, foreign trade, or local administration. [HW]

12.199 E. Herbert Norman. *Origins of the modern Japanese state: selected writings of E. H. Norman.* John W. Dower, ed. New York: Pantheon, 1975. ISBN 0-394-49413-X (cl), 0-394-70927-6 (pbk). ‣ Convenient reprinting of some of author's most important writings with hard-hitting reassessment by Dower claiming place for Norman as major historian of modern Japanese development. [HW]

12.200 Shinzaburō Ōishi. "The *bakuhan* system." In *Tokugawa Japan: the social and economic antecedents of modern Japan.* Chie Nakane and Shinzaburō Ōishi, eds., pp. 11–36. Tokyo: Tokyo University Press, 1990. ISBN 0-86008-447-7. ‣ Brief overview of Tokugawa system of rule. [MC]

12.201 Herman Ooms. *Charismatic bureaucrat: a political biography of Matsudaira Sadanobu, 1758–1829.* Chicago: University of Chicago Press, 1975. ISBN 0-226-63031-5. ‣ Applies notion of charisma to political and intellectual biography of major domain and *bakufu* (shogunate) bureaucrat-reformer. Probably last effective defender of Tokugawa order, Matsudaira invigorated faltering regime. [HW]

12.202 Robert K. Sakai. "The consolidation of power in Satsuma-han." In *Studies in the institutional history of early modern Japan.* John Whitney Hall and Marius B. Jansen, eds., pp. 131–39. Princeton: Princeton University Press, 1968. ISBN 0-691-03071-5 (cl), 0-691-00013-1 (pbk). ‣ Study of rule by Shimazu *daimyō* (family of "outside" feudal lords) house in Kyushu and its articulation within *baku-han* (combined shogunal-domainal) system. [HW]

12.203 Donald H. Shively. "Tokugawa Tsunayoshi, the *genroku* shogun." In *Personality in Japanese history.* Albert M. Craig and Donald H. Shively, eds., pp. 85–126. Berkeley: University of California Press, 1970. ISBN 0-520-01699-8. ‣ Places Tsunayoshi, fifth shogun, in context of *genroku* era (1688–1704) and discusses his reform policies and edicts enforcing Compassion for Living Beings that earned him title of "dog shogun." [MC]

12.204 Ronald P. Toby. *State and diplomacy in early modern Japan: Asia in the development of the Tokugawa bakufu.* 1984 ed. Stanford: Stanford University Press, 1991. ISBN 0-8047-1951-9 (cl), 0-8047-1952-7 (pbk). ‣ Pathbreaking study emphasizing East Asian diplomacy as vital element in *bakufu* (shogunate) legitimation. Paperback edition contains revised introduction. [HW]

12.205 Conrad Totman. *Early modern Japan.* Berkeley: University of California Press, 1993. ISBN 0-520-08026-2. ‣ Comprehensive (597-page) survey of Japan's early modern period (1568–1868). Blends political, economic, intellectual, literary, and cultural history. Introduces new ecological perspective covering natural disasters, resource use, demographics, and river control. [MC]

12.206 Conrad Totman. *Politics in the Tokugawa bakufu, 1600–1843.* 1967 ed. Berkeley: University of California Press, 1988. ISBN 0-520-06313-9 (pbk). ‣ Still best guide to workings of Tokugawa *bakufu* (shogunate). Describes *bakufu* as "working institution" and examines how regime kept peace for so long. Main weaknesses are its rather static descriptive character and its imputation of steady "bureaucratic rationalization" to *bakufu* leadership and decision making. Paperback edition contains new preface that addresses these flaws and contains useful updated bibliographical supplement. [HW]

12.207 Conrad Totman. *Tokugawa Ieyasu, shogun: a biography.*

San Francisco: Heian, 1983. ISBN 0-89346-210-1. ‣ Nicely written biography of Tokugawa Ieyasu, founder of Tokugawa shogunate. For general readers; draws heavily on work of Nakamura Kōya and other Japanese Ieyasu specialists. [MC]

12.208 Tsuji Tatsuya. "Politics in the eighteenth century." In *The Cambridge history of Japan.* John Whitney Hall and James L. McClain, eds., vol. 4, pp. 425–77. Cambridge: Cambridge University Press, 1991. ISBN 0-521-22355-5. ‣ Close look at reigns of Tokugawa shoguns Tsunayoshi and Yoshimune and successive *bakufu* (shogunate) reform efforts of eighteenth century by distinguished Japanese specialist. [HW]

12.209 T. G. Tsukahira. *Feudal control in Tokugawa Japan: the sankin kōtai system.* Cambridge, Mass.: East Asian Research Center; distributed by Harvard University Press, 1966. ‣ Standard descriptive account of Tokugawa hostage system of alternate-year attendance by *daimyō* (feudal lords) in Edo. [HW]

SEE ALSO

13.73 Herschel Webb. *The Japanese imperial institution in the Tokugawa period.*

Law and Legal Institutions

12.210 William H. Coaldrake. "Edo architecture and Tokugawa law." *Monumenta Nipponica* 36.3 (1981) 235–84. ISSN 0027-0741. ‣ Groundbreaking study relating architecture to its social and legal environment. Focuses on legal methods used by *bakufu* (shogunate) to curb ostentation and prevent fires. [MC]

12.211 Dan Fenno Henderson. *Conciliation and Japanese law: Tokugawa and modern.* 2 vols. Seattle: University of Washington Press for the Association for Asian Studies, 1965. ‣ Standard account of development of Japanese legal principles and practice. Stresses tendency to reach compromise agreements prior to trial. Extensive bibliography. [HW]

12.212 Dan Fenno Henderson. "Contracts in Tokugawa villages." *Journal of Japanese studies* 1 (1974) 51–81. ISSN 0095-6848. ‣ Useful study of nature of contract in villages and shogunal attitude to nonpenal law enforcement. [MC]

12.213 Dan Fenno Henderson. "The evolution of Tokugawa law." In *Studies in the institutional history of early modern Japan.* John Whitney Hall and Marius B. Jansen, eds., pp. 203–30. Princeton: Princeton University Press, 1968. ISBN 0-691-03071-5 (cl), 0-691-00013-1 (pbk). ‣ Still best introduction to legal institutions and practices of Edo period. Stresses that Tokugawa administration was authoritarian and efficient at all levels, that justiciable law was undeveloped, and that tendencies to individualize decisions and to press for conciliation were both antilegal features of Tokugawa justice. [HW]

12.214 Dan Fenno Henderson. *Village "contracts" in Tokugawa Japan: fifty specimens with English translations and comments.* Seattle: University of Washington Press, 1975. ISBN 0-295-95405-1. ‣ Useful discussion of legal practice and notion of contract in Tokugawa villages. Provides insight into family and kinship, taxation, labor, and status system as well as legal issues. [MC]

Status System

Samurai

12.215 Bonnie F. Abiko. "Watanabe Kazan: the man and his times." Ph.D. dissertation. Princeton: Princeton University, 1982. ‣ Biographical study of Kazan focusing on his art and harsh treatment by *bakufu* (shogunate). [MC]

12.216 Arai Hakuseki. *Told round a brushwood fire: the autobiography of Arai Hakuseki.* Joyce Ackroyd, trans. Princeton: Princeton University Press, 1980. ISBN 0-691-04671-9. ‣ First scholarly translation of one of most revealing Edo period autobiographies of scholar, statesman, and shogunal advisor. Fascinating autobiography; uneven translation. [MC]

12.217   Ronald P. Dore. "Talent and social order in Tokugawa Japan." In *Studies in the institutional history of early modern Japan.* John Whitney Hall and Marius B. Jansen, eds., pp. 349–61. Princeton: Princeton University Press, 1968. ISBN 0-691-03071-5 (cl), 0-691-00013-1 (pbk). ▸ Discussion of both obstacles to and avenues for literate, able samurai administrators to rise in *bakufu* (shogunate) and domain bureaucracies. [HW]

12.218   Charles J. Dunn. *Everyday life in imperial Japan.* 1969 ed. New York: Dorset, 1989. ISBN 0-88029-352-7. ▸ Illustrated survey of daily life during Tokugawa period. Describes lives of people in Japan's four social classes—samurai, farmers, craftsmen, and merchants—and of several nonclass groups—courtiers and courtesans of imperial court at Kyoto, Shintō and Buddhist priests, doctors and intellectuals, actors, and outcasts and outlaws. Earlier title: *Everyday Life in Traditional Japan.* [HW]

12.219   Torao Haraguchi et al., eds. *The status system and social organization of Satsuma: a translation of the Shūmon Tefuda Aratame Jōmoku.* Honolulu: University Press of Hawaii, 1975. ISBN 0-8248-0390-6. ▸ Translation of set of regulations dealing with registration and investigation of religious sects. Provides invaluable insight into politics, social life, and religion of one most powerful *tozama* ("outside") domains of Edo period. [HW]

12.220   Kokichi Katsu. *Musui's story: the autobiography of a Tokugawa samurai.* Teruko Craig, trans. Tucson: University of Arizona Press, 1988. ISBN 0-8165-1035-0. ▸ Limpid translation of unique autobiography of Edo samurai, shogunal vassal of low rank who lived on fringes of proper samurai society and made his way among lower-class townsmen of Edo. As revealing in its way as Arai Hakuseki's autobiography (12.216). [MC]

12.221   Chie Nakane. "Tokugawa society." In *Tokugawa Japan: the social and economic antecedents of modern Japan.* Chie Nakane and Shinzaburō Ōishi, eds. Conrad Totman, trans., pp. 213–31. Tokyo: University of Tokyo Press, 1990. ISBN 0-86008-447-7. ▸ Discussion of essential characteristics of Tokugawa social structure stressing enduring influence on modern Japan. [MC]

12.222   Chie Nakane and Shinzaburō Ōishi, eds. *Tokugawa Japan: the social and economic antecedents of modern Japan.* Conrad Totman, trans. Tokyo: University of Tokyo Press, 1990. ISBN 0-86008-447-7. ▸ Lively collection of essays by prominent Japanese scholars looking at aspects of Tokugawa society including governing system, village society, commerce, growth of cities, transportation, communications networks, art, and *kabuki* theater. [MC]

12.223   Donald H. Shively. "Sumptuary regulation and status in early Tokugawa Japan." *Harvard journal of Asiatic studies* 25 (1964–65) 123–64. ISSN 0073-0548. ▸ Valuable account of *bakufu*'s (shogunate) efforts to enforce social-status distinctions through sumptuary legislation. Gives good sense of workings of Tokugawa status system. [MC]

12.224   Kōzō Yamamura. "The increasing poverty of the samurai in Tokugawa Japan, 1600–1868." *Journal of economic history* 31.2 (1971) 378–406. ISSN 0022-0507. ▸ Shows how samurai were, relatively, losing ground to merchants and even some villagers during period. [MC]

12.225   Kōzō Yamamura. "Samurai income and demographic change: the genealogies of Tokugawa bannermen." In *Family and population in East Asian history.* Susan B. Hanley and Arthur P. Wolf, eds., pp. 62–80. Stanford, Calif.: Stanford University Press, 1985. ISBN 0-8047-1232-8. ▸ Demographic analysis of samurai families serving the Tokugawa shoguns. [MC]

Rural Society and Peasant Protest

12.226   Tatsurō Akai. "The common people and agriculture." In *Tokugawa Japan: the social and economic antecedents of modern Japan.* Chie Nakane and Shinzaburō Ōishi, eds. Conrad Totman, trans., pp. 167–91. Tokyo: University of Tokyo Press, 1990. ISBN 0-86008-447-7, 4-13-027024-9. ▸ Illustrations of rural life and agricultural change. [MC]

12.227   Harumi Befu. "Village autonomy and articulation with the state." In *Studies in the institutional history of early modern Japan.* John Whitney Hall and Marius B. Jansen, eds., pp. 301–16. Princeton: Princeton University Press, 1968. ISBN 0-691-03071-5 (cl), 0-691-00013-1 (pbk). ▸ Stresses relative autonomy of Tokugawa villages, at least while annual taxes were paid by villagers. [HW]

12.228   Hugh Borton. "Peasant uprisings in Japan of the Tokugawa period." *Transactions of the Asiatic Society of Japan,* Second series, 16 (May 1938) 1–219. ▸ Early study of peasant protest. [MC]

12.229   David Luke Howell. "Hard times in the Kantō: economic change and village life in late Tokugawa Japan." *Modern Asian studies* 23.2 (1988) 349–71. ISSN 0026-749X. ▸ Analysis of pressures on village life brought about by famine and economic change. [MC]

12.230   Arne Kalland. "A credit institution in Tokugawa Japan: the Ura-Tamegi Fund of Chikuzen province." In *Europe interprets Japan.* Gordon Daniels, ed., pp. 3–12. Tenterden, England: Norbury, 1984. ISBN 0-904404-42-0 (pbk). ▸ Close look at fairly sophisticated credit union. [MC]

12.231   Arne Kalland and Jon Pedersen. "Famine and population in Fukuoka domain during the Tokugawa period." *Journal of Japanese studies* 10.1 (1984) 31–72. ISSN 0095-6848. ▸ Closely focused demographic study of impact of famine on one domain. [HW]

12.232   William W. Kelly. *Water control in Tokugawa Japan: irrigation organization in a Japanese river basin, 1600–1870.* Ithaca, N.Y.: Cornell University Press, China-Japan Program, 1982. (Cornell University East Asia papers, 31.) ISSN 8756-5293. ▸ Useful study of cooperative allocation and organization of irrigation rights. [MC]

12.233   J. Victor Koschmann. "Action as text: ideology in the Tengu insurrection." In *Conflict in modern Japanese history: the neglected tradition.* Tetsuo Najita and J. Victor Koschmann, eds., pp. 81–106. Princeton: Princeton University Press, 1982. ISBN 0-691-05364-2 (cl), 0-691-10137-X (pbk). ▸ Thoughtful, theoretical analysis of major protest movement. [MC]

12.234   Satoru Nakamura. "The development of rural industry." In *Tokugawa Japan: the social and economic antecedents of modern Japan.* Chie Nakane and Shinzaburō Ōishi, eds., pp. 81–97. Tokyo: University of Tokyo Press, 1990. ISBN 0-86008-447-7. ▸ Examination of evolution of cotton industry to illustrate long-term patterns of change that characterized rural economy as a whole. [MC]

12.235   Satō Tsuneo. "Tokugawa villages and agriculture." In *Tokugawa Japan: the social and economic antecedents of modern Japan.* Chie Nakane and Shinzaburō Ōishi, eds. Conrad Totman, trans., pp. 37–80. Tokyo: University of Tokyo Press, 1990. ISBN 0-86008-447-7. ▸ Concise description of organization of rural society, village life and work, and changing conditions in countryside. [MC]

12.236   Irwin Scheiner. "Benevolent lords and honorable peasants: rebellion and peasant consciousness in Tokugawa Japan."

In *Japanese thought in the Tokugawa period, 1600–1868: methods and metaphors.* 1978 ed. Tetsuo Najita and Irwin Scheiner, eds., pp. 39–62. Chicago: University of Chicago Press, 1988. ISBN 0-226-56801-6 (cl, 1978), 0-226-56802-4 (pbk). ▸ Examines traditions of benevolent rule and honorable protest in Tokugawa society. [HW]

12.237 Robert J. Smith. "Transformation of commoner households in Tennōji Mura, 1757–1858." In *Family and population in East Asian history.* Susan B. Hanley and Arthur P. Wolf, eds., pp. 247–76. Stanford, Calif.: Stanford University Press, 1985. ISBN 0-8047-1232-8. ▸ Anthropological study of change at village level. [MC]

12.238 Thomas C. Smith. *The agrarian origins of modern Japan.* 1959 ed. New York: Atheneum, 1966. ▸ Still best study of history of Japanese agriculture and village life. Stresses importance of transition from society based on status to one based on contract. Change partly result of commercialization of agriculture which contributed to Japan's rapid modernization during Meiji period. [MC]

12.239 Thomas C. Smith. "The Japanese village in the seventeenth century." In *Studies in the institutional history of early modern Japan.* John Whitney Hall and Marius B. Jansen, eds., pp. 263–82. Princeton: Princeton University Press, 1968. ISBN 0-691-03071-5 (cl), 0-691-00013-1 (pbk). ▸ Study of accommodation of villages to *bakufu* (shogunate) and domain rule. [HW]

12.240 Thomas C. Smith. *Nakahara: family farming and population in a Japanese village, 1717–1830.* Stanford, Calif.: Stanford University Press, 1977. ISBN 0-8047-0928-9. ▸ Analysis of population and tax registers of pseudonymous village of Nakahara to reconstruct relationship between demography and economic development. [MC]

12.241 Michiko Tanaka. "Village youth organizations (*wakamono nakama*) in late Tokugawa politics and society." Ph.D. dissertation. Princeton: Princeton University, 1983. ▸ Study of young men's and women's village organizations. [MC]

12.242 Ronald P. Toby. "Both a borrower and a lender be: from village moneylender to rural banker in the *tempō* era." *Monumenta Nipponica* 46.4 (1991) 483–512. ISSN 0027-0741. ▸ Excellent study of how Nishimatsu family of rural bankers responded to economic pressures and changes of early nineteenth century to transform themselves from moneylenders to bankers and from village landlords to rural entrepreneurs. [MC]

12.243 Conrad Totman. *The origins of Japan's modern forests: the case of Akita.* Honolulu: University of Hawaii Press, 1985. ISBN 0-8248-0954-8. ▸ Study of recovery of timber resources in northeastern Japan. [HW]

12.244 Conrad Totman. "Tokugawa peasants: win, lose, or draw." *Monumenta Nipponica* 41.4 (1986) 457–76. ISSN 0027-0741. ▸ Review of Western literature on Tokugawa peasants and peasant protest. Excellent bibliography; extensive list of works in English on Tokugawa peasants and their political activity. [MC]

12.245 Constantine N. Vaporis. "Overland communications in Tokugawa Japan." Ph.D. dissertation. Princeton: Princeton University, 1987. ▸ One of best studies of travel and barriers to travel in Tokugawa Japan. [MC]

12.246 Constantine N. Vaporis. "Post station and assisting villages: *corvée* labor and peasant contention." *Monumenta Nipponica* 41.4 (1986) 377–414. ISSN 0027-0741. ▸ Study of how growing demand for transport assistance led to constant contention between peasants and post stations that demanded *corvée* labor. [HW]

12.247 Anne Walthall. "Japanese *gimin*: peasant martyrs in popular memory." *American historical review* 91.5 (1986) 1–85. ISSN

0002-8762. ▸ Introduction to literature and actions of Tokugawa period peasants who were killed in their opposition to authority. [MC]

12.248 Anne Walthall. "Narratives of peasant uprisings in Japan." *Journal of Asian studies* 42.3 (1983) 571–88. ISSN 0021-9118. ▸ Structuralist study of narratives representing peasant protests in Tokugawa period. Relates protest literature to war tales, folk tales, and local legends. [HW]

12.249 Anne Walthall. "Peripheries: rural culture in Tokugawa Japan." *Monumenta Nipponica* 39.4 (1984) 371–92. ISSN 0027-0741. ▸ Rare, serious examination of cultural life at village level. [HW]

12.250 Anne Walthall. *Social protest and popular culture in eighteenth-century Japan.* Tucson: University of Arizona Press for the Association for Asian Studies, 1986. (Association for Asian Studies monographs, 43.) ISBN 0-8165-0961-1. ▸ Study of mentality of peasants based on peasant writings. Finds no obvious antifeudal consciousness or religious mentality of type stressed by Bix 13.83. [MC]

12.251 Anne Walthall. "Village networks: *sōdai* and the sale of Edo nightsoil." *Monumenta Nipponica* 43 (1988) 279–303. ISSN 0027-0741. ▸ Study of village cooperatives and their impact on Edo economy. [MC]

12.252 James W. White. "State growth and popular protest in Tokugawa Japan." *Journal of Japanese studies* 14.1 (1988) 1–25. ISSN 0095-6848. ▸ Examination of how Tokugawa *bakufu* (shogunate), sought to circumscribe peasant life and protest by controlling use of physical force. [MC]

12.253 Kären Wigen. "The geographic imagination in early modern Japanese history: retrospect and prospect." *Journal of Asian studies* 51.1 (1992) 3–29. ISSN 0021-9118. ▸ Sparkling essay on relationship between geography and regional economic development. [MC]

SEE ALSO

13.64 William W. Kelly. *Deference and defiance in nineteenth-century Japan.*

13.90 Stephen Vlastos. *Peasant protests and uprisings in Tokugawa Japan.*

13.91 Anne Walthall, ed. and trans. *Peasant uprisings in Japan.*

Merchants and Urban Society

12.254 Sydney Crawcour. "Some observations on merchants: a translation of Mitsui Takafusa's *Chōnin Kōken Roku.*" *Transactions of the Asiatic Society of Japan,* Third series, 8 (1961) 1–139. ▸ Translation of merchant's code providing insight into Tokugawa merchant ethic and early history of Mitsui commercial enterprise. [HW]

12.255 John Whitney Hall. "The castle town and Japan's modern urbanization." In *Studies in the institutional history of early modern Japan.* John Whitney Hall and Marius B. Jansen, eds., pp. 169–88. Princeton: Princeton University Press, 1968. ISBN 0-691-03071-5 (cl), 0-691-00013-1 (pbk). ▸ Fine study of role of castle towns as major urban centers of Edo period, many of which survive as leading modern cities. [HW]

12.256 Hiroshi Irie. "Apprenticeship training in Tokugawa Japan." *Acta Asiatica* 54 (1988) 1–23. ISSN 0567-7254. ▸ Interesting look at lower levels of Tokugawa merchant society. [MC]

12.257 Hidenobu Jinnai. "The spatial structure of Edo." In *Tokugawa Japan: the social and economic antecedents of modern Japan.* Chie Nakane and Shinzaburō Ōishi, eds. Conrad Totman, trans., pp. 81–97. Tokyo: University of Tokyo Press, 1990. ISBN 0-86008-447-7, 4-13-027024-9. ▸ Tour of Edo, from its bustling waterfronts and waterways and merchant quarters to elegant *yaskiki* residences of *daimyō* (feudal lords). [MC]

12.258 Gary P. Leupp. *Servants, shophands, and laborers in the cities of Tokugawa Japan.* Princeton: Princeton University Press, 1992. ISBN 0-691-03139-8. ▸ First study in English to explore urban underclass in Tokugawa Japan. [HW]

12.259 James L. McClain. "Castle towns and *daimyo* authority: Kanazawa in the years 1583–1630." *Journal of Japanese studies* 6.2 (1980) 267–99. ISSN 0095-6848. ▸ Introduces early history of castle town of Kanazawa emphasizing political aspects. Close study of *daimyō* (feudal lord) entry into and rule over Kanazawa, castle town of Maeda *daimyō* family, in transition from Toyotomi to Tokugawa *bakufu* (shogunates). [HW]

12.260 James L. McClain. *Kanazawa: a seventeenth-century Japanese castle town.* New Haven: Yale University Press, 1982. ISBN 0-300-02736-2. ▸ Evaluation of interaction and contribution of Maeda *daimyō* (feudal lord) family, its samurai-staffed bureaucracy, and local merchants and artisan to Kanazawa's rapid growth, 1583–1700. [MC]

12.261 Takeshi Moriya. "*Yūgei* and *chōnin* society in the Edo period." *Acta Asiatica* 33 (1977) 32–54. ISSN 0567-7254. ▸ Perceptive essay on cultural activities of Tokugawa period merchants. [HW]

12.262 Tetsuo Najita. "Ōshio Heihachiro (1793–1837)." In *Personality in Japanese history.* Albert M. Craig and Donald H. Shively, eds., pp. 155–79. Berkeley: University of California Press, 1970. ISBN 0-520-01699-8. ▸ Examination of hardship in Ōsaka and surrounding countryside that provoked revolt led by Ōshio, samurai official. [HW]

12.263 Gilbert Rozman. "Edo's importance in the changing Tokugawa society." *Journal of Japanese studies* 1.1 (1974) 113–26. ISSN 0095-6848. ▸ Explores Edo's vital contribution to and its impact on surrounding economy as huge center of consumption. [HW]

12.264 Gilbert Rozman. *Urban networks in Ch'ing China and Tokugawa Japan.* Princeton: Princeton University Press, 1974. ISBN 0-691-03082-0. ▸ Valuable comparative study stressing importance of interconnections of various levels of urban centers to striking urban development of Edo period. Networks approach. [HW]

12.265 Charles D. Sheldon. *The rise of the merchant class in Tokugawa Japan, 1600–1868.* 1958 ed. New York: Russell & Russell, 1973. ISBN 0-8462-1725-2. ▸ Dated, early study of some of great merchant houses of Edo and Ōsaka. [HW]

12.266 Robert J. Smith. "Small families, small households, and residential instability: town and city in 'pre-modern' Japan." In *Household and family in past time.* Peter Laslett, ed., pp. 429–71. Cambridge: Cambridge University Press, 1972. ISBN 0-521-08473-3. ▸ One of few studies of family life in Edo period. [HW]

SEE ALSO
13.434 Takeo Yazaki. *Social change and the city in Japan.*

Social History and Demographic Change

12.267 Joyce Ackroyd. "Women in feudal Japan." *Transactions of the Asiatic Society of Japan,* Third series, (1959) 31–68. ▸ Argues that ease with which women could be divorced in Tokugawa Japan was indicative of women's miserable social status in premodern period. [MC]

12.268 Laurel L. Cornell. "The deaths of old women: folklore and mortality in nineteenth-century Japan." In *Recreating Japanese women, 1600–1945.* Gail Lee Bernstein, ed., pp. 71–87. Berkeley: University of California Press, 1991. ISBN 0-520-07015-

I (cl), 0-520-07017-8 (pbk). ▸ Interesting study of female mortality. [MC]

12.269 Laurel L. Cornell. "Peasant women and divorce in preindustrial Japan." *Signs* 15.4 (1990) 710–32. ISSN 0097-9740. ▸ Examination of circumstances and effects of divorce. Questions view presented by Ackroyd (12.267) and others that divorce in preindustrial Japan was always arbitrary and ruthless. [MC]

12.270 Laurel L. Cornell and Akira Hayami. "The *shūmon aratame chō*: Japan's population registers." *Journal of family history* 11.4 (1986) 311–28. ISSN 0363-1990. ▸ Helpful introduction to basic source for Edo period social and demographic history. [MC]

12.271 Susan B. Hanley. "Tokugawa society: material culture, standard of living, and life-styles." In *The Cambridge history of Japan.* John Whitney Hall and James L. McClain, eds., vol. 4, pp. 660–705. Cambridge: Cambridge University Press, 1991. ISBN 0-521-22355-5. ▸ One of first in-depth studies of Tokugawa material culture in English. [HW]

12.272 Akira Hayami. "The myth of primogeniture and impartible inheritance in Tokugawa Japan." *Journal of family history* 8.1 (1983) 3–29. ISSN 0363-1990. ▸ Japan's leading demographic historian challenges received wisdom on prevalence of primogeniture. [MC]

12.273 Akira Hayami and Nobuko Uchida. "Size of household in a Japanese county throughout the Tokugawa era." In *Household and family in past time.* Peter Laslett, ed., pp. 473–515. Cambridge: Cambridge University Press, 1972. ISBN 0-521-08473-3. ▸ Polished, technical demographic study of household size. [HW]

12.274 Ryōsuke Ishii. "The status of women in traditional Japanese society." *Japanese annual of international law* 29 (1986) 10–22. ISSN 0448-8806. ▸ Brief but helpful introduction to changing legal status of women, antiquity to Tokugawa. [MC]

12.275 Ann Bowman Jannetta. *Epidemics and mortality in early modern Japan.* Princeton: Princeton University Press, 1987. ISBN 0-691-05484-3. ▸ Demographic study of impact of epidemic disease, especially smallpox, on population growth. Argues abortion and infanticide, rather than disease-induced mortality, may account for stagnation in population growth in late eighteenth and nineteenth centuries. [HW]

12.276 Ann Bowman Jannetta and Samuel H. Preston. "Two centuries of mortality change in central Japan: the evidence from a temple death register." *Population studies: a journal of demography* 45 (1991) 417–36. ▸ Well-documented study of village mortality in Tokugawa period. [MC]

12.277 Emiko Hayashi Kirk. "Divorce in Tokugawa Japan: a study of Nishijō village, 1773–1868." M.A. thesis. Ithaca, N.Y.: Cornell University, 1987. ▸ Rare, detailed study of divorce in village society. [MC]

12.278 Carl Mosk. "Fecundity, infanticide, and food consumption in Japan." *Explorations in economic history* 15 (July 1978) 269–89. ISSN 0014-4983. ▸ Careful demographic study. [HW]

12.279 Kikue Yamakawa. *Women of the Mito domain: recollections of samurai family life.* Kate Wildman Nakai, trans. Tokyo: University of Tokyo Press, 1992. ISBN 0-86008-477-9. ▸ Revealing, elegant translation of reflections of lower-ranking samurai woman. Fascinating addition to social history of late Tokugawa and Meiji periods. Chapters on education, dress, abortion, infanticide, samurai stipends, grooming, dwellings, amusements, food, marriage, and divorce. [HW]

Economic History

12.280 William Atwell. "Some observations on the 'seventeenth-century crisis' in China and Japan." *Journal of Asian studies* 45.2 (1986) 223–44. ISSN 0021-9118. ▸ Strong argument that silver flow was important link between China and Japan and that economic developments in one country affected other in late sixteenth and early seventeenth century. Places China and Japan in global economic picture. [MC]

12.281   Philip C. Brown. "The mismeasure of land: land surveying in the Tokugawa period." *Monumenta Nipponica* 42.2 (1987) 115–55. ISSN 0027-0741. ‣ Demonstrates Tokugawa period tax rates were often based on inaccurate land surveys. [MC]

12.282   Philip C. Brown. "Practical constraints on early Tokugawa land taxation: annual versus fixed assessments in Kaga domain." *Journal of Japanese studies* 14 (1988) 369–401. ISSN 0095-6848. ‣ Shows why domain rulers found it hard to squeeze as much tax as they would have liked out of peasantry. [MC]

12.283   Sydney Crawcour. "Changes in Japanese commerce in the Tokugawa period." In *Studies in the institutional history of early modern Japan*. John Whitney Hall and Marius B. Jansen, eds., pp. 189–202. Princeton: Princeton University Press, 1968. ISBN 0-691-03071-5 (cl), 0-691-00013-1 (pbk). ‣ Somewhat dated but still useful overview of vigorous commercial development and its impact on Tokugawa economy. [HW]

12.284   Sydney Crawcour. "Economic change in the nineteenth century." In *The Cambridge history of Japan*. Marius B. Jansen, ed., vol. 5, pp. 569–617. Cambridge: Cambridge University Press, 1989. ISBN 0-521-22356-3. ‣ Assesses mixed state of *bakufu* (shogunate) and domain economies and painful economic transition to open ports under Western pressure. [HW]

12.285   William B. Hauser. *Economic institutional change in Tokugawa Japan: Osaka and the Kinai cotton trade*. Cambridge: Cambridge University Press, 1974. ISBN 0-521-20302-3. ‣ Case study of growth and decline of cotton industry during eighteenth and early nineteenth centuries in most economically advanced areas of Tokugawa Japan: the city of Ōsaka and three provinces of surrounding Kinai region. Enumerates implications for understanding Tokugawa period economic and social change. [HW]

12.286   David Luke Howell. "Capitalist transformation of the Hokkaido fishery, 1672–1935." Ph.D. dissertation. Princeton: Princeton University, 1989. ‣ Excellent study of struggle between big and small net owners in rich herring fishery of Hokkaido during early modern and modern eras. [MC]

12.287   Nobuhiko Nakai and James L. McClain. "Commercial change and urban growth in early modern Japan." In *The Cambridge history of Japan*. John Whitney Hall and James L. McClain, eds., vol. 4, pp. 519–95. Cambridge: Cambridge University Press, 1991. ISBN 0-521-22355-5. ‣ Both overview of urban development and introduction to recent research on urban commerce. [HW]

12.288   Luke S. Roberts. "The merchant origins of national prosperity thought in eighteenth-century Tosa." Ph.D. dissertation. Princeton: Princeton University, 1991. ‣ Argues local merchants in Tosa developed economic philosophy, known as national prosperity (*kokueki*), aimed at benefiting themselves and domain or country. [MC]

12.289   Thomas C. Smith. "The land tax in the Tokugawa period." In *Studies in the institutional history of early modern Japan*. John Whitney Hall and Marius B. Jansen, eds., pp. 283–99. Princeton: Princeton University Press, 1968. ISBN 0-691-03071-5 (cl), 0-691-00013-1 (pbk). ‣ One of several studies debating levels of taxation borne by peasants in Tokugawa period. Tax rates probably higher in early Tokugawa period, but *bakufu* (shogunate) and domain governments unable to squeeze as much tax from villages as official statistics suggest. Reprint of 1958 article. [HW]

SEE ALSO
13.30 Susan B. Hanley and Kōzō Yamamura. *Economic and demographic change in preindustrial Japan, 1600–1868.*

Education

12.290   Ronald P. Dore. *Education in Tokugawa Japan.* 1965 ed. Ann Arbor: University of Michigan Press, 1992. ISBN 0-485-12086-0. ‣ Pathbreaking, enduring work discussing aims of samurai education, organization of schools, atmosphere that prevailed therein, and traditional curriculum. Shows how these educational institutions created social change by promoting respect for ability and achievement that ran counter to and gradually undermined principle of hereditary status. Also examines education among commoners. [HW]

12.291   John Whitney Hall. "The Confucian teacher in Tokugawa Japan." In *Confucianism in action*. 1959 ed. David S. Nivison and Arthur F. Wright, eds., pp. 268–301. Stanford: Stanford University Press, 1966. ISBN 0-8047-0554-2. ‣ Provides clear picture of activities and status of *daimyō* (feudal lord)–sponsored Confucian scholars (*jusha*). [HW]

12.292   Richard Rubinger. *Private academies of Tokugawa Japan.* Princeton: Princeton University Press, 1982. ISBN 0-691-05352-9. ‣ Discussion of role of private academies (*shijuku*) that provided basic education for commoners and low-ranking samurai. [HW]

Religion

12.293   Robert N. Bellah. *Tokugawa religion: the cultural roots of modern Japan.* 1957 ed. New York: Free Press, 1985. ISBN 0-02-902460-9 (pbk). ‣ Classic study, still much cited in Japan. Stresses counterpart of Weberian ethic emerging from shingaku ethical movement. Earlier title: *Tokugawa Religion: The Values of Preindustrial Japan.* [HW]

12.294   Nam-lin Hur. "Popular Buddhist culture in the Edo period: a case study of Sensōji." Ph.D. dissertation. Princeton: Princeton University, 1992. ‣ Revealing study of Sensōji (Asakusa Kannon) temple and its role as devotional center for Edo townspeople and pilgrims. [MC]

12.295   Hartmut O. Rotermund. *Hōsōgami ou la petite vérole aisément: matériaux pour l'étude de épidémies dans le Japon des dix-huitième, dix-neuvième siècles.* Paris: Maisonneuve & Larose, 1991. ISBN 2-7068-1033-5. ‣ Fascinating study of materials on religious and popular traditions used to counter threat of epidemic disease in late Edo period, seen through worship of Hōsōgami, smallpox god. [MC]

12.296   Paul B. Watt. "Jiun Sonja (1718–1804): a response to Confucianism within the context of Buddhist reform." In *Confucianism and Tokugawa culture.* Peter Nosco, ed., pp. 188–214. Princeton: Princeton University Press, 1984. ISBN 0-691-07286-8. ‣ Through Jiun, Watt shows how Buddhists sought to answer critique of Buddhism mounted by Confucian scholars and advocates of National Learning. [HW]

Cultural History

12.297   C. Andrew Gerstle, ed. *Eighteenth-century Japan: culture and society.* Boston: Allen & Unwin, 1989. ISBN 0-04-380031-9. ‣ Uses popular literature and theater as focus for lively study of urban culture. [MC]

12.298   Isao Kumakura. "Kan'ei culture and *chanoyu*." In *Tea in Japan: essays on the history of chanoyu.* H. Paul Varley and Kumakura Isao, eds. H. Paul Varley, trans., pp. 135–60. Honolulu: University of Hawaii Press, 1989. ‣ Locates tea ceremony and its aesthetics in context of early seventeenth-century culture and politics. [MC]

12.299 Donald H. Shively. *"Bakufu versus kabuki."* In *Studies in the institutional history of early modern Japan.* John Whitney Hall and Marius B. Jansen, eds., pp. 231–62. Princeton: Princeton University Press, 1968. ISBN 0-691-03071-5 (cl), 0-691-00013-1 (pbk). ▸ Lively essay on frequently frustrated efforts of *bakufu* (shogunate) to regulate actors of burgeoning *kabuki* theater. Reprint of 1955 article. [HW]

12.300 Donald H. Shively. "Popular culture." In *The Cambridge history of Japan.* John Whitney Hall and James L. McClain, eds., vol. 4, pp. 706–70. Cambridge: Cambridge University Press, 1991. ISBN 0-521-22355-5. ▸ Excellent survey of cultural world of great urban centers of Tokugawa Japan. [HW]

Intellectual History

12.301 W. G. Beasley and Carmen Blacker. "Japanese historical writing in the Tokugawa period." In *Historians of China and Japan.* W. G. Beasley and Edwin G. Pulleyblank, eds., pp. 245–63. London: Oxford University Press, 1961. ▸ Introduction to historical writings of Arai Hakuseki and other Tokugawa period historians. [MC]

12.302 Robert N. Bellah. "Baigan and Sorai: continuities and discontinuities in eighteenth-century Japanese thought." In *Japanese thought in the Tokugawa period, 1600–1868: methods and metaphors.* 1978 ed. Tetsuo Najita and Irwin Scheiner, eds., pp. 137–52. Chicago: University of Chicago Press, 1988. ISBN 0-226-56801-6 (cl, 1978), 0-226-56802-4 (pbk). ▸ Reassessment of earlier interpretation of Ishida Baigan (in Bellah 12.293). Contrasts conceptual consciousness of Ogyū Sorai with symbolic consciousness of Baigan, arguing kind of attitude displayed by Sorai had negative consequences for modern Japan. [HW]

12.303 Masahide Bito. "Ogyū Sorai and the distinguishing features of Japanese Confucianism." In *Japanese thought in the Tokugawa period, 1600–1868: methods and metaphors.* 1978 ed. Tetsuo Najita and Irwin Scheiner, eds., pp. 153–60. Chicago: University of Chicago Press, 1988. ISBN 0-226-56801-6 (cl, 1978), 0-226-56802-4 (pbk). ▸ Challenges common notion that Sorai was excessive Sinophile. [HW]

12.304 Willem Jan Boot. *The adoption and adaptation of Neo-Confucianism in Japan: the role of Fujiwara Seika and Hayashi Razan.* Netherlands: Proefschrift, Rijksuniversiteit te Leiden, 1982. ▸ Careful introduction to early development of Neo-Confucianism and its self-conscious separation from Buddhism. [HW]

12.305 John S. Brownlee. *Political thought in Japanese historical writing: from Kojiki (712) to Tokushi Yoron (1712).* Waterloo, Ont.: Wilfrid Laurier University Press, 1991. ISBN 0-88920-997-9. ▸ Examination of twenty-two historical texts from thousand-year period, treating some strategies of premodern Japanese historians on issues of political power and imperial institutions. Not definitive. [MC]

12.306 Albert M. Craig. "Science and Confucianism in Tokugawa Japan." In *Changing Japanese attitudes toward modernization.* 1965 ed. Marius B. Jansen, ed., pp. 133–60. Princeton: Princeton University Press, 1971. ISBN 0-691-03007-3 (cl), 0-691-00009-2 (pbk). ▸ Interesting essay assessing Confucianism's potential for encouragement of rational scientific inquiry. [HW]

12.307 Wm. Theodore De Bary. *Neo-Confucian orthodoxy and the learning of the mind-and-heart.* New York: Columbia University Press, 1981. ISBN 0-231-05228-6. ▸ Positive assessment of Neo-Confucian contribution to Japanese thought. [HW]

12.308 David Magarey Earl. *Emperor and nation in Japan: political thinkers of the Tokugawa period.* 1964 ed. Westport, Conn.: Greenwood, 1981. ISBN 0-313-23105-2. ▸ Examination of imperial institution as locus for national self-identity. Focuses especially on ideas and actions of Yoshida Shoin, samurai scholar and leading exponent of imperial loyalism. [HW]

12.309 Harry D. Harootunian. "The consciousness of archaic form in the new realism of *kokugaku.*" In *Japanese thought in the Tokugawa period, 1600–1868: methods and metaphors.* 1978 ed. Tetsuo Najita and Irwin Scheiner, eds., pp. 63–104. Chicago: University of Chicago Press, 1988. ISBN 0-226-56801-6 (cl, 1978), 0-226-56802-4 (pbk). ▸ Methodological study using metaphor of archaism and Foucauldian theory to expose "eruption" of nativist thought (*kokugaku*) as new mode of discourse in late eighteenth and early nineteenth centuries. [HW]

12.310 Harry D. Harootunian. "Late Tokugawa culture and thought." In *The Cambridge history of Japan.* Marius B. Jansen, ed., vol. 5, pp. 168–258. Cambridge: Cambridge University Press, 1989. ISBN 0-521-22356-3. ▸ Study of nineteenth-century thought in such categories as culture of play, play of culture, good doctrine and governance, restoration of worship and work, religions of relief, and defense and wealth. [HW]

12.311 Harry D. Harootunian. *Things seen and unseen: discourse and ideology in Tokugawa nativism.* Chicago: University of Chicago Press, 1988. ISBN 0-226-31706-4 (cl), 0-226-31707-2 (pbk). ▸ Challenging, at times opaque, theoretical discussion of late Tokugawa nativist thought. [HW]

12.312 J. Victor Koschmann. *The Mito ideology: discourse, reform, and insurrection in late Tokugawa Japan, 1790–1864.* Berkeley: University of California Press, 1987. ISBN 0-520-05768-6. ▸ Easily accessible structural analysis revising previous conceptions of role and action of samurai activists of Mito domain in late Tokugawa thought. Topics include domain reform, criticism of Tokugawa *bakufu* (shogunate), and leadership in movement to "revere the emperor and expel the barbarians." Argues activists may not have directly led Meiji Restoration, but writings and actions were ideological texts to be read by others who played more direct role. [HW]

12.313 Olof G. Lidin. *The life of Ogyū Sorai: a Tokugawa Confucian philosopher.* Lund, Sweden: Studentlitteratur, 1973. (Scandinavian Institute of Asian Studies monograph series, 19.) ISBN 91-44-10181-3. ▸ Basic biography of one of most influential and enduring Tokugawa thinkers. Offers positive assessment. [HW]

12.314 Masao Maruyama. *Studies in the intellectual history of Tokugawa Japan.* Mikiso Hane, trans. Princeton: Princeton University Press, 1974. ISBN 0-691-07566-2 (cl), 0-691-00832-9 (pbk). ▸ Pioneering studies; assessment of Ogyū Sorai as most creative political thinker of period remains important reference point. [HW]

12.315 Shigeru Matsumoto. *Motoori Norinaga, 1730–1801.* Cambridge, Mass.: Harvard University Press, 1970. ISBN 0-674-58775-8. ▸ Psychobiography of leading eighteenth-century nativist thinker. [HW]

12.316 J. R. McEwan. *The political writings of Ogyū Sorai.* Cambridge: Cambridge University Press, 1962. ISBN 0-521-05627-6. ▸ Translation and commentary of Sorai's most important political writings. [HW]

12.317 I. J. McMullin. "Non-agnatic adoption: a Confucian controversy in seventeenth- and eighteenth-century Japan." *Harvard journal of Asiatic studies* 35 (1975) 133–88. ISSN 0073-0548. ▸ Interesting study of Confucian attitudes toward adoption. [MC]

12.318 Tetsuo Najita. "History and nature in eighteenth-century Tokugawa thought." In *The Cambridge history of Japan.* John Whitney Hall and James L. McClain, eds., vol. 4, pp. 596–659. Cambridge: Cambridge University Press, 1991. ISBN 0-521-22355-5. ▸ Excellent introduction to major movements and issues in eighteenth-century thought and what author sees as century's moral crisis. [HW]

12.319 Tetsuo Najita. "Method and analysis in the conceptual portrayal of Tokugawa intellectual history." In *Japanese thought in the Tokugawa period, 1600–1868: methods and metaphors.* 1978 ed. Tetsuo Najita and Irwin Scheiner, eds., pp. 3–38. Chicago: University of Chicago Press, 1988. ISBN 0-226-56801-6 (cl, 1978), 0-226-56802-4 (pbk). ▸ Introductory discussion of importance of ideological pattern and historical metaphor in study of Tokugawa intellectual history, followed by application of methods to thought of Kaihō Seiryō through analysis of his discourse on past and present, *Keiko dan.* [HW]

12.320 Tetsuo Najita and Irwin Scheiner, eds. *Japanese thought in the Tokugawa period, 1600–1868: methods and metaphors.* 1978 ed. Chicago: University of Chicago Press, 1988. ISBN 0-226-56801-6 (cl, 1978), 0-226-56802-4 (pbk). ▸ Eight essays employing variety of metaphors in search for "structural comparabilities" in Tokugawa thought. Attempt to clarify methodological issues and suggest future approaches. [HW]

12.321 Kate Wildman Nakai. "The naturalization of Confucianism in Tokugawa Japan: the problem of Sinocentrism." *Harvard journal of Asiatic studies* 40.1 (1980) 157–99. ISSN 0073-0548. ▸ Excellent discussion of changing meaning of China and eventual rejection of Sinocentrism in Tokugawa thought. [HW]

12.322 E. Herbert Norman. *Andō Shōeki and the anatomy of Japanese feudalism.* Washington, D.C.: University Publications of America, 1979. (Transactions of the Asiatic Society of Japan, Third series, 2.) ▸ Seeks in Andō Shōeki's thought basis for challenge to Tokugawa rule. Publication of 1949 article. [HW]

12.323 Peter Nosco. *Remembering paradise: nativism and nostalgia in eighteenth-century Japan.* Cambridge, Mass.: Council on East Asian Studies, Harvard University; distributed by Harvard University Press, 1990. ISBN 0-674-76007-7. ▸ Discussion of Tokugawa nativist thought (*kokugaku*) in terms of nostalgia for purer Japanese past. [MC]

12.324 Peter Nosco, ed. *Confucianism and Tokugawa culture.* 1984 ed. Princeton: Princeton University Press, 1989. ISBN 0-691-07286-8 (cl, 1984), 0-691-00839-6 (pbk). ▸ Important collection of essays on Tokugawa intellectual and religious history. [HW]

12.325 Herman Ooms. *Tokugawa ideology: early constructs, 1570–1680.* Princeton: Princeton University Press, 1985. ISBN 0-691-05444-4. ▸ Questions idea of clear-cut Tokugawa support for Neo-Confucianism as ideology. Argues Tokugawa Ieyasu veiled himself in web of Shintō–Buddhist–Confucian ideology. Challenging study of intellectual foundations of Tokugawa rule. [MC]

12.326 Samuel Hideo Yamashita. "Nature and artifice in the writings of Ogyū Sorai." In *Confucianism and Tokugawa culture.* Peter Nosco, ed., pp. 138–65. Princeton: Princeton University Press, 1984. ISBN 0-691-07286-8 (cl, 1984), 0-691-00839-6 (pbk). ▸ Thoughful study of fundamental dichotomy in philosopher's thought. [HW]

SEE ALSO

10.16 William G. Beasley and Edwin G. Pulleyblank, eds. *Historians of China and Japan.*

13.72 Bob Tadashi Wakabayashi. *Anti-foreignism and Western learning in early modern Japan.*

Foreign Relations

12.327 Anthony Farrington. *The English factory in Japan, 1613–1623.* 2 vols. London: British Library, 1991. ISBN 0-7123-0642-0 (set), 0-7123-0644-7 (v. 1), 0-7123-0645-5 (v. 2). ▸ Compilation of wide array of archival material relating to Hirado factory and its abortive role in East India trade. Most important source of information on sadly mismanaged venture. [MC]

12.328 Grant Goodman. *Japan: the Dutch experience.* Rev. ed. London: Athlone, 1986. ISBN 0-485-11262-0. ▸ Demonstrates nature and extent of impact Dutch had on Japanese intellectual life during Edo period. Earlier title: *The Dutch Impact on Japan.* [MC]

12.329 Marius B. Jansen. "*Rangaku* and westernization." *Modern Asian studies* 18 (October 1984) 541–53. ISSN 0026-749X. ▸ Stresses contribution of Dutch studies (*rangaku*) to acceptance of Western learning and institutions in Meiji period. [HW]

12.330 Peter Kapitza, ed. *Japan in Europa: Texte und Bilddokumente zur europäischen Japankenntnis von Marco Polo bis Wilhelm von Humboldt.* 2 vols. Munich: Iudicium, 1990. ISBN 3-89129-990-7. ▸ Encyclopedia of European reports on Japan from Marco Polo to Wilhelm von Humboldt. Interesting reading and helpful in understanding how Western discovery of Japan developed. Preference given to German translations of texts; where translation not available, published in original language. [MC]

12.331 Donald Keene. *The Japanese discovery of Europe, 1720–1830.* 1952 ed. Stanford, Calif.: Stanford University Press, 1969. ▸ Account of growth of Western learning in Tokugawa Japan with particular emphasis on career and writings of political economist and navigator Honda Toshiaki (1744–1821). Examines mid-Tokugawa period views of Europe and of European knowledge as well as penetration of Western ideas and culture into Japan and its impact on Japanese intellectual life. Translations of Honda's chief works in appendix. [HW]

12.332 Derek Massarella. *A world elsewhere: Europe's encounter with Japan in the sixteenth and seventeenth centuries.* New Haven: Yale University Press, 1990. ISBN 0-300-04633-2. ▸ History of English East India Company in Japan. Skillful use of surviving company records. [MC]

12.333 Kazui Tashiro. "Foreign relations during the Edo period: *sakoku* reexamined." *Journal of Japanese studies* 8.2 (1982) 283–306. ISSN 0095-6848. ▸ Important contribution to discussion of seclusion (*sakoku*). [MC]

12.334 Kazui Tashiro. "Tsushima *han*'s Korean trade, 1684–1710." *Acta Asiatica* 30 (1976) 85–105. ISSN 0567-7254. ▸ Detailed study of island of Tsushima's trade with Korea revealing its important intermediary role in Korean-Japanese relations. [MC]

12.335 Ronald P. Toby. "Reopening the question of *sakoku*: diplomacy in the legitimation of the Tokugawa *bakufu*." *Journal of Japanese studies* 3.2 (1977) 323–64. ISSN 0095-6848. ▸ Essay that challenged prevailing view of seclusion (*sakoku*) by stressing vitality of Japan's Asian contacts in Tokugawa period. [HW]

F. G. NOTEHELFER

Modern Japan

Japan is one of the most dynamic nations in the world today. Its rise to power from what was an isolated feudal state in the mid-nineteenth century to world prominence and leadership by the latter half of the twentieth century has been little short of extraordinary. Few observers looking at Japan in the 1860s sensed the scale and speed of the transformation that lay ahead. Few Japanese, it should be added, were fully conscious of the costs that such a transformation entailed for the Japanese people, who were forced to jettison much of their past in the name of modernity. Indeed, few Japanese had any inkling that the challenges of the catch-up game with the West on which Japan embarked with the Meiji Restoration in 1868 would lead not only to early successes and world-power status by the first decade of this century, but also to tragedy and vast destruction four decades later. Nor were there many, either from without or within, who dared to imagine the scale and scope of Japan's phoenixlike reemergence to world prominence in the decades after World War II.

It is the speed and scale of change in Japan's modern history, its remarkable successes, and its equally poignant and tragic failures that have intrigued students of the past on both sides of the Pacific Ocean. For if history still essentially wrestles with the questions of how and why, then Japan poses an important set of such questions. And it is precisely the search for answers to these questions that has energized historians of the Japanese experience, be they American or Japanese.

In approaching these questions the nature of the Meiji Restoration has been of primary concern. How was Japan able to restructure its political, economic, and social system as quickly as it did? How were the vast changes initiated under the modern state perceived? What, if any, was the legacy of these changes? Nowhere were these issues more carefully researched and passionately debated than in Japan itself. By the 1920s and 1930s, Japanese academic historians, heavily influenced by Marxism, concluded that the Restoration represented an aborted revolution that had ended in a new form of absolutism. Japan's counterrevolution, they insisted, had opened the way to imperialism, totalitarianism, and an aggressive military posture that set Japan on the road to war with China in the 1930s and with the United States in 1941. Struggling against the imperial state and its head, the emperor, such historians rejected the official, popular interpretation of the Restoration as a spontaneous resurgence of loyalty to the throne. Less concerned with the emperor and the emerging loyalism that placed him at the focal center of the Restoration, such historians dedicated their spadework to the economic transformation of the late Tokugawa period (1600–1868). In doing so, they

379

assembled a rich treasure trove of historical documents that would subsequently serve both Japanese and Western historians to new ends.

In the 1920s, when the Japanese initiated their all-important debates on the nature of modern Japanese history, there was as yet little serious American scholarship on Japan. While several American universities tried to fill this lacuna in the 1930s, American studies on Japan were still woefully inadequate during this critical decade. It was not until World War II that this field rapidly and dramatically expanded. A crash program on the Japanese language produced a substantial group of men and women with language skills. Tours of duty as occupationnaires honed these skills and aroused a genuine interest in Japan and the Japanese people. Fueled by such interest, university programs focusing on language and area studies developed and expanded, and by the 1950s and 1960s, a new generation of American historians joined their prewar colleagues in actively pursuing a reevaluation of Japanese history. Placed in important history departments around the country, these men and women also trained graduate students who then built on and enlarged their visions of the modern Japanese past.

Like their Japanese counterparts in the twenties and thirties, American (and other Western) historians felt compelled to reconsider the Restoration, which confronted them, as it did the Japanese, as the seminal event of the modern Japanese experience. While the responses of some, including the important Canadian historian E. H. Norman, shadowed the concerns of their earlier Japanese colleagues, and while many of those who had experienced the war remained preoccupied with the question of what had gone wrong, others soon stepped out on bolder and more productive paths. By the 1960s, a distinct contrast separated most American and Japanese historians. The Japanese, weighed down by the memory of the war and the pessimistic assessment of their Marxist methodology, continued to focus on Japan's backwardness, on the persistence of feudal hangovers, and on an essentially negative assessment of Japan's modern experience; American historians, however, became increasingly positive and optimistic in their evaluation of Japan's modern past.

As the immediacy of war faded into the background, American modernization scholars, including E. O. Reischauer, J. W. Hall, M. B. Jansen, and A. M. Craig, began to shift their inquiry away from unfulfilled promises and toward the causes of Japan's rapid nineteenth- and early twentieth-century transformation. Influenced by the postwar American preoccupation with development, they saw in Japan a useful case study to be explored. Trying to counter the strong role that ideology played in the Japanese academic community, these scholars sought to establish a less value-laden approach to Japanese history that stressed process over politics. Once again the key question became: how was Japan able to transform itself so quickly during the Meiji period (1868–1912)? As in the case of earlier Japanese studies, the focus was placed not only on the Meiji experience but also on the Tokugawa era that preceded it. The result was a reevaluation of what had once been seen as a static and stagnant world. Using archival materials gathered by their Japanese predecessors and new spadework of their own, American historians showed that Japan was far more educated, agriculturally productive, commercially advanced, and bureaucratically prepared for modernity than the well-established "feudal" image suggested. The Tokugawa period, these scholars concluded, was clearly early modern, and its accomplishments were directly linked to the Meiji Restoration.

For modernization historians the essence of modern Japanese history focused on a high degree of continuity rather than on radical change. The Meiji Restoration, once a distinct break, came to be seen largely as a bridge that united modern with early modern Japan. As they pictured it, twentieth-century Japan represented a further continuation of the modernizing process. Japan, as Reischauer saw it, was on a steady upward course toward a more open and democratic society. Even the thirties and

World War II came to be seen largely as temporary aberrations on a course of development that achieved ultimate fulfillment in the post–World War II or late Showa era.

Dedicated as they were to a new vision of Japanese history, postwar American scholars were equally dedicated to the preparation of a new generation of historians to carry on their efforts. Almost all major American universities trained such scholars in the postwar years. The result was a dramatic proliferation of scholarly works on Japanese history. A comparison of this *Guide* with its 1961 predecessor indicates the scope of this expansion. Of the 350 works selected by H. Borton and J. Hall for the earlier volume, 200 were in the Japanese language. These, it must be added, still constitute some of the best surveys of Japanese scholarship in the field and should be consulted by all students familiar with the Japanese language. By contrast, the current list, which concentrates on English-language works, was selected from more than a thousand volumes. Behind such numbers lies not only the growing significance of Japan, but also the effective preparation of scholars and researchers by the earlier generation.

A growing diversity has come to mark the field of Japanese studies in the past two decades. Younger scholars have rejected the established interpretations of their elders as often as they have chosen to follow them. Modernization, once the dominant theme of the older generation, has been modified, revised, and in some cases, rejected for diverse, new, and eclectic approaches. While many American historians of Japan retain a semblance of the optimism that inspired their teachers, that optimism is often considerably muted. Younger scholars have been less inclined to substitute process for politics, and some have questioned the earlier tendency to regard as given that which had to be. Such scholars argue that there were alternative paths to modernity, that choices had to be made, and that these choices were made by individuals and groups who were concerned with power and its uses. A renewed interest in politics and ideology has provided a revised view of that process. At the same time, the disenfranchised—women, minorities, industrial workers, and even certain religious and intellectual groups—have received new attention. Social history has placed its focus as much on the bottom as on the top layers of Japanese economic, political, and social systems. Winners have been paired with losers, not only in the human, but also in the industrial and environmental realms. Accepted cultural, social, and religious values, which, since the days of Ruth Benedict, have been regarded as essential for understanding modern Japan, have also been questioned. Consensus and harmony have been challenged by studies of conflict and violence. Japan's much touted love of nature has been reexamined from the perspective of befouled air and seas and the wanton destruction of domestic and even foreign ecologies.

The diversity of modern scholarship on Japan demonstrates the many ways in which Japan, as Ezra Vogel wrote in 1979, has to be regarded as "number one." Recent scholarship confirms at least one aspect of the success story pursued by the earlier generation of historians. Indeed, there are those who argue that Japan represents not only the epitome of the postindustrial society but also the quintessential postmodern society. Needless to say only history can confirm such judgments, but few would deny that contemporary Japan remains one of the most dynamic nations in the world today.

The bibliography that follows has been designed to present as broad a perspective on modern Japanese history as is possible within the restrictions posed by the editors. If the criteria of selecting only the most important works has tended to increase the coverage of some topics, to the neglect of others, it also can be used as an indicator of where future work is needed. While we know a good deal more about Japanese history today than we did thirty years ago, there are gaps. One of the most important areas that deserves further, careful reexamination is the interwar period, particularly the 1930s. Japan's "dark valley," as some have labeled it, cannot simply be discarded as an aberration. In the end no really complete assessment of modern Japanese history can be written until both Japanese and Western historians come to grips with this crucial age and link its complex dual faces of democracy and militarism. It may well be that our lack of a definitive history of modern Japan is the result of our inability to explain (or failure to wrestle with) this dilemma.

Finally, a few words need to be added about periodization. The Japanese have long used official reign names to designate periods. Accordingly, the modern age can be divided into the following periods: Meiji (1868–1912), Taisho (1912–1926), Showa (1926–1989), and Heisei (1989–). While the Meiji period forms a complete historical unit, the Taisho and Showa do not. In many instances it is more effective to link Taisho, or that portion of Taisho that follows World War I, with early Showa, which ended with Japan's defeat in World War II (1945). Late Showa (1945–1989) can then be used effectively to cover the postwar period.

[Contributors: FGN = F. G. Notehelfer, GMB = Gordon M. Berger, JSH = John S. Hill, NR = Norman Rich, RRM = Ralph R. Menning, SM = Sally Marks]

REFERENCE WORKS

Dictionaries and Encyclopedias

13.1 Ainslie T. Embree, ed. *Encyclopedia of Asian history.* 4 vols. New York: Scribner's, 1988. ISBN 0-684-18619-5 (set). ▸ Covers broad sweep of Asian history, geography, politics, art, religion, philosophy, law, and literature. Japan broadly represented. Extensively illustrated; reliable and up to date. [FGN]

13.2 Janet E. Hunter, comp. *Concise dictionary of modern Japanese history.* Berkeley: University of California Press, 1984. ISBN 0-520-04390-1 (cl), 0-520-04557-2 (pbk). ▸ Guide to people, places, events, and movements of modern Japanese history. Most entries include short bibliographies. Useful appendix lists all cabinets and their members from 1885–1980. [FGN]

13.3 Gen Itaska et al., eds. *Kodansha encyclopedia of Japan* and *Supplement.* 10 vols. Tokyo: Kodansha; distributed by Harper & Row, 1983–86. ISBN 0-87011-620-7 (set), 0-80711-814-5 (suppl.). ▸ Leading English-language reference work on Japanese matters. Excellent essays on historical periods and historical problems by prominent scholars. Essential tool for students dealing with Japan. [FGN]

Atlases and Geographies

13.4 David Kornhauser. *Japan: geographical background to urban-industrial development.* 2d ed. New York: Longman, 1982. ISBN 0-582-30081-9. ▸ Focuses on cultural, political, and historical elements that have transformed Japan's modern landscape from villages to modern industrial cities. Good introductory volume. Earlier title: *Urban Japan.* [FGN]

13.5 Glenn T. Trewartha. *Japan: a geography.* 1965 ed. Madison: University of Wisconsin Press, 1970. ISBN 0-299-03440-5. ▸ Most complete survey of Japan's geography and geographically related subjects. Still standard work. [FGN]

SEE ALSO
  12.8 Martin Collcutt, Marius B. Jansen, and Isao Kumakura. *A cultural atlas of Japan.*

Bibliographies

13.6 Roberta Abraham. *Bibliography on technology and social change in China and Japan.* Ames: Iowa State University, Committee on Technology and Social Change in Foreign Cultures, 1974. ISBN 0-945271-21-2. ▸ Bibliography addressing technological literature on Chinese and Japanese development, tracing native sources as well as Western imports. Cross-spectrum of literature of social change also included. [FGN]

13.7 Association for Asian Studies. *Cumulative bibliography of Asian studies, 1941–1965.* 8 vols. *1966–1970.* 6 vols. Boston: Hall, 1969–73. ISBN 0-8161-0127-2 (set), 0-8161-0959-1 (set). ▸ Multivolume author and subject bibliography, covering both books and articles on Japan and Asia. See also *Bibliography of Asian Studies* (11.1). [FGN]

13.8 Rex Coleman and John Owen Haley, comps. *An index to Japanese law: a bibliography of Western-language materials, 1867–1973.* Tokyo: Japanese American Society for Legal Studies, 1975. (*Law in Japan: an annual,* Special issue, 1975.) ▸ Comprehensive guide to Western-language materials on Japanese law and legal history. Includes some 4,000 books, pamphlets, articles, and essays covering all aspects of Japanese law. [FGN]

13.9 John W. Dower. *Japanese history and culture from ancient to modern times: seven basic bibliographies.* New York: Wiener, 1986. ISBN 0-910129-20-7 (cl), 0-910129-36-3 (pbk). ▸ Personalized bibliography covering breadth of Japanese history. Particularly detailed and useful for modern period. Focuses on scholarly studies and monographs. Excellent for graduate students. [FGN]

13.10 H. Byron Earhart. *The new religions of Japan: a bibliography of Western-language materials.* 2d ed. Ann Arbor: University of Michigan, Center for Japanese Studies, 1983. (Michigan papers in Japanese studies, 9.) ISBN 0-939512-13-0. ▸ Bibliographical guide to new religions that emerged in modern Japan. Covers primary and secondary materials. Organized by author and by religious grouping (Shintō, Buddhist, Christian, etc.). [FGN]

13.11   Peter Grilli, ed. *Japan in film: a comprehensive annotated catalogue of documentary and theatrical films on Japan available in the United States.* New York: Japan Society Gallery, 1984. ISBN 0-913304-20-4. ‣ Annotated guide to films relating to Japan available in the United States. [FGN]

13.12   Fujio Ikado and James R. McGovern. *A bibliography of Christianity in Japan: Protestantism in English sources (1859–1959).* Tokyo: International Christian University, Committee on Asian Cultural Studies, 1966. ‣ Useful guide to English-language literature on Protestant Christianity in modern Japan. Includes over 1,000 annotated entries. [FGN]

13.13   Japan Foundation, comp. *Catalogue of books in English on Japan, 1945–1981.* Tokyo: Japan Foundation, 1986. ISBN 0-10-36645-5. ‣ Catalog of approximately 9,000 English-language books about Japan in humanities, social sciences, and fine arts. [FGN]

13.14   Hesung Chun Koh, ed. and comp. *Korean and Japanese women: an analytic bibliographical guide.* Westport, Conn.: Greenwood, 1982. ISBN 0-313-23387-X. ‣ Annotated entries dealing with English-language literature on Japanese and Korean women up to 1980s. Critical exploration of issues relating to women. [FGN]

13.15   James W. Morley, ed. *Japan's foreign policy, 1868–1941: a research guide.* New York: Columbia University Press, 1974. ISBN 0-231-08996-X. ‣ Research guide designed for graduate students, including superb critical essays on Japanese foreign and military policies as well as bibliography on Japan's foreign relations in English- and Japanese-language sources. [FGN/NR]

13.16   G. Raymond Nunn, comp. *Japanese periodicals and newspapers in Western languages: an international union list.* London: Mansell, 1979. ISBN 0-7201-0934-5. ‣ Comprehensive catalog of 3,500 Western-language titles of magazines, newspapers, society transactions, bulletins, reports, handbooks, yearbooks, directories, from 1860s to 1978. [FGN]

13.17   Frank Joseph Shulman. *Japan.* Santa Barbara, Calif.: Clio, 1990. (World bibliographical series, 103.) ISBN 1-85109-074-6. ‣ Most extensive critically annotated bibliography on Japan currently available. Covers some 1,900 popular and academic English-language books and monographs on Japan dealing with wide variety of fields and subjects. [FGN]

13.18   Frank Joseph Shulman, ed. and comp. *Japan and Korea: an annotated bibliography of doctoral dissertations in Western languages, 1877–1969.* Chicago: American Library Association, 1970. ISBN 0-8389-0085-2. ‣ Annotated guide to 2,077 doctoral dissertations dealing with Japan and Korea. Indexed by author, degree-granting institution, and subject. Virtually all academic subjects covered. *Supplement* available from Seattle: University of Washington Press, 1982. ISBN 0-295-95895-2 (cl), 0-295-95961-4 (pbk). [FGN]

13.19   Bernard S. Silberman. *Japan and Korea: a critical bibliography.* 1962 ed. Westport, Conn.: Greenwood, 1982. ISBN 0-313-23594-5. ‣ Annotated bibliography consisting of 1,600 books and articles on Japan and 300 entries on Korea. Covers variety of topics and fields. Good for Western scholarship dealing with Japan to 1962. Now seriously dated. [FGN]

13.20   *The United States in East Asia: a historical bibliography.* Santa Barbara, Calif.: ABC-Clio Information Services, 1985. (ABC-Clio research guides, 14.) ISBN 0-87436-452-3. ‣ Annotated bibliography covering periodical articles published in American, European, and Asian journals between 1973 and 1984 on history of United States–East Asian relations. [FGN]

13.21   Robert E. Ward and Frank Joseph Shulman. *The Allied occupation of Japan, 1945–1952: an annotated bibliography of Western-language materials.* Chicago: American Library Association, 1974. ISBN 0-8389-0127-1. ‣ Comprehensive survey of materials covering Allied occupation of Japan. Annotates 3,176 books, articles, dissertations, and government publications dealing with this event. [FGN]

13.22   William D. Wray, ed. *Japan's economy: a bibliography of its past and present.* New York: Wiener, 1989. ISBN 0-910129-79-7. ‣ Extensive guide to English-language literature covering Japanese economy from Tokugawa period (1600–1867) to 1980s. Arranged chronologically by major topic. Detailed and up to date. [FGN]

Historiography

13.23   Hugh Borton. "A survey of Japanese historiography." *American historical review* 43 (1938) 489–99. ISSN 0002-8762. ‣ Leading survey of Japanese historiography in prewar period. [FGN]

13.24   Peter Duus. "Whig history, Japanese style: the Min'yusha historians and the Meiji Restoration." *Journal of Asian studies* 33.3 (1974) 415–36. ISSN 0021-9118. ‣ Discussion of interpretation of Meiji Restoration as incomplete revolution developed by Minyusha historians such as Tokutomi Soho. Important on conception of Meiji Restoration. [FGN]

13.25   Carol Gluck. "The people in history: recent trends in Japanese historiography." *Journal of Asian studies* 38.1 (1978) 25–50. ISSN 0021-9118. ‣ Review of recent Japanese historical scholarship that has come to emphasize role of common people as important contributors to development of modern Japan. Excellent exploration of bottom-up history. [FGN]

13.26   John Whitney Hall. "Historiography in Japan." In *Teachers of history: essays in honor of Laurence Bradford Packard.* 1954 ed. H. Stuart Hughes, ed., pp. 284–304. Freeport, N.Y.: Books for Libraries, 1971. ‣ Early postwar view of Japanese historiography; still useful. [FGN]

13.27   John Whitney Hall. *Japanese history: new dimensions of approach and understanding.* 2d ed. Washington, D.C.: Service Center for Teachers of History, 1966. (Service Center for Teachers of History publication, 4.) ‣ Well-organized discussion of Japanese history including historiographical interpretations and bibliography. [FGN]

13.28   Sue Henny and Jean-Pierre Lehmann, eds. *Themes and theories in modern Japanese history: essays in memory of Richard Storry.* London: Athlone, 1988. ISBN 0-485-11242-6. ‣ Useful overview. Explores various interpretations of modern Japanese history. Modern Japanese development treated from diverse historiographic perspectives. [FGN]

13.29   James W. Morley. "Historical writing in modern Japan." In *The development of historiography.* Matthew A. Fitzsimons, Alfred G. Pundt, and Charles E. Nowell, eds., pp. 381–89. Harrisburg, Pa.: Stackpole, 1954. ‣ Discussion of twentieth-century Japanese historiography. Brief and to the point. [FGN]

Demography

13.30   Susan B. Hanley and Kōzō Yamamura. *Economic and demographic change in preindustrial Japan, 1600–1868.* Princeton: Princeton University Press, 1977. ISBN 0-691-03111-8 (cl), 0-691-10055-1 (pbk). ‣ Excellent analysis of Tokugawa economic change through demographic lenses. Gradually rising living standards attributed to expanding production coupled with population growth, controlled by abortion and infanticide. [FGN]

13.31   Irene B. Taeuber. *The population of Japan.* Princeton: Princeton University Press, 1958. ‣ Still definitive study on population of Japan. Outstanding analysis of demographic change in

Japan from premodern times to 1950s. Thorough and comprehensive; includes massive bibliography of English and Japanese works. [FGN]

GENERAL STUDIES

13.32 G. C. Allen. *A short economic history of modern Japan.* 4th ed. New York: St. Martin's, 1981. ISBN 0-312-71771-7. ‣ Overview of Japanese economic development from Meiji Restoration (1868–1912) to 1980. Focuses on industrial and financial development as well as on governmental policy. Best introductory survey. [FGN]

13.33 Michiko Y. Aoki and Margaret B. Dardess, eds. *As the Japanese see it: past and present.* Honolulu: University of Hawaii Press, 1981. ISBN 0-8248-0759-6 (cl), 0-8248-0760-X (pbk). ‣ Anthology containing thirty-one selections concentrating on religion, family, community, and state in twentieth-century Japan. Oriented toward general reader. [FGN]

13.34 William G. Beasley. *The rise of modern Japan.* New York: St. Martin's, 1990. ISBN 0-312-04078-4 (cl), 0-312-04077-6 (pbk). ‣ Standard textbook on modern Japanese history written by one of Britain's leading Japanese historians. Emphasizes political and economic developments. [FGN]

13.35 Hugh Borton. *Japan's modern century: from Perry to 1970.* 2d ed. New York: Ronald, 1970. ‣ History of Japan from 1853 to 1955. At time of publication best single-volume history of modern Japan. Now somewhat dated though still valuable for wealth of information on prewar Japan. [FGN]

13.36 Albert M. Craig, ed. *Japan: a comparative view.* Princeton: Princeton University Press, 1979. ISBN 0-691-05271-9. ‣ Well-documented essays on Japan, China, and Korea dealing with urbanization, modernization, culture, personality, economy, and society. Stresses comparative approach. [FGN]

13.37 Peter Duus. *The rise of modern Japan.* Boston: Houghton-Mifflin, 1976. ISBN 0-395-20665-0. ‣ Sensitive analytical treatment of modern Japanese history focusing on nineteenth-century westernization, pursuit and failure of imperialism, and Japan's post–World War II economic achievements. [FGN]

13.38 Peter Duus, ed. *The Cambridge history of Japan: the twentieth century.* Cambridge: Cambridge University Press, 1989. ISBN 0-521-22357-1. ‣ Comprehensive examination of Japan's political development, economic growth, and intellectual and social movements through 1970s. Explores Japan's rise and fall as twentieth-century military power, and details first phase of Japan's postwar economic recovery. [FGN]

13.39 Frank Gibney. *Japan, the fragile super-power.* 2d rev. ed. New York: New American Library, 1985. ISBN 0-452-00776-3 (pbk). ‣ Panoramic view of post–World War II Japan. Study focuses on social, political, and economic changes that have made Japan into world power in second half of twentieth century. [FGN]

13.40 John Whitney Hall and Richard K. Beardsley. *Twelve doors to Japan.* New York: McGraw-Hill, 1965. ‣ Interdisciplinary introduction to Japan focusing on how different academic disciplines have come to interpret Japanese culture and society. [FGN]

13.41 Mikiso Hane. *Modern Japan, a historical survey.* 2d ed. Boulder: Westview, 1992. ISBN 0-8133-1367-8 (cl), 0-8133-1368-6 (pbk). ‣ Well-written and comprehensive survey of modern Japanese history. Strength of work lies in its insights into history of Japan's economically deprived classes, women, and minorities. Challenges prior optimistic interpretations of Japanese development. [FGN]

13.42 Marius B. Jansen. *Japan and China: from war to peace, 1894–1972.* Chicago: Rand McNally, 1975. ‣ History of Japan

and China concentrating on interaction between these nations at diplomatic and developmental levels. Useful comparative study that explores emergence of both China and Japan as Asian powers. [FGN]

13.43 Marius B. Jansen. *Japan and its world: two centuries of change.* 1980 ed. Ann Arbor: University Microfilms International, 1992. ISBN 0-8357-6927-5 (pbk). ‣ Three highly informative lectures on Japan's relationship to the outside world. Explores Confucianism, Meiji search for knowledge from abroad, and Japan's quest for role in twentieth century. [FGN]

13.44 Marius B. Jansen, ed. *The Cambridge history of Japan: the nineteenth century.* Cambridge: Cambridge University Press, 1989. ISBN 0-521-22356-3. ‣ Explores Japan's transformation from feudal society to modern nation-state. Economic and demographic changes paired with political, cultural, and foreign policy issues led to Restoration and emergence of Meiji state. [FGN]

13.45 Marius B. Jansen, ed. *Changing Japanese attitudes toward modernization.* 1965 ed. Princeton: Princeton University Press, 1971. ISBN 0-691-03007-3 (cl), 0-691-00009-2 (pbk). ‣ Essays by leading scholars on modern Japanese history. Publication of series initiated modernization debate between Japanese and American scholars on nature of Meiji Restoration and subsequent Japanese development. [FGN]

13.46 Masataka Kosaka. *A history of postwar Japan.* 1972 ed. New York: Kodansha; distributed by Harper & Row, 1982. ISBN 0-87011-513-8 (pbk). ‣ Concise history of Japan since 1945. One of few works addressing postwar period as separate historical age. Originally published as *100 Million Japanese.* [FGN]

13.47 Jon Livingston, Joe Moore, and Felicia Oldfather, eds. *The Japan reader.* Vol. 1: *Imperial Japan, 1800–1945.* Vol. 2: *Postwar Japan, 1945 to the present.* New York: Pantheon, 1973–74. ISBN 0-394-48437-1 (v. 1, cl), 0-394-48903-9 (v. 2, cl), 0-394-70668-4 (v. 1, pbk), 0-394-70669-2 (v. 2, pbk). ‣ Collected readings in primary sources for undergraduate courses in modern Japanese history. Well-balanced, comprehensive selection including fiction, autobiography, documents, and scholarly arguments. [FGN]

13.48 David John Lu, comp. *Sources of Japanese history.* Vol. 2. New York: McGraw-Hill, 1974. ISBN 0-07-038903-9 (v. 2, cl), 0-07-038905-5 (v. 2, pbk). ‣ Well-selected collection of primary source materials about Japan from late Tokugawa period through contemporary Japan. Emphasizes social, economic, and political documents. [FGN]

13.49 Tetsuo Najita. *Japan.* Englewood Cliffs, N.J.: Prentice-Hall, 1974. ISBN 0-13-509455-0 (cl), 0-13-509448-8 (pbk). ‣ Important historical essay covering development of modern Japan. Focuses on themes of bureacracy and political idealism to explain Japan's remarkable achievements in twentieth century. [FGN]

13.50 Kenneth B. Pyle. *The making of modern Japan.* Lexington, Mass.: Heath, 1978. ISBN 0-669-84657-0. ‣ Brief overview of Japanese history from 1600 to 1970. Strength of work lies in author's ability to present sophisticated arguments and complex interpretations in simple, lucid, and readable manner. [FGN]

13.51 Edwin O. Reischauer. *Japan: the story of a nation.* 1989 4th ed. New York: McGraw-Hill, 1990. ISBN 0-07-557074-2. ‣ Concise, well-balanced survey stressing positive elements that allowed Japan to utilize its traditional society and values to build modern state. Presents modernization viewpoint. [FGN]

13.52 Edwin O. Reischauer. *The Japanese.* 1977 ed. Cambridge, Mass.: Belknap, 1981. ISBN 0-674-47176-8 (cl, 1977), 0-674-47178-4 (pbk). ‣ Excellent portrait of Japan and Japanese, analyzing historical background to explain contemporary achievements. Follow up on author's popular *The United States and Japan* (40.639). [FGN]

13.53 Edwin O. Reischauer and Albert M. Craig. *Japan: tradition and transformation*. Rev. ed. Boston: Houghton-Mifflin, 1989. ISBN 0-395-49696-9 (pbk). ▸ Detailed, comprehensive history of Japan. Japan sections of this well-documented text are revised and updated from *East Asia: Tradition and Transformation*, developed at Harvard in late 1950s. [FGN]

13.54 G. B. Sansom. *The Western world and Japan: a study in the interaction of European and Asiatic cultures*. 1949 ed. New York: Knopf, 1962. ▸ Excellent analysis of Western impact on Japan from 1600–1894 in part 2. Focus on how Japan perceived West and how it responded to Western influences. [FGN]

13.55 Richard Storry. *A history of modern Japan*. 1960 ed. New York: Penguin, 1983. ISBN 0-14-020475-X. ▸ Brief historical survey of modern Japanese development. Particularly insightful coverage of 1920s and 1930s, showing process by which Japan moved steadily toward confrontation and war with West. [FGN]

13.56 Arthur E. Tiedemann, ed. *An introduction to Japanese civilization*. New York and Lexington, Mass.: Columbia University Press and Heath, 1974. ISBN 0-231-03651-5 (cl), 0-669-52878-1 (pbk). ▸ Introductory overview. First half presents narrative of Japanese history; second half includes essays by leading scholars on topics such as religion, art, literature, economics, political institutions, etc. [FGN]

13.57 Ryusaku Tsunoda, Wm. Theodore De Bary, and Donald Keene, eds. *Sources of Japanese tradition*. Vol. 2. 1958 ed. New York: Columbia University Press, 1971. ISBN 0-231-08605-9 (v. 2). ▸ Still standard collection of source materials dealing with Japan from Tokugawa period to World War II. In addition to political and economic questions, selections address religious, philosophical, and aesthetic issues. [FGN]

13.58 Harry Wray and Hilary Conroy, eds. *Japan examined: perspectives on modern Japanese history*. Honolulu: University of Hawaii Press, 1983. ISBN 0-8248-0806-1 (cl), 0-8248-0839-8 (pbk). ▸ Introductory study exploring diverse interpretations applied to modern Japanese history on chronological and topical basis. Leading historians debate major themes of Japanese development. [FGN]

TOKUGAWA ROOTS OF MODERNIZATION, 1600–1867

13.59 Robert N. Bellah. *Tokugawa religion: the cultural roots of modern Japan*. 1957 ed. New York: Free Press, 1985. ISBN 0-02-902460-9 (pbk). ▸ Important application of Weberian theory to show how Buddhism, Confucianism, Shintō, and Shingaku thought fostered values and behavior essential for Japan's modernization. [FGN]

13.60 Ronald P. Dore. *Education in Tokugawa Japan*. 1965 ed. London: Athlone, 1992. ISBN 0-485-12086-0. ▸ Excellent study showing dramatic expansion of education during latter half of Tokugawa period. Education seen as source of mobility and basis for emerging meritocracy in early modern Japan. [FGN]

13.61 John Whitney Hall and Marius B. Jansen, eds. *Studies in the institutional history of early modern Japan*. Princeton: Princeton University Press, 1968. ISBN 0-691-03071-5 (cl), 0-691-00013-1 (pbk). ▸ Twenty-one significant essays dealing with political, social, and economic structures as they responded to changes in latter half of Tokugawa period. Focuses on Tokugawa institutional development. [FGN]

13.62 Harry D. Harootunian. *Toward restoration: the growth of political consciousness in Tokugawa Japan*. 1970 ed. Berkeley: University of California Press, 1991. ISBN 0-520-07403-3. ▸ Major exploration of late Tokugawa thought in effort to locate dynamics leading to Meiji Restoration. Shows how thinkers of Mito school turned ethical tradition into theory of action through process of politicization. [FGN]

13.63 Ann Bowman Jannetta. *Epidemics and mortality in early modern Japan*. Princeton: Princeton University Press, 1987. ISBN 0-691-05484-3. ▸ Pathbreaking study of epidemic diseases of Tokugawa period and their impact on population growth. Concludes infanticide and abortion were greater factors in population control than diseases. [FGN]

13.64 William W. Kelly. *Deference and defiance in nineteenth-century Japan*. Princeton: Princeton University Press, 1985. ISBN 0-691-09417-9. ▸ Insightful examination of rural protest movements in North Japan. Popular consciousness and political action linked in transition from tributary polity to nation-state and from mercantilism to capitalism. [FGN]

13.65 Masao Maruyama. *Studies in the intellectual history of Tokugawa Japan*. 1974 ed. Mikiso Hane, trans. Princeton: Princeton University Press, 1989. ISBN 0-691-07566-2 (cl, 1974), 0-691-00832-9 (pbk). ▸ Brilliant analysis of intellectual roots of modern Japan by leading theorist of Japanese modes of thought and behavior through exploration of transformation of late Tokugawa thought. [FGN]

13.66 Tetsuo Najita. *Visions of virtue in Tokugawa Japan: the Kaitokudo Merchant Academy of Osaka*. Chicago: University of Chicago Press, 1987. ISBN 0-226-56804-0 (cl), 0-226-56805-9 (pbk). ▸ Sees merchants as active participants in intellectual history of Tokugawa politics; denies earlier interpretations of merchant passivity. Impressive new reading of social thought in Tokugawa Japan. [FGN]

13.67 Tetsuo Najita and J. Victor Koschmann, eds. *Conflict in modern Japanese history: the neglected tradition*. Princeton: Princeton University Press, 1982. ISBN 0-691-05364-2 (cl), 0-691-10137-X (pbk). ▸ Provocative essays by eighteen American and Japanese scholars, challenging concepts of consensus and harmony usually associated with Japanese society. Focuses on conflict as major theme in modern Japanese development. [FGN]

13.68 Thomas C. Smith. *The agrarian origins of modern Japan*. 1959 ed. Stanford, Calif.: Stanford University Press, 1984. ISBN 0-8047-0530-5 (cl), 0-8047-0531-3 (pbk). ▸ Seminal work on Tokugawa agriculture, tracing transformation of Japanese villages from subsistence to commercialized farming during last half of Tokugawa age. [FGN]

13.69 Thomas C. Smith. *Native sources of Japanese industrialization, 1750–1920*. Berkeley: University of California Press, 1988. ISBN 0-520-05837-2 (cl), 0-520-06293-0 (pbk). ▸ Distinguished historian of Japan explores factors that helped Japanese to industrialize. Rich and provocative, challenging some accepted notions about emergence of modern industrial societies. [FGN]

13.70 Ronald Toby. *State and diplomacy in early modern Japan: Asia in the development of the Tokugawa bakufu*. 1984 ed. Stanford, Calif.: Stanford University Press, 1991. ISBN 0-8047-1951-9 (cl), 0-8047-1952-7 (pbk). ▸ Major reinterpretation challenging view of early modern Japan as isolated or closed nation. Argues Tokugawa shoguns conducted active foreign policy with China and Korea. [FGN]

13.71 Conrad Totman. *The collapse of the Tokugawa bakufu, 1862–1868*. Honolulu: University of Hawaii Press, 1980. ISBN 0-8248-0614-X. ▸ Examination of disintegration of Tokugawa shogunate in final decade of its rule. Massive and detailed in its treatment. Masterly reconstruction of period utilizing vast array of primary sources. [FGN]

13.72 Bob Tadashi Wakabayashi. *Anti-foreignism and Western learning in early modern Japan: the New Theses of 1825*. Cambridge, Mass.: Harvard University, Council on East Asian Studies, 1986. (Harvard East Asian monographs, 126.) ISBN 0-674-04025-2. ▸ Traces relationship between Dutch studies and emergence of antiforeign thought in late Tokugawa Japan.

Focuses on Mito scholar Aizawa's *Shinron* (New Thesis). Shows paradox: those who knew most about West were most antiforeign. [FGN]

13.73 Herschel Webb. *The Japanese imperial institution in the Tokugawa period.* New York: Columbia University Press, 1968. ISBN 0-231-03120-3. ▸ Best analysis of character and status of imperial institution during Tokugawa period. Shows how imperial house became rallying point for anti-Tokugawa ideology. [FGN]

13.74 Kōzō Yamamura. *A study of samurai income and entrepreneurship: quantitative analysis of economic and social aspects of the samurai in Tokugawa and Meiji, Japan.* Cambridge, Mass.: Harvard University Press, 1974. ISBN 0-674-85322-5. ▸ Quantitative analysis of economic and social aspects of samurai in Tokugawa and Meiji Japan. Well-documented exploration of transition of samurai from feudal to modern Japan. [FGN]

SEE ALSO
  12.222 Chie Nakane and Shinzaburō Ōishi, eds. *Tokugawa Japan.*
  12.313 J. Victor Koschmann. *The Mito ideology.*

MEIJI RESTORATION, 1868–1912

13.75 Paul Akamatsu. *Meiji 1868: revolution and counter-revolution in Japan.* Miriam Kochan, trans. New York: Harper & Row, 1972. ISBN 0-06-010044-3. ▸ Clearest statement of Marxist position on Meiji Restoration. Argues revolutionary potential of Restoration was aborted by late Meiji absolutism. Reflects earlier Japanese interpretations of Restoration. [FGN]

13.76 William G. Beasley. *The Meiji Restoration.* Stanford, Calif.: Stanford University Press, 1972. ISBN 0-8047-0815-0. ▸ Life-work of major British historian of Japan. Massive treatment arguing Restoration was nationalist revolution. Comprehensive and well documented. [FGN]

13.77 Albert M. Craig. *Choshu in the Meiji Restoration.* Cambridge, Mass.: Harvard University Press; distributed by University Microfilms, 1961. ISBN 0-674-12850-8. ▸ Major study accounting for Choshu's leading role in Restoration. Traces domain's financial resources and presents good picture of late Tokugawa *han* (domain) in transition. [FGN]

13.78 Thomas M. Huber. *The revolutionary origins of modern Japan.* 1981 ed. Stanford, Calif.: Stanford University Press, 1990. ISBN 0-8047-1048-1 (cl), 0-8047-1755-9 (pbk). ▸ Challenges earlier interpretations of Restoration by reexamining Choshu role. Argues that much of incentive for change in Choshu came from development of service aristocracy that favored new order. [FGN]

13.79 Marius B. Jansen. *Sakamoto Ryoma and the Meiji Restoration.* 1961 ed. Stanford, Calif.: Stanford University Press, 1971. ISBN 0-8047-0784-7. ▸ One of seminal works on Meiji Restoration. Very good on role played by restoration activists (*shishi*), such as Sakamoto. Major source on Tosa domain's role in Restoration. [FGN]

13.80 E. Herbert Norman. *Japan's emergence as a modern state: political and economic problems in the Meiji period.* 1940 ed. Westport, Conn.: Greenwood, 1973. ISBN 0-8371-6573-3. ▸ Early well-written study of Meiji Restoration, emphasizing merchant–lower samurai alliance as causal. Classic postwar interpretation of Restoration based on Kyoto and Marxist schools. [FGN]

13.81 Michio Umegaki. *After the Restoration: the beginnings of Japan's modern state.* New York: New York University Press, 1988. ISBN 0-8147-8552-2. ▸ Reinterpretation of Restoration from perspective of continuity rather than change, with result that Restoration largely portrayed as nonevent. [FGN]

13.82 Neil L. Waters. *Japan's local pragmatists: the transition from bakumatsu to Meiji in the Kawasaki region.* Cambridge, Mass.: Harvard University, Council on East Asian Studies, 1983. (Harvard East Asian monographs, 105.) ISBN 0-674-47192-X. ▸ Thoughtful reexamination of significance of Restoration at local level, exploring elements of continuity and change witnessed in region just south of city of Edo. Suggests considerable continuities. [FGN]

SEE ALSO
  12.219 Torao Haraguchi et al., eds. *The status system and social organization of Satsuma.*

Peasant Protests and Popular Uprisings: Before and During Meiji Restoration

13.83 Herbert P. Bix. *Peasant protest in feudal Japan, 1590–1884.* New Haven: Yale University Press, 1986. ISBN 0-300-03485-7. ▸ Series of chronologically organized case studies of peasant uprisings with particular focus on class struggle and emerging peasant consciousness. Good example of revised Marxist approach. [FGN]

13.84 Hugh Borton. "Peasant uprisings in Japan of the Tokugawa period." *Transactions of the Asiatic Society of Japan,* Second series, 15 (1938) 1–219. ▸ Best prewar study in English of Japanese peasant uprisings. Still useful. [FGN]

13.85 Roger W. Bowen. *Rebellion and democracy in Meiji Japan: a study of commoners in the popular rights movement.* Berkeley: University of California Press, 1980. ISBN 0-520-03665-4 (cl), 0-520-05230-7 (pbk). ▸ Revisionist appraisal of grassroots democratic movement in Meiji Japan that found expression in Fukushima, Kabasan, and Chichibu rebellions of 1870s and 1880s. Provides good bottom-up view of Restoration and popular rights movement. [FGN]

13.86 Nobutaka Ike. *Beginnings of political democracy in Japan.* 1950 ed. New York: Greenwood, 1969. ISBN 0-8371-1802-5. ▸ Important early study of political activities and theories of popular rights movement in Meiji Japan. Traces emergence of political parties within socioeconomic environment of 1870s and 1880s. [FGN]

13.87 Augustus H. Mounsey. *The Satsuma rebellion: an episode of modern Japanese history.* 1879 ed. Washington, D.C.: University Publications of America, 1979. ISBN 0-89093-259-X. ▸ Account of great rebellion in Japan; still one of basic sources of information on this uprising. [FGN]

13.88 E. Herbert Norman. *Soldier and peasant in Japan: the origins of conscription.* 1943 ed. New York: AMS Press, 1978. ISBN 0-404-59549-9. ▸ Although somewhat dated, still important study on emergence of concept of conscription in late Tokugawa and early Meiji periods. [FGN]

13.89 Irwin Scheiner. "Benevolent lords and honorable peasants: rebellion and peasant consciousness in Tokugawa Japan." In *Japanese thought in the Tokugawa period, 1600–1868: methods and metaphors.* 1978 ed. Tetsuo Najita and Irwin Scheiner, eds., pp. 39–62. Chicago: University of Chicago Press, 1988. ISBN 0-226-56801-6 (cl, 1978), 0-226-56802-4 (pbk). ▸ Thoughtful examination of unwritten social compact tying lords and peasants into dynamic symbiotic relationship in Tokugawa Japan. Shows how covenant gave way to new forces in final Tokugawa years. [FGN]

13.90 Stephen Vlastos. *Peasant protests and uprisings in Tokugawa Japan.* Berkeley: University of California Press, 1986. ISBN 0-520-04614-5. ▸ Excellent reevaluation of peasantry. Argues peasant protest directed against traditional village leaders and commercial elite rather than feudal ruling classes. Shows peasant role in Restoration restricted both ideologically and organizationally. [FGN]

13.91 Anne Walthall, ed. and trans. *Peasant uprisings in Japan: a critical anthology of peasant histories.* Chicago: University of Chicago Press, 1991. ISBN 0-226-87233-5 (cl), 0-226-87234-3 (pbk). ▸ Pioneering study introducing voices of rural Japan into discussion of resistance to domination by Tokugawa authorities. Rich compendium of peasant martyrs, uprisings, and riots, filled with insights into politics of peasant protest. See also Walthall 12.260. [FGN]

Meiji Leadership

13.92 Roger F. Hackett. *Yamagata Aritomo in the rise of modern Japan, 1838–1922.* Cambridge, Mass.: Harvard University Press, 1971. ISBN 0-674-96301-6. ▸ Biography of one of central leaders of Meiji Restoration and founder of modern Japanese army. Subsequently Japan's most powerful elder statesman. Careful study of Yamagata's official career. [FGN]

13.93 Ivan Parker Hall. *Mori Arinori.* Cambridge, Mass.: Harvard University Press, 1973. ISBN 0-674-58730-8. ▸ Biography of Japan's first envoy to United States and minister of education in Meiji government who was assassinated in 1889. Fine study of maverick Meiji leader, brilliant scholar, and westernizer. [FGN]

13.94 Masakazu Iwata. *Okubo Toshimichi: the Bismarck of Japan.* Berkeley: University of California Press, 1964. ▸ Somewhat dated study of leading figure in early years of Meiji Restoration and one of most powerful oligarchs who attempted to steer middle course in guiding Japan toward modernization. [FGN]

13.95 Kido Takayoshi. *The diary of Kido Takayoshi.* 3 vols. Sidney D. Brown and Akiko Hirota, trans. Tokyo: University of Tokyo Press, 1983–86. ISBN 0-86008-328-4 (v. 1), 0-86008-350-0 (v. 2), 0-86008-386-1 (v. 3). ▸ Translation of diary of one of most important early Meiji leaders covering years 1868–71. Major historical source for Meiji Restoration. [FGN]

13.96 Joyce C. Lebra. *Okuma Shigenobu: statesman of Meiji Japan.* Canberra: Australian National University Press, 1973. ISBN 0-7081-0400-2. ▸ Well-researched biography of one of significant Meiji oligarchs and founder of Progressive party. [FGN]

13.97 Yoshitake Oka. *Five political leaders of modern Japan: Ito Hirobumi, Okuma Shigenobu, Hara Takashi, Inukai Tsuyoshi, and Saionji Kimmochi.* Andrew Fraser and Patricia Murray, trans. Tokyo: University of Tokyo Press, 1986. ISBN 0-86008-379-9. ▸ Diverse study of careers of five prominent politicians including Meiji leaders Ito and Okuma. Case-study approach to leadership in Japan. [FGN]

13.98 Bernard S. Silberman and Harry D. Harootunian, eds. *Modern Japanese leadership: transition and change.* 1966 ed. Tucson: University of Arizona Press, 1989. ▸ Volume of conference papers (1963) by various authors, exploring emergence of new leadership in Meiji Japan; emphasizes individuals and groups. Approaches vary from individual studies to social-demographic analyses of political elite. Contains several important essays. [FGN]

Foreign Observer Accounts

13.99 Erwin O. E. von Baelz. *Awakening Japan: the diary of a German doctor.* 1932 ed. Toku Baelz, ed. Bloomington: University of Indiana Press, 1974. ISBN 0-253-31090-3. ▸ Highly informative account of life in Japan and detailed portrait of many important government figures with whom author was associated in his role as physician-in-waiting to imperial house. Excellent on life and politics in Meiji Japan. [FGN]

13.100 Isabella L. Bird. *Unbeaten tracks in Japan: an account of travels on horseback in the interior including visits to the Aborigines of Yezo and the shrines of Nikko and Ise.* 1881 ed. 2 vols. Boston: Beacon, 1987. ISBN 0-8070-7015-7. ▸ Observations on and broad, perceptive description of Japanese customs and rural life by excellent observer and ethnographer who traveled widely in Japan (1878). Also available on microfilm from New Haven: Research Publications, 1976 (History of Women). [FGN]

13.101 John R. Black. *Young Japan: Yokohama and Yedo, 1858–1879.* 1883 ed. 2 vols. Grace Fox, Introduction. New York: Oxford University Press, 1968. ▸ Detailed history of Yokohama and Edo (Tokyo) by British newspaper editor and publisher who resided in Japan, 1861–79. Useful firsthand source on life in Japan as perceived by Western eye. [FGN]

13.102 Basil Hall Chamberlain. *Things Japanese, being notes on various subjects connected with Japan for the use of travellers and others.* 1939 6th rev. ed. Rutland, Vt.: Tuttle, 1970. ISBN 0-8048-0713-2. ▸ Collection of materials on various Japanese topics, presented by direct observer and one of most knowledgable writers about Japan in nineteenth century. Still useful. [FGN]

13.103 Mary Crawford Fraser. *A diplomat's wife in Japan: sketches at the turn of the century.* 1899 ed. Hugh Cortazzi, ed. New York: Weatherhill, 1982. ISBN 0-8348-0172-8. ▸ Perceptive, informative account of life in Japan, 1889–94, by wife of British diplomat. Initially published as *A Diplomatist's Wife in Japan: Letters from Home to Home.* Also available on microform from New Haven: Research Publications, 1976. History of Women, Reel 544, no. 4190. [FGN]

13.104 William Elliot Griffis. *The Mikado's empire.* 1895 8th ed. Wilmington, Del.: Scholarly Resources, 1973. ▸ Important firsthand account of history of Japan and Griffis's personal experiences. Written by American educator and clergyman who taught in Japan, 1870–74. [FGN]

13.105 Francis Hall. *Japan through American eyes: the journal of Francis Hall, Kanagawa and Yokohama, 1859–1866.* F. G. Notehelfer, ed. Princeton: Princeton University Press, 1992. ISBN 0-691-03181-9. ▸ Annotated biography and diary of Francis Hall, leading American merchant in Yokohama, 1859–66, who also served as Japan correspondent for Horace Greely's *New York Tribune.* Fine description of Japan before Restoration. [FGN]

13.106 Lafcadio Hearn. *Japan: an attempt at interpretation.* New York: Macmillan, 1904. ▸ Author's final effort to sum up his perceptions of Japan and Japanese culture; published posthumously. Often critical of development of modern Japan. More analytical than literary. [FGN]

13.107 Edward S. Morse. *Japan, day by day, 1877, 1878–79, 1882–83.* Boston: Houghton-Mifflin, 1917. ▸ Carefully documented, illustrated account of life in Japan by eminent American zoologist who lived in Japan, 1877–83, taught at Tokyo University, and helped establish Japanese Imperial Museum. [FGN]

13.108 Algernon Bertram Freeman-Mitford Redesdale. *Mitford's Japan: the memoirs and recollections, 1866–1906, of Algernon Bertram Mitford, the first lord Redesdale.* Hugh Cortazzi, ed. London: Athlone, 1985. ISBN 0-485-11275-2. ▸ Memoirs of important nineteenth-century British diplomat-scholar who was in Japan in late 1860s and observed civil war between Tokugawa and imperial forces. [FGN]

13.109 Robert A. Rosenstone. *Mirror in the shrine: American encounters with Meiji Japan.* Cambridge, Mass.: Harvard University Press, 1988. ISBN 0-674-57641-1. ▸ Examination of perceptions of Japan held by Griffis (13.104), Hearn (13.106), and Morse (13.107) and how Japanese experiences altered their cultural identities as Westerners. Important effort to produce new form of biography. [FGN]

13.110 Clara A. N. Whitney. *Clara's diary: an American girl in Meiji Japan.* M. William Steele and Tamiko Ichimata, eds. Tokyo: Kodansha, 1979. ISBN 0-87011-341-0. ▸ Charming portrait of Meiji life and society presented through eyes of American girl who arrived in Japan in 1875 at age of fifteen and later married son of prominent Japanese statesman. [FGN]

13.111   Toshio Yokoyama. *Japan in the Victorian mind: a study of stereotyped images of a nation, 1850–80*. Basingstoke: Macmillan, 1987. ISBN 0-333-40472-6. ▸ Thorough analysis of British stereotypes of Japan that emerged out of perceptions that British writers and observers of Japan presented to public. Shows large gap between Japanese reality and British perceptions. [FGN]

Political History

13.112   George Akita. *Foundations of constitutional government in modern Japan, 1868–1900*. Cambridge, Mass.: Harvard University Press, 1967. ▸ Standard work on writing of Meiji constitution. Rejects earlier interpretation that leaders of oligarchy opposed constitution. Rather, while oligarchs questioned democracy as way to strong state, they favored constitutional rule. [FGN]

13.113   George M. Beckmann. *The making of the Meiji constitution: the oligarchs and the constitutional development of Japan, 1868–1891*. 1957 ed. Westport, Conn.: Greenwood, 1975. ISBN 0-8371-6553-9. ▸ Study of conflicts and compromises out of which Meiji constitution emerged in 1889. Older, but still valuable, examination of Meiji political history. [FGN]

13.114   John W. Dower, ed. *Origins of the modern Japanese state: selected writings of E. H. Norman*. New York: Pantheon, 1975. ISBN 0-394-49413-X (cl), 0-394-70927-6 (pbk). ▸ Reprint of Norman's "Japan's Emergence as a Modern State" as well as several other works. Introductory essay, "E. H. Norman, Japan, and the Uses of History," serves as useful introduction to important historian's thought. [FGN]

13.115   James L. Huffman. *Politics of the Meiji press: the life of Fukuchi Gen'ichiro*. Honolulu: University of Hawaii Press, 1980. ISBN 0-8248-0679-4. ▸ Fine exploration of relationship between Meiji press and politics, focusing on career of Fukuchi Gen'ichiro, editor of influential *Tokyo Nichi Nichi Shimbun*. [FGN]

13.116   Hirobumi Ito. *Commentaries on the constitution of the empire of Japan*. 1906 2d ed. Miyoji Ito, trans. Washington, D.C.: University Publications of America, 1979. ISBN 0-89093-212-3. ▸ Authoritative exposition of Meiji constitution and its conceptual framework by principal architect of document. [FGN]

13.117   R.H.P. Mason. *Japan's first general election: 1890*. Cambridge: Cambridge University Press, 1969. ISBN 0-521-07147-X. ▸ Concludes government bureaucrats and upholders of popular rights were central to election. Former wanted statism; latter, more liberal forms of organization and government. Resulting compromise undergirded weak but emerging constitutional order. Best study on early Diets in action. [FGN]

13.118   Walter Wallace McLaren. *A political history of Japan during the Meiji era, 1867–1912*. Rev. ed. London: Cass; distributed by Biblio, 1966. ISBN 0-7146-2018-1. ▸ Early but still useful political history of Meiji period, concentrating on emergence of Japan's modern parliamentary system. Detailed coverage of events and personalities. [FGN]

13.119   Walter Wallace McLaren, ed. *Japanese government documents of the Meiji era*. 1914 ed. 2 vols. Westport, Conn.: Greenwood, 1979. ISBN 0-313-26912-2 (v. 1), 0-313-26913-0 (v. 2). ▸ Still best English-language collection of Meiji period legislation. Invaluable source. [FGN]

13.120   Shigenobu Okuma, comp. *Fifty years of new Japan*. 1909 2d ed. 2 vols. Marcus B. Huish, ed. of English version. New York: Kraus Reprint, 1970. ISBN 0-527-68280-2. ▸ Important essays by leading participants in Meiji Restoration and Meiji government. Ito on constitution, Yamagata on army, Matsukata on finance, and Yamamoto on navy of particular interest. Also available on microfiche from Chicago: Library Resources, 1970. [FGN]

13.121   Joseph Pittau. *Political thought in early Meiji Japan, 1868–1889*. Ann Arbor: University Microfilms, 1967. ISBN 0-317-09172-7. ▸ Well-balanced treatment of political thought of early Meiji years, culminating in writing of Meiji constitution. Shows dynamic interaction of traditional Japanese and German constitutional ideas. [FGN]

13.122   Robert A. Scalapino. *Democracy and the party movement in prewar Japan*. 1953 ed. Berkeley: University of California Press, 1975. ISBN 0-520-02914-3. ▸ One of most thorough treatments of Japanese political development from Meiji period through World War II. Somewhat pessimistic, sees party movement and Japanese democracy as failing in prewar period. [FGN]

13.123   Johannes Siemes. *Hermann Roesler and the making of the Meiji state: an examination of his background and his influence on the founders of modern Japan and the complete text of the Meiji constitution accompanied by his personal commentaries and notes*. Tokyo: Tuttle, 1968. ▸ Important exploration of role of German constitutional scholar who assisted Ito Hirobumi in writing Meiji constitution in Japan; effect of his ideas on modern Japanese state. [FGN]

13.124   Bernard S. Silberman. *Ministers of modernization: elite mobility in the Meiji Restoration, 1868–1873*. Tucson: University of Arizona Press, 1964. ▸ Pioneering exploration of role of samurai during early years of new Meiji government. Demonstrates post-1868 elite drawn almost entirely from strata of pre-1868 elite. [FGN]

13.125   Robert E. Ward, ed. *Political development in modern Japan*. 1968 ed. Princeton: Princeton University Press, 1973. ISBN 0-691-00017-4 (pbk). ▸ Collection of articles including important studies on Meiji politics: Hall on throne; Hackett on Meiji *genro* (elder statesmen); Craig on Fukuzawa's nationalism; Jansen on foreign policy; and Ike on war and modernization. [FGN]

13.126   Robert A. Wilson. *Genesis of the Meiji government in Japan, 1868–1871*. 1957 ed. Westport, Conn.: Greenwood, 1978. ISBN 0-8371-9091-6. ▸ Description of first efforts to create centralized administration in opening years of Meiji period. Only English-language work addressing this period in detail. [FGN]

Thought and Culture

13.127   Carmen Blacker. *The Japanese enlightenment: a study of the writings of Fukuzawa Yukichi*. Cambridge: Cambridge University Press, 1964. ISBN 0-521-04267-4. ▸ Important study of thought of Japan's leading westernizer and chief exponent of enlightenment in Meiji Japan. Critic of traditional learning, Fukuzawa advocated new approaches to values, family, and history. [FGN]

13.128   Richard John Bowring. *Mori Ogai and the modernization of Japanese culture*. Cambridge: Cambridge University Press, 1979. ISBN 0-521-21319-3. ▸ Significant analysis of life and thought of Mori Ogai, Meiji writer and bureaucrat who, as one of leading literary figures of age, played important role in intellectual transformation of Meiji Japan. [FGN]

13.129   William Reynolds Braisted, ed. and trans. *Meiroku Zasshi: journal of the Japanese enlightenment*. Cambridge, Mass.: Harvard University Press, 1976. ISBN 0-674-56467-7. ▸ Translation of major journal of Japanese enlightenment, published 1873–75. Invaluable primary source dealing with early Meiji thought and Japanese attitudes toward West. [FGN]

13.130   Yukichi Fukuzawa. *The autobiography of Yukichi Fukuzawa*. 1966 ed. Eiichi Kiyooka, revised translation. New York: Columbia University Press, 1966. ISBN 0-231-08373-4 (pbk). ▸ Fascinating view of transition from Tokugawa to modern Japan as experienced by one of Japan's most important nineteenth-century thinkers and educators. Highly readable, informative autobiography. [FGN]

13.131 Carol Gluck. *Japan's modern myths: ideology in the late Meiji period.* 1985 ed. Princeton: Princeton University Press, 1987. ISBN 0-691-05449-5 (cl, 1985), 0-691-00812-4 (pbk). ‣ Important study of evolution of ideology in Meiji Japan, showing that process by which new civic values were formulated and inculcated was far more haphazard than previously assumed. [FGN]

13.132 Thomas R. H. Havens. *Nishi Amane and modern Japanese thought.* Princeton: Princeton University Press, 1970. ISBN 0-691-03080-4. ‣ Study of leading interpreter of Western positivism and utilitarianism in nineteenth-century Japan. Excellent portrait of Meiji intellectual wrestling with foreign ideas. [FGN]

13.133 Daikichi Irokawa. *The culture of the Meiji period.* 1985 ed. Marius B. Jansen, ed. and trans. Princeton: Princeton University Press, 1988. ISBN 0-691-06634-5 (cl, 1985), 0-691-00030-1 (pbk). ‣ Provocative cultural history by one of most critical and creative Japanese historians. Reveals vital and rich political life in countryside that was betrayed by emperor system. [FGN]

13.134 Marius B. Jansen and Gilbert Rozman, eds. *Japan in transition: from Tokugawa to Meiji.* Princeton: Princeton University Press, 1986. ISBN 0-691-05459-2 (cl), 0-691-10245-7 (pbk). ‣ Discussion, by fifteen authors, of aspects of crucial Japanese transition from Tokugawa state to emergence of Meiji transformation. Several important essays focus on administration, organization, urbanization, and material culture. [FGN]

13.135 Earl H. Kinmonth. *The self-made man in Meiji Japanese thought: from samurai to salary man.* Berkeley: University of California Press, 1981. ISBN 0-520-04159-3. ‣ Exploration of development of ideal of self-advancement through education and white-collar employment that spread from samurai to general populace during Meiji years. Gives due consideration to consequences. Excellent portrait of social advancement through education. [FGN]

13.136 Masaaki Kosaka, ed. *Japanese thought in the Meiji era.* 1958 ed. David Abosch, trans. Tokyo: Toyo Bunko, 1969. (Centenary Cultural Council series: Japanese culture in the Meiji era, 9.) ‣ Informative, well-organized introduction to main themes of late nineteenth- and early twentieth-century Japanese thought. [FGN]

13.137 Inazo Nitobe. *Bushido, the soul of Japan: an exposition of Japanese thought.* 1905 ed. William Elliot Griffis, Introduction. Rutland, Vt.: Tuttle, 1991. ISBN 0-8048-0693-4. ‣ Reinterpretation of Japan's classical warrior ethos to fit needs of modern state. Highly influential work explaining Japanese values to West. [FGN]

13.138 F. G. Notehelfer. *American samurai: Captain L. L. Janes and Japan.* Princeton: Princeton University Press, 1985. ISBN 0-691-05443-6. ‣ Study of teacher of Western learning who converted large number of students to Christianity. Provides insights into Japanese acceptance of Christianity and role of Western employees in Meiji Japan. [FGN]

13.139 F. G. Notehelfer. *Kotoku Shusui: portrait of a Japanese radical.* Cambridge: Cambridge University Press, 1971. ISBN 0-521-07989-6. ‣ Examines life and thought of Japan's leading left-wing thinker at turn of century, whose ideas had decisive influence on subsequent radical movements in Japan and China. Important analysis of relationship of nationalism to socialism. [FGN]

13.140 Kakuzo Okakura. *The awakening of Japan.* 1905 ed. New York: Japan Society Gallery, 1921. ‣ Interpretation of Japanese culture and civilization within context of Japan's emergence as modern state. Somewhat idealistic but important statement by major intellectual figure of his age. [FGN]

13.141 John D. Pierson. *Tokutomi Soho, 1863–1957: a journalist for modern Japan.* Princeton: Princeton University Press, 1980. ISBN 0-691-04674-3. ‣ Thorough study of thought and career of one of Japan's most important journalists, publicists, social critics, and historians. Explains his movement from youthful liberalism to conservatism and ultranationalism. [FGN]

13.142 Kenneth B. Pyle. *The new generation in Meiji Japan: problems in cultural identity, 1885–1895.* Stanford, Calif.: Stanford University Press, 1969. ‣ Study of Meiji intellectuals such as Tokutomi Soho, Shiga Shigetaka, Miyake Setsurei, and Kuga Katsunan focusing on how they saw direction of Japan's modernization. [FGN]

13.143 Donald Roden. *Schooldays in imperial Japan: a study of the culture of a student elite.* Berkeley: University of California Press, 1980. ISBN 0-520-03910-6. ‣ Discussion of development of university preparatory academies as center of distinctive cultural experience that defined status and honor in prewar Japan. Well-documented study describing how schools eased transition to new middle class. [FGN]

13.144 Jay Rubin. *Injurious to public morals: writers and the Meiji state.* Seattle: University of Washington Press, 1984. ISBN 0-295-96043-4. ‣ Significant new exploration of Meiji government's system of censorship, particularly in relation to modern novel. Examines leaders' distrust of writers who attempted to deal with human experience in open and honest manner. [FGN]

13.145 Edward Seidensticker. *Low city, high city: Tokyo from Edo to the earthquake.* 1983 ed. Cambridge, Mass.: Harvard University Press, 1991. ISBN 0-674-53939-7. ‣ Cultural history of development of Tokyo (earlier name, Edo) in modern age by leading scholar of Japanese literature. Excellent portrait of modern Japan in transition from Edo to Meiji-Taisho culture (1603–1923). [FGN]

13.146 Toson Shimazaki. *Before the dawn.* 1987 ed. William E. Naff, trans. Honolulu: University of Hawaii Press, 1988. ISBN 0-8248-0914-9 (cl, 1987), 0-8248-1164-X (pbk). ‣ Reconstruction of social and economic transition from late Tokugawa to early Meiji rule in villages along Kiso River. Important grassroots study; based on autobiographies. [FGN]

13.147 Donald H. Shively, ed. *Tradition and modernization in Japanese culture.* Princeton: Princeton University Press, 1971. ISBN 0-691-03072-3 (cl), 0-691-00020-4 (pbk). ‣ Excellent collection of essays on culture of Meiji period covering art, music, and literature. Each area presented in relation to main themes of Japanese modernization. [FGN]

13.148 D. Eleanor Westney. *Imitation and innovation: the transfer of Western organizational patterns to Meiji Japan.* Cambridge, Mass.: Harvard University Press, 1987. ISBN 0-674-44437-X. ‣ Insightful study of impact of Western organizational models on Meiji police, postal system, and newspapers. Finds Japanese reshaped tradition to fit foreign organizational stuctures rather than vice versa. [FGN]

13.149 Kunio Yanagida, ed. and comp. *Japanese manners and customs in the Meiji era.* Charles S. Terry, trans. Tokyo: Pan-Pacific Press, 1957. (Centenary Cultural Council series: Japanese culture in the Meiji era, 4.) ‣ Important essays on Japanese social and religious customs edited by Japan's most important twentieth-century folklorist. Emphasizes changes in customs as Japan entered modern age. [FGN]

Section 13: Modern Japan

TAISHO AND EARLY SHOWA JAPAN, 1912–1941

Political History

13.150 George M. Beckmann and Genji Okubo. *The Japanese Communist party, 1922–1945.* Stanford, Calif.: Stanford University Press, 1969. ISBN 0-8047-0674-3. ▸ Important study of Japanese Communist party exploring its origins, development, and suppression in prewar period and its reorganization to meet postwar challenge after Japan's surrender. [FGN]

13.151 Gordon Mark Berger. *Parties out of power in Japan, 1931–1941.* Princeton: Princeton University Press, 1977. ISBN 0-691-03106-1. ▸ Excellent examination of role of political parties in 1930s. Challenges interpretation that party power was destroyed by rise of militarism. Argues parties preserved power in 1930 and war years and reemerged as major players after World War II. [FGN]

13.152 Lesley Connors. *The emperor's adviser: Saionji Kinmochi and pre-war Japanese politics.* London: Croom Helm, 1987. ISBN 0-7099-3449-1. ▸ Career of major prewar political figure and one of emperor's chief advisers. Traces his liberalism and internationalism as well as acute political sense. Excellent on 1920s and 1930s. [FGN]

13.153 Peter Duus. *Party rivalry and political change in Taisho Japan.* Ann Arbor: University Microfilms, 1968. ISBN 0-317-08420-8. ▸ Pathbreaking study exploring growth of two-party system and its effect on politics in Taisho Japan. Examines roles of Hara Kei (prime minister, 1918–21, Seiyukai party) and Kato Komei (prime minister, 1924–26, Kenseikai party) in expanding party influence and power. Also available on microfilm from Ann Arbor: University Microfilms International, 1989. [FGN]

13.154 William Miles Fletcher III. *The Japanese business community and national trade policy, 1920–1942.* Chapel Hill: University of North Carolina Press, 1989. ISBN 0-8078-1847-X. ▸ Examination of how *zaikai* (world of finance) developed relations with and influenced bureaucracy to develop trade controls in prewar period. Interpretation differs sharply from Johnson's focus on bureaucracy (Ministry of Trade and Industry) as initiating force (13.195). [FGN]

13.155 William Miles Fletcher III. *The search for a new order: intellectuals and fascism in prewar Japan.* Chapel Hill: University of North Carolina Press, 1982. ISBN 0-8078-1514-4. ▸ Important new study of thought of Royama Masamichi, Ryu Shintaro, and Miki Kiyoshi, intellectuals and members of Showa Kenkyukai (Prime Minister Konoe Fujimaro's brain trust), active during 1930s. Focuses on reform ideas. [FGN]

13.156 Joshua A. Fogel. *Politics and Sinology: the case of Naito Konan (1866–1934).* Cambridge, Mass.: Harvard University, Council on East Asian Studies, 1984. ISBN 0-674-68790-6. ▸ Important effort, examining Japanese visions of China through lens of one of Japan's leading twentieth-century Sinologists. Addresses link between scholarly research and political ideology (and action). [FGN]

13.157 Andrew Gordon. *Labor and imperial democracy in prewar Japan.* Berkeley: University of California Press, 1991. ISBN 0-520-06783-5. ▸ Significant reexamination of political role of working men and women in early twentieth-century Japan. Sees in labor struggles movement for imperial democracy which flowered in 1920s but came to naught in growing labor-capital polarization of 1930s. [FGN]

13.158 Jon Halliday. *A political history of Japanese capitalism.* 1975 ed. New York: Monthly Review Press, 1978. ISBN 0-85345-471-X. ▸ Well-documented examination from Marxist perspective of development of Japanese capitalism and of relationships between military expansion and Japanese economy. [FGN]

13.159 Gregory J. Kasza. *The state and the mass media in Japan, 1918–1945.* Berkeley: University of California Press, 1988. ISBN 0-520-05943-3. ▸ Revealing examination of state's control of public media during period of Taisho democracy associated with party governments, 1918–32, and military dominated governments, 1937–45. [FGN]

13.160 J. Victor Koschmann, ed. *Authority and the individual in Japan: citizen protest in historical perspective.* Tokyo: University of Tokyo Press; distributed by ISBS, 1978. ISBN 0-86008-238-5. ▸ Interpretive, polemical essays by twelve Japanese and American scholars and critics, exploring Japanese patterns of obedience and acceptance of authority for prewar and postwar periods. [FGN]

13.161 Michael Lewis. *Rioters and citizens: mass protest in imperial Japan.* Berkeley: University of California Press, 1990. ISBN 0-520-06642-1. ▸ Comprehensive examination of 1918 rice riots in Japan, questioning standard interpretations. Describes and analyzes different patterns of urban and rural violence that accompanied outbreak of popular protest. [FGN]

13.162 Masao Maruyama. *Thought and behavior in modern Japanese politics.* 1963 ed. Ivan Morris, ed. New York: Oxford University Press, 1969. ▸ Classic study of Japan's modern political tradition presented in series of cogent essays addressing specific issues. Provocative on such topics as development of nationalism, ultranationalism, and Japan's political psychology during 1930s and 1940s. [FGN]

13.163 Frank O. Miller. *Minobe Tatsukichi: interpreter of constitutionalism in Japan.* Berkeley: University of California Press, 1965. ▸ Biography of Japan's leading constitutional scholar whose theories of the state were widely accepted in 1920s, but who was purged in 1930s for liberal tendencies. Standard work on prewar constitutional thought. [FGN]

13.164 Sharon Minichiello. *Retreat from reform: patterns of political behavior in interwar Japan.* Honolulu: University of Hawaii Press, 1984. ISBN 0-8248-0778-2. ▸ Cogent discussion of Nagai Ryutaro's transition from liberal democrat to spokesman for military totalitarianism as characteristic of interwar political reformists, illustrating continuities between Taisho progressivism and early Showa imperialism. [GMB]

13.165 Richard H. Mitchell. *Censorship in imperial Japan.* Princeton: Princeton University Press, 1983. ISBN 0-691-05384-7. ▸ Traces development of system of censorship initiated by Japanese government from 1868 to 1945. Carefully explores methods used to control speech and publication and to encourage self-censorship. [FGN]

13.166 Richard H. Mitchell. *Thought control in prewar Japan.* Ithaca, N.Y.: Cornell University Press, 1976. ISBN 0-8014-1002-9. ▸ Balanced examination of effort to control thought that emerged in wake of passage of Peace Preservation Law of 1925. [FGN]

13.167 James W. Morley, ed. *Dilemmas of growth in prewar Japan.* Princeton: Princeton University Press, 1971. ISBN 0-691-03074-X. ▸ Fourteen scholars address interwar years from perspective of political and military affairs, economic and social systems, and intellectual world. Concluding section compares Japan and Germany. Important collection of essays. [FGN]

13.168 Tetsuo Najita. *Hara Kei in the politics of compromise, 1905–1915.* Cambridge, Mass.: Harvard University Press, 1967. ▸ Very important study of career, to 1915, of Hara Kei, Japan's first party prime minister in 1918. Shows how Hara built up Seiyukai by manipulating patronage and challenging established order. Reveals adroit use of compromise as path to new form of Taisho politics. [FGN]

13.169 Sharon H. Nolte. *Liberalism in modern Japan: Ishibashi Tanzan and his teachers, 1905–1960.* Berkeley: University of California Press, 1987. ISBN 0-520-05707-4. ‣ Sound analysis of pre-war Japanese liberalism focusing on leading politician and post-war prime minister. Traces roots linking late Meiji and early Taisho liberal thought with post–World War II expressions. [FGN]

13.170 Robert A. Scalapino. *The Japanese communist movement, 1920–1966.* Berkeley: University of California Press, 1967. ‣ Traces origins and development of Japanese Communist party from Russian Revolution to postwar Japan. Careful examination of party organization, strategy, and tactics in difficult prewar years and party's rise to prominence in 1950s and 1960s. [FGN]

13.171 Bernard S. Silberman and Harry D. Harootunian, eds. *Japan in crisis: essays on Taisho democracy.* Princeton: Princeton University Press, 1974. ISBN 0-691-03094-4. ‣ Fifteen works by major scholars: interpretive essays; case studies on Yoshino Sakuzo, Natsume Soseki, and Kawakami Hajime; essays on both left-wing and nationalist thought; and analysis of economy and bureaucracy. Wide ranging and informative. [FGN]

13.172 Rodger Swearingen and Paul Langer. *Red flag in Japan: international communism in action, 1919–1951.* 1952 ed. Westport, Conn.: Greenwood, 1968. ISBN 0-8371-0242-1. ‣ Standard pre-war history of Japanese Communist party analyzing its postwar prospects for success as political movement. [FGN]

13.173 Elise K. Tipton. *The Japanese police state: the Tokko in interwar Japan.* Honolulu: University of Hawaii Press, 1990. ISBN 0-8248-1328-6. ‣ Well-written analysis of Japan's Special Higher Police (Tokko) and role it played in controlling prewar dissidents, such as leftists, and in setting political values and behavior patterns for broad spectrum of Japanese. [FGN]

13.174 David Anson Titus. *Palace and politics in prewar Japan.* Ann Arbor: University Microfilms, 1974. ISBN 0-317-08627-8. ‣ Careful examination of position and role of imperial institution in Japan's prewar political order. Analyzes complex relationship between emperor, palace leaders, palace bureaucracy, and political leaders outside palace. [FGN]

13.175 George O. Totten. *The social democratic movement in pre-war Japan.* New Haven: Yale University Press, 1966. ‣ Left-wing party development in prewar period, examining party factions, ideology, leadership, and support organizations, as well as tactics and policies. Still standard work on subject. [FGN]

13.176 A. Morgan Young. *Imperial Japan, 1926–1938.* New York: Morrow, 1938. ‣ General history of early Showa Japan by resident newspaperman. Gives on-the-scene view of major political, social, and economic events of 1930s. Dated but still useful. [FGN]

13.177 A. Morgan Young. *Japan in recent times, 1912–1926.* 1929 ed. Westport, Conn.: Greenwood, 1973. ISBN 0-8371-5480-4. ‣ One of few general histories of Taisho period, written from perspective of editor of *Kobe Chronicle.* Earlier title: *Japan under Taisho Tenno, 1912–1926.* [FGN]

Thought and Culture

13.178 Tatsuo Arima. *The failure of freedom: a portrait of modern Japanese intellectuals.* Cambridge, Mass.: Harvard University Press, 1969. ISBN 0-674-29130-1. ‣ Early provocative examination of Taisho intellectuals' efforts to escape from political involvement into realm of spiritual and aesthetic freedom. Discusses figures such as Uchimura Kanzo, Arishima Takeo, and Akutagawa Ryunosuke. [FGN]

13.179 Nobuya Bamba and John F. Howes, eds. *Pacifism in Japan: the Christian and socialist tradition.* Vancouver: University of British Columbia Press, 1978. ISBN 0-7748-0072-0 (cl), 0-7748-0088-7 (pbk). ‣ Japanese, American, and Canadian scholars effectively explore roots of pacifism in Japan by examining ideas of important Japanese thinkers such as Uchimura Kanzo, Kinoshita Naoe, Kotoku Shusui, Kagawa Toyohiko, and Yanaihara Tadao. [FGN]

13.180 Andrew E. Barshay. *State and intellectual in imperial Japan: the public man in crisis.* Berkeley: University of California Press, 1988. ISBN 0-520-06017-2. ‣ Examination of limits of intellectual freedom and pressures of social and institutional conformity confronting Japanese intellectuals of prewar years. Good on role of intellectual in modern society. [FGN]

13.181 Gail Lee Bernstein. *Japanese Marxist: a portrait of Kawakami Hajime, 1879–1946.* 1976 ed. Cambridge, Mass.: Harvard University, Council on East Asian Studies, 1990. (Harvard East Asian monographs, 152.) ISBN 0-674-47194-6. ‣ Study of life and thought of important Japanese economist and Marxist thinker who taught economics at Kyoto Imperial University in 1920s and 1930s. Excellent, well-written study, rich in insights. [FGN]

13.182 George B. Bickle, Jr. *The new Jerusalem: aspects of utopianism in the thought of Kagawa Toyohiko.* Tucson: University of Arizona Press, 1976. (Monographs of the Association for Asian Studies, 30.) ISBN 0-8165-0550-0 (cl), 0-8165-0531-4 (pbk). ‣ Detailed study of utopian thought of one of Japan's major twentieth-century Christian leaders and social activists. Traces sources and development of Kagawa's Christian socialist ideas. [FGN]

13.183 Germaine A. Hoston. *Marxism and the crisis of development in prewar Japan.* Princeton: Princeton University Press, 1986. ISBN 0-691-07722-3 (cl), 0-691-10206-6 (pbk). ‣ In-depth analysis of Marxist debate in Japan over how capitalism developed in that country. Reveals originality of Japanese Marxist theoreticians and their efforts to deal with questions of economic growth in late-developing nation. [FGN]

13.184 Hyman Kublin. *Asian revolutionary: the life of Sen Katayama.* Princeton: Princeton University Press, 1964. ‣ Biography of one of Japan's leading left-wing activists and Marxist expatriates. Founding member of Japanese socialist and labor movement. Comprehensive, thorough study of Katayama's life and thought. [FGN]

13.185 Richard H. Minear. *Japanese tradition and Western law: emperor, state, and law in the thought of Hozumi Yatsuka.* Cambridge, Mass.: Harvard University Press, 1970. ISBN 0-674-47252-7. ‣ Perceptive study of life and thought of one of Japan's leading constitutional scholars and conservatives, whose ideas were important in establishing Meiji-Taisho orthodoxy. [FGN]

13.186 J. Thomas Rimer, ed. *Culture and identity: Japanese intellectuals during the interwar years.* Princeton: Princeton University Press, 1990. ISBN 0-691-05570-X. ‣ More than a dozen leading scholars explore search for personal identity and freedom among Taisho and early Showa intellectuals against backdrop of rapidly transforming industrial and mass society. Important examination of Taisho culture. [FGN]

13.187 Miriam Silverberg. *Changing song: the Marxist manifestos of Nakano Shigeharu.* Princeton: Princeton University Press, 1990. ISBN 0-691-06816-X. ‣ Study of life and literature of leading twentieth-century Japanese poet and social critic. Addresses Nakano's use of Marxism as critique of mass culture. Superb analysis of Japanese culture in 1920s and 1930s. [FGN]

13.188 Henry Dewitt Smith II. *Japan's first student radicals.* Cambridge, Mass.: Harvard University Press, 1972. ISBN 0-674-47185-7. ‣ Careful examination of prewar Japanese student movement focusing on Shinjinkai, left-wing student association, at Tokyo University. Follows course of radical student activity from 1918 into early 1930s. [FGN]

13.189 Thomas A. Stanley. *Osugi Sakae, anarchist in Taisho*

Japan: the creativity of the ego. Cambridge, Mass.: Harvard University, Council on East Asian Studies, 1982. (Harvard East Asian monographs, 102.) ISBN 0-674-64493-X. ‣ Life and thought of pioneer Japanese anarchist and social reformer, killed by Japanese police at time of 1923 Tokyo earthquake. Well-written study tracing relationship between thought and action among Japanese radicals. [FGN]

13.190 George M. Wilson. *Radical nationalist in Japan: Kita Ikki, 1883–1937.* Cambridge, Mass.: Harvard University Press, 1969. ‣ Good portrait of Japan's leading radical right-wing reformer whose ideas fueled call for Showa Restoration and led to February 26th Incident of 1936. Reveals complex interweaving of traditional and Western thought. [FGN]

ECONOMIC DEVELOPMENT SINCE 1868

13.191 Jerome Bernard Cohen. *Japan's economy in war and reconstruction.* Minneapolis: University of Minnesota Press, 1949. ‣ Thoroughly documented study of Japanese economy in World War II and immediate postwar period. Still best English-language study of Japanese economy of late 1930s and early 1940s. [FGN]

13.192 W. Mark Fruin. *Kikkoman: a company, clan, and community.* Cambridge, Mass.: Harvard University Press, 1983. ISBN 0-674-50340-6. ‣ Examination of transformation of one of Japan's traditional brewers into modern twentieth-century corporation. Focuses on how traditional values and community structures were utilized to build modern firm. [FGN]

13.193 Johannes Hirschmeier. *The origins of entrepreneurship in Meiji Japan.* Cambridge, Mass.: Harvard University Press, 1964. ‣ Presents careful, detailed evaluation of samurai and commoner contributions to commercial and industrial expansion in immediate post-Restoration years. Good on dynamics leading to successful industrialization. [FGN]

13.194 Johannes Hirschmeier and Tsunehiko Yui. *The development of Japanese business, 1600–1980.* 2d ed. Boston: Allen & Unwin, 1981. ISBN 0-04-330322-6 (pbk). ‣ Broad-based, perceptive study of four historical models of Japanese business leaders: merchants of Tokugawa, Meiji entrepreneurs, college graduate business leaders (1896–1945), and men who organized Japan's postwar economic miracle. [FGN]

13.195 Chalmers A. Johnson. *MITI and the Japanese miracle: the growth of industrial policy, 1925–1975.* 1982 ed. Tokyo: Tuttle, 1986. ISBN 0-8047-1128-3 (cl, 1982), 0-8047-1206-9 (pbk). ‣ Important, influential study of Ministry of Trade and Industry whose carefully planned industrial policy played important role in Japanese economic growth since 1920s. Major study of how Japanese bureaucracy managed Japanese economy. [FGN]

13.196 Solomon B. Levine and Hisashi Kawada. *Human resources in Japanese industrial development.* Princeton: Princeton University Press, 1980. ISBN 0-691-03952-6. ‣ Historical examination of Japanese development of and investment in human resources, providing manpower base for rapid industrialization and modern economic growth. [FGN]

13.197 William W. Lockwood. *The economic development of Japan: growth and structural change.* 1954 ed. Princeton: Princeton University Press, 1968. ISBN 0-691-03014-6 (cl), 0-691-00001-8 (pbk). ‣ Detailed analysis of Japanese economic development from Meiji to post–World War II era. Important structural analysis of Japan's economic growth; postwar classic, balanced and thorough. [FGN]

13.198 William W. Lockwood, ed. *The state and economic enterprise in Japan: essays in the political economy of growth.* Princeton: Princeton University Press, 1965. ISBN 0-691-02162-7. ‣ Excellent essays tracing sources of Japanese industrialization and examin-

ing process by which Japan transformed economy from traditional agriculture to modern industrial state. [FGN]

13.199 Byron K. Marshall. *Capitalism and nationalism in prewar Japan: the ideology of the business elite, 1868–1941.* Stanford, Calif.: Stanford University Press, 1967. ISBN 0-8047-0325-6. ‣ Study of close relationship between nationalist ideals and economic growth in prewar Japan. Effectively analyzes how concern for nation and group values often took precedence over individuated capitalist ideals. [FGN]

13.200 Ryoshin Minami. *The economic development of Japan: a quantitative study.* Ralph Thomson, Ryoshin Minami, and David Merriman, trans. New York: St. Martin's, 1986. ISBN 0-312-22876-7. ‣ Thorough quantitative analysis of Japanese economic development addressing why and how Japan achieved modern economic growth, sustained above-average growth levels, and prospects for future growth. [FGN]

13.201 Michio Morishima. *Why has Japan succeeded? Western technology and the Japanese ethos.* Cambridge: Cambridge University Press, 1982. ISBN 0-521-24494-3 (cl), 0-521-26903-2 (pbk). ‣ Study of relationship between traditional Japanese value system, including Confucianism, and development of modern economy. Good example of school of thought that emphasizes values as core of Japan's postwar economic strength. [FGN]

13.202 Yasusuke Murakami and Hugh T. Patrick, gen. eds. *The political economy of Japan.* Vol. 1: *The domestic transformation.* Vol. 2: *The changing international context.* Vol. 3: *Cultural and social dynamics.* Kōzō Yamamura (v. 1), Yasukichi Yasuba (v. 1), Takashi Inoguchi (v. 2), Daniel I. Okimoto (v. 2), Shumpei Kumon (v. 3), and Henry Rosovsky (v. 3), eds. Stanford, Calif.: Stanford University Press, 1987–92. ISBN 0-8047-1380-4 (v. 1, cl), 0-8047-1448-7 (v. 2, cl), 0-8047-1991-8 (v. 3, cl), 0-8047-1381-2 (v. 1, pbk), 0-8047-1481-9 (v. 2, pbk), 0-8047-1992-6 (v. 3, pbk). ‣ Essays on postwar Japanese economy with particular concern for implications of Japanese economic development for 1990s. Series represents most thorough and comprehensive treatment of postwar Japanese economy to date. [FGN]

13.203 Takafusa Nakamura. *Economic growth in prewar Japan.* Robert A. Feldman, trans. New Haven: Yale University Press, 1983. ISBN 0-300-02451-7. ‣ Survey of Japanese economic development from Meiji period to World War II. Contrasts balanced economic growth in agriculture, industry, and service sectors during Meiji with imbalances in these areas during Taisho and early Showa years. [FGN]

13.204 Takafusa Nakamura. *The postwar Japanese economy: its development and structure.* 1981 ed. Jacqueline Kaminski, trans. Tokyo: University of Tokyo Press, 1983. ISBN 0-86008-284-9 (cl, 1981), 0-86008-355-1 (pbk). ‣ Description of development of Japanese economy after World War II by one of Japan's leading economists. Covers broad spectrum of economic change, private initiative, and government cooperation. [FGN]

13.205 Kazushi Ohkawa and Henry Rosovsky. *Japanese economic growth: trend acceleration in the twentieth century.* Stanford, Calif.: Stanford University Press, 1973. ISBN 0-8047-0833-9. ‣ Important study of Japanese economic development employing standard economic growth models to determine how Japanese economy grew at ever increasing rates, particularly after World War II. [FGN]

13.206 Kazushi Ohkawa and Miyohei Shinohara. *Patterns of Japanese economic development: a quantitative appraisal.* New Haven: Yale University Press, 1979. ISBN 0-300-02183-6. ‣ Presents best sets of statistical data on crucial aspects of Japanese economic development in modern period. Important reference source for students of modern Japanese economy. [FGN]

13.207 Hugh T. Patrick, ed. *Japanese industrialization and its* *social consequences.* Berkeley: University of California Press, 1976. ISBN 0-520-03000-1. ‣ Insightful essays on social effects of rapid industrialization in Japan. Explores evolving characteristics of workers and changing occupational structure, welfare, and environment. [FGN]

13.208 Hugh T. Patrick and Henry Rosovsky, eds. *Asia's new giant: how the Japanese economy works.* Washington, D.C.: Brookings Institution, 1976. ISBN 0-8157-6934-2 (cl), 0-8157-6933-4 (pbk). ‣ Acclaimed examination, by twenty-three American and Japanese scholars, of how Japanese economy was managed in 1950s and 1960s. [FGN]

13.209 John G. Roberts. *Mitsui: three centuries of Japanese business.* 1973 2d ed. Tokyo: Weatherhill, 1989. ISBN 0-8348-0080-2. ‣ Well-written study of Tokugawa merchant house that transformed itself into one of pre- and post–World War II giants. Examines traditional and modern business strategies pursued by firm. [FGN]

13.210 Henry Rosovsky. *Capital formation in Japan, 1865–1940.* New York: Free Press, 1961. ‣ Important work; pioneering application of quantitative analysis to question of capital formation in Japan. Traces prewar historical trends in private and government sectors. Remains significant for students of economic history. [FGN]

13.211 Thomas C. Smith. *Political change and industrial development in Japan: governmental enterprise, 1868–1880.* 1955 ed. Stanford, Calif.: Stanford University Press, 1974. ISBN 0-8047-0469-4. ‣ Excellent analysis of role played by government in early industrialization of Meiji period: government initiative combined with private entrepreneurship to build foundations of industrial state. [FGN]

13.212 William D. Wray. *Mitsubishi and the N.Y.K., 1870–1914: business strategy in the Japanese shipping industry.* Cambridge, Mass.: Harvard University, Council on East Asian Studies, 1984. (Harvard East Asian monographs, 108.) ISBN 0-674-57665-9. ‣ Emergence and development of Mitsubishi and its shipping line, Nippon Yusen Kaisha. Analyzes strategy of Mitsubishi's leaders and their use and support of Meiji government to further firm's interests. Thorough and detailed. [FGN]

Labor and Industrial Relations

13.213 James C. Abegglen. *Management and worker: the Japanese solution.* Tokyo: Sophia University with Kodansha, 1973. ISBN 0-87011-199-X. ‣ Extends interpretation to 1970s that Japanese organize labor resources differently from Western nations. Revision of 1958 classic: *The Japanese Factory: Aspects of Its Social Organization.* [FGN]

13.214 Gary D. Allinson. *Japanese urbanism: industry and politics in Kariya, 1872–1972.* Berkeley: University of California Press, 1975. ISBN 0-520-02842-2. ‣ Pathbreaking social and demographic study of Kariya, home of Toyota Motors Corporation. Examines social, political, and labor relations accompanying transformation of minor loom producer into Japan's leading automobile firm. [FGN]

13.215 Iwao F. Ayusawa. *A history of labor in modern Japan.* 1966 ed. Westport, Conn.: Greenwood, 1976. ISBN 0-8371-8991-8. ‣ Good overview of development of Japanese labor from Meiji period through postwar Japan. Examines how labor adapted to pressures of industrialization and explores efforts of Japanese workers to improve their conditions vis-à-vis management. [FGN]

13.216 John W. Bennett and Iwao Ishino. *Paternalism in the Japanese economy: anthropological studies of oyabun-kobun patterns.* 1963 ed. Westport, Conn.: Greenwood, 1972. ISBN 0-8371-6424-9. ‣ Leading study of role that traditional boss-follower relations

played in modern Japan. Seeks to identify reciprocal dependency relations between workers and managers as essential labor-management pattern in Japan. [FGN]

13.217 Robert E. Cole. *Japanese blue collar: the changing tradition.* 1971 ed. Berkeley: University of California Press, 1973. ISBN 0-520-01681-5 (cl), 0-520-02354-4 (pbk). ‣ Sociologist's examination of working conditions, values, and attitudes of Japan's blue-collar workers. Utilizes data collected in 1960s to indicate how Japan's work force and management system is changing. Important contribution to understanding Japanese work force. [FGN]

13.218 Ronald P. Dore. *British factory—Japanese factory: the origins of national diversity in employment relations.* 1973 ed. Berkeley: University of California Press, 1990. ISBN 0-520-02268-8 (cl), 0-520-02495-8 (pbk). ‣ Very important examination by leading sociologist of Japan of social organization of factory in Japan and Great Britain, comparing English Electric and Hitachi. Challenges convergence theory (industrialization brings convergence) and argues for national diversity in industrial management systems. [FGN]

13.219 Sheldon Garon. *The state and labor in modern Japan.* Berkeley: University of California Press, 1988. ISBN 0-520-05983-2. ‣ Thorough, sophisticated examination of evolution of Japanese government's policies toward labor from late nineteenth century to present. Revises previous concepts of state-labor relationships. [FGN]

13.220 Andrew Gordon. *The evolution of labor relations in Japan: heavy industry, 1853–1955.* Cambridge, Mass.: Harvard University, Council on East Asian Studies, 1985. (Harvard East Asian monographs, 117.) ISBN 0-674-27130-0 (cl), 0-674-27131-9 (pbk). ‣ Argues that contemporary labor system in Japan emerged out of decades of bitter struggle between labor and management. Concludes traditional Japanese employment system, including lifetime employment, is largely postwar product. [FGN]

13.221 W. Dean Kinzley. *Industrial harmony in modern Japan: the invention of a tradition.* London: Routledge, 1991. ISBN 0-415-05167-3. ‣ Informative study of origins, role, and legacy of Kyochokai (Cooperation and Harmony Society), founded in 1919 by Shibusawa Eiichi and Tokonami Takejiro. Originated ideas of factory as moral community and industrial paternalism as means of countering labor unrest. [FGN]

13.222 Stephen S. Large. *Organized workers and socialist politics in interwar Japan.* Cambridge: Cambridge University Press, 1981. ISBN 0-521-23675-4. ‣ Well-documented study of relationship between labor organizations and left-wing political movements in 1920s and 1930s. [FGN]

13.223 Robert M. Marsh and Hiroshi Mannari. *Modernization and the Japanese factory.* Princeton: Princeton University Press, 1976. ISBN 0-691-09365-2 (cl), 0-691-10037-3 (pbk). ‣ Revisionist examination of postwar Japanese factory system. Less product of traditional values and paternalism than utilization of modern organizational structures. [FGN]

13.224 Keiichiro Nakagawa, ed. *Labor and management: proceedings of the Fourth Fuji Conference/International Conference on Business History.* Tokyo: University of Tokyo Press, 1979. ISBN 0-86008-243-1. ‣ Broad, diverse examination, by leading Japanese scholars, of emergence of Japanese labor and management system over modern century. [FGN]

13.225 Kazuo Okochi, Bernard Karsh, and Solomon B. Levine, eds. *Workers and employers in Japan: the Japanese employment relations system.* 1973 ed. Princeton: Princeton University Press, 1974. ISBN 0-691-03097-9. ‣ Twelve essays focusing on post–World War II industrial relations in Japan, especially management, labor, government, and legal and social aspects. Emphasizes role of government in all sectors. [FGN]

13.226 Robert A. Scalapino. *The early Japanese labor movement: labor and politics in a developing society.* Berkeley: University of California, Institute of East Asian Studies, 1983. ISBN 0-912966-65-3 (pbk). ▸ Study of emergence of labor movement in Japan; first as failed radical movement and second as successful moderate and middle-of-road organization. Careful exploration and analysis of link between unions and political activity. [FGN]

13.227 Mikio Sumiya. *Social impact of industrialization in Japan.* [Tokyo]: Japanese National Commission for UNESCO, 1963. ▸ Traces social consequences of industrialization of Japanese society. Particular attention to impact of emerging factory system on workers and their lives. Detailed and useful on Meiji period. [FGN]

13.228 Koji Taira. *Economic development and the labor market in Japan.* New York: Columbia University Press, 1970. ISBN 0-231-03272-2. ▸ Examination of Japanese labor market in Japan's modern century. Argues Japanese labor market has always shown narrow wage differentials and high degree of efficiency in allocating human resources. [FGN]

13.229 E. Patricia Tsurumi. *Factory girls: women in the thread mills of Meiji Japan.* Princeton: Princeton University Press, 1990. ISBN 0-691-03138-X. ▸ Exploration of lives of female textile workers who played dominant role in work force of nineteenth- and early twentieth-century Japan. Vivid description of factory life in Meiji Japan based on many primary sources. [FGN]

13.230 Thomas O. Wilkenson. *The urbanization of Japanese labor, 1868–1955.* Amherst: University of Massachusetts Press, 1965. ▸ Study of transformation of Japanese worker from rural-agrarian to urban-industrial context. Explores demographic shift and its social and political consequences. [FGN]

13.231 Michael Yoshino. *Japan's managerial system: tradition and innovation.* Cambridge, Mass.: MIT Press, 1968. ISBN 0-262-24004-1 (cl), 0-262-74006-0 (pbk). ▸ Study of Japanese managerial practices in Tokugawa, Meiji, and post-Meiji eras. Good on ideologies of post–World War II Japan and how Japanese business leaders met challenges of 1950s and 1960s. [FGN]

Agriculture, Villages, and Rural Society

13.232 Richard K. Beardsley, John W. Hall, and Robert E. Ward. *Village Japan.* 1959 ed. Chicago: University of Chicago Press, 1969. ▸ Interdisciplinary study of rural life in Japan based on fieldwork carried out in village in Okayama prefecture in 1950s. Valuable description and insights into village society in immediate postwar years. [FGN]

13.233 John F. Embree. *Suye mura: a Japanese village.* 1939 ed. Chicago: University of Chicago Press, 1964. ▸ Classic study of Japanese village in mid-1930s by first American anthropologist to address Japanese rural life and its institutions. Still best portrait of village society in prewar Japan. [FGN]

13.234 Penelope Francks. *Technology and agricultural development in pre-war Japan.* New Haven: Yale University Press, 1984. ISBN 0-300-02927-6. ▸ Study of effects of technological improvements on agricultural output, 1880s to 1930s, in northwest Kyūshū. Demonstrates output tripled through use of improved irrigation methods, better seeds, and electric pumps. [FGN]

13.235 Tadashi Fukutake. *Japanese rural society.* 1967 ed. Ronald P. Dore, trans. Ithaca, N.Y.: Cornell University Press, 1972. ISBN 0-8014-9127-4. ▸ Examination of nature of Japanese rural society before World War II and in immediate postwar period. Explores kinship, family life, and *ie* (household) system and provides analysis of political authority structure. [FGN]

13.236 Mikiso Hane. *Peasants, rebels, and outcastes: the underside of modern Japan.* New York: Pantheon, 1982. ISBN 0-394-51963-9 (cl), 0-394-71040-1 (pbk). ▸ Examination of what modernization meant for peasants and other minority groups in years following Meiji Restoration. Critical evaluation balancing general optimism of modernization scholars. [FGN]

13.237 Thomas R. H. Havens. *Farm and nation in modern Japan: agrarian nationalism, 1870–1940.* Princeton: Princeton University Press, 1974. ISBN 0-691-03101-0. ▸ Excellent study of agrarianist (*nohonshugi*) thought in Meiji-Taisho period. Analyzes government policy toward agriculture and responses that such policies elicited among villagers and their ideological spokesmen. [FGN]

13.238 James I. Nakamura. *Agricultural production and the economic development of Japan, 1873–1922.* Princeton: Princeton University Press, 1966. ▸ Careful examination of agricultural development in Meiji and early Taisho periods. Challenges accepted interpretations of early Meiji agricultural statistics. [FGN]

13.239 Edward Norbeck. *Country to city: the urbanization of a Japanese hamlet.* Salt Lake City: University of Utah Press, 1978. ISBN 0-87480-119-2. ▸ Study of transformation of Inland Sea village, Takashima, into modern suburb of city of Kurashiki. Important insight on urbanization of rural Japan. [FGN]

13.240 Takekazu Ogura, ed. *Agricultural development in modern Japan.* 1963 rev. ed. Tokyo: Fuji, 1970. ▸ Broad survey of transformation of Japanese agriculture in modern period. [FGN]

13.241 J. W. Robertson-Scott. *The foundations of Japan: notes made during journeys of 6,000 miles in rural districts as a basis for a sounder knowledge of the Japanese.* New York: Appleton, 1922. ▸ Early but still useful account of Japanese rural life and village setting in Meiji and early Taisho eras. [FGN]

13.242 Richard J. Smethurst. *Agricultural development and tenancy disputes in Japan, 1870–1940.* Princeton: Princeton University Press, 1986. ISBN 0-691-05468-1. ▸ Well-documented revisionist study arguing development of rural market economy after Meiji period led to general rise, rather than decline, of rural standard of living. Reinterprets issue of tenancy. [FGN]

13.243 Robert J. Smith. *Kurusu: the price of progress in a Japanese village, 1951–1975.* Stanford, Calif.: Stanford University Press, 1978. ISBN 0-8047-0962-9 (cl), 0-8047-1060-0 (pbk). ▸ Anthropological study exploring dramatic changes in typical Japanese village from 1950s to 1970s. Important study of rural change in postwar period. [FGN]

13.244 Ann Waswo. *Japanese landlords: the decline of a rural elite.* Berkeley: University of California Press, 1977. ISBN 0-520-03217-9. ▸ Examination of landlord-tenant conflicts in 1920s. Argues Japanese landlords were neither as powerful nor as reactionary as previously assumed. [FGN]

DIPLOMACY AND FOREIGN RELATIONS, 1868–1941

13.245 Rutherford Alcock. *The capital of the tycoon: a narrative of a three years' residence in Japan.* 1863 ed. 2 vols. New York: Greenwood, 1969. ISBN 0-8371-1865-4. ▸ Firsthand account of Japan on eve of Meiji Restoration by one of Great Britain's leading East Asian diplomats. Useful insights. [FGN]

13.246 Asahi Shimbun Staff. *The Pacific rivals: a Japanese view of Japanese-American relations.* New York: Weatherhill and Asahi, 1972. ISBN 0-8348-0070-5. ▸ Articles by Japanese authors dealing with foreign relations issues involving United States and Japan. Both prewar and postwar problems treated, often by principals involved. Largely anecdotal in approach. [FGN]

13.247 Nobuya Bamba. *Japanese diplomacy in a dilemma: new light on Japan's China policy, 1924–1929.* Vancouver: University of British Columbia Press, 1972. ISBN 0-7748-0018-6. ▸ Careful, sensitive examination of Japan's increasingly troubled relationship with China during period of expanding Chinese nationalism and rise of Chiang Kai-shek and Kuomintang (Nationalist party). [FGN]

13.248 Michael A. Barnhart. *Japan prepares for total war: the search for economic security, 1919–1941.* Ithaca, N.Y.: Cornell University Press, 1987. ISBN 0-8014-1915-8 (cl), 0-8014-9529-6 (pbk). ▸ Discussion of economic roots of Japanese expansionism in quest for secure resource base. Fine partial explanation of origins of Pacific War. [JSH]

13.249 William G. Beasley. *Great Britain and the opening of Japan, 1834–1858.* London: Luzac, 1951. ▸ Still the basic study of official British policy toward Japan in years leading to opening of Japan and signing of commercial treaties. Maintains China central to Britain's Japan policy. [FGN]

13.250 William G. Beasley. *Japanese imperialism, 1894–1945.* 1987 ed. New York: Oxford University Press, 1991. ISBN 0-19-821575-4 (cl, 1987), 0-19-822168-1 (pbk). ▸ Thorough exploration of sources and development of Japanese imperialism. Argues Japan's rapid industrialization led to imperial expansion, which changed in nature as Japan increased in economic and military power. [FGN]

13.251 William G. Beasley, ed. *Select documents on Japanese foreign policy, 1853–1868.* London: Oxford University Press, 1955. ▸ Collection of many crucial documents dealing with opening of Japan. Excellent introduction elucidates main debates of late Tokugawa domestic and foreign policy. [FGN]

13.252 Warren I. Cohen, ed. *New frontiers in American–East Asian relations: essays presented to Dorothy Borg.* New York: Columbia University Press, 1983. ISBN 0-231-05630-3 (cl), 0-231-05631-1 (pbk). ▸ Eight historiographical essays surveying and analyzing American cultural, military, economic, and political relations with China, Japan, and Korea in nineteenth and twentieth centuries. Comprehensive and up to date. [FGN]

13.253 Hilary Conroy. *The Japanese seizure of Korea, 1868–1910: a study of realism and idealism in international relations.* Philadelphia: University of Pennsylvania Press, 1960. ▸ Traces Japanese policy toward Korea from Restoration to Japanese annexation. Well documented and thorough with important insights into domestic and foreign policy. [FGN]

13.254 James B. Crowley. *Japan's quest for autonomy: national security and foreign policy, 1930–1938.* Princeton: Princeton University Press, 1966. ▸ Most important 1960s reevaluation of Japanese national policies in 1930s. Reexamines role of military and other groups in national security debates that shaped domestic and foreign policy. [FGN]

13.255 Tyler Dennett. *Americans in eastern Asia: a critical study of United States' policy in the Far East in the nineteenth century.* New York: Barnes & Noble, 1963. ▸ Comprehensive overview of American interests in and United States policy toward Japan and East Asia in nineteenth century. [FGN]

13.256 Peter Duus, Ramon H. Myers, and Mark R. Peattie. *The Japanese informal empire in China, 1895–1937.* Princeton: Princeton University Press, 1989. ISBN 0-691-05561-0. ▸ Study addresses expansion of Japanese economic, social, political, and military influence in China during pre–World War II period. Fourteen essays address different aspects of how Japan was able to replace West as dominant outside force in China. [FGN]

13.257 Grace Fox. *Britain and Japan, 1858–1883.* Oxford: Clarendon, 1969. ▸ Analysis of British-Japanese interaction, based on British, American, and Japanese archival sources. Emphasis on Anglo-Japanese diplomacy, including British efforts to mediate Sino-Japanese crisis (1871–74) and Britain's role in modernization of Japan. Discusses British influence on trade, finance, currency, newspapers, and medicine. [RRM]

13.258 Townsend Harris. *The complete journal of Townsend Harris, first American consul general and minister to Japan.* 1930 rev. ed. Mario Emilio Cosenza, ed. Rutland, Vt.: Tuttle, 1959. ▸ Journal of America's first consul to Japan who negotiated commercial treaties of 1858. Important source. [FGN]

13.259 Henry Heusken. *Japan journal, 1855–1861.* Robert A. Wilson and Jeannette C. van der Corput, eds. and trans. Ann Arbor: University Microfilms, 1964. ISBN 0-317-11275-9. ▸ English translation of journal of secretary to Townsend Harris, first American consul general in Japan. Firsthand American account of late Tokugawa Japan. [FGN]

13.260 Frank Ikle. *German-Japanese relations, 1936–1940.* New York: Bookman, 1956. ▸ Background of troubled alliance, tracing complex nature of German-Japanese relations in late 1930s. Reveals degree to which Japan was outmaneuvered by Nazi Germany's efforts to contain Soviet Union. Somewhat dated but still best work on topic. [FGN]

13.261 Akira Iriye. *After imperialism: the search for a new order in the Far East, 1921–1931.* 1965 ed. Chicago: Imprint, 1990. ISBN 1-879176-00-9 (pbk). ▸ Best explanation of Japan's foreign policy in 1920s in wake of Wilson's New Diplomacy. With breakdown of earlier imperialist models, Japan and West sought cooperative approach to China with little success. [FGN]

13.262 Akira Iriye. *Pacific estrangement: Japanese and American expansion, 1897–1911.* Cambridge, Mass.: Harvard University Press, 1972. ISBN 0-674-65075-1. ▸ Wide-ranging examination of Japanese-American interaction, influence of American example on Japanese policies, and American and European reactions to Japanese imperialism. Focus on problems that arose as result of physical and cultural-intellectual encounters. [NR/FGN]

13.263 Akira Iriye, ed. *Mutual images: essays in American-Japanese relations.* Cambridge, Mass.: Harvard University Press, 1975. ISBN 0-674-59550-5. ▸ Study of Japanese and American perceptions of one another. Series of essays focusing on mutual images that emerged from sources as diverse as fairs, books, and travel accounts. Diverse and interesting approaches. [FGN]

13.264 Marius B. Jansen. *The Japanese and Sun Yat-sen.* Cambridge, Mass.: Harvard University Press, 1954. ▸ Carefully researched study of Sino-Japanese relations focusing on career of Chinese revolutionary Sun Yat-sen. Explores links between revolutionary nationalism in Meiji Japan and Asian idealists. [FGN]

13.265 F. C. Jones. *Extraterritoriality in Japan and the diplomatic relations resulting in its abolition, 1853–1899.* 1931 ed. New York: AMS Press, 1970. ISBN 0-404-03598-1. ▸ Standard work on system of unequal treaties which subjected Japan to treaty-port structure. Elaborates Japanese struggles to rid country of this system. [FGN]

13.266 F. C. Jones. *Japan's new order in East Asia: its rise and fall, 1937–1945.* New York: Oxford University Press, 1954. ▸ Thorough, comprehensive exploration of Japan's military expansion from outbreak of China War in 1937 through Pacific War. Standard early history of World War II in Asia and Pacific. [FGN]

13.267 Malcolm D. Kennedy. *The estrangement of Great Britain and Japan, 1917–1935.* Berkeley: University of California Press, 1969. ▸ Good study of growing rift that developed between Great Britain and Japan in years following World War I, largely involving policies of both nations toward China and Pacific. [FGN]

13.268 Joyce Lebra, ed. *Japan's greater East Asia co-prosperity sphere in World War II: selected readings and documents.* New York: Oxford University Press, 1975. ISBN 0-19-638265-3. ▸ Informative collections of selected readings and documents dealing with Japan's effort to develop and integrate Asian economic "co-prosperity" in early 1940s. [FGN]

13.269 George A. Lensen. *The Russian push toward Japan: Russo-Japanese relations, 1697–1875.* Princeton: Princeton University Press, 1959. ▸ Comprehensive history of Japanese-Russian relations to end of nineteenth century. Probes both Russian advances and Japanese responses. [FGN]

13.270 Toten Miyazaki. *My thirty-three years' dream: the autobiography of Miyazaki Toten.* Marius B. Jansen and Etō Shinkichi, trans. Princeton: Princeton University Press, 1982. ISBN 0-691-05348-0. ▸ Important autobiography of Japanese continental adventurer who sought to extend Japanese influence in China by supporting Chinese revolutionaries such as Sun Yat-sen and K'ang Yu'wei. [FGN]

13.271 James W. Morley. *The Japanese thrust into Siberia, 1918.* 1957 ed. Freeport, N.Y.: Books for Libraries, 1972. ISBN 0-8369-9966-5. ▸ Excellent study of Japan during 1918 Siberian intervention. Shows internal factional debate over control of Japan's foreign policy and treats Japan's transition from imperialism to new diplomacy. [FGN]

13.272 James W. Morley, ed. *Japan's road to the Pacific War.* 4 vols. New York: Columbia University Press, 1976–1984. ISBN 0-231-05782-2 (v. 1), 0-231-05522-6 (v. 2), 0-231-08969-4 (v. 3), 0-231-04804-1 (v. 4). ▸ Translations from important seven-volume series on outbreak of Pacific War, published by *Asahi* newspaper in 1963, which incorporated most important Japanese scholarship on topic. See also at 47.169–72. [FGN]

13.273 William Fitch Morton. *Tanaka Giichi and Japan's China policy.* New York: St. Martin's, 1980. ISBN 0-312-78500-3. ▸ Analysis of Japan's China policy under Prime Minister Tanaka Giichi, 1927–29. Careful examination of Tanaka's aggressive posture; shows that 1927 Tanaka Memorial (plan for Japanese expansion) has been wrongly attributed to him. [FGN]

13.274 Mutsu Munemitsu. *Kenkenroku: a diplomatic record of the Sino-Japanese War, 1894–95.* Gordon Mark Berger, ed. and trans. Princeton: Princeton University Press, 1982. ISBN 0-691-03106-1. ▸ Memoirs of Japan's foreign minister during and immediately after Sino-Japanese War. Justifies and explains Japan's decision to accept European demands to return Liaotung Peninsula to China following war. Essential for understanding Sino-Japanese War. [FGN]

13.275 Ramon H. Myers and Mark R. Peattie, eds. *The Japanese colonial empire, 1895–1945.* 1984 ed. Princeton: Princeton University Press, 1987. ISBN 0-691-05398-7 (cl, 1984), 0-691-10222-8 (pbk). ▸ Important collection examining origin and development of Japan's colonial empire in Taiwan, Korea, Kwantung, and South Pacific. Treats various topics relating to management of colonial territories in fourteen essays. [FGN]

13.276 Charles E. Neu. *The troubled encounter: the United States and Japan.* 1975 ed. Huntington, N.Y.: Krieger, 1979. ISBN 0-88275-951-5. ▸ Traces development of American relations with Japan, 1890–1941. Explores assumptions and perspectives held by both nations that led to growing confrontation. Relies heavily on Western sources. [FGN]

13.277 Ian H. Nish. *Alliance in decline: a study in Anglo-Japanese relations, 1908–23.* London: Athlone; distributed by Oxford University Press, 1972. ISBN 0-485-13133-1. ▸ Best available study of alliance's final decade. Attributes end to differences over China, British dissatisfaction at Japanese expansionism, danger to relations with Australia, Canada, and United States, and American intervention. [SM/NR]

13.278 Ian H. Nish, ed. *Anglo-Japanese alienation, 1919–1952: papers of the Anglo-Japanese Conference on the History of the Second*

World War. Cambridge: Cambridge University Press, 1982. ISBN 0-521-24061-1. ▸ Series of essays dealing with Anglo-Japanese relations from end of World War I to San Francisco Peace Treaty. Explores various dimensions of confrontation that brought both nations into Pacific War. Contains number of important insights into crises of Pacific War. [FGN]

13.279 Shumpei Okamoto. *The Japanese oligarchy and the Russo-Japanese War.* New York: Columbia University Press, 1970. ISBN 0-231-03404-0. ▸ Examines diplomacy of Russo-Japanese War from perspective of Japanese oligarchy and its consciousness of Japan's military and financial vulnerability. Shows oligarchs as astute realists. [FGN]

13.280 Laurence Oliphant. *Narrative of the earl of Elgin's mission to China and Japan in the years 1857, 1858, 1859.* 1860 ed. New York: Praeger, 1970. ▸ Standard account of British mission to East Asia resulting in signing of Anglo-Japanese treaty of 1858 (Treaty of Yedo), which opened Japan to trade and commerce with Great Britain. [FGN]

13.281 Mark R. Peattie. *Nan'yo: the rise and fall of the Japanese in Micronesia, 1885–1945.* Honolulu: University of Hawaii Press, 1988. (Pacific Island monograph series, 4.) ISBN 0-8248-1087-2. ▸ Examination of Japan's late nineteenth- and twentieth-century interests in Micronesia and her post–World War I administration of region as League of Nations mandate. Thorough and comprehensive. [FGN]

13.282 Stephen E. Pelz. *Race to Pearl Harbor: the failure of the Second London Naval Conference and the onset of World War II.* Cambridge, Mass.: Harvard University Press, 1974. ISBN 0-674-74575-2. ▸ Excellent study of breakdown of naval disarmament negotiations between United States and Japan in 1930s that led to naval arms buildup culminating in Pearl Harbor. Shows Japanese naval expansion in 1930s. [FGN]

13.283 Matthew Calbraith Perry. *Narrative of the expedition of an American squadron to the China seas and Japan, performed in the years 1852, 1853, and 1854, under the command of Commodore M.C. Perry, United States Navy, by order of the government of the United States.* 1856 ed. 3 vols. Francis L. Hawks, ed. New York: AMS Press, 1967. (United States. 33d Congress, Second session, 1854–1855, Senate executive document, 79.) ISBN 0-404-05060-3 (set). ▸ Official record of Perry expedition compiled from notes and journals of Perry and his officers. Important primary source. Also available on microfilm from Woodbridge, Conn.: Research Publications, 1980. [FGN]

13.284 Klaus H. Pringsheim. *Neighbors across the Pacific: the development of economic and political relations between Canada and Japan.* Westport, Conn.: Greenwood, 1983. ISBN 0-313-23507-4. ▸ Good survey of Canadian-Japanese relations since late nineteenth century. [FGN]

13.285 Ernest Satow. *A diplomat in Japan: an inner history of the critical years in the evolution of Japan.* 1921 ed. Rutland, Vt.: Tuttle, 1983. ISBN 0-8048-1447-3. ▸ Important firsthand account of Anglo-Japanese relations in last years of Tokugawa regime by member of British diplomatic corps. Excellent observations. [FGN]

13.286 Oliver Statler. *Shimoda story.* 1969 ed. Honolulu: University of Hawaii Press, 1986. ISBN 0-8248-1059-7 (pbk). ▸ Impressive effort to integrate Harris and Heusken's diaries (13.258, 13.259) with Japanese historical documents surrounding arrival of America's first consul general in Japan. Highly readable yet detailed. [FGN]

13.287 Richard Storry. *Japan and the decline of the West in Asia, 1894–1943.* New York: St. Martin's, 1979. ISBN 0-312-44050-2. ▸ Japan's emergence as world power viewed against backdrop of diminishing European influence in Asia. Leading British historian's interpretation of Japan's role in Asia. [FGN]

13.288 Tatsuji Takeuchi. *War and diplomacy in the Japanese empire.* 1935 ed. New York: Russell & Russell, 1967. ▸ General survey of Japanese foreign relations leading to emergence as world power. Objective, realistic assessment of prewar Japan. [FGN]

SEE ALSO

RISE OF MILITARISM AND WORLD WAR II IN THE PACIFIC, 1941–1945

13.289 Hiroyuki Agawa. *The reluctant admiral: Yamamoto and the Imperial Navy.* John Bester, trans. Tokyo: Kodansha, 1979. ISBN 0-87011-355-0 (cl), 0-87011-512-X (pbk). ▸ Excellent biography of Yamamoto Isoroku, admiral who headed Japan's combined fleet during first half of Pacific War. Portrayal of complex character; contrasts leadership style in army and navy. [FGN]

13.290 Dorothy Borg and Shumpei Okamoto, eds. *Pearl Harbor as history: Japanese-American relations, 1931–1941.* New York: Columbia University Press, 1973. ISBN 0-231-03734-1. ▸ Twenty-six Japanese and American scholars examine fateful decade of 1930s from variety of perspectives. Sheds new light on complex interaction between Japan and United States that led to war in 1941. [FGN]

13.291 Robert J. C. Butow. *Japan's decision to surrender.* Stanford, Calif.: Stanford University Press, 1954. ▸ Important analysis of forces that combined to bring about Japan's surrender in World War II. Explores various Japanese peace feelers and emperor's role in final decision to accept Potsdam Declaration. [FGN]

13.292 Robert J. C. Butow. *Tojo and the coming of the war.* 1961 ed. Stanford, Calif.: Stanford University Press, 1969. ▸ Detailed study of wartime prime minister and his role as leading general in Japanese army in Japan's decision to go to war with United States in 1941. Massive, thorough, comprehensive. [FGN]

13.293 Hugh Byas. *Government by assassination.* New York: Knopf, 1942. ▸ Study of rise of nationalism and militarism in 1930s written by on-the-scene observer. Particularly graphic in its description of trials following 1932 assassination of Prime Minister Inukai (May 15th Incident). [FGN]

13.294 Alvin D. Coox. *Nomonhan: Japan against Russia, 1939.* 1985 ed. 2 vols. Stanford, Calif.: Stanford University Press, 1990. ISBN 0-8047-1160-7 (cl, set, 1985), 0-8047-1835-0 (pbk, 2 vols. in 1). ▸ Massive account of Japan's five-month undeclared war with Soviet Union, fought in 1939, which resulted in decisive Soviet victory. Rich in detail and thoroughly documented. [FGN]

13.295 Robert Craigie. *Behind the Japanese mask.* London: Hutchinson, 1945. ▸ Memoirs of British ambassador to Japan from 1937–42. Vivid description of life in wartime Japan. Also

available on microform: Harvard University Microproduction Service. [FGN]

13.296 Frederick W. Deakin and Richard Storry. *The case of Richard Sorge.* New York: Harper & Row, 1966. ▸ Intriguing study of Sorge's career as Nazi journalist and trusted adviser of German embassy staff in Tokyo, while head of one of greatest espionage networks in modern history. [FGN]

13.297 John W. Dower. *War without mercy: race and power in the Pacific War.* New York: Pantheon, 1986. ISBN 0-394-50030-X (cl), 0-394-75172-8 (pbk). ▸ Explores American and English, as well as Japanese, stereotypes of enemy in Pacific War and shows how such denigration of "other" affected policies and planning. Searches for linkages between racism and war. [FGN]

13.298 Paul S. Dull. *A battle history of the Imperial Japanese Navy (1941–1945).* Annapolis, Md.: Naval Institute Press, 1978. ISBN 0-87021-097-1. ▸ History of Japanese navy's involvement in Pacific War from perspective of Japanese naval participants. Essentially narrative of major engagements of war. [FGN]

13.299 David C. Evans, ed. and trans. *The Japanese navy in World War II: in the words of former Japanese naval officers.* 2d ed. Annapolis, Md.: Naval Institute Press, 1986. ISBN 0-87021-316-4. ▸ Translation of seventeen important essays by Japanese participants covering naval strategy, tactics, and operations. Analyzes and reexamines successes such as Pearl Harbor and defeats such as Midway. [FGN]

13.300 Joseph C. Grew. *Turbulent era: a diplomatic record of forty years, 1904–1945.* 1952 ed. 2 vols. Freeport, N.Y.: Books for Libraries, 1970. ISBN 0-8369-5284-7. ▸ Complete memoirs of United States ambassador to Japan in years preceeding World War II. Well connected in Japan and insightful, Grew warned United States government of impending Japanese attack. [FGN]

13.301 Harada Kumao. *Fragile victory: Prince Saionji and the 1930 London Treaty issue, from the memoirs of Baron Harada Kumao.* 1955 ed. Thomas Francis Mayer-Oakes, ed. and trans. Ann Arbor: University Microfilms, 1968. ISBN 0-685-16247-8. ▸ London Naval Conference and its outcome explored from perspective of domestic politics and rise of military power. Incorporates major portions of Saionji's and Harada's memoirs. Essential primary source. [FGN]

13.302 Thomas R. H. Havens. *Valley of darkness: the Japanese people and World War Two.* 1978 ed. Lanham, Md.: University Press of America, 1986. ISBN 0-8191-5495-4 (pbk). ▸ Examination of impact of World War II on Japanese society. Good on social changes induced by war. Vivid, textured portrait of life in wartime Japan. [FGN]

13.303 Saburo Hayashi. *Kogun: the Japanese army in the Pacific War.* Westport, Conn.: Greenwood, 1978. ISBN 0-313-20291-5. ▸ History of Japanese army in World War II as portrayed by member of Japanese General Staff. Projects Japanese military perceptions, campaigns; critically assesses their successes and failures. [FGN]

13.304 John Hersey. *Hiroshima.* 1946 rev. ed. New York: Bantam, 1985. ISBN 0-553-26058-8. ▸ Moving and powerful examination of lives of six individuals involved in Hiroshima bombing, following their experiences in hours and days after event. [FGN]

13.305 Shigeru Honjo. *Emperor Hirohito and his chief aide-de-camp: the Honjo diary, 1933–36.* Mikiso Hane, trans. Tokyo: University of Tokyo Press, 1982. ISBN 0-86008-319-5. ▸ Portrait of emperor during mid-1930s seen through diary of General Honjo who served as liaison officer between throne and army. Gives important insights into Hirohito's thoughts and actions. [FGN]

13.306 Saburo Ienaga. *The Pacific War, 1931–1945: a critical perspective on Japan's role in World War II.* New York: Pantheon,

1979. ISBN 0-394-73496-3. ‣ Major Japanese historian's unsugarcoated version of Japan's role in World War II in Pacific. Eloquent, angry, blunt reminder of war as disaster filled with suffering on all sides. [FGN]

13.307   Nobutaka Ike, ed. and trans. *Japan's decision for war: records of the 1941 policy conferences*. Stanford, Calif.: Stanford University Press, 1967. ISBN 0-8047-0305-1. ‣ Inside view of Japanese decision to go to war with United States. Translation of crucial records of sixty-two policy conferences held in 1941 that culminated in Japan's fateful choice. [FGN]

13.308   Akira Iriye. *Power and culture: the Japanese-American war, 1941–1945*. Cambridge, Mass.: Harvard University Press, 1981. ISBN 0-674-69580-1 (cl), 0-674-69582-8 (pbk). ‣ Study of Pacific War through interplay of culture and foreign relations. Sees war as part of Japanese and American search for new international order, not power confrontation. Revisionist argument. [FGN]

13.309   Chalmers A. Johnson. *An instance of treason: Ozaki Hotsumi and the Sorge spy ring*. 1964 ed. Stanford, Calif.: Stanford University Press, 1990. ISBN 0-8047-1766-4 (cl), 0-8047-1767-2 (pbk). ‣ Engrossing study of leading Japanese member of this century's most important spy ring. By informing Russians of Japan's decision to advance west—not east—Ozaki and Sorge changed history. Good on Ozaki's idealism. [FGN]

13.310   Robert Jay Lifton. *Death in life: survivors of Hiroshima*. 1967 ed. Chapel Hill: University of North Carolina Press, 1991. ISBN 0-8078-4344-X. ‣ Study of psychological consequences of exposure to atomic bombing of Hiroshima based on extensive interview data. Important study of survivor guilt. [FGN]

13.311   Hillis Lory. *Japan's military masters: the army in Japanese life*. 1943 ed. Westport, Conn.: Greenwood, 1973. ISBN 0-8371-6581-4. ‣ One of few studies of Japanese army in prewar period. Useful but dated. [FGN]

13.312   Richard H. Minear, ed. and trans. *Hiroshima: three witnesses*. Princeton: Princeton University Press, 1990. ISBN 0-691-05573-4 (cl), 0-691-00837-X (pbk). ‣ Moving translation of writings of three Japanese authors (Tamiki Hara, Yoko Ota, and Sankichi Toge) who experienced atomic bombing of Hiroshima and incorporated their experiences into their literary work. [FGN]

13.313   Sadako N. Ogata. *Defiance in Manchuria: the making of Japanese foreign policy, 1931–1932*. 1964 ed. Westport, Conn.: Greenwood, 1984. ISBN 0-313-24428-6. ‣ Argues Manchurian Incident of 1931 was directly attributable to struggles in Japanese army between junior and senior officers, not military-civilian tensions. Depicts army as increasingly irresponsible and out of control. [FGN]

13.314   Yoshitake Oka. *Konoe Fumimaro: a political biography*. 1983 ed. Shumpei Okamoto and Patricia Murray, trans. Lanham, Md.: Madison Books; distributed by National Book Network, 1992. ISBN 0-8191-8292-3. ‣ Study of political career of man who served as Japan's prime minister on three occasions from 1937 to 1941. Complex and enigmatic figure who failed in efforts to prevent outbreak of war with United States. Excellent biography by leading Japanese historian. [FGN]

13.315   Mark R. Peattie. *Ishiwara Kanji and Japan's confrontation with the West*. Princeton: Princeton University Press, 1975. ISBN 0-691-03099-5. ‣ Perceptive, revealing examination of career and thought of Ishiwara Kanji who played central role in Manchurian Incident, Young Officers' Rebellion of 1936, and China War of 1937. [FGN]

13.316   Gordon W. Prange. *At dawn we slept: the untold story of Pearl Harbor*. 1981 ed. New York: Penguin, 1982. ISBN 0-14-006455-9 (pbk). ‣ First volume of Prange's posthumous trilogy (with 13.317 and 13.319). Together these volumes constitute

definitive work to date on Japanese attack on United States. [FGN]

13.317   Gordon W. Prange. *December 7, 1941: the day the Japanese attacked Pearl Harbor*. New York: McGraw-Hill, 1988. ISBN 0-07-050682-5. ‣ Third volume of Prange's trilogy (with 13.316 and 13.319). Examines in detail the events of December 7, 1941, on various military installations in Hawaii. [FGN]

13.318   Gordon W. Prange. *Miracle at Midway*. New York: McGraw-Hill, 1982. ISBN 0-07-050672-8. ‣ Examination of strategies, planning, and decision making behind United States' decisive victory at Battle of Midway by leading American historian of Pearl Harbor. Fine analysis of Nimitz's remarkable success. [FGN]

13.319   Gordon W. Prange. *Pearl Harbor: the verdict of history*. New York: McGraw-Hill, 1986. ISBN 0-07-050668-X. ‣ Second volume of Prange's trilogy (with 13.316 and 13.317). Attempts to assign responsibility on United States side. [FGN]

13.320   Paul W. Schroeder. *The Axis-alliance and Japanese-American relations, 1941*. Ithaca, N.Y.: Cornell University Press, 1958. ‣ Basic study of role of Tripartite Pact between Germany, Italy, and Japan and its effect on United States–Japanese relations and outbreak of war in Pacific. [FGN]

13.321   Mamoru Shigemitsu. *Japan and her destiny: my struggle for peace*. F.S.G. Piggott and Oswald White, eds. and trans. New York: Dutton, 1958. ‣ Review of Japanese foreign policy from 1931 to 1945 by Japan's foreign minister and ambassador to Great Britain. Explores inner workings of Japan's liberal diplomatic community. Subjective but revealing. [FGN]

13.322   Ben-Ami Shillony. *Politics and culture in wartime Japan*. 1981 ed. New York: Oxford University Press, 1991. ISBN 0-19-820260-1. ‣ Provocative exploration of political and cultural developments in Japan during World War II. Suggests Japanese government, while repressive, was less totalitarian than others due to institutional and cultural constraints. [FGN]

13.323   Ben-Ami Shillony. *Revolt in Japan: the young officers and the February 26, 1936 Incident*. Princeton: Princeton University Press, 1973. ISBN 0-691-07548-4. ‣ Study of failed coup of 1936. Radical young officers under influence of Kita Ikki sought to purge Japan of its parliament and return power to emperor. Marked demise of radical Right and Showa Restoration. Best work on topic. [FGN]

13.324   Saburo Shiroyama. *War criminal: the life and death of Hirota Koki*. John Bester, trans. Tokyo: Kodansha, 1977. ISBN 0-87011-275-9. ‣ Biography of Japan's foreign minister and prime minister in 1930s who was only civilian sentenced to death in Tokyo war crimes trials. Sympathetic account of Hirota's life. [FGN]

13.325   Richard J. Smethurst. *A social basis of prewar Japanese militarism: the army and the rural community*. Berkeley: University of California Press, 1974. ISBN 0-520-02552-0. ‣ Well-documented study of Japanese army's penetration of countryside through its reservist organization. Shows rural roots of Japanese militarism in the 1930s. [FGN]

13.326   John J. Stephan. *Hawaii under the rising sun: Japan's plans for conquest after Pearl Harbor*. Honolulu: University of Hawaii Press, 1984. ISBN 0-8248-0872-X. ‣ Explores Japanese plans for invasion and occupation of Hawaiian Islands which were foiled by defeat at Midway. Also examines plans for Japanese-Americans in islands' subsequent development. Important contribution to understanding Japanese war aims. [FGN]

13.327   Richard Storry. *The double patriots: a study of Japanese nationalism*. 1957 ed. Westport, Conn.: Greenwood, 1973. ISBN 0-8371-6643-8. ‣ Study of rise of militarism in 1930s from Manchurian Incident (1931) to outbreak of China War (1937) and Pearl Harbor (1941). One of first postwar efforts to explain forces that led Japan to war. [FGN]

13.328 John Toland. *The rising sun.* 1970 ed. New York: Bantam, 1982. ISBN 0-553-26435-4 (pbk). ▸ Balanced history of World War II in Pacific based on extensive interviews of participants on both sides. Highly readable and instructive. [FGN]

13.329 George M. Wilson, ed. *Crisis politics in prewar Japan: institutional and ideological problems of the 1930s.* Tokyo: Sophia University Press, 1970. ▸ Collection of essays on Japan in 1930s. Good articles by Wilson on renovation, Shillony on military radicals, and Spaulding on renovationist bureaucrats. [FGN]

13.330 Takehiko Yoshihashi. *Conspiracy at Mukden: the rise of the Japanese military.* 1963 ed. Westport, Conn.: Greenwood, 1980. ISBN 0-313-22443-9. ▸ Detailed study of Manchurian Incident which launched Japanese army on expansionism in 1930s. Demonstrates event engineered by both military activists and civilian politicians. [FGN]

SEE ALSO
44.788 Ronald H. Spector. *Eagle against the sun.*
44.794 Herbert Feis. *The atomic bomb and the end of World War II.*
48.171 James W. Morley, ed. *Deterrent diplomacy.*
48.268 Christopher Thorne. *Allies of a kind.*

OCCUPATION

13.331 Hans H. Baerwald. *The purge of Japanese leaders under the occupation.* Berkeley: University of California Press, 1959. ▸ Still the best examination of occupation efforts to purge Japanese leaders from official positions. Studies controversial aspects of policy which often purged individuals not for personal record but for positions they held. [FGN]

13.332 T. A. Bisson. *Zaibatsu dissolution in Japan.* 1954 ed. Westport, Conn.: Greenwood, 1976. ISBN 0-8371-8816-4. ▸ Examination of United States efforts to reorganize Japanese industrial enterprises during occupation by breaking apart *zaibatsu* (financial clique) firms. Analyzes attempt at and failure of trustbusting in Japan. [FGN]

13.333 Ronald P. Dore. *Land reform in Japan.* 1959 ed. New York: Schocken, 1985. ISBN 0-8052-3948-0. ▸ Examination of land reforms carried out under American occupation in postwar Japan. Excellent portrait of rural society and effects that American induced reforms had on villages and their inhabitants. [FGN]

13.334 John W. Dower. *Empire and aftermath: Yoshida Shigeru and the Japanese experience.* Cambridge, Mass.: Harvard University, Council on East Asian Studies, 1979. (Harvard East Asian monographs, 84.) ISBN 0-674-25125-3. ▸ Significant study of career of Japan's most important postwar prime minister who guided nation through difficult years of American occupation and postwar reconstruction. Explains how Conservatives reestablished control in postwar Japan. [FGN]

13.335 Robert Fearey. *The occupation of Japan: second phase, 1948–1950.* 1950 ed. Westport, Conn.: Greenwood, 1972. ISBN 0-8371-6271-8. ▸ Concentrates on changes in occupation policy and attempted reforms in Japan that emerged with cold war and with "reversed course," occupation policy designed to reestablish Japan as economically viable state and Western ally in Asia. [FGN]

13.336 Richard B. Finn. *Winners in peace: MacArthur, Yoshida, and postwar Japan.* Berkeley: University of California Press, 1992. ISBN 0-520-06909-9. ▸ Young participant examines course of occupation, 1945–52, focusing on interaction of General Douglas MacArthur and Prime Minister Yoshida Shigeru. Balanced presentation of occupation reforms. [FGN]

13.337 Mark Gayn. *Japan diary.* 1948 ed. Rutland, Vt.: Tuttle, 1981. ISBN 0-8048-1369-8 (pbk). ▸ Most detailed, best journalistic account of early occupation years in Japan. Excellent in capturing feeling of occupation from 1945 to 1947. [FGN]

13.338 Eleanor M. Hadley. *Antitrust in Japan.* Princeton: Princeton University Press, 1970. ISBN 0-691-04194-6. ▸ Important examination of American occupation policy to carry out *zaibatsu* (financial clique) dissolution in Japan. Shows how early efforts to reform Japanese industrial structure gave way under cold war pressures to preservation of status quo. [FGN]

13.339 Kyoko Inoue. *MacArthur's Japanese constitution: a linguistic and cultural study of its making.* Chicago: University of Chicago Press, 1991. ISBN 0-226-38391-1. ▸ Well-argued linguistic analysis of Japan's postwar constitution. Rejects accepted interpretations of how document was derived and calls for new translation and explanation of how Japanese document differs from official English text. [FGN]

13.340 D. Clayton James. *Triumph and disaster, 1945–1964.* Vol. 3 of *The years of MacArthur.* Boston: Houghton-Mifflin, 1985. ISBN 0-395-36004-8 (v. 3). ▸ Final volume in James's authoritative trilogy covering General MacArthur's life. Covers role as proconsul in Japan. Thoroughly researched, detailed, and informative. Best biography on MacArthur to date. [FGN]

13.341 Kazuo Kawai. *Japan's American interlude.* 1960 ed. Chicago: University of Chicago Press, 1979. ISBN 0-226-42775-7. ▸ Balanced, well-written discussion of American occupation and attempted reforms by on-the-scene observer who served as editor of *Nippon Times.* Excellent overview of Japan under United States control. [FGN]

13.342 William Manchester. *American Caesar: Douglas MacArthur, 1880–1964.* 1978 ed. New York: Dell, 1983. ISBN 0-440-30424-5 (pbk). ▸ One of major postwar studies of MacArthur evaluating career as general and proconsul in Japan. Useful but not as authoritative as James's biography (13.340). [FGN]

13.343 John Curtis Perry. *Beneath the eagle's wings: Americans in occupied Japan.* New York: Dodd Mead, 1980. ISBN 0-396-07876-1. ▸ Revealing examination of first years of occupation in Japan from perspective of occupiers who attempted to reform Japan from within. [FGN]

13.344 Robert E. Ward and Sakamoto Yoshikazu, eds. *Democratizing Japan: the Allied occupation.* Honolulu: University of Hawaii Press, 1987. ISBN 0-8248-0883-5. ▸ More than a dozen Western and Japanese scholars explore Allied efforts to democratize Japanese political system and evaluate successes and failures of this effort. Best reassessment to date. [FGN]

13.345 Harry Emerson Wildes. *Typhoon in Tokyo: the occupation and its aftermath.* 1954 ed. New York: Octagon Books, 1978. ISBN 0-374-98572-3. ▸ Vivid description of American reform efforts in Japan under occupation. Early evaluation of degree to which United States–inspired changes were taking root in Japan. [FGN]

13.346 Justin Williams, Sr. *Japan's political revolution under MacArthur: a participant's account.* Athens: University of Georgia Press, 1979. ISBN 0-8203-0452-2. ▸ Head of legislative division in General MacArthur's Government Section describes implementation of American policies designed to democratize Japan. Candid if opinionated firsthand perspective on American efforts. [FGN]

13.347 Yoshida Shigeru. *The Yoshida memoirs: the story of Japan in crisis.* 1962 ed. Kenichi Yoshida, trans. Westport, Conn.: Greenwood, 1973. ISBN 0-8371-6733-7. ▸ Memoirs of Japan's most important postwar prime minister who headed several cabinets, 1946–54. Candid Japanese assessment of American occupation and its policies. Good descriptions of General MacArthur and men around him. [FGN]

13.348   Michael M. Yoshitsu. *Japan and the San Francisco peace settlement.* New York: Columbia University Press, 1983. ISBN 0-231-05514-5. ▸ Well-researched study of political and diplomatic process leading to San Francisco Peace Treaty. Examines Japanese efforts and compromises that returned sovereignty to Japan in wake of World War II. [FGN]

POSTWAR JAPAN

Politics, Parties, and Parliament

13.349   Gary D. Allinson. *Suburban Tokyo: a comparative study in politics and social change.* Berkeley: University of California Press, 1979. ISBN 0-520-03768-5. ▸ Major study of growth of opposition party strength in western Tokyo suburbs. Examines social, economic, and demographic dynamics in these two cities that have caused voters to shift away from conservative Liberal Democratic party politics. [FGN]

13.350   David E. Apter and Nagayo Sawa. *Against the state: politics and social protest in Japan.* Cambridge, Mass.: Harvard University Press, 1984. ISBN 0-674-00920-7 (cl), 0-674-00921-5 (pbk). ▸ Thorough treatment of massive protest movement against government's efforts to construct New Tokyo International Airport at Narita. Describes nature and organization of struggle pitting local farmers and urban leftists against government officials. [FGN]

13.351   Hans H. Baerwald. *Japan's parliament: an introduction.* London: Cambridge University Press, 1974. ISBN 0- 521-20387-2. ▸ Best survey of Japanese parliament. Examines historical development and current workings of bicameral legislature, party system, system of governance within Diet, and periodic confrontations marking its development. [FGN]

13.352   Hans H. Baerwald. *Party politics in Japan.* Boston: Allen & Unwin, 1986. ISBN 0-04-320183-0 (cl), 0-04-320184-9 (pbk). ▸ Account of Japanese party politics for general reader. Focuses on nature of Japanese party system (particularly its proclivity to factionalism), Diet, and recent trends. [FGN]

13.353   Ardath W. Burks. *The government of Japan.* 1964 2d ed. Westport, Conn.: Greenwood, 1982. ISBN 0-313-23575-9. ▸ General survey of Japanese government, political parties, and postwar Japanese Diet. [FGN]

13.354   John Creighton Campbell. *Contemporary Japanese budget politics.* Berkeley: University of California Press, 1977. ISBN 0-520-02573-3. ▸ Classic study of process of budget making in postwar Japan. Focuses on complex interrelationship between parties and bureaucracy that has pitted political interests against those of Ministry of Finance. Addresses crucial issue of who ran postwar Japan. [FGN]

13.355   Allan B. Cole, George O. Totten, and Cecil H. Uyehara. *Socialist parties in postwar Japan.* New Haven: Yale University Press, 1966. ▸ Detailed exploration of Japan's postwar noncommunist socialist parties. Traces growth and development in period after 1945. Both a history and study of party structure, organization, and tactics. [FGN]

13.356   Gerald L. Curtis. *Election campaigning Japanese style.* 1971 ed. Tokyo: Kodansha, 1983. ISBN 0-87011-630-4. ▸ Important description of successful campaign by new Liberal Democratic party candidate, Sato Bunsei, who ran for rural seat in 1967 election. One of best firsthand accounts of campaign practices, strategy, and organization at local level. [FGN]

13.357   Gerald L. Curtis. *The Japanese way of politics.* New York: Columbia University Press, 1988. ISBN 0-231-06680-5 (cl), 0-231-06681-3 (pbk). ▸ Leading political scientist's excellent study of evolution of Japanese politics in postwar period. Concentrates on how Japan's most important party, Liberal Democratic party, has combined conservative stability with change and innovation to remain in power. [FGN]

13.358   Haruhiro Fukui. *Party in power: the Japanese Liberal-Democrats and policy-making.* Berkeley: University of California Press, 1970. ISBN 0-520-01646-7. ▸ Thorough, informative analysis of Liberal Democratic party, examining crucial points in its development from perspective of policy formulation over controversial issues. Presents three case studies. [FGN]

13.359   Nobutaka Ike. *Japanese politics: patron-client democracy.* 2d ed. New York: Knopf, 1972. ISBN 0-394-316995-9. ▸ Updates author's earlier study, *Japanese Politics: An Introductory Survey*, arguing for close business-government relationship that became central to Liberal Democratic party's management of postwar politics. Significant analysis of postwar Japanese political system. [FGN]

13.360   Takeshi Ishida. *Japanese political culture: change and continuity.* New Brunswick, N.J.: Transaction, 1983. ISBN 0-87855-465-3. ▸ Leading Japanese political sociologist examines elements of Japanese value system and organizational structures that undergird modern politics. Series of insightful essays sheds light on broad range of topics. [FGN]

13.361   Chalmers A. Johnson. *Japan's public policy companies.* Washington, D.C.: American Enterprise Institute for Public Policy Research, 1978. (Hoover Institution studies, 60.) ISBN 0-8447-3272-9. ▸ Important study of public corporations and public-private enterprises that constitute important sector of government's economic bureaucracy. Traces history of such enterprises and their role in Japan's political economy. [FGN]

13.362   Paul S. Kim. *Japan's civil service system: its structure, personnel, and politics.* New York: Greenwood, 1988. ISBN 0-313-26150-4. ▸ Thorough examination of Japanese civil service system, including administrative structure, management, recruiting, and retention systems. [FGN]

13.363   George R. Packard III. *Protest in Tokyo: the security treaty crisis of 1960.* 1966 ed. Westport, Conn.: Greenwood, 1978. ISBN 0-313-20532-9. ▸ Thorough examination of May–June 1960 struggle over revisions in United States–Japan mutual security treaty, which led to fall of Prime Minister Kishi's government and cancellation of President Eisenhower's visit to Japan. [FGN]

13.364   T. J. Pempel. *Policy and politics in Japan: creative conservatism.* Philadelphia: Temple University Press, 1982. ISBN 0-87722-249-5 (cl), 0-87722-250-9 (pbk). ▸ Concentrates on creative but conservative ways in which Japan's Liberal Democratic party has addressed changing conditions in economic, social, educational, environmental, and commercial fields. Major cogent analysis. [FGN]

13.365   T. J. Pempel, ed. *Policymaking in contemporary Japan.* Ithaca, N.Y.: Cornell University Press, 1977. ISBN 0-8014-1048-7. ▸ Variety of case studies of policy making in postwar period. Chapters by American and Japanese scholars range from rice price supports to decision to have Prime Minister Tanaka visit Peking in 1972. [FGN]

13.366   Susan J. Pharr. *Losing face: status politics in Japan.* Berkeley: University of California Press, 1990. ISBN 0-520-06050-4 (cl), 0-520-08092-0 (pbk). ▸ Important new study linking Japanese culture to politics and micro- to macroprocesses. Analyzes interaction between protest and social structure in postwar Japan, looking at how struggles over equality are waged. [FGN]

13.367   Bradley M. Richardson and Scott C. Flanagan. *Politics in Japan.* Boston: Little, Brown, 1984. ISBN 0-316-74432-8. ▸ Good example of structural-functional approach studying performance of Japanese political institutions and examining interaction between politics and society in 1960s and 1970s. [FGN]

13.368   Robert A. Scalapino and Junnosuke Masumi. *Parties and politics in contemporary Japan*. Berkeley: University of California Press, 1962. ▸ Study of party development in postwar period and analysis of political crisis of May–June 1960. Designed for broad student audience, approach both descriptive and analytical. [FGN]

13.369   William E. Steslicke. *Doctors in politics: the political life of the Japan Medical Association*. New York: Praeger, 1973. ▸ Best study to date of Japanese interest group, examining Japan Medical Association's efforts to influence government policy in 1960–61 on several key issues related to Japan's system of health insurance. [FGN]

13.370   James Arthur Ainscow Stockwin. *Japan, divided politics in a growth economy*. 2d ed. New York: Norton, 1982. ISBN 0-393-95235-5. ▸ Text on contemporary Japanese politics emphasizing close relationship between government and big business. Revision of author's 1975 book on same topic. [FGN]

13.371   James Arthur Ainscow Stockwin. *The Japanese Socialist party and neutralism: a study of a political party and its foreign policy*. London: Cambridge University Press, 1968. ISBN 0-522-83838-3. ▸ Thorough scholarly presentation of political and ideological history of Japan Socialist party, Japan's major opposition party. Traces party's ideas on neutral foreign policy in 1950s and 1960s. [FGN]

13.372   Nathaniel B. Thayer. *How the Conservatives rule Japan*. Princeton: Princeton University Press, 1969. ISBN 0-691-03029-4. ▸ Carefully documented analysis of organization, internal structure, and functioning of Liberal Democratic party. Evaluates party factions, ties to big business and industry, and intricate balancing of factional versus party organizational power. [FGN]

Prefectural and Local Government

13.373   Steven R. Reed. *Japanese prefectures and policymaking*. Pittsburgh: University of Pittsburgh Press, 1986. ISBN 0-8229-3527-9. ▸ Study of relationship between central government and local (prefectural) administrations on policy issues. Several revealing case studies presented. Emphasis on pollution, education, and housing policies. [FGN]

13.374   Richard J. Samuels. *The politics of regional policy in Japan: localities incorporated?* Princeton: Princeton University Press, 1983. ISBN 0-691-07657-X (cl), 0-691-10152-3 (pbk). ▸ Study of local government participation in regional policy making during 1970s. Challenges some widely held perceptions about degree of national centralization in Japan. Emphasizes horizontal rather than vertical relationships. [FGN]

13.375   Kurt Steiner. *Local government in Japan*. Stanford, Calif.: Stanford University Press, 1965. ▸ Best, most comprehensive treatment of local government in Japan covering field from prefectural and metropolitan administrations down to ward level. Historical analysis employed to examine contemporary political structures. [FGN]

13.376   Kurt Steiner, Ellis S. Krauss, and Scott C. Flanagan, eds. *Political opposition and local politics in Japan*. Princeton: Princeton University Press, 1980. ISBN 0-691-07625-1 (cl), 0-691-02201-1 (pbk). ▸ Essays analyzing political opposition in local politics during 1960s and 1970s. Particularly good on locally based citizen's movements and effects they had on variety of reform issues, ranging from pollution to urban development. [FGN]

Foreign Relations

13.377   Tsuneo Akaha. *Japan in global ocean politics*. Honolulu: University of Hawaii Press and Law of the Sea Institute, 1985. ISBN 0-8248-0898-3. ▸ Perceptive study of Japan's position on law of the sea and growing concern of nations to claim jurisdiction

over ocean areas bordering their shores for economic exploitation. [FGN]

13.378   Gordon Daniels and Reinhard Drifte, eds. *Europe and Japan: changing relationships since 1945*. Ashford, England: Norbury, 1986. ISBN 0-904404-44-7. ▸ Eight essays by British, German, and Japanese scholars studying emergence of new relationships and ties between Europe, Japan, and United States in past three decades. Includes important essays by European scholars. [FGN]

13.379   I. M. Destler et al. *Managing an alliance: the politics of U.S.-Japanese relations*. Washington, D.C.: Brookings Institution, 1976. ISBN 0-8157-1820-9 (cl), 0-8157-1819-5 (pbk). ▸ Study of bureaucratic and political forces that combined in United States and Japan to determine foreign policy decisions. Best on how officials in each government perceived each other's actions. [FGN]

13.380   I. M. Destler, Haruhiro Fukui, and Hideo Sato. *The textile wrangle: conflict in Japanese-American relations, 1969–1971*. Ithaca, N.Y.: Cornell University Press, 1979. ISBN 0-8014-1120-3. ▸ Thorough examination of Nixon administration's efforts, between 1969 and 1971, to get Japan to control textile exports to United States. Treats problem as political, not economic, issue. [FGN]

13.381   John K. Emmerson and Harrison M. Holland. *The eagle and the rising sun: America and Japan in the twentieth century*. Reading, Pa.: Addison-Wesley, 1988. ISBN 0-201-08891-6. ▸ Discussion of United States–Japanese relations in modern period by two career diplomats who spent much of postwar period in Tokyo. New perspective on growing trade and security frictions between United States and Japan. [FGN]

13.382   Thomas R. H. Havens. *Fire across the sea: the Vietnam War and Japan, 1965–1975*. Princeton: Princeton University Press, 1987. ISBN 0-691-05491-6 (cl), 0-691-00811-6 (pbk). ▸ Revealing study of Japanese government's treaty-related support of Vietnam War and Japanese public's vigorous antiwar reactions. Suggests Japanese leaders linked war aid to reversion of Okinawa to Japanese sovereignty. [FGN]

13.383   Donald C. Hellmann. *Japanese foreign policy and domestic politics: the peace agreement with the Soviet Union*. Berkeley: University of California Press, 1969. ▸ Well-documented examination of how Liberal Democratic party managed to play dominant role in Ministry of Foreign Affairs' efforts to normalize relations between Japan and Soviet Union in 1956. [FGN]

13.384   Frank Langdon. *The politics of Canadian-Japanese economic relations, 1952–1983*. Vancouver: University of British Columbia Press, 1983. ISBN 0-7748-0188-3. ▸ Analysis of major issues affecting postwar Canadian-Japanese relations. After historical introduction, focuses on economic questions of trade, manufacturing, investment, and natural resources. Essential for understanding postwar Canadian-Japanese relations. [FGN]

13.385   Chae-Jin Lee. *China and Japan: new economic diplomacy*. Stanford, Calif.: Hoover Institution Press, 1984. ISBN 0-8179-7971-9 (cl), 0-8179-7972-7 (pbk). ▸ Study of increasingly important economic relationship between mainland China and Japan. Discusses economic negotiations of 1970s and 1980s and economic diplomacy that led Japan to invest heavily in several important Chinese construction programs. Good on Japan's postwar China policy. [FGN]

13.386   Chong-Sik Lee. *Japan and Korea: the political dimension*. Stanford, Calif.: Hoover Institution Press, 1985. ISBN 0-8179-8181-0. ▸ Study of Korean-Japanese relations during post–World War II period. Most effective in treating fundamental differences in political structures, economic policies, and psychological perceptions and explains how these affected relations of both countries. [FGN]

13.387 Lawrence Olson. *Japan in postwar Asia.* New York: Praeger, 1970. ▸ Discussion of Japan's shift from Asian foreign policy of "low posture" (1952–64) to one of increasing Asian visibility (1964–69). Early effort to explain Japan's reemergence as Asian power. [FGN]

13.388 Alan Rix. *Japan's economic aid: policy-making and politics.* New York: St. Martin's, 1980. ISBN 0-312-44063-4. ▸ Timely study of Japan's aid and economic assistance policies, which were heavily influenced by Japanese bureaucratic interests. Argues aid policy based on certain key bilateral relationships. [FGN]

13.389 Myles L. C. Robertson. *Soviet policy towards Japan: an analysis of trends in the 1970s and 1980s.* Cambridge: Cambridge University Press, 1988. ISBN 0-521-35131-6. ▸ Thorough analysis of Soviet-Japanese relations in past two decades based heavily on Soviet viewpoint. Stresses issues of ideology, economic relations, Soviet strategy for Northeast Asia, and perceptions of United States–Japanese and Japanese-Chinese relations. [FGN]

13.390 Robert A. Scalapino, ed. *The foreign policy of modern Japan.* Berkeley: University of California Press, 1977. ISBN 0-520-03196-2. ▸ Conference volume; thirteen American and Japanese scholars address wide cross-spectrum of issues relating to Japan's foreign policy. Focus on how policy is made, by whom, and how it is implemented. Presents variety of views. [FGN]

13.391 William Watts. *The United States and Japan: a troubled partnership.* Cambridge, Mass.: Ballinger, 1984. ISBN 0-88410-993-3. ▸ Argues United States–Japanese relationship both strong and fragile. Shows how bilateral frictions affect perceptions on both sides of Pacific. Based on public opinion survey data. Cautiously optimistic. [FGN]

13.392 John Welfield. *An empire in eclipse: Japan in the postwar American alliance system; a study in the interaction of domestic politics and foreign policy.* Atlantic Highlands, N.J.: Athlone, 1988. ISBN 0-485-11334-1. ▸ Balanced discussion of United States–Japanese relationship between end of World War II and collapse of United States–Soviet détente in 1978. Explains Japanese foreign policy after 1978 as effort to continue special relationship with United States that marked earlier period. [FGN]

13.393 Endymion Wilkinson. *Japan versus Europe: a history of misunderstanding.* New York: Penguin Books, 1983. ISBN 0-14-022469-6. ▸ Examination of development of European images of Japan and Japanese images of Europe. Effectively argues Japanese have clearer understanding of Europe than vice versa. Explores relationship of mutual images to current frictions. [FGN]

13.394 Dennis T. Yasutomo. *The manner of giving: strategic aid and Japanese foreign policy.* Lexington, Mass.: Lexington Books, 1986. ISBN 0-669-12894-5. ▸ Revealing study of Japan's foreign aid policies. Argues Japan uses foreign aid as political tool in relations with Third World. Use of foreign aid therefore geared to pursue political and security interests as much as to gain economic goals. [FGN]

SEE ALSO
  48.537 Robert S. Ozaki and Walter Arnold, eds. *Japan's foreign relations.*

Security and Defense

13.395 James E. Auer. *The postwar rearmament of Japanese maritime forces, 1945–71.* New York: Praeger, 1973. ▸ Useful study on Japanese naval forces. After discussion of immediate postwar naval demobilization, explores early history of Japan's maritime Self-Defense Force (1953–71). [FGN]

13.396 Robert W. Barnett. *Beyond war: Japan's concept of comprehensive national security.* Washington, D.C.: Brassey's, 1984. ISBN 0-08-031617-4 (cl), 0-08-031952-1 (pbk). ▸ Study of American and Japanese responses to report on comprehensive national security prepared for Japanese government by task force headed by Masamichi Inoki. Report addresses how to forestall, prevent, or limit war. Important insights into Japanese strategic planning. [FGN]

13.397 James H. Buck, ed. *The modern Japanese military system.* Beverly Hills, Calif.: Sage, 1975. ISBN 0-8039-0513-0 (cl), 0-8039-0514-9 (pbk). ▸ Examination of history and organization of Japan's postwar Self-Defense Forces by nine American scholars. Essays treat variety of defense-related topics. Useful portrait of Japanese army in postwar period. [FGN]

13.398 Reinhard Drifte. *Arms production in Japan: the military applications of civilian technology.* Boulder: Westview, 1986. ISBN 0-8133-7258-5. ▸ Careful study of arms production capabilities of Japanese economy in 1980s with emphasis on Japanese research and development in shipbuilding, aircraft production, space and missile industry, and supporting high-tech industries. [FGN]

13.399 John K. Emmerson. *Arms, yen, and power: the Japanese dilemma.* New York: Nellen, 1971. ISBN 0-8424-0057-5. ▸ Important examination, by distinguished American diplomat in Japan, of complex interrelationship between expanding economic power and Japan's postwar decision to maintain minimum military forces. [FGN]

13.400 John K. Emmerson and Leonard A. Humphreys. *Will Japan rearm? A study in attitudes.* Washington, D.C.: American Enterprise Institute for Public Policy Research, 1973. (Hoover Institution studies, 44.) ISBN 0-8447-3114-5. ▸ Early effort to wrestle with question of Japan's future defense policy. Argues Japanese sentiment, while supporting minimum defense expenditures, remains vigorously opposed to remilitarization of Japan and abolition of Article 9 of Japan's postwar constitution. [FGN]

13.401 Malcolm McIntosh. *Japan re-armed.* New York: St. Martin's, 1986. ISBN 0-312-44055-3. ▸ Critical evaluation of Japan's current rearmament policy, arguing Japan has been rearming at dramatic rate. Gives historical overview of postwar defense considerations and policies. [FGN]

13.402 Richard L. Sneider. *U.S.-Japanese security relations: a historical perspective.* New York: Columbia University, East Asian Institute, 1982. ISBN 0-913418-01-3. ▸ Thoughtful consideration of history and future of United States–Japanese security relationship by important government official active in East Asian affairs. Argues Americans need to pay attention to internal Japanese debates over security matters. [FGN]

13.403 Taketsugu Tsurutani. *Japanese policy and East Asian security.* New York: Praeger, 1981. ISBN 0-03-059806-0. ▸ Exploration of Japanese defense policy focusing on nation's role in promoting and maintaining regional security in East Asia in 1980s. Effective examination of defense-related issues; makes policy recommendations. [FGN]

13.404 Martin E. Weinstein. *Japan's postwar defense policy, 1947–1968.* New York: Columbia University Press, 1971. ISBN 0-231-63447-4. ▸ Best of early postwar studies of Japan's emerging defense policy. Shows how Japanese government leaders maintained clear and distinct perception of defense issues and pursued own course, independent of domestic and foreign distractions. [FGN]

SOCIETY, SOCIAL SYSTEM, AND VALUES

13.405 Lewis Austin, ed. *Japan—the paradox of progress.* New Haven: Yale University Press, 1976. ISBN 0-300-01957-2. ▸ Exploration of aspects of Japan's postwar political and social culture by eleven American scholars. Covers wide cross-spectrum of topics dealing with growth-inspired conflict and challenges that they spring from rapid development. [FGN]

13.406 Harumi Befu. *Japan: an anthropological introduction.* San Francisco: Chandler, 1971. ISBN 0-8102-0430-4. ‣ Traces cultural origins and historical background of Japanese institutions such as kinship, marriage, and family, as well as contemporary organizational structures. Introductory survey for uninitiated. [FGN]

13.407 Robert N. Bellah. "Values and social change in modern Japan." *Asian cultural studies* 3 (1962) 13–56. ‣ Important essay treating historical development of political values in Japan. Values analyzed in comparative context with similar developments in West. [FGN]

13.408 Ruth Benedict. *The chrysanthemum and the sword: patterns of Japanese culture.* 1946 ed. Boston: Houghton-Mifflin, 1989. ISBN 0-395-50075-3. ‣ Pioneering work on Japanese social system and value structure produced at time of World War II by a leading American cultural anthropologist. Now somewhat dated though interpretation still works well for traditional Japanese society. [FGN]

13.409 Peter N. Dale. *The myth of Japanese uniqueness.* 1986 ed. New York: St. Martin's, 1990. ISBN 0-312-55872-4 (cl, 1986), 0-312-04629-4 (pbk). ‣ Significant analysis of Japanese fondness for *nihonjinron* (interpretations of Japanese uniqueness). Attributes such interests to psychological and sociological roots. [FGN]

13.410 George A. De Vos. *Socialization for achievement: essays on the cultural psychology of the Japanese.* 1973 ed. Berkeley: University of California Press, 1975. ISBN 0-520-01827-3 (cl, 1973), 0-520-02893-7 (pbk). ‣ Series of important essays concentrating on normative role behavior, motivation for achievement, alienation, and deviancy. Examines Japanese values and psychology in variety of contexts. [FGN]

13.411 Takeo Doi. *The anatomy of dependence.* 1973 ed. John Bester, trans. Tokyo: Kodansha, 1981. ISBN 0-87011-494-8. ‣ Important exploration of dependency patterns among modern Japanese tracing back to childhood socialization. Leading Japanese psychiatrist's interpretation of *amae* (indulgence) as source of adult reliance and its role in shaping modern Japanese social organizations. [FGN]

13.412 Takeo Doi. *The anatomy of self: the individual versus society.* 1986 ed. Mark A. Harbison, trans. Tokyo: Kodansha, 1988. ISBN 0-87011-761-0 (cl, 1986), 0-87011-902-8 (pbk). ‣ Follow-up to 13.411 addressing relationship between individual psyche and group-oriented behavior. Addresses important Japanese concepts of *omote/ura* (front/back) and *tatemae/honne* (external appearance/true essence). Essential for understanding Japanese psychology. [FGN]

13.413 Ronald P. Dore, ed. *Aspects of social change in modern Japan.* Princeton: Princeton University Press, 1967. ‣ Excellent series of essays by seventeen Japanese and American authors analyzing elements of social change that have influenced Japanese modernization. [FGN]

13.414 Tadashi Fukutake. *The Japanese social structure: its evolution in the modern century.* 1982 2d ed. Ronald P. Dore, trans. Tokyo: University of Tokyo Press, 1989. ISBN 0-86008-446-9. ‣ Important study of Japan's rapid social transformation in pre- and postwar periods, examining changes in patriarchal family system, group-oriented behavior, individualism, and social relations. Explores social consequences of industrial mass society. [FGN]

13.415 Tadashi Fukutake. *Japanese society today.* 1974 2d ed. Tokyo: University of Tokyo Press, 1981. ISBN 0-86008-113-3 (cl, 1974), 0-86008-291-1 (pbk). ‣ Fine survey concentrating on con-

temporary scene. Examines Japanese society from perspective of urbanization, industrialization, and demographic shifts. Analyzes problems attendant to mass society. [FGN]

13.416 Matthews Masayuki Hamabata. *Crested kimono: power and love in the Japanese business family.* Ithaca, N.Y.: Cornell University Press, 1990. ISBN 0-8014-2333-3 (cl), 0-8014-9975-5 (pbk). ‣ Sociologist's inside view of female networks supporting Japan's family-owned business enterprises. Insightful look at Japanese society and gender relations. [FGN]

13.417 Takeshi Ishida. *Japanese society.* New York: Random House, 1971. ISBN 0-394-31011-X. ‣ Survey examining contemporary Japanese cultural values and social structure as they emerged out of Japan's traditional society. Contrasts rapid economic transformation with slow social change. [FGN]

13.418 Donald Keene. *Landscapes and portraits, appreciations of Japanese culture.* New York: Kodansha, 1971. ISBN 0-87011-146-9. ‣ Personal interpretation of Japanese culture written by one of America's premier translators and literary scholars. Rich and sensitively nuanced. [FGN]

13.419 Dorinne K. Kondo. *Crafting selves: power, gender, and discourses of identity in a Japanese workplace.* Chicago: University of Chicago Press, 1990. ISBN 0-226-45043-0 (cl), 0-226-45044-9 (pbk). ‣ Anthropologist's portrayal of life in Japanese confectionary factory. Describes intricate interpersonal relationships among artisans and explains how individuals establish and preserve personal identities. [FGN]

13.420 Ellis S. Krauss, Thomas P. Rohlen, and Patricia G. Steinhoff, eds. *Conflict in Japan.* Honolulu: University of Hawaii Press, 1984. ISBN 0-8248-0948-3 (cl), 0-8248-0867-3 (pbk). ‣ Analysis by Japanese and American scholars of aspects of conflict and conflict resolution in postwar Japanese society. Important challenge to notion of Japan as consensus society. [FGN]

13.421 Takie Sugiyama Lebra. *Japanese patterns of behavior.* Honolulu: University of Hawaii Press, 1976. ISBN 0-8248-0396-5 (cl), 0-8248-0460-0 (pbk). ‣ Study of contemporary Japanese behavior patterns through analysis of commonly held beliefs and attitudes. Reveals how proper social conduct incorporates values of dependency, place, reciprocity, belonging, and selfhood. [FGN]

13.422 Robert Jay Lifton, Shuichi Kato, and Michael R. Reich. *Six lives, six deaths: portraits from modern Japan.* New Haven: Yale University Press, 1979. ISBN 0-300-02266-2 (cl), 0-300-02600-5 (pbk). ‣ Team of scholars, including psychiatrist and literary specialist, examines Japanese attitudes toward life and death through series of biographical essays. Thought-provoking. [FGN]

13.423 Jeannie Lo. *Office ladies, factory women: life and work at a Japanese company.* Armonk, N.Y.: Sharpe, 1990. ISBN 0-87332-598-2. ‣ Informative ethnographical account describing life of female workers in Nagoya manufacturing firm. Studies women on factory floor and in sales office and observes their lives in company dormitories. [FGN]

13.424 Fosco Maraini. *Meeting with Japan.* 1959 ed. Tokyo: Kodansha, 1971. ‣ Well-written presentation of modern Japanese culture, society, and history by established Italian scholar and longtime student of Japan. Somewhat sentimental. [FGN]

13.425 Erdman B. Palmore and Daisaku Maeda. *The honorable elders revisited: a revised crosscultural analysis of aging in Japan.* 1975 rev. ed. Durham, N.C.: Duke University Press, 1985. ISBN 0-8223-0261-6 (cl), 0-8223-0263-2 (pbk). ‣ Revision of Palmore's important *The Honorable Elders* (1975). Comparative study of social status and integration of elderly in Japan and in Western societies. Examines variety of topics including health, medical care, and living conditions, etc. [FGN]

13.426 David W. Plath. *The after hours: modern Japan and the search for enjoyment.* 1964 ed. Westport, Conn.: Greenwood, 1984. ISBN 0-313-24297-6. ‣ Rich and textured ethnographic treatment of work and leisure in 1950s Japan. Examines changing entertainment patterns accompanying Japan's emergence as advanced industrial society. [FGN]

13.427 David W. Plath. *Long engagements: maturity in modern Japan.* Stanford, Calif.: Stanford University Press, 1980. ISBN 0-8047-1054-6 (cl), 0-8047-1176-3 (pbk). ‣ Sensitive treatment of aging in Japan. Examines how meaningful long-term relationships among cohorts develop and are sustained by exploring set of real-life case studies and fictional characters. [FGN]

13.428 Jennifer Robertson. *Native and newcomer: making and remaking a Japanese city.* Berkeley: University of California Press, 1991. ISBN 0-520-07296-0. ‣ Ethnographic study of Kodaira, a Tokyo suburb, showing how citizens of this community have both restructured the past and imagined the future. Effectively combines history with critical theory and ethnography. [FGN]

13.429 Thomas P. Rohlen. *For harmony and strength: Japanese white-collar organization in anthropological perspective.* Berkeley: University of California Press, 1974. ISBN 0-520-02674-8. ‣ Pathbreaking examination of work relationships and social structure in Japanese bank. Participant-observer's description of lifetime commitment, wage structure, promotions, and daily interactions among Japanese office workers. [FGN]

13.430 Kurt Singer. *Mirror, sword, and jewel: the geometry of Japanese life.* 1973 ed. Richard Storry, ed. Tokyo: Kodansha, 1981. ISBN 0-87011-460-3. ‣ Reflections of German Jew who taught in Japan during 1930s. Important insights into nature of Japanese psychology and workings of Japanese social system. Still impressive. [FGN]

13.431 Robert J. Smith. *Japanese society: tradition, self, and the social order.* 1983 ed. Cambridge: Cambridge University Press, 1987. ISBN 0-521-25843-X (cl, 1983), 0-521-31552-2 (pbk). ‣ Important study of transformation of Japanese society into mass industrial society. Argues Japan adopted significantly different pattern in this transition than did West. [FGN]

13.432 Robert J. Smith and Richard K. Beardsley, eds. *Japanese culture: its development and characteristics.* Chicago: Aldine, 1963. ‣ Cultural anthropological examination of Japanese culture and its transformation in modern period. [FGN]

13.433 Kazuko Tsurumi. *Social change and the individual: Japan before and after defeat in World War II.* Princeton: Princeton University Press, 1970. ISBN 0-691-09347-4. ‣ Excellent exploration of socialization patterns in various Japanese groups over pre- and postwar periods. Relationship of societal change and personality development are central themes. [FGN]

13.434 Takeo Yazaki. *Social change and the city in Japan: from earliest times through the Industrial Revolution.* David L. Swain, trans. Tokyo: Japan Publications, 1968. ‣ Traces close relationship between changes in political and economic structure of Japanese cities and their ecological and demographic conditions. Examines cities such as Edo, Tokyo, Ōsaka, and Kyoto. Still best work on topic. [FGN]

Women

13.435 Alice Mabel Bacon. *Japanese girls and women.* 1891 ed. New York: Gordon, 1975. ISBN 0-87968-253-1. ‣ Early history of women in Japan. Still useful for information on late nineteenth century. Also available on microfilm from New Haven: Research Publications, 1977 (History of Women). [FGN]

13.436 Gail Lee Bernstein. *Haruko's world: a Japanese farm woman and her community.* Stanford, Calif.: Stanford University Press, 1983. ISBN 0-8047-1174-7 (cl), 0-8047-1287-5 (pbk).

‣ Important study of changing gender relationships in postwar rural Japan focusing on middle-aged farm woman in Shikoku. Broad insights into role of women in agriculture. [FGN]

13.437 Gail Lee Bernstein, ed. *Re-creating Japanese women, 1600–1945.* Berkeley: University of California Press, 1991. ISBN 0-520-07015-1 (cl), 0-520-07017-8 (pbk). ‣ Thirteen contributors address issues of women and family in Tokugawa period and modern discourse on family, gender, and work. Argues gender is not biological, rather socially constructed and culturally transmitted. Many insights. [FGN]

13.438 Jane Condon. *A half a step behind: Japanese women in the eighties.* New York: Dodd Mead, 1985. ISBN 0-396-08665-9. ‣ Balanced portrait of contemporary Japanese women in family, work place, and educational system. Highlights women's contributions to Japanese society. Focuses on recent changes affecting women's lives. [FGN]

13.439 Alice H. Cook and Hiroko Hayashi. *Working women in Japan: discrimination, resistance, reform.* New York: ILR Press, 1980. ISBN 0-87546-079-8 (cl), 0-87546-079-8 (pbk). ‣ Critical study of exploitation and discrimination faced by women workers under contemporary employment system in Japan. Documents problem and shows what steps are being taken to resolve it. [FGN]

13.440 Liza Crihfield Dalby. *Geisha.* Berkeley: University of California Press, 1983. ISBN 0-520-04742-7. ‣ Ethnography of Japan's traditional female entertainers in context of their modern existence. Historical and contemporary portrait; intimate, revealing, and entertaining. [FGN]

13.441 Mikiso Hane, ed. and trans. *Reflections on the way to the gallows: voices of Japanese rebel women.* 1988 ed. New York: Pantheon, 1990. ISBN 0-679-72273-4. ‣ Presentation of women radicals in context of modern Japanese development. Includes important statements by such figures as Fukuda Hideko, Kanno Sugako, Kaneko Fumiko, Yamakawa Kikue. [FGN]

13.442 Anne E. Imamura. *Urban Japanese housewives: at home and in the community.* Honolulu: University of Hawaii Press, 1987. ISBN 0-8248-1082-1. ‣ Focuses on daily life, family role, and public involvement of urban, middle-class, Japanese housewife. Sociological approach, particularly informative on effect of housing on behavior and perceptions. [FGN]

13.443 Shidzue Ishimoto. *Facing two ways: the story of my life.* 1935 ed. Stanford, Calif.: Stanford University Press, 1984. ISBN 0-8047-1239-5 (cl), 0-8047-1240-9 (pbk). ‣ Classic autobiography of one of Japan's feminist pioneers and political activists. Excellent introduction to gender issues in early twentieth-century Japan. [FGN]

13.444 Takashi Koyama. *The changing social position of women in Japan.* Paris: UNESCO, 1961. ‣ Examination of transformation of women's roles in modern Japan. Well-documented official presentation of subject. [FGN]

13.445 Joyce C. Lebra, Joy Paulson, and Elizabeth Powers, eds. *Women in changing Japan.* 1976 ed. Stanford, Calif.: Stanford University Press, 1978. ISBN 0-8047-0971-8 (pbk). ‣ Essays on women in various occupational roles, examining Japanese ideals of femininity, work patterns, and social problems such as suicide. Effectively contrasts traditional expectations with modern opportunities. [FGN]

13.446 Takie Sugiyama Lebra. *Japanese women: constraint and fulfillment.* Honolulu: University of Hawaii Press, 1984. ISBN 0-8248-0868-1. ‣ Ethnographic study of fifty-seven Japanese women from various backgrounds and ages in central Japanese city. Challenges stereotypical conceptions of women in home and office. [FGN]

13.447 Susan J. Pharr. *Political women in Japan: the search for a* *place in political life.* Berkeley: University of California Press, 1981. ISBN 0-520-04071-6 (cl), 0-520-04453-3 (pbk). ▸ Explores role that women have come to play in postwar Japanese politics, based on extensive interviews with participants, activists, and supporters. Best on political socialization of contemporary Japanese women. [FGN]

13.448 Dorothy Robins-Mowry. *The hidden sun: women of modern Japan.* Boulder: Westview, 1983. ISBN 0-86531-421-7 (cl), 0-86531-437-3 (pbk). ▸ Survey treating women in pre- and postwar periods. Comprehensive overview, including useful chronology of events involving women. [FGN]

13.449 Sharon L. Sievers. *Flowers in salt: the beginnings of feminist consciousness in modern Japan.* Stanford, Calif.: Stanford University Press, 1983. ISBN 0-8047-1165-8 (cl), 0-8047-1382-0 (pbk). ▸ Pioneering work dealing with women who were outspoken critics of Meiji Japan and who developed gender-based political consciousness as part of Japan's modernization process. Important and insightful. [FGN]

13.450 Robert J. Smith and Ella Lury Wiswell. *The women of Suye Mura.* Chicago: University of Chicago Press, 1982. ISBN 0-226-76344-7 (cl), 0-226-76345-5 (pbk). ▸ Follow-up on Embree's classic account (13.233). Incorporates materials on women from field notes of Wiswell. Perceptive portrait of women in rural Japan. [FGN]

13.451 Etsu Inagaki Sugimoto. *A daughter of the samurai: how a daughter of feudal Japan, living hundreds of years in one generation, became a modern American.* 1928 ed. Rutland, Vt.: Tuttle, 1966. ISBN 0-8048-1655-7. ▸ Insightful autobiography of Japanese woman born in late Tokugawa years who lived through Japan's modernization in Meiji period and eventually came to United States. Vivid account. [FGN]

Minorities and Minority Issues

13.452 John Batchelor. *Ainu life and lore: echoes of a departing race.* 1927 ed. New York: Johnson Reprint, 1971. ▸ Pioneering study of Ainu, indigenous people of northern Japan. Presents history, customs, and community life of Ainu in Hokkaido. Also records many of their oral tales. Available on microfilm from Ann Arbor: University Microfilms International. [FGN]

13.453 George A. De Vos and Hiroshi Wagatsuma. *Japan's invisible race: caste in culture and personality.* 1966 rev. ed. Berkeley: University of California Press, 1972. ▸ Classic examination of issues of untouchability and caste segregation in Japan with reference to *burakumin*, a class of pariahs existing in Japan from ancient times and currently including some two million Japanese. Analyzes Japanese racist ideology. [FGN]

13.454 M. Inez Hilger. *Together with the Ainu: a vanishing people.* Norman: University of Oklahoma Press, 1971. ISBN 0-8061-0950-5. ▸ Study of Ainu based on fieldwork carried out in Japan in 1965–66 by American cultural anthropologist and two Japanese assistants. Excellent ethnography of Ainu culture. [FGN]

13.455 Changsoo Lee and George A. De Vos. *Koreans in Japan: ethnic conflict and accommodation.* Berkeley: University of California Press, 1981. ISBN 0-520-04258-1. ▸ Interdisciplinary examination of Korean minority in Japan focusing on perception and treatment of community by mainstream Japanese. Treats legal, educational, and occupational status of this minority, as well as its historical origins. Raises important questions of race and ethnicity. [FGN]

13.456 Richard H. Mitchell. *The Korean minority in Japan.* Berkeley: University of California Press, 1967. ▸ Historical study of Korean community in Japan tracing its origins and analyzing Korean-Japanese interactions in twentieth century. Examines political involvement of minority community as well as its contributions to Korean nationalism. Balanced historical treatment. [FGN]

13.457 I. Roger Yoshino and Sueo Murakoshi. *The invisible visible minority: Japan's burakumin.* Ōsaka: Buraku Kaiho Kenkyusho, 1977. ▸ Description of *burakumin* life and discrimination suffered by this community. Sympathetic and informative account by leading figure in *burakumin* liberation movement. [FGN]

Education

13.458 Ronald S. Anderson. *Education in Japan: a century of modern development.* Washington, D.C.: United States Department of Health, Education, and Welfare, Office of Education, 1975. ▸ Comprehensive overview of history and development of education in Japan from feudal to modern times. First part historical, second addresses nature of contemporary educational system, kindergarten through high school. [FGN]

13.459 William K. Cummings. *Education and equality in Japan.* Princeton: Princeton University Press, 1980. ISBN 0-691-09385-7 (cl), 0-691-10088-8 (pbk). ▸ Well-documented examination of relationship between Japanese school system, its commitment to egalitarian values, and transformation of Japanese society. [FGN]

13.460 Benjamin C. Duke. *Japan's militant teachers: a history of the left-wing teachers' movement.* Honolulu: University of Hawaii Press, 1973. ISBN 0-8248-0237-3. ▸ Standard history of Japan's most active left-wing labor union, Nikkyoso, which represents majority of nation's public school teachers. Discusses and analyzes past and present confrontations between Nikkyoso and government. [FGN]

13.461 Benjamin C. Duke, ed. *Ten great educators of modern Japan: a Japanese perspective.* Tokyo: University of Tokyo Press, 1989. ISBN 0-86008-442-6. ▸ Examination of development of modern Japanese ideas on education through careers and philosophies of ten of Japan's leading educators. Insights into how values were reflected in educational structures they created. [FGN]

13.462 Hugh L. Keenleyside and A. F. Thomas. *History of Japanese education and present educational system.* Tokyo: Hokuseido Press, 1937. ▸ One of few studies of prewar Japanese educational system available in English. Important source for understanding Japanese education before World War II. [FGN]

13.463 Ellis S. Krauss. *Japanese radicals revisited: student protest in postwar Japan.* Berkeley: University of California Press, 1974. ISBN 0-520-02467-2. ▸ Study of generation of Japanese student-radicals (1950s to 1960s) examining how their beliefs, Marxist ideology, and activism were sustained or altered by jobs, peer pressure, and other social forces following graduation. Rich in information and detail. [FGN]

13.464 Michio Nagai. *Higher education in Japan: its takeoff and crash.* Jerry Dusenbury, trans. Tokyo: University of Tokyo Press, 1971. ISBN 0-86008-067-6. ▸ Frank and revealing exploration of strengths and weaknesses of pre- and postwar Japanese educational system, by former minister of education. Treats both historical roots and contemporary problems. [FGN]

13.465 Herbert Passin. *Society and education in Japan.* 1965 ed. New York: Kodansha, 1982. ISBN 0-87011-554-5. ▸ Classic study of role of education in modernization of Japan. Traces Tokugawa sources, Meiji restructuring based on foreign models, and prewar use of education for indoctrination. Introduces many primary sources. [FGN]

13.466 T. J. Pempel. *Patterns of Japanese policymaking: experiences from higher education.* Boulder: Westview, 1978. ISBN 0-89158-270-3. ▸ Critical analysis and examination of distinct policy-making patterns characteristic of Japanese government's efforts to deal with higher education in postwar years. [FGN]

13.467   Thomas P. Rohlen. *Japan's high schools*. Berkeley: University of California Press, 1983. ISBN 0-520-04801-6 (cl), 0-520-04863-6 (pbk). ‣ Anthropological examination of five secondary schools in Kōbe area. Perceptive and informative examination and assessment of strengths and weaknesses of contemporary Japanese high school system. [FGN]

13.468   Barbara Rose. *Tsuda Umeko and women's education in Japan*. New Haven: Yale University Press, 1992. ISBN 0-300-05177-8. ‣ Tsuda Umeko came to United States as young girl with Iwakura Mission (1871) and eventually returned to Japan to become founder of Ms. Tsuda's College. Balanced evaluation of her career and ideas on female education. [FGN]

13.469   Donald R. Thurston. *Teachers and politics in Japan*. Princeton: Princeton University Press, 1973. ISBN 0-691-07553-0. ‣ Study of Japan teachers union (Nikkyoso). Argues that, while lacking influence at national policy-making level, union has considerable power to affect implementation of policy at prefectural and local levels. [FGN]

SEE ALSO

11.730 E. Patricia Tsurimi. *Japanese colonial education in Taiwan, 1895–1945*.

LAW

13.470   Lawrence Ward Beer. *Freedom of expression in Japan: a study of comparative law, politics, and society*. Tokyo: Kodansha, 1984. ISBN 0-87011-632-0. ‣ Traces development of freedom of expression in Japan from 1860s to 1980s and analyzes how concept came to be interpreted in Japanese legal system. Various legal issues involving personal freedoms explored in social and historical contexts. Important and standard work on topic. [FGN]

13.471   John Braithwaite. *Crime, shame, and reintegration*. Cambridge: Cambridge University Press, 1989. ISBN 0-521-35567-2 (cl), 0-521-35668-7 (pbk). ‣ Important study contributing to Western social science ideas on crime and criminology. Uses theoretical model based on Japanese system of role of community participation in crime control. Emphasizes Japanese concept of reintegrative shaming. [FGN]

13.472   A. Didrick Castberg. *Japanese criminal justice*. New York: Praeger, 1990. ISBN 0-275-93355-5. ‣ Detailed description of formal process of criminal law enforcement in Japan. Covers all aspects from legal education to Japanese prison system. Most complete study currently available in English. [FGN]

13.473   *The constitution and criminal statutes of Japan*. Tokyo: Ministry of Justice, 1960. ‣ Translation of postwar constitution and criminal code of Japan. Important primary source. [FGN]

13.474   J. E. De Becker. *The annotated civil code of Japan*. 1909–10 ed. 4 vols. Tadasu Hayashi, trans. and annotator. Washington, D.C.: University Publications of America, 1979. ISBN 0-89093-215-8. ‣ Translation and annotation of Meiji civil code. Basic source. [FGN]

13.475   Julian Gresser, Koichiro Fujikura, and Akio Morishima. *Environmental law in Japan*. Cambridge, Mass.: MIT Press, 1981. ISBN 0-262-07076-6. ‣ Examines development and implementation of Japan's environmental law in wake of serious pollution problems that emerged in Japan in 1960s and 1970s. Good description of how moral outrage over pollution was transformed into legal remedies. [FGN]

13.476   John Owen Haley. *Authority without power: law and the Japanese paradox*. New York: Oxford University Press, 1991. ISBN 0-19-505583-7. ‣ Important interpretive study of role of law in contemporary Japan arguing that historical separation of power from authority in Japan resulted in system that relies heavily on strengths of informal community controls, backed by custom and consensus, to maintain order. [FGN]

13.477   John Owen Haley, ed. *Law and society in contemporary Japan: American perspectives*. Dubuque: Kendall/Hunt, 1988. ISBN 0-8403-4719-7 (pbk). ‣ Essays by thirteen American scholars and practitioners on Japanese law and role and functioning of Japanese legal system. Important insights into how law can serve as instrument for social change or social control. [FGN]

13.478   Dan Fenno Henderson. *Conciliation and Japanese law: Tokugawa and modern*. 2 vols. Seattle: University of Washington Press, 1964. (Association for Asian Studies monographs and papers, 13.) ‣ Classic examination of role that mediation or conciliation has played in Japanese society and Japanese approach to law and conflict resolution. Traces historical roots and modern expressions of these social values. [FGN]

13.479   Dan Fenno Henderson. *Foreign enterprise in Japan: laws and policies*. Chapel Hill: University of North Carolina Press, 1973. ISBN 0-8078-1210-2. ‣ Detailed examination of legal institutions governing introduction and participation of foreign capital and technology in Japanese economy. Critical study treating legal problems faced by foreign enterprises in Japan. [FGN]

13.480   Nobushige Hozumi. *Ancestor-worship and Japanese law*. 1940 2d rev. ed. New York: Books for Libraries, 1973. ISBN 0-8369-7163-9. ‣ Important interpretation of relationship between traditional family system values and modern legal institutions, by one of Japan's leading Meiji-Taisho legal scholars. [FGN]

13.481   Hiroshi Itoh and Lawrence Ward Beer, comp. and trans. *The constitutional case law of Japan: selected Supreme Court decisions, 1961–70*. Seattle: University of Washington Press, 1978. ISBN 0-295-95571-6. ‣ Translations of thirty-two Supreme Court decisions from 1960s. Follows Maki's earlier study of such cases from occupation through 1960 (13.482). Assesses role of Supreme Court in changing postwar environment. Basic source. [FGN]

13.482   John M. Maki. *Court and constitution in Japan: selected Supreme Court decisions, 1948–60*. Ikeda Masaaki, David C. S. Sissons, and Kurt Steiner, trans. Seattle: University of Washington Press, 1964. ‣ Twenty-six translations of representative Japanese Supreme Court decisions covering postwar period to 1960. Wide range of significant cases with analysis of role of new Supreme Court. [FGN]

13.483   William J. Sebald, trans. *The criminal code of Japan*. Kōbe: Japan Chronicle Press, 1936. ‣ Translation of Meiji criminal code. [FGN]

13.484   Frank K. Upham. *Law and social change in postwar Japan*. Cambridge, Mass.: Harvard University Press, 1978. ISBN 0-674-51786-5. ‣ Study of manner in which political elite of Japan and aggrieved parties use legal system to manage, alleviate, and direct sources of social conflict and change in postwar Japan. Important insights into social role of courts and legal system in Japan. [FGN]

13.485   Arthur Taylor Von Mehren, ed. *Law in Japan: the legal order in a changing society*. Cambridge, Mass.: Harvard University Press, 1964. ‣ Incorporates seventeen essays by Japanese legal scholars on various aspects of Japanese law. Explores changing nature of law in Japan in wake of World War II. Broad overview. [FGN]

ENVIRONMENT

13.486   Allen Hershkowitz and Eugene Salerni. *Garbage management in Japan: leading the way*. New York: INFORM, 1987. ISBN 0-91878-043-8. ‣ Study of Japan's municipal solid waste management system and practices. Sees problems of waste management as largely political and cultural rather than technical. Focuses attention on Japanese successes. [FGN]

13.487   Norie Huddle and Michael R. Reich. *Island of dreams:*

environmental crisis in Japan. Cambridge, Mass.: Schenkman, 1987. ISBN 0-87047-027-2 (cl), 0-87047-028-0 (pbk). ▸ Discussion of severe environmental problems Japan suffered in 1960s and early 1970s, including Yokkaichi asthma, Minamata disease, PCB poisoning, itai itai disease, and red tides. Studies these problems within context of rapid economic growth. [FGN]

13.488 Margaret A. McKean. *Environmental protest and citizen politics in Japan.* Berkeley: University of California Press, 1981. ISBN 0-520-04115-1. ▸ Study of citizens' movements that emerged out of Japan's massive industrial pollution problems of 1960s and 1970s. Not only protested national policy, but also significantly altered local politics. [FGN]

13.489 W. Eugene Smith and Aileen M. Smith. *Minamata, words and photos.* New York: Holt, Rinehart & Winston, 1975. ISBN 0-03-013631-8 (cl), 0-03-013636-9 (pbk). ▸ Examination of disaster that befell small fishing and farming town of Minamata, when its citizens' health was destroyed by methyl-mercury pollution of Chisso Corporation. Severe indictment of major polluter, dramatically illustrated. [FGN]

13.490 Kenneth Strong. *Ox against the storm: a biography of Tanaka Shozo, Japan's conservationist pioneer.* Vancouver: University of British Columbia Press, 1977. ISBN 0-7748-0067-4. ▸ Well-written biography of Tanaka Shozo (1841–1913), Japan's first modern environmental crusader. Led movement against Ashio Copper Mine, major source of pollution that destroyed lives and livelihoods of thousands of Japanese in Meiji period. [FGN]

SCIENCE AND TECHNOLOGY

13.491 Alun M. Anderson and John Sigurdson. *Science and technology in Japan.* 2d ed. New York: Longman, 1991. ISBN 0-582-03684-4. ▸ Comprehensive overview of state of Japanese science and technology in postwar period. Examines Japan's government-industry research projects in field of science and technology. [FGN]

13.492 James R. Bartholomew. *The formation of science in Japan: building a research tradition.* New Haven: Yale University Press, 1989. ISBN 0-300-04261-2. ▸ Pioneering study of formation of Japan's modern scientific tradition. Argues Japan drew on late Tokugawa tradition as well as Western sources to create dynamic synthesis of ideas and highly creative scientific community. [FGN]

13.493 Christopher Freeman. *Technology, policy, and economic performance: lessons from Japan.* London: Pinter, 1987. ISBN 0-86187-928-7. ▸ Study of development of postwar Japanese technology and its relationship to economic growth. Compares long-term trends in national levels of scientific and technological research and development in Japan, United States, and Western Europe. Useful comparative overview. [FGN]

13.494 Yoshio Mikami and David Eugene Smith. *A history of Japanese mathematics.* Chicago: Open Court, 1914. ▸ Traces history and development of traditional mathematics (*wasan*) in Japan and shows how system was replaced by European mathematics after Meiji Restoration. Dated but still important. [FGN]

13.495 Shigeru Nakayama. *Academic and scientific traditions in China, Japan, and the West.* Tokyo: University of Tokyo Press, 1984. ISBN 0-86008-339-X. ▸ Historical examination of scientific traditions of East Asia and West. Focuses on how scientific traditions evolved and how cultural differences pushed them in separate directions. Informative on national differences. [FGN]

13.496 Shigeru Nakayama. *A history of Japanese astronomy: Chinese background and Western impact.* Cambridge, Mass.: Harvard University Press, 1969. ▸ Study of development of Japanese astronomy from its continental roots until late nineteenth century

when it came to be dominated by Western ideas. Describes gradual growth of Western scientific ideas in Japan after sixteenth century. Standard work on topic. [FGN]

13.497 Shigeru Nakayama, David L. Swain, and Eri Yagi, eds. *Science and society in modern Japan: selected historical sources.* Cambridge, Mass.: MIT Press, 1974. ISBN 0-262-14022-5. ▸ Collection of essays by prominent historians of science introducing representative postwar writings on science in Japan. Contains Soichi Oya's "Reflections on the History of Science in Japan" and Eri Yagi's "Statistical Approaches to the History of Science." [FGN]

MEDICINE AND HEALTH

13.498 John Z. Bowers. *Western medical pioneers in feudal Japan.* Baltimore: Johns Hopkins University Press, 1970. ISBN 0-8018-1081-7. ▸ Fascinating study of Western physicians who lived in Japan and taught European medical ideas and practices to Japanese during Tokugawa and modern periods. Considers five physicians who lived and worked on Deshima. [FGN]

13.499 John Z. Bowers. *When the twain meet: the rise of Western medicine in Japan.* Baltimore: Johns Hopkins University Press, 1980. (Henry Sigerist supplements to the *Bulletin of the History of Medicine*, n.s., 5.) ISBN 0-8018-2432-X. ▸ One of few studies addressing importance of German medicine in nineteenth-century Japan. Discusses activities of number of German (and British) physicians who lived and worked in Japan during and after Meiji Restoration. [FGN]

13.500 Margaret M. Lock. *East Asian medicine in urban Japan: varieties of medical experience.* Berkeley: University of California Press, 1980. ISBN 0-520-03820-7. ▸ Rich, detailed study of role and importance of East Asian medicine (*kanpo*) in modern Japanese cities. Studies popularity of herb medicines, acupuncture, moxibustion, and massage among city dwellers. Essentially an ethnography. [FGN]

13.501 Edward Norbeck and Margaret M. Lock, eds. *Health, illness, and medical care in Japan: cultural and social dimensions.* Honolulu: University of Hawaii Press, 1987. ISBN 0-8428-1102-X. ▸ Study addressing Japanese social, political, and cultural elements that influenced Japanese conception of health, illness, and medical care. Six essays focus on role cultural values play in illness and health care. [FGN]

13.502 Emiko Ohnuki-Tierney. *Illness and culture in contemporary Japan: an anthropological view.* Cambridge: Cambridge University Press, 1984. ISBN 0-521-25982-7 (cl), 0-521-27786-8 (pbk). ▸ Examination of cultural meaning of health and health care in Japan. Explores Japanese attitudes toward illness and its causes, death, the body, and Eastern, as well as Western, medical practices. Important, provocative insights. [FGN]

13.503 David K. Reynolds. *The quiet therapies: Japanese pathways to personal growth.* Honolulu: University of Hawaii Press, 1980. ISBN 0-8248-0690-5. ▸ Introduction to five clinically successful Japanese psychotherapies, including Morita therapy, *naikan* (introspection therapy), *shadan* (isolation therapy), *seiza* (quiet sitting therapy), and *zen* (meditation therapy). [FGN]

RELIGION

General Studies

13.504 Masaharu Anesaki. *History of Japanese religion with special reference to the social and moral life of the nation.* 1930 ed. Rutland, Vt.: Tuttle, 1963. ▸ Classic treatment of religion in Japan. Addresses Buddhism, Shintō, and later additions of Confucianism and modern religions such as Christianity. Now somewhat dated. [FGN]

13.505 Robert S. Ellwood and Richard Pilgrim. *Japanese reli-*

gion: a cultural perspective. Englewood Cliffs, N.J.: Prentice-Hall, 1985. ISBN 0-13-509282-5 (pbk). ‣ Introductory work focusing both on history of Japanese religion and on role of religion in contemporary Japanese life. [FGN]

13.506 Hideo Kishimoto. *Japanese religion in the Meiji era.* John F. Howes, trans. Tokyo: Obunsha, 1956. (Centenary Cultural Council series: Japanese culture in the Meiji era, 2.) ‣ Older but still useful analysis of historical and religious context from which modern Japanese religious positions developed. Examines role of government in molding and controlling religious movements. [FGN]

13.507 Joseph M. Kitagawa. *Religion in Japanese history.* 1966 ed. New York: Columbia University Press, 1990. ISBN 0-231-02838-5. ‣ Excellent overview by major figure in the field. Historical and structural analysis of role of religion in Japanese history. Traces history of religion in Japan from early Shintō to postwar new religions. [FGN]

13.508 William P. Lebra. *Okinawan religion: belief, ritual, and social structure.* Honolulu: University of Hawaii Press, 1966. ‣ Rare examination of Okinawan religion. Essentially study of folk religious ideas central to Okinawa that predate and transcend later religions such as Buddhism and Shintō. [FGN]

13.509 Shigeyoshi Murakami. *Japanese religion in the modern century.* H. Byron Earhart, trans. Tokyo: University of Tokyo Press, 1980. ISBN 0-86008-260-1. ‣ Religious history of modern Japan. Traces interrelationship between religion and social, economic, and political organizations. Critical of government's efforts to control religious freedoms before World War II. [FGN]

13.510 Edward Norbeck. *Religion and society in modern Japan: continuity and change.* Houston: Tourmaline, 1970. ‣ Cultural anthropologist's sensitive assessment of role and function of religion in modern Japan. Addresses major changes that have had impact on Japanese religious perceptions and movements since 1868. [FGN]

13.511 Ian Reader. *Religion in contemporary Japan.* Honolulu: University of Hawaii Press, 1991. ISBN 0-8248-1353-7 (cl), 0-8248-1354-5 (pbk). ‣ One of best available discussions on religion in modern Japanese life. Follows historical sources and traces how religion works within social context of contemporary society. [FGN]

SEE ALSO
  12.10 H. Byron Earhart. *Japanese religion.*

Buddhism

13.512 Masao Abe. *Zen and Western thought.* 1985 ed. William R. LaFleur, ed. Honolulu: University of Hawaii Press, 1989. ISBN 0-8248-0952-1 (cl, 1985), 0-8248-1214-X (pbk). ‣ Sixteen essays by Abe on various aspects of Zen Buddhism. Discusses meaning and nature of Zen and its interrelationship with Western philosophical ideas. [FGN]

13.513 Heinrich Dumoulin. *Japan.* Vol. 2 of *Zen Buddhism: a history.* James W. Heisig and Paul Knitter. New York: Macmillan, 1988–90. 2 vols. ISBN 0-02-908250-1 (v. 2, cl), 0-02-908240-4 (v. 2, pbk). ‣ Standard work on historical development of Zen Buddhism in Japan. Definitive study of role of Zen in Japanese culture and how Zen ideas have molded Japanese life and art. [FGN]

13.514 Charles Eliot. *Japanese Buddhism.* 1935 ed. London: Routledge & Kegan Paul, 1969. ‣ Still standard work on Buddhism in Japan. Covers historical development of Buddhist religion, its sects, teachings, and organizations. Useful historical source for contemporary Buddhism in Japan. [FGN]

13.515 James Edward Ketelaar. *Of heretics and martyrs in Meiji Japan: Buddhism and its persecution.* Princeton: Princeton Uni-

versity Press, 1990. ISBN 0-691-05599-8. ‣ Study of how Buddhism became target of severe persecution in early Meiji years. Explains it survived by reconstituting itself as coherent belief system and bastion of Japanese values. [FGN]

13.516 Stuart D. B. Picken. *Buddhism, Japan's cultural identity.* Tokyo and New York: Kodansha, 1982. ISBN 0-87011-499-9. ‣ Popular and lavishly illustrated work showing how Buddhism developed and merged with Shintō to play role of guarantor of social continuity and identity of Japanese people. Treats contemporary as well as traditional Japan. [FGN]

13.517 Daisetz T. Suzuki. *The essentials of Zen Buddhism: selected from the writings of Daisetz T. Suzuki.* 1962 ed. Bernard Phillips, ed. Westport, Conn.: Greenwood, 1973. ISBN 0-8371-6649-7. ‣ Collection of Suzuki's articles and essays on Zen Buddhism arranged to serve as introduction to subject. Brings together some of most important writings of leading exponent of Zen to West in twentieth century. [FGN]

13.518 Daisetz T. Suzuki. *Zen and Japanese culture.* 1959 rev. 2d ed. Princeton: Princeton University Press, 1970. ISBN 0-691-09848-2 (cl), 0-691-01770-0 (pbk). ‣ Republication of important essays on role of Zen in cultural life and art of Japanese people. Also addresses role of Zen as shaper of moral values and character. [FGN]

13.519 Notto R. Thelle. *Buddhism and Christianity in Japan: from conflict to dialogue, 1854–1899.* Honolulu: University of Hawaii Press, 1987. ISBN 0-8248-1006-6. ‣ Exploration of confrontation of Buddhism and Christianity within broad cultural and sociopolitical context. Demonstrates influence of social and ideological upheavals of early Meiji Japan on both religions. [FGN]

Shintō

13.520 Wilhelmus H. M. Creemers. *Shrine Shinto after World War II.* Leiden: Brill, 1968. ‣ History of termination during occupation of government support for Japan's 100,000 Shintō shrines. Also, how these shrines reorganized and eventually sought to regain some of their prewar social, political, and economic status. Important for understanding occupation's religious policies. [FGN]

13.521 Wilbur Fridell. *Japanese shrine mergers, 1906–1912: state Shinto moves to the grassroots.* Tokyo: Sophia University Press, 1973. ‣ Transition from Shintō as folk cult to Shintō as state religion studied from institutional perspective. Important for understanding emergence of state orthodoxy in late Meiji Japan. [FGN]

13.522 Helen Hardacre. *Shinto and the state, 1868–1988.* Princeton: Princeton University Press, 1991. ISBN 0-691-07348-1 (cl), 0-691-02052-3 (pbk). ‣ Explores state's involvement in and manipulation of Shintō from Meiji Restoration to present. Raises fundamental questions about state sponsorship of religion. Best recent study on Shintō religion. [FGN]

13.523 Jean Herbert. *Shinto: at the fountain-head of Japan.* New York: Stein & Day, 1967. ‣ Massive, detailed study of Shintō based on interview data derived between 1935 and 1964. Covers its history, metaphysics, ethics, spiritual discipline, aesthetics, and rituals. Shintō mythology thoroughly covered. [FGN]

13.524 Daniel C. Holtom. *Modern Japan and Shinto nationalism: a study of present-day trends in Japanese religions.* 1947 rev. ed. New York: Paragon Book Reprint, 1963. ‣ Older but still important examination of role played by Shintō as state religion in wake of Meiji Restoration and relationship between it and prewar Japanese nationalism. Examines altered position of Shintō in immediate postwar years. Counterposes Shintō particularism with universalism of teachings such as Christianity and Buddhism. [FGN]

13.525 Stuart D. B. Picken. *Shinto, Japan's spiritual roots.*

Tokyo: Kodansha, 1980. ISBN 0-87011-410-7. ▸ Survey of Shintō; extensively illustrated. Covers Shintō mythology, community festivals, and shrines as well as rituals, festivals, and Shintō's role in cultural and aesthetic life of Japan. Shintō's role in Japan's most popular sport, Sumo wrestling, also documented. [FGN]

Christianity

13.526 Ernest E. Best. *Christian faith and cultural crisis, the Japanese case.* Leiden: Brill, 1966. ▸ Excellent discussion of effects of environment of cultural confrontation and rapid social change on Christianity in modern Japan. Particularly raises issues of acculturation and political, economic, and social pressures that molded this foreign teaching. [FGN]

13.527 Carlo Caldarola. *Christianity, the Japanese way.* Leiden: Brill, 1979. ISBN 90-04-05842-7. ▸ Examines Japanese response to Christianity in modern period by exploring development of two distinct Japanese Christian movements: Mukyokai or non-church Christianity, and Makuya or tabernacle sect. [FGN]

13.528 Otis Cary. *A history of Christianity in Japan: Roman Catholic, Greek Orthodox, and Protestant missions.* 1909 ed. Rutland, Vt.: Tuttle, 1976. ISBN 0-8048-1177-6. ▸ Classic work on Roman Catholic, Protestant, and Greek Orthodox Christianity in Japan. Dated but still invaluable for its detail and thoroughness. [FGN]

13.529 Richard Henry Drummond. *A history of Christianity in Japan.* Grand Rapids, Mich.: Eerdmans, 1971. ▸ Comprehensive survey of Christianity in Japan covering Roman Catholic, Protestant, and Russian Orthodox churches. Traces Christian movement in Japan from sixteenth century to contemporary times. [FGN]

13.530 Charles W. Iglehart. *A century of Protestant Christianity in Japan.* Tokyo: Tuttle, 1959. ▸ Survey of Protestant Christianity in modern Japan. [FGN]

13.531 Stuart D. B. Picken. *Christianity and Japan: meeting, conflict, hope.* Tokyo: Kodansha, 1983. ISBN 0-87011-589-8. ▸ Descriptive account of Christianity in Japan highlighting Christians' contributions to Japanese society and culture. Evaluates successes and failures of church over centuries. Good general overview. [FGN]

13.532 Irwin Scheiner. *Christian converts and social protest in Meiji Japan.* Berkeley: University of California Press, 1970. ISBN 0-520-01585-1. ▸ Significant study of relationship between déclassé samurai and emergence of Christianity in Meiji Japan. Argues many Japanese Christian leaders attempted to use Christianity to regain lost status. [FGN]

13.533 Kanzo Uchimura. *The complete works of Kanzo Uchimura.* Vol. 1: *How I became a Christian: out of my diary.* Vol. 2: *Representative men of Japan.* Taijiro Yamamoto and Yoichi Muto, eds. Tokyo: Kyobunkan, 1971–73. ▸ First two volumes of seven-volume collection of works of one of Japan's most important Christian leaders. Volume 1 contains autobiography. Volume 2 contains short biographies of important men; especially interesting are portraits of Saigo Takamori, Uesugi Yozan, Ninomiya Sontoku, Nakai Toju, and Nichiren. [FGN]

Postwar New Religions

13.534 Winston Davis. *Dojo: magic and exorcism in modern Japan.* Stanford, Calif.: Stanford University Press, 1980. ISBN 0-8047-1053-8. ▸ Revealing sociological examination of Sukyo Mahikari, Japanese new religion founded in 1960, which uses magical amulets and ritual to exorcise spirits possessing its members. [FGN]

13.535 Stewart Guthrie. *A Japanese new religion: Rissho Kosei-*

kai in a mountain hamlet. Ann Arbor: University of Michigan, Center for Japanese Studies, 1988. ISBN 0-939512-33-5 (cl), 0-939512-34-3 (pbk). ▸ Study of Risshō Kōseikai, Society for Virtuous Human Relations, which split from Nichiren Buddhism and became second largest new religion in Japan. Interesting ethnography of this sect in village in Gumma prefecture. [FGN]

13.536 Helen Hardacre. *Lay Buddhism in contemporary Japan: Reiyukai Kyodan.* Princeton: Princeton University Press, 1984. ISBN 0-691-07284-1. ▸ Important study of lay Buddhist movement, Reiyūkai Kyōdan (Society of Friends of the Spirits), which emerged as one of most dynamic new religions of postwar Japan. Traces history of sect from 1920s to 1980s. [FGN]

13.537 H. Neill McFarland. *The rush hour of the gods: a study of new religious movements in Japan.* 1967 ed. New York: Harper & Row, 1970. ▸ Examines religious ferment of postwar years that spawned numerous new religions. Identifies chief characteristics and social functions of these sects and analyzes environment that produced them. Best work on broad spectrum of new religions. [FGN]

13.538 Daniel Metraux. *The history and theology of Soka Gakkai: a Japanese new religion.* Lewiston, N.Y.: Mellen, 1988. ISBN 0-88946-055-8. ▸ Thorough study of leading postwar new religion, Sōka Gakkai, Nichiren Buddhist–based order that has become powerful not only in religious arena but also in politics. Examines theology as well as social organization. [FGN]

13.539 Harry Thomsen. *The new religions of Japan.* 1963 ed. Westport, Conn.: Greenwood, 1978. ISBN 0-8371-9878-X. ▸ Treats fourteen of most influential new religions of Japan. Gives history, founding, worship practices, and doctrines of these religions. Good survey of topic. [FGN]

13.540 James W. White. *The Sokagakkai and mass society.* Stanford, Calif.: Stanford University Press, 1970. ISBN 0-8047-0728-6. ▸ Political scientist's analysis of membership and ideology of Sōka Gakkai, Japan's most militant new postwar religion. Attempts to apply Kornhauser's theory of mass society (13.4) to emergence of this religious and political movement. [FGN]

Folk Religion

13.541 Carmen Blacker. *The catalpa bow: a study of shamanistic practices in Japan.* 1975 ed. London: Allen & Unwin, 1986. ISBN 0-04-398008-2. ▸ Excellent study of shamans and shamanistic beliefs and practices in Japan. Treats both historical sources of shamanistic beliefs and their contemporary manifestations in folk religions in Japan. [FGN]

13.542 Geoffrey Bownas. *Japanese rainmaking and other folk practices.* London: Allen & Unwin, 1963. ▸ Informative study of historical sources and current expressions of number of Japanese folk practices and festivals. These include New Year's and Bon celebrations; Gion festival; births, marriages, deaths; rainmaking; and taboos. [FGN]

13.543 Ichiro Hori. *Folk religion in Japan: continuity and change.* 1968 ed. Joseph M. Kitagawa and Alan L. Miller, eds. Chicago: University of Chicago Press, 1983. ISBN 0-226-35335-4. ▸ Six lectures delivered at University of Chicago addressing chief characteristics of Japanese folk religion. Main contribution lies in tracing folk religious components of Buddhism and Shintō. [FGN]

13.544 Robert J. Smith. *Ancestor worship in contemporary Japan.* Stanford, Calif.: Stanford University Press, 1974. ISBN 0-8047-0873-8. ▸ Modern anthropological analysis of ancestor worship in Japan. After tracing historical roots of concept, seeks to determine role in modern social, religious, and political life. Excellent overview of important topic. [FGN]

PHILOSOPHY

13.545 Frederick Franck, ed. *The Buddha eye: an anthology of the Kyoto school.* 1982 ed. New York: Crossroad, 1991. ISBN 0-8245-1071-2. ▸ Seventeen essays by five members of important Kyoto school of philosophy founded by Nishida Kitaro, Japan's leading twentieth-century philosopher. Study of close linkage between Kyoto school ideas and Mahayana Buddhism. Important source. [FGN]

13.546 Charles A. Moore, ed. *The Japanese mind: essentials of Japanese philosophy and culture.* Honolulu: East-West Center Press, 1967. ▸ Essays by scholars and thinkers dealing with philosophical and religious attitudes of Japanese people. Attempts to establish how Japanese have adapted philosophical perspectives introduced from outside world. Informative anthology. [FGN]

13.547 Hajime Nakamura. *A history of the development of Japanese thought, from 592–1868.* 2d ed. 2 vols. Tokyo: Kokusai Bunka Shinkokai, 1969. ▸ Leading scholar and philosopher of twentieth-century Japan rethinks Japanese philosophical tradition. Addresses not only individual thinkers and movements but also problem of philosophical thought in Japan. Important presentation of Japanese perspective. [FGN]

13.548 Kitaro Nishida. *Fundamental problems of philosophy: the world of action and the dialectical world.* David A. Dilworth, trans. Tokyo: Sophia University Press, 1970. ▸ Translation of Nishida's important *Tetsugaku no konpon mondai*, written 1933–34. [FGN]

13.549 Keiji Nishitani. *Religion and nothingness.* 1982 ed. Jan van Bragt, trans. Berkeley: University of California Press, 1983. ISBN 0-520-04329-4 (cl, 1982), 0-520-04946-2 (pbk). ▸ Leading member of Kyoto school addresses fundamental meaning of existence, arguing man must come to understand life from perspective of two fundamental Mahayana concepts, absolute nothingness and emptiness. [FGN]

13.550 Gino K. Piovesana. *Contemporary Japanese philosophical thought.* New York: St. John's University Press, 1969. ▸ Revision of earlier *Recent Japanese Philosophical Thought, 1862–1962: A Survey.* Summarizes Japanese philosophical thought over modern century. Covers variety of schools from empiricism to neo-Kantianism. Native Japanese philosophies developed by Nishida Kitaro, Watsuji Tetsuro, Tanabe Hamime, and others also explored. Good overview. [FGN]

13.551 Warren W. Smith. *Confucianism in modern Japan: a study of conservatism in Japanese intellectual history.* 1959 2d ed. Tokyo: Hokuseido Press, 1973. ▸ Older but still-useful study of role of Confucian thought in modern Japan and role Confucian ideas played in establishing Japanese political, social, and economic institutions since Meiji Restoration. Argues for direct ties between Confucianism and Japan's conservative values. [FGN]

LITERATURE

13.552 Robert Lyons Danly. *In the shade of spring leaves: the life and writings of Higuchi Ichiyo, a woman of letters in Meiji Japan.* New Haven: Yale University Press, 1981. ISBN 0-300-02614-5. ▸ Biography of Japan's first modern woman writer. Includes translations of nine of her most important stories. Fine portrait of Meiji writer and sensibilities that emerged in her effort to deal with modern Japan. [FGN]

13.553 Takeo Doi. *The psychological world of Natsume Soseki.* William Jefferson Tyler, trans. Cambridge, Mass.: Harvard University, East Asian Research Center, 1976. (Harvard East Asian monographs, 68.) ISBN 0-674-72116-0. ▸ Revealing examination of inner world of Natsume Soseki and his characters by leading Japanese psychiatrist. Treats ten of Soseki's major novels. [FGN]

13.554 Edward Fowler. *The rhetoric of confession: shishosetsu in early twentieth-century Japanese fiction.* Berkeley: University of California Press, 1988. ISBN 0-520-06064-4. ▸ Critical, historical analysis of development of I-novel, form of autobiographical fiction popular in modern Japan. Shows Japanese roots and foreign influences that shaped this form of literature. [FGN]

13.555 International House of Japan Library, comp. *Modern Japanese literature in translation: a bibliography.* Tokyo: Kodansha, 1979. ISBN 0-87011-339-9. ▸ Lists of some 9,000 works by 1,500 Japanese authors translated into Western languages. Useful and comprehensive. [FGN]

13.556 Shuichi Kato. *A history of Japanese literature.* Vol. 3: *The modern years.* Don Sanderson, trans. New York: Kodansha, 1983. ▸ Important Japanese scholar's evaluation of writings of many figures who contributed to development of modern Japanese literature and thought. Analyzes response to Western ideas and literary movements. [FGN]

13.557 Dennis Keene. *Yokomitsu Riichi: modernist.* New York: Columbia University Press, 1980. ISBN 0-231-04938-2. ▸ Critical evaluation of Japan's leading modernist writer of interwar years. Analysis of Yokomitsu's work documenting impact of European literary ideas on Japanese modernist movement. [FGN]

13.558 Donald Keene. *Dawn to the West: Japanese literature of the modern era.* Vol. 1: *Fiction.* Vol. 2: *Poetry, drama, criticism.* New York: Holt, Rinehart & Winston, 1984. ISBN 0-03-062814-8 (v. 1), 0-03-062816-4 (v. 2). ▸ Distinguished scholar's comprehensive history of modern Japanese literature. Covers all aspects of Japan's modern literary tradition. Essential for students of twentieth-century thought and literature. [FGN]

13.559 Arthur G. Kimball. *Crisis in identity and contemporary Japanese novels.* Rutland, Vt.: Tuttle, 1973. ISBN 0-8048-1090-7. ▸ Exploration and analysis of contemporary Japanese preoccupation with problem of identity, which finds expression in many postwar novels, through series of specific case studies. Raises important issues about Japanese postwar identity. [FGN]

13.560 Phyllis I. Lyons. *The saga of Dazai Osamu: a critical study with translations.* Stanford, Calif.: Stanford University Press, 1985. ISBN 0-8047-1197-6. ▸ Careful psychological examination of one of modern Japan's most intensely personal writers. Explores childhood and development of Dazai as writer and analyzes how his autobiographical novels reflect his troubled psyche. [FGN]

13.561 Edwin McClellan. *Two Japanese novelists: Soseki and Toson.* 1969 ed. Chicago: University of Chicago Press, 1987. ▸ Biographical sketches of two early twentieth-century Japanese writers and examination of role played by each in development of Meiji-Taisho literature and emergence of popular I-novel, form of fictionalized autobiography. [FGN]

13.562 Masao Miyoshi. *Accomplices of silence: the modern Japanese novel.* Berkeley: University of California Press, 1974. ISBN 0-520-02540-7. ▸ Study raising fundamental questions about Japanese language and its ability to sustain modern Western narrative tradition associated with the novel. Shows how Japanese writers wrestled with this problem. [FGN]

13.563 James A. O'Brien. *Dazai Osamu.* Boston: Twayne, 1975. ISBN 0-8057-2664-0. ▸ Literary biography of Dazai Osamu (1909–48) addressing his perceptions of self and troubled and passionate forms in which his characters express these perceptions. Includes critical discussion of major works. [FGN]

13.564 Irena Powell. *Writers and society in modern Japan.* London: Macmillan, 1983. ISBN 0-333-27593-4. ▸ Well-documented examination of rise and fall of *bundan* (literary establishment) of prewar Japan. Links writings of members of this elite circle to social context and literary network that produced them. [FGN]

13.565 J. Thomas Rimer. *Mori Ogai.* Boston: Twayne, 1975. ISBN 0-8057-2636-5. ▸ Excellent study of life and literature of one of Meiji Japan's leading writers, critics, and translators. Focuses on Ogai's literary career; analyzes his major works. See also Rimer's other studies of Ogai's works. [FGN]

13.566 Marleigh Grayer Ryan. *The development of realism in the fiction of Tsubouchi Shoyo.* Seattle: University of Washington Press, 1975. (Publications on Asia of the Institute for Comparative Foreign Area Studies, 26.) ISBN 0-295-95382-9. ▸ Important study of emergence of realism in late nineteenth-century Japanese fiction through writings of Tsubouchi Shoyo, pioneer in introducing Western literary techniques in 1880s. [FGN]

13.567 Marleigh Grayer Ryan, ed. and trans. *Japan's first modern novel: "Ukigumo" of Futabatei Shimei.* 1967 ed. Ann Arbor, Mich.: University of Michigan, Center for Japanese Studies, 1990. ISBN 0-939512-44-0. ▸ Excellent analysis and translation of *Ukigumo* (Drifting Cloud), published in late 1880s and often regarded as Japan's first modern novel. [FGN]

13.568 William F. Sibley. *The Shiga hero.* Chicago: University of Chicago Press, 1979. ISBN 0-226-75620-3. ▸ Important analytical study of central character of Shiga Naoya's fiction. Author reconstructs and compares Shiga's life to life of fictional hero and explores inner psyche of Japan's leading writer of I-novel (fictional autobiography). [FGN]

13.569 Janet A. Walker. *The Japanese novel of the Meiji period and the ideal of individualism.* Princeton: Princeton University Press, 1979. ISBN 0-691-06400-8. ▸ Well-researched study of contribution that Western idea of individualism made toward development of novel in Meiji period. Shows how Meiji writers such as Kitamura Tokoku and Shimazaki Toson emphasized new role for individual. [FGN]

ART AND ARCHITECTURE

13.570 Botand Bognar. *Contemporary Japanese architecture: its development and challenge.* New York: Van Nostrand Reinhold, 1985. ISBN 0-442-21174-0. ▸ Traces dynamic development of postwar Japanese architecture to its traditional roots. Good in describing synthesis between Japanese and Western values. [FGN]

13.571 Philip Drew. *The architecture of Arata Isozaki.* New York: Harper & Row, 1982. ISBN 0-06-431550-9. ▸ Thorough presentation of work of Japan's leading contemporary architect. Analyzes Isozaki's style and attempts to place it within context of modern and postmodern ideas. [FGN]

13.572 Walter Gropius and Kenzo Tange. *Katsura: tradition and creation in Japanese architecture.* Charles S. Terry, trans. New Haven: Yale University Press, 1960. ▸ Two of this century's leading architects consider role and influence of Katsura Imperial Villa as wellspring of architectural ideas and source of contemporary considerations of space and form. [FGN]

13.573 Minoru Harada. *Meiji Western painting.* Akiko Murakata, trans. New York: Weatherhill, 1974. ISBN 0-8348-2708-5 (cl), 0-8348-2709-3 (pbk). ▸ Useful study of development of Western-style painting in Meiji period. Focuses on evolution of oil painting under foreign tutelage and as it was developed by Japanese painters who studied this new medium at home and abroad. [FGN]

13.574 Thomas R. H. Havens. *Artist and patron in postwar Japan: dance, music, theater, and the visual arts, 1955–1980.* Princeton: Princeton University Press, 1982. ISBN 0-691-05363-4. ▸ Revealing exploration of *iemoto* (patronage system) in various fields, including visual and performance arts. Examines how traditional social structure has been used to undergird contemporary arts in Japan. [FGN]

13.575 Japan Photographers Association. *A century of Japanese photography.* New York: Pantheon, 1980. ISBN 0-394-51232-4. ▸ Excellent history of photography in late nineteenth- and twentieth-century Japan. [FGN]

13.576 Michiaki Kawakita. *Modern currents in Japanese art.* Charles S. Terry, trans. New York: Weatherhill, 1974. ISBN 0-8348-1028-X. ▸ History and development of modern Japanese art from Meiji Restoration to 1950s. Examines Tokugawa antecedents, Nihonga school (style of painting) advocated by Okakura Tenshin, and modern Western schools and their impact in Japan. Good overview. [FGN]

13.577 Udo Kultermann, ed. *Kenzo Tange, 1946–1969: architecture and urban design.* New York: Praeger, 1970. ▸ International edition of work of one of Japan's greatest twentieth-century architects. Illustrates and analyzes Tange's contributions to modern architecture. Fine portrait. [FGN]

13.578 David Kung. *The contemporary artist in Japan.* Honolulu: East-West Center Press, 1966. ▸ Survey of contemporary artists in Japan including painters, sculptors, and printmakers. Focuses on abstract and international school painters working in postwar Japan. [FGN]

13.579 Julia Meech-Pekarik. *The world of the Meiji print: impressions of a new civilization.* New York: Weatherhill, 1986. ISBN 0-8348-0209-0. ▸ Fascinating portrayal of "civilization and enlightenment" prints that marked early Meiji period. Emphasizing new realism, prints focused on urban and Western subjects using bright colors. [FGN]

13.580 Hugo Munsterberg. *The art of modern Japan: from the Meiji restoration to the Meiji centennial, 1868–1968.* New York: Hacker, 1978. ISBN 0-87817-187-8. ▸ Survey of modern Japanese art covering painting, printmaking, sculpture, architecture, and crafts during modern period. Traces Japanese traditional and modern Western interrelationships. [FGN]

13.581 Robert Treat Paine and Alexander Coburn Soper. *The art and architecture of Japan.* 1981, 3d ed. Baltimore: Penguin, 1985. ISBN 0-14-056108-0. ▸ Still most thorough and comprehensive work on history of Japanese art and architecture. Treats both traditional and modern periods. Extensively illustrated. [FGN]

13.582 Oliver Statler. *Modern Japanese prints: an art reborn.* 1956 ed. Rutland, Vt.: Tuttle, 1980. ISBN 0-8048-0406-0. ▸ Looks at twentieth-century Japanese printmakers exploring how contemporary artists have used and adapted print tradition to new ends. Useful insights on Japanese art in transition. [FGN]

13.583 David B. Stewart. *The making of a modern Japanese architecture: 1868 to the present.* Tokyo: Kodansha, 1987. ISBN 0-87011-844-7. ▸ Thorough examination of development of modern Japanese architecture from Victorian-influenced Meiji period to postmodernism of 1980s. [FGN]

13.584 Shuji Takashina and J. Thomas Rimer. *Paris in Japan: the Japanese encounter with European painting.* St. Louis: Washington University Press, 1987. ISBN 0-936316-11-X (pbk). ▸ Essays accompanying exhibition catalog, offering first comprehensive overview of influence that French, especially Parisian, painters had on development of Western-style painting in Japan. [FGN]

13.585 Clark Worswick, ed. *Japan: photographs, 1854–1905.* New York: Knopf, 1979. ISBN 0-394-50836-X. ▸ Photographs by some of major photographers active in Japan in late nineteenth century. Includes work of Felice Beato, Kusakabe Kinbei, and Baron Raimund von Stillfried. Brief history accompanies illustrations. [FGN]

MUSIC

13.586 Eta Harich-Schneider. *A history of Japanese music.* London: Oxford University Press, 1973. ISBN 0-19-316203-2. ▸ Thorough, encyclopedic survey of history of music in Japan. Traces development of music over Japan's historic ages and includes development of Western-based music in modern age. Includes three 33 1/3 rpm phonodiscs. [FGN]

13.587 William P. Malm. *Japanese music and musical instruments.*

1959 ed. Rutland, Vt.: Tuttle, 1968. ▸ Most authoritative scholarly survey of history of Japanese music and construction of Japanese musical instruments. Standard work for all interested in Japanese instruments and traditional music. [FGN]

JOHN B. DUNCAN AND YŎNG-HO CH´OE

Korea

As a nation and a state, Korea has one of the world's longest histories. References to Korean states in Manchuria and the northern part of the Korean peninsula appear in Chinese sources in the final centuries BCE, and Korea fully emerged on the stage of history with the rise of the Three Kingdoms of Koguryŏ, Paekche, and Silla in the early centuries CE. The Korean people have lived under one government since Silla's unification of the Korean peninsula in 668 CE, except for a brief hiatus at the beginning of the tenth century and the tragic division of the country since 1945. The Korean people's historical experience is of vital importance for our understanding of East Asia, but there are also aspects of Korean history that are of universal historical interest, including the early development of a bureaucratic political system and the long Korean experience in importing and adapting foreign cultural influences.

The study of Korean history is a comparatively new field in Western academic circles. There was a spate of English-language books produced mostly by Western missionaries around the turn of the century and occasional books in the 1920s and 1930s, but serious studies of Korea's past did not begin to appear in Western languages until the 1940s and it was not until the 1970s that significant numbers of book-length studies on Korea began to be published in the West. The growth of the field in recent years has been encouraging, especially with regard to scholarship on modern Korea.

Western historical scholarship on traditional Korea has inquired into a comparatively broad spectrum. We have a number of significant studies in such areas as politics, foreign relations, social history, the fine arts, Buddhism, and Neo-Confucianism, although virtually nothing has been published in English on premodern economic history. Such overall diversity notwithstanding, Western-language historical scholarship on traditional Korea is very thin. Fewer than twenty-five quality book-length English-language monographs have been published on premodern Korean history. For that reason, we have chosen to supplement the subsection on traditional Korea by selecting a number of articles from scholarly journals that treat exceptionally important issues or fill particularly salient gaps.

Despite Korea's rich tradition of Confucian historiography, early modern study of Korea's history was dominated by Japanese historians of the colonial era, who tended to portray Korea as a historically stagnant and backward society. Post-1945 Korean-language historical scholarship has, as a consequence, striven to rebut the stagnation thesis and depict Korean history as a story of progressive internal development (*nae-jaejŏk palchŏn*) that would, had it not been interrupted by foreign aggression, have led to the rise of a modern industrial society. Western historians, while rejecting the stagnation thesis, have generally been more cautious of the internal development theory and have focused on other issues and approaches to explain the dynamics that sustained traditional Korean society.

Studies on traditional Korean political history have emphasized the domination of the relatively weak kingship throughout the premodern era by powerful social and political elites, or have focused on the influence of Confucian ideology on government and politics. Most studies on Confucian politics stress how elites used Confucian dogma against the throne, but there is also an alternative view arguing that the king, in at least one instance, was able to use Confucian ideas to strengthen the royal prerogative. Scholarship on premodern foreign relations is limited and centers on Korea's position in the traditional East Asian international order and its effect on internal politics and society or on early Korean-Japanese relations, especially the controversy over whether Japan exercised control over part of southern Korea in ancient times.

Significant themes in English-language studies of Korean social history focus on social mobility in the Chosŏn dynasty (1392–1910). One debate centers around the question of commoners rising to hold official status through the examination system in the early years of the dynasty; another focuses on the issue of social mobility in the countryside during the later years of the dynasty. Another important theme, prominent in Western scholarship, is the influence of Confucianism on Chosŏn dynasty Korean society in relation to both the formation and maintenance of late traditional elites and the status of women in family and society.

Works on religion and thought in the early traditional period, from the rise of the Three Kingdoms in the third and fourth centuries CE to the fall of the Koryŏ dynasty in 1392, deal primarily with Buddhism (both the influence of Buddhism on Korean society and the development of Buddhist doctrine in Korea) and emphasize ecumenical tendencies in Korean Buddhist thought. Studies on religion and thought during the Chosŏn dynasty focus largely on the sophisticated metaphysical discourse of the mid-Chosŏn or on the Korean reaction to Western Catholicism in the seventeenth and eighteenth centuries. There are also a number of works dealing with premodern Korean achievements in science and the fine arts, most notably ceramics.

Modern Korea has attracted the attention of many historians and historically oriented scholars in recent decades in part because of the high drama of the past century. As a result, there are a number of fine studies on such topics as the opening of Korea to the outside world and its colonization by Japan, the country's division into northern and southern regimes after 1945, the Korean War, and the recent, rapid economic growth of South Korea. Other, less dramatic aspects of the modern Korean experience have, however, received scant attention from historians, with the consequence that little has been published on such topics as modern Korean social or cultural history.

Among the most frequently examined topics in modern Korean political and diplomatic history has been the failure of Korea to resist imperialism in the late nineteenth and early twentieth centuries. Some scholars have emphasized the inability of Korean elites to transcend their own social and political interests in order to carry out needed reforms, while others have stressed the difficulties Korea had making the transition from the old China-centered, East Asian international order to the modern nation-state system. Studies on Korean politics during the period of Japanese colonial rule from 1910 to 1945 focus on the rise of nationalism and the debilitating effects of factional infighting and internal divisions between leftist and rightist forces. The causes of the division of the country after 1945, along with the origins and nature of the Korean War, have formed a focal point of scholarly controversy, with opinions divided between those who see the division and the mid-twentieth-century outbreak of hostilities on the Korean Peninsula primarily in terms of a clash between Cold War superpowers and those who argue that the Korean War also had domestic origins and was as much a civil war as it was a conflict between Eastern and Western blocs. Historians and political scientists concerned with the difficulties South Korea has experienced in trying to establish a democratic political system have tended to focus on internal factors, although a number of scholars have also argued that American policies toward Korea inhibited the growth of democracy. Korean communism and the North Korean state have also received considerable attention, with several scholars examining the Korean communist movement during the colonial period, the rise to power of Kim Il Sung in North Korea, and North Korea's unique Kim-centered political system.

Studies of economic development have focused on South Korea as an example of late industrialization in which the state has played a major role in economic development rather than as a model of successful free market policies. Some more recent writings, echoing themes in scholarship on other East Asian newly industrializing countries, argue that the Confucian cultural heritage has been a major factor in the rise of South Korea's economy. The significance of Japanese colonial rule for Korean economic development has been a source of controversy, with some scholars downplaying the colonial legacy while others contend that the foundation for South Korea's rapid postwar industrialization was laid during the colonial period.

Historical scholarship on other aspects of the modern Korean experience has been meager. One area that has received some attention is religion, with studies on the rise of the indigenous Eastern Learning (*tonghak*) in the late nineteenth century as well as on the activities of Western missionaries in Korea in the late nineteenth and early twentieth centuries and the growth of Korean Christianity in the twentieth century. There are a number of fine studies on modern society and culture that have been produced in other academic disciplines, most notably anthropology, which have not been included here because they are essentially nonhistorical.

The section on Korea is divided into two major subsections, traditional and modern, each of which is subdivided into a number of periods. The traditional period has two divisions: the early traditional, which begins with prehistory and includes the Three Kingdoms, Unified Silla (668–935), and Koryŏ (936–1392), and the late traditional period, which covers the establishment of the Chosŏn dynasty in 1392 to the death of King Ch'ŏljong in 1863. The 1392 dynastic change from Koryŏ to Chosŏn forms a conventional and, for our purposes, a convenient breaking point. It should not, however, be taken as an authoritative statement regarding the periodization of Korean history; there are still too many unanswered questions about the nature of the Koryŏ-Chosŏn transition. The modern subsection begins with a group of works that deal with the entire modern period, but then is separated into three periods: the opening of Korea to the outside world, from the enthronement of King Kojong and the regency of the Taewŏn'gun in 1864 to the annexation of Korea by Japan in 1910; the period of Japanese colonial rule, from 1910 to 1945; and the post-1945 period. This periodization is based on major political events and does not necessarily reflect underlying social and cultural trends.

The materials for each period within the traditional and modern subsections are presented in three major subject groupings: politics and foreign relations; society and economy; and religion, thought, and culture. Again, these classifications are somewhat arbitrary and derive in part from what the editors perceive as integral relationships, as between domestic politics and foreign relations, and in part from the simple dearth of English-language research on some topics, which, under more abundant circumstances, could be treated separately.

An additional useful source of Western-language historical scholarship on Korea, both traditional and modern, not included here are unpublished Ph.D. dissertations.

For that reason, the reader should consult F. J. Shulman's annotated bibliographies of Western-language doctoral dissertations (11.17, 13.18, 14.5).

For Korean-language scholarship, a prodigious amount of historical research is being published in South Korea. Important periodicals include *Yŏksa hakpo* (Korean Historical Review) by Yŏksa Hakhoe (Korean Historical Association), *Hanguksa yŏngu* (Journal of Korean History) by Hanguksa Yŏnguhoe (Association for Korean Historical Studies), *Hanguk saron* (Studies of Korean History) by Seoul National University, *Hanguk sahak* (Historical Studies of Korea) by Hanguk Chŏngsin Munhwa Yŏnguwŏn (Academy of Korean Studies), and *Kuksagwan nonch'ong* (Studies from the National History Compilation Committee). There are two useful guides to historical publications in South Korea. *Yŏksa hakpo* periodically reviews recent historical scholarship. Kuksa P'yŏnch'an Wiwŏnhoe (National History Compilation Committee) puts out a quarterly publication *Hanguksa yŏngu hwibo* (Bulletin for Korean Historical Studies), listing the latest books and articles on Korean history along with their tables of contents. Chang Tŭk-chin compiled *Hanguksa nonjŏ ch'ong mongnok* (Comprehensive Bibliography of Korean History) in three volumes, providing a comprehensive list of books and articles with their tables of contents published in South Korea from 1945 to 1984.

North Korean scholars have also published a number of monographs and articles (mostly in *Ryŏksa kwahak* [Historical Science]), that unfortunately are not easily available to Western scholars. Although North Korean scholars have produced many important new findings, their scholarship is often marred by ideological idiosyncrasies.

For studies of Korean history in Japan, *Chōsen gakuhō* (Journal of the Academic Association of Koreanology in Japan) and *Chōsenshi kenkyūkai rombunshū* (Studies of Korean History Research Society) are the two most important periodicals. For a comprehensive listing of studies of Korean history after 1945, the forthcoming *Sengo Nihon ni okeru Chōsenshi bunken mokuroku* (Postwar Japanese Bibliography of Korean History) will be very useful.

Entries are arranged under the following headings:

Reference Works

General Studies

Historiography

Early Traditional Korea: Three Kingdoms, Silla, and Koryŏ Periods
 Politics and Foreign Relations
 Society and Economy
 Religion, Thought, and Culture

Late Traditional Korea: Chosŏn Dynasty, 1392–1864
 Politics and Foreign Relations
 Society and Economy
 Religion, Thought, and Culture

Late Chosŏn and Modern Korea Since 1864
 Politics and Foreign Relations
 Religion, Thought, and Culture

Opening of Korea, 1864–1910
 Politics and Foreign Relations
 Society and Economy
 Religion, Thought, and Culture

Colonial Korea, 1910–1945
 Politics and Foreign Relations
 Society and Economy
 Religion, Thought, and Culture

Korea Since 1945
 Politics and Foreign Relations
 Society and Economy

[Contributors: CJE = Carter J. Eckert, JBD = John B. Duncan, JSH = John S. Hill, MR = Michael Robinson, YC = Yŏng-ho Ch'oe]

REFERENCE WORKS

14.1 Chang Tŭk-chin, ed. *Hanguksa nonjŏ ch'ong mongnok* (Comprehensive bibliography of Korean history). 3 vols. Seoul: Minjok Munhwasa, 1985. ▸ Lists Korean monographs and articles with their table of contents published in South Korea between 1945 and 1984. Volume 1, from antiquity to Koryŏ; volume 2, Chosŏn dynasty; volume 3, modern period up to 1945. [YC]

14.2 Owen Nickerson Denny. *American advisor in late Yi Korea: the letters of Owen Nickerson Denny.* Robert R. Swartout, Jr., ed. University: University of Alabama Press, 1984. ISBN 0-8173-0189-5. ▸ Observations on Korean and East Asian situation in late nineteenth century. Useful introduction by editor. [JBD]

14.3 Han-kyo Kim, ed. *Studies on Korea: a scholar's guide.* Honolulu: University of Hawaii Press, 1980. ISBN 0-8248-0673-5. ▸ Best available English-language bibliography on Korea. Comprehensive treatment of works in Western languages up through 1976. Includes introductory essays for each section. [JBD]

14.4 George McCune et al., eds. *Korean-American relations: documents pertaining to the Far Eastern diplomacy of the United States.* Vol. 1: *The initial period, 1883–1886.* Vol. 2: *The period of growing influence, 1887–1895.* Vol. 3: *The period of diminishing influence.* Berkeley: University of California Press, 1951–89. ISBN 0-8248-1202-6 (v. 3). ▸ Compilation of official American records. Useful for study of United States policy but limited by lack of private American records and documents from Korean side. [JBD]

14.5 Frank Joseph Shulman. *Doctoral dissertations on Japan and Korea, 1969–1979: an annotated bibliography of studies in Western languages.* Seattle: University of Washington Press, 1982. ISBN 0-295-95895-2 (cl), 0-295-95961-4 (pbk). ▸ Update of Shulman's 1877–1969 bibliography of Ph.D. dissertations (13.18). [JBD]

SEE ALSO
13.18 Frank Joseph Shulman. *Japan and Korea.*

GENERAL STUDIES

14.6 Hochin Choi. *The economic history of Korea: from the earliest times to 1945.* Seoul: Freedom Library, 1971. ▸ Well-known general economic history covering all periods through 1940. Outdated, sometimes inaccurate, but contains much factual information not found in other general histories. [CJE]

14.7 Carter J. Eckert et al. *Korea old and new: a history.* Seoul: Ilchokak for Korea Institute, Harvard University, 1990. ISBN 0-967713-0-9. ▸ Rewritten, condensed version of Ki-baik Lee's *A New History of Korea* (14.16). New chapters on late nineteenth century, colonial period, and post–World War II added. Lacks treatment of North Korea. Useful as one-volume general history, college text. [MR]

14.8 James Huntley Grayson. *Korea: a religious history.* New York: Oxford University Press, 1989. ISBN 0-19-826186-1. ▸ Historical survey of Korean Buddhism, Confucianism, and Christianity. Emphasis more on social and political context than on internal development of religious and intellectual traditions. Also describes modern folk religions. [JBD]

14.9 Woo-keun Han. *History of Korea.* Grafton K. Mintz, ed. Kyung-shik Lee, trans. Honolulu: University of Hawaii Press, 1971. ISBN 0-8248-0334-5. ▸ Balanced, detailed history of Korea up through 1960 by leading South Korean historian. Somewhat dated. [JBD]

14.10 Takashi Hatada. *A history of Korea.* Warren W. Smith and Benjamin H. Hazard, eds. and trans. Santa Barbara, Calif.: ABC-Clio, 1969. ISBN 0-87436-065-X. ▸ Representative of post-1945 Japanese scholarship on Korea. Somewhat dated. [JBD]

14.11 William E. Henthorn. *A history of Korea.* New York: Free Press, 1971. ISBN 0-02-914460-4 (cl), 0-02-914610-0 (pbk). ▸ Somewhat dated but evenhanded college survey course textbook. Stops with nineteenth century. [JBD]

14.12 Wanne J. Joe. *Traditional Korea: a cultural history.* Vol. 1 of *A history of Korean civilization.* Seoul: Chungang University Press, 1972. ▸ Cultural history up to end of traditional period. Useful introductory sections on Confucianism, Taoism, and Buddhism. Marred by poor editing. [JBD]

14.13 Chewon Kim and Lena Kim Lee. *Arts of Korea.* Tokyo: Kodansha; distributed by Harper & Row, 1974. ISBN 0-87011-206-6. ▸ Comprehensive history of Korean art. Nicely illustrated. [JBD]

14.14 Kim Won-yong et al. *The arts of Korea.* 6 vols. Seoul: Dong Hwa, 1979. ▸ Comprehensive treatment of various Korean art forms in six volumes. [JBD]

14.15 Ki-baik Lee. *A new history of Korea.* Edward W. Wagner and Edward J. Shultz, trans. Cambridge: Harvard University Press for Harvard-Yenching Institute, 1984. ISBN 0-674-61575-1. ▸ Translation of widely used Korean college textbook. Reflects generally accepted South Korean view of history, emphasizing role of dominant socioeconomic groups. Sketchy treatment of post-1945 period; neglects North Korea. [JBD]

14.16 Donald Stone Macdonald. *The Koreans: contemporary politics and society.* 2d ed. Boulder: Westview, 1990. ISBN 0-8133-0966-2 (cl), 0-8133-0967-0 (pbk). ▸ Reliable, comprehensive overview of contemporary history, society, and politics; covers both North and South Korea. Widely used as survey textbook on modern Korea. [JBD]

14.17 Evelyn McCune. *The arts of Korea: an illustrated history.* Tokyo: Tuttle, 1961. ▸ Outdated but still most comprehensive and useful study of Korean arts, including sculpture, ceramics, architecture, and painting from ancient times to end of Chosŏn (1910). [YC]

14.18 Shannon Boyd-Bailey McCune. *Korea's heritage: a regional and social geography.* Rutland, Vt.: Tuttle, 1956. ISBN 0-8048-0351-X. ▸ Dated but still best general geography on Korea. Illustrated; includes valuable bibliographic notes and statistical appendixes. [JBD]

14.19 Andrew C. Nahm. *Korea tradition and transformation: a history of the Korean people.* Elizabeth, N.J.: Hollym International, 1988. ISBN 0-930878-56-6. ▸ General survey history. Weak on traditional Korea, detailed treatment of modern period. [JBD]

HISTORIOGRAPHY

14.20 Yŏng-ho Ch'oe. "An outline history of Korean historiography." *Korean studies* 4 (1980) 1–27. ISSN 0145-840X. ▸ Discussion of main aspects of historical writings on Korea including characteristics and roles from antiquity to modern times. [YC]

14.21 Yŏng-ho Ch'oe. "Reinterpreting traditional history in North Korea." *Journal of Asian studies* 40.3 (1981) 503–23. ISSN 0021-9118. ▸ Examines salient characteristics of North Korean historical scholarship, especially issues related to periodization of traditional history. [YC]

14.22 Hugh H. W. Kang. "Images of Korean history." In *Traditional Korea—theory and practice.* Andrew C. Nahm, ed. Kalamazoo: Center for Korean Studies, Western Michigan University, 1974. (Korean studies series, 3.) ▸ Critical study of major Japanese historians of pre-1945 Korea analyzing how they distorted Korean history. [YC]

14.23 Fujiya Kawashima. "Historiographic development in South Korea: state and society from the mid-Koryŏ to the mid-Yi dynasty." *Korean studies* 2 (1978) 29–56. ISSN 0145-840X. ▸ Survey of historical writings in South Korea between 1945 and 1975 pointing out salient characteristics and significant findings in South Korean historiography on Korea (935–1910). [YC]

EARLY TRADITIONAL KOREA: THREE KINGDOMS, SILLA, AND KORYŎ PERIODS

Politics and Foreign Relations

14.24 Gina Lee Barnes. "Early Korean states: a review of historical interpretation." In *Bibliographic reviews of Far Eastern archaeology.* Oxbow Books and Gina L. Barnes, eds., pp. 113–62. Cambridge: Oxbow Books, 1990. ISBN 0-946897-19-0. ▸ Critical survey of various interpretations of rise of states in early Korea. Argues for relatively late formation of state. [JBD]

14.25 Ch'ŏn Kwan-u. "A new interpretation of the problems of Mimana." *Korea journal* 14.2, 14.4 (1974) 9–23, 31–44. ISSN 0023-3900. ▸ Examination of Japanese and Korean historical sources to refute claim that Japan established control over some part of southern Korea in ancient times. Interesting view of controversial issue by Korean scholar. [YC]

14.26 John B. Duncan. "The formation of the central aristocracy in early Koryŏ." *Korean studies* 12 (1988) 39–61. ISSN 0145-840X. ▸ Good scholarly examination of policy of centralization that led to change in social makeup of central officialdom, which in turn led to political instability toward end of eleventh century. [YC]

14.27 K.H.J. Gardiner. *The early history of Korea: the historical development of the peninsula up to the introduction of Buddhism in the fourth century.* Honolulu and Canberra: University of Hawaii Press and Centre of Oriental Studies with Australia National University Press, 1969. ISBN 0-7081-0257-3. ▸ Short synthesis of modern studies; uncritically accepts some Japanese interpretations disputed by Koreans. [YC]

14.28 Takashi Hatada. "An interpretation of the King Kwanggaet'o Inscription." V. Dixon Morris, trans. *Korean studies* 3 (1979) 1–17. ISSN 0145-840X. ▸ After reviewing different Japanese and Korean readings of inscriptions, author offers interpretation of controversial inscription regarding Japan's military presence in southern Korea. Thoughtful, imaginative essay. [YC]

14.29 William E. Henthorn. *Korea: the Mongol invasions.* Leiden: Brill, 1963. ▸ Largely chronological narrative of Mongol invasions of Korea during thirteenth century with analysis of Mongol demands on Koryŏ. [YC]

14.30 Hugh H. W. Kang. "The first succession struggle of Koryŏ in 945: a reinterpretation." *Journal of Asian studies* 36.3 (1977) 411–28. ISSN 0021-9118. ▸ Examination of clash between former Silla aristocracy and upstart maritime interests for control of Koryŏ state, resulting in narrowing power bases. Important scholarly study. [YC]

14.31 Hugh H. W. Kang. "Institutional borrowing: the case of the Chinese civil service examination system in early Koryŏ." *Journal of Asian studies* 34.1 (1974) 109–25. ISSN 0021-9118. ▸ Role of Chinese adviser, Shuang Chi, in introducing examination system and circumstances and objectives of King Kwangjong's acceptance of Chinese institution. Interesting, scholarly study of institutional diffusion. [YC]

14.32 Byong-ik Koh. "Korea's contacts with 'the western regions' in pre-modern times." *Sahoe kwahak* 2 (1958) 55–73. ▸ Narrative survey of Korea's religious and cultural contacts with regions west of China from Three Kingdoms period (313–668) to fall of Mongols in fourteenth century. [YC]

14.33 Seong-Rae Park. "Portents in Korean history." *Journal of social sciences and humanities* 47 (1978) 31–92. ISSN 0023-4044. ▸ Study of recordings and interpretations of unusual natural phenomena, such as eclipses, halos, comets, meteors, etc., from tenth to sixteenth century. [YC]

14.34 Michael C. Rogers. "National consciousness in medieval Korea: the impact of Liao and Chin on Koryŏ." In *China among equals.* Morris Rossabi, ed., pp. 151–72. Berkeley: University of California Press, 1983. ISBN 0-520-04383-9 (cl), 0-520-04562-9 (pbk). ▸ Stimulating study of Koryŏ Korea's place in international order of Northeast Asia and how its transformation from China-centered order to multistate system affected Koreans. [JBD]

14.35 Edward J. Shultz. "Ch'oe Ch'unghŏn: his rise to power." *Korean studies* 8 (1984) 58–82. ISSN 0145-840X. ▸ Examination of major issues and political situation leading Ch'oe Ch'unghŏn to seize power in 1196. Analyzes power base of Ch'oe house that dominated Koryŏ until 1259. Careful study of Koryŏ military rule. [YC]

14.36 Edward J. Shultz. "Military revolt in Koryŏ: the 1170 coup d'état." *Korean studies* 3 (1979) 19–48. ISSN 0145-840X. ▸ Examination of diverse political forces surrounding throne, based on thesis that military revolt of 1170 result of power struggles. Important new interpretation. [YC]

14.37 Edward J. Shultz. "Twelfth-century Koryŏ politics: the rise of Han Anin and his partisans." *Journal of Korean studies* 6 (1988–89) 3–38. ISSN 0731-1613. ▸ Study of how Han Anin, a political leader, and his followers fared in political turmoil of twelfth century while advocating political and intellectual reform. [YC]

14.38 Yasukazu Suematsu. "Japan's relations with the Asian continent and the Korean peninsula (before 900 A.D.)." *Cahiers d'histoire mondiale* 4.3 (1958) 671–87. ISSN 0379-3702. ▸ Narrative account of Japan's contacts with Chinese colonies in Korea and efforts to import Chinese culture. Contends Japan controlled area in southern Korea called Mimana. [YC]

Society and Economy

14.39 Jeong-hak Kim. *The prehistory of Korea.* Richard J. Pearson and Kazue Pearson, trans. Honolulu: University of Hawaii Press, 1979. ISBN 0-8248-0552-6. ▸ Nicely translated version of somewhat dated study on prehistoric Korea by leading Korean archaeologist. [JBD]

14.40 James B. Palais. "Land tenure in Korea: tenth to twelfth centuries." *Journal of Korean studies* 4 (1982–83) 73–205. ISSN 0731-1613. ▸ Extensive review and scholarly discussion of Korean and Japanese studies on land-tenure system in early Koryŏ. [YC]

14.41 James B. Palais. "Slavery and slave society in the Koryŏ period." *Journal of Korean studies* 5 (1984) 173–90. ISSN 0731-1613. ▸ Examination of scholarship on slavery in Koryŏ. Provocative thesis that Koryŏ was slave society. [JBD]

Religion, Thought, and Culture

14.42 Robert Buswell, Jr. *The formation of Ch'an ideology in China and Korea: the "Vajrasamadhi-Sutra," a Buddhist apocryphon.* Princeton: Princeton University Press, 1989. ISBN 0-691-07336-8. ▸ Stimulating new study on origins of Ch'an (Korean, Sŏn; Japanese, Zen) Buddhism. Advances thesis that seminal Ch'an text was written in Korea, rather than China. Important implications for study of East Asian Buddhism as discrete national traditions. [JBD]

14.43 Chinul. *The Korean approach to Zen: the collected works of Chinul.* Robert E. Buswell, Jr., trans. Honolulu: University of Hawaii Press, 1983. ISBN 0-8248-0785-5. ▸ Authoritative translation accompanied by thoughtful introduction on life and thought of Chinul, great Korean Buddhist philosopher of Koryŏ. [YC]

14.44 Byŏng-hŏn Choi. "Tosŏn's geomantic theories and the foundation of Koryŏ dynasty." *Seoul journal of Korean studies* 2 (1989) 65–92. ▸ Discussion of geomantic theories of Tosŏn, founder of geomancy in Korea, and how he influenced Wang Kŏn, first king of Koryŏ dynasty. [YC]

14.45 K.H.J. Gardiner. "The *Samguk-sagi* and its sources." *Papers on Far Eastern history* 2 (1970) 1–42. ISSN 0048-2870. ▸ Study of sources Kim Pusik used in compiling *Samguk-sagi* (History of the Three Kingdoms), in twelfth century, evaluating reliability of some entries on Koguryŏ, Paekche, and Silla periods. [YC]

14.46 Godfrey St. G. M. Gompertz. *Korean celadon and other wares of the Koryŏ period.* London: Faber & Faber, 1963. ▸ Basic study of ceramic arts of Koryŏ period with emphasis on Korean achievements in production of green celadon ware. [JBD]

14.47 Kakhun. *Lives of eminent Korean monks: the Haedong Kosŭng Chŏn.* Peter H. Lee, trans. Cambridge, Mass.: Harvard University Press, 1969. (Harvard-Yenching Institute studies, 25.) ISBN 0-674-53662-2. ▸ Translation with good introduction and notes of two extant chapters of work compiled in 1215. Useful source of information on early Korean Buddhism. [YC]

14.48 Lewis R. Lancaster and C. S. Yu, eds. *The introduction of Buddhism to Korea: new cultural patterns.* Berkeley: Asia Humanities Press, 1989. ISBN 0-89581-877-9 (cl), 0-89581-888-4 (pbk). ▸ Collection of papers, some excellent, on early Buddhist history in Korea. Covers such topics as indigenization of Buddhism, Buddhism's influence on Korean society, and social and political factors in Korean acceptance of Buddhism. [JBD]

14.49 Ki-baik Lee. "Confucian political ideology in the Silla unification and early Koryŏ period." *Journal of social sciences and humanities* 42 (1975) 1–23. ISSN 0023-4044. ▸ Analysis of problems and tensions confronting those with Confucian education in society dominated by bone-rank system, castelike social structure of Silla. [YC]

14.50 Michael C. Rogers. "P'yŏnnyŏn T'ongnok: the foundation legend of the Koryŏ state." *Journal of Korean studies* 4 (1982–83) 3–72. ISSN 0731-1613. ▸ Compiled in twelfth century, foundation legend justified geomantic superiority of capital city Kaesŏng and primacy of Silla tradition. Analyzed within context of changes in international situation of Northeast Asia. [YC]

14.51 Richard Rutt. "The Flower Boys of Silla." *Transactions of the Royal Asiatic Society, Korea Branch* 37 (1961) 1–66. ISSN 0035-869X. ▸ Examination of various interpretations. Concludes Hwarang (Flower Boys) was band of adolescents organized for high moral purpose, essentially religious in nature, with certain quasi-military characteristics. [YC]

LATE TRADITIONAL KOREA: CHOSŎN DYNASTY, 1392–1864

Politics and Foreign Relations

14.52 Ching Young Choe. "Kim Yuk (1580–1658) and the *taedongbŏp.*" *Journal of Asian studies* 23.1 (1963) 21–35. ISSN 0021-9118. ▸ Examination of how Uniform Land Tax law (*taedongbŏp*) was adopted, shedding light on tribute tax system and decision-making processes of Chosŏn (Yi) dynasty. Scholarly study of important measure. [YC]

14.53 Chun Hae-jong. "Sino-Korean tributary relations in the Ch'ing period." In *The Chinese world order: traditional China's foreign relations.* John K. Fairbank, ed., pp. 90–111. Cambridge, Mass.: Harvard University Press, 1968. ISBN 0-674-12600-9. ▸ Meticulous study of Korea's tributary missions sent to Ch'ing China (1644–1912), including economic aspects. [YC]

14.54 Donald N. Clark. "Chosŏn's founding fathers: a study of merit subjects in the early Yi dynasty." *Korean studies* 6 (1982) 17–40. ISSN 0145-840X. ▸ Examination of personal and social ties of merit subjects (men rewarded by king for exceptional service) of early rulers of Chosŏn dynasty, concluding dynastic transition from Koryŏ to Chosŏn not a radical change in ruling stratum. [YC]

14.55 John B. Duncan. "The social background to the founding of the Chosŏn dynasty: change or continuity?" *Journal of Korean studies* 6 (1988–89) 39–79. ISSN 0731-1613. ▸ Analysis of clan affiliations of officialdom showing, contrary to widely held belief, remarkable continuity in ruling stratum in transition from middle Koryŏ to early Chosŏn. [YC]

14.56 JaHyun Kim Haboush. "Confucian rhetoric and ritual and techniques of political dominance: Yŏngjo's use of the Royal Lecture." *Journal of Korean studies* 5 (1984) 39–62. ISSN 0731-1613. ▸ Scholarly study of how institution of Royal Lecture, which bureaucracy often used to point out royal deficiencies, was utilized by King Yŏngjo to dominate bureaucracy. [YC]

14.57 JaHyun Kim Haboush. *A heritage of kings: one man's monarchy in the Confucian world.* New York: Columbia University Press, 1988. ISBN 0-231-06656-2. ▸ Important, stimulating study of Confucian kingship, ideology, and politics focusing on rule of King Yŏngjo. [YC]

14.58 Pyong-Choon Hahm. *The Korean political tradition and law: essays in Korean law and legal history.* 1967 ed. Seoul: Seoul Computer Press for Royal Asiatic Society, Korea Branch, 1987. ▸ Collection of essays by legal specialist, including important essays on political tradition and law, rule of royal succession, and discrimination against descendants of concubines. Argues law subordinate to Confucian ethical values. [YC]

14.59 Yŏnung Kwŏn. "The Royal Lecture and Confucian politics in early Yi Korea." *Korean studies* 6 (1982) 41–62. ISSN 0145-840X. ▸ Examines how Royal Lecture evolved from Confucian institution of royal indoctrination to forum for political debate.

Important study of peculiar Korean institution shedding much light on decision making. [YC]

14.60 Gari K. Ledyard. "Confucianism and war: the Korean security crisis of 1598." *Journal of Korean studies* 6 (1988–89) 81–119. ISSN 0731-1613. ▸ Study of crisis surrounding kingship of Korea following accusations on conduct of war made by Chinese official during Hideyoshi invasions. Fascinating study of Korea's relationship to China. [YC]

14.61 James B. Palais. "Stability in Yi dynasty Korea: equilibrium systems and marginal adjustment." *Occasional papers on Korea: the Joint Committee on Korean Studies of the American Council of Learned Societies and the Social Science Research Council* 3 (1975) 1–18. ISSN 0364-7676. ▸ Reflections on what enabled Chosŏn state, polity, and society to be so self-sufficient and stable for over five hundred years in spite of maladies that beset dynasty. Provocative essay. [YC]

14.62 Seong-Rae Park. "Portents and Neo-Confucian politics in Korea, 1392–1519." *Journal of social sciences and humanities* 49 (1979) 53–117. ISSN 0023-4044. ▸ Changing attitudes in interpreting portents affecting politics and ideology of early Chosŏn (Yi) dynasty. Important study offering new dimension in study of early Chosŏn state. [YC]

14.63 William Shaw. *Legal norms in a Confucian state.* Berkeley: University of California Press, Institute of East Asian Studies, 1981. (Korean research monographs, 5.) ISBN 0-912966-32-7 (pbk). ▸ Three-part study: introduction to Chosŏn (Yi) dynasty law; Korean society, government, and legal thought in eighteenth-century case records; and cases from Simnirok (trial records). Disputes contention that law was subordinate to Confucian ethical values. [YC]

14.64 Sohn Pow-key. "The concept of history and Korean *yangban.*" *International journal of Korean studies* 1 (1973) 93–115. ▸ Stimulating study of perception and role of history as well as recordkeeping under Chosŏn (Yi) dynasty. Finds historical recordkeeping had effect of limiting monarchical power. [YC]

14.65 Sohn Pow-key. "Power versus status: the role of ideology during the early Yi dynasty." *Tongbang hakchi* 10 (1969) 209–53. ▸ Analysis and discussion of debate within Korean court on issue of whether Korean kings had authority to give sacrificial offerings to heaven. Important study of balance of power between monarchy and *yangban* (class of scholar-officials). [YC]

14.66 Edward Willett Wagner. *The literati purges: political conflict in early Yi Korea.* Cambridge, Mass.: Harvard University, East Asian Research Center, 1974. (Harvard East Asian monographs, 58.) ISBN 0-674-53618-5. ▸ Examination of purges of 1498, 1504, and 1519 that resulted from sustained conflict between censorial organs and higher authority of kings and high ministers. Stimulating study of important subject. [YC]

Society and Economy

14.67 Yŏng-ho Ch'oe. *The civil examinations and the social structure in early Yi dynasty Korea, 1392–1600.* Seoul: Korean Research Center, 1987. ▸ Analysis of structure of examination system's recruiting of civil officials and its effect on social status with emphasis on whether commoners were admitted. [YC]

14.68 Ch'oe Pu. *Ch'oe Pu's diary: a record of drifting across the sea.* John Meskill, trans. Tucson: University of Arizona Press, 1965. (Association for Asian Studies, Monographs and papers, 17.) ▸ Detailed record of Ch'oe Pu's experiences and observations as castaway traveling through China before returning to Korea. Valuable information on customs and life styles of both China and Korea. [YC]

14.69 Martina Deuchler. *The Confucian transformation of Korea: a study of society and ideology.* Cambridge, Mass.: Harvard University, Council on East Asian Studies, 1992. (Harvard-Yenching Institute monograph series, 36.) ISBN 0-674-16088-6. ▸ Analysis of impact of Neo-Confucianism on Korean society and emergence of patrilineality in Chosŏn (Yi) dynasty showing how change narrowed membership of ruling elite. Uses historical and socioanthropological methodology. [YC]

14.70 Martina Deuchler. " 'Heaven does not discriminate': a study of secondary sons in Chosŏn Korea." *Journal of Korean studies* 6 (1988–89) 121–63. ISSN 0731-1613. ▸ Study of discrimination against secondary sons ritual succession and holding of government office and of movement to end discrimination. Scholarly analysis of peculiar Korean custom. [YC]

14.71 Fujiya Kawashima. "A study of the Hyangan: kin groups and aristocratic localism in the seventeenth- and eighteenth-century Korean countryside." *Journal of Korean studies* 5 (1984) 3–38. ISSN 0731-1613. ▸ Fascinating study of evolution of local elite organization that functioned as kin group to promote and preserve local traditions and culture. [YC]

14.72 Laurel Kendall and Mark Peterson, eds. *Korean women: view from the inner room.* New Haven: East Rock Press, 1983. ISBN 0-9108250-2-5 (pbk). ▸ Useful collection of papers on status of women in Korean society with focus on Chosŏn period. [JBD]

14.73 Gari K. Ledyard. *The Dutch come to Korea.* Seoul: Royal Asiatic Society, Korea Branch, 1971. (Royal Asiatic Society, Korea Branch, Monograph series, 3.) ▸ Account of adventures and experiences of Dutch sailors who reached Korea following shipwreck in seventeenth century. Useful for Korea's political and social conditions at time. [YC]

14.74 James B. Palais. "Confucianism and the aristocratic-bureaucratic balance in Korea." *Harvard journal of Asiatic studies* 44.2 (1984) 427–68. ISSN 0073-0548. ▸ Learned essay on salient characteristics of state and society of Chosŏn (Yi) dynasty with comparative perspectives on Chinese history. Important, thought-provoking study. [YC]

14.75 Jin-Young Ro. "Demographic and social mobility trends in early seventeenth-century Korea: an analysis of Sanŭm county census registers." *Korean studies* 7 (1983) 77–113. ISSN 0145-840X. ▸ Careful study of two census registers of county in southern Korea applying demographic methodology. Throws light on population structure and largely downward social mobility. [YC]

14.76 Susan Shin. "The social structure of Kŭmhwa county in the seventeenth century." *Occasional papers on Korea: the Joint Committee on Korean Studies of the American Council of Learned Societies and the Social Science Research Council* 1 (1974) 9–35. ISSN 0364-7676. ▸ Scholarly analysis of 1672 census register of Kŭmhwa (Kimhwa) county focusing on status system and social mobility. Pioneering study. [YC]

14.77 T'ae-jin Yi. "The socio-economic background of Neo-Confucianism in Korea of the fifteenth and sixteenth centuries." *Seoul journal of Korean studies* 2 (1989) 39–63. ▸ Examination of successful introduction of new agricultural technology that enabled Neo-Confucian scholar-officials to emerge as new political force who initiated various self-serving reforms. Interesting study of potentially far-reaching significance. [YC]

Religion, Thought, and Culture

14.78 Donald L. Baker. "Jesuit science through Korean eyes." *Journal of Korean studies* 4 (1982–83) 207–39. ISSN 0713-1613. ▸ Study of Korean reaction to introduction of Western instruments and ideas on astronomy and calendar making during seventeenth and eighteenth centuries. [YC]

14.79 Donald L. Baker. "The martyrdom of Paul Yun: Western religion and Eastern ritual in eighteenth-century Korea." *Transactions of the Royal Asiatic Society, Korea Branch* 54 (1979) 33–

58. ▸ Good account of introduction of Catholicism into Korea and conflict it created with Confucian practices of ancestral services. [YC]

14.80 Donald L. Baker. "Sirhak medicine: measles, smallpox, and Chŏng Tasan." *Korean studies* 14 (1990) 134–66. ISSN 0145-840X. ▸ Examination of place of Chŏng Yag-yong in Sirhak (Practical Learning) tradition focusing on his medical work as it related to Neo-Confucian medical theory. Erudite study of Sirhak school's approach to medicine. [YC]

14.81 Chai-sik Chung. "Christianity as heterodoxy: an aspect of general cultural orientation in traditional Korea." In *Korea's response to the West*. Yung-hwan Jo, ed., pp. 57–86. Kalamazoo: Korea Research & Publications, 1977. ▸ Analysis of how and why some Korean Confucian scholars rejected Christianity and upheld orthodoxy of Confucianism. [YC]

14.82 Wm. Theodore De Bary and JaHyun Kim Haboush, eds. *The rise of Neo-Confucianism in Korea*. New York: Columbia University Press, 1985. ISBN 0-231-06052-1. ▸ Collection of fifteen studies on various aspects of Neo-Confucianism during Chosŏn (Yi) dynasty by scholars from the West, Korea, and Japan. Includes excellent introduction. [YC]

14.83 Godfrey St. G. M. Gompertz. *Pottery and porcelain of the Yi period*. London: Faber & Faber, 1968. ▸ Basic survey of ceramic arts during Chosŏn period. [JBD]

14.84 Sang-woon Jeon. *Science and technology in Korea: traditional instruments and techniques*. Cambridge, Mass.: MIT Press, 1974. ISBN 0-262-10014-2. ▸ Survey of historical development in fields of astronomy, meteorology, physics, chemistry, and geography. Scholarly, authoritative study. [YC]

14.85 Michael C. Kalton. "Chŏng Tasan's philosophy of man: a radical critique of the Neo-Confucian world view." *Journal of Korean studies* 3 (1981) 3–38. ISSN 0731-1613. ▸ Study of Chŏng Tasan's (Chŏng Yag-yong) view of man and universe in contrast to prevailing Neo-Confucian vision. Important study of Sirhak (Practical Learning) scholar of Chosŏn Korea. [YC]

14.86 Michael C. Kalton. "T'oegye's *Ten Diagrams on Sage Learning*: a Korean view of the essence of Chu Hsi's teachings." *Journal of Korean studies* 7 (1990) 97–114. ISSN 0713-1613. ▸ Study of how Yi Hwang (T'oegye) compressed essence of Chu Hsi's teachings into his famous Ten Diagrams, and analysis of structure of Ten Diagrams. [YC]

14.87 King Seijong Memorial Society. *King Seijong the Great: a biography of Korea's most famous king*. Seoul: King Seijong Memorial Society, 1970. ▸ Old-fashioned hagiography of King Sejong (r. 1418–50) but contains much useful information on achievements of great Chosŏn king: promotion of scholarship, invention of Korean alphabet, and development of science and technology. [YC]

14.88 Peter H. Lee, ed. and trans. *Songs of flying dragons: a critical reading*. Cambridge, Mass.: Harvard University Press, 1975. (Harvard-Yenching Institute monograph series, 22.) ISBN 0-674-82075-4. ▸ Annotated translation and study of eulogy cantos composed in fifteenth century to celebrate founding of Chosŏn (Yi) dynasty. Erudite study of literature shedding much light on history as well. [YC]

14.89 Yi Hwang. *To become a sage: the "Ten Diagrams on Sage Learning" by Yi T'oegye*. Michael C. Kalton, ed. and trans. New York: Columbia University Press, 1988. ISBN 0-231-06410-1. ▸ Translation of *Sŏnghak sipto*, regarded as summation of what Yi Hwang (Yi T'oegye) considered to be essential in understanding Neo-Confucianism. Translator provides good introduction and helpful commentaries. [YC]

LATE CHOSŎN AND MODERN KOREA SINCE 1864

Politics and Foreign Relations

14.90 Gregory Henderson. *Korea: the politics of the vortex*. Cambridge, Mass.: Harvard University Press, 1968. ▸ Argues postcolonial politics represented continuation of traditional pattern of atomized individual mobility. Flawed thesis but much useful information, especially on colonial and postcolonial periods. Engaging style. [JBD]

14.91 Chong-sik Lee. *The Korean Workers' party: a short history*. Stanford, Calif.: Hoover Institution Press, 1978. ISBN 0-8179-6852-0. ▸ Concise survey of communist movement in colonial Korea and of development of Kim Il Sung's regime in North Korea after 1945. [JBD]

14.92 Chong-sik Lee. *The politics of Korean nationalism*. Berkeley: University of California Press, 1965. ▸ Standard treatment of Korean nationalist movement from late nineteenth century through end of colonial period in 1945. [JBD]

14.93 Yur-bok Lee and Wayne Patterson, eds. *One hundred years of Korean-American relations, 1882–1982*. University: University of Alabama Press, 1986. ISBN 0-8173-0265-4. ▸ Collection of papers on history of Korean-American relations. Treats entire one-hundred-year span but particularly good on 1882–1905 period. [JBD]

14.94 Andrew C. Nahm, ed. *The United States and Korea: American-Korean relations, 1866–1976*. Kalamazoo: Western Michigan University, Center for Korean Studies, 1979. (Korean studies series, 6.) ▸ Uneven collection of ten articles on Korean-American relations. Focus on late nineteenth century and post-1945 era. [JBD]

Religion, Thought, and Culture

14.95 Donald N. Clark. *Christianity in modern Korea*. Lanham, Md.: University Press of America, 1986. ISBN 0-8191-5384-2 (cl), 0-8191-5385-0 (pbk). ▸ Brief but useful study of growth of Christianity in Korea. Shows relationship between Christianity and historical situation. [JBD]

14.96 Yong Choon Kim. *The Chondogyo concept of man: an essence of Korean thought*. Seoul: Pan Korea, 1978. ▸ Laudatory introduction to history and doctrinal development of native religion (Ch'ŏndogyo) that arose in mid-nineteenth century in response to domestic crisis and challenge of Catholicism. [JBD]

OPENING OF KOREA, 1864–1910

Politics and Foreign Relations

14.97 Vipan Chandra. *Imperialism, resistance, and reform in late nineteenth-century Korea: enlightenment and the Independence Club*. Berkeley: University of California Press, Institute of East Asian Studies, 1988. (Korean research monographs, 13.) ISBN 0-912966-99-8. ▸ Carefully researched, well-written, and detailed study of Independence Club in context of Korean movement for political reform inspired by Western models around turn of century. [CJE]

14.98 Jongsuk Chay. *Diplomacy of asymmetry: Korean-American relations to 1910*. Honolulu: University of Hawaii Press, 1990. ISBN 0-8248-1236-0. ▸ Sound study arguing American policy toward Korea, 1866–1910, characterized not by imperialistic designs but rather by disinterest and passivity resulting from Korea's overall lack of importance to United States. [JBD]

14.99 Ching Young Choe. *The rule of the Taewŏn'gun, 1864–1873: restoration in Yi Korea*. Cambridge, Mass.: Harvard University, East Asian Research Center, 1972. (Harvard East Asian monographs, 45.) ISBN 0-674-78030-2. ▸ Rebuts conventional negative assessments of Hŭngsŏn Taewŏn'gun (Grand Prince

Hŭngsŏn), argues rule was restoration that arrested dynasty's socioeconomic decline. Asserts Taewŏn'gun influenced by Practical Learning movement. [JBD]

14.100 Hilary Conroy. *The Japanese seizure of Korea, 1868–1910: a study of realism and idealism in international relations.* Philadelphia: University of Pennsylvania Press, 1960. ▸ Contends Japanese takeover of Korea not due to expansionist imperialism but rather to combination of realistic needs for modern, stable Korea as prerequisite for Japanese national security and idealistic impulse to reform Korea. [JBD]

14.101 Harold F. Cook. *Korea's 1884 incident: its background and Kim Ok-kyun's elusive dream.* Seoul: Royal Asiatic Society, Korea Branch, 1972. (Royal Asiatic Society, Korea Branch, Monograph series, 4.) ▸ Study of abortive attempt by Enlightenment party to modernize Korea following model of Meiji Japan. Somewhat limited by focus on reform advocate Kim Ok-kyun. [JBD]

14.102 Martina Deuchler. *Confucian gentlemen and barbarian envoys: the opening of Korea, 1875–1885.* Seattle: University of Washington Press for Royal Asiatic Society, Korea Branch, 1977. ISBN 0-295-95552-X. ▸ Well-researched study of efforts toward reform after Korea opened to outside world in second half of nineteenth century. Argues reforms generally unsuccessful because of inability of elites to transcend traditional sociopolitical interests. [JBD]

14.103 Fred Harvey Harrington. *God, mammon, and the Japanese: Dr. Horace N. Allen and Korean-American relations, 1884–1905.* 1944 ed. Stuart Bruchey, ed. New York: Arno, 1980. ISBN 0-405-13357-X. ▸ Valuable study of diverse roles of American missionary turned diplomat in Korea at end of Chosŏn dynasty. [JBD]

14.104 Homer B. Hulbert. *The passing of Korea.* 1906 ed. Seoul: Yonsei University, 1990. ▸ Sympathetic eyewitness account of Korean society and Korea's international difficulties in late nineteenth and early twentieth centuries. [JBD]

14.105 C. I. Eugene Kim and Han-Kyo Kim. *Korea and the politics of imperialism, 1876–1910.* Berkeley: University of California Press, 1967. ▸ Well-researched study of period from opening of Korea to annexation by Japan. Attributes loss of independence to late nineteenth-century convergence of imperialist ambitions on Korea and inability of Koreans to respond effectively. [JBD]

14.106 Key-Hiuk Kim. *The last phase of the East Asian world order: Korea, Japan, and the Chinese empire, 1860–1882.* Berkeley: University of California Press, 1980. ISBN 0-520-03556-9. ▸ Informative discussion of Korea's place in traditional East Asian international system and how Korea affected by destruction of that system. Emphasis on transformation of China from benign suzerain to occupier. [JBD]

14.107 Yur-bok Lee. *Diplomatic relations between the United States and Korea, 1861–1887.* Atlantic Highlands, N.J.: Humanities Press, 1970. ISBN 0-391-00084-5. ▸ Argues East Asian diplomatic behavior in late nineteenth century based less on traditional Sinitic familial international order than on practical political and economic interests. Good discussion of activities of American diplomats in Korea. [JBD]

14.108 Yur-bok Lee. *West goes East: Paul Georg von Mollendörff and great power imperialism in late Yi Korea.* Honolulu: University of Hawaii Press, 1988. ISBN 0-8248-1150-X. ▸ Comprehensive study of diplomatic role of German adviser to Korean throne within broader context of changing international order as result of imperialism in East Asia. Focuses on von Mollendörff's controversial attempt to enlist Russian support for Korea. [JBD]

14.109 Frederick A. McKenzie. *Korea's fight for freedom.* 1920 ed. New York: AMS Press, 1970. ISBN 0-404-04137-X. ▸ Sympathetic narrative of Korean efforts to maintain or regain independence from Japan in late nineteenth and early twentieth centuries. [JBD]

14.110 Frederick A. McKenzie. *The tragedy of Korea.* London: Hodder & Stoughton, 1908. ▸ Informative eyewitness account of Japanese takeover (1905) and Korean resistance. [JBD]

14.111 M. Frederick Nelson. *Korea and the old orders in Asia.* 1945 ed. New York: Russell & Russell, 1967. ▸ Examination of Korea's position in traditional East Asian international system. Argues Korean (and Chinese) diplomatic behavior of late nineteenth century can only be understood within informal familial East Asian system of international relations. Still standard treatment but compare Kim (14.106) and Lee (14.107). [JBD]

14.112 James B. Palais. *Politics and policy in traditional Korea.* Cambridge, Mass.: Harvard University Press, 1975. ISBN 0-674-68770-1. ▸ Thoroughly researched analysis of Korean inability to respond positively to challenge of outside world in nineteenth century in terms of social, economic, and political interests of traditional elites. Best study to date of late traditional sociopolitical history. [JBD]

14.113 Robert R. Swartout, Jr. *Mandarins, gunboats, and power politics: Owen Nickerson Denny and the international rivalries in Korea.* Honolulu: University of Hawaii Press, Asian Studies Program, 1980. (Asian studies at Hawaii, 25.) ISBN 0-8248-0681-6. ▸ Useful examination of late nineteenth-century Sino-Korean relations through activities of American adviser to Korean throne. Argues American adviser ultimately failed to incorporate Korea into modern nation-state system because of his inability to operate within traditional East Asian system of international relations. [JBD]

SEE ALSO
  13.386 Chong-sik Lee. *Japan and Korea.*

Society and Economy

14.114 Isabella L. Bird Bishop. *Korea and her neighbours: a narrative of travel with an account of the recent vicissitudes and present condition.* 1897 ed. Rutland, Vt.: Tuttle, 1986. ISBN 0-8048-1489-9. ▸ Interesting account of conditions in Korea in late nineteenth century. Orientalist but often sympathetic view of Korea and Koreans. [JBD]

Religion, Thought, and Culture

14.115 Lak-Geoon George Paik. *The history of Protestant missions in Korea, 1832–1910.* 1971 2d ed. Seoul: Korea Yonsei University Press, 1980. ▸ Interesting account of early Protestant activities in Korea by leading Korean Christian and intellectual. [JBD]

14.116 Benjamin B. Weems. *Reform, rebellion, and the heavenly way.* Tucson: University of Arizona Press, 1964. (Association for Asian Studies, Monographs and papers, 15.) ISBN 0-8165-0144-0. ▸ Brief, evenhanded study of historical evolution of indigenous religion with emphasis on its role as reform movement. [JBD]

COLONIAL KOREA, 1910–1945
Politics and Foreign Relations

14.117 C. I. Eugene Kim and Doretha E. Mortimore, eds. *Korea's response to Japan: the colonial period, 1910–1945.* Kalamazoo: Western Michigan University, Center for Korean Studies, 1977. ▸ Uneven collection of articles on Korean response to Japanese rule. Articles arranged topically: socioeconomic change, religious responses, nationalism and cultural movements, independence movements, and issues of identity. [MR]

14.118 Andrew C. Nahm, ed. *Korea under Japanese colonial rule: studies of the policy and techniques of Japanese colonialism.* Kalamazoo: Western Michigan University, Center for Korean Studies, 1973. (Korean studies series, 2.) ▸ Useful compilation of articles on Japanese colonial period. Analysis skewed by nationalist bias. General coverage of all aspects of Japanese colonial rule and Korean response. [MR]

14.119   Suh Dae-sook. *Documents of Korean communism, 1918–1948*. Princeton: Princeton University Press, 1970. ISBN 0-691-08723-7. ▸ Translation and compilation of basic documents of Korean communist movement. Useful research tool. [JBD]

14.120   Suh Dae-sook. *The Korean communist movement, 1918–1948*. Princeton: Princeton University Press, 1967. ▸ Definitive study of Korean communist movement from its beginnings to rise to power in North Korea. Examines failure of old domestic Communists and rise in North Korea of Kim Il Sung's new communist group. [JBD]

SEE ALSO
48.158 Ramon H. Myers and Mark R. Peattie, eds. *The Japanese colonial empire, 1895–1945*.

Society and Economy

14.121   Carter J. Eckert. *Offspring of empire: the Koch'ang Kims and the colonial origins of Korean capitalism*. Seattle: University of Washington Press, 1991. ISBN 0-295-97065-0. ▸ Well-written, thoroughly researched study refuting "sprouts of capitalism" thesis (incipient capitalism). Argues Korean capitalism first arose during colonial period; shows close cooperation between Korean entrepreneurs and Japanese colonial rulers. Strong implications for study of post–World War II economic development. [JBD]

14.122   Andrew J. Grajdanzev. *Modern Korea*. 1944 ed. New York: Octagon Books, 1978. ISBN 0-374-93226-3. ▸ Classic, critical survey of Japanese colonial administration of Korea, based on published government sources in Japanese and English. [CJE]

14.123   Hoon Koo Lee. *Land utilization of rural economy in Korea*. Chicago: University of Chicago Press, 1936. ▸ Valuable study of Korean rural economy under Japanese colonial rule. [JBD]

14.124   Dennis L. McNamara. *The colonial origins of Korean enterprise, 1910–1945*. Cambridge: Cambridge University Press, 1990. ISBN 0-521-38565-2. ▸ Somewhat thin description of entrepreneurship in colonial Korea. Focuses on Hanil/Tongil Bank, Hwasin retailers, and Kyŏngsŏng Spinning, concluding they were dependent, not comprador, enterprises. [MR]

14.125   Sang Chul Suh. *Growth and structural changes in the Korean economy, 1910–1940*. Cambridge, Mass.: Harvard University, Council on East Asian Studies, 1978. ISBN 0-674-36439-2. ▸ Generally negative assessment of colonial legacy based on statistical analysis of various sectors of colonial economy. Suffers from narrowly defined conception of economic growth and occasionally faulty interpretation of statistics. [CJE]

Religion, Thought, and Culture

14.126   Wi Jo Kang. *Religion and politics under the Japanese rule*. Lewiston, N.Y.: Mellen, 1987. ISBN 0-88946-056-6. ▸ Argues Japanese policies in colonial Korea created divisive tendencies within religious movements. Strong on Christianity and Buddhism, slights Confucianism and indigenous religions. Marred by poor editing and occasional inaccuracies. [JBD]

14.127   Michael Edson Robinson. *Cultural nationalism in colonial Korea, 1920–1925*. Seattle: University of Washington Press, 1988. ISBN 0-295-96600-9. ▸ Well-researched study of nationalist intellectuals in colonial Korea. Analyzes development of rightist and leftist varieties and argues Left-Right split was major debilitating factor for Korean independence movement. [JBD]

14.128   Kenneth M. Wells. *New God, new nation: Protestants and*

self-reconstruction nationalism in Korea, 1896–1937. Honolulu: University of Hawaii Press, 1990. ISBN 0-8248-1338-3. ▸ Examination of relationship between Korean nationalism and Protestant Christianity. Flawed but useful study for intellectual history of early Korean nationalist leaders. [MR]

KOREA SINCE 1945
Politics and Foreign Relations

14.129   Richard C. Allen. *Korea's Syngman Rhee: an unauthorized portrait*. Rutland, Vt.: Tuttle, 1960. ▸ Critical biography of South Korea's first president. [JBD]

14.130   Bruce Cumings. *The origins of the Korean War*. Vol. 1: *Liberation and the emergence of separate regimes, 1945–1947*. Vol. 2: *The roaring of the cataract, 1947–1950*. 2 vols. Princeton: Princeton University Press, 1981–90. ISBN 0-691-09383-0 (v. 1, cl), 0-691-07843-2 (v. 2, cl), 0-691-10113-2 (v. 1, pbk), 0-691-02538-X (v. 2, pbk). ▸ Sharply revisionist account based on massive study of documents. Important study. [JSH/JBD]

14.131   Bruce Cumings, ed. *Child of conflict: the Korean-American relationship, 1943–1953*. Seattle: University of Washington Press, 1983. (Publications on Asia of the School of International Studies, University of Washington, 37.) ISBN 0-295-95995-9. ▸ Critical reassessment of United States–Korean relations during crucial years of liberation, division, and war in Korea. [JBD]

14.132   Sungjoo Han. *The failure of democracy in South Korea*. Berkeley: University of California Press, 1974. ISBN 0-520-02437-0. ▸ Scholarly study of South Korean political history in post-1945 period with focus on weakness of Second Republic headed by Chang Myŏn. [JBD]

14.133   Young Whan Kihl. *Politics and policy in divided Korea: regimes in contest*. Boulder: Westview, 1984. ISBN 0-86531-700-3 (cl), 0-86531-701-1 (pbk). ▸ Informative, comparative study of North and South Korean political systems. Short history of both political systems since 1948. [MR]

14.134   Ilpyong J. Kim and Young Whan Kihl. *Political change in South Korea*. New York: Korean PWPA; distributed by Paragon House, 1988. ISBN 0-943852-59-5 (cl), 0-943852-60-9 (pbk). ▸ Thorough examination of various issues surrounding 1987 democratization movement in South Korea. Topics such as constitution, party politics, military, voting behavior, and student activism discussed as they relate to Korea's transition to democracy. [MR]

14.135   Kwan Bong Kim. *The Korea-Japan treaty crisis and the instability of the Korean political system*. New York: Praeger, 1971. ▸ Most comprehensive discussion of political furor surrounding normalization of relations between South Korea and Japan. Discusses political motivations for normalization and why treaty provoked such strong anti-Japanese protest. [MR]

14.136   Kim Se-jin. *The politics of military revolution in Korea*. Chapel Hill: University of North Carolina Press, 1971. ISBN 0-8078-1168-8. ▸ Only study in English of 1961 military coup in South Korea. Focuses on development and factionalism of South Korean army and on planning and aftermath of coup itself. [CJE]

14.137   Lee Chong-sik. *Materials on Korean communism, 1945–1947*. Honolulu: University of Hawaii, Center for Korean Studies, 1977. (University of Hawaii, Center for Korean Studies, Occasional papers, 7.) ISBN 0-917536-11-8. ▸ Collection of translated rare documents pertaining to Korean communist movement, 1945–47. Bulk of documents from *Haebang Ilbo*, official organ of Korean Communist party, published in Seoul. Other documents relate to publications of left-wing organizations. [MR]

14.138   James Irving Matray. *The reluctant crusade: American foreign policy in Korea, 1941–1950*. Honolulu: University of Hawaii

Press, 1985. ISBN 0-8248-0973-4. ▸ Detailed analysis of American foreign policy toward Korea from Japanese attack on Pearl Harbor to decision to enter Korean War. Places United States policy in larger context of Soviet-American relations and as test case of evolving containment policy. [MR]

14.139 James Irving Matray, ed. *Historical dictionary of the Korean War.* Westport, Conn.: Greenwood, 1991. ISBN 0-313-25924-0. ▸ Comprehensive dictionary of Korean War. Includes biography, battles, place names, maps, and political events. Limited by reliance on Western-language sources. [MR]

14.140 E. Grant Meade. *American military government in Korea.* New York: King's Crown, 1951. ▸ Basic history of United States occupation government in Korea, 1945–48. Particularly important as reference work to main actors, United States policies, domestic Korean political strife, and evolution of First Republic of Korea (established 1948). [MR]

14.141 John Merrill. *Korea: the peninsular origins of the war.* Newark: University of Delaware Press, 1989. ISBN 0-87413-300-9. ▸ Convincing argument that Korean War was civil and revolutionary as well as international in character. Emphasizes Third World nationalism and desire by both regimes, North and South, to unify country. [JBD]

14.142 Harold Joyce Noble. *Embassy at war: an account of the early weeks of the Korean War and United States relations with South Korean president Syngman Rhee.* Frank Baldwin, ed. Seattle: University of Washington Press, 1975. ISBN 0-295-95341-1. ▸ Embassy staffer's account of crucial events of summer, 1950, with useful introduction by editor. [JBD]

14.143 John Kie-chiang Oh. *Korea: democracy on trial.* Ithaca, N.Y.: Cornell University Press, 1968. ▸ Concise yet very useful scholarly study of political development in South Korea, 1948–61. [YC]

14.144 Robert T. Oliver. *Syngman Rhee and American involvement in Korea, 1942–1960: a personal narrative.* Seoul: Panmun, 1979. ▸ Background to United States–Korean relations as related by personal friend and adviser of Syngman Rhee. [JBD]

14.145 Robert T. Oliver. *Syngman Rhee: the man behind the myth.* 1954 ed. Westport, Conn.: Greenwood, 1973. ISBN 0-8371-6759-0. ▸ Laudatory biography by American adviser to Rhee. Interesting and useful personal insights. [JBD]

14.146 Robert A. Scalapino and Chong-sik Lee. *Communism in Korea.* Berkeley: University of California Press, 1972. ISBN 0-520-02080-4. ▸ Two-volume history of Korean communism. Standard reference tool to biography, organizational history, factions, and ideology within Korean communist movement. Volume 1 covers early history and development of Korean communism to 1945; volume 2 devoted to first two decades of communist rule in North Korea. [MR]

14.147 I. F. Stone. *The hidden history of the Korean War.* 1952 ed. Boston: Little, Brown, 1988. ISBN 0-316-81773-2 (cl), 0-316-81770-8 (pbk). ▸ Radical journalist's alternative account of immediate causes of outbreak of hostilities. Challenges official United States–South Korean version of unprovoked North Korean aggression. [JBD]

14.148 Dae-sook Suh. *Kim Il Sung: the North Korean leader.* New York: Columbia University Press, 1988. ISBN 0-231-06572-8. ▸ Well-written and most objective biography to date. Debunks both North and South Korean propaganda regarding Kim's life and achievements. [JBD]

Society and Economy

14.149 Alice Amsden. *Asia's next giant: South Korea and late industrialization.* New York: Oxford University Press, 1989. ISBN 0-19-505852-6. ▸ Excellent account of Korean economic development since early 1960s. Develops theory that Korea represents late industrialization, in which technology (learned rather than developed) and strong government played leading role in economic development. [MR]

14.150 Sung Hwan Ban, Pal Yong Moon, and Dwight H. Perkins. *Rural development.* Cambridge, Mass.: Harvard University, Council on East Asian Studies, 1980. (Harvard East Asian monographs, 89.) ISBN 0-674-78042-6. ▸ Best general survey to date on South Korean rural development with emphasis on 1960s and 1970s. Includes chapters on role of central and local government and off-farm migration. Useful bibliography of English and Korean sources. [CJE]

14.151 Lee-Jay Cho and Yoon Hyun Kim, eds. *Economic development in the Republic of Korea: a policy perspective.* Honolulu: East-West Center; distributed by University of Hawaii Press, 1990. ISBN 0-86638-131-7. ▸ Broad, well-researched volume on South Korea's economic development from neoclassical economists, many of whom served in key bureaucratic posts during period of rapid growth. In-depth analyses of Korea's economic policies from 1960s to 1980s, including currency and prices, taxation, population, agricultural and industrial policies. [MR]

14.152 David C. Cole and Princeton N. Lyman. *Korean development: the interplay of politics and economics.* Cambridge, Mass.: Harvard University Press, 1971. ISBN 0-674-50563-8. ▸ Detailed account, based on English-language sources, of early years of South Korea's rapid economic growth and political development under Park Chung Hee. Examines modernization paradigm suggesting correlation between economic growth and democratic development. [CJE]

14.153 Frederic C. Deyo, ed. *The political economy of the new Asian industrialism.* Ithaca, N.Y.: Cornell University Press, 1987. ISBN 0-8014-9449-4 (cl), 0-8014-9449-4 (pbk). ▸ Excellent collection of articles providing rich analysis of rapid economic development in Asian nations. Several chapters by leading scholars devoted to Korea's economic development, focusing on issues such as role of state, foreign capital, export-oriented industrialization, labor, and world system. [MR]

14.154 Leroy P. Jones and Il Sakong. *Government, business, and enterpreneurship in economic development: the Korean case.* Cambridge, Mass.: Harvard University, Council on East Asian Studies, 1980. ISBN 0-674-35791-4. ▸ Important early study of government-business relationship in South Korea, including growth of *chaebŏl* (corporations). Focuses largely on 1960s and 1970s and uses variety of Korean and English source materials, as well as personal interviews and questionnaires. [CJE]

14.155 Paul W. Kuznets. *Economic growth and structure in the Republic of Korea.* New Haven: Yale University Press, 1977. ISBN 0-300-02019-8. ▸ Careful, thoughtful analysis of South Korean economy through mid-1970s based primarily on official economic statistics. [CJE]

14.156 Edward S. Mason et al. *The economic and social modernization of the Republic of Korea.* Cambridge: Harvard University, Council on East Asian Studies, 1980. (Harvard East Asian monographs, 92.) ISBN 0-674-23175-9. ▸ General summary of Harvard-Korean Development Institute series on modernization of Korea. Chapters on Korea and Third World, history, industrialization, foreign trade, foreign assistance, and government-business relations. [MR]

14.157 Sandra Mattielli, ed. *Virtues in conflict: tradition and the Korean woman today.* Seoul: Samhwa for the Royal Asiatic Society, Korea Branch, 1977. ▸ Stimulating collection of articles treating influence of historical traditions on lives of contemporary Korean women. [JBD]

14.158 Cornelius Osgood. *The Koreans and their culture.* New York: Ronald, 1951. ‣ Fascinating account of village life in Korea in mid-twentieth century. Dated, sometimes inaccurate historical introduction. [JBD]

14.159 Byung-nak Song. *The rise of the Korean economy.* Hong Kong: Oxford University Press, 1990. ISBN 0-19-583979-X. ‣ Argues Korean economic development a combination of government policy and sociocultural factors deriving from Confucian tradition. [JBD]

14.160 Jung- en Woo. *Race to the swift: state and finance in Korean industrialization.* New York: Columbia University Press, 1991. ISBN 0-231-07146-9. ‣ Stimulating study of role of state in South Korean economic development with emphasis on financial control and rise of *chaebŏl* (corporation) entrepreneurs. [JBD]

14.161 Yu Eui-Young and Earl H. Phillips, eds. *Korean women in transition: at home and abroad.* Los Angeles: California State University, Center for Korean-American and Korean Studies, 1987. (Korean-American and Korean Studies publications series, 5.) ISBN 0-9428310-04 (cl), 0-9428310-12 (pbk). ‣ Overview of life of Korean women in North and South Korea and United States. Features such topics as women in professions, women in low-income families, in work force, changing status of women, and women in immigrant families and organizations. [MR]

DAVID LELYVELD AND SANJAY SUBRAHMANYAM

South Asia

Bⱼritish imperial rule and political movements to create the modern nation states of India, Pakistan, Sri Lanka, Bangladesh, and Nepal have dominated academic studies of South Asian history. These studies, as well as modern works on the precolonial millennia, draw in large measure on the common international vocabulary of social science and history writing that has developed over the course of the nineteenth and twentieth centuries. Much of the most influential work has been written in English. Although there is a significant body of work in South Asian languages, before, during, and after the colonial period, a form of intellectual dualism ensures that these writings are relegated to secondary status. Most South Asian historians who can write in English prefer to do so in order to reach a more influential and international audience, if not a larger one. The contrast with China, Japan, and much of the Middle East is instructive here. Furthermore, for the period after about 1750, a large, even preponderant, number of historians, including South Asians who know at least one South Asian language, have confined their research to English-language sources.

The case is very different when one turns to the period before 1750, for here much depends on access to sources in other languages and scripts. Given the daunting number of vernacular and classical languages relevant to South Asian history, it is not surprising that more recent periods receive more attention. Many scholars trained outside South Asia, notably in the United Kingdom, have been particularly dependent on translations and secondary materials in English even when dealing with precolonial history. On the other hand, the legacies of Orientalism and classical Indology in the rest of Europe have resulted in somewhat different traditions of historiography. In the United States, the linking of South Asian studies to aid and development programs has encouraged more culturally and linguistically demanding training for scholars, particularly since the 1960s.

Other traditions of historiography already existed before the last quarter of the eighteenth century, when attempts were made under English East India Company rule in Bengal to develop a systematic construct of South Asian history appropriate to European ideologies and interests. The common assertion that precolonial India lacked a sense of history derives from anachronistic assumptions. Precolonial historiography included genealogies of communities and ruling houses and, after about 1000 CE, chronicles and histories that drew from both indigenous and Perso-Arabic literary traditions. Historians such as Kalhana, Juzjani, Zia al-Din Barani, Abu'l Fazl, 'Abd al-Qadir al-Badayuni, and 'Abd al-Hamid Lahori and anonymous chroniclers in Telugu, Malayalam, and Sinhala all produced voluminous works in the eight hundred years before the foundation of the Asiatic Society of Bengal. What is significant is the extent to which these indigenous traditions were discredited and displaced by the 1850s to make way for a new, often colonially sponsored, historiography.

The task of early colonial historiography was to establish a narrative framework in terms of political regimes and religious institutions, including what British officials took to be authoritative legal norms. Much of this writing sought to evaluate South Asia in contrast to European society, either as a place of classic stability or decadent stagnation, with few autonomous possibilities for change. Writers of varying persuasions, ranging from James Mill and Henry Maine to Karl Marx, described and propounded an India defined in terms of permanent beliefs and practices, crystallized in institutions such as caste, village community, and sect. Colonial historians developed a three-fold classification of historical eras that continues to dominate the field: Hindu, to about 1200 CE; Mohammedan (that is, Muslim), to about 1750; and British, inaugurated by the British seizure of power in Bengal. Later these periods became known respectively as ancient, medieval, and modern.

Much important work was done in the nineteenth and early twentieth centuries with respect to the first of these loosely defined blocks, the ancient. Archaeological findings, together with comparative linguistics, helped define a conception of early North Indian civilization associated with Aryans and a body of texts known as Vedas. Starting in 1922, archaeologists brought to light the pre-Vedic civilization of the Indus Valley, a subject that remains controversial with respect to language, date, and relationship to subsequent South Asian history. Archaeology, linguistics, epigraphy, and literary and religious studies all helped define and celebrate a classical Indian civilization from the third century BCE to the sixth century CE.

The worshipful attitude expressed in Orientalist scholarship toward classical India often carried with it a disparaging judgment of the period associated with Muslim rule, a period characterized by foreign conquest, indiscriminate pillage, and the atrophy of classical Indian institutions. Nationalist scholars, particularly those associated with Aligarh Muslim University, sought to redress the balance with respect to this period by focusing on the systematic and paternalistic character of administration and on the development of a rich cultural syncretism that flourished in this epoch.

In the postindependence period, the influence of Marxist historiography has led some South Asian writers to pose the entire historical process in terms of evolutionary stages, thus taking the sting out of the predominantly religious periodization imposed by colonial historians. Most ambitious was D. D. Kosambi (15.119), whose encyclopedic mind sought to systematize all Indian history into Marxian categories. Such work has generated a fierce debate about the appropriateness of such terms as "slavery" and "feudalism" in precolonial India, both among Marxist historians and between them and scholars guided by other traditions and ideologies.

The transition into colonialism has also been the subject of much debate, once the civilizing mission of the colonial power had been called into question. Soviet, Indian, and a few Western scholars tried to establish whether or not India had been on the brink of an autonomous transition to industrial capitalism, cut short by the British seizure of power. The focus here, as in much of the important work dealing with the period from 1500 to 1800, was on economic and political processes; the social and cultural consequences of the transition received far less attention. In this controversy, not all attitudes and positions have been predictable. The stand taken by South Asian scholars, particularly the Aligarh school, posited a relatively stagnant South Asian technology, stemming from elite indifference to change. In contrast, some Soviet scholars saw India in 1750 as on the verge of autonomous industrialization.

The colonial period, state policy, and the establishment of British power were the dominant themes in South Asian studies until a generation ago. Justification and condemnation of imperialism and concern with the possible formation of India as a modern nation-state overwhelmed other possible areas of historical investigation. Economic and social history was concerned with the ways in which British rule aided or hampered Indian progress toward wealth and power in the modern world or why supposedly stagnant Indian institutions remained impervious to foreign influence. Many historians were motivated by concern over the national unity of India: whether it was rooted in an ancient past that could be identified as Hindu and whether it excluded non-Hindus, notably Muslims, as essentially separate. In the years just before and after the partition of India and the creation of Pakistan in 1947, the issue of the place of Muslims in South Asian history and their relationship to the Mughals and other ruling dynasties that preceded British rule became a matter of intense historical debate. From the mid–1980s much of this debate over the place of Muslims as citizens of the modern Indian state has been revived.

Second only to issues of national unity have been questions concerned with India's economic development and the extent to which India's relative deprivation in modern times is a result of indigenous institutions or foreign exploitation. Various models of economic development, most often Marxian, have been tried particularly by historians who are themselves South Asians, against South Asian data and have resulted in vigorous theoretical and historiographic debate.

Outside South Asia itself, Britain has continued to be a major center of South Asian historical studies. The so-called Cambridge school, initiated by Anil Seal and brought to fruition in the work of C. A. Bayly and D. Washbrook, argued that British rule established structures of competition among self-serving elites. Private ambition gave rise to unintended institutional transformations in the form of voluntary associations and finally Indian nationalism and Muslim separatism. Most British historical studies of modern India have relied on British archival sources and have paid little attention to South Asian sources, particularly those that are only available in South Asian languages. In recent years, Cambridge school historians have turned to the role of precolonial formations and world history in their discussions of the modern period.

There have, however, been contrasting efforts to see South Asians as actors in a history that has not necessarily been driven by British models. Although South Asia has often been relegated to episodic appearances in the historical narratives of other societies, there is a continuous historical tradition, mostly associated with Indological studies, to account for indigenous institutions and conceptual systems. In contrast to the subcontinental framework, often inspired by nationalist aspirations, much historical work, especially in more recent years, has looked to local and regional history. This approach has been supported by the creation in the postindependence period of a federal-state system in India, demarcated according to modern standard languages. In contrast to most historians trained in Britain, historians trained in North America since the 1960s, such as the Chicago school associated with Bernard S. Cohn, have emphasized the study of South Asian consciousness while calling into question the colonial construction of knowledge about India.

A large body of historical studies has been concerned with agrarian society and economy, often in relation to the history of peasant movements and the possibilities of social revolution. Led by Ranajit Guha, the subaltern studies collective of scholars in India, Britain, and Australia has developed new research strategies in an effort to document the consciousness and agency of the great majority of the Indian population. During the same period there has been an important new literature on the history of women. Often set in the framework of older narratives of nationalism, it increasingly seeks to establish alternative historical perspectives. Other new tendencies have drawn upon the world-systems approach of Immanuel Wallerstein (22.275) and postmodernist skepticism about the identification of systematic and continuous historical institutions. Current South Asian historiography has fully entered the debates of contemporary cultural and social theory in much of the rest of the world.

[Contributors: AAY = Anand A. Yang, DEL = David E. Ludden, DSL = David S. Lelyveld, FFC = Frank F. Conlon, GLP = Gregory L. Possehl, PKO = Philip K. Oldenburg, RSN = Richard S. Newell, SS = Sanjay Subrahmanyam.]

REFERENCE WORKS

South Asia General

15.1 M. S. Andronov. *Dravidian languages.* D. M. Segal, trans. Moscow, Russia: Nauka, Central Department of Oriental Literature, 1970. ▸ Authoritative, succinct work from viewpoint of comparative linguistics but addressing issues of historicity. [SS]

15.2 V. D. Divekar, ed. *Annotated bibliography on the economic history of India (1500 A.D. to 1947 A.D.)* 4 vols. in 5. Poona and New Delhi: Gokhale Institute of Politics and Economics and Indian Council of Social Science Research, 1977–80. ▸ Official papers and reports with selections from records, gazetteers, cen-

sus reports, legislation, books, articles, and theses. Multiple sectional indexes and categories require close attention. [FFC]

15.3 N. N. Gidwani and K. Navalani, eds. and comps. *A guide to reference materials on India.* 2 vols. Jaipur, India: Saraswati, 1974. ▸ Multidisciplinary guide to bibliographies, yearbooks, and gazetteers with extensive listings in volume 2 to Indian- and European-language sources in history, literature, art, and social sciences. Needs updating and lacks annotation but nonetheless useful. [DSL]

15.4 D. A. Low, J. C. Iltis, and Mary Doreen Wainwright, eds. *Government archives in South Asia: a guide to national and state archives in Ceylon, India, and Pakistan.* London: Cambridge University Press, 1969. ISBN 0-521-07507-6. ▸ Detailed listing of categories, locations, and nature of holdings at state and national level, with some indication of history of their establishment and rules of access. Outdated and incomplete, but still most useful preliminary overview. [DSL]

15.5 Colin P. Masica. *The Indo-Aryan languages.* Cambridge: Cambridge University Press, 1991. ISBN 0-521-23420-4. ▸ Comparative analysis of linguistic features of Indo-Aryan languages of northern India, Pakistan, Nepal, Bangladesh, and Sri Lanka. Not historically oriented. [DSL]

15.6 Martin Moir. *A general guide to the India Office records.* London: British Library, 1988. ISBN 0-7123-0629-3. ▸ Administrative organization and background of East India Company and Government of India supplements descriptive inventory of India Office records under post-1967 classifications. Essential scholarly companion for research. [FFC]

15.7 Maureen L. P. Patterson. *South Asian civilizations: a bibliographic synthesis.* Chicago: University of Chicago Press, 1981. ISBN 0-226-64910-5. ▸ Modern bibliography on all aspects of South Asian history, culture, arts, and contemporary affairs with emphasis on books available in North America. Modern and contemporary materials organized in regionally defined sections requiring care for subcontinental searches. [FFC]

15.8 J. D. Pearson, ed. *South Asian bibliography: a handbook and guide.* South Asia Library Group, comp. Hassocks, England and Atlantic Highlands, N.J.: Harvester and Humanities, 1979. ISBN 0-391-00819-6. ▸ Wide-ranging handbook compiled by librarians and scholars on manuscripts, archives, theses, and printed books. Efficient access to very useful information hindered by uneven presentation and indexing. [FFC]

15.9 Francis Robinson, ed. *The Cambridge encyclopedia of India, Pakistan, Bangladesh, Sri Lanka, Nepal, Bhutan, and the Maldives.* Cambridge: Cambridge University Press, 1989. ISBN 0-521-33451-9. ▸ South Asian and Western specialists offer major reference on subcontinent's history, culture, economy, and society. Utility of excellent articles slightly limited by absence of extended cross-references or alternative topical indexing apparatus. [FFC]

15.10 Carol Sakala. *Women of South Asia: a guide to resources.* Maureen L. P. Patterson, Foreword. Millwood, N.Y.: Kraus International, 1980. ISBN 0-527-78574-1. ▸ Comprehensive bibliography of materials on South Asian women. Limited by its appearance prior to recent expansion of women-centered research, but still best introduction to literature. [FFC]

15.11 Joseph E. Schwartzberg, ed. *A historical atlas of South Asia.* 1978 ed. New York: Oxford University Press, 1992. (Association for Asian Studies, Reference series, 2.) ISBN 0-19-506869-6. ▸ Comprehensive atlas of subcontinental history presenting mappable geographic features and relationships. Monument of scholarly endeavor presenting rich documentation and insights with revisions and corrections in map plates and text. [FFC]

15.12 O.H.K. Spate and A. T. Learmonth. *India and Pakistan: a general and regional geography.* 1967 3d rev. ed. London:

Methuen, 1972. ▸ Standard geography of South Asia, including Sri Lanka and what is now Bangladesh, with period-piece analyses of peoples, history, and economy. Political and social information now outdated but of historical significance. [PKO]

15.13 Henry Yule and A. C. Burnell. *Hobson-Jobson: a glossary of colloquial Anglo-Indian words and phrases, and kindred terms, etymological, historical, geographical, and discursive.* 1903 2d ed. William Crooke, ed. London: Routledge & Kegan Paul, 1985. ISBN 0-7100-2886-5. ▸ Historical dictionary, documented with literary quotations, of words, often loosely derived from South Asian languages, that appear in English texts germane to South Asian studies. Indispensable and often entertaining guide to European knowledge and perceptions. [DSL]

SEE ALSO
11.1 *Bibliography of Asian studies.*
11.17 Frank Joseph Shulman, ed. and comp. *Doctoral dissertations on Asia.*
13.1 Ainslie T. Embree, ed. *Encyclopedia of Asian history.*
17.12 J. D. Pearson, ed. *Index Islamicus.*
18.29 J. D. Pearson, et al., eds. *Index Islamicus.*

Afghanistan, Nepal, and Sri Lanka

15.14 Ludwig W. Adamec, ed. *Historical and political gazetteer of Afghanistan.* 6 vols. Graz: Akademische Druck- & Verlagsanstalt, 1972–85. ISBN 3-201-00857-5 (v. 2), 3-201-00942-3 (v. 3), 3-201-01089-8 (v. 4), 3-201-01125-8 (v. 5), 3-201-01272-6 (v. 6). ▸ Extensively revised edition of original Government of India gazetteer of Afghanistan published in 1914. Unique reference for study of Afghanistan's geographic features, regions, tribes and communities, localities, and social conditions at beginning of twentieth century. [RSN]

15.15 L. Boulnois and H. Millot. *Bibliographie du Népal.* Vol. 1 and Supplement: *Science humaines, référence en langues européenes* and *Science humaines, référence en langues européenes, supplement, 1967–73.* Paris: Centre National de la Recherche Scientifique, 1969–75. ISBN 2-222-01893-5 (suppl.) ▸ Copious listing of references to history, religion, anthropology, politics, and economics of Nepal. Unannotated and unselective but relatively complete to 1973. [DSL]

15.16 H.A.I. Goonetileke. *A bibliography of Ceylon: a systematic guide to the literature on the land, people, history, and culture published in Western languages from the sixteenth century to the present day.* 5 vols. to date. Zug, Switzerland: Inter Documentation, 1970–. ISBN 3-85750-015-8 (v. 3), 3-85750-051-4 (v. 4), 3-85750-054-4 (v. 5). ▸ Comprehensive bibliographical project of works published in European languages. Useful organization with valuable annotations in later two volumes. [DSL]

15.17 Schuyler Jones, comp. *Afghanistan.* Oxford: Clio, 1992. (World bibliographical series, 135.) ISBN 1-85109-140-8. ▸ Up-to-date, general bibliography, including history, of works available in English dealing with geographical area of Afghanistan. Introductory rather than comprehensive work, well organized with informative annotations. [DSL]

15.18 Patrick Peebles. *Sri Lanka: a handbook of historical statistics.* Boston: Hall, 1982. ISBN 0-8161-8160-8. ▸ Statistical tables, with brief introductions, of population, migration, commerce, agriculture, and government administration. Data drawn entirely from nineteenth and twentieth centuries. [DSL]

HISTORIOGRAPHY

South Asia General

15.19 Sarvepalli Gopal, ed. *Anatomy of a confrontation: the Babri Masjid–Ramjanmbhumi issue.* New Delhi, India: Viking, 1991. ISBN 0-670-83984-1. ▸ Collection of essays dealing with contem-

porary political controversy over site claimed by both Hindus and Muslims. Excellent essays, from secular perspective, on political uses of history. [DSL]

15.20 Ronald B. Inden. *Imagining India.* Oxford: Blackwell, 1990. ISBN 0-631-16923-7. ▸ Critique of dominant historiographic constructions of religion, kingship, caste, and village community. Presents alternative historical approach to institutions of monarchy. Complex, controversial, and stimulating work covering critical theory to practical historical scholarship. [DSL]

15.21 C. H. Philips, ed. *Historians of India, Pakistan, and Ceylon.* 1961 ed. London: Oxford University Press, 1967. ▸ Good introduction to historical writing in India to 1947, especially on role of British imperial and nationalist writing that deals with more geographically dominant political regimes. [FFC]

15.22 *Problems of historical writing in India: proceedings of the seminar held at the India International Centre, New Delhi, 21st–25th January 1963.* New Delhi, India: India International Centre, 1963. ▸ Brief statements of broad interdisciplinary historiographic agenda, predominantly by leading young Indian historians early in their careers. Significant introduction to their work. [DSL]

15.23 Siba Pada Sen, ed. *Historians and historiography in modern India.* Calcutta, India: Institute of Historical Studies, 1973. ▸ Essays on pioneering Indian historians since nineteenth century. Collection argues for separate Indian nationalist historiographic tradition. Particularly strong on historians of ancient India, a useful antidote to Philips, ed. 15.21, but limited by biographical emphasis and exclusion of Muslim writers. [DSL]

15.24 Romila Thapar. *The past and prejudice.* New Delhi, India: Ministry of Information and Broadcasting, Publications Division, 1973. ▸ Concise critique of "stereotypes" of South Asian history, including notions of caste, Oriental despotism, Aryan race, Asian mode of production, and absence of change. Written for general audience; pioneering effort to liberate historiography of India from Orientalist preconceptions. [DSL]

15.25 Romila Thapar, Harbans Mukhia, and Bipan Chandra. *Communalism and the writing of Indian history.* Delhi: People's, 1969. ▸ Three essays critical of conventional construction of South Asian history in terms of ancient (Hindu), medieval (Muslim), and modern (British and nationalist). By three Indian scholars whose work deals with these periods and who are secular and nationalist in orientation. [DSL]

Sri Lanka

15.26 R.A.L.H. Gunawardana. "The people of the lion: Sinhala consciousness in history and historiography." In *Ethnicity and social change in Sri Lanka: papers presented at a seminar organized by the Social Scientists' Association, December 1979,* pp. 1–53. Colombo: Social Scientists' Association, 1984. ▸ Historical survey of term Sinhala in relation to ruling dynasties, religion, language, territory, and physical appearance. Calls into question racist and nationalist concepts of group identity. Essential historiographic critique of dominant literature on Sri Lanka. [DSL]

15.27 Steven Kemper. *The presence of the past: chronicles, politics, and culture in Sinhala life.* Ithaca, N.Y.: Cornell University Press, 1991. ISBN 0-8014-2395-3. ▸ Study of how twentieth-century nationalists used ancient myths and chronicles to establish ideology of nationalism based on Buddhism, Sinhalese language, and racial theory. Nonreductionist argument for historically dynamic concept of culture in relation to power. [DSL]

HISTORICAL SURVEYS

South Asia General

15.28 K. Antonova, G. M. Bongard-Levin, and G. Kostovsky. *A history of India.* 2 vols. Katharine Judelson, trans. Moscow,

Russia: Progress, 1979. ‣ Important work of Soviet school, representing collaboration among specialists. Particularly strong on early India, Islam, and North Indian medieval states (from materialist perspective); unsatisfactory on colonial period. [SS]

15.29 *The Cambridge history of India.* Edition varies. 5 vols. in 6. Delhi: Chand, 1963–68. ‣ Chapters and volumes by diverse hands, all British, heavily weighted to historical role of foreign conquerors and rise and fall of imperial state formations, from Aryans to Greeks to Turks and ultimately to establishment of British rule and its exercise to 1918. First published 1922. Good coverage of military history. Volume 2 on first millennium CE never appeared. Culminating work of British colonial historiography. [DSL]

15.30 Damodar Dharmanand Kosambi. *An introduction to the study of Indian history.* 1975 2d rev. ed. London: Sangam, 1985. ISBN 0-86132-065-4 (pbk). ‣ General work of Marxist interpretation, widely used as introductory text in India. Important insights, especially into ancient period, but often too sweeping in generalization. [SS]

15.31 Hermann Külke and Dietmar Rothermund. *A history of India.* 1986 ed. London: Routledge, 1990. ISBN 0-415-04799-4. ‣ Great strengths of this survey are first three chapters, covering early civilizations to early Middle Ages. Much of post-1500 materials should be used with caution. [SS]

15.32 R. C. Majumdar, ed. *The history and culture of the Indian people.* 11 vols. Bombay, India: Bharatiya Vidya Bhavan, 1951–77. ‣ Major postindependence historical project by leading nationalist historians, supplanting older *Cambridge History of India* (15.29). Places great emphasis on Indian cultural and political unity and continuity based on brahmanic norms. Gives achievement or decline of large-scale imperial formations exaggerated prominence. Uneven in quality, apologetic in tone, biased on role of Muslims in Indian civilization; weak on modern period. [DSL]

15.33 Jawaharlal Nehru. *The discovery of India.* 1946 ed. Delhi: Oxford University Press, 1989. ISBN 0-19-562394-0 (cl), 0-19-562359-2 (pbk). ‣ Written by great Indian nationalist in prison during early 1940s. Broad, inclusive vision of South Asian history. Weak in scholarship and ideologically much contested, but most influential argument for India's fundamental unity. [DSL]

15.34 H. L. Seneviratne, ed. "Identity, consciousness, and the past: the South Asian scene." *Social analysis* 25 (September 1989). ISSN 0155-977X. ‣ Anthropological studies in construction of historical consciousness with respect to religious, ethnic, and national identities in southern India, Sri Lanka, and Nepal. Using variety of textual sources, demonstrates ways histories are continually refashioned. [DSL]

15.35 Vincent A. Smith. *The Oxford history of India.* 4th ed. Percival Spear, ed. Delhi: Oxford University Press, 1981. ISBN 0-19-561297-3 (pbk). ‣ Summary of findings and interpretations of British imperial historiography. Largely useful as strawman; tone and interpretations still echo, not least in postcolonial South Asia. Corrected version of 1958 revision of 1919 survey of South Asian history. [DSL]

15.36 Romila Thapar and Percival Spear. *A history of India.* 1966 ed. 2 vols. Baltimore: Penguin, 1982. ISBN 0-14-020769-4 (v. 1, pbk), 0-14-020770-8 (v. 2, pbk). ‣ Wisely but somewhat unconventionally divided at sixteenth century. Concise two-volume survey concerned with history of social institutions. Volume 1 by Thapar is outstanding work of synthesis and interpretation; volume 2 by Spear, undistinguished. [DSL]

Regional and Local Surveys

15.37 Olaf Caroe. *The Pathans, 550 B.C.–A.D. 1957.* 1958 ed. Karachi, Pakistan: Oxford University Press, 1983. ISBN 0-19-

577221-0. ‣ Historical survey of Pashtun tribes on both sides of what is now border between Afghanistan and Pakistan. Classic British account by colonial offical. [RSN]

15.38 Louis Dupree. *Afghanistan.* 1973 ed. Princeton: Princeton University Press, 1980. ISBN 0-691-00023-9 (pbk). ‣ Encyclopedic discussion of landscape, history, culture, politics, arts, and social organization, centering on Afghan monarchy and its demise in 1970s. Standard reference with personalized touch. [RSN]

15.39 Robert Eric Frykenberg, ed. *Delhi through the ages: studies in urban history, culture, and society.* Delhi: Oxford University Press, 1986. ISBN 0-19-561728-2. ‣ Collection of essays arranged in chronological sections presenting wide range of Indian social and cultural history, particularly since establishment of Muslim dynastic rule, from perspective of what has often been great capital city. Not to be read as single narrative, but rich for particularity of research presented here. [DSL]

15.40 K. A. Nilakanta Sastri. *A history of South India from prehistoric times to the fall of Vijayanagar.* 4th ed. Madras, India: Oxford University Press, 1976. ‣ Valuable reference work, particularly for political history in dynastic mode; less convincing on cultural and socioeconomic aspects. Author was major mid-century authority on South Indian history and doyen of University of Madras school. [SS]

15.41 Rishikesh Shaha. *Ancient and medieval Nepal.* New Delhi, India: Manohar, 1992. ISBN 81-85425-69-8. ‣ Broad survey of Nepal's history from Licchavis (fifth century CE) to late eighteenth century. Chronological organization, with brief chapters on social, religious, and architectural history. Old-fashioned work. [SS]

15.42 K. M. de Silva. *A history of Sri Lanka.* Delhi: Oxford University Press, 1981. ISBN 0-19-561371-6. ‣ Historical survey from fifth century BCE to 1981 with greatest emphasis on European, particularly British, domination. Comprehensive introduction but best as political history; Sinhalese nationalist perspective. [DSL]

Topical Studies

15.43 A. L. Basham, ed. *A cultural history of India.* Oxford: Clarendon, 1975. ISBN 0-19-821914-8. ‣ Thirty-five chapters by specialists surveying aspects of ancient, medieval, and modern South Asian culture and institutions. Some contributions retained from original *Legacy of India* (1937) which it succeeds. [FFC]

15.44 Madeleine Biardeau. *Hinduism: the anthropology of a civilization.* Richard Nice, trans. Delhi: Oxford University Press, 1989. ISBN 0-19-562409-2. ‣ Combines anthropological insights with textual material. Influenced by author's training as textual scholar. [SS]

15.45 J. Duncan M. Derrett. *Religion, law, and the state in India.* New York: Free Press, 1968. ‣ Analytic and historical essays on history of religious codes and legal systems based on Sanskrit and, to lesser extent, Islamic sources and their institutionalized interpretation by British colonial and postcolonial Indian authorities. Major work on South Asian legal history. [DSL]

15.46 Madhav M. Deshpande. *Sociolinguistic attitudes in India: an historical reconstruction.* Ann Arbor: Karoma, 1979. ISBN 0-89720-007-1 (cl), 0-89720-008-X (pbk). ‣ Wide-ranging survey of prestige of Sanskrit and linguistic forms of resistance in development of alternative literary languages associated with non-brahmanical religious movements, Jainism, Buddhism, and Islam. Concludes with history of Marathi language. Brief but stimulating treatment. [DSL]

15.47 Louis Dumont. *Homo hierarchicus: the caste system and its implications.* 1980 rev. ed. Mark Sainsbury, Louis Dumont, and

Basia Gulati, trans. Delhi: Oxford University Press, 1988. ISBN 0-19-562133-6. ▸ Effort to present all-encompassing structural theory of South Asian civilization dominated by religious ideology of hierarchy and subordination of worldly power and individual motivation. Utterly ahistorical, but seminal text of European Indology that has inspired much scholarship, often by way of refutation. [DSL]

15.48 Louis Dumont. *Religion, politics, and history in India: collected papers in Indian sociology.* Paris: Mouton, 1970. ▸ Important essays on individual identity, caste, marriage, religion, and nationalism by major anthropologist and theoretician of South Asian culture. Provocative attempt at unified theory; read alongside 15.47. [DSL]

15.49 Ainslie T. Embree, ed. *Sources of Indian tradition.* Vol. 1: *From the beginning to 1800.* 2d ed. New York: Columbia University Press, 1988. ISBN 0-231-06650-3 (v. 1, cl), 0-231-06651-1 (v. 1, pbk). ▸ Selected texts of major religious traditions of South Asia with brief introductions and commentary. Lucid presentation for beginning students, but confined to narrow concept of high culture. [DSL]

15.50 Jean Filliozat. *India: the country and its traditions.* Margaret Ledesert, trans. Englewood Cliffs, N.J.: Prentice-Hall, 1962. ▸ Work of century's leading French Indologist. Characteristic mix of anthropology and textual tradition. Weak on medieval and early modern developments. [SS]

15.51 Madhav Gadgil and Ramachandra Guha. *This fissured land: an ecological history of India.* Berkeley: University of California Press, 1993. ISBN 0-520-07621-4 (cl), 0-520-08296-6 (pbk). ▸ Ambitious attempt to analyze gamut of Indian history from ecological perspective. Pre-1800 section is highly schematic, at times mechanistic, and occupies half book; post-1800 section more conventional study of state policy and ecological debates. [SS]

15.52 Hermann Goetz. *The art of India: five thousand years of Indian art.* 2d ed. New York: Crown, 1964. ▸ Magisterial survey by great art historian of India. Useful as introduction but clearly dated on many specific topics. [SS]

15.53 J. C. Heesterman. *The inner conflict of tradition: essays in Indian ritual, kingship, and society.* Chicago: University of Chicago Press, 1985. ISBN 0-226-32297-1 (cl), 0-226-32299-8 (pbk). ▸ Indologist's interpretation of Indian institutions as dominated by brahmanical rituals and ideologies that subordinate political and economic realms. Dubious attempt to use ancient textual materials to interpret later, including modern, historical regimes and social practices. [DSL]

15.54 *A history of Indian literature.* Wiesbaden: Harrassowitz, 1973–. ▸ Ongoing multivolume series issued in fascicles on history of literatures in major South Asian languages and particular genres. Monument of recent European Indological scholarship. [DSL]

15.55 David Ludden. *Peasant history in South India.* Princeton: Princeton University Press, 1985. ISBN 0-691-05456-8. ▸ Peasant history of Tirunelveli region of Tamil Nadu from 900 CE to early nineteenth century. Combines technological and institutional history, internal dynamics, and external influences. Well-focused, but broadly significant, long-duration history. [DSL]

15.56 Barbara Stoler Miller, ed. *The powers of art: patronage in Indian culture.* Delhi: Oxford University Press, 1992. ISBN 0-19-562842-X. ▸ Nineteen papers on various aspects of patronage organized in four broadly chronological sections: ancient India, South India, Mughal and Hindu courts, and British rule. [SS]

15.57 K. M. Panikkar. *Geographical factors in Indian history.* 3d ed. Bombay, India: Bharatiya Vidya Bhavan, 1969. ▸ Firm nationalist perspective stressing geographic coherence of India. Revisits same arguments elsewhere on land versus sea, etc. [SS]

15.58 R. Ramachandran. *Urbanization and urban systems in India.* Delhi: Oxford University Press, 1989. ISBN 0-19-562140-9. ▸ Survey of India's urban system and urbanization process, both historical and in terms of contemporary geographical theory. Historical materials tend toward generality, yet suggestive in light of concentration on modern conditions. [FFC]

15.59 John F. Richards, ed. *Kingship and authority in South Asia.* 2d ed. Madison: South Asian Studies, University of Wisconsin-Madison, 1981. ▸ Papers on kingship, antiquity to eighteenth-century precolonial period, primarily from perspective of variety of religious ideologies and practices. Suggestive comparative study from diverse chronological, regional, and theoretical perspectives. [DSL]

15.60 Dietmar Rothermund. *An economic history of India: from pre-colonial times to 1986.* London: Croom Helm with Methuen, 1988. ISBN 0-7099-4228-1. ▸ Extremely useful, sound survey of economic history touching most major themes and updating debates in many specialized fields. Especially valuable for its handling of transition to national economic development in context of long-term economic history. [DEL]

15.61 Susie Tharu and K. Lalita, eds. *Women writing in India: 600 B.C. to the present.* Vol. 1: *600 B.C. to the early twentieth century.* New York: Feminist Press at the City University of New York; distributed by Talman, 1991. ISBN 1-55861-026-X (v. 1, cl), 1-55861-027-8 (v. 1, pbk). ▸ Literary anthology with translations from major South Asian languages and extensive commentary on historical contexts. Important cooperative research effort opening large new territory. [DSL]

ARCHAEOLOGICAL STUDIES TO ca. 600 CE

Prehistory

15.62 Bridget Allchin, Andrew Goudie, and Karunarkara Hegde. *The prehistory and palaeogeography of the Great Indian desert.* London: Academic, 1978. ISBN 0-12-050450-2. ▸ Geological, geographical, and archaeological survey of Thar desert, synthesizing all previous work. Especially strong on Upper Pleistocene. [GLP]

15.63 Shashi Asthana. *History and archaeology of India's contacts with other countries, from earliest times to 300 B.C.* Delhi: B. R. Publishing; distributed by D. K. Publishers' Distributors, 1976. ▸ Survey of transregional contacts focusing most prominently on maritime contacts with Mesopotamia during Mature Harappan period. Well documented. [GLP]

15.64 Shashi Asthana. *Pre-Harappan cultures of India and the borderlands.* New Delhi, India: Books & Books, 1985. ISBN 81-85016-13-5. ▸ Survey of archaeology on which mature, urban-phase Harappan culture rests. Strong on descriptive issues, rather than theory. Good bibliography. [GLP]

15.65 Warwick Ball and Jean-Claude Gardin. *Archaeological gazetteer of Afghanistan/Catalogue des sites archeologiques d'Afghanistan.* 2 vols. Paris: Éditions Recherches sur les Civilisations, 1982. (Synthese, 8.) ISBN 2-86538-040-8 (set). ▸ Annotated gazetteer, articles, maps, and bibliography on archaeological sites of Afghanistan. Excellent coverage. [GLP]

15.66 N. R. Banerjee. *The Iron Age in India.* Robert Heine-Geldern, Foreword. Delhi: Munshiram Manoharlal, 1965. ▸ Useful, very careful archaeologist's summary of evidence on Iron Age. Current to date of publication. Meticulous historiographical summary. Somewhat dated in relation to new findings, but nevertheless significant marker. [SS]

15.67 Dilip K. Chakrabarti. *The early use of iron in India.* Delhi: Oxford University Press, 1992. ISBN 0-19-562992-2. ▸ Brief work in six chapters, recapitulating earlier papers by same author.

Argues for full-fledged Iron Age in North India ca. 1000 BCE. Uses archaeological and literary sources. [SS]

15.68 Dilip K. Chakrabarti. *A history of Indian archaeology: from the beginning to 1947*. New Delhi, India: Munshiram Manoharlal, 1988. ISBN 81-215-0079-6. ‣ History of development of archaeology as scholarly discipline with respect to South Asia. Strong on eighteenth- and nineteenth-century archaeology. [GLP]

15.69 R. N. Dandekar. *Harappan bibliography*. Poona: Bhandarkar Oriental Research Institute, 1987. (Government Oriental series, Class B, 15.) ‣ Comprehensive annotated compilation, arranged topically. Best available bibliography. [GLP]

15.70 Walter A. Fairservis, Jr. *The Harappan civilization and its writing: a model for the decipherment of the Indus script*. Delhi: Oxford University Press and IBH, 1992. ISBN 81-204-0491- 2. ‣ Most recent effort to decipher first South Asian form of writing. Like all other attempts, suggestive but unprovable. [GLP]

15.71 Walter A. Fairservis, Jr. *The roots of ancient India*. 2d ed. Chicago: University of Chicago Press, 1975. ISBN 0-226-23429-0 (pbk). ‣ Comprehensive survey of prehistoric archaeology of South Asia from Paleolithic to early Iron Age. Especially strong on Harappan civilization. [GLP]

15.72 Michael Jansen. *Die Indus-Zivilisation: Wiederentdeckung einer frühen Hochkultur*. Cologne: DuMont, 1986. ISBN 3-7701-1435-3. ‣ Most recent comprehensive study by head of project to resurvey site of Mohenjo-daro. Especially strong on history of archaeological studies of Harappan civilization. [GLP]

15.73 B. B. Lal and S. P. Gupta, eds. *Frontiers of the Indus civilization: Sir Mortimer Wheeler commemoration volume*. New Delhi, India: Books & Books for Indian Archaeological Society with Indian History and Culture Society, 1984. ISBN 0-85672-231-6. ‣ Compilation of recent studies by prominent authorities on broad range of Harappan topics. Well illustrated, good bibliographies. [GLP]

15.74 Giancarlo Ligabue and Sandro Salvatori, eds. *Bactria: an ancient oasis civilization from the sands of Afghanistan*. Venice, Italy: Erizzo, 1988. ISBN 88-7077-025-7. ‣ Survey of recent archaeological finds from Bronze Age Bactria. Excellent chapters by specialists. Beautifully illustrated. [GLP]

15.75 John Marshall, ed. *Mohenjo-daro and the Indus civilization: being an official account of archaeological excavations at Mohenjo-daro carried out by the Government of India between the years 1922 and 1927*. 1931 ed. 3 vols. Delhi: Indological Book House, 1973. ‣ Classic report edited by person chiefly responsible for initial work at Mohenjo-daro. Much, especially Marshall's contributions, has not yet been eclipsed. [GLP]

15.76 Gregory L. Possehl, ed. *Ancient cities of the Indus*. Durham, N.C.: Carolina Academic, 1979. ISBN 0-89089-093-5. ‣ Reprints older, but still useful classical literature on Indus Valley archaeology with good bibliography. [GLP]

15.77 Gregory L. Possehl, ed. *Harappan civilization: a contemporary perspective*. Warminster, Pa.: Aris & Phillips with American Institute of Indian Studies, 1982. ISBN 0-85668-211-X. ‣ Collection of recent work on first South Asian urban societies. Wide range of topics, good bibliographies; well illustrated. [GLP]

15.78 Gregory L. Possehl and Paul C. Rissman. "The chronology of prehistoric India: from earliest times to the Iron Age." In *Chronologies in Old World archaeology*. 3d ed. Robert W. Ehrich, ed., vol. 1, pp. 465–90. Chicago: University of Chicago Press, 1992. ISBN 0-226-19447-7 (set), 0-226-19445-0 (v. 1). ‣ Extensive paper establishing chronological framework for prehistoric South Asia. Copious radiocarbon data contextualized within general view of Indian history. [GLP]

15.79 Shereen Ratnagar. *Encounters: the westerly trade of Harappa civilization*. Delhi: Oxford University Press, 1981. ISBN 0-19-561253-1. ‣ Survey of commerce and contacts between Harappan civilization and Mesopotamia. Excellent research, well documented and illustrated. [GLP]

15.80 Jim G. Shaffer. "The Indus Valley, Baluchistan, and Helmand traditions: Neolithic through Bronze Age." In *Chronologies in Old World archaeology*. 3d ed. Robert W. Ehrich, ed., vol. 1, pp. 441–64. Chicago: University of Chicago Press, 1992. ISBN 0-226-19445-0 (v. 1). ‣ Chronology of prehistoric materials from what is now Pakistan and Afghanistan. Most recent and authoritative discussion. [GLP]

15.81 Vibha Tripathi. *The painted grey ware, an Iron Age culture of northern India*. 1975 ed. Delhi: Concept, 1976. ‣ Report of evidence from archaeological sites after Hastinapura excavation. Discusses beginning of Iron Age in middle Gangetic plain. Plates and figures. [SS]

15.82 Mortimer Wheeler. *The Indus civilization: supplementary volume to the Cambridge History of India*. 3d ed. Cambridge: Cambridge University Press, 1968. ISBN 0-521-06958-0 (cl), 0-521-09538-7 (pbk). ‣ Classic, influential work by archaeologist of early excavations at both Mohenjo-daro and Harappa. Concise, well written, but weak bibliography and illustrations. [GLP]

SEE ALSO
2.36 Viktor I. Sarianidi. *Die Kunst des alten Afghanistan*.
2.37 D. P. Agrawal. *The archaeology of India*.
2.38 Bridgit Allchin and Raymond Allchin. *The rise of civilization in India and Pakistan*.
2.39 F. Raymond Allchin and N. Hammond, eds. *The archaeology of Afghanistan from the earliest times to the Timurid period*.
2.40 A. Ghosh, ed. *An encyclopaedia of Indian archaeology*.
2.41 Catherine Jarrige, ed. *South Asian archaeology, 1989*.
2.42 Gregory L. Possehl. "Revolution in the urban revolution."
2.43 H. D. Sankalia. *The prehistory and protohistory of India and Pakistan*.
2.44 Maurizio Taddei, ed. *South Asian archaeology 1987*.

Dravidian, Indo-Aryan, and the Vedic Era

15.83 T. Balakrishnan Nayar. *The problem of Dravidian origins: a linguistic, anthropological, and archaeological approach*. Madras, India: University of Madras, 1977. ‣ Wide-ranging, multidisciplinary approach to origins of Dravidians, recapitulating earlier articles by same author. [SS]

15.84 G. M. Bongard-Levin. *The origin of Aryans: from Scythis to India*. Harish C. Gupta, trans. New Delhi, India: Arnold-Heinemann, 1980. ‣ Brief, lucid work by Russian authority in five chapters. Uses comparative linguistics and other evidence to trace Aryans' trajectory to their arrival in North India. [SS]

15.85 Haran Chandra Chaklador. *The Aryan occupation of eastern India*. Nirmal Kumar Basu, ed. Calcutta, India: Maitra; distributed by Mukhopadhyay, 1962. ‣ Brief study, tracing evidence on Aryan presence and aryanization of eastern India, including Bengal. [SS]

15.86 V. Gordon Childe. *The Aryans: a study of Indo-European origins*. 1926 ed. New York: Dorset, 1987. ISBN 0-88029-139-7. ‣ Classic early work, by general and comparative historian of ancient world, summing up main hypotheses as well as evidence—literary, linguistic, and archaeological—on Aryans. [SS]

15.87 R. N. Dandekar. *Vedic bibliography*. 4 vols. Bombay, India and Poona: Karnatak and University of Poona, 1946–85. ‣ Massive work, over 2,000 pages, tracing work done since 1930. Continues earlier bibliography prepared by Renou (15.99). Includes work on Indus Valley civilization. [SS]

15.88 Madhav M. Deshpande and Peter Edwin Hook. *Aryan*

and non-Aryan in India. Ann Arbor: University of Michigan, Center for South and Southeast Asian Studies, 1979. ISBN 0-89148-014-5. ‣ Edited volume, including eight papers mainly on lexical, linguistic, and literary matters. Useful introductory chapter by Basham. [SS]

15.89 C. von Fürer-Haimendorf. "When, how, and from where did the Dravidians come to India." *Indo-Asian culture* 2.3 (1954) 238–47. ISSN 0019-7203. ‣ Brief but important statement by major ethnologist and anthropologist of India addressing problem of Dravidian origins. [SS]

15.90 U. N. Ghoshal. *A history of Hindu public life.* Vol. 1: *Period of the Vedic samhitas, the brahmanas, and the older Upanishads.* Calcutta, India: Ghoshal, 1945–66. ‣ Interesting, somewhat antiquarian approach to public institutions and social history by extremely prolific Indian historian of wide interests. [SS]

15.91 G. S. Ghurye. *Vedic India.* Bombay, India: Bhaktal for Popular Prakashan; distributed by Banarsidas, 1979. ‣ Voluminous work, published by leading Indian sociologist late in life. Applies sociological insights to textual study of mainly Sanskrit materials. [SS]

15.92 Jan Gonda. *Vedic literature (samhitas and brahmanas).* Vol. 1.1 of *A history of Indian literature.* Wiesbaden: Harrassowitz, 1975. ISBN 3-447-01603-5. ‣ Voluminous work by leading authority on early Sanskrit literature. Provides extensive and accessible approach to these writings. [SS]

15.93 P. Joseph. *The Dravidian problem in the South Indian culture complex.* Madras, India: Orient Longman, 1972. ‣ Brief statement outlining nature of problem of Dravidian origins from largely social anthropological and linguistic viewpoint. [SS]

15.94 N. N. Law. *Age of the "Rgveda."* Calcutta, India: Mukhopadhyay, 1965. ‣ One of several brief studies devoted to nature of society and social relations, largely from internal Vedic evidence. [SS]

15.95 Arthur Anthony Macdonell and Arthur Berriedale Keith. *Vedic index of names and subjects.* 1912 ed. 2 vols. Delhi: Motilal Banarsidass, 1967. ‣ Useful research tool, but criticized for anachronistic parallels with terminology from European history. Entries on major and minor substantives in Vedic texts with extensive Sanskrit term index and index for English. [SS]

15.96 D. D. Mehta. *Positive sciences in the Vedas.* New Delhi, India: Heinemann, 1974. ‣ Discussion of nature of scientific, mathematical, and applied scientific knowledge in Vedic textual tradition. Eschews extravagant claims often made for Vedic science. [SS]

15.97 Asko Parpola. "The coming of the Aryans to Iran and India and the cultural and ethnic identity of the Dasas." *Orientalia,* n.s., 64 (1988) 194–302. ISSN 0030-5367. ‣ Extensive article reopening key questions of Aryan arrival in South and Southwest Asia and relations with earlier settlers. [SS]

15.98 Wilhelm Rau. *The meaning of "pur" in Vedic literature.* Munich: Fink, 1976. ISBN 3-7705-1280-4. ‣ Careful textual examination of Vedic literature follows changing meaning of term *pur* (used to indicate a geographical locus) and its historical significance. [SS]

15.99 Louis Renou. *Vedic India.* Vol. 3 of *Classical India.* Philip Spratt, trans. Delhi: Indological Book House, 1971. ‣ Brief work by celebrated French Indologist examining Vedic texts, nature of belief and speculation therein, and Vedic ritual. [SS]

15.100 James A. Santucci. *An outline of Vedic literature.* Missoula, Mont.: Scholars' Press for American Academy of Religion, 1976. ISBN 0-89130-085-6. ‣ Brief handbook providing succinct outline of major Vedic texts and their content. [SS]

15.101 Sarva Daman Singh. *Ancient Indian warfare, with special reference to the Vedic period.* Leiden: Brill, 1965. ‣ Interesting but brief monographic work, based largely on textual references, on area where little serious research—but many extravagant claims—exists. [SS]

15.102 Andree F. Sjoberg, ed. *Symposium on Dravidian civilization.* Austin: Jenkins, 1971. ‣ Five essays, on different aspects of Dravidian civilization; particularly relevant are papers by Sjoberg and Emeneau. Each paper followed by record of discussion. [SS]

Age of Epics and the Establishment of Indian Kingship

15.103 Prem Nath Bazaz. *The role of "Bhagavad Gita" in Indian history.* New Delhi, India: Sterling, 1975. ‣ Eclectic and at times eccentric work on central text of Vaisnava-Krishnaite cult, revived in twentieth century by M. K. Gandhi as guide to ethical action. Strongly critical of Gandhian use and interpretation of text. [SS]

15.104 J. L. Brockington. *Righteous Rama: the evolution of an epic.* 1984 ed. Delhi: Oxford University Press, 1985. ISBN 0-19-561710-X (cl, 1984), 0-19-815463-1 (pbk). ‣ Comprehensive study, based on Baroda edition of Sanskrit epic, *Ramayana* (1960–75), of boyhood of hero Rama. Attempts through linguistic analysis to establish chronology of stages of textual development. Relates text to social context in ancient India. [SS]

15.105 S. C. De. *Historicity of "Ramayana" and the Indo-Aryan society in India and Ceylon.* Delhi: Ajanta, 1976. ‣ Somewhat speculative attempt to place *Ramayana* in context of other evidence concerning settlement and acculturation in epic age society. [SS]

15.106 Georges Dumezil. *The destiny of a king.* Alf Hiltebeitel, trans. Chicago: University of Chicago Press, 1973. ISBN 0-226-16975-8. ‣ Brief, classic work by structurally oriented French theorist of myth and Indo-Aryan culture. [SS]

15.107 Robert P. Goldman. *Gods, priests, and warriors: the Bhrgus of the "Mahabharata."* New York: Columbia University Press, 1977. ISBN 0-231-03941-7. ‣ Brief monographic study of particular set of warrior-priests from Sanskrit *Mahabharata* epic; interesting implications for social history. [SS]

15.108 Robert P. Goldman, ed. and trans. *The "Ramayana" of Valmiki: an epic of ancient India.* Vol. 1: *Balakanda.* Vol. 2: *Ayodhyakanda.* Vol. 3: *Aranyakanda.* Princeton: Princeton University Press, 1984–91. ISBN 0-691-06561-6 (v. 1), 0-691-01485-X (v. 2), 0-691-06660-4 (v. 3). ‣ Important modern translation of first section of Sanskrit epic of boyhood of hero Rama; includes critical apparatus and extensive introductions. Particularly useful section, "History and Historicity," in volume 1. [SS]

15.109 Damodar Dharmanand Kosambi. *Myth and reality: studies in the formation of Indian culture.* Bombay, India: Popular Prakashan, 1962. ‣ Short collection of essays by iconoclastic Marxist historian on wide-ranging subjects including village community in Goa, mother-goddess cult sites, prehistory of western Deccan, and social and economic aspects of *Bhagavad Gita.* [SS]

15.110 F. Max Muller, trans. *The Upanisads.* 1879–84 ed. 2 vols. Delhi: Motilal Banarsidass, 1965. (The sacred books of the East, 1, 15.) ‣ Classic translations from pre-Buddhist esoteric Sanskrit philosophical treatises by German Indologist, who dated them to between 800 and 600 BCE. [SS]

15.111 Wendy Doniger O'Flaherty. *Hindu myths: a sourcebook.* Harmondsworth: Penguin, 1975. ISBN 0-14-044306-1. ‣ Compendium of selections from wide variety of Hindu myths in easily accessible format for wide audience. [SS]

15.112 Romila Thapar. *Exile and the kingdom: some thoughts on the "Ramayana."* Bangalore, India: Mythic Society, 1978. ‣ Concise attempt at historicization of *Ramayana* epic, in largely materialistic framework of interpretation. Analyzes epic's conflicts in terms of social divisions. [SS]

15.113 J.A.B. Van Buitenen, ed. and trans. *The Mahabharata.* 3 vols. Chicago: University of Chicago Press, 1973–80. ISBN 0-226-84648-2. ▸ Massive translation from Sanskrit of second great Indian epic. Flawed by use of European terminology to translate Indian institutions and uneven literary quality. [SS]

15.114 R. C. Zaehner. *Bhagavad-Gita with commentary based on the original sources.* Oxford: Clarendon, 1969. ISBN 0-19-826522-0. ▸ Important, standard translation of great Vaishnava text by authority on Indian religious studies. Useful, extensive commentary and critical apparatus; introduction largely from philosophical viewpoint. [SS]

ANCIENT INDIA, ca. 600 BCE–600 CE
General Studies

15.115 A. L. Basham. *The wonder that was India: a study of the history and culture of the Indian subcontinent before the coming of the Muslims.* 1963 3d rev. ed. London: Sidgwick & Jackson, 1985. ISBN 0-283-35457-7 (cased), 0-283-99257-3 (pbk). ▸ Survey of high culture and civilization of classical India, prehistory to end of first millennium, organized in thematic chapters on state, society, everyday life, religion, arts, language, and literature. Useful introductory text with large bibliography. [SS]

15.116 Balkrishna Govind Gokhale. *Ancient India: history and culture.* 1959 4th ed. Bombay, India: Asia Publishing House, 1970. ▸ Competently written general survey from empiricist perspective. Focus on chronology, elite politics, and high culture. [SS]

15.117 Susan L. Huntington. *The art of ancient India: Buddhist, Hindu, Jain.* New York: Weatherhill, 1985. ISBN 0-8348-0183-3. ▸ Illustrated survey of Hindu and Buddhist art and architecture in context of religious thought and institutions. Well-informed, frequently original scholarship and interpretations. [DSL]

15.118 D. N. Jha. *Ancient India: an introductory outline.* New Delhi, India: People's Publishing House, 1977. ▸ Introductory text, written from explicitly Marxist perspective. Discussion of ancient Indian society in terms of class tension; focuses on institutions such as slavery. [SS]

15.119 Damodar Dharmanand Kosambi. *The culture and civilisation of ancient India in historical outline.* 1965 ed. New Delhi, India: Vikas, 1970. ▸ Based on textual, numismatic, and archaeological evidence, chronological account from primitive life and prehistory, through first cities, Aryans, transition from tribe to society, Mauryas and Magadha, ending with rise of "feudalism." Pioneering Marxist analysis; no footnotes. [SS]

15.120 R. C. Majumdar, ed. *The classical accounts of India: being a compilation of the English translations of the accounts left by Herodotus, Megasthenes, Arrian, Strabo, Quintus, Diodorus, Siculus, Justin, Plutarch, Frontinus, Nearchus, Apollonius, Pliny, Ptolemy, Aelian, and others with maps.* 1961 ed. Calcutta, India: Mukhopadhyay, 1981. ▸ Compendium of translations from Greek and Roman accounts; may be used as handbook to accompany introductory courses on this period. Not comprehensive in coverage, but useful. [SS]

15.121 S. C. Malik, ed. *Indian civilization: the first phase, problems of a sourcebook.* Simla, India: Indian Institute of Advanced Study, 1971. (Transactions of the Indian Institute of Advanced Study, 17.) ▸ Proceedings of seminar from 1970 on creating sourcebook. Useful essays and reflections by various participants and editor. [SS]

15.122 Dineschandra Sircar. *Studies in the geography of ancient and medieval India.* 2d rev. ed. Delhi: Motilal Banarsidass, 1971. ▸ Marshals evidence from inscriptions and epigraphs to examine specific issues of historical geography. Useful in absence of proper historical atlas for period. Twenty-nine brief chapters, each on different place. [SS]

Religious and Intellectual History

15.123 André Bareau. *Les premiers conciles bouddhiques.* Paris: Presses Universitaires de France, 1955. (Annales du Musée Guimet, Bibliotheque d'études, 60.) ▸ Coherent and comprehensive summary of evidence on early Buddhist councils, with particular attention to historicity and character of conclave or "communal recitation" at Magadha capital of Rajagrha after Buddha's death. [SS]

15.124 A. L. Basham. *The origins and development of classical Hinduism.* Kenneth G. Zysk, ed. Boston: Beacon, 1989. ISBN 0-8070-7300-8. ▸ Brief, posthumous work by celebrated historian of ancient India. Begins with Indus culture and ends in first centuries CE. Contains list of author's principal works. [SS]

15.125 Colette Caillat. *Atonements in the ancient ritual of the Jaina monks.* Ahmedabad, India: L. D. Institute of Indology, 1975. ▸ Technical study of Jaina texts on atonement by leading French authority. Sheds light on early history of Jainism. [SS]

15.126 Asim Kumar Chatterjee. *A comprehensive history of Jainism.* Vol. 1: *Up to 1000 A.D.* Calcutta, India: Mukhopadhyay, 1978. ▸ Conventional, chronologically organized work tracing history of Jainism and its relations with political power centers, from origins to 1000 CE. Useful as reference work; based on some original sources. [SS]

15.127 D. P. Chattopadhyaya. *Science and society in ancient India.* 1977 ed. Amsterdam: Grüner, 1978. (Philosophical Currents, 22.) ISBN 90-6032-098-0. ▸ Intelligent attempt to use Marxist materialist historical analysis to reexamine evidence on scientific knowledge and its social context in ancient India. Particular focus on medicine, and on Caraka-Samhita text (possibly of pre-Buddhist origin). [SS]

15.128 Edward Conze. *Buddhist thought in India: three phases of Buddhist philosophy.* 1962 ed. London: Allen & Unwin, 1983. ISBN 0-04-294128-8. ▸ Textual philosophical study, identifying three phases as archaic Buddhism, Sthaviras, and Mahayana. [SS]

15.129 Mircea Eliade. *Patanjali and yoga.* 1969 ed. Charles Lam Markmann, trans. New York: Schocken, 1975. ISBN 0-8052-0491-1. ▸ Study of Ashtanga (Eight-fold) Yoga of Patanjali (ca. second century BCE) by leading authority on yoga and yogic spiritualism. [SS]

15.130 A.C.A. Foucher. *The life of the Buddha: according to the ancient texts and monuments of India.* 1963 ed. Simone Brangier Boas, trans. Westport, Conn.: Greenwood, 1972. ISBN 0-8371-6476-1. ▸ Important work by French archaeologist and specialist of Buddhist literature. May need revision in light of new interpretations. [SS]

15.131 Erich Frauwallner. *The earliest Vinaya and the beginnings of Buddhist literature.* Luciano Petech, trans. Rome: Istituto Italiano per il Medio ed Extremo Oriente, 1956. ▸ Important, influential work examining six surviving versions of second (Khandhaka) section of Buddhist Vinaya and arguing they derive from same basic text, composed soon after Second Council at Vesali. Important for Buddhist sect formation, usually attributed to geographical dispersion. [SS]

15.132 Jan Gonda. *Aspects of early Visnuism.* 2d ed. Delhi: Motilal Banarsidass, 1969. ▸ Brief, somewhat loosely structured, but nevertheless useful study from prolific scholar. Largely textual-empirical in orientation. [SS]

15.133 Jan Gonda. *Visnuism and Sivaism: a comparison.* London: University of London and Athlone, 1970. ISBN 0-485-17409-X. ▸ Short monograph, based on textual sources, on emergence of theistic Hinduism in ancient period. Comparative framework. [SS]

15.134 Suvira Jaiswal. *The origin and development of Vaisnavism: Vaisnavism from 200 B.C. to A.D. 500.* 1980 2d rev. ed. Delhi: Munshiram Manoharlal, 1981. ▸ Monographic study, from Marxist materialist perspective, analyzing origins and early history of worship of Vishnu as sectarian religion. [SS]

15.135 J. Przyluski. *The legend of Emperor Asoka in Indian and Chinese texts.* Dilip Kumar Biswas, trans. Calcutta, India: Mukhopadhyay, 1967. ▸ Study of Pali and Chinese materials on Mauryan ruler Aśoka, by leading French Buddhist studies specialist of interwar period. [SS]

15.136 Benoychandra Sen. *Studies in the Buddhist Jatakas: tradition and polity.* Calcutta, India: Saraswat Library, 1974. ▸ Loosely knit work on Jataka tales, stories of former lives of Buddha, emphasizing their politico-historical significance. [SS]

15.137 Vishwanath Prasad Varma. *Early Buddhism and its origins.* 1971 ed. New Delhi, India: Munshiram Manoharlal, 1973. ▸ Wide-ranging study placing history of early Buddhism in relation to Vedic tradition. [SS]

Social and Economic History

15.138 Anant Sadashiv Altekar. *Education in ancient India.* 6th ed. Varanasi, India: Nand Kishore, 1965. ▸ Old-fashioned, conventional work with useful data gathered from classical sources. Can be consulted as encyclopedia and for textual information. [SS]

15.139 Jeannine Auboyer. *Daily life in ancient India, from approximately 200 B.C. to 700 A.D.* 1965 ed. Simon Watson Taylor, trans. New York: Macmillan, 1968. ▸ Structurally oriented descriptions of elite and nonelite social structure, politics and administration, trade and production, individual and collective existence, and royal and aristocratic life styles. Lightly referenced; intended for wide readership. [SS]

15.140 Dev Raj Chanana. *Slavery in ancient India as depicted in Pali and Sanskrit texts.* New Delhi, India: People's, 1960. ▸ Concise study, treating slavery (and categories of Dasa and Dasi) as depicted in Sanskrit epics, *Arthasastra*, and in Buddhist Tipitaka, Vinaya, and Sutta literature. Well argued and presented; influenced by Marxist historiography. [SS]

15.141 Moti Chandra. *Trade and trade routes in ancient India.* New Delhi, India: Abhinav, 1977. ▸ Wide-ranging attempt (extending as late as eleventh century CE) at discussion of trade and historical geography, albeit from somewhat antiquarian perspective. Useful as reference work but lacks focus or argument. Mainly based on Buddhist and Jain sources. [SS]

15.142 U. N. Ghoshal. *The agrarian system in ancient India.* 2d ed. Calcutta, India: Saraswat Library, 1973. ▸ Brief text, ranging chronologically well into first millennium CE, based largely on normative texts on statecraft and inheritance. Closing discussion of state versus private ownership of land. [SS]

15.143 D. N. Jha. *Studies in early Indian economic history.* Delhi: Anupama, 1980. ▸ Collection of essays with largely Marxist and neo-Marxist focus. Useful approach to social and economic stratification; data on trade and agriculture. [SS]

15.144 Bimala Churn Law. *Tribes in ancient India.* 2d ed. Poona: Bhandarkar Oriental Research Institute, 1973. ▸ Empiricist, encyclopedic work, surveying textual and epigraphic evidence on tribes without, however, addressing vexed question of defining

"tribe." Useful in terms of data collected; organized as roughly seventy-five brief chapters, each on separate "tribe." [SS]

15.145 Sachindra Kumar Maity. *Economic life in northern India in the Gupta period, cir. A.D. 300–550.* 2d rev. ed. Delhi: Motilal Banarsidass, 1970. ▸ Brings together wide range of data on urban and rural economic life; lacks explicit theoretical argument. Supplemented and modified by subsequent works, particularly on trade. [SS]

15.146 R. C. Majumdar. *Corporate life in ancient India.* 3d ed. Calcutta, India: Mukhopadhyay, 1969. ▸ Discussion of corporate activities, divided into economic, political, religious, and social life. Perspective intended to show that corporate republican sentiments and practice found in ancient India. [SS]

15.147 A. K. Narain, ed. *Seminar papers on the local coins of northern India, c. 300 B.C. to 300 A.D.* Varanasi, India: Department of Ancient Indian History, Culture, and Archaeology, College of Indology, Banaras Hindu University, 1968. ▸ Useful work on numismatics, but lacks systematic analysis of coin hoards or quantitative sophistication. Nevertheless, useful for survey of museum coin collections of period. [SS]

15.148 R. N. Saletore. *Early Indian economic history.* 1973 ed. London and Totowa, N.J.: Curzon and Rowman & Littlefield, 1975. ISBN 0-87471-599-7. ▸ Massive study, almost compendium, with, at times, undigested data on variety of economic and fiscal subjects. Due weight, at times disproportionate, to state-generated normative texts. [SS]

15.149 S. C. Sarkar. *Educational ideas and institutions in ancient India.* 1928 ed. Patna, India: Janaki Prakashan, 1979. ▸ Brief study which may be used in conjunction with Altekar (15.138), which it supplements without surpassing. At times derivative in construction. [SS]

15.150 Ram Sharan Sharma. *Perspectives in social and economic history of early India.* New Delhi, India: Munshiram Manoharlal, 1983. ▸ Brief collection of author's essays, proposing theory of stages of evolution in ancient India. Strongly Marxist materialist in orientation. Revised edition of *Light on Early Indian Society and Economy* (1966). [SS]

15.151 Ram Sharan Sharma. *Sudras in ancient India: a social history of the lower orders down to c. A.D. 600.* 2d rev. ed. Delhi: Motilal Banarsidass, 1980. ▸ Early monographic study of underprivileged social group (*varna*) by prolific Marxist author. Close attention to textual evidence; generalizations less sweeping than in author's later work. [SS]

15.152 Dineschandra Sircar. *Social life in ancient India.* Calcutta, India: University of Calcutta, 1971. (Centre of Advanced Study in Ancient Indian History and Culture, Lectures and seminars, 6B.2.) ▸ Slim, edited volume with essays on different aspects of social history. Focus on issues such as slavery as well as state and government. [SS]

15.153 Romila Thapar. *Ancient Indian social history: some interpretations.* New Delhi, India: Orient Longman, 1978. ▸ Important, extensive collection of papers of prolific and leading neo-Marxist Indian historian. Contains anthropologically inspired reflections on gift, status, and stratification. [SS]

15.154 N. K. Wagle. *Society at the time of the Buddha.* 1966 ed. New York: Humanities, 1967. ▸ Useful, accessibly written, approach to society in mid-first millennium BCE. Neither sophisticated nor theoretically informed. [SS]

SEE ALSO
3.258 Xinru Liu. *Ancient India and ancient China.*

Political Systems and Ideologies

15.155   Anant Sadashiv Altekar. *State and government in ancient India.* 4th ed. Delhi: Motilal Banarsidass, 1962. ▸ Defense of idea of unitary, protonational state and orderly government in ancient India. Indian nationalist perspective, originally written 1949. [SS]

15.156   Charles Drekmeier. *Kingship and community in early India.* Stanford, Calif.: Stanford University Press, 1962. ▸ Important attempt to examine relative importance of community-based polity versus idea of ruler, based on careful examination of textual materials on statecraft. Discusses decline of "tribal culture," emergence of *varna*, and classical Hindu theory of kingship. Contrast Marxist formulation of similar problem by Sharma (15.165). [SS]

15.157   U. N. Ghoshal. *A history of Indian political ideas: the ancient period and the period of transition into the Middle Ages.* 1959 ed. Madras, India: Oxford University Press, 1968. ▸ Characteristic attempt, from Indian nationalist perspective, to project origins of modern institutions and ideas into ancient past. Nevertheless important as representative of this school. [SS]

15.158   Jan Gonda. *Ancient Indian kingship from the religious point of view.* Leiden: Brill, 1966. ▸ Brief but influential monograph exploring religious bases of Indian kingship and notion of temporal power. Influence on subsequent research and on ideas of ritual kingship, result of its focus on Raja-Purohita relationship and concept of *cakravartin* (universal sovereign). [SS]

15.159   J. C. Heesterman. *The ancient Indian royal consecration: the "Rajasuya" described according to the Yajus texts and annotated.* The Hague: Mouton, 1957. ▸ Textual treatment of Vedic consecration ritual in tradition of Dutch Sanskrit studies. Identifies some structural constants that determine and circumscribe royal power. [SS]

15.160   P. V. Kane. *History of Dharmasastra (ancient and mediaeval religious and civil law in India).* 2d rev. ed. 5 vols. in 8. Poona: Bhandarkar Oriental Research Institute, 1968–77. ▸ Standard, authoritative work on legal texts and compendia of ancient period. Relationship between precept and practice remains vexed question. [SS]

15.161   R. P. Kangle. *The Kautilya Arthasastra.* 1969–72 2d ed. 3 vols. Delhi: Motilal Banarsidass, 1986. ISBN 81-208-0039-7 (v. 1), 81-208-0040-0 (v. 2), 81-208-0041-9 (v. 3). ▸ Standard translation of Machiavellian treatise on statecraft attributed to Kautilya (or Canakya), minister of Mauryan ruler Chandragupta, and probably originating between fourth century BCE and the third century CE. [SS]

15.162   I. W. Mabbett. *Truth, myth, and politics in ancient India.* New Delhi, India: Thomson, 1971. ▸ Brief work in thirteen chapters on political institutions and concepts, largely from time of Mauryas. Includes discussions of bureaucracy, treasury, divinity and contract, foreign relations, etc. [SS]

15.163   Radhakumud Mookerji. *Local government in ancient India.* 1920 2d rev. ed. Delhi: Motilal Banarsidass, 1958. ▸ Early monograph by well-known, prolific historian of ancient India. Based on original, largely normative texts. Seeks to identify structure of local (as distinct from central) government. [SS]

15.164   J. P. Sharma. *Republics in ancient India, c. 1500 BC–500 BC.* Leiden: Brill, 1968. ▸ Concise study focusing on Northeast Republics, located roughly north and east of Benares, before emergence of Mauryas. Organized in separate chapters on principal republics or corporate confederacies such as Licchavis, Videhas, Nayas, Mallas, Sakyas, Koliyas, etc. [SS]

15.165   Ram Sharan Sharma. *Aspects of political ideas and institutions in ancient India.* 2d ed. Delhi: Motilal Banarsidass, 1968.

▸ Loosely structured work, first published 1959, examining state formation in early India from Marxist perspective. [SS]

15.166   Romila Thapar. *From lineage to state: social formations in the mid-first millennium B.C. in the Ganga valley.* 1984 ed. Delhi: Oxford University Press, 1990. ISBN 0-19-562675-3 (pbk). ▸ Brief, schematic, and Marxist-inflected presentation of transition from lineage-based political systems to state systems in northern India, ca. 500 BCE. Useful as introduction to area, extensive bibliography. [SS]

15.167   Thomas R. Trautmann. *Kautilya and the "Arthasastra": a statistical investigation of the authorship and evolution of the text.* Leiden: Brill, 1971. ▸ Careful study using computer analysis of *Arthasastra*, text on statecraft, usually attributed to period of Mauryas or after. Analysis of economic and other data available therein, even on such issues as forestry. [SS]

Regional Regimes and Societies

Nepal

15.168   K. P. Jayaswal. *Chronology and history of Nepal.* Varanasi, India: Bharati-Prakashan, 1976. ▸ Reprint of long article first published 1936. Establishes basic chronology and elements for early history of Nepal. [SS]

15.169   D. R. Regmi. *Ancient Nepal.* 3d ed. Calcutta, India: Mukhopadhyay, 1969. ▸ Useful monograph, based on original sources and archaeological reports. Conventional in approach; largely empiricist and chronological in orientation. [SS]

Indo-Greeks

15.170   P.H.L. Eggermont. *Alexander's campaigns in Sind and Baluchistan and the siege of the Brahmin town of Harmatelia.* Louvain: Leuven University Press, 1975. (Orientalia Lovaniensia analecta, 3.) ISBN 90-6186-037-7. ▸ Closely documented work on later campaigns in India of Alexander the Great, after his crossing of Indus in 326 BCE, and capitulation of Taxila. [SS]

15.171   Olivier Guillaume. *Analysis of reasonings in archaeology: the case of Graeco-Bactrian and Indo-Greek numismatics.* Osmund Bopearuchchi, trans. Delhi: Oxford University Press, 1990. (French studies in South Asian culture, 4.) ISBN 0-19-562626-5. ▸ Methodological exercise, examining materials and historiography on Indo-Greek kingdoms of Indian northwest frontier and Afghanistan. Critique of both Narain 9.107 and Tarn 9.108. [SS]

15.172   George Woodcock. *The Greeks in India.* London: Faber, 1966. ▸ Relatively brief synthetic account for wide readership. Summarizes evidence used by Narain (9.107) and Tarn (9.108) and some later findings. [SS]

SEE ALSO
  9.106 Frank L. Holt. *Alexander the Great and Bactria.*
  9.107 A. K. Narain. *The Indo-Greeks.*
  9.108 William W. Tarn. *The Greeks in Bactria and India.*

Mauryan Era

15.173   Sudhakar Chattopadhyaya. *Bimbisara to Asoka: with an appendix on the later Mauryas.* Calcutta, India: Roy & Chowdhury, 1977. ▸ Useful, conventional political history, setting out main features of received wisdom on Mauryas. May be consulted as supplement to more interpretative works. [SS]

15.174   Balkrishna Govind Gokhale. *Asoka Maurya.* New York: Twayne, 1966. ▸ Readable, conventional account, presenting main elements in Mauryan ruler Asoka's career (third century BCE); nationalist Indian perspective. [SS]

15.175   Radhakumud Mookerji. *Chandragupta Maurya and his times.* 1966 4th ed. Delhi: Motilal Banarsidass, 1988. ISBN 81-208-

0405-8. ‣ Covers administration of Mauryan kingdom, save for first two chapters on ruler's origins, early life, and conquests. Gazetteerlike chapters on administration, land system, urban administration, law, army, and social and economic conditions. First published 1943. [SS]

15.176 M.G.S. Narayanan. "The Mauryan problem in Sangam works in historical perspective." *Journal of Indian history* 53.2 (1975) 243–54. ISSN 0022-1775. ‣ Interesting attempt to place mention of Mauryas in early southern Indian (Sangam) literature in context of hypotheses of contact and conflict. [SS]

15.177 K. A. Nilakanta Sastri, ed. *Age of the Nandas and Mauryas.* 2d ed. New Delhi, India: Motilal Banarsidass, 1967. ‣ Substantial collaborative work presenting materials on Mauryas and their predecessors. Useful as reference work. First published 1952. [SS]

15.178 Vishuddhanand Pathak. *History of Kosala up to the rise of the Mauryas.* Delhi: Motilal Banarsidass, 1963. ‣ Discussion of Kosala kingdom using historical sources and epics, in particular *Ramayana.* Useful chapters on historical geography and religion. [SS]

15.179 V. R. Ramachandra Dikshitar. *The Mauryan polity.* 2d ed. Madras, India: University of Madras, 1953. ‣ Standard monograph of Madras school; conventional organization and careful in approach to sources. Some interesting insights into political organization. [SS]

15.180 Niharranjan Ray. *Maurya and post-Maurya art: a study in social and formal contrasts.* New Delhi, India: Indian Council of Historical Research; distributed by Thomson, 1975. ‣ Interesting, brief social history by leading Indian art historian. Succinct summary of specialized research. [SS]

15.181 Dineschandra Sircar. *Aśokan studies.* Calcutta, India: Indian Museum, 1979. ‣ Slim, late collection of studies by prolific historian of ancient India and translator of inscriptions of emperor Aśoka. Plates and illustrations. [SS]

15.182 Romila Thapar. *Aśoka and the decline of the Mauryas.* 2d ed. Delhi: Oxford University Press, 1973. ‣ Examination of administration and polity under Aśoka. Concludes that excessive centralization of power around ruler and absence of sense of nationhood caused empire to crumble. [SS]

Central Asians and North Indian Kingdoms

15.183 Bhaskar Chattopadhyay. *Kushana state and Indian society: a study in post-Mauryan polity and society.* Calcutta, India: Punthi Pustak, 1975. ‣ Conventional study of social and political order and religious synthesis under Kushans (Kuei-Shang), dynasty of Central Asian origin which flourished between first and third centuries CE. Focus on reign of Kanishka, best known of Kushan rulers and major patron of Buddhism. [SS]

15.184 Sudhakar Chattopadhyaya. *The Sakas in India.* 2d ed. Santiniketan, India: Visva-Bharati, 1967. ‣ Political history of Sakas (Sai Wang) of Central Asia (northwestern, northern, and western India), from first century BCE to the first century CE, and emergence of Indo-Parthians and Kushans. Some of its conclusions, especially chronology, remain hotly debated. [SS]

15.185 Bela Lahiri. *Indigenous states of northern India, circa 200 B.C. to 320 A.D.* Calcutta, India: University of Calcutta, 1974. ‣ Useful study of neglected area: local indigenous dynasties of northern India, such as Sungas and Kanvas, after Mauryan decline, and Saka and Kushan dominance, to emergence of the Guptas. Even if methodologically not innovative, fills gap in historiography. [SS]

15.186 Dineschandra Sircar. *Ancient Malwa and the Vikramaditya tradition.* 1966 ed. Delhi: Munshiram Manoharlal, 1969.

‣ Monograph by prolific Indian historian on (probably) mythical ruler of first-century BCE Malwa, focus of many legends on kingship and supposed founder of Vikrama era. [SS]

15.187 Dineschandra Sircar. *Some problems concerning the Kusanas.* Hubli-Dharwar, India: Kannada Research Institute, Karnatak University, 1971. ‣ Brief reconsideration of Kushan history with respect to unresolved problems of chronology and nature of power and political institutions. [SS]

SEE ALSO
9.109 A. L. Basham, ed. *Papers on the date of Kanishka.*
9.110 B. G. Gafurov et al., eds. *Tsentral'naia Aziia v Kushanskuiu epokhu.*
9.111 John Rosenfield. *The dynastic arts of the Kushans.*

Gupta India

15.188 Balkrishna Govind Gokhale. *Samudra Gupta: life and times.* New York: Asia Publishing House, 1962. ‣ Political history of Samudra Gupta, (r. ca. 335–375), known as expansionist monarch. Based on inscriptional and other evidence, including numismatic evidence. Extremely conventional account. [SS]

15.189 Sachindra Kumar Maity. *The imperial Guptas and their times, cir. A.D. 330–550.* New Delhi, India: Munshiram Manoharlal, 1975. ‣ Standard account of Gupta dynasty of Magadha from its foundation by Chandragupta in early fourth century to its decline after Budhagupta (d. 497). Useful for chronology, political history, and outline of administrative institutions. [SS]

15.190 Radhakumud Mookerji. *The Gupta empire.* 4th ed. Delhi: Motilal Banarsidass, 1969. ‣ Brief monographic discussion of Gupta with particular attention to political history. Largely from nationalist, golden age–oriented perspective. [SS]

15.191 V. R. Ramachandra Dikshitar. *The Gupta polity.* Madras, India: University of Madras, 1952. ‣ Detailed, extensive study by traditionalist historian; based on original sources. Highlights political and administrative institutions under Guptas. [SS]

15.192 Bardwell L. Smith, ed. *Essays on Gupta culture.* Columbia, Mo.: South Asia Books, 1983. ISBN 0-8364-0871-3. ‣ Well-intergrated, multidisciplinary symposium on art, literature, religion, and political authority of Gupta and contemporary and succeeding kingdoms both in northern and southern India, ca. fourth to seventh centuries CE. Accessible to nonspecialist, with excellent bibliographical essays. [DSL]

15.193 Joanna Gottfried Williams. *The art of Gupta India: empire and province.* Princeton: Princeton University Press, 1982. ISBN 0-691-03988-7 (cl), 0-691-10126-4 (pbk). ‣ Art historian's study of sculpture and architecture of northern and central India of fourth to seventh centuries CE. Relates art to institutions and cultural prestige of Gupta dynasty well beyond time and place of its actual ruling power. [DSL]

Middle and South India

15.194 K. G. Sesha Aiyar. *Cera kings of the Sangam period.* London: Luzac, 1937. ‣ Brief monographic discussion of major South Indian Cera dynasty of Sangam epoch from ca. second century CE. Based on literary evidence such as patronage to poets. [SS]

15.195 Sudhakar Chattopadhyaya. *Some early dynasties of South India.* Delhi: Motilal Banarsidass, 1974. ‣ Useful monographic account of Andhra-Satavahanas and other dynasties of early South India. Largely conventional politico-dynastic history. [SS]

15.196 G. S. Ghurye. *Indian acculturation: Agastya and Skanda.* Bombay, India: Popular Prakashan, 1977. ‣ Important, argumentative work, partly from anthropological viewpoint. Uses mythic and folklore materials on nature of acculturation and settlement at edge of Aryan and Dravidian culture complexes. [SS]

15.197 George L. Hart III. *The poems of ancient Tamil: their milieu and their Sanskrit counterparts.* Berkeley: University of California Press, 1975. ISBN 0-520-02672-1. ‣ Important work on Sangam and other literature (ca. first to fourth centuries CE) examines differences and mutual influences between North and South Indian cultures. Large sampling of translations. [SS]

15.198 T. V. Mahalingam. *Kancipuram in early South Indian history.* New York: Asia Publishing House, 1969. ‣ Loosely chronologically organized work on role of important center of Kancipuram, in northcentral Tamilnadu. Particularly important early sections on Pallava dynasty. [SS]

15.199 M.G.S. Narayanan. *Aspects of aryanisation in Kerala.* Trivandrum, India: Kerala Historical Society, 1973. ‣ Brief summary of legendary and historical materials on aryanization/sanskritization of Kerala from neo-Marxist perspective. [SS]

15.200 K. A. Nilakanta Sastri. *Cultural contacts between Aryans and Dravidians.* Bombay, India: Manaktalas, 1967. ‣ Useful but brief survey touching on historical evidence and also on legendary figure of Agastya, sage who migrated south. [SS]

15.201 Himanshu Prabha Ray. *Monastery and guild: commerce under the Satavahanas.* Delhi: Oxford University Press, 1986. ISBN 0-19-561941-2. ‣ Expansion of agricultural wealth and commercial capital in western Deccan under Satavahana dynasty, which patronized both Buddhist and brahmin monasteries until its decline in third century CE. Based on archaeological, literary, and inscriptional data. [SS]

15.202 N. Subrahmanian. *Sangam polity: the administration and social life of the Sangam Tamils.* Rev. ed. Madurai, India: Ennes, 1980. ‣ Weighty, authoritative, but rather conventional approach to Sangam period society in southern India. Largely based on literary record. [SS]

Sri Lanka

15.203 A. L. Basham. "Prince Vijaya and the aryanisation of Ceylon." *Ceylon historical journal* 1.3 (1952) 163–71. ISSN 0577-4691. ‣ Discussion of scanty evidence on figure of Prince Vijaya, semi-mythical figure associated with early political process in Sri Lanka. [SS]

15.204 H. W. Codrington. *Ancient land tenure and revenue in Ceylon.* 1939 ed. Colombo: Ceylon Government Press, 1950. ‣ Succinct account of early land tenure in Sri Lanka. Example of British colonial historiography. Anachronistically constructed, but remains useful point of reference. Available on microfilm from Berkeley, Calif.: University of California (1983). [SS]

15.205 S. D. De Lanerolle. *Origins of Sinhala culture.* Colombo: Lake House Investments, 1976. ‣ Brief, useful survey of evidence on early Sri Lanka. Read with Basham 15.203, Gunawardana 15.26, and others. Translated from Sinhala; controversial and sensitive subject. [SS]

15.206 Wilhelm Geiger. *The Dipavamsa and Mahavamsa and their historical development in Ceylon.* Ethel M. Coomaraswamy, trans. Colombo: H.C. Cottle, Government Printer, 1908. ‣ Discussion of two major Buddhist chronicles of Sri Lanka, *Dipavamsa*, history of Buddhism on the island, and *Mahavamsa*, history of Mahavihara, major monastery, compiled from earlier oral traditions, ca. 500 CE. [SS]

15.207 Tilak Hettiarachchy. *History of kingship in Ceylon up to the fourth century A.D.* Colombo: Lake House Investments, 1972. ‣ Study of ideas and concepts relating to kingship and the state in early Sri Lanka. Emphasizes relation to Buddhism and religious currents and institutions. Competent monographic survey. [SS]

"MEDIEVAL" INDIA, ca. 600–1500
General Studies and Historiography

15.208 H. M. Elliott. *The history of India, as told by its own historians: the Muhammadan period.* 1867–77 ed. 8 vols. John Dowson, ed. New York: AMS Press, 1966. ‣ First published 1867–77, collection of imperfectly translated excerpts mostly from Persian and Arabic texts, frequently racist commentary. Although some texts now available in more complete and correct translations, this collection is all that is available for many others. [SS/DSL]

15.209 J. S. Grewal. *Medieval India: history and historians.* Amritsar, India: Guru Nanak University, 1975. ‣ Brief overview of major lines of development and historiography in medieval India, particularly in North. Relatively strong on vernacular materials compared to other similar works. [SS]

15.210 Peter Hardy. *Historians of medieval India: studies in Indo-Muslim historical writing.* 1960 ed. London: Luzac, 1966. ‣ Important, controversial interpretation of Indo-Persian writings of sultanate and Mughals. Argues for role of patronage and absence of Western-style historical tradition. [SS]

15.211 Mohibbul Hasan, ed. *Historians of medieval India.* 1968 ed. Meerut, India: Meenakshi Prakashan, 1983. ‣ Edited collection mostly focusing on Islamic and Indo-Persian writings and on northern India. [SS]

15.212 Shahpurshah Hormasji Hodivala. *Studies in Indo-Muslim history: a critical commentary on Elliott and Dowson's "History of India as Told by Its Own Historians."* 1939–57 ed. 2 vols. Lahore: Islamic Book Service, 1979. ‣ Consideration and critique of selections and translations in Elliott 15.208. Partly constitutes a nationalist critique. [SS]

15.213 Achut Dattatraya Pusalker. *Studies in the epics and Puranas.* 1955 ed. Bombay, India: Bharatiya Vidya Bhavan, 1963. ‣ Empiricist study, limited largely to Sanskrit sources, lacking well-defined theoretical apparatus. Useful as introduction to texts and sources. [SS]

15.214 M. A. Stein, ed. and trans. *Kalhana's "Rajatarangini": a chronicle of the kings of Kasmir.* 1900 ed. 2 vols. Delhi: Motilal Banarsidass, 1979. ‣ Classic translation of major chronicle from mid-twelfth century. Invaluable source for history of medieval Kashmir. [SS]

SEE ALSO
9.249 Zahiruddin Muhammad Babur. *The Babur-Nama.*

Hindu and Buddhist Societies

Northern and Middle India

15.215 Anant Sadashiv Altekar. *Rashtrakutas and their times.* 2d rev. ed. Poona: Oriental Book Agency, 1967. ‣ Standard work based on epigraphic and other sources, concerning dynasty of western India, mid-eighth to late tenth century. Conventional in format; area not yet treated in more modern studies. [SS]

15.216 Atreyi Biswas. *The political history of the Hunas in India.* 1971 ed. New Delhi, India: Munshiram Manoharlal, 1973. ‣ Narrowly conceived political history of Central Asian Hunas (Hsiung-nu), sometimes associated with collapse of Gupta empire and process of urban decay in late fifth to early sixth century. Chronological organization by ruler with emphasis on Mihirakula; appendix on coinage. [SS]

15.217 D. Devahuti. *Harsha: a political study.* 2d ed. Oxford: Oxford University Press, 1983. ISBN 0-19-561392-9. ‣ Standard monograph devoted to important North Indian ruler (606–647), examining general political context as well. Useful appendixes on coinage; use of Indian and Chinese sources. [SS]

15.218 John S. Deyell. *Living without silver: the monetary history* *of early medieval North India.* Delhi: Oxford University Press, 1990. ISBN 0-19-562216-2. ▸ Numismatic study of northern and western Indian coin hoards and limited textual materials. Describes persistence of money in era often described as moneyless. Valuable study, of greater general significance than title suggests. [SS]

15.219 Hermann Goetz. *Studies in the history, religion, and art of classical and mediaeval India.* Hermann Külke, ed. Wiesbaden: Steiner, 1974. ISBN 3-515-01817-4. ▸ Collected essays on variety of themes, ranging from classical period to medieval Deccan and North India. [SS]

15.220 Lallanji Gopal. *The economic life of northern India, c. A.D. 700–1200.* 2d rev. ed. Delhi: Motilal Banarsidass, 1989. ISBN 81-208-0302-7. ▸ Useful alternative perspective to Sharma 15.226 and proponents of Indian feudalism. More descriptive than analytical. [SS]

15.221 Lal Mani Joshi. *Studies in the Buddhistic culture of India during the seventh and eighth centuries A.D.* 2d rev. ed. Delhi: Motilal Banarsidass, 1977. ▸ Useful study of late Buddhism in India. More important for subject matter than treatment. Descriptive and hampered by availability of limited source materials. [SS]

15.222 Vibhuti Bhushan Mishra. *The Gurjara-Pratiharas and their times.* Delhi: Chand, 1966. ▸ Political history of late pre-sultanate dynasty of North India. Conventional organization covering range of areas, but no new perspectives or arguments. [SS]

15.223 Barrie M. Morrison. *Political centers and cultural regions in early Bengal.* Tucson: University of Arizona Press; for Association of Asian Studies, 1970. ISBN 0-8165-0154-8. ▸ Brief, dense monograph examining Bengal at time of Palas and Senas. Important attempt to go beyond conventional dynastic history to examine bases of regional coherence. [SS]

15.224 Ramendra Nath Nandi. *Religious institutions and cults in the Deccan, c. AD 600–AD 1000.* Delhi: Motilal Banarsidass, 1973. ▸ Useful counterpoint to standard political histories, based on textual as well as epigraphic sources. Useful background to works on popular devotionalism (*bhakti*) in region. [SS]

15.225 Akhowri Braj Ballav Prasad. *Political organisation of North India, A.D. 950–1194.* Patna, India: Janaki Prakashan, 1979. ▸ Conventional political history of North India in phase of fragmentation prior to Muhammad of Ghur and his satraps' establishment at Delhi. Useful data. [SS]

15.226 Ram Sharan Sharma. *Indian feudalism, c. A.D. 300–1200.* 2d ed. Delhi: Macmillan Company of India, 1980. ISBN 0-333-90343-9. ▸ Marxist interpretation arguing for period of ruralization, cessation of commerce, and thus feudalism in North India before sultanate. Based on numismatic evidence and land-grant texts. [SS]

15.227 Dineschandra Sircar, ed. *Land system and feudalism in ancient India.* Calcutta, India: University of Calcutta, 1966. (Centre of Advanced Study in Ancient Indian History and Culture, Lectures and seminars, 1.B.) ▸ Variant to Sharma 15.226 which may be seen as representing independent and parallel development. Similar influences, though thesis less monocausal and more empiricist. [SS]

15.228 Sidney Toy. *Strongholds of India.* Melbourne: Heinemann, 1957. ▸ Brief descriptions, accompanied by sketches (sometimes inaccurate) of medieval fortifications in India. Based on received archaeological wisdom and field surveys. Little reconciliation with textual materials. [SS]

15.229 Ghulam Yazdani. *The early history of the Deccan.* 2 vols. London: Oxford University Press under authority of Government of Andhra Pradesh, 1960. ▸ Edited two-volume history of Deccan to foundation of Bahmani state, mid-fourteenth century. ▸

Important articles on Calukyas, Kakatiyas, and other dynasties. Rich in political and dynastic information; also useful for architecture, arts, and literature. [SS]

Himalayan Societies

15.230 Michael Aris. *Bhutan: the early history of a Himalayan kingdom.* Warminster: Aris & Phillips, 1979. ISBN 0-85668-082-6 (cl), 0-85668-199-7 (pbk). ▸ Valuable treatment of otherwise obscure area based on archaeological and limited textual evidence. Standard work, well written even if not greatly innovative in methodology or presentation. [SS]

15.231 Luciano Petech. *Mediaeval history of Nepal (c. 750–1482).* 2d ed. Rome: Istituto Italiano per il Medio ed Extremo Oriente, 1984. (Serie orientale Roma, 54.) ▸ Important work using archaeological evidence, presenting medieval history of Nepal to emergence of kingdom of Kathmandu. In some respects supersedes early twentieth-century study by Sylvain Levi. [SS]

15.232 Mary Shepherd Slusser. *Nepal mandala: a cultural study of the Kathmandu Valley.* 2 vols. Princeton: Princeton University Press, 1982. ISBN 0-691-03128-2 (set). ▸ Comprehensive, well-illustrated cultural history of Kathmandu Valley. Strongest in its presentation of archaeological findings for period before 1200. Narrative history, overly concerned with establishing continuities. [DSL]

South India

15.233 A. Appadorai. *Economic conditions in southern India, 1000–1500 AD.* 2 vols. Madras, India: University of Madras, 1936. ▸ Survey of largely inscriptional evidence on land tenure, fiscal system, coinage, economic organization, trading guilds, etc., in peninsular India. Assumes static structure for period. [SS]

15.234 S. R. Balasubrahmanyam. *Middle Chola temples: Rajaraja I to Kulottunga I, A.D. 985–1070.* 1975 ed. Amsterdam: Oriental Press, 1977. ISBN 90-6023-607-6. ▸ Survey with plans and line drawings of extremely significant phase of temple construction in Tamil country. Covers major sites such as Tanjavur and Gangaikondacolapuram. [SS]

15.235 B. D. Chattopadhyaya. *Coins and currency systems in South India, c. A.D. 225–1300.* 1976 ed. New Delhi, India: Munshiram Manoharlal, 1977. ▸ Survey of largely numismatic, and to more limited extent, textual and epigraphic evidence. Encyclopedic rather than analytic in character. [SS]

15.236 J. Duncan M. Derrett. *The Hoysalas, a medieval Indian royal family.* Madras, India: Oxford University Press, 1957. ▸ Best monographic study of South Indian political structure of pre-1500 period, using detailed epigraphic evidence. Eschews model or explicit theorizing. [SS]

15.237 Kenneth R. Hall. *Trade and statecraft in the age of the Colas.* New Delhi, India: Abhinav, 1980. ▸ Controversial attempt to apply theories of G. William Skinner on marketing and Karl Polanyi on administered trade to the Cola dynasty inscriptions, tenth to thirteenth century. Focuses on marketing center (*nagaram*). [SS]

15.238 Noboru Karashima. *South Indian history and society: studies from inscriptions, A.D. 850–1800.* Delhi: Oxford University Press, 1984. ISBN 0-19-561586-7. ▸ Collected essays, based on Tamil inscriptions, largely focusing on Cola dynasty of Tanjavur. Argues for limited form of private property in land, through institution of *kani*, combination of land and water rights, as well as status in rural society. [SS]

15.239 C. Minakshi. *Administration and social life under the Pallavas.* 2d rev. ed. Madras, India: University of Madras, 1977. ▸ Well-documented study, based on inscriptions, of early (pre-

Cola) dynasty of Tamilnadu. Empiricist, more resource than monograph. [SS]

15.240 M. S. Nagaraja Rao. *The Chalukyas of Badami: seminar papers.* Bangalore, India: Mythic Society, 1978. ▸ Edited volume of largely archaeological and architectural perspectives on great temple-building dynasty of Deccan, sixth to eighth century. [SS]

15.241 K. A. Nilakanta Sastri. *The Colas: with over 100 illustrations.* 1955 2d rev. ed. Madras, India: University of Madras, 1975. ▸ Massive study of political, cultural, and social history based largely on inscriptions. Sees Colas of Tanjavur as "Byzantine" state with sophisticated bureaucracy. [SS]

15.242 Viyaya Ramaswamy. *Textiles and weavers in medieval South India.* Delhi: Oxford University Press, 1985. ISBN 0-19-561705-3. ▸ Long-term study, running from Colas to eighteenth century, of weaver communities in Tamil country. Underlying neo-Marxist theory of emergence of master weaver. Uses inscriptional and European documentation. [SS]

15.243 George W. Spencer. *The politics of expansion: the Chola conquest of Sri Lanka and Sri Vijaya.* Madras, India: New Era, 1983. ▸ Reworking of essays, mostly published in 1960s and 1970s. Shows Colas as raiders rather than stable empire builders in South Asian and Southeast Asian context. [SS]

15.244 Burton Stein. *Peasant state and society in medieval South India.* 1980 ed. Delhi: Oxford University Press, 1985. ISBN 0-19-561830-0 (cl, 1980), 0-19-561065-2 (pbk). ▸ Major, controversial, revisionist work, applying anthropologists' model of segmentary state to South India between eighth and seventeenth centuries. Based largely on secondary literature. [SS]

15.245 Y. Subbarayalu. *Political geography of the Chola country.* Madras, India: State Department of Archaeology, Government of Tamilnadu, 1973. ▸ Careful mapping of inscriptional evidence to show existence of well-defined geographical entities (*nadus*) that formed basis of Cola territories. Poorly written and hence much underrated work. Forms empirical basis of "segmentary" interpretations. [SS]

15.246 K. Sundaram. *Studies in the social and economic conditions of medieval Andhra, A.D. 1100–1600.* Machilipatnam, India: Triveni, 1968. ▸ Summary of economic and social bases of states in medieval Andhra, based largely on Telugu (rather than Persian or European) materials. Stresses role of temples and merchant guilds; important in particular for Kakatiya dynasty of Warangal. [SS]

15.247 Thomas R. Trautmann. *Dravidian kinship.* Cambridge: Cambridge University Press, 1981. ISBN 0-521-23703-3. ▸ Important semi-anthropological, semi-historical work. Exhaustive examination of peculiarities of kinship system in south. Some chapters focus on political implications and use historical, especially inscriptional, materials. [SS]

15.248 N. Venkataramanayya. *The eastern Calukyas of Vengi.* Madras, India: Vedam Venkataraya Sastry, 1950. ▸ Political study of dynasty of Telugu country, seventh to thirteenth century, based on inscriptional and other material. [SS]

Sri Lanka

15.249 Wilhelm Geiger. *Culture of Ceylon in mediaeval times.* 1960 ed. Heinz Bechert, ed. Stuttgart: Steiner, 1986. ISBN 3-515-04447-7. ▸ Translated work by early twentieth-century German Orientalist and Pali scholar. Dated but nevertheless important; strong textual basis. [SS]

15.250 R.A.L.H. Gunawardana. *Robe and plough: monasticism and economic interest in early medieval Sri Lanka.* Tucson: University of Arizona Press for Association for Asian Studies, 1979. ISBN 0-8165-0648-5 (cl), 0-8165-0647-7 (pbk). ▸ Explores inter-

relationship between Buddhist monasteries and kingship in medieval Sri Lanka, with sidelights on irrigation, trade, and urbanization. Well informed both on materials and theoretical constructs. [SS]

15.251 S. Pathmanathan. *The kingdom of Jaffna.* Colombo: Rajendran, 1978. ▸ Largely political history of northern Sri Lankan kingdom, whose rulers, Arya Cakravartis, sought to control channel between southern India and Sri Lanka. [SS]

15.252 Bardwell L. Smith, ed. *Religion and legitimation of power in Sri Lanka.* Chambersburg, Penn.: Anima, 1978. ISBN 0-89012-008-0. ▸ Collected papers, not all concerned with medieval period. Important entry point into historiography; many papers remain state-of-the-art. [SS]

15.253 Ginota Parana Vidanage Somaratne. *The political history of the kingdom of Kotte, 1400–1521.* Nugegoda, Sri Lanka: Deepani, 1975. ▸ Political history of western Sri Lankan kingdom, which dominated fifteenth-century politics and where Portuguese set up fort of Colombo. Useful data, conventional format. [SS]

Religion and Society

15.254 Richard Barz. *The Bhakti sect of Vallabhacarya.* Faridabad, India: Thomson, 1976. ▸ Treats sect (*sampradaya*) founded by Telugu brahman Vallabhacarya (1479–1531?), particularly powerful among mercantile communities in North India and Gujarat. [SS]

15.255 John Braisted Carman. *The theology of Ramanuja: an essay in interreligious understanding.* New Haven: Yale University Press, 1974. ISBN 0-300-01521-6. ▸ Analysis of theological aspects of qualified nondualistic philosophy of eleventh- to early twelfth-century South Indian religious reformer, associated with Srirangam temple. [SS]

15.256 Hermann Goetz. *Mira Bai: her life and times.* Bombay, India: Bharatiya Vidya Bhavan, 1966. ▸ Semi-popular work, attempting to come to grips with biography and context of Mira, reputedly Sisodia Rajput, princess of Mewar, in Rajasthan, from early sixteenth century. Figure of Mira herself remains shrouded in obscurity, as does textual tradition for her songs. [SS]

15.257 Jan Gonda. *Medieval religious literature in Sanskrit.* Vol. 2.1 of *A history of Indian literature.* Wiesbaden: Harrassowitz, 1977. ISBN 3-447-01743-0. ▸ Survey of medieval religious literature in Sanskrit with useful bibliography and brief comments on extensive range of texts. Not always strong on historical context. [SS]

15.258 Friedhelm Hardy. *Viraha-bhakti: the early history of Krsna devotion in South India.* Delhi: Oxford University Press, 1983. ISBN 0-19-561251-5. ▸ Rich study of Vaisnava devotional material, based on Tamil and Sanskrit sources. Argues for different, more eclectic, social and cultural basis for such devotionalism than usually offered. [SS]

15.259 Ronald B. Inden. *Marriage and rank in Bengali culture: a history of caste and clan in middle period Bengal.* Berkeley: University of California Press, 1976. ISBN 0-520-02569-5. ▸ Important work of Chicago school, applying anthropological method to historical sources to examine issues of hierarchy via descent and marriage in early medieval Bengal. [SS]

15.260 W. H. McLeod. *Guru Nanak and the Sikh religion.* 1968 ed. Delhi: Oxford University Press, 1976. ▸ Life and thought of Guru Nanak (1469–1539), founder of Sikh religious tradition, in context of popular North Indian religious devotionalism. Historically informed, sympathetically presented. [DSL]

15.261 S. G. Mudgal. *"Advaita" of Sankara, a reappraisal: impact of Buddhism and Samkhya on Sankara's thought.* Delhi:

Motilal Banarsidass, 1975. ISBN 0-8426-0737-4. ‣ Examination of *Advaita Vedanta* of this influential ninth-century philosopher and religious reformer in context of other contemporary philosophical trends, particularly Buddhism, to which Sankara was inimical, but from which he borrowed. [SS]

15.262 T. S. Narayana Sastri. *The age of Sankara.* 2d rev. ed. T. N. Kumaraswamy, ed. Madras, India: Paul, 1971. ‣ Attempt to reconstruct historical context of Nambudiri Brahman from Kerala. Sankara (ca. 788–820 CE) established pan-Indian religious network of resurgent ascetic Hinduism. Somewhat hagiographic in treatment but nevertheless useful work. [SS]

15.263 Kanti Chandra Pandey. *Abhinavagupta: an historical and philosophical study.* 2d rev. ed. Varanasi, India: Chowkhamba Sanskrit Series Office, 1963. ‣ Vast, encyclopedic work, at times somewhat impenetrable, on Abhinavagupta (ca. 1000), major exponent of Saivism from Kashmir and also aesthetician and proponent of idea of "*Santarasa.*" [SS]

15.264 V. Raghavan. *The great integrators: the saint-singers of India.* Delhi: Ministry of Information and Broadcasting, Publications Division, 1966. ‣ General and popular work by authority on Sanskrit literature and South Indian devotionalism. General introduction written from Indian nationalist perspective. [SS]

15.265 Rajendra Ram. *A history of Buddhism in Nepal, A.D. 704–1396.* Patna, India: Janabharati Prakashana; distributed by Motilal Banarsidass, 1978. ‣ Concise work on important but neglected theme. Empiricist and descriptive in orientation, but useful as reference work. [SS]

15.266 A. K. Ramanujan, ed. and trans. *Speaking of Siva.* Baltimore: Penguin, 1973. ISBN 0-14-044270-7. ‣ Brilliant translations from Kannada language of devotional poets of medieval period in Saiva mold. Useful historical and literary-historical insights in appended essay. [SS]

15.267 Bhasker Anand Saletore. *Mediaeval Jainism, with special reference to the Vijayanagara empire.* Bombay, India: Karnatak, 1939. ‣ Study of Jaina communities, mostly in Karnataka, and their relations with Vijayanagara, based largely on inscriptional record. Useful material, largely empiricist approach. Focus on shrine of Sravanabelagola. [SS]

15.268 David Dean Shulman. *The king and the clown in South Indian myth and poetry.* Princeton: Princeton University Press, 1985. ISBN 0-691-05457-6. ‣ Analysis of South Indian kingship, drawing largely on Tamil, Sanskrit, and Telugu materials, using structural and psychological approach. Excellent translations and comparisons with classical materials. [SS]

15.269 James Silverberg, ed. *Social mobility in the caste system in India: an interdisciplinary symposium.* The Hague: Mouton, 1968. ‣ Largely inspired by Indian sociologist M. N. Srinivas's idea of "sanskritization," collection of essays attempts to define nature and scope of vertical mobility in caste system through series of historical studies. [SS]

15.270 Bardwell L. Smith, ed. *Hinduism: new essays in the history of religions.* 1976 ed. Leiden: Brill, 1982. (Studies in the history of religion; supplements to *Numen,* 33.) ISBN 90-04-06788-4. ‣ Useful essays on Hinduism in social and political perspective, not merely textual and theological analysis. Now somewhat dated but nevertheless significant benchmark. [SS]

15.271 Ch. Vaudeville, ed. and trans. *Kabir.* Vol. 1. Oxford: Clarendon, 1974. ISBN 0-19-826526-3 (v. 1). ‣ Biography and legend of fifteenth-century North Indian poet and mystic and his language and religious context, with translations from his *Sakhis.* Influential work on major theme of medieval cultural history. [SS]

15.272 Kamil V. Zvelebil. *The poets of the powers.* London: Rider, 1973. ISBN 0-09-115900-8 (cl), 0-09-115901-6 (pbk). ‣ Introduc-

tion to and selections from works of early medieval Tamil Siddhas, Tantric Yogis reputed to possess supernatural powers; tradition continued into early modern period. [SS]

Muslims in South Asia

Rule of Muslim Dynasties

15.273 K. M. Ashraf. *Life and conditions of the people of Hindustan.* 3d ed. New Delhi, India: Munshiram Manoharlal, 1988. ISBN 81-215-0092-3. ‣ Study written in 1930s of Delhi sultanate, from early thirteenth century. Title misleading; not purely political narrative, but largely focused on court. [SS]

15.274 Muhammad ᶜAziz Ahmad. *Political history and institutions of the early Turkish empire of Delhi, 1206–1290 A.D.* Rev. ed. Lahore: University of Punjab, Research Society of Pakistan, 1987. ISBN 969-425-069-2. ‣ Account of so-called slave kings (Mamluks), from Qutb al-Din to Balban. Use of Persian sources; close to chroniclers' own perspective in terms of organization. [SS]

15.275 Clifford Edmund Bosworth. *The later Ghaznavids: splendour and decay; the dynasty in Afghanistan and northern India, 1040–1186.* New York: Columbia University Press, 1977. ISBN 0-231-04428-3. ‣ Good use of sparse documentation on late Ghaznavids in Punjab; read with 9.160. Contains useful chronology and appendix. [SS]

15.276 Upendra Nath Day. *Medieval Malwa: a political and cultural history, 1401–1562.* Delhi: Munshiram Manoharlal, 1965. ‣ Regional history, from Persian sources, of Ghuri and Khalji sultans of Malwa to Mughal conquest of area. Mostly chronological by reign, three chapters on administrative, economic, and cultural aspects. Major focus on Sultan Mahmud Khalji (d. 1469). [SS]

15.277 Simon Digby. *War-horse and elephant in the Delhi sultanate: a study of military supplies.* Oxford: Orient Monographs, 1971. ‣ Succinct, lucid monographic treatment of trade in and use of war materials, especially horses and elephants in sultanate warfare. Uses wealth of Persian materials. Questions conventional view of Turk-Rajput military balance. [SS]

15.278 Mohammad Habib. *Sultan Mahmud of Ghaznin.* 2d ed. Delhi: Chand, 1967. ‣ Revisionist when it first appeared in 1961, arguing that celebrated Afghanistan-based sultan raided India for economic gain rather than to further Islam. Important polemically, but supplanted historiographically by Bosworth (15.275). [SS]

15.279 A.B.M. Habibullah. *The foundation of Muslim rule in India: a history of the establishment and progress of the Turkish sultanate of Delhi, 1206–1290 A.D.* 2d rev. ed. Allahabad, India: Central Book Depot, 1961. ‣ Old-fashioned political narrative, setting out main dynastic and political twists and turns of thirteenth century; based on Persian chronicles. Important sections on law, judiciary, and provincial administration. Useful on currency and finance. [SS]

15.280 Abdul Halim. *History of the Lodi sultans of Delhi and Agra.* 1961 ed. Delhi: Idarah-i Adabiyat-i Delli, 1974. ‣ History of these Afghan rulers of Delhi and Agra. Wide range of sources cited; interesting insights into cultural patronage. Old-fashioned, careful work focusing on latter half of fifteenth and early sixteenth century. [SS]

15.281 Agha Mahdi Husain. *Tughluq dynasty.* Calcutta, India: Thacker, Spink, 1963. ‣ General account of Tughluqs; some useful appendixes, but inaccurate on some details especially with reference to Muhammad Shah Tughluq. Uses range of sources, but lacks integration and analysis. [SS]

15.282 S. C. Misra. *The rise of Muslim power in Gujarat: a history* *of Gujarat from 1209 to 1442.* 1981 2d ed. New Delhi, India: Munshiram Manoharlal, 1982. ‣ Useful, largely political account of emergence of Gujarat sultanate from under shadow of Delhi sultanate; largely based on Persian sources. Still standard work on subject; does not address last hundred years of Gujarat sultanate. [SS]

15.283   W. H. Moreland. *The agrarian system of Moslem India: a historical essay with appendices.* 1929 ed. Delhi: Low Price, 1990. ISBN 81-85395-00-4. ‣ Detailed assessment by British civil servant of sultanate and Mughal fiscal systems and institutions. [SS]

15.284   R. Nath. *History of sultanate architecture.* New Delhi, India: Abhinav, 1978. ‣ Useful, largely empiricist survey of major sultanate monuments; fails to draw links with general historical trends. Line drawings and some photographs. [SS]

15.285   S.B.P. Nigam. *Nobility under the sultans of Delhi, A.D. 1206–1398.* 1967 ed. Delhi: Munshiram Manoharlal, 1968. ‣ Examination of shifting composition of nobility under sultanate, but falls short of genuine prosopographical study. Weak on source materials. [SS]

15.286   K. A. Nilakanta Sastri. *A comprehensive history of India.* Vol. 5: *The Delhi sultanate, A.D. 1206–1526.* New Delhi, India: People's, 1982. ‣ Useful reference work with much detail. Somewhat naive in assumptions and old-fashioned in organization. Sections are direct paraphrases of medieval chronicles. [SS]

15.287   Pushpa Prasad. *Sanskrit inscriptions of Delhi sultanate, 1191–1526.* Delhi: Centre of Advanced Study in History, Aligarh Muslim University and Oxford University Press, 1990. ISBN 0-19-562123-9. ‣ Sourcebook, providing texts and translations of Sanskrit inscriptions from North India over period 1191–1526. Translations should be used with caution. Useful as compendium in place of hitherto scattered materials. [SS]

15.288   Ishtiaq Husain Qureshi. *The administration of the sultanate of Delhi.* 5th rev. ed. New Delhi, India: Oriental Books Reprint; distributed by Munshiram Manoharlal, 1971. ‣ Examination of major fiscal, juridical, and other institutions that existed and evolved under sultans of Delhi. Coherent presentation but unsophisticated in treatment. [SS]

15.289   Mian Muhammad Saeed. *The Sharqi sultanate of Jaunpur: a political and cultural history.* Karachi, Pakistan: University of Karachi, 1972. ‣ Study of regional sultanate located in modern-day Uttar Pradesh, ca. 1394–1505. Initial sections on political history, followed by extended discussion of architecture, literature, and fine arts; mystics and Ṣūfīs; useful appendixes. Only serious treatment of this important area. [SS]

15.290   Iqtidar Husain Siddiqi. *Afghan despotism in India, 1451–1555.* New Delhi, India: Indian Institute of Islamic Studies, 1966. ‣ Consideration of Lodi and Sur dynasties, including Sher Shah Sur and his successors. Largely political and administrative history; well documented but few novel insights. [SS]

15.291   M. R. Tarafdar. *Husain Shahi Bengal, 1495–1538 A.D.: a socio-political study.* Dacca, Bangladesh: Asiatic Society of Pakistan, 1965. (Asiatic Society of Pakistan, 16.) ‣ Voluminous, valuable study of brief period in history of pre-Mughal Bengal, using Persian, Arabic, and vernacular sources. Standard reference work on politics and administration, though weak on external trade and Portuguese presence. Not yet superseded. [SS]

15.292   R. P. Tripathi. *Some aspects of Muslim administration.* 1959 2d rev. ed. Allahabad, India: Central Book Depot, 1966. ‣ General approach to sultanate and Mughal rule, as seen from nationalist perspective. Discusses centralizing versus decentralizing tendencies in these regimes and posits Turko-Mongol theory of kingship. [SS]

15.293   H. Nelson Wright. *The coinage and metrology of the sultans of Delhi: incorporating a catalogue of the coins in the author's cabinet now in the Delhi Museum.* 1936 ed. New Delhi, India: Oriental Books Reprint, 1974. ‣ Pioneering work on numismatics and related matters, incorporating earlier catalog by same author. [SS]

15.294   Ghulam Yazdani. *Bidar: its history and monuments.* London: Oxford University Press, 1947. ‣ Pioneering study of fifteenth-century capital of Bahmani sultans of Deccan, with major monuments including *madrasa* constructed by vizier, Khwaja Mahmud Gawan Gilani (d. 1481). [SS]

Religion and Society

15.295   Aziz Ahmad. *Studies in Islamic culture in the Indian environment.* 1964 ed. Lahore: Oxford University Press, 1970. ‣ Disparate essays on religious and political interaction of Muslims and Hindus in northern India, eighth to twentieth century. Argue for abiding cultural and social separation. Learned but written under influence of partition of India and creation of Pakistan. [DSL]

15.296   Muhammad ibn Ahmad al-Biruni. *Alberuni's India: an account of the religion, philosophy, literature, geography, chronology, astronomy, customs, laws, and astrology of India about A.D. 1030.* 1910 ed. 2 vols. in 1. Edward C. Sachau, ed. and trans. New Delhi, India: Munshiram Manoharlal, 1992. ‣ Standard two-volume translation of great encyclopedic work by al-Biruni (ca. 973–1051), intellectual courtier of Sultan Muhammad of Ghaznin. Examines elite Indic civilization from cosmopolitan Muslim perspective. [SS/DSL]

15.297   P. M. Currie. *The shrine and cult of Mu'in al-Din Chishti of Ajmer.* Delhi: Oxford University Press, 1989. ISBN 0-19-562202-2. ‣ Examination of shrine and cult of one of earliest Indian Ṣūfī saints (1142–1236); born in Sistan, buried in Ajmer. Good use of hagiographic materials in general; interesting photographs and map. [SS]

15.298   Richard Maxwell Eaton. "Approaches to the study of conversion to Islam in India." In *Approaches to Islam in religious studies.* Richard C. Martin, ed., pp. 106–23. Tucson: University of Arizona Press, 1985. ISBN 0-8165-0868-2. ‣ Critique of and set of hypotheses for study of conversion to Islam in South Asia that seeks to correlate religious change to ecological and social contexts. Lucid, provocative discussion of crucial and controversial subject that requires further research. [DSL]

15.299   Richard Maxwell Eaton. *Sufis of Bijapur, 1300–1700: social roles of Sufis in medieval India.* Princeton: Princeton University Press, 1978. ISBN 0-691-03110-X. ‣ Role of Ṣūfīs in Deccan region, long the southern frontier of Indian Islam, under Bahmani and Adil Shahi sultans of Bijapur. Intersperses political and cultural history. Imaginative use of Ṣūfī hagiographic sources, as well as Persian chronicles. [SS]

15.300   Carl W. Ernst. *Eternal garden: mysticism, history, and politics at a South Asian Sufi center.* Albany: State University of New York Press, 1992. ISBN 0-7914-0883-3 (cl), 0-7914-0884-1 (pbk). ‣ Study of relationship of Ṣūfī Islam to Muslim ruling power, non-Muslim culture, and religious conversion centering on career and shrine of Shaikh Burhan al-din Gharib (d. 1337). Richly researched, convincingly argued revision of much previous scholarship on Islam in premodern India. [DSL]

15.301   Peter Hardy. "Modern European and Muslim explanations of conversion to Islam in South Asia." In *Conversion to Islam.* Nehemia Levtzion, ed., pp. 68–99. New York: Holmes & Meier, 1979. ISBN 0-8419-0343-3. ‣ Historiographic study of how scholars, particularly those associated with British rule in India, have dealt with question of conversion. Useful for fresh approaches that emphasize long-term and collective rather than individual perspectives. [DSL]

15.302 S. M. Jaffar. *Education in Muslim India: being an enquiry into the state of education during the Muslim period of Indian history, 1000–1800 A.D.* 1936 ed. Delhi: Idarah-i Adabiyat-i Delli, 1973. ▸ Examination of Islamic learning and educational institutions in India within chronological framework. Unexciting, but theme is important and little examined. [SS]

15.303 Bruce B. Lawrence. *An overview of Sufi literature in the sultanate period, 1206–1526 A.D.* Patna, India: Khuda Bakhsh Oriental Public Library, 1979. ▸ Useful survey of Ṣūfī materials, by leading authority on early Indian Ṣūfism. Far more careful approach to historicity than Rizvi 15.312. [SS]

15.304 Derryl N. Maclean. *Religion and society in Arab Sind.* Leiden: Brill, 1989. (Monographs and theoretical studies in sociology and anthropology in honour of Nels Anderson, 25.) ISBN 90-04-08551-3 (pbk). ▸ Study of eighth-century Arab conquest and gradual establishment of Islam in Sind in relation to prior religious and social history of political and economic division along Hindu-Buddhist lines. Creative use of chronicles and genealogies; original and provocative contribution to study of Islam in South Asia. [DSL]

15.305 Mohammad Wahid Mirza. *Life and works of Amir Khusrau.* 1935 ed. Delhi: Idarah-i Adabiyat-i Delli, 1974. ▸ Useful biographical introduction to Khusrau (d. 1325), his career under later slave kings, Khaljis, and early Tughluqs, and his works in Persian and Hindvi. Old-fashioned, somewhat hagiographical study. [SS]

15.306 M. Mujeeb. *The Indian Muslims.* 1967 ed. New Delhi, India: Munshiram Manoharlal, 1985. ▸ Narrative, often anecdotal history of North Indian Indo-Muslim literary and political history from Delhi sultanate to partition of India. Written from nationalist Indian perspective in opposition to pro-Pakistani historiography. [DSL]

15.307 Mohammad Noor Nabi. *Development of Muslim religious thought in India from 1200 AD. to 1450 AD.* Aligarh, India: Aligarh Muslim University, 1962. ▸ Study of Islamic thought in India, mainly under Delhi sultanate. Examines relatively orthodox as well as heterodox trends, staying close to and often little more than paraphrasing texts themselves. [SS]

15.308 Azim Nanji. *The Nizari Isma'ili tradition in the Indo-Pakistan subcontinent.* Delmar, N.Y.: Caravan, 1978. ISBN 0-88206-020-1. ▸ Study of history and textual sources for important community of Isma'ili Muslims, who recognize Agha Khan as spiritual leader and have integrated Indic language and culture into their religious way of life. Raises issues of religious diversity and syncretism in South Asian environment. [DSL]

15.309 Khaliq Ahmad Nizami. *Some aspects of religion and politics in India during the thirteenth century.* 1974 2d ed. Mohammad Habib, Introduction. Delhi: Idarah-i Adabiyat-i Delli, 1978. ▸ Loosely structured study addressing nexus between religion and politics, largely under sultans Iltutmish and Balban. Encyclopedic rather than analytical, using wide range of sources. [SS]

15.310 Khaliq Ahmad Nizami. *Studies in medieval Indian history and culture.* Allahabad, India: Kitab Mahal, 1966. ▸ Collected essays in empiricist mode, tinged with pro-Islamic perspective. Useful as entry point into wide range of Persian texts, but not always critical of sources. [SS]

15.311 Abdul Qaiyum Rafiqi. *Sufism in Kashmir from the fourteenth to the sixteenth century.* Varanasi, India: Bharatiya, 1972. ▸ Work mainly focusing on Kubravi and Rishi orders of Ṣūfīs in Kashmir. Extensive paraphrasing and direct citation from sources; lacks analytical focus. [SS]

15.312 Saiyid Athar Abbas Rizvi. *A history of Sufism in India.* Vol. 1: *Early Sufism and its history in India to 1600 A.D.* 1975 ed. New Delhi, India: Munshiram Manoharlal, 1978. ▸ Encyclopedic

but not always historically sound. Covers major Ṣūfī orders in India, as well as traditions of Qalandars and martyrs, with long excursus on relations between Ṣūfīs and Hindu mystics. [SS]

15.313 Asim Roy. *The Islamic syncretistic tradition in Bengal.* Princeton: Princeton University Press, 1983. ISBN 0-691-05387-1. ▸ Discussion of elements of syncretism among Islam, Buddhism, and popular Hinduism in Bengal of medieval and modern period. Based largely on vernacular sources. Well written but somewhat repetitive in argument. [SS]

15.314 Mehrdad Shokoohy. *Bhadresvar, the oldest Islamic monuments in India.* Leiden: Brill, 1989. ISBN 90-04-08341-3. ▸ Valuable illustrated treatment of remains of early Islamic trading site in coastal Gujarat, largely from perspective of architectural historian. [SS]

15.315 H. C. Verma. *Medieval routes to India, Baghdad to Delhi: a study of trade and military routes.* Calcutta, India: Naya Prokash, 1978. ▸ Useful reference work, little analysis. Traces trade routes between northern India and Central Asia and Iranian world at time of Delhi sultanate. Based on translated sources. [SS]

15.316 Andre Wink. *Al-Hind, the making of the Indo-Islamic world.* Vol. 1: *Early medieval India and the expansion of Islam (7th–11th centuries).* Leiden: Brill, 1990. ISBN 90-04-09249-8. ▸ Part polemical and part encyclopedic work, first in projected series. Argues for economic expansion in India, based on growing trade with Middle East and denies Indian feudalism thesis. Extensive dependence on secondary literature in English and European languages. [SS]

EARLY MODERN EMPIRES AND GLOBAL ECONOMY, ca. 1500–ca. 1800

General Studies and Historiography

15.317 Satish Chandra, ed. *Essays in medieval Indian economic history.* New Delhi, India: Munshiram Manoharlal, 1987. ISBN 81-215-0085-0. ▸ Selection of twenty-nine brief papers presented to Indian History Congress, 1941–83. In two sections, "Agriculture and Revenue" and "Trade, Market, and Currency." [SS]

15.318 A. I. Chicherov. *India, economic development in the sixteenth–eighteenth centuries: outline history of crafts and trade.* Rev. ed. Moscow, Russia: Nauka, Central Department of Oriental Literature, 1971. ▸ Revisonist Soviet work arguing that India in three centuries before colonial rule was developing seeds of capitalism, which were destroyed by colonial impact. Focuses largely on crafts, textile production, and internal and external trade. Very large but little-utilized bibliography. [SS]

15.319 Chandra Richard De Silva and D. De Silva. "The history of Ceylon (c. 1500–1658): a historiographical and bibliographical survey." *Ceylon journal of historical and social sciences* 3.1 (1973) 52–77. ▸ Relatively comprehensive, competent coverage focusing largely on so-called Portuguese period. Omits some recent works. [SS]

15.320 Irfan Habib. *An atlas of the Mughal empire: political and economic maps with detailed notes, bibliography, and index.* Aligarh, India and Delhi: Centre of Advanced Study in History, Aligarh Muslim University and Oxford University Press, 1982. ISBN 0-19-560379-6. ▸ Valuable summary of political and economic data from Persian chronicles and documents and European materials available in English translation. Post-1700 materials have not been incorporated and data on Deccan and South India relatively weak. [SS]

15.321 Dirk H. A. Kolff. *Naukar, Rajput, and Sepoy: the ethnohistory of the military labour market in Hindustan, 1450–1850.* Cambridge: Cambridge University Press, 1990. ISBN 0-521-38132-0. ▸ Study of military recruitment and migration of peasants in precolonial North India. Argues for importance of seasonal employment in armies for peasants, their wide spatial mobility in pursuit of army wages, and critical role of service to military commanders in process of social mobility. Critical for revisionist understandings of precolonial rural society. [DEL]

15.322 K. M. Panikkar. *Asia and Western dominance: a survey of the Vasco da Gama epoch of Asian history, 1498–1945.* 1959 rev. ed. New York: Collier, 1969. ▸ Important polemical work, from Indian nationalist perspective. Stresses dominance of sea power over continental polities after 1498. [SS]

15.323 Frank Perlin. "Proto-industrialisation and pre-colonial South Asia." *Past and present* 98 (1983) 30–95. ISSN 0031-2746. ▸ Examination of utility of concept of protoindustrialization for understanding economic changes in early modern South Asia. Proposes idea of protocapitalism for period. [SS]

15.324 Tapan Raychaudhuri and Irfan Habib, eds. *The Cambridge economic history of India.* Vol. 1: *C. 1200–c. 1750.* 1982 ed. Cambridge: Cambridge University Press, 1987. ISBN 0-521-22692-9 (v. 1). ▸ Summary of collective wisdom of 1970s on Delhi sultanate, Vijayanagara, Mughals, and Deccan sultanates. Major chapters by editors and Burton Stein. Central work in subsequent debates. [SS]

15.325 John F. Richards. "Mughal state finance and the premodern world economy." *Comparative studies in society and history* 23.2 (1981) 285–308. ISSN 0010-4175. ▸ Argues that Mughal fiscal system was highly centralized and operated independently of banking networks. Argues for symbiosis between Mughals and East India companies in seventeenth century. [SS]

15.326 Jagadish Narayan Sarkar. *History of history writing in medieval India: contemporary historians, an introduction to medieval Indian historiography.* Calcutta, India: Ratna Prakashan, 1977. ▸ Useful summation of major chronicles and histories of medieval period; weak on southern India, better on North India and Deccan. [SS]

15.327 Sanjay Subrahmanyam. *Merchants, markets, and the state in early modern India.* Delhi: Oxford University Press, 1990. ISBN 0-19-562569-2. ▸ Collection of articles ranging from Kanara coast in seventeenth century to late eighteenth- and early nineteenth-century Bengal and Tamilnadu. Fresh perspectives on peasant production, marketing, weaving, and revenue economy. [SS]

SEE ALSO
3.250 K. N. Chaudhuri. *Trade and civilisation in the Indian Ocean.*

Mughal Empire and Late Deccan Sultanates

15.328 Catherine B. Asher. *Architecture of Mughal India.* Part 1. Vol. 4 of *The new Cambridge history of India.* Cambridge: Cambridge University Press, 1992. ISBN 0-521-26728-5. ▸ Handsomely illustrated survey of both major and many minor monuments of Mughal period. Predictably, much of focus is on periods of emperors Akbar, Jahangir, and Shah Jahan, but also deals with Mughal successor states more extensively than is usual. [SS]

15.329 M. Athar Ali. *The Mughal nobility under Aurangzeb.* Bombay, India: Asia Publishing House for Department of History, Aligarh Muslim University, 1966. ▸ Study of nobility under Mughal ruler Aurangzeb (1658–1707), based almost exclusively on Persian sources. Largely statistical approach designed to show balance between different ethnic groups, as well as effects of incorporation of nobles from Deccan sultanates. [SS]

15.330 Milo Cleveland Beach. *Mughal and Rajput painting.* Part 1. Vol. 3 of *The new Cambridge history of India.* Cambridge: Cambridge University Press, 1992. ISBN 0-521-40027-9. ▸ Focuses on rise of Mughal painting between 1540 and 1660, rise thereafter of local and regional styles, and eighteenth-century dominance of Rajput painting. Includes some 200 plates, mostly black and white. [SS]

15.331 Stephen P. Blake. *Shahjahanabad: the sovereign city in Mughal India, 1639–1739.* Cambridge: Cambridge University Press, 1991. ISBN 0-521-39045-1. ▸ Based largely on Persian sources, book examines structure of city of Shahjahanabad (Old Delhi), built by Mughal emperor Shah Jahan. Structure of sovereign city linked to Weberian theory of patrimonial-bureaucratic state, dominated by ruler and handful of nobles. [SS]

15.332 Satish Chandra. *Parties and politics at the Mughal court, 1707–1740.* 2d ed. New Delhi, India: People's Publishing House, 1972. ▸ Study of politics of Mughal state, in phase of "decline," identified with death of Aurangzeb (1707). Focuses on crumbling of institutions that had earlier dominated, particularly prebendal-assignment (*jagirdari*) and on growing sense of crisis that emerged. [SS]

15.333 Irfan Habib. *The agrarian system of Mughal India (1556–1707).* London: Asia Publishing House, 1963. ▸ Examination of fiscal system under Mughals using a wide range of principally Persian sources. Traces relations between centrally controlled lands, prebends, and local potentates (*zamindars*). Last chapter is Marxist analysis of Mughal decline, seen as result of peasant rebellion against excessive fiscal pressure. Widely cited, especially by Indian historians. [SS]

15.334 Gavin Hambly. *Cities of Mughul India: Delhi, Agra, and Fatehpur Sikri.* 1968 ed. New Delhi, India: Vikas, 1977. ISBN 0-7069-0627-6. ▸ Useful general introduction to history of three major Mughal centers in North India; illustrations, and some plans. More specialized studies of single centers are now available, but work retains its general importance. [SS]

15.335 Mohibbul Hasan. *Babur: founder of the Mughal empire in India.* New Delhi, India: Manohar, 1985. ▸ Largely political history of Babur, Timurid prince who founded Mughal state in northern India. Uses Persian sources, including some relatively underutilized materials. Conventional in approach, with useful chapter on administrative structure under early Mughals. [SS]

15.336 Ibn Hasan. *The central structure of the Mughal empire and its practical working up to the year 1657.* 1936 ed. New Delhi, India: Munshiram Manoharlal, 1970. ▸ Considers key administrative and financial institutions of Mughals in reigns of Akbar, Jahangir, and Aurangzeb. Intermediate step between Moreland 15.342 and later works of Habib (15.333), Raychaudhuri (15.344), and others. [SS]

15.337 Ibrahim Adil Shah II. *Kitab-i Nauras.* Nazir Ahmad, ed. New Delhi, India: Bharatiya Kala Kendra, 1956. ▸ Valuable edition and English translation of collection of lyric poems in Deccani, attributed to a sultan of Deccan kingdom of Bijapur (r. 1580–1627). Long historical introduction by Ahmad makes edition particularly useful. [SS]

15.338 Ahsan Raza Khan. *Chieftains in the Mughal empire during the reign of Akbar.* Simla, India: Indian Institute of Advanced Study, 1977. ▸ Questions notion of Mughal empire in late sixteenth century as highly centralized state, using evidence of main Mughal chronicles of epoch. Provides region-by-region listing of chieftains, their domains and military strength. Underlying purpose is to see Akbar's empire as comprising small core region with extensive and unruly periphery. [SS]

15.339 Iqtidar Alam Khan. *Mirza Kamran: a bibliographical study.* Bombay, India: Asia Publishing House, 1964. ▸ Study of Kamran, son of Babur and half-brother of Mughal ruler Humayun. Between late 1530s and early 1550s, Kamran was great thorn in Humayun's flesh as challenger and rival contender with base at Kabul. Mainly conventional political analysis with close attention to detail based on Persian sources. [SS]

15.340 D. N. Marshall. *Mughals in India: a bibliographical survey of manuscripts.* 1967 ed. London: Mansell, 1985. ISBN 0-7201-1772-0. ▸ Invaluable guide to published and unpublished texts on Mughal period, in Persian, but also other languages. Over 2,000 entries arranged by author. [SS]

15.341 Shireen Moosvi. *The economy of the Mughal empire, c. 1595: a statistical study.* Aligarh, India and Delhi: Centre of Advanced Study in History, Aligarh Muslim University and Oxford University Press, 1987. ISBN 0-19-561725-8. ▸ Controversial analysis of economy of Akbar's empire, positing high level of revenue and centralization, with population estimate for all of India of between 140 and 150 million in 1600. Weak on trade and on social underpinnings of economic history; based on very limited Persian materials. [SS]

15.342 W. H. Moreland. *From Akbar to Aurangzeb: a study in Indian economic history.* 1923 ed. New York: AMS Press, 1975. ISBN 0-404-56298-1. ▸ Pioneering attempt to study seventeenth century in India using combination of Persian and European (Dutch and English) materials. Overstates extent of Mughal oppression and European dominance over maritime trade, but unsurpassed as synthesis of Indian economic history between 1605 and 1707. [SS]

15.343 M. A. Nayeem. *External relations of the Bijapur kingdom, 1489–1686 A.D.: a study in diplomatic history.* Hyderabad, India: Bright for Sayeedia Research Institute, 1974. ▸ 'Adilshahi kingdom of Bijapur was strategically located in sixteenth and seventeenth centuries, to deal with Mughals, Portuguese, Iran, and other powers. Focuses on diplomatic exchanges, based largely on Persian sources. Distressing number of typographic errors. [SS]

15.344 Tapan Raychaudhuri. *Bengal under Akbar and Jahangir: an introductory study in social history.* 1966 2d ed. Delhi: Munshiram Manoharlal, 1969. ▸ Early attempt to study regional society under Mughal rule in relation to changes in fabric of Bengal society, in particular socioreligious reform movements under general banner of Vaishnavism. Limited access to source material and relatively weak treatment of economy. [SS]

15.345 John F. Richards. *Mughal administration in Golconda.* Oxford: Clarendon, 1975. ISBN 0-19-821561-4. ▸ Analysis of Qutb Shahi sultanate of Golconda in seventeenth century, its takeover by Mughals and emergence of Hyderabad in eighteenth century as semi-independent state. Extensive detail on local administration and fiscal relations, 1687–1724. Based on new Persian documentation. [SS]

15.346 John F. Richards, ed. *The imperial monetary system of Mughal India.* Delhi: Oxford University Press, 1987. ISBN 0-19-561953-6. ▸ Papers on economy of India, sixteenth to eighteenth century; not all papers focus on imperial monetary system. Substantial contribution by Perlin and other important papers by Prakash and Habib. [SS]

15.347 Saiyid Athar Abbas Rizvi. *Religious and intellectual history of the Muslims in Akbar's reign, with special reference to Abu'l Fazl, 1556–1605.* New Delhi, India: Munshiram Manoharlal, 1975. ▸ Richly documented, though poorly argued study of Shaikh Abu'l Fazl (1551–1602), chief ideologue and chronicler of Mughal emperor Akbar. Also examines reaction of orthodox Muslims to Akbar's religious experimentation. [SS]

15.348 Jadunath Sarkar. *History of Aurangzib, mainly based on Persian sources.* 1925–52 ed. 5 vols. in 4. Bombay, India: Orient Longman, 1972–74. ▸ Most important contribution of Jadunath Sarkar, who dominated Mughal studies in his generation. Sharply critical of Aurangzeb, portrayed as bigoted Sunni Muslim. Work has since fallen into disrepute in eyes of neo-Marxist Indian historians, who argue that author's sectarian prejudices overwhelmed his historical judgment. [SS]

15.349 G. D. Sharma. *Rajput polity, a study of politics and administration of the state of Marwar, 1638–1749.* New Delhi, India: Manohar, 1977. ▸ Study of western Indian kingdom of Marwar under Mughal suzerainty, based largely on Rajasthani literature and archival papers. Largely concerned with political details, but also useful insights into fiscal assignment system (*patta*). [SS]

15.350 H. K. Sherwani. *History of the Qutb Shahi dynasty.* 1969 ed. New Delhi, India: Munshiram Manoharlal, 1974. ▸ Massive study by doyen of medieval Deccan studies in India. Using extremely wide range of Persian, Arabic, and vernacular sources, addresses political and cultural history of Hyderabad-Golconda state between early sixteenth and late seventeenth centuries. Makes up in richness what it lacks in coherence. [SS]

15.351 Radhey Shyam. *The kingdom of Ahmadnagar.* New Delhi, India: Motilal Banarsidass, 1966. ▸ General political, military, and diplomatic history of this Deccan sultanate between late fifteenth and early seventeenth century. Mostly translated Persian sources, supplemented by a few in Portuguese; weak on fiscal and economic affairs and on social and cultural history. [SS]

15.352 Som Prakash Verma. *Art and material culture in the paintings of Akbar's court.* New Delhi, India: Vikas, 1978. ISBN 0-7069-0595-4. ▸ Materialist interpretation of art from Mughal court with focus on realism and aspect as mirror of period. Useful details on instruments and artisanal products under heading "material culture." [SS]

15.353 Mark Zebrowski. *Deccani painting.* London and Berkeley: Sotheby and University of California Press, 1983. ISBN 0-520-04878-4. ▸ Richly illustrated book describing specificity of Deccani painting, and its historical evolution. Sultanates of Deccan in sixteenth and seventeenth centuries produced important body of painting, with mix of Persian, other West Asian, and even European influences, but at same time distinct from Mughal school. [SS]

SEE ALSO
18.89 Yohanan Friedmann. *Shaykh Ahmad Sirhindi.*

Vijayanagar, South India, and Sri Lanka

15.354 Anna Libera Dallapiccola, ed. *Vijayanagara, city and empire: new currents of research.* 2 vols. Stuttgart: Steiner, 1985. ISBN 3-515-04554-6 (set). ▸ Rich on architectural and bibliographic information, with number of detailed plans of city. Economic and political history not as well treated, with exception of articles by Külke and Breckenridge. [SS]

15.355 Henry Heras. *South India under the Vijayanagara empire: the Aravidu dynasty.* 1927 ed. 2 vols. New Delhi, India: Cosmo, 1980. ▸ Political history of late sixteenth and early seventeenth century. Use of extensive missionary and Portuguese sources, with excerpts reproduced in valuable appendix. Also treats Nayaka states of Senji, Madurai, Tanjavur and to lesser extent Ikkeri. Previously published as *The Aravidu Dynasty of Vijayanagara* (1927). [SS]

15.356 A. P. Ibrahim Kunju. *Rise of Travancore: a study of the life and times of Martanda Varma.* Trivandrum, India: Kerala Historical Society, 1976. ▸ Political history of Travancore or Venad kingdom in southern Kerala, focusing on reign of its most famous eighteenth-century ruler, who promoted state centralization, trade monopolies, and far-reaching military changes. [SS]

15.357 Noboru Karashima. *Towards a new formation: South Indian society under Vijayanagar rule.* Delhi: Oxford University Press, 1992. ISBN 0-19-562861-6. ▸ Defends view that Nayaka rulers of period were "feudatories" of Vijayanagara and emerged from fifteenth-century centralized bureaucratic formation. Based largely on epigraphic sources. [SS]

15.358 A. Krishnaswami. *The Tamil country under Vijayanagar.*

Annamalainagar, India: Annamalai University, 1964. ▸ Early proponent of view that Vijayanagara in fifteenth and sixteenth centuries was feudal state. Political narrative and some epigraphic and literary evidence; unreliable on European materials. [SS]

15.359 T. V. Mahalingam. *Administration and social life under Vijayanagar.* 2d rev. ed. 2 vols. Madras, India: University of Madras, 1969–75. ▸ Summary of received wisdom on administrative institutions and economy and society in style of Madras school. Conventional in format, based largely on epigraphy and translated travel accounts. [SS]

15.360 George Michell. *The Vijayanagara courtly style: incorporation and synthesis in the royal architecture of southern India, fifteenth–seventeenth centuries.* New Delhi, India: Manohar and American Institute of Indian Studies, 1992. ISBN 81-85425-29-9. ▸ Brief text, followed by extensive black-and-white photographs and line drawings. Focuses on Vijayanagara itself and Penugonda and Candragiri, two other sites in Andhra Pradesh. [SS]

15.361 K. M. Panikkar. *A history of Kerala, 1498–1801.* Annamalainagar, India: Annamalai University, 1960. ▸ Overview of Kerala's political history, with focus on relations between indigenous states (especially Cochin, Calicut, and Travancore) and the Portuguese, Dutch, and English. Useful for chronological detail and broad political phases; unreliable on many details. [SS]

15.362 Velcheru Narayana Rao, David Dean Shulman, and Sanjay Subrahmanyam. *Symbols of substance: court and state in Nayaka-period Tamilnadu.* Delhi: Oxford University Press, 1992. ISBN 0-19-563021-1. ▸ Ambitious attempt to combine literary materials in Telugu, Tamil, and Sanskrit with more conventional historical materials, to provide view of political culture in Tamil country, 1500–1700. [SS]

15.363 Bhasker Anand Saletore. *Social and political life in the Vijayanagara empire (A.D. 1346–A.D. 1646).* 2 vols. Madras, India: Paul, 1934. ▸ View of Vijayanagara based mostly on materials from western, Kannada-speaking regions; stresses continuity with earlier institutions. Still important for its coverage of materials. [SS]

15.364 R. Sathianathaier. *Tamilaham in the seventeenth century.* Madras, India: University of Madras, 1956. ▸ Consideration of history of political relations between Tamil Nayakas and Aravidu dynasty, with extensive use of Jesuit letters. Largely narrative in character. [SS]

15.365 H. L. Seneviratne. *Rituals of the Kandyan state.* Cambridge: Cambridge University Press, 1978. ISBN 0-521-21736-9. ▸ Buddhist rituals of sacred tooth relic of kingdom of Kandy, ca. 1500–1800, as representation of royal power and agrarian relations as well as modern transformations since 1948. Methodologically adventurous effort to use ethnographic observation to document distant past. [DSL]

15.366 Robert Sewell. *A forgotten empire, Vijayanagar: a contribution to the history of India.* 1900 ed. Shannon, Ireland and New York: Irish University Press and Barnes & Noble, 1972. ▸ Classic account of Vijayanagara, using epigraphic and European sources; very valuable appendix with translations of Portuguese accounts. No rigid theoretical model or well-defined framework. [SS]

15.367 Burton Stein. *Vijayanagara.* Cambridge: Cambridge University Press, 1989. ISBN 0-521-26693-9. ▸ Summary of historiographical trends to mid-1980s on Vijayanagara. Largely political narrative with some economic and social history content; weak on cultural and literary aspects. [SS]

15.368 K. D. Swaminathan. *The Nayakas of Ikkeri.* Madras, India: Varadachary, 1957. ▸ Origins and development of Keladi state in Karnataka, from late sixteenth century to eighteenth century. Largely political narrative; only coherent political account of region to date. [SS]

15.369 N. Venkataramanayya. *Studies in the history of the third dynasty of Vijayanagara.* 1935 ed. Delhi: Gian, 1986. ▸ Focus on sixteenth century and on Telugu-speaking regions of empire; with very wide use of epigraphic, literary, and semi-literary sources in that language. With Saletore 15.363, best of pre-1980s studies of Vijayanagara. [SS]

European Outposts and Regimes

15.370 Tikiri Abeyasinghe. *Portuguese rule in Ceylon, 1594–1612.* Colombo: Lake House Investments, 1966. ▸ Political narrative, with some fiscal details, of establishment of Portuguese power in Sri Lanka by Dom Jerónimo de Azevedo and his successors. Published materials, some archival sources. [SS]

15.371 Sinnappah Arasaratnam. *Dutch power in Ceylon, 1658–1687.* 1958 ed. Delhi: Navrang, 1988. ▸ Account of Dutch control of coastal regions of Sri Lanka from 1658 and their conflict with rulers of Kandy, particularly Raja Sinha. Based largely on Dutch sources. [SS]

15.372 Sinnappah Arasaratnam. *Merchants, companies, and commerce on the Coromandel coast, 1650–1740.* Delhi: Oxford University Press, 1986. ISBN 0-19-561873-4. ▸ Account of trade on southeastern coast of India, with attention to both Asian and European traders. Argues for decline of trade as result of internal political anarchy. Not very rich on source material. [SS]

15.373 Genevieve Bouchon. *"Regent of the Sea": Cannanore's response to Portuguese expansion, 1507–1528.* Louise Shackley, trans. Delhi: Oxford University Press, 1988. ISBN 0-19-562062-3. ▸ Account of Mappila leader Mammale and his relations with Portuguese on Malabar coast and in Maldives and Laccadives. Close attention to detail; based on Portuguese sources. [SS]

15.374 C. R. Boxer. *Portuguese India in the mid-seventeenth century.* Delhi: Oxford University Press, 1980. ▸ Brief account of Portuguese India in phase of most intense competition with Dutch East India Company (VOC). Focus on intra-Asian trade routes and decline of trade on Cape route. [SS]

15.375 K. N. Chaudhuri. *The trading world of Asia and the English East India Company, 1660–1760.* Cambridge: Cambridge University Press, 1978. ISBN 0-521-21716-4. ▸ Wide-ranging, ambitious work, based on extensive research in archives of English East India Company; much quantitative material. Burdened with theoretical framework of systems analysis, which may be ignored. [SS]

15.376 Ashin Das Gupta. *Malabar in Asian trade, 1740–1800.* Cambridge: Cambridge University Press, 1967. ▸ Succinct examination, based on Dutch and English sources, of struggle over maritime trade of Kerala at time of Travancore's consolidation. Largely narrative; little quantification. Very well written. [SS]

15.377 Chandra Richard De Silva. *The Portuguese in Ceylon, 1617–1638.* Colombo: Cave, 1972. ▸ Political and economic account of Portuguese trade and military struggles in Sri Lanka. Useful details of cinnamon and other commodities based to large extent on published Portuguese sources. [SS]

15.378 Teotonio R. De Souza. *Medieval Goa: a socio-economic history.* New Delhi, India: Concept, 1979. ▸ Account from nationalist Indian perspective of Portuguese presence in Goa; uses extensive Portuguese and Konkani sources, some samples of which may be found in appendixes. Weak on economic analysis. [SS]

15.379 A. R. Disney. *Twilight of the pepper empire: Portuguese trade in southwest India in the early seventeenth century.* Cambridge, Mass.: Harvard University Press, 1978. ISBN 0-674-91429-5. ▸ Brief but extensively documented account of Portuguese trade on Kerala and Kanara coasts, focusing on period of

Portuguese East India Company (1628–33). Analyzes reasons for failure of company. [SS]

15.380 Ole Feldbæk. *India trade under the Danish flag, 1772–1808: European enterprise and Anglo-Indian remittance and trade.* Copenhagen: Studentlitteratur, 1969. ▸ Uses Danish archives to study mutuality of interests between English private traders (or company officials in unofficial capacity) and Danish Company, which remitted their money to Europe by way of trade. [SS]

15.381 P. J. Marshall. *East Indian fortunes: the British in Bengal in the eighteenth century.* Oxford: Clarendon, 1976. ISBN 0-19-821566-5. ▸ Account of British trade in Bengal before and after battle of Plassey (1757); traces rise of Calcutta private trading fleet, up-country trade, making of fortunes, and political repercussions. [SS]

15.382 M. N. Pearson. *Merchants and rulers in Gujarat: the response to the Portuguese in the sixteenth century.* Berkeley: University of California Press, 1976. ISBN 0-520-02809-0. ▸ Largely based on printed Portuguese sources, brief but important Weberian analysis of political responses in Gujarat to Portuguese threat. Materials from seventeenth and eighteenth centuries also used. [SS]

15.383 M. N. Pearson. *The Portuguese in India.* Part 1. Vol. 1 of *The new Cambridge history of India.* Cambridge: Cambridge University Press, 1987. ISBN 0-521-25713-1. ▸ Short account of Portuguese trade and Luso-Indian society between 1500 and 1961. Weak on post-1650 period, somewhat strident for earlier period, and uneven in historiographical coverage. [SS]

15.384 Om Prakash. *The Dutch East India Company and the economy of Bengal, 1630–1720.* Princeton: Princeton University Press, 1985. ISBN 0-691-05447-9. ▸ Extensive quantitative data on Dutch trade from Bengal, based almost exclusively on Dutch sources. Argues company trade was net contribution to trade in region and promoted economic expansion. [SS]

15.385 Ahsan Jan Qaisar. *The Indian response to European technology and culture (A.D. 1498–1707).* Delhi: Oxford University Press, 1982. ISBN 0-19-561313-9. ▸ Sector-by-sector analysis of how Indians adapted to, ignored, or imitated European technology; discusses clockwork, shipbuilding, glassmaking, and military technology. Useful, somewhat fragmentary work, lacking general cultural analysis. [SS]

15.386 Tapan Raychaudhuri. *Jan Company in Coromandel, 1605–1690: a study in the interrelations of European commerce and traditional economies.* The Hague: Nijhoff, 1962. ▸ Early, influential study of company trade with useful quantitative data in chronological and narrative framework. Based on Dutch archival data. [SS]

15.387 Siba Pada Sen. *The French in India, first establishment and struggle.* Calcutta, India: University of Calcutta, 1947. ▸ Narrative account of political circumstances and some economic aspects of French presence in India in late seventeenth and early eighteenth century. Somewhat thin on primary material. [SS]

15.388 Sanjay Subrahmanyam. *Improvising empire: Portuguese trade and settlement in the Bay of Bengal, 1500–1700.* Delhi: Oxford University Press, 1990. ISBN 0-19-562570-6. ▸ Collection of essays, with few translated documents in appendix, based largely on Portuguese, some Italian and Dutch, materials. Bulk of essays focus on sixteenth century. [SS]

15.389 Sanjay Subrahmanyam. *The Portuguese empire in Asia, 1500–1700: a political and economic history.* London: Longman, 1993. ISBN 0-582-05069-3 (cl), 0-582-05068-5 (pbk). ▸ Survey of recent literature on Portuguese in Asia organized around argument about changing nature of their presence. Stresses political and economic change in both Asia and Europe as contributing factors. [SS]

15.390 Ian Bruce Watson. *Foundation for empire: English private trade in India, 1659–1760.* New Delhi, India: Vikas, 1980. ISBN 0-7069-1038-9. ▸ Argues English private trade from about 1659 set stage for political intervention. Useful details of private trade of English East India Company officials in Madras, then Calcutta and Bombay. [SS]

SEE ALSO
    3.188 Holden Furber. *Rival empires of trade in the Orient, 1600–1800.*
    3.252 Ashin Das Gupta and M. N. Pearson, eds. *India and the Indian Ocean, 1500–1800.*

Sikh, Maratha, and Other Anti-Mughal Regimes

15.391 Indu Banga. *Agrarian system of the Sikhs, late eighteenth and early nineteenth century.* New Delhi, India: Manohar, 1978. ▸ Study of fiscal system of Sikh state under Ranjit Singh and his successors and creative adaptation of Mughal practices, such as revenue assignment. Based on Punjabi sources and some travel accounts. [SS]

15.392 V. G. Dighe. *Peshwa Bajirao I and the Maratha expansion.* Bombay, India: Karnatak, 1944. ▸ Political narrative based on Marathi sources of Peshwa government of Marathas and consequent marginalization of Bhonsles. Useful details of Baji Rao's relations with Maratha *sardars* (warrior chiefs). [SS]

15.393 Hiroshi Fukazawa. *The medieval Deccan: peasants, social systems, and states, sixteenth to eighteenth centuries.* Delhi: Oxford University Press, 1991. ISBN 0-19-562309-6. ▸ Collection of scattered essays focusing on Deccan sultanates and Marathas, with strong emphasis on fiscal and economic relations. Important insights into corvée labor, revenue assignment, and village servants. [SS]

15.394 Balkrishna Govind Gokhale. *Poona in the eighteenth century.* New Delhi, India: Oxford University Press, 1988. ISBN 0-19-562137-9. ▸ Broad outlines of administration and economic and social life in capital of Peshwas; based on Marathi records from Poona itself. Useful as introduction; not very richly textured. [SS]

15.395 Stewart N. Gordon. "The slow conquest: the administrative integration of Malwa into the Maratha empire, 1720–1760." *Modern Asian studies* 11.1 (1977) 1–40. ISSN 0026-749X. ▸ Pioneering study of transition from Mughal to Maratha rule in Malwa, from vantage point of Marathi sources. Argues against stereotype of Marathas as marauders, and makes case for institutional continuity. [SS]

15.396 J. S. Grewal. *The Sikhs of the Punjab.* Part 2. Vol. 3 of *The new Cambridge history of India.* Cambridge: Cambridge University Press, 1990. ISBN 0-521-26884-2. ▸ Useful summary of main historical stages in emergence of Sikh community and determinants of its identity to present day. Stronger for precolonial period to ca. 1830. [SS]

15.397 Vithal Trimbak Gune. *The judicial system of the Marathas: a detailed study of the judicial institutions in Maharashtra, from 1600–1818 A.D., based on original decisions called mahzars, nivadpatras, and official orders.* Poona: Deccan College Postgraduate and Research Institute, 1953. ▸ Argues for elements of both centralization and local autonomy, latter embodied in *gota*, gathering of privilege-holding *vatandars*. Rare study of judicial intervention and structure of judiciary in precolonial Indian state. [SS]

15.398 A. R. Kulkarni. *Maharashtra in the age of Shivaji.* Poona: Deshmukh, 1969. ▸ Useful study of social and economic conditions in late seventeenth-century Maharashtra, based on Marathi records, often of great detail and yielding minute information. Disappointing on cultural history. [SS]

15.399 Jadunath Sarkar. *House of Shivaji: studies and documents* *on Maratha history, royal period.* 1955 3d ed. Calcutta, India: Orient Longman, 1978. ▸ Pioneering though loosely structured work on Maratha history in period up to emergence of Peshwas. Somewhat biased in its treatment of Maratha-Mughal relations. [SS]

15.400 Surendra Nath Sen. *Administrative system of the Marathas.* 1925 2d ed. Calcutta, India: Bagchi, 1976. ▸ Useful work setting out main administrative and fiscal institutions of Marathas and thus redressing notion of their state as one built on predatory raiding. [SS]

15.401 Surendra Nath Sen. *Early career of Kanhoji Angria and other papers.* Calcutta, India: University of Calcutta, 1941. ▸ Collected papers, including several based on French and Portuguese sources, concerning eighteenth-century history. [SS]

15.402 Surendra Nath Sen. *The military system of the Marathas.* 1958 2d rev. ed. Calcutta, India: Bagchi, 1979. ▸ Study of Maratha military mobilization in late eighteenth and early nineteenth centuries, focusing on roles of European mercenary captains and using European records. Useful detail of some figures and of salaries, structure of organization, etc. Somewhat exaggerates European role. [SS]

15.403 C. K. Srinivasan. *Maratha rule in the Carnatic.* C. S. Srinivasachari, ed. Surendra Nath Sen, Introduction. Annamalainagar, India: Annamalai University, 1944. ▸ Mostly political and military narrative on Maratha involvement in Carnatic from late seventeenth century (under chieftains Shahaji, Shivaji, and Vyamkoji), emergence of Tanjore state, and later Maratha interventions in Jinji, and then in eighteenth century under Peshwas. [SS]

15.404 Andre Wink. *Land and sovereignty in India: agrarian society and politics under the eighteenth-century Maratha svarajya.* Cambridge: Cambridge University Press, 1986. ISBN 0-521-32064-X. ▸ Ambitious study of Maratha state building, seen in context of long view of Islamic history and using concept of *fitna,* which author defines as sedition. Large sections are narratives, concerning specific Maratha magnate and princely families; useful closing discussion on revenue farming. [SS]

Late Mughal Era and Successor States

15.405 Muzaffar Alam. *The crisis of empire in Mughal North India: Awadh and the Punjab, 1707–1748.* Delhi: Oxford University Press, 1986. ISBN 0-19-561892-0. ▸ Study of politics and political economy in context of Mughal North India after reign of Aurangzeb; based on wide range of Persian sources. Argues for contrasting experiences in Awadh and Punjab; modifies received view of Mughal decline. [SS]

15.406 J.M.S. Baljon. *Religion and thought of Shah Wali Allah Dihlawi, 1707–1762.* Leiden: Brill, 1986. ISBN 90-04-07684-0. ▸ Well-researched, lucid analysis of Arabic and Persian works of major Sunnī theologian of eighteenth-century Delhi. [DSL]

15.407 Richard B. Barnett. *North India between empires: Awadh, the Mughals, and the British, 1720–1801.* Berkeley: University of California Press, 1980. ISBN 0-520-03787-1. ▸ Analysis of political structure and events in transition between central Mughal rule in early reign of Muhammad Shah and British dominance over this northern Indian region. Influential work though largely based on English and translated Persian sources, to neglect of others. [SS]

15.408 C. A. Bayly. "The pre-history of 'communalism'? Religious conflict in India, 1770–1860." *Modern Asian studies* 19.2 (1985) 177–203. ISSN 0026-749X. ▸ Study of incidents of sectarian violence predating consolidation of British rule. Important and controversial riposte to subaltern studies interpretation. [SS]

15.409 Susan Bayly. *Saints, goddesses, and kings: Muslims and Christians in South Indian society, 1700–1900.* Cambridge: Cambridge University Press, 1989. ISBN 0-521-37201-1. ▸ Argues three

great world religions produced politically mediated forms of syncretism in South India. Focuses on Islam in eighteenth century and Christianity in ninteenth century. [SS]

15.410 Stephen F. Dale. *Islamic society on the South Asian frontier: the Mappilas of Malabar, 1498–1922.* Oxford: Oxford University Press, 1980. ISBN 0-19-821571-1. ▸ Attempt to establish continuity of militant South Indian Muslim anti-British movement in nineteenth and early twentieth century with violence directed at Portuguese in sixteenth century. Useful long-term view, if somewhat oversimplified in its categories. [SS]

15.411 Ashin Das Gupta. *Indian merchants and the decline of Surat, c. 1700–1750.* Wiesbaden: Steiner, 1979. ISBN 3-515-02718-1. ▸ Examination of fate of merchants of Surat, vis-à-vis growing Dutch and English commercial ambitions and declining Mughal polity. Focuses on Muslim Bohra family of merchant Mulla Abdul Ghafur. Extensive reliance on English and Dutch sources. [SS]

15.412 Kalikinkar Datta. *Alivardi and his times.* 2d rev. ed. Calcutta, India: World Press, 1963. ▸ Examines career and context of second nawab of Bengal in eighteenth century, successor of Murshid Quli Khan. Consideration of changing political alliances and relations with Mughals and Marathas. [SS]

15.413 Richard G. Fox. *Kin, clan, raja, and rule: state-hinterland relations in pre-industrial India.* Berkeley: University of California Press, 1971. ISBN 0-520-01807-9. ▸ Brilliant effort to reconstruct changing rural power relations that resulted from varyingly successful efforts by Mughal sultans to control land revenue and power structures in parts of North India ruled by Rajput Rajas. Never surpassed as heuristic for historical political sociology of pre-British North India. [DEL]

15.414 Hermann Goetz. *The crisis of Indian civilization in the eighteenth and early nineteenth centuries: the genesis of the Indo-Muslim civilization.* Calcutta, India: University of Calcutta, 1938. ▸ Two essays, the more important one on eighteenth century, contrasting material decline and political chaos in this period with cultural efflorescence that accompanied it. Author's perspective largely art historical. [SS]

15.415 M. H. Gopal. *Tipu Sultan's Mysore, an economic study.* Bombay, India: Popular Prakashan, 1971. ▸ Examination of fiscal and financial basis of Mysore state under Tipu Sultan (1782–99), using mostly British records. Useful details on military organization, mercenaries, and fiscal changes. [SS]

15.416 Mohibbul Hasan. *History of Tipu Sultan.* 2d ed. Calcutta, India: World Press, 1971. ▸ Political history of Tipu Sultan, based on European accounts, but also on major Persian sources (particularly those from Tipu's own library). Result is somewhat hagiographical, but very valuable account. [SS]

15.417 William Irvine. *Later Mughals.* 1921–22 ed. 2 vols. in 1. Jadunath Sarkar, ed. New Delhi, India: Oriental Books Reprint; distributed by Munshiram Manoharlal, 1971. ▸ Standard work of political history on Mughals after death of Aurangzeb. Closely follows and often paraphrases accounts in Persian chronicles. Somewhat whiggish in flavor. Jadunath Sarkar's afterword pertains to invasion of Delhi by Nadir Shah (1739). [SS]

15.418 Abdul Karim. *Murshid Quli Khan and his times.* Dacca: Asiatic Society of Pakistan, 1963. ▸ Biographical, historical account of first nazir of Bengal to exercise autonomy in early eighteenth century. Also useful as study of British political penetration of region. [SS]

15.419 Yusuf Husain Khan. *The first Nizam: the life and times of Nizamu'l-Mulk Asaf Jah I.* 2d rev. ed. Bombay, India: Asia Publishing House, 1963. ▸ Revision of pioneering work, largely of political history, concerning reemergence of Hyderabad as political center in eighteenth century. Uses Persian chronicles, but not vast administrative papers available from period. [SS]

15.420 L. Lockhart. *Nadir Shah: a critical study based mainly upon contemporary sources.* 1938 ed. New York: AMS Press, 1973. ISBN 0-404-56290-6. ‣ Political narrative of decline of Safavid power and emergence of Turkoman "tribal" power under Tahmasp Quli Khan, who took title Nadir Shah. Uses Persian chronicles and French, English, and Portuguese accounts. Not yet superseded as account of Nadir Shah. [SS]

15.421 Zahir Uddin Malik. *The reign of Muhammad Shah, 1719–1748.* Bombay, India: Asia Publishing House for Centre of Advanced Study, Department of History, Aligarh Muslim University, 1977. ISBN 0-210-40598-8. ‣ Useful political narrative of first half of eighteenth century, using Persian sources, and organized as conventional study of Mughal empire in "decline." Focuses on personalities but without particular psychological insights. [SS]

15.422 Jadunath Sarkar. *Fall of the Mughal empire.* Edition varies. 4 vols. Bombay, India: Orient Longman, 1971–72. ‣ Reprints of scattered essays, largely concerning Mughal empire in late eighteenth century. Particularly useful as study of Afghan power in Delhi and period of dominance by Maratha Shinde (Sindhia) family at Mughal court. [SS]

15.423 Noman Ahmad Siddiqi. *Land revenue administration under the Mughals, 1700–1750.* Bombay, India: Asia Publishing House for Centre of Advanced Study, Department of History, Aligarh Muslim University, 1970. ‣ Fiscal and economic history, intended to elaborate concept of agrarian crisis of over-exaction in Mughal North India in early eighteenth century. Can be read as extension of Habib 15.333; unfortunately rather poorly organized and written. [SS]

15.424 Dilbagh Singh. *The state, landlords, and peasants: Rajasthan in the eighteenth century.* New Delhi, India: Manohar, 1990. ISBN 81-85425-05-1. ‣ Focuses on regional economy that formed part of Jaipur state in latter half of eighteenth century. Argues political instability and Maratha tribute exactions caused decline in area under cultivation and general agrarian depression. [SS]

15.425 Percival Spear. *Twilight of the Mughuls: studies in late Mughul Delhi.* 1951 ed. Oxford: Oxford University Press, 1980. ISBN 0-19-577288-1. ‣ Informative, but largely anecdotal approach to Delhi under later Mughals, but before emergence of Pax Britannica. Read with Sarkar 15.422 for general political context in northern India. [SS]

SEE ALSO
18.99 Nehemia Levtzion and John O. Voll, eds. *Eighteenth-century renewal and reform in Islam.*
18.110 S.A.A. Rizvi. *Shah Wali-Allah and his times.*

MODERN SOUTH ASIA

British Rule in South Asia

General Studies

15.426 C. A. Bayly, ed. *The Raj: India and the British, 1600–1947.* London: National Portrait Gallery, 1990. ISBN 1-85514-026-8 (cased), 1-85514-027-6 (pbk). ‣ Art exhibition catalog with essays and reproductions encapsulating British contacts with India. Beyond brilliant reproductions, essayists provide sophisticated introductions to issues of colonialism and cultural contact. [FFC]

15.427 Sugata Bose, ed. *South Asia and world capitalism.* Delhi: Oxford University Press, 1990. ISBN 0-19-562544-7. ‣ Papers from 1986 conference aimed at reconceptualizing South Asian history by engaging world-systems theory. Makes persuasive case for recognizing links between regional and world systems. [AAY]

15.428 Bernard S. Cohn. *An anthropologist among the historians and other essays.* 1987 ed. Ranajit Guha, Introduction. Delhi: Oxford University Press, 1988. ISBN 0-19-561875-0. ‣ Collected studies on Indian history and society from perspective of cultural anthropology, including construction of British knowledge about India. Influential and wide ranging, these studies have stimulated a generation of American scholarship on South Asia. [DSL]

15.429 Parshotam Mehra. *A dictionary of modern Indian history, 1707–1947.* Delhi: Oxford University Press, 1985. ISBN 0-19-561552-2. ‣ Large collection of articles, alphabetically arranged, on persons, events, legislation, and institutions. Useful as document of received ideas, information, and bibliography. [DSL]

15.430 Penderel Moon. *British conquest and dominion of India.* London: Duckworth, 1989. ISBN 0-7156-2169-6. ‣ Colonial history as retold by former civil servant. History portrayed as drama of events largely played out by British actors, although lesser administrations share spotlight here with governors-general and viceroys. [AAY]

15.431 L.S.S. O'Malley, ed. *Modern India and the West: a study of the interaction of their civilizations.* 1941 ed. London: Oxford University Press, 1968. ‣ Major summary statement of role of British rule in transforming Indian institutions, society, and culture. Important as historical document though limited by its wholly British perspective. [DSL]

15.432 Edward Thompson and G. T. Garrett. *Rise and fulfillment of British rule in India.* Allahabad, India: Central Book Depot, 1962. ‣ Classic liberal survey of Indian political and administrative history to 1933. Although centered on British policies and activities, treatment of Indian response and initiatives is balanced and fair. [FFC]

15.433 D. A. Washbrook. "Law, state, and agrarian society in colonial India." *Modern Asian studies* 15.3 (1981) 649–721. ISSN 0026-749X. ‣ Critical article repositioning study of legal history as means to investigate dynamics of power in countryside. Perhaps most frequently cited article in studies of colonial law in last decade. [DEL]

Establishment of British Rule in India

15.434 C. A. Bayly. "English-language historiography on British expansion in India and Indian reactions since 1945." In *Reappraisals in overseas history: essays on post-war historiography about European expansion.* P. C. Emmer and H. L. Wesseling, eds., pp. 21–53. Leiden: Leiden University Press; distributed by Kluwer Boston, 1979. ISBN 90-6021-444-7 (cl), 90-6021-447-1 (pbk). ‣ Thoughtful survey of postwar and postindependence investigative and interpretive trends in historiography of South Asia. Considerate celebration of diversity of approaches and schools. [FFC]

15.435 C. A. Bayly. *Indian society and the making of the British empire.* Part 2. Vol. 1 of *The new Cambridge history of India.* Cambridge: Cambridge University Press, 1988. ISBN 0-521-25092-7. ‣ Wide-ranging synthetic essay arguing that colonization of India in eighteenth century must be seen in relation to indigenous developments in subcontinent and not simply as imposition of external force. Marred by several slips on chronology, dates, and names; useful bibliographical essay. [SS]

15.436 Henry Dodwell. *Dupleix and Clive: the beginning of empire.* 1920 ed. Hamden, Conn.: Archon, 1968. ‣ Reprint of classic political narrative on Anglo-French rivalry in southern and, to lesser extent, eastern India. Defends view that rivalry propelled English East India Company into political arena. [SS]

15.437 Holden Furber. *Bombay presidency in the mid-eighteenth century.* Bombay, India: Asia Publishing House, 1965. ‣ Brief monograph based on Heras Memorial Lectures. Portrays society of Bombay city and dependent mercantile networks using mainly English and Dutch sources. [SS]

15.438 Holden Furber. *John Company at work: a study of European expansion in India in the late eighteenth century.* 1948 ed. New York: Octagon, 1970. ▸ Important study of public and private face of English East India Company as power in country trade and politics. Pioneering use of Dutch sources in systematic fashion. [SS]

15.439 Brijen K. Gupta. *Sirajuddaulah and the East India Company, 1756–1757, background to the foundation of British power in India.* 1962 ed. Leiden: Brill, 1966. ▸ Study of transition in mid-eighteenth-century Bengal and contest of years 1756–57 culminating in Battle of Plassey. Largely political history and based mostly on English sources. [SS]

15.440 H. T. Lambrick. *Sir Charles Napier and Sind.* Oxford: Clarendon, 1952. ▸ Study of circumstances surrounding conquest of Sind (1842–43) and career of its conqueror. Writing with personal knowledge of province, author offers evenhanded historical judgment of events. [FFC]

15.441 P. J. Marshall. *Bengal—the British bridgehead: eastern India, 1740–1828.* Part 2. Vol. 2 of *The new Cambridge history of India.* Cambridge: Cambridge University Press, 1987. ISBN 0-521-25330-6. ▸ Study of British expansion into Bengal, focusing on balance of power in Nawabi state, into late eighteenth century. Traditional study based on English sources. [SS]

SEE ALSO
    47.95 M. E. Yapp. *Strategies of British India.*

British Policy and Administration

15.442 David Arnold. *Police power and colonial rule: Madras, 1859–1947.* Delhi: Oxford University Press, 1986. ISBN 0-19-561893-9. ▸ Combines institutional history of police force, established under British colonial rule, with account of increasingly pervasive political order, "Police Raj," founded on violent coercion and suppression of subaltern resistance movements in southern India. [DEL]

15.443 Christopher John Baker, Gordon Johnson, and Anil Seal, eds. *Power, profit, and politics: essays on imperialism, nationalism, and twentieth-century India.* Cambridge: Cambridge University Press, 1981. (*Modern Asian studies,* 15.3.) ▸ Studies in twentieth-century politics from Indian and British perspectives, both local and more general. Cambridge school with greater emphasis on economic history as motive in political development. [DSL]

15.444 Stephen P. Cohen. *The Indian army: its contribution to the development of a nation.* Rev. ed. Delhi: Oxford University Press, 1990. ISBN 0-19-562757-1. ▸ Study of role and involvement of military in creation of nation-state. Uses modernization framework to emphasize nonpolitical character of British Indian Army and its subordination to interests of the state. [AAY]

15.445 Bernard S. Cohn. *The development and impact of British administration in India: a bibliographic essay.* New Delhi, India: Indian Institute of Public Administration, 1961. ▸ Review of literature on British India. Dated, but one of first accounts to point to unanticipated effects of British policies and actions in India. [AAY]

15.446 Robert I. Crane and N. Gerald Barrier, eds. *British imperial policy in India and Sri Lanka, 1858–1912: a reassessment.* Columbia, Mo.: South Asia Books, 1981. ▸ Collection of essays on British imperial policy and administration. Attempts to treat familiar issues in new ways by looking at various levels of decision making and at specific bureaucrats, policies, and legislation. [AAY]

15.447 M. N. Das. *India under Morley and Minto: politics behind*

revolution, repression, and reforms. London: Allen & Unwin, 1964. ▸ Analysis of role of secretary of state for India and viceroy in shaping early twentieth-century events. Claims their policies and responses to political developments had far-reaching consequences. [AAY]

15.448 Robert Eric Frykenberg. *Guntur district, 1788–1848: a history of local influence and central authority in South India.* Oxford: Clarendon, 1965. ▸ Seminal work on local politics in early colonial rule. Argues for continuity of local elites across colonial transition. Documents their ability to undermine British power. [DEL]

15.449 Sarvepalli Gopal. *British policy in India, 1858–1905.* Cambridge: Cambridge University Press, 1965. ▸ Broad-ranging survey of colonial administrative policies and politics at subcontinental level. Useful framework for overview of British initiatives offering links to local and regional studies. [FFC]

15.450 Briton Martin. *New India, 1885: British official policy and the emergence of the Indian National Congress.* Berkeley: University of California Press, 1969. ISBN 0-520-01580-0. ▸ Study of British official policy relating to establishment of Indian National Congress in 1885. Concentrates on evaluating this founding nationalist movement in terms of competing colonial and national interests. [AAY]

15.451 Thomas R. Metcalf. *The aftermath of revolt: India, 1857–1870.* Princeton: Princeton University Press, 1964. ▸ Effect of 1857 Great Mutiny on colonial policies and practices relating to social reform, education, land settlement, agrarian relations, Indian states, government structure, and racism. Views aftermath as watershed period. [AAY]

15.452 B. B. Misra. *The central administration of the East India Company, 1773–1834.* Manchester: Manchester University Press, 1959. ▸ Detailed account of evolution of central organs of colonial rule in India, documented according to subject; based on extensive use of India Office records and other official documentation. [FFC]

15.453 R. J. Moore. *Endgames of empire: studies of Britain's Indian problem.* Delhi: Oxford University Press, 1988. ISBN 0-19-562143-3. ▸ Collection of author's articles on political and constitutional problems and stratagems behind transfer of power in India. Sober analysis of British perspectives leading to independence and partition. [FFC]

15.454 B. N. Pandey. *The introduction of English law into India: the career of Elijah Impey in Bengal, 1774–83.* Bombay, India: Asia Publishing House, 1967. ▸ Development of English legal system in late eighteenth century through career of controversial British judge. Lauds introduction of rule of law for its positive contributions, but pays little attention to its local workings. [AAY]

15.455 Peter G. Robb. *The government of India and reform: policies towards politics and the constitution, 1916–1921.* Oxford: Oxford University Press, 1976. ISBN 0-19-713590-0. ▸ Analysis of policy making at viceregal level of government. Traces development of policy and decision making in eventful years leading to rise of nationalist mass movement. [AAY]

15.456 John Rosselli. *Lord William Bentinck: the making of a liberal imperialist, 1774–1839.* Berkeley: University of California Press, 1974. ISBN 0-520-02299-8. ▸ Career of notable governor-general characterized as liberal imperialist. Detailed biography of his Italian and Indian experiences. Views Bentinck as forerunner of Indian nationalism. [AAY]

15.457 Hugh Tinker. *The foundations of local self-government in India, Pakistan, and Burma.* 1954 ed. New York: Praeger, 1968. ▸ Basic introduction to evolution of institutions of local self-government in British India. Highlights colonial purposes and policies with recognition of variations in realized results. Photocopy available from Ann Arbor: University Microfilms International, 1973. [FFC]

15.458 P.H.M. van den Dungen. *The Punjab tradition: influence and authority in nineteenth-century India.* London: Allen & Unwin, 1972. ISBN 0-04-954016-5. ▸ Colonial administration and ideology as embodied in so-called Punjab tradition. Attempts to delineate and contextualize this official tradition by focusing on government debates over Punjab Land Alienation Act of 1900. [AAY]

British Ideology and Society in India

15.459 Charles Allen, ed. *Plain tales from the raj: images of British India in the twentieth century.* 1975 ed. New York: Holt, Rinehart & Winston, 1985. ISBN 0-03-005862-7 (pbk). ▸ Oral history, originally prepared for British Broadcasting Company, of British social life in India in final phase of colonial period. Beginning of empire nostalgia, valuable as documentation. [DSL]

15.460 Kenneth Ballhatchet. *Race, sex, and class under the raj: imperial attitudes and policies and their critics, 1793–1905.* New York: St. Martin's, 1980. ISBN 0-312-66144-4. ▸ Study of racism and its intersection with gender through policies toward control of venereal disease among British military personnel, and prostitution. Despite misleading title, insightful documentation of anxieties of colonial rule. [DSL]

15.461 Bernard S. Cohn. "Cloth, clothes, and colonialism: India in the nineteenth century." In *Cloth and human experience.* Annette B. Weiner and Jane Schneider, eds., pp. 303–53. Washington, D.C.: Smithsonian Institution, 1989. ISBN 0-87474-986-7 (cl), 0-87474-995-6 (pbk). ▸ History of British attitudes toward India as revealed in styles of colonial dress; used to differentiate ruling class and protect outsiders from tropical conditions. Classic study of imperialist ideology and practice. [DSL]

15.462 Bernard S. Cohn. "The command of language and the language of command." In *Subaltern studies 4: writings on South Asian history and society.* Ranajit Guha, ed., pp. 276–329. Delhi: Oxford University Press, 1985. ISBN 0-19-561840-8. ▸ British study of Indian vernacular languages and institutionalization of standardized forms of these languages and subordinate instruments of imperial power. Important study of formulation of colonial knowledge and consequent cultural practices. [DSL]

15.463 Ketaki Kushari Dyson. *A various universe: a study of the journals and memoirs of British men and women in the Indian subcontinent, 1765–1856.* Delhi: Oxford University Press, 1978. ISBN 0-19-561074-1. ▸ Survey of writing on India by British residents; treats diversity of cultural themes. Most useful for lengthy quotations and guide to further reading. [DSL]

15.464 Ainslie T. Embree. *Charles Grant and British rule in India.* New York: AMS Press, 1962. ISBN 0-404-51606-8. ▸ Study of English East India Company man and evangelical, subsequently involved in shaping India policy in London. Emphasizes his maverick position on many policy issues to assess his role in consolidating colonial rule. [AAY]

15.465 Helen Fein. *Imperial crime and punishment: the massacre at Jallianwala Bagh and British judgement, 1919–1920.* Honolulu, Hawaii: University of Hawaii Press, 1977. ISBN 0-8248-0506-2. ▸ Correlates British public approval or condemnation of 1919 Amritsar massacre with differing conceptions of universe of obligation. Sociological study of British attitudes toward India. [AAY]

15.466 Ranajit Guha. *A rule of property for Bengal: an essay on the idea of permanent settlement.* 1981 2d ed. New Delhi, India: Orient Longman; distributed by Apt Books, 1982. ISBN 0-86131-289-9. ▸ Formulation and experimental application of conflicting theories of property and authority among British rulers of Bengal, 1773–93, culminating in so-called permanent settlement. Profound work of intellectual history for period of major ideological

transformations that are arguably related to establishment of colonial rule. [DSL]

15.467 Francis G. Hutchins. *The illusion of permanence: British imperialism in India.* Princeton: Princeton University Press, 1967. ▸ Lively analytical narrative utilizing literature, memoirs, and official papers to determine imperialist attitudes in colonial India, from missionaries to viceroys. [FFC]

15.468 Robert Grant Irving. *Indian summer: Lutyens, Baker, and imperial Delhi.* 1981 ed. New Haven: Yale University Press, 1984. ISBN 0-300-02422-3. ▸ Illustrated exploration of architectural and cultural politics and aesthetics in design of British imperial capital at Delhi. Effectively places architectural history in wider context. [FFC]

15.469 Raghavan Iyer. "Utilitarianism and all that (the political theory of British imperialism in India)." In *South Asian affairs 1.* Raghavan Iyer, ed., pp. 9–71. London: Chatto & Windus, 1966. (St. Antony's papers, 8.) ▸ Analysis of conflicting ideologies justifying British colonial rule in India and their varying attitudes toward authoritarianism and ultimate possibilities of Indian self-rule. Important both to study of South Asia and influence of colonial encounter on British thought. [DSL]

15.470 Margaret MacMillan. *Women of the raj.* New York: Thames & Hudson, 1988. ISBN 0-500-01420-5. ▸ Charts experiences of European women (*memsahibs*) in India, from their voyage out to their everyday routines. Somewhat successful in adding texture and complexity to *memsahib* stereotype. [AAY]

15.471 P. J. Marshall, ed. *The British discovery of Hinduism in the eighteenth century.* Cambridge: Cambridge University Press, 1970. ISBN 0-521-07737-0. ▸ Selection of early British writings on Hindu religious and legal texts by first British administrators of Bengal in late eighteenth century. Excellent introduction points to ideological and institutional significance of colonial knowledge. [DSL]

15.472 Thomas R. Metcalf. *An imperial vision: Indian architecture and Britain's raj.* Berkeley: University of California Press, 1989. ISBN 0-520-06235-3. ▸ Representation of British authority and British concepts of their place in Indian history as revealed in public architecture. Handsomely illustrated, historically well informed. [DSL]

15.473 Partha Mitter. *Much maligned monsters: history of European reactions to Indian art.* 1977 ed. Chicago: University of Chicago Press, 1992. ISBN 0-226-53239-9 (pbk). ▸ Study of creation of enduring stereotypes from demonization to romanticization of Indian art. Ranging from European Middle Ages to present but concentrating on eighteenth and nineteenth century. Important as historiography of art as well as general issues of Orientalist ideologies. [DSL]

15.474 S. N. Mukherjee. *Sir William Jones: a study in eighteenth-century British attitudes to India.* 2d ed. Hyderabad, India: Orient Longman, 1987. ▸ Biographical analysis of major British Orientalist scholar in Britain and India. Emphasis on ideas and legacies of scholarly discoveries. [FFC]

15.475 Sten Nilsson. *European architecture in India, 1750–1850.* 1968 ed. Agnes George and Eleonore Zettersten, trans. New York: Taplinger, 1969. ▸ Description of Danish, French, and British architecture and urban planning; illustrated. Unique application of classical architectural principles to European Indian architecture through analysis of colonial buildings, materials, designs, and methods. [FFC]

15.476 Pratapaditya Pal and Vidya Dehejia. *From merchants to emperors: British artists and India, 1757–1930.* Ithaca, N.Y.: Cornell University Press, 1986. ISBN 0-8014-1907-7 (cl), 0-8014-9386-2 (pbk). ▸ Catalog of museum exhibit surveying work of

British artists, particularly representations of Indian life during nineteenth century. Handsomely illustrated with text chiefly useful for information about artists and patronage. [DSL]

15.477 Benita Parry. *Delusions and discoveries: studies on India in the British imagination, 1880–1930.* Berkeley: University of California Press, 1972. ISBN 0-520-02215-7. ‣ Wide-ranging study of fictional representations of India under British rule by British authors as study of ideologies and anxieties of colonialism. Subtle and historically well-informed work of literary history. [DSL]

15.478 Eric Stokes. *The English utilitarians and India.* 1959 ed. Delhi: Oxford University Press, 1989. ISBN 0-19-562355-X. ‣ Classic study in intellectual and administrative trends in colonial India. Applies Benthamite theories to English East India Company land tenure, revenue, judicial, and administrative policies and practices, and their effects. [FFC]

15.479 Sara Suleri. *The rhetoric of English India.* Chicago: University of Chicago Press, 1992. ISBN 0-226-77982-3 (cl), 0-226-77983-1 (pbk). ‣ Studies of how India has been imagined in English literature, including Edmund Burke, Rudyard Kipling, and E. M. Forster, as well as postcolonial writers. Important contribution to study of complex inner contradictions of colonial discourse. [DSL]

15.480 Gauri Viswanathan. *Masks of conquest: literary study and British rule in India.* New York: Columbia University Press, 1989. ISBN 0-231-07084-5. ‣ Argues formulation of English literary studies as academic field was bound up with effort to legitimate British rule in India. Subtle contribution to study of colonial education that reaches out to larger English-speaking world. [DSL]

15.481 Lewis D. Wurgaft. *The imperial imagination: magic and myth in Kipling's India.* Middletown, Conn.: Wesleyan University Press; distributed by Harper & Row, 1983. ISBN 0-8195-5082-5. ‣ Psychohistorical analysis of British perceptions and anxieties in late nineteenth-century Punjab after 1857 rebellion. Informed by object-relations theory, treats British imperialism as psychopathology. [DSL]

Indirect Rule and the Indian Princes

15.482 Nicholas B. Dirks. *The hollow crown: ethnohistory of an Indian kingdom.* Cambridge: Cambridge University Press, 1987. ISBN 0-521-32604-4. ‣ Account of transformation of social and cultural authority of kingship in Padukkottai, a "little kingdom" of Tamilnadu overtaken by British imperial domination. Combines historical and ethnographic research with complex cultural analysis. [DSL]

15.483 Michael H. Fisher. *A clash of cultures: Awadh, the British, and the Mughals.* Riverdale, Md.: Riverdale, 1987. ISBN 0-913215-27-9. ‣ History of Awadh from early eighteenth to mid-nineteenth century. Especially effective in offering rich portrait of urban culture of area between Mughal and British interests. [AAY]

15.484 Michael H. Fisher. *Indirect rule in India: residents and the residency system, 1764–1858.* Delhi: Oxford University Press, 1991. ISBN 0-19-562676-1. ‣ Comprehensive study of evolution of British residency supervision of Indian princely states. Cogent survey of problems of indirect rule with sophisticated analysis of general policy and individual practice. [FFC]

15.485 Björn Hettne. *Political economy of indirect rule: Mysore, 1881–1947.* London: Curzon, 1978. (Scandanavian Institute of Asian Studies, 32.) ISBN 0-7007-0106-0. ‣ Study of development of political and economic strategies for British indirect rule of princely state of Mysore and effects on society into postcolonial period. [DEL]

15.486 Robin Jeffrey. *Decline of Nayar dominance: society and politics in Travancore, 1847–1908.* New York: Holmes & Meier, 1976. ISBN 0-8419-0184-8. ‣ Study of social change in Travancore

(Kerala), focusing on diminishing power and erosion of matriarchy among Nayers in context of caste-community competition. Strong regional social history with limited theoretical perspectives. [FFC]

15.487 Robin Jeffrey, ed. *People, princes, and paramount power: society and politics in the Indian princely states.* Delhi: Oxford University Press, 1978. ‣ Case studies of some of more than five hundred princely states, largely showing that their diverse political histories partake of patterns in those parts of India directly ruled by British. Uneven collection with some excellent studies. [DSL]

15.488 S. V. Kothekar. *The Gaikwads of Baroda and the East India Company, 1770–1820.* Nagpur, India: Nagpur University, 1977. ‣ Study of transition of Gaikwads from independent power to dependent rulers under aegis of company; based on Marathi and English documents. Unfortunately weak on economic aspects. [SS]

15.489 Rosie Llewellyn-Jones. *A fatal friendship: the nawabs, the British, and the city of Lucknow.* Delhi: Oxford University Press, 1985. ISBN 0-19-561706-1. ‣ Analysis of architecture, cultural encounter, and power struggles in Awadh in its transition from Mughal successor state to British annexation, 1775–1856. Lively and perceptive, particularly with regard to political meanings of buildings. [DSL]

15.490 V. P. Menon. *The story of the integration of the Indian states.* 1956 ed. New York: Arno, 1972. ISBN 0-405-04575-1. ‣ Classic account of termination of princely states as separate entities at time of Indian independence from British rule. Written by Indian civil servant and major participant in much of political maneuvering and negotiation. [DSL]

15.491 Barbara N. Ramusack. *The princes of India in the twilight of empire: dissolution of a patron-client system, 1914–1939.* Columbus: Ohio State University Press for University of Cincinnati, 1978. ISBN 0-8142-0272-1. ‣ Study of stirrings of political ambition and action among princely rulers during era of constitutional change. Insightful, objective analysis of working of Chamber of Princes and princes' limited political potential. [FFC]

15.492 Edward Thompson. *The making of the Indian princes.* 1943 ed. London: Curzon, 1978. ISBN 0-7007-0124-9. ‣ Narrative history of establishment of regional Maratha regimes in eighteenth century and their conquest and absorption as princely states by British in early nineteenth century. Classic work on origins of indirect rule. [DSL]

Economy and Society under British Imperialism

Agrarian Economy and Society

15.493 Shahid Amin. *Sugarcane and sugar in Gorakhpur: an inquiry into peasant production for capitalist enterprise in colonial India.* Delhi: Oxford University Press, 1984. ISBN 0-19-561545-X. ‣ Study of socioeconomic and political dynamics underlying present cash-crop production in eastern Uttar Pradesh. Nuanced analysis of fate of peasant producers, increasingly tied to capitalist market system. [AAY]

15.494 David Arnold. "Famine in peasant consciousness and peasant action: Madras, 1876–8." In *Subaltern studies 3: writings on South Asian history and society.* Ranajit Guha, ed., pp. 62–115. Delhi: Oxford University Press, 1984. ISBN 0-19-561653-7. ‣ Best account of famine in colonial India. Reconstructs experience of famine from rural perspective, partly based on folklore and anecdote. [DEL]

15.495 B. H. Baden-Powell. *The land systems of British India: being a manual of the land-tenures and of the systems of land-revenue administration prevalent in the several provinces.* 1892 ed. 4 vols. in 3. New York: Johnson Reprint, 1972. ‣ Monumental codification of land-tenure systems as legal forms institutionalized in British

India. Evolutionary account exemplifying how colonial discourse justified its own political creations. [DEL]

15.496 Gita Bajpai. *Agrarian urban economy and social change: the socio-economic profile of select districts of Gujarat, 1850–1900.* Delhi: Daya, 1989. ISBN 81-7035-053-0. ‣ Reconsideration of what constitutes "agrarian" in highly urbanized and commercial economy of western India. Good data but no argument. Presents type of data that will enrich future studies of politics and cultural history. [DEL]

15.497 Christopher John Baker. *An Indian rural economy, 1880–1955: the Tamilnad countryside.* Oxford: Clarendon, 1984. ISBN 0-19-821572-X. ‣ Analysis of agricultural, manufacturing, commercial, credit, transportation, and political components of regional economy during late colonial and early national period. Generates fullest available understanding of what "rural" means historically in India, including towns and cities in rural landscape. [DEL]

15.498 B. M. Bhatia. *Famines in India: a study in some aspects of the economic history of India with special reference to food problem, 1860–1990.* 3d rev. ed. Delhi: Konark, 1991. ISBN 81-220-0211-0. ‣ Concludes uneven development of country was cause of scarcity. Best in detailing government responses to famine and better on nineteenth than on twentieth century. [AAY]

15.499 George Blyn. *Agricultural trends in India, 1891–1947: output, availability, and productivity.* Philadelphia: University of Pennsylvania Press, 1966. ‣ Seminal study of agricultural price trends in relation to output and productivity. Serves as basis for all subsequent work on commercialization, peasant responsiveness to prices, and effects of productivity. [DEL]

15.500 Sugata Bose. *Agrarian Bengal: economy, social structure, and politics, 1919–1947.* Cambridge: Cambridge University Press, 1986. ISBN 0-521-30448-2. ‣ Sophisticated attempt to understand regional rural economy in relation to its economic context within British empire. Seeks to demonstrate that shifts from property to debt relations generated regional divergences within greater Bengal that help to account for shifting political trends. [DEL]

15.501 Jan Breman. *Patronage and exploitation: changing agrarian relations in South Gujarat, India.* Wil van Gulik, trans. Berkeley: University of California Press, 1974. ISBN 0-520-02197-5. ‣ Historically supported sociological reconstruction of changing relations of agrarian production during rise of commercial agriculture and private-property rights. Alternative to classic Marxian theory, focusing on power in production process in relation to distribution of benefits and household differentiation. [DEL]

15.502 I. J. Catanach. *Rural credit in western India, 1875–1930: rural credit and the co-operative movement in the Bombay presidency.* Berkeley: University of California Press, 1970. ISBN 0-520-01595-9. ‣ Study of cooperative credit societies in Bombay Deccan, ca. 1875–1920, in context of policy debates on peasant indebtedness. Balanced, unpolemical analysis of social and economic trends; heavy on administrative details. [FFC]

15.503 Neil Charlesworth. *Peasants and imperial rule: agriculture and agrarian society in the Bombay presidency, 1850–1935.* Cambridge: Cambridge University Press, 1985. ISBN 0-521-23206-6. ‣ Effects of imperial policies on rural economy and society in western India. Presents clear summation of debates and evidence. [DEL]

15.504 Benoy Choudhury. *Growth of commerical agriculture in Bengal, 1757–1901.* Calcutta, India: Maitra for Indian Studies, Past and Present, 1964. ‣ Example of author's extensive work on commercial crop production, export, prices, and financing in eastern India. Fullest account of commodity crop production at aggregate level. [DEL]

15.505 Robert Eric Frykenberg, ed. *Land control and social structure in Indian history.* Madison: University of Wisconsin Press, 1969. ISBN 0-299-05240-0. ‣ Studies in agrarian history, primarily in British period and representing cross-section of regional economies. Virtually every essay critical of previous historiography. [DEL]

15.506 Robert Eric Frykenberg, ed. *Land tenure and peasant in South Asia.* 1977 ed. New Delhi, India: Manohar, 1984. ‣ Essays on relations of land tenure, politics, and agrarian conditions. One of better efforts to link specific historical studies of regions with current policy issues in rural development. [DEL]

15.507 Arun Ghosh, ed. and comp. *Agrarian structure and peasant movements in colonial and post-independence India: an annotated bibliography.* Calcutta, India: Bagchi, 1990. ISBN 81-7074-065-7. ‣ Small, selective volume with basic annotation focused on land-tenure struggles from perspective of policy and peasant politics. Good representation of linkage between land-revenue and land-tenure systems and peasant politics in historiography and social science literature. [DEL]

15.508 Kathleen Gough. *Rural society in southeast India.* Cambridge: Cambridge University Press, 1981. ISBN 0-521-23889-7. ‣ Reconstruction of long-range agrarian history of Tanjavur district, Tamilnadu, organized as sequence of modes of production, particularly nature of agricultural labor. Contextualizes author's anthropological fieldwork. [DEL]

15.509 Paul R. Greenough. *Prosperity and misery in modern Bengal: the famine of 1943–1944.* New York: Oxford University Press, 1982. ISBN 0-19-503082-6. ‣ Study of famine in cultural context. Seeks to discern culturally specific meanings of scarcity and plenty to uncover implicit rules underlying patterns of "famine victimization and mortality." [AAY]

15.510 Sumit Guha. *The agrarian economy of the Bombay Deccan, 1818–1941.* Delhi: Oxford University Press, 1985. ISBN 0-19-561786-X. ‣ Well-documented but controversial study, especially in its use of economic theory. Argues population growth, cultivation of marginal lands, and entrenchment of unfavorable credit systems responsible for economic stagnation under British rule. [FFC]

15.511 Stephen Henningham. *A great estate and its landlords in colonial India: Darbhanga, 1860–1942.* Delhi: Oxford University Press, 1990. ISBN 0-19-562559-5. ‣ Brief biography of great estate of Darbhanga in Bihar and its proprietors. Concentrates largely on public activities of Darbhanga rajas and on their estate administration and organization. [AAY]

15.512 Benedict Hjejle. "Slavery and agricultural bondage in South India in the nineteenth century." *Scandinavian economic history review* 15.1–2 (1967) 71–126. ISSN 0358-5522. ‣ One of first publications to consider in detail history of bonded labor in South India and colonial efforts to abolish it in favor of labor-market system organized around legally free workers. Now superseded but critical as historiographic baseline for later work. [DEL]

15.513 M. Mufakharul Islam. *Bengal agriculture, 1920–1946: a quantitative study.* Cambridge: Cambridge University Press, 1978. ISBN 0-521-21579-X. ‣ Applies statistical methods to measure agricultural output of region. Makes persuasive case for agricultural stagnation in early twentieth century. [AAY]

15.514 Sirajul Islam. *Bengal land tenure: the origin and growth of intermediate interests in the nineteenth century.* 1985 ed. Calcutta, India: Bagchi, 1988. ISBN 81-7074-037-1. ‣ Study of rise of intermediate tenures, between *zamindars* (local powerholders) and cultivators, in Bengal presidency; important for role such intermediaries played in accounts of modern agrarian politics in region. Regional comparisons from local records as well as land-tenure reforms under colonial regime before electoral politics. [DEL]

15.515   N. K. Jit. *The agrarian life and economy of Orissa: a survey, 1833–1897*. Calcutta, India: Punthi Pustak, 1984. ▸ Only substantial study of agrarian conditions in Orissa in nineteenth century. Useful primarily as reference. [DEL]

15.516   Tom G. Kessinger. *Vilyatpur, 1848–1968: social and economic change in a North Indian village*. Berkeley: University of California Press, 1974. ISBN 0-520-02340-4. ▸ Classic attempt to link historical method with anthropological conceptions of village society and peasant farming. Demonstrates changing conditions of peasant family farmers and their relations with workers during rise of commercial production and early stages of Green Revolution. Based on records from village in Indian Punjab. [DEL]

15.517   Dharma Kumar. *Land and caste in South India: agricultural labour in the Madras presidency during the nineteenth century*. 1965 ed. New Delhi, India: Manohar, 1992. ISBN 81-7304-005-2. ▸ First major work on South Indian agrarian history, with new introduction. Argues no major proportional increase in size of landless laborer population or decline in its living conditions statistically demonstrable in nineteenth century. [DEL]

15.518   Ravinder Kumar. *Western India in the nineteenth century: a study in the social history of Maharashtra*. London and Toronto: Routledge & Kegan Paul and University of Toronto Press, 1968. ISBN 0-7100-4568-9. ▸ Study of impact of colonial policy on rural society in Bombay presidency. Argues break-up of village society and shifts in rural power toward moneylenders accounts for ruptures revealed in Deccan riots of 1875. [DEL]

15.519   David Ludden. "Productive power in agriculture: a survey of work on the local history of British India." In *Agrarian power and agricultural productivity in South Asia*. Meghnad Desai, Susanne Hoeber Rudolph, and Ashok Rudra, eds., pp. 51–99. Berkeley: University of California Press, 1984. ISBN 0-520-05369-9. ▸ Review of literature on agrarian history highlighting issues, concepts, and methodologies. Ambitious, thought-provoking attempt to assess literature with specific conceptual grids. [AAY]

15.520   Michelle Burge McAlpin. *Subject to famine: food crises and economic change in western India, 1860–1920*. Princeton: Princeton University Press, 1983. ISBN 0-691-05385-5. ▸ Revisionist argument that severity of famines declined in western India from 1870 to 1920 and minimum level of life security improved as result of British policies. Conclusions have been vehemently rejected by numerous scholars. [DEL]

15.521   Thomas R. Metcalf. *Land, landlords, and the British raj: northern India in the nineteenth century*. Berkeley: University of California Press, 1979. ISBN 0-520-03575-5. ▸ Case study of nature and effects of colonial power on rural society of northwestern provinces and Oudh, present-day Uttar Pradesh. Especially informative on changing role of large estate holders (*taluqdars*). [AAY]

15.522   Walter C. Neale. *Economic change in rural India: land tenure and reform in the Uttar Predesh, 1800–1955*. 1962 ed. Port Washington, N.Y.: Kennikat, 1973. ISBN 0-8046-1704-X. ▸ Classic work in debates about economic development under British rule and during Green Revolution. Argues limited effectiveness of land tenure and development policies in spurring economic progress derived from nonmarket character of agrarian social organization in India. [DEL]

15.523   Utsa Patnaik, ed. *Agrarian relations and accumulation: the "mode of production" debate in India*. Bombay, India: Oxford University Press for Sameeksha Trust, 1990. ISBN 0-19-562565-X. ▸ Meeting of Marxian theory and Indian agrarian society in debate on appropriate definition and historical location of feu-

dalism, caste, colonialism, and capitalism. Intensely argued among Indian historians. [DSL]

15.524   Utsa Patnaik and Manjari Dingwaney, eds. *Chains of servitude: bondage and slavery in India*. Madras, India: Sangam; distributed by Orient Longman, 1985. ISBN 0-86131-490-5. ▸ Valuable general essays and specific case studies of various forms of bondage labor and service and exploitative employer-laborer relations, historically and in the present. Important volume. [AAY]

15.525   Jacques Pouchepadass. *Paysans de la plaine du Gange: croissance agricole et société dans le district Champaran (Bihar), 1860–1950*. Paris: École Française d'Extrême-Orient, 1989. (Publications de l'École Française d'Extrême-Orient, 157.) ISBN 2-85539-757-X. ▸ Investigation of roots of Bihar's agrarian underdevelopment in specific setting of Champaran, site of one of Gandhi's major nonviolent struggles. Annales-like in its reconstruction of economic and social trends; careful, magisterial study. [AAY]

15.526   Gyan Prakash. *Bonded histories: genealogies of labor servitude in colonial India*. Cambridge: Cambridge University Press, 1990. ISBN 0-521-36278-4. ▸ Genealogy of notion and practice of bonded labor through study of Bhuinyas of South Bihar. Imaginative delineation of discursive field in which this institution developed as colonial "invention." [AAY]

15.527   Gyan Prakash, ed. *The world of the rural labourer in colonial India*. Delhi: Oxford University Press, 1992. ISBN 0-19-562832-2. ▸ Diverse essays on agricultural laborers. Mostly about economic and social conditions but some attention to cultural contours of their lived experiences. [AAY]

15.528   Ratnalekha Ray. *Change in Bengal agrarian society, c. 1760–1850*. New Delhi, India: Manohar, 1979. ▸ Critical revisionist work, which first demonstrated limits of agrarian transformation caused by Permanent Settlement of Bengal in 1793, and rise within colonial system of intermediary agrarian powers between small-holding peasants and elite *zamindars* (local powerholders). [DEL]

15.529   Dietmar Rothermund. *Government, landlord, and peasant in India: agrarian relations under British rule, 1865–1935*. Wiesbaden: Steiner, 1978. ISBN 3-515-02764-5. ▸ Best overview of land law and agrarian legislation and the official cognition of peasant conditions in colonial India. Rich in references. [DEL]

15.530   Asiya Siddiqi. *Agrarian change in a northern Indian state: Uttar Pradesh, 1819–1833*. Oxford: Clarendon, 1973. ISBN 0-19-821553-3. ▸ History of land revenue in one region of North India. Looks at both policy and its implementation at local level to analyze its workings in and effects on agrarian society. [AAY]

15.531   Ian Stone. *Canal irrigation in British India: perspectives on technological change in a peasant society*. Cambridge: Cambridge University Press, 1984. ISBN 0-521-25023-4. ▸ Study of canal irrigation policies and their impact in Uttar Pradesh, North India. Argues against Whitcombe 15.533 that benefits of canal irrigation outweighed damage they did. Solid contribution to continuing debates on ecological and economic impact of large irrigation projects. [DEL]

15.532   Daniel Thorner and Alice Thorner. *Land and labour in India*. 1962 ed. New York: Asia Publishing House, 1974. ▸ Classic essays on political economy of development. Connects colonial and independence periods. [DEL]

15.533   Elizabeth Whitcombe. *Agrarian conditions in northern India*. Vol. 1: *The United Provinces under British rule, 1860–1900*. Berkeley: University of California Press, 1972. ISBN 0-520-01706-4. ▸ Seeks to demonstrate negative impact of British land laws and irrigation technology in region of North India. Established ground for subsequent debates. [DEL]

15.534 Anand A. Yang. *The limited raj: agrarian relations in colonial India, Saran district, 1793–1920.* Berkeley: University of California Press, 1989. ISBN 0-520-05711-2. ▸ Detailed study of single *zamindari* landlord estate in Bihar. Traces its development as arena for organization of rural power, economic stagnation, and social relations. Excellent as account of limited role of colonial state in formulating conditions for agrarian life in *zamindar* estates. [DEL]

Imperialism, Capitalism, and Industry

15.535 Amiya Kumar Bagchi. *Private investment in India, 1900–1939.* Cambridge: Cambridge University Press, 1972. ISBN 0-521-07641-2. ▸ Patterns and determinants of investment especially in industrial sector with case studies of selected industries. Instructive analysis and argument regarding impacts of colonial tariff, commercial, industrial, and monetary policies. [FFC]

15.536 Henry T. Bernstein. *Steamboats on the Ganges: exploration in the history of India's modernization through science and technology.* 1960 ed. Calcutta, India: Orient Longman, 1987. ISBN 0-86131-757-2. ▸ Study of steamboats and their use on Ganges river between 1819 and 1840. Outdated modernization framework, but still useful information. [AAY]

15.537 Sabyasachi Bhattacharya, ed. *The South Indian economy: agrarian change, industrial structure, and state policy, c. 1914–1947.* Delhi: Oxford University Press, 1991. ISBN 0-19-562642-7. ▸ Solid chapters on Andhra, Tamilnadu, and Kerala and one chapter on tea plantations in Karnataka. No overarching argument, but central focus on commodity production. All chapters very substantial. [DEL]

15.538 Dipesh Chakrabarty. *Rethinking working-class history: Bengal, 1890–1940.* Princeton: Princeton University Press, 1989. ISBN 0-691-05548-3. ▸ Explorations of problems of worker solidarity in Calcutta jute mills in terms of continuities of precapitalist culture. Rich empirical and theoretical development of Marxian analysis and cultural theory. [DSL]

15.539 Neil Charlesworth. *British rule and the Indian economy, 1800–1914.* London: Macmillan, 1982. ISBN 0-333-27966-2 (pbk). ▸ Introductory overview of impact of British rule on Indian economy, 1800–1914. Judicious, balanced synthesis of significant research in economic history with useful suggestions for further reading. [FFC]

15.540 K. N. Chaudhuri. *The economic development of India under the East India Company, 1814–58: a selection of contemporary writings.* Cambridge: Cambridge University Press, 1971. ISBN 0-521-07933-0. ▸ Documents showing policy disputes and their intellectual foundations in Britain, conflicts pertaining to charter renewals of English East India Company, linked to empirical evidence concerning Indian economic development. Demonstrates foundation of development discourse in India. [DEL]

15.541 K. N. Chaudhuri and Clive J. Dewey, eds. *Economy and society: essays in Indian economic and social history.* Delhi: Oxford University Press, 1979. ISBN 0-19-561073-3. ▸ Most useful collection of articles produced in 1970s on agrarian history of colonial India. Contains many classics that have been subsequently reprinted. [DEL]

15.542 D. R. Gadgil. *The industrial evolution of India in recent times, 1860–1939.* 5th ed. Bombay, India: Oxford University Press, Indian Branch, 1971. ▸ Traditional survey of economic conditions in British India, including agriculture. Text for 1860–1914 is unrevised Cambridge thesis; for 1914–39, revised narrative of developments. First published 1944. [FFC]

15.543 Peter Harnetty. *Imperialism and free trade: Lancashire and India in the mid-nineteenth century.* Vancouver, Canada: University of British Columbia Press, 1972. ISBN 0-7748-0005-4. ▸ How British trade policy, having crushed Indian textile export production, fostered growth of commercial cotton production to supply British textile mills. Basic source on imperial economic policy. [DEL]

15.544 Hameeda Hossain. *The Company weavers of Bengal: The East India Company and the organization of textile production in Bengal, 1750–1813.* Delhi: Oxford University Press, 1988. ISBN 0-19-562043-7. ▸ Excellent, well-documented economic history. Examines changes in textile production and lives of artisans who supplied English East India Company in Bengal. [DEL]

15.545 Gordon Johnson, ed. "Review of *The Cambridge Economic History of India.*" *Modern Asian studies* 19.3 (1985). ISSN 0026-749X. ▸ Volume of essays in response to publication of volume 2 of *Cambridge Economic History of India,* on modern period. Includes debates, rebuttals, and essays to represent kind of economic history left out of Cambridge volume. [DEL]

15.546 Blair B. Kling. *Partner in empire: Dwarkanath Tagore and the age of enterprise in eastern India.* Berkeley: University of California Press, 1976. ISBN 0-520-02927-5. ▸ Biographical study of Indian entrepreneur and development of Indo-British collaborations in commerce, industry, and "managing agencies" in Bengal. Valuable insights on limits of early modern British-Indian economic and social relations. [FFC]

15.547 Dharma Kumar, ed. *The Cambridge economic history of India.* Vol. 2: *C. 1757–c. 1970.* Cambridge: Cambridge University Press, 1983. ISBN 0-521-22802-6 (v. 2). ▸ Massive accumulation of data on trade, manufacture, demography, policies, prices, money, technological change, and development issues in colonial India. Basic text for any study of modern Indian economic history. See also Johnson, ed. 15.545. [DEL]

15.548 Morris David Morris. *The emergence of an industrial labor force in India: a study of the Bombay cotton mills, 1854–1947.* Berkeley: University of California Press, 1965. ▸ Recruitment and organization of textile labor in Bombay. Pioneering analysis of cotton-mill industry and its workers over period of ninety years, their discipline, wages, and commitment. Blends history, sociology, and economics. [FFC]

15.549 Morris David Morris et al. *Indian economy in the nineteenth century: a symposium.* Delhi: Indian Economic and Social History Association; distributed by Hindustan, 1969. ▸ Critique of standard nationalist account of effects of British rule on Indian economy by Morris and responses of leading, mostly Indian historians. Seminal debate on data and methodology for determining economic history. [DSL]

15.550 Tapan Mukerjee. "The theory of economic drain: the impact of British rule on the Indian economy, 1840–1900." In *Economic imperialism: a book of readings.* Kenneth E. Boulding and Tapan Mukerjee, eds., pp. 195–212. Ann Arbor: University of Michigan Press, 1972. ISBN 0-472-16830-4 (cl), 0-472-08170-5 (pbk). ▸ Study of effects of British rule on economy of India in nineteenth century. Particularly concerned with role of government policy in promoting or retarding Indian development. [DEL]

15.551 Brij Narain. *Indian economic life, past and present.* 1929 ed. Delhi: Neeraj Publishing House; distributed by D. K. Publishers' Distributors, 1984. ▸ Study of different aspects of economic history. Much superseded by current research, but extensive coverage of such topics as price trends, currency, industries, banking, and finance still worth perusing. [AAY]

15.552 Richard Newman. *Workers and unions in Bombay, 1918–1929: a study of organisation in the cotton mills.* Canberra: Australian National University, South Asia History Section, 1981. ISBN 0-908070-04-7. ▸ Study of organization of production and control of Bombay textile mills, jobbers, and their workers during period of labor unrest. Well-documented analysis of mill and union structures and politics. [FFC]

15.553 Rajat Kanta Ray. *Industrialization in India: growth and conflict in the private corporate sector, 1914–47*. Delhi: Oxford University Press, 1979. ISBN 0-19-561463-1 (pbk). ‣ Study of constraints placed on industrialization through lack of domestic markets, technological supplies, and especially role of British regime in inhibiting development, mostly by inaction. Excellent research on major Indian entrepreneurs. [DSL]

15.554 Rajat Kanta Ray, ed. *Entrepreneurship and industry in India, 1800–1947*. Delhi: Oxford University Press, 1992. ISBN 0-19-562806-3. ‣ Essays analyzing European and Indian groups involved in business and industry. Interesting and suggestive approach seeks to link organized business sector and bazaar world of indigenous bankers and traders. [AAY]

15.555 Radhe Shyam Rungta. *Rise of business corporations in India, 1851–1900*. London: Cambridge University Press, 1970. ISBN 0-521-07354-5. ‣ Economic, legal, and policy contexts of emergence of managing agencies and corporations in India as vehicles for industrial enterprises. Closely documented monograph that also intervenes in broader debates on India's colonial economy. [FFC]

15.556 N. K. Sinha. *The economic history of Bengal*. Vols. 1 and 2: *From Plassey to the Permanent Settlement*. Edition varies. Calcutta, India: Mukhopadhyay, 1965–68. ‣ Economic conditions in Bengal during latter half of eighteenth century. Still authoritative in coverage of revenue history and European commercial activities. [AAY]

15.557 Daniel Thorner. *Investment in empire: British railway and steam shipping enterprise in India, 1825–1849*. Philadelphia: University of Pennsylvania Press, 1950. ‣ Pioneering monograph in economic history and colonial policies. Examines promotion of steamship and railway facilities to and in India through official initiatives and private investments. [FFC]

15.558 Thomas A. Timberg. *The Marwaris: from traders to industrialists*. New Delhi, India: Vikas, 1978. ISBN 0-7069-0528-8. ‣ Collection of essays looking at various aspects of history of highly successful commercial community. Informative sections on their history and entrepreneurial and industrial activities. [AAY]

15.559 B. R. Tomlinson. *The political economy of the raj, 1914–1947: the economics of decolonization in India*. London: Macmillan, 1979. ISBN 0-333-22361-6. ‣ Examination of difficulty in maintaining India as paying proposition for both British manufacturers and investors, while paying administrative and military costs out of Indian revenues. Insightful analysis from perspective of Britain's conflicting economic interests. [DSL]

15.560 D. A. Washbrook. "Progress and problems: South Asian economic and social history, c. 1720–1860." *Modern Asian studies* 22.1 (1988) 57–96. ISSN 0026-749X. ‣ Historiography of modern Indian social and economic change, examines ethnohistorical, world history, and Marxian approaches. Highly prescriptive call for giving South Asia its due in consolidated historiographic enterprise. [DSL]

Demography and Urbanization

15.561 Indu Banga, ed. *The city in Indian history: urban demography, society, and politics*. Columbia, Mo.: South Asia Publications, 1991. ISBN 0-945921-17-9. ‣ Sixteen essays from Urban History Group emphasizing conceptual and historiographical issues in study of cities in India from ancient to modern times. Illustrative of diversity of approaches and influences. [FFC]

15.562 Indu Banga, ed. *Ports and their hinterlands in India, 1700–1950*. New Delhi, India: Manohar, 1992. ISBN 81-85425-86-8. ‣ Nineteen essays on Indian ports, their economic and social functions, and hinterland relations. Not all contributions reflect

conceptual and methodological issues, but provide useful summations of recent research. [FFC]

15.563 N. Gerald Barrier, ed. *The census in British India: new perspectives*. New Delhi, India: Manohar, 1981. ‣ Essays based on census research or on limitations of census as source. Betrays limited appreciation of how census was itself instrument of power and stimulus to manipulation and resistance. [DSL]

15.564 Dilip K. Basu, ed. *The rise and growth of the colonial port cities in Asia*. Lanham, Md.: University Press of America with University of California, Center for South and Southeast Asia Studies, 1985. ISBN 0-8191-4761-3 (cl), 0-8191-4762-1 (pbk). ‣ Brief papers exploring city-hinterland relations, role of mercantile elites, and urban morphology. Insightful and provocative in raising questions and providing some answers regarding colonial port cities. [AAY]

15.565 Sukanta Chaudhuri, ed. *Calcutta: the living city*. Vol. 1: *The past*. Calcutta, India: Oxford University Press, 1990. ISBN 0-19-562585-4 (v. 1), 0-19-562718-0 (set). ‣ Well-illustrated but brief essays highlighting rich history of Calcutta. Coverage extends to key historical episodes, prominent inhabitants, neighborhoods, ethnic communities, architecture, theater, music, and art. [AAY]

15.566 Kingsley Davis. *The population of India and Pakistan*. 1951 ed. New York: Russell & Russell, 1968. ‣ Summary of South Asian demographic research, based primarily on extensive census operations carried on by British authorities. Lucid introduction to field at dawn of Indian national independence. [DSL]

15.567 Mariam Dossal. *Imperial designs and Indian realities: the planning of Bombay city, 1845–1875*. Bombay, India: Oxford University Press, 1991. ISBN 0-19-562583-8. ‣ Policy and practice in "improving" Bombay city during period of economic and demographic growth. Well-documented conflicts and constraints governing applications of urban technology between colonial rulers and Indian citizens. [FFC]

15.568 Tim Dyson, ed. *India's historical demography: studies in famine, disease, and society*. London and Riverdale, Md.: Curzon and Riverdale, 1989. ISBN 0-7007-0206-7, 0-913215-43-0. ‣ Aggregate and regional studies of social impact of famine, seasonal mortality, and interactions between inequality, disease, and life expectancy. Includes several articles of critical importance to social and economic history. [DEL]

15.569 Kenneth L. Gillion. *Ahmedabad: a study in Indian urban history*. Berkeley: University of California Press, 1968. ‣ Study of transformation of premodern administrative and trading city into industrial center under British rule. Analysis of politics of urban self-government and social life predominate over economics of industrialization. [FFC]

15.570 Anthony D. King. *Colonial urban development: culture, social power, and environment*. London: Routledge & Kegan Paul, 1976. ISBN 0-7100-8404-8. ‣ Influential sociological study of colonial urban space and built environments of British rule. Examines growth of Indian urban forms such as cantonments and hill stations and expressions of British power and social separation. [FFC]

15.571 Susan Lewandowski. *Migration and ethnicity in urban India: Kerala migrants in the city of Madras, 1870–1970*. New Delhi, India: Manohar, 1980. ‣ Description of patterns of urban migration to Madras from Kerala region with attention to migration stimuli and problems of identity and social change in the city. Persuasive analysis combining history, anthropology, and demography. [FFC]

15.572 Veena Talwar Oldenburg. *The making of colonial Lucknow, 1856–1877*. Princeton: Princeton University Press, 1984. ISBN 0-691-06590-X. ‣ Study of Lucknow in aftermath of mutiny and its development into colonial urban space dominated by issues of safety, sanitation, and loyalty. Vivid account of urban transformation projected "from above" on city's Indian citizens. [FFC]

15.573 Pradip Sinha. *Calcutta in urban history*. Calcutta, India: KLM, 1978. ▸ Calcutta from its village beginnings to mid-nineteenth-century prominence as major political and economic center. Impressionistic and suggestive essays on city conceptualized as bazaar. [AAY]

15.574 K. C. Zachariah. *A historical study of internal migration in the Indian sub-continent, 1901–1931*. New York: Asia Publishing House, 1964. ▸ Statistical study based on census returns, focused on interstate and urban-rural migration patterns. Basis of all subsequent work in this field. [DEL]

Gender, Caste, and Identity

15.575 Meredith Borthwick. *The changing role of women in Bengal, 1849–1905*. Princeton: Princeton University Press, 1984. ISBN 0-691-05409-6. ▸ Survey of changing definitions and situations of women, based on Bengali-language journals, autobiographies, and biographies. Sophisticated analysis of consequences of reforms illuminating modernity's positive and negative impact on women. [FFC]

15.576 Frank F. Conlon. *A caste in a changing world: the Chitrapur Saraswat brahmans, 1700–1935*. Berkeley: University of California Press, 1977. ISBN 0-520-02998-4. ▸ Long-range history of formation of social group from localized nexus of marriage arrangements and ritual status to dispersed, organized, and politically active "caste." Important revision of standard, ahistorical interpretations of Indian society. [DSL]

15.577 Ranajit Guha. "Chandra's death." In *Subaltern studies 5: writings on South Asian history and society*. Ranajit Guha, ed., pp. 135–65. Delhi: Oxford University Press, 1987. ISBN 0-19-562004-6. ▸ Exegesis of Bengali depositions regarding abortion that resulted in mother's death in 1849. Masterly analysis of intersection of religion, patriarchy, economic exploitation, and judicial intervention. [DSL]

15.578 Robert L. Hardgrave, Jr. *The Nadars of Tamilnad: the political culture of a community in change*. Berkeley: University of California Press, 1969. ▸ Connects history of group mobility and differentiation with emergence of reform efforts, urbanization, and nationalist politics in Tamilnadu since early nineteenth century. Influential for many subsequent studies of caste and politics. [DEL]

15.579 Charles H. Heimsath. *Indian nationalism and Hindu social reform*. Princeton: Princeton University Press, 1964. ▸ Exploration of dynamics and contradictions of movements for social reform during nationalist period. Superseded in some instances by more recent, detailed research; still reliable introduction. Photocopy available from Ann Arbor: University Microfilms International, 1977. [FFC]

15.580 Paul Hockings. *Ancient Hindu refugees: Badaga social history, 1550–1975*. The Hague: Mouton, 1980. ISBN 90-279-7798-4. ▸ Historical anthropology of ethnic and linguistic community in Nilgiri hills using official, missionary, and mythic sources to reconstruct demographic, economic, and social history, particularly for nineteenth and twentieth centuries. Treatment of earlier period more speculative. [DSL]

15.581 J. Krishnamurty, ed. *Women in colonial India: essays on survival, work, and the state*. Delhi: Oxford University Press, 1989. ISBN 0-19-562347-9. ▸ Eleven essays from *Indian Economic and Social History Review* on economic, educational, social, and political status of Indian women during British colonial rule. Useful compendium with potential for comparative studies. [FFC]

15.582 Edmund Leach and S. N. Mukherjee, eds. *Elites in South Asia*. Cambridge: Cambridge University Press, 1970. ISBN 0-521-07710-9. ▸ Eleven essays on wide range of subjects, seventeen to twentieth century, with multiple disciplinary perspectives. Discussion of specific elites rather than contribution to elite theory. [FFC]

15.583 Karen Isaksen Leonard. *Social history of an Indian caste: the Kayasths of Hyderabad*. Berkeley: University of California Press, 1978. ISBN 0-520-03431-7. ▸ Two centuries of Hyderabad Kayasth family history and social change. Convincing argument that families, kin groups, and marriage networks (and not only caste) constituted appropriate and effective units of social analysis. [AAY]

15.584 Gail Minault, ed. *The extended family: women and political participation in India and Pakistan*. Columbia, Mo.: South Asia Books, 1981. ISBN 0-8364-0765-2. ▸ Collection of essays treating women's participation in formal organizations devoted to nationalism, social reform, and women's concerns in twentieth-century South Asia, before and after colonial rule. [DSL]

15.585 B. B. Misra. *The Indian middle classes: their growth in modern times*. 1961 ed. Delhi: Oxford University Press, 1978. ISBN 0-19-560599-3. ▸ Attempts to identify commercial, industrial, agricultural and, most of all, professional sections of population as "middle classes" created by British economic, administrative, and educational policies from late eighteenth to beginning of twentieth century. Relies on administrative reports and statistics. [DSL]

15.586 Ghulam Murshid. *Reluctant debutant: response of Bengali women to modernization, 1849–1905*. Rajshahi, Bangladesh: Sahitya Samsad, Rajshahi University, 1983. ▸ Early work in rapidly growing field. Looks at effects of modernization on Bengali women, particularly their own responses. Includes useful documentation. [DEL]

15.587 Ashis Nandy. *The intimate enemy: loss and recovery of self under colonialism*. Delhi: Oxford University Press, 1983. ISBN 0-19-561505-0 (cl), 0-19-562237-5 (pbk). ▸ Study of psychology of colonialism focusing on British categorizations of Indians by gender and age, conflicted responses of Indians, and achievement of Gandhi. Seminal essay on culture of British India. [DSL]

15.588 Rosalind O'Hanlon. *Caste, conflict, and ideology: Mahatma Jotirao Phule and low-caste protest in nineteenth-century western India*. Cambridge: Cambridge University Press, 1985. ISBN 0-521-26615-7. ▸ Career and teachings of Maharashtrian non-brahman leader emphasizing ideology and popular culture in mass protest against traditional social and religious hierarchies. Persuasive analysis grounded in unusually sensitive reading of indigenous sources. [FFC]

15.589 Gail Omvedt. *Cultural revolt in a colonial society: the non-brahman movement in western India, 1873 to 1930*. Bombay, India: Scientific Socialist Education Trust, 1976. ▸ Examination of cultural and political mobilizations among non-brahmans of Maharashtra against social, religious, and economic privileges. Analysis of political and economic protests from Marxist perspective. [FFC]

15.590 Kumkum Sangari and Sudesh Vaid, eds. *Recasting women: essays in Indian colonial history*. 1989 ed. New Brunswick, N.J.: Rutgers University Press, 1990. ISBN 0-8135-1579-3 (cl), 0-8135-1580-7 (pbk). ▸ Ten essays on women in state, society, and culture of colonial India nominally linked by questions of regulation and reproduction of patriarchy. Diverse topics and approaches suggest potentials for further reading and research. [FFC]

15.591 Sumit Sarkar. *Bibliographical survey of social reform movements in the eighteenth and nineteenth century*. New Delhi, India: Indian Council of Historical Research; distributed by Motilal

Banarsidas, 1975. ▸ Review of literature on movements concerned with caste, gender, and social equality and relevance of colonial rule. Outdated but still one of best examples of historical bibliography. [DSL]

15.592 Sumit Sarkar. "The Kalki-Avatar if Bikrampur: a village scandal in early twentieth century Bengal." In *Subaltern studies 6: writings on South Asian history and society.* Ranajit Guha, ed., pp. 1–53. Delhi: Oxford University Press, 1989. ISBN 0-19-562278-2. ▸ Study in historical memory and forgetting, inspired by work of recent historians of early modern Europe. Class, caste, and gender reversals and popular religious concepts of messianic redemption revealed in obscure scandal in early twentieth-century rural Bengal. [DSL]

15.593 Asok Sen. *Iswar Chandra Vidyasagar and his elusive milestones.* Calcutta, India: Riddhi-India, 1977. ▸ Examination of frustrations and disappointments of noted Indian educator and reformer. Nuanced, empathetic portrayal coexists uneasily with stark emphasis on contradictions and inadequacies of colonial situation. [FFC]

15.594 Henny Sender. *The Kashmiri pandits: a study of cultural choice in North India.* New York: Oxford University Press, 1988. ISBN 019-561726-6. ▸ Social, cultural, and political traditions of elite caste's transition from participation in Mughal culture to emergence of modern identity. Sensitive, pragmatic analysis of social and cultural change. [FFC]

15.595 Anthony R. Walker. *The Toda of South India: a new look.* Delhi: Hindustan Publishing, 1986. ▸ Reconstruction of changing environment faced by Todas since 1819, based on oral evidence and other ethnographic fieldwork. Fullest description of this tribal group in Nilgiris made famous by earlier ethnographers and linguists. [DEL]

15.596 D. A. Washbrook. "'To each a language of his own': language, culture, and society in colonial India." In *Language, history, and class.* Penelope J. Corfield, ed., pp. 179–203. Oxford: Blackwell, 1991. ISBN 0-631-16732-3 (cl), 0-631-16733-1 (pbk). ▸ Brief, well-balanced introduction to problem of linguistic subnationalisms and rise of linguisitic politics. Examines British concepts of linguistic populations as clearly bounded groups that could be counted in censuses. [DSL]

15.597 Anand A. Yang, ed. *Crime and criminality in British India.* Tucson: University of Arizona Press for Association for Asian Studies, 1985. ISBN 0-8165-0951-4. ▸ Studies in British definitions of crime and ascriptive "criminal tribes," and of crime as popular resistance. Lively, original exploration of colonial theory and institutions, as well as social history. [DSL]

15.598 Eleanor Zelliot. *From untouchable to dalit: essays on the Ambedkar movement.* New Delhi, India: Manohar, 1992. ISBN 81-85425-37-X. ▸ Studies of untouchables, especially Mahars, of western India, Ambedkar's religious and political leadership, and emergence of *dalit* (oppressed) sociocultural identity. Convenient collection of sensitive, significant scholarship by recognized authority. [FFC]

Religious Communities and Institutions

15.599 Rafiuddin Ahmed. *The Bengal Muslims, 1871–1906: a quest for identity.* 2d ed. Delhi: Oxford University Press, 1988. ISBN 0-19-562203-0. ▸ Valuable analysis from Bangladesh national perspective of ethnicity formation and conflict. Contrasts development of Islamic consciousness among rural Bengalis with urban reform movements. Pioneering use of folk literature. [FFC]

15.600 Arjun Appadurai. *Worship and conflict under colonial rule: a South Indian case.* Cambridge: Cambridge University Press, 1981. ISBN 0-521-23122-1. ▸ Study of changing symbols, prac-

tices, and organization of South Indian temple from precolonial contexts to those of British rule. Exemplary combination of anthropological insights and historical research. [DSL]

15.601 Aziz Ahmad. *Islamic modernism in India and Pakistan, 1857–1964.* London: Oxford University Press for Royal Institute of International Affairs, 1967. ▸ History of religious thought of major South Asian Muslim writer-thinkers dealing with issues raised by European power, South Asian nationalism, and modernity. Methodologically conventional but well-informed introduction to ideological roots of Pakistan. [DSL]

15.602 Leslie Brown. *The Indian Christians of St. Thomas: an account of the ancient Syrian church of Malabar.* Rev. ed. Cambridge: Cambridge University Press, 1982. ISBN 0-521-21258-8. ▸ History of transformations of ancient Christian community of Kerala in response to European rule and influence and coercions by British clergyman of Anglican church. Particular emphasis on colonial period. [DSL]

15.603 J.R.I. Cole. *Roots of North Indian Shi'ism in Iran and Iraq: religion and state in Awadh, 1722–1859.* Berkeley: University of California Press, 1988. ISBN 0-520-05641-8. ▸ Studies of ideological and political conflict among Shī'ī Muslim religious leaders in context of princely state of Awadh to time of British annexation. Impressive research combined with somewhat rigid Weberian analytic framework. [DSL]

15.604 J. N. Farquhar. *Modern religious movements in India.* 1915 ed. Delhi: Munshiram Manoharlal, 1967. ▸ Detailed survey of religious and religion-related reform and revivalist movements in India to early twentieth century by Christian missionary. Balanced, reliable introductory survey. [FFC]

15.605 Duncan B. Forrester. *Caste and Christianity: attitudes and policies on caste of Anglo-Saxon Protestant missions in India.* London and Atlantic Highlands, N.J.: Curzon and Humanities, 1980. ISBN 0-7007-0129-X, 0-391-01785-3. ▸ Ideological and institutional history of missionary interpretations of caste and responses by Hindus and Indian Christians in context of British imperial rule, Indian nationalism, and movements for social reform. Subtle, highly differentiated study. [DSL]

15.606 Yohanan Friedmann. *Prophecy continuous: aspects of Ahmadi religious thought and its medieval background.* Berkeley: University of California Press, 1989. ISBN 0-520-05772-4. ▸ Scholarly combination of history and theological analysis. Examines messianic and reformist Ahmadi movement, founded by Mirza Ghulam Ahmad in 1889, and subsequently object of intense opposition among dominant Muslim groups, especially in Pakistan. [DSL]

15.607 Kenneth W. Jones. *Arya dharm: Hindu consciousness in nineteenth-century Punjab.* Berkeley: University of California Press, 1976. ISBN 0-520-02920-8. ▸ Analysis of religious and political content and impact of Arya Samaj of Dayananda Saraswati. Strong analysis of institutional activities and impact of movement in Punjab politics and culture. [FFC]

15.608 Kenneth W. Jones. *Socio-religious reform movements in British India.* Part 3. Vol. 1 of *The new Cambridge history of India.* Cambridge: Cambridge University Press, 1989. ISBN 0-521-24986-4. ▸ Geographically organized survey primarily of religious reform or revitalization movements during colonial rule. Subcontinental analysis generalizes socioreligious forms and functions, without emphasis on contestations within traditions of meanings and beliefs. [FFC]

15.609 Kenneth W. Jones, ed. *Religious controversy in British India: dialogues in South Asian languages.* Albany: State University of New York Press, 1992. ISBN 0-7914-0827-2 (cl), 0-7914-0828-0 (pbk). ▸ Literary, journalistic, theatrical, and oratorical disputation between and among Hindus, Muslims, Christians, and Sikhs in nineteenth and early twentieth century. Well-focused collection making welcome use of popular publications in South Asian languages. [DSL]

15.610 J.T.F. Jordens. *Dayananda Sarasvati: his life and ideas.* Delhi: Oxford University Press, 1978. ISBN 0-19-560995-6. ‣ Substantial biography of major nineteenth-century Hindu teacher and publicist combined with history of his ideas and theories. Careful scholarly analysis of development of Dayananda's thought and reformist Hindu Arya Samaj movement. [FFC]

15.611 Muin-ud-din Ahmad Khan. *History of the Fara ᶜidi movement in Bengal, 1818–1906.* Karachi, Pakistan: Pakistan Historical Society, 1965. ‣ Pioneering study of Muslim religious movements in nineteenth-century Bengal associated with peasant rebellion against predominantly Hindu landowners in colonial context. Notable for its use of Bengali sources. [DSL]

15.612 Gregory C. Kozlowski. *Muslim endowments and society in British India.* Cambridge: Cambridge University Press, 1985. ISBN 0-521-25986-X. ‣ How British judicial system construed South Asian variation of Muslim institution of *waqf* (endowment) and political initiatives taken by organized Muslim groups. Well-focused, lucid monograph of legal and political processes in colonial situation. [DSL]

15.613 Eckehard Külke. *The Parsees in India: a minority as agent of social change.* Munich: Weltforum, 1974. ISBN 3-8039-0070-0. ‣ Social and cultural change among Parsis, Zoroastrian community of colonial Bombay, and their role as minority in society and politics. Detailed narrative informed by sociological theory; good bibliography. [FFC]

15.614 Matthew Lederle. *Philosophical trends in modern Maharashtra.* Bombay, India: Popular Prakashan, 1976. ‣ Study of intellectual and philosophical trends in social and religious thought among Marathi speakers. Regional intellectual history introducing important Maharashtrian thinkers and writers. Helpful translations but relatively little analysis. [FFC]

15.615 David Lelyveld. *Aligarh's first generation: Muslim solidarity in British India.* Princeton: Princeton University Press, 1978. ISBN 0-691-03112-6. ‣ History of Sayyid Ahmad's college for Muslims, its conception, creation, curriculum, and student politics, weaving strands of Muslim identity, social backgrounds, subsequent careers, and community politics. Elegant, well-documented narrative. [FFC]

15.616 Barbara Daly Metcalf. *Islamic revival in British India: Deoband, 1860–1900.* Princeton: Princeton University Press, 1982. ISBN 0-691-05343-X. ‣ Study of religious culture and institutional achievements of leaders of reformist Muslim movement centered in major educational establishment at Deoband. Sensitive study of attempts to carve out meaningful Muslim way of life in context of colonialism and nationalism. [DSL]

15.617 Harjot Oberoi. "Brotherhood of the pure: the poetics and politics of cultural transgression." *Modern Asian studies* 26.1 (1992) 157–97. ISSN 0026-749X. ‣ Lucid, refreshing approach to modern Sikh history. Focuses on Kuka millenarian movement among Sikhs in late nineteenth-century Punjab and broader problems of religious identity in midst of economic change. [DSL]

15.618 Geoffrey A. Oddie. *Hindu and Christian in South-East India.* London and Wellesley Hills, Mass.: Curzon and Riverdale, 1991. ISBN 0-7007-0224-5, 0-913215-55-4. ‣ Analysis of cases of Hindu conversions to Christianity in Tamilnadu. Qualifies assumptions concerning social and cultural change associated with religious conversion. [FFC]

15.619 Geoffrey A. Oddie, ed. *Religion in South Asia: religious conversion and revival movements in South Asia in medieval and modern times.* 2d rev. ed. New Delhi, India: Manohar, 1991. ISBN

81-85425-46-9. ‣ Essays on proselytization and conversion (and reconversion) events and experiences of or among Muslims, Christians, Buddhists, and others in India and Sri Lanka. Suggestive lines for comparative study of religious encounter. [FFC]

15.620 Franklin A. Presler. *Religion under bureaucracy: policy and administration for Hindu temples in South India.* Cambridge: Cambridge University Press, 1987. ISBN 0-521-32177-8. ‣ Role of modern Indian state bureaucracy in controlling religious institutions as economic and social centers, set against long-term historical analysis of relation of Hindu temple to earlier political regimes. Well-researched work of political scientist concerned with long-term historical change. [DSL]

15.621 Joan G. Roland. *Jews in British India: identity in a colonial era.* Hanover, N.H.: University Press of New England for Brandeis University, 1989. (Tauber Institute for the Study of European Jewry, 9.) ISBN 0-87451-457-6. ‣ Study of political and cultural strategies among Indian Jews in relation to nationalism, Zionism, and internal cohesion. Richly documented analysis emphasizing Bene-Israel and Baghdadi Jews in Bombay. [FFC]

15.622 Christian W. Troll. *Sayyid Ahmad Khan: a reinterpretation of Muslim theology.* New Delhi, India: Vikas, 1978. ISBN 0-7069-0626-8. ‣ Intellectual biography of seminal figure in development of modern Muslim intellectual and institutional responses to challenges of modernity, colonialism, and Indian nationalism. Emphasis on religious thought through close reading of relevant texts. [DSL]

Education, Literature, and Art

15.623 Sumanta Banerjee. *The parlour and the streets: elite and popular culture in nineteenth-century Calcutta.* Calcutta, India: Seagull, 1989. ISBN 81-7046-063-8. ‣ Urban cultural reflections of emerging alienation between *bhadralok* (elite) and lower classes of Calcutta. Exposition and analysis of folk song, poetry, drama, and street entertainment informed by contemporary Bengal's problems. [FFC]

15.624 N. Gerald Barrier. *Banned: controversial literature and political control in British India, 1907–1947.* Columbia: University of Missouri Press, 1974. ISBN 0-8262-0159-8. ‣ History of press control and censorship with attention to legislation and application, followed by annotated bibliography of banned publications. Fascinating study of imperial anxieties and role of press in cultures of resistance. [DSL]

15.625 Erik Barnouw and S. Krishnaswamy. *Indian film.* 2d ed. New York: Oxford University Press, 1980. ISBN 0-19-502682-9 (cl), 0-19-502683-7 (pbk). ‣ Study of Indian cinema in colonial and early independence periods with attention to technological change, economic imperatives, politics, state control, censorship, and cultural traditions. Lucid, reliable introduction to major institution of modern India. [DSL]

15.626 S. Theodore Baskaran. *The message bearers: the nationalist politics and the entertainment media in South India, 1880–1945.* Christopher Baker, Introduction. Madras, India: Cre-A, 1981. ‣ History of modern theater, popular song, silent and sound motion pictures, primarily Tamil, in context of nationalism, social conflict, and colonial censorship. Pioneering research on mass media and popular culture. [DSL]

15.627 Aparna Basu. *The growth of education and political development in India, 1898–1920.* Delhi: Oxford University Press, 1974. ISBN 0-19-560352-4. ‣ Study of education under assault from colonial reform initiatives and as ground of Western-educated political classes. Careful analysis of issues and institutions revealing new chapter in immobility of colonial bureaucracy. [FFC]

15.628 Sudhir Chandra. *The oppressive present: literature and social consciousness in colonial India.* Delhi: Oxford University

Press, 1992. ISBN 0-19-562797-0. ▸ Study of ways North Indian Hindu writers of late nineteenth century negotiated conflicting attitudes toward British rule, women's status, caste, and Muslims. Complex reading of wide variety of sources in Hindi and other languages. [DSL]

15.629 Sisir Kumar Das. *A history of Indian literature.* Vol. 8: *1800–1910: Western impact, Indian response.* New Delhi, India: Sahitya Akademi, 1991. ISBN 81-7201-006-0 (v. 8). ▸ Analysis of Indian literatures in colonial era by genre and theme in subcontinental overview supplemented by detailed chronological tables and indexing. Informed more by literary history than critical theory. [FFC]

15.630 Sisir Kumar Das. *Sahibs and munshis: an account of the College of Fort William.* New Delhi, India: Orion; distributed by Rupa, 1978. ▸ Study of Indian literati who taught and prepared teaching materials in modern Indian languages at Fort William College, Calcutta, in first decade of nineteenth century. Clear, well-informed history of important cultural episode. [DSL]

15.631 Barun De. "A historical critique of Renaissance analogues for nineteenth-century India." In *Perspectives in social sciences 1: historical dimensions.* Barun De, ed., pp. 178–218. Calcutta, India: Oxford University Press for Centre for Studies in Social Sciences, Calcutta, 1977. ISBN 0-19-560778-3. ▸ Critique of influential concept that introduction of British intellectual thought and practices were in some way analogous to European Renaissance. Major revision, effectively argued, of historiographic orthodoxy. [DSL]

15.632 Judith Mara Gutman. *Through Indian eyes.* New York: Oxford University Press for International Center of Photography, 1982. ISBN 0-19-503135-0 (cl), 0-19-503136-9 (pbk). ▸ Illustrated history of achievement of Indian photographers arguing for continuities with pre-photographic principles of composition and perception. Pioneering, provocative work treating culture and technology in context of colonialism. [DSL]

15.633 David Kopf. *British Orientalism and the Bengal renaissance: the dynamics of Indian modernization, 1773–1835.* Berkeley: University of California Press, 1969. ▸ Analysis of interactions between British institutions and Bengali intelligentsia in Calcutta that produced concepts of renaissance and revitalization. Valuable insights into sociocultural encounter and change attached to optional theoretical perspective. [FFC]

15.634 Nita Kumar. *The artisans of Banaras: popular culture and identity, 1880–1986.* Princeton: Princeton University Press, 1988. ISBN 0-691-05531-9. ▸ Historical and ethnographic exploration of Banaras citizen's concepts of place, time, leisure, and change. Richly detailed description of life and festivals of city augments analysis of constitution of popular culture. [FFC]

15.635 Bruce Tiebout McCully. *English education and the origins of Indian nationalism.* 1940 ed. Gloucester, Mass.: Smith, 1966. ▸ Links development of British educational institutions and curricula to rise of demands for representative institutions and national independence. Influential, now largely superseded, cause-and-effect argument; oblivious to indigenous Indian perspectives. [DSL]

15.636 Ellen E. McDonald and Craig M. Stark. *English education, nationalist politics and elite groups in Maharashtra, 1885–1915.* Berkeley: Center for South and Southeast Asian Studies, University of California, 1969. (Occasional Paper, 5.) ▸ Pioneering and rare attempt at cliometrics. Relation of English education to nationalist politics as revealed in statistical analysis of college students in late nineteenth-century Maharashtra compared to membership during following decades of Indian National Congress. [DSL]

15.637 Ashis Nandy. *Alternative sciences: creativity and authen-* ticity in two Indian scientists. New Delhi, India: Allied, 1980. ▸ Scientific culture in colonial context through biographical studies of physicist J. C. Bose (1858–1937) and mathematician S. Ramanujan (1887–1920). Essay in social-psycholological conflicts of colonial situation. [DSL]

15.638 Tapan Raychaudhuri. *Europe reconsidered: perceptions of the West in nineteenth-century Bengal.* Delhi: Oxford University Press, 1988. ISBN 0-19-562066-6. ▸ Comparative study of three major Bengali intellectuals—Bhudev Mukhopadhyay, Bankimchandra, and Vivekananda—to show their independence from colonial ideological domination and how they sharply disagreed in their interpretation of European culture. Orientalism in reverse. [DSL]

Modern Political Movements

Primary Anti-Colonial and Peasant Resistance

15.639 F. W. Buckler. *Legitimacy and symbols: the South Asian writings of F. W. Buckler.* M. N. Pearson, ed. Ann Arbor: University of Michigan, Center for South and Southeast Asian Studies, 1985. ISBN 0-89148-032-3 (cl), 0-89148-033-1 (pbk). ▸ Includes "The Political Theory of the Indian Mutiny" (1922) and contemporary criticisms to this bold attempt to explain 1857 Rebellion in terms of religion-based theories of Mughal legitimacy. [DSL]

15.640 Adrienne Cooper. *Sharecropping and sharecroppers' struggles in Bengal, 1930–1950.* Calcutta, India: Bagchi, 1988. ISBN 81-7074-039-8. ▸ Descriptive account of sharecropping and struggles involving tenants, most importantly Tebhaga movement. Proceeds from premise that revolts are resistance to dependency. [DEL]

15.641 A. R. Desai, ed. *Peasant struggles in India.* Bombay, India: Oxford University Press, 1979. ISBN 0-19-560803-8. ▸ Analysis of vast array of conflicts involving farmers, tenants, landowners, tribals, and state in British India and since independence. Fundamental for understanding intellectual and empirical basis of subaltern studies and related historiographic trends. [DEL]

15.642 D. N. Dhanagare. *Peasant movements in India, 1920–1950.* Delhi: Oxford University Press, 1983. ISBN 0-19-561390-2. ▸ Monograph that puts peasant uprisings at heart of Indian politics in late colonial and early nationalist period. Valuable primarily for its vast listing of movements and references to documents and secondary work. [DEL]

15.643 Stephen Fuchs. *Rebellious prophets: a study of messianic movements in Indian religions.* 2d ed. Delhi: Anthropos Institute, 1973. ▸ Examination of messianic movements of so-called primitive and backward groups that were triggered by socioeconomic tensions. Problematic but provocative discussion connecting diverse social movements. [AAY]

15.644 Ramachandra Guha. *The unquiet woods: ecological change and peasant resistance in the Himalaya.* 1989 ed. Berkeley: University of California Press, 1990. ISBN 0-520-06501-8. ▸ Study of ecological politics during colonial and national periods, focusing on forest policy, resource exploitation, and popular resistance. Formative text for ecological history of modern South Asia. [DEL]

15.645 Ranajit Guha. *Elementary aspects of peasant insurgency in colonial India.* 1983 ed. Delhi: Oxford University Press, 1985. ISBN 0-19-561517-4. ▸ Resistance to capitalist exploitation in Indian countryside and relative absence of full-scale revolutionary movements. Foundational text of subaltern school of Indian historiography, which seeks to theorize forms of insurgency that characterized rural India during colonial period. [DEL]

15.646 David Hardiman. *The coming of the Devi: adivasi assertion in western India.* Delhi: Oxford University Press, 1987. ISBN 0-19-

561957-9. ▸ Study of religiously inspired political movement among so-called tribal peoples in 1920s and 1930s. Fascinating, often insightful analysis relating *adivasi* struggles with Gandhi-led nationalist movement. [AAY]

15.647 David Hardiman, ed. *Peasant resistance in India, 1858–1914.* Delhi: Oxford University Press, 1992. ISBN 0-19-562725-3. ▸ Discussion of peasant resistance after 1857 Rebellion and before rise of nationalist mass movement. Attempts to show different acts of resistance shared common sense of peasant community. [AAY]

15.648 Douglas E. Haynes and Gyan Prakash, eds. *Contesting power: resistance and everyday social relations in South Asia.* Berkeley: University of California Press, 1992. ISBN 0-520-07585-4. ▸ Disparate forms of resistance in everyday social life in rural and urban India and Sri Lanka from perspectives of class and gender. Theoretical discussion by Scott unifies volume, but strength is its richness of detail and diversity of locations discussed. [DEL]

15.649 Stephen Henningham. *Peasant movements in colonial India: North Bihar, 1917–1942.* Canberra: Australian National University, 1982. ISBN 0-908070-08-X. ▸ Examination of six peasant movements in Northeast India. Attributes limited success to inherent weaknesses structured by subordination to Indian National Congress–led national movement. [AAY]

15.650 Jagdish Chandra Jha. *The tribal revolt of Chotanagpur, 1831–1832.* Patna, India: Kashi Prasad Jayaswal Research Institute, 1987. ▸ Most detailed account of event in history of tribal rebellions. Situates it well in its agrarian setting. One of few accounts in agrarian history of Chota Nagpur. [DEL]

15.651 Blair B. Kling. *The blue mutiny: the indigo disturbances in Bengal, 1859–1862.* Philadelphia: University of Pennsylvania Press, 1966. ▸ Survey of social and economic developments that resulted in "indigo disturbances" in mid-nineteenth-century Bihar. Emphasis on relating disturbances to colonial administration and policies rather than on events and actors. [AAY]

15.652 Joyce Lebra-Chapman. *The rani of Jhansi: a study in female heroism in India.* Honolulu, Hawaii: University of Hawaii Press, 1986. ISBN 0-8248-0984-X. ▸ Biography of Indian Joan of Arc figure of 1857 Rebellion. Attempts, with some success, to negotiate between historical figure and legend to recover biographical information and subsequent mythology. [AAY]

15.653 K. N. Panikkar. *Against lord and state: religion and peasant uprisings in Malabar, 1836–1921.* Delhi: Oxford University Press, 1989. ISBN 0-19-562139-5. ▸ Addresses core question under debate: to what extent do religious community and class oppression explain origin and conduct of Moplah [Mapilla] rebellions? Based on overview of considerable historiography and massive documentation. [DEL]

15.654 Surendra Nath Sen. *Eighteen fifty-seven.* New Delhi, India: Ministry of Information and Broadcasting, Publications Division, 1957. ▸ Government of India–sponsored centenary volume on 1857 Rebellion. Attempts to present balanced picture but has more to say about government actions than rebel roles in movement. [AAY]

15.655 K. S. Singh. *Birsa Munda and his movement, 1874–1901: a study of a millenarian movement in Chotanagpur.* Calcutta, India: Oxford University Press, 1983. ISBN 0-19-561424-0. ▸ History of late nineteenth-century movement among Munda people of Chotanagpur led by religious prophet. Emphatic assertion that "tribal" culture is alien to neighboring peasant society. Earlier title: *The Dust Storm and the Hanging Mist.* [DEL]

15.656 K. S. Singh, ed. *Tribal movements in India.* 2 vols. New Delhi, India: Manohar, 1982–83. ▸ Diverse studies of tribal movements in modern South Asia. Varying quality exemplifies state of field of tribal studies until early 1980s. [DEL]

15.657 Eric Stokes. *The peasant and the raj: studies in agrarian society and peasant rebellion in colonial India.* Cambridge: Cambridge University Press, 1978. ISBN 0-521-21684-2 (cl), 0-521-29770-2 (pbk). ▸ Twelve essays exploring complex and subtle changes in agrarian society ushered in by colonial rule. Especially provocative in ideas on change in agrarian society in nineteenth century. [DEL]

15.658 Eric Stokes. *The peasant armed: the Indian rebellion of 1857.* C. A. Bayly, ed. Oxford: Clarendon, 1986. ISBN 0-19-821570-3. ▸ Analysis of 1857 Rebellion in terms of rural participation, geography, timing, as well as larger administrative, economic, and military contexts. Explains larger project of utilizing Mutiny documentation to contribute to general agrarian and social history. [DEL]

Nationalist Politics, 1886–1947

15.659 Paul R. Brass and Francis Robinson, eds. *The Indian National Congress and Indian society, 1885–1985: ideology, social structure, and political dominance.* Delhi: Chanakya, 1987. ISBN 81-7001-026-8. ▸ Studies by historians and political scientists of major organization of Indian nationalism and dominant party after independence. Particularly good on rural localities and constraints on Muslim participation. [DSL]

15.660 Michael Brecher. *Nehru: a political biography.* London: Oxford University Press, 1959. ▸ Examination of Jawaharlal Nehru's public career in nationalist politics prior to independence and as prime minister to 1958. Good synthesis based on documentary material available at time of writing. [FFC]

15.661 Emily C. Brown. *Har Dayal: Hindu revolutionary and rationalist.* Tucson: University of Arizona Press, 1975. ISBN 0-8165-0422-9 (cl), 0-8165-0512-8 (pbk). ▸ Biography of nationalist leader whose political activities extended across Europe and United States. Especially informative in portraying involvement in formation of Ghadr party in California in 1913. [AAY]

15.662 Judith M. Brown. *Gandhi and civil disobedience: the mahatma in Indian politics, 1928–34.* Cambridge: Cambridge University Press, 1977. ISBN 0-521-21279-0. ▸ Indian politics and political leadership during and after civil disobedience movements. Framed as collision of British constitutional and Gandhian political strategies; analysis emphasizes pragmatic politics over ideologies. [FFC]

15.663 Judith M. Brown. *Gandhi's rise to power: Indian politics, 1915–1922.* Cambridge: Cambridge University Press, 1985. ISBN 0-521-08353-2. ▸ Study of changing nature of Indian politics framed in Gandhi's mobilizations following his return to India. Emphasis on Gandhi's mobilization of constituencies with consequent deemphasis of ideology or charisma. [FFC]

15.664 Judith M. Brown. *Modern India: the origins of an Asian democracy.* Oxford: Oxford University Press, 1985. ISBN 0-19-913124-4 (cl), 0-19-822859-7 (pbk). ▸ India from eighteenth to twentieth century with focus on political development. Also addresses ideas and institutions. Particularly useful on social and political movements leading to independence. [FFC]

15.665 Bipan Chandra. *The rise and growth of economic nationalism in India: economic policies of Indian national leadership, 1880–1905.* New Delhi, India: People's Publishing House, 1966. ▸ Comprehensive history of economic thought associated with Indian nationalist movement. Sympathetically presented, but within Marxist framework. [DSL]

15.666 Partha Chatterjee. *Nationalist thought and the colonial world: a derivative discourse?* London: Zed for United Nations University; distributed by Biblio Distribution Center, 1986. ISBN 0-86232-552-8 (cl), 0-86232-553-6 (pbk). ▸ Critical analysis of major formulations of Indian nationalist ideologies in relation to their role in establishing dominant model of social order and class interest. Stimulating analysis informed by theories of Antonio Gramsci. [DSL]

15.667 Ainslie T. Embree. *India's search for national identity.* New York: Knopf, 1972. ISBN 0-394-31642-8. ▸ Succinct introduction to mainstream issues of Indian nationalism. Argues political processes and institutions more than essential cultural unities are at heart of nation formation in South Asia. [DSL]

15.668 Erik H. Erikson. *Gandhi's truth: on the origins of militant nonviolence.* New York: Norton, 1969. ISBN 0-393-01049-X. ▸ Classic of psychohistory uses Freudian theory and method to analyze personality and leadership of Mahatma Gandhi, centering on Ahmedabad textile strike of 1918 and Gandhi's first fast. [DSL]

15.669 John Gallagher, Gordon Johnson, and Anil Seal, eds. *Locality, province, and nation: essays on Indian politics, 1870–1940, reprinted from "Modern Asian Studies" 1973.* Cambridge: Cambridge University Press, 1973. ISBN 0-521-09811-4. ▸ Politics, nationalism, and British power in colonial India. Early product of so-called Cambridge school interpretation, yet already diversifying analyses pointing to further critiques and new directions for research. [FFC]

15.670 Sarvepalli Gopal. *Jawaharlal Nehru: a biography.* 3 vols. Cambridge, Mass.: Harvard University Press, 1976–1984. ISBN 0-674-47310-8 (v.1), 0-674-47311-6 (v.2), 0-674-47312-4 (v.3). ▸ Semi-official, comprehensive biography of India's first prime minister, nationalist leader, and political intellectual. Emphasizes complex contexts of Nehru's activities and policies in place of apologias. [FFC]

15.671 A.D.D. Gordon. *Businessmen and politics: rising nationalism and a modernizing economy in Bombay, 1918–33.* Columbia, Mo.: South Asia Books, 1978. ISBN 0-8364-0194-8. ▸ Influential interpretation occasionally obscured by detail. Links variable Bombay business support for Gandhi and Indian National Congress to differential experiences of economic change and urban politics. [FFC]

15.672 Leonard A. Gordon. *Brothers against the raj: a biography of Indian nationalists Sarat and Subhas Chandra Bose.* New York: Columbia University Press, 1990. ISBN 0-231-07442-5 (cl), 0-231-07443-3 (pbk). ▸ Thorough biography of prominent nationalist leader and his brother. Subhas Bose's involvement with Germany and Japan in World War II carefully chronicled. [AAY]

15.673 John Patrick Haithcox. *Communism and nationalism in India: M. N. Roy and Comintern policy, 1920–1939.* Princeton: Princeton University Press, 1971. ISBN 0-691-08722-9. ▸ Study of communism and socialism in India and abroad and their role in nationalist movement. Develops theme by looking at Indian and international career of Communist International leader, M. N. Roy. [AAY]

15.674 Ravinder Kumar, ed. *Essays on Gandhian politics: the Rowlatt satyagraha of 1919.* Oxford: Clarendon, 1971. ISBN 0-19-827176-X. ▸ Studies in organization and local manifestations of Mahatma Gandhi's first all-India nonviolent campaign against British authoritarianism. Valuable for its detailed accounts of how *satyagraha* actually worked. [DSL]

15.675 D. A. Low, ed. *Congress and the raj: facets of the Indian struggle, 1917–47.* London: Heinemann, 1977. ISBN 0-435-99580-4. ▸ Sixteen case studies of Indian National Congress politics in regions of subcontinent. Recruitment to nationalism of previously marginal actors such as dominant peasants and its consequences emphasized, but Muslim majority areas omitted. [FFC]

15.676 D. A. Low, ed. *The Indian National Congress: centenary*

hindsights. Delhi: Oxford University Press, 1988. ISBN 0-19-562142-5. ▸ Diverse set of essays commemorating Congress' centenary in 1985. Informative in revealing party's strengths and weaknesses in mobilizing different communities and groups. [AAY]

15.677 D. A. Low, ed. *Soundings in modern South Asian history.* Berkeley: University of California Press, 1968. ▸ Eleven contributions by eight scholars on topics of political and social history of nineteenth- and twentieth-century India. Some essays superseded by author's monographs, but collection remains influential milestone. [FFC]

15.678 Claude Markovits. *Indian business and nationalist politics, 1931–1939: the indigenous capitalist class and the rise of the Congress party.* Cambridge: Cambridge University Press, 1985. ISBN 0-521-26551-7. ▸ Study of indigenous Indian capitalism's confrontations and conjunctions with nationalism and nationalist politics. Clear analysis of business support of Indian National Congress and resistance to Left's policy initiatives. [FFC]

15.679 J. C. Masselos. *Towards nationalism: group affiliations and the politics of public associations in nineteenth-century western India.* Bombay, India: Popular Prakashan, 1974. ▸ Detailed evolution of public affairs, political action, nationalist sentiment, and ideology in Bombay presidency. Most reliable guide to regional roots of Indian nationalism. [FFC]

15.680 John R. McLane. *Indian nationalism and the early Congress.* Princeton: Princeton University Press, 1977. ISBN 0-691-03113-4 (cl), 0-691-10056-X (pbk). ▸ Insufficiently informed by local perspectives, but best organizational history of early Congress as whole. Concludes first phase of Indian National Congress, 1885–1905, concerned with its leadership, organization, and controversies regarding class interest and Hindu-Muslim unity. [DSL]

15.681 S. R. Mehrotra. *The emergence of the Indian National Congress.* Delhi: Vikas, 1971. ISBN 0-7069-0080-4. ▸ Presentation of major personalities, organizations, and issues relevant to formulation of Indian nationalism between 1857 Rebellion and founding of Congress in 1885. Straightforward, well-researched narrative history represents state of field before Cambridge and subaltern schools. [DSL]

15.682 R. J. Moore. *The crisis of Indian unity, 1917–1940.* Oxford: Clarendon, 1974. ISBN 0-19-821560-6. ▸ Careful, clear analysis of major chapters in Indian freedom struggle from perspective of constitutional and political history. Finds politics and processes in devolution of power eroded potential for Indian unity. [FFC]

15.683 B. R. Nanda. *Gokhale, the Indian moderates and the British raj.* Princeton: Princeton University Press, 1977. ISBN 0-691-03115-0. ▸ Biographical study of Indian moderate political leader with description of nationalist politics and Indo-British relations of period. Exceptionally able use of private papers illuminating dilemmas and contributions of pre-Gandhian nationalism. [FFC]

15.684 Gyanendra Pandey, ed. *The Indian nation in 1942.* Calcutta, India: Bagchi for Centre for Studies in Social Sciences, 1988. ISBN 81-7074-024-X. ▸ Study of Quit India movement as it unfolded in various parts of country. Best at showing extent to which it was led by Gandhi even as it followed agendas often at odds with Gandhian principles. [AAY]

15.685 Lloyd I. Rudolph and Susanne Hoeber Rudolph. *The modernity of tradition: political development in India.* 1967 ed. Chicago: University of Chicago Press, 1984. ISBN 0-226-73137-5. ▸ Stimulating treatment of theme of continuity and change. Explores ways in which institutional forms and ideological beliefs adapt to new contexts: rise of caste associations, Gandhi's charisma, and legal institutions. [DSL]

15.686 Sumit Sarkar. *Modern India, 1885–1947.* 1983 ed. D. A. Low, Foreword. Basingstoke, England: Macmillan, 1989. ISBN 0-333-43805-1 (cased), 0-333-43806-X (pbk). ▸ Marxian, nonelitist narrative history and analysis of social roots of political mobilization and course of Indian nationalism. Best overview of subject. [DSL]

15.687 Anil Seal. *The emergence of Indian nationalism: competition and collaboration in the later nineteenth century.* Cambridge: Cambridge University Press, 1968. ISBN 0-521-06274-8. ▸ Interpretation of early nationalist politics in terms of private ambitions of regional elites within framework of colonial institutions. Founding manifesto of Namierite Cambridge school of modern Indian history. [DSL]

15.688 Mike Shepperdson and Colin Simmons, eds. *The Indian National Congress and the political economy of India, 1885–1985.* Aldershot, England: Avebury, 1988. ISBN 0-566-05076-5. ▸ Large, diverse collection of papers addressing 100-year history of Indian National Congress from generally Marxist perspective. Includes some substantial contributions along with more ephemeral efforts. [DSL]

15.689 Stanley A. Wolpert. *Tilak and Gokhale: revolution and reform in the making of modern India.* 1961 ed. Delhi: Oxford University Press, 1989. ISBN 0-19-562392-4. ▸ Examination of Indian nationalism through contrasting ideas and contributions of "moderate" and "extremist" nationalists of Maharashtra. While these rubrics are outmoded, narrative remains vigorous and insightful. [FFC]

Regional and Local Politics

15.690 Syed Nur Ahmad. *From martial law to martial law: politics in the Punjab, 1919–1958.* Craig Baxter, ed. Mahmud Ali, trans. Boulder: Westview, 1985. ISBN 0-86531-845-X (pbk). ▸ Political history of undivided Punjab in final decades of British rule and Pakistani Punjab in decade following partition. History of events and personalities. Originally published in Urdu, 1965. [DSL]

15.691 Imran Ali. *The Punjab under imperialism: 1885–1947.* Princeton: Princeton University Press, 1988. ISBN 0-691-05527-0. ▸ Concludes growth in production as result of British irrigation systems concentrated wealth in hands of privileged military elite to detriment of general economic development. Important in part for implications for independent Pakistan. [DEL]

15.692 Shahid Amin. "Approver's testimony, judicial discourse: the case of Chauri Chaura." In *Subaltern studies 5: writings on South Asian history and society.* Ranajit Guha, ed., pp. 166–202. Delhi: Oxford University Press, 1987. ISBN 0-19-562004-6. ▸ Analysis of ways in which British judicial rules determined nature of evidence in Chauri Chaura incident of 1922 and tended to erase its political import. Exemplary use of discourse theory in subaltern studies project. [DSL]

15.693 Shahid Amin. "Gandhi as mahatma: Gorakhppur district, eastern UP, 1921–2." In *Subaltern studies 3: writings in South Asian history and society.* Ranajit Guha, ed., pp. 1–61. Delhi: Oxford University Press, 1984. ISBN 0-19-561653-7. ▸ Local transformation of Gandhi's noncooperation movement into one of empowerment, often violent, of rural populace. Brilliant reading of unexpected sources, such as reports of rumors, to articulate popular ideologies of resistance. [DSL]

15.694 David Arnold. *Congress in Tamilnad: nationalist politics in South India, 1919–1937.* Columbia, Mo.: South Asia Books, 1977. ISBN 0-88386-958-6. ▸ Analysis of regional manifestations of Indian nationalist politics and politicians in Madras with emphasis on Tamilnadu. Detailed review of transition from elite to mass political mobilizations. [FFC]

15.695 Christopher John Baker. *The politics of South India, 1920–1937.* Cambridge: Cambridge University Press, 1976. ISBN 0-521-20755-X. ▸ Account of successes and failures of anti-brahmin Justice party and nationalist Congress in development of patron-client relations that reached beyond localities. Overly reliant on English, especially official British sources. [DSL]

15.696 Christopher John Baker and D. A. Washbrook, eds. *South India: political institutions and political change, 1880–1940.* New Delhi, India: Macmillan, 1975. ▸ Essays on politics in late colonial Madras presidency. Formative contributions to what became Cambridge school of Indian political historiography. Concentrates on local bases of nationalist politics in agrarian power relations. [DEL]

15.697 D.E.U. Baker. *Changing political leadership in an Indian province: the Central Provinces and Berar, 1919–1939.* Delhi: Oxford University Press, 1979. ISBN 0-19-561135-7. ▸ Study of nationalist politics in linguistically heterogeneous province during Gandhian era. Carefully documents erosion of Marathi elite's domination in competition with emergent Gandhian and Hindi politicians. [FFC]

15.698 Marguerite Ross Barnett. *The politics of cultural nationalism in South India.* Princeton: Princeton University Press, 1976. ISBN 0-691-07577-8. ▸ Examines Tamil cultural nationalism of Justice party and Dravidian Progressive Federation (D.M.K.) party as ideology of mass mobilization and modernization. Excellent introduction to trends of modern Tamilnadu politics. [FFC]

15.699 C. A. Bayly. *The local roots of Indian politics: Allahabad, 1880–1920.* Oxford: Clarendon, 1975. ISBN 0-19-821562-2. ▸ Study of Indian nationalism's emergence in North Indian city. Emphasizes transformations of dominant urban elite interest groups' parochial politics of trade, local government, and language into wider national arena. [FFC]

15.700 J. H. Broomfield. *Elite conflict in a plural society: twentieth-century Bengal.* Berkeley: University of California Press, 1968. ▸ Examination of provincial politics and social conflict in early twentieth-century Bengal. Analysis grounded on contested concept of self-conscious regional elite (*bhadralok*). At once influential and problematic. [FFC]

15.701 Richard I. Cashman. *The myth of the Lokamanya: Tilak and mass politics in Maharashtra.* Berkeley: University of California Press, 1975. ISBN 0-520-02407-9. ▸ Analysis of political career of nationalist leader Bal Gangadhar Tilak focusing on his several major mobilizations and movements. Significant revisionist assessment of Tilak as mass leader and his nationalist movement in Maharashtra. [FFC]

15.702 Partha Chatterjee. *Bengal, 1920–1947.* Vol. 1: *The land question.* Calcutta, India: Bagchi for Centre for Studies in Social Sciences, 1984. ▸ Meticulous study of land-reform politics in Bengal entangled with imperial and nationalist disputations. Establishes connections between agrarian economy and politics. [DEL]

15.703 Christine Dobbin. *Urban leadership in western India: politics and communities in Bombay city, 1840–1885.* London: Oxford University Press, 1972. ISBN 0-19-821841-9. ▸ Discussion of roots of public culture and nationalism as displayed in dynamics of Bombay local urban politics and intracaste and community leadership. Analysis depends largely on problematic socioeconomic categories. [FFC]

15.704 S.J.M. Epstein. *The earthy soil: Bombay peasants and the Indian nationalist movement, 1919–1947.* Delhi: Oxford University Press, 1988. ISBN 0-19-562214-6. ▸ Clearly argued monograph that presents new view of agrarian politics at work in nationalist movement. Shows extent to which involvement in commercialized agriculture and opposition to taxes rather than opposition to British rule motivated farmers who rallied behind Gandhi and Indian National Congress. [DEL]

15.705   Leonard A. Gordon. *Bengal: the nationalist movement, 1876–1940.* 1973 ed. New York: Columbia University Press, 1974. ISBN 0-231-03753-8. ‣ Study of three generations of Bengali political leaders' careers, ideas, and activities reveals weakening of regional priorities under emergent nationalism. Sensitive analysis of Indian nationalism in regional context through biographical perspective. [FFC]

15.706   Amalendu Guha. *Planter-raj to swaraj: freedom struggle and electoral politics in Assam, 1826–1947.* New Delhi, India: People's Publishing House for Indian Council of Historical Research, 1977. ‣ Discussion of provincial legislature of Assam and its involvement in nationalist movement of region. Valuable as both socioeconomic and political history of little-studied region. [AAY]

15.707   David Hardiman. *Peasant nationalists of Gujarat: Kheda district, 1917–34.* Delhi: Oxford University Press, 1981. ISBN 0-19-561255-8. ‣ Analysis of uses of matrimonial networks, nationalist politics, and British colonial legal system to achieve caste and class dominance in rural district. Contributed to formulation of subaltern school of Indian history. [DSL]

15.708   Zoya Hasan. *Dominance and mobilization: rural politics in western Uttar Pradesh, 1930–1980.* New Delhi, India: Sage, 1989. ISBN 0-8039-9588-1. ‣ Analysis of politics in Aligarh district viewed over period straddling pre- and postindependence eras. Best at illuminating relationship between socioeconomic conditions and power and politics. [AAY]

15.709   Douglas E. Haynes. *Rhetoric and ritual in colonial India: the shaping of a public culture in Surat city, 1852–1928.* Berkeley: University of California Press, 1991. ISBN 0-520-06725-8. ‣ Narrative of public life in Gujarat city illuminates dynamics and dilemmas of Indian appropriation of British civic rhetoric. History intelligently informed by discursive analysis. [FFC]

15.710   Eugene F. Irschick. *Politics and social conflict in South India: the non-brahman movement and Tamil separatism, 1916–1929.* Berkeley: University of California Press, 1969. ISBN 0-520-00596-1. ‣ Study of emergence of counter-nationalism in colonial South Indian non-brahman, Dravidian movement. Useful introduction to varied manifestations of South Indian separatism. [FFC]

15.711   Gyanendra Pandey. *The ascendancy of the Congress in Uttar Pradesh, 1926–34: a study in imperfect mobilization.* Delhi: Oxford University Press, 1978. ISBN 0-19-560969-7. ‣ Role of peasantry and elite in nationalist and agrarian issues in specific areas of Uttar Pradesh. Particularly illuminating in locating and establishing peasant initiative and involvement in agrarian reforms. [AAY]

15.712   Gyanendra Pandey. "Peasant revolt and Indian nationalism: the peasant movement in Awadh, 1919–1922." In *Subaltern studies 1: writings on South Asian history and society.* Ranajit Guha, ed., pp. 143–97. Delhi: Oxford University Press, 1982. ISBN 0-19-561355-4. ‣ Detailed study of one region focusing on leadership, its relations with peasantry, and its alienation from Gandhian Congress during first effort at Congress mass mobilization. Argues for autonomous origins of peasant mobilization in Uttar Pradesh and its essential separation from elitist politics of Indian nationalism. [DEL]

15.713   Rajat Kanta Ray. *Social conflict and political unrest in Bengal, 1875–1927.* Delhi: Oxford University Press, 1984. ISBN 0-19-561654-5. ‣ Relationship between European elite and Indian business and professional groups in period of rising nationalism. Careful analysis of social and economic bases of political developments. [AAY]

15.714   Rajat Kanta Ray. *Urban roots of Indian nationalism: pres-*

sure groups and conflict of interests in Calcutta city politics, 1875–1939. New Delhi, India: Vikas, 1979. ISBN 0-7069-0808-2. ‣ Study of opposition between European imperial interests and Indian nationalist aspirations played out in urban politics of Calcutta. Illuminates Congress party's decline, emergence of social tensions, and Muslim separatism. [FFC]

15.715   Peter Reeves. *Landlords and governments in Uttar Pradesh: a study of their relations until zamindary abolition.* Bombay, India: Oxford University Press, 1991. ISBN 0-19-562778-8. ‣ Study of relations between colonial government and landlords in early twentieth century. Concentrates on revealing shifts in their relationships in decades leading up to abolition of landlords. [AAY]

15.716   Sumit Sarkar. *"Popular" movements and "middle-class" leadership in late colonial India: perspectives and problems of a "history from below."* Calcutta, India: Bagchi for Centre for Studies in Social Sciences, 1983. ‣ Argues that divorce between popular resistance and political leadership of Indian nationalist cause brought independence without substantial social change. Marxian perspective, by major scholar of modern social movements. [DSL]

15.717   Sumit Sarkar. *Swadeshi movement in Bengal, 1903–1908.* New Delhi, India: People's Publishing House, 1973. ‣ Excellent account of strengths and weaknesses of early twentieth-century phase of nationalist movement in Bengal that emphasized boycott of British goods and of its ties to other political developments. [AAY]

15.718   Tanika Sarkar. *Bengal, 1928–1934: the politics of protest.* Delhi: Oxford University Press, 1987. ISBN 0-19-562076-3. ‣ Examination of Bengal worker and peasant protests in coherent interpretive framework ranging from rural Gandhians to Jitu Santal's tribal hinduization movement to carters' strike. Blends subaltern school perspectives with objective historical analysis. [FFC]

15.719   Majid Hayat Siddiqi. *Agrarian unrest in North India: the United Provinces, 1918–22.* New Delhi, India: Vikas, 1978. ISBN 0-7069-0592-X. ‣ Analysis of peasant mobilization in context of early Congress effort to build mass following. Should be read in contrast with subaltern studies and especially work of Gyan Pandey for its treatment of relations between agrarian politicians and Congress. [DEL]

15.720   R. Suntharalingam. *Politics and nationalist awakening in South India, 1852–1891.* Tucson: University of Arizona Press for Association for Asian Studies, 1974. ISBN 0-8165-0447-4 (cl), 0-8165-0468-7 (pbk). ‣ Social and institutional background to rise and spread of nationalism in Madras presidency. Best detailed introduction to issues of education, elites, and politics before emergence of non-brahman movement. [FFC]

15.721   D. A. Washbrook. *The emergence of provincial politics: the Madras presidency, 1870–1920.* Cambridge: Cambridge University Press, 1976. ISBN 0-521-20982-X. ‣ Traces movement of power from hinterland to Madras city through political channels established by colonial state. First to link agrarian political economy to nationalist politics at regional level. [DEL]

Religion, Politics, and the Partition of India

15.722   Sara F. D. Ansari. *Sufi saints and state power: the pirs of Sind, 1843–1947.* Cambridge: Cambridge University Press, 1992. ISBN 0-521-40530-0. ‣ Portrait of Muslim religious leaders of Sind as "collaborators" with British rule and participants in electoral politics leading to creation of Pakistan. Pure "Cambridge school" in its reliance on British official perspective and dismissal of indigenous culture. [DSL]

15.723   Bipan Chandra. *Communalism in modern India.* New

Delhi, India: Vikas, 1984. ISBN 0-7069-2510-6. ‣ Argues rise of political loyalties along Hindu versus Muslim lines is result of modern institutions and class interests in context of colonial rule rather than long-term cultural or religious difference. Strong statement of secular nationalist historiography. [DSL]

15.724 Partha Chatterjee. "Agrarian relations and communalism in Bengal, 1926–1935." In *Subaltern studies 1: writings on South Asian history and society.* Ranajit Guha, ed., pp. 9–38. Delhi: Oxford University Press, 1982. ISBN 0-19-561355-4. ‣ Argues for clear relation between property and social conflict that generated politics of antagonism between Hindus and Muslims in Bengal. Presents strong case for primacy of material subordination and conflict in this process. [DEL]

15.725 Suranjan Das. *Communal riots in Bengal, 1905–1947.* Delhi: Oxford University Press, 1991. ISBN 0-19-562840-3. ‣ Attributes changes in character of Hindu-Muslim riots and growing communalization in Bengal to better organization and closer ties to institutional politics. [AAY]

15.726 Veena Das, ed. *Mirrors of violence: communities, riots, and survivors in South Asia.* Oxford: Oxford University Press, 1990. ISBN 0-10-562547-1. ‣ Historical and more recent studies and interpretive essays on religious and ethnic violence in India, Pakistan, and Sri Lanka. Marshalls psychological, political, and cultural theoretical perspectives to understand nature of group conflict. [DSL]

15.727 Richard G. Fox. *Lions of the Punjab: culture in the making.* Berkeley: University of California Press, 1985. ISBN 0-520-05491-1. ‣ Anthropologist's interpretation of twentieth-century Sikh separatism as derived from differential growth of agricultural commodity production fostered under British rule along with military recruitment policies and racist ideologies. Painted in bold strokes, provocative critique of historical interpretations that are founded on static concepts of culture. [DSL]

15.728 Sandria B. Freitag. *Collective action and community: public arenas and the emergence of communalism in North India.* Berkeley: University of California Press, 1989. ISBN 0-520-06439-9. ‣ Development of politicized religious conflict between North Indian Hindus and Muslims in context of new public arenas and colonial institutions. Draws from example of European social historiography to achieve new insights into relation of religion and politics. [DSL]

15.729 David Gilmartin. *Empire and Islam: Punjab and the making of Pakistan.* Berkeley: University of California Press, 1988. ISBN 0-520-06249-3. ‣ Identifies foundations of Pakistan not in Hindu-Muslim conflict, but at regional level in conflicts and combinations of Ṣūfī institutions, rural lineages, reformist Islam, urban-based political leadership, and power of colonial state in British Punjab. Lucid analysis and exemplary archival research in wide variety of English and Urdu sources. [DSL]

15.730 Peter Hardy. *The Muslims of British India.* London: Cambridge University Press, 1972. ISBN 0-521-08488-1 (cl), 0-521-09783-5 (pbk). ‣ Argues that roots of Muslim separatism are to be found in precolonial history of Muslim rule and political thought and continued dominance of traditional elites. Work of scholar of premodern Islamic intellectual history, largely confined to northern India. [DSL]

15.731 Mushirul Hasan. *Nationalism and communal politics in India, 1885–1930.* New Delhi, India: Manohar, 1991. ISBN 81-85425-30-9. ‣ Detailed political history emphasizing great variation among Muslim political tendencies and role of short-term tactical errors on part of Indian National Congress in creation of nationalist unity. Thorough archival research, motivated by Indian nationalist perspective. [DSL]

15.732 Mushirul Hasan, ed. *Communal and pan-Islamic trends in colonial India.* Rev. ed. New Delhi, India: Manohar, 1985. ‣ Collected articles on political definition of Muslim identity in early twentieth-century India, with special attention to issues and leadership in selected regions and India as whole. Excellent introduction to current research by scholars in India. [DSL]

15.733 Anita Inder Singh. *The origins of the partition of India, 1936–1947.* Delhi: Oxford University Press, 1987. ISBN 0-19-561955-2. ‣ Useful if conventional political history. High politics of political calculation and maneuver among British, Congress, Muslim League, and provincial politicians in which short-term advantage overwhelms long-term goals. [DSL]

15.734 Ayesha Jalal. *The sole spokesman: Jinnah, the Muslim League, and the demand for Pakistan.* Cambridge: Cambridge University Press, 1985. ISBN 0-521-24462-5. ‣ Study of founder of Pakistan as political strategist for whom partition was reluctantly accepted substitute for decentralized India. Well researched and closely argued, but narrow in focus; accounts for Jinnah's motives but not larger movement that he lead. [DSL]

15.735 Rajiv A. Kapur. *Sikh separatism: the politics of faith.* London: Allen & Unwin, 1986. ISBN 0-04-320179-2. ‣ Examination of formation and conflicts of voluntary associations designed to unify and mobilize Sikhs in Punjab for sake of political autonomy. Useful political narrative but lacking depth in either cultural or socioeconomic analysis. [DSL]

15.736 Gail Minault. *The Khilafat movement: religious symbolism and political mobilization in India.* New York: Columbia University Press, 1982. ISBN 0-231-05072-0. ‣ Careful study of political motivation of major anticolonial movement, 1919–24, that combines Muslim solidarity with Indian nationalism. Serious consideration of religious symbolism. [DSL]

15.737 B. R. Nanda. *Gandhi: pan-Islamism, imperialism, and nationalism in India.* Bombay, India: Oxford University Press, 1989. ISBN 0-19-562299-5. ‣ Perceptive study of political and ideological motives and their limitations. Examines Gandhi's role in the Khilafat movement, 1919–24, working on behalf of pan-Islamic cause in order to foster national unity. [DSL]

15.738 David Page. *Prelude to partition: the Indian Muslims and the imperial system of control, 1920–1932.* Delhi: Oxford University Press, 1982. ISBN 0-19-561303-1. ‣ Namierite study of British and Indian political maneuvers that established political regime in Punjab dominated by mostly Muslim rural magnates with little interest in Indian nationalist project. [DSL]

15.739 Gyanendra Pandey. *The construction of communalism in colonial North India.* Delhi: Oxford University Press, 1990. ISBN 0-19-562552-8 (cl), 0-19-563010-6 (pbk). ‣ One of best studies of colonial discourse. Localized, historically dispersed conflicts between Muslims and Hindus in nineteenth century were reified by colonial analysis into chronic conditions of Indian society in general. [DSL]

15.740 Gyanendra Pandey. "Rallying round the cow: sectarian strife in the Bhojpuri region, c. 1888–1917." In *Subaltern studies 2: writings on South Asian history and society.* Ranajit Guha, ed., pp. 60–129. Delhi: Oxford University Press, 1983. ISBN 0-19-561990-0. ‣ Examination of economic and social tensions among particular groups that intersected with religious concerns in particular locality to create violent confrontations between Hindus and Muslims. Breaks down more monolithic explanations of Hindu-Muslim conflict. [DSL]

15.741 C. H. Philips and Mary Doreen Wainwright, eds. *The partition of India: policies and perspectives, 1935–1947.* 1969 ed. Cambridge, Mass.: MIT Press, 1970. ISBN 0-262-16043-9. ‣ Collection of academic articles, memoirs, journalistic essays, and other documents, largely dealing with high political negotiations, major personalities, and ideological statements relevant to partition of India. Mixed bag, but essential to historiography of seminal event. [DSL]

15.742 Francis Robinson. *Separatism among Indian Muslims: the politics of the United Provinces' Muslims, 1860–1923*. London: Cambridge University Press, 1974. ISBN 0-521-20432-1. ‣ Attempt to explain rise of Muslim separatist politics in terms of private ambitions of unscrupulous elite. Based on English sources, reflects official British perceptions. [DSL]

15.743 Khalid B. Sayeed. *Pakistan: the formative phase, 1857–1948*. 2d ed. George Cunningham, Foreword. London: Oxford University Press, 1968. ‣ History of political events and negotiations among the Indian National Congress, Muslim League, and British government with respect to Muslim separatism and partition of India. Standard work, lucid and politically astute with respect to elite political history. [DSL]

15.744 Farzana Shaikh. *Community and consensus in Islam: Muslim representation in colonial India, 1860–1947*. Cambridge: Cambridge University Press, 1989. ISBN 0-521-36328-4. ‣ Ideological and institutional history of Muslim responses to introduction of representative government, nationalism, and democratic movements. Controversial analysis from perspective of political theory, particularly with respect to relationship of Islam to challenges of modernity. [DSL]

Sri Lanka

15.745 Asoka Bandarage. *Colonialism in Sri Lanka: the political economy of the Kandyan highlands, 1833–1886*. Berlin: Mouton, 1983. ISBN 90-279-3080-5. ‣ Study of British colonial impact on Kandyan Ceylon during nineteenth century, especially with respect to agricultural development and political economy. Valuable for theoretical interpretation as well as useful maps and tables. [DEL]

15.746 C. S. Blackton. "The 1915 riots in Ceylon: a symposium." *Journal of Asian studies* 29.2 (1970) 219–66. ISSN 0021-9118. ‣ Examination of Ceylon's transition from peace to violence in 1915. Combines detailed account of events with contemporary interpretations. [DEL]

15.747 K. M. De Silva. *Social policy and missionary organizations in Ceylon, 1840–1855*. London: Longman for Royal Commonwealth Society, 1965. ‣ Study of missionary groups and their role in social policies of Ceylon's colonial government. Special attention to colonial policy with respect to Buddhist and Hindu institutions. [DEL]

15.748 K.N.O. Dharmadasa. *Language, religion, and ethnic assertiveness: the growth of Sinhalese nationalism in Sri Lanka*. Ann Arbor: University of Michigan Press, 1992. ISBN 0-472-10288-5. ‣ Study of literary and political movements that reinterpreted history and made Sinhalese language and Buddhist religion central to modern nationalism in colonial Ceylon in nineteenth and early twentieth centuries. Much original research, largely from within Sinhalese nationalist perspective. [DSL]

15.749 James S. Duncan. *The city as text: the politics of landscape interpretation in the Kandyan kingdom*. Cambridge: Cambridge University Press, 1990. ISBN 0-521-35305-X. ‣ Analysis of conflicting political symbolism and economic and political constraints involved in planning of royal capital of Kandy in early nineteenth century. Stimulating, though overly schematic in its long-term generalizations on Sri Lankan history. [DSL]

15.750 Richard Gombrich and Gananath Obeyesekere. *Bud-

dhism transformed: religious change in Sri Lanka*. Princeton: Princeton University Press, 1988. ISBN 0-691-07333-3. ‣ Study of transformations in beliefs, rituals, and emotional character of Sinhalese Buddhism since nineteenth century, influenced by Protestant Christianity, devotional Hinduism, and social change. Combines ethnography, history, and social commentary. [DSL]

15.751 Kitsiri Malalgoda. *Buddhism in Sinhalese society, 1750–1900: a study of religious revival and change*. Berkeley: University of California Press, 1976. ISBN 0-520-02873-2. ‣ Sophisticated analysis linking revival of Sri Lankan Buddhism to internal conditions and colonial intrusions. Useful corrective to views crediting Buddhist renaissance primarily to European Theosophical Society. [FFC]

15.752 Mick Moore. *The state and peasant politics in Sri Lanka*. Cambridge: Cambridge University Press, 1985. ISBN 0-521-26550-9. ‣ Detailed study of state development policy in Sri Lanka and its impact on agrarian politics. Essential for any study of current conflicts on island. [DEL]

15.753 Michael Roberts. *Caste conflict and elite formation: the rise of the Karava elite in Sri Lanka, 1500–1931*. Cambridge: Cambridge University Press, 1982. ISBN 0-521-23210-4. ‣ Study of status change and identity formation in Sri Lanka through emergence of entrepreneurial elites within originally low-status caste. Insightful analysis of Sinhalese socioeconomic conditions occasionally flawed by retrospective, essentialist interpretations. [FFC]

15.754 Michael Roberts, ed. *Collective identities, nationalisms, and protest in modern Sri Lanka*. Colombo: Marga Institute, 1979. ISBN 0-86-13158-12. ‣ Fifteen essays with extended introduction on issues of identity, nationalism, and resistance in colonial and postcolonial Sri Lanka. Valuable symposium reflecting perspectives of mid-1970s. [FFC]

15.755 John D. Rogers. *Crime, justice, and society in colonial Sri Lanka*. London and Riverdale, Md.: Curzon and Riverdale, 1987. ISBN 0-7007-0192-3, 0-913215-24-4. ‣ Discussion of crime in its economic, political, social, and cultural settings during British rule in Sri Lanka. Well-researched analysis of judicial ideology as well as social history. [DEL]

Nepal

15.756 Lionel Caplan. *Land and social change in East Nepal: a study of Hindu-tribal relations*. Berkeley: University of California Press, 1970. ISBN 0-520-01400-6. ‣ Historical and anthropological study of relationship between Limbus and brahman migrants since late eighteenth century. Traces changing relationships over time. [AAY]

15.757 Sherry B. Ortner. *High religion: a cultural and political history of Sherpa Buddhism*. Princeton: Princeton University Press, 1989. ISBN 0-691-09439-X (cl), 0-691-02843-5 (pbk). ‣ Study of Buddhist community that migrated from Tibet in sixteenth century and responses to Nepali state interventions and British imperialism in nineteenth and twentieth centuries. Uses oral history and speculative interpretation of limited documents to advance theory of structural continuity and historical change. [DSL]

15.758 Kumar Pradhan. *The Gorkha conquests: the process and consequences of the unification of Nepal, with particular reference to eastern Nepal*. Calcutta, India: Oxford University Press, 1991. ISBN 0-19-562723-7. ‣ Study of expansion of Gorkha kingdom into eastern Nepal and its affects on nature of state and society in context of British imperialism. [DEL]

15.759 D. R. Regmi. *Modern Nepal*. Vol. 1: *Rise and growth in the eighteenth century*. 2d ed. Calcutta, India: Mukhopadhyay, 1975. ISBN 0-88386-491-6 (set). ‣ Straightforward narrative account of events and personalities. First volume chronicles late eighteenth-century emergence of kingdom of Nepal; second volume, its early nineteenth-century clash with British. [AAY]

15.760 Mahesh C. Regmi. *An economic history of Nepal, 1846–1901.* Varanasi, India: Nath, 1988. ▸ Economic data and description organized into chapters on fiscal, agrarian, mining, forests, trade, taxation, and state regulation. Reads like gazetteer but contains useful data and references. [DEL]

15.761 Mahesh C. Regmi. *Landownership in Nepal.* Berkeley: University of California Press, 1976. ISBN 0-520-02750-7. ▸ Informative study of landholding patterns over period of two centuries and of effects of land reforms on traditional system of land tenure and on agrarian society. Examines categories of landholding and taxation systems. Clear descriptions and excellent references; best place to begin agrarian studies of Nepal. [AAY/DEL]

15.762 Mahesh C. Regmi. *A study in Nepali economic history, 1768–1846.* New Delhi, India: Manjusri, 1971. (Bibliotheca Himalayica, Series 1, 14.) ▸ Economic history of country during decisive period of territorial unification. Surveys economic and agrarian conditions paying special attention to administration, government policies, and land tenure. [AAY]

15.763 Mahesh C. Regmi. *Thatched huts and stucco palaces: peasants and landlords in nineteenth-century Nepal.* New Delhi, India: Vikas, 1978. ISBN 0-7069-0672-1. ▸ Agrarian relations and economic history of Nepal in nineteenth century. Concentrates on state's relations with landowning elite and elite's relations with peasants. [AAY]

15.764 Rishikesh Shaha. *Modern Nepal: a political history, 1769–1955.* Vol. 1: *1769–1885.* Vol. 2: *1885–1955.* New Delhi, India: Manohar, 1990. ISBN 81-85425-02-7 (set), 81-85425-03-5 (v. 1), 81-85425-04-3 (v. 2). ▸ Running account of political trends and developments in Nepal from 1769 to 1955. Structured according to government regimes with useful chronological index. [DEL]

15.765 Ludwig F. Stiller. *The rise of the house of Gorkha: a study in the unification of Nepal, 1768–1816.* New Delhi, India: Manjusri, 1973. ▸ Unification of Nepal, with special attention to geographic, geopolitical, and economic concerns. Valuable analysis of tactics used to overcome formidable Himalayan barriers to unity. [DEL]

15.766 Ludwig F. Stiller. *The silent cry: the people of Nepal, 1816–1839.* Kathmandu, Nepal: Sahayogi Prakashan, 1976. ▸ Account of aftermath of Treaty of Sagauli (1816) with British and establishment of Gorkha dominance in Nepal. Particularly concerned with state's economic penetration of village society. Sensitive if somewhat speculative history. [DSL]

15.767 Ludwig F. Stiller, ed. *Letters from Kathmandu: the Kot massacre.* Kathmandu, Nepal: Research Centre for Nepal and Asian Studies, Tribhuvan University, Kiritipur, 1981. ▸ Story of fall of Samrajya Laxmi Devi, Nepali queen, in 1846. Provides foundation from which other historical accounts of nineteenth-century political history have been written. [DEL]

15.768 John Whelpton. *Kings, soldiers, and priests: Nepalese politics and the rise of Jang Bahadur Rana, 1830–1857.* New Delhi, India: Manohar, 1991. ISBN 81-85425-64-7. ▸ Excellent political history, informed by theoretical issues on nature of South Asian monarchy. Examines intersection of Hindu kingship, British imperialism, and nation-state in nineteenth-century Nepal. [DSL]

SEE ALSO
9.332 Alistair Lamb. *Tibet, China, and India, 1914–1950.*

Afghanistan

15.769 Ludwig W. Adamec. *Afghanistan, 1900–1923: a diplomatic history.* Berkeley: University of California Press, 1967.

▸ Narrative of Afghan diplomacy leading to assertion of full national independence from Great Britain. Concentrates on Afghanistan's status during World War I. Well documented, widely cited. [RSN]

15.770 C. Collin Davies. *The problem of the north-west frontier, 1890–1908, with a survey of policy since 1849.* 2d rev. ed. London and New York: Curzon and Barnes & Noble, 1974. ISBN 0-06-491613-8. ▸ Analysis of British efforts to stabilize region adjoining Afghanistan at peak of Government of India's anxiety over tsarist Russian expansion. Definitive account of "Great Game." [RSN]

15.771 Mountstuart Elphinstone. *An account of the kingdom of Caubul.* 1839 3d ed. 2 vols. Olaf Caroe, Introduction. Karachi, Pakistan: Oxford University Press, 1972. ISBN 0-19-636062-5. ▸ Early nineteenth-century British official's examination of Afghan society during early Durrani monarchy. Still extensively quoted; perhaps most brilliant description of Afghanistan in English. [RSN]

15.772 W. K. Fraser-Tytler. *Afghanistan: a study of political developments in central and southern Asia.* 3d ed. M. C. Gillett, ed. London: Oxford University Press, 1967. ▸ Thorough historical survey emphasizing period of British involvement. Standard work on Durrani dynasty. [RSN]

15.773 Vartan Gregorian. *The emergence of modern Afghanistan: politics of reform and modernization, 1880–1946.* Stanford, Calif.: Stanford University Press, 1969. ISBN 0-8047-0706-5. ▸ Encyclopedic analyisis of recent Afghan history. Outstanding source on politics and society founded on remarkable command of highly varied language sources. [RSN]

15.774 Abd al-Rahman Khan. *The life of Abdur Rahman, amir of Afghanistan.* 1900 ed. 2 vols. Sultan Mahomed Khan, ed. M. E. Yapp, Introduction. Karachi, Pakistan: Oxford University Press, 1980. ISBN 0-19-577258-X (set). ▸ Autobiography, partly transcribed from dictation, of ruler who forcefully united Afghanistan at end of nineteenth century. Comprehensive apologia for brutal but epic reign. [RSN]

15.775 Charles Masson. *Narrative of various journeys in Balochistan, Afghanistan, and the Panjab, 1826–1838.* 1842–44 ed. 4 vols. Karachi, Pakistan: Oxford University Press, 1974–77. ISBN 0-19-577160-5 (set). ▸ Description of countryside, customs, society, and politics prior to the first Anglo-Afghan war. Classic of travel literature, unrivaled in detail and accuracy concerning Afghanistan and its region in early nineteenth century. [RSN]

15.776 Leon B. Poullada. *Reform and rebellion in Afghanistan, 1919–1929: King Amanullah's failure to modernize a tribal society.* Ithaca, N.Y.: Cornell University Press, 1973. ISBN 0-8014-0772-9. ▸ Study of Amanullah's foreign policy and reforms introduced to modernize Afghan society and economy. Argues tribal politics dominant factor in reaction that overwhelmed king's government. [RSN]

15.777 May Schinasi. *Afghanistan at the beginning of the twentieth century: nationalism and journalism in Afghanistan, a study of "Serâj ul-Akhbâr" (1911–1918).* Naples, Italy: Instituto Universitario Orientale, 1979. (Seminario di studi asiatici, 3.) ▸ Study of Mahmud Tarzi (1865–1933) and influence of Ottoman modernism and pan-Islamic movements in formulation of Afghan national identity through press. Significant examination of elite perspective and its selective response to European challenge. [DSL]

POSTCOLONIAL SOUTH ASIA

Comparative Studies and International Relations

15.778 James Warner Björkman, ed. *Fundamentalism, revivalists, and violence in South Asia.* Riverdale, Md.: Riverdale, 1988. ISBN 0-913215-06-6. ▸ Collected essays that span colonial and postcolonial eras and deal with politics of Hindu, Muslim, Buddhist, and Sikh identities in various South Asian settings. Useful overview of contemporary debates and research. [DSL]

15.779 Paul R. Brass and Marcus F. Franda, eds. *Radical politics in South Asia*. Cambridge, Mass.: MIT Press, 1973. ISBN 0-262-02099-8. ▸ Description of indigenous roots of radicalism in Bangladesh, Sri Lanka, and India, where various communist parties have been strongest. Nonpolemical, comprehensive treatment of institutionalized radicalism written by non-Marxists. [PKO]

15.780 Sisir Gupta. *Kashmir: a study in India-Pakistan relations*. 1966 ed. Bombay, India: Asia Publishing House, 1967. ▸ Detailed, exhaustive narrative history of Kashmir dispute in period up to 1964. Most persuasively documented and argued Indian view; balanced and still relevant. [PKO]

15.781 Ronald J. Herring. *Land to the tiller: the political economy of agrarian reform in South Asia*. New Haven: Yale University Press, 1983. ISBN 0-300-02725-7. ▸ Best account of agrarian reform; comparative analysis assessing prospects and accomplishments in different political climates in South Asia. Rich in detail and analytically sound; reference point for all subsequent work on subject. [DEL]

15.782 Steven A. Hoffmann. *India and the China crisis*. Berkeley: University of California Press, 1990. ISBN 0-520-06537-9. ▸ Thorough detailed analysis of 1962 border conflict. Balanced critique of earlier work makes this definitive account—pending release of all Indian and Chinese documents. [PKO]

15.783 Donald Eugene Smith, ed. *South Asian politics and religion*. 1966 ed. Princeton: Princeton University Press, 1969. ▸ Twenty-four essays on contemporary and historical aspects of relations between religion and political life in India, Pakistan, and Ceylon. Benchmark documentation of continuing significant issues for South Asian states and societies. [FFC]

Republic of India

15.784 Walter K. Andersen and Shridhar D. Damle. *Brotherhood in saffron: Rashtriya Swayamsevak Sangh and Hindu revivalism*. Boulder: Westview, 1987. ISBN 0-8133-7358-1 (pbk). ▸ Detailed though not exhaustive discussion of history and social background of keystone organization of 1990s emergence of Hindu nationalism. Strictly scholarly, avoids calling movement fascist. [PKO]

15.785 Donald W. Attwood. *Raising cane: the political economy of sugar in western India*. 1991 ed. Boulder: Westview, 1992. ISBN 0-8133-1287-6 (1991, cl), 0-8133-1428-3 (pbk). ▸ Historically sensitive village-centered study of impact of emergence of sugarcane economy and politics on farmer family mobility. Questions standard assertions on class relations, commercialization of peasant economy, and global political economy. [PKO]

15.786 Granville Austin. *The Indian Constitution: cornerstone of a nation*. Oxford: Clarendon, 1966. ▸ Clearly written, detailed account of making of constitution. Analysis of critical issues of federalism and fundamental rights using Constituent Assembly debates, other documents, and interviews with participants. Remains definitive treatment. [PKO]

15.787 Sumanta Banerjee. *India's simmering revolution: the Naxalite Uprising*. London: Zed; distributed by Biblio Distribution Center, 1984. ISBN 0-86232-037-2 (cl), 0-86232-038-0 (pbk). ▸ Careful, nuanced narrative of localized peasant uprisings of 1967–72, and accompanying split in Communist party of India (Marxist). Highly sympathetic account. [PKO]

15.788 Amrita Basu. *Two faces of protest: contrasting modes of women's activism in India*. Berkeley: University of California Press, 1992. ISBN 0-520-06506-9. ▸ Comparison of women's political dependency and autonomous action in two states in early

1980s, using micro- and state-level field and documentary sources. Major contribution for its firm empirical foundation. [PKO]

15.789 Paul R. Brass. *Language, religion, and politics in North India*. London: Cambridge University Press, 1974. ISBN 0-521-20324-4. ▸ Political scientist's attempt to explain successes and failures of religious and linguistic definitions of political solidarity—Muslims and Sikhs, Hindi, Urdu, Punjabi, and Maithili—before and after 1947. Important, though somewhat lacking in cultural analysis. [DSL]

15.790 Paul R. Brass. *Politics of India since independence*. Part 4. Vol. 1 of *The new Cambridge history of India*. Cambridge: Cambridge University Press, 1990. ISBN 0-521-26613-0 (cl), 0-521-39651-4 (pbk). ▸ Comprehensive survey of India's political development incorporating problems of national integration, ethnicity, and political economy. Emphasizes systemic crisis arising from excessive political centralization and ethnic mobilizations. [FFC]

15.791 Michael Brecher. *Succession in India: a study in decision-making*. London: Oxford University Press, 1966. ▸ Day-by-day account of political maneuvering during two transitions in aftermath of Nehru's death: to prime ministership of Lal Bahadur Shastri (1964) and Indira Gandhi (1966). Uses interviews with major participants and then presents semi-insider's but impartial view. Earlier title: *Nehru's Mantle: The Politics of Succession in India*. [PKO]

15.792 Jan Breman. *Of peasants, migrants, and paupers: rural labour circulation and capitalist production in West India*. Delhi: Oxford University Press, 1985. ISBN 0-19-561649-9. ▸ Historically informed sociology of rural labor relations, mobility, and living conditions, grounded in fieldwork and archival research. Model for historical interactions with social science technique and of labor studies. [DEL]

15.793 Jyotirindra Das Gupta. *Language conflict and national development: group politics and national language policy in India*. Berkeley: University of California Press, 1970. ▸ Political scientist's history and analysis of reformulation of India's internal boundaries along linguistic lines since independence. Somewhat undermined by unproblematic acceptance of standardized languages as social facts. [DSL]

15.794 Richard G. Fox. *From zamindar to ballot box: community change in a North Indian market town*. Ithaca, N.Y.: Cornell University Press, 1969. ▸ Analysis of change in agrarian North India from political system sustained by landlord property rights to one sustained by vote banks and electioneering. Political anthropology grounded in historical data and argumentation. [DEL]

15.795 Marcus F. Franda. *Radical politics in West Bengal*. Cambridge, Mass.: MIT Press, 1971. ISBN 0-262-06040-X. ▸ Detailed descriptive analysis of rise of radicalism in one of its two major strongholds as well as splits in Communist party. Thorough, non-Marxist account. [PKO]

15.796 Francine R. Frankel. *India's green revolution: economic gains and political costs*. Princeton: Princeton University Press, 1971. ISBN 0-691-07536-0. ▸ Case study of initial stages of changed seed and fertilizer agriculture in five far-flung districts. Attempts to establish correlation between transformations and rising discontent. [DSL]

15.797 Francine R. Frankel. *India's political economy, 1947–1977: the gradual revolution*. Princeton: Princeton University Press, 1978. ISBN 0-691-03120-7 (cl), 0-691-10072-7 (pbk). ▸ Best starting place for politics of economic development in independent India. Work to which scholars return repeatedly for information and insight. Most useful on political struggles surrounding Jawaharlal Nehru that laid basis for India's development regime. [DEL]

15.798 Francine R. Frankel and M.S.A. Rao, eds. *Dominance and state power in modern India: decline of a social order.* 2 vols. Delhi: Oxford University Press, 1989–90. ISBN 0-19-562098-4 (v. 1), 0-19-562261-8 (v. 2). ‣ Arguments on emergence of dominant class from among landowning castes midway in caste hierarchy. Full spectrum of Marxist to modernization approaches provide rich empirical accounting of caste politics in various states in all major regions of country. Locates origins deep within colonial history. [PKO]

15.799 James M. Freeman. *Untouchable: an Indian life history.* Stanford, Calif.: Stanford University Press, 1979. ISBN 0-8047-1001-5. ‣ Oral history construction of biography of marginal and disreputable individual in rural Orissa. Sympathetic but unromanticized. [DSL]

15.800 Marc Galanter. *Competing equalities: law and the backward classes in India.* Berkeley: University of California Press, 1984. ISBN 0-520-04289-1. ‣ Analysis of compensatory discrimination policies of independent India in historical, political, and legal frameworks. Thorough, sober exploration of sociolegal experiments and their results. [FFC]

15.801 Kathleen Gough. *Rural change in Southeast India: 1950s to 1980s.* Delhi: Oxford University Press, 1989. ISBN 0-19-562216-6. ‣ Summation of fieldwork in Tanjavur district, Tamilnadu, conducted over three decades. Comparative study of agrarian subregions, focusing on labor relations, especially on living conditions of landless agricultural laborers. History of labor in intensely cultivated rice region documented by fieldwork data. [DEL]

15.802 B. D. Graham. *Hindu nationalism and Indian politics: the origins and development of the Bharatiya Jana Sangh.* Cambridge: Cambridge University Press, 1990. ISBN 0-521-38348-X. ‣ Biography of party as institution focusing on organizational and leadership maneuvers of its ancestor, Bharatiya Janata party. Discusses political consequences of ideology, electoral tactics, and interest group links, but only to 1967. [PKO]

15.803 Akhil Gupta. "Revolution in Telengana, 1946–1951." *Social science probings* 3.1 (1986) 3–72. ‣ Overview and analysis of revolutionary movement in former state of Hyderabad, now part of Andhra Pradesh. Contributes to understanding of constraints on peasant revolution in South Asian setting. [DSL]

15.804 Henry C. Hart, ed. *Indira Gandhi's India: a political system reappraised.* Boulder: Westview, 1976. ISBN 0-89158-042-5 (cl), 0-89158-109-X (pbk). ‣ Examination of civil service, military, and Congress party during twenty-one-month emergency interlude (1975–77) of quasi-authoritarian rule. Also essays on historical precedent and social dynamics. Nuanced, durable analysis. [PKO]

15.805 Mark Juergensmeyer. *Religious rebels in the Punjab: the social vision of untouchables.* Rev. ed. Delhi: Ajanta, 1988. ISBN 81-202-0208-2. ‣ Study of lower-caste social reform movements and reevaluation of Hindu ideology in twentieth-century Punjab. Extensive bibliography to support further research. First published as *Religion as Social Vision: The Movement against Untouchability in Twentieth-Century Punjab.* [DEL]

15.806 Mary Fainsod Katzenstein. *Ethnicity and equality: the Shiv Sena party and preferential politics in Bombay.* Ithaca, N.Y.: Cornell University Press, 1979. ISBN 0-8014-1205-6. ‣ Emergence in linguistic ethnic-based economic grievances in Bombay of militant right-wing nativist political movement and party. Strong documentary and interview basis for analysis of Shiv Sena before reorientation to Hindu communalism. [FFC]

15.807 Stanley A. Kochanek. *The Congress party of India: dynamics of one-party democracy.* Princeton: Princeton University Press, 1968. ISBN 0-691-03013-8. ‣ Intimate history and ethnog-raphy of Congress in its period of dominance. Careful description. [PKO]

15.808 Atul Kohli. *Democracy and discontent: India's growing crisis of governability.* New York: Cambridge University Press, 1990. ISBN 0-521-39161-X (cl), 0-521-39692-1 (pbk). ‣ Non-apocalyptic, duly hedged argument that weakening institutions of Indian state are seriously challenged by multiplying demands. Empirical foundations mainly in 1980s restudy of Congress party politics in five districts studied by Weiner in 1960s (15.824). [PKO]

15.809 Atul Kohli, ed. *India's democracy: an analysis of changing state-society relations.* Rev. ed. Princeton: Princeton University Press, 1990. ISBN 0-691-07760-6 (cl), 0-691-02333-6 (pbk). ‣ Study of significant state institutions (parties, military), socio-economic actors (proprietary classes, middle class, and castes), and ethnic-separatist and grassroots movements as simultaneously constituents and challengers of democratic regime. Analytically provocative, diverse perspectives. [PKO]

15.810 H. R. Luthra. *Indian broadcasting.* New Delhi, India: Ministry of Information and Broadcasting, Publications Division, 1986. ‣ Narrative history of broadcasting from its origins in 1920s to rapid spread of television after 1982. Based on extensive archival research as well as insider experience. [DSL]

15.811 Baldev Raj Nayar. *India's mixed economy: the role of ideology and interest in its development.* Bombay, India: Popular Prakashan, 1989. ISBN 0-86132-217-7. ‣ Exhaustive analysis of emergence and strength of public-sector enterprises in postindependence era. Argues for primacy of politics and ideology. Powerful, thoroughly scholarly, nonradical, nonstatist critique. [PKO]

15.812 Baldev Raj Nayar. *Minority politics in the Punjab.* Princeton: Princeton University Press, 1966. ‣ Detailed narrative of Sikh political activity in Punjab before its breakup into Sikh and Hindu majority states in 1966. Political analysis uninfluenced by tragic turn of events since 1983. [PKO]

15.813 T. J. Nossiter. *Communism in Kerala: a study in political adaptation.* Berkeley: University of California Press for Royal Institute of International Affairs, London, 1982. ISBN 0-520-04667-6. ‣ Political scientist's history of Marxist political movements in Kerala and their relative success in democratic politics since 1957. Complex, well-documented analysis. [DSL]

15.814 T. J. Nossiter. *Marxist state governments in India: politics, economics, and society.* London: Pinter, 1988. ISBN 0-86187-456-0 (cased), 0-86187-457-9 (pbk). ‣ Concise overview of Communist party politics in Kerala, West Bengal, and Tripura. Marxist perspective giving full credit to accomplishments of those ministries. [PKO]

15.815 Lloyd I. Rudolph and Susanne Hoeber Rudolph. *In pursuit of Lakshmi: the political economy of the Indian state.* Chicago: University of Chicago Press, 1987. ISBN 0-226-73138-3 (cl), 0-226-73139-1 (pbk). ‣ Analysis of interplay of command politics of state institutions and Congress and Janata parties, whose historical development and electoral support until 1985 are analyzed, with "demand groups" located in economy. Interpretive political history that stakes out powerful non-Marxist position. [PKO]

15.816 Susanne Hoeber Rudolph and Lloyd I. Rudolph, eds. *Education and politics in India: studies in organization, society, and policy.* Cambridge, Mass.: Harvard University Press, 1972. ISBN 0-674-23865-6. ‣ Major synoptic introductory essay by editors and narrowly focused articles on social and political environment of rural through university education. Remains benchmark study. [PKO]

15.817 Milton Singer. *When a great tradition modernizes: an anthropological approach to Indian civilization.* New York: Praeger,

1972. ‣ Anthropological study of transformations of South Asian cultural forms in modern urban setting of Madras. Lucid discussion of theory and research helped set groundwork for later studies by scholars more familiar with language and culture. [DSL]

15.818 Donald Eugene Smith. *India as a secular state.* Princeton: Princeton University Press, 1963. ‣ Comprehensive exploration of issues and institutions of state-religion relations in India to 1960. Events have moved beyond narrative, but analysis is illuminating and historically relevant. [FFC]

15.819 M. N. Srinivas. *The remembered village.* Berkeley: University of California Press, 1976. ISBN 0-520-02997-6. ‣ Detailed description and analysis of social dynamics of Mysore village. Reconstructed from memory, has fluid ease of story told rather than society dissected, but with all profundity intact. Superb. [PKO]

15.820 Stree Shakti Sanghatana, comp. *"We were making history": life stories of women in the Telangana people's struggle.* New Delhi, India and London: Kali for Women and Zed, 1989. ISBN 0-86232-678-8 (cl), 0-86232-679-6 (pbk). ‣ Oral history, gathered by collective of feminist historians, of women who participated in Maoist peasant uprising, 1948–51, shortly after newly independent India annexed former Hyderabad state. [DSL]

15.821 Shashi Tharoor. *Reasons of state: political development and India's foreign policy under Indira Gandhi, 1966–1977.* New Delhi, India: Vikas, 1982. ISBN 0-7069-1275-6. ‣ Analytic, nondiplomatic history, locating foreign policy institutions firmly within domestic political system. Most thorough study of period and of Indira Gandhi's contribution. [PKO]

15.822 Achin Vanaik. *The painful transition: bourgeois democracy in India.* London: Verso, 1990. ISBN 0-86091-288-4 (cl), 0-86091-504-2 (pbk). ‣ Best articulated left-wing analysis of role of Indian state in postindependence economic development. Links India's rise to dominance in South Asia with internal economic transformation. [PKO]

15.823 Myron Weiner. *The child and the state in India: child labor and education policy in comparative perspective.* Princeton: Princeton University Press, 1991. ISBN 0-691-07868-8 (cl), 0-691-01898-7 (pbk). ‣ Account of nonimplementation of compulsory primary education policies, and consequences for persistence of child labor. Comparisons with United States, Europe, and developing countries to India's discredit. Scathing attack on elitist attitudes of government officials and others. [PKO]

15.824 Myron Weiner. *Party politics in India: the development of a multi-party system.* 1957 ed. Port Washington, N.Y.: Kennikat, 1972. ISBN 0-8046-1651-5. ‣ Ethnographies of parties opposed to Indian National Congress in mid-1950s and analysis of party system as dominated by Congress party. [PKO]

15.825 Myron Weiner. *The politics of scarcity: public pressure and political response in India.* Chicago: University of Chicago Press, 1962. ‣ Balanced, broad description of 1950s landscape of demand groups, within modernization perspective of interest groups. [PKO]

15.826 Myron Weiner. *Sons of the soil: migration and ethnic conflict in India.* Princeton: Princeton University Press, 1978. ISBN 0-691-09379-2. ‣ Study of nativism and ethnic conflicts arising from internal migration with case studies from Assam, tribal Bihar, and Andhra Pradesh and useful all-India theoretical discussion. Rational analysis of irrational phenomenon to 1970s. [FFC]

15.827 Myron Weiner and Mary Fainsod Katzenstein. *India's preferential policies: migrants, the middle classes, and ethnic equality.* Chicago: University of Chicago Press, 1981. ISBN 0-226-88577-1. ‣ Compares policies favoring "locals" over other Indian citizens in polity and struggles to introduce them in Bombay,

Andhra Pradesh, and Assam. Nuanced discussion of actual and potential conflict between democratic ideology of equality and group identity in multiethnic country. [PKO]

Pakistan and the Breakaway of Bangladesh

15.828 Akbar S. Ahmed. *Pakistan society: Islam, ethnicity, and leadership in South Asia.* Karachi, Pakistan: Oxford University Press, 1986. ISBN 0-19-577350-0. ‣ Anthropological essays on social solidarity in Pakistan that seek to establish long-range structural continuities and links to larger Islamic world. Non-Muslim South Asian connections (India and Hindus) notably absent. [DSL]

15.829 Akbar S. Ahmed. *Resistance and control in Pakistan.* 1983 ed. London: Routledge, 1991. ISBN 0-415-05797-3 (pbk). ‣ Account by Pakistani anthropologist and civil servant involved in pacifying tribal rivalry and resistance against state in Waziristan during 1970s. Remarkable for continuity with British colonial forms of knowledge and their political agenda. Earlier title: *Religion and Politics in Muslim Society.* [DSL]

15.830 James K. Boyce. *Agrarian impasse in Bengal: institutional constraints to technological change.* Oxford: Oxford University Press, 1987. ISBN 0-19-828532-9 (cl), 0-19-828567-1 (pbk). ‣ Historical argumentation for dynamics of immobility and poverty in Bangladesh today. Excellent connections between politics, social organization, inequality, and investment in development. Critical for historians of agriculture and development. [DEL]

15.831 Shahid Javed Burki. *Pakistan under Bhutto, 1971–1977.* 2d ed. London: Macmillan, 1988. ISBN 0-333-45085-X (cased), 0-333-45086-8 (pbk). ‣ Interpretive history of Zulfikar Ali Bhutto's impact on Pakistan's political development. Sound, sober assessment by economist. [PKO]

15.832 Keith B. Callard. *Pakistan: A political study.* London: Allen & Unwin, 1957. ‣ Careful narrative of first phase of undivided Pakistan's history. Has enormous advantage of lack of hindsight. [PKO]

15.833 Herbert Feldman. *The end and the beginning: Pakistan, 1969–1971.* 1975 ed. London: Oxford University Press, 1978. ISBN 0-19-215809-0. ‣ Spare narrative of breakup of Pakistan and emergence of Bangladesh. Superior to other accounts for its disinterested balance. [PKO]

15.834 Marcus F. Franda. *Bangladesh, the first decade.* New Delhi, India and Hanover, N.H.: South Asian Publishers and Universities Field Staff International, 1982. ISBN 0-88333-006-7. ‣ Contemporaneous snapshot views of events and forces that shaped new country in its first years. Covers politics, international relations, economy, and population. Careful if quasi-journalistic scholarship. [PKO]

15.835 Rounaq Jahan. *Pakistan: failure in national integration.* New York: Columbia University Press, 1972. ISBN 0-231-03625-6. ‣ Political history of Pakistan emphasizing exploitation of East Wing and emergence of Bengali nationalism. Persuasive analysis, moderate in tone (author is Bangladeshi); good use of then-available scholarship. [PKO]

15.836 Talukder Maniruzzaman. *The Bangladesh Revolution and its aftermath.* 2d ed. Dacca, Bangladesh: Bangladesh University Press, 1988. ‣ Detailed, sober narrative of liberation war of 1971, framed by historical background and postindependence developments. Well-informed, scholarly account. [PKO]

15.837 Omar Noman. *Pakistan: a political and economic history since 1947.* Rev. ed. London: Kegan Paul International; distributed by Routledge, Chapman & Hall, 1990. ISBN 0-7103-0389-0. ‣ Focus on Zulfikar Ali Bhutto and Zia eras (1971–88). Left-wing perspective carefully evaluating links between economic and political factors. Earlier title: *The Political Economy of Pakistan.* [PKO]

15.838 Richard Sisson and Leo E. Rose. *War and secession: Pakistan, India, and the creation of Bangladesh.* Berkeley: University of California Press, 1990. ISBN 0-520-06280-9 (cl), 0-520-07665-6 (pbk). ▸ Based, to significant extent, on interviews with participants including United States government officials. Untangles complex foreign relations dimension of breakup of Pakistan. Needs to be complemented by definitive Bangladeshi view, as yet unwritten. [PKO]

15.839 Anwar Hussain Syed. *The discourse and politics of Zulfikar Ali Bhutto.* Basingstoke, England: Macmillan, 1992. ISBN 0-333-56478-2 (cased), 0-333-57665-9 (pbk). ▸ Analysis of populist, authoritarian leadership in Pakistani politics when Bhutto was prime minister (1971–77) and its aftermath. Politically and culturally astute. [DSL]

15.840 Anwar Hussain Syed. *Pakistan: Islam, politics, and national solidarity.* Rev. ed. Lahore: Vanguard, 1984. ▸ Historical study of role of Islam in Pakistani politics, casting doubt on viability of national solidarity founded on religious injunctions. Concise, lucid analysis of limits of ideology. [DSL]

Sri Lanka

15.841 Radhika Coomaraswamy. *Sri Lanka: the crisis of the Anglo-American constitutional traditions in a developing society.* New Delhi, India: Vikas, 1984. ISBN 0-7069-2472-X. ▸ Politics of Sri Lanka as affected by Anglo-American constitutional ideals. Outlined account of cause, effect, and possible solutions to current ethnic conflict. [DEL]

15.842 K. M. De Silva and W. Howard Wriggins. *J. R. Jayewardene of Sri Lanka: a political biography.* Vol. 1: *1906–1956.* Honolulu, Hawaii: University of Hawaii Press, 1988. ISBN 0-8248-1183-6 (v. 1). ▸ Political biography of Sri Lanka's first president, with some attention to family history. Chronologically detailed study of important leader. [DEL]

15.843 Robert N. Kearney and Barbara Diane Miller. *Internal migration in Sri Lanka and its social consequences.* Boulder: Westview, 1987. ISBN 0-8133-7321-2 (pbk). ▸ Small, statistical demography linking settlement patterns and population variables to emergence of ethnic conflict. Useful for its data. [DEL]

15.844 James Manor. *The expedient utopian: Bandaranaike and Ceylon.* Cambridge: Cambridge University Press, 1989. ISBN 0-521-37191-0. ▸ Account of impact of S.W.R.D. Bandaranaike, prime minister in 1950s, on Sri Lankan society and politics through his quest for preeminence and power. [DEL]

15.845 James Manor, ed. *Sri Lanka in change and crisis.* New York: St. Martin's, 1984. ISBN 0-312-75452-3. ▸ Analysis of 1982–83 crisis from wide range of perspectives, from scholars to active (pseudonymous) participants. Covers 1982 elections and 1983 riots. Vivid, generally honest and agonized appraisal. [PKO]

15.846 A. Jeyaratnam Wilson. *The break-up of Sri Lanka: the Sinhalese-Tamil conflict.* Honolulu, Hawaii: University of Hawaii Press, 1988. ISBN 0-8248-1211-5. ▸ Account of disintegration of Sri Lanka concentrating on state policy and power with respect to Sinhalese-Tamil conflict. [DEL]

15.847 W. Howard Wriggins. *Ceylon: dilemmas of a new nation.* Princeton: Princeton University Press, 1960. ▸ Historical, economic, and constitutional background to postindependence politics and detailed analysis of religion and political change to 1959. Most exhaustive and balanced treatment of initial politics and transformative change. [PKO]

Afghanistan, Nepal, and Bhutan

15.848 Anthony Arnold. *Afghanistan's two-party communism: Parcham and Khalq.* Stanford, Calif.: Hoover Institution Press, Stanford University, 1983. ISBN 0-8179-7792-9 (pbk). ▸ Origin of

People's Democratic party and its factional rivalries, which materially complicated Soviet Union's effort to defeat Afghan resistance. Soundly documented and argued. [RSN]

15.849 Henry S. Bradsher. *Afghanistan and the Soviet Union.* Rev. ed. Durham, N.C.: Duke University Press, 1985. ISBN 0-8223-0556-9 (cl), 0-8223-0690-5 (pbk). ▸ Analysis of seizure of power by Afghan Communists, Soviet involvement leading to military intervention in 1979, early course of Afghan-Soviet war, and international responses. Definitive account so far, largely based on United States intelligence documents. [RSN]

15.850 Richard Burghart. "The formation of the concept of a nation-state in Nepal." *Journal of Asian studies* 44.1 (1984) 101–25. ISSN 0021-9118. ▸ Valuable interpretive analysis of ways in which indigenous culture and external pressures, notably British imperialism, converged to move Nepal in direction of nation-state polity. [DSL]

15.851 Pierre Centlivres. *Un bazar d'Asie centrale: forme et organisation du bazar de Tashqurghan.* Wiesbaden: Reichert with Harrassowitz, 1972. ISBN 3-920153-07-3. ▸ Geography, history, and social and economic account of Tashkurgan, strategically located trading center studied during 1960s. Major work of leading specialist on northern Afghanistan. [RSN]

15.852 Anthony Hyman. *Afghanistan under Soviet domination, 1964–91.* 3d ed. Basingstoke, England: Macmillan Academic and Professional, 1992. ISBN 0-333-49290-0 (cl), 0-333-49291-9 (pbk). ▸ Closely researched account of social and political conditions that enabled Afghanistan's Marxists to seize and squander power. Mixes journalistic reports with analysis of social dynamics shaping anti-Marxist resistance. [RSN]

15.853 Nancy Peabody Newell and Richard S. Newell. *The struggle for Afghanistan.* Ithaca, N.Y.: Cornell University Press, 1981. ISBN 0-8014-1389-3. ▸ Overview of Afghan politics leading to 1978 coup, Soviet invasion, and early phase of Afghan-Soviet war. Disputes general assumption in early 1980s that Soviet victory was inevitable. [RSN]

15.854 Richard S. Newell. *The politics of Afghanistan.* Ithaca, N.Y.: Cornell University Press, 1972. ISBN 0-8014-0688-9. ▸ Study of political and economic developments during experiment with constitutional monarchy, 1963–73. Examines cultural and demographic factors and changes in social dynamics. [RSN]

15.855 Leo E. Rose. *The politics of Bhutan.* Ithaca, N.Y.: Cornell University Press, 1977. ISBN 0-8014-0909-8. ▸ Overview of foreign relations, Constitution, and public administration of Himalayan kingdom with useful historical introduction. Poltical science from American cold war perspective. [DSL]

15.856 Olivier Roy. *Islam and resistance in Afghanistan.* 2d ed. Cambridge: Cambridge University Press, 1990. ISBN 0-521-39308-6 (cl), 0-521-39700-6 (pbk). ▸ Analysis of Islam as critical factor determining Afghan response to Soviet invasion and occupation. Widely influential interpretation of varieties of religious leadership that have dominated politics of Afghan resistance movement. [RSN]

15.857 Amin Saikal and William Maley. *Regime change in Afghanistan: foreign policy and the politics of legitimacy.* Boulder: Westview, 1991. ISBN 0-8133-1326-0. ▸ Examination of Afghan Marxist regime, politics of resistance and its foreign supporters, and military-political stalemate that led to Soviet withdrawal. Well-documented argument that overcomes urge to theorize. [RSN]

15.858 Rishikesh Shaha. *Politics in Nepal, 1980–1990: referendum, stalemate, and triumph of people power.* 2d rev. ed. New Delhi, India: Manohar, 1990. ISBN 81-85425-21-3. ▸ Political innovations established by King Birendra to shore up institution of monarchy against political parties; king overthrown by popular movement for democracy and human rights in 1990. Narrative history of recent events. [DEL]

15.859 M. Nazif Shahrani and Robert L. Canfield, eds. *Revolutions and rebellions in Afghanistan: anthropological perspectives.* Berkeley: Institute of Internal Studies, University of California, 1984. ISBN 0-87725-157-6. ▸ Fourteen anthropological accounts of context and responses to Marxist government and Soviet occupation of Afghanistan. Offers regional and ethnic perspectives that diverge sharply from metropolitan perspective of Kabul. [RSN]

DAVID K. WYATT

Southeast Asia

The term "Southeast Asia" came into general usage only after World War II and especially during the Vietnam War of the 1960s and 1970s. It is generally understood to comprise that corner of the Asian continent lying between India, China, and Australia, including the contemporary nation-states of Burma, Thailand, Laos, Cambodia, Vietnam, Malaysia, Singapore, Brunei, Indonesia, and the Philippines, in which a total of nearly half a billion people now live. It does not include Sri Lanka, Taiwan, or even the Andaman and Nicobar islands; nor does the region conventionally include neighboring portions of China and India, even though these regions, until quite recent times, often can most intelligibly be understood in a Southeast Asian context. As late as the 1950s, the study of Southeast Asia was an adjunct of colonial history and, like the region itself, was fragmented between the colonial powers—Britain, France, the Netherlands, Spain, and the United States. It tended to focus on archaeology and ancient history and on the activities of the colonial powers themselves in earlier centuries. It was supported primarily by the need to prepare colonial officials for careers in the region, for which purpose major centers of "colonial" scholarship developed in Paris, London, and Leiden, as well as within the region itself, most notably at Hanoi, where the venerable École Française d'Extrême-Orient was centered.

In the previous edition of this *Guide*, the section on Southeast Asia, edited by the late John M. Echols, included only two-thirds as many items as this new edition, and most of the items earlier listed are no longer included. The difference between the two editions says a great deal about the maturation of the field of Southeast Asian history over the past three decades. Thirty years ago, Southeast Asian history was hardly taught in American universities, and the few centers of such studies in the former colonial metropoli—Paris, London, Leiden—were winding down with the old colonial empires. At the same time, in the context of the latter stages of the Cold War and of a new globalism that were to bring intensified political, economic, and cultural contacts between the North Atlantic world and the former colonial and now newly independent nations, the cultures and histories of large portions of the world were becoming "relevant" and "interesting" in ways they never had been before. As a new generation of scholars were trained to staff expanding university systems, Southeast Asia became a major focus of attention, all the more as war in Vietnam came to engage the attention of much of the world for almost two decades.

From the early 1960s onward, a new generation of scholars was shaped by three abiding concerns. First, these historians rejected the monoculturalism and monolingualism of their predecessors and took seriously the cultures and languages of Southeast Asia. Whereas an earlier generation had preferred "objective" or "scientific" Western-language sources to indigenous ones, they now reversed the colonial hierarchy. Second, they were profoundly influenced by the social sciences, especially anthropology and political science, which at that time claimed to hold the key to an understanding of this Third World. Third, especially because of their fascination with colonialism and nationalism and with the dramatic and rapid manner in which so many Southeast Asian nations had attained independence from colonial rule, their interests were focused— excessively, as it turned out—on modern history, to the neglect of what they came to see as the antiquarianism and philologism of the colonial study of ancient and (for lack of a better word) medieval history. These commitments and prejudices also led them to concentrate especially on national, as opposed to subnational or regional, cultures and entities and to be far less concerned than they might have been with the history of the region as a whole. Some of the deficiencies of this new wave of Southeast Asian historiography have begun to be repaired in recent years, but far more remains to be done. There has been no major new synthetic view of Southeast Asian history as a whole since D.G.E. Hall's *A History of South-East Asia* (16.16), which defined the field in 1955. The existing historiography is extremely weak in intellectual and cultural history. Only bits and pieces of the economic history of the region have been produced, and even the diplomatic history of relations between Southeast Asian rulers and European and Asian countries is spotty. Social and gender history are poorly developed, with a few notable exceptions. Much of the work currently under way is (surely excessively) shaped by the enduring bitterness and battles of the 1960s and 1970s produced by the Indochina War, and continuing unevenness will result from the difficulties outside scholars face in trying to conduct serious archival research in Burma and Indochina. At least, as the research of the next generation of Southeast Asian historians proceeds, both in the region and abroad, scholars will be able to build upon a base much more solid and extensive than that existing only three decades ago.

The works listed below represent only a small sampling of the scholarship produced over the past three decades, or, for that matter, by a century of colonial scholarship. These underrepresent not only major contributions in other Western languages (notably French, Dutch, and Spanish) but also a substantial and growing body of work in the indigenous languages of the region. This listing overwhelmingly privileges publications in book form and slights an important body of scholarship that has appeared in article form. By now it should be powerfully clear that serious scholarship in Southeast Asian history is not possible without deep, serious study of the indigenous languages of the region, not only because of the abundant indigenous source material but also because of the significant scholarship produced within the region itself.

Of the scholarship described below, approximately one-tenth is general in nature, covering the whole region. Of the remainder, roughly three-fourths concerns the modern period (since 1750), while only one-fourth deals with earlier periods. The material is geographically unbalanced as well. English-language scholarship is most extensive on the largest country of the region, Indonesia, which in this respect also benefits from its proximity to lively scholarly traditions in Australia, and on the Philippines and Malaysia, where much higher education and scholarship has been conducted in English. English-language scholarship is much less well-developed on those countries where it has been difficult to conduct research over the past three decades—Burma and the countries of Indochina (Vietnam, Cambodia, and Laos).

No major bibliographies of Southeast Asian history have been produced within the past decade. Excellent scholarly aids are to be found in the World Bibliographical Series of country bibliographies produced by various authors, often historians, and published by the Clio Press. Excellent facilities now are established in the United States, Europe, and Australia for the study of Southeast Asia. The best library collections are to be found at Cornell University, the Library of Congress, Ohio University, and the Universities of Michigan, Wisconsin, Washington, and Hawaii, as well as in Kyoto, Canberra, Paris, London, and Leiden. Many of these libraries are linked electronically, facilitating interlibrary loans. Language programs are regularly held for all the major languages of the region, including a national summer intensive program in the United States.

Entries are arranged under the following headings:

Reference Works

General Studies

Early History to ca. 1300

Middle Period, ca. 1300–ca. 1750
General Studies
Mainland Southeast Asia: Burma, Siam, and Indochina
Island Southeast Asia: Malaysia, Indonesia,
and the Philippines

Modern Period, since 1750
General Studies
Burma
Thailand
Indochina
Vietnam
Cambodia
Laos
Malaysia, Singapore, and Brunei
Indonesia
Philippines

[Contributors: DKW = David K. Wyatt]

REFERENCE WORKS

16.1 *Atlas of South-East Asia.* D.G.E. Hall, Introduction. New York: St. Martin's, 1964. ‣ Excellent though increasingly dated. Historical maps on endpapers. [DKW]

16.2 J. G. de Casparis. *Indonesian chronology.* Leiden: Brill, 1978. (Handbuch der Orientalistik, Dritte Abteilung: Indonesien, Malaysia, und die Philippinen; Erster Band: Geschichte, Lieferung, 1.) ISBN 90-04-05752-8. ‣ Careful, detailed explanation of complex early and modern chronological systems in Indonesia, especially Java. Includes tables and guides to conversion. [DKW]

16.3 W. Ph. Coolhaas. *A critical survey of studies on Dutch colonial history.* 2d rev. ed. G. J. Schutte, ed. The Hague: Nijhoff, 1980. (Koninklijk Instituut voor Taal-, Land-, en Volkenkunde, Bibliographical series, 4.) ISBN 90-247-2307-8. ‣ Narrative-form bibliography of Dutch East and West India companies, dealing primarily but not exclusively with Indonesia. First published in Dutch in 1957 and twice updated. [DKW]

16.4 J. C. Eade. *Southeast Asian ephemeris: solar and planetary positions, AD 638–2000.* Ithaca, N.Y.: Cornell University, Southeast Asia Program, 1989. ISBN 0-87727-704-4. ‣ Essential reference for dealing with dates from Burma, Thailand, Cambodia, and Laos. Mainly tables; some extrapolation required; not for the fainthearted. Other volumes of tables in press. [DKW]

16.5 M. B. Hooker, ed. *Laws of South-East Asia.* 2 vols. Saint Paul: Legal, 1986–88. ISBN 0-409-99528-2 (set). ‣ Volume 1 contains selection of premodern legal texts; volume 2 covers European laws of colonial era. Good reference source. [DKW]

16.6 Jan M. Pluvier. *A handbook and chart of South-East Asian history.* Kuala Lumpur: Oxford University Press, 1967. ‣ Covers period since 1782 only. Lists of names of rulers and colonial authorities, plus prime ministers and heads of government. Useful chart demonstrating synchronisms. [DKW]

16.7 Than Tun, ed. *The royal orders of Burma, AD 1598–1885.* 10 vols. Kyoto: Kyoto University, Center for Southeast Asian Studies, 1983–90. ‣ Monumental compilation of decrees issued by successive kings of Burma from end of sixteenth century to end of indigenous rule in Burma in 1885. Each has full, annotated Burmese text, introduction, and summary in English. Summaries not always as full as users might wish, but give flavor of premodern government. [DKW]

GENERAL STUDIES

16.8 Barbara Watson Andaya and Leonard Y. Andaya. *A history of Malaysia.* New York: St. Martin's, 1982. ISBN 0-312-38120-4. ‣ Balanced and authoritative history from earliest times. Authors most at home in seventeenth and eighteenth centuries, but cover earlier and later periods intelligently. Best introduction to subject. [DKW]

16.9 *Bali: studies in life, thought, and ritual.* J. L. Swellengrebel, Introduction. Dordrecht: Foris, 1984. ISBN 90-6765-061-7. ‣ Translations of important Dutch scholarship on Bali. Introduction includes lengthy history of island. Other articles (especially by Goris and Korn) explore aspects of culture and history particularly useful for historians. Excellent bibliography. [DKW]

16.10 Harry J. Benda. *Continuity and change in Southeast Asia: collected journal articles of Harry J. Benda.* New Haven: Yale University, Southeast Asia Studies, 1972. (Southeast Asia Studies, Monograph series, 18.) ‣ Excellent collection of Benda's articles on modern political history, which helped define field in United States in 1960s. Note particularly articles on elites, popular rebellion, and World War II. [DKW]

16.11 Paul J. Bennett. *Conference under the tamarind tree: three essays in Burmese history.* New Haven: Yale University, Southeast Asia Studies, 1971. (Southeast Asia Studies, Monograph series, 15.) ‣ Three penetrating essays: northern Burma in fourteenth century, Burmese politics (1878–82), and comparison of mid-nineteenth-century Burmese minister Kinwun Mingyi and Vietnamese minister Phan Thanh Gian. [DKW]

16.12 David P. Chandler. *A history of Cambodia.* 2d ed. Boulder: Westview, 1992. ISBN 0-8133-0926-3. ‣ Modern standard history of Cambodia covers period only to 1954. Some parts very thin, especially fourteenth and fifteenth centuries. Short but well researched; very useful bibliographical essay. [DKW]

16.13 Renato Constantino. *A history of the Philippines: from the Spanish colonization to the Second World War.* New York: Monthly Review, 1975. ISBN 0-85345-394-2. ‣ Perhaps most popular of histories of Philippines, not without reason, but tends to see collective resistance to colonialism as primary motive force of history. [DKW]

16.14 Angel Martinez Cuesta. *History of Negros.* Alfonso Felix, Jr., and Caritas Sevilla, trans. Manila: Historical Conservation Society, 1980. ‣ Extensive work covering long span of Philippine history from perspective of sugar-growing island of Negros. Translated from Spanish; based primarily on Spanish archive sources. [DKW]

16.15 Lorraine Gesick, ed. *Centers, symbols, and hierarchies: essays on the classical states of Southeast Asia.* New Haven: Yale University, Southeast Asia Studies, 1983. (Southeast Asia Studies, Monograph series, 26.) ISBN 0-938692-04-6. ‣ Six long essays treat kingship and nature of the state in premodern Southeast Asia. Authors represent much of best in recent American scholarship on earlier Southeast Asian history. [DKW]

16.16 D.G.E. Hall. *A history of South-East Asia.* 4th ed. New York: St. Martin's, 1981. ISBN 0-312-38641-9 (cl), 0-312-38642-7 (pbk). ‣ Good synopses of history prior to 1300, and good coverage of European activities after 1511. Defined field of Southeast Asian history; little changed from 1955 first edition, when serious studies had hardly begun. [DKW]

16.17 G. E. Harvey. *History of Burma from the earliest times to 10 March 1824, the beginning of the English conquest.* 1925 ed. London: Cass, 1967. ‣ Still standard, although beginning to be superseded by modern monographs. Based on wealth of indigenous sources. Remarkable achievement by civil servant writing in his spare time, covering extensive range of Burmese sources. [DKW]

16.18 M. B. Hooker. *A concise legal history of South-East Asia.* New York: Oxford University Press, 1978. ISBN 0-19-825344-3. ‣ Excellent survey of legal traditions in Southeast Asia, which are extremely complex under pressures of Indian, Chinese, Islamic, and European colonial influences. Good bibliographical references to extensive literature. [DKW]

16.19 Htin Aung. *A history of Burma.* New York: Columbia University Press, 1967. ‣ Readable, general history, flawed by inconsistent scholarship and partisan tone. Coverage of sources superficial and neglect of European sources weakens argument. [DKW]

16.20 Le Thanh Khoi. *Histoire du Viet Nam, des origines à 1858.* Paris: Sudestasie, 1981. ISBN 2-85881-001-X. ‣ Standard general history of Vietnam up to beginnings of French colonial rule in 1858, based especially on Vietnamese sources. First published in 1955; this edition revised with new title. [DKW]

16.21 Adhémard Leclère. *Histoire du Cambodge depuis les première siècle de notre ère; d'après les inscriptions lapidaires, les annales chinoises et annamites, et les documents européen des six derniers siècles.* 1914 ed. New York: AMS Press, 1975. ISBN 0-404-54845-8. ‣ Extremely full and detailed, but not completely reliable; author tended to use sources uncritically. See Cœdès's review in *Bulletin de l'École Française d'Extrême-Orient* 14 (1914) 47–54. [DKW]

16.22 J. C. van Leur. *Indonesian trade and society: essays in Asian social and economic history.* James S. Holmes and A. van Marle, trans. The Hague: van Hoeve, 1955. ‣ Four seminal essays that first called for looking at Southeast Asian history, not from deck of European trading ship, but from wharves and shores. [DKW]

16.23 Anthony Reid, ed. *Slavery, bondage, and dependency in Southeast Asia.* St. Lucia: University of Queensland Press, 1983. ISBN 0-7022-1873-1. ‣ Fifteen essays on various forms of slavery and dependency found in Southeast Asia in premodern times. Uncommonly useful and interesting volume. [DKW]

16.24 Anthony Reid and David G. Marr, eds. *Perceptions of the past in Southeast Asia.* Singapore: Heinemann Educational Books for the Asian Studies Association of Australia, 1979. (Asian Studies Association of Australia, Southeast Asia publications series, 4.) ISBN 0-7081-1759-7 (cl), 0-7081-1760-0 (pbk). ‣ Careful, thoughtful review of indigenous historiography in premodern and modern Southeast Asia, presented at Australian conference. Twenty-two authors, primarily antipodean or Southeast Asian. Best book on subject. [DKW]

16.25 M. C. Ricklefs. *A history of modern Indonesia since c. 1300.* 2d ed. Stanford, Calif.: Stanford University Press, 1993. ISBN 0-8047-2194-7 (cl), 0-8047-2195-5 (pbk). ‣ Short and readable general history with extensive bibliography. Much stronger on Java than on outer islands. [DKW]

16.26 Alfredo R. Roces, ed. *Filipino heritage: the making of a nation.* 10 vols. Manila: Lahing Pilipino; distributed by Felta Book Sales, 1977–78. ‣ Massive, encyclopedic, well-illustrated compendium of articles by almost 200 authors (writing on their areas of expertise) on cultural topics, from prehistory through Spanish and American periods to World War II and independence. Very useful. [DKW]

16.27 Kernial Singh Sandhu and Paul Wheatley, eds. *Melaka: the transformations of a Malay capital, c. 1400–1980.* 2 vols. Kuala Lumpur: Oxford University Press, 1983. ISBN 0-19-580491-0 (set). ‣ Forty–six papers touching all aspects of long history of Malacca, port city that was among greatest in world in fifteenth century and has lived on in central position in Malay memory. [DKW]

16.28 John R. W. Smail. "On the possibility of an autonomous history of modern Southeast Asia." *Journal of Southeast Asian history* 2.2 (1961) 72–102. ISSN 0022-4634. ‣ Probably key article

in reshaping definition and methodologies of Southeast Asian history that began in early 1960s. [DKW]

16.29 Nicholas Tarling, ed. *The Cambridge history of Southeast Asia.* 2 vols. Cambridge: Cambridge University Press, 1992. ISBN 0-521-35505-2 (v. 1), 0-521-35506-0 (v. 2). ‣ Long-awaited, general history by distinguished contributors. Organized thematically and regionally, rather than chronologically; first volume covers to ca. 1800; second volume, nineteenth and twentieth centuries. [DKW]

16.30 G. R. Tibbetts. *A study of the Arabic texts concerning material on South-East Asia.* Leiden: Brill, 1979. (Oriental Translation Fund, n.s., 44.) ISBN 90-04-05783-8. ‣ Extremely dull but important examination of all classical Arabic texts concerning Southeast Asia. Established relations between these texts, dating from the ninth to the sixteenth century. [DKW]

16.31 C. M. Turnbull. *A history of Malaysia, Singapore, and Brunei.* Rev. ed. Boston: Allen & Unwin, 1989. ISBN 0-04-364025-7. ‣ General history by an acknowledged expert (first edition published 1979). Good bibliography. [DKW]

16.32 O. W. Wolters. *History, culture, and region in Southeast Asian perspectives.* Singapore: Institute of Southeast Asian Studies, 1982. ISBN 9971-902-42-7. ‣ Sage collection of essays on whether Southeast Asia bound together solely by geography or whether region distinguished by commonalities of culture and intraregional relationships translating into shared historical identity. Essential introduction to the field. [DKW]

16.33 David K. Wyatt. *Thailand: a short history.* New Haven: Yale University Press, 1984. ISBN 0-300-03054-1 (cl), 0-300-03582-9 (pbk). ‣ Standard history of Thailand from prehistoric period to the early 1980s. [DKW]

EARLY HISTORY TO ca. 1300

16.34 Michael Aung-Thwin. *Pagan: the origins of modern Burma.* Honolulu: University of Hawaii Press, 1985. ISBN 0-8248-0960-2. ‣ Major synthetic treatment of earliest history (in eleventh to thirteenth centuries). Includes much material on economic bases of Burma's civilization in agricultural landholdings; has engendered much debate. [DKW]

16.35 Lawrence Palmer Briggs. *The ancient Khmer empire.* Philadelphia: American Philosophical Society, 1951. (Transactions of the American Philosophical Society, n.s. 41, pt. 1.) ‣ Extended, well-illustrated study of ancient Cambodian history, based primarily on work of Cœdès and other French scholars. Better on arts, architecture, and monumental remains than on social and economic developments. [DKW]

16.36 Adhir Chakravarti. *The Sdok Kak Thom inscription.* 2 vols. Calcutta: Sanskrit College, 1978–80. (Calcutta Sanskrit College research series, 111–112.) ‣ Magisterial two-volume translation and exposition of one of most important inscriptions of ancient kingdom of Angkor; provides key evidence concerning foundation of *devarāja* (god-king) institution. [DKW]

16.37 Chou Ta-kuan. *Mémoires sur les coutumes du Cambodge de Tcheou Ta-kouan.* Rev. ed. Paul Pelliot, ed. and trans. Paris: Adrien-Maisonneuve, 1951. (Œuvres posthumes de Paul Pelliot, 3.) ‣ Classical account on ancient Angkor by Chinese envoy who visited there in 1296–97. Extremely detailed and thorough, though incomplete. English translation (by J. Gilman d'Arcy Paul) published under title, *Notes on the Customs of Cambodia,* 1967 ed. (1987); lacks Pelliot's extensive annotation. [DKW]

16.38 George Cœdès. *The indianized states of Southeast Asia.* Walter F. Vella, ed. Susan Brown Cowing, trans. Honolulu: University of Hawaii Press, 1968. ‣ Magisterial account of earliest history, to 1300, virtually devoid of analysis. Extraordinary accomplishment, demonstrating enormous range and erudition of author's scholarship. Translation of his classic, *Les états hindouises de l'Asie du sud-est*, first published in 1944 and 1948 and last revised in 1964. [DKW]

16.39   George Cœdès, ed. and trans. *Inscriptions du Cambodge*. 8 vols. Paris: de Boccard, 1937–66. (École Française d'Extrême-Orient, Collection de textes et documents sur l'Indochine, 3.7.) ▸ Monumental collection of most of lithic inscriptions of ancient Cambodia, geographical extent of which spills over into modern Thailand, Laos, and Vietnam. Edition is not complete or self-contained, as many additional inscriptions edited by Cœdès were published in *Bulletin de l'École Française d'Extrême-Orient*. Available on microfilm from Ithaca, N.Y.: Cornell University Libraries (1987). [DKW]

16.40   Juan R. Francisco. *Philippine palaeography*. Quezon City: Linguistic Society of the Philippines, 1973. (*Philippine journal of linguistics*, Special monograph issue, 3.) ISSN 0048-3796. ▸ Modest but thorough and systematic examination of pre-Hispanic writing systems of Philippines. Author argues for Sumatran (Indonesia) origins, perhaps in twelfth to fourteenth centuries. [DKW]

16.41   Juan R. Francisco. *The Philippines and India: essays in ancient cultural relations*. Manila: National Book Store, 1971. ▸ Concern for cultural relations, not directly with India but rather with "indianized" Java, Sumatra, and Malay Peninsula, mainly in tenth to twelfth centuries. [DKW]

16.42   Bernard Philippe Groslier and Jacques Arthaud. *Angkor: art and civilization*. Rev. ed. Eric Ernshaw Smith, trans. New York: Praeger, 1966. ▸ Classic coffee-table book on Angkor, Cambodia's great capital, ninth to thirteenth century, by conservator (Groslier) long in charge of French archaeological service's efforts to excavate and renovate old city. [DKW]

16.43   Kenneth R. Hall. *Maritime trade and state development in early Southeast Asia*. Honolulu: University of Hawaii Press, 1985. ISBN 0-8248-0843-6 (cl), 0-8248-0959-9 (pbk). ▸ Innovative attempt to build on work of Cœdès by examining relationship between movements in international trade and growth and decline of political systems. Somewhat careless in editing of sources and rather more assertive than evidence allows. [DKW]

16.44   Friedrich Hirth and W. W. Rockhill, eds. and trans. *Chau Ju-kua: his work on the Chinese and Arab trade in the twelfth and thirteenth centuries, entitled Chu-fan-chi*. 1911 ed. Amsterdam: Oriental Press, 1966. ▸ Lovely account of trading countries of Asia, and especially Southeast Asia, based on merchants' testimony in Canton in early thirteenth century. Durable translation. Standard work of Southeast Asian and Chinese maritime history. [DKW]

16.45   Karl L. Hutterer. *An archaeological picture of a pre-Spanish Cebuano community*. Cebu City, Philippines: University of San Carlos, 1973. ▸ Based on archaeological excavations on Cebu, where Magellan landed in 1521. Describes thriving, complex pre-Hispanic culture that had much in common with other sites elsewhere in Southeast Asia. [DKW]

16.46   Karl L. Hutterer, ed. *Economic exchange and social interaction in Southeast Asia: perspectives from prehistory, history, and ethnography*. Ann Arbor: University of Michigan, Center for South and Southeast Asian Studies, 1977. (Michigan papers on South and Southeast Asia, 13.) ISBN 0-89148-013-7. ▸ Based on evidence from wide variety of sources, traces central importance of regional trade in stimulating cultural and economic change in first millennium CE (and before). Excellent collection of essays. [DKW]

16.47   F. Landa Jocano. *Philippine prehistory: an anthropological overview of the beginnings of Filipino society and culture*. Quezon City: University of the Philippines, Center for Advanced Studies, 1975. ▸ Adventurous and original examination of pre-Hispanic

Philippines. Stresses local innovations and adoptions, minimizes significance of cultural influences from outside archipelago. [DKW]

16.48   Antoinette M. Barrett Jones. *Early tenth-century Java from the inscriptions: a study of economic, social, and administrative conditions in the first quarter of the century*. Dordrecht: Foris, 1984. (Verhandelingen van het Koninklijk Instituut voor Taal-, Land-, en Volkenkunde, 107.) ISBN 90-6765-062-5 (pbk). ▸ Conventional treatment of trade, religious institutions, administration, and taxation and revenue in tenth-century Java, based on close reading of extensive epigraphic evidence. [DKW]

16.49   N. J. Krom. "Indo-Javanese history." *Journal of the Greater India Society* 16 (1957) 1–82. ▸ Very conservative, old treatment of relationship between Java and Indonesia in ancient times, taking very narrow view of subject. Based on his work from 1920s and 1930s; translated from Dutch. [DKW]

16.50   Hermann Külke. *The devaraja cult*. I. W. Mabbett, trans. Ithaca, N.Y.: Cornell University, Southeast Asia Program, 1978. (Southeast Asia Program, Data paper, 108.) ISBN 0-88727-108-9. ▸ Major reinterpretation of *devarāja* (god-king) concept in ancient Cambodia, based on rereading of old epigraphic evidence. First published in German in 1974. [DKW]

16.51   G. H. Luce. "The early Syam in Burma's history." *Journal of the Siam Society* 46.2, 47.1 (1958–59) 123–214, 59–101. ISSN 0304-226X. ▸ Superb analysis of Chinese sources for what they reveal about developments in Siam. Definitive account. [DKW]

16.52   G. H. Luce. *Old Burma—early Pagán*. 3 vols. Locust Valley, N.Y.: Augustin for Artibus Asiae and New York University, Institute of Fine Arts, 1969–70. (Artibus Asiae, Supplementum, 25.) ISBN 0-686-92654-4. ▸ *Magnum opus* of one of great modern historians of Burma. Careful, detailed treatment of kingdom of Pagan, eleventh to thirteenth century. [DKW]

16.53   R. C. Majumdar. *Champā: history and culture of an Indian colonial kingdom in the Far East, second to sixteenth century AD*. 1927 ed. Delhi: Gian, 1985. ▸ Author's claim of "Indian colonial empire" in Southeast Asia largely outdated but much material on ancient Champa, on central and southern coast of Vietnam, unavailable elsewhere in English. Includes text of many Cham inscriptions. [DKW]

16.54   Georges Maspero. *Le royaume de Champa*. Paris: van Oest, 1928. ▸ Lamentably only full treatment of the vitally important history of Champa, arguably first indianized state of Southeast Asia, that flourished on Vietnamese coast in the first millennium CE. Dated but not yet superseded. [DKW]

16.55   Pe Maung Tin and G. H. Luce, trans. *The "Glass Palace Chronicle" of the kings of Burma*. 1923 ed. New York: AMS Press, 1976. ▸ Classic translation of premodern Burmese historiography, covering empire of Pagan in eleventh through thirteenth centuries. English prose accurate, though pretending to medievalism. [DKW]

16.56   Paul Pelliot. "Deux itinéraires de Chine en Inde à la fin du huitième siècle." *Bulletin de l'École Française d'Extrême-Orient* 4 (1904) 131–413. ISSN 0336-1519. ▸ Classical mining of Chinese sources for information concerning early Southeast Asian polities at end of eighth century. Basic Chinese material comes from pilgrims who traversed region en route to India. [DKW]

16.57   Paul Pelliot. "Le Fou-nan." *Bulletin de l'École Française d'Extrême-Orient* 3 (1903) 248–303. ISSN 0336-1519. ▸ Scholarship for almost a century referred to kingdom of "Funan," in general area of Cambodia and southern Vietnam, citing invariably this article based on Chinese reports. Admirably presented evidence has been reread by Claude Jacques in Smith and Watson, eds. 16.62. [DKW]

16.58 H. G. Quaritch Wales. *Dvâravatî, the earliest kingdom of Siam (sixth to eleventh century AD)*. London: Quaritch, 1969. ‣ Dry, cultural approach to polity that controlled central Thailand in centuries before Angkor's power extended into region. Evidence entirely epigraphic, archaeological, and numismatic. Later scholarship, primarily in Thai, has gone beyond Wales. [DKW]

16.59 Sachchidanand Sahai. *Les institutions politiques et l'organisation administrative du Cambodge ancien (sixième à treizième siècles)*. Paris: L'École Française d'Extrême-Orient, 1970. (Publications de l'École Française d'Extrême-Orient, 75.) ‣ Synoptic, synthetic, and detailed epigraphic analysis of ancient Cambodian institutions by one of George Cœdès's last students. [DKW]

16.60 Himansu Bhusan Sarkar. *Corpus of the inscriptions of Java (Corpus inscriptionum Javanicarum) up to 928 AD*. 2 vols. Calcutta: Mukhopadhyay, 1971–72. ‣ Massive collection of 112 Old Javanese and Sanskrit inscriptions from Java, expertly translated and explicated. Contains wealth of information on virtually all subjects. [DKW]

16.61 William Henry Scott. *Prehispanic source materials for the study of Philippine history*. Rev. ed. Quezon City: New Day, 1984. ISBN 971-10-0226-4 (pbk, bookprint), 971-10-0227-2 (pbk, newsprint). ‣ Refreshing and original approach to pre-Hispanic Philippines that cuts through several generations of speculation and deals with hard data, notably early Chinese accounts and fruits of archaeological and prehistoric research. [DKW]

16.62 R. B. Smith and W. Watson, eds. *Early South East Asia: essays in archaeology, history, and historical geography*. New York: Oxford University Press, 1979. ISBN 0-19-713587-0. ‣ Weighty collection of papers from conference (London, 1973). First half deals with prehistory; second half with first millennium CE. Jacques's article on "Funan" particularly important, but almost all profitable for readers. [DKW]

16.63 Keith Weller Taylor. *The birth of Vietnam*. Berkeley: University of California Press, 1983. ISBN 0-520-04428-2 (cl), 0-520-07417-3 (pbk). ‣ Treats earliest phase of Vietnamese history, to tenth century, from Chinese and Vietnamese sources. Sensibly sifts fact from legends in extremely rich written tradition dating back more than a millennium. Pioneering work. [DKW]

16.64 Paul Wheatley. *The Golden Khersonese: studies in the historical geography of the Malay Peninsula before AD 1500*. Kuala Lumpur: University of Malaya Press, 1961. ‣ Classic account of early history of Malay Peninsula (including areas now in Thailand), employing sources from broad range of languages, especially Chinese. Marvelous maps. Careful, thorough study; not yet superseded. [DKW]

16.65 Paul Wheatley. *Nagara and commandery: origins of the Southeast Asian urban traditions*. Chicago: University of Chicago, Department of Geography, 1983. (Department of Geography research papers, 207–208.) ISBN 0-89065-113-2. ‣ Detailed, erudite treatment of differing origins of urban traditions in Vietnam, in indianized portions of Indochina (including Burma), and in island world (Malay Peninsula and Java) in first millennium CE. [DKW]

16.66 O. W. Wolters. *Early Indonesian commerce: a study of the origins of Srivijaya*. Ithaca, N.Y.: Cornell University Press, 1967. ‣ Classic study of western Indonesia in first millennium CE, based primarily on Chinese sources. Model of reasoning and presentation. Locates ancient empire of Śrīvijaya on southeast coast of Sumatra. [DKW]

SEE ALSO

2.58 Charles Higham. *The archaeology of mainland Southeast Asia*.

MIDDLE PERIOD, ca. 1300–ca. 1750
General Studies

16.67 Thome Pires. *The "Suma Oriental" of Tomé Pires, an account of the East, from the Red Sea to Japan, written in Malacca and India in 1512–1515, and "The book of Francisco Rodrigues," rutter of a voyage in the Red Sea, nautical rules, almanack, and maps, written and drawn in the East before 1515*. 2 vols. Armando Cortesao, ed. and trans. London: Hakluyt Society, 1944. (Works issued by the Hakluyt Society, Second series, 89–90.) ‣ Extraordinary account of Asia as seen by Portuguese apothecary in Malacca; particularly full on Southeast Asia. Useful for all scholars working on fifteenth and sixteenth centuries. [DKW]

16.68 H. G. Quaritch Wales. *Ancient South-East Asian warfare*. 1900 ed. London: Quaritch, 1952. ‣ Anthropologist's extended treatment of premodern warfare. Treats primitive warfare, Chinese influence, and warfare as possibly influenced by Indian military theory in Burma, Siam, Cambodia, and Indonesia. [DKW]

16.69 Anthony Reid. *Southeast Asia in the age of commerce, 1450–1680*. Vol. 1: *The lands below the winds*. Vol. 2: *Expansion and crisis*. New Haven: Yale University Press, 1988–93. ISBN 0-300-03921-2 (v. 1, cl), 0-300-04750-9 (v. 1, pbk), 0-300-05412-2 (v. 2, cl). ‣ Braudelian overview of this long period based primarily on European travelers' accounts and records. [DKW]

SEE ALSO
10.378 Ma Huan. *Ying-yai sheng-lan*.

Mainland Southeast Asia: Burma, Siam, and Indochina

16.70 Charles Archaimbault. *Contribution à l'étude d'un cycle de légendes Lau*. Paris: L'École Française d'Extrême-Orient, 1980. (Publications de l'École Française d'Extrême-Orient, 119.) ISBN 2-85539-719-7. ‣ Superb translation and analysis of various versions (manuscripts reproduced in appendix) of chronicles and historical legends of That Phanom region of middle Mekong River. Author's erudition formidable. [DKW]

16.71 Aroonrut Wichienkeeo and Gehan Wijeyewardene, eds. *The Laws of King Mangrai (Mangrayathammasart): the "Wat Chang Kham," Nan manuscript from the Richard Davis Collection*. Aroonrut Wichienkeeo, trans. Canberra: Richard Davis Fund, 1986. ISBN 0-9589029-0-9 (cl), 0-86784-775-1 (pbk). ‣ Traditional law code from kingdom of Lan Na, at Chiangmai in northern Thailand used until twentieth century, dated by tradition to beginning of fourteenth century. Argument that core may be that old, but most is somewhat later. [DKW]

16.72 Michael Aung-Thwin. *Irrigation in the heartland of Burma: foundations of the pre-colonial Burmese state*. DeKalb: Northern Illinois University, Center for Southeast Asian Studies, 1990. (Center for Southeast Asian Studies, Occasional paper, 15.) ISBN 1-877979-15-5. ‣ Careful, well-illustrated analysis of precolonial irrigation system of northern Burma, in what is called Dry Zone. Based especially on epigraphic sources. [DKW]

16.73 Mabel Haynes Bode. *The Pali literature of Burma*. 1909 ed. London: Royal Asiatic Society; distributed by Luzac, 1966. ‣ Old, still valuable examination of premodern Burma's intellectual life, focusing primarily on Pali-language works, both religious and secular, found in Buddhist monasteries. [DKW]

16.74 Charnvit Kasetsiri. *The rise of Ayudhya: a history of Siam in the fourteenth and fifteenth centuries*. Kuala Lumpur: Oxford University Press, 1976. ISBN 0-19-580313-2. ‣ First detailed treatment of subject. Emergence of Thai political power in what was later to become Thailand. Argument for utility of indigenous historical sources and continuities before and after foundation of Ayudhya in 1351. [DKW]

16.75 O. Frankfurter, trans. "Translation of events in Ayuddhya, 686–966." *Journal of the Siam Society* 6.3 (1909) 1–21. ISSN 0304-226X. ‣ Translation of so-called Luang Prasœt edition of royal chronicles of Ayudhya (Siam) from 1324 to 1604 CE. Original written in 1680. [DKW]

16.76 Bernard Philippe Groslier. *Angkor et le Cambodge au seizième siècle d'aprés les sources portugaises et espagnoles*. Paris: Presses Universitaires de France, 1958. (Annales du Musée Guimet, Bibliothèque d'études, 63.) ‣ Introductory section on historical background since 1431, followed by sections on Angkor and Cambodia as described in sixteenth-century Spanish and Portuguese sources. Interesting plates and maps, including maps superimposed on aerial views of region's irrigation system. [DKW]

16.77 D.G.E. Hall. *Early English intercourse with Burma, 1587–1743*. 1928 rev. ed. New York: Barnes & Noble, 1968. ISBN 0-389-01075-8. ‣ Old-fashioned but thorough and unsuperseded account, based entirely on English sources, with "The Tragedy of Negrais" as new appendix. Available on microfilm from Boulder: University of Colorado, Library Reproduction Service (1980). [DKW]

16.78 E. W. Hutchinson. *Adventurers in Siam in the seventeenth century*. 1940 ed. Bangkok: DD Books, 1985. ISBN 974-405-475-1. ‣ Still definitive account of complex doings in late seventeenth century involving various French, Dutch, English, Greek, and other figures. Based entirely on careful, thorough examination of Western archives and published sources. [DKW]

16.79 Victor B. Lieberman. *Burmese administrative cycles: anarchy and conquest, c. 1580–1760*. Princeton: Princeton University Press, 1984. ISBN 0-691-05407-X. ‣ Innovative, provocative examination of almost completely neglected period using primarily Burmese-language sources. Argues cyclicality of premodern Burmese history, in which successive administrations sowed seeds of their own decline. [DKW]

16.80 Mak Phoen and Khin Sok, eds. and trans. *Chroniques royales du Cambodge*. 3 vols. Paris: École française d'Extrême-Orient, 1981–88. (L'École Française d'Extrême-Orient, Collection de textes et documents sur l'Indochine, 13.) ISBN 2-85539-537-2 (v. 2–3). ‣ Careful edition of Cambodian chronicles over very difficult period; comparisons with variant editions. [DKW]

16.81 Nguyen Ngoc Huy, Ta Van Tai, and Tran Van Liem, trans. *The Lê Code: law in traditional Vietnam, a comparative Sino-Vietnamese legal study with historical-juridical analysis and annotations*. 3 vols. Athens: Ohio University Press, 1987. ISBN 0-8214-0630-2. ‣ Discussion of Lê dynasty law code, compiled in fifteenth century, widely believed to be most Vietnamese, as opposed to Chinese, of Vietnamese law codes. Beautiful edition, major asset to scholarship on history of period. [DKW]

16.82 Camille Notton, trans. *Annales du Siam*. 4 vols. Paris: Lavazelle, 1926–39. ‣ Careful translations of various early chronicles by then-French consul in Chiang Mai. Volume 1 includes legendary chronicles, volume 2 the chronicle of Lamphun, volume 3 the important chronicle of Chiang Mai, and volume 4 historical legends of central Thailand. Exceptionally well done. [DKW]

16.83 Prasert na Nagara and Alexander B. Griswold. *Epigraphic and historical studies*. Bangkok: Historical Society, 1992. ISBN 974-88735-5-2. ‣ Enormously erudite study of inscriptions of kingdom of Sukhōthai from thirteenth through fifteenth centuries. Sets standard for all future work. Supersedes all Cœdès's translations of same inscriptions in his *Recueil des inscriptions du Siam*. [DKW]

16.84 Ratanapañña Thera. *The sheaf of garlands of the epochs of the conqueror, being a translation of Jinakâlamâlîpakaranam of Ratanapanna Thera of Thailand*. 1968 ed. Saeng Manavidura, Introduction. N. A. Jayawickrama, ed. and trans. London: Luzac

for the Pali Text Society, 1978. (UNESCO collection of representative works, Translation series, 36.) ‣ Chronicle written at Chiang Mai (northern Thailand), early sixteenth century by local monk; history of Buddhism. Useful chiefly for accurate observations on local history and for revealing principles of local historiography. [DKW]

16.85 Sao Saimong Mangrai. *The "Pädæng Chronicle" and the "Jengtung State Chronicle" translated*. Ann Arbor: University of Michigan, Center for South and Southeast Asian Studies, 1981. (Michigan papers on South and Southeast Asia, 19.) ISBN 0-89148-020-X (cl), 0-89148-021-8 (pbk). ‣ Two indigenous chronicles from Khön Shan region of extreme northeastern Burma, old Keng Tung state, translated with extensive introduction and annotation. First text given also in facsimile. [DKW]

16.86 George Vinal Smith. *The Dutch in seventeenth-century Thailand*. DeKalb: Northern Illinois University, Center for Southeast Asian Studies, 1977. (Center for Southeast Asian studies, Special report, 16.) ‣ Thorough mining of Dutch and Thai sources on complex relations between European commercial power and old Thai kingdom during seventeenth century. Concludes with defense of Dutch historical sources. [DKW]

16.87 Jeremias van Vliet. *The short history of the kings of Siam*. David K. Wyatt, ed. Leonard Y. Andaya, trans. Bangkok: Siam Society, 1975. ‣ Originally composed in 1640 by Dutch merchant, long resident at Siamese capital, Ayudhya; apparently based on now lost Thai chronicles. Needs to be considered in conjunction with Luang Prasœt chronicle (16.83) and fuller Ayudhya chronicles (synoptic English version planned for 1995). [DKW]

16.88 John K. Whitmore. *Vietnam, Ho Quy Ly, and the Ming (1371–1421)*. New Haven: Yale Center for International and Area Studies, Council on Southeast Asia Studies, 1985. (Lac-Viet series, 2.) ISBN 0-938692-22-4. ‣ Detailed study of critical period when new dynasty seized power and was replaced by long Chinese occupation. Based on difficult research in Chinese and Vietnamese sources. [DKW]

16.89 Yu Insun. *Law and society in seventeenth- and eighteenth-century Vietnam*. Seoul: Korea University, Asiatic Research Center, 1990. ‣ Modest monograph focuses on family, property, and village relationships as encapsulated in Lê dynasty law code. [DKW]

Island Southeast Asia: Malaysia, Indonesia, and the Philippines

16.90 Raja Ali al-Haji Riau. *The precious gift (Tuhfat al-nafis): an annotated translation*. Barbara Watson Andaya and Virginia Matheson, trans. Kuala Lumpur: Oxford University Press, 1982. ISBN 0-19-582507-1. ‣ Mid-nineteenth-century account of events in Malay world since late seventeenth century, as seen from area at tip of Malay Peninsula. Most important local source for its period. [DKW]

16.91 Barbara Watson Andaya. *Perak, the abode of grace: a study of an eighteenth-century Malay state*. Kuala Lumpur: Oxford University Press, 1979. ISBN 0-19-580385-X. ‣ Fine historical monograph on history of important tin-mining state of Perak, especially in late eighteenth century, based on both indigenous and Dutch sources. [DKW]

16.92 Leonard Y. Andaya. *The heritage of Arung Palakka: a history of South Sulawesi (Celebes) in the seventeenth century*. The Hague: Nijhoff, 1981. (Verhandelingen van het Koninklijk Instituut voor Taal-, Land-, en Volkenkunde, 91.) ISBN 90-247-2463-5 (pbk). ‣ Pioneering effort to relate Dutch to indigenous historical sources in tracing extension of Dutch power and extinction of local rulers in seventeenth-century Sulawesi. One of few histories of its kind; offers rare look outside Java in early Dutch period. [DKW]

16.93 Leonard Y. Andaya. *The kingdom of Johor, 1641–1728.* Kuala Lumpur: Oxford University Press, 1975. ISBN 0-19-580262-4. ▸ Innovative study of critical locale and important developments at southern tip of Malay Peninsula when successive waves of external influence, particularly from Bugis, Minangkabau, and Dutch, reshaped Johore's political patterns. [DKW]

16.94 Emma Helen Blair. *The Philippine Islands, 1493–1898: explorations by early navigators, descriptions of the islands and their peoples, their history, and the records of the Catholic missions, as related in contemporaneous manuscripts, showing the political, economic, commercial, and religious conditions of these islands from the earliest relations with European nations to the close of the nineteenth century.* 55 vols. Cleveland: Clark, 1903–1909. ▸ Monumental collection of translations of Spanish documents and books from Spanish colonial period in Philippines, arranged roughly chronologically, but much more extensive on sixteenth and seventeenth centuries than on eighteenth and nineteenth. Volume 53 a bibliography, and volumes 54–55 an index. [DKW]

16.95 C. R. Boxer. *The Dutch seaborne empire, 1600–1800.* New York: Knopf, 1965. ▸ Elegantly written survey by old master of history of Portuguese and Dutch empires. Analytically old-fashioned, but even specialists consult it with profit. [DKW]

16.96 C. R. Boxer. *The Portuguese seaborne empire, 1415–1825.* New York: Knopf, 1969. ▸ Standard general introduction to subject, by leading authority. Good bibliography. [DKW]

16.97 C. C. Brown, trans. *Sejarah Melayu or Malay annals.* Rev. ed. R. Roolvink, Introduction. Kuala Lumpur: Oxford University Press, 1970. ISBN 0-19-580356-6 (pbk). ▸ Classical Malay history, written probably at beginning of seventeenth century by author(s) unknown. Literate and faithful translation. Useful introduction on "The Variant Versions of the Malay Annals." [DKW]

16.98 Nicholas P. Cushner. *Spain in the Philippines: from conquest to revolution.* Rutland, Vt.: Tuttle, 1971. (Institute of Philippine Culture monographs, 1.) ▸ Best general treatment of Spanish colonial period prior to nineteenth century in Philippines. Judicious and careful, based primarily on Spanish archives in Seville. [DKW]

16.99 G.W.J. Drewes. "New light on the coming of Islam to Indonesia?" *Bijdragen van het Koninklijk Instituut voor Taal-, Land-, en Volkenkunde* 124.4 (1968) 433–59. ISSN 0006-2294. ▸ Excellent summary of contemporary state of art concerning islamization of Southeast Asia. Written mainly to discount several earlier contributions to field. [DKW]

16.100 Denys Lombard. *Le sultanat d'Atjeh au temps d'Iskandar Muda, 1607–1636.* Paris: L'École Française d'Extrême-Orient, 1967. (Publications de l'École Française d'Extrême-Orient, 61.) ▸ Best and fullest account of this important seventeenth-century state on northwestern tip of Sumatra, based on wide range of sources. [DKW]

16.101 Ferdinand E. Marcos. *Tadhana (destiny): the history of the Filipino people.* 4 vols. to date. Manila: Ferdinand E. Marcos, 1976–80. ▸ Though attributed to late president, and certainly edited by him, volumes reportedly ghost-written by many others, including some excellent scholars. Best essays in three parts of volume 2, covering period from 1565 to 1815. Excellent bibliographical essays. [DKW]

16.102 M.A.P. Meilink-Roelofsz. *Asian trade and European influence in the Indonesian archipelago between 1500 and about 1630.* The Hague: Nijhoff, 1962. ▸ First general overview of period based on Dutch records, taking up where van Leur left off (16.22) three decades earlier. Excellent account of pre-1600

trading system, and judicious examination of first three decades of Dutch activities. [DKW]

16.103 Luis Merino. *The Cabildo secular or municipal government of Manila: social component, organization, economics.* Iloilo, Philippines: University of San Agustin, Research Center, 1980. (Studies on the municipality of Manila, 1.) ▸ Careful, and at times dreary, detailed examination of administration of Manila in first century (seventeenth century) as colonial capital of Philippines. Good information on colonial political, economic, and social structures. [DKW]

16.104 A. C. Milner. *Kerajaan: Malay political culture on the eve of colonial rule.* Tucson: University of Arizona Press for the Association for Asian Studies, 1982. (Association for Asian Studies, Monographs, 40.) ISBN 0-8165-0772-4 (cl), 0-8165-0774-0 (pbk). ▸ Attempt to expand on Gullick's pregnant synthesis (16.243). Defines Malay world more broadly; includes both sides of Straits of Malacca, considers Malay documents in addition to colonial British ones, and extends consideration further back in time. [DKW]

16.105 Soemarsaid Moertono. *State and statecraft in old Java: a study of the later Mataram period, sixteenth to nineteenth century.* Ithaca, N.Y.: Cornell University, Modern Indonesia Project, 1968. ▸ Perceptive and critical survey of premodern Javanese statecraft and administration from Dutch and Javanese sources. Athough an M.A. thesis, an enduring work. [DKW]

16.106 Antonio de Morga. *Sucesos de las Islas Filipinas.* J. S. Cummins, ed. and trans. Cambridge: Cambridge University Press for the Hakluyt Society, 1971. (Works issued by the Hakluyt Society, Second series, 140.) ISBN 0-521-01035-7. ▸ Still an extraordinary work for early seventeenth-century publication. Covers Spanish activities in Philippines in detail, also considerable information about rest of Southeast Asia, including Cambodia. [DKW]

16.107 F. H. van Naerssen and R. C. de Iongh. *The economic and administrative history of early Indonesia.* Leiden: Brill, 1977. (Handbuch der Orientalistik, Dritte Abteilung: Indonesien, Malaysia, und die Philippinen, 7.) ISBN 90-04-04918-5. ▸ Naerssen's essay concerns institutional and administrative history, mainly on Java and Bali, in earliest period. De Iongh's essay deals more briefly with Portuguese and Dutch activities in sixteenth and early seventeenth centuries. Useful and brief overview. [DKW]

16.108 J. Noorduyn. "Majapahit in the fifteenth century." *Bijdragen van het Koninklijk Instituut voor Taal-, Land-, en Volkenkunde* 134 (1978) 207–74. ISSN 0006-2294. ▸ Skillful use of wide range of indigenous sources in tracing Javanese history through turbulent and murky period. [DKW]

16.109 John Leddy Phelan. *The hispanization of the Philippines: Spanish aims and Filipino responses, 1565–1700.* Madison: University of Wisconsin Press, 1959. ▸ Long classic survey of Spanish colonial policy in Philippines and how it was modified to suit local circumstances. Based on Spanish archival sources. [DKW]

16.110 Theodore G. Th. Pigeaud, ed. *Islamic states in Java, 1500–1700: eight Dutch books and articles by H. J. de Graaf.* The Hague: Nijhoff, 1976. (Verhandelingen van het Koninklijk Instituut voor Taal-, Land-, en Volkenkunde, 70.) ISBN 90-247-1876-7. ▸ Handy and useful summary in English of massive scholarly output of de Graaf over many years. Sources not indicated and must be sought in original Dutch versions. [DKW]

16.111 Theodore G. Th. Pigeaud, ed. and trans. *Java in the fourteenth century, a study in cultural history: the "Nagara-Kertagama" by Rakawi Prapañca of Majapahit, 1365 AD.* 3d ed. The Hague: Nijhoff, 1960. 5 vols. (Koninklijk Instituut voor Taal-, Land-, en Volkenkunde, Translation series, 1–5). ▸ Prapañca's epic poem written at Javanese Majapahit court in 1365, with original text, translation, and annotations. Central text for study of medieval Java. [DKW]

16.112 Serafin D. Quiason. *English "country trade" with the Philippines, 1644–1765.* Quezon City: University of the Philippines Press, 1966. ▸ Study of integration of Philippines into Asia-wide "country trade" conducted under aegis of English East India Company, despite Spanish efforts to restrict trade with other European powers. Somewhat over-detailed and under-analyzed. [DKW]

16.113 Vicente L. Rafael. *Contracting colonialism: translation and Christian conversion in Tagalog society under early Spanish rule.* Ithaca, N.Y.: Cornell University Press, 1988. ISBN 0-8014-2065-2. ▸ Conceptually very innovative and complex. Examination of transformations of Spanish colonial and evangelizing effort under exigencies of operating in local vernaculars by focusing on fields of meaning in vocabulary of power relationships in colonial context. [DKW]

16.114 J. J. Ras. *Hikajat Bandjar: a study in Malay historiography.* The Hague: Nijhoff, 1968. (Bibliotheca Indonesica, 1.) ▸ The Malay chronicle of old Malay state of Banjarmasin, on south coast of Borneo. Lengthy text with translation from area otherwise little represented in literature of Southeast Asian history. [DKW]

16.115 Robert R. Reed. *Colonial Manila: the context of Hispanic urbanism and the process of morphogenesis.* Berkeley: University of California Press, 1978. ISBN 0-520-09579-0. ▸ Somewhat technical but stimulating examination of Spanish policies and practices that gave rise to rapid growth and shape of Manila. [DKW]

16.116 Anthony Reid and Lance Castles, eds. *Pre-colonial state systems in Southeast Asia: the Malay Peninsula, Sumatra, Bali-Lombok, South Celebes.* Kuala Lumpur: Malaysian Branch of the Royal Asiatic Society, 1975. (Malaysian Branch of the Royal Asiatic Society, Monographs, 6.) ▸ Twelve essays on nature of pre-modern state by scholars working on islands of Southeast Asia. Focuses primarily on seventeenth to nineteenth century. [DKW]

16.117 M. C. Ricklefs. *Modern Javanese historical tradition: a study of an original Kartasura chronicle and related materials.* London: University of London, School of Oriental and African Studies, 1978. ISBN 0-7286-0045-5. ▸ Important study of short Javanese chronicle with text and translation. Text is concerned mainly with eighteenth century. Best example of this genre of Javanese historical writing in English. [DKW]

16.118 S. O. Robson. "Java at the crossroads: aspects of Javanese cultural history in the fourteenth and fifteenth centuries." *Bijdragen van het Koninklijk Instituut voor Taal-, Land-, en Volkenkunde* 137 (1981) 259–92. ISSN 0006-2294. ▸ Argument for necessity of placing Java in broader Asian context based on examination of number of fragmentary texts from this dark period. [DKW]

16.119 Najeeb M. Saleeby. *The history of Sulu.* 1908 ed. Manila: Filipiniana Book Guild, 1963. (Philippine Islands Bureau of Science Division of Ethnology Publications, 4.2. Publications of the Filipiniana Book Guild, 4.) ▸ Extraordinary early account by American official of early history (fifteenth to nineteenth century) of Sulu sultanate in extreme southeast of archipelago, region best known for Islam and organized piracy and smuggling. [DKW]

16.120 B.J.O. Schrieke. *Indonesian sociological studies: selected writings.* 2 vols. The Hague: van Hoeve, 1955–57. ▸ Collection of important, masterly essays, many previously unpublished, ranging over wide areas and subjects. Of particular note: "The Shifts in Political and Economic Power in the Indonesian Archipelago in the Sixteenth and Seventeenth Century," "The Causes and

Effects of Communism on the West Coast of Sumatra," and, in volume 2, the massive "Ruler and Realm in Early Java." [DKW]

16.121 William Henry Scott. *"Cracks in the Parchment Curtain" and other essays in Philippine history.* Rev. ed. Quezon City: New Day, 1985. ISBN 971-10-0073-3 (bookprint), 971-10-0074-1 (newsprint). ▸ Stimulating, often brilliant essays on earlier history, especially Spanish period. Author, in Philippines for more than thirty years, best known for extracting local history from seemingly intractable foreign sources buried in archives around world. [DKW]

16.122 A. Teeuw and David K. Wyatt. *Hikayat Patani: the story of Patani.* 2 vols. The Hague: Nijhoff, 1970. (Bibliotheca Indonesica, 5.) ▸ Edition, annotation, and translation of eighteenth-century annals of old Malay state of Patani (South Thailand). Interesting example both of traditional historiography and of conceptions of political power. [DKW]

16.123 Richard O. Winstedt, A. E. Coope, and D. Ismail Hussain. *A history of Johore (1365–1895).* Kuala Lumpur: Malaysian Branch of the Royal Asiatic Society, 1979. (Malaysian Branch of the Royal Asiatic Society, Reprints, 6.) ▸ Excellent combination of long articles previously published (1932, 1936) dealing with history of Johore. "Hikayat Negeri Johor" in Malay, but useful introduction in English. [DKW]

16.124 O. W. Wolters. *The fall of Srivijaya in Malay history.* Ithaca, N.Y.: Cornell University Press, 1970. ISBN 0-8014-0595-5. ▸ Brilliant, innovative study of Straits of Malacca region (fourteenth and fifteenth centuries): fall of old maritime empire of Śrīvijaya on Sumatran coast and rise of new empire of Malacca. Ingeniously combines Malay and Chinese sources to solve long-standing puzzles. [DKW]

MODERN PERIOD, SINCE 1750

General Studies

16.125 Benedict R. O'G. Anderson. *Imagined communities: reflections on the origin and spread of nationalism.* Rev. ed. London: Verso, 1991. ISBN 0-86091-329-5 (cl), 0-86091-546-8 (pbk). ▸ Political scientist's sage reflections on origins of modern nationalism, based especially on his thorough knowledge of Indonesia and other Southeast Asian cases. [DKW]

16.126 John F. Cady. *The history of post-war Southeast Asia.* Athens: Ohio University Press, 1974. ISBN 0-8214-0160-2 (cl), 0-8214-0175-0 (pbk). ▸ Handiest and fullest account of Southeast Asian history since World War II. Extremely detailed account of politics; weaker in analysis and generalization. [DKW]

16.127 C. D. Cowan, ed. *The economic development of South-East Asia: studies in economic history and political economy.* London: Allen & Unwin, 1964. (University of London, School of Oriental and African Studies, Studies on modern Asia and Africa, 3.) ▸ Eight important early essays on economic history and historical demography of Southeast Asia focused mainly on twentieth century. [DKW]

16.128 Jennifer Wayne Cushman. *Family and state: the formation of a Sino-Thai tin-mining dynasty, 1797–1932.* Craig J. Reynolds, ed. Singapore: Oxford University Press, 1991. ISBN 0-19-588966-5 (cl). ▸ Fascinating examination of changing fortunes of Khaw family based in southern Thailand and on island of Penang. Based on Thai, Chinese, and Western sources. Prepared for publication by Reynolds following author's death. [DKW]

16.129 John S. Furnivall. *Colonial policy and practice: a comparative study of Burma and Netherlands India.* 1948 ed. New York: New York University Press, 1956. ▸ Classic comparative study of British and Dutch colonial rule. Historical chapters deal with nineteenth- and twentieth-century evolution of colonial system. Based on Western-language sources only. [DKW]

16.130 Alfred W. McCoy, ed. *Southeast Asia under Japanese occupation.* New Haven: Yale University, Southeast Asian Studies, 1980. (Southeast Asia Studies, Monograph series, 22.) ISBN 0-938692-08-9. ▸ Fine collection of essays on wartime Southeast Asia, dealing with resistance, collaboration, and economic and social change as well as political preparations for independence in postwar period. Good representation of best of recent scholarship. [DKW]

16.131 Ruth T. McVey, ed. *Southeast Asian transitions: approaches through social history.* New Haven: Yale University Press, 1978. (Southeast Asia Studies, Monograph series, 8.) ISBN 0-300-02184-4. ▸ Six essays exploring relations between regional and national (and international) history in Southeast Asia (nineteenth and twentieth centuries). Volume improves on usual festschrift by having unifying themes and shared vision. [DKW]

16.132 Victor Purcell. *The Chinese in Southeast Asia.* 1965 2d ed. Kuala Lumpur: Oxford University Press, 1980. ISBN 0-19-580463-5. ▸ Account that helped define study of Overseas Chinese in Southeast Asia at height of cold war. More detail on many issues available in first edition published in 1951. [DKW]

16.133 James C. Scott. *The moral economy of the peasant: rebellion and subsistence in Southeast Asia.* New Haven: Yale University Press, 1976. ISBN 0-300-01862-2 (cl), 0-300-02190-9 (pbk). ▸ Argument that agrarian rebellions in Burma and Vietnam in 1930s best understood in terms of traditional moral order that changes of colonial era violated. Began debate with Popkin (16.220). [DKW]

16.134 Josef Silverstein, ed. *Southeast Asia in World War II, four essays.* New Haven: Yale University, Southeast Asia Studies, 1966. (Southeast Asian studies, Monograph series, 7.) ▸ Now standard group of essays focusing particularly on Burma and Philippines under Japanese occupation during World War II. See also McCoy's collection on same subject (16.130). [DKW]

16.135 David J. Steinberg, ed. *In search of Southeast Asia: a modern history.* Rev. ed. Honolulu: University of Hawaii Press, 1987. ISBN 0-8248-1110-0 (pbk). ▸ Pathbreaking redefinition of modern Southeast Asian history stressing common themes and benefiting from authors' combined expertise on diverse cultures of region. Large portions extensively revised since first published in 1970. Excellent bibliographical essay. [DKW]

16.136 Nicholas Tarling. *Anglo-Dutch rivalry in the Malay world, 1780–1824.* Cambridge: Cambridge University Press, 1962. ▸ Anglo-Dutch tensions centering on trade and political dominance in western portion of Indonesian archipelago, ultimately issuing in Anglo-Dutch Treaty of 1824, partitioning Indonesia and Malaysia. Based entirely on colonial archives. [DKW]

16.137 David K. Wyatt and Alexander B. Woodside, eds. *Moral order and the question of change: essays on Southeast Asian thought.* New Haven: Yale University, Southeast Asia Studies, 1982. (Southeast Asia Studies, Monograph series, 24.) ISBN 0-938692-02-X (pbk). ▸ Seven pioneering attempts at intellectual history of eighteenth and nineteenth centuries. Very long and meaty essays on Siam, Cambodia, Burma, Vietnam, Java, and Philippines deal with topics not found elsewhere. [DKW]

Burma

16.138 Michael Adas. *The Burma delta: economic development and social change on an Asian rice frontier, 1852–1941.* Madison: University of Wisconsin Press, 1974. ISBN 0-299-06490-5. ▸ Detailed systematic analysis of process by which nearly empty delta of Irrawaddy River became vast rice plain under British rule. Based primarily on settlement reports compiled by British officials. [DKW]

16.139 Richard A. Butwell. *U Nu of Burma.* Stanford, Calif.: Stanford University Press, 1963. ▸ Almost journalistic biography of this key figure through first fifteen years of Burma's postcolonial history by political scientist with long experience in Burma. [DKW]

16.140 John F. Cady. *A history of modern Burma.* 1958 ed. with 1960 supplement. Ithaca, N.Y.: Cornell University Press, 1963. ISBN 0-8014-0059-7. ▸ Mammoth, conventional political narrative covering period from end of eighteenth century to onset of army rule in 1960. Based entirely on Western-language sources by author who taught in Burma in 1930s. [DKW]

16.141 John F. Cady. *The United States and Burma.* Cambridge, Mass.: Harvard University Press, 1976. ISBN 0-674-92320-0. ▸ Balanced, brief history of Burma; sure-handed and succinct. Not based on reading of Burmese sources. [DKW]

16.142 W. S. Desai. *History of the British Residency in Burma, 1826–1840.* 1939 ed. Farnborough, Hants.: Gregg International, 1972. ISBN 0-576-03152-6. ▸ Old and dated, but still useful examination of British relations with kingdom of Burma in a critical period, based on archives of English East India Company. [DKW]

16.143 John S. Furnivall. *The fashioning of Leviathan: the beginnings of British rule in Burma.* Gehan Wijeyewardene, ed. Canberra: Australian National University, Research School of Pacific Studies, 1991. ISBN 0-7315-1196-4. ▸ First published as long article (1939); classic essay for study of early British rule along southeast coast of Burma (1820s and 1830s). Based primarily on British administrative records. [DKW]

16.144 D.G.E. Hall. *Henry Burney: a political biography.* London: Oxford University Press, 1974. ISBN 0-19-713583-8. ▸ Long career of Burney in Penang and Siam and then in Burma through 1820s and 1830s. Based on Burney's papers and on archives of English East India Company. More important for Burma than for Siam. [DKW]

16.145 Maung Htin Aung. *The stricken peacock: Anglo-Burmese relations, 1752–1948.* The Hague: Nijhoff, 1965. ▸ Nationalistic review of Burmese relations with Britain over two centuries with heaviest emphasis on nineteenth century. [DKW]

16.146 Charles Lee Keeton III. *King Thebaw and the ecological rape of Burma: the political and commercial struggle between British India and French Indo-China in Burma, 1878–1886.* Delhi: Manohar Book Service, 1974. ▸ First relatively full study of reign of Thibaw (1878–85) based on British and British Indian, but not Burmese, sources. Curiously broad definition of ecology. Obvious focus on economic relations between British India and Burma. [DKW]

16.147 William J. Koenig. *The Burmese polity, 1752–1819: politics, administration, and social organization in the early Kon-baung period.* Ann Arbor: University of Michigan, Center for South and Southeast Asian Studies, 1990. (Michigan papers on South and Southeast Asia, 34.) ISBN 0-89148-056-0 (cl), 0-89148-057-9 (pbk). ▸ Dense, detailed study, one of first to be based on Burmese-language sources. Achieves comprehensive coverage of most aspects of Burmese society in period immediately preceding Anglo-Burmese war (1824–26). [DKW]

16.148 Maung Maung. *From sangha to laity: nationalist movements of Burma, 1920–1940.* Columbia, Mo.: South Asia Books, 1980. (Australian National University, Monographs on South Asia, 4.) ▸ Mature and full examination of Burmese nationalism in period, flawed by author's lack of extensive Burmese sources when writing this (as M.A. thesis) in Australia. [DKW]

16.149 E. Michael Mendelson. *Sangha and state in Burma: a study of monastic sectarianism and leadership.* John P. Ferguson, ed. Ithaca, N.Y.: Cornell University Press, 1975. ISBN 0-8014-0875-X. ▸ Extensive coverage of Burmese Buddhist history prior to and during colonial rule by British anthropologist who studied

Burmese Buddhism intensively, then abandoned Burma studies for literature. Work rescued by Ferguson. [DKW]

16.150   Mya Sein. *The administration of Burma.* 1938 ed. Josef Silverstein, Introduction. Kuala Lumpur: Oxford University Press, 1973. ▸ Overview of local and central administration in pre-colonial Burma, based on indigenous sources. [DKW]

16.151   Oliver B. Pollak. *Empires in collision: Anglo-Burmese relations in the mid-nineteenth century.* Westport, Conn.: Greenwood, 1979. ISBN 0-313-20824-7. ▸ Political collision between British India and still-independent Burma (1840s to 1860s). Flawed by limitations of Western-language sources and much too brief. Period still needs better treatment. [DKW]

16.152   E. Sarkisyanz. *Buddhist backgrounds of the Burmese revolution.* The Hague: Nijhoff, 1965. ▸ Idiosyncratic history of modern Burma tracing developments in ideological and religious terms. Very influential. [DKW]

16.153   Josef Silverstein. *Burma: military rule and the politics of stagnation.* Ithaca, N.Y.: Cornell University Press, 1977. ISBN 0-8014-0911-X (cl), 0-8014-9863-5 (pbk). ▸ Much dealing with Burmese political, economic, and social history, primarily since independence in 1948 in this political science book. Good bibliography. [DKW]

16.154   Donald Eugene Smith. *Religion and politics in Burma.* Princeton: Princeton University Press, 1965. ▸ Good examination of checkered history of Buddhism in century of British rule and in first decades of independence. Based entirely on English sources. Best read in conjunction with Mendelson 16.149. [DKW]

16.155   Nicholas Tarling. *The fourth Anglo-Burmese War: Britain and the independence of Burma.* Gaya, India: Centre for South East Asian Studies, 1987. ▸ First thorough mining of British archives for materials on post–World War II relationship between Britain and Burma, which culminated in independence of Burma in 1948. [DKW]

16.156   Robert H. Taylor. *The state in Burma.* Honolulu: University of Hawaii Press, 1987. ISBN 0-8248-1141-0. ▸ Thoughtful, analytical examination of modern Burmese politics from late colonial times to present. Tends toward excessive sympathy for post-1962 military regime. [DKW]

16.157   Hugh Tinker. *The Union of Burma: a study of the first years of independence.* 4th ed. London: Oxford University Press for the Royal Institute of International Affairs, 1967. ▸ Long the standard account of politics in newly independent Burma. [DKW]

16.158   Frank N. Trager. *Burmese sit-tàns, 1764–1826: records of rural life and administration.* William J. Koenig, trans. Tucson: University of Arizona Press for the Association for Asian Studies, 1979. (Association for Asian Studies, Monographs, 36.) ISBN 0-8165-0672-8 (cl), 0-8165-0658-2 (pbk). ▸ Major and fascinating collection of rural administrative documents from Burma dating from eighteenth and early nineteenth centuries. Long introduction sets them in context. [DKW]

Thailand

16.159   M. R. Akin Rabibhadana. *The organization of Thai society in the early Bangkok period, 1782–1873.* Ithaca, N.Y.: Cornell University, Southeast Asia Program, 1969. (Thailand Project, Interim reports series, 12. Southeast Asia Program, Data paper, 74.) ▸ Perceptive analysis of Siamese society based primarily on traditional laws and on genealogical information on leading families. Now standard work in field. [DKW]

16.160   Benjamin A. Batson. *The end of the absolute monarchy in Siam.* Singapore: Oxford University Press, 1984. (Asian Studies Association of Australia, Southeast Asia publications series, 10.) ISBN 0-19-582612-4 (pbk). ▸ Definitive account of reign of King

Prajadhipok (r. 1925–35) of Siam and revolution of 1932, based on Western and Thai sources. Prajadhipok victim of forces beyond his control. [DKW]

16.161   Benjamin A. Batson, ed. and comp. *Siam's political future: documents from the end of the absolute monarchy.* Ithaca, N.Y.: Cornell University, Southeast Asia Program, 1974. (Southeast Asia Program, Data paper, 96.) ISBN 0-87727-096-1. ▸ Collection of important documents from 1925 to 1935 documenting royal and official indecision about political reform prior to military coup that ended absolute monarchy in 1932. Excellent introductions. [DKW]

16.162   Ian Brown. *The élite and the economy in Siam, c. 1890–1920.* Singapore: Oxford University Press, 1988. ISBN 0-19-588877-4. ▸ One of first detailed economic histories of Thailand based on archival sources. Strong especially on economic relations with major European powers and on development of export agriculture. [DKW]

16.163   Tej Bunnag. *The provincial administration of Siam, 1892–1915: the Ministry of the Interior under Prince Damrong Rajanubhab.* Kuala Lumpur: Oxford University Press, 1977. ISBN 0-19-580343-4. ▸ Elegant, thorough study of major reforms of internal and local administration under Prince Damrong's direction. Damrong was important and influential figure in his own right. [DKW]

16.164   *The Burney papers.* 1910–14 ed. 5 vols. Farnborough, England: Gregg International, 1971. ISBN 0-576-03311-1 (set), 0-576-03945-4 (v. 1), 0-576-03946-2 (v. 2), 0-576-03947-0 (v. 3), 0-576-03948-9 (v. 4), 0-576-03949-7 (v. 5). ▸ Massive collection of documents on Anglo-Siamese relations between 1822 and 1849 which, read carefully, sheds much light on poorly documented Thai politics during this period. [DKW]

16.165   Chandran Jeshurun. *The contest for Siam, 1889–1902: a study in diplomatic rivalry.* Kuala Lumpur: Penerbit Universiti Kebangsaan Malaysia, 1977. ▸ Classic, definitive diplomatic history of Anglo-French rivalry over Siam (Thailand) based on British and French archives. Elegantly written and tightly argued, but focused entirely on European actions and discussion. [DKW]

16.166   Chatthip Nartsupha, Suthy Prasartset, and Montri Chenvidyakarn, eds. *The political economy of Siam.* Vol. 1: *1851–1910.* Vol. 2: *1910–1932.* 1978 ed. 2 vols. Bangkok: Social Science Association of Thailand Press, 1981. ▸ Collection of documents translated from Thai, critiquing royal failures in last decades of absolute monarchy. Argues that traditional sociopolitical order (so-called *sakdina* system) and Western imperialism prevented formation of independent bourgeois class, without which true capitalism and industrialism could not develop. Extremely influential, spawning much similar work. [DKW]

16.167   Direk Jayanama. *Siam and World War II.* Jane Godrey Keyes, ed. and trans. Bangkok: Social Science Association of Thailand Press, 1978. ▸ Unusual, enthralling account of Thailand's complex history during World War II by man who was Thai foreign minister during much of period. Apt translation. [DKW]

16.168   John B. Haseman. *The Thai resistance movement during the Second World War.* DeKalb: Northern Illinois University, Center for Southeast Asian Studies; distributed by Cellar Book Shop, 1978. (Center for Southeast Asian Studies, Special report, 17.) ▸ Interesting account of wartime Thai efforts to aid Allies in war against Japan. So far, only serious study in English of most important episode. [DKW]

16.169   Kevin Hewison. *Bankers and bureaucrats: capital and the role of the state in Thailand.* New Haven: Yale University, Southeast Asia Studies, 1989. (Southeast Asia Studies, Monograph series, 34.) ISBN 0-938692-41-0. ▸ Political economy of modern

Thailand, primarily since 1932. Rise of agrarian, commercial, industrial, and banking capital in context of state policy; rise of Sarit Thanarat (1957) a significant turning point. Best read with Suehiro 16.182 and with Chatthip et al. 16.166. [DKW]

16.170 Hong Lysa. *Thailand in the nineteenth century: evolution of the economy and society.* Singapore: Institute of Southeast Asian Studies, 1984. ISBN 9971-902-82-6, 9971-902-72-9 (pbk). ▸ Political economy of nineteenth-century Thailand, focusing particularly on economic organization and nature of precapitalist society. Based primarily on Thai sources. [DKW]

16.171 James C. Ingram. *Economic change in Thailand, 1850–1970.* Rev. ed. Stanford, Calif.: Stanford University Press, 1971. ISBN 0-8047-0782-0. ▸ Long the standard treatment of Thai economic history; balanced and detailed study not completely superseded by Suehiro 16.182, Sompop 16.179, and Hewison 16.169, and should be read in conjunction with them. Earlier title: *Economic Change in Thailand since 1850.* [DKW]

16.172 Yoneo Ishii. *Sangha, state, and society: Thai Buddhism in history.* Peter Hawkes, trans. Honolulu: University of Hawaii Press, 1986. (Kyoto University Center for Southeast Asian Studies, Monographs, 15.) ISBN 0-8248-0993-9 (cl), 0-8248-0994-7 (pbk). ▸ Short history of Thai Buddhism by Japan's leading historian of Thailand. Based primarily on Thai sources. [DKW]

16.173 David Morell and Chai-anan Samudavanija. *Political conflict in Thailand: reform, reaction, revolution.* Cambridge, Mass.: Oelgeschlager Gunn & Hain, 1981. ISBN 0-89946-044-5. ▸ Most authoritative account of turbulent 1970s in Thailand, based especially on Thai sources. [DKW]

16.174 H. G. Quaritch Wales. *Ancient Siamese government and administration.* 1934 ed. New York: Paragon Book Reprint, 1965. ▸ Classic treatment of subject, based primarily on old Thai laws and administrative documents. Romanizes as if originals were Sanskrit. [DKW]

16.175 Craig J. Reynolds, ed. and trans. *Thai radical discourse: "The Real Face of Thai Feudalism Today."* Ithaca, N.Y.: Cornell University, Southeast Asia Program, 1987. (Studies on Southeast Asia, 3.) ISBN 0-87727-702-8 (pbk). ▸ Complex, sophisticated translation and lengthy analysis of key book for Thai Left in 1970s by Jit Poumisak. Lengthy introduction and analysis puts Jit and his work into perspective. [DKW]

16.176 Viraphol Sarasin. *Tribute and profit: Sino-Siamese trade, 1652–1853.* Cambridge, Mass.: Harvard University Press for the Council on East Asian Studies, 1977. (Harvard East Asian monographs, 76.) ISBN 0-674-80915-7. ▸ Examination of major period of growth in trade between China and Siam, particularly in rice, and impact on parties concerned. Based primarily on Chinese sources. [DKW]

16.177 Lauriston Sharp and Lucien M. Hanks. *Bang Chan: social history of a rural community in Thailand.* Ithaca, N.Y.: Cornell University Press, 1978. ISBN 0-8014-0858-X. ▸ Delightful account based on oral testimony covering period from 1840s to 1950s. No other book so treats nature of peasant life over this period. [DKW]

16.178 G. William Skinner. *Chinese society in Thailand: an analytical history.* Ithaca, N.Y.: Cornell University Press, 1957. ▸ Classic account, based on oral and written Chinese evidence, of immigrant Chinese community in Thailand, focusing on century between 1850 and 1950. [DKW]

16.179 Sompop Manarangsan. *Economic development of Thailand, 1850–1950: response to the challenge of the world economy.* Bangkok: Chulalongkorn University, Institute of Asian Studies, 1989. (Institute of Asian Studies monograph, 42.) ISBN 974-576-830-8. ▸ Dry, methodical analysis of economic change since opening of Siam to world trade in 1855. Includes controversial

assertion of relative economic stasis from World War I to 1950s. [DKW]

16.180 Judith A. Stowe. *Siam becomes Thailand: a story of intrigue.* Honolulu: University of Hawaii Press, 1991. ISBN 0-8248-1393-6 (cl), 0-8248-1394-4 (pbk). ▸ Straight, useful narrative history of period from end of absolute monarchy in 1932 to end of World War II. Fills need in absence of much else on this period. [DKW]

16.181 Suchit Bunbongkarn. *The military in Thai politics, 1981–1986.* Singapore: Institute of Southeast Asian Studies, 1987. ISBN 9971-988-61-5. ▸ Best introduction to byzantine world of intersection between military and political power in Thailand in recent years. [DKW]

16.182 Akira Suehiro. *Capital accumulation in Thailand, 1855–1985.* Tokyo: Centre for East Asian Cultural Studies, 1989. ISBN 4-89656-105-8. ▸ Pathbreaking economic history with special attention to rise of moneyed interests and their relationship to state and to political power in each period. Breathtaking detail. Should be read with Hewison 16.169 and with Chattip et al. 16.166. [DKW]

16.183 Thak Chaloemtiarana. *Thailand: the politics of despotic paternalism.* Bangkok: Social Science Association of Thailand and Thammasat University, Thai Khadi Institute, 1979. ▸ Detailed analysis of Field Marshal Sarit Thanarat's tenure (1958–63) as prime minister and dictator. Grounds rule in search for new ideology for authoritarianism; sees success of economic development in government's new relations with business community. [DKW]

16.184 Chaophraya Thiphakarawong (Kham Bunnag). *The Dynastic Chronicles, Bangkok era, the first reign.* 1 vol. to date. Thadeus Flood and Chadin Flood, eds. and trans. Tokyo: Centre for East Asian Cultural Studies, 1978–. ▸ Excellent translation of vitally important chronicle of first reign of Chakri dynasty, 1782–1809. Following format adopted in fourth reign chronicles, text translated literally with annotations to follow in a second volume. [DKW]

16.185 Chaophraya Thiphakarawong (Kham Bunnag). *The Dynastic Chronicles, Bangkok era, the fourth reign, B.E. 2394–2411 (AD 1851–1868).* 4 vols. to date. Chadin Flood, trans. Tokyo: Centre for East Asian Cultural Studies, 1965–. ▸ Literal translation of Chao Phraya Thiphakorawong's chronicle of reign of King Mongkut (r. 1851–68), written in early 1870s. Translation in first two volumes, followed by annotations, commentary, appendixes, and bibliography in volumes 3 and 4. Index planned for volume 5 not yet published. Good expression of nineteenth-century indigenous historiography by Mongkut's foreign minister. [DKW]

16.186 Vajirananavarorasa (Prince-Patriarch of Siam). *Autobiography: the life of Prince-Patriarch Vajirañana of Siam, 1860–1921.* Craig J. Reynolds, ed. and trans. Athens: Ohio University Press, 1979. ISBN 0-8214-0376-1 (cl), 0-8214-0408-3 (pbk). ▸ Short autobiography of arguably most famous Thai Buddhist monk; sheds light on life during absolute monarchy as well as on formative stage in growth of modern Thai Buddhism. Long introduction especially useful. [DKW]

16.187 Walter F. Vella. *Chaiyo! King Vajiravudh and the development of Thai nationalism.* Honolulu: University of Hawaii Press, 1978. ISBN 0-8248-0493-7. ▸ Sympathetic treatment of epochal period, reign of King Vajiravudh (r. 1910–25). Vajiravudh credited with creation of Thai nationalism, which Vella describes without clearly defining concept. [DKW]

16.188 Walter F. Vella. *Siam under Rama III, 1824–1851.* Locust Valley, N.Y.: Augustin for the Association for Asian Studies, 1957. (Association for Asian Studies, Monographs and papers,

4.) ▸ First historical monograph to appear using primarily (printed) Thai-language sources. Strongest in extended treatment of relations between Bangkok and various vassal states that surrounded Siam. [DKW]

16.189 Constance M. Wilson. *Thailand: a handbook of historical statistics.* Boston: Hall, 1983. ISBN 0-8161-8115-2. ▸ Varied collection of statistics on wide range of subjects, accurate as far as sources allow. [DKW]

16.190 Joseph J. Wright, Jr. *The balancing act: a history of modern Thailand.* Oakland, Calif.: Pacific Rim, 1991. ISBN 974-8206-62-9. ▸ Detailed narrative history of half-century since end of absolute monarchy in 1932 based on English sources. Much information found nowhere else. [DKW]

16.191 David K. Wyatt. "Family politics in nineteenth-century Thailand." *Journal of Southeast Asian history* 9.2 (1968) 208–28. ISSN 0022-4634. ▸ Innovative examination of family lineages in high office in early Bangkok period (1782–1868), especially using genealogical information. [DKW]

16.192 David K. Wyatt. *The politics of reform in Thailand: education in the reign of King Chulalongkorn.* New Haven: Yale University Press, 1969. (Yale Southeast Asia studies, 4.) ISBN 0-300-01156-3. ▸ First monograph based primarily on Thai-language archival records. Modestly discusses educational reform, but in process constructs outline of its political context. [DKW]

Indochina

16.193 Philippe Devillers and Jean Lacouture. *End of a war: Indochina, 1954.* Rev. ed. Alexander Lieven and Adam Roberts, trans. New York: Praeger, 1969. ▸ Collaboration between academic and veteran journalist with extensive experience of Indochina during First Indochina War (1946–54). Conveys immediacy lacking in later accounts. [DKW]

16.194 Ellen J. Hammer. *The struggle for Indochina, 1940–1955.* Stanford, Calif.: Stanford University Press, 1966. ▸ Examination mainly of First Indochina War (1946–54) from Western-language sources. Can almost be read as antiwar tract, though written decade before Second Indochina War. [DKW]

16.195 Donald Lancaster. *The emancipation of French Indochina.* 1961 ed. New York: Octagon Books, 1975. ISBN 0-374-94719-8. ▸ Balanced examination of history of French Indochina from late nineteenth century, particularly wartime period, postwar struggle of Lao, Cambodians, and Vietnamese for independence, and Geneva Conference of 1954. Based primarily on published French materials. [DKW]

16.196 Alfred W. McCoy. *The politics of heroin: CIA complicity in the global drug trade.* Rev. ed. Brooklyn: Lawrence Hill Books, 1991. ISBN 1-55652-126-X (cl), 1-55652-125-1 (pbk). ▸ Revised and expanded edition of *The Politics of Heroin in Southeast Asia* (1972). Deals especially with Laos in 1960s, but ranges much more broadly in space and time. [DKW]

16.197 Milton E. Osborne. *River road to China: the Mekong River expedition, 1866–1873.* New York: Liveright, 1975. ISBN 0-87140-578-4. ▸ Well-written account of Lagrée-Garnier Expedition which ascended Mekong River from Cambodia through Laos into China between 1866 and 1868, setting stage for later French moves into region. [DKW]

16.198 Georges Taboulet, ed. *La geste française en Indochine: histoire par les textes de la France en Indochine des origines à 1914.* 2 vols. Paris: Adrien-Maisonneuve, 1955. ▸ Massive collection of French documents concerning Indochina (but mainly Vietnam). Volume 1 covers period from mid-seventeenth century to 1858 and focuses on activities of French Catholic missionaries; volume 2 to 1914. [DKW]

Vietnam

16.199 Georges Boudarel, trans. "Mémoires de Phan Boi Chau (Phan Boi Chau nien bieu): traduction de la version en *quoc ngu.*" *France-Asie* 22.3–4 (1968) 263–470. ISSN 0338-5264. ▸ Elegant, fascinating memoirs of leading Vietnamese nationalist and revolutionary from first quarter of twentieth century. [DKW]

16.200 Joseph Buttinger. *The smaller dragon: a political history of Vietnam.* New York: Praeger, 1958. ▸ Earliest full history of Vietnam in English, to beginning of French rule in 1880s. Suffers from reliance on Western-language sources and from staunch anticommunist perspective. [DKW]

16.201 Joseph Buttinger. *Vietnam: a dragon embattled.* 2 vols. New York: Praeger, 1967. ▸ Picks up where *The Smaller Dragon* (16.200) leaves off, covers beginnings of French rule through colonial period and warfare of 1940s to 1960s. Staunchly anticommunist and based exclusively on Western-language sources. Useful nonetheless. [DKW]

16.202 John F. Cady. *The roots of French imperialism in eastern Asia.* Ithaca, N.Y.: Cornell University Press for the American Historical Association, 1954. ▸ Focusing primarily on period from 1815 to 1870s, study concerned only incidentally with Vietnam. Uses French records exclusively to trace stages by which France came to establish colonial empire in Vietnam. [DKW]

16.203 Dang Phu'o'ng-Nghi. *Les institutions publiques du Vietnam au dix-huitième siècle.* Paris: L'École Française d'Extrême-Orient, 1969. (L'École Française d'Extrême-Orient, Publications, 64.) ▸ Central power and local institutions in Vietnam in eighteenth century; necessary for an understanding of what followed. Succinct and clear, based on careful reading of indigenous sources. [DKW]

16.204 Philippe Devillers. *Histoire du Viet-Nam de 1940 à 1952.* 3d rev. ed. Paris: Seuil, 1952. ▸ Impassioned account of First Indochina War based in large measure on firsthand knowledge. Especially rich in detail. [DKW]

16.205 William J. Duiker. *The communist road to power in Vietnam.* Boulder: Westview, 1981. ISBN 0-89158-794-2. ▸ Political history of Vietnam from 1900 to 1975. Focuses on leadership and policies of Communist party. Based mainly on French and American archival materials and on writings of some Vietnamese scholars. [DKW]

16.206 William J. Duiker. *The rise of nationalism in Vietnam, 1900–1941.* Ithaca, N.Y.: Cornell University Press, 1976. ISBN 0-8014-0951-9. ▸ Early general account of rise of Vietnamese nationalism, somewhat more conservative approach than Marr 16.214, 16.215. Treats scholar-patriots (1900–20), urban nationalists (1920–40), and social revolutionaries who created Communist party of Indochina. [DKW]

16.207 Bernard B. Fall. *Hell in a very small place: the siege of Dien Bien Phu.* 1967 ed. New York: Da Capo, 1985. ISBN 0-306-802317 (pbk). ▸ Vivid account of last great, disastrous (for French) battle of First Indochina War in 1953–54. Based in part on French military archives. [DKW]

16.208 Gerald Cannon Hickey. *Free in the forest: ethnohistory of the Vietnamese Central Highlands, 1954–1976.* New Haven: Yale University Press, 1982. ISBN 0-300-02437-1. ▸ Continuation of 16.209, treats period when hill peoples of southern Vietnam caught up in Second Indochina War (1960–75). Pays increasing attention to ethnonationalism, drive for autonomy among some hill peoples. [DKW]

16.209 Gerald Cannon Hickey. *Sons of the mountains: ethnohistory of the Vietnamese central highlands to 1954.* New Haven: Yale University Press, 1982. ISBN 0-300-02453-3. ▸ Almost unique to historical literature on Southeast Asia (with Hickey 16.208).

Material slender until French arrival in 1870s and 1880s, after which detail much fuller. Much more attention to Austroasiatic-speaking than to Austronesian-speaking ethnic groups. [DKW]

16.210 Thomas Lionel Hodgkin. *Vietnam: the revolutionary path.* New York: St. Martin's, 1981. ISBN 0-312-84588-X. ‣ Endeavors to cover all of history from prehistoric times to 1945; sympathetic to Vietnamese Revolution, interprets all of Vietnamese history as leading up to it. Based on discussions with modern Vietnamese scholars. [DKW]

16.211 Huynh Kim Khanh. *Vietnamese communism, 1925–1945.* Ithaca, N.Y.: Cornell University Press for Institute of Southeast Asian Studies, 1982. ISBN 0-8014-1369-9 (cl), 0-8014-9397-8 (pbk). ‣ Chronicles internal developments of Indochinese Communist party and assesses reasons for communism's success in 1945. Notable discussion of Vietnamese ideological flexibility vis-à-vis China and Soviet Union. [DKW]

16.212 George McT. Kahin. *Intervention: how America became involved in Vietnam.* 1986 ed. Garden City, N.Y.: Anchor/Doubleday, 1987. ISBN 0-385-24099-6 (pbk). ‣ Magisterial, exhaustive examination of why and how United States became involved in Vietnam, concentrating particularly on 1950s and 1960s. Based on close reading of declassified United States documents. [DKW]

16.213 Jean Lacouture. *Ho Chi Minh, a political biography.* Jane Clark Seitz, ed. Peter Wiles, trans. New York: Random House, 1968. ‣ One of earliest, and still among best, biographies of Ho Chi Minh, by veteran French journalist. [DKW]

16.214 David G. Marr. *Vietnamese anticolonialism, 1885–1925.* Berkeley: University of California Press, 1971. ISBN 0-520-01813-3 (cl), 0-520-02046-4 (pbk). ‣ Examines Vietnamese resistance to French colonial rule from Vietnamese sources. Felicitous contrasts between older generation resisting French by traditional means in late nineteenth century and beginnings of modern nationalism in early twentieth century. [DKW]

16.215 David G. Marr. *Vietnamese tradition on trial, 1920–1945.* Berkeley: University of California Press, 1981. ISBN 0-520-04180-1. ‣ Topical essays, all revolving around how Vietnamese both preserved and transformed their national culture and identity in late years of French colonial rule. Based almost entirely on Vietnamese sources. [DKW]

16.216 Nguyen Thanh Nha. *Tableau économique du Viet-Nam aux dix-septième et dix-huitième siècles.* 1966 ed. Paris: Cujas, 1970. ‣ Study of Vietnamese economy in seventeenth and eighteenth centuries based on Vietnamese annals, laws, European accounts, and other documentary materials. [DKW]

16.217 Nguyen The Anh. *The withering days of the Nguyen dynasty.* Singapore: Institute of Southeast Asian Studies, 1978. (Institute of Southeast Asian Studies, Research notes and discussions series, 7.) ‣ Study of the Vietnamese monarchy during years when France gained control over it (1883–88). Serious attention to factional politics at Vietnamese court. [DKW]

16.218 Milton E. Osborne. *The French presence in Cochinchina and Cambodia: rule and response (1859–1905).* Ithaca, N.Y.: Cornell University Press, 1969. ISBN 0-8014-0512-2. ‣ Comparative study of early French colonial capture and administration of Cochinchina (southernmost portion of Vietnam) and Cambodia. Based primarily on French-language sources. [DKW]

16.219 *The Pentagon Papers: the Defense Department history of United States decisionmaking on Vietnam.* Senator Gravel ed. 5 vols. Boston: Beacon, 1971–72. ISBN 0-8070-0526-6 (v. 1–4, cl), 0-8070-0522-3 (v. 5, cl), 0-8070-0527-4 (v. 1–4, pbk), 0-8070-0523-1 (v. 5, pbk). ‣ Best of three different editions of Pentagon Papers: volumes 1–4 consist of analysis, followed by documents. Volume 5 consists of essays, edited by antiwar activists Howard

Zinn and Noam Chomsky, that present an alternative reading of documents and analysis. [DKW]

16.220 Samuel L. Popkin. *The rational peasant: the political economy of rural society in Vietnam.* Berkeley: University of California Press, 1979. ISBN 0-520-03561-5 (cl), 0-520-03954-8 (pbk). ‣ Disputes Scott 16.133 on issue of peasant conditions and incentives to revolt. [DKW]

16.221 Hue Tam-Ho Tai. *Millenarianism and peasant politics in Vietnam.* Cambridge, Mass.: Harvard University Press, 1983. ISBN 0-674-57555-5. ‣ Interpretation of background to and rise of Hoa-hao religious movement in southern Vietnam during 1930s and 1940s; covers last half of nineteenth century and first half of twentieth century. [DKW]

16.222 Hue Tam-Ho Tai. *Radicalism and the origins of the Vietnamese Revolution.* Cambridge, Mass.: Harvard University Press, 1992. ISBN 0-674-74612-0. ‣ Innovative attempt to distinguish radicalism of early 1920s in Vietnamese nationalism from Marxism that soon followed. [DKW]

16.223 Truong Buu Lam. *Patterns of Vietnamese response to foreign intervention, 1858–1900.* New Haven: Yale University, Southeast Asia Studies, 1967. (Yale Southeast Asian studies, Monograph series, 11.) ‣ Close reading of small selection of Vietnamese documents from period of resistance against imposition of French colonial rule. [DKW]

16.224 Walter F. Vella, ed. *Aspects of Vietnamese history.* Honolulu: University of Hawaii Press, 1973. ISBN 0-8248-0236-5. ‣ Includes six useful essays, five of which deal with twentieth century, by R. B. Smith, Vu Duc Bang, William H. Frederick, Milton Osborne, Hoang Ngoc Thanh, and Truong Buu Lam. [DKW]

16.225 Alexander B. Woodside. *Community and revolution in modern Vietnam.* Boston: Houghton-Mifflin, 1976. ISBN 0-395-20367-8. ‣ For its time, very calm and reasonable book, grounded in deep knowledge of Vietnamese history. Examines early nationalists, confrontation with French colonialism in search for identity, and shaping of intellectuals and ideology in twentieth century. [DKW]

16.226 Alexander B. Woodside. *Vietnam and the Chinese model: a comparative study of Vietnamese and Chinese.* 1971 ed. Cambridge, Mass.: Harvard University Press for the Council on East Asian Studies, 1988. (Harvard East Asian monographs, 140.) ISBN 0-674-93721-X. ‣ Brilliant study of nineteenth-century Vietnam. Unusual for attempting sophisticated comparisons with contemporary China. Heart of volume is longstanding problem of Vietnamese identity vis-à-vis China. Original subtitle: *Nguyen and Ch'ing Civil Government in the First Half of the Nineteenth Century.* [DKW]

Cambodia

16.227 David P. Chandler. *The tragedy of Cambodian history: politics, war, and revolution since 1945.* New Haven: Yale University Press, 1991. ISBN 0-300-04919-6. ‣ Definitive treatment of recent Cambodian history based on extensive archival research and interviews. Covers period only to Vietnamese invasion of 1979. [DKW]

16.228 David P. Chandler and Ben Kiernan, eds. *Revolution and its aftermath in Kampuchea: eight essays.* New Haven: Yale University, Southeast Asia Studies, 1983. (Southeast Asian studies, Monograph series, 25.) ISBN 0-938692-05-4 (pbk). ‣ Excellent collection of essays by world's leading Cambodia specialists not long after fall of Pol Pot regime. Some especially historical articles by Serge Thion and Gareth Porter. [DKW]

16.229 Alain Forest. *Le Cambodge et la colonisation française: histoire d'une colonisation sans heurts (1897–1920).* Paris: L'Harmattan, 1980. ISBN 2-85802-139-2. ‣ Very lengthy, detailed treatment of heart of French colonial era, based on French sources including archival materials. [DKW]

16.230 Ben Kiernan. *How Pol Pot came to power: a history of communism in Kampuchea.* London: Verso, 1985. ISBN 0-86091-097-0 (cl), 0-86091-805-X (pbk). ▸ History of Cambodia since World War I, concentrating especially on period since 1954. Grapples with question of how an apparently weak Khmer Communist party came to power. [DKW]

16.231 Ben Kiernan and Chanthou Boua, eds. *Peasants and politics in Kampuchea, 1942–1981.* Armonk, N.Y.: Sharpe, 1982. ISBN 0-87332-217-7 (cl), 0-87332-224-X (pbk). ▸ Some excellent historical articles on history of Cambodia during little studied periods, by acknowledged experts. [DKW]

Laos

16.232 René de Berval. *Kingdom of Laos: the land of the million elephants and of the white parasol.* Mrs. Teissier du Cros, trans. Saigon: France-Asie, 1959. ▸ Collection of essays covering everything from geography and history to arts, ethnography, religion, medicine, language, literature, education, and folklore. Includes many translated excerpts from Lao historical works. [DKW]

16.233 Paul Le Boulanger. *Histoire du Laos français: essai d'une étude chronologique des principautés laotiennes.* Paris: Plon, 1931. ▸ Regrettably outdated and old-fashioned but no real alternative. Considers that an "objective" Lao past actually exists; documents simply do not lend themselves to certainties he purveys. Within limits, a reasonable and useful book. English translation available on microtransparency: C. A. Messner, trans., *A History of French Laos* (Human Relations Area Files, 1955). [DKW]

16.234 MacAlister Brown and Joseph J. Zasloff. *Apprentice revolutionaries: the communist movement in Laos, 1930–1985.* Stanford, Calif.: Hoover Institution Press, 1986. ISBN 0-8179-8122-5 (pbk). ▸ Very detailed and very cautious history of communist movement by experienced political scientists. Benefits from excellent documentation, much of it not public domain. Key tension is question of Laotian independence vis-à-vis Vietnam. [DKW]

16.235 Geoffrey C. Gunn. *Political struggles in Laos (1930–1954): Vietnamese communist power and the Lao struggle for national independence.* Bangkok: Duang Kamol, 1988. ISBN 974-210-447-6, 974-210-459-5. ▸ Monographic narrative begins to fill dark hole in Lao history, where there had been almost no previous work. Poorly written, but very informative. Good bibliography of materials in Western languages. [DKW]

16.236 Maha Sila Viravong. *History of Laos.* 1959 ed. New York: Paragon Book Reprint, 1964. ▸ Represents conventional Lao thinking about their own history. Based on broad range of traditional manuscript sources. First published in Lao in 1957. [DKW]

Malaysia, Singapore, and Brunei

16.237 R. Bonney. *Kedah, 1771–1821: the search for security and independence.* Kuala Lumpur: Oxford University Press, 1971. ▸ Systematic and thoughtful study of excruciating history of Kedah, caught between its Malay, Thai, and Burmese neighbors, through difficult years of late eighteenth and early nineteenth centuries. [DKW]

16.238 Donald E. Brown. *Brunei: the structure and history of a Bornean Malay sultanate.* Brunei: Brunei Museum, 1970. (Brunei Museum journal, Monograph, 2.2.) ▸ Still strongest and one of richest accounts of Brunei sultanate, by anthropologist. Takes a social and structural approach often preferable to drier listings of names and events. [DKW]

16.239 Cheah Boon Kheng, ed. and comp. *From PKI to the*

Comintern, 1924–1941: the apprenticeship of the Malayan Communist party, selected documents and discussion. Ithaca, N.Y.: Cornell University, Southeast Asia Program, 1992. (Southeast Asia Program series, 8.) ISBN 0-87727-125-9. ▸ Major compilation of documents at last gives distinctive identity to Malayan Communist party in decades before World War II. Materials primarily from police files. [DKW]

16.240 C. D. Cowan. *Nineteenth-century Malaya: the origins of British political control.* London: Oxford University Press, 1961. ▸ Careful examination of conditions leading up to establishment of British colonial control in west coast Malayan states in 1870s. Lays particular stress on European rivalries. [DKW]

16.241 John H. Drabble. *Malayan rubber: the interwar years.* Houndmills: Macmillan, 1991. ISBN 0-333-53436-0. ▸ Studies phenomenal growth of Malayan rubber industry from nothing to world leadership before World War II. Based on British and company archives. [DKW]

16.242 N. John Funston. *Malay politics in Malaysia: a study of the United Malays National Organisation and Party Islam.* Kuala Lumpur: Heinemann Educational Books, 1980. ▸ Close examination of Malay politics in late colonial period (to 1957) and first decades of independence, based on wide range of sources. [DKW]

16.243 J. M. Gullick. *Indigenous political systems of western Malaya.* Rev. ed. London: Athlone, 1988. ISBN 0-485-19417-1. ▸ Perhaps Southeast Asian historians' favorite anthropological work. Analysis of political systems of west coast of Malay Peninsula in nineteenth century: strained by burgeoning tin industry and gave way to British colonial "protection" in 1870s. [DKW]

16.244 J. M. Gullick. *Malay society in the late nineteenth century: the beginnings of change.* Singapore: Oxford University Press, 1987. ISBN 0-19-588850-2. ▸ Traces changes especially on west coast of Malay Peninsula as tin industry developed, Chinese immigration accelerated, and Malay-Chinese conflict erupted. Beautifully illustrated. [DKW]

16.245 Graham W. Irwin. *Nineteenth-century Borneo: a study in diplomatic rivalry.* Singapore: Moore, 1955. ▸ Examines competition between Dutch and English for control over island resulting in present-day partition between Malaysia and Indonesia. Based on colonial archives. [DKW]

16.246 Khoo Kay Kim. *The western Malay states, 1850–1873: the effects of commercial development on Malay politics.* Kuala Lumpur: Oxford University Press, 1972. ▸ Major contribution to study of relationship between Malay states and British by examining commercial and other economic ties that bound British Straits settlements (Singapore, Penang, Malacca) to west coast Malay states before onset of British control in 1873. [DKW]

16.247 Lim Teck Ghee. *Peasants and their agricultural economy in colonial Malaya, 1874–1941.* Kuala Lumpur: Oxford University Press, 1977. ISBN 0-19-580338-8. ▸ Excellent survey account, focusing on peasants and peasant agriculture in period during which most attention usually falls on immigrant communities and export production of tin and rubber. [DKW]

16.248 W. Linehan. *A history of Pahang.* Kuala Lumpur: Malaysian Branch of the Royal Asiatic Society, 1973. (Malaysian Branch of the Royal Asiatic Society, Reprints, 2.) ▸ Remains sole detailed account of whole history of east coast Malay state of Pahang. Very unanalytical. [DKW]

16.249 Craig Alan Lockard. *From kampung to city: a social history of Kuching, Malaysia, 1820–1970.* Athens: Ohio University, Center for Southeast Asian Studies, 1987. (Monographs in international studies, Southeast Asia series, 75.) ISBN 0-89680-136-5. ▸ Readable urban history of Sarawak's chief town over long period. Interesting final section places Kuching in wider comparative context, especially in matters concerning overseas Chinese. [DKW]

16.250 Hendrik M. J. Maier. *In the center of authority: the Malay "Hikayat Marong Mahawangsa."* Ithaca, N.Y.: Cornell University, Southeast Asia Program, 1988. ISBN 0-87727-703-6. ▸ Written by literary scholar, tracing curious history of changing interpretations and taming of indigenous legendary chronicle of old Malay state of Kedah, from 1820s. [DKW]

16.251 S. M. Middlebrook. *Yap Ah Loy, 1837–1885.* Rev. ed. Kuala Lumpur: Art Printing Works for the Malaysian Branch of the Royal Asiatic Society, 1983. (Malaysian Branch of the Royal Asiatic Society, Reprints, 9.) ISBN 967-994824-5. ▸ Classic study of Chinese headman of Kuala Lumpur region first published in 1951 and revised here by Gullick. Underlines importance of Chinese immigration and industry in foundation of modern Malaya. Introduction and final three chapters by J. M. Gullick. [DKW]

16.252 Robert Pringle. *Rajahs and rebels: the Ibans of Sarawak under Brooke rule, 1841–1941.* Ithaca, N.Y.: Cornell University Press, 1970. ISBN 0-8014-0552-1. ▸ Careful examination of changing position and conditions of Iban—major tribal people of Sarawak—during century of rule by Brooke family, "White Rajahs." Excellent bibliography. [DKW]

16.253 Victor Purcell. *The Chinese in Malaya.* 1948 ed. London: Oxford University Press, 1967. ▸ Written by man who spent most of his career in Malayan Civil Service (1921–46) in positions of responsibility for Chinese affairs. Remains historically useful. [DKW]

16.254 Margaret Clark Roff. *The politics of belonging: political change in Sabah and Sarawak.* Kuala Lumpur: Oxford University Press, 1974. ISBN 0-19-580264-0. ▸ Study of political integration of East Malaysian territories into Malaysian polity in decade following union in 1963. [DKW]

16.255 William R. Roff. *The origins of Malay nationalism.* New Haven: Yale University Press, 1967. (Southeast Asia Studies, Monograph series, 2.) ▸ Examines differential impact of British colonial control on different elements within Malay society and their growing responses, especially in years just before World War II. Based primarily on Malay-language materials, especially newspapers and periodicals. [DKW]

16.256 William R. Roff, ed. *Kelantan: religion, society, and politics in a Malay state.* Kuala Lumpur: Oxford University Press, 1974. ISBN 0-19-638239-4. ▸ Unusually good collection of essays on history, religion, and politics of Kelantan, small old sultanate on northeast coast of Malaya. Focuses on nineteenth and twentieth centuries and on Malay-language sources. [DKW]

16.257 Emily Sadka. *The protected Malay states, 1874–1895.* Kuala Lumpur: University of Malaya Press, 1968. ▸ Detailed examination of first two decades of British influence and power under fiction of "protection" in Perak and Selangor, less so in Negri Sembilan and Pahang. [DKW]

16.258 Benedict Sandin. *The Sea Dayaks of Borneo before White Rajah rule.* 1967 ed. East Lansing: Michigan State University Press, 1968. ▸ Reconstruction of precolonial history of the Sarawak Dayaks based on oral evidence; unconventional treatment. Focus on pre-Sarawak migrations, period of clearing and settling, and turmoil of mid and late nineteenth-century piracy and rebellions. [DKW]

16.259 Sharom Ahmat. "Kedah-Siam relations, 1821–1905." *Journal of the Siam Society* 59.1 (1971) 97–118. ISSN 0304-226X. ▸ Through this period (and to 1909), Kedah remained vassal of kings of Siam. Author traces relationship over almost century, using mainly Malay sources. [DKW]

16.260 Sharom Ahmat. "The political structure of the state of Kedah, 1879–1905." *Journal of Southeast Asian studies* 1.2 (1970) 115–28. ISSN 0022-4634. ▸ Traces particularly interesting succession patterns and structural responses to external stimuli during period of intense colonial pressure. [DKW]

16.261 Anthony Short. *The communist insurrection in Malaya, 1948–1960.* New York: Crane, Russack, 1975. ISBN 0-8448-0306-5. ▸ Official backing and access to classified documents withdrawn following disagreements with sponsors; published independently by author after long delays. Very rich study of turbulent period. [DKW]

16.262 Michael R. Stenson. *Industrial conflict in Malaya: prelude to the communist revolt of 1948.* London: Oxford University Press, 1970. ISBN 0-19-212957-0. ▸ Careful study of labor movement and strikes in Malaya immediately preceding communist insurrection that broke out in 1948. Definitive. [DKW]

16.263 A. J. Stockwell. *British policy and Malay politics during the Malayan Union experiment, 1945–1948.* Kuala Lumpur: Art Printing Works for the Malaysian Branch of the Royal Asiatic Society, 1979. (Malaysian Branch of the Royal Asiatic Society, Monographs, 8.) ▸ Examination of chaotic formative period in Malay politics immediately following World War II, centering on events leading up to and following creation of Malayan Union. Nice sequel to Roff 16.255. [DKW]

16.264 Nicholas Tarling. *Britain, the Brookes, and Brunei.* Kuala Lumpur: Oxford University Press, 1971. ▸ Conventional account, from British archives, of mid-nineteenth-century turbulence that ended with Brooke rule in Sarawak and precarious independence of sultanate of Brunei. [DKW]

16.265 Nicholas Tarling. *Piracy and politics in the Malay world: a study of British imperialism in nineteenth-century Southeast Asia.* Melbourne: Cheshire, 1963. ▸ Conventional account of British encounters with various pirates including turbulence on northwest coast of Brunei and in southern Philippines. Underappreciates complex political and social dimensions of piracy in period. [DKW]

16.266 Eunice Thio. *British policy in the Malay Peninsula, 1886–1910.* Vol. 1: *The southern and central states.* Singapore: University of Malaya Press, 1968. ▸ Careful, documented account of revived British forward policy that brought Negri Sembilan, Johore, and Pahang under British paramountcy and in succeeding period during which British control was consolidated (1890–1910). [DKW]

16.267 K. G. Tregonning. *A history of modern Sabah: North Borneo, 1881–1963.* 2d ed. Singapore: University of Malaya Press for the University of Singapore, 1965. ▸ Workmanlike general history of Sabah over relatively brief period, written at time of independence from Britain and subsequent incorporation into Malaysia. [DKW]

16.268 Carl A. Trocki. *Opium and empire: Chinese society in colonial Singapore, 1800–1910.* Ithaca, N.Y.: Cornell University Press, 1990. ISBN 0-8014-2390-2. ▸ Examines role of opium in colonial state, including financing of colonial rule. Bears useful comparison with Rush 16.312. [DKW]

16.269 Carl A. Trocki. *Prince of pirates: the Temenggongs and the development of Johor and Singapore, 1784–1885.* Singapore: Singapore University Press, 1979. ▸ Development of Johore (at southern tip of Malay Peninsula) and neighboring Singapore, focusing on particular family involved in both places. [DKW]

16.270 C. M. Turnbull. *A history of Singapore, 1819–1988.* 2d ed. Singapore: Oxford University Press, 1989. ISBN 0-19-588911-8 (cl), 0-19-588943-6 (pbk). ▸ Standard history of Singapore with lengthy bibliographical references. Very straightforward. [DKW]

16.271 C. M. Turnbull. *The Straits settlements, 1826–67: Indian* *presidency to crown colony.* London: Athlone, 1972. ISBN 0-485-13132-3. ▸ Clear focus on British administration in Singapore, Penang, and Malacca over half-century before British power expanded onto Malay Peninsula, based entirely on colonial records. [DKW]

16.272 Karl von Vorys. *Democracy without consensus: communalism and political stability in Malaysia.* Princeton: Princeton University Press, 1975. ISBN 0-691-07571-9. ▸ Detailed analysis and description of West Malaysian politics from Japanese occupation to early 1970s, but especially on period since independence in 1957. Stresses Malaysian commitment to democratic rule. [DKW]

16.273 R. J. Wilkenson, ed. *Papers on Malay subjects.* P. L. Burns, reprint ed. Kuala Lumpur: Oxford University Press, 1971. ▸ Selected papers, edited by Wilkinson, published 1907–17. Include Wilkinson's "History of the Peninsular Malays" and various historical papers on states of Perak and Negri Sembilan, mainly but not exclusively dealing with nineteenth century. [DKW]

16.274 Richard O. Winstedt. *A history of Malaya.* 1935 ed. Singapore: Marican, 1982. ▸ First published in 1935. Betrays view of one who served more than thirty years as British colonial official in Malaya but also extremely well versed in Malay literature. Not as well disposed toward Chinese immigrant community as Purcell 16.253. [DKW]

16.275 Richard O. Winstedt. "A history of Selangor." *Journal of the Malaysian Branch of the Royal Asiatic Society* 12.3 (1934) 1–34. ISSN 0085-5774. ▸ Brief history of Selangor, Malay state in which modern capital, Kuala Lumpur, is situated. [DKW]

16.276 Richard O. Winstedt. "Negri Sembilan: the history, polity, and beliefs of the nine states." *Journal of the Malaysian Branch of the Royal Asiatic Society* 12.3 (1934) 35–111. ISSN 0085-5774. ▸ Standard, classical history of nine states near Malacca on west coast of Malay Peninsula, based primarily on indigenous sources. [DKW]

16.277 Richard O. Winstedt, R. J. Wilkinson, and W. E. Maxwell. *A history of Perak.* Kuala Lumpur: Malaysian Branch of the Royal Asiatic Society, 1974. (Malaysian Branch of the Royal Asiatic Society, Reprints, 3.) ▸ Winstedt and Wilkinson history first published in 1934 accompanies three articles by Maxwell from 1878, 1882, and 1883. Very handy reprint pulls them together with informative introductions, notes, and appendixes. Provides excellent introduction to history of Perak, one of most important west coast Malay states. [DKW]

16.278 Wong Lin Ken. *The Malayan tin industry to 1914.* Tucson: University of Arizona Press for the Association of Asian Studies, 1965. (Association for Asian studies, Monographs, 14.) ▸ Standard account of tin industry on west coast of Malay Peninsula, especially in nineteenth century. Very specialized and detailed work. [DKW]

Indonesia

16.279 Taufik Abdullah. *Schools and politics: the Kaum Muda movement in West Sumatra (1927–1933).* Ithaca, N.Y.: Cornell University, Modern Indonesia Project, 1971. ▸ Examination of how schools became political in late colonial period when Dutch rule encountered Islamic modernism in West Sumatra. Excellent scholarship. [DKW]

16.280 Susan Abeyasekere. *Jakarta: a history.* Rev. ed. Singapore: Oxford University Press, 1989. ISBN 0-19-588947-9. ▸ Four-century progress from small fishing village to megalopolis. Uncommonly good attempt at both urban and national history. [DKW]

16.281 Benedict R. O'G. Anderson. *Java in a time of revolution:* *occupation and resistance, 1944–1946.* Ithaca, N.Y.: Cornell University Press, 1972. ISBN 0-8014-0687-0. ▸ Analytical approach to early stages of Indonesian Revolution by political scientist with strong cultural sensitivities. Establishes primary importance of youth, army, and communist and socialist elements in forming revolution. [DKW]

16.282 Benedict R. O'G. Anderson. *Language and power: exploring political cultures in Indonesia.* Ithaca, N.Y.: Cornell University Press, 1990. ISBN 0-8014-2354-6 (cl), 0-8014-9758-2 (pbk). ▸ Eight stimulating essays about Indonesian politics and history. Historians find especially useful his seminal article on "The Idea of Power in Javanese Culture," first published in 1972. [DKW]

16.283 Benedict R. O'G. Anderson and Ruth T. McVey. *A preliminary analysis of the October 1, 1965 coup in Indonesia.* Ithaca, N.Y.: Cornell University, Modern Indonesia Project, 1971. ▸ First published within months of coup; analysis of bloody events of 1965 remains controversial, arguing that postcoup regime bears considerable responsibility for what happened. [DKW]

16.284 Harry J. Benda. *The crescent and the rising sun: Indonesian Islam under the Japanese occupation, 1942–1945.* The Hague: van Hoeve; distributed by the Institute of Pacific Relations, 1958. ▸ Sensitive account of Indonesian Islam in wartime conditions by one who was himself caught up in events he analyzes. Excellent introductory section on prewar developments. [DKW]

16.285 Peter Boomgaard. *Children of the colonial state: population growth and economic development in Java, 1795–1880.* Amsterdam: Free University Press, 1989. (Centre for Asian Studies, Amsterdam, Monographs, 1.) ISBN 90-6256-783-5, 90-72765-04-4, ISSN 0293-4659. ▸ Iconoclastic monograph wrestles with old saws about nineteenth-century Java, represented particularly by Geertz 16.294. On basis of colonial documentation offers new explanations of Java's nineteenth-century population explosion. [DKW]

16.286 Harold A. Crouch. *The army and politics in Indonesia.* Rev. ed. Ithaca, N.Y.: Cornell University Press, 1988. ISBN 0-8014-2297-3 (cl), 0-8014-9506-7 (pbk). ▸ Incisive, critical examination of rise of military to power in Indonesia from days of Indonesian Revolution (1945–49). [DKW]

16.287 Bernhard Dahm. *History of Indonesia in the twentieth century.* P. S. Falla, trans. London: Praeger, 1971. ISBN 0-269-02734-3. ▸ Thorough, persuasive account of Indonesian history, focusing primarily on Java in twentieth century to fall of Sukarno in 1965. Somewhat outdated. [DKW]

16.288 C. van Dijk. *Rebellion under the banner of Islam: the Darul Islam in Indonesia.* The Hague: Nijhoff, 1981. (Verhandelingen van het Koninklijk Instituut voor Taal-, Land-, en Volkenkunde, 94.) ISBN 90-247-6172-7 (pbk). ▸ Key work on orthodox Islamic political movements in independent Indonesia, based on indigenous sources. [DKW]

16.289 Christine Dobbin. *Islamic revivalism in a changing peasant economy: Central Sumatra, 1784–1847.* London: Curzon, 1983. (Scandinavian Institute of Asia Studies, Monograph series, 47.) ISBN 0-7007-0155-9 (pbk). ▸ How modernist Islam thrived and grew, becoming political force on west coast of Sumatra in eighteenth and nineteenth centuries. [DKW]

16.290 R. E. Elson. *Javanese peasants and the colonial sugar industry: impact and change in an East Java residency, 1830–1940.* Singapore: Oxford University Press for Asian Studies Association of Australia, 1984. (Southeast Asia publications series, 9.) ISBN 0-86861-608-7 (cl), 0-86861-616-8 (pbk), 0-19-582619-1. ▸ Detailed agrarian history of East Java district, looking at how rise and fall of plantation sugar industry shaped peasant life. Questions Geertz's thesis of "agricultural involution" (16.294). [DKW]

16.291 C. Fasseur. *The politics of colonial exploitation: Java, the Dutch, and the cultivation system.* R. E. Elson and Ary Kraal, eds. and trans. Ithaca, N.Y.: Cornell University, Southeast Asia Program, 1992. ISBN 0-87727-707-9. ▸ One of first truly fresh looks at system of colonial revenue practiced by Dutch in Indonesia, 1830–70; central to understanding of Java in nineteenth century. [DKW]

16.292 Herbert Feith. *The decline of constitutional democracy in Indonesia.* Ithaca, N.Y.: Cornell University Press, 1962. ▸ Detailed examination of politics between independence (end of 1949) and beginning of end of parliamentary democracy (1957). Written close to events described and analyzed, not yet superseded. [DKW]

16.293 William H. Frederick. *Visions and heat: the making of the Indonesian Revolution.* Athens: Ohio University Press, 1989. ISBN 0-8214-0905-0 (cl), 0-8214-0906-9 (pbk). ▸ Thoughtful, considered examination of complex interplay of forces during Indonesian Revolution (1945–49) through developments in important Javanese city of Surabaya. Admittedly weak in coverage of Left. [DKW]

16.294 Clifford Geertz. *Agricultural involution: the process of ecological change in Indonesia.* 1963 ed. Berkeley: University of California Press, 1966. ISBN 0-520-00459-2 (cl), 0-520-00459-0 (pbk). ▸ Anthropologist's examination of how nineteenth-century Java's exploding population pressed against finite agricultural resources; comparisons with swidden-farming regions of Outer Islands of Indonesia. Enormously influential essay; but see Bloomgaard 16.285 and Elson 16.290. [DKW]

16.295 Elizabeth E. Graves. *The Minangkabau response to Dutch colonial rule in the nineteenth century.* Ithaca, N.Y.: Cornell University, Modern Indonesia Project, 1981. (Southeast Asia Program, Monograph series, 60.) ISBN 0-87763-000-3 (pbk). ▸ A sort of counterpoint to Abdullah 16.279, covering earlier period and different region of Sumatra, but also involving education, economics, colonial rule, and religion. [DKW]

16.296 Donald Hindley. *The Communist party of Indonesia, 1951–1963.* Berkeley: University of California Press, 1964. ▸ Deals especially with puzzle of how the Communist Party of Indonesia (PKI) recovered so rapidly from its disintegration in 1948 to its position of major power by early 1960s. [DKW]

16.297 John Ingleson. *Road to exile: the Indonesian Nationalist movement, 1927–1934.* Singapore: Heinemann Educational Books for the Asian Studies Association of Australia, 1979. (Southeast Asia publications series, 1.) ISBN 0-7081-0309-X. ▸ Nicely balanced study of transition between radicalism of 1927 and concerted nationalist pressure against Dutch by new Indonesian Nationalist party (PNI) by mid-1930s. [DKW]

16.298 Audrey R. Kahin, ed. *Regional dynamics of the Indonesian Revolution: unity from diversity.* Honolulu: University of Hawaii Press, 1985. ISBN 0-8248-0982-3. ▸ Excellent collection of articles on the revolution (1945–49) in locales all over archipelago. Gives national depth to what otherwise often seems overly Javanese phenomenon. [DKW]

16.299 George McT. Kahin. *Nationalism and revolution in Indonesia.* Ithaca, N.Y.: Cornell University Press, 1952. ▸ Exceptionally durable, early account of Indonesian Revolution (1945–49) by American political scientist, firsthand observer and participant. Later accounts, though perhaps more broadly based, cannot match immediacy of this account. [DKW]

16.300 J. Kathirithamby-Wells. *The British West Sumatran presidency, 1760–1785: problems of early colonial enterprise.* Kuala Lumpur: Penerbit Universiti Malaya, 1977. ▸ Conventional examination of classic backwater of British colonial rule, distinguished especially by quality of scholarship. [DKW]

16.301 J. D. Legge. *Sukarno: a political biography.* 1972 ed. Boston: Allen & Unwin, 1984. ISBN 0-86861-463-7. ▸ Straightforward yet sophisticated biographical account, by Australian historian who spent entire career working on postwar Indonesia. [DKW]

16.302 Ruth T. McVey. *The rise of Indonesian communism.* Ithaca, N.Y.: Cornell University Press, 1965. ▸ Massive, 500-page account of first decade or so (to 1927) of Indonesian Communist party (PKI), based on Indonesian, Dutch, Russian, and other sources. [DKW]

16.303 Rex Mortimer. *Indonesian communism under Sukarno: ideology and politics, 1959–1965.* Ithaca, N.Y.: Cornell University Press, 1974. ISBN 0-8014-0825-3. ▸ Focuses primarily on early 1960s, when Indonesian Communist party (PKI) was one of main props of Sukarno's power. Written in aftermath of party's decimation in massacres of 1965 to 1966. [DKW]

16.304 Akira Nagazumi. *The dawn of Indonesian nationalism: the early years of the Budi Utomo, 1908–1918.* Tokyo: Institute of Developing Economies, 1972. (Ajia Keizai Kenkyujo, Occasional papers series, 10.) ISBN 4-495-85201-9. ▸ Very early work of scholarship; best work on earlier years of Budi Utomo, commonly regarded as forerunner of Indonesian nationalist organizations. [DKW]

16.305 Rob Nieuwenhuys. *Mirror of the Indies: a history of Dutch colonial literature.* E. M. Beekman, ed. Frans van Rosevelt, trans. Amherst: University of Massachusetts Press, 1982. ISBN 0-87023-368-8. ▸ Engagingly written history of Dutch and Eurasian-Dutch fiction emanating from Dutch East Indies in colonial (and postcolonial) period. [DKW]

16.306 Anthony Reid. *The blood of the people: revolution and the end of traditional rule in northern Sumatra.* Kuala Lumpur: Oxford University Press, 1979. ISBN 0-19-580399-X. ▸ Comparative examination of social revolutions which accompanied Indonesian national revolution (1945–49) in two North Sumatra provinces of Aceh and East Coast. [DKW]

16.307 Anthony Reid. *The Indonesian national revolution, 1945–1950.* Hawthorn, Victoria: Longman, 1974. ISBN 0-582-71046-4 (cl), 0-582-71047-2 (pbk). ▸ Excellent, brief overview of Indonesian Revolution, distinguished by how it pulls together broad range of scholarship. Helpful bibliographical essay. [DKW]

16.308 G. J. Resink. *Indonesia's history between the myths: essays in legal history and historical theory.* The Hague: van Hoeve, 1968. ▸ Stimulating essays on Indonesian history by Dutch legal scholar. Topics include Eurocentrism, regiocentrism, and Indocentrism. Questions myth of 350 years of Dutch colonialism; most of Indonesia was not controlled by Dutch until late nineteenth century or later. [DKW]

16.309 M. C. Ricklefs. *Jogjakarta under Sultan Mangkubumi, 1749–1792: a history of the division of Java.* London: Oxford University Press, 1974. ISBN 0-19-713578-1. ▸ Exhaustive coverage of both Dutch and Javanese sources for very complex period when Dutch presided over division of Javanese power, which they then dominated for almost two centuries. [DKW]

16.310 Richard Robison. *Indonesia: the rise of capital.* North Sydney: Allen & Unwin for the Asian Studies Association of Australia, 1986. (Southeast Asia publications series, 13.) ISBN 0-04-909024-0. ▸ Pioneering, influential attempt to trace lineage of Indonesian capitalism, primarily focuses on Soeharto's New Order era. [DKW]

16.311 J. Eliseo Rocamora. *Nationalism in search of ideology: the Indonesian Nationalist party, 1946–1965.* Quezon City: University of the Philippines, Center for Advanced Studies, 1975. ▸ Careful, detailed study of Indonesian Nationalist party, party of Indonesian Revolution, in first two decades of Indonesian independence. [DKW]

16.312 James R. Rush. *Opium to Java: revenue farming and Chinese enterprise in colonial Indonesia, 1860–1910.* Ithaca, N.Y.: Cornell University Press, 1990. ISBN 0-8014-2218-3. ▸ Seminal work on Chinese in nineteenth-century Java. Role of opium in financing colonial state and in providing foundation for immigrant Chinese economic activity in Java. Based on colonial archives and indigenous sources. [DKW]

16.313 Sartono Kartodirdjo. *The peasants' revolt of Banten in 1888: its conditions, course, and sequel, a case study of social movements in Indonesia.* The Hague: Nijhoff, 1966. (Verhandelingen van het Koninklijk Instituut voor Taal-, Land-, en Volkenkunde, 50.) ▸ Very lengthy and detailed study of single peasant revolt against Dutch rule in rural East Java in 1888, based on Dutch colonial records. [DKW]

16.314 Sartono Kartodirdjo. *Protest movements in rural Java: a study of agrarian unrest in the nineteenth and early twentieth centuries.* 1973 ed. Singapore: Oxford University Press, 1988. ▸ General work attempting to make sense of peasant movements in Java in terms of what are now passé social science categories. Based primarily on Dutch records. [DKW]

16.315 Takashi Shiraishi. *An age in motion: popular radicalism in Java, 1912–1926.* Ithaca, N.Y.: Cornell University Press, 1990. ISBN 0-8014-2188-8. ▸ Brilliant examination of early years of Indonesian Nationalist movement focusing on Java. Based on full range of sources, internal and external. Insists on wholeness of "movement," comprising labor, religious, and ideological groups. [DKW]

16.316 Soedjatmoko et al., eds. *An introduction to Indonesian historiography.* Ithaca, N.Y.: Cornell University Press, 1965. ▸ Twenty-two essays on aspects of historiography of Indonesia. Much attention paid to premodern indigenous historical writing and to external (Dutch, Chinese, Japanese, Portuguese, etc.) sources. [DKW]

16.317 Heather Sutherland. *The making of a bureaucratic elite: the colonial transformation of the Javanese priyayi.* Singapore: Heinemann Educational Books for the Asian Studies Association of Australia, 1979. (Southeast Asia publications series, 2.) ISBN 0-7081-1814-3 (cl), 0-7081-1815-1 (pbk). ▸ Concentrating mainly on nineteenth century, shows how Javanese elite was as much product of Dutch policy and education as of Javanese tradition. Significantly influenced subsequent writing. [DKW]

16.318 Jean Gelman Taylor. *The social world of Batavia: European and Eurasian in Dutch Asia.* Madison: University of Wisconsin Press, 1983. ISBN 0-299-09470-7. ▸ Slim, synthetic analysis of urban society in Jakarta from beginning to end of Dutch rule; growth and disappearance of mestizo society. [DKW]

16.319 Robert Van Niel. *The emergence of the modern Indonesian elite.* The Hague: van Hoeve; distributed by University of British Columbia Publications Centre, 1970. ▸ Early, and now substantially superseded, account of origins of Indonesian nationalist movement, emphasizing social and educational change and growing confrontation with Dutch authority. [DKW]

16.320 W. F. Wertheim. *Indonesian society in transition: a study of social change.* 1956 2d rev. ed. Westport, Conn.: Hyperion, 1979. ISBN 0-88355-823-8. ▸ Excellent analytical approach to understanding of twentieth-century Indonesia by Dutch Marxist sociologist. [DKW]

Philippines

16.321 Jose Veloso Abueva. *Ramon Magsaysay: a political biography.* Manila: Solidaridad, 1971. ▸ Probably best among biographies of Philippine presidents. Full on details of events and personalities; not as satisfying in its handling of issues and analysis of developments. [DKW]

16.322 Pedro S. de Achutegui and Miguel A. Bernad. *Aguinaldo and the Revolution of 1896: a documentary history.* Quezon City: Ateneo de Manila University Press, 1972. ▸ Marvelous, rich collection of documents (with parallel translations) from archives, newspapers, and contemporary books concerning Emilio Aguinaldo (first Philippine president) and Philippine Revolution. Good introductions and annotations. [DKW]

16.323 Teodoro A. Agoncillo. *The fateful years: Japan's adventure in the Philippines, 1941–1945.* 2 vols. Quezon City: Garcia, 1965. ▸ Best and fullest account of Japanese period in Philippine history, paying full attention both to general political and economic movements and to details of daily life. [DKW]

16.324 Teodoro A. Agoncillo. *Malolos: the crisis of the republic.* Quezon City: University of the Philippines Press, 1960. ▸ Covers the later years (1897–1901) of Philippine republic, when insurgent government headquartered in Malolos, Bulacan province. Major themes of growing factionalism within elite and increasing tensions with newly arriving American forces. [DKW]

16.325 Teodoro A. Agoncillo. *The revolt of the masses: the story of Bonifacio and the Katipunan.* 1956 ed. Quezon City: University of the Philippines Press, 1974. ▸ Long saga of Andres Bonifacio (1863–97), key leader of revolutionary Katipunan society, whose execution at hands of Aguinaldo's elite government launched Philippine Revolution in 1896. Available on microfilm from New Haven: Yale University Library, Photographic Services. [DKW]

16.326 Teodoro A. Agoncillo and Milagros C. Guerrero. *History of the Filipino people.* 7th ed. Quezon City: Garcia, 1986. ▸ Popular general history by recognized authorities; tends to emphasize recent history and deemphasize pre-1762 developments. Especially good on American period (1902–46) and World War II. [DKW]

16.327 Raymond Bonner. *Waltzing with a dictator: the Marcoses and the making of American policy.* New York: Vintage, 1987. ISBN 0-394-75835-8. ▸ Very full, well-researched study of Marcos dictatorship, making ample use of American documents obtained under Freedom of Information Act. [DKW]

16.328 Bernadita Reyes Churchill. *The Philippine independence missions to the United States, 1919–1934.* Manila: National Historical Institute, 1983. ▸ Careful chronicling of successive Filipino missions to Washington seeking Philippine independence, succeeding only in 1934 with plan for commonwealth government and promise of independence in 1946. Well balanced and judiciously written. [DKW]

16.329 Renato Constantino and Letizia R. Constantino. *The Philippines: the continuing past.* Quezon City: Foundation for Nationalist Studies, 1978. ▸ Best general treatment of Philippines since independence. Primarily political history, 1941–65. Rethinking of recent developments in terms of "people's history," to argue that older patterns of control and hierarchy persist. [DKW]

16.330 Bruce Cruikshank. *Samar, 1768–1898.* Manila: Historical Conservation Society, 1985. (Historical Conservation Society series, 41.) ▸ Detailed, meticulous rare study of island of Samar, based on exhaustive coverage of colonial archives, with particular attention to work of Franciscan friars, who took responsibility for Samar in 1768. [DKW]

16.331 Edilberto C. De Jesus. *The tobacco monopoly in the Philippines: bureaucratic enterprise and social change, 1766–1880.* Quezon City: Ateneo de Manila University Press, 1980. ▸ Examines monopoly's creation and role in underpinning Philippine prosperity through most of its existence and its effects particularly on main tobacco growing area, Cagayan Valley, in mid-nineteenth century. Excellent archival research. [DKW]

16.332 Maria Lourdes Diaz-Trechuelo. "The economic development of the Philippines in the second half of the eighteenth century." *Philippine studies* 11.2 (1963) 195–231. ISSN 0031-7837. ▸ First in pathbreaking series of five articles on Philippine economic and colonial history, based on Spanish archival sources. Shows how colonial government moved from deficit-financing to turning profit in islands. [DKW]

16.333 Daniel F. Doeppers. *Manila, 1900–1941: social change in a late colonial metropolis.* New Haven: Yale University, Southeast Asia Studies, 1984. (Southeast Asia Studies, Monograph series, 27.) ISBN 0-938692-06-2. ▸ Geographer's careful and incisive examination of dry statistical sources to trace colonial economy in its social dimensions and to examine social change in late colonial period. [DKW]

16.334 Theodore Friend. *Between two empires: the ordeal of the Philippines, 1929–1946.* New Haven: Yale University Press, 1965. ▸ Well-regarded account deals with years between promise of independence and actual fulfillment in 1946; United States held islands, but would not act decisively to defend them against Japan in years immediately preceding World War II. [DKW]

16.335 Peter Gordon Gowing. *Mandate in Moroland: the American government of Muslim Filipinos, 1899–1920.* 1977 ed. Quezon City: New Day; distributed by Cellar Book Shop, 1983. ISBN 971-10-0101-2, 971-10-0102-0. ▸ Administrative and political history of southernmost islands of Philippines, with substantial Muslim population, during period of American military occupation (1899–1903), military government (1903–13), and Christian Filipino takeover (1913–20). Based on American colonial archives. [DKW]

16.336 Leon Ma. Guerrero. *The first Filipino: a biography of José Rizal.* Manila: National Heroes Commission, 1963. ▸ Beautifully written and organized, by far best biography of José Rizal (1861–96), literary man and patriot. Skeptical of Philippine Revolution but, nonetheless, blamed for it by Spanish colonial regime and executed. [DKW]

16.337 Reynaldo Clemeña Ileto. *Pasyon and revolution: popular movements in the Philippines, 1840–1910.* Quezon City: Ateneo de Manila University Press; distributed by Cellar Book Shop, 1979. ▸ Brilliant attempt to relate popular movements (from peasant rebellions to Philippine Revolution) to imagery and vocabulary inculcated in nineteenth-century Filipino mind by annual replaying of last days of Christ (the "Pasyon" [Passion]). [DKW]

16.338 Felix M. Keesing. *The ethnohistory of northern Luzon.* Stanford, Calif.: Stanford University Press, 1962. ▸ Excellent, suggestive synthesis of history of ethnically complex region in northern Philippines, where eight major lowland and ten major upland groups have forged relationships over many centuries. Based especially on Spanish-era accounts. [DKW]

16.339 Benedict J. Kerkvliet. *The Huk rebellion: a study of peasant revolt in the Philippines.* Berkeley: University of California Press, 1977. ISBN 0-520-03106-7. ▸ Landmark study of famous Huk movement of immediate post–World War II period, episode of rural protest against continuing exploitation that has never fully died out. Excellent introduction to subject. [DKW]

16.340 John A. Larkin. *The Pampangans: colonial society in a Philippine province.* Berkeley: University of California Press, 1972. ISBN 0-520-02076-6. ▸ Pioneering study of single Philippine province (1565–1921) that began wave of similar studies, making Philippines best-studied area of Southeast Asia on provincial level. [DKW]

16.341 Cesar Adib Majul. *Muslims in the Philippines.* 2d ed. Quezon City: University of the Philippines Press for the Asian Center, 1973. ▸ Focuses particularly on so-called Moro Wars, but much broader in coverage and sympathies, examining gradual decline of Muslim sultanates and political institutions of southern Philippines. Handsome and impressive work. [DKW]

16.342 Cesar Adib Majul. *The political and constitutional ideas of the Philippine Revolution.* 2d ed. Quezon City: University of the Philippines Press for the Asian Center, 1973. ▸ Somewhat old-fashioned but still useful analysis of political thought of key figures in politics of 1890s. Essentially concerned only with elite thought. [DKW]

16.343 Glenn Anthony May. *Social engineering in the Philippines: the aims, execution, and impact of American colonial policy, 1900–1913.* Westport, Conn.: Greenwood, 1980. ISBN 0-313-20978-2. ▸ Critical view of early American colonial policy as self-deluded, arguing that much-vaunted social engineering of American policy more words than action. Based on American archives. [DKW]

16.344 Alfred W. McCoy and Edilberto C. De Jesus, eds. *Philippine social history: global trade and local transformations.* Honolulu: University of Hawaii Press, 1982. ISBN 0-8248-0803-7. ▸ Thirteen excellent essays focusing on nineteenth and twentieth centuries, each dealing with different area. Represents best of recent scholarship, particularly centering on new attention given to local, social, and economic history. [DKW]

16.345 Stuart Creighton Miller. *"Benevolent assimilation": the American conquest of the Philippines, 1899–1903.* New Haven: Yale University Press, 1982. ISBN 0-300-02697-8 (cl), 0-300-03081-9 (pbk). ▸ Nicely written account of the Philippine-American war, written with eye on what author sees as comparable experience in Vietnam. [DKW]

16.346 Resil B. Mojares. *Theater in society, society in theater: social history of a Cebuano village, 1840–1940.* Quezon City: Ateneo de Manila University Press, 1985. ISBN 971-113-045-9 (cl), 971-113-044-0 (pbk). ▸ Ingenious study of relationship between folk theater and local history in town of Valladolid, south of island of Cebu, in nineteenth and twentieth centuries. [DKW]

16.347 Norman G. Owen. *Prosperity without progress: Manila hemp and material life in the colonial Philippines.* Berkeley: University of California Press, 1984. ISBN 0-520-04470-3. ▸ Impressive, careful study of how Bikol region prospered by specializing in production of Manila hemp (or *abaca*) for export but failed to develop strengths to survive collapse of world market for *abaca*. Focuses on period 1850 to 1910. [DKW]

16.348 Norman G. Owen, ed. *Compadre colonialism: studies on the Philippines under American rule.* Ann Arbor: University of Michigan, Center for South and Southeast Asian Studies, 1971. (Michigan papers on South and Southeast Asia, 3.) ▸ Six impressive papers on American rule in Philippines between turn of century and World War II. Most contributors completing doctoral dissertations at time of publication; book represented new wave of scholarship in United States. [DKW]

16.349 Eliodoro G. Robles. *The Philippines in the nineteenth century.* Quezon City: Malaya Books, 1969. ▸ Well-organized, persuasive account of nineteenth-century Philippines. Goes far toward accounting for early success of Philippine Revolution in terms of successes of Spanish rule, rather than inefficiencies and failures. [DKW]

16.350 Ma. Fe Hernaez Romero. *Negros Occidental between two foreign powers (1888–1909).* Manila: Negros Occidental Historical Commission, 1974. ▸ Curious study of refusal of sugar elite of Negros Occidental to ally with fledgling Philippine republic and of efforts of a lower-class rebellion to challenge them. Unusual and worthwhile book. [DKW]

16.351 David A. Rosenberg, ed. *Marcos and martial law in the Philippines.* Ithaca, N.Y.: Cornell University Press, 1979. ISBN 0-8014-1195-5. ▸ Careful academic studies of period of martial law in Philippines under Marcos, written without benefit of knowing outcome. [DKW]

16.352 Dennis Morrow Roth. *The Friar estates of the Philippines.* Albuquerque: University of New Mexico Press, 1977. ISBN

0-8263-0429-X. ‣ Standard account of amassing of large landed estates by Catholic religious orders in Philippines. Focuses especially on late nineteenth century and on area around Manila. [DKW]

16.353 John N. Schumacher. *The Propaganda movement, 1880–1895.* Manila: Solidaridad, 1973. ‣ Standard work on elite political reform movement culminating in Philippine Revolution of 1896. Concerned primarily with young members of elite abroad, mainly in Madrid and Barcelona. [DKW]

16.354 John N. Schumacher. *Revolutionary clergy: the Filipino clergy and the Nationalist movement, 1850–1903.* Quezon City: Ateneo de Manila University Press, 1981. ‣ Based on exhaustive research in numerous archives in Philippines and abroad. Argues that role of Roman Catholic clergy in politics of late nineteenth century much more important than previously thought. [DKW]

16.355 William Henry Scott. *Ilocano responses to American aggression, 1900–1901.* Quezon City: New Day, 1986. ISBN 971-10-0336-8. ‣ Important recent study reopens question of Filipino resistance to imposition of American colonial rule in 1890s; non-Tagalog (away from Manila) resistance much more important than thought. [DKW]

16.356 Peter W. Stanley. *A nation in the making: the Philippines and the United States, 1899–1921.* Cambridge, Mass.: Harvard University Press for the Department of History, Committee on American–East Asia Relations and Council on East Asian Studies, 1974. (Harvard studies in American–East Asian relations, 4.) ISBN 0-674-60125-4. ‣ Finely researched and written examination of relations between American colonial rulers and leaders of Filipino elite during first two decades of American rule. [DKW]

16.357 Peter W. Stanley, ed. *Reappraising an empire: new perspectives on Philippine-American history.* Cambridge, Mass.: Harvard University Press for the Department of History, Committee on American–East Asia Relations and Council on East Asian Studies, 1984. (Harvard studies in American–East Asian relations, 10.) ISBN 0-674-74975-8. ‣ Yet another reappraisal of American rule in Philippines with hindsight of another generation of historical research. Several exemplify growing emphasis on collaborative compromise reached between colonial governors and indigenous elite. [DKW]

16.358 David J. Steinberg. *Philippine collaboration in World War II.* Ann Arbor: University of Michigan Press, 1967. ‣ Account of wartime period very different from that of Agoncillo 16.323. Concerned with issues important at time, including moral dilemma of those who had to choose between Americans, Japanese, and Filipino nation. [DKW]

16.359 David J. Steinberg. *The Philippines: a singular and a plural place.* 2d rev. ed. Boulder: Westview, 1990. ISBN 0-8133-0766-X (cl), 0-8133-8060-X (pbk). ‣ Solid, engaging general introduction to Philippines. Excellent bibliography. [DKW]

16.360 David R. Sturtevant. *Popular uprisings in the Philippines, 1840–1940.* Ithaca, N.Y.: Cornell University Press, 1976. ISBN 0-8014-0877-6. ‣ Original attempt to generalize about popular resistance to Spanish and American colonial rule. At times overgeneralized; insufficient attention to different contexts of rebellions and problems of sources deriving from those who suppressed rebellions. Still, a useful introduction. [DKW]

16.361 John R. M. Taylor, ed. and comp. *The Philippine insurrection against the United States.* 5 vols. Renato Constantino, ed. Pasay City: Eugenio Lopez Foundation, 1971. ‣ Massive collection of translated documents selected from papers captured in course of long (1898–1902) American military campaign to secure control of Philippines. Collection runs to 600 pages of introductory material and more than 2,000 pages of documents. Complete documents, running to 643 rolls of microfilm, available from United States National Archives. [DKW]

16.362 James Francis Warren. *The Sulu zone, 1768–1898: the dynamics of external trade, slavery, and ethnicity in the transformation of a Southeast Asian maritime state.* Singapore: Singapore University Press, 1981. ISBN 9971-69-004-7. ‣ Conceptually very stimulating. Examines complex interrelationships between long independence of Sulu, in extreme south of Philippines, its basis in trade with English East India Company and in use of slave labor, and strains that economic exigencies placed on ethnic relations. [DKW]

16.363 Edgar Wickberg. "The Chinese mestizo in Philippine history." *Journal of Southeast Asian history* 5.1 (1964) 62–100. ISSN 0022-4634. ‣ Seminal article, essential to understanding of modern Philippine history. [DKW]

16.364 Edgar Wickberg. *The Chinese in Philippine life, 1850–1898.* New Haven: Yale University Press, 1965. ‣ Excellent account of subject and one of best earlier monographs on Philippine history. Good bibliography and sensible handling of very complex phenomenon. [DKW]

16.365 David Wurfel. *Filipino politics: development and decay.* Ithaca, N.Y.: Cornell University Press, 1988. ISBN 0-8014-0872-0. ‣ Focus mainly on recent structures of political and economic power, especially during Marcos martial law regime. Useful for understanding of recent history. [DKW]

Islamic World to 1500

Study of the Islamic Middle East began with religion and philology, not with history. Oriental studies acquired an institutionalized identity in European universities over the course of the nineteenth century at the same time that France, Britain, and Russia were gaining or consolidating dominion over most of the Muslim Middle East and North Africa. Some of the roots of Oriental studies were fed from this imperialist vein, as Edward Said has persuasively argued in his landmark book *Orientalism* (17.50). But there were other roots, as well. Some went back to a preimperialist polemic against Islam that dated to the late medieval period when Christian thinkers both feared Ottoman advances in eastern Europe and, in a post-Crusading reverie, dreamt of the mass conversion of the infidels. Still other roots pursued the freshly perceived linkages within the Semitic and Indo-European language families, with their increasingly racist overtones. While in today's politicized academic environment few Arabists move on to the study of Hebrew, it was considered natural in the nineteenth century for students of one Semitic language to familiarize themselves with several others. On the Indo-European side, Persian was seen not just as a tongue related to those of Europe, but as one with possibly closer affinity to Aryan origins. Needless to say, concepts of Semite and Aryan, partially supporting themselves on Orientalist philology, acquired increasing and chilling significance as time progressed.

The scholarly agenda in Oriental studies faculties focused heavily on editing texts, and scholars from different countries exhibited a good deal of collegiality, reflecting the notion that they were collectively engaged in a noble enterprise, to wit, discovering the Muslim East. Although some historical chronicles were among the earliest works edited, there was very little concern with distilling a sophisticated historical narrative from these raw materials. Books on history in European languages were often little more than condensations of one chronicle or another. History as an independent discipline was scarcely in evidence.

A few landmark works early in the twentieth century—Wellhausen's *Das Arabische Reich und sein Sturz* (cf. 17.133) and I. Goldziher's *Vorlesungen über den Islam* (cf. 17.383), to name but two—introduced a higher level of synthesis and analytical insight into the field. Wellhausen provided a model for empirically sound political narrative and Goldziher for grand conceptualization about medieval Islam as a whole. Both of these tendencies grew as text editing continued, but the field as a whole remained decidedly uncritical, both in the scholarly sense and in a reluctance to diminish collegiality by attacking each other's work.

World War II was a watershed. Orientalism in Germany was grievously wounded by emigration, Nazi intolerance, and postwar turmoil. Its recovery did not fully begin until the 1970s. French Orientalism, relying heavily on field experience in colonial territories, became implicated and politically polarized in the Algerian war of independence. Britain's loss of empire was followed by a slow academic retreat from heavy commitment to Oriental studies. But, for the first time, the United States became a significant force. Led by such notable émigrés as Gustave von Grunebaum and Sir Hamilton Gibb, and with funding from the United States government and private foundations, the field of Middle East studies was invented. With its declared objective the training of Middle East specialists to support new worldwide commitments, Middle East studies disdained the medieval and text-editing focus of European Orientalism and saw history as a useful background discipline. Students and faculty alike were encouraged to concentrate their talents on the modern world. Sweeping generalizations about Islam and its medieval history became required reading, but serious work on history was rarely undertaken. Significantly, European Orientalist programs retained their medieval focus and generally did not meld purely academic pursuits with concern for contemporary issues.

A turning point came in the 1970s; as the founding fathers passed from the scene and the influence of the European tradition of Oriental studies dwindled, the outcry over scholarly complicity in American imperialism in Vietnam seeped into the Middle East field. Although never clearly dividing along left- or right-wing lines, partly because of crosscutting allegiances along the Arab-Israeli divide, the new critical attitude found many targets. The field of Middle East studies was portrayed as a stagnant, self-congratulatory men's club, wedded to broad and stereotyping generalizations and dubious theories of modernization and political development. At the same time, a substantial shift in student attention from master's degree programs in Middle East studies to doctoral programs in disciplinary departments began to produce a growing cadre of scholars who had some awareness of what was happening in the discipline of history generally, even if the actual historical work remained methodologically retrograde with respect to the discipline as a whole.

Edward Said's famous critique *Orientalism* (17.50), published in 1978, brought the ferment to a head and made "Orientalism" a byword for racist, imperialist fantasizing. It also fueled a religious and ethnically based critique that would grow in later years into substantial suspicion on the part of Muslims and people of Middle Eastern ethnic identity that Western scholarship was irredeemably biased. Old ideas from the nineteenth and early twentieth centuries were exposed to scathing criticism, and new ideas were scrutinized for hidden or overt tendentiousness.

Medieval Middle Eastern history as a field of study sharing methods, concerns, and philosophical underpinnings with history in general does not much antedate the 1970s. Coming on the scene in a period of intensifying critical debate—focused primarily on the modern period, and on its selective use of the past—the new medievalists experimented with a wide variety of hitherto unused historiographical approaches. Sociology, prosopography, *annaliste* history, gender studies, narrative theory, economic history, quantitative history, and anthropology have all been utilized in a few works, but no new subfield has gained enough practitioners or demonstrated sufficiently unequivocal excellence to constitute a major school. At the same time, important new works of a more traditional nature—political narrative, institutional history, and legal history—have opened up new areas of study and revised earlier opinions in a still underpopulated discipline.

Overshadowing the current wave of experimentation has been controversy over the earliest period of Islamic history. Skepticism concerning religious lore pertaining to the first century of Islam, preserved almost exclusively in later texts, was voiced in the first half of the century by Ignaz Goldziher, Joseph Schacht, and Carl Becker. Lack of Muslim familiarity with Western scholarship, however, and the disinclination of Western scholars to listen to criticism emanating from the Muslim world prevented a significant outcry from arising at the time. It was not until the 1970s that the debate was truly joined following the publication of books by J. Wansbrough (17.65, 17.102), and P. Crone and M. Cook (17.379) who revived the earlier skepticism and took it to the point of rejecting virtually all Muslim accounts of Islamic origins. They proposed that early Muslim religious history was based on pious forgeries designed to conceal the true origins of the faith. Basing their argument on Christian and Jewish sources, and on methods developed with respect to those sources, they maintained that Muhammad may never have existed, that the Qur'ān was constructed over time by ordinary human device, and that Islam's roots lay in Jewish sectarianism.

Given the politicized nature of Middle East scholarship at the time and the growing popularity of Said's notion that Western Orientalists habitually invent an "Orient" to suit their own psychological and political needs, it is hardly surprising that this sharply argued revision of Islamic origins met with severe protest. Not only did many Muslims take offense, but many Western scholars were dismayed by the wholesale dismissal of sources they had relied on throughout their careers. Ferocious reviews and rebuttals appeared in normally staid scholarly journals, enlivening the field considerably.

The Wansbrough–Crone–Cook manifesto, like Said's polemic a bit earlier, proved a stimulus to new and more critical scholarship. But, it tended to draw attention to the earliest period in Islamic history, already the most intensively studied part of the field, and thus drained scarce talent from other regions, periods, and topics starved for attention. Where the debate will go in the future is unpredictable, but it stands as a prime example of the close connection between medieval history and contemporary political and cultural engagement.

At present, the study of the medieval Islamic world is uneven, both in quality and coverage. Traditional political history dictated a focus on the central institution of the caliphate and tended toward a comparative neglect of the period after 945, when the caliphate lost temporal power. Today, however, there is a healthy and growing interest in provincial history and outlooks. The history of Islamic Spain is fairly robust, receiving a good deal of attention from Spanish historians, but the history of North Africa still lags, dominated by a traditional French interpretive approach that new historians will ultimately have to escape. Mamluk Egypt is enjoying a good deal of attention, but Iran remains understudied, partly because Arabists are often disinclined to study the non-Arab world and few Iranists choose to study the period 600–1100 for which most sources are in Arabic. Although a number of important works have been devoted to early Turkish history in the Middle East and the islamization of Anatolia, this field, too, remains understudied. The same is true of outlying areas such as India, West Africa, and the Sudan. In all areas, the balance between traditional religious, cultural, and political history and social and economic history still weighs heavily in favor of the former.

The bibliography that follows focuses on the more recent trends in the historiography of the period, but an effort has been made to include all major areas of historical work, both topically and regionally. Readers who gain from this an overall impression of conservatism and lack of historiographical adventure and sophistication will not be far off the mark. But also included here are a number of more innovative works that should be seen as harbingers of a more lively future in a field where the number of workers is few and the opportunity for interesting new work almost unlimited.

Entries are arranged under the following headings:

Reference Works

General Histories

Islam and Europe

Historiography

Pre-Islamic Arabia and the Origins of Islam
   Mecca and Arabia
   Life of Muhammad
   Qurʾān
   Traditions of the Prophet (Ḥadīth)

The Caliphate in Power
   The Rashidun and Umayyad Caliphates, 632–750
   Abbasid Caliphate
   The Abbasid Revolution, 647–754
   The Abbasids from al-Mansur through al-Maʾmun, 754–833
   The Abbasids from al-Muʿtasim to the Buyid Seizure of
      Baghdad, 833–945

The Fragmentation of Caliphal Power
   Iran and the East down to the Seljuq Takeover, 1037
   Egypt to 1171 and North Africa
   Islamic Spain and Sicily
   The Crusaders and Their Opponents
   The Seljuqs and Their Contemporaries

Mongol and Post-Mongol Periods
   The East from Chinggis Khan to Tamerlane, 1218–1400
   The Mamluks in Egypt and Syria, 1250–1517
   Islam in Anatolia, 1071–1402

Social and Economic History
   Social Structure and Daily Life
   Women and Gender
   Economics, Trade, Taxation, and Administration
   Technology
   Urban Studies
   Numismatics

Religion
   Islam
   Non-Muslims in Islamic Lands
   Islamic Law
   Theology and Education
   Ṣūfism
   Shiism

Literature, Philosophy, Science, and Art
   Arabic and Persian Literature
   Islamic Philosophy
   Science and Medicine
   Art, Architecture, and Music

[Contributors: RWB = Richard Williams Bulliet]

REFERENCE WORKS

17.1   Aziz Suryal Atiya, ed. *The Coptic encyclopedia.* 8 vols. New York: Macmillan, 1991. ISBN 0-02-897025-X (set). ‣ Primary reference work dealing with history and culture of Christian minority in Egypt. Signed articles contributed by established scholars. [RWB]

17.2   Jere L. Bacharach. *A Middle East studies handbook.* Rev. ed. Seattle: University of Washington Press, 1984. ISBN 0-295-96138-4 (cl), 0-295-96144-9 (pbk). ‣ Useful student handbook containing basic dynasty charts, date conversion tables, chronology, and glossary. [RWB]

17.3   C. E. Bosworth. *The Islamic dynasties: a chronological and genealogical handbook.* Edinburgh: Edinburgh University Press, 1980. ISBN 0-85224-402-9. ‣ Convenient handbook for checking dates and sequence of Islamic rulers. Arranged by dynasty, each section introduced by brief account of location and duration of rule. More extensive data available in von Zambaur 17.16. [RWB]

17.4   William C. Brice, ed. *An historical atlas of Islam.* Leiden: Brill, 1981. ISBN 90-04-06116-9. ‣ Best atlas available with good coverage of medieval Islam. Scale and detail of maps, however, inadequate for many reference purposes. [RWB]

17.5   Eckart Ehlers. *Iran: ein bibliographischer Forschungsbericht mit Kommentaren und Annotationen/A bibliographic research survey with comments and annotation.* Munich: Saur, 1980. ISBN 3-598-21132-5. ‣ Bibliography on historical, economic, archaeological, anthropological, and geographic aspects of Iranian studies. Not very complete, particularly in coverage of history, but useful for ancillary disciplines. [RWB]

17.6   *Encyclopaedia of Islam.* 2d ed. 7 vols. to date. Leiden: Brill, 1960–. ISBN 90-04-05745-5 (v. 4), 90-04-07819-3 (v. 5), 90-04-08112-7 (v. 6), 90-04-09419-9 (v. 7). ‣ New edition of key scholarly reference work for Islamic studies. Difficult to use without knowledge of Arabic (subjects are commonly listed by transliterated Arabic term) but highly authoritative with extensive bibliographies. [RWB]

17.7   *Encyclopaedia of Islam.* 1913–36 ed. 9 vols. Leiden: Brill, 1987. ISBN 90-04-08265-4 (set). ‣ For many decades the primary scholarly reference for Islamic history, now being replaced by new edition which has reached letter R (17.6). This edition still essential for later part of alphabet although many articles outdated, particularly in bibliography. In English, but non-Arabists may have difficulty since most entries are based on Arabic words. [RWB]

17.8   Gerhard Endress. *An introduction to Islam.* New York: Columbia University Press, 1988. ISBN 0-231-16580-9 (cl), 0-231-16580-9 (pbk). ‣ Brief summary chapters with extensive bibliography and good chronological table. Chapters too short, but bibliography well selected with brief annotations. Absence of index covering authors is lamentable. [RWB]

17.9   G.S.P. Freeman-Grenville. *The Muslim and Christian calendars, being tables from the conversion of Muslim and Christian dates from the Hijra to the year A.D. 2000.* 2d ed. London: Collings; distributed by Rowman & Littlefield, 1977. ISBN 0-86036-059-8. ‣ Useful little book containing tables for converting Muslim years to Gregorian years and instructions on how to calculate specific days. Convenient for deskside reference, but computer users will prefer ease and precision of *Taqwim: A Multi-Calendar Display* (University of Chicago, 1990). [RWB]

17.10   Abu al-Qasim Muhammad Ibn Hawqal. *Configuration de la terre.* 2 vols. J. H. Kramers and Gaston Wiet, trans. Paris: Maisonneuve & Larose, 1964. ‣ Complete translation of important medieval Arab geographer. Makes available to non-Arabists the style and content of this important genre of historical source. No comparable translation in English. [RWB]

17.11   Guy Le Strange. *The lands of the eastern caliphate: Mesopotamia, Persia, and Central Asia from the Moslem conquest to the time of Timur.* 1905 ed. New York: AMS Press, 1976. ISBN 0-404-56287-6. ‣ Geographical survey based closely on medieval Arabic geographies. Very good for brief notices on specific places and routes, but lacking in sophistication as work of geography. [RWB]

17.12   James Douglas Pearson, comp. *Index Islamicus, 1906–1955: a catalogue of articles on Islamic subjects in periodicals and other collective publications* and *Supplements, 1956–60, 1961–65, 1966–70, 1971–75, 1976–80.* Wolfgang H. Behn, Monographs, 1976–80. Cambridge and London: Heffer and Mansell, 1958–80. ISSN 0306-9524. ‣ Essential, comprehensive list of articles in all languages contained in specialized Orientalist publications. Supplement for 1976–80 lists monographs as well as articles. [RWB]

17.13 G. J. Roper, ed. *Index Islamicus*. London: Mansell, 1983. ISBN 0306-9524. ‣ Continuation of Pearson 17.12. Quarterly supplements continue to present. [RWB]

17.14 Jean Sauvaget. *Introduction to the history of the Muslim East: a bibliographical guide, based on the second edition as recast by Claude Cahen*. 1965 ed. Claude Cahen, ed. Westport, Conn.: Greenwood, 1982. ISBN 0-313-23488-4. ‣ Translation of author's excellent bibliographical guide, expanded by important French historian Claude Cahen, long recognized as best bibliography for students. Covers sources and auxiliary disciplines as well as major studies in European languages. [RWB]

17.15 Ehsan Yarshater, ed. *Encyclopaedia Iranica*. 6 vols. to date. Costa Mesa, Calif.: Mazda, 1982–. ISBN 0-939214-75-X (v. 1), 0-939214-76-8 (v. 2), 0-939214-77-6 (v. 3), 0-939214-78-4 (v. 4), 0-939214-79-2 (v. 5), 1-56859-007-5 (v. 6). ‣ Superb new reference work still in early volumes. Covers pre-Islamic and Islamic periods with long articles of impeccable scholarship. Compares favorably in many instances with *Encyclopaedia of Islam* (17.6, 17.7). [RWB]

17.16 Eduard von Zambaur. *Manuel de généalogie et de chronologie pour l'histoire de l'Islam*. 1927 ed. Bad Pyrmont: Lafaire, 1955. ‣ Much more detailed than Bosworth 17.3 and therefore necessary for detailed historical work. Includes extensive genealogy charts as well as lists of rulers. Epigraphic or numismatic character of documentation included. Out of date for some dynasties. [RWB]

SEE ALSO
13.1 Ainslie T. Embree, ed. *Encyclopedia of Asian history*.
18.6 Wolfgang H. Behn, comp. *Index Islamicus, 1665–1905*.

GENERAL HISTORIES

17.17 Carl Brockelmann. *History of the Islamic peoples*. 1960 ed. Joel Carmichael and Moshe Perlmann, trans. New York: Capricorn, 1980. ISBN 0-7100-0521-0 (pbk). ‣ Old but always in print general history. Deals more extensively and authoritatively with medieval period than most textbooks in Middle East history. Good chronological tables. [RWB]

17.18 Douglas Morton Dunlop. *Arab civilization to A.D. 1500*. New York: Praeger, 1971. ‣ Valuable compendium of lore derived from long career of reading Arabic sources. Analytical side poorly developed, but useful when tracking down particular source or author. [RWB]

17.19 Ross E. Dunn. *The adventures of Ibn Battuta, a Muslim traveller of the fourteenth century*. 1986 ed. Berkeley: University of California Press, 1989. ISBN 0-250-05771-6 (cl, 1986), 0-250-06743-6 (pbk). ‣ Excellent study of career and travels of Ibn Battuta, who traversed Muslim world from West Africa to China. Good companion to published abridged version of his travels (17.27). [RWB]

17.20 H.A.R. Gibb. *Studies on the civilization of Islam*. Stanford J. Shaw and William R. Polk, eds. Boston: Beacon, 1962. ‣ Collection of essays by most influential Islamic medievalist of last generation in English-speaking world. Author's works influential for later scholars and thus important even when superseded by later analyses or sources. [RWB]

17.21 G. R. Hawting. *The first dynasty of Islam: the Umayyad caliphate, AD 661–750*. Carbondale: Southern Illinois University Press, 1987. ISBN 0-8093-1324-3. ‣ Short analytical history of Umayyad caliphate incorporating recent ideas and approaches. Supplants Wellhausen 17.133 conceptually, but lacks wealth of detail. Best general history of Umayyads. [RWB]

17.22 Marshall G. S. Hodgson. *The classical age of Islam*. Vol. 1 of *The venture of Islam: conscience and history in a world civilization*. Chicago: University of Chicago Press, 1974. ISBN 0-226-34678-1 (pbk). ‣ First of three-volume study covering history of Islamic civilization. Important synthesis noted for its innovative terms and periodization, concentration on moral and intellectual values, and critique of European tradition of Islamic studies. [RWB]

17.23 Marshall G. S. Hodgson. *The expansion of Islam in the middle period*. Vol. 2 of *The venture of Islam: conscience and history in a world civilization*. Chicago: University of Chicago Press, 1974. ISBN 0-226-34680-3 (pbk). ‣ Continues author's grand synthesis for period 1000–1500. [RWB]

17.24 Peter Malcolm Holt. *The age of the Crusades: the Near East from the eleventh century to 1517*. New York: Longman, 1986. ISBN 0-582-49303-X. ‣ Highly detailed political history with heavy concentration on political intricacies of Crusader states. Little insight into social, economic, or even political complexities of Islamic states. [RWB]

17.25 Peter Malcolm Holt, Ann K. S. Lambton, and Bernard Lewis, eds. *The central Islamic lands*. Vol. 1 of *The Cambridge history of Islam*. Cambridge: Cambridge University Press, 1970. ISBN 0-521-07567-X. ‣ Collection of essays covering Middle East and North Africa. Other parts of Islamic world covered in volume 2 (17.26). Criticized for overconcentration on political history, but contains many good articles. [RWB]

17.26 Peter Malcolm Holt, Ann K. S. Lambton, and Bernard Lewis, eds. *The further Islamic lands, Islamic society, and civilization*. Vol. 2 of *The Cambridge history of Islam*. Cambridge: Cambridge University Press, 1970. ISBN 0-521-07601-3. ‣ Covers non–Middle Eastern regions and also includes good general essays on cultural topics such as science, literature, and art. [RWB]

17.27 Ibn Battuta. *Travels in Asia and Africa, 1325–1354*. 1929 ed. H.A.R. Gibb, trans. London: Routledge & Kegan Paul, 1983. ISBN 0-7100-9568-6. ‣ Excellent abridged translation of greatest travel account in Islamic history. From China to West Africa, Ibn Battuta made detailed observations providing unique insight into fourteenth-century society. [RWB]

17.28 Muhammad ibn Ahmad Ibn Jubayr. *The travels of Ibn Jubayr*. R.J.C. Broadhurst, trans. London: Cape, 1952. ‣ Next to Ibn Battuta, Ibn Jubayr is most famous traveler in Islamic history. Twelfth-century journey gives vivid depiction of most Islamic countries of Mediterranean basin. [RWB]

17.29 Shams al-Din Ibn Khallikan. *Ibn Khallikan's biographical dictionary*. 1841–71 ed. 4 vols. William MacGuckin, baron de Slane, trans. New York: Johnson Reprint, 1961. ‣ Translation of most literary of medieval Arabic biographical dictionaries. Anecdotes and information about hundreds of rulers and religious and cultural figures, much of it drawn from earlier biographical dictionaries. Important for form as well as content. [RWB]

17.30 Hugh N. Kennedy. *The prophet and the age of the caliphates: the Islamic Near East from the sixth to the eleventh century*. New York: Longman, 1986. ISBN 0-582-49312-9 (cl), 0-582-49313-7 (pbk). ‣ Conceived within framework of a series; but little coordination of style or approach. Good but slow history stops at tenth century for Iran but continues down to Crusades for Arab lands. Volumes by Morgan (17.35) and Holt (17.24) pick up where this leaves off. [RWB]

17.31 Tarif Khalidi. *Classical Arab Islam: the culture and heritage of the golden age*. Princeton: Darwin, 1985. ISBN 0-87850-047-2. ‣ Series of short essays on major topics painting portrait of Arab Islamic culture. [RWB]

17.32 Bernard Lewis. *The Arabs in history*. 6th ed. New York: Oxford University Press, 1993. ISBN 0-19-285258-2 (pbk). ‣ Readily available short historical survey. Scholarship superseded in some places, but still popular as introductory work. [RWB]

17.33 Bernard Lewis, ed. and trans. *Islam, from the Prophet Muhammad to the capture of Constantinople.* 1974 ed. 2 vols. New York: Oxford University Press, 1987. ISBN 0-19-505087-8 (v. 1), 0-19-505088-6 (v. 2). ▸ Useful collection of translated excerpts from medieval Islamic sources dealing, in particular, with issues of government and its relationship to religion. Excerpts and introductory paragraphs brief, but many passages otherwise unavailable in translation. [RWB]

17.34 André Miquel. *La géographie humaine du monde musulman jusqu'au milieu de onzième siècle.* Edition varies. 3 vols. Paris: Éditions de l'École des Haute Études en Sciences, 1973–88. ISBN 2-7132-0044-X (v. 2), 2-7132-0885-8 (v. 3). ▸ Massive study, not just of medieval Arabic geographers, but also of natural historians, travelers, and others whose works may be included under rubric of human geography. Not systematic reference book, but sensitive, sophisticated exploration of how medieval authors saw their world. Essential starting point for work on Islamic geography. [RWB]

17.35 David O. Morgan. *Medieval Persia, 1040–1797.* New York: Longman, 1988. ISBN 0-582-01483-2 (cl), 0-582-49324-2 (pbk). ▸ Short survey history in series with little congruity of style or approach among authors (see also Holt 17.24). Follows Kennedy's volume on earlier history (17.30). Good on Mongol period, sketchy on earlier dynasties. [RWB]

17.36 Francis E. Peters. *Allah's commonwealth: a history of Islam in the Near East, 600–1100 A.D.* New York: Simon & Schuster, 1973. ISBN 0-671-21564-7. ▸ Good readable history of medieval Islam concentrating on religious and philosophical matters. [RWB]

17.37 D. S. Richards, ed. *Islamic civilisation, 950–1150.* Oxford: Cassirer, 1973. ISBN 0-85181-006-3 (cl), 0-85181-017-9 (pbk). ▸ Conference essays on wide variety of subjects. Most important are contributions disproving Louis Massignon's longstanding hypothesis that guilds existed in medieval Islamic times. [RWB]

17.38 Franz Rosenthal, ed. and trans. *The classical heritage in Islam.* Emile Marmorstein and Jenny Marmorstein, trans. Berkeley: University of California Press, 1975. ISBN 0-520-01997-0. ▸ Anthology of translations from texts on medicine, philosophy, science, music, etc., designed to show influence of classical thought in building of Islamic civilization. [RWB]

17.39 J. J. Saunders. *History of medieval Islam.* 1965 ed. New York: Routledge, 1990. ISBN 0-415-05914-3. ▸ Somewhat dated but excellent short introductory survey to medieval Islamic history from Muhammad through Mongol invasions. Fluent narrative style rather than incisive scholarly analysis. [RWB]

17.40 Dominique Sourdel and Janine Sourdel-Thomine. *La civilisation de l'Islam classique.* Paris: Arthaud, 1968. ▸ Unusually good survey containing excellent coverage of social and artistic topics along with customary political narrative. [RWB]

17.41 Bertold Spuler. *The Muslim world: a historical survey.* Part 1: *The age of the caliphs.* Leiden: Brill, 1960. ▸ Adequate but dull survey history. [RWB]

17.42 Bertold Spuler. *The Muslim world: a historical survey.* Part 2: *The Mongol period.* Leiden: Brill, 1960. ▸ Survey history; gains authority because of author's major work *Die Mongolen in Iran.* [RWB]

17.43 Gustave E. Von Grunebaum. *Classical Islam: a history, 600–1258.* Katherine Watson, trans. Chicago: Aldine, 1970. ▸ General history by scholar noted and sometimes criticized for stress on Islam as sole explanatory source of medieval cultural development. [RWB]

17.44 Gustave E. Von Grunebaum. *Medieval Islam: a study in cultural orientation.* 1953 2d ed. Chicago: University of Chicago Press, 1961. ▸ Important synthesis by leading scholar of last generation. Has endured attack as prime exemplar of "Orientalism." [RWB]

17.45 Gustave E. Von Grunebaum. "The sources of Islamic civilization." *Der Islam* 46.1–2 (1970) 1–54. ISSN 0021-1818. ▸ Good example of noted author's sweeping philhellenic view of Islamic civilization as a whole. Viewpoint and method provide good text for discussions of Said's concept of Orientalism (17.50). [RWB]

17.46 Bernard G. Weiss and Arnold H. Green. *A survey of Arab history.* Rev. ed. Cairo: American University in Cairo Press, 1987. ISBN 977-424-180-0. ▸ Textbook focusing exclusively on Arab world from Muhammad to present. Unattractively produced but good history with more detail than Hourani's work (18.59) on same subject. [RWB]

SEE ALSO
    18.59 Albert Hourani. *A history of the Arab peoples.*
    18.68 Ira Marvin Lapidus. *A history of Islamic societies.*

ISLAM AND EUROPE

17.47 Norman Daniel. *Islam and the West: the making of an image.* 2d rev. ed. Oxford: Oneworld, 1992. ISBN 1-85168-043-8. ▸ Extensive treatment of European views of Islam. More substantial but less readable than Southern 17.51. Sequel, *Islam, Europe, and Empire,* describes how medieval stereotypes endured and were augmented in nineteenth century. [RWB]

17.48 James Kritzeck. *Peter the Venerable and Islam.* Princeton: Princeton University Press, 1964. ▸ Study of twelfth-century abbot of Cluny whose views of Islam played major part in shaping European thinking. For more general context of European thought about Islam see Daniel 17.47. [RWB]

17.49 Maxime Rodinson. *Europe and the mystique of Islam.* Roger Veinus, trans. Seattle: University of Washington Press, 1987. ISBN 0-295-96485-5 (pbk). ▸ Two essays by major French Orientalist on history of European studies of Islam. Favorably portrays tradition attacked by Said 17.50. [RWB]

17.50 Edward W. Said. *Orientalism.* 1978 ed. New York: Vintage, 1979. ISBN 0-394-74067-X (pbk). ▸ Biting analysis of systematic stereotyping and imperialistic bias in European and American scholarship devoted to Islam and Middle East. Landmark work in critique of historiography. [RWB]

17.51 R. W. Southern. *Western views of Islam in the Middle Ages.* 1962 ed. Cambridge, Mass.: Harvard University Press, 1978. ISBN 0-674-95055-0. ▸ Elegant set of lectures on how medieval Europeans viewed Islam. Essential reading for appreciating roots of later biases and stereotypes. [RWB]

17.52 Bryan S. Turner. *Weber and Islam: a critical study.* Boston: Routledge & Kegan Paul, 1974. ISBN 0-7100-8942-2 (pbk). ▸ Critique of Max Weber's comments on Islam (scattered throughout his works). Valuable contribution to debate on Orientalism. [RWB]

HISTORIOGRAPHY

17.53 Aziz al-Azmeh. *Ibn Khaldun, an essay in reinterpretation.* Totowa, N.J.: Cass, 1982. ISBN 0-7146-3130-2. ▸ Stands out among mass of writing on famous Muslim historian and sociologist. Should be compared with Muhsin Mahdi's earlier work (17.61). [RWB]

17.54 Abd al-Aziz Duri. *The rise of historical writing among the Arabs.* Fred M. Donner, trans. Princeton: Princeton University Press, 1983. ISBN 0-691-05388-X. ▸ Monograph treating earliest emergence of Arabic historical writing from stage of oral transmission of lore. Does not deal with important chroniclers like al-Tabari. [RWB]

17.55 Ernest Gellner. *Muslim society: a sociological interpretation.* Cambridge: Cambridge University Press, 1981. ISBN 0-521-23160-9 (cl), 0-521-27407-9 (pbk). ▸ Long title essay proposes grand theory for understanding alleged oscillation between rural religiosity and urban legalism in Islamic history. Author's distinguished background in philosophy and anthropology and deep interest in Ibn Khaldûn make for strongly argued hypothesis, but one that accords poorly with empirical record. [RWB]

17.56 Shlomo Dov Goitein. "A plea for the periodization of Islamic history." *Journal of the American Oriental Society* 88.2 (1968) 224–27. ISSN 0003-0279. ▸ Sensible statement, based largely on ethnicity, on still debated question of periodization. Compares favorably with Hodgson's more elaborate scheme (17.22, 17.23, 18.55). [RWB]

17.57 R. Stephen Humphreys. *Islamic history: a framework for inquiry.* Rev. ed. Princeton: Princeton University Press, 1991. ISBN 0-691-03145-2 (cl), 0-691-00856-6 (pbk). ▸ Best introduction to current issues and bibliography in Islamic historiography. Chapters on reference works and sources followed by twelve penetrating essays on major areas of historical inquiry. Not comprehensive; many topics covered. [RWB]

17.58 Ibn Khaldûn. *The Muqaddimah: an introduction to history.* Franz Rosenthal, trans. Princeton: Princeton University Press, 1969. ISBN 0-691-09946-4 (cl), 0-691-01754-9 (pbk). ▸ Good scholarly translation of most important work of sociological and historical speculation of Muslim world. Considered one of great thinkers of all time, Ibn Khaldûn ruminated on rise and fall of dynasties, his most famous theory, and also on whole gamut of human activity. Better than one-volume abridgment (1.155) that omits much of latter. [RWB]

17.59 Tarif Khalidi. *Islamic historiography: the histories of Mas'udi.* Albany: State University of New York Press, 1975. ISBN 0-87395-282-0. ▸ Study of writings of early tenth-century historian particularly noted for knowledge about and interest in non-Islamic world. Nature of sources used and selection of material revealing of attitude toward historiography. [RWB]

17.60 Bernard Lewis and Peter Malcolm Holt, eds. *Historians of the Middle East.* London: Oxford University Press, 1962. ▸ Collection of essays on genres of history and individual historians. Coverage includes Arab, Turkish, Iranian, Byzantine, and European historians. [RWB]

17.61 Muhsin Mahdi. *Ibn Khaldûn's philosophy of history: a study in the philosophic foundation of the science of culture.* 1957 ed. Chicago: University of Chicago Press, 1971. ISBN 0-226-50183-3. ▸ Standard starting point for modern studies of seminal Islamic thinker. Emphasis on philosophy and effect on Ibn Khaldûn's personal career. Later works challenge some of Mahdi's conclusions (cf. al-Azmeh 17.53). [RWB]

17.62 Fedwa Malti-Douglas. "Dreams, the blind, and the semiotics of the biographical notice." *Studia Islamica* 51 (1980) 137–62. ISSN 0585-5292. ▸ Sophisticated contribution to question of how to use biographical dictionaries. Semiotic approach is bold and novel in medieval Islamic field. [RWB]

17.63 Franz Rosenthal. *A history of Muslim historiography.* 2d rev. ed. Leiden: Brill, 1968. ISBN 90-04-01906-5. ▸ Listing and discussion of major historical writings and of key Arabic works dealing with writers of history. Not particularly concerned with historiography in sense of intellectual foundation and method of writing history. [RWB]

17.64 Marilyn Robinson Waldman. *Toward a theory of historical narrative: a case study in Perso-Islamicate historiography.* Colum-

bus: Ohio State University Press, 1980. ISBN 0-8142-0297-7. ▸ Study of work of eleventh-century Persian historian Bayhaqi. Approaches his work as structured by personal and stylistic considerations more than by factual narrative. Not convincing, but significant contribution to new forms of text criticism in Islamic history. [RWB]

17.65 John E. Wansbrough. *The sectarian milieu: content and composition of Islamic salvation history.* New York: Oxford University Press, 1978. ISBN 0-19-713596-X. ▸ Extension of controversial argument for nonhistoricity of early Islam begun in 17.102. Early Islamic tradition rejected as historical source and interpreted in light of Old Testament salvation history. [RWB]

SEE ALSO

1.155 Ibn Khaldûn. *The Muqaddimah: an introduction to history.*

PRE-ISLAMIC ARABIA AND THE ORIGINS OF ISLAM

Mecca and Arabia

17.66 Joseph Chelhod. *Introduction à la sociologie de l'Islam: de l'animisme à l'universalisme.* Paris: Éditions Besson-Chantemerle, 1958. ▸ Little-known but important sociological approach to origins of Islam stressing changes in personal values and spiritual outlook. [RWB]

17.67 Patricia Crone. *Meccan trade and the rise of Islam.* Princeton: Princeton University Press, 1987. ISBN 0-691-05480-0. ▸ Revisionist history challenging view of W. Montgomery Watt (17.91), from Lammens that Mecca was major entrepôt for Oriental goods and spices. Persuasive but for effort to deny Mecca any significant economic role. [RWB]

17.68 Fred M. Donner. "The Bakr b. Wa'il tribes and politics in northeastern Arabia on the eve of Islam." *Studia Islamica* 51 (1980) 5–38. ISSN 0585-5292. ▸ Good example of complexity of studying Arab tribal politics at time of conquests. Addresses question of method directly. [RWB]

17.69 Dale F. Eickelman. "Musaylima: an approach to the social anthropology of seventh-century Arabia." *Journal of the economic and social history of the Orient* 10.1 (1967) 17–52. ISSN 0022-4995. ▸ Excellent study of one "false prophet" contemporary with Muhammad. Appraisal of social and economic background of his movement helps understand origins of Islam. [RWB]

17.70 Hisham Ibn al-Kalbi. *The book of idols: being a translation from the Arabic of the "Kitāb al-Aṣnām."* Nabih Amin Faris, trans. Princeton: Princeton University Press, 1952. ▸ Short treatise cataloging shrines and pilgrimage sites in Arabia, naming gods, and describing rituals. [RWB]

17.71 Mahmood Ibrahim. *Merchant capital and Islam.* Austin: University of Texas Press, 1990. ISBN 0-292-75107-9. ▸ Experiment in applying Marxian approach to political economy to pre-Islamic history and rise of Islam. Contrasts sharply with portrayal of period in Crone 17.67. [RWB]

17.72 M. J. Kister. *Studies in jāhiliyya and early Islam.* London: Variorum, 1980. ISBN 0-86078-068-6. ▸ Collected essays by scholar known for his profound knowledge of sources on Arabia at time of Muhammad. Good in conjunction with interpretive biographies of the Prophet to discover how much simplification and generalization is required to produce seemingly coherent narrative. [RWB]

17.73 Fazlur Rahman. "Pre-foundations of the Muslim community in Mecca." *Studia Islamica* 43 (1976) 5–24. ISSN 0585-5292. ▸ Focus on Qur'ānic passages linking Muhammad to earlier prophets of Judaism and Christianity, particularly in context of shifts in attitude and policy before and after migration to Medina.

Characteristic of author's deep understanding of Islamic tradition. [RWB]

17.74 Sidney Smith. "Events in Arabia in the sixth-century A.D." *Bulletin of the School of Oriental and African Studies* 16.3 (1954) 425–68. ISSN 0041-977X. ▸ Sound effort to establish Arabian chronology for pre-Islamic period. Superseded in some respects (see Holt et al., eds. 17.25) but worth consulting. [RWB]

17.75 Gustave E. Von Grunebaum. "The nature of Arab unity before Islam." *Arabica: revue d'études arabes* 10.1 (1963) 5–23. ISSN 0570-5398. ▸ Succinct but suggestive discussion, based largely on language and literature, of whether Arabs constituted cultural nation before rise of Islam. Complements other works that concentrate on social, economic, and political aspects of pre-Islamic Arabia. [RWB]

17.76 Erich Wolf. "The social organization of Mecca and the origins of Islam." *Southwest journal of anthropology* 7 (1951) 329–56. ▸ Interpretation of social roots of Islam by noted anthropologist. Approach may be compared with Chelhod 17.66, devoted to same subject. [RWB]

Life of Muhammad

17.77 Tor Andrae. *Mohammed: the man and his faith.* 1936 ed. Theophil Menzel, trans. New York: Harper, 1960. ▸ Brief biography of Muhammad stressing Christian viewpoint. Such religious approaches to Prophet's life now largely superseded by social and economic interpretations. Still worth reading. [RWB]

17.78 Michael A. Cook. *Muhammad.* New York: Oxford University Press, 1983. ISBN 0-19-287606-6 (cl), 0-19-287605-8 (pbk). ▸ Less a biography of Muhammad than penetrating examination of problems and approaches of such biographies. Short but provocative. [RWB]

17.79 Fred M. Donner. "Mecca's food supplies and Muhammad's boycott." *Journal of the social and economic history of the Orient* 20.3 (1977) 249–66. ISSN 0022-4995. ▸ Excellent analysis of economic underpinnings of Muhammad's campaign to bring Mecca into submission to Islam. Read with Kister 17.83 and Rubin 17.89. [RWB]

17.80 Fred M. Donner. "Muhammad's political consolidation in Arabia up to the conquest of Mecca." *Muslim world* 69.4 (1979) 229–47. ISSN 0027-4909. ▸ Good study of how Muhammad extended his power over Arabia during his years in Medina. Read with Shoufani 17.130. [RWB]

17.81 Muhammad Husayn Haykal. *The life of Muhammad.* 1976 ed. Ismail Ragi al-Faruqi, trans. London: Shorouk, 1983. ▸ Biography by eminent Egyptian Muslim historian. Preferred by many Muslims. [RWB]

17.82 Muhammad Ibn Ishāq. *The life of Muhammad: a translation of Ishāq's "Sirat Rasul Allah."* 1955 ed. Alfred Guillaume, trans. New York: Oxford University Press, 1970. ISBN 0-19-636034-X. ▸ Full English translation of essential early history of Muhammad and his community. All interpretive biographies of Prophet depend on this work. [RWB]

17.83 M. J. Kister. "'O God, tighten thy grip on Mudar': some socio-economic and religious aspects of an early *hadīth.*" *Journal of the economic and social history of the Orient* 24.3 (1981) 242–73. ISSN 0022-4995. ▸ With articles by Donner 17.79 and Rubin 17.89, contributes to understanding specific policy attributed to Muhammad with respect to his enemies in Mecca. [RWB]

17.84 Martin Lings. *Muhammad: his life based on the earliest sources.* Rev. ed. London: Islamic Texts Society, 1991. ISBN 0-946621-25-X. ▸ Good biography of Muhammad from conventional Muslim standpoint. Avoids psychological and sociological

theorizing that Muslims find objectionable in biographies by Europeans. [RWB]

17.85 Gordon Darnell Newby. *The making of the last Prophet: a reconstruction of the earliest biography of Muhammad.* Columbia: University of South Carolina Press, 1989. ISBN 0-87249-552-3. ▸ Study concentrating not on life of the Prophet, but on sacred history of earlier prophets. Helps understanding of complications in studying Ibn Ishāq's traditional biography (17.82). [RWB]

17.86 Francis E. Peters. "The quest of the historical Muhammad." *International journal of Middle East studies* 23.3 (1991) 291–315. ISSN 0020-7438. ▸ Comparison of how New Testament scholars study life of Jesus and how Islamicists study life of Muhammad. Survey article illuminating problem of source authenticity rather than effort to resolve problem. [RWB]

17.87 Hannah Rahman. "The conflicts between the Prophet and the opposition in Madina." *Der Islam* 62.2 (1985) 260–97. ISSN 0021-1818. ▸ Good study of crucial but little-examined period in Muhammad's career. Brings fresh analysis to issues addressed in Watt 17.92. [RWB]

17.88 Maxime Rodinson. *Mohammed.* Anne Carter, trans. New York: Pantheon, 1971. ISBN 0-394-47110-5. ▸ Eminently readable biography from avowedly psychological, atheistic standpoint. Appeals to secular mind but offends Muslims (and some non-Muslims) for atheism and simplistic application of Freudian theories. [RWB]

17.89 Uri Rubin. "Muhammad's curse of Mudar and the blockade of Mecca." *Journal of the economic and social history of the Orient* 31.3 (1988) 249–64. ISSN 0022-4995. ▸ With articles by Donner 17.79 and Kister 17.83, contributes to understanding of specific policy attributed to Muhammad with respect to his enemies in Mecca. [RWB]

17.90 Muhammad ibn Jarir al-Tabari. *The history of al-Tabari.* Vol. 1: *General introduction and from the creation to the flood.* Vol. 2: *Prophets and patriarchs.* Vol. 3: *The children of Israel.* Vol. 4: *The ancient kingdoms.* Vol. 6: *Muhammad at Mecca.* Vol. 7: *Foundation of the community.* Vol. 9: *The last years of the Prophet: the formation of the state, A.D. 630–632/A.H. 8–11.* Albany: State University of New York Press, 1985–. ISBN 0-88706-563-5 (v. 1, cl), 0-87395-921-3 (v. 2, cl), 0-7914-1687-3 (v. 3, cl), 0-88706-181-8 (v. 4, cl), 0-88706-706-9 (v. 6, cl), 0-88706-344-6 (v. 7, cl), 0-88706-691-7 (v. 9, cl), 0-88706-562-7 (v. 1, pbk), 0-88706-313-6 (v. 2, pbk), 0-88706-182-6 (v. 4, pbk), 0-88706-707-7 (v. 6, pbk), 0-88706-345-4 (v. 7, pbk), 0-88706-692-5 (v. 9, pbk). ▸ Monumental translation of most important medieval Arabic chronicle (with 17.131 and 17.137). Covers pre-Islamic period, including stories of prophets known in Judaeo-Christian tradition, and the life of Muhammad. Individual volumes translated by experts. [RWB]

17.91 W. Montgomery Watt. *Muhammad at Mecca.* Oxford: Clarendon, 1953. ▸ Most influential recent biography of the Prophet. Socioeconomic approach criticized, but discussions of individual events and numerous appendixes constitute valuable collations of material regardless of viewpoint. [RWB]

17.92 W. Montgomery Watt. *Muhammad at Medina.* 1956 ed. New York: Oxford University Press, 1981. ISBN 0-19-577307-1. ▸ Sequel to *Muhammad at Mecca* (17.91). Greater complexity of situation after the Hijrah (flight to Medina) in 622 makes for more difficult and disjointed presentation. [RWB]

17.93 W. Montgomery Watt. *Muhammad's Mecca: history in the Qur'ān.* Edinburgh: Edinburgh University Press, 1988. ISBN 0-85224-565-3. ▸ Attempt to portray Mecca on basis of Qur'ānic text. Stands as rebuttal to Crone's challenge (17.67). [RWB]

17.94 W. Montgomery Watt. *Muhammad: prophet and statesman.* London: Oxford University Press, 1974. ISBN 0-19-881078-

4. ▸ Narrative biography based on two-volume study of Muhammad's life organized by discrete episodes and topics. Lacks valuable empirical infrastructure of longer works (17.91, 17.92). [RWB]

Qur'ān

Interpretations

17.95 Arthur J. Arberry, trans. *The Koran interpreted*. 1955 ed. 2 vols. in 1. New York: Macmillan, 1986. ISBN 0-02-083260-5. ▸ Interpretation—Muslims regard accurate translations as theologically impossible—of Qur'ān stressing poetic qualities and accessibility for English readers. Not noted for philological precision. [RWB]

17.96 Richard Bell, trans. *The Qur'an: translated with a critical re-arrangement of the surahs by Richard Bell*. 2 vols. Edinburgh: T & T Clark, 1937–39. ▸ Rearrangement of Qur'ān according to principles author thought went into its collation after Muhammad's death; effort challenged as arbitrary and unconvincing. Resulting translation, however, makes many obscure sections seem understandable. [RWB]

17.97 M. M. Khatib, trans. *The bounteous Koran: a translation of meaning and commentary*. 1984 ed. London: Macmillan, 1986. ISBN 0-333-34738-2. ▸ One of several excellent Qur'ān interpretations by Muslim scholars; authorized by al-Azhar mosque in Cairo. Contains Arabic in facing columns. [RWB]

17.98 J. M. Rodwell, trans. *The Koran*. 1861 ed. New York: Dutton, 1953. ▸ Mid-nineteenth-century interpretation notable only for its rearrangement of chapters in putative chronological order. Scholars disagree on precise sequence, but this version gives useful impression. [RWB]

Studies

17.99 Mahmoud Ayoub. *The Qur'an and its interpreters*. 1984 ed. 2 vols. to date. Albany: State University of New York Press, 1992–. ISBN 0-87395-727-X (v. 1), 0-7914-0994-5 (v. 2). ▸ Series promises to open up field of Qur'ān interpretation (*tafsīr*) to those who do not read Arabic. Presents and discusses excerpts from different *tafsīr* works. Volumes treat different chapters of Qur'ān. [RWB]

17.100 Helmut Gätje. *The Qur'an and its exegesis: selected texts with classical and modern Muslim interpretations*. Alford T. Welch, trans. Berkeley: University of California Press, 1976. ISBN 0-520-02833-3. ▸ Introduction to Muslim science of Qur'ān interpretation (*tafsīr*) with brief extracts from commentaries of different periods on topics of interest to historians. [RWB]

17.101 Robert Roberts. *The social laws of the Qoran: considered and compared with those of the Hebrew and other ancient codes*. 1925 ed. London and Atlantic Highlands, N.J.: Curzon and Humanities Press, 1990. ISBN 0-7007-0204-0 (cl), 0-391-03661-0 (pbk). ▸ Convenient analysis of Qur'ānic verses on marriage, divorce, adultery, children, slaves, inheritance, charity, crime, commerce, and food. [RWB]

17.102 John E. Wansbrough. *Quranic studies: sources and methods of scriptural interpretation*. Oxford: Oxford University Press, 1977. ISBN 0-19-713588-9. ▸ Provocative, highly controversial analysis designed to show Qur'ān not composed during Muhammad's time but rather developed out of later controversies, and that both Islamic belief and Muhammad, viewed as a fictitious figure, arise from Jewish prototypes. Crone's writings, particularly *Hagarism* (17.379) written with Michael Cook, reflect same school of thought. [RWB]

17.103 W. Montgomery Watt, ed. *Bell's introduction to the Qur'ân*. Edinburgh: Edinburgh University Press, 1977. ISBN 0-85224-171-2. ▸ Excellent handbook for learning about Qur'ān

with good topic index. Watt's rewriting softens some of Bell's views (17.96). [RWB]

Traditions of the Prophet (Ḥadīth)

17.104 Muhammad ibn Ismaᶜil al-Bukhari. *A manual of hadith*. 1951 ed. Muhammad Ali, trans. New York: Olive Branch, 1988. ISBN 0-940793-20-2. ▸ Translated selections from major ninth-century collection of traditions (*ḥadīth*) of Muhammad. [RWB]

17.105 G.H.A. Juynboll. *Muslim tradition: studies in chronology, provenance, and authorship of early ḥadīth*. New York: Cambridge University Press, 1983. ISBN 0-521-25382-9. ▸ Difficult work attempting to determine manner and extent to which traditions of the Prophet derive from Muhammad himself. Essential for anyone seeking to understand longstanding controversy over genuineness of *ḥadīth*. [RWB]

17.106 Muhammad ibn ᶜAbd Allah al-Hakim al-Nisaburi. *An introduction to the science of tradition*. James Robson, ed. and trans. London: Royal Asiatic Society; distributed by Luzac, 1953. (Oriental translation fund, n.s., 39.) ▸ Handbook on classification of "strong" and "weak" traditions of the Prophet (*ḥadīth*). Excellent illustration of how medieval Muslim specialists viewed these texts. [RWB]

17.107 Arent Jan Wensinck. *A handbook of early Muhammadan tradition, alphabetically arranged*. 1927 ed. Leiden: Brill, 1971. ▸ Major ninth-century collections of sound traditions. Arranged alphabetically by subject. [RWB]

THE CALIPHATE IN POWER

The Rashidun and Umayyad Caliphates, 632–750

17.108 K. Athamina. "Aᶜrāb and muhājirūn in the environment of amṭār." *Studia Islamica* 66 (1987) 5–26. ISSN 0585-5292. ▸ Consideration of second-class treatment of Arabs who did not participate fully in early Islamic army and society. Valuable contribution to understanding complexity of conquest period. [RWB]

17.109 Ahmad ibn Yahya Baladhuri. *The origins of the Islamic state: being a translation from the Arabic . . . of the "Kitāb Futūḥ al-Buldān."* 2 vols. Philip K. Hitti (v. 1) and Francis Murgotten (v. 2), trans. New York: Columbia University Press, 1916–24. ▸ Translation of important early Arabic chronicle covering Arab conquests. Geographical arrangement makes campaigns and treaties in different regions easy to find, but must be compared with other sources to obtain complete picture. [RWB]

17.110 Alfred J. Butler. *The Arab conquest of Egypt and the last thirty years of Roman dominion*. Oxford: Clarendon, 1902. ▸ History of transition to Islamic rule making full use of Christian sources. Where to find out what happened to library of Alexandria. [RWB]

17.111 Patricia Crone. *Roman, provincial, and Islamic law: the origins of the Islamic patronate*. New York: Cambridge University Press, 1987. ISBN 0-521-32253-7. ▸ Thorough case study of laws of clientage. Proposes major features of Islamic law stem from pre-Islamic provincial law, primarily Jewish. Contribution to author's controversial theory of Jewish origins of Islam (see 17.379). [RWB]

17.112 Patricia Crone. *Slaves on horses: the evolution of the Islamic polity*. New York: Cambridge University Press, 1980. ISBN 0-521-22961-8. ▸ Excellent study of Umayyad period correcting tendency of earlier historians to see it as continually dominated by tribal politics. Less successful attempt to explain thereby rise of Mamluks in Abbasid times. [RWB]

17.113 Patricia Crone and Martin Hinds. *God's caliph: religious authority in the first centuries of Islam*. New York: Cambridge University Press, 1986. ISBN 0-521-32185-9. ▸ Challenging revisionist history claiming importance for Umayyad use of title "caliph of God," as opposed to "caliph (successor) of the messenger of God." Disagreement with hypothesis centers not on evidence of title being used, but on political significance of contexts in which it appears. [RWB]

17.114   Daniel C. Dennett, Jr. *Conversion and the poll tax in early Islam.* Cambridge, Mass.: Harvard University Press, 1950. ▸ Short provocative monograph challenging portrayal of Islamic taxation system in legal texts as anachronistic and inflexible; reality more diverse and inconsistent. Raises question of role of taxes in conversion. [RWB]

17.115   Fred M. Donner. *The early Islamic conquests.* Princeton: Princeton University Press, 1981. ISBN 0-691-05327-8. ▸ Best history of Arab conquests. Revises earlier accounts by taking closer look at sources and accepting impossibility of recovering neat, coherent narrative. Essential reading for method as well as content. [RWB]

17.116   Francesco Gabrieli. *Muhammad and the conquests of Islam.* Virginia Luling and Rosamund Linell, trans. New York: McGraw-Hill, 1968. ▸ Popular account of early Islamic history focusing on Arab conquests. Readable but lacks scholarly precision. Example of standard account of period that Donner challenges in 17.115. [RWB]

17.117   H.A.R. Gibb. *The Arab conquests of Central Asia.* London: Royal Asiatic Society, 1923. ▸ Superseded in much of its analysis, but still starting point of extensive historical discussion on Arab frontier in Central Asia. Read with Shaban 17.139, Frye 17.182, and Daniel 17.145. [RWB]

17.118   H.A.R. Gibb. "The fiscal rescript of ʿUmar II." *Arabica: revue d'études arabes* 2.1 (1955) 1–16. ▸ Translation and brief analysis of key document touching on status of non-Arab converts to Islam as well as on fiscal matters. Crucial to understanding administrative evolution of early Islamic state. [RWB]

17.119   Saleh K. Hammarneh. "Marwan b. al-Hakam and the caliphate." Eugene Rogan, trans. *Der Islam* 65.2 (1988) 200–25. ISSN 0021-1818. ▸ Revisionist view of standard opinion that eponym of Marwanid phase of Umayyad caliphate had no political ambition; portrayed instead as active aspirant for office. Translation of 1981 Arabic article. [RWB]

17.120   Donald R. Hill. *The termination of hostilities in the early Arab conquests, A.D. 634–656.* London: Luzac, 1971. ISBN 0-7189-1051-7. ▸ Compilation of brief texts from many sources, arranged by province, giving details of treaties and other arrangements terminating hostilities. Convincingly demonstrates substantial local variation and absence of consistent pattern stemming from central government's policies. [RWB]

17.121   Martin Hinds. "Kufan political alignments and their background in the mid-seventh century A.D." *International journal of Middle East studies* 2.4 (1971) 346–67. ISSN 0020-7438. ▸ Dense but insightful examination of tribal allegiances and political groupings at time of first Civil War, 656–661. Essential reading on topic. [RWB]

17.122   Martin Hinds. "The murder of the caliph ʿUthman." *International journal of Middle East studies* 3.4 (1972) 450–69. ISSN 0020-7438. ▸ Important, detailed examination of event that sparked first Civil War in 656. [RWB]

17.123   Martin Hinds. "The Siffin arbitration agreement." *Journal of Semitic studies* 17 (1972) 93–129. ISSN 0022-4480. ▸ Careful reconstruction of crucial agreement ending Civil War and marking commencement of Umayyad dynasty. Establishes text as one of few early Arabic prose documents that seems to be firmly known. [RWB]

17.124   G.H.A. Juynboll. "The *qurrāʾ* in early Islamic history." *Journal of the economic and social history of the Orient* 16.2–3 (1973) 113–29. ISSN 0022-4995. ▸ Acute analysis of and contribution to debate over seventh-century political terminology. Read with Shaban 17.129 and Hinds 17.121. [RWB]

17.125   Walter Emil Kaegi. *Byzantium and the early Islamic conquests.* New York: Cambridge University Press, 1992. ISBN 0-521-41172-6. ▸ Good analytical portrayal of Arab conquests from Byzantine point of view. [RWB]

17.126   Keith Lewinstein. "The Azariqa in Islamic heresiography." *Bulletin of the School of Oriental and African Studies* 54.2 (1991) 251–68. ISSN 0041-977X. ▸ Valuable study of early Islamic schismatic group. As Kharijites, Azariqa belong to important but little known branch of Islam. [RWB]

17.127   Michael G. Morony. *Iraq after the Muslim conquest.* Princeton: Princeton University Press, 1984. ISBN 0-691-05395-2. ▸ Major study utilizing great variety of non-Muslim sources in conjunction with Arabic texts. Shows that much that is considered typically Islamic carried over from period of Sasanian rule. [RWB]

17.128   Erling L. Petersen. *ʿAli and Muʿawiya in early Arabic tradition: studies on the genesis and growth of Islamic historical writing until the end of the ninth century.* P. Lampe Christiansen, trans. Copenhagen: Munksgaard, 1964. ▸ Painstaking study of contradictory Arabic accounts of first Civil War (656–661). Excellent illustration of care and effort required to rescue historical plausibility from layers of oral tradition. [RWB]

17.129   M. A. Shaban. *Islamic history: a new interpretation.* Vol. 1: *A.D. 600–750 (A.H. 132).* Cambridge: Cambridge University Press, 1971. ISBN 0-521-08137-8 (v. 1). ▸ Controversial, challenging interpretation of early Islamic history, largely from standpoint of economic interests. Unwillingness to entertain rival opinions and casual citation of sources has limited book's scholarly acceptance. See also volume 2 (17.154). [RWB]

17.130   Elias Shoufani. *Al-Riddah, and the Muslim conquest of Arabia.* Toronto: University of Toronto Press, 1973. ISBN 0-8020-1915-3. ▸ Short revisionist treatment of years immediately following death of Muhammad, 632–634. Argues wars of period should be seen as effectively conquering Arabian peninsula and foreshadowing subsequent conquests in Iraq and Syria. [RWB]

17.131   Muhammad ibn Jarir al-Tabari. *The history of al-Tabari.* Vol. 10: *The conquest of Arabia, A.D. 632–633/A.H. 11.* Vol. 11: *The challenge to the empires.* Vol. 12: *The battle of al-Qadisiyyah and the conquest of Syria and Palestine.* Vol. 13: *The conquest of Iraq, southwestern Persia, and Egypt: the middle years of Umar's caliphate, A.D. 636–642/A.H. 15–21.* Vol. 15: *The crisis of the early caliphate: the reign of ʿUthman, A.D. 644–656/A.H. 24–35.* Vol. 18: *Between civil wars.* Vol. 19: *The caliphate of Yazid b. Muʿawiyah, A.D. 680–683/A.H. 60–64.* Vol. 20: *The collapse of Sufyanid authority and the coming of the Marwanids: the caliphates of Muʿawiyah II and Marwan I and the beginning of the caliphate of ʿAbd al-Malik, A.D. 683–685/A.H. 64–66.* Vol. 21: *The victory of the Marwanids, A.D. 685–693/A.H. 66–73.* Vol. 22: *The Marwanid restoration: the caliphate of ʿAbd al-Malik, A.D. 693–701/A.H. 74–81.* Vol. 23: *The zenith of the Marwanid house: the last years of ʿAbd al-Malik and the caliphate of al-Walid, A.D. 700–715/A.H. 81–86.* Vol. 24: *The empire in transition: the caliphates of Sulayman, ʿUmar, and Yazid, A.D. 715–724/A.H. 96–105.* Vol. 25: *The end of expansion: the caliphate of Hisham, A.D. 724–738/A.H. 105–120.* Vol. 26: *The waning of the Umayyad caliphate: prelude to revolution, A.D. 738–745/A.H. 121–127.* Albany: State University of New York Press, 1985–. ISBN 0-7914-1071-4 (v. 10), 0-7914-0851-5 (v. 11), 0-7914-0733-0 (v. 12), 0-88706-876-6 (v. 13, cl), 0-7914-0155-3 (v. 15, cl), 0-87395-933-7 (v. 18), 0-7914-0040-9 (v. 19), 0-88706-855-3 (v. 20, cl), 0-7914-0221-5 (v. 21, cl), 0-88706-975-

4 (v. 22), 0-88706-721-2 (v. 23), 0-7914-0072-7 (v. 24, cl), 0-88706-569-4 (v. 25, cl), 0-88706-810-3 (v. 26, cl), 0-7914-1072-2 (v. 10, pbk), 0-7914-0852-3 (v. 11, pbk), 0-7914-0733-0 (v. 12, pbk), 0-88706-877-4 (v. 13, pbk), 0-7914-0155-3 (v. 15, pbk), 0-88706-314-4 (v. 18, pbk), 0-7914-0041-7 (v. 19, pbk), 0-88706-857-X (v. 20, pbk), 0-88706-722-0 (v. 21, pbk), 0-7914-0222-3 (v. 22, pbk), 0-88706-722-0 (v. 23, pbk), 0-7914-0073-5 (v. 24, pbk), 0-88706-570-8 (v. 25, pbk), 0-88706-812-X (v. 26, pbk). ▸ Monumental translation of most important medieval Arabic chronicle (with 17.90 and 17.137). Covers first four caliphs, known as Rashidun caliphs, and succeeding Umayyad dynasty. Individual volumes translated by experts. [RWB]

17.132 W. F. Tucker. "ᶜAbd Allah Ibn Muᶜawiya and the Janahiyya: rebels and ideologies of the late Umayyad period." *Studia Islamica* 51 (1980) 39–58. ISSN 0585-5292. ▸ Sets in perspective victory of Abbasid movement in ferment of mid-eighth-century revolutionary politics by detailed examination of contemporary Shīᶜī revolt that failed. [RWB]

17.133 Julius Wellhausen. *The Arab kingdom and its fall.* 1927 ed. Margaret Graham Weir, trans. Beirut: Khayats, 1963. ▸ Major study of Umayyad dynasty from which all later discussions ultimately derive. Vision of caliphate as Arab national achievement very influential. [RWB]

17.134 Julius Wellhausen. *The religio-political factions in early Islam.* R. C. Ostle and S. M. Walzer, trans. New York: American Elsevier, 1975. ISBN 0-444-10872-6. ▸ Still valuable study of second Civil War and of messianic revolt of al-Mukhtar (685–687) in particular. Originally published in German, 1901. [RWB]

17.135 Abd al-Husain Zarrinkub. "The Arab conquest of Iran and its aftermath." In *The Cambridge history of Iran.* Richard N. Frye, ed., vol. 4, pp. 1–56. Cambridge: Cambridge University Press, 1975. ISBN 0-521-20093-8. ▸ Excellent presentation of Arab conquests. Makes available in English views and approach of important Iranian historian. [RWB]

Abbasid Caliphate

Sources

17.136 Bayard Dodge, trans. *The fihrist of al-Nadīm: a tenth-century survey of Muslim culture.* 2 vols. New York: Columbia University Press, 1970. ISBN 0-231-02925-X. ▸ Valuable translation of Baghdad bookseller's detailed inventory of available texts. Arranged by topic, gives names of authors and book titles for many lost works and indicates cultural tendencies of the period. [RWB]

17.137 Muhammad ibn Jarir al-Tabari. *The history of al-Tabari.* Vol. 27: *The ᶜAbbasid revolution, A.D. 743–786/A.H. 126–132.* Vol. 29: *Al-Mansur and al-Mahdi, A.D. 763–786/A.H. 126–132.* Vol. 30: *The ᶜAbbasid caliphate in equilibrium: the caliphates of Musa al-Hadi and Harun al-Rashid, A.D. 785–809/A.H. 169–193.* Vol. 31: *The war between brothers, A.D. 809–813/A.H. 193–198.* Vol. 32: *The reunification of the ᶜAbbasid caliphate.* Vol. 33: *Storm and stress along the northern frontiers of the ᶜAbbasid caliphate: the caliphate of al-Muᶜtasim, A.D. 833–863/A.H. 227–248.* Vol. 34: *The roots of decay, A.D. 841–863/A.H. 227–248.* Vol. 35: *The crisis of the ᶜAbbasid caliphate.* Vol. 36: *The revolt of the Zanj, A.D. 869–879/A.H. 255–265.* Vol. 37: *The ᶜAbbasid recovery.* Vol. 38: *The return of the caliphate to Baghdad.* Albany: State University of New York Press, 1985–. ISBN 0-87395-884-5 (v. 27), 0-7914-0142-1 (v. 29, cl), 0-88706-564-3, (v. 30, cl), 0-7914-1085-4 (v. 31), 0-88706-058-7 (v. 32), 0-7914-0494-3 (v. 33), 0-88706-874-X (v. 34), 0-87395-883-7 (v. 35), 0-7914-0763-2 (v. 36), 0-88706-054-4 (v. 37), 0-87395-876-4 (v. 38), 0-7914-0143-X (v. 29, pbk), 0-88706-566-X (v. 30, pbk), 0-7914-1086-2 (v. 31, pbk), 0-88706-057-9 (v. 32, pbk), 0-7914-0494-3 (v. 33, pbk), 0-88706-875-8 (v. 34, pbk), 0-7914-0764-0 (v. 36, pbk), 0-88706-053-6 (v. 37, pbk).

▸ Monumental translation of most important medieval Arabic chronicle (with 17.90 and 17.131). Covers history of Abbasid caliphate to death of author. Individual volumes translated by experts. [RWB]

17.138 Al-Mahassin ibn Ali al-Tanukhi. *The table-talk of a Mesopotamian judge.* D. S. Margoliouth, trans. London: Royal Asiatic Society, 1922. (Oriental translation fund, 28.) ▸ Essays and ruminations of tenth-century judge and litterateur. Good example of sophisticated literary taste. [RWB]

The Abbasid Revolution, 647–754

17.139 M. A. Shaban. *The ᶜAbbasid Revolution.* Cambridge: Cambridge University Press, 1970. ISBN 0-521-07849-0. ▸ Solid account of Arab conquests and subsequent revolts in eastern Iran and Central Asia culminating in movement that overthrew Umayyad caliphate. Assertion that revolution almost entirely Arab affair strongly challenged by Daniel 17.145 among others. [RWB]

17.140 Moshe Sharon. *Black banners from the east: the establishment of the ᶜAbbasid state—incubation of a revolt.* Jerusalem: Magnes Press with Hebrew University, 1983. ISBN 965-223-501-6. ▸ Lively history of Abbasid Revolution largely based on anonymous chronicle detailing conspiratorial antecedents. Chronicle was not available to Shaban 17.139 when he wrote on same subject. [RWB]

17.141 Gerlof van Vloten. *Recherches sur la domination arabe, le chiitisme, et les croyances messianiques sous le khalifat des Omayades.* 1894 ed. Ankara: Ankara Universitesi Basimevi, 1986. (Verhandelingen der Koninklijke Akademie van Wetenschappen te Amsterdam; Afdeeling Letterkunde, 1.3.) ▸ Pays great scholarly attention to revolution that brought Abbasid dynasty to power; remains worthy of consultation for introduction of idea of messianism into debate. [RWB]

The Abbasids from al-Mansur through al-Ma'mun, 754–833

17.142 Christopher I. Beckwith. "Aspects of the early history of the Central Asian guard corps in Islam." *Archivum Eurasiae medii aevi* 4 (1984) 29–43. ▸ Explores connections between pre-Islamic Central Asian tradition of royal guards and appearance of special military forces under Umayyad and early Abbasid caliphs. Contributes to ongoing debate on origin of Abbasid Mamluk corps. [RWB]

17.143 Irit Bligh-Abramski. "Evolution versus revolution: Umayyad elements in the ᶜAbbasid regime, 133/750–320/932." *Der Islam* 65.2 (1988) 226–43. ISSN 0021-1818. ▸ Rare study dealing with Syria, capital of province of Umayyads, during caliphate of their successors, the Abbasids. [RWB]

17.144 Harold Bowen. *The life and times of ᶜAli ibn ᶜIsa, "the good vizier."* 1928 ed. New York: AMS Press, 1975. ISBN 0-404-56215-9. ▸ Excellent monograph detailing bureaucratic politics of Abbasid caliphate during period of weakening in early tenth century. Rich in anecdote and detail, vividly portrays human side of competition between vizierial factions. [RWB]

17.145 Elton Daniel. *The political and social history of Khurasan under Abbasid rule, 747–820.* Minneapolis: Bibliotheca Islamica, 1979. ISBN 0-88297-025-9. ▸ Best history of Iran during this period; see also shorter account by Mottahedeh 17.191. Stresses distinctively Iranian issues rather than concentrating on caliphal politics. [RWB]

17.146 Tayyeb El-Hibri. "Harun al-Rashid and the Mecca protocol of 802: a plan for division or succession?" *International journal of Middle East studies* 24.3 (1992) 461–80. ISSN 0020-7438. ▸ Excellent revisionist article challenging authenticity of documents by which Harun al-Rashid allegedly divided caliphate between his two sons. Argues historians sympathetic to al-Ma'mun, who won ensuing civil war, altered text of one document to fit outcome of conflict. [RWB]

17.147 Hugh N. Kennedy. "Central government and provincial élites in the early ʿAbbasid caliphate." *Bulletin of the School of Oriental and African Studies* 44.1 (1981) 26–38. ISSN 0041-977X. ▸ Complements author's general history of early Abbasid period (17.148). Issue of provincial elites eventually became crucial when caliphate began to dissolve. [RWB]

17.148 Hugh N. Kennedy. *The early Abbasid caliphate: a political history.* Totowa, N.J.: Barnes & Noble, 1981. ISBN 0-389-20018-2. ▸ Best narrative history of early Abbasid period. [RWB]

17.149 Jacob Lassner. *Islamic revolution and historical memory: an inquiry into the art of ʿAbbasid apologetics.* New Haven: American Oriental Society, 1986. (American Oriental Series, 66.) ISBN 0-940490-66-8. ▸ Penetrating study of myth making in stories of origins of Abbasid political movement given in various chronicles. Best example of author's technique of intensively criticizing narrative sources. [RWB]

17.150 Jacob Lassner. "Provincial administration under the early ʿAbbasids: Abu Jaʿfar al-Mansur and the governors of the Haramayn." *Studia Islamica* 49 (1979) 39–54. ISSN 0585-5292. ▸ Control of Mecca and Medina, *ḥaramain* or "Two Holy Places," essential to legitimacy of Abbasid rule. Examines Abbasid approach to problem. [RWB]

17.151 Jacob Lassner. "Provincial administration under the early ʿAbbasids: the ruling family and the *amṭār* of Iraq." *Studia Islamica* 50 (1980) 21–36. ISSN 0585-5292. ▸ Discussion of Abbasid method of solidifying control in provincial governorships after overthrow of Umayyad dynasty. *Amṭār* were major cities in Iraq that new regime had to control to maintain power. [RWB]

17.152 Jacob Lassner. *The shaping of ʿAbbasid rule.* Princeton: Princeton University Press, 1980. ISBN 0-691-05281-6. ▸ Author is leading exponent of close, critical reading of sources to uncover tendentiousness and propaganda. Practices his method on several specific topics with interesting but sometimes confusing results. [RWB]

17.153 Farouk Omar. *The Abbasid caliphate, 132/750–170/786.* Baghdad: National Printing and Publishing, 1969. ▸ Useful survey of Abbasid revolution and early decades of Abbasid rule. [RWB]

17.154 M. A. Shaban. *Islamic history: a new interpretation.* Vol. 2: *A.D. 750–1055 (A.H. 132–448).* Cambridge: Cambridge University Press, 1976. ISBN 0-521-21198-0 (v. 2). ▸ Portrayal of economic interests as primary motor of Islamic history. Imprecise use of sources and espousal of extreme views makes book even more controversial than its predecessor (17.129). [RWB]

17.155 Dominique Sourdel. *Le vizirat ʿabbaside de 749 à 936 (132 à 324 de l'hégire).* 2 vols. Damascus: Institut Français de Damas, 1960. ▸ Essential monograph covering origin and development of office of vizier. Chronological treatment with specific discussion of each vizier during period of Abbasid independence. [RWB]

The Abbasids from al-Muʿtasim to the Buyid Seizure of Baghdad, 833–945

17.156 H.A.R. Gibb. "Government and Islam under the early ʿAbbasids: the political collapse of Islam." In *L'élaboration de l'Islam: colloque de Strasbourg, 12–13–14 Juin 1959,* pp. 115–27. Paris: Presses Universitaires de France, 1961. ▸ Reflections on weakening of Abbasid caliphate and occupation of Baghdad by Buyids in 945. Question of why Shīʿī Buyids retained Sunnī caliph in office touches on broader issues of nature of authority in medieval Islam. [RWB]

17.157 Ira Marvin Lapidus. "The separation of state and religion in the development of early Islamic society." *International journal of Middle East studies* 6.4 (1975) 363–420. ISSN 0020-7438. ▸ Valuable study by leading social historian of political-religious controversy in Baghdad before and during inquisition *(miḥna)* decreed by caliph al-Ma'mun in effort to force religious conformity. [RWB]

17.158 Reuben Levy. *A Baghdad chronicle.* Cambridge: Cambridge University Press, 1929. ▸ Narrative history of Abbasids and their capital city during period of growing weakness in late ninth and tenth centuries. Assembled from Arabic chronicles of period, more a pastiche of summary translations than analytical history. [RWB]

17.159 Roy P. Mottahedeh. "The *shuʿūbiyah* controversy and the social history of early Islamic Iran." *International journal of Middle East studies* 7.2 (1976) 161–82. ISSN 0020-7438. ▸ Adds to discussions of pro-Iranian literary movement begun by Goldziher 17.382 and Gibb 17.20. Considers Qur'ān commentary as important but neglected source. [RWB]

17.160 Walter Melville Patton. *Ahmed ibn Hanbal and the mihna: a biography of the imam, including an account of the Mohammedan inquisition called the mihna, 218–234 A.H.* Leiden: Brill, 1897. ▸ Surprisingly, still only monograph on crucial episode in ninth-century Islamic history. Many of author's views of inquisition and of Ahmad ibn Hanbal have been published in other contexts, but can still be consulted for full story. [RWB]

17.161 David Waines. "The third-century internal crisis of the Abbasids." *Journal of the economic and social history of the Orient* 20.3 (1977) 282–306. ISSN 0022-4995. ▸ Detailed account of catastrophic fall in tax revenues under Abbasid rule. Crucial for understanding decay of Abbasid power in late ninth and early tenth centuries. [RWB]

17.162 C. T. Hartley Walker. "Jahiz of Basra to al-Fath ibn Khaqan on the 'Exploits of the Turks and the Army of the Khalifate in General.'" *Journal of the Royal Asiatic Society* (1915) 631–97. ▸ Early text on role of Turks as soldiers in service of caliph. [RWB]

THE FRAGMENTATION OF CALIPHAL POWER

Iran and the East down to the Seljuq Takeover, 1037

Sources

17.163 Milton Gold, trans. *The Tarikh-e Sistan* (The history of Sistan). Rome: Istituto Italiano per il Medio ed Estremo Oriente, 1976. ▸ Anonymous chronicle, one of earliest Persian prose works in Arabic script, focusing on Saffarid dynasty that broke away from Abbasid caliphal rule. Rare sympathetic view of independent dynasty of tenth century. [RWB]

17.164 Ahmad ibn Muhammad Miskawayh. *The eclipse of the Abbasid caliphate.* 7 vols. H. F. Amedroz and D. S. Margoliouth, eds. and trans. London: Oxford University Press, 1920–21. ▸ Translated portion (volumes 4–6) of this major tenth-century Arabic chronicle affords best source for studying Buyid period from vantage point of Baghdad. Author writes about events of his own lifetime; gives more lively account than many other chroniclers. [RWB]

17.165 Abu Bakr Muhammad ibn Jaʿfar Narshakhî. *The history of Bukhara.* Richard N. Frye, ed. and trans. Cambridge, Mass.: Mediaeval Academy of America, 1954. (Mediaeval Academy of America, Publications, 61.) ISBN 0-910956-35-9. ▸ Translation of important early Persian source on history of Central Asia. Extensive erudite notes illuminate particular problems and help understand differences between Islam in frontier region and more common story of centralized caliphate. [RWB]

Studies

17.166 Vasilii Vladimirovich Bartol'd. *An historical geography of Iran.* Svat Soucek, trans. Princeton: Princeton University Press, 1984. ▸ Excellent, accessible introduction to historical geography of Iran. [RWB]

17.167 Vasilii Vladimirovich Bartol'd. *Turkestan down to the Mongol invasion.* 3d ed. London: Luzac, 1968. ▸ Starting point for all work on medieval Islamic Central Asia down to Mongol invasion by acknowledged master. Dense, authoritative, not yet superseded, although later scholars have modified or expanded on certain findings. [RWB]

17.168 Thierry Bianquis. *Damas et la Syrie sous la domination fatimide (359–468/969–1076): essai d'interprétation de chroniques arabes médiévales.* 2 vols. Damascus: Institut Français de Damas, 1986–89. ▸ Major dynasty-centered monograph comparable to those by Canard 17.180 and Elisséeff 17.242. Essential reading for history of Arabs of Syria prior to Crusades. [RWB]

17.169 C. E. Bosworth. "The armies of the Saffarids." *Bulletin of the School of Oriental and African Studies* 31.3 (1968) 534–54. ISSN 0041-977X. ▸ One of a series of articles by Bosworth bringing together material relating to size, recruitment, and activities of military forces in medieval Iran. See also his articles on Buyid and Ghaznavid military (17.171, 17.173). [RWB]

17.170 C. E. Bosworth. "The early Islamic history of Ghur." *Central Asiatic journal* 6.2 (1961) 116–33. ISSN 0008-9192. ▸ Rulers of Ghur, obscure region in northwest Afghanistan, played important role in Islamic conquest of India. Covers beginnings of Islam among these remote mountain tribespeople. [RWB]

17.171 C. E. Bosworth. "Ghaznevid military organisation." *Der Islam* 36.1–2 (1960) 37–77. ISSN 0578-6967. ▸ One of series of articles by Bosworth bringing together material relating to size, recruitment, and activities of military forces in medieval Iran. See also his articles on Buyid and Saffarid military (17.169, 17.173). [RWB]

17.172 C. E. Bosworth. "The heritage of rulership in early Islamic Iran and the search for dynastic connections with the past." *Iranian studies* 11 (1978) 7–34. ISSN 0021-0862. ▸ Suggestive discussion of real and artificial genealogies of independent Iranian dynasties of ninth and tenth centuries. Explores question of continuity and legitimacy of pre-Islamic Iranian royal tradition within Islam. [RWB]

17.173 C. E. Bosworth. "Military organisation under the Buyids of Persia and Iraq." *Oriens* 18–19 (1967) 143–67. ISSN 0078-6527. ▸ One of series of articles by Bosworth bringing together material relating to the size, recruitment, and activities of military forces in medieval Iran. See also his articles on Saffarid and Ghaznavid military (17.169, 17.171). [RWB]

17.174 C. E. Bosworth. "The rulers of Chaghaniyan in early Islamic times." *Iran* 19 (1981) 1–20. ▸ Account of early Islamic penetration into isolated river valley north of Afghanistan. Provides useful background for one prince from this general region who became major political figure in Abbasid politics in ninth century. [RWB]

17.175 C. E. Bosworth. *Sistan under the Arabs from the Islamic conquest to the rise of the Saffarids (30–250/651–864).* Rome: Istituto Italiano per il Medio ed Estremo Oriente, 1968. (Reports and memoirs, 11.) ▸ Important monograph on southern Iran during early Islamic period. Corrects customary bias favoring history of northeastern Iran and shows importance of southern region. [RWB]

17.176 C. E. Bosworth. "The Tahirids and Saffarids." In *The Cambridge history of Iran.* Richard N. Frye, ed., vol. 4, pp. 90–135. Cambridge: Cambridge University Press, 1975. ISBN 0-521-

20093-8. ▸ Best narratives of two of earliest independent dynasties in history of Islamic Iran. Dense and detailed with minimum of historical analysis; excellent resource for further work on various aspects of ninth- and tenth-century Iran. [RWB]

17.177 Richard Williams Bulliet. "A quantitative approach to medieval Muslim biographical dictionaries." *Journal of the economic and social history of the Orient* 13 (1970) 195–211. ISSN 0022-4995. ▸ Experimental effort to determine degree of interconnection between parts of Iran along major routes by counting frequency of place names borne by members of religious elite. [RWB]

17.178 Heribert Busse. *Chalif und Grosskönig: die Buyiden im Iraq (945–1055).* Wiesbaden: Steiner, 1969. ▸ Major monograph on Buyid dynasty, Iranian tribal chieftains who carved out state in Iran and took control of Baghdad, Abbasid capital, in 945. [RWB]

17.179 Heribert Busse. "Iran under the Buyids." In *The Cambridge history of Iran.* Richard N. Frye, ed., vol. 4, pp. 250–304. Cambridge: Cambridge University Press, 1975. ISBN 0-521-20093-8. ▸ Article drawn from author's large monograph on Buyids (17.178). Best starting point for political history of Buyid dynasty. [RWB]

17.180 Marius Canard. *Histoire de la dynastie des Hamdanides de Jazira et de Syrie.* Paris: Presses Universitaires de France, 1953. ▸ Major monograph on important tenth-century Arab tribal kingdom in northern Mesopotamia. Contemporary with Iranian Buyid, Saffarid, and Samanid kingdoms, Shī'ī Hamdanid dynasty primary example of parallel devolution of Abbasid power in Arab territory. [RWB]

17.181 Jamsheed K. Choksy. "Zoroastrians in Muslim Iran: select problems of coexistence and interaction during the early medieval period." *Iranian studies* 20.1 (1987) 17–30. ISSN 0021-0862. ▸ Excellent exploratory article concerning largely unstudied interaction between Zoroastrians and Muslims in Iran. Longer work on subject anticipated from same author. [RWB]

17.182 Richard N. Frye. *The golden age of Persia: the Arabs in the East.* New York: Barnes & Noble, 1975. ISBN 0-06-492288-X. ▸ Interesting but sometimes frustrating book concentrating on first three centuries of Islamic rule in Iran. Characteristically exhibits immense erudition but eschews both broad conceptualization and clear narration. [RWB]

17.183 Richard N. Frye. "The Samanids." In *The Cambridge history of Iran.* Richard N. Frye, ed., vol. 4, pp. 136–61. Cambridge: Cambridge University Press, 1975. ISBN 0-521-20093-8. ▸ Best introduction to history of important tenth-century Iranian dynasty ruling from Bukhara. Less thorough, however, than comparable dynastic histories in same volume. [RWB]

17.184 Moshe Gil. *A history of Palestine, 634–1099.* Ethel Broido, trans. Cambridge: Cambridge University Press, 1992. ISBN 0-521-40437-1. ▸ Extensive narrative history of Palestine up to beginning of Crusades followed by topical chapters, including discussions of Jews, Christians, Samaritans, and Karaites. Translated from Hebrew. [RWB]

17.185 Hafizullah Kabir. *The Buwayhid dynasty of Baghdad.* Calcutta: Iran Society, 1964. ▸ Basic narrative of dynasty that took over Baghdad in 945 and ended independence of Abbasid caliphate. Busse 17.178 preferable. [RWB]

17.186 Joel L. Kraemer. *Humanism in the renaissance of Islam: the cultural revival during the Buyid age.* Leiden: Brill, 1986. ISBN 90-04-07259-4. ▸ Broadens and deepens Mez's concept of renaissance of Islam (17.190). Lively portrayal of scholars, critics, patrons, and other tenth-century cultural figures. [RWB]

17.187 Wilferd Madelung. "The assumption of the title *shahan-*

shah by the Buyids and 'the reign of Daylam (Dawlat al-Day-lam).'" *Journal of Near Eastern studies* 28 (1969) 84–108, 168–83. ▸ Study of revival of symbols of Iranian kingship by Shīʿī Iranian dynasty that took over Baghdad in 945. Read with articles by Busse (17.178 and 17.179). [RWB]

17.188 Wilferd Madelung. "The minor dynasties of northern Iran." In *The Cambridge history of Iran.* Richard N. Frye, ed., vol. 4, pp. 198–249. Cambridge: Cambridge University Press, 1975. ISBN 0-521-20093-8. ▸ Terse, fact-filled account of small princi-palities in Elburz mountains of northern Iran. Region important for development of Shiism, particularly Zaydī Shiism. [RWB]

17.189 Wilferd Madelung. *Religious trends in early Islamic Iran.* Albany: Persian Heritage Foundation, 1988. ISBN 0-88706-700-X (cl), 0-88706-701-8 (pbk). ▸ Excellent survey of Islamic religious developments in Iran and intersection with social and political structures. [RWB]

17.190 Adam Mez. *The Renaissance of Islam.* 1937 ed. Salahud-din Khuda-Bukhsh and D. S. Margoliouth, trans. New York: AMS Press, 1975. ▸ Potpourri of information on cultural matters in ninth and tenth centuries drawn from Arabic *belles lettres*, chronicles, etc. Treatment of topics like urban life and economic activities anecdotal rather than analytical, but anecdotes are well worth reading. [RWB]

17.191 Roy P. Mottahedeh. "The ʿAbbasid caliphate in Iran." In *The Cambridge history of Iran.* Richard N. Frye, ed., vol. 4, pp. 57–89. Cambridge: Cambridge University Press, 1975. ISBN 0-521-20093-8. ▸ Good general essay on Abbasid caliphate with reference to Iran. For more extensive and assertive approach see Daniel 17.145. [RWB]

17.192 Roy P. Mottahedeh. *Loyalty and leadership in an early Islamic society.* Princeton: Princeton University Press, 1980. ISBN 0-691-05296-4. ▸ Brief but methodologically important study of types of dependency and affiliation, particularly in governing cir-cles, in tenth-century Iran. Argues categories derived from exam-ination of vocabulary actually in use are preferable to exogenous analytical categories. [RWB]

17.193 Peter Von Sivers. "Taxes and trade in the ʿAbbasid *thughūr*, 750–962/133–351." *Journal of the economic and social his-tory of the Orient* 25.1 (1982) 71–99. ISSN 0022-4995. ▸ Political economy approach to provincial history of northern Iraq and Syria during period of Abbasid independence. [RWB]

SEE ALSO
9.160 C. E. Bosworth. *The Ghaznavids.*
9.162 Richard N. Frye. *Bukhara.*

Egypt to 1171 and North Africa

17.194 B. J. Beshir. "Fatimid military organization." *Der Islam* 55.1 (1978) 37–56. ISSN 0021-1818. ▸ Solid study of Fatimid mil-itary issues. Useful to read with articles by Bosworth on contem-porary military organization of various Iranian dynasties (17.169, 17.171, 17.173). [RWB]

17.195 Michael Brett. "The spread of Islam in Egypt and North Africa." In *Northern Africa: Islam and modernization.* Michael Brett, ed., pp. 1–12. London: Cass, 1973. ISBN 0-7146-2972-3. ▸ Good brief analysis of extension of Islam into North Africa. Discusses conversion as well as invasion. [RWB]

17.196 Robert Brunschvig. *La Berbérie orientale sous les Hafsides, des origines à la fin du quinzième siècle.* 2 vols. Paris: Adrien-Mai-sonneuve, 1940–47. ▸ Major work in French tradition of North African historical studies. Concentrates on thirteenth to fifteenth century Tunis-based dynasty. Thorough discussion of sources. [RWB]

17.197 Richard Williams Bulliet. "Botr et baranès: hypothèses

sur l'histoire des Berbères." *Annales: économies, sociétés, civilisa-tions* 36.1 (1981) 104–16. ISSN 0395-2649. ▸ Argues origin of major division among Berbers, as perceived by Arab conquerors, dates from Roman empire. Argument based on history of agri-cultural technology and camel utilization. [RWB]

17.198 Vincent J. Cornell. "Socioeconomic dimensions of *recon-quista* and *jihad* in Morocco: Portuguese Dukkala and the Saʿdid Sus, 1450–1557." *International journal of Middle East studies* 22.4 (1990) 379–418. ISSN 0020-7438. ▸ Good study of extension of Iberian drive to expel Muslims. Understanding Portuguese designs on Morocco essential to history of voyages of discovery along African coast. [RWB]

17.199 P. F. de Moraes Farias. "The Almoravids: some ques-tions covering the character of the movement during its period of closest contact with the western Sudan." *Bulletin de l'Institut Français d'Afrique Noire* 29 (1967) 794–878. ▸ Reconsideration of semi-legendary origins of Almoravid dynasty. Challenging new approach to problem. [RWB]

17.200 Hans Gottschalk. *Die Mādārāʾijun: ein Beitrag zur Ge-schichte Ägyptens unter dem Islam.* Berlin: de Gruyter, 1931. ▸ Unusual monograph detailing history of family of finance offi-cials involved in Abbasid and Egyptian political affairs. [RWB]

17.201 Ulrich Haarmann. "Regional sentiment in medieval Islamic Egypt." *Bulletin of the School of Oriental and African Stud-ies* 43.1 (1980) 55–66. ISSN 0041-977X. ▸ Good example of new tendency to explore regional approaches to medieval Islamic his-tory and escape overconcentration on caliphal capital. [RWB]

17.202 Zaky Mohamed Hassan. *Les Tulunides: étude de l'Egypte à la fin du dix-neuvième siècle, 868–905.* Paris: Busson, 1933. ▸ Only full treatment of Tulunid dynasty, first independent Islamic dynasty of Egypt. Connections with Abbasids in Baghdad are well treated in Gottschalk 17.200. [RWB]

17.203 Harry W. Hazard. "Moslem North Africa, 1049–1394." In *A history of the Crusades.* Harry W. Hazard, ed., vol. 3, pp. 457–85. Madison: University of Wisconsin Press, 1975. ISBN 0-299-06670-3. ▸ Essay gives thorough coverage of final phase of Crusades which saw shift of focus to Egypt, Tunisia, and other locales remote from Holy Land. [RWB]

17.204 J.F.P. Hopkins. *Medieval Muslim government in Barbary until the sixth century of the hijra.* London: Luzac, 1958. ▸ One of few monographs on Islamic history of North Africa written in English. Very good for Almohad period; sources for administra-tive history of earlier dynasties are scarce, however. [RWB]

17.205 Hady Roger Idris. *La Berbérie orientale sous les Zirides, Xe–XIIe siècles.* Paris: Adrien-Maisonneuve, 1962. ▸ Thorough dynastic history in French tradition of North African studies. Zirids, who came to power as North African provincial governors after Fatimids departed Tunisia for Egypt in 969, achieved inde-pendence and switched allegiance to the Sunnī Abbasid caliph-ate. [RWB]

17.206 Charles-André Julien. *History of North Africa: Tunisia, Algeria, Morocco, from the Arab conquest to 1830.* R. Le Tourneau and C. C. Stewart, eds. John Petrie, trans. New York: Praeger, 1970. ▸ English translation of second volume of standard French survey of North African history. Better than Abun-Nasr 18.347 for medieval history. [RWB]

17.207 Ira Marvin Lapidus. "The conversion of Egypt to Islam." *Israel Oriental studies* 2 (1972) 248–62. ISSN 0334-4401. ▸ Important contribution to debate over chronology of conversion to Islam and method of determining conversion. [RWB]

17.208 Abd Allah Laroui. *The history of the Maghrib: an inter-pretive essay.* Ralph Manheim, trans. Princeton: Princeton Uni-versity Press, 1977. ISBN 0-691-03109-6. ▸ Revisionist general history; read with Julien 17.206. Seeks to decolonialize North African history by challenging standard approach of French historians. Often interesting although seldom provides exciting alternative vision. [RWB]

17.209 Roger Le Tourneau. *The Almohad movement in North Africa in the twelfth and thirteenth centuries.* Princeton: Princeton University Press, 1969. ▸ Good short survey of most important dynasty in history of North Africa. Almohads rose to power in twelfth century and extended control over Muslim Spain as well as North Africa. Regrettably, no full-length monograph on subject available in English. [RWB]

17.210 Roger Le Tourneau. *Fez in the age of the Marinides.* Besse Alberta Clement, trans. Norman: University of Oklahoma Press, 1961. ▸ Small but valuable history and portrait of Fez during its heyday in fourteenth century. Draws on author's long and masterly *Fès avant le protectorat*, minutely describing largely unchanged "old" city in nineteenth century. [RWB]

17.211 Yaacov Lev. "Army, regime, and society in Fatimid Egypt, 358–487/968–1094." *International journal of Middle East studies* 19.3 (1987) 337–66. ISSN 0020-7438. ▸ Detailed look at various ethnic and functional components of Fatimid army from initial invasion of Egypt using Berber troops to heavy reliance on Turkish and African slave troops later. Should be compared with articles on army composition by Bosworth (17.169, 17.171, 17.173), Beshir (17.194), and Bacharach (17.307). [RWB]

17.212 Yaacov Lev. "The career of Ya'qub ibn Killis and the beginning of the Fatimid administration in Egypt." *Der Islam* 58.2 (1981) 237–49. ISSN 0021-1818. ▸ Study of key figure in early administrative history of Fatimid Egypt. [RWB]

17.213 James E. Lindsay. "Prophetic parallels in Abu 'Abd Allah al-Shi'i's mission among the Kutama Berbers, 893–910." *International journal of Middle East studies* 24.1 (1992) 39–56. ISSN 0020-7438. ▸ Study of missionary career that led to rise of Fatimid regime in Tunisia in 909. Argues primary narrative account tacitly compares Abu 'Abd Allah with Muhammad. Valuable historiographical inquiry. [RWB]

17.214 H. T. Norris. *The Berbers in Arabic literature.* New York: Longman, 1982. ISBN 0-582-78303-8. ▸ Valuable collection of excerpts from Arabic texts dealing with Berber matters. [RWB]

17.215 Mohamed Talbi. *L'émirat aghlabide, 184–296/800–909.* Paris: Librairie d'Amerique et d'Orient, 1966. ▸ Fine monograph on Aghlabid dynasty of Tunisia, first part of Abbasid caliphate to acquire independence. Also important for Sicily since Aghlabids carried out conquest. No English-language substitute. [RWB]

17.216 Gaston Wiet. *L'Égypte arabe de la conquête arabe à la conquête ottomane, 642–1517.* Vol. 4 of *Histoire de la nation égyptienne.* Paris: Société de l'Histoire National, Librairie Plon, 1938. ▸ Only good survey of Islamic history of Egypt. Out of date in many parts but still useful for gaining sweeping view of sequence of Egyptian history. [RWB]

SEE ALSO
18.347 Jamil M. Abun-Nasr. *History of the Maghrib in the Islamic period.*

Islamic Spain and Sicily

17.217 Michele Amari. *Storia dei musulmani di Sicilia.* 2d ed. 12 pts. Carlo Alfonso Nallino, ed. Catania: Prampolini, 1933–39. ▸ Massive nineteenth-century work, essential starting point for work on Muslims in Sicily even though much of it is general Islamic history. [RWB]

17.218 Rachel Arié. *L'Espagne musulmane au temps des Nasrides, 1232–1492.* 1976 ed. Paris: de Boccard, 1990. ISBN 2-7018-0052-

8. ▸ Major monograph on last dynasty of Islamic Spain. No comparable English-language work on these rulers who beautified Alhambra and gave rise to a rich literary tradition dealing with end of Muslim rule. With new afterword by author. [RWB]

17.219 Aziz Ahmad. *A history of Islamic Sicily.* Edinburgh: Edinburgh University Press, 1975. ISBN 0-85224-274-3. ▸ Brief history of Islamic Sicily in series devoted to introductory books. Serious students will need to refer back to Amari's voluminous but partially dated study (17.217). [RWB]

17.220 Charles Julian Bishko. "The Spanish and Portuguese reconquest, 1095–1492." In *A history of the Crusades.* Harry W. Hazard, ed., vol. 3, pp. 396–456. Madison: University of Wisconsin Press, 1975. ISBN 0-299-06670-3. ▸ Good account, from Christian perspective, of *riconquista* in Spain in context of Crusading movement. [RWB]

17.221 Anwar G. Chejne. *Muslim Spain: its history and culture.* Minneapolis: University of Minnesota Press, 1974. ISBN 0-8166-0688-9. ▸ Broad survey stressing cultural achievements, discussed in topical chapters. Lacks separate coverage of Christians and Jews. [RWB]

17.222 Thomas F. Glick. *Irrigation and society in medieval Valencia.* Cambridge, Mass.: Harvard University Press, 1970. ISBN 0-674-46675-6. ▸ Innovative study of continuity between Muslim and Christian agrarian systems in Spain, combining archaeological and documentary sources. Important contribution both to study of agriculture and medieval technology and to development of method in these fields. [RWB]

17.223 Thomas F. Glick. *Islamic and Christian Spain in the early Middle Ages.* Princeton: Princeton University Press, 1979. ISBN 0-691-05274-3. ▸ Major work on Islamic Spain by medievalist with background in geography. Challenges dominant approaches traditional to field; proposes new ways of looking, politically and culturally, at Christian-Muslim relations. [RWB]

17.224 Andrew Handler. *The Zirids of Granada.* Coral Gables, Fla.: University of Miami Press, 1974. ISBN 0-87024-216-4. ▸ Small monograph on local dynasty in southern Spain following breakup of caliphate in eleventh century. Wasserstein 17.231 gives broader picture, but still useful, detailed study. [RWB]

17.225 Leonard Patrick Harvey. *Islamic Spain, 1250 to 1500.* Chicago: University of Chicago Press, 1990. ISBN 0-226-31960-1. ▸ Best study in English focusing on Arabs and Christians in Aragon, Valencia, and Navarre in period of reconquest and on political history of Granada, last Muslim kingdom. [RWB]

17.226 S. M. Imamuddin. *Muslim Spain, 711–1492 A.D.: a sociological study.* 2d ed. Leiden: Brill, 1981. ISBN 90-04-06131-2. ▸ Survey with topical chapters in social, economic, administrative, and cultural history. More compilation of lore than sophisticated analysis. [RWB]

17.227 Salma Khandra Jayyusi, ed. *The legacy of Muslim Spain.* Leiden: Brill, 1992. (Handbuch der Orientalistik, Erste Abteilung: der nahe und mittlere Osten, 12.) ISBN 90-04-09599-3. ▸ Thousand-page collection of articles on all aspects of Islamic Spain. Particularly valuable for articles in English by scholars who usually write in French or Spanish. Essential update. [RWB]

17.228 Évariste Levi-Provençal. *Histoire de l'Espagne musulmane.* Rev. ed. 3 vols. Paris: Maisonneuve, 1950–67. ▸ Essential starting point for study of history of Islamic Spain from eighth through tenth centuries. Superseded in some specific areas but still largest, most thorough history of period. [RWB]

17.229 Robert S. Lopez. "The Norman conquest of Sicily." In *A history of the Crusades.* 2d ed. Marshall W. Baldwin, ed., vol. 1, pp. 54–67. Madison: University of Wisconsin Press, 1969.

‣ Story of end of Muslim rule in Sicily focusing on Norman side. [RWB]

17.230 Ahmad ibn Muhammad al-Maqqari. *The history of the Mohammedan dynasties in Spain.* 1840–43 ed. 2 vols. Pascual de Gayangos y Arce, trans. New York: Johnson Reprint, 1964. ‣ General history, somewhat romantic in character, by seventeenth-century author. Only extensive Arabic chronicle for Muslim Spain available in English translation. [RWB]

17.231 David Wasserstein. *The rise and fall of the party-kings: politics and society in Islamic Spain, 1002–1086.* Princeton: Princeton University Press, 1985. ISBN 0-691-05436-3. ‣ Detailed narrative history of period of fragmented rule following fall of caliphate in Spain. Sequel to monumental work of Levi-Provençal (17.228). [RWB]

17.232 W. Montgomery Watt and Pierre Cachia. *A history of Islamic Spain.* 1965 ed. Chicago: Aldine, 1967. ‣ Brief general work on Islamic Spain with separate discussion of Arabic literature in Spain (by Cachia). Too short to be more than introduction. [RWB]

17.233 Benjamin W. Wheeler. "The reconquest of Spain before 1095." In *A history of the Crusades.* 2d ed. Marshall W. Baldwin, ed., vol. 1, pp. 31–39. Madison: University of Wisconsin Press, 1969. ‣ Early stages of *riconquista* seen largely from Christian viewpoint. [RWB]

The Crusaders and Their Opponents

Sources

17.234 Gregory Bar Hebraeus. *The chronography of Gregory Abu'l-Faraj, 1225–1286.* 1932 ed. 2 vols. E.A.W. Budge, trans. Amsterdam: APA, 1976. ISBN 90-6022-411-6. ‣ Translation from Syriac of Syrian Christian chronicle covering period of late Crusades. [RWB]

17.235 Ibn al-Qalanisi. *The Damascus chronicle of the Crusades.* H.A.R. Gibb, trans. London: Luzac, 1967. ‣ Translated excerpts from Damascus-oriented chronicle of early twelfth century. Omits passages dealing with internal Muslim politics. For fuller, but not complete, translation of work, see 17.236. [RWB]

17.236 Ibn al-Qalanisi. *Damas de 1075 à 1154.* Roger Le Tourneau, trans. Damascus: Institut Français de Damas, 1952. ‣ Complete translation of work partially translated by Gibb (17.235). Gibb's extensive introduction important for understanding work. [RWB]

17.237 Usamah ibn Munqidh. *An Arab-Syrian gentleman and warrior in the period of the Crusades: memoirs of Usamah ibn-Munqidh.* 1929 ed. Philip K. Hitti, trans. Princeton: Princeton University Press, 1987. ISBN 0-691-87746-0 (cl), 0-691-02269-0 (pbk). ‣ Vivid, readable autobiography of Syrian knight. Shows how Arabs viewed coarseness of unsophisticated Crusaders as well as what life was like. [RWB]

17.238 William of Tyre. *A history of deeds done beyond the sea.* 1941 ed. New York: Octagon Books, 1976. ISBN 0-374-90320-4. ‣ Essential chronicle of Crusades by churchman living in Crusader kingdom. [RWB]

Studies

17.239 Aziz Suryal Atiya. *Crusade, commerce, and culture.* 1962 ed. New York: Wiley, 1966. ‣ Brief but stimulating interpretation of interchange in eastern Mediterranean at time of Crusades. [RWB]

17.240 Aharon Ben-Ami. *Social change in a hostile environment: the Crusaders' kingdom of Jerusalem.* Princeton: Princeton University Press, 1969. ‣ Alternating historical and analytical chapters examining impact on feudal state of location amidst Muslim

adversaries. Brief and pointed, valuable for focus on Middle Eastern dimension of Crusades. [RWB]

17.241 Andrew S. Ehrenkreutz. *Saladin.* Albany: State University of New York Press, 1972. ISBN 0-87395-095-X. ‣ Demythologizing biography of heroic foe of Crusaders. Contrary to image conveyed by Gibb and earlier writers (e.g., 17.245), Saladin (Salah al-Din) shown as fortunate opportunist of only modest talent. [RWB]

17.242 Nikita Elisséeff. *Nur ad-Din, un grand prince musulman de Syrie au temps des croisades (511–569 h./1118–1174).* 3 vols. Damascus: Institut Français de Damas, 1967. ‣ Major monograph on key figure in Syrian history during Crusades. Predecessor and patron of Saladin (Salah al-Din), Nur al-Din first to rally Muslims successfully and showed how to defeat the invaders. [RWB]

17.243 H.A.R. Gibb. "The Aiyubids." In *A history of the Crusades.* 2d ed. Robert Lee Wolff and Harry W. Hazard, ed., vol. 2, pp. 693–714. Madison: University of Wisconsin Press, 1969. ‣ Good short history of rulers of Egypt and Syria descending from Saladin (Salah al-Din). Superseded for Syria by Humphreys 17.247. [RWB]

17.244 H.A.R. Gibb. "The career of Nur-ad-Din." In *A history of the Crusades.* 2d ed. Marshall W. Baldwin, ed., vol. 1, pp. 513–27. Madison: University of Wisconsin Press, 1969. ‣ Short account of major ruler, patron of Saladin (Salah al-Din), to which Elisséeff devoted three-volume monograph (17.242). See also Humphreys's discussion of Nur al-Din (17.247). [RWB]

17.245 H.A.R. Gibb. *Saladin: studies in Islamic history.* Beirut: Arab Institute for Research and Publication, 1974. ‣ Collection of previously dispersed essays covering career of Saladin (Salah al-Din). Presents Saladin as strong moral leader. View strongly revised in biography by Ehrenkreutz (17.241). [RWB]

17.246 H.A.R. Gibb. "Zengi and the fall of Edessa." In *A history of the Crusades.* Marshall W. Baldwin, ed., vol. 1, pp. 449–62. Philadelphia: University of Pennsylvania Press, 1958. ‣ History of first major setback to Crusades. Zengi's career set pattern for accomplishments of his son Nur al-Din. [RWB]

17.247 R. Stephen Humphreys. *From Saladin to the Mongols: the Ayyubids of Damascus, 1193–1260.* Albany: State University of New York Press, 1977. ISBN 0-87395-263-4. ‣ Excellent monograph on rule of Ayyubids in Syria. Focus on political history with special topics, such as religious patronage and military organization, addressed by author in separate articles. [RWB]

17.248 R. Stephen Humphreys. "Politics and architectural patronage in Ayyubid Damascus." In *The Islamic world from classical to modern times: essays in honor of Bernard Lewis.* C. E. Bosworth et al., eds., pp. 151–74. Princeton: Darwin, 1989. ISBN 0-87850-066-9. ‣ Quantified study demonstrating utilization of patronage as instrument of control. [RWB]

17.249 M. C. Lyons and David Jackson. *Saladin: the politics of the holy war.* New York: Cambridge University Press, 1982. ISBN 0-521-22358-X. ‣ Study avoiding both romanticization and harsh demythologization of most famous foe of Crusaders. Narrower in scope than works by Gibb (17.245) and Ehrenkreutz (17.241). [RWB]

17.250 Joshua Prawer. *The history of the Jews in the Latin kingdom of Jerusalem.* Oxford: Clarendon, 1988. ISBN 0-19-822557-1. ‣ Specialized study offering contrast to other works on Jews in Islamic world. Valuable for explicating situation of Jews in Jerusalem in medieval period. [RWB]

17.251 Steven Runciman. "The pilgrimages to Palestine before 1095." In *A history of the Crusades.* 2d ed. Marshall W. Baldwin, ed., vol. 1, pp. 68–78. Madison: University of Wisconsin Press,

1969. ▸ Crusades thought of as armed pilgrimages and history of pilgrimage to Holy Land essential to understanding them. Written by superb historian. [RWB]

17.252 Maya Schatzmiller. "The Crusades and Islamic warfare—a re-evaluation." *Der Islam* 55.1 (1992) 247–88. ISSN 0021-1818. ▸ Inquiry into content and historical context of Islamic texts on military affairs, variously dated to Abbasid era and Crusading era. [RWB]

17.253 Emmanuel Sivan. *L'Islam et la croisade: idéologie et propagande dans les réactions musulmanes aux croisades.* Paris: Maisonneuve, 1968. ▸ Thorough, chronologically organized account of Muslim reactions to Crusades. [RWB]

The Seljuqs and Their Contemporaries

Sources

17.254 Kai Ka'us ibn Iskandar. *A mirror for princes: the "Qabus Nama."* Reuben Levy, trans. New York: Dutton, 1951. ▸ Readable translation of interesting document presented as ruler's advice to his son. Gives vivid impression of worldview of eleventh-century Iranian ruler. [RWB]

17.255 Nizam al-Mulk. *The book of government or rules for kings: the Siyar al-muluk or Siyasat-nama of Nizam al-Mulk.* Rev. ed. Hubert Darke, trans. Boston: Routledge & Kegan Paul, 1978. ▸ Good translation of major work on government in genre of Mirrors for Princes. Nizam al-Mulk, most powerful vizier of the Seljuq empire, writes from practical experience, not just from theory. [RWB]

17.256 Khass-hajib Yusuf. *Wisdom of royal glory: a Turko-Islamic "Mirror for Princes."* Robert Dankoff, trans. Chicago: University of Chicago Press, 1983. ISBN 0-226-97179-1. ▸ Translation of one of earliest books written in Turkic. Good discussion of connections with Islamic and Indian antecedents for Mirror for Princes genre (see 17.254). [RWB]

Studies

17.257 C. E. Bosworth. *The later Ghaznavids, splendour and decay: the dynasty in Afghanistan and northern India, 1040–1186.* New York: Columbia University Press, 1977. ISBN 0-231-04428-3. ▸ Brief sequel to author's major monograph on earlier Ghaznavid rulers. Of greater interest for history of Islam in India than for significant involvement with other dynasties in Iran and Central Asia. [RWB]

17.258 Harold Bowen. "Notes on some early Seljuqid viziers." *Bulletin of the School of Oriental and African Studies* 20 (1957) 105–10. ISSN 0041-977X. ▸ Brief discussion of very beginnings of Seljuq rule in Iran after 1037. Illuminates some problems, personalities, and ambiguities involved in transition of Seljuqs from tribal raiders to imperial rulers. [RWB]

17.259 Richard Williams Bulliet. "Local politics in eastern Iran under the Ghaznavids and Seljuks." *Iranian studies* 11 (1978) 35–56. ISSN 0021-0862. ▸ Description of series of political events in Iran, Afghanistan, and Central Asia in tenth to twelfth centuries. Argues local religious elites enjoyed great power and occasionally sought independence of imperial rule. [RWB]

17.260 Claude Cahen. "The Turkish invasion: the Selchükids." In *A history of the Crusades.* 2d ed. Marshall W. Baldwin, ed., vol. 1, pp. 135–76. Philadelphia: University of Pennsylvania Press, 1958. ▸ General article by major French historian of last generation. Concentrates on Seljuqs of Syria and Anatolia more than Seljuq sultans in Iran. [RWB]

17.261 Claude Cahen. "The Turks in Iran and Anatolia before the Mongol invasions." In *A history of the Crusades.* 2d ed. Robert Lee Wolff, ed., vol. 2, pp. 661–92. Philadelphia: University of

Pennsylvania Press, 1969. ▸ Good survey of complicated political history of Turks. Longer but more opaque treatment available in author's *Pre-Ottoman Turkey* (17.299). [RWB]

17.262 Angelika Hartmann. *An-Nāṣir li-Dīn Allāh (1180–1225): Politik, Religion, Kultur in die späten Abbasidenzeit.* Berlin: de Gruyter, 1975. ISBN 3-11-004179-0. ▸ Comprehensive study of caliphate of most important late Abbasid ruler. Essential for understanding important changes of twelfth to thirteenth centuries. [RWB]

17.263 Axel Havemann. "The vizier and the *ra'īs* in Saljuq Syria: the struggle for urban self-representation." *International journal of Middle East studies* 21.2 (1989) 233–42. ISSN 0020-7438. ▸ Exploration of functions of two positions in Seljuq government. Focuses on ambiguous nature of urban chief (*ra'īs*) in Syrian context. [RWB]

17.264 Carole Hillenbrand. "The career of Najm ad-Din Il-Ghazi." *Der Islam* 58.2 (1981) 250–92. ISSN 0021-1818. ▸ Study of minor Turkish ruler in northern Iraq during Seljuq period. Valuable corrective to histories that concentrate on rulers from major dynasties. Helps explain broader political environment and illuminate careers of better-known figures. [RWB]

17.265 Carole Hillenbrand. "The establishment of Artuqid power in Diyar Bakr in the twelfth century." *Studia Islamica* 54 (1981) 129–54. ISSN 0585-5292. ▸ Contribution to history of little studied Turkoman principality contemporary with Seljuq sultanate. Based on local history of Diyar Bakr in eastern Anatolia. [RWB]

17.266 Carla L. Klausner. *The Seljuk vezirate: a study of civil administration, 1055–1194.* Cambridge, Mass.: Center for Middle Eastern Studies, 1973. (Harvard Middle Eastern monographs, 22.) ISBN 0-674-80095-8. ▸ Useful but unexciting history of Seljuq vizierate. For more general consideration of Seljuq administration see Lambton 17.267. [RWB]

17.267 Ann K. S. Lambton. *Continuity and change in medieval Persia: aspects of administrative, economic, and social history, eleventh to fourteenth century.* New York: Bibliotheca Persica, 1988. ISBN 0-88706-133-8 (cl), 0-88706-134-6 (pbk). ▸ Lecture series combining materials from author's unpublished doctoral dissertation on Seljuq administration with comparative perspective on Mongol period. Excellent study but narrowly focused on administrative practice rather than overall nature of government and society. [RWB]

17.268 Gary Leiser, ed. and trans. *A history of the Seljuks: Ibrahim Kafesoğlu's interpretation and the resulting controversy.* Carbondale: Southern Illinois University Press, 1988. ISBN 0-8093-1414-2. ▸ Translation from Turkish of article on Seljuqs in major Turkish reference work *Islam Ansiklopedisi*, accompanied by documents detailing complex charges of plagiarism and double-dealing surrounding article. Sordid controversy aside, best on political history, particularly of Rum Seljuqs of Konya, but superficial on social and cultural matters. [RWB]

17.269 P. A. MacKay. "Patronage and power in sixth–twelfth-century Baghdad: the life of the vizier ʿAdud Al-Din ibn al-Muzaffar." *Studia Islamica* 34 (1971) 27–56. ISSN 0585-5292. ▸ Unusual study of vizier from late Abbasid period. Read with Klausner 17.266 and Mason 17.271. [RWB]

17.270 George Makdisi. *Ibn ʿAqil et la resurgence de l'Islam traditionaliste au onzième siècle.* Damascus: Institut Français de Damas, 1963. ▸ Major monograph from which all of author's later works originate. Extensive portrayal of religious and intellectual world of eleventh century but with very narrow focus on Baghdad. Frequent implication that events outside Baghdad are comparatively insignificant is serious limitation. [RWB]

17.271 Herbert Mason. *Two statesmen of mediaeval Islam: Vizir*

Ibn Hubayra (499–560 AH/1105–1165 AD) and Caliph an-Nasir li Din Allah (553–622 AH/1158–1225 AD). The Hague: Mouton, 1972. ▸ Only extensive treatment in English on last important Abbasid caliph, al-Nasir; Ibn Hubayra, figure of less importance. Longer work by Hartmann in German is preferable (17.262). [RWB]

SEE ALSO

9.161 C. E. Bosworth. "The political and dynastic history of the Iranian world (A.D. 1000–1217)."

MONGOL AND POST-MONGOL PERIODS

The East from Chinggis Khan to Tamerlane, 1218–1400

Sources

17.272 ᶜAta-Malik al-Juvayni. *The history of the world-conqueror.* 2 vols. John Andrew Boyle, trans. Cambridge, Mass.: Harvard University Press, 1958. ▸ Vivid translation of major Persian chronicle covering early Mongol history and conquests of Chinggis Khan. [RWB]

17.273 Fadlallah Rashid al-Din. *The successors of Genghis Khan.* John Andrew Boyle, trans. New York: Columbia University Press, 1971. ISBN 0-231-03351-6. ▸ Sequel to Boyle's translation of ᶜAta-Malik al-Juvani's chronicle of Chinggis Khan's career (17.272). Excerpt from much longer work gives good example of style of important Persian historian. [RWB]

Studies

17.274 David Ayalon. "The great *yasa* of Chingiz Khan: a reexamination (parts A, B, C1, C2)." *Studia Islamica* 33–34, 36, 38 (1971–73) 97–140, 151–80, 113–58, 107–56. ISSN 0585-5292. ▸ Important reexamination of understanding of Mongol law preserved in medieval Arabic texts; shown to distort actual legal picture. Valuable understanding of impact of Mongol rule on Islamic world. [RWB]

17.275 John Andrew Boyle. "The death of the last ᶜAbbasid caliph: a contemporary Muslim account." *Journal of Semitic studies* 6.2 (1961) 145–62. ISSN 0022-4480. ▸ End of Abbasid caliphate after five centuries a traumatic event in Islamic history. Stories about demise of last caliph as captive of Mongol invader Hülegü contribute to appreciating this trauma. [RWB]

17.276 Claude Cahen. "The Mongols and the Near East." In *A history of the Crusades.* 2d ed. Robert Lee Wolff, ed., vol. 2, pp. 715–34. Philadelphia: University of Pennsylvania Press, 1969. ▸ Major French historian of last generation and specialist on history of Anatolia. Overlaps his book *Pre-Ottoman Turkey* (17.299). [RWB]

17.277 David O. Morgan. "The 'great *yasa* of Chingiz Khan' and Mongol law in the Ilkhanate." *Bulletin of the School of Oriental and African Studies* 49.1 (1986) 163–76. ISSN 0041-977X. ▸ Discussion of Mongol law. Read with Ayalon 17.274 on same subject. [RWB]

17.278 David O. Morgan. "The Mongol armies in Persia." *Der Islam* 56.1 (1979) 81–96. ISSN 0021-1818. ▸ Good article on organization of Mongol armies. Compare with articles by Bosworth on military organization of earlier dynasties in Iran (17.169, 17.171, 17.173). [RWB]

17.279 I. P. Petrushevsky. "The socio-economic condition of Iran under the Il-khans." In *Cambridge history of Iran.* John Andrew Boyle, ed., vol. 5, pp. 483–537. Cambridge: Cambridge University Press, 1968. ISBN 0-521-06936-X. ▸ Makes available in English views of important Soviet economic historian otherwise writing in Russian. [RWB]

17.280 John Masson Smith, Jr. *The history of the Sarbadar dynasty, 1336–1381 A.D., and its sources.* The Hague: Mouton,

1970. ▸ History of anomalous state, important as precursor of Safavid dynasty, based on religious zealotry of mixed Ṣūfī and Shīᶜī character. Difficult for nonspecialist. [RWB]

17.281 John Masson Smith, Jr. "Mongol manpower and Persian population." *Journal of the economic and social history of the Orient* 18 (1975) 271–99. ISSN 0022-4995. ▸ Ingenious but not entirely convincing effort to relate Mongol army size to population of provinces responsible for army units. Good exploration of problems facing demographic historians in this period. [RWB]

17.282 Bertold Spuler, comp. *History of the Mongols, based on Eastern and Western accounts of the thirteenth and fourteenth centuries.* Helga Drummond and Stuart Drummond, trans. Berkeley: University of California Press, 1972. ISBN 0-520-01960-1. ▸ Translated excerpts from many languages, woven together to present composite portrayal of Mongols as seen by adversaries and subject peoples. [RWB]

17.283 John E. Woods. *The Aqquyunlu: clan, confederation, empire, a study in fifteenth/ninth-century Turko-Iranian politics.* Minneapolis: Bibliotheca Islamica, 1976. (Studies in Middle Eastern history, 3.) ISBN 0-88297-011-9. ▸ Dry but valuable study of Turkic tribal state in Mesopotamia and eastern Anatolia in fifteenth century. Essential for understanding development of Safavid dynasty in Iran after 1500 and for contemporary Ottoman history. [RWB]

SEE ALSO

9.237 John Andrew Boyle. "Dynastic and political history of the Il-khans."

The Mamluks in Egypt and Syria, 1250–1517

17.284 David Ayalon. "Aspects of the Mamluk phenomenon." *Der Islam* 54.2, 55.1 (1975, 1977) 196–225, 1–32. ISSN 0021-1818. ▸ Important article bringing together many of author's thoughts on Mamluks from long career focusing on subject. Topics range from Abbasid period onward and go well beyond Egypt and Syria. [RWB]

17.285 David Ayalon. "The auxiliary forces of the Mamluk sultanate." *Der Islam* 65.1 (1988) 260–97. ISSN 0021-1818. ▸ Unchanged translation of author's original 1945 publication in Hebrew. Treats Arabs, Kurds, and other military forces used by Mamluks. [RWB]

17.286 David Ayalon. "The Circassians in the Mamluk kingdom." *Journal of the American Oriental Society* 69.3 (1949) 135–47. ISSN 0003-0279. ▸ Study of role of Circassian Mamluks is basic to understanding rise to dominance in sultanate during fourteenth century. [RWB]

17.287 David Ayalon. *Gunpowder and firearms in the Mamluk kingdom: a challenge to a mediaeval society.* 2d ed. Totowa, N.J.: Cass, 1978. ISBN 0-7146-3090-X. ▸ Brief monograph investigating Mamluks' comparative disinclination to use firearms, failing that contributed to their defeat by more innovative Ottomans in 1516–17. Discusses siege weapons, personal firearms, and coastal defenses. [RWB]

17.288 David Ayalon. "Names, titles, and 'nisbas' of the Mamluks." *Israel Oriental studies* 5 (1975) 189–232. ISSN 0334-4401. ▸ One of author's several studies of social origins and status of Mamluk slave caste in Egypt and Syria. Islamic personal names are elaborate and informative; demonstrates utility for historical analysis. [RWB]

17.289 David Ayalon. "Studies on the structure of the Mamluk army." *Bulletin of the School of Oriental and African Studies* 15.1–2, 16.3 (1953–54) 203–28, 448–76, 57–90. ISSN 0041-977X. ▸ All discussions of Mamluk phenomenon begin with work of Ayalon. Compare with works by Bosworth (17.169, 17.171, 17.173), Beshir

(17.194), and others on organization of the military under various Islamic dynasties. [RWB]

17.290 Jean-Claude Garcin. "The Mamluk military system and the blocking of medieval Moslem society." In *Europe and the rise of capitalism*. Jean Baechler, John A. Hall, and Michael Mann, eds., pp. 114–35. New York: Blackwell, 1988. ISBN 0-631-15006-4. ▸ Discussion, by French scholar little published in English, of possible relationship between Mamluk military system and comparative expansion of European economy vis-à-vis Islam after twelfth century. Critical response by Michael Cook. [RWB]

17.291 R. Stephen Humphreys. "The emergence of the Mamluk army." *Studia Islamica* 45–46 (1977) 67–100, 147–82. ISSN 0585-5292. ▸ Study of development of Mamluk soldiery that culminated in Mamluk commanders supplanting Ayyubid sultans, by specialist on Ayyubid period. [RWB]

17.292 Abu al-Mahasin Yusuf Ibn Taghribirdi. *History of Egypt, 1382–1469.* 1954–60 ed. 7 vols. William Popper, ed. and trans. New York: AMS Press, 1976. ISBN 0-404-58800-X. ▸ Translation, with notes and indexes, of major chronicle of Mamluk period. [RWB]

17.293 Robert Irwin. *The Middle East in the Middle Ages: the early Mamluk sultanate, 1250–1382.* Carbondale: Southern Illinois University Press, 1986. ISBN 0-8093-1286-7. ▸ Brief general history of period poorly covered but abundantly documented. Best starting point for Mamluk history. [RWB]

17.294 Carl F. Petry. *The civilian elite of Cairo in the later Middle Ages.* Princeton: Princeton University Press, 1981. ISBN 0-691-05329-4. ▸ Exhaustive quantitative study of religious and civil personages registered in biographical dictionaries of Mamluk period. Many maps and tables order material but tend to overwhelm analytical framework and interpretation. [RWB]

17.295 Carl F. Petry. *Twilight of majesty: the reigns of the Mamluk sultans al-Ashraf Qaytbay and Qansuh al-Ghawri in Egypt.* Seattle: Middle East Center, Jackson School of International Studies, University of Washington, 1993. (Occasional papers, 4.) ISBN 0-295-97307-2. ▸ Invaluable study of late Mamluk period. [RWB]

17.296 Hassanein Rabie. *The financial system of Egypt, A.H. 564–741/A.D. 1169–1341.* New York: Oxford University Press, 1972. ISBN 0-19-713564-1. ▸ Excellent presentation of Egypt's land-grant system during Ayyubid and early Mamluk periods. [RWB]

17.297 Mustafa M. Ziada. "The Mamluk sultans to 1293." In *A history of the Crusades.* 2d ed. Robert Lee Wolff, ed., vol. 2, pp. 735–58. Philadelphia: University of Pennsylvania Press, 1969. ▸ Somewhat dull narrative history of early Mamluk sultanate. [RWB]

17.298 Mustafa M. Ziada. "The Mamluk sultans, 1291–1517." In *A history of the Crusades.* Harry W. Hazard, ed., vol. 3, pp. 486–512. Madison: University of Wisconsin Press, 1975. ISBN 0-299-06670-3. ▸ Lackluster narrative of later Mamluk sultanate but no better alternative in English. [RWB]

Islam in Anatolia, 1071–1402

17.299 Claude Cahen. *Pre-Ottoman Turkey: a general survey of the material and spiritual culture and history, c. 1071–1330.* New York: Taplinger, 1968. ▸ Major monograph on Muslim Anatolia from Battle of Manzikert (1071) to end of Mongol period. Complements work by Vryonis on Christians in Anatolia (17.302). Dense, data-packed reading. [RWB]

17.300 Mehmet Fuat Köprülü. *The origins of the Ottoman empire.* Gary Leiser, ed. and trans. Albany: State University of New York Press, 1992. ISBN 0-7914-0819-1. ▸ Important interpretation of

Ottoman origins focusing on tribal background. Read as counterpoint to Wittek 17.304, who stresses religious factors. [RWB]

17.301 Rudi Paul Lindner. *Nomads and Ottomans in medieval Anatolia.* Bloomington: Indiana University, Research Institute for Inner Asian Studies, 1983. (Uralic and Altaic series, 144.) ISBN 0-933070-12-8. ▸ Study of nomadism in Anatolia challenging Wittek's theory of origin of Ottoman empire (17.304). Skillful refutation but does not adequately replace Wittek. [RWB]

17.302 Speros Vryonis, Jr. *The decline of medieval Hellenism in Asia Minor and the process of islamization from the eleventh through the fifteenth century.* Berkeley: University of California Press, 1971. ISBN 0-520-01597-5. ▸ Important, thorough study of Islam's progress and Christianity's recession in Anatolia after defeat of Byzantines in 1071. Uses many types of documentation, mostly from Christian side. Should be balanced by Cahen 17.299. [RWB]

17.303 Paul Wittek. "De la défaite d'Ankara à la prise de Constantinople." *Revue des études islamiques* 12 (1938) 1–34. ISSN 0336-156X. ▸ Second half of Wittek's general thesis on rise of Ottoman empire. Less influential than his *Rise of the Ottoman Empire* (17.304) but essential for understanding his complete vision. [RWB]

17.304 Paul Wittek. *The rise of the Ottoman empire.* 1938 ed. New York: Franklin, 1971. (Royal Asiatic Society monographs, 23.) ISBN 0-8337-3855-0. ▸ Short but extremely influential work focusing on rise of Ottoman empire through support of Muslim religious warriors battling on Christian frontier. For challenge to theory see Lindner 17.301. [RWB]

SOCIAL AND ECONOMIC HISTORY
Social Structure and Daily Life

17.305 M. Manazir Ahsan. *Social life under the Abbasids, 170–289 A.H./786–902 A.D.* New York: Longman, 1979. ISBN 0-582-78079-9. ▸ Collection of data on social and economic life, primarily in Baghdad, gleaned from variety of sources. Valuable detail but little useful analysis. [RWB]

17.306 David Ayalon. "Regarding population estimates in the countries of medieval Islam." *Journal of the economic and social history of the Orient* 28.1 (1985) 1–19. ISSN 0022-4995. ▸ Attempts to derive population estimates for Egypt and Syria in Mamluk period from specific textual sources; criticizes more casual estimates by other scholars. [RWB]

17.307 Jere L. Bacharach. "African military slaves in the medieval Middle East: the cases of Iraq (869–955) and Egypt (868–1171)." *International journal of Middle East studies* 13.4 (1981) 471–95. ISSN 0020-7438. ▸ Study of attitudes toward black African as opposed to Turkish slave soldiery. Argues decline of former not necessarily result of racist views. [RWB]

17.308 C. E. Bosworth. *The mediaeval Islamic underworld.* Vol. 1: *The Banu Sasan in Arabic society and literature.* Leiden: Brill, 1976. ISBN 90-04-04392-6 (v.1). ▸ Edition, translation, and careful philological study of two long poems (tenth and fourteenth centuries) dedicated to jargon of Islamic fraternity of beggars and their various activities. Good introductory essay on beggars and other underworld groups, but otherwise difficult for nonspecialist to penetrate. [RWB]

17.309 Richard W. Bulliet. *Islam: the view from the edge.* New York: Columbia University Press, 1993. ISBN 0-231-08218-5. ▸ Short, general synthesis of Islamic social history. Argues for studying local developments rather than central political history. [RWB]

17.310 Claude Cahen. "Tribes, cities, and social organization." In *The Cambridge history of Iran.* Richard N. Frye, ed., vol. 4, pp. 305–28. Cambridge: Cambridge University Press, 1975. ISBN

0-521-20093-8. ‣ Short article by pioneer in social history of medieval Islam. Summarizes some hypotheses of author's important article in French on urban autonomy. [RWB]

17.311 Hayyim J. Cohen. "The economic background and the secular occupations of Muslim jurisprudents and traditionists in the classical period of Islam (until the middle of the eleventh century)." *Journal of the economic and social history of the Orient* 13 (1970) 16–61. ISSN 0022-4995. ‣ Pioneering attempt to extract socioeconomic data from medieval biographical dictionaries. Unrefined methodology makes conclusions questionable. [RWB]

17.312 Benjamin R. Foster. "*Agoranomos* and *muḥtasib.*" *Journal of the economic and social history of the Orient* 13.2 (1970) 128–44. ISSN 0022-4995. ‣ Comparison of Byzantine office of market inspector with very similar office of *muḥtasib* in Islamic law. Raises but does not completely resolve question of whether Islamic institution derives from Byzantine model. [RWB]

17.313 Avner Giladi. "Concepts of childhood and attitudes towards children in medieval Islam." *Journal of the economic and social history of the Orient* 32.2 (1989) 121–52. ISSN 0022-4995. ‣ Initial inquiry into medical and religious attitudes toward children in society with high infant mortality. Data taken largely from medical works. [RWB]

17.314 Shlomo Dov Goitein. *Studies in Islamic history and institutions.* 1966 ed. Leiden: Brill, 1968. ‣ Collected articles of important scholar written before he undertook his monumental study of Cairo Geniza papers (17.392). Stress on social and institutional history. [RWB]

17.315 Reuben Levy. *The social structure of Islam.* 1957 ed. Cambridge: Cambridge University Press, 1965. ‣ Broad survey of Islamic religious and political institutions. Lacking sophistication in terms of sociology and social history, more useful for general reference than interpretation. [RWB]

17.316 Bernard Lewis. *Race and slavery in the Middle East: an enquiry.* New York: Oxford University Press, 1990. ISBN 0-19-505326-5. ‣ Recognizing emphasis on equality in Islamic law and theology, author concentrates on Muslim practice and gives evidence, including good color illustrations, of racial conflict. Much of slavery discussion deals with later periods. [RWB]

17.317 Franz Rosenthal. *Gambling in Islam.* Leiden: Brill, 1975. ISBN 90-04-04314-4. ‣ Examination of selection of key texts to divine how medieval Islamic society dealt with gambling. [RWB]

17.318 Franz Rosenthal. *The herb: hashish versus medieval Muslim society.* Leiden: Brill, 1971. ISBN 90-04-02563-4. ‣ Exploration of how hashish is discussed in Arabic texts and impact of hashish on society. [RWB]

17.319 Franz Rosenthal. "On suicide in Islam." *Journal of the American Oriental Society* 66.3 (1946) 239–59. ISSN 0003-0279. ‣ Review of attitudes toward suicide in Qur'ān and traditions of the Prophet followed by list of suicides and circumstances under which they occurred. [RWB]

17.320 Peter Von Sivers. "Military, merchants, and nomads: the social evolution of the Syrian cities and countryside during the classical period, 780–969/164–358." *Der Islam* 56.2 (1979) 212–44. ISSN 0021-1818. ‣ Provocative effort to tie together main elements of medieval Islamic society in evolutionary fashion. Seeks to explain growth of influence of urban elites and isolation and impoverishment of countryside during post-Umayyad/pre-Fatimid period; era rarely studied in Syria. [RWB]

17.321 David Waines. *In a caliph's kitchen.* London: Riad El-Rayyes, 1989. ISBN 1-869844-60-2. ‣ Cookbook drawn from recipes of Abbasid period, studied and tested by expert Arabist. Pioneering work in Islamic food history. [RWB]

Women and Gender

17.322 Amr ibn Bahr Jahiz. *The "Epistle of Singing-girls" of Jahiz.* A.F.L. Beeston, ed. and trans. Warminster: Aris & Phillips, 1980. ‣ Translation of short book by premier belle lettrist of Abbasid period. Gives good impression of ribald-type conversation favored by men and helps understanding of their view of women. [RWB]

17.323 Huda Lutfi. "Al-Sakhawi's '*Kitāb al-Nisā*' as a source for the social and economic history of Muslim women during the fifteenth century A.D." *Muslim world* 71.2 (1981) 104–24. ISSN 0027-4909. ‣ One of first efforts to explore medieval Islamic women's history from social and economic instead of ideological viewpoint. Utilizes one of few biographical dictionaries that concentrates on women. [RWB]

17.324 Huda Lutfi. "A study of six fourteenth-century *iqrār*s from al-Quds relating to Muslim women." *Journal of the economic and social history of the Orient* 26.3 (1983) 246–94. ISSN 0022-4995. ‣ Arabic text, translation, and analysis of legal documents from Jerusalem. Such documents rare; those relating to women rarer. [RWB]

17.325 Fedwa Malti-Douglas. *Woman's body, woman's word: gender and discourse in Arabo-Islamic writing.* Princeton: Princeton University Press, 1991. ISBN 0-691-06856-9 (cl), 0-691-01488-4 (pbk). ‣ Sophisticated analysis of portrayal of women in various types of sources, including the Arabian Nights, the philosophy of Ibn Tufail, and religious texts. Final third deals with modern texts. [RWB]

17.326 Basim Musallam. *Sex and society in Islamic civilization.* New York: Cambridge University Press, 1983. ISBN 0-521-24874-4. ‣ Important study of methods, legal status, and social acceptability of contraception. Demonstrates major difference between Islamic and Judaic or Christian practices. [RWB]

17.327 Maya Shatzmiller. "Aspects of women's participation in the economic life of later medieval Islam: occupations and mentalities." *Arabica* 35 (1988) 36–58. ISSN 0570-5398. ‣ Product of author's long-term interest in exploring labor issues and social history. Pioneering empirical work on Islamic women's history. [RWB]

17.328 William Robertson Smith. *Kinship and marriage in early Arabia.* 1903 ed. London: Darf, 1990. ISBN 1-85077-188-X. ‣ Old but still valuable for trying to understand position of women in pre-Islamic Arabia, crucial issue in view of disagreement over whether Islamic strictures freed or limited women. [RWB]

Economics, Trade, Taxation, and Administration

17.329 Eliyahu Ashtor. *Levant trade in the later Middle Ages.* Princeton: Princeton University Press, 1983. ISBN 0-691-05386-3. ‣ Minutely documented but often rather confusing monograph on trade in eastern Mediterranean. Uses both Arabic and European sources used. [RWB]

17.330 Eliyahu Ashtor. *A social and economic history of the Near East in the Middle Ages.* Berkeley: University of California Press, 1976. ISBN 0-520-02962-3. ‣ Summarizes and refers to many individual studies by this erratic pioneer of Islamic social and economic history. Ideas expressed should not be taken at face value but traced back to original study, usually in French, for direct appraisal of sources and techniques. [RWB]

17.331 C. E. Bosworth. "Abu ʿAbdallah al-Khwarazmi on the technical terms of the secretary's art." *Journal of the economic and social history of the Orient* 12.2 (1969) 113–64. ISSN 0022-4995. ‣ Annotated translation of chapter on administration from tenth-century encyclopedic work. Provides valuable insight into workings of Islamic chanceries. [RWB]

17.332 Jamsheed K. Choksy. "Loan and sales contracts in ancient and early medieval Iran." *Indo-Iranian journal* 31 (1988) 191–218. ISSN 0019-7246. ▸ Careful study of differences between Zoroastrian and Muslim practices in area of loans and contracts. Representative of author's broader concern with relations between Muslims and Zoroastrians in early Islamic Iran. [RWB]

17.333 Richard S. Cooper. "The assessment and collection of *kharāj* tax in medieval Egypt." *Journal of the American Oriental Society* 96.3 (1976) 365–82. ISSN 0003-0279. ▸ Detailed study of methods and associated terminology of land-tax collection in Egypt. As primary tax for medieval Islamic governments, article is suggestive for other areas of Middle East as well. [RWB]

17.334 Gladys Frantz-Murphy. "A new interpretation of the economic history of medieval Egypt: the role of the textile industry 254–567/868–1171." *Journal of the economic and social history of the Orient* 24.3 (1981) 274–97. ISSN 0022-4995. ▸ Argues textiles formed backbone of Egyptian economy in pre-Fatimid and Fatimid periods. Example of use of papyri for economic history. [RWB]

17.335 Ziaul Haque. *Landlord and peasant in early Islam: a study of the legal doctrine of mazra°a or sharecropping.* 1977 ed. Islamabad: Islamic Research Institute Press, 1986. ▸ Thorough examination of classic legal texts on issue of sharecropping. Data primarily legal with little indication of actual practice. Dense work designed for specialists. [RWB]

17.336 Hilmar C. Krueger. "The Italian cities and the Arabs before 1095." In *A history of the Crusades.* 2d ed. Marshall W. Baldwin, ed., vol. 1, pp. 40–53. Philadelphia: University of Pennsylvania Press, 1969. ▸ Early contacts between Italian cities and Arabs less studied than major trading links that developed later. [RWB]

17.337 Subhi Labib. "Egyptian commercial policy in the Middle Ages." In *Studies in the economic history of the Middle East.* Michael A. Cook, ed., pp. 63–77. New York: Oxford University Press, 1970. ISBN 0-19-713561-7. ▸ Survey article based on 17.338; basic work on commercial history during this period. [RWB]

17.338 Subhi Labib. *Handelsgeschichte Ägyptens im Spätmittelalter, 1171–1517.* Wiesbaden: Steiner, 1965. ▸ Major monograph on commercial history of Egypt during flowering of trade relations with Italy. [RWB]

17.339 Ann K. S. Lambton. "The evolution of *iqtā°* in medieval Iran." *Iran: journal of the British Institute of Persian Studies* 5 (1967) 41–50. ISSN 0578-6967. ▸ Short inquiry into medieval Iranian grants of land usufruct. Important contribution to debate over nature of landholding in Islam. [RWB]

17.340 Ira Marvin Lapidus. "The grain economy of Mamluk Egypt." *Journal of the economic and social history of the Orient* 12.1 (1969) 1–15. ISSN 0022-4995. ▸ Brief but perceptive analysis of state and private dimensions of grain marketing. [RWB]

17.341 Frede Løkkegaard. *Islamic taxation in the classic period, with special reference to circumstances in Iraq.* 1950 ed. Philadelphia: Porcupine, 1978. ISBN 0-87991-459-9. ▸ Study of taxation system contained in Abbasid period texts translated by A. Ben Shemesh and of degree to which it applied in Iraq. [RWB]

17.342 Kosei Morimoto. *The fiscal administration of Egypt in the early Islamic period.* Michael Robbins, trans. Kyoto, Japan: Dohosha, 1981. ISBN 4-8104-0212-6. ▸ Discussion of taxation and fiscal administration; read with Dennett 17.114. Goes beyond Dennett chronologically to include early Abbasid and even Fatimid topics. [RWB]

17.343 Richard T. Mortel. "Prices in Mecca during the Mamluk period." *Journal of the social and economic history of the Orient* 32.3 (1989) 279–334. ISSN 0022-4995. ▸ Heavily documented price lists

for basic commodities. Mecca supplied by caravan, thus prices reflect broader economic conditions. [RWB]

17.344 Maxime Rodinson. *Islam and capitalism.* Brian Pearce, trans. Austin: University of Texas Press, 1978. ISBN 0-292-73816-1. ▸ Investigation by important Marxist scholar of apparent incongruity between Islam and capitalism. Valuable contribution to understanding whole sweep of Islamic economic history. [RWB]

17.345 Tsugitaka Sato. "The evolution of the *iqtā°* system under the Mamluks: an analysis of 'al-Rawk al-Husami' and 'al-Rawk al-Nasiri.'" *Memoirs of the Research Department of the Toyo Bunko* 37 (1979) 99–131. ISSN 0082-562X. ▸ Important contribution to evolution of fiscal administration in Islam. Study of cadastral surveys of Egypt during Mamluk period. [RWB]

17.346 Tsugitaka Sato. "The *iqtā°* system under the Buwayhids." *Orient (Tokyo)* 18 (1982) 83–105. ▸ Useful study of land-grant administration after Buyid (Buwayhid) takeover of Baghdad in 945. [RWB]

17.347 Maya Shatzmiller. *Labour in the medieval Islamic world.* Leiden: Brill, 1993. ISBN 90-04-09896-8. ▸ Pioneering work discussing status of professions and crafts and organization of labor. [RWB]

17.348 Abraham L. Udovitch. *Partnership and profit in medieval Islam.* Princeton: Princeton University Press, 1970. ISBN 0-691-03084-7. ▸ Fundamental study of Islamic legal attitudes toward business and partnership. Each school of law discussed and compared with types of partnership in Christian Mediterranean lands. [RWB]

17.349 Abraham L. Udovitch. "Reflections on the institutions of credit and banking in the medieval Islamic Near East." *Studia Islamica* 41 (1975) 5–22. ISSN 0585-5292. ▸ Explores why banking did not develop in Islamic world as it did in Europe. Proposes answers on basis of theoretical writings and contemporary documents. [RWB]

17.350 Abraham L. Udovitch, ed. *The Islamic Middle East, 700–1900: studies in economic and social history.* Princeton: Darwin, 1981. ISBN 0-87850-030-8. ▸ Collection of essays on wide variety of topics. Solid contribution in sparsely covered field. [RWB]

17.351 David Waines. "Bread and society: an essay on the staff of life in medieval Iraq." *Journal of the economic and social history of the Orient* 30.3 (1987) 255–85. ISSN 0022-4995. ▸ Far-reaching essay on history and role of bread in Mesopotamian history and on its composition, preparation, and economic significance in Islamic Iraq in particular. Pioneering work on food history in Islam. [RWB]

Technology

17.352 Richard Williams Bulliet. "Medieval Arabic *ṭarsh:* a forgotten chapter in the history of printing." *Journal of the American Oriental Society* 107.3 (1987) 427–38. ISSN 0003-0279. ▸ Connects surviving specimens of block printing dating as early as tenth century with poems devoted to practices of fraternity of beggars. Argues beggars developed printing for purpose of forging amulets and that this restricted spread of invention, which eventually fell into disuse and was forgotten. [RWB]

17.353 Shlomo Dov Goitein. "Urban housing in Fatimid and Ayyubid times." *Studia Islamica* 47 (1978) 5–24. ISSN 0585-5292. ▸ Study based on documentary sources from Jewish community of Cairo. Compare with data in Marcus 18.205 dealing with eighteenth-century Aleppo. [RWB]

17.354 W. F. Paterson. "The archers of Islam." *Journal of the economic and social history of the Orient* 9.1–2 (1966) 69–87. ISSN 0022-4995. ▸ Technology of Middle Eastern and Central Asian warfare focusing on design and mechanics of compound bow. [RWB]

17.355 Andrew M. Watson. *Agricultural innovation in the early Islamic world: the diffusion of crops and farming techniques, 700–1100.* New York: Cambridge University Press, 1983. ISBN 0-521-24711-X. ▸ First half devoted to specific plants whose cultivation spread in early Islamic period and second half to theory of "green revolution." Former discussion forms valuable contribution, but latter has met mixed reception. [RWB]

17.356 Hans E. Wulff. *The traditional crafts of Persia: their development, technology, and influence on Eastern and Western civilizations.* Cambridge, Mass.: MIT Press, 1966. ▸ Indispensable work on traditional craft technology. Historical reflections much less important than careful documentation of machinery and technique acquired from traditional craftsmen while living in Iran. Many descriptions apply to entire Middle East. [RWB]

SEE ALSO
4.379 Ahmad Y. Al-Hassan and Donald R. Hill. *Islamic technology.*
4.467 Richard Williams Bulliet. *The camel and the wheel.*

Urban Studies

17.357 Richard Williams Bulliet. "Medieval Nishapur: a topographic and demographic reconstruction." *Studia Iranica* 5 (1976) 67–89. ISSN 0221-5004. ▸ Maps major Iranian city, destroyed in twelfth century, on basis of textual references, aerial photography, and site observation. Discusses demographic history. [RWB]

17.358 Richard Williams Bulliet. *The patricians of Nishapur: a study in medieval Islamic social history.* Cambridge, Mass.: Harvard University Press, 1972. ISBN 0-674-65792-6. ▸ Pioneering study on history of the ʿulamaʾ based on biographical dictionaries. Valuable both as study of major medieval city in northeast Iran and as example of possible approaches to history of ʿulamaʾ. [RWB]

17.359 Claude Cahen. "Mouvements populaires et autonomisme urbain dans l'Asie musulmane du moyen âge." *Arabica* 5, 6 (1958, 1959) 225–50, 25–56, 233–65. ISSN 0570-5398. ▸ Seminal study in social history suggesting links between young men's organizations, local militias, and underworld groups in Islamic cities from eleventh to thirteenth century. Difficult to follow and inadequate in documentation, but necessary reading in field of urban social structure. [RWB]

17.360 Hichem Djaït. *Al-Kufa, naissance de la ville islamique.* Paris: Maisonneuve & Larose, 1986. ISBN 2-7068-0927-2. ▸ Less urban study of early Islamic garrison city of Kufa than inquiry into various aspects of early Islamic urbanization in general. Primary historical monograph by Tunisian thinker whose books on more general philosophical and historical subjects have attracted attention. [RWB]

17.361 Lisa Golombek. "Urban patterns in pre-Safavid Isfahan." *Iranian studies* 7.1 (1974) 18–44. ISSN 0021-0862. ▸ Discussion of earliest development and expansion of major Iranian city in Islamic period. Based on texts and maps. [RWB]

17.362 Albert H. Hourani and Samuel M. Stern, eds. *The Islamic city: a colloquium.* Oxford: Cassirer, 1970. ISBN 0-571-09085-0. ▸ Collection of essays on Islamic cities compiled at peak of interest in idea that Islam generated unique urban form. No general conclusions reached. [RWB]

17.363 Al Khatib al-Baghdadi. *The topography of Baghdad in the early Middle Ages: text and studies.* Jacob Lassner, trans. Detroit: Wayne State University Press, 1970. ISBN 0-8143-1391-4. ▸ Translation of introductory volume, devoted to topography, of massive eleventh-century biographical dictionary dealing with religious scholars of Baghdad. Appended essays elaborate on specific topics, such as determining exact units of measurement. [RWB]

17.364 Wladyslaw B. Kubiak. *Al-Fustat: its foundation and early urban development.* Cairo: American University in Cairo Press, 1987. ISBN 977-424-168-1 (pbk). ▸ Precursor to neighboring Cairo as Islamic capital of Egypt, Fustat is poorly described in surviving texts. Based on archaeological excavations, attempts to answer questions historians often ask about demography and topography. [RWB]

17.365 Ira Marvin Lapidus. *Muslim cities in the later Middle Ages.* New York: Cambridge University Press, 1984. ISBN 0-521-26231-1 (cl), 0-521-27762-0 (pbk). ▸ Highly influential synthesis of urban social and political structure based mostly on Syrian cities of Mamluk period. Model has been adopted, sometimes with poor results, well beyond area and period of immediate relevance. [RWB]

17.366 Ira Marvin Lapidus, ed. *Middle Eastern cities: a symposium on ancient, Islamic, and contemporary Middle Eastern urbanism.* 1969 ed. Berkeley: University of California Press, 1979. ISBN 0-520-03850-9. ▸ Collection of essays compiled during heyday of scholarly discussion of theory of "Islamic city." Constructively goes beyond Islamic limitation and draws comparisons with non-Islamic urban histories. [RWB]

17.367 Jacob Lassner. "Massignon and Baghdad: the complexities of growth in an imperial city." *Journal of the economic and social history of the Orient* 9.1–2 (1966) 1–27. ISSN 0022-4995. ▸ Reflections on development of Abbasid capital by author who also translated major work on city's geography. [RWB]

17.368 Guy Le Strange. *Baghdad during the Abbasid caliphate from contemporary Arabic and Persian sources.* 1900 ed. Westport, Conn.: Greenwood, 1983. ISBN 0-313-23198-2. ▸ Still only book to attempt general history of medieval Islam's greatest city. Maps in particular have not been improved upon. For specific periods, however, work by Makdisi 17.369 and Lassner 17.367 has superseded descriptive content. [RWB]

17.369 George Makdisi. "The topography of eleventh-century Baghdad: materials and notes." *Arabica: revue d'études arabes* 6.2–3 (1959) 178–97, 281–309. ▸ Excellent depiction of Baghdad a century after Abbasid loss of power. Corrects misimpressions often entertained by those who read only about Baghdad in its early phases. Sources used go well beyond those available to Le Strange 17.368. [RWB]

17.370 Jean Sauvaget. *Alep: essai sur le développement d'une grande ville syrienne, des origines au milieu du dix-neuvième siècle.* 2 vols. Paris: Geuthner, 1941. ▸ Pioneering work in Islamic urban history. Second volume contains plates and maps to illustrate text, concentrating heavily on Aleppo's physical growth and structure. Social history comparatively weak and overall approach unsophisticated by today's standards of urban history. Nevertheless, no better monograph of similar extent on a medieval Arab city has been written. [RWB]

17.371 Susan J. Staffa. *Conquest and fusion: the social evolution of Cairo, A.D. 642–1850.* Leiden: Brill, 1977. ISBN 90-04-04774-3. ▸ Solid history of city's development with strong emphasis on Ayyubid and Mamluk times in section devoted to pre-Ottoman period. [RWB]

17.372 Gustave E. Von Grunebaum. "The structure of the Muslim town." In *Islam: essays in the nature and growth of a cultural tradition,* pp. 141–58. Menasha, Wis.: American Anthropological Association, 1955. ▸ Most influential essay in volume of articles by prominent Islamicist of last generation. Proposes universal type of Islamic city according to which Islamic doctrinal and legal views determined physical, economic, and social forms of urban life. Work established "Islamic city" as focus for many later scholars. [RWB]

Numismatics

17.373 Michael L. Bates. "Islamic numismatics." *Middle East Studies Association bulletin* 12.2–3, 13.1–2 (1978–79) 1–16, 2–18; 3–21, 1–9. ISSN 0026-3184. ▸ Excellent bibliographical survey of field of Islamic numismatics. Covers collections, catalogs, and research tools as well as major interpretive works. [RWB]

17.374 K. Jahn. "Paper currency in Iran: a contribution to the cultural and economic history of Iran in the Mongol period." *Journal of Asian history* 4 (1970) 101–35. ISSN 0021-910X. ▸ Informative study of attempt by Ilkhan ruler in Iran to introduce paper currency on Chinese model and of experiment's failure. [RWB]

17.375 Ronald A. Messier. "The Almoravids: West African gold and the gold currency of the Mediterranean basin." *Journal of the economic and social history of the Orient* 17.1 (1974) 31–47. ISSN 0022-4995. ▸ Uses trace-metal analysis to investigate West African sources of gold coinage in eleventh-century Mediterranean basin. Good example of how technique can produce valuable results for historians. [RWB]

17.376 George C. Miles. *The numismatic history of Rayy.* New York: American Numismatic Society, 1938. (Numismatic studies, 2.) ▸ Most important work on Islamic numismatics as tool for building historical narrative. Northern Iranian mint city of Rayy better presented through its coins than through any other means. Excellent model for numismatic work. [RWB]

17.377 George C. Miles. "Numismatics." In *The Cambridge history of Iran.* Richard N. Frye, ed., vol. 4, pp. 364–77. Cambridge: Cambridge University Press, 1975. ISBN 1-521-20093-8. ▸ Short survey of Iranian numismatics by leading expert of last generation. For more extensive, but also more specialized, treatment see Miles 17.376. [RWB]

RELIGION

Islam

General

17.378 Richard Williams Bulliet. *Conversion to Islam in the medieval period: an essay in quantitative history.* Cambridge, Mass.: Harvard University Press, 1979. ISBN 0-674-17035-0. ▸ Innovative attempt to use onomastic materials from medieval biographical dictionaries to project quantitative pattern of conversion to Islam in different parts of medieval Islamic world. Conclusions have not met with universal agreement. [RWB]

17.379 Patricia Crone and Michael A. Cook. *Hagarism: the making of the Islamic world.* New York: Cambridge University Press, 1977. ISBN 0-521-21133-6. ▸ Highly controversial book proposing early Islamic religious tradition should be jettisoned. True story of Islam, pieced together from Christian and Jewish fragments, indicates that Muhammad and Qur'ān were historical fictions. [RWB]

17.380 Christian Décobert. *Le mendiant et le combattant.* Paris: Seuil, 1991. ISBN 2-02-012231-6. ▸ Major reinterpretation of origins of Islam. Argues against major theses of Patrica Crone (17.67) and Crone and Cook (17.379) and stresses relationship between almsgiving, conquest, and sanctuaries. [RWB]

17.381 H.A.R. Gibb. *Mohammedanism: an historical survey.* 2d ed. New York: Oxford University Press, 1969. ISBN 0-19-888017-0. ▸ Classic introductory book on Islam. Many similar books published, but none so useful for novice reader interested in medieval period. [RWB]

17.382 Ignaz Goldziher. *Introduction to Islamic theology and law.* Andras Hamori and Ruth Hamori, trans. Princeton: Princeton University Press, 1981. ISBN 0-691-07257-4 (cl), 0-691-10099-3 (pbk). ▸ Most influential Western synthesis of Islamic intellectual history. Essential starting point for understanding agenda of twentieth-century Islamic studies in Europe and North America. [RWB]

17.383 Ignaz Goldziher. *Muslim studies.* 2 vols. Samuel M. Stern, ed. Albany: State University of New York Press, 1967–71. ISBN 0-87395-234-0 (v. 1), 0-87395-235-9 (v. 2). ▸ Collection of essays by famous Orientalist. Most important and controversial contribution in volume 2 concerning traditions of the Prophet (*ḥadīth*). Author's skepticism lays foundation for still continuing debate. [RWB]

17.384 Duncan Black Macdonald. *The religious attitude and life in Islam: being the Haskell lectures on comparative religion delivered before the University of Chicago in 1906.* 1912 ed. Beirut: Khayats, 1965. ▸ Still useful portrayal of popular side of Islamic religion, including dreams, local pilgrimage, etc., by one of founders of Islamic studies in United States. [RWB]

17.385 Fazlur Rahman. *Islam.* 2d ed. Chicago: University of Chicago Press, 1979. ISBN 0-226-70280-4 (cl), 0-226-70281-2 (pbk). ▸ Sophisticated survey of Islamic religion by prominent Muslim modernist. More advanced and intellectually demanding than most general books on Islam. [RWB]

17.386 Gustave E. Von Grunebaum. *Muhammadan festivals.* 1951 ed. New York: Olive Branch, 1988. ISBN 0-940793-11-3. ▸ Useful manual describing main Muslim religious festivals, rites pertaining to them, and their historical roots. [RWB]

Non-Muslims in Islamic Lands

17.387 Aziz Suryal Atiya. *A history of Eastern Christianity.* Rev. ed. Millwood, N.Y.: Kraus Reprint, 1980. ISBN 0-527-03703-6. ▸ Introduction to complicated history of Eastern Christian sects and doctrines by important Coptic scholar. [RWB]

17.388 Salo Wittmayer Baron. *A social and religious history of the Jews.* Vol. 17: *Late Middle Ages and era of European expansion: Byzantines, Mamelukes, Maghribians.* 18 vols. New York: Columbia University Press, 1983. ISBN 0-231-08856-6. ▸ Part of Baron's monumental work on social and economic history of Jews. Offers broader perspective than Goitein's (17.392, 21.32) and Cohen's work on Egypt (21.25) or Fischel 17.390 on Jews in earlier Islamic times. [RWB]

17.389 Richard Williams Bulliet. "Naw Bahar and the survival of Iranian Buddhism." *Iran* 14 (1976) 140–45. ISSN 0578-6967. ▸ Proposes on basis of toponyms and medieval texts that Buddhism once extended well into Iran. Helps understand rise of Barmak family, of Buddhist origin, as viziers of Abbasid caliphs. [RWB]

17.390 Walter J. Fischel. *Jews in the economic and political life of medieval Islam.* 1937 ed. New York: KTAV, 1969. ISBN 0-87068-047-1. ▸ Study of Jewish participation in medieval Islamic politics and society drawn mostly from non-Jewish sources. Gives different perspective from Goitein's work on Jewish Geniza documents (17.392). [RWB]

17.391 Michael Gervers and Ramzi Jibran Bikhazi, eds. *Conversion and continuity: indigenous Christian communities in Islamic lands, eighth to eighteenth centuries.* Toronto: Pontifical Institute of Mediaeval Studies, 1990. (Papers in mediaeval studies, 9.) ISBN 0-88844-809-2. ▸ Good collection of essays on neglected subject of Christians under Islamic rule. Coverage and approaches vary. Synthesis article by Bulliet attempts unification of volume. [RWB]

17.392 Shlomo Dov Goitein. *A Mediterranean society: the Jewish* communities of the Arab world as portrayed in the documents of the *Cairo Geniza*. Vol. 1: *Economic foundations*. Vol. 2: *The community*. Vol. 3: *The family*. Vol. 4: *Daily life*. Vol. 5: *The individual: portrait of a Mediterranean personality as reflected in the Cairo Geniza*. Vol. 6: *Cumulative indices*. 6 vols. Berkeley: University of California Press, 1967–. ISBN 0-520-01867-2 (v. 2), 0-520-03265-9 (v. 3), 0-520-04869-5 (v. 4), 0-520-05647-7 (v. 5). ‣ Monumental work delineating every aspect of life in Jewish community of Egypt during Fatimid, Ayyubid, and Mamluk periods. Geniza manuscript storeroom of synagogue of Fustat, sealed until nineteenth century, supplies vast body of documentation; systematically and magisterially drawn upon. [RWB]

SEE ALSO
21.25 Mark R. Cohen. *Jewish self-government in medieval Egypt*.
21.44 Norman A. Stillman, comp. *The Jews of Arab lands*.

Islamic Law

Sources

17.393 Malik ibn Anas. *"Al-Muwatta" of Imam Malik ibn Anas: the first formulation of Islamic law*. A. A. Bewley, trans. New York: Kegan Paul International, 1989. ISBN 0-7103-0361-0. ‣ Foundation work of Maliki school of law, one of four major approaches to Sunnī law. Essential primary source for work on Islamic law and on legal history of North Africa where Maliki law predominates to present day. [RWB]

17.394 Muhammad ibn Idris al Shaficī. *Islamic jurisprudence: Shaficī's "Risala."* Majid Khadduri, trans. Baltimore: Johns Hopkins University Press, 1961. ‣ Translation of major work by eponymous founder of Shaficī law school of Sunnī Islam. Basic text for Islamic law. [RWB]

17.395 Muḥammad ibn al-Hasan al-Shaybani. *The Islamic law of nations: Shaybani's "Siyar."* Majid Khadduri, trans. Baltimore: Johns Hopkins University Press, 1966. ‣ Important text in perspective on Western concern with Islam's perspective of international relations. [RWB]

17.396 Abu Yusuf Ya'qub. *Yahyā ben Ādam's Kitāb Al-Kharāj: taxation in Islam*. Vol. 1, rev. ed. 3 vols. Ben-Shemesh Aharon, ed. and trans. London: Luzac, 1967–70. ISBN 0-7189-0138-X (v. 1). ‣ Translations of most important legal treatises on taxation from Abbasid period. Brief introductions are adequate but do not offer extensive treatment of taxation history. [RWB]

Studies

17.397 Noel J. Coulson. *A history of Islamic law*. Pakistan ed. Lahore: Lahore Law Times Publications, 1979. ‣ Standard, readable introduction. Best initiation to subject. [RWB]

17.398 Ignaz Goldziher. *The zāhiris: their doctrine and their history*. Wolfgang H. Behn, ed. and trans. Leiden: Brill, 1971. ISBN 90-04-02632-0. ‣ Insightful study of Sunnī school of law that became extinct. Though Zahiris few, with only one great figure, Ibn Hazm of Spain, analysis illuminates much broader array of issues dealing with foundations of Islamic law. [RWB]

17.399 Wael B. Hallaq. "Considerations on the function and character of Islamic legal theory." *Journal of the American Oriental Society* 104.4 (1984) 679–90. ISSN 0003-0279. ‣ Together with author's other articles, constitutes broad and insightful reevaluation of character and function of medieval Islamic jurisprudence. Read with earlier survey works by Schacht (17.407, 17.408) and Coulson (17.397). [RWB]

17.400 Wael B. Hallaq. "On the authoritativeness of Sunni consensus." *International journal of Middle East studies* 18.4 (1986) 427–454. ISSN 0020-7438. ‣ Part of author's reappraisal of major bases of Sunnī law. [RWB]

17.401 Wael B. Hallaq. "Was the gate of *ijtihād* closed?" *International journal of Middle East studies* 16.1 (1984) 3–41. ISSN 0020-7438. ‣ Revisionist, controversial article challenging assumption that individual decision making in Sunnī law gave way to total ossification in late medieval period. Inquires into "Orientalist" approach to legal history. [RWB]

17.402 Ann K. S. Lambton. *State and government in medieval Islam: an introduction to the study of Islamic political theory; the jurists*. London: Oxford University Press, 1981. ISBN 0-19-713600-1. ‣ Best introduction to political theory as seen by Islamic jurists, by one of major figures of last generation. More extensive in this area than Rosenthal 17.480, who deals largely with philosophers. [RWB]

17.403 Gary Leiser. "Hanbalism in Egypt before the Mamluks." *Studia Islamica* 54 (1981) 155–82. ISSN 0585-5292. ‣ Study of extension of Hanbali law school to Egypt. Hanbali school rose and flourished in Baghdad before spreading to Syria and Egypt in twelfth century. Topic little studied for Egypt. [RWB]

17.404 Wilferd Madelung. "The early *murji'a* in Khurasan and Transoxania and the spread of Hanafism." *Der Islam* 59.1 (1982) 32–39. ISSN 0021-1818. ‣ Study of Islamic beliefs in Iran during first three Islamic centuries. Lays groundwork for addressing later, bitter rivalry between Hanafi and Shaficī law schools in Iran. [RWB]

17.405 George Makdisi. "The juridical theology of Shaficī: origins and significance of *uṣūl al-fiqh*." *Studia Islamica* 59 (1984) 5–48. ISSN 0585-5292. ‣ Reappraisal of contribution of al-Shaficī to Islamic law. Tends to favor rival Hanbali school. [RWB]

17.406 J. S. Nielsen. "Sultan al-Zahir Baybars and the appointment of four chief *qadis* (663/1265)." *Studia Islamica* 60 (1984) 167–76. ISSN 0585-5292. ‣ Discussion of appointment of chief judges from all four Sunnī law schools is part of conciliation between formerly hostile rivals; important feature of later Islamic history. [RWB]

17.407 Joseph Schacht. *An introduction to Islamic law*. New York: Oxford University Press, 1982. ISBN 0-19-825473-3 (pbk). ‣ Standard text on Islamic law. Not as readable as Coulson 17.397, but Schacht one of major figures in field and noted proponent of theory that most traditions of the Prophet were fabricated. [RWB]

17.408 Joseph Schacht. *The origins of Muhammadan jurisprudence*. New York: Clarendon, 1979. ‣ Classic exposition of early Islamic law arguing traditions of the Prophet were mostly fabricated in process of legal evolution. Sharply challenged by Muslim scholars. [RWB]

17.409 Émile Tyan. *Histoire de l'organisation judiciaire en pays d'Islam*. 2d ed. 2 vols. Leiden: Brill, 1960. ‣ Unlike other general works on Islamic law, concentrates on how law courts functioned and evolved. Dated in some respects but best introduction to subject. [RWB]

Theology and Education

Sources

17.410 Muhammad Mustafa Aczami. *On Schacht's "Origins of Muhammadan jurisprudence."* New York: Wiley, 1985. ISBN 0-471-89145-2. ‣ Challenge by Muslim author to Schacht's influential theory (17.407) that traditions of the Prophet largely fabricated long after his death. [RWB]

17.411 cAbd al-Qahir al-Baghdadi. *Moslem schisms and sects*. 2 vols. Kate Seelye (v. 1) and A. S. Halkin (v. 2), trans. New York and Tel Aviv: Columbia University Press and Palestine Publishing, 1920–35. ‣ Translation of one of two key books on Islamic sects (see 17.414). Both date to eleventh century. [RWB]

17.412 Abu Hamid al-Ghazzali. *The faith and practice of al-*

Ghazzali. 1967 ed. W. Montgomery Watt, trans. Chicago: Kazi, 1982. ▸ Translation of short, readable autobiographical work by foremost Islamic theologian (d. 1111). Superb text for understanding integration of Sūfism into other streams of religious thought. [RWB]

17.413   Richard J. McCarthy. *The theology of al-Ashʿari: the Arabic text of al-Ashʿari's "Kitab al-lumaʿ" and "Risala Istihsan al-Khawd fi ʿilm al-Kalam."* Beirut: Imprimeries Catholiques, 1953. ▸ Translation and analysis of works by eponymous founder of dominant approach to Islamic theology. Gives good example of type of questions considered and method of argument. [RWB]

17.414   Muhammad ibn Abd al-Karim al-Shahristani. *Muslim sects and divisions.* A. K. Kazi and J. G. Flynn, trans. Boston: Kegan Paul International, 1984. ISBN 0-7103-0063-8. ▸ Translation of part 1 of *Kitāb al-Milal wa'l-Nihal,* one of two major treatises, along with that of al-Baghdadi (17.411), on divisions within Islam as a whole. [RWB]

17.415   Arent Jan Wensinck. *The Muslim creed: its genesis and historical development.* 1932 ed. New Delhi: Oriental Books Reprint, 1979. ▸ Discusses content of credal statements (e.g., faith versus works, God and creation) and translates three creeds attributed to eighth-century legist Abu Hanifa. [RWB]

Studies

17.416   Jonathan Berkey. *The transmission of knowledge in medieval Cairo: a social history of Islamic education.* Princeton: Princeton University Press, 1992. ISBN 0-691-03191-6. ▸ First major exploration of education in medieval Egypt. For different approach to religious elite see Petry 17.294. [RWB]

17.417   Richard Williams Bulliet. "The age structure of medieval Islamic education." *Studia Islamica* 57 (1983) 105–18. ISSN 0585-5292. ▸ Quantitative study based on biographical dictionaries of northeast Iranian city of Nishapur. Asks when students began studies of traditions of Muhammad, how many years they studied, when teachers of traditions began to teach, etc. [RWB]

17.418   Richard Williams Bulliet. "The *shaikh al-Islam* and the evolution of Islamic society." *Studia Islamica* 35 (1972) 53–68. ISSN 0585-5292. ▸ Discussion of wide-spread use of term *shaikh al-Islām,* ultimately highest religious post in Ottoman empire. Proposes origin in educational milieu of northeastern Iran. [RWB]

17.419   Michael A. Cook. *Early Muslim dogma: a source-critical study.* New York: Cambridge University Press, 1981. ISBN 0-521-23379-8. ▸ Attack on positions taken by important German scholar Josef van Ess in 17.420. Argues against early dating of works involved in theological debates. [RWB]

17.420   Josef van Ess. *Zwischen Hadit und Theologie: Studien zum entstehen prædestinatianisher Überlieferung.* Berlin: de Gruyter, 1975. ▸ Important study of origins of theological speculation in Islam. See critique by Cook (17.419). [RWB]

17.421   Joan Gilbert. "Institutionalization of Muslim scholarship and professionalization of the ʿulamā' in medieval Damascus." *Studia Islamica* 52 (1980) 105–34. ISSN 0585-5292. ▸ Excellent examination of beginnings of *madrasah* (college) education in Damascus in eleventh to thirteenth centuries. Extracted from unpublished doctoral dissertation. [RWB]

17.422   Gary Leiser. "The *madrasa* and the islamization of the Middle East: the case of Egypt." *Journal of the American Research Center in Egypt* 22 (1985) 29–47. ISSN 0065-9991. ▸ Argues rise of Islamic colleges in Egypt since twelfth century contributed to shrinking of Christian minority. Hypothesis suggestive but not proven. Based on author's unpublished doctoral dissertation. [RWB]

17.423   George Makdisi. "Ashʿari and the Ashʿarites in Islamic

religious history." *Studia Islamica* 17–18 (1962–1963) 37–80, 19–40. ISSN 0585-5292. ▸ Author, primary exponent of theory of "Sunnī revival" led by Hanbalis, tends to depreciate role of rival Ashʿarites. Other scholars portray Ashʿarism as new orthodox theology of Islam. [RWB]

17.424   George Makdisi. *The rise of colleges: institutions of learning in Islam and the West,* Edinburgh: Edinburgh University Press, 1981. ISBN 0-85224-375-8. ▸ Not a narrative history, rather exposition of institutional form—funding, curricula, style of learning, etc.—of Islamic college (*madrasah*) and comparison with early European universities. [RWB]

17.425   George Makdisi. *The rise of humanism in classical Islam and the Christian West, with special reference to scholasticism.* Edinburgh: Edinburgh University Press, 1990. ISBN 0-85224-630-7. ▸ Discussion of institutions and techniques of Muslim higher education after eleventh century. Argues great similarity with Europe. [RWB]

17.426   A. L. Tibawi. "Origin and character of *al-madrasah.*" *Bulletin of the School of Oriental and African Studies* 25.2 (1962) 225–38. ISSN 0041-977X. ▸ Erudite, combative challenge to Makdisi's theory of origin of Islamic colleges (17.425). Issue of *madrasah's* origin and function still not resolved. [RWB]

17.427   Dominique Urvoy. *Le monde des ulemas andalous du VI/XIe au VII/XIIIe siècle.* Geneva: Droz, 1978. ▸ Quantitative study of ʿulamā of Muslim Spain describing geographical patterns of study, fields of study, scholarly networks, etc. Complicated tables make work primarily for specialists, but illustrates new directions in quantitative history of medieval Islam. [RWB]

17.428   W. Montgomery Watt. *The formative period of Islamic thought.* Edinburgh: Edinburgh University Press, 1973. ISBN 0-85224-245-X. ▸ Most extensive statement of development of early Islamic theological views about which author wrote several earlier works. [RWB]

17.429   M.J.L. Young, ed. *Religion, learning, and science in the ʿAbbasid period.* New York: Cambridge University Press, 1990. ISBN 0-521-32763-6. ▸ Collection of essays on major literary fields. Most extensive and up-to-date treatment of Arabic literature. [RWB]

Ṣūfism

Sources

17.430   Farid al-Din ʿAttar. *The conference of the birds.* Afkham Darbandi and Dick Davis, trans. and Introduction. Harmondsworth: Penguin, 1984. ISBN 0-14-044434-3 (pbk). ▸ One of great works of Ṣūfī spiritual writing at time of Mongol invasion. Recounts mystic journey of thirty birds searching for ultimate bird, Simurg (literally, in Persian, "thirty birds"). Model for Salman Rushdie's first novel *Grimus* (anagram of Simurg). [RWB]

17.431   Farid al-Din ʿAttar. *Muslim saints and mystics: episodes from the "Tadhkirat al-Auliya'" (Memorial of the Saints).* 1966 ed. Arthur J. Arberry, trans. New York: Penguin, 1988. ISBN 0-14-019114-3 (pbk). ▸ Excellent example of genre of saintly anecdotes so popular in early Ṣūfī literature. Author died in Mongol invasion. [RWB]

17.432   Muhammad ibn Ibrahim Kalabadhi. *The doctrine of the Sufis: "Kitab a-ʿarruf li-Madhhab Ahl al-Tasawwuf."* 1935 ed. Arthur J. Arberry, trans. New York: Cambridge University Press, 1977. ISBN 0-521-21647-8 (cl), 0-521-29218-2 (pbk). ▸ Influential tenth-century manual of Islamic mystical thought emphasizing conformity with Islamic law. Outlines main line of development of moderate Ṣūfism. [RWB]

17.433   Abu al-Qasim al-Qushayri. *Principles of Sufism.* B. R. von Schlegell, trans. Berkeley: Mizan, 1992. ISBN 0-933782-21-7 (cl),

0-933782-20-9 (pbk). ▸ Translation from Arabic of one of most important manuals of Ṣūfī thought and practice. [RWB]

17.434 Abu al-Najib al-Suhrawardi. *A Sufi rule for novices: "Kitab Adab al-Muridin" of Abu al-Najib al-Suhrawardi.* Menahem Milson, trans. Cambridge, Mass.: Harvard University Press, 1975. ISBN 0-674-85403-9. ▸ Concise statement of rules both for Ṣūfīs and for Ṣūfī admirers who wanted to keep company with them. Superb portrayal of twelfth-century manners and morals. [RWB]

17.435 Muhammad ibn al-Husayn al-Sulami. *The book of Sufi chivalry: lessons to a son of the moment.* Tosun Bayrak al-Jerrahi al-Halveti, trans. New York: Inner Traditions, 1983. ISBN 0-86692-128-9. ▸ Earliest treatise on ideal of young manhood (*futūwa*) in Ṣūfī thought. General and aphoristic but nevertheless important as precursor of organized young men's organizations in following centuries, on which see Cahen 17.359. [RWB]

Studies

17.436 Arthur J. Arberry. *Sufism: an account of the mystics of Islam.* London: Allen & Unwin, 1979. ▸ General work on Ṣūfism by scholar noted for appreciation of mystic poetry. Emphasizes pre-fifteenth-century period and personalities and aesthetic appreciation. [RWB]

17.437 Gerhard Böwering. "The *adab* literature of classical Sufism: Ansari's code of conduct." In *Moral conduct and authority: the place of adab in South Asian Islam.* Barbara Daly Metcalf, ed., pp. 62–87. Berkeley: University of California Press, 1984. ISBN 0-520-04660-9. ▸ Study of one of first codes of conduct that marked transition of Ṣūfism toward organization by brotherhood. Work by important mystic and poet from Afghanistan should be compared with more extensive and detailed code by Suhrawardi (17.434). [RWB]

17.438 William C. Chittick. *The Sufi path of knowledge: Ibn al-ʿArabi's "Metaphysics of Imagination."* Albany: State University of New York Press, 1989. ISBN 0-88706-884-7 (cl), 0-88706-885-5 (pbk). ▸ Long, difficult monograph analyzing major work by most important Ṣūfī thinker of thirteenth century. Important work for understanding illuminationist approach to Islamic mysticism. [RWB]

17.439 Vincent J. Cornell. "The logic of analogy and the role of the Sufi *shaykh* in post-Marinid Morocco." *International journal of Middle East studies* 15.1 (1983) 67–93. ISSN 0020-7438. ▸ Study of Moroccan Ṣūfism by foremost specialist. Important reading for later Moroccan history because Ṣūfism contributed to rise of Alawi dynasties still in power. [RWB]

17.440 Leonard Lewisohn, ed. *The legacy of mediæval Persian Sufism.* New York: Khaniqahi Nimatullahi, 1992. ISBN 0-933546-45-9 (cl) 0-933546-47-5 (pbk). ▸ Large number of essays on many aspects of Ṣūfism in Iran. Collection uneven but contains valuable detailed studies. [RWB]

17.441 Louis Massignon. *The passion of al-Hallaj: mystic martyr of Islam.* 4 vols. Herbert Mason, trans. Princeton: Princeton University Press, 1983. ISBN 0-691-09910-3 (set). ▸ Masterwork of Islamic studies; massive study of Ṣūfī mystic crucified in Baghdad in 922. Approval or disapproval of free ways and extreme views used to classify Ṣūfī thinkers and movements in general. [RWB]

17.442 Reynold A. Nicholson. *Studies in Islamic mysticism.* Cambridge: Cambridge University Press, 1978. ISBN 0-521-29546-7. ▸ Several essays on Ṣūfism including, in particular, analysis and partial translation of biography of Abu Saʿid ibn Abi al-Khair, flamboyant Iranian mystic of early eleventh century. [RWB]

17.443 Jalal al-Din Rumi. *The Sufi path of love: the spiritual teachings of Rumi.* William C. Chittick, trans. Albany: State University of New York Press, 1983. ISBN 0-87395-723-7 (cl), 0-87395-724-5 (pbk). ▸ Translations with commentary from various works by great thirteenth-century Ṣūfī poet, topically organized and designed to show pattern of mystical thought. Other translations available by Arberry (17.436) and Nicholson (17.442). [RWB]

17.444 Annemarie Schimmel. *Mystical dimensions of Islam.* Chapel Hill: University of North Carolina Press, 1975. ISBN 0-8078-1223-4 (cl), 0-8078-1271-4 (pbk). ▸ Sensitive appreciation of early Islamic Ṣūfism stressing poetic and ecstatic dimensions. [RWB]

17.445 Margaret Smith. *An early mystic of Baghdad: a study of the life and teaching of Harith b. Asad al-Muhasibi, A.D. 781–A.D. 857.* 1935 ed. New York: AMS Press, 1973. ISBN 0-404-56324-4. ▸ Biography of one of most important early Ṣūfīs by prominent scholar of mysticism. [RWB]

17.446 Margaret Smith. *Rabiʿa the mystic and her fellow-saints in Islam: being the life and teachings of Rabiʿa al-ʿAdawiyya al-Qaysiyya of Basra together with some account of the place of the women saints in Islam.* New York: Cambridge University Press, 1984. ISBN 0-521-26779-X (cl), 0-521-31863-7 (pbk). ▸ Biography of one of few well-known women in Islamic history, noted for mysticism and frank manner toward men. [RWB]

17.447 J. Spencer Trimingham. *The Sufi orders in Islam.* Oxford: Oxford University Press, 1971. ISBN 0-19-501662-9. ▸ Serviceable but unexciting survey of Islamic Ṣūfī orders. More descriptive than analytical. [RWB]

Shiism

17.448 Farhad Daftary. *The Ismaʿilis: their history and doctrines.* New York: Cambridge University Press, 1990. ISBN 0-521-37019-1. ▸ Best history of Ismaʿili Shiism. Summarizes many studies by various scholars. [RWB]

17.449 Marshall G. S. Hodgson. "How did the early Shiʿa become sectarian?" *Journal of the American Oriental Society* 75.1 (1955) 1–13. ISSN 0003-0279. ▸ Study of transformation of Shiism from political movement into group of religious sects in period 656–786. Early contribution to ongoing debate on Shīʿī sectarianism. [RWB]

17.450 Marshall G. S. Hodgson. *The order of Assassins.* New York: AMS Press, 1980. ISBN 0-404-17018-8. ▸ Thorough study of Nizari branch of Ismaʿili Shiism, notorious as order of Assassins. Concentrates on sect origins and vagaries of its theology. Political history better covered by Lewis 17.453. [RWB]

17.451 S. H. M. Jafri. *The origins and early development of Shiʿa Islam.* London: Longman, 1979. ISBN 0-582-78080-2. ▸ Sound, extensive treatment of problem that has interested many historians: how Shiism, which originated in political dispute in 650s, became religious movement with wide variety of sects. [RWB]

17.452 Etan Kohlberg. "From *Imamiyya* to *Ithna-ʿashariyya*." *Bulletin of the Journal of Oriental and African Studies* 39.3 (1976) 521–34. ISSN 0041-977X. ▸ Insightful study of evolution of majority viewpoint in Shiism and occlusion of twelfth imam. [RWB]

17.453 Bernard Lewis. *The Assassins: a radical sect in Islam.* 1968 ed. New York: Oxford University Press, 1987. ISBN 0-19-520550-2 (pbk). ▸ Best introductory book on Ismaʿili Shīʿī sect that gained notoriety in eleventh and twelfth centuries for political violence. More readable and less theologically detailed than Hodgson's monograph (17.450). [RWB]

17.454 Bernard Lewis. *The origins of Ismaʿilism: a study of the historical background of the Fatimid caliphate.* New York: AMS Press, 1975. ISBN 0-404-56289-2. ▸ Good introduction to peculiar problems connected with antecedents of Fatimid dynasty. Ancestors of Fatimid caliphs lived in secrecy, perhaps using pseudonyms; who they actually were has been debated for centuries. For more recent survey work see Daftary 17.448. [RWB]

17.455 Wilferd Madelung. "Some notes on non-Isma⁽ili Shiism in the Maghrib." *Studia Islamica* 44 (1976) 87–98. ISSN 0585-5292. ▸ Isma⁽ili Fatimid dynasty most important Shī⁽ī state in North African history; other Shī⁽ī tendencies have been little studied. This study begins to fill lacuna. [RWB]

17.456 Hossein Modarressi. *Crisis and consolidation in the formative period of Shī⁽ite Islam: Abu Ja⁽far ibn Qiba al-Razi and his contribution to Imamite Shī⁽ite thought.* Princeton: Darwin, 1993. ISBN 0-87850-095-2. ▸ Key study of political and religious evolution of Shiism in period before occultation of Twelfth Imam. [RWB]

17.457 Richard T. Mortel. "Zaydi Shi⁽ism and the Hasanid *sharīfs* of Mecca." *International journal of Middle East studies* 19.4 (1987) 455–72. ISSN 0020-7438. ▸ Provincial history of governors of Mecca from tenth to fifteenth century. Stress on Zaydī Shiism revises conventional viewpoint. [RWB]

17.458 Abdulaziz Abdulhussein Sachedina. *Islamic messianism: the idea of the mahdi in Twelver Shī⁽ism.* Albany: State University of New York Press, 1981. ISBN 0-87395-442-4 (cl), 0-87395-458-0 (pbk). ▸ Stresses importance of messianism in early development of Shiism. Revises conventional view that only twelfth imam was object of messianic contemplation. [RWB]

SEE ALSO
18.104 Moojan Momen. *An introduction to Shī⁽ī Islam.*

LITERATURE, PHILOSOPHY, SCIENCE, AND ART

Arabic and Persian Literature

17.459 Julia Ashtiany, ed. *⁽Abbasid belles lettres.* New York: Cambridge University Press, 1990. (Cambridge history of Arabic literature.) ISBN 0-521-24016-6. ▸ Collection of specialist essays offering most extensive and up-to-date scholarship on Arabic prose and poetry of Abbasid period. [RWB]

17.460 A.F.L. Beeston et al., eds. *Arabic literature to the end of the Umayyad period.* New York: Cambridge University Press, 1983. (Cambridge history of Arabic literature.) ISBN 0-521-24015-8. ▸ New series offering essays by different authors on many aspects of Arabic literature. Most up-to-date scholarship in field. [RWB]

17.461 Edward Granville Browne. *A literary history of Persia.* 4 vols. Cambridge: Cambridge University Press, 1929. ▸ Classic turn-of-century survey of Persian history and literature. Great influence on later studies of Iran in Islamic period; should be consulted although now largely superseded. [RWB]

17.462 Victor Danner. "Arabic literature in Iran." In *The Cambridge history of Iran.* Richard N. Frye, ed., vol. 4, pp. 566–94. Cambridge: Cambridge University Press, 1975. ISBN 0-521-21193-8. ▸ Excellent article treating Iranians writing in Arabic. Topic sometimes neglected or glossed over in general works by Arabists. [RWB]

17.463 Abu al-Qasim Firdawsi. *The epic of the kings: "Shahnama," the national epic of Persia.* Reuben Levy, ed. and trans. London: Routledge & Kegan Paul, 1967. ▸ Greatly abridged, prose translation of Persian national epic. Satisfactory introduction to main story cycles of original, but only distantly reflects scope and grandeur. No full English-language translation available. [RWB]

17.464 H.A.R. Gibb. *Arabic literature: an introduction.* 2d rev. ed. Oxford: Clarendon, 1963. ISBN 0-19-881332-5. ▸ Short, accessible

history of Arabic literature. Lacks specimen texts; better for conceptualization of genres and historical sequence than for getting feel of literature. [RWB]

17.465 Dmitri Gutas. "Classical Arabic wisdom literature: nature and scope." *Journal of the American Oriental Society* 101.1 (1981) 49–86. ISSN 0003-0279. ▸ Excellent study of character and sources, including pre-Islamic and foreign, of proverbial wisdom in medieval Arabic sources. Provides foundation for studying abundant later collections of proverbs. [RWB]

17.466 James Kritzeck, ed. *Anthology of Islamic literature from the rise of Islam to modern times.* 1964 ed. New York: New American Library, 1975. ISBN 0-452-00783-6 (pbk). ▸ Broadly conceived anthology containing many types of poetry and prose from Arabic, Persian, and Turkish. Concentration on medieval period. [RWB]

17.467 Reuben Levy. *An introduction to Persian literature.* New York: Columbia University Press, 1969. ISBN 0-231-03177-7. ▸ Brief survey of history of Persian literature. Primarily describes genres and major authors. [RWB]

17.468 George Morrison, ed. *History of Persian literature from the beginning of the Islamic period to the present day.* Leiden: Brill, 1981. (Handbuch der Orientalistik, Erste Abteilung, Der nahe und der mittlere Osten, Band 4, Iranistik, 2/2.) ISBN 90-04-06481-8 (pbk). ▸ Recent survey of Persian literary history with contributions by several specialists. [RWB]

17.469 Reynold A. Nicholson. *A literary history of the Arabs.* 1956 ed. London: Curzon, 1992. ISBN 0-7007-0261-X. ▸ Standard history of Arabic literature. Longer and more detailed than Gibb 17.464. For more recent and extensive treatment, see volumes of *Cambridge History of Arabic Literature* as they appear (e.g., 17.459, 17.460). [RWB]

17.470 Charles Pellat, ed. *The life and works of Jahiz: translations of selected texts.* D. M. Hawke, trans. Berkeley: University of California Press, 1969. ▸ Jahiz, premier writer of *belles lettres* during period of Abbasid greatness; only a few of his many works have been translated. Excellent overview by foremost Western student of his work, through brief excerpts, of topics he wrote about, along with good account of his life. [RWB]

17.471 Lutz Richter-Bernburg. "Linguistic *shu⁽ūbiya* and early neo-Persian prose." *Journal of the American Oriental Society* 94.1 (1974) 55–64. ISSN 0003-0279. ▸ Contribution to longstanding debate on rise of Persian national sentiment—and defenders of Arab tradition—among writers in Arabic and Persian during Abbasid period. [RWB]

17.472 Al-Tha⁽alibi. *The book of curious and entertaining information.* C. E. Bosworth, trans. Edinburgh: Edinburgh University Press, 1968. ▸ Delightful potpourri of lore. Excellent example of medieval Arabic *belles lettres.* [RWB]

Islamic Philosophy

17.473 Henry Corbin. *History of Islamic philosophy.* Liadain Sherrard and Philip Sherrard, trans. London: Kegan Paul International, 1992. ISBN 0-7103-0416-1. ▸ Translation of key work in Islamic philosophy bringing Neoplatonic tradition into conjunction with Aristotelian tradition. Author and his followers have strongly challenged traditional views of Islamic philosophy; excellent introduction to this school of thought. [RWB]

17.474 Majid Fakhry. *A history of Islamic philosophy.* 2d ed. New York: Columbia University Press, 1983. ISBN 0-231-05532-3. ▸ Sound general history of philosophy in medieval Islam. Emphasizes Aristotelian rather than Neoplatonic tradition emphasized by Corbin and his school (17.473). [RWB]

17.475 Miriam Galston. *Politics and excellence: the political phi-*

losophy of Alfarabi. Princeton: Princeton University Press, 1990. ISBN 0-691-07808-4. ‣ Exploration of Aristotelian roots of Islamic political philosophy. [RWB]

17.476 Lenn Evan Goodman. *Avicenna.* New York: Routledge, 1992. ISBN 0-415-01929-X (cl), 0-415-07409-6 (pbk). ‣ Good introduction to work of Avicenna, properly known as Ibn Sina, seminal Persian figure in philosophy and medicine and probably most important thinker in Aristotelian tradition in Arabic. [RWB]

17.477 Muhammad ibn Abd al-Malik Ibn Tufayl. *Ibn Tufayl's "Hayy ibn Yaqzan": a philosophical tale.* Lenn Evan Goodman, trans. New York: Twayne, 1972. ‣ Good, readable translation of classic twelfth-century story of man on desert island using his reason to probe universe. Excellent example of Islamic thought in Aristotelian tradition. [RWB]

17.478 Oliver Leaman. *An introduction to medieval Islamic philosophy.* New York: Cambridge University Press, 1985. ISBN 0-521-24707-1 (cl), 0-521-28911-4 (pbk). ‣ Brief book analyzing content of Islamic philosophy: types of questions addressed, method of argument, etc. For more descriptive approach see Fakhry 17.474. [RWB]

17.479 Ian Richard Netton. *Al-Farabi and his school.* New York: Routledge, 1992. ISBN 0-415-03594-5 (cl), 0-415-03595-3 (pbk). ‣ Good survey of work and influence of al-Farabi, leading exponent of Aristotelian tradition. [RWB]

17.480 Erwin I. J. Rosenthal. *Political thought in medieval Islam: an introductory outline.* 1958 ed. Westport, Conn.: Greenwood, 1985. ISBN 0-313-25094-4. ‣ Rather dull work concentrating on philosophical tradition. Little convergence with actual political or administrative history. [RWB]

17.481 Dominique Urvoy. *Ibn Rushd: Averroes.* Olivia Stewart, trans. London: Routledge, 1991. ISBN 0-415-02141-3 (cl), 0-415-05567-9. ‣ Good introduction to work of Ibn Rushd, North African thinker, important in evolution of European scholasticism under Latin name Averroës. Culminates Aristotelian tradition in Islamic philosophy. [RWB]

17.482 Richard Walzer. *Greek into Arabic: essays on Islamic philosophy.* 1962 ed. Columbia: University of South Carolina Press, 1982. ISBN 0-87249-176-5. ‣ Study of passage of Greek thought, through Syriac, into Arabic world and of careers of major translators. [RWB]

Science and Medicine

17.483 J. L. Berggren. "History of mathematics in the Islamic world: the present state of the art." *Middle East Studies Association bulletin* 19 (1985) 9–33. ISSN 0026-3184. ‣ Excellent brief introduction to history of mathematics with up-to-date bibliography. [RWB]

17.484 Lawrence I. Conrad. "Arabic plague chronologies and treatises: social and historical factors in the formation of a literary genre." *Studia Islamica* 54 (1981) 51–94. ISSN 0585-5292. ‣ Complements Dols 17.486 on content of plague treatises and overall incidence and impact of plague. More concerned with genre of texts than history of plague. [RWB]

17.485 Lawrence I. Conrad. "*Ta'un* and *waba'*: conceptions of plague and pestilence in early Islam." *Journal of the economic and social history of the Orient* 25.3 (1982) 225–67. ISSN 0022-4995. ‣ Perceptive appraisal of meaning of crucial Arabic terms denoting epidemic disease. Should be read with Dols 17.486, but concentrates on earlier period. [RWB]

17.486 Michael W. Dols. *The Black Death in the Middle East.* Princeton: Princeton University Press, 1977. ISBN 0-691-03107-X. ‣ Only extensive study of Black Death and plague in general in Islamic world, though focuses mostly on Syria, Egypt, and

North Africa. Data come from plague treatises and variety of other sources. Full discussion of demographic as well as medical issues. [RWB]

17.487 Michael W. Dols. *Majnun: the madman in medieval Islamic society.* New York: Clarendon, 1992. ISBN 0-19-820221-0. ‣ Long study of how mental aberration (*majnūn*) was viewed in medieval Islam. Full discussion of medical and religious views, idea of spirit possession, and basic conception of what constitutes mental disorder. [RWB]

17.488 E. S. Kennedy. "The exact sciences." In *The Cambridge history of Iran.* Richard N. Frye, ed., vol. 4, pp. 378–95. Cambridge: Cambridge University Press, 1975. ISBN 0-521-20093-8. ‣ Specialized essay by leading scholar of Islamic science of past generation. [RWB]

17.489 E. S. Kennedy. "The exact sciences in Iran under the Saljuqs and Mongols." In *Cambridge history of Iran.* John Andrew Boyle, ed., vol. 5, pp. 659–79. Cambridge: Cambridge University Press, 1968. ISBN 0-521-06936-X. ‣ Specialized essay by leading scholar of Islamic science of past generation. [RWB]

17.490 David A. King. "The exact sciences in medieval Islam: some remarks on the present state of research." *Middle East Studies Association bulletin* 14 (1980) 10–26. ISSN 0026-3184. ‣ Excellent, brief introduction with useful bibliography of scholarship on Islamic science. [RWB]

17.491 Seyyed Hossein Nasr. "Life sciences, alchemy, and medicine." In *The Cambridge history of Iran.* Richard N. Frye, ed., vol. 4, pp. 396–441. Cambridge: Cambridge University Press, 1975. ISBN 0-521-20093-8. ‣ Extensive essay designed for specialists who already have understanding of field. [RWB]

17.492 George Saliba. *A history of Arabic astronomy: planetary theories during the golden age of Islam.* New York: New York University Press, 1994. ISBN 0-8147-7962-X. ‣ Major contribution concentrating on eleventh to fifteenth centuries. Some parts for specialists only, but with good historical introduction. [RWB]

17.493 Manfred Ullmann. *Islamic medicine.* Jean Watt, trans. Edinburgh: Edinburgh University Press, 1978. ISBN 0-85224-325-1. ‣ Short, dense survey covering diet and pharmacology as well as pathology and anatomy. Best introduction in English. [RWB]

Art, Architecture, and Music

17.494 K.A.C. Cresswell. *Early Muslim architecture.* 2d ed. 2 vols. New York: Hacker, 1979. ISBN 0-87817-176-2. ‣ Revision of extensive standard work on Islamic architecture down to ca. 900. Coverage based both on archaeology and texts. [RWB]

17.495 K.A.C. Cresswell. *The Muslim architecture of Egypt.* 1952–59 ed. 2 vols. New York: Hacker, 1979. ISBN 0-87817-175-4. ‣ Extensive standard work on Egyptian architecture stressing period 939–1326. [RWB]

17.496 Richard Ettinghausen. *Arab painting.* Lausanne: Skira, 1962. ‣ Basic book on Arab painting, particularly miniature painting, by paramount Islamic art scholar of last generation. [RWB]

17.497 Henry George Farmer. *A history of Arabian music to the twelfth century.* 1929 ed. London: Luzac, 1973. ‣ Standard history dealing with theory and anecdotal material from early texts. [RWB]

17.498 Oleg Grabar. *The formation of Islamic art.* 2d rev. ed. New Haven: Yale University Press, 1987. ISBN 0-300-03969-7 (cl), 0-300-04046-6 (pbk). ‣ Influential study by prominent historian of Islamic art. Addresses question of how distinctively Islamic art came into being, using motifs and techniques already common in pre-Islamic cultures. [RWB]

17.499 Harry W. Hazard, ed. *The art and architecture of Crusader*

states. Vol. 4 of *A history of the Crusades*. Madison: University of Wisconsin Press, 1977. ISBN 0-299-06820-x. ▸ Extensive collection of essays on many aspects of art and architecture in Crusader kingdoms. [RWB]

17.500 Derek Hill and Oleg Grabar. *Islamic architecture and its decoration, A.D. 800–1500: a photographic survey*. Chicago: University of Chicago Press, 1964. ▸ Superbly illustrated study of Islamic architecture, mostly in Iran and Anatolia. Best analysis of evolution of decorative brickwork and tile, major artistic feature of period after 1000. [RWB]

17.501 Arthur Upham Pope and Phyllis Akkerman, eds. *A survey of Persian art from prehistoric times to the present*. Rev. ed. 16 vols. Ashiya, Japan: SOPA; distributed by Tuttle, 1981. ISBN 4-89360-011-7 (set). ▸ Enormous compilation of illustrated studies by various authors on every aspect of Persian art. Superseded in many sections, but still place to start in particular subfields. [RWB]

17.502 George Dimitri Sawa. *Music performance practice in the early ʿAbbasid era, 132–320 AH/750–932 AD*. Toronto: Pontifical Institute of Mediaeval Studies, 1989. (Studies and texts, 92.) ISBN 0-88844-092-8. ▸ Divided into two parts: theory of performance and practice of performance. Main sources are al-Farabi and Abu al-Faraj al-Isbahani. Excellent introduction to medieval Islamic music. [RWB]

CARTER VAUGHN FINDLEY

Middle East and North Africa since 1500

While scholarly definitions vary, the Middle East is commonly understood to consist, in terms of late twentieth-century political geography, of Turkey, Iran, Israel, the Arab countries of Southwest Asia, and Egypt. North Africa includes Morocco, Algeria, and Tunisia; Libya is assigned to either the Middle East or North Africa. Although Islamic civilization had spread far beyond the Middle East, flourishing for centuries as the pre–da Gaman world's most widely diffused civilization (and remaining one of the most widespread to this day), the Middle East forms a justifiable unit of analysis. This is the historical heartland of Islamic civilization and the primary setting for development and diffusion of the three "classic" Islamic high cultures, conveyed through the linguistic media of Arabic, Persian, and Turkish. The interactions among these cultures and the integrity of the region have varied in intensity across time but never disappeared. North Africa is an extension of the Middle East, united with it by ties of religion, history, and shared Arabic culture.

The terms "Middle East" and the roughly synonymous "Near East" are of course objectionable in that they name the region from the vantage point of Europeans and Americans. The muddle reflected in scholarly vacillation between "Middle East," "Near East," or even "Near and Middle East," partly results from a history of shifting preferences, with occasional attempts at compromise. The confusion, however, also implicitly signals the difficulty of finding a value-neutral designator for a region that lies mainly in Southwest Asia but also includes Egypt as one of its key constituents. Constructed on the analogy of East Asia or South Asia, the name for the Middle East and North Africa would become Southwest Asia and North Africa. This has so far not gained wide acceptance. Moreover, even this does not solve the problem of finding an unobjectionable name for the core region, the Middle East, consisting of Southwest Asia plus Egypt. The term "Middle East" remains in use, then, for want of a better. The peoples of the region have appropriated this term and use it freely in their own languages.

When the second edition of the *Guide* was published in 1961, the study of the Islamic world was at a turning point. It was moving beyond the tradition of Orientalism into the new mode of area studies. The scholarly tradition of Orientalism had been founded on the study of language and philology and implicitly assumed the readiness of the linguistically competent scholar to study history, literature, or other topics, without further training in the relevant discipline. Influenced in its origins by classical studies, scholarly Orientalism also concentrated on the formative phases of the civilizations it studied. The Orientalist tradition produced many valuable contributions to scholarship, but World War II, in particular, spotlighted the limitations of this approach.

The creation of area-studies programs in the 1950s and 1960s, therefore, launched a new approach to the study of the cultures of the Middle East and other major regions. Area studies would focus more on the contemporary world and gain in sophistication by combining language and area expertise with systematic formation in disciplines like history and the social sciences. The training of sizable numbers of scholars who were both historians and experts on Islamic cultures began with the area-studies programs. Area studies also drew inspiration from modernization theory. An outgrowth of political and economic-development studies, modernization theory aimed to identify the stages by which modern Western societies had risen and to analyze the progress of other societies along a presumably identical developmental path.

By the early 1960s, scholars who had either explicitly adopted the modernization approach or had assimilated elements of it from their intellectual environment were producing work that gave direction to a new generation of scholars. A number of these works clustered in Turkish studies, where the vast Ottoman archives continue to provide rich opportunities for historians. Between 1959 and 1964, N. Berkes (18.261), R. Davison (18.263), K. Karpat (18.278), B. Lewis (18.281), and Ş. Mardin (18.283) all published seminal works on nineteenth- and twentieth-century Ottoman and Turkish history. About the same time, A. Hourani's work in intellectual history (18.57) and C. Issawi's in economic history (18.62) imparted a comparable new stimulus to historical study of the Arab world.

Since these pioneering works, the historiography of the Middle East and North Africa has grown explosively in quality and in quantity. The *American Historical Review* devoted its December 1991 issue (vol. 96.5) to historiographical articles on a number of topics relevant to the crisis in the Arab-Persian Gulf; these articles illustrate some aspects of this development. To a degree, the growth has paralleled that in the major traditional fields of historical study. To some degree, too, it has taken its bearings from the close association with the social sciences that characterizes area studies in general. With this growth in the scholarship came shifts of interest, partly stimulated by economic and political events. While productivity in Turkish studies continued, growth in the study of the Arab world and Iran was accelerating more rapidly by the 1980s. Zionism, the state of Israel, and the Palestinian national movement have remained perennial foci of interest.

Today, the historical study of the Middle East is again at a turning point. The implications for the future are not yet as clear as those of the transition thirty years ago, but two major dimensions of change are apparent. First, interest in the modernization paradigm declined by the 1970s with the realization that development eliminated neither dependency nor traditional structures and values. Second, while the growth in volume of publication led to the opening of many new lines of inquiry, the same process led scholars increasingly into the minutely focused scholarship that is commonplace in the more highly developed fields of historical study. Responding to this problem and to questions about the modernization paradigm, several senior scholars opted for reintegrative approaches that challenge the limits of the area-studies framework—spatially, temporally, and conceptually—and point in some cases toward a globalist approach. This reintegrative trend found its great precursor in M. Hodgson, whose three-volume *Venture of Islam* (18.55) remains a highly provocative attempt at a comprehensive history of Islamic civilization. Hodgson's *Venture* is world-historical in conception, and he also left another unfinished work on world history at his death in 1968. More recently, I. Lapidus's *History of Islamic Societies* (18.68) again takes an integral approach to the history of Islamic civilization, from the rise of Islam to the present and from West

Africa to China. A. Hourani's *History of the Arab Peoples* (18.59) offers the kind of masterly summation and interpretation that enlightens both nonspecialists and experts. The volumes that C. Issawi has produced on economic history since 1966 perform a reintegrative function in a different sense, spanning all levels of analysis, from the locally focused to a region-wide synthesis.

One factor paving the way for such large-scale syntheses has been the proliferation of monographic approaches, despite the risks of hyper-specialization that this trend implies. Albert Hourani has characterized these approaches in terms of successive but overlapping trends in political, intellectual, and social history, plus an emerging emphasis on collective mentalities.

As scholars have worked their way more deeply into archival collections in the region—the richest being those of Turkey, Egypt, and Syria—and tapped new categories of nonarchival sources as well, these trends have led to the opening of whole new subfields. Social and intellectual history has gained with the discovery of more extensive autobiographical sources than earlier scholars had thought existed, as evidenced by the contributions of R. Dankoff (18.177, 18.178, 18.179) and C. Kafadar (18.198) to premodern Ottoman studies. The opening of Islamic religious court records from the Ottoman empire enabled scholars for the first time to study Islamic law, not from normative sources but in terms of application. The result has been major new insights into the artisanal and merchant economy, credit, family life, and women's roles in particular, as exemplified in the works of R. Jennings (18.197) on Kayseri in Anatolia, J. Tucker (18.166) on women in nineteenth-century Egypt, A. Marcus (18.205) on Aleppo, or A. Raymond (18.211) on eighteenth-century Cairo. For the period prior to 1800, a major trend has been to challenge long-standing ideas of decline, either rejecting them or presenting more nuanced views that emphasize development in some respects, if decline in others. Cornell Fleisher's work in Ottoman intellectual history (18.182) exemplifies this revisionist trend.

With the growth of the field, historians of both the premodern and modern periods have made major advances in the study of elites and classes, occupational groups, social networks, and factions. This trend has greatly stimulated the development of social history and has also exerted a much wider impact. P. Khoury's works on Syria (18.407, 18.408) and H. Batatu's monumental study of Iraq (18.433) exemplify this trend at the intersection of political and social history. The growth of scholarship has enabled historians to examine a wide spectrum of groups, from the highest Ottoman *'ulamā'* (18.219), to Iranian tribesmen (18.576), to Tunisian peasants (18.388). A long-standing interest in religious thought and leadership has gained strength with the decline of the teleologically secularist modernization paradigm and with events such as the Iranian revolution. Here there are many works to cite, from N. Keddie's study of Jamal al-Din al-Afghani (18.94), to Ş. Mardin's study of Said Nursi (18.101), O. Carré's work on Sayyid Qutb (18.83), or the debate among H. Algar (18.560), S. Arjomand (18.561), and others on the role of religion in the history of Iran. Now also notable among emerging subfields are urban history, pioneered by A. Raymond (18.72, 18.211), and demographic history, represented by the work of J. McCarthy (18.284, 18.515) on the populations of Anatolia and Palestine or A. Duben and C. Behar (18.268) on Istanbul.

With such works, the historiography of the Middle East has become much more inclusive. Women's historians have contributed greatly to this change, both through their substantive findings and through debate about the Islamic gender system and the relevance of Western feminist concerns to Islamic societies. The study of Middle Eastern women is part of a wider growth of interest in nonelite groups, including slaves (18.294) and industrial workers (18.290, 18.301).

These examples and the following bibliography suffice to illustrate the dynamism of Middle Eastern historiography in Europe and North America. It remains to note, however, that much significant scholarship also appears in the languages of the region. Given the editorial policy and intended audience of the *Guide*, such works are not included in the following listings unless available in translation (works that historians from the Middle East have published in Western languages of course are included here). Much of the scholarship discussed above would not have been possible, however, without the extensive contributions of scholars in the region. Attentive readers of the works listed below will become vicariously acquainted, not only with major archives and libraries of the region but also with such leading historians as Halil Inalcik and Ömer Lutfi Barkan of Turkey, Abd al-Aziz Duri in Iraq, Abd al-Karim Rafeq of Syria, and Firidun Adamiyyat and Abd al-Husayn Zarrinkub in Iran. Doing research in the region and enjoying the colleagueship of its scholars are among the most rewarding experiences awaiting Middle East historians.

Mastery of one or more Middle Eastern languages, not to speak of major European languages, is essential, not just for original research but also for unrestrained reading of the scholarly literature on Middle Eastern history. The works listed here nonetheless suffice to introduce interested readers to the substantive accomplishments of scholars in the field and to the challenges and opportunities that it offers for further research.

ACKNOWLEDGMENTS   *Compilation of this section benefited from the advice and assistance of Charles Issawi and the late Albert Hourani.*

Entries are arranged under the following headings:

Reference Works

General Studies

Topical Fields
Islam
Women

Islamic Empires, 1500–1800
Ottoman Empire
Safavid Empire and Eighteenth-Century Iran
Peripheral Regions, 1500–1800: Arabian Peninsula

The Modern Era
Late Ottoman Empire and Turkish Republic
Egypt
Sudan
Libya
Tunisia, Algeria, and Morocco
Syria, Lebanon, and Jordan
Iraq
Zionist Movement and the State of Israel
Palestine and the Palestinian National Movement
Arabian Peninsula
Iran

[Contributors: Contributors: AG = Arthur Goldschmidt, Jr., AR = Aron Rodrigue, CK = Cemal Kafadar, CVF = Carter Vaughn Findley, DSS = Dona S. Straley, EM = Ezra Mendelsohn, GRG = Gene R. Garthwaite, IB = Israel Bartal, JET = Judith E. Tucker, JOV = John O. Voll, JSH = John S. Hill, JW = John E. Woods, LV = Lucette Valensi, MCW = Mary C. Wilson, MS = Marlène Shamay, PM = Philip Mattar, PSK = Philip S. Khoury, PWS = Paul W. Schroeder, RS = Reeva S. Simon, WLO = William L. Ochsenwald]

REFERENCE WORKS

18.1 *Abstracta Iranica.* Tehran: Département d'Iranologie de l'Institut Français de Téhéran, 1978–. (*Studia Iranica*, Supplement.) ISSN 0240-8910. ▸ Primary bibliography for subject. Includes references to and summaries in French of books and articles on Iranian culture from prehistoric times to present. Publications in Western and Iranian languages cited. Published annually. [DSS]

18.2 *Al-Fihrist: quarterly index to Arabic periodical literature.* Beirut, 1981–. ISSN 0257-439X. ▸ Only major index to Arabic journals. Cites articles from Arabic journals on Arab world and Islam. Emphasis on modern politics and development but includes arts and culture. [DSS]

18.3 *Annuaire de l'Afrique du Nord.* Paris: Centre National de la Recherche Scientifique, 1962–. ISSN 0066-2607. ▸ Excellent annual summary. Includes essays on individual topics, review of events in each country, and bibliography of journal articles and books published about and in area. Published annually, includes Mauritania but not Egypt. [DSS]

18.4 Jere L. Bacharach. *A Middle East studies handbook.* Rev. ed. Seattle: University of Washington Press, 1984. ISBN 0-295-96138-4 (cl), 0-295-96144-9 (pbk). ▸ Handy, single volume for ready reference, featuring dynastic charts, historical maps, Islamic calendar conversion table, abbreviations of periodicals, reference works, and chronology. [DSS]

18.5 Ali Banuazizi. *Social stratification in the Middle East and North Africa: a bibliographic survey.* London: Mansell, 1984. ISBN 0-7201-1711-9. ▸ Basic, introductory guide lists books, articles, and theses in English and French concerning socioeconomic change, status, and values. Arranged by country with useful subject index. [DSS]

18.6 Wolfgang H. Behn. *Index Islamicus, 1665–1905: a bibliography of articles on Islamic subjects in periodicals and other collective publications.* Millersville, Pa.: Adiyok, 1989. ISBN 3-9800467-5-3. ▸ Cites articles in Western languages on historical, linguistic, political, and cultural topics. Extends coverage of Pearson et al., eds. *Index Islamicus* (18.29). Massive achievement, only publication to cover pre-twentieth century. [DSS]

18.7 *Bibliyughrafiya al-wahdah al-ʿArabiyah, 1908–1980* (Bibliography of Arabic unity, 1908–1980). 3 vols. in 7. Beirut: Markaz Dirasat al-Wahdah al-'Arabiyah, 1983–86. ▸ Cites books, articles, dissertations, book reviews, and government reports. Comprehensive coverage much wider than title indicates, embracing most subjects except natural sciences. English, French, and Arabic titles. [DSS]

18.8 Gerald H. Blake, John Dewdney, and Jonathan Mitchell, eds. *Cambridge atlas of the Middle East and North Africa.* Cambridge: Cambridge University Press, 1987. ISBN 0-521-24243-6. ▸ Contains fifty-eight maps treating wide range of historical, political, social, economic, and environmental subjects. Emphasizes region as whole not individual countries. [CVF]

18.9 Jody Boudreault et al., eds. *United Nations resolutions on Palestine and the Arab-Israeli conflict.* Rev. ed. 4 vols. Washington, D.C.: Institute for Palestine Studies, 1987. ISBN 0-88728-161-3 (v. 1), 0-88728-162-1 (v. 2), 0-88728-163-X (v. 3), 0-88728-240-7 (v. 4). ▸ Convenient compilation of texts of all resolutions passed between 1947 and 1986 by United Nations and related international organizations. Includes voting information. [DSS]

18.10 Moshe Brawer, ed. *Atlas of Israel: cartography, physical and human geography.* 3d ed. Tel Aviv and New York: Survey of Israel and Macmillan, 1985. ISBN 0-02-905950-X. ▸ Includes subject maps, tables, and charts illustrating text. Excellent treatment of human and physical geography. [DSS]

18.11 Thomas A. Bryson. *United States/Middle East diplomatic relations, 1784–1978: an annotated bibliography.* Metuchen, N.J.: Scarecrow, 1979. ISBN 0-8108-1197-9. ▸ Includes English-language books, articles, and dissertations. Emphasis on twentieth century. Fewer entries than Silverburg 18.34 but has annotations which Silverburg lacks. [DSS]

18.12 *Encyclopaedia of Islam.* 2d ed. 7 vols. to date. Leiden: Brill, 1960–. ISBN 90-04-05745-5 (v. 4), 90-04-07819-3 (v. 5), 90-04-08112-7 (v. 6), 90-04-09419-9 (v. 7). ▸ Premier scholarly reference work. Ongoing; consult first edition for entries planned for future publication. [DSS]

18.13 Martin Gilbert. *The Arab-Israeli conflict: its history in maps.* 5th rev. ed. London: Weidenfeld & Nicolson, 1992. ISBN 0-297-82113-X. ▸ Shows the political, military, and demographic changes from 1900 to 1991 in 126 maps arranged chronologically, each with inset notes. Unusual treatment. [DSS]

18.14 Yvonne Yazbeck Haddad, John O. Voll, and John L. Esposito. *The contemporary Islamic revival: a critical survey and bibliography.* New York: Greenwood, 1991. ISBN 0-313-24719-6, ISSN 0742-6836. ▸ General introduction lists publications in English, some with annotations, divided by geographic area with subject index. Introductory essays discuss historical framework, types and themes of literature, and specific case studies. [DSS]

18.15 J. C. Hurewitz. *The Middle East and North Africa in world politics: a documentary record.* 2d rev. ed. 2 vols. New Haven: Yale University Press, 1975. ISBN 0-300-01294-2. ▸ Texts of treaties, commercial agreements, and statements of policy in English translation, each with commentary and bibliography. Generally excludes Balkan provinces of Ottoman empire. Only available compilation in English translation. [DSS]

18.16 *Islamic book review index.* Berlin: Adiyok, 1982. ISSN 0724-2263. ▸ Includes citations for reviews of books on all aspects of

Islamic world, compiled mostly from Western-language journals. Published annually. Only work of its kind. [DSS]

18.17 Jamil E. Jreisat and Zaki R. Ghosheh. *Administration and development in the Arab world: an annotated bibliography.* New York: Garland, 1986. ISBN 0-8240-8593-0. ▸ Includes books, articles, and dissertations in English with annotations for each entry. Topics are interpreted broadly including social and economic aspects and human resources. Good starting point; use with Banuazizi 18.5. [DSS]

18.18 Walid Khalidi and Jill Khaddouri, eds. *Palestine and the Arab-Israeli conflict: an annotated bibliography.* Beirut: Institute for Palestine Studies, 1974. ISBN 0-88728-121-4. ▸ Includes books, articles, and other published and unpublished materials largely in English, Arabic, and Hebrew with annotations, divided topically and chronologically. Still most useful despite its age. [DSS]

18.19 *Kiryat sefer.* Jerusalem: Jewish National & University Library Press and Bet ha-Sefarim, 1924–. ISSN 0023-1851. ▸ Comprehensive quarterly bibliography listing all Israeli publications on all subjects and all publications on Judaica from throughout the world. Citations in language of publication; all other material in Hebrew. [DSS]

18.20 Hans-Jürgen Kornrumpf. *Osmanische Bibliographie mit besonderer Berücksichtigung der Türkei in Europa.* Leiden: Brill, 1973. (Handbuch der Orientalistik, Erste Abteilung: der nahe und der mittlere Osten, Ergänzungsband, 8.) ISBN 90-04-03549-4. ▸ Books and articles, including Balkan and Turkish publications. Outdated, but useful for extending the coverage of *Turkologischer Anzeiger* (18.36) backward in time. [CVF]

18.21 Yehuda Lukacs, ed. *The Israeli-Palestinian conflict: a documentary record.* Rev. ed. Cambridge: Cambridge University Press, 1992. ISBN 0-521-37561-4 (cl), 0-521-37597-5 (pbk). ▸ Useful collection of over 200 Arab, Palestinian, Israeli, American, and international documents pertaining to Palestinian-Israeli and Arab-Israeli conflicts. [PM]

18.22 *The Middle East: abstracts and index.* Pittsburgh: Northumberland Press and Library Information and Research Service, 1978–. ISSN 0162-766X. ▸ Includes references and summaries for books, book reviews, journal articles, government documents, dissertations, editorials, and statistical publications, mostly in English; volumes cover works published five to six years earlier. Especially good for items not covered in other indexes. [DSS]

18.23 *The Middle East and North Africa.* London: Europa, 1948–. ISSN 0076-8502. ▸ Includes essays on political and economic topics, section on regional organizations, and surveys of individual countries containing information and statistics on economy, government, media, religion, and education. Standard, invaluable reference. [DSS]

18.24 *Middle East contemporary survey.* New York: Holmes & Meier, 1978–. ISSN 0163-5476. ▸ Annual volumes of political and economic essays on current topics, especially intra- and interregional affairs. Individual country surveys emphasize domestic and foreign policy. Does not include Morocco, Algeria, or Tunisia. Convenient annual survey. [DSS]

18.25 *The Middle East in conflict: a historical bibliography.* Santa Barbara, Calif.: ABC-Clio, 1985. ISBN 0-87436-381-0. ▸ Abstracts of over 3,000 articles in many languages published from 1973 to 1982 covering twentieth-century history. Must be used in conjunction with other indexes. [DSS]

18.26 Trevor Mostyn and Albert H. Hourani, eds. *The Cambridge encyclopedia of the Middle East and North Africa.* Cambridge: Cambridge University Press, 1988. ISBN 0-521-32190-5. ▸ Thematic essays and studies of individual countries with emphasis on culture and social and economic change; includes short bibliographies for each topic and country. [CVF]

18.27 Assia Neuberg, Yaakov Rothschild, and Hadasa Rothschild. *The state of Israel: an annotated bibliography.* 3 vols. Jerusalem: Bet sefer le-safranut a.y. ha-Universitah ha-Ivrit, Merkaz ha-hadrakah le-sifriyot tsiburiyot, 1988. ISBN 965-231-010-7. ▸ Includes books in Western languages, Hebrew, and Yiddish on all subjects from Balfour Declaration to 1988. Annotations in Hebrew. Most complete bibliography for period covered. [IB/DSS]

18.28 Veronica S. Pantelidis. *Arab education, 1956–78: a bibliography.* London: Mansell; distributed by Wilson, 1982. ISBN 0-7201-1588-4. ▸ Best available bibliography for period covered. Includes English-language books, articles, dissertations, reports, and working papers with descriptive annotations. [DSS]

18.29 James Douglas Pearson, Ann Walsh, and Julia F. Ashton, eds. and comps. *Index Islamicus: a catalogue of articles on Islamic subjects in periodicals and other collective publications.* 5 vols. with various supplements. Cambridge: Heffer, 1958–. ISSN 0306-9524. ▸ Cites articles (and, since 1976, books) in Western languages published since 1906 on historical, linguistic, political, and cultural topics. Current updates provided by *Quarterly Index Islamicus.* Premier index for scholars. [DSS]

18.30 Donald Edgar Pitcher. *An historical geography of the Ottoman empire, from earliest times to the end of the sixteenth century.* Leiden: Brill, 1972. ISBN 90-04-03828-0. ▸ Contains thirty-six maps with corresponding essays, illustrating foundation, expansion, and political organization of Ottoman empire. [CVF]

18.31 Bernard Reich, ed. *Political leaders of the contemporary Middle East and North Africa: a biographical dictionary.* New York: Greenwood, 1990. ISBN 0-313-26213-6. ▸ Interpretive biographies of seventy persons who have significantly influenced political developments in the region since World War II. Includes short bibliography of important works after each entry. Excellent overviews of careers; especially important for figures little known in West. [DSS]

18.32 Francis Robinson. *Atlas of the Islamic world since 1500.* New York: Facts on File, 1982. ISBN 0-87196-629-8. ▸ Contains maps, essays, and illustrations on religious, political, and cultural history. Excellent introduction suitable for general or scholarly reader. [DSS]

18.33 Walid I. Sharif. *Oil and development in the Arab Gulf States: a selected annotated bibliography.* London: Croom Helm, 1985. ISBN 0-7099-3368-1. ▸ Only bibliography of its kind; cites books, articles, dissertations, reports, and unpublished papers, largely in English and Arabic and mostly annotated. Concentrates on economic, political, and social impact. [DSS]

18.34 Sanford R. Silverburg. *United States foreign policy and the Middle East/North Africa: a bibliography of twentieth-century research.* New York: Garland, 1990. ISBN 0-8240-4613-7. ▸ Lists books, articles, dissertations, theses, and government publications in English. Emphasis on Israel and Persian Gulf region. Unsophisticated subject index and uneven treatment of countries and regions. [DSS]

18.35 *Tübinger Atlas des vorderen Orients.* Wiesbaden: Reichert, 1977–. ISBN 3-88226-610-4. ▸ Single sheet, folio-sized maps covering physical and human geography and history from prehistory to present. Massive, detailed undertaking. [DSS]

18.36 *Turkologischer Anzeiger.* Vienna: Institut für Orientalistik der Universität Wien, 1975–. ISSN 0084-0076. ▸ Indispensable bibliography of books, articles, and reviews in all languages on all phases of Turkish studies. Published annually, originally as supplement to *Wiener Zeitschrift für die Kunde des Morgenlandes.* [CVF]

18.37 *World bibliographical series.* Santa Barbara, Calif.: Clio, 1977–. ▸ Subject bibliographies for the following countries, each volume devoted to particular country: Algeria, Bahrain, Egypt, Iran, Iraq, Israel, Jordan, Kuwait, Lebanon, Libya, Morocco, Oman, Sudan, Tunisia, Turkey, Saudi Arabia, Sudan, Syria, United Arab Emirates, the Yemens. Introductory, mainly in English. [DSS]

18.38 Ehsan Yarshater, ed. *Encyclopaedia Iranica*. 5 vols. to date. London: Routledge & Kegan Paul, 1982. ISBN 0-7100-9099-4 (v. 1), 0-7100-9131-1 (v. 4). ‣ Comprehensive and detailed, treats all aspects of Iranian culture from prehistory to present. Complements and updates *Encyclopedia of Islam* (18.12). In progress. [DSS]

GENERAL STUDIES

18.39 Fouad Ajami. *The Arab predicament: Arab political thought and practice since 1967*. Rev. ed. Cambridge: Cambridge University Press, 1992. ISBN 0-521-43243-X, 0-521-43833-0 (pbk). ‣ Major political ideas and trends after 1967. Provocative analysis of responses to 1967 defeat, Egypt as mirror of Arab world, and Islamic fundamentalism. [CVF]

18.40 Ami Ayalon. *Language and change in the Arab Middle East: the evolution of modern political discourse*. New York: Oxford University Press, 1987. ISBN 0-19-504140-2. ‣ Monograph on development of modern political concepts and vocabulary in Arabic language. [CVF]

18.41 Gabriel Baer. *Fellah and townsman in the Middle East: studies in social history*. Totowa, N.J.: Cass, 1982. ISBN 0-7146-3126-4. ‣ Specialized essays by pioneer social historian on peasants and townspeople in Egypt and Syria, village shaykh in Palestine, Ottoman guilds, and urban and rural revolt. [CVF]

18.42 Robin L. Bidwell, ed. *British documents on foreign affairs: reports and papers from the Foreign Office confidential print*. Part 2: *From the First to the Second World War*. Series B: *Turkey, Iran, and the Middle East, 1918–39*. 25 vols. to date. Frederick, Md.: University Publications of America, 1985–. ISBN 0-89093-603-X (set). ‣ Diplomatic dispatches, telegrams, and other reports, including articles, speeches, pamphlets, statistics, interviews, and discussions with political leaders. Valuable primary sources for political and diplomatic history. [DSS]

18.43 Issa J. Boullata. *Trends and issues in contemporary Arab thought*. Albany: State University of New York Press, 1990. ISBN 0-7914-0194-4 (cl), 0-7914-0195-2 (pbk). ‣ Provocative survey of "neglected trends and issues in contemporary Arab thought." Emphasizes innovative thinking on Arab heritage, Islam, dependency, women's status as seen by women, and contemporary Arab society and politics. Read with Hourani 18.57, 18.58, 18.59. [DSS]

18.44 L. Carl Brown. *International politics and the Middle East: old rules, dangerous game*. Princeton: Princeton University Press, 1984. ISBN 0-691-05410-X (cl), 0-691-10159-0 (pbk). ‣ Original, influential analysis arguing for existence of distinctive international relations subsystem in region; historic legacy of Eastern question going back to late eighteenth century. [CVF]

18.45 M. van Bruinessen. *Agha, shaikh, and state: the social and political structures of Kurdistan*. 1978 ed. London: Zed, 1992. ISBN 1-85649-018-1 (cl), 1-85649-019-X (pbk). ‣ Monograph on twentieth-century Kurdish history. Analysis of social and political relations in terms of tribal, religious, and state organization, based on historical sources and fieldwork. Provides most comprehensive background for understanding Kurdish history and society. [GRG]

18.46 Edmund Burke III, and Ira Marvin Lapidus. *Islam, politics, and social movements*. Berkeley: University of California Press, 1988. ISBN 0-520-05758-9 (cl), 0-520-06868-8 (pbk). ‣ Original essays on social protest and political resistance movements in Islamic societies, nineteenth and twentieth centuries. Cultural and social analyses of movements in North Africa, Egypt, Fertile Crescent, Iran, and India. [LV/CVF]

18.47 Adeed I. Dawisha. *The Arab radicals*. New York: Council on Foreign Relations, 1986. ISBN 0-87609-020-X (cl), 0-87609-019-6 (pbk). ‣ Study of forces opposing status quo in Arab world and Arab-Israeli relations. Radical states include Libya, Iraq, Syria, Algeria; movements include Palestine Liberation Organization, Hizbollah, Islamic Jihad, and Muslim Brotherhood. Neglects terrorism. [CVF]

18.48 Alasdair Drysdale and Gerald H. Blake. *The Middle East and North Africa: a political geography*. New York: Oxford University Press, 1985. ISBN 0-19-503537-2 (cl), 0-19-503538-0 (pbk). ‣ Evolution of regional state system, problems of land boundaries and waterways, national and regional integration, Arab-Israeli conflict, and petroleum. Valuable insights into ecological bases of region's modern history. [CVF]

18.49 Abd al-Aziz Duri. *The historical formation of the Arab nation: a study in identity and consciousness*. Lawrence I. Conrad, trans. London: Croom Helm, 1987. ISBN 0-7099-3471-8. ‣ One of few studies by major Arab historian available in English. Interpretation of growth of nationalism as based in language and culture, including Islam. Deemphasizes Western influences. Translation of *Al-Takwin al-tarikhi lil ummah al-ʿArabiyah*. [DSS]

18.50 Haim Gerber. *The social origins of the modern Middle East*. Boulder: Rienner, 1987. ISBN 0-931477-63-8. ‣ Provocative analysis of socioagrarian structure of Ottoman empire and its role in formation of twentieth-century nations. [CVF]

18.51 David Gillard, ed. *British documents on foreign affairs: reports and papers from the Foreign Office confidential print*. Part 1: *From the mid-nineteenth century to the First World War*. Series B: *The Near and Middle East, 1856–1914*. 20 vols. Frederick, Md.: University Publications of America, 1984–85. ISBN 0-89093-602-1 (set). ‣ Important compilation for study of the period. Diplomatic dispatches, telegrams, and other reports, including articles, speeches, pamphlets, statistics, interviews, and discussions with political leaders. Valuable primary sources for political and diplomatic history. [DSS]

18.52 Bent Hansen. *The political economy of poverty, equality, and growth: Egypt and Turkey*. Oxford: Oxford University Press for the World Bank, 1991. ISBN 0-19-520825-0. ‣ Sophisticated comparative analysis of major countries, combining methods of analytical economic history and political economy. Important work by prominent economist with much experience in the region. [CVF]

18.53 Z. Y. Hershlag. *The economic structure of the Middle East*. Leiden: Brill, 1975. ISBN 90-04-04214-8. ‣ Topical survey of regional economy: human resources, structure of production, finance, international sector, and growth processes. [CVF]

18.54 Z. Y. Hershlag. *Introduction to the modern economic history of the Middle East*. 2d rev. ed. Leiden: Brill, 1980. ISBN 90-04-06061-8. ‣ Valuable, comprehensive study of social and institutional structural changes and their relationship to economic processes, noting distinctive change after World War I. [DSS]

18.55 Marshall G. S. Hodgson. *The gunpowder empires and modern times*. Vol. 3 of *The venture of Islam: conscience and history in a world civilization*. Chicago: University of Chicago Press, 1974. ISBN 0-226-34677-3 (set), 0-226-34681-1 (v. 3, cl), 0-226-34685-4 (v. 3, pbk). ‣ History of Islamic civilization in Middle East and South Asia. Comprehensive study of Islamic empires, 1500–1800, and Islam and Western impact, 1800–ca. 1950. Innovative, influential, idiosyncratic. Underlying globalist perspective. [CVF/JOV]

18.56 Peter Malcolm Holt, Ann K. S. Lambton, and Bernard

Lewis, eds. *Cambridge history of Islam*. 1970 ed. 2 vols. in 4. Cambridge: Cambridge University Press, 1978. ISBN 0-521-22310-5 (cl, set). ‣ Essays on history and culture of Islamic countries of Africa, Middle East, and South and Southeast Asia. Encyclopedic coverage; useful as reference work. Standard introduction but uneven treatment. [DSS]

18.57   Albert Hourani. *Arabic thought in the liberal age, 1798–1939*. 1962 ed. Cambridge: Cambridge University Press, 1983. ISBN 0-521-25837-5 (cl), 0-521-27423-0 (pbk). ‣ Classic study of European influence on modern Arab thought. Emphasizes interrelationships between seemingly disparate streams of Islamist and secular thought. [CVF]

18.58   Albert Hourani. *The emergence of the modern Middle East*. Berkeley: University of California Press, 1981. ISBN 0-520-03862-6. ‣ Highly regarded essays on selected topics: Ottoman antecedents; Islamic thinkers and movements; and ideology and revolution, especially in Lebanon. [CVF]

18.59   Albert Hourani. *A history of the Arab peoples*. Cambridge, Mass.: Harvard University Press, 1991. ISBN 0-674-39565-4. ‣ Magisterial, panoramic view of Arabs and their culture from rise of Islam to present. [CVF]

18.60   *International documents on Palestine*. Beirut and Kuwait City: Institute for Palestine Studies and University of Kuwait, 1967–. ‣ Important original sources in English, including interviews, press conferences, resolutions, and other statements of policy by individual governments and of intra- and interregional organizations. Compilation of widely dispersed material. [DSS]

18.61   Tareq Y. Ismael. *International relations of the contemporary Middle East: a study in world politics*. Syracuse: Syracuse University Press, 1986. ISBN 0-8156-2381-X (cl), 0-8156-2382-8 (pbk). ‣ Comprehensive study of regional system of international relations and its global context. Emphasizes regional and domestic influences on international behavior of Middle Eastern states. [CVF]

18.62   Charles P. Issawi. *An economic history of the Middle East and North Africa*. New York: Columbia University Press, 1982. ISBN 0-231-03443-1 (cl), 0-231-08377-7 (pbk). ‣ Synthesizes author's earlier works. Expansionist Europe's impact; Middle Eastern societies' response. Well-informed analysis of and introduction to demographics, trade, transport, agriculture, manufactures, institutional and policy factors, and petroleum. [CVF/LV]

18.63   Charles P. Issawi, ed. *The economic history of the Middle East, 1800–1914: a book of readings*. 1966 ed. Chicago: University of Chicago Press, 1975. ISBN 0-226-38609-0. ‣ Collection of primary and secondary sources covering infrastructure, trade, manufacturing, agriculture, land tenure, and finance with analysis and commentary. Groundbreaking work by premier economic historian of region. [CVF]

18.64   Kemal H. Karpat, ed. *Political and social thought in the contemporary Middle East*. Rev. ed. New York: Praeger, 1982. ISBN 0-03-057609-1 (cl), 0-03-057608-3 (pbk). ‣ Extensive collection of source extracts in translation; insightful commentary and analysis. [CVF]

18.65   Elie Kedourie. *Politics in the Middle East*. Oxford: Oxford University Press, 1992. ISBN 0-19-219167-5 (cl), 0-19-289154-5 (pbk). ‣ Insightful essays on political culture of modern Middle East. Distinguished scholar's last work. [CVF]

18.66   Tarif Khalidi, ed. *Land tenure and social transformation in the Middle East*. Beirut: American University of Beirut, 1984. ISBN 0-8156-6071-5. ‣ Essays representing recent scholarship on land tenure in Middle East, from ancient times to present. Important for agrarian and socioeconomic history. [CVF]

18.67   Martin S. Kramer. *Islam assembled: the advent of the Mus-* *lim congresses*. New York: Columbia University Press, 1986. ISBN 0-231-05994-9. ‣ Study of Muslim efforts to foster unity by convening congresses from late nineteenth century through World War II. Important topic in growth of modern Islamic internationalism. [CVF]

18.68   Ira M. Lapidus. *A history of Islamic societies*. Cambridge: Cambridge University Press, 1988. ISBN 0-521-22552-3. ‣ Comprehensive survey of Islamic civilization and societies, from Middle Eastern beginnings through diffusion into northern and sub-Saharan Africa, Balkans, Central Asia, India, China, and Southeast Asia up to present. [CVF]

18.69   Bernard Lewis. *The Muslim discovery of Europe*. New York: Norton, 1982. ‣ Ambitious, wide-ranging study of development of Muslim attitudes toward and knowledge of Europe across the centuries. Extensive discussion of and quotations from original sources. [CVF]

18.70   Roger Owen. *The Middle East in the world economy, 1800–14*. London: Methuen, 1981. ISBN 0-416-14270-2. ‣ Comprehensive economic history emphasizing rise in incomes, primarily of landowners; growth in seaborne trade; integration into world economy; role of local governments in economic change; and national reactions among local elites. [CVF]

18.71   Yehoshua Porath. *In search of Arab unity, 1930–1945*. Totowa, N.J.: Cass, 1986. ISBN 0-7146-3264-3 (cl), 0-7146-4051-4 (pbk). ‣ Examination of Arab efforts to promote unity; attempts to solve Palestine problem in context of Arab unity and related British policy. Specialized study based on British and Jewish archival sources and Arabic memoir literature. [CVF]

18.72   André Raymond. *Grandes villes arabes à l'époque ottomane*. Paris: Sindbad, 1985. ISBN 2-7274-0107-8. ‣ Major work by leading urban historian. Chapters on urban evolution during Ottoman period: population, institutions, spatial organization, economy, and built environment. Partial translation published as *The Great Arab Cities in the Sixteenth–Eighteenth Centuries: An Introduction*. [CVF]

18.73   Alan Richards and John Waterbury. *A political economy of the Middle East: state, class, and economic development*. Boulder: Westview, 1990. ISBN 0-8133-0155-6 (cl), 0-8133-0156-4 (pbk). ‣ Extremely insightful, comprehensive analysis of transformation of political economy of Middle Eastern nations. Interrelation of politics and development strategies; impact of different strategies on class formation. [CVF]

18.74   Hisham Sharabi. *Neopatriarchy: a theory of distorted change in Arab society*. New York: Oxford University Press, 1988. ISBN 0-19-505141-6. ‣ Provocative analysis; seeks explanation of many of Arab world's contemporary problems in modernization (strengthening, deformation) of traditional patriarchalism under impact of European hegemony. Concludes liberation cannot be a quick fix. [CVF]

18.75   Bassam Tibi. *Arab nationalism: a critical enquiry*. 2d ed. Marion Farouk-Sluglett and Peter Sluglett, eds. and trans. New York: St. Martin's, 1990. ISBN 0-312-04234-5. ‣ Arab nationalism as case study in Third World nationalisms. Emphasizes Sati‘ al-Husri (1882–1968) and origins of his ideas in German romantics and Ibn Khaldûn. Critiques of pan-Islamism and local nationalisms. Insightful analysis. [CVF]

18.76   Bassam Tibi. *Islam and the cultural accommodation of social change*. Clare Krojzl, trans. Boulder: Westview, 1990. ISBN 0-8133-0917-4. ‣ Provocative argument that Muslims must take critical view of their past and depoliticize their religion in order to adjust to modern world. [DSS]

18.77   Malcolm E. Yapp. *The making of the modern Near East, 1792–1923*. New York: Longman, 1987. ISBN 0-582-01366-6 (cl), 0-582-49380-3 (pbk). ‣ Introductory general history of modern

Middle East; emphasis on politics. Extensive coverage of developments in outlying regions as well as political centers and of British policy. [CVF]

18.78 Malcolm E. Yapp. *The Near East since the First World War*. London: Longman, 1990. ISBN 0-582-49500-8 (cl), 0-582-49499-0 (pbk). ▸ General history of modern Middle East and North Africa; emphasis on politics and international relations. [CVF]

TOPICAL FIELDS

Islam

18.79 Akbar S. Ahmed. *Discovering Islam: making sense of Muslim history and society*. London: Routledge & Kegan Paul, 1988. ISBN 0-7102-1049-3 (cl), 0-415-03930-4 (pbk). ▸ Islamic ideal defined by Qur'ān and life of Muhammad as basis for understanding Muslim history; tension between ideal and reality major dynamic. Scholarly, revivalist Muslim perspective. [JOV]

18.80 Georges Anawati and Maurice Borrmans. *Tendances et courants de l'Islam arabe contemporain*. Vol. 1: *Egypte et Afrique du Nord*. Munich and Mainz: Kaiser and Matthias Grünewald Verlag, 1982. (Entwicklung und Frieden, Wissenschatliche Reihe, 26.) ISBN 3-459-01471-7, 3-7867-1013-9. ▸ Detailed survey covering Egypt and North Africa of thinkers and trends in different realms of Islamic thought. [CVF]

18.81 J. N. D. Anderson. *Islamic law in the modern world*. New York: New York University Press, 1959. ▸ Influential discussion of displacement of Islamic law by westernized codes and legal reform efforts within Islamic societies. Presents views of 1950s regarding inevitable success of secularism in Islamic societies. [JOV]

18.82 Leonard Binder. *Islamic liberalism: a critique of development ideologies*. Chicago: University of Chicago Press, 1988. ISBN 0-226-05146-3 (cl), 0-226-05147-1 (pbk). ▸ Contemporary discourse among Muslims involves debate between liberals and fundamentalists. Major Muslim intellectuals show the options but indigenous liberalism difficult. Foucauldian perspective; intellectually ambitious analysis. [JOV]

18.83 Olivier Carré. *Mystique et politique: lecture révolutionnaire du Coran par Sayyid Qutb, frère musulman radical*. Paris: Presses de la Fondation Nationale des Sciences Politiques, 1984. ISBN 2-7246-0496-2, 2-204-02169-5. ▸ Monograph on Qur'ān commentary of Sayyid Qutb (1906–66), leading twentieth-century Islamic thinker and Muslim Brotherhood activist. Emphasizes Qutb's method and ideal sociopolitical order. [CVF]

18.84 Juan Ricardo I. Cole and Nikki R. Keddie, eds. *Shiᶜism and social protest*. New Haven: Yale University Press, 1986. ISBN 0-300-03550-0 (cl), 0-300-03553-5 (pbk). ▸ Transformation of Twelver Shiism from quietism to political activism. Collection of essays with case studies of Iran, Persian Gulf, Lebanon, Iraq, Afghanistan, and Saudi Arabia. [JOV]

18.85 Kenneth Cragg. *Counsels in contemporary Islam*. Edinburgh: Edinburgh University Press, 1965. ▸ Internal counsels shape Muslim prospects in coping with challenges of modernization. Abduh, Iqbal, Muslim Brotherhood, and others provide broad spectrum of Muslim approaches. History of religions perspective. [JOV]

18.86 Hamid Enayat. *Modern Islamic political thought*. Austin: University of Texas Press, 1982. ISBN 0-292-75069-2 (cl), 0-292-75070-6 (pbk). ▸ Insightful study of ideas and issues in twentieth-century Islamic political thought, Sunnī and Shīᶜī: caliphate, concept of Islamic state, nationalism, democracy, socialism, Shīᶜī modernism. Emphasizes Sunnī-Shīᶜī cross-fertilization. [CVF]

18.87 Werner Ende and Udo Steinbach, eds. *Der Islam in der*

Gegenwart. Munich: Beck, 1984. ISBN 3-406-09740-5. ▸ Voluminous collection of essays on history of Islam, its contemporary political role, and contemporary Islamic culture. Includes treatment of Islamic societies outside Middle East. [CVF]

18.88 John L. Esposito. *Islam and politics*. 3d ed. Syracuse, N.Y.: Syracuse University Press, 1991. ISBN 0-8156-2544-8. ▸ Different roles of Islam in development of political structures and ideologies in modern era. Contemporary Islamic resurgence response of dynamic Islam to West. History of religions perspective. [JOV]

18.89 Yohanan Friedmann. *Shaykh Ahmad Sirhindi: an outline of his thought and a study of his image in the eyes of posterity*. Montreal: McGill University, Institute of Islamic Studies, 1971. (McGill Islamic studies, 2.) ISBN 0-7735-0068-5. ▸ Analysis of major seventeenth-century Indian Muslim thinker concluding that later historians overemphasized reformism of Sirhindi. His later image reportedly more influential than his actions. [JOV]

18.90 H.A.R. Gibb. *Modern trends in Islam*. 1947 ed. New York: Octagon Books, 1978. ISBN 0-374-93046-5. ▸ Discussion of serious weaknesses in Islamic modernism and liberalism in first half of twentieth century as response to West. Standard Western critique of Islamic modernism; shaped much subsequent scholarship. [JOV]

18.91 Michael Gilsenan. *Recognizing Islam: religion and society in the modern Arab world*. 1982 ed. London: Taurus, 1990. ISBN 1-85043-297-X. ▸ Analysis of Islamic diversity as response to varying social conditions in modern world. Complex role of religion in urban, village, and tribal societies from perspective of historian-anthropologist. [JOV]

18.92 Yvonne Yazbeck Haddad. *Contemporary Islam and the challenge of history*. Albany: State University of New York Press, 1982. ISBN 0-87395-543-9 (cl), 0-87395-544-7 (pbk). ▸ Discussion of Muslim responses to challenges of modernization as reflected in historical scholarship; neonormative Islamic perspective seen as heart of contemporary Islamic resurgence. History of religions perspective. [JOV]

18.93 F. de Jong. *Turuq and Turuq-linked institutions in nineteenth-century Egypt: a historical study in organizational dimensions of Islamic mysticism*. Leiden: Brill, 1978. ISBN 90-04-05704-8. ▸ Specialized study of Egypt's mystical societies (*turuq*) and related institutions arguing that they reached historic high point of influence in nineteenth century. Based on private papers, religious court archives, and interviews. [CVF]

18.94 Nikki R. Keddie. *Sayyid Jamal ad-Din "al-Afghani": a political biography*. Berkeley: University of California Press, 1972. ISBN 0-520-01986-5. ▸ Important, authoritative study of life of enigmatic, important political leader and intellectual who resisted European encroachment; based on contemporary sources. Argues his opposition to imperialism more important than his reformist goals. [GRG]

18.95 Nikki R. Keddie, ed. *Scholars, saints, and Sufis: Muslim religious institutions since 1500*. 1972 ed. Berkeley: University of California Press, 1978. ISBN 0-520-02027-8 (cl, 1972), 0-520-03644-1 (pbk). ▸ Argument that secularization and modernization have not eliminated importance of ᶜulamā' and Ṣūfī institutions. Significant collection of essays on these institutions in Middle East and Islamic Africa. [JOV]

18.96 Gilles Kepel. *Muslim extremism in Egypt: the prophet and pharaoh*. Jon Rothschild, trans. Berkeley: University of California Press, 1985. ISBN 0-520-05687-6. ▸ Examination of major organizations and movements of Islamic revival in Egypt in twentieth century. Covers small radical movements, popular preachers, major groups such as Muslim Brotherhood. Ideological content and political dimensions emphasized. [JOV]

18.97 Adel-Théodore Khoury. *Tendances et courants de l'Islam* *arabe contemporain.* Vol. 2: *Une modèle d'état islamique: l'Arabie saoudite.* Munich and Mainz: Kaiser and Matthias Grünewald Verlag, 1983. (Entwicklung und Frieden, Wissenschaftliche Reihe, 30.) ISBN 3-459-01524-1, 3-7867-1060-0. ▸ Study of Saudi state as Islamic model; its historical genesis, governmental system and institutions, law and justice, culture, international policy toward Muslims and non-Muslims. [CVF]

18.98   Jacob M. Landau. *The politics of pan-Islam: ideology and organization.* New York: Oxford University Press, 1990. ISBN 0-19-827709-1. ▸ Study of modern leaders and movements advocating political unity of Islamic world; not confined to Middle East. [JOV]

18.99   Nehemia Levtzion and John O. Voll, eds. *Eighteenth-century renewal and reform in Islam.* Syracuse, N.Y.: Syracuse University Press, 1987. ISBN 0-8156-2402-6. ▸ Islamic revivalism in different forms throughout Islamic world. Essays examine groups in Africa, Middle East, and South Asia. [JOV]

18.100   Charles Malik, ed. *God and man in contemporary Islamic thought: proceedings.* Beirut: Syracuse University Press for American University of Beirut, 1972. ISBN 0-8156-6035-9. ▸ Perceptions of human condition based on nature of Islamic faith. Collection of addresses by major Muslim thinkers and non-Muslim scholars with extensive thematic introduction showing diversity of views. [JOV]

18.101   Şerif Mardin. *Religion and social change in modern Turkey: the case of Bediüzzaman Said Nursi.* Albany: State University of New York Press, 1989. ISBN 0-88706-996-7 (cl), 0-88706-997-5 (pbk). ▸ Study of most controversial religious leader in republican Turkey. Sees his appeal in popular malaise over official secularism. [CVF]

18.102   B. G. Martin. *Muslim brotherhoods in nineteenth-century Africa.* Cambridge: Cambridge University Press, 1976. ISBN 0-521-21062-3. ▸ Şūfī brotherhoods as focus of Islamic revivalism in nineteenth-century Africa. Holy wars and puritanical reforms basic core, laying foundations for later nationalisms in Nigeria, Algeria, Libya, and Somalia. [JOV]

18.103   Richard P. Mitchell. *The society of the Muslim Brothers.* London: Oxford University Press, 1969. ▸ Influential interpretation of modern Islamic resurgence. Muslim Brotherhood in Egypt as exemplar of modern Muslim revivalism. Standard source for rise and development of Brotherhood. [JOV/AG]

18.104   Moojan Momen. *An introduction to Shīʿī Islam: the history and doctrines of Twelver Shīʿism.* New Haven: Yale University Press, 1985. ISBN 0-300-03499-7 (cl), 0-300-03531-4 (pbk). ▸ Survey of doctrine, practice, theology, popular religion, and religious scholars and individuals from seventh century to present. Important background for understanding contemporary role of religion and society in Iran. [GRG]

18.105   Thomas Naff and Roger Owen, eds. *Studies in eighteenth-century Islamic history.* Carbondale: Southern Illinois University Press, 1977. ISBN 0-8903-0819-3. ▸ Eighteenth century as dynamic, not simply corrupt period of Islamic history. Collection of essays on Ottoman and Iranian history, especially strong on ʿulamāʾ institutions and Islamic culture. [JOV]

18.106   Seyyed Hossein Nasr. *Traditional Islam in the modern world.* 1987 ed. London: Kegan Paul; distributed by Routledge Chapman and Hall, 1990. ISBN 0-7103-0177-4 (cl, 1987), 0-7103-0332-7 (pbk). ▸ Explanation of apologetic and fundamentalist Muslim approaches as simply reactions to West; authentic expressions of Islam involve more effective traditionalist interaction with modernity. By historian of Islamic science and philosopher. [JOV]

18.107   R. S. O'Fahey. *Enigmatic saint: Ahmad Ibn Idris and the Idrisi tradition.* Evanston, Ill.: Northwestern University Press, 1990. ISBN 0-8101-0910-7 (cl), 0-8101-0911-5 (pbk). ▸ Revivalist Islamic tradition of nineteenth century built on Şūfī teachings of North African scholar. Important reinterpretation of origins of African Islamic brotherhoods and modern development of Şūfism. [JOV]

18.108   James P. Piscatori. *Islam in a world of nation-states.* Cambridge: Cambridge University Press, 1986. ISBN 0-521-32985-X (cl), 0-521-33867-0 (pbk). ▸ Traditional Muslim political theory limits sovereignty of separate states, but territorial pluralism and nation-states developed in Islamic historical experience. Authoritative presentation of state formation in Islamic history. [JOV]

18.109   Fazlur Rahman. *Islam and modernity: transformation of an intellectual tradition.* Chicago: University of Chicago Press, 1982. (Publications of the Center for Middle Eastern Studies, 15.) ISBN 0-226-70283-9 (cl), 0-226-70284-7 (pbk). ▸ Assessment that traditionalist Muslim rigidity limits capacity for constructive modern intellectualism; flexible educational systems and broad moral principles based on Qurʾān needed. Liberal modernist Muslim perspective. [JOV]

18.110   Saiyid Athar Abbas Rizvi. *Shah Wali-Allah and his times: a study of eighteenth-century Islam, politics, and society in India.* Canberra: Maʿrifat, 1980. ISBN 0-949830-01-1. ▸ Standard work on major eighteenth-century thinker. Comprehensive in coverage, emphasizing impact on Islamic law and intellectual traditions. Notes impact of Wali-Allah's ideas from an Islamic scholarly perspective. [JOV]

18.111   Erwin I. J. Rosenthal. *Islam in the modern national state.* Cambridge: Cambridge University Press, 1965. ▸ Western secular nationalism created intellectual problems for Muslims. Impact of westernization on Islamic politics with country studies and discussions of constitutions, role of women, and education. Classic Western Orientalist approach. [JOV]

18.112   Reinhard Schulze. *Islamischer Internationalismus im zwanzigsten Jahrhundert: Untersuchungen zur Geschichte der islamischen Weltliga.* Leiden: Brill, 1990. ISBN 90-04-08286-7, ISSN 0085-6193. ▸ Ambitious study of Islamic internationalism as cultural phenomenon; Muslim World League (*Rabitat al-ʿalam al-Islami*), founded 1962 as organizational expression of internationalism. Discusses theological and ideological issues debated within league. [CVF]

18.113   Emmanuel Sivan. *Radical Islam: medieval theology and modern politics.* Rev. ed. New Haven: Yale University Press, 1990. ISBN 0-300-04914-5. ▸ Discussion of development of radical Sunnī Muslim fundamentalism with special emphasis on medieval ideological foundations laid by Ibn Taymiyyah. Relates rise to failure of secular socialist states and leftist ideologies. [JOV]

18.114   Wilfred Cantwell Smith. *Islam in modern history.* 1957 ed. Princeton: Princeton University Press, 1977. ISBN 0-691-03030-8 (cl), 0-691-01991-6 (pbk). ▸ Examination of issues of modernization in Muslim world. Very influential analysis of role of history in Islamic consciousness with case studies of Arab world, Turkey, Pakistan, and India. [JOV]

18.115   Tamara Sonn. *Between Qurʾan and crown: the challenge of political legitimacy in the Arab world.* Boulder: Westview, 1990. ISBN 0-8133-7579-7. ▸ Political legitimacy in modern Arab world involves clash between secular and Islamic systems, but synthesis possible. Historical approach presents traditional and contemporary conditions. [JOV]

18.116   Bassam Tibi. *The crisis of modern Islam: a preindustrial culture in the scientific-technological age.* Judith von Sivers, trans. Salt Lake City: University of Utah Press, 1988. ISBN 0-87480-299-7. ▸ Argument for replacing Western technological domination of Muslims with culturally pluralistic world society. Emphasis on belief systems as well as economic factors. Important modernist, secularist perspective. [JOV]

18.117 John O. Voll. *Islam: continuity and change in the modern world.* Boulder: Westview, 1982. ISBN 0-89158-931-7 (cl), 0-89158-983-x (pbk). ▸ Comprehensive introduction to Islamic movements in Middle East and beyond, from eighteenth century through Iranian Revolution. Interprets developments in terms of conservative, fundamentalist, and adaptationalist modes of experience. [JOV]

18.118 Gustave E. von Grunebaum. *Modern Islam: the search for cultural identity.* 1962 ed. Westport, Conn.: Greenwood, 1983. ISBN 0-313-24087-6. ▸ Clash between modern Western and traditional Islamic values. Standard source in Orientalist perspective, emphasizing dilemmas and problems. [JOV]

18.119 Michael Winter. *Society and religion in early Ottoman Egypt: studies in the writing of ʿAbd al-Wahhab al- Shaʿrani.* New Brunswick, N.J.: Transaction, 1982. ISBN 0-87855-351-7. ▸ Specialized study of al-Shaʿrani (1493–1565), major religious figure of early Ottoman Egypt, and his writings as source on religious, intellectual, and social history. [CVF]

Women

18.120 Nermin Abadan-Unat, Deniz Kandiyoti, and Mübeccel R. Kıray, eds. *Women in Turkish society.* Leiden: Brill, 1981. ISBN 90-04-06346-3 (pbk). ▸ Representative articles on gender issues: demographic, educational, occupational, religious, political, and class related. Extent and limits of progress after fifty years of official egalitarianism. [CVF]

18.121 Leila Ahmed. *Women and gender in Islam: historical roots of a modern debate.* New Haven: Yale University Press, 1992. ISBN 0-300-04942-0. ▸ Traces development of Islamic discourse on gender from rise of Islam. Focus on critical periods in elaboration of sex roles. Historicizes discussion of gender and Islam; welcome antidote to essentialist approach. [JET]

18.122 Lamya Al-Faruqi. *Women, Muslim society, and Islam.* Indianapolis: American Trust, 1988. ISBN 0-89259-068-8. ▸ Meaning of Islam for women. Overview of Islamic history and gender; gloss on Islamic texts. Islamist perspective arguing for Islamic feminism; good introduction. [JET]

18.123 Malek Alloula. *The colonial harem.* Myrna Godzich and Wlad Godzich, trans. Barbara Harlow, Introduction. Minneapolis: University of Minnesota Press, 1986. ISBN 0-8166-1383-4 (cl), 0-8166-1384-2 (pbk). ▸ Uses picture postcards, ca. 1900–25, of Algerian women to study French colonial vision of Algeria and indigenous reaction to that vision. Numerous illustrations, harem-veil-sexuality themes. Valuable demonstration of French Orientalism. [JET]

18.124 Ayad Al-Qazzaz. *Women in the Middle East and North Africa: an annotated bibliography.* Austin: University of Texas at Austin, Center for Middle Eastern Studies, 1977. (Middle Eastern monographs, 2.) ISBN 0-292-79009-0. ▸ Bibliography of Middle Eastern women; all English-language titles. Indexed by country and subject. Brief annotations for each title. [JET]

18.125 Soraya Altorki. *Women in Saudi Arabia: ideology and behavior among the elite.* New York: Columbia University Press, 1986. ISBN 0-231-06182-X (cl), 0-231-06183-8 (pbk). ▸ Groundbreaking study of family relationships and gender roles among elites in Jiddah. Focus on social changes over three generations since 1930s in household, social life, and sex roles. Rare insider view of Arabian family life. [WLO/JET]

18.126 Nayra Atiya. *Khul Khaal: five Egyptian women tell their stories.* Syracuse, N.Y.: Syracuse University Press, 1982. ISBN 0-8156-0177-8 (cl), 0-8156-0181-6 (pbk). ▸ First-person life narratives of five Egyptian women of different backgrounds, urban and rural, lower and middle class. Childhood, marriage, work, family life, beliefs, and aspirations. Lively and immediate. [JET]

18.127 Margot Badran. "Dual liberation: feminism and nationalism in Egypt, 1870s–1925." *Feminist issues* 8 (1988) 15–34. ISSN 0270-6679. ▸ Pioneering study of early Egyptian feminism, focusing on interaction of feminism and nationalism in Egypt, among upper- and middle-class Egyptian women. Connection between women in nationalist movement and erosion of harem. [JET]

18.128 Margot Badran and Miriam Cooke, eds. *Opening the gates: a century of Arab feminist writing.* Bloomington: Indiana University Press, 1990. ISBN 0-253-31121-7 (cl), 0-253-20577-8 (pbk). ▸ Anthology of Arab women's writing from 1880s to present, including essays, memoirs, short stories, and poems about women's experiences and gender relations. Indigenous feminism highlighted. Unique spectrum of women's writing. [JET]

18.129 Beth Baron and Nikki R. Keddie, eds. *Women in Middle Eastern history: shifting boundaries in sex and gender.* New Haven: Yale University Press, 1991. ISBN 0-300-05006-2. ▸ Seventeen papers on various aspects of sex and gender in Middle East history. Early Islamic and Mamluk periods, early modern and modern Turkey, Iran, and Arab world. Representative of current research. [JET]

18.130 Lois Beck and Nikki R. Keddie, eds. *Women in the Muslim world.* Cambridge, Mass.: Harvard University Press, 1978. ISBN 0-674-95480-7 (cl), 0-674-95481-5 (pbk). ▸ Pioneering papers discussing Muslim women in Arab world, Iran, Turkey, Pakistan, and China. Legal and social change, women and work, and religion and ideology. Historical and contemporary case studies. Good representation of work of 1970s. [GRG/JET]

18.131 Herbert L. Bodman, Jr., comp. *Women in the Muslim world: a bibliography of books and articles primarily in the English language.* Providence: Association for Middle East Women's Studies, 1991. ▸ Bibliography on women in Muslim world. Over 1,200 entries on women and Islam; Arab world; Turkey; Iran; Soviet Union; and South, Southeast, and East Asia. No annotations; index. [JET]

18.132 Juan Ricardo I. Cole. "Feminism, class, and Islam in turn-of-the-century Egypt." *International journal of Middle East studies* 13 (1981) 387–407. ISSN 0020-7438. ▸ Pathbreaking analysis of indigenous factors in Egyptian feminism. Emergence of indigenous feminism in late nineteenth-century Egypt in context of social change. Divergence of upper and lower middle classes on women's issues reflects different needs and responsibilities. [JET]

18.133 Fanny Davis. *The Ottoman lady: a social history from 1718 to 1918.* New York: Greenwood, 1986. ISBN 0-313-24811-7. ▸ Upper-class Ottoman women in eighteenth and nineteenth centuries. Family life, education, dress, political involvement, and contributions to architecture, arts, and literature. Wealth of empirical material, little analysis. [JET]

18.134 Nawal El Saadawi. *The hidden face of Eve: women in the Arab world, a personal account.* 1980 ed. Sherif Hetata, ed. and trans. Irene L. Gendzier, Introduction. Boston: Beacon, 1982. ISBN 0-8070-6701-6 (pbk). ▸ Collection of essays by prominent Egyptian feminist on history of female sexuality, clitoridectomy, women's movement, women's work, and the family. Provocative and personal. [JET]

18.135 John L. Esposito. *Women in Muslim family law.* Syracuse, N.Y.: Syracuse University Press, 1982. ISBN 0-8156-2256-2. ▸ Explores definition of women, gender in classical Muslim family law, and development of legal reform in modern period; specifics governing marriage, divorce, child custody, and inheritance. Pro-reform position of author evident. Useful summary of main developments. [JET]

18.136 Elizabeth Warnock Fernea, ed. *Women and the family in the Middle East: new voices of change.* Austin: University of Texas Press, 1985. ISBN 0-292-75528-7 (cl), 0-292-75529-5 (pbk). ▸ Papers, short stories, poetry, and interviews covering women, family, health, education, politics, law, religion, work, identity. Features voice of indigenous woman. Good broad selection. [JET]

18.137 Elizabeth Warnock Fernea and Basima Qattan Bezirgan, eds. *Middle Eastern Muslim women speak.* Austin: University of Texas Press, 1977. ISBN 0-292-75033-1 (cl), 0-292-75041-2 (pbk). ▸ Anthology of documents relevant to history, roles, and status of Muslim women. Good selection of primary materials including excerpts from Qur'ān, women's poetry, oral culture, interviews, and essays. [JET]

18.138 Erika Friedl. *Women of Deh Koh: lives in an Iranian village.* Washington, D.C.: Smithsonian Institution Press, 1989. ISBN 0-87474-400-8 (pbk). ▸ Insightful narrative of village life and views from women's perspective. Changing political context of Iran in 1970s and 1980s. [GRG]

18.139 Haim Gerber. "Social and economic position of women in an Ottoman city: Bursa, 1600–1700." *International journal of Middle East studies* 12 (1980) 231–44. ISSN 0020-7438. ▸ Position of women in seventeenth-century Anatolian town. Belies notion of all-oppressive patriarchal family; describes high economic profile of women in Ottoman towns and cities. Pioneering work in Islamic court records. [JET]

18.140 David C. Gordon. *Women of Algeria: an essay on change.* Cambridge, Mass.: Harvard University, Center for Middle Eastern Studies, 1968. (Harvard Middle Eastern monographs, 19.) ▸ Survey of women in modern Algerian history. French colonial policies, women in Algerian revolution, problems of independence. Much empirical material; modernization framework. [JET]

18.141 Lucie Duff Gordon. *Letters from Egypt.* 1946 rev. ed. London: Virago, 1983. ISBN 0-86068-379-3 (cl), 0-86068-379-6 (pbk). ▸ Letters of Englishwoman written 1862–69, during stay in Egypt. Rare record of male and female daily life in Lower and Upper Egypt. Good travel account describing women and gender issues. [JET]

18.142 Sarah Graham-Brown. *Images of women: the portrayal of women in photography of the Middle East, 1860–1950.* New York: Columbia University Press, 1988. ISBN 0-231-06826-3. ▸ History of photography of Middle Eastern women in contexts of Western domination; indigenous class, gender domination. Female as symbol of Orientalism, nationalism, westernization, and religion. Many striking photographs. [JET]

18.143 Mervat Hatem. "The politics of sexuality and gender in segregated patriarchal systems: the case of eighteenth- and nineteenth-century Egypt." *Feminist studies* 12.2 (1986) 251–74. ISSN 0046-3663. ▸ Comparative study of patriarchal systems. Argues nineteenth century gradually changed eighteenth-century system as colonialism added external source of tension. Original argument for unique gender system. [JET]

18.144 Lesley Hazleton. *Israeli women: the reality behind the myths.* New York: Simon & Schuster, 1977. ISBN 0-671-22531-6. ▸ Attack on myth of gender equality in discussion of Jewish Israeli women, early Zionist days to 1970. Focuses on women and sexuality, religion, marriage, procreation, and politics. Good general introduction. [JET]

18.145 Nadia Hijab. *Womanpower: the Arab debate on women at work.* Cambridge: Cambridge University Press, 1988. ISBN 0-521-26443-X (cl), 0-521-26992-X (pbk). ▸ History of integration of Arab women into labor force in twentieth century: legal status, development policies, and political rights. Highlights internal debates on women's roles and status. Strong overview of women's public roles. [JET]

18.146 Ronald C. Jennings. "Women in early seventeenth-century Ottoman judicial records." *Journal of the economic and social history of the Orient* 18 (1975) 53–114. ISSN 0022-4995. ▸ Path-breaking study of women's activities in Islamic court in seventeenth-century Anatolian city of Kayseri. Women's prominent role in property transactions, inheritance, and family problems. Some involvement in *waqf* (charitable foundations) and trade. [JET]

18.147 Çiğdem Kâğıtçıbaşı, ed. *Sex roles, family, and community in Turkey.* Bloomington: Indiana University, Turkish Studies, 1982. (Indiana University Turkish studies, 3.) ▸ Studies of family structure, sex roles, and change in familial and communal relations, urban and rural. [CVF]

18.148 Deniz Kandiyoti. "Emancipated but unliberated? Reflections on the Turkish case." *Feminist studies* 13.2 (1987) 317–38. ISSN 0046-3663. ▸ Methodological discussion of Islam as ideological system supporting corporate control of female sexuality. Culturally specific experience of gender modified by diversity and specificity of women's experiences in different Islamic societies. Stimulating new approach. [JET]

18.149 Deniz Kandiyoti, ed. *Women, Islam, and the state.* Philadelphia: Temple University Press, 1991. ISBN 0-87722-785-3 (cl), 0-87722-786-1 (pbk). ▸ Collection of papers on relationship between Islam, modern nation-states of Middle East and South Asia, and women. Includes Turkey, Iran, Egypt, Yemen, Iraq, Lebanon, Pakistan, and Bangladesh. Unique contribution to neglected topic. [JET]

18.150 Marnia Lazreg. "Feminism and difference: the perils of writing as a woman on women in Algeria." *Feminist studies* 14.1 (1988) 81–107. ISSN 0046-3663. ▸ Feminist discourse on women in Algeria. Problematic of representation of Eastern women in context of domination. General discussion of female intellectuals' roles in defining indigenous feminism. [JET]

18.151 Abraham Marcus. "Men, women, and property: dealers in real estate in eighteenth-century Aleppo." *Journal of the economic and social history of the Orient* 26 (1983) 137–63. ISSN 0022-4995. ▸ Confirms impressions of active female participation in urban real-estate market. Argues participation was search for security. Based on sound research in Islamic court records from Aleppo. [JET]

18.152 Fatima Mernissi. *Beyond the veil: male-female dynamics in a modern Muslim society.* Rev. ed. Bloomington: Indiana University Press, 1987. ISBN 0-253-31162-4 (cl), 0-253-20423-2 (pbk). ▸ Traditional Muslim views of women and female sexuality as seen through Islamic texts. Pre-Muslim social order more favorable to women. Explores gender relations in context of change in modern Morocco. Provocative view of a Moroccan feminist. [JET]

18.153 Fatima Mernissi, ed. *Doing daily battle: interviews with Moroccan women.* 1988 ed. Mary Jo Lakeland, trans. New Brunswick, N.J.: Rutgers University Press, 1989. ISBN 0-8135-1417-7 (cl), 0-8135-1418-5 (pbk). ▸ Based on oral histories of Moroccan women of different backgrounds: life in harem, factory, and countryside. Portraits of strong, self-assured women with powerful voices. [JET]

18.154 Mary Wortley Montagu. *The complete letters of Lady Mary Wortley Montagu.* Vol. 1: *1708–1720.* 3 vols. Robert Halsband, ed., pp. 304–427. Oxford: Clarendon, 1965–67. ▸ Most scholarly edition of letters from Englishwoman and traveler containing rare first-person descriptions of harems, including those of Ottoman dignitaries. One of better travel accounts for women's and gender issues. [JET]

18.155 Guity Nashat, ed. *Women and revolution in Iran.* Boulder: Westview, 1983. ISBN 0-86531-931-6 (pbk). ▸ Papers on women's role in 1979 Iranian Islamic Revolution; discusses historical and religious context of women, participation in Revolution, and condition under new regime in early 1980s. Broad treatment of critical events. [JET]

18.156 Cynthia Nelson. "The voices of Doria Shafik: feminist consciousness in Egypt, 1940–60." *Feminist issues* 6.2 (1986) 15–32. ISSN 0270-6679. ▸ Brief biography of Egyptian feminist of 1940s and 1950s and founder of journal *Bint al-Nil*. Feminism in relation to Islam and nationalism. Rare look at neglected period in women's history. [JET]

18.157 Michelle Raccagni. *The modern Arab woman: a bibliography.* Metuchen, N.J.: Scarecrow, 1978. ISBN 0-8108-1165-0. ▸ Bibliography of nearly three thousand titles on Arab women, including modern history. Titles in English, French, and Arabic. Includes Arabic periodical and newspaper articles; index. [JET]

18.158 Fatna A. Sabbah. *Woman in the Muslim unconscious.* New York: Pergamon, 1984. ISBN 0-08-031626-3 (cl), 0-08-031625-5 (pbk). ▸ Explores gender discourses shaping unconscious image of women in Muslim society. Fourteenth- and fifteenth-century erotica and Islamic texts used to delineate erotic and orthodox discourse on women and gender. Creative, original typology of gender discourse. [JET]

18.159 Eliz Sanasarian. *The women's rights movement in Iran: mutiny, appeasement, and repression from 1900 to Khomeini.* New York: Praeger, 1982. ISBN 0-275-90894-1 (cl), 0-275-91587-5 (pbk). ▸ Informative study of Iranian women's rights movement, including that of 1919–32 under Reza Shah; antishah movement; and first years of Islamic Republic. Mainly institutional and political narrative. [JET]

18.160 Rosemary Sayigh. "Roles and functions of Arab women: a reappraisal." *Arab studies quarterly* 3 (1981) 258–74. ISSN 0271-3519. ▸ Critique of Orientalist approach to study of Arab women among both Western and Arab scholars. Calls for new approach studying change in social formations and political and economic forces. [JET]

18.161 Huda Shaarawi. *Harem years: the memoirs of an Egyptian feminist (1879–1924).* 1986 ed. Margot Badran, ed. and trans. New York: Feminist Press at the City University of New York, 1987. ISBN 0-935-31271-4 (cl), 0-935-31270-6 (pbk). ▸ Memoirs of early Egyptian feminist: childhood in affluent harem; early married life; and first forays into politics, feminism, and nationalism. Good primary source. [JET]

18.162 Linda Usra Soffan. *The women of the United Arab Emirates.* New York: Barnes & Noble, 1980. ISBN 0-06-496396-9. ▸ Best available short account of law, tradition, education, economy, and government in relation to women of Gulf region. [WLO]

18.163 Barbara Swirski and Marilyn P. Safir, eds. *Calling the equality bluff: women in Israel.* New York: Teachers College Press, 1991. ISBN 0-8077-6250-4. ▸ Wide range of essays and documentation on problems of Jewish and non-Jewish women in Israel. Treats divorce and other issues of personal status under religious law, reproductive issues, political participation, military service, and women in the work force. [CVF]

18.164 Azar Tabari and Nahid Yeganeh, eds. *In the shadow of Islam: the women's movement in Iran.* London: Zed; distributed by Lawrence Hill, 1982. ISBN 0-86232-022-4 (cl), 0-86232-039-9 (pbk). ▸ Articles comprising feminist criticism of Islamic ideology and Islamic Republic. Discusses Islam and women's oppression, women's movement in Islamic Republic, and Khomeini on women. Includes rare documents from government, political parties, and women's groups. [GRG/JET]

18.165 Germaine Tillion. *The republic of cousins: women's oppression in Mediterranean society.* Quintin Hoare, trans. London: Al-

Saqi, 1983. ISBN 0-86356-100-4 (cl), 0-86356-010-5 (pbk). ▸ Attributes female oppression to endogamous marriage in Mediterranean cultural area. Sweeping survey of Paleolithic, ancient, Islamic, and contemporary Mediterranean society. [JET]

18.166 Judith E. Tucker. *Women in nineteenth-century Egypt.* Cambridge: Cambridge University Press, 1985. ISBN 0-521-30338-9 (cl), 0-521-31420-8 (pbk). ▸ Important, trailblazing treatment of women and gender in nineteenth-century rural and urban Egypt. Developments in female occupations, property holdings, women in protest politics, women and rise of the state, and slavery. Based on Islamic court records. [AG/JET]

ISLAMIC EMPIRES, 1500–1800

Ottoman Empire

18.167 Rifa'at Ali Abou-el-Haj. *The 1703 rebellion and the structure of Ottoman politics.* Leiden: Nederlands Historisch-Archaeologisch Instituut te Istanbul, 1984. (Uitgaven van het Nederlands Historisch-Archaeologisch Instituut te Istanbul, 52.) ISBN 90-6258-052-1 (pbk). ▸ Of numerous uprisings in Ottoman Istanbul, only one studied in English. Involved Janissaries, 'ulamā', and guilds. Prosopographic analysis of factional politics. Questions notions of decline and corruption in later Ottoman history. [CK]

18.168 Abdulhak Adnan Adivar. *La science chez les Turcs Ottomans.* Paris: Maisonneuve, 1939. ▸ Encyclopedic survey of rational sciences from fifteenth to nineteenth century. Dated but still useful. Only such work in any language. [CK]

18.169 Mustafa Âli. *Mustafa Âli's counsel for sultans of 1581.* 2 vols. Andreas Tietze, ed. and trans. Vienna: Verlag der Österreichischen Akademie der Wissenschaften, 1979–82. (Forschungen zur islamischen Philologie und Kulturgeschichte, 6–7. Denkschriften-Österreichische Akademie der Wissenschaften, Philosophisch-historische Klasse, 137, 158.) ISBN 3-7001-0288-7 (v. 1, pbk), 3-001-0518-5 (v. 2, pbk). ▸ Important forerunner of decline-reform treatises, listing disorders and remedies. Focus on abuse of authority and deviation from established rules, mixed with author's personal complaints and self-promotion. Excellent critical edition and translation. [CK]

18.170 Walter G. Andrews. *Poetry's voice, society's song: Ottoman lyric poetry.* Seattle: University of Washington Press, 1985. ISBN 0-295-96153-8. ▸ Pioneering literary criticism of classical poetry. Applies contemporary criticism to classical Ottoman poetry, including *ghazal* form (short lyric poem). Questions unbridged separation between elite and folk poetry on conceptual grounds rather than research. [CK]

18.171 Franz Babinger. *Mehmed the Conqueror and his time.* William C. Hickman, ed. Ralph Manheim, trans. Princeton: Princeton University Press, 1978. ISBN 0-691-09900-6. ▸ Exhaustive study of political and military events and Mehmed II's character. Extraordinary breadth of sources. Strong bias weakens analysis; to be read in conjunction with Inalcik's review in *Speculum* (1960). [CK]

18.172 Gabriel Baer. "The administrative, economic, and social functions of Turkish guilds." *International journal of Middle East studies* 1.1 (1970) 28–50. ISSN 0020-7438. ▸ Brief, broad, comprehensive look at different functions of Ottoman guilds, primarily those of Istanbul. Role in serving state and lack of autonomy emphasized here, challenged by others. [CK]

18.173 Karl K. Barbir. *Ottoman rule in Damascus, 1708–1758.* Princeton: Princeton University Press, 1980. ISBN 0-691-95297-2. ▸ Revisionist thesis arguing Ottoman rule in Damascus declined only from mid-1700s rather than throughout century. Based on Ottoman archival sources. [PSK/MCW]

18.174 Ömer Lutfi Barkan. "The price revolution of the sixteenth century: a turning point in the economic history of the

Near East." Justin McCarthy, trans. *International journal of Middle East studies* 6.1 (1975) 3–28. ISSN 0020-7438. ▸ Abbreviated translation of 1970 article. Establishes price series from late fifteenth to early seventeenth century, based on account books of religious foundations. Points to price revolution from 1584–85. Contested but still seminal. [CK]

18.175 Nicoara Beldiceanu. *Le timar dans l'État ottoman (debut XIVe–debut XVIe siècle).* Wiesbaden: Harrassowitz, 1980. ISBN 3-447-02103-9. ▸ Best available monograph on *timar*—type of landholding used mainly to compensate cavalry officers for services rendered—origins, evolution, and varieties. Thorough study of pivotal institution of classical Ottoman land tenure; almost no discussion of social life. [CK]

18.176 Benjamin Braude and Bernard Lewis, eds. *Christians and Jews in the Ottoman empire: the functioning of a plural society.* 2 vols. New York: Holmes & Meier, 1982. ISBN 0-8419-0519-3 (v. 1), 0-8419-0520-7 (v. 2). ▸ Collection of articles on various aspects of Jewish and Christian communities in Ottoman empire. Controversial period from fifteenth to twentieth century. Revises conventional ideas about interfaith relations (millet system). [AR/CK/CVF]

18.177 Evliya [Çelebi]. *Evliya Çelebi in Bitlis: the relevant section of the "Seyahatname."* Robert Dankoff, ed. and trans. Leiden: Brill, 1990. (Evliya Çelebi's *Book of Travels*: the land and people of Ottoman empire in the seventeenth century: a corpus of partial editions, 2.) ISBN 90-04-09242-0. ▸ Fascinating account of eastern Anatolian town by seventeenth-century traveler. Informative on social life of town, its trades, and languages and on local (Kurdish) ruler, his cultural patronage, and relations with central state. [CK]

18.178 Evliya [Çelebi]. *Evliya Çelebi in Diyarbekir: the relevant section of the "Seyahatname."* Martin van Bruinessen and Hendrik Boeschoten, eds. and trans. Leiden: Brill, 1988. (Evliya Çelebi's *Book of Travels*: the land and people of the Ottoman Empire in the seventeenth century; a corpus of partial editions, 1.) ISBN 90-04-08165-8. ▸ Valuable seventeenth-century account of eastern Anatolia, with much information on physical description, government, society, economy, and languages. [CVF]

18.179 Evliya [Çelebi]. *The intimate life of an Ottoman statesman, Melek Ahmed Pasha (1588–1662): as portrayed in Evliya Çelebi's "Book of Travels" (Seyahat-name).* Robert Dankoff, trans. Rhoads Murphey, Introduction. Albany: State University of New York Press, 1991. ISBN 0-7914-0640-7 (cl), 0-7914-0641-5 (pbk). ▸ Rare detailed biography of a vizier. Glimpses into intimate life of Melek Ahmed Pasha, relative and patron of Evliya. Details of marriage to princess and records of dreams. [CK]

18.180 Suraiya Faroqhi. *Men of modest substance: house owners and house property in seventeenth-century Ankara and Kayseri.* Cambridge: Cambridge University Press, 1987. ISBN 0-521-32629-X. ▸ Pioneering social history of housing in two Anatolian towns based on court records, mostly sale contracts. Shape and units of residences, prices, owners; ethnic, gender, and class factors. [CK]

18.181 Suraiya Faroqhi. *Towns and townsmen in Ottoman Anatolia: trade, crafts, and food production in an urban setting, 1520–1650.* Cambridge: Cambridge University Press, 1984. ISBN 0-521-25447-7. ▸ Detailed, informative tableau of production and exchange of various goods in Anatolian towns: roads, ports, communications, and markets. Relations to agricultural hinterland. [CK]

18.182 Cornell F. Fleischer. *Bureaucrat and intellectual in the Ottoman empire: the historian Mustafa Âli (1541–1600).* Princeton: Princeton University Press, 1986. ISBN 0-691-05464-9. ▸ Unique intellectual biography covering career and writings of bureaucrat-writer and pioneer of decline discourse. Discussion of major

related issues, e.g., relations between religious and dynastic law and Islamic and Turco-Mongol traditions. [CK]

18.183 Haim Gerber. *Economy and society in an Ottoman city: Bursa, 1600–1700.* Jerusalem: Hebrew University, Institute of Asian and African Studies, 1988. ISBN 965-223-388-9. ▸ Socioeconomic life of western Anatolian town, based on court records. Demographics, guilds, industries, agricultural investment, trade, credit relations, and pious foundations. Enlightening examination of legal system and different principles of law in practice. [CK]

18.184 Daniel Goffman. *Izmir and the Levantine world, 1550–1650.* Seattle: University of Washington Press, 1990. ISBN 0-295-96932-6. ▸ Convincing description of emergence of Izmir as important link in Middle Eastern–Mediterranean commerce. Role of administration and different communities. Based on Ottoman and European archival records. [CK]

18.185 Godfrey Goodwin. *A history of Ottoman architecture.* 1971 ed. New York: Thames & Hudson, 1987. ISBN 0-500-27429-0 (pbk). ▸ Extensive survey of Ottoman architecture. Chronologically organized; ground plans and photographs of major buildings. [CK]

18.186 William J. Griswold. *The great Anatolian rebellion, 1000–1020/1591–1611.* Berlin: Schwarz, 1983. (Islamkundliche Untersuchungen, 83.) ISBN 3-922968-34-1. ▸ Only monograph in English on cataclysmic Jelali revolts in late sixteenth- and early seventeenth-century Anatolian–North Syrian countryside. Emphasizes political, administrative, and military aspects. [CK]

18.187 Alexander H. de Groot. *The Ottoman empire and the Dutch Republic: a history of the earliest diplomatic relations, 1610–1630.* Leiden: Nederlands Historisch-Archaeologisch Instituut te Istanbul, 1978. (Uitgaven van het Nederlands Historisch-Archaeologisch Instituut te Istanbul, 43.) ISBN 90-6258-043-2. ▸ Political-diplomatic history of establishment of Ottoman-Dutch relations; turning point, along with slightly earlier arrival of English, in commercial history of eastern Mediterranean. Contains texts of treaties. Somewhat old fashioned but very useful. [CK]

18.188 Frederick William Hasluck. *Christianity and Islam under the sultans.* 1929 ed. 2 vols. New York: Octagon Books, 1973. ISBN 0-374-93747-8. ▸ Collection of studies on religious beliefs and practices among Muslims and Christians in Anatolia and Balkans. Pioneering study combining history and ethnography. Focus on popular cults and syncretism. [CK]

18.189 Ralph S. Hattox. *Coffee and coffeehouses: the origins of a social beverage in the medieval Near East.* 1985 ed. Seattle: University of Washington Press, 1988. ISBN 0-295-96231-3 (pbk). ▸ Traces evolution from plant to beverage to social custom and institution. Focus on Arab cities and Istanbul. Analyzes ensuing legal-ethical discussion. Original, though not deeply researched, account of fascinating subject. [CK]

18.190 Andrew C. Hess. *The forgotten frontier: a history of the sixteenth-century Ibero-African frontier.* Chicago: University of Chicago Press, 1978. (Publications of the Center for Middle Eastern Studies, 10.) ISBN 0-226-33028-1. ▸ Emergence of Turco-Muslim and Latin Christian cultural-political spheres in Mediterranean emphasizing difference and separation; contra Braudel 6.26. Impact of firearms on North Africa and Ottoman-Habsburg struggles. [CK]

18.191 Uriel Heyd. *Studies in old Ottoman criminal law.* V. L. Ménage, ed. Oxford: Clarendon, 1973. ISBN 0-19-825312-5. ▸ Useful introduction to Ottoman legal system, particularly criminal law. Texts (and translations) of samples from various codes (*kanunname*). Only work on subject in any European language. [CK]

18.192 Wolf-Dieter Hütteroth and Kamal Abdulfattah. *Historical geography of Palestine, Transjordan, and southern Syria in the late sixteenth century.* Erlangen: Selbstverlag der fränkischen geographischen Gesellschaft in Kommission bei Palm & Enke, 1977. (Erlanger Geographische Arbeiten, Sonderband, 5.) ISBN 3-920-40541-2. ‣ Innovative geographical study based on detailed registers (*defter-i mufassal*) of Ottoman land registry system. [CVF]

18.193 Colin Imber. *The Ottoman empire, 1300–1481.* Istanbul: Isis, 1990. ISBN 975-428-015-0. ‣ Basic work; attempts to establish chronology for early Ottoman history. [CVF]

18.194 Halil Inalcik. *The Ottoman empire: the classical age, 1300–1600.* 1973 ed. Norman Itzkowitz and Colin Imber, trans. New Rochelle, N.Y.: Caratzas, 1989. ISBN 0-89241-388-3. ‣ Surveys rise and expansion, classical administration; military, land regime, legal system, and social structure; and beginnings of postclassical transformation by dean of Ottoman historians. [CK]

18.195 Halil Inalcik. *The Ottoman empire: conquest, organization, and economy.* London: Variorum, 1978. ISBN 0-86078-032-5. ‣ Seminal articles (published 1954–76) on methods of conquest, Mehmed II's policy toward Istanbul after conquest, taxation and land regime, law under Suleyman the Lawgiver, economy and commerce, firearms, and decline and reform. [CK]

18.196 Halil Inalcik. *Studies in Ottoman social and economic history.* London: Variorum, 1985. ISBN 0-86078-162-3. ‣ Collection of seminal articles (published 1969–84) on emergence of Ottoman state, Crimean khanate, impact of Annales school, military-fiscal transformation, rice cultivation, servile labor, *chiftliks* (estates), markets, and metrology. [CK]

18.197 Ronald C. Jennings. "Loans and credit in early seventeenth-century Ottoman judicial records: the *sharia* court of Anatolian Kayseri." *Journal of the economic and social history of the Orient* 16.2 (1973) 168–216. ISSN 0022-4995. ‣ Study of mechanisms and networks of credit in Anatolian town, treating class, gender, and ethnic factors. One of author's numerous, pioneering explorations among Islamic court records. [CK]

18.198 Cemal Kafadar. "Self and others: the diary of a dervish in seventeenth-century Istanbul and first-person narratives in Ottoman literature." *Studia Islamica* 69 (1989) 121–50. ISSN 0585-5292. ‣ Introduction to and analysis of unusual source: dervish's diary, detailed record of his social life for four years (1660–64). Surveys other first-person narratives before westernization. Cultural history. [CK]

18.199 M. Fuad Köprülü. *The origins of the Ottoman empire.* Gary Leiser, ed. and trans. Albany: State University of New York Press, 1992. ISBN 0-7914-0819-1. ‣ Seminal work by major Turkish scholar of early twentieth century. Important for ongoing controversy about origins of Ottoman empire. Originally published as *Les origines de l'Empire ottoman* (1935). [CVF]

18.200 I. Metin Kunt. *The sultan's servants: the transformation of Ottoman provincial government, 1550–1650.* New York: Columbia University Press, 1983. ISBN 0-231-05578-1. ‣ Transformation of Ottoman provincial administration and its relations with center, traced by analyzing appointment registers. Recruitment, promotion, and conditions of service of governors. Rise of household networks to dominance in political life. Succinct and convincing. [CK]

18.201 Aptullah Kuran. *Sinan: the grand old master of Ottoman architecture.* Ara Güler and Mustafa Niksarli, Photographers. Washington, D.C.: Institute of Turkish Studies, 1987. ISBN 0-941469-00-X. ‣ First comprehensive treatment of most famous Ottoman architect, including discussion of stylistic development. Accurate plans and photographs; catalog of hundreds of buildings built by and attributed to Sinan in appendix. [CK]

18.202 Rudi Paul Lindner. *Nomads and Ottomans in medieval Anatolia.* Bloomington: Indiana University, Research Institute for Inner Asian Studies, 1983. (Uralic and Altaic series, 144.) ISBN 0-933070-12-8. ‣ Revisionist study of rise of Ottoman state with analysis of Ottoman policy vis-à-vis pastoralists. Stimulating but not always convincing case study of horse drovers of Central Anatolia. Explains appeal of Safavids in sixteenth century. Challenges Gaza (holy war) thesis. [CK]

18.203 Robert Mantran. *Istanbul dans la seconde moitié du dix-septième siècle.* Paris: Maisonneuve, 1962. (Bibliothèque de l'Institut Français d'Études Anatoliennes d'Istanbul, 12.) ‣ Detailed study of Istanbul's population, ethnosocial structure, administration, economy, and trade in latter part of seventeenth century. Shorter, more popular version (also in French) focuses on daily life. [CK]

18.204 Robert Mantran, ed. *Histoire de l'Empire ottoman.* Paris: Fayard, 1989. ISBN 2-213-01956-8. ‣ Most recent attempt at comprehensive history of empire. Chapters by France's Ottomanists, examining political, diplomatic, institutional, regional, intellectual, and cultural history; chapters uneven in quality. [CVF]

18.205 Abraham Marcus. *The Middle East on the eve of modernity: Aleppo in the eighteenth century.* New York: Columbia University Press, 1989. ISBN 0-231-06594-9. ‣ Innovative social history of Aleppo in eighteenth century, based on court records. Population, social structure, administration, economy, industries, guilds, popular culture, charity, health, public services, and neighborhood life. [CK]

18.206 Bruce Masters. *The origins of Western economic dominance in the Middle East: mercantilism and the Islamic economy in Aleppo, 1600–1750.* New York: New York University Press, 1988. ISBN 0-8147-5435-X. ‣ Heyday of Aleppo as trade entrepôt until its decline. Discusses vitality of Asian caravan trade, trading communities and commercial practices. Interesting thesis concerning differences between mercantilist and "Islamic" approaches to economy. [CK]

18.207 Bruce McGowan. *Economic life in Ottoman Europe: taxation, trade, and the struggle for land, 1600–1800.* Cambridge and Paris: Cambridge University Press and Éditions de la Maison des Sciences de l'Homme, 1981. ISBN 0-521-25208-8. ‣ Annales-influenced economic history of Ottoman Balkans, discussing international trade, land use, estate formation, taxation, and demography. Case study of Macedonian town based on court records. Sheds light on several unresolved issues in agrarian and demographic history of postclassical age. [CK]

18.208 Gülru Necipoğlu. *Architecture, ceremonial, and power: the Topkapı palace in the fifteenth and sixteenth centuries.* Cambridge, Mass.: MIT Press, 1991. ISBN 0-262-14050-0. ‣ Reconstructs original design and sixteenth-century evolution of main palace as royal residence and seat of government. Analyzes meaning in original context and in relation to state ideology and ceremony. [CK]

18.209 Omeljan Pritsak. "Das erste türkisch-ukrainische Bündnis (1648)." *Oriens* 6 (1953) 266–98. ISSN 0078-6527. ‣ Background and sources for crucial juncture in Ottoman involvement in northern Black Sea. Provides context of relations with Poland, Ukraine, Crimea, and Russia. [CK]

18.210 Abdul-Karim Rafeq. *The province of Damascus, 1723–1783.* Beirut: Khayat, 1966. ‣ Pioneering examination of decline of Ottoman rule in Damascus province in eighteenth century and emergence of local power groups in city and countryside. Based on wide variety of local Arabic chronicles and biographical dictionaries. [PSK/MCW]

18.211 André Raymond. *Artisans et commerçants au Caire au dix-huitième siècle.* 2 vols. Damascus: Institut Français de Damas, 1973–74. ‣ Exhaustive, reliable study of Cairene crafts and commerce in eighteenth century. Traces larger trends in Red Sea and Mediterranean commerce. Statistical analyses of prices, currencies, and commodities, especially coffee. Also discusses guild structure and relations between artisans and military. [CK]

18.212 Richard C. Repp. *The mufti of Istanbul: a study of the development of the Ottoman learned hierarchy.* London: Ithaca Press for the Oxford Board of the Faculty of Oriental Studies; distributed by Humanities Press, 1986. (Oxford Oriental Institute monographs, 8.) ISBN 0-86372-041-2. ▸ Evolution of top office in Ottoman scholarly hierarchy from mid-fifteenth to late sixteenth century. Focus on individual careers, often with excessive detail on specifics. Glimpses into higher education and linkages between scholarly and administrative functions. [CK]

18.213 Michael Rogers. "The state and the arts in Ottoman Turkey. *Part 1:* The stones of Süleymaniye. *Part 2:* The furniture and decoration of Süleymaniye." *International journal of Middle East studies* 14 (1982) 71–86, 283–313. ISSN 0020-7438. ▸ Analyzes issues raised by Barkan's monumental work in Turkish on construction of Süleymaniye mosque complex (1550–57). Rigorous institutional, technological, and terminological discussion of building activity and architectural practice. [CK]

18.214 Clarence Dana Rouillard. *The Turk in French history, thought, and literature (1520–1660).* 1936 ed. New York: AMS Press, 1973. ISBN 0-404-56321-X. ▸ Broadly researched, detailed study of image of Turks in early modern French culture. [CK]

18.215 Stanford J. Shaw. *Empire of the gazis: the rise and decline of the Ottoman empire, 1280–1808.* Vol. I of *History of the Ottoman empire and modern Turkey.* Cambridge: Cambridge University Press, 1976. 2 vols. ISBN 0-521-21280-4 (v. I). ▸ General history of the period. [CVF]

18.216 Stanford J. Shaw. *The financial and administrative organization and development of Ottoman Egypt, 1517–1798.* 1958 ed. Princeton: Princeton University Press, 1962. ▸ Detailed analysis of Egyptian treasury revenues and expenditures over three centuries. Surplus as revenues of the Istanbul government (Sublime Porte). Informative on governors, military, administrative structures, and changes. [CK]

18.217 Lewis V. Thomas. *A study of Naima.* Norman Itzkowitz, ed. New York: New York University Press, 1972. ISBN 0-8147-8150-0. ▸ Study of life and ideas of Ottoman historian Naima (d. 1716), author of important six-volume chronicle spanning late sixteenth to early eighteenth century. Pioneering intellectual history. Sample translations. [CK]

18.218 Speros Vryonis, Jr. *The decline of medieval Hellenism in Asia Minor and the process of islamization from the eleventh through the fifteenth century.* Berkeley: University of California Press, 1971. (UCLA publications of the Center for Medieval and Renaissance Studies, 4.) ISBN 0-520-01597-5. ▸ Transformation of Anatolia from Byzantine core province into Turkish heartland; elimination of unified Christian rule, nomadic incursions, and recurrent warfare as major factors. [CVF]

18.219 Madeline C. Zilfi. *The politics of piety: the Ottoman ulema in the post classical age, 1600–1800.* Minneapolis: Bibliotheca Islamica, 1988. ISBN 0-88297-042-9. ▸ Successful demonstration of emergence of ʿulamā' aristocracy through monopolization of top legal-scholarly offices by a few families. Includes analysis of Kadizadeli phenomenon, seventeenth-century ultra-Orthodox movement. [CK]

SEE ALSO
21.220 Amnon Cohen. *Jewish life under Islam.*

Safavid Empire and Eighteenth-Century Iran

18.220 Adel Allouche. *The origins and development of the Ottoman-Safavid conflict (906–962/1500–1555).* Berlin: Schwarz,

1983. (Islamkundliche Untersuchungen, 91.) ISBN 3-922968-31-7. ▸ Essay on first phase of Ottoman-Safavid relations down to Peace of Amasya (1555). Conflict viewed in regional context. [JW]

18.221 Said Amir Arjomand. *The shadow of God and the hidden imam: religion, political order, and societal change in Shiite Iran from the beginning to 1890.* Chicago: University of Chicago Press, 1984. (Publications of the Center for Middle Eastern Studies, 17.) ISBN 0-226-02782-1 (cl), 0-226-02784-8 (pbk). ▸ Sociological and historical study of rise and development of Safavid Shiism based on rigorous analysis of religious and political normative and narrative sources. [JW]

18.222 Jean-Louis Bacqué-Grammont. *Les Ottomans, les Safavides, et leurs voisins: contribution à l'histoire des relations internationales dans l'Orient islamique de 1514 à 1524.* Istanbul: Nederlands Historisch-Archaeologisch Instituut te Istanbul, 1987. (Publications de l'Institut Historique et Archéologique Néerlandais de Stamboul, 56.) ISBN 90-6258-056-4. ▸ Ottoman-Safavid relations, 1514–24. Uses previously unpublished documents from Ottoman archives. [JW]

18.223 L. L. Bellan. *Chah ʿAbbas I: sa vie, son histoire.* Paris: Paul Guethner, 1932. ▸ Political biography of most outstanding Safavid ruler. Heavily dependent on official court chronicle of period. [JW]

18.224 Edward Granville Browne. *A literary history of Persia.* Vol. 4: *Modern times, 1500–1924.* 1928 ed. Cambridge: Cambridge University Press, 1969. ISBN 0-521-04346-8. ▸ Neither political history nor literary history. Useful survey of literary and intellectual developments in context of politics and history. [JW]

18.225 Elke Eberhard. *Osmanische Polemik gegen die Safawiden im sechzehnten Jahrhundert nach arabischen Handschriften.* Freiburg: Schwarz, 1970. (Islamkundliche Untersuchungen, 3.) ▸ Study of political-religious ideology of Ottoman-Safavid conflict. [JW]

18.226 Masashi Haneda. *Le chah et les qizilbas: le système militaire safavide.* 1986 ed. Berlin: Schwarz, 1987. (Islamkundliche Untersuchungen, 119.) ISBN 3-922968-61-9. ▸ Analysis of internal struggle between centralizing administration and decentralizing tribally-based military. [JW]

18.227 Walther Hinz. *Irans Aufstieg zum Nationalstaat im fünfzehnten Jahrhundert.* Berlin: de Gruyter, 1936. ▸ Dated but well-documented and useful study of social and religious prehistory of Safavids. [JW]

18.228 *The Houghton Shahnameh.* 2 vols. Martin B. Dickson and Stuart Cary Welch, Introductions. Cambridge, Mass.: Harvard University, Fogg Art Museum, 1981. ISBN 0-674-40854-3. ▸ Remarkable collaboration between historian and art historian to introduce especially outstanding illuminated manuscript of Firdawsi's *Shahnameh* (Book of Kings), Iranian national epic. [JW]

18.229 Peter Jackson and Laurence Lockhart, eds. *The Timurid and Safavid periods.* Vol. 6 of *The Cambridge history of Iran.* Cambridge: Cambridge University Press, 1986. ISBN 0-521-20094-6 (v. 6). ▸ Standard introductory work; uneven treatment. Chapters on all aspects of Iranian history, fifteenth to seventeenth centuries: diplomacy, politics, society, economy, religion, and culture. [DSS]

18.230 Mehdi Keyvani. *Artisans and guild life in the later Safavid period: contribution to the social-economic history of Persia.* Berlin: Schwarz, 1982. (Islamkundliche Untersuchungen, 65.) ISBN 3-922968-10-4 (pbk). ▸ Survey of basic practices, institutions, and forms of trade and industry. Emphasis on political and social roles of voluntary organizations. [JW]

18.231 Ann K. S. Lambton. *Landlord and peasant in Persia: a*

study of land tenure and land revenue administration. 1969 rev. ed. London: Taurus; distributed by St. Martin's, 1991. ISBN 1-85043-293-7. ▸ Classic study of Iranian agrarian regime and forms of taxation. [JW]

18.232 Laurence Lockhart. *The fall of the Safavi dynasty and the Afghan occupation of Persia.* Cambridge: Cambridge University Press, 1958. ▸ Discussion of internal and external factors in collapse of Safavid power. [JW]

18.233 Laurence Lockhart. *Nadir Shah: a critical study based mainly upon contemporary sources.* 1938 ed. New York: AMS Press, 1973. ISBN 0-404-56290-6. ▸ Political biography of founder of Afshars, first Safavid successor state. Political, military, and religious factors emphasized. [JW]

18.234 Michel M. Mazzaoui. *The origins of the Safawids: Šīʿism, Sufism, and the Ghulat.* Wiesbaden: Steiner, 1972. (Freiburger Islamstudien, 3.) ▸ Sectarian developments leading up to establishment of Safavid state. [JW]

18.235 Robert W. Olson. *The siege of Mosul and Ottoman-Persian relations, 1718–1743: a study of rebellion in the capital and war in the provinces of the Ottoman empire.* Bloomington: Indiana University Press, 1975. ISBN 0-87750-183-1. ▸ Later period of Ottoman-Safavid relations. Nadir Shah's campaigns against Ottomans shown primarily from Ottoman viewpoint. [JW]

18.236 Barbara von Palombini. *Bündniswerben abendländischer Mächte um Persien, 1453–1600.* Wiesbaden: Steiner, 1968. (Freiburger Islamstudien, 1.) ▸ Europe's search for allies in East to aid in struggle against Ottoman empire. [JW]

18.237 John R. Perry. *Karim Khan Zand: a history of Iran, 1747–1779.* Chicago: University of Chicago Press, 1979. (Publications of the Center for Middle Eastern Studies, 12.) ISBN 0-226-66098-2. ▸ Comprehensive picture of complex situation in post–Nadir Shah period. [JW]

18.238 James J. Reid. *Tribalism and society in Islamic Iran, 1500–1629.* Malibu, Calif.: Undena, 1983. ISBN 0-89003-125-8 (cl), 0-89003-124-X (pbk). ▸ Flawed but useful study of social dynamics of Safavid state to death of Shah ʿAbbas I. Prosopographical data important. [JW]

18.239 Riazul Islam. *Indo-Persian relations: a study of the political and diplomatic relations between the Mughul empire and Iran.* Tehran: Iran Culture Foundation, 1970. (Publications of the Iranian Culture Foundation, 93. Sources of the history and geography of Iran, 32.) ▸ Account of Safavid-Mughal relations during reign of each emperor. [JW]

18.240 K. M. Röhrborn. *Provinzen und Zentralgewalt Persiens im sechzehnten und siebzehnten Jahrhundert.* Berlin: de Gruyter, 1966. (Studien zur Sprache, Geschichte und Kultur des islamischen Orients, Beihefte zur *Zeitschrift der Islam*, n.F., 2.) ▸ Survey of Safavid central and provincial administration based on normative and narrative sources. [JW]

18.241 Ghulam Sarwar. *History of Shah Ismaʿil Safawi.* 1939 ed. New York: AMS Press, 1975. ISBN 0-404-56322-8. ▸ Political biography of founder of Safavid dynasty, based mainly on official narrative sources. [JW]

18.242 Roger M. Savory. *Iran under the Safavids.* Cambridge: Cambridge University Press, 1980. ISBN 0-521-22483-7. ▸ Superficial but useful survey of politics, administration, religion, foreign relations, and culture in Safavid period. [JW]

18.243 Sibylla Schuster-Walser. *Das safawidische Persien im Spiegel europäischer Reiseberichte (1502–1722).* Baden-Baden: Grim, 1970. ▸ Overview of European attitudes toward Safavids expressed in travel literature. Important source for synthetic studies of period. [JW]

Peripheral Regions, 1500–1800: Arabian Peninsula

18.244 Ahmad Mustafa Abu Hakima. *History of eastern Arabia, 1750–1800: the rise and development of Bahrain and Kuwait.* Beirut: Khayat, 1965. ▸ Persian Gulf region from 1700 to 1800 with emphasis on tribal and commercial factors. Best available study on domestic rather than foreign events. [WLO]

18.245 Husayn ibn Abdullah al-Amri. *The Yemen in the eighteenth and nineteenth centuries: a political and intellectual history.* London: Ithaca Press for the University of Durham, Centre for Middle Eastern and Islamic Studies, 1985. (Durham Middle East monographs, 1.) ISBN 0-86372-032-3. ▸ North Yemen from 1753 to 1835, including study of thought of Muhammad ibn Ali ibn Muhammad al-Shawkani (1760–1834). Thorough examination of traditional politics and religion. [WLO]

18.246 Robin L. Bidwell. *Travellers in Arabia.* London: Hamlyn, 1976. ISBN 0-600-32900-3. ▸ Introduction to all major European visitors to Arabia. Valuable summaries of their observations and useful illustrations. [WLO]

18.247 Juan Ricardo I. Cole. "Rival empires of trade and Imami Shiʿism in eastern Arabia, 1300–1800." *International journal of Middle East studies* 19.2 (1987) 177–204. ISSN 0020-7438. ▸ Political and religious competition between Portuguese, Ottomans, Safavids, and indigenous groups in Persian Gulf region. Concentrates on Bahrain. Welcome synthesis of scattered sources on neglected period and region. [WLO]

18.248 Gerald De Gaury. *Rulers of Mecca.* 1954 ed. New York: AMS Press, 1982. ISBN 0-404-16517-6. ▸ Hashimite emirs of Mecca from 1185 to 1925. Political intrigues and some information on Egyptian and Ottoman involvement. Traditional political narrative. [WLO]

18.249 John Hansman. *Julfar, an Arabian port: its settlement and Far Eastern ceramic trade from the fourteenth to the eighteenth centuries.* London: Royal Asiatic Society of Great Britain and Ireland, 1985. ISBN 0-947593-01-2. ▸ Archaeological survey of Ra's al-Khaimah, United Arab Emirates, and trade contacts with China. Important example of use of archaeology for early modern Middle Eastern history. [WLO]

18.250 Eric Macro. *Yemen and the Western world since 1571.* New York: Praeger, 1968. ▸ Summary of European–North Yemeni relations to 1967. Basic, substantial discussion of Ottoman-British border dispute. [WLO]

18.251 Jon E. Mandaville. "The Ottoman province of al-Hasa in the sixteenth and seventeenth centuries." *Journal of the American Oriental Society* 90.3 (1970) 486–513. ISSN 0003-0279. ▸ Ottoman rule in eastern Arabia from 1550 to 1670 based on Istanbul archives. Covers Portuguese relations, local groups, imperial administration. Pioneering work showing value of Ottoman sources for Arab history. [WLO]

18.252 Sultan ibn Muhammad al-Qasimi. *The myth of Arab piracy in the Gulf.* 2d ed. London: Routledge, 1988. ISBN 0-415-02973-2. ▸ Provocative, revisionist review of eighteenth-century Persian Gulf history, British and Indian involvements, and destruction of Qasimi naval power in early nineteenth century. Based on British and Indian documents. [WLO]

18.253 Patricia Risso. *Oman and Muscat: an early modern history.* New York: St. Martin's, 1986. ISBN 0-312-58434-2. ▸ Emergence of relatively secular government at Muscat, 1749–1804. Examines commercial wealth and Al Bu Saʿid dynasty. Stimulating reexamination of eighteenth-century decline paradigm for lower Persian Gulf. [WLO]

18.254 Kamal S. Salibi. *A history of Arabia.* Delmar, N.Y.: Caravan, 1980. ISBN 0-88206-036-8. ▸ Introductory survey of Arabian peninsula history from antiquity through rise of Islam, Ottoman period, and independence. Valuable short bibliography. Best beginning work for study of Arabian history. [WLO]

18.255 Robert B. Serjeant. *The Portuguese off the South Arabian coast: Hadrami chronicles with Yemeni and European accounts of Dutch pirates off Mocha in the seventeenth century.* 1963 ed. Beirut: Librairie du Liban, 1974. ISBN 0-8426-0708-0. ‣ Specialist description of South Arabian society and history, contacts with Portuguese, and traditional chroniclers' views of this interaction. [WLO]

18.256 Abd al-Qadir ibn Ahmad al-Shafiʿi [Ibn Faraj]. *Bride of the Red Sea: a tenth/sixteenth-century account of Jeddah.* G. Rex Smith and Ahmad Umar al-Zaylaʿi, eds. and trans. Durham, England: University of Durham, Centre for Middle Eastern and Islamic Studies, 1984. (Centre for Middle Eastern and Islamic Studies, Occasional papers series, 22.) ISSN 0307-0654. ‣ English and Arabic texts of manuscript on city of Jiddah, its mosques, and fortifications. One of few translations available for this time and region. Useful as introduction to traditional history. [WLO]

18.257 John O. Voll. "Hadith scholars and *tariqahs*: an *ulama* group in the eighteenth-century Haramayn and their impact in the Islamic world." *Journal of Asian and African studies* 15.3–4 (1980) 264–73. ISSN 0021-9096. ‣ Islamic religious thought in Mecca and Medina and its spread to other regions. Significant revision of eighteenth-century decline hypothesis for Islamic societies through analysis of neo-Ṣūfī Islamic mysticism. [WLO]

18.258 John C. Wilkinson. *The imamate tradition of Oman.* Cambridge: Cambridge University Press, 1987. ISBN 0-521-32713-X. ‣ Wide-ranging treatment of theory and practice of imamate. Combination of sociological history, tribal analysis, and Islamic political theories; includes end of imamate institution in twentieth century. [WLO]

THE MODERN ERA

Late Ottoman Empire and Turkish Republic

18.259 Nermin Abadan-Unat et al. *Turkish workers in Europe, 1960–1975: a socio-economic reappraisal.* Leiden: Brill, 1976. ISBN 90-04-04478-7. ‣ Valuable range of studies of factors influencing migration, its economic impact on Turkey, social issues faced by migrants and their families, and socioeconomic significance of migration for European countries. [CVF]

18.260 Feroz Ahmad. *The Turkish experiment in democracy, 1950–1975.* Boulder: Westview for the Royal Institute of International Affairs, 1977. ISBN 0-89158-629-6. ‣ Highly detailed history of Turkish politics from end of single-party era (1945) through mid-1970s. Stress and destabilization resulted from institutional rigidities, economic growth, and political mobilization and polarization. [CVF]

18.261 Niyazi Berkes. *The development of secularism in Turkey.* Montreal: McGill University Press, 1964. ‣ Provocative, wide-ranging study of westernization and secularization in late Ottoman empire and republican Turkey. Social and cultural change; especially full on Young Turk and Atatürk periods. [CVF]

18.262 Robert Bianchi. *Interest groups and political development in Turkey.* Princeton: Princeton University Press, 1984. ISBN 0-691-07653-7 (cl), 0-691-10149-3 (pbk). ‣ Comparative analysis of roles of interest groups at different stages of political development and tensions between pluralist and corporatist interest groups. Important for study of Turkish politics since 1960. [CVF]

18.263 Roderic H. Davison. *Reform in the Ottoman empire, 1856–1876.* Princeton: Princeton University Press, 1963. ISBN 0-877-52135-2. ‣ Major study of Ottoman reform in second half of Tanzimat period. [CVF]

18.264 Selim Deringil. *Turkish foreign policy during the Second*

World War: an "active" neutrality. Cambridge: Cambridge University Press, 1989. ISBN 0-521-34466-2. ‣ Most recent study of Turkey's controversial policy of neutrality. Tactical acumen of Turkish statesmen in guarding republic's independence and avoiding mistakes made in World War I. [CVF]

18.265 C. H. Dodd. *The crisis of Turkish democracy.* 2d rev. ed. Huntingdon: Eothen, 1990. ISBN 0-906719-16-X (pbk). ‣ Detailed study of collapse of democracy and military intervention of 1980. Background of coup; how 1982 constitution attempted to balance order with democracy and government by people. [CVF]

18.266 C. H. Dodd. *Democracy and development in Turkey.* North Humberside: Eothen, 1979. ISBN 0-906719-01-1 (cl), 0-906719-00-3 (pbk). ‣ Turkey's attempt to combine economic development with democracy. Comprehensive analysis of political system: institutions, ideas, political culture, elites, and pressure groups. [CVF]

18.267 C. H. Dodd. *Politics and government in Turkey.* Berkeley: University of California Press, 1969. ‣ Major study of politics and administration under Second Turkish Republic. [CVF]

18.268 Alan Duben and Cem Behar. *Istanbul households: marriage, family, and fertility, 1880–1940.* Cambridge: Cambridge University Press, 1991. ISBN 0-521-38375-7. ‣ First Muslim city to experience fertility decline and related changes in family life. Highly original study, combining methods of social anthropology, historical demography, and social history. Based on 1885 and 1907 census registers. [CVF]

18.269 Carter Vaughn Findley. *Bureaucratic reform in the Ottoman empire: the Sublime Porte, 1789–1922.* Princeton: Princeton University Press, 1980. ISBN 0-691-05288-3. ‣ Major study of administrative reform and development in Ottoman empire and of rise of Ottoman civil bureaucracy. Organizational history of Sublime Porte (administrative headquarters under grand vizier). [CVF]

18.270 Carter Vaughn Findley. *Ottoman civil officialdom: a social history.* Princeton: Princeton University Press, 1989. ISBN 0-691-05545-9. ‣ Social history, including related topics in cultural and economic history, of Ottoman civil officialdom, 1789–1922. Combines quantitative analysis of personnel records with narrative analysis of literary sources. Complements Findley 18.269. [CVF]

18.271 Frederick W. Frey. *The Turkish political elite.* Cambridge, Mass.: MIT Press, 1965. ‣ Analysis of membership of Grand National Assembly (1920–60). Transition to multiparty politics as reflected in composition of elite, political rise of legal profession, and spread of localism. Important study in collective biographical analysis. [CVF]

18.272 William Hale. *The political and economic development of modern Turkey.* New York: St. Martin's, 1981. ISBN 0-312-62059-4. ‣ Valuable overview of Turkey's political economy, from founding of republic, through era of statism and import substitution, to transition to market-oriented policy. [CVF]

18.273 Z. Y. Hershlag. *The contemporary Turkish economy.* London: Routledge, 1988. ISBN 0-415-00388-1. ‣ Recent work by well-known authority on Turkish economy. Includes historical survey of economic history under Turkish Republic; emphasis on 1980s. [CVF]

18.274 Z. Y. Hershlag. *Turkey: the challenge of growth.* 2d rev. ed. Leiden: Brill, 1968. ‣ Pioneering study of economic development in Turkey, chronologically and topically organized. Title of first edition: *Turkey: an economy in transition.* [CVF]

18.275 Charles P. Issawi. *The economic history of Turkey, 1800–1914.* Chicago: University of Chicago Press, 1980. (Publications of the Center for Middle Eastern Studies, 13.) ISBN 0-226-38603-

1. ▸ Surveys social structure, trade, transport, agriculture, industry, and finance. Extracts from many sources, primary and secondary, combined with analysis and commentary by leading economic historian of Middle East. [CVF]

18.276 Kemal H. Karpat. *The gecekondu: rural migration and urbanization.* Cambridge: Cambridge University Press, 1976. ISBN 0-521-20954-4. ▸ Valuable historical, socioeconomic, and political study, based on fieldwork in Istanbul shantytowns (*gecekondu*). Turkey's experience with Third World's rapid rural-to-urban migration and superurbanization. [CVF]

18.277 Kemal H. Karpat. *Ottoman population, 1830–1914: demographic and social characteristics.* Madison: University of Wisconsin Press, 1985. ISBN 0-299-09160-0. ▸ Analyzes Ottoman archival sources to study demographic change. Noteworthy emphasis on impact of border shifts and population movements in transition to primarily Muslim population. Separate chapter on Istanbul. [CVF]

18.278 Kemal H. Karpat. *Turkey's politics: the transition to a multi-party system.* Princeton: Princeton University Press, 1959. ▸ Study of transformation of Turkish Republic, from single-party to multiparty system. Major work on Republic's politics through 1950s. [CVF]

18.279 Jacob M. Landau. *Pan-Turkism in Turkey: a study of irredentism.* London: Hurst, 1981. ISBN 0-905838-57-2. ▸ Valuable study of pan-Turkish nationalism, from its origins among Turks in tsarist Russia through its resurgence in Turkish politics of 1970s. Attributes limited impact to socioeconomic factors, among others. [CVF]

18.280 Jacob M. Landau. *Radical politics in modern Turkey.* Leiden: Brill, 1974. ISBN 90-04-04016-1. ▸ Detailed study of radicalization of Turkish politics in 1960s. Expanding political mobilization led to polarization, violence, and military intervention of 1971. [CVF]

18.281 Bernard Lewis. *The emergence of modern Turkey.* 2d ed. London: Oxford University Press for the Royal Institute of International Affairs, 1968. ▸ Pioneering study of Ottoman reform and rise of Turkish Republic. [CVF]

18.282 Raymond Lifchez, ed. *The dervish lodge: architecture, art, and Sufism in Ottoman Turkey.* Berkeley: University of California Press, 1992. ISBN 0-520-07060-7. ▸ Essays on dervish meeting halls and dervish milieu in Ottoman empire, ca. 1836–1925; valuable for architectural history and sociocultural history of Islamic mysticism. [CVF]

18.283 Şerif Mardin. *The genesis of Young Ottoman thought: a study in the modernization of Turkish political ideas.* Princeton: Princeton University Press, 1962. ▸ Study of major Ottoman ideological movement of 1860s and 1870s. Valuable for emphasizing Islamic as well as European sources of Young Ottoman ideas. Trailblazing study in history of political thought. [CVF]

18.284 Justin McCarthy. *Muslims and minorities: the population of Ottoman Anatolia and the end of the empire.* New York: New York University Press, 1983. ISBN 0-8147-5390-6. ▸ Pioneering demographic history of Anatolia from late Ottoman times through founding of Turkish Republic. Emphasizes war-related demographic disaster of 1914–23. Compares impact on Muslims, Greeks, Armenians, and other groups. [CVF]

18.285 Zehra Önder. *Die türkische Aussenpolitik im Zweiten Weltkrieg.* Munich: Oldenbourg, 1977. (Südosteuropäische Arbeiten, 73.) ISBN 3-486-48211-4. ▸ Study of Turkey's neutrality policy during World War II. Predates Deringil's study (18.264), but uses German as well as British sources. [CVF]

18.286 Ergun Özbudun. *Social change and political participation in Turkey.* Princeton: Princeton University Press, 1976. ISBN

0-691-07580-8. ▸ Monograph analyzing voting patterns, 1960–70. Rapid socioeconomic change coincided with declining voter turnout. Seeks explanation in combination of democracy and development, leading to increase in autonomous, as opposed to mobilized, participation. [CVF]

18.287 Şevket Pamuk. *The Ottoman empire and European capitalism, 1820–1913: trade, investment, and production.* Cambridge: Cambridge University Press, 1987. ISBN 0-521-33194-3. ▸ Very useful examination of consequences of European economic penetration. Long-term trends in Ottoman foreign trade and European investment. Commercialization of agriculture. Decline and resistance of handicrafts. [CVF]

18.288 Daniel Panzac. *La peste dans l'Empire ottoman, 1700–1850.* Louvain: Peeters for Association pour le Developpement des Études Turques, 1985. (Collection Turcica, 5.) ISBN 90-6831-033-X. ▸ Innovative study of period when plague had disappeared from northern and Central Europe but persisted in Ottoman empire. Disappearance of Ottoman plague predated quarantines; speculation as to causes. [CVF]

18.289 Daniel Panzac. *Quarantaines et lazarets: l'Europe et la peste d'Orient: XVIIe–XXe siècles.* Aix-en-Provence: Edisud, 1986. ISBN 2-85744-266-1. ▸ Quarantines established to prevent spread of plague from Ottoman empire to Europe. Valuable study of international collaboration in public health. Complements Panzac 18.288. [CVF]

18.290 Donald Quataert. *Social disintegration and popular resistance in the Ottoman empire, 1881–1908: reactions to European economic penetration.* New York: New York University Press, 1983. ISBN 0-8147-6950-0. ▸ Examines reactions of nonelite groups to impact of European-dominated world economy. Pioneering work on Ottoman labor history. [CVF]

18.291 Richard D. Robinson. *The First Turkish Republic: a case study in national development.* Cambridge, Mass.: Harvard University Press, 1963. ▸ Broad-ranging analysis of Turkey's national development under First Republic (1923–60). Emphasizes both Turkey's success compared to other underdeveloped countries and problems highlighted by 1960 coup. [CVF]

18.292 Stanford J. Shaw. *Between old and new: the Ottoman empire under Selim III, 1789–1807.* Cambridge, Mass.: Harvard University Press, 1971. ISBN 0-674-06830-0. ▸ Detailed study of reign of Selim III and his reforms, the *Nizam-i Cedid* or New Order. [CVF]

18.293 Stanford J. Shaw and Ezel Kural Shaw. *Reform, revolution, and republic: the rise of modern Turkey, 1808–1975.* Vol. 2 of *History of the Ottoman empire and modern Turkey.* Cambridge: Cambridge University Press, 1977. ISBN 0-521-21449-1 (cl), 0-521-29166-6 (pbk). ▸ Comprehensive history of period; emphasis on Ottoman reforms. [CVF]

18.294 Ehud R. Toledano. *The Ottoman slave trade and its suppression, 1840–1890.* Princeton: Princeton University Press, 1982. ISBN 0-691-05369-3. ▸ Study of differences in traffic in African and Circassian slaves. Key role of British in ending African trade and of Ottomans in ending Black Sea trade. Important work for history of slavery. [CVF]

18.295 Vamik D. Volkan and Norman Itzkowitz. *The immortal Atatürk: a psychobiography.* Chicago: University of Chicago Press, 1984. ISBN 0-226-86388-3. ▸ Insightful recent biography in English of founder of modern Turkey. Seeks explanation for his career in his personality traits. [CVF]

18.296 Walter F. Weiker. *The modernization of Turkey: from Ataturk to the present day.* New York: Holmes & Meier, 1981. ISBN 0-8419-0503-7. ▸ Good overview of political development, emphasizing tensions between democracy, on one hand, and economic growth, urbanization, political polarization, and religious and social conflict, on the other hand. [CVF]

18.297   Erik Jan Zürcher. *Political opposition in the early Turkish Republic: the Progressive Republican party, 1924–1925.* Leiden: Brill, 1991. ISBN 90-04-09341-9, ISSN 0085-6193. ‣ Revisionist history of Turkish Republic's first opposition party, seen also as last serious center of opposition to Mustafa Kemal Atatürk. [CVF]

18.298   Erik Jan Zürcher. *The unionist factor: the role of the Committee of Union and Progress in the Turkish national movement, 1905–1926.* Leiden: Brill, 1984. ISBN 90-04-07262-4. ‣ Important revisionist history of Young Turk and early Republican periods. Uses sources from political opposition to cast new light on relations between Mustafa Kemal Atatürk and Committee of Union and Progress. [CVF]

Egypt

18.299   Gabriel Baer. *A history of landownership in modern Egypt, 1800–1950.* London: Oxford University Press for the Royal Institute of International Affairs, 1962. (Royal Institute of International Affairs, Middle Eastern monographs, 4.) ‣ Classic study of evolution of land tenure and land management practices in Egypt under Muhammad Ali dynasty; now being corrected by more detailed research. [AG]

18.300   Gabriel Baer. *Studies in the social history of modern Egypt.* Chicago: University of Chicago Press, 1969. (Publications of the Center for Middle Eastern Studies, 4.) ‣ Collected essays on many aspects of Egypt's social and economic history in nineteenth and twentieth centuries, meticulously researched and useful for period 1800–1950. [AG]

18.301   Joel Beinin and Zachary Lockman. *Workers on the Nile: nationalism, communism, Islam, and the Egyptian working class, 1882–1954.* Princeton: Princeton University Press, 1987. ISBN 0-691-05506-8. ‣ Detailed, heavily documented account of evolution of Egyptian industrial workers during period of British occupation, written from Marxist perspective. [AG]

18.302   Selma Botman. *Egypt from independence to revolution, 1919–1952.* Syracuse, N.Y.: Syracuse University Press, 1991. ISBN 0-8156-2530-8 (cl), 0-8156-2531-6 (pbk). ‣ Concise treatment of twentieth-century Egypt's political, economic, social, and intellectual development leading up to 1952 Revolution, correcting previous surveys by stressing nonmainstream groups. [AG]

18.303   Kenneth M. Cuno. *The pasha's peasants: land, society, and economy in Lower Egypt, 1740–1858.* Cambridge: Cambridge University Press, 1992. ISBN 0-521-40478-9. ‣ Revisionist study of agrarian history. In contrast to old view of sharp break between Ottoman and modern periods, shows that cash-crop agriculture, commoditization of land, and stratified rural society were not new developments of nineteenth century. [CVF]

18.304   Marius K. Deeb. *Party politics in Egypt: the Wafd and its rivals.* London: Ithaca Press for Oxford St. Antony's College, Middle East Centre, 1979. (St. Antony's Middle East monographs, 9.) ISBN 0-903729-40-7. ‣ Detailed, well-documented study of Wafd party in relation to other political parties, factions, and leaders within Egypt from 1919 to 1939. [AG]

18.305   R. Hrair Dekmejian. *Egypt under Nasir, a study in political dynamics.* Albany: State University of New York Press, 1971. ISBN 0-87395-080-1. ‣ Perceptive analysis of Egypt's politics under Gamal Abdel Nasser, stressing his charismatic authority as instrument for popular mobilization. [AG]

18.306   Gilbert Delanoue. *Moralistes et politiques musulmans dans l'Egypte du dix-neuvième siècle (1798–1882).* 2 vols. Cairo: Institut Français d'Archéologie Orientale du Caire, 1982. (Textes arabes et études islamiques, 15.) ‣ Major study of leading political and

social thinkers; lives and ideas of both traditionalists and modernists. [CVF]

18.307   Arthur E. Goldschmidt, Jr. *Modern Egypt: the formation of a nation-state.* Boulder: Westview, 1988. ISBN 0-86531-182-X (cl), 0-86531-183-8 (pbk). ‣ Short, introductory history of Egypt, mainly political, stressing period since 1750. [AG]

18.308   Raymond A. Hinnebusch, Jr. *Egyptian politics under Sadat: the post-populist development of an authoritarian-modernizing state.* Rev. ed. Boulder: Rienner, 1988. ISBN 1-55587-124-0. ‣ Objective treatment of political changes in Egypt under presidents Anwar al-Sadat and Husni Mubarak. [AG]

18.309   Derek Hopwood. *Egypt: politics and society, 1945–1990.* 3d ed. London: HarperCollins, 1991. ISBN 0-04-956014-X (pbk). ‣ Concise, well-written history of political, economic, social, and intellectual changes in Egypt from World War II up to era of Husni Mubarak. [AG]

18.310   F. Robert Hunter. *Egypt under the khedives, 1805–1879: from household government to modern bureaucracy.* Pittsburgh: University of Pittsburgh Press, 1984. ISBN 0-8229-3808-1. ‣ Evolution of Egypt's government from rise of Muhammad Ali to fall of Khedive Isma'il with biographical sketches of leading officials. Heavily documented from Egyptian and European archival sources. [AG]

18.311   James P. Jankowski and Israel Gershoni. *Egypt, Islam, and the Arabs: the search for Egyptian nationhood, 1900–1930.* New York: Oxford University Press, 1986. ISBN 0-19-504096-1. ‣ Detailed account of intellectual transition in Egypt from pan-Islamism to pharaonic Egyptian nationalism and then to pan-Arabism, making use of writings by leading Egyptian thinkers. Important contribution to study of nationalism in Egypt. [AG]

18.312   LaVerne Kuhnke. *Lives at risk: public health in nineteenth-century Egypt.* Berkeley: University of California Press, 1990. ISBN 0-520-06364-3. ‣ Pathbreaking study of evolution of Egyptian government policy regarding containment and treatment of epidemic diseases. [AG]

18.313   David S. Landes. *Bankers and pashas: international finance and economic imperialism in Egypt.* 1958 ed. Cambridge, Mass.: Harvard University Press, 1979. ISBN 0-674-06165-9. ‣ Well-written account of European (especially French) investment banking and its operation in Egypt during reign of Khedive Isma'il, using private papers and archival sources. [AG]

18.314   E. W. Lane. *Manners and customs of the modern Egyptians.* M. Saad el-Din, Introduction. New York: Dutton, 1966. ‣ Detailed description of social customs, beliefs, and attitudes prevalent among Muslims of early nineteenth-century Egypt, especially Cairo. One of first ethnographic studies, originally published 1836. [AG]

18.315   Wm. Roger Louis and Roger Owen, eds. *Suez 1956: the crisis and its consequences.* New York: Oxford University Press, 1989. ISBN 0-19-820141-9 (cl), 0-19-820241-5 (pbk). ‣ Important anthology containing introduction, twenty-two contributions on specialized topics related to 1956 Suez War, and bibliography. Representing several viewpoints, heavily documented from government documents, memoirs, and secondary sources. [AG]

18.316   Robert Mabro and Samir Radwan. *The industrialization of Egypt, 1939–1973: policy and performance.* Oxford: Clarendon, 1976. ISBN 0-19-828405-5. ‣ Detailed, heavily documented study of role of foreign and domestic capitalists and of state in industrializing Egypt during and after World War II. [AG]

18.317   Roger Owen. *Cotton and the Egyptian economy, 1820–1914: a study in trade and development.* Oxford: Clarendon, 1969. ISBN 0-19-821643-2. ‣ Well-written, perceptive account of spread of cultivation of long-staple cotton and its effect on Egyptian economic and social life. [AG]

18.318 Donald M. Reid. *Cairo University and the making of a modern Egypt.* Cambridge: Cambridge University Press, 1990. ISBN 0-521-36641-0. ‣ Study of origin and development of Egypt's first modern national university. Important for understanding higher education in Egypt and other Arab countries. [AG]

18.319 Alan Richards. *Egypt's agricultural development, 1800–1980: technical and social change.* Boulder: Westview, 1982. ISBN 0-86531-099-8. ‣ Detailed, well-documented study of Egypt's agricultural evolution and its social consequences. [AG]

18.320 Afaf Lutfi al-Sayyid-Marsot. *Egypt and Cromer: a study in Anglo-Egyptian relations.* New York: Praeger, 1968. ‣ Balanced treatment of British occupation of Egypt during period of Lord Cromer's proconsulship (1883–1907), discussing policies of Khedive Abbas Hilmi II (r. 1892–1914) and of Egyptian nationalists. [AG]

18.321 Afaf Lutfi al-Sayyid-Marsot. *Egypt in the reign of Muhammad Ali.* Cambridge: Cambridge University Press, 1984. ISBN 0-521-24795-0 (cl), 0-521-28968-8 (pbk). ‣ History of Muhammad Ali's reign, based heavily on archival sources, stressing his many contributions to Egypt's westernization. Excellent scholarship; Egyptian-Arab nationalist viewpoint, anti-British. Although well-written, criticized for understating Ottoman Turkish influences. [AG/PWS]

18.322 Afaf Lutfi al-Sayyid-Marsot. *Egypt's liberal experiment, 1922–1936.* Berkeley: University of California Press, 1977. ISBN 0-520-03109-1. ‣ Interesting, sometimes anecdotal account clarifying complicated history of royal and parliamentary Egyptian politics between Britain's unilateral declaration of Egypt's independence and 1936 Anglo-Egyptian Treaty. [AG]

18.323 Alexander Schölch. *Egypt for the Egyptians! The sociopolitical crisis in Egypt, 1878–1882.* London: Ithaca Press for St. Antony's College, Middle East Centre, 1981. (St. Antony's Middle East monographs, 14.) ISBN 0-903729-82-2. ‣ Revisionist treatment of Egyptian nationalist movement in period of Urabi Revolution, correcting earlier misinterpretations by Egyptian and Western writers. [AG]

18.324 Robert L. Tignor. *Modernization and British colonial rule in Egypt, 1882–1914.* Princeton: Princeton University Press, 1966. ‣ Topical treatment of various aspects of British rule during era of veiled protectorate. Classic study, well written; needs revision. [AG]

18.325 Robert L. Tignor. *State, private enterprise, and economic change in Egypt, 1918–1952.* Princeton: Princeton University Press, 1984. ISBN 0-691-05416-9. ‣ Detailed study of role of government and of domestic and foreign capitalists in Egypt's economic development during period between 1919 and 1952 revolutions. Critiques application of dependency theory to Egypt. [AG]

18.326 Ehud R. Toledano. *State and society in mid-nineteenth-century Egypt.* New York: Cambridge University Press, 1990. ISBN 0-521-37194-5. ‣ Reexamination of Egypt's government under Abbas and Saʿid, correcting earlier treatments of this period of Egyptian history. Stresses essentially Ottoman Turkish character of Egypt's rulers. [AG]

18.327 Panayiotis J. Vatikiotis. *The history of modern Egypt, from Muhammad Ali to Mubarak.* 4th rev. ed. Baltimore: Johns Hopkins University Press, 1991. ISBN 0-8018-4214-x (cl), 0-8018-4215-8 (pbk). ‣ Detailed survey of Egypt's political and intellectual history since 1750. Now partly superseded by recent monographic studies; needs revision. [AG]

18.328 Panayiotis J. Vatikiotis. *Nasser and his generation.* New York: St. Martin's, 1978. ISBN 0-312-55938-0. ‣ Detailed, insightful treatment of President Nasser's background, rise to power, internal policies, role as Arab nationalist leader and opponent of Israel, personality, and impact on Egyptian life. [AG]

18.329 Gabriel R. Warburg. *Egypt and the Sudan, studies in history and politics.* London: Cass, 1985. ISBN 0-7146-3247-3. ‣ Collection of author's essays on various aspects of modern Egyptian and Sudanese history, carefully analyzing relationship between British imperial power and local elites. [AG]

18.330 Gabriel R. Warburg and Uri M. Kupferschmidt, eds. *Islam, nationalism, and radicalism in Egypt and the Sudan.* New York: Praeger, 1983. ISBN 0-03-063812-7. ‣ Collection of essays, written by Israeli, Egyptian, European, and American scholars on intellectual and political trends in Egypt and Sudan during nineteenth and twentieth centuries. Includes several important studies of role of Islam in Egyptian and Sudanese politics. [AG]

18.331 John Waterbury. *The Egypt of Nasser and Sadat: the political economy of two regimes.* Princeton: Princeton University Press, 1983. ISBN 0-691-07650-2 (cl), 0-691-10147-7 (pbk). ‣ Meticulous analysis of attempted socialist transformation of Egypt under presidents Nasser and Sadat. Heavily documented. [AG]

Sudan

18.332 Carolyn Fluehr-Lobban, Richard A. Lobban, and John O. Voll. *Historical dictionary of the Sudan.* 3d ed. Metuchen, N.J.: Scarecrow, 1992. ISBN 0-8108-2547-3. ‣ Chronology, introduction, dictionary, bibliography, and appendixes. Useful reference tool for historians of Sudan. [AG]

18.333 Richard L. Hill. *Egypt in the Sudan, 1820–1881.* 1956 ed. Westport, Conn.: Greenwood, 1986. ISBN 0-313-25116-9. ‣ Classic account of conquest and government of Sudan under rule of Muhammad Ali dynasty, leading up to Mahdiyah period. Makes good use of Egyptian and British sources. [AG]

18.334 Peter Malcolm Holt. *The Mahdist state in the Sudan, 1881–1898: a study of its origins, development, and overthrow.* 2d ed. Oxford: Clarendon, 1970. ISBN 0-19-821660-2. ‣ Well-documented, thoroughly researched political history of Mahdist rebellion and of Sudanese history during Mahdiyah era. [AG]

18.335 Peter Malcolm Holt and Michael W. Daly. *A history of the Sudan from the coming of Islam to the present day.* 4th ed. London: Longman, 1988. ISBN 0-582-00406-3 (pbk). ‣ Concise history of those regions of Upper Nile that now comprise Sudan; mainly political and military, but also economic and social, stressing nineteenth and twentieth centuries. Excellent introduction. [AG]

18.336 Tim Niblock. *Class and power in the Sudan: the dynamics of Sudanese politics, 1898–1985.* Albany: State University of New York Press, 1987. ISBN 0-88706-480-9 (cl), 0-88706-481-7 (pbk). ‣ Cogent analysis of socioeconomic determinants of Sudanese political behavior in modern times. [AG]

18.337 Gabriel R. Warburg. *Islam, nationalism, and communism in a traditional society: the case of the Sudan.* London: Cass, 1978. ISBN 0-7146-3080-2. ‣ Detailed treatment of ideological currents in modern history of Sudan. Stresses British policies and Sudanese parties and personalities. [AG]

18.338 Gabriel R. Warburg. *The Sudan under Wingate: administration in the Anglo-Egyptian Sudan, 1899–1916.* London: Cass, 1971. ISBN 0-7146-2612-0. ‣ Detailed, objective study of Sudan's government after suppression of Mahdists. Based on British government archives and papers of Sir Francis Reginald Wingate. [AG]

18.339 Peter Woodward. *Sudan, 1898–1989: the unstable state.*

Boulder: Rienner, 1990. ISBN 1-55587-193-3. ‣ Analytical survey of political history in colonial and independence periods. Emphasizes weakness of state structure because of its clientalist nature. [JOV]

Libya

18.340 Lisa Anderson. *The state and social transformation in Tunisia and Libya, 1830–1980.* Princeton: Princeton University Press, 1986. ISBN 0-691-05462-2. ‣ Innovative comparative study, contrasting divergent paths of political development of two neighboring states. Attributes differences to divergent impacts of French and Italian rule on precolonial administrative and social systems. Rigorous political study. [CVF/AG/MS]

18.341 John Davis. *Libyan politics, tribe and revolution: an account of the Zuwaya and their government.* Berkeley: University of California Press, 1987. ISBN 0-520-06294-9. ‣ Describes how tribal peoples accustomed to freedom and autonomy had to adjust to new conditions under revolutionary regime. [MS]

18.342 Marius K. Deeb and Mary Jane Deeb. *Libya since the revolution: aspects of social and political development.* New York: Praeger, 1982. ISBN 0-03-058308-X. ‣ Analysis of tensions and upheavals that have resulted from conflict between traditional mores and socialist-implemented structures, institutions, values, and technology. [MS]

18.343 Edward Evan Evans-Pritchard. *The Sanusi of Cyrenaica.* 1949 ed. Oxford: Clarendon, 1973. ‣ Classic study of development among Libyan Bedouin of Sanusi Order, neo-Ṣūfī movement that evolved under impact of Italian occupation into nationalist political movement. Available on microfilm from New Haven: Human Relations Area Files, 1974. [CVF]

18.344 Ronald Bruce St. John. *Historical dictionary of Libya.* Metuchen, N.J.: Scarecrow, 1991. ISBN 0-8108-2451-5. ‣ Useful reference tool, includes chronology, introduction, definitions, and bibliography. Especially detailed on period since 1969. [AG/LV]

18.345 John L. Wright. *Libya: a modern history.* Baltimore: Johns Hopkins University Press, 1982. ISBN 0-8018-2767-1. ‣ Concise, objective account of Libya's history in nineteenth and twentieth centuries. [AG/LV]

SEE ALSO
28.330 Claudio G. Segré. *Fourth shore.*

Tunisia, Algeria, and Morocco

18.346 Janet L. Abu-Lughod. *Rabat: urban apartheid in Morocco.* Princeton: Princeton University Press, 1980. ISBN 0-691-05315-4 (cl), 0-691-10098-5 (pbk). ‣ Polemical study of policy of segregation introduced by French in twentieth-century Moroccan city planning. [LV/MS]

18.347 Jamil M. Abun-Nasr. *History of the Maghrib in the Islamic period.* Cambridge: Cambridge University Press, 1987. ISBN 0-521-33184-6 (cl), 0-521-33767-4 (pbk). ‣ Most comprehensive survey in English of history of North Africa from Arab conquest to postindependence states. [LV/MS]

18.348 Charles-Robert Ageron. *Modern Algeria: a history from 1830 to the present.* Michael Brett, ed. and trans. London: Hurst, 1991. ISBN 1-85065-027-6. ‣ Basic book on colonial Algeria. [LV/MS]

18.349 Allal Al-Fasi. *The independence movements in Arab North Africa.* 1954 ed. Hazem Zaki Nuseibeh, trans. New York: Octagon Books, 1970. (American Council of Learned Societies, Near Eastern translation program, 8.) ‣ History of nationalism by one of major leaders of movement for independence in Morocco. [LV/MS]

18.350 Jacques Berque. *French North Africa: the Maghrib between two world wars.* Jean Stewart, trans. London: Faber & Faber, 1967. ‣ Stimulating though hard to read description and analysis of North Africa under French rule and rise of nationalism by leading French scholar of North Africa. [LV/MS]

18.351 Robin L. Bidwell. *Morocco under colonial rule: French administration of tribal areas, 1912–1956.* London: Cass, 1973. ISBN 0-7146-2877-8. ‣ Argues that cooptation of native leaders in tribal administration led to initial successes but ultimately failed. Describes how tribal customs not harmful to European interests were preserved. [LV/MS]

18.352 Pierre Bourdieu. *The Algerians.* Alan C. M. Ross, trans. Boston: Beacon, 1962. ‣ Good introduction to structure of Algerian society and colonial impact analyzed by major French social scientist. [LV/MS]

18.353 Kenneth L. Brown. *People of Salé: tradition and change in a Moroccan city, 1830–1930.* Cambridge, Mass.: Harvard University Press, 1976. ISBN 0-674-66155-9. ‣ Pioneering social history of traditional Moroccan city. [LV/MS]

18.354 L. Carl Brown. *The Tunisia of Ahmad Bey, 1837–1855.* Princeton: Princeton University Press, 1974. ISBN 0-691-03100-2. ‣ Classic case study in modernization and survey of European-inspired political and military reforms in nineteenth-century Tunisia. [LV/MS]

18.355 L. Carl Brown, ed. and trans. *The surest path: the political treatise of a nineteenth-century Muslim statesman.* Cambridge, Mass.: Harvard University, Center for Middle Eastern Studies, 1967. (Harvard Middle Eastern monographs, 16.) ‣ Translation of and introduction to political treatise by Khayr al-Din al-Tunisi, major reformist statesman in Tunisia. Important source for history of political reforms in nineteenth-century Middle East. [LV/MS]

18.356 Edmund Burke III. *Prelude to protectorate in Morocco: precolonial protest and resistance, 1860–1912.* Chicago: University of Chicago Press, 1976. ISBN 0-226-08075-7. ‣ Pioneering study showing how incorporation of Morocco into world capitalist system and European intervention disrupted its society and created new social forces. Comparison with Middle East. [LV/MS]

18.357 Mohamed-Hédi Chérif. *Pouvoir et société dans la Tunisie de Husayn bin ⁽Ali, 1705–1740.* Tunis: Université de Tunis, 1984. (Publications de l'Université de Tunis, Faculté des lettres et sciences humaines de Tunis, Quatrième série: histoire, 29.) ‣ Intensively researched study of state and society under dynasty that ruled in Tunisia from eighteenth through twentieth centuries. [LV/MS]

18.358 Allan Christelow. *Muslim law courts and the French colonial state in Algeria.* Princeton: Princeton University Press, 1985. ISBN 0-691-05438-X. ‣ Examines how colonial state intervention into Algerian society through its traditional judicial system created heritage of bitterness that was captured by moderate Algerian nationalists. [LV/MS]

18.359 David Corcos. *Studies in the history of the Jews of Morocco.* Jerusalem: Mass, 1976. ‣ Anthology of studies on Jewish community in Morocco during later Middle Ages. [LV/MS]

18.360 Raphael Danziger. *Abd al-Qadir and the Algerians: resistance to the French and internal consolidation.* E. Ashor, Introduction. New York: Holmes & Meier, 1977. ISBN 0-8419-0236-4. ‣ Well-documented study of most prominent figure of Algerian resistance to French colonization; organization of his state and its evolution. [LV/MS]

18.361 Ross E. Dunn. *Resistance in the desert: Moroccan responses to French imperialism, 1881–1912.* Madison: University of Wisconsin Press, 1977. ISBN 0-299-07360-2. ‣ Valuable analysis of rural political institutions and action in colonial challenge. Study concentrates on southeastern tribes and oasis communities. [LV/MS]

18.362 Jean Duvignaud. *Change at Shebika: report from a North African village*. Frances Frenaye, trans. Austin: University of Texas Press, 1977. ISBN 0-292-71041-0. ‣ Vivid, readable description of Tunisian village after independence. [LV/MS]

18.363 Frantz Fanon. *The wretched of the earth*. 1963 ed. Constance Farrington, trans. New York: Grove Weidenfeld, 1991. ISBN 0-8021-5083-7. ‣ Controversial description of Algerian movement for independence by radical thinker and protagonist. [LV/MS]

18.364 Nancy Elizabeth Gallagher. *Medicine and power in Tunisia, 1780–1900*. Cambridge: Cambridge University Press, 1983. ISBN 0-521-25124-9. ‣ Argues that epidemics elicited responses from entire society and that shift from Arabic to European medicine was fundamental part of colonial experience. [LV/MS]

18.365 Ernest Gellner. *Saints of the Atlas*. Chicago: University of Chicago Press, 1969. ISBN 0-226-28699-1. ‣ Seminal study of basic structures of Moroccan rural society and political organization by major British social scientist. [LV/MS]

18.366 Ernest Gellner and C. Micaud, eds. *Arabs and Berbers: from tribe to nation in North Africa*. London: Duckworth, 1973. ISBN 0-7156-0639-5. ‣ Collection of original case studies in political science and anthropology on ethnic groups. [LV/MS]

18.367 Arnold H. Green. *The Tunisian ulama, 1873–1915: social structure and response to ideological currents*. Leiden: Brill, 1978. ISBN 90-04-05687-4. ‣ Valuable social and intellectual history of Tunisian scholars in period of accelerated change. [LV/MS]

18.368 Alistair Horne. *A savage war of peace: Algeria, 1954–1962*. Rev. ed. New York: Penguin, 1987. ISBN 0-14-010191-8 (pbk). ‣ Vivid, well-written chronicle of war for independence in Algeria. [LV/MS]

18.369 Martha Crenshaw Hutchinson. *Revolutionary terrorism: the FLN in Algeria, 1954–1962*. Stanford, Calif.: Hoover Institution Press, 1978. (Hoover Institution publications, 196.) ISBN 0-8179-6961-6. ‣ Detailed analytical case study of National Liberation Front (FLN). Includes bibliographical note on most relevant sources for subject. [LV/MS]

18.370 Henry F. Jackson. *The FLN in Algeria: party development in a revolutionary society*. Westport, Conn.: Greenwood, 1977. ISBN 0-8371-9401-6. ‣ Study of development of the Front de Libération Nationale from 1954 to 1964. Includes interviews, unpublished primary sources, and field observations in 1963 and 1966 on events discussed in book. [LV/MS]

18.371 Charles-André Julien. *La conquête et les débuts de la colonisation, 1827–1871*. Vol. I of *Histoire de l'Algérie contemporaine*. 3d ed. Paris: Presses Universitaires de France, 1986. ISBN 2-13-037763-7. ‣ Standard work on history of modern Algeria, mostly from French point of view. [LV/MS]

18.372 Charles-André Julien. *History of North Africa: Tunisia, Algeria, Morocco, from the Arab conquest to 1830*. R. Le Tourneau and C. C. Stewart, eds. John Petrie, trans. New York: Praeger, 1970. ‣ Traditional history of kings and battles; remains standard textbook for history of Maghreb. First published in French in 1926. [LV/MS]

18.373 Abd Allah Laroui. *The crisis of the Arab intellectuals: traditionalism or historicism?* Diarmid Cammell, trans. Berkeley: University of California Press, 1976. ISBN 0-520-02971-2. ‣ Provocative analysis of Maghribī intellectuals by one of their most prominent representatives. [LV/MS/JOV]

18.374 Abd Allah Laroui. *The history of the Maghrib: an inter-

pretive essay*. Ralph Manheim, trans. Princeton: Princeton University Press, 1977. ISBN 0-691-03109-6. ‣ Pioneering revision of colonial historiography from nationalist point of view. [LV/MS]

18.375 Mohamed el-Mansour. *Morocco in the reign of Mawley Sulayman*. Wisbech, Cambridgeshire: Middle East and North African Studies Press, 1988. ISBN 0-906559-32-4. ‣ Well-balanced reevaluation of social structures, state organization, economic life, and sultan's role in maintaining stability. Based on Moroccan Royal Archives and European sources. [LV/MS]

18.376 Henry Munson, Jr., ed. and trans. *The House of Si Abd Allah: the oral history of a Moroccan family*. New Haven: Yale University Press, 1984. ISBN 0-300-03084-3. ‣ Readable social and cultural history of Moroccan family over past century. Tensions between fundamentalist Islam and westernization. [LV/MS]

18.377 C. R. Pennell. *A country with a government and a flag: the Rif War in Morocco, 1921–1926*. Wisbech, Cambridgeshire: Middle East and North African Studies Press; distributed by Rienner, 1986. ISBN 0-906559-23-5. ‣ Political, social, and economic history of five years of anticolonial struggle. Relies on untapped archival material. [LV/MS]

18.378 Kenneth J. Perkins. *Historical dictionary of Tunisia*. Metuchen, N.J.: Scarecrow, 1989. ISBN 0-8108-2226-1. ‣ Focuses on recent events and figures, but also considers by whom and how country formed. Includes important selected bibliography. [LV/MS]

18.379 Kenneth J. Perkins. *Qaids, captains, and colons: French military administration in the colonial Maghrib, 1844–1934*. New York: Africana, 1981. ISBN 0-8419-0564-9. ‣ Compares Bureaux Arabes in Algeria, Service des Renseignements in Tunisia, and Service des Affaires Indigènes in Morocco. French military officers' evolving administrative roles relating to local populace and French settlers. [LV/MS/CVF]

18.380 Kenneth J. Perkins. *Tunisia: crossroads of the Islamic and European worlds*. Boulder: Westview, 1986. ISBN 0-86531-591-4. ‣ Chronological history from pre-Islamic times to 1956. Discusses postindependence political and governmental structures and role of Habib Bourguiba and other nationalist leaders since independence. [LV/MS]

18.381 David Prochaska. *Making Algeria French: colonialism in Bône, 1870–1920*. Cambridge and Paris: Cambridge University Press and Éditions de la Maison des Sciences de l'Homme, 1990. ISBN 0-521-34303-8. ‣ Lively, revisionist account of European colonial settlement. Discusses colonial Algerian historiography, theories of settler colonization, and the colonial city. Uses large computerized census sample. [LV/MS]

18.382 Paul Rabinow. *French modern: norms and forms of the social environment*. Cambridge, Mass.: MIT Press, 1989. ISBN 0-262-18134-7. ‣ Includes chapter on colonial city planning in Morocco entitled "Techno-Cosmopolitanism: Governing Morocco." [LV/MS]

18.383 David Seddon. *Moroccan peasants: a century of change in the eastern Rif, 1870–1970*. Folkstone, Kent: Dawson, 1981. ISBN 0-7129-0930-3. ‣ Specialized study in socioeconomic microhistory. Local developments in broader context of Moroccan history. Examines changes in local class structure and ideology in relation to political economy of Moroccan state. [CVF/LV/MS]

18.384 Will D. Swearingen. *Moroccan mirages: agrarian dreams and deceptions, 1912–1986*. Princeton: Princeton University Press, 1987. ISBN 0-691-05505-X (cl), 0-691-10236-8 (pbk). ‣ Analysis of colonial policymaking. Demonstrates present Moroccan leaders fulfill colonial vision with disastrous results. [LV/MS]

18.385 John Talbott. *The war without a name: France in Algeria, 1954–1962*. New York: Knopf; distributed by Random House,

1980. ISBN 0-394-50909-9. ‣ History of Algerian war of independence and its impact on French public life. [LV/MS]

18.386 Ann Thomson. *Barbary and Enlightenment: European attitudes towards the Maghrib in the eighteenth century.* Leiden: Brill, 1987. ISBN 90-04-08273-5. ‣ Investigation of European literature of eighteenth century concerning Western attitudes toward North Africa. [LV/MS]

18.387 Lucette Valensi. *On the eve of colonialism: North Africa before the French conquest.* Kenneth J. Perkins, trans. New York: Africana, 1977. ISBN 0-8419-0322-0 (cl), 0-8419-0360-3 (pbk). ‣ Sound, original overview of social and economic conditions in precolonial Maghrib, 1790–1830. Inspired by Annales school. [LV/MS]

18.388 Lucette Valensi. *Tunisian peasants in the eighteenth and nineteenth centuries.* Beth Archer, trans. Cambridge and Paris: Cambridge University Press and Éditions de la Maison des Sciences de l'Homme, 1985. ISBN 0-521-25558-9. ‣ Blends methods of history and anthropology to portray Tunisian countryside in eighteenth and nineteenth centuries and changes that affected both peasantry and Tunisian state. Pioneering study. [LV/MS]

18.389 Lucette Valensi and Nathan Wachtel. *Jewish memories.* Barbara Harshav, trans. Berkeley: University of California Press, 1991. ISBN 0-520-06637-5. ‣ Includes lively accounts of Sefardi Jews who migrated from Egypt, Libya, Tunisia, Algeria, and Morocco to France. Contribution to study of collective memory and ethnicity in Arab world. [LV/MS]

18.390 John Waterbury. *The commander of the faithful: the Moroccan political elite, a study in segmented politics.* New York: Columbia University Press, 1970. ISBN 0-231-03326-5. ‣ Classic, major study of political system and of political life of independent Morocco. [LV/MS]

Syria, Lebanon, and Jordan

18.391 Raouf Sad Abujaber. *Pioneers over Jordan: the frontier of settlement in Transjordan, 1860–1914.* London: Taurus, 1989. ISBN 1-85043-116-7. ‣ Family papers, interviews, local archives, and secondary sources in English and Arabic supplement author's personal knowledge in fascinating account of land settlement and agricultural development in pre–World War I Jordan. [PSK/MCW]

18.392 Dominique Chevallier. *La société du Mont Liban: à l'époque de la révolution industrielle en Europe.* Paris: Librarie Orientaliste Paul Geuthner, 1971. ‣ Detailed economic and social history of nineteenth-century Lebanon and transformations created by dramatic growth of European commercial influence. Methodological and thematic concerns influenced by Annales school. For specialists. [PSK/MCW]

18.393 David Dean Commins. *Islamic reform: politics and social change in late Ottoman Syria.* New York: Oxford University Press, 1990. ISBN 0-19-506103-9. ‣ Intellectual and social history of Islamic modernism in Syria offering new insights into decline of Muslim religious scholars and leaders in relation to emerging secular elites with ties to Istanbul. [PSK/MCW]

18.394 Uriel Dann. *King Hussein and the challenge of Arab radicalism: Jordan, 1955–1967.* New York: Oxford University Press, 1989. ISBN 0-19-505498-9. ‣ Study of King Hussein's personality to assess his political resiliency. Based on newspapers and journals from critical but neglected period. [PSK/MCW]

18.395 C. Ernest Dawn. *From Ottomanism to Arabism: essays on the origins of Arab nationalism.* Urbana: University of Illinois Press, 1973. ISBN 0-252-00202-4. ‣ Influential work examining rise of most important Arab ideological and political movement of twentieth century. Argues Arab nationalism appealed to minority of urban elites before World War I. [PSK/MCW]

18.396 John F. Devlin. *The Baʿth party: a history from its origins to 1966.* Stanford, Calif.: Hoover Institution Press, 1976. (Hoover Institution publications, 156.) ISBN 0-8179-6561-3. ‣ First comprehensive history of party from its origins to schism that led to expulsion of its founders from Syria. [PSK/MCW]

18.397 Claude Dubar and Salim Nasr. *Les classes sociales au Liban.* Paris: Presses de la Fondation Nationale des Sciences Politiques, 1976. (Cahiers de la Fondation Nationale des Sciences Politiques, 204.) ISBN 2-7246-0367-2, 2-7246-0368-0. ‣ Study of historical formation of social classes in Lebanon and character of class consciousness in context of multiconfessional society. Historical sociology illuminates tensions between class and confessional identity. [PSK/MCW]

18.398 Leila Tarazi Fawaz. *Merchants and migrants in nineteenth-century Beirut.* Cambridge, Mass.: Harvard University Press, 1983. ISBN 0-674-56925-3. ‣ Monograph examining European commercial impact and regional migration patterns that made Beirut leading seaport of eastern Mediterranean. Suggests how sectarianism rent previously harmonious relations among Muslim and Christian communities. [PSK/MCW]

18.399 Peter Gubser. *Jordan: crossroads of Middle Eastern events.* Boulder: Westview, 1983. ISBN 0-89158-986-4. ‣ Introduction to society, economy, and history of Jordan. Based mainly on secondary sources, newspapers and journals, and Jordanian official publications. [PSK/MCW]

18.400 Raymond A. Hinnebusch, Jr. *Authoritarian power and state formation in Baʿthist Syria: army, party, and peasant.* Boulder: Westview, 1990. ISBN 0-8133-7590-8. ‣ Analysis of rise and consolidation of military-party state in post-1958 era and pillars of Hafiz al-Asad's authority: military, Baʿth party, and peasantry. Sophisticated neo-Marxist methodology. [PSK/MCW]

18.401 Derek Hopwood. *Syria 1945–1986: politics and society.* London: Unwin Hyman, 1988. ISBN 0-04-445039-7 (cl), 0-04-445046-x (pbk). ‣ Readable introductory text interpreting how people of modern Syria see history and goals of their society. Blends economic, social, and cultural analysis with political and diplomatic history. [PSK/MCW]

18.402 Albert Hourani. *Syria and Lebanon, a political essay.* New York: Oxford University Press, 1946. ‣ Classic and still best overview of French mandate theory and practice; interwar period. [PSK/MCW]

18.403 Michael C. Hudson. *The precarious republic: political modernization in Lebanon.* 1968 ed. Boulder: Westview, 1985. ISBN 0-8133-30105-x. ‣ Detailed analysis of bargaining among major confessional communities necessary to enable fragile state based on consociational politics to operate after independence. Situated within modernization school of political analysis. [PSK/MCW]

18.404 Charles P. Issawi, ed. *The Fertile Crescent, 1800–1914: a documentary history.* New York: Oxford University Press, 1988. ISBN 0-19-504951-9. ‣ Covers social change, trade, transport, agriculture, manufacturing, and finance. Pioneering economic history of region, combining Issawi's extensive essays and commentaries with extracts from widely varied primary and secondary sources. [CVF]

18.405 Michael Johnson. *Class and client in Beirut: the Sunni Muslim community and the Lebanese state, 1840–1985.* London: Ithaca Press, 1986. ISBN 0-86372-062-5. ‣ Class and patron-client analysis of central role of Sunnī Muslim community in postindependence politics and reasons for its decline in 1975 civil war. For specialist. [PSK/MCW]

18.406 Rashid I. Khalidi. *British policy towards Syria and Palestine, 1906–1914: a study of the antecedents of the Hussein-McMahon corespondence, the Sykes-Picot Agreement, and the Balfour Declaration.* London: Ithaca Press for St. Antony's College, Middle

East Centre, 1980. (St. Antony's Middle East monographs, 11.) ISBN 0-903729-57-1. ▸ Detailed monograph using British archives to reveal basis for wartime division of power in Middle East between Britain and France in period just prior to World War I. [PSK/MCW]

18.407 Philip S. Khoury. *Syria and the French mandate: the politics of Arab nationalism, 1920–1945*. Princeton: Princeton University Press, 1987. ISBN 0-691-05486-X. ▸ Comprehensive history emphasizing continuity of interwar Syrian politics with Ottoman period. Examines conflicts between Syrian elites and French and between liberal and radical nationalism. Cast in framework of political sociology. [MCW]

18.408 Philip S. Khoury. *Urban notables and Arab nationalism: the politics of Damascus, 1860–1920*. Cambridge: Cambridge University Press, 1983. ISBN 0-521-24796-9. ▸ Explains how Ottoman reform and agrarian commercialization produced class whose factional struggles gave rise to Arab nationalism. Complements ideological studies of Arab nationalism. [MCW]

18.409 Norman N. Lewis. *Nomads and settlers in Syria and Jordan, 1800–1980*. Cambridge: Cambridge University Press, 1987. ISBN 0-521-26548-7. ▸ Focus on expansion of state control in countryside and concomitant expansion of agriculture. Complements urban-based political studies. [PSK/MCW]

18.410 Stephen Hemsley Longrigg. *Syria and Lebanon under French mandate*. London: Oxford University Press, 1958. ▸ Political chronicle of interwar years by former British military officer and oil company representative. Especially critical of French failures of governance, echoing Anglo-French rivalry of period. [PSK/MCW]

18.411 James D. Lunt. *Hussein of Jordan: a political biography*. London: Macmillan, 1989. ISBN 0-333-41272-9. ▸ Admiring portrait of King Hussein focusing on major political events: expulsion of Glubb Pasha, 1957 attempted coup, Iraqi Revolution, 1967 War, Black September, 1973 War, and relations with Palestinians. [PSK/MCW]

18.412 Moshe Maʿoz. *Ottoman reform in Syria and Palestine, 1840–1861: the impact of the Tanzimat on politics and society*. Oxford: Clarendon, 1968. ISBN 0-19-821537-1. ▸ Detailed monograph studies implementation, impact of, and local resistance to Ottoman reform in Syrian provinces. Focus on changing relations between Muslim majority and religious minorities (Christians and Jews). [PSK/MCW]

18.413 Shaul Mishal. *West Bank/East Bank: the Palestinians in Jordan, 1949–1967*. New Haven: Yale University Press, 1978. ISBN 0-300-02191-7. ▸ Study of large, dissatisfied community of Palestinians under Jordanian rule. Uses Jordanian archives captured in 1967 War, but informed by Israeli perspective. [PSK/MCW]

18.414 Samir A. Mutawi. *Jordan in the 1967 War*. Cambridge: Cambridge University Press, 1987. ISBN 0-521-34352-6. ▸ Study of 1967 War from Jordanian perspective. Illuminates backdrop of war, especially inter-Arab rivalries and Syrian-Israeli military escalation. Based on interviews with King Hussein and other Jordanian participants. [PSK/MCW]

18.415 Augustus Richard Norton. *Amal and the Shiʿa: struggle for the soul of Lebanon*. Austin: University of Texas Press, 1987. ISBN 0-292-73039-X (cl), 0-292-73040-3 (pbk). ▸ Emergence of Shiʿi political power in postindependence Lebanon and career of Imam Musa Sadr during early years of Civil War. Reinterpretation of modernization's impact on countryside based on fieldwork in southern Lebanon. [PSK/MCW]

18.416 Tabitha Petran. *The struggle over Lebanon*. New York: Monthly Review Press, 1987. ISBN 0-85345-651-8 (cl), 0-85345-652-6 (pbk). ▸ Detailed history of class and confessional conflict

during twentieth century. Argues that reform movement of progressive Lebanese national movement provoked Civil War of 1975. [PSK/MCW]

18.417 Itamar Rabinovich. *Syria under the Baʿth, 1963–66: the army-party symbiosis*. Jerusalem: Israel Universities Press, 1972. ISBN 0-7065-1266-9. ▸ Detailed monograph examining formative phase of first Baʿthist regime in Syria and relationship between leaders of Syrian army and Baʿth party. Concentrates on role of sectarian loyalties in Syrian politics. [PSK/MCW]

18.418 Itamar Rabinovich. *The war for Lebanon, 1970–1985*. Rev. ed. Ithaca, N.Y.: Cornell University Press, 1985. ISBN 0-8014-1870-4 (cl), 0-8014-9313-7 (pbk). ▸ Balanced, well-informed narrative account of origins of Lebanese Civil War. Concentrates on rivalries between major confessional communities. [PSK/MCW]

18.419 André Raymond, ed. *La Syrie d'aujourd'hui*. Paris: Éditions du Centre National de la Recherche Scientifique, 1980. ISBN 2-222-02624-5. ▸ Important collection on modern Syrian history, politics, society, economy, and culture with special attention to relations between urban and rural life by new generation of French scholars. [PSK/MCW]

18.420 Kamal S. Salibi. *A house of many mansions: the history of Lebanon reconsidered*. Berkeley: University of California Press, 1988. ISBN 0-520-06517-4. ▸ Examination of mythical histories behind conflicting visions of Lebanese nation by Lebanon's leading historian. Suggests myths have obscured common experiences that could help foster reconstitution of society. [PSK/MCW]

18.421 Kamal S. Salibi. *The modern history of Lebanon*. 1965 ed. Delmar, N.Y.: Caravan, 1977. ISBN 0-88206-015-5. ▸ Classic narrative of politics, society, and culture in nineteenth and twentieth centuries explaining Lebanon's disproportionate influence in region. Maronite community highlighted at expense of other important confessional groups. [PSK/MCW]

18.422 Linda Schatkowski Schilcher. *Families in politics: Damascene factions and estates of the eighteenth and nineteenth centuries*. Stuttgart: Steiner, 1985. (Berliner Islamstudien, 2.) ISBN 3-515-03146-4 (pbk). ▸ Examination of society in Ottoman Damascus emphasizes political factionalism and changing power relations between local elites and Ottoman state. Neo-Weberian analysis of religious and military status groups; complements political narratives. [PSK/MCW]

18.423 Patrick Seale. *Asad of Syria: the struggle for the Middle East*. 1988 ed. Berkeley: University of California Press, 1989. ISBN 0-520-06667-7. ▸ Sympathetic biography based on interviews with key participants, including Asad. How Asad and his ʿAlawi coreligionists gained power through military and Baʿth party. Especially informative on Syrian-American relations. [PSK/MCW]

18.424 Patrick Seale. *The struggle for Syria: a study of post-war Arab politics, 1945–1958*. Rev. ed. New Haven: Yale University Press, 1987. ISBN 0-300-03944-1 (cl), 0-300-03970-0 (pbk). ▸ Examines complexities of Syrian politics in regional context, rise of radical movements, and fall of traditional elite. Vivid narrative based on interviews with numerous participants in events. [PSK/MCW]

18.425 Avi Shlaim. *Collusion across the Jordan: King Abdullah, the Zionist movement, and the partition of Palestine*. New York: Columbia University Press, 1988. ISBN 0-231-06838-7 (cl), 0-231-07365-8 (pbk). ▸ Provocative, revisionist narrative of secret relations between Jordanian king and Zionists. Proves that Abdullah agreed with Zionists to divide Palestine between them. Abridged paperback edition published as *The Politics of Partition*, New York: Columbia University Press, 1990. ISBN 0-231-07365-8. [PSK/MCW/PM]

18.426 William I. Shorrock. *French imperialism in the Middle East: the failure of policy in Syria and Lebanon, 1900–1914*. Madison: University of Wisconsin Press, 1976. ISBN 0-299-07030-1. ▸ French and British archival material informs author's pioneering thesis that while France's claim to Syria and Lebanon was consolidated prior to World War I, so was France's unpopularity in region. [PSK/MCW]

18.427 John P. Spagnolo. *France and Ottoman Lebanon, 1861–1914*. London: Ithaca Press for St. Antony's College, Middle East Centre, 1977. (St. Antony's Middle East monographs, 7.) ISBN 0-903729-23-7. ▸ Studies political change in complex society subjected to interaction of powerful European influences and Ottoman interests. Examines foundations of modern Lebanon. For specialists. [PSK/MCW]

18.428 Abdul Latif Tibawi. *A modern history of Syria, including Lebanon and Palestine*. New York: St. Martin's, 1969. ISBN 0-333-10066-2. ▸ Comprehensive study of Syria from Ottoman times 1960s treats political history in conjunction with social, economic, and cultural developments. Narrative integrates study of ruling elites with popular classes. [PSK/MCW]

18.429 Mary C. Wilson. *King Abdullah, Britain, and the making of Jordan*. Cambridge: Cambridge University Press, 1987. ISBN 0-521-32421-1 (cl), 0-521-39987-4 (pbk). ▸ Comprehensive political biography of founder of Jordan and analysis of state formation in historical context of Ottoman decline, extension of British power in region, and rise of Arab nationalism. [PSK]

18.430 Meir Zamir. *The formation of modern Lebanon*. 1985 ed. Ithaca, N.Y.: Cornell University Press, 1988. ISBN 0-8014-9523-7 (pbk). ▸ Demonstrates how local Christians influenced French creation of Greater Lebanon and French-supported domination that ultimately clashed with expanding Muslim population. Focus on confessional intractability needs balance. [PSK/MCW]

Iraq

18.431 Ghassan al-Atiyah. *Iraq, 1908–1921: a socio-political study*. Beirut: Arab Institute for Research and Publishing, 1973. ▸ Development of political parties and Arab nationalist groups in Mesopotamia. Iraq under Ottoman and Young Turk rule. Local reactions to post–World War I British plans resulting in 1920 revolt. [RSS]

18.432 Amatzia Baram. *Culture, history, and ideology in the formation of Baʿthist Iraq, 1968–89*. New York: St. Martin's, 1991. ISBN 0-312-04805-X. ▸ Process of deliberate institution of Mesopotamian-focused art, folklore, archaeology, theater, poetry, and history in Saddam Husayn's pan-Arab Baʿthist Iraq. Conflict and/or reconciliation of pan-Arabism, Mesopotamian myth, and Islam. [RSS]

18.433 Hanna Batatu. *The old social classes and the revolutionary movements of Iraq: a study of Iraq's old landed and commercial classes and of its Communists, Baʿthists, and Free Officers*. Rev. ed. Princeton: Princeton University Press, 1982. ISBN 0-691-05241-7 (cl, 1978), 0-691-02198-8 (pbk). ▸ Class analysis from Ottoman to Baʿth period based on detailed coverage of civilian and military personalities, Shīʿī, minority groups, and economic, educational, and social factors. [RSS]

18.434 Christopher B. B. Birdwood. *Nuri as-Said: a study in Arab leadership*. London: Cassell, 1959. ▸ Sympathetic portrayal of the perennial politician from his Ottoman army service through mandate and monarchy periods, 1920–58. Emphasizes post–World War II period and Iraqi-British relations. [RSS]

18.435 Stuart A. Cohen. *British policy in Mesopotamia, 1903–1914*. London: Ithaca Press for St. Antony's College, Middle East Centre, 1976. (St. Antony's Middle East monographs, 5.) ISBN 0-903729-17-2. ▸ British commercial and strategic interests in

pre–World War I Ottoman Iraq, reflecting British defense of India and fear of German-dominated Berlin-to-Baghdad railroad. Diplomatic history. [RSS]

18.436 Uriel Dann. *Iraq under Qassem: a political history, 1958–1963*. New York: Praeger, 1969. ISBN 0-269-67064-5. ▸ Detailed account drawn from press, radio, and personal accounts of coup that overthrew monarchy in 1958. Discussion of emergence of Communist party, Kurdish problem, and Qasim-Nasir (Nasser) competition in Arab world. [RSS]

18.437 Gerald De Gaury. *Three kings in Baghdad, 1921–1958*. London: Hutchinson, 1961. ▸ Personal, anecdotal portrayal of kings Faysal I, Ghazi, and Faysal II and regent Abd al-Ilah. Reminiscences by British officer who served in Iraq during monarchy. [RSS]

18.438 Marion Farouk-Sluglett and Peter Sluglett. *Iraq since 1958: from revolution to dictatorship*. 1987 ed. London: Taurus, 1990. ISBN 1-85043-317-8. ▸ Political history of regimes of Abd al-Karim Qasim, Abd al-Salam Arif, Abd al-Rahman Arif, and Baʿth, with analysis of Shīʿīs, Kurds, Iraqi Communist party, Iran-Iraq War, and oil. [RSS]

18.439 Elizabeth Warnock Fernea. *Guests of the sheik: an ethnography of an Iraqi village*. 1965 ed. New York: Doubleday, 1989. ISBN 0-385-01485-6. ▸ American woman's experience living traditional life of Iraqi woman in rural village in southern Iraq in late 1950s. [RSS]

18.440 Fritz Grobba. *Männer und Mächte im Orient: fünfundzwanzig Jahre diplomatischer Tätigkeit im Orient*. Zurich: Musterschmidt, 1967. ▸ Memoirs of German ambassador to Iraq and Saudi Arabia in 1930s; his views on Arab nationalism, Rashid Ali, Nuri as-Said, and Iraqi political history, 1921–41. [RSS]

18.441 Efraim Karsh and Inari Rautsi. *Saddam Hussein: a political biography*. New York: Free Press, 1991. ISBN 0-02-917063-X. ▸ Development of Iraqi Baʿth party, emergence of Saddam Husayn and Tikriti relatives in control of regime. Political and economic motivations for Iran-Iraq War and Gulf crisis of 1990–91. [RSS]

18.442 Abbas Kelidar, ed. *The integration of modern Iraq*. New York: St. Martin's, 1979. ISBN 0-312-41891-4. ▸ Anthology includes articles on Faysal I, development of Iraqi army, rural-urban migration, political elites, regional development and industrial policy after 1958, Kurds, and Iraqi Communist party. [RSS]

18.443 Majid Khadduri. *Independent Iraq, 1932–1958: a study in Iraqi politics*. 1960 2d ed. New York: AMS Press, 1981. ISBN 0-404-18972-5. ▸ Political history of monarchy with emphasis on interwar period. [RSS]

18.444 Majid Khadduri. *Republican Iraq: a study in Iraqi politics since the revolution of 1958*. London: Oxford University Press, 1969. ▸ Regimes of Abd al-Karim Qasim, Abd al-Salam Arif, and Abd al-Rahman Arif, 1958–68. Oil negotiations, Kurdish questions, and rivalries between pan-Arabs, Communists, Baʿthists, and Iraqi nationalists. [RSS]

18.445 Stephen Hemsley Longrigg. *Four centuries of modern Iraq*. 1925 ed. Beirut: Librairie du Liban, 1968. ▸ Political, economic, social, and diplomatic history emphasizing nineteenth century, Ottoman and Young Turk regimes, and World War I. [RSS]

18.446 Stephen Hemsley Longrigg. *Iraq, 1900 to 1950: a political, social, and economic history*. London: Oxford University Press, 1953. ▸ Based on newspapers, and British and Iraqi official reports; written by British official. Detailed pro-British view of Iraqi politics. [RSS]

18.447 Phebe Marr. *The modern history of Iraq*. Boulder: Westview, 1985. ISBN 0-86531-119-6. ▸ Political, social, diplomatic, economic, cultural history from 1920 to Iran-Iraq War with detail on education, emergence of new elites, and process of urbanization. [RSS]

18.448 Helen Chapin Metz, ed. *Iraq: a country study.* 4th ed. Washington, D.C.: Library of Congress, Federal Research Division; distributed by United States Government Printing Office, 1990. ▸ Historical survey of twentieth-century Iraq including solid bibliography of English-language sources and statistical appendixes on population, education, agriculture, trade, and military. [RSS]

18.449 Tim Niblock, ed. *Iraq: the contemporary state.* New York: St. Martin's, 1982. ISBN 0-312-43585-1. ▸ Collection of articles covering economic and foreign policy in Gulf. Topics include oil, women, Kurds, industrialization, and rural development after 1958. [RSS]

18.450 Edith T. Penrose and E. F. Penrose. *Iraq: international relations and national development.* Boulder: Westview, 1978. ISBN 0-89158-804-3. ▸ Political and economic development of Iraq, 1920 to Baʿth period, with emphasis on urban development, agrarian reform, and oil policy. [RSS]

18.451 Daniel Silverfarb. *Britain's informal empire in the Middle East: a case study of Iraq, 1929–1941.* New York: Oxford University Press, 1986. ISBN 0-19-503997-1. ▸ Analysis of Anglo-Iraqi relations emphasizing British economic and strategic goals via indirect rule of Iraq and newly independent state's attempt at independent policy making. [RSS]

18.452 Reeva S. Simon. *Iraq between the two world wars: the creation and implementation of a nationalist ideology.* New York: Columbia University Press, 1986. ISBN 0-231-06074-2. ▸ Development of system of education and textbooks that helped mold ideology of pan-Arab movement. Emergence of Arab nationalist military clique that ruled Iraq, 1920–41. [RSS]

18.453 Peter Sluglett. *Britain in Iraq, 1914–1932.* London: Ithaca Press for St. Antony's College, Middle East Centre, 1976. (St. Antony's Middle East monographs, 4.) ISBN 0-903729-16-4. ▸ Narrative history focusing on British tribal policy, defense, education, Shiʿis, land, and role of King Faysal I and Iraqi politicians during mandate period. [RSS]

18.454 Mohammad A. Tarbush. *The role of the military in politics: a case study of Iraq to 1941.* London: Kegan Paul, 1982. ISBN 0-7103-0036-0. ▸ Development of Iraqi military elite and its participation in Iraqi pan-Arab politics from World War I to Rashid Ali coup. [RSS]

18.455 Geoffrey Warner. *Iraq and Syria, 1941.* 1974 ed. Newark: University of Delaware Press, 1979. ISBN 0-87413-155-3. ▸ Diplomatic and military accounts of World War II campaigns in Iraq and Syria including relations with Axis powers and Iraqi revolt of 1941. [RSS]

SEE ALSO
  47.365 Briton Cooper Busch. *Britain, India, and the Arabs, 1914–1921.*

Zionist Movement and the State of Israel

18.456 Shmuel Almog, ed. *Zionism and the Arabs: essays.* Jerusalem: Historical Society of Israel and the Zalman Shazar Center, 1983. ISBN 965-227-010-5. ▸ Collection of articles discussing main attitudes of Zionist political movements toward Palestinians before 1948. Refutes contention that Jewish settlers ignored Arab presence in area. [IB]

18.457 Michael Avi-Yonah. "Israel." In *Encyclopaedia Judaica.* Vol. 9, pp. 106–1045. Jerusalem: Keter, 1971. ▸ Covers geography, history, politics, society, and culture; includes maps and tables. Post-1967 optimistic presentation, highlighting Zionist historiography of early years of state. [IB]

18.458 Arieh L. Avneri. *The claim of dispossession: Jewish land settlement and the Arabs, 1878–1948.* 1982 ed. New Brunswick, N.J.: Transaction, 1984. ISBN 0-87855-964-7 (pbk). ▸ Examines Arab presence in Palestine, population growth during seventy years of Jewish settlement, numbers of refugees, and Zionist policy of land purchase. Zionist perspective. [IB]

18.459 Sydney D. Bailey. *Four Arab-Israeli wars and the peace process.* Basingstoke, England: Macmillan, 1990. ISBN 0-333-48225-5 (cl), 0-333-48226-3 (pbk). ▸ Recounts political origins, courses, and consequences of Arab-Israeli wars of 1948, 1956, 1967, and 1973 and postwar mediation. Critical analysis of conventions about political negotiations and mediation. [IB]

18.460 Yehoshua Ben-Arieh. *Jerusalem in the nineteenth century: emergence of the new city.* New York: St. Martin's, 1986. ISBN 0-312-44188-6. ▸ Study in historical geography, focusing on transformation of society and urban development concommitant with evolution of Jerusalem from walled city to modern metropolis. [IB]

18.461 Yehoshua Ben-Arieh. *Jerusalem in the nineteenth century: the old city.* New York: St. Martin's, 1984. ISBN 0-312-44187-8. ▸ Reconstructs urban growth of Jerusalem as depicted in contemporary Western writings; special focus on Jewish community, 1800–14. Major product of Israeli historical-geographical school. [IB]

18.462 Uri Bialer. *Between East and West: Israel's foreign policy orientation, 1948–1956.* Cambridge: Cambridge University Press, 1990. ISBN 0-521-36249-0. ▸ Historical study of early Israeli policy making and administration; analyzes internal debates over foreign policy options (pro-Soviet, pro-Western, or nonaligned) and development of policy preference toward West. [IB]

18.463 Mitchell Cohen. *Zion and state: nation, class, and the shaping of modern Israel.* Oxford: Blackwell, 1987. ISBN 0-631-15243-1. ▸ Critical interpretation from labor-Zionist perspective. Analyzes transformation of Zionism and Israeli politics from revolutionary vision of regenerating Jewish society to compromises of statehood. [IB]

18.464 Richard I. Cohen, ed. *Vision and conflict in the Holy Land.* New York: St. Martin's, 1985. ISBN 0-312-84967-2. ▸ Major topics in history of Palestine from early Middle Ages to present: relationship of Diaspora Jews to land, messianism, nationalism, and modern political conflicts. Mainstream Israeli historiography. [IB]

18.465 Shmuel Noah Eisenstadt. *The transformation of Israeli society: an essay in interpretation.* Boulder: Westview, 1985. ISBN 0-8133-0306-0. ▸ Crystallization of institutional molds of Israeli society. Change, transition, and confrontation in postrevolutionary community. Sociological analysis of major aspects and trends of development to mid-1980s. [IB]

18.466 Amos Elon. *The Israelis: founders and sons.* 1971 ed. New York: Penguin, 1983. ISBN 0-14-022476-9 (pbk). ▸ Polemic from liberal Israeli perspective on evolution of Israeli society from radical Zionist pioneers into community marked by political clashes and ethnic tensions. [IB]

18.467 ESCO Foundation for Palestine. *Palestine, a study of Jewish, Arab, and British policies.* 1947 ed. 2 vols. Millwood, N.Y.: Kraus Reprint, 1980. ISBN 0-527-27750-9 (set). ▸ Main pre-1948, pro-Zionist document on subject. Monographs on various phases of Palestine problem: Jewish local self-government, Zionist aims and policies, land relations, and other aspects of Jewish-Arab conflict. [IB]

18.468 Shmuel Ettinger and Israel Bartal. "The first *aliyah*: ideological roots and practical accomplishments." In *The Jerusalem cathedra.* Levine I. Lee, ed., vol. 2, pp. 197–227. Detroit: Wayne State University Press, 1982. ISSN 0333-7618. ▸ Historical interpretation of roots of modern Jewish society before 1948. Emergence of Jewish nationalism from mid-nineteenth century to first stage of settlement in Palestine, combination of traditional and modern elements. [IB]

18.469 Itamar Even-Zohar. "The emergence of a native Hebrew culture in Palestine, 1882–1948." *Studies in Zionism* 4 (1981) 167–84. ISSN 0334-1771. ▸ Crystallization of unique local culture, distinct from Jewish cultures of Diaspora. Study of Israeli language, literature, and popular culture between ideology and multiethnic influences. Semiotics of modern Jewish society, pre-1948 community as cultural system. [IB]

18.470 Yehoshua Freundlich et al., eds. *Teudot li-mediniyut hahuts shel medinat Yisrael.* (Documents on the foreign policy of Israel). 6 vols. Jerusalem: Government Printer at Hamaker Press, 1948–1991. ISBN 965-279-002-8 (v. 2), 965-279-000-1 (v. 3), 965-279-005-2 (v. 4), 965-279-006-0 (v. 5), 965-279-008-7 (v. 6). ▸ Collection of materials pertaining to establishment of state, from war of independence to peace negotiations with Jordan. Covers foreign relations with United States and Soviet Union, armistices with Arab countries, and emergence of Israeli foreign relations. Authoritative publication of primary sources in English, French, and Hebrew. [IB]

18.471 Ben Halpern. *The idea of the Jewish state.* 1969 2d ed. Cambridge, Mass.: Harvard University Press, 1972. ISBN 0-674-44201-6. ▸ Traces evolution of Zionism from vaguely defined aspiration toward sovereignty to realization of statehood; analyzes its relationship to Israeli state. Zionist perspective. [IB]

18.472 Arthur Hertzberg, ed. *The Zionist idea: a historical analysis and reader.* 1959 ed. Westport, Conn.: Greenwood, 1975. ISBN 0-8371-2565-0. ▸ Zionist writings from early religious forerunners of Jewish nationalism to socialist Zionism and leaders of political struggle in Palestine. Provides broad spectrum of Jewish nationalist thought rooted in modern Europe. [IB]

18.473 Lawrence A. Hoffman, ed. *The land of Israel: Jewish perspectives.* Notre Dame, Ind.: Notre Dame University Press, 1986. ISBN 0-268-01280-6. ▸ Post-1967 collection of studies on Jewish attitudes toward Palestine through the ages. Wide variety of religious trends explicating Jewish longing for land. History of ideas and theology. [IB]

18.474 *Israel government yearbook.* Jerusalem: Government Printer, 1950–1990. ISSN 0578-8218. ▸ Major documentary source on Israeli government, political system, demography, and economic conditions. Presents official perspective which accommodates political changes in administration. Contains statistics, diagrams, and maps. [IB]

18.475 Ruth Kark, ed. *The land that became Israel: studies in historical geography.* Michael Gordon, trans. New Haven: Yale University Press, 1990. ISBN 0-300-04718-5. ▸ Discussion of infrastructure, entrepreneurship, and settlement. Treats human geography of Palestine to 1950s. Studies of Israeli historical-geographical school, dealing with all sectors of population. [IB]

18.476 Baruch Kimmerling. *Zionism and territory: the socio-territorial dimensions of Zionist politics.* Berkeley: University of California, Institute of International Studies, 1983. (Berkeley Institute of International Studies, Research series, 51.) ISBN 0-87725-151-7 (pbk), ISSN 0068-6093. ▸ Impact of land and territory on evolution of Jewish community in Palestine. Sociological analysis of roots of Arab-Jewish conflict from early Zionist settlement to present. [IB]

18.477 Baruch Kimmerling, ed. *The Israeli state and society: boundaries and frontiers.* Albany: State University of New York Press, 1989. ISBN 0-88706-849-9 (cl), 0-88706-850-2 (pbk). ▸ Mosaic of social and political phenomena arising from confrontation of Zionist ideology with reality. Offers conceptual framework for sociopolitical analysis of relationship between state and society. [IB]

18.478 Neville J. Mandel. *The Arabs and Zionism before World War I.* Berkeley: University of California Press, 1976. ISBN 0-520-02466-4 (cl), 0-520-03940-8 (pbk). ▸ Historical account of early roots of Arab antagonism toward Zionism. Describes Arab opposition to Zionist aims and activities in Palestine in late Ottoman period and relations among Turks, Arab nationalists, and Zionists. [IB]

18.479 Moshe Mossek. *Palestine immigration policy under Sir Herbert Samuel: British, Zionist, and Arab attitudes.* London: Cass; distributed by Biblio Distribution Centre, 1978. ISBN 0-7146-3096-9. ▸ Examination of immigration policy during first five years of British civil administration. Analyzes different approaches, patterns, procedures, and schemes of immigration. [IB]

18.480 Tudor Parfitt. *The Jews in Palestine, 1800–1882.* Wolfeboro, N.H.: Boydell, 1987. (Royal Historical Society studies in history, 52.) ISBN 0-86193-209-9, ISSN 0269-2244. ▸ Social and demographic transformation of pre-Zionist Jewish community centered in four holy cities: Jerusalem, Safed, Tiberias, and Hebron. Traces emergence of Jewish polity in Palestine to nineteenth century. [IB]

18.481 Raphael Patai, ed. *Encyclopedia of Zionism and Israel.* 2 vols. New York: Herzl, 1971. ISBN 0-07-079635-1. ▸ Covers places in Israel; biographies; history of Israel and Zionism; social, economic, agricultural, cultural, and religious development. Fervent pro-Zionist tone. Valuable reference to pre-1973 scholarship. [IB]

18.482 Derek J. Penslar. *Zionism and technocracy: the engineering of Jewish settlement in Palestine, 1870–1918.* Bloomington: Indiana University Press, 1991. ISBN 0-253-34290-2. ▸ Social, intellectual, and institutional history tracing origins of Zionism's first settlement engineering, from French Jewish philanthropies, German colonial models, and East European radical pioneering. Revises conventional histories from new perspective. [IB]

18.483 Itamar Rabinovich and Jehuda Reinharz, eds. *Israel in the Middle East: documents and readings on society, politics, and foreign relations, 1948–present.* New York: Oxford University Press, 1984. ISBN 0-19-503362-0 (cl), 0-19-503363-9 (pbk). ▸ Annotated sources encompassing political and diplomatic history; economic, legal, and social aspects since 1948. Selective collection of many documents otherwise unavailable in English. [IB]

18.484 Jehuda Reinharz. *Chaim Weizmann: the making of a Zionist leader.* New York: Oxford University Press, 1985. ISBN 0-19-503446-5. ▸ Authoritative scholarly biography of early career of Israel's first president, from Belorusian town of 1870s to World War I. [IB]

18.485 Susan Hattis Rolef, ed. *Political dictionary of the state of Israel.* New York and London: Macmillan and Collier Macmillan, 1987. ISBN 0-02-916421-4. ▸ Five hundred entries on all aspects of politics including biographies of statesmen and politicians. Comprehensive reference source, compiled by Israeli historians, political and social scientists, journalists, and government officials. [IB]

18.486 Norman Rose. *Chaim Weizmann, a biography.* 1986 ed. New York: Penguin, 1989. ISBN 0-14-012230-3. ▸ Comprehensive, compelling biography of central Zionist, diplomat, and politician who contributed to creation of state of Israel. Spans East European childhood to presidency of Jewish state. [IB]

18.487 Nadav Safran. *Israel: the embattled ally; with a new preface and postscript.* 1978 ed. Cambridge, Mass.: Belknap, 1981. ISBN 0-674-46881-3 (cl), 0-674-46882-1 (pbk). ▸ Comprehensive portrait of modern Israel as background to analysis of United States–Israeli relations. Dynamics and implications of change and evolution. History of international relations combined with contemporary politics and diplomacy. [IB]

18.488 Simon Schama. *Two Rothschilds and the land of Israel.* New York: Knopf; distributed by Random House, 1978. ISBN 0-394-50137-3. ▸ Surveys philanthropy of Baron Edmond de Rothschild and James Rothschild that made Jewish settlements in Palestine possible. A first study, based on family archives; laudatory tone. [IB]

18.489 Gershon Shafir. *Land, labor, and the origins of the Israeli-Palestinian conflict, 1882–1914.* Cambridge: Cambridge University Press, 1989. ISBN 0-521-35300-9. ▸ Post-1967 sociological, non-Zionist interpretation of early Jewish colonization. Highlights efforts of East European settlers to gain control of land and labor markets formative to Israeli society. [IB]

18.490 Leonard Stein. *The Balfour Declaration.* 1961 ed. Jerusalem: Magnes, 1983. ISBN 965-223-448-6. ▸ Detailed reconstruction of Zionist political activity, 1914–20, leading to British mandate in Palestine. Most authoritative documented work on subject. Political history by active Zionist leader. Classic of diplomatic history. [IB/EM]

18.491 Shabtai Teveth. *Ben-Gurion, the burning ground, 1886–1948.* Boston: Houghton-Mifflin, 1987. ISBN 0-395-35409-9. ▸ Definitive biography of predominant leader who shaped nascent Israeli nation, spanning early Zionist career in Ottoman Palestine to aftermath of Holocaust. [IB]

18.492 Ronald W. Zweig, ed. *David Ben-Gurion: politics and leadership in Israel.* London: Cass, 1991. ISBN 0-7146-3423-9. ▸ Critical essays examining Ben-Gurion's pivotal role at turning points in Israeli history, from early Jewish colonization to war of independence and early years of Jewish state. [IB]

SEE ALSO
47.378 Isaiah Friedman. *The question of Palestine.*

Palestine and the Palestinian National Movement

18.493 Ibrahim Abu-Lughod, ed. *The transformation of Palestine: essays on the origin and development of the Arab-Israeli conflict.* 2d ed. Evanston, Ill.: Northwestern University Press, 1987. ISBN 0-8101-0744-9. ▸ Sixteen basic essays, written from Palestinian perspective, mostly about mandate period including colonization, land, Palestinian resistance, Arab-Israeli issues, and international involvement. [PM]

18.494 Geoffrey Aronson. *Israel, Palestinians, and the Intifada: creating facts on the West Bank.* Washington, D.C.: Institute for Palestine Studies and Kegan Paul, 1990. ISBN 0-7103-0336-X. ▸ Detailed study of Israeli policies regarding West Bank and Palestinian responses from 1967 to 1988. Based on Israeli press and official statements. Revised edition of *Creating Facts* (1987). [PM]

18.495 Laurie A. Brand. *Palestinians in the Arab world: institution building and the search for state.* New York: Columbia University Press, 1988. ISBN 0-231-06722-4. ▸ Pioneering study of origins and evolution of Palestinian social and political institutions in Egypt, Kuwait, and Jordan that contributed to reemergence of Palestinian nationalism after 1948. [PM]

18.496 Neil Caplan. *Futile diplomacy.* Vol. 1: *Early Arab-Zionist negotiation attempts, 1913–1931.* Vol. 2: *Arab-Zionist negotiations and the end of the mandate.* 2 vols. London: Cass, 1983–86. ISBN 0-7146-3214-7 (v. 1), 0-7146-3215-5 (v. 2). ▸ Balanced analysis of fruitless attempts between 1913 and 1948 by Arabs, including Palestinians and Zionists, to resolve Palestine conflict. Includes over seventy documents. [PM]

18.497 Helena Cobban. *The Palestinian Liberation Organization: people, power, and politics.* Cambridge: Cambridge University Press, 1984. ISBN 0-521-25128-1 (cl), 0-521-27216-5 (pbk).

▸ Empathetic analysis of Palestine Liberation Organization (PLO), 1964–83, including Fatah leaders, internal opposition, Arab milieu, and performance in occupied territories. [PM]

18.498 Beshara B. Doumani. "Rediscovering Ottoman Palestine: writing Palestinians into history." *Journal of Palestine studies* 21.2 (1992) 5–28. ISSN 0377-919X. ▸ Critical analysis of Palestinian and Israeli historiography of late Ottoman Palestine. [PM]

18.499 Simha Flapan. *Birth of Israel: myths and realities.* 1987 ed. New York: Pantheon, 1992. ISBN 0-394-55588-X. ▸ Controversial revisionist work by Israeli scholar and peace activist, challenging official Israeli accounts of partition and Palestinian exodus. Based on primary sources. [PM]

18.500 Geoffrey W. Furlonge. *Palestine is my country: the story of Musa Alami.* New York: Praeger, 1969. ▸ More than a biography, recounts Palestine history during first half of twentieth century from viewpoint of moderate Palestinian political figure. [PM]

18.501 Alain Gresh. *The PLO, the struggle within: towards an independent Palestinian state.* Rev. ed. A. M. Berrett, trans. London: Zed, 1988. ISBN 0-86232-754-7 (cl), 0-86232-755-5 (pbk). ▸ Comprehensive history of Palestine Liberation Organization, discussing trends in Palestinian political thinking and internal debates. Based on PLO documents and interviews with PLO leaders. [PM]

18.502 Yehoshafat Harkabi. *Israel's fateful hour.* New York: Harper & Row, 1988. ISBN 0-06-016039-X. ▸ Critical analysis of Israel's position on Palestinian issue by authority and formerly hawkish head of Israeli military intelligence. [PM]

18.503 Alan Hart. *Arafat: a political biography.* Bloomington: Indiana University Press, 1989. ISBN 0-253-32711-3 (cl), 0-253-20516-6 (pbk). ▸ Sympathetic, detailed political biography of most important Palestinian leader since late 1960s, based on interviews with top Palestine Liberation Organization officials. [PM]

18.504 J. C. Hurewitz. *The struggle for Palestine.* Rev. ed. New York: Schocken, 1976. ISBN 0-8052-0524-1. ▸ One of earliest attempts to write nonpartisan history; still reliable account of Palestine problem between 1936 and 1948. [PM]

18.505 Abu Iyad and Eric Rouleau. *My home, my land: a narrative of the Palestinian struggle.* Linda Butler Koseoglu, trans. New York: Times Books, 1981. ISBN 0-8129-0936-4. ▸ Political story of Salah Khalaf, code named Abu Iyad, founder of Fatah and for years number-two leader of Palestine Liberation Organization under Yasir Arafat. Unique for its inside account of PLO and advocacy of accommodation with Israel. Based on interviews with Abu Iyad. [PM]

18.506 Tarif Khalidi. "Palestinian historiography, 1900–1948." *Journal of Palestine studies* 10.3 (1981) 59–76. ISSN 0377-919X. ▸ Useful discussion from Arab perspective of research and writing in Arabic by Palestinian writers; constraints on them, their preoccupations, and value of their works. [PM]

18.507 Walid Khalidi. *Before their diaspora: a photographic history of the Palestinians, 1876–1948.* Washington, D.C.: Institute for Palestine Studies, 1991. ISBN 0-88728-219-0 (cl), 0-88728-228-8 (pbk). ▸ Photographic essay on Palestinians by a foremost authority; includes almost 500 photographs, long chronology, and scholarly introduction covering period from 1876 to 1948. [PM]

18.508 Walid Khalidi, ed. *From haven to conquest: readings in Zionism and the Palestine problem until 1948.* 1971 ed. Washington, D.C.: Institute for Palestine Studies, 1987. ISBN 0-88728-155-9 (cl), 0-88728-156-7 (pbk). ▸ Anthology of over eighty selections, including maps and statistics on population, land tenure, etc., and on Palestine problem before 1948. Includes excellent synthesis and interpretation from Palestinian perspective. [PM]

18.509 Fred J. Khouri. *The Arab-Israeli dilemma.* 3d ed. Syracuse, N.Y.: Syracuse University Press, 1985. ISBN 0-8156-2339-9 (cl), 0-8156-2340-2 (pbk). ▸ Well-documented, balanced, and comprehensive work. Standard survey of conflict. [PM]

18.510 Uri M. Kupferschmidt. *The Supreme Muslim Council: Islam under the British mandate for Palestine.* Leiden: Brill, 1987. ISBN 90-04-07929-7. ▸ Well-documented analysis, from Israeli perspective, of Supreme Muslim Council; its administration of Muslim courts and religious endowments; and political participation of its members. [PM]

18.511 Ann Mosely Lesch. *Arab politics in Palestine, 1917–1939: the frustration of a nationalist movement.* Ithaca, N.Y.: Cornell University Press, 1979. ISBN 0-8014-1237-4. ▸ Authoritative, dispassionate history of constraints on Palestinian national movement. Based on British, Arab, and Zionist primary sources. Best concise study on subject. [PM]

18.512 Wm. Roger Louis and Robert W. Stookey, eds. *The end of the Palestine mandate.* Austin: University of Texas Press, 1986. ISBN 0-292-72052-1. ▸ Seven essays ranging from balanced and valuable (Hurewitz and Khalidi) to partisan (Cohen) about British, United States, and Soviet policies and Arab and Jewish leaders in late 1940s. [PM]

18.513 Ian Lustick. *Arabs in the Jewish state: Israel's control of a national minority.* Austin: University of Texas Press, 1980. ISBN 0-292-70347-3 (cl), 0-292-70348-1 (pbk). ▸ Dispassionate, systematic; best analysis of Israel's policies that have led to highly effective system of control over its Palestinian citizens. [PM]

18.514 Philip Mattar. *Mufti of Jerusalem: Al-Hajj Amin al-Husayni and the Palestinian national movement.* Rev. ed. New York: Columbia University Press, 1992. ISBN 0-231-06462-4. ▸ First scholarly biography of controversial Palestinian leader; revisionist, balanced account. Based on archival sources and interviews. [PM]

18.515 Justin McCarthy. *The population of Palestine: population history and statistics of the late Ottoman period and the mandate.* New York: Columbia University Press, 1990. ISBN 0-231-07110-8. ▸ Short scholarly study of controversial population statistics of Palestine from 1850 to 1948. Based on Ottoman archives and British statistics. Includes tables. [PM]

18.516 Ylana N. Miller. *Government and society in rural Palestine, 1920–1948.* Austin: University of Texas Press, 1985. ISBN 0-292-72728-3. ▸ Introductory study of constraining effects of British policy on Palestinian village life. Based largely on archival sources. [PM]

18.517 Benny Morris. *Birth of the Palestinian refugee problem, 1947–1949.* Cambridge: Cambridge University Press, 1987. ISBN 0-521-33028-9. ▸ Detailed, balanced, and myth-debunking scholarly work (Israeli and Arab). Definitive history of 1948 exodus based on Israeli, British, and United States sources. [PM]

18.518 Muhammad Y. Muslih. *The origins of Palestinian nationalism.* New York: Columbia University Press, 1988. ISBN 0-231-06508-6. ▸ Pioneering scholarly analysis of internal Arab factors that contributed to emergence of Palestinian nationalism. Based on interviews and Arab, British, and Zionist archives. [PM]

18.519 Roger Owen, ed. *Studies in the economic and social history of Palestine in the nineteenth and twentieth centuries.* Carbondale: Southern Illinois University Press, 1982. ISBN 0-8093-1089-9. ▸ Collection of four basic scholarly socioeconomic studies of Palestine covering 1856–82, 1920–48, and post-1948. [PM]

18.520 Don Peretz. *Intifada: the Palestinian uprising.* Boulder: Westview, 1990. ISBN 0-8133-0859-3 (cl), 0-8133-0860-7 (pbk).

▸ Systematic overview; origins and effects on Palestinians, Israel, and international opinion by one of few nonpartisan scholars on Palestine problem. [PM]

18.521 Avi Plascov. *Palestinian refugees in Jordan, 1948–1957.* London: Cass, 1981. ISBN 0-7146-3120-5. ▸ Groundbreaking, thoroughly researched study of Palestinian refugee community in Jordan from Israeli perspective. Based on archival sources, interviews, and Arabic publications. [PM/PSK/MCW]

18.522 Yehoshua Porath. *The emergence of the Palestinian-Arab national movement.* Vol. 1: *1918–1929.* Vol 2: *The Palestinian-Arab national movement: from riots to rebellion, 1929–1939.* London: Cass, 1974–77. ISBN 0-7146-2939-1 (v. 1), 0-7146-3070-5 (v. 2). ▸ Most comprehensive scholarly history of Palestinian nationalism, 1917–39. Based on Arab, Zionist, and British documents and Arabic works. Volume 2 more readable but less balanced. Indispensable works. [PM/JSH]

18.523 William B. Quandt. *Decade of decisions: American policy toward the Arab-Israeli conflict, 1967–1976.* Berkeley: University of California Press, 1977. ISBN 0-520-03469-4 (cl), 0-520-03536-4 (pbk). ▸ Analysis of formulation of United States policy toward Arab-Israeli conflict by scholar and former member of National Security Council. [PM]

18.524 Emile Sahliyeh. *In search of leadership: West Bank politics since 1967.* Washington, D.C.: Brookings Institution, 1988. ISBN 0-8157-7698-5 (cl), 0-8157-7697-7 (pbk). ▸ First comprehensive examination of changes in Palestine political elite, from pro-Jordanian traditional leaders to mass-supported pro-Palestine Liberation Organization politicians, resulting from social and political trends, 1967–87. [PM]

18.525 Edward W. Said. *Question of Palestine.* 1979 ed. New York: Vintage, 1980. ISBN 0-394-74527-2. ▸ Powerful Palestinian interpretation of history of Palestine problem written for Western audience by one of foremost Palestinian intellectuals. [PM]

18.526 Rosemary Sayigh. *Palestinians, from peasants to revolutionaries: a people's history.* Noam Chomsky, Introduction. London: Zed, 1979. ISBN 0-905762-24-X (cl), 0-905762-25-8 (pbk). ▸ Pro-Palestinian account of transformation of Palestinian peasant refugees into militants and revolutionaries. Based on interviews with camp Palestinians in Lebanon. [PM]

18.527 Alexander Schölch. *Palestine in transformation, 1856–1882: studies in social, economic, and political development.* William C. Young and Michael Gerrity, trans. Washington, D.C.: Institute for Palestine Studies, 1992. ISBN 0-88728-234-2. ▸ Groundbreaking study of impact of European penetration and Ottoman reforms on socioeconomic developments in Palestine, 1856–82. Based on British, German, and Israeli documents. For specialists. [PM]

18.528 Charles D. Smith. *Palestine and the Arab-Israeli conflict.* 2d ed. New York: St. Martin's, 1992. ISBN 0-312-06557-4 (cl), 0-312-04904-8 (pbk). ▸ One of best surveys of modern history of Palestine and the conflict. Comprehensive narrative with sound conclusions based on wide resources. [PM]

18.529 Pamela Ann Smith. *Palestine and the Palestinians, 1876–1983.* New York: St. Martin's, 1984. ISBN 0-312-59487-9 (cl), 0-312-59488-7 (pbk). ▸ Attempt to write concise history of Palestinian politics and society, 1876–1983. [PM]

18.530 Kenneth W. Stein. *The land question in Palestine, 1917–1939.* Chapel Hill: University of North Carolina Press, 1984. ISBN 0-8078-1579-9 (cl), 0-8078-4178-1 (pbk). ▸ Comprehensive sociopolitical history, from Zionist perspective, of land tenure and sales. Based on extensive British and Zionist archival material. [PM]

18.531 *Survey of Palestine.* 1946 ed. 3 vols. Washington, D.C.:

Institute for Palestine Studies, 1991. ISBN 0-88728-211-3 (v. 1, cl), 0-88728-214-8 (v. 2, cl), 0-88728-216-4 (v. 3, cl), 0-88728-213-X (v. 1, pbk), 0-88728-215-6 (v. 2, pbk), 0-88728-217-2 (v. 3, pbk). ▸ Authoritative, dispassionate, comprehensive source on Palestine's government, politics, demographics, and economy. Compiled by British mandatory administration, 1945–47. [PM]

Arabian Peninsula

18.532 Ahmad Mustafa Abu Hakima. *The modern history of Kuwait, 1750–1965.* London: Luzac, 1983. ISBN 0-7189-0259-9. ▸ Comprehensive discussion of Kuwait from internal as well as British perspective. Best summary in English on subject. [WLO]

18.533 Calvin H. Allen, Jr. *Oman: the modernization of the sultanate.* Boulder: Westview, 1987. ISBN 0-8133-0125-4. ▸ Equal coverage of events before 1970; basic introduction to changes with new political order thereafter. Emphasis on internal political history with some discussion of economic and foreign matters. [WLO]

18.534 Mohammed Almana. *Arabia unified: a portrait of Ibn Saud.* Rev. ed. London: Hutchinson Benham, 1982. ISBN 0-09-147290-3 (cl), 0-09-147291-1 (pbk). ▸ Account of Saudi royal court before impact of oil. Personal memoir by admirer of King Abd al-Aziz (Ibn Saʿud). [WLO]

18.535 Ayman Al-Yassini. *Religion and state in the kingdom of Saudi Arabia.* Boulder: Westview, 1985. ISBN 0-8133-0058-4. ▸ Covers all aspects of Wahhābī movement, establishment of Saʿudi power, and involvement of ʿulamāʾ in government. Valuable in regard to practical connections of Islam and state administration. [WLO]

18.536 Irvine H. Anderson. *ARAMCO, the United States, and Saudi Arabia: a study of the dynamics of foreign oil policy, 1933–1950.* Princeton: Princeton University Press, 1981. ISBN 0-691-04679-4. ▸ Discusses Arabian American Oil Company, oil industry, and diplomatic relations of United States with Saudi Arabia. More useful for American perspectives and actions than Middle East. [WLO]

18.537 Robin L. Bidwell. *The two Yemens.* Boulder: Westview, 1983. ISBN 0-86531-295-8. ▸ Comprehensive history of both North and South Yemen with emphasis on modern times. Valuable especially for British perspective. [WLO]

18.538 Robert D. Burrowes. *The Yemen Arab Republic: the politics of development, 1962–1986.* Boulder: Westview, 1987. ISBN 0-8133-0435-0. ▸ After introduction, mostly standard political history for period 1967 to 1984. [WLO]

18.539 Alvin J. Cottrell, ed. *The Persian Gulf states: a general survey.* Baltimore: Johns Hopkins University Press, 1980. ISBN 0-8018-2204-1. ▸ Massive study of early and recent times for Arabia, Iran, and Iraq. Covers social, cultural, economic, and political events. [WLO]

18.540 Jill Crystal. *Oil and politics in the Gulf: rulers and merchants in Kuwait and Qatar.* Cambridge: Cambridge University Press, 1990. ISBN 0-521-36639-9. ▸ Political and economic factors in twentieth-century Persian Gulf history. Brief, stimulating revisionist examination of political impact of oil on power especially starting in 1930s. [WLO]

18.541 Gerald De Gaury. *Faisal: king of Saudi Arabia.* London: Barker, 1966. ▸ Favorable biography of Faisal before he became king. [WLO]

18.542 R. J. Gavin. *Aden under British rule, 1839–1967.* New York: Barnes & Noble, 1975. ISBN 0-06-492337-1. ▸ Emphasis on Aden but includes hinterland and also relations with North Yemen. Traditional political work; deals chiefly with pre-1919 period. [WLO]

18.543 A. Reza S. Islami and Rostam Mehraban Kavoussi. *The political economy of Saudi Arabia.* Seattle: University of Washington Press, 1984. ISBN 0-295-96139-2 (pbk). ▸ Critical examination of Saudi history and government. One of few leftist critiques of Saudi affairs available in English. [WLO]

18.544 John B. Kelly. *Britain and the Persian Gulf, 1795–1880.* Oxford: Clarendon, 1968. ISBN 0-19-821360-3. ▸ Best available discussion of British contacts with all Persian Gulf countries for this period. [WLO]

18.545 Robert Geran Landen. *Oman since 1856: disruptive modernization in a traditional Arab society.* Princeton: Princeton University Press, 1967. ▸ Outstanding pioneering work on Omani history, concentrating on diplomacy, imperialism, and political development. [WLO]

18.546 William L. Ochsenwald. *The Hijaz railroad.* Charlottesville: University Press of Virginia, 1980. ISBN 0-8139-0825-6. ▸ Impact on Arabia, Syria, Jordan, and Lebanon. Based chiefly on European archives and Arab newspapers. Reassesses impact of T. E. Lawrence (Lawrence of Arabia) on Middle Eastern history. Only substantial study on subject in English. [WLO]

18.547 William L. Ochsenwald. *Religion, society, and the state in Arabia: the Hijaz under Ottoman control, 1840–1908.* Columbus: Ohio State University Press, 1984. ISBN 0-8142-0366-3. ▸ Innovative study of Ottoman administration in western Arabia including socioeconomic and political analysis. Based on Ottoman and European archives. Emphasizes religion as determinative force, follows Braudelian examples. [WLO]

18.548 John E. Peterson. *Defending Arabia.* New York: St. Martin's, 1986. ISBN 0-312-19114-6. ▸ Twentieth-century military history of Arabia, especially involving great powers. Security aspects, as locally perceived, contrasted with foreign views. Most important of many works on this subject. [WLO]

18.549 John E. Peterson. *Oman in the twentieth century: political foundations of an emerging state.* New York: Barnes & Noble, 1978. ISBN 0-06-495522-2. ▸ Geographical introduction, followed by specialist analysis of institutions, government, tribes, and changes since 1970. [WLO]

18.550 John E. Peterson. *Yemen: the search for a modern state.* Baltimore: Johns Hopkins University Press, 1982. ISBN 0-8018-2784-1. ▸ Brief political history of North Yemen with emphasis on institutions following historical introduction; useful for political scientists. [WLO]

18.551 H. St. John B. Philby. *Arabia of the Wahhabis.* 1928 ed. London: Cass, 1977. ISBN 0-7146-3073-X. ▸ One of many brilliant accounts by famous European traveler. Focuses on formation of Saudi Arabia and description of region. [WLO]

18.552 H. St. John B. Philby. *Saʿudi Arabia.* 1955 ed. New York: Arno, 1972. ISBN 0-405-04581-6. ▸ Descriptions corresponding to reigns, from rise of Wahhābī movement in eighteenth century to death of King Abd al-Aziz (Ibn Saʿud). Author was adviser to king and strongly favorable to him. [WLO]

18.553 Robert W. Stookey. *South Yemen: a Marxist republic in Arabia.* Boulder: Westview, 1982. ISBN 0-86531-024-6. ▸ Short but influential discussion of sole thoroughly Marxist regime in Middle East in twentieth century. [WLO]

18.554 Manfred W. Wenner. *Modern Yemen, 1918–1966.* Baltimore: Johns Hopkins University Press, 1967. (Johns Hopkins University studies in historical and political science, 84.1.) ▸ Includes opposition movements, foreign relations, and civil war. One of first Western scholarly examinations of Yemeni political history. [WLO]

18.555 John C. Wilkinson. *Arabia's frontiers: the story of Britain's boundary drawing in the desert.* London: Taurus; distributed by

St. Martin's, 1991. ISBN 1-85043-319-4. ▸ Brilliant investigation of amorphousness of boundaries in Arabian peninsula. Diplomatic history of boundary negotiating process. [WLO]

18.556 R. Bayly Winder. *Saudi Arabia in the nineteenth century.* 1965 ed. New York: Octagon Books, 1980. ISBN 0-374-98676-2. ▸ Detailed political history based on Arabic sources. Most important work on subject with profound implications for later Saudi developments. [WLO]

Iran

18.557 Ervand Abrahamian. *Iran between two revolutions.* Princeton: Princeton University Press, 1982. ISBN 0-691-05342-1 (cl), 0-691-00790-X (pbk). ▸ Influential analysis of Iranian politics and society, 1905–79. Detailed examination of communist Tudeh party and nationalism, with emergence of class identities crosscut by group, ethnic, and religious factors. [GRG]

18.558 Ervand Abrahamian. *The Iranian Mojahedin.* New Haven: Yale University Press, 1989. ISBN 0-300-04423-2. ▸ Important analysis of failure of radical Islamic Socialists in Iranian Revolution. Set in political, social, and intellectual context; based on interviews and survey of radical Islamic literature. [GRG]

18.559 Shahrough Akhavi. *Religion and politics in contemporary Iran: clergy-state relations in the Pahlavi period.* Albany: State University of New York Press, 1980. ISBN 0-87395-408-4. ▸ Basic description of political interaction of state and religion in mid-twentieth-century Iran. Sociology of religion and examination of religious scholars' role within religious institution and state. [GRG]

18.560 Hamid Algar. *Religion and state in Iran, 1785–1906: the role of the ulama in the Qajar period.* 1969 ed. Berkeley: University of California Press, 1980. ISBN 0-520-04100-3. ▸ Pioneering survey of political interaction of state and 'ulamā' in nineteenth-century Iran. Describes 'ulamā' as leaders of opposition to Western impact and to government. [GRG/JW]

18.561 Said Amir Arjomand. *The turban for the crown: the Islamic revolution in Iran.* New York: Oxford University Press, 1988. ISBN 0-19-504257-3 (cl), 0-19-504258-1 (pbk). ▸ Analyzes historic change in Shīʿī thought and practice under Khomeini that resulted in clerical success and Islamic government with politicized Shīʿī population. [GRG]

18.562 Peter Avery, Gavin Hambly, and Charles Melville, eds. *From Nadir Shah to the Islamic Republic.* Vol. 7 of *The Cambridge history of Iran.* Cambridge: Cambridge University Press, 1991. ISBN 0-521-20095-4. ▸ Chapters on all aspects of Iranian history since mid-sixteenth century: diplomacy, politics, society, economy, and religious and cultural life. [GRG]

18.563 Shaul Bakhash. *The reign of the ayatollahs: Iran and the Islamic revolution.* Rev. ed. New York: Basic Books, 1990. ISBN 0-465-06890-1 (pbk). ▸ Balanced overview, by prominent scholar and journalist, of 1979 Iranian Revolution and subsequent Islamic Republic, clergy's success in establishing its power. [GRG]

18.564 Amin Banani. *The modernization of Iran, 1921–41.* 1961 ed. Stanford, Calif.: Stanford University Press, 1969. ▸ Classic account of centralization, modernization, and westernization under Reza Shah. Describes major military, administrative, and cultural reforms initiated. [GRG]

18.565 Mangol Bayat. *Iran's first revolution: Shīʿism and the constitutional revolution of 1905–1909.* New York: Oxford University Press, 1991. ISBN 0-19-506822-X. ▸ Critical revisionist analysis of role and attitudes of religious elite toward early twentieth-century modernization. Asserts that religious elite, not challenging government, was coopted and that revolution represented secularist victory. [GRG]

18.566 Lois Beck. *The Qashqa'i of Iran.* New Haven: Yale University Press, 1986. ISBN 0-300-03212-9. ▸ Influential survey of history of important tribal confederation. Analyzes its political system, interaction with state, and impact of rapid change. Analysis combines anthropology and history. [GRG]

18.567 Julian Bharier. *Economic development in Iran, 1900–1970.* London: Oxford University Press, 1971. ISBN 0-19-215342-0. ▸ Clear, comprehensive survey of all aspects of Iran's economy. Descriptive, includes valuable data and tables. [GRG]

18.568 Carol Bier, ed. *Woven from the soul, spun from the heart: textile arts of Safavid and Qajar Iran, sixteenth-nineteenth centuries.* Washington, D.C.: Textile Museum, 1987. ISBN 0-87405-027-8 (cl), 0-87405-026-X (pbk). ▸ Nine articles with illustrations, including surveys and analyses of much-neglected Qajar period. Art history encompassing technology and social and economic history. [GRG]

18.569 James A. Bill. *The eagle and the lion: the tragedy of American-Iranian relations.* New Haven: Yale University Press, 1988. ISBN 0-300-04097-0 (cl), 0-300-04412-7 (pbk). ▸ Clear analysis of complexities of American-Iranian relations. Sharply criticizes United States government's willful ignorance of Iran and incompetence, especially from 1953 through Iran-Contra scandal. [GRG]

18.570 James A. Bill and Wm. Roger Louis. *Musaddiq, Iranian nationalism, and oil.* Austin: University of Texas Press, 1988. ISBN 0-292-75100-1. ▸ Survey of oil nationalization and constitutional crisis and Prime Minister Musaddiq's role. Examines nationalism, religion, oil, Iranian politics, and United States and British roles. [GRG]

18.571 Michael E. Bonine and Nikki R. Keddie, eds. *Modern Iran: the dialectics of continuity and change.* Albany: State University of New York Press, 1981. ISBN 0-87395-465-3 (cl), 0-87395-641-9 (pbk). ▸ Provocative analysis of nineteenth- and twentieth-century economic, social, and political change. Focus on key aspects of society, urban and rural, and on culture; by twenty specialists. [GRG]

18.572 Richard Cottam. *Nationalism in Iran, updated through 1978.* Rev. ed. Pittsburgh: University of Pittsburgh Press, 1979. ISBN 0-8229-3396-7 (cl), 0-8229-5299-8 (pbk). ▸ Analysis of Iranian nationalism in response to foreign intervention, especially cold war. Describes Musaddiq crisis and United States misunderstanding of it as reinforcing Iranian nationalism and cynicism. [GRG]

18.573 George N. C. Curzon. *Persia and the Persian question.* 1892 ed. 2 vols. New York: Barnes & Noble, 1966. ▸ Classic late nineteenth-century account of all aspects of Persian society. Despite imperialist perspective, invaluable encyclopedic accumulation of contemporary detail and anecdotes by leading British statesman. [GRG]

18.574 Ronald W. Ferrier. *The developing years, 1901–1932.* Vol. 1 of *The history of the British Petroleum Company.* Cambridge: Cambridge University Press, 1982. ISBN 0-521-24647-4 (pbk). ▸ Authoritative, lucid study of key economic factor and company. Utilizes British Petroleum archives from company's perspective but within context of expanding energy needs of industrialized world. [GRG]

18.575 Willem M. Floor. "The guilds in Iran: an overview from the earliest beginnings till 1972." *Zeitschrift der deutschen morgenländischen Gesellschaft* 75 (1975) 99–116. ISSN 0341-0137. ▸ Surveys important institutions critical to economic and social role of the bazaar. Neglected but important area of study by one of few urban social historians of Iran. [GRG]

18.576 Gene R. Garthwaite. *Khans and shahs: a documentary analysis of the Bakhtiyari in Iran.* Cambridge: Cambridge University Press, 1983. ISBN 0-521-24235-5. ▸ Pioneering history of political and socioeconomic organization of important tribal confederation in regional and national context. Historical anthropology; based on contemporary documents included with translations. [GRG]

18.577 G. G. Gilbar. "The big merchants (*tujjar*) and the Persian constitutional revolution of 1906." *Asian and African studies* 11 (1977) 275–303. ISSN 0571-2472. ▸ Important analysis of neglected group. Argues merchant participation in 1906 Revolution reflected growing trade and confidence on their part. [GRG]

18.578 G. G. Gilbar. "Demographic developments in late Qajar Persia, 1810–1906." *Asian and African studies* 2 (1976) 125–56. ISSN 0571-2472. ▸ Best available survey of population changes, based on close textual analysis. [GRG]

18.579 Shahla Haeri. *Law of desire: temporary marriage in Iran.* Syracuse, N.Y.: Syracuse University Press, 1989. ISBN 0-8156-2465-4 (cl), 0-8156-2483-2 (pbk). ▸ Unique survey and analysis of temporary marriage through interviews and legal texts. Useful insights into marriage, roles of women, and their interaction with religious scholars, society, and culture as a whole. [GRG]

18.580 Eric J. Hooglund. *Land and revolution in Iran, 1960–1980.* Austin: University of Texas Press, 1982. ISBN 0-292-74633-4. ▸ Critical survey of land redistribution policies and their impact. Includes peasant attitudes toward land reform and changes that led to 1979 Revolution. Based on extensive fieldwork and knowledge. [GRG]

18.581 Charles P. Issawi, ed. and comp. *The economic history of Iran, 1800–1914.* Chicago: University of Chicago Press, 1971. (Publications of the Center for Middle Eastern Studies, 8.) ISBN 0-226-38606-6. ▸ Survey of nineteenth- and early twentieth-century economic and social history reproducing primary contemporary sources. Succinct background, introductions, and summaries of key economic categories. [GRG]

18.582 Hassan Kamshad. *Modern Persian prose literature.* Cambridge: Cambridge University Press, 1966. ▸ Survey of key nineteenth- and twentieth-century writers that provides framework for understanding intellectual history and attitudes of intelligentsia. Part 2 focuses on most important writer of twentieth century, Sadeq Hidayat. [GRG]

18.583 Homa Katouzian. *Musaddiq and the struggle for power in Iran.* London: Taurus; distributed by St. Martin's, 1990. ISBN 1-85043-210-4. ▸ Political biography of Mohammad Musaddiq (1882–1967), leading democratic politician and prime minister (1951–53). Includes history of Popular movement of Iran, which he led. [CVF]

18.584 Farhad Kazemi and Ervand Abrahamian. "The nonrevolutionary peasantry of modern Iran." *Iranian studies* 11.1–4 (1978) 259–304. ISSN 0021-0862. ▸ Critical examination of absence of peasant rebellions in Iran. Lack of middle peasantry with persistence of traditional village insularity prevented cross-regional class consciousness and revolts. [GRG]

18.585 Nikki R. Keddie. *Roots of revolution: an interpretive history of modern Iran.* New Haven: Yale University Press, 1981. ISBN 0-300-02606-4 (cl), 0-300-02611-0 (pbk). ▸ Best available overview and analysis of historic nineteenth- and twentieth-century factors such as imperialism and internal economic, social, political, and ideological changes leading to clerical success of revolution. [GRG]

18.586 Ann K. S. Lambton. *Qajar Persia: eleven studies.* Austin: University of Texas Press, 1987. ISBN 0-292-76900-8. ▸ Wide-ranging essays on nineteenth- and early twentieth-century Iran by leading authority. Narratives on important topics, based on careful textual reading. [GRG]

18.587 John Malcolm. *A history of Persia from the most early period to the present time, containing an account of the religion, government, usages, and character of the inhabitants of that kingdom.* Rev. ed. London: Murray, 1829. ▸ Valuable as classic contemporary account of early nineteenth-century Qajar Iran with firsthand anecdotes by British diplomat, whose attitudes are characteristic of subsequent travelers and observers. [GRG]

18.588 Roy P. Mottahedeh. *The mantle of the prophet: religion and politics in Iran.* New York: Pantheon, 1985. ISBN 0-394-74865-4 (pbk). ▸ Description and analysis of traditional culture and education of cleric and his values in changing twentieth-century Iran. Compelling imaginative interpretation with historical and biographical bases. [GRG]

18.589 Misagh Parsa. *Social origins of the Iranian Revolution.* New Brunswick, N.J.: Rutgers University Press, 1989. ISBN 0-8135-1411-8 (cl), 0-8135-1412-6 (pbk). ▸ Analysis of Iranian Revolution in comparative context. Important revisionist argument that structural factors and group action, rather than religious ideology, drove revolution. Emphasizes central role of bazaar merchants. [GRG]

18.590 Rouhollah K. Ramazani. *Iran's foreign policy, 1941–1973: a study of foreign policy in modernizing nations.* Charlottesville: University Press of Virginia, 1975. ISBN 0-8139-0594-X. ▸ Survey of Iran as factor in cold war and issues of oil and nationalism. Authoritative analysis by specialist on foreign policy. [GRG]

18.591 Rouhollah K. Ramazani. *Revolutionary Iran: challenge and response in the Middle East.* Baltimore: Johns Hopkins University Press, 1986. ISBN 0-8018-3377-9. ▸ Careful analysis of postrevolutionary Iranian foreign policy and regional role. Argues that revolutionary rhetoric obscures continuity of historical, geographical, and sociopolitical factors in determining policy. [GRG]

18.592 Richard Tapper. *Pasture and politics: economics, conflict, and ritual among Shahsevan nomads of northwestern Iran.* London: Academic Press, 1979. ISBN 0-12-683660-4. ▸ Description of pastoral nomads and their interaction with sedentary society. Rich ethnographic data, especially on ritual. Critical analysis in comparative and theoretical context. [GRG]

18.593 Donald N. Wilber. *Riza Shah Pahlavi: the resurrection and reconstruction of Iran.* Hicksville, N.Y.: Exposition, 1975. ISBN 0-682-48206-4. ▸ Best available narrative biography of rise to power and role of critical, centralizing, and secularizing nationalist ruler in twentieth century. [GRG]

SEE ALSO
47.279 Firuz Kazemzadeh. *Russia and Britain in Persia, 1864–1914.*

Section 19

MARGARET JEAN HAY AND JOSEPH C. MILLER

Sub-Saharan Africa

Africans have, as other peoples, always thought about their past, though in distinctive ways that arose from the social and cultural milieux particular to their lives. For most, living without written means of preserving their recollections of things past, efforts to conserve the lessons of accumulated experience focused on memory, as enhanced by the careful structuring of verbal representations of it: songs and other rhymed or rhythmic language; intensely dramatic metaphors that Westerners saw as "mythical" or "magical"; sharply and therefore memorably contrasted and overlapping conceptual categories of the sort celebrated by structuralist anthropology; woven, carved, and scarified visual representations of inspired artistry (J. Vansina 19.100); and regular performances ("ritual" in the language of the classical ethnographers). These lessons from experience were worked out collectively and preserved through the participation of many people in their construction, recitation, and performance.

The poet Jonathon Swift (1667–1745) acerbically observed his European contemporaries' ignorance of an Africa viewed as mysterious, wild, and savage and concluded that they filled the gaps in real knowledge of the people with "elephants, for want of towns." Far more mythical than the Africans' own chronicles were the reports of most early outsiders—traders, travelers, and later, missionaries, soldiers, and colonial administrators—who ventured there and wrote about what they thought they saw.

Renaissance "arm-chair historians" in their studies back in Europe, used these travelers' reports to satisfy their own growing curiosity about distant parts of the world and adapted them to fit pet theories. The respect with which the Europeans on the scene in the sixteenth and seventeenth centuries quite realistically treated their African counterparts began to erode in their hands, as they incorporated their sources' uncomprehending repulsion at some of the Africans' customs they described into systematic theories of European superiority and African inferiority, expressed increasingly in terms of biological determinism. As Europe moved toward becoming "the modern West," the growing differences between its own civilization and those of most of the rest of the world found an explanation in racism. The racialist dismissal of all things in Africa worthy of Europeans' respect dominated the Western image of Africa throughout the nineteenth century and during much of the first half of the twentieth. The crudest racist assumption about Africa's past was that it had none, at least no record or accomplishment recognizable to Western progressives, and certainly none recoverable by the narrowly positivist documentary canon of the newly professionalized field of history at that time.

Academic countertendencies, of course, grew apace with the triumph of pseudo-scientific racism. A kind of paternalistic liberalism had sounded a counterpoint within even the most racist condemnations of African life since the debates over abolition. Africans took the lead toward the end of the nineteenth century in writing carefully considered, sympathetic, historical studies of their own lands, mostly in English. These were men descended from earlier generations of slaves in the 1820s and 1830s educated by Christian missionaries in Sierra Leone, the Gold Coast, and elsewhere in coastal western Africa; the works they composed remain essential to the field today (e.g., R. W. July 19.74). The most scholarly of the first generation of colonial mandarins, particularly the French, wrote magnificent studies of the lands they ruled. In South Africa, the generation that spanned the turn of the century also collected major compilations of African oral traditions and European documents and wrote the first synthetic histories of Dutch and English settlers and the imperial rulers of the region (G. McC. Theal, ed. 19.715, 19.716, 19.717).

Both administrative and scholarly writing assumed their classical colonial forms with the consolidation of European governments in Africa after World War I. Colonial governments began to sponsor research, scientific in style, on economic, natural, and human aspects of territories that they still barely knew, and their expanding bureaucracies began to generate sometimes vast collections of day-to-day records that now form an important basis of historical research. In South Africa, polarization between people of British and Dutch descent, the crystallization of an Afrikaner cultural and political identity, and the development of a comprehensive university system divided into English- and Afrikaans-speaking segments, motivated divergent historical searches for the origins of the nation's troubled character. By World War II, South Africa had the most structured and divided historiography of any part of the continent (C. Saunders 19.92; K. Smith 19.95).

Most influential for later historians in colonial tropical Africa were social anthropologists. Though generally intending to discover, understand, and appreciate Africans on their own terms, they inevitably contributed to justification and rationalization of colonial power structures. Anthropology in the 1930s and 1940s thus retained the contrast that their racist counterparts had drawn between the modern West and a savage Africa, but they implicitly identified the African ethnographic present, of which they wrote, with some vaguely pleasant past, later characterized as a romanticized "merrie Africa" (A. G. Hopkins 19.217), that they dismissed as utterly unknowable in any scientifically reliable way.

An academic historiography distinct from anthropology and from administrative reports began to take shape as Africans claimed political authority for themselves in the 1950s. It arose in part from the university colleges that were created in several colonies at that time to educate future rulers of the independent nations that would, in time, take their rightful places on the world stage. It also came from European museums and schools of "Oriental" studies and from the training academies for colonial officials, converted to academic centers, in Britain, France, Belgium, and—though more faintly—Portugal. A primary mission was to endow Africans with political and moral legitimacy in the eyes of the West through recovery of Africa's true, dynamic record of achievement in the past. Drawing on the political inspiration of the times, as party after party emerged in the waning colonies of Africa, professional historians trained in imperial history or in the colonial history of European activities in Africa, along with academically inclined former administrators and missionaries, drew on the established emphasis on ancient African kingdoms and empires and on the political orientation of colonial anthropology to start to replace old "elephants" with thriving towns and states.

The seminal products of their efforts appeared simultaneously with the lowering of the flags of empire, with 1960 as both the "year of independence" in Africa and the year in which both the *Journal of African History* and the *Cahiers d'études africaines* established themselves as the principal Anglo- and Francophone historical journals. The new African historians writing in them focused on discovering the sources from which one might reconstruct a verifiable past for Africa, including metropolitan archives and a few colonial collections, earlier European and Islamic writings about Africa in up-to-then unappreciated scope and variety (J. D. Fage 19.57; J.F.P. Hopkins and N. Levtzion, eds. 19.131), historical archaeology, the Africans' own histories ("oral traditions," but seen largely as primary sources analogous to written documents [D. P. Henige 1.113; J. Vansina 1.116], rather than as the synthetic products of communal and individual historical composition that they were), the ethnographic corpus, and linguistic evidence. African "history" was assumed from the beginning to include early times accessible only through archaeological techniques and a productive—although not always comforting—dialog continues today between the two disciplines.

The 1960s were thus the decade in which African historiography assumed its classical form: highly resourceful in methodology, morally charged with commitment to the dignity of Africa and Africans, determined to replace the presentistic static villages of the anthropologists with a long record of dynamic states and other achievements recognizable to the Western world, seeing the past—as these scholars fancied themselves—on "African terms." Some of the key contributions came from African scholars trained in London and Paris and teaching at the new institutions of higher education in West Africa (e.g., R. A. Adeleye 19.193; J.F.A. Ajayi 19.194; E. A. Ayandele 19.199; O. Ikime 19.218).

The creation of federally funded African area studies centers at ten or more universities in North America, where very little experience with Africa was available, attracted a modest immigration of European specialists as the founding generation of African historians, converted a few Americans specialized in other fields, and pushed the first graduates of the new Ph.D. programs rapidly into positions of responsibility for the subject in major departments of history. African history in the United States therefore showed few tendencies distinct from its European colonial roots and drew only occasionally on the characteristically American academic styles of folklore, cultural anthropology, or ethnohistory. African history had almost no connection to the established field of "Negro (American) history," as taught in the still segregated black colleges and universities.

In France, history was less clearly distinguished from the *sciences humaines*—geography, anthropology, politics, sociology—and generally less developed for Africa than in Anglophone countries. Theoretical fashions in Paris—Lévi-Straussian structuralism, Althusserian neo-Marxism, Annales-style social history, Braudelian breadth, and, later, Foucauldian and other poststructuralist philosophies—in turn spread throughout the discipline, and monumental French *doctorats d'État* made definitive contributions to the history—as well as to the geography and sociology—of the Francophone colonies and countries. The French, owing to their colonial connections with North Africa, had a particular concern with Islam and were also active in archaeology. In Belgium, professional history meant "Europe," but valuable linguistic, ethnographic, and other scientific studies came from the Museum at Tervuren devoted to Zaire, Rwanda, and Burundi and from the Académie Royale des Sciences d'Outre-Mer. Portugal, which clung tenaciously to its African possessions against the currents flowing everywhere else toward independence, also held its rich, deep documentary collections closely to its chest. Isolated scholars in Italy, Germany, the Netherlands, and elsewhere took up studies on Africa, but they were too few to establish styles of their own.

The dominant themes of this first generation of historians have been characterized as "trade and politics," with reference to its tendency to emphasize Africans' long-distance trade with Europeans, or across the Sahara Desert with North Africa, as the sources from which rulers in Africa built their celebrated centralized states. More creative than definitive, nationalist historiography implicitly invented an African past that featured the political and military achievements of the sort in which Europe itself took particular pride during the 1950s.

The search for a more Afrocentric vision of the past grew at this time from literary and philological roots established among Francophone scholars, some in Africa—particularly Senegal, the pinnacle of France's educational enterprise in Africa—and some of African descent but of West Indian birth. They drew on an established literary celebration of *négritude*, a cultural and psychological humaneness associated with Africa, and centered at the Paris publishing house and Francophone African cultural center, Présence Africaine. Usually expressed in literary modes, *négritude* found its most effective extension in historical terms in the writings of the Senegalese scholar Cheikh Anta Diop.

There were also European efforts to find alternatives to the prejudicial tone of most Western thinking about Africa. These mostly emerged from socialist and self-consciously Marxist thinking, focusing on the exploitive aspects of the slave trade of the seventeenth and eighteenth centuries, of imperialism in the nineteenth century, and of colonial rule in the twentieth. In the United States, only the most visionary African American scholars found publishers for their thinking about Africa, but more as background to the experiences of the population of African descent in the Americas than on its own terms. African American thinking about the African past, insofar as it had a distinct coherence, retained less scholarly, often romanticized, overtones. African American scholars who studied the subject at the new area studies centers contributed to all the established strains of thought in the general field.

Three books published at the end of the decade, rooted in the forward-looking style from which they had emerged, struck chords that still resonate. T. O. Ranger's *Revolt in Southern Rhodesia* (19.709) was a triumphal destruction of a lingering myth that Africans had seldom resisted the imposition of colonial rule and that those who had fought had done so in blind defense of older, doomed ways of living. Dozens of scholars then elaborated Ranger's argument (e.g., A. F. Isaacman and B. Isaacman 19.765) in every part of the continent over the following decade. Ranger had added a populist African initiative to the colonial era, up to that point a time known mostly in terms of government policies and political reaction by European-educated elites.

The second watershed book was Philip D. Curtin's *The Atlantic Slave Trade: A Census* (22.243), which offered a masterfully comprehensive overview of the numbers of Africans taken as captives to the Americas. Dozens of other historians ransacked archives throughout the Atlantic world for a decade, to refine, though not substantially to raise, Curtin's totals. It was a project that had profound implications for American and European history, as well as that of Africa, but for Africa this "numbers game" made it possible for the first time to use quantitative evidence to infer conditions otherwise undocumented along the African coasts and, with effort, in parts of the interior. "Trade and politics" from the sixteenth through the nineteenth centuries henceforth were often understood also as destruction and depopulation.

The third work was Walter Rodney's *How Europe Underdeveloped Africa* (3.211), a passionate attribution of the twentieth-century differences of wealth and technology between Europe and Africa to the economic and human losses that Africa had suffered through trading—gold and its human wealth for relatively valueless, cheap goods, guns, and gin—with Europe. This perspective, in spite of its implicit minimizing of African agency and accomplishment even in contact with larger and technologically more powerful parts of the world, tapped deep-running resentment in many quarters, as the political optimism of the 1960s faded in recognition of Africa's underlying economic problems. Many "underdevelopment" studies during the following decade attempted to work out the processes by which Africa had declined (e.g., J. E. Inikori, ed. 19.904).

Rodney set the critical tone for the 1970s. New approaches, often "radical" in tone, gained momentum from the glaring failures of the nationalist governments of the independence era in Africa, as regime after regime twisted electoral processes in their own favor and then fell to popular indifference and military *coups d'état*. Governments under extreme pressure found the universities politically suspect and neglected and sometimes closed the institutions to disperse the youthful educated opponents studying at them. African institutions of higher education lost the momentum they had gained toward taking prominent roles in defining the historiography of the continent (B. Jewsiewicki and D. Newbury, eds. 19.70).

Africa had no lack of scholarly sympathizers abroad. Historians in Europe and the United States substituted economics and "underdevelopment" for "states and trade" at the center of their studies, and they identified peasants and workers as important agents of historical change. Social history and conflict took over the main stage from chiefs and politics, undifferentiated Africans, and functional consensus. States were discredited, and colonial rule was revealed as merely the superficial form in which world capitalism had "penetrated" Africa. Foreign exploitation, unequal exchange, became a significant "African" perspective in the historiography, and political-economic struggle among opposed African class interests structured the innovative narratives in the field. Socialist perspectives and political economy required elaborate theorization, often from French sources, to convert the scattered and inchoate remarks on Africa in the writings of Marx and Engels to the historical circumstances as understood from the existing, decidedly non-Marxist literature, on the continent. Competing conceptualizations of earlier periods arose, in the forms of proposed "African," "slave," "lineage," or "tributary modes of production," but attention shifted sharply to the modern period, from colonial conquest (1880s) through independence. There a principal debate pitted the world-systems theorists and students of "underdevelopment" concerned with the external sources of Africa's evident poverty against more orthodox Marxists who examined the internal class dynamics between workers and "fractions" of capital (e.g., B. Freund 19.17, 19.18).

Non-Marxist historians took up economic history, the liberal analog of the political economists. Their manifesto was A. G. Hopkins's *Economic History of West Africa* (19.217), and Curtin's quantitative work on the slave trade (19.154) had originally grown from a footnote in what became a masterly economic history of far western Africa. Writing in a new journal, *African Economic History*, quantitative historians with formal economic and demographic training applied the theorems of market economics to nineteenth-century African commerce throughout the continent, though particularly to the merchants prominent in western Africa (see especially R. A. Austen 19.826).

A quest for professional respectability stimulated historians committed to more classical standards of scholarship to eschew theory and to embrace a full and formal critique of the sources for the African past. This critical impulse subjected oral traditions, in particular, to objections that reliable chronologies would never emerge from these sources, and that orally transmitted recollections about the past changed constantly through time, thus invalidating attempts to use them as historical sources based on analogies to documentary method. The same critical facility directed at understanding written sources quickly revealed the great complexity of the older European accounts about Africa and the misguided innocence with which the first generation of historians to use them as sources had written. The scholarly journal through which this impulse found its principal outlet was an annual journal of historical method, *History in Africa*.

Studies published there have since provided both a steady conscience for and often highly original contributions to the field.

The precolonial counterpart to the modern historians' emphasis on labor was the discovery of slavery, certainly widespread in nineteenth-century Africa and arguably crucial to the consideration of large African political systems long before then (C. Meillassoux 19.914; S. Miers and I. Kopytoff, eds. 19.915). Debate flared on several fronts, including the extent to which slavery in Africa grew from stimuli emanating from the Atlantic trade, the degree to which the institution had served to assimilate outsiders in local communities or had resembled the exclusive and openly exploitive system prevalent in the New World, whether the condition had fallen more heavily on men or women, and the many roles played by slaves in the African past; so ubiquitous and central did the institution appear that it was possible to write a general survey in terms of the history of the institution (P. E. Lovejoy 19.908).

An even more profound deepening of historians' understanding of Africans' experience took the form of recognizing the implications of the continent's highly gendered societies and cultures and the differential impact of colonial rule on women and men (N. R. Hunt 19.64; A. Wipper and H. Lyons, eds. 19.885). Earlier work had lingered in Orientalist fascination with powerful women who had violated Western norms for the "gentler sex," for example, the women labeled "Amazons" who had served the kings of the west African state of Dahomey. The new work recognized the broad constraints of patriarchy and explored its implications for women of all stations, though sometimes with an implicit tendency to allow its subjects to appear passive within the limitations on their lives. The principal challenges lay in developing a historical perspective of significant time depth, finding the meanings that women had given to their own lives, uncovering the broader influence that they had wielded through events still understood largely in terms of what men had done, and extending insights arising from examination of women to a fully gendered history of men as well.

Africa south of the Limpopo River developed a historiography of its own, distinct from imperial history or the history of Europeans in South Africa, during the 1970s. The distinctive presence there of large communities of Dutch and English descent and the substantial development of industry, transportation infrastructure, and cities drew South African history in directions different from those in which historians of tropical Africa had moved. Historians deeply opposed to the injustices of racial separation and to government repression of speech and inquiry congregated in exile, principally in London and secondarily in the United States, around Leonard M. Thompson, first at the University of California, Los Angeles, and then at Yale. There they applied lessons learned from colleagues working on tropical Africa and in European social history to recover the past of all the people in their own country. A new *Journal of Southern African Studies* made its appearance as the forum in which many of the most important questions in the field were debated. Politicized as the historiography of other parts of Africa sometimes became, the suffering of so many and the drama of a confrontation then already growing, gave South African historiography an even greater intensity and productivity.

By the early 1980s focus shifted from the countryside to the city. Research conditions in many rural areas of Africa had deteriorated with economic decline and political instability, and the naiveté of the claims of classical village ethnography to scientific objectivity had been exposed by scholars from areas formerly subject to anthropological objectification as exotically different from, "other" than, the Western scholar. Even as older styles of research in Africa became less attractive, new opportunities appeared. Rural Africans, reacting to the hardships of life in local economies drained of men and morale, had in fact moved to the cities. Urban cultures and economies, some of them building on bases established in the nineteenth century, became prime subjects of research for Africanist historians. Urban histories—of food provisioning systems, of dockworkers, textile workers, and other laboring groups, of prostitutes, of merchants and professional people, of culture—appeared in growing profusion. In addition, the voluminous written primary record of the mature colonial period, the 1930s through the 1950s, became increasingly available as time passed and the advancing limit of the thirty-year rule opened judicial files, police reports, government intelligence records, and the archives of colonial medical and other service agencies. Detailed day-to-day working documentation of modern African life, supplemented by recollections collected from its survivors, both African and European, enabled historians to dig far below the summary impressions and deceptions found in the formal reports on which they had previously based their understanding of it. These research opportunities also brought them face to face, more so than in the past, with the people whom they studied.

Identifying the barrier to understanding created by lingering tendencies to treat Africa as "other" than Europe has provided the distinctive tone in the historiography of the continent since the late 1980s. Though a few scholars have hesitated to venture beyond lamenting past misrepresentations and contemplating the formidability of the challenge, others employed discourse analysis and other techniques to write about the minds of Africans they studied (D. W. Cohen and E. S. Atieno Odhiambo 19.473). Oral "traditions," after rejection as "objective" windows on the African past, returned to favor as valuable expressions of African *mentalités*, key sources for what could become intellectual and cultural histories in Africa.

In the rural areas, the breakdown of the 1950s and 1960s illusion of village isolation moved beyond the themes of depletion and destruction that characterized the 1970s to reexamine rural people as peasants, communities determined to maintain cultural and economic autonomy in the face of increasing intrusions by outsiders (A. F. Isaacman 19.66). The stereotype of the "tribe"—long rejected by African historians as pejorative and ahistorical, owing to its implication of unchanging and anachronistic attitudes, but never examined as a construct of the human imagination—has been replaced with historical reconstructions of its invention and its political and personal utility to its creators (L. Vail, ed. 19.810). Historians now see village Africans in complex ways that highlight the interaction of received wisdom with novel circumstances, of ideological preferences with material constraints, of change with continuity, of the individual with the community.

Postmodernist scholarship in Africa—if it can surmount the hesitancy created by the chasm between self and other—may thus represent a culmination of the liberal urge, underlying African historiography from the start, to find "African perspectives," to understand Africans on their own terms, multiple and conflicting as they are now understood to be. In this context, so-called "Afrocentric" perspectives of the sort widely discussed in nonprofessional circles in the United States during the early 1990s, represent a countercurrent dedicated to projecting modern, Western values into ancient Africa. "Afrocentric" studies draw selectively on the results of the scholarship of academic historians of Africa, if often uncritically, and present their thoughts in scholarly style. However much these advocates intend thus to bring Africa within the charmed circle of world respectability, they effectively renew the impulse recurrent in the older historiography of the field to interpret Africa by modern Western cultural, especially technological, criteria, in contrast to professional African historians' search for the universality of the human experience in Africa, beyond cultural and individual idiosyncrasies. The two missions parallel each other in seeking to integrate Africans into world history on terms that each would use to study their own pasts. They differ in the forms of difference that they acknowledge: cultural or racial; both aim to add the African experience to the emerging emphasis on global historical patterns.

Economic weakness since about 1970 has depleted the creativity of historians based in African institutions, with the major exception of South Africa, where the field has moved in the opposite direction, toward locally rooted, socially and culturally energized historical study. Historians living and working abroad inevitably subordinate local sensitivities to broader themes. Those teaching in African institutions, of whom there have been many, have drifted into other posts. Expatriates, often prominent in the 1960s and still in some cases in the 1970s, returned to their own countries. African nationals left to join history departments in Europe and North America or moved into responsible positions in government and business at home, and those remaining in the universities have faced substandard salaries, state intrusiveness, lack of access to foreign books and journals that require scarce hard currency to import, and other obstacles to assuming positions of leadership in the field. Most history in Africa, outside the Republic of South Africa, relies on local archives and contributes to primary knowledge of local circumstances. The United States—now by far the world leader in terms of numbers of historians studying Africa—Canada, and Europe dominate research, teaching, and publication. Anglophone scholarship accounts for approximately 84 percent of the monographs published, with French a distant second at 10 percent and smaller numbers of contributions in German, Italian, and other world languages. The foreigners' postmodern agenda of overcoming their own alienness has come to structure the field. Intellectually, as well as ethically and politically, further historiographical development of Africa is poised to receive the contributions of Africa-based scholars, financially enabled to draw on the scholarship of their colleagues abroad and to contribute their thinking to it.

Entries are arranged under the following headings:

Reference Works and General Studies

Historiography and Historical Method

Western Africa
  To 600 CE
  Seventh to Sixteenth Century
  Seventeenth and Eighteenth Centuries
  Nineteenth Century
  Twentieth Century

Northeastern Africa

Eastern Africa
  Early Eastern Africa
  Nineteenth Century
  Twentieth Century

Central Africa
  To ca. 1850
  Since ca. 1850

Southern Africa
  Early Southern Africa
  Nineteenth Century
  Twentieth Century

Topical Studies
  General Studies
  Women
  Slavery
  Health and Disease

[Contributors: AMcD = E. Ann McDougall, CHA = Charles Ambler, DSN = David S. Newbury, DMA = David M. Anderson, DO'C = David O'Connor, DPH = David P. Henige, DSN = David S. Northrup, DWR = David W. Robinson, EAE = Elizabeth A. Eldredge, JCM = Joseph C. Miller, JJL = Joseph J. Lauer, JKT = John K. Thornton, JLS = Jay L. Spaulding, KDP = K. David Patterson, LNS = Lynda Norene Shaffer, MJH = Margaret Jean Hay, NRH = Nancy Rose Hunt, PMM = Phyllis M. Martin, RCL = Robin C. Law, RHE = Richard H. Elphick, RJM = Roderick J. McIntosh, RRR = Richard R. Roberts, SSG = Stephen S. Gosch, TTS = Thomas T. Spear, WHW = William H. Worger]

REFERENCE WORKS AND GENERAL STUDIES

19.1 *Africa bibliography.* Manchester: Manchester University Press, 1984–. ISSN 0266-6731. ▸ Annual listing of scholarly work about the continent; arranged by geographic area and country. Indexes. Best printed source to start search for recent references. [JJL]

19.2 *Africa contemporary record: annual survey and documents.* New York: Africana, 1968–. ISSN 0065-3845. ▸ Annual survey mainly of political events; includes overview essays, country-by-country review, and documents. Early volumes published in London and edited by Colin Legum. [JJL]

19.3 *Africa since 1914: a historical bibliography.* Santa Barbara, Calif.: ABC-Clio, 1985. (Clio bibliography series, 17.) ISBN 0-87436-395-0. ▸ Abstracts (some lengthy) of 4,329 periodical articles, published 1973–82. [JJL]

19.4 *Africa south of the Sahara.* London: Europa, 1971–. ISBN 0065-3896. ▸ Annually updated summary of current information. Includes signed historical overviews that are periodically revised. Best source of brief information. [JJL]

19.5 *African historical demography.* Vol. 2. Edinburgh: University of Edinburgh, African Studies Centre, 1981. ▸ More than thirty papers dealing with population size, distribution, mobility, and effects of epidemics, slave raiding, and labor migration on African societies. Displays range of reasonable possibilities in this area of research. [DPH]

19.6 *African historical dictionaries.* Edition varies. 54 vols. Metuchen, N.J.: Scarecrow, 1974–93. ISBN 0-8108-2413-2 (v. 47), 0-8108-2547-3 (v. 53), 0-8108-2768-9 (v. 54). ▸ Series of volumes, one per country, with many second editions; each with chronology, alphabetical listing of topics and names, and extensive bibliography. Some very good but most stronger on current affairs than on history. [JJL]

19.7 Jacob F. Ade Ajayi and Michael Crowder, eds. *Historical atlas of Africa.* Cambridge: Cambridge University Press, 1985. ISBN 0-521-25353-5. ▸ Elegant, coffee-table quality, multiauthored maps and accompanying essays on geography, climate, diseases, archaeological eras, and history through contemporary social statistics (education, urbanization, industrialization, etc.) Text contributions from fifty-seven prominent historians; 300 maps in seventy-two sections; index of over 4,000 names. [JJL/JCM]

19.8 Paul Bohannan and Philip D. Curtin. *Africa and Africans.* 3d ed. Prospect Heights, Ill.: Waveland, 1988. ISBN 0-88133-347-6 (pbk). ▸ New edition of very accessible introduction to African history, through American myths about African past to brief synthetic historical chapters, supported by anthropological survey (in classic terms) of cultures and social institutions, especially rural. [JCM]

19.9 Elizabeth W. Böhmer, comp. *Left-radical movements in South Africa and Namibia, 1900–1981: a bibliographical and historical study.* 2 vols. Cape Town: South African Library, 1986. (Grey bibliographies, 14.) ISBN 0-86968-055-4 (set). ▸ Over 5,000 references to unions, political parties, black consciousness movements, and church movements. [JJL]

19.10 Ian Brownlie. *African boundaries: a legal and diplomatic encyclopaedia.* Berkeley: University of California Press for Royal Institute of International Affairs, 1979. ISBN 0-520-03795-2. ▸ Detailed examination of boundaries, complete with sketch maps and legal documents. [JJL]

19.11 Robert O. Collins. *African history: text and readings.* Vol. 1: *Western Africa.* Vol. 2: *Eastern and Central Africa.* Vol. 3: *Southern Africa.* 3 vols. New York: Wiener, 1990. ISBN 1-55876-015-6 (v. 1), 1-55876-016-4 (v. 2), 1-55876-017-2 (v. 3). ▸ Three volumes of short excerpts from primary sources, prehistory through modern period. Most comprehensive and current resource of this type for field. [JCM]

19.12 Catherine Coquery-Vidrovitch. "Process of urbanization in Africa (from the origins to the beginning of independence)." *African studies review* 34.1 (1991) 1–98. ISSN 0002-0206. ▸ Bibliographic essay on urban and social change. [JJL]

19.13 Basil Davidson. *Africa in history: themes and outlines.* 4th ed. New York: Macmillan/Collier, 1991. ISBN 0-02-042791-3. ▸ From journalist-historian, master interpreter of continent. Readable tribute to African values and internal dynamic of Africa's history. New edition of one of author's many works. [JCM]

19.14 Basil Davidson. *African civilization revisited: from antiquity to modern times.* Trenton, N.J.: Africa World, 1991. ISBN 0-86543-123-X (cl), 0-86543-124-8 (pbk). ▸ Anthology of mostly primary sources (over 125 selections), most very short and weighted toward antiquity and early times, with brief general introduction to historical contexts and types of contributors, African, Asian, and European. Valid, illustrative starting point. [JCM]

19.15 Peter Duignan, ed. *Guide to research and reference works on sub-Saharan Africa.* Helen F. Conover and Peter Duignan, comps. Stanford, Calif.: Hoover Institution on War, Revolution, and Peace, 1971–72. (Hoover Institution bibliographical series, 46.) ISBN 0-8179-2461-2. ▸ Sound but dated overview; critical annotations for most of the 3,127 titles listed. [JJL]

19.16 Tore Linne Eriksen and Richard Moorson. *The political* *economy of Namibia: an annotated critical bibliography*. 2d ed. Uppsala: Scandinavian Institute of African Studies with United Nations Institute for Namibia, 1989. (Norwegian foreign policy studies, 69.) ISBN 9-17-106297-1. ‣ Lengthy critical annotations; indexes. [JJL]

19.17 Bill Freund. "Labor and labor history in Africa: a review of the literature." *African studies review* 27.2 (1984) 1–58. ISSN 0002-0206. ‣ Explores labor as part of history of ideas; includes labor migration. [JJL]

19.18 Bill Freund. *The making of contemporary Africa: the development of African society since 1800*. Bloomington: Indiana University Press, 1984. ISBN 0-253-33660-0 (cl), 0-253-28600-X (pbk). ‣ Nineteenth- and twentieth-century Africa from systematically materialist perspective reflecting social and economic historiography of 1970s and early 1980s. Covers modern African workers and peasants; skeptical view of nationalist politicians. [JCM]

19.19 Peter S. Garlake. *The kingdoms of Africa*. 1978 ed. New York: Bedrick, 1990. ISBN 0-87226-305-3 (cl), 0-87226-234-0 (pbk). ‣ Lavishly illustrated archaeological approach to social history of famous African kingdoms, fourth to sixteenth centuries; Meroë (Upper Nile), Aksum (Ethiopia), Zimbabwe, Swahili cities (east coast), Ghana, Mali, Songhai, and other western African states. [JCM]

19.20 *General history of Africa: UNESCO International Scientific Committee for the Drafting of a General History of Africa*. 8 vols. to date. Paris, Berkeley, and London: UNESCO, University of California Press, and Heinemann, 1981–. ISBN 0-520-03912-2 (v. 1), 0-520-03913-0 (v. 2), 0-520-03914-9 (v. 3), 0-520-03915-7 (v. 4), 0-520-03916-5 (v. 5), 0-520-03917-3 (v. 6), 0-520-03918-1 (v. 7), 0-520-03920-3 (v. 8). ‣ International—especially African—scholarship with emphasis on resistance and other historical themes of 1960s. Chapters by many authors, organized by period and by region. Strengths include Islamic perspectives on western and northern Africa and illustrations. [JCM]

19.21 Jean E. Meeh Gosebrink, ed. and comp. *African studies information resources directory*. Oxford: Zell for African Studies Association, 1986. ISBN 0-9054503-0-2. ‣ Identifies sources of information and documentation in United States; notes on 437 libraries, special collections, publishers, etc. For specialists. [JJL]

19.22 David P. Henige. *A union list of African archival materials in microform*. 2d ed. Madison: University of Wisconsin, Memorial Library, 1984. ‣ Bibliography of 299 entries from eighteen United States libraries. [JJL]

19.23 David P. Henige. *Works in African history: an index to reviews, 1978–1982*. Los Angeles: Crossroads, 1984. ISBN 0-9184564-9-5. ‣ Most recent volume in series indexing 5,000 reviews (from about 500 journals) for 1,003 books. [JJL]

19.24 Robert L. Hess and Dalvan M. Coger. *Semper ex Africa: a bibliography of primary sources for nineteenth-century tropical Africa as recorded by explorers, missionaries, traders, travelers, administrators, military men, adventurers, and others*. Stanford, Calif.: Hoover Institution on War, Revolution, and Peace, 1972. (Hoover Institution bibliographical series, 47.) ISBN 0-817-92471-x. ‣ List of 7,732 books and articles, arranged by place visited. See Fage, ed. 19.57 and others for better editions of these sources. [JJL]

19.25 Peter C. Hogg. *African slave trade and its suppression: a classified and annotated bibliography of books, pamphlets, and periodical articles*. London: Cass, 1973. ISBN 0-7146-2775-5. ‣ Emphasizes contemporary accounts, 4,675 entries, now somewhat dated. See bibliographies by Joseph C. Miller for more recent work. [JJL]

19.26 *International African bibliography*. London: Mansell,

1971–. ISBN 0020-5877. ‣ Quarterly listing of new books, articles, and papers. Geographic arrangement; sometimes cumulated. [JJL]

19.27 International Council on Archives and UNESCO. *Guide to the sources of the history of nations, B: Africa*. Vol. 3. Zug, Switzerland: Inter Documentation, 1970–. (Collectanea Archivi Vaticani.) ‣ Covers archives of France, Italy, Scandinavia, Spain, the Vatican, and West Germany. [JJL]

19.28 Robert W. July. *A history of the African people*. 4th ed. Prospect Heights, Ill.: Waveland, 1992. ISBN 0-88133-631-9. ‣ Standard general text, regularly revised, emphasizing politics of early African states and especially colonial rule, nationalism, and independence. Strongest on nationalist ideologies and postindependence dilemmas. [JCM]

19.29 M. A. Kwamena-Poh et al. *African history in maps*. Burnt Mill, England: Longman, 1982. ISBN 0-582-60331-5. ‣ Accessible, affordable, general historical atlas; now slightly dated, but recommended choice in this category. Thirty-six two-color maps, useful index. [JCM]

19.30 Joseph J. Lauer, Gregory V. Larkin, and Alfred Kagan, comps. *American and Canadian doctoral dissertations and master's theses on Africa, 1974–1987*. Atlanta: Crossroads, Emory University, 1989. ISBN 0-918456-63-0. ‣ Lists over 8,000 titles, arranged by country and discipline. Supplements appear in *African Studies Association News*. [JJL]

19.31 Mark R. Lipschutz and R. Kent Rasmussen. *Dictionary of African historical biography*. 2d ed. Berkeley: University of California Press, 1987. ISBN 0-520-05179-3. ‣ Best biographical dictionary. Some 850 entries for individuals prominent before 1980. Includes bibliographical references. [JJL]

19.32 Phyllis M. Martin and Patrick O'Meara, eds. *Africa*. 2d ed. Bloomington: Indiana University Press, 1986. ISBN 0-253-30211-0 (cl), 0-253-20392-9 (pbk). ‣ Six updated historical chapters by specialists, together with surveys of recent work in other disciplines (demography, economics, thought, arts, urban society, popular culture, and recent politics). Sound, current introduction to continent. Third edition in preparation. [JCM]

19.33 Noel Matthews and M. Doreen Wainwright, comps. *A guide to manuscripts and documents in the British Isles relating to Africa*. J. D. Pearson, ed. London: Oxford University Press, 1971. ISBN 0-19-713567-6. ‣ Lists both official and unofficial papers; arranged by location. [JJL]

19.34 Paulos Milkias. *Ethiopia: a comprehensive bibliography*. Boston: Hall, 1989. ISBN 0-8161-9066-6. ‣ Over 19,000 entries arranged in broad subject categories; not comprehensive and poorly indexed. [JJL]

19.35 Naomi Musiker and Reuben Musiker. *South African history: a bibliographical guide with special reference to territorial expansion and colonization*. New York: Garland, 1984. ISBN 0-8240-9174-4. ‣ Lengthy summary annotations of 1,028 books; limited by emphasis on people of European descent. [JJL]

19.36 L. H. Ofosu-Appiah, ed. *Dictionary of African biography*. 2 vols. New York: Reference Publications, 1977–79. ISBN 0-917256-00-X (set). ‣ Scholarly biographies covering Ethiopia, Ghana, Sierra Leone, and Zaire. Plan for twenty volumes unfulfilled. [JJL]

19.37 Roland Oliver. *The African experience*. New York: Icon, 1991. ISBN 0-06-435850-X (cl), 0-06-430218-0 (pbk). ‣ Insightful updating of classic of African history from one of the creators and masters of field. Short, readable chapters from earliest times through independence, particularly distinctive for ancient eras. [JCM]

19.38 Roland Oliver and John D. Fage, eds. *Cambridge history*

of Africa. 8 vols. Cambridge: Cambridge University Press, 1975–86. ISBN 0-521-22215-X (v. 1), 0-521-21592-7 (v. 2), 0-521-20981-1 (v. 3), 0-521-20413-5 (v. 4), 0-521-20701-0 (v. 5), 0-521-22803-4 (v. 6), 0-521-22505-1 (v. 7), 0-521-22409-8 (v. 8). ‣ Comprehensive multiauthored general history, prehistory to ca. 1975. Represents best of British scholarship on 1970s Africa. Useful reference work with index and bibliography of works to dates of publication. [JCM]

19.39 T. O. Ranger. "Religious movements and politics in sub-Saharan Africa." *African studies review* 29.2 (1986) 1–69. ISSN 0002-0206. ‣ Bibliographic essay on traditional and Christian religious movements focusing on rural areas. [JJL]

19.40 Yvette Scheven. *Bibliographies for African studies, 1970–1986.* London: Zell, 1988. ISBN 0-9054503-3-7. ‣ Carefully annotated bibliography of 3,277 bibliographies in social sciences and humanities; extensive indexes. Updated by "Africana Reference Works" in *African Book Publishing Record,* number 2 of each year. [JJL]

19.41 Kevin W. Shillington. *History of Africa.* New York: St. Martin's, 1989. ISBN 0-312-03178-5 (cl), 0-312-03179-3 (pbk). ‣ Introductory text with numerous illustrations and maps, reflecting current scholarship at date of publication; chronological balance among pre-1600 period, seventeenth–eighteenth (slave trade), nineteenth (commercial development), and twentieth (colonial period to independence) centuries. Recommended starting point. [JCM]

19.42 Aloha South. *Guide to federal archives relating to Africa.* Waltham, Mass.: Crossroads, 1977. ‣ Detailed descriptions of known Africa-related records in National Archives; indexes of subjects, places, and names. [JJL]

19.43 Aloha South, comp. *Guide to non-federal archives and manuscripts in the United States relating to Africa.* 2 vols. London: Zell, 1989. ISBN 0-905450-55-8 (set), 0-905450-56-6 (v. 1), 0-905450-57-4 (v. 2). ‣ Lists textual and nontextual records in about 442 depositories. [JJL]

19.44 Ruth M. Stone and Frank J. Gillis. *African music and oral data: a catalog of field recordings, 1902–1975.* Bloomington: Indiana University Press, 1976. ISBN 0-253-30262-5. ‣ Listing of oral data gathered by historians and others; some tapes deposited with Archives of Traditional Music (Bloomington). [JJL]

19.45 Ralph Uweche, ed. *Makers of modern Africa: profiles in history.* Vol. 3 of *Know Africa.* 2d ed. London: Africa Books, 1991. ISBN 0-903274-18-3. ‣ Biographies of 680 deceased individuals, limited to nineteenth and twentieth centuries. Supplemented by publisher's *Africa Who's Who.* [JJL]

19.46 David S. Wiley and Robert Cancel, eds. *Africa on film and videotape, 1960–1981: a compendium of reviews.* East Lansing: Michigan State University, African Studies Center, 1982. ‣ Lengthy descriptions and critiques of available material; includes notes on stereotypes. [JJL]

19.47 Julian W. Witherell, comp. *The United States and Africa: guide to U.S. official documents and government-sponsored publications on Africa, 1785–1975.* Washington, D.C.: Library of Congress, for sale by United States Government Printing Office, 1978. ISBN 0-8444-0261-3. ‣ Lists and indexes over 8,800 items, mostly since 1951. [JJL]

19.48 *World bibliographical series.* Santa Barbara, Calif.: Clio, 1977–. ‣ Detailed annotations on major works of history; good introductory bibliographies, when relatively recent. Series will cover every country, each in separate volume. [JJL]

HISTORIOGRAPHY AND HISTORICAL METHOD

19.49 David N. Beach. "The Rozvi in search of their past." *History in Africa* 10 (1983) 13–34. ISSN 0361-5413. ‣ Discussion of how twentieth-century renditions of Rozvi (Shona, modern Zimbabwe) oral tradition were invented to suit ambient circumstances. Suggests particular attention to latter-day contexts of such materials [DPH]

19.50 Belinda Bozzoli and Peter Delius, eds. "Radical history and South African history." *Radical history review* 46–47 (1990). ISSN 0163-6545. ‣ Excellent overview illustrating range of interests and key debates in recent South African historiography; articles on labor, agriculture, squatter movements, literature, African political organization, popular history, and comparative historiography (with United States South). [DSN]

19.51 David William Cohen. "The undefining of oral tradition." *Ethnohistory* 33.1 (1989) 9–18. ISSN 0014-1801. ‣ Argues against formalist definitions of oral tradition, using Soga of Uganda to show that knowledge of past resides in everyday discourse and can be ferreted out only through understanding its norms. [DPH]

19.52 David William Cohen, comp. *Towards a reconstructed past: historical texts from Busoga, Uganda.* Oxford: Oxford University Press for British Academy, 1986. ISBN 0-19-726039-X. ‣ Rare collection of documents illuminating Soga (Uganda) historical thought. More than a dozen traditional texts, some collected by compiler, others written years ago. [DPH]

19.53 Dennis D. Cordell and Joel W. Gregory. "Earlier African historical demographies." *Canadian journal of African studies* 23.1 (1989) 5–27. ISSN 0008-3968. ‣ Survey of recent studies discussing sources and methods, including travelers' accounts, paleodemography, archaeology, and genealogies. Suggests several approaches susceptible to existing evidence. [DPH]

19.54 Dennis D. Cordell and Joel W. Gregory. "Historical demography and demographic history in Africa: theoretical and methodology considerations." *Canadian journal of African studies* 14.3 (1980) 389–416. ISSN 0008-3968. ‣ Plea for sufficiency of data to write formal demographic history in Africa with interdisciplinary approach emphasizing theory. Supports position by collating various source types: censuses, vital registration data, tax rolls, etc. [DPH]

19.55 Donald Denoon and Adam Kuper. "Nationalist historians in search of a nation: the 'new historiography' in Dar es Salaam." *African affairs* 69.277 (1970) 329–49. ISSN 0001-9909. ‣ Seminal critique of nationalist history as excessively privileging initiatives of African elites and excluding wider regional trends and broader social processes. Focuses on postcolonial historiography at University of Dar es Salaam. [DSN]

19.56 Christopher Ehret and Merrick Posnansky, eds. *The archaeological and linguistic reconstruction of African history.* Berkeley: University of California Press, 1982. ISBN 0-520-04593-9. ‣ Thirteen studies suggesting ways to correlate evidence for protohistoric period. Concentrates on Bantu expansion question and on linguistic methods for discerning pastoralist and agriculturalist societies. [DPH/TTS]

19.57 John D. Fage, ed. *A guide to original sources for precolonial western Africa published in European languages.* Madison: University of Wisconsin, African Studies Program, 1987. (Studies in African sources, 2.) ISBN 0-942615-01-8. ‣ Chronologically arranged listing of all known travel accounts published before 1870. Exemplary tracing of works through editions and translations to show how texts changed in the process. [DPH/JJL]

19.58 Colin Flight. "The Bantu expansion and the SOAS network." *History in Africa* 15 (1988) 261–301. ISSN 0361-5413. ‣ Traces evolution of well-known debate over Bantu origins and expansion through records of discussion seminars at School of Oriental and African Studies (London). Reveals sociopsychological and political dimensions invisible in published record. [DPH]

19.59 Christopher Fyfe, ed. *African studies since 1945: a tribute* *to Basil Davidson.* London: Longman, 1976. ISBN 0-582-64207-8 (cl), 0-582-64208-6 (pbk). ▸ African historiography from World War II to early 1970s; essays on diverse fields (administrative and economic history, anthropology, archaeology, education, Islam, literature) and regional characteristics (South Africa, Britain, France, Germany, Lusophone Africa). [DSN]

19.60 Beatrix Heintze and Adam Jones, eds. "European sources for sub-Saharan Africa before 1900: use and abuse." *Paideuma* 33 (1987). ISSN 0078-7809. ▸ Twenty-two textual and historiographical studies of various sources, with emphasis on contexts, influence, interrelationships, and editing; intended as exemplars of critical standards for similar sources. [DPH]

19.61 David P. Henige. "In quest of error's sly imprimatur: the concept of 'authorial intent' in modern textual criticism." *History in Africa* 14 (1987) 87–112. ISSN 0361-5413. ▸ Discussion of applicability of methods of literary criticism with regard to creating and understanding texts for historians. Reminds readers that all texts have more than face value. [DPH]

19.62 David P. Henige. "The problem of feedback in oral tradition: four examples from the Fante coastlands." *Journal of African history* 14.2 (1973) 223–35. ISSN 0021-8537. ▸ Examples from southern Ghana illustrating how oral tradition recasts material borrowed from written sources in oral structure. Concludes historians must search for feedback mechanisms in so-called oral tradition. [DPH]

19.63 David P. Henige. "Truths yet unborn? Oral tradition as a casualty of cultural contact." *Journal of African history* 23.3 (1982) 395–412. ISSN 0021-8537. ▸ Examples from Africa and elsewhere illustrate ease with which historical sources, both written and oral, absorbed and reused newly acquired information. Discusses circumstances in which this is likely to occur and suggests analytical alternatives. [DPH]

19.64 Nancy Rose Hunt. "Placing women's history and locating gender." *Social history* 14.3 (1989) 359–73. ISSN 0307-1022. ▸ Review of questions, sources, and periods in studies on women in recent African historiography. Notes insufficient attention to symbolic and cultural representations of womanhood; critical of projecting Western concepts onto African political actions. Extensive bibliography. [DSN]

19.65 Paul Irwin. *Liptako speaks: history from oral tradition in Africa.* Princeton: Princeton University Press, 1981. ISBN 0-691-05309-X. ▸ Restudy of Mossi society (Burkina Faso) during two separate periods of fieldwork. Cautionary tale of need to reinterview informants for consistency, illustrates how purposely inconsistent oral testimony can be. [DPH]

19.66 Allen F. Isaacman. "Peasants and rural social protest in Africa." *African studies review* 33.2 (1990) 1–120. ISSN 0002-0206. ▸ Historiography of peasants and rural protest in African agrarian history, emphasizing peasant agency. Very broad definition of resistance. [JJL]

19.67 Clinton M. Jean. *Behind the Eurocentric veils: the search for African realities.* Amherst, Mass.: University of Massachusetts Press, 1992. ISBN 0-87023-757-8. ▸ Argues for Afrocentric historiography challenging Weberian/Parsonian and Marxist assumptions of lineal sequence and hierarchy of different civilizations. Theoretical work with only generalized reference to Africa. [DSN]

19.68 Bogumil Jewsiewicki. "African historical studies: academic knowledge as 'usable past' and radical scholarship." *African studies review* 32.3 (1989) 1–77. ISSN 0002-0206. ▸ Seminal work on social production of knowledge on Africa. Stresses similarities between radical and African–African American perspectives and liberal paradigms as common products of shared nineteenth-century Western epistemes. [DSN/JJL]

19.69 Bogumil Jewsiewicki, ed. *Modes of production: the challenge*

of Africa. Ottawa: Canadian Association of African Studies, 1985. (*Canadian journal of African studies,* 19). ISSN 0008-3968. ▸ More than twenty short papers on perennial but controversial topic of Marxist theory as it relates to African historiography. All sides of debate represented. Most papers by historians. Useful bibliography. [DPH]

19.70 Bogumil Jewsiewicki and David Newbury, eds. *African historiographies: what history for which Africa?* Beverly Hills, Calif.: Sage, 1986. ISBN 0-8039-2498-4. ▸ Distinguishes trends in national historiographies on Africa, both within Africa (Nigeria, Senegal, Tanzania, Zaire, South Africa) and outside (France, Belgium, Britain, United States). Valuable for particular approaches, schools, and oral methods. [DSN/DPH]

19.71 Adam Jones. "Four years in Asante: one source or several?" *History in Africa* 18 (1991) 173–203. ISSN 0361-5413. ▸ Exemplary source criticism. Shows 1875 account by Ramseyer, German missionary in Asante, once thought unproblematical, underwent several revisions. Standard English translation is misleading; best text remains in manuscript. [DPH]

19.72 Adam Jones, ed. *German sources for West African history, 1599–1699.* Wiesbaden: Steiner, 1983. ISBN 3-515-03728-4 (pbk). ▸ Model translation-edition of several works on West African coast (Lübeling, Ulsheimer, Brun, Hemmersam, Müller, Zur Eich), with full editorial apparatus, maps, indexing, and introductions. [DPH]

19.73 Adam Jones, ed. *Raw, medium, well done: a critical review of editorial and quasi-editorial work on pre-1885 European sources for sub-Saharan Africa, 1960–1986.* Madison: University of Wisconsin, African Studies Program, 1987. ISBN 0-942615-00-X. ▸ Analysis of several hundred recent editions of pre-1885 accounts. Finds editorial standards seldom high and defines criteria that prospective editors must meet to produce valid work. [DPH]

19.74 Robert W. July. *The origins of modern African thought: its development in West Africa during the nineteenth and twentieth centuries.* New York: Praeger, 1967. ▸ Comprehensive introduction to context and content of West African and diaspora scholars writing on Africa. Focuses on Anglophone work, including Edward Wilmot Blyden, Africanus Horton, Samuel Johnson, Casely Hayford, and others. [DSN]

19.75 Steven Kaplan. "Hagiographies and the history of medieval Ethiopia." *History in Africa* 8 (1981) 107–23. ISSN 0361-5413. ▸ Hagiographies—once conventions are understood (forms and reasons for and circumstances of their creation)—reveal aspects of medieval Ethiopia not recoverable from secular sources. Important for monasticism, church influence in secular affairs, and ecclesiastical politics. [DPH]

19.76 Lidwien Kapteijns. *African historiography written by Africans, 1955–1973: the Nigerian case.* Leiden: Afrika-Studiecentrum, 1977. ISBN 90-7011-021-0. ▸ Detailed consideration of major contributors to efflorescence of historical writing by Nigerians, 1955–75. Highlights common themes—nationalism, resistance, elites—and debates; useful bibliography. [DSN]

19.77 Joseph Ki-Zerbo, ed. *Methodology and African prehistory.* Vol. 1 of *General history of Africa: UNESCO International Scientific Committee for the Drafting of a General History of Africa.* Berkeley: University of California Press, 1981. ISBN 0-520-03912-2. ▸ Three notable surveys of historiography: Fage on written sources before 1950, Hama/Ki-Zerbo on concepts of time in African societies, and Curtin on transformations from national focus to global perspectives. [DSN]

19.78 Robin C. C. Law. "Early Yoruba historiography." *History in Africa* 3 (1976) 69–89. ISSN 0361-5413. ▸ Survey of late nineteenth- and early twentieth-century historical writing among

Yoruba (Nigeria). Shows reliance on non-Yoruba sources and modern historians' need for awareness of Yoruba historiographical conventions. [DPH]

19.79 Nehemia Levtzion and J.F.P. Hopkins, eds. *Corpus of early Arabic sources for West African history.* Cambridge: Cambridge University Press, 1981. ISBN 0-521-22422-5. ▸ Sixty-five annotated translations from Arabic-language authors (ninth to seventeenth centuries) on West and North Africa. Emphasizes interrelationships among sources and massive but unacknowledged borrowing typical of period. Editors provide information about authors and excellent bibliography. [DPH/LNS]

19.80 John M. Lonsdale. "Explanations of the Mau Mau Revolt." In *Resistance and ideology in settler societies.* Tom Lodge, ed., pp. 168–78. Johannesburg: Ravan, 1986. ISBN 0-86975-304-5 (pbk). ▸ Eight penetrating explanations—all characteristic of continental historiography—of Mau Mau Revolt in 1950s Kenya, differing on Kikuyu (rebels') society, colonial power, and political leadership: official/psychological, nationalist, elite cooptation; political personalities; rural stratification; peasant resistance; urban violence; and Kikuyu ethnicity. [DSN]

19.81 Paul E. Lovejoy, Igor Kopytoff, and Frederick Cooper. "Indigenous African slavery." In *Roots and branches: current directions in slave studies.* Michael Craton, ed., pp. 19–83. Toronto: Pergamon, 1979. ISBN 0-08-025367-9. ▸ Valuable symposium on distinctive forms of slavery in Africa with useful references to historiography. Lovejoy considers diversity and relates internal changes to external commerce; Kopytoff stresses social incorporation; and Cooper examines class interactions and ideologies. [DSN]

19.82 Joseph C. Miller, ed. *The African past speaks: essays on oral tradition and history.* Hamden, Conn.: Archon, 1980. ISBN 0-208-01784-4. ▸ Nine case studies, largely from East and Central Africa, essay on memory, and editorial introduction that lays out general taxonomy for oral historical materials and ways to treat them. [DPH]

19.83 Caroline Neale. *Writing "independent" history: African historiography, 1960–1980.* Westport, Conn.: Greenwood, 1985. ISBN 0-313-24652-1. ▸ Thoughtful critique of effort to liberate colonial historiography by "bringing Africans into human history," seeing emphasis on human initiative as innocent of political constraints. Excellent introduction to African as well as European authors of 1960s and 1970s. [DSN]

19.84 David Newbury. "Bushi and the historians: historiographical themes in eastern Kivu." *History in Africa* 5 (1978) 132–52. ISSN 0361-5413. ▸ Shows crystallization over time and application of themes in colonial histories of precolonial Central Africa, but widely applicable elsewhere. Themes include origins, migration, conquest, cultural impermeability, social stratification, and state hierarchy. [DSN]

19.85 Sharon E. Nicholson. "The methodology of historical climate reconstruction and its application to Africa." *Journal of African history* 20.1 (1979) 31–49. ISSN 0021-8537. ▸ Classic climate history using documentary sources to trace patterns over western and northern Africa. Concludes that climate can be combined with archaeological and geological evidence to reveal environmental influences. [DPH]

19.86 Derek Nurse. "A linguistic consideration of Swahili origins." *Azania* 18 (1983) 127–50. ISSN 0067-270X. ▸ Finds very old vocabularies of cultivation and pastoralism in several Swahili dialects depict scenario for ancestral Swahili diaspora before external Arabo-Islamic cultural influence. Draws support from archaeological record. [DPH]

19.87 Claude-Hélène Perrot, Gilbert Gonnin, and Ferdinand Nahimana, eds. *Sources orales de l'histoire de l'Afrique.* Paris: Centre National de la Recherche Scientifique, 1989. ISBN 2-222-04244-5. ▸ Latest extended attempt to rehabilitate oral tradition as source for all periods and aspects of African history. Supports argument with more than fifteen studies from throughout Francophone Africa. [DPH]

19.88 Ian Phimister. "Zimbabwean economic and social historiography since 1970." *African affairs* 78.311 (1979) 253–68. ISSN 0001-9909. ▸ Early review of confrontation between liberal and radical approaches. Focuses on Zimbabwe, but early insights into social and political roles under colonialism applicable to wider literature on Africa. [DSN]

19.89 Andrew D. Roberts. "The earlier historiography of colonial Africa." *History in Africa* 5 (1978) 153–67. ISSN 0361-5413. ▸ Survey of amateur attempts by colonial officials to write history and ethnography of areas they administered. Points out how these works are of value to historians in spite of deficiencies by today's professional standards. [DPH]

19.90 Peter Robertshaw, ed. *A history of African archaeology.* Portsmouth, N.H.: Heinemann, 1990. ISBN 0-435-08040-7 (cl), 0-435-08041-5 (pbk). ▸ Informative overviews of African archaeology including personal memoirs, regional surveys and thematic essays. Thoughtful introductory and concluding essays (Robertshaw and Trigger) situating African archaeology within wider discipline. Excellent bibliography. [DSN]

19.91 Peter Rosa. "Physical anthropology and the reconstruction of recent precolonial history in Africa." *History in Africa* 12 (1985) 281–305. ISSN 0361-5413. ▸ Argues for including concepts from physical anthropology (e.g., gene flow, random genetic shift) to complement conventional historical sources. Suggests vulnerability of current theories of race and ethnicity to these data. [DPH]

19.92 Christopher Saunders. *The making of the South African past: major historians on race and class.* Totowa, N.J.: Barnes & Noble, 1989. ISBN 0-389-20785-3. ▸ Solid, well-written introduction to South African historiography, centered on liberal tradition—Theal, MacMillan, De Kiewiet, and (less so) Walker (see 19.716, 19.700, 19.745, 19.721). Also discusses 1970s radical challenge. [DSN]

19.93 David Schoenbrun. "Treating an interdisciplinary allergy: methodological approaches to pollen studies for the historian of early Africa." *History in Africa* 18 (1991) 323–48. ISSN 0361-5413. ▸ Suggests how historians can use palynological data from interlacustrine area (modern Uganda) to infer demographic and culture change antedating written or oral records. [DPH]

19.94 Jarle Simensen. "Value orientation in historical research and writing: the colonial period in African history." *History in Africa* 17 (1990) 267–82. ISSN 0361-5413. ▸ Reminder of how seldom historical writing can be regarded as objective exercise; examples from historiography of colonial Africa. Relates historical and scientific discourse. [DPH]

19.95 Ken Smith. *The changing past: trends in South African historical writing.* 1988 ed. Athens: Ohio University Press, 1989. ISBN 0-8214-0926-3 (cl), 0-8214-0927-1 (pbk). ▸ Identifies five traditions: British imperial, settler, Afrikaans, liberal, and radical. Focuses on latter two; broader range of themes and individuals than Saunders 19.92, but more a catalog than coherent analysis. [DSN]

19.96 Elinor Sosne. "Of biases and queens: the Shi past through an androgynous looking-glass." *History in Africa* 6 (1979) 225–52. ISSN 0361-5413. ▸ Discussion of benefits of interviewing women and studying historical roles of women in African societies. Examples from Shi people of eastern Zaire demonstrate that even when focus not specifically on gender or domestic matters, women's perspectives complemented and illuminated other field data. [DPH]

19.97 A. J. Temu and Bonaventure Swai. *Historians and Africanist history: a critique.* London: Zed, 1981. ISBN 0-905762-78-9 (cl), 0-905762-79-7 (pbk). ‣ Most complete radical critique of liberal postcolonial historiography for Africa as a whole. Concerned with themes of 1970s: nationalism, peasants, resistance, and African initiative. Full consideration of writing by Africans. [DSN]

19.98 Michael Twaddle. "On Ganda historiography." *History in Africa* 1 (1974) 325–63. ISSN 0361-5413. ‣ Notes outpouring of historical writings by Africans (of Ganda ethnic background) in early colonial period; derived from intensity of politics of indirect rule, they significantly influenced colonial policy. Argues that written mode froze fluid oral sources while intensifying debate over their meaning. [DSN]

19.99 Michael Twaddle. "Towards an early history of the East African interior." *History in Africa* 2 (1975) 147–84. ISSN 0361-5413. ‣ Seeks to throw light on tangled East African social and political origins by drawing together written, oral, and archaeological evidence. Broad-gauged and critically informed approach allows diverse interpretations. [DPH]

19.100 Jan Vansina. *Art history in Africa: an introduction to method.* London: Longman, 1984. ISBN 0-582-64367-8 (cl), 0-582-64368-6 (pbk). ‣ Treats art from historian's viewpoint, concentrating on context, interrelationships, and change rather than aesthetics. Extends discussion of art as manifestation of intellectual history. [DPH]

19.101 Jan Vansina. "Bantu in the crystal ball." *History in Africa* 6, 7 (1979, 1980) 287–333, 293–325. ISSN 0361-5413. ‣ Thorough overview of linguistics and history through a century of studies on Bantu language groups. Illustrates durability of diffusion theories, importance of personal outlooks, and difficulty of transforming established paradigms. [DSN]

19.102 Jan Vansina. "Is elegance proof?" *History in Africa* 9 (1982) 307–48. ISSN 0361-5413. ‣ Criticizes Luc de Heusch and other structural anthropologists for failure to understand full range of historical and ethnographic material available for study of more remote African past. [DPH]

19.103 Jan Vansina. "The power of systematic doubt in historical enquiry." *History in Africa* 1 (1974) 109–27. ISSN 0361-5413. ‣ Discussion of scientific method of inquiry by verification and falsification developed in nineteenth century and how and why it should be applied to African historiography, with case study of origins of Kuba of Zaire. Concludes constant recourse to evidence vital to test interpretation. [DPH]

19.104 Ivor Wilks, Nehemia Levtzion, and Bruce M. Haight, eds. *Chronicles from Gonja: a tradition of West African Muslim historiography.* Cambridge: Cambridge University Press, 1986. ISBN 0-521-26041-8. ‣ Translation-edition of four major Arabic recensions (script included) of so-called Gonja chronicle. Valuable historical introduction and extensive apparatus; model for Arabic sources for West and East Africa. [DPH]

SEE ALSO
1.113 David P. Henige. *Oral historiography.*
1.116 Jan Vansina. *Oral tradition as history.*

WESTERN AFRICA

To 600 CE

19.105 Suzanne Bernus et al. *La région d'In Gall—Tegidda n Tesemt: programme archéologique d'urgence.* 4 vols. Niamey, Niger: Institut de Recherches en Sciences Humaines, 1977–81. (Études Nigériennes, 47–50.) ISBN 2-85920-47-4 (v. 47), 2-85920-48-2 (v.

48), 2-85920-49-0 (v. 49), 2-85920-50-4 (v. 50). ‣ Regional survey of Saharan copper zone at Azelik, Agadez, and Marandet. Examines transformations from late Neolithic, local, small-scale society to metal-using complex institutions with long-distance trade. [RJM]

19.106 Gabriel Camps. *Les civilisations préhistoriques de l'Afrique du Nord et du Sahara.* Paris: Doin, 1974. ISBN 2-7040-0030-1. ‣ Synthesis of Saharan–North African lithic industries, populations, and rock art. Classic in comprehensiveness on Stone Age Sahara, but dated emphasis on tools rather than people. [RJM]

19.107 Graham Connah. *Three thousand years in Africa: man and his environment in the Lake Chad region of Nigeria.* Cambridge: Cambridge University Press, 1981. ISBN 0-521-22848-4. ‣ Regional survey and excavation at Daima on southern Lake Chad floodplain; ecological approach to late Neolithic and early Iron Age adaptations gives environmental, if not social, context of adaptations. [RJM]

19.108 Jack R. Harlan, Jan M. J. de Wet, and Ann B. L. Stemler, eds. *Origins of African plant domestication.* Chicago: Mouton; distributed by Aldine, 1976. ISBN 0-202-90033-9. ‣ Best available discussion of archaeological evidence for climate change, population pressures, and plant-human interactions behind domestication of cereal and root crops; heavy on plant genetics and ecologies. [RJM]

19.109 Henri J. Hugot. "The prehistory of the Sahara." In *General history of Africa: UNESCO International Scientific Committee for the Drafting of a General History of Africa.* 1981 ed. Joseph Ki-Zerbo, ed., vol. 1, pp. 585–610. Berkeley: University of California Press, 1989. ISBN 0-520-06696-0 (cl), 0-85255-092-8 (pbk). ‣ Sahara as cradle of multiple Stone Age cultures and processes such as crop domestication. Change attributed to climatic deterioration and migration. More comprehensive than Mauny 19.111, but older, typological approach to prehistory. [RJM]

19.110 François J. Kense. "The initial diffusion of iron to Africa." In *African iron working, ancient and traditional.* Randi Haaland and Peter Shinnie, eds., pp. 11–27. Oslo: Norwegian University Press; distributed by Oxford University Press, 1985. ISBN 8-200-07292-4. ‣ Theories and recent evidence for early iron technology; diversity of technology and spread of furnace types as clues to origin, diffusion, and social context of innovation. Readable general synthesis. [RJM]

19.111 Raymond Mauny. *Tableau géographique de l'Ouest Africain au moyen âge d'après les sources écrites, la tradition, et l'archéologie.* Dakar: Institut Fondamental d'Afrique Noire, 1961. (Mémoires de l'Institut Fondamentale d'Afrique Noire, 61.) ‣ Basic sourcebook of Iron Age and historical artifacts and sites in Sahara and West Africa. Comprehensive at date of publication, with enormous amounts of unpublished material; little interpretation beyond perspective of Arabic sources. [RJM]

19.112 Susan Keech McIntosh. *Excavation at Jenne-jeno, Hambarketolo, and Kaniana (inland Niger Delta, Mali).* Berkeley: University of California Press, 1993. ‣ Most current synthesis of Middle Niger prehistory. Latest excavations show regional and pan-West African contexts of emerging urbanism, long-distance trade, and artisan production, early Iron Age through historic period. [RJM]

19.113 Susan Keech McIntosh and Roderick James McIntosh. "From stone to metal: new perspectives on the later prehistory of West Africa." *Journal of world prehistory* 2.1 (1988) 89–133. ISSN 0892-7537. ‣ Historical synthesis of origins of Saharan and West African urbanism, long-distance trade, and iron production. Highlights innovative nature of these stratified societies, Stone Age to eleventh century. [RJM]

19.114 Susan Keech McIntosh and Roderick James McIntosh.

Prehistoric investigations in the region of Jenne, Mali: a study in the development of urbanism in the Sahel. 2 vols. Oxford: British Archaeological Reports, 1980. (Cambridge monographs in African archaeology, 2.) ISBN 0-86054-103-7 (set, pbk). ‣ Middle Niger excavations and survey in Jenne vicinity. Places origins and maturation of early urban site and regional network well before trans-Saharan commerce. [RJM]

19.115 Nicole Petit-Maire and J. Riser, eds. *Sahara ou Sahel?* Paris: Laboratoire de Géologie du Quaternaire du Centre National de la Recherche and Librairie du Museum, 1983. ISBN 2-904894-00-4. ‣ Study of Holocene lakes and lakeside communities in vast Malian Sahara. Best example of multidisciplinary collaboration on palaeoecology and human responses to environmental stress. [RJM]

19.116 C. Thurstan Shaw. *Igbo-Ukwu: an account of archaeological discoveries in eastern Nigeria.* Evanston, Ill.: Northwestern University Press, 1970. ISBN 0-8101-0304-0. ‣ Eighth-century ritual and art site showing early long-distance trade, artistic, and bronze-working capacity. Goes beyond conventional use of state structure to interpret altars and burial as part of nonhereditary secret society. [RJM]

19.117 C. Thurstan Shaw. *Nigeria: its archaeology and early history.* London: Thames & Hudson, 1978. ISBN 0-500-02086-8. ‣ Summary of major archaeological finds for nonspecialists using excavation and ethnography to reconstruct Iron Age society. Comprehensive coverage of early Yoruba materials, Nok, Igbo-Ukwu, Ife, and Benin finds. [RJM]

19.118 C. Thurstan Shaw. "The prehistory of West Africa." In *Methodology and African pre-history.* 1981 ed. Joseph Ki-Zerbo, ed., pp. 611–33. Berkeley: University of California Press, 1990. ISBN 0-520-06696-0 (cl), 0-85255-092-8 (pbk). ‣ Overview of prehistoric sub-Saharan West African expansion in scale and regional integration as adaptation to climatic changes and resulting new environmental possibilities. Accents human agency and opportunism. [RJM]

19.119 Nikolaas Van der Merwe. "The advent of iron in Africa." In *The coming of the age of iron.* Theodore A. Wertime and James D. Muhly, eds., pp. 463–506. New Haven: Yale University Press, 1980. ISBN 0-300-02425-8. ‣ Comprehensive, still up-to-date synthesis of social needs and resource distribution behind iron introduction across Africa. Acknowledges external sources (possibly North Africa) but stresses local adaptation to overcome crude dichotomy common in this debate. [RJM]

19.120 Martin A. J. Williams and Hugues Faure, eds. *The Sahara and the Nile: Quarternary environments and prehistoric occupation in northern Africa.* Rotterdam: Balkema, 1980. ISBN 9-06-191012-9. ‣ Best accounts of peoples who made Saharan stone tools and their ecological adaptations. Reviews evolution and paleoclimate of Sahara and Nile leading to crop domestication, often under desiccating conditions. [RJM]

Seventh to Sixteenth Century

19.121 George E. Brooks. *Landlords and strangers: ecology, society, and trade in western Africa, 1000–1630.* Boulder: Westview, 1993. ISBN 0-8133-1262-0 (cl), 0-8133-1263-9 (pbk). ‣ Study of cultural and geographical focus around Mande diaspora and landlord-stranger relations. Controversial linkage of climate changes (drying 1000–1500, wetter 1500–1630) to slaving, trading, and migration. Interdisciplinary, wide range of written sources. [AMcD]

19.122 George E. Brooks. *Western Africa to c. 1860 A.D.: a provisional historical schema based on climate periods.* Bloomington: Indiana University, African Studies Program, 1985. (Working papers, 1.) ISBN 0-317-39359-6. ‣ Reconstructs two millennia of major climate oscillations in far-western Africa (wetter and drier)

to suggest influences on political development, ethnic identities, trade patterns, and social institutions. Highly suggestive and controversial. [JCM]

19.123 Stephen Bulman. "The buffalo-woman tale: political imperatives and narrative constraints in the Sunjata Epic." In *Discourse and its disguises: the interpretation of African oral texts.* Karin Barber and P. F. de Moraes Farias, eds. Birmingham: University of Birmingham, Centre of West African Studies, 1989. (Birmingham University African studies series, 1.) ISBN 0-7044-1042-7. ‣ Gendered discourse analysis of Sunjata Epic (founding legend, Mali empire). Integrated historical-mythical analysis revealing Islamic and local hunter-stranger folklore and society and politics of imperial Mali (ca. fourteenth century). [AMcD]

19.124 Sheryl L. Burkhalter. "Listening for silences in Almoravid history: another reading of 'The Conquest That Never Was.'" *History in Africa* 19 (1992) 103–31. ISSN 0361-5413. ‣ Provocative rebuttal to Conrad and Fisher 19.127 criticizing their reading of Arabic sources; informed by recent work on discourse and voice appropriation. Significant departure from traditional views. [AMcD/DPH]

19.125 S. M. Cissoko. "The Songhay from the twelfth to the sixteenth century." In *General history of Africa: UNESCO International Scientific Committee for the Drafting of a General History of Africa.* D. T. Niane, ed., vol. 4, pp. 187–210. Berkeley: University of California Press, 1984. ISBN 0-520-03915-7. ‣ Authoritative survey of Songhai empire, reflecting urban-rural, Islamic-animist, and external-internal dichotomies of Arabic and oral sources. Now superseded by recent archaeology showing early urban development (Jenne-Jeno, Gao-Sane). [AMcD]

19.126 David C. Conrad. "Islam in the oral traditions of Mali: Bilali and Surakata." *Journal of African history* 26.1 (1985) 33–50. ISSN 0021-8537. ‣ Discussion of Mali (empire) founding epic, centered on Sunjata, as influenced by Arabic literature. Discourse analysis makes major contribution in showing role of evolving local traditions in conversion to Islam. [AMcD]

19.127 David C. Conrad and Humphrey J. Fisher. "The conquest that never was: Ghana and the Almoravids, 1076. Part 1: The external Arabic sources. Part 2: The local oral sources." *History in Africa* 9, 10 (1982, 1983) 21–59, 53–78. ISSN 0361-5413. ‣ Meticulous examination of sources, both written Arabic and oral traditions, to challenge eleventh-century Almoravid "conquest" of Ghana. Subsequent writings (Conrad 19.126, McDougall 19.134, McIntosh and McIntosh 19.136, and Burkhalter 19.124) question force and external influence. [AMcD/DPH]

19.128 Jean Devisse. "Trade and trade routes in West Africa." In *General history of Africa.* Abr. ed. M. Elfasi and I. Hrbek, eds., vol. 3, pp. 367–435. Berkeley: University of California Press, 1992. ISBN 0-520-03914-9 (cl), 0-520-06698-7 (pbk). ‣ Superb overview utilizing recent archaeology and emphasizing Saharan and Sahelian commercial links along east-west as well as north-south axes. Emphasis on regional sub-Saharan economic integration replaces older accent on trans-Saharan gold trade. [AMcD]

19.129 John D. Fage. "Upper and lower Guinea." In *The Cambridge history of Africa.* Roland Oliver, ed., vol. 3, pp. 463–518. Cambridge: Cambridge University Press, 1977. ISBN 0-521-20981-1. ‣ Masterly sketch integrating diverse histories of coast and hinterland from Senegal to Cameroon. Dated discussion of sources but relevant methodology and research orientation. Excellent introduction to first European contact. [AMcD]

19.130 P. F. de Moraes Farias. "Silent trade: myth and historical evidence." *History in Africa* 1 (1974) 9–24. ISSN 0361-5413. ‣ Imaginative debunking of widely held belief that silent trade characterized ancient long-distance exchange; includes comparative examples. Discourse analysis shows that mythological idiom masked varied economic realities. [AMcD]

19.131 J.F.P. Hopkins and Nehemia Levtzion, eds. *Corpus of early Arabic sources for West African history.* Cambridge: Cambridge University Press, 1981. ISBN 0-521-22422-5. ‣ Essential collection of sixty-five translated Arabic source excerpts; accessible for general reader through extensive annotations, author biographies, notes on historical context, and full indexing. Perspectives limited to Arab interests in Islam, morality, and commerce. [AMcD]

19.132 I. Hrbek and Jean Devisse. "The Almoravids." In *General history of Africa: UNESCO International Scientific Committee for the Drafting of a General History of Africa.* M. Elfasi and I. Hrbek, eds., vol. 3, pp. 336–66. Berkeley: University of California Press, 1988. ISBN 0-520-03914-9 (cl), 0-520-06698-7 (pbk). ‣ Current overview of controversial Muslim dynasty in twelfth-century Morocco and western Sahara, emphasizing contributions to Moroccan economy, trans-Saharan trade, and mineral production, rather than destruction. Also stresses regional differences, not homogeneity. [AMcD]

19.133 Nehemia Levtzion. *Ancient Ghana and Mali.* 2d ed. New York: Africana, 1980. ISBN 0-8419-0431-6 (cl), 0-8419-0432-4 (pbk). ‣ Defining synthesis of these famous ancient polities using Arabic sources. Sees state growth as stimulated by Arab trans-Saharan trade and Islam. Subsequent work stresses oral sources (Conrad 19.126, Bulman 19.123), sub-Saharan regional economy (McIntosh and McIntosh 19.136, McDougall 19.134, 19.135), and pre-Islamic culture (Burkhalter 19.124, Conrad and Fisher 19.127). [AMcD]

19.134 E. Ann McDougall. "The Sahara reconsidered: pastoralism, politics, and salt from the ninth through the twelfth centuries." *History in Africa* 12 (1983) 263–86. ISSN 0361-5413. ‣ Southern Saharan pastoralism generated wealth in herds, oasis agriculture, commerce, and salt, transforming it into power through religious and family alliances, relations with Sahel (sub-desert) region. Salt, not gold, base of ancient Ghana's political economy. [AMcD]

19.135 E. Ann McDougall. "The view from Awdaghust: war, trade, and social change in the southwestern Sahara from the eighth to the fifteenth century." *Journal of African history* 26.1 (1985) 1–31. ISSN 0021-8537. ‣ Southern Saharan trading center (Awdagust) reflecting social and economic evolution in southern Sahara; agriculture and salt generated wealth supporting specialized warriors, cultivators, and traders. Downplays trans-Saharan commerce (see Levtzion 19.133). [AMcD]

19.136 Roderick James McIntosh and Susan Keech McIntosh. "From *'siècles obscures'* to revolutionary centuries on the Middle Niger." *World archaeology* 20.1 (1988) 141–65. ISSN 0043-8243. ‣ Provocative overview to 1400 CE, illustrating relevance of climate, archaeology, and cross-cultural anthropology for understanding emergence of urban societies and large states. Rejects Arab-stimulus development model (see Levtzion 19.133). [AMcD]

19.137 D. T. Niane. "Mali and the second Mandingo expansion." In *General history of Africa: UNESCO International Scientific Committee for the Drafting of a General History of Africa.* D. T. Niane, ed., vol. 4, pp. 117–70. Berkeley: University of California Press, 1984. ISBN 0-520-03915-7. ‣ Conventional account of the rise of Mali and birth of Mande culture as spread through commercial and religious networks. Critical use of oral tradition (Sunjata Epic), Arabic sources, archaeology, and art. Drawings, maps, and excellent photographs (see Conrad 19.126, Bulman 19.123). [AMcD]

19.138 H. T. Norris. *Saharan myth and saga.* Oxford: Clarendon, 1972. ISBN 0-19-815139-X. ‣ Brilliant unveiling of oral and

written sources with detailed textual and contextual analysis and nuanced understanding of diffusion of Arab culture; Almoravids feature prominently. Extensive appendixes, notes, and glossary. [AMcD]

19.139 Ade Obayemi. "The Yoruba and Edo-speaking peoples and their neighbours before 1600." In *History of West Africa.* 3d ed. Jacob F. Ade Ajayi and Michael Crowder, eds., vol. 1, pp. 196–263. Burnt Mill, England: Longman, 1985. ISBN 0-582-64683-9. ‣ Comprehensive history of these diverse regions reconstructed largely through oral tradition and archaeology. State-centralization theme is dated, but historians will benefit from intellectual enthusiasm and interdisciplinary insights. [AMcD]

19.140 A.F.C. Ryder. "From the Volta to Cameroon." In *General history of Africa: UNESCO International Scientific Committee for the Drafting of a General History of Africa.* D. T. Niane, ed., vol. 4, pp. 339–70. Berkeley: University of California Press, 1984. ISBN 0-520-03915-7. ‣ Good introduction to modern Nigeria's Delta societies, extending to social and economic development. Discussion and photographs of exquisite Benin and Nupe bronzes, as well as famous Igbo-Ukwu archaeological excavation. [AMcD]

19.141 Abdullahi Smith. "The early states of Central Sudan." In *History of West Africa: UNESCO International Scientific Committee for the Drafting of a General History of Africa.* 3d ed. Jacob F. Ade Ajayi and Michael Crowder, eds., vol. 1, pp. 152–95. Burnt Mill, England: Longman, 1985. ISBN 0-582-64683-9. ‣ Authoritative account of climatic, cultural, and political history of Sahelian Niger, Chad, and Nigeria. Critical of Arab sources and northern influences; explains Kanuri development through local migrations. Traces pre-Islamic regional religions. [AMcD]

19.142 Tal Tamari. "The development of caste systems in West Africa." *Journal of African history* 32.2 (1991) 221–49. ISSN 0021-8537. ‣ Argues West African artisan and musician castes originated among Mande, Soninke, and Wolof peoples in thirteenth to fourteenth centuries. Innovative use of Sunjata Epic (Mali foundation legend), Arabic, and oral sources. [AMcD/DWR]

SEE ALSO
2.20 Susan Keech McIntosh and Roderick James McIntosh. "The early city in West Africa."

Seventeenth and Eighteenth Centuries

19.143 Michel Abitbol. *Tombouctou et les Arma de la conquête marocaine du Soudan nigérien en 1591 à l'hégémonie de l'empire Peul du Maçina en 1833.* Paris: Maisonneuve et Larose, 1979. ISBN 2-7068-0770-9. ‣ Study of Moroccan conquest of Songhai and independent Arma state based on Timbuktu which emerged out of it. Meticulously detailed regional history emphasizing economic background to political events. [RCL]

19.144 Mahdi Adamu. *The Hausa factor in West African history.* Zaria, Nigeria: Ahmadu Bello University Press; distributed by Oxford University Press, 1978. ISBN 978-125-006-2, 0-19-575442-5. ‣ Study of Hausa (northern Nigerian people) commercial diaspora and spread of Hausa culture throughout eastern West Africa, mostly nineteenth century. Well researched, if theoretically unadventurous. [RCL]

19.145 Jacob F. Ade Ajayi and Michael Crowder, eds. *History of West Africa.* 3d ed. 2 vols. Burnt Mill, England: Longman, 1985. ISBN 0-582-64683-9. ‣ Chapters mainly regional, give reasonably detailed and comprehensive coverage of West African history. [RCL]

19.146 I. A. Akinjogbin. *Dahomey and its neighbours, 1708–1818.* Cambridge: Cambridge University Press, 1967. ‣ Interpretation of rise and character of Dahomey (eighteenth-century West

African kingdom) as response to problems of order posed by Atlantic slave trade. Superseded in detail by Law 19.173 but still worth reading as provocative introduction to controversy. [RCL]

19.147 E. J. Alagoa. *A history of the Niger Delta: an historical interpretation of Ijo oral tradition*. Ibadan: Ibadan University Press, 1972. ‣ Detailed, case-by-case study of Ijo communities of Niger Delta, based principally on local oral traditions. Difficult but illuminating for questions of state formation and impact of long-distance trade. [RCL]

19.148 Bawuro Mubi Barkindo. *The sultanate of Mandara to 1902: history of the evolution, development, and collapse of a Central Sudanese kingdom*. Stuttgart: Steiner, 1989. ISBN 3-515-04416-7. ‣ Study of minor Central Sudan kingdom, but set in wider regional context, including conversion to Islam. Main emphasis on evolution of political institutions. [RCL]

19.149 Abdoulaye Bathily. *Les Portes de l'Or: le royaume de Galam (Sénégal) de l'ère musulmane au temps des négriers (VIIe–XVIIe siècle)*. Paris: Harmattan, 1989. ISBN 2-7384-0276-3. ‣ Assessment of impact of involvement in trans-Saharan and Atlantic trades. Stresses destructive impact of Atlantic slave trade, to which Galam's decline in eighteenth century is attributed. [RCL]

19.150 William Bosman. *A new and accurate description of the coast of Guinea, divided into the Gold, the Slave, and the Ivory coasts*. 4th ed. John D. Fage and R. E. Bradbury, eds. New York: Barnes & Noble, 1967. ‣ Classic, original account of European trade and indigenous societies on West African coast in late seventeenth century. Essential source for local organization and impact of Atlantic trade. [RCL]

19.151 Jean Boulègue. *Le Grand Jolof, XIIe–XVIe siècle*. Blois and Paris: Facades and Karthala, 1987. ISBN 2-907233-00-9. ‣ Study of nature and social basis of major Islamic state to earliest period of European trade. Analytical rather than narrative history; ambitious in purpose and persuasive in its conclusions. [RCL]

19.152 E. W. Bovill. *The golden trade of the Moors*. 2d ed. Robin Hallett, additional material. London: Oxford University Press, 1968. ‣ General history of Sahara and western Sudan as well as trans-Saharan trade. Outdated (originally published 1933), but still best general introductory survey in English. [RCL]

19.153 S. M. Cissoko. *Tombouctou et l'empire Songhay: épanouissement du Soudan nigérien aux XVe–XVIe siècles*. Dakar: Nouvelles Éditions Africaines, 1975. ISBN 2-7236-0087-4. ‣ Comprehensive, detailed account of Songhai empire (sixteenth century) with attention to economic and social basis of political institutions. [RCL]

19.154 Philip D. Curtin. *Economic change in pre-colonial Africa: Senegambia in the era of the slave trade*. 2 vols. Madison: University of Wisconsin Press, 1975. ISBN 0-299-06640-1 (v. 1), 0-299-06650-9 (suppl.) ‣ Detailed study of organization and impact of European trade in one area of West Africa. Pioneering, and still virtually unique, in application of detailed quantitative data to these issues. [RCL/DAN]

19.155 Kwame Yeboa Daaku. *Trade and politics on the Gold Coast, 1600–1720: a study of the African reaction to European trade*. London: Clarendon, 1970. ISBN 0-19-821653-X. ‣ Solid but analytically limited account of operation and impact of early European trade. Superseded by Kea 19.169, but remains useful as more readable introduction. [RCL]

19.156 Archibald Dalzel. *The history of Dahomy, an inland kingdom of Africa*. 1793 ed. John D. Fage, comp. London: Cass, 1967. ‣ One of first European histories of indigenous African state, written as defense of morality of slave trade. Despite pro-slavery biases, invaluable historical source. [RCL]

19.157 K. G. Davies. *The Royal African Company*. 1957 ed. New York: Octagon Books, 1975. ISBN 0-374-92074-5. ‣ History of chartered company that held monopoly of English trade with Africa, 1672–98, and managed British possessions on West African coast until 1750. Very informative on company's West African operations. [RCL]

19.158 Mahmadou Diawara. *La graine de la parole: dimension sociale et politique des traditions orales du royaume de Jaara (Mali) du quinzième au milieu du dix-neuvième siècle*. Stuttgart: Steiner, 1990. ISBN 3-515-05021-3. ‣ Study of representations of history in oral traditions, stressing variety of perspectives and their use to define identities and support claims for power. Innovative in directing attention away from state and toward society. [RCL]

19.159 Kenneth Onwuka Dike and Felicia Ekejiuba. *The Aro of South-eastern Nigeria, 1650–1980: a study of socio-economic transformation in Nigeria*. Ibadan: Ibadan University Press, 1990. ISBN 978-154-912-2. ‣ Study of major trading diaspora, which dominated supply of slaves for Atlantic trade in southeastern Nigeria, based mainly on oral traditions. Contentious in interpreting Aro as "state." [RCL]

19.160 Olaudah Equiano. *Equiano's travels: his autobiography, the interesting narrative of the life of Olaudah Equiano or Gustavus Vasa the African*. ed. London: Heinemann, 1967. ISBN 3-435-90010-2. ‣ Autobiography (first published 1789) of Igbo exported as slave in 1756. Classic of abolitionist literature; most informative of such eighteenth-century slave narratives. [RCL]

19.161 E. O. Erim. *The Idoma nationality, 1600–1900: problems of studying the origin and development of ethnicity*. Enugu, Nigeria: Fourth Dimension, 1981. ISBN 978-15-6182-3. ‣ Virtually only published history of any part of neglected Middle Belt of Central Nigeria before nineteenth century. Principal emphasis on processes of ethnic and state formation. [RCL]

19.162 John D. Fage. *A history of West Africa: an introductory survey*. 4th ed. Cambridge: Cambridge University Press, 1969. ISBN 0-521-07406-1. ‣ Revised from pioneering survey (published 1955), covering entire period from prehistory to independence. Still best single-volume, short introductory survey of West African history. [RCL]

19.163 J. K. Fynn. *Asante and its neighbours, 1700–1807*. Evanston, Ill.: Longman and Northwestern University Press, 1971. ISBN 0-8101-0369-9. ‣ Rise and expansion of one of major West African states in context of Atlantic slave trade. Analytically unadventurous but offers sound historical narrative. [RCL]

19.164 Nicoué Lodjou Gayibor. *Le Genyi: un royaume oublié de la Côte de Guinée au temps le la traite des Noirs*. Lomé, Togo and Paris: Haho and Karthala, 1990. ISBN 2-906718-28-9. ‣ Detailed study of minor coastal state (Togo area) involved in Atlantic slave trade. Illuminating as complement to better studied history of neighboring larger states such as Dahomey. [RCL]

19.165 Mervyn Hiskett. *The development of Islam in West Africa*. New York: Longman, 1984. ISBN 0-582-64692-8 (cl), 0-582-64694-4 (pbk). ‣ Best-balanced (chronologically and geographically) survey of subject available. Gives adequate coverage to period before 1800 and to peripheral areas where Islam remained minority religion. [RCL]

19.166 Jan S. Hogendorn and Marion Johnson. *The shell money of the slave trade*. Cambridge: Cambridge University Press, 1986. ISBN 0-521-32086-0. ‣ Analysis of cowry shells, imported from Indian Ocean and widely used as currency in West Africa. Critically important for understanding of West African domestic economies, as well as trade with Europeans. [RCL/DWR]

19.167 Samuel Johnson. *The history of the Yorubas from the earliest times to the beginning of the British Protectorate*. 1921 ed.

O. Johnson, ed. Westport, Conn.: Negro University Press, 1970. ISBN 0-8371-5670-X. ‣ Pioneering account (written 1890s) by Christian Yoruba, based mainly on oral traditions. Classic of African historiography, and still most important single source for precolonial Yoruba history. [RCL]

19.168 Adam Jones. *From slaves to palm oil: a history of the Galinhas Country (West Africa), 1730–1890.* Wiesbaden: Steiner, 1983. ISBN 3-515-03878-7. ‣ Case study of operation and impact of European trade, including slave trade, emphasizing effects on social and political change. [RCL]

19.169 Ray A. Kea. *Settlements, trade, and polities in the seventeenth-century Gold Coast.* Gregory Chu, illustrator. Baltimore: Johns Hopkins University Press, 1982. ISBN 0-8018-2310-2. ‣ Analysis of transformation of socioeconomic structures by Atlantic slave trade, applying Marxist theory and stressing rise of new military states. Difficult but sophisticated, persuasive analysis. [RCL/DAN]

19.170 M. A. Kwamena-Poh. *Government and politics in the Akuapem state, 1730–1850.* Evanston, Ill.: Northwestern University Press, 1973. ISBN 0-8101-03826. ‣ Rise and decline of minor state of Gold Coast. Mainly narrative history, but usefully illuminates processes of state formation and interaction with European influences. [RCL]

19.171 A.J.H. Latham. *Old Calabar, 1600–1891: the impact of the international economy upon a traditional society.* Oxford: Clarendon, 1973. ISBN 0-19-821687-4. ‣ Case study of impact of European trade on coastal trading community in Niger Delta, stressing transformation of sociopolitical structures. Massive detail, sometimes confusing in presentation, gives analysis solid support. [RCL/DAN]

19.172 Robin C. C. Law. *The horse in West African history: the role of the horse in the societies of pre-colonial West Africa.* Oxford: Oxford University Press for International African Institute, 1980. ISBN 0-19-724206-5. ‣ Discussion of introduction and use of horses throughout West Africa, especially in warfare. Argues for cavalry-related revolution in military tactics and organization, also affecting sociopolitical structures. [RCL]

19.173 Robin C. C. Law. *The Oyo empire, c. 1600–c. 1836: a West African imperialism in the era of the Atlantic slave trade.* Oxford: Clarendon, 1977. ISBN 0-19-822709-4. ‣ Study of major Yoruba state of coastal region, concentrating mainly on evolution of political structures. Also assesses significance of empire's involvement in Atlantic slave trade. [RCL/DWR]

19.174 Nehemia Levtzion. *Muslims and chiefs in West Africa: a study of Islam in the Middle Volta Basin in the pre-colonial period.* Oxford: Clarendon, 1968. ISBN 0-19-821639-4. ‣ Rare study of Islam in more southerly (and less well-documented) regions of West Africa, where Muslim clerics and traders had to accommodate to authority of pagan rulers. [RCL/DWR]

19.175 Eveline Christiana Martin. *The British West African settlements, 1750–1821: a study in local administration.* 1927 ed. New York: Negro University Press, 1970. ISBN 0-8371-3612-1. ‣ Study of British possessions on West African coast, relating mainly to the Company of Merchants Trading to Africa. Despite age, still the definitive study. [RCL]

19.176 Georg Norregård. *Danish settlements in West Africa, 1658–1850.* Sigurd Mammen, trans. Boston: Boston University Press, 1966. ‣ Study of activities of Danish African Company in West Africa, especially Gold Coast. Invaluable distillation of material in Danish archives; illuminates African history as well as Danish enterprise. [RCL]

19.177 Duarte Pacheco Pereira. *Esmeraldo de situ orbis.* George T. Kimble, ed. and trans. London: Hakluyt Society, 1937. (Works issued by the Hakluyt Society, Second series, 79.) ‣ Classic description of West African coast at beginning of sixteenth century. Essential source for coastal societies in early years of European trade. [RCL]

19.178 Mungo Park. *Travels in the interior districts of Africa.* New York: Arno, 1971. ISBN 0-405-01718-9. ‣ Account by first European explorer to penetrate West African interior in 1795–97. Classic of European exploration, but also invaluable source for conditions in African societies. [RCL]

19.179 Karl Polanyi. *Dahomey and the slave trade: an analysis of an archaic economy.* Seattle: University of Washington Press, 1966. (American Ethnological Society monographs, 2.) ‣ Treats Dahomey as case study of precapitalist economic organization, including domestic as well as overseas trade. Stresses nonmarket character and state control. Inaccurate in detail, but still fruitfully provocative analysis. [RCL]

19.180 Carl Christian Reindorf. *The history of the Gold Coast and Asante, based on traditions and facts comprising a period of more than three centuries from about 1500 to 1860.* 2d ed. Accra, Ghana: Ghana Universities Press, 1966. ‣ Pioneering local history by Christian African, based on oral tradition (first published 1895). Classic of West African historiography and valuable historical source. [RCL]

19.181 Walter Rodney. *History of the Upper Guinea coast, 1545–1800.* 1970 ed. New York: Monthly Review, 1982. ISBN 0-85344-5546-5. ‣ Concentrates on effects of European trade. Negative assessment of slave trade; controversial claim that slavery did not exist in region prior to slave trade. [RCL/DAN]

19.182 A.F.C. Ryder. *Benin and the Europeans, 1485–1897.* New York: Humanities, 1969. ‣ Meticulously detailed analysis of changing patterns of European trade, but does not venture far in assessing its significance for African kingdom. [RCL/DWR]

19.183 Elias Saad. *Social history of Timbuktu: the role of Muslim scholars and notables, 1400–1900.* Cambridge: Cambridge University Press, 1983. ISBN 0-521-24603-2. ‣ Intellectual and social history of principal center of Islamic scholarship, based mainly on local Islamic sources. Arguably exaggerates autonomy of Timbuktu and continuity of social structures, but work of enormous erudition. [RCL]

19.184 Lamin O. Sanneh. *The Jakhanke Muslim clerics: a religious and historical study of Islam in Senegambia.* Lanham, Md.: University Press of America, 1989. ISBN 0-81-917481-5 (cl), 0-04-276001-1 (pbk). ‣ Study of influential Islamic diaspora, emphasizing clerical rather than commercial aspects and spread of Islam by peaceful methods. Useful antidote to general concentration on militant Islam. [RCL]

19.185 Lamin O. Sanneh. *West African Christianity: the religious impact.* London: Orbis, 1983. ISBN 0-88344-703-7. ‣ Only general survey of history of Christianity in West Africa giving adequate coverage to pre-nineteenth-century Roman Catholic missionary enterprise. [RCL]

19.186 Robert S. Smith. *Kingdoms of the Yoruba.* 3d ed. Madison: University of Wisconsin Press, 1988. ISBN 0-299-11600-X (cl), 0-299-11604-X (pbk). ‣ Summary of literature on Yoruba history. Conservative but not uncritical treatment, based mainly on oral traditions. Invaluable for dealing with kingdoms other than Oyo and before nineteenth century. [RCL]

19.187 J. S. Trimingham. *A history of Islam in West Africa.* 1962 ed. New York: Oxford University Press for University of Glasgow, 1970. ISBN 0-19-285038-5 (pbk). ‣ More a history of West Africa written from Islamic sources than a history of Islam. Overtaken by much recent work on Islam but remains useful as accessible summary of West Africa. [RCL]

19.188 Albert Van Dantzig. *Les hollandais sur la Côte de Guinée*

Français à l'époque de l'essor de l'Ashanti et du Dahomey, 1680–1740. Paris: Société d'Histoire d'Outre-mer, 1980. (Bibliothèque d'histoire d'Outre-mer, Nouvelle série travaux, 3.) ISBN 2-85970-0033-X. ▸ Mainly history of Dutch West India Company's activities on West African coast, but provides detailed information on indigenous African history during critical period. [RCL]

19.189 Pierre Verger. *Trade relations between the Bight of Benin and Bahia from the seventeenth to nineteenth centuries.* Evelyn Crawford, trans. Ibadan: Ibadan University Press, 1976. ISBN 978-121-019-2. ▸ Treats history of indigenous African societies, especially Dahomey, as well as Brazilian trade. Analytically unambitious but valuable for extensive quotation of contemporary sources. [RCL]

19.190 John Vogt. *Portuguese rule on the Gold Coast, 1469–1682.* Athens: University of Georgia Press, 1979. ISBN 0-8203-0443-3. ▸ Essentially narrative account of rise and fall of Portuguese power on West African coast. History of Europeans in Africa rather than of Africa itself. [RCL]

Nineteenth Century

19.191 Sa'ad Abubakar. *The Lamibe of Fombina: a history of Adamawa.* Zaria, Nigeria: Ahmadu Bello University Press, 1977. ISBN 9-7812-50119. ▸ Rare study of one constituent emirate of Sokoto caliphate in nineteenth century. Shows process of Fulbe colonization and takeover in Nigeria-Cameroon border area. [DWR]

19.192 Mahdi Adamu and A.H.M. Kirk-Greene, eds. *Pastoralists of the West African savannah.* Manchester: Manchester University Press with International African Institute, 1986. ISBN 0-7190-2200-2. ▸ Introduction and papers presented at seminar of International African Institute. Some excellent anthropological and historical studies of enduring value. [DWR]

19.193 Remi A. Adeleye. *Power and diplomacy in northern Nigeria, 1804–1906.* New York: Humanities, 1971. ISBN 0-391-00169-8. ▸ Most complete account of political and military history of Sokoto caliphate with special emphasis on increasing European influence and British conquest in early twentieth century. [DWR]

19.194 Jacob F. Ade Ajayi. *Christian missions in Nigeria, 1841–91: the making of a new elite.* 1965 ed. Evanston, Ill.: Northwestern University Press, 1969. ▸ One of most complete studies of European and African missionaries in southern Nigeria and African response. Emphasizes emergence of new westernized elite. [DWR]

19.195 Jacob F. Ade Ajayi and Robert S. Smith. *Yoruba warfare in the nineteenth century.* 1964 ed. Cambridge: Cambridge University Press with University of Ibadan, Institute of African Studies, 1971. ISBN 0-521-04012-4. ▸ Most complete military history of Yoruba civil wars of nineteenth century. [DWR]

19.196 Stephen Adebanji Akintoye. *Revolution and power politics in Yorubaland, 1840–1893: Ibadan expansion and the rise of the Ekitiparapo.* New York: Humanities, 1971. ▸ Useful exploration of Civil War period in Yoruba history, centered around rise of state of Ibadan and its opponents. [DWR]

19.197 Umar Al-Naqar. *The pilgrimage tradition in West Africa: an historical study with specific reference to the nineteenth century.* Khartoum: Khartoum University Press, 1972. ▸ General description of Muslim pilgrimage by land from West Africa, eleventh to nineteenth century, based primarily on Arabic records. [DWR/SSG]

19.198 Kwame Arhin. *West African traders in Ghana in the nineteenth and twentieth centuries.* New York: Longman, 1979. ISBN 0-582-64650-2. ▸ Series of essays focusing mainly on nineteenth-century Asante and its northern trade, trading structure, interaction of stranger and indigenous traders, and of both with the state. [DWR]

19.199 Emmanuel Ayankami Ayandele. *The missionary impact on modern Nigeria, 1842–1914: a political and social analysis.* London: Longman, 1966. ▸ Covers same ground as Ajayi 19.194, but with more attention to negative consequences, links of missionary and imperial activity, and rise of independent-thinking Nigerian Christians. [DWR]

19.200 Amadou Hampate Bâ and Jacques Daget. *L'empire peul du Macina, 1818–53.* 3d ed. Abidjan: Nouvelles Éditions Africaines, Éditions de l'École des Hautes Études en Sciences Sociales, 1984. ISBN 2-7236-0626-0. ▸ Study of reform Muslim state of Macina based on oral traditions and Arabic documents. Stops short of heated conflict with Senegalese forces led by al-Hajj Umar. [DWR]

19.201 Stephen Baier. *An economic history of Central Niger.* New York: Oxford University Press, 1980. ISBN 0-19-822717-5. ▸ Pioneering study of Central Niger, flexibility of its producers and traders, and economic change in nineteenth and twentieth centuries. Describes large network of relations in Niger and Nigeria. [DWR]

19.202 Stephen Baier and Paul E. Lovejoy. "The desert-side economy of the Central Sudan." *International journal of African historical studies* 8.4 (1975) 551–81. ISSN 0361-7882. ▸ Important article about economic relations between Sahara desert and Sahelian regions along north-south axis. Shows connections between areas usually considered separately. [DWR]

19.203 Boubacar Barry. *La Sénégambie du quinzième au dix-neuvième siècle: traite négrière, Islam, et conquête coloniale.* Paris: Harmattan, 1988. ISBN 2-85802-670-X. ▸ Synthesis of secondary and unpublished works on history of Senegambia, stressing economic integration, impact of Atlantic slave trade, and exploitation by ruling classes. [DWR]

19.204 Heinrich Barth. *Travels and discoveries in North and Central Africa: being a journal of an expedition undertaken under the auspices of H.B.M.'s government in the years, 1849–1855.* 1857 ed. 3 vols. London: Cass, 1965. ▸ Seminal, detailed record of travels of German explorer through Sahelian regions. Essential source for interior West Africa in mid-nineteenth century. [DWR]

19.205 Saburi Biobaku, ed. *Sources of Yoruba history.* Oxford: Clarendon, 1973. ISBN 0-19-821669-6. ▸ Collective work by specialists in various fields relative to history of southwestern Nigeria or Yorubaland. [DWR]

19.206 Louis Brenner. *The shehus of Kukawa: a history of the al-Kanemi dynasty of Bornu.* Oxford: Clarendon, 1973. ▸ Study of shehus (shaikhs) of Bornu in nineteenth century, when it came under control of scholar and political leader Muhammad al-Kanemi and his successors. [DWR]

19.207 Donald Crummey and C. C. Stewart, eds. *Modes of production in Africa: the precolonial era.* Beverly Hills, Calif.: Sage, 1981. ISBN 0-8039-1133-5 (cl), 0-8039-1134-3 (pbk). ▸ Pioneering studies of major African states and economies from Marxist perspective. Not widely used, but good example of mode-of-production literature current in 1970s. [DWR]

19.208 Philip D. Curtin, ed. *Africa remembered: narratives by West Africans from the era of the slave trade.* Madison: University of Wisconsin Press, 1967. ▸ Biographical or autobiographical narratives about West Africans, most of whom were slaves, containing valuable recollections on African societies, enslavement, and passage to Americas. [DWR]

19.209 Kwamina Dickson. *A historical geography of Ghana.* Cambridge: Cambridge University Press, 1969. ISBN 0-521-07102-X. ▸ Analysis of different regions of Ghana and their resource capacities in relation to agricultural and mineral production and trade in different historical periods. [DWR]

19.210 Kenneth Onwuka Dike. *Trade and politics in the Niger Delta, 1830–1885: an introduction to the economic and political history of Nigeria.* 1956 ed. Westport, Conn.: Greenwood, 1981. ISBN 0-313-23297-0. ▸ One of earliest studies of trade and politics along West African coast, showing importance of initiatives of African political and economic leaders. [DWR]

19.211 Daryll Forde and Phyllis Kaberry, eds. *West African kingdoms in the nineteenth century.* London: Oxford University Press, 1967. ▸ Useful set of articles on enduring, medium-sized kingdoms from Senegambia to Cameroon, written by specialists. [DWR]

19.212 Christopher Fyfe. *A history of Sierra Leone.* London: Oxford University Press, 1962. ▸ Useful historical summary of Sierra Leone, from eighteenth century when British arrived to mid-twentieth century. [DWR]

19.213 G. O. Gbadamosi. *The growth of Islam among the Yoruba, 1841–1908.* Atlantic Highlands, N.J.: Humanities, 1978. ISBN 0-391-00834-X. ▸ Only study of expansion of Islam among Yoruba, beginning roughly with collapse of Oyo empire and ending with early colonial period. [DWR]

19.214 Timothy Gerrard. *Akan weights and the gold trade.* New York: Longman, 1980. ISBN 0-582-64631-6. ▸ Meticulous study by art historian of Akan (Ghana) gold trade over some 500 years, using informants and written record. Attempts to trace origins of weights to Islamic and Portuguese standards. [DWR]

19.215 Odile Goerg. *Commerce et colonisation en Guinée, 1850–1913.* Paris: Harmattan, 1986. ISBN 2-85802-473-9. ▸ Only study of areas that came to constitute colony of Guinée during period of French penetration and exploitation. [DWR]

19.216 Mervyn Hiskett. *The sword of truth: the life and times of the Shehu Usuman dan Fodio.* New York: Oxford University Press, 1973. ISBN 0-19-501648-3. ▸ Well-written biography of founder of Sokoto caliphate. Gives good sense of Usuman's scholarly and pastoral milieu and content of Islamic teaching and poetry. [DWR]

19.217 Anthony G. Hopkins. *An economic history of West Africa.* New York: Columbia University Press, 1973. ISBN 0-231-03739-2. ▸ Ambitious effort to describe economic history of West Africa from formalist perspective. Still basis for debates about nature of economy and conditions of entrepreneurship. [DWR]

19.218 Obaro Ikime. *Merchant prince of the Niger Delta: the rise and fall of Nana Olomu, last governor of the Benin River.* New York: Africana, 1968. ▸ Study of one of entrepreneurial princes who acquired considerable wealth and influence immediately prior to British conquest. [DWR]

19.219 Marion Johnson. "The economic foundations of an Islamic theocracy: the case of Masina." *Journal of African history* 17.4 (1976) 481–95. ISSN 0021-8537. ▸ Economic historian's approach to highly regimented economy established by Islamic state in Middle Niger Delta in early nineteenth century. [DWR]

19.220 G. I. Jones. *Trading states of the Oil Rivers: a study of political development in eastern Nigeria.* London: Oxford University Press for International African Institute, 1963. ▸ Anthropologist's view of history of small, commercially oriented states of Niger Delta coast and changing relationships of kingship, secret societies, canoe houses, and slavery. [DWR]

19.221 Idrissa Kimba. *Guerres et servitude: les populations du Niger occidental au dix-neuvième siècle et leurs réactions face à la colonisation (1896–1906).* Niamey, Niger: Institut de Recherches en Sciences Humaines, 1981. ISBN 2-85921-046-6. ▸ Studies of reactions of societies of southwestern Niger to European pressure and French conquest at turn of century. [DWR]

19.222 A.H.M. Kirk-Greene and S. J. Hogben. *The emirates of northern Nigeria: a preliminary survey of their historical traditions.* London: Oxford University Press, 1966. ▸ Useful emirate-by-emirate survey of written and oral traditions, especially of eighteenth and nineteenth centuries. [DWR]

19.223 Martin A. Klein. *Islam and imperialism in Senegal: Sine-Saloum, 1847–1914.* Stanford, Calif.: Stanford University Press for Hoover Institution on War, Revolution, and Peace, 1968. ISBN 0-85224-029-5. ▸ Study of key region of Senegal amid struggles of traditional authorities, Muslim reformers, and French imperialists in late nineteenth century. [DWR/RRR]

19.224 Martin A. Klein. "Social and economic factors in the Muslim revolutions in Senegambia." *Journal of African history* 13.3 (1972) 419–41. ISSN 0021-8537. ▸ Role of Muslims and especially Muslim reform movements amid escalating conditions of violence in late nineteenth-century Senegambia. [DWR]

19.225 Jean Kopytoff. *Preface to modern Nigeria: the "Sierra Leoneans" in Yoruba, 1830–1890.* Madison: University of Wisconsin Press, 1965. ▸ Liberated Africans of Sierra Leone were ex-slaves who came originally from Yoruba area and returned there in mid-nineteenth century as missionaries, traders, and officials. [DWR]

19.226 Murray Last. *The Sokoto caliphate.* New York: Humanities, 1967. ▸ Careful study based primarily on Arabic documentation of reform movement of Usuman dan Fodio and regime he created. Definitive statement of this important phenomenon. [DWR]

19.227 Peter Lloyd. *The political development of Yoruba kingdoms in the eighteenth and nineteenth centuries.* London: Royal Anthropological Institute, 1971. (Occasional paper, Royal Anthropological Institute of Great Britain and Ireland, 31.) ISBN 0-9006320-3-8. ▸ Anthropologist's exploration of development of six Yoruba states and their failure to produce enduring centralized institutions, especially because of entrenched and competing kinship structures. [DWR]

19.228 Paul E. Lovejoy. *Caravans of kola: the Hausa kola trade, 1700–1900.* Zaria, Nigeria: Ahmadu Bello University Press and Oxford University Press, 1980. ISBN 978-12-5009-7 (cl), 978-15-4568-2 (pbk). ▸ Explores kola trade between Asante and Hausaland, combining written and oral data. Focuses on trading firms or family corporations that dominated this trading diaspora. [DWR]

19.229 Paul E. Lovejoy. *Salt of the desert sun: a history of salt production and trade in the Central Sudan.* Cambridge: Cambridge University Press, 1986. ISBN 0-521-30182-3. ▸ Enduring study of different kinds of salt traded between desert and Sahel, their uses, and trading corporations involved, all set within regional economy of Nigeria-Niger-Chad area. [DWR]

19.230 Akin Mabogunje. *Urbanization in Nigeria.* New York: Africana, 1968. ▸ Studies of selected Nigerian cities, traditional and modern, and processes of urbanization in the country; special attention to Lagos and Ibadan. [DWR]

19.231 B. G. Martin. *Muslim brotherhoods in nineteenth-century Africa.* New York: Cambridge University Press, 1976. ISBN 0-521-21062-3. ▸ Biographies of seven Muslim leaders, ranging from Algeria to East Africa. Emphasizes militant reform and resistance and synthesizes published European literature and indigenous Arabic sources. [DWR]

19.232 Tom McCaskie. "Accumulation, wealth, and belief in Asante history. Part 1: To the close of the nineteenth century. Part 2: The twentieth century." *Africa* 53–56 (1983–86) 23–43, 3–23. ISSN 0001-9720. ▸ Pioneering effort to study interrelationship of economy and cognition by leading authority in Asante intellectual history. [DWR]

19.233 Tom McCaskie. "Death and the Asantehene: a historical meditation." *Journal of African history* 30.3 (1989) 417–44. ISSN 0021-8537. ‣ Provocative essay based on intense familiarity with Asante sources. Focuses on events surrounding death of king in 1867, but reflects back across all of Asante history. [DWR]

19.234 Tom McCaskie. "Komo Anokye of Asante: meaning, history, and process in an African society." *Journal of African history* 27.2 (1986) 315–39. ISSN 0021-8537. ‣ Provocative exploration of meaning of founding myth of Asante nation by leading intellectual historian of Asante. [DWR]

19.235 Gustav Nachtigal. *Sahara and Sudan.* Vol. 1: *Tripoli, the Fezzan, and Tibesti.* Vol. 2: *Kawar, Bornu, Kanem, Borku, Tibesti.* Vol. 3: *Borno* (not yet translated). Vol. 4: *Wadai and Darfur.* Allan G. B. Fisher and Humphrey J. Fisher, eds. and trans. Berkeley: University of California Press, 1974–87. ISBN 0-520-01789-7 (v. 1), 0-903983-996-6 (v. 2), 0-391-03415-4 (v. 3), 0-520-01789-7 (v. 4). ‣ Invaluable detailed descriptions of history, anthropology, and flora and fauna of whole region around Lake Chad in late nineteenth century. [DWR]

19.236 Don C. Ohadike. *The Ekumeku movement: western Igbo resistance to the British conquest of Nigeria.* Athens: Ohio University Press, 1991. ISBN 0-8214-0985-9. ‣ Lively, detailed, and accessible account of one region's experience with British explorers and missionaries, imposition of colonial rule, and violent resistance. [MJH]

19.237 Yves Person. *Samori: une révolution dyula.* 3 vols. Dakar: Mémoires de l'Institut Fondementale d'Afrique Noire, 1968–75. ‣ Exhaustive study of career of Samori, who constructed vast Islamic empire in late nineteenth-century West Africa. Invaluable reference for scholars, not very accessible for general reader. [DWR]

19.238 John Peterson. *Province of freedom: a history of Sierra Leone, 1787–1870.* Evanston, Ill.: Northwestern University Press, 1969. ISBN 0-8101-0264-1. ‣ Important study of first century of British experiment at Freetown, superseding in part older work of Fyfe (19.212), especially in exploration of nineteenth-century social history. [DWR]

19.239 Margaret Priestley. *West African trade and coast society: a family study.* London: Oxford University Press, 1969. ISBN 0-19-215638-1. ‣ Careful but narrowly focused research on descendants of Richard Brew, Irish trader, and his Fante wife and their fortunes over three centuries. [DWR]

19.240 Richard Roberts. *Warriors, merchants, and slaves: the state and the economy in the Middle Niger valley, 1700–1914.* Stanford, Calif.: Stanford University Press, 1987. ISBN 0-8047-1378-2. ‣ Useful study of Middle Niger region across three political regimes. Shows relation of commercial and political specialists and effect of state systems on production and trade. [DWR/DAN]

19.241 David Wallace Robinson. *Chiefs and clerics: Abdul Bokar Kan and the history of Futa Toro, 1853 to 1891.* Oxford: Clarendon, 1975. ISBN 0-19-822701-9. ‣ Primarily political and military history, based on oral, archival, and Arabic materials. Presents complex picture of resistance to French conquest. One of few studies of this regime in English. [DWR]

19.242 David Wallace Robinson. *The holy war of Umar Tal: the western Sudan in the mid-nineteenth century.* New York: Oxford University Press, 1985. ISBN 0-19-822720-5. ‣ Carefully documented study of life and military career of important Muslim reformer who has been portrayed as hero of resistance. Based on Arabic, French, and oral materials. [DWR]

19.243 Enid Schildkrout and Carol Gelber, eds. *The golden stool: studies of the Asante center and periphery.* New York: American Museum of Natural History, 1987. ISSN 0865-9452. ‣ Valuable collection of articles by specialists in art history, art, and history

summarizing present state of knowledge about kingdom and society of Asante. [DWR]

19.244 Tom W. Shick. *Behold the promised land: a history of Afro-American settler society in nineteenth-century Liberia.* Baltimore: Johns Hopkins University Press, 1980. ISBN 0-8018-2309-9. ‣ One of few studies of Americo-Liberian experiment in Liberia. Does not illuminate relations with native Liberians, but gives good sense of American community. [DWR]

19.245 Robert S. Smith. *Warfare and diplomacy in pre-colonial West Africa.* 2d ed. Madison: University of Wisconsin Press, 1989. ISBN 0-299-12330-8 (cl), 0-299-12334-0 (pbk). ‣ Useful exploration of how West African states used warfare and diplomacy; special attention to horses, guns, and slaves. Second edition only lightly modified, but bibliography is up to date. [DWR]

19.246 C. C. Stewart and E. K. Stewart. *Islam and social order in Mauritania: a case study from the nineteenth century.* Oxford: Clarendon, 1973. ISBN 0-19-821688-2. ‣ Pioneering study of Shaykh Sidia al-Kabir (1775–1868), whose career combined Islamic scholarship with dispute mediation, application of Islamic law, Ṣūfī orders, and production and trade. [DWR]

19.247 Ivor Wilks. *Asante in the nineteenth century.* 1975 ed. Cambridge: Cambridge University Press, 1989. ISBN 0-521-37994-6. ‣ Exploration of politics and geography of kingship in powerful Asante state, based on extensive research. Uses Weberian model to show elaboration of bureaucracy. [DWR]

19.248 John Ralph Willis, ed. *The cultivators of Islam.* London: Cass, 1979. ISBN 0-7146-1737-6. ‣ Somewhat dated biographies of Islamic holy men in nineteenth-century Senegambian region. Introduction links Islamic ideals with particular ethnic groups or phases of islamization. [DWR]

19.249 John Ralph Willis, ed. *Slaves and slavery in Muslim Africa.* Vol. 1: *Islam and the ideology of enslavement.* Vol. 2: *The servile estate.* Totowa, N.J.: Cass, 1985. ISBN 0-7146-3142-6 (v. 1), 0-7146-3201-5 (v. 2). ‣ Some useful biographical and institutional papers on neglected subject from 1977 conference, but largely unrevised with ineffective introduction. [DWR]

19.250 Larry Yarak. *Asante and the Dutch, 1744–1873.* New York: Oxford University Press, 1990. ISBN 0-19-822156-8. ‣ Pioneering, careful study of Asante-Dutch relations and their importance for Asante state, by acknowledged specialist who challenges many of Wilks's assumptions (19.247) about bureaucratic procedures. [DWR]

Twentieth Century

19.251 Omoniyi Adewoye. *The judicial system in southern Nigeria, 1854–1954: law and justice in a colonial dependency.* Atlantic Highlands, N.J.: Humanities, 1977. ISBN 0-391-00735-1. ‣ Pathbreaking study of law in colonial Africa. Provides historical overview of evolving British policy and changing nature of various courts which served to adjudicate disputes between Africans and Europeans. [RRR]

19.252 Adiele Eberechukwu Afigbo. *The warrant chiefs: indirect rule in southeastern Nigeria, 1891–1929.* New York: Humanities, 1972. ISBN 0-582-64539-5. ‣ Detailed case study of British colonial policy of indirect rule and establishment of native administration. Provides ethnographic background to Igbo society and explores briefly 1929 Aba Women's War. [RRR]

19.253 S.K.B. Asante. *Pan-African protest: West Africa and the Italo-Ethiopian crisis.* London: Longman, 1977. ISBN 0-582-64194-2. ‣ Useful study on development of West African nationalism during interwar period, with special reference to West African diplomatic and popular protests against Italian invasion of Ethiopia. [RRR]

19.254 Dennis Austin. *Politics in Ghana, 1946–1960.* 1964 ed. New York: Oxford University Press with Royal Institute of International Affairs, 1970. ▸ Enduring early study of politics of decolonization in Gold Coast. Excellent analysis of nationalism and politics of transition to independence. [RRR]

19.255 Peter Tamas Bauer. *West African trade: a study of competition, oligopoly, and monopoly in a changing economy.* 1954 ed. New York: Kelley, 1963. ▸ Detailed macroeconomic study of British West African economy, with particular concern to demonstrate effects of monopolies on structure and performance of economy. [RRR]

19.256 Sara Shepherd Sweezy Berry. *Cocoa, custom, and socioeconomic change in rural western Nigeria.* Oxford: Clarendon, 1975. ISBN 0-19-821697-1. ▸ Excellent history of evolution of cash-crop production in three major regions of western Nigeria. Provides detailed socioeconomic analysis of origins and impact of expanding cocoa production. [RRR]

19.257 Sara Shepherd Sweezy Berry. *Fathers work for their sons: accumulation, mobility, and class formation in an extended Yoruba community.* Berkeley: University of California Press, 1985. ISBN 0-520-05164-5. ▸ Important sequel to first book on cocoa (19.256). Details social and economic changes, move away from agriculture, and changing political economy in Yoruba cocoa regions after 1945. [RRR]

19.258 Denise Bouche. *L'enseignement dans les territoires français de l'Afrique occidentale de 1817 à 1920: mission civilisatrice ou formation d'une élite?* Lille and Paris: Atelier Reproduction des Thèses, Université Lille III and Champion, 1975. ISBN 2-252-01690-6. ▸ Very detailed study of history and politics of education in colonial French West Africa concentrating on Senegal. Examines making of Western-educated elite. [RRR]

19.259 Denise Bouche. *Les villages de liberté en Afrique noire française, 1887–1910.* The Hague: Mouton, 1968. (Le monde d'Outre-mer, passé et présente, Première série, 28.) ▸ Pathbreaking study of French antislavery policies in West Africa with particular attention to development of freed slave villages. Examines tensions between policy and practice. [RRR]

19.260 Louis Brenner. *West African Sufi: the religious heritage and spiritual search of Cerno Bokar Saalif Taal.* Berkeley: University of California Press, 1984. ISBN 0-520-05008-8 (cl), 0-520-05009-6 (pbk). ▸ Biography of Muslim leader and his spiritual growth during period of French colonial rule. Includes much of interest on spread of West African Islam during twentieth century. [MJH]

19.261 Raymond Leslie Buell. *The native problem in Africa.* 1928 ed. 2 vols. Hamden, Conn.: Archon, 1965. ▸ Massive two-volume study by American of European colonialism in Africa, based on data assembled in 1918. Remains excellent resource for detailed study of colonial policy and practice. [RRR]

19.262 William B. Cohen. *The rulers of empire: the French colonial service in Africa.* Stanford, Calif.: Hoover Institution Press, 1971. ISBN 0-8179-1951-1. ▸ Critical study of theory and practice of French colonial administration and its administrators. [RRR]

19.263 James Smoot Coleman. *Nigeria: background to nationalism.* 1958 ed. Berkeley: University of California Press, 1971. ISBN 0-520-02070-7. ▸ Enduring, masterly study of nationalism in Nigeria, by leading American political scientist. Important introduction to contemporary Nigerian history. [RRR]

19.264 Dennis D. Cordell and Joel W. Gregory, eds. *African population and capitalism: historical perspectives.* Boulder: Westview, 1987. ISBN 0-8133-7408-1. ▸ Broad theory and sixteen well-documented, innovative studies in historical demography. Special emphasis on role of colonial capitalism in shaping African populations and in creating poverty. [RRR/PMM]

19.265 Michael Crowder. *Revolt in Bussa: a study of British "native administration" in Nigerian Borgu, 1902–1935.* Evanston, Ill.: Northwestern University Press, 1973. ISBN 0-8101-0416-4. ▸ Detailed case study of revolt against colonial occupation in one region of Nigeria. Examines forms of resistance to and collaboration with colonial administration in Nigeria. [RRR]

19.266 Michael Crowder. *Senegal: a study in French assimilation policy.* New York: Oxford University Press, 1962. ▸ Introductory essay on French colonial policy in Senegal. Provides useful framework for examination of changing colonial native policy. [RRR]

19.267 Michael Crowder. *West Africa under colonial rule.* Evanston, Ill.: Northwestern University Press, 1968. ▸ Comparison of British and French colonialism and colonial policies in West Africa. Useful guide for teachers. [RRR]

19.268 Michael Crowder, ed. *West African resistance: the military response to colonial occupation.* 2d ed. London: Hutchinson, 1978. ISBN 0-09-134031-4. ▸ Celebratory but uneven studies of West African forms of military resistance to European colonial conquest. [RRR]

19.269 Michael Crowder and Obaro Ikime, eds. *West African chiefs: their changing status under colonial rule and independence.* Brenda Packman, trans. New York: Africana, 1970. ISBN 0-8419-0046-9. ▸ Collection of essays on changes in French and British colonial policy toward African chiefs. Several excellent essays on social history of native administration. [RRR]

19.270 Donal Brian Cruise O'Brien. *The Mourides of Senegal: the political and economic organization of an Islamic brotherhood.* Oxford: Clarendon, 1971. ISBN 0-19-821662-9. ▸ Pathbreaking study of social, economic, and ideological factors in development of Mouride Islamic brotherhood in rural and urban Senegal. Demonstrates how Islamic ideologies adapted to local conditions. [RRR]

19.271 Basil Davidson. *Black star: a view of the life and times of Kwame Nkrumah.* Boulder: Westview, 1989. ISBN 0-8133-302928-X. ▸ Sympathetic account of Ghana's first president, written in context of Ghana's independence. [RRR]

19.272 John De St. Jore. *The Nigerian Civil War.* London: Hodder & Stoughton, 1972. ISBN 0-340-12640-X. ▸ Detailed day-to-day account of Nigerian Civil War in late 1960s; written contemporaneously. Particularly valuable for detail and narrative account of war. [RRR]

19.273 Myron J. Echenberg. *Colonial conscripts: the Tirailleurs Sénégalais in French West Africa, 1857–1960.* Portsmouth, N.H.: Heinemann, 1991. ISBN 0-435-0848-2 (cl), 0-435-08052-0 (pbk). ▸ Fine historical study devoted to African soldier in French West African history. Provides evidence on neglected part of African history. [RRR]

19.274 Adamu Mohammed Fika. *The Kano Civil War and British over-rule, 1882–1940.* New York: Oxford University Press, 1978. ISBN 0-19-575448-2. ▸ Study of economic and political change in Kano emirate (Nigeria), late precolonial era to 1940. Argues internal crisis of 1893–95 facilitated British conquest and subsequent colonial rule. [RRR]

19.275 John E. Flint. *Sir George Goldie and the making of Nigeria.* London: Oxford University Press, 1960. ▸ Study of British colonial policy in Nigeria, with special reference to Royal Niger Company and Sir George Goldie. Demonstrates importance of merchant capitalism in scramble for Africa. [RRR]

19.276 Bill Freund. *Capital and labour in the Nigerian tin mines.* Atlantic Highlands, N.J.: Humanities, 1981. ISBN 0-391-02155-9. ▸ Detailed case study of political economy of colonialism in Nigeria through examination of colonial capital and labor policies of colonial state. [RRR]

19.277 Lewis H. Gann and Peter Duignan, eds. *Colonialism in Africa, 1870–1960.* 5 vols. London: Cambridge University Press, 1969–75. ISBN 0-521-07373-1 (v. I), 0-521-07844-X (v. 3), 0-521-08641-8 (v. 4), 0-521-07859-8 (v. 5). ▸ Five volumes of essays written by leading scholars during first decade of African independence. Several essays provide excellent syntheses on history and politics of colonialism, 1870–1914 (volume I); on social change in African societies (volume 3); and on economics of colonialism (volume 4). Volume 5 is bibliographic guide to literature on colonialism as of 1973. [RRR]

19.278 Prosser Gifford and Wm. Roger Louis, eds. *Decolonization and African independence: the transfers of power, 1960–1980.* New Haven: Yale University Press, 1988. ISBN 0-300-04070-9 (cl), 0-300-04388-0 (pbk). ▸ Important collection of essays on politics of decolonization in Africa. Focuses largely on European side of the story. [RRR]

19.279 William Malcolm Hailey. *An African survey: a study of problems arising in Africa south of the Sahara.* 2d rev. ed. New York: Oxford University Press, 1957. ▸ Massive survey of colonialism in Africa on eve of decolonization. Clear and accessible, contains rich detailed data on politics and socioeconomic conditions of late colonial period. [RRR]

19.280 William Malcolm Hailey. *Native administration and political development in British tropical Africa, 1872–1969.* 1944 ed. A.H.M. Kirk-Greene, Introduction. Nendeln, Liechtenstein: Krause, 1979. ISBN 3-262-00205-4. ▸ Important reprint of original British Colonial Office study of British colonial administration in Africa; detailed, thorough, accessible. [RRR]

19.281 John D. Hargreaves. *The end of colonial rule in West Africa: essays in contemporary history.* New York: Barnes & Noble, 1979. ISBN 0-06-492705-9. ▸ Series of essays on decolonization written by leading scholar of colonialism in West Africa. [RRR]

19.282 John D. Hargreaves. *West Africa partitioned.* Vol. 1: *The loaded pause, 1885–1889.* Vol. 2: *The elephants and the grass.* Madison: University of Wisconsin Press, 1974–85. ISBN 0-299-06720-3. ▸ Two-volume history of scramble in West Africa. Remains one of best histories of period of colonial conquest because of its sensitivity to African roles. [RRR]

19.283 Christopher Harrison. *France and Islam in West Africa, 1860–1960.* New York: Cambridge University Press, 1988. ISBN 0-521-35230-4. ▸ Broad overview of French Islamic policies in West Africa. Useful insights but uneven in coverage. [RRR]

19.284 Polly Hill. *The migrant cocoa-farmers of southern Ghana: a study in rural capitalism.* Cambridge: Cambridge University Press, 1963. ▸ Pathbreaking study of rural capitalism in Ghana, including role of kinship structures. Demonstrates author's distinctive approach to indigenous economies. [RRR]

19.285 Polly Hill. *Rural Hausa: a village and a setting.* Cambridge: Cambridge University Press, 1972. ISBN 0-521-08242-0. ▸ Detailed study of one northern Nigerian village and its economic and social changes during twentieth century. Applies both historical and survey methods to explain change. [RRR]

19.286 Thomas Lionel Hodgkin. *Nationalism in colonial Africa.* 1957 ed. New York: New York University Press, 1960. ▸ Excellent contemporary study of emerging nationalism and decolonization in Africa. Sensitive to ideologies and contradictions of emergent African nationalism. [RRR]

19.287 Jan S. Hogendorn. *Nigerian groundnut exports: origins and early development.* Zaria, Nigeria: Ahmadu Bello University Press, 1978. ISBN 9-7812-5005-4. ▸ Important application of vent-for-surplus theory to colonial economic development in Nigeria.

Demonstrates African initiatives in face of colonial efforts to promote exports. [RRR]

19.288 Richard P. S. Jeffries. *Class, power, and ideology in Ghana: the railwaymen of Sekondi.* Cambridge: Cambridge University Press, 1978. ISBN 0-521-21806-3. ▸ One of first major case studies of working-class experience in colonial Africa. Examines trade unionism and politics in Ghana with special reference to railway workers. [RRR]

19.289 G. Wesley Johnson, Jr. *The emergence of black politics in Senegal: the struggle for power in the Four Communes, 1900–1920.* Stanford, Calif.: Stanford University Press for Hoover Institution on War, Revolution, and Peace, 1971. ISBN 0-8047-0783-9. ▸ Political history of Africans in enfranchised Four Communes of colonial Senegal and their quest for political empowerment within colonial regime. Focus on electoral politics. [RRR]

19.290 Lansine Kaba. *The Wahhabiyya: Islamic reform and politics in French West Africa.* Evanston, Ill.: Northwestern University Press, 1974. ISBN 0-8101-0427-X. ▸ Study of rise and diffusion of Muslim Wahhabiyya movement, 1945 to early 1960s, by historian and member of this movement. [RRR]

19.291 Martin Kilson and Harvard University, Center for International Affairs. *Political change in a West African state: a study of the modernization process in Sierra Leone.* 1966 ed. New York: Atheneum, 1969. ▸ Political science approach to decolonization and independence in Sierra Leone. Contains much material of interest to historians of this period. [RRR]

19.292 David Kimble. *A political history of Ghana: the rise of Gold Coast nationalism, 1850–1928.* Oxford: Clarendon, 1963. ▸ Somewhat dated but detailed study of African nationalism in Gold Coast during early colonial period. [RRR]

19.293 A.H.M. Kirk-Greene, ed. *The principles of native administration in Nigeria: selected documents, 1900–1947.* London: Oxford University Press, 1965. ▸ Important selection of colonial documents on debates concerning development of British indirect rule policy in Nigeria and place of native administration in British colonialism. [RRR]

19.294 J. Ayodele Langley. *Pan-Africanism and nationalism in West Africa, 1900–1945: a study in ideology and social classes.* Oxford: Clarendon, 1973. ISBN 0-19-821689-0. ▸ Still best study of pan-Africanism in British West Africa, with special attention to African ideologies and expressions of pan-Africanism. [RRR]

19.295 Paul M. Lubeck. *Islam and urban labor in northern Nigeria: the making of a Muslim working class.* New York: Cambridge University Press, 1986. ISBN 0-521-30942-5. ▸ Detailed study of how political economy and Islam in northern Nigeria combined to shape ideology and practice of urban working class. Original theoretical orientation uses both historical and social science methodologies. [RRR]

19.296 Frederick John Dealtry Lugard. *The diaries of Lord Lugard.* 4 vols. Margery Freda Perham, ed. Evanston, Ill.: Northwestern University Press, 1959–63. (Northwestern University African Studies, 3.) ▸ Diaries of one of foremost British colonial governors in Nigeria and architect of British native policy of indirect rule. [RRR]

19.297 Kristin Mann. *Marrying well: marriage, status, and social change among the educated elite in colonial Lagos.* New York: Cambridge University Press, 1985. ISBN 0-521-30701-5. ▸ Original study of African elite in colonial Lagos with special focus on impact of Christianity on elite Yoruba urban women. Uses correspondence and court records as well as archives and interviews. [RRR]

19.298 Patrick Manning. *Francophone sub-Saharan Africa, 1880–1985.* New York: Cambridge University Press, 1988. ISBN 0-521-

33024-6 (cl), 0-521-33886-7 (pbk). ▸ Survey of Francophone African countries during colonialism and independence. Important comparative perspectives. [RRR]

19.299 Jacques Marseille. *Empire colonial et capitalisme français: histoire d'un divorce.* 1984 ed. Paris: Michel and Seuil, 1989. ISBN 2-02-010894-1. ▸ Major reassessment of economic aspects and benefits of French colonialism in Africa, although focused more from metropolitan perspective. [RRR]

19.300 Susan M. Martin. *Palm oil and protest: an economic history of the Ngwa region, south-eastern Nigeria, 1800–1980.* New York: Cambridge University Press, 1988. ISBN 0-521-34376-3. ▸ Detailed study of impact of palm-oil exports on society and economy of small Igbo community over period of 200 years, with special emphasis on changing gender and generational relations. [RRR]

19.301 Marc Michel. *L'appel à l'Afrique: contributions et réactions à l'effort de guerre en A.O.F. (1914–1919).* Paris: Publications de la Sorbonne, 1982. (Institut d'Histoire des Relations Internationales Contemporaines, Série Afrique, 6.) ISBN 2-85944-046-1. ▸ Massive, detailed study of French military recruitment and African reactions in West Africa, with special attention to recruitment revolts. [RRR]

19.302 Colin Walter Newbury, comp. *British policy towards West Africa: select documents, 1875–1914, with statistical appendices, 1800–1914.* 2d rev. ed. Oxford: Clarendon, 1971. ISBN 0-19-821663-7. ▸ Important collection of documents cataloging changing British colonial policy in West Africa. Statistical appendixes provide useful long-term view of changing terms of trade. [RRR]

19.303 Kwame Nkrumah. *Ghana: the autobiography of Kwame Nkrumah.* 1957 ed. New York: International Publishers, 1971. ISBN 0-7178-0293-0. ▸ Life story of first prime minister of independent Ghana. Provides important insights into development of key African nationalist and political theorist. [RRR]

19.304 John David Yeadon Peel. *Aladura: a religious movement among the Yoruba.* London: Oxford University Press for International African Institute, 1968. ▸ Pathbreaking study of independent African church, its breaking away from European-dominated mission churches, and meaning of religious conversion among Yoruba. [RRR]

19.305 John David Yeadon Peel. *Ijeshas and Nigerians: the incorporation of a Yoruba kingdom, 1890s–1970s.* New York: Cambridge University Press, 1983. ISBN 0-521-22545-0. ▸ Historical sociology of transformation of Nigerian precolonial kingdom into administrative unit of colonial Nigeria, with special attention to education and religious change. [RRR/DWR]

19.306 Paul Pélissier. *Les paysans du Sénégal: les civilisations agraires du Cayor à la Casamance.* Saint-Yrieix, France: Fabrègue, 1966. ▸ Detailed, original historical geography of rural life in Casamance. Example of broad-ranging French human-geography approach. [RRR]

19.307 Margery Freda Perham. *The colonial reckoning.* New York: Knopf, 1962. ▸ Self-reflections on African nationalism and decolonization by one of Britain's leading woman scholars and activists in colonial issues. [RRR]

19.308 Margery Freda Perham. *Native administration in Nigeria.* 2d rev. ed. New York: Oxford University Press, 1962. ▸ Key historical document on British colonialism in Nigeria, written in 1930s by leading scholar and teacher of colonial administration. Wealth of data on Nigerian societies. [RRR]

19.309 Claire C. Robertson. *Sharing the same bowl: a socioeconomic history of women and class in Accra, Ghana.* 1984 ed. Ann Arbor: University of Michigan Press, 1990. ISBN 0-472-09444-0

(cl), 0-472-06444-4 (pbk). ▸ Interdisciplinary study of women and their changing positions in Ga society of Ghana. Raises significant but controversial methodological and conceptual questions. [RRR]

19.310 Elliott Percival Skinner. *The Mossi of the Upper Volta: the political development of a Sudanese people.* Stanford, Calif.: Stanford University Press, 1964. ▸ Important but somewhat dated political ethnology of Mossi of Burkina Faso (formerly Upper Volta). [RRR]

19.311 Mary Felice Smith, ed. *Baba of Karo: a woman of the Muslim Hausa.* 3d ed. Michael Garfield Smith, Introduction. New Haven: Yale University Press, 1981. ISBN 0-300-02734-6 (cl), 0-300-32741-9 (pbk). ▸ Unique life history of privileged Muslim Hausa woman. Provides rich detail about female life cycle, kinship, friendships, and marriage. Unintentionally raises important issues about methods of collecting life histories. [RRR/NRH]

19.312 Michael Garfield Smith. *Government in Zazzau, 1800–1950.* New York: Oxford University Press for International African Institute, 1960. ▸ Detailed, dense study of political change among Hausa of northern Nigeria from precolonial through colonial times. One of earliest examples of author's political anthropology and his methodology. [RRR]

19.313 Francis G. Snyder. *Capitalism and legal change: an African transformation.* New York: Academic Books, 1981. ISBN 0-12-654220-1. ▸ Original, important effort by legal scholar to study law and social change in colonial Senegal. Difficult but with rich insights into political economy of rural change. [RRR]

19.314 Leo Spitzer. *The creoles of Sierra Leone: responses to colonialism, 1870–1945.* Madison: University of Wisconsin Press, 1974. ISBN 0-299-06590-1. ▸ Detailed study of African elite under British colonialism. Rich insights into ideology and challenges facing Western-educated African elite. [RRR]

19.315 Martin Staniland. *The lions of Dagbon: political change in northern Ghana.* New York: Cambridge University Press, 1975. ISBN 0-521-20682-0. ▸ Detailed political anthropology of Dagomba of northern Ghana and their changing politics under colonial rule and independence. [RRR]

19.316 Ibrahim K. Sundiata. *Black scandal: America and the Liberian labor crisis, 1929–36.* Philadelphia: Institute for the Study of Human Issues, 1980. ISBN 0-915980-96-7. ▸ Political history of labor crisis surrounding Liberian export of unfree labor and involving Americo-Liberian ruling elite, League of Nations, and United States government. [RRR]

19.317 Jean Suret-Canale. *French colonialism in tropical Africa, 1900–1945.* Till Gottheiner, trans. New York: Pica, 1971. ISBN 0-87663-702-0. ▸ Magnificent but idiosyncratic study of French colonialism in sub-Saharan Africa, with emphasis on economic aspects of colonialism and colonial capitalism. [RRR]

19.318 Virginia McLean Thompson and Richard Adloff. *French West Africa.* 1957 ed. New York: Greenwood, 1969. ▸ Encyclopedic but narrow study of African political parties and politics in French West Africa during decolonization. [RRR]

19.319 William Tordoff. *Ashanti under the Prempehs, 1888–1935.* London: Oxford University Press, 1965. ▸ Useful political study of impact of British colonialism on Asante (or Ashanti) politics and government in Gold Coast. Read with Wilks 19.247. [RRR]

19.320 Immanuel Wallerstein and Peter C. W. Gutkind, eds. *The political economy of contemporary Africa.* 1976 ed. Beverly Hills, Calif.: Sage, 1985. ISBN 0-8039-2096-2 (cl), 0-8039-2097-0 (pbk). ▸ Uneven collection of essays on newly independent Africa, most useful in representing ideological debates in African studies during early 1970s. [RRR]

19.321 Michael Watts. *Silent violence: food, famine, and peasantry in northern Nigeria.* Berkeley: University of California Press, 1983. ISBN 0-520-04323-5. ▸ Masterly but dense study of political economy of colonialism and its impact on environment and food production of peasantry in northern Nigeria. [RRR]

19.322 Timothy C. Weiskel. *French colonial rule and the Baule peoples: resistance and collaboration.* New York: Oxford University Press, 1980. ISBN 0-19-822715-9. ▸ Detailed study of Baule resistance to colonial conquest and subsequent social and economic responses. [RRR]

19.323 Aristide R. Zolberg. *Creating political order: the party-states of West Africa.* 1966 ed. Chicago: University of Chicago Press, 1985. ISBN 0-226-98901I. ▸ Insightful political science study of African politics of decolonization and tendency toward one-party states in West Africa. Still best overview and useful for historians of 1945–60 period. [RRR]

SEE ALSO
47.205 Henri Brunschwig. *French colonialism, 1871–1914.*

NORTHEASTERN AFRICA

19.324 Mordechai Abir. *Ethiopia: the era of the princes, 1769–1855.* New York: Praeger, 1968. ▸ During age of feudal disunity, Christian kingdom threatened by convergence of expanding Islamic and Oromo interests. Emphasizes ethnicity, religion, and trade. [JLS]

19.325 William Yewdale Adams. *Nubia: corridor to Africa.* Princeton: Princeton University Press, 1977. ISBN 0-691-09370-9. ▸ Standard survey of northern Sudan, fourth millennium BCE to ca. 1300 CE: Kerma, Kush, Meroë, Christian era. Sensible interpretations based largely on archaeological evidence. [JLS/DO'C]

19.326 Randi R. Balsvik. *Haile Sellassie's students: the intellectual and social background to revolution, 1952–1957.* East Lansing: Michigan State University, African Studies Center, 1985. ▸ Underground scholar disguised as housewife chronicles rise of increasingly militant student opposition to repressive imperial regime. Impressionistic but persuasive social, intellectual, and political profile of movement. [JLS]

19.327 Gerd Baumann. *National integration and local integrity: the Miri of the Nuba Mountains in the Sudan.* Oxford: Oxford University Press, 1987. ISBN 0-19-823401-5. ▸ Modern nationalist consensus history on micro scale. Methodologically innovative use of popular music texts. Weak conceptualization of earlier periods. [JLS]

19.328 Anders Björkelo. *Prelude to the Mahdiyya: peasants and traders in the Shendi region, 1821–1885.* Cambridge: Cambridge University Press, 1988. ISBN 0-521-35336-X. ▸ Regional socioeconomic history based largely upon travel literature. Emphasizes rise to prosperity of northern Sudanese merchant diaspora under Turkish colonial auspices. [JLS]

19.329 Lee V. Cassanelli. *The shaping of Somali society: reconstructing the history of a pastoral people, 1600–1900.* Philadelphia: University of Pennsylvania Press, 1982. ISBN 0-8122-7832-1. ▸ Pioneering exploration of central themes in modern precolonial experience of culturally coherent but politically decentralized nation. Emphasis on oral sources and ecological determinants of historical process. [JLS]

19.330 Christopher Clapham. *Haile-Selassie's government.* New York: Praeger, 1969. ▸ Lucid description of government of Haile Selassie, 1941–67, despite somewhat dated rhetorical idiom. Exemplary attention to career trajectories of elite and to architecture of rivalry among courtiers. [JLS]

19.331 Christopher Clapham. *Transformation and continuity in*

revolutionary Ethiopia. Cambridge: Cambridge University Press, 1988. ISBN 0-521-334441-1. ▸ Discussion of revolutionary years, 1974–87. Emphasizes growth of state power, benefits of land reform, and literacy campaigns. Rising opposition movements, subsequently victorious, modeled themselves on revolutionary regime. [JLS]

19.332 Robert O. Collins. *Land beyond the rivers: the southern Sudan, 1898–1918.* New Haven: Yale University Press, 1971. ISBN 0-300-01406-6. ▸ Sympathetic survey based largely on European archival sources. Emphasizes activities of intrusive ruling institution. [JLS]

19.333 Robert O. Collins. *Shadows in the grass: Britain in the southern Sudan, 1918–1956.* New Haven: Yale University Press, 1983. ISBN 0-300-02922-5. ▸ Sympathetic survey based largely on European archival sources and interviews of former colonial officials. Emphasizes activities of intrusive ruling institution. [JLS]

19.334 Robert O. Collins. *The southern Sudan, 1883–1898: a struggle for control.* New Haven: Yale University Press, 1962. ▸ Sympathetic survey based largely on European archival sources. Emphasizes activities of competing sets of foreign intruders. [JLS]

19.335 Donald Crummey. *Priests and politicians: Protestant and Catholic missions in Orthodox Ethiopia, 1830–1868.* Oxford: Clarendon, 1972. ISBN 0-19-821677-7. ▸ Study of alien missionaries whose arrival exacerbated religious, cultural, and political tensions and tied diverse indigenous factions to rival foreign patrons. Sensitive use of European sources to illuminate African realities. [JLS]

19.336 Martin W. Daly. *Empire on the Nile: the Anglo-Egyptian Sudan, 1898–1934.* Cambridge: Cambridge University Press, 1986. ISBN 0-521-30878-X. ▸ Analysis of first decades of second colonial period, based largely on British, Egyptian, and Sudanese archival sources and papers of officials. Emphasizes activities of foreign ruling institution. [JLS]

19.337 Martin W. Daly. *Imperial Sudan: the Anglo-Egyptian condominium, 1934–1956.* Cambridge: Cambridge University Press, 1991. ISBN 0-521-39163-6. ▸ Analysis of later decades of second colonial period, based largely upon British, Egyptian, and Sudanese archival sources and papers of officials. Emphasizes activities of foreign ruling institution. [JLS]

19.338 Francis Mading Deng. *The man called Deng Majok: a biography of power, polygyny, and change.* New Haven: Yale University Press, 1986. ISBN 0-300-03385-0. ▸ Uniquely valuable orally based biography of gifted Sudanese leader who achieved unprecedented eminence under colonial rule and who sought to reconcile Islamic and African cultures. [JLS]

19.339 Donald L. Donham. *Work and power in Maale, Ethiopia.* Ann Arbor: University Microfilms International Research, 1985. ISBN 0-8357-1557-4. ▸ Microstudy of subordinate imperial southern community. History at one point in time—the revolutionary years, 1974–75. [JLS]

19.340 Donald L. Donham and Wendy James, eds. *The southern marches of imperial Ethiopia: essays in history and social anthropology.* Cambridge: Cambridge University Press, 1986. ISBN 0-521-32237-5. ▸ Collection of diverse but uniformly perceptive microstudies concerning incorporation of peripheral peoples into Ethiopian empire. Exemplary collaboration between history and anthropology. [JLS]

19.341 Hagai Erlikh. *Ethiopia and Eritrea during the scramble for Africa: a political biography of Ras Alula, 1875–1897.* East Lansing: Michigan State University, African Studies Center, 1982. (Northeast African Studies monograph, 11.) ▸ Life of governor whose province first fell to European colonizers. Illuminates complex interplay between internal politics and intrusive foreign ambitions. Useful corrective to reductionist nationalist interpretations. [JLS]

19.342 Janet J. Ewald. *Soldiers, traders, and slaves: state formation and economic transformation in the greater Nile valley, 1700–1885.* Madison: University of Wisconsin Press, 1990. ISBN 0-299-12600-5 (cl), 0-299-12604-8 (pbk). ▸ Royalist consensus history of the Nuba Mountains kingdom of Taqali under Jayli dynasty. Skillful integration of oral and written indigenous sources, archival materials, and travelers' accounts. [JLS]

19.343 Richard Gray. *A history of the southern Sudan, 1839–1889.* 1961 ed. Westport, Conn.: Greenwood, 1978. ISBN 0-313-20402-0. ▸ Survey of invasions by Turks, Egyptians, Europeans, and northern Sudanese, and rivalry between central government and autonomous warlords enriched by trade in slaves, guns, and ivory. Uses European archival sources and travelers' accounts. [JLS]

19.344 John W. Harbeson. *The Ethiopian transformation: the quest for the post-imperial state.* Boulder: Westview, 1988. ISBN 0-8133-7418-9. ▸ Critical, institutional analysis of social change, 1974–88. Finds transformation—not revolution—in which autocratic military regime served its own interests. [JLS]

19.345 Yusuf Fadl Hasan. *The Arabs and the Sudan from the seventh to the early sixteenth century.* Edinburgh: Edinburgh University Press, 1967. ISBN 0-85224-023-6. ▸ Study of Egyptian invasions of late medieval Nubia. Emphasizes Arab immigration; based largely on Arabic historical and geographical works written outside Sudan. [JLS]

19.346 Mohammed Hassen. *The Oromo of Ethiopia: a history, 1570–1860.* Cambridge: Cambridge University Press, 1990. ISBN 0-521-38011-1. ▸ Rectification of historiography of early *völkerwanderungen* (migrations), with detailed treatment of settlement and rise of states in the Gibé Valley. Exceptionally perceptive discussion of state formation, commerce, and Islam. [JLS]

19.347 Robert L. Hess. *Italian colonialism in Somalia.* Chicago: University of Chicago Press, 1966. ▸ Study of foreign ruling institution of colonial age, seen as minimal and comparatively benign regime. Useful background to Somali historiography for this period yet to be written. [JLS]

19.348 Richard L. Hill. *Egypt in the Sudan, 1820–1881.* New York: Oxford University Press with Royal Institute of Colonial Affairs, 1959. (Middle Eastern monographs, 2.) ▸ Standard survey of central institutions of Ottoman period. Unequaled in its command of complex source literature and sensitive to range of Sudanese responses to colonial rule. [JLS]

19.349 Peter Malcolm Holt. *The Mahdist state in the Sudan, 1881–1898: a study of its origins, development, and overthrow.* 2d ed. Oxford: Clarendon, 1970. ISBN 0-19-821660-2. ▸ Perceptive, appreciative study of millennial regime that ousted Turks and restored independence. Draws significantly on state archives. [JLS]

19.350 Wendy James. *"Kwanim Pa": the making of the Uduk people.* Oxford: Oxford University Press, 1979. ISBN 0-19-823194-6. ▸ Microhistory of small but ancient linguistic group culturally reconstituted as intentional community of twentieth century. Emphasizes period before independence. Exemplary synthesis of oral and archival sources. [JLS]

19.351 Wendy James. *The listening ebony: moral knowledge, religion, and power among the Uduk of Sudan.* Oxford: Clarendon, 1988. ISBN 0-19-823403-1. ▸ Microhistory of small southern Sudanese community since independence, emphasizing defense of key cultural values amid strong pressures from outsiders. Exemplary synthesis of oral and archival sources. [JLS]

19.352 Steven Kaplan. *The monastic holy man and the christian-*

ization of early Solomonic Ethiopia. Wiesbaden: Steiner, 1984. ISBN 3-515-03934-1. ▸ Discussion of rise of medieval monasticism among Christians and Jews, emphasizing social, political, and religious contributions of tradition. Based on astute analysis of hagiography, much of it unpublished. [JLS]

19.353 Lidwien Kapteijns. *Mahdist faith and Sudanic tradition: the history of the Masalit sultanate, 1870–1930.* London: Kegan Paul International, 1985. ISBN 0-7103-0090-5. ▸ Political and social history of small border kingdom strategically vital to ambitions of Mahdists and Europeans. Based on oral sources supported by Mahdist and European archives. [JLS]

19.354 Lidwien Kapteijns and Jay L. Spaulding. *After the millennium: diplomatic correspondence from Wadai and Dar Fur on the eve of colonial conquest, 1885–1916.* East Lansing: Michigan State University, African Studies Center, 1988. ▸ Diplomatic history of western sultanates from Mahdist movement to World War I. Based on state correspondence of sultanates. [JLS]

19.355 Raymond C. Kelly. *The Nuer conquest: the structure and development of an expansionist system.* Ann Arbor: University of Michigan Press, 1985. ISBN 0-472-10064-5 (cl), 0-472-08056-3 (pbk). ▸ Sophisticated, venturesome ethnohistory of nineteenth century. Applies anthropological modeling techniques to ecological and archival data and to orally derived information. [JLS]

19.356 David D. Laitin and Said S. Samatar. *Somalia: nation in search of a state.* Boulder: Westview, 1987. ISBN 0-86531-555-8. ▸ Affectionate general introduction in nationalist tradition emphasizing events since independence. Offers perceptive (but now dated) assessment of accomplishments and failures of regime of Siyaad Barre. [JLS]

19.357 Ioan M. Lewis. *A modern history of Somalia.* 2d ed. Boulder: Westview, 1988. ISBN 0-8133-7402-2 (pbk). ▸ Standard political and diplomatic survey, ca. 1850–1976, with notes on 1980s. Perceptive and informed but monodimensional; emphasizes role of clans to exclusion of other processes. [JLS]

19.358 Harold Marcus. *Ethiopia, Great Britain, and the United States, 1941–1974: the politics of empire.* Berkeley: University of California Press, 1983. ISBN 0-520-04613-7. ▸ Informed, perceptive study of post–World War II diplomacy. Concludes British influence gave way to American, newcomers allowed themselves to be drawn into deepening commitment to controversial regime. [JLS]

19.359 Harold Marcus. *Haile Sellassie I: the formative years, 1892–1936.* Berkeley: University of California Press, 1987. ISBN 0-520-05601-9. ▸ Traces rule of absolutist king who saw himself as embodying Ethiopian sovereignty; interprets period as transition between feudalism and capitalism. [JLS]

19.360 Harold Marcus. *A history of Ethiopia.* Berkeley: University of California Press, 1993. ISBN 0-520-08121-8. ▸ Standard introductory survey with sensible interpretations in nationalist tradition. Based on secondary literature about olden times and author's familiarity with modern period. [JLS]

19.361 Harold Marcus. *The life and times of Menelik II: Ethiopia, 1844–1913.* Oxford: Clarendon, 1975. ISBN 0-19-821674-2. ▸ Political history of monarch's career, including brief and troubled reign of his successor. Best in treatment of last decade of reign, for which oral sources were available. [JLS]

19.362 John Markakis. *Ethiopia: anatomy of a traditional polity.* Oxford: Clarendon, 1974. ISBN 0-19-821691-2. ▸ Perceptive survey of state and society on eve of revolution. Interpretation follows nationalist tradition, but incorporates telling critiques of imperial regime. [JLS]

19.363 John Markakis. *National and class conflicts in the horn of Africa.* New York: Cambridge University Press, 1987. ISBN 0-521-

33362-8. ▸ Concludes that since World War II dominant, urban-based military and merchant elites supported by diverse foreign interests have been challenged repeatedly by desperate revolts of increasingly impoverished subsistence producers. [JLS]

19.364 James McCann. *From poverty to famine in northeast Ethiopia: a rural history, 1900–1935.* Philadelphia: University of Pennsylvania Press, 1987. ISBN 0-8122-8038-5. ▸ Regional social history of agricultural impoverishment in northern highlands. Treats interactions among technology, demography, institutions, and environment. [JLS]

19.365 Charles C. McClellan. *State transformation and national integration: Gedeo and the Ethiopian empire, 1895–1935.* East Lansing: Michigan State University, African Studies Center, 1988. ▸ Perceptive analysis of incorporation of Gedeo into Ethiopian empire and rise of coffee production. Based substantially on wealth of oral information, astutely controlled through written sources. [JLS]

19.366 S. C. Munro-Hay. *An African civilization: the Axumite kingdom of northern Ethiopia.* Edinburgh: Edinburgh University Press, 1989. ISBN 0-7486-0106-6. ▸ Deft introductory survey of ancient kingdom. Incorporates recent archaeological discoveries; draws also on numismatic, epigraphic, and literary sources. [JLS]

19.367 R. S. O'Fahey. *State and society in Dar Fur.* New York: St. Martin's, 1980. ISBN 0-312-75606-2. ▸ Institutional survey of Dar Fur government and economy in consensus history tradition, emphasizing integrative role of Islam. Draws on Dar Fur government records, travel accounts and orally derived colonial archival information. [JLS]

19.368 R. S. O'Fahey and Jay L. Spaulding. *Kingdoms of the Sudan.* London: Methuen; distributed by Harper & Row, Barnes & Noble Import Division, 1974. ISBN 0-416-77450-4 (cl), 0-416-77460-1 (pbk). ▸ Survey of Sinnar and Dar Fur political history. Based largely on travel literature and orally preserved information recorded in writing by colonial officials. [JLS]

19.369 Philippe Oberlé and Pierre Hugot. *Histoire de Djibouti des origines à la république.* Paris: Présence Africaine, 1985. ISBN 2-7087-0442-7. ▸ Survey of political events in small, improbable modern state born of mutual antipathies of its neighbors. Emphasis on career trajectories of leading politicians. [JLS]

19.370 Sven Rubenson. *King of kings: Tewodros of Ethiopia.* Addis Ababa: Haile Sellassie I University Press, 1966. (Historical Studies [Addis Ababa], 2.) ▸ Sensitive, sympathetic biography of enigmatic founder of modern Ethiopian state. Draws on contemporary chronicles, diplomatic records, and modern legend. [JLS]

19.371 Sven Rubenson. *The survival of Ethiopian independence.* London: Heinemann, 1976. (Lund studies in international history, 7.) ISBN 0-435-94240-9 (cl), 0-435-94241-7 (pbk). ▸ Standard nineteenth-century, nationalist diplomatic history. Based primarily on Ethiopian government documents, but benefits from author's broad command of diverse sources. [JLS]

19.372 Abdi Ismail Samatar. *The state and rural transformation in northern Somalia, 1884–1986.* Madison: University of Wisconsin Press, 1989. ISBN 0-299-11990-4 (cl), 0-299-11994-7 (pbk). ▸ Keen, perceptive analysis of rise to political hegemony of merchant class, socioeconomic grounds for failure of democracy, and political economy of dictatorship. [JLS]

19.373 Ahmed I. Samatar. *Socialist Somalia: rhetoric and reality.* Atlantic Highlands, N.J., and London: Institute for African Alternatives and Zed, 1988. ISBN 0-86232-589-7 (cl), 0-86232-588-9 (pbk). ▸ Pioneering social history traces disintegration of viable precolonial society into modern "basket case." Emphasis on failures of colonialism and of dictatorship of Siyaad Barre. [JLS]

19.374 Said S. Samatar. *Oral poetry and Somali nationalism: the case of Sayyid Mohammad 'Abdille Hasan.* Cambridge: Cambridge University Press, 1982. ISBN 0-521-23833-1. ▸ Troubled age of founding father of modern Somalia. Sympathetic but not uncritical study rests primarily on orally preserved, poetic literature of period. [JLS]

19.375 Alberto Sbacchi. *Ethiopia under Mussolini: fascism and the colonial experience.* London: Zed, 1985. ISBN 0-86232-254-5 (cl), 0-86232-255-3 (pbk). ▸ Study of Italian colonial venture in Ethiopia. Based largely on European published and archival sources, but perceptive in assessment of at present poorly documented contemporary Ethiopian realities. [JLS]

19.376 Ahmad Alawad Sikainga. *The western Bahr al-Ghazal under British rule, 1898–1956.* Athens: Ohio University, Center for International Studies, 1991. (Monographs in international studies, Africa series, 57.) ISBN 0-89680-161-6. ▸ Regional study of controversial colonial policies concerning ethnically and religiously heterogeneous congeries of small-scale communities long battered by slavers. Based largely on Sudanese archival sources. [JLS]

19.377 Jay L. Spaulding. *The heroic age in Sinnar.* East Lansing: Michigan State University, African Studies Center, 1985. (Northeast African Studies monographs, 15.) ▸ Social history of decline and fall of kingdom, ca. 1750–ca. 1850, with concomitant assertion of Arab identity by many northern Sudanese. Based largely on indigenous Arabic sources. [JLS]

19.378 Irma Taddia. *L'Eritrea—colonia, 1890–1952: paessaggi, strutture, uomini del colonialismo.* Milan: Angeli, 1986. ▸ Balanced, perceptive social history of colonial era, in which institutional foundations of new state were laid. Skillful use of comparative legal analysis to integrate ethnographic and administrative sources. [JLS]

19.379 Tadesse Tamrat. *Church and state in Ethiopia, 1270–1577.* Oxford: Clarendon, 1972. ISBN 0-19-821671-8. ▸ Pioneering study of expansion of medieval state under Solomonic dynasty, emphasizing political and monastic institutions. Draws on Ethiopian hagiography and chronicles. [JLS]

19.380 Gabru Tareke. *Ethiopia, power, and protest: peasant revolts in the twentieth century.* Cambridge: Cambridge University Press, 1991. ISBN 0-521-40011-2. ▸ Pioneering study of peasantry emphasizing self-assertion through revolt during period 1941–70; serves as basis for a critical reassessment of Haile Selassie's state. Skillful integration of oral and archival sources. [JLS]

19.381 Virginia McLean Thompson and Richard Adloff. *Djibouti and the Horn of Africa.* Stanford, Calif.: Stanford University Press, 1968. ▸ Factual survey of country's institutions and preoccupations at independence. Now somewhat dated, but reliable background. Weak conceptualization of precolonial period. [JLS]

19.382 Alessandro Triulzi. *Salt, gold, and legitimacy: prelude to the history of a no-man's land, Belá Shangul, Wallagga, Ethiopia (ca. 1800–1898).* Naples: Instituto Universitario Orientale, 1981. ▸ Discussion of exploitation of Bertha and neighboring peoples of western Ethiopia by intrusive northern Sudanese elite. Exceptionally skillful integration of oral and written sources. [JLS]

19.383 Bahru Zewde. *A history of modern Ethiopia, 1885–1974.* Athens: Ohio University Press, 1992. ISBN 0-8214-0971-9 (cl), 0-8214-0972-7 (pbk). ▸ Critical reassessment of modern history tracing evolution of political discontent and social catastrophe under sequence of repressive modernizing regimes supported by foreigners. [JLS]

EASTERN AFRICA

Early Eastern Africa

19.384 John Beattie. *The Nyoro state.* Oxford: Clarendon, 1971. ISBN 0-19-823171-7. ▸ Early functionalist analysis of important interlacustrine state; focus on political structures and impact of colonialism on them. [TTS]

19.385 Iris Berger. *Religion and resistance: East African kingdoms in the precolonial period.* Tervuren, Belgium: Musée Royale de l'Afrique Centrale, 1981. (Musée Royale de l'Afrique Centrale Annales Série in-8° Sciences Humaines, 105.) ‣ Important essay on regional cults, resistance, and state formation in interlacustrine area, based on modern interpretation of oral traditions; includes information about women's role in resistance. [TTS]

19.386 H. Neville Chittick. *Kilwa: an Islamic trading city on the East African coast.* Nairobi: British Institute in Eastern Africa, 1974. (Memoir of the British Institute in Eastern Africa, 5.) ‣ Classic archaeological study of Swahili trading town stressing foreign influences. See also Nurse and Spear 19.405 and Pouwels 19.414. [TTS]

19.387 David William Cohen. *The historical tradition of Busoga: Mukama and Kintu.* Oxford: Clarendon, 1972. ISBN 0-19-821673-4. ‣ Early history of related interlacustrine states based on oral traditions. Assesses significance of origin traditions for ethnicity and state formation. [TTS]

19.388 Christopher Ehret. *Southern Nilotic history: linguistic approaches to the study of the past.* Evanston, Ill.: Northwestern University Press, 1971. ISBN 0-8101-0315-X. ‣ Pioneering study of early history of southern Nilotic-speaking peoples based on linguistic evidence. [TTS]

19.389 Steven Feierman. *The Shambaa kingdom: a history.* Madison: University of Wisconsin Press, 1974. ISBN 0-299-06360-7. ‣ Important structuralist analysis of oral traditions combined with documentary data to reconstruct founding of Shambaa state, its structure, and impact of trade. [TTS]

19.390 G.S.P. Freeman-Grenville, ed. *The East African coast: select documents from the first to the earlier nineteenth century.* 2d ed. London: Collings, 1975. ISBN 0-901720-85-2. ‣ Useful, standard collection of early recorded traditions and travelers' accounts of coast. [TTS]

19.391 Ann E. Frontera. *Persistence and change: a history of Taveta.* Los Angeles: Crossroads, 1978. ISBN 0-918456-19-3. ‣ Socioeconomic history of Kenyan society from seventeenth century through colonial period. Important study of formation of multiethnic community based on oral and written data. [TTS]

19.392 Peter S. Garlake. *Early Islamic architecture of the East African coast.* London: Oxford University Press for British Institute of History and Archaeology in East Africa, 1966. ‣ Remains basic reference, though somewhat dated by subsequent work. [TTS]

19.393 Luc de Heusch. *Le Rwanda et la civilisation interlacustre.* Brussels: Université Libre de Bruxelles, Institute de Sociologie, 1966. ‣ Examines important interlacustrine state in regional context. [TTS]

19.394 Douglas H. Johnson and David M. Anderson, eds. *The ecology of survival: case studies from northeast African history.* Boulder: Westview, 1988. ISBN 0-8133-0727-9. ‣ Important, innovative sociohistorical studies of ecological change, based largely on original fieldwork. Articles explore historical changes that led to environmental decline and impoverishment. [TTS]

19.395 Apolo Kaggwa. *The kings of Buganda.* M.S.M. Semakula Kiwanuka, ed. and trans. Nairobi: East African Publishing House, 1971. ‣ Extensive early collection of Buganda oral traditions gathered by Sir Apolo Kaggwa, prime minister of Buganda, in late nineteenth century. [TTS]

19.396 Samwiri Rubaraza Karugire. *A history of the kingdom of Nkore in western Uganda to 1896.* Oxford: Clarendon, 1971. ISBN 0-19-821670-X. ‣ Fundamental revision of earlier, static interpre-

tation showing how elites mobilized wealth and patronage to achieve power; based on careful analysis of oral sources. Fine example of precolonial political history. [TTS]

19.397 Samwiri Rubaraza Karugire. *A political history of Uganda.* Nairobi: Heinemann, 1980. ISBN 0-435-94524-6 (cl), 0-435-94525-4 (pbk). ‣ Ostensibly a general political history, this text reflects author's deep despair over state of Ugandan politics in aftermath of colonial rule and regimes of Obote and Amin. [TTS]

19.398 Israel K. Katoke. *The Karagwe kingdom: a history of the Abanyambo of north western Tanzania, c. 1400–1915.* Nairobi: East African Publishing House, 1975. ‣ Basic, accessible history of interlacustrine kingdom, focusing on nineteenth century; based on oral traditions, adheres closely to traditional evidence. Selection of oral texts appended. [TTS/CHA]

19.399 I. N. Kimambo. *A political history of the Pare of Tanzania, c. 1500–1900.* Nairobi: East African Publishing House, 1969. ‣ Early history of political development based on oral traditions. Reflects nationalist approach of Dar es-Salaam school of 1960s. [TTS/CHA]

19.400 I. N. Kimambo and A. J. Temu, eds. *A history of Tanzania.* Evanston, Ill.: Northwestern University Press for the Historical Association of Tanzania, 1969. ‣ General text reflecting nationalist orientation of Dar es-Salaam school in 1960s. [TTS]

19.401 M. S. M. Semakula Kiwanuka. *A history of Buganda: from the foundation of the kingdom to 1900.* New York: Africana, 1971. ISBN 0-8419-0114-7. ‣ Accessible, early account of traditional political history of important interlacustrine kingdom, based on oral traditions. Emphasis on writings of nineteenth-century official, Sir Apollo Kaggwa, prime minister of Buganda. [TTS/CHA]

19.402 John Lamphear. *The traditional history of the Jie of Uganda.* Oxford: Clarendon, 1976. ISBN 0-19-821692-0. ‣ Pioneering study of early history of agro-pastoral people. Careful analysis of local traditions and rituals to show how Jie emerged as creative amalgam of previous groups. [TTS]

19.403 Godfrey Muriuki. *A history of the Kikuyu, 1500–1900.* Nairobi: Oxford University Press, 1974. ISBN 0-19-572314-7. ‣ Pioneering study of Kikuyu peoples based on oral traditions. Shows how Kikuyu social and political institutions developed in context of their expansion across highlands of central Kenya and their interaction with other peoples. [TTS]

19.404 Émile Mworoha. *Histoire du Burundi.* Paris: Hatier, 1987. ISBN 2-218-06009-4. ‣ Collected articles on history of important interlacustrine kingdom. [TTS]

19.405 Derek Nurse and Thomas T. Spear. *The Swahili: reconstructing the history and language of an African society, 800–1500.* Philadelphia: University of Pennsylvania Press, 1985. ISBN 0-8122-7928-X (cl), 0-8122-1207-X (pbk). ‣ Early history of Swahili coast based on linguistic, oral, archaeological, and documentary accounts. Argues for indigenous origins of Swahili culture. [TTS]

19.406 John W. Nyakatura. *Anatomy of an African kingdom: a history of Bunyoro-Kitara.* Teopista Muganwa, trans. Garden City, N.Y.: Anchor, 1973. ISBN 0-385-06966-9. ‣ Example of traditional history of interlacustrine kingdom, written by early Nyoro historian. Based on literal interpretation of oral tradition. [TTS]

19.407 William Robert Ochieng'. *A pre-colonial history of the Gusii in western Kenya from c. 1500 to 1914.* Kampala: East African Literature Bureau, 1974. ‣ Early history of decentralized Kenyan people based on rather literal interpretation of oral traditions, emphasizing population movements and political evolution. [TTS]

19.408 Bethwell A. Ogot. *History of the southern Luo.* Vol. 1:

Migration and settlement, 1500–1900. Nairobi: East African Publishing House, 1967. ‣ Dense history of Luo migrations from Sudan into Uganda and Kenya. Classic study of patrilineal segmentary society based on oral traditions, one of first such accounts by African historian. [TTS]

19.409 Bethwell A. Ogot, ed. *Kenya before 1900: eight regional studies.* Nairobi: East African Publishing House, 1976. ‣ Case studies of early history of Kalenjin, Okiek, Gusii, Kikuyu, Meru, Kamba, and Mijikenda peoples based largely on oral traditions. [TTS]

19.410 Bethwell A. Ogot and John A. Kieran, eds. *Zamani: a survey of East African history.* 2d ed. London: Longman, 1974. ISBN 0-582-60293-9. ‣ East Africa from early man to 1971. Authoritative text but now somewhat dated. Value to beginners hindered somewhat by organizational emphasis on differences between ethnic groupings rather than regional similarities. [TTS]

19.411 Roland Oliver and Gervase Mathew, eds. *History of East Africa.* Vol. 1. 1963 ed. Oxford: Clarendon, 1966–76. ‣ East Africa from Stone Age to 1898. Comprehensive text and bibliography, but now very dated. See Harlow and Chilver, eds. 19.484 and Low and Smith, eds. 19.505 for volumes 2 and 3. [TTS]

19.412 Bridglal Pachai, ed. *The early history of Malawi.* Evanston, Ill.: Northwestern University Press, 1972. ISBN 0-8101-0372-9. ‣ Uneven collection of papers posed uneasily between prevailing nationalist historiography and emergent studies of political economy, such as Palmer and Parsons, eds. 19.793 and Mandala 19.614. Covers prehistory to nineteenth century. [TTS]

19.413 D. W. Phillipson. *The later prehistory of eastern and southern Africa.* New York: Africana, 1977. ISBN 0-8419-0347-6 (cl), 0-8419-0348-4 (pbk). ‣ Archaeological survey, Stone Age through Iron Age. Good synthesis of archaeological data, but weak on linguistic interpretation. [TTS]

19.414 Randall L. Pouwels. *Horn and crescent: cultural change and traditional Islam on the East African coast, 800–1900.* Cambridge: Cambridge University Press, 1987. ISBN 0-521-32308-8. ‣ Authoritative study of indigenous Swahili culture and influence of Islam on local tradition. Sensitive, well-informed study; unusual in taking seriously both local forms and foreign influences. [TTS]

19.415 Andrew D. Roberts, ed. *Tanzania before 1900.* 1968 ed. Nairobi: East African Publishing House for Historical Association of Tanzania, 1974. ‣ Case studies of seven Tanzanian peoples, among first to be based extensively on original fieldwork and collections of oral traditions. Focus on expansion of trade and political changes in nineteenth century. [TTS]

19.416 Peter Robertshaw, ed. *Early pastoralists of south-western Kenya.* Nairobi: British Institute in Eastern Africa, 1990. (Memoirs of the British Institute in Eastern Africa, 11.) ISBN 1-87256-601-4. ‣ Reports on recent archaeological work that pushes back origins of pastoralism in area and conveys more dynamic picture of its subsequent development. [TTS]

19.417 Peter Ridway Schmidt. *Historical archaeology: a structural approach in an African culture.* Westport, Conn.: Greenwood, 1978. ISBN 0-8371-9849-6. ‣ Innovative use of oral traditions and archaeology to reconstruct early history of ironworking in central Tanzania. [TTS]

19.418 Aylward Shorter. *Chiefship in western Tanzania: a political history of Kimbu.* Oxford: Clarendon, 1972. ISBN 0-19-823178-4. ‣ Detailed historical and anthropological study of series of chiefdoms in western Tanzania, linking political development to expanding trade in nineteenth century. [TTS]

19.419 Thomas T. Spear. *The kaya complex: a history of the Mijikenda peoples of the Kenya coast to 1900.* Nairobi: Kenya Literature

Bureau, 1978. ‣ Socioeconomic history of nine Kenya peoples based on oral, ethnographic, and linguistic data. Links settlement and political development with trade and relations with coast. [TTS]

19.420 Thomas T. Spear. *Kenya's past: an introduction to historical method in Africa.* London: Longman, 1981. ISBN 0-582-64696-0 (cl), 0-582-64695-2 (pbk). ‣ Regional synthesis demonstrating how archaeological, linguistic, oral, and ethnographic data are used to reconstruct African history from early mankind to late nineteenth century. [TTS]

19.421 Thomas T. Spear and Richard Waller, eds. *Being Maasai: ethnicity and identity in East Africa.* London: Currey, 1993. ISBN 0-85255-216-5 (cl), 0-85255-215-7 (pbk). ‣ Historical, anthropological, and contemporary case studies stressing fluid and instrumental nature of ethnicity among Maasai and neighboring peoples. [TTS]

19.422 Kathleen M. Stahl. *History of Chagga people of Kilimanjaro.* The Hague: Mouton, 1964. ‣ Historical study of chiefship on Kilimanjaro based on dated, literal interpretation of Chagga traditions. [TTS]

19.423 Justus Strandes. *The Portuguese period in East Africa.* 2d ed. J. S. Kirkman, ed. Jean F. Wallwork, trans. Nairobi: East African Literature Bureau, 1968. ‣ Translation of classic German study of Portuguese influence on East Africa, first published in 1899. Somewhat dated, but remains most complete account today. [TTS]

19.424 John Edward Giles Sutton. *The archaeology of the western highlands of Kenya.* Nairobi: British Institute in Eastern Africa, 1973. (Memoirs of the British Institute in Eastern Africa, 3.) ‣ Historical archaeology of southern Nilotic speakers. Like Robertshaw, ed. 19.416, proposes fundamental reassessment of development of pastoralism and agriculture in central and western Kenya as dynamic processes. [TTS]

19.425 Jan Vansina. *L'évolution du royaume Rwanda dès origines à 1900.* Brussels: Académie Royale des Sciences d'Outre-mer, 1962. (Mémoires in-8° Académie Royale des Sciences d'Outre-mer: classe des sciences morales et politiques, 26.) ‣ Early history of important interlacustrine state based on pioneering use of oral traditions. [TTS]

19.426 James Bertin Webster, ed. *Chronology, migration, and drought in interlacustrine Africa.* New York: Africana, 1979. ISBN 0-8419-0377-8 (cl), 0-8419-0388-3 (pbk). ‣ Narrowly focused articles seek chronology for precolonial societies through analysis of kinglists and references to drought and migration in oral tradition and measurement of Nile water levels. [MJH]

19.426 Gideon S. Were. *A history of the Abaluyia of western Kenya, c. 1500–1930.* Nairobi: East African Publishing House, 1967. ‣ Early history of small-scale Kenyan peoples based on somewhat literal use of oral traditions. Emphasizes population movements and political evolution. [TTS]

19.428 Roy Willis. *A state in the making: myth, history, and social transformation in pre-colonial Ufipa.* Bloomington: Indiana University Press, 1981. ISBN 0-253-19537-3. ‣ Historical anthropology of political economy and state formation based on structuralist approach to traditions. [TTS]

Nineteenth Century

19.429 Charles H. Ambler. *Kenyan communities in the age of imperialism: the central region in the late nineteenth century.* New Haven: Yale University Press, 1988. ISBN 0-300-03957-3. ‣ Well-regarded case study of small-scale societies in context of development of local and long-distance trade, imperial expansion, and famine. Regional approach challenges established ethnic perspective. [CHA]

19.430 Norman Robert Bennett. *Arab versus European: diplomacy and war in nineteenth-century East Central Africa.* New York: Africana, 1986. ISBN 0-8419-0861-3. ▸ Detailed archival study of political and economic struggles between Europeans and Arabs in nineteenth-century eastern Africa; redresses earlier tendency to focus on European-African conflicts, neglecting Arab role. Lack of bibliography limits usefulness. [CHA]

19.431 Norman Robert Bennett. *Mirambo of Tanzania, 1840?–1884.* New York: Oxford University Press, 1971. ▸ Accessible account of man who built a Nyamwezi chiefdom into powerful military state by exploiting long-distance trade and British contacts. Paucity of evidence leaves portrait unfinished. [CHA]

19.432 Roger Botte. "Rwanda and Burundi, 1889–1930: chronology of a slow assassination." *International journal of African historical studies* 18.1–2 (1985) 53–91, 289–314. ISSN 0361-7882. ▸ Describes impact of natural disasters. Among few works in English for period. Notes provide guide to unpublished and foreign-language works. [CHA]

19.433 Enid M. Burke. "African and Seychellois socio-cultural ties, mid-eighteenth century to present day." In *History and social change in East Africa: proceedings of the 1974 conference of the Historical Association of Kenya.* Bethwell A. Ogot, ed., pp. 86–110. Nairobi: East African Literature Bureau, 1976. (Hadith, 6.) ▸ Brief overview of Seychelles history. Footnotes provide guide to basic sources. [CHA]

19.434 Carolyn M. Clark. "Land and food, women and power in nineteenth-century Kikuyu." *Africa* 50.4 (1980) 357–70. ISSN 0001-9720. ▸ Examines Kikuyu women's economic roles within larger political economy. Sophisticated analysis of tension between female autonomy and male domination. [CHA]

19.435 David William Cohen. *Womunafu's Bunafu: a study of authority in a nineteenth-century African community.* Princeton: Princeton University Press, 1977. ISBN 0-691-03093-6. ▸ Innovative work on role of leadership in Busoga, in present-day Uganda. Critical analysis of oral evidence. One of most important studies of small-scale precolonial African society. [CHA]

19.436 Frederick Cooper. "Islam and cultural hegemony: the ideology of slaveowners on the East African coast." In *The ideology of slavery in Africa.* Paul E. Lovejoy, ed., pp. 270–307. Beverly Hills, Calif.: Sage, 1981. ISBN 0-8039-1664-7 (cl), 0-8039-1665-5 (pbk). ▸ Acute study by leading historian of East African slavery that draws on Gramsci to challenge Orientalist assumptions. Focuses on generalized role of Islam in defining subordination. [CHA]

19.437 Reginald Coupland. *East Africa and its invaders: from the earliest times to the death of Seyyid Said in 1856.* 1938 ed. New York: Russell & Russell, 1965. ▸ Orientalist imperial history focusing on European actions and convinced of righteousness of British antislavery mission. Still useful for detailed record of trade and diplomacy. [CHA]

19.438 Reginald Coupland. *The exploitation of East Africa, 1856–1890: the slave trade and the scramble.* 2d ed. Jack Simmons, Introduction. London: Faber & Faber, 1968. ▸ British imperial and antislavery actions on East African coast. Focuses on career of proconsul John Kirk. Dated but still valuable as thorough, readable record of events. [CHA]

19.439 Jeffrey A. Fadiman. *An oral history of tribal warfare: the Meru of Mt. Kenya.* Athens: Ohio University Press, 1982. ISBN 0-8214-0632-9 (cl), 0-8214-0633-7 (pbk). ▸ Traditions of warfare and raiding in Mt. Kenya region. Uncritical use of oral evidence and static perspective, but useful introduction to Meru history and cosmology and to organization of violence. [CHA]

19.440 Jim Freedman. *Nyabingi: the social history of an African divinity.* Tervuren, Belgium: Musée Royal de l'Afrique Centrale,

1984. (Annales, série in-8°, Sciences humaines, 115.) ▸ Interpretive essay on transformation of cult of female god, Nyabingi, in northern Rwanda and southern Uganda. Discusses conflict between farmers and herders and resistance to and impact of colonialism. [CHA]

19.441 James L. Giblin. *The politics of environmental control in northeastern Tanzania, 1840–1940.* Philadelphia: University of Pennsylvania Press, 1992. ISBN 0-8122-3177-5. ▸ Important regional study of interconnections among economic transformation, imperial expansion, and environmental change. Systematic use of oral and documentary evidence in in-depth exploration of issues raised by Koponen 19.447 and Kjekshus 19.446. [CHA/DMA]

19.442 Peter C. W. Gutkind. *The royal capital of Buganda: a study of internal conflict and external ambiguity.* The Hague: Mouton, 1963. (Publications of the Institute of Social Studies, 12.) ▸ Sociological study of development of Buganda's capital under colonialism. Includes substantial material on nineteenth century. [CHA]

19.443 Hamed bin Muhammed. *L'autobiographie de Hamed ben Mohammed el-Murjebi Tippo Tip (ca. 1840–1905).* 1966 ed. François Bontinck, trans. Brussels: Académie Royale des Sciences d'Outre-mer, 1974. (Académie Royale des Sciences d'Outre-mer: classe des sciences morales et politiques, 42.4.) ▸ Autobiographical recollections of most important coastal merchant active in trade across Tanganyika, who became political force in eastern Zaire. One of few memoirs by nineteenth-century African. [CHA]

19.444 Gerald W. Hartwig. *The art of survival in East Africa: the Kerebe and long-distance trade, 1800–1895.* New York: Africana, 1976. ISBN 0-8419-0182-1. ▸ Commercial initiative and social change in small state of southeastern Lake Victoria. Useful study of impact of larger forces on society. Controversial reliance on encyclopedic oral informants. [CHA]

19.445 Gerald W. Hartwig. "Demographic considerations in East Africa during the nineteenth century." *International journal of African historical studies* 12.4 (1979) 653–72. ISSN 0361-7882. ▸ Useful compilation of information relating to drought, famine, disease, and mortality for entire region. Suggests demographic trends through the 1800s. Critical of Kjekshus 19.446. [CHA]

19.446 Helge Kjekshus. *Ecology control and economic development in East African history: the case of Tanganyika, 1850–1950.* Berkeley: University of California Press, 1977. ISBN 0-520-03384-1. ▸ Sweeping study of commercial and economic history in relationship to environment and disease. Challenges underdevelopment theory, but idealizes precolonial society. Lacks detailed local evidence. [CHA/DMA]

19.447 Juhani Koponen. *People and production in late precolonial Tanzania: history and structures.* Helsinki: Finnish Society for Development Studies; distributed by Scandinavian Institute of African Studies, 1988. (Monographs of the Finnish Society for Development Studies, 2. Studia historica, 28.) ISBN 951-96-1560-1. ▸ Well-informed materialist analysis of impact of trade on small, independent societies. Evidence, from travelers' accounts, does not sustain assertions of prosperity of precolonial rural economies. [CHA/TTS]

19.448 John Lamphear. "The Kamba and the northern Mrima coast." In *Pre-colonial African trade: essays on trade in central and eastern Africa before 1900.* Richard Gray and David Birmingham, eds., pp. 75–101. London: Oxford University Press, 1970. ISBN 0-19-215639-X. ▸ Somewhat dated, but still most thorough account of development of long-distance commerce into Kenya interior. Based on written sources. [CHA]

19.449 Donald Anthony Low, ed. *The mind of Buganda: docu-*

ments of the modern history of an African kingdom. Berkeley: University of California Press, 1971. ISBN 0-520-01969-5. ▸ Some sixty documents selected by leading historian representing local and European perspectives. Charts Buganda history from 1850s to 1960s. Introductory overview and index, but little annotation. [CHA]

19.450 Fred Morton. *Children of Ham: freed slaves and fugitive slaves on the Kenya coast, 1873 to 1907.* Boulder: Westview, 1990. ISBN 0-8133-8002-2. ▸ Thorough account of struggles of Christian freed slaves and fugitives to preserve freedom. Larger revisionist claims regarding East African slavery are not convincing. [CHA]

19.451 Christine Stephanie Nicholls. *The Swahili coast: politics, diplomacy, and trade on the East African littoral, 1798–1856.* New York: Africana, 1971. ISBN 0-8419-0099-X. ▸ Sober account, based on English, French, and Swahili archives, of diplomatic relations between Omanis and Europeans. Analysis of local society and politics superseded by subsequent studies. [CHA]

19.452 Arye Oded. *Islam in Uganda: islamization through a central state in pre-colonial Africa.* New York: Wiley, 1974. ISBN 0-470-65260-8. ▸ Thorough account of efforts of Muslim party in mid-nineteenth-century kingdom of Buganda. Lacks analytical insight, but remains one of few treatments of topic. [CHA]

19.453 Bethwell A. Ogot, ed. *Kenya in the nineteenth century.* Nairobi: Bookwise, 1985. (Hadith, 8.) ▸ Seven disparate essays, including notable pieces by Waller on Maasai, Sperling on spread of Islam, Ehret on linguistic analysis, Gold on Nandi women, and Cooper on slavery. [CHA]

19.454 J. M. Onyango-ku-Odongo and James Bertin Webster, eds. *The central Lwo during the Aconya.* Nairobi: East African Literature Bureau, 1976. ▸ One of series of works compiled by teams of researchers collecting oral traditions of Ugandan societies. Intentionally uncritical presentation of traditional accounts by academic and local historians. [CHA]

19.455 Randall M. Packard. *Chiefship and cosmology: an historical study of political competition.* Bloomington: Indiana University Press, 1981. ISBN 0-253-30831-3. ▸ Important study of ideology as shaping political roles and conflict among Bashu people of Zaire-Uganda border region. Sophisticated analysis of oral tradition and ritual in change in nineteenth and twentieth centuries. [CHA]

19.456 Benjamin C. Ray. *Myth, ritual, and kingship in Buganda.* New York: Oxford University Press, 1991. ISBN 0-19-506436-4. ▸ Comparative analysis of precolonial institutions, interpretations of them, and their subsequent evolution. Evaluation of possible connections to ancient Egypt. Religious studies perspective. [CHA]

19.457 John Rowe. "The purge of Christians at Mwanga's court: a reassessment of this episode in Buganda history." *Journal of African history* 5.1 (1964) 55–71. ISSN 0021-8537. ▸ Places purge within king's larger policy of challenging traditional chiefs. Author's important dissertation on Buganda remains unpublished. [CHA]

19.458 Ahmed I. Salim, ed. *State formation in eastern Africa.* Nairobi: Heinemann, 1984. ISBN 0-435-94364-2. ▸ Eleven case studies of societies from Ethiopia to Zimbabwe. Focusing attention on development of state institutions in smaller-scale societies. [CHA]

19.459 Edward I. Steinhart. *Conflict and collaboration: the kingdoms of western Uganda, 1890–1907.* Princeton: Princeton University Press, 1977. ISBN 0-691-03114-2. ▸ Comparative study of response of African leaders in Ankole, Toro, and Bunyoro to British imperialism. Excellent on roles of indigenous structures in shaping resistance and accommodation. Somewhat strained theoretical framework. [CHA]

19.460 John Tosh. *Clan leaders and colonial chiefs in Lango: the political history of an East African stateless society, c. 1800–1939.* Oxford: Clarendon, 1978. ISBN 0-19-822711-6. ▸ Impressively researched account of small-scale societies in central Uganda facing neighboring states and British imperialism. Dated interpretation but still one of few works not focused on a major state. [CHA]

19.461 Richard Waller. "Ecology, migration, and expansion in East Africa." *African affairs* 84 (1985) 347–70. ISSN 0001-9909. ▸ Detailed examination of pastoralists of Rift Valley and Lake Turkana. Draws on local studies to explore connections between population movement, environment, and development of ethnic groups and identities. [CHA]

19.462 Marcia Wright. "Women in peril: a commentary on the life stories of captives in nineteenth-century East-central Africa." *African social research* 20 (1975) 800–19. ISSN 0002-0168. ▸ Influential approach to study of histories of women and slavery by leading scholar of region. Uses autobiographical narratives to reconstruct shifting definitions of gender and servitude. [CHA]

19.463 Michael Wright. *Buganda in the heroic age.* Nairobi: Oxford University Press, 1971. ▸ Study of internal struggle for power in Buganda, 1884–1900. Substantial use of oral sources. Focuses attention on actions of Muslim faction. [CHA]

19.464 C. C. Wrigley. "The Christian revolution in Buganda." *Comparative studies in society and history* 2.1 (1959–60) 33–48. ISSN 0010-4175. ▸ Still useful study of religious politics in Ugandan kingdom in late nineteenth century. Argues Christian successes permitted Buganda to preserve distinctiveness under colonialism. [CHA]

19.465 Marguerite Ylvisaker. *Lamu in the nineteenth century: land, trade, and politics.* Boston: Boston University, African Studies Center, 1979. (African research studies, 13.) ▸ Description extends beyond coastal elite and emphasizes local economy and contacts along coast and inland. Complements studies focusing on Indian Ocean diplomacy and trade. [CHA]

Twentieth Century

19.466 David M. Anderson. "Depression, dust bowl, demography, and drought: the colonial state and soil conservation in East Africa during the 1930s." *African affairs* 83.332 (1984) 321–44. ISSN 0001-9909. ▸ Examines emergence of British colonial conservation policies, using examples from Kenya, Tanganyika, and Uganda. Important for emphasis on 1930s origin of rural development schemes implemented after 1945. [DMA]

19.467 David E. Apter. *The political kingdom in Uganda: a study in bureaucratic nationalism.* 2d ed. Princeton: Princeton University Press, 1967. ▸ Still best available guide to politics of nationalism in colonial Uganda, with much valuable detail on organization of government and management of political change. [DMA]

19.468 Ralph A. Austen. *Northwest Tanzania under German and British rule: colonial policy and tribal politics, 1889–1939.* New Haven: Yale University Press, 1968. ▸ Deals with German conquest of region around Lake Nyanza and subsequent transfer to British control in 1916, then provides examination of workings of indirect rule to 1939. [DMA]

19.469 Bruce Berman and John M. Lonsdale. *Unhappy valley: conflict in Kenya and Africa.* London: Currey, 1992. ISBN 0-85255-021-9 (cl), 0-85255-022-7 (pt. 1, pbk), 0-85255-099-5 (pt. 2, pbk). ▸ Twelve thematic essays, eight dealing specifically with colonial Kenya. Includes several classic pieces, especially chapters on colonial conquest and moral economy of Mau Mau. Essential reading. [DMA]

19.470 Cynthia Brantley. *The Giriama and colonial resistance in*

Kenya, 1800–1920. Berkeley: University of California Press, 1981. ISBN 0-520-04216-6. ‣ Useful monograph on process of colonial conquest in coastal region of Kenya. Resistance culminated in uprising, led by the prophetess Mekatalili. Combines oral histories with documentary sources. [DMA]

19.471 E. A. Brett. *Colonialism and underdevelopment in East Africa: the politics of economic change, 1919–1939.* 1973 ed. London: Heinemann, 1981. ISBN 0-435-94510-6 (pbk). ‣ Important comparative study of economics of British colonial policies in Kenya, Uganda, and Tanganyika, elaborating dependency model. [DMA]

19.472 Anthony Clayton and Donald C. Savage. *Government and labour in Kenya, 1895–1963.* London: Cass, 1974. ISBN 0-7146-3025-X. ‣ Meticulous study of colonial labor policies, especially strong on labor law and African political reactions, notably emergence of trade unions. [DMA]

19.473 David William Cohen and E. S. Atieno Odhiambo. *Siaya: the historical anthropology of an African landscape.* Athens: Ohio University Press, 1989. ISBN 0-821-40901-8 (cl), 0-821-40902-6 (pbk). ‣ Innovative collection of essays on local conceptions and representations of history in Luo district of Siaya, in western Kenya. Easy, narrative style but intellectually complex. [DMA]

19.474 Frederick Cooper. *From slaves to squatters: plantation labor and agriculture in Zanzibar and coastal Kenya, 1890–1925.* New Haven: Yale University Press, 1980. ISBN 0-300-02454-1. ‣ Second, and arguably best, of author's trilogy of important books (with 19.475 and 19.895) on coastal East Africa. Study of postemancipation class struggle, with focus on labor in agricultural economy. [DMA]

19.475 Frederick Cooper. *On the African waterfront: urban disorder and the transformation of work in colonial Mombasa.* New Haven: Yale University Press, 1987. ISBN 0-300-03618-3. ‣ History of worker consciousness among Kenya dockworkers, 1930s to early 1960s. Sensitive to wider colonial labor problems in Africa. Excellent, elegantly written book. [DMA]

19.476 Andrew Coulson. *Tanzania: a political economy.* Oxford: Clarendon, 1982. ISBN 0-19-828292-3 (cl), 0-19-828293-1 (pbk). ‣ Outline of history to Arusha Declaration (1967), with final section on 1970s. Good summaries of basic data on economic performance. Emphasizes neglect of peasantry and expansion of state bureaucracy. [DMA]

19.477 Martin R. Doornbos. *Not all the king's men: inequality as a political instrument in Ankole, Uganda.* The Hague: Mouton, 1978. ISBN 90-279-7707-0. ‣ Response to earlier assertions of dominance of centralized authority; emphasizes importance of social inequality in determining local politics. Much useful detail, if somewhat narrow in focus. [DMA]

19.478 Steven Feierman. *Peasant intellectuals: anthropology and history in Tanzania.* Madison: University of Wisconsin Press, 1990. ISBN 0-299-12520-3 (cl), 0-299-12524-6 (pbk). ‣ Ambitious survey of peasant responses to colonial policies in Shambaa region, revealed through shifting idioms of local discourse and discussed in terms of hegemony. Extensive use of oral materials. [DMA]

19.479 Marcus Franda. *The Seychelles: unquiet islands.* Boulder: Westview, 1982. ISBN 0-86531-266-4. ‣ Basic historical, political, and social background to Seychelles. Useful starting point. [DMA]

19.480 Joseph Gahama. *Le Burundi sous administration belge: la période du mandat, 1919–1939.* Paris: Karthala, 1983. ISBN 2-86537-089-5. ‣ Detailed account of mandate period, especially strong on chiefly power, agriculture, famine, Christian missions,

and social protest. Very useful study, based on wide range of documentary and oral sources. [DMA]

19.481 Cherry Gertzel. *Party and locality in northern Uganda, 1945–1962.* London: Athlone for Institute of Commonwealth Studies, 1974. (Commonwealth papers, 16.) ISBN 0-485-17616-5. ‣ Examination of growth of nationalist politics at local level in Lango and Acholi. Excellent on character of urban-rural and center-regional links. [DMA]

19.482 David Goldsworthy. *Tom Mboya: the man Kenya wanted to forget.* Nairobi: Heinemann, 1982. ISBN 0-8419-0787-0 (cl), 0-8419-0788-9 (pbk). ‣ Evocative political biography of one of Kenya's most significant (and controversial) modern figures, key figure in trade union movement. Balanced, clearsighted account. [DMA]

19.483 Holger Bernt Hansen. *Mission, church, and state in a colonial setting: Uganda, 1890–1925.* London: Heinemann, 1984. ISBN 0-435-94518-1. ‣ Massive study of Church Missionary Society and establishment of its Native Anglican church; concentrates on Buganda. Essential for all students of religion in Africa. [DMA]

19.484 Vincent Harlow and E. M. Chilver, eds. *History of East Africa.* Vol. 2. Oxford: Clarendon, 1965. ISBN 0-19-078902-5. ‣ Multiauthored general history of Kenya, Uganda, and Tanganyika, 1895–1945. Now dated, but still offers useful introduction. See Oliver and Mathew, eds. 19.411 and Low and Smith, eds. 19.505 for volumes 1 and 3. [DMA]

19.485 Elspeth Huxley. *White-man's country: Lord Delamere and the making of Kenya.* 1967 2d ed. 2 vols. New York: Praeger, 1968. ISBN 0-19-354621-2. ‣ Laudatory biography of Kenya's most famous white settler, first published 1935. Vivid prose with much valuable detail on colonial politics. [DMA]

19.486 John Iliffe. *A modern history of Tanganyika.* Cambridge: Cambridge University Press, 1979. ISBN 0-521-22024-6 (cl), 0-521-29611-0 (pbk). ‣ First and only comprehensive history of mainland Tanzania, organized around well-chosen themes within broad chronological framework. Masterpiece of scholarship, written in easy style. Highly recommended. [DMA]

19.487 John Iliffe. *Tanganyika under German rule, 1905–1912.* Cambridge: Cambridge University Press, 1969. ISBN 0-521-05371-4. ‣ Indispensable work on German colonialism during period of considerable change, in wake of Maji Maji uprising (1905–1907). Especially vivid portayal of Governor Rechenberg. [DMA]

19.488 John Iliffe, ed. *Modern Tanzanians: a volume of biographies.* Nairobi: East African Publishing House for Historical Association of Tanzania, 1973. ‣ Collection of short political biographies of prominent Tanzanians, mostly written by local historians. Contributions vary in quality, but all are informative. [DMA]

19.489 Martin H. Y. Kaniki, ed. *Tanzania under colonial rule.* 1979 ed. London: Longman for Historical Association of Tanzania, 1980. ISBN 0-582-64649-9 (pbk). ‣ Political economy approach to colonial history stressing underdevelopment theme. Twelve essays; those by Rodney, Bowles, and Iliffe strongly recommended. [DMA]

19.490 Tabitha Kanogo. *Squatters and the roots of Mau Mau, 1905–63.* Athens: Ohio University Press, 1987. ISBN 0-8214-0873-9 (cl), 0-8214-0874-7 (pbk). ‣ History of Kikuyu who took up residence as laborers (squatters) on European-owned farmland, only to be evicted in 1940s. Their struggle contributed significantly to Mau Mau Rebellion (1952–56). [DMA]

19.491 Dane Kennedy. *Islands of white: settler society and culture in Kenya and Southern Rhodesia, 1890–1939.* Durham, N.C.: Duke University Press, 1987. ISBN 0-8223-0708-1. ‣ Comparative study of two British settler societies, dealing with social origins as well as cultural behavior on frontier. Unusual approach and good reading. [DMA]

19.492 Jomo Kenyatta. *Facing Mount Kenya: the tribal life of the Gikuyu.* 1953 ed. B. Malinowski, Introduction. New York: AMS, 1978. ISBN 0-404-14676-7. ‣ Important statement on Kikuyu ethnography. Written in 1938 by man who was to be first president of independent Kenya. Offers historical insights on himself. [DMA]

19.493 Isaria N. Kimambo. *Penetration and protest in Tanzania: the impact of the world economy on the Pare, 1860–1960.* Athens: Ohio University Press, 1991. ISBN 0-8214-0967-0 (cl), 0-8214-0997-2 (pbk). ‣ Examination of impact of colonial capital on Pare Hills region, stressing reaction of peasantry to enforced rural change. Treatment of post-1945 development projects especially useful. [DMA/TTS]

19.494 B. E. Kipkorir, ed. *Biographical essays on imperialism and collaboration in colonial Kenya.* Nairobi: Kenya Literature Bureau, 1980. ‣ Eight biographical essays exploring ambiguities of collaboration and resistance in colonial context. Valuable studies of controversial individuals—three Europeans, five Africans. [DMA]

19.495 Gavin Kitching. *Class and economic change in Kenya: the making of an African petite bourgeoisie, 1905–1970.* New Haven: Yale University Press, 1980. ISBN 0-300-02385-5. ‣ Award-winning study of rural social and economic differentiation, with emphasis on importance of changes in agricultural production. Combines theoretical skill with empirical rigor. Highly recommended. [DMA]

19.496 John Lamphear. *The scattering time: Turkana responses to colonial rule.* Oxford: Clarendon, 1992. ISBN 0-19-820226-1. ‣ Comprehensive study of Turkana armed resistance to conquest, 1890s to 1920s, with military history theme, in which leadership of diviner Loolel Kokoi features prominently. Effective use of oral sources. [DMA]

19.497 René Lemarchand. *Rwanda and Burundi.* New York: Praeger, 1970. ‣ Historical survey, mostly devoted to 1960s. Powerfully written; reflects author's outrage at ethnic conflicts and political genocide. [DMA]

19.498 Colin Leys. *Underdevelopment in Kenya: the political economy of neo-colonialism, 1964–71.* Berkeley: University of California Press, 1975. ISBN 0-520-02741-0 (cl), 0-520-02770-1 (pbk). ‣ Modern history viewed in light of underdevelopment theory. One of most important books on modern Kenya, but gives too little attention to internal dynamics of social change. [DMA]

19.499 Ian Linden and Jane Linden. *Church and revolution in Rwanda.* Manchester: Manchester University Press, 1977. ISBN 0-7190-0671-6. ‣ Study of influence of Catholic church (White Fathers) on political relations between Tutsi and Hutu, nineteenth century to independence. Thorough, complex book based on close reading of primary sources. [DMA]

19.500 Michael F. Lofchie. *Zanzibar: background to revolution.* Princeton: Princeton University Press, 1965. ‣ Detailed study of political history of Zanzibar Revolution, written very close to events. [DMA]

19.501 John M. Lonsdale. "Mau Maus of the mind: making Mau Mau and remaking Kenya." *Journal of African history* 31.3 (1990) 393–422. ISSN 0021-8537. ‣ Critical survey of meanings given to and interpretations of Mau Mau. Shatters many stereotypes and challenges easy assumptions. Most important essay on Mau Mau in print. [DMA]

19.502 Wm. Roger Louis. *Ruanda-Urundi, 1884–1919.* 1963 ed. Westport, Conn.: Greenwood, 1979. ISBN 0-313-20905-7. ‣ Diplomatic history of dispute between Germany, Britain, and Bel-

gian Congo State over control of Ruanda-Urundi. Important for history of European partition of region. [DMA]

19.503 Donald Anthony Low. *Buganda in modern history.* Berkeley: University of California Press, 1971. ISBN 0-520-01640-8. ‣ Remains best introduction to impact of imperialism and colonialism on politics of kingdom of Buganda. [DMA]

19.504 Donald Anthony Low and R. Cranford Pratt. *Buganda and British overrule, 1900–1955: two studies.* 1960 ed. Nairobi: Oxford University Press for Makerere Institute of Social Research, 1970. ‣ Low's contribution on Uganda Agreement is seminal work on topic. Pratt deals with politics, 1900 to Kabaka crisis (1953–55). Still remarkably useful volume. [DMA]

19.505 Donald Anthony Low and Alison Smith, eds. *History of East Africa.* Vol. 3. Oxford: Clarendon, 1976. ISBN 0-19-821680-7. ‣ General history of colonialism's last phase (1945–65), organized by territory and dealing mainly with political and economic themes. Additional chapters on immigrant communities, Christianity, and social change. Introduction especially useful. See Oliver and Mathew, eds. 19.411 and Harlow and Chilver, eds. 19.484 for volumes 1 and 2. [DMA]

19.506 G. Andrew Maguire. *Toward "Uhuru" in Tanzania: the politics of participation.* London: Cambridge University Press, 1969. ISBN 0-521-07652-8. ‣ Examination of rise of African politics in Sukumaland, 1940s to independence. One of best books on local mobilization of politics in nationalist era. [DMA]

19.507 J. S. Mangat. *A history of the Asians in East Africa, c. 1886–1945.* Oxford: Clarendon, 1969. ISBN 0-19-821647-5. ‣ Although based on relatively narrow range of documentary sources, still best general history of economically important Asian immigrant community. [DMA]

19.508 Ali A. Mazrui. *Soldiers and kinsmen in Uganda: the making of a military ethnocracy.* Beverly Hills, Calif.: Sage, 1975. ISBN 0-8039-0427-4. ‣ Important study of rise of military rule in Uganda, written in midst of Idi Amin's reign of terror. Scholarly and informative. [DMA]

19.509 Sally Falk Moore. *Social facts and fabrications: "customary" law on Kilimanjaro, 1880–1980.* Cambridge: Cambridge University Press, 1986. ISBN 0-521-30938-7 (cl), 0-521-31201-9 (pbk). ‣ Anthropological account of formation of African customary law during colonial period among Chagga. Crucial for social and legal change. [DMA]

19.510 H. F. Morris and James S. Read. *Indirect rule and the search for justice: essays in East African legal history.* Oxford: Clarendon, 1972. ISBN 0-19-821675-0. ‣ Essays on implementation of colonial legal system and its interaction with African customary law to 1939. Remains most important work on East African legal history, despite whiggish overtones. [DMA]

19.511 G. H. Mungeam. *British rule in Kenya, 1895–1912: the establishment of administration in the East Africa Protectorate.* Oxford: Clarendon, 1966. ‣ Now rather dated but still authoritative work on administrative conquest of Kenya, seen from colonial record. Emphasizes power of man-on-the-spot to dictate colonial policy. [DMA]

19.512 J. Forbes Munro. *Colonial rule and the Kamba: social change in the Kenya highlands, 1889–1939.* Oxford: Clarendon, 1975. ISBN 0-19-821-699-8. ‣ Meticulous local history of colonial impact in central Kenya, combining oral and archival sources. Important in marking shift in Kenyan historiography away from political themes and toward social history. [DMA]

19.513 Jeremy Murray-Brown. *Kenyatta.* 2d ed. London: Allen & Unwin, 1979. ISBN 0-04-920059-3. ‣ Best available biography of Jomo Kenyatta, Kenya's first president, up to first decade of his presidency. Sympathetic yet also critical. [DMA]

19.514 Catharine Newbury. *The cohesion of oppression: clientship and ethnicity in Rwanda, 1860–1960.* New York: Columbia University Press, 1988. ISBN 0-231-06256-7. ‣ Substantial revisionary social and political history focusing on transformations in social relations in southwestern Rwanda. One of best works on Rwanda available in English. [DMA]

19.515 Malyn Newitt. *The Comoro Islands: struggle against dependency in the Indian Ocean.* Boulder: Westview, 1984. ISBN 0-86531-292-3. ‣ Standard introduction to Comoro history concentrating on difficulties of developing modern state. Footnotes provide guide to basic sources. [DMA/CHA]

19.516 Bethwell A. Ogot, ed. *Politics and nationalism in colonial Kenya.* Nairobi: East African Publishing House for Historical Association of Kenya, 1972. (Hadith, 4.) ‣ First selection of critical essays to examine idea of Kenyan nationalism, edited by Kenya's most distinguished historian. Richly varied contributions. [DMA]

19.517 Roland Oliver. *The missionary factor in East Africa.* 1965 2d ed. London: Longman, 1970. ‣ First scholarly work on Christian missions in East Africa. Now rather dated, but still only work to relate metropolitan developments with events in mission field. [DMA]

19.518 R. Cranford Pratt. *The critical phase in Tanzania, 1945–1968: Nyerere and the emergence of a socialist strategy.* Cambridge: Cambridge University Press, 1976. ISBN 0-521-20824-6. ‣ Combines biography of Julius Kambarage Nyerere with broader contemporary political history. Two aims sometimes at odds, but valuable for discussion of links between socialism and nationalism. [DMA]

19.519 Terence O. Ranger. *Dance and society in eastern Africa, 1890–1970: the Beni Ngoma.* Berkeley: University of California Press, 1975. ISBN 0-520-02799-9. ‣ Pioneering study in African social history stressing role of dance groups as focus for ethnic and social cohesion. Imaginative use of sources. [DMA]

19.520 Audrey I. Richards. *East African chiefs: a study of political development in some Ugandan and Tanganyika tribes.* 1959 ed. New York: Praeger, 1960. ‣ Political biographies of African chiefs from Uganda and Northwest Tanganyika, set within context of indirect rule and development of government. [DMA]

19.521 Carl G. Rosberg, Jr., and John Nottingham. *The myth of "Mau Mau": nationalism in Kenya.* 1966 ed. Stanford, Calif.: Hoover Institution on War, Revolution, and Peace, 1975. ‣ Pioneering study of Mau Mau Rebellion (1952–59) by an academic and former colonial administrator. Basic conclusions remain largely unchallenged, despite much subsequent work on topic. Still essential reading. [DMA]

19.522 Ahmed I. Salim. *The Swahili-speaking peoples of Kenya's coast, 1895–1965.* Nairobi: East African Publishing House, 1973. ‣ Political history of Kenya's coastal region. Weak on socioeconomic background, but good coverage of ethnic political mobilization between 1918 and 1939 and Swahili activities during nationalist phase. [DMA]

19.523 Issa G. Shivji. *Law, state, and the working class in Tanzania, c. 1920–1964.* Portsmouth, N.H.: Heinemann, 1986. ISBN 0-435-08013-X (pbk). ‣ Examines development of industrial relations and labor law within Marxist framework. Treatment of evidence sometimes wayward, but many valuable analytical insights. [DMA]

19.524 Makhan Singh. *Kenya's trade unions, 1952–56.* Bethwell A. Ogot, ed. Nairobi: Uzima, 1980. ‣ Second of two volumes by leading trade union activist, this dealing with Mau Mau period. Posthumously published, it is virtually a primary source, with extensive extracts from documents. Much valuable detail. [DMA]

19.525 M.P.K. Sorrenson. *Land reform in the Kikuyu country: a study of government policy.* Nairobi: Oxford University Press for East African Institute of Social Research, 1967. ‣ Examination of implementation of colonial land-use and resettlement policies in central Kenya during and after Mau Mau Emergency. Detail sometimes daunting, but indispensable work. [DMA]

19.526 John Spencer. *The Kenya African Union.* London: Kegan Paul International, 1985. ISBN 0-7103-0100-6. ‣ Only available history of Kenya's most important pre–Mau Mau political party. Vivid portraits of personalities and keen analysis of motive, informed by wide-ranging interviews with participants. [DMA]

19.527 Sharon Stichter. *Migrant labour in Kenya: capitalism and African response, 1895–1975.* Harlow, England: Longman, 1982. ISBN 0-582-64326-0. ‣ Labor history viewed within dependency framework, but with detailed coverage of evolution of Kenya's migrant labor system. Good general survey. [DMA]

19.528 Robert W. Strayer. *The making of mission communities in East Africa: Anglicans and Africans in colonial Kenya, 1875–1935.* Albany: State University of New York Press, 1978. ISBN 0-873952-45-6. ‣ Essays on history of Church Missionary Society in Kenya, based on mission archives. Includes important chapter (with Jocelyn Murray) on Kikuyu female circumcision crisis. [DMA]

19.529 Nicola Swainson. *The development of corporate capitalism in Kenya, 1918–1977.* 1979 ed. Berkeley: University of California Press, 1980. ISBN 0-520-03988-2 (cl), 0-520-04019-8 (pbk). ‣ Best available empirical study of emergence of corporate capital. Weak on specifics of colonial policy toward industrialization, but still very valuable. [DMA]

19.530 David W. Throup. *Economic and social origins of Mau Mau, 1945–53.* Athens: Ohio University Press, 1988. ISBN 0-8214-0883-6 (cl), 0-8214-0884-4 (pbk). ‣ Comprehensive study of causes of Mau Mau Rebellion focusing on impact of colonial policies on African politics. Updates earlier work with substantial documentation. [DMA]

19.531 Meredeth Turshen. *Political ecology of disease in Tanzania.* New Brunswick, N.J.: Rutgers University Press, 1984. ISBN 0-8135-1030-9. ‣ Sets history of disease and public health in political economy analysis of colonial rule in Tanzania. [MJH]

19.532 G. N. Uzoigwe, ed. *Uganda: the dilemma of nationhood.* New York: NOK Publications International, 1982. ISBN 0-88357-038-6. ‣ Polemical study of creation of modern Ugandan state examining themes of nation-building, neocolonialism, and politics. [DMA]

19.533 Roger M. A. Van Zwanenberg and Anne King. *An economic history of Kenya and Uganda, 1800–1970.* London: Macmillan, 1975. ISBN 0-333-17671-5. ‣ General introductory economic history giving weight to production as well as exchange and to themes of demography, agricultural change, and social differentiation. Aimed at student readership. [DMA]

19.534 Gary Wasserman. *Politics of decolonization: Kenya Europeans and the land issue, 1960–65.* Cambridge: Cambridge University Press, 1976. ISBN 0-521-20838-6. ‣ Comprehensive study of bargaining over fate of European-owned farmland in politics of decolonization and implementation of settlement scheme. Based on primary sources. Important study. [DMA]

19.535 Frederick Burkewood Welbourn. *Religion and politics in Uganda, 1952–62.* Nairobi: East African Publishing House, 1965. ‣ Episodic, but useful early statement on importance of religion in determining political affiliations in last phase of colonialism in Uganda. [DMA]

19.536 Luise White. *The comforts of home: prostitution in colonial Nairobi.* Chicago: Chicago University Press, 1990. ISBN 0-226-

89506-8 (cl), 0-226-89507-6 (pbk). ▸ Presents prostitution as element of labor history. Contains much incidental material on general history of Nairobi. Key text on social history and gender studies. [DMA]

19.537 Audrey Wipper. *Rural rebels: a study of two protest movements in Kenya.* Nairobi: Oxford University Press, 1977. ISBN 0-19-572430-5 (cl), 0-19-572387-2 (pbk). ▸ Portraits of two anticolonial protest movements, Mumbo (among Gusii) and Diniya-Msambwa (among Luyia and Pokot), both involving cults of spirit possession and prophecy. Still useful, although interpretation now dated. [DMA]

19.538 Marcia Wright. *German missions in Tanganyika, 1891–1941: Lutherans and Moravians in the southern highlands.* Oxford: Clarendon, 1971. ISBN 0-19-821665-3. ▸ Pioneering study of German mission activity under both German and British administration. Only account of topic available in English. [DMA]

19.539 C. C. Wrigley. *Crops and wealth in Uganda: a short agrarian history.* 2d ed. Nairobi: Oxford University Press, 1970. ▸ Economic history of agricultural production in Uganda, written with splendid clarity and offering good blend of empiricism and analysis. Essential reading. [DMA]

CENTRAL AFRICA

To ca. 1850

19.540 David Birmingham. "Early African trade in Angola and its hinterland." In *Pre-colonial African trade: essays on trade in central and eastern Africa before 1900.* Richard Gray and David Birmingham, eds., pp. 163–74. London: Oxford University Press, 1970. ISBN 0-19-215639-X. ▸ Preliminary study emphasizing African commercial acumen in context of better-known European Atlantic system. Uses early documentation to relate inter-African trade patterns to European penetration. [JKT]

19.541 David Birmingham. "Society and economy before A.D. 1400." In *History of Central Africa.* David Birmingham and Phyllis M. Martin, eds., vol. 1, pp. 1–29. London: Longman, 1983. ISBN 0-582-64673-1 (cl), 0-582-64674-X (pbk). ▸ Study of ecological and material conditions from archaeological evidence. Treats early migrations and development of state systems with special focus on both interregional and local trade as resources for political development. [JKT]

19.542 David Birmingham. *Trade and conflict in Angola: the Mbundu and their neighbours under the influence of the Portuguese, 1483–1790.* Oxford: Clarendon, 1966. ▸ Social structure and early history of Kongo and Ndongo, Portuguese invasion of Angola, African reactions, and development of slave trade; early attempt to integrate oral tradition and documents around trade-driven Africanist approach. [JKT]

19.543 François Bontinck. "Un mausolée pour les Jaga." *Cahiers d'études africaines* 20.3 (1980) 387–89. ISSN 0008-0055. ▸ Supports Miller in debate on Jaga (19.561 and 19.563) by noting that new Kongo royal dynasty, of dubious legitimacy, might have sought Portuguese support by labeling domestic rebels as cannibal invaders. See also Thornton 19.574 and Hilton 19.555. [JKT]

19.544 António Brásio. *Monumenta missionaria africana.* 15 vols. Lisbon: Agência Geral do Ultramar, Divisão de Publicaçoes e Biblioteca, 1952–88. ▸ Large, basic collection of primary sources, all in original language but with partially modernized orthography. Focuses mostly on shorter documents, with brief summaries and occasional critical notes. [JKT]

19.545 Susan H. Broadhead. "Beyond decline: the kingdom of Kongo in the eighteenth and nineteenth centuries." *International journal of African historical studies* 12.4 (1979) 615–50. ISSN 0361-7882. ▸ Best treatment of generally neglected eighteenth- and

early nineteenth-century period; Kongo society, political factions, local Catholic church, and noble title associations after civil wars. [JKT]

19.546 Dennis D. Cordell. "The savanna belt of North-Central Africa." In *History of Central Africa.* David Birmingham and Phyllis M. Martin, eds., vol. 1, pp. 30–74. London: Longman, 1983. ISBN 0-582-64673-1 (cl), 0-582-64674-X (pbk). ▸ Three-stage approach to history of region: ecology, settlement of ethnic groups, and external trade north through Muslim states and south to Atlantic. Concludes with intensified late eighteenth-century Muslim penetration from north. [JKT]

19.547 Kajsa Ekholm. *Power and prestige: the rise and fall of the old Kongo kingdom.* Uppsala: Skriv Service AB, 1972. ▸ Study of Kongo social and economic structures, 1400–1800, with anthropological emphasis on kinship politics to explain factionalism and eventually seventeenth-century civil wars. Focus on theoretical issues more than on documentary support for thesis. [JKT]

19.548 Brian M. Fagan. "Early trade and raw materials in South Central Africa." In *Pre-colonial African trade: essays on trade in central and eastern Africa before 1900.* Richard Gray and David Birmingham, eds., pp. 24–38. London: Oxford University Press, 1970. ISBN 0-19-215639-X. ▸ Use of archaeological data to show items traded over long distances from early centuries CE. Correlates trade with political centralization. [JKT]

19.549 António Custódio Gonçalves. *Le lignage contre l'état: dynamique politique Kongo du seizième au dix-septième siècle.* Lisbon: Universidade de Evora, 1985. ▸ Study using anthropological kinship-based model of pre-1500 Kongo political structure, similar to Ekholm 19.547. Concludes seventeenth-century foreign trade strengthened nonlineage leaders, but elders reemerged with new ideology in eighteenth century. [JKT]

19.550 Richard Gray and David Birmingham. "Some economic and political consequences of trade in central and eastern Africa in the pre-colonial period." In *Pre-colonial African trade: essays on trade in central and eastern Africa before 1900.* Richard Gray and David Birmingham, eds., pp. 1–23. London: Oxford University Press, 1970. ISBN 0-19-215639-X. ▸ Introductory overview emphasizing long-distance trade as stimulus to political centralization, both in formation of African states and in interactions among them. [JKT]

19.551 Richard Gray and David Birmingham, eds. *Pre-colonial African trade: essays on trade in central and eastern Africa before 1900.* London: Oxford University Press, 1970. ISBN 0-19-215639-X. ▸ Pioneering essays documenting trade in Central Africa, with emphasis on monopolization by political leaders. Larger volume of commerce from overseas intensified centralization of power. See Birmingham 19.542, Fagan 19.548, Gray and Birmingham 19.550, and Martin 19.558. [JKT]

19.552 Robert W. Harms. *River of wealth, river of sorrow: the central Zaire basin in the era of the slave and ivory trade, 1500–1891.* New Haven: Yale University Press, 1981. ISBN 0-300-02616-1. ▸ Contrasts untransformed inland societies with transformed riverine society using nineteenth- and twentieth-century data to identify competitive forces, increased use of slaves, and attempts at enlargement of political scale. [JKT/DAN]

19.553 Beatrix Heintze. "Written sources, oral traditions, and oral traditions as written sources: the steep and thorny way to early Angolan history." *Paideuma* 33 (1987) 263–88. ISSN 0078-7809. ▸ Comparison of various written versions of oral traditions for sixteenth-century Ndongo state in Angola to distinguish differences among texts owing to perspectives of European authors and to variation among informants. [JKT]

19.554 Anne Hilton. "European sources for the study of religious change in sixteenth- and seventeenth-century Kongo."

Paideuma 33 (1987) 289–312. ISSN 0078-7809. ▸ Analysis of prejudices evident in reports of European missionaries to Kongo which limit historians' abilities to reconstruct religious history. But finds it possible to confirm argument (Hilton 19.556) that Kongo religion changed to support monarchy. [JKT]

19.555 Anne Hilton. "The Jaga reconsidered." *Journal of African history* 22.2 (1981) 191–202. ISSN 0021-8537. ▸ Study of development of palm-cloth trade from eastern Kongo and wars in area set off by invasion of Jaga, identified as people from east. Intervention in debate among Miller 19.561, 19.563, Thornton 19.574, and Bontinck 19.543. [JKT]

19.556 Anne Hilton. *The Kingdom of Kongo.* Oxford: Clarendon, 1985. ISBN 0-19-822719-1. ▸ Political and social history, 1500–1700, with extensive discussion of religious change. Finds external trade promoted centralization and, through christianization, focused religious system on monarchy but also prompted regional reactions. [JKT]

19.557 Mutumba Mainga. *Bulozi under the Luyana kings: political evolution and state formation in pre-colonial Zambia.* London: Longman, 1973. ISBN 0-582-64073-3 (cl), 0-582-64088-1 (pbk). ▸ Social and economic structures and chronicle-style political history of Lozi state in western Zambia to Kololo conquest (1830s). Based largely on literal interpretation of Lozi oral traditions. [JKT/TTS]

19.558 Phyllis M. Martin. "The trade of Loango in the seventeenth and eighteenth centuries." In *Pre-colonial African trade: essays on trade in central and eastern Africa before 1900.* Richard Gray and David Birmingham, eds., pp. 139–62. London: Oxford University Press, 1970. ISBN 0-19-215639-X. ▸ Concludes merchants of Loango state (coast north of Zaire River mouth) reorganized to supply external trade from seventeenth to eighteenth centuries; preview and summary of arguments developed in Martin 19.913. [JKT]

19.559 Joseph C. Miller. *Kings and kinsmen: early Mbundu states in Angola.* Oxford: Clarendon, 1976. ISBN 0-19-822704-3. ▸ Pioneering nonliteral reading of oral traditions against documentary sources. Focuses on Imbangala mercenary warriors, whose assaults on older Mbundu kingdoms after 1575 blended with Portuguese invasion of Angola. [JKT]

19.560 Joseph C. Miller. "The paradoxes of impoverishment in the Atlantic zone." In *History of Central Africa.* David Birmingham and Phyllis M. Martin, eds., vol. 1, pp. 118–59. London: Longman, 1983. ISBN 0-582-64673-1 (cl), 0-582-64674-X (pbk). ▸ General introduction using droughts to frame social changes stimulated by African elites who initially took advantage of Portuguese commerce. Concludes slave trading eventually created other more destructive tendencies and impoverishment. [JKT]

19.561 Joseph C. Miller. "Requiem for the Jaga." *Cahiers d'études africaines* 13.1 (1973) 121–49. ISSN 0008-0055. ▸ Origin of debate concerning origin and impact of Jaga, rootless warriors said to have invaded Kongo in 1568. Argues invasion was domestic rebellion and Portuguese officials used it to justify intervention in dynastic politics (cf. Thornton 19.574, Miller 19.563, Hilton 19.555, and Bontinck 19.543). [JKT]

19.562 Joseph C. Miller. "The significance of drought, disease, and famine in the agriculturally marginal zones of West-Central Africa." *Journal of African history* 23.1 (1982) 17–61. ISSN 0021-8537. ▸ Summarizes documentation on climate and disease history of Angola, ca. 1560s to 1830, and links episodes of drought, famine, and disease to wars and slave trading in region. [JKT/DPH]

19.563 Joseph C. Miller. "Thanatopsis." *Cahiers d'études africaines* 18.2 (1978) 223–31. ISSN 0008-0055. ▸ Reply to Thornton 19.574; argues Thornton's analysis of 1568 Jaga invasion of

Kongo does not eliminate possibilities raised earlier (19.561) and warns against literal use of secondhand source material. [JKT]

19.564 Joseph C. Miller and John K. Thornton. "The chronicle as source, history, and hagiography: the Catálogo dos Governadores de Angola." *Paideuma* 33 (1987) 359–90. ISSN 0078-7809. ▸ Identifies military service records of locally born Portuguese Angolans as sources for well-known chronicle of Portuguese conquest. Chronicle defends military prowess in era of commercial domination from Portugal and Brazil. [JKT]

19.565 Thomas Q. Reefe. *The rainbow and the kings: a history of the Luba empire to 1891.* Berkeley: University of California Press, 1981. ISBN 0-520-04140-2. ▸ Combines oral traditions of Luba people (southern Zaire) with documentary evidence ca. 1880 to reconstruct political history, ca. 1600 to beginning of colonial period. Valuable demonstration of limitations of oral tradition for historical purposes. [JKT]

19.566 Thomas Q. Reefe. "The societies of the eastern savanna." In *History of Central Africa.* David Birmingham and Phyllis M. Martin, eds., vol. 1, pp. 160–204. London: Longman, 1983. ISBN 0-582-64673-1 (cl), 0-582-64674-X (pbk). ▸ Uses anthropology to hypothesize older social patterns and draws on oral sources to build political history of major states. Finds rich ecology and rivers facilitated production and transport and enabled early consolidation of political authority. [JKT]

19.567 Andrew D. Roberts. *A history of the Bemba: political growth and change in north-eastern Zambia before 1900.* Madison: University of Wisconsin Press, 1973. ISBN 0-299-06450-6. ▸ Uses oral tradition and written documentation to reconstruct history of multiple, small Bemba states and trading activity, particularly in nineteenth century. Revises earlier ideas of single, large Bemba empire. [JKT/TTS]

19.568 John K. Thornton. "The art of war in Angola, 1575–1680." *Comparative studies in society and history* 30.2 (1988) 360–78. ISSN 0010-4175. ▸ Reconstructs armaments, tactics, and logistics of tightly organized, professional, sixteenth-century African armies. Argues Portuguese invaders adapted African art of war and European arms were marginal factors. [JKT]

19.569 John K. Thornton. "The correspondence of the Kongo kings, 1614–35: problems of internal written evidence on a Central African kingdom." *Paideuma* 33 (1987) 407–22. ISSN 0078-7809. ▸ African documents reveal perspectives different from those of European sources, but finds kings' political situation with respect to nature of Kongo kingship more influential than nationality. [JKT]

19.570 John K. Thornton. "Demography and history in the kingdom of Kongo, 1550–1750." *Journal of African history* 18.4 (1977) 507–30. ISSN 0021-8537. ▸ Pioneering attempt to develop quantitative data from missionary baptismal records to reconstruct demography of Kongo. Contends, against previous assumptions, that Kongo population did not decline precipitously during slave trade and civil wars. [JKT]

19.571 John K. Thornton. "The development of an African Catholic church in the kingdom of Kongo, 1491–1750." *Journal of African history* 25.1 (1984) 147–67. ISSN 0021-8537. ▸ Christianity was widely accepted, elite staved off Portuguese attempts to exert political control through church, and financial need kept church dependent on state. Nineteenth-century missionary rejection of Kongo Christianity concealed these facts, evident from original documents. [JKT]

19.572 John K. Thornton. "The kingdom of Kongo, ca. 1390–1678: the development of an African social formation." *Cahiers d'études africaines* 22.3–4 (1982) 325–42. ISSN 0008-0055. ▸ Marxist periodization for African state in terms of alterations in primary mode of production. Oral sources show traditionally defined periods matched those based on analysis of social formation. [JKT]

19.573 John K. Thornton. *The kingdom of Kongo: civil war and transition, 1641–1718.* Madison: University of Wisconsin Press, 1983. ISBN 0-299-09290-9. ▸ Wealth concentrated in capital was key to centralization in Kongo; civil wars after 1665 over royal succession destroyed the city, making restoration of monarchy after 1718 possible only on basis of less centralized, unstable rural politics. [JKT]

19.574 John K. Thornton. "A resurrection for the Jaga." *Cahiers d'études africaines* 18.2 (1978) 223–28. ISSN 0008-0055. ▸ Reassesses Miller 19.561 concerning origins of Jaga invaders of Kongo state; identifies Jagas as Yaka coming from east and proposes likely origin in Kwango basin. See also Miller 19.563. [JKT]

19.575 John K. Thornton. "The slave trade in eighteenth-century Angola: effects on demographic structures." *Canadian journal of African studies* 14.3 (1980) 417–27. ISSN 0008-3968. ▸ Analysis of unique 1777–78 Portuguese census showing losses of young adult males to slave trade, unbalanced sex ratios among adults, but insignificant reduction in fertility. Slave trade altered structure of population, not its size. [JKT]

19.576 Jan Vansina. *The children of Woot: a history of the Kuba peoples.* Madison: University of Wisconsin Press, 1978. ISBN 0-299-07490-0. ▸ Use of ethnographic data and less literal use of oral traditions (see Vansina 19.577 and Miller 19.559) to reconstruct history of Kuba kingdom (southwest Zaire), 1500 to late nineteenth century. Focus on development of authority and interregional conflict. [JKT/PMM]

19.577 Jan Vansina. *Kingdoms of the savanna.* Madison: University of Wisconsin Press, 1966. ISBN 0-299-03660-X (cl), 0-299-03664-2 (pbk). ▸ Seminal synthesis of documents, comparative ethnography, and oral traditions from Angola to Malawi to reconstruct history of larger states, 1500–1900. Overly literal use of oral data leaves detailed conclusions somewhat open to question. [JKT]

19.578 Jan Vansina. *Paths in the rainforests: toward a history of political tradition in Equatorial Africa.* Madison: University of Wisconsin Press, 1990. ISBN 0-299-12570-X (cl), 0-299-12574-2 (pbk). ▸ Study of ancient Bantu culture through innovative linguistic method in small-scale commercial societies and small early states. External trade promoted political centralization after 1500, but basic patterns eroded only after late nineteenth-century colonial conquest. [JKT]

19.579 Jan Vansina. "The peoples of the forest." In *History of Central Africa.* David Birmingham and Phyllis M. Martin, eds., vol. 1, pp. 75–117. London: Longman, 1983. ISBN 0-582-64673-1 (cl), 0-582-64674-X (pbk). ▸ Forest ecology conditioned social development from small-scale organizations through trading societies organized by "big men" and early states. Summary of evidence and argument in Vansina 19.578. [JKT]

19.580 Jean-Luc Vellut. "Notes sur le Lunda et la frontière luso-africaine." *Études d'histoire africaine* 3 (1972) 61–166. ISSN 0071-1993. ▸ Discussion of Lunda empire, early eighteenth-century state in southern Zaire that expanded toward Portuguese trade from west, incorporated intermediate peoples of eastern Angola, and stimulated Cokwe traders and raiders to overthrow Lunda authority. [JKT]

Since ca. 1850

19.581 Roger T. Anstey. *King Leopold's legacy: the Congo under Belgian rule, 1908–1960.* London: Oxford University Press for Institute of Race Relations, 1966. ▸ Reviews colonial policy, emphasizing Belgian pragmatism; economic policy; close relations of church, state, and business; growth of towns; and pro-

phetic movements. Strong orientation to political rather than social history. [PMM]

19.582 Ralph A. Austen and Rita Headrick. "Equatorial Africa under colonial rule." In *History of Central Africa.* David Birmingham and Phyllis M. Martin, eds., vol. 2, pp. 27–94. London: Longman, 1983. ISBN 0-582-64675-8 (cl), 0-582-64676-6 (pbk). ▸ Comprehensive overview of French Equatorial Africa, with particular emphasis on economic and social history. Discusses weakness of French colonial state, demography, disease, colonial health policies, education, and new social formations. [PMM]

19.583 Georges Balandier. *Sociology of black Africa: social dynamics in Central Africa.* Douglas Garman, trans. London: Deutsch, 1970. ISBN 0-233-96121-6. ▸ Influential study for its analysis of precolonial social organization and belief systems, colonial rule, and African social and cultural adaptations; main focus on Gabon and Congo. Based on 1950s research. [PMM]

19.584 Sylvain Bemba. *Cinquante ans de musique du Congo-Zaire, 1920–1970: de Paul Kamba à Tabu-Ley.* Paris: Présence Africaine, 1984. ISBN 2-7087-0434-6. ▸ Authoritative cultural history of popular music in Congo and Zaire, focusing mainly on 1945–70 and covering Latin American influences, recording industry, and bands and singers. By leading Congolese intellectual, writing from experience. [PMM]

19.585 Gerald J. Bender. *Angola under the Portuguese: the myth and the reality.* Berkeley: University of California Press, 1978. ISBN 0-520-03221-7. ▸ Critical analysis of ideology of racial tolerance (lusotropicalism) that justified Portuguese rule in Angola over five centuries. Also examines late colonial white settlement and antiguerrilla strategies. [PMM]

19.586 David Birmingham and Phyllis M. Martin, eds. *History of Central Africa.* 2 vols. London: Longman, 1983. ISBN 0-582-64675-8 (cl), 0-582-64676-6 (pbk). ▸ Only comprehensive survey of Central Africa from Chad to Zimbabwe. Volume 2 (ca. 1900–80) takes up colonialism, capitalist penetration, African responses, class formation, urbanization, ethnicity, and religious and liberation movements. [PMM]

19.587 Edouard Bustin. *The Lunda under Belgian rule: the politics of ethnicity.* Cambridge, Mass.: Harvard University Press, 1975. ISBN 0-674-53953-2. ▸ Dynamics of precolonial Lunda (southern Zaire, Shaba Province) imperial ideology, tribute, international trade, and political integration. Discusses interaction of these structures with Belgian colonial administration and reinvention of ethnicity in nationalist politics. [PMM]

19.588 Martin Chanock. *Law, custom, and social order: the colonial experience in Malawi and Zambia.* Cambridge: Cambridge University Press, 1985. ISBN 0-521-30137-8. ▸ Study of codification and interpretation of customary law as invented by chiefs and white officials in British Central Africa to control social change (age and gender roles) brought by colonialism and capitalism. [PMM]

19.589 William Gervase Clarence-Smith. *Slaves, peasants, and capitalists in southern Angola, 1840–1926.* Cambridge: Cambridge University Press, 1979. ISBN 0-521-22406-3. ▸ Radical account of Portuguese colonialism, slavery, and social banditry and consequences of capitalism and world economy, including poor white settlement, labor migration, rural impoverishment, and development of peasant class. [PMM]

19.590 Catherine Coquery-Vidrovitch. "The colonial economy of the former French, Belgian, and Portuguese zones, 1914–35." In *Africa under colonial domination, 1880–1935.* A. Adu Boahen, ed., pp. 351–81. Berkeley: University of California Press, 1985. (General history of Africa: UNESCO International Scientific Committee for the Drafting of a General History of Africa, 7.) ISBN 0-520-03918-1. ▸ Survey of capitalist exploitation, from

World War I boom to Great Depression, by respected French economic historian. Comparative statistics on colonial investment, trade, taxation, and food production. [PMM]

19.591 Catherine Coquery-Vidrovitch. *Le Congo au temps des grandes compagnies concessionaires, 1898–1930.* Paris: Mouton, 1972. ▸ Defines early colonial rule in French Equatorial Africa as exploitation by some thirty concessionary companies, reliant on forced-labor policies and taxation. Discusses African responses. Rich economic data from colonial archives. [PMM]

19.592 Samuel Decalo. *Historical dictionary of Chad.* 2d ed. Metuchen N.J.: Scarecrow, 1987. (African historical dictionaries, 13.) ISBN 0-8108-1937-6. ▸ Useful reference work and bibliography for Francophone country with little literature in English. Entries on people, places, political parties, economic institutions; mainly recent history. [PMM]

19.593 Jill R. Dias. "Famine and disease in the history of Angola, c. 1830–1930." *Journal of African history* 22.3 (1981) 349–78. ISSN 0021-8537. ▸ Excellent analysis of climatic instability, especially rainfall, and relationship to food resources, famine, demography, and malnutrition-derived and contagious diseases. Resulting population weakness and malnutrition motivated revolts against Portuguese colonialism. [PMM]

19.594 Johannes Fabian. *Language and colonial power: the appropriation of Swahili in the former Belgian Congo, 1880–1938.* 1986 ed. Berkeley: University of California Press, 1991. ISBN 0-520-07625-7. ▸ Pioneering study of connections between colonial expansion and use of language to achieve power. Discussion of historical evolution of Swahili as means of communication for military, religious, ideological, and economic purposes. [PMM]

19.595 Johannes Fabian. "Popular culture in Africa: findings and conjectures." *Africa* 48.4 (1978) 315–34. ISSN 0001-9720. ▸ Early, influential definition of popular culture as secular and religious expressions of life experiences, usually pioneered by urban masses. Explores popular music, religion, and painting in Shaba province, Zaire. [PMM]

19.596 Bruce Fetter. *The creation of Elisabethville, 1910–1940.* Stanford, Calif.: Hoover Institution on War, Revolution, and Peace, 1976. (Hoover Institution publications, 155.) ISBN 0-8179-6551-3. ▸ Belgian colonial society and institutions in regional capital from viewpoint of European administrators and mining interests more than that of African workers. One of few accounts of urban Central Africa in English. [PMM]

19.597 Karen E. Fields. *Revival and rebellion in colonial Central Africa.* Princeton: Princeton University Press, 1985. ISBN 0-691-09409-8. ▸ Study of millennial Watchtower movement in British Central Africa. Transcends older interpretations of such religious movements as political rebellion or religious revival by focusing on context of mundane social relations and beliefs. [PMM]

19.598 David E. Gardinier. *Historical dictionary of Gabon.* Metuchen, N.J.: Scarecrow, 1981. (African historical dictionaries, 30.) ISBN 0-8108-1435-8. ▸ Excellent reference work and bibliography for Francophone country with few sources in English. Especially good for entries on political parties and leaders, churches, and education. [PMM]

19.599 Jane I. Guyer. "The food economy and French colonial rule in central Cameroun." *Journal of African history* 19.4 (1978) 177–97. ISSN 0021-8537. ▸ Case study of French colonial food policy in Cameroon, including forced requisitions, retardation of rural economic institutions, landowning class using political force, and disparities in rural wealth. Shows need for indigenous-oriented investment. [PMM]

19.600 Joseph Hanlon. *Beggar your neighbours: apartheid power in southern Africa.* Bloomington: Indiana University Press, 1986. ISBN 0-253-33131-5. ▸ Analysis of South Africa's efforts at de-

stablizing eight African nations, ca. 1975–85, to ensure internal security and regional economic and geopolitical dominance; responses of these states; and nationalist guerrilla struggles. [PMM]

19.601 Robert W. Harms. *Games against nature: an eco-cultural history of the Nunu of Equatorial Africa.* Cambridge: Cambridge University Press, 1987. ISBN 0-521-34373-9. ▸ Uses game theory, oral and colonial records, to reconstruct adaptation to changing environments by riverain peoples of Central African rain forests. Discusses adaptation to colonial rule. Innovative and readable. [PMM]

19.602 Franz-Wilhelm Heimer, ed. *Social change in Angola.* Munich: Weltforum, 1973. ISBN 3-8039-0075-1. ▸ Nine essays based on pioneering social science research, dealing with slave trade, Portuguese colonialism, education, ecology, peasant farming, urbanization, and nationalism. Only English-language collection on these subjects for twentieth-century Angola. [PMM]

19.603 Lawrence W. Henderson. *Angola: five centuries of conflict.* Ithaca, N.Y.: Cornell University Press, 1979. ISBN 0-8014-1247-1. ▸ Country survey dealing with human and natural resources, slave trade and transition to colonialism, missionaries, nationalism, and liberation struggle. Balanced treatment, especially of politically contentious recent past. [PMM]

19.604 John Higginson. *A working class in the making: Belgian colonial labor policy, private enterprise and the African mineworker, 1907–1951.* Madison: University of Wisconsin Press, 1991. ISBN 0-299-12070-8 (cl), 0-299-12074-0 (pbk). ▸ Roots of worker consciousness in Belgian Congo mining industry; associations, Watchtower movement, workplace resistance, and rural-urban linkages. Criticizes earlier structural analyses that neglect informal popular culture. [PMM]

19.605 Tony Hodges and Malyn Newitt. *Sao Tomé and Príncipe: from plantation colony to microstate.* Boulder: Westview, 1988. ISBN 0-8133-0380-X. ▸ Readable historical overview of little-known country emphasizing Portuguese colonialism, sugar and cocoa production, labor history, nationalism, and political change since independence, from Marxist authoritarianism to multiparty democracy. [PMM]

19.606 Bogumil Jewsiewicki. "La contestation sociale et la naissance du prolétaire au cours de la première moitié du vingtième siècle." *Canadian journal of African studies* 10.1 (1976) 47–70. ISSN 0008-3968. ▸ Early, influential article in urban social history relating African popular responses to colonialism in Belgian Congo to religious movements, emerging ethnicity, and working-class consciousness. [PMM]

19.607 Bogumil Jewsiewicki. "The Great Depression and the making of the colonial economic system in the Belgian Congo." *African economic history* 4 (1977) 153–76. ISSN 0145-2258. ▸ Classic core-periphery analysis, both within colony and in relation to world economy. Shows how Great Depression increased colonial domination of indigenous economies in Belgian Congo. [PMM]

19.608 Pierre Kalck. *Central African republic: a failure in de-colonisation.* Barbara Thomson, trans. New York: Praeger, 1971. ISBN 0-269-02801-3. ▸ Country survey emphasizing French colonial period (Ubangi-Shari-Chad), growth of African nationalism, political leaders, independence, and national politics. Largely political history, one of few accounts in English. [PMM]

19.609 S. E. Katzenellenbogen. *Railways and the copper mines of Katanga.* Oxford: Clarendon, 1973. ISBN 0-19-821676-9. ▸ International business interaction with British, Belgian, Portuguese, German, French, and South African imperial interests, creating island of industrial development in Central Africa. Strong on personalities and politics. [PMM]

19.610 Ian Linden and Jane Linden. *Catholics, peasants, and*

Chewa resistance in Nyasaland, 1889–1939. Berkeley: University of California Press, 1974. ISBN 0-520-02500-8. ▸ Places Catholic mission church in context of indigenous belief systems, rural farming interests, and British colonial policies. Complements other mission histories that emphasize African educated elites. [PMM]

19.611 Maryinez Lyons. *The colonial disease: a social history of sleeping sickness in northern Zaire, 1900–1940*. Cambridge: Cambridge University Press, 1992. ISBN 0-521-40350-2. ▸ Study of disease in African society under colonial rule, including ecological crises, forced population movement, Belgian health policy, and economic priorities. Exemplary medical history by social historian. [PMM]

19.612 Elikia M'Bokolo. "French colonial policy in Equatorial Africa in the 1940s and the 1950s." In *Transfer of power in Africa: decolonization, 1940–1960*. Gifford Prosser and Wm. Roger Louis, eds., pp. 173–210. New Haven: Yale University Press, 1982. ISBN 0-300-02568-8. ▸ Discussion of interaction of local conditions and metropolitan policies in decolonization process, leading to national independence through alliance of African political elites and French administration rather than mass protest. [PMM]

19.613 Wyatt MacGaffey. *Religion and society in Central Africa: the BaKongo of Lower Zaire*. Chicago: University of Chicago Press, 1986. ISBN 0-226-50029-2 (cl), 0-226-50030-6 (pbk). ▸ Kongo religious history stressing social context and continuities of cosmology over five centuries; interaction with foreigners (slave trade, colonial rule); ritual, religious specialists, and Christianity and prophetic movements. Remarkable for time depth. [PMM]

19.614 Elias C. Mandala. *Work and control in a peasant economy: a history of the Lower Tchiri Valley in Malawi, 1859–1960*. Madison: University of Wisconsin Press, 1990. ISBN 0-299-12490-8 (cl), 0-299-12494-0 (pbk). ▸ Study of peasant communities struggling against colonial state to control labor. Considers human agency, local priorities, world market demands, and environmental constraints. Radical analysis emphasizing production forces. [PMM]

19.615 John A. Marcum. *The anatomy of an explosion, 1950–1962*. Vol. 1 of *The Angolan revolution*. Cambridge, Mass.: MIT Press, 1969. ▸ Detailed political origins of modern Angolan nationalism and clandestine formation of three major political parties under Portuguese dictatorship. Focuses on leadership and organization rather than popular roots of struggle. [PMM]

19.616 John A. Marcum. *Exile politics and guerrilla warfare, 1962–1976*. Vol. 2 of *The Angolan revolution*. Cambridge, Mass.: MIT Press, 1978. ▸ Classic, rural-based armed conflict against Portuguese by three liberation groups. Emphasizes political organization, economic issues, and internationalization of struggle within Africa and through cold war. [PMM]

19.617 Marvin D. Markowitz. *Cross and sword: the political role of Christian missions in the Belgian Congo, 1908–1960*. Stanford, Calif.: Stanford University for Hoover Institution on War, Revolution, and Peace, 1973. (Hoover Institution publications, 114.) ISBN 0-8179-1141-3. ▸ Mostly factual study of colonial state relations with Catholic and Protestant missions, especially education policy and formation of African clergy; voluntary associations and syncretic churches as African responses to domination. [PMM]

19.618 Phyllis M. Martin. "Colonialism, youth, and football in French Equatorial Africa." *International journal of the history of sport* 8.1 (1991) 56–71. ISSN 0264-9373. ▸ French introduction of football and its appropriation by urban Africans for their own purposes. Focuses on sport as arena for negotiating colonial experience. Represents growing field of social history. [PMM]

19.619 John McCracken. *Politics and Christianity in Malawi, 1875–1940: the impact of Livingstonia Mission in the northern province*. Cambridge: Cambridge University Press, 1977. ISBN 0-521-21444-0. ▸ Discussion of influence of Scottish missionaries and businessmen in development of artisanal class and educated African elite, labor migration to South Africa and consequent social differentiation, and growth of independent churches. [PMM]

19.620 David Newbury. *Kings and clans: Ijwi Island and the Lake Kivu Rift, 1780–1840*. Madison: University of Wisconsin Press, 1992. ISBN 0-299-12890-3 (cl), 0-299-12894-6 (pbk). ▸ Innovative approach to precolonial state formation focusing on dynamic social context for emerging kingship in Zaire-Rwanda borderlands. Treats relationship between ritual and royalty, changing clan identities, and political transformation. [PMM/TTS]

19.621 David Northrup. *Beyond the bend in the river: African labor in eastern Zaire, 1865–1940*. Athens: Ohio University, Center for International Studies, 1988. (Monographs in international studies: Africa series, 52.) ISBN 0-89680-151-9. ▸ Considers continuous disruption from coercive labor systems imposed by foreign powers, from nineteenth-century Arab entrepreneurs to Belgian colonial state and private capital. Limited emphasis on African context. [PMM]

19.622 Jane L. Parpart. *Labor and capital on the African copperbelt*. Philadelphia: Temple University Press, 1983. ISBN 0-87722-325-4. ▸ Radical analysis of African worker consciousness in midst of employer paternalism in Northern Rhodesian mining industry. Focus on unionization and industrial action rather than on popular roots of action. [PMM]

19.623 K. David Patterson. *The northern Gabon coast to 1875*. Oxford: Clarendon, 1975. ISBN 0-19-821696-3. ▸ Relations of African coastal populations with European and American traders, missionaries, and administrators, mainly nineteenth century. Examines political impact and African initiatives. [PMM]

19.624 Charles Perrings. *Black mineworkers in Central Africa: industrial strategies and the evolution of an African proletariat in the copperbelt, 1911–41*. New York: Africana, 1979. ISBN 0-8419-0462-6. ▸ Marxist rejection of previous liberal interpretations of mining industry in Belgian Congo and Northern Rhodesia in terms of precapitalist and capitalist modes of production. Critiques state and company policies, labor initiatives, and class formation. [PMM]

19.625 Gwyn Prins. *The hidden hippopotamus: reappraisal in African history, the early colonial experience in western Zambia*. Cambridge: Cambridge University Press, 1980. ISBN 0-521-22915-4. ▸ Rich historical reconstruction of African kingdom stressing economic strategies of production, distribution and exchange, cosmology, and ritual and royal power. Examines early interaction with British missionaries in this context. [PMM]

19.626 Terence O. Ranger and Isaria N. Kimambo, eds. *The historical study of African religion*. Berkeley: University of California Press, 1972. ISBN 0-520-02206-8. ▸ Landmark collection of essays placing African religion in historical context. Reconstructs early religious history through linguistic and archaeological analysis of cults. Also treats indigenous religion, Christianity, and Islam. [PMM]

19.627 Terence O. Ranger and John Weller, eds. *Themes in the Christian history of Central Africa*. Berkeley: University of California Press, 1975. ISBN 0-520-02536-9. ▸ Influential collection of essays moving away from Eurocentric mission history to study interaction of indigenous religion with Christianity. Integrates religion with social and political change in colonial and immediate postcolonial periods. [PMM]

19.628 Andrew D. Roberts. *A history of Zambia*. 1976 ed. New York: Africana, 1979. ISBN 0-8419-0291-7. ▸ Country study important for discussion of cultural continuity from Iron Age to disruptions of slave and ivory trades and British colonial conquest. Topics include settler agriculture, mining, independent churches, and political nationalism. [PMM/TTS]

19.629 Robert I. Rotberg. *The rise of nationalism in Central Africa: the making of Malawi and Zambia, 1873–1964.* Cambridge, Mass.: Harvard University Press for the Center for International Affairs, 1965. ISBN 0-674-77191-5. ▸ Classic nationalist historiography. Richly informative on political history, personalities, and interaction with colonial authorities; short on interpretation and African social context. [PMM]

19.630 William J. Samarin. *The black man's burden: African colonial labor on the Congo and Ubangi rivers, 1880–1900.* Boulder: Westview, 1989. ISBN 0-8133-7740-4. ▸ Study of early colonization of Equatorial Africa by agents of France and Léopold II. Examines how European capitalist and Christian work ethic influenced perceptions and management of African labor, based on linguistic evidence. [PMM]

19.631 Enid Schildkrout and Curtis A. Keim. *African reflections: art of northeastern Zaire.* Seattle: University of Washington Press, 1990. ISBN 0-295-96961-x (cl), 0-295-96962-8 (pbk). ▸ Stunningly illustrated exhibition catalog; important text puts art in context of cosmology, daily life, social and political institutions, and historical change since mid-nineteenth century. Relates European myths of Africa to museum collections. [PMM]

19.632 George Shepperson and Thomas Price. *Independent African: John Chilembwe and the origins, setting, and significance of the Nyasaland native rising of 1915.* 1958 ed. Edinburgh: Edinburgh University Press, 1987. ISBN 0-85224-540-8 (pbk). ▸ Striking, well-written story about mission-educated Africans, African American missionaries, millennarian ideas, oppressive British taxation and labor policies, and rebellion against colonial rule. Classic early work on African resistance. [PMM]

19.633 Ibrahim K. Sundiata. *Equatorial Guinea: colonialism, state terror, and the search for stability.* Boulder: Westview, 1990. ISBN 0-8133-0429-6. ▸ Historical overview of Fernando Póo (Bioko) and Río Muni, emphasizing twentieth century, economic development, ethnic division, migrant labor, and dictatorship. Accessible survey of little-known country. [PMM]

19.634 Robert Farris Thompson and Joseph Cornet. *The four moments of the sun: Kongo art in two worlds.* Washington, D.C.: National Gallery of Art, 1981. ISBN 0-89468-003-x. ▸ Beautifully illustrated exhibition catalog with important text placing Kongo pottery, textiles, architecture, and sculpture in historical context. Treats cosmology, law, and medicine dating back to sixteenth century. [PMM]

19.635 Virginia McLean Thompson and Richard Adloff. *The emerging states of French Equatorial Africa.* Stanford, Calif.: Stanford University Press, 1960. ▸ Encyclopedic account of late colonial period. Excellent reference for political institutions, judicial system, foreign relations, commerce, industry and transportation, education, social welfare, religion, and mass communication. [PMM]

19.636 Leroy Vail. "Ecology and history: the example of eastern Zambia." *Journal of southern African studies* 3.2 (1977) 129–155. ISSN 0305-7070. ▸ Early, influential discussion showing disastrous impact of South African capitalism and British colonial rule on regional ecology, soil erosion, and disease. Also treats game laws and gun control. Less emphasis on African strategies. [PMM]

19.637 Jan Vansina. *The Tio kingdom of the middle Congo, 1880–1892.* London: Oxford University Press for International African Institute, 1973. ISBN 0-19-724189-1. ▸ Comprehensive historical ethnography of society on eve of French colonial conquest. Detailed treatment of daily life, material culture, political and social institutions, cosmology, and local and international trade. [PMM]

19.638 Megan Vaughan. *The story of an African famine: gender and famine in twentieth-century Malawi.* Cambridge: Cambridge University Press, 1987. ISBN 0-521-32917-5. ▸ Pathbreaking agricultural and social history exploring multiple experiences of 1949 famine, including interconnections of climatic instability, failed colonial policies, demography, kinship strategies, and vulnerability of women and children. [PMM]

19.639 Brian Weinstein. *Éboué.* New York: Oxford University Press, 1972. ▸ Highly readable biography of black Guyanese French colonial officer who became governor-general of Equatorial Africa in de Gaulle's wartime administration. Éboué's career highlights ambiguities of black colonial elites. [PMM]

19.640 Brian Weinstein. *Gabon: nation-building on the Ogooué.* Cambridge, Mass.: MIT Press, 1966. ▸ Study of forging national identity in newly independent country through communications, education, ideology, government policy, and international relations. Mixture of scholarship and personal experience, written during optimistic phase of African nationalism. [PMM]

19.641 Douglas L. Wheeler and René Pélissier. *Angola.* 1971 ed. Westport, Conn.: Greenwood, 1978. ISBN 0-313-20011-4. ▸ Particularly useful for informed discussion of Portuguese background to colonial rule. Discusses harsh labor policies, coffee, oil, diamonds, elite nationalism through journalism, political parties, and organization of guerrilla warfare. [PMM]

19.642 M. Crawford Young. "The northern republics, 1960–1980." In *History of Central Africa.* David Birmingham and Phyllis M. Martin, eds., vol. 2, pp. 291–335. London: Longman, 1983. ISBN 0-582-64675-8 (cl), 0-582-64676-6 (pbk). ▸ Comparative overview of political differentiation, continued economic dependency, class formation, and new political ethnicity in Francophone republics during first two decades of independence, showing drift toward authoritarian rule. [PMM]

SOUTHERN AFRICA
Early Southern Africa

19.643 David N. Beach. *The Shona and Zimbabwe, 900–1850: an outline of Shona history.* New York: Holmes & Meier, 1980. ISBN 0-8419-0624-6. ▸ Precolonial political history of plateau between Zambezi and Limpopo rivers, based on Portuguese sources, oral traditions, and synthesis of archaeological findings. Also treats culture, economy, and speculations on everyday life. [RHE]

19.644 H.H.K. Bhila. *Trade and politics in a Shona kingdom: the Manyika and their African and Portuguese neighbours, 1575–1902.* Burnt Mill, England: Longman, 1982. ISBN 0-582-64354-6 (pbk). ▸ Study of gold-producing Manyika kingdom, its break away from Munhumutapa empire, and its relations with other African states and Portuguese at Sofala (see Elkiss 19.646). Dates market-oriented underdevelopment well before nineteenth century. [RHE]

19.645 David Birmingham and Shula Marks. "Southern Africa." In *The Cambridge history of Africa.* Roland Oliver, ed., vol. 3, pp. 567–620. Cambridge: Cambridge University Press, 1977. ISBN 0-521-20981-1 (v. 3). ▸ Overview of area of modern Zimbabwe, Mozambique, and South Africa before 1600, drawing on archaeological findings. Now dated but useful bibliography, bibliographic essay, and maps. [RHE]

19.646 T. H. Elkiss. *The quest for an African Eldorado: Sofala, southern Zambezia, and the Portuguese, 1500–1865.* Waltham, Mass.: Crossroads, 1981. ISBN 0-918456-41-x. ▸ Short, readable history of Portuguese entrepôt at Sofala, legendary for its alleged association with King Solomon's mines. Treats commercial and political relations with its African neighbors, chiefly from Portuguese sources. [RHE]

19.647   Richard Elphick. *Khoikhoi and the founding of white South Africa.* 2d ed. Johannesburg: Ravan, 1985. ISBN 0-86975-230-8 (pbk). ▸ Precolonial cattle-keeping Khoikhoi and relations with hunter-gatherer San. Socioeconomic analysis of subordination of both groups by Dutch at Cape of Good Hope, 1652–1715. Incorporates recent archaeological findings on precolonial era. [RHE]

19.648   Richard Elphick and Hermann Giliomee, eds. *The shaping of South African society, 1652–1840.* Rev. 2d ed. Middletown, Conn.: Wesleyan University Press, 1989. ISBN 0-8195-5209-7 (cl), 0-8195-6211-4 (pbk). ▸ Twelve specialists analyze legal, economic, and demographic history of Dutch (later British) colony at Cape of Good Hope for origins of South Africa's modern racial order. Deemphasizes religion and ideology (contra Gerstner 19.649); substantially updates earlier (1979) edition. [RHE]

19.649   Jonathan Neil Gerstner. *The thousand generation covenant: Dutch Reformed covenant theology and group identity in colonial South Africa, 1652–1814.* Leiden: Brill, 1991. ISBN 90-04-09361-3. ▸ Recent version of classic thesis attributing white exclusivism and domination in early South Africa to Calvinist Dutch Reformed theology. Ideological interpretation alternative to Elphick and Giliomee, eds. 19.648. [RHE]

19.650   Martin Hall. *The changing past: farmers, kings, and traders in southern Africa, 200–1860.* Cape Town: Philip, 1987. ISBN 0-86486-065-X. ▸ Ambitious synthesis of archaeological, written, and linguistic evidence on precolonial southern Africa. Indian Ocean commerce replaced agriculture and cattle as sources of power. Diagrams, photographs, sketches, sidebars, and extensive bibliography. [RHE]

19.651   Raymond K. Kent. *Early kingdoms in Madagascar, 1500–1700.* New York: Holt, Rinehart & Winston, 1970. ISBN 0-03-084171-2. ▸ Vigorous, controversial argument for early formation of African-Indonesian culture in Madagascar and on adjacent African coast. Also argues importance of African influence on earliest Madagascan kingdoms. [RHE]

19.652   Conrad Phillip Kottack et al., eds. *Madagascar: society and history.* Durham, N.C.: Carolina Academic, 1986. ISBN 0-89089-252-0 (cl), 0-89089-253-9 (pbk). ▸ Twenty-one articles on contemporary and historic Madagascar, with particular emphasis on migrations, social structure, royalty, and kinship. Individual and cumulative bibliographies useful for further study. [RHE]

19.653   I. D. MacCrone. *Race attitudes in South Africa: historical, experimental, and psychological studies.* 1937 ed. Johannesburg: Witwatersrand University Press, 1957. ▸ Influential though dated account by psychologist, attributing origins of South African racial order in Dutch Cape Colony, 1652–1795, to replacement of religious by racial discrimination under frontier conditions. [RHE]

19.654   Shula Marks. "Southern Africa and Madagascar." In *The Cambridge history of Africa.* Richard Gray, ed., vol. 4, pp. 384–468. Cambridge: Cambridge University Press, 1975. ISBN 0-521-33460-8 (set), 0-521-20413-5 (v. 4). ▸ Portuguese and Dutch colonialism situated within broader developments in African societies of southern Africa and Madagascar; based on first generation of Africanist studies with useful bibliographic essay. [RHE]

19.655   Susan Newton-King and V. C. Malherbe. *The Khoikhoi rebellion in the eastern Cape (1799–1803).* Cape Town: University of Cape Town, 1981. (Communications of the Centre for African Studies, University of Cape Town, 5.) ISBN 0-7992-0411-0. ▸ Sets final phase of Khoisan military resistance to European colonists within transition from Dutch to British rule, dissolution of independent Khoisan polities into rural proletariat, and complex Xhosa-Khoisan relations. [RHE]

19.656   J. B. Peires. *The house of Phalo: a history of the Xhosa people in the days of their independence.* Berkeley: University of California Press, 1982. ISBN 0-520-04663-3 (cl), 0-520-04793-1 (pbk). ▸ Precolonial history of Xhosa, followed by lengthy conflict with white settlers and British government up to 1850. Useful appendix on Xhosa historiography. Early, successful Africanist study. [RHE]

19.657   Nigel Penn. "Land, labour, and livestock in the Western Cape during the eighteenth century." In *The angry divide: social and economic history of the Western Cape.* Wilmot G. James and Mary Simons, eds., pp. 2–19. Cape Town: Philip with University of Cape Town, Centre for African Studies, 1989. ISBN 0-86486-116-8. ▸ Leading historian of eighteenth-century Khoisan synthesizes entire period in generally materialist interpretation, drawing on extensive archival research; footnotes to author's other articles. [RHE]

19.658   Robert Ross. *Beyond the pale: essays on the history of colonial South Africa.* Middletown, Conn.: Wesleyan University Press, 1993. ISBN 0-8195-5258-5. ▸ Eleven essays, five new, on Dutch and early British colonization at Cape of Good Hope. Includes translation of author's essay emphasizing influence of global economy on origins of white supremacy. [RHE]

19.659   Robert Ross. *Cape of torments: slavery and resistance in South Africa.* London: Routledge & Kegan Paul, 1983. ISBN 0-7100-9407-8. ▸ Early but well-researched survey of slavery at the Cape of Good Hope, based largely on court records. Cape slaves lacked class consciousness and were thus less rebellious than slaves elsewhere. [RHE]

19.660   Carmel Schrire, ed. *Past and present in hunter-gatherer societies.* Orlando, Fla.: Academic Press, 1984. ISBN 0-12-629180-2. ▸ Anthropologists and archaeologists attempt to move hunter-gatherers from timeless ethnographic theory to historical contexts; also conflicting views on possible continuities between ancient hunter-gatherers and the modern San. Useful bibliographies. [RHE]

19.661   Robert Carl-Heinz Shell. *Children of bondage: a social history of the slave society at the Cape of Good Hope, 1652–1838.* Hanover, N.H.: Wesleyan University Press and University Press of New England, 1993. ISBN 0-8195-5273-9. ▸ Major treatment of Cape slavery emphasizing reasons why Cape developed slave economy. Includes discussion of slave trade, family and slavery, Cape Town slave lodge, architecture, women, and civic status conferred by baptism. [RHE]

19.662   Alan K. Smith. "The Indian Ocean zone." In *History of Central Africa.* David Birmingham and Phyllis M. Martin, eds., vol. 1, pp. 205–44. London: Longman, 1983. ISBN 0-582-64673-1 (cl), 0-582-64674-X (pbk). ▸ Brief survey of region of modern Malawi and Mozambique emphasizing disruptive effects of growing international commercial contacts, especially slave trade in period before 1800. [RHE]

19.663   Jacqueline S. Solway and Richard B. Lee. "Foragers, genuine or spurious? Situating the Kalahari San in history." *Current anthropology* 31.2 (1990) 109–46. ISSN 0011-3204. ▸ Good introduction to whether Kalahari hunter-gatherers are isolated remnants of ancient past or creations of recent local and international economies. Authors moving from isolationist school to intermediate position; vigorous responses from other scholars. [RHE]

19.664   Pieter Van Duin and Robert Ross. *The economy of the Cape Colony in the eighteenth century.* Leiden: Centre for the History of European Expansion, 1987. (Intercontinenta, 7.) ▸ Best overall quantitative analysis of Dutch Cape Colony economy.

Argues, against earlier writers, that economy was dynamic, steadily growing, and not subject to chronic overproduction. [RHE]

19.665 Pierre Vérin. *The history of civilisation in North Madagascar*. David Smith, trans. Rotterdam, Holland: Balkema, 1986. ISBN 90-6191-021-8. ▸ Overview by archaelogist of coastal northern Madagascar, islamized communities, and Sakalava from earliest times to the nineteenth century. Discusses contacts with Indonesia, Islamic Asia, African coast, and later with Portuguese, Dutch, and French, particularly through slave trade. [RHE]

19.666 Pierre Vérin. *Madagascar*. Paris: Karthala, 1990. ISBN 2-86537-255-3. ▸ Semi-popular introduction (in French) to Madagascar history and culture by eminent archaeologist; strongest on precolonial period. [RHE]

19.667 Nigel Worden. *Slavery in Dutch South Africa*. Cambridge: Cambridge University Press, 1985. ISBN 0-521-25875-8. ▸ First comprehensive analysis of Cape slavery, based largely on quantitative data, as more like ancient Roman slavery than contemporary slavery in America but not thereby benign. Also synthesizes views of previous authors. [RHE]

Nineteenth Century

19.668 David N. Beach. "Ndebele raiders and Shona power." *Journal of African history* 15.4 (1975) 633–51. ISSN 0021-8537. ▸ Political and economic competition inspired raids of Ndebele kingdom against declining Changamire-Rozvi state of Shona-speaking peoples of Zimbabwe, 1830s to 1890s. Argues extent of raiding previously exaggerated. [EAE]

19.669 William Beinart and Colin Bundy. *Hidden struggles in rural South Africa: politics and popular movements in the Transkei and eastern Cape, 1890–1930*. Berkeley: University of California Press, 1987. ISBN 0-520-05779-1 (cl), 0-520-05780-5 (pbk). ▸ Case studies of African resistance in rural areas of Cape Colony/Province stressing socioeconomic differentiation, divergent African roles, and conscious intellectual responses to political constraints under European rule. [EAE]

19.670 William Beinart, Peter Delius, and Stanley Trapido, eds. *Putting a plough to the ground: accumulation and dispossession in rural South Africa, 1850–1930*. Johannesburg: Ravan, 1986. ISBN 0-86975-283-9. ▸ Case studies of rise of white agricultural capitalistic enterprises and changes in labor status of dispossessed Africans, tracing concomitant struggles between Europeans, Africans, and the state. [EAE]

19.671 Gerald M. Berg. "Riziculture and the founding of monarchy in Imerina." *Journal of African history* 22.3 (1981) 289–308. ISSN 0021-8537. ▸ Links rise of rigid social hierarchy to control over water and irrigated land for rice cultivation. Challenges previous emphasis on role of cooperative labor in rise of Imerina dynasty. [EAE]

19.672 Helmut Bley. *South-west Africa under German rule, 1894–1914*. Hugh Ridley, ed. and trans. Evanston, Ill.: Northwestern University Press, 1971. ISBN 0-8101-0346-X. ▸ Brutal imposition of policies of land expropriation and population relocation designed to support German settler economy provoked African revolts (1904–1907) and German military repression. Important narrative history. [EAE]

19.673 Philip Bonner. *Kings, commoners, and concessionaires: the evolution and dissolution of the nineteenth-century Swazi state*. Cambridge: Cambridge University Press, 1983. ISBN 0-521-24270-3. ▸ Internal sociopolitical relations, regional politics, and Swazi diplomacy as Swazi struggled against European expansion. Authoritative analysis based on oral and archival sources. [EAE]

19.674 Colin Bundy. *The rise and fall of the South African peasantry*. 2d ed. Cape Town: Philip, 1988. ISBN 0-86486-088-9 (pbk). ▸ Seminal study. Late nineteenth-century African peasant responsiveness to European market curtailed by dispossession, land deterioration, and declining terms of trade. Insufficient attention to rural differentiation, debatable chronology. [EAE]

19.675 Sandra B. Burman. *Chiefdom politics and alien law: Basutoland under Cape rule, 1872–1884*. New York: Africana, 1981. ISBN 0-8419-0591-6. ▸ Political and diplomatic history documenting disarmament policy leading to BaSotho rebellion of 1880–81 and disannexation of Basutoland (Lesotho) from Cape Colony. Only authoritative study of period. [EAE]

19.676 Gwyn Campbell. "The adoption of autarky in imperial Madagascar, 1820–1835." *Journal of African history* 28.3 (1987) 395–411. ISSN 0021-8537. ▸ Fear of British imperialism inspired policy to foster rapid internal economic growth under King Radama I and Queen Ranavalona I following curtailment of export slave trade and British failure to open legitimate trade. [EAE]

19.677 Gwyn Campbell. "Slavery and *fanompoana*: the structure of forced labor in Imerina (Madagascar), 1790–1861." *Journal of African history* 29.3 (1988) 463–86. ISSN 0021-8537. ▸ Important economic and political reinterpretation. *Fanompoana*, form of compulsory tribute labor from free subjects to crown, was more important than slavery in Imerina empire's economy and political expansion. [EAE]

19.678 Julian Cobbing. "The absent priesthood: another look at the Rhodesian risings of 1896–1897." *Journal of African history* 18.1 (1977) 61–84. ISSN 0021-8537. ▸ Refutes argument that Mwari priests led Ndebele and Shona risings (see Ranger 19.709). Argues 1820s to 1830s Venda origins of Mwari cult, disputing possible appeal based on ancient connections to Rozvi state or Great Zimbabwe. [EAE]

19.679 Julian Cobbing. "The evolution of the Ndebele *amabutho*." *Journal of African history* 15.4 (1974) 607–31. ISSN 0021-8537. ▸ Reinterpretation of kingdom's sociopolitical organization, previously defined as hierarchy of military regiments, divisions, and provinces. Young men composed residential military regiments, *amabutho*, which became demilitarized villages following marriage of men. [EAE]

19.680 Julian Cobbing. "The *mfecane* as alibi: thoughts on Dithakong and Mbolompo." *Journal of African history* 29.3 (1988) 487–519. ISSN 0021-8537. ▸ Delagoa Bay slave trade expansion and two battles reinterpreted to attribute early nineteenth-century southern African conflicts to European slaving activities. Overthrows conventional Zulucentric interpretations; strongly challenged on other grounds. See Eldredge 19.687 and Hamilton 19.694. [EAE]

19.681 Jean Comaroff and John Comaroff. *Of revelation and revolution: Christianity, colonialism, and consciousness in South Africa*. Chicago: University of Chicago Press, 1991. ISBN 0-226-11441-4 (cl), 0-226-11442-2 (pbk). ▸ Ambitious, insightful study of cultural and religious interaction between British missionaries and Tswana people they sought to convert. [MJH]

19.682 C. Clifton Crais. *White supremacy and black resistance in preindustrial South Africa: the making of colonial order in the eastern Cape, 1770–1865*. Cambridge: Cambridge University Press, 1991. ISBN 0-521-40479-7. ▸ Postmodernist perspective of conquest, dispossession, and African resistance. Emphasizes emergence and reinforcement of social boundaries and identities as Europeans asserted their dominance. Interpreted in terms of culture, representation, and discourse. [EAE]

19.683 Peter Delius. *The land belongs to us: the Pedi polity, the Boers, and the British in the nineteenth-century Transvaal*. 1983 ed. Berkeley: University of California Press, 1984. ISBN 0-520-05148-3. ▸ African kingdom struggles against competing white societies for land and autonomy. Documents politics and diplomacy, missionary role, land dispossession, African tribute labor to whites, rise of farm labor tenancy, and labor migration. [EAE]

19.684 Leslie Clement Duly. *British land policy at the Cape, 1795–1844: a study of administrative procedures in the empire.* Durham, N.C.: Duke University Press, 1968. ‣ Only thorough study of land policies and practices that greatly aggravated early Anglo-Boer relations and drove Dutch expansionism leading up to and during Great Boer Trek from Cape. [EAE]

19.685 Andrew Duminy and Bill Guest, eds. *Natal and Zululand from earliest times to 1910: a new history.* Pietermaritzburg: University of Natal Press, 1989. ISBN 0-86980-695-5. ‣ Collected articles representing recent scholarship; coverage from Stone Age onward, especially African sociopolitical consolidation from late eighteenth century, Zulu kingdom, white settlement and expansion, British colonial policies, Christianity, immigrant Indians, and South African (Boer) War and aftermath. [EAE]

19.686 Elizabeth A. Eldredge. "Drought, famine, and disease in nineteenth-century Lesotho." *African economic history* 16 (1987) 61–93. ISSN 0145-2258. ‣ Links drought-induced conflicts over land between BaSotho and Europeans and associated famines to food entitlements; correlates epidemics to famines. Disproportionate suffering of poor demonstrates socioeconomic determinants of effects of droughts. [EAE]

19.687 Elizabeth A. Eldredge. "Sources of conflict in southern Africa, ca. 1800–1830: the *mfecane* reconsidered." *Journal of African history* 33.1 (1992) 1–35. ISSN 0021-8537. ‣ Delagoa Bay ivory trade fostered socioeconomic differentiation; ecological crises precipitated conflict and allowed wealthy to consolidate power. Challenges attribution of slave-raiding to missionaries, and Cobbing's chronology of slave trade (19.680). [EAE]

19.688 Elizabeth A. Eldredge. *A South African kingdom: the pursuit of security in nineteenth-century Lesotho.* Cambridge: Cambridge University Press, 1993. ISBN 0-521-44067-X. ‣ Links internal sociopolitical consolidation to rise and decline of agriculture, local industries, craft production, and local and regional trade. Also discusses gender relations, women's political and economic roles, colonial policies, rise of labor migrancy. [EAE]

19.689 Elizabeth A. Eldredge. "Woman in production: the economic role of women in nineteenth-century Lesotho." *Signs* 16.4 (1991) 707–31. ISSN 0097-9740. ‣ Women's predominant roles in agriculture and craft production allowed them to trade surpluses, increase household wealth, and provide economic security. Labor burden increased as men were drawn into labor migrancy. [EAE]

19.690 Stephen Ellis. *The rising of the red shawls: a revolt in Madagascar, 1895–1899.* Cambridge: Cambridge University Press, 1985. ISBN 0-521-26287-9. ‣ Survey of Imerina history and provincial government examining social and religious factors underlying insurrection against Europeans and local collaborators which influenced French colonial policy and Malagasy resistance to colonialism. [EAE]

19.691 John S. Galbraith. *Reluctant empire: British policy on the South African frontier, 1834–1854.* 1963 ed. Westport, Conn.: Greenwood, 1978. ISBN 0-313-20087-4. ‣ Important work tracing economic, political, and humanitarian influences shaping British policy in period marked by frontier wars, land annexation and frontier retraction, Great Trek, and British imperial advances into interior. [EAE]

19.692 Robert J. Gordon. *The Bushman myth: the making of a Namibian underclass.* Boulder: Westview, 1992. ISBN 0-8133-1173-X (cl), 0-8133-1381-3 (pbk). ‣ Examination of European construction of false negative and positive stereotypes, mid-nineteenth century to present. Bushmen were social bandits resisting

genocide; participated in regional trade. Destroys myth of isolation and stasis. [EAE]

19.693 Jeff Guy. *The destruction of the Zulu kingdom: the civil war in Zululand, 1879–1884.* London: Longman, 1979. ISBN 0-582-64686-3. ‣ Narrative of later history of Zulu kingdom as it confronted British imperialism, experienced internal strife and partition, and the loss of independence, land, and economic viability. [EAE]

19.694 Carolyn Anne Hamilton. " 'The character and objects of Chaka': a reconsideration of the making of Shaka as Mfecane motor." *Journal of African history* 33.1 (1992) 37–63. ISSN 0021-8537. ‣ Demonstrates Europeans represented Shaka as benign until local atrocity stories emerged from African sources soon after his death. Important challenge to Cobbing's analysis (19.680) of role of Europeans in myth-making surrounding Shaka. [EAE]

19.695 Patrick Harries. "Slavery, social incorporation, and surplus extraction: the nature of free and unfree labour in South-East Africa." *Journal of African history* 22.3 (1981) 309–30. ISSN 0021-8537. ‣ Seminal study of labor relations. Rise of Delagoa Bay slave trade from late 1820s and domestic slavery in Gaza empire from 1860s. Falsely accuses earlier historians of covering up Portuguese slave trade involvement (Eldredge 19.687). [EAE]

19.696 Allen F. Isaacman. *Mozambique: the africanization of a European institution, the Zambesi prazos, 1750–1902.* Madison: University of Wisconsin Press, 1972. ISBN 0-299-06110-8. ‣ Imposition of Portuguese landed estates in Zambezi valley; social and economic organization, racial assimilation; expansion into larger Africanized political units which resisted Portuguese colonial expansion in late nineteenth century. [EAE/RHE/TTS]

19.697 Margaret Kinsman. "Beasts of burden: the subordination of southern Tswana women, ca. 1800–1840." *Journal of southern African studies* 10.1 (1983) 39–54. ISSN 0305-7070. ‣ Legal and material dependence on male kin made women vulnerable to physical deprivation and violence. Argues dependence caused women to accept and rationalize their own subordination in glorification of servitude. [EAE]

19.698 Gerhard Liesegang. "Nguni migrations between Delagoa Bay and the Zambezi, 1821–1839." *African historical studies* 3.2 (1970) 317–37. ISSN 0001-9992. ‣ Uses oral traditions and Portuguese sources to reconstruct routes of four emigrant groups dislodged from vicinity of emerging Zulu state. Traces conflicts with local population and Portuguese in Mozambique and Zimbabwe. [EAE]

19.699 William F. Lye. "The Ndebele kingdom south of the Limpopo River." *Journal of African history* 10.1 (1969) 87–104. ISSN 0021-8537. ‣ Kingdom prior to 1837 expulsion into Zimbabwe; Ndebele migration and raiding was motivated by search for secure settlement; once established, Mzilikazi (king) pursued restrained policies of interaction with his neighbors. [EAE]

19.700 William M. MacMillan. *Bantu, Boer, and Briton: the making of the South African native problem.* 1963 ed. Westport, Conn.: Greenwood, 1979. ISBN 0-313-20906-5. ‣ Classic liberal narrative history centered on British frontier policy through 1854. Discusses missionary influences, 1835 frontier war with Xhosa, colonial intervention, and Great Boer Trek. Information on African societies unreliable. [EAE]

19.701 William M. MacMillan. *The Cape colour question: a historical survey.* 1927 ed. London: Hurst, 1969. ‣ Classic, liberal study of European perspectives on race, slavery, and demand for labor; missionary humanitarian influence; and changing legal status of Khoi and their emancipation as result of missionary efforts. [EAE]

19.702 J. S. Marais. *The Cape coloured people, 1652–1937.* 1939 ed. New York: AMS Press, 1978. ISBN 0-404-12106-3. ▸ Narrative history of mixed population of imported slaves, Khoi, San, and Europeans. Settlements beyond Cape frontier, servitude within colony, missionary involvement, and emancipation of 1828. Dated perspective and terminology. [EAE]

19.703 Shula Marks and Anthony Atmore, eds. *Economy and society in pre-industrial South Africa.* London: Longman, 1980. ISBN 0-582-64655-3 (cl), 0-582-64656-1 (pbk). ▸ Important Marxist case studies of nineteenth-century African societies, integration into regional market economy, internal transformations, white societies in Cape and Transvaal, and rise of labor migrancy. Characteristic of 1970s historiography. [EAE]

19.704 Colin Murray. *Black mountain: land, class, and power in the eastern Orange Free State, 1880s–1980s.* Washington, D.C.: Smithsonian Institution, 1992. ISBN 1-56098-227-6. ▸ Examination of survival of Barolong elite from remnant of chiefdom in Thaba Nchu district. Treats perpetuation of class and ethnic divisions following land dispossession and forced resettlement in huge rural Bantustan slums. [EAE]

19.705 S. Daniel Neumark. *Economic influences on the South African frontier, 1652–1836.* Stanford, Calif.: Stanford University Press, 1957. (Stanford University Food Research Institute, Miscellaneous publications, 12.) ▸ Important work exploring production and trade in frontier districts. Overturns myth of Dutch-speaking frontier farmers as economically self-sufficient. [EAE]

19.706 Malyn Newitt. *Portuguese settlement on the Zambesi: exploration, land tenure, and colonial rule in East Africa.* New York: Africana, 1973. ISBN 0-8419-0132-5. ▸ Study of system of crown land grants (*prazos*) which gave rise to independent *prazo* rulers, their nineteenth-century struggles for supremacy, and eventual conquest by Portuguese in late nineteenth and early twentieth centuries. [EAE/TTS]

19.707 J. D. Omer-Cooper. *The Zulu aftermath: a nineteenth-century revolution in Bantu Africa.* 1966 ed. London: Longman, 1980. ISBN 0-582-64531-X. ▸ Zulucentric interpretation of early nineteenth-century conflicts. Since overturned but still basic narrative coverage of African leaders and politics to mid-nineteenth century. See also Cobbing 19.680, Eldredge 19.687, and Hamilton 19.694. [EAE]

19.708 J. B. Peires. *The dead will arise: Nongqawuse and the Great Xhosa cattle-killing movement of 1856–7.* Bloomington: Indiana University Press, 1989. ISBN 0-253-34388-0 (cl), 0-253-20524-7 (pbk). ▸ Decades of wars with Europeans, land dispossession, and cattle epidemics fostered socioeconomic differentiation and sociopolitical disintegration among Xhosa, leading to revival of prophecies, destruction of food resources, and mass starvation. [EAE]

19.709 Terence O. Ranger. *Revolt in Southern Rhodesia, 1896–97: a study in African resistance.* Evanston, Ill.: Northwestern University Press, 1967. ▸ Organization and outbreak of dramatic rebellions in Matabeleland and Mashonaland against new settler administration; violent suppression of uprisings. Asserts leadership role of Mwari priests; later challenged by Cobbing 19.678. [EAE]

19.710 R. Kent Rasmussen. *Migrant kingdom: Mzilikazi's Ndebele in South Africa.* London: Collings, 1978. ISBN 0-86036-06-1. ▸ Narrative political history of kingdom and its leader; revises previous works with regard to chronology and directions of conquest and expansion. Based on close reexamination of written sources. [EAE]

19.711 Robert Ross. *Adam Kok's Griquas: a study in the development of stratification in South Africa.* Cambridge: Cambridge University Press, 1976. ISBN 0-521-21199-0. ▸ Study of rise and decline of autonomous frontier societies of mixed descendants of

imported slaves, Europeans, and KhoiSan. Traces external relations, internal politics, land, authority, and economy and discusses eventual removal to Nomansland followed by rebellion and disintegration. [EAE]

19.712 Stanlake Samkange. *Origins of Rhodesia.* New York: Praeger, 1968. ▸ Detailed political and diplomatic history of Ndebele/Matabele state from its inception under leadership of Mzilikazi in 1820s until its invasion and conquest by British forces in 1893. [EAE]

19.713 Peter Sanders. *Moshoeshoe: chief of the Sotho.* London: Heinemann, 1975. ISBN 0-435-32793-3. ▸ Analysis of personalities, socioeconomic relations, missionary roles, and conflicts with Europeans that shaped political and diplomatic history of Ba-Sotho under rule of nation's founder, Moshoeshoe, until his death in 1870. [EAE]

19.714 Kevin W. Shillington. *The colonisation of the southern Tswana, 1870–1900.* Braamfontein, South Africa: Ravan, 1985. ISBN 0-86975-270-7 (pbk). ▸ Narrates annexation of BaTlhaping, BaRolong, and BaTlharo chieftaincies to Cape Colony following discovery of diamonds. Traces Bechuanaland Wars of 1881–84, Cecil Rhodes's interventions, and role of mining capital. [EAE]

19.715 George McCall Theal, comp. *Records of south-eastern Africa: collected in various libraries and archive departments in Europe.* 1898–1903 ed. 9 vols. Cape Town: Struik, 1964. ▸ Critical primary sources including early shipwreck accounts, Portuguese official records, and British reports, 1506–1825; arbitration records concerning British-Portuguese dispute over control of Delagoa Bay, 1872–75. [EAE]

19.716 George McCall Theal, ed. *Basutoland records.* 1883 ed. 3 vols. in 4. Cape Town: Struik, 1964. ▸ Indispensable collection of official documents and correspondence produced between 1833 and 1869, retrieved for colonial administration; letters from Moshoeshoe and other BaSotho, missionaries in Lesotho, and colonial officials. [EAE]

19.717 George McCall Theal, ed. *Records of the Cape Colony.* 36 vols. London: Clowes for Government of the Cape Colony, 1897–1905. ▸ Reproduces materials relevant to Cape Colony, 1793–1828. Critical primary sources on British governance in Cape Colony, laws, slavery, settlers, land, crime, frontier relations. Available on microfilm from Washington, D.C.: Library of Congress Photoduplication Service, 1986, 9 reels. [EAE]

19.718 Leonard M. Thompson. *Survival in two worlds: Moshoeshoe of Lesotho, 1786–1870.* Oxford: Clarendon, 1975. ISBN 0-19-821693-9 (cl), 0-19-822702-7 (pbk). ▸ Biography of founder of Sotho nation, with emphasis on Christian missionaries and Moshoeshoe's diplomatic defense of his people from European imperial expansiveness. Classic, based on oral and archival research. [EAE]

19.719 Leonard M. Thompson, ed. *African societies in southern Africa: historical studies.* New York: Praeger, 1969. ISBN 0-435-94803-2. ▸ Seminal studies by key scholars that marked new historiographic attention to internal historical dynamics of African societies to mid-nineteenth century. Treats settlement patterns, social structure, oral traditions, trade, politics, and diplomacy among Sotho-Tswana– and Nguni-speaking peoples. [EAE]

19.720 Robert Vicat Turrell. *Capital and labour on the Kimberley diamond fields, 1871–1890.* Cambridge: Cambridge University Press, 1987. ISBN 0-521-33354-7. ▸ Careful study of struggles between small independent diggers and large mining companies. Discusses emergence of colonial capitalism, restriction of Africans to wage labor, and introduction of closed compounds. [EAE]

19.721 Eric A. Walker. *The Great Trek.* London: Black, 1965. ▸ Classic study of flight of Dutch-speaking farmers from British-ruled Cape Colony, motives, and fate of Voortrekkers in conflicts with Africans and British in Natal and Transvaal. Unreliable treatment of African societies. [EAE]

19.722 R. L. Watson. *The slave question: liberty and property in South Africa.* Middletown, Conn.: Wesleyan University Press, 1990. ISBN 0-8195-5221-6. ▸ Explores conflicting principles of personal freedom and sanctity of property rights in weak Cape Colony antislavery movement. Finds absence of principled abolitionist movement left legacy of harsh race relations in South Africa. [EAE]

19.723 Edwin N. Wilmsen. *Land filled with flies: a political economy of the Kalahari.* Chicago: University of Chicago Press, 1989. ISBN 0-226-90014-2 (cl), 0-226-90015-0 (pbk). ▸ Demonstrates hunter-gatherer societies have complicated history involving pastoralism, trade, dispossession, and impoverishment and did not exist in isolation from surrounding African and European communities. Controversial argument and imprecise use of evidence. [EAE]

19.724 William H. Worger. *South Africa's city of diamonds: mine workers and monopoly capitalism in Kimberley, 1867–1895.* New Haven: Yale University Press, 1987. ISBN 0-300-03716-3. ▸ Overview of African labor migrancy, imposition of controls over African workers, and rise of white worker consciousness, followed by narrative of company amalgamation and emergence of monopoly capitalism. [EAE]

19.725 Diana Wylie. *A little god: the twilight of patriarchy in a southern African chiefdom.* Middletown, Conn.: Wesleyan University Press, 1990. ISBN 0-8195-5228-3. ▸ Analysis of political crises among ruling BamaNgwato of Botswana, particularly under Tshekedi Khama (regent 1925–49). Reveals power relationships among chiefs, dynastic rivalries, legal change, and erosion of popular support. [EAE]

Twentieth Century

19.726 Hoyt Alverson. *Mind in the heart of darkness: value and self-identity among the Tswana of southern Africa.* New Haven: Yale University Press, 1978. ISBN 0-300-02244-1. ▸ Account of Tswana (people of Botswana) migrant laborers in South Africa by anthropologist. Finds high level of self-worth and sense of autonomy, in spite of hardships of colonialism. Based on extensive oral interviews and on folklore, proverbs, etc. [WHW]

19.727 William Beinart. *The political economy of Pondoland, 1860–1930.* Cambridge: Cambridge University Press, 1982. ISBN 0-521-24393-9. ▸ Examination of indebtedness and other forces behind migrant labor and chiefs as recruiting agents. Argues that South African industrialization impoverished rural areas. Combines archival and oral sources on Pondoland (African homeland, Transkei). [WHW]

19.728 Iris Berger. *Threads of solidarity: women in South African industry, 1900–1980.* Bloomington: Indiana University Press, 1992. ISBN 0-253-31173-X (cl), 0-253-20700-2 (pbk). ▸ Study of political consciousness and trade unions among women workers (white and black) in range of South African industries (garment, food, and canning) and domestic servants. Finds origins in workplace, race, and gender discrimination. [WHW/NRH]

19.729 Philip Bonner. "Family, crime, and political consciousness on the East Rand, 1939–1955." *Journal of southern African studies* 14.3 (1988) 393–420. ISSN 0305-7070. ▸ Innovative utilization of municipal records to study African urban culture on Witwatersrand (Johannesburg, South Africa), showing crime and youth gangs as efforts to create autonomous spaces within confines of apartheid. [WHW]

19.730 Belinda Bozzoli, ed. *Class, community, and conflict: South African perspectives.* Johannesburg: Ravan, 1987. ISBN 0-86975-281-2 (pbk). ▸ Witwatersrand History Workshop (major radical popular history forum) papers (1984) examining material bases of community consciousness among diverse groups (rural African women, Afrikaner factory workers, etc.). Extends 1978 workshop; see 19.731. [WHW]

19.731 Belinda Bozzoli, ed. *Town and countryside in the Transvaal: capitalist penetration and popular response.* Johannesburg: Ravan, 1983. ISBN 0-86975-139-5. ▸ Witwatersrand History Workshop (major radical popular history forum) papers (1978) on African and Indian reactions to implementation of apartheid. Innovative focus on immiseration of daily life (groups ranging from flower sellers to sharecroppers) and strikes and boycotts as responses See also 19.730. [WHW]

19.732 Helen Bradford. *A taste of freedom: the ICU in rural South Africa, 1924–1930.* New Haven: Yale University Press, 1987. ISBN 0-300-03873-9. ▸ Rural bases of support for South Africa's largest African trade union in 1920s (Industrial and Commercial Workers Union [ICU]), with emphasis on millennial appeal. Extensive archival and oral research, replaces simpler notions of consciousness. [WHW]

19.733 Jon M. Bridgman. *The revolt of the Hereros.* Berkeley: University of California Press, 1981. ISBN 0-520-04113-5. ▸ Study of resistance to German colonialism in South West Africa (Namibia) among Herero people, concentrating on German policy, perceived fundamental threat to colonial control, military strategies, and harsh repression of uprising. [WHW]

19.734 Jeffrey Butler, Richard Elphick, and David Welsh, eds. *Democratic liberalism in South Africa: its history and prospect.* Middletown, Conn.: Wesleyan University Press, 1987. ISBN 0-8195-5165-1 (cl), 0-8195-6197-5 (pbk). ▸ Conference papers with liberal overviews of history, politics, and economics, reflecting white English-speaking South Africans' views of apartheid as product of Afrikaner racial ideology. Written self-consciously against radical historiography's stress on economic bases of white supremacy. [WHW]

19.735 Gwendolen M. Carter. *The politics of inequality: South Africa since 1948.* 1959 2d rev. ed. New York: Octagon Books, 1977. ISBN 0-374-91300-5. ▸ First and still most thorough study of apartheid as it was implemented in 1950s. Valuable as chronicle of nationalist government policies of racial separation now justified as valid in concept but flawed in execution. [WHW]

19.736 John Cell. *The highest stage of white supremacy: the origins of segregation in South Africa and the American South.* Cambridge: Cambridge University Press, 1982. ISBN 0-521-24096-4 (cl), 0-521-27061-8 (pbk). ▸ Comparative study of segregation in South Africa and American South during late nineteenth and early twentieth centuries. Emphasizes industrialization as cause, unlike Fredrickson's liberal focus on Afrikaner racial ideology (19.752). [WHW]

19.737 Nancy Clark. "South Africa's state corporations: the death knell of economic colonialism?" *Journal of southern African studies* 14.1 (1987) 99–122. ISSN 0305-7070. ▸ Finds state intervention in South African economy went beyond favoring Afrikaners to provide cheap black labor to gold-mining industry. Official records substantiate state responsiveness to struggles in workplace. [WHW]

19.738 Jean Comaroff. *Body of power, spirit of resistance: the culture and history of a South African people.* Chicago: University of Chicago Press, 1985. ISBN 0-226-11422-8. ▸ Analysis of history and symbolism of Zionist (African spiritual) churches among Tshidi (or Tswana) in terms of articulation of cultures and forms of resistance among marginalized populations, especially women. [MJH]

19.739 Jean Comaroff and John Comaroff. *Ethnography and the historical imagination.* Boulder: Westview, 1992. ISBN 0-8133-

1304-X (cl), 0-8133-1305-8 (pbk). ‣ Influential post-modernist anthropologists show how study of history and culture is critical for understanding of Tswana society. Emphasis on historical imagination still neglects indigenous perspectives. [MJH]

19.740 Vincent Crapanzano. *Waiting: the whites of South Africa.* New York: Random House, 1985. ISBN 0-394-50986-2. ‣ Extensive use of interviewees' own words (small-town whites, teenagers to octogenarians) to reveal harsh attitudes toward blacks, moral justifications for supremacy of whites, and anxiety over maintenance of white control. [WHW]

19.741 Jonathan Crush. *The struggle for Swazi labour, 1890–1920.* Kingston, Ont.: McGill-Queen's University Press, 1987. ISBN 0-7735-0569-5. ‣ Examination of transformation of Swaziland from rural autonomy to supplier of migrant labor for South Africa's mines and target for land speculators. Chiefs, in collaboration with labor recruiters, created stratified and largely impoverished society. [WHW]

19.742 Jonathan Crush, Alan Jeeves, and David Yudelman, eds. *South Africa's labor empire: a history of black migrancy to the gold mines.* Boulder: Westview, 1991. ISBN 0-8133-7417-0. ‣ Extends accounts by Beinart (19.727) and Crush (19.741) to show continuing dependence of South African mines on foreign sources of labor from 1940s. Also discusses development of trade unions among migrant miners in 1980s. [WHW]

19.743 T.R.H. Davenport. *South Africa: a modern history.* 4th ed. Toronto: University of Toronto Press, 1991. ISBN 0-8020-5940-6 (cl), 0-8020-6880-4 (pbk). ‣ Detailed general history of South Africa emphasizing political developments from Dutch settlement (1652) onward. Self-consciously liberal stress on eighteenth-century slavery and frontier experiences in creating modern Afrikaner racism. [WHW]

19.744 Stephen M. Davis. *Apartheid's rebels: inside South Africa's hidden war.* New Haven: Yale University Press, 1987. ISBN 0-300-03991-3 (cl), 0-300-03992-1 (pbk). ‣ Study of African National Congress' adoption of violent means—especially sabotage and guerrilla war—to seek political ends during 1970s and 1980s. Also discusses South African Nationalist government's counterinfiltration strategies. [WHW]

19.745 C. W. De Kiewiet. *A history of South Africa, social and economic.* 1957 ed. London: Oxford University Press, 1966. ‣ Masterly narrative with emphasis on white farmers' and industrialists' demand for cheap black labor that prefigures later radical critique. Classic general history of South Africa; early breakthrough to liberal social and economic interpretation. [WHW]

19.746 W. J. De Kock, ed. *Dictionary of South African biography.* 5 vols. to date. Pretoria: Tafelberg-Vitgewers, 1968–. ISBN 0-624-00856-8 (v. 1), 0-624-00369-8 (v. 2), 0-624-00849-5 (v. 3). ‣ Ongoing multivolume series of biographies (now numbering in thousands), primarily of white male politicians with occasional African chiefs. Basic repository of biographical information otherwise not accessible. [WHW]

19.747 Donald Denoon and Balam Nyeko. *Southern Africa since 1800.* 2d ed. London: Longman, 1984. ISBN 0-582-72707-3 (pbk). ‣ Accessible undergraduate-level overview of social, economic, and political developments in South Africa from end of Cape slavery to crumbling of apartheid. Strives to focus on African initiatives rather than white actions. [WHW]

19.748 Saul Dubow. *Racial segregation and the origins of apartheid in South Africa, 1919–36.* New York: St. Martin's, 1989. ISBN 0-312-02774-5. ‣ Examination of white policy makers within South African Department of Native Affairs who shaped segregationist thought and policies. Radical emphasis on economic sources of racism in industrializing country, rather than post-1948 Afrikaner nationalism. [WHW]

19.749 William Finnegan. *Crossing the line: a year in the land of apartheid.* 1986 ed. New York: Harper & Row, 1987. ISBN 0-06-091430-0 (pbk). ‣ Vivid autobiographical account of American surfer's year teaching in South African school for coloureds. Reveals students' acute political consciousness. Clear, lived accounts of apartheid, causes, and counterstrategies make this useful classroom text. [WHW]

19.750 Ruth First and Ann Scott. *Olive Schreiner: a biography.* 1980 ed. New Brunswick, N.J.: Rutgers University Press, 1990. ISBN 0-8135-1621-8 (cl), 0-8135-1622-6 (pbk). ‣ Definitive biography of South Africa's first and most important novelist and feminist. Traces political opposition to Cecil Rhodes's harsh treatment of blacks and literary focus on difficulties women faced in South Africa and England. [WHW]

19.751 Julie Frederikse. *The unbreakable thread: non-racialism in South Africa.* Bloomington: Indiana University Press, 1990. ISBN 0-253-32473-4 (cl), 0-253-20619-7 (pbk). ‣ Lavishly illustrated—posters, graffiti, etc.—journalistic account of popular resistance to implementation of apartheid in 1970s and 1980s. Valuable in classroom for primary sources detailing mass-based people's war against apartheid. [WHW]

19.752 George Frederickson. *White supremacy: a comparative study in American and South African history.* 1980 ed. New York: Oxford University Press, 1981. ISBN 0-19-502759-0. ‣ Original, historical (seventeenth century to present) comparison of racial discrimination in South Africa and United States. Liberal stress on parallel preindustrial experience (Cape Colony slavery, frontier) in formation of Afrikaner racial ideology. [WHW]

19.753 Gail M. Gerhart. *Black power in South Africa: the evolution of an ideology.* Berkeley: University of California Press, 1978. ISBN 0-520-03022-2 (cl), 0-520-03933-5 (pbk). ‣ Study of Africanist and black-consciousness political thought in South Africa since World War II. Uniquely detailed discussion of Anton Lembede, Robert Sobukwe, and Stephen Biko stresses primacy of African interests, countering multiracialism of African National Congress. [WHW]

19.754 Ian Goldin. *Making race: the politics and economics of colonial identity in South Africa.* London: Longman, 1987. ISBN 0-582-01979-6. ‣ Economic bases of racial/political identity of mixed-race residents of Cape Colony, so-called coloureds. Focuses on 1948–84 (apartheid) period in which government encouraged distinct coloured identity to divide black opposition. [WHW]

19.755 Bonar Gow. "Madagascar." In *The Cambridge history of Africa.* Michael Crowder, ed., vol. 8, pp. 674–97. Cambridge: Cambridge University Press, 1985. ISBN 0-521-22409-8. ‣ Brief survey of impact of French colonialism, development of nationalist movement, and economic and political problems of independence in modern Madagascar. Annotated guide to historical literature (mostly in French). [WHW]

19.756 Stanley B. Greenberg. *Legitimating the illegitimate: states, markets, and resistance in South Africa.* Berkeley: University of California Press, 1987. ISBN 0-520-06010-5 (cl), 0-520-06011-3 (pbk). ‣ Discussion of contradictions of apartheid, especially restriction of domestic consumer market by mining industry's use of low-wage migrant workers. Finds resultant labor conflict and high unemployment weakened business support for apartheid, 1970s to 1980s. [WHW]

19.757 Stanley B. Greenberg. *Race and state in capitalist development: comparative perspectives.* New Haven: Yale University Press, 1980. ISBN 0-300-02444-4 (cl), 0-300-02527-0 (pbk). ‣ Broad comparative study of labor policy in South Africa, Alabama, Northern Ireland, and Israel. Shows recurrent business use of racial/ethnic feelings to divide and weaken workers in class (not racial) analysis. Little focus on the state, despite title. [WHW]

19.758 Albert Grundlingh. *Fighting their own war: South African blacks and the First World War.* Johannesburg: Ravan, 1987. ISBN 0-86975-321-5 (pbk). ‣ Documents African participation in World War I, overturning older view that only whites played role. Treats recruitment and experiences of noncombatant blacks in South West Africa, East Africa, and France, including raised political expectations. [WHW]

19.759 Kenneth W. Grundy. *The militarization of South African politics.* Bloomington: Indiana University Press, 1986. ISBN 0-253-31678-2. ‣ Study of growth of military influence within South Africa's government during 1970s and 1980s as blacks' resistance to apartheid posed increasing threat to public order. Finds government strategic concerns led to centralization and preponderant influence of security apparatus. [WHW]

19.760 Kenneth W. Grundy. *Soldiers without politics: blacks in the South African armed forces.* Berkeley: University of California Press, 1983. ISBN 0-520-04710-9. ‣ Concludes increasing incorporation of Africans into South African military ironically made black collaboration vital to maintenance of white government control. Contradictions unrecognized by white officials in early 1980s. [WHW]

19.761 W. K. Hancock. *Smuts.* 1962 ed. 2 vols. Cambridge: Cambridge University Press, 1968. ‣ Definitive, though near-hagiographic, biography of Jan Smuts (Boer leader in South African War 1899–1902, politician 1910–48). Stresses Smuts's opposition to extreme Afrikaner nationalism and role as world statesman, but misses contributions to segregationist policies. [WHW]

19.762 Baruch Hirson. *Year of fire, year of ash: the Soweto Revolt, roots of a revolution?* London: Zed, 1979. ISBN 0-905762-28-2 (cl), 0-905762-29-0 (pbk). ‣ Most thorough study of 1976 black schoolchildren's revolt in Soweto against required instruction in Afrikaans language. Shows poverty and desperation of youth spreading black-consciousness–inspired national rebellion. See Gerhart 19.753. [WHW]

19.763 Muriel Horrell, comp. *Laws affecting race relations in South Africa (to the end of 1976).* 4th ed. Johannesburg: South African Institute of Race Relations, 1978. ISBN 0-86982-168-7. ‣ Comprehensive compilation of texts of apartheid legislation, together with information on implementation of racially discriminatory practices. Use with annual surveys of race relations produced by liberal watchdog South African Institute of Race Relations. Earlier title: *Legislation and Race Relations.* [WHW]

19.764 D. Hobart Houghton. *The South African economy.* 4th ed. Cape Town: Oxford University Press, 1976. ISBN 0-19-570080-5 (cl), 0-19-570081-3 (pbk). ‣ Basic university text by leading liberal economist; chapters on farming, manufacturing, gold mining, and migrant labor. Assumes economic growth will end racial discrimination. Appendix gives figures current to 1975. [WHW]

19.765 Allen F. Isaacman and Barbara Isaacman. *The tradition of resistance in Mozambique: the Zambesi Valley, 1850–1921.* Berkeley: University of California Press, 1976. ISBN 0-520-03065-6. ‣ Social, economic, and political bases of African resistance to Portuguese colonialism, based on extensive archival and oral research. Resistance struggles, primarily over control of African labor, inhibited conquest (1890s) and continued through World War I. [WHW]

19.766 Barbara Isaacman and Allen F. Isaacman. *Mozambique: from colonialism to revolution, 1900–1982.* Boulder: Westview, 1983. ISBN 0-86531-210-9 (cl), 0-86531-211-7 (pbk). ‣ Best general history of twentieth-century Mozambique, concentrating on African activities rather than Portuguese colonizers. Emphasizes economic motivation of Portuguese colonialism and African nationalist strategy to control land and labor. [WHW]

19.767 Sheridan Johns and R. Hunt Davis, Jr. *Mandela, Tambo, and the African National Congress: the struggle against apartheid, 1948–1990—a documentary survey.* New York: Oxford University Press, 1991. ISBN 0-19-505783-X (cl), 0-19-505784-8 (pbk). ‣ Well-selected documents relating to post-1948 history of African National Congress (ANC). Illustrates ideas of Nelson Mandela, Oliver Tambo, and other ANC leaders, but limited to political elite rather than rank-and-file members. [WHW]

19.768 Frederick A. Johnstone. *Class, race, and gold: a study of class relations and racial discrimination in South Africa.* 1976 ed. Lanham, Md.: University Press of America, 1987. ISBN 0-8191-5743-0 (pbk). ‣ Key radical text establishing economic bases of racial discrimination in South Africa: cheap black labor essential to profitability of gold-mining industry. Also documents labor struggles in mines, 1900 to mid-1920s. [WHW]

19.769 Thomas Karis and Gwendolen M. Carter, eds. *From protest to challenge: a documentary history of African politics in South Africa, 1882–1964.* 4 vols. Stanford, Calif.: Hoover Institution on War, Revolution, and Peace, 1972–77. (Hoover Institution publications, 89, 122–23, 161.) ISBN 0-8179-1891-4 (v. 1, cl), 0-8179-1221-5 (v. 2, cl), 0-8179-1892-2 (v. 1, pbk), 0-8179-1222-3 (v. 2, pbk), 0-8179-6232-8 (v. 3, pbk), 0-8179-6612-9 (v. 4, pbk). ‣ Primary materials documenting development of black politics in South Africa, ranging from newspaper extracts to 1955 Freedom Charter, with more than 100 biographies of anti-apartheid whites and blacks (volume 4). [WHW]

19.770 Peter Katjavivi. *A history of resistance in Namibia.* 1988 ed. Trenton, N.J.: Africa World, 1990. ISBN 0-86543-143-4 (cl), 0-86543-144-2 (pbk). ‣ Overview of black resistance to German and South African colonialism in Namibia (South West Africa). Continuous struggle against forced labor and land alienation under leadership of SWAPO (South West Africa People's Organisation). [WHW]

19.771 Norma J. Kriger. *Zimbabwe's guerrilla war: peasant voices.* Cambridge: Cambridge University Press, 1992. ISBN 0-521-39254-3. ‣ Examination of regional and tribal divisions within African resistance to white rule in Southern Rhodesia (Zimbabwe) during 1970s. Extensive archival research and fieldwork in Zimbabwe. Against standard emphasis on nationalist unity. See Ranger 19.709, Lan 19.772. [WHW]

19.772 David Lan. *Guns and rain: guerrillas and spirit mediums in Zimbabwe.* Berkeley: University of California Press, 1985. ISBN 0-520-05557-8 (cl), 0-520-05589-6 (pbk). ‣ Study of African resistance to white rule in Southern Rhodesia (Zimbabwe) in 1960s and 1970s, as unified and led by spirit mediums. Supports Ranger's emphasis on long-term continuity of struggle and essential unity of nationalists (19.709); see Kriger 19.771. [WHW]

19.773 Joseph Lelyveld. *Move your shadow: South Africa, black and white.* 1985 ed. New York: Penguin, 1986. ISBN 0-14-009326-5 (pbk). ‣ Insightful discussions of contemporary South Africa by *New York Times* correspondent, from contradictions of Afrikaner nationalism to corruption of homeland (dependent African enclave states) politics. Accessible text for classroom use. [WHW]

19.774 Gavin Lewis. *Between the wire and the wall: a history of South African "coloured" politics.* New York: St. Martin's, 1987. ISBN 0-312-00857-0. ‣ Analysis of coloured political organizations between late nineteenth century and 1948 as inspiration for structures, strategies, and ideologies developed by African National Congress. Brief overview of events since 1948 (apartheid era). [WHW]

19.775 Tom Lodge. *Black politics in South Africa since 1945.* London: Longman, 1983. ISBN 0-582-64328-7 (cl), 0-582-64327-9 (pbk). ‣ Basic overview of black politics in South Africa since 1910, with detailed coverage from 1945, especially black protest movements in 1950s. Stronger on grassroots community protests (bus boycotts, etc.) than on formal political organizations (e.g., African National Congress). [WHW]

19.776 Nelson Mandela. *No easy walk to freedom.* 1965 ed. London: Mandarin, 1990. ISBN 0-7493-0504-5 (pbk). ▸ Speeches and writings of Nelson Mandela, most important contemporary leader of African National Congress (ANC), jailed for alleged treason, 1962–91. Testimony given at treason trial reveals ANC turn to controlled violence. Useful in classroom for eloquent prose. [WHW]

19.777 Shula Marks. *The ambiguities of dependence in South Africa: class, nationalism, and the state in twentieth-century Natal.* Baltimore: Johns Hopkins University Press, 1986. ISBN 0-8018-3267-5. ▸ Examines contradictions faced by early twentieth-century Africans through case studies of leaders of diverse political movements (African National Congress [ANC], Industrial and Commercial Workers' Union [ICU], Zulu kingdom). Demonstrates wide range of strategies necessary to oppose racially discriminatory practices. [WHW]

19.778 Shula Marks. *Reluctant rebellion: the 1906–08 disturbances in Natal.* Oxford: Clarendon, 1970. ISBN 0-19-821655-6. ▸ Detailed examination of social, economic, and political contexts behind last Zulu revolt against British rule (Bambatha Rebellion). Strong archival research on colonial policies, but lack of oral research shortchanges coverage of African motivations. [WHW]

19.779 Shula Marks and Richard Rathbone, eds. *Industrialisation and social change in South Africa: African class formation, culture, and consciousness, 1870–1930.* New York: Longman, 1982. ISBN 0-582-64338-4. ▸ First detailed case studies of impact of industrialization on both rural and urban African communities. Shows qualitative change in race relations with development of gold and diamond mining and struggles between Africans and Europeans over labor and land. [WHW]

19.780 Shula Marks and Stanley Trapido, eds. *The politics of race, class, and nationalism in twentieth-century South Africa.* London: Longman, 1987. ISBN 0-582-64490-9 (pbk). ▸ Studies of development of class and ethnic identities as products of current social, economic, and political struggles, not self-evident categories. Focus on language, literature, and political discourse reflecting competing nationalisms. [WHW]

19.781 Mark Mathabane. *Kaffir boy: the true story of a black youth's coming of age in apartheid South Africa.* 1986 ed. New York: Penguin, 1987. ISBN 0-452-26471-5 (pbk). ▸ Autobiography of young South African growing up in 1970s provides insight into harsh impact of apartheid on black urban life. Detailed narrative shows why Soweto uprising sparked widespread political unrest among blacks, especially youth; see Frederikse 19.751 and Hirson 19.762. [WHW]

19.782 Paul Maylam. *A history of the African people of South Africa: from the early Iron Age to the 1970s.* New York: St. Martin's, 1986. ISBN 0-312-37511-5. ▸ General history of South Africa concentrating on experiences of Africans since 1830. Summarizes both liberal and radical approaches but overly schematic and lacking strong interpretive argument. Undergraduate textbook. [WHW]

19.783 Fatima Meer. *Higher than hope: the authorized biography of Nelson Mandela.* 1988 ed. New York: Harper & Row, 1990. ISBN 0-06-016146-9. ▸ Fullest biography of Nelson Mandela currently available, written with family approval; more detail than interpretation. Good information; read with speeches and more analytical studies of modern South Africa. [WHW]

19.784 Francis Meli. *South Africa belongs to us: a history of the ANC.* 1988 ed. Bloomington: Indiana University Press, 1989. ISBN 0-253-33740-2 (cl), 0-253-28591-7 (pbk). ▸ General synthesis of secondary literature on modern South Africa by spokesman

for African National Congress (ANC). Liberation struggles of black South Africans interpreted from ANC nationalist viewpoint, little attention to rival organizations or local or regional issues. [WHW]

19.785 William Minter. *King Solomon's mines revisited: Western interests and the burdened history of southern Africa.* New York: Basic Books, 1986. ISBN 0-465-03723-2 (cl), 0-465-03724-0 (pbk). ▸ Dissects European and American investment in southern African mining and finance as contributing to development of racial discrimination. Close economic ties softened British and United States government criticism of apartheid in 1960s to 1980s. [WHW]

19.786 Naboth Mokgatle. *The autobiography of an unknown South African.* Berkeley: University of California Press, 1971. ISBN 0-520-01845-1 (cl), 0-520-02903-8 (pbk). ▸ Autobiography of African life spanning much of twentieth century. Shows strong links that migrant workers retained with rural homes, poverty, and discrimination before apartheid (1950s) and strength of family and community ties in facing adversity. [WHW]

19.787 T. Dunbar Moodie. "The political economy of the black miners' strike of 1946." *Journal of southern African studies* 13.1 (1986) 1–35. ISSN 0305-7070. ▸ Study of key strike in black worker organization in gold mines. Shows union leading migrant workers to unite, overcoming temporary nature of employment through moral outrage at sub-subsistence wage levels and harsh treatment by employers. [WHW]

19.788 T. Dunbar Moodie. *The rise of Afrikanerdom: power, apartheid, and the Afrikaner civil religion.* Berkeley: University of California Press, 1975. ISBN 0-520-03943-2 (pbk). ▸ Calvinism and Dutch Reformed Church involved in consolidation of Afrikaner nationalism and, ultimately, political strength. Rigorous research in primary documents shows how Afrikaners justified racially exclusivist nationalism. See Murray 19.789. [WHW]

19.789 Colin Murray. *Families divided: the impact of migrant labour in Lesotho.* Cambridge: Cambridge University Press, 1981. ISBN 0-521-23501-4. ▸ Intimate study of destructive impact of male labor migration on family life and structure in Lesotho from late nineteenth century to 1970s; based on extensive fieldwork. Treats women as household heads and food producers in increasingly impoverished countryside. [WHW]

19.790 Dan O'Meara. *Volkskapitalisme: class, capital, and ideology in the development of Afrikaner nationalism, 1934–1948.* Cambridge: Cambridge University Press, 1983. ISBN 0-521-24285-1. ▸ Marxist analysis of economic and class bases of Nationalist party. Identifies petty bourgeois clerks, teachers, and lawyers as seeking to improve own positions; against Moodie's emphasis on religious underpinnings (19.788). [WHW]

19.791 Andre Odendaal. *Vukani bantu! The beginnings of black protest politics in South Africa to 1912.* Cape Town: Philip with University of Cape Town, Centre for African Studies, 1984. ISBN 0-908396-73-2. ▸ Only thorough examination of African politics in South Africa up to founding of African National Congress, based on extensive documentary research. Story continued in Walshe's history of African nationalism after 1912 (19.818). [WHW]

19.792 J. D. Omer-Cooper. *A history of southern Africa.* London: Heinemann, 1987. ISBN 0-435-08010-5 (pbk). ▸ Well-illustrated general history of South Africa for undergraduates and secondary schools. Liberal approach with emphasis on African societies and formation of racial attitudes in colonial times. Despite title, focus on South Africa, with brief appendixes on Botswana, Lesotho, and Swaziland. [WHW]

19.793 Robin Palmer and Neil Parsons, eds. *The roots of rural poverty in central and southern Africa.* Berkeley: University of California Press, 1977. ISBN 0-520-03318-3 (pbk). ‣ Seminal collection of radical studies showing impoverishment of African communities in southern Africa. Inaugurated massive rejection of earlier optimistic assessments of colonial capitalism, but claim that African opposition was quelled by 1930s subsequently rejected. [WHW/EAE]

19.794 Ian Phimister. *An economic and social history of Zimbabwe, 1890–1948: capital accumulation and class struggle.* London: Longman, 1988. ISBN 0-582-64423-2. ‣ Marxist analysis examining power of gold-mining industry and settler agriculture to fashion colonial economic policies. Concludes forced African migrant labor and land confiscations stimulated African resistance, e.g., by Watchtower Society. [WHW]

19.795 Solomon T. Plaatje. *Native life in South Africa: before and since the European war and the Boer Rebellion.* 1916 ed. Brian Willan, Introduction. Athens: Ohio University Press, 1991. ISBN 0-8214-0986-7. ‣ Vividly detailed account by famous journalist and founder of African National Congress of discrimination suffered by Africans in South Africa, particularly as result of 1913 land act. Stress on economic levels of racial discrimination prefigures later radical interpretations. See Willan 19.822. [WHW]

19.796 Benjamin Pogrund. *Sobukwe and apartheid.* 1990 ed. New Brunswick, N.J.: Rutgers University Press, 1991. ISBN 0-8135-1692-7 (cl), 0-8135-1693-5 (pbk). ‣ Detailed journalistic biography of Robert Sobukwe, key founder of Pan Africanist Congress (PAC). Focus on personal beliefs and actions; useful approach to philosophy subsequently appealing to young blacks. See Gerhart 19.753. Earlier title: *How Can Man Die Better?* [WHW]

19.797 Deborah Posel. *The making of apartheid, 1948–1961: conflict and compromise.* Oxford: Oxford University Press, 1991. ISBN 0-19-827334-7 (cl), 0-19-827772-5. ‣ Nationalists had no blueprint for apartheid when elected in 1948; segregationist policies developed in 1950s out of government concern to regulate black urban influx; against liberal view of apartheid as reflecting heritage of Afrikaner racism. [WHW]

19.798 Robert M. Price. *The apartheid state in crisis: political transformation in South Africa, 1975–1990.* New York: Oxford University Press, 1991. ISBN 0-19-506749-5 (cl), 0-19-506750-9 (pbk). ‣ Analysis of internal contradictions of apartheid as government repression provoked black militancy that business interests and officials found too costly to contain. Sees weakening of apartheid as pragmatic compromise with African labor rather than rejection of racism. [WHW]

19.799 Terence O. Ranger. *Peasant consciousness and guerrilla war in Zimbabwe: a comparative study.* Berkeley: University of California Press, 1985. ISBN 0-520-05555-1 (cl), 0-520-05588-8 (pbk.) ‣ Study of grassroots bases of African resistance to colonial capitalism in Southern Rhodesia (Zimbabwe). Emphasizes regional and local peasant consciousness of exploitation and adoption of progressively militant tactics, culminating in guerrilla war. [WHW]

19.800 Robert I. Rotberg. *The founder: Cecil Rhodes and the pursuit of power.* 1988 ed. New York: Oxford University Press, 1990. ISBN 0-19-504968-3 (cl, 1988), 0-19-506668-5 (pbk). ‣ Definitive biography of most prominent mining magnate and politician in late nineteenth-century southern Africa; prodigious research, but more detail than success with attempted psychohistorical interpretation of Rhodes's character. [WHW]

19.801 Edward Roux. *Time longer than rope: a history of the black man's struggle for freedom in South Africa.* 2d ed. Madison: University of Wisconsin Press, 1966. ISBN 0-299-03204-3 (pbk). ‣ Classic, contemporary account of African resistance to racial discrimination to ca. 1948. Often anecdotal and overly detailed,

but emphasis on workers' economic issues anticipated later radical studies. [WHW]

19.802 H. J. Simons and R. E. Simons. *Class and colour in South Africa, 1850–1950.* Harmondsworth: Penguin, 1969. ISBN 0-14-041025-2. ‣ Important early account, by white African National Congress activists, of African resistance to racial discrimination in South Africa. Introduced class analysis of segregation and apartheid, inspiring later radical interpretations. [WHW]

19.803 Newell Stultz. *Afrikaner politics in South Africa, 1934–1948.* Berkeley: University of California Press, 1974. ISBN 0-520-02452-4. ‣ Taking Afrikaner unity as given, follows Nationalist party politics in decade preceding implementation of apartheid. Compare with Moodie's emphasis on religion (19.788) and O'Meara on class divisions (19.790). [WHW]

19.804 Maureen Swan. *Gandhi: the South African experience.* Johannesburg: Ravan, 1985. ISBN 0-86975-232-4. ‣ Study of formative years of famous Indian nationalist in South Africa. Shows protests against government extension of discrimination to Indian community, but demythologizes by showing Gandhi's responsiveness to business backers rather than laborers and prominent roles of other Indian politicians. [WHW]

19.805 Leonard M. Thompson. *A history of South Africa.* 1990 ed. New Haven: Yale University Press, 1992. ISBN 0-300-04815-7 (cl, 1990), 0-300-05171-9 (pbk). ‣ Fluid writing, apt detail, consistent (liberal) argument make this best short history of South Africa, by leading scholar of his generation. Emphasis on Africans as makers of own history; particularly strong on period before 1900. [WHW]

19.806 Leonard M. Thompson. *The political mythology of apartheid.* New Haven: Yale University Press, 1985. ISBN 0-300-03368-0 (cl), 0-300-03512-8 (pbk). ‣ Close examination of myths manufactured by Afrikaner nationalists to justify apartheid, extending liberal stress on importance of ideology in sustaining racism. Concludes stories of alleged African savagery and British oppression embellished without regard to factual details. [WHW]

19.807 Leonard M. Thompson. *The unification of South Africa, 1902–1910.* Oxford: Clarendon, 1960. ‣ Definitive on political foundations of modern South Africa, confirmed in Union Agreement of 1910. Focuses on constitutional debates on excluding blacks from franchise and on including Afrikaans as official language. [WHW]

19.808 Virginia McLean Thompson and Richard Adloff. *The Malagasy Republic: Madagascar today.* Stanford, Calif.: Stanford University Press, 1965. ‣ Attempt to explain movement from bloody revolt to peaceful decolonization. Concentrates on politics, but also population growth, economic stagnation, religion, education, and Malagasy literature since World War II. [WHW]

19.809 Thomas Tlou and Alec Campbell. *History of Botswana.* Gaborone: Macmillan, 1984. ISBN 0-333-36531-3 (pbk). ‣ Basic survey (secondary school, first-year university) covering Botswana from origins of mankind to present. Superficial but only integrated history of country and useful compendium of basic information. [WHW]

19.810 Leroy Vail, ed. *The creation of tribalism in southern Africa.* Berkeley: University of California Press, 1989. ISBN 0-520-06284-1 (cl), 0-520-06415-1 (pbk). ‣ Fourteen studies of historical development of modern ethnicity (national, racial, and tribal) in southern Africa. Treats economic and political motivations, particularly colonial governments' urge to find tribes through exaggeration of distinctions not important to Africans. [WHW]

19.811 Leroy Vail and Landeg White. *Capitalism and colonialism in Mozambique: a study of Quelimane district.* 1980 ed. Minneapolis: University of Minnesota Press, 1981. ISBN 0-8166-1039-8. ‣ Exhaustive study of devastation of colonial capitalism (British sugar firms) in Portuguese Mozambique. Details colonial demands for African labor and land; innovative use of African songs to reveal African experience of forced exactions. [WHW]

19.812 Leroy Vail and Landeg White. *Power and the praise poem: South African voices in history.* Charlottesville: University Press of Virginia, 1991. ISBN 0-8139-1339-X (cl), 0-8139-1340-3 (pbk). ‣ Innovative study of African songs as vehicles for popular critique of political authority. Demonstrates continuity from early nineteenth-century states through modern African resistance to authoritarianism, colonial and independent. [WHW]

19.813 Floris A. van Jaarsveld. *The Afrikaner's interpretation of South African history.* Cape Town: Simondium, 1964. ‣ Insider's account of Afrikaners' historical sense of persecution by British, fears of black "savagery," and religious sources of national consciousness. Explains why Afrikaners believed they had to adopt apartheid policies. [WHW]

19.814 Charles van Onselen. *Chibaro: African mine labour in Southern Rhodesia, 1900–1933.* 1976 ed. Johannesburg: Ravan, 1980. ISBN 0-902818-96-1 (pbk). ‣ First major study of African mine labor. Social history of mine compounds in which workers were confined as locales where consciousness of exploitation and identity as workers emerged, resulting in resistance through go-slows, sabotage, and abandonment of work. [WHW]

19.815 Charles van Onselen. "Race and class in the South African countryside." *American historical review* 95.1 (1990) 99–123. ISSN 0002-8762. ‣ Study of harsh impact of industrialization on South Africa's countryside, through personal experiences of Kas Maine, African sharecropper. Moves beyond Marxist structural dichotomies of race and class to show nuanced human relationships. [WHW]

19.816 Charles van Onselen. *Studies in the social and economic history of the Witwatersrand, 1886–1914.* 2 vols. London: Longman, 1982. ISBN 0-582-64382-1 (v. 1, cl), 0-582-64384-8 (v. 2, cl), 0-582-64383-X (v. 1, pbk), 0-582-64385-6 (v. 2, pbk). ‣ Essays on growth of Johannesburg finding development in breaking of older African communities and formation of new classes—laundrymen, bootleggers, prostitutes, and cart drivers. Sees lives of all, including racial divisions, forced into conformity with economic needs of mining capitalists. [WHW]

19.817 Cherryl A. Walker, ed. *Women and gender in southern Africa to 1945.* Bloomington: Indiana University Press, 1991. ISBN 0-253-20665-0 (pbk). ‣ Basic, and only, collection of essays documenting experiences of women in nineteenth- and twentieth-century South Africa. Topics range from gender oppression in precapitalist African societies to white women's suffrage movement. [WHW]

19.818 Peter Walshe. *The rise of African nationalism in South Africa: the African National Congress, 1912–1952.* Berkeley: University of California Press, 1971. ISBN 0-520-01810-9. ‣ Innovative (for its time) focus on political organization of African opposition to racial discrimination; small, elite ANC founded 1912, transformed into mass movement only in 1950s. Still most exhaustive coverage of ANC throughout this period. [WHW]

19.819 Peter Warwick. *Black people and the South African War, 1899–1902.* Cambridge: Cambridge University Press, 1983. ISBN 0-521-25216-4. ‣ South African War (1899–1902), usually depicted as white man's (Anglo-Boer) conflict, involved many Africans, ready to take up arms to end racial discrimination. Although war raised African expectations of political emancipation, white man's peace dashed them. [WHW]

19.820 Peter Warwick, ed. *The South African War: the Anglo-Boer War, 1899–1902.* Harlow, England: Longman, 1980. ISBN 0-582-78526-X. ‣ Detailed studies of South African War (1899–1902), moving beyond conventional military/political perspec-

tives. Topics range from gold-mining industry's provocation of conflict, to social history of Boer commandos, and poetry of the war. [WHW]

19.821 Landeg White. *Magomero: portrait of an African village.* 1987 ed. Cambridge: Cambridge University Press, 1989. ISBN 0-521-32182-4 (cl, 1987), 0-521-38909-7 (pbk). ‣ Evocative study of changing impact of colonialism in Malawian village from time of David Livingstone (mid-nineteenth century) to author's visits in 1970s and 1980s. Archival and oral research reveals forced labor, increasing poverty, but also persistence of African ideals of independence. [WHW]

19.822 Brian Willan. *Sol Plaatje: South African nationalist, 1876–1932.* Berkeley: University of California Press, 1984. ISBN 0-520-05274-9 (cl), 0-520-05334-6 (pbk). ‣ Definitive biography of journalist and African National Congress founder, as ambivalent believer in moral and material superiority of West but critic of racial discrimination. Exemplifies Western-educated, Christian Africans who replaced chiefs as politicians in early twentieth century. See Plaatje 19.795. [WHW]

19.823 Monica Wilson and Leonard M. Thompson, eds. *The Oxford history of South Africa.* 1969 ed. 2 vols. New York: Oxford University Press, 1971. ISBN 0-19-821641-6 (v. 1). ‣ Major collaborative history of South Africa. Defined "liberal" focus on political oppression of Africans, interpreted as result of Afrikaner racism, with economic development the solution; lightning rod for subsequent radical (Marxist) critique. [WHW]

19.824 David Yudelman. *The emergence of modern South Africa: state, capital, and the incorporation of organized labor on the South African gold fields, 1902–1939.* Westport, Conn.: Greenwood, 1983. ISBN 0-313-23170-2. ‣ Rejects Marxist structuralism and naive liberal views to explain failure of white and black working classes to unite against employers as product of state and capitalist cooptation of majority of white workers through higher wages and job protection at expense of white radicals and blacks. [WHW]

TOPICAL STUDIES

General Studies

19.825 David A. Anderson and Richard Grove, eds. *Conservation in Africa: people, policies, and practice.* Cambridge: Cambridge University Press, 1987. ISBN 0-521-34199-X. ‣ Sixteen accounts of past conservation experiences in Africa that go beyond preservation of exotic wildlife to consider conservation ideology and to link conservation to agrarian and pastoralist development. [MJH]

19.826 Ralph A. Austen. *African economic history: internal development and external dependency.* Portsmouth, N.H.: Heinemann, 1987. ISBN 0-435-08017-2 (pbk). ‣ Broad overview of African economic history. Tries to find middle ground between liberal and Marxist interpretations. Particularly useful for analysis of trade and interpretation of regional economies. [MJH]

19.827 W. G. Clarence-Smith. *The third Portuguese empire, 1825–1975: a study in economic imperialism.* Manchester: Manchester University Press, 1985. ISBN 0-7190-1719-X. ‣ Summary of 150 years of Portuguese colonialism, based on secondary sources. Focuses on economic impact and importance of colonies for Portuguese domestic economy. [JCM/MJH]

19.828 Anthony Clayton and David Killingray. *Khaki and blue: military and police in British colonial Africa.* Athens: Ohio University, Center for International Studies, 1989. (Monographs in International Studies, Africa series, 51.) ISBN 0-89680-147-0. ‣ Personal reminiscences of British men tell how military and police were organized in African colonies and reflected white attitudes to African crime and to Africans themselves. [MJH]

19.829 Catherine Coquery-Vidrovitch and Paul E. Lovejoy, eds. *The workers of African trade.* Beverly Hills, Calif.: Sage, 1985. ISBN 0-8039-2472-0. ‣ Collection of essays concerning transport workers (porters, teamsters) of long-distance trade in different regions of Africa. Broadly and convincingly illuminates economic history. [MJH]

19.830 Donald Crummey, ed. *Banditry, rebellion, and social protest in Africa.* Portsmouth, N.H.: Heinemann, 1986. ISBN 0-435-08011-3 (pbk). ‣ Collection of scholarly articles on bandits and rebels in African history, some quite lively and accessible. Editor's introduction is useful overview of literature, inspired by Eric Hobsbawm. [MJH]

19.831 Bill Freund. *The African worker.* Cambridge: Cambridge University Press, 1988. ISBN 0-521-30758-9 (cl), 0-521-31491-7 (pbk). ‣ Balanced, thoughtful synthesis of labor historiography in Africa, largely radical in tone. Looks forward to conceptualization broadened beyond conventional wage-paid workplaces to fields, families, and forests. [JCM/DSN]

19.832 Jane I. Guyer, ed. *Feeding African cities: studies in regional social history.* Bloomington: Indiana University Press with International African Institute, 1987. ISBN 0-253-32102-6. ‣ Rich essays link urban and agricultural history by focusing on problems of maintaining food supply to Kano, Dar es Salaam, Yaounde, and Harare. Editor's comparative epilogue is superb. [MJH]

19.833 Randi Haaland and Peter Shinnie, eds. *African iron working, ancient and traditional.* Oslo: Norwegian University Press; distributed by Oxford University Press, 1985. ISBN 82-00-07292-4. ‣ Essays by archaeologists that move beyond conventional technical studies to social and economic implications of technology. Some case studies, some suggestive interpretations; relatively current thinking on perennial conundrum in early African history. [JCM]

19.834 Adrian Hastings. *A history of African Christianity, 1950–1975.* Cambridge: Cambridge University Press, 1979. ISBN 0-521-22212-5 (cl), 0-521-29397-9 (pbk). ‣ Thorough institutional history of African Christianity in late colonial and early independence periods. Includes separatist as well as established mission churches. Emphasis on English-speaking Africa. [MJH]

19.835 Eugenia W. Herbert. *Red gold of Africa: copper in precolonial history and culture.* Madison: University of Wisconsin Press, 1984. ISBN 0-299-09600-9. ‣ Wide-ranging, thorough, and imaginative reconstruction of copper production and copper artifacts in African history, showing economic and symbolic value of Africa's primary prestige metal. Based on secondary literature. [MJH]

19.836 John Iliffe. *The African poor: a history.* Cambridge: Cambridge University Press, 1987. ISBN 0-521-34415-8 (cl), 0-521-34877-3 (pbk). ‣ Broad, accessible portrayal of poverty and poor throughout African history. Emphasizes description rather than theoretical insights, but broadly contrasts earlier circumstantial with modern structural poverty. [MJH]

19.837 David Killingray and Richard Rathbone, eds. *Africa and the Second World War.* New York: St. Martin's, 1986. ISBN 0-312-00941-0. ‣ Interesting, accessible collection of scholarly papers analyzing involvement of African men in World War II. Focus on British colonies; discussion of war's economic impact on rural societies. [MJH]

19.838 Martin A. Klein, ed. *Peasants in Africa: historical and contemporary perspectives.* Beverly Hills, Calif.: Sage, 1980. ISBN 0-8039-1406-7 (cl), 0-8039-1407-5 (pbk). ‣ Scholarly articles, usually from Marxist perspective, on peasants and peasant societies presenting historical views of rural impoverishment through colonial domination in western and southern Africa. [MJH]

19.839 Igor Kopytoff, ed. *The African frontier: the reproduction of traditional African societies.* Bloomington: Indiana University Press, 1987. ISBN 0-253-30252-8. ‣ Fascinating, controversial introduction applies frontier thesis to traditional (i.e., anthropological) Africa, seeing change originating on borders of African societies as conventionally defined. Case studies strong on their own terms. [MJH]

19.840 Gerhard Liesegang, Helma Pasch, and Adam Jones, eds. *Figuring African trade: proceedings of the Symposium on the Quantification and Structure of the Import and Export and Long-Distance Trade in Africa, 1800–1913.* Berlin: Reimer, 1986. (Kolmer Beiträge zur Afrikanistik, 11.) ISBN 3-496-00819-9 (cl), 3-496-00815-6 (pbk). ‣ Scholarly papers in English and French presenting very specific, detailed, and largely quantitative case studies of African trade up to World War I, mostly external. [MJH]

19.841 John M. MacKenzie. *The empire of nature: hunting, conservation, and British imperialism.* Manchester: Manchester University Press, 1988. ISBN 0-7190-2227-4. ‣ British cult of hunting at core of predatory early colonialism in Africa, followed by conservationist response, and modern safari tourism. Effects on African societies largely negative. [JCM]

19.842 Kristin Mann and Richard Roberts, eds. *Law in colonial Africa.* Portsmouth, N.H.: Heinemann, 1991. ISBN 0-435-08053-9 (cl), 0-435-08055-5 (pbk). ‣ Multiple case studies illuminating interaction between law and social history in African colonies. Advocates studies of law as changing construct born in struggles over resources and authority. [MJH]

19.843 V. Y. Mudimbe. *The invention of Africa: gnosis, philosophy, and the order of knowledge.* Bloomington: Indiana University Press, 1988. ISBN 0-253-33126-9 (cl), 0-253-20468-2 (pbk). ‣ Influential, Foucauldian analysis attempts to uncover African epistemology. Regrets that dominant tension between tradition and modernity derives from Western concepts. [MJH]

19.844 Malyn Newitt. *Portugal in Africa: the last hundred years.* London: Longman, 1981. ISBN 0-582-64379-1 (cl), 0-582-64377-5 (pbk). ‣ Study of Angola, Mozambique, São Tomé/Príncipe, Guinée, and Cape Verde Islands under Portuguese rule, with emphasis on African resistance but less control of economic issues. Best introduction to Portuguese colonial Africa. [JCM]

Women

19.845 Agnes Aidoo. "Asante queen mothers in government and politics in the nineteenth century." In *The black woman cross-culturally.* 1981 ed. Filomina Chioma Steady, ed., pp. 65–77. Rochester, Vt.: Schenkman, 1985. ISBN 0-87073-345-1 (cl), 0-87073-346-X (pbk). ‣ Pioneering historical sketch of three queen mothers' political careers. Argues ritual constraints imposed on all women limited scope of queen mothers' authority until after menopause. [NRH]

19.846 Edward A. Alpers. " 'Ordinary household chores': ritual and power in a nineteenth-century Swahili women's spirit possession cult." *International journal of African historical studies* 17.4 (1984) 677–702. ISSN 0361-7882. ‣ Detailed review of evidence on women's participation in spirit possession cults on Zanzibar Island. Interprets cult as female compensatory, domesticating activity related to declining status of Swahili women. [NRH]

19.847 Bolanle Awe et al., eds. "Women, family, state, and economy in Africa." *Signs* 16 (1991). ISSN 0097-9740. ‣ Excellent collection combining state-of-art theoretical insights into relationships between economic change and intrahousehold gender struggles with topics reflecting new trends in historical research. [NRH]

19.848 Sandra T. Barnes. "Ritual, power, and outside knowledge." *Journal of religion in Africa* 20.3 (1990) 248–68. ISSN 0022-

4200. ‣ How precolonial women-outsiders achieved prominence in Lagos because they bore outside knowledge of religious ideas and practices. Significant interpretation focusing on intermediary roles of in-marrying women. [NRH]

19.849   Edna G. Bay, ed. *Women and work in Africa*. Boulder: Westview, 1982. ISBN 0-86531-312-1. ‣ Interdisciplinary anthology including two notable historical contributions: Muntemba on women and agricultural change in Zambia, 1930–70, and Yates on gender and education in colonial Zaire. [NRH]

19.850   Jean Boyd. *The caliph's sister: Nana Asma'u, 1793–1865, teacher, poet, and Islamic leader*. Totowa, N.J.: Cass, 1989. ISBN 0-7146-3319-4 (cl), 0-7146-4067-0 (pbk). ‣ Illustrated, highly accessible, engaging biography of prolific, influential Muslim woman scholar. Masterfully integrates analysis of literary writings, political history of Sokoto caliphate, and social history of women and religious life. [NRH]

19.851   Jean Boyd and Murray Last. "The role of women as 'agents religieux' in Sokoto." *Canadian journal of African studies* 19.2 (1985) 283–300. ISSN 0008-3968. ‣ Calls for African women's intellectual history; outlines policies on Muslim women's education, assesses writings of female scholars, and explores mobilization of women in Islamic instruction in nineteenth-century northern Nigeria. [NRH]

19.852   Belinda Bozzoli with Mmantho Nkotsoe. *Women of Phokeng: consciousness, life strategy, and migrancy in South Africa, 1900–1983*. Portsmouth, N.H.: Heinemann, 1991. ISBN 0-435-08054-7 (cl), 0-435-08056-3 (pbk). ‣ Examination of consciousness and experiences of twenty-two women born before 1916. Treats peasant backgrounds, mission education, township migration, domestic service, beer brewing, and political protest. Superb analytical privileging of women's voices. [NRH]

19.853   George Chauncey, Jr. "The locus of reproduction: women's labour in the Zambian Copperbelt, 1927–1953." *Journal of southern African studies* 7.2 (1981) 135–64. ISSN 0305-7070. ‣ Influential classic; how gender structured labor processes in colonial mining industry. Reveals complex alliances and contradictions. Economic independence of women in mine compounds threatened rural African leaders and colonial state. [NRH]

19.854   Mona Étienne. "Women and men, cloth, and colonization: the transformation of production-distribution relations among the Baule (Ivory Coast)." *Cahiers d'études africaines* 27.65 (1977) 41–64. ISSN 0008-0055. ‣ Pivotal analysis of female subordination under colonialism. Finds expanding commodity economy resulted in alienation of women's labor and loss of gender interdependency in cloth production and distribution. [NRH]

19.855   Deborah Gaitskell, comp. *Special issue on women in southern Africa*. Oxford: Oxford University Press, 1983. (*Journal of southern African studies*, 10.) ISSN 0305-7070. ‣ Many important contributions to southern African women's history, including Wright on technology, marriage, and women's work among Tonga and Peters on gender and development cycles in Botswana. [NRH]

19.856   Susan Geiger. "Women in nationalist struggle: TANU activists in Dar es Salaam." *International journal of African historical studies* 20.1 (1987) 1–26. ISSN 0361-7882. ‣ Pioneering treatment of women and nationalism. Origins and development of Muslim women's participation in Tanganyika African National Union in Dar es Salaam in 1950s, using life histories. [NRH]

19.857   Jane I. Guyer. *Family and farm in southern Cameroon*. Boston: Boston University, African Studies Center, 1984. (African research studies, 15.) ISBN 0-915118-13-0. ‣ Theoretically remarkable study of family, agricultural, and dietary change among Beti from precolonial period, highlighting changes in divi-

sion of labor, colonial expansion of polygyny, and feminization of food production. [NRH]

19.858   Nancy J. Hafkin and Edna G. Bay, eds. *Women in Africa: studies in social and economic change*. Stanford, Calif.: Stanford University Press, 1976. ISBN 0-8047-0906-8 (cl), 0-8047-1011-2 (pbk). ‣ Still best available historical anthology on African women, with broad coverage. Effective classroom text. Includes eighteenth-century women entrepreneurs in Senegal (Brooks), Luo women and colonialism (Hay), and Aba Women's War (van Allen). [NRH]

19.859   Karen Tranberg Hansen, ed. *African encounters with domesticity*. New Brunswick, N.J.: Rutgers University Press, 1992. ISBN 0-8135-1803-2 (cl), 0-8135-1804-0 (pbk). ‣ Imaginative collection explores multiple meanings of domesticity in colonial and postcolonial life. Stimulating essays embrace mission encounters, domestic science training, hygiene, and historical change in gendering of work. [NRH]

19.860   Margaret Jean Hay and Sharon Stichter, eds. *African women south of the Sahara*. London: Longman, 1984. ISBN 0-582-64373-2 (pbk). ‣ Best available introductory classroom text on African women, with many historically minded contributions. Emphasis on changing gender division of labor in household, economy, politics, religion, art, and literature. [NRH]

19.861   Margaret Jean Hay and Marcia Wright, eds. *African women and the law: historical perspectives*. Boston: Boston University, African Studies Center, 1982. (Boston University Papers on Africa, 7.) ISBN 0-915118-11-4 (pbk). ‣ Essays on importance of legal records for African women's history. Original essays with broad chronological and geographic coverage consider women's rights regarding property, mobility, and marriage. Highlights colonial creation of customary law. [NRH]

19.862   Nancy Rose Hunt. "'Le bébé en brousse': European women, African birth spacing, and colonial intervention in breast feeding in the Belgian Congo." *International journal of African historical studies* 21.3 (1988) 401–32. ISSN 0361-7882. ‣ Pioneering study of colonial pronatalism examines efforts since 1920s to reduce prolonged breast-feeding and postpartum abstinence to increase natality. Examines European colonial women as maternal figures. [NRH]

19.863   Nancy Rose Hunt. "Noise over camouflaged polygamy, colonial morality taxation, and a woman-naming crisis in Belgian Africa." *Journal of African history* 32.3 (1991) 471–94. ISSN 0021-8537. ‣ Study of how Belgian antipolygamy measures had unintended consequences. Analyzes 1950s Bujumbura Revolt against taxation of urban single women in light of etymology and unruly manipulation of female tax categories. [NRH]

19.864   Caroline Ifeka-Moller. "Female militancy and colonial revolt: the Women's War of 1929, eastern Nigeria." In *Perceiving women*. Shirley Ardener, ed., pp. 127–57. New York: Wiley, 1975. ISBN 0-470-03309-6. ‣ Culturally sensitive interpretation of Aba women's tax revolt in terms of change in gender division of labor under colonial rule, where women achieved unprecedented commercial power and were taxed as men. [NRH]

19.865   Birgitta Larsson. *Conversion to greater freedom? Women, church, and social change in north-western Tanzania under colonial rule*. Uppsala: Acta Universitatis Upsaliensis, 1991. (Studia historica Upsaliensia, 162.) ISBN 91-554-2684-0. ‣ Richly documented study of Haya women as social actors in context of court life, Christian missions, cash-crop economy, and colonial demographic crisis. Includes nuns, prostitutes, revival movement, and girls' education. [NRH]

19.866   Shula Marks, ed. *Not either an experimental doll: the separate worlds of three South African women*. Bloomington: Indiana University Press, 1987. ISBN 0-253-34843-9 (cl), 0-253-28640-9 (pbk). ‣ Extraordinary collection of letters among English Fabian, Zulu social worker, and Xhosa school girl, 1949–51. Compelling introduction and epilogue situate intimate aspects of these lives in broader context. [NRH]

19.867 Shula Marks and Richard Rathbone, eds. "The history of the family in Africa." *Journal of African history* 24 (1983). ISSN 0021-8537. ‣ Exceptional contributions to history of gender include Gaitskell on domesticity and Christianity in Johannesburg, Hilton on changes in Kongo women's position, and Vaughan on women's relationships in Malawi. [NRH]

19.868 Nina Emma Mba. *Nigerian women mobilized: women's political activity in southern Nigeria, 1900–1965.* Berkeley: University of California, Institute of International Studies, 1982. (Research series, 48.) ISBN 0-87725-148-7 (pbk). ‣ Broad history of political activities organized by Igbo, Egba, and Yoruba women in colonial and postcolonial periods. Coverage includes Aba Women's War, Abeokuta Women's Union, and women in Lagos politics. [NRH]

19.869 Joseph C. Miller. "Nzinga of Matamba in a new perspective." *Journal of African history* 26.2 (1975) 201–16. ISSN 0021-8537. ‣ Pioneering biography of precolonial African woman leader. Reconciles conflicting historical images of this extraordinary seventeenth-century queen; stresses her cultural position as woman and outsider. [NRH/JKT]

19.870 Sarah Mirza and Margaret Strobel, eds. and trans. *Three Swahili women: life histories from Mombasa, Kenya.* Bloomington: Indiana University Press, 1989. ISBN 0-253-36012-9 (cl), 0-253-28854-1 (pbk). ‣ Captivating life histories of three Muslim Swahili women born between 1890 and 1920. Emphasizes impact of slavery, strategies of Swahili women of diverse backgrounds, and women's ceremonies and rituals. [NRH]

19.871 Randall M. Packard. "Social change and the history of misfortune among the Bashu of eastern Zaire." In *Explorations in African systems of thought.* 1980 ed. Ivan Karp and Charles S. Bird, eds., pp. 237–67. Washington, D.C.: Smithsonian Institution, 1987. ISBN 0-87474-591-8 (pbk). ‣ Groundbreaking study linking Bashu social change and emergence of gendered idioms of misfortune and witchcraft. Analyzes history of female witches in light of strains in gender relations in colonial period. [NRH]

19.872 Denise Paulme, ed. *Women of tropical Africa.* 1963 ed. H. M. Wright, trans. Berkeley: University of California Press, 1971. ISBN 0-520-00989-4 (cl), 0-520-02052-9 (pbk). ‣ Classic anthropological anthology on women in Francophone Africa, including women's precolonial political roles (Lebeaf), life histories of five Nzakara women (Laurentin), and extensive annotated bibliography. [NRH]

19.873 Claire C. Robertson and Iris Berger, eds. *Women and class in Africa.* New York: Africana, 1986. ISBN 0-8419-0979-2. ‣ Significant essays consider relationship between class and gender, including anticolonial activity among Yoruba women (Johnson), education and class formation (Robertson), and labor unrest among Kikuyu women (Presley). [NRH]

19.874 Patricia W. Romero, ed. *Life histories of African women.* Atlantic Highlands, N.J.: Ashfield, 1988. ISBN 0-948660-04-x (cl), 0-948660-05-8 (pbk). ‣ Seven biographies or autobiographies of women from various regions of Africa, finely rendered by prominent Africanists; many show colonial influence. Effective introductory text. [NRH]

19.875 Elizabeth Schmidt. *Peasants, traders, and wives: Shona women in the history of Zimbabwe, 1870–1939.* Portsmouth, N.H.: Heinemann, 1992. ISBN 0-435-08064-4 (cl), 0-435-08066-0 (pbk). ‣ Rigorous feminist history of colonial Zimbabwe highlighting how women's labor and struggle to control sexuality were central

to political economy and formation of peasantries. Includes discussion of precolonial women's roles. [NRH]

19.876 Margaret Strobel. *Muslim women in Mombasa, 1890–1975.* New Haven: Yale University Press, 1979. ISBN 0-300-02302-2. ‣ Unrivaled cultural history of African women highlighting Swahili dances, rituals, and celebrations. Analyzes relationship between slavery and gender asymmetry and impact of colonialism on female subculture. [NRH]

19.877 John K. Thornton. "Legitimacy and political power: Queen Njinga, 1624–1663." *Journal of African history* 32.1 (1991) 25–40. ISSN 0021-8537. ‣ Specialist study bringing important new evidence to bear on Njinga's (Nzinga's) career and legacy. Interesting gender analysis of her dramatic assertions of maleness to overcome opponents' contentions concerning illegitimacy of female rule. Compare Miller 19.869. [NRH/JKT]

19.878 Leroy Vail and Landeg White. "The possession of the dispossessed: songs as history among Tumbuka women." In *Power and the praise poem: southern African voices in history,* pp. 231–77. Charlottesville: University Press of Virginia, 1991. ISBN 0-8139-1339-x (cl), 0-8139-1340-3 (pbk). ‣ Exquisite analysis of women's spirit possession songs as female reading of historical changes in balance of power between sexes as colonial capitalism superseded Ngoni domination. [NRH]

19.879 Megan Vaughan. *Curing their ills: colonial power and African illness.* Stanford, Calif.: Stanford University Press, 1991. ISBN 0-8047-1970-5 (cl), 0-8047-1971-3 (pbk). ‣ Imaginative history of colonial medical practice and writing as gendered, sexualized discourse. Relies on European sources; astutely engages feminist and critical theory. [NRH]

19.880 Cherryl A. Walker. *Women and resistance in South Africa.* 1982 ed. New York: Monthly Review, 1991. ISBN 0-85345-830-8 (cl), 0-85345-829-4 (pbk). ‣ Basic political history tracing women's organizations and antipass protests in South Africa, in context of national liberation movement and economic changes restructuring women's position in society. [NRH]

19.881 E. Frances White. *Sierra Leone's settler women traders: women on the Afro-European frontier.* Ann Arbor: University of Michigan Press, 1987. ISBN 0-472-10080-7. ‣ Best available study of Krio women merchants' changing economic status and roles as culture brokers. Based on interviews; several biographies included. [NRH]

19.882 Luise White. "Separating the men from the boys: constructions of gender, sexuality, and terrorism in central Kenya, 1939–1959." *International journal of African historical studies* 23.1 (1990) 1–25. ISSN 0361-7882. ‣ Groundbreaking analysis of colonialism and male gender reconstruction. Compelling use of autobiographies of Mau Mau Rebellion participants to demonstrate integral role of struggles over masculinity, sexuality, marriage, and housework. [NRH]

19.883 Ann Whitehead. "Rural women and food production in sub-Saharan Africa." In *The political economy of hunger.* Vol. 1: *Entitlement and well-being.* Jean Dreze and Amartya Sen, eds., pp. 425–73. Oxford: Clarendon, 1990. ISBN 0-19-828635-x. ‣ Critical review of literature on gender and agrarian change in Africa. Important synthesis of twentieth-century transformation of rural women's work. Explodes myth of female farming systems; stresses key analytical variables. [NRH]

19.884 Audrey Wipper, ed. "Rural women: development or underdevelopment?" *Rural Africana* 29 (1975–76). ISSN 0085-5839. ‣ Interdisciplinary special issue. Historical treatments include women in Kenya labor force, children born out of wedlock among Toro, colonial tax riots among Pare women, and Kenya's Maendeleo ya Wanawake movement. [NRH]

19.885 Audrey Wipper and Harriet Lyons, eds. "Current

research on African women." *Canadian journal of African studies* 22 (1988). ISSN 0008-3968. ‣ Special issue on African women's studies reviews sixteen years of interdisciplinary research. Includes Hay on historical perspectives on African women and Presley on women and Mau Mau. [NRH]

19.886 Marcia Wright. *Strategies of slaves and women: life-stories from East/Central Africa.* New York: Barber, 1993. ISBN 0-936508-27-2 (cl), 0-936508-28-0 (pbk). ‣ Six exceptional life histories; penetrating historical commentaries on female survival strategies from mid-nineteenth-century servitude and social dislocation to twentieth-century social reconstruction in mission communities. [NRH]

19.887 Sherilynn Young. "Fertility and famine: women's agricultural history in southern Mozambique." In *The roots of rural poverty in central and southern Africa.* Robin Palmer and Neil Parsons, eds., pp. 66–81. Berkeley: University of California Press, 1977. ISBN 0-520-03318-3. ‣ Pioneering essay on sexual division of labor, from sixteenth century, among Tsonga and Chopi peoples, highlighting women's agricultural innovations and ritual roles during twentieth-century ecological disasters. [NRH]

Slavery

19.888 Jacob F. Ade Ajayi and B. O. Oloruntimehin. "West Africa in the anti-slave trade era." In *Cambridge history of Africa.* John E. Flint, ed., vol. 5, pp. 200–21. New York: Cambridge University Press, 1986. ISBN 0-521-20701-0. ‣ Nigerian historians place end of Atlantic slave trade in its larger West African historical context, stressing role of international economy, Christian missionaries, and Muslim *jihads* (holy wars). [DAN]

19.889 Edward A. Alpers. *Ivory and slaves: changing patterns of international trade in East Central Africa to the later nineteenth century.* Berkeley: University of California Press, 1975. ISBN 0-520-02689-6. ‣ Traces expansion of trade in northern Mozambique and adjacent areas from Portuguese arrival over several centuries. Emphasizes African participation and destructive effects of international capitalism. [DAN]

19.890 Johnson U. J. Asiegbu. *Slavery and the politics of liberation, 1787–1861: a study of liberated African emigration and British anti-slavery policy.* New York: Africana, 1969. ISBN 0-8419-0027-2. ‣ Review of fate of Africans liberated from slaving vessels who were indentured to labor in West Indies. [DAN]

19.891 Gwyn Campbell. "Madagascar and Mozambique in the slave trade of the western Indian Ocean, 1800–1861." *Slavery and abolition* 9.3 (1988) 166–93. ISSN 0144-039X. ‣ Mozambique slave exports rose after 1820 Britanno-Merina Treaty ended slave exports from Imerina-controlled areas of Madagascar. French slave trade participation spurred by demand in Merina empire and French islands. [EAE]

19.892 Gwyn Campbell. "Madagascar and the slave trade, 1810–95." *Journal of African history* 22.2 (1981) 203–27. ISSN 0021-8537. ‣ Links internal politics to rising export slave trade and intensification of slave use in Merina empire until slavery was abolished by French in 1895. [EAE]

19.893 W. G. Clarence-Smith, ed. *The economics of the Indian Ocean slave trade in the nineteenth century.* London: Cass, 1989. ISBN 0-7146-3359-3. ‣ Collection of original case studies on slave trade from eastern Africa to Middle East, India, Madagascar, and Indian Ocean islands, primarily in nineteenth century. [DAN]

19.894 Frederick Cooper. *Plantation slavery on the east coast of Africa.* New Haven: Yale University Press, 1977. ISBN 0-300-02041-4. ‣ Examination of growth of plantation slavery in Arab- and Swahili-controlled territories in East Africa in nineteenth century. Frequent comparisons with slavery in Americas. Also examines role of Islam in slavery. [DAN]

19.895 Frederick Cooper. "The problem of slavery in African studies." *Journal of African history* 20.1 (1979) 103–25. ISSN 0021-8537. ‣ Important critique and summary of recent works on slavery in Africa, evaluating its role as labor system and impact of colonial era. Comparisons with slavery in Americas. [DAN]

19.896 Dennis D. Cordell. *Dar al-Kuti and the last years of the trans-Saharan slave trade.* Madison: University of Wisconsin Press, 1985. ISBN 0-299-09520-7. ‣ Examination of Muslim commercial penetration in Central Africa, with focus on local as well as regional and international economies. Discusses effects of slave raids and trade, demography, and depopulation. [DAN/DWR]

19.897 Philip D. Curtin. *The tropical Atlantic in the age of the slave trade.* Washington, D.C.: American Historical Association, 1991. ISBN 0-87229-048-4. ‣ Brief summary of Curtin 3.349. [DAN]

19.898 Basil Davidson. *The African slave trade.* Rev. ed. Boston: Little, Brown, 1980. ISBN 0-316-17439-4 (cl), 0-316-17438-6 (pbk). ‣ Readable, comprehensive popular survey of African participation in Atlantic slave trade, evaluating impact of slave trade on African history. Emphasizes strengths of African culture and impact of European powers. [DAN]

19.899 David Eltis and James Walvin, eds. *The abolition of the Atlantic slave trade: origins and effects in Europe, Africa, and the Americas.* Stanley L. Engerman, Introduction. Madison: University of Wisconsin Press, 1981. ISBN 0-299-08490-6. ‣ Original scholarly articles on specialized topics. Abolitionist campaigns and impact of abolition in Africa, illegal slave trade, and demographic and cultural effects of abolition in West Indies and United States. [DAN]

19.900 John D. Fage. "African societies and the Atlantic slave trade." *Past and present* 125 (1989) 97–115. ISSN 0031-2746. ‣ Review of historiography since 1969, focusing on demographic, economic, and social consequences of Atlantic slave trade in West Africa. By leading British scholar. [DAN]

19.901 Allan G. B. Fisher and Humphrey J. Fisher. *Slavery and Muslim society in Africa: the institution in Saharan and Sudanic Africa and the trans-Saharan trade.* Garden City, N.Y.: Doubleday, 1971. ‣ Popular account of slavery in West Africa and of slave trade to North Africa, mostly in nineteenth century. Scope limited by heavy reliance on observations of German explorer Gustav Nachtigal. [DAN]

19.902 Christopher Fyfe. "Freed-slave colonies in West Africa." *Cambridge history of Africa.* John E. Flint, ed., vol. 5, pp. 170–99. New York: Cambridge University Press, 1976. ISBN 0-521-20701-0. ‣ Summary by leading specialist of origins and development of Sierra Leone, settled by ex-slaves from Americas and recaptives from Atlantic slave trade. Similar for colonies of Liberia and Libreville (Gabon). [DAN]

19.903 Henry A. Gemery and Jan S. Hogendorn, eds. *The uncommon market: essays in the economic history of the Atlantic slave trade.* New York: Academic Press, 1979. ISBN 0-12-279850-3. ‣ Original scholarly papers on economic operation of slave trade in sub-Saharan Africa; Atlantic and trans-Saharan export trade in slaves, role of various European nations, and abolition in Americas. [DAN]

19.904 J. E. Inikori, ed. *Forced migration: the impact of the export slave trade on African societies.* New York: Africana, 1982. ISBN 0-8419-0795-1 (cl), 0-8419-0799-4 (pbk). ‣ Edited collection reprinting scholarly essays on slavery and slave trade in sub-Saharan Africa from different perspectives. Emphasis on social and economic effects of Atlantic slave trade. [DAN]

19.905 J. E. Inikori and Stanley L. Engerman, eds. *The Atlantic slave trade: effects on economies, societies, and peoples in Africa, the*

Americas, and Europe. Durham, N.C.: Duke University Press, 1992. ISBN 0-8223-1230-1 (cl), 0-8223-1243-3 (pbk). ‣ Scholarly articles examining impact of slave trade in western Sudan, northern Nigeria, Angola, England, New England, and West Indies. Topics include demography, epidemiology, industrial economy, and racism. [DAN]

19.906   Herbert S. Klein. "Economic aspects of the eighteenth-century Atlantic slave trade." In *The rise of the merchant empires: long-distance trade in the early modern world, 1350–1750.* James D. Tracy, ed., pp. 287–310. Cambridge: Cambridge University Press, 1990. ISBN 0-521-38210-6. ‣ Readable, authoritative summary of recent scholarship treating merchandise exchanged for slaves in Africa, terms of trade and profits, demographic issues, and Middle Passage. [DAN]

19.907   Robin C. C. Law. *The slave coast of West Africa, 1550–1750: the impact of the Atlantic slave trade on an African society.* Oxford: Clarendon, 1991. ISBN 0-19-820228-8. ‣ Critical study of role of Atlantic slave trade in rise of Dahomey discussing increased warfare in region, political disintegration, and commercialization of violence (cf. Akinjogbin 19.146). [DAN/RCL]

19.908   Paul E. Lovejoy. *Transformations in slavery: a history of slavery in Africa.* Cambridge: Cambridge University Press, 1983. ISBN 0-521-24369-6 (cl), 0-521-28646-8 (pbk). ‣ Exceptionally comprehensive synthesis of history of slavery and slave trading within and from sub-Saharan Africa, including both Atlantic and Middle Eastern slave trades. [DAN]

19.909   Paul E. Lovejoy, ed. *The ideology of slavery in Africa.* Beverly Hills, Calif.: Sage, 1981. ISBN 0-8039-1664-7 (cl), 0-8039-1665-5 (pbk). ‣ Edited collection of original scholarly studies of slavery in West and West Central Africa, mostly in nineteenth and early twentieth centuries, emphasizing role of indigenous African ideologies. [DAN]

19.910   Patrick Manning. "Contours of slavery and social change in Africa." *American historical review* 88.4 (1983) 835–57. ISSN 0002-8762. ‣ Analysis of demographic, social, and economic impact of external slave trade on Africa, price of slaves, and African systems of slavery. Readable summary of scholarly schools of interpretation by leading authority. [DAN]

19.911   Patrick Manning. *Slavery and African life: Occidental, Oriental, and African slave trades.* Cambridge: Cambridge University Press, 1990. ISBN 0-521-34396-8 (cl), 0-521-34867-6 (pbk). ‣ Evaluation of impact of Atlantic and Middle Eastern slave trades in Africa based on computer model and price analysis. Treats growth of slavery in Africa. [DAN/PMM]

19.912   Patrick Manning. *Slavery, colonialism, and economic growth in Dahomey, 1640–1960.* Cambridge: Cambridge University Press, 1982. ISBN 0-521-23544-8. ‣ Detailed examination of economic development in West African state of Dahomey (now Benin), including era of Atlantic slave trade, its abolition, and French colonial rule. [DAN/DWR]

19.913   Phyllis M. Martin. *The external trade of the Loango coast, 1576–1870: the effects of changing commercial relations on the Vili kingdom of Loango.* Oxford: Clarendon, 1972. ISBN 0-19-821685-8. ‣ Case study of role of Atlantic commerce, including slave trade, on African polity over long term; emphasizes African response. [DAN/JKT]

19.914   Claude Meillassoux. *The anthropology of slavery: the womb of iron and gold.* Alide Dasnois, trans. Chicago: University of Chicago Press, 1991. ISBN 0-226-51911-2 (cl), 0-226-51912-0 (pbk). ‣ Highly analytical and theoretical analysis of social, political, and economic reasons for expansion of slavery and slave trade in western and Central Sudan of West Africa. [DAN]

19.915   Suzanne Miers and Igor Kopytoff, eds. *Slavery in Africa: historical and anthropological perspectives.* Madison: University of

Wisconsin Press, 1977. ISBN 0-299-07330-0 (cl), 0-299-07334-3 (pbk). ‣ Seminal theoretical introduction and original case studies of slavery in sub-Saharan Africa, late nineteenth and early twentieth centuries. Emphasizes importance of slave roles in kinship networks rather than economic production. [DAN]

19.916   Suzanne Miers and Richard Roberts, eds. *The end of slavery in Africa.* Madison: University of Wisconsin Press, 1988. ISBN 0-299-11550-X (cl), 0-299-11554-2 (pbk). ‣ Theoretical and historical introduction and original case studies of ending of slavery in sub-Saharan Africa during early colonial era and its social impact. Discusses transition to wage labor. [DAN]

19.917   Joseph C. Miller. *Way of death: merchant capitalism and the Angolan slave trade, 1730–1830.* Madison: University of Wisconsin Press, 1988. ISBN 0-299-11560-7. ‣ Comprehensive history of slave trade between Angola and Brazil stressing African perceptions and motives for participation, role of European capitalism, experiences of those enslaved, and effects on Africa and Brazil. Presents largest segment of African slave trade through powerful metaphors of death. [DAN/JKT/PMM]

19.918   David Northrup. *Trade without rulers: precolonial economic development in south-eastern Nigeria.* Oxford: Clarendon, 1978. ISBN 0-19-822712-4. ‣ Places slave trade from Bight of Biafra in larger context of area's social and economic development, stressing mechanisms and motives of African merchants. [DAN/RCL]

19.919   François Renault. *Lavigerie, l'esclavage africain, et l'Europe, 1868–1892.* 2 vols. Paris: de Boccard, 1971. ‣ Comprehensive study of campaign against slavery in East and Central Africa stressing, activities of Catholic missionaries, Congo Free State, and European governments. [DAN]

19.920   François Renault. *Libération d'esclaves et nouvelle servitude: les rachats de captifs africains pour le compte des colonies françaises après l'abolition de l'esclavage.* Abidjan: Nouvelles Éditions Africaines, 1976. ISBN 2-7236-0501-9. ‣ Wide-ranging account of end of slavery in French colonies, with emphasis on use and abuse of liberated Africans as forced labor in West Africa and Indian Ocean. [DAN]

19.921   Edward Reynolds. *Stand the storm: a history of the Atlantic slave trade.* 1985 ed. London: Allison & Busby; distributed by Carol, 1989. ISBN 0-85031-586-7 (cl), 0-95031-586-7 (pbk). ‣ Brief, popular survey of origin, organization, and abolition of Atlantic slave trade and its effects on Africa and Atlantic world. Explains historiographical development. [DAN]

19.922   Claire C. Robertson and Martin A. Klein, eds. *Women and slavery in Africa.* Madison: University of Wisconsin Press, 1983. ISBN 0-299-09460-X. ‣ Original case studies of female slaves and slave traders in Africa and in slave trade. Argues slave women's productive, not reproductive, functions most valued in Africa. [DAN]

19.923   Abdul Sheriff. *Slaves, spices, and ivory in Zanzibar: integration of an East African commercial empire into the world economy, 1770–1873.* Athens: Ohio University Press, 1987. ISBN 0-8214-0871-2 (cl), 0-8214-0872-0 (pbk). ‣ Revisionist economic study of international commerce from Zanzibar and eastern Africa, stressing growth of African dependence in face of expanding European capitalism. [DAN/TTS]

19.924   John K. Thornton. *Africa and Africans in the making of the Atlantic world, 1400–1680.* Cambridge: Cambridge University Press, 1992. ISBN 0-521-39233-0 (cl), 0-521-39864-9 (pbk). ‣ Wide-ranging scholarly contribution to early Atlantic slave trade. Topics include slavery in Africa, commerce with Europe, African labor and resistance in New World slavery, and African cultural traditions in the Americas. [DAN]

SEE ALSO

3.349 Philip D. Curtin. *The rise and fall of the plantation complex.*

22.243 Philip D. Curtin. *The Atlantic slave trade.*

22.252 David Eltis. *Economic growth and the ending of the trans-atlantic slave trade.*

22.270 James A. Rawley. *The transatlantic slave trade.*

22.273 Barbara L. Solow, ed. *Slavery and the rise of the Atlantic system.*

37.223 Herbert S. Klein. *The Middle Passage.*

Health and Disease

19.925 Z. A. Ademuwagun et al., eds. *African therapeutic systems.* Waltham, Mass.: Crossroads, 1979. ▸ Forty-one essays, mostly reprinted journal articles in English, on traditional medicine and its interactions with modern medicine in West Africa; bibliography and filmography. Convenient, somewhat dated, introduction to topic. [KDP]

19.926 Dauril Alden and Joseph C. Miller. "Unwanted cargoes: the origins and dissemination of smallpox via the slave trade from Africa to Brazil, c. 1560–1830." In *The African exchange: toward a biological history of black people.* Kenneth F. Kiple, ed., pp. 35–109. Durham, N.C.: Duke University Press, 1988. ISBN 0-8223-0731-6. ▸ Excellent analysis of unintended biological byproduct of slave trade, transportation of destructive diseases from Africa to Americas. Correlates timing of African droughts and epidemics with Brazilian pandemics. [KDP]

19.927 David Arnold, ed. *Imperial medicine and indigenous societies.* Manchester: Manchester University Press, 1988. ISBN 0-7190-2495-1. ▸ Ten state-of-the-art essays on imperial medicine, including Africa, India, New Zealand, and Philippines. Valuable for comparative work on social and political aspects of colonial health policies. [KDP]

19.928 Ahmed Bayoumi. *The history of Sudan health services.* Nairobi: Kenya Literature Bureau, 1979. ▸ Competent administrative history notable for range of topics covered: campaigns against major diseases, nineteenth-century developments, medical research, and training health workers. Graphs, charts, and references essential for work on this country. [KDP]

19.929 Ann Beck. *Medicine, tradition, and development in Kenya and Tanzania, 1920–1970.* Waltham, Mass.: Crossroads, 1981. ISBN 0-918456-44-4. ▸ Argues traditional medicine will continue to have appeal in new African states in spite of clinic-based medical policies of colonial period and independent governments. Author has published extensively on East African medical history. [KDP]

19.930 Leland V. Bell. *Mental and social disorder in sub-Saharan Africa: the case of Sierra Leone, 1787–1990.* Westport, Conn.: Greenwood, 1991. ISBN 0-313-27942-X. ▸ Pioneering monograph on care of mentally ill; institutional history of Kissy Hospital (fairly successful custodial asylum), with some attention to broader social issues based on patient case histories, archival sources, and mental health literature. [KDP]

19.931 Réné Collignon and Charles Becker. *Santé et population en Sénégambie des origines à 1960: bibliographie annotée.* Paris: Institut National d'Études Démographiques, 1989. ISBN 2-7332-7011-7. ▸ Bibliography of 2,908 citations with good annotations for nineteenth- and twentieth-century materials on Senegal and Gambia. Broad coverage of health and demography with subject and author indexes. [KDP]

19.932 Philip D. Curtin. "Epidemiology and the slave trade." *Political science quarterly* 83.2 (1968) 190–216. ISSN 0032-3195. ▸ Seminal study of health, demographic, and socioeconomic consequences of intermixing of disease environments as unanticipated byproducts of European conquest in Americas and slave trade. Nonimmune European, African, and American populations exposed to new pathogens. [KDP]

19.933 Philip D. Curtin. *The image of Africa: British ideas and action, 1780–1850.* 1964 ed. Madison: University of Wisconsin Press, 1973. ▸ Thorough study of British intellectual encounter with Africa; contains still valuable material on development of European knowledge of tropical diseases and devastating impact of disease on European lives and health in Africa. [KDP]

19.934 Danielle Domergue-Cloarec. *Politique coloniale française et réalités coloniales: la santé en Côte d'Ivoire, 1905–1958.* 2 vols. Paris: Académie des Sciences d'Outre-mer, 1986. (Publications de l'Université de Toulouse-LeMirail, C–1.) ISBN 2-7227-0005-0 (set). ▸ Detailed study of health conditions and public health in major French colony, with rich data notably on trypanosomiasis (sleeping sickness). Although limited comparisons with other colonies, one of very few works on Francophone Africa. [KDP]

19.935 John Farley. *Bilharzia: a history of imperial tropical medicine.* Cambridge: Cambridge University Press, 1991. ISBN 0-521-40086-4. ▸ Excellent introduction to one of most damaging diseases of developing countries. Well-written and researched global study with critical attention particularly to unsuccessful control programs in southern Africa. [KDP]

19.936 Steven Feierman. "Struggles for control: the social roots of health and healing in modern Africa." *African studies review* 28.2/3 (1985) 73–147. ISSN 0002-0206. ▸ Review essay on social determinants of health and health care over past century, valuable for references as well as an analysis. [JJL]

19.937 Steven Feierman, comp. *Health and society in Africa: a working bibliography.* Waltham, Mass.: Crossroads, 1979. ISBN 0-9184-5616-9. ▸ Valuable source for works on medical care, both traditional and modern. Emphasis on social aspects of disease and health care complements more clinical epidemiological approach of Patterson (19.948). [KDP]

19.938 John Ford. *The role of the trypanosomiases in African ecology: a study of the tsetse fly problem.* Oxford: Oxford University Press, 1971. ISBN 0-19-854375-1. ▸ Highly technical, sometimes misinterpreted, but influential work on social and economic histories of 1970s. Argues colonial conquest upset equilibrium that Africans had established with disease environment; science now dated. [KDP]

19.939 James L. Giblin. "Trypanosomiasis control in African history: an evaded issue?" *Journal of African history* 31.1 (1990) 59–80. ISSN 0021-8537. ▸ Argues Ford's stress (19.938) on acquired immunity to sleeping sickness is critical for disease control in precolonial and modern times. Based on detailed study in Northeast Tanzania. [KDP]

19.940 Joel W. Gregory, Dennis D. Cordell, and Raymond Gervais. *African historical demography: a multidisciplinary bibliography.* Los Angeles: Crossroads, 1984. ISBN 0-918456-51-7. ▸ Bibliography of 2,550 items classified by region and by subject (fertility, mortality, migration, and slave trade) with author and subject indexes. Unique guide to population explosion in post-1945 Africa. [KDP]

19.941 Gerald W. Hartwig and K. David Patterson, eds. *Disease in African history: an introductory survey and case studies.* Durham, N.C.: Duke University Press, 1978. (Duke University Center for Commonwealth and Comparative Studies, 44.) ISBN 0-8223-0410-4. ▸ General introduction and nine pioneering essays extending Curtin's stress (19.932) on growing intercommunication to show changing disease environments (relapsing fever, river blindness) in East Africa, Ghana, Cameroon, Chad, and Sudan. [KDP]

19.942 August Hirsch. *Handbook of geographical and historical pathology.* 2d German ed. 3 vols. Charles Creighton, trans. London: New Sydenham Society, 1883–86. (New Sydenham Society publications, 106, 112, 117.) ‣ Classic, heavily documented, late nineteenth-century global description of known disease distribution, history, and cause, with surprisingly rich material on Africa. Essential guide to pre–twentieth-century studies. Originally published 1859–62. [KDP]

19.943 Charles C. Hughes and John M. Hunter. "Disease and 'development' in Africa." *Social science and medicine* 3 (1970) 443–93. ISSN 0037-7856. ‣ Classic discussion of unexpected and damaging health consequences of water projects and other development schemes. Although examples dated, demonstrates importance of health-planning aspects of development projects. [KDP]

19.944 Kenneth F. Kiple. "A survey of recent literature on the biological past of the black." In *The African exchange: toward a biological history of black people.* Kenneth F. Kiple, ed., pp. 7–34. Durham, N.C.: Duke University Press, 1988. ISBN 0-8223-0731-6. ‣ Review of recent literature on biomedical history of Africans and their descendants in the Americas. Strong historical synthesis of technical fields, especially genetics and nutrition; excellent bibliography. [KDP]

19.945 John J. McKelvey, Jr. *Man against tsetse: struggle for Africa.* Ithaca, N.Y.: Cornell University Press, 1973. ISBN 0-8014-0768-0. ‣ Vivid, accessible account of trypanosomiasis (sleeping sickness) campaigns in various territories, including Príncipe, showing successes and failures of entomological and chemoprophylactic measures in colonial era. More accessible than Ford 19.938. [KDP]

19.946 Randall M. Packard. "Maize, cattle, and mosquitoes: the political economy of malaria epidemics in colonial Swaziland." *Journal of African history* 25.2 (1984) 189–212. ISSN 0021-8537. ‣ Significant effort to show human factors as well as natural conditions behind outbreaks of disease. Links malaria epidemics to decline in Swazi economic independence, failed rains, and nutritional deficiencies. [KDP]

19.947 Randall M. Packard. *White plague, black labor: tuberculosis and the political economy of health and disease in South Africa.* Berkeley: University of California Press, 1989. ISBN 0-520-06574-3 (cl), 0-520-06575-1 (pbk). ‣ Provocative study of social causes and consequences of tuberculosis and of medical attempts to understand and control it in context of rapid change under harsh system of racial domination and migrant labor. [KDP]

19.948 K. David Patterson. *Health in colonial Ghana: disease, medicine, and socio-economic change, 1900–1955.* Waltham, Mass.: Crossroads, 1981. ISBN 0-918456-42-8. ‣ Survey of changing disease conditions as influenced by medical knowledge, improve-

ments in health-care delivery, economic change, urbanization, education, and nutrition in relatively favored colony. Extensive tabular data facilitates comparative studies. [KDP]

19.949 K. David Patterson, comp. *Infectious diseases in twentieth-century Africa: a bibliography of their distribution and consequences.* Waltham, Mass.: Crossroads, 1979. ISBN 0-918456-29-0 (pbk). ‣ Covers sub-Saharan Africa to early 1979, excluding North Africa; 3,481 citations with author and subject indexes. Clinical/epidemiological focus complements Feierman 19.937; stress on social environment. [KDP]

19.950 Howard Phillips. *"Black October": the impact of the Spanish influenza epidemic of 1918 on South Africa.* Pretoria: Department of National Education, 1990. ISBN 0-7970-1580-9. ‣ Detailed study of epidemic that caused worst single demographic disaster in African history, setting social cooperation and conflict and political consequences for more centralized health policy in context of complex South African ethnic and racial situation. [KDP]

19.951 E. E. Sabben-Clare, D. J. Bradley, and K. Kirkwood, eds. *Health in tropical Africa during the colonial period.* Oxford: Oxford University Press, 1980. ISBN 0-19-858165-3. ‣ Memoirs of colonial medical personnel and essays on variety of topics, mostly for British territories. Good flavor of times and problems from health officers' perspectives. [KDP]

19.952 Ralph Schram. *A history of the Nigerian health services.* Ibadan: Ibadan University Press, 1971. ‣ Pioneering study of major country from early times to 1960. Unlike similar works, stresses missionary medicine as well as government health measures. [KDP]

19.953 Charles Tettey. *Medicine in British West Africa, 1880–1956: an annotated bibliography.* Accra: University of Ghana, Medical School Library, 1975. ‣ Comprehensive bibliography on health problems and medical services during colonial era. Dated but still useful for access to earlier medical and historical literature. [KDP]

19.954 Charles Wilcocks. *Aspects of medical investigation in Africa.* London: Oxford University Press, 1962. ‣ Valuable survey of history of research efforts on tuberculosis, schistosomiasis (bilharzia), and trypanosomiasis (sleeping sickness), primarily in British territories. Gives sense of medical possibilities of time and colonial health priorities. [KDP]

SEE ALSO
4.724 Roy M. MacLeod and Milton Lewis, eds. *Disease, medicine, and empire.*

FREDRIC L. CHEYETTE AND MARCIA L. COLISH

Medieval Europe

The following section on the Middle Ages, the largest single section in the *Guide*, is arranged in two distinct parts. The first, edited by Fredric L. Cheyette, encompasses political, social, and economic history; the second, edited by Marcia L. Colish, treats church and intellectual history (p. 676).

In the years since the publication of the last edition of the *Guide*, there have been major, even dramatic, shifts in the historiography of medieval Europe. Some of these changes have resulted from publication of new primary materials, providing researchers with new evidence and making it possible, and in some cases necessary, to pose new kinds of questions. Other changes have come in response to movements in the wider intellectual and social context which historians operate and thus are specific to the changing culture of the late twentieth century. In the bibliography that follows, we have given almost exclusive attention to works published since 1961 in order to provide the user with the most reliable and up-to-date scholarship. Earlier works have been listed when they continue to exercise a substantial influence on current scholarship either because of the questions they raised or the methods they pioneered. Many of these titles will also serve users who are interested in reconstructing the changing interpretations of the last generation.

Scholarship since the publication of the 1961 *Guide* has most notably altered our conception of the political, social, and economic history of medieval Europe. In the earlier edition, studies of feudalism, chivalry, and constitutional history took pride of place. The studies of social history listed there were primarily anecdotal in content; only G. Duby's monograph (20.354) on the society of the Mâconnais region of Burgundy and J. Russell's pioneering work (20.103) on medieval demography marked what were about to become two of the most vigorous and transforming kinds of scholarship. Economic history was divided among the history of medieval cities, money, banking, and the manorial economy. Apart from the history of medieval cities and their commerce, the late Middle Ages—especially north of the Alps—was hardly represented. The period between antiquity and the Carolingians likewise was little represented. Peasants appeared only as subjects of the manorial economy. They along with women were "people without history."

All this has changed. Subjects hardly visible then occupy a large space in this bibliography, while subjects that assumed large importance then have been reduced to modest proportion. This is a reflection not of an historiographical bias on the part of the editor or the contributors, but rather of the direction scholarship has taken in the last three decades.

In part, the new topics and methods, the scholarly colonization of new areas, have been simply the consequence of the arrival of a new generation of historians eager to move into fields where neglected archives could be explored, where the chances of making an interesting discovery, of saying something new, were greater than in fields long plowed by earlier generations. To some extent, it has also been ideologically driven. Marxist theory, with its emphasis on class conflict and changes in the social relations of production, has been a powerful stimulus to investigate particular aspects of social history, even among those who are not philosophical or political adepts of Marxism. (Interestingly, very little work of significance in this field has come out of Eastern Europe and the former Soviet Union, even as concerns the countries of Eastern Europe themselves. The demand for ideological correctness in those countries seems to have deadened rather than stimulated the historical imagination.) More recently, the feminist movement has not only opened up the history of medieval women—whose activities have turned out to be far more visible than earlier historiography would have suggested—but also pointed to the construction of gender itself as a topic of historical investigation. It has likewise given fresh impetus to the history of the family, household, and private life, in contrast to the public world of politics: the world of sentiment and eroticism, of informal social networks, of noninstitutional piety, of informal play of power and status through marriage, female dress, rituals, and codes of behavior.

Far more powerful than ideology in the transformation of medieval historical studies has been the application of new tools to old tasks and old tools to new tasks. Statistical analysis is now commonly applied to medieval economic and demographic data; it is also (more problematically) sometimes applied to data drawn from criminal court records or collections of land conveyances. Computers now enable medieval historians to organize and manipulate not only numerical data but also name lists for studies of prosopography and the reconstruction of social groups and kinship networks; they enhance the historian's ability to study the changing vocabulary of medieval texts; they have even been used to reconstruct historical land-use patterns from modern maps and aerial photographs. Archaeology, once reserved for the study of cultures that left little or no written record, is now a major subfield of medieval historical scholarship. It has opened a vast new body of evidence for the study of economic exchange, settlement patterns, and even politics (since from the tenth century onward, castles played an essential role in the exercise of power). Equally important has been the adaptation of theories, concepts, and research strategies drawn from the neighboring social sciences—especially ethnology and anthropology—in social history and of development, monetarist, and various forms of demographic theory in economic history. Particularly striking examples have been signaled in the comments in the bibliography, but the practice is now pervasive.

This introduction surveys only a small portion of this abundant historiographical harvest.

Though its subject matter is separated from us by a vast expanse of time, historical writing about the Middle Ages has never been totally free of political considerations. The constitutional and institutional histories of an earlier generation of Anglo-American scholars sprang from a pride in the success of parliamentary government. Its leading questions were, why haven't the French been more like the English? Or alternatively, why haven't the Germans been more like the French and the English? Nazism and World War II were clearly the driving force behind Barraclough's survey of medieval German politics and institutions, *The Origins of Modern Germany* (20.610). On the other side, the racial theories of National Socialism spurred German historians of the

1930s to seek out the historic "folk-leaders" of the German peoples and to find them in the medieval German aristocracy. Some of these concerns of the inter- and postwar years have become mere vestiges of their former selves or have been absorbed into more encompassing issues that spring from concerns of the late twentieth century: the process of state formation, for example, or of economic development. Preoccupations with the nobility, and thus with issues of family and kinship and the structures of power that do not derive from the state and its institutions, have been powerfully reinforced by the major impetus for change in the last generation—the new social history.

The focus of the older social history was the curious and the picturesque and thus strikingly anecdotal. In contrast, the central concern of the new social history has been the systematic study of social classes, especially their origins, membership, ideologies, and cultures. Medieval historians quickly realized that the very notion of social class as it came out of modern sociology (of whatever ideological bent) presented grave problems when applied to medieval evidence. Wealth, a standard criterion of modern class analysis, turned out to be an inadequate diagnostic indicator. Should we call the medieval nobility a class, or was the distance between the great aristocrats and their poor household knights (some of whom, in Germany, were legally serfs) so great as to make them distinct social groups? Were medieval city dwellers a bourgeoisie in the nineteenth-century sense of that term? Were the peasants a social class? And where did the clergy fit into a class structure? How were each of these groups within medieval society constituted? Who belonged to them? And how was membership determined? Did they come into being at particular times? And, if so, under what circumstances? And above all, how should we overlay our own ideas of social class on the medieval concept of estates, a concept eventually institutionalized in late medieval representative assemblies? Because these problems concern, among other things, the constitution of the medieval ruling elite, they also impinge strongly on the concerns of political history. They remain among the central problems of medieval social history.

In their search for the origins and structure of medieval classes, especially the nobility, historians have paid particular attention to the hierarchical ties of patronage and clientage (of which feudalism in its several forms now seems to be a subspecies) that made them cohere. They have also looked at other practices that held groups together, for instance, the structure of the courts that surrounded kings and great lords and the dynamics of social life in cities and villages. They have studied styles of feuding and rituals of conflict resolution, religious processions and royal entries, and marriage negotiations and funeral processions. The shared ideologies of medieval people also served to articulate and cement their class structure. It is in this context that the study of subjects as varied as chivalry, crusading ideas, and attitudes toward marriage have received fresh impetus. And from ideology it has been only a short step to shared culture—to the particular forms of literature, art, religious practice, dress, and food consumption that helped to define and delineate social groups.

Another major topic of investigation and debate of the last generation has been the source or sources of the dynamic population growth and economic and social development that occurred after the year 1000 and of the economic and demographic crisis of the fourteenth and fifteenth centuries. Two different groups of historians have attempted to link the beginning and end of this great medieval cycle. One group is usually termed neo-Malthusian; the other is more or less Marxist in inspiration.

The neo-Malthusians (M. M. Postan, G. Duby, R. Fossier, E. Le Roy Ladurie, and others) argue that the great medieval expansion was agricultural before it was commercial, that it depended on the conversion of new land into arable. To explain the timing of the expansion, these historians have sometimes pointed to such technological innovations as the invention of the heavy wheeled plow (L. T. White, Jr. 20.43) or the greater availability of iron (G. Duby 20.66, 20.120; R. Fossier 20.280) or to a warmer climate (G. Duby 20.66, 20.120). Population continued to expand, and an increasingly complex economy developed, they argue, as long as additional land was available; but eventually the only available new land was of marginal productive quality, while the productivity of land already under plow declined from overuse and insufficient fertilizer. When population outran food production, famine was inevitable, and a weakened population was more prone to disease.

The alternative view (argued variously by G. Bois, R. Brenner, P. Toubert, and Fossier at times) finds the source of dynamism after the year 1000 in the way that a new group of lords reshaped the landscape and peasant settlements in order to exploit them more easily. This seignorial control long supported growth; but in the fourteenth century, they argue, it began to act as a brake, as the demands of war financing and changing noble consumption patterns forced peasants to pay out an increasing portion of what they produced. It is this rural impoverishment, Bois and Brenner argue, caused by landlords and kings, that caused the late medieval crisis to last for over a century.

A few large, overarching themes—three centuries of economic expansion followed by a century and a half of crisis and decline; the elaboration of a social world based on village agriculture and dominated by a warrior elite; and the development of urban commercial networks that eventually involved village agriculturalists, noble landlords, and kings and their administrations—now provide the framework even for traditional subjects, such as the development of governmental institutions, the relations of church and state, and the Crusades. Studies of institutions now view them as places where political transactions occur. They describe the dynamics of institutional change rather than the fixity of rules, rights, obligations, and procedures. This tendency has been most notable in studies of the Crusading states and of the areas where late medieval governments were most innovative—war finance and justice.

At the same time, many themes drawn from social history, political anthropology, and more recent historical studies have reshaped the study of political history. Lewis B. Namier's work on eighteenth-century British politics and studies of patron-client relations in modern Mediterranean countries have led medieval historians to look at patronage networks and factionalism, and in that way to bring together two worlds once thought to be quite different from each other—late medieval England and Renaissance Italy. Studies of formal political theory have grown to encompass many other manifestations of political culture and ideology—in historiography and literature, religious and political rituals, music, art, and architecture.

Some of these issues—most notably the origins of the medieval nobility—have preoccupied historians of the early as well as late Middle Ages. German historians working on early kinship structures and on the self-conception of aristocratic families here have led the way. The major transformations of early medieval scholarship, however, have stemmed from archaeology. Excavations at a multitude of sites from England to the Persian Gulf have reopened the old question of continuity or discontinuity between antiquity and the Middle Ages. Strong arguments have been advanced for a long agony of the Mediterranean economy from the third to the eighth century, and a concomitant restructuring of exchanges around the northern seas. The role of the Vikings as raiders and traders linking the Carolingian world with the Black Sea, Byzantium, and Persia, has been brought into clearer focus. A greater appreciation of their positive contribution to Western economic growth has replaced an older stereotype of violent plunderers. At the same time, institutional studies of the eighth and ninth centuries have suggested a strong continuity of governmental practices from late antiquity to the Carolingians, and even to the Saxon kings.

All these problems and studies have profoundly recast the geographical framework of medieval historical scholarship. The older constitutional focus, with its emphasis on governmental, especially monarchical, institutions, fit snugly into the boundaries of the modern nation-state. The new questions, however, easily and sometimes necessarily overflow those boundaries. Questions about the structure of the noble class, chivalric culture, urban factionalism, or popular revolts, concern phenomena that are European wide, even if monographs often treat these phenomena in a particular country. At the same time, many of the questions raised by social historians can best be studied by focusing on a particular region, where there can be some hope of mastering all the surviving evidence. Thus we have witnessed the proliferation of regional monographs in France and more recently in Spain, studies of shire gentry in England, studies of territorial principalities in Germany, and urban studies all over Europe. Even in political and institutional history new regional configurations are emerging: England and northwestern France from the twelfth to the fifteenth century, Catalonia, Mediterranean France, and Genoa and Pisa in the eleventh and twelfth centuries.

The fields of church and intellectual history have also seen two massive historiographical changes during the past generation: the waning of confessionalism as a motive for the study of church history, and its replacement by two alternative approaches to the subject, ecumenism and the mode of bottom-up history derived from the Annales school of French medieval studies. Even at the point when the 1961 *Guide* was published, there was no lack of confessionally inspired studies of medieval church history. On the one side stood the Roman Catholic apologists and triumphalists, extolling the period as the Age of Faith and holding up the architects of its ecclesiastical institutions and theological systems and the authors of its devotional and mystical classics as saints and heroes to be venerated and imitated. On the other side stood the Protestant and secular anti-Catholics, eager to expose the actual or perceived vices, corruptions, errors, and superstitions of the medieval church, or, alternatively, to seek out the heresiarchs or intellectuals persecuted for their teachings who could be hailed as forerunners of the Reformation or as morning stars of the Enlightenment.

The combined arrival of the ecumenical movement and the increasing shift of research in this field out of the hands of divinity professors charged with representing a particular brand of Christianity and into the hands of historians and professors of religious studies, who typically regard the writing of proselytizing church history as an abuse of their professional duties, has contributed to two notable features of the church history written in the past few decades. First, readers will find that much of the recent church history and history of canon law is remarkably bland, straightforward, and free of ideological flag-waving. This is because the historians, regardless of their own religious persuasions, if any, have simply recognized that the church was a major medieval institution, whose structures, functions, laws, and theories were important in their own right and for the influence they exercised on secular government and political theory in the Middle Ages and beyond. A second mandate flowing from the new, irenic spirit attributable to ecumenism has been the search for connections between medieval Christian thought and the Reformation. What is new and different here is that recent scholars have not turned to the medieval heretics and rebels, as before, but have sought continuities between the mainstream orthodox scholastic theologians and mystics of the Middle Ages and those of the Reformation. Indeed, in some quarters, the effort to ask medieval Christian thinkers to answer the questions posed by the magisterial reformers has led to a distorted, or anachronistic, interpretation of medieval thought. A reaction to this type of analysis has already set in, arguing, in particular, that the later centuries of medieval theology and church history need to be understood in their own historical context and not just as a prelude to the Reformation.

The second major current that has had a powerful effect on medieval church history is the influence of the Annales school. This influence can be seen in the study of ritual and liturgy, which seeks to uncover the religious beliefs, orthodox or heterodox, of participants who left no written records reporting their opinions, and, above all, in the study of lay patronage of churches or monasteries, religious confraternities, and such popular cultic practices as the veneration of saints and their relics and the belief in magic and witchcraft. A strongly populist inspiration is at work in many of these studies, reflecting the view that "real" history concerns itself with the outlook of ordinary people and not with the doctrines and theories of church leaders, canonists, and theologians. In some parts of this field, recourse to models from psychohistory or anthropology has had the effect of reducing medieval religious ideas and practices to mere behaviors, significant only for their psychopathology or social content, while ignoring their religious meanings to medieval people themselves. Similarly, the impact of women's studies and women's history has led to many new studies. Here, too, ideological positions, in this case derived from feminism, have sometimes led to an anachronistic or tendentious reading of the role of women in medieval religious culture that sees only the marginalization or disempowerment of women and that ignores the opportunities that medieval religion provided them for power and authority and intellectual, literary, and artistic roles. Thus, in some of the new research one can find church historians who are really social historians in disguise, informed by certain social, political, or intellectual agendas. But, in the best of the new research inspired by these insights there is also a subtle and sophisticated use of models drawn from sister disciplines that at the same time reflects the authors' historical imagination and ability to take seriously the religious beliefs and practices of medieval Christians, however much they may be a foreign country to the modern researcher and his or her audience.

The interest in history from the bottom up has redrawn the lines of controversy in other ways as well. Some medievalists take this approach to mean that there were two distinct religious and intellectual cultures in the Middle Ages, elite and popular, and that they remained fundamentally separate and self-contained. Others, while ready to acknowledge that the flow of doctrine from church leaders to laypeople was never automatic or total and that christianization meant different things to different people, have found, nonetheless, that there was a percolation up as well as trickle down, and that the traffic between intellectuals and laypersons was a two-way street. Another issue that has both clarified and complicated this debate is literacy. Recent studies have shown that medieval literacy was more widespread, in Latin as well as the vernaculars, than hitherto suspected. At the same time, other studies have noted that a highly oral component remained in the dissemination of ideas at the decidedly high end of the educational and literary spectrum. From this perspective, illiteracy emerges as less of a barrier obstructing a medieval person's access to elite culture than what one might otherwise have supposed. This whole area is very much in a state of flux at the present writing. Whether or not a consensus will emerge, and, if so, what it will look like, is by no means clear.

Two other fundamental historiographical shifts address elite culture primarily, taking us from church history and religious culture to intellectual history and its adjuncts in art history and literary history more specifically. When the second edition of the *Guide* was published, there was considerable consensus among medieval intellectual historians. They agreed that the major battle still to be fought was the one inherited from the earlier, twentieth-century "revolt of the medievalists" against Renaissance scholars who continued to follow Jakob Burckhardt's influential portrayal of the Middle Ages as Dark Ages that lacked the individualism, the "discovery of the world and of man," and the appreciation of the classics that, in his view, entitled the Renaissance to be regarded as the beginning of modern Europe. In taking up arms against this claim, they attacked it in terms of the same classical bias in which it was framed by the

Burckhardtians. Mid-century medievalists succeeded in showing that medieval thinkers, jurists, scientists, artists, and writers had indeed known, preserved, copied, studied,
and taken seriously the classical legacy; and there are fairly recent titles in the bibliography below that continue to define medieval culture, or some subsection of it, such
as political theory or literature, primarily or exclusively in terms of this classical orientation. But, within the past generation, many medievalists have rejected this earlier
scenario for two reasons: it fails to pay adequate attention to nonclassical elements,
and, more important, it treats medieval thinkers as passive recipients of the classics
while ignoring their own creative, original, and postclassical achievements. Efforts to
document this originality extend from art history to literary history to the history of
philosophy and science. In the latter two fields, much attention during the past two
decades has been devoted to the history of medieval logic, semantics, and speculative
grammar. This is partly because these subjects represent fields of genuine advance in
medieval philosophy; it also reflects the perspectives of some late twentieth-century
philosophers, who find antecedents or parallels in this period to the kind of logic that
interests them. In the case of science, scholars have pointed out that medieval thinkers
were not content to imitate or replicate the Greco-Arabic tradition they inherited.
Rather, in such areas as the physics of local motion or the mathematization of physics,
they sought to go beyond and to criticize their sources, thus, many would argue, paving
the way for the scientific revolution of the sixteenth and seventeenth centuries.

These developments are related to the final major historiographical shift of the past
generation to be noted here, the collapse of neo-Thomism and the demise of the storyline it had long provided for the history of medieval speculative thought. According
to that interpretation, the high point was the synthesis of Christianity and Greek philosophy, largely Aristotelianism, by Thomas Aquinas in the late thirteenth century.
Developments prior to that moment were included and evaluated in terms of whether
and how they contributed to the eventual Thomistic synthesis of reason and revelation.
If a particular thinker was simply marching to a different drummer, he was only taken
seriously for the light he shed on the Thomistic project, by comparison with it. As for
the speculative thought of the late Middle Ages, it was condemned under the heading
of "the decline of medieval thought" for its departures from Thomism and for the
greater popularity of the thought of the later scholastics. Now, many of the newly edited
and published texts referred to at the beginning of this introduction have provided the
means for fleshing out the non-Thomist or post-Thomist chapters of medieval intellectual history. In this connection, research on the late thirteenth and fourteenth centuries and, to a lesser extent, on the twelfth century, have become new frontier areas,
decentering the monumental importance of Aquinas and the allegedly perennial truth
of his teachings and seeking a more accurate historical estimate of which thinkers were
influential in the high Middle Ages and why. A post–neo-Thomist appraisal of Aquinas
himself has even begun to emerge. These developments have promoted some of the
fastest moving and most influential changes in our understanding of high and late
medieval speculative thought. The agenda before medieval intellectual historians is
clear. They agree that important fresh light has now been shed on many figures and
themes that had remained obscure and that much more work is needed along the same
lines. The mood is one of the excitement of discovery. But, it must be noted that there
is also a negative aspect to this phenomenon, one felt just as keenly by a medieval
historian looking for a solid and reliable introductory textbook on the history of medieval philosophy to assign to undergraduates as by a nonmedievalist user of this part of
the *Guide* seeking enlightenment on the same subject. Scholarship has been moving so
fast that no new synthesis of the state of our present knowledge exists that can be
recommended without serious reservations. There are, to be sure, some recent titles in
this field listed below. But they all leave much to be desired, being too thin and super-

ficial or too driven by a single theme or issue to do full justice to the assignment. In any event, to the extent that a new storyline has begun to emerge in this part of the field, it is one that accents diversity, eclecticism, and debate within the orthodox consensus rather than the privileging of any one school of medieval thought as the main theme.

In the following bibiography, areas of research are represented by English-language publications wherever possible. At the same time, we have endeavored to present scholarship on all the regions of Europe and on all the major questions that have attracted historians' attention. This has meant of necessity including works in languages other than English when there is little or no significant English-language scholarship. In areas where foreign-language research abounds, such as in French regional social history, citations are limited to a few exemplary works. The lack of symmetry that may be evident is thus a consequence of our commitment to making this section as user-friendly as possible. We hope that readers will receive our efforts in the collegial spirit in which they are offered, and we encourage the user to explore the bibliographical guides and above all the bibliographies included in most of the works listed here; they will guide the reader to the vast literature beyond.

Social, Economic, and Political History

[Contributors: ACM = Alexander C. Murray, CMW = Colin M. Wells, DJO = Duane J. Osheim, DMH = Derek M. Hirst, FLC = Fredric L. Cheyette, JBF = John B. Freed, JFP = James F. Powers, JJC = John J. Contreni, JMB = János M. Bak, JSCRS = Jonathan S. C. Riley-Smith, KP = Kenneth Pennington, LAP = Linda A. Pollock, LCA = Lorraine C. Attreed, MLC = Marcia L. Colish, PHF = Paul H. Freedman, PJG = Patrick J. Geary, PPR = Peep Peter Rebane, RMK = Ruth M. Karras, RWB = Richard W. Bulliet, RWK = Richard W. Kaeuper, SDW = Stephen D. White, TFXN = Thomas F. X. Noble, WJC = William J. Courtenay]

REFERENCE WORKS

Bibliographies

20.1 János M. Bak. *Medieval narrative sources: a chronological guide (with a list of major letter collections).* New York: Garland, 1987. ISBN 0-8240-8440-3. ▸ Very useful listing of chronicles, selection of saints' lives with historical information, epics, historical sagas, and letter collections. Covers Latin Europe and Byzantium, fifth century to ca. 1500. Also lists translations. [FLC]

20.2 Gray Cowan Boyce, ed. and comp. *Literature of medieval history, 1930–1975: a supplement to Louis John Paetow's "A Guide to the Study of Medieval History."* 5 vols. Paul Meyvaert, Introduction. Millwood, N.Y.: Kraus International, 1981. ISBN 0-527-10462-0 (set, cl), 0-527-69101-1 (set, pbk). ▸ Though outdated even when first published, helpful starting point. Lists half-century of scholarship; arranged by general works, then topically. Primary emphasis on political and elite history. [FLC]

20.3 R. C. van Caenegem. *Guide to the sources of medieval history.* Amsterdam: North-Holland; distributed by Elsevier North-Holland, 1978. ISBN 0-7204-0743-5. ▸ Bibliography of traditionally defined sources: chronicles, letter collections, legal codes, etc. Useful guide to libraries and archives with listing of major collections of sources. Also includes dictionaries and encyclopedias, prosopography, place names, chronology, diplomatics, heraldry, seals, and epigraphy. Translation of *Encyclopedie van de Geschiedenis der Middeleeuwen* (1962), revised and updated. [FLC]

20.4 Everett U. Crosby, Charles Julian Bishko, and Robert L. Kellogg. *Medieval studies: a bibliographical guide.* New York: Garland, 1983. ISBN 0-8240-9107-8. ▸ Annotated general bibliography; arranged topically and by country with a guide to libraries and archives. More up to date than Boyce, ed. 20.2. [FLC]

20.5 Bruno Gebhardt. *Handbuch der deutschen Geschichte.* Vol. 1: *Frühzeit und Mittelalter.* 10th ed. Herbert Grundmann, ed. Stuttgart: Klett-Cotta, 1991. ISBN 3-12-902510-3 (v. 1). ▸ Each of 256 sections contains summary of established facts, major issues, and annotated bibliography. Extremely useful. [JBF]

20.6 Léopold Genicot, ed. *Typologie des sources du moyen âge occidental.* 67 vols. to date. Turnhout, Belgium: Brepols, 1972–. ISBN 2-503-36000-9 (set). ▸ Broad interpretation of sources: from law codes to liturgical books, armor to tree rings. Each type of source is subject of separate volume containing both bibliography and commentary on nature and use of source type in question. Index to volumes 1–50 published 1992. [FLC]

20.7 *International medieval bibliography.* Leeds: University of Leeds. ISSN 0020-7950 ▸ Semi-annual listing of articles from over 900 journals and *Festschriften*. Arranged by subject. Most complete current guide to scholarship. [FLC]

20.8 Hans Eberhard Mayer. *Bibliographie zur Geschichte der Kreuzzüge.* 1960 ed. Hanover: Hahnsche, 1965. ▸ Standard bibliography of Crusades in the East and Latin kingdoms of East, including 5,362 titles to late 1950s. Continued (for 1958–67) in *Historische Zeitschrift*, Sonderheft, 3 (1969) 641–731. Narrow, traditional conception of Crusades. [JSCRS]

20.9   Hans Eberhard Mayer, Joyce McLellan, and Harry W. Hazard. "Select bibliography of the Crusades." In *The impact of the Crusades on Europe*. Harry W. Hazard and Norman P. Zacour, eds., pp. 511–664. Madison: University of Wisconsin Press, 1989. ISBN 0-299-10740-X. ▶ Bibliography of Crusades to late 1980s. More selective than Mayer 20.8, but includes titles on theaters of war other than the East. [JSCRS]

20.10   James M. Powell, ed. *Medieval studies: an introduction*. 2d ed. Syracuse, N.Y.: Syracuse University Press, 1992. ISBN 0-8156-2555-3 (cl), 0-8156-2556-1 (pbk). ▶ Manual for beginning students. Bibliography and discussion of technical issues of paleography, diplomatics, numismatics, prosopography, and chronology. Also brief surveys of medieval art, English literature, music, and philosophy. [FLC]

20.11   *Repertorium fontium historiae medii aevi, primum ab Augusto Potthast digestum, nunc cura collegii historicorum e pluribus nationibus emendatum et auctum*. 6 vols. to date. Rome: Istituto Storico Italiano per il Medio Evo, 1962–. ▶ Cooperative international bibliography of primary sources other than archival documents. Volume one lists individual titles in series publications. Succeeding volumes list sources alphabetically by author and anonymous works by title. In 1993, complete to letter K. [FLC]

20.12   Joel T. Rosenthal, ed. *Medieval women and the sources of medieval history*. Athens: University of Georgia Press, 1990. ISBN 0-8203-1214-2 (cl), 0-8203-1226-6 (pbk). ▶ Studies of how medieval sources, familiar and not, can be read for women's history; includes seals, preachers' *exempla*, canon law, charters, sagas, medical literature, saints' lives, coins, and legal texts. Substantial bibliography. Fundamental work. [FLC]

20.13   Michael M. Sheehan and Jacqueline Murray, comps. *Domestic society in medieval Europe: a select bibliography*. Toronto: Pontifical Institute of Mediaeval Studies, 1990. ISBN 0-88844-413-3. ▶ Selective bibliography of 453 titles, briefly annotated, including general studies, family, marriage, attitudes toward sexuality and marriage, the celibate state, women, children, elderly, outcasts, and dress. [FLC]

20.14   Société des Historiens Médiévistes de l'Enseignement Supérieur. *Bibliographie de l'histoire médiévale en France (1965–1990)*. Michel Balard, comp. Paris: Publications de la Sorbonne, 1992. ISBN 2-85944-214-6. ▶ Selective but vast bibliography of medieval studies by French scholars, arranged topically. Includes research on all of Europe, Byzantium, Turkic world, Islam, and sub-Saharan Africa. Also includes auxiliary sciences and computer use. [FLC]

20.15   Jonathan W. Zophy, comp. *An annotated bibliography of the Holy Roman Empire*. New York: Greenwood, 1986. ISBN 0-313-24028-0. ▶ Annotated bibliography of 3,023 titles on rulers, church, nobility, peasantry, economic and social history, war, culture, and Reformation. [FLC]

SEE ALSO

31.5 F. C. Dahlmann et al., eds. *Dahlmann-Waitz Quellenkunde der deutschen Geschichte*.

Dictionaries and Encyclopedias

20.16   Ian H. Adams. *Agrarian landscape terms: a glossary for historical geography*. Rev. ed. London: Institute of British Geographers, 1977. (Institute of British Geographers, Special publication, 9.) ISSN 0073-9006. ▶ Defines numerous land terms that appear in medieval and early modern documents. [FLC]

20.17   Robert Auty et al., eds. *Lexikon des Mittelalters*. 5 vols. to date. Munich: Artemis, 1977–. ISBN 3-7608-8901-8 (v. 1), 3-7608-8902-6 (v. 2), 3-7608-8903-4 (v. 3), 3-7608-8904-2 (v. 4), 3-7608-8905-0 (v. 5). ▶ Intended to be medieval Pauly-Wissowa. Extensive coverage; lengthy articles on major subjects; bibliographies. In 1992, complete only to letter M. [FLC]

20.18   Johannes Brøndsted, John Danstrup, and Lis Rubin Jacobsen, eds. *Kulturhistorisk leksikon for nordisk middelalder fra vikingetid til reformationstid* (Cultural-historical dictionary for the Scandinavian Middle Ages from the Viking age to the Reformation). 22 vols. Copenhagen: Rosenkilde og Bagger, 1956–. ▶ Indispensible standard reference for most aspects of medieval Scandinavian history. Includes articles in all Scandinavian languages with extensive bibliographies. Particularly useful entries on individual primary sources. [RMK]

20.19   Anne Echols and Marty Williams. *An annotated index of medieval women*. New York: Wiener, 1992. ISBN 0-910129-27-4. ▶ About 1,500 entries. Information drawn from secondary works in English and French. Useful for Western Europe; less so for Central and Mediterranean Europe. Better for later than for earlier Middle Ages. [FLC]

20.20   Joseph Reese Strayer, ed. *Dictionary of the Middle Ages*. 13 vols. New York: Scribner's, 1982–89. ISBN 0-684-19073-7 (set). ▶ From Aachen to Zwart'noc' (Armenian church). For less specialized audience than *Lexikon* (20.17), and thus less comprehensive, but complete. Good place to begin for almost any subject. [FLC]

Manuals and Research Aids

20.21   Pierre Alexandre. *Le climat en Europe au moyen âge: contribution à l'histoire des variations climatiques de 1000 à 1425, d'après les sources narratives de l'Europe occidentale*. Paris: École des Hautes Études en Sciences Sociales, 1987. (Recherches d'histoire et de sciences sociales, 24.) ISBN 2-7132-0852-1. ▶ Tables of weather events, 1000–1425, drawn from narrative sources. Covers continental Europe from Atlantic to Silesia and Austria, south to Rome and Pyrenees. Dates "medieval climate optimum" (i.e. period of maximum warming) at ca. 900–1300. [FLC]

20.22   Alain de Boüard. *Manuel de diplomatique française et pontificale*. 2 vols. and portfolio of plates. Paris: Picard, 1929–52. ▶ Standard handbook describing structure of public acts—royal and papal letters and diplomas—and private acts—legal documents such as land conveyances and wills. [FLC]

20.23   Harry Bresslau. *Handbuch der Urkundenlehre für Deutschland und Italien*. 1958–60 2d ed. 2 vols. Hans-Walter Klewitz, ed. Berlin: de Gruyter, 1968–69. ▶ Standard technical work on medieval written documents and official and legal diplomatics for Germany and Italy. [FLC]

20.24   Christopher R. Cheney, ed. *Handbook of dates for students of English history*. 1945 corr. ed. London: Royal Historical Society, 1991. (Royal Historical Society, Guides and handbooks, 4.) ISBN 0-901050-10-5. ▶ Useful manual for dating English documents: royal and papal regnal dates, court terms, saints' days, and perpetual calendar. [FLC]

20.25   Arthur Giry. *Manuel de diplomatique*. 1894 ed. Hildesheim: Olms, 1972. ISBN 3-487-04513-3. ▶ Thorough account of diplomatics superseded by de Boüard 20.22 for France and Bresslau 20.23 for Germany. Still very useful for technicalities of medieval dating. [FLC]

20.26   David C. Nicolle. *Arms and armour of the Crusading era, 1050–1350*. 2 vols. White Plains, N.Y.: Kraus International, 1988. ISBN 0-527-67128-2 (set). ▶ Over 1,700 line drawings of arms and armor. Taken from material from eastern Eurasian steppes to western Europe. Includes dictionary of terms. [JSCRS]

20.27 Peter Spufford. *Money and its use in medieval Europe.* Cambridge: Cambridge University Press, 1988. ISBN 0-521-30384-2. ‣ Fluent introduction to complex, technical subject of history of money, ca. 400–ca. 1500. Focuses on commercial revolution of thirteenth century and monetary crisis of later Middle Ages. [FLC]

20.28 Ronald Edward Zupko. *A dictionary of weights and measures for the British Isles: the Middle Ages to the twentieth century.* Philadelphia: American Philosophical Society, 1985. (Memoirs of the American Philosophical Society, 168.) ISBN 0-87169-168-x. ‣ Gives metric equivalents for all documented weights and measures with local and regional variations. Comprehensive. Other handbooks of weights and measures by same author for France and Italy. [FLC]

GENERAL STUDIES

20.29 Robert-Henri Bautier. *The economic development of medieval Europe.* Heather Karolyi, trans. New York: Harcourt Brace Jovanovich, 1971. ISBN 0-15-127438-X. ‣ Traditionally organized, introductory text covering standard topics: revivals and collapses, sixth to ninth century; Mediterranean revival; agriculture and rise of European commerce; fairs and trade with Asia; famines, plagues, and other calamities of later Middle Ages; and attendant economic changes. Lacks theoretical framework. [FLC]

20.30 R. C. van Caenegem. *An historical introduction to private law.* D.E.L. Johnston, trans. New York: Cambridge University Press, 1992. ISBN 0-521-40514-9 (cl) 0-521-42745-2 (pbk). ‣ Basic narrative from late antiquity to nineteenth century from perspective of traditional European legal history. "External history" of law: lawgivers, jurists, judges, and texts they produced. Translation of *Introduction historique au droit privé.* [FLC]

20.31 Carlo M. Cipolla, ed. *The Middle Ages.* Vol. 1 of *Fontana economic history of Europe.* 1972 ed. New York: Barnes & Noble for Fontana, 1976. ISBN 0-06-492176-X (pbk). ‣ Basic history for general reading public. Major United States, British, and French historians contribute chapters on specialties: Duby on agriculture, Le Goff on cities, Thrupp on industry, and White on technology. Disparate rather than unifying point of view. [FLC]

20.32 Philippe Contamine. *War in the Middle Ages.* Michael Jones, trans. Oxford: Blackwell, 1984. ISBN 0-631-13142-6. ‣ Comprehensive overview, early Middle Ages to fifteenth century. Discusses social, political, and technical aspects of warfare: arms, strategy, and tactics; history of courage; knighthood; just war; and law of arms. Extensive bibliography. Translation of *La guerre au moyen âge* (1980). [RWK]

20.33 *Culture et idéologie dans la genèse de l'état moderne: actes de la table ronde organisée par le Centre National de la Recherche Scientifique et l'École Française de Rome, Rome, 15–17 Octobre 1984.* Rome: École Française de Rome, 1985. (Collection de l'École Française de Rome, 82.) ISBN 2-7283-0104-2. ‣ Conference papers on ideology and the state, antiquity to seventeenth century. Topics include literacy, education, images, music, architecture, propaganda, and political theory. [FLC]

20.34 Robert Fossier, ed. *The Cambridge illustrated history of the Middle Ages.* Vol. 1: *350–950.* Vol. 2: *950–1250.* Vol. 3: *1250–1520.* 3 vols. to date. Janet Sondheimer and Sarah Hanbury-Tenison, trans. Cambridge: Cambridge University Press, 1986–. ISBN 0-521-26644-0 (v. 1), 0-521-26646-7 (v. 3). ‣ Imaginative and untraditional history. Translation of *Le moyen âge* (1982–83). Brings best current French medieval scholarship to English-reading audience. Emphasis on West but substantial attention to Byzantium and Islam. [FLC]

20.35 Aron Gurevich. *Categories of medieval culture.* G. L. Campbell, trans. London: Routledge & Kegan Paul, 1985. ISBN 0-7100-9578-3. ‣ Imaginative attempt to establish medieval worldview, written in reaction to strictures of Marxist historiography. Discussion focuses on categories of space, time, macrocosm and microcosm, law, wealth, labor, and property. Work of brilliant outsider. Translation of *Kategorii srednevekovoi kul'tury* (1981). [FLC]

20.36 Aron Gurevich. *Medieval popular culture: problems of belief and perception.* 1988 ed. János M. Bak and Paul A. Hollingsworth, trans. Cambridge and Paris: Cambridge University Press and Éditions de la Maison des Sciences de l'Homme, 1990. ISBN 0-521-30369-9 (cl, 1988), 0-521-38658-6 (pbk). ‣ Provocative, pioneering attempt to study peasant culture as "interaction of traditional folklore and Christianity," sixth to thirteenth century. Uses penitentials, saints' lives, vision literature, and *Elucidarium* of Honorius of Autun. Translation of *Problemy srednevekovoi narodnoi kul'tury* (1981). [FLC]

20.37 Jacques Le Goff. *Medieval civilization, 400–1500.* 1988 ed. Julia Barrow, trans. Oxford: Blackwell, 1989. ISBN 0-631-15512-0 (cl), 0-631-17566-0 (pbk). ‣ Survey with emphasis on social, economic, and cultural history. Ahead of its time when published; addresses questions that remain pertinent to current scholarship. Major attention to material culture, class structure and sociability, and mentalities. Translation of *La civilisation de l'Occident médiévale* (1965). [FLC]

20.38 Jacques Le Goff. *Time, work, and culture in the Middle Ages.* 1980 ed. Arthur Goldhammer, trans. Chicago: University of Chicago Press, 1982. ISBN 0-226-47080-6 (cl, 1980), 0-226-47081-4 (pbk). ‣ Eighteen essays, including often cited "Merchant's Time and Church's Time," "Licit and Illicit Trades," "Clerical Culture and Folklore," "Melusina: Mother and Pioneer." Translation of *Pour un autre moyen âge* (1977). [FLC]

20.39 Michael Moissey Postan. *The medieval economy and society: an economic history of Britain in the Middle Ages.* 1972 ed. New York: Penguin, 1984. ISBN 0-14-020896-8. ‣ Introductory history arguing author's neo-Malthusian theory: medieval economy expanded by opening new land; eventually population outgrew resources, leading to crisis. Focus on rural economy; only brief attention to towns and trade. [FLC]

20.40 Michael Moissey Postan, ed. *The Cambridge economic history of Europe.* Vol. 1: *The agrarian life of the Middle Ages.* Vol. 2: *Trade and industry in the Middle Ages.* Vol. 3: *Economic organization and policies in the Middle Ages.* Edition varies. Cambridge: Cambridge University Press, 1966–87. ISBN 0-521-04505-3 (v. 1), 0-521-08709-0 (v. 2), 0-521-04506-1 (v. 3), ISSN 0068-6646. ‣ Classic articles reprinted with new ones on a number of subjects, with updated bibliographies. Essential starting point. [FLC]

20.41 Timothy Reuter, ed. and trans. *The medieval nobility: studies on the ruling classes of France and Germany from the sixth to the twelfth century.* 1978 ed. Amsterdam: North-Holland; distributed by Elsevier North-Holland, 1979. ISBN 0-444-85136-4. ‣ Translation of major articles; Continental scholarship made accessible to anglophone readers. [JBF]

20.42 Joseph Reese Strayer. *On the medieval origins of the modern state.* 1970 ed. Princeton: Princeton University Press, 1973. ISBN 0-691-05183-6 (pbk). ‣ Terse essay on medieval state building. Argues sovereign state emerged by 1300 as dominant political form in Western Europe. Articulates premises underlying both older and modern studies of royal institutions. [RWK/SDW]

20.43 Lynn T. White, Jr. *Medieval technology and social change.* 1962 ed. London: Oxford University Press, 1980. ISBN 0-19-500266-0 (pbk). ‣ Studies relationship of technological development to medieval social change. Although major arguments (that wheeled plow allowed agricultural expansion; that stirrup was responsible for feudalism) now discounted, still valuable. See also White 20.1312. [FLC]

National and Regional Histories

20.44 Edouard Baratier, ed. *Histoire de la Provence.* 1969 ed. Toulouse: Privat, 1987. ISBN 2-7089-1649-1. ▸ Readable, comprehensive history of region between Alps and Rhône River, from prehistory to present. Two chapters on Middle Ages. Each chapter by expert on period or topic. For region to west, see Wolff, ed. 20.63. [TFXN]

20.45 Edward Burman. *Emperor to emperor: Italy before the Renaissance.* London: Constable, 1991. ISBN 0-09-469490-7. ▸ Wide-ranging popular history; readable, reasonably reliable, well illustrated. Not up to date but recommended for treatment of southern Italy, region poorly served by literature in English. [TFXN]

20.46 Thomas Durham. *Serbia: the rise and fall of a medieval empire.* York: Sessions, 1989. ISBN 1-85072-060-6 (pbk). ▸ Introduction to Serbian history stressing cultural identity of Serbs and their complex relations with neighboring peoples. Written for nonspecialists. [TFXN]

20.47 Günter P. Fehring. *The archaeology of medieval Germany: an introduction.* Ross Samson, trans. London: Routledge, 1991. ISBN 0-415-04062-0. ▸ Survey of excavations of churches, cemeteries, fortifications, and settlements in Germany. Translation of *Einführung in die Archäologie des Mittelalters* (1987). [FLC]

20.48 David Marshall Lang. *The Bulgarians: from pagan times to the Ottoman conquest.* Boulder: Westview, 1976. ISBN 0-89158-530-3. ▸ Brief introduction with strong attention to cultural developments. Useful bibliography; excellent illustrations. [TFXN]

20.49 A. W. A. Leeper. *A history of medieval Austria.* 1941 ed. R. W. Seton-Watson and C. A. Macartney, eds. New York: AMS Press, 1978. ISBN 0-404-15347-X. ▸ Dated, but only history of Austria available in English. [JBF]

20.50 Jean-François Lemarignier. *La France médiévale: institutions et société.* 1970 ed. Paris: Colin, 1989. ▸ Survey of French political and legal institutions, late antiquity to end of fifteenth century. Valuable both as reference work and as example of institutional history in French tradition. [SDW]

20.51 John Edward Lloyd. *A history of Wales from the earliest times to the Edwardian conquest.* 1939 3d ed. 2 vols. New York: Longmans, Green, 1967. ▸ Romantic, narrative Welsh history, from Paleolithic to 1278. Largely superseded for later period by works of Davies 20.515, but remains classic introduction to subject. First published 1911. [SDW]

20.52 Ferdinand Lot and Robert Fawtier, eds. *Histoire des institutions françaises au moyen âge.* 3 vols. Paris: Presses Universitaires de France, 1957–62. ▸ Standard work on French institutions representing legalistic point of view common at mid-century. Volume 1 treats institutions of great fiefs; volume 2, king, courts, finance, and army; and volume 3, French church. [RWK]

20.53 Bryce Lyon. *A constitutional and legal history of medieval England.* 2d ed. New York: Norton, 1980. ISBN 0-393-95132-4. ▸ History of administration and law, Anglo-Saxons to Tudors. Discusses Parliament, chancery, household, exchequer, and councils. Last great American homage to Stubbs's constitutionalism (20.58). [RWK]

20.54 David Nicholas. *Medieval Flanders.* London: Longman, 1992. ISBN 0-582-01679-7 (cl), 0-582-01678-9 (pbk). ▸ Basic introduction, early Middle Ages to incorporation into Habsburg empire, focusing on politics, industry, and trade. Brief surveys of agrarian economy and cultural life. Substantial bibliography. No equivalent in any language. [FLC]

20.55 Joseph F. O'Callaghan. *A history of medieval Spain.* 1975 ed. Ithaca, N.Y.: Cornell University Press, 1983. ISBN 0-8014-9264-5 (pbk). ▸ Best introduction in English to history of medieval Spain. Balanced account covering all regions, strongest on political history. Good bibliography. [TFXN]

20.56 Michael Richter. *Medieval Ireland: the enduring tradition.* Brian Stone and Adrian Keogh, trans. New York: St. Martin's, 1988. ISBN 0-312-02338-3. ▸ Brief introduction to Irish history by German scholar thoroughly at home in Irish history, but intended for those who are not. Translation of *Irland im Mittelalter* (1983). [PJG]

20.57 John M. Steane. *The archaeology of medieval England and Wales.* 1984 ed. Athens: University of Georgia Press, 1985. ISBN 0-8203-0755-6. ▸ History through eyes of field archaeologist, examining impact of man on urban and rural landscape. Covers topics from archaeology of medieval government to production of necessities of life. More technical than Clarke 20.352. [FLC]

20.58 William Stubbs. *The constitutional history of England.* 1883–87 3d–4th ed. 3 vols. Buffalo: Hein, 1987. ISBN 0-89941-559-8 (set). ▸ Classic presentation of nineteenth-century English constitutionalism; viewpoint dominated English medieval scholarship until 1960s. Worth reading for that reason. [RWK]

20.59 Peter F. Sugar and Péter Hanák, eds. *A history of Hungary.* Bloomington: Indiana University Press, 1990. ISBN 0-253-35578-8. ▸ Collection of essays, six on prehistory and Middle Ages. Treats Hungarian raids, conversion to Christianity, development of Western-type state, emergence of nobility, and growth of representative institutions. [JMB]

20.60 Seppo Suvanto. "Medieval studies in Finland: a survey." *Scandinavian journal of history* 4 (1979) 287–304. ISSN 0346-8755. ▸ Survey of work on medieval Finnish history, addressing whether, given its domination by Sweden, Finland had separate medieval history. Focus on interdisciplinary work. [RMK]

20.61 Giovanni Tabacco. *The struggle for power in medieval Italy: structures of political rule.* Rosalind Brown Jensen, trans. Cambridge: Cambridge University Press, 1989. ISBN 0-521-33469-1 (cl), 0-521-33680-5 (pbk). ▸ Draws on social science theories and Gramscian Marxism; difficult but highly original and challenging. Emphasizes transformation of ruling classes and structures through which power was exercised and role of nobility and towns in formation of regional states. Translation of part of "Einaudi" history (28.2). [TFXN/DJO/JFP]

20.62 Giovanni Tabacco and Paul Renucci, eds. *Dalla caduta dell'Impero romano al secolo XVIII.* Vol. 2 of *Storia d'Italia.* Turin: Einaudi, 1974. ▸ Part of multivolume history of Italy written by numerous specialists. Tabacco's chapters translated as *The struggle for power* (20.61), but nearly 2,000 pages remain untranslated. Narrative more complex than Galasso's *Storia d'Italia* (28.2, v. 1) and more stimulating on cultural and social history. [TFXN]

20.63 Philippe Wolff, ed. *Histoire du Languedoc.* Rev. ed. Toulouse: Privat, 1988. ISBN 2-7089-1609-2. ▸ General history of region, prehistory to present. Useful chapters on seigneurial regime, counts of Toulouse, Albigensian crusade, and impact of French conquest. [PHF]

SEE ALSO
33.697 Stanko Guldescu. *History of medieval Croatia.*

Rural World

20.64 Roland Bechmann. *Trees and man: the forest in the Middle Ages.* Katharyn Dunham, trans. New York: Paragon, 1990. ISBN 1-55778-034-X. ▸ Popular history of forests as ecosystem, as place for agriculture and stock rearing, as source of fuel and lumber, and in law and politics. Translation of *Des arbres et des hommes* (1984). [FLC]

20.65 Jean Chapelot and Robert Fossier. *The village and house in the Middle Ages.* Henry Cleere, trans. Berkeley: University of

California Press, 1985. ISBN 0-520-04669-2. ▸ Technical account of building techniques in context of social and economic history: first sketch by Fossier of his theory of "regrouping" of European population into villages, fortified settlements, parishes, lordships, ca. 1000, and formation of seigneurial regime. See also Fossier 20.280. Translation of *Le village et la maison au moyen âge* (1980). [FLC]

20.66 Georges Duby. *Rural economy and country life in the medieval West.* 1968 ed. Cynthia Postan, trans. Columbia: University of South Carolina Press, 1990. ISBN 0-87249-347-4 (pbk). ▸ Survey of rural economy from Carolingian period to fourteenth century. Discussion of technical poverty of early economy, expansion leading to overpopulation by 1300, transformation of seigneury, and Malthusian crisis. Dated in part but still best general introduction. Includes representative documents. Translation (not always accurate) of *L'économie rurale et la vie des campagnes dans l'occident médiéval* (1962). [FLC]

20.67 Georges Duby and Armand Wallon, eds. *Histoire de la France rurale.* 1975–77 ed. 4 vols. Paris: Seuil, 1992. ISBN 2-02-013706-2 (set), 2-02-017332-8 (v. 1), 2-02-017333-6 (v. 2), 2-02-017334-4 (v. 3), 2-02-017335-2 (v. 4). ▸ Survey of scholarship (as of early 1970s) on French rural history. Volume 1, prehistory to 1340; volume 2, 1340–1789. Written for general readership. [FLC]

20.68 Charles-Emmanuel Dufourcq and Jean Gautier-Dalché. *Histoire économique et sociale de l'Espagne chrétienne au moyen âge.* Paris: Colin, 1976. ▸ Introductory survey of social and commercial history of Spain, beginning in eighth century but emphasizing period 1200 to 1500. Classical rather than Annales approach, strongest on municipal trade and agriculture. [JFP]

20.69 Klaus Fehn et al. *Genetische Siedlungsforschung in Mitteleuropa und seinen Nachbarräumen.* 2 vols. Peter Burggraaff, ed. Bonn: Siedlungsforschung, 1988. ▸ Conference reports on archaeology, geography, and history of settlements throughout Europe. Up-to-date guide to research problems and bibliography. [FLC]

20.70 H.P.R. Finberg and Joan Thirsk, eds. *The agrarian history of England and Wales.* Vol. 1.2: *A.D. 43–1042.* Vol. 2: *1042–1350.* Vol. 3: *1348–1500.* 8 vols. to date. London: Cambridge University Press, 1967–. ISBN 0-521-08423-7 (v. 1.2), 0-521-20073-3 (v. 2), 0-521-20074-1 (v. 3). ▸ Region-by-region encyclopedic survey. Volume 1 treats post-Roman Wales and Anglo-Saxon England; volumes 2 and 3, Domesday England, settlement, techniques, demography, social structure, prices and wages, diet, housing, marketing, landlords, forms of landholding, and peasant rebellions. [FLC]

20.71 Vito Fumagalli and Gabriella Rossetti Pepe, eds. *Medioevo rurale: sulle tracce della civilta contadina.* Bologna: Il Mulino, 1980. ▸ Stimulating collection of articles devoted mainly to northern and central Italy, using place names, maps, legal texts, and saints' lives to study rural life throughout Middle Ages. Includes history of cultivated plants and settlements. [FLC]

20.72 Léopold Genicot. *Rural communities in the medieval West.* Baltimore: Johns Hopkins University Press, 1990. ISBN 0-8018-3870-3. ▸ General introductory survey. Sees emergence of community as complex work of aristocracy, church, and free peasants. Studies organization of village economy, legal structure, and parish. [FLC]

20.73 Jean Guilaine, ed. *Pour une archéologie agraire: à la croisée des sciences de l'homme et de la nature.* Paris: Colin, 1991. ISBN 2-200-37189-2 (cl), 2-200-37189-6 (jacket). ▸ Important discussions by specialists of techniques for archaeological study of landscape: aerial photography, phytohistory, geo-archaeology; soil, and pollen, charcoal, and seed remains. Relates fauna to human occupation. Fundamental for advanced techniques. [FLC]

20.74 David Hall. *Medieval fields.* Aylesbury, England: Shire, 1982. ISBN 0-85263-599-0 (pbk). ▸ Best brief introduction to study of English open fields. Particular attention to remains of medieval fields that can still be seen. [FLC]

20.75 W. G. Hoskins. *The making of the English landscape.* Rev. ed. Christopher Taylor, Introduction. London: Hodder & Stoughton, 1992. ISBN 0-340-56648-5 (pbk). ▸ Classic study describing major problems of landscape history: nature of settlements (farmsteads, villages, towns); changing population densities; land use; and relationship to soils, geology, and native vegetation. Introduction to series of shire landscape histories. [FLC/LCA]

20.76 Hans-Jürgen Nitz, ed. *Historisch-genetische Siedlungsforschung: Genese und Typen ländlicher Siedlungen und Flurformen.* Darmstadt: Wissenschaftliche Buchgesellschaft, 1974. ISBN 3-534-05071-1. ▸ Handy collection of major contributions to German debate over origins of open fields and division of holdings into long strips. Introduction sets out problems. [FLC]

20.77 Ghislaine Noyé, ed. *Structures de l'habitat et occupation du sol dans les pays méditerranéens: les méthodes et l'apport de l'archéologie extensive.* Rome and Madrid: École Française de Rome and Casa de Velázquez, 1988. (Castrum, 2. Collection de l'École Française de Rome, 105. Publications de la Casa de Velázquez, Série archéologie, 9.) ISBN 2-7283-0148-4, 84-86839-05-X. ▸ Conference papers (French, Spanish, Italian) describing landscape survey archaeology in Spain, Italy, North Africa, Greece, and Syria. Focuses on problem of locating and dating settlement sites. Important for demography, history of land use, and social organization of peasantry. [FLC]

20.78 T. W. Potter. *The changing landscape of South Etruria.* New York: St. Martin's, 1979. ISBN 0-312-12953-X. ▸ Presents results of long-term collective archaeological survey of settlement patterns north of Rome, prehistory to 1300 CE. One of few major studies of transition from antique to medieval landscape. [FLC]

20.79 Oliver Rackham. *Ancient woodland: its history, vegetation, and uses in England.* London: Arnold, 1980. ISBN 0-7131-2723-6. ▸ Technical analysis of ecology and historical ecology of woodland in England. Historical sections summarized for general reader in 20.80. [FLC]

20.80 Oliver Rackham. *Trees and woodland in the British landscape.* Rev. ed. London: Dent, 1990. ISBN 0-460-04786-8. ▸ Description of woodland as ecosystem. Prehistory to present with considerable attention to Middle Ages. For more technical presentation see author's *Ancient Woodland* (20.79). [FLC]

20.81 B. H. Slicher van Bath. *The agrarian history of Western Europe, A.D. 500–1850.* 1963 ed. Olive Ordish, trans. London: Arnold, 1966. ▸ General history of agricultural practices in Europe before industrialization. Best known for calculation of variations in productivity of premodern agriculture. [FLC]

20.82 Christopher Taylor. *Village and farmstead: a history of rural settlement in England.* London: Philip, 1983. ISBN 0-540-01071-5. ▸ Brief discussion of Middle Ages, but of fundamental importance for understanding medieval land use. Insists on mobility of rural settlements and continuities in landscape since Neolithic. [FLC]

SEE ALSO
  30.191 Wilhelm Abel. *Geschichte der deutschen Landwirtschaft vom frühen Mittelalter bis zum neunzehnten Jahrhundert.*

Urban World, Commerce, and Industry

20.83 John Blair and Nigel Ramsay, eds. *English medieval industries: craftsmen, techniques, products.* London: Hambledon, 1991. ISBN 0-907628-87-7. ▸ Collection of essays on stone cutting and stone construction and on crafts of metal-, glass-, textile-, and leather-making. Based on both literary and archaeological evidence. Technical. [FLC]

20.84 Carlrichard Brühl. *Palatium und Civitas: Studien zur Profantopographie spätantiker Civitates vom dritten bis dreizehnten Jahrhundert.* 2 vols. to date. Cologne: Böhlau, 1975–. ISBN 3-412-11375-1 (v. 1), 3-412-21788-3 (v. 2). ‣ Study of monumental buildings and defensive walls in cities of Roman origin. [FLC]

20.85 André Chédeville, Jacques Le Goff, and Jacques Rossiaud. *Histoire de la France urbaine.* Vol. 2: *La ville médiévale: des Carolingiens à la Renaissance.* Paris: Seuil, 1980. ISBN 2-02-005666-6 (v. 2), 2-02-005591-0 (set). ‣ Profusely illustrated introduction. Cities seen as centers of exchange and artisanal production inserted in feudal system. Copious attention to culture and daily life, as well as to institutions and economy. [FLC]

20.86 Pierre Couperie. *Paris through the ages: an illustrated historical atlas of urbanism and architecture.* 1968 ed. Marilyn Low, trans. New York: Braziller, 1971. ISBN 0-8076-0556-5. ‣ History of city seen through creation of buildings and development of topography. Numerous maps and photographs. Translation of *Paris au fil du temps* (1968). [LCA]

20.87 E. A. Gutkind. *International history of city development.* 8 vols. to date. New York: Free Press, 1964–. ISBN 0-02-913340-8 (set), 0-02-913260-6 (v. 2), 0-02-913270-3 (v. 3), 0-02-913280-0 (v. 4), 0-02-913300-9 (v. 5), 0-02-913310-6 (v. 6), 0-02-913320-3 (v. 7), 0-02-913330-0 (v. 8). ‣ Survey of town planning and urban development covering western, central, and eastern Europe with wealth of plans and aerial photographs. Bold if occasionally dubious generalizations. Town selection uneven. [LCA/JFP]

20.88 A. R. Hall and H. K. Kenward, eds. *Environmental archaeology in the urban context.* London: Council for British Archaeology, 1982. (Council for British Archaeology research report, 43.) ISBN 0-906780-12-8. ‣ Technical discussions of problems reconstructing environment of ancient and medieval British urban areas: climate, rubbish, human parasites, insects, and wild and domestic animals. [FLC]

20.89 Richard Krautheimer. *Rome: profile of a city, 312–1308.* 1980 ed. Princeton: Princeton University Press, 1983. ISBN 0-691-03947-X (cl), 0-691-00319-X (pbk). ‣ Magisterial, lavishly illustrated history of city from architectural perspective by greatest student of medieval Roman architecture. Marred by occasional errors of fact on political matters. [TFXN/JFP]

20.90 Robert S. Lopez. *The shape of medieval monetary history.* London: Variorum Reprints, 1986. ISBN 0-86078-195-X. ‣ Collection of author's works. Includes his classic articles "An Aristocracy of Money in the Early Middle Ages," "Back to Gold, 1252," "Une Histoire à Trois Niveaux: la Circulation Monétaire," and "Moneta e Monetieri nell'Italia Barbarica." [FLC]

20.91 Robert S. Lopez and Irving W. Raymond, eds. and trans. *Medieval trade in the Mediterranean world: illustrative documents translated with introduction and notes.* 1955 ed. New York: Columbia University Press, 1990. ISBN 0-231-01865-7 (cl), 0-231-09626-7 (pbk). ‣ Study of Byzantine, Muslim, and Western trade: markets, merchandise, exchange, contracts, routes, insurance, litigation, manuals, and accounting. Brings trade and traders alive using potpourri of texts from three continents with elaborate notes. [FLC]

20.92 A.E.J. Morris. *A history of urban form: before the industrial revolutions.* 1979 2d ed. London: Godwin, 1991. ISBN 0-7114-5512-0. ‣ Study of urban growth from Ireland to Bohemia. Chapter on medieval towns distinguishes three types of urban form resulting from organic growth and two types of new town plans. Extensive maps, plans, and aerial photographs. [LCA]

20.93 Hans Planitz. *Die deutsche Stadt im Mittelalter von der*

Römerzeit bis zu den Zunftkämpfen. 1954 ed. Vienna: Böhlau, 1980. ‣ General survey of German urban development from Roman and Merovingian period to thirteenth century. Focuses on topography, political and economic relationships, and burgher society. [LCA]

20.94 Leopoldo Torres Balbás. "La Edad Media." In *Resumen histórico del urbanismo en España.* 3d ed. Leopoldo Torres Balbás and Antonio García y Bellido, eds., pp. 67–149. Madrid: Instituto de Estudios de Administración Local, 1987. ‣ Discursive and unsystematic, nonetheless creates vital picture of contrast between urban spaces in northern and southern Spain: Christian royal and military functionalism versus Muslim persistent tribalism. [JFP]

20.95 Richard Unger. *The ship in the medieval economy, 600–1600.* Toronto: McGill-Queens University Press, 1980. ISBN 0-7735-0526-1. ‣ Technical account of changes in shipbuilding. Evokes social and economic environment of technological change and technical limitations imposed by tools and materials. [FLC]

20.96 Charles Verlinden. *L'esclavage dans l'Europe médiévale.* 2 vols. Bruges: De Tempel, 1955–77. (Rijksuniversiteit te Gent, Werken uitgegeven door de Faculteit van de Letteren en Wijsbegeerte, 119, 162.) ‣ Vast panorama of European Mediterranean slavery and barbarian kingdoms during fifteenth century. Volume 1 covers Iberian world (Christian, Muslim) and France; volume 2, Italy. Slaves are North Africans, Greeks, Turks, Circassians, Slavs, and black Africans. [FLC]

20.97 Philippe Wolff, ed. *Histoire de Toulouse.* Toulouse: Privat, 1988. ISBN 2-7089-4709-5. ‣ Overview from prehistory to present; half devoted to medieval period. Popular in style and social-economic in approach with useful bibliographical survey. One of many French urban histories published by Privat. [JFP]

Demography, Family, and Household

20.98 Philippe Ariès and Georges Duby, eds. *A history of private life.* Vol. 2: *Revelations of the medieval world.* Arthur Goldhammer, trans. Cambridge, Mass.: Belknap, 1988. ISBN 0-674-39976-5 (v. 2). ‣ Assumes family and material world of household is by definition private space; but opens finally to issue of individual withdrawal from public world and to emergence of intimate thought cultivated and fixed in private writing. Better discussion of family in *Historie de la famille* (20.99). Translation of *Histoire de la vie privée* (1985–). [FLC]

20.99 André Burguière et al., eds. *Histoire de la famille.* 2 vols. Paris: Colin, 1986. ISBN 2-200-37106-3 (v. 1), 2-200-37104-7 (v. 2). ‣ About one-third of volume 1 concerns Middle Ages. Full account of debates on family structure and ideology and functions of marriage. Uses wide range of studies from many countries. Best introduction to current issues. [FLC]

20.100 Georges Duby and Jacques Le Goff, eds. *Famille et parenté dans l'occident médiéval: actes du Colloque de Paris (6–8 juin 1974), organise per l'École Pratique des Hautes Études (sixième section) en collaboration avec le College de France et l'École Française de Rome, communications et debats.* Rome: École Française de Rome, 1977. (Collection de l'École Française de Rome, 30.) ‣ Conference papers explore varieties of perceptions of kinship, late antiquity to 1500 CE. Particular attention to personal names and relationship of family to property and to church. Treats Germany, Italy, and Poland. Dated but still important. [FLC]

20.101 Jack Goody. *The development of the family and marriage in Europe.* 1983 ed. Cambridge: Cambridge University Press, 1990. ISBN 0-521-24739-X (cl), 0-521-28925-4 (pbk). ‣ Family structure and marriage rules from late antiquity to Reformation, by African ethnologist turned medieval historian. Argues church doctrine, linked to political and economic interests, transformed rules. Fundamental but difficult. [FLC]

20.102 David Herlihy. *Medieval households.* Cambridge, Mass.: Harvard University Press, 1985. ISBN 0-674-56375-1 (cl), 0-674-56376-x (pbk). ‣ Basic introduction to history of household unit (domestic family), antiquity to 1500 CE. Traces rise of agnatic kinship lines and emotional ties within larger kindreds. Uses data from study of Tuscany to outline problems for research. [FLC]

20.103 Josiah Cox Russell. *The control of late ancient and medieval population.* Philadelphia: American Philosophical Society, 1985. (Memoirs of the American Philosophical Society, 160.) ISBN 0-87169-160-4. ‣ Far broader than title indicates. Thorough review of techniques and problems of historical demography before tax records and parish registers. Supersedes his *Late Ancient and Medieval Population* (1958). Vast bibliography. [FLC]

20.104 Shulamith Shahar. *Childhood in the Middle Ages.* London: Routledge, 1990. ISBN 0-415-02624-5. ‣ Argues against Ariès 22.234 that people were aware of childhood and invested emotionally and materially in children. Anecdotal history, from Carolingians to fifteenth century with leavening of psychological theory. [FLC]

Women

20.105 Bonnie S. Anderson and Judith P. Zinsser. *A history of their own: women in Europe from prehistory to the present.* 1988 ed. 2 vols. New York: Perennial Library, 1989. ISBN 0-06-091452-1 (v. 1, pbk), 0-06-091563-3 (v. 2, pbk). ‣ Textbook-style history. Volume 1 largely devoted to Middle Ages. Balanced treatment of empowerment and subordination. Substantial attention to rural as well as urban women. [FLC]

20.106 Clarissa W. Atkinson. *The oldest vocation: Christian motherhood in the Middle Ages.* Ithaca, N.Y.: Cornell University Press, 1991. ISBN 0-8014-2071-7. ‣ Treats motherhood as ideology and institution. Sees legacy of early Christianity, physiological assumptions derived from Greek medicine, spiritual motherhood, cult of Virgin, and female sainthood. Insists on ambiguity of role. For general reader. [FLC]

20.107 Georges Duby and Michelle Perrot, eds. *A history of women in the West.* 2 vols. to date. Cambridge, Mass.: Belknap, 1992–. ISBN 0-674-40370-3 (v. 1), 0-674-40371-1 (v. 2). ‣ Chapters on preaching about and to women, women's medicine, clothing, the "good wife," women and family strategies, and women's space and voices. Concerned more with women as social category than with definitions of gender. Translation of *Storia delle donne in Occidente* (1990–92). [FLC]

20.108 Mary Erler and Maryanne Kowaleski, eds. *Women and power in the Middle Ages.* Athens: University of Georgia Press, 1988. ISBN 0-8203-0957-5 (cl), 0-8203-0958-3 (pbk). ‣ Essays on women in countryside and cities of northern Europe and Venice. Discuss exercise of power through family and informal networks; female piety and women in literature. Make useful distinctions among power, authority, and influence. [FLC]

20.109 Margaret Wade Labarge. *A small sound of the trumpet: women in medieval life.* Boston: Beacon, 1986. ISBN 0-8070-5626-x. ‣ Classic popular account. Treats queens, noblewomen, townswomen, nuns and recluses, peasant women, prostitutes, and criminals. [FLC]

Other Topics

20.110 David Austin and Leslie Alcock, eds. *From the Baltic to the Black Sea: studies in medieval archaeology.* London: Unwin Hyman, 1990. ISBN 0-04-445119-9. ‣ Conference papers include major theoretical arguments about relationship of archaeology to written evidence and problems of interpretation. Also technical reports on Scandinavia, Poland, Hungary, Denmark, and Czechoslovakia. [FLC]

20.111 Jean-Noel Biraben. *Les hommes et la peste en France et dans les pays européens et méditerranéens.* 2 vols. Paris: Mouton, 1975–76. ISBN 2-7193-0930-3 (v. 1), 2-7193-3078-8 (v. 2). ‣ Volume 1 includes epidemiology of *Pasteurella pestis*, brief survey of "Justinianic" plagues, and extensive account of "plague era," 1348–1860. Volume 2 covers reactions to disease—ideas of divine punishment, cataclysm, and contagion and development of public health measures. [FLC]

20.112 Jim Bradbury. *The medieval siege.* Woodbridge, England: Boydell, 1992. ISBN 0-8511-5312-7. ‣ Enthusiastic popular history based on wide reading. Anecdotal narratives of sieges from late antiquity to Hundred Years' War. Useful for description of siege weapons and conventions of siege warfare. [FLC]

20.113 Jean Devisse. *From the early Christian era to the "age of discovery."* Vol. 2 of *The image of the black in Western art.* William Granger Ryan, trans. New York: Morrow, 1979. 2 vols. ISBN 0-688-03543-4 (v. 2.1), 0-688-03548-5 (v. 2.2). ‣ Massive survey tracing inheritance of ancient Mediterranean ideas of negritude into Christian Middle Ages (both Byzantine and Latin). Images associate blackness with evil or with Saracens, but ambiguities emerged in later Middle Ages with black Magus and St. Maurice. [FLC]

20.114 Archibald R. Lewis and Timothy J. Runyan. *European naval and maritime history, 300–1500.* 1985 ed. Bloomington: Indiana University Press, 1990. ISBN 0-253-32082-8. ‣ Popular introduction treating Byzantine, Muslim, and Western seamen; vessels on Mediterranean and Northern seas; and development of English and Iberian fleets. Primarily narrative of naval warfare, piracy, and commerce. [FLC]

20.115 Michel Mollat. *The poor in the Middle Ages: an essay in social history.* Arthur Goldhammer, trans. New Haven: Yale University Press, 1986. ISBN 0-300-02789-3. ‣ General history of attitudes of powerful toward poor and institutions created to care for them (charitable, hospitals) and police them. Synthesis of many of author's smaller studies. For general audience but based on extensive scholarship. Translation of *Les pauvres au moyen âge* (1978). [FLC]

20.116 Michel Pastoureau. *Couleurs, images, symboles: études d'histoire et d'anthropologie.* Paris: Léopard d'or, 1989. ISBN 2-86377-085-3. ‣ Social history of symbols, mainly in medieval context, treating colors, clothing, heraldry, medals, Arthurian names, and the pig. [FLC]

20.117 Michel Pastoureau, ed. *Le vêtement: histoire, archéologie, et symbolique vestimentaires au moyen âge.* Paris: Léopard d'or, 1989. ISBN 2-86377-089-6. ‣ Collection of essays treating clothing of children and workers, of relics, and of dream worlds. Addresses clothing as sign, morality of clothing, and revolution in male dress in fourteenth century. [FLC]

SEE ALSO
4.230 John B. Harley and David Woodward, eds. *The history of cartography.*
4.504 John H. Pryor. *Geography, technology, and war.*

EARLY MIDDLE AGES, ca. 400–ca. 1000

General Studies

20.118 Irving A. Agus. *Urban civilization in pre-Crusade Europe: a study of organized town-life in northwestern Europe during the tenth and eleventh centuries based on the Responsa literature.* 2 vols. New York: Yeshiva Universiy Press, 1965. ‣ Rich collection of sources in translation, with commentary. Topics include travel, business, money lending, trades, family, and education. Based on rabbinic answers to Talmudic legal and moral questions. Illuminates dark period of urban life. [FLC]

20.119 Roger Collins. *Early medieval Europe, 300–1000.* New

York: St. Martin's, 1991. ISBN 0-312-06037-8 (cl), 0-312-06198-6 (pbk). ▸ Sound, up-to-date introduction stressing institutional and political developments. Has no rival in English at present. [TFXN]

20.120   Georges Duby. *The early growth of the European economy: warriors and peasants from the seventh to the twelfth century.* 1974 ed. Howard B. Clarke, trans. Ithaca, N.Y.: Cornell University Press, 1978. ISBN 0-8014-9169-X. ▸ Sees economy, sixth to tenth century, as one of plunder and gift giving; transformed into seigneurial economy ca. 1000. First part against Pirenne 20.129; second, major statement of author's vision of seigneurial regime. Translation of *Guerriers et paysans, VIIe–XIIe siècle* (1973). [FLC]

20.121   Patrick J. Geary. *Before France and Germany: the creation and transformation of the Merovingian world.* New York: Oxford University Press, 1988. ISBN 0-19-504457-6 (cl), 0-19-504458-4 (pbk). ▸ Brief introduction to Merovingian history from perspective of late Roman provincial society. [PJG]

20.122   Judith Herrin. *The formation of Christendom.* 1987 ed. Princeton: Princeton University Press, 1989. ISBN 0-691-00831-0 (pbk). ▸ Fascinating parallel accounts of Byzantium, Islam, and West, fifth to ninth century. Tries to explain fate of Roman world without privileging West. Stronger on Byzantium than Islam; idiosyncratic on West. [TFXN]

20.123   Richard Hodges. *Dark Age economics: the origins of towns and trade, A.D. 500–1000.* 2d ed. London: Duckworth, 1989. ISBN 0-7156-1666-8. ▸ Anthropological approach to early medieval economic history. Argues noncommercial exchange existed among elites, channeled through trading centers (labeled emporia to compare with trading ports in pre-colonial Africa and Asia). [FLC]

20.124   Richard Hodges and David Whitehouse. *Mohammed, Charlemagne, and the origins of Europe: archaeology and the Pirenne thesis.* Ithaca, N.Y.: Cornell University Press, 1983. ISBN 0-8014-1615-9 (cl), 0-8014-9262-9 (pbk). ▸ Uses archaeology and economic anthropology to reverse thesis of Pirenne (20.129), arguing grave decline in population and economy, fourth to eighth centuries, followed by revived trade links through Scandinavia to Persia supporting Carolingian renaissance. Second part elaborated in Hodges 20.123. [FLC]

20.125   Herbert Jankuhn, Walter Schlesinger, and Heiko Steuer, eds. *Vor- und Frühformen der europäischen Stadt im Mittelalter: Bericht über ein Symposium in Reinhausen bei Göttingen in der Zeit vom 18. bis 24. April 1972.* 2 vols. Göttingen: Vandenhoeck & Ruprecht, 1975. (Abhandlungen der Akademie der Wissenschaften in Göttingen, Philologisch-historische Klasse, dritte Folge, 83–84.) ▸ Technical conference papers in English, French, and German. Topics include concept of town, continuity of Roman towns, and studies of individual sites in Germany, Scandinavia, Castile, England, Baltic region, and Eastern Europe. Based on archaeology. [FLC]

20.126   Lucien Musset. *The Germanic invasions: the making of Europe, AD 400–600.* Edward James and Columba James, trans. University Park: Pennsylvania State University Press, 1975. ISBN 0-271-01198-X. ▸ Combines narrative synthesis of history of successor kingdoms with discussion of historiographical problems. Still valuable guide, although selection of problems now seems dated. Translation of *Les invasions: les vagues germaniques* (1965). [ACM]

20.127   Janet L. Nelson. *Politics and ritual in early medieval Europe.* London: Hambledon, 1986. ISBN 0-907628-59-1. ▸ Collected essays, mainly on Carolingian and Anglo-Saxon kingship and coronation ritual. Other topics include law, women, saints, and historiography. Tour of recent scholarly interests. [ACM]

20.128   Thomas F. X. Noble and John J. Contreni, eds. *Religion,*

culture, and society in the early Middle Ages: studies in honor of Richard E. Sullivan. Kalamazoo, Mich.: Western Michigan University, Medieval Institute Publications, 1987. ISBN 0-918720-83-4 (cl), 0-918720-84-2 (pbk). ▸ Collection of specialized essays, largely by American scholars, on late antique, Merovingian, and Carolingian cultural and political history. Topics include Gregory of Tours, iconoclasm, kingship, religious ideas, and institutions. [PJG]

20.129   Henri Pirenne. *Mohammed and Charlemagne.* 1939 ed. Totowa, N.J.: Barnes & Noble, 1980. ISBN 0-389-20134-0. ▸ Last and greatest of Pirenne's works; set fundamental problem of early Middle Ages for two generations. Thesis—that ancient Roman world continued uninterrupted to ca. 700 when Islam broke connections to East—now abandoned, but still essential starting point for discussions of period's economy. See Duby 20.120, Hodges and Whitehouse 20.124, Bois 20.258, Grierson 20.269, and Lopez 20.90. Translation of *Mahomet et Charlemagne* (1936). [FLC]

20.130   Klavs Randsborg, ed. *The birth of Europe: archaeology and social development in the first millennium A.D.* Rome: L'Erma di Bretschneider, 1989. (Analecta Romana Instituti Danici supplementum, 16.) ISBN 88-7062-662-8. ▸ Conference papers focusing on Italy and Scandinavia in first millenium CE. Mainly general essays on European-wide and regional changes, especially in settlement patterns and trade, as seen through archaeology. [FLC]

20.131   P. H. Sawyer and I. N. Wood, eds. *Early medieval kingship.* Leeds: University of Leeds, School of History, 1977. ISBN 0-906200-00-8. ▸ Papers of conference on kingship in British Isles, Spain, and Frankish kingdom. Specialized essays on royal succession, inauguration rituals, genealogies, law, and merchants. [ACM]

20.132   Pauline Stafford. *Queens, concubines, and dowagers: the king's wife in the early Middle Ages.* Athens: University of Georgia Press, 1983. ISBN 0-8203-0639-8. ▸ Study of interrelationship of social norms, politics, and still-fluid institutions of monarchy, showing important role of royal consorts, fifth to eleventh century. [ACM]

20.133   Gerd Tellenbach. *Ausgewählte Abhandlungen und Aufsätze.* 4 vols. Stuttgart: Hiersemann, 1988–. ISBN 3-7772-8820-9 (set), 3-7772-8821-7 (v. 1), 3-7772-8822-5 (v. 2), 3-7772-8823-3 (v. 3). ▸ Collected articles by founder of Freiburg school. Volume 3 has most important work on imperial nobility. Other subjects include historiography, liturgy, and Carolingian empire and successor kingdoms. [JBF]

20.134   J. M. Wallace-Hadrill. *Early Germanic kingship in England and on the Continent: the Ford lectures, delivered in the University of Oxford in Hilary term 1970.* Oxford: Clarendon, 1971. ISBN 0-19-821491-X. ▸ Study of influence, first of Roman empire and then of Christian church on ideology rather than royal government. Roman period to ninth century. [ACM]

20.135   Suzanne Fonay Wemple. *Women in Frankish society: marriage and the cloister, 500 to 900.* 1981 ed. Philadelphia: University of Pennsylvania Press, 1985. ISBN 0-8122-1209-6 (pbk). ▸ Discussion of factors affecting status of women: forms of marriage and rise of monogamy. Particularly strong on religious life. [ACM/JJC]

20.136   Karl Ferdinand Werner. *Vom Frankenreich zur Entfaltung Deutschlands und Frankreichs: Ursprünge, Strukturen, Beziehungen, ausgewählte Beiträge, Festgabe zu seinem sechzigsten Geburtstag.* Sigmaringen, Germany: Thorbecke, 1984. ISBN 3-7995-7027-6. ▸ Twelve articles in German and French on Frankish administrative and political history. Original examinations of aristocracy, regional administration, and territorial organization, eighth to tenth century. [PJG]

20.137   Patrick Wormald, Donald A. Bullough, and Roger Collins, eds. *Ideal and reality in Frankish and Anglo-Saxon society: studies presented to J. M. Wallace-Hadrill*. Oxford: Blackwell, 1983. ISBN 0-631-12661-9. ▸ Specialized essays on Merovingian, Carolingian, and Anglo-Saxon monarchy, religious literature, practices, and politics stressing comparison of insular and Continental developments. Several essays on Bede the Venerable. [ACM]

Late Roman World

20.138 P. S. Barnwell. *Emperor, prefects, and kings: the Roman West, 395–565*. Chapel Hill: University of North Carolina Press, 1992. ISBN 0-8078-2071-7. ▸ Study of changes in administration of western empire as prefects replaced by barbarian kings. Argues changes fit traditional Roman repertory; new kings were half masters of soldiers and half Roman prefects, more fully dependent on Roman system than their predecessors. [FLC]

20.139 Peter Brown. *The cult of the saints: its rise and function in Latin Christianity*. 1981 ed. Chicago: University of Chicago Press, 1982. ISBN 0-226-07621-0 (cl, 1981), 0-226-07622-9 (pbk). ▸ Imaginative examination of cult of saints through sixth century. Emphasizes role of bishops in organizing and promoting saints' cults. [PJG]

20.140 John F. Drinkwater and Hugh Elton, eds. *Fifth-century Gaul: a crisis of identity?* Cambridge: Cambridge University Press, 1992. ISBN 0-521-41485-7. ▸ Conference papers focusing on reaction of Gaul to barbarian invasion and settlement. Topics include sources, Gothic settlement, social and cultural history, and archaeology. Emphasizes disruption of ancient world. [ACM]

20.141 Jean Durliat. *Les finances publiques de Dioclétien aux Carolingiens (284–889)*. Sigmaringen: Thorbecke, 1990. (Beihefte der Francia, 21.) ISBN 3-7995-7321-6. ▸ Radical argument for continuity in form and scale of taxation from Roman to Carolingian period. Redefines technical vocabulary of landholding and social status. Argues for public character of Carolingian polyptychs. [ACM]

20.142 Walter Goffart. *Rome's fall and after*. London: Hambledon, 1989. ISBN 1-85285-001-9. ▸ Collected articles of important specialist in early medieval historiography and administrative history. Downplays distinctiveness of barbarians and role in fall of the empire. Also studies of taxation, seigneury, polyptychs, and historians. [ACM]

20.143 Raymond Van Dam. *Leadership and community in late antique Gaul*. Berkeley: University of California Press, 1985. ISBN 0-520-05162-9. ▸ Examination of fusion of Gallic aristocratic society and Christian leadership in fifth century, primarily through episcopal office. [PJG]

Germanic Peoples

20.144 Bernard S. Bachrach. *A history of the Alans in the West: from their first appearance in the sources of classical antiquity through the early Middle Ages*. Minneapolis: University of Minnesota Press, 1973. ISBN 0-8166-0678-1. ▸ Brief, readable account of Alans from formation as people outside Roman frontier, through peregrinations across Rome's western provinces, to final settlement in Spain. [TFXN]

20.145 Thomas S. Burns. *A history of the Ostrogoths*. 1984 ed. Bloomington: Indiana University Press, 1991. ISBN 0-253-32831-4 (cl), 0-253-20600-6 (pbk). ▸ Readable history of Ostrogoths from first encounters with Romans to fall of their Italian kingdom in mid-sixth century. Draws on archaeological evidence. Good bibliography. [TFXN]

20.146 Walter Goffart. *Barbarians and Romans, A.D. 418–584: the techniques of accommodation*. Princeton: Princeton University Press, 1980. ISBN 0-691-05303-0. ▸ Stimulating account of Roman use of tax mechanisms and *hospitalitas* regime (quartering sol-diers in private homes) to incorporate barbarian peoples into framework of empire's western provinces. [TFXN]

20.147 Peter Heather. *Goths and Romans, 332–489*. New York: Oxford University Press, 1991. ISBN 0-19-820234-2. ▸ Major reappraisal of Jordanes's history of the Goths, arguing that Visigoths and Ostrogoths emerged as distinct groupings only after Hunnic invasions. Stresses Roman intervention and Gothic response. [CMW]

20.148 Edward James. *The Franks*. Oxford: Blackwell, 1991. ISBN 0-631-17936-4 (pbk). ▸ Combines history of archaeology with emphasis on fifth and sixth centuries and northern Gaul. Discusses meaning of name "Frank." [ACM]

20.149 Alexander Callander Murray. *Germanic kinship structure: studies in law and society in antiquity and in the early Middle Ages*. Toronto: Pontifical Institute of Mediaeval Studies, 1983. (Studies and texts, 65.) ISBN 0-88844-065-0 (pbk). ▸ Challenges notion of early Germanic society as clan-based; emphasizes role of cognation. About half the book on Frankish sources, especially *Lex Salica*. [ACM]

20.150 E. A. Thompson. *Romans and barbarians: the decline of the western empire*. Madison: University of Wisconsin Press, 1982. ISBN 0-299-08700-X. ▸ Twelve essays on West in fifth and sixth centuries, primarily from point of view of Germanic invaders. [CMW]

20.151 Reinhard Wenskus. *Stammesbildung und Verfassung: das Werden der frühmittelalterlichen Gentes*. 2d ed. Cologne: Böhlau, 1977. ISBN 3-412-00177-5. ▸ Process-oriented examination of Germanic tribes, arguing for their constitutional rather than ethnic nature. [PJG]

20.152 Herwig Wolfram. *Die Geburt Mitteleuropas: Geschichte Österreichs vor seiner Entstehung, 378–907*. Berlin: Siedler, 1987. ISBN 3-88680-263-9. ▸ Original discussion of transformation of Danubian and Alpine regions of modern Austria and their peoples. [PJG]

20.153 Herwig Wolfram. *History of the Goths*. Rev. from 2d German ed. Thomas Dunlap, trans. Berkeley: University of California Press, 1988. ISBN 0-520-05259-5 (cl), 0-520-06983-8 (pbk). ▸ Magisterial history of Goths (Visigoths and Ostrogoths) from formation as peoples to creation of Gothic kingdoms in Italy, Gaul, and Spain. Extensive treatment of Goths in Balkans. [TFXN]

Italy

20.154 Gian Piero Bognetti. *Castelseprio: artistic and historical guide*. Vittoria Bradshaw Cozzi, trans. Venice, Italy: Neri Pozza Editore, 1960. ▸ Important introduction to Lombard culture through major monument—a small church—by greatest expert on Lombard art, architecture, and culture. Only work by this author translated into English. [TFXN]

20.155 Paolo Delogu, Andre Guillou, and Gherardo Ortalli. *Langobardi e Bizantini*. Vol. 1 of *Storia d'Italia*. Turin: UTET, 1980. ISBN 88-02-03510-5. ▸ Expert, up-to-date general history, sixth to ninth century. Delogu on Lombard Italy, Guillou on Byzantium, and Ortalli on Venice; weak on south. This and "Einaudi" history (28.2) starting point for those who read Italian. [TFXN]

20.156 Wilhelm Ensslin. *Theoderich der Grosse*. 1947 ed. Munich: Bruckmann, 1959. ▸ Only substantial biography of most important of early Germanic kings. Also superb history of Italy, 480–526. [TFXN]

20.157 Vito Fumagalli. *Il regno italico*. Vol. 2 of *Storia d'Italia*. Turin: UTET, 1978. ISBN 88-02-02538-X. ▸ Clear, comprehensive account of precommunal Italy by master historian. Strikes balance between political narrative and social-institutional analysis. [TFXN]

20.158 Ferdinand Gregorovius. *History of the city of Rome in the Middle Ages.* 1903–12 ed., Edition varies. 8 vols. in 13. Annie Hamilton, trans. New York: AMS Press, 1967. ▸ Grand narrative history in nineteenth-century style. Volumes 1–3: detailed account of city's political, social, and cultural development from late Roman empire to eleventh century. [TFXN]

20.159 Jan T. Hallenbeck. *Pavia and Rome: the Lombard monarchy and the papacy in the eighth century.* Philadelphia: American Philosophical Society, 1982. (Transactions of the American Philosophical Society, 72.4.) ISBN 0-87169-724-6 (pbk). ▸ Detailed, sympathetic account of Lombard relations with Rome from high point of Lombard monarchy to its conquest by Charlemagne. Almost only significant treatment of Lombards in English. [TFXN]

20.160 Thomas Hodgkin. *Italy and her invaders.* 1880–99 ed. 8 vols. New York: Russell & Russell, 1967. ▸ Classic narrative of barbarian invasions. Vigorous; filled with anecdotes and quotations from primary sources. Observes each people, from Huns to Franks, as they pass through Italy. Corrected by modern scholarship but never superseded. [TFXN]

20.161 Barbara M. Kreutz. *Before the Normans: southern Italy in the ninth and tenth centuries.* Philadelphia: University of Pennsylvania Press, 1991. ISBN 0-8122-3101-5. ▸ Only significant book in English on southern Italy before eleventh century. Stresses political developments, but short sections treat society and culture. Reliable and readable. [TFXN]

20.162 Peter Llewellyn. *Rome in the Dark Ages.* New York: Praeger, 1971. ISBN 0-571-08972-0. ▸ Wide-ranging history of Rome and central Italy, late fifth through tenth centuries. Emphasizes politics. [TFXN]

20.163 Thomas F. X. Noble. *The Republic of St. Peter: the birth of the papal state, 680–825.* Philadelphia: University of Pennsylvania Press, 1984. ISBN 0-8122-7917-4 (cl), 0-8122-1239-8 (pbk). ▸ Detailed account of papal temporal rule in Italy with attention to local institutions, social structures, and diplomacy. Lengthy bibliography. [TFXN/JJC]

20.164 Franklin K. Toker. "Early medieval Florence: between history and archaeology." In *Medieval archaeology: papers of the Seventeenth Annual Conference of the Center for Medieval and Early Renaissance Studies.* Charles L. Redman, ed., pp. 261–83. Binghamton: State University of New York at Binghamton, 1989. (Medieval and Renaissance texts and studies, 60.) ISBN 0-86698-044-X. ▸ Story of Florentine topography, antiquity to 1000 CE, based on archaeology, primarily author's excavations under city's cathedral. [FLC]

20.165 Otto G. Von Simson. *Sacred fortress: Byzantine art and statecraft in Ravenna.* 1948 ed. Princeton: Princeton University Press, 1987. ISBN 0-691-04038-9 (cl), 0-691-00276-2 (pbk). ▸ Penetrating discussion of ritual and propagandistic significance of mosaics of sixth-century Ravenna. Forty-eight very good black-and-white plates. [TFXN]

20.166 Bryan Ward-Perkins. *From classical antiquity to the Middle Ages: urban public building in northern and central Italy, AD 300–850.* Oxford: Oxford University Press, 1984. ISBN 0-19-821898-2. ▸ Survey stressing continuity in building practices, techniques, and patronage, late antiquity to Carolingian conquest of Italy. [TFXN]

20.167 Chris Wickham. *Early medieval Italy: central power and local society, 400–1000.* 1981 ed. Ann Arbor: University of Michigan Press, 1989. ISBN 0-472-08099-7 (pbk). ▸ Analytical history emphasizing social and economic forces that built local com-

munities. Stronger on northern and central Italy than on Rome and South. [TFXN]

20.168 Chris Wickham. *The mountains and the city: the Tuscan Appenines in the early Middle Ages.* Oxford: Clarendon, 1988. ISBN 0-19-821966-0. ▸ Microhistory of two mountain communities in Tuscany, local development and connections with outside world. Based on brilliant analysis of charter evidence. [TFXN]

SEE ALSO
8.325 Thomas S. Brown. *Gentlemen and officers.*

Spain and Southern Gaul

20.169 Roger Collins. *The Arab conquest of Spain, 710–797.* Oxford: Blackwell, 1989. ISBN 0-631-15923-1. ▸ Learned, readable account of Muslim conquest. Discusses reasons why it happened and foundations it laid for subsequent Spanish history. [TFXN]

20.170 Roger Collins. *The Basques.* 2d ed. Oxford: Blackwell, 1990. ISBN 0-631-17565-2 (pbk). ▸ Illustrated history of Basque peoples and culture, prehistory to twelfth century. Considerable attention to impact of outside peoples on Basques. [TFXN]

20.171 Roger Collins. *Early medieval Spain: unity in diversity, 400–1000.* 1983 ed. New York: St. Martin's, 1987. ISBN 0-312-01354-X (pbk). ▸ Thorough introduction to early medieval Spain. Stresses continuities from Roman to Visigothic periods and from Visigoths to age of divided Muslim and Christian rule. [TFXN]

20.172 Paul-Albert Février et al. *La Provence des origines à l'an mille: histoire et archéologie.* Rennes, France: Société d'Éditions Ouest-France, 1989. ISBN 2-7373-0456-3. ▸ Detailed, scholarly survey of region's geography and history. Chapters on classical antiquity (Février), late antiquity (Guyon) and early Middle Ages (Fixot) informed by most recent archaeology. Not for novices. [FLC]

20.173 Patrick J. Geary. *Aristocracy in Provence: the Rhône basin at the dawn of the Carolingian age.* Philadelphia: University of Pennsylvania Press, 1985. ISBN 0-8122-7999-9. ▸ Specialized regional study of lower Rhône basin in eighth century. Emphasizes assimilation of local elites into wider Frankish social and political structures. [PJG]

20.174 Thomas F. Glick. *Islamic and Christian Spain in the early Middle Ages.* Princeton: Princeton University Press, 1979. ISBN 0-691-05274-3. ▸ Avoids political narrative to compare society and economy of both Muslim and Christian regions of Spain from eighth to eleventh centuries. Challenges dominant approaches and proposes new ways of looking at Christian-Muslim political and cultural relations. [TFXN/RWB]

20.175 Edward James, ed. *Visigothic Spain: new approaches.* Oxford: Clarendon, 1980. ISBN 0-19-822543-1. ▸ Collection of research papers by English and Continental scholars on many aspects of history of Spain, fifth to eighth century. [TFXN]

20.176 P. D. King. *Law and society in the Visigothic kingdom.* Cambridge: Cambridge University Press, 1972. ISBN 0-521-08421-0. ▸ Careful analyses of Visigothic institutions, social structures, and values based on close readings of surviving law codes. [TFXN]

20.177 Archibald R. Lewis. *The development of southern French and Catalan society, 718–1050.* Austin: University of Texas Press, 1965. ▸ Focuses on political history and institutions of lands lying on either side of eastern Pyrenees. Good account of development and behavior of aristocracy. [TFXN]

20.178 José Orlandis. *Historia del reino visigodo español.* Madrid: Rialp, 1988. ISBN 84-321-2417-6. ▸ Sound, comprehensive treatment by best Spanish specialist on subject. First place to begin for Spanish readers. [TFXN]

20.179   Claudio Sanchez-Albornoz. *La España cristiana de los siglos VIII al XI.* Vol. 1: *El reino Astur-Leonas (772 a 1037).* Madrid: Espasa-Calpe, 1980. ISBN 84-239-4981-8 (v. 1), 84-239-4800-5 (set). ▸ Best history of Christian Spain between Muslim conquest and beginning of *Reconquista;* by this century's foremost historian of medieval Spain. Nothing comparable in English. [TFXN]

20.180   E. A. Thompson. *The Goths in Spain.* Oxford: Clarendon, 1969. ISBN 0-19-814271-4. ▸ Not a full survey. Contains interesting and challenging perspectives, from Marxist point of view. [TFXN]

20.181   W. Montgomery Watt and Pierre Cachia. *A history of Islamic Spain.* 1965 ed. Edinburgh: Edinburgh University Press, 1977. ISBN 0-85224-332-4 (pbk). ▸ Brief yet comprehensive; remains standard introduction in English to history of al-Andalus. Political narrative by Watt still sound; section on literature by Cachia needs updating. [TFXN]

Merovingian Francia

20.182   Hartmut Atsma, ed. *La Neustrie, les pays au nord de la Loire de 650 à 850: Colloque historique international.* 2 vols. Karl Ferdinand Werner, Introduction. Sigmaringen, Germany: Thorbecke, 1989. (Beihefte der *Francia,* 16.) ISBN 3-7995-7316-X. ▸ Collection of specialized conference papers in English, French, and German on all aspects of northern Francia in early Middle Ages. Presents state of scholarship as of 1985. [PJG]

20.183   Bernard S. Bachrach. *Merovingian military organization, 481–751.* Minneapolis: University of Minnesota Press, 1972. ISBN 0-8166-0621-8. ▸ Survey of Frankish military history. Stresses importance of military organization for political history. [PJG]

20.184   Horst Ebling. *Prosopographie der Amtsträger des Merowingerreiches: von Chlothar II. (613) bis Karl Martell (741).* Munich: Fink, 1974. (Beihefte der *Francia,* 2.) ▸ Indispensible if occasionally incomplete prosopographical listing of persons identified by contemporary sources as secular office holders in later Merovingian kingdoms. [PJG]

20.185   Eugen Ewig. *Spätantikes und fränkisches Gallien: gesammelte Schriften (1952–1973).* 2 vols. Hartmut Atsma, ed. Munich: Artemis, 1976–79. (Beihefte der *Francia,* 3.1–2.) ISBN 3-7608-4652-1 (v. 1). ▸ Collection of most important essays by leading scholar of Merovingian Europe. Many focus on political and religious institutions, particularly of Rhineland. [PJG]

20.186   Paul Fouracre. "Observations on the outgrowth of Pippinid influence in the 'regnum Francorum' after the battle of Tertry (687–715)." *Medieval prosopography* 5.2 (1984) 1–31. ISSN 0198-9405. ▸ Prosopographical study of Neustrian officials, arguing Pippin II's consolidation of power was gradual and built on consensus of magnate and royal interests. [PJG]

20.187   Richard A. Gerberding. *The rise of the Carolingians and the "Liber Historiae Francorum."* Oxford: Clarendon, 1987. ISBN 0-19-822940-2. ▸ Argues for value of *Liber Historiae Francorum* as historical source for period from 650s to rule of Charlemagne. Discusses provenance and political conceptions of its author. Gives translated extracts. [ACM]

20.188   František Graus. *Volk, Herrscher, und Heiliger im Reich der Merowinger: Studien zur Hagiographie der Merowinger.* Prague: Nakladatelství Československé Akademie, 1965. ▸ Presents Merovingian hagiography as ideological literature. [PJG]

20.189   Edward James. *The origins of France: from Clovis to the Capetians, 500–1000.* New York: St. Martin's, 1982. ISBN 0-312-58862-3. ▸ Study of Gaul after collapse of Roman empire. Topics include regional history as well as monarchy; organized around themes of community and authority. Annotated bibliography of English- and foreign-language works. [ACM]

20.190   Archibald R. Lewis. "The dukes in the 'regnum Francorum,' A.D. 550–751." *Speculum* 51 (1976) 381–410. ISSN 0038-7134. ▸ Survey of ducal office and evolution of dukes from military and administrative officers to hereditary *principes.* [PJG]

20.191   Alexander Callander Murray. "From Roman to Frankish Gaul: *Centenarii* and *Centenae* in the administration of the Merovingian kingdom." *Traditio* 44 (1988) 59–100. ISSN 0362-1529. ▸ Discussion of Roman background to Merovingian officeholding, the hundred (subdivision of the county), and local police associations. [ACM]

20.192   I. N. Wood. *The Merovingian North Sea.* Alingsås, Sweden: Viktoria, 1983. ISBN 91-86708-00-7. ▸ Discussion of Merovingian hegemony on North Sea coast. Makes case for including Kent within Merovingian rule. [ACM]

Carolingian Francia

20.193   Wolfgang Braunfels, ed. *Karl der Grosse: Lebenswerk und Nachleben.* 5 vols. Dusseldorf: Schwann, 1965–68. ▸ Collection of essays by international team of experts on all aspects of Carolingian history. Some essays dated; but still point of departure for subject. [PJG]

20.194   Karl Brunner. *Oppositionelle Gruppen im Karolingerreich.* Vienna: Böhlau, 1979. (Veröffentlichungen des Instituts für Österreichische Geschichtsforschung, 25.) ISBN 3-205-08531-0. ▸ Pathbreaking prosopographical study of aristocratic opposition to Carolingians. [PJG]

20.195   Wendy Davies. *Small worlds: the village community in early medieval Brittany.* Berkeley: University of California Press, 1988. ISBN 0-520-06483-6. ▸ Microhistory of region in ninth-century Brittany, based on archives of monastery of Redon. Describes transformation of free peasant landowners into tenants of aristocrats and monastery. [PJG]

20.196   F. L. Ganshof. *The Carolingians and the Frankish monarchy: studies in Carolingian history.* Janet Sondheimer, trans. Ithaca, N.Y.: Cornell University Press, 1971. ISBN 0-8014-0635-8. ▸ Sixteen articles on administrative history by foremost mid-twentieth-century specialist in Carolingian law and institutions. [PJG]

20.197   F. L. Ganshof. *Frankish institutions under Charlemagne.* 1968 ed. Bryce Lyon and Mary Lyon, trans. New York: Norton, 1970. ▸ Basic, wide-ranging synthesis of administrative, judicial, and military institutions. Richly documented, though controversy muted. Translation of part of author's contribution to Braunfels, ed. 20.193. [ACM]

20.198   Pierre Riché. *Daily life in the world of Charlemagne: with expanded footnotes.* 1978 ed. Jo Ann McNamara, trans. Philadelphia: University of Pennsylvania Press, 1988. ISBN 0-8122-1096-4 (pbk). ▸ Rich in information and observation on all aspects of aristocratic clerical life, including material culture (and thus artisans, merchants, and rustics). No other comparable book for Frankish world. Translation of *La vie quotidienne dans l'Empire carolingien* (1973). [ACM]

20.199   Julia M. H. Smith. *Province and empire: Brittany and the Carolingians.* Cambridge: Cambridge University Press, 1992. ISBN 0-521-38285-8. ▸ Analyzes development of Brittany by focusing on royal and imperial hegemony, lordship, aristocratic rivalries, ecclesiastical jurisdictions, and cultural traditions. Invites reflection on themes of integration and unity in Carolingian world. [PJG]

20.200   J. M. Wallace-Hadrill. "The Vikings in Francia." In *Early medieval history.* 1975 ed. J. M. Wallace-Hadrill, pp. 217–36. New York: Barnes & Noble, 1976. ISBN 0-06-497393-X. ▸ Defense of traditional view of Viking raids and activities in Carolingian realms; argues recent scholars wrong to think monastic chronicles exaggerated them. [RMK]

Britain

20.201 Richard P. Abels. *Lordship and military obligation in Anglo-Saxon England*. Berkeley: University of California Press, 1988. ISBN 0-520-05794-5. ▸ Study of composition and recruitment of Anglo-Saxon armies; presents lordship and land tenure as twin bases of military obligation. In tradition of John 20.215; in contrast to commonwealth of low-ranking freemen (ceorls) of Stenton 20.222. [ACM/SDW]

20.202 Frank Barlow. *Edward the Confessor.* 1970 ed. Berkeley: University of California Press, 1984. ISBN 0-520-05319-2 (pbk). ▸ Detailed narrative of reign and analysis of royal government, finance, royal succession, and king's reputation for sanctity. Treats reign as period of political consolidation, not disintegration. [SDW]

20.203 Steven Bassett, ed. *The origins of Anglo-Saxon kingdoms.* London: Leicester University Press, 1989. ISBN 0-7185-1317-7. ▸ Interdisciplinary essays representing new interest in Anglo-Saxon origins and British antecedents. Studies on individual kingdoms, kingship, and social conditions. Articles mix sound observation with speculation. [ACM]

20.204 James Campbell. *Essays in Anglo-Saxon history, 400–1200.* London: Hambledon, 1986. ISBN 0-907628-32-X (cl), 0-907628-33-8 (pbk). ▸ Collected essays by major scholar. Topics include institutional framework of government, Bede the Venerable, church, conversion to Christianity, and Continental context for Anglo-Saxon history. [ACM]

20.205 James Campbell, Eric John, and Patrick Wormald, eds. *The Anglo-Saxons.* 1982 ed. London: Penguin, 1991. ISBN 0-14-014395-5. ▸ Survey by leading Anglo-Saxonists; trenchant scholarship. Political narrative; analysis of local and central government, church, Vikings, Normans, coinage, and lawmaking. Profusely illustrated; useful bibliography. [ACM/SDW]

20.206 Colin Chase, ed. *The dating of "Beowulf."* Toronto: University of Toronto Press in association with Centre for Medieval Studies, University of Toronto, 1981. ISBN 0-8020-5576-1. ▸ Conference papers challenging traditional dating of *Beowulf* to age of Bede and arguing poem dates to late ninth century or even later. [ACM]

20.207 Wendy Davies. *Patterns of power in early Wales.* Oxford: Clarendon, 1990. ISBN 0-19-820153-2. ▸ General introduction. Sees growing chaos ninth to eleventh century. Viking and English raids crucial in promoting rulers who could raise troops to fight in England or hire Vikings to fight in Wales. Counters traditional nationalist story. [FLC]

20.208 David N. Dumville. "Sub-Roman Britain: history and legend." *History* 62 (1977) 173–92. ISSN 0361-2759. ▸ Critical review of British sources purportedly of value for fifth and sixth centuries and modern reconstructions based on them. Consigns King Arthur to legend. [ACM]

20.209 Gillian Fellows Jensen. "The Vikings in England: a review." *Anglo-Saxon England* 4 (1975) 181–206. ISSN 0263-6751. ▸ Survey of scholarship, as of 1975, providing benchmark of received opinion against which to measure more recent work. [RMK]

20.210 H.P.R. Finberg. *Lucerna: studies of some problems in the early history of England.* New York: St. Martin's, 1964. ▸ Influential work combining broad synthesis with detailed local history attentive to charters, toponymy, and language. Argues for continuity between Roman Britain and Anglo-Saxon England. [ACM]

20.211 Margaret Gelling. *The West Midlands in the early Middle Ages.* Leicester: Leicester University Press; distributed by St. Martin's, 1992. ISBN 0-7185-1170-0 (cl), 0-7185-1395-9 (pbk). ▸ Geographic, archaeological history of region that is notable for presence of Saxon, British, and Welsh populations and for Offa's Dyke. One of series planned to cover all English regions. [FLC]

20.212 John Godfrey. *The church in Anglo-Saxon England.* Cambridge: Cambridge University Press, 1962. ▸ Broad survey, Roman period to eleventh century. Topics include conversion, institutions, culture, and missions to the Continent. [ACM]

20.213 Richard Hodges. *The Anglo-Saxon achievement: archaeology and the beginnings of English society.* Ithaca, N.Y.: Cornell University Press, 1989. ISBN 0-8014-2398-8. ▸ Seeks origins of distinct English personality in settlement patterns and economic structures of Anglo-Saxon period. Combative rewriting of cultural history from material remains within theoretical framework of new archaeology. [FLC]

20.214 Della Hooke, ed. *Anglo-Saxon settlements.* Oxford: Blackwell, 1988. ISBN 0-631-15454-X. ▸ Collection of specialized essays on churches, place names, Anglo-Scandinavian settlements, villages, and fields with comparative essays on Carolingian Central Europe. [FLC]

20.215 Eric John. *"Orbis Britanniae" and other studies.* Leicester: Leicester University Press, 1966. (Studies in early English history, 4.) ▸ Essays by leading revisionist of Anglo-Saxon social and political history. Topics include Anglo-Saxon kingship, landholding, feudalism, tenth-century monastic reform, Anglo-Saxon charters, and response to critics. [ACM]

20.216 H. R. Loyn. *The governance of Anglo-Saxon England, 500–1087.* Stanford, Calif.: Stanford University Press, 1984. ISBN 0-8047-1217-4. ▸ Treats royal government to 899; formation of English kingdom, 899–1066; and Norman conquest. Emphasizes precocious development of Anglo-Saxon state; argues continuity between late Anglo-Saxon and Norman England. Informative if unoriginal survey. [SDW]

20.217 Frederic William Maitland. *Domesday Book and beyond: three essays in the early history of England.* 1897 ed. J. C. Holt, Foreword. Cambridge: Cambridge University Press, 1987. ISBN 0-521-34112-4 (cl), 0-521-34918-4 (pbk). ▸ Masterpiece of historical detective work, reconstructing late Saxon social structure, tenurial practice, and the "hide" from Domesday Book. Often criticized but never replaced. [FLC]

20.218 Henry Mayr-Harting. *The coming of Christianity to Anglo-Saxon England.* 3d ed. University Park: Pennsylvania State University Press, 1991. ISBN 0-271-00769-9. ▸ Linked essays on conversion to Christianity and political and cultural character of new church (up to mid-eighth century). Gives equal, imaginative weight to Roman and Irish missions. [ACM]

20.219 P. H. Sawyer, ed. *Medieval settlement: continuity and change.* London and New York: Arnold and Crane Russak, 1976. ISBN 0-8448-1092-4. ▸ Conference papers employing disciplines of history, place-name study, archaeology, palaeobotany, and blood-group research (among others) to show complexity of development, in contrast to simple models of traditional historiography. Emphasis mainly on England. [ACM]

20.220 Alan Small, ed. *The Picts: a new look at old problems.* Dundee, Scotland: University of Dundee, Department of Geography, 1987. ISBN 0-903674-09-2. ▸ Up-to-date, general and specialized conference papers. [ACM]

20.221 Alfred P. Smyth. *Warlords and holy men: Scotland, A.D. 80–1000.* 1984 ed. Edinburgh: Edinburgh University Press, 1989. ISBN 0-7486-0100-7 (pbk). ▸ Pointed argument and synthesis of current scholarly views. Topics include Britons, Picts, Scots,

Columba, Adomnàn, Vikings, kingdom of Scotland, and conquest of southern Uplands. Annotated bibliography. [ACM]

20.222 Frank Stenton. *Anglo-Saxon England.* 1971 3d ed. New York: Oxford University Press, 1989. ISBN 0-19-282237-3 (pbk). ‣ Though some corrections made for third edition, represents state of knowledge at mid-century (1955 2d edition). Provides benchmark by which to measure growth in knowledge and changing conceptions in last forty-five years. [FLC]

20.223 Alan Vince. *Saxon London: an archaeological investigation.* London: Seaby, 1990. ISBN 1-85264-019-7. ‣ Results of thirty years of archaeological work; shows how much of city's early history, from rebirth in seventh century to Norman conquest, remains a mystery. [FLC]

Ireland

20.224 Lisa M. Bitel. *Isle of the saints: monastic settlement and Christian community in early Ireland.* Ithaca, N.Y.: Cornell University Press, 1990. ISBN 0-8014-2471-2. ‣ Survey presents social and cultural context of Irish monasticism, as seen in hagiographical texts. [PJG]

20.225 Nancy Edwards. *The archaeology of early medieval Ireland.* Philadelphia: University of Pennsylvania Press, 1990. ISBN 0-8122-3085-X. ‣ Survey of research on period between christianization and Norman conquest. Topics include settlements, food production, crafts and exchange, churches, fortifications, art, and Vikings. [FLC]

20.226 Michael J. Enright. *Iona, Tara, and Soissons: the origin of the royal anointing ritual.* New York and Berlin: de Gruyter, 1985. ISBN 0-89925-118-8. ‣ Challenging revisionist thesis concerning origins of royal unction. Argues for Irish origins. [PJG]

20.227 Kathleen Hughes. *Early Christian Ireland: introduction to the sources.* Ithaca, N.Y.: Cornell University Press, 1972. ISBN 0-8014-0721-4. ‣ Introduction to major sources of Irish history to 1100. Invaluable for understanding types and limitations of Irish archaeological, legal, religious, and narrative sources. [PJG]

20.228 Heinz Löwe, ed. *Die Iren und Europa im früheren Mittelalter.* 2 vols. Stuttgart: Klett-Cotta, 1982. ISBN 3-12-915470-1 (set). ‣ Scholarly conference papers in English, French, German, and Italian discuss aspects of relationship between Irish and Continental cultures. [PJG]

20.229 Alfred P. Smyth. *Scandinavian kings in the British Isles, 850–880.* Oxford: Oxford University Press, 1977. ISBN 0-19-821865-6. ‣ Argues kingdom of Dublin closely linked to Viking kingdoms in Britain. Serious consideration of literary works that other scholars dismiss as legendary. Important thesis about significance of kingship in Viking activity. [RMK]

Vikings

20.230 Thorsten Andersson and Karl Inge Sandred, eds. *The Vikings: proceedings of the symposium of the faculty of arts of Uppsala University, June 6–9, 1977.* Uppsala: Uppsala Universitet; distributed by Almqvist & Wiksell, 1978. (Symposia Universitatis Uppsaliensis annum quingentesimum celebrantis, 8.) ISBN 91-554-0706-4. ‣ Topics include Viking seamanship in literature and archaeology, Scandinavian influence on language and place-names in British Isles, and administrative organization of Viking Scandinavia. [RMK]

20.231 M. A. S. Blackburn and D. M. Metcalf, eds. *Viking age coinage in the northern lands: the Sixth Oxford Symposium on Coinage and Monetary History.* 2 vols. Oxford: British Archaeological Reports, 1981. (British Archaeological Reports, International series, 122.) ISBN 0-86054-150-9. ‣ Both introductory and more technical articles on coinage in Scandinavia and elsewhere and its relevance to economic history of Viking age. [RMK]

20.232 Helen Clarke and Björn Ambrosiani. *Towns in the Viking age.* New York: St. Martin's, 1991. ISBN 0-312-06086-6. ‣ Discussion of economic structures and trade largely based on archaeology. Leaves open controversial question of royal influence on urban development. Covers towns in Scandinavia, Britain, and Slavonic-Baltic region. [RMK/LCA]

20.233 Carol J. Clover and John Lindow, eds. *Old Norse-Icelandic literature: a critical guide.* Ithaca, N.Y.: Cornell University Press, 1985. ISBN 0-8014-1755-4. ‣ Review articles and bibliographies by leading authorities on major types of Old Norse written sources for study of Viking age. Topics include mythology, poetry, and sagas. [RMK]

20.234 R. T. Farrell, ed. *The Vikings.* London: Phillimore, 1982. ISBN 0-85033-436-5. ‣ Collection of articles by leading scholars; useful to nonspecialists. Topics include history, art history, archaeology, and literature with geographical spread from Scandinavia to North America. Extensive bibliography. [RMK]

20.235 Peter Foote and David M. Wilson. *The Viking achievement: the society and culture of early medieval Scandinavia.* 1970 ed. London and New York: Sidgwick & Jackson and St. Martin's, 1990. ISBN 0-312-03510-1. ‣ Best introductory survey available although now slightly dated, especially on archaeology. Concentrates on Scandinavia and on society and culture; less attention to Viking expansion and politics. [RMK]

20.236 James Graham-Campbell and Dafydd Kidd. *The Vikings.* New York: Metropolitan Museum of Art and Morrow, 1980. ISBN 0-87099-219-8 (cl), 0-688-03603-1 (cl), 0-87099-220-1 (pbk). ‣ Exhibition catalogue. Photographic illustration of artifacts and sites with extended commentaries. [RMK]

20.237 Judith Jesch. *Women in the Viking age.* Woodbridge, England: Boydell, 1991. ISBN 0-85115-278-3. ‣ Thorough, sophisticated survey takes into account masculine origins of surviving texts. Organized around different types of sources: archaeology, runic inscriptions, and literary texts. [RMK]

20.238 Gwyn Jones. *A history of the Vikings.* Rev. ed. Oxford: Oxford University Press, 1984. ISBN 0-19-285139-X (pbk). ‣ Good introduction. Thorough political narrative with sections on society and culture. Covers both Scandinavia and overseas expansion. Criticized for too readily using literature as historical evidence. [RMK]

20.239 Gwyn Jones. *The Norse Atlantic saga, being the Norse voyages of discovery and settlement to Iceland, Greenland, and North America.* 2d ed. Oxford: Oxford University Press, 1986. ISBN 0-19-215886-4 (cl), 0-19-285160-8 (pbk). ‣ Norse discovery and colonization of Iceland, Greenland, and Vinland. Includes translations of major sources with appendixes on archaeological material from Greenland, Newfoundland, and arctic Canada. [RMK]

20.240 Sven-Olof Lindquist and Birgitta Radhe, eds. *Society and trade in the Baltic during the Viking age: papers of the seventh Visby Symposium held at Gotlands Fornsal, Gotland's Historical Museum, Visby, August 15th–19, 1983.* Visby, Sweden: Gotlands Fornsal, 1985. (Acta Visbyensia, 7.) ‣ Papers in English and German on history, geography, archaeology, and numismatics; narrowly focused but based on latest empirical and theoretical work. [RMK]

20.241 Klavs Randsborg. *The Viking age in Denmark: the formation of a state.* New York: St. Martin's, 1980. ISBN 0-312-84650-9. ‣ Argues for early formation of Danish state, based on archaeological evidence combined with Marxist-influenced theoretical perspective. Not for beginners. [RMK]

20.242 Else Roesdahl. *Viking age Denmark.* Susan Margeson and Kirsten Williams, trans. London: British Museum Publications, 1982. ISBN 0-7141-8027-0. ‣ More survey than interpretation. Particularly good on archaeological data. Translation of *Danmarks Vikingetid* (1980). [RMK]

20.243 P. H. Sawyer. *Kings and Vikings: Scandinavia and Europe, A.D. 700–1100.* New York: Methuen, 1982. ISBN 0-416-74180-0 (cl), 0-416-74190-8 (pbk). ‣ Interpretive essay with strong emphasis on sources. Relates Viking raids to growth of royal power. Excellent bibliography. If you only read one book on Vikings, read this one. [RMK]

20.244 Knud Rahbek Schmidt, ed. *Varangian problems: report of the first international symposium of the theme, "the eastern connections of the Nordic peoples in the Viking period and early Middle Ages," Moesgaard, University of Aarhus, 7th–11th October 1968.* Copenhagen: Munksgaard, 1970. (*Scando-Slavica*, Supplementum, 1.) ISBN 87-16-00456-6. ‣ Papers on Scandinavian activity and influence in early Russia, from historical, archaeological, and linguistic viewpoints. Useful background to debate; superseded in part by recent archaeology. [RMK]

Holy Roman Empire

20.245 Gerd Althoff. *Verwandte, Freunde, und Getreue: zum politischen Stellenwert der Gruppenbindungen im frühen Mittelalter.* Darmstadt: Wissenschaftliche Buchgesellschaft, 1990. ISBN 3-534-04125-9. ‣ Analysis of formation and structure of kinship, peer, and lordship groups among nobility in Carolingian and Ottonian Germany. Synthesizes author's previous work on noble self-consciousness and conflict resolution. [JBF]

20.246 Heinrich Fichtenau. *Living in the tenth century: mentalities and social orders.* Patrick J. Geary, trans. Chicago: University of Chicago Press, 1991. ISBN 0-226-24620-5. ‣ Annales-style investigation of late and post-Carolingian culture. Topics include ordering of society, family (in classical and modern senses), nobility, religious life, and disorder. Translation of *Lebensordnungen des zehnten Jahrhunderts* (1984). [JBF/JJC]

20.247 Josef Fleckenstein. *Early medieval Germany.* Bernard S. Smith, trans. Amsterdam: North-Holland; distributed by Elsevier North-Holland, 1978. ISBN 0-444-85134-8. ‣ Brief introductory chapters on clan and household, nobility, king, church, manor and peasants, and cultural revival, followed by an extended political narrative, Charlemagne to Conrad II. Presupposes some prior knowledge. Translation of *Grundlagen und Beginn der deutschen Geschichte* (1976). [JBF]

20.248 Eduard Hlawitschka, comp. *Königswahl und Thronfolge in ottonisch-frühdeutscher Zeit.* Darmstadt: Wissenschaftliche Buchgesellschaft, 1971. ISBN 3-534-04166-6. ‣ Collection of important articles on royal elections (particularly those of 911, 919, and 936), Saxon dynasty, indivisibility of kingdom, and aristocracy. Good introduction. [JBF]

20.249 Hellmut Kämpf. *Die Entstehung des deutschen Reiches (Deutschland um 900).* 5th ed. Darmstadt: Wissenschaftliche Buchgesellschaft, 1980. ‣ Articles (written mainly during Third Reich) on role of king and aristocracy in formation of Germany. Debate inspired Tellenbach's interest in imperial aristocracy (20.133). [JBF]

20.250 Karl J. Leyser. *Rule and conflict in an early medieval society: Ottonian Saxony.* Bloomington: Indiana University Press, 1979. ISBN 0-253-17525-9. ‣ Collection of studies on topics such as Otto I and his enemies, women of Saxon aristocracy, and sacral kingship, using insights of social anthropology. Best work in any language on tenth-century women. [JBF]

20.251 Timothy Reuter. *Germany in the early Middle Ages, c. 800–1056.* London: Longman, 1991. ISBN 0-582-08156-4 (cl), 0-582-49034-0 (pbk). ‣ Largely political history incorporating recent scholarship, but drawing own conclusions on major issues

such as election of Henry I. For English-language readers, replaces Barraclough 20.610 for this period. [JBF]

20.252 Walter Schlesinger. *Die Entstehung der Landesherrschaft: Untersuchungen vorwiegend nach mitteldeutschen Quellen.* 1941 ed. Darmstadt: Wissenschaftliche Buchgesellschaft, 1983. ISBN 3-534-05184-X. ‣ Using Thuringian evidence, argues lordship based not on usurpation of royal rights but on nobility's innate right to rule. Nazi overtones. [JBF]

20.253 Percy Ernst Schramm. *Kaiser, Rom, und Renovatio: Studien zur Geschichte des römischen Erneuerungsgedankens vom Ende des karolingischen Reiches bis zum Investiturstreit.* 1929 ed. Darmstadt: Wissenschaftliche Buchgesellschaft, 1984. ISBN 3-534-00442-6. ‣ Study of imperial ideology, particularly during reign of Otto III. Brilliant example of interwar German intellectual history. Reprint of 1929 edition with bibliography of 1957 edition. [JBF]

20.254 Wilhelm Störmer. *Früher Adel: Studien zur politischen Führungsschicht im fränkisch-deutschen Reich vom achten bis elften Jahrhundert.* 2 vols. Stuttgart: Hiersemann, 1973. ISBN 3-7772-7314-7 (set), 3-7772-7308-2 (v. 1), 3-7772-7307-4 (v. 2). ‣ Synthesis of specialized research. Discusses idea of nobility, naming practices, family structure, marriage patterns, landholding, military service, colonization, relations with monarchy and church, and constitutional issues. [JBF]

Balkans

20.255 Centro Italiano di Studi Sull'alto Medioevo, ed. *Gli slavi occidentali e meridionali nell'alto Medioevo: 15–21 aprile 1982.* 2 vols. Spoleto: Presso la sede del Centro, 1983. (Settimane di Studio del Centro Italiano di Studi Sull'alto Medioevo, 30.) ISSN 0528-5666. ‣ Conference papers in English, French, German, and Italian survey current state of scholarship. Topics include migration, settlement, early state formation, ethnology, economy, paganism, conversions to Christianity, literacy, and art. [FLC]

20.256 John V. A. Fine, Jr. *The early medieval Balkans: a critical survey from the sixth to the late twelfth century.* 1983 ed. Ann Arbor: University of Michigan Press; distributed by Manchester University Press, 1991. ISBN 0-472-08149-7 (pbk). ‣ Detailed account stressing political developments and relations with Byzantium but does not neglect society and culture. [TFXN]

SEE ALSO
33.136 Steven Runciman. *A history of the first Bulgarian empire.*
33.320 Antal Bartha. *Hungarian society in the ninth and tenth centuries.*

Rural World

20.257 Heinrich Beck, Dietrich Denecke, and Herbert Jankuhn, eds. *Untersuchungen zur eisenzeitlichen und frühmittelalterlichen Flur in Mitteleuropa und ihrer Nutzung: Bericht über die Kolloquien der Kommission für die Altertumskünde Mittel- und Nordeuropas in den Jahren 1975 und 1976.* 2 vols. Göttingen: Vandenhoeck & Ruprecht, 1979–. (Abhandlungen der Akademie der Wissenschaften in Göttingen, Philologisch-historische Klasse, Dritte folge, 115, 116.) ISBN 3-525-82395-9 (v. 1), 3-525-82396-7 (v. 2). ‣ Technical study of field forms from Iron Age to early Middle Ages, using literary and archaeological evidence. Volume 1 includes local and regional studies, fields in law codes, and retrospective method; volume 2, ecological and technical studies of soil and tools and place-name studies. [FLC]

20.258 Guy Bois. *The transformation of the year one thousand: the village of Lournand from antiquity to feudalism.* Jean Birrell, trans. Manchester: Manchester University Press; distributed by St. Martin's, 1992. ISBN 0-7190-3565-1 (cl), 0-7190-3566-X (pbk). ‣ Discussion of profound sources of medieval growth sees origin of feudal society in revolutionary tenth-century break with antique slave economy. Combative Marxist history. Translation of *La mutation de l'an mil* (1989). [FLC]

20.259 Michel Fixot and Elisabeth Zadora-Rio, eds. *L'église, le terroir.* Paris: Centre National de la Recherche Scientifique, 1989. (Monographie du CRA, 1.) ISBN 2-222-04356-5. ‣ Conference reports describing fortified cemeteries and inhabited cemeteries and protected spaces of asylum. Part of emerging problem in early medieval settlements. [FLC]

20.260 Vito Fumagalli. *Terra e società nell'Italia padana: i secoli IX e X.* 2d ed. Turin: Einaudi, 1976. ‣ Description of social organization of rural Po valley in period when other areas of Europe ill documented. Discusses land clearing, creation of small holdings, emergence of new nobility, and incidence of servitude. [FLC]

20.261 Walter Janssen and Dietrich Lohrmann, ed. *Villa-Curtis-Grangia: Landwirtschaft zwischen Loire und Rhein von der Römerzeit zum Hochmittelalter; sechzehntes Deutsch-Französisches Historikerkolloquium des Deutschen Historischen Instituts Paris, Xanten 28.9–1.10.1980/Économie rurale entre Loire et Rhin de l'époque gallo-romaine au douzième–treizième siècle.* Munich: Artemis, 1983. ISBN 3-7608-4661-0. ‣ Conference papers (French, German) including major studies of continuities and discontinuities of antique/early medieval agrarian establishments and of monastic estates, tenth to thirteenth century. Major revisionist views of early medieval great estates. [FLC]

20.262 Massimo Montanari. *L'alimentazione contadina nell'alto medioevo.* Naples: Liguori, 1979. ISBN 88-207-0774-8. ‣ Using early documentation reconstructs ninth- and tenth-century landscape of northern Italy; discusses production of grains, pastoralism, hunting and gathering, fishing, wine and beer, gardening, and cooking methods. Examines problem of hunger and food as social symbol. Engaging and novel. [FLC]

20.263 Werner Rösener, ed. *Strukturen der Grundherrschaft im frühen Mittelalter.* Göttingen: Vandenhoeck & Ruprecht, 1989. (Veröffentlichungen des Max-Planck-Institut für Geschichte, 92.) ISBN 3-525-35628-5. ‣ Local and general studies reflecting current scholarly opinion on organization of landed estates in early Middle Ages. [PJG]

20.264 William H. TeBrake. *Medieval frontier: culture and ecology in Rijnland.* College Station: Texas A&M University Press, 1985. ISBN 0-89096-204-9. ‣ Highly original study of ecology and early occupation of coastal Holland. Discusses Frisian reclamation, process of settlement, forms of agriculture and pastoralism. [FLC]

20.265 Adriaan Verhulst, ed. *Le grand domaine aux époques mérovingienne et carolingienne/Die Grundherrschaft im frühen Mittelalter: actes du colloque international, Gand, 8–10 septembre 1983.* Ghent: Belgisch Centrum voor Landelijke Geschiedenis, 1985. (Belgisch Centrum voor Landelijke Geschiedenis, Publikatie/Centre Belge d'Histoire Rurale, Publication, 81.) ‣ Conference proceedings on subject of estate formation in Frankish period. Studies argue that bipartite manor appears in northern Gaul only in seventh century. For advanced students. [PJG]

20.266 Chris Wickham. "Problems of comparing rural societies in early medieval western Europe." *Transactions of the Royal Historical Society,* Series 6, 2 (1992) 221–46. ISSN 0080-4401. ‣ Provocative "musing about the methodological problems" of surveying early medieval rural world. Forceful polemic against national and legal-historical paradigms. Advances "peasant society" paradigm as alternative. [FLC]

Other Topics

20.267 Wendy Davies and Paul Fouracre, eds. *The settlement of disputes in early medieval Europe.* 1986 ed. Cambridge: Cam-

bridge University Press, 1992. ISBN 0-521-42895-5 (pbk). ‣ Essays challenging traditional picture of early medieval law given by legal historians. Using evidence of charters, emphasizes law as process and rational character of procedure. [ACM]

20.268 N. Gauthier and J.-Ch. Picard, eds. *Topographie chrétienne des cités de la Gaule, des origines au milieu du huitième siècle.* 8 vols. to date. Paris: Edition-Diffusion de Boccard, 1986–. ISBN 2-7018-0026-9 (v. 1), 2-7018-0027-7 (v. 2), 2-7018-0029-3 (v. 3), 2-7017-0030-7 (v. 4), 2-7018-0035-8 (v. 5), 2-7018-0047-1 (v. 6), 2-7018-0051-X (v. 7), 2-7018-0071-4 (v. 8). ‣ Each volume covers one ecclesiastical province. Description of topography of churches and monasteries in each *civitas.* Bibliography; references to excavations. [FLC]

20.269 Philip Grierson. *Dark Age numismatics: selected studies.* London: Variorum Reprints, 1979. ISBN 0-86078-041-4. ‣ Collection of articles by foremost medieval numismatist of this generation, including major critiques of Pirenne 20.129: "Commerce in the Dark Ages," "Carolingian Europe and the Arabs," and "The Monetary Reforms of Abd al-Malik." [FLC]

20.270 Maurice Lombard. *Les métaux dans l'ancien monde du cinquième au onzième siècle.* Paris: Mouton, 1974. ‣ Fundamental study of metallurgy and precious metals in Europe, West Asia, and Africa. Emphasizes technical contributions of Goths, Franks, Lombards, and Avars to European technology. Production of metals in Islamic world. [FLC]

20.271 Frederick S. Paxton. *Christianizing death: the creation of a ritual process in early medieval Europe.* Ithaca, N.Y.: Cornell University Press, 1990. ISBN 0-8014-2492-5. ‣ Study of rituals of death and dying from late antiquity through mid-ninth century. Sees unified understanding of death emerging in later Carolingian period that combines traditions of penance and triumph. [PJG]

20.272 Pierre Riché. *Education and culture in the barbarian West: from the sixth through the eighth century.* John J. Contreni, trans. Columbia: University of South Carolina Press, 1976. ISBN 0-87249-376-8 (pbk). ‣ Classic study of high culture and schooling in early Middle Ages. Translation of *Éducation et culture dans l'occident barbare, VIe–VIIIe siècles* (1962). [PJG/JJC]

SEE ALSO
   21.50 Bernard S. Bachrach. *Early medieval Jewish policy in western Europe.*

EUROPE, ca. 1000–ca. 1500

General Studies

20.273 Robert Bartlett. *Trial by fire and water: the medieval judicial ordeal.* 1986 ed. Oxford: Clarendon, 1988. ISBN 0-19-822735-3 (pbk). ‣ Argues ordeal spread with Christianity as form of proof in hard cases. After clerical involvement withdrawn in 1214, replaced by jury (England, Denmark) and torture but continued in witchcraft trials. Sees ordeal as part of belief system. Controversial. [FLC]

20.274 Paolo Brezzi and Egmont Lee, eds. *Sources of social history: private acts of the late Middle Ages.* Toronto: Pontifical Institute of Mediaeval Studies, 1984. (Papers in mediaeval studies, 5.) ISBN 0-88844-805-8 (pbk). ‣ Conference papers (Italian, French, English) describing notarial records of Italy, Provence, and Barcelona; their use for reconstructing social practices (dowries, testaments); also for study of piety, literacy, and linguistic practices. [FLC]

20.275 Christopher Brooke. *Europe in the central Middle Ages, 962–1154.* 2d ed. London: Longman, 1987. ISBN 0-582-00533-7 (cl), 0-582-49391-9 (pbk). ‣ One of best current textbook treatments of formative period of medieval Europe, arranged topically. Emphasis on politics; one chapter each on economy and society. [FLC]

20.276 Elizabeth A. R. Brown. "The tyranny of a construct: feudalism and historians of medieval Europe." *American historical review* 79 (1974) 1063–88. ISSN 0002-8762. ▸ Vigorously argues that concept of feudalism has outlived usefulness and should be abandoned by both professional and student historians. [FLC]

20.277 J. H. Burns. *Lordship, kingship, and empire: the idea of monarchy, 1400–1525.* Oxford: Clarendon, 1992. ISBN 0-19-820206-7. ▸ Study of ideas of lordship in France, England, Spain, Papacy, and Holy Roman Empire through writings of theologians and lawyers; in particular, Jean de Terrevermeille, Sir John Fortescue, Don Alvaro de Luna, Rodrigo Sanchez de Arévalo, Antonio de Roselli, and fifteenth-century conciliarists. [FLC]

20.278 Fredric L. Cheyette. "The invention of the state." In *Essays in medieval civilization.* Bede Karl Lackner and Kenneth R. Philp, eds., pp. 143–78. Austin: University of Texas Press, 1978. ISBN 0-292-72023-8. ▸ Reconceptualization of early history of medieval state, arguing state a cultural construct as well as political institution. Gregorian Reform critical period for rethinking political relationships. Daring alternative to institutional histories of state. [SDW]

20.279 Georges Duby. *The three orders: feudal society imagined.* Arthur Goldhammer, trans. Chicago: University of Chicago Press, 1980. ISBN 0-226-16771-2 (cl), 0-226-16772-0 (pbk). ▸ Explores interaction of ideology and social practice through analysis of mode of representing society as three interdependent orders. Fullest and most theoretically well-developed version of author's vision of French history. Translation of *Les trois ordres ou l'imaginaire du féodalisme* (1978). [SDW]

20.280 Robert Fossier. *Enfance de l'Europe, Xe–XIIe siècle: aspects économiques et sociaux.* 1982 ed. 2 vols. Paris: Presses Universitaires de France, 1989. ISBN 2-13-042346-9 (v. 1), 2-13-042536-4 (v. 2). ▸ Argues economic growth was demographically driven and shaped by reorganization of basic elements of human community: kinship groups, parishes, lordships, noble solidarities, and villages. Sees rural economic revolution preceeding commercial revolution. Kings figure little in Fossier's picture. [FLC]

20.281 Guy Fourquin. *The anatomy of popular rebellion in the Middle Ages.* Anne Chesters, trans. Amsterdam: North-Holland; distributed by Elsevier North-Holland, 1978. ISBN 0-444-85006-6. ▸ Critiques idea of class conflict, emphasizing elite leadership. Treats medieval rebellions as messianic, peasant, and urban disturbances in time of crisis, to achieve social mobility. Longer on theory than on narrative. Translation of *Les soulèvements populaires au moyen âge.* [FLC]

20.282 Jean-Philippe Genet, ed. *L'état moderne, genèse: bilans et perspectives, actes du colloque au Centre National de la Recherche Scientifique à Paris, les 19–20 septembre 1989.* Paris: Centre National de la Recherche Scientifique, 1990. ISBN 2-222-04445-6. ▸ Collection of papers summarizing five years of research and conferences on theme. Treats Spain, France, central and eastern Europe; taxation; administrators and judges; nobility; prophecy; and iconography. Bibliography of recent research. [FLC]

20.283 Thomas Head and Richard Landes, eds. *The peace of God: social violence and religious response in France around the year 1000.* Ithaca, N.Y.: Cornell University Press, 1992. ISBN 0-8014-2741-X (cl), 0-8014-8021-3 (pbk). ▸ Essays by major United States, French, and German historians on peace movement in central and southern France and Flanders. Treats peace and relics, heresy, and church reform. Different, sometimes conflicting approaches. Includes review of historiography. [SDW]

20.284 Johan Huizinga. *The waning of the Middle Ages: a study of the forms of life, thought, and art in France and the Netherlands*

in the fourteenth and fifteenth centuries. 1924 ed. F. Hopman, trans. New York: St. Martin's, 1985. ISBN 0-312-85540-0. ▸ One of century's great works of medieval history. Analyzes chivalry, love, and religious thought as types of formal language, "crystallizing into images." Influential even among those who dispute his view of late medieval culture as a decline. Translation of *Herfsttij der Middeleeuwen* (1919). [FLC]

20.285 Internationaler Kongress Krems an der Donau. *Frau und spätmittelalterlicher Alltag: Internationaler Kongress Krems an der Donau 2 bis 5 Oktober 1984.* Vienna: Österreichische Akademie der Wissenschaften, 1986. (Veröffentlichungen des Instituts für mittelalterliche Realienkunde Österreichs, 9.) ISBN 3-7001-0782-X. ▸ Conference papers on women's daily life in later Middle Ages. Discusses ecclesiastical and medical literature and iconography. Women in late medieval France, Poland, Italy, Serbia, Flanders, and Austria. [FLC]

20.286 Michel Mollat and Philippe Wolff. *The popular revolutions of the late Middle Ages.* A. L. Lytton-Sells, trans. London: Allen & Unwin, 1973. ISBN 0-04-940040-1 (cl), 0-04-940041-X (pbk). ▸ Narrative of peasant and urban revolts of later thirteenth through fifteenth centuries. Moderately Marxist in emphasis on class conflict. Translation of *Ongles Bleus, Jacques et Ciompi* (1970). [FLC]

20.287 John H. Mundy. *Europe in the High Middle Ages, 1150–1309.* 2d ed. London: Longman, 1991. ISBN 0-582-08016-9 (cl), 0-582-49395-1 (pbk). ▸ Unconventional, stimulating study defining insiders and outsiders. Discusses development of towns and commerce, gender roles, status groups, forms of government, intellectual life, popular culture, heresy, and church and state. [FLC]

20.288 Jean-Pierre Poly and Eric Bournazel. *The feudal transformation, 900–1200.* Caroline Higgitt, trans. New York: Holmes & Meier, 1991. ISBN 0-8419-1167-3 (cl), 0-8419-1168-1 (pbk). ▸ Original synthesis of political, legal, and social development, mainly in France. Discusses lordship, fidelity, nobility, serfdom, peace movements, church, kingship, political ideology, heretics, and women. Good introduction to French scholarship to 1980. Valuable bibliography. Translation of *La mutation féodale, Xe–XIIe siècle* (1980). [SDW]

20.289 Susan Reynolds. *Kingdoms and communities in Western Europe, 900–1300.* 1984 ed. Oxford: Clarendon, 1986. ISBN 0-19-821999-7 (pbk). ▸ Revisionist view of medieval politics in England, France, Germany, and Italy. Stresses horizontal ties within local, regional, and national communities, rather than hierarchical structures. Valuable effort to reconceptualize medieval politics. [SDW]

20.290 R. W. Southern. *The making of the Middle Ages.* 1953 ed. New Haven: Yale University Press, 1992. ISBN 0-300-00230-0 (pbk). ▸ One of great works of twentieth-century medieval scholarship. Explores "secret and momentous changes in thought and feeling," 972–1204. Gently engages reader in conversation with medieval men. [FLC]

20.291 Philip Ziegler. *The Black Death.* 1969 ed. Harmondsworth: Penguin, 1982. ISBN 0-14-006076-6. ▸ History of 1348 plague written for general public. Emphasis on British Isles. [FLC]

SEE ALSO

22.80 Denys Hay. *Europe in the fourteenth and fifteenth centuries.*
22.236 T. H. Aston and C.H.E. Philpin, eds. *The Brenner debate.*

Economies and the Urban World

20.292 Philip Abrams and E. A. Wrigley. *Towns in societies: essays in economic history and historical sociology.* Cambridge:

Cambridge University Press, 1978. ISBN 0-521-21826-8. ‣ Collection of essays including studies of urban patriciates, poverty, family structure, and patterns of wealth. Often-cited works by leading urban and social historians. [LCA]

20.293 M. W. Barley, ed. *European towns: their archaeology and early history.* London: Academic Press for Council for British Archaeology, 1977. ISBN 0-12-078850-0. ‣ Conference papers wed archaeology to urban history, examining physical remains in relation to social, political, and ecclesiastical history of towns in British Isles, northern Europe, and Italy. [LCA]

20.294 Jean-Louis Biget, Jean-Claude Hervé, and Yvon Thébert. *Les cadastres anciens des villes et leur traitement par l'informatique: actes de la table ronde.* Rome and Paris: École Française de Rome and Edition-Diffusion de Boccard, 1989. (Collection de l'École Française de Rome, 120.) ISBN 2-7283-0164-6. ‣ Conference papers on computer processing of data from medieval and early modern lists of urban property holdings (*catasto, compoix, cadastre*), mainly in Italy and southern France. Includes analyzing family structure and distribution of wealth as well as map-making. [FLC]

20.295 Carlo M. Cipolla. *Before the Industrial Revolution: European society and economy, 1000–1700.* 2d ed. New York: Norton, 1980. ISBN 0-393-01343-X (cl), 0-393-95115-4 (pbk). ‣ Economist's history; analyzes demand, factors of production, and productivity, demographic trends, technological development, credit, and money supply. Treats Middle Ages as part of long preindustrial economy. Translation of *Storia economica dell'Europa preindustriale* (1975). [FLC]

20.296 John Day. *The medieval market economy.* Oxford: Blackwell, 1987. ISBN 0-631-15479-5. ‣ Collected essays (many translated from French and Italian) including both technical essays on money supply and general introductory essays on merchants, bankers, and late medieval economic crises. Important monetarist view of structural problems in economy. [FLC]

20.297 Robert Fossier. *Peasant life in the medieval West.* Juliet Vale, trans. New York: Blackwell, 1988. ISBN 0-631-14363-7. ‣ General introduction to current issues in demography, fixing of village sites, marriage and family, labor, sociability, law, and lordship. Claims European coverage, but mainly French; omits recent English debates. Translation of *Paysans d'occident* (1984). [FLC]

20.298 International Commission for the History of Towns. *Guide international d'histoire urbaine.* Vol. 1: *Europe.* Philippe Wolff, ed. Paris: Klincksieck, 1977. ISBN 2-252-01837-2 (v. 1), 2-252-01836-4 (set). ‣ Very brief historical essays in French and English followed by survey of archives and types of sources and substantial bibliographies (to 1975). Covers all European countries (in 1977) from Albania to Yugoslavia with additional essays on ancient and Byzantine cities. [FLC]

20.299 William Chester Jordan. "Women and credit in the Middle Ages: problems and directions." *Journal of European economic history* 17 (1988) 33–62. ISSN 0391-5115. ‣ Pathbreaking survey enriched by ethnographic comparisons focusing on women, Christian and Jewish, as borrowers and lenders. Surveys entire subject of urban and rural pawnbroking. Critical attention to needed research. [FLC]

20.300 Robert S. Lopez. *The commercial revolution of the Middle Ages, 950–1350.* 1971 ed. Cambridge: Cambridge University Press, 1976. ISBN 0-521-21111-5 (cl), 0-521-29046-5 (pbk). ‣ Original statement of what has become commonplace. Traces how underdeveloped society developed, mostly by its own efforts. Emphasis on Mediterranean. [FLC]

20.301 Harry A. Miskimin. *The economy of early Renaissance Europe, 1300–1460.* 1969 ed. Cambridge: Cambridge University

Press, 1975. ISBN 0-521-21017-8 (cl), 0-521-29021-X (pbk). ‣ Complex interpretation in textbook format of complex period. Accepts Postan thesis of Malthusian crisis (see section introduction, 20.39, 20.388), but emphasizes rise in living standards after plague, shift in demand, growth of industry, and change in north-south balance of trade toward south. [FLC]

20.302 John T. Noonan, Jr. *The scholastic analysis of usury.* Cambridge, Mass.: Harvard University Press, 1957. ‣ Detailed analysis of theological writing on credit from Thomas Aquinas to eighteenth century. Important for understanding context of early commerce and banking. [FLC]

20.303 Henri Pirenne. *Medieval cities: their origins and the revival of trade.* 1952 ed. Frank D. Halsey, trans. Princeton: Princeton University Press, 1969. ISBN 0-691-00760-8. ‣ Classic thesis of urban revival, arguing it began with resurgence of trade and creation of new burgher class and new political order. Often criticized but still fundamental starting point. [LCA]

20.304 Josiah Cox Russell. *Medieval regions and their cities.* Bloomington: Indiana University Press, 1972. ISBN 0-253-33735-6. ‣ Thought-provoking, debatable, regional thesis framed in demographic terms providing framework for survey of thirteenth- and fourteenth-century urban regions. [JFP]

20.305 Peter Spufford. *Handbook of medieval exchange.* London: Royal Historical Society; distributed by Boydell & Brewer, 1986. (Royal Historical Society guides and handbooks, 13.) ISBN 0-86193-105-X. ‣ Compilation of rates of exchange for coins, twelfth through fifteenth century, allowing medieval prices to be reduced to common unit. Includes brief survey of medieval money changing and international banking. Essential reference book. [FLC]

20.306 Jean-Claude Maire Vigueur. *D'une ville à l'autre: structures matérielles et organisation de l'espace dans les villes européennes (XIIIe–XVIe siècle).* Rome: École Française de Rome, 1989. (Collection de l'École Française de Rome, 122.) ISBN 2-7283-0187-5. ‣ Conference papers in English, French, and Italian focusing on urban topography, distribution of people by status and occupation, property market, urbanization, houses, public and private space, and architecture. Reflects contemporary scholarly interests. [FLC]

SEE ALSO
22.30 Paul M. Hohenberg and Lynn Hollen Lees. *The making of urban Europe, 1000–1950.*
22.257 Barbara A. Hanawalt, ed. *Women and work in pre-industrial Europe.*

Lordship, Nobility, and Government

20.307 Peter F. Ainsworth. *Jean Froissart and the fabric of history: truth, myth, and fiction in the "Chroniques."* Oxford: Clarendon, 1990. ISBN 0-19-815864-5. ‣ Treats chronicle as literary text, reading Froissart as moralist, ideologue, and writer of romance. Theoretically complex analysis of narrative structure. Reading knowledge of French required. [FLC]

20.308 Marc Bloch. *Feudal society.* 2 vols. L. A. Manyon, trans. Chicago: University of Chicago, 1964. ISBN 0-226-05978-2 (v. 1, pbk), 0-226-05979-0 (v. 2, pbk). ‣ Considers feudalism as form of society passing through two ages. Much criticized and revised but still basic. Focus on lordship, serfdom, nobility, and politics. Also treats culture, material life, kinship, and law. Translation of *La société féodale* (1949). [SDW]

20.309 Philippe Contamine, ed. *La noblesse au moyen âge, XIe–XVe siècles: essais à la mémoire de Robert Boutruche.* Paris: Presses Universitaires de France, 1976. ‣ Collection of specialized articles on regional and urban nobilities and noble culture, mainly in France. [FLC]

20.310 Jean-Philippe Genet and Michel Le Mené, eds. *Genèse de l'état moderne: prélèvement et redistribution, actes du colloque de Fontevrand, 1984.* Paris: Centre National de la Recherche Scientifique, 1987. ISBN 2-222-03828-6. ▸ Conference papers on fiscal systems of European states, antiquity to seventeenth century. Ten concern later Middle Ages in Castile, Sweden, Germany, Low Countries, France, and England. Relationship between lordship and taxation, warfare, and resistance. [FLC]

20.311 Bernard Guenée. *States and rulers in later Medieval Europe.* Juliet Vale, trans. Oxford: Blackwell, 1985. ISBN 0-631-13673-8 (cl), 0-631-136746-6 (pbk). ▸ Focuses on idea of nation, ideology of princely government, resources and function of state (=prince), and representative institutions, rather than on government as social process. Extensive bibliography to 1984. Excellent introduction. Translation of *L'occident aux quatorzième et quinzième siècles: l'état* (1971). [RWK/FLC]

20.312 John R. Hale, J.R.L. Highfield, and B. Smalley, eds. *Europe in the late Middle Ages.* Evanston, Ill.: Northwestern University Press, 1965. ISBN 0-8101-0112-2. ▸ Introductory essays on variety of topics, mainly political. Covers Italy, France, Spain, Germany, and Low Countries. [RWK]

20.313 Jacques Heers. *Parties and political life in the medieval West.* David Nicholas, trans. Amsterdam: North-Holland; distributed by Elsevier North-Holland, 1977. ISBN 0-7204-0539-4. ▸ Survey of recruitment, structure, and activities of political action groups, especially in medieval Italy, defined neither by economic condition, nor social status, nor ideology. Traces connections to families and clienteles. [FLC]

20.314 Maurice Keen. *Chivalry.* New Haven: Yale University Press, 1984. ISBN 0-300-03150-5. ▸ Classic study emphasizing lay origins of chivalry. Argues, against Huizinga 20.284, that it retained vigor and meaning through later Middle Ages as code of conduct for nobility. Eclectic in method. Good bibliography. [RWK/SDW]

20.315 Maurice Keen. *The laws of war in the late Middle Ages.* London: Routledge & Kegan Paul, 1965. ▸ Analysis of law of arms as developed during Hundred Years' War including code regulating practical aspects such as ransom and loot. Argues law of arms paved way for law of nations. [RWK]

20.316 Edward Peters. *Torture.* 1985 ed. New York: Blackwell, 1986. ISBN 0-631-13164-7 (cl), 0-631-13723-8 (pbk). ▸ Essential story of revival of torture in thirteenth century with end of ordeals and revival of Roman law; only one chapter on Middle Ages. Brief discussion of modes of proof. [FLC/KP]

The Crusades

20.317 Paul Alphandéry and Alphonse Dupront, eds. *La Chrétienté et l'idée de Croisade.* 2 vols. Paris: Michel, 1954–59. ▸ Influential when published but limitations of evidence have since become apparent. Stresses actions and ideas of popular elements in Crusades. [JSCRS]

20.318 Penny J. Cole. *The preaching of the Crusades to the Holy Land, 1095–1270.* Cambridge, Mass.: Mediaeval Academy of America, 1991. (Mediaeval Academy books, 98.) ISBN 0-915651-03-3. ▸ First major examination of Crusade sermons, analyzed in historical contexts. [JSCRS]

20.319 Giles Constable. *Monks, hermits, and Crusaders in medieval Europe.* London: Variorum Reprints, 1988. ISBN 0-86078-221-2. ▸ Collection includes two important essays— "Medieval Charters as a Source for the History of Crusades" and "Financing of the Crusades in the Twelfth Century"—show significance of European cartularies for history of Crusades and especially financing of expeditions. [JSCRS]

20.320 Giles Constable. "The Second Crusade as seen by contemporaries." *Traditio* 9 (1953) 213–79. ISSN 0362-1529. ▸ Discussion of contemporary perceptions of Crusade. Pluralist approach, giving equal weight to expeditions in Spain and Baltic region. [JSCRS]

20.321 H. E. John Cowdrey. "Pope Urban II's preaching of the First Crusade." *History* 55.184 (1970) 177–88. ISSN 0018-2648. ▸ First effective challenge to Erdmann's view (20.326) that Jerusalem originally a secondary, devotional goal. Argues Jerusalem central to Pope Urban's strategy from start. [JSCRS]

20.322 Étienne Delaruelle. *L'idée de croisade au moyen âge.* Jean Richard, Introduction. Turin: Bottega d'Erasmo, 1980. ▸ Theological account of origins of Crusading idea (originally published in articles 1941–54). Overshadowed by Erdmann 20.326, but now increasingly seen as important in its own right. [JSCRS]

20.323 Alain Demurger. *Vie et mort de l'ordre du Temple, 1118–1314.* Rev. ed. Paris: Seuil, 1989. ISBN 2-02-010482-2. ▸ General history of Knights Templars. Semipopular but with sensible conclusions, based on up-to-date reading. [JSCRS]

20.324 Gary Dickson. "The advent of the Pastores, 1251." *Revue belge de philologie et d'histoire* 66 (1988) 249–67. ISSN 0035-0818. ▸ Origins and course of Shepherds' crusade (1251) by leading scholar of popular Crusades. [JSCRS]

20.325 Verena Epp. *Fulcher von Chartres: Studien zur Geschichtsschreibung des ersten Kreuzzuges.* Düsseldorf: Droste, 1990. ISBN 3-7700-0819-7. ▸ Dense study of *Historia Hierosolymitana* of Fulcher of Chartres; treats Fulcher as theologian, historian, natural scientist, commentator, and Latin stylist. [JSCRS]

20.326 Carl Erdmann. *The origin of the idea of Crusade.* Marshall W. Baldwin and Walter Goffart, trans. Princeton: Princeton University Press, 1977. ISBN 0-691-05251-4. ▸ Sees Crusading ideology springing from reform movement, papal diplomacy, and spirituality. Highly influential view, which though now challenged, still has adherents. Translation of *Die Entstehung des Kreuzzugsgedankens* (1935). [JSCRS/MLC]

20.327 Alan Forey. *The military orders from the twelfth to the early fourteenth centuries.* Toronto: University of Toronto Press, 1992. ISBN 0-8020-2805-5 (cl), 0-8020-7680-7 (pbk). ▸ General history of all military orders up to suppression of Templars. Compares orders and sets church's other religious orders in context. [JSCRS]

20.328 Michael Gervers, ed. *The Second Crusade and the Cistercians.* New York: St. Martin's, 1992. ISBN 0-312-05607-9. ▸ Conference papers demonstrating new directions being taken by historians of Crusades. Subjects include St. Bernard of Clairvaux, art, music, and European preliminaries to and consequences of Crusade. [JSCRS]

20.329 John T. Gilchrist. "The Erdmann thesis and the canon law, 1083–1141." In *Crusade and settlement: papers read at the first conference of the Society for the Study of the Crusades and the Latin East and presented to R. C. Smail.* Peter W. Edbury, ed., pp. 37–45. Cardiff: University College Cardiff Press; distributed by Humanities Press, 1985. ISBN 0-906449-78-2. ▸ Examination of canon law texts, concluding—against Erdmann 20.326—that ethical justification of warfare did not quickly replace older, more ambiguous attitude among churchmen to violence. [JSCRS]

20.330 Norman Housley. *The Avignon papacy and the Crusades, 1305–1378.* Oxford: Clarendon, 1986. ISBN 0-19-821957-1. ▸ Role of Avignon papacy in Crusading movement. Considers all aspects of Crusading movement in fourteenth century, including all theaters of war. [JSCRS]

20.331 Norman Housley. *The later Crusades, 1274–1580: from Lyons to Alcazar.* Oxford: Oxford University Press, 1992. ISBN 0-19-822137-1 (cl), 0-19-822136-3 (pbk). ▸ Comprehensive history of later Crusades. Takes story to late sixteenth century. Likely to be standard work for many years. [JSCRS]

20.332 Peter Jackson. "The Crusade against the Mongols (1241)." *Journal of ecclesiastical history* 42 (1991) 1–18. ISSN 0022-0469. ▸ Crusade launched to resist Mongol invasion of Europe. Draws attention to neglected but important thirteenth-century Crusade. [JSCRS]

20.333 Benjamin Z. Kedar. *Crusade and mission: European approaches toward the Muslims.* 1984 ed. Princeton: Princeton University Press, 1988. ISBN 0-691-05424-X. ▸ Discusses Christian attitudes to Islam and relationship between missions and Crusades. More judicious than Daniel 20.1159. Demonstrates that ideas of missionary war underlay Crusades. [JSCRS]

20.334 Hans Eberhard Mayer. *The Crusades.* 2d ed. John B. Gillingham, trans. Oxford: Oxford University Press, 1988. ISBN 0-19-873098-5 (cl), 0-19-873097-7 (pbk). ▸ General history of Crusades in the East until 1291 and informative introduction to history of kingdoms of Latin East. By leading exponent of traditional, restricted conception of Crusades. [JSCRS]

20.335 James M. Powell. *Anatomy of a Crusade, 1213–1221.* Philadelphia: University of Pennsylvania Press, 1986. ISBN 0-8122-8025-3. ▸ Detailed account of Fifth Crusade. Informative on role of Pope Innocent III and on recruitment and preparations. Draws attention to effects of Frederick II's failure to join expedition. [JSCRS]

20.336 Donald E. Queller. *The Fourth Crusade: the conquest of Constantinople, 1201–1204.* Philadelphia: University of Pennsylvania Press, 1977. ISBN 0-8122-7730-9. ▸ Detailed account arguing diversion of Crusade unforeseen and unplanned. [JSCRS]

20.337 Jonathan Riley-Smith. *The Crusades: a short history.* New Haven: Yale University Press, 1987. ISBN 0-300-03905-0. ▸ General history viewing Crusades in many theaters and over very long time span. Sees end of Crusading movement in 1798. [JSCRS]

20.338 Jonathan Riley-Smith. *The First Crusade and the idea of Crusading.* Philadelphia: University of Pennsylvania Press, 1986. ISBN 0-8122-8026-1. ▸ Discusses early development of Crusading thought. Argues, in opposition to Erdmann 20.326, that Crusading idea evolved out of first Crusaders' experiences, which were then written up by theologians. [JSCRS]

20.339 Helmut Roscher. *Papst Innocenz III und die Kreuzzüge.* Göttingen: Vandenhoeck & Ruprecht, 1969. ▸ Detailed study of Crusading policies of one of most enthusiastic popes. Broad view of Crusades. [JSCRS]

20.340 Steven Runciman. *A history of the Crusades.* 1951–54 ed. 3 vols. Cambridge: Cambridge University Press, 1987. ISBN 0-521-20554-9 (set), 0-521-06161-X (v. 1), 0-521-06162-8 (v. 2), 0-521-06163-6 (v. 3). ▸ Classic history of Crusades to East to 1291 with brief treatment of later Crusades to 1464. Favors Greeks. Regarded as dated when first appeared, but had inspirational effect on later generations of historians. [JSCRS]

20.341 Sylvia Schein. *Fideles Crucis: the papacy, the West, and the recovery of the Holy Land, 1274–1314.* Oxford: Clarendon, 1991. ISBN 0-19-822165-7. ▸ Crusade strategy in late thirteenth and early fourteenth centuries. Challenges belief that loss of Acre in 1291 marked watershed in Crusade planning. [JSCRS]

20.342 Kenneth M. Setton, ed. *A history of the Crusades.* 2d ed. 6 vols. Madison: University of Wisconsin Press, 1969–89. ISBN 0-299-04831-4 (v. 1), 0-299-04841-1 (v. 2), 0-299-06670-3 (v. 3), 0-299-06820-X (v. 4), 0-299-09140-6 (v. 5), 0-299-10740-X (v. 6). ▸ Collaborative history to 1522. "Pluralist," covering most theaters of war. Has some of failings of great collaborative projects, but many useful contributions. Gives proper regard to fourteenth

century and to Latin Greece. Useful gazetteers and indexes. [JSCRS]

20.343 Elizabeth Siberry. *Criticism of Crusading, 1095–1274.* Oxford: Clarendon, 1985. ISBN 0-19-821953-9. ▸ Looking closely at thirteenth-century critics, undermines argument that contemporaries distinguished between Crusades to East and other Crusades. Demonstrates fundamental criticism rare. [JSCRS]

20.344 Christopher Tyerman. *England and the Crusades, 1095–1588.* Chicago: University of Chicago Press, 1988. ISBN 0-226-82012-2. ▸ Examines English experience of Crusading up to Spanish Armada. Adopts broader conception of Crusading here than in earlier works. [JSCRS]

SEE ALSO
   21.56 Robert Chazan. *European Jewry and the First Crusade.*
   28.87 Kenneth M. Setton. *The papacy and the Levant, 1204–1571.*

Europe and the World

20.345 C. F. Beckingham. *Between Islam and Christendom: travellers, facts, and legends in the Middle Ages and the Renaissance.* London: Variorum Reprints, 1983. ISBN 0-86078-123-2. ▸ Classic lectures on Prester John, accounts of European travelers to Arabia, Africa, and Islamic travelers and geographers. [FLC]

20.346 Valerie I. J. Flint. *The imaginative landscape of Christopher Columbus.* Princeton: Princeton University Press, 1992. ISBN 0-691-05681-1. ▸ Lively survey describes Old World Columbus carried in his head: imagined geography, cosmology, prophetic visions, sea stories (Sinbad, classical), marvels of the East, and Terrestrial Paradise. [FLC]

20.347 J.R.S. Phillips. *The medieval expansion of Europe.* Oxford: Oxford University Press, 1988. ISBN 0-19-219232-9 (cl), 0-19-289123-5 (pbk). ▸ Broad introductory survey of medieval Europe's contacts with Asia, Africa, and North America. Treats commerce, Mongol missions, and geographical knowledge. Sets fifteenth-century transformations in long tradition. [FLC]

20.348 Folker E. Reichert. *Begegnungen mit China: die Entdekkung Ostasiens im Mittelalter.* Sigmaringen, Germany: Thorbecke, 1992. ISBN 3-7995-5715-6. ▸ Detailed account of western travelers and residents in China, thirteenth century to ca. 1450. Studies perceptions and misperceptions of travelers, nature of reports, reflections in epics and romances, hagiography, and historiography. Includes list of known Westerners in China. [FLC]

SEE ALSO
   3.158 Felipe Fernández-Armesto. *Before Columbus.*
   17.47 Norman Daniel. *Islam and the West.*

NORTHWESTERN EUROPE, ca. 1000–ca. 1500

General Studies

20.349 Maurice Beresford and J.K.S. St. Joseph. *Medieval England: an aerial survey.* 2d ed. Cambridge: Cambridge University Press, 1979. ISBN 0-521-21961-2 (cl), 0-521-21861-2 (pbk). ▸ Collection of photographs taken since 1940s of fields, villages, and towns; many new photographs and better quality reproductions in second edition. Commentary and maps indicate historical information in images. [FLC]

20.350 J. L. Bolton. *The medieval English economy, 1150–1500.* London and Totowa, N.J.: Dent and Rowman & Littlefield, 1980. ISBN 0-8476-6234-9 (cl), 0-8476-6235-7 (pbk). ▸ Thematically organized discussion of settlement patterns, demand, supply, population, markets, and pre- and post-plague economies. Insists on complexity and regional variations. Clear but technical discussion of major issues; not for the novice. Substantial bibliography. [FLC]

20.351 Bruce M. S. Campbell, ed. *Before the Black Death: studies in the "crisis" of the early fourteenth century.* Manchester: Manchester University Press; distributed by St. Martin's, 1991. ISBN 0-7190-3208-3. ‣ Conference papers; a major effort to reassess economy of early fourteenth century, around which swirl fundamental debates on structural failure of medieval economy. Treats demography, agrarian economy, textile industry, royal finance, and natural catastrophes. [FLC]

20.352 Helen Clarke. *The archaeology of medieval England.* 1984 ed. Oxford: Blackwell, 1986. ISBN 0-631-15293-8 (pbk). ‣ Popular introduction to medieval archaeology, 1066–1500. Covers rural world, churches and monasteries, castles, crafts, towns, and trade. [FLC]

20.353 Georges Duby. *France in the Middle Ages, 987–1460: from Hugh Capet to Joan of Arc.* Juliet Vale, trans. Oxford: Blackwell, 1991. ISBN 0-631-17026-x. ‣ Description of slow emergence of French state out of seigneurial order. Situates genesis of state in early thirteenth century. Cursory treatment of later Middle Ages. Translation of *Le moyen âge, 987–1460* (1987). [SDW]

20.354 Georges Duby. *La société aux onzième et douzième siècles dans la région mâconnaise.* 1971 rev. ed. Paris: École des Hautes Études en Sciences Sociales, 1988. ISBN 2-7132-0371-6. ‣ Social and political history of small region laying basis for argument on emerging new social order, ca. 1000, and subsequent development. Influential model for many subsequent studies of other regions. First published 1953. [SDW]

20.355 Jean Dunbabin. *France in the making, 843–1180.* Oxford: Oxford University Press, 1985. ISBN 0-19-873030-6 (cl), 0-19-873031-4 (pbk). ‣ Survey, well-grounded in recent scholarship. Covers politics, government, lordship, nobility, and church viewed from regional rather than national perspective. Good bibliography. Best introduction in English. [SDW]

20.356 Christopher Dyer. *Standards of living in the later Middle Ages: social change in England, c. 1200–1520.* Cambridge: Cambridge University Press, 1989. ISBN 0-521-25127-3 (cl), 0-521-27215-7 (pbk). ‣ Massive assemblage of evidence on aristocratic, peasant, and urban incomes and consumption patterns. Focus on material objects and possessions rather than statistics. Also discusses weather and living standards. [FLC]

20.357 Theodore Evergates. *Feudal society in the bailliage of Troyes under the counts of Champagne, 1152–1284.* Baltimore: Johns Hopkins University Press, 1975. ISBN 0-8018-1663-7. ‣ Study of peasants and rural communities as well as lordships of counts, castellans, and knights. Includes both statistical and genealogical data. [SDW]

20.358 Jean-Michel Mehl. *Les jeux au royaume de France: du treizième au début du seizième siècle.* France: Fayard, 1990. ‣ Description of variety, social makeup, location, and professionalization of games using pardons, criminal proceedings, and literature. Analyzes attitude of authorities and psychology, sociology, and symbolic and ritual function of games. [FLC]

20.359 William Ian Miller. *Bloodtaking and peacemaking: feud, law, and society in saga Iceland.* Chicago: University of Chicago Press, 1990. ISBN 0-226-52679-8. ‣ Excellent social and anthropological analysis of legal norms and practices structuring power relations. Best introduction to medieval Icelandic society. [RMK]

20.360 Colin Platt. *The parish churches of medieval England.* London: Secker & Warburg, 1981. ISBN 0-436-37553-2 (cl), 0-436-37554-0 (pbk). ‣ Introduction to buildings, furnishings, parish clergy, popular piety, and organization of parish community. Many illustrations. [FLC]

20.361 Josiah Cox Russell. *British medieval population.* Albuquerque: University of New Mexico Press, 1948. ‣ Pioneering study setting out fundamental problems of reconstructing medieval population structure and change using Domesday Book, "extents," and poll taxes. Conclusions disputed, but study remains necessary starting point. Also available from Ann Arbor: University Microfilms International. [FLC]

20.362 Margaret Wood. *The English mediaeval house.* 1965 ed. London: Bracken, 1983. ISBN 0-946495-02-5. ‣ Detailed history of English domestic architecture, ca. 1100–ca. 1500. Based on detailed examination of standing structures. [FLC]

Rural World

20.363 Grenville Astill and Annie Grant, eds. *The countryside of medieval England.* Oxford: Blackwell, 1988. ISBN 0-631-15091-9. ‣ Survey of rural material culture, using both documents and archaeology, with special emphasis on methodological problems. Treats use of resources, settlement, fields, equipment, plants, woodland, animals, and demography. [FLC]

20.364 T. H. Aston, ed. *Landlords, peasants, and politics in medieval England.* New York: Cambridge University Press, 1987. ISBN 0-521-32403-3. ‣ Collection of articles from *Past and Present*. Includes studies of landholding, horse hauling, agrarian capitalism, serfdom, and royal taxation; many now considered classics. [FLC]

20.365 W. O. Ault. *Open-field farming in medieval England: a study of village by-laws.* New York and London: Barnes & Noble and Allen & Unwin, 1972. ISBN 0-04-942104-2 (cl), 0-04-942105-0 (pbk). ‣ Study of village regulation of open fields. Detailed record of agricultural techniques and day-to-day problems of community beyond fields. Includes translated documents. More technical discussion in "Open-Field Husbandry and the Village Community," *Transactions of the American Philosophical Society* 55 (1965). [FLC]

20.366 David Bates. *A bibliography of Domesday Book.* 1985 ed. Woodbridge, England: Boydell for Royal Historical Society, 1986. ISBN 0-85115-433-6. ‣ Includes 4,684 items, arranged under "General Studies" and then locally by shire. [FLC]

20.367 George T. Beech. *A rural society in medieval France: the Gâtine of Poitou in the eleventh and twelfth centuries.* Baltimore: Johns Hopkins University Press, 1964. ‣ Brief, well-researched study of small region treating rural economy, castellans and other nobles, and serfdom. Argues region radically transformed by rise of independent castellans and development of rural economy. Rare example of French regional study in English. [SDW]

20.368 Maurice Beresford and John G. Hurst. *Wharram Percy: deserted medieval village.* New Haven: Yale University Press, 1991. ISBN 0-300-04978-1. ‣ Presentation of major village excavation in Yorkshire. Narrative of process of discovery brings life to findings; model of the genre. For general audience. [FLC]

20.369 Maurice Beresford and John G. Hurst, eds. *Deserted medieval villages: studies.* 1971 ed. Gloucester: Sutton, 1989. ISBN 0-86299-655-4. ‣ Review of historical and archaeological research (to 1968) on depopulation and village desertion with gazetteers of excavations and known sites in England, Scotland, Wales, and Ireland. Still useful, though much work has been done since. [FLC]

20.370 Kathleen Biddick. *The other economy: pastoral husbandry on a medieval estate.* Berkeley: University of California Press, 1989. ISBN 0-520-06388-0. ‣ Study of economy of Peterborough Abbey, concentrating on nature and use of pastoral resources. Much technical economic work including calculations of production and consumption. [FLC]

20.371 John Blair, ed. *Ministers and parish churches: the local church in transition, 950–1200.* Oxford: Oxford University Committee for Archaeology, 1988. (Oxford University Committee for Archaeology, Monograph, 17.) ISBN 0-947816-17-8. ‣ Conference papers on major issues, both organizational and architectural, in study of eleventh- and twelfth-century parishes. Covers period when large minster parishes divided into local parochial system; fundamental problem in organization of countryside. [FLC]

20.372   Guy Bois. *The crisis of feudalism: economy and society in eastern Normandy c.1300–1550*. Cambridge and Paris: Cambridge University Press and Éditions de la Maison des Sciences de l'Homme, 1984. ISBN 0-521-25483-3. ▸ Revisionist Marxist history of late medieval economic crisis. Technical analysis of demography, prices, and income. Argues crisis prolonged by royal-seigneurial "appropriation of peasant income" and "destabilization of productive capacity." Translation of *Crise du féodalisme* (1976). [FLC]

20.373   Monique Bourin[-Derruau] and Robert Durand. *Vivre au village au moyen âge: les solidarités paysannes du onzième au treizième siècles*. Paris: Messidor and Temps Actuels, 1984. ISBN 2-209-05630-6. ▸ Looks at village as social system, rather than economic or production system. Treats family and household, church, festivals and charities, lordship in the village, outsiders, communal work, justice and finance, and peasant revolts. Materials almost exclusively French. [FLC]

20.374   H. C. Darby. *Domesday England*. 1977 ed. Cambridge: Cambridge University Press, 1986. ISBN 0-521-31026-1 (pbk). ▸ Summary of findings published, region by region, in five-volume *Domesday Geography* (1952–67). Elaborate numerical analysis with many maps. Basic. [FLC]

20.375   R. A. Donkin. *The Cistercians: studies in the geography of medieval England and Wales*. Toronto: Pontifical Institute of Mediaeval Studies, 1978. (Studies and texts, 38.) ISBN 0-88844-039-1. ▸ Demonstrates Cistercians often depopulated agricultural land as well as clearing and draining. Studies practice of animal husbandry, marketing of meat and wool, and use of mills. [FLC]

20.376   Barbara A. Hanawalt. *Crime and conflict in English communities, 1300–1348*. Cambridge, Mass.: Harvard University Press, 1979. ISBN 0-674-17580-8. ▸ Study of legal mechanisms for detecting and prosecuting crime; also living conditions, kinship, and community networks of criminals and victims. Applies conflict theory to analyze crime and justice as ways of gaining and maintaining power. [FLC]

20.377   Barbara A. Hanawalt. *The ties that bound: peasant families in medieval England*. 1986 ed. New York: Oxford University Press, 1989. ISBN 0-19-503649-2 (cl, 1986), 0-19-504564-5 (pbk). ▸ Statistical but literate study of material environment, kinship ties, economy, childhood, marriage, old age and death, neighborhoods and brotherhoods in and around the peasant household. [FLC]

20.378   P.D.A. Harvey. *The peasant land market in medieval England*. Oxford: Clarendon, 1984. ISBN 0-19-822661-6. ▸ Four regional studies analyzing what happens when lords of men become lords of land, and tenants become holders of specific pieces of land. Describes buying and selling, division of holdings, and widening gap between rich and poor after plague of 1348. Technical. [FLC]

20.379   Charles Higounet. *Défrichements et villeneuves du Bassin Parisien (XIe–XIVe siècles)*. Paris: Centre National de la Recherche Scientifique, 1990. ISBN 2-222-04210-0. ▸ Painstaking historical geography, result of voyage through archives and on foot, by car, and airplane across landscape of Paris region. Studies process of land clearance: who promoted it, who did the work, and who profited. [FLC]

20.380   R. H. Hilton. *Bond men made free: medieval peasant movements and the English rising of 1381*. 1973 ed. London: Routledge, 1988. ISBN 0-415-01880-3. ▸ Sees peasants as social class, and

rebellion inherent in "feudal" class structure. Analytical account of events of 1381 focusing on social composition, leadership, aims, and beliefs. Sets revolt in European context. A classic. [FLC]

20.381   R. H. Hilton. *A medieval society: the West Midlands at the end of the thirteenth century*. 1966 ed. Cambridge: Cambridge University Press, 1983. ISBN 0-521-25374-8. ▸ Description of society of peasants, towns, knights, and clergy at end of thirteenth and beginning of fourteenth century. Descriptive rather than analytical; emphasis on incomes and economic institutions. Pioneering regional history. [FLC]

20.382   George Caspar Homans. *English villagers of the thirteenth century*. 1941 ed. New York: Norton, 1975. ISBN 0-393-00765-0. ▸ Pioneering work of historical sociology, by sociologist, attempting to portray "social order as a whole," including organization of agriculture, family life, ceremonies, and rituals. A generation ahead of medieval scholarship. [FLC]

20.383   Paul R. Hyams. *King, lords, and peasants in medieval England: the common law of villeinage in the twelfth and thirteenth centuries*. Oxford: Clarendon, 1980. ISBN 0-19-821880-X. ▸ Thorough study of common law of villeinage (peasant land tenure) in thirteenth century. [FLC]

20.384   William Chester Jordan. *From servitude to freedom: manumission in the Sénonais in the thirteenth century*. Philadelphia: University of Pennsylvania Press, 1986. ISBN 0-8122-8006-7. ▸ Study of problem of servile manumission in thirteenth century through exacting analysis of case involving St.-Pierre-le-Vif in Sens. Seeks emotional meaning of freedom beyond economic motives and possibilities. [FLC]

20.385   Edmund King. *Peterborough Abbey, 1086–1310: a study in the land market*. Cambridge: Cambridge University Press, 1973. ISBN 0-521-20133-0. ▸ Economic study of agricultural activity, especially twelfth to thirteenth centuries. Discusses labor services, tenants, manors, pastoral economy, forest, and marketing for both clerical and lay landholdings. [KP]

20.386   Reginald Lennard. *Rural England, 1086–1135: a study of social and agrarian conditions*. 1959 ed. Oxford: Clarendon, 1966. ▸ Detailed study of estate management with brief consideration of villages and their peasant inhabitants. [FLC]

20.387   L. R. Poos. *A rural society after the Black Death: Essex, 1350–1525*. Cambridge: Cambridge University Press, 1991. ISBN 0-521-38260-2. ▸ Important example of new social history. Focuses on demography and marriage patterns, also industry, houses, servants, rebellion, and religious nonconformity. Denies fifteenth-century break in continuity. Emphasizes population mobility in search of opportunity. [FLC]

20.388   Michael Moissey Postan. *Essays on medieval agriculture and general problems of the medieval economy*. Cambridge: Cambridge University Press, 1973. ISBN 0-521-08744-9. ▸ Collection of seminal essays by master of English economic history. Detailed research used to support theory of medieval population crisis. [FLC]

20.389   J. A. Raftis. *The estates of Ramsey Abbey: a study in economic growth and organization*. Toronto: Pontifical Institute of Mediaeval Studies, 1957. (Studies and texts, 3.) ▸ Traces monastic economy, twelfth to fifteenth century. Administrative organization, land management, production of livestock and grain, and wages and prices. [KP]

20.390   J. A. Raftis. *Tenure and mobility: studies in the social history of the mediaeval English village*. Toronto: Pontifical Institute of Mediaeval Studies, 1981. (Studies and texts, 8.) ISBN 0-88844-008-1 (pbk). ▸ Pioneering study by founder of Toronto school of English village history. Examines forms of landholding, leasing and selling, village government, and out- and in-migration. Emphasizes integration of village community. [FLC]

20.391 Zvi Razi. *Life, marriage, and death in a medieval parish: economy, society, and demography in Halesowen, 1270–1400.* Cambridge: Cambridge University Press, 1980. ISBN 0-521-23252-X. ‣ Tests Malthusian theory of dating and causes of late medieval demographic change. Argues population controlled by sharp differential in fertility and mortality because of differences in wealth. Finds widening gap post-1348. [FLC]

20.392 Trevor Rowley, ed. *The origins of open-field agriculture.* London and Totowa, N.J.: Croom Helm and Barnes & Noble, 1981. ISBN 0-389-20102-2. ‣ Collection of articles debating origins of open fields based on archaeology, charters, and interpretation of late medieval documents and maps. Demonstrates existence of open fields in late Saxon period. [FLC]

20.393 Eleanor Searle. *Lordship and community: Battle Abbey and its banlieu, 1066–1538.* Toronto: Pontifical Institute of Mediaeval Studies, 1974. (Studies and texts, 26.) ISBN 0-88844-018-9. ‣ History of abbey founded by William I on site of Battle of Hastings, its lordships, lands, revenues, customs, and tenures. [KP]

20.394 Richard M. Smith, ed. *Land, kinship, and life-cycle.* Cambridge: Cambridge University Press, 1984. ISBN 0-521-26611-4. ‣ Collection of local studies of demography, inheritance patterns, land market, and changes in land-family bonds. Half of articles on Middle Ages, half on early modern period. Major introductory survey of problems. Several fundamental essays on attachment to and inheritance of land, on kinship, and on poverty as phase of life cycle. [FLC/DMH]

20.395 J. Z. Titow. *Winchester yields: a study in Medieval agricultural productivity.* Cambridge: Cambridge University Press, 1972. ISBN 0-521-08349-4. ‣ Masterly technical interpretation of account books of estates of Winchester to establish productivity of land in terms of return on seed sown. Shows declining yields at end of thirteenth century. [FLC]

Urban World, Commerce, and Industry

20.396 J. N. Bartlett. "The expansion and decline of York in the later Middle Ages." *Economic history review,* Second series, 12 (1959) 17–33. ISSN 0013-0117. ‣ Describes expansion of economy through fourteenth century, then decline as clothmaking migrated to countryside. Early quantitative study of urban decline; remains required reading. [LCA]

20.397 Maurice Beresford. *New towns of the Middle Ages: town plantation in England, Wales, and Gascony.* 1967 ed. Gloucester: Sutton, 1988. ISBN 0-86299-430-6. ‣ Description of towns' plantation: economic and military purposes, communication networks, and relations with older towns. Includes maps, plans, and gazetteer of sites. General survey. [LCA]

20.398 Jacques Boussard, Raymond Cazelles, and Jean Favier. *Nouvelle histoire de Paris: de la fin du siège de 885–886 à la mort de Phillippe Auguste. Nouvelle histoire de Paris: de la fin du regne de Phillippe Auguste à la mort de Charles V, 1223–1380. Nouvelle histoire de Paris: Paris au quinzième siècle, 1380–1500.* Paris: Association pour la Publication d'une Histoire de Paris et Diffusion Hachette, 1972–. ISBN 2-85962-000-1 (v. 1), 2-01-001847-8 (v. 3). ‣ Political, economic, social, and cultural role of city and environs from advent of Capetian dynasty to end of Middle Ages. Scholarly popular history. [LCA]

20.399 Elizabeth Chapin. *Les villes de foires de Champagne: des origines au début du quatorzième siècle.* 1937 ed. Geneva: Slatkine Reprints, 1976. ‣ Classic work on urban trade fairs of northeastern France. Discusses individual towns, cloth industry, mercantile activities, and financial operations. Extensive maps and tables. [LCA]

20.400 Bernard Chevalier. *Les bonnes villes de France du quatorzième au seizième siècle.* Paris: Aubier-Montaigne, 1982. ISBN 2-7007-0291-3. ‣ Survey of French urban life in later Middle Ages. Topics include plague, war, depopulation, expansion of royal control, economic and industrial development, enforcement of law, and cultural and religious change. [LCA]

20.401 Raymond Adrien De Roover. *Money, banking, and credit in mediaeval Bruges: Italian merchant-bankers, Lombards, and money-changers, a study in the origins of banking.* Cambridge, Mass.: Mediaeval Academy of America, 1948. ‣ Description of emergence of professional Italian money dealers in Flanders, 1300 onward, with decline of fairs of Champagne. Treats development of bills of exchange, public finance, pawnbroking and usury, trade in bullion, and deposit banking. Remains fundamental. [FLC]

20.402 Virginia Wylie Egbert. *On the bridges of mediaeval Paris: a record of early fourteenth-century life.* Princeton: Princeton University Press, 1974. ISBN 0-691-03906-2. ‣ Thirty illuminations from "Life of Saint Denis" manuscript revealing society and economy as it flourished on Seine and on Paris bridges in fourteenth century. Unique source for everyday life. [LCA]

20.403 Elizabeth Ewan. *Townlife in fourteenth-century Scotland.* Edinburgh: Edinburgh University Press, 1990. ISBN 0-7486-0128-7 (cased), 0-7486-0151-1 (pbk). ‣ Description of urban behavior, sense of community, and relations with other communities and power centers. Briefer examinations of government and economy. Benefits from recent work in archaeology. [LCA]

20.404 William Fitzstephen. *Norman London.* 1934 ed. F. M. Stenton, ed. and trans. New York: Italica Press, 1990. ISBN 0-934977-19-4. ‣ Twelfth-century description of topography and social activities with useful map and glossary. Editor's introductory essay discusses royal relations with city and development of governmental institutions. [LCA]

20.405 E. B. Fryde. *William de la Pole: merchant and king's banker (d. 1366).* Ronceverte, W.V.: Hambledon, 1988. ISBN 0-907628-35-4. ‣ Biography of merchant and war financier whose son became lord chancellor and earl of Suffolk. [RWK]

20.406 R. A. Griffiths, ed. *Boroughs of mediaeval Wales.* Cardiff: University of Wales Press, 1978. ISBN 0-7083-0681-0. ‣ Study of eleven selected towns with special emphasis on relations with English overlords. Political and legal focus supported by archival material and topographical data. [LCA]

20.407 R. H. Hilton. *English and French towns in feudal society: a comparative study.* Cambridge: Cambridge University Press, 1992. ISBN 0-521-41352-4. ‣ Comparative study along Marxist lines of class differences in medieval towns and sociopolitical influence of feudal ruling class within them. Simplistic arguments of social relations; useful bibliography. [LCA]

20.408 Urban Tigner Holmes, Jr. *Daily living in the twelfth century based on the observations of Alexander Neckham in London and Paris.* 1952 ed. Westport, Conn.: Greenwood, 1980. ISBN 0-313-22796-9. ‣ Social history based particularly on Neckham's *De nominibus utensilium.* Wealth of descriptions of London and Paris, university curricula, urban mercantile activities, and daily life. [LCA]

20.409 Richard Holt and Gervase Rosser, eds. *The English medieval town: a reader in English urban history, 1200–1540.* London: Longman, 1990. ISBN 0-582-05129-0 (cased), 0-582-05128-2 (pbk). ‣ Collection of articles, published 1960s–80s, on leading questions of English urban history in later Middle Ages. Selections treat relations to countryside, demographic crisis, impoverishment, industry and guilds, politics, and ritual activities; represent new scholarly trends. [FLC]

20.410 Henry Kraus. *Gold was the mortar: the economics of cathe-*

dral building. London: Routledge & Kegan Paul, 1979. ISBN 0-7100-8728-4. ▸ Description of "monetary adventure" of building seven French and one English Gothic cathedrals: Paris, Amiens, Toulouse, Lyon, Strasbourg, Poitiers, Rouen, and York. Popular history at its best. [FLC]

20.411 T. H. Lloyd. *The English wool trade in the Middle Ages.* Cambridge: Cambridge University Press, 1977. ISBN 0-521-21239-1. ▸ Narrative, institutional rather than economic history of trade, twelfth to fifteenth century. Discusses Flemings, Cahorsins, Italians, and English "staple" (privileged wool-exporters), and Edward III as a wool dealer. Counts a lot of sheep. [FLC]

20.412 M. D. Lobel. *Historic towns: maps and plans of towns and cities in the British Isles, with historical commentaries, from earliest times to 1800.* 3 vols. Oxford: Lovell Johns-Cook, 1969–89. ISBN 0-902134-00-0 (v. 1), 0-85967-185-2 (v. 2), 0-19-822979-8 (v. 3). ▸ In addition to maps, contains political and social history and history of topographic development of thirteen British cities. Basic. [LCA]

20.413 G. H. Martin and Sylvia McIntyre. *A bibliography of British and Irish municipal history.* 1 vol. to date. Leicester: Leicester University Press; distributed by Humanities, 1972–. ISBN 0-7185-1093-3 (v. 1). ▸ Updates Charles Gross's *Bibliography of British Municipal History* (1897). Annotated entries for Roman, medieval, and modern periods; historiographical introduction to urban history since nineteenth century. Essential guide. [LCA]

20.414 Michel Mollat, ed. *Le rôle du sel dans l'histoire.* Paris: Presses Universitaires de France, 1968. (Publications de la Faculté des Lettres et Sciences Humaines de Paris-Sorbonne, Serie recherches, 37.) ▸ Collection of essays on salt commerce covering western France, Portugal, North Sea, and Mediterranean; mainly medieval. Includes interesting essay on salt as metaphor in Christian literature and liturgy. [FLC]

20.415 John H. Munro. *Wool, cloth, and gold: the struggle for bullion in Anglo-Burgundian trade, 1340–1478.* Brussels and Toronto: Editions de l'Université de Bruxelles and University of Toronto Press, 1972. ISBN 0-8020-1897-1. ▸ Description of destruction of Flemish wool industry and shift in commerce from Bruges to Antwerp through attempts to control flow of specie between England and Low Countries. Technical. [FLC]

20.416 A. R. Myers. *London in the age of Chaucer.* Norman: University of Oklahoma Press, 1972. ISBN 0-8061-0997-1. ▸ Vivid social history anchored in primary sources. Examines physical appearance of fourteenth-century city, governmental and administrative structures, and social classes. Annotated bibliography. [LCA]

20.417 David Nicholas. *The domestic life of a medieval city: women, children, and the family in fourteenth-century Ghent.* Lincoln: University of Nebraska Press, 1985. ISBN 0-8032-3310-8. ▸ Social history of urban family life demonstrating women's active role in urban economy. Discusses emotional feelings toward children, marital choices, and family-clans' role in peacekeeping. For general readers. [LCA]

20.418 David Nicholas. *The metamorphosis of a medieval city: Ghent in the age of the Arteveldes, 1302–1390.* Lincoln: University of Nebraska Press, 1987. ISBN 0-8032-3314-0. ▸ Factual examination of political and economic problems of Ghent during century of plague and warfare, when difficulties of its cloth industry forced city to reorient economy. [LCA]

20.419 David Nicholas. *Town and countryside: social, economic, and political tensions in fourteenth-century Flanders.* Bruges: De Tempel, 1971. (Rijksuniversiteit te Gent, Werken uitgegeven door de Faculteit van de Letteren en Wijsbegeerte, 152.) ▸ Analysis of political, demographic, economic, and legal relations between towns and countryside focusing on Bruges, Ghent, and

Ypres. Particular attention to migration and textile manufacture. Theory free. [LCA]

20.420 D. M. Palliser. *Tudor York.* Oxford: Oxford University Press, 1979. ISBN 0-19-821878-8. ▸ Study of important provincial city and northern ecclesiastical capital from 1460s, treating relations with royal government, internal affairs, local government, economy, poverty, and oligarchy. [LCA]

20.421 Charles Petit-Dutaillis. *The French communes in the Middle Ages.* Joan Vickers, trans. Amsterdam: North-Holland; distributed by Elsevier North-Holland, 1978. ISBN 0-7204-0550-5. ▸ Classic study defining communes as sworn urban associations. Based on founding charters. Examines role in royal politics. For contrary views, see Vermeesch 20.431 and Stephenson 20.425. Partial translation of *Les communes françaises* (1947). [LCA]

20.422 Charles Phythian-Adams. *Desolation of a city: Coventry and the urban crisis of the late Middle Ages.* Cambridge: Cambridge University Press, 1979. ISBN 0-521-22604-X. ▸ Description of economic troubles of important provincial town. Although basic assumption of decline not always proven by sources, work remains essential to debate over late medieval economic crisis. [LCA/DMH]

20.423 Susan Reynolds. *An introduction to the history of English medieval towns.* 1977 ed. Oxford: Clarendon, 1982. ISBN 0-19-822697-7 (pbk). ▸ Essential guide for beginners with meticulous attention to definition of terms and concepts. Discusses limitations and potentials of sources and opportunities for further study. Extensive bibliography. [LCA]

20.424 Michael Spearman, Michael Lynch, and Geoffrey Stell, eds. *The Scottish medieval town.* Edinburgh: Donald, 1988. ISBN 0-85976-170-3. ▸ Conference papers placing Scottish towns in ecclesiastical, economic, legal, and social contexts. Extensive bibliography; maps, plates, and plans culled from primary sources. [LCA]

20.425 Carl Stephenson. *Borough and town: a study of urban origins in England.* Cambridge, Mass.: Mediaeval Academy of America, 1933. (Monographs of the Mediaeval Academy of America, 7.) ▸ Although outdated and often criticized, a landmark in the field. Adopts Pirenne's thesis on town origins (20.303), relating English development to that of Continent. [LCA]

20.426 Heather Swanson. *Medieval artisans: an urban class in late medieval England.* Oxford: Blackwell, 1989. ISBN 0-631-16161-9. ▸ Discussion of major crafts, place of artisans in town government, relations with merchant class, and political subordination until ca. 1400. [LCA]

20.427 James Tait. *The medieval English borough: studies on its origins and constitutional history.* 1936 ed. Manchester and New York: Manchester University Press and Barnes & Noble, 1968. ISBN 0-7190-0339-3. ▸ Classic legal-constitutional view of town origins. Against Stephenson 20.425, traces towns to early Anglo-Saxon period, focusing on burgage tenure and royal grants. Magisterial argument in graceful prose. [LCA]

20.428 John A. F. Thomson, ed. *Towns and townspeople in the fifteenth century.* Gloucester: Sutton, 1988. ISBN 0-86299-469-1. ▸ Conference papers exploring recent topics in urban history. Treats oligarchies, role of women, place of church, and urban decay in later Middle Ages. Represents current scholarly interests. [LCA]

20.429 Sylvia L. Thrupp. *The merchant class of medieval London, 1300–1500.* 1948 ed. Ann Arbor: University of Michigan Press, 1989. ISBN 0-472-09072-0 (cl), 0-472-06072-4 (pbk). ▸ Focuses on economic and social positions of merchants, involvement in municipal government, and standards of living. Documents generalizations of economic historians. Criticized for absence of interpretation. [LCA]

20.430 Hilary L. Turner. *Town defences in England and Wales: an architectural and documentary study, A.D. 900–1500.* Hamden, Conn.: Archon, 1971. ISBN 0-208-91167-6. ▸ Gazetteer of remains of urban ramparts, complemented by examination of political and economic context of urban defenses. Valuable maps, plans, and plates. [LCA]

20.431 Albert Vermeesch. *Essai sur les origines et la signification de la commune dans le nord de la France (onzième et douzième siècles).* Heule, France: UGA, 1966. (Studies presented to the International Commission for the History of Representative and Parliamentary Institutions, 30.) ▸ Argues communes originally organizations of Peace of God (see Head and Landes, eds. 20.283), gradually differentiated from diocesan peace associations (contra Petit-Dutaillis 20.421). [FLC]

20.432 Gwyn A. Williams. *Medieval London from commune to capital.* 1963 ed. London: University of London, Athlone Press, 1970. ▸ Focuses on administrative patriciate, patterns of mercantile interests, and constitutional developments in thirteenth and fourteenth centuries as monarchy changed from feudal regime to impersonal bureaucracy. Factual. [LCA]

20.433 Charles R. Young. *The English borough and royal administration, 1130–1307.* Durham, N.C.: Duke University Press, 1961. ▸ Integrates towns into larger political world by describing administrative responsibilities towns undertook at behest of royal government and political and administrative relationship that followed. Informative. [LCA]

SEE ALSO
27.115 Herman van der Wee. *The growth of the Antwerp market and the European economy (XIV–XVI centuries).*

Lordship, Nobility, and Other Elites

20.434 Michael Altschul. *A baronial family in medieval England: the Clares, 1217–1314.* 1965 ed. New York: AMS Press, 1986. ISBN 0-404-61349-7. ▸ Multifaceted study of wealthy, influential thirteenth-century baronial family whose political and economic interests extended over western England, Wales, and Ireland. Focuses primarily on landed wealth. [RWK]

20.435 J.M.W. Bean. *From lord to patron: lordship in late medieval England.* Philadelphia: University of Pennsylvania Press, 1989. ISBN 0-8122-8196-9. ▸ Closely argued analysis of creation of noble retinues through use of contracts of indenture. Attacks idea that practice constituted "bastard feudalism." [RWK]

20.436 H. S. Bennett. *The Pastons and their England: studies in an age of transition.* 1932 ed. Cambridge: Cambridge University Press, 1990. ISBN 0-521-39826-6. ▸ Anecdotal social history based on letters of fifteenth-century gentry family. Topically arranged under headings such as love and marriage, houses and furniture, wayfaring, etc. [RWK]

20.437 Constance Brittain Bouchard. *Sword, miter, and cloister: nobility and the church in Burgundy, 980–1198.* Ithaca, N.Y.: Cornell University Press, 1987. ISBN 0-8014-1974-3. ▸ Analysis of relations between secular nobles and religious communities in Burgundy. Treats social origins of religious leaders, role of nobles in monastic reform, and noble patronage of monasteries. Reflects recent scholarly questions. [SDW/KP]

20.438 D'Arcy Jonathan Dacre Boulton. *The knights of the crown: the monarchical orders of knighthood in later medieval Europe, 1325–1520.* New York: St. Martin's, 1987. ISBN 0-312-45842-8. ▸ Detailed account of knightly orders founded by monarchs from England and Castile to Hungary. Connects them to elaboration of courtly display and invention of institutions to promote loyalty among fighting elite. [FLC]

20.439 R. Allen Brown. *Castles from the air.* Cambridge: Cambridge University Press, 1989. ISBN 0-521-32932-9. ▸ Aerial photographs of castles, mainly British, with commentary on history of structures. [FLC]

20.440 Marie-Thérèse Caron. *La noblesse dans le duché de Bourgogne, 1315–1477.* Lille, France: Presses Universitaires de Lille, 1987. ISBN 2-85939-296-3. ▸ Massive study of noble hierarchy, estates, lordship, family structure and family life, religious sentiment, and social mobility. Includes portrait of Pierre de Beffremont, count of Charny. [FLC]

20.441 Christine Carpenter. *Locality and polity: a study of Warwickshire landed society, 1401–1499.* Cambridge: Cambridge University Press, 1992. ISBN 0-521-37016-7. ▸ Most elaborate of all studies of medieval gentry inspired by McFarlane 20.461. Treats social mobility, regional identity, estates, family, lineage, ambitions, and networks, but also political beliefs. Ultimate objective is definition of "body politic." [FLC]

20.442 Philippe Contamine, ed. *L'état et les aristocraties (France, Angleterre, Ecosse), XIIe–XVIIe siècle: actes de la table ronde organiseé par le Centre National de la Recherche Scientifique, Maison Française d'Oxford, 26 et 27 septembre 1986.* Paris: Presses de l'École Normale Supérieur, 1989. ISBN 2-7288-0140-1. ▸ Conference papers, nine on fourteenth and fifteenth centuries. Brief synthetic views of nobility in Burgundy, Brittany, England, and Scotland. Studies of idea of nobility in literature. [FLC]

20.443 David Crouch. *The Beaumont twins: the roots and branches of power in the twelfth century.* Cambridge: Cambridge University Press, 1986. ISBN 0-521-30215-3. ▸ Study of nature of baronial power in England and Normandy through lives of twin brothers, Waleran, count of Meulan, and Robert, earl of Leicester, analyzing exploitation of estates. Provides model for future studies. [SDW]

20.444 David Crouch. *William Marshal: court, career, and chivalry in the Angevin empire, 1147–1219.* London: Longman, 1990. ISBN 0-582-03787-5 (cl), 0-582-03786-7 (pbk). ▸ Narrative biography of William the Courtier from childhood, through career as household knight, to regent of kingdom. Discusses relations with associates, participation in war and tournaments, and religious patronage. Compare Duby 20.448. [SDW]

20.445 Georges Duby. *The chivalrous society.* 1977 ed. Cynthia Postan, trans. Berkeley: University of California Press, 1980. ISBN 0-520-04271-9. ▸ Fifteen articles by dean of French medievalists, many from *Hommes et structures du moyen âge* (1973). Topics include nobility, kinship, knighthood, Peace of God, and judicial institutions. Good introduction to Duby's work. [SDW]

20.446 Georges Duby. *The knight, the lady, and the priest: the making of modern marriage in medieval France.* Barbara Bray, trans. New York: Pantheon, 1983. ISBN 0-394-52445-4. ▸ Complex argument placing medieval secular and religious views of upper-class marriage into broader theory of social, political, and cultural change in eleventh- and twelfth-century northern France. Translation of *Le chevalier, la femme et le prêtre* (1981). [SDW]

20.447 Georges Duby. *Medieval marriage: two models from twelfth-century France.* 1978 ed. Elborg Forster, trans. Baltimore: Johns Hopkins University Press, 1991. ISBN 0-8018-2049-9 (cl), 0-8018-4319-7 (pbk). ▸ Most forceful statement of author's theory on women's role in seigneurial society, where husbanding of patrimony was paramount. Formation and gradual victory of lay conception of marriage that was very different from ecclesiastical conception. [FLC]

20.448 Georges Duby. *William Marshal: the flower of chivalry.* Richard Howard, trans. New York: Pantheon, 1985. ISBN 0-394-54309-2. ▸ Uses biographical narrative of prominent Anglo-French nobleman to study knighthood and chivalry. Written for general audience. Compare Crouch 20.444. Translation of *Guillaume le Maréchal* (1984). [SDW]

20.449 Steven Fanning. *A bishop and his world before the Gregorian Reform: Hubert of Angers, 1006–1047.* Philadelphia: American Philosophical Society, 1988. (Transactions of the American Philosophical Society, 78.1.) ISBN 0-87169-781-5 (pbk). ▸ Portrait of bishop treating ecclesiastical and secular politics and noble families in eleventh-century Anjou. Provides introduction to early Angevin history. Excellent bibliography. [SDW/JJC]

20.450 Chris Given-Wilson. *The English nobility in the late Middle Ages: the fourteenth-century political community.* London: Routledge & Kegan Paul, 1987. ISBN 0-7102-0491-4. ▸ Synthesis of current scholarship examining all of privileged society, gentry to dukes. Topics include war, politics, land, and family. [RWK]

20.451 J. C. Holt. *Robin Hood.* Rev. ed. London: Thames & Hudson, 1989. ISBN 0-500-27541-6 (pbk). ▸ Locates origins of Robin Hood legend in noble and gentry households in late thirteenth century and follows its course. [RWK]

20.452 Michael Jones, ed. *Gentry and lesser nobility in late medieval Europe.* New York: St. Martin's, 1986. ISBN 0-312-32117-1. ▸ Comparative essays on elite social groups: Carpenter on England, Van Winter on Netherlands, Du Boulay on Germany, McKay on Castile, Wormald on Scotland, Contamine on France, and Dockray on gentry marriages. [RWK]

20.453 Maurice Keen. "Chaucer's knight, the English aristocracy, and the Crusade." In *English court culture in the later Middle Ages.* V. J. Scattergood and J. W. Sherborne, eds., pp. 45–61. New York: St. Martin's, 1983. ISBN 0-312-25412-1. ▸ Demonstrates that biography of knight in prologue to Chaucer's *Canterbury Tales* is record of Crusader. Highlights English experience in different fourteenth-century theaters of war. [JSCRS]

20.454 John R. Kenyon. *Medieval fortifications.* New York: St. Martin's, 1990. ISBN 0-312-04842-4. ▸ Architectural archaeology from earth and timber castles of 1066 to elaborate stone constructions of fifteenth century. Describes both defensive and residential aspects. [FLC]

20.455 David J. Cathcart King. *Castellarium Anglicanum: an index and bibliography of the castles in England, Wales, and the islands.* 2 vols. Millwood, N.Y.: Kraus International, 1983. ISBN 0-527-50110-7 (set). ▸ Massive listing of sites mentioned in texts, visible in landscape, or discovered by excavation. Bibliography. Valuable introduction presents summary history of castles in Britain. [FLC]

20.456 Geoffrey Koziol. *Begging pardon and favor: ritual and political order in early medieval France.* Ithaca, N.Y.: Cornell University Press, 1992. ISBN 0-8014-2369-4. ▸ Highly original study of political ritual and culture, looking at eleventh-century supplications in order to explore construction of political relationships among nobles and reproduction of political and religious culture. [SDW]

20.457 Agathe Lafortune-Martel. *Fête noble en Bourgogne au quinzième siècle: le banquet du Faisan (1454), aspects politiques, sociaux, et culturels.* Montreal and Paris: Bellarmin and Vrin, 1984. ISBN 2-89007-547-8. ▸ Unique study of chivalric banquet-festival illuminating its theatrical entertainments as political discourse (promoting Burgundian "state"), social display, religious propaganda, and carnival. [FLC]

20.458 Simon Lloyd. *English society and the Crusade, 1216–1307.* Oxford: Clarendon, 1988. ISBN 0-19-822949-6. ▸ Examination of English response to Crusading appeals in thirteenth century. Reveals how recruitment operated at local level. [JSCRS]

20.459 Philippa C. Maddern. *Violence and social order: East Anglia, 1422–1442.* Oxford: Clarendon, 1992. ISBN 0-19-

820235-0. ▸ Imaginative, strongly revisionist study questioning easy assumptions about nature of violence, especially equation of violence with bad government. Examines what fifteenth-century people thought of violence and its significance for quarrels, government, and piety. [FLC]

20.460 J. R. Maddicott. "The birth and setting of the ballads of Robin Hood." *English historical review* 93.367 (1978) 276–99. ISSN 0013-8266. ▸ Shows how Robin Hood stories fit fourteenth-century social and political conditions and perhaps even particular persons. [RWK]

20.461 K. B. McFarlane. *The nobility of later medieval England: the Ford lectures for 1953 and related studies.* Oxford: Clarendon, 1980. ISBN 0-19-822657-8 (pbk). ▸ Seminal for all subsequent study of later Middle Ages in England. View of social relations applicable to Continent as well. Argues importance of nobility undervalued by historians. [RWK]

20.462 Jean Mesqui. *Châteaux et enceintes de la France médiévale: de la défense à la résidence.* 2 vols. Paris: Picard, 1991–. ISBN 2-7084-0419-9 (v. 1). ▸ Architectural history of French castles, mainly after spread of stone construction in eleventh century. Volume one arranged by architectural feature rather than site. Includes index of monuments. [FLC]

20.463 Charlotte A. Newman. *The Anglo-Norman nobility in the reign of Henry I: the second generation.* Philadelphia: University of Pennsylvania Press, 1988. ISBN 0-8122-8138-1. ▸ Study of role of new nobles, those who owed status to royal patronage rather than inheritance, in Anglo-Norman politics and society. Discusses organization of families, service to king, and exploitation of royal patronage. [SDW]

20.464 J.J.N. Palmer, ed. *Froissart: historian.* Totowa, N.J.: Rowman & Littlefield, 1981. ISBN 0-85115-146-9. ▸ Collection of papers by English, French, and American scholars assessing Jean Froissart's accuracy as historian of contemporary events. Most conclude he was not a modern positivist concerned with relating "how things really happened." [FLC]

20.465 Michel Pastoureau. *Traité d'héraldique.* Paris: Picard, 1979. ISBN 2-7084-00363-3. ▸ History of adoption of coats of arms in Europe. Discusses methodology for identifying, dating, and placing arms; symbolism of colors and figures; rules of composition; and arms as cultural phenomenon. [FLC]

20.466 Simon Payling. *Political society in Lancastrian England: the greater gentry of Nottinghamshire.* New York: Oxford University Press, 1991. ISBN 0-19-820209-1. ▸ Study of county community focusing on wealthiest families. Shows disappearance of old families and concentration of wealth among those favored by baronial and royal patronage. Also discusses officeholding, crime, and conflict resolution. [FLC]

20.467 Edouard Perroy. "Social mobility among the French noblesse in the later Middle Ages." *Past and present* 21 (1962) 25–38. ISSN 0031-2746. ▸ Unique study quantifying disappearance of noble families in region of Forez and rate of replacement by newcomers. Argues no distinction between England and Continent in social mobility. [FLC]

20.468 Françoise Piponnier. *Costume et vie sociale: la cour d'Anjou, XIVe–XVe siècle.* Paris: Mouton, 1970. ▸ Pioneering social and economic history of dress. Discusses language of display, language of colors and materials, dress and social hierarchy, and service and uniforms; also economy of production, purchase, and consumption. [FLC]

20.469 Colin Richmond. *John Hopton: a fifteenth-century Suffolk gentleman.* Cambridge: Cambridge University Press, 1981. ISBN 0-521-23434-4. ▸ Amicable gentleman of minor virtues and vices, in contrast to litigious Paston family and the violent Sir John

Fastolf. Rarely documented, commonly ignored side of fifteenth-century gentry. [FLC]

20.470 Colin Richmond. *The Paston family in the fifteenth century: the first phase.* Cambridge: Cambridge University Press, 1990. ISBN 0-521-38502-4. ▸ First volume of "thick narrative" of life of gentry family, based on famous Paston letters. [RWK]

20.471 Joel T. Rosenthal. *Patriarchy and families of privilege in fifteenth-century England.* Philadelphia: University of Pennsylvania Press, 1991. ISBN 0-8122-3072-8. ▸ Series of related essays on family forms and structures, emphasizing diversity and complexity, finding them at once patriarchal and horizontal. Reflective, in-depth approach. [RWK/LAP]

20.472 Joel T. Rosenthal. *The purchase of paradise: gift giving and the aristocracy, 1307–1485.* London: Routledge & Kegan Paul, 1972. ISBN 0-7100-7262-7. ▸ Discussion of charitable giving by aristocrats treating changing styles of piety, ecclesiastical foundations, prayers and masses for the dead, and gifts to burial churches. Statistical presentation of evidence. [RWK]

20.473 Barbara H. Rosenwein. *To be the neighbor of Saint Peter: the social meaning of Cluny's property, 909–1049.* Ithaca, N.Y.: Cornell University Press, 1989. ISBN 0-8014-2206-X. ▸ Studies gifts to Cluny in order to analyze social relationships between abbey and neighbors. Reaches new understanding of meanings of land and gifts. Combines quantitative methods, social history, and anthropological history. [SDW/JJC]

20.474 Nigel Saul. *Knights and esquires: the Gloucestershire gentry in the fourteenth century.* Oxford: Clarendon, 1981. ISBN 0-19-821883-4. ▸ One of earliest, still one of the best, studies of "county communities." Topics include estates, "bastard feudalism" and military service, office holding, lawlessness, and transformation of knights and esquires into gentry as aristocracy becomes parliamentary peerage. [FLC]

20.475 E.L.G. Stones. "The Folvilles of Ashby-Folville, Leicestershire, and their associates in crime, 1326–1347." *Transactions of the Royal Historical Society,* Fifth series, 7 (1957) 117–36. ISSN 0080-4401. ▸ Classic account of activities of a medieval gang. [RWK]

20.476 Emily Zack Tabuteau. *Transfers of property in eleventh-century Norman law.* Chapel Hill: University of North Carolina Press, 1988. ISBN 0-8078-1774-0. ▸ Important revisionist study of land transfers in early Norman law. Shows relations between lords and followers not rigidly hierarchical or systematized before 1066. Critique of older views of feudalism. Complements Bates 20.578. [SDW]

20.477 D. A. Trotter. *Medieval French Literature and the Crusades, 1100–1300.* Geneva: Droz, 1988. ▸ Detailed survey. Plays down any specifically Crusading element in literature, arguing it reflects general literary trends and is poor guide to public opinion. [JSCRS]

20.478 Anthony Tuck. *Crown and nobility, 1272–1461: political conflict in late medieval England.* Totowa, N.J.: Barnes & Noble, 1985. ISBN 0-389-20612-1. ▸ Basic reign-by-reign analysis of emergence of particular English pattern of royal power, noble politics, and war. [RWK]

20.479 Malcolm Vale. *War and chivalry: warfare and aristocratic culture in England, France, and Burgundy at the end of the Middle Ages.* Athens: University of Georgia Press, 1981. ISBN 0-8203-0571-5. ▸ Discussion of practice of war and ideals of chivalry as transmitted to Renaissance Europe. [RWK]

20.480 Simon Walker. *The Lancastrian affinity, 1361–1399.* Oxford: Oxford University Press, 1990. ISBN 0-19-820174-5. ▸ Study of retainers of John of Gaunt, looking at "affinity" from viewpoint of retainers and treating careers, wealth, marriages,

and roles in local communities. Critical view of generalizations about magnate control and sources of local violence. [FLC]

20.481 Scott L. Waugh. *The lordship of England: royal wardships and marriages in English society and politics, 1217–1327.* Princeton: Princeton University Press, 1988. ISBN 0-691-05509-2. ▸ Original, meticulously researched monograph. Shows how royal exploitation of rights of feudal lordship over nobles were harmonized with strategies nobles used to promote power of own families. [SDW]

20.482 W. E. Wightman. *The Lacy family in England and Normandy, 1066–1194.* Oxford: Clarendon, 1966. ▸ Study of two branches of family, in Yorkshire and in Herefordshire. Also discusses family's lands in Normandy. Shows how twelfth-century English politics can be viewed from perspective of baronial family. [SDW]

POLITICS AND GOVERNMENT
General Studies

20.483 Christopher Allmand. *The Hundred Years' War: England and France at war, ca. 1300–ca. 1450.* Cambridge: Cambridge University Press, 1988. ISBN 0-521-26499-5 (cl), 0-521-31923-4 (pbk). ▸ Splendid, concise narrative of Hundred Years' War. Also brief thematic chapters on land and naval forces, recruitment and supply, war and administrative and political institutions, social change, and developing national identities. [RWK]

20.484 Christopher Allmand. *Lancastrian Normandy, 1415–1450: the history of a medieval occupation.* Oxford: Clarendon, 1983. ISBN 0-19-822642-X. ▸ Synthesis of scholarship, adding much new material from archives, especially from Paris Parlement and private papers of Sir John Fastolf. Particular attention to English settlement, administration, Norman estates, and social and economic conditions. [FLC]

20.485 John W. Baldwin. *Masters, princes, and merchants: the social views of Peter the Chanter and his circle.* 2 vols. Princeton: Princeton University Press, 1970. ISBN 0-691-05178-X (set). ▸ Informative discussion of late twelfth-century French political culture, based on writings of Parisian theologian (d. 1197). Topics include kingship, court life, usury, taxation, trial by ordeal, marriage, and capital punishment. [SDW/WJC]

20.486 Jacques Boussard. *Le gouvernement d'Henry II Plantagenêt.* Paris: Librairie d'Argences, 1956. ▸ Combines political narrative of reign with detailed examination of central and local political institutions in Continental and English territories of Angevin empire. Supplements studies of reign by Warren 20.541 and Gillingham 20.492. [SDW]

20.487 R. Allen Brown. *The Normans and the Norman conquest.* 2d ed. Dover, N.H.: Boydell, 1985. ISBN 0-8511-5427-1. ▸ Learned, polemical study of England and Normandy before 1066, relations with Scandinavia, Norman conquest of England, and Norman England. Emphasizes Norman political achievements and Anglo-Saxon weakness. Represents old but influential school of historiography. [SDW]

20.488 Fredric L. Cheyette. "The sovereign and the pirates, 1332." *Speculum* 45 (1970) 40–68. ISSN 0038-7134. ▸ Discussion of piracy, development of law of marque and reprisal in relation to growing ideas of sovereignty, just war, and royal monopoly of violence. [FLC]

20.489 Congrès National des Sociétés Savantes. *La "France anglaise" au moyen âge: colloque des historiens medievistes français et britanniques.* Paris: Comité des Travaux Historiques et Scientifiques, 1988. (Actes du 111e Congrès National des Sociétés Savantes, Poitiers, 1986, Section d'histoire medievale et de philologie, 1.) ISBN 2-7355-0136-1. ▸ Conference papers by French and English historians on political ideologies, nobility and service, diplomacy, warfare, administration, and finances. Excellent summary statements by Lewis, Leguai, Thompson, and Contamine. [FLC]

20.490   David C. Douglas. *The Norman achievement, 1050–1100.* Berkeley: University of California Press, 1969. ISBN 0-520-01383-2. ▸ Comprehensive account of Norman influence on Europe, treating Norman invasions of England, Southern Italy, and Holy Land. Discusses Norman political institutions in different areas. [SDW]

20.491   David C. Douglas. *The Norman fate, 1100–1154.* Berkeley: University of California Press, 1976. ISBN 0-520-03027-3. ▸ Sequel to 20.490. Treats Norman kingdoms in England and Sicily, Norman political influence on Europe, and Norman participation in Crusades. [SDW]

20.492   John B. Gillingham. *The Angevin empire.* New York: Holmes & Meier, 1984. ISBN 0-8419-1011-1 (cl), 0-8419-1012-X (pbk). ▸ Brief survey of Angevin politics and government in Britain and France from Henry II to John (1154–1216). Treats empire as distinctive, viable political formation. Best introduction to Angevin history. [SDW]

20.493   J.R.L. Highfield and Robin Jeffs, eds. *The crown and local communities in England and France in the fifteenth century.* Gloucester: Sutton, 1981. ISBN 0-904387-67-4 (cl), 0-904387-79-8 (pbk). ▸ Scholarly conference papers by British and French historians on relations among magnates, city and town governments, and royal institutions. Focuses on both theory and practice. Treats England, Brittany, Burgundy, London, and Rouen. [FLC]

20.494   Michael Jones. *Ducal Brittany, 1364–1399: relations with England and France during the reign of Duke John IV.* London: Oxford University Press, 1970. ISBN 0-19-821835-4. ▸ Thorough and detailed diplomatic and military history. [RWK]

20.495   Richard W. Kaeuper. *War, justice, and public order: England and France in the later Middle Ages.* Oxford: Clarendon, 1988. ISBN 0-19-822873-2. ▸ Comparative study emphasizing costs of war and judicial overextension as problems in state building and public order. [RWK]

20.496   John Keegan. *The face of battle.* 1976 ed. New York: Dorset, 1986. ISBN 0-88029-083-8. ▸ Fine introductory essay on practice of military history followed by studies of four battles; account of battle of Agincourt is superb. [RWK]

20.497   John Le Patourel. *Feudal empires: Norman and Plantagenet.* London: Hambledon, 1984. ISBN 0-907628-22-2. ▸ Ten articles on Norman, Anglo-Norman, and Angevin politics and government, eight on later medieval England and France. Consistently emphasizes interconnections between England and France. [SDW]

20.498   John Le Patourel. *The Norman empire.* Oxford: Clarendon, 1976. ISBN 0-19-822525-3. ▸ Study of noble families, landholding, government, finance, and politics in areas ruled by Normans (1066–1144). Considers territories a coherent unit. Valuable explanation of Norman political expansion. Major work of research and synthesis. [SDW]

20.499   James Lydon, ed. *The English in medieval Ireland: proceedings of the first joint meeting of the Royal Irish Academy and the British Academy, Dublin, 1982.* Dublin: Royal Irish Academy, 1984. ISBN 0-901714-31-3. ▸ Scholarly conference papers on politics, law, Anglo-Irish nobility, warfare, language and literature, and Ireland's relations with English kings. Focus on assimilation of Norman, Welsh, Flemish, and English settlers into Irish society. [SDW]

20.500   Jonathan Sumption. *The Hundred Years' War: trial by battle.* Philadelphia: University of Pennsylvania Press, 1991. ISBN 0-8122-3147-3. ▸ Sprawling narrative of war, based on unpublished archives in England and France as well as chronicles. Volume carries story only to 1347. When completed will supersede all previous accounts. Massive bibliography. [FLC]

20.501   Malcolm Vale. *The Angevin legacy and the Hundred Years' War, 1250–1340.* Oxford: Blackwell, 1990. ISBN 0-631-13243-0. ▸ Sets Plantagenet-Capetian dynastic conflict into context of interests of inhabitants of "non-royal France." Rejects view that war was a consequence of transformation from feudalism to nationalism; sees it as dispute over authority in Aquitaine. [FLC]

20.502   Charles T. Wood. *Joan of Arc and Richard III: sex, saints, and government in the Middle Ages.* New York: Oxford University Press, 1988. ISBN 0-19-504060-0. ▸ Uses lives of French martyr and English king to delineate crucial differences between governance of England and France by fifteenth century. [RWK]

British Isles, 1066–1307

20.503   John H. Baker. *An introduction to English legal history.* 3d ed. London: Butterworths, 1990. ISBN 0-406-53101-3. ▸ Useful manual covering procedure (origins of common law, growth of courts, forms of action, jury, pleading), substantive law (real and personal property, torts, crime), legal profession, legal literature, and lawmaking. Bibliography; translated documents. [SDW]

20.504   Frank Barlow. *William Rufus.* Berkeley: University of California Press, 1983. ISBN 0-520-04936-5. ▸ Authoritative, detailed narrative of reign analyzing royal court, government, and finance. Argues William maintained royal power in England and restored ducal rights in Normandy. [SDW]

20.505   G.W.S. Barrow. *The Anglo-Norman era in Scottish history.* Oxford: Clarendon, 1980. ISBN 0-19-822473-7. ▸ Shows how kingdom of Scots formed between 1090s and 1296, through fusion of Celtic, Anglo-Saxon, Scandinavian, and French elements. Treats settlement patterns and early Scottish feudalism. Informative if not analytically well focused. [SDW]

20.506   G.W.S. Barrow. *The kingdom of the Scots: government, church, and society from the eleventh to the fourteenth century.* New York: St. Martin's, 1973. ▸ Valuable set of specialized essays on Scottish politics, government, law, and church history. [SDW]

20.507   G.W.S. Barrow. *Kingship and unity: Scotland, 1000–1306.* 1981 ed. Edinburgh: Edinburgh University Press, 1989. ISBN 0-7486-0104-X. ▸ Brief survey. Topics include kings, kingship, feudalism, church, towns, rural economy, and foreign relations. Good introduction with notes on further reading. [SDW]

20.508   Paul Brand. *The origins of the English legal profession.* Cambridge, Mass.: Blackwell, 1992. ISBN 0-631-15401-9. ▸ History of emergence of paid legal specialists, especially in reign of Edward I. Argues development began with continuing service of royal judges, regular written records, and development of writ system, all demanding expert knowledge. [FLC]

20.509   D. A. Carpenter. *The minority of Henry III.* Berkeley: University of California Press, 1990. ISBN 0-520-07239-1. ▸ Detailed study of English politics and government, 1216–ca. 1225. Argues period saw refashioning of English state through recovery of royal rights, establishment of internal peace, and maintenance of royal control over French possessions. Compare Stacey 20.538. [SDW]

20.510   Marjorie Chibnall. *Anglo-Norman England, 1066–1166.* New York: Blackwell, 1987. ISBN 0-631-13234-1. ▸ Lucid, well-documented survey tracing development of royal government. Treats royal finance, common law, canon law, villeinage, and relations between English and Normans. [SDW]

20.511   Marjorie Chibnall. *The empress Matilda: queen consort, queen mother, and lady of the English.* 1991 ed. Oxford: Blackwell,

1992. ISBN 0-631-15737-9. ‣ Analysis of role of female ruler in feudal society through account of disputed royal succession (1135–1153), Matilda's position as lord and political patron, and efforts to promote interests of her son Henry II. [SDW]

20.512 M. T. Clanchy. *England and its rulers, 1066–1272: foreign lordship and national identity.* Totowa, N.J.: Barnes & Noble, 1983. ISBN 0-389-20423-4. ‣ Best survey of English history from Norman conquest to death of Henry III. Treats royal politics and government, nobility, law, and political culture. Emphasizes influence of Continental political and cultural movements on England. [SDW]

20.513 M. T. Clanchy. *From memory to written record: England, 1066–1307.* 2d ed. Cambridge, Mass.: Blackwell, 1992. ISBN 0-631-17823-6 (cased), 0-631-16857-5 (pbk). ‣ Study of production of written records, political uses of literacy, and development of literate mentality to illuminate medieval law and government. Literacy now important topic for students of state formation in European and non-European societies. [SDW]

20.514 Art Cosgrove, ed. *Medieval Ireland, 1169–1534.* Oxford: Clarendon, 1987. ISBN 0-19-821741-2. ‣ Best introduction; twenty-nine chapters by different contributors providing continuous narrative of Irish political history. Discusses politics, society, economy, and culture. Immense topical bibliography. [SDW]

20.515 R. R. Davies. *The age of conquest: Wales, 1063–1415.* 1987 ed. Oxford: Oxford University Press, 1991. ISBN 0-19-820198-2 (pbk). ‣ Outstanding introduction and valuable reference work. Places Wales in context of European history focusing on Welsh resistance to English rule. Also treats many other topics. Excellent bibliography. Earlier title: *Conquest, Coexistence, and Change: Wales, 1063–1415.* [SDW]

20.516 R.H.C. Davis. *King Stephen, 1135–1154.* 3d ed. London: Longman, 1990. ISBN 0-582-04000-0. ‣ Combines biographical study with analysis of politics and royal government. Discusses establishment of hereditary tenure and formation of noble class. Too brief to be definitive, but good introduction to so-called "anarchy of Stephen." [SDW]

20.517 Michael Dolley. *Anglo-Norman Ireland, ca. 1100–1318.* Dublin: Gill and Macmillan, 1972. ISBN 0-7171-0560-X. ‣ Brief narrative of twelfth- and thirteenth-century Irish history by leading scholar. Useful bibliography. [SDW]

20.518 David C. Douglas. *William the Conqueror: the Norman impact upon England.* 1964 ed. London: Methuen, 1977. ISBN 0-413-24320-6 (cl), 0-413-38380-6 (pbk). ‣ Biography of William and study of politics and government in Normandy and England. Emphasizes both distinctiveness of Norman political institutions and extent of influence on England. Major work. [SDW]

20.519 A.A.M. Duncan. *Scotland: the making of the kingdom.* New York: Barnes & Noble, 1975. ISBN 0-06-491830-0. ‣ Surveys Scottish history from prehistoric times, but focuses on gradual formation of kingdom, 1058–ca. 1300. Good introduction to Scottish politics and government; valuable bibliography. [SDW]

20.520 Robin Frame. *The political development of the British Isles, 1100–1400.* Oxford: Oxford University Press, 1990. ISBN 0-19-219202-7 (cl), 0-19-289183-9 (pbk). ‣ Integrated picture of kingship, government, nobility, political relations, church, and border societies in England, Wales, Scotland, and Ireland, 1100–1400. Emphasizes Anglo-Norman and Plantagenet expansion into Celtic areas and Celtic resistance. [SDW]

20.521 John B. Gillingham. *Richard the Lionheart.* 1989 2d ed. New York: New Amsterdam, 1991. ISBN 1-56131-024-7. ‣ Revisionist narrative of king and crusader's early life and reign, reconceptualizing history of Angevin politics: Richard effective ruler

of Angevin empire, not irresponsible absentee king of England. Good bibliography, but lacks annotation. [SDW]

20.522 Judith A. Green. *The government of England under Henry I.* Cambridge: Cambridge University Press, 1986. ISBN 0-521-32321-5. ‣ Dense, well-documented discussion of king's retinue, servants, finance, justice, and local government. Portrays reign as era of remarkable growth of English state power stimulated by war abroad and facilitated by peace at home. [SDW]

20.523 C. Warren Hollister. *Monarchy, magnates, and institutions in the Anglo-Norman world.* London: Hambledon, 1986. ISBN 0-907628-50-8. ‣ Collection of previously published essays; some broadly discuss twelfth-century government, others focus more narrowly on royal politics, government, and nobility under Henry I. Introductions discuss scholarship since each essay's first publication. [SDW]

20.524 J. C. Holt. *Magna Carta.* 2d ed. Cambridge: Cambridge University Press, 1992. ISBN 0-521-25970-3 (cl), 0-521-27778-7 (pbk). ‣ Fullest, most analytically coherent discussion of political background, drafting of document, meaning of each clause, and subsequent revisions. Treats document as something more than expression of baronial interests. [SDW]

20.525 J. C. Holt. *The northerners: a study in the reign of King John.* 1961 ed. Oxford: Clarendon, 1992. ISBN 0-19-820309-8 (pbk). ‣ Study of formation of baronial opposition to Angevin rule in England, 1167–1216. Valuable both as analysis of baronial politics and as background to issuance of Magna Carta. [SDW]

20.526 Richard W. Kaeuper. *Bankers to the crown: the Riccardi of Lucca and Edward I.* Princeton: Princeton University Press, 1973. ISBN 0-691-05204-2. ‣ Detailed study of connection between money lending and wool trade, discussing role of Riccardi as "king's merchants" and growth of loans to king secured by tax revenues, especially wool customs, mint profits, and shire revenues. [FLC]

20.527 William E. Kapelle. *The Norman conquest of the North: the region and its transformation, 1000–1135.* Chapel Hill: University of North Carolina Press, 1979. ISBN 0-8078-1371-0. ‣ Description of transformation of northern English politics and northern nobility, 1100–1135. Discusses Norman conquest of region and resistance of Northumbrians. Argues oat-bread line determined pattern of Norman settlement. Good example of regional political history. [SDW]

20.528 J. R. Lander. *Conflict and stability in fifteenth-century England.* 3d ed. London: Hutchinson, 1977. ISBN 0-09-129190-9 (cl), 0-09-129191-7 (pbk). ‣ Short, highly readable account, both narrative and topical, of broader social developments. Covers areas that Keen's textbook (20.559) does not. [RWK]

20.529 H. R. Loyn. *The Norman conquest.* 3d ed. London: Hutchinson, 1982. ISBN 0-09-149530-X (cl), 0-09-149531-8 (pbk). ‣ Brief introductory synthesis for nonspecialists of politics and government from late Anglo-Saxon to post-conquest England and Normandy. Acknowledges Norman innovations while emphasizing continuity between pre- and postconquest England. [SDW]

20.530 James Lydon. *The lordship of Ireland in the Middle Ages.* Toronto: University of Toronto Press, 1972. ISBN 0-8020-1883-1 (cl), 0-8020-0224-2 (microfiche). ‣ Essay on conflict between Anglo-Irish and Gaelic political traditions, 1169–1500, treating establishment of lordship of Ireland, thirteenth-century feudalism, Edwardian Ireland, early fourteenth-century Gaelic revival, and later medieval decline. Index and bibliography; lacks notes. [SDW]

20.531 S.F.C. Milsom. *Historical foundations of the common law.* 2d ed. Boston: Butterworth, 1981. ISBN 0-406-62502-6 (cl), 0-406-62503-4 (pbk). ‣ Basic textbook covering both medieval and modern periods. Focuses on procedure and substantive rules: property in land, personal actions, and trespass and case. Brief chapter on criminal law. [FLC]

20.532 S.F.C. Milsom. *The legal framework of English feudalism: the Maitland lectures given in 1972.* Cambridge: Cambridge University Press, 1976. ISBN 0-521-20947-1. ▸ Radical reinterpretation of origins of common law arguing changes in royal judicial procedures accidentally transformed feudal ideas about relations between lords and vassals into legal doctrines about real property. Difficult but rewarding. [SDW]

20.533 Donnchadh ó Corráin. *Ireland before the Normans.* 1972 ed. Dublin: Gill and Macmillan. ▸ Brief survey of Irish political and social history, ninth century to 1169. Focuses on Viking invasions and conflicts among Irish kings. Useful genealogies, good bibliography. [SDW]

20.534 A. J. Otway-Ruthven. *A history of medieval Ireland.* 2d ed. New York: St. Martin's, 1980. ISBN 0-312-38139-5. ▸ Detailed narrative history of Irish politics, 1169–1495. Surveys early medieval Ireland and analyzes high medieval social structure, ecclesiastical history, and political organization. Good bibliography. [SDW]

20.535 Robert C. Palmer. *The county courts of medieval England, 1150–1350.* Princeton: Princeton University Press, 1982. ISBN 0-691-05341-3. ▸ Demonstrates importance of county courts by analyzing legal procedure, personnel, and jurisdiction. Discusses early history of legal profession. Good example of recent work on medieval English law. [SDW/RWK]

20.536 Maurice Powicke. *The thirteenth century, 1216–1307.* 1962 2d ed. Oxford: Oxford University Press, 1991. ISBN 0-19-285249-3 (pbk). ▸ Older, still-useful survey of English politics and state institutions under Henry III and Edward I. Compare more recent work of Carpenter 20.509, Prestwich 20.537, and Stacey 20.538. [SDW]

20.537 Michael Prestwich. *English politics in the thirteenth century.* New York: St. Martin's, 1990. ISBN 0-312-04527-1. ▸ Brief, valuable survey of thirteenth-century government. Treats kingship, nobility, local government, church, military service, taxation, and Parliament to describe transformation of feudal kingdom into political nation. [SDW]

20.538 Robert C. Stacey. *Politics, policy, and finance under Henry III, 1216–1245.* Oxford: Clarendon, 1987. ISBN 0-19-820086-2. ▸ Reevaluation of royal politics and administration during first half Henry's reign. Argues changes in policies after 1245 provoked baronial reaction. Based on meticulous study of narrative and record sources. Compare Carpenter 20.509. [SDW]

20.539 F. M. Stenton. *The first century of English feudalism, 1066–1166.* 2d ed. Oxford: Clarendon, 1961. ▸ Reconstruction of internal organization of English baronies, 1066–1166. Treats organization, households, thanes, knights, knights' fees and service, castles, and castle guard. Influential on later views of baronage and feudalism. [SDW]

20.540 W. L. Warren. *The governance of Norman and Angevin England, 1086–1272.* Stanford, Calif.: Stanford University Press, 1987. ISBN 0-8047-1307-3. ▸ Revisionist, original argument on development of English government emphasizing influence of local political practices and ideas on royal government, rather than power of state to control local communities. [SDW]

20.541 W. L. Warren. *Henry II.* 1973 ed. Berkeley: University of California Press, 1977. ISBN 0-520-02282-3 (pbk). ▸ Detailed reappraisal combining narrative of Henry's life with close analysis of royal politics and government and relations with church. Focuses more on England than on French territories. Compare Boussard 20.486. [SDW]

20.542 W. L. Warren. *King John.* Rev. ed. Berkeley: University of California Press, 1978. ISBN 0-520-03643-3. ▸ Both biography and study of Angevin royal government. Scholarly account portrays king as inventive administrator and poor political strategist. [SDW]

British Isles, 1307–1485

20.543 G.W.S. Barrow. *Robert Bruce and the community of the realm of Scotland.* 3d ed. Edinburgh: Edinburgh University Press, 1988. ISBN 0-8522-4539-4 (cl), 0-8522-4604-8 (pbk). ▸ Thorough exploration of career of Scottish king and evolution of concept of Scottish nation. [RWK]

20.544 John G. Bellamy. *Crime and public order in England in the later Middle Ages.* London: Routledge & Kegan Paul, 1973. ISBN 0-7100-7421-2. ▸ Early attempt to survey criminal activity and system of criminal justice. Must now be supplemented by more recent research in England and comparative materials from Continent (e.g., Hanawalt 20.376, Gauvard 20.600). [RWK]

20.545 J. G. Bellamy. *The law of treason in England in the later Middle Ages.* Cambridge: Cambridge University Press, 1970. ISBN 0-521-07830-X. ▸ Interprets treason law as barometer of political attitudes of those in royal administration and in country at large. [RWK]

20.546 S. B. Chrimes. *An introduction to the administrative history of mediaeval England.* 1966 3d ed. Oxford: Blackwell, 1981. ISBN 0-631-12141-2. ▸ Traditional conception of administration as abstract, rule-based set of governmental institutions. Concise and clear. [RWK/FLC]

20.547 G. P. Cuttino. *English diplomatic administration, 1259–1339.* 2d ed. Oxford: Clarendon, 1971. ISBN 0-19-822348-X. ▸ Painstaking administrative history of diplomacy. Particular attention to legal aspects of Anglo-French relations before Hundred Years' War. [RWK]

20.548 R. G. Davies and Jeffrey H. Denton, eds. *The English Parliament in the Middle Ages.* Philadelphia: University of Pennsylvania Press, 1981. ISBN 0-8122-7802-X. ▸ Six essays by leading specialists covering parliamentary history, "prehistory" to 1509. Discusses internal organization and procedures; also Parliament as site of political conflict and social negotiation. Best introduction. [RWK/SDW]

20.549 Kenneth Fowler. *The king's lieutenant: Henry of Grosmont, first duke of Lancaster, 1310–1361.* New York: Barnes & Noble, 1969. ISBN 0-389-01003-0. ▸ Biography of leading knight, diplomat, and administrator, and account of his clients and retainers. Based on voluminous surviving Lancastrian records. [RWK]

20.550 E. B. Fryde. *Studies in medieval trade and finance.* London: Hambledon, 1983. ISBN 0-907628-10-9. ▸ Selected articles, including important "Financial Policies and Popular Resistance," "Parliament and Peasant Revolts," and numerous essays on finances of Edward III. [RWK]

20.551 E. B. Fryde and Edward Miller, eds. *Historical studies of the English Parliament.* 2 vols. Cambridge: Cambridge University Press, 1970. ISBN 0-521-07613-7 (v. 1), 0-521-07733-8 (v. 2). ▸ Twenty-three classic studies, 1893–1969, by Jolliffe, Maitland, Edwards, Cam, Wilkinson, and others giving detailed, if disjointed, narrative of parliamentary history to 1603. Represent different approaches to subject. [RWK/SDW]

20.552 Natalie Fryde. *The tyranny and fall of Edward II, 1321–1326.* Cambridge: Cambridge University Press, 1979. ISBN 0-521-22201-X. ▸ Interpretation of reign based on close reading of sources, especially unpublished manuscripts. Financial evidence particularly strong. [RWK]

20.553 Alan Harding. *The law courts of medieval England.* London and New York: Allen & Unwin and Barnes & Noble, 1973. ISBN 0-04-942106-9 (cl), 0-04-942107-7 (pbk). ▸ Technical but concise history of growth of royal jurisdiction with emphasis on social and political setting. Includes seventy pages of documents. [RWK]

20.554 G. L. Harriss. *Cardinal Beaufort.* New York: Oxford University Press, 1988. ISBN 0-19-820135-4. ▸ Biography of elder statesman and mentor of three kings, active 1403–46. Emphasizes effects of human passions and failings on events. [FLC]

20.555 G. L. Harriss. *King, Parliament, and public finance in medieval England to 1369.* Oxford: Clarendon, 1975. ISBN 0-19-8221435-4. ▸ Thorough analysis of growth of ideas of public obligation to pay taxes, as well as growth of governmental finance and administration, especially under stress of war. [RWK]

20.556 G. L. Harriss. "War and the emergence of the English Parliament, 1297–1360." *Journal of medieval history* 2 (1976) 35–57. ISSN 0304-4181. ▸ Clear account of connection between growth of Parliament's role in government and first phase of Hundred Years' War. [RWK]

20.557 Ernest F. Jacob. *The fifteenth century, 1399–1485.* 1961 ed. Oxford: Clarendon, 1978. ISBN 0-19-821714-5. ▸ Thorough summary of scholarship as of 1961 by pioneer. Political narrative with separate chapters on church, magnates, townspeople, and government institutions. Written when study of social history of period just beginning. New edition in preparation. [RWK]

20.558 Michael Jones and Malcolm G. Underwood. *The king's mother: Lady Margaret Beaufort, countess of Richmond and Derby.* Cambridge: Cambridge University Press, 1992. ISBN 0-521-34512-X. ▸ Thematic biography of mother of Henry VII. Extensive treatment of estate management, household, and university patronage. "No recluse, but a veteran of bruising political battles." [RWK]

20.559 Maurice Keen. *England in the later Middle Ages: a political history.* 1973 ed. London: Routledge, 1988. ISBN 0-415-02783-7 (pbk). ▸ Readable textbook summarizing scholarship as of 1970. Emphasis on politics and institutions rather than social history. [RWK]

20.560 J. R. Maddicott. *Law and lordship: royal justices as retainers in thirteenth- and fourteenth-century England.* Oxford: Past and Present Society, 1978. (*Past and present*, Supplement, 4.) ISSN 0031-2746. ▸ Shows how magnates' retention of royal justices produced widespread dissatisfaction with law and justice. Pioneering study. [RWK]

20.561 Gervase Mathew. *The court of Richard II.* 1968 ed. New York: Norton, 1969. ▸ Deftly written account of writers (Geoffrey Chaucer, John Gower, Adam of Usk, Thomas Hoccleve), painters, and other craftsmen and artists at royal court. Superb introduction to courtly culture. [FLC]

20.562 May McKisack. *The fourteenth century, 1307–1399.* 1959 ed. Oxford: Clarendon, 1976. ▸ Summary of scholarship as of 1959. Political narrative with chapters on Parliament, chivalry, church, rural society, towns, learning, and Lollardy. New edition in preparation. [RWK]

20.563 Ranald Nicholson. *Scotland: the later Middle Ages.* New York: Barnes & Noble, 1974. ISBN 0-06-495147-2. ▸ Large-scale synthesis of scholarship covering late thirteenth through fifteenth centuries. [RWK]

20.564 W. M. Ormrod. *The reign of Edward III: crown and political society in England, 1327–1377.* New Haven: Yale University Press, 1990. ISBN 0-300-04875-0. ▸ Detailed study presents positive evaluation of Edward III as restorer of monarchical power and prestige. [RWK]

20.565 Edward Powell. *Kingship, law, and society: criminal justice in the reign of Henry V.* Oxford: Clarendon, 1989. ISBN 0-19-820082-X. ▸ Argues later Middle Ages not chaotic or lawless. Henry V, by adroit political management and mediation, fulfilled subjects' expectations of public order despite limited crown resources. [RWK]

20.566 Michael Prestwich. *Edward I.* Berkeley: University of California Press, 1988. ISBN 0-520-06266-3. ▸ Contrasts relative success of first half of reign with difficulties of second half. Chronological narrative and chapters on household, statutes, and Parliament. Based on profound knowledge of sources. Detailed, authoritative. [RWK/SDW]

20.567 Michael Prestwich. *The three Edwards: war and state in England, 1272–1377.* New York: St. Martin's, 1980. ISBN 0-312-80251-X. ▸ Narrative of reigns interspersed with chapters on Parliament, nobility, Hundred Years' War, "Profits and Chivalry," and economy. As strong on social history as on political. Best introduction to England in fourteenth century. [RWK]

20.568 J. S. Roskell. *The commons and their speakers in English parliaments, 1376–1523.* New York: Barnes & Noble, 1965. (Studies presented to the International Commission for the History of Representative and Parliamentary Institutions, 28.) ▸ Describes emergence of effective Speaker and concurrent growth in power of House of Commons. Thorough. [RWK]

20.569 Charles D. Ross. *Edward IV.* Berkeley: University of California Press, 1974. ISBN 0-520-02781-7. ▸ Survey describing restoration of monarchy after weakness of Henry VI. Stresses financial innovation and creation of institutional base later exploited by Tudors. [RWK/DMH]

20.570 Charles D. Ross. *Richard III.* Berkeley: University of California Press, 1981. ISBN 0-520-04589-0. ▸ Places Richard in context of power politics of his age. Supplemented, though not replaced, by Horrox 23.37. More analytical than narrative. [RWK]

20.571 T. F. Tout. *Chapters in the administrative history of mediaeval England: the wardrobe, the chamber, and the small seals.* 1920–33 ed. 6 vols. Manchester and New York: Manchester University Press and Barnes & Noble, 1967. ▸ Most thorough study of institutional development and procedures of central royal administration. Dense, packed with information. Classic of English institutional history. [RWK]

20.572 Juliet Vale. *Edward III and chivalry: chivalric society and its context, 1270–1350.* Woodbridge, England: Boydell, 1982. ISBN 0-85115-170-1. ▸ After presentation of late thirteenth-century tournament narratives, discusses urban festivals, cultural patronage, tournaments at court of Edward III, and Order of the Garter. [FLC]

20.573 Scott L. Waugh. *England in the reign of Edward III.* Cambridge: Cambridge University Press, 1991. ISBN 0-521-32510-2 (cl), 0-521-31090-3 (pbk). ▸ Clearly written introduction. Sets Edward's accomplishments in context of his difficult times. [RWK]

20.574 James Willard et al. *The English government at work, 1327–1336.* 3 vols. Cambridge, Mass.: Mediaeval Academy of America, 1940–50. ▸ Collection of studies by English, Canadian, and American scholars. Volume 1 discusses king, council, Parliament, chancery, household, diplomacy, military, and forests; volume 2, fiscal administration; and volume 3, manors and shire officials. Classic institutional history. [RWK]

20.575 Bertram Percy Wolffe. *Henry VI.* 1981 ed. London: Methuen, 1983. ISBN 0-413-52240-7 (pbk). ▸ Chronological account presenting Henry as incompetent king and no saint. [RWK]

SEE ALSO
23.37 Rosemary Horrox. *Richard III.*

France, 987–1315

20.576 John W. Baldwin. *The government of Philip Augustus: foundations of French royal power in the Middle Ages.* 1986 ed. Berkeley: University of California Press, 1991. ISBN 0-520-07391-6 (pbk). ‣ Political narrative, institutional history, and study of political ideology. Studies royal justice and finance, feudal lordship, king's relations with church, and theories of kingship. Definitive study of important phase in French state formation. [SDW]

20.577 Dominique Barthélemy. *L'ordre seigneurial, XIe–XIIe siècle.* Paris: Seuil, 1990. ISBN 2-02-011554-9. ‣ Survey of regional and royal politics, church, and economy. Represents eleventh through twelfth centuries as period of seigneurial order, not feudal anarchy. Outstanding introduction to French scholarship. Extensive bibliography. [SDW]

20.578 David Bates. *Normandy before 1066.* London: Longman, 1982. ISBN 0-582-48492-8 (pbk). ‣ Well-researched study of politics, ducal government, church, economy, and society of pre-conquest Normandy. Radical, convincing reinterpretation of early Norman history, stressing resemblances to other French regions, rather than uniqueness of political institutions. [SDW]

20.579 Robert-Henri Bautier, ed. *La France de Philippe Auguste, le temps des mutations: actes du colloque international organise par le Centre National de la Recherche Scientifique, Paris, 29 septembre–4 octobre.* Paris: Centre National de la Recherche Scientifique, 1982. (Colloques internationaux du Centre National de la Recherche Scientifique, 602.) ISBN 2-222-02824-8. ‣ Fifty articles in French by leading experts on royal government and politics, political ideology, ecclesiastical politics, economic history, intellectual history, and art. Supplements Baldwin's study of reign (20.576). [SDW]

20.580 Thomas N. Bisson. *Assemblies and representation in Languedoc in the thirteenth century.* Princeton: Princeton University Press, 1964. ISBN 0-691-09201-X. ‣ Shows how kings and lords used different types of regional assemblies, 1080–1302. Views assemblies and representation from administrative, rather than political or ideological, perspective. [SDW]

20.581 Monique Bourin-Derruau. *Temps d'équilibres, temps de ruptures: treizième siècle.* Paris: Seuil, 1990. ISBN 2-02-012220-0. ‣ Nuanced survey combining intellectual, cultural, economic, and social history with political narrative. Sound introduction to recent French work. Useful bibliography of 234 books and articles. [SDW]

20.582 Eric Bournazel. *Le gouvernement capétien au douzième siècle, 1108–1180: structures sociales et mutations institutionnelles.* Paris: Presses Universitaires de France, 1975. ‣ Uses royal charters to reconstruct methods of royal government under Louis VI and Louis VII. Particular attention to composition and activities of royal councils. Continues Lemarignier's work on early Capetians (20.586). [SDW]

20.583 Olivier Guillot. *Le comte d'Anjou et son entourage au onzième siècle.* 2 vols. Paris: Picard, 1972. ‣ Detailed reconstruction of central and local government, 960–1109. Treats count's powers, officials, relations with Saint Aubin d'Angers and other monasteries, bishops of Angers, and local castellans. Significant supplement to scholarship in English. [SDW]

20.584 Elizabeth M. Hallam. *Capetian France, 987–1328.* London: Longman, 1980. ISBN 0-582-48909-1. ‣ Survey of royal and regional politics under early Capetians, revival of royal power (1108–1226), and consolidation and apogee of royal government

(1226–1328). Reference work rather than original interpretation of Capetian history. [SDW]

20.585 William Chester Jordan. *Louis IX and the challenge of the Crusade: a study in rulership.* Princeton: Princeton University Press, 1979. ISBN 0-691-05285-9. ‣ Discusses influence of Crusading on Louis IX's kingship and government. Draws attention to importance of financial arrangements and effects on Louis IX of defeat on Crusade in 1250. [JSCRS]

20.586 Jean-François Lemarignier. *Le gouvernement royal aux premiers temps capétiens (987–1108).* Paris: Picard, 1965. ‣ Influential study of early Capetian kingship using royal charters to trace decline of royal power under early Capetians and beginning of recovery at end of eleventh century. For twelfth century see Bournazel 20.582. [SDW]

20.587 Andrew W. Lewis. *Royal succession in Capetian France: studies on familial order and the state.* Cambridge, Mass.: Harvard University Press, 1981. ISBN 0-674-77985-1. ‣ Original study of medieval kingship. Compares royal to princely and baronial successions; using French and German examples, identifies similarities and differences between royal and noble models of family. [SDW]

20.588 Paul Ourliac and Jean-Louis Gazzaniga. *Histoire du droit privé français de l'an mil au code civil.* Paris: Michel, 1985. ISBN 2-226-02209-0. ‣ Conventional handbook. Topics include legal procedure, influence of Roman law, customary law, law of persons and property, marriage and family, and succession. Large bibliography. Good reference work. [SDW]

20.589 Jean Richard. *Saint Louis: Crusader king of France.* Simon Lloyd, ed. Jean Birrell, trans. Cambridge: Cambridge University Press, 1992. ISBN 0-521-38156-8. ‣ Detailed narrative celebrating Louis as ruler, peacemaker, reformer of governmental institutions, and Crusader. Informative, rather than insightful or analytically compelling. Includes select English-language bibliography. Abridged translation of *Saint Louis* (1983). [SDW]

20.590 Eleanor Searle. *Predatory kinship and the creation of Norman power, 840–1066.* Berkeley: University of California Press, 1988. ISBN 0-520-06276-0. ‣ Original interpretation of early Norman history arguing Norman political organization based on malleable form of Germanic kinship rather than feudal or Carolingian institutions. Interesting alternative to institutional history. [SDW]

20.591 Joseph Reese Strayer. *Medieval statecraft and the perspectives of history: essays by Joseph R. Strayer.* Princeton: Princeton University Press, 1971. ISBN 0-691-04602-6. ‣ Collected essays. Topics include Normandy, feudalism, Crusades, state-building, and reign of Philip IV. Author influential in American study of French institutional history. [SDW]

France, 1315–1500

20.592 Françoise Autrand. *Charles VI: la folie du roi.* Paris: Fayard, 1986. ISBN 2-213-01703-4. ‣ Colorful large-scale narrative for general reader. Major reevaluation of reign based on profound knowledge of personnel, political ideas, language of costume, ritual, and art. [FLC]

20.593 Françoise Autrand. *Naissance d'un grand corps de l'état: les gens du Parlement de Paris, 1345–1454.* Paris: Université de Paris I, Pantheon Sorbonne, 1981. (Publications de la Sorbonne, Nouvelle series, Recherche, 46.) ISBN 2-85944-032-1. ‣ Pioneering study of origins of nobility "of the robe," based on prosopographical study of members of Paris Parlement during Hundred Years' War. Shows importance of court as center of family strategies. [FLC]

20.594 Colette Beaune. *The birth of an ideology: myths and symbols of nation in late medieval France.* Fredric L. Cheyette, ed.

Susan Ross Huston, trans. Berkeley: University of California Press, 1991. ISBN 0-520-05941-7. ‣ Comprehensive study of late medieval forms of nationalism: national saints, festivals, idea of "Most Christian King," historical myths of origins, "Salic law," and symbols joining king to nascent idea of nation. Translation of *Naissance de la nation France* (1985). [FLC]

20.595 Raymond Cazelles. *La société politique et la crise de la royauté sous Philippe de Valois.* Paris: Librairie d'Argences, 1958. ‣ Detailed study of politics in royal court and high administration. Describes origins and recruitment of personnel, careers, rewards, and how they shaped political networks. Pioneering political prosopography. [RWK/FLC]

20.596 Raymond Cazelles. *Société politique, noblesse et couronne sous Jean le Bon et Charles V.* Geneva: Droz, 1982. (Mémoires et documents publiés par la Société de l'École des Chartres, 28.) ‣ Extends author's work on Philip of Valois to reigns of son and grandson. Detailed attention to taxation and finance, estates, Jacquerie, and development of political ideology—in particular, idea of crown. [RWK/FLC]

20.597 Bernard Chevalier and Philippe Contamine, eds. *La France de la fin du quinzième siècle: renouveau et apogée, économie, pouvoirs, arts, culture, et conscience nationales, colloque international du Centre National de la Recherche Scientifique, Tours, Centre d'Études Superieures de la Renaissance, 3–6 octobre 1983.* Paris: Centre National de la Recherche Scientifique, 1985. ISBN 2-222-03612-7. ‣ Conference papers primarily concerned with reign of Louis XI. Includes detailed studies of prosopography of political class and late fifteenth-century historiography. [FLC]

20.598 Esther Cohen. *The crossroads of justice: law and culture in late medieval France.* New York: Brill, 1992. ISBN 90-04-09569-1. ‣ Studies myths of law, especially criminal law, and role of rituals and folklore. Rituals of exclusion and inclusion (animal trials), of power and disgrace. Novel use of anthropological theory to plumb mysteries of trial and punishment. [FLC]

20.599 S. H. Cuttler. *The law of treason and treason trials in later medieval France.* Cambridge: Cambridge University Press, 1981. ISBN 0-521-23968-0. ‣ Traces slow development of treason as crime against public authority. Treats theory, legal formulation, political context, and specific trials. [RWK]

20.600 Claude Gauvard. *"De Grace Especial": crime, état, et société en France à la fin du moyen âge.* 2 vols. Paris: Publications de la Sorbonne, 1991. ISBN 2-85944-209-X (set). ‣ Broad methodological introduction with special attention to computer processing of data. Emphasizes justice was less to punish than to restore honor. Treats crime statistically but also in larger social matrix. [FLC]

20.601 Bernard Guenée. *Tribunaux et gens de justice dans le bailliage de Senlis à la fin du moyen âge (vers 1380–vers 1550).* Paris: Belles Lettres, 1963. (Publications de la Faculté des Lettres de l'Université de Strasbourg, 144.) ‣ Explores functioning of local courts, both royal and lordly, from village on up; how disputes came to court, cost, procedures, effectiveness, officialdom, and relations to Parisian courts. Only study of its kind for France. [FLC]

20.602 John Bell Henneman. *Royal taxation in fourteenth-century France: the captivity and ransom of John II, 1356–1370.* Philadelphia: American Philosophical Society, 1976. (Memoirs of the American Philosophical Society, 116.) ISBN 0-87169-116-7. ‣ Continuing history of French taxation (with 20.603). Shows how regular peacetime taxation emerged after crisis of 1350s. [RWK]

20.603 John Bell Henneman. *Royal taxation in fourteenth-century France: the development of war financing, 1322–1356.* Princeton: Princeton University Press, 1971. ISBN 0-691-05188-7. ‣ Detailed

chronological account of developing theory and practice of French taxation up to crisis of 1350s. Particular attention to local negotiations and experiments with representative assemblies. [RWK]

20.604 Yvonne Labande-Mailfert. *Charles VIII: le vouloir et la destinée.* Paris: Fayard, 1986. ISBN 2-213-01773-5. ‣ History in grand style for general public by leading French specialist in period. Political narrative with extensive quotations from contemporary documents. Particular attention to ideological implications of art. [FLC]

20.605 P. S. Lewis. *Later medieval France: the polity.* London and New York: Macmillan and St. Martin's, 1968. ‣ Best work in English on subject. Social history rather than political narrative. Covers sentiment and feeling as well as warfare and taxation, little on institutions other than representative assemblies. [FLC]

20.606 Nadia Margolis, comp. *Joan of Arc in history, literature, and film: a select, annotated bibliography.* New York: Garland, 1990. ISBN 0-8240-4638-2. ‣ Vast, thorough bibliography including primary sources, manuscript and printed, and histories and biographies from fifteenth century to the present. Treats special and controversial topics. Includes many items mentioning Joan only in passing. [FLC]

20.607 Joseph Reese Strayer. *The reign of Philip the Fair.* Princeton: Princeton University Press, 1980. ISBN 0-691-05302-2 (cl), 0-691-10089-6 (pbk). ‣ Analytical rather than narrative portrait of apogee of medieval French monarchy, interpreted as critical stage in emergence of secular, sovereign state. Positive interpretation of Philip's motives and actions. [RWK/SDW]

20.608 Richard Vaughan. *Valois Burgundy.* Hamden, Conn.: Archon, 1975. ISBN 0-208-01511-6. ‣ Reign-by-reign summary of author's four detailed studies of fourteenth- and fifteenth-century Burgundian dukes. Topical chapters on political relations with other powers, administration, warfare, court, and arts. [RWK]

SCANDINAVIA, CENTRAL AND EASTERN EUROPE, ca. 1000–ca. 1500

General Studies

20.609 Adam of Bremen. *History of the archbishops of Hamburg-Bremen.* Francis Joseph Tschan, ed. and trans. New York: Columbia University Press, 1959. ‣ Primary account of extension of Christianity into Scandinavia. Describes political, social, and religious milieus of Scandinavia, North Germany, and Baltic area. [PPR]

20.610 Geoffrey Barraclough. *The origins of modern Germany.* 3d ed. Oxford: Blackwell, 1988. ISBN 0-631-16106-6. ‣ Written under impact of World War II utilizing best interwar German scholarship. Long the standard English-language work on political and constitutional history of medieval empire. [JBF]

20.611 Geoffrey Barraclough, trans. *Mediaeval Germany, 911–1250: essays by German historians.* 1938 ed. 2 vols. New York: AMS Press, 1979. ISBN 0-404-14800-X. ‣ Volume 2 contains translations of articles by major German historians that formed basis for *The Origins of Modern Germany* (20.610). Introduction has comments on empire and papacy, duchies, monarchy, principalities, and Hohenstaufen state. [JBF]

20.612 Franz Brunhölzl and Max Spindler. *Handbuch der bayerischen Geschichte.* 2d ed. 4 vols. Munich: Beck, 1981–. ISBN 3-406-07322-0 (v. 1). ‣ General reference work. Volume 1 covers pre-Wittelsbach period; volume 2, Wittelsbach duchy, 1180–1800; volume 3, Franconia, Swabia, and Upper Palatinate before incorporation into Bavaria; and volume 4, modern Bavaria. Extensive bibliography. [JBF]

20.613 Colloquio Internazionale di Storia Ecclesiastica in Occasione dell'VI Centenario della Lituania Cristiana: 1387–1987. *La cristianizzazione della Lituania: atti del Colloquio Internazionale di Storia Ecclesiastica in occasione del VI centenario della Lituania Cristiana (1387–1987), Roma, 24–26 Giugno 1987.* Paulus Rabikauskas, ed. Vatican City: Libreria Editrice Vaticana, 1989. (Pontificio Comitato di Scienze Storiche: atti e documenti, 2.) ISBN 88-209-1648-7. ▸ Detailed, scholarly conference papers, some in English, on conversion of Lithuania to Christianity. [PPR]

20.614 Colloquio Internazionale di Storia Ecclesiastica in Occasione dell'VIII Centenario della Chiesa in Livonia: 1186–1986. *Gli inizi del cristianesimo in Livonia-Lettonia: atti del Colloquio Internazionale de Storia Ecclesiastica in occasione dell'VIII centenario della Chiesa in Livonia (1186–1986), Roma, 24–25 Giugno 1986.* Vatican City: Libreria Editrice Vaticana, 1989. (Pontificio Comitato di Scienze Storiche: atti e documenti, 1.) ISBN 88-209-1598-7. ▸ Conference papers in English, German, and Italian focusing on story of conversion of Estonia and Latvia to Christianity. Treats myths and pre-Christian religion, Crusading orders, and missionaries. [PPR]

20.615 F.R.H. Du Boulay. *Germany in the later Middle Ages.* New York: St. Martin's, 1983. ISBN 0-312-32625-4. ▸ Topics covered include language and forms of communication, individual kings, principalities, towns, rural communities, and church. Written as introductory text for English-language readers. Valuable bibliography. [JBF/LCA]

20.616 Odilo Engels et al. *Die Salier und das Reich.* 3 vols. Sigmaringen, Germany: Thorbecke, 1991. ISBN 3-7995-4133-0 (set). ▸ Published for exhibit on Salian dynasty. Volume 1 contains articles on nobility and imperial constitution; volume 2, on the church; and volume 3, on social and intellectual history. Synthesis of recent scholarship for general audience. [JBF]

20.617 P. Feldbauer et al. *Herrschaftsstruktur und Ständebildung: Beiträge zur Typologie der österreichischen Länder aus ihren mittelalterlichen Grundlagen.* 3 vols. to date. Vienna: Verlag für Geschichte und Politik, 1973–. ISBN 3-486-43991-X (set), 3-7028-0063-8 (v. 1). ▸ Comparative studies of late medieval social groups in territories comprising modern Austria. Volume 1 treats lords and knights; volume 2, cities; and volume 3, peasants and clergy. [JBF]

20.618 Josef Fleckenstein. *Ordnungen und formende Kräfte des Mittelalters: ausgewählte Beiträge.* 1989 ed. Göttingen: Vandenhoeck & Ruprecht, 1991. ISBN 3-525-36221-8. ▸ Collected articles by scholar of Freiburg school best known for work on imperial court chapel and on chivalry. Topics include Carolingian Europe, church, knighthood, and historiography. [JBF]

20.619 Johannes Fried. "Deutsche Geschichte im früheren und hohen Mittelalter: Bemerkungen zu einigen neuen Gesamtdarstellungen." *Historische Zeitschrift* 245.3 (1987) 625–59. ISSN 0018-2613. ▸ Discussion of problem of defining Germany and its political history in light of regional differences and problem of integrating that history into European context. Stresses Carolingian origins and questions idea that German institutional development lagged behind western Europe. [JBF]

20.620 Horst Fuhrmann. *Germany in the high Middle Ages, ca. 1050–1200.* Timothy Reuter, trans. Cambridge: Cambridge University Press, 1986. ISBN 0-521-26638-6 (cl), 0-521-31980-3 (pbk). ▸ Good introduction to period. Contrasts gradual decline of monarchy to contemporary developments elsewhere, setting these in context of political, social, economic, and cultural transformation of Central Europe. Translation of *Deutsche Geschichte im hohen Mittelalter* (1983). [JBF]

20.621 Marija Alseikaite Gimbutas. *The Balts.* New York: Praeger, 1963. ▸ Standard description of life among pre-Christian Baltic peoples; omits Estonians. Good, if dated, bibliography. [PPR]

20.622 Reiner Haussherr, ed. *Die Zeit der Staufer: Geschichte, Kunst, Kultur, Katalog der Ausstellung, Stüttgart, Altes Schloss und Kunstgebande, 26. März–5. Juni 1977.* 5 vols. Stuttgart: Wirtembergisches Landesmuseum, 1977–79. ▸ Published for exhibit on Hohenstaufen dynasty. Volume 1 is exhibition catalog; volume 2, illustrations of exhibit; volume 3, scholarly articles; volume 4, maps and genealogies; and volume 5, additional articles. Synthesis of recent scholarship for general audience. [JBF]

20.623 Alfred Haverkamp. *Medieval Germany, 1056–1273.* 2d ed. Helga Braun and Richard Mortimer, trans. Oxford: Oxford University Press, 1992. ISBN 0-19-822132-0 (cl), 0-19-822172-X (pbk). ▸ Places history of Germany from accession of Henry IV to end of interregnum into European context. Representative of recent trend to deemphasize distinctive aspects of German history. Translation of *Aufbruch und Gestaltung Deutschland, 1056–1273* (1984). [JBF]

20.624 Charles Higounet. *Les Allemands en Europe centrale et orientale au moyen âge.* Paris: Aubier, 1989. ISBN 2-7007-2223-X. ▸ General account of Germany's relations with eastern neighbors and spread and impact of German settlement in different regions. Balanced, non-nationalistic treatment. [JBF]

20.625 Hagen Keller. *Zwischen regionaler Begrenzung und universalem Horizont: Deutschland im Imperium der Salier und Staufer, 1024 bis 1250.* Berlin: Propyläen, 1986. ISBN 3-549-05812-8. ▸ Lavishly illustrated cultural, intellectual, social, religious, and political history of Germany in European context; deemphasizes politics. Best of recent general histories, but presupposes some knowledge of period. [JBF]

20.626 David Kirby. *Northern Europe in the early modern period: the Baltic world, 1492–1772.* London: Longman, 1990. ISBN 0-582-00410-1 (cl), 0-582-00411-X (pbk). ▸ Introductory chapter on Old Livonia and discussion of Hansa and Teutonic order providing brief introduction to medieval Baltic region. [PPR]

20.627 Karl J. Leyser. *Medieval Germany and its neighbours, 900–1250.* London: Hambledon, 1982. ISBN 0-907628-08-7 (cl), 0-907628-09-5 (pbk). ▸ Collection of author's articles on Ottonian and Hohenstaufen Germany, imperial relations with Byzantium and England, and aristocracy. Significant critique of Schmid and Freiburg school. [JBF]

20.628 Alphons Lhotsky. *Geschichte Österreichs: seit der Mitte des dreizehnten Jahrhunderts (1281–1358).* Vienna: In Kommission bei Böhlau, 1967. (Veröffentlichungen der Kommission für Geschichte Österreichs, 1, Geschichte Österreichs, 2.1.) ▸ Introductory history of eastern Alpine territories from establishment of Habsburgs to accession of Rudolf IV. Continuation of Lechner 20.724. [JBF]

20.629 Peter Moraw. *Von offener Verfassung zu gestalteter Verdichtung: das Reich im späten Mittelalter, 1250 bis 1490.* Berlin: Propyläen, 1985. ISBN 3-549-05813-6. ▸ Lavishly illustrated general history. Deemphasizes politics; stresses modernization, development of German identity, and intensification of contacts beyond empire. Best of new histories of later Middle Ages, but presupposes some knowledge of period. [JBF]

20.630 Otto of Freising. *The two cities: a chronicle of universal history to the year 1146 A.D.* 1928 ed. Austin P. Evans and Charles Knapp, eds. Charles Christopher Mierow, trans. New York: Octagon Books, 1966. ▸ Pessimistic account of late Salian and early Hohenstaufen periods by Cistercian bishop, grandson of Henry IV. Classic example of application of Augustinian theology to medieval historical writing. [JBF]

20.631 Gustav Ränk. *Old Estonia, the people and culture.* Betty Oinas and Felix J. Oinas, eds. and trans. Bloomington: Indiana University Press, 1976. (Uralic and Altaic series, 112.) ISBN 0-87750-190-4. ▸ Based mostly on pre–World War II research, and thus dated, but still best available work in English on pre-Christian Estonia. Translation of *Vana Eesti Rahvas ja Kultuur* (1949). [PPR]

SEE ALSO
33.20 John V. A. Fine, Jr. *The late medieval Balkans.*
33.337 Erik Fügedi. *Kings, bishops, nobles, and burghers in medieval Hungary.*
33.465 Norman Davies. *God's playground.*

Rural World

20.632 Wilhelm Abel. *Die Wüstungen des ausgehenden Mittelalters.* 3d rev. ed. Stuttgart: Fischer, 1976. ISBN 3-437-50185-2. ▸ First brought scholarly attention to late medieval deserted villages. Links desertion to fall of population and to agrarian depression. Brief summary in English in Abel 30.190. [FLC]

20.633 Karl S. Bader. *Studien zur Rechtsgeschichte des mittelalterlichen Dorfes.* Edition varies. 3 vols. Vienna: Böhlau, 1973–81. ISBN 3-412-06981-7 (v. 1), 3-205-00014-5 (v. 2), 3-205-07102-6 (v. 3). ▸ Village as legal entity and possessor of own "peace." Treats right of asylum, legal organization of community, and village law of real property. Detailed, thorough study based on South German and Swiss documentation. [FLC]

20.634 Philippe Dollinger. *L'évolution des classes rurales en Bavière depuis la fin de l'époque carolingienne jusqu'au milieu du treizième siècle.* Paris: Belles Lettres, 1949. (Publications de la Faculté des Lettres de l'Université de Strasbourg, 112.) ▸ Study of origins of manorial economy and peasantry in Bavaria where different groups long retained their distinct status. Rare example of Annales-style regional monograph of a German territory. [JBF]

20.635 Günther Franz, ed. *Deutsches Bauerntum im Mittelalter.* Darmstadt: Wissenschaftliche Buchgesellschaft, 1976. ISBN 3-534-06405-4. ▸ Collection of articles representing principal strands of German scholarship on peasantry through 1960s. Treats peasant freedom, lordship and servitude as instrument of territorial power. [FLC]

20.636 Richard C. Hoffmann. *Land, liberties, and lordship in a late medieval countryside: agrarian structures and change in the duchy of Wrocław.* Philadelphia: University of Pennsylvania Press, 1989. ISBN 0-8122-8090-3. ▸ Unique study of agrarian conditions in Eastern Europe. Shows how duchy escaped fourteenth-century crisis only to succumb to violence spawned by Hussites and reimposition of serfdom. [JBF]

20.637 Werner Rösener. *Peasants in the Middle Ages.* Alexander Stutzer, trans. Urbana: University of Illinois Press, 1992. ISBN 0-252-06289-2. ▸ Study of domestic life and material culture of Central European peasants. Treats settlement, house and farmyard, clothing, food, labor, sociability, kinship structure, status distinctions, relation to lords, legal status, peasant rebellions, and late medieval crisis. Colorful, anecdotal. [FLC]

Urban World, Commerce, and Industry

20.638 Reinhard Barth. *Argumentation und Selbstverständnis der Bürgeropposition in städtischen Auseinandersetzungen des Spätmittelalters: Lübeck 1403–1408, Braunschweig 1374–1376, Mainz 1444–1446, Köln 1396–1400.* 1974 ed. Cologne: Böhlau, 1976. ISBN 3-412-11176-7. ▸ Study of town chronicles of Lübeck, Braunschweig, Mainz, and Cologne. Analyzes conflict of viewpoints on nature and distribution of urban power and special interests as burgher authors criticized patrician rulers. [LCA]

20.639 F. L. Carsten. "Medieval democracy in the Brandenburg towns and its defeat in the fifteenth century." *Transactions of the Royal Historical Society, Fourth series* 25 (1943) 73–91. ISSN 0080-4401. ▸ Describes how plans of new towns east of Elbe River for self-government and independent jurisdiction thwarted by mar-

graves outside towns and aristocrats within. Shows influence of external politics on urban development. [LCA]

20.640 Philippe Dollinger. *The German Hansa.* D. S. Ault and S. H. Steinberg, ed. and trans. Stanford, Calif.: Stanford University Press, 1970. ISBN 0-8047-0742-1. ▸ Traces Hansa's development from merchant associations to loosely organized association of cities. May overstate cities' role. Documents and statistics in appendixes. Translation of *La Hanse* (1964). [JBF/LCA]

20.641 Heinz Dopsch and Hans Spatzenegger, eds. *Geschichte Salzburgs: Stadt und Land.* Vol. 1: *Vorgeschichte, Altertum, Mittelalter.* Salzburg: Universitätsverlag Pustet, 1981–. ISBN 3-7025-0197-5 (set), 3-7025-0121-5 (v. 1.1), 3-7025-0214-9 (v. 1.2). ▸ Multiauthored political, social, cultural, religious, and intellectual history of principality and modern province of Salzburg. Volume 1 covers ancient and medieval periods. Detailed local history at its finest. [JBF]

20.642 F.R.H. Du Boulay. "The German town chroniclers." In *The writing of history in the Middle Ages: essays presented to Richard William Southern.* R. H. C. Davis and J. M. Wallace-Hadrill, eds., pp. 445–69. Oxford: Clarendon, 1981. ISBN 0-19-822556-3. ▸ Survey of vernacular chronicles of later Middle Ages from large and small towns, showing ideas of civic identity, descriptions of constitutional growth, and urban role in national events. [LCA]

20.643 Edith Ennen. *The medieval town.* Natalie Fryde, trans. Amsterdam: North-Holland; distributed by Elsevier North-Holland, 1979. ISBN 0-444-85133-X. ▸ Comprehensive survey, antiquity to later Middle Ages, with emphasis on Italian and German urbanism. Describes demographic and economic development. Extensive bibliography. Translation of *Die europäische Stadt des Mittelalters* (1972). [LCA]

20.644 Gordon S. Harrison. "The Hanseatic League in historical interpretation." *The historian* 33 (1971) 385–97. ISSN 0018-2370. ▸ Survey of German studies of Hansa towns finding many ethnocentric and provincial. Includes annotated bibliography of English-language sources. [LCA]

20.645 Martha C. Howell. *Women, production, and patriarchy in late medieval cities.* 1986 ed. Chicago: University of Chicago Press, 1988. ISBN 0-226-35504-7 (pbk). ▸ Evidence from Leiden and Cologne used to trace women workers in urban economy, participation in family-owned shops and craft guilds, and failure to gain influence in capitalistic ventures. [LCA]

20.646 Paul Johansen and Heinz von Zur Mühlen. *Deutsch und undeutsch im mittelalterlichen und frühneuzeitlichen Reval.* Cologne: Böhlau, 1973. ISBN 3-412-96172-8. ▸ Seminal work on urban life in Hansa town of Tallinn (Revel). Discusses occupations, rights, and privileges of German and non-German residents. Based on manuscript sources. For advanced students. [PPR]

20.647 Werner Lenk. *Das Nürnberger Fastnachtspiel des fünfzehnten Jahrhunderts: ein Beitrag zur Theorie und zur Interpretation des Fastnachtspiels als Dichtung.* Berlin: Akademie-Verlag, 1966. (Deutsche Akademie der Wissenschaften zu Berlin, Veröffentlichungen des Instituts für deutsches Sprache und Literatur, 33.) ▸ Mentality of Nuremberg citizens measured and analyzed in context of annual Shrovetide carnival. Participation and characterization of Jews, Turks, and peasants and nobles reveal urban concepts of self-identity and ceremony. [LCA]

20.648 Wilhelm Rausch, ed. *Die Stadt am Ausgang des Mittelalters.* Linz/Donau: Österreichischer Arbeitskreis für Stadtgeschichtsforschung, 1974. (Beiträge zur Geschichte der Städte Mitteleuropas, 3.) ▸ Conference papers on political and social history of German and Swiss towns. Basic and often-cited studies with extensive references to further reading. [LCA]

20.649 Fritz Rörig. *The medieval town.* 1967 ed. Berkeley: University of California Press, 1969. ‣ Major older survey of northern European towns. Stresses role of trade, rise of burgher class, and government. Focus on Flemish, Baltic, and German towns. Translation of *Die europäische Stadt und die Kultur des Bürgertums im Mittelalter* (1964). [LCA]

20.650 Rhiman A. Rotz. "Investigating urban uprisings with examples from Hanseatic towns, 1374–1416." In *Order and innovation in the Middle Ages: essays in honor of Joseph R. Strayer.* William Chester Jordan, Bruce McNab, and Teófilo F. Ruíz, eds., pp. 215–33, 483–94. Princeton: Princeton University Press, 1976. ISBN 0-691-05231-X. ‣ Review of historiography of medieval insurrections across Europe including prosopography of participants and nature of power threatened and coveted. Special emphasis on social organizations of Lübeck and Brunswick. Extensive references. [LCA]

20.651 Johannes Schildhauer. *The Hansa: history and culture.* Katherine Vanovitch, trans. New York: Dorset, 1988. ISBN 0-88029-182-6. ‣ Brief survey of history of Hansa towns, stressing material culture. Extensive photographs document chapters on housing, town planning, crafts, art, and music. Passages from primary sources included. Translation of *Die Hanse* (1984). [LCA]

20.652 Paul Strait. *Cologne in the twelfth century.* Gainesville: University Presses of Florida, 1974. ISBN 0-8130-0448-9. ‣ Describes relations of patriciate to archbishop, and gradual consolidation of their control during first century of constitutional growth. Stresses connections between urban community and landed society and open nature of town patriciate. [LCA]

SEE ALSO
30.14 Thomas A. Brady, Jr. *Turning Swiss.*

Lordship, Nobility, and Other Elites

20.653 Gerd Althoff. *Adels- und Königsfamilien im Spiegel ihrer Memorialüberlieferung: Studien zum Totengedenken der Billunger und Ottonen; Bestandteil des Quellenwerkes, Societas et fraternitas.* Munich: Fink, 1984. ISBN 3-7705-2267-2. ‣ Examination of self-consciousness of Billung dukes of Saxony and of Saxon dynasty. Example of Freiburg school's use of necrology for prosopography and investigation of mental attitudes. [JBF]

20.654 Carl Göran Andrae. *Kyrka och frälse i Sverige under äldre medeltid* (Church and nobility in Sweden during the early Middle Ages). Stockholm: Svenska Bokförlaget, 1960. ‣ Discussion of role of church and its privileges in development of Swedish aristocracy. Summary in German. [RMK]

20.655 Benjamin Arnold. *German knighthood, 1050–1300.* Oxford: Clarendon, 1985. ISBN 0-19-821960-1. ‣ Only modern general study of ministerials, group of unfree knights unique to medieval Germany. Application of Bloch's thesis about origins of nobility to Germany (20.308). [JBF]

20.656 Sverre Bagge. *Society and politics in Snorri Sturluson's "Heimskringla."* Berkeley: University of California Press, 1991. ISBN 0-520-06887-4. ‣ Argues that historiography was key to power relations in Snorri's society. [RMK]

20.657 Karl Bosl. *Frühformen der Gesellschaft im mittelalterlichen Europa: ausgewählte Beiträge zu einer Strukturanalyse der mittelalterlichen Welt.* Munich: Oldenbourg, 1964. ‣ Collection of articles stressing connections among freedom, service, and social mobility within ministerial class. Author's theories have informed postwar discussion of ministerials. [JBF]

20.658 Karl Bosl. *Die Reichsministerialität der Salier und Staufer: ein Beitrag zur Geschichte des hochmittelalterlichen deutschen Volkes, Staates, und Reiches.* 2 vols. Stuttgart: Hiersemann, 1950–51. (Schriften der Monumenta Germaniae Historica, Deutsches Institut für Erforschung des Mittelalters, 10.) ‣ Prosopographical, topographical, and genealogical study of imperial ministerials, chief instruments of Hohenstaufen imperial revival. Detailed investigation of administration of imperial domain. [JBF]

20.659 Otto Brunner. *Land and lordship: structures of governance in medieval Austria.* Howard Kaminsky and James Van Horn Melton, trans. Philadelphia: University of Pennsylvania Press, 1992. ISBN 0-8122-8183-7. ‣ Examination of relationship between *Land* (community), bearers of justice and peace, and ruler. Influential but controversial for Nazi overtones. Translation of *Land und Herrschaft,* 4th rev. ed. (1939). [JBF]

20.660 Joachim Bumke. *The concept of knighthood in the Middle Ages.* W.T.H. Jackson and Erika Jackson, trans. New York: AMS Press, 1982. ISBN 0-404-18034-5. ‣ Based on analysis of Middle High German texts, supplemented by findings of historians. Rejects view, popularized by Bloch 20.308, that knights shared common lay culture. Translation of *Studien zum Ritterbegriff im zwölften und dreizehnten Jahrhundert,* 2d ed. (1977). [JBF]

20.661 Jesse L. Byock. *Medieval Iceland: society, sagas, and power.* Berkeley: University of California Press, 1988. ISBN 0-520-05420-2. ‣ Social history of power relations in Iceland based on sagas. Focuses on stateless nature of Icelandic society. [RMK]

20.662 Josef Fleckenstein. *Herrschaft und Stand: Untersuchungen zur Sozialgeschichte im dreizehnten Jahrhundert.* Göttingen: Vandenhoeck & Ruprecht, 1977. (Veröffentlichungen des Max-Planck-Institut für Geschichte, 51.) ISBN 3-525-35364-2. ‣ Symposium papers summarizing German scholarship on transformation of "estates" of nobles, ministerials, knights, and burghers in various territories of empire. [JBF]

20.663 John B. Freed. *The counts of Falkenstein: noble self-consciousness in twelfth-century Germany.* Philadelphia: American Philosophical Society, 1984. (Transactions of the American Philosophical Society, 74.6.) ISBN 0-87169-746-7 (pbk). ‣ Uses *Codex Falkensteinensis,* oldest German collection of documents from noble family, to examine formation of patrilineal lineage and its consequences. Critical response to Schmid 20.681. [JBF]

20.664 John B. Freed. "The crisis of the Salzburg ministerialage, 1270–1343." *Studies in medieval and Renaissance history* 11 (1989) 111–71. ISSN 0081-8224. ‣ Examination of political, economic, and familial factors leading to impoverishment of ministerials. Only work in English on origins of later medieval German lower nobility. [JBF]

20.665 John B. Freed. "The formation of the Salzburg ministerialage in the tenth and eleventh centuries: an example of upward social mobility in the early Middle Ages." *Viator* 9 (1978) 67–102. ISSN 0083-5897, ISBN 0-520-03608-5. ‣ Traces evolution of elite group, functional precursors of later ministerials, among servile population. Only detailed study in English on origins of ministerials. [JBF]

20.666 John B. Freed. "Nobles, ministerials, and knights in the archdiocese of Salzburg." *Speculum* 62.3 (1987) 575–611. ISSN 0038-7134. ‣ Examination of changes in concept of knighthood between tenth and fourteenth centuries. Challenges Arnold's equation of ministerials and knights (20.655). [JBF]

20.667 John B. Freed. "The origins of the European nobility: the problem of the ministerials." *Viator* 7 (1976) 211–41. ISSN 0083-5897, ISBN 0-520-03136-9. ‣ Discussion of theories of social origins of ministerials, their upward mobility, and fate after 1200. Useful guide to literature. [JBF]

20.668 John B. Freed. "Reflections on the medieval German nobility." *American historical review* 91.3 (1986) 553–75. ISSN 0002-8762. ‣ Introduction to post–World War II German studies of nobility, specifically work of Tellenbach 20.133, Schmid 20.681, and Bosl 20.657, 20.658. Argues underlying premises originated during Third Reich. [JBF]

20.669 Karol Górski. "Origins of the Polish *sejm.*" *Slavonic and East European review* 44 (1965–66) 122–38. ISSN 0037-6795. ▸ Description of transformation of meetings of ducal courts, royal curia, and local nobility into diets (*sejm*) of medieval Poland. Focuses on role of military service as well as social development of nobility. [JMB]

20.670 Internationaler Kongress Krems an der Donau. *Adelige Sachkultur des Spätmittelalters: Internationaler Kongress Krems an der Donau 22. bis 25. September 1980.* Vienna: Österreichische Akademie der Wissenschaften, 1982. (Veröffentlichungen des Instituts für mittelalterliche Realienkunde Österreichs, 5; Sitzungsberichte: Österreichische Akademie der Wissenschaften, Philosophisch-historische Klasse, 400.) ISBN 3-7001-0467-7. ▸ Collection of articles in German, French, English, and Italian on daily life of late medieval nobility, particularly in Germanic countries. Emphasizes material culture. [JBF]

20.671 C. Stephen Jaeger. *The origins of courtliness: civilizing trends and the formation of courtly ideals, 939–1210.* 1985 ed. Philadelphia: University of Pennsylvania Press, 1989. ISBN 0-8122-1307-6 (pbk). ▸ Argues courtesy originated among Ottonian court clerics who revived classical ideals of civic virtue. Good introduction to imperial episcopate, but anachronistic view of state. [JBF]

20.672 Nada Klaić. "Postanak plemstva 'dvanaestero plemena' kraljevine Hrvatske (The nobility of the 'twelve clans' of the kingdom of Croatia)." *Historijski zbornik* 11–12 (1958–59) 121–63. ISSN 0351-2193. ▸ Most recent summary of controversy over existence of autochthonous nobility in early medieval Croatia and relationship to kingdom of Hungary after Croatia's incorporation ca. 1100. [JMB]

20.673 John Martin Klassen. *The nobility and the making of the Hussite Revolution.* Boulder: East European Quarterly; distributed by Columbia University Press, 1978. ISBN 0-914710-40-0. ▸ Statistical and qualitative analysis of landowning nobility in Bohemia and Moravia around 1400, discussing role played and gains and losses of nobility during Hussite Revolution. [JMB]

20.674 Thomas Lindkvist. "Swedish medieval society: previous research and recent developments." *Scandinavian journal of history* 4 (1979) 253–68. ISSN 0346-8755. ▸ Broad historiographical overview focusing on emergence of Swedish state and rise of aristocratic class. [RMK]

20.675 F. Maksay. *Les pays de la noblesse nombreuse.* Budapest: Akadémiai Kiadó, 1980. (Magyar Tudomanyos Akademia: studia historica Academiae Scientiarum Hungaricae, 139.) ISBN 963-05-2552-6 (pbk). ▸ Comparative study of nobility in Hungary and Poland treating property, privileges, and political role. Emphasizes military role and decline of royal domain. Attempts statistical analysis. [JMB]

20.676 Karol Modzelewski. "The system of the *ius ducale* and the idea of feudalism: comments on the earliest class society in medieval Poland." *Quaestiones Medii Aevi* 1 (1977) 71–99. ISSN 0137-4001. ▸ Summary of author's studies of decline of "state serfdom" and emergence of landed nobility. Emphasizes differences between Poland, western Europe, and so-called Asiatic despotism. See also Russocki 20.680. [JMB]

20.677 Helge Paludan. "Conceptions of Danish society during the high Middle Ages." *Scandinavian journal of history* 4 (1979) 269–85. ISSN 0346-8755. ▸ Historiography of Danish social structure discussing scholarly concern over whether or not Denmark was "feudal." [RMK]

20.678 Hans Patze, ed. *Die Burgen im deutschen Sprachraum: ihre rechts- und verfassungsgeschichtliche Bedeutung.* 2 vols. Sigmaringen, Germany: Thorbecke, 1976. ISBN 3-7995-6619-8 (set). ▸ General articles and regional studies on castles and relations to other power centers. Studies key element in rise of territorial lordship. [JBF]

20.679 Miloslav Polivka. "The Bohemian lesser nobility at the turn of the fourteenth and fifteenth century." *Historica* 25 (1985) 121–75. ISSN 0440-9205. ▸ Analysis of role of noble and knightly families in royal and local government and status differences within noble estate. Underscores number of poor nobles. Extensive bibliography and historiographical discussion. [JMB]

20.680 Stanisław Russocki. "Le 'féodalism centralisé' dans le centre-est de l'Europe." *Acta Poloniae historica* 66 (1992) 31–37. ISSN 0001-6829. ▸ Critical review of Marxist theories on development of feudalism in Poland. [JMB]

20.681 Karl Schmid. *Gebetsgedenken und adliges Selbstverständnis im Mittelalter, ausgewählte Beiträge: Festgabe zu seinem sechzigsten Geburtstag.* Sigmaringen, Germany: Thorbecke, 1983. ISBN 3-7995-7023-3. ▸ Contains author's most important articles on formation of patrilineal lineage, noble self-consciousness, and prayer fraternities. Very influential in German historiography. See Freed 20.663 and Leyser 20.627 for critical assessment. [JBF]

20.682 Aloys Schulte. *Der Adel und die deutsche Kirche im Mittelalter: Studien zur Sozial-, Rechts- und Kirchengeschichte.* 1922 2d ed. Amsterdam: Schippers, 1966. ▸ Classic study of noble domination of German church. Argues membership in church foundations limited to free nobility. Celibacy major factor in extinction of noble lines. [JBF]

20.683 Julius Gyula Szekfü. "Die Servienten und Familarien im ungarischen Mittelalter." *Ungarische Rundschau der historischen Wissenschaften* 2 (1912) 524–57. ▸ Description of Hungarian feudalism; less formalized than Western version and rarely lasted beyond retainer's lifetime. Describes legal and social status of dependent noblemen who took service with magnates. [JMB]

20.684 Friedrich-Wilhelm Wentzlaff-Eggebert. *Kreuzzugsdichtung des Mittelalters: Studien zu ihrer geschichtlichen und dichterischen Wirklichkeit.* Berlin: de Gruyter, 1960. ▸ Places French and German Crusading poetry in historical and conceptual contexts. Argues songs and poems followed developments in Crusading thought. [JSCRS]

SEE ALSO
33.336 Erik Fügedi. *Castle and society in medieval Hungary, 1000–1437.*

POLITICS AND GOVERNMENT

German Empire

20.685 David Abulafia. *Frederick II: a medieval emperor.* 1988 ed. New York: Oxford University Press, 1992. ISBN 0-19-508040-8 (pbk). ▸ Best biography in any language. Emphasizes traditional nature of ideas and policies and attempts to cooperate with popes and German princes. Rejects Kantorowicz's view of Frederick II as medieval superman (20.697). [JBF/DJO]

20.686 Charles Calvert Bayley. *The formation of the German college of electors in the mid-thirteenth century.* Toronto: University of Toronto Press, 1949. ▸ Places double election of 1257 in political, constitutional, legal, and diplomatic context. Represents older view stressing rise of princes at expense of monarchy. [JBF]

20.687 Uta-Renate Blumenthal. *The investiture controversy: church and monarchy from the ninth to the twelfth century.* Philadelphia: University of Pennsylvania Press, 1988. ISBN 0-8122-8112-8. ▸ Traces church reform movement from beginnings through conflict between Gregory VII and Henry IV to Concordat of Worms. Useful bibliography. Author's translation of *Der Investiturstreit* (1982). [JBF/KP]

20.688 Lutz Fenske. *Adelsopposition und kirchliche Reformbewegung im östlichen Sachsen: Entstehung und Wirkung des sächsischen*

Widerstandes gegen des salische Königtum während des Investitur-streits. Göttingen: Vandenhoeck & Ruprecht, 1977. (Veröffentli-chungen des Max-Planck-Instituts für Geschichte, 47.) ISBN 3-525-35356-1. ▸ Prosopographical study of Saxon opposition to Henry IV. Argues that reform movement politically important only after 1076. Important for understanding Investiture Conflict, but presupposes knowledge of Saxon history. [JBF]

20.689 Josef Fleckenstein, ed. *Investiturstreit und Reichsverfassung.* Sigmaringen, Germany: Thorbecke, 1973. (Konstanzer Arbeitskreis für Mittelalterliche Geschichte, Vorträge und Forschungen, 17.) ISBN 3-7995-6617-1. ▸ Collection of articles on church reform movement and Investiture Conflict, papacy, nobility, monarchy, cities, and Concordat of Worms. Synthesis of German scholarship as of date of publication. [JBF]

20.690 Werner Goez. *Der Leihezwang: eine Untersuchung zur Geschichte des deutschen Lehnrechtes.* Tübingen: Mohr, 1962. ▸ Argues German kings not legally obligated to re-enfeoff vacant fief. Rejects Mitteis's view (20.700) that *Leihezwang* (forced enfeoffment) major factor in royal failure to create centralized state. [JBF]

20.691 Werner Goez. *Translatio imperii: ein Beitrag zur Geschichte des Geschichtsdenkens und der politischen Theorien im Mittelalter und in der frühen Neuzeit.* Tübingen: Mohr, 1958. ▸ History of idea of "transfer of empire." Shows it was fully developed by Otto of Freising and utilized by Innocent III to justify intervention in disputed election of 1198. Sophisticated analysis. [JBF]

20.692 Karl Hampe. *Germany under the Salian and Hohenstaufen emperors.* R. F. Bennett, trans. Totowa, N.J.: Rowman & Littlefield, 1973. ISBN 0-87471-173-8. ▸ History of individual reigns from Conrad II (1024–1039) to Frederick II (1194–1250). First published in 1908 and for many years the classic history of medieval Germany. Translation of *Deutsche Kaisergeschichte in der Zeit der Salier und Staufer,* 11th ed. (1963). [JBF]

20.693 Boyd H. Hill, Jr. *Medieval monarchy in action: the German empire from Henry I to Henry IV.* London and New York: Allen & Unwin and Barnes & Noble, 1972. ISBN 0-389-04652-3. ▸ Translation of fifty important or representative documents with brief introduction to reign of each monarch, 918–1106. Gives English-language readers flavor of royal government. [JBF]

20.694 Eduard Hlawitschka. *Vom Frankenreich zur Formierung der europäischen Staaten- und Völkergemeinschaft, 840–1046: ein Studienbuch zur Zeit der späten Karolinger, der Ottonen, und der frühen Salier in der Geschichte Mitteleuropas.* Darmstadt: Wissenschaftliche Buchgesellschaft, 1986. ISBN 3-534-03566-6. ▸ Political history by member of Freiburg school. Places origins of Germany into European context. Discusses current status of and literature about specific problems, such as county structure. [JBF]

20.695 Karl Jordan. *Henry the Lion: a biography.* P. S. Falla, trans. Oxford: Clarendon, 1986. ISBN 0-19-821969-5. ▸ Biography of most famous twelfth-century German prince, duke of Saxony and Bavaria, and Frederick Barbarossa's cousin and rival. Popular history by expert. Translation of *Heinrich der Löwe* (1979). [JBF]

20.696 Hellmut Kämpf, ed. *Canossa als Wende: ausgewählte Aufsätze zur neueren Forschung.* 1963 ed. Darmstadt: Wissenschaftliche Buchgesellschaft, 1969. ▸ Collection of major articles on most dramatic incident in Investiture Conflict, Henry IV's penance at Canossa. Important for historiography but becoming dated. [JBF]

20.697 Ernst Kantorowicz. *Frederick the Second, 1194–1250.* Edith O. Lorimer, trans. New York: Smith, 1931. ▸ Classic portrait presenting emperor as heroic figure towering above his age. Compare Abulafia 20.685. [FLC]

20.698 Joachim Leuschner. *Germany in the late Middle Ages.* Sabine MacCormack, trans. Amsterdam: North-Holland, 1980.

ISBN 0-444-85135-6. ▸ Brief political history of Germany from double election of 1198 to mid-fifteenth century. Useful introduction. Translation of *Deutschland im späten Mittelalter* (1975). [JBF]

20.699 Heinrich Mitteis. *Lehnrecht und Staatsgewalt: Untersuchungen zur mittelalterlichen Verfassungsgeschichte.* 1933 ed. Darmstadt: Wissenschaftliche Buchgesellschaft, 1974. ▸ Comparative study of feudal law from German perspective. Argues that in Germany, in contrast to France and England, proprietary element stronger than personal ties. Views challenged by Goez 20.691. [JBF]

20.700 Heinrich Mitteis. *The state in the Middle Ages: a comparative constitutional history of feudal Europe.* H. F. Orton, trans. Amsterdam and New York: North-Holland and American Elsevier, 1975. ISBN 0-444-10825-4. ▸ Dated, but reveals how leading German legal historian in interwar period approached medieval political history. Emphasizes German political developments. Translation of *Der Staat des hohen Mittelalters* (1940). [JBF]

20.701 Theodor Ernst Mommsen. *Imperial lives and letters of the eleventh century.* 1962 ed. Karl F. Morrison, trans. Robert L. Benson, ed. New York: Columbia University Press, 1967. ▸ Translations of Wipo's *Deeds of Conrad II,* an anonymous life of Henry IV, and Henry's letters. Illustrates important aspects of imperial ideology at empire's zenith. [JBF]

20.702 Eckhard Müller-Mertens. *Regnum Teutonicum: Aufkommen und Verbreitung des deutschen Reichs- und Königsauffassung im früheren Mittelalter.* Vienna: Böhlau, 1970. ISBN 3-205-00502-3. ▸ Argues concept of German *Reich* and king was developed by Pope Gregory VII and Henry IV's princely opponents to deprive emperor of sacral status. Marxist challenge to nationalistic German history. [JBF]

20.703 Peter Munz. *Frederick Barbarossa: a study in medieval politics.* Ithaca, N.Y.: Cornell University Press, 1969. ▸ Presents emperor as astute, flexible politician who pursued long-term plans. Best available account, but concept of Barbarossa's "grand design" has gained little acceptance. [JBF]

20.704 Otto of Freising. *The deeds of Frederick Barbarossa.* 1953 ed. Charles Christopher Mierow, ed. and trans. New York: Norton, 1966. ▸ Major source on early years of emperor's reign, written by his uncle. Most important work of foremost medieval German historian. [JBF]

20.705 Timothy Reuter. "The 'imperial church system' of the Ottonian and Salian rulers: a reconsideration." *Journal of ecclesiastical history* 33.3 (1982) 347–74. ISSN 0022-0469. ▸ Argues kings did not consciously use church as counterweight to nobility; bishops sought on their own to rule counties. See Fleckenstein's critical response in his collected essays (20.689). [JBF]

20.706 Gerd Tellenbach. *Church, state, and Christian society at the time of the investiture contest.* 1940 ed. R. F. Bennett, trans. Toronto: University of Toronto Press with Medieval Academy of America, 1991. (Medieval Academy reprints for teaching, 27.) ISBN 0-8020-6857-X. ▸ Classic interpretation of Investiture Conflict. Argues Church abandoned traditional subordination to divinely instituted kings in order to impose own conception of right order on world. Emphasizes transformation of Christian society by church reform. Translation of *Libertas, Kirche, und Weltordnung im Zeitalter des Investiturstreites* (1936). [JBF/KP]

20.707 Thomas Van Cleve. *The Emperor Frederick II of Hohenstaufen, immutator mundi.* Oxford: Clarendon, 1972. ISBN 0-19-822513-X. ▸ Detailed study of emperor, portrayed as "transformer of the world." For more conventional view of medieval monarch see Abulafia 20.685. [JBF]

20.708 Thomas Van Cleve. *Markward of Anweiler and the Sicilian regency: a study of Hohenstaufen policy in Sicily during the* *minority of Frederick II.* Princeton: Princeton University Press, 1937. ▸ Biography of most famous imperial ministerial, Henry IV's tutor, who became duke. Places Markward's spectacular career in broader context than Bosl's *Reichsministerialität* (20.658). [JBF]

Scandinavian Kingdoms

20.709 Sverre Bagge. "Borgerkrig og statsudvikling i Norge i middelalderen (Civil war and the development of the state in Norway during the Middle Ages)." *Historisk Tidsskrift* 65 (1986) 145–97. ISSN 0018-263X. ▸ Argues period of civil wars, 1130–1240, crucial for formation of Norwegian state. Resource crisis among aristocracy led to war and was resolved by emergence of stronger central monarchy. English summary. [RMK]

20.710 Aksel Erhardt Christensen. *Kongemagt og aristokrati: epoker i middelalderlig dansk statsopfattelse indtil unionstiden* (Royal power and aristocracy: stages in the medieval Danish conception of the state to the period of the Union). 1945 ed. Copenhagen: Akademisk Forlag, 1976. ▸ Discussion of building of monarchy and state. Argues feudal relations existed in Denmark between nobility and monarchy and between peasants and nobility, even without feudal legal arrangements. [RMK]

20.711 Knut Helle. "Norway in the high Middle Ages." *Scandinavian journal of history* 6 (1981) 161–89. ISSN 0346-8755. ▸ Historiographical survey, sharply critiquing Marxist perspective that king and aristocracy had common interests. [RMK]

20.712 Jenny Jochens. "The politics of reproduction: medieval Norwegian kingship." *American historical review* 92 (1987) 329–32. ISSN 0002-8762. ▸ Analysis of how Norwegian kings used marriage alliances to bolster royal power. [RMK]

20.713 Claus Krag and Jørn Sandnes. *Nye middelalderstudier.* Vol. 2: *Kongedomme, kirke, stat* (New studies on the Middle Ages. Vol. 2: Kingdom, church, state). Oslo: Universitetsforlaget, 1983. ISBN 82-00-06529-4 (v. 2). ▸ Selections from leading Norwegian scholars over last several decades on medieval Norwegian kingship, church, and state. Useful introductory essays. [RMK]

20.714 Erik Lönnroth. *Statsmakt och statsfinans i det medeltida Sverige: studier över skatteväsen och länsförvaltning* (State power and state finance in medieval Sweden). 1940 ed. Göteborg: Acta Universitatis Gothoburgensis, 1984. (Goteborgs hogskolas arsskrift, 46.3.) ISBN 91-7346-134-2. ▸ Sees Swedish history as struggle between crown and aristocracy for control of resources. Influential, though criticized on details. Summary in German. [RMK]

20.715 Thomas Riis. *Les institutions politiques centrales du Danemark, 1100–1332.* Odense, Denmark: Odense University Press, 1977. ISBN 87-7492-214-9. ▸ Constitutional developments from end of Viking age until interregnum of 1330s. Discusses ideology of kingship and nature of various political assemblies. [RMK]

20.716 P. H. Sawyer. *The making of Sweden.* Alingsås, Sweden: Viktoria, 1989. ISBN 91-86708-08-2. ▸ Discussion of rise of kingship in Sweden in light of other regions of Europe, how development of Swedish kingdom influenced by Denmark. Suggests Sweden not unified until twelfth century. [RMK]

20.717 Elsa Sjöholm. "Sweden's medieval laws: European legal tradition—political change." *Scandinavian journal of history* 15 (1990) 65–87. ISSN 0346-8755. ▸ Summary of author's controversial Swedish work. Argues medieval Swedish law not derived from oral tradition but solely from external European tradition. Uses law as evidence for power relations in late thirteenth-century Sweden. [RMK]

German Principalities

20.718 Benjamin Arnold. *Count and bishop in medieval Germany: a study of regional power, 1100–1350.* Philadelphia: University of Pennsylvania Press, 1992. ISBN 0-8122-3084-1. ▸ Case study of themes author explores in 20.719. Bishops of Eichstätt, relying on ministerials, outlasted their comital neighbors and created, after 1305, a modest principality. [JBF]

20.719 Benjamin Arnold. *Princes and territories in medieval Germany.* Cambridge: Cambridge University Press, 1991. ISBN 0-521-39085-0. ▸ Argues princes utilized traditional manorial rights, economic expansion, and peace movement to create lordships. In contrast to Barraclough 20.610, stresses princes' abilities rather than royal failure. [JBF]

20.720 Friedrich Benninghoven. *Der Orden der Schwertbrüder (Fratres milicie Christi de Livonia).* Cologne: Böhlau, 1965. ▸ Classic work on Sword Brothers of Livonia. Thorough and meticulous with excellent bibliography, maps, and photographs. [PPR]

20.721 Eric Christiansen. *The northern Crusades: the Baltic and the Catholic frontier, 1100–1525.* Minneapolis: University of Minnesota Press, 1980. ISBN 0-8166-0994-2. ▸ Best introduction in English to medieval history of Baltic region. Avoids detailed discussion of theory but argues campaigns were true Crusades. Lively and broad in coverage. Excellent bibliography. [PPR/JSCRS]

20.722 Henry J. Cohn. *The government of the Rhine palatinate in the fifteenth century.* 1965 ed. Aldershot, England: Gregg Revivals, 1991. ISBN 0-7512-0005-0. ▸ Examination of tranformation of government from complex of feudal rights to territorial state with relatively uniform administration. Influenced by work of Carsten on German estates in modern period (30.107). [JBF]

20.723 Lawrence G. Duggan. *Bishop and chapter: the governance of the bishopric of Speyer to 1552.* New Brunswick, N.J.: Rutgers University Press, 1978. (Studies presented to the International Commission for the History of Representative and Parliamentary Institutions, 62.) ISBN 0-8135-0857-6. ▸ Concludes cathedral chapter served as functional diet of ecclesiastical principality, a dependency of Rhine palatinate. Applies Carsten's work on estates to institutions of medieval bishopric (30.107). [JBF/KP]

20.724 Karl Lechner. *Die Babenberger: Markgrafen und Herzöge von Österreich, 976–1246.* 1976 ed. Vienna: Böhlau, 1985. (Veröffentlichungen des Instituts für Österreichische Geschichtsforschung, 23.) ISBN 3-205-00018-8. ▸ History of duchy of Austria and dynasty that created it. Best introduction to principality that became core of separate nation. [JBF]

20.725 Helmut Maurer. *Der Herzog von Schwaben: Grundlagen, Wirkungen, und Wesen seiner Herrschaft in ottonischer, salischer, und staufischer Zeit.* Sigmaringen, Germany: Thorbecke, 1978. ISBN 3-7995-7007-1. ▸ Examination of transformation of duchy from royal office into complex of lands and rights held in fief from crown. Case study of territorialization of lordship. [JBF]

20.726 Hans Patze, ed. *Der deutsche Territorialstaat im vierzehnten Jahrhundert.* 2 vols. Sigmaringen, Germany: Thorbecke, 1970–71. ISBN 3-7995-6613-9 (v. 13) 3-7995-6614-7 (v. 14). ▸ General articles and regional studies. Most comprehensive account of late medieval principalities. Synthesis left to reader. [JBF]

20.727 Hans Patze, ed. *Die Grundherrschaft im späten Mittelalter.* 2 vols. Sigmaringen, Germany: Thorbecke, 1983. ISBN 3-7995-6627-9 (set). ▸ General and local studies of late medieval manorial structures by major German scholars. Important because, as Arnold has argued (20.719), traditional manorial rights were at heart of territorial lordship. [JBF]

20.728 Brian A. Pavlac. "Excommunication and territorial politics in high medieval Trier." *Church history* 60.1 (1991) 20–36. ISSN 0009-6407. ▸ Argues spiritual censure was effective weapon against archbishop's opponents, especially as technique for creating new territorial lordship. [JBF]

20.729 Ferdinand Seibt. "Land und Herrschaft in Böhmen." *Historische Zeitschrift* 200 (1965) 284–315. ISSN 0018-2613. ▸ Discussion of role of noble landowners in establishment of territorial government and estates. Follows studies on Austria by Brunner 20.659. Based on Czech studies. [JMB]

20.730 William Urban. *The Livonian crusade.* Washington, D.C.: University Press of America, 1981. ISBN 0-8191-1683-1 (cl), 0-8191-1684-X (pbk). ▸ Covers events in Livonia from 1290s to 1560s. Concentrates, more than Christiansen 20.721, on military and political events with more details for advanced student. [PPR]

20.731 William Urban. *The Samogitian Crusade.* Chicago: Lithuanian Research and Studies Center, 1989. ISBN 0-929700-03-1. ▸ Best English-language work on conversion of Lithuania. Takes neutral position between those who see Baltic crusades as wars of conquest and plunder and those who believe they were justified. Covers to 1400. [PPR]

Kingdoms of Eastern Europe

20.732 János M. Bak. *Königtum und Stände in Ungarn im vierzehnten–sechzehnten Jahrhundert.* Wiesbaden: Steiner, 1973. ▸ Summary of Hungarian research on late medieval kingdom, investigating role of nobility in royal elections, during interregna, and in establishment of "dualist-corporative" polity around 1500. [JMB]

20.733 György Bónis. "The Hungarian feudal diet (thirteenth to eighteenth centuries)." *Recueils de la Société Jean Bodin pour l'histoire comparative des institutions* 20 (1965) 287–307. ISSN 0998-0601. ▸ Overview of development of noble diet in kingdom of Hungary. Critical of romantic-nationalist views of earlier scholars. Treats mainly formal and legal aspects of government of estates. [JMB]

20.734 František Graus. "Die Entstehung der mittelalterlichen Staaten in Mitteleuropa." *Historica* 10 (1965) 5–65. ISSN 0440-9205. ▸ Overview of transformation of armed retinues of powerful leaders into service nobility and then an Estate of landed nobles. Explores parallels to neighboring countries. Polemic against idea of "ancient nobilities." [JMB]

20.735 Zoltán J. Kosztolnyik. *From Coloman the Learned to Béla III, 1095–1196: Hungarian domestic policies and their impact upon foreign affairs.* Boulder: East European Monographs; distributed by Columbia University Press, 1987. (East European monographs, 220.) ISBN 0-88033-116-X. ▸ Political narrative and legal-administrative history. Discusses Investiture Controversy, policies toward Byzantium and Rome, canonization of Ladislas I, and ideas of kingship. [FLC]

20.736 Stanisław Russocki. "Structures politiques dans l'Europe des Jagellon." *Acta Poloniae historica* 29 (1979) 101–42. ISSN 0001-6829. ▸ Analysis of rule of Jagellon brothers, 1490–1526, showing absence of coordinated politics but spread of common influences through courts. Weak monarchy in Poland paralleled by growth of Estates in Bohemia, Moravia, and Hungary. [JMB]

20.737 Zygmunt Wojciechowski. *L'état polonais au moyen âge: histoire des institutions.* Bernard Hamel, trans. Paris: Sirey, 1949. ▸ Despite age, still best overview of medieval Polish state; extensive bibliography. French institutional history approach, better on systematic than on dynamic description of political development. [JMB]

SEE ALSO

33.382 Steven Béla Várdy, Géza Grosschmid, and L. S. Domonkos, eds. *Louis the Great, king of Hungary and Poland.*

MEDITERRANEAN EUROPE, ca. 1000–ca. 1500

General Studies

20.738 David Abulafia. *The two Italies: economic relations between the Norman kingdom of Sicily and the northern communes.* 1976 ed. Cambridge: Cambridge University Press, 1977. ISBN 0-521-21211-1. ▸ Describes growth of Italian commerce in twelfth century. Suggests Norman kings allowed northern merchants to control exports of raw materials to detriment of southern industries. [DJO]

20.739 Pierre Bonnassie. *From slavery to feudalism in south-western Europe.* Jean Birrell, trans. Cambridge and Paris: Cambridge University Press and Editions de la Maison des Sciences de l'Homme, 1991. ISBN 0-521-36324-1. ▸ Collected articles on end of ancient slavery, aristocratic assertiveness in eleventh century, and imposition of new forms of servitude. Shows strength of feudal institutions in Mediterranean contradicting views of older scholarship. [PHF]

20.740 Charles T. Davis. *Dante's Italy, and other essays.* Philadelphia: University of Pennsylvania Press, 1984. ISBN 0-8122-7883-6. ▸ Collection of specialized essays on education, political thought, and concept of commune in thirteenth-century Italy. [DJO]

20.741 *Structures féodales et féodalisme dans l'occident méditerranéen, dixième–treizième siècles: bilan et perspectives de recherches, colloque international organisé par le Centre National de la Recherche Scientifique et l'École Française de Rome, Rome 10–13 octobre 1978.* 1978 ed. Rome: École Française de Rome, 1980. (Collection de l'École Française de Rome, 44.) ISBN 2-7283-0000-3. ▸ Conference papers in French and Italian. Includes important articles on establishment of castles and imposition of seigneurial regime in southern France and Christian Spain. [PHF]

20.742 Helene Wieruszowski. *Politics and culture in medieval Spain and Italy.* Rome: Storia e Letteratura, 1971. ▸ Collection of specialized essays focusing on political and intellectual life, especially civic context of literature and art. [DJO]

Rural World

20.743 Bruno Andreolli, Vito Fumagalli and Massimo Montanari, eds. *Le campagne italiane prima e dopo il Mille: una società in trasformazione.* Bologna: Cooperativa Libraria Universitaria Editrice Bologna, 1985. ▸ Collection of articles on agricultural techniques, free peasants, land reclamation, material culture, and forms of lordship. [FLC]

20.744 Constance Hoffman Berman. *Medieval agriculture, the Southern French countryside, and the early Cistercians: a study of forty-three monasteries.* Philadelphia: American Philosophical Society, 1986. (Transactions of the American Philosophical Society, 76.5.) ISBN 0-87169-765-3 (pbk). ▸ Shows, with others (such as Donkin 20.375), that Cistercians not pioneers, but reshapers of acquired agrarian landscape. Studies managerial practice, labor recruitment, tithe acquisition, and marketing. Ascribes profitability to privileges and lower labor costs. [FLC]

20.745 Robert Boutruche. *La crise d'une société: seigneurs et paysans du Bordelais pendant la Guerre de cent ans.* 1947 ed. Paris: Belles Lettres, 1963. (Publications de la Faculté des Lettres de l'Université de Strasbourg, 110.) ▸ Pioneering study of noble rural life during late medieval "crisis." Describes decline in seigneurial revenues, changes in economic organization of lords' estates; alternate sources of income in pillage, pensions, commerce, and church; decline of old families and rise of new. [FLC]

20.746 Henri Bresc. *Un monde méditerranéen: économie et société en Sicile, 1300–1450.* 2 vols. Rome: École Française de Rome, 1986. (Bibliothèque des Écoles Française d'Athènes et de Rome, 262.) ISBN 2-7283-0103-4 (set), 2-7283-0128-X (v. 1), 2-7283-

0129-8 (v. 2). ▸ Uses underdevelopment theory of colonialism and dependency to argue Norman policy led to specialization in grain export, locking region into unequal exchange for manufactures from north. Vast, Annales-style thesis. [FLC]

20.747 Giovanni Cherubini. *L'Italia rurale del basso medioevo.* Rome: Laterza, 1985. ISBN 88-420-2537-2. ▸ Study of enlargement and intensification of agriculture, conquest of rural world by cities, and transfer of ownership and reorganization. Sees southern dependence and rural impoverishment beginning in later Middle Ages. For the general reader. [FLC]

20.748 Gabrielle Démians d'Archimbaud. *Les fouilles de Rougiers (Var): contribution à l'archéologie de l'habitat rural médiéval en pays méditerranéen.* Paris and Valbonne: Centre National de la Recherche Scientifique and Centre Regional de Publications de Sophia Antipolis, 1980. (Publication de l'U.R.A., 6. Archéologie médiévale méditerranéenne, Mémoires, 2.) ISBN 2-222-02604-0. ▸ Excavation report of village, occupied twelfth to fourteenth century. Detailed description of fortified habitat. Refined technical analysis of difficult stratigraphy. Model excavation. [FLC]

20.749 Robert Durand. *Les campagnes portugaises entre Douro et Tage aux douzième et treizième siècles.* Lisbon and Paris: Fundação Calouste Gulbenkian and Centro Cultural Português, 1982. (Civilização Portuguesa, 9.) ▸ Insists on peasant initiative in shaping structures of countryside, strength of village community, and peasant mastery of technology and money. Peasants protected by counts for fiscal reasons. Rural lordships creations of later twelfth century. Annales-style regional history. [FLC]

20.750 Stephan R. Epstein. *An island for itself: economic development and social change in late medieval Sicily.* Cambridge: Cambridge University Press, 1991. ISBN 0-521-38518-0. ▸ Shows fifteenth century was period of demographic and economic upsurge, based on regional specialization and access to markets. Develops large theory of relation of political-institutional to socioeconomic change. Response to Abulafia 20.738 and Bresc 20.746. [FLC]

20.751 Paul Freedman. *The origins of peasant servitude in medieval Catalonia.* Cambridge: Cambridge University Press, 1991. ISBN 0-521-39327-2. ▸ Description of gradual subjugation of free frontier peasantry by lords, weakening lordship in plague era, and agitation and civil war. Sets conclusions against wide range of studies from England to Eastern Europe. Major work with implications far beyond Catalonia. [FLC]

20.752 Jean-Marie Pesez, ed. *Brucato: histoire et archéologie d'un habitat médiéval en Sicile.* 2 vols. Rome: École Française de Rome, 1984. (Collection de l'École Française de Rome, 78.) ISBN 2-7283-0074-7 (set), 2-7283-0075-5 (v. 1), 2-7283-0076-3 (v. 2). ▸ Technical excavation report of Sicilian "agro-town" of late thirteenth to early fourteenth century. [FLC]

Urban World, Commerce, and Industry

20.753 Robert Brentano. *Rome before Avignon: a social history of thirteenth-century Rome.* Berkeley: University of California Press, 1991. ISBN 0-520-06952-8. ▸ Lively description of life of city, families, and social groups, especially those depending on papal court for status. Numerous illustrations. [DJO/JFP]

20.754 María del Carmen Carlé. *Del concejo medieval castellano-leonés.* Buenos Aires: Instituto de Historia de España, 1968. ▸ Survey of emergence and growth of Leónese-Castilian municipalities from twelfth through mid-fourteenth centuries. Draws extensively on town codes (*fueros*). General but useful introduction to municipal government. [JFP]

20.755 Claude Carrère. *Barcelone, centre économique à l'époque des difficultés: 1380-1462.* 2 vols. Paris: Mouton, 1967. ▸ Detailed study of city and region in period of critical social unrest. Indus-

trial, commercial, and social background to 1462 civil war. Explores conflict between rentiers and merchant-craftsmen alliance. [JFP]

20.756 Stanley Chojnacki. "Dowries and kinsmen in early Renaissance Venice." *Journal of interdisciplinary history* 5 (1975) 571-600. ISSN 0022-1953. ▸ Study of who financed inflated dowries of fourteenth and fifteenth centuries. Based on wills; shows role of mothers, grandparents, and uncles, and how "distinctive feminine social impulse" influenced patrician social relations. [FLC]

20.757 Samuel Kline Cohn, Jr. *The cult of remembrance and the Black Death: six Renaissance cities in central Italy.* Baltimore: Johns Hopkins University Press, 1992. ISBN 0-8018-4303-0. ▸ Dense, difficult study tracing shifts in piety, charity, funeral rituals, and control of property after death using 3,389 wills. Finds major change after second (1361-62) rather than first plague period. Important social and religious context of early Renaissance art. [FLC]

20.758 Antonio Collantes de Terán Sánchez. *Sevilla en la Baja Edad Media: la ciudad y sus hombres.* 2d ed. Seville: Servicio de Publicaciones del Excmo. Ayuntamiento, 1984. ISBN 84-500-2380-7. ▸ Cautious, thoughtful, detailed history of city from later fourteenth to early sixteenth century. Stresses demography, topography, and class structures based on census lists and other sources. [JFP]

20.759 Mario Del Treppo. *I mercanti catalani e l'espansione della corona aragonese nel secolo XV.* Naples: Libreria Scientifica Editrice, 1968. ▸ Study of Catalan business classes with focus on political background. Against Vicens Vives 20.963 and Carrère 20.755, argues economic climate favorable in fifteenth century, but notes limitations leading to 1462 crisis. [JFP]

20.760 Mario Del Treppo and Alfonso Leone. *Amalfi medioevale.* Naples: Giannini, 1977. ▸ Useful historical survey, 900-1500, blending two monographs. Focus on social and economic history giving special attention to fourteenth-century decline wrought by nature and Aragonese. [JFP]

20.761 Heath Dillard. *Daughters of the reconquest: women in Castilian town society, 1100-1300.* 1984 ed. Cambridge: Cambridge University Press, 1989. ISBN 0-521-38737-X (pbk). ▸ Depicts status, legal standing, and activities of urban women in Castile in variety of social groups. Emphasizes how women gave stability to frontier settlements and the economic and legal power that came from this. [PHF/JFP]

20.762 Edward D. English. *Enterprise and liability in Sienese banking, 1230-1350.* Cambridge, Mass.: Mediaeval Academy of America, 1988. (*Speculum* anniversary monographs, 12.) ISBN 0-910956-94-4 (cl), 0-910956-95-2 (pbk). ▸ Study of rise and fall of Bonsignori and Tolomei banks as result of dependence on papal patronage, problems of liability in bankruptcy, and complicity of commune. Emphasizes difficulties of organizing credit around 1300. [FLC]

20.763 Steven Epstein. *Wills and wealth in medieval Genoa, 1150-1250.* Cambridge, Mass.: Harvard University Press, 1984. ISBN 0-674-95356-8. ▸ Study of family structure and charity as shaped by urbanization and commercial revolution. Also discusses funeral ceremonies and burial choices. Based on 632 surviving wills. [FLC]

20.764 Carlos Estepa Díez. *Estructura social de la ciudad de León (siglos XI-XIII).* León, Spain: Centro de Estudios e Investigación "San Isidoro," 1977. (Fuentes y estudios de historia Leonesa, 19.) ISBN 84-00-03668-9. ▸ Description of emerging capital city of kingdom of León. Focuses primarily on social structures, governmental system, economic activity, and role of minorities. [JFP]

20.765 Carlos Estepa Díez et al. *Burgos en la Edad Media.* Valladolid: Junta de Castilla y León, Consejería de Educación y Cultura, 1984. ISBN 84-500-9692-8. ▸ Several monographs blended into effective narrative history, ninth through fifteenth centuries. Best on social and economic conditions, most incisive from 1250–1500. Some subjects, like Black Death, slighted. [JFP]

20.766 José María Font Rius. *Orígenes del régimen municipal de Cataluña.* Madrid: Instituto Nacional de Estudios Jurídicos, 1946. (Publicaciones del Instituto Nacional de Estudios Jurídicos, Serie 1, Publicaciones periódicas, 7.) ▸ Reviews theories of town origins and development, European and peninsular. Focuses on institutional development of legal freedoms and group identity, beginning in late twelfth century. [JFP]

20.767 David Friedman. *Florentine new towns: urban design in the late Middle Ages.* New York and Cambridge, Mass.: Architectural History Foundation and MIT Press, 1988. (Architectural History Foundation books, 12.) ISBN 0-262-06113-9. ▸ Clearly written examination of new towns of Florentine *contado* (region), 1250–1350. Describes balance between idealism and pragmatic local interests reflecting city's own internal conflicts. Interdisciplinary methodology. [JFP]

20.768 Alberto García Ulecia. *Los factores de diferenciación entre las personas en los fueros de la Extremadura castellano-aragonesa.* Seville: Publicaciones de la Universidad de Sevilla, 1975. (Anales de la Universidad Hispalense, Serie Derecho, 26.) ISBN 84-600-6644-4. ▸ Study of class relationships in Castilian municipalities and attached territories, eleventh through thirteenth centuries. Finds class differences based on gender, family, office, residence, and property. [JFP]

20.769 Richard A. Goldthwaite. *The building of Renaissance Florence: an economic and social history.* 1980 ed. Baltimore: Johns Hopkins University Press, 1990. ISBN 0-8018-2977-1 (pbk). ▸ Study of Florentine architecture and social structure that sustained it in fifteenth century. Good on building industry and architectural style, but concept of wealth distribution countered by other scholars. [JFP]

20.770 Julio González. *Repartimiento de Sevilla.* 2 vols. Madrid: Consejo Superior de Investigaciones Científicas, Escuela de Estudios Medievales, 1951. (Textos, 15–16.) ▸ Study of repopulating Seville in mid-thirteenth century showing how colonists reshaped Muslim city. Pattern of repopulation repeated elsewhere. Many documents printed in full. [JFP]

20.771 Julio González. *Repoblación de Castilla la Nueva.* 2 vols. Madrid: Universidad Complutense, Facultad de Filosofía y Letras, 1975–76. ▸ Study of advancing frontier and population resettlement in León-Castile, eleventh to thirteenth century. Discusses military role of towns in territorial expansion. Volume 1, narrative; volume 2, methodology. [JFP]

20.772 Angel González Palencia. *Los mozárabes de Toledo en los siglos XII y XIII.* 4 vols. Madrid: Instituto de Valencia de Don Juan, 1926–30. ▸ Classic study of Christian minority living in Muslim-occupied Toledo, before and after Christian conquest of 1085. Played crucial role in mediating among cultures. Dated social history but still valuable. Includes translated documents. [JFP]

20.773 Louis Green. *Chronicle into history: an essay on the interpretation of history in Florentine fourteenth-century chronicles.* Cambridge: Cambridge University Press, 1972. ISBN 0-521-08517-9. ▸ Analysis of tradition and innovation in writings of Giovanni and Matteo Villani and Goro Dati placed in larger context of Renaissance ideas. Sees movement from emphasis on divine justice to workings of fortune. [FLC]

20.774 Jacques Heers. *Gênes au quinzième siècle: activité économique et problèmes sociaux.* Paris: Service d'Édition et de Vente des Publications de l'Education, 1961. ▸ Survey of Genoa's busi-

ness, commercial, and social life focusing on 1440–60. Stronger on large-scale economic organization than individual craft workers. [JFP]

20.775 Jacques Heers, ed. *Fortifications, portes de villes, places publiques, dans le monde méditerranéen.* Paris: Presses de l'Université de Paris-Sorbonne, 1985. ▸ Conference papers on urban fortifications and impact on municipal spaces, mainly focusing on thirteenth to fifteenth centuries, in both Muslim and Christian Mediterranean. [JFP]

20.776 Etienne Hubert. *Espace urbain et habitat à Rome du dixième siècle à la fin du treizième siècle.* Rome: Istituto Storico Italiano per il Medio Evo and École Française de Rome, 1990. (Nuovi studi storici, 7. Collection de l'École Française de Rome, 135.) ▸ Study of development of urban space, streets, domestic architecture and interior space, property rights, and social organization of urban space. Archival supplement to Brentano's imaginative reconstruction (20.753). [FLC]

20.777 Diane Owen Hughes. "Sumptuary law and social relations in Renaissance Italy." In *Disputes and settlements: law and human relations in the West.* John Bossy, ed., pp. 69–100. Cambridge: Cambridge University Press, 1983. ISBN 0-521-25283-0. ▸ Examines laws against excess in women's dress (seeing them as metaphors for social distinctions) which attacked splendor that disrupted social order. Italian laws less hierarchical, more antifeminist than those of Northern Europe. [FLC]

20.778 Benjamin Z. Kedar. *Merchants in crisis: Genoese and Venetian men of affairs and the fourteenth-century depression.* New Haven: Yale University Press, 1976. ISBN 0-300-01941-6. ▸ Novel attempt to measure mood and mentality on basis of changes in contract formulae, names of persons and ships, and chronicles. Set against measurement of business difficulties. [FLC]

20.779 Francis William Kent and Patricia Simon, eds. *Patronage, art, and society in Renaissance Italy.* Canberra and New York: Humanities Research Centre Australia and Oxford University Press, 1987. ISBN 0-19-821978-4. ▸ Conference papers distinguish political clientelism from art patronage, then show overlap. Anthropological perspective in introductory essays by editors and those of Weissman and Lytle. Local studies cover fourteenth to fifteenth century. Important, fresh views. [FLC]

20.780 David I. Kertzer and Richard P. Saller, eds. *The family in Italy from antiquity to the present.* New Haven: Yale University Press, 1991. ISBN 0-300-05037-2. ▸ Includes articles on medieval ideas about procreation and kinship; Christian legal and moral guides to sexuality; kinship and politics; and adultery law. [FLC]

20.781 Julius Kirschner. *Pursuing honor while avoiding sin: the "Monte delle Doti" of Florence.* Milan: Giuffre, 1978. ▸ Discusses development of dowry fund, its operations and fiscal troubles after 1452; problematic moral status. For related study see Kirschner and Molho 20.782. [FLC]

20.782 Julius Kirschner and Anthony Molho. "The dowry fund and the marriage market." *Journal of modern history* 50 (1978) 403–38. ISSN 0022-2801. ▸ Preliminary quantitative analysis of records from Florentine dowry fund. Results used in Kirschner 20.781. [FLC]

20.783 Thomas Kuehn. "Some ambiguities of female inheritance ideology in the Renaissance." *Continuity and change* 2 (1987) 11–36. ISSN 0268-4160. ▸ Complex, theoretically innovative study. Denies clear dichotomy between male and female senses of kinship. Shows agnation sometimes dysfunctional for patrilines. Example of rule complexity and ambiguity that framed but did not limit family strategies. [FLC]

20.784 José María Lacarra. *El desarrollo urbano de las ciudades de Navarra y Aragon en la Edad Media.* Zaragoza: Consejo Superior de Investigaciones Científicas, Instituto de Estudios Pirenaicos,

1950. (Publicaciones del Instituto de Estudios Piernaicos, Historia, 17.2.) ‣ Overview of emergence of towns in two northern kingdoms of Spain during eleventh and twelfth centuries, by preeminent historian of medieval Aragon. Focuses on influence of warfare and pilgrimage routes. [JFP]

20.785 Miguel Angel Ladero Quesada. *La ciudad medieval, 1248–1492.* Vol. 2 of *Historia de Sevilla.* 2d rev. ed. F. Morales Padrón, ed. Seville: Secretariado de Publicaciones de la Universidad de Sevilla, 1980. (Publicaciones de la Universidad de Sevilla, Coleccion de bolsillo, 49). ISBN 84-7405-163-0 (v. 2). ‣ Study of economic and social life of city from Christian occupation to conquest of Granada. Treats Christian colonization, evolution of class structures, and changes in urban topography. [JFP]

20.786 Robert S. Lopez. *Genova marinara nel duecento: Benedetto Zaccaria, ammiraglio e mercante.* Milan: Principato, 1933. ‣ Classic account of Genoese admiral and merchant in age of Byzantine restoration (1260–1310), active from Cyclades to Castile, who combined commerce with piracy and conquest. Represents Genoese activity in person of renowned individual. [JFP]

20.787 Robert S. Lopez. *Su e giù per la storia di Genova.* Genoa: Università di Genova, Istituto di Paleografia e Storia Medievale, 1975. (Collana storica di fonti e studi, 20.) ‣ Collection of articles in French, English, and Italian devoted primarily to Genoa and its East and West trade relationships in thirteenth and fourteenth centuries. [JFP]

20.788 Antonio Henrique R. de Oliveira Marques. *Daily life in Portugal in the late Middle Ages.* S. S. Wyatt, trans. Madison: University of Wisconsin Press, 1971. ISBN 0-299-05580-9. ‣ Introduction to late medieval Portuguese social history, much pertaining to towns. Interdisciplinary use of legal, narrative, literary, and artistic sources. Many instructive contemporary illustrations. Translation of *A sociedade medieval portuguesa* (1964). [JFP]

20.789 Maureen Fennell Mazzaoui. *The Italian cotton industry in the later Middle Ages, 1100–1600.* Cambridge: Cambridge University Press, 1981. ISBN 0-521-23095-0. ‣ Description of Italy's pivotal role as bridge between Islam and West. Discusses trade on Mediterranean, spread of cotton manufacture in twelfth century, and technological innovation to allow mass production, marketing, and international trade. [FLC]

20.790 Salvador de Moxó. *Repoblación y sociedad en la España cristiana medieval.* Madrid: Rialp, 1979. ISBN 84-321-1983-0. ‣ Thorough overview of Christian occupation of Castile and Aragon, 800–1350. Discusses impact of settlement, nature of frontier towns, their expropriation of countryside, and impact of reconquest on urban population. [JFP]

20.791 Lynn H. Nelson. "The foundation of Jaca (1076): urban growth in early Aragon." *Speculum* 53.4 (1978) 688–708. ISSN 0038-7134. ‣ Careful study of early growth of nascent capital of Aragon, based on extensive liberties in its 1076 *fuero* (town code). Describes interaction of royal and ecclesiastical policy, and importance of pilgrimage route. [JFP]

20.792 Leah Lydia Otis. *Prostitution in medieval society: the history of an urban institution in Languedoc.* Chicago: University of Chicago Press, 1985. ISBN 0-226-64032-9 (cl), 0-226-64033-7 (pbk). ‣ Narrates how thirteenth-century tolerance turned into later medieval regulation: creation of official red-light districts and municipally owned brothels. Discusses origins and status of "public women" and legal organization of trade. [FLC]

20.793 Jean Passini. *Villes médiévales du chemin de Saint-Jacques-de-Compostelle: de Pampelune à Burgos; villes de fondation et villes d'origine romaine.* Paris: Éditions Recherche sur les Civilisations, 1984. (Mémoire, 47.) ISBN 2-86538-115-3. ‣ Survey of urban development along pilgrimage route to Santiago de Compostela

in Navarre and eastern Castile. Special attention to ecclesiastical structures. Many maps, charts, and plates. [JFP]

20.794 Carmela Pescador. "La caballería popular en León y Castilla." *Cuadernos de historia de España* 33–34, 35–36, 37–38, 39–40 (1961, 1962, 1963, 1964) 101–238, 56–201, 88–198, 169–260. ISSN 0325-1195. ‣ Extended discussion of lower order of knights, major participants in Castilian *Reconquista.* Important for urban history and characteristic military structures of Castile. [PHF/JFP]

20.795 James F. Powers. "Frontier municipal baths and social interaction in thirteenth-century Spain." *American historical review* 84.3 (1979) 649–67. ISSN 0002-8762. ‣ Examination of social problems created by mixed use of municipal bath houses by men and women, Christians, Muslims, and Jews in newly conquered towns of Hispanic frontier. Studies impact of segregation. [JFP]

20.796 James F. Powers. *A society organized for war: the Iberian municipal militias in the central Middle Ages, 1000–1284.* Berkeley: University of California Press, 1988. ISBN 0-520- 05644-2. ‣ Description of evolution of municipal armies, beginning with military role of towns on frontier of Iberian Christian kingdoms. Emphasizes impact on urban societies and economies. [JFP]

20.797 Yves Renouard. *Les hommes d'affaires italiens du moyen âge.* 1968 rev. ed. Bernard Guillemain, ed. Paris: Colin, 1972. ‣ Attention primarily on commercial institutions: family companies, partnerships, companies with branch offices, and banking, 500–1500. Focus primarily on Venice, Genoa, and Florence. Classic summary of half-century of scholarship. [FLC]

20.798 Kathryn L. Reyerson. *Business, banking, and finance in medieval Montpellier.* Toronto: Pontifical Institute of Mediaeval Studies, 1985. (Studies and texts, 75.) ISBN 0-88844-075-8 (pbk). ‣ Study of financial techniques and credit before 1350. Treats business partnerships, loans, deposit banking, foreign exchange, and activities of merchants, artisans, and peasants. Based on notarial archives. [FLC]

20.799 Dennis Romano. *Patricians and popolani: the social foundations of the Venetian Renaissance state.* Baltimore: Johns Hopkins University Press, 1987. ISBN 0-8018-3513-5. ‣ Explores sense of community and presence of conflict through private lives and personal associations. Views city as network of kinship, artisanal, religious, and patron-client networks that prevented easy division into status and economic groups. [FLC]

20.800 Adeline Rucquoi. *Valladolid en la Edad Media.* 2 vols. Valladolid: Junta de Castilla y León, Consejería de Educación y Cultura, 1987. ISBN 84-505-5564-7 (set), 84-505-5563-9 (v. 1), 84-505-5565-5 (v. 2). ‣ Focuses on city's maturity and subsequent decline as royal center under Trastámara dynasty. Discusses growing dominance of royal officialdom, landed aristocracy, and church disruption of socioeconomic balance of earlier system. Creative scholarship. [JFP]

20.801 Teofilo F. Ruiz. *Sociedad y poder real en Castilla (Burgos en la baja Edad Media).* Barcelona: Ariel, 1981. ISBN 84-344-0812-0. ‣ Examination of town's social and economic evolution in wake of conquest of Seville, 1248–1350. Consolidation of power by municipal knightly class, who, with church and king, sought to exploit countryside. [JFP]

20.802 Rafael Sánchez Saus. *Caballeria y linaje en la Sevilla medieval: estudio genealógico y social.* Cádiz: Servicio de Publicaciones, Universidad de Cádiz, 1989. ISBN 8-4779-8022-5 (cl), 8-4778-6976-6 (pbk). ‣ Exhaustive genealogical investigation of twenty-five families of Seville. Revisionist thesis. Concludes urban elites adopted family structure and lineage patterns of nobility; finds boundaries between urban and rural elites fluid. [PHF]

20.803 Armando Sapori. *The Italian merchant in the Middle Ages.* Patricia Ann Kennen, trans. New York: Norton, 1970. ISBN 0-393-05417-9. ‣ Masterly synopsis of lifetime of study, written for beginner. Describes merchant at work, solidarity abroad, religion, culture, development of contracts, and accounting. For notes and bibliography, consult original French edition: *Le marchand italien au moyen âge* (1952). [FLC]

20.804 Armando Sapori. *Studi di storia economica: secoli XIII, XIV, XV.* 1955–67 3d ed. 3 vols. Florence: Sansoni, 1982–. ‣ Collected shorter studies by leading Italian specialist of first half of century. Studies on money lending, real estate, international commerce, and major merchant banks of thirteenth and fourteenth centuries, principally in Florence. [FLC]

20.805 Randolph Starn. *Contrary commonwealth: the theme of exile in medieval and Renaissance Italy.* Berkeley: University of California Press, 1982. ISBN 0-520-04615-3. ‣ Discussion of reasons for exile. Examines exiles' legal status, strategies, organizations, and voice in poetry, letters, and fiction. Traces emergence of concentrated urban political power conjoined with atomized individual self-interest. New-style cultural history. [FLC]

20.806 Louis Stouff. *Arles à la fin du moyen âge.* 2 vols. Aix-en-Provence and Lille: Université de Provence and Atelier National Reproduction des Thèses, Université de Lille III, 1986. ISBN 2-85399-122-9. ‣ Social and economic history of city, focusing primarily on thirteenth and fourteenth centuries. Special attention to exploitation of countryside by city. [JFP]

20.807 Louis Stouff. *Ravitaillement et alimentation en Provence aux quatorzième et quinzième siècles.* Paris: Mouton, 1970. ‣ Investigation of Provençal food supply, 1300–1500. Demonstrates consumption, especially of meat, at near-present levels. Insightful discussion of connections of rural to urban economies with special attention to transport. [JFP]

20.808 Luis G. de Valdeavellano. *Orígenes de la burguesía en la España medieval.* 4th ed. José Manuel Perez-Prendes y Munoz de Arraco, ed. Madrid: Espasa-Calpe, 1991. ‣ Valuable overview of theories about origins of northern Castilian urbanization and commercial class. Emphasis on pilgrimage road to Santiago de Compostela and on fortress theory of town origins. [JFP]

SEE ALSO

28.99 David Herlihy. *Medieval and Renaissance Pistoia.*
28.100 David Herlihy and Christiane Klapisch-Zuber. *Tuscans and their families.*
28.114 Frederic C. Lane. *Venice.*
28.129 Lauro Martines, ed. *Violence and civil disorder in Italian cities, 1200–1500.*
28.138 Frederic C. Lane. *Andrea Barbarigo.*
28.153 Richard C. Trexler. *Public life in Renaissance Florence.*
29.33 John Edwards. *Christian Córdoba.*

Lordship, Nobility, and Other Elites

20.809 Martin Aurell. *Une famille de la noblesse provençale au moyen âge: les Porcelet.* Avignon: Aubanel, 1986. ISBN 2-7006-0116-5. ‣ Narrates rise and fall of important aristocratic family of Arles between tenth and fourteenth centuries. Describes profits from urban lordship and subsequent decline once Capetian conquest consolidated. [PHF]

20.810 Isabel Beceiro Pita and Ricardo Córdoba de la Llave. *Parentesco, poder y mentalidad: la nobleza castellana siglos XII–XV.* Madrid: Consejo Superior de Investigaciones Científicas, 1990. ISBN 84-00-07066-6. ‣ Discussion of internal structure, mental attitudes, and relation of individual to lineage within noble families. Traces establishment of lineages, triumph of primogeniture, marriage, inheritance, and family sentiment. [PHF]

20.811 Stanley Chojnacki. "In search of the Venetian patriciate: families and faction in the fourteenth century." In *Renaissance Venice.* John R. Hale, ed., pp. 47–90. Totowa, N.J.: Rowman & Littlefield, 1973. ISBN 0-87471-166-5. ‣ Demonstrates fluidity of patrician status in fourteenth century, tracing expansion of class and contrasting situation with more closed group of later centuries. [DJO]

20.812 Congreso de Estudios Medievales (1987: León, Spain). *En torno al feudalismo hispánico: I Congreso de Estudios Medievales.* Avila: Fundación Sánchez Albornoz, 1988. ISBN 84-505-8598-8. ‣ Conference papers forming excellent survey of recent work throughout Iberia. Feudalism here includes resettlement, seigneurial exploitation, warfare, civil order, and habits of thought. [PHF]

20.813 Enrico Fiumi. *Fioritura e decadenza dell'economia fiorentina.* Florence: Olschki, 1977. ‣ Classic discussion of development of Florence in thirteenth century, arguing population growth fueled prosperity until early fourteenth century. Demonstrates fluidity of aristocratic and lower classes. [DJO]

20.814 Richard A. Fletcher. *The quest for El Cid.* 1989 ed. New York: Knopf, 1990. ISBN 0-394-57447-8. ‣ Historical background of El Cid and Christian Spain of early *Reconquista.* Describes way of life and ethos of nobility. Popular history at its best. [PHF]

20.815 Marie-Claude Gerbet. *La noblesse dans le royaume de Castille: étude sur ses structures sociales en Estrémadure de 1454 à 1516.* Paris: Publications de la Sorbonne, 1979. (Publications de la Sorbonne, n.s.: recherches, 32.) ISBN 2-85944-014-3. ‣ Description of late medieval nobility of Estremadura, family structures, alliances, and power. Emphasizes importance of royal favor for families to develop national role. Notes disparity among levels of nobles and between elder and cadet family branches. [PHF]

20.816 Ralph E. Giesey. *If not, not: the oath of the Aragonese and the legendary laws of Sobrabe.* Princeton: Princeton University Press, 1968. ‣ Intricate study of historical myth making and images of kingship and liberty. Aragonese traditions of nobles' autonomy justified by layers of legend, developing primarily fourteenth through sixteenth centuries. [PHF]

20.817 David Herlihy. *Pisa in the early Renaissance: a study of urban growth.* 1958 ed. Port Washington, N.Y.: Kennikat, 1973. ISBN 0-8046-1698-1. ‣ Description of thirteenth-century urbanization emphasizing effects of economic and demographic growth, especially development of livestock raising, on traditional urban and rural social groups. Based on notarial archives. [DJO/JFP]

20.818 Carol Lansing. *The Florentine magnates: lineage and faction in a medieval commune.* Princeton: Princeton University Press, 1991. ISBN 0-691-03154-1. ‣ Focus on thirteenth-century. Shows importance of joint property in towers, palaces, and ecclesiastical rights for noble lineages. Urban origins of many nobles. Discusses role of women, knighthood, violence and factions, and debate over "true nobility." [DJO]

20.819 G. A. Loud. *Church and society in the Norman principality of Capua, 1058–1197.* Oxford: Clarendon, 1985. ISBN 0-19-822931-3. ‣ Argues principality's response to political and religious issues defined by Lombard and Norman families dominating region (on edge of Norman kingdom, close to Rome). Interests of lay and ecclesiastical officials closely intertwined. [DJO]

20.820 Pascual Martínez Sopena. *El estado señorial de Medina de Rioseco bajo el Almirante Alfonso Enriquez (1389–1430).* Valladolid: Universidad de Valladolid, Secretariado de Publicaciones, 1977. ISBN 84-600-0811-8. ‣ Description of development of seigneury in northern Meseta; importance of royal favor in aristocratic aggrandizement under Trastámara dynasty. Effectively depicts connection of state building to private power. [PHF]

20.821 José Mattoso. *Portugal medieval: novas interpretaçoes.* 2d ed. Lisbon: Impresa Nacional-Casa de Moneda, 1992. ISBN 972-27-0511-3. ▸ Collection of essays. Important for understanding status and power of Portuguese nobles, their relation to monastic foundations, formation of seigneuries, and culture. [PHF]

20.822 Ramón Menéndez Pidal. *The Cid and his Spain*. 1934 ed. Harold Sunderland, trans. London: Cass, 1971. ISBN 0-7146-1508-0. ▸ Evocative if not always reliable. Still useful introduction to reconquest, culture, and peculiar conditions of eleventh-century Spain. On historical figure of Cid, see Fletcher 20.814. [PHF]

20.823 Emilio Mitre Fernández. *Evolución de la nobleza en Castilla bajo Enrique III (1396–1406)*. Valladolid: Universidad de Valladolid, Secretariado de Publicaciones, 1968. ▸ Investigation of period of relative peace and effective royal rule marking crucial stage in crystallization of new service nobility. Class would later participate in severe crises following Enrique's death. [PHF]

20.824 Salustiano Moreta Velayos. *Malhechores-feudales: violéncia, antagonismos, y alianzas de clases en Castilla, siglos XIII–XIV*. Madrid: Catedra, 1978. ISBN 84-376-0129-0. ▸ Examination of violence of Castilian nobility in late Middle Ages in terms of economic and ritualized behavior. [PHF]

20.825 Salvador de Moxó. "La nobleza castellano-leonesa en la Edad Media." *Hispania* 114 (1970) 5–68. ISSN 0018-2133. ▸ Description of changes in fourteenth-century nobility in direction of patrimonialization, greater seigneurial exploitation, and displays of power. Contrasts earlier emphasis on military activity and reputation. [PHF]

20.826 Salvador de Moxó. "De la nobleza vieja a la nobleza nueva: la transformación nobiliaria castellana en el siglo XIV." *Cuadernos de historia* 3 (1969) 1–271. ISSN 0590-1928. ▸ Discussion of Castilian Civil War; shifts in aristocratic power; extinction of old families through endogamy, war, and plague; emergence of knightly families allied with Trastámara dynasty; and fourteenth-century zenith of nobles' power. [PHF]

20.827 Donald E. Queller. *The Venetian patriciate: reality versus myth*. Urbana: University of Illinois Press, 1986. ISBN 0-252-01144-9. ▸ Study of Venetian ruling class, ca. 1200–ca. 1500, emphasizing manipulation of friendship, status, and power to evade laws and prosecution. Argues myth of civic harmony in city was self-serving propaganda. Shows many nobles poor. [DJO]

20.828 Martin Riquer. *Caballeros andantes españoles*. Madrid: Espasa-Calpe, 1967. ▸ Brief, authoritative discussion of waning of Spanish Middle Ages. Treats life, culture, ceremony, and ethos of Iberian nobility as reflected in literature and history. [PHF]

20.829 J. E. Ruiz Doménec. "Système de parenté et théorie d'alliance dans la société catalane (env. 1000–env. 1240)." *Revue historique* 262 (1979) 305–25. ISSN 0035-3264. ▸ Anthropological approach to history of Catalan nobility, based on theoretical and comparative literature. Develops paradigm of family alliances, showing socioeconomic ramifications, strategies, and persistence over time. [PHF]

20.830 John C. Shideler. *A medieval Catalan noble family: the Montcadas, 1000–1230*. Berkeley: University of California Press, 1983. (Publications of the Center for Medieval and Renaissance Studies, University of California at Los Angeles, 20.) ISBN 0-520-04578-5. ▸ Narrates emergence of minor castle-holding family to prominence as royal seneschals. Important case study of aristocratic strategies for advancement and of power of lineage through female line. [PHF]

20.831 Santiago Sobrequés Vidal. *Els barons de Catalunya*. 4th ed. Barcelona: Vicens-Vives, 1980. ISBN 84-316-1806-X. ▸ Important investigation of noble families in Catalonia (for which considerably less work exists than for Castile). Strongest on late Mid-

dle Ages. For Montcada family, superseded by Shideler 20.830. [PHF]

20.832 Santiago Sobrequés Vidal. "La nobleza catalana en el siglo XIV." *Anuario de estudios medievales* 7 (1970–71) 513–31. ISSN 0066-5061. ▸ Emphasizes divisions between lower donzells (drawn from townsmen, even wealthy peasants) and grandees who dominated over one-third of territory and constituted parliamentary opposition to kings. [PHF]

20.833 Luis Suárez Fernández. *Nobleza y monarquía: puntos de vista sobre la historia política castellana del siglo XV*. 2d ed. Valladolid: Universidad de Valladolid, Facultad de Filosofia y Letras, Departamento de Historia Medieval, 1975. (Estudios y documentos, 15.) ISBN 84-600-1777-X. ▸ Description of aristocratic domination of Castile between civil wars of 1368 and 1474. While monarchy survived and was restored, period originated long-term seigneurialization of royal revenues. [PHF]

20.834 Pierre Toubert. *Les structures du Latium médiéval: le Latium méridional et la Sabine du neuvième siècle à la fin du douzième siècle*. 2 vols. Ottorino Bertolini, Preface. Rome: École Française de Rome, 1973. (Bibliotheque des Écoles Française d'Athens et de Rome, 221.) ▸ Classic regional study tracing regrouping of rural population in fortified hilltop villages. Argues process motivated by considerations of production and power rather than defense from foreign invaders. [DJO]

20.835 Stephen Weinberger. "Aristocratic families and social stability in eleventh-century Provence." *Journal of medieval history* 8.5 (1982) 149–57. ISSN 0304-4181. ▸ Argues aristocratic families disrupted eleventh-century society, but also solidified it by stabilizing family structure, property transfers, and by interest in maintaining civil order. [PHF]

20.836 Stephen Weinberger. "Nobles et noblesse dans la Provence médiévale (ca. 850–1100)." *Annales* 36 (1981) 913–21. ISSN 0395-2649. ▸ Meaning of "noble" and "nobility" in Provence depended on personal characteristics as well as lineage and military or governmental role. Character (and ultimately chivalry) emphasized by monastic chroniclers. [PHF]

Latin East

20.837 Michel Balard. *La Romanie gênoise: douzième–début du quinzième siècle*. 2 vols. Rome: École Française de Rome, 1978. (Atti della Societa ligure di storia patria, Nuova serie, 18 (92), 1. Bibliothèque des Écoles Française d'Athènes et de Rome, 235.) ▸ Monumental study of Genoese politics and colonization in eastern Mediterranean, 1204–1409: Pera, Caffa, Chios, Black Sea. Detailed description of colonial society and economy based on notarial records. [FLC]

20.838 Meron Benvenisti. *The Crusaders in the Holy Land*. 1970 ed. New York: Macmillan, 1972. ▸ Survey of surviving secular and ecclesiastical buildings of Latin settlers in "Israeli" Palestine. Draws attention to wealth of agricultural remains, including farms, mills, sugar and olive presses, stables, and aqueducts. [JSCRS]

20.839 Paul Deschamps. *Les châteaux des croisés en Terre-Sainte*. 3 vols. René Dussand, Preface. Paris: Geuthner, 1934–77. ▸ First volume describes Crac des Chevaliers; second and third survey castles in kingdom of Jerusalem, county of Tripoli, and principality of Antioch. Standard work on Crusader castles; now rather dated. [JSCRS]

20.840 Peter W. Edbury. *The kingdom of Cyprus and the Crusades, 1191–1374*. Cambridge: Cambridge University Press, 1991. ISBN 0-521-26876-1. ▸ Political history covering first two centuries of kingdom's existence. Brings study of Cypriot politics into line with research concerning other Crusader states of eastern Mediterranean. [JSCRS]

20.841 Peter W. Edbury and John Gordon Rowe. *William of Tyre: historian of the Latin East.* Cambridge: Cambridge University Press, 1988. ISBN 0-521-26766-8. ▸ Review of William of Tyre's life and work, examining especially his approach to writing of history. [JSCRS]

20.842 Bernard Hamilton. *The Latin church in the Crusader states: the secular church.* London: Variorum, 1980. ISBN 0-86078-072-4. ▸ Describes relations of Latin church with Eastern churches in patriarchates of Antioch and Jerusalem. Does not cover monastic or religious communities. [JSCRS]

20.843 David Jacoby. *La féodalité en Grèce médiévale: les "Assises de Romanie"; sources, application, et diffusion.* Paris: Mouton, 1971. (École Pratique des Hautes Études, 6 section: documents et recherches sur l'économie des pays Byzantins, Islamiques et Slaves et leurs relations commerciales au moyen âge, 10.) ▸ Analysis of laws of Latin settlers in southern Greece and Aegean. Brings constitutional history of Latin Greece into line with that of Jerusalem. [JSCRS]

20.844 David Jacoby. *Studies on the Crusader states and on Venetian expansion.* Northampton, England: Variorum, 1989. ISBN 0-86078-249-2. ▸ Collected articles. Particularly important for cultural and commercial history, and for topography of Acre. [JSCRS]

20.845 Michael A. Köhler. *Allianzen und Verträge zwischen fränkischen und islamischen Herrschern im vorderen Orient: eine Studie über das zwischenstaatliche Zusammenleben vom zwölften bis ins dreizehnten Jahrhundert.* Berlin: de Gruyter, 1991. ISBN 3-11-011959-5. ▸ Concentrates on Christian-Muslim treaties in twelfth century. Argues Islamic forms, based on eleventh-century commercial agreements, predominate. Pleads for integrated history of region. [JSCRS]

20.846 Ralph-Johannes Lilie. *Byzanz und die Kreuzfahrerstaaten: Studien zur Politik des byzantinischen Reiches gegenüber den Staaten der Kreuzfahrer in Syrien und Palästina bis zum Vierten Kreuzzug (1096–1204).* Munich: Fink, 1981. ISBN 3-7705-2042-4. ▸ Study of relations between Byzantine empire and Crusaders and Crusader states of Latin East in context of Mediterranean politics. Less Greek-centered than most histories. [JSCRS]

20.847 Anthony Luttrell. *The Hospitallers in Cyprus, Rhodes, Greece, and the West (1291–1440): collected studies.* London: Variorum, 1978. ISBN 0-86078-022-8. ▸ Collected articles, mainly on Hospitallers on Rhodes and in West. Best guide to Hospitaller occupation of Rhodes. [JSCRS]

20.848 Anthony Luttrell. *The Hospitallers of Rhodes and their Mediterranean world.* Aldershot, England: Variorum Ashgate, 1992. ISBN 0-86078-307-3. ▸ Further studies of Hospitallers role in later Crusades and in West. [JSCRS]

20.849 Amin Maalouf. *The Crusades through Arab eyes.* 1984 ed. Jon Rothschild, trans. New York: Schocken, 1989. ISBN 0-8052-0898-4 (cl), 0-8052-0833-X (pbk). ▸ Popular account of Crusades in East to 1291. Conventional history from Muslim point of view. [JSCRS]

20.850 Christopher Marshall. *Warfare in the Latin East, 1192–1291.* Cambridge: Cambridge University Press, 1992. ISBN 0-521-39428-7. ▸ Description of thirteenth-century warfare in Palestine, Syria, and Cyprus. Takes over where Smail 20.862 left off. Points to overriding factor of manpower shortage on Christian side. [JSCRS]

20.851 Hans Eberhard Mayer. *Bistümer, Klöster, und Stifte im Königreich Jerusalem.* Stuttgart: Hiersemann, 1977. (Schriften der Monumenta Germaniae Historica, Deutsches Institut für Erforschung des Mittelalters, 26.) ISBN 3-7772-7719-3. ▸ Study of bishoprics and religious communities in kingdom of Jerusalem. Unrivaled knowledge of documentary material. [JSCRS]

20.852 Hans Eberhard Mayer. *Probleme des lateinischen Königreichs Jerusalem.* London: Variorum, 1983. ISBN 0-86078-126-7. ▸ Selected articles on kingship and lordship in Latin East. Marks change in approach from broad constitutional history to detailed studies of workings of government at all levels in Latin Palestine. [JSCRS]

20.853 Hans Eberhard Mayer. "The wheel of fortune: seignorial vicissitudes under kings Fulk and Baldwin III of Jerusalem." *Speculum* 65 (1990) 860–77. ISSN 0038-7134. ▸ Genealogical study of Brisebarre family, lords of Beirut, revealing new evidence on royal policy. Typical revisionist work by leading historian of kingdom of Jerusalem. [JSCRS]

20.854 Joshua Prawer. *Crusader institutions.* Oxford: Clarendon, 1980. ISBN 0-19-822536-9. ▸ Collected studies on government, law, society, and economy. Author, with Richard 20.858, renewed historiography of kingdom of Jerusalem. Influential approach now being revised by Mayer 20.851, 20.852, 20.853. [JSCRS]

20.855 Joshua Prawer. *The Latin kingdom of Jerusalem: European colonialism in the Middle Ages.* London: Weidenfeld & Nicolson, 1972. ISBN 0-297-99397-6. ▸ Concentrates on government and society. Argues Jerusalem a European colony. Controversial, but widely accepted by Israeli scholars. [JSCRS]

20.856 Denys Pringle. *The red tower (al-Burj al-Ahmar): settlement in the plain of Sharon at the time of the Crusaders and Mamluks, A.D. 1099–1516.* London: British School of Archaeology in Jerusalem, 1986. (British School of Archaeology in Jerusalem, Monograph series, 1.) ISBN 0-9500542-6-7 (pbk). ▸ Excavation report. New approach to archaeology of Crusader East, here studying castle in context of its environment. [JSCRS]

20.857 Jean Richard. *The Latin kingdom of Jerusalem.* 2 vols. Janet Shirley, trans. Amsterdam: North-Holland; distributed by Elsevier North-Holland, 1979. ISBN 0-444-85092-9 (v. 1), 0-444-85262-X (v. 2). ▸ Best general introductory history of kingdom. Author, with Prawer 20.855, shaped modern scholarly approach to Latin Jerusalem. Translation of *Le royaume latin de Jerusalem* (1953). [JSCRS]

20.858 Jean Richard. *Orient et Occident au moyen âge: contacts et relations (XIIe–XVe siècles).* London: Variorum, 1976. ISBN 0-902089-93-5. ▸ Thirty-one articles on crusading, Latin East, and missions, including some studies of 1950s that began to revise history of Latin Kingdom of Jerusalem. [JSCRS]

20.859 Jonathan Riley-Smith. *The feudal nobility and the kingdom of Jerusalem, 1174–1277.* Hamden, Conn.: Archon, 1973. ISBN 0-208-01348-2. ▸ Narrates struggle between crown and nobility and emergence of school of noble jurists in thirteenth century. Constitutional history in mold established by Richard 20.858 and Prawer 20.855. [JSCRS]

20.860 Jonathan Riley-Smith. *The Knights of St. John in Jerusalem and Cyprus, c. 1050–1310.* London and New York: Macmillan and St. Martin's, 1967. ▸ General history ending with capture of Rhodes. Emphasis on Order of the Hospital as religious institution in Latin East. Topics include organization, privileges, economic activity, and lordships. [JSCRS/KP]

20.861 Emmanuel Sivan. *L'Islam et la croisade: idéologie et propagande dans les réactions musulmanes aux croisades.* Paris: Maissonneuve, 1968. ▸ Muslim attitudes to Crusades and Latin settlement of Levantine coastline. Examines Muslim concepts and reemergence of *jihad* (holy war). [JSCRS]

20.862 R. C. Smail. *Crusading warfare, 1097–1193.* 1956 ed. Cambridge: Cambridge University Press, 1989. ISBN 0-521-09730-4 (pbk). ▸ Survey of armies, castles, and tactics employed by all sides in warfare in Latin East. Classic study. For sequel, see Marshall 20.850. [JSCRS]

20.863 Freddy E. Thiriet. *La Romanie vénitienne au moyen âge: le développement et l'exploitation du domaine colonial vénitien (XIIIe–XVe siècles).* 1959 ed. Paris: de Boccard, 1975. (Bibliothèque des Écoles Française d'Athènes et de Rome, 193.) ▸ Political history of Venice in Byzantine world. Discusses creation of "empire," origins of colonies, commerce, defense, finance, and first contact with Ottomans. Based on Venetian archives. [FLC]

20.864 Steven Tibble. *Monarchy and lordships in the Latin kingdom of Jerusalem, 1099–1291.* Oxford: Clarendon, 1989. ISBN 0-19-822731-0. ▸ Shows royal manipulation of feudal structures and resources at disposal of magnates. Demonstrates weakness of lords by later twelfth century. [JSCRS]

SEE ALSO
17.250 Joshua Prawer. *The history of the Jews in the Latin kingdom of Jerusalem.*

POLITICS AND GOVERNMENT
Italy

20.865 Sarah Rubin Blanshei. "Crime and law enforcement in medieval Bologna." *Journal of social history* 16 (1982) 121–38. ISSN 0022-4529. ▸ Traces uneven transition from vendetta and payment of composition to harsher, depersonalized, public-oriented conception of crime. Linked to changes in city's politics and growing factionalism. Rare study, in English, of medieval criminal law outside of England. [FLC]

20.866 William M. Bowsky. *A medieval Italian commune: Siena under the Nine, 1287–1355.* Berkeley: University of California Press, 1981. ISBN 0-520-04256-5. ▸ Study of rule of banking-merchant oligarchy who controlled city with help of magnate class. Emphasizes civic pride and economic restraint. Clearest description in English of functioning of Italian urban government ca. 1300. [DJO/JFP]

20.867 O. Capitani, G. Galasso, and R. Salvini. *The Normans in Sicily and southern Italy.* Oxford: Oxford University Press for British Academy, 1977. ISBN 0-19-725865-0. ▸ Essays on impact of Norman migration and conquest, emphasizing social and political diversity of South before arrival of Normans. Other topics include chronicles and architecture. [DJO]

20.868 Giorgio Chittolini. *La formazione dello Stato regionale e le istituzioni del contado: secoli XIV e XV.* Turin: Einaudi, 1979. ▸ Examination of emergence of regionalism in Italy, 1300–1500, through city rule of *contado* (smaller towns, rural lords, and countryside around it); concentrates on Lombardy and Tuscany. Interesting description of rural and aristocratic measures to counter urban encroachment. [JFP]

20.869 Eugene L. Cox. *The eagles of Savoy: the House of Savoy in thirteenth-century Europe.* Princeton: Princeton University Press, 1974. ISBN 0-691-05216-6. ▸ Study of family that came to rule Piedmont, following diplomatic and marital connections throughout Italy and rest of Europe. Pedestrian but thorough. [DJO]

20.870 George W. Dameron. *Episcopal power and Florentine society, 1000–1320.* Cambridge, Mass.: Harvard University Press, 1991. ISBN 0-674-25891-6. ▸ Investigation of political role of Florentine bishops, describing importance of episcopal lands and offices to magnate families who were competing for influence in communal government. [DJO]

20.871 Gerald W. Day. *Genoa's response to Byzantium, 1155–1204: commercial expansion and factionalism in a medieval city.* Urbana: University of Illinois Press, 1988. ISBN 0-252-01496-0. ▸ Study of privileges granted to Genoese aristocratic merchants, rivalry with Venice, and alliance with marquis of Montferrat. Connects Byzantine trade to developing factionalism in city. Per-

ceptive views of differences in political culture East and West. [FLC]

20.872 Trevor Dean. *Land and power in late medieval Ferrara: the rule of the Este, 1350–1450.* Cambridge: Cambridge University Press, 1988. ISBN 0-521-33127-7. ▸ Studies feudal society—reemergence of fief and its obligations—in d'Este patrimony, including vassals, legal relationships, new families and old, and the transformation of territorial nobility. Corrects exclusively urban vision of late medieval–Renaissance Italy. [FLC]

20.873 Marie-Luise Favreau-Lilie. *Die Italiener im Heiligen Land vom ersten Kreuzzug bis zum Tode Heinrichs von Champagne (1098–1197).* Amsterdam: Hakkert, 1989. ISBN 90-256-0953-8. ▸ Description of relations of Venice, Genoa, and Pisa with Latin rulers in Syria and Palestine and cities' privileges. Fullest account to date. [JSCRS]

20.874 Louis Green. *Castruccio Castracani: a study on the origins and character of a fourteenth-century Italian despotism.* Oxford: Clarendon, 1986. ISBN 0-19-821992-X. ▸ Biography of famous despot of early fourteenth century. Emphasizes state of war in Lombardy and Flanders as training ground for military adventurers. [DJO]

20.875 Jacques Heers. *Family clans in the Middle Ages: a study of political and social structures in urban areas.* Barry Herbert, trans. Amsterdam: North-Holland; distributed by Elsevier North-Holland, 1977. ISBN 0-7204-9009-X. ▸ Seminal study of kinship lines and clienteles and their control of towns and surrounding countryside. Concerned mainly with Italy; less material from Germany and France. Translation often faulty. Translation of *Le clan familial au moyen âge* (1974). [JFP]

20.876 Norman Housley. *The Italian Crusades: the papal-Angevin alliance and the Crusades against Christian lay powers, 1254–1343.* Oxford: Clarendon, 1982. ISBN 0-19-821925-3. ▸ Description of "political" Crusades in Italy, demonstrating how these Crusades can be treated in conventional terms, as equivalents to Crusades in Holy Land. [JSCRS]

20.877 J. K. Hyde. *Padua in the age of Dante.* Manchester and New York: Manchester University Press and Barnes & Noble, 1966. ▸ Shows protohumanist leaders succumbing to class interests as republicanism declined. Emphasizes dominance of jurists and fluidity of social groups. Discusses communal offices. Difficult reading. [DJO/JFP]

20.878 J. K. Hyde. *Society and politics in medieval Italy: the evolution of the civil life, 1000–1350.* New York: St. Martin's, 1973. ▸ Survey of political and social history focusing on formation of autonomous urban governments. Emphasizes creation of ideology of civic life that would be important in Renaissance. Good bibliography. [DJO/JFP]

20.879 Evelyn M. Jamison. *The Norman administration of Apulia and Capua: more especially under Roger II and William I, 1127–1166.* 1913 ed. Dione Clementi and Theo Kölzer, eds. Aalen: Scientia Verlag, 1987. ISBN 3-511-09200-0. ▸ Essential work on politics and administration in Norman kingdom of southern Italy–Sicily. Focuses on political tensions between kings and local nobilities. [DJO]

20.880 Hagen Keller. *Adelsherrschaft und städtische Gesellschaft in Oberitalien, 9.–12. Jahrhundert.* Tübingen: Niemeyer, 1979. ISBN 3-484-80088-7. ▸ Identifies background and interests of upper and lower nobilities—*cattanei* (captains) and *valvassori* (vassals)—and nonnoble townsmen active in early governments in most North Italian towns in central Middle Ages. [DJO]

20.881 John Larner. *Italy in the age of Dante and Petrarch, 1216–1380.* London: Longman, 1980. ISBN 0-582-48366-2. ▸ Political narrative from Frederick II to 1380 followed by chapters on family structures, nobility, party conflict in urban governments, countryside, merchants and workers, and religious life. [DJO]

20.882   Donald Matthew. *The Norman kingdom of Sicily.* Cambridge: Cambridge University Press, 1992. ISBN 0-521-26284-4 (cl), 0-521-26911-3 (pbk). ‣ Most recent survey in English. Emphasizes local interests and papal, Greek, and Muslim challengers as limits on royal power. [DJO]

20.883   John Julius Norwich. *The kingdom in the sun, 1130–1194.* 1970 ed. London: Faber, 1976. ISBN 0-571-10903-9. ‣ Narrative of Hauteville rule in southern Italy until succession of Hohenstaufen. Emphasizes role of family and court in development of region. Popular history. Follows on story told in 20.884. [DJO]

20.884   John Julius Norwich. *The Normans in the South, 1016–1130.* 1967 ed. London: Solitaire, 1981. ISBN 0-907387-00-4. ‣ Narrative of arrival of Normans in southern Italy and first years of Norman kings. Earlier title: *The Other Conquest.* [DJO]

20.885   Peter Partner. *The lands of St. Peter: the Papal State in the Middle Ages and the early Renaissance.* Berkeley: University of California Press, 1972. ISBN 0-520-02181-9. ‣ Political and diplomatic history of papacy and of towns and nobles of central and northern Italy. Focuses on development of papal administration in thirteenth and fourteenth centuries. [DJO/TFXN/KP]

20.886   Reinhold Schumann. *Authority and the commune, Parma, 833–1133 (Impero e comune, Parma, 833–1133).* Parma, Italy: Deputazione di Storia Patria per le Province Parmensi, 1973. (Fonti e studi, 2 serie, 8.) ‣ Description of amalgamation of Lombard and Roman townsmen with grand feudatories to form local governing class. Emphasizes close connections of great rural aristocrats to non-noble townsmen. [DJO]

20.887   Daniel Waley. *The Italian city-republics.* 3d ed. New York: Longman, 1988. ISBN 0-582-55388-1. ‣ Overview of city-states in Italy concentrating on twelfth to fourteenth centuries. Orientation primarily political and institutional. Third edition includes essay on recent historiography. [JFP]

20.888   Daniel Waley. *Mediaeval Orvieto: the political history of an Italian city-state, 1157–1334.* Cambridge: Cambridge University Press, 1952. ‣ Study of small but strategically important town in Papal States, emphasizing dominance of factions formed by local nobility. Discusses Guelf-Ghibelline dispute and rise of despotic government. [DJO/JFP]

20.889   Daniel Waley. *The Papal State in the thirteenth century.* London and New York: Macmillan and St. Martin's, 1961. ‣ History of formation of tightly administered papal government in central Italy, insisting on role of region in papal diplomatic calculations, especially in conflict between pope and emperor. [DJO/KP]

20.890   Daniel Waley. *Siena and the Sienese in the thirteenth century.* Cambridge: Cambridge University Press, 1991. ISBN 0-521-40312-X. ‣ Survey of period 1250–1310, arguing (against Bowsky 20.866) continuity with earlier thirteenth century. Describes natural evolution into era of commercial and oligarchical Nine. Economic, social, and institutional focus. [JFP]

SEE ALSO
   28.10 Hans Baron. *The crisis of the early Italian Renaissance.*
   28.93 Gene A. Brucker. *Renaissance Florence.*
   28.104 Christine Meek. *Lucca, 1369–1400.*

Provence and Occitania

20.891   Ramon d'Abadal i de Vinyals. "A propos de la 'domination' de la maison comtale de Barcelona sur le Midi de la France." *Annales du Midi* 76 (1964) 315–45. ISSN 0003-4398. ‣ Argues Catalan rulers had no consistent policy of expansion in Occitania; from 1082 to 1179 ignored region in favor of New

Catalonia. Only Alfonso I and Peter I had ambitions there. Compare Higounet 20.897. [PHF]

20.892   Martin Aurell. *La vielle et l'épée: troubadours et politique en Provence au treizième siècle.* Paris: Aubier, 1989. ISBN 2-7007-2222-1. ‣ Detailed biographical and ethnographic investigation of troubadours in social-historical context. Argues troubadours reflect ethos of nobility; songs are documents of social as well as political propaganda. [PHF]

20.893   Xavier Barral i Altet et al., eds. *Catalunya i França meridional a l'entorn de l'any mil, Barcelona, 2–5 Juliol 1987/La Catalogne et la France meridionale autour de l'an mil: colloque international Centre National de la Recherche Scientifique, Generalitat de Catalunya Hugues Capet, 987–1987, la France de l'an mil.* Barcelona: Generalitat de Catalunya, Departament de Cultura, 1991. (Colleccio actes de congressos, 2.) ISBN 84-393-1690-9. ‣ Conference papers commemorating coronation of Hugh Capet. Topics include government, settlement patterns, formation of noble classes, and local and regional identity. [PHF]

20.894   Thomas N. Bisson. *Medieval France and her Pyrenean neighbours: studies in early institutional history.* London: Hambledon, 1989. (Studies presented to the International Commission for the History of Representative and Parliamentary Institutions, 70.) ISBN 0-907628-69-9. ‣ Pathbreaking articles on Catalonia, Aragon, Languedoc, representation, feudal monarchy, and coinage. Especially notable: "Feudalism in Twelfth-Century Catalonia," "The Organized Peace," and "The Rise of Catalonia." [PHF/SDW]

20.895   Jacqueline Caille. "Les seigneurs de Narbonne dans le conflit Toulouse-Barcelone au douzième siècle." *Annales du Midi* 97 (1985) 227–44. ISSN 0003-4398. ‣ Description of how rivalry among Toulouse, Barcelona, and Trencavals permitted archbishops and viscounts of Narbonne to profit and build up substantial and virtually independent principality. [PHF]

20.896   James Given. *State and society in medieval Europe: Gwynedd and Languedoc under outside rule.* Ithaca, N.Y.: Cornell University Press, 1990. ISBN 0-8014-2439-9 (cl), 0-8014-9774-4 (pbk). ‣ Story of differing fates of two conquered territories: Languedoc remained autonomous and Gwynedd became colonized. Places fate of both (with difficulty) into comparative state building and post-Marxist theory of state frameworks. [PHF]

20.897   Charles Higounet. "Un grand chapitre de l'histoire du douzième siècle: la rivalité des maisons de Toulouse et de Barcelone pour la prépondérance méridionale." In *Mélanges d'histoire du moyen âge dédiés à la mémoire de Louis Halphen.* Robert-Henri Bautier et al., pp. 313–22. Paris: Presses Universitaires de France, 1951. ‣ Description of twelfth-century ambitions of counts of Barcelona until alliances and ambitions of rival counts of Toulouse destroyed by Albigensian crusades. Compare Abadal i de Vinyals 20.891. [PHF]

20.898   Archibald R. Lewis. "The development of town government in twelfth-century Montpellier." *Speculum* 22.1 (1947) 51–67. ISSN 0038-7134. ‣ Shows role of burghers and emerging guild organizations in reducing power of city's lord and capturing instruments of government, largely accomplished by 1204–1205. [JFP]

20.899   Elisabeth Magnou-Nortier. *La société laïque et l'église dans la province ecclésiastique de Narbonne (zone cispyrénéenne) de la fin du huitième à la fin du onzième siècle.* Toulouse: Association des publications de l'Université de Toulouse-Le Mirail, 1974. (Publications de l'Université de Toulouse-Le Mirail, Serie A, 20.) ‣ Detailed, controversial regional study of lay society and church. Judges pre-Gregorian conditions favorably; reform had disastrous impact. Argues this was largely allodial rather than feudal society. [PHF]

20.900 John H. Mundy. *Liberty and political power in Toulouse, 1050–1230*. New York: Columbia University Press, 1954. ▸ Surveys evolution of municipal consulate and gradual conquest of power from count of Toulouse. Describes social origins of consular families and conquest of countryside by urban militia. Also available from Ann Arbor: University Microfilms International. [JFP]

20.901 Suzanne Nelli. *Les Durfort de Languedoc au moyen âge*. Toulouse: Privat, 1989. ISBN 2-7089-8619-8. ▸ History of noble family established in Visigothic era, its control over numerous castles and baronial jurisdictions, and its eclipse after Albigensian crusade. [PHF]

20.902 Jean-Pierre Poly. *La Provence et la société féodale, 879–1166: contribution à l'étude des structures dites féodales dans le Midi*. Paris: Bordas, 1976. ISBN 2-04-007740-5. ▸ Regional study that shows difficulty fitting Provence into French models of feudalism. Finds break in traditional forms of social organization occurred 1000–1030. [PHF]

20.903 Michel Roquebert. *L'epopée Cathare*. Edition varies. 4 vols. Toulouse: Privat, 1970–90. ISBN 2-7089-2344-7 (v. 2), 2-7089-9036-5 (v. 3), 2-7089-9044-6 (v. 4). ▸ Detailed account of the Albigensian crusade. Treats Catharism in social as well as religious terms. [JSCRS]

20.904 Joseph Reese Strayer. *Les gens de justice du Languedoc sous Philippe le Bel*. Toulouse: Association Marc Bloch, 1970. (Cahiers de l'Association Marc Bloch de Toulouse: études d'historie méridionale, 5.) ▸ Examination of careers of about two hundred lawyers. Concludes Roman law not in itself a contributor to royal centralization, as most Languedocian lawyers did not aspire to royal administrative careers. [PHF]

20.905 Jonathan Sumption. *The Albigensian crusade*. London: Faber, 1978. ISBN 0-571-11064-9. ▸ Detailed, unsentimental account of religious dissent and conquest of Languedoc (1208–29). Emphasizes weakness of Occitan institutions and delineates competing interests seeking to supplant counts of Toulouse. [PHF/KP]

The Spanish Kingdoms

20.906 Ramon d' Abadal i de Vinyals. *Els primers comtes catalans*. 3d ed. Barcelona: Vicens-Vives, 1980. ISBN 84-316-1804-3. ▸ Best account of political formation of Catalan states in post-Carolingian era (despite somewhat anachronistic idea of what constitutes a "nation"). Also describes patterns of resettlement and establishment of monasteries. [PHF]

20.907 Cesar Alvárez Alvárez. *El condado de Luna en la baja edad media*. León, Spain: Colegio Universitario de León, Institución "Fray Bernardino de Sahagùn", C.E.C.E.L, 1982. (Publaciones Colegio Universitario de León, Unidad de Investigación, Serie Filosofia y Letras, 25.) ISBN 84-300-7668-9. ▸ Case study of new noble family allied with Trastámara dynasty. Quiñones family became counts of Luna in 1462. Describes politics, alliances, and estate management. [PHF]

20.908 Antonio Ballesteros Beretta. *Alfonso X el Sabio*. 1963 ed. Barcelona: El Albir, 1984. ISBN 84-7370-069-4. ▸ Compendious, somewhat dated account of complex monarch, his cultural and political ambitions, and disastrous end to his reign. Work published posthumously. [PHF]

20.909 Charles Julian Bishko. *Studies in medieval Spanish frontier history*. London: Variorum Reprints, 1980. ISBN 0-86078-069-4. ▸ Collected essays, including survey of Reconquest, studies of ranching and pastoralism, and major monograph on Leonese-Castilian alliance with Cluny. [JFP]

20.910 Thomas N. Bisson. *The medieval crown of Aragon: a short history*. 1986 ed. Oxford: Clarendon, 1991. ISBN 0-19-820236-9 (pbk). ▸ History of Catalonia and Aragon from ninth to late fifteenth century. Traces institutional and political development, Mediterranean expansion, and cultural accomplishments. [PHF]

20.911 Thomas N. Bisson, ed. *Fiscal accounts of Catalonia under the early count-kings, 1151–1213*. 2 vols. Berkeley: University of California Press, 1984. ISBN 0-520-04388-2 (set), 0-520-04719-2 (set, jacket). ▸ Extensive introduction showing how revenue was collected and accounted. Edition of archival records demonstrates precocious growth of bureaucratic administration in Catalonia. [PHF]

20.912 Pierre Bonnassie. *La Catalogne au tournant de l'an mil: croissance et mutations d'une société*. Paris: Michel, 1990. ISBN 2-226-03672-5. ▸ Fundamental account of crisis and restoration of Catalan comital authority under pressure of aristocratic rebellion. Sees mid-eleventh century as time of disintegration. Important comparative implications for Iberia and France. Revised version of *La Catalogne du milieu de dixième à la fin du onzième siècle* (1975–76). [PHF]

20.913 John Boswell. *The royal treasure: Muslim communities under the crown of Aragon in the fourteenth century*. New Haven: Yale University Press, 1977. ISBN 0-300-02090-2. ▸ Focuses on Aragonese-Castilian war, 1355–66, to study royal exploitation and favoritism toward Muslim communities. Discusses internal organization of communities, military duties, tax obligations, legal rights, and forms of oppression. Based on royal registers. [FLC]

20.914 Robert I. Burns. *The Crusader kingdom of Valencia: reconstruction on a thirteenth-century frontier*. 2 vols. Cambridge, Mass.: Harvard University Press, 1967. ▸ Description of consolidation and governance of Valencia after conquest by Aragon-Catalonia in 1238. Focus on ecclesiastical divisions and administration. [PHF]

20.915 Robert I. Burns. *Medieval colonialism: postcrusade exploitation of Islamic Valencia*. Princeton: Princeton University Press, 1975. ISBN 0-691-05227-1. ▸ Examination of process of change in wake of Christian occupation of Valencia in 1238, with particular emphasis on monarchy's fiscal management of newly won city and territory. Excellent bibliography and illustrations. [JFP]

20.916 Robert I. Burns, ed. *Emperor of culture: Alfonso X the Learned of Castile and his thirteenth-century Renaissance*. Philadelphia: University of Pennsylvania Press, 1990. ISBN 0-8122-8116-0. ▸ Collection of essays by various authors concerning Alfonso's cultural enterprises, politics, and administration. Most suggestive contributions by Burns and O'Callaghan. Bibliography of Alfonsine material. [PHF]

20.917 Robert I. Burns, ed. *The worlds of Alfonso the Learned and James the Conqueror: intellect and force in the Middle Ages*. Princeton: Princeton University Press, 1985. ISBN 0-691-05451-7. ▸ Somewhat uneven collection of articles on kingship, society, and culture in thirteenth-century Spain. Articles by Bisson, O'Callaghan, and Lewis important for royal politics and administration. [PHF]

20.918 Joseph Calmette. *Louis XI, Jean II, et la révolution catalane (1461–1473)*. 1902 ed. Geneva: Slatkine Reprints, 1977. ▸ Basic work on course of Catalan civil war and its political ramifications, especially efforts of Louis XI to establish control over Catalonia. [PHF]

20.919 Americo Castro. *The structure of Spanish history*. Edmund L. King, trans. Princeton: Princeton University Press, 1954. ▸ Famous polemical interpretation of Spain's greatness and decline. Emphasizes Islamic and Jewish influence and consequences of their subsequent extirpation. Discusses source of dispute with Sánchez-Albornoz 20.960 over Islam and source of Iberian backwardness. [PHF]

20.920 Rita Costa Gomes. "L'émergence du politique dans le Portugal du bas moyen âge: perspectives récents." In *La recherche en histoire du Portugal*. 1 vol. to date. Jean Aubin et al., pp. 25–32. Paris: Centre d'Études Portugaises, École des Hautes Études en Sciences Sociales, and Société Française d'Histoire du Portugal, 1989–. ‣ Excellent summary of recent work on medieval Portugal and slowly growing impact of new approaches and methodologies, especially in study of kingship. [PHF]

20.921 Odilo Engels. *Reconquista und Landesherrschaft: Studien zur Rechts- und Verfassungsgechichte Spaniens im Mittelalter*. Paderborn: Schöningh, 1989. (Rechts- und Staatswissenschafliche Veröffentlichungen der Görres-Gesellschaft, Neue Folge, 53.) ISBN 3-506-73353-2. ‣ Collection of articles on lordship, monarchy, and reconquest. Based on close and legalistic reading of documents, with particular attention to conflicting lordships in Aragon-Catalonia. [PHF]

20.922 Richard A. Fletcher. "Reconquest and Crusade in Spain, c. 1050–1150." *Transactions of the Royal Historical Society*, Fifth series, 37 (1987) 31–47. ISSN 0080-4401. ‣ Maintains that idea of Crusade did not take root in Spain until second quarter of twelfth century. Convincing, but probably not end of argument. [JSCRS]

20.923 Alan Forey. *The Templars in the Corona de Aragón*. London: Oxford University Press, 1973. ISBN 0-19-713137-9. ‣ Account of establishment and spread of Templars, 1130 to dissolution. Discusses role of order in frontier expansion, focusing on administration of local convents and exploitation of property. [PHF/JSCRS]

20.924 Manuel González Jiménez. "Frontier and settlement in the kingdom of Castile (1085–1350)." In *Medieval frontier societies*. Robert Bartlett and Angus McKay, eds., pp. 49–74. Oxford: Clarendon, 1989. ISBN 0-19-822881-3. ‣ Most useful survey of settlement of Islamic frontier during period of royal expansion. Considers geography, privileges, local institutions, and effects on Castilian lordship and governance. [PHF]

20.925 César González Mínguez. *Fernando IV de Castilla (1295–1312): la guerra civil y el predominio de la nobleza*. Valladolid: Universidad de Valladolid, Secretariado de Publicaciones, 1976. ISBN 8-4600-2301-X. ‣ Ferdinand's reign (1295–1312) beset by civil war over disputed succession. Argues settlement in 1305 marked advance in independence of nobility, paving way for Trastámara era and near eclipse of monarchy. [PHF]

20.926 Alexandre Herculano. *História de Portugal desde o começo da monarquia até o fim do reinado de Afonso III*. 8 vols. in 4. José Mattoso, ed. Lisbon: Livaria Bertrand, 1980–81. ‣ Grand nineteeth-century comprehensive history of medieval Portugal; nationalistic and anticlerical. This edition has critical notes and bibliography by José Mattaso. [PHF]

20.927 J. N. Hillgarth. *The problem of a Catalan Mediterranean empire, 1229–1327*. London: Longman, 1975. (*English historical review*, Supplement, 8.) ISBN 0-443-09504-3. ‣ Disputes notion of organized Catalan imperial expansion, arguing trade was strong but political control less so; junior branches of ruling family (Sicily, Majorca, etc.) not subordinate to Barcelona. [PHF]

20.928 J. N. Hillgarth. *The Spanish kingdoms, 1250–1516*. 2 vols. Oxford: Clarendon, 1976–78. ISBN 0-19-822530-X (v. 1), 0-19-822531-8 (v. 2). ‣ More a varied, fascinating compendium than chronological narrative. Well-balanced between Aragon and Castile. Incisive, learned, and opinionated. [PHF]

20.929 José María Lacarra. *Historia política del reino de Navarra: desde sus orígenes hasta su incorporacion a Castilla*. 3 vols. Pamplona: Aranzadi, 1972–73. (Biblioteca Caja de Ahorros de Navarra, 3.) ISBN 84-500-5699-3. ‣ Most comprehensive and detailed history of Navarre. Discusses Navarre's emergence in

ninth century, brief political splendor in eleventh, and position between Castile and France during Hundred Years' War. [PHF]

20.930 Miguel Angel Ladero Quesada. *Castilla y la conquista del reino de Granada*. 1967 ed. Granada: Diputación Provincial de Granada, 1988. (Biblioteca de ensayo, 14.) ISBN 84-505-5489-6. ‣ Remains fundamental account of conquest of Granada (1482–92). Discusses economic background and composition of army. [PHF]

20.931 Miguel Angel Ladero Quesada. *El siglo XV en Castilla: fuentes de renta y política fiscal*. Barcelona: Ariel, 1982. ISBN 84-344-6538-8. ‣ Synthesis of author's studies of royal finance. Describes establishment of fiscal system and role in formation of modern state. Interprets fiscal history in terms of social and political conditions. [PHF]

20.932 Jesús Lalinde Abadía. *La gobernación general en la corona de Aragón*. Madrid: Consejo Superior de Investigaciones Cientificas, 1963. ‣ Discusses development of administration in crown of Aragon: legal theory and practice of officials acting in name of king, thirteenth to eighteenth century. Shows peculiar constitutional structure of realm. [PHF]

20.933 Albert Lecoy de la Marche. *Les relations politiques de la France avec le royaume de Majorque (îles Baléares, Roussillon, Montpellier, etc.)* 2 vols. Paris: Leroux, 1892. ‣ Still most thorough treatment of kingdom ruled by junior branch of house of Barcelona, which included Roussillon and Montpellier as well as Majorca. [PHF]

20.934 Béatrice Leroy. *La Navarre au moyen âge*. Paris: Michel, 1984. ISBN 2-226-01883-2. ‣ Considerably more compact than Lacarra 20.929. Good general history of Navarre from Roncevaux to 1512. Equal consideration given to both sides of Pyrenees and to French and Spanish periods of influence. [PHF]

20.935 Béatrice Leroy. *Pouvoirs et sociétés politiques en péninsule ibérique, XIVe–XVe siècles*. Paris: Centre de Documentation Universitaire et Société d'Édition d'Enseignement Superieur, 1991. (Regards sur l'histoire, Histoire medievale, 71.) ISBN 2-7181-3363-5. ‣ Collection of texts and commentary. Shows internal conditions of Portugal, Navarre, Castile, and Aragon, emphasizing formal and informal mechanisms of order and administration. Good balance between political theory and practice. [PHF]

20.936 Derek W. Lomax. *La orden de Santiago, 1170–1275*. Madrid: Consejo Superior de Investigaciones Cientificas, Escuela de Estudios Medievales, 1965. (Estudios, 38.) ‣ Description of religious and political life of Order of Santiago; role in reconquest and resettlement; seigneurial administration; and internal organization and sources of wealth. [PHF]

20.937 Derek W. Lomax. *The reconquest of Spain*. London: Longman, 1978. ISBN 0-582-50209-8. ‣ Introductory history of expansion of Christian Spain from eighth century to 1492. Emphasizes period of rapid expansion of Castile, 1086–1252. [PHF]

20.938 Elena Lourie. *Crusade and colonisation: Muslims, Christians, and Jews in medieval Aragon*. Aldershot, England and Brookfield, Vt.: Variorum and Gower, 1990. ISBN 0-86078-266-2. ‣ Collected studies. Includes important article "A Society Organised for War"—on creation of large military class—and essays on Jews and Muslims in Catalonia, Aragon, and Valencia. [FLC]

20.939 Marvin Lunenfeld. *Keepers of the city: the corregidores of Isabella I of Castile, 1474–1504*. Cambridge: Cambridge University Press, 1987. ISBN 0-521-32930-2. ‣ Discussion of administration of towns by royal officials during period of consolidation and reform. Finds variation among towns and changes over time in corregidors' powers and degree of royal control. [PHF]

20.940 Angus MacKay. *Spain in the Middle Ages: from frontier to empire, 1000–1500.* 1977 ed. New York: St. Martin's, 1989. ISBN 0-312-74978-3. ▸ Best single-volume account of Spain in central and later Middle Ages. Emphasis on Castile and influence of frontier. Cultural relations among Jews, Muslims, and Christians treated without sentimentality or exaggeration. [PHF]

20.941 José Antonio Maravall. *El concepto de España en la Edad Media.* 3d ed. Madrid: Centro de Estudios Constitucionales, 1981. (Colección estudios politicos, 2.) ISBN 84-259-0650-4. ▸ Traces idea of Spain within different medieval kingdoms. Brilliant study of historiography, cultural history, myth making, and ideology of state. [PHF]

20.942 Jesús Ernesto Martínez Ferrando. *Jaime II de Aragón: su vida familiar.* Barcelona: Consejo Superior de Investigaciones Científicas, Escuela de Estudios Medievales, 1948. (Publicaciones de la Sección de Barcelona, 10–11. Estudios, 9–10.) ▸ Unusual account of political intrigue intertwined with family conflict. Concentrates on sons' education, Jaime's relations with wife and children, and aspects of everyday life: ceremony, piety, consumption, recreation. [PHF]

20.943 José Mattoso. *Identificaçao de um país: ensaio sobre as origens de Portugal, 1096–1325.* 3d ed. 2 vols. Lisbon: Editorial Estampa, 1988. ▸ Synthesis of medieval Portuguese political formation. Argues for early sense of unity despite contrast between North and South. Treats social history, especially class distinctions in absence of feudalism. [PHF]

20.944 Roger Bigelow Merriman. *The rise of the Spanish empire in the Old World and in the New.* 1918–34 ed. 4 vols. New York: Cooper Square, 1962. ▸ Traces rise of Spain from reconquest to Philip II. More restrained and broader than Prescott 29.48 but equally magisterial. Reflects early twentieth-century interest in empire and political and military expansion. [PHF]

20.945 José Manuel Nieto Soria. *Fundamentos ideológicos del poder real en Castilla (siglos XIII–XVI).* Madrid: Eudema, 1988. ISBN 84-7754-024-1. ▸ Description of images and symbols of royal power. Argues Castilian monarchy sacralized and ministerial, in contrast to Ruiz 20.956 who emphasizes secular power. Rather defensively favorable judgment of monarchy. Compare Linehan 20.1099. [PHF]

20.946 Joseph F. O'Callaghan. *The Córtes of Castile-León, 1188–1350.* Philadelphia: University of Pennsylvania Press, 1989. ISBN 0-8122-8125-X. ▸ Optimistic survey of place of Córtes in medieval Castilian government. Emphasizes precocious development, especially inclusion of towns. [PHF]

20.947 Bonifacio Palacios Martín. *La coronación de los reyes de Aragón, 1204–1410: aportación al estudio de las estructuras políticas medievales.* Valencia: Anubar, 1975. ISBN 84-7013-066-8. ▸ Description of ceremonial and ideological significance of coronation of Aragonese kings from Peter II's homage, to Innocent III, to extinction of House of Barcelona. Monarchs eventually dispensed with ecclesiastical mediation and crowned themselves. [PHF]

20.948 Rogelio Pérez-Bustamante. *El gobierno y la administración de los reinos de la corona de Castilla (1230–1474).* 2 vols. Madrid: Universidad Autónoma, 1976. (Antiqua et mediaevalia, 2.) ISBN 84-7009-027-5 (v. 1), 84-7009-188-3 (v. 2). ▸ Study of all levels of Castilian royal administration during period of territorial expansion and increasing internal violence. Includes extensive lists of personnel and register of 573 documents. [PHF]

20.949 Evelyn S. Procter. *Curia and Córtes in León and Castile, 1072–1295.* Cambridge: Cambridge University Press, 1980. ISBN 0-521-22639-2. ▸ Discusses royal court and formation of consultative assemblies. With O'Callaghan 20.946, emphasizes urban

participation. More on early Córtes than O'Callaghan but ends before period of decline. [PHF]

20.950 Bernard F. Reilly. *The kingdom of León-Castilla under King Alfonso VI, 1065–1109.* Princeton: Princeton University Press, 1988. ISBN 0-691-05515-7. ▸ Detailed account of important reign that saw reconquest of Toledo, Almoravid counterattack, and consolidation of several realms under Castilian hegemony. [PHF]

20.951 Bernard F. Reilly. *The kingdom of León-Castilla under Queen Urraca, 1109–1126.* Princeton: Princeton University Press, 1982. ISBN 0-691-05344-8. ▸ Reconstruction of political events of turbulent era when Uracca ruled León-Castile. Favorable account of what others have considered disastrous reign. Large use of archival sources. [PHF]

20.952 Nicholas Round. *The greatest man uncrowned: a study of the fall of don Alvaro de Luna.* London: Tamesis; distributed by Longwood, 1986. ISBN 0-7293-0211-3. ▸ Political biography of leading aristocrat and royal minister, friend of John II of Castile for forty years. Execution (1453) crucial moment in relationship of crown and nobility. [PHF]

20.953 Adeline Rucquoi, ed. *Genèse médiévale de l'Espagne moderne: du refus à la révolte, les résistances.* Nice and Paris: Université de Nice and Diffusion, Les Belles Lettres, 1991. (Publication de la Faculté des Lettres, Arts, et Sciences Humaines de Nice, Nouvelle serie, 4.) ISBN 2-251-62159-8. ▸ Conference papers in French and Spanish on themes of royal power, symbols, and centralization and resistance to royal authority by nobles, towns, and peasants. Discusses indirect means of noncooperation as well as armed revolt. [PHF]

20.954 Adeline Rucquoi, ed. *Genèse médiévale de l'Espagne moderne, 1370–1516: realidad e imágenes del poder, España a fines de la edad media.* Valladolid: Ambito, 1988. ISBN 84-86770-13-0. ▸ Conference papers in French and Spanish on Castilian monarchy, its ideological basis, and interaction of king, nobles, and towns. [PHF]

20.955 Adeline Rucquoi, ed. *Genesis medieval del estado moderno: Castilla y Navarra (1250–1370).* Valladolid: Ambito, 1987. ISBN 84-8604-793-5. ▸ Collection of articles in French and Spanish. Focuses on development of centralized institutions despite, or in relation to, violence and disorder. [PHF]

20.956 Teófilo F. Ruiz. "Unsacred monarchy: the king of Castile in the late Middle Ages." In *Rites of power: symbolism, ritual, and politics since the Middle Ages.* Sean Wilentz, ed., pp. 109–44. Philadelphia: University of Pennsylvania Press, 1985. ISBN 0-8122-7948-4. ▸ Argues secular basis for Castilian kingship, absence of anointment, ecclesiastical coronation, other attributes common to European kingship. [PHF]

20.957 P. E. Russell. *The English intervention in Spain and Portugal in the time of Edward III.* Oxford: Clarendon, 1955. ISBN 0-19-80085-5. ▸ Definitive account of claims, diplomacy, and war stemming from Castilian dynastic disputes and consequent extension of Hundred Years' War into Iberia. [PHF]

20.958 A.F.C. Ryder. *Alfonso the Magnanimous: king of Aragon, Naples, and Sicily, 1396–1458.* Oxford: Clarendon, 1990. ISBN 0-19-821954-7. ▸ Biography of humanist king whose energies were chiefly bestowed on Italy to detriment of Aragon-Catalonia. Favorable treatment of cultivated but often maligned ruler. [PHF]

20.959 Claudio Sánchez-Albornoz. *Una ciudad de la España Cristiana hace mil años: estampas de la vida en León.* 10th ed. Madrid: Rialp, 1984. ISBN 84-321-1876-1. ▸ Classic, pioneering study of emerging capital of fledgling state of León in early eleventh century. Many illustrations of daily life. [JFP]

20.960 Claudio Sánchez-Albornoz. *España: un enigma histórico.*

10th ed. Barcelona: EDASA, 1985. ISBN 84-350-1702-8 (cl), 84-350-1705-2 (pbk, set). ‣ Essay on why Spain is different from Europe. Answers with grand but dubious polemic against Castro 20.919 over Spanish "backwardness." Argues no permanent Arab or Jewish influence. English translation unreliable. [PHF]

20.961 Julio Valdeón Baruque. *Alfonso X el Sabio*. Valladolid: Junta de Castilla y León, Consejería de Educación y Cultura, 1986. (Colección Villalar, 1.) ISBN 84-505-3366-x. ‣ Brief, balanced assessment of cultural achievements and political ambitions. Includes excerpts from *Partidas, Cantigas,* and other works showing Alfonso's interests, talents, and ideology. [PHF]

20.962 Julio Valdéon Baruque. *Enrique II de Castilla: la guerra civil y la consolidación del régimen, 1366–1371*. Valladolid: Universidad de Valladolid, Secretariado de Publicaciones, 1966. ‣ Civil war of 1366–71 seen as evidence of recovery of Castile's vitality and beginning of expansion sustained over next century. [PHF]

20.963 Jaime Vicens Vives. *Fernando el Católico príncipe de Aragón, rey de Sicilia, 1458–1478: Sicilia en la política de Juan II de Aragón*. Madrid: Consejo Superior de Investigaciones Científicas, 1952. (Biblioteca "Reyes católicos," Estudios, 3.) ‣ Study of crisis of crown of Aragon and relation of Sicily to Catalonia-Aragon. Important for formative years of Ferdinand who would resolve war and join Aragon to Castile. [PHF]

20.964 Jaime Vicens Vives. *Els Trastámares: el segle XV*. Barcelona: Vicens-Vives, 1974. ‣ Summary of author's many works on era. Discussion of Trastámara dynasty's succession to throne of Aragon. Shows discontent of nobles, ambitions of Alfonso the Magnanimous in Italy, and problem of servile peasantry. [PHF]

20.965 Johannes Bernhard Vincke. *Staat und Kirche in Katalonien und Aragon während des Mittelalters*. Münster: Aschendorff, 1931. ‣ Discussion of public authority of church and rights of kings over it. Emphasis on thirteenth and fourteenth centuries and ability of state to extract revenue from church. [PHF]

SEE ALSO
29.35 Felipe Fernández-Armesto. *Ferdinand and Isabella.*
29.47 William D. Phillips, Jr. *Enrique IV and the crisis of fifteenth-century Castile, 1425–1480.*
29.48 William H. Prescott. *History of the reign of Ferdinand and Isabella.*

Church and Intellectual History

❧

[Contributors: BSH = Bert S. Hall, FHS = Fiona Harris Stoertz, JJC = John J. Contreni, JS = John Scarborough, KP = Kenneth Pennington, MHS = Michael H. Shank, MLC = Marcia L. Colish, PJG = Patrick J. Geary, TFXN = Thomas F. X. Noble, WJC = William J. Courtenay]

REFERENCE WORKS

20.966 Geoffrey Barraclough. *The medieval papacy.* 1968 ed. New York: Norton, 1979. ISBN 0-393-95100-6. ▸ Good general introduction to history of papacy. Emphasizes both growth of papal institutions and interactions of popes and secular rulers. [KP]

20.967 Carl T. Berkhout and Jeffrey Burton Russell, eds. *Medieval heresies: a bibliography, 1960–1979.* Toronto: Pontifical Institute of Mediaeval Studies, 1981. (Subsidia mediaevalia, 11.) ISBN 0-88844-360-9. ▸ Extensive annotated bibliography on medieval heresies. Treats heretical doctrines, movements, Crusades, religious orders, and repression of heresy, 700–1500. Includes over 2,000 entries in twenty-five groupings. [KP/FHS]

20.968 Mary Ann Bowman, ed. *Western mysticism: guide to the basic works.* Chicago: American Library Association, 1978. ISBN 0-8389-0266-9. ▸ Fully annotated bibliography, organized into sections on philosophy, history, practice, experience, literature of mysticism, and oriental mysticism in Western context. Includes guide for library acquisitions. Recommended for general reader. [FHS]

20.969 Rosalind B. Brooke and Christopher Brooke. *Popular religion in the Middle Ages: western Europe, 1000–1300.* London:

Thames & Hudson, 1984. ISBN 0-500-25087-1 (cl), 0-500-27381-2 (pbk). ▸ Popularly written and brief but provides useful synthesis of more specialized works. Treats religious aspirations, beliefs, hopes, and fears of ordinary lay people in Western Christendom. [FHS]

20.970 J. H. Burns, ed. *The Cambridge history of medieval political thought, c. 350–c. 1450.* Cambridge: Cambridge University Press, 1988. ISBN 0-521-24324-6. ▸ Collection of essays by leading scholars treating major aspects of political and legal theory and ecclesiology across Middle Ages. [MLC]

20.971 Catholic University of America, Staff, eds. *New Catholic encyclopedia.* 1967–79 ed. 17 vols. and supplement. New York: McGraw-Hill, 1989. ISBN 0-07-010235-X (v. 17). ▸ General reference work covering church history, theology, religious orders, religious life, and related matters from foundation of church to present. All entries include bibliographical orientations. [MLC]

20.972 Alan B. Cobban. *The medieval universities: their development and organization.* London: Methuen, 1975. ISBN 0-416-81250-3. ▸ Survey of institutional development of medieval universities. Provides good synthesis of state of research as of date of publication. [WJC]

20.973 Giles Constable, ed. *Medieval monasticism: a select bibliography.* Toronto: University of Toronto Press, 1976. ISBN 0-8020-2200-6 (cl), 0-8020-6280-6 (pbk). ▸ General annotated bibliography covering monasticism and religious orders in Western and Eastern churches, religious women, hermits, canons, monastic government, and relations of religious orders with papacy. [KP]

20.974 Frederick C. Copleston. *A history of philosophy.* Vol. 2: *Mediaeval philosophy: Augustine to Scotus.* Vol. 3: *Late mediaeval and Renaissance philosophy: Ockham to Suarez.* 1950–53 ed. 9 vols. New York: Image, 1985. ISBN 0-385-23032-X (v. 2, pbk), 0-385-23033-8 (v. 3, pbk). ▸ Standard introduction to history of medieval philosophy from Augustine to fifteenth century. Dated but more detailed and better balanced than its alternatives. [WJC]

20.975 Ernst Robert Curtius. *European literature and the Latin Middle Ages.* 1953 ed. Willard R. Trask, trans. Princeton: Princeton University Press, 1990. ISBN 0-691-09969-3 (cl), 0-691-01899-5 (pbk). ▸ Learned defense of continuity of classical literary tradition across Middle Ages, studied thematically, as part of larger argument opposing view of period as literary Dark Age. Edition has new epilogue. [WJC/MLC]

20.976 Irenée Henri Dalmais. *Principles of the liturgy.* Vol. 1 of *The church at prayer: an introduction to the liturgy.* Aimé Georges J. Martimort et al., eds. Matthew O'Connnell, trans. Collegeville, Minn.: Liturgical Press, 1986. ISBN 0-8146-1363-2. ▸ First of four-volume comprehensive, collaborative work containing wealth of information about liturgy, sacraments, monastic rites, and religious profession. Best general reference in its field. [FHS]

20.977 Peter Dronke. *Women writers of the Middle Ages: a critical study of texts from Perpetua (d. 203) to Marguerite Porete (d. 1310).* New York: Cambridge University Press, 1984. ISBN 0-521-25580-5 (cl), 0-521-27573-3 (pbk). ▸ Insightful explication of texts written 200–1300 CE, by eighty-four women. Focuses on language, thought, and emotion. Seminal study of medieval female authors. [JJC]

20.978 W.T.H. Jackson. *Medieval literature: a history and a guide.* New York: Collier, 1966. ▸ Introductory survey of medieval literature, treating Latin and vernacular tradition in major European languages. Covers all important genres and authors, seventh through sixteenth centuries. [WJC]

20.979 J.N.D. Kelly. *The Oxford dictionary of popes.* 1986 ed. New York: Oxford University Press, 1988. ISBN 0-19-282085-0 (pbk). ▸ Biographies of popes to John Paul II. Provides valuable biographical orientation after each entry. [KP]

20.980 Richard Kieckhefer. *Magic in the Middle Ages.* Cambridge: Cambridge University Press, 1989. ISBN 0-521-30941-7 (cl), 0-521-31202-7 (pbk). ▸ Excellent introduction to natural and demonic magic in medieval culture, 500–1500, and its relationship to other cultural forms. Argues magic point of intersection between popular and elite cultures. [FHS]

20.981 David Knowles and Dimitri Obolensky. *The Middle Ages.* Vol. 2 of *The Christian centuries.* New York: McGraw-Hill, 1968. ▸ Treats conversion of Western Europe to Christianity, development of Christian institutions and doctrine in early Middle Ages, eleventh-century reform movement, and ecclesiastical history of high Middle Ages. [JJC]

20.982 Norman A. Kretzmann, Anthony Kenny, and Jan Pinborg, eds. *The Cambridge history of later medieval philosophy: from the rediscovery of Aristotle to the disintegration of scholasticism, 1100–1600.* 1982 ed. New York: Cambridge University Press, 1988. ISBN 0-521-22605-8 (cl, 1982), 0-521-36933-9 (pbk). ▸ Collected essays providing detailed studies on most aspects of high and late medieval philosophy with extensive bibliography. History of logic emphasized. [WJC]

20.983 G.W.H. Lampe, ed. *The Cambridge history of the Bible.* Vol. 2: *The West from the fathers to the Reformation.* Cambridge: Cambridge University Press, 1969. ISBN 0-521-04255-0. ▸ Collection of essays surveying most aspects of biblical study and commentary from Jerome to Reformation, including numerous studies of vernacular scriptures as well as Latin exegesis. [WJC]

20.984 C. H. Lawrence. *Medieval monasticism: forms of religious life in Western Europe in the Middle Ages.* 2d ed. New York: Longman, 1989. ISBN 0-582-01727-0 (pbk). ▸ Excellent introduction to development of monasticism and monastic institutions from third to fourteenth century. Accents variety of forms of monastic life in medieval Western church. [JJC/KP]

20.985 Gabriel Le Bras, Charles Lefebvre, and Jacqueline Rambaud. *L'âge classique, 1140–1378: sources et théorie du droit.* Paris: Sirey, 1965. ▸ Standard introduction to history of medieval canon law, teaching of law at Bologna, literature of canon law, and creation of canonical jurisprudence, types of canon law, and relationship to ecclesiastical institutions. [KP]

20.986 C. S. Lewis. *The discarded image: an introduction to medieval and Renaissance literature.* 1964 ed. Cambridge: Cambridge University Press, 1967. ISBN 0-521-09450-X. ▸ Valuable background on classical, Christian, and vernacular worldviews and beliefs about other world that informed literatures and literary audiences of period. [MLC]

20.987 Bernard McGinn, John Meyendorff, and Jean Leclercq, eds. *Christian spirituality: origins to the twelfth century.* 1985 ed. New York: Crossroad, 1992. ISBN 0-8245-0681-2 (cl), 0-8245-0681-9 (pbk). ▸ Nineteen studies on practice and theory of Christian spiritual life from perspectives of monks, laypersons, and theologians; spirituality as manifested in art, liturgy, theology, and reform movements. [JJC]

20.988 Martin Rawson Patrick McGuire, ed. *Introduction to medieval Latin studies: a syllabus and bibliographical guide.* 2d ed. Washington, D.C.: Catholic University of America Press, 1977. ISBN 0-8132-0542-5. ▸ Covers both Christian and secular Latin authors and subjects from early church through thirteenth century. Provides excellent bibliographical orientation through publication date. [MLC]

20.989 John A. Nicholas and Lillian Thomas Shank, eds. *Medieval religious women.* 3 vols. Kalamazoo, Mich.: Cistercian, 1984–92. ISBN 0-87907-871-5 (v. 1, cl), 0-87907-887-1 (v. 2, cl), 0-87907-613-5 (v. 3, cl), 0-87907-971-1 (v. 1, pbk), 0-87907-986-X (v. 2, pbk), 0-87907-913-4 (v. 3, pbk). ▸ Each volume contains chronologically ordered articles by different authors. Volume 1 explores variety of lifestyles open to religious women; volume 2 describes spirituality, experiences, and values of individual women; and volume 3 focuses on Cistercian nuns. Excellent introduction to medieval women and religion. [FHS]

20.990 Jaroslav Pelikan. *The Christian tradition: a history of the development of doctrine.* Vol. 1: *The emergence of the Catholic tradition (100–600).* Vol. 3: *The growth of medieval theology (600–1300).* Vol. 4: *The reformation of church and dogma (1300–1700).* 5 vols. to date. Chicago: University of Chicago Press, 1971–89. ISBN 0-226-65370-6 (v. 1, cl), 0-226-65374-9 (v. 3, cl), 0-226-65376-5 (v. 4, cl), 0-226-65371-4 (v. 1, pbk), 0-226-65375-7 (v. 3, pbk), 0-226-65377-3 (v. 4, pbk). ▸ Systematic treatment of Christian teachings, 100–1700, accenting consensus positions. Beginning with biblical roots of Christianity, arrives at orthodox consensus of sixth century. Continues with challenges to Augustinian synthesis and emergence of high medieval consensus and positions of late medieval theologians, their continuities and discontinuities with Reformation theology. [JJC/MLC]

20.991 Richard William Pfaff, ed. *Medieval Latin liturgy: a select bibliography.* Toronto: University of Toronto Press, 1982. ISBN 0-8020-5564-8 (cl), 0-8020-6488-4 (pbk). ▸ Excellent reference work for Christian liturgy, fourth to sixteenth century. Organized topically with detailed annotations accompanying each entry. Covers scholarship to 1977. [FHS]

20.992 Jill Raitt, Bernard McGinn, and John Meyendorff, eds. *Christian spirituality: the high Middle Ages and Reformation.* New York: Crossroad, 1989. ISBN 0-8245-0765-7 (cl, 1987), 0-685-17332-1 (pbk). ▸ Essays by various authors treating mysticism, Marian devotion, liturgy, and religious women. Extremely useful collection. [FHS/WJC]

20.993 Jeffrey Burton Russell. *A history of medieval Christianity: prophesy and order.* New York: Crowell, 1968. ▸ Charts creative tension between Christian imperative to transform world and countervailing tendency to accommodate religion to society as it animated church history through fifteenth century. [JJC]

20.994 Jeffrey Burton Russell. *Witchcraft in the Middle Ages.* Ithaca, N.Y.: Cornell University Press, 1972. ISBN 0-8014-0697-8. ▸ Examination of emergence and development of witch phenomenon and degree to which it was accepted, 300–1486. Links witchcraft to heresy. Best introduction to subject. [FHS/JJC]

20.995 Beryl Smalley. *The study of the Bible in the Middle Ages.* 3d ed. Oxford: Blackwell, 1983. ISBN 0-631-13168-X (pbk). ▸ How Bible was studied from fourth to thirteenth century. Emphasizes changes in interpretive methods and centrality of biblical scholarship to medieval intellectual history. [JJC/WJC]

20.996 R. W. Southern. *Western society and the church in the Middle Ages.* 1970 ed. Harmondsworth: Penguin, 1990. ISBN 0-14-020503-9 (pbk). ▸ General history of church from 1050 to 1300. Treats growth of papal authority, episcopal government, development of religious orders, and role of church in society. [KP]

20.997 Marilyn Stokstad. *Medieval art.* New York: Harper & Row, 1986. ISBN 0-06-438555-8 (cl), 0-06-430132-X (pbk). ▸ Excellent general introduction to medieval art from early Christian to late Gothic period. Balanced coverage of all styles, regions, and genres. [MLC]

20.998 Walter Ullmann. *Medieval political thought.* 1965 ed. Harmondsworth: Penguin, 1975. ISBN 0-14-055102-6. ▸ Survey of political thought from late Roman times to fifteenth century, emphasizing clericalization of political theory. Theme is descending concepts of power giving way to ascending theories of political authority. Earlier title: *A History of Political Thought: The Middle Ages.* [JJC/WJC]

20.999 John Van Engen. "The Christian Middle Ages as an historiographical problem." *American historical review* 91.3 (1986) 519–52. ISSN 0002-8762. ▸ Essay on changing historiographical perspectives of past twenty years on relationship between Christianity and Middle Ages. Urges attention to process of christianization and to social meanings of Christian practices to medieval people. [JJC]

20.1000 Paul Vinogradoff. *Roman law in medieval Europe.* New York: Barnes & Noble, 1968. ISBN 0-904676-06-4. ▸ Classic account of revival of Roman law in medieval Europe and influence of Roman law on English, French, and German legal systems. [KP]

SEE ALSO
4.54 David C. Lindberg. *The beginnings of Western science.*

CHURCH AND INTELLECTUAL HISTORY, 300–1050

General Studies

20.1001 Jean Daniélou and Henri-Irenée Marrou. *The first six hundred years.* Vincent Cronin, trans. New York: McGraw-Hill, 1964. ▸ Study of origins and emergence of Christianity, confrontation with Roman empire, and internal doctrinal disputes. [JJC]

20.1002 W.H.C. Frend. *The rise of Christianity.* 1984 ed. Philadelphia: Fortress, 1985. ISBN 0-8006-1931-5. ▸ Development of Christianity from origins to death of Gregory I (604). Evolution of doctrine and Christian institutions and relationship of new religion to Roman state and to barbarian Europe. [JJC]

SEE ALSO
8.135 Judith Herrin. *The formation of Christendom.*

Church in Late Antiquity and the Early Middle Ages

20.1003 Ludwig Bieler. *Ireland, harbinger of the Middle Ages.* 1963 ed. New York: Oxford University Press, 1966. ▸ Authoritative, lavishly illustrated study of Irish culture in early Middle Ages. Surveys ecclesiastical life, education, literature, and art. [MLC]

20.1004 Peter Brown. *Augustine of Hippo: a biography.* 1967 ed. New York: Dorset, 1986. ISBN 0-88029-098-6. ▸ Traces religious and intellectual odyssey of Augustine (354–430) against backdrop of political crisis and religious tension. Finely nuanced discussion of Augustine's thought. [JJC]

20.1005 Eleanor Shipley Duckett. *The wandering saints of the early Middle Ages.* New York: Norton, 1964. ISBN 0-393-00266-7. ▸ Studies of Celtic, Anglo-Saxon, and Frankish missionaries and pilgrims. Examines their intellectual and religious formation and charts their impact on medieval society from fifth to ninth century. [JJC]

20.1006 J.N.D. Kelly. *Jerome: his life, writings, and controversies.* New York: Harper & Row, 1975. ISBN 0-06-064333-1. ▸ Life of Jerome (331–420) as scholar, scriptural commentator, monk, and controversialist. Emphasizes Jerome's role in establishment of Latin Bible and as proponent of sexual asceticism. [JJC]

20.1007 Robert A. Markus. *The end of ancient Christianity.* New York: Cambridge University Press, 1990. ISBN 0-521-32716-4 (cl), 0-521-33949-9 (pbk). ▸ Charts changes in intellectual and spiritual horizons within Christian world, 400–600. Treats lived experience of religion as well as theological culture. [MLC]

20.1008 Rosamond McKitterick. *The Frankish church and the Carolingian reforms, 789–895.* London: Royal Historical Society, 1977. ISBN 0-901050-32-6. ▸ Examination of practical application of Carolingian reforms at level of bishops, priests, and people. Teaching, preaching, and praying in Frankish kingdom. [JJC]

20.1009 John T. McNeill. *The Celtic churches: a history, A.D. 200 to 1200.* Chicago: University of Chicago Press, 1974. ISBN 0-226-56095-3. ▸ General study of church in Celtic lands. Surveys institutions, culture, and religious life. [MLC]

20.1010 Angelo Paredi. *Saint Ambrose: his life and times.* M. Joseph Costelloe, trans. Notre Dame, Ind.: University of Notre Dame Press, 1964. ▸ Interweaves political and doctrinal controversies of fourth century with biography of bishop of Milan. [JJC]

20.1011 Jeffrey Richards. *Consul of God: the life and times of Gregory the Great.* London: Routledge & Kegan Paul, 1980. ISBN 0-7100-0346-3. ▸ Biography of pope with special focus on politics and discussion of Gregory's relationships with Italian and Sicilian bishops. [JJC]

20.1012 Jeffrey Richards. *The popes and the papacy in the early Middle Ages, 476–752.* Boston: Routledge & Kegan Paul, 1979. ISBN 0-7100-0098-7. ▸ Papal history in light of doctrinal and jurisdictional confrontations largely with Byzantine empire. Influence of political climate in Rome and Italy for papal development. [JJC]

20.1013 Birgit Sawyer, Peter H. Sawyer, and Ian Wood, eds. *The christianization of Scandinavia: report of a symposium held at Kungalo, Sweden, 4–9 August 1986.* Alingsås, Sweden: Viktoria, 1987. ISBN 91-86708-04-X (pbk). ▸ Analysis of meanings and methods of conversion from paganism to Christianity from ninth to eleventh century. Discusses missionary activity and effects of conversion on Scandinavians. [JJC]

20.1014 Charles Thomas. *Christianity in Roman Britain to A.D. 500.* Berkeley: University of California Press, 1981. ISBN 0-520-04392-8. ▸ Study of christianization of Britain using archaeological evidence. Stresses significance of local, insular practices in shaping early British Christianity. [JJC]

20.1015 Walter Ullmann. *The growth of papal government in the Middle Ages: a study in the ideological relation of clerical to lay power.* 3d ed. London: Methuen, 1970. ISBN 0-416-15890-0. ▸ Growth of papal authority from fourth to mid-twelfth century. Development of concept of church as institution and competing papal and imperial notions of authority. [JJC]

20.1016 J. M. Wallace-Hadrill. *The Frankish church.* Oxford: Clarendon, 1983. ISBN 0-19-826906-4. ▸ Christianity in Frankish kingdoms from fifth through ninth centuries. Church as institution and as cultural and reforming agent. [JJC]

Early Medieval Monasticism

20.1017 Herbert Bloch. *Monte Cassino in the Middle Ages.* 3 vols. Cambridge, Mass.: Harvard University Press, 1986. ISBN 0-674-58655-7 (set). ▸ History of monastery, eighth to fifteenth century. Situates Monte Cassino and its possessions in Italian countryside and world of the Byzantines, Carolingians, and Holy Roman Empire. [JJC]

20.1018 H. B. Clarke and Mary Brennan, eds. *Columbanus and Merovingian monasticism.* Oxford: British Archaeological Reports, 1981. (British archaeological reports, International series, 113.) ISBN 0-86054-135-5. ▸ View of relationship between Ireland and Continent, 500–750, through career and influence of Irish missionary, Columbanus. Monasticism, intellectual and religious life in Frankish realms. [JJC]

20.1019 Jean Décarreaux. *Monks and civilization from the barbarian invasions to the reign of Charlemagne.* Charlotte Haldane, trans. Garden City, N.Y.: Doubleday, 1964. ▸ Study of monks as civilizing agents contributing to shaping of Europe and fashioning of common modes of thinking and living. Haphazard development of monastic institutions and traditions in various countries. [JJC]

20.1020 Marilyn Dunn. "Mastering Benedict: monastic rules and their authors in the early medieval West." *English historical* *review* 105 (1990) 567–94. ISSN 0013-8266. ▸ Review of scholarship on Benedictine rule and its relationship to other rules. Suggests that Rule of the Master composed after that of Benedict. [JJC]

20.1021 Jean Leclercq. *The love of learning and the desire for God: a study of monastic culture.* 3d ed. Catharine Misrahi, trans. New York: Fordham University Press, 1982. ISBN 0-8232-0407-3 (pbk). ▸ Discussion of monastic culture and intellectual life as animated by spiritual concerns. Biblical interpretation, liberal studies, and monastic literature developed in environment emphasizing spiritual perfection and quest for mystical union. [JJC/WJC]

20.1022 Paul Meyvaert. *Benedict, Gregory, Bede, and others.* London: Variorum, 1977. ISBN 0-86078-005-8. ▸ Sixteen studies investigating history of monasticism and early medieval Latin-Christian authors. [JJC]

20.1023 Friedrich Prinz. *Frühes Mönchtum im Frankenreich: Kultur und Gesellschaft in Gallien, den Rheinlanden, und Bayern am Beispiel der monastischen Entwicklung (vierte bis achte Jahrhundert).* 2d ed. Munich: Oldenbourg, 1988. ▸ Development of monasticism in early Frankish kingdoms from fourth to eighth century. Most important survey of pre-Benedictine monasticism across western Europe. [JJC/PJG]

20.1024 John J. Ryan. *Irish monasticism: origins and early development.* 1931 ed. Ithaca, N.Y.: Cornell University Press, 1972. ISBN 0-8014-0613-7. ▸ Irish monasticism in fifth and sixth centuries; compares Irish monastic life and ritual to other forms of monasticism in West. [JJC]

Topics in Early Medieval Church History

20.1025 Peter Brown. *The body and society: men, women, and sexual renunciation in early Christianity.* New York: Columbia University Press, 1988. ISBN 0-231-06100-5 (cl), 0-231-06101-3 (pbk). ▸ Finely nuanced study of ascetic renunciation of sexuality in early Christianity to fifth century, development of doctrine of virginity and sexual restraint against background of pagan versions of sexual asceticism. [JJC]

20.1026 Peter Brown. *The cult of the saints: its rise and function in Latin Christianity.* Chicago: University of Chicago Press, 1981. ISBN 0-226-07621-0 (cl), 0-226-07622-9 (pbk). ▸ Study of theory and practice of belief in dead as intercessors between living human beings and God and of understood meaning and benefits of veneration of saints for medieval Christians. [JJC]

20.1027 Peter Brown. *Society and the holy in late antiquity.* Berkeley: University of California Press, 1989. ISBN 0-520-06800-9. ▸ Essays on religious life from fourth to seventh century with original studies on holiness, paganism, Christianity, and supernatural, emphasizing social functions and implications of religious belief and practice. [JJC]

20.1028 James A. Brundage. *Law, sex, and Christian society in medieval Europe.* Chicago: University of Chicago Press, 1987. ISBN 0-226-07783-7. ▸ Charts development of canon law and theology on sexual morality from early Christian times to sixteenth century, arguing that efforts of churchmen to regulate sexual conduct actually informed lay attitudes. [JJC/KP]

20.1029 Patrick J. Geary. *Furta sacra: thefts of relics in the central Middle Ages.* Rev. ed. Princeton: Princeton University Press, 1990. ISBN 0-691-00862-0. ▸ Study of theft of saints' relics, ninth to eleventh century, seen as means of capturing the sacred. Treats methods of theft, use of relics, and justification of their theft. [JJC/FHS]

20.1030 Josef A. Jungmann. *The early liturgy to the time of Gregory the Great.* Francis A. Brunner, trans. Notre Dame, Ind.: University of Notre Dame Press, 1959. ▸ Outline of history of Chris-

tian modes of worship through sixth century. Shows influence of pagan ritual and christological disputes in early church on development of early medieval liturgy. [JJC]

20.1031 Joseph H. Lynch. *Godparents and kinship in early medieval Europe.* Princeton: Princeton University Press, 1986. ISBN 0-691-05466-5. ▸ Study of baptismal sponsorship, 200–1000, emphasizing liturgical practices, theological underpinnings of godparenting, enduring spiritual kinship relations among those involved, and their significant political, social, and juridical consequences. [JJC]

20.1032 Joseph H. Lynch. *Simoniacal entry into religious life from 1000 to 1260: a social, economic, and legal study.* Columbus: Ohio State University Press, 1976. ISBN 0-8142-0222-5. ▸ Study of practice of associating membership in religious houses with payment and emergence of reform movements critical of simony. [JJC]

20.1033 Karl F. Morrison. *The mimetic tradition of reform in the West.* Princeton: Princeton University Press, 1982. ISBN 0-691-05350-2. ▸ Argues tradition renewed itself by creative imitation and reform; Augustine, Gregory I, Paschasius Radbertus, and Hincmar of Reims thus engaged in self-critical imitation to improve self and society. [JJC]

20.1034 Karl F. Morrison. *Tradition and authority in the Western church, 300–1140.* Princeton: Princeton University Press, 1969. ISBN 0-691-07155-1. ▸ While churchmen often invoked authority of tradition, attempts to address common problems engendered multiple traditions; far from monolithic, medieval Christian tradition conditioned by temporal and local exigencies. [JJC/KP]

20.1035 Karl F. Morrison. *The two kingdoms: ecclesiology in Carolingian political thought.* Princeton: Princeton University Press, 1964. ▸ How study of legal and patristic texts led Carolingian clerics to formulate political ideologies offering alternative ways (royalist, papalist, and episcopal) of viewing church and state as distinct if interrelated institutions. [JJC]

20.1036 Pierre J. Payer. *Sex and the penitentials: the development of a sexual code, 550–1150.* Toronto: University of Toronto Press, 1984. ISBN 0-8020-5649-0. ▸ Reconstruction of sexual behavior of Europeans (sixth to twelfth century) and attitudes and pastoral strategies of religious leaders in addressing sexual practices and offenses using handbooks of penance. [JJC]

Early Medieval Intellectual History

20.1037 Walter Berschin. *Greek letters and the Latin Middle Ages from Jerome to Nicholas of Cusa.* Rev. ed. Jerold C. Frakes, trans. Washington, D.C.: Catholic University of America Press, 1988. ISBN 0-8132-0606-5. ▸ Demonstration of how continuous contact with Byzantium stimulated Greek learning in medieval West. Living contacts as well as book learning explain persistence of Greek studies in Europe. [JJC]

20.1038 George Hardin Brown. *Bede the Venerable.* Boston: Twayne, 1987. ISBN 0-8057-6940-4. ▸ Introduction to life, times, scriptural commentaries, pedagogical treatises, sermons, poems, and letters of great Northumbrian scholar (d. 735). Emphasis on historical work, especially *Ecclesiastical History of the English People.* [JJC]

20.1039 Franz Brunhölzl. *De Cassiodore: à la fin de la renaissance carolingienne.* Vol. 1 of *Histoire de la littérature latine du moyen âge.* Henri Rochais, trans. Jean-Paul Bouhot, collab. Turnhout: Brepols, 1990. ISBN 2-503-50041-2 (pt. 1), 2-503-50049-8 (pt. 2). ▸ Survey of history of Latin literature from sixth through ninth centuries, cultural developments in England, Spain, Italy, Gaul, and, especially, Carolingian renaissance. [JJC]

20.1040 Henry Chadwick. *Augustine.* Oxford: Oxford University Press, 1986. ISBN 0-19-287535-3 (cl). ▸ Excellent brief introduction accenting Augustine's philosophy as well as his theology and areas in which his thought was most influential. Organized thematically. [MLC]

20.1041 Henry Chadwick. *Boethius: the consolations of music, logic, theology, and philosophy.* 1981 ed. Oxford: Clarendon, 1990. ISBN 0-19-826549-2 (pbk). ‣ Readable biographic account of last great ancient philosopher, followed by helpful, understandable discussions of major writings. [TFXN]

20.1042 Charles Norris Cochrane. *Christianity and classical culture: a study of thought and action from Augustus to Augustine.* 1957 ed. London: Oxford University Press, 1974. ‣ Revolution in thought and religion as Roman paganism and Christianity collided in third and fourth centuries. Positive treatment of emergence of Christianity as state religion and of new Christian view of history. [JJC]

20.1043 Marcia L. Colish. *Stoicism in Christian Latin thought through the sixth century.* Vol. 2 of *The Stoic tradition from antiquity to the early Middle Ages.* New York: Brill, 1990. 2 vols. ISBN 90-04-09328-1 (v. 2), 90-04-09330-3 (set). ‣ Only general study of appropriation of Stoic doctrine by Latin Christian thinkers, third through sixth centuries, who viewed it both positively and negatively in addressing own Christian concerns. [JJC]

20.1044 Pierre Courcelle. *Late Latin writers and their Greek sources.* Harry E. Wedeck, trans. Cambridge, Mass.: Harvard University Press, 1969. ‣ Study of influence of Greek tradition in North Africa, Gaul, and Italy from fourth to sixth centuries, weighing impact of Greek thought on Western philosophy, theology, and scriptural studies. [JJC]

20.1045 Allen J. Frantzen. *King Alfred.* Boston: Twayne, 1986. ISBN 0-8057-6918-8. ‣ Introductory survey of patronage of religion and education by West Saxon king, Alfred the Great (849–899), and his translations of classical and patristic texts from Latin to Old English. [MLC]

20.1046 Stephen Gersh. *From Iamblichus to Eriugena: an investigation of the prehistory and evolution of the Pseudo-Dionysian tradition.* Leiden: Brill, 1978. ISBN 90-04-05396-4. ‣ Traces antecedents of thought of Pseudo-Dionysius the Areopagite, his influence on early medieval philosophy, and transmission and development of Christian Neoplatonism through ninth century. [JJC]

20.1047 Stephen Gersh. *Middle Platonism and Neoplatonism: the Latin tradition.* 2 vols. Notre Dame, Ind.: University of Notre Dame Press, 1986. ISBN 0-268-01363-2. ‣ Maps transmission of Platonic tradition to early Middle Ages. Only general study of Neoplatonism in works of Latin thinkers such as Boethius, Servius, Macrobius, and Martianus Capella. [JJC]

20.1048 Margaret T. Gibson, ed. *Boethius: his life, thought, and influence.* Oxford: Blackwell, 1981. ISBN 0-631-11141-7. ‣ Fourteen studies on educational, philosophical, and literary works of Roman statesman and philosopher (480–524), especially his *Consolation of Philosophy.* Assesses influence of his thought on Middle Ages. [JJC]

20.1049 Walter Goffart. *The narrators of barbarian history (A.D. 550–800): Jordanes, Gregory of Tours, Bede, and Paul the Deacon.* Princeton: Princeton University Press, 1988. ISBN 0-691-05514-9. ‣ Examination of four major early medieval historians. Discusses literary aspects of each author's work and demonstrates how local and contemporary concerns helped to shape their narratives. [JJC]

20.1050 Michael Haren. *Medieval thought: the Western intellectual tradition from antiquity to the thirteenth century.* 2d ed. Toronto: University of Toronto Press, 1993. ISBN 0-8020-2868-3. ‣ Reception and influence of Plato, Aristotle, and Neoplatonists in medi-

eval thought from Augustine to thirteenth-century scholastics. Sees theme of medieval speculative thought as absorption of classical legacy. [JJC]

20.1051 Michael W. Herren, ed. *The sacred nectar of the Greeks: the study of Greek in the West in the early Middle Ages.* London: King's College London Medieval Studies, 1988. (King's College London medieval studies, 2.) ISBN 0-9513085-1-3 (pbk). ‣ Eight essays examining evidence for study of Greek from seventh to ninth century. Finds Greek studies influenced Latin grammatical studies, biblical exegesis, and Christian theology. [JJC]

20.1052 Gerhart B. Ladner. *The idea of reform: its impact on Christian thought and action in the age of the fathers.* Rev. ed. New York: Harper & Row, 1967. ‣ Magisterial study of Christian notions of reform stressing personal rebirth from sin into state of grace. Reform understood as improvement oriented to future, not to past golden age. [JJC]

20.1053 John Marenbon. *Early medieval philosophy (480–1150): an introduction.* New York: Routledge, 1988. ISBN 0-415-00070-x (pbk). ‣ Stresses relationship between philosophical speculation, grammar, theology, and science, arguing that theology stimulated philosophical reflection. [JJC]

20.1054 Giselle de Nie. *Views from a many-windowed tower: studies of imagination in the works of Gregory of Tours.* Amsterdam: Rodopi, 1987. ISBN 90-6203-719-4 (pbk). ‣ Advanced stylistic analysis of Frankish historian and bishop's work (538–594). Apparently random style becomes coherent when works read as expressions of nonverbal thought. Sensitivity to images and dreams, and discontinuities in nature inform his work. [JJC]

20.1055 James J. O'Donnell. *Cassiodorus.* Berkeley: University of California Press, 1979. ISBN 0-520-03646-8. ‣ Study of political, monastic, historiographical, educational, philosophical, and theological writings and activities of Roman author and monk against backdrop of sixth-century Ostrogothic Italy. Perspective more literary than doctrinal. [JJC]

20.1056 Edward Kennard Rand. *Founders of the Middle Ages.* 1928 ed. New York: Dover, 1957. ISBN 0-486-20369-7 (pbk). ‣ Dated but still classic study of preservation and use of classical tradition by Western Christian writers from Jerome through Boethius. Benchmark in anti-Burckhardtian revisionist movement. [MLC]

20.1057 Pierre Riché. *Écoles et enseignement dans le haut moyen âge, fin du cinquième siècle–milieu du onzième siècle.* Paris: Picard, 1989. ISBN 2-7084-0378-8. ‣ Introductory survey of schools, masters, pedagogy, and curricula from sixth to eleventh century. Treats education of clergy and laypersons. [JJC]

20.1058 Carole Straw. *Gregory the Great: perfection in imperfection.* Berkeley: University of California Press, 1988. ISBN 0-520-05767-8. ‣ Examination of key figure in transformation of late antique thought and beginning of early medieval intellectual patterns. Nuanced treatment of scriptural and theological bases of church father's outlook. [JJC]

20.1059 Warren Treadgold, ed. *Renaissances before the Renaissance: cultural revivals of late antiquity and the Middle Ages.* Stanford, Calif.: Stanford University Press, 1984. ISBN 0-8047-1198-4. ‣ Seven essays on phenomenon of cultural revival from second through twelfth centuries, especially Carolingian period, Anglo-Saxon monastic revival, and twelfth-century renaissance. [JJC]

Carolingian and Post-Carolingian Culture

20.1060 Bernhard Bischoff. *Latin paleography: antiquity and the Middle Ages.* David O'Cróinín and David Ganz, trans. Cambridge: Cambridge University Press, 1990. ISBN 0-521-36473-6 (cl), 0-521-36726-3 (pbk). ‣ History of handwriting in its cultural context in late Roman empire and Middle Ages. Authoritative treatment of production and cultural function of books in medieval society. [JJC]

20.1061 Bernhard Bischoff. "Turning points in the history of Latin exegesis in the early Middle Ages." In *Biblical studies: the medieval Irish contribution.* Martin McNamara, ed. Colm O'Grady, article trans., pp. 73–160. Dublin: Dominican, 1975. (Proceedings of the Irish Biblical Association, 1.) ▸ How work of Irish commentators on Bible influenced Continental biblical studies in seventh, eighth, and ninth centuries. Magisterial delineation of characteristics of Hiberno-Latin biblical exegesis. [JJC]

20.1062 Donald A. Bullough. *The age of Charlemagne.* 1965 ed. New York: Exeter Books; distributed by Bookthrift, 1980. ISBN 0-89673-045-X. ▸ Survey of scholarship, learning, art, architecture, and political theory during reign of Charlemagne (768–814). Sees Charlemagne as catalyst of European change. [JJC]

20.1063 Donald A. Bullough. *Carolingian renewal: sources and heritage.* Manchester: Manchester University Press, 1991. ISBN 0-7190-3354-3. ▸ Eight studies tracing inspiration and impact of Carolingian intellectual and cultural efforts from eighth to tenth century. Sees Carolingian renaissance as inspired by both religious and dynastic concerns. [JJC]

20.1064 Donald A. Bullough. "*Europae pater*: Charlemagne and his achievement in the light of recent scholarship." *English historical review* 75 (1970) 59–105. ISSN 0013-8266. ▸ Ostensibly review of Wolfgang Braunfels et al., eds., *Karl der Grosse: Lebenswerk und Nachleben* (1965–68); essay sheds own light on Carolingian religious and intellectual life. [JJC]

20.1065 Marcia L. Colish. *The mirror of language: a study in the medieval theory of knowledge.* 2d ed. Lincoln: University of Nebraska Press, 1983. ISBN 0-8032-1418-9. ▸ Groundbreaking semiotic study of theological work of saints Augustine, Anselm, and Thomas Aquinas and of Dante. Discusses role of grammar, rhetoric, and dialectic in shaping their verbal thinking about God. [JJC/WJC]

20.1066 John J. Contreni. *The Cathedral School of Laon from 850 to 930: its manuscripts and masters.* Fahrenzhausen-Bachenhausen: Arbeo-Gesellschaft, 1978. (Münchener Beiträge zur Mediävistik und Renaissance Forschung, 29.) ISBN 3-920128-30-3. ▸ Study of Carolingian school where three generations of masters taught liberal arts, medicine, Greek, and theology using library resources they collected. Laon's bishops patronized school and Irish masters taught there. [JJC]

20.1067 Eleanor Shipley Duckett. *Death and life in the tenth century.* 1967 ed. Ann Arbor: University of Michigan Press, 1971. ▸ Overview of highs and lows in tenth-century culture. Second part of book treats monastic reforms, poetry, historiography, liturgical and nonliturgical drama, learning, and art. [MLC]

20.1068 Bruce S. Eastwood. "Plinian astronomical diagrams in the early Middle Ages." In *Mathematics and its applications to science and natural philosophy in the Middle Ages: essays in honor of Marshall Clagett.* Edward Grant and John Emery Murdoch, eds., pp. 141–72. Cambridge: Cambridge University Press, 1987. ISBN 0-521-32260-X. ▸ How pedagogical concerns led masters who taught astronomy to create diagrams to convey complex astronomical data in graphic form. Original study of emergence of visual aids to complement verbal learning. [JJC]

20.1069 David Ganz. *Corbie in the Carolingian renaissance.* Sigmaringen: Thorbecke, 1990. (Beihefte zu *Francia*, 20.) ISBN 3-7995-7320-8. ▸ Careful study of eighth- and ninth-century manuscripts of Corbie, showing that monastery was major center of theological and philosophical study. [JJC]

20.1070 Margaret T. Gibson and Janet L. Nelson, eds. *Charles the Bald: court and kingdom.* 2d ed. Aldershot: Variorum, 1990. ISBN 0-86078-265-4. ▸ Twenty-one studies on reign of Charlemagne's grandson, Charles (844–877), focusing especially on church and world of scholarship. [JJC]

20.1071 Peter Godman. *Poets and emperors: Frankish politics and Carolingian poetry.* Oxford: Clarendon, 1987. ISBN 0-19-812820-7. ▸ Poets enjoyed patronage of powerful political figures. Shows political poems an important gauge of texture of Carolingian political as well as intellectual life. [JJC]

20.1072 Peter Godman and Roger Collins, eds. *Charlemagne's heir: new perspectives on the reign of Louis the Pious (814–840).* Oxford: Clarendon, 1990. ISBN 0-19-821994-6. ▸ Thirty-one studies of neglected reign treating church, empire, law, learning, literature, art, architecture, and historiography in time of Frankish emperor. [JJC]

20.1073 Ernst H. Kantorowicz. *Laudes regiae: a study in liturgical acclamations and mediaeval ruler worship.* 1946 ed. Millwood, N.Y.: Kraus Reprint, 1974. ▸ Classic investigation of royal acclamations in coronation liturgies of medieval rulers from early Carolingians to thirteenth century. Pioneering study of ritual as source for political theory and popular belief. [JJC]

20.1074 M.L.W. Laistner. *Thought and letters in western Europe, A.D. 500 to 900.* 1957 rev. ed. Ithaca, N.Y.: Cornell University Press, 1966. ▸ Survey of Latin-Christian culture from fourth through eighth century providing in-depth study of education, libraries, literature, theology, philosophy, and historical writing in Carolingian age. [MLC]

20.1075 Wilhelm Levison. *England and the Continent in the eighth century.* 1946 ed. Oxford: Clarendon, 1949. ▸ Dated but useful study of Anglo-Saxon missionaries, reforming Frankish church and establishing links between Franks and popes, and their revival of learning and scholarship in Frankish kingdoms. [JJC]

20.1076 John Marenbon. *From the circle of Alcuin to the school of Auxerre: logic, theology, and philosophy in the early Middle Ages.* Cambridge: Cambridge University Press, 1981. ISBN 0-521-23428-X. ▸ Study showing how logical studies transformed theology in ninth century. Evidence of tradition of philosophical glossing and abstract speculation revises place of ninth century in medieval philosophy. [JJC]

20.1077 Rosamond McKitterick. *The Carolingians and the written word.* Cambridge: Cambridge University Press, 1989. ISBN 0-521-30539-X (cl), 0-521-31565-4 (pbk). ▸ Revisionist investigation of uses of writing in eighth and ninth centuries. Employment of written word in government and law argues for literacy at all levels of Carolingian society. [JJC]

20.1078 Rosamond McKitterick, ed. *The uses of literacy in early mediaeval Europe.* Cambridge: Cambridge University Press, 1990. ISBN 0-521-34409-3. ▸ Eleven revisionist studies on literacy in different geographical and cultural settings, fifth to tenth century, including use of writing in law, in secular and ecclesiastical administration, and among laypersons. [JJC]

20.1079 John J. O'Meara. *Eriugena.* Oxford: Clarendon, 1988. ISBN 0-19-826674-X. ▸ Discussion of poetry, biblical exegesis, Greek-Latin translations, controversies, and especially philosophy of ninth-century Irish scholar. Establishes Eriugena's place in Carolingian culture and his immediate philosophical and theological influence. [JJC]

20.1080 Wesley M. Stevens. "*Compotistica et astronomica* in the Fulda school." In *Saints, scholars, and heroes: studies in mediaeval culture in honour of Charles W. Jones.* 2 vols. Margot H. King and Wesley M. Stevens, eds., vol. 2, pp. 27–63. Collegeville, Minn.: Saint John's Abbey & University, Hill Monastic Manuscript Library, 1979. ISBN 0-8357-0480-7. ▸ Study of early medieval science as exemplified by education at Carolingian monastery of Fulda. Original treatment of geometry, astronomy, and arithmetical computation. [JJC]

20.1081 Richard E. Sullivan. "The Carolingian age: reflections on its place in the history of the Middle Ages." *Speculum* 64.2 (1989) 267–306. ISSN 0038-7134. ▸ Review of scholarship on Carolingian period. Challenges historians to recognize essential pluralism of Carolingian world. [JJC]

20.1082 Walter Ullmann. *The Carolingian renaissance and the idea of kingship.* London: Methuen, 1969. ISBN 0-4161-1770-8. ▸ Sees Carolingian renaissance as effort to renew Frankish society. Treats political theory from standpoint of recovery of classical thought, downplaying influence of Germanic and Christian traditions. [JJC]

20.1083 Walter Ullmann. *Law and politics in the Middle Ages: an introduction to the sources of medieval political ideas.* Ithaca, N.Y.: Cornell University Press, 1975. ISBN 0-8014-0940-3. ▸ Introductory examination of development of law between sixth and fifteenth centuries, noting origins and sources of Roman, canon, and nonsecular Roman law. [JJC]

20.1084 Luitpold Wallach. *Alcuin and Charlemagne: studies in Carolingian history and literature.* 1959 rev. ed. New York: Johnson Reprint, 1968. (Cornell studies in classical philology, 32.) ▸ Essays focusing on Charlemagne's adviser, especially his intellectual influence on Frankish court in late eighth and early ninth centuries, relationship with Charlemagne, and literary method. [JJC]

INSTITUTIONAL HISTORY OF THE CHURCH, 1050–1500

General Church History and the Papacy

20.1085 Marshall W. Baldwin. *Alexander III and the twelfth century.* Glen Rock, N.J.: Newman, 1968. ▸ Introduction to Alexander III's early years, cardinalate, election as pope, beginnings of schism of 1159, Thomas Becket affair and relations with England, and Alexander's concept of papal monarchy. [KP]

20.1086 Geoffrey Barraclough. *Papal provisions: aspects of church history, constitutional, legal, and administrative in the later Middle Ages.* Westport, Conn.: Greenwood, 1971. ISBN 0-8371-4198-2. ▸ Traces development of rules governing bestowal of benefices in church, papal authority to grant benefices, and canon law of benefices. [KP]

20.1087 Anne Llewellyn Barstow. *Married priests and the reforming papacy: the eleventh-century debates.* Lewiston, N.Y.: Mellen, 1982. ISBN 0-88946-976-8. ▸ Presentation of debate over clerical celibacy, legislation enforcing it, and defense of clerical marriage. Discusses social implications of unmarried priests after eleventh century. [KP]

20.1088 Thomas S. R. Boase. *Boniface VIII.* London: Constable, 1933. ▸ Dated but still readable account of important late medieval pope. Discusses Boniface's election as pope, dispute with King Philip IV of France and Colonna cardinals, and bulls asserting papal authority. [KP]

20.1089 Christopher R. Cheney. *The papacy and England, twelfth–fourteenth centuries: historical and legal studies.* London: Variorum, 1982. ISBN 0-86078-099-6. ▸ Specialized studies on relations of papacy with King John, popes' reactions to Magna Carta, and papal letters sent to English recipients and their legal forms and contents. [KP]

20.1090 Christopher R. Cheney. *Pope Innocent III and England.* Stuttgart: Hiersemann, 1976. ISBN 3-7772-7623-5. ▸ Accessible discussion of influence of pope on English politics and ecclesiastical affairs in early thirteenth century. Analyzes King John's

difficulties with Innocent and pope's reaction to Magna Carta. [KP]

20.1091 H.E.J. Cowdrey. *The age of Abbot Desiderius: Montecassino, the papacy, and the Normans in the eleventh and early twelfth centuries.* Oxford: Clarendon, 1983. ISBN 0-19-821939-3. ▸ Study of papacy under Victor III. Treats Victor's goals as abbot of Monte Cassino and as pope in context of contemporary Italian politics. Not for beginners. [KP/WJC]

20.1092 John R. Eastman. *Papal abdication in later medieval thought.* Lewiston, N.Y.: Mellen, 1990. ISBN 0-88946-831-1. ▸ History of actual and legendary abdications of popes. Treats theological and canonical literature dealing with question of papal abdication in later Middle Ages. [KP]

20.1093 Joseph Gill. *Personalities of the Council of Florence, and other essays.* 1964 ed. New York: Barnes & Noble, 1965. ▸ Specialized studies of churchmen who participated in Council of Florence. Discussion of reaction of both papacy and Greek Orthodox clerics to goal of ecclesiastical union. [KP]

20.1094 James Heft. *John XXII and papal teaching authority.* Lewiston, N.Y.: Mellen, 1986. ISBN 0-88946-815-X. ▸ Analysis of conflict of John XXII (1316–34) with Franciscans and his legislation. Focuses on emergence, in this context, of doctrine of papal sovereignty and infallibility. [KP]

20.1095 Hubert Jedin and John T. Dolan, eds. *Handbook of church history.* Vol. 3: *The church in the age of feudalism.* Vol. 4: *From the high Middle Ages to the eve of the Reformation.* 10 vols. Anselm Biggs, trans. New York: Herder & Herder, 1965–70. ▸ General handbook and collaborative effort, giving balanced coverage of all aspects of church life from early Middle Ages to eve of Reformation. Treats structure and function of ecclesiastical institutions, religious orders, reform movements, worship, theology, and heresy. Volumes 5–10 published under title: *History of the Church.* [KP]

20.1096 Howard Kaminsky. *Simon de Cramaud and the Great Schism.* New Brunswick, N.J.: Rutgers University Press, 1983. ISBN 0-8135-0949-1. ▸ Study of French prelate's role during Great Schism at councils of Paris (1394) and Pisa (1409) as advocate of cession as way to unify church. [KP]

20.1097 Eric Waldram Kemp. *Canonization and authority in the Western church.* 1948 ed. Westport, Conn.: Hyperion, 1979. ISBN 0-88355-852-1. ▸ Discussion of canonization of saints from ancient church to present, growth of papal authority as sole power to recognize saints, and development of canonization procedures. [KP]

20.1098 C. H. Lawrence, ed. *The English church and the papacy in the Middle Ages.* New York: Fordham University Press, 1965. ▸ Specialized essays on ecclesiastical, political, and financial relations between popes and English clergy. Description of papal curia, ecclesiastical jurisdiction, and court cases. Reform movements in England and Rome. [KP]

20.1099 Peter Linehan. *The Spanish church and the papacy in the thirteenth century.* Cambridge: Cambridge University Press, 1971. ISBN 0-521-08039-8. ▸ Study of relations between Rome and Iberian churches. Treats reform movement in Spain, economic conditions of churches, and influence of Spaniards in Rome. [KP]

20.1100 William E. Lunt. *Financial relations of the papacy with England, 1327–1534.* 2 vols. Cambridge, Mass.: Mediaeval Academy of America, 1939–62. (Studies in Anglo-papal relations during the Middle Ages, 1–2. Mediaeval Academy of America publications, 33, 74.) ▸ Study of papal taxes and revenues in England to 1534. Analysis of procurations of papal legates and collectors of taxes, royal and Crusade taxes. [KP]

20.1101 Horace K. Mann. *The lives of the popes in the early Mid-*

dle Ages. 1925–32 2d ed. 19 vols. Wilmington, N.C.: Consortium, 1979. ISBN 0-8434-0691-7. ▸ History of papacy from Gregory I to Boniface VIII (590–1305). Dated but only detailed narrative of papal history for period. Also available on microfilm from Howard University Microreproduction Service. [KP]

20.1102 Rosamond Joscelyne Mitchell. *The laurels and the tiara: Pope Pius II, 1458–1464.* 1962 ed. Garden City, N.Y.: Doubleday, 1963. ▸ Biography of humanist, patron of arts, bishop, cardinal, and pope; his reign and achievements. [KP]

20.1103 Guillaume Mollat. *The popes at Avignon, 1305–1378.* 1963 ed. Janet Love, trans. New York: Harper & Row, 1965. ▸ Standard account of papacy at Avignon. Popes' relations with secular rulers and operation of papal court, including administration and finance. [KP]

20.1104 Colin Morris. *The papal monarchy: the Western church from 1050 to 1250.* Oxford: Clarendon, 1989. ISBN 0-19-826907-2. ▸ General history of Western church. Covers investiture controversy, growth of papal monarchy, friars, structure of ecclesiastical government, and church-state relations. Annotated bibliographies. [KP]

20.1105 Francis C. Oakley. *The Western church in the later Middle Ages.* 1979 ed. Ithaca, N.Y.: Cornell University Press, 1985. ISBN 0-8014-1208-0 (cl, 1979), 0-8014-9347-1 (pbk). ▸ Fourteenth- and fifteenth-century church history viewed in its own right rather than as mere prelude to Reformation. Covers papacy, conciliar movement, and theological, spiritual, heretical, and institutional developments. [KP/FHS]

20.1106 Yves Renouard. *The Avignon papacy, 1305–1403.* Denis Bethell, trans. Hamden, Conn.: Archon, 1970. ISBN 0-208-01156-0. ▸ Study of papacy at Avignon to end of Great Schism. Discusses administrative centralization, bureaucracy, patronage, and relations between popes and secular rulers. [KP]

20.1107 I. S. Robinson. *The papacy, 1073–1198: continuity and innovation.* Cambridge: Cambridge University Press, 1990. ISBN 0-521-26498-7 (cl), 0-521-31922-6 (pbk). ▸ Detailed history at introductory level of evolution of papal government during critical stage in development. Treats politics and church-state relations. [KP]

20.1108 I. S. Robinson. "Pope Gregory VII: bibliographical survey." *Journal of ecclesiastical history* 36 (1985) 439–83. ISSN 0022-0469. ▸ Guide to literature on eleventh century's most important pope (1073–85) and his role in reform of church and in controversy between popes and lay rulers. [KP]

20.1109 Robert Somerville. *Pope Alexander III and the Council of Tours (1163): a study of ecclesiastical politics and institutions in the twelfth century.* Berkeley: University of California Press, 1977. (Publications of the Center for Medieval and Renaissance Studies, 12.) ISBN 0-520-03184-9. ▸ Detailed study of important church council. Examines calling, organization, and legislation of council. Illustrates significance of conciliar decrees. [KP]

20.1110 Joachim W. Stieber. *Pope Eugenius IV, the Council of Basel, and the secular and ecclesiastical authorities in the empire: the conflict over supreme authority and power in the church.* Leiden: Brill, 1978. ISBN 90-04-05240-2. ▸ Eugenius's struggle to overcome conciliarist movement at Council of Basel and to reassert papal supremacy over church councils. Not for beginners. [MLC]

20.1111 Mary Stroll. *The Jewish pope: ideology and politics in the papal schism of 1130.* Leiden: Brill, 1987. ISBN 90-04-08590-4. ▸ Detailed examination of papal schism of 1130 and motives of both papal chancellor Haimeric and of Innocent II's supporters. Also treats Gregorian reform movement and growth of juridical papacy. [KP]

20.1112 R. N. Swanson. *Universities, academics, and the Great*

Schism. Cambridge: Cambridge University Press, 1979. ISBN 0-521-22127-7. ▸ Specialized analysis of learned debate surrounding Great Schism, emergence of conciliarist solution to split between Roman and Avignonese popes, and the Council of Constance. [KP/WJC]

20.1113 John A. F. Thomson. *Popes and princes, 1417–1517: politics and polity in the late medieval church.* London: Allen & Unwin, 1980. ISBN 0-04-901027-1. ▸ Examination of church in postconciliar period. Discusses conflict between papal monarchy and nationalism, between Roman centralization and local control, and economic problems within church. [KP]

20.1114 Helene Tillmann. *Pope Innocent III.* Walter Sax, trans. Amsterdam: Elsevier, 1980. ISBN 0-444-85137-2. ▸ Biography of most important pope of Middle Ages. Studies Innocent's reform policies, concept of papal authority, role in Crusades, and relations with European monarchs. [KP]

20.1115 Walter Ullmann. *The origins of the Great Schism: a study in fourteenth-century ecclesiastical history.* 1948 ed. Hamden, Conn.: Archon, 1972. ISBN 0-208-01277-X. ▸ Dated but still useful introductory history of beginnings of Great Schism, 1378 to ca. 1383, and reactions of secular monarchs, theologians, and canonists to schism within church. [KP]

20.1116 Diana Wood. *Clement VI: the pontificate and ideas of an Avignon pope.* Cambridge: Cambridge University Press, 1989. ISBN 0-521-35460-9. ▸ Study of reign of Avignonese pope. Analyzes Clement's conception of his office, relationship with cardinals, and connections to France. Insightful study of fourteenth-century religious attitudes. [KP]

SEE ALSO
22.144 Ludwig von Pastor. *The history of the popes from the close of the Middle Ages.*
28.131 Peter Partner. *The pope's men.*
28.155 Joseph Gill. *The Council of Florence.*

National Churches, Bishoprics, and Institutions

20.1117 Frank Barlow. *The English church, 1000–1066: a history of the later Anglo-Saxon church.* 2d ed. London: Longman, 1979. ISBN 0-582-49049-9. ▸ Accessible examination of English church before Norman conquest. Treats episcopal government, relations between kings and bishops, church organization, and education of clergy. [KP]

20.1118 Frank Barlow. *Thomas Becket.* 1986 ed. Berkeley: University of California Press, 1990. ISBN 0-520-05920-4 (cl, 1986), 0-520-07175-1 (pbk). ▸ Biography of Becket with evenhanded treatment of issues, events, and outcome of his clash with Henry II. Careful examination of legal and political background. [KP]

20.1119 Constance Brittain Bouchard. *Spirituality and administration: the role of the bishop in twelfth-century Auxerre.* Cambridge, Mass.: Mediaeval Academy of America, 1979. (*Speculum* anniversary monographs, 5.) ISBN 0-910956-67-7. ▸ Study of administration of seven French bishops. Uses biographies to illustrate spirituality and administrative talents as perceived by contemporaries. [KP]

20.1120 Catherine E. Boyd. *Tithes and parishes in medieval Italy: the historical roots of a modern problem.* Ithaca, N.Y.: Cornell University Press, 1952. ▸ Dated, but only survey of ecclesiastical taxation in Italy from earliest times to twentieth century. Discusses Italian parish structure, transformation of lay tithes, and distribution and city-state regulation of tithes. [KP]

20.1121 Robert Brentano. *Two churches: England and Italy in the thirteenth century.* 1968 ed. Berkeley: University of California Press, 1988. ISBN 0-520-06098-9 (pbk). ▸ Comparison of institutional structure of Italian and English church governments, discussing relationship of each church to central authority and to local interests. [KP]

20.1122   Martin Brett. *The English church under Henry I.* London: Oxford University Press, 1975. ISBN 0-19-821861-3. ▸ Study of English church in early twelfth century. Examines bishops and archbishops in church and state; functions of cathedral chapters; life, duties, and social status of parish clergy; and relations with Rome. [KP]

20.1123   Mark Buck. *Politics, finance, and the church in the reign of Edward II: Walter Stapeldon, treasurer of England.* Cambridge: Cambridge University Press, 1983. ISBN 0-521-25025-0. ▸ Case study of role clerics played in secular as well as church government in early fourteenth century. Description of upheavals in Edward II's reign that led to Stapeldon's murder. [KP]

20.1124   Norman F. Cantor. *Church, kingship, and lay investiture in England, 1089–1135.* 1958 ed. New York: Octagon Books, 1969. ▸ Study of church and state in England during investiture controversy. Discusses ecclesiastical policies of Anglo-Norman kings and relations between England and papacy. [KP]

20.1125   Christopher R. Cheney. *English bishops' chanceries, 1100–1250.* Manchester: Manchester University Press, 1950. (Publications of the Faculty of Arts of the University of Manchester, 3.) ▸ Study of administration of English bishops' households using documents produced by episcopal government and collected in episcopal archives. [KP]

20.1126   Christopher R. Cheney. *The English church and its laws, twelfth–fourteenth centuries.* London: Variorum, 1982. ISBN 0-86078-108-9. ▸ Specialized institutional and legal studies of English church. Focuses on content and form of synodal legislation and relations between England and Rome. [KP]

20.1127   Christopher R. Cheney. *From Becket to Langton: English church government, 1170–1213.* 1956 ed. Manchester: Manchester University Press, 1965. ▸ Analysis of structure of English church, its relations with Rome and king, episcopal authority, description of dioceses, and role of canon law. [KP]

20.1128   Irene Josephine Churchill. *Canterbury administration: the administrative machinery of the archbishopric of Canterbury, illustrated from original records.* 2 vols. London: Society for Promoting Christian Knowledge, 1933. ▸ Detailed description of structure of government in archdiocese of Canterbury, thirteenth to fifteenth century. Treats elections, visitations, provincial assemblies, ecclesiastical courts, papal judges delegate, and financial administration. [KP]

20.1129   Joseph H. Dahmus. *William Courtenay: archbishop of Canterbury, 1381–1396.* University Park: Pennsylvania State University Press, 1966. ▸ Life of influential bishop of London and archbishop of Canterbury. Discussion of role in trial of John Wyclif and suppression of Lollards and relations with crown. [KP]

20.1130   Jeffrey H. Denton. *Philip the Fair and the ecclesiastical assemblies of 1294–1295.* Philadelphia: American Philosophical Society, 1991. (Transactions of the American Philosophical Society, 81.1.) ISBN 0-87169-811-0 (pbk). ▸ Discussion of French king and assemblies that raised funds for war against England by imposing 10 percent tax on church property and conditions under which French clergy granted subsidies to the crown. [KP]

20.1131   Jeffrey H. Denton. *Robert Winchelsey and the crown, 1294–1313: a study in the defense of ecclesiastical liberty.* Cambridge: Cambridge University Press, 1980. ISBN 0-521-22963-4. ▸ Analysis of career of Winchelsey, archbishop of Canterbury, illustrating church-state relations on issue of clerical taxation during reigns of King Edward I and Pope Boniface VIII. [KP]

20.1132   J. C. Dickinson. *The later Middle Ages: from the Norman conquest to the eve of the Reformation.* Vol. 2 of *An ecclesiastical history of England.* New York: Barnes & Noble, 1979. 8 vols. ISBN 0-06-491678-2 (v. 2). ▸ General history of English church. Structure of bishoprics, monasteries, and parishes; relationship between Rome and England; and decline of ecclesiastical institutions in later Middle Ages. [KP]

20.1133   Kathleen Edwards. *The English secular cathedrals in the Middle Ages: a constitutional study with special reference to the fourteenth century.* 2d ed. Manchester: Manchester University Press, 1967. ▸ Study of structure of cathedral chapters of secular canons, duties of their officers (dean, cantor, chancellor, treasurer, archdeacon), and jurisdiction of bishops over chapters of canons. [KP]

20.1134   Bernard Guenée. *Between church and state: the lives of four French prelates in the late Middle Ages.* Arthur Goldhammer, trans. Chicago: University of Chicago Press, 1991. ISBN 0-226-31032-9. ▸ Biographies of four French bishops, thirteenth to fifteenth century, focusing on roles in government of church and in rule of secular state. Church history through biography. [KP]

20.1135   Roy Martin Haines. *The church and politics in fourteenth-century England: the career of Adam Orleton, 1275–1345.* Cambridge: Cambridge University Press, 1978. ISBN 0-521-21544-7. ▸ Career of Orleton as lawyer, diplomat, bishop of Hereford, Worcester, and Winchester. Discussion of his political role in revolt against King Edward II led by his wife Queen Isabella and her lover Roger Mortimer. [KP]

20.1136   Margaret Howell. *Regalian right in medieval England.* London: Athlone, 1962. (University of London historical studies, 9.) ▸ Analysis of right claimed by English kings to collect revenue from vacant bishoprics in twelfth and thirteenth centuries. Studies exercise and significance of royal and feudal rights and royal ecclesiastical patronage. [KP]

20.1137   Peter Linehan. *Spanish church and society, 1150–1300.* London: Variorum, 1983. ISBN 0-86078-132-1. ▸ Specialized essays on structure of Spanish church in twelfth and thirteenth centuries. Topics include rise of nationalism, Spain as frontier society, and reform of church. [KP]

20.1138   Duane J. Osheim. *An Italian lordship: the bishopric of Lucca in the late Middle Ages.* Berkeley: University of California Press, 1977. (Publications of the Center for Medieval and Renaissance Studies, 11.) ISBN 0-520-03005-2. ▸ Study of governance and administration of bishopric of Lucca from eleventh to fourteenth century. Examines episcopal rights, wealth, and landholdings and relations between city-state and bishop. [KP]

20.1139   W. A. Pantin. *The English church in the fourteenth century.* 1953 ed. Toronto: University of Toronto Press, 1980. ISBN 0-8020-6411-6 (pbk). ▸ Survey of church government, pastoral roles and social structure of clergy, intellectual life, royal and aristocratic patronage, papal provisions, and relations between English church and papacy. [KP/WJC]

20.1140   Avrom Saltman. *Theobald, archbishop of Canterbury.* 1956 ed. New York: Greenwood, 1969. ▸ Biography of Thomas Becket's predecessor at Canterbury. Treats Theobald's relations with other bishops, with monasteries in Canterbury province, and with Henry II. Discussion of structure of archbishop's household. [KP]

20.1141   Beryl Smalley. *The Becket conflict and the schools: a study of intellectuals in politics.* Totowa, N.J.: Rowman & Littlefield, 1973. ISBN 0-87471-172-X. ▸ Study of major figures involved in controversy between Henry II and Thomas Becket. Focuses on masters of theology who supported Becket and the case against him. [KP]

20.1142   R. W. Southern. *Saint Anselm and his biographer: a study of monastic life and thought, 1059–c. 1130.* Cambridge: Cambridge

University Press, 1963. ▸ Biography of St. Anselm as abbot and theologian as well as archbishop. Treats conflict with William II and Henry I, monastic community at Canterbury, and his biographer, Eadmer. [KP/WJC]

20.1143 R. N. Swanson. *Church and society in late medieval England.* Oxford: Blackwell, 1989. ISBN 0-631-14659-8. ▸ Study of English church and lay society, including careers of clerics, politics and church, canon and English law, ecclesiastical and secular courts, economic activity of church, heresy, and reform. [KP/FHS]

20.1144 A. Hamilton Thompson. *The English clergy and their organization in the later Middle Ages.* Oxford: Clarendon, 1966. ▸ General history of English church in fifteenth century. Covers episcopal government, cathedral chapters, collegiate churches, parsons, vicars, curates, chantries, and monasteries. [KP]

20.1145 Sally N. Vaughn. *Anselm of Bec and Robert of Meulan: the innocence of the dove and the wisdom of the serpent.* Berkeley: University of California Press, 1987. ISBN 0-520-05674-4. ▸ Analysis of church-state relations in England in late eleventh and early twelfth centuries. Focuses on role of bishops, especially St. Anselm of Canterbury, and nobles in affairs of Anglo-Norman realm. [KP]

20.1146 Katherine Walsh. *Richard FitzRalph in Oxford, Avignon, and Armagh: a fourteenth-century scholar and primate.* Oxford: Clarendon, 1981. ISBN 0-19-822637-3. ▸ Study of mid-fourteenth-century Irish archbishop; his dealings with independence and reform of Irish church, Black Death, pastoral care, and mendicant controversy. [KP/WJC]

20.1147 John Watt. *The church and the two nations in medieval Ireland.* Cambridge: Cambridge University Press, 1970. ISBN 0-521-07738-9. ▸ Analysis of effects of English conquest on Irish church. Treats structure of Irish church, status of clergy in common law, role of episcopate, and Statute of Kilkenny and church. [KP]

20.1148 K. L. Wood-Legh. *Perpetual chantries in Britain.* Cambridge: Cambridge University Press, 1965. ▸ Study of establishment and function of chantries (endowments for singing of masses or prayers) in England, their relationships with bishops, abbots, and lay society, and duties of chaplains attached to them. [KP]

20.1149 Charles R. Young. *Hubert Walter, lord of Canterbury and lord of England.* Durham, N.C.: Duke University Press, 1968. ▸ Biography of bishop, archbishop, royal justiciar, and chancellor, studying role in politics, disputes with monks of Canterbury, and episcopal and provincial administration. [KP]

SEE ALSO
28.156 Denys Hay. *The church in Italy in the fifteenth century.*

Religious Orders

20.1150 Charles Julian Bishko. *Spanish and Portuguese monastic history, 600–1300.* London: Variorum, 1984. ISBN 0-86078-136-4. ▸ Specialized essays on establishment and growth of monasticism in Iberian peninsula, spread of Cluniac order between eleventh and thirteenth centuries, and Spanish church councils. [KP]

20.1151 Thomas S. R. Boase. *St. Francis of Assisi.* Bloomington: Indiana University Press, 1968. ▸ Still useful biography of St. Francis, treating chronology of his life, spread of Franciscan order, its organization and early rules, relationship to papacy, and Franciscan missions in Palestine and Egypt. [KP]

20.1152 Rosalind B. Brooke. *The coming of the friars.* New York: Barnes & Noble, 1975. ISBN 0-06-490700-7. ▸ Useful introduction to historical situation antedating establishment of Franciscans and Dominicans, new religious orders and heresies of twelfth

century, lives of saints Francis and Dominic, and relations with papacy. [KP]

20.1153 Rosalind B. Brooke. *Early Franciscan government, Elias to Bonaventure.* Cambridge: Cambridge University Press, 1959. ▸ Groundbreaking history of governance of Franciscan order to 1260. Treats sources and legislation of early Franciscans, lives of ministers general, and tension between Franciscan ideals and growth of order. [KP]

20.1154 David Burr. *Olivi and Franciscan poverty: the origins of the usus pauper controversy.* Philadelphia: University of Pennsylvania Press, 1989. ISBN 0-8122-8151-9. ▸ Specialized study of importance of Peter John Olivi in formation of Franciscan ideas of poverty before split in order between spirituals and conventuals. [KP/WJC]

20.1155 Giles Constable. *Cluniac studies.* London: Variorum, 1980. ISBN 0-86078-054-6. ▸ Specialized essays on abbey of Cluny, Cluniac order, and Peter the Venerable, treating monastic legislation, administration, and relationship of Cluniacs to lay authorities. [KP]

20.1156 Giles Constable. *Monastic tithes, from their origins to the twelfth century.* Cambridge: Cambridge University Press, 1964. ▸ Dated but valuable study of taxation by monasteries ministering to lay congregations and related papal legislation for and privileges to various religious orders. [KP]

20.1157 H.E.J. Cowdrey. *The Cluniacs and the Gregorian reform.* Oxford: Clarendon, 1970. ISBN 0-19-826429-1. ▸ Most recent, general study of Cluny's exemptions from episcopal control in eleventh and twelfth centuries; order's expansion into France, Germany, and Spain; and relationship to papacy and reform movement. [KP]

20.1158 F. G. Cowley. *The monastic order in South Wales, 1066–1349.* Cardiff: University of Wales Press, 1977. ISBN 0-7083-0648-1. ▸ General treatment of Welsh monasticism, surveying monastic recruitment, discipline, economy, literary production, and relations with bishops and lay society. [KP]

20.1159 E. Randolph Daniel. *The Franciscan concept of mission in the high Middle Ages.* Lexington: University Press of Kentucky, 1975. ISBN 0-8131-1315-6. ▸ Outlines fusion of Joachim of Fiore's thought with Franciscan doctrines of mission and conversion. Argues for continuity of Franciscan missionary ideology from Francis to fifteenth century. [KP]

20.1160 Omer Englebert. *Saint Francis of Assisi: a biography.* 2d ed. Eve Marie Cooper, trans. Ignatius Brady and Raphael Brown, revising eds. Chicago: Franciscan Herald Press, 1966. ▸ Biography of St. Francis of Assisi with detailed appendixes on sources, chronology, family, and early followers. Extensive bibliography for 1939–63. [KP]

20.1161 John B. Freed. *The friars and German society in the thirteenth century.* Cambridge, Mass.: Mediaeval Academy of America, 1977. (Mediaeval Academy of America publications, 86.) ISBN 0-910956-60-X. ▸ Study of expansion of Franciscan order into eastern Germany, establishment of their priory in Cologne, social origins of friars, and their involvement in German imperial politics. [KP]

20.1162 Bernard Hamilton. *Monastic reform, Catharism, and the crusades (900–1300).* London: Variorum, 1979. ISBN 0-86078-042-2. ▸ Specialized essays on monasticism in Italy and Latin kingdom of Jerusalem, Albigensian heresy and Albigensian crusade, and relations between Latin and Greek churches. [KP]

20.1163 Bennett D. Hill. *English Cistercian monasteries and their patrons in the twelfth century.* Urbana: University of Illinois Press, 1968. ▸ Leading detailed account of spread of Cistercians in England, patrons and reform policies, and compromises with original ideals that led to intense economic activity and acquisition of wealth. [KP]

20.1164 William A. Hinnebusch. *The early English friars preachers*. Rome: Ad S. Sabinae, 1951. (Dissertationes historicae, 14.) ‣ Study of spread of Dominican order in England in thirteenth century. Includes geographical survey of episcopal, royal, and noble Dominican foundations with attention to architecture, economic activities, and governance of their houses. [KP]

20.1165 William A. Hinnebusch. *The history of the Dominican order*. Vol. 1: *Origins and growth to 1500*. Vol. 2: *The intellectual and cultural life to 1500*. 2 vols. New York: Alba House, 1966–73. ISBN 0-8189-0266-3 (v. 1). ‣ Detailed general history of Dominican order from foundation to 1500. Topics include life of St. Dominic, spread of order geographically, its governance and legislation, and intellectual influence of Dominicans on high medieval culture. [KP]

20.1166 Noreen Hunt. *Cluniac monasticism in the central Middle Ages*. Hamden, Conn.: Archon, 1971. ISBN 0-208-01247-8. ‣ Study of constitution of Cluniac order, its impact on monastic reform in eleventh and twelfth centuries, and spread to Iberian peninsula. [KP]

20.1167 Noreen Hunt. *Cluny under Saint Hugh, 1049–1109*. 1967 ed. Notre Dame, Ind.: University of Notre Dame Press, 1968. ‣ Basic study of constitution of Cluny, 1049–1109: government, monastic structure, exemptions, economy, and spread of order into France, Spain, Portugal, Italy, Germany, and Low Countries. [KP]

20.1168 Bruno S. James. *Saint Bernard of Clairvaux: an essay in biography*. New York: Harper, 1957. ‣ Dated but valuable biography of Bernard (1090–1153), leading Cistercian of his day; relations with kings of France, papacy, and other Cistercian leaders; and spread of order in France. [KP/WJC]

20.1169 Penelope D. Johnson. *Prayer, patronage, and power: the abbey of la Trinité, Vendôme, 1032–1187*. New York: New York University Press, 1981. ISBN 0-8147-4162-2. ‣ Specialized case study of establishment of monasteries in West Central France, their organization and economic activities, lay patrons, and relations with other monasteries and with Rome. [KP]

20.1170 Benjamin Z. Kedar. *Crusade and mission: European approaches toward the Muslims*. Princeton: Princeton University Press, 1984. ISBN 0-691-05424-X. ‣ Discussion of Franciscan missions to convert Muslims and tension between this policy and that of Crusade and conquest in twelfth and thirteenth centuries. [KP]

20.1171 David Knowles. *The monastic order in England: a history of its development from the times of St. Dunstan to the Fourth Lateran Council, 940–1216*. 2d ed. Cambridge: Cambridge University Press, 1963. ‣ Survey of monasticism in England, focusing on influence of Norman conquest, spread of Cluniacs, and rise of Cistercians. Describes monastic governance and administration; weighs economic and intellectual importance of monasticism. [KP]

20.1172 David Knowles. *The religious orders in England*. Vol. 1: *The old orders, 1216–1340*. Vol. 2: *The end of the Middle Ages*. 2 vols. Cambridge: Cambridge University Press, 1948–55. ‣ Remains leading overview of Benedictines, Augustinians, Cistercians, and friars in England, 1216–1480, charting orders' governance, economy, administration, relations with bishops, schools, libraries, intellectual life, and late medieval decline. [KP]

20.1173 Bede K. Lackner. *The eleventh-century background of Cîteaux*. Washington, D.C.: Cistercian, 1972. ISBN 0-87907-808-1. ‣ Sees crisis in eleventh-century monasticism, foundation of Cluny and other new religious orders in response to crisis, as context for beginnings of Cistercians. [KP]

20.1174 Malcolm D. Lambert. *Franciscan poverty: the doctrine of the absolute poverty of Christ and the apostles in the Franciscan order, 1210–1323*. London: Society for Promoting Christian Knowledge, 1961. ‣ Study of Franciscan conceptions of poverty from St. Francis to condemnation of doctrine of absolute poverty by Pope John XXII, and of split between spiritual and conventual Fransciscans. [KP]

20.1175 Louis J. Lekai. *The Cistercians: ideals and reality*. Kent, Ohio: Kent State University Press, 1977. ISBN 0-87338-201-3. ‣ General account of Cistercian order from its foundation in eleventh century to modern times. Surveys Cistercian contributions to learning, art, liturgy, and economy. [KP]

20.1176 Henrietta Leyser. *Hermits and the new monasticism: a study of religious communities in Western Europe, 1000–1150*. New York: St. Martin's, 1984. ISBN 0-312-36999-9. ‣ Only general study of hermits in Italy, France, and England. Treats organization, role of female hermits, liturgy, labor, relationship to laity, and preaching. [KP/JJC]

20.1177 Lester K. Little. *Religious poverty and the profit economy in medieval Europe*. 1978 ed. Ithaca, N.Y.: Cornell University Press, 1983. ISBN 0-8014-9247-5. ‣ Description of new and old religious orders of twelfth and thirteenth centuries. Based on thesis that they accented voluntary poverty in reaction to urban economy. Treats heretical movements in that same light. [KP/FHS]

20.1178 Donald Matthew. *The Norman monasteries and their English possessions*. 1962 ed. Westport, Conn.: Greenwood, 1979. ISBN 0-313-20847-6. ‣ Overview of Norman-French monastic holdings in England, relationship between priories and mother houses, and dissolution and suppression of holdings in fourteenth century. [KP]

20.1179 Ernest W. McDonnell. *The beguines and beghards in medieval culture with special emphasis on the Belgian scene*. 1954 ed. New York: Octagon Books, 1969. ‣ Still valuable study of devout Christians who formed communities outside of existing religious orders, thirteenth to fifteenth century; their relations with local bishops and papacy; and legislation outlawing and persecuting them in fourteenth century. [KP/FHS]

20.1180 John H. Moorman. *A history of the Franciscan order from its origins to the year 1517*. Oxford: Clarendon, 1968. ISBN 0-19-826425-9. ‣ Basic introduction to life of St. Francis, spread of Franciscan order outside Italy, dispute between spirituals and conventuals, missions outside Europe, and development of several branches of order in late Middle Ages. [KP]

20.1181 Joseph F. O'Callaghan. *The Spanish military order of Calatrava and its affiliates*. London: Variorum, 1975. ISBN 0-902089-75-7. ‣ Specialized essays treating foundation and spread of Spanish military religious orders, twelfth to fifteenth century; covers their functions, governing statutes, and relations with Spanish ecclesiastical hierarchy. [KP]

20.1182 Colin Platt. *The abbeys and priories of medieval England*. New York: Fordham University Press, 1984. ISBN 0-8232-1117-7 (cl), 0-8232-1118-5 (pbk). ‣ Survey of monastic foundations in England from 1066 to Reformation. Religious, economic, and social importance of monasteries; special attention to building programs. [KP]

20.1183 Williell R. Thomson. *Friars in the cathedral: the first Franciscan bishops, 1226–1261*. Toronto: Pontifical Institute of Mediaeval Studies, 1975. (Studies and texts, 33.) ISBN 0-88844-033-2. ‣ Study of effect and influence of Franciscan bishops on church. Prosopographical study of each Franciscan bishop. Analyzes Franciscan activities in frontier areas of Christianity. [KP]

20.1184 Richard C. Trexler. *Naked before the father: the renunciation of Francis of Assisi*. New York: Lang, 1989. ISBN 0-8204-

0931-6. ▸ Examination of Francis's renunciation of his father and worldly career—using literary and artistic sources—both as family drama and as assertion of spiritual versus mercantile values. Psychohistorical approach. [KP]

20.1185 John Van Engen. "The 'crisis of cenobitism' reconsidered: Benedictine monasticism in the years 1050–1150." *Speculum* 61 (1986) 269–304. ISSN 0038-7134. ▸ Survey of literature on problems of monastic development and reform in eleventh and twelfth centuries. Challenges view that Benedictine order was in state of decline. [KP]

20.1186 Sally N. Vaughn. *The abbey of Bec and the Anglo-Norman state, 1034–1136.* Woodbridge, England: Boydell & Brewer; distributed by Biblio, 1981. ISBN 0-85115-140-X. ▸ Founding of abbey of Bec, its relations with Norman dukes and, after 1066, with English kings. Discusses role of archbishops of Canterbury Lanfranc and Anselm in shaping its monastic life. [KP]

20.1187 M. H. Vicaire. *Saint Dominic and his times.* Kathleen Pond, trans. New York: McGraw-Hill, 1964. ▸ Detailed and still useful life and times of St. Dominic. Study of founding and spread of order, and relationship to church, papacy, and other contemporary reform movements. [KP]

20.1188 Ann K. Warren. *Anchorites and their patrons in medieval England.* Berkeley: University of California Press, 1985. ISBN 0-520-05278-1. ▸ Study of hermits in England, twelfth to sixteenth century, documenting royal, aristocratic, mercantile, and clerical patronage; actual and perceived religious and social roles. [KP/FHS]

Heresy and the Inquisition

20.1189 Malcolm Barber. *The trial of the Templars.* Cambridge: Cambridge Univerity Press, 1978. ISBN 0-521-21896-9. ▸ Account of persecution and condemnation of Knights Templars as heretics in early fourteenth century. Role of papacy and French monarchy; description of trial and Inquisitorial procedures. [KP]

20.1190 Norman Cohn. *The pursuit of the millennium: revolutionary millenarians and mystical anarchists of the Middle Ages.* 1970 rev. ed. New York: Oxford University Press, 1972. ISBN 0-19-500456-6 (pbk). ▸ Classic if controversial psychosocial account of medieval radical religious movements. Relates such movements to social and political change and inability of movements' adherents to cope with change. [KP/FHS]

20.1191 Joseph H. Dahmus. *Prosecution of John Wyclyf.* 1952 ed. Hamden, Conn.: Archon, 1970. ISBN 0-208-00953-1. ▸ Older but still useful study of Wyclif's education and academic career at Oxford, involvement in politics and political polemics, persecution by papacy, and trial for heresy. [KP]

20.1192 Decima L. Douie. *The nature and the effect of the heresy of the Fraticelli.* 1932 ed. New York: AMS Press, 1978. ISBN 0-404-16121-9. ▸ Dated but still useful discussion of split between spiritual and conventual Franciscans in thirteenth and fourteenth centuries, influence of Joachism on spirituals, and dispute between spirituals and Pope John XXII over apostolic poverty. [KP]

20.1193 Anthony Kenny, ed. *Wyclif in his times.* Oxford: Clarendon, 1986. ISBN 0-19-820088-9. ▸ Specialized essays on English reformer's impact on literature, philosophy, theology, and history; career as Oxford professor; and influence on John Hus and later thinkers. [KP/WJC]

20.1194 Richard Kieckhefer. *Repression of heresy in medieval Germany.* 1978 ed. Philadelphia: University of Pennsylvania Press, 1979. ISBN 0-8122-7758-9. ▸ Comparative study of activities of papal and episcopal Inquisitors in Germany. Treats persecution of beghards, beguines, and Waldensians. Sees Inquisition as neither monolithic nor exclusively papal. [KP/FHS]

20.1195 Malcolm D. Lambert. *Medieval heresy: the Gregorian reform to the Reformation.* 2d ed. Cambridge, Mass.: Blackwell, 1992. ISBN 0-631-17431-1 (cl), 0-631-17432-X (pbk). ▸ Popular, not learned, heretical movements, 1000–1450. Treats appeal of heresy, response of official church, and evangelical heresy of late Middle Ages and its relation to Reformation. Earlier title: *Medieval Heresy: Popular Movements from Bogomil to Hus.* [KP/FHS]

20.1196 Emmanuel Le Roy Ladurie. *Montaillou: the promised land of error.* 1978 ed. Barbara Bray, trans. New York: Vintage, 1979. ISBN 0-394-72964-1 (pbk). ▸ Heterodox theology and mentalities of villagers in southern France in early fourteenth century, elicited by Inquisitors hunting suspected heretics, as filtered through Inquisitors' outlook and interrogatory procedures. [KP/FHS]

20.1197 Henry Charles Lea. *A history of the Inquisition in the Middle Ages.* 1955 ed. 3 vols. New York: Russell & Russell, 1958. ▸ Classic description of institutional workings of Inquisition, its rules of evidence, trial procedures, penalties, and much information about medieval heresies. Although dated, remains very valuable. Also available as one-volume summary from New York: Harper & Row, 1963. [KP]

20.1198 Gordon Leff. *Heresy in the later Middle Ages: the relation of heterodoxy to dissent, c. 1250–c. 1450.* 2 vols. Manchester: Manchester University Press, 1967. ▸ Comprehensive treatment of heretical movements. Discusses doctrines, spread of heresy, importance of mysticism and voluntary poverty in heterodox thought, reaction of papacy to heresy, and creation and use of Inquisition. [KP/FHS]

20.1199 Robert E. Lerner. *The heresy of the free spirit in the later Middle Ages.* Notre Dame, Ind.: University of Notre Dame Press, 1992. ISBN 0-268-01094-3 (pbk). ▸ Leading study of fourteenth-century heretical movement, effectiveness of Inquisition against it, and importance of mysticism in late medieval heterodox and orthodox religious thought. [KP/FHS]

20.1200 K. B. McFarlane. *John Wycliffe and the beginnings of English Nonconformity.* 1952 ed. London: English University Press, 1972. ▸ Biography of most important English theologian-heretic of fourteenth century. Treats Wyclif's relationship to and influence on Lollards, and persecution of Wyclif and suppression of his followers. [KP/WJC]

20.1201 R. I. Moore. *The formation of a persecuting society: power and deviance in western Europe, 950–1250.* 1987 ed. Oxford: Blackwell, 1990. ISBN 0-631-13746-7 (cl), 0-631-17145-2 (pbk). ▸ Controversial study of emergence of attitudes and institutions for detection and punishment of religious dissenters as well as Jews and lepers. Argues these groups were marginalized for social not religious reasons. [FHS]

20.1202 R. I. Moore. *The origins of European dissent.* 1977 ed. New York: Blackwell, 1985. ISBN 0-631-14721-7 (cl), 0-631-14404-8 (pbk). ▸ Argues popular heresy was vehicle for expressing alienation and economic distress as well as spiritual dissatisfaction with established church. Focuses on eleventh and twelfth centuries. [KP/FHS]

20.1203 Peter Partner. *The murdered magicians: the Templars and their myth.* 1981 ed. London: Aquarian, 1982. ISBN 0-85030-534-9. ▸ History of Knights Templars from their foundation to trial for heresy that led to dissolution. Examines and seeks to dispel myths surrounding order. [KP]

20.1204 Edward Peters. *Inquisition.* 1988 ed. Berkeley: University of California Press, 1989. ISBN 0-520-06630-8. ▸ Survey of law, procedure, and legislation of Inquisition, its persecution of heretics in Spain, Italy, and New World. Treats and seeks to dispel myth of Inquisition in history, art, and literature. [KP]

20.1205 Marjorie Reeves. *Joachim of Fiore and the prophetic* *future.* 1976 ed. New York: Harper & Row, 1977. ISBN 0-06-131924-4 (pbk). ► Seminal study of life and thought of twelfth-century Italian visionary and influence of his apocalyptic teachings on spiritual Franciscans and on other heretical movements of thirteenth and fourteenth centuries. [KP/WJC]

20.1206 Steven Runciman. *The medieval Manichee: a study of the Christian dualist heresy.* 1947 ed. Cambridge: Cambridge University Press, 1988. ISBN 0-521-06166-0 (cl), 0-521-28926-2 (pbk). ► Discussion of dualist heresy from Manichaean origins to eastern Mediterranean and spread from Balkans to France and Italy in twelfth century. [KP]

20.1207 Jeffrey Burton Russell. *Dissent and reform in the early Middle Ages.* 1965 ed. New York: AMS Press, 1982. (Publications of the Center for Medieval and Renaissance Studies, 1.) ISBN 0-404-16196-0. ► Survey of heresies, 700–1150. Analyzes social, doctrinal, economic, and, above all, moral motivations for dissent. Considers geographical differences in spread of heresy. [KP/FHS]

20.1208 Albert Clement Shannon. *The popes and heresy in the thirteenth century.* New York: AMS Press, 1980. ISBN 0-404-16228-2. ► Study of establishment of papal Inquisition at beginning of thirteenth century. Suppression of heresy by church, procedure in Inquisitorial courts, penalties for heresy, and appeals to Rome. [KP]

20.1209 Arthur Stanley Turberville. *Mediaeval heresy and the Inquisition.* 1920 ed. Hamden, Conn.: Archon, 1964. ► Older but still useful overview of heretical movements from eleventh to fifteenth century. Surveys origin, procedures, and spread of Inquisition. [KP]

20.1210 Walter L. Wakefield. *Heresy, crusade, and Inquisition in southern France, 1100–1250.* Berkeley: University of California Press, 1974. ISBN 0-520-02380-3. ► Discussion of Catharist and Waldensian heresies, ecclesiastical persecution of heretics, Albigensian crusade, and establishment of Inquisition by Pope Innocent III. [KP]

20.1211 Daniel Walther. "A survey of recent research on the Albigensian Cathari." *Church history* 34 (1965) 146–77. ISSN 0009-6407. ► Reviews literature, ca. 1940–65, on Albigensian heresy and its religious beliefs. [KP]

SEE ALSO
33.174 Howard Kaminsky. *A history of the Hussite revolution.*
33.220 M. Spinka. *John Hus.*

Roman and Canon Law

20.1212 Robert L. Benson. *The bishop-elect: a study in medieval ecclesiastical office.* Princeton: Princeton University Press, 1968. ► Classic study of canonical status of men elected to bishoprics but not yet installed, their authority, power, and jurisdiction; rules governing episcopal elections; and relations between bishops-elect and secular rulers. [KP]

20.1213 Robert L. Benson. " '*Plenitudo potestatis*': evolution of a formula from Gregory IV to Gratian." In *Studia Gratiana: post octava Decreti saeculari.* Alfons Stickler, ed., vol. 14, pp. 195–217. Bologna: Institutum Iuridicum Universitatis Studiorum Bononiensis, 1967. ► Specialized study of early development of theory of fullness of power as most significant term describing papal authority. Term used also to characterize imperial and royal authority. [KP]

20.1214 Harold J. Berman. *Law and revolution: the formation of the Western legal tradition.* Cambridge, Mass.: Harvard University Press, 1983. ISBN 0-674-51774-1 (cl), 0-674-51776-8 (pbk). ► Survey of legal history from investiture controversy in eleventh century to end of Middle Ages, stressing influence of canon law on European legal systems. [KP]

20.1215 Uta-Renate Blumenthal. *The early councils of Pope Paschal II (1100–1110).* Toronto: Pontifical Institute of Mediaeval Studies, 1978. (Studies and texts, 43.) ISBN 0-88844-043-X. ► Analysis of content, reforming intentions, and importance of legislation of Pope Paschal II's councils. Not for beginners. [KP]

20.1216 James A. Brundage. *Medieval canon law and the Crusader.* Madison: University of Wisconsin Press, 1969. ISBN 0-299-05480-2. ► Thorough survey of legal foundations for instituting Crusades, canonical force of Crusade vow, and Crusaders' status, privileges, and obligations according to canon law. [KP]

20.1217 Joseph Canning. *The political thought of Baldus de Ubaldis.* Cambridge: Cambridge University Press, 1987. ISBN 0-521-32521-8. ► Study of canon lawyer Baldus's conception of monarchical sovereignty, idea of the state, and theory of corporate independence as applied to Italian city-states. Appendix contains valuable short biographies of jurists. [KP]

20.1218 Christopher R. Cheney. *English synodalia of the thirteenth century.* Rev. ed. London: Oxford University Press, 1968. ► Study of constitutional structure of English episcopal synods treating procedure, judicial business, participants, contents of statutes, and importance as historical sources. [KP]

20.1219 Stanley Chodorow. *Christian political theory and church politics in the mid-twelfth century: the ecclesiology of Gratian's "Decretum."* Berkeley: University of California Press, 1972. (Publications of the Center for Medieval and Renaissance Studies, 5.) ISBN 0-520-01850-8. ► Study of Gratian, father of medieval canon law. Most extensive treatment in English of Gratian's theory of laws, sacraments, church, and state. [KP]

20.1220 Helmut Coing, ed. *Handbuch der Quellen und Literatur der neueren europäischen Privatrechtsgeschichte.* Vol. 1: *Mittelalter (1100–1500): die gelehrten Rechte und die Gesetzgebung.* 3 vols. Munich: Beck, 1973–88. ISBN 3-406-03631-7 (v. 1). ► Most recent history of development and growth of medieval Roman and canon law. History of sources, literature, and doctrines of these legal traditions. Extensive bibliographies. [KP]

20.1221 Charles Donahue, Jr., ed. *The records of the medieval ecclesiastical courts: reports of the working group on church court records.* Vol. 1: *The Continent.* Berlin: Duncker & Humbolt, 1989. ISBN 3-428-06619-7. ► Compilation and discussion of ecclesiastical archival records preserving court proceedings, with detailed bibliographical guide to secondary literature and comparisons among different European churches. [KP]

20.1222 Charles Duggan. *Twelfth-century decretal collections and their importance in English history.* London: Athlone, 1963. (University of London historical studies, 12.) ► Specialized discussion of papal legislation in England during twelfth century and canonists' use of collections of papal letters in teaching and practice. [KP]

20.1223 Clarence Gallagher. *Canon law and the Christian community: the role of law in the church according to the Summa aurea of Cardinal Hostiensis.* Rome: Gregorian University Press, 1978. (Analecta Gregoriana, 208.) ► Study of canon lawyer Henricus of Segusio's theories of ecclesiastical government, showing importance of corporation theory for medieval institutional and ecclesiological ideas. [KP]

20.1224 Jean Gaudemet. *Le gouvernement de l'église à l'époque classique.* Vol. 1: *Le gouvernement local.* Paris: Cujas, 1979. ► Basic investigation of structure of local church governments in twelfth and thirteenth centuries, studying role of bishop, institutions of diocese and parish, and officials of local church. [KP]

20.1225 John T. Gilchrist. *The church and economic activity in the Middle Ages.* London: Macmillan, 1969. ISBN 0-333-05496-2. ► Good general study of canonical rules and institutions that attempted to govern merchants, bankers, pawnbrokers, and craftsmen. Discusses doctrines regarding usury, just price, credit, profit, charity, and church property. [KP]

20.1226 R. H. Helmholz. *Canon law and the law of England.* London: Hambledon, 1987. ISBN 0-907628-93-1. ▪ Specialized essays on relationship between canon law and English law covering procedure, family law, bankruptcy, debt, usury, and barriers to litigation in ecclesiastical courts. [KP]

20.1227 R. H. Helmholz. *Marriage litigation in medieval England.* Cambridge: Cambridge University Press, 1974. ISBN 0-521-20411-9. ▪ Fundamental study of litigation involving marriage contracts, separation, and annulment in English courts. Treats procedure; roles of judges, attorneys, and witnesses; and influence of canon law on English law. [KP]

20.1228 Ernst H. Kantorowicz. *The king's two bodies: a study in mediaeval political theology.* 1957 ed. Princeton: Princeton University Press, 1981. ISBN 0-691-07120-9 (cl), 0-691-02018-3 (pbk). ▪ Classic study of theory of medieval kingship; influence of corporate structures of thought derived from theology and Roman and canon law in understanding nature of royal authority. [KP]

20.1229 Stephan Kuttner. *Gratian and the schools of law, 1140–1234.* London: Variorum, 1983. ISBN 0-86078-133-x. ▪ Essays on first century of canon law studies at Bologna, Gratian's role in development of canon law, and influence of Roman law on his *Decretum.* [KP]

20.1230 Stephan Kuttner. *The history of ideas and doctrines of canon law in the late Middle Ages.* London: Variorum, 1980. ISBN 0-86078-058-9. ▪ Specialized essays treating influence of canon law on legal theory and ecclesiastical institutions, teaching of canon law at Bologna in twelfth century, and canonists' views of papal authority. [KP]

20.1231 Stephan Kuttner. *Medieval councils, decretals, and collections of canon law: selected essays.* 2d rev. ed. London: Variorum, 1992. ISBN 0-86078-336-7. ▪ Specialized essays on importance of canon law collections in twelfth and early thirteenth centuries, and on thirteenth-century church councils and their legislation. [KP]

20.1232 Gerhart B. Ladner. "The concepts of ecclesia and Christianitas and their relation to the idea of *plenitudo potestatis* from Gregory VII to Boniface VIII." In *Sacerdozio e regno da Gregorio VII a Bonifazio VII,* pp. 49–77. Rome: Universitas Gregoriana, 1954. (Miscellanea historiae pontificiae, 18.) ▪ Fundamental study of canonical doctrine of pope's fullness of power from eleventh to early fourteenth century and relation of concept to ideas of reform. [KP]

20.1233 F. Donald Logan. *Excommunication and the secular arm in medieval England: a study in legal procedure from the thirteenth to the sixteenth century.* Toronto: Pontifical Institute of Mediaeval Studies, 1968. (Studies and texts, 15.) ▪ Technical study of authority of popes, bishops, and lesser clergy to excommunicate; impact of excommunication on persons' status; procedures for enforcing penalties and obtaining readmission to communion; and excommunication in English law. [KP]

20.1234 James M. Moynihan. *Papal immunity and liability in the writings of the medieval canonists.* Rome: Gregorian University Press, 1961. (Analecta Gregoriana, 120.) ▪ Specialized studies of canon law on papal immunity from prosecution for crimes, and canonical argument that pope may be prosecuted for heresy. [KP]

20.1235 James Muldoon. *Popes, lawyers, and infidels: the church and the non-Christian world, 1250–1550.* Philadelphia: University of Pennsylvania Press, 1979. ISBN 0-8122-7770-8. ▪ Most important overview of papacy's relationship with Muslims, Mongols, and other non-Christians. Examines justifications in canon law for waging war against infidels. [KP]

20.1236 Wolfgang Peter Müller. "The recovery of Justinian's *Digest* in the Middle Ages." *Bulletin of medieval canon law* 20 (1990) 1–29. ISSN 0146-2989. ▪ Review of chronology of reconstruction of *Digest* in late eleventh and early twelfth centuries, showing it was recovered at Bologna in three stages from 1075 to 1125. [KP]

20.1237 Francis C. Oakley. *Natural law, conciliarism, and consent in the late Middle Ages.* London: Variorum, 1984. ISBN 0-86078-137-2. ▪ Specialized essays on conciliar movement, leading proponents of representative government for church in fourteenth and fifteenth centuries, and importance of natural law theory in medieval jurisprudence. [KP]

20.1238 Kenneth Pennington. *Pope and bishops: the papal monarchy in the twelfth and thirteenth centuries.* Philadelphia: University of Pennsylvania Press, 1984. ISBN 0-8122-7918-2. ▪ Learned analysis of terminology and theory of papal authority in church, Pope Innocent III's influence on both theory and practice of church government, and relationship between papal and episcopal power. [KP]

20.1239 Gaines Post. *Studies in medieval legal thought: public law and the state, 1100–1322.* Princeton: Princeton University Press, 1964. ▪ Seminal study emphasizing importance of Roman and canon law in shaping medieval institutions, including representative assemblies. Argues jurists first to conceptualize idea of the state. [KP/WJC]

20.1240 Charles M. Radding. *The origins of medieval jurisprudence: Pavia and Bologna, 850–1150.* New Haven: Yale University Press, 1988. ISBN 0-300-03909-3. ▪ Controversial argument for importance of Pavia over Bologna in rebirth of Roman law and development of medieval jurisprudence in Italy. Thesis challenged by Müller (20.1236). [KP]

20.1241 Roger Reynolds. "Law, canon: to Gratian." In *Dictionary of the Middle Ages.* Joseph Reese Strayer, ed., vol. 7, pp. 395–413. New York: Scribner's, 1986. ISBN 0-684-18169-x. ▪ Short history of canon law to 1140, discussing sources, canonical collections, and individual canonists. [KP]

20.1242 Frederick H. Russell. *The just war in the Middle Ages.* Cambridge: Cambridge University Press, 1975. ISBN 0-521-20690-1. ▪ Single best study of doctrine of just war in medieval theological and legal thought from Augustine to Thomas Aquinas. Notes contribution of canonists to just war theories. [KP]

20.1243 John J. Ryan. *Saint Peter Damiani and his canonical sources: a preliminary study in the antecedents of the Gregorian reform.* Toronto: Pontifical Institute of Mediaeval Studies, 1956. (Studies and texts, 2.) ▪ Study of important eleventh-century reformer. Discusses career and contribution to canon law; analyzes reform principles. [KP]

20.1244 Friedrich Carl von Savigny. *Geschichte der römischen Rechts im Mittelalter.* 5th ed. 7 vols. Aalen: Scientia, 1986. ISBN 3-511-07250-6. ▪ Complete listing of jurists who wrote on Roman law in period from 1075 to 1500. Biographical sketches and references to manuscripts and printed sources. [KP]

20.1245 Jane E. Sayers. *Papal judges delegate in the province of Canterbury, 1198–1254: a study in ecclesiastical jurisdiction and administration.* London: Oxford University Press, 1971. ISBN 0-19-821836-2. ▪ Case study of origins and development of papal-delegated jurisdiction to bishops; procedure, administration, and personnel of their courts; and types of cases heard by these ecclesiastical courts. [KP]

20.1246 Johann Friedrich von Schulte. *Die Geschichte der Quellen und Literatur des canonischen Rechts.* Vol. 1: *Von Gratian bis auf Papst Gregor IX.* Vol. 2: *Vom Papst Gregor IX bis zum Concil von Trient.* 1875–80 ed. 2 vols. in 1. Graz: Akademische Druck- & Verlagsanstalt, 1956. ▪ Most complete listing of canon lawyers,

1140–1500. Combines biographical sketches with lists of their works. [KP]

20.1247 Robert Somerville. *The councils of Urban II.* Vol. 1: *Decreta Claromontensia.* Amsterdam: Hakkert, 1972. (Annuarium historiae conciliorum, Supplementum, 1.) ‣ History of Council of Clermont and its place in eleventh-century conciliar legislation. Analyzes forms of conciliar legislation. Not for beginners. [KP]

20.1248 Robert Somerville. *Papacy, councils, and canon law in the eleventh–twelfth centuries.* London: Variorum, 1990. ISBN 0-86078-260-3. ‣ Specialized essays on early twelfth-century church councils and their legislation. Canon law in age of investiture controversy. [KP]

20.1249 Brian Tierney. *Church law and constitutional thought in the Middle Ages.* London: Variorum, 1979. ISBN 0-86078-036-8. ‣ Specialized essays on influence of canon law on medieval political theory and constitutional thought, theory of papal sovereignty and conciliarism, jurisprudence, and development of representative assemblies and parliaments. [KP]

20.1250 Brian Tierney. *Foundations of the conciliar theory: the contribution of the medieval canonists from Gratian to the Great Schism.* 1955 ed. London: Cambridge University Press, 1968. ISBN 0-521-07399-5. ‣ Groundbreaking analysis of canonists' contributions to theories of representative government for church and debates on this issue, ca. 1150–1450. Appendix gives biographies of canonists discussed. [KP/WJC]

20.1251 Brian Tierney. *Medieval poor law: a sketch of canonical theory and its application in England.* Berkeley: University of California Press, 1959. ‣ Groundbreaking study of poverty and relief in canonical jurisprudence and ecclesiastical institutions; theory and practice, 1140–1500. Sees origins of social welfare thinking in twelfth century. [KP]

20.1252 Brian Tierney. *Origins of papal infallibility, 1150–1350: a study on the concepts of infallibility, sovereignty, and tradition in the Middle Ages.* 1972 ed. Leiden: Brill, 1988. ISBN 90-04-08884-9 (cl), 90-04-03440-4 (pbk). ‣ Well-documented study of emergence of theories of papal sovereignty and infallibility. More sharply defined formulations of these principles linked to papacy's role in dispute between spiritual and conventual Franciscans. [KP/WJC]

20.1253 Brian Tierney. *Religion, law, and the growth of constitutional thought, 1150–1650.* Cambridge: Cambridge University Press, 1982. ISBN 0-521-23495-6. ‣ Outstanding study of impact of canon law on ideas of sovereignty, jurisdiction, corporate theory, and representative government, influencing both limited and absolutist theories of government and fueling tension between them. [KP]

20.1254 Richard C. Trexler. *Synodal law in Florence and Fiesole, 1306–1518.* Vatican: Biblioteca Apostolica Vaticana, 1971. (Studi e testi, 268.) ‣ Study of ecclesiastical legislation in Florence and Fiesole analyzing statutes and describing local synodal practice, structure of Tuscan ecclesiastical councils, and relationship of episcopal to urban secular law. [KP]

20.1255 Walter Ullmann. *Law and jurisdiction in the Middle Ages.* George Garnett, ed. London: Variorum, 1988. ISBN 0-86078-231-X. ‣ Specialized essays on law in relation to governmental institutions, empire, and papacy in thirteenth century; on procedure of Inquisition; and on jurisprudence in later Middle Ages. [KP]

20.1256 Elisabeth Vodola. *Excommunication in the Middle Ages.* Berkeley: University of California Press, 1986. ISBN 0-520-04999-3. ‣ Fundamental survey of origins, development, and decline of excommunication as means of canonical censure, ca. 1050–1300, and doctrine of excommunication and its impact on courtroom procedure. [KP]

20.1257 John Watt. *The theory of papal monarchy in the thirteenth century: the contribution of the canonists.* New York: Fordham University Press, 1965. ‣ Study of understanding of papal authority from early church to thirteenth century, emphasizing and analyzing contribution of canonists to language of papal sovereignty. [KP]

20.1258 Michael Wilks. *The problem of sovereignty in the later Middle Ages: the papal monarchy with Augustinus Triumphus and the publicists.* 1963 ed. Cambridge: Cambridge University Press, 1964. ‣ Theory of papal authority showing contribution of canonists and publicists, treating problems of church and state; of figures studied to theories of both; of limited monarchy, absolutism, and corporate government. [KP]

SEE ALSO
28.109 Richard C. Trexler. *The spiritual power.*

INTELLECTUAL HISTORY, 1050–1500
General Studies

20.1259 E. J. Ashworth, ed. *The tradition of medieval logic and speculative grammar from Anselm to the end of the seventeenth century: a bibliography from 1836 onwards.* Toronto: Pontifical Institute of Mediaeval Studies, 1978. (Subsidia mediaevalia, 9.) ISBN 0-88844-3587-7. ‣ Detailed, thorough, and fully annotated bibliography of medieval logic by leading contributor to field. [MLC]

20.1260 Aldo S. Bernardo and Saul Levin, eds. *The classics in the Middle Ages: papers of the twentieth annual conference of the Center for Medieval and Early Renaissance Studies.* Binghamton, N.Y.: Center for Medieval & Early Renaissance Studies, 1990. (Medieval and Renaissance texts and studies, 69.) ISBN 0-86698-078-4. ‣ Twenty-six papers exploring classicism in medieval culture, mainly in literature and philosophy. Illustrates range of scholarly understandings of medieval classicism from passive reception to creative reworking of ancient legacy. [MLC]

20.1261 I. M. Bochenski. *A history of formal logic.* 2d ed. Ivo Thomas, ed. and trans. New York: Chelsea, 1970. ISBN 0-8284-0238-8. ‣ Part 3, covering scholastic logic, considered basic introduction to that subject at time of publication, although much new scholarship has emerged since. [WJC]

20.1262 Edgar de Bruyne. *The esthetics of the Middle Ages.* Eileen B. Hennessy, trans. New York: Ungar, 1969. ‣ Basic survey of medieval aesthetic theory, treating beauty as transcendental and also considering relations between aesthetics and Neoplatonic and Aristotelian currents of thought. [MLC]

20.1263 G. L. Bursill-Hall. *Speculative grammars of the Middle Ages: the doctrine of partes orationis of the Modistae.* 1971 ed. The Hague: Mouton, 1972. ‣ Basic study of speculative grammar and semantics in high Middle Ages, exemplifying recent interest of both modern philosophers and medievalists in this subject. [MLC]

20.1264 G. L. Bursill-Hall, Sten Ebbesen, and Konrad Koerner, eds. *De ortu grammaticae: studies in medieval grammar and linguistic theory in memory of Jan Pinborg.* Amsterdam: Benjamins, 1990. ISBN 90-272-4526-6. ‣ Collected essays reflecting newest discoveries and debated issues in history of medieval semantics and speculative grammar. [MLC]

20.1265 Richard C. Dales. *The intellectual life of western Europe in the Middle Ages.* 2d. rev. ed. Leiden: Brill, 1992. ISBN 90-04-09622-1 (cl), 0-8191-0900-2 (1980, pbk). ‣ Examination of medieval thought from late antiquity to fourteenth century, accenting seminal role of period before twelfth century. Stresses reception of classical heritage, as adapted by Christianity, as main theme. [MLC]

20.1266 Étienne Gilson. *History of Christian philosophy in the Middle Ages.* New York: Random House, 1955. ‣ Long-standard guide to medieval philosophy and classic example of Neo-Thomistic treatment. Remains useful for perspectives of great medievalist and rich bibliographical notes. [WJC]

20.1267 Étienne Gilson. *Reason and revelation in the Middle Ages.* 1938 ed. New York: Scribner's, 1950. ▸ Classic statement of earlier understanding of thrust of medieval speculative thought as synthesis of reason and revelation attained most fully by Thomas Aquinas. [MLC]

20.1268 Martin Grabmann. *Die Geschichte der scholastischen Methode: nach den gedruckten und ungedruckten Quellen.* 1909 ed. 2 vols. Berlin: Akademie-Verlag, 1988. ISBN 3-05-000593-9 (v. 1), 3-05-000594-7 (v. 2). ▸ Pioneering work on development of scholasticism, rich in documentation. Based on author's extensive familiarity with manuscript sources. Remains essential authority in the field. [WJC]

20.1269 Martin Grabmann. *Mittelalterliches Geistesleben: Abhandlungen zur Geschichte der Scholastik und Mystik.* 3 vols. Munich: Hueber, 1926–56. ▸ Collected papers on scholastic philosophy and mysticism by major authority. Especially useful for studies of speculative grammar, Thomistic and Dominican theology, and German mysticism. [WJC]

20.1270 Friedrich Heer. *The intellectual history of Europe.* Vol. 1: *From the beginnings of Western thought to Luther.* 1966 ed. Jonathan Steinberg, trans. New York: Doubleday, 1968. ▸ Introductory textbook, also designed for general reader, with good blend of intellectual, social, and religious history. [WJC]

20.1271 Richard William Hunt. *The history of grammar in the Middle Ages: collected papers.* G. L. Bursill-Hall, ed. Amsterdam: Benjamins, 1980. ISBN 90-272-0896-4. ▸ Collected essays on theory and teaching of grammar in Middle Ages, emphasizing twelfth and thirteenth centuries, and grammar as literary as well as logical art. [MLC]

20.1272 William C. Kneale and Martha Kneale. *The development of logic.* 1962 ed. Oxford: Clarendon, 1984. ISBN 0-19-824773-7 (pbk). ▸ Survey remains standard reference work in field. Dated on medieval logic and must be used with caution in that area. [WJC]

20.1273 John Marenbon. *Later medieval philosophy (1150–1350): an introduction.* London: Routledge, 1987. ISBN 0-7102-0286-5. ▸ Short, sometimes overly swift and cursory, survey of philosophy from St. Anselm to William of Ockham, accenting psychology. [WJC]

20.1274 James J. Murphy. *Rhetoric in the Middle Ages: a history of rhetorical theory from St. Augustine to the Renaissance.* Berkeley: University of California Press, 1974. ISBN 0-520-02439-7. ▸ Excellent introduction to theory and practice of rhetoric in medieval schools and in medieval society more widely. [WJC]

20.1275 Jan Pinborg. *Medieval semantics: selected studies on medieval logic and grammar.* Sten Ebbesen, ed. London: Variorum, 1984. ISBN 0-86078-143-7. ▸ Posthumously collected papers, many of which have had seminal impact on subsequent research, by one of twentieth century's most outstanding contributors to field of medieval logic and semantics. [MLC]

20.1276 B. B. Price. *Medieval thought: an introduction.* Oxford: Blackwell, 1992. ISBN 0-631-17508-3 (cl), 0-631-17509-1 (pbk). ▸ Survey of medieval thought from origins of Christianity through fifteenth century. Treats vernacular traditions, philosophy, and science, but emphasizes continuity of Christianity as period's main theme. [MLC]

20.1277 Gerard Verbeke. *The presence of Stoicism in medieval thought.* Washington, D.C.: Catholic University of America Press, 1983. ISBN 0-8132-0572-7 (cl), 0-8132-0573-5 (pbk). ▸ Small but important book charting knowledge and use of Stoi-

cism by medieval thinkers through thirteenth century. Accents ethics, free will and fatalism, and challenge of Stoic materialism to Christian thinkers. [MLC]

20.1278 Julius R. Weinberg. *A short history of medieval philosophy.* Princeton: Princeton University Press, 1964. ▸ Chronologically and thematically selective; serves as excellent introduction to subject. Notable for how it interweaves Muslim and Jewish philosophy. [WJC]

Growth of Learning

20.1279 Karl Barth. *Anselm, "Fides Quaerens Intellectum": Anselm's proof of the existence of God in the context of his theological scheme.* 1960 ed. Ian W. Robinson, trans. Pittsburgh: Pickwick, 1985. ISBN 0-915138-75-1. ▸ Highly personal, provocative analysis of St. Anselm's ontological argument for God's existence. Controversial, influential interpretation. [WJC]

20.1280 Robert L. Benson, Giles Constable, and Carol D. Lanham, eds. *Renaissance and renewal in the twelfth century.* 1982 ed. Toronto: University of Toronto Press, 1991. (Mediaeval Academy reprints for teaching, 26.) ISBN 0-8020-6850-2 (pbk). ▸ Conference papers assessing most areas of twelfth-century culture on fiftieth anniversary of Haskins's seminal work (20.1293). Treats education, literature, Roman and canon law, philosophy, theology, science, and art. [WJC]

20.1281 M. D. Chenu. *Nature, man, and society in the twelfth century: essays on new theological perspectives in the Latin West.* 1968 ed. Jerome Taylor and Lester K. Little, eds. and trans. Chicago: University of Chicago Press, 1983. ISBN 0-226-10256-4 (pbk). ▸ Insightful study of twelfth-century grammar, theology, philosophy, science, biblical study, and religion. Argues for discovery of world and of man in this period. [WJC]

20.1282 Marshall Clagett, Gaines Post, and Robert Reynolds, eds. *Twelfth-century Europe and the foundations of modern society.* Madison: University of Wisconsin Press, 1966. ▸ Conference papers covering institutional as well as intellectual history. Those in latter group treat education, liberal arts, school of Chartres, law, and influence of non-Western cultures. [WJC]

20.1283 Philippe Delhaye. *Enseignement et morale au douzième siècle.* Fribourg: Éditions Universitaires de Fribourg, 1988. ISBN 2-8271-0375-3. ▸ Collected papers of noted authority dealing with history of education in twelfth century and teaching of moral philosophy in particular. [MLC]

20.1284 Peter Dronke, ed. *A history of twelfth-century Western philosophy.* Cambridge: Cambridge University Press, 1988. ISBN 0-521-25896-0. ▸ Collected essays studying Platonic and Stoic thought, Arabic influence, science, logic, beginnings of reception of Aristotle, and a number of individual thinkers; extensive bibliographies. [WJC]

20.1285 G. R. Evans. *Alan of Lille: the frontiers of theology in the later twelfth century.* Cambridge: Cambridge University Press, 1983. ISBN 0-521-24618-0. ▸ Most extensive treatment in English of important theologian and poet, studied thematically and from standpoint of history of theology, not literary criticism. [WJC]

20.1286 G. R. Evans. *Anselm and a new generation.* Oxford: Clarendon, 1980. ISBN 0-19-826651-0. ▸ Assesses St. Anselm's influence, or lack of it, in context of changing philosophical methods and theological agendas through middle of twelfth century. [WJC]

20.1287 G. R. Evans. *Anselm and talking about God.* Oxford: Clarendon, 1978. ISBN 0-19-826647-2. ▸ Fine study of language and argumentation in St. Anselm's thought, focusing on proofs for God's existence, rationale for incarnation of Christ, and treatment of free will. [WJC]

20.1288 G. R. Evans. *The mind of St. Bernard of Clairvaux.*

Oxford: Clarendon, 1983. ISBN 0-19-826667-7. ▸ Exploration of Bernard's activities as preacher and controversialist, treating selected themes rather than essaying full-scale study. [WJC]

20.1289 G. R. Evans. *Old arts and new theology: the beginnings of theology as an academic discipline.* Oxford: Clarendon, 1980. ISBN 0-19-826653-7. ▸ Outline of emergence of differing kinds of theology in twelfth century and rise of scholastic theology, accenting impact of study of liberal arts in its development. [WJC]

20.1290 Stephen C. Ferruolo. *The origins of the university: the schools of Paris and their critics, 1100–1215.* Stanford, Calif.: Stanford University Press, 1985. ISBN 0-8047-1266-2. ▸ Study of clash between developing Parisian schools and older monastic educational ideals: emergence of scholasticism viewed from standpoint of thinkers who deplored trend. [WJC]

20.1291 Joseph de Ghellinck. *L'essor de la littérature latine au douzième siècle.* Brussels: Desclée de Brouwer, 1955. ▸ Standard, dated survey of scholarly, monastic, and poetic literature written in Latin in twelfth century. [WJC]

20.1292 Margaret T. Gibson. *Lanfranc of Bec.* Oxford: Clarendon, 1978. ISBN 0-19-822462-1. ▸ Best full-scale study of Lanfranc's career as abbot, schoolmaster, and archbishop of Canterbury and of his thought, by editor of his letters. [WJC]

20.1293 Charles Homer Haskins. *The Renaissance of the twelfth century.* 1927 ed. Cambridge, Mass.: Harvard University Press, 1976. ISBN 0-674-76075-1. ▸ Seminal work on twelfth-century culture, arguing against Dark Ages view of Middle Ages on basis of classicism manifested in its intellectual traditions. [WJC]

20.1294 Desmond P. Henry. *The logic of Saint Anselm.* Oxford: Clarendon, 1967. ▸ Best study to date of Anselm's contribution to logic and speculative grammar. Thorough, solid, and detailed. [WJC]

20.1295 C. Warren Hollister, ed. *The twelfth-century Renaissance.* New York: Wiley, 1969. ISBN 0-471-40693-7. ▸ Collection of papers debating Haskins's thesis (20.1293) and discussing state of question to date. Focuses on political theory, humanism, rationalism, literature, and art. [WJC]

20.1296 Jean Jolivet. *Arts du langage et théologie chez Abélard.* 2d ed. Paris: Vrin, 1982. ▸ Major exposition of twelfth-century thinker's philosophy and theology, giving pride of place to semantics as key to his thought. Extremely influential study. [WJC]

20.1297 Artur Michael Landgraf. *Dogmengeschichte der Frühscholastik.* 4 vols. in 9. Regensburg: Pustat, 1952–56. ▸ Collected studies of major topics in twelfth-century theology, particularly those remaining of interest in thirteenth century, based mostly on manuscript evidence. Fundamental, indispensable work. [WJC]

20.1298 Jean Leclercq. *Monks and love in twelfth-century France: psycho-historical essays.* Oxford: Clarendon, 1979. ISBN 0-19-822546-6. ▸ Draws on psychohistory and contemporary courtly love tradition in vernacular literature to explain spirituality of monks in reformed twelfth-century orders, especially Cistercians. [WJC]

20.1299 D. E. Luscombe. *The school of Peter Abelard: the influence of Abelard's thought in the early scholastic period.* Cambridge: Cambridge University Press, 1969. ISBN 0-521-07337-5. ▸ Standard work on diffusion and influence of theological writings of Abelard and his disciples across twelfth century. [WJC]

20.1300 John C. Moore. *Love in twelfth-century France.* Philadelphia: University of Pennsylvania Press, 1972. ISBN 0-8122-7648-5. ▸ Comparative study of views of love in monastic and secular writers of twelfth-century France. Sees fewer parallels between them than does Leclercq 20.1298. [WJC]

20.1301 Colin Morris. *The discovery of the individual, 1050–1200.* 1972 ed. Toronto: University of Toronto Press, 1987. (Mediaeval Academy reprints for teaching, 19.) ISBN 0-8020-6665-8. ▸ Study of concepts of selfhood, primarily in twelfth century. Controversial effort to push Burckhardtian individualism back into Middle Ages. [WJC]

20.1302 Alexander Murray. *Reason and society in the Middle Ages.* Oxford: Clarendon, 1978. ISBN 0-19-822540-7. ▸ Insightful interpretation of social, economic, and intellectual change, ninth to twelfth century. Accents nobles' patronage of religious reform and growth of more mathematical and analytical outlook. [WJC]

20.1303 Lauge Olaf Nielsen. *Theology and philosophy in the twelfth century: a study of Gilbert Porreta's thinking and the theological exposition of the doctrine of the incarnation during the period 1130–1180.* Leiden: Brill, 1982. (Acta theologica Danica, 15.) ISBN 90-04-06545-8. ▸ Study of twelfth-century discussions of Christ's incarnation with special attention to Gilbert of Poitiers, his followers and critics. Densely written, but only treatment of subject in English. [WJC]

20.1304 Alvin Plantinga, ed. *The ontological argument, from St. Anselm to contemporary philosophers.* Richard Taylor, Introduction. Garden City, N.Y.: Anchor, 1965. ▸ Collection of essays giving sense of continuing debates over Anselm's famous argument, from his own day to mid-twentieth century. Some debates framed anachronistically and some not. [MLC]

20.1305 R. W. Southern. *Medieval humanism and other studies.* New York: Harper & Row, 1970. ▸ Important collection of essays on twelfth-century humanism and humanism in England. Includes controversial paper arguing against existence of school of Chartres. [WJC]

20.1306 R. W. Southern. *Saint Anselm: a portrait in a landscape.* Cambridge: Cambridge University Press, 1990. ISBN 0-521-36262-8. ▸ Originally intended to replace earlier study of Anselm (20.1142), this work is separate and more extensive assessment of Anselm's life and thought. [WJC]

20.1307 Fernand van Steenberghen. *Aristotle in the West: the origins of Latin Aristotelianism.* 1955 2d ed. New York: Humanities Press, 1970. ▸ Classic study of chronology and philosophical impact of translation of Aristotle's works into Latin and their reception by Western thinkers in twelfth and thirteenth centuries. [WJC]

20.1308 Brian Stock. *The implications of literacy: written language and models of interpretation in the eleventh and twelfth centuries.* Princeton: Princeton University Press, 1983. ISBN 0-691-05368-5. ▸ Provocative, broad-based study of relationship between literacy and oral culture and use of texts as balance between oral and literate culture shifted toward greater literacy. [WJC]

20.1309 Brian Stock. *Myth and science in the twelfth century: a study of Bernard Silvester.* Princeton: Princeton University Press, 1972. ISBN 0-691-05201-8. ▸ Study of Bernard's *Cosmographia* as exemplar of new rationalism and explanatory framework. Emphasizes mythopoetic form and context of cosmogony; use of Platonic, Neoplatonic, and Christian sources; and originality. Major figure in school of Chartres. [MLC/MHS]

20.1310 Martin M. Tweedale. *Abailard on universals.* Amsterdam: Elsevier, 1976. ISBN 0-7204-8040-X. ▸ In-depth and controversial study of theologian's position on universal concepts in its historical setting. [WJC]

20.1311 Winthrop Wetherbee. *Platonism and poetry in the twelfth century: the literary influence of the school of Chartres.* Princeton: Princeton University Press, 1972. ISBN 0-691-06219-6. ▸ Analysis of philosophy of members of twelfth-century school of Chartres, accenting concerns and methods as well as conclusions and literary expression of ideas. [MLC]

20.1312 Lynn T. White, Jr. *Medieval religion and technology: collected essays.* Berkeley: University of California Press, 1978. (Publications of the Center for Medieval and Renaissance Studies, 13.) ISBN 0-520-03566-6. ‣ Collection of author's essays on religion and magic in medieval society and their relationship to technological change. [BSH]

Schools and Universities

20.1313 Louis J. Bataillon, Bertrand G. Guyot, and Richard H. Rouse, eds. *La production du livre universitaire au moyen âge: exemplar et pecia.* Paris: Centre National de la Recherche Scientifique, 1988. ISBN 2-222-0499-fl. ‣ Important group of studies on books and book production in thirteenth and fourteenth centuries, especially at university centers. [WJC]

20.1314 Gray Cowan Boyce. *The English-German nation in the University of Paris during the Middle Ages.* Bruges: Saint Catherine Press, 1927. ‣ Groundbreaking but dated study of origins and operation of nations in arts faculty at University of Paris. Should be used in conjunction with more recent scholarship. [WJC]

20.1315 Leonard E. Boyle. *Pastoral care, clerical education, and canon law, 1200–1400.* London: Variorum, 1981. ISBN 0-86078-081-3. ‣ Collected essays on clerical education and effects of decree of Pope Boniface VIII concerning education of clergy in early fourteenth century. [WJC]

20.1316 J. I. Catto, ed. *The early Oxford schools.* Vol. 1 of *The history of the university of Oxford.* Oxford: Clarendon, 1984. ISBN 0-19-951011-3. ‣ In-depth studies of institutional and intellectual history of Oxford University in thirteenth century. [WJC]

20.1317 M. T. Clanchy. *From memory to written record: England, 1066–1307.* Cambridge, Mass.: Harvard University Press, 1979. ISBN 0-674-32510-9. ‣ Important study of impact of growing literacy on largely oral culture of medieval England, its effects in law, politics, church life, and literature. [MLC]

20.1318 Alan B. Cobban. *The medieval English universities: Oxford and Cambridge to c. 1500.* Berkeley: University of California Press, 1988. ISBN 0-520-06244-2. ‣ Thorough account of origins, governmental structures, curriculum, organization of teaching, and student life at medieval Oxford and Cambridge. [WJC]

20.1319 William J. Courtenay. *Schools and scholars in fourteenth-century England.* Princeton: Princeton University Press, 1987. ISBN 0-691-05500-9. ‣ Detailed study of English educational structures and intellectual developments from late thirteenth century through age of Chaucer. Extensive bibliography. [WJC]

20.1320 Astrik L. Gabriel. *Garlandia: studies in the history of the mediaeval university.* Notre Dame, Ind.: Mediaeval Institute, 1969. ‣ Collected articles on important aspects of medieval university life and structure accenting administrative history of universities and subcorporations within them. [WJC]

20.1321 Charles Homer Haskins. *The rise of universities.* 1923 ed. Ithaca, N.Y.: Cornell University Press, 1979. ISBN 0-8014-9015-4. ‣ Brief, eminently readable overview of medieval universities, concentrating on status and activities of professors and students. [WJC]

20.1322 K. W. Humphreys. *The book provisions of the medieval friars, 1215–1400.* Amsterdam: Erasmus, 1964. ‣ Excellent study of book production and library collections among mendicant orders. [WJC]

20.1323 Jozef Ijsewijn and Jacques Paquet, eds. *The universities in the late Middle Ages.* Louvain: Louvain University Press, 1978. ISBN 90-6186-055-5. ‣ Collected papers representing some of newest research on intellectual, social, and institutional aspects of late medieval universities. [WJC]

20.1324 Ernest F. Jacob. "English university clerks in the later Middle Ages: the problem of maintenance." *Bulletin of the John Rylands University Library of Manchester* 29 (1946) 304–25. ISSN 0021-7239. ‣ Seminal essay on financing of English university education in later Middle Ages. [WJC]

20.1325 Pearl Kibre. *The nations in the mediaeval universities.* Cambridge, Mass.: Mediaeval Academy of America, 1948. (Mediaeval Academy of America publications, 49.) ‣ Standard work on development and operation of national subunits within arts faculties and universities of medieval Europe, their origin, status, and privileges. [WJC]

20.1326 Pearl Kibre. *Scholarly privileges in the Middle Ages: the rights, privileges, and immunities of scholars and universities at Bologna, Padua, Paris, and Oxford.* Cambridge, Mass.: Mediaeval Academy of America, 1962. (Mediaeval Academy of America publications, 72.) ‣ Classic study of origin and administration of scholarly privileges at medieval universities. [WJC]

20.1327 James M. Kittelson and Pamela J. Transue, eds. *Rebirth, reform, and resilience: universities in transition, 1300–1700.* Columbus: Ohio State University Press, 1984. ISBN 0-8142-0356-6. ‣ Important collection of essays on social, intellectual, and political aspects of late medieval universities. [WJC]

20.1328 Damian Riehl Leader. *A history of the university of Cambridge.* Vol. 1: *The university to 1546.* Christopher Brooke, ed. Cambridge: Cambridge University Press, 1988. ISBN 0-521-32882-9. ‣ Most recent history of university of Cambridge, based in part on early statutes recovered and edited by M. B. Hackett. [WJC]

20.1329 Gordon Leff. *Paris and Oxford universities in the thirteenth and fourteenth centuries: an institutional and intellectual history.* New York: Wiley, 1968. ‣ Introduction to origins, structure, and development of universities of Paris and Oxford. Covers both institutional and intellectual history. [WJC]

20.1330 Guy Fitch Lytle. "Patronage patterns and Oxford colleges, c. 1300–c. 1500." In *The university in society.* Lawrence Stone, ed., vol. 1, pp. 111–49. Princeton: Princeton University Press, 1974. ISBN 0-691-05213-1. ‣ Study of institutional, financial, and social effects of changing patterns of patronage on late medieval education at Oxford. Argues for crisis in educational patronage; controversial thesis. [WJC]

20.1331 Jo Ann Hoeppner Moran. *The growth of English schooling, 1340–1548: learning, literacy, and laicization in pre-Reformation York Diocese.* Princeton: Princeton University Press, 1985. ISBN 0-691-05430-4. ‣ In-depth study of elementary and secondary education in archdiocese of York in late Middle Ages, showing lay literacy more prevalent than hitherto thought. [WJC]

20.1332 Nicholas Orme. *Education and society in medieval and Renaissance England.* London: Hambledon, 1989. ISBN 1-85285-003-5. ‣ Specialized essays on English schools in high and late Middle Ages, several focused on school books, lay literacy, and education of literary figures such as Chaucer and Langland. [WJC]

20.1333 Nicholas Orme. *English schools in the Middle Ages.* London: Methuen, 1973. ISBN 0-416-16080-0. ‣ Major work on development of elementary and secondary education in medieval England. [WJC]

20.1334 Frank Pegues. "Royal support of students in the thirteenth century." *Speculum* 31 (1956) 454–62. ISSN 0038-7134. ‣ Examination of forms and extent of royal patronage of university students in medieval England and France. [WJC]

20.1335 Gaines Post. "Masters' salaries and student fees in the mediaeval universities." *Speculum* 7 (1932) 181–98. ISSN 0038-

7134. ▸ Fundamental study of financial structure of university education on Continent. [WJC]

20.1336 Hastings Rashdall. *The universities of Europe in the Middle Ages.* 1936 rev. ed. 3 vols. F. M. Powicke and A. B. Emden, eds. Oxford: Clarendon, 1987. ISBN 0-19-822981-X (v. 1), 0-19-822982-8 (v. 2), 0-19-822983-6 (v. 3). ▸ Standard introduction to history of medieval universities. Extremely useful although dated. [WJC]

20.1337 H. de Ridder-Symoens, ed. *Universities in the Middle Ages.* Vol. 1 of *A history of the university in Europe.* Walter Rueg, ed. Cambridge: Cambridge University Press, 1992. ISBN 0-521-36105-2. ▸ Collaborative work with chapters by specialists on university origins, institutional structures, student life, career patterns of masters, and related topics. Most up-to-date account available. [WJC]

20.1338 Joel T. Rosenthal. "English medieval education since 1970: so near and yet so far." *History of education quarterly* 22 (1982) 499–511. ISSN 0018-2680. ▸ Bibliography and critical analysis of recent scholarship on medieval English education. [WJC]

20.1339 Nancy G. Siraisi. *Arts and sciences at Padua: the studium of Padua before 1350.* Toronto: Pontifical Institute of Mediaeval Studies, 1973. ISBN 0-88844-025-1. ▸ Thorough examination of institutional structure and curriculum in arts and medicine at University of Padua in thirteenth and early fourteenth centuries. [WJC]

20.1340 Nancy G. Siraisi. *Taddeo Alderotti and his pupils: two generations of Italian medical learning.* Princeton: Princeton University Press, 1981. ISBN 0-691-05313-8. ▸ Discussion of reception of Aristotle and Greco-Arabic science in medical faculty of University of Bologna and its increasing acceptance and use during this period. Brilliantly evokes late thirteenth-century teaching and practice of medicine; gender-neutral study. [MLC/JS]

20.1341 Cyril Eugene Smith. *The University of Toulouse in the Middle Ages.* Milwaukee: Marquette University Press, 1958. ▸ Good introduction to structure and development of University of Toulouse in context of history of universities in southern France. Should be used in conjunction with more recent studies. [WJC]

20.1342 Sven Stelling-Michaud. *L'Université de Bologne et la pénétration des droits romain et canonique en Suisse aux treizième et quatorzième siècles.* Geneva: Droz, 1955. ▸ Early chapters cover development and influence in Switzerland of legal study at University of Bologna, its most important medieval center. [WJC]

20.1343 D.E.R. Watt. "Scottish masters and students at Paris in the fourteenth century." *Aberdeen University review* 36 (1955–56) 169–80. ISSN 0001-320X. ▸ Study of national group important in faculties of arts and theology in fourteenth-century University of Paris. [WJC]

20.1344 James A. Weisheipl. "Curriculum of the faculty of arts at Oxford in the early fourteenth century." *Mediaeval studies* 26 (1964) 143–85. ISSN 0076-5872. ▸ Discussion of textbooks used, courses of study offered, and disputations held at early fourteenth-century university of Oxford. [WJC]

20.1345 James A. Weisheipl. "Developments in the arts curriculum at Oxford in the early fourteenth century." *Mediaeval studies* 28 (1966) 151–75. ISSN 0076-5872. ▸ Charts introduction of new subjects, textbooks, and types of disputations, especially in field of logic. [WJC]

SEE ALSO
30.301 James H. Overfield. *Humanism and scholasticism in late medieval Germany.*

Thirteenth-Century Philosophy and Theology

20.1346 David Burr. *The persecution of Peter John Olivi.* Philadelphia: American Philosophical Society, 1976. (Transactions of the American Philosophical Society, n.s., 66.5.) ISBN 0-87169-665-7. ▸ Biography of Franciscan theologian of critical importance to theological issues of late thirteenth century, especially debate on apostolic poverty among Franciscans. [WJC]

20.1347 M. D. Chenu. *Toward understanding Saint Thomas.* A. M. Landry and D. Hughes, eds. and trans. Chicago: Regnery, 1964. ▸ Excellent reconstruction of educational context in which Thomas Aquinas developed his corpus of writings. Emphasizes methodology and outlook more than doctrinal content. [WJC]

20.1348 Werner Dettloff. *Die Entwicklung der Akzeptations- und Verdienstlehre von Duns Scotus bis Luther, mit besonderer Berücksichtigung der franziskaner Theologen.* Münster: Aschendorff, 1963. (Beiträge zur Geschichte der Philosophie und Theologie des Mittelalters: Texte und Untersuchungen, 40.2.) ▸ Pioneering study of influence of thirteenth-century philosopher's theory of merit and divine acceptation in late medieval thought, particularly among other members of Franciscan order. [WJC]

20.1349 Étienne Gilson. *The Christian philosophy of St. Thomas Aquinas.* 1956 ed. L. K. Shook, trans. New York: Octagon Books, 1983. ▸ Clear, precise account of thought of Thomas Aquinas, interpreted from strongly Neo-Thomist perspective. [WJC]

20.1350 Étienne Gilson. *Jean Duns Scot: introduction à ses positions fondamentales.* Paris: Vrin, 1952. ▸ Dated but still one of most important studies of philosopher's thought. Treats him more as philosopher than theologian. [WJC]

20.1351 Étienne Gilson. *The philosophy of St. Bonaventure.* 1938 ed. Illtyd Trethowan and Frank J. Sheed, trans. Paterson, N.J.: St. Anthony Guild Press, 1965. ▸ Older but still basic appraisal of Bonaventure's place in philosophical currents of thirteenth century. Treats Bonaventure's mysticism as well as philosophy and discursive theology, presenting constant comparisons with Aquinas. [WJC]

20.1352 Roland Hissette. *Enquête sur les 219 articles condamnés à Paris le 7 mars 1277.* Louvain: Publications Universitaires, 1977. ISBN 2-8017-0086-X. ▸ Thorough examination of background and meaning of individual articles in famous condemnation of 1277, whose subsequent chilling effect on speculative thought has been contested. [WJC]

20.1353 Mark D. Jordan. *Ordering wisdom: the hierarchy of philosophical discourses in Aquinas.* Notre Dame, Ind.: University of Notre Dame Press, 1986. ISBN 0-268-01500-7. ▸ Post–Neo-Thomist analysis of Thomas Aquinas's semantics and philosophical discourse, whose semiotic capacity depends on its objects of knowledge, from physics to psychology to metaphysics to theology. [MLC]

20.1354 Bernard J. Lonergan. *Verbum: word and idea in Aquinas.* David B. Burrell, ed. Notre Dame, Ind.: University of Notre Dame Press, 1967. ▸ Important study of philosophical and theological epistemology of St. Thomas Aquinas. [WJC]

20.1355 Steven P. Marrone. *Truth and scientific knowledge in the thought of Henry of Ghent.* Cambridge, Mass.: Mediaeval Academy of America, 1985. (Speculum anniversary monographs, 11.) ISBN 0-910956-91-X (cl), 0-910956-92-8 (pbk). ▸ Examination of epistemology of Henry of Ghent, major figure in late thirteenth-century scholasticism, whose views, presenting radically alternative positions, could not be ignored by his contemporaries and successors. [WJC]

20.1356 Steven P. Marrone. *William of Auvergne and Robert Grosseteste: new ideas of truth in the early thirteenth century.* Princeton: Princeton University Press, 1983. ISBN 0-691-05383-9.

▸ Study of epistemologies of William of Auvergne and Robert Grosseteste and their significance for science as well as for philosophy. [WJC]

20.1357 James McEvoy. *The philosophy of Robert Grosseteste.* Oxford: Clarendon, 1982. ISBN 0-19-824645-5. ▸ In-depth study of philosophical and scientific thought of theologian and scientist. Reappraises his contributions to reception of Aristotelianism and to cosmogony based on light. Preferred interpretation. [WJC/MHS]

20.1358 Walter H. Principe. *The theology of the hypostatic union in the early thirteenth century.* 4 vols. Toronto: Pontifical Institute of Mediaeval Studies, 1963–75. (Studies and texts, 7, 12, 19, 32.) ▸ Fundamental study of central Christian doctrine in thought of William of Auxerre, Alexander of Hales, Hugh of St. Cher, and Philip the Chancellor; much research based on unpublished sources. Solid and original. [MLC]

20.1359 Frederick J. Roensch. *Early Thomistic school.* Dubuque, Iowa: Priory Press, 1964. ▸ Biographical and philosophical study of Dominican defenders of thought of St. Thomas Aquinas at Paris and Oxford in late thirteenth century. [WJC]

20.1360 R. W. Southern. *Robert Grosseteste: the growth of an English mind in medieval Europe.* 2d ed. Oxford: Clarendon, 1992. ISBN 0-19-820310-1 (cl), 0-19-820145-9 (pbk). ▸ Grosseteste's life and thought as theologian and scientific thinker treating him as English scholar uninfluenced by Continental currents of thought; thesis concerning his intellectual insularity has been challenged. [WJC/KP]

20.1361 Fernand van Steenberghen. *Maître Siger de Brabant.* Louvain: Publications Universitaires, 1977. (Philosophes médiévaux, 21.) ISBN 2-8017-0063-0. ▸ Regarded as definitive study of Siger of Brabant, thirteenth-century leader of Latin Averroist movement at University of Paris, and his place in Aristotelian tradition. [WJC]

20.1362 Fernand van Steenberghen. *The philosophical movement in the thirteenth century.* Edinburgh: Nelson, 1955. ▸ Controversial but still useful account of currents of philosophy in late thirteenth century and reactions to reception of Aristotle. [WJC]

20.1363 Fernand van Steenberghen. *La philosophie au treizième siècle.* 2d ed. Louvain: Institut Superieur de Philosophie, 1991. (Philosophes médiévaux, 28.) ISBN 90-683-1370-3. ▸ Detailed study of development of scholastic philosophy from reception of Aristotle to Raymond Lull. Sees Thomas Aquinas as high point of story. Dated but still important. [WJC]

20.1364 James A. Weisheipl. *Friar Thomas d'Aquino: his life, thought, and works.* 1974 ed. Washington, D.C.: Catholic University of America Press, 1983. ISBN 0-8132-0590-5 (pbk). ▸ Detailed biographical study of Aquinas sorting fact from fiction and legend. Best available treatment of his life. [WJC]

20.1365 John F. Wippel. *The metaphysical thought of Godfrey of Fontaines: a study in late thirteenth-century philosophy.* Washington, D.C.: Catholic University of America Press, 1981. ISBN 0-8132-0556-5. ▸ Thorough examination of main features of metaphysics of Godfrey of Fontaines, leading late thirteenth-century theologian. [WJC]

20.1366 Allan B. Wolter. *The philosophical theology of John Duns Scotus.* Marilyn McCord Adams, ed. Ithaca, N.Y.: Cornell University Press, 1990. ISBN 0-8014-2385-6. ▸ Solid overview of thought of philosopher and theologian by leading Scotistic authority of our time. Major synthesis of work of Wolter's scholarly lifetime. [WJC]

Late Medieval Thought

20.1367 Marilyn McCord Adams. *William Ockham.* 2 vols. Notre Dame, Ind.: University of Notre Dame Press, 1987. ISBN

0-268-01940-1 (set). ▸ Exhaustive analysis and commentary on Ockham's philosophy and theology; omits political theory. Book-length section on natural philosophy, including views on substance, matter, quantity, time, motion, and causality. Currently regarded as standard treatment. [WJC/MHS]

20.1368 Philotheus Boehner. *Collected articles on Ockham.* Eligius M. Buytaert, ed. St. Bonaventure, N.Y.: Franciscan Institute, 1958. (Philosophy series, 12.) ▸ Collection of seminal studies on assorted aspects of Ockham's thought by one of foremost Ockham authorities of twentieth century. [WJC]

20.1369 Philotheus Boehner. *Medieval logic: an outline of its development from 1250 to c. 1400.* 1952 ed. Westport, Conn.: Hyperion, 1979. ISBN 0-88355-682-0. ▸ Standard introduction covering development of speculative grammar, supposition, theory of consequences, and logical contributions of Peter of Spain, William of Ockham, John Buridan, Walter Burley, and Albert of Saxony. [WJC]

20.1370 William J. Courtenay. *Capacity and volition: a history of the distinction of absolute and ordained power.* Bergamo: Lubrina, 1990. ISBN 88-7766-103-8. ▸ History of this distinction from eleventh century to end of Middle Ages, showing its applications by philosophers and theologians and its role in development of covenant theology. [MLC]

20.1371 Neal W. Gilbert. "Ockham, Wyclif, and the 'via moderna.'" In *Antiqui und moderni: Traditionsbewusstsein und Fortschrittsbewusstsein im späten Mittelalter.* Albert Zimmerman, ed., pp. 85–125. Berlin: de Gruyter, 1974. ISBN 3-11-004538-9. ▸ Revisionist study of meaning of "modern" and origins of conflict between *via moderna* and *via antiqua* in late Middle Ages. [WJC]

20.1372 J. N. Hillgarth. *Ramon Lull and Lullism in fourteenth-century France.* Oxford: Clarendon, 1971. ISBN 0-19-824348-0. ▸ Definitive study of thought of Ramon Lull and his influence in France in century after his death. [WJC]

20.1373 Anne Hudson and Michael Wilks, eds. *From Ockham to Wyclif.* Oxford: Blackwell, 1987. ISBN 0-631-15055-2. ▸ Specialized conference papers on important aspects of scholasticism and religious thought as well as ecclesiastical institutions in fourteenth-century England. [WJC]

20.1374 Zénon Kaluza. *Les querelles doctrinales à Paris: nominalistes et réalistes aux confines du quatorzième et du quinzième siècles.* Bergamo: Lubrina, 1988. ISBN 88-7766-034-1. ▸ One of best studies of controversies leading to separation of *via moderna* and *via antiqua* in late medieval scholasticism. [WJC]

20.1375 Paul Oskar Kristeller. *Medieval aspects of Renaissance learning: three essays.* 1974 ed. Edward P. Mahoney, ed. and trans. New York: Columbia University Press, 1992. ISBN 0-231-07950-8 (cl), 0-231-07951-6 (pbk). ▸ Essays exploring connections between medieval and Renaissance thought, especially Thomism and contributions of mendicant orders. Argues for continuity of scholasticism in Renaissance. [WJC]

20.1376 Gordon Leff. *Bradwardine and the Pelagians: a study of his "De Causa Dei" and its opponents.* Cambridge: Cambridge University Press, 1957. ▸ Basic study of major fourteenth-century philosopher, theologian, scientific thinker, and churchman. [MLC]

20.1377 Gordon Leff. *The dissolution of the medieval outlook: an essay on intellectual and spiritual change in the fourteenth century.* New York: Harper & Row, 1976. ISBN 0-06-131897-3 (pbk). ▸ Outline of shifts between thirteenth- and fourteenth-century thought in theology, philosophy, and science. Argues paradigm shift creating new outlook did not develop. [MLC]

20.1378 Gordon Leff. *Gregory of Rimini: tradition and innovation in fourteenth-century thought.* Manchester: Manchester University

Press, 1961. ‣ Study of important scholastic philosopher and theologian whose thought was highly controversial in his own day. [MLC]

20.1379 Gordon Leff. *William of Ockham: the metamorphosis of scholastic discourse.* Totowa, N.J.: Rowman & Littlefield, 1975. ISBN 0-87471-679-9. ‣ Extended examination of most areas of fourteenth-century philosopher's thought. Remains useful although predates complete critical edition of Ockham's works and is regarded as unreliable on some points. [WJC]

20.1380 John Emery Murdoch and Edith Dudley Sylla, eds. *The cultural context of medieval learning: proceedings of the first international colloquim on philosophy, science, and theology in the Middle Ages, September 1973.* Dordrecht: Reidel, 1975. ISBN 90-277-0560-7 (cl), 90-277-0587-9 (pbk). ‣ Collection of seminal essays on interrelation of philosophy, theology, and science in late Middle Ages. [WJC/MHS]

20.1381 Francis C. Oakley. *Omnipotence, covenant, and order: an excursion in the history of ideas from Abelard to Leibniz.* Ithaca, N.Y.: Cornell University Press, 1984. ISBN 0-8014-1631-0. ‣ Study of medieval understanding of theology, physical world, and politics, based on distinction between God's absolute and ordained power, with defense of intellectual history against would-be detractors. [WJC]

20.1382 Heiko A. Oberman. *The harvest of medieval theology: Gabriel Biel and late medieval nominalism.* 1963 ed. Durham, N.C.: Labyrinth, 1983. ISBN 0-939464-05-5 (pbk). ‣ Seminal study of leading German theologian on eve of Reformation, important for pioneering idea of studying continuities between late medieval theology and Protestantism. [WJC]

20.1383 John Herman Randall, Jr. *The school of Padua and the emergence of modern science.* Padua: Antenore, 1961. ‣ Major contribution to history of Aristotelianism and Averroism in Renaissance Italy. Charts links to and differences from medieval versions of these traditions. [WJC]

20.1384 Herman Shapiro. *Motion, time, and place according to William Ockham.* St. Bonaventure, N.Y.: Franciscan Institute, 1957. (Philosophy series, 13.) ‣ Important study of one of most influential and controversial aspects of Ockham's philosophy. [WJC]

20.1385 Katherine H. Tachau. *Vision and certitude in the age of Ockham: optics, epistemology, and the foundations of semantics, 1250–1345.* Leiden: Brill, 1988. ISBN 90-04-08552-1 (pbk). ‣ Sophisticated examination of epistemology of Ockham and contemporaries, especially Roger Bacon. Charts sources and influence on next generation, and relates science of optics to philosophy. Makes notable use of unpublished sources. [WJC/MHS]

20.1386 Roberto Weiss. *Humanism in England during the fifteenth century.* 3d ed. Oxford: Blackwell, 1967. ‣ Study of individual English humanists and English contacts of Poggio Bracciolini. Treats Renaissance humanism as alternative to medieval scholasticism with no continuities between them. Compare Ozment 22.95. [WJC]

20.1387 Adolar Zumkeller. "Die Augustinerschule des Mittelalters: Vertreter und philosophisch-theologische Lehre." *Analecta Augustiniana* 27 (1964) 167–262. ‣ Biographical register of theologians belonging to Augustinian order, thirteenth to fifteenth century, indicating their major writings. Useful research tool. [WJC]

SEE ALSO
22.95 Steven E. Ozment. *The age of reform, 1250–1550.*

History of Science in the High and Late Middle Ages

20.1388 Marshall Clagett. *Archimedes in the Middle Ages.* 4 vols. in 1. Madison: University of Wisconsin Press, 1964. ‣ Funda-

mental study of reception of third-century BCE mathematician into medieval scientific thought and his impact on physics in high and late Middle Ages. [MLC]

20.1389 Marshall Clagett. *The science of mechanics in the Middle Ages.* Madison: University of Wisconsin Press, 1959. ‣ Classic treatment of medieval mechanics that, although dated, remains basis for subsequent studies. [MLC]

20.1390 Alistair C. Crombie. *Augustine to Galileo.* 1959 2d rev. ed. 2 vols. in 1. Cambridge, Mass.: Harvard University Press, 1979. ISBN 0-674-05273-0. ‣ Long-standard history of medieval science, remains valuable today although views on experimental science and some other issues have been called into question by later research. [WJC]

20.1391 Richard C. Dales. *Medieval discussions of the eternity of the world.* Leiden: Brill, 1990. ISBN 90-04-9215-3. ‣ Detailed investigation of eternity thesis, interest in which was triggered by reception of Aristotle in its Averroist form, and which was debated by medieval theologians, philosophers, and scientific thinkers. [MLC/MHS]

20.1392 Stewart Copinger Easton. *Roger Bacon and his search for a universal science: a reconsideration.* New York: Columbia University Press, 1952. ‣ Dated but still important, pioneering study relating thirteenth-century scholar's scientific research into optics and physics to his theology and program for church reform. [MLC]

20.1393 Edward Grant. *Physical science in the Middle Ages.* 1971 ed. New York: Cambridge University Press, 1977. ISBN 0-521-21862-4 (cl), 0-521-29294-8 (pbk). ‣ Study of theories of motion and cosmology from early Middle Ages to fourteenth century. Emphasizes late scholastics' critique of Aristotle's theory of local motion. [WJC]

20.1394 Anneliese Maier. *On the threshold of exact science: selected writings of Anneliese Maier on late medieval natural philosophy.* Steven D. Sargent, ed. and trans. Philadelphia: University of Pennsylvania Press, 1982. ISBN 0-8122-7831-3. ‣ Collection of most important papers of extremely influential historian of late medieval science, treating motion, causation, impetus theory, physics, and general achievements of late medieval natural philosophers. Central for understanding differences between fourteenth- and seventeenth-century approaches to natural philosophy. [MLC/MHS]

20.1395 Nicholas H. Steneck. *Science and creation in the Middle Ages: Henry of Langenstein (d. 1397) on Genesis.* Notre Dame, Ind.: University of Notre Dame Press, 1976. ISBN 0-268-01672-0. ‣ Study of scientific views, especially on cosmogenesis, of important late medieval scholastic. Excellent introduction to full range and key theories of late medieval science and natural philosophy. [WJC/MHS]

20.1396 C. H. Talbot. *Medicine in medieval England.* London: Oldbourne, 1967. ‣ General introduction to study and practice of medicine in medieval England. [WJC]

20.1397 James A. Weisheipl, ed. *Albertus Magnus and the sciences: commemorative essays.* Toronto: Pontifical Institute of Mediaeval Studies, 1980. (Studies and texts, 49.) ISBN 0-88844-049-9 (pbk). ‣ Collected papers exploring Dominican scholar and saint's contributions to wide range of issues in natural sciences. [WJC]

20.1398 Curtis Wilson. *William Heytesbury: medieval logic and the rise of mathematical physics.* 1956 ed. Madison: University of Wisconsin Press, 1960. ‣ Excellent introduction to interrelation of late medieval logic and physics in thought of Oxford scholastic. [WJC]

SEE ALSO
4.55 David C. Lindberg, ed. *Science in the Middle Ages.*

4.56 David C. Lindberg. *Theories of vision from al-Kindi to Kepler.*

4.687 Nancy G. Siraisi. *Medieval and early Renaissance medicine.*

Biblical Studies

20.1399 William J. Courtenay. "The Bible in the fourteenth century: some observations." *Church history* 54 (1985) 176–87. ISSN 0009-6407. ▸ Survey of developments in biblical exegesis in fourteenth and early fifteenth centuries, especially on Continent. [WJC]

20.1400 G. R. Evans. *The language and logic of the Bible.* Vol. 1: *The earlier Middle Ages.* Vol. 2: *The road to Reformation.* 2 vols. Cambridge: Cambridge University Press, 1984–85. ISBN 0-521-26371-9 (v. 1), 0-521-30548-9 (v. 2). ▸ Study of methods of biblical exegesis from monastic culture of eleventh century through scholastic culture of high and late Middle Ages. Accents impact of grammatical and logical studies rather than theological issues on exegesis. [WJC]

20.1401 Henri de Lubac. *L'exégèse médiévale: les quatres sens de l'écriture.* 2 vols. in 4. Paris: Aubier, 1959–64. ▸ Standard study of biblical exegesis from early church to Reformation, especially for medieval exegetes who gave biblical text polysemous rather than literal reading. [WJC]

20.1402 Beryl Smalley. *English friars and antiquity in the early fourteenth century.* Oxford: Blackwell, 1960. ▸ Study of biblical exegesis in fourteenth century with special attention to English Dominican authors. Sees work of these scholastics as compatible with their interest in classical antiquity. [WJC]

20.1403 Beryl Smalley. *The Gospels in the schools, c. 1100–c. 1280.* London: Hambledon, 1985. ISBN 0-907628-49-4. ▸ Collection of specialized essays expanding author's earlier studies (cf. 20.995) here emphasizing New Testament exegesis on part of scholastic theologians. [WJC]

20.1404 Katherine Walsh and Diana Wood, eds. *The Bible in the medieval world: essays in memory of Beryl Smalley.* Oxford: Blackwell, 1985. ISBN 0-631-14275-4. ▸ Essays centering on biblical exegesis from eighth to fifteenth century in memory of Beryl Smalley. [WJC]

Political Theory

20.1405 R. W. Carlyle and Alexander J. Carlyle. *A history of mediaeval political theory in the West.* 1903–36 ed. 6 vols. Edinburgh: Blackwood & Sons, 1970. ▸ Early but still basic and very detailed work on medieval political theory that continues to merit consultation. [WJC]

20.1406 Thomas Gilby. *The political thought of Thomas Aquinas.* 1958 ed. Chicago: University of Chicago Press, 1973. ▸ Useful introduction to political thought of saint, accenting his appeal to Aristotelianism as basis for political life, seen as natural end for man. [WJC]

20.1407 Arthur Stephen McGrade. *The political thought of William of Ockham: personal and institutional principles.* Cambridge: Cambridge University Press, 1974. ISBN 0-521-20284-1. ▸ Solid analysis of Ockham's theories of law, society, and political authority. Sees these ideas as more or less distinct from Ockham's philosophy. [WJC]

20.1408 Charles Howard McIlwain. *The growth of political thought in the West from the Greeks to the end of the Middle Ages.* 1932 ed. New York: Cooper Square, 1968. ▸ Despite date, provides fundamental introduction and orientation to medieval political theory. [WJC]

20.1409 Jürgen Miethke. *Ockhams Weg zur Sozialphilosophie.* Berlin: de Gruyter, 1969. ▸ Among best studies of William of Ockham's political and social thought in wider context of his philosophy. [WJC]

20.1410 John B. Morrall. *Political thought in medieval times.* 1958 ed. Toronto: University of Toronto Press, 1980. (Mediaeval Academy reprints for teaching, 7.) ISBN 0-8020-6413-2 (pbk). ▸ Brief introduction focusing only on major figures in history of medieval political thought. Accents reception of classical political philosophy and emergence of secular rationales for political life. [WJC]

20.1411 Francis C. Oakley. "Celestial hierarchies revisited: Walter Ullmann's vision of medieval politics." *Past and present* 60 (1973) 3–48. ISSN 0031-2746. ▸ Trenchant critique of conflict of ascending and descending models of political authority found repeatedly in Ullmann's many publications on medieval political thought. [WJC]

20.1412 Francis C. Oakley. *The political thought of Pierre d'Ailly: the voluntarist tradition.* New Haven: Yale University Press, 1964. ▸ Careful study of political theory and ecclesiology of leading fourteenth-century scholastic thinker. [WJC]

20.1413 Alessandro Passerin d'Entrèves. *The medieval contribution to political thought: Thomas Aquinas, Marsilius of Padua, Richard Hooker.* 1939 ed. New York: Humanities, 1959. ▸ Good introduction to political thought of Aquinas and Marsilius, emphasizing contributions to grounding of politics on natural sanctions and to principle of representation and consent. [MLC]

Latin and Vernacular Literatures

20.1414 William Anderson. *Dante the maker.* London: Routledge & Kegan Paul, 1980. ISBN 0-7100-0322-6. ▸ Detailed biography of writer-poet. Treats writing of *Commedia*, and places it in social context. [WJC]

20.1415 Thomas Goddard Bergin. *Dante.* 1965 ed. Westport, Conn.: Greenwood, 1976. ISBN 0-8371-7973-4. ▸ Study of Dante's life, political setting, and profile of all his works before devoting several chapters to *Commedia*. Best general introduction to Dante. [WJC]

20.1416 Roger Boase. *The origin and meaning of courtly love: a critical study of European scholarship.* Totowa, N.J.: Rowman & Littlefield, 1977. ISBN 0-87471-950-X. ▸ Helpful guide to intense scholarly debates on origins of courtly love and its literary, social, and religious significance. [MLC]

20.1417 Joachim Bumke. *Courtly culture: literature and society in the high Middle Ages.* Thomas Dunlap, trans. Berkeley: University of California Press, 1991. ISBN 0-520-06634-0. ▸ Study of courtly love literature in social setting generally, but emphasizing Germany and reflecting influence of Jaeger's thesis (20.1423). [MLC]

20.1418 J. A. Burrow. *Medieval writers and their work: Middle English literature and its background, 1100–1500.* Oxford: Oxford University Press, 1982. ISBN 0-19-219135-7 (cl), 0-19-289122-7 (pbk). ▸ Survey of Middle English literature from its beginnings through generation after Chaucer, placing authors in social and intellectual contexts. Highly useful introduction. [MLC]

20.1419 Peter Dronke. *Dante and medieval Latin traditions.* 1986 ed. Cambridge: Cambridge University Press, 1988. ISBN 0-521-32152-2 (cl, 1986), 0-521-37960-1 (pbk). ▸ Provides important literary, philosophical, theological, and scientific backgrounds for particular ideas, images, and symbols in Dante's *Commedia*. [WJC]

20.1420 Peter Dronke. *Medieval Latin and the rise of European love-lyric.* 2d ed. 2 vols. Oxford: Clarendon, 1968. ISBN 0-19-814346-X. ▸ Learned attack on view that medieval poets merely received and imitated classical models. Also argues for widespread incidence of attitudes that some scholars associate preclusively with medieval courtly love literature. [MLC]

20.1421 Peter Dronke. *Poetic individuality in the Middle Ages: new departures in poetry, 1000–1150.* 2d ed. London: Westfield College, University of London, Committee for Medieval Studies, 1986. (Westfield publication in medieval studies, 1.) ISBN 1-870059-00-X, ISSN 0269-9699. ▸ Includes studies of Ruodlieb, poetry of Peter Abelard, Hildegard of Bingen, and other texts. Argues forcefully for authors' creative rather than merely imitative use of sources. [WJC]

20.1422 John H. Fisher. *The importance of Chaucer.* Carbondale: Southern Illinois University Press, 1992. ISBN 0-8093-1741-9. ▸ Up-to-date assessment of Chaucer's place in history of medieval English literature and of European literature more widely. Good general introduction to writer and his works. [MLC]

20.1423 C. Stephen Jaeger. *The origins of courtliness: civilizing trends and the formation of courtly ideals, 939–1210.* Philadelphia: University of Pennsylvania Press, 1985. ISBN 0-8122-7936-0. ▸ Revisionist, influential interpretation of origins of courtly love attitudes; seen arising in German ecclesiastical courtly settings rather than in secular courts of southern France. [MLC]

20.1424 George Kane. *Chaucer and Langland: historical and textual approaches.* Berkeley: University of California Press, 1989. ISBN 0-520-06316-3. ▸ Places these two major fourteenth-century English authors in historical setting of age and considers textual issues in their works. [MLC]

20.1425 Max Manitius. *Geschichte der lateinischen literatur des Mittelalters.* 1911–31 ed. 3 vols. Munich: Beck, 1964–65. (Handbuch der Altertumswissenschaft, 9.2.) ▸ Despite age, remains important survey and reference work. Lists authors and works; provides bibliographical orientation. [WJC]

20.1426 Charles Muscatine. *The Old French fabliaux.* New Haven: Yale University Press, 1986. ISBN 0-300-03527-6. ▸ Excellent, spirited introduction to important and often bawdy genre of medieval vernacular literature. Reveals humorous and irreverent side of medieval literary imagination. [MLC]

20.1427 F.J.E. Raby. *A history of Christian Latin poetry: from the beginnings to the close of the Middle Ages.* 1953 2d ed. Oxford: Oxford University Press, 1966. ▸ Still main work providing overview of Latin Christian poetry throughout Middle Ages. [WJC]

20.1428 F.J.E. Raby. *A history of secular Latin poetry in the Middle Ages.* 1957 2d ed. 2 vols. Oxford: Clarendon, 1967. ▸ Companion volume to Raby's work on Christian Latin poetry (20.1427), providing analogous survey of secular Latin literature of all genres throughout Middle Ages. [WJC]

20.1429 L. D. Reynolds and N. G. Wilson. *Scribes and scholars: a guide to the transmission of Greek and Latin literature.* 3d ed. Oxford: Clarendon, 1991. ISBN 0-19-872145-5 (cl), 0-19-872146-3 (pbk). ▸ Study of transmission and reception of classical literary texts by focusing on manuscripts, scriptoria, and centers of learning. Treats classics as principal source of medieval literary inspiration. [WJC]

20.1430 Olive Sayce. *The medieval German lyric, 1150–1300: the development of its themes and forms in their European context.* Oxford: Clarendon, 1982. ISBN 0-19-815772-X. ▸ Sound recent survey of lyric poetry in Middle High German, written accessibly for English-speaking reader and organized by genres and themes. [MLC]

20.1431 L. T. Topsfield. *Troubadours and love.* London: Cambridge University Press, 1975. ISBN 0-521-20596-4. ▸ Survey of poets who wrote about love in twelfth and thirteenth centuries showing wide variation in attitudes toward subject. Courtly love does not exhaust phenomenon. [MLC]

20.1432 Maurice O'Connell Walshe. *Medieval German literature, a survey.* Cambridge, Mass.: Harvard University Press, 1962. ▸ Overview of history of medieval German literature, treated both chronologically, thematically, and in terms of literary genres. Best introduction in English. [MLC]

20.1433 Karl Young. *The drama of the medieval church.* 1933 ed. 2 vols. Oxford: Clarendon, 1967. ▸ Still standard introduction to medieval religious drama, covering liturgical, mystery, and miracle plays from Latin origins in early Middle Ages to vernacularization at end of period. [WJC]

Art and Architecture

20.1434 Jean Bony. *The English decorated style: Gothic architecture transformed, 1250–1350.* Ithaca, N.Y.: Cornell University Press, 1979. ISBN 0-8014-1243-9. ▸ Major work on late medieval Gothic architecture and architectural decoration in England, charting development of England's unique national approach to Gothic style. [WJC]

20.1435 Jean Bony. *French Gothic architecture of the twelfth and thirteenth centuries.* Berkeley: University of California Press, 1983. ISBN 0-520-02831-7. ▸ Excellent, well-illustrated overview of development and spread of French Gothic architecture within France and in other countries influenced by France. [WJC]

20.1436 Adolf Katzenellenbogen. *Allegories of the virtues and vices in medieval art: from early Christian times to the thirteenth century.* 1939 ed. Alan J. P. Crick, trans. Toronto: University of Toronto Press, 1989. (Mediaeval academy reprints for teaching, 24.) ISBN 0-8020-6706-9 (pbk). ▸ Iconographical analyses of art works, both painting and sculpture, showing connection with moral schemata taught by Christian thinkers across period studied. [MLC]

20.1437 Adolf Katzenellenbogen. *The sculptural programs of Chartres cathedral: Christ, Mary, ecclesia.* 1959 ed. New York: Norton, 1964. ▸ Detailed analysis of sculptural programs of west, north, and south portals of Chartres cathedral, relating iconography to theology, Mariology, ecclesiology, and spirituality of twelfth century. [MLC]

20.1438 Erwin Panofsky. *Renaissance and renascences in Western art.* 1960 ed. New York: Harper & Row, 1972. ISBN 0-06-430026-9. ▸ Controversial, even tendentious, comparison between medieval and Renaissance classicism in art. Argues it was only in latter age that classicism was appropriated with chemical purity. Historiographically important. [MLC]

20.1439 Whitney S. Stoddard. *Monastery and cathedral in France: medieval architecture, sculpture, stained glass, manuscripts, the art of the church treasuries.* 1966 ed. New York: Harper & Row, 1972. ISBN 0-06-430022-6. ▸ Survey of art in France from Romanesque to Gothic, concentrating on Gothic cathedrals but with broad attention to all genres of art in high and late Middle Ages. [WJC]

20.1440 Geoffrey F. Webb. *Architecture in Britain: the Middle Ages.* 1956 ed. Harmondsworth: Penguin, 1965. ▸ General overview of architecture in England from Anglo-Saxons to late Gothic architecture, from major cathedrals to secular buildings and parish churches. [WJC]

TOPICS IN CHURCH HISTORY

Popular Religion

20.1441 Kathleen Ashley and Pamela Sheingorn, eds. *Interpreting cultural symbols: Saint Anne in late medieval society.* Athens: University of Georgia Press, 1990. ISBN 0-8203-1262-2 (cl), 0-8203-1263-0 (pbk). ▸ Extensive introduction prefaces essays on aspects of late medieval cult of mother of Virgin Mary. Employs interdisciplinary approaches, incorporating insights from cultural and gender studies. [FHS]

20.1442   James R. Banker. *Death in the community: memorialization and confraternities in an Italian commune in the late Middle Ages.* Athens: University of Georgia Press, 1988. ISBN 0-8203-1034-4. ‣ Treats lay confraternities created to provide corporal and spiritual aid to moribund in context of contemporary beliefs and social structures, charting changes in attitudes toward death and charity, 1250–1450. [FHS]

20.1443   Frank Barlow. "The king's evil." *English historical review* 95 (1980) 3–27. ISSN 0013-8266. ‣ Careful reappraisal of Bloch's thesis (20.1444) arguing no continuous established custom of royal touching emerged before thirteenth century. Argues Bloch misled by few isolated incidences. [FHS]

20.1444   Marc Bloch. *The royal touch: sacred monarchy and scrofula in England and France.* J. E. Anderson, trans. New York: Dorset, 1989. ISBN 0-88029-408-6. ‣ Social, religious, and political meaning of royal authority in Middle Ages as seen in belief that sovereign's touch cures scrofula and related diseases. Annales-school classic. [FHS]

20.1445   Renate Blumenfeld-Kosinski and Timea Szell, eds. *Images of sainthood in medieval Europe.* Ithaca, N.Y.: Cornell University Press, 1991. ISBN 0-8014-2507-7 (cl), 0-8014-9745-0 (pbk). ‣ Collection of essays emphasizing language of hagiography and ways in which gender was factored into sanctity in Middle Ages. Exciting new perspectives. [FHS]

20.1446   William A. Christian, Jr. *Apparitions in late medieval and Renaissance Spain.* Princeton: Princeton University Press, 1981. ISBN 0-691-05326-x. ‣ Study of apparitions of Virgin Mary in Spain and their importance in popular religion and for cult of Virgin more specifically. [MLC]

20.1447   D. L. D'Avray. *The preaching of the friars: sermons diffused from Paris before 1300.* Oxford: Clarendon, 1985. ISBN 0-19-822772-8. ‣ Argues character of mendicant preaching cannot be fully explained by urban social context; audience not purely urban or commercial. Attempts to contextualize sermon evidence more broadly. [FHS]

20.1448   Sharon Farmer. *Communities of Saint Martin: legend and ritual in medieval Tours.* Ithaca, N.Y.: Cornell University Press, 1991. ISBN 0-8014-2391-0. ‣ Investigation of how three medieval communities in region of Tours defined themselves through cult of St. Martin. Innovative analysis of relationship between group identity and religious expression. [FHS]

20.1449   Ronald C. Finucane. *Miracles and pilgrims: popular beliefs in medieval England.* Totowa, N.J.: Rowman & Littlefield, 1977. ISBN 0-87471-831-7. ‣ Collective biographies of beneficiaries of miracles at particular English shrines. Considers social class, personality type, gender, and illness to find distinct patterns. Complements Ward 20.1465. [FHS]

20.1450   Maureen Flynn. *Sacred charity: confraternities and social welfare in Spain, 1400–1700.* Ithaca, N.Y.: Cornell University Press, 1989. ISBN 0-8014-2227-2. ‣ Examination of lay religious culture of Spanish confraternities and how it shaped religious life, moral community, and poor relief. Useful for religious and social historians. [FHS]

20.1451   Michael Goodich. *Vita perfecta: the ideal of sainthood in the thirteenth century.* Stuttgart: Hiersemann, 1982. ISBN 3-7772-8201-4. ‣ Highlights saints' formative years up to conversion or admission to religious order, giving profiles and statistical analyses of various kinds of saints. Excellent list of sources in appendix. [FHS]

20.1452   Aron Gurevich. *Medieval popular culture: problems of belief and perception.* Janos M. Bak and Paul A. Hollingsworth,

trans. Cambridge: Cambridge University Press, 1988. ISBN 0-521-30369-9 (cl), 0-521-38658-6 (pbk). ‣ Fascinating, original discussion of relationship between learned and popular culture, particularly religion, as revealed in six literary genres. Argues for interaction and interpenetration. Anthropologically influenced. [FHS]

20.1453   Thomas Head. *Hagiography and the cult of saints: the diocese of Orléans, 800–1200.* Cambridge: Cambridge University Press, 1990. ISBN 0-521-36500-7. ‣ Development of role of saints' cults in Orléanaise society and religion. Shows how veneration of saints reflected society's changing needs. [FHS]

20.1454   Richard Kieckhefer. *Unquiet souls: fourteenth-century saints and their religious milieu.* Chicago: University of Chicago Press, 1984. ISBN 0-226-43509-1. ‣ Anecdotal study of fifty-five late medieval saints. Emphasizes their contemporary biographers and their conceptions of holiness. Situates study in context of popular piety. [FHS]

20.1455   Jacques Le Goff. *Your money or your life: economy and religion in the Middle Ages.* Patricia M. Ranum, trans. New York: Zone Books, 1988. ISBN 0-942299-14-0 (cl), 0-942299-15-9 (pbk). ‣ Study of how European society developed ways of coping with problem of usury as new commercial economy threatened old Christian values. Useful if less comprehensive than Little 20.1177. [FHS]

20.1456   Daniel R. Lesnick. *Preaching in medieval Florence: the social world of Franciscan and Dominican spirituality.* Athens: University of Georgia Press, 1989. ISBN 0-8203-1047-6. ‣ Study of how friars guided new urban classes of bankers, merchants, and artisans through social upheaval and spiritual dilemmas created by commercial revolution. Analysis of sermons in terms of audience's concerns. [FHS]

20.1457   Lester K. Little. *Liberty, charity, fraternity: lay religious confraternities at Bergamo in the age of the commune.* Sandro Buzzetti, ed. Northampton, Mass.: Smith College, 1988. ISBN 0-87391-0400. ‣ Good introduction to lay confraternities in context of medieval Italian society. Treats emergence of self-regulating lay corporate entities concerned with prayer, fraternity, and charity. [FHS]

20.1458   Raoul Manselli. *La religion populaire au moyen âge: problèmes de méthode et d'histoire.* Montreal: Institut d'Études Médiévales Albert-le-Grand, 1975. ‣ Brief but useful consideration of relationship between popular and learned religion. Includes discussions of heresy, saints, and miracles. Emphasis on historical methodology in this field. [FHS]

20.1459   Gerald R. Owst. *Literature and pulpit in medieval England: a neglected chapter in the history of English letters and of the English people.* 2d rev. ed. New York: Barnes & Noble, 1966. ‣ Seminal study of English literature's debt to sermons and tractates of medieval church. Addresses many aspects of popular religion. Important for historians as well as students of literature. [FHS]

20.1460   Jean-Claude Schmitt. *The holy greyhound: Guinefort, healer of children since the thirteenth century.* Martin Thomas, trans. Cambridge: Cambridge University Press, 1983. ISBN 0-521-24434-x. ‣ Explores complex relationship between popular and learned cultures by examining cult of French dog-saint mentioned in exemplum of Stephen of Bourbon. Anthropologically influenced analysis. [FHS]

20.1461   Jonathan Sumption. *Pilgrimage: an image of mediaeval religion.* 1975 ed. Totowa, N.J.: Rowman & Littlefield, 1976. ISBN 0-87471-677-2. ‣ Comprehensive, useful introduction to pilgrimage as expression of piety and related topics. Concentrates on France, 1050–1250, but occasionally goes beyond. [FHS]

20.1462   Charles Trinkaus and Heiko A. Oberman, eds. *The pur-

suit of holiness in late medieval and Renaissance religion: papers from the University of Michigan conference. Leiden: Brill, 1974. ISBN 90-04-03791-8. ▸ Essays on theology, mysticism, practice of confession, lay piety, and cult of youth, humanism, and the arts. Useful articles on popular religion, both Renaissance and medieval. [FHS/WJC]

20.1463 André Vauchez. *Les laïcs au moyen âge: pratiques et expériences religieuses.* Paris: du Cerf, 1987. ISBN 2-204-02710-3. ▸ Study of selected aspects of popular religion, 1100-1450. Covers emergence of lay devotion including mysticism, confraternities, and heresy. Large section devoted to women and religion. [FHS]

20.1464 André Vauchez. *La sainteté en occident au derniers siècles du moyen âge: d'après les procès de canonisation et les documents hagiographiques.* Rev. ed. Rome: Écoles Françaises de Rome, 1988. ISBN 2-7283-0171-9. ▸ Most complete discussion of saints, cults, and canonization in later Middle Ages, including statistical analysis. Outstanding lists of sources, especially canonization procedures; important scholarly resource. [FHS]

20.1465 Benedicta Ward. *Miracles and the medieval mind: theory, record, and event, 1000–1215.* Rev. ed. Philadelphia: University of Pennsylvania Press, 1987. ISBN 0-8122-1228-2 (pbk). ▸ Useful introduction to miracles and cults of saints. Examines theoretical concept of miracles associated with shrines of saints and their meaning in medieval religious thought and practice. [FHS]

20.1466 Marina Warner. *Alone of all her sex: the myth and the cult of the Virgin Mary.* 1976 ed. New York: Vintage, 1983. ISBN 0-394-71155-6 (pbk). ▸ Study of veneration of Virgin Mary and understanding of her religious and theological importance since New Testament period. Emphasizes importance of Marian symbolism and devotion in Middle Ages. [FHS]

20.1467 Donald Weinstein and Rudolph M. Bell. *Saints and society: the two worlds of Western Christendom, 1000–1700.* 1982 ed. Chicago: University of Chicago Press, 1986. ISBN 0-226-89056-2. ▸ Collective study of 864 saints' lives, treated quantitatively, to chart trends reflecting social status, gender, geography, age, type of calling, and motivation. Reveals intriguing patterns. [FHS]

20.1468 Stephen D. White. *Custom, kinship, and gifts to saints: the laudatio parentum in Western France, 1050–1150.* Chapel Hill: University of North Carolina Press, 1988. ISBN 0-8078-1779-1. ▸ Analysis of lay gifts of property to churches and monasteries, seen as gifts to patron saints, in legal, social, and religious contexts. Gifts and countergifts created enduring social relationships. [FHS]

20.1469 Stephen Wilson, ed. *Saints and their cults: studies in religious sociology, folklore, and history.* Cambridge: Cambridge University Press, 1983. ISBN 0-521-24978-3. ▸ Collection of essays, several on medieval Europe. Includes extremely valuable one-hundred-page annotated bibliography of secondary sources for saints and their cults. [FHS]

SEE ALSO
28.154 Ronald F. E. Weissman. *Ritual brotherhood in Renaissance Florence.*

Mysticism

20.1470 Edward A. Armstrong. *Saint Francis, nature mystic: the derivation and significance of the nature stories in the Franciscan legend.* 1973 ed. Berkeley: University of California Press, 1976. ISBN 0-520-03040-0 (pbk). ▸ Analysis of particularly Franciscan approach to nature mysticism developed by Francis of Assisi; his sources and his influences within his own order. [MLC]

20.1471 Stephanus Gerard Axters. *The spirituality of the old Low Countries.* Donald Attwater, trans. London: Blackfriars, 1954. ▸ Flemish spirituality and mysticism through Hadewych, John Ruysbroeck, and followers, especially Denis the Carthusian and

participants in Devotio Moderna. Accents early medieval origins, not mystics' response to later religious practice. [FHS]

20.1472 James M. Clark. *The great German mystics: Eckhart, Tauler, and Suso.* 1949 ed. New York: Russell & Russell, 1970. ▸ Overview of fourteenth-century mysticism including other German mystics besides Dominican Rhineland mystics mentioned in title. Good bibliography. [FHS]

20.1473 Ewert H. Cousins. *Bonaventure and the coincidence of opposites.* Jacques Guy Bougerol, Introduction. Chicago: Franciscan Herald Press, 1978. ISBN 0-8199-0580-1. ▸ Study of mystical doctrine of thirteenth-century Franciscan scholastic, minister general, and cardinal, noting his use of Franciscan sources as well as ideas drawn from wider mystical tradition. [MLC]

20.1474 Oliver Davies. *God within: the mystical tradition of northern Europe.* New York: Paulist Press, 1988. ISBN 0-8091-3041-6. ▸ Using comparative analysis, argues fourteenth-century Flemish mystical writers form distinctive spiritual movement differing from other schools of Christian mysticism in other ages. [FHS]

20.1475 Jean Dechanet. *William of St. Thierry: the man and his work.* Richard Strachan, trans. Spencer, Mass.: Cistercian, 1972. ISBN 0-87907-810-3. ▸ Only English-language study of life and teachings of twelfth-century mystic in Cistercian tradition, including his criticisms of contemporary scholastic theologians. [MLC]

20.1476 Gervais Dumeige. *Richard de Saint-Victor et l'idée chrétienne de l'amour.* Paris: Presses Universitaires de France, 1952. ▸ Study of most important, influential mystic in twelfth-century school of St. Victor, his sources and teachings. [MLC]

20.1477 Étienne Gilson. *The mystical theology of Saint Bernard.* A.H.C. Downs, trans. Kalamazoo, Mich.: Cistercian, 1990. ISBN 0-87907-960-6. ▸ Fundamental discussion of sources of mystical doctrine of Bernard of Clairvaux and his union of mysticism with active life. Viewed in context of events and personalities influencing him. [WJC]

20.1478 Marion Glasscoe, ed. *The medieval mystical tradition in England: papers read at the Exeter symposium, July 1980.* Exeter: University of Exeter Press, 1980. ISBN 0-95989-141-0. ▸ Collection of articles including wide variety of topics concerning mystics and mysticism. No unifying themes or approaches. [FHS]

20.1479 C. F. Kelley. *Meister Eckhart on divine knowledge.* New Haven: Yale University Press, 1977. ISBN 0-300-02098-8. ▸ Mysticism as quest for suprarational knowledge of deity, rather than as affective experience, as main theme of contemplative teachings of influential fourteenth-century Dominican spiritual master. [MLC]

20.1480 David Knowles. *The English mystical tradition.* 1961 ed. New York: Harper & Row, 1965. ▸ Places English mystics in larger context of Continental Christian mystical tradition and England of later Middle Ages, when most lived. [FHS]

20.1481 Valerie Marie Lagorio and Ritamary Bardley, eds. *The fourteenth-century English mystics: a comprehensive annotated bibliography.* New York: Garland, 1981. ISBN 0-8240-9535-9. ▸ Includes important scholarship on mysticism for past century, for England and beyond. Comprehensive sections on individual mystics. Good annotations. Very useful for medievalists and general readers. [FHS]

20.1482 J. M. Perrin. *Catherine of Siena.* Paul Barrett, trans. Westminster, Md.: Newman, 1965. ▸ Life, teachings, and influence of fourteenth-century Dominican tertiary; her mystical theology, spirituality, and efforts at church reform. [MLC]

20.1483 R. R. Post. *The modern devotion: confrontation with Reformation and humanism.* Leiden: Brill, 1968. ▸ Study of Brethren and Sisters of Common Life and lay religious movement of Devotio Moderna. Nuanced analysis of relations with Renaissance Christian humanism and Reformation. Compare with Hyma 22.134. [WJC]

20.1484 Marjorie Reeves. *The influence of prophecy in the later Middle Ages: a study in Joachimism.* Oxford: Clarendon, 1969. ‣ Reception, development, and wide influence of millenarian teachings of Joachim of Fiore in both orthodox and heterodox applications. Argues decisive change in European opinion toward millenarianism came only in seventeenth century. [FHS/WJC]

20.1485 Wolfgang Riehle. *The Middle English mystics.* Bernard Standring, trans. London: Routledge & Kegan Paul, 1981. ISBN 0-7100-0612-8. ‣ Comparative approach to mystics, accenting development of metaphorical mystical language. Focuses on language and use of imagery rather than theology. [FHS]

20.1486 Michael E. Sawyer, comp. *A bibliographical index of five English mystics: Richard Rolle, Julian of Norwich, the author of the "Cloud of Unknowing," Walter Hilton, Margery Kempe.* Pittsburgh: Pittsburgh Theological Seminary, Clifford E. Barbour Library, 1978. (Bibliographia tripotamopolitana, 10.) ‣ Comprehensive bibliography on individual English mystics. Useful annotations for many but not all entries. Good for specialist and general reader. [FHS]

20.1487 Umesh Sharma and John Arndt, eds. and comps. *Mysticism: a select bibliography.* Waterloo, Ont.: Waterloo Lutheran University, 1973. ISBN 0-9690998-8-6. ‣ Unannotated listing of selected works in English or English translation since 1900. Includes literary, psychological, and philosophical as well as historical aspects of Eastern and Western religions. [FHS]

20.1488 Paul E. Szarmach, ed. *An introduction to the medieval mystics of Europe: fourteen original essays.* Albany: State University of New York Press, 1984. ISBN 0-87395-834-9 (cl), 0-87395-835-7 (pbk). ‣ Collected essays providing introductory overview of important medieval mystics with useful bibliographical suggestions for further study. [FHS]

20.1489 Evelyn Underhill. *Jacopone da Todi, poet and mystic, 1228–1306: a spiritual biography.* New York: Dutton, 1919. ‣ Classic study of important Franciscan mystic and poet, important for translating distinctive Franciscan form of spirituality into vernacular literary form. [MLC]

20.1490 Evelyn Underhill. *The mystics of the church.* 1925 ed. Wilton, Conn.: Morehouse-Barlow, 1988. ISBN 0-8192-1435-3. ‣ Classic study of Christian mysticism across ages. Dated but still important for extremely influential classification of different types of mystics. [MLC]

20.1491 Evelyn Underhill. *Ruysbroeck.* London: Bell, 1915. ‣ Seminal, still-important study of fourteenth-century Flemish mystic, important for synthesis of most of currents of Christian mysticism known in his time. [MLC]

20.1492 James Walsh, ed. *Pre-Reformation English spirituality.* New York: Fordham University Press, 1965. ‣ Twenty articles, each examining a different medieval English spiritual writer; most were solitaries or wrote for solitaries. [FHS]

20.1493 E. I. Watkin. *On Julian of Norwich, and in defense of Margery Kempe.* Exeter: University of Exeter Press, 1979. ISBN 0-85989-054-6 (pbk). ‣ Study of two late medieval English visionaries, one (Julian) an anchoress and the other (Margery) a wife, mother, and indefatigable pilgrim. Contrasts spiritual lives and writings. [MLC]

SEE ALSO
22.134 Albert Hyma. *The Christian renaissance.*

Witchcraft, Magic, and Diabology

20.1494 Valerie I. J. Flint. *The rise of magic in early medieval Europe.* Princeton: Princeton University Press, 1991. ISBN 0-691-03165-7. ‣ How early medieval churchmen baptized some forms

of pagan magic and developed their own magic, based on miracles and cult of saints. Christianization seen as accommodation, not just conversion, of pagans. [MLC]

20.1495 Richard Kieckhefer. *European witch trials: their foundation in popular and learned culture, 1300–1500.* Berkeley: University of California Press, 1976. ISBN 0-520-02967-4. ‣ Study focusing on later medieval witch trials and distinctions and intersections between popular and learned notions of witchcraft that they reveal. Discusses literature and legislation on witchcraft only peripherally. [FHS]

20.1496 Edward Peters. *The magician, the witch, and the law.* Philadelphia: University of Pennsylvania Press, 1978. ISBN 0-8122-7746-5 (cl), 0-8122-1101-4 (pbk). ‣ Study of medieval conceptions of witchcraft and attitudes toward it, emphasizing definition and condemnation of witchcraft by theologians, moralists, and jurists rather than social or gender-related aspects. [FHS]

20.1497 Jeffrey Burton Russell. *Lucifer: the devil in the Middle Ages.* 1984 ed. Ithaca, N.Y.: Cornell University Press, 1988. ISBN 0-8014-1503-9 (cl), 0-8014-9429-X (pbk). ‣ Third of author's four studies of concept of the devil, here treating fifth through fifteenth centuries. Suggests main points of diabology remained stable during period, despite minor refinements. [FHS]

SEE ALSO
22.168 Norman Cohn. *Europe's inner demons.*

Women in Religion

20.1498 Derek Baker, ed. *Medieval women.* Oxford: Blackwell, 1978. ISBN 0-631-19260-3. ‣ Unsystematic but interesting collection of essays on women in ecclesiastical history, including female saints; nuns; and women in Crusader states, in heretical movements, and in lay piety. [FHS]

20.1499 Rudolph M. Bell. *Holy anorexia.* Chicago: University of Chicago Press, 1985. ISBN 0-226-04204-9. ‣ Study of extreme fasting in lives of 261 Italian nuns. Unlike Bynum 20.1501, takes psychohistorical approach, viewing behavior as anorexic protest against patriarchal society. Controversial, even anachronistic, interpretation. [FHS]

20.1500 Caroline Walker Bynum. *Fragmentation and redemption: essays on gender and the human body in medieval religion.* New York: Zone Books, 1991. ISBN 0-942299-63-9 (cl), 0-942299-62-0 (pbk). ‣ Collection of highly original, thought-provoking essays, many previously published. Uses sociological, gender, and anthropological theory in analysis of symbolism of human body in medieval religion and art. [FHS]

20.1501 Caroline Walker Bynum. *Holy feast and holy fast: the religious significance of food to medieval women.* Berkeley: University of California Press, 1987. ISBN 0-520-05722-8 (cl), 0-520-06329-5 (pbk). ‣ Persuasive exploration of importance of food and food imagery to women and recognized value of fasting in medieval Christian culture as explanation for extreme fasting and eucharistic mysticism among women. [FHS]

20.1502 Caroline Walker Bynum. *Jesus as mother: studies in the spirituality of the high Middle Ages.* Berkeley: University of California Press, 1982. (Publications of the Center for Medieval and Renaissance Studies, 16.) ISBN 0-520-04194-1 (cl), 0-520-05222-6 (pbk). ‣ Five insightful essays analyzing language and symbolism employed in spiritual writings of twelfth and thirteenth centuries. Explains image of Jesus as mother and mystical piety of nuns of Helfta. [FHS]

20.1503 Graciela S. Daichman. *Wayward nuns in medieval literature.* Syracuse, N.Y.: Syracuse University Press, 1986. ISBN 0-8156-2372-0 (cl), 0-8156-2379-8 (pbk). ‣ Discussion of misconduct in nunneries. Attempts to validate portrayal of nuns in medieval literature by using historical evidence drawn from contemporary society. Concludes canards had some basis in fact. [FHS]

20.1504 Lina Eckenstein. *Women under monasticism: chapters on saint-lore and convent life between A.D. 500 and A.D. 1500.* 1896 ed. New York: Russell & Russell, 1963. ▸ Influential, pioneering work on women in religious orders. Also available on microfilm from New Haven: Research Publications. Dated but still useful. [FHS]

20.1505 Sharon K. Elkins. *Holy women of twelfth-century England.* Chapel Hill: University of North Carolina Press, 1988. ISBN 0-8078-1775-9. ▸ Examination of eremitic and cenobitic forms of English female religious life, 1066–1215, treating geographical, social, and chronological patterns of recruitment of women into religious orders and rules governing their lives. [FHS/KP]

20.1506 Sharon Farmer. "Persuasive voices: clerical images of medieval wives." *Speculum* 61.3 (1986) 517–43. ISSN 0038-7134. ▸ Despite increasing misogyny and decreasing economic power for women in later Middle Ages, perceptive and practical churchmen encouraged women to influence their husbands. Emphasizes wives' perceived capacity for moral persuasion. [FHS]

20.1507 Mary Jeremy Finnegan. *The women of Helfta: scholars and mystics.* Athens: University of Georgia Press, 1991. ISBN 0-8203-1291-6. ▸ Detailed study of three thirteenth-century mystics of Saxon monastery of Helfta: Gertrude the Great, Mechtild of Hakeborn, and Mechtild of Magdeburg. [FHS]

20.1508 Sabina Flanagan. *Hildegard of Bingen, 1098–1179: a visionary life.* New York: Routledge, 1990. ISBN 0-415-01340-2 (cl), 0-415-05793-0 (pbk). ▸ Up-to-date intellectual biography of twelfth-century Benedictine abbess, scientific writer, and visionary, accenting interconnections among her works rather than her sources or contemporary influences. [MLC]

20.1509 Penny Schine Gold. *The lady and the virgin: image, attitude, and experience in twelfth-century France.* Chicago: University of Chicago Press, 1985. ISBN 0-226-30087-0. ▸ Exploration of relationship between secular and religious images of women and reality of women's lives in medieval France. Finds ambivalence, not progress or decline in treatment of women. [FHS]

20.1510 Penelope D. Johnson. *Equal in monastic profession: religious women in medieval France.* Chicago: University of Chicago Press, 1991. ISBN 0-226-40185-5. ▸ Study of organization of twenty-six French nunneries, eleventh to thirteenth century, treating nuns' social origins and relationships with bishops and male monasteries. Draws on visitation records of Eudes Rigaud. [FHS/KP]

20.1511 Barbara Newman. *Sister of wisdom: St. Hildegard's theology of the feminine.* Berkeley: University of California Press, 1987. ISBN 0-520-05810-0. ▸ Detailed analysis of feminine imagery and symbols in thought of prominent and influential visionary and spiritual writer. Places Hildegard firmly in twelfth-century milieu and in tradition of wisdom theology. [FHS]

20.1512 Eileen Power. *Medieval English nunneries, c. 1275–1535.* 1922 ed. New York: Biblo & Tannen, 1964. ▸ Classic, comprehensive, careful picture of all aspects of English nunnery life; remains unsurpassed. Excellent reference tool but omits Gilbertine order. Also available on microfiche from Ann Arbor: University Microfilms International. [FHS]

20.1513 Shulamith Shahar. *The fourth estate: a history of women in the Middle Ages.* Chaya Galai, trans. London: Methuen, 1983. ISBN 0-416-35410-6 (cl), 0-416-36810-7 (pbk). ▸ Useful overview of roles of women in society, twelfth through fifteenth centuries. Includes sections on nuns, witches, and women in heretical movements. [FHS]

20.1514 Susan Mosher Stuard, ed. *Women in medieval history and historiography.* Philadelphia: University of Pennsylvania Press, 1987. ISBN 0-8122-8048-2 (cl), 0-8122-1290-8 (pbk). ▸ Overview of history and historiography for England, Italy, France, and Germany at time of publication. Excellent research tool with very valuable bibliographies. [FHS]

20.1515 Sally Thompson. *Women religious: the founding of English nunneries after the Norman conquest.* Oxford: Clarendon, 1991. ISBN 0-19-820095-1. ▸ Examination of early history of 139 English convents, 1066–1275, their relationship to Continental orders, and roles of founders and patrons. Major theme is effects of nuns' dependence on men. [FHS]

Liturgy

20.1516 Suitbert Baumer. *Histoire du bréviaire.* 1905 ed. 2 vols. Reginald Biron, trans. Rome: Herder & Herder, 1967. ▸ Dated but still standard work. French translation and revision of original German work on history of monastic breviary from earliest times to present. [FHS]

20.1517 John Bossy. "The mass as a social institution, 1200–1700." *Past and present* 100 (1983) 29–61. ISSN 0031-2746. ▸ Examination of supersession of mass as central act of Christian worship in much of Western Christendom by other ritual forms, showing social impact of Reformation, Protestant and Catholic, on this development. [FHS]

20.1518 Gregory Dix. *The shape of the liturgy.* 1945 2d ed. London: Dacre, 1975. ▸ Deals mostly, but not exclusively, with liturgy of the Eucharist. Influential study; helped determine lines of controversy since first published in 1945. [FHS]

20.1519 John Harper. *The forms and orders of Western liturgy from the tenth to the eighteenth century: a historical introduction and guide for students and musicians.* Oxford: Clarendon, 1991. ISBN 0-19-316128-1 (cl), 0-19-816279-0 (pbk). ▸ Introductory practical and scholarly guide to Christian public worship. Focuses on medieval liturgy, providing straightforward outline of its rites. More descriptive than explanatory in historical terms. Glossary; good bibliography. [FHS]

20.1520 Andrew Hughes. *Medieval manuscripts for mass and office: a guide to their organization and terminology.* Toronto: University of Toronto Press, 1982. ISBN 0-8020-5467-6. ▸ Introduction to liturgical codices, use in research, and variability according to liturgical season and local church rites. Provides helpful explanations of terms and practices. [FHS]

20.1521 Edwin Oliver James. *Seasonal feasts and festivals.* 1961 ed. New York: Barnes & Noble, 1963. ▸ Brief introduction to history of rituals and festivals, Christian and pre-Christian, from Paleolithic period through Middle Ages and beyond. Provides useful background for medieval liturgical feasts. [FHS]

20.1522 Cheslyn Jones et al., eds. *The study of liturgy.* New York: Oxford University Press, 1978. ISBN 0-19-520075-6 (cl), 0-19-520076-4 (pbk). ▸ Collection of essays by various authors treating baptism, Eucharist, ordination, monastic office, and liturgical calendar chronologically. Strongest on early church, but excellent introduction to study of medieval liturgy. [FHS]

20.1523 Josef A. Jungmann. *The mass of the Roman rite: its origins and development.* 1951–55 ed. 2 vols. Francis A. Brunner, trans. Westminster, Md.: Christian Classics, 1986. ISBN 0-87061-129-1 (pbk, set). ▸ Comprehensive study of history of all aspects of Western mass, following its development chronologically and topically. Remains standard work although subsequent scholarship has modified some details. [FHS]

20.1524 Henry Charles Lea. *A history of auricular confession and indulgences in the Latin church.* 1896 ed. 3 vols. New York: Greenwood, 1968. ▸ Pioneering study of history of sacrament of penance and theory and practice of indulgences in medieval Europe. Rich in detail and lack of sympathy for religious culture portrayed. [FHS]

20.1525   Gary Macy. *Theologies of the Eucharist in the early scholastic period: a study of the salvific function of the sacrament according to the theologians, c. 1080–c. 1220.* Oxford: Clarendon, 1984. ISBN 0-19-826669-3. ▸ Popular eucharistic devotion and scholastic theology interacting to produce new eucharistic doctrine and ritual. Accents religious significance of rite to communicants. Compare Rubin 20.1527. [MLC]

20.1526   Richard William Pfaff. *New liturgical feasts in later medieval England.* Oxford: Clarendon, 1970. ISBN 0-19-826704-5. ▸ History of development of new feasts in English church calendar in later Middle Ages. Convincingly shows origins to be litur-

gical or derived from devotions in private manuals of prayer. [FHS]

20.1527   Miri Rubin. *Corpus Christi: the Eucharist in late medieval culture.* Cambridge: Cambridge University Press, 1991. ISBN 0-521-35605-9. ▸ Controversial functionalist approach to eucharistic ritual from anthropological and behavioral perspective. Shows little interest in or sympathy for religious meaning for medieval Christians. [FHS]

20.1528   S.J.P. Van Dijk and J. Hazelden Walker. *The origins of the modern Roman liturgy: the liturgy of the papal court and the Franciscan order in the thirteenth century.* Westminster, Md.: Newman, 1960. ▸ Authoritative study of formation of Romano-Franciscan liturgy, basis of late medieval Roman use and of subsequent Tridentine rite. [FHS]

DAVID B. RUDERMAN

Medieval and Modern
Jewish History

There has been a virtual explosion of scholarly writing on Jewish history in the medieval and modern periods during the last thirty years. One rough measure of this development is to compare the present entries on Jewish history in this *Guide* with the previous edition published in 1961. Of the hundred and twenty items on Jewish history listed in the earlier *Guide*, less than half actually pertain to the medieval and modern periods. This compares with some 325 items alloted to this section of the present *Guide* dealing exclusively with postancient Jewish history. But the sheer number of cited works is only the beginning of the story. Among the entries in the 1961 edition, the number of individual authors is relatively small; Salo W. Baron is listed several times, as are Cecil Roth, Jacob Marcus, and Guido Kisch. This obviously reflects the relatively small number of professional historians in the field as of 1961 and an even smaller number holding full-time positions in North American universities.

Even more telling is the manner in which Jewish history is organized. The only separate section on the Jews is a subdivision of a unit on the history of religions. Within this unit, one finds three pages on the history of Judaism, some sixty-seven items, of which the majority consist of general guides, surveys, or periodicals with the primary focus on Judaism in the biblical or rabbinic periods. In contrast, only eight books on the Jews are clustered together within a larger section on medieval history, with all the remaining works scattered throughout the entire volume.

The reader of this section of the present *Guide* will surely be impressed by the remarkable transformation that has taken place. I refer first to the vast quantity of works in English and other Western languages; the fact that most are published by university and academic presses; the emerging specializations within the subfields of Jewish history (e.g., Jews under medieval Islam, Jewish social history in modern Western Europe, Jewish intellectual history in the Renaissance); and the actual emergence of an international community of scholars from North America, Europe, and Israel engaged in the regular publication of books and periodicals, in holding academic conferences, and in training graduate students in specialized fields. I refer also to the quality of the work, its nonparochial nature, its comparative thrust, its systematic engagement with archival and manuscript research, its range of methodologies and interpretive schemes, its inner- and outer-directed nature that examines the Jewish experience both on its own cultural terms and in its dialogue and negotiation with host societies.

By way of an explanation for this sweeping expansion of the field, I offer one more example of the state of Jewish historical study during the period of the previous *Guide*.

Five years after its appearance, Gavin Langmuir published an essay in the *Journal of the History of Ideas* (27 [1966] 343–64; and republished in G. Langmuir, *Toward a Definition of Antisemitism*, pp. 21–41 [Berkeley, 1990]) entitled "Majority History and Postbiblical Jews." Langmuir bitterly complained about "the scanty and erratic attention" Jewish history received. He attributed this neglect to a traditional Christian reading of history in which the first-century Jews were of great historical significance, until the coming of Christ, when their ancestors and descendants became irrelevant and uninteresting: "After the emergence of Christianity, a reprobation falls on the Jews, and a dark night of ignorance conceals their activities from the historical consciousness of most of Western society until Dreyfus, the Balfour Declaration, or Hitler once more draws historical attention to the Jews." Even when secular historians abandoned this theological position, they continued to remain faithful to its historiographical perspective, either consciously or unconsciously. Examining a wide array of contemporary surveys of Western history, Langmuir concluded that the historiographic tradition hostile to or ignorant of Jews still predominated and that most historians were "little inspired to read the work of Jewish historians, let alone study the matter for themselves."

Langmuir acknowledged that a significant historical literature on postbiblical Jewish history already existed, written for the most part by Jewish historians. His major complaint revolved around their relative isolation from the historical community, their lack of impact on general treatments of Western history, and the reluctance of the historical establishment to integrate their findings into larger pictures of the medieval and modern worlds. Langmuir's concern, of course, reflected a situation that had prevailed for well over a hundred years since the beginnings of modern historical scholarship in the early nineteenth century. Despite the considerable achievements of several generations of Jewish scholars, publishing their results in Hebrew, German, French, Yiddish, and other European languages, they were read primarily by other Jewish scholars in books and journals devoted exclusively to Jewish topics and produced under Jewish auspices. The isolated nature of these publications reflected directly the social circumstances under which their authors labored. While trained in European universities, they were unable to teach their fields or engage in scholarly work within the university community. Thus they worked on the fringes of academia, as teachers within Jewish-sponsored institutions or as librarians or rabbis. With the establishment of the Hebrew University of Jerusalem in 1925, with its heavy emphasis on Judaic studies, there finally emerged an institutional base for Jewish historical scholarship within a secular, university setting. And during the last sixty-five years, universities throughout Israel have established major centers of scholarship, assembling massive archives and manuscript holdings, instituting impressive structures of academic conferences and publications, and training hundreds of graduate students in every field of Jewish history.

Within an American context, similar development was rather slow. Despite the prestige achieved by a few holders of academic chairs in Jewish history or thought at leading universities, most American universities were impervious to the idea of teaching Judaica beyond the traditional courses in Bible and Semitic languages. The Christian perspective on postbiblical Jewish history prevailed until the mid-1960s, the period in which the last *Guide* was produced and when Gavin Langmuir wrote the aforementioned essay.

The enlargement of this section thus reflects a much greater social and cultural development than the mere proliferation of publications on Jewish history. In the first place, the last thirty years have witnessed the widespread acceptance of Judaic studies in most major universities in North America. Individual courses have led to permanent faculty positions, interdisciplinary programs, undergraduate and graduate fields of specialization, the augmentation of library resources, and ultimately the growing and increasingly lively interest in publishing in all fields of Judaica on the part of university and trade presses.

While the first stage of this process in the 1960s and 1970s focused on the establishment of positions and the institution of new courses, the 1980s and 1990s have moved steadily into another stage: the integration of Judaic studies within the larger curriculum of the humanities and social sciences. In many universities, Jewish history is taught within history departments or in departments with other historians of religion. Jewish historians and their students are accustomed to engaging in intellectual conversations with their colleagues in other historical fields; new methodological and interpretive discourses constantly encourage them to ask new and bold questions of their material, to question conventional treatments of their subjects, and to examine the dynamics of the Jewish experience through wider and sharper lenses. Conversely, students of medieval history, or early modern and modern history can no longer afford to ignore this "orphaned" minority of Western civilization; the Jews and their cultural legacy increasingly inform and enrich discussions of the history of Christian and Muslim majorities. And the publication of articles and books closely mirror the radical changes in the new university environments. Subjects of Jewish historical interest are regularly discussed in periodicals in European or American history, in the scholarly forums of historians. Thirty years ago, Jewish historians most often submitted their books to Jewish publishers such as the Jewish Publication Society of America. In today's market, the latter have been eclipsed with the regular publication of Jewish studies by such prestigous university presses as Harvard, Yale, California, Indiana, SUNY, Oxford, Cambridge, and many others.

Along with the dramatic changes on this continent, Israeli historians have continued their scholarly activity and have even expanded it, producing an extraordinary array of articles, monographs, and edited texts dealing with every aspect of the Jewish past. This academic community has the enthusiastic support of a Hebrew-reading public with a vociferous appetite for devouring books on even the most arcane historical subjects. Israeli scholarship has also produced important scholarly work in subjects generally neglected by their European ancestors or their American counterpart especially in areas such as Zionism, history of the Yishuv, Israeli history, and history of the Jews in Islamic countries. Israeli historians have also pioneered other areas, such as the history of Jewish art and music, Jewish mysticism, and the political history of diaspora Jewish communities.

In recent years, the university teaching of Jewish history has experienced a revival in Europe as well, especially in countries such as Great Britain, France, Spain, Germany, Italy, and even in Eastern Europe. With the diminution of the European Jewish community since World War II, many of those holding university posts and publishing books and articles in Jewish history are themselves non-Jews. And with the growth of scholarly opportunities for pursuing research outside of Israel, the contact between European, American, and Israeli historians has been greatly enhanced in recent years. American and European historians regularly visit and utilize the resources of Israeli libraries and archives; Israelis regularly work in Europe and North America, teach in universities abroad, and engage in intense dialogue with scholars trained outside of Israel. The result has been a mutually fructifying experience for both sides. Historians outside of Israel are exposed to the high linguistic and paleographical standards of Israeli scholarship and to the intense scrutiny of their work by highly critical and exacting specialists in their fields. Israeli historians now regularly interact with colleagues in the United States and Europe who sometimes raise methodological issues and questions of a comparative nature that are somewhat different than their own. One result of these new contacts is the increasing number of Israeli scholars publishing in English through North American or English university presses, conceptualizing and presenting their material to conform more to the tastes and standards of a reading audience untutored in Jewish culture but generally sophisticated in historical research.

To the peruser of the inventory that follows, the results of this notable emergence of a significant cadre of scholars, trained in diverse approaches and specialities and integrated into the larger community of historical scholarship to an unprecedented degree, are patently self-evident. While earlier scholarly writing in Jewish history was predominantly concerned with philological or intellectual questions, reflecting both the regnant tastes of classical Jewish and European scholarship, the new writing is increasingly more diverse. Novel subjects are treated and new approaches have been introduced: the social history of nonelites, family and women's history, political history, cultural history and the history of mentalities, economic history, and the history of education, to name only a few. Fields where writing has been especially prolific and intense include Jewish social history in modern Europe, the restructuring of Jewish culture and society in early modern Europe, Jewish culture under medieval Christendom, Jewish messianism, the history of the Conversos, antisemitism and the Holocaust, the history of Zionism, and American Jewish history. With the emergence of a younger generation of scholars literate in rabbinic sources and trained in the requisite languages of the region, and with the opening of previously closed archives and repositories, the fields of East European and Russian Jewish history are receiving new attention after years of neglect. Israel's systematic collecting and cataloguing of governmental and communal archives along with Hebrew manuscripts from all over the world have opened up untold possibilities for Jewish cultural and social history in all periods and localities.

There are undoubtedly some weaknesses that accompany all these new advances. New approaches and historical fashions usually take longer "to catch fire" among traditionally trained Jewish historians. The impact of social anthropology, the intersection between history and literary criticism, psychoanalysis and history, or quantitative history, for example, have touched contemporary historical writing only slightly. On the other hand, there is always the danger that "fashionable" historiography might replace the philological tools and exhaustive and exacting knowledge displayed by an earlier generation of Jewish historians. Attaining the proper balance between methodological sophistication and proper textual grounding offer a formidable challenge to would-be Jewish historians of the future. There remain many uncharted areas for future research. Vast bodies of literary sources such as rabbinic responsa, sermons, communal ledgers, popular moral and mystical literature, as well as archival documents, still remain untapped and need to be integrated with each other and within the larger social and cultural contexts from which they emerge.

Despite the gaps and challenges that still remain, this bibliography provides ample testimony to the enormous scholarly output of the past three decades. The reader should be aware of the severe limitation of selecting books and articles primarily written in English. For anyone wishing to engage more deeply in the subject, Hebrew is a prerequisite along with several other European languages, depending on the field of specialization. Nevertheless, because of the accelerated pace of translations into English in recent years, the lists that follow still offer a rich and representative sampling of current achievements and future expectations.

Entries are arranged under the following headings:

Reference Works and General Studies

Jews Under Medieval Islam

Jews Under Medieval Christendom

Jews in Early Modern Europe

Jews of Western and Central Europe, 1750–1914

Jews of Eastern Europe, 1750–1914

Jews in Islamic Lands, 1492–1948

American Jewish History

European Jewry Since 1914

[Contributors: AG = Arthur Goldschmidt, Jr., APK = Alexander P. Kazhdan, AR = Aron Rodrigue, CK = Cemal Kafadar, CVF = Carter Vaughn Findley, DBR = David B. Ruderman, DEF = David E. Fishman, EM = Ezra Mendelsohn, GJM = Gary J. Marker, HEA = Howard E. Adelman, JBK = Jonathan B. Knudsen, JCB = Joseph C. Bradley, JSG = Jeffrey S. Gurock, KESZ = Kristin E. S. Zapalac, KRS = Kenneth R. Stow, LV = Lucette Valensi, MR = Mieczysław Rozbicki, MRC = Mark R. Cohen, MS = Marlène Shamay, PEH = Paula E. Hyman, SBV = Steven Béla Várdy, SLH = Steven L. Hoch, WLB = William Lee Blackwood]

REFERENCE WORKS AND GENERAL STUDIES

21.1 Salo W. Baron. *A social and religious history of the Jews.* 2d rev. ed. 18 vols. New York and Philadelphia: Columbia University Press and Jewish Publication Society of America, 1952–83. ISBN 0-231-08838-8 (v. 1), 0-231-08839-6 (v. 2), 0-231-08840-X (v. 3), 0-231-08841-8 (v. 4), 0-231-08842-6 (v. 5), 0-231-08843-4 (v. 6), 0-231-08844-2 (v. 7), 0-231-08845-0 (v. 8), 0-231-08846-9 (v. 9), 0-231-08847-7 (v. 10), 0-231-08848-5 (v. 11), 0-231-08849-3 (v. 12), 0-231-08850-7 (v. 13), 0-231-08851-5 (v. 14), 0-231-08852-3 (v. 15), 0-231-08853-1 (v. 16), 0-231-08854-X (v. 17), 0-231-08855-8 (v. 18). ▸ Political, social, and cultural history in synthetic chapters crossing geographical boundaries with exhaustive bibliographical annotation. Ancient through early-modern times. Useful for overview; enormous detail in notes but difficult reading. [DBR]

21.2 Judith Baskin, ed. *Jewish women in historical perspective.* Detroit: Wayne State University Press, 1991. ISBN 0-8143-2091-0 (cl), 0-8143-2092-9 (pbk). ▸ Collection of articles by different specialists on history of women and their place in Jewish culture from antiquity to the present. Only anthology of its kind written from historical perspective. [DBR]

21.3 Haim Beinart. *The atlas of medieval Jewish history.* New York: Simon & Schuster, 1992. ISBN 0-13-050691-5. ▸ Maps and accompanying texts on Jewish history from fifth to seventeenth century. Useful and informative for students. [DBR]

21.4 Hayyim Hillel Ben Sasson, ed. *A history of the Jewish people.* Cambridge, Mass.: Harvard University Press, 1976. ISBN 0-674-39730-4 (cl), 0-674-39731-2 (pbk). ▸ Overview of Jewish history written by team of specialists from Hebrew University in Jerusalem. Chapters on medieval and modern history often insightful and original with strong Israel-centered orientation. [DBR]

21.5 Evyatar Friesel. *Atlas of modern Jewish history.* New York: Oxford University Press, 1990. ISBN 0-19-505393-1. ▸ Maps and accompanying text on modern Jewish experience based on Hebrew edition. Useful and informative for students. [DBR]

21.6 Julius Guttman. *Philosophies of Judaism: the history of Jewish philosophy from biblical times to Franz Rosenzweig.* 1964 ed. David W. Silverman, trans. New York: Schocken, 1973. ISBN 0-8052-0402-4 (pbk). ▸ Comprehensive introduction to Jewish philosophy with focus on medieval and modern periods. Classic work; still useful but outdated in many respects. [DBR]

21.7 Gershon D. Hundert and Gershon C. Bacon. *The Jews in Poland and Russia: bibliographical essays.* Bloomington: Indiana University Press, 1984. ISBN 0-253-33158-7. ▸ Two extensive bibliographical surveys of East European Jewry in medieval, early modern, and modern periods. [HEA/DBR]

21.8 Moshe Idel. *Kabbalah: new perspectives.* New Haven: Yale University Press, 1988. ISBN 0-300-03860-7 (cl), 0-300-04699-5 (pbk). ▸ New, bold reconstruction of kabbalah, first since Scholem's classic account (21.13). Use of many new sources with emphasis on mystical experience. Major rewriting that provoked fascinating scholarly controversy. [DBR]

21.9 Paul R. Mendes-Flohr and Jehuda Reinharz, ed. *The Jew in the modern world: a documentary history.* New York: Oxford University Press, 1980. ISBN 0-19-502631-4 (cl), 0-19-502632-2 (pbk). ▸ Valuable collection of sources documenting cultural, social, and political history of Jews in modern world. Wise and useful selection. Ideal for teaching modern Jewish history and thought. [DBR]

21.10 Michael A. Meyer, ed. *Ideas of Jewish history.* 1974 ed. Detroit: Wayne State University Press, 1987. ISBN 0-8143-1950-5 (cl), 0-8143-1951-3 (pbk). ▸ Synthesis and source reader of Jewish historical writing from antiquity to twentieth century with emphasis on modern period. Only anthology in English of its kind. [DBR]

21.11 Léon Poliakov. *The history of anti-Semitism.* 4 vols. Richard Howard, trans. New York: Vanguard, 1965–85. ISBN 0-8149-0186-7 (v. 1), 0-8149-0701-6 (v. 2), 0-8149-0762-8 (v. 3), 0-8149-0872-1 (v. 4). ▸ Grand overview of antisemitism from first century to Holocaust translated from French. Hardly final word on subject but generally good introduction to vast subject. Ample citations from rich literary sources. [DBR]

21.12 Howard Morley Sachar. *The course of modern Jewish history.* Rev. ed. New York: Vintage, 1990. ISBN 0-679-72746-9. ▸ Standard survey of modern Jewish history from eighteenth century to present. Well written and lucid; new, up-to-date edition corrected and revised. [DBR]

21.13 Gershom G. Scholem. *Major trends in Jewish mysticism.* 1954 3d. rev. ed. New York: Schocken, 1961. ISBN 0-8052-0005-3. ▸ Overview of Jewish mystical thought from late antiquity to Sabbatianism and Hasidism. Classic and seminal treatment of subject. [KRS/DBR]

21.14 Robert M. Seltzer. *Jewish people, Jewish thought: the Jewish experience in history.* New York: Macmillan, 1980. ISBN 0-02-408950-8 (cl), 0-02-408940-0 (pbk). ▸ Broad historical survey of Jewish history from antiquity to present. Attempt to integrate history and thought; effort not fully successful but still fine one-volume introduction. [DBR]

21.15 Frank E. Talmage, ed. *Disputation and dialogue: readings in the Jewish-Christian encounter.* New York: KTAV, 1975. ISBN 0-87068-284-9. ▸ Rich collection of materials on interaction between Jews and Christians from first to twentieth century. Well-introduced selections with comprehensive bibliographical essays. [DBR]

21.16 Yosef H. Yerushalmi. *Zakhor: Jewish history and Jewish memory.* Seattle: University of Washington Press, 1982. ISBN 0-295-95939-8. ▸ Interpretive essay on place of collective memory in Jewish thought and its dialectical relationship to writing of history. Eloquent and provocative reading of Jewish history in medieval and modern times. [DBR]

21.17 Yosef H. Yerushalmi et al., eds. *Bibliographical essays in medieval Jewish studies.* New York: KTAV, 1976. ISBN 0-87068-486-8. ▸ Collection of essays on Jews of medieval Europe under Islam and Christendom, church and Jews, and Jewish philosophy and mysticism. Each chapter written by a specialist. [KRS]

JEWS UNDER MEDIEVAL ISLAM

21.18 Eliyahu Ashtor. *The Jews of Moslem Spain.* 3 vols. Aaron Klein and Jenny Malchowitz Klein, trans. Philadelphia: Jewish Publication Society of America, 1973–84. ISBN 0-8276-0237-5 (v. 1), 0-8276-0100-X (v. 2), 0-8276-0237-5 (v. 3). ▸ Overview of Jewish life from Arab conquest in 711 to Christian reconquest of Toledo in 1085. Fascinating but often fanciful reconstruction of lives and doings of important figures. Omits developments late eleventh and in twelfth centuries. [MRC]

21.19 Bat Ye'or [pseudonym]. *The Dhimmi: Jews and Christians under Islam.* Rev. ed. David Maisel, Paul Fenton, and David Littman, trans. Rutherford, N.J.: Fairleigh Dickinson University Press, 1985. ISBN 0-8386-3233-5 (cl), 0-8386-3262-9 (pbk). ▸ Survey of Muslim–non-Muslim (Jewish, Christian) relations to modern times. Tendentious historical overview with useful, large selection of primary documents translated from 1980 French original. [MRC]

21.20 Ross Brann. *The compunctious poet: cultural ambiguity and Hebrew poetry in Muslim Spain.* Baltimore: Johns Hopkins University Press, 1991. ISBN 0-8018-4073-2. ▸ Study of theme of discomfort with Spanish-Jewish intellectual values as expressed in poetry of Golden Age. Good general introduction to intellectual life of period. [MRC]

21.21 T. Carmi. *The Penguin book of Hebrew verse.* New York: Viking, 1981. ISBN 0-670-36507-6. ▸ Useful anthology of poems from all periods (Hebrew with accompanying English translation), with many representative selections from Islamic world. [MRC]

21.22 Gerson D. Cohen. "The reconstruction of Gaonic history." Introduction to *Texts and studies in Jewish history and literature.* 2d ed. 2 vols. Jacob Mann, ed., vol. 1, pp. xiii–xcvi. New York: KTAV, 1972. ISBN 0-87068-085-4. ▸ Excellent introduction to Gaonic period (seventh to thirteenth centuries) and its literature. Historiographical with extensive bibliography appended. [MRC]

21.23 Gerson D. Cohen. "The soteriology of R. Abraham Maimuni." *Proceedings of the American Academy for Jewish Research* 35, 36 (1967, 1968) 75–98, 33–56. ISSN 0065-6798. ▸ Excellent article on this important legal authority, thinker, head of Jews in Egypt, and son of Moses Maimonides drawn to Sufism, attempted to incorporate it into Judaism. [MRC]

21.24 Mark R. Cohen. "Islam and the Jews: myth, countermyth, history." *Jerusalem quarterly* 38 (1986) 125–37. ISSN 0334-4800. ▸ Addresses conflicting extreme views on Islamic-Jewish relations in Middle Ages. Attempts to present subject in balanced manner through comparison with medieval Christian-Jewish relations. [MRC]

21.25 Mark R. Cohen. *Jewish self-government in medieval Egypt: the origins of the office of Head of the Jews, ca. 1065–1126.* Princeton: Princeton University Press, 1980. ISBN 0-691-05307-3. ▸ Origins of central institution, the *nagidate* (in Hebrew) or Headship of the Jews (in Arabic). Based mainly on documents from Cairo Genizah. Comparison drawn with patriarchate of the Coptic church. [MRC]

21.26 Antoine Fattal. *Le statut légal des non-Musulmans en pays d'Islam.* Beirut: Catholique, 1958. (Recherches publiées sous la direction de l'Institut de Lettres Orientales de Beyrouth, 10.) ▸ Standard work on legal status of non-Muslim minorities, mainly Jews, Christians, and Zoroastrians; organized by juridical categories. Notes Roman and Sāsānid antecedents of many laws. [MRC]

21.27 Walter J. Fischel. *Jews in the economic and political life of medieval Islam.* 1937 ed. New York: KTAV, 1969. ISBN 0-87068-047-1. ▸ Portraits of Jewish notables who played important roles

in Islamic administration or in economic affairs during the Abbasid, Fatimid, and Mongol periods. [MRC]

21.28 Abraham Geiger. *Judaism and Islam.* 1898 ed. F. M. Young, trans. Moshe Perlmann, Introduction. New York: KTAV, 1970. ISBN 0-87068-058-7. ▸ Classic, pioneering, comparative study of Jewish roots of Islam. Published in German (1833) and subsequently augmented by literature identifying other inspirations from Muḥammad's religious ideas. Revisions well summarized (with bibliography) in new introduction by Perlmann. [MRC]

21.29 Moshe Gil. *A history of Palestine, 634–1099.* Ethel Broido, trans. Cambridge: Cambridge University Press, 1992. ISBN 0-521-40437-1. ▸ Features history, institutions, and economic activities of the Jews, but also includes much on Christians and covers general political developments from Arab conquest to First Crusade. Hebrew original includes two additional volumes of documents. [MRC]

21.30 S. D. Goitein. *Jews and Arabs: their contacts through the ages.* 3d rev. ed. New York: Schocken, 1974. ISBN 0-8052-0464-4 (pbk). ▸ Overview of history, Jewish-Arab relations, and Jewish civilization under Islam. Partially superseded by voluminous subsequent publications by same author based on documents from Cairo Genizah, most importantly, *A Mediterranean Society* (21.31). [MRC]

21.31 S. D. Goitein. *A Mediterranean society: the Jewish communities of the Arab world as portrayed in the documents of the Cairo Geniza.* 5 vols. Berkeley: University of California Press, 1967–88. ISBN 0-520-00484-1 (v. 1), 0-520-01867-2 (v. 2), 0-520-03265-9 (v. 3), 0-520-04869-5 (v. 4), 0-520-05647-7 (v. 5), 0-520-08136-6 (v. 6). ▸ Magisterial depiction of life in Mediterranean Islamic world in eleventh through thirteenth centuries. Indispensable for Islamic as well as Jewish history. Volume 1: economic life; volume 2: the community; volume 3: the family; volume 4: daily life; volume 5: the individual; and volume 6: indexes. [MRC]

21.32 S. D. Goitein, comp. and trans. *Letters of medieval Jewish traders.* Princeton: Princeton University Press, 1973. ISBN 0-691-05212-3 (pbk). ▸ Eighty documents from Cairo Genizah, translated from Arabic with introductions and notes. Relates to trade in Mediterranean and to India during eleventh to thirteenth centuries reflecting general, not simply Jewish, economic life. [MRC]

21.33 Abraham Halkin, ed. and trans. *Crisis and leadership: epistles of Maimonides.* David Hartman, Discussant. Philadelphia: Jewish Publication Society of America, 1985. ISBN 0-8276-0238-3. ▸ Three important works of Maimonides providing entrance to intellectual and communal activities of this great figure of Jewish history. [MRC]

21.34 Haim Zeev Hirschberg. *A history of the Jews in North Africa. Vol. 1: From antiquity to the sixteenth century.* 2d rev. ed. M. Eichelberg, trans. Leiden: Brill, 1974. ISBN 90-04-03820-5 (v. 1). ▸ Standard survey treating political, social, economic, and intellectual developments (the latter, up to ca. 1200 only). See 21.228 for volume 2. [MRC]

21.35 Abraham Ibn Daud. *Sefer ha-qabbalah: a critical edition with a translation and notes of the "Book of Tradition."* Gerson D. Cohen, ed. and trans. Philadelphia: Jewish Publication Society of America, 1967. ▸ Introduction to and literary and historical analysis of important text from twelfth-century Spain. Superb introduction to Jewish intellectual history and courtier life in Muslim Spain. English and Hebrew. [MRC]

21.36 Bernard Lewis. *The Jews of Islam.* Princeton: Princeton University Press, 1984. ISBN 0-691-05419-3 (cl), 0-691-00807-8 (pbk). ▸ Jewish-Islamic relations to modern times. Excellent and unbiased introduction to subject. Treats status of other religions in Islam and Judeo-Islamic tradition. [MRC]

21.37 Obadiah ben Abraham ben Moses Maimonides. *The treatise of the pool.* Paul Fenton, ed. and trans. London: Octagon Press for the Sufi Press, 1981. ISBN 0-900860-87-1. ▸ Good introduction to an important trend in Jewish mysticism (Jewish Sufism) in Arab-Islamic Middle Ages. Accompanied by translation of representative Jewish text. [MRC]

21.38 Vera B. Moreen. *Iranian Jewry's hour of peril and heroism: a study of Babai ibn Lutf's chronicle (1617–1662).* New York: American Academy for Jewish Research, 1987. (Texts and studies, 6.) ISBN 0-231-06578-7. ▸ Historical commentary on Judeo-Persian (Safavid) chronicle of persecution. One of few works on medieval Iranian Jewry in English. [MRC]

21.39 Leon Nemoy, ed. and trans. *A Karaite anthology: excerpts from the early literature.* New Haven: Yale University Press, 1952. ISBN 0-300-00792-2 (cl), 0-300-03929-8 (pbk). ▸ Good introduction to most important Jewish sectarian movement in Middle Ages. Selected texts with informative introduction. [MRC]

21.40 Gordon D. Newby. *A history of the Jews of Arabia: from ancient times to their eclipse under Islam.* Columbia: University of South Carolina Press, 1988. ISBN 0-87249-558-2. ▸ Fresh and thorough study providing important background for relations between Jews, Judaism, and nascent Islam. [MRC]

21.41 Raymond P. Scheindlin. *The gazelle: medieval Hebrew poems on God, Israel, and the soul.* Philadelphia: Jewish Publication Society of America, 1991. ISBN 0-8276-0384-3. ▸ Excellent introduction to Hebrew religious poetry of Jews in Muslim Spain. Hebrew texts with elegant English translations and literary commentary. Companion to 21.42. [MRC]

21.42 Raymond P. Scheindlin. *Wine, women, and death: medieval Hebrew poems on the good life.* Philadelphia: Jewish Publication Society of America, 1986. ISBN 0-8276-0266-9. ▸ Excellent introduction to secular Hebrew poetry of Jews of Muslim Spain. Hebrew texts with elegant English translations and literary commentary. Companion to 21.41. [MRC]

21.43 Collette Sirat. *A history of Jewish philosophy in the Middle Ages.* Cambridge and Paris: Cambridge University Press and Éditions de la Maison des Sciences de l'Homme, 1985. ISBN 0-521-26087-6 (cl), 0-521-39727-8 (pbk). ▸ Comprehensive survey of philosophical trends and major figures in both Islamic world and Mediterranean Christendom (Provence, Christian Spain, and Italy) through fifteenth century. [MRC]

21.44 Norman A. Stillman, comp. *The Jews of Arab lands: a history and source book.* Philadelphia: Jewish Publication Society of America, 1979. ISBN 0-8276-0116-6 (cl), 0-8276-0198-0 (pbk). ▸ Concise, up-to-date survey (in introduction) of Jewish history under Islam to nineteenth century, accompanied by large and useful selection of illustrative primary sources in English translation. [MRC]

21.45 Eli Strauss [Eliyahu Ashtor]. *Toledot ha-yehudim be-Miẓrayim ve-Suriah taḥat shilton ha-mamlukim (History of the Jews in Egypt and Syria under Mamluk rule).* 3 vols. Jerusalem: Mossad Harav Kook, 1944–70. ▸ Standard work for period 1250–1517. Editing flawed; no English translation available, and no similar work in English exists. Volume 3 contains seventy-four texts from the Cairo Genizah utilized in book. [MRC]

21.46 Isadore Twersky. *Introduction to the Code of Maimonides (Mishneh Torah).* New Haven: Yale University Press, 1980. ISBN 0-300-02319-7 (cl), 0-300-02846-6 (pbk). ▸ Critical examination of historical, literary, and legal contexts of major code of Jewish law of Middle Ages. First volume of projected translation of entire fourteen-volume code; almost complete. [DBR]

21.47 Isadore Twersky, ed. *A Maimonides reader.* New York: Behrman House, 1972. ISBN 0-87441-200-5 (cl), 0-87441-206-4 (pbk). ▸ Excellent introduction to legal, philosophical, and epis-

tolary writings of Maimonides. Selected texts preceded by informative introduction. [MRC]

21.48 Israel Zinberg. *A history of Jewish literature.* Vol. 1: *The Arabic-Spanish period.* Bernard Martin, ed. and trans. Cleveland: Press of Case Western Reserve University, 1972. 12 vols. ISBN 0-82950-228-9 (v. 1). ▸ Useful survey of major literary developments, containing generous selections in translation. Updated by translator with bibliographical notes at end. [MRC]

JEWS UNDER MEDIEVAL CHRISTENDOM

21.49 Zvi Ankori. *Karaites in Byzantium: the formative years, 971–1100.* 1959 ed. New York: AMS Press, 1983. ISBN 0-404-51597-5. ▸ Sole in-depth study of development of Karaite community and learning in Byzantium and eventual reconciliation between Karaite and Rabbinite factions. Views Karaism as movement of urban intellectuals in revolt. [KRS]

21.50 Bernard S. Bachrach. *Early medieval Jewish policy in western Europe.* Minneapolis: University of Minnesota Press, 1977. ISBN 0-8166-0814-8. ▸ Arguable claim to Jewish political power and influence in Visigothic Spain and Carolingian France. Discusses Jews as military allies of selected rulers, relationship between finance and power, and Jews as recognized early medieval nationality. [KRS]

21.51 Yizhak Fritz Baer. *A history of the Jews in Christian Spain.* 2 vols. Louis Schoffman, trans. Philadelphia: Jewish Publication Society of America, 1971. ISBN 0-8276-0115-8 (v. 1), 0-8276-0338-X (v. 2). ▸ Classic but controversial study of rise and fall of Jewish communities in Christian Spain. Focuses on conflicts between Jews over communal power, piety, and learning and uncertain role of kings and Inquisition as agents of persecution and expulsion. [KRS]

21.52 David Berger. *The Jewish-Christian debate in the high Middle Ages: a critical edition of the "Nizzahon Vetus" with introduction, translation, and commentary.* Philadelphia: Jewish Publication Society of America, 1979. (Judaica, texts and translations, 4.) ISBN 0-8276-0104-2. ▸ Succinct introduction to medieval religious polemic. Translation of highly developed example of Jewish-Christian argumentation about biblical meaning; extensively annotated. [KRS]

21.53 Bernhard Blumenkranz. *Juifs et Chrétiens dans le monde occidental, 430–1096.* Paris: Mouton, 1960. (École Pratique des Hautes Études, Paris, Section des sciences économiques et sociales, Études juives, 2.) ▸ Exhaustive examination of Jewish-Christian relations, legal status of Jews, and missionary competition in early Middle Ages. Concludes that Jews at first acceptable if not powerful members of early medieval society, but eventually legally degraded. [KRS]

21.54 Steven Bowman. *The Jews of Byzantium (1204–1453).* Tuscaloosa: University of Alabama Press, 1985. ISBN 0-8173-0198-4. ▸ Sole study of Jews in Byzantium between Fourth Crusade and Ottoman conquest. Imperial and ecclesiastical policy toward Jews, Jewish settlements, and organization of community's intellectual life. Second part contains extracts from texts, Jewish and non-Jewish. [KRS/APK]

21.55 Robert Chazan. *Daggers of faith: thirteenth-century Christian missionizing and Jewish response.* Berkeley: University of California Press, 1989. ISBN 0-520-06297-3. ▸ Study of various tactics employed by Christian missionaries and contemporaneous lines of Jewish defense. Covers familiar ground on Christian side and less familiar Jewish response. [DBR]

21.56 Robert Chazan. *European Jewry and the First Crusade.* Berkeley: University of California Press, 1987. ISBN 0-520-05566-7. ▸ Reevaluation claiming Crusades not turning point in Jewish history based on descriptive reading of Hebrew Crusade chronicles. Includes translations of central texts. [KRS]

21.57 Jeremy Cohen. *The friars and the Jews: the evolution of medieval anti-Judaism.* 1982 ed. Ithaca, N.Y.: Cornell University Press, 1984. ISBN 0-8014-1406-7 (cl), 0-8014-9266-1 (pbk). ‣ Controversial rereading of Dominican and Franciscan efforts in thirteenth century to create demonic image of Jews; attacked Talmud as vehicle of an allegedly false Judaism, no longer the true one of Bible. [KRS]

21.58 Jeremy Cohen, ed. *Essential papers on Judaism and Christianity in conflict: from late antiquity to the Reformation.* New York: New York University Press, 1991. ISBN 0-8147-1442-0 (cl), 0-8147-1443-9 (pbk). ‣ Collection of recent articles by contemporary scholars on historical relations between Jews and Christians primarily in Middle Ages. Very useful, up-to-date collection, especially for students. [KRS/DBR]

21.59 Richard Barrie Dobson. *The Jews of medieval York and the massacre of March, 1190.* 1974 ed. York, England: University of York, 1976. ‣ Penetrating diplomatic reconstruction of massacre, examining roles of king, his ministers, clergy, and rebellion of king's borrowers. [KRS]

21.60 Douglas Morton Dunlop. *The history of the Jewish Khazars.* New York: Schocken Books, 1967. ‣ History, conversion to Judaism of the Khazars royal family, and others; reactions and eventual Khazar demise, ninth to twelfth centuries. Khazar origins, enemies, and state. [KRS]

21.61 Louis Finkelstein. *Jewish self-government in the Middle Ages.* 1924 rev. ed. New York: Feldheim, 1964. ‣ Indispensable collection of decrees of Jewish local and regional councils. Examines common goals of Jewish self-governing bodies in France, Spain, Germany and Italy, Corfu, and Crete. Texts of synodal decrees with Hebrew and English translation and commentary. [KRS]

21.62 Benjamin R. Gampel. *The last Jews on Iberian soil: Navarrese Jewry, 1479–1498.* Berkeley: University of California Press, 1989. ISBN 0-520-06509-3. ‣ Engaging study of survival of Navarrese Jewry between 1492 and expulsion of 1498. Considers political, economic, and religious issues, especially clash with Spanish Inquisition. [KRS]

21.63 Solomon Grayzel. *The church and the Jews in the thirteenth century.* 1966–89 rev. ed. Kenneth R. Stow, ed. and annotator. New York and Detroit: Jewish Theological Seminary of America and Wayne State University Press, 1989–. ISBN 0-8143-2254-9. ‣ Classic, annotated documentation with analytical introduction of papal-Jewish relations at time of papacy's greatest power. Legal restrictions on Jews paralleled by legal protection. [KRS]

21.64 Moshe Idel. *The mystical experience in Abraham Abulafia.* Albany: State University of New York Press, 1988. ISBN 0-88706-552-X (cl), 0-88706-553-8 (pbk). ‣ Study of one of major mystics of medieval Judaism, founder of school of ecstatic Kabbalah. First of planned four-volume work on Abulafia and his influence. Critical for author's reconstruction of history of Jewish mysticism. [KRS/DBR]

21.65 William C. Jordan. *The French monarchy and the Jews: from Philip Augustus to the last Capetians.* Philadelphia: University of Pennsylvania Press, 1989. ISBN 0-8122-8175-6. ‣ Meticulous examination of decline of Jewish status and final expulsion, 1182–1394, against setting of increasingly exploitative yet piously motivated Capetian religious and administrative policies. Suspect attempts of monarchy to move Jews from lending to crafts. [KRS]

21.66 Guido Kisch. *The Jews in medieval Germany: a study of their legal and social status.* 2d ed. New York: KTAV, 1970. ISBN 0-87068-017-X. ‣ Difficult but essential legal history of Jews in various systems of medieval German law. Discusses decline of

their legal status to chamber serfdom and integrity of legal opinions about them. [KRS]

21.67 Gavin I. Langmuir. *History, religion, and antisemitism.* Berkeley: University of California Press, 1990. ISBN 0-520-06141-1. ‣ Controversial new interpretation of link between late ancient–early medieval anti-Judaism and late medieval and modern antisemitism. Discusses antisemitism and irrational thinking, irrational myth of Jew, religion and religiosity, and historical definition of religion. [KRS]

21.68 Gavin I. Langmuir. *Toward a definition of antisemitism.* Berkeley: University of California Press, 1990. ISBN 0-520-06144-6. ‣ Important essays on aspects of medieval antisemitism: Jewish legal status, Jews of England and France, libel of ritual murder, crucifixion libels, and First Crusade assaults. [KRS]

21.69 Amnon Linder, ed. *The Jews in Roman imperial legislation.* Detroit: Wayne State University Press, 1987. ISBN 0-8143-1809-6. ‣ Intensive study with translations of texts of Roman imperial law concerning Jews and their immediate meanings and implications for Middle Ages. [KRS]

21.70 Ivan G. Marcus. *Piety and society: the Jewish Pietists of medieval Germany.* Leiden: Brill, 1981. (Études sur le judaisme médiéval, 10.) ISBN 90-04-06345-5. ‣ Essential, reevaluative study of ethos of Pietists of Germany, their social program, and eventual reconciliation with Ashkenazic Jewish society. [KRS]

21.71 James William Parkes. *The conflict of the church and the synagogue: a study of the origins of antisemitism.* 1934 ed. New York: Atheneum, 1974. ISBN 0-689-70151-9. ‣ Initial study of Jewish-Christian conflict from Apostle Paul to Visigothic Spain and Carolingian France. Examination of theology and law in service of religious antipathy and division. [KRS]

21.72 Henry Gerald Richardson. *The English Jewry under Angevin kings.* 1960 ed. Westport, Conn.: Greenwood, 1983. ISBN 0-313-24247-X. ‣ Exclusively archival perspective on Jews as instruments of medieval English royal financial and fiscal manipulation, from settlement (1066) to explusion (1290). [KRS]

21.73 Cecil Roth. *The history of the Jews in England.* 3d ed. Oxford: Clarendon, 1964. ISBN 0-19-822488-5. ‣ Old-fashioned history of English Jews from their arrival in 1066 to expulsion of 1290, readmission in 1654, and emancipation in 1858. Discusses royal exploitation, relations between Jews and Christians, and tenor of Jewish life. [KRS]

21.74 Cecil Roth. *The history of the Jews of Italy.* Philadelphia: Jewish Publication Society of America, 1946. ‣ Eloquent but dated study of Jews of Italy from late antiquity through fascist period: cultural and economic life, relations with authorities, and Christian intellectual figures. Renaissance light, ghetto darkness. [KRS]

21.75 Cecil Roth, ed. *The Dark Ages: Jews in Christian Europe, 711–1096.* Rev. ed. I. H. Levine, revising editor. New Brunswick, N.J.: Rutgers University Press, 1976. ‣ Collected, uneven essays on Jewish settlement in France, Germany, and Italy, on Jewish cultural and religious life, and on royal and ecclesiastical policies. [KRS]

21.76 Bernard Septimus. *Hispano-Jewish culture in transition: the career and controversies of Ramah.* Cambridge, Mass.: Harvard University Press, 1982. ISBN 0-674-39230-2. ‣ Excellent intellectual biography of career of Me'ir Halevi Abulafia (1165–1244), communal leader, rabbi, and central figure of Maimonidean controversy. Moderate philosopher, opponent of Averroism, and Andalusian conservative. [KRS]

21.77 Andrew Sharf. *Byzantine Jewry, from Justinian to the Fourth Crusade.* New York: Schocken, 1971. ISBN 0-8052-3387-3. ‣ Useful survey of Jews under Byzantine rule in Byzantium and southern Italy. Examines policies of church and emperors, persecutions of ninth century, and flowering of Jewish culture. [KRS/APK]

21.78 Joseph Shatzmiller. *Shylock reconsidered: Jews, moneylending, and medieval society.* Berkeley: University of California Press, 1990. ISBN 0-520-06635-9. ‣ Provocative reevaluation of Christian opinion of Jewish lenders and theological and royal attitudes toward lending. Explores problem of indebtedness in medieval society and special situation of southern France. [KRS]

21.79 Haim Soloveitchik. "Religious law and change: the medieval Ashkenazic example." *Association for Jewish Studies review* 12.2 (1987) 205–21. ISSN 0364-0094. ‣ Insightful study of role of *halakhah* (Jewish law) and its interpretation in shaping medieval Jewish life. Contrasts legal theory with custom and popular practice. [KRS]

21.80 Haim Soloveitchik. "Three themes in the 'Sefer Hasidim.' " *Association for Jewish Studies review* 1 (1976) 311–57. ISSN 0364-0094. ‣ Novel interpretation of origin and character of German Jewish Pietism that flourished in high Middle Ages. Argues that Pietism was reaction to growing dominance of French-Jewish school of rabbinic commentators. [KRS/DBR]

21.81 Shalom Spiegel. *The last trial: on the legends and lore of the command to Abraham to offer Isaac as a sacrifice, the akedah.* 1967 ed. Judah Goldin, trans. and Introduction. New York: Behrman House, 1979. ISBN 0-87441-290-0. ‣ Eloquent essay on Jewish concept and poetry of martyrdom, *qiddush ha-shem*, in Middle Ages, its arguably Christian medieval stimulus, and ancient pagan parallels. Translation of *The Akedah* (Binding of Isaac) by Ephraim of Bonn. [KRS]

21.82 Kenneth R. Stow. *Alienated minority: the Jews of medieval Latin Europe.* Cambridge, Mass.: Harvard University Press, 1992. ISBN 0-674-01592-4. ‣ Comprehensive overview of Jews of Latin Europe from St. Paul through Pope Paul IV. Topics include ecclesiastical consistency and royal vacillation, Jews as medieval other, exegesis as cement of culture and society, and Jewish political theory. [KRS]

21.83 Kenneth R. Stow. "The Jewish family in the Rhineland in the high Middle Ages: form and function." *American historical review* 92.5 (1987) 1085–1110. ISSN 0002-8762. ‣ First study of medieval Jewish family as small, essentially conjugal unit motivated by affection, in a homogeneous northern European Jewish society. Demographic calculations based on martyr lists from First Crusade. [KRS]

21.84 Kenneth R. Stow. *The 1007 anonymous and papal sovereignty: Jewish perceptions of the papacy and papal policy in the high Middle Ages.* Cincinnati: Hebrew Union College, Jewish Institute of Religion, 1984. (Hebrew Union College annual supplements, 4.) ISBN 0-87820-603-5, ISSN 0275-9993. ‣ Innovative study of Jewish views of pope as protector and of medieval king as arbitrary menace expressed in thirteenth-century narrative masquerading as tale of (fictitious) eleventh-century events. [KRS/DBR]

21.85 Edward A. Synan. *The popes and the Jews in the Middle Ages.* New York: Macmillan, 1965. ‣ Informed overview of papal attitudes and policies toward Jews from late Roman empire to late Middle Ages. Extensive analysis of papal documents. [KRS]

21.86 Joshua Trachtenberg. *The devil and the Jews: a medieval conception of the Jews and its relation to modern antisemitism.* 2d pbk. ed. Philadelphia: Jewish Publication Society of America, 1983. ISBN 0-8276-0227-8. ‣ Classic study of demonic vision of Jews, especially in later Middle Ages, characterized by blood libels and similar accusations. [KRS]

21.87 Arthur J. Zuckerman. *A Jewish princedom in feudal France, 768–900.* New York: Columbia University Press, 1972. ISBN 0-231-03298-6. ‣ Controversial study of purported Jewish prince-

dom in southern France, Narbonne. Discusses Jewish aid in overthrowing Muslim rule and Jewish relations and marriage with Christian nobility in early Middle Ages. [KRS]

JEWS IN EARLY MODERN EUROPE

21.88 Robert Bonfil. *Rabbis and Jewish communities in Renaissance Italy.* Jonathan Chipman, trans. Oxford: Oxford University Press for the Littman Library, 1989. ISBN 0-19-710064-3. ‣ Social, cultural, and religious history of major institution in early modern Italy. Brilliant combination of primary research and theoretical conceptualization that challenges most conventional wisdom about the rabbis and the Renaissance. [HEA]

21.89 Marianne Calmann. *The carrière of Carpentras.* Oxford: Oxford University Press for the Littman Library, 1984. ISBN 0-19-710037-6. ‣ Most up-to-date study of one of few French Jewish communities surviving into early modern period under protection of popes of Rome who controlled four ghettos (*carrière*) in northern Provence. [HEA]

21.90 Elisheva Carlbach. *The pursuit of heresy: Rabbi Moses Hagiz and the Sabbatian controversies.* New York: Columbia University Press, 1990. ISBN 0-231-07190-6. ‣ Pioneering work on western European Jewish life in eighteenth century. Includes story of rabbi who battled heretics and Sabbatians in some of most fascinating communal and intellectual struggles of this period in Jewish history. [HEA]

21.91 Mark R. Cohen, ed. and trans. *The autobiography of a seventeenth-century Venetian rabbi: Leon Modena's "Life of Judah."* Mark R. Cohen et al., Introductory Essays. Howard E. Adelman and Benjamin C. I. Ravid, Historical Notes. Princeton: Princeton University Press, 1988. ISBN 0-691-05529-7 (cl), 0-691-00824-8 (pbk). ‣ Intimate look at social, religious, cultural, and political life in ghetto through autobiography of versatile rabbi (gambler and alchemist). Introductions and notes provide background and analysis. [HEA]

21.92 Bernard Dov Cooperman, ed. *Jewish thought in the sixteenth century.* Cambridge, Mass.: Harvard University, Center for Jewish Studies, 1983. (Harvard Judaic texts and studies, 2.) ISBN 0-674-47461-9 (cl), 0-674-47462-7 (pbk). ‣ Specialized articles in early modern Jewish intellectual history by some of major researchers in field. Topics include rhetoric, historiography, theology, philosophy, ethics, mysticism, and messianism. [HEA]

21.93 John Edwards. *The Jews in Christian Europe, 1400–1700.* Rev. ed. London: Routledge, 1988. ISBN 0-415-00864-6. ‣ Nuanced synthesis of early modern Jewish history focusing on complexities of Jewish-Christian relations. Complements Israel 21.97. [HEA]

21.94 Jerome Friedman. *The most ancient testimony: sixteenth-century Christian Hebraica in the age of Renaissance nostalgia.* Athens: Ohio University Press, 1983. ISBN 0-8214-0700-7. ‣ Analysis of role of Christian Hebraists, including Reuchlin and Luther, in major controversies and function of Jewish sources in general orientation of major Christian scholars. Discusses relationship between Charles V and Jews. Only overview of its kind in English. [HEA/KESZ]

21.95 Glückel of Hameln. *The life of Glückel of Hameln, 1646–1724: written by herself.* 1962 ed. Beth-Zion Abrahams, ed. and trans. New York: Yoseloff, 1963. ‣ Autobiography of German Jewish woman of early modern period. Extensive personal discussion of economic, political, religious, and social life. Full critical edition or translation remains desideratum. [HEA]

21.96 R. Po-Chia Hsia. *The myth of ritual murder: Jews and magic in Reformation Germany.* New Haven: Yale University Press, 1988. ISBN 0-300-04120-9. ‣ Important analysis that sheds light on values and mentality of society in general and relations between Jews and Christians at many levels of society, from popular folklore to leading figures of Reformation. [HEA]

21.97 Jonathan I. Israel. *European Jewry in the age of mercantilism, 1550–1750.* 2d ed. New York: Oxford University Press, 1989. ISBN 0-19-821136-8. ‣ Essential synthesis of early modern Jewish history emphasizing economic aspect. Includes important revisions on impact of Thirty Years' War on Jews. Provocative argument on pattern of Jewish exclusion and cultural revival. Complements Edwards 21.93. [HEA/JBK]

21.98 Yosef Kaplan. *From Christianity to Judaism: the story of Isaac Orobio de Castro.* Raphael Loewe, trans. Oxford: Oxford University Press for the Littman Library, 1989. ISBN 0-19-710060-0. ‣ New perspective on crypto-Jewry. Brilliantly reconstructed life of Portuguese New Christian who reverted to Judaism. Major study of intellectual life and spiritual world of Dutch Sefardim, including Jewish-Christian relations, Sabbatianism, and Jewish heresy. [HEA]

21.99 Yosef Kaplan, Henry Mechoulan, and Richard Popkin, eds. *Menasseh ben Israel and his world.* Leiden: Brill, 1989. ISBN 90-04-08516-5. ‣ Collection of papers by leading scholars presenting new information and interpretations of life, work, and times of major Dutch rabbi of seventeenth century. Important studies of Iberian New Christians and rise of heresy and messianism. [HEA]

21.100 David S. Katz. *Philo-Semitism and the readmission of the Jews to England, 1603–1655.* Oxford: Clarendon, 1982. ISBN 0-19-821885-0. ‣ Definitive study of attitudes toward Jews, Hebrew, and ten lost tribes in Puritan England. Events and attitudes that led to eventual acceptance of Jews after their expulsion in 1290. [HEA]

21.101 David S. Katz and Jonathan I. Israel, eds. *Sceptics, millenarians, and Jews.* Leiden: Brill, 1990. ISBN 90-04-09160-2. ‣ Collection of essays in honor of Richard Popkin that tie together important themes in early modern general and Jewish history: development of Jewish doctrines and history of philosophy and theology. [HEA]

21.102 Jacob Katz. *Exclusiveness and tolerance: studies in Jewish-Gentile relations in medieval and modern times.* 1961 ed. Westport, Conn.: Greenwood, 1980. ISBN 0-313-22387-4. ‣ Classic study of transition of Jews from medieval to modern times. Integration of primary rabbinic texts and sociological categories of historical analysis. Jewish-Christian relations and Jewish ambivalence in early modern period. [HEA]

21.103 Jacob Katz. *Tradition and crisis: Jewish society at the end of the Middle Ages.* New York: Schocken, 1971. ISBN 0-8052-0316-8. ‣ Classic study of Jewish life in Poland, Lithuania, and Germanic lands. Description of communal and intercommunal institutions of Jewish community, including family and creation of neutral society. [HEA]

21.104 Shimon P. Markish. *Erasmus and the Jews.* Anthony Olcott, trans. Chicago: University of Chicago Press, 1986. ISBN 0-226-50590-1. ‣ Analysis of Erasmus's writings on Mosaic law, Judaism, and Jews concluding that no evidence sustains recent accusations that Erasmus was antisemite. Afterword by Arthur A. Cohen challenges Markish's conclusions. [HEA]

21.105 André Neher. *Jewish thought and the scientific revolution of the sixteenth century: David Gans (1541–1613) and his times.* David Maisel, trans. Oxford: Oxford University Press for the Littman Library, 1986. ISBN 0-19-710057-0. ‣ Relationship of Jewish thought to thinking of Renaissance in Prague, Posen, Cracow, and Frankfurt. Life and thought of Jewish historian, mathematician, geographer, and astronomer. Useful study, although uneven and unreliable at times. [HEA]

21.106 Benzion Netanyahu. *Don Isaac Abravanel: statesman and philosopher.* 3d ed. Philadelphia: Jewish Publication Society of America, 1972. ‣ Politically powerful Jewish statesman in Spain who went into exile with Jews in 1492, eventually settling in Venice. His involvement in finance, diplomacy, scholarship, and messianism. Classic work. [HEA]

21.107 Heiko A. Oberman. *The roots of anti-Semitism in the age of Renaissance and Reformation.* James I. Porter, trans. Philadelphia: Fortress Press, 1984. ISBN 0-8006-0709-0. ‣ Compelling survey of relations between Jews and Christian reformers. Revision of conventional view on attitudes of Erasmus, Reuchlin, and Luther toward the Jews. [HEA]

21.108 Léon Poliakov. *Jewish bankers and the Holy See from the thirteenth to the seventeenth century.* Miriam Kochan, trans. London: Routledge & Kegan Paul, 1977. ISBN 0-7102-8256-8. ‣ Useful study of role of Jews in money trade: protections granted to Jews by papacy, doctrine of usury and Jews, techniques of Jewish loan banks, and Jewish money trade in Milan, Florence, Venice, and Rome. [HEA]

21.109 Brian S. Pullan. *The Jews of Europe and the Inquisition of Venice, 1550–1670.* Totowa, N.J.: Barnes & Noble, 1983. ISBN 0-389-20414-5. ‣ Venetian Inquisitorial documents about people who were neither Jewish nor Christian or were both. Engaging and well-written study of growing lack of boundaries between Jews and Christians in conversion, mixed marriage, and sexual contact. [HEA]

21.110 Brian S. Pullan. *Rich and poor in Renaissance Venice: the social institutions of a Catholic state, to 1620.* Cambridge, Mass.: Harvard University Press, 1971. ISBN 0-674-76940-6. ‣ Includes a detailed, archival study of Venetian Jewry, the establishment of the ghetto, and Jewish moneylending in the larger context of the Catholic *scuole grandi* and trends in Christian philanthropy. [HEA]

21.111 Benjamin C. I. Ravid. *Economics and toleration in seventeenth-century Venice: the background and context of the "Discorso" of Simone Luzzatto.* Jerusalem: American Academy for Jewish Research, 1978. (American Academy for Jewish Research monograph series, 2.) ‣ Seminal exploration of mercantilistic justifications for tolerating Jews in early modern Europe. Study of legal status and commercial activities of Jewish merchants of Venice based on archival work on their charters. [HEA]

21.112 Cecil Roth. *The Jews in the Renaissance.* 1959 ed. New York: Harper & Row, 1965. ‣ Although extensive and eloquent, in need of much revision. Nevertheless, provides great deal of information, but not always fully documented or properly nuanced. Influenced by classic Renaissance interpretation of Jacob Burckhart (28.4). [HEA]

21.113 David B. Ruderman. *Kabbalah, magic, and science: the cultural universe of a sixteenth-century Jewish physician.* Cambridge, Mass.: Harvard University Press, 1988. ISBN 0-674-49660-4. ‣ More than an intellectual biography of versatile Abraham Yagel, sixteenth-century physician and Kabbalist. Intellectual overview of Italian Jewry in late Renaissance and Baroque periods, especially interrelationship between Kabbalah, magic, science, and rabbinic Judaism. [HEA]

21.114 David B. Ruderman, ed. *Essential papers on Jewish culture in Renaissance and Baroque Italy.* New York: New York University Press, 1991. ISBN 0-8147-7419-9 (cl), 0-8147-7420-2 (pbk). ‣ Anthology of recent articles focusing on intellectual and cultural history and on interaction between Jewish and Italian civilizations. Introduction provides overview and differing interpretations. Only collection of its kind. [DBR]

21.115 David B. Ruderman, ed. *Preachers of the Italian ghetto.* Berkeley: University of California Press, 1992. ISBN 0-520-07735-0. ‣ Study of Renaissance-Baroque Jewish sermons as source for

Jewish cultural and social history in matters such as Jewish-Christian relations, mysticism, and community politics. Fresh essays written by team of specialists with introduction by editor. [HEA]

21.116 Gershom G. Scholem. *Sabbatai Sevi: the mystical messiah, 1626–1676.* R. J. Zwi Werblowsky, trans. Princeton: Princeton University Press, 1973. ISBN 0-691-09916-2 (cl), 0-691-01809-x (pbk). ‣ Definitive biography of most famous early modern Jewish messianic pretender and his movement. Finds roots of movement in Jewish mysticism. [HEA]

21.117 Lester A. Segal. *Historical consciousness and religious tradition in Azariah de' Rossi's "Meor 'einayim."* Philadelphia: Jewish Publication Society of America, 1989. ISBN 0-8276-0316-9. ‣ Emergence of Jewish historiography in sixteenth century. Careful study of aspects of its most erudite figure and his work. [HEA]

21.118 Stephen Sharot. *Messianism, mysticism, and magic: a sociological study of Jewish religious movements.* Chapel Hill: University of North Carolina Press, 1982. ISBN 0-8078-1491-1. ‣ Theoretical study of Jewish history using categories from social sciences; complements studies of Scholem (21.13, 21.116). Topics include medieval messianic movements, Sabbatians, Hasidim, and religious Zionism. [HEA]

21.119 Byron L. Sherwin. *Mystical theology and social dissent: the life and works of Judah Loew of Prague.* Rutherford, N.J.: Fairleigh Dickinson University Press and Associated University Presses, 1982. ISBN 0-8386-3028-6. ‣ Intellectual biography of a major central European religious figure. Overview of his voluminous writings on Jewish nationhood and religious thought. [HEA]

21.120 Moses A. Shulvass. *The Jews in the world of the Renaissance.* Elvin I. Kose, trans. Leiden: Brill, 1973. ISBN 90-04-03646-6. ‣ Translation of 1955 work preceding Roth 21.112 and also influenced by Burckhart 28.4. Surveys by Shulvass and Roth cover same basic ground, complementing and differing from each other in many ways. [HEA]

21.121 Shlomo Simonsohn. *History of the Jews in the duchy of Mantua.* Jerusalem: KTAV, 1977. (Publications of the Disapora Research Institute, 17.) ISBN 0-87068-341-1. ‣ Exhaustive history of early modern Jewish community. Covers its historical development, demography, economy, communal and intercommunal relations, social history, and cultural history, including literature, art, science, and famous rabbis. [HEA]

21.122 Selma Stern. *The court Jew: a contribution to the history of the period of absolutism in Europe.* 1950 ed. Ralph Wiemar, trans. Egon Mayer, Introduction. New Brunswick, N J : Transaction, 1985. ISBN 0-88738-019-0. ‣ Overview of experiences of powerful yet vulnerable Jews in early modern Central Europe. Based on archival work in almost all of German *Staats-* and *Stadtarchiven* from 1920 to 1938. [HEA]

21.123 Selma Stern. *Josel of Rosheim: commander of Jewry in the Holy Roman Empire and of the German nation.* Gertrude Hischler, trans. Philadelphia: Jewish Publication Society of America, 1965. ‣ Classic biography of German Jew who represented his coreligionists before emperors, kings, electors, dukes, and bishops during sixteenth century and whose life and thought intersected with Luther's and Charles V's. [HEA]

21.124 Kenneth R. Stow. *Catholic thought and papal Jewry policy, 1555–1593.* New York: Jewish Theological Seminary of America, 1977. (Moreshet, 5.) ISBN 0-87334-001-9. ‣ The year 1555 as a watershed in papal attitudes toward and treatment of Jews with issuance of *Cum nimis absurdum* by Pope Paul IV. Important work considering changes within context of papacy's conversionary program. [HEA]

21.125 Isadore Twersky and Bernard Septimus, eds. *Jewish thought in the seventeenth century.* Cambridge, Mass.: Harvard University, Center for Jewish Studies, 1987. (Harvard Judaic texts and studies, 6.) ISBN 0-674-47465-1 (cl), 0-674-47466-x (pbk). ‣ Important specialized studies in early modern Jewish intellectual history: mysticism, philosophy, philology, apologetics, historiography, theology, and polemics. [HEA]

21.126 Bernard D. Weinryb. *The Jews of Poland: a social and economic history of the Jewish community in Poland from 1100 to 1800.* Philadelphia: Jewish Publication Society of America, 1973. ISBN 0-8276-0016-X. ‣ Nuanced survey from fifteenth to eighteenth century: legal, economic, social, and religious trends. Major revision stressing limited impact of massacres of 1648 and of influence of messianic pretender Sabbatai Sevi in Poland (contra Scholem 21.116). [HEA]

21.127 R. J. Zwi Werblowsky. *Joseph Karo: lawyer and mystic.* 2d ed. Philadelphia: Jewish Publication Society of America, 1977. ISBN 0-8276-0090-9. ‣ Sensitive study of mystical side of major codifier of Jewish law in sixteenth century. Attempt to probe his psychological makeup and to demonstrate complexity of Jewish culture in early modern Europe. [HEA]

21.128 Chaim Wirszubski. *Pico della Mirandola's encounter with Jewish mysticism.* Paul Oskar Kristeller, Introduction. Cambridge, Mass.: Harvard University Press, 1990. ISBN 0-674-66730-1. ‣ Careful and detailed study of Christian use of Jewish mysticism during Renaissance, focusing on kabbalistic content of Pico della Mirandola's major works, sources, understanding of magic, ancient texts, and influence on subsequent Christian kabbalists. [HEA]

21.129 Myriam Yardeni. *Anti-Jewish mentalities in early modern Europe.* Lanham, Md.: University Press of America, 1990. ISBN 0-8191-7559-5. ‣ Collection of essays that helps fill lacuna in Jewish history in early modern France. Includes studies of Jews in travelers' accounts. [HEA]

21.130 Yosef H. Yerushalmi. *From Spanish court to Italian ghetto: Isaac Cardoso, a study in seventeenth-century Marranism and Jewish apologetics.* 1971 ed. Seattle: University of Washington Press, 1981. ISBN 0-295-95824-3. ‣ Masterful reconstruction of life and thought of man who moved from Catholicism to Judaism, from Portugal to Italy, and from philosophy to messianic enthusiasm. One of best discussions of use of Inquisitional documents for reconstruction of history. [HEA]

JEWS OF WESTERN AND CENTRAL EUROPE, 1750–1914

21.131 Phyllis Cohen Albert. *The modernization of French Jewry: consistory and community in the nineteenth century.* Hanover, N.H.: Brandeis University Press; distributed by University Press of New England, 1977. ISBN 0-87451-139-9. ‣ Massive study of role of state-recognized Jewish communal institutions in socioeconomic and cultural development of French Jewry. Particularly good on emergence of modern French rabbinate. [PEH]

21.132 Alexander Altmann. *Moses Mendelssohn: a biographical study.* Tuscaloosa: University of Alabama Press for the Jewish Publication Society of America, 1973. ISBN 0-8173-6860-4. ‣ Classic biography of most important philosopher of German Jewish Enlightenment. Restores Mendelsohn's place in German Enlightenment. [PEH/JBK]

21.133 Steven E. Aschheim. *Brothers and strangers: the East European Jew in German and German Jewish consciousness, 1800–1923.* Madison: University of Wisconsin Press, 1982. ISBN 0-299-09110-4. ‣ Cultural and intellectual history of encounter of Germans and German Jews with Jews from eastern Europe. Pioneering study. [PEH]

21.134 Salo W. Baron. "Ghetto and emancipation." *Menorah journal* 14 (1928) 515–26. ‣ Frames discourse about traditional

European Jewry and its emancipation. A classic. Companion to 21.135. [PEH]

21.135 Salo W. Baron. "Newer approaches to Jewish emancipation." *Diogenes* 29 (1960) 56–81. ISSN 0392-1921. ▸ Reexamination of issue of emancipation by dean of Jewish historians in United States. Companion to 21.134. [PEH]

21.136 Jay R. Berkovitz. *The shaping of Jewish identity in nineteenth-century France.* Detroit: Wayne State University Press, 1989. ISBN 0-8143-2011-2. ▸ Study of role of French Jewish leaders in constructing new basis for Jewish identity and religious expression in postemancipation France. Important contribution to understanding of ideology of emancipation. [PEH]

21.137 Vicki Caron. *Between France and Germany: the Jews of Alsace-Lorraine, 1871–1918.* Stanford, Calif.: Stanford University Press, 1988. ISBN 0-8047-1443-6. ▸ Social and political history of Jews of Alsace-Lorraine under German rule. Innovative linkage of socioeconomic change and issue of national identification. [PEH]

21.138 David H. Ellenson. *Rabbi Esriel Hildesheimer and the creation of a modern Jewish Orthodoxy.* Tuscaloosa: University of Alabama Press, 1990. ISBN 0-8173-0485-1. ▸ Exploration of development of modern Orthodoxy in Germany as aspect of denominationalism in modern Judaism. Splendid use of sociological methods to address issues of legitimation of authority, tradition, and innovation. [PEH]

21.139 Todd M. Endelman. *The Jews of Georgian England, 1714–1830: tradition and change in a liberal society.* Philadelphia: Jewish Publication Society of America, 1979. ISBN 0-8276-1119-0. ▸ Important social history of acculturation of Jews in Georgian England. Challenges focus of previous historiography on intellectual currents and on Germany as model for modernization of Jewry. [PEH]

21.140 Todd M. Endelman. *Radical assimilation in English Jewish history, 1656–1945.* Bloomington: Indiana University Press, 1990. ISBN 0-253-31952-8. ▸ Broad social history of Anglo-Jewry in modern times. Focuses on factors in British society facilitating assimilation. [PEH]

21.141 Todd M. Endelman, ed. *Jewish apostasy in the modern world.* New York: Holmes & Meier, 1987. ISBN 0-8419-1029-4. ▸ Collection of original and comparative essays on conversion from Judaism in modern period in Central and West Europe, Russia, and United States; central issue in understanding of social and cultural contexts of assimilation. [PEH]

21.142 Lloyd P. Gartner. *The Jewish immigrant in England, 1870–1914.* 2d ed. London: Simon, 1973. ISBN 0-903620-00-6. ▸ Classic study of East European Jewish immigrant community in London. Includes discussion of immigrant quarter and its socioeconomic structure, labor politics, religion, and cultural expressions. [PEH]

21.143 Michael Graetz. *Les juifs en France au dix-neuvième siècle: de la Révolution française à l'Alliance Israélite Universelle.* Salomon Malka, trans. Paris: Seuil, 1989. ISBN 2-02-010032-0. ▸ Innovative examination of intellectual and socioeconomic factors that shaped leadership of French Jewry in nineteenth century and stimulated foundation of major Jewish self-defense and educational agency active internationally. [PEH]

21.144 Nancy L. Green. *The pletzl of Paris: Jewish immigrant workers in the "belle epoque."* New York: Holmes & Meier, 1985. ISBN 0-8419-0995-4. ▸ Authoritative analysis of socioeconomic and political experience of East European immigrant Jewish workers in Paris. Situates Jewish experience within general labor and migration history. [PEH]

21.145 Deborah Hertz. *Jewish high society in Old Regime Berlin.* New Haven: Yale University Press, 1988. ISBN 0-300-03775-9. ▸ Examination of social and cultural contexts of salon Jewesses of Berlin. Sophisticated consideration of gender in assimilation of German Jewry. Also contributes to understanding of generational changes ca. 1800. [PEH/JBK]

21.146 Arthur Hertzberg. *The French Enlightenment and the Jews.* New York: Columbia University Press, 1968. ▸ Classic and controversial study in intellectual history that argues for origins of modern antisemitism within Enlightenment. Also includes examination of status and activity of Jews in eighteenth-century France. [PEH]

21.147 Paula E. Hyman. *The emancipation of the Jews of Alsace: acculturation and tradition in the nineteenth century.* New Haven: Yale University Press, 1991. ISBN 0-300-04986-2. ▸ Study of the impact of emancipation upon a traditional village-based society. Uses methodologies of social history to explore interaction of elites and broad strata of Jewish population. [PEH]

21.148 Marion A. Kaplan. *The making of the Jewish middle class: women, family, and identity in imperial Germany.* New York: Oxford University Press, 1991. ISBN 0-19-503952-1. ▸ How women contributed to shaping of German Jewish middle class and also expanded their nondomestic roles. First work to fully incorporate gender into our understanding of acculturation and identity formation among European Jewry. [PEH]

21.149 Jacob Katz. *Jews and Freemasons in Europe, 1723–1939.* Leonard Oschry, trans. Cambridge, Mass.: Harvard University Press, 1970. ISBN 0-674-47480-5. ▸ Exploration of social relations as well as representation of Jews and Freemasons in Europe. Classic case study. [PEH]

21.150 Jacob Katz. *Out of the ghetto: the social background of Jewish emancipation, 1770–1870.* 1973 ed. New York: Schocken, 1978. ISBN 0-8052-0601-9. ▸ Classic study of processes of acculturation and integration of Jews into West and Central European societies in age of emancipation. Broad social and intellectual overview. [PEH]

21.151 Jacob Katz, ed. *Toward modernity: the European Jewish model.* New Brunswick, N.J.: Transaction, 1987. ISBN 0-88738-092-1. ▸ Useful comparison of German model of acculturation with historical experience of Jews in ten other countries. Essays on Italy, the Netherlands, and Hungary included. [PEH]

21.152 Hillel J. Kieval. *The making of Czech Jewry: national conflict and Jewish society in Bohemia, 1870–1918.* New York: Oxford University Press, 1988. ISBN 0-19-504057-0. ▸ Social, cultural, and political development of Czech Jewry in its multiethnic context. Particularly good discussion of Czech-Jewish movement and Prague Zionism. [PEH]

21.153 Marjorie Lamberti. *Jewish activism in imperial Germany: the struggle for civil equality.* New Haven: Yale University Press, 1978. ISBN 0-300-02163-1. ▸ Political history of Jews in imperial Germany with special attention to self-defense activities. Especially strong on interaction of German and Jewish history. [PEH]

21.154 Robert Liberles. *Religious conflict in social context: the resurgence of Orthodox Judaism in Frankfurt am Main, 1838–1877.* Westport, Conn.: Greenwood, 1985. ISBN 0-313-24806-0. ▸ Superb study of emergence of neo-Orthodoxy in Germany. Special attention to social and political factors in Jewish community and German society. [PEH]

21.155 Frances Malino. *The Sephardic Jews of Bordeaux: assimilation and emancipation in Revolutionary and Napoleonic France.* Tuscaloosa: University of Alabama Press, 1978. ISBN 0-8173-6903-1. ▸ Examination of Sefardic Jewish community of Bordeaux and its role in emancipation of French Jewry. Synthesizes intellectual, social, and political history to present a portrait of preemancipation assimilation. [PEH]

21.156 Michael R. Marrus. *The politics of assimilation: the French Jewish community at the time of the Dreyfus Affair.* 1971 ed. New York: Oxford University Press, 1980. ISBN 0-19-822591-1 (pbk). ▸ Examination of culture and ideology of French Jewry as it confronted antisemitism of the Dreyfus Affair. Includes interesting discussion of Bernard Lazare and beginnings of Zionism in France. [PEH]

21.157 William O. McCagg, Jr. *A history of Habsburg Jews, 1670–1918.* Bloomington: Indiana University Press, 1989. ISBN 0-253-33189-7. ▸ Major comprehensive study of Jews of Habsburg empire. Focuses on processes of assimilation against backdrop of imperial politics. [PEH]

21.158 Michael Meyer. *The origins of the modern Jew: Jewish identity and European culture in Germany, 1749–1824.* Detroit: Wayne State University Press, 1967. ISBN 0-8143-1470-8 (pbk). ▸ Exploration of main currents of modern Jewish thought in Germany under impact of German Enlightenment. [PEH]

21.159 Michael Meyer. *Response to modernity: a history of the reform movement in Judaism.* New York: Oxford University Press, 1988. ISBN 0-19-505167-X. ▸ Definitive history of reform movement worldwide from its origins to present. Basic source written from perspective of intellectual history. [PEH]

21.160 Werner E. Mosse, Arnold Paucker, and Reinhard Rürup, eds. *Revolution and evolution: 1848 in German-Jewish history.* Tübingen: Mohr, 1981. (Schriftenreihe wissenschaftlicher Abhandlungen des Leo-Baeck-Instituts, 39.) ISBN 3-16-743752-9, ISSN 0459-097X. ▸ Important collection on political, economic, social, religious, and cultural features of emancipation at time of 1848 Revolution. International roster of authors represent range of voices in historiography of German Jewry. [PEH]

21.161 Jehuda Reinharz. *Fatherland or promised land: the dilemma of the German Jew, 1893–1914.* Ann Arbor: University of Michigan Press, 1975. ISBN 0-472-76500-0. ▸ Exploration of conflict between Jewish liberalism and Zionism in Germany against backdrop of rise of political antisemitism. Important in debate about nature of Jewish consciousness in imperial Germany. [PEH]

21.162 Marsha L. Rozenblit. *The Jews of Vienna, 1867–1914: assimilation and identity.* Albany: State University of New York Press, 1983. ISBN 0-87395-844-6 (cl), 0-87395-845-4 (pbk). ▸ Innovative study of social characteristics of Viennese Jewry and their relation to Jewish identity. Quantified history at its most informative. [PEH]

21.163 M.C.N. Salbstein. *The emancipation of the Jews in Britain: the question of the admission of the Jews to Parliament, 1828–1860.* Rutherford, N.J.: Fairleigh Dickinson University Press, 1982. ISBN 0-8386-3110-X. ▸ Detailed analysis of process by which Jews received full political rights in Great Britain. Full attention paid both to Jewish activists and to British political context. [PEH]

21.164 Ismar Schorsch. *Jewish reactions to German anti-Semitism, 1870–1914.* New York: Columbia University Press, 1972. ISBN 0-231-03643-4. ▸ Development of German Jewish defense organizations and their impact on Jewish identity. Must reading for understanding of Jewish culture in imperial Germany. [PEH]

21.165 Simon Schwarzfuchs. *Napoleon, the Jews, and the Sanhedrin.* London: Routledge & Kegan Paul, 1979. ISBN 0-7100-8955-4. ▸ Comprehensive analysis of Napoleonic Sanhedrin that redefined terms of Jewish emancipation in France. Best account in English. [PEH]

21.166 David J. Sorkin. *The transformation of German Jewry, 1780–1840.* New York: Oxford University Press, 1987. ISBN 0-19-504992-6. ▸ Emergence of new German Jewish identity based on *Bildung* (cultivation). Explores interaction of factors internal and external to Jewish community and situates ideas in their social context. [PEH]

21.167 Uriel Tal. *Christians and Jews in Germany: religion, politics, and ideology in the Second Reich, 1870–1914.* Noah Jonathan Jacobs, trans. Ithaca, N.Y.: Cornell University Press, 1975. ISBN 0-8014-0879-2. ▸ Important exploration of Christian and Jewish religious thought as foundation for understanding Christian-Jewish relations in Germany and evolution of antisemitism. Classic of intellectual history. [PEH]

21.168 Jack Wertheimer. *Unwelcome strangers: East European Jews in imperial Germany.* New York: Oxford University Press, 1987. ISBN 0-19-504893-8. ▸ Comprehensive social and political history of East European Jews in Germany. Comparative perspective with other Jewish communities. [PEH]

21.169 Bill Williams. *The making of Manchester Jewry, 1740–1875.* New York: Holmes & Meier, 1976. ISBN 0-8419-0252-6. ▸ Examination of social history of Jewish community of Manchester within context of urban history of Manchester. Model communal study. [PEH]

21.170 Robert S. Wistrich. *The Jews of Vienna in the age of Franz Joseph.* Oxford: Oxford University Press for the Littman Library, 1989. ISBN 0-19-710070-8. ▸ Magisterial synthesis of political and cultural history of Viennese Jewry. Emphasis on struggle against antisemitism, rise of Zionism, and Jewish culture and identity. [PEH]

21.171 Robert S. Wistrich. *Socialism and the Jews: the dilemmas of assimilation in Germany and Austria-Hungary.* Rutherford, N.J. and East Brunswick, N.J.: Fairleigh Dickinson University Press and Associated University Presses, 1982. ISBN 0-8386-3020-6. ▸ Exploration of role of socialism in defining Jewish Question in nineteenth-century Central Europe and relation of Jews to socialist movement. Detailed political history. [PEH]

JEWS OF EASTERN EUROPE, 1750–1914

21.172 Chimen Abramsky, Maciej Jachimczyk, and Antony Polonsky, eds. *The Jews in Poland.* Oxford: Blackwell, 1986. ISBN 0-631-14857-4. ▸ Studies focusing on economic and legal position of Jews, Polish-Jewish relations, and assimilation. Ideal source for balanced introductory information. [DEF/WLB]

21.173 I. Michael Aronson. *Troubled waters: the origins of the 1881 anti-Jewish pogroms in Russia.* Pittsburgh: University of Pittsburgh Press, 1990. ISBN 0-8229-3656-9. ▸ Comprehensive examination of events and attitudes of different segments of Russian government and society toward Jews. Original and thorough. [DEF]

21.174 Shlomo Avineri. *The making of modern Zionism: intellectual origins of the Jewish state.* New York: Basic Books, 1981. ISBN 0-465-04328-3. ▸ Portraits of major figures and trends in Zionist thought. Excellent introduction. Complements Hertzberg, ed. 21.183. [DEF]

21.175 Salo W. Baron. *The Russian Jew under tsars and Soviets.* 1976 ed. New York: Schocken, 1987. ISBN 0-8052-0838-0. ▸ Survey of Russian-Jewish history. Valuable reference work; notes serve as excellent guide to the literature on the subject. [DEF]

21.176 Władysław T. Bartoszewski and Antony Polonsky, eds. *The Jews in Warsaw: a history.* Oxford: Institute for Polish-Jewish Studies and Blackwell, 1991. ISBN 0-631-17074-X. ▸ Studies of economic, political, and to lesser extent cultural history. Meticulous scholarship. [DEF]

21.177 Stephen D. Corrsin. *Warsaw before the First World War: Poles and Jews in the third city of the Russian empire, 1880–1914.* Boulder: East European Monographs; distributed by Columbia University Press, 1989. (East European monographs, 274.) ISBN

0-88033-166-6. ▸ Rigorous socioeconomic analysis. Productive use of comparative approach. [DEF]

21.178 Lucy S. Dawidowicz, ed. *The golden tradition: Jewish life and thought in eastern Europe.* 1967 ed. Northvale, N.J.: Aronson, 1989. ISBN 0-87668-852-0. ▸ Biographical and autobiographical selections illuminating cultural and political currents of nineteenth and early twentieth centuries. Splendid introduction. [DEF]

21.179 Jonathan Frankel. *Prophecy and politics: socialism, nationalism, and the Russian Jews, 1862–1917.* Cambridge: Cambridge University Press, 1981. ISBN 0-521-23028-4. ▸ Examination of Jewish political ideologies in their historical and intellectual context. Magisterial in scope, rigorous in analysis. [DEF]

21.180 Arthur Green. *Tormented master: a life of Nahman of Bratslav.* 1979 ed. Woodstock, Vt.: Jewish Lights, 1992. ISBN 1-879045-11-7. ▸ Biography of one of most original and enigmatic figures in history of Hasidism. Modern psychological tools used fruitfully in conjunction with analysis of religious ideas. [DEF]

21.181 Louis Greenberg. *The Jews in Russia: the struggle for emancipation.* 2 vols. in 1. New York: Schocken, 1976. ISBN 0-8052-0525-X. ▸ Survey of Russian Jewish history from late eighteenth century to World War I. Focus on "Jewish question" in Russia and on ideological trends within Jewish intelligentsia. Dated but still useful. [DEF]

21.182 Alexander Hertz. *The Jews in Polish culture.* Lucjan Dobroszycki, ed. Richard Lourie, trans. Evanston, Ill.: Northwestern University Press, 1988. ISBN 0-8101-0758-9. ▸ Reflections on image of Jews and their role in development of Polish culture. Sophisticated, balanced appraisal of Polish-Jewish cohabitation. [DEF/MR]

21.183 Arthur Hertzberg, ed. *The Zionist idea: a historical analysis and reader.* 1959 ed. Westport, Conn.: Greenwood, 1970. ISBN 0-8371-2565-0. ▸ Selections from works of major Zionist thinkers. Stimulating introductory essay. Complements Avineri 21.174. [DEF]

21.184 Gershon D. Hundert. *The Jews in a Polish private town: the case of Opatow in the eighteenth century.* Baltimore: Johns Hopkins University Press, 1992. ISBN 0-8018-4273-5. ▸ Pioneering study of single community in prepartition Poland, leading to reassessment of conventional wisdom. Lucid presentation based on extensive archival sources. Focus on Jewish society and communal institutions. [DEF]

21.185 Gershon D. Hundert, ed. *Essential papers on Hasidism: origins to present.* New York: New York University Press, 1991. ISBN 0-8147-3470-7 (cl), 0-8147-3469-3 (pbk). ▸ Selection of studies on history, religious ideas, and institutions of Hasidism. Indispensable anthology of best historiography on subject since turn of century. [DEF]

21.186 Louis Jacobs. *Hasidic prayer.* New York: Schocken, 1973. ISBN 0-8052-0604-3 (pbk). ▸ Reviews Hasidic philosophy of prayer, mystical techniques, and rituals. Useful introduction to key aspect of Hasidic religion. [DEF]

21.187 Arkadius Kahan. *Essays in Jewish social and economic history.* Roger Weiss, ed. Jonathan Frankel, Introduction. Chicago: University of Chicago Press, 1986. ISBN 0-226-42240-2. ▸ Studies on Jewish entrepreneurship and industrialization in tsarist Russia. State-of-the-art economic history. [DEF]

21.188 John D. Klier. *Russia gathers her Jews: the origins of the "Jewish question" in Russia, 1772–1825.* Dekalb: Northern Illinois University Press, 1986. ISBN 0-87580-117-X. ▸ Official Russian policies and attitudes toward Jews in period after partition of Poland. Careful and subtle analysis. [DEF]

21.189 Walter Laqueur. *History of Zionism.* New York:

Schocken, 1976. ISBN 0-8052-0523-3. ▸ Single-volume history of Zionist movement from its beginnings until establishment of state of Israel. Comprehensive, insightful, lucid. [DEF]

21.190 Eli Lederhendler. *The road to modern Jewish politics: political tradition and political reconstruction in the Jewish community of tsarist Russia.* New York: Oxford University Press, 1989. ISBN 0-19-505891-7. ▸ Transformation of Jewish political institutions and ideas during eighteenth and nineteenth centuries. Excellent synthetic study utilizing models from social sciences. [DEF]

21.191 Isaac Levitats. *The Jewish community in Russia, 1772–1844.* 1943 ed. Jerusalem: Posner, 1981. ISBN 965-219-000-4. ▸ Institutions and activities of self-governing Jewish community (*kahal*) in Russia. Topics include rabbinate, taxation, philanthropy, and relations with tsarist government. Clear and comprehensive. [DEF]

21.192 Ehud Luz. *Parallels meet: religion and nationalism in the early Zionist movement.* Lenn J. Schramm, trans. Philadelphia: Jewish Publication Society of America, 1988. ISBN 0-8276-0297-9. ▸ Conflicting visions of role of religion in Jewish national revival at turn of century. Topics include anti-Zionist Orthodoxy, religious Zionism, and secular-cultural Zionism. [DEF]

21.193 Vasilii Lvov-Rogachevsky. *A history of Russian Jewish literature.* Arthur Levin, ed. and trans. Ann Arbor: Ardis, 1979. ISBN 0-88233-271-6. ▸ Only broad treatment of subject. A classic. [DEF]

21.194 Raphael Mahler. *Hasidism and the Jewish Enlightenment: their confrontation in Galicia and Poland in the first half of the nineteenth century.* Eugene Orenstein, Aaron Klein, and Jenny Machlowitz Klein, trans. Philadelphia: Jewish Publication Society of America, 1985. ISBN 0-8276-0233-2. ▸ Aspects of Jewish *Kulturkampf* between enlightened and pious and involvement of imperial authorities. Interesting Marxist approach. [DEF]

21.195 Ezra Mendelsohn. *Class struggle in the Pale: the formative years of the Jewish Workers' movement in tsarist Russia.* Cambridge: Cambridge University Press, 1970. ISBN 0-521-07730-3. ▸ Emergence of Jewish working class in Russia and coalescence of distinct Jewish labor movement. Focus on social and cultural dimensions. Outstanding study; a classic. [DEF]

21.196 Dan Miron. *A traveler disguised: a study in the rise of modern Yiddish fiction in the nineteenth century.* New York: Schocken, 1973. ISBN 0-8052-3499-3. ▸ Conflicted attitude of Jewish writers toward Yiddish and tensions of Yiddish literary creativity. Works of Mendele Moykher Seforim, grandfather of Yiddish literature, viewed with keen eye to their cultural, historical, and literary background. [DEF]

21.197 Alexander Orbach. *New voices of Russian Jewry: a study of the Russian Jewish press in Odessa in the era of the great reforms, 1860–1871.* Leiden: Brill, 1980. ISBN 90-04-06175-4. ▸ Intelligent study of Russian Jewish intelligentsia of 1860s and its attitudes toward issues of enlightenment, emancipation, and antisemitism. [DEF]

21.198 David Patterson. *The Hebrew novel in czarist Russia.* Edinburgh: Edinburgh University Press, 1964. ▸ Useful survey of Hebrew literature of Haskalah (Jewish Enlightenment). Attention paid to historical background and role of ideology. [DEF]

21.199 Yoav Peled. *Class and ethnicity in the Pale: the political economy of Jewish workers' nationalism in late imperial Russia.* New York: St. Martin's, 1989. ISBN 0-312-03098-3. ▸ Sociological models used to illuminate emergence of Bundism. Original and stimulating. [DEF]

21.200 Hans Rogger. *Jewish policies and right-wing politics in imperial Russia.* Berkeley: University of California Press, 1986. ISBN 0-520-04596-3. ▸ Antisemitism viewed in historical setting at turn of century. Early pogroms inspired by local police and patriotic press. Only after 1905 did relationship between antisemites and central authorities deepen. Thought-provoking interpretation. [DEF/JCB/GJM]

21.201 David Roskies. *Against the Apocalypse: responses to catastrophe in modern Jewish culture.* Cambridge, Mass.: Harvard University Press, 1984. ISBN 0-674-00915-0. ‣ Suggestive, sweeping examination of central theme in Jewish literature. Focus on Yiddish literature from nineteenth century through Holocaust. [DEF]

21.202 Murray J. Rosman. *The lords' Jews: magnate Jewish relations in the Polish-Lithuanian Commonwealth during the eighteenth century.* Cambridge, Mass.: Harvard Center for Jewish Studies and Harvard Ukrainian Research Institute, 1990. (Harvard Ukrainian Research Institute monograph series. Harvard University, Center for Jewish Studies, Harvard Judaic texts and studies, 7.) ISBN 0-916458-18-0. ‣ Role of Jews in Poland's economic system and their complex relationship with nobility. Meticulous study based on archival materials. [DEF]

21.203 Isaac M. Rubinow. *Economic condition of the Jews in Russia.* 1907 ed. New York: Arno, 1975. ISBN 0-405-06744-5. ‣ United States Bureau of Labor; valuable for statistical information. [DEF]

21.204 Michael Stanislawski. *For whom do I toil? Judah Leib Gordon and the crisis of Russian Jewry.* New York: Oxford University Press, 1988. ISBN 0-19-504290-5. ‣ Biographical study of Hebrew poet and leading figure of Russian-Jewish Enlightenment. Focus on Gordon's career as publicist and social critic. Lucid and compelling. [DEF]

21.205 Michael Stanislawski. *Tsar Nicholas I and the Jews: the transformation of Jewish society in Russia, 1825–1855.* Philadelphia: Jewish Publication Society of America, 1983. ISBN 0-8276-0216-2. ‣ Definitive study of tsarist policy toward Jews. State intervention motivated less by antisemitism than by conservatism, bureaucratic inefficiency, and other reasons of state. Also discusses emergence of enlightened Jewish intelligentsia and internal social tensions and conflicts. [DEF/SLH]

21.206 Henry J. Tobias. *The Jewish Bund in Russia from its origins to 1905.* Stanford, Calif.: Stanford University Press, 1972. ISBN 0-8047-0764-2. ‣ Ideological and organizational development of major Jewish Socialist party. Thorough and comprehensive. [DEF]

21.207 David Vital. *The origins of Zionism.* 1975 ed. Oxford: Clarendon, 1980. ISBN 0-19-827439-4 (pbk). ‣ Analysis of emergence of Zionism in East European context. Best synthesis available. First of three-volume study (with 21.208 and 21.317). [DEF]

21.208 David Vital. *Zionism: the formative years.* New York: Oxford University Press, 1982. ISBN 0-19-827443-2 (cl), 0-19-827715-6 (pbk). ‣ Well-written and well-conceived organizational and political history of Zionist movement in Herzlian and post-Herzlian periods until World War I. Second of three-volume study (with 21.207 and 21.317). [DEF]

21.209 Israel Zinberg. *History of Jewish literature.* 12 vols. Bernard Martin, ed. and trans. Cleveland: Press of Case Western Reserve University, 1972–78. ISBN 0-82950-228-9 (v. 1), 0-82950-231-0 (v. 2). ‣ Volumes nine through twelve deal with Hasidism and Jewish Enlightenment (Haskalah) in eastern Europe. Classic, still valuable work of scholarship. [DEF]

21.210 Steven Zipperstein. *The Jews of Odessa: a cultural history, 1794–1881.* Stanford, Calif.: Stanford University Press, 1985. ISBN 0-8047-1251-4 (cl), 0-8047-1962-4 (pbk). ‣ Social conditions and cultural institutions of modernizing community. Unrestricted by traditional features of Jewish communities in Pale, new city represented model of future. Lucid and sensitive presentation. [DEF/SLH]

JEWS IN ISLAMIC LANDS, 1492–1948

21.211 Michel Abitbol. *The Jews of North Africa during the Second World War.* Detroit: Wayne State University Press, 1989. ISBN 0-8143-1824-X. ‣ Study of treatment of Jews of Morocco, Algeria, and Tunisia by Vichy regime. Also reactions within Jewish communities and resistance activities. Important contribution to study of Holocaust period. Translation from French original: *Les Juifs d'Afrique du Nord sous Vichy.* [AR]

21.212 Reuben Ahroni. *Yemenite Jewry: origins, culture, and literature.* Bloomington: Indiana University Press, 1986. ISBN 0-253-36807-3. ‣ Overview of history and culture of Jews of Yemen; emphasis on literary creativity of community. [AR]

21.213 Marc D. Angel. *The Jews of Rhodes: the history of a Sephardic community.* New York: Sepher-Hermon, 1978. ISBN 0-87203-072-5. ‣ Study of history and culture of Sefardic community of island of Rhodes. Surveys developments from its origins in the sixteenth century to its annihilation by Nazis in World War II. [AR]

21.214 Marc D. Angel. *Voices in exile: a study in Sephardic intellectual history.* Hoboken, N.J.: KTAV and Sephardic House, 1991. ISBN 0-88125-370-7. ‣ Survey of rabbinical and popular culture of Sefardim. Focus on Judeo-Spanish communities of the Levant. [AR]

21.215 Mair Jose Benardete. *Hispanic culture and character of the Sephardic Jews.* 2d rev. ed. Marc D. Angel, ed. New York: Sepher-Harmon for the Foundation for the Advancement of Sephardic Studies and Culture and Sephardic House, 1982. ISBN 0-87203-100-4. ‣ Collection of essays on history and culture of Sefardic communities of Levant; emphasis on survival of Hispanic heritage. While outdated in parts, offers some important insights into Judeo-Spanish culture. [AR]

21.216 Esther Benbassa. *Un grand Rabbin sepharade en politique, 1892–1923.* Paris: Presses du Centre National de la Recherche Scientifique, 1990. ISBN 2-87682-041-2. ‣ Letters to Alliance Israélite Universelle written by Haim Nahum, last chief rabbi of Ottoman empire. Introductory section discusses his life and times. [AR]

21.217 Benjamin Braude and Bernard Lewis, eds. *Christians and Jews in the Ottoman empire: the functioning of a plural society.* 2 vols. New York: Holmes & Meier, 1982. ISBN 0-8419-0519-3 (v. 1), 0-8419-0520-7 (v. 2). ‣ Collection of articles on various aspects of Jewish and Christian communities in Ottoman empire. Covers period from fifteenth to twentieth century. Revises conventional ideas about interfaith relations (millet system). [AR/CK/CVF]

21.218 André Chouraqui. *Between East and West: a history of the Jews of North Africa.* Michael M. Bernet, trans. Philadelphia: Jewish Publication Society of America, 1968. ‣ Brief survey of history of Jews of Maghrib. Discusses political and cultural developments from earliest times to mid-twentieth century. [AR/LV]

21.219 André Chouraqui. *Histoire des Juifs en Afrique du Nord.* Paris: Hachette, 1985. ISBN 2-01-011533-3. ‣ Detailed study of cultural, social, and political history of Jews of Maghrib; emphasis on modern period. [AR]

21.220 Amnon Cohen. *Jewish life under Islam: Jerusalem in the sixteenth century.* Cambridge, Mass.: Harvard University Press, 1984. ISBN 0-674-47436-8. ‣ Focuses on Jewish community of Jerusalem in sixteenth century. History reconstructed through documentation of Muslim courts of law: relations with authorities, internal administration of community, social relations, and economic activities. Translation of *Yehudim be-shilton ha-Islam.* [AR/CK]

21.221 Hayyim J. Cohen. *The Jews of the Middle East, 1860–*

1972. New York: Wiley, 1973. ISBN 0-470-16424-7. ▸ Overview of political history of Middle Eastern Jewry in contemporary period; emphasis on relations with non-Jewish world. [AR]

21.222 Shlomo A. Deshen. *The Mellah Society: Jewish community life in Sherifian Morocco.* Chicago: University of Chicago Press, 1989. ISBN 0-226-14339-2 (cl), 0-226-14340-6 (pbk). ▸ Study of traditional Jewish society in Morocco; makes extensive use of rabbinical sources. Important exposition of Jewish communal existence in North Africa. [AR]

21.223 Shlomo A. Deshen and Walter P. Zenner, eds. *Jewish societies in the Middle East: community, culture, and authority.* Washington, D.C.: University Press of America, 1982. ISBN 0-8191-2578-4 (cl), 0-8191-2579-2 (pbk). ▸ Collection of essays on history and culture of Jewish communities; emphasis on modern period. Useful articles on little-studied communities. [AR]

21.224 Mark Alan Epstein. *The Ottoman Jewish communities and their role in the fifteenth and sixteenth centuries.* Freiburg: Schwarz, 1980. (Islamkundliche Untersuchungen, 56.) ISBN 3-87997-077-7 (pbk). ▸ Study of history of Jewish communities of Ottoman empire during first two centuries of Ottoman rule based on Ottoman archival sources. Especially important for Ottoman-Jewish relations. [AR]

21.225 Renzo de Felice. *Jews in an Arab land: Libya, 1835–1970.* Judith Roumani, trans. Austin: University of Texas Press, 1985. ISBN 0-292-74016-6. ▸ Detailed history of Jewish community of Libya in modern period. Focuses in particular on period under Italian rule. Translation of *Ebrei in un paese arabo.* [AR]

21.226 Jane S. Gerber. *Jewish society in Fez, 1450–1700: studies in communal and economic life.* Leiden: Brill, 1980. ISBN 90-04-05820-6. ▸ History of internal life of Jewish community of Fez in early modern period. Covers relations with surrounding Moroccan society. Significant case study. [AR]

21.227 Harvey E. Goldberg. *Jewish life in Muslim Libya: rivals and relatives.* Chicago: University of Chicago Press, 1990. ISBN 0-226-30091-9 (cl), 0-226-30092-7 (pbk). ▸ Collection of essays of historical anthropology discussing various facets of Jewish social life in Libya in nineteenth and twentieth centuries. Original and innovative approach to study of Jewish society in Muslim country in period of transition and change. [AR]

21.228 Haim Zeev Hirschberg. *A history of the Jews of North Africa.* Vol. 2: *From the Ottoman conquests to the present time.* 2d rev. ed. M. Eichelberg, trans. Leiden: Brill, 1981. ISBN 90-04-06295-5 (v. 2). ▸ General history of Jews of Maghrib. Based primarily on rabbinical sources. For volume 1, see 21.34. [AR]

21.229 Gudrun Krämer. *The Jews in modern Egypt, 1914–1952.* Seattle: University of Washington Press, 1989. ISBN 0-295-96795-1. ▸ Detailed history of Egyptian Jewry in final decades of British control and period of Egyptian independence. Special attention to effects of Arab nationalism, Zionism, and communism. [AR/AG]

21.230 Jacob M. Landau. *Jews in nineteenth-century Egypt.* New York: New York University Press, 1969. ▸ Collection of articles on Egyptian Jewry in modern period; emphasis on politics and culture. Useful, but lacking central theme. [AR]

21.231 Michael M. Laskier. *The Alliance Israélite Universelle and the Jewish communities of Morocco, 1862–1962.* Albany: State University of New York Press, 1983. (SUNY series in modern Jewish history. Tel-Aviv University Diaspora Research Institute, Publications, 45.) ISBN 0-87395-656-7 (cl), 0-87395-655-9 (pbk). ▸ Study of educational work of Alliance Israélite Universelle in Morocco, site of largest Jewish community and largest network of Alliance schools in any Arab country. Focuses on political activities of organization and on relations with Jewish communities. Important institutional history. [AR/CK]

21.232 Nissim Rejwan. *The Jews of Iraq: 3000 years of history and culture.* London: Weidenfeld & Nicholson, 1985. ISBN 0-297-78713-6. ▸ Overview of history of Jews of Iraq; emphasis on modern period, but first ninety pages deal somewhat cursorily with Middle Ages. Reviews major developments and personalities. Only such survey available in English. [AR/MRC]

21.233 Aron Rodrigue. *French Jews, Turkish Jews: the Alliance Israélite Universelle and the politics of Jewish schooling in Turkey, 1860–1925.* Bloomington: Indiana University Press, 1990. ISBN 0-253-35021-2. ▸ Study of politics of relationship between Alliance Israélite Universelle and Turkish Jewry. Analyzes role played by Alliance school network in westernization of Turkish Jewry. [AR]

21.234 Aron Rodrigue. *De l'instruction à l'émancipation: les enseignants de l'Alliance Israélite Universelle et les Juifs d'Orient, 1860–1939.* Paris: Calmann-Levy, 1989. ISBN 2-7021-1757-0. ▸ Survey of political and cultural activities of Alliance Israélite Universelle in North Africa and the Middle East. Selection of letters from Alliance archives. [AR]

21.235 Cecil Roth. *Dona Gracia of the House of Nasi.* Philadelphia: Jewish Publication Society of America, 1948. ISBN 0-8276-0099-2. ▸ Study of life and times of Mendes/Nasi family in sixteenth century. Focuses on family matriarch, Dona Gracia Nasi, her financial, political, and cultural activities and her boycott of port of Ancona, Italy. Romanticized image, but useful information. [AR]

21.236 Cecil Roth. *The House of Nasi: the duke of Naxos.* Philadelphia: Jewish Publication Society of America, 1948. ▸ Study of life of Marrano financier, Don Joseph Nasi. Discusses life in Europe as well as subsequent activities in Ottoman empire. Highly romantic account. [AR]

21.237 David Solomon Sassoon. *A history of the Jews in Baghdad.* 1949 ed. New York: AMS Press, 1982. ISBN 0-404-16427-7. ▸ Study of social, political, and cultural history of Jews of Baghdad; emphasis on modern period. Somewhat outdated, but still useful. [AR]

21.238 Daniel J. Schroeter. *Merchants of Essaouira: urban society and imperialism in southwestern Morocco, 1844–1886.* Cambridge: Cambridge University Press, 1988. ISBN 0-521-32455-6. ▸ Perceptive and significant study of economic activities of largely Jewish mercantile elite of Essaouira (Mogador). Discusses place of this elite in economic relations between Morocco and Europe. Portrays Moroccan seaport and trading community at time of integration into world capitalist system. [AR/LV/MS]

21.239 Shimon Shamir, ed. *The Jews of Egypt: a Mediterranean society in modern times.* Boulder: Westview, 1987. ISBN 0-8133-7290-9. ▸ Collection of articles on political, economic, and cultural life of Jews of Egypt; focus mostly on twentieth century. Full of important information. [AR]

21.240 Aryeh Shmuelevitz. *The Jews of the Ottoman empire in the late fifteenth and sixteenth centuries: administrative, economic, legal, and social relations as reflected in the responsa.* Leiden: Brill, 1984. ISBN 90-04-07071-0. ▸ History of Jews of Ottoman empire in early modern period. Emphasis on internal and external legal history based on rabbinical *responsa.* Good communal history. [AR]

21.241 Norman A. Stillman. *The Jews of Arab lands in modern times.* Philadelphia: Jewish Publication Society of America, 1991. ISBN 0-8276-0370-3. ▸ Documents illustrating various aspects of Jewish existence in Arab lands in nineteenth and twentieth centuries preceded by long introductory essay. Sequel to 21.44. [AR]

21.242 Abraham L. Udovitch and Lucette Valensi. *The last Arab Jews: the communities of Jerba, Tunisia.* Chur: Harwood Academic, 1984. ISBN 3-7186-0135-4, ISBN 0275-7524. ▸ Work of historical anthropology studying life and culture of two Jewish communities of Tunisian island of Djerba; focus on contemporary period. [AR/LV/MS]

AMERICAN JEWISH HISTORY

21.243 Salo W. Baron. *Steeled by adversity: essays and addresses on American Jewish life.* Jeanette Meisel Baron, ed. Philadelphia: Jewish Publication Society of America, 1971. ▸ Anthology of influential historiographical contributions by major interpreter of American Jewish history; particularly useful for tracing evolution of discipline. Overview of East European Jewish migration to America. [JSG]

21.244 Nathan C. Belth. *A promise to keep: a narrative of the American encounter with anti-Semitism.* New York: Times Books, 1979. ISBN 0-8129-0814-7. ▸ Only extant narrative overview and survey of antisemitism in United States. Focus on social discrimination and interethnic tensions and Jewish response over past century. [JSG]

21.245 Joseph Blau and Salo W. Baron, eds. *The Jews in the United States, 1790–1840: a documentary history.* 3 vols. New York: Columbia University Press, 1963. ▸ Three-volume anthology of documents illuminating American Jewish life during period for which there is no comprehensive scholarly treatment. Emphasizes both internal and external life of community. [JSG]

21.246 Naomi W. Cohen. *American Jews and the Zionist idea.* New York: KTAV, 1975. ISBN 0-87068-272-5. ▸ Comprehensive overview of history of Zionism in United States. Concerned both with emergence of American Zionist ideology and evolution of constituency supportive of Zionism in America. [JSG]

21.247 Naomi W. Cohen. *Encounter with emancipation: the German Jews in the United States, 1830–1914.* Philadelphia: Jewish Publication Society of America, 1984. ISBN 0-8276-0236-7. ▸ Comprehensive history of migration, settlement, mobility, and acculturation of Jews from Central Europe over three generations. Reception of Jews in nineteenth-century America and evolution of intergroup relationships. [JSG]

21.248 Naomi W. Cohen. *Not free to desist: the American Jewish Committee, 1906–1966.* Philadelphia: Jewish Publication Society of America, 1972. ▸ History of oldest Jewish defense organization in America. Very useful in providing context for interpreting antisemitism in United States between 1900 and 1960s. [JSG]

21.249 Moshe Davis. *The emergence of Conservative Judaism: the historical school in nineteenth-century America.* 1963 ed. Westport, Conn.: Greenwood, 1977. ISBN 0-8371-9792-9. ▸ Evolution of variety of nineteenth-century Jewish religious denominations in America. Over-ambitious attempt to link that century's traditional, Americanized Jewish activities with twentieth-century Conservative Judaism. [JSG]

21.250 Henry Feingold. *Zion in America: the Jewish experience from colonial times to the present.* Rev. ed. New York: Hippocrene, 1981. ISBN 0-88254-307-5. ▸ Survey of American Jewish history from seventeenth century to 1970s. Emphasis on uniqueness of American Jewish history within both American ethnic and world Jewish history. [JSG]

21.251 Nathan Glazer. *American Judaism.* 2d rev. ed. Chicago: University of Chicago Press, 1989. ISBN 0-226-29843-4. ▸ Introduction to development of Jewish religious and ethnic life over three centuries. This edition takes note of significant recent historiographical contributions to Jewish denominational history. [JSG]

21.252 Arthur A. Goren. *New York Jews and the quest for community: the kehillah experiment, 1908–1922.* New York: Columbia University Press, 1970. ISBN 0-231-03422-9. ▸ Groundbreaking study of attempts of early twentieth-century German and East European Jews in New York to create organized community in

voluntaristic America. Explores limits of Jewish intraethnic cooperation. [JSG]

21.253 Jeffrey S. Gurock. *American Jewish history: a bibliographical guide.* New York: Anti-Defamation League of B'nai B'rith, 1983. ISBN 0-88464-037-X (pbk). ▸ Best available compilation and classification of some 800 books and articles. Includes essay on evolution of American Jewish historiography from nineteenth century to 1980. [JSG]

21.254 Oscar Handlin. "American views of the Jew at the opening of the twentieth century." *Publication of the American Jewish Historical Society* 40 (June 1951) 323–44. ISSN 0164-0178. ▸ Classic examination of ideological and popular roots of 1890s' antisemitism. Compares levels of toleration for Jews and other American ethnic minorities. [JSG]

21.255 Will Herberg. "The Jewish labor movement in the United States." *American Jewish year book* 53 (1952) 3–74. ISSN 0065-8987. ▸ Basic introduction to evolution of unions among Jews and Jewish labor history from 1880s to 1950s. Particular emphasis on Jewish union and radical life on Lower East Side under impact of East European migration. [JSG]

21.256 Will Herberg. *Protestant-Catholic-Jew: an essay in American religious sociology.* Rev. ed. Garden City, N.Y.: Anchor, 1960. ▸ Pioneering historical study of Jewish religious and ethnic identification over three generations, 1880–1950. Sociology of postwar Jewish life, emphasizing patterns of assimilation and emergence of Jewish civic religion. [JSG]

21.257 John Higham. *Send these to me: immigrants in urban America.* Rev. ed. Baltimore: Johns Hopkins University Press, 1984. ISBN 0-8018-2473-7(cl), 0-8018-2438-9 (pbk). ▸ Examination of social roots of late nineteenth-century American antisemitism and other nativist reactions to ethnic and minority groups. Consideration of wealth and status issues as sources of discrimination. [JSG]

21.258 Irving Howe. *World of our fathers.* 1983 ed. New York: Schocken, 1989. ISBN 0-8052-0928-X. ▸ Well-written treatment of processes of arrival, adjustment, and mobility of East European Jews, particularly during the 1880 to 1920 period. Major emphasis on radical culture and lifestyle on Lower East Side. Companion volume to Howe and Libo 21.259. [JSG]

21.259 Irving Howe and Kenneth Libo, eds. *How we lived: a documentary history of immigrant Jews in America, 1880–1930.* New York: Marek, 1979. ISBN 0-399-90051-9 (cl). ▸ Useful companion volume to Howe 21.258. Documents illuminate processes of migration, settlement, and advancement of East European Jews with particular focus on Lower East Side community. [JSG]

21.260 Leon A. Jick. *The americanization of the synagogue.* Hanover, N.H.: University Press of New England for Brandeis University Press, 1976. ISBN 0-87451-119-4. ▸ Social history of evolution of Jewish denominational life in nineteenth-century America. Persuasive analysis of impact of americanization upon immigrant German Jews in emergence of Reform Judaism. [JSG]

21.261 Abraham J. Karp. *Haven and home: a history of the Jews in America.* New York: Schocken, 1985. ISBN 0-8052-3920-0 (cl), 0-8052-0817-8 (pbk). ▸ Introductory narrative and documentary history of American Jewish life from colonial period to present. Particular emphasis on Jewish religious, intellectual, and cultural life. [JSG]

21.262 Abraham J. Karp. "New York chooses a chief rabbi." *Publication of the American Jewish Historical Society* 44.3 (1955) 129–98. ISSN 0164-0178. ▸ Influential study of attempts in nineteenth century by immigrant Orthodox Jews to recreate East European religious civilization on Lower East Side. Adjustment of Judaism to American environment. [JSG]

21.263 Thomas Kessner. *The golden door: Italian and Jewish immigrant mobility in New York City, 1880–1915.* New York: Oxford University Press, 1977. ISBN 0-19-502116-9. ▸ Pathbreaking quantitative study of economic and residential mobility among Jews and Italians over two immigrant generations. Comparisons of levels of advancement and interpretation of factors contributing to rate of mobility. [JSG]

21.264 Bertram Wallace Korn. *American Jewry and the Civil War.* New York: Atheneum, 1961. ▸ Classic examination of involvement and attitudes of American Jews toward slavery and Civil War. Political and social antisemitism during Civil War and thereafter. [JSG]

21.265 Charles Liebman. "Orthodoxy in American Jewish life." *American Jewish year book* 66 (1965) 21–97. ISSN 0065-8987. ▸ Seminal study establishing system for classifying types of Orthodox attitudes and behavior in nineteenth- to twentieth-century America. Considers status of denomination as of mid-1960s. [JSG]

21.266 Charles Liebman. "Reconstructionism in American Jewish life." *American Jewish year book* 71 (1970) 3–99. ISSN 0065-8987. ▸ Useful overview of history of Reconstructionism in America, its social and ideological roots. Impact of Reconstructionism on other Jewish denominations and Jewish communal life. [JSG]

21.267 Steven M. Lowenstein. *Frankfurt on the Hudson, the German Jewish community of Washington Heights, 1933–1983: its structure and culture.* Detroit: Wayne State University Press, 1988. ISBN 0-8143-1960-2. ▸ Stimulating social history of migration, settlement, and adjustment of Jewish refugees from Nazi Germany. Acculturation and patterns of ethnic-religious persistence in Washington Heights, New York. Model communal history. [JSG]

21.268 Jacob Rader Marcus. *The American Jewish woman, 1654–1980.* New York: KTAV, 1981. ISBN 0-87068-751-4. ▸ Descriptive narrative of contributions of Jewish women and women's organization to development of American Jewish life from colonial period to present. Written in Marcus's encyclopedic style. [JSG]

21.269 Jacob Rader Marcus. *The colonial American Jew, 1492–1776.* 3 vols. Detroit: Wayne State University Press, 1970. ISBN 0-8143-1403-1. ▸ Basic introduction of encyclopedic dimension detailing Jewish communal life in America from first seventeenth-century arrivals until Revolutionary War. Areas of settlement, internal developments, process of emancipation, relationships with other groups, and interaction with Jewry worldwide. [JSG]

21.270 Jacob Rader Marcus and Abraham J. Peck, eds. *The American rabbinate: a century of continuity and change, 1883–1983.* Hoboken, N.J.: KTAV, 1985. ISBN 0-88125-076-7. ▸ Pathbreaking essay analyzing evolution of Orthodox, Conservative, and Reform rabbinates from late nineteenth century to present. Definition of continuity, tradition, and change within each denomination. [JSG]

21.271 Deborah Dash Moore. *At home in America: second generation New York Jews.* New York: Columbia University Press, 1981. ISBN 0-231-05062-3. ▸ Thoughtful, well-written study of ethnic persistence, forms of communal life, and interaction with urban environment among second-generation Jews in New York City, ca. 1920–40. Migration patterns from Lower East Side. [JSG]

21.272 Marc Lee Raphael. *Profiles in American Judaism: the Reform, Conservative, Orthodox, and Reconstructionist traditions in historical perspective.* 1985 ed. San Francisco: Harper & Row, 1985. ISBN 0-06-066802-4 (pbk). ▸ Useful introduction to history, ideology, institutional framework, and belief system of Reform, Conservative, Orthodox, and Reconstructionist denominations

from nineteenth century to present. Identification of leading rabbinical and lay leaders. [JSG]

21.273 Moses Rischin. *The promised city: New York's Jews, 1870–1914.* 1962. ed. Cambridge, Mass.: Harvard University Press, 1977. ISBN 0-674-71501-2 (pbk). ▸ Classic examination of conditions of settlement for East European Jews on Lower East Side, 1870 to World War I. Urban environment, process of acculturation, interaction with German Jews and wider New York political and social world. [JSG]

21.274 Jonathan Sarna, ed. *The American Jewish experience.* New York: Holmes & Meier, 1986. ISBN 0-8419-0934-2 (cl), 0-8419-0935-0 (pbk). ▸ Anthology of important scholarly articles and sections of books produced over past thirty years covering history of American Jewry. Complemented with historiographical notes and bibliography. [JSG]

21.275 Jonathan Sarna, ed. and trans. *People walk on their heads: Moses Weinberger's Jews and Judaism in New York.* New York: Holmes & Meier, 1982. ISBN 0-8419-0707-2 (cl), 0-8419-0731-5 (pbk). ▸ Fascinating expression of late nineteenth-century American Orthodox rabbinical protest against modernization and secularization by East European Jews. Efforts to reconstitute European religious civilization in America. [JSG]

21.276 Marshall Sklare. *Conservative Judaism: an American religious movement.* 1972 rev. ed. Lanham, Md.: University Press of America, 1985. ISBN 0-8191-4480-0. ▸ Pioneering treatment of acculturation and assimilation of second- and third-generation East European Jews in post–World War II America. Role of Conservative Jewish ideology and institutions in maintenance of Jewish religious and social identification. [JSG]

21.277 Melvin I. Urofsky. *American Zionism from Herzl to the Holocaust.* Garden City, N.Y.: Anchor, 1975. ISBN 0-385-03639-6. ▸ Best introduction to emergence of distinctive American Zionist ideology, rise of indigenous leadership, and rise of support among American Jews. Role of Louis Brandeis as leader and ideologue. [JSG]

21.278 Chaim I. Waxman. *America's Jews in transition.* Philadelphia: Temple University Press, 1983. ISBN 0-87722-321-1 (cl), 0-87722-329-7 (pbk). ▸ Social structure and history of Jewish life in America, early twentieth century to 1980s. Particularly important treatments of patterns of identifications and assimilation and of communal issues of 1960s to 1970s. [JSG]

21.279 Jack Wertheimer, ed. *The American synagogue: a sanctuary transformed.* Cambridge: Cambridge University Press, 1987. ISBN 0-521-33290-7. ▸ Very useful anthology of specialized studies on development and change within Orthodox, Conservative, and Reform synagogues from eighteenth century to present. Governance, aesthetics, and leadership issues within synagogue life. [JSG]

21.280 David Wyman. *The abandonment of the Jews: America and the Holocaust, 1941–1945.* 1984 ed. New York: Pantheon, 1985. ISBN 0-394-42813-7 (1984, cl), 0-394-74077-7 (pbk). ▸ Most comprehensive study of United States government policies toward American Jews, rescue, and refugees during World War II. Relationship of American Jewish leadership to Franklin D. Roosevelt. Minority group status during wartime. [JSG]

EUROPEAN JEWRY SINCE 1914

21.281 Mordechai Altshuler. *Soviet Jewry since the Second World War: population and social structure.* New York: Greenwood, 1987. ISBN 0-313-24494-4, ISSN 0147-1104. ▸ Rigorous statistical approach employed to illuminate trends in Jewish life. Essential for understanding the subject. [EM]

21.282 Yehuda Bauer. *Flight and rescue: Brichah.* New York: Random House, 1970. ▸ Emigration from Europe to Palestine of

Holocaust survivors in immediate post–World War II period. Oral history used to good effect. [EM]

21.283 Randolph L. Braham. *The politics of genocide: the Holocaust in Hungary.* 2 vols. New York: Columbia University Press, 1981. ISBN 0-231-04496-8 (set). ▸ Meticulous and exhaustive chronicle of subject of great interest and importance by greatest authority. Includes invaluable background material on interwar period. Definitive work. [EM/SBV]

21.284 David Cesarani, ed. *The making of modern Anglo-Jewry.* Cambridge, Mass: Blackwell, 1990. ISBN 0-631-16776-5. ▸ Subjects covered include Jewish politics, antisemitism, Jewish trade unionism, Jewish immigration, and Jewish culture. State of art scholarship on subject. [EM]

21.285 Richard I. Cohen. *The burden of conscience: French Jewish leadership during the Holocaust.* Bloomington: Indiana University Press, 1987. ISBN 0-253-31263-9. ▸ Jewish leaders react to unprecedented situation. Excellent case study; complements Marrus and Paxton 21.303. [EM]

21.286 Stuart Cohen. *English Zionists and British Jews: the communal politics of Anglo-Jewry, 1895–1920.* Princeton: Princeton University Press, 1982. ISBN 0-691-05361-8. ▸ For and against Jewish nationalism within integrated but changing Jewish community. Splendid case study. [EM]

21.287 Lucy S. Dawidowicz. *The war against the Jews, 1933–1945.* 10th anniversary ed. Toronto: Bantam, 1986. ISBN 0-553-34302-5. ▸ Old standard synthesis; still useful and recommended for classroom use. [EM]

21.288 Lucjan Dobroszycki, ed. *The chronicle of the Łódź ghetto, 1941–1944.* Richard Lourie et al., trans. New Haven: Yale University Press, 1984. ISBN 0-300-03208-0. ▸ Well-edited, well-translated version of one of most important primary sources on Polish Holocaust. Interweaves mundane and tragic observations, providing unique perspective on conditions imposed upon Jews in occupied Poland. [EM/WLB]

21.289 Jonathan Frankel, ed. *The Jews and the European crises, 1914–1921.* New York: Oxford University Press, 1988. ISBN 0-19-505113-0, ISSN 0740-8625. ▸ Collection of scholarly articles on impact of World War I on Jews in Russia, Germany, England, and elsewhere. Excellent introductory essay by editor. [EM]

21.290 Jonathan Frankel, ed. *The Soviet government and the Jews, 1948–1967: a documented study.* Cambridge: Cambridge University Press, 1984. ISBN 0-521-24713-6. ▸ Wealth of primary material on all aspects of subject. Introductory sections provide necessary historical background. [EM]

21.291 Zvi Y. Gitelman. *Jewish nationality and Soviet politics: the Jewish sections of the CPSU, 1917–1930.* Princeton: Princeton University Press, 1972. ISBN 0-691-07542-5. ▸ Efforts of Jewish communism to transform Jewish life in accordance with Leninist doctrine. Pioneering study, objective and penetrating. [EM]

21.292 Israel Gutman. *The Jews of Warsaw, 1939–1943: ghetto, underground, revolt.* Ina Friedman, trans. Bloomington: Indiana University Press, 1982. ISBN 0-253-33174-9. ▸ German policy, Jewish-Polish relations, and Jewish politics in largest of all Polish ghettos. Thorough and objective, indispensable guide to one of most dramatic chapters of Holocaust history. [EM]

21.293 Israel Gutman, ed. *Encyclopaedia of the Holocaust.* 4 vols. New York: Macmillan, 1990. ISBN 0-02-896090-4 (set). ▸ Four-volume work including articles on all imaginable aspects of subject. Indispensable reference. [EM]

21.294 Israel Gutman et al., eds. *The Jews of Poland between two world wars.* Hanover, N.H.: University Press of New England for Brandeis University Press, 1989. (Tauber Institute for the Study of European Jewry, 10.) ISBN 0-87451-446-0. ▸ Collection of articles. Up-to-date research and comprehensiveness makes this best

single-volume treatment; particularly noteworthy contributions on Jewish culture and religion. [EM]

21.295 Raul Hilberg. *The destruction of the European Jews.* Rev. ed. 3 vols. New York: Holmes & Meier, 1985. ISBN 0-8419-0832-x (set). ▸ How Germans and their allies organized and implemented Final Solution. New three-volume edition of magisterial work, exhaustive and authoritative; controversial on Jewish role. [EM]

21.296 Paula E. Hyman. *From Dreyfus to Vichy: the remaking of French Jewry, 1906–1939.* New York: Columbia University Press, 1979. ISBN 0-231-04722-3. ▸ Evolution of one of Europe's major communities during period of political flux, rising antisemitism, and East European Jewish immigration. Standard work. [EM]

21.297 Oscar Isaiah Janowsky. *The Jews and minority rights (1898–1919).* New York: AMS Press, 1966. ▸ Debate on how to define Jews' status and guarantee international protection. Emphasis on "Jewish question" at Versailles Peace Conference. Classic, still not superseded. [EM]

21.298 *The Jews of Czechoslovakia: historical studies and surveys.* 3 vols. Philadelphia: Jewish Publication Society of America, 1968–84. ▸ Three volumes covering interwar period and Holocaust in Czech lands, Slovakia, and sub-Carpathian Rus'. Many contributors, not all scholars, but nothing comparable on subject. [EM]

21.299 Marion A. Kaplan. *The Jewish feminist movement in Germany: the campaigns of the Jüdischer Frauenbund, 1904–1938.* Westport, Conn.: Greenwood, 1979. ISBN 0-313-20736-4. ▸ Unusual and important subject attractively presented. [EM]

21.300 Otto Dov Kulka and Paul R. Mendes-Flohr, eds. *Judaism and Christianity under the impact of National Socialism.* Jerusalem: Historical Society of Israel and Zalman Shazar Center, 1987. ISBN 965-227-041-5. ▸ Essays on attitude of various churches to Jews, mostly in Germany, but also Europe. Covers interwar, Holocaust, and post–World War II periods. Excellent collection on extremely important subject. [EM]

21.301 Joseph Marcus. *Social and political history of the Jews in Poland, 1919–1939.* Berlin: Mouton, 1983. (New Babylon, Studies in the social sciences, 37.) ISBN 90-279-3239-5. ▸ Most systematic overview of Jewish history in interwar period. Highlights crucial interrelationship between socioeconomic standing and political development. Eccentric, opinionated, biased, but well worth reading. [EM/WLB]

21.302 Michael R. Marrus. *The Holocaust in history.* Hanover, N.H.: University Press of New England for Brandeis University Press, 1987. (Tauber Institute for the Study of European Jewry, 7.) ISBN 0-87451-425-8. ▸ How different historians and historical schools cope with impossible subject. Best treatment of highly contentious subject. [EM]

21.303 Michael R. Marrus and Robert O. Paxton. *Vichy France and the Jews.* New York: Basic Books, 1981. ISBN 0-465-09005-2. ▸ Liberal France betrays her citizens of Jewish faith. Classic study. Complement to Cohen 21.285. [EM]

21.304 Ezra Mendelsohn. *The Jews of East Central Europe between the world wars.* Bloomington: Indiana University Press, 1983. ISBN 0-253-33160-9. ▸ Survey includes chapters on Poland, Romania, Czechoslovakia, Hungary, and Baltic states. Only attempt in English at synthesis of Jewish history in this region in interwar period. [EM]

21.305 Ezra Mendelsohn. *Zionism in Poland: the formative years, 1915–1926.* New Haven: Yale University Press, 1981. ISBN 0-300-02448-7. ▸ Very detailed study of manifold activities of this Jewish nationalist movement in country where it was particularly influential. [EM]

21.306 Peter Meyer, ed. *The Jews in the Soviet satellites.* 1953 ed.

Westport, Conn.: Greenwood, 1971. ISBN 0-8371-2621-5. ▸ Work by several hands covers Jewish communities of Czechoslovakia, Poland, Hungary, Romania, and Bulgaria from end of war to 1950s. Old standby, but nothing better. [EM]

21.307 Meir Michaelis. *Mussolini and the Jews: German-Italian relations and the Jewish Question in Italy, 1922-1945.* Oxford: Clarendon for the Institute of Jewish Affairs, 1978. ISBN 0-19-822542-3. ▸ How Italian fascism dealt with Jewish Question in land of little antisemitism. Masterly treatment of fascinating subject. [EM]

21.308 George L. Mosse. *Germans and Jews: the Right, the Left, and the search for a "third force" in pre-Nazi Germany.* New York: Grosset & Dunlap, 1971. ISBN 0-448-00257-4. ▸ "Jewish question" in thought and politics and Jewish attitudes toward motherland. Leading social historian raises important questions. [EM]

21.309 Donald L. Niewyk. *The Jews in Weimar Germany.* Baton Rouge: Louisiana State University Press, 1980. ISBN 0-8071-0661-5. ▸ Tragic last chapter in history of Central Europe's most creative and most important Jewish community. Concise synthesis. [EM]

21.310 Benjamin Pinkus. *The Jews of the Soviet Union: the history of a national minority.* Cambridge: Cambridge University Press, 1988. ISBN 0-521-34078-0. ▸ Surveys major trends since Revolution. Already somewhat out-of-date, given recent dramatic events, but best available synthesis. [EM]

21.311 Jehuda Reinharz, ed. *Living with antisemitism: modern Jewish responses.* Hanover, N.H.: University Press of New England for Brandeis University Press, 1987. (Tauber Institute for the Study of European Jewry, 6.) ISBN 0-87451-388-X (cl), 0-87451-412-6 (pbk). ▸ Discusses different Jewish strategies for coping with hostility of neighbors. Collection of scholarly articles covers many European countries in pre–World War II and Holocaust periods. [EM]

21.312 Yaacov Ro'i and Avi Beker, eds. *Jewish culture and identity in the Soviet Union.* New York: New York University Press, 1991. ISBN 0-8147-7408-3. ▸ Scholars and activists on various aspects of subject from 1917 to 1980s. Special emphasis on Jewish nationalism, Judaism, and state policy in pre-Gorbachev era. [EM]

21.313 Jacob Shavit. *Jabotinsky and the revisionist movement, 1925-1948.* London: Cass, 1988. ISBN 0-7146-3325-9. ▸ Genesis of Zionism of antisocialist, integral nationalist variety. Important for understanding current Israeli politics. [EM]

21.314 Jonathan Steinberg. *All or nothing: the Axis and the Holocaust, 1941-1943.* London: Routledge, 1990. ISBN 0-415-04757-

9, 0-415-00773-9. ▸ New, fascinating material on Italy's Jewish policy in occupied Yugoslavia, Greece, and France. Italy's policy compared to that of Germany. [EM]

21.315 Isaiah Trunk. *Judenrat: the Jewish councils in eastern Europe under Nazi occupation.* 1972 ed. Jacob Robinson, Introduction. New York: Stein & Day, 1977. ISBN 0-8128-2170-X. ▸ Role of Nazi-appointed Jewish organizations during period of mass murder. Classic analysis of one of most controversial of all subjects. [EM]

21.316 Bela Vago and George L. Mosse, eds. *Jews and non-Jews in eastern Europe, 1918–1945.* New York: Wiley, 1974. ISBN 0-471-89760-0. ▸ Collection of articles, most dealing with worsening of Jewish-Christian relations as result of rise of East European fascism. Especially useful for coverage of Romania and Hungary. [EM]

21.317 David Vital. *Zionism: the crucial phase.* New York: Oxford University Press, 1987. ISBN 0-19-821932-6. ▸ Mostly on dramatic World War I period when Zionist movement made its greatest breakthrough. Third volume of masterly history of subject (with 21.207 and 21.208). [EM]

21.318 David H. Weinberg. *A community on trial: the Jews of Paris in the 1930s.* Chicago: University of Chicago Press, 1977. ISBN 0-226-88507-0. ▸ Established community and new immigrants react to political and economic crisis. Instructive case study of important community. [EM]

21.319 Leni Yahil. *The Holocaust: the fate of European Jewry, 1932-1945.* Ina Friedman and Haya Galai, trans. New York: Oxford University Press, 1990. ISBN 0-19-504522-X. ▸ One-volume abridgment of well-received two-volume Hebrew study. Latest effort at synthesis by leading scholar of subject. Extremely thorough. [EM]

21.320 Leni Yahil. *The rescue of Danish Jewry: test of a democracy.* Morris Gradel, trans. Philadelphia: Jewish Publication Society of America, 1983. ISBN 0-8276-0232-4 (pbk). ▸ Famous Danish exception to lack of initiative by European governments in protecting Jews from Nazis. Best book on subject. [EM]

21.321 Susan Zuccotti. *The Italians and the Holocaust: persecution, rescue, and survival.* New York: Basic Books, 1987. ISBN 0-465-03622-8. ▸ Best account of Italian Jewish struggle to survive Holocaust, including conflicted roles of government, Catholic church, and Italian citizenry, along with Jewish response. [EM]

SEE ALSO
18.490 Leonard Stein. *The Balfour Declaration.*
33.411 Nathaniel Katzburg. *Hungary and the Jews, 1897–1918.*
33.542 David J. Engel. *In the shadow of Auschwitz.*

PEREZ ZAGORIN

Modern Europe, General

Conventional American and English historiographical usage has long designated the entire expanse of five hundred years of European history, from the Renaissance to the present, as modern history. Within it, however, historians now commonly distinguish between the early modern and modern periods: the first covers the Renaissance (formally the year 1500, but extending back also into the fifteenth century) to the Enlightenment and the eve of the French Revolution in 1789; and the second, the era from the French Revolution, an event of wide European significance, through the two world wars and beyond to the present. This periodization is the basis of the chronological categories that order the following bibliography. The topical headings within each chronological category are designed to take in the salient aspects of each period and to include the literature of both the more traditional fields of general European history and others that have developed so remarkably during the past thirty years or so. The bibliography contains works dealing with various aspects of the history of modern Europe as a whole or of large regions or parts of Europe transcending national boundaries. It focuses on Western Europe, since Eastern Europe, Russia, and the Soviet Union are covered by separate sections of the *Guide*; and is complemented by those sections that are devoted to the modern national histories of the countries of Western Europe. Moreover, the *Guide* contains two separate sections on international relations from 1815 to the present. Accordingly, for the period after 1815, most of the works dealing with diplomacy, interstate relations, and wars between the countries of Europe will be found listed in these sections. What we have retained here pertaining to these subjects are a small number of works that also shed essential light on broader themes and on the life of Europe as a whole in the nineteenth and twentieth centuries and are therefore appropriate to this section. The reader will likewise note the presence in this section of books dealing with individuals, their lives, thought, and influence. Although such individuals also belong to a more local historical context (e.g., Martin Luther and Karl Marx to Germany and Sigmund Freud to Vienna and Austria), they are also figures of European importance and for this reason are essential to this section. The reader can and should consult the relevant national histories for additional works on these figures.

The compilation of a historical bibliography provides an opportunity to take stock of the intellectual and scholarly developments in a particular field of historical study. At the present time, consciousness of the unity of Europe has never been greater in the minds of Europeans and non-Europeans alike. The countries of Western Europe have expressed their common interest in peace and economic well being by joining in a supranational economic and political community, while many in Russia and the countries of Eastern Europe, recently liberated from Soviet domination, also aspire to membership in a single, united Europe reaching from the Atlantic Ocean to the Urals. Historiographically, however, we live in an age of intense specialization; scholars no longer feel able to tackle the task of writing the history of modern Europe singlehandedly, and apart from the potted narratives found in textbooks which make no pretense of originality or insight, such works are scarcely to be found. Books such as the British historian H.A.L. Fisher's three-volume *History of Europe*, an attempt at historical interpretation published nearly sixty years ago, are largely a thing of the past. In their place we have numerous collaborative works on European history enlisting the efforts of different specialists and limited to specific periods. Among the outstanding examples in this section are the series of volumes by individual authors in the French collection, *Peuples et civilizations*, and *The New Cambridge Modern History* in thirteen volumes, each of its chapters written by a separate author, which is centered on, though not exclusively concerned with, Europe, and deals with the whole era from the Renaissance, to post–World War II. One of the most notable recent trends in the historiography of modern Europe is the great increase of works relating to the early modern era. This has been motivated, in part, by the conception of the early modern period as a distinct epoch, which, despite significant changes and developments, still retained many continuities with the past. The resulting literature, especially on the Renaissance, the Reformation, and the sixteenth and seventeenth centuries, includes many brilliant and original works that have not only deepened but in some cases transformed historical understanding of major aspects of this period. One of the most important contributions to early modern historiography has been the writings and research program of the scholars gathered round the French journal *Annales: économies, sociétés, civilisations* and the Centre de Recherches Historiques of the École Pratique des Hautes Études, VIe Section, whose mentors were Lucien Febvre, Marc Bloch, and Fernand Braudel. These historians sought a "total history" that would integrate diverse aspects of the past: they focused on the long-term trends (*la longue durée*) dominating the life of a society rather than on political history and specific events, and they strove to identify and analyze enduring social and economic structures, utilizing quantitative methods whenever possible. For some years the Annales school was the strongest single influence in the historiography of early modern Europe. Braudel's book, *The Mediterranean and the Mediterranean World in the Age of Philip II* (6.26), is one of the chief examples of the aims and methods of this school.

Another trend in the historiography of modern Europe is the expansion of old fields, their differentiation into subdisciplines, and the explosion of newly created historical fields. The history of political thought and intellectual history generally intensively cultivated in the past generation, continues to produce important original work, endeavoring more than ever before to view these subjects in close relation to their political and social contexts. Large ensembles or bodies of ideas such as humanism, republicanism, liberalism, Marxism, and fascism, and the work of major thinkers of European significance such as Machiavelli, Erasmus, Hobbes, Locke, Hegel, Nietzsche, and Max Weber, have been studied and exhibited in fresh perspectives. Social history, while not a new field, has been revitalized and extended by sophisticated methods and close investigation of social groups, classes, and structures, urban and rural communities, professions, political parties, and other collectivities, often making use of hitherto unexploited evidence. Partly in consequence of the development of social history and the sweep of its ambition, old-fashioned narrative political history has declined. Many historians have come to believe that an exclusively narrative approach does not lend itself to the comprehension of the complexity of the historical process and the deeper forces that shape society. At the same time, however, historical interest in politics remains high, and students of political history have sought to enrich their understanding of political developments, institutions and structures, parties, nationalist and other movements, and modern revolutionary phenomena by engaging in comparative studies as well as by drawing closer to social history and utilizing some of its techniques and findings. A noticeable characteristic of the work in the political history of the nineteenth and twentieth centuries, and especially of the interwar and post–World War II period, is the blending of politics, diplomacy, and economics with the study of interest groups, economic ideologies, the welfare state, and the institutional effects of war and of post-war reconstruction.

Historical demography, a relative of social history, has developed into an independent discipline taking advantage of computer technology to mine large new bodies of evidence that shed significant new light on the fundamental facts of demographic change and their varied and complex effects on European society. Economic history has striven to turn itself into an increasingly quantitative discipline closely associated with economic theory, and has brought new techniques to the historical investigation of the Industrial Revolution and other economic developments and activities. One of the most striking changes in European historiography has been the emergence of women's history as a separate and prolific area of study. The earlier edition of this *Guide* neither included women's history as a distinctive field nor did it contain many works on the subject. Today the situation is entirely different, and women's or gender history is a continually expanding area that attracts an increasing number of scholars. Other historiographical fields that have made their appearance include psychohistory, the attempt to apply psychological methods of analysis to historical phenomena ranging from individual biographies to mass movements; the history of sexuality, which seeks to understand sexual relations, practices, and ideas about sex as socially and culturally determined facts; the history of marriage and the family, which investigates family and household structures and relationships across time; the history of popular culture, concerned with the beliefs, customs, rituals, mentalities, and forms of associations of the masses of people not part of the elite and ruling groups of their society. All of these and other innovative developments in the historiography of modern Europe are represented among the works listed in this section.

In addition to witnessing the emergence of new fields of study, recent European historiography has also become increasingly interdisciplinary. Many historians have attempted to take advantage of the methods and work done in anthropology, linguistics, literary criticism, sociology, and political science in order to broaden and deepen their investigations into the past. The anthropological and sociological concept of culture also influences the work of some historians who seek to investigate the shared culture of particular groups. In place of considering class as an abstract economic entity, for example, such historians are apt to regard it as a cultural phenomenon reflecting the lives of people who possess a common experiential background, linguistic traits, rituals, symbols, and values that need to be studied in their distinctiveness.

The vast, unceasing quantity of publication and the expansion of historical fields relating to modern Europe have made even the specialist's task a daunting one. Their main consequence has been to make syntheses more difficult and to encourage further specialization and increasing narrowness in scholarship. Admirable works of considerable breadth on modern European history continue to be written, of course; but even these do not attempt to sum up a whole era in the life of Europe, but select some lesser though significant aspect or theme on which to concentrate. If the movement toward European unification continues to grow with the goal of realizing durable political and economic institutions binding the countries and peoples of Europe together, then historiography will probably respond in due course by rethinking the concept of Europe and attempting to provide synthetic accounts of modern European history as a whole.

ACKNOWLEDGMENTS   *The selection of books for this section from the mass of existing literature has been in many ways a delicate and complicated one. I have sought to provide adequate representation of works of all kinds on modern European history on subjects ranging from politics to the arts. I wish to express my appreciation to the scholars whom I asked to serve as contributors and whose specialized knowledge has helped to assure the quality and usefulness of the selection in the many domains it covers. Special thanks are owed to Dr. Donald S. Cloyd and Dr. Jennifer Lloyd, who worked closely with me and gave great assistance in choosing many of the bibliographical entries and in preparing this section for publication.*

Entries are arranged under the following headings:

Reference Works
> Bibliographies and Guides
> Important Series, Collective Works, and Broad Perspectives
> Geographies and Atlases

Western Europe, 1500–1789
> General Studies and Political, Diplomatic, and
> Military History
> The Reformation, Churches, and Religion
> Cultural and Intellectual History and Political Thought
> Economic, Social, and Women's History
> The Arts

Western Europe, 1789–1914
> General Studies and Political, Diplomatic, and
> Military History
> Cultural and Intellectual History and Political Thought
> Economic, Social, and Women's History
> The Arts

Twentieth-century Europe and the Two World Wars, 1914–1945
> General Studies
> World War I
> Politics, Economy, and Society between the Wars
> Cultural and Intellectual History and Political Thought
> World War II in Europe: Origins and Impact
> The Holocaust
> The Arts

Postwar Europe, 1945–1989
> General Studies and Political History
> Cultural and Intellectual History and the Arts
> Social and Economic History

[Contributors: BSH = Bert S. Hall, BYK = Bonnelyn Young Kunze, CKF = Carole K. Fink, DMH = Derek M. Hirst, DSC = Donald Stephen Cloyd, FHS = Fiona Harris Stoertz, FLC = Fredric L. Cheyette, GS = Grace Seiberling, JBK = Jonathan B. Knudsen, JH = John Higham, JJS = James J. Sheehan, JKS = John K. Smith, JML = Jennifer M. Lloyd, JS = Jonathan Sperber, JSH = John S. Hill, KP = Katharine Park, KZ = Kristin E. S. Zapalac, LCA = Lorraine C. Attreed, LMB = Lawrence M. Bryant, LP = Linda A. Pollock, MAB = Mark A. Burkholder, MHS = Michael H. Shank, MM = Mark Motley, MW = Merry E. Wiesner-Hanks, PFG = Paul F. Grendler, PZ = Perez Zagorin, RMG = Richard M. Golden, RPL = Ralph P. Locke, SEK = Sharon E. Kingsland, SLE = Stanley L. Engerman, TAB = Thomas A. Brady, Jr., WJC = William J. Courtenay]

REFERENCE WORKS

Bibliographies and Guides

22.1 Derek H. Aldcroft and Richard Rodger, comps. *Bibliography of European economic and social history.* Manchester: Manchester University Press, 1984. ISBN 0-7190-0944-8. ▸ Bibliography of English-language titles arranged topically by region and country with sections on Europe as a whole. Stronger on modern period and economic history; less helpful on Germany. Outdated on women's and gender studies. [JML]

22.2 *Annual bulletin of historical literature.* London: Historical Association, 1911–. ▸ Selective, annotated bibliography, published annually, covering modern Europe and other subject areas. [PZ]

22.3 Roland H. Bainton and Eric W. Gritsch, eds. *Bibliography of the continental Reformation: materials available in English.* 2d rev. ed. Hamden, Conn.: Archon, 1972. ISBN 0-208-01219-0. ▸ Lists many different kinds of works, including printed sources, general histories, monographs, and materials on Counter-Reformation. [PZ]

22.4 Gwyn M. Bayless. *Bibliographic guide to the two world wars:* an annotated survey of English language reference materials. London: Bowker, 1977. ISBN 0-85935-013-4. ▸ Comprehensive bibliography of bibliographies; now somewhat dated. [JML]

22.5 *Beiläge der Vierteljahreshefte für Zeitgeschichte.* Stuttgart: Deutsche-Verlags-Anstalt, 1953–. ISSN 0042-5702. ▸ Annual bibliography emphasizing Germany but containing much useful material on more general topics in twentieth-century history, notably two world wars, fascism, and national socialism. [DSC]

22.6 J. S. Bromley and Albert Goodwin, eds. *A select list of works on Europe and Europe overseas, 1715–1815.* Oxford: Clarendon, 1956. ▸ Somewhat dated but still useful. Excludes works on English domestic history. [PZ]

22.7 Alan Bullock and A.J.P. Taylor. *A select list of books on European history, 1815–1914.* 2d ed. Oxford: Clarendon, 1957. ▸ Somewhat dated but still useful. Does not include English domestic history. [PZ]

22.8 Ronald J. Caldwell. *The era of the French Revolution: a bibliography of the history of Western civilization, 1789–1799.* 2 vols. New York: Garland, 1985. ISBN 0-8240-8794-1. ▸ Extensive, partly annotated listings, including theses and dissertations. Not confined to France; includes sections on general and national European history. [JML/DSC]

22.9 Ronald J. Caldwell. *The era of Napoleon: a bibliography of the history of Western civilization, 1799–1815.* 2 vols. New York: Garland, 1991. ISBN 0-8240-5644-2. ▸ Extensive, partly annotated topical listings, including theses and dissertations. Sections on general history and national histories of all European nations. [JML/DSC]

22.10 Cheryl Cline. *Women's diaries, journals, and letters: an annotated bibliography.* New York: Garland, 1989. ISBN 0-8240-6637-5. ▸ Citations chosen for historical and linguistic content not literary merit. Mostly English writing, but also French, Spanish, German, and Portuguese. Diaries reveal attitudes toward historical events and rituals of everyday life. [BYK]

22.11 Fédération International des Sociétés et Instituts pour l'Étude de la Renaissance. *Bibliographie internationale de l'humanisme et de la Renaissance.* Geneva: Librairie Droz, 1965–. ISSN 0067-7000. ▸ Comprehensive bibliography, published annually, of new work on Renaissance in many languages, including English. [JML]

22.12 Linda Frey, Marsha Frey and Joanne Schneider, eds. *Women in western European history: a select chronological and topical bibliography.* Vol. 1: *Antiquity to the French Revolution.* Vol. 2: *Nineteenth and twentieth centuries.* Supplement: *Works recently published and works recently discovered.* Westport, Conn.: Greenwood, 1982–86. ISBN 0-313-22858-2 (v. 1), 0-313-22859-0 (v. 2), 0-313-25109-6 (suppl.) ▸ General reference work to teacher and student in uncovering women's experiences within western European historical framework. Organized into geographical, political, and topical divisions, subdivided into narrower topics and biographies. [BYK]

22.13 Harvard University, Henry Adams History Club. *A select bibliography of history.* 4th ed. David D. Grose, ed. Cambridge, Mass.: Henry Adams History Club, 1970. ▸ Bibliography covering forty-two fields of historical scholarship. Somewhat dated but still useful, mostly on western Europe; includes some primary sources. [JML]

22.14 B. R. Mitchell. *European historical statistics, 1750–1975.* 2d rev. ed. New York: Facts on File, 1981. ISBN 0-87196-329-9. ▸ Useful, comprehensive compendium of statistics on climate, population, labor, agriculture, industry, trade, transportation, commerce, finance, prices, education, and national accounting. [JML]

22.15 Gerd Muehsam. *Guide to basic information sources in the visual arts.* Santa Barbara, Calif.: ABC-Clio, 1978. ISBN 0-87436-278-4. ▸ Bibliography and guide to reference and research tools with emphasis on works in English. Presented in chapters on how to do research on particular topics including historical periods, media (e.g., prints), and technical phenomena (e.g., color). [GS]

22.16 Steven E. Ozment, ed. *Reformation Europe: a guide to research.* St. Louis: Center for Reformation Research, 1982. ISBN 0-910345-01-5. ▸ Up-to-date bibliographic essays and bibliographies by various Reformation scholars. Wide ranging, including sections on Counter-Reformation, art, humanism, witchcraft, and women, and cites both English and foreign-language works. European in focus but concentrates on Germany. [JML/TAB]

22.17 John Roach, ed. *A bibliography of modern history.* Cambridge: Cambridge University Press, 1968. ISBN 0-521-07191-7. ▸ Companion volume to *The New Cambridge Modern History* (22.32), following same plan of organization by volumes and chapters. Includes printed primary sources as well as wide selection of secondary literature. [PZ]

SEE ALSO
    47.14 Daniel H. Thomas and Lynn M. Case, eds. *The new guide to the diplomatic archives of Western Europe.*

Important Series, Collective Works, and Broad Perspectives

22.18 Bonnie S. Anderson and Judith P. Zinsser. *A history of their own: women in Europe from prehistory to the present.* Vol. 2: *Fifteenth century to the present.* New York: Harper & Row, 1988. ISBN 0-06-015899-9 (cl), 0-06-091563-3 (pbk). ▸ Standard survey with special focus on woman's place and function in European society. Maintains that gender similarities outweighed differences according to period, nationality, and class, and that this held true over time. [BYK]

22.19 Ernest Barker, G. N. Clark, and P. Vaucher, eds. *The European inheritance.* 3 vols. Oxford: Clarendon, 1954. ▸ Interesting interpretive essays dealing with various aspects of European history since Renaissance. [PZ]

22.20 Marilyn J. Boxer and Jean H. Quataert, eds. *Connecting spheres: women in the Western world, 1500 to the present.* New York: Oxford University Press, 1987. ISBN 0-19-504123-2 (cl), 0-19-504133-X (pbk). ▸ Good introductory collection exploring race, class, religion, sexual preference, language, and culture. Divided into three topical and chronological sections: age of religious upheaval and political centralization, period of European industrialization and liberalization, and era of interventionist state. [BYK]

22.21 Renate Bridenthal, Claudia Koonz, and Susan Mosher Stuard, eds. *Becoming visible: women in European history.* 2d ed. Boston: Houghton-Mifflin, 1987. ISBN 0-395-41950-6 (pbk). ▸ Classic collection of essays on women's history, antiquity to twentieth-century welfare state. Brief general introductions, useful bibliographies. [BYK]

22.22 Whitney Chadwick. *Women, art, and society.* New York: Thames & Hudson, 1990. ISBN 0-500-20241-9 (cl), 0-500-18194-2 (pbk). ▸ Discussion of women as producers of art from early times to twentieth century. Draws on feminist research on representation and notions of femininity as well as rediscovery of women artists. [GS]

22.23 Carlo M. Cipolla, ed. *The Fontana economic history of Europe.* 6 vols. London: Collins and Fontana, 1972–76. ▸ Substantial essays by European scholars on European economic history from Middle Ages to present. Uses both topical and national approaches, includes Scandinavia and eastern Europe. [JML]

22.24 J. H. Clapham et al., eds. *The Cambridge economic history*

of Europe. Edition varies. 10 vols. Cambridge: Cambridge University Press, 1941–89. ▸ Major collective reference work for European economic history. Pertinent volumes listed separately. [PZ]

22.25 Carl Dahlhaus. *Foundations of music history.* J. B. Robinson, trans. Cambridge: Cambridge University Press, 1983. ISBN 0-521-23281-3 (cl), 0-521-29890-3 (pbk). ▸ Sophisticated introduction, by influential musicologist, to various philosophies of music history. Special attention to competing claims of Marxist determinism and formalist history of styles. [RPL]

22.26 John Fleming and Hugh Honour, eds. *Style and civilization.* Edition varies. 9 vols. Harmondsworth: Penguin, 1967–91. ▸ Accessible, provocative series aimed at interpreting European styles of art in their contemporary context; for general reader. Pertinent titles listed separately. [JML]

22.27 Egon Friedell. *A cultural history of the modern age: the crisis of the European soul from the Black Death to the world war.* Edition varies. 3 vols. Charles Francis Atkinson, trans. Alfred Polgar, Introduction. New York: Knopf, 1954–64. ▸ Interesting, wide-ranging study of European culture from Renaissance through World War I; many suggestive discussions and insights. [PZ]

22.28 Louis Halphen and Philippe Sagnac, eds. *Peuples et civilisations.* Paris: Presses Universitaires de France, 1926–. ▸ Well-known series covering many historical periods from antiquity to twentieth century. Some volumes rather old, but contain helpful narratives and bibliographies. Pertinent titles listed separately. [PZ]

22.29 Arnold Hauser. *The social history of art.* 1951 ed. 4 vols. Stanley Godman, trans. New York: Vintage, 1985. ISBN 0-394-70114-3 (v. 1, pbk), 0-394-70115-1 (v. 2, pbk), 0-394-70116-X (v. 3, pbk), 0-394-70117-8 (v. 4, pbk). ▸ Massive survey from prehistory to present. Deals primarily with visual arts, but includes all arts in economic and social context. Marxist approach. [JML]

22.30 Paul M. Hohenberg and Lynn Hollen Lees. *The making of urban Europe, 1000–1950.* Cambridge, Mass.: Harvard University Press, 1985. ISBN 0-674-54360-2. ▸ Broad synthesis in Annales tradition. Describes cities as part of international network transcending local connections; links agricultural productivity and urban expansion. First four chapters on medieval towns. [JML/LCA]

22.31 William L. Langer, ed. *The rise of modern Europe.* 20 vols. New York: Harper, 1936–85. ▸ Useful series of volumes covering successive periods of European history from Renaissance to mid-twentieth century. Individual titles listed separately. [PZ]

22.32 *The new Cambridge modern history.* Edition varies. 14 vols. Cambridge: Cambridge University Press, 1957–90. ▸ Collective work, with volumes organized chronologically, by international body of contributors, shorter than its predecessor (22.43). Indispensable reference. Individual titles listed separately. [PZ]

22.33 Jean F. O'Barr, Deborah Pope, and Mary Wyer, eds. *Ties that bind: essays on mothering and patriarchy.* Chicago: University of Chicago Press, 1990. ISBN 0-226-61545-6 (cl), 0-226-61546-4 (pbk). ▸ Useful collection investigating Western ideology of mothering through variety of sources, including children's books, medical writings, and psychological theory. [BYK]

22.34 Rozsika Parker and Griselda Pollock. *Old mistresses: woman, art, and ideology.* New York: Pantheon, 1981. ISBN 0-394-52430-6 (cl), 0-394-70814-8 (pbk). ▸ History of women artists from Middle Ages to modern times, as well as discussion of their historical treatment and ideological implications of their exclusion from canon. [GS]

22.35 Nikolaus Pevsner. *An outline of European architecture.* 1968 7th ed. Harmondsworth: Penguin, 1990. ISBN 0-14-013524-3.

‣ Concise illustrated survey of major buildings from ancient Greece to early twentieth century. [GS]

22.36 Nikolaus Pevsner, Peter Lasko, and Judy Nairn, eds. *The Pelican history of art.* 40 vols. London: Penguin, 1953–. ‣ Wide-ranging series by established scholars, many specific to individual areas or nations. Pertinent titles listed separately. [JML]

22.37 Stanley Sadie, ed. *Music and society.* 8 vols. Manchester and Englewood Cliffs, N.J.: Manchester University Press and Prentice-Hall, 1987–. ‣ Authoritative sociohistorical overviews of music and musical life, representing music history as series of responses to social, economic, and political circumstances, including religious and intellectual developments. Volumes treat chronological eras; chapters mainly examine single region, country, or city. Rich visual and bibliographical documentation; little discussion of musical style. Pertinent titles listed below. Some volumes published under British title, *Man and Music.* [RPL]

22.38 Stanley Sadie, ed. *The new Grove dictionary of musical instruments.* 3 vols. London: Macmillan, 1984. ISBN 0-943818-05-2. ‣ Greatly expanded entries from Sadie, ed. 22.39 on instrument manufacture and repertoire, plus many new entries. [RPL]

22.39 Stanley Sadie, ed. *The new Grove dictionary of music and musicians.* 1980 ed. 20 vols. London: Macmillan, 1985. ISBN 0-333-23111-2 (set). ‣ Fundamental reference work for historical information on musical life in various countries and cities at various times. Reliable composer biographies include lists of works and selective bibliographies. Articles on genres, aesthetics, instrument manufacture, repertoire, and historiography. [RPL]

22.40 Stanley Sadie, ed. *The new Grove dictionary of opera.* 4 vols. London: Macmillan, 1992. ISBN 0-935859-92-6 (set, cl), 0-333-48552-1 (set, pbk). ‣ Greatly expanded entries from Sadie, ed. 22.39 plus many new entries. [RPL]

22.41 Lawrence Stone, ed. *The university in society.* Vol. 1: *Oxford and Cambridge from the fourteenth to the early nineteenth century.* Vol. 2: *Europe, Scotland, and the United States from the sixteenth to the twentieth century.* Princeton: Princeton University Press, 1974. ISBN 0-691-05213-1 (v. 1), 0-691-05214-X (v. 2). ‣ Interesting essays on reform, resistance to change, and student rebellions. Traces vast increases in university enrollments after wars and revolutions. [DSC]

22.42 Marvin Trachtenberg and Isabelle Hyman. *Architecture, from prehistory to post-modernism: the Western tradition.* New York: Abrams, 1986. ISBN 0-8109-1077-2. ‣ Liberally illustrated survey focusing on buildings and formal issues rather than on architecture in its societal role. [GS]

22.43 A. W. Ward, G. W. Prothero, and Stanley Leathes, eds. *The Cambridge modern history.* 13 vols. Cambridge: Cambridge University Press, 1902–12. ‣ Famous collective work. Though largely outdated, some chapters may still be consulted for detailed narratives and historical insights. Full bibliographies. [PZ]

22.44 Piero Weiss and Richard Taruskin, eds. *Music in the Western world: a history in documents.* New York: Schirmer Books, 1984. ISBN 0-02-872910-2 (cl), 0-02-872900-5 (pbk). ‣ Primary sources, expertly translated and annotated, on musical life in court, church, concert hall, opera house, and bourgeois home. Especially rich on European composers after ca. 1600; their letters, polemical writings, and reactions to their work in press. [RPL]

22.45 J. A. Westrup et al., eds. *The new Oxford history of music.* Edition varies. 10 vols. London: Oxford University Press, 1954–90. ISBN 0-19-316329-2 (v. 2), 0-19-316305-5 (v. 5), 0-19-316306-3 (v. 6), 0-19-316307-1 (v. 7), 0-19-316308-X (v. 8), 0-19-316309-8 (v. 9), 0-19-316310-1 (v. 10). ‣ Standard multivolume history of music, mainly European. Specialist authors using copi-

ous musical examples to illustrate points about style. Pertinent titles listed separately. Companion *History of Music in Sound* available from same publisher (ten two-disc sets). [RPL]

22.46 Philip P. Wiener, ed. *Dictionary of the history of ideas: studies of selected pivotal ideas.* 5 vols. New York: Scribner's, 1973–74. ISBN 0-684-13293-1 (set). ‣ Essential reference work for both early modern and modern periods, containing useful entries with full bibliographies by expert contributors. Main emphasis on European ideas, especially since Enlightenment. [JML]

Geographies and Atlases

22.47 H. C. Darby and Harold Fullard, eds. *The new Cambridge modern history atlas.* Vol. 14 of *The new Cambridge modern history.* Rev. ed. Cambridge: Cambridge University Press, 1978. ISBN 0-521-09908-0 (pbk). ‣ Excellent atlas of comprehensive coverage, designed to accompany *The New Cambridge Modern History* (22.32). [PZ]

22.48 N.J.G. Pounds. *An historical geography of Europe.* Cambridge: Cambridge University Press, 1990. ISBN 0-521-32217-0 (cl), 0-521-31109-8 (pbk). ‣ Useful reference work combining economic, demographic, and environmental history in geographic presentation. [DSC]

22.49 F. W. Putzger. *Historischer Weltatlas.* 1961 rev. ed. Alfred von Hansel and Walter Leisering, eds. Bielefeld: Velhagen & Klasing, 1965. ‣ Standard reference, regularly updated in successive editions. [PZ]

22.50 William R. Shepherd. *Shepherd's historical atlas.* 9th rev. ed. Totowa, N.J.: Barnes & Noble, 1980. ISBN 0-389-20155-3. ‣ One of best historical atlases. Contains maps relating mainly to period prior to World War I with small number of additional maps for interwar and post–World War II years. [PZ]

WESTERN EUROPE, 1500–1789

General Studies and Political, Diplomatic, and Military History

22.51 Matthew S. Anderson. *Europe in the eighteenth century, 1713–1783.* 3d ed. London: Longman, 1987. ISBN 0-582-00115-3 (cl), 0-582-49389-7 (pbk). ‣ Excellent study, embracing society, economy, political history, education, Enlightenment, and religion. [PZ]

22.52 Perry Anderson. *Lineages of the absolutist state.* 1974 ed. London: Verso, 1979. ISBN 0-86091-710-X. ‣ Stimulating Marxist account of development of absolutism in Europe, stressing its organic relationship to late stage of feudal society. [PZ]

22.53 Edward Armstrong. *The emperor Charles V.* 1910 2d ed. 2 vols. London: Macmillan, 1929. ‣ Scholarly political biography of Charles V and account of his reign over his many realms; now somewhat dated. [PZ]

22.54 T. H. Aston, ed. *Crisis in Europe.* 1965 ed. Garden City, N.Y.: Anchor, 1967. ‣ Interesting group of essays by various scholars, debating question of crisis of economy, society, and state as explanation of revolutions that occurred in number of countries in mid-seventeenth century. [PZ]

22.55 J.N.L. Baker. *A history of geographical discovery and exploration.* Rev. ed. New York: Cooper Square, 1967. ‣ Scholarly survey devoted mainly to Western discovery and exploration from fifteenth to twentieth century, describing advance of geographical knowledge and many voyages of exploration in all parts of world. Well provided with maps. [PZ]

22.56 Jeremy Black. *The rise of the European powers, 1679–1793.* London: Arnold, 1990. ISBN 0-7131-6537-5. ‣ Interesting survey arguing for diversity and unpredictability of forces shaping diplomacy and international relations. [MM]

22.57 Richard Bonney. *The European dynastic states, 1494–1660.* Oxford: Oxford University Press, 1991. ISBN 0-19-873022-5 (cl), 0-19-873023-3 (pbk). ▸ Survey, mainly political, of states of early modern Europe. [PZ]

22.58 Fernand Braudel. *The Mediterranean and the Mediterranean world in the age of Philip II.* 2d rev. ed. 2 vols. Siân Reynolds, trans. New York: Harper & Row, 1977. ISBN 0-06-090566-2 (v. 1, pbk), 0-06-090567-0 (v. 2, pbk). ▸ Landmark study in originality and scope by leading scholar of French Annales school which attempts to embrace geography, economies, societies, states, and political history of sixteenth century Mediterranean world in a total synthesis. Although parts fail to cohere into single whole, still one of most important contributions to historiography of early modern Europe. [PZ]

22.59 J. S. Bromley, ed. *The rise of Great Britain and Russia, 1688–1715/25.* Vol. 6 of *The new Cambridge modern history.* Cambridge: Cambridge University Press, 1970. ▸ Wide-ranging collaborative work of reference an ' interpretation, treating evolving pattern of European power as well as economy, religion, cultural change, and science in late seventeenth and early eighteenth centuries. [PZ]

22.60 F. L. Carsten, ed. *The ascendancy of France, 1648–1688.* Vol. 5 of *The new Cambridge modern history.* Cambridge: Cambridge University Press, 1964. ▸ Essential work of reference and interpretation covering many aspects of seventeenth century. Centers on emergence of France in reign of Louis XIV as paramount European power. [PZ]

22.61 Charles Carter. *The western European powers, 1500–1700.* Ithaca, N.Y.: Cornell University Press, 1971. ISBN 0-8014-0631-5. ▸ Helpful guide to archival and printed sources of western European diplomacy and state relations in early modern period. [PZ]

22.62 G. N. Clark. *The seventeenth century.* 1947 2d ed. Westport, Conn.: Greenwood, 1981. ISBN 0-313-22765-9. ▸ Pioneering synthesis examining many aspects of seventeenth-century European civilization; now rather dated. [PZ]

22.63 J. P. Cooper, ed. *The decline of Spain and the Thirty Years' War, 1609–1648/59.* Vol. 4 of *The new Cambridge modern history.* Cambridge: Cambridge University Press, 1971. ▸ Basic work of reference and interpretation. Specialists discuss crisis of seventeenth century, politics, war, international relations, and other important aspects of earlier seventeenth century. [PZ]

22.64 Walter Louis Dorn. *Competition for empire, 1740–1763.* Vol. 9 of *The rise of modern Europe.* 1940 ed. New York: Harper & Row, 1963. ▸ Solid older account of rivalry of major European powers, emphasizing comparative constitutional history, military developments, and war. Includes discussion of Enlightenment. [PZ]

22.65 William Doyle. *The old European order, 1660–1800.* Oxford: Oxford University Press, 1978. ISBN 0-19-913073-6 (cl), 0-19-913131-7 (pbk). ▸ Survey of eighteenth-century society up to and including French Revolution, focusing on general economic, social, intellectual, and political changes that led to end of Old Regime. [PZ]

22.66 Richard S. Dunn. *The age of religious wars, 1559–1715.* 2d ed. New York: Norton, 1979. ISBN 0-393-05694-5 (cl), 0-393-09021-3 (pbk). ▸ Brief survey of religious conflicts in Europe unleashed by Reformation. Includes chapters on economic, political, and intellectual developments. [PZ]

22.67 John H. Elliott. *Europe divided, 1559–1598.* 1968 ed. Ithaca, N.Y.: Cornell University Press, 1982. ISBN 0-8014-9233-5 (pbk). ▸ Excellent account of international conflicts and religious divisions of later sixteenth century. [PZ]

22.68 John H. Elliott. *The Old World and the New, 1492–1650.* 1970 ed. Cambridge: Cambridge University Press, 1992. ISBN 0-521-42709-6 (pbk). ▸ Short, incisive discussion of intellectual, political, and economic impact of discovery of New World on Europe. [PZ/MAB]

22.69 G. R. Elton, ed. *The Reformation.* Vol. 2 of *The new Cambridge modern history.* 2d ed. Cambridge: Cambridge University Press, 1990. ISBN 0-521-34536-7. ▸ Basic reference work by number of specialists covering major aspects of religion, politics, and culture during first period of Reformation in various countries of Europe. [PZ]

22.70 Carl J. Friedrich. *The age of the baroque, 1610–1660.* Vol. 5 of *The rise of modern Europe.* 1952 ed. New York: Harper & Row, 1962. ▸ Survey of earlier part of seventeenth century. Overworks concept of baroque, applying it to politics, state, philosophy, and other subjects. [PZ]

22.71 Eduard Fueter. *Geschichte des europäischen Staatensystems von 1492 bis 1559.* 1919 ed. Osnabruck, Germany: Zeller, 1972. ▸ Valuable survey of emergent system of European state and great-power relations in earlier part of sixteenth century. [PZ]

22.72 Samuel R. Gardiner. *The Thirty Years' War, 1618–1648.* 1874 ed. St. Clair Shores, Mich.: Scholarly Press, 1972. ISBN 0-403-00604-X. ▸ Long outdated, but helpful as clear, brief account of origins, international complications, and main stages of Thirty Years' War. [PZ]

22.73 Leo Gershoy. *From despotism to revolution, 1763–1789.* Vol. 10 of *The rise of modern Europe.* 1944 ed. New York: Harper & Row, 1962. ▸ Excellent older account of enlightened despotism and political, social, and economic developments in France and Europe leading up to French Revolution. Needs to be supplemented by later scholarship on background and origins of French Revolution, subject of much new research and reinterpretation. [PZ]

22.74 Myron Gilmore. *The world of humanism, 1453–1517.* Vol. 2 of *The rise of modern Europe.* 1952 ed. Westport, Conn.: Greenwood, 1983. ISBN 0-313-24081-7. ▸ Perceptive survey of Renaissance culture, religion, and politics to eve of Reformation. [PZ]

22.75 John Francis Guilmartin, Jr. *Gunpower and galleys: changing technology and Mediterranean warfare at sea in the sixteenth century.* London: Cambridge University Press, 1974. ISBN 0-521-20272-8. ▸ Important account of nature and changing character of sea warfare in Mediterranean, including technical details on ships, ballistics, ordnance, and crews with accounts of major engagements such as Battle of Lepanto. [PZ]

22.76 John R. Hale. *War and society in Renaissance Europe, 1450–1620.* 1985 ed. Baltimore: Johns Hopkins University Press, 1986. ISBN 0-8018-3196-2 (pbk). ▸ Interesting discussion of effects of chronic warfare on society, government, technology, and military developments from Renaissance to beginning of seventeenth century. [PZ]

22.77 Fritz Hartung. *Enlightened despotism.* Geoffrey Barraclough, ed. H. Otto, trans. London: Routledge & Kegan Paul for Historical Association, 1957. (General series of the Historical Association, 36.) ▸ Short discussion of concept of enlightened despotism or absolutism in eighteenth-century Europe. Clarifies its meaning, which associates it with development of Enlightenment, and considers some of its manifestations and consequences in France, Prussia, and Austria. [PZ]

22.78 Henri Hauser. *La préponderance espagnole (1559–1660).* 1948 3d ed. Paris: Mouton, 1973. (Peuples et civilisations, 9.) ▸ Broad scholarly survey of century of Spanish monarchy's preponderance in Europe. Dated but may be consulted for reference. [PZ]

22.79 Henri Hauser and Augustin Renaudet. *Les débuts de l'âge moderne: la Renaissance et la Réforme.* 4th ed. Paris: Presses Universitaires de France, 1956. (Peuples et civilisations, 8.) ‣ Scholarly, comprehensive survey of emergence of modern world in Renaissance and Reformation. Dated in parts, but worth consulting as reference. [PZ]

22.80 Denys Hay. *Europe in the fourteenth and fifteenth centuries.* 2d ed. London: Longman, 1989. ISBN 0-582-48343-3 (cl), 0-582-49179-7 (pbk). ‣ Good survey by specialist in Renaissance history. Primarily concerned with northern Europe, theory and practice of government. Briefer coverage of social groups, religion, culture, and trade. [PZ/FLC]

22.81 Max Immich. *Geschichte des europäischen Staatensystems von 1660 bis 1789.* 1905 ed. Munich: Oldenbourg, 1967. ‣ Excellent survey of diplomatic history and European state system from mid-seventeenth century to eve of French Revolution. [PZ]

22.82 H. G. Koenigsberger, George L. Mosse, and G. Q. Bowler. *Europe in the sixteenth century.* 2d ed. London: Longman, 1989. ISBN 0-582-04615-7 (cl), 0-582-49390-0 (pbk). ‣ Broad survey of political, religious, and economic developments. [PZ]

22.83 Leonard Krieger. *Kings and philosophers, 1689–1789.* New York: Norton, 1970. ISBN 0-393-05415-2 (cl), 0-393-09905-9 (pbk). ‣ Survey of European states and monarchies and of thought and thinkers of Enlightenment. Focuses on enlightened despotism as last phase of prerevolutionary era in Europe. [PZ]

22.84 Donald L. Lach. *Asia in the making of Europe.* 2 vols. Chicago: University of Chicago Press, 1965. ‣ Remarkable original synthesis describing intellectual, cultural, and artistic consequences of European encounter with Asian societies and culture. [PZ]

22.85 Charles de Lannoy and Herman Van der Linden. *Histoire de l'expansion coloniale des peuples européens.* 3 vols. Brussels: Lamertin, 1907–21. ‣ Broad treatment of colonial expansion by Portugal, Spain, Netherlands, Denmark, and Sweden, including administration and economic life of colonies and effects of expansion on home countries. [PZ]

22.86 J. O. Lindsay, ed. *The Old Regime, 1713–1763.* Vol. 7 of *The new Cambridge modern history.* 1957 ed. Cambridge: Cambridge University Press, 1966. ‣ Basic work of reference and interpretation. Specialists cover economic and social change, governmental institutions, political history, diplomacy, religion, cultural developments, and Enlightenment. [PZ]

22.87 Garrett Mattingly. *Renaissance diplomacy.* 1955 ed. New York: Dover, 1988. ISBN 0-486-25570-0 (pbk). ‣ Important study of great power relations in Renaissance Italy and northern Europe and of evolution of diplomatic institutions, including resident ambassadors and international law. [PZ]

22.88 John Miller, ed. *Absolutism in seventeenth-century Europe.* New York: St. Martin's, 1990. ISBN 0-312-04930-7. ‣ Survey of fortunes of absolute monarchy in principal states by various scholars. Emphasis on diversity of situations. [MM]

22.89 Roland Mousnier. *Les seizième et dix-septième siècles: les progrès de la civilisation européene et le declin de l'Orient (1492–1715).* 2d rev. ed. Paris: Presses Universitaires de France, 1956. ‣ Wide survey; includes considerable social and economic history, emphasizing factors leading to Europe's world supremacy. [PZ]

22.90 Roland Mousnier and Ernest Labrousse. *Le dix-huitième siècle: révolution intellectuelle, technique et politique (1715–1815).* 2d ed. Paris: Presses Universitaires de France, 1955. ‣ Survey of great breadth, encompassing Asia and America as well as Europe. Describes economic, technological, scientific, intellectual, and

political developments in century culminating in French Revolution and Napoleonic empire. [PZ]

22.91 Pierre Muret. *La prépondérance anglaise (1715–1763).* 3d rev. ed. Paris: Presses Universitaires de France, 1949. (Peuples et civilisations, 11.) ‣ Largely political survey of states of Europe, especially England and France, and of diplomatic and international relations to end of Seven Years' War. [PZ]

22.92 Frederick L. Nussbaum. *The triumph of science and reason, 1660–1685.* Vol. 6 of *The rise of modern Europe.* 1953 ed. New York: Harper Torchbooks, 1962. ‣ Wide treatment of later seventeenth century emphasizing economic change and development of science and scientific thought. [PZ]

22.93 Marvin O'Connell. *The Counter-Reformation, 1559–1610.* Vol. 4 of *The rise of modern Europe.* New York: Harper & Row, 1974. ISBN 0-06-013233-7. ‣ Good overview of religious and political response of Catholic church to challenge of Protestantism. [PZ]

22.94 David Ogg. *Europe in the seventeenth century.* 1960 8th rev. ed. New York: Collier, 1962. ‣ Admirable political history. Somewhat dated but still useful as survey. [PZ]

22.95 Steven E. Ozment. *The age of reform, 1250–1550: an intellectual and religious history of late medieval and Reformation Europe.* New Haven: Yale University Press, 1980. ISBN 0-300-02477-0 (cl), 0-300-02760-5 (pbk). ‣ Broad, learned study emphasizing religious and theological developments. First five chapters offer insightful interpretation of theology and religion from fourteenth to sixteenth century, arguing for continuities in how medieval and Reformation thinkers posed theological questions. [PZ/WJC]

22.96 Geoffrey Parker. *The military revolution: military innovation and the rise of the West, 1500–1800.* Cambridge: Cambridge University Press, 1988. ISBN 0-521-32607-9 (cl), 0-521-37680-7 (pbk). ‣ Discussion of debated concept of military revolution and scholarly study of changing methods and weapons of war on land and sea in early modern Europe, China, Japan, and India, which gave West military superiority and dominance in world. [PZ]

22.97 Geoffrey Parker, ed. *The Thirty Years' War.* 1987 rev. ed. New York: Military Heritage, 1988. ISBN 0-88029-296-2. ‣ Collection of studies by editor and nine other contributors. Analyzes and describes antecedents and stages of Thirty Years' War and sets conflict in its international context. Includes substantial bibliography. [PZ]

22.98 J. H. Parry. *The age of reconnaissance.* 2d ed. Berkeley: University of California Press, 1981. ISBN 0-520-04234-4 (cl), 0-520-04235-2 (pbk). ‣ Excellent, detailed study of European geographical discovery, trade, and settlement outside bounds of Europe from fifteenth to seventeenth century. Discusses conditions making expansion of Europe possible, including ships and seamanship. Account of discoveries and resulting creation of European and Western empires and colonies. Revision of 1963 classic by author who defined period. [PZ/MAB]

22.99 J. H. Parry. *Europe and a wider world, 1415–1715.* 3d rev. ed. London: Hutchinson University Library, 1966. ‣ Brief account of European discovery, exploration, and commerce in both Eastern and Western Hemispheres, together with development of European colonization and empire, trade wars, and introduction of slavery into the Americas. [PZ]

22.100 D. H. Pennington. *Europe in the seventeenth century.* 2d ed. London: Longman, 1989. ISBN 0-582-03449-3 (cl), 0-582-49388-9 (pbk). ‣ Wide treatment of political, religious, intellectual, and socioeconomic history of seventeenth-century Europe. Includes discussion of war, political thought, and science. [PZ]

22.101 Boies Penrose. *Travel and discovery in the Renaissance, 1420–1620.* 1952 ed. New York: Atheneum, 1962. ‣ Useful history of exploration and discovery recounting journeys of European travelers to remote and little-known places. Also discusses cartography and navigation. [PZ]

22.102 Walter Platzhoff. *Geschichte des europäischen Staatensystems von 1559 bis 1660.* Munich: Oldenbourg, 1928. ‣ Good study of European state system and international relations during century of Spain's preponderance and beginning of its decline. [PZ]

22.103 G. R. Potter, ed. *The Renaissance, 1493–1520.* Vol. 1 of *The new Cambridge modern history.* Cambridge: Cambridge University Press, 1957. ‣ Important reference work containing synthesis and interpretation of various aspects of Renaissance in Italy and northern Europe by a number of specialists. [PZ]

22.104 Theodore K. Rabb. *The struggle for stability in early modern Europe.* New York: Oxford University Press, 1975. ISBN 0-19-501956-3. ‣ Well-informed review and discussion of controversial issue of crisis in seventeenth century. Argues crisis consisted of major changes in politics, economy, and thought, precipitating breakdown of authority and stability; resolved through emergence of new equilibrium toward end of century. Good bibliographical notes. [PZ]

22.105 Leopold von Ranke. *History of the Latin and Teutonic nations, 1494–1514.* 1909 ed. G. R. Dennis, trans. New York: AMS Press, 1976. ISBN 0-404-09258-6. ‣ First work (1824) on modern European history by master of nineteenth-century historiography. Contains famous appendix on sources. [PZ]

22.106 Eugene F. Rice, Jr. *The foundations of early modern Europe, 1460–1559.* New York: Norton, 1970. ISBN 0-393-05420-9 (cl), 0-393-09898-2 (pbk). ‣ Brief survey of Renaissance and Reformation discussing major aspects of period and tracing main lines of change. [PZ]

22.107 Penfield Roberts. *The quest for security, 1715–1740.* Vol. 8 of *The rise of modern Europe.* 1947 ed. New York: Harper & Row, 1963. ‣ Survey of period of transition from end of Louis XIV's reign. Discussions of politics, economics, ideas, arts, and balance of power. [PZ]

22.108 Philippe Sagnac. *La fin de l'ancien régime et la Révolution Americaine (1763–1789).* 3d rev. ed. Paris: Presses Universitaires de France, 1952. (Peuples et civilisations, 12.) ‣ Broad political and diplomatic survey of Europe and American Revolution. Final chapter on economy, culture, art, and ideas. [PZ]

22.109 Philippe Sagnac. *Louis XIV (1661–1714): la prépondérance française.* 3d ed. Paris: Presses Universitaires de France, 1949. (Peuples et civilisations, 10.) ‣ Old-fashioned comprehensive treatment of European history during reign of Louis XIV and French ascendancy. [PZ]

22.110 Lewis W. Spitz. *The Protestant Reformation, 1517–1559.* Vol. 3 of *The rise of modern Europe.* 1985 ed. New York: Harper, 1987. ISBN 0-06-132069-2 (pbk). ‣ Solid account of background, beginning, and spread of Reformation in Europe. Includes chapter on Catholic revival. [PZ]

22.111 Franco Venturi. *The end of the Old Regime in Europe, 1768–1776.* 2 vols. R. Burr Litchfield, trans. Princeton: Princeton University Press, 1989–91. ISBN 0-691-03156-8 (v. 1), 0-691-03157-6 (v. 2). ‣ Important scholarship by leading Italian historian of eighteenth century and Enlightenment. Discusses conflicts and other developments in many states of Europe, from Russia to Britain, in last years of Old Regime. [PZ]

22.112 R. B. Wernham, ed. *The Counter-Reformation and the price revolution, 1559–1610.* Vol. 3 of *The new Cambridge modern history.* Cambridge: Cambridge University Press, 1968. ‣ Essential reference work by number of specialists, providing wide survey of religious, political, intellectual, and economic developments in second half of sixteenth century. [PZ]

22.113 John B. Wolf. *The emergence of the great powers, 1685–1715.* Vol. 7 of *The rise of modern Europe.* 1951 ed. Westport, Conn.: Greenwood, 1983. ISBN 0-313-24088-4. ‣ Useful survey focusing on war and diplomacy; discussions also of science, religion, and culture. [PZ]

22.114 Isser Woloch. *Eighteenth-century Europe: tradition and progress, 1715–1789.* New York: Norton, 1982. ISBN 0-393-01506-8 (cl), 0-393-95214-2 (pbk). ‣ Brief survey of European states and society in eighteenth century. Considerable attention to economic changes, culture, intellectual developments, and dynamic elements of the time that led to crisis of Old Regime and French Revolution. [PZ]

22.115 Perez Zagorin. *Rebels and rulers.* 2 vols. Cambridge: Cambridge University Press, 1982. ISBN 0-521-24472-2 (v. 1, cl), 0-521-24473-0 (v. 2, cl), 0-521-28711-1 (v. 1, pbk), 0-521-28712-x (v. 2, pbk). ‣ Comparative history of revolutions in early modern Europe centered on England, France, and Spanish empire. Proposes typology of revolutions; discusses political, social, economic, and ideological contexts of early modern revolutions; and presents account of some of greater revolutionary struggles of period. [PZ]

22.116 Gaston Zeller. *Le temps modernes.* Vol. 1: *De Christophe Colombe à Cromwell.* Paris: Hachette, 1953. ‣ Good survey of European international relations and conflicts from 1492 to 1660. [PZ]

22.117 Gaston Zeller. *Les temps modernes.* Vol. 2: *De Louis XIV à 1789.* Paris: Hachette, 1955. ‣ Lucid, precise account of rivalries, conflicts, and diplomacy of European states from France's ascendancy under Louis XIV to eve of French Revolution. [PZ]

SEE ALSO
  30.15 Karl Brandi. *The emperor Charles V.*
  30.98 C.B.A. Behrens. *Society, government, and the Enlightenment.*

The Reformation, Churches, and Religion

22.118 Roland H. Bainton. *The Reformation of the sixteenth century.* Rev. ed. Boston: Beacon, 1985. ISBN 0-8070-1301-3. ‣ Short, well-informed survey of Protestant Reformation by one of foremost twentieth-century historians of subject. [PZ]

22.119 Roland H. Bainton. *The travail of religious liberty: nine biographical studies.* 1951 ed. Hamden, Conn.: Archon, 1971. ISBN 0-208-01085-8. ‣ Brief account of religious persecution and development of ideas of religious toleration, centering on number of writers of sixteenth and seventeenth centuries, including Castellio, Milton, Williams, and Locke. [PZ]

22.120 Heinrich Boehmer. *The Jesuits: an historical study.* 1928 4th rev. ed. Paul Zeller Strodach, trans. New York: Gordon, 1975. ISBN 0-87968-199-3. ‣ Short account of Jesuit order and its character in sixteenth and seventeenth centuries by German Protestant scholar. [PZ]

22.121 William J. Bouwsma. *John Calvin: a sixteenth-century portrait.* New York: Oxford University Press, 1988. ISBN 0-19-504394-4. ‣ Attempt by prominent scholar to set Calvin's life in context of his times. Provocative psychological thesis. [JML]

22.122 James Brodrick. *The origin of the Jesuits.* 1940 ed. Chicago: Loyola University Press, 1986. ISBN 0-8294-0522-4. ‣ Jesuit historian's short account of beginning of Jesuit order and of its founder, Loyola, and its first members. [PZ]

22.123 James Brodrick. *The progress of the Jesuits (1556–1579).* 1947 ed. Chicago: Loyola University Press, 1986. ISBN 0-8294-0523-2. ‣ Sequel to preceding work (22.122), surveying various activities of Jesuit order and some of its leading figures. [PZ]

22.124 John Calvin. *Institutes of the Christian religion.* 2 vols. John

T. McNeill, ed. Ford Lewis Battles, trans. Philadelphia: Westminster Press, 1960. ▸ Best English-language edition of basic document of sixteenth-century Protestantism, crucially important as systematization of Protestant doctrine by greatest reformer of generation following Luther. [PZ]

22.125 Euan Cameron. *The European Reformation*. Oxford: Clarendon, 1991. ISBN 0-19-873094-2 (cl), 0-19-873093-4 (pbk). ▸ Overview of Protestant Reformation in Europe during sixteenth century. Excellent introduction to current debates. [PZ/TAB]

22.126 Owen Chadwick. *The Reformation*. 1972 rev. ed. Harmondsworth: Penguin, 1990. ISBN 0-14-020504-7. ▸ Discussion of religious change during Reformation and Counter-Reformation. Stresses doctrine and developments in church. [PZ]

22.127 Jean Delumeau. *Catholicism between Luther and Voltaire: a new view of the Counter-Reformation*. Philadelphia: Westminster, 1977. ISBN 0-664-21341-3. ▸ Study of Counter-Reformation focusing on developments within Catholic church. Distinctive approach; conceives revival of Catholicism as spread of christianization and gives considerable attention to religious sociology and collective psychology in estimating effect of these changes on average believer. [PZ/RMG]

22.128 A. G. Dickens. *The Counter-Reformation*. New York: Harcourt Brace & World, 1969. ▸ Brief survey of Catholic revival in sixteenth century, seen as product of internal impulsion toward reform and as response to challenge of Protestantism. [PZ]

22.129 A. G. Dickens. *Reformation and society in sixteenth-century Europe*. New York: Harcourt Brace & World, 1966. ▸ Concise introductory account by leading scholar of social, political, and intellectual aspects of Reformation. [JML]

22.130 A. G. Dickens and John Tonkin. *The Reformation in historical thought*. Cambridge, Mass.: Harvard University Press, 1985. ISBN 0-674-75311-9. ▸ Valuable survey of historical interpretations of Reformation from sixteenth century to present. [PZ]

22.131 Jane Dempsey Douglass. *Women, freedom, and Calvin*. Philadelphia: Westminster, 1985. ISBN 0-664-24663-x. ▸ Elegant analysis of Calvin's thought; takes Calvin to task for not pursuing implications of ideas. Treats question of women's proper role in church, based on Calvin's idea of Christian freedom. Only sixteenth-century theologian to view women's roles as matters pertaining to human, not divine, law. [BYK/MW]

22.132 H. Outram Evennett. *The spirit of the Counter-Reformation*. 1968 ed. John Bossy, ed. Notre Dame, Ind.: University of Notre Dame Press, 1970. ISBN 0-268-00425-0 (pbk). ▸ Excellent lectures defining character of Counter-Reformation and discussing some of its manifestations in internal reform and religious life of Catholic church. [PZ]

22.133 Philip Hughes. *The revolt against the church: Aquinas to Luther*. Vol. 3 of *A history of the church*. 1947 ed. London: Sheed & Ward, 1979. ISBN 0-7220-7983-4 (v. 3). ▸ Well-informed, fair-minded treatment of Reformation by Catholic scholar. [PZ]

22.134 Albert Hyma. *The Christian renaissance*. 2d ed. Hamden, Conn.: Archon, 1965. ▸ Examination of Dutch Brethren of the Common Life's insistence on return to simple apostolic life. Five chapters respond to controversy initially raised by author's inclusion of Protestant Reformation within his account of Devotio Moderna, late medieval lay pietistic movement. [JML/FHS]

22.135 Joyce L. Irwin. *Womanhood in radical Protestantism, 1525–1675*. New York: Mellen, 1979. ISBN 0-88946-549-5 (cl), 0-88946-547-9 (pbk). ▸ Collection of documents and commentary on women's active role in sectarian Protestantism. Explores why sectarian tendencies toward leveling of social distinctions did not change overall attitudes toward status of women. Good sur-

vey of ideas from wing of Reformation for whom position and role of women were most problematic. [BYK/MW]

22.136 Hubert Jedin. *A history of the Council of Trent*. 2 vols. Ernest Graf, trans. London: Nelson, 1957–61. ▸ Major scholarly study of origin, background, and earlier phases of Council of Trent, one of major events of Catholic and Counter-Reformation. [PZ]

22.137 B. J. Kidd, ed. *Documents illustrative of the continental Reformation*. 1911 ed. Oxford: Clarendon, 1967. ▸ Large, useful collection of sources, many untranslated, covering careers of Luther, Zwingli, and Calvin and Protestant Reformation in Germany, Switzerland, Netherlands, Scotland, and other countries of northern Europe. Excludes England. [PZ]

22.138 Joseph Lecler. *Toleration and the Reformation*. 2 vols. T. L. Westow, trans. London: Longman, 1960. ▸ Standard, detailed account of development of principle and practice of religious toleration in sixteenth and seventeenth centuries. Includes discussion of many different writers. [PZ/TAB]

22.139 Émile G. Léonard. *A history of Protestantism*. 2 vols. H. H. Rowley, ed. Joyce M. H. Reid, trans. Indianapolis: Bobbs Merrill, 1967–68. ▸ Scholarly account of Protestantism from emergence and spread of Lutheranism and Calvinism in sixteenth century through its establishment and subsequent fortunes in seventeenth century, including its situation in France and during Thirty Years' War. [PZ]

22.140 Ignatius Loyola. *The spiritual exercises of St. Ignatius: based on studies in the language of the autograph*. Louis J. Puhl, trans. Chicago: Loyola University Press, 1951. ▸ Work of Catholic spiritual instruction by founder of Jesuit order. Important as historical document because of its use in training members of order, as well as for its role in religious life of lay Catholics. [PZ]

22.141 Martin Luther. *Three treatises*. 1970 2d rev. ed. Charles M. Jacobs, A.T.W. Steinhauser, and W. A. Lambert, eds. Philadelphia: Fortress, 1988. ISBN 0-8006-1639-1. ▸ Translation of essential source in development of Protestantism, three treatises written by Luther in 1520: "To the Christian Nobility of the German Nation," "The Babylonian Captivity of the Church," and "The Freedom of the Christian." [PZ]

22.142 Sherrin Marshall, ed. *Women in Reformation and Counter-Reformation Europe: public and private worlds*. Bloomington: Indiana University Press, 1989. ISBN 0-253-33678-3 (cl), 0-253-20527-1 (pbk). ▸ Studies of women's experience of religious change extracted from legal records and other sources. Covers variety of social groups, periods, and locales. Essays vary from descriptive to analytical but all are accessible to general reader. [BYK/MW]

22.143 John T. McNeill. *The history and character of Calvinism*. 1954 ed. New York: Oxford University Press, 1967. ▸ Important synthesis and interpretation of Calvin's career and beliefs and spread of Calvinism in Europe and North America. Attempts to understand spirit and significance of Calvinism both in past and in twentieth century. [PZ]

22.144 Ludwig von Pastor. *The history of the popes from the close of the Middle Ages, drawn from the secret archives of the Vatican and other original sources*. 1891–1953 ed. 40 vols. Frederick I. Antrobus et al., eds. Nendeln, Liechtenstein: Kraus Reprint, 1969. ▸ Indispensable work by German Catholic historian based on many sources in Vatican and other collections. Detailed account of activity of popes within church and in role as sovereigns in politics and international relations of Italy and Europe. Much information on personalities and on theological and ecclesiastical controversies. [PZ]

22.145 Menna Prestwich, ed. *International Calvinism, 1541–1715*. Oxford: Clarendon, 1985. ISBN 0-19-821933-4. ▸ Scholarly essays, by various authors, surveying history of Calvinism in certain countries from its beginnings in Geneva to early eighteenth century. Important essays on French Calvinism, French Calvinist political thought, and revocation of the Edict of Nantes. [PZ/RMG]

22.146 Leopold von Ranke. *History of the popes: their church and state.* Rev. ed. 3 vols. E. Fowler, trans. New York: Colonial, 1901. ▸ Classic (first published 1830s) by famous German historian. Learned account of individual popes and their religious and political activities during Reformation and Counter-Reformation, written in spirit of objectivity and based on extensive critical use of sources. [PZ]

22.147 Ernst Troeltsch. *The social teachings of the Christian churches.* 1931 ed. 2 vols. Olive Wyon, trans. Louisville, Ky.: Westminster and John Knox, 1992. ISBN 0-664-25320-2 (set), 0-664-25318-0 (v. 1), 0-664-25319-9 (v. 2). ▸ Profound, learned study of sociology and social doctrines of Christian churches and denominations in Middle Ages and early modern era. Reflects influence of Max Weber and contrasts church and sect as distinctive types of religious association and organization. [PZ]

22.148 Paul Van Dyke. *Ignatius Loyola, the founder of the Jesuits.* 1926 ed. Port Washington, N.Y.: Kennikat, 1968. ▸ Fair and discerning biography by Protestant scholar of one of foremost figures of Catholic Reformation and Counter-Reformation. [PZ]

22.149 Earl M. Wilbur. *A history of Unitarianism.* 1945–62 ed. 2 vols. Boston: Beacon, 1965. ▸ Scholarly study of origins, development, and theological conceptions of anti-Trinitarian groups such as Socinians that were part of Protestant Reformation and gave rise to modern Unitarianism. [PZ]

22.150 Leopold Willaert. *Après le Concile de Trent: la restauration Catholique, 1563–1648.* Paris: Bloud & Gay, 1960. ▸ Catholic scholar's synthesis of history of Catholic church and revival of Catholicism in century following Council of Trent. [PZ]

22.151 George Huntston Williams. *The radical Reformation.* 3d rev. ed. Kirksville, Mo.: Sixteenth Century Journal, 1992. ISBN 0-940474-15-8. ▸ Important scholarly work, presenting typology and survey of evangelical, spiritualist, and sectarian groups, denominations, and individual thinkers that were outside mainstream Protestantism and comprised radical wing of Reformation. [PZ/TAB]

22.152 George Huntston Williams and Angel M. Mergal, eds. *Spiritual and Anabaptist writers: documents illustrative of the radical Reformation and evangelical Catholicism.* Philadelphia: Westminster, 1957. ▸ Valuable collection of writings, preceded by good introduction, of several sixteenth-century authors whose unorthodox beliefs placed them outside mainstream of Protestant Reformation. Includes selections from Thomas Müntzer, Sebastian Franck, Menno Simons, Juan de Valdés, and others. [PZ]

SEE ALSO
27.294 G. R. Potter. *Zwingli.*
30.8 Roland H. Bainton. *Here I stand.*
30.36 Steven E. Ozment. *Mysticism and dissent.*

Cultural and Intellectual History and Political Thought

22.153 J. W. Allen. *History of political thought in the sixteenth century.* Rev. ed. Totowa, N.J.: Rowman & Littlefield, 1977. ISBN 0-87471-885-6. ▸ Discussion of work of major and lesser-known figures based on careful readings of texts. Sections on Lutheranism, Calvinism, England, France, and Italy; does not include Spanish thinkers. [JML]

22.154 P. S. Allen. *The age of Erasmus: lectures delivered in the universities of Oxford and London.* 1914 ed. New York: Russell & Russell, 1963. ▸ Classic reconstruction of Erasmus's social world by great Erasmus scholar. Sections on educational and religious

institutions, private life, and pilgrimages. Identifies Renaissance as major turning point. [JML]

22.155 Roland H. Bainton. *Erasmus of Christendom.* 1969 ed. New York: Crossroad, 1982. ISBN 0-8245-0415-1 (pbk). ▸ Straightforward, approachable biography emphasizing Erasmus's place in Reformation. Analyses of his major works. [JML]

22.156 Carl L. Becker. *The heavenly city of the eighteenth-century philosophers.* 1932 ed. New Haven: Yale University Press, 1977. ISBN 0-300-00017-0 (pbk). ▸ Stimulating discussion advancing doubtful thesis that utopian vision of philosophy of Enlightenment represented reformulation of Augustinian-medieval idea of city of God. [PZ]

22.157 Isaiah Berlin, ed. *The age of Enlightenment: the eighteenth-century philosophers.* 1956 ed. New York: Oxford University Press, 1979. ISBN 0-19-215857-0. ▸ Selections from John Locke, Voltaire, George Berkeley, David Hume, Thomas Reid, Étienne Bonnot de Mably de Condillac, Julien Offray de La Mettrie, Johann Georg Hamann, and Georg Christoph Lichtenberg, with commentary. Emphasis on British empiricists, their disciples, and critics. Useful, basic collection. [JML]

22.158 R. R. Bolgar. *The classical heritage and its beneficiaries: from the Carolingian age to the end of the Renaissance.* 1954 ed. New York: Harper & Row, 1964. ▸ Traces influence of Greco-Roman heritage on Byzantium, Middle Ages, and Renaissance. Stresses importance of needs of education in response to that heritage. Argues for uniqueness of Renaissance approach to classics. [JML]

22.159 Peter Burke. *Popular culture in early modern Europe.* 1978 ed. Aldershot, England: Wildwood House; distributed by Gower, 1988. ISBN 0-7045-0596-7. ▸ Wide-ranging history of popular meanings, attitudes, values, and symbolic forms, tracing interaction and eventual separation of elite and nonelite traditions. Deals with effects of Puritanism, literacy, and commercial revolution on popular culture. [JML]

22.160 John Burns and Mark Goldie, ed. *The Cambridge history of political thought, 1450–1700.* Cambridge: Cambridge University Press, 1991. ISBN 0-521-24716-0. ▸ Basic reference work with valuable bibliography and chapters by various authors discussing many major and minor political thinkers and ideas of early modern era, including Machiavelli, Jean Bodin, Hugo Grotius, Thomas Hobbes, Benedict de Spinoza, and John Locke. [PZ]

22.161 Edwin Arthur Burtt. *The metaphysical foundations of modern physical science.* 1952 rev. ed. Atlantic Highlands, N.J.: Humanities Press, 1989. ISBN 0-391-01742-X. ▸ Lucid discussion of philosophical underpinnings of early modern science and evolution of Newtonian metaphysics from Copernicus to Newton. [JML]

22.162 J. B. Bury. *The idea of progress: an inquiry into its origin and growth.* 1932 rev. ed. Charles A. Beard, Introduction. New York: Dover, 1987. ISBN 0-486-25421-6 (pbk). ▸ Classic, still useful, placing origin of idea of progress in Enlightenment; ranges over European thought from Machiavelli to twentieth century. [JML]

22.163 Pierce Butler. *The origin of printing in Europe.* Chicago: University of Chicago Press, 1940. ▸ Detailed look at determining effects of mechanical process on early stages of printing. Useful account of early printing technology. [JML]

22.164 Herbert Butterfield. *The origins of modern science, 1300–1800.* 1957 rev. ed. New York: Free Press, 1966. ▸ Classic, pioneering work, identifying scientific revolution as locus of transition to modernity. Concentration on pivotal events that changed mentality. History of ideas approach. [JML]

22.165 Ernst Cassirer. *The individual and the cosmos in Renais-*

sance philosophy. 1963 ed. Mario Domandi, trans. Philadelphia: University of Pennsylvania Press, 1972. ISBN 0-8122-1036-0. ‣ Classic discussion of philosophical thought of Renaissance, giving particular attention to ideas of Nicholas of Cusa. [PZ]

22.166 Ernst Cassirer. *The philosophy of the Enlightenment.* 1951 ed. Fritz C. A. Koelln and James P. Pettegrove, trans. Princeton: Princeton University Press, 1979. ISBN 0-691-07150-0 (cl), 0-691-01963-0 (pbk). ‣ Philosophical and historical discussion of Enlightenment as turning point in development of modern consciousness. Sections on natural science, psychology and epistemology, religion, historiography, political science, and aesthetics. In-depth, rather than broad, survey. [JML]

22.167 Ernst Cassirer, Paul Oskar Kristeller, and John Herman Randall, Jr., eds. *The Renaissance philosophy of man.* 1948 ed. Chicago: University of Chicago Press, 1967. ‣ Valuable source collection, consisting of short treatises by six Renaissance thinkers, Petrarch, Marsilio Ficino, Pico della Mirandola, Lorenzo Valla, Pietro Pomponazzi, and Juan Luis Vives. Includes valuable introduction and prefaces by editors and translators. [PZ]

22.168 Norman Cohn. *Europe's inner demons: an enquiry inspired by the great witch-hunt.* New York: Basic Books, 1975. ISBN 0-465-02131-X. ‣ Provocative, controversial study of witchcraft to fifteenth century. Identifies and evaluates claim that witch hunters attacked certain social groups. Argues marginalization of abhorrent social groups predates Middle Ages and that medieval witch hunters expressed own fears and anxieties in this framework. [JML/FHS]

22.169 Gerald R. Cragg. *The church and the age of reason, 1648–1789.* Rev. ed. Harmondsworth: Penguin, 1970. ISBN 0-14-020505-5 (pbk). ‣ Brief survey of church history covering Europe, Catholicism, and Protestant denominations. Stresses encroachment made on Christianity by rationalism and Enlightenment. [PZ]

22.170 Robert Darnton. *The business of enlightenment: a publishing history of the Encyclopédie, 1775–1800.* Cambridge, Mass.: Belknap, 1979. ISBN 0-674-08785-2. ‣ Detailed information on eighteenth-century publishing and book trades, centering on publication of great French *Encyclopedia.* Discussion of relationship of publishing to early modern economy and politics, penetration of Enlightenment ideas, and their connection with French Revolution. [JML]

22.171 Jean Delumeau. *Sin and fear: the emergence of a Western guilt culture, 13th–18th centuries.* 1990 ed. Eric Nicholson, trans. New York: St. Martin's, 1991. ISBN 0-312-03582-9 (cl, 1990), 0-312-05800-4 (pbk). ‣ Examination of unprecedented emphasis on guilt and shame in early modern period as part of movement toward introspection and development of new moral conscience. Discusses both Catholic and Protestant thought in massive, wide-ranging study. [JML]

22.172 Elizabeth L. Eisenstein. *The printing press as an agent of change: communications and cultural transformations in early modern Europe.* 2 vols. Cambridge: Cambridge University Press, 1979. ISBN 0-521-22044-0 (set). ‣ Comprehensive study of printing press as chief agent of revolutionary change in Renaissance, Reformation, and Scientific Revolution. Narrow in focus; omits reciprocal effects of events on printing. Despite much criticism, worth exploring. [JML/KZ/BSH]

22.173 Desiderius Erasmus. *The correspondence of Erasmus.* 11 vols. to date. R.A.B. Mynors and D.F.S. Thomson, trans. Ann Arbor and Toronto: UMI Books on Demand and University of Toronto Press, 1974–. ISBN 0-8357-4724-7 (v. 1), 0-8020-1983-8 (v. 2), 0-8020-2202-2 (v. 3), 0-8020-5366-1 (v. 4), 0-8020-5429-3 (v. 5), 0-8020-5500-1 (v. 6), 0-8020-5607-5 (v. 7), 0-8020-2607-9 (v. 8), 0-8020-2604-4 (v. 9), 0-8020-5976-7 (v. 10), 0-8020-0536-5 (v. 11). ‣ Scholarly English-language edition of

essential documentary source for life and activities of greatest humanist scholar of sixteenth century and for many aspects of humanistic culture of his time. Work in progress. [PZ]

22.174 Lucien Febvre. *The problem of unbelief in the sixteenth century: the religion of Rabelais.* Beatrice Gottlieb, trans. Cambridge, Mass.: Harvard University Press, 1982. ISBN 0-674-70825-3 (cl), 0-674-70826-1 (pbk). ‣ Classic Annales reconstruction of mentality of sixteenth century, arguing for impossibility of religious unbelief at that time. Suggests scientific revolution as watershed between medieval and modern mentalities. [JML]

22.175 Margaret W. Ferguson, Maureen Quilligan, and Nancy J. Vickers, eds. *Rewriting the Renaissance: the discourses of sexual difference in early modern Europe.* Chicago: University of Chicago Press, 1986. ISBN 0-226-24313-3 (cl), 0-226-24314-1 (pbk). ‣ Stimulating collection of revisionist feminist scholarship focusing on relations between men and women of Renaissance era, and featuring differences according to gender, race, and class. Explores literary texts and art to identify coded language and visual symbols pertaining to women, gender, and sexual difference. [BYK]

22.176 Wallace K. Ferguson. *The Renaissance in historical thought: five centuries of interpretation.* Boston: Houghton-Mifflin, 1948. ‣ Essential discussion of formation and development of historical concept of Renaissance in work of many different scholars and thinkers. [PZ]

22.177 John Neville Figgis. *The divine right of kings.* 1965 2d rev. ed. Gloucester, Mass.: Smith, 1970. ‣ History of ideas of divinely ordained monarchy, hereditary right, and nonresistance from Middle Ages to eighteenth century. Argues idea of divine right arose from necessity and had beneficial effect on politics. Classic work. [JML]

22.178 John Neville Figgis. *Political thought from Gerson to Grotius, 1414–1625.* New York: Harper, 1960. ‣ Old but still valuable discussion of major thinkers and bodies of ideas on nature of authority and on relationships between church and state, individual and society. Focuses on transition of initiative from church to state. [JML]

22.179 Michel Foucault. *Madness and civilization: a history of insanity in the age of reason.* 1965 ed. Richard Howard, trans. New York: Vintage, 1973. ISBN 0-394-71914-X. ‣ History of madness, 1500 to early nineteenth century. Traces idea of madness from medieval acceptance through Renaissance "ship of fools" to modern separation of insane in asylums. Influential, controversial thesis that each age's culture is defined by limits of its language and its consciousness of the unspeakable. Also inspired extensive scholarship in history of psychiatry. [JML/CH]

22.180 Peter Gay. *The Enlightenment: an interpretation.* 1966–69 ed. 2 vols. New York: Norton, 1977. ISBN 0-393-00870-3 (v. 1, pbk), 0-393-00875-4 (v. 2, pbk). ‣ Enlightenment as precursor of modernity. Criticizes Becker's thesis (22.156). Examination of relationship between Enlightenment thinkers and wider culture. Emphasis on progress as both idea and practical program. Witty and provocative. [JML]

22.181 Otto Gierke. *Natural law and the theory of society, 1500–1800.* 1934 ed. 2 vols. Ernest Barker, trans. Boston: Beacon, 1957. ‣ Work by great German scholar tracing influence of idea of natural law on general theories of human nature and society. Organicist approach to state development. [JML]

22.182 Lucien Goldmann. *The philosophy of the Enlightenment: the Christian burgess and the Enlightenment.* Henry Maas, trans. Cambridge, Mass.: MIT Press, 1973. ISBN 0-262-07060-X. ‣ Marxian study of tension between Enlightenment individualism and Christian doctrine. Traces connection between Christianity,

Enlightenment thought, and Marxism. Brief but stimulating analysis. [JML]

22.183 Anthony Grafton and Lisa Jardine. *From humanism to the humanities: education and the liberal arts in fifteenth- and sixteenth-century Europe.* Cambridge, Mass.: Harvard University Press, 1986. ISBN 0-674-32460-9. ▸ History of humanist education from Guarino to Justus Lipsius; chapters on selected figures and aspects of Italian and European schools. Argues that success came from its attraction for ruling elites rather than intrinsic worth or utility. Polemical work; view not widely accepted. [JML/PFG]

22.184 A. Rupert Hall. *The revolution in science, 1500–1750.* 3d ed. London: Longman, 1983. ISBN 0-582-49133-9 (pbk). ▸ Third edition of 1954 textbook. Traces shift from magic to rational science. Treats natural sciences topically and chronologically; omits mathematics and medicine. Unabashed positivist interpretation of scientific revolution as progress of value-free knowledge of nature. [JML/MHS]

22.185 Norman Hampson. *A cultural history of the Enlightenment.* New York: Pantheon, 1968. ▸ Enlightenment as way of life; emphasis on France. Analysis of its concepts of time and its political impact. Encyclopedic range. [JML]

22.186 E. Harris Harbison. *The Christian scholar in the age of the Reformation.* New York: Scribner's, 1956. ▸ Erasmus, Luther, and Calvin as Christian intellectuals. Written from Protestant perspective. [JML]

22.187 Paul Hazard. *The European mind: the critical years, 1680–1715.* 1953 ed. J. Lewis May, trans. New York: Fordham University Press, 1990. ISBN 0-8232-1274-2. ▸ Learned, stimulating discussion, locating genesis of Enlightenment and intimations of romantic thinking in erosion of classicism and rise of individualism. Emphasis on Pierre Bayle, Jacques Benique Bossuet, Gottfried Wilhelm von Leibnitz, and John Locke. [JML]

22.188 Paul Hazard. *European thought in the eighteenth century: from Montesquieu to Lessing.* 1954 ed. J. Lewis May, trans. Gloucester, Mass.: Smith, 1973. ISBN 0-8446-2226-5. ▸ Discussion of collapse of traditional values and transition from age of faith to age of reason to age of feeling. Emphasis on France. Classic work. [JML]

22.189 J. H. Hexter. *The vision of politics on the eve of the Reformation: More, Machiavelli, and Seyssel.* New York: Basic Books, 1973. ISBN 0-465-09043-5. ▸ Identifies three modes of political thought, all originating in early modern period: predatory, utopian, and constitutional. Stimulating discussion of work of three representative thinkers. [JML]

22.190 Albert O. Hirschman. *The passions and the interests: political arguments for capitalism before its triumph.* 1977 ed. Princeton: Princeton University Press, 1981. ISBN 0-691-00357-2. ▸ Study of changes in moral and political perceptions of human acquisitive instinct from sixteenth to eighteenth centuries. Includes account of emergence of interest theory. Emphasis on Thomas Hobbes, Montesquieu, and Scottish thinkers. [JML]

22.191 R. A. Houston. *Literacy in early modern Europe: culture and education, 1500–1800.* New York: Longman, 1988. ISBN 0-582-03080-3 (cl), 0-582-55266-4 (pbk). ▸ Survey of spread of literacy, education, and print. Stresses role of culture and society in determining their influence. [MM]

22.192 Johan Huizinga. *Erasmus and the age of Reformation.* 1957 ed. F. Hopman and Barbara Flower, trans. Princeton: Princeton University Press, 1984. ISBN 0-691-05421-5 (cl), 0-691-00801-9 (pbk). ▸ Readable, critical biography by distinguished Dutch scholar, portraying Erasmus as gifted, perceptive scholar with no capacity for action. [JML]

22.193 Margaret Hunt et al. *Women and the Enlightenment.* New York: Haworth Press for the Institute for Research in History, 1984. ISBN 0-86656-190-0. ▸ Specialized essays on women's responses to Enlightenment. Includes women outside high culture; places them in social and intellectual context. [BYK]

22.194 Donald R. Kelley. *Foundations of modern historical scholarship: language, law, and history in the French Renaissance.* New York: Columbia University Press, 1970. ISBN 0-231-03141-6. ▸ Essential study of major stage of development of historical thinking when historical methods used in philological critiques of Roman law by Italian humanists were applied to French history. Focuses on French intellectuals. [JML/LMB]

22.195 Donald R. Kelley. *Renaissance humanism.* Boston: Twayne, 1991. ISBN 0-8057-8606-6 (cl), 0-8057-8631-7 (pbk). ▸ Brief, incisive survey of humanism as intellectual and cultural movement in Italy and northern Europe, explaining its origins, range of interests, relationship to philosophy and arts, and the social and educational context that sustained it. [PZ]

22.196 Joan Kelly-Gadol. "Did women have a Renaissance?" In *Becoming visible: women in European history.* 2d ed. Renate Bridenthal, Claudia Koonz, and Susan Mosher Stuard, eds., pp. 175–202. Boston: Houghton-Mifflin, 1987. ISBN 0-395-41950-6 (pbk). ▸ Influential article questioning standard interpretations of Renaissance from women's and gender perspective. [BYK]

22.197 Alexandre Koyré. *From the closed world to the infinite universe.* 1957 ed. Baltimore: Johns Hopkins University Press, 1968. (Publications of the Institute of the History of Medicine, Third series: The Hideyo Noguchi lectures, 7.) ▸ History of cosmology from Giordano Bruno and Johann Kepler to Isaac Newton and Gottfried Wilhelm von Leibniz. Traces destruction of medieval finite universe and geometrization of space. Influential study of early modern physical science, informed and accessible. [JML]

22.198 A. J. Krailsheimer and William A. Coupe, eds. *The continental Renaissance, 1500–1600.* 1971 ed. Atlantic Highlands, N.J.: Humanities Press, 1978. ISBN 0-391-00816-1. ▸ Survey of Renaissance literature in Western continental Europe. Sections on cultural and historical backgrounds. Straightforward literary history. [JML]

22.199 Thomas Walter Laqueur. *Making sex: body and gender from the Greeks to Freud.* Cambridge, Mass.: Harvard University Press, 1990. ISBN 0-674-54349-1. ▸ Controversial statement that sex as well as gender is constructed by culture. Contrasts two historical views: female as lesser male (one-sex model) and male and female (two-sex model) as fundamentally different. Traces history of understanding of sexual difference and transition from one-sex to two-sex model. [JML/SEK]

22.200 Christina Larner. *Witchcraft and religion: the politics of popular belief.* New York: Blackwell, 1984. ISBN 0-631-13447-6. ▸ Stimulating examination of relationship between witchcraft prosecutions and political ideology of Christianity. Deemphasizes social explanations and pagan survivals. Important collection by major scholar. [JML]

22.201 Brian P. Levack. *The witch-hunt in early modern Europe.* New York: Longman, 1987. ISBN 0-582-49122-3 (cl), 0-582-49123-1 (pbk). ▸ Coherent introduction to and synthesis of recent scholarship. Multicausal approach emphasizing complexity and diversity. [JML]

22.202 Arthur O. Lovejoy. *The great chain of being: a study of the history of an idea.* 1964 2d ed. Cambridge, Mass.: Harvard University Press, 1982. ISBN 0-674-36153-9 (pbk). ▸ Discussion of traditional view of world in ethics, aesthetics, astronomy, and biology from antiquity to eighteenth century. Classic history of ideas. [JML]

22.203 Ian Maclean. *The Renaissance notion of woman: a study in* *the fortunes of scholasticism and medical science in European intellectual life.* Cambridge: Cambridge University Press, 1980. ISBN 0-521-22906-5 (cl), 0-521-27436-2 (pbk). ▸ Compact, dense survey of Renaissance notion of woman, idea of sex difference, relationship between gender difference and other differences, and attitudes toward women in sixteenth-century medical, legal, theological, and ethical texts. [BYK/KP/LP]

22.204   Friedrich Meinecke. *Machiavellism: the doctrine of raison d'état and its place in modern history.* 1957 ed. Douglas Scott, trans. Boulder: Westview, 1984. ISBN 0-8133-0046-0 (pbk). ▸ Classic work tracing influence and history of Machiavelli's idea of state in European politics and culture and examining its amoral implications. Concentrates on Germany. [JML]

22.205   Pierre Mesnard. *L'essor de la philosophie politique au seizième siècle.* 3d ed. Paris: Librairie Philosophique J. Vrin, 1969. ▸ Traces development of ideas of sovereignty and resistance. Useful sections on Poland and on Spanish thinkers. Standard history of political thought. [JML]

22.206   Michael Mullett. *Popular culture and popular protest in late medieval and early modern Europe.* New York: Croom Helm, 1987. ISBN 0-7099-3566-8. ▸ Analysis of causes and nature of early modern popular rebellions. Posits reformist rather than revolutionary mentality, identifies towns as agents of cultural change, rejects monolithic definition of popular culture. Useful overview. [JML]

22.207   Anthony Pagden, ed. *The languages of political theory in early modern Europe.* Cambridge: Cambridge University Press, 1987. ISBN 0-521-32087-9. ▸ Wide-ranging collection of essays. Topics include political thought in Spain, Netherlands, and Naples; work of Thomas More, James Harrington, Thomas Hobbes, Samuel Pufendorf, and Jean-Baptiste Rousseau. Emphasis on social and intellectual context. [JML]

22.208   Alessandro Passerin d'Entrèves. *Natural law: an introduction to legal philosophy.* 1970 2d rev. ed. London: Hutchinson University Library, 1972. ISBN 0-09-102600-8. ▸ History of concept of natural law from Justinian to twentieth century. Combines historical and philosophical views to understand lasting appeal of idea of natural law. Valuable synthesis. [JML]

22.209   Rudolf Pfeiffer. *History of classical scholarship from 1300 to 1850.* Oxford: Clarendon, 1976. ISBN 0-19-814364-8. ▸ Useful survey, focusing on Italy, Netherlands, Germany, and England. Sections on Lorenzo Valla, Angelo Politian, Erasmus, Richard Bentley, Johann Joachim Winckelmann, and Friedrich August Wolf. [JML]

22.210   Margaret Mann Phillips. *Erasmus and the northern Renaissance.* Rev. ed. Woodbridge, England: Boydell & Brewer, 1981. ISBN 0-85115-151-5. ▸ Reissue of standard biography with useful summary and analysis of major works. Balanced assessment of Erasmus's influence. [JML]

22.211   J.G.A. Pocock. *The Machiavellian moment: Florentine political thought and the Atlantic republican tradition.* Princeton: Princeton University Press, 1975. ISBN 0-691-07560-3. ▸ History of idea of civic humanism, early modern republicanism, and republican virtue. Discusses formulation of key paradigms in Florence, their reworking by James Harrington, and their use by opposition groups in England and British colonies in North America. Influential thesis. [JML]

22.212   Richard Henry Popkin. *The history of scepticism from Erasmus to Spinoza.* Rev. ed. Berkeley: University of California Press, 1979. ISBN 0-520-03876-2 (pbk). ▸ Traces revival of ancient skepticism and its effects on rationalism and religion; argues it undermined each in turn. Shows importance of religious and theological issues, especially in England. Concludes with discussion of René Descartes's attempt to overcome skepticism. [JML]

22.213   Albert Rabil, Jr., ed. *Renaissance humanism: foundations,*

forms, and legacy. 3 vols. Philadelphia: University of Pennsylvania Press, 1988. ISBN 0-8122-8066-0 (set). ▸ Valuable collection of essays addressing all aspects of humanism in Italy and northern Europe. Forty-one chapters by authorities; comprehensive bibliography. Best survey of field in any language. [PZ/PFG]

22.214   Adolf Reichwein. *China and Europe: intellectual and artistic contacts of the eighteenth century.* J. C. Powell, trans. New York: Knopf, 1925. ▸ Describes European adoption and adaptation of Chinese influences. Focuses on rococo style, Enlightenment thought, Physiocrats, Johann Wolfgang von Goethe, and gardening. Old but not superseded. [JML]

22.215   James Bruce Ross and Mary Martin McLaughlin, eds. *The portable Renaissance reader.* New York: Viking, 1953. ▸ Large anthology of selections from Renaissance writers on many topics such as society, power, dignity of man, arts, nature, and religion. [PZ]

22.216   Charles B. Schmitt. *Aristotle and the Renaissance.* Cambridge, Mass.: Harvard University Press for Oberlin College, 1983. ISBN 0-674-04525-4. ▸ Survey of how Aristotle was studied and interpreted during Renaissance, arguing for originality, diversity, and importance of Renaissance Aristotelian thought. Discussion of translations of Aristotle's works and varieties of Aristotelianism; emphasis on Greek rather than medieval tradition. [JML/PFG]

22.217   Charles B. Schmitt, Quentin Skinner, and Eckhard Kessler, eds. *The Cambridge history of Renaissance philosophy.* Cambridge: Cambridge University Press, 1988. ISBN 0-521-25104-4. ▸ Comprehensive survey and synthesis by numerous contributors, arranged topically rather than by individual philosopher. International focus. [JML]

22.218   Jean Seznec. *The survival of the pagan gods: the mythological tradition and its place in Renaissance humanism and art.* 1953 ed. Barbara F. Sessions, trans. Princeton: Princeton University Press, 1972. ISBN 0-691-09829-8 (cl), 0-691-01783-2 (pbk). ▸ History of European ideas of Greek gods and myths to eighteenth century. Emphasis on continuity. Well illustrated with little-known material. [JML]

22.219   Quentin Skinner. *Foundations of modern political thought.* 2 vols. Cambridge: Cambridge University Press, 1978. ISBN 0-521-22023-8 (v. 1, cl), 0-521-22284-2 (v. 2, cl), 0-521-29337-5 (v. 1, pbk), 0-521-29435-5 (v. 2, pbk). ▸ Thorough, detailed summary of major and minor thinkers. Places theorists in social and intellectual context; especially strong on humanism, Thomas More, and consequences of Reformation. Aims to show evolution of modern concept of state. Influential standard work. [JML/DH]

22.220   J. L. Talmon. *The origins of totalitarian democracy.* 1952 ed. Boulder: Westview, 1985. ISBN 0-8133-0165-3 (pbk). ▸ Classic study tracing origins of both liberal and totalitarian democracy to tensions in Enlightenment thought between desire for liberty and search for utopia. Follows totalitarian tradition through to twentieth century. [JML]

22.221   R. H. Tawney. *Religion and the rise of capitalism: a historical study.* 1926 ed. Harmondsworth: Penguin, 1984. ISBN 0-14-055144-1 (pbk). ▸ Classic study of possible connection between Protestant doctrine and emergence of capitalist economy. Focus on English Puritanism. [JML]

22.222   H. R. Trevor-Roper. "The European witch craze of the sixteenth and seventeenth centuries and other essays." In *Religion, the Reformation, and social change and other essays.* 3d rev. ed, pp. 90–192. London: Secker & Warburg, 1984. ISBN 0-436-42510-6. ▸ Wide-ranging attempt to explain witch craze as result of early modern intellectual and social conditions. Emphasis on persecution of outsiders, connected to return of religious wars. Lucid argument for connection with Inquisition mentality. [JML]

22.223   Franco Venturi. *Utopia and reform in the Enlightenment.* Cambridge: Cambridge University Press, 1971. ISBN 0-521-07845-8. ▸ Useful historiographical introduction by major scholar of Enlightenment. Examines political context, including assessment of impact of republican tradition. Includes section on chronology and geography and case study of rights of punishment. [JML]

22.224   Brian Vickers, ed. *Occult and scientific mentalities in the Renaissance.* Cambridge: Cambridge University Press, 1984. ISBN 0-521-25879-0 (cl), 0-521-33836-0 (pbk). ▸ Collection of papers by various authors reexamining place of magic in Renaissance and Newtonian science. Major papers by Vickers on magic in scientific revolution and by Westfall on Newton. [JML]

22.225   D. P. Walker. *Spiritual and demonic magic from Ficino to Campanella.* 1958 ed. Notre Dame, Ind.: University of Notre Dame Press, 1975. ISBN 0-268-01670-4. ▸ Excellent introduction to Neoplatonic magic in sixteenth century and its connections with music, physiology, medicine, astrology, and philosophical assumptions. Claims that Tomaso Campanella's work united two traditions, natural spiritual and demonic, both inimical to religion. [JML/MHS]

22.226   Alan Watson. *The making of the civil law.* Cambridge, Mass.: Harvard University Press, 1981. ISBN 0-674-54310-6. ▸ History of legal systems of Western continental Europe from Justinian to Napoleon, showing how they developed distinctive features from common base in Roman law. Argues differences arose from differing legal histories, not external circumstances. Wide-ranging specialist study. [JML]

22.227   Max Weber. *The Protestant ethic and the spirit of capitalism.* 1976 2d ed. Talcott Parsons, trans. London: Unwin Hyman, 1989. ISBN 0-04-331101-6. ▸ Classic thesis arguing Calvinist idea of a calling formed moral base and driving force of capitalist entrepreneurs. Applies concept of ideal type to economic history. [JML]

22.228   Alfred N. Whitehead. *Science and the modern world.* 1925 ed. New York: Macmillan, 1967. ▸ Famous philosopher's account of effects of growth of modern science on mentalities and modes of thought from seventeenth century. Claims new ways of thinking transcend limits of scientific mind. Accessible and nontechnical. [JML]

22.229   Basil Willey. *The eighteenth-century background: studies on the idea of nature in the thought of the period.* 1940 ed. London: Ark, 1986. ISBN 0-7448-0042-0 (pbk). ▸ Study of changes in ideas of nature in religion, ethics, philosophy, and politics, to show harmony of religion and natural science. Old but still useful. [JML]

22.230   Frances A. Yates. *Giordano Bruno and the hermetic tradition.* 1964 ed. Chicago: University of Chicago Press, 1991. ISBN 0-226-95007-7 (pbk). ▸ Pioneering investigation of influence of Renaissance magic on Florentine academy and Bruno's work. Sets Bruno's life in context. Shows him as attempting synthesis of magic and religion. [JML]

22.231   Frances A. Yates. *The Rosicrucian enlightenment.* 1972 ed. London: Ark, 1986. ISBN 0-7448-0051-X (pbk). ▸ Discusses mysterious Rosicrucean brotherhood and identification of style of thinking between Renaissance and scientific revolution founded on combination of Protestant religious feeling, alchemy, Kabala, and medicine. Traces its influence in England and at court of Elizabeth of Bohemia, daughter of James I of England. Stimulating and controversial. [JML]

22.232   Perez Zagorin. *Ways of lying: dissimulation, persecution, and conformity in early modern Europe.* Cambridge, Mass.: Har-

vard University Press, 1990. ISBN 0-674-94834-3. ▸ Argues for importance of theory and practice of dissimulation in early modern religion and culture. Examines relationship between casuistry and dissimulation, as a response to persecution, its use by Catholics, Protestants, Jews, religious sectarians, and philosophers. Stimulating specialist work. [JML]

SEE ALSO
4.80 Marie Boas [Hall]. *The scientific Renaissance, 1450–1630.*
4.93 Thomas S. Kuhn. *The Copernican revolution.*
28.17 Paul Oskar Kristeller. *Renaissance thought.*
28.179 Carlo Ginzburg. *The cheese and the worms.*
30.73 Gerhard Oestreich. *Neostoicism and the early modern state.*
37.149 Edmundo O'Gorman. *The invention of America.*

Economic, Social, and Women's History

22.233   Bengt Ankarloo. "Agriculture and women's work: directions of change in the West, 1700–1900." *Journal of family history* 4.2 (1979) 111–36. ISSN 0363-1990. ▸ Influential discussion of issues relating to women's work during transition from feudal to capitalist mode of agricultural production and from rural to urban patterns of life. [BYK]

22.234   Philippe Ariès. *Centuries of childhood: a social history of family life.* 1962 ed. Robert Baldick, trans. London: Cape, 1973. ISBN 0-02-460001-7. ▸ History of concepts of childhood, family, and home from Middle Ages to French Revolution. Emphasis on role of education and development of private life in defining childhood as distinct phase. Claims early modern period as one of transition between medieval and modern ideas of childhood and family. Pioneering, important study. [JML/BYK]

22.235   Philippe Ariès. *The hour of our death.* 1981 ed. Helen Weaver, trans. New York: Oxford University Press, 1991. ISBN 0-19-507364-9. ▸ Exercise in history of mentalities, tracing relationship between attitudes toward death in Western culture and awareness of self, defense of society against untamed nature, belief in afterlife, and belief in existence of evil. Massive synthesis of huge range of material. [JML]

22.236   T. H. Aston and C.H.E. Philpin, eds. *The Brenner debate: agrarian class structure and economic development in pre-industrial Europe.* 1985 ed. Cambridge: Cambridge University Press, 1987. ISBN 0-521-34933-8 (pbk). ▸ Collection of papers by various scholars criticizing Robert Brenner's Marxist thesis of relationship between class structure and agrarian economic growth (reprinted here). No synthesis, but useful for specific local examples of agrarian development and stagnation in early modern Europe. [JML]

22.237   Salo W. Baron. *A social and religious history of the Jews.* Vol. 13–15. 2d rev. ed. New York: Columbia University Press, 1970–73. ISBN 0-231-08850-7 (v. 13), 0-231-08851-5 (v. 14), 0-231-08852-3 (v. 15). ▸ Important, broad synthesis starting in antiquity. Volumes 13–14 deal with effects of Inquisition, Renaissance, Reformation, Counter-Reformation, wars of religion, and Thirty Years' War on western European Jewish communities. Volume 15 treats resettlement and exploration. [JML]

22.238   Fernand Braudel. *Civilization and capitalism, fifteenth to eighteenth centuries.* Vol. 1: *The structures of everyday life: the limits of the possible.* Vol. 2: *The wheels of commerce.* Vol. 3: *The perspective of the world.* Siân Reynolds, trans. New York: Harper & Row, 1981–84. ISBN 0-06-014845-4 (v. 1), 0-06-015091-2 (v. 2), 0-06-015372-2 (v. 3). ▸ Economic history on grand scale in accord with global focus of Annales school. Study of basic forms of economic and social life, commercial relationships, and development of international capitalism. Approach very different from that of specialist economic historians. [PZ]

22.239   M. L. Bush. *Noble privilege.* Vol. 1 of *The European nobility.* New York: Holmes & Meier, 1983. ISBN 0-8419-0873-7.

‣ Intended as framework for national and regional studies. Describes noble privileges through time and across national boundaries; argues for their effects on emergence of modern democratic state. [JML]

22.240 Carlo M. Cipolla, ed. *The sixteenth and seventeenth centuries.* Vol. 2 of *Fontana economic history of Europe.* 1974 ed. New York: Barnes & Noble, 1977. ISBN 0-06-492177-8. ‣ Substantial essays on population, demand, technology, rural Europe, manufacturing, trade, and finance by specialists. Useful collection of diverse expertise. [JML]

22.241 Alice Clark. *Working life of women in the seventeenth century.* 3d ed. London: Routledge, 1992. ISBN 0-415-06668-9. ‣ Examines women's productivity in domestic industry, family industry, and capitalist industry. Classic, older description of women's work. [BYK]

22.242 André Corvisier. *Armies and societies in Europe, 1494–1789.* Abigail T. Siddall, trans. Bloomington: Indiana University Press, 1979. ISBN 0-253-12985-0. ‣ Social history of armies in Old Regime, divided into three sections: nation and army; state and army; and military society. Covers social composition, military ranking, and all aspects of army life. Classic study. [JML]

22.243 Philip D. Curtin. *The Atlantic slave trade: a census.* Madison: University of Wisconsin Press, 1969. ISBN 0-299-05400-4. ‣ Examination of slave trade from fifteenth to nineteenth centuries. Includes estimated geographical distribution of slaves over time and numbers of slaves involved. Fundamental work. [SLE/MAB]

22.244 Ralph Davies. *The rise of the Atlantic economies.* Ithaca, N.Y.: Cornell University Press, 1973. ISBN 0-8014-0801-6. ‣ Comparative economic history of England, France, Netherlands, Iberia, and New World colonies in early modern period. Sections on population, income, commerce, agriculture, and capital. Standard work. [JML]

22.245 Jan De Vries. *The economy of Europe in an age of crisis, 1600–1750.* Cambridge: Cambridge University Press, 1976. ISBN 0-521-21123-9 (cl), 0-521-29050-3 (pbk). ‣ Useful digest of information on western and Central Europe emphasizing regional and commercial exchange. Advances thesis that early modern economy was stagnant but unstable. [JML]

22.246 Jan De Vries. *European urbanization, 1500–1800.* Cambridge, Mass.: Harvard University Press, 1984. ISBN 0-674-27015-0. ‣ Pathbreaking study of early modern transnational urban system as precondition for urban industrialization. Cliometric approach. [JML]

22.247 Noel Deerr. *The history of sugar.* 2 vols. London: Chapman & Hall, 1949–50. ‣ Broad survey concerning production and trade in sugar from ancient times, including discussion of sugar and slavery in various slave colonies of New World. [SLE]

22.248 A. G. Dickens, ed. *The courts of Europe: politics, patronage, and royalty, 1400–1800.* 1977 ed. New York: Greenwich House; distributed by Crown, 1984. ISBN 0-517-43575-6. ‣ Comprehensive survey by various scholars of kings and their courts, including their influence on politics and art. Best general introduction to subject. [MM]

22.249 Elizabeth Donnan. *Documents illustrative of the history of the slave trade to America.* 1930–35 ed. 4 vols. New York: Octagon Books, 1965. ‣ Major collection of documents ranging from fifteenth to nineteenth centuries, dealing primarily with English slave trade to British West Indies and mainland colonies. [SLE]

22.250 Richard Ehrenberg. *Capital and finance in the age of the Renaissance: the Fuggers and their connections.* 1928 ed. H. M. Lucas, trans. Fairfield, N.J.: Kelley, 1985. ISBN 0-678-00015-8. ‣ Classic study of early modern finance with wider scope than title suggests. Includes Fuggers, other German financiers, Flor-

entines, Tuscans, international bourses, and growth of national debts. [JML]

22.251 Norbert Elias. *The history of manners.* 1978 ed. Edmund Jephcott, trans. New York: Pantheon, 1982. ISBN 0-394-71133-5 (pbk). ‣ Discussion of development of manners as part of European civilization. Original thesis arguing for close connection between growth of individual self-control and expanding power of state. [MM]

22.252 David Eltis. *Economic growth and the ending of the transatlantic slave trade.* New York: Oxford University Press, 1987. ISBN 0-19-504135-6. ‣ Detailed examination of slave trade's role in expansion into Americas and of causes and effects of British suppression and abolition of slave trade. [SLE]

22.253 Jean-Louis Flandrin. *Families in former times: kinship, household, and sexuality.* Richard Southern, trans. New York: Cambridge University Press, 1979. ISBN 0-521-22323-7 (cl), 0-521-29449-5 (pbk). ‣ Best introduction to kinship, household, and family life. Integrates demography with other sources. [MM]

22.254 Michael W. Flinn. *The European demographic system, 1500–1800.* Baltimore: Johns Hopkins University Press, 1981. ISBN 0-8018-2426-5 (cl), 0-8018-3155-5 (pbk). ‣ Survey and synthesis of recent work on family reconstruction from parish registers, including trends in fertility, mortality, and migration and analysis of preindustrial changes. Concentrates on Britain, France, Germany, and Scandinavia; statistical appendix. [JML]

22.255 Robert Forster and Elborg Forster, eds. *European society in the eighteenth century.* New York: Walker, 1969. ‣ Extracts from primary source material on poor, family, aristocracy, kings and courts, towns, countryside, agriculture, trade and commerce, guilds, religion, and age of reform. Does not cover Scandinavia, Iberia, or Low Countries. [JML]

22.256 Albert Goodwin, ed. *The European nobility in the eighteenth century: studies of the nobilities of the major European states in the pre-reform era.* 1953 ed. New York: Harper & Row, 1967. ‣ Useful essay collection including both western and eastern Europe; draws no general conclusions. Helpful bibliography. [JML]

22.257 Barbara Hanawalt, ed. *Women and work in pre-industrial Europe.* Bloomington: Indiana University Press, 1986. ISBN 0-253-36610-0 (cl), 0-253-20367-8 (pbk). ‣ Working experiences of slaves, domestic servants, wet nurses, respectable widows, professional midwives, and women in the crafts. [BYK]

22.250 Eli F. Heckscher. *Mercantilism.* 1955 2d rev. ed. 2 vols. Mendel Shapiro, trans. New York: Garland, 1983. ISBN 0-8240-5363-X. ‣ Classic work describing mercantilism as both system and doctrine in early modern Europe. Emphasis on England and France; comparative approach. Rejects materialist interpretation and argues for intervention as facet of emerging nation-state. [JML]

22.259 Bridget Hill, comp. *Eighteenth-century women: an anthology.* London: Allen & Unwin, 1984. ISBN 0-04-909013-5 (cl), 0-04-909014-3 (pbk). ‣ Useful reappraisal of female education, marriage, women's legal position, poor, women in agriculture, textile industries, domestic service, and women's protest. Based on eighteenth-century documents. [BYK]

22.260 George Huppert. *After the Black Death: a social history of early modern Europe.* Bloomington: Indiana University Press, 1986. ISBN 0-253-30406-6 (cl), 0-253-30446-6 (pbk). ‣ Synthesis in Annales tradition, incorporating recent research. Focus on France, Britain, Italy, and Germany. Limited but useful overview. [JML]

22.261 Pierre Jeannin. *Merchants of the sixteenth century.* Paul Fittingoff, trans. New York: Harper & Row, 1972. ISBN 0-06-

138878-5. ▸ Reconstructs world of urban merchant, with emphasis on structural differences from modern period. Notes end of urban autonomy and social ambition of many bourgeois as court replaced city as prime social focus. [JML]

22.262 Henry Kamen. *European society, 1500–1700.* 1984 ed. Boston: Unwin Hyman, 1989. ISBN 0-04-445644-1. ▸ Valuable survey illustrating thesis that collaboration between state and producing elite broadened state's power base and generated stability by end of period. Useful bibliography. [JML]

22.263 Henry Kamen. *The iron century: social change in Europe, 1550–1660.* Rev. ed. London: Sphere, 1976. ISBN 0-351-17055-3. ▸ Wide-ranging discussion of social consequences of economic recession and nature of seventeenth-century crisis. Quantitative, Annales approach. [JML]

22.264 Hermann Kellenbenz. *The rise of the European economy: an economic history of continental Europe from the fifteenth to the eighteenth century.* Rev. ed. Gerhard Benecke, ed. New York: Holmes & Meier, 1976. ISBN 0-8419-0273-9. ▸ General survey, focusing on France, Russia, Switzerland, and Scandinavia. Strongest on industry, trade, and commerce. Offers no general theory. [JML]

22.265 Gerard Kent and Gert Hekma, eds. *The pursuit of sodomy: male homosexuality in Renaissance and Enlightenment Europe.* New York: Harrington Park, 1989. (Journal of homosexuality, 16.) ISBN 0-918393-49-3. ▸ Comprehensive anthology of recent scholarship, suggesting early modern period transitional in construction of homosexuality. [JML]

22.266 Margaret L. King. *Women of the Renaissance.* Chicago: University of Chicago Press, 1991. ISBN 0-226-43617-9 (cl), 0-226-43618-7 (pbk). ▸ Synthesis of recent work showing women as wives, mothers, and widows. Includes women in church and notable women. Extensive bibliography. [BYK]

22.267 Peter Laslett and Richard Wall, eds. *Household and family in past time: comparative studies in the size and structure of the domestic group.* Cambridge: Cambridge University Press, 1972. ISBN 0-521-08473-3. ▸ Comparative studies by leading scholars of period from 1600 to present in Europe, colonial North America, and Japan. Case-study approach. Controversial editorial essay argues nuclear family was norm in all cases. [JML]

22.268 Fréderic Mauro. *Le seizième siècle européen: aspects économiques.* 3d ed. Paris: Presses Universitaires de France, 1981. (Nouvelle Clio, 32.) ISBN 2-13-037139-6. ▸ Useful survey of sources with complete bibliography. Anti-quantitative; now dated economic theory. [JML]

22.269 Roger Mols. *Introduction à la démographie historique des villes de l'Europe du quatorzième au dix-huitième siècle.* 3 vols. Gambloux: Duculot, 1954–56. (Université Catholique de Louvain: recueil de travaux d'histoire et de philologie, Quatrième serie, Fasc. 1–3.) ▸ Synthesis of available data for western Europe. Summarizes results of previous research; indicates areas for further study. Comprehensive bibliography. [JML]

22.270 James A. Rawley. *The transatlantic slave trade: a history.* New York: Norton, 1981. ISBN 0-393-01471-1. ▸ General history of slave trades of European countries and British North American colonies, encompassing economic, demographic, social, and political aspects. [SLE]

22.271 E. E. Rich and Charles Wilson, eds. *The economic organization of early modern Europe.* Vol. 5 of *Cambridge economic history of Europe.* Cambridge: Cambridge University Press, 1977. ISBN 0-521-08710-4. ▸ Discussion of concepts and methods in economic history and authoritative survey of agriculture, fishing, trade, banking, nature of enterprise, industry, government, and society. Full bibliographies. [JML]

22.272 E. E. Rich and Charles Wilson, eds. *The economy of expanding Europe in the sixteenth and seventeenth centuries.* Vol. 4 of *Cambridge economic history of Europe.* Cambridge: Cambridge University Press, 1967. ▸ Comprehensive, expert survey by numerous contributors. Includes sections on scientific method and colonial settlement. Extensive bibliography. [JML]

22.273 Barbara Solow, ed. *Slavery and the rise of the Atlantic system.* Cambridge and Cambridge, Mass.: Cambridge University Press and Harvard University, W.E.B. DuBois Institute for Afro-American Research, 1991. ISBN 0-521-40090-2. ▸ Essays on various aspects of slavery in the New World and their impact on Africa and Europe between sixteenth and nineteenth centuries. [SLE]

22.274 Louise A. Tilly and Joan Wallach Scott. *Women, work, and family.* 1978 ed. New York: Methuen, 1987. ISBN 0-416-01681-2 (pbk). ▸ Standard study of family economy in early modern England and France, tracing effects of industrialization and occupational and demographic change. Includes single and married women. [BYK]

22.275 Immanuel Wallerstein. *The modern world system.* Vol. 1: *Capitalist agriculture and the origins of the European world economy in the sixteenth century.* Vol. 2: *Mercantilism and the consolidation of the European world economy, 1600–1750.* Vol. 3: *The second era of great expansion of the capitalist world-economy, 1730–1840s.* Edition varies. New York: Academic Press, 1974–89. ISBN 0-12-785920-9 (v. 1, cl), 0-12-785923-3 (v. 2, cl), 0-12-785925-X (v. 3, cl), 0-12-785919-5 (v. 1, pbk), 0-12-785924-1 (v. 2, pbk), 0-12-785926-8 (v. 3, pbk). ▸ Emergence of single social system, from Peru to Danube, grounded in competition between powerful states. How system perpetuated itself while allowing power to shift within. Neo-Marxist historical sociology on grand scale. [JH]

22.276 Charles Wilson. "Mercantilism: some vicissitudes of an idea." *Economic history review* 10.2 (1957) 181–88. ISSN 0013-0117. ▸ Brief history of definition of mercantilism from Smith to Heckscher. Argues against Heckscher's thesis (22.258) for interdependence of economic and political motives and for historical perspective. [JML]

22.277 Charles Wilson and Geoffrey Parker, eds. *Introduction to the sources of European economic history, 1500–1800.* Ithaca, N.Y.: Cornell University Press, 1977. ISBN 0-8014-1109-2. ▸ Very useful compilation and synthesis of source material for southern and western Europe. Short essays for each country or area, divided topically. Many tables and figures. [JML]

SEE ALSO
4.369 Charles Joseph Singer et al., eds. *A history of technology.*
20.295 Carlo M. Cipolla. *Before the Industrial Revolution.*
37.223 Herbert S. Klein. *The Middle Passage.*

The Arts

22.278 Gerald Abraham, ed. *The age of humanism, 1540–1630.* Vol. 4 of *The new Oxford history of music.* London: Oxford University Press, 1968. ISBN 0-19-316304-7. ▸ Balanced, well-informed overview of increasing importance of secular vocal genres in various countries of Europe; musical examples and good illustrations. Attention also given to instrumental music and response of sacred polyphony to Martin Luther and Counter-Reformation. [RPL]

22.279 Gerald Abraham, ed. *Concert music, 1630–1750.* Vol. 6 of *The new Oxford history of music.* London: Oxford University Press, 1986. ISBN 0-19-316306-3. ▸ Begins, despite title, with genres related to sacred music and opera, then traces rise of baroque instrumental music. Good illustrations and musical examples. [RPL]

22.280 Arts Council of Great Britain. *The age of neo-classicism.*

London: Victoria and Albert Museum, 1972. ISBN 0-900085-72-x (pbk). ‣ Exhibition catalog presenting painting, sculpture, prints, architecture, decorative arts, and stage design from 1750s to early nineteenth century. Gives sense of pervasiveness of neo-classical phenomenon. Includes short biographies of many artists. [GS]

22.281 Otto Benesch. *The art of the Renaissance in northern Europe: its relation to the contemporary spiritual and intellectual movements.* Rev. ed. London: Phaidon, 1965. ‣ Examination of effects of coincidence of Renaissance, religious revolution, and new science in France, Germany, and Netherlands. Finds correspondences in aims and methods of all three and uncovers cosmological meanings in art. Provocative specialist study, now a classic. [JML]

22.282 Manfred F. Bukofzer. *Music in the baroque era: from Monteverdi to Bach.* New York: Norton, 1947. ‣ European-wide study, including sections on musical form, thought, and sociology. Thorough, comprehensive treatment, requiring some musical knowledge. Good bibliography. [JML/JBK]

22.283 Charles D. Cuttler. *Northern painting from Pucelle to Breugel: fourteenth, fifteenth, and sixteenth centuries.* New York: Holt, Rinehart & Winston, 1968. ISBN 0-03-089476-X. ‣ Survey, with many illustrations, of northern Renaissance art in Germany, Austria, Spain, Switzerland, and France with emphasis on Netherlands. [GS]

22.284 Iain Fenlon, ed. *The Renaissance: from the 1470's to the end of the sixteenth century.* Englewood Cliffs, N.J.: Prentice-Hall, 1989. ISBN 0-13-773409-3 (cl), 0-13-773417-4 (pbk). ‣ Extensive overview of music's place in society and society's influence on music, including rise of music printing and religious changes, followed by chapters on individual European areas, countries, or topics. [RPL]

22.285 Creighton Gilbert. *History of Renaissance art: painting, sculpture, architecture throughout Europe.* New York: Abrams, 1973. ISBN 0-8109-0169-2. ‣ Liberally illustrated survey on European art from thirteenth to sixteenth century with emphasis on Italy. [GS]

22.286 Arnold Hauser. *Mannerism: the crisis of the Renaissance and the origin of modern art.* 1965 ed. 2 vols. Eric Mosbacher, trans. Cambridge, Mass.: Belknap, 1986. ISBN 0-674-54815-9 (pbk). ‣ Finds keys to mannerism in alienation and instability. Sets arts in economic, social, religious, political, and scientific contexts. Classic study. [JML]

22.287 Julius S. Held and Donald Posner. *Seventeenth- and eighteenth-century art: baroque painting, sculpture, architecture.* New York: Abrams, 1971. ISBN 0-8109-0032-7. ‣ Abundantly illustrated survey text. [GS]

22.288 Elizabeth Gilmore Holt, ed. *A documentary history of art.* Rev. ed. 3 vols. Princeton and New Haven: Princeton University Press and Yale University Press, 1981–86. ISBN 0-691-00333-5 (v. 1, pbk), 0-691-00344-0 (v. 2, pbk), 0-300-03358-3 (v. 3, pbk). ‣ Useful collection of sources from Middle Ages to eighteenth century, mainly from Italy, but also Spain and northern Europe. Emphasis on theory and technique but with few examples of artists' contracts or legal documents. [JML]

22.289 Hugh Honour. *Neo-classicism.* 1968 ed. Harmondsworth: Penguin, 1977. (Style and civilization.) ISBN 0-14-020978-6 (pbk). ‣ Enlightenment art set in contemporary context; includes painting, architecture, and design. Focus on France but with wide range of examples from Europe and America. [JML]

22.290 Dom Anselm Hughes and Gerald Abraham, eds. *Ars nova and the Renaissance, 1300–1540.* Vol. 3 of *The new Oxford history of music.* 1960 ed. New York: Oxford University Press, 1986. ISBN 0-19-316303-9. ‣ Focus on later medieval music, but

useful chapters on secular vocal music, instrumental music, and musical instruments in Renaissance. Full bibliographies and many musical examples. [JML]

22.291 Rensselaer W. Lee. *Ut pictura poesis: the humanistic theory of painting.* New York: Norton, 1967. ‣ Study of themes of ideal imitation of human action and comparison of painting with poetry in art theory between fifteenth and eighteenth centuries. Useful for pointing out important texts, but does not subject them to critical analysis. [GS]

22.292 Michael Levey. *Early Renaissance.* 1967 ed. Harmondsworth: Penguin, 1978. (Style and civilization.) ISBN 0-14-020914-x (pbk). ‣ Renaissance as age of transition, achieving realism that surpassed reality, and brief period of synthesis of faith and reason. Wide-ranging synthesis with examples from northern and southern Europe. [JML]

22.293 Michael Levey. *High Renaissance.* Harmondsworth: Penguin, 1975. (Style and civilization.) ISBN 0-14-021823-8 (pbk). ‣ Wide range of examples of sixteenth-century virtuosity in painting, architecture, and design from all over Europe. Characterizes High Renaissance style by its accomplishment and confidence. Dazzling synthesis. [JML]

22.294 Anthony Lewis and Nigel Fortune, eds. *Opera and church music, 1630–1750.* Vol. 5 of *The new Oxford history of music.* Oxford: Oxford University Press, 1975. ISBN 0-19-316305-5. ‣ With Volume 6 (22.279) covers baroque era. Treats two genres that were grandest and most basic to musical livelihood. Good illustrations and musical examples; direct and engaging style. [RPL]

22.295 Emile Mâle. *Religious art: from the twelfth to the eighteenth centuries.* 1949 ed. Princeton: Princeton University Press, 1982. ISBN 0-691-04000-1. ‣ Classic art history, condensed from three volumes to one. Emphasis on iconography. Assesses influences of Counter-Reformation and mysticism. [JML]

22.296 John Rupert Martin. *Baroque.* New York: Harper & Row, 1977. ISBN 0-06-435332-X (cl), 0-06-430077-3 (pbk). ‣ Introduction to art of seventeenth century, organized thematically rather than chronologically. [GS]

22.297 Erwin Panofsky. *Renaissance and renascences in Western art.* 1960 ed. New York: Harper & Row, 1972. ISBN 0-06-430026-9. ‣ Distinguishes Renaissance from earlier revivals of classical influence as total and permanent change that distanced and rationalized classical past. Important and influential thesis. [JML]

22.298 Erwin Panofsky. *Studies in iconology: humanistic themes in the art of the Renaissance.* 1939 ed. New York: Harper & Row, 1972. ISBN 0-06-430025-0. ‣ Influential approach to interpretation assuming high literary culture in which classic texts underlay important visual images. [GS]

22.299 Nikolaus Pevsner. *Academies of art, past and present.* 1940 ed. New York: Da Capo, 1973. ISBN 0-306-71603-8. ‣ Informed account of nature and role of art academies from ancient Greece to present. Connects academicism with mannerism and absolutism. [JML]

22.300 Robert Rosenblum. *Transformations in late eighteenth-century art.* 1969 2d ed. with additional bibliography. Princeton: Princeton University Press, 1974. ISBN 0-691-03846-5. ‣ Thematic discussion of international neoclassicism. [GS]

22.301 John Shearman. *Mannerism.* 1967 ed. Harmondsworth: Penguin, 1978. (Style and civilization.) ISBN 0-14-020808-9. ‣ Mannerism as style of confident excess, not restlessness or neurosis. Main focus on Italy, but some consideration of France and Germany. Stimulating overview for general reader. [JML]

22.302 Roy Strong. *Art and power: Renaissance festivals, 1450–1650.* Berkeley: University of California Press, 1984. ISBN 0-520-

05479-2. ▸ Survey of growing importance of arts as political spectacle and propaganda. [MM]

22.303 H. R. Trevor-Roper. *Princes and artists: patronage and ideology at four Habsburg courts, 1517–1633.* 1976 ed. New York: Thames & Hudson, 1991. ISBN 0-500-27623-4. ▸ Survey of function of art at courts of Charles V, Philip II, Rudolf II, and Spanish Netherlands. Inquiry into art as prestige and as reflection of prevailing values. [JML]

22.304 Giorgio Vasari. *Lives of the most eminent painters, sculptors, and architects.* 1912–15 rev. ed. 10 vols. Gaston du C. de Vere, trans. New York: AMS Press, 1976. ISBN 0-404-09730-8 (set). ▸ Indispensable source for lives and work of Renaissance painters by sixteenth-century Florentine artist. Classic biography and art history. [JML]

22.305 Egon Wellesz and Frederick Sternfeld, eds. *The age of Enlightenment, 1745–1790.* Vol. 7 of *The new Oxford history of music.* London: Oxford University Press, 1973. ISBN 0-19-316307-1. ▸ Authoritative overview of growth of serious and comic opera, sacred music, secular song, and especially new instrumental genres, all culminating in works of Haydn and Mozart. Copious musical examples and bibliography. [RPL]

22.306 Neal Zaslaw, ed. *The classical era: from the 1740's to the end of the eighteenth century.* Englewood Cliffs, N.J.: Prentice-Hall, 1989. ISBN 0-13-136920-2 (cl), 0-13-136938-5 (pbk). ▸ Introduction treats music and society in classical era, followed by chapters by experts on major musical centers in Europe. In particular, careers and work of Mozart and Haydn discussed in their social setting. Extensive overview of period. [JML]

WESTERN EUROPE, 1789–1914

General Studies and Political, Diplomatic, and Military History

22.307 Eugene N. Anderson and Pauline R. Anderson. *Political institutions and social change in continental Europe in the nineteenth century.* Berkeley: University of California Press, 1967. ▸ Immensely useful examination of political institutions including central, intermediate, and local government; parties; bureaucracies; and civil rights by two social historians. Broadly conceived and well written with much historical detail. [DSC]

22.308 Frederick B. Artz. *Reaction and revolution, 1814–1832.* Vol. 13 of *The rise of modern Europe.* 1934 ed. New York: Harper & Row, 1968. ▸ Survey of society, politics, and culture. Focuses on justification of authority and liberalism, states, revolutionary disturbances, and disintegration of restoration. [DSC]

22.309 Maurice Baumont. *L'essor industriel et l'impérialisme coloniale (1878–1904).* 3d rev. ed. Paris: Presses Universitaires de France, 1965. (Peuples et civilisations, 18.) ▸ Survey of power politics, imperialism, industrial expansion, Great Depression, return to protectionism, social conflicts, and culture. [DSC]

22.310 Geoffrey Best. *War and society in revolutionary Europe, 1770–1870.* New York: St. Martin's, 1982. ISBN 0-312-85551-6. ▸ Up-to-date survey of Old Regime armies, French nation in arms and its opponents' responses, guerrilla war in Spain, post-Napoleonic deliberalization and depoliticization, and role of armies in revolutions and insurrections to 1860s. [DSC]

22.311 Robert C. Binkley. *Realism and nationalism, 1852–1871.* Vol. 15 of *The rise of modern Europe.* 1935 ed. New York: Harper & Row, 1963. ▸ Helpful survey of ideas and culture as well as politics. [DSC]

22.312 Brian Bond. *War and society in Europe, 1870–1970.* 1984 ed. New York: Oxford University Press, 1986. ISBN 0-19-520502-2 (pbk). ▸ Survey and synthesis examining growing violence of war, new militarism from 1870s, technical and economic trans-

formation, and loss of distinction between combatants and civilians. [DSC]

22.313 Julius Braunthal. *History of the International, 1864–1914.* Vol. 1. Henry Collins and Kenneth Mitchell, trans. New York: Praeger, 1967. ▸ Most comprehensive history of organizations and politics of socialism by single author. First of three-volume work covers the First and Second Internationals. Not as lively as Joll 22.339. [DSC]

22.314 Crane Brinton. *A decade of revolution, 1789–1799.* Vol. 11 of *The rise of modern Europe.* 1934 ed. New York: Harper & Row, 1963. ▸ Compact and still useful survey. [DSC]

22.315 Geoffrey Bruun. *Europe and the French imperium, 1799–1814.* Vol. 12 of *The rise of modern Europe.* 1938 ed. Westport, Conn.: Greenwood, 1983. ISBN 0-313-24078-7. ▸ Useful short survey of French rule in Europe, examining economy, society, culture, and national aspirations. [DSC]

22.316 J.P.T. Bury, ed. *The zenith of European power, 1830–1870.* Vol. 10 of *The new Cambridge modern history.* Cambridge: Cambridge University Press, 1964. ISBN 0-521-04548-7. ▸ Valuable collaborative work of synthesis and interpretation. Surveys period of rapid economic, scientific, religious, and cultural change. Liberal constitutional reforms, rise of nationalism, revolutions of 1848 and their aftermath, Crimean War, and background to unification in Germany and Italy. Glances at American Civil War and European relations with rest of world. [DSC]

22.317 David Calleo. *The German problem reconsidered: Germany and the world order, 1870 to the present.* 1978 ed. Cambridge: Cambridge University Press, 1982. ISBN 0-521-29966-7 (pbk). ▸ Essays surveying German question in broad context of nineteenth- and twentieth-century European history and in international system. Controversial, stimulating but not totally convincing. Good introduction to contexts in which question has been discussed. [DSC/JJS/CKF/JSH]

22.318 Clive H. Church. *Europe in 1830: revolution and political change.* London: Allen & Unwin, 1983. ISBN 0-04-940067-3. ▸ Shows that although impulses of political and social protest did not quite coalesce, 1830 was important revolution. Reveals political complexity that models of social revolution ignore. [DSC]

22.319 C. W. Crawley, ed. *War and peace in an age of upheaval, 1793–1830.* Vol. 9 of *The new Cambridge modern history.* Cambridge: Cambridge University Press, 1965. ISBN 0-521-04547-9. ▸ Valuable work of synthesis and interpretation by number of collaborators. Surveys revolutionary wars; Napoleon and aftermath in political economic and social change in major nations; relations with Near East, Asia, Africa, United States, and Latin America; and Congress of Vienna and European relations thereafter. [DSC]

22.320 Benedetto Croce. *History of Europe in the nineteenth century.* 1933 ed. Henry Furst, trans. New York: Harcourt Brace & World, 1963. ▸ Philosophic history and classic exposition of century's liberal faith. Writing in dark times, great Italian thinker sought to show that ideas and moral dispositions of liberalism inevitably triumphed over their enemies. [DSC]

22.321 Otto Dann and John Dinwiddy, eds. *Nationalism in the age of the French Revolution.* London: Hambledon, 1988. ISBN 0-907628-97-4. ▸ Essays by different historians offering country-by-country survey with useful bibliography for each. [DSC]

22.322 Hans Delbrück, Jr. *History of the art of war within the framework of political history.* 4 vols. Walter J. Renfroe, trans. Westport, Conn.: Greenwood, 1975–85. ISBN 0-8371-6365-X (v. 1), 0-8371-8163-1 (v. 2), 0-8371-8164-X (v. 3), 0-8371-8165-8 (v. 4). ▸ Despite some defects, considered classic history of art of warfare through Napoleonic wars. [DSC]

22.323 Milorad M. Drachkovitch, ed. *The revolutionary Inter-*

nationals, 1864–1943. Stanford, Calif.: Stanford University Press for the Hoover Institution on War, Revolution, and Peace, 1966. ▸ Concise essays offer synthesis and interpretation of three Internationals, anarchism, social democracy, and Comintern as Soviet instrument. Useful introduction to these topics. [DSC]

22.324 François Fejtő, ed. *The opening of an era, 1848: an historical symposium.* 1948 ed. A.J.P. Taylor, Introduction. New York: Fertig, 1966. ▸ Essays on most of western and eastern Europe. Older but good coverage of politics. [DSC]

22.325 Franklin L. Ford. *Europe, 1780–1830.* 2d ed. London: Longman, 1989. ISBN 0-582-03378-0 (cl), 0-582-49392-7 (pbk). ▸ Best introductory survey of period, summing up social, political, economic, and cultural transformation. Includes essay on sources used by historians of period and bibliographic notes. [DSC]

22.326 André Fugier. *La Révolution française et l'empire napoléonien.* Paris: Hachette, 1954. ▸ Brief treatment of political, economic, and psychological aspects of Napoleonic policy and empire. [DSC]

22.327 Robert Gildea. *Barricades and borders: Europe, 1800–1914.* Oxford: Oxford University Press, 1987. ISBN 0-19-873028-4 (cl), 0-19-873029-2 (pbk). ▸ Well-organized, up-to-date survey with useful general bibliography. [DSC]

22.328 Jacques Léon Godechot. *La grande nation: l'expansion révolutionnaire de la France dans le monde de 1789 à 1799.* 2d ed. Paris: Aubier Montaigne, 1983. ISBN 2-7007-0310-3. ▸ Analysis of how revolution expanded across Europe through popular agitation, ideological influence, government action, and military conquest. Second volume addresses deeper changes wrought by events. [DSC]

22.329 Albert Goodwin, ed. *The American and French Revolutions.* Vol. 8 of *The new Cambridge modern history.* Cambridge: Cambridge University Press, 1965. ISBN 0-521-04546-0. ▸ Essential work of reference and interpretation covering political and diplomatic history, economic and cultural developments, American Revolution, and French Revolution to 1793. [PZ]

22.330 Jürgen Habermas. *The structural transformation of the public sphere: an inquiry into a category of bourgeois society.* Thomas Burger and Frederick Lawrence, trans. Cambridge, Mass.: MIT Press, 1989. ISBN 0-262-08180-6. ▸ Historical and sociological account of emergence of liberal public sphere, its transformation and disintegration in welfare state. Demanding but influential work. [DSC]

22.331 Theodore S. Hamerow. *The birth of a new Europe: state and society in the nineteenth century.* Chapel Hill: University of North Carolina Press, 1983. ISBN 0-8078-1548-9. ▸ Discussion of economic and social change, change in structure of politics and functions of government, and international relations in industrializing Europe. Much admired comparative study reflecting trends of recent scholarship. [DSC]

22.332 Carlton J. H. Hayes. *A generation of materialism, 1871–1900.* Vol. 15 of *The rise of modern Europe.* 1941 ed. Westport, Conn.: Greenwood, 1983. ISBN 0-313-24082-5. ▸ Older survey. Overview of materialist culture and power politics after Franco-Prussian war. [DSC]

22.333 F. H. Hinsley, ed. *Material progress and world-wide problems, 1870–1898.* Vol. 11 of *The new Cambridge modern history.* Cambridge: Cambridge University Press, 1962. ISBN 0-521-04549-5. ▸ Valuable work of synthesis and interpretation by various specialists. Describes contradictory impulses in age of rapid industrialization and urbanization and increasing organization of interests within state. Covers domestic politics and decline of liberalism, rise of socialism, national protectionism, European power rivalries, and imperialism. [DSC]

22.334 Eric J. Hobsbawm. *The age of capital, 1848–1875.* 1979 2d ed. New York: New American Library, 1984. ISBN 0-452-00696-1. ▸ Marxist historian's account of commerce, industry, politics, and culture in golden age of bourgeoisie. [DSC]

22.335 Eric J. Hobsbawm. *The age of empire, 1875–1914.* 1987 ed. New York: Vintage, 1989. ISBN 0-679-72175-4 (pbk). ▸ Marxist historian's interpretation of origins of First World War. As mass labor movements arose, new middle classes rejected liberalism, and pursuit of empires prepared Europe's self-destruction. Overlooks specifics of Germany's role. [DSC]

22.336 Eric J. Hobsbawm. *The age of revolution: Europe, 1789–1848.* 1962 ed. London: Sphere, 1978. ISBN 0-349-11693-8. ▸ Introductory survey examining how French and industrial revolutions changed European society. Surveys politics, economic and social change, ideology, science, and arts. [DSC]

22.337 John A. Hobson. *Imperialism, a study.* 1938 3d rev. ed. London: Unwin Hyman, 1988. ISBN 0-04-325019-X (pbk). ▸ Classic that influenced Lenin, Karl Kautsky, Rosa Luxembourg, and others. Radical-liberal critique arguing imperialism served to perpetuate unequal division of wealth in Britain by guaranteeing profitable investment of surplus capital abroad. [DSC]

22.338 Michael Howard. *The Franco-Prussian war.* 1961 ed. London: Methuen, 1981. ISBN 0-416-30750-7 (pbk). ▸ Shows how war reflected technical, economic, and social changes and anticipated wars to come. Explores political as well as military significance of battles recounted. Much admired, standard account. [DSC]

22.339 James Joll. *The Second International, 1889–1914.* Rev. ed. London: Routledge & Kegan Paul, 1974. ISBN 0-7100-7966-4. ▸ Description of golden age of international socialism and weaknesses that led to disaster of summer 1914 and rise of communism. [DSC]

22.340 V. G. Kiernan. *From conquest to collapse: European empires from 1815 to 1960.* New York: Pantheon, 1982. ISBN 0-394-50959-5. ▸ Military history of European forces and conquests, and native responses and rebellion. Broad survey with interesting detail by Marxist historian. [DSC]

22.341 Hans Kohn. *Prelude to nation-states: the French and German experience, 1789–1815.* Princeton: Van Nostrand, 1967. ▸ Comparative intellectual history of crucial period in which nationalism took shape in both countries. Good introduction to topic. [DSC]

22.342 Laurence Lafore. *The long fuse: an interpretation of the origins of World War I.* 2d ed. Philadelphia: Lippincott, 1971. ▸ Focuses on interstate relations and chain of events in Central and eastern Europe that allowed Serb nationalism to ignite world war. Very readable survey. [DSC]

22.343 William L. Langer. *Political and social upheaval, 1832–1852.* Vol. 14 of *The rise of modern Europe.* New York: Harper & Row, 1969. ISBN 0-06-131582-6. ▸ Survey of all Europe at time when political and social impulses of French and industrial revolutions began to coalesce. [DSC]

22.344 Georges Lefebvre. *The French Revolution.* 2 vols. Elizabeth Moss Evanson, John Hall Stewart, and James Friguglietti, trans. New York: Columbia University Press, 1962–64. ▸ Great French historian puts Revolution in strong European context. Emphasizes economic and social history. [DSC]

22.345 Vladimir I. Lenin. *Imperialism, the highest stage of capitalism.* Rev. ed. New York: International, 1939. ▸ Written in 1916, study became communist orthodoxy. Expanded Hobson's arguments (22.337) that imperialism served protectionist, financial, and militarist interests to portray capitalism as inevitably ending in cataclysmic conflict between European powers. [DSC]

22.346 Fernand L'Huillier et al. *Nationalité et nationalisme (1860–1878)*. Rev. ed. Paris: Presses Universitaires de France, 1968. (Peuples et civilisations, 17.) ‣ Study of period that began with resurgence of liberalism, which revealed its contradictions and laid foundations of Europe dominated by nationalism and great power rivalry. [DSC]

22.347 Albert S. Lindemann. *A history of European socialism*. 1983 ed. New Haven: Yale University Press, 1984. ISBN 0-300-02797-4 (cl, 1983), 0-300-03246-3 (pbk). ‣ Broad synthesis of institutional and social history with history of ideas. Emphasizes socialists' democratic aspirations. Best introduction to this topic; annotated chapter bibliographies provide guides to further reading. [DSC]

22.348 Wm. Roger Louis, ed. *Imperialism: the Robinson and Gallagher controversy*. New York: New Viewpoints, 1976. ISBN 0-531-05375-X (cl), 0-531-05582-5 (pbk). ‣ Essay collection introduces and clarifies controversy (47.249) over relative importance of European and non-European factors evaluating imperialism. [DSC]

22.349 Wolfgang J. Mommsen. *Der europäische Imperialismus: Aufsätze und Abhandlungen*. Göttingen: Vandenhoeck & Ruprecht, 1979. ISBN 3-525-01321-3. ‣ Essays on how political, social, and economic factors fueled imperialism within European metropoles, and how imperialism helped to undermine liberal and democratic movements there. Balanced portrayal of ties between domestic politics and foreign policies. [DSC]

22.350 Wolfgang J. Mommsen. *Theories of imperialism*. 1980 ed. P. S. Falla, trans. Chicago. University of Chicago Press: 1982. ISBN 0-226-53396-4 (pbk). ‣ Superb survey, moving from classic texts, which took Eurocentric view of origins of imperialism—still an important perspective—to more recent recognition of role of periphery. [DSC]

22.351 Werner E. Mosse. *The European powers and the German question, 1848–1871, with special reference to England and Russia*. 1958 ed. New York: Octagon Press, 1969. ‣ Comprehensive diplomatic history. [DSC]

22.352 Lewis B. Namier. *1848: the revolution of the intellectuals*. 1946 ed. Oxford: Oxford University Press for British Academy, 1992. ISBN 0-19-726111-6. ‣ Classic discussion focused on Central Europe. Argues revolution had ideological but no concrete political results in that it heralded dangers of nationalist radicalism, rather than approaching social revolution. [DSC]

22.353 R. R. Palmer. *The age of democratic revolution: a political history of Europe and America, 1760–1800*. 1959–64 ed. 2 vols. Princeton: Princeton University Press, 1969–70. ISBN 0-691-00569-9 (v. 1), 0-691-00570-2 (v. 2). ‣ Important reinterpretation and synthesis, arguing French Revolution not unique event but part of general movement toward democracy in America and many countries of western Europe in late eighteenth century; justifies describing period as one of Atlantic democratic revolution. Offers comprehensive survey of revolutionary politics in all countries. [DSC]

22.354 Peter Paret, ed. *Makers of modern strategy from Machiavelli to the nuclear age*. Princeton: Princeton University Press, 1986. ISBN 0-691-09235-4 (cl), 0-691-02764-1 (pbk). ‣ Up-to-date essays by distinguished historians. Essential commentary on and guide to subject, strongest on nineteenth and twentieth centuries. Excellent bibliography. [DSC]

22.355 Maurice Pearton. *The knowledgeable state: diplomacy, war, and technology since 1830*. London: Burnett, 1982. ISBN 0-09-147230-X. ‣ Indispensable guide to how industrialization and technology changed relationship between war and peace and civil government and military by necessitating more advanced planning and more total economic committment. [DSC]

22.356 Léon Poliakov. *The history of anti-Semitism*. Vol. 3: *From Voltaire to Wagner*. Vol. 4: *Suicidal Europe, 1870–1933*. Miriam Kochan and George Klim, trans. New York: Vanguard, 1975–85. ISBN 0-8149-0762-8 (v. 3), 0-8149-0872-1 (v. 4). ‣ Richly detailed, exploring connections with nationalism. Final volume includes Russia but emphasizes France. [DSC]

22.357 Felix Ponteil. *L'éveil des nationalités et le mouvement libéral, 1815–1848*. Rev. ed. Paris: Presses Universitaires de France, 1960. (Peuples et civilisations, 15.) ‣ Detailed synthesis examining progress of liberalism and its impact from Congress of Vienna to eve of revolutions of 1848. Covers industrialization, social tensions, nationalism, and early imperialism. Emphasizes political history. [DSC]

22.358 Charles H. Pouthas. *Démocraties et capitalisme (1848–1860)*. 3d ed. Paris: Presses Universitaires de France, 1961. (Peuples et civilisations, 16.) ‣ Survey of revolutions of 1848 and ways that liberalism and nationalism continued to reshape politics in authoritarian regimes thereafter. [DSC]

22.359 Pierre Renouvin. *La crise européenne et la Première Guerre Mondiale*. 5th rev. ed. Paris: Presses Universitaires de France, 1969. (Peuples et civilisations, 19.) ‣ Survey emphasizing military and diplomatic history of World War I and integrating this with domestic politics, economics, culture, and examination of Europe's place in world. [DSC]

22.360 Pierre Renouvin. *Le dix-neuvième siècle*. Vol. 1: *De 1815 à 1871: l'Europe des nationalités et l'éveil de nouveaux mondes*. Vol. 2: *De 1871 à 1914: l'apogée de l'Europe*. 1954–55 ed. Paris: Hachette, 1965–67. ‣ Survey of nineteenth-century treaties, European domestic and international politics, and relations with new world and imperialism. [DSC]

22.361 Priscilla S. Robertson. *Revolutions of 1848: a social history*. 1952 ed. Princeton: Princeton University Press, 1967. ISBN 0-691-00756-X (pbk). ‣ Not social history as now understood, but narrative, anecdotal account by historian stressing futility of revolutions' outcome. Captures drama of events better than motives of participants. [DSC]

22.362 George Rudé. *Debate on Europe, 1815–1850*. New York: Harper & Row, 1972. ISBN 0-06-131702-0. ‣ Survey of historians' debates on history of Europe from settlement of Napoleonic wars to revolutions of 1848. Focused mostly on English and French literature. [DSC]

22.363 George Rudé. *Revolutionary Europe, 1783–1815*. 1964 ed. New York: Harper & Row, 1966. ‣ Excellent brief survey of society, government, interstate conflicts in prerevolutionary Europe, French Revolution, its impact and echoes in rest of Europe, Napoleonic era, and new legends, myths, and traditions. [DSC]

22.364 Guido Ruggiero. *The history of European liberalism*. 1959 ed. R. G. Collingwood, trans. Gloucester, Mass.: Smith, 1981. ‣ Study of background and historical forms of liberalism in England, France, Germany, and Italy. Views liberalism in context of European institutions and ideologies. Standard history that helped define European liberalism. [DSC]

22.365 Hagen Schulze, ed. *Nation-building in Central Europe*. Leamington Spa, England: Berg; distributed by St. Martin's, 1987. ISBN 0-85496-529-7. ‣ Short essays on rise of German nationalism, nationality problems, French and Polish relations with Germany, and German problem in European context. Good bibliography. [DSC]

22.366 Joseph Alois Schumpeter. *Imperialism and social classes*. 1951 ed. Paul M. Sweezy, ed. Heinz Norden, trans. Fairfield, N.J.: Kelley, 1989. ISBN 0-678-00020-4. ‣ Work by great economist, written in 1918, arguing imperialism not direct consequence of capitalism, but rather result of deformation of capitalist economies by interests of premodern feudal elites. [DSC]

22.367 Albert Sorel. *L'Europe et la Révolution française.* Edition varies. 8 vols. Paris: Plon, 1946–49. ▸ Long considered classic on Europe during French Revolution. Despite age, retains usefulness as most detailed treatment of high politics and diplomacy. [DSC]

22.368 Peter N. Stearns. *1848: the revolutionary tide in Europe.* New York: Norton, 1974. ISBN 0-393-05510-8 (cl), 0-393-09311-5 (pbk). ▸ Recent introduction to subject, treating social causes, social impact, and ideology. Revolutions of 1848 seen as learning experience for all classes. [DSC]

22.369 Norman Stone. *Europe transformed, 1878–1919.* Cambridge, Mass.: Harvard University Press, 1984. ISBN 0-674-26922-5 (cl), 0-674-26923-3 (pbk). ▸ Chronicle of death of liberalism throughout continent after 1870s. Survey incorporates findings of recent scholarship in social history. [DSC]

22.370 Hew Strachan. *European armies and the conduct of war.* Boston: Allen & Unwin, 1983. ISBN 0-04-940069-X (cl), 0-04-940070-3 (pbk). ▸ Best single-volume survey of theory and practice of land warfare in Europe, 1700 to present. Includes guide to further reading. [DSC]

22.371 A.J.P. Taylor. *The struggle for mastery in Europe, 1848–1918.* 1954 ed. New York: Oxford University Press, 1971. ISBN 0-19-501408-1. ▸ Standard work, provocative in its interpretations. Discusses European great-power diplomacy and relations with Russia as shifting definitions and justifications of national power, German unification, new alliances, and dissolution of Ottoman empire led to World War I. [DSC]

22.372 Jean Tulard. *Le grand empire, 1804–1815.* Paris: Albin-Michel, 1982. ISBN 2-226-01628-7. ▸ Examination of Napoleon's empire, which appeared as new, progressive Europe, but collapsed because it pursued economic policies that favored France alone. Sees empire's immediate legacy in that vision of Europe. [DSC]

22.373 E. L. Woodward. *Three studies in European conservatism: Metternich, Guizot, the Catholic church in the nineteenth century.* 1929 ed. Hamden, Conn.: Archon, 1963. ▸ Influential account by liberal historian of three instances in long defeat of conservatism. [DSC]

22.374 Stuart Woolf. *Napoleon's integration of Europe.* London: Routledge, 1991. ISBN 0-415-04961-X. ▸ Best synthesis examining intentions, tools of conquest, administration, exploitation, responses of the occupied, and legacies that shaped nineteenth century's expectations of state and desires to limit state power. Bibliography. [DSC]

SEE ALSO
18.313 David S. Landes. *Bankers and pashas.*
31.185 Hans-Ulrich Wehler. *The German empire, 1871–1918.*
31.208 Geoff Eley. *Reshaping the German Right.*
47.49 Henry A. Kissinger. *A world restored.*
47.184 Paul M. Kennedy. *The rise of the Anglo-German antagonism, 1860–1914.*
47.213 Herbert Feis. *Europe, the world's banker, 1870–1914.*
47.249 Ronald E. Robinson and John Gallagher. *Africa and the Victorians.*
47.301 George F. Kennan. *The decline of Bismarck's European order.*
47.302 George F. Kennan. *The fateful alliance.*
47.340 Imanuel Geiss, ed. *July 1914, the outbreak of the First World War.*
47.344 James Joll. *The origins of the First World War.*
47.346 Paul M. Kennedy, ed. *The war plans of the great powers, 1880–1914.*
47.348 John W. Langdon. *July 1914.*

Cultural and Intellectual History and Political Thought

22.375 M. H. Abrams. *Natural supernaturalism: tradition and revolution in romantic literature.* 1971 ed. New York: Norton, 1973. ISBN 0-393-00609-3. ▸ Romanticism as turning point for Western civilization. As mind of man replaced heaven and hell, theological feelings assimilated to nature. Treats works of William Wordsworth, Friedrich Schiller, G.W.F. Hegel, Friedrich Hölderlin, Goethe, William Blake, Samuel Coleridge, Percy Bysshe Shelley, and Thomas Carlyle, among others. Standard account. [DSC]

22.376 Raymond Aron. *Main currents in sociological thought.* Vol. 1: *Montesquieu, Comte, Marx, Tocqueville: the sociologists and the Revolution of 1848.* Vol. 2: *Durkheim, Pareto, Weber.* 1965–67 ed. 2 vols. Richard Howard and Helen Weaver, trans. Garden City, N.Y.: Anchor, 1968–70. ▸ Classic study of thinkers' contrasting views of relative importance of rational objective factors and subjective moral ones in understanding and explaining social facts; explains how their personalities and national cultures shaped their positions. [DSC]

22.377 Shlomo Avineri. *The social and political thought of Karl Marx.* 1968 ed. Cambridge: Cambridge University Press, 1990. ISBN 0-521-09619-7 (pbk). ▸ One-volume survey conveniently organized around major themes. Emphasizes continuing influence of Hegel and unity of Marx's thought. [DSC]

22.378 Jacques Barzun. *Classic, romantic, and modern.* 1961 2d rev. ed. Chicago: University of Chicago Press, 1975. ISBN 0-226-03852-1. ▸ Defends Romanticism when it was under attack, arguing it reinvigorated European culture, widening its emotional and intellectual horizons. Carefully distinguishes romanticism as cultural movement from anticultural subjectivism. [DSC]

22.379 Jacques Barzun. *Darwin, Marx, Wagner: critique of a heritage.* 1958 2d rev. ed. Chicago: University of Chicago Press, 1981. ISBN 0-226-03859-9 (pbk). ▸ Classic interpretation of three of nineteenth century's most influential thinkers. Suggests their legacy was one of dogmatism, mechanism, and intellectual and artistic imposture. [DSC]

22.380 James H. Billington. *Fire in the minds of men: origins of the revolutionary faith.* New York: Basic Books, 1980. ISBN 0-465-02405-X. ▸ Broad synthesis and entertaining narrative account of evolving faiths and intricately interconnected underworlds of nineteenth-century nationalist and social revolutionaries by historian drawing on Slavic as well as European sources. [DSC]

22.381 Roger Boesche. *The strange liberalism of Alexis de Tocqueville.* Ithaca, N.Y.: Cornell University Press, 1987. ISBN 0-8014-1964-6. ▸ How Tocqueville saw liberalism's impact on European politics and culture, his reasoning in trying to give it conservative and democratic ballast, and his influence. Essential work on seminal thinker. [DSC]

22.382 Marilyn J. Boxer and Jean H. Quataert, eds. *Socialist women: socialist feminism in the nineteenth and twentieth century.* New York: Elsevier, 1978. ISBN 0-444-99042-9 (cl), 0-444-99050-X (pbk). ▸ Essays presenting broad survey of major European socialists on relationship between socialism and feminism. [BYK]

22.383 Georg M. C. Brandes. *Main currents in nineteenth-century literature.* 1923 ed. 6 vols. Diana White and Mary Morison, trans. New York: Haskell, 1975. ISBN 0-8383-1574-7. ▸ Treats mainly romantic authors and poets to 1848. So rich in detail, it sometimes approaches social history. [DSC]

22.384 John Breuilly. *Nationalism and the state.* 1982 ed. Chicago: University of Chicago Press, 1985. ISBN 0-226-07412-9 (pbk). ▸ Theories of nationalism and comparative studies of different types, beginning in early modern Europe. Looks at unification, separatist, anticolonial, and reform nationalism worldwide. Most comprehensive historical sociology. [DSC]

22.385 Owen Chadwick. *The secularization of the European mind in the nineteenth century.* 1975 ed. Cambridge: Cambridge University Press, 1990. ISBN 0-521-39829-0. ▸ Superb introduction and survey. Examines wide range of intellectuals, placing them carefully in broader social contexts of urbanization, socialism, and anticlericalism. Demonstrates importance of religion in forming self-understanding even of those who chose irreligion. [DSC]

22.386 G.D.H. Cole. *A history of socialist thought.* Edition varies. 5 vols. London: Macmillan, 1953–67. ▸ Classic on movement and its thought by British guild socialist who thought that both Social Democrats and Communists depended too much on state. [DSC]

22.387 Frederick C. Copleston. *A history of philosophy.* Vol. 6: *Wolff to Kant.* Vol. 7: *Fichte to Nietzsche.* Vol. 8: *Bentham to Russell.* Edition varies. 9 vols. in 3. New York: Doubleday, 1985–. ISBN 0-385-23032-X (v. 2 [vols. 4–6], pbk), 0-385-23033-8 (v. 3 [vols. 7–9], pbk). ▸ Useful general reference covering Immanuel Kant, various idealists and materialists, Friedrich Nietzsche, utilitarianism, realism, John Dewey, and Bertrand Russell among others. [DSC]

22.388 Peter Gay. *Freud: a life for our time.* 1988 ed. New York: Anchor, 1989. ISBN 0-385-26256-6 (pbk). ▸ Important general biography. [DSC]

22.389 Ernest Gellner. *Nations and nationalism.* Ithaca, N.Y.: Cornell University Press, 1983. ISBN 0-8014-1662-0 (cl), 0-8014-9263-7 (pbk). ▸ Critical of Kedourie 22.409, arguing nationalism not merely ideology, but emerged in answer to requirements of social and cultural system created with industrialization. Influential, easily understood statement of this argument. [DSC]

22.390 Martin Green. *The mountain of truth: the counter-culture begins, Ascona, 1900–1920.* Hanover, N.H.: University Press of New England for Tufts University, 1988. ISBN 0-87451-365-0. ▸ Discussion of first counterculture and its commune, its international fame, visitors, and influences; also "first hippies," Otto Gross, Gusto Gräser, and Rudolf Laban. [DSC]

22.391 Martin Green. *The von Richthofen sisters: the triumphant and tragic modes of love, Else and Frieda von Richthofen, Otto Gross, Max Weber, and D. H. Lawrence in the years 1870–1970.* 1974 ed. Albuquerque: University of New Mexico Press, 1988. ISBN 0-8263-1038-9 (pbk). ▸ Sisters' relationships with Max Weber and D. H. Lawrence helped shape both mens' views and established terrain of profound conflict between intellectual styles of ascetic responsibility and literary romanticism. [DSC]

22.392 Élie Halévy. *The growth of philosophic radicalism.* Rev. ed. Mary Morris, trans. Clifton, N.J.: Kelley, 1972. ISBN 0-678-08005-4. ▸ Standard work on English utilitarianism. Treats David Hume, Jeremy Bentham, Adam Smith, Edmund Burke, Thomas Godwin, William R. Malthus, J. S. Mill, and David Ricardo among others. [DSC]

22.393 Geoffrey Hawthorn. *Enlightenment and despair: a history of sociology.* 2d ed. Cambridge: Cambridge University Press, 1987. ISBN 0-521-33101-3 (cl), 0-521-33721-6 (pbk). ▸ Very useful synthesis with concise analyses of individual thinkers. Presents history of social theorizing since Enlightenment as history of failure to reckon with practical contexts. [DSC]

22.394 Carlton J. H. Hayes. *The historical evolution of modern nationalism.* 1931 ed. New York: Russell & Russell, 1968. ▸ Still useful, broad survey of nationalist ideas. [DSC]

22.395 Friedrich Heer. *Europe, mother of revolutions.* Charles Kessler and Jennetta Adcock. London: Weidenfeld & Nicolson, 1971. ISBN 0-297-99382-8. ▸ General survey of thought in nineteenth century. Some chapters very weak, but stronger ones on Germany, Catholic social thought, and Russia in Europe. [DSC]

22.396 Erich Heller. *The artist's journey into the interior and other essays.* 1965 ed. New York: Harcourt Brace Jovanovich, 1976. ISBN 0-15-607950-X. ▸ Collection of essays. Famous title essay sums up hubris and despair of nineteenth- and early twentieth-century poets in Central Europe and beyond. Another portrays Friedrich Schiller's transfer of theological desires to art as spiritual catastrophe for European civilization. Read with 22.397. [DSC]

22.397 Erich Heller. *The disinherited mind: essays in modern German literature and thought.* 4th ed. New York: Harcourt Brace Jovanovich, 1975. ISBN 0-15-626100-6. ▸ This book and its companion (22.396) essential for understanding contribution of Central European poets and philosophers to modern mind. Discusses bitter retreat of culture into the mind, where it cannot survive. [DSC]

22.398 Erich Heller. *The importance of Nietzsche: ten essays.* Chicago: University of Chicago Press, 1988. ISBN 0-226-32637-3 (cl), 0-226-32638-1 (pbk). ▸ Seminal, widely admired essays on Friedrich Nietzsche and Western tradition and his influence on later thinkers and poets. Places him in relation to Johann Wolfgang von Goethe, Jacob Burckhardt, Rainer Maria Rilke, William Butler Yeats, Ludwig Wittgenstein, and postmodernists. [DSC]

22.399 Wilhelm Hennis. *Max Weber: essays in reconstruction.* Keith Tribe, trans. London: Allen & Unwin, 1988. ISBN 0-04-301301-5. ▸ Important reconstruction of Weber's intentions and ideas, distinguishing them sharply from those of modern social science and emphasizing his cultural and historical concerns. Stresses Friedrich Nietzsche's influence. [DSC]

22.400 Eric J. Hobsbawm. *Nations and nationalism since 1780: programme, myth, reality.* 2d ed. Cambridge: Cambridge University Press, 1992. ISBN 0-521-43961-2. ▸ Argues French and German cases anomalous. Offers good account of new era of nationalism after 1870; especially strong on popular proto-nationalism and linguistic aspects. [DSC]

22.401 Stephen Holmes. *Benjamin Constant and the making of modern liberalism.* New Haven: Yale University Press, 1984. ISBN 0-300-03083-5. ▸ Essential for understanding origins of modern liberalism. Contributes to debate over how much modern political thought has learned from ancient republics, emphasizing limits of this debt. [DSC]

22.402 Sidney Hook. *From Hegel to Marx: studies in the intellectual development of Karl Marx.* 1936 ed. Ann Arbor: University of Michigan Press, 1968. ▸ Important, first work in English to take account of discovery of young Marx's manuscripts. Examines G.W.F. Hegel's influence on Marx and Marx's relations with young Hegelians, including Arnold Ruge, Max Stirner, Moses Hess, and especially Ludwig Feuerbach. [DSC]

22.403 H. Stuart Hughes. *Consciousness and society: the reorientation of European social thought, 1890–1930.* Rev. ed. New York: Vintage, 1977. ISBN 0-394-70201-8. ▸ Analysis of how thinkers responded as new psychological and historical knowledge imposed limits on their faith in reason. Classic account of how social thought shaped modern mind. [DSC]

22.404 Richard N. Hunt. *The political ideas of Marx and Engels.* Vol. 1: *Marxism and totalitarian democracy, 1818–1850.* Vol. 2: *Classical Marxism, 1850–1895.* 2 vols. Pittsburgh: University of Pittsburgh Press, 1974–84. ISBN 0-8229-3285-7 (v. 1), 0-8229-3496-5 (v. 2). ▸ Valuable for attention to historical context of ideas, especially in first volume. Sees both men as decidedly more democratic than many of their followers. [DSC]

22.405 Gerald N. Izenberg. *Impossible individuality: romanticism, revolution, and the origins of modern selfhood, 1787–1802.* Princeton: Princeton University Press, 1992. ISBN 0-691-06926-3. ▸ Writers in Germany, France, and England and political, social, and psychological origins of modern concept of selfhood. Provocative interpretation rooted in biographical detail. [DSC]

22.406 Hubert Jedin and John T. Dolan, eds. *History of the church.* Vols. 7–10. New York: Crossroad, 1980–81. ISBN 0-8245-0318-X (set), 0-8245-0004-0 (v. 7), 0-8245-0011-3 (v. 8), 0-8245-0012-1 (v. 9), 0-8245-0013-X (v. 10). ▸ Collaborative work of reference and standard, official history of Catholicism covering modernism controversy and other aspects of confrontation with industrial age. Dense scholarly apparatus. [DSC]

22.407 James Joll. *The anarchists.* 1979 2d ed. Cambridge, Mass.: Harvard University Press, 1980. ISBN 0-674-03641-7 (cl), 0-674-03642-5 (pbk). ▸ Best introduction to nineteenth-century anarchists and movements. [DSC]

22.408 Ernest Jones. *The life and work of Sigmund Freud.* 3 vols. New York: Basic Books, 1953–57. ▸ Written by one of Freud's disciples. Rich in information, but tries to put Freud and his circle in best possible light. [DSC]

22.409 Elie Kedourie. *Nationalism.* 4th rev. ed. London: Hutchinson, 1985. ISBN 0-09-053444-1 (pbk). ▸ Essential essay on how Europeans invented doctrine of nationalism at beginning of nineteenth century. [DSC]

22.410 Hans Kohn. *Prophets and peoples: studies in nineteenth-century nationalism.* 1946 ed. New York: Octagon Books, 1975. ▸ Brief survey of what J. S. Mill, Jules Michelet, Giuseppe Mazzini, Heinrich von Treitschke, and Fyodor Dostoevsky had to say about nationalism. [DSC]

22.411 Leszek Kolakowski. *Main currents of Marxism: its origins, growth, and dissolution.* 1978 ed. 3 vols. P. S. Falla, trans. Oxford: Oxford University Press, 1981. ISBN 0-19-285107-1 (v. 1, pbk), 0-19-285108-X (v. 2, pbk), 0-19-285109-8 (v. 3, pbk). ▸ Standard general reference. Penetrating, philosophically informed account of thought of Marx and Friedrich Engels, its intellectual roots and influence, and indispensable survey of later Marxism. [DSC]

22.412 Kenneth Scott Latourette. *The nineteenth century in Europe: background and the Roman Catholic phase.* Vol. 1 of *Christianity in a revolutionary age: a history of Christianity in the nineteenth and twentieth centuries.* New York: Harper & Brothers, 1958. ▸ Addresses political as well as religious themes: revolution and Catholic responses, and institutional, devotional, intellectual, and national transformation throughout nineteenth century. Protestant scholar's account offers valuable overview and detail. [DSC]

22.413 Kenneth Scott Latourette. *The nineteenth century in Europe: the Protestant and Eastern churches.* Vol. 2 of *Christianity in a revolutionary age: a history of Christianity in the nineteenth and twentieth centuries.* New York: Harper & Brothers, 1959. ▸ Invaluable overview. Country-by-country examination of theology, biblical and historical studies, awakenings and revivals, and organization and squabbles. [DSC]

22.414 Émile G. Léonard. *Déclin et renouveau: dix-huitième-vingtième siècle.* Vol. 3 of *Histoire générale du Protestantisme.* 1964 ed. Paris: Presses Universitaires de France, 1988. ISBN 2-13-041888-0 (v. 3). ▸ Well-regarded work, covers eighteenth to twentieth century. [DSC]

22.415 Wolf Lepenies. *Between literature and science: the rise of sociology.* 1988 ed. R. J. Hollingdale, trans. New York: Cambridge University Press, 1992. ISBN 0-521-32852-7. ▸ Penetrating study showing how and why social science and literature, in French, English, and German contexts, have fought with and needed each other, in each case for reasons embedded in national culture. [DSC]

22.416 George Lichtheim. *Marxism: an historical and critical study.* 1964 2d rev. ed. New York: Columbia University Press, 1982. ISBN 0-231-05424-6 (cl), 0-231-05425-4 (pbk). ▸ One-volume survey, critical but sympathetic. Focuses on Friedrich Engels's role in creating scientist Marxism that emasculated vital elements of socialism. [DSC]

22.417 George Lichtheim. *The origins of socialism.* New York: Praeger, 1969. ▸ Concise, well-written introduction. Surveys radical responses to French Revolution and English critics of early Industrial Revolution, explaining how Marx built on these traditions. [DSC]

22.418 Karl Löwith. *From Hegel to Nietzsche: the revolution in nineteenth-century thought.* 1964 ed. David E. Green, trans. New York: Columbia University Press, 1991. ISBN 0-231-07498-0 (cl), 0-231-07499-9 (pbk). ▸ Study of reception of G.W.F. Hegel in works of Ludwig Feuerbach, Arnold Ruge, Bruno Bauer, Max Stirner, Marx, and Sören Kierkegaard in context that stretches from Jean-Jacques Rousseau to Friedrich Nietzsche. Discusses how nineteenth-century thinkers replaced Christianity with humanism, then lost faith in humanity. Classic work. [DSC]

22.419 Maurice Mandelbaum. *History, man, and reason: a study in nineteenth-century thought.* 1971 ed. Baltimore: Johns Hopkins University Press, 1974. ISBN 0-8018-1608-4. ▸ Standard work on historicism in nineteenth-century philosophical movements. How historicism interacted with and helped shape ideas about malleability of man, views of limits of reason, and rebellion against reason. [DSC]

22.420 Herbert Marcuse. *Reason and revolution: Hegel and the rise of social theory.* 1955 2d ed. Atlantic Highlands, N.J.: Humanities Press, 1989. ISBN 0-391-02999-1. ▸ Romantic Marxist's view of philosopher's work as summons to perpetual revolution. Influential study among leftists that helped resurrect outlook associated with younger Marx. [DSC]

22.421 William J. McGrath. *Freud's discovery of psychoanalysis: the politics of hysteria.* Ithaca, N.Y.: Cornell University Press, 1986. ISBN 0-8014-1770-8. ▸ Essential, detailed account of cultural origins of Freud's ideas, focusing on role of Freud's inner life and responses to political, religious, and scientific controversies in *fin-de-siècle* Vienna in shaping his theories. [DSC]

22.422 John T. Merz. *A history of European thought in the nineteenth century.* 1904–12 ed. 4 vols. New York: Dover, 1965. ▸ First two volumes survey science, second two philosophy. [DSC]

22.423 Arthur Mitzman. *The iron cage: an historical interpretation of Max Weber.* 1969 ed. New Brunswick, N.J.: Transaction, 1985. ISBN 0-87855-984-1 (pbk). ▸ Standard biographical introduction. How Weber's theoretical concerns mirrored tensions between bourgeois virtues embodied in ascetic rationality and ethics of responsibility and erotic, mystical, neoromantic currents of *fin-de-siècle*. [DSC]

22.424 Wolfgang J. Mommsen. *The age of bureaucracy: perspectives on the political sociology of Max Weber.* 1974 ed. New York: Harper & Row, 1977. ISBN 0-06-131862-0. ▸ Influential scholar's concise essays portraying historical context of Weber's ideas: relation to Marx, support for imperialism, view of democracy, and troubled identity as German liberal. [DSC]

22.425 Wolfgang J. Mommsen and Jürgen Osterhammel, eds. *Max Weber and his contemporaries.* 1987 ed. London: Unwin Hyman for German Historical Institute, 1989. ISBN 0-04-445148-2 (pbk). ▸ Essays address Weber's relations with social science and social scientists, with theologians and historians, with politicians and activists, and with philosophers. Illustrates range of Weber's influence. [DSC]

22.426 Maurice Olender. *The languages of paradise: race, religion, and philology in the nineteenth century.* Arthur Goldhammer, trans. Cambridge, Mass.: Harvard University Press, 1992. ISBN 0-674-51052-6. ▸ History of philology key to understanding modern racial and ethnic myths. Rich account of scholars' myth making. [DSC]

22.427 Daniel Pick. *Faces of degeneration: a European disorder, c. 1848–c. 1918.* Cambridge: Cambridge University Press, 1989. ISBN 0-521-36021-8. ‣ Study of anxieties and ideas that provided cultural basis and content of social Darwinism in France, Italy, and England. For Germany see Weindling 4.742. [DSC]

22.428 Karl Pribram. *A history of economic reasoning.* Baltimore: Johns Hopkins University Press, 1983. ISBN 0-8018-2291-2. ‣ Study of how economic reasoning unfolded as integral part of Western thought. Published posthumously, unfinished; but a monumental work of scholarship. [DSC]

22.429 Bernard M. G. Reardon. *Religion in the age of romanticism: studies in early nineteenth-century thought.* Cambridge: Cambridge University Press, 1985. ISBN 0-521-30088-6 (cl), 0-521-31745-2 (pbk). ‣ Discusson of essential themes and Continental thinkers, including Friedrich Daniel Ernst Schleiermacher and G.W.F. Hegel, Catholic theologians influenced by Friedrich Wilhelm Joseph von Schelling, Félicité Robert de Lamennais, and Ernest Renan among others. Particularly useful for understanding conflicts within Catholic church in Germany. [DSC/JS]

22.430 Hans Rogger and Eugen Weber, eds. *The European Right: a historical profile.* 1965 ed. Berkeley: University of California Press, 1966. ‣ Fine introduction to developing ideologies and parties of extreme Right in western Europe, Germany, Russia, Finland, and Romania in late nineteenth and twentieth centuries. See also Sternhell's work (26.183) on topic, now considered fundamental. [DSC]

22.431 Eric Roll. *A history of economic thought.* 5th rev. ed. London: Faber & Faber, 1992. ISBN 0-571-16553-2. ‣ Standard general introduction. [DSC]

22.432 Lawrence Scaff. *Fleeing the iron cage: culture, politics, and modernity in the thought of Max Weber.* Berkeley: University of California Press, 1989. ISBN 0-520-06435-6 (cl), 0-520-07547-1 (pbk). ‣ Close reading of Weber on quality of modern humanity and on living in modern subjectivist culture. Builds on Hennis 22.399. [DSC]

22.433 Joseph Alois Schumpeter. *The history of economic analysis.* 1954 ed. Elizabeth Boody Schumpeter, ed. London: Allen & Unwin, 1986. ISBN 0-04-330086-3 (cl), 0-04-330376-5 (pbk). ‣ Classic work on internal history of science of economics. [DSC]

22.434 Jerrold Seigel. *Marx's fate: the shape of a life.* Princeton: Princeton University Press, 1978. ISBN 0-691-05259-X. ‣ Interesting scholarly biography of Marx. Somewhat Freudian, but very strong on other contexts of his thought and political activities. Footnotes serve as good bibliography. [DSC]

22.435 George Steiner. *In Bluebeard's castle: some notes toward the redefinition of culture.* New Haven: Yale University Press, 1971. (T. S. Eliot memorial lectures, 1970.) ISBN 0-300-01501-1 (cl), 0-300-01710-3 (pbk). ‣ Broad interpretation of nineteenth-century culture. Western culture's destructive conception of truth and ennui of long, slow nineteenth century incubated violence of twentieth. [DSC]

22.436 Frank J. Sulloway. *Freud, biologist of the mind: beyond the psychoanalytic legend.* New York: Basic Books, 1979. ISBN 0-465-02559-5. ‣ Argues Freud drew heavily on contemporary scientific knowledge in biology and psychology, and although his contribution was respectable, work reflected limits of those fields at that time. Standard general reference. [DSC]

22.437 Charles Taylor. *Hegel.* 1975 ed. Cambridge: Cambridge University Press, 1977. ISBN 0-521-29199-2 (pbk). ‣ One of most lucid studies of Georg Wilhelm Friedrich Hegel. Sets Hegel firmly in context of times and demonstrates importance in shap-

ing later accounts, including Marx's, of situation and meaning of freedom. [DSC]

22.438 Robert C. Tucker. *The Marxian revolutionary idea.* 1969 ed. New York: Norton, 1970. ISBN 0-393-00539-9. ‣ Short essay comparing Marxist social theory with Marxist ideology. Argues Marx can be viewed as revolutionary, but not as successful social theorist. [DSC]

22.439 Robert C. Tucker. *Philosophy and myth in Karl Marx.* 2d ed. Cambridge: Cambridge University Press, 1972. ISBN 0-521-08455-5 (cl), 0-521-09701-0 (pbk). ‣ Important critique of Marx. Argues young Marx's moralistic focus on problems of alienation distorted his later thinking; as consequence he lacked empirical interest in economics and failed to develop adequate conception of freedom. [DSC]

22.440 Alec R. Vidler. *The church in an age of revolution, 1789 to the present day.* 1971 rev. ed. Harmondsworth: Penguin, 1985. ISBN 0-14-020506-3. ‣ Survey of major developments in both Catholic and Protestant churches. [DSC]

22.441 René Wellek. *A history of modern criticism: 1750–1950.* Vol. 2: *The romantic age.* Vol. 3: *The age of transition.* Vol. 5: *English criticism, 1900–1950.* Vol. 7: *German, Russian, and eastern European criticism, 1900–1950.* New Haven: Yale University Press, 1955–92. ISBN 0-300-03378-8 (v. 5), 0-300-05039-9 (v. 7). ‣ Standard history of literary criticism, touching on every important critic and movement. [DSC]

22.442 George Woodcock. *Anarchism: a history of libertarian ideas and movements.* Rev. ed. Harmondsworth: Penguin, 1986. ISBN 0-14-022697-4 (pbk). ‣ Comprehensive history touching on every aspect of philosophy and all movements. Good bibliography. [DSC]

22.443 Bernard Yack. *The longing for total revolution: philosophic sources of social discontent from Rousseau to Marx and Nietzsche.* Princeton: Princeton University Press, 1986. ISBN 0-691-07712-6. ‣ Seminal account. Argues social critics, especially Kantian Left who rejected role of institutions in conditioning people, could not pursue any particular conception of freedom, only objects of hatred. Claims G.W.F. Hegel, despite defects, offered better approach. [DSC]

SEE ALSO
  26.266 Roger Shattuck. *The banquet years.*
  28.416 Jack J. Roth. *The cult of violence.*
  30.323 Karl Barth. *Protestant theology in the nineteenth century.*
  31.268 Wolfgang J. Mommsen. *Max Weber and German politics, 1890–1920.*
  31.315 Carl E. Schorske. *Fin-de-siècle Vienna.*

Economic, Social, and Women's History

22.444 Samuel J. Behrman, Leslie Corsa, Jr., and Ronald Freedman, eds. *Fertility and family planning: a world view.* Ann Arbor: University of Michigan Press, 1969. ISBN 0-472-14200-3 (cl), 0-472-08126-8 (pbk). ‣ Illuminating analysis of global fertility trends from eighteenth to twentieth century, including causes, consequences, biological aspects, and programs for family planning. [BYK]

22.445 Susan Groag Bell and Karen M. Offen, eds. *Women, the family, and freedom: the debate in documents, 1750–1950.* 2 vols. Stanford, Calif.: Stanford University Press, 1983. ISBN 0-8047-1170-4 (v. 1, cl), 0-8047-1172-0 (v. 2, cl), 0-8047-1171-2 (v. 1, pbk), 0-8047-1173-9 (v. 2, pbk). ‣ Analysis of women's position in European society relative to men from Enlightenment to mid-twentieth century. Thematic organization based on contemporary documents stating and challenging prevailing ideas concerning family roles and education, employment, political life, and women's legal status. [BYK]

22.446 Jerome Blum. *The end of the old order in rural Europe.* Princeton: Princeton University Press, 1978. ISBN 0-691-05266-2 (cl), 0-691-10067-5 (pbk). ▸ Justly admired work, examining demographic, economic, technological, and social change, and politics from late eighteenth to early nineteenth century. Finds common pattern in agrarian change and peasant emancipation across Europe and Russia. [DSC]

22.447 Carlo M. Cipolla, ed. *Contemporary economies.* Vol. 6 of *The Fontana economic history of Europe.* 1976 ed. New York: Barnes & Noble with Fontana, 1977. ISBN 0-06-492183-2 (v. 6.1), 0-06-492184-0 (v. 6.2). ▸ Country-by-country survey of twentieth-century economies. [DSC]

22.448 Carlo M. Cipolla, ed. *The emergence of industrial societies.* Vol. 4 of *The Fontana economic history of Europe.* 1973 ed. New York: Barnes & Noble with Fontana, 1976. ISBN 0-06-492179-4 (v. 4.1), 0-06-492180-8 (v. 4.2). ▸ Country-by-country survey of developments from early Industrial Revolution to 1914 with concluding chapter on emergence of world economy centered on Europe. [DSC]

22.449 Carlo M. Cipolla, ed. *The Industrial Revolution, 1700–1914.* Vol. 3 of *The Fontana economic history of Europe.* 1973 ed. New York: Barnes & Noble with Fontana, 1976. ISBN 0-06-492178-6. ▸ Concision and variety of perspectives distinguish this series from others. [DSC]

22.450 Carlo M. Cipolla, ed. *The twentieth century.* Vol. 5 of *The Fontana economic history of Europe.* 1976 ed. New York: Barnes & Noble with Fontana, 1977. ISBN 0-06-492181-6 (v. 5.1), 0-06-492182-4 (v. 5.2). ▸ Concise essays by specialists surveying population, demand, labor, management, Keynesian economics, agriculture, national planning, environment, investment policies, and money supply in European economies. [DSC]

22.451 J. H. Clapham. *The economic development of France and Germany, 1815–1914.* 1936 4th ed. Cambridge: Cambridge University Press, 1968. ▸ Old but still rewarding comparative economic history. [DSC]

22.452 Ansley J. Coale and Susan Cotts Watkins, eds. *The decline of fertility in Europe: the revised proceedings of a conference on the Princeton European Fertility Project.* Princeton: Princeton University Press for Office of Population Research, 1986. ISBN 0-691-09416-0 (cl), 0-691-10176-0 (pbk). ▸ Summary of findings of study of fertility, eighteenth century to 1980s, assessing social, economic, and cultural factors. This study of Office of Population Research at Princeton University generated many articles and monographs; see, for example, Anderson 34.247, Knodel 31.247, Livi-Bacci 29.187, Van de Walle 26.319, and Watkins 22.495. [DSC]

22.453 Geoffrey Crossick and Heinz-Gerhard Haupt, eds. *Shopkeepers and master artisans in nineteenth-century Europe.* London: Methuen, 1984. ISBN 0-416-35660-5. ▸ Examination of group with considerable but varied political influence, treating political, economic, and social aspects. Excellent introduction; notes provide good bibliography. Includes German, British, French, Belgian, and Austrian case studies. [DSC]

22.454 François Crouzet. *Britain ascendant: comparative studies in Franco-British economic history.* Martin Thom, trans. Cambridge: Cambridge University Press, 1990. ISBN 0-521-34434-4. ▸ Essays providing good general orientation and bibliography on number of topics including capital formation, Napoleon's continental system, and western Europe's attempts to catch up with Britain. [DSC]

22.455 François Crouzet, W. H. Challoner, and W. M. Stern, eds. *Essays in European economic history, 1789–1914.* London: Arnold for Economic History Society, 1969. ISBN 0-7131-5461-6. ▸ Useful essays on important topics including liberal agrarian

reforms' impact on social structure in Central Europe, new banks, and German cartels. [DSC]

22.456 Phyllis Deane. *The first Industrial Revolution.* 2d ed. Cambridge: Cambridge University Press, 1979. ISBN 0-521-22667-8 (cl), 0-521-29609-9 (pbk). ▸ Excellent study of breakthrough to modern pattern of economic growth in British economy, 1750–1850. [DSC]

22.457 Jacques Donzelot. *The policing of families.* Robert Hurley, trans. New York: Pantheon, 1979. ISBN 0-394-50338-4 (cl), 0-394-73752-0 (pbk). ▸ Influential, follows Foucault 22.460; examines charity, social welfare, and psychoanalysis in nineteenth and twentieth centuries. Argues state's use of social welfare to control individuals encouraged moral values to float in equilibrium with social norms. [DSC]

22.458 Jacques Dupâquier et al., eds. *Marriage and remarriage in populations of the past.* New York: Academic Press, 1981. ISBN 0-12-224660-8. ▸ Detailed studies of effects of marriage and remarriage on fertility, inheritance, and family structure from seventeenth to nineteenth century showing different gender patterns of remarriage in French, Nordic, Asian, and Islamic cultures. [BYK]

22.459 Lewis S. Feuer. *The conflict of generations: the character and significance of student movements.* New York: Basic Books, 1969. ▸ Unable to overcome limited perspectives of university life, emerging movements usually chose self-destructive means of authoritarian Left or Right. Opinionated but essential for catastrophic politics of German, Bosnian, Russian, and other movements. [DSC]

22.460 Michel Foucault. *Discipline and punish: the birth of the prison.* 1977 ed. Alan Sheridan [-Smith], trans. New York: Vintage, 1979. ISBN 0-394-72767-3 (pbk). ▸ Influential study of how technologies of social discipline reshaped society and remade visions of self at time of Industrial Revolution. [DSC]

22.461 Michel Foucault. *History of sexuality.* 1978–86 ed. 3 vols. Robert Hurley, trans. New York: Vintage, 1988–90. ISBN 0-394-74026-2 (v. 1, pbk), 0-394-75122-1 (v. 2, pbk), 0-394-74155-2 (v. 3, pbk). ▸ Provocative and very influential investigation into regulation of sexuality in Greek and Roman culture and in western Europe since seventeenth century. Based on theory that power in modern society is exercised through professional definition of knowledge; maintains that growing discourse on sexuality indicates desire to control not repress. [BYK/JML]

22.462 Peter Gay. *The bourgeois experience: Victoria to Freud.* Vol. 1: *The education of the senses.* Vol. 2: *The tender passion.* New York: Oxford University Press, 1984, 1986–87. ISBN 0-19-503352-3 (v. 1, cl), 0-19-503741-3 (v. 2, cl), 0-19-503728-6 (v. 1, pbk), 0-19-505183-1 (v. 2, pbk). ▸ Ambitious study of European and American middle classes, including sexuality, private life, erotic feeling and conduct, and experience of love. [JML]

22.463 Dick Geary. *European labor protest, 1848–1939.* New York: St. Martin's, 1981. ISBN 0-312-26974-9. ▸ Brief survey of issues that arise when labor history focuses on motives and experiences of ordinary workers. Represents move away from institutional histories of parties and unions. Useful bibliographic notes. [DSC]

22.464 John R. Gillis. *Youth and history: tradition and change in European age relations, 1770–present.* Rev. ed. New York: Academic Press, 1981. ISBN 0-12-785264-6. ▸ Survey of youth cultures, movements, and experiences from eighteenth to twentieth century. Author a 1968er who believes adolescents make their own history. [DSC]

22.465 H. J. Habakkuk and Michael Moissey Postan, eds. *The industrial revolutions and after: incomes, population, and technological change.* Vol. 6 of *The Cambridge economic history of Europe.*

Cambridge: Cambridge University Press, 1965. ▸ Discussion of national incomes, population, transport, and changes in technology and agriculture across Europe. Separate treatment of Russian industrialization with brief surveys of United States and Far East. [DSC]

22.466   Eli F. Heckscher. *The Continental system: an economic interpretation.* 1922 ed. Harald Westergaard, ed. C. S. Fearenside, trans. Gloucester, Mass.: Smith, 1964. ISBN 0-8446-1230-8. ▸ Classic study of Napoleon's self-blockade of Continent. [DSC]

22.467   W. O. Henderson. *Britain and industrial Europe, 1750–1870: studies in British influence on the Industrial Revolution in western Europe.* 3d ed. Leicester: Leicester University Press, 1972. ISBN 0-7185-1116-6. ▸ Older but standard work on British influence and transmission of technical knowledge and entrepreneurial skills and investment in France, Belgium, Holland, Germany, Habsburg empire, and Switzerland. [DSC]

22.468   Miroslav Hroch. *Social preconditions of national revival in Europe: a comparative analysis of the social composition of patriotic groups among the smaller European nations.* Ben Fowkes, trans. Cambridge: Cambridge University Press, 1985. ISBN 0-521-22891-3. ▸ Important structural study comparing groups in nineteenth and twentieth centuries in Norway, Bohemia, Finland, Slovakia, Belgium (Flemish groups), and Schleswig (Danes). [DSC]

22.469   Konrad H. Jarausch, ed. *The transformation of higher learning, 1860–1930: expansion, diversification, social opening, and professionalization in England, Germany, Russia, and the United States.* Chicago: University of Chicago Press, 1983. ISBN 0-226-39367-4. ▸ Dense essays with statistics on enrollment, social recruitment, gender of students, fees, disciplines, institutional types, and career choices chart emergence of modern systems of higher education. [DSC]

22.470   Hartmut Kaelble. *Industrialisation and social inequality in nineteenth-century Europe.* Bruce Little, trans. Leamington Spa, England: Berg, 1986. ISBN 0-907582-37-0 (cl), 0-907582-38-9 (pbk). ▸ Study of inequality in wealth and income, in workplace, in housing, in health care, between social classes, and in strata within classes. Compact, rigorous survey of current literature on question. [DSC]

22.471   David S. Landes. *The unbound Prometheus: technological change and industrial development in western Europe from 1750 to the present.* Cambridge: Cambridge University Press, 1969. ISBN 0-521-07200-X (cl), 0-521-09418-6 (pbk). ▸ Standard work on how technological change, social organization, and other factors influenced timing and different characteristics of Industrial Revolution and later development in Britain, France, and Germany. [DSC/JKS]

22.472   Peter Mathias and Sidney Pollard, eds. *The industrial economies: the development of economic and social policies.* Vol. 8 of *The Cambridge economic history of Europe.* Cambridge: Cambridge University Press, 1989. ISBN 0-521-22504-3. ▸ Collection of studies surveying trade policies and politics in nineteenth century, world trade and its disintegration in 1930s, currencies, national fiscal policies, taxation and public finance, labor-state relations, and economic and social policy making in major and some peripheral powers to 1940s. [DSC]

22.473   Peter Mathias and Michael Moissey Postan, eds. *The industrial economies: capital, labor, and enterprise.* Part 1: *Britain, France, Germany, and Scandinavia.* Part 2: *The United States, Japan, and Russia.* Vol. 7 of *The Cambridge economic history of Europe.* Cambridge: Cambridge University Press, 1978. ISBN 0-521-21124-7 (set), 0-521-21590-0 (v. 7.1), 0-521-21591-9 (v. 7.2). ▸ Essential work of synthesis and interpretation by number of specialists. European chapters examine capital formation, labor market, entrepreneurs, and management from the Indus-

trial Revolution through World War II. Stops short of important restructuring of 1950s. [DSC]

22.474   Arno J. Mayer. *The persistence of the Old Regime: Europe to the Great War.* New York: Pantheon, 1981. ISBN 0-394-51141-7. ▸ Polemical essay arguing premodern elites continued to rule until World War I. Simplistic view of political culture ignores populism and much else. Essential and more nuanced perspectives provided by national studies. See Eley 31.227 and Blackbourn and Eley 31.174 on Germany and Dangerfield 24.51 on Britain. [DSC]

22.475   Mary Jo Maynes. *Schooling in western Europe: a social history.* Albany: State University of New York Press, 1985. ISBN 0-87395-976-0 (cl), 0-87395-977-9 (pbk). ▸ Brief synthesis of reforms and social motives from early modern period through Industrial Revolution. Uses French, German, and English literature and sources. Useful bibliography. [DSC]

22.476   John M. Merriman, ed. *Consciousness and class experience in nineteenth-century Europe.* New York: Holmes & Meier, 1979. ISBN 0-8419-0444-8. ▸ Representative of social historians' concern with class conflict, studies examine experience of labor in Industrial Revolution and address theoretical controversies about proletarianization. Covers England and France only. [DSC]

22.477   Alan S. Milward and S. B. Saul. *The development of the economies of Continental Europe, 1850–1914.* Cambridge, Mass.: Harvard University Press, 1977. ISBN 0-674-20023-3. ▸ Continues 22.478, arguing real forces of development were at first far removed from technology. Changes in social and economic structures preceded and balanced technological innovation; relative autonomy of industry came late. Accessible and important corrective to technological determinism. [DSC]

22.478   Alan S. Milward and S. B. Saul. *The economic development of Continental Europe, 1780–1870.* 2d ed. London: Allen & Unwin, 1979. ISBN 0-04-330299-8. ▸ First of two volumes (with 22.477) offering broad synthesis and interpretation of relationship between economic and social change and technology. Overview of changes in late eighteenth century, influence of British economy, population, technological changes, and French Revolution; surveys major powers and regions to 1870. [DSC]

22.479   Harvey Mitchell and Peter N. Stearns. *Workers and protest: the European labor movement, the working classes, and the origins of social democracy, 1890–1914.* Itasca, Ill.: Peacock, 1971. ▸ Informative debate between two historians on relative roles of ideology, labor elites, and attitudes of rank and file in development of reformist and revisionist tendencies in British, French, and German labor movements. [DSC]

22.480   Wolfgang J. Mommsen and Gerhard Hirschfeld, eds. *Social protest, violence, and terror in nineteenth- and twentieth-century Europe.* New York: St. Martin's for German Historical Institute, 1982. ISBN 0-312-73471-9. ▸ Wide-ranging collection giving good overview of protest, political murder, leftist and rightist terrorism in Europe, including Russia and Spain, from 1800 through fascism. Final essay on late twentieth-century developments. [DSC]

22.481   Wolfgang J. Mommsen and Hans-Gerhard Husung, eds. *The development of trade unionism in Great Britain and Germany, 1880–1914.* London: Allen & Unwin for German Historical Institute, 1985. ISBN 0-04-940080-0. ▸ Essays by Hobsbawm, Cronin, and Boll provide guide to international comparison of union organization and strikes. Others deal with narrower British and German topics. [DSC]

22.482   Wolfgang J. Mommsen and Wolfgang Mock, ed. *The emergence of the welfare state in Britain and Germany, 1850–1950.* London: Croom Helm for German Historical Institute, 1981. ISBN 0-7099-1710-4. ▸ Essays by various authors survey historical background in nineteenth-century social legislation, social security and unemployment before World War I, interwar welfare crisis, breakthrough of welfare state after World War II, and unintended consequences of welfare system. [DSC]

22.483 Roderick Phillips. *Putting asunder: a history of divorce in Western society.* Cambridge: Cambridge University Press, 1988. ISBN 0-521-32434-3. ‣ Excellent comprehensive treatment of three themes: divorce legislation and attitudes to divorce, experience of divorce, and question of marriage breakdown from Middle Ages to present. Detects clear but uneven trend toward liberalization. [BYK]

22.484 Pamela M. Pilbeam. *The middle classes in Europe, 1789–1914: France, Germany, Italy, and Russia.* Chicago: Lyceum, 1990. ISBN 0-925065-29-3 (cl), 0-925065-26-9 (pbk). ‣ Comparative survey introducing recent scholarship. Reflects realization that traditional elites and middle class of professionals and state servants, rather than entrepreneurs, shaped nineteenth-century political culture. [DSC]

22.485 Ivy Pinchbeck. *Women workers and the Industrial Revolution, 1750–1850.* 3d ed. Kerry Hamilton, Introduction. London: Virago, 1981. ISBN 0-86068-170-X (pbk). ‣ Pioneering, still useful older study of women in agriculture, as day laborers, in industry, and in trade and crafts. Includes impact of agrarian revolution and growth of textile industries. [BYK]

22.486 Sidney Pollard. *Peaceful conquest: the industrialization of Europe, 1760–1970.* 1981 ed. Oxford: Oxford University Press, 1982. ISBN 0-19-877093-6 (cl), 0-19-877095-2 (pbk). ‣ Dense, detailed regional economic history covering agriculture, resources, leading industries, population, labor, transmission of technology, investment, and intrusive aspects of war and of events in expanding world economy. [DSC]

22.487 William M. Reddy. *Money and liberty in modern Europe: a critique of historical understanding.* Cambridge: Cambridge University Press, 1987. ISBN 0-521-30445-8 (cl), 0-521-31509-3 (pbk). ‣ Sympathetic assessment of forty years of scholarship on European social history, but showing concept of class obscured understanding of social conflicts. Outlines more demanding cultural history of economics and social conflict. [DSC]

22.488 Fritz K. Ringer. *Education and society in modern Europe.* Bloomington: Indiana University Press, 1979. ISBN 0-253-31929-3. ‣ Examination of German and French educational systems from late eighteenth century to 1960s. Final chapter compares European with English and American systems. [DSC]

22.489 Bonnie G. Smith. *Changing lives: women in European history since 1700.* Lexington, Mass.: Heath, 1989. ISBN 0-669-14561-0 (pbk). ‣ Comprehensive recent survey, tracing effects of nationality, class, economics, politics, culture, and reproduction on gender relationships. Both topical and chronological narratives. [BYK]

22.490 Peter N. Stearns. *Lives of labour: work in a maturing industrial society.* New York: Holmes & Meier, 1975. ISBN 0-8419-0192-9. ‣ General comparative social history examining changing structure of employment and character of labor and how workers responded in Britain, Belgium, Germany, and France, 1890–1914. Best available survey of its kind. [DSC]

22.491 Anthony Sutcliffe. *Towards the planned city: Germany, Britain, the United States, France, 1780–1914.* New York: St. Martin's, 1981. ISBN 0-312-81039-3. ‣ Focuses on late nineteenth and early twentieth centuries when Germany was acknowledged leader in planning. Discusses diffusion of ideas and planning as international movement. See Schorske 31.315 for important Viennese efforts. [DSC]

22.492 Klaus Tenfelde, ed. *Arbeiter und Arbeiterbewegung im Vergleich: Berichte zur internationalen historischen Forschung.*

Munich: Oldenbourg, 1986. (Historische Zeitschrift, Sonderheft, 15.) ISBN 3-486-61750-8. ‣ Includes comparative essays in English on local research on working-class history, petite bourgeoisie, workers' culture, and collective action. Treats important research themes. [DSC]

22.493 Charles Tilly, Louise Tilly, and Richard Tilly. *The rebellious century, 1830–1930.* Cambridge, Mass.: Harvard University Press, 1975. ISBN 0-674-74955-3. ‣ Comparative analysis arguing collective violence in France, Italy, and Germany reflected solidarity and consciously articulated interests rather than breakdown of society and uprooting of individuals. Important argument, but not convincing. [DSC]

22.494 Clive Trebilcock. *The industrialization of the Continental powers, 1780–1914.* London: Longman, 1981. ISBN 0-582-49119-3 (cl), 0-582-49120-7 (pbk). ‣ Best overall introduction to comparative study of commonly used models for explaining industrialization. Untangles with ease topics such as changing role of cartels in German economy and peculiar pattern of French investment. [DSC]

22.495 Susan Cotts Watkins. *From provinces into nations: demographic integration in western Europe, 1870–1960.* Princeton: Princeton University Press, 1991. ISBN 0-691-09451-9. ‣ Study of how cultural influences shaping demographic behavior have shifted. Careful, well-received study with lucid exposition of complex material. [DSC]

22.496 Heinrich August Winkler, ed. *Organisierter Kapitalismus: Voraussetzungen und Anfänge.* Göttingen: Vandenhoeck & Ruprecht, 1974. ISBN 3-525-35960-8. ‣ Essential, often-cited essays refine concept of organized capitalism and survey politics and social consequences of evolution of concentrated, bureaucratically organized, cartelized European industrial economies from late nineteenth century. [DSC]

SEE ALSO
30.164 Michael Mitterauer and Reinhard Seider. *The European family.*

The Arts

22.497 Gerald Abraham, ed. *The age of Beethoven, 1790–1830.* Vol. 8 of *The new Oxford history of music.* 1982 ed. Oxford: Oxford University Press, 1985. ISBN 0-19-316308-X. ‣ Rich summary of social, political, and institutional contexts of musical life, followed by masterful discussion of French opera, as well as chapters on genres in which Ludwig Beethoven and Franz Schubert were particularly active, and on important operatic developments in Italy (Gioacchino Antonio Rossini) and elsewhere. Excellent bibliography and numerous musical examples. [RPL]

22.498 Gerald Abraham, ed. *Romanticism, 1830–1890.* Vol. 9 of *The new Oxford history of music.* Oxford: Oxford University Press, 1990. ISBN 0-19-316309-8. ‣ Study of genres of Beethoven-Schubert-Rossini era continued to dominate, but new developments included character piece, programmatic orchestral works, and distinctive national traditions in opera and other genres. Rich biography and many musical examples. [RPL]

22.499 Bojan Bujic, ed. *Music in European thought, 1851–1912.* Cambridge: Cambridge University Press, 1988. ISBN 0-521-23050-0. ‣ Useful excerpts from writings by Richard Wagner, Friedrich Nietzsche, Stéphane Mallarmé, Spencer, Charles Darwin, and lesser-known figures. [RPL]

22.500 Carl Dahlhaus. *Nineteenth-century music.* J. Bradford Robinson, trans. Berkeley: University of California Press, 1989. ISBN 0-520-05291-9. ‣ Thoughtful account of European art music, 1814–1914, and its lighter derivatives (parlor and park-bandstand music), focusing on problematic cross-currents underlying greatest works. Better informed on Austro-German music. Essay chapters offer challenging approaches. [RPL]

22.501 Helmut Gernsheim and Alison Gernsheim. *The history of photography from the camera obscura to the beginning of the modern era.* 2d ed. New York: McGraw-Hill, 1969. ▸ Comprehensive history of photography, especially in Europe. [GS]

22.502 George Heard Hamilton. *Nineteenth- and twentieth-century art: painting, sculpture, architecture.* New York: Abrams, 1970. ISBN 0-8109-0346-6. ▸ Survey of nineteenth- and twentieth-century art to about mid-century. [GS]

22.503 Henry-Russell Hitchcock. *Architecture: nineteenth and twentieth centuries.* 4th ed. Harmondsworth: Penguin, 1977. ISBN 0-14-056115-3. ▸ Standard history of architecture in Europe and America up to mid-twentieth century. [GS]

22.504 Werner Hofmann. *The earthly paradise: art in the nineteenth century.* Brian Battershaw, trans. New York: Braziller, 1961. ▸ Stimulating, if not always convincing, attempt to see themes in art of entire century and throughout Europe. [GS]

22.505 Elizabeth Gilmore Holt, ed. *From the classicists to the impressionists: a documentary history of art and architecture in the nineteenth century.* Garden City, N.Y.: Anchor, 1966. ▸ Selection of documents, including writings by artists, shows contribution of geniuses and also highlights new forms. [GS]

22.506 Hugh Honour. *Romanticism.* New York: Harper & Row, 1979. (Style and civilization.) ISBN 0-06-433336-1 (cl), 0-06-430089-7 (pbk). ▸ Thematic treatment of romanticism as complex, pan-European historical phenomenon rather than as subjective experience. [GS]

22.507 David Clay Large, William Weber, and Anne Dzamba Sessa, eds. *Wagnerism in European culture and politics.* Ithaca, N.Y.: Cornell University Press, 1984. ISBN 0-8014-1646-9 (cl), 0-8014-9283-1 (pbk). ▸ Overview of Wagnerian ideals as seen in wide range of cultural, not just musical, phenomena in Germany, France, Italy, Russia, Britain, and United States. [RPL]

22.508 Peter Le Huray and James Day, eds. *Music and aesthetics in the eighteenth and early nineteenth centuries.* Abr. ed. Cambridge: Cambridge University Press, 1988. ISBN 0-521-35901-5 (pbk). ▸ Excerpts from Jean-Jacques Rousseau, Immanuel Kant, August Wilhelm von Schlegel, Arthur Schopenhauer, G.W.F. Hegel, and lesser-known figures. [RPL]

22.509 Jean-Claude Lemagny and André Rouille, eds. *A history of photography: social and cultural perspectives.* Janet Lloyd, trans. Cambridge: Cambridge University Press, 1987. ISBN 0-521-34407-7. ▸ Series of chronologically arranged essays by a number of contributors who focus on social issues as corrective to more formally and technically oriented histories of photography. [GS]

22.510 Beaumont Newhall. *The history of photography from 1839 to the present.* Rev. ed. New York: Museum of Modern Art; distributed by New York Graphic Society Books, 1982. ISBN 0-87070-380-3 (cl), 0-87070-381-1 (pbk). ▸ Updated version of standard concise history of photography. [GS]

22.511 Linda Nochlin. *Realism.* 1971 ed. Harmondsworth: Penguin, 1978. (Style and civilization.) ISBN 0-14-021305-8. ▸ Discussion of concept of realism in general and very specific concerns for representation of modern life in mid-nineteenth century. Usefully links visual arts with literary and intellectual currents. [GS]

22.512 Fritz Novotny. *Painting and sculpture in Europe, 1780–1880.* 1971 2d ed. Harmondsworth: Penguin, 1980. (Style and civilization.) ISBN 0-14-056120-X (pbk). ▸ Most internationally oriented survey of nineteenth-century art; little mention of British artists. [GS]

22.513 Alexander Ringer, ed. *The early Romantic era: between revolutions, 1789 and 1848.* Englewood Cliffs, N.J.: Prentice-Hall, 1991. ISBN 0-13-222332-5 (pbk). ▸ Comprehensive overview of urban musical life and related changes in musical genres and styles, followed by chapters on Paris, Vienna, Berlin, Dresden, London, and Leipzig, Italian opera, London, Russia, United States, and Latin America. [RPL]

22.514 Robert Rosenblum and W. H. Janson. *Nineteenth-century art.* New York: Abrams, 1984. ISBN 0-8109-1362-3. ▸ Account of nineteenth-century painting (Rosenblum) and sculpture (Janson) avoiding evolutionary approach, but including greater variety of artists and themes than earlier histories. Useful bibliography. [GS]

22.515 Jim Samson, ed. *The late Romantic era: from the mid-nineteenth century to World War I.* Englewood Cliffs, N.J.: Prentice-Hall, 1991. ISBN 0-13-524174-X (cl), 0-13-524182-0 (pbk). ▸ Introductory editorial synthesis, formed by chapters treating music in political, social, and cultural contexts in individual countries or cities of Europe, United States, and Latin America. Focuses on such issues as political absolutism, nationalism, modernism, and conflicting notions of progress. [RPL]

TWENTIETH-CENTURY EUROPE AND THE TWO WORLD WARS, 1914–1945

General Studies

22.516 Hannah Arendt. *The origins of totalitarianism.* 1973 3d rev. ed. San Diego, Calif.: Harcourt Brace Jovanovich, 1979. ISBN 0-15-670153-7. ▸ Classic and most influential treatment of concept of totalitarianism. Treats rise of antisemitism, European imperialism, and state organization and terror under nazism and Stalinism. [DSC]

22.517 Raymond Aron. *The century of total war.* 1954 ed. Boston: Beacon, 1955. ▸ Perceptive, sometimes brilliant interpretive essay by famous French intellectual linking origins and progress of politics of absolutes in twentieth century to industrialized war. [DSC]

22.518 Gail Braybon and Penny Summerfield. *Out of the cage: women's experiences in two world wars.* New York: Pandora, 1987. ISBN 0-86358-046-7 (cl), 0-86358-228-1 (pbk). ▸ Gender issues in wartime, using oral sources, photographs, and sociologists' Mass Observation archive. Focuses on new opportunities and problems and women who experienced both wars. [BYK]

22.519 Oron James Hale. *The great illusion, 1900–1914.* Vol. 17 of *The rise of modern Europe.* New York: Harper & Row, 1971. ▸ Title refers to illusion that general war between enlightened European powers was impossible. Serves as review of facts but interpretation dated. [DSC]

22.520 Margaret Randolph Higonnet et al., eds. *Behind the lines: gender and the two world wars.* New Haven: Yale University Press, 1987. ISBN 0-300-03687-6. ▸ Pathbreaking study of gender system in two world wars. Shows importance of wartime transformations in social roles of women, but also demonstrates and tries to account for women's failure to hold on to temporary gains in status. [JML]

22.521 James Joll. *Europe since 1870: an international history.* 4th ed. London: Penguin, 1990. ISBN 0-14-013843-9. ▸ Best single-volume survey of high politics and diplomacy. Examines role of state, ideas, and individual actors in making European politics; covers to 1980s. [DSC]

22.522 Charles S. Maier. *In search of stability: explorations in historical political economy.* Cambridge: Cambridge University Press, 1987. ISBN 0-521-23001-2 (cl), 0-521-34698-3 (pbk). ▸ Essential set of essays on role of economic beliefs and ideologies, some imported from United States, in breakdown and reconstruction of political and social stability in twentieth-century Europe. [DSC]

22.523 Arthur Marwick. *War and social change in the twentieth century: a comparative study of Britain, France, Germany, Russia, and the United States.* London: Macmillan, 1974. ISBN 0-333-11238-5 (cl), 0-333-11248-2 (pbk). ▸ Almost a social history of twentieth-century Europe; weaker on United States. Examines destruction and disruption, how war tested institutions and brought about wider economic and political participation, and psychological legacies. [DSC]

22.524 C. L. Mowat, ed. *The shifting balance of world forces, 1898–1945.* Vol. 12 of *The new Cambridge modern history.* Cambridge: Cambridge University Press, 1968. ISBN 0-521-04551-7. ▸ Valuable collective work of synthesis and interpretation examining Europe's role in world history in this period. Includes social and cultural history but emphasizes economics, politics and diplomacy, two world wars, and changes in European relations with other regions. [DSC]

22.525 Karl Polanyi. *The great transformation.* 1944 ed. Boston: Beacon, 1985. ISBN 0-8070-5679-0 (pbk). ▸ Brilliant interpretation of deep roots of twentieth-century disaster. Nineteenth-century civilization, resting on self-regulating market, was destroyed in twentieth century as society sought measures to defend itself from annihilation by that market. [DSC]

22.526 Bernadotte E. Schmitt and Harold C. Vedeler. *The world in the crucible, 1914–1919.* Vol. 21 of *The rise of modern Europe.* New York: Harper & Row, 1984. ISBN 0-06-015268-0. ▸ Most thorough survey of war and its consequences. Extensive account of campaigns, politics, diplomacy, and resulting revolutions in Russia, Germany, eastern Europe, and Balkans. [DSC]

22.527 Raymond J. Sontag. *A broken world, 1919–1939.* Vol. 19 of *The rise of modern Europe.* 1971 ed. New York: Harper & Row, 1972. ISBN 0-06-131651-2 (pbk). ▸ Survey of interwar Europe emphasizing political history and international relations. [DSC]

World War I

22.528 Modris Eksteins. *Rites of spring: the Great War and the birth of the modern age.* 1989 ed. Toronto: Lester & Orpen Dennys, 1990. ISBN 0-88619-202-1 (pbk). ▸ Analysis of war as psychological event. Shows how modern avant-garde's attack on moral constraints was joined, through experience of war, to roots of fascism and national socialism. Penetrating reassessment of modernism. [DSC]

22.529 Marc Ferro. *The Great War, 1914–1918.* 1973 ed. Nicole Stone, trans. New York: Military Heritage, 1989. ISBN 0-88029-449-3. ▸ Study of anticipation of war and its approach, how it was fought and experienced, its politics and economics, and its legacies in social and political tensions. Unconventional but sparkling brief review. [DSC]

22.530 Gerd Hardach. *The First World War, 1914–1918.* 1977 ed. Berkeley: University of California Press, 1981. ISBN 0-520-04397-9. ▸ Thorough economic history. Treats blockade, commercial warfare, armaments, finances and currencies, food supply, labor relations in Europe, and legacies of war in international economy. [DSC]

22.531 Eric J. Leed. *No man's land: combat and identity in World War I.* Cambridge: Cambridge University Press, 1979. ISBN 0-521-22471-3 (cl), 0-521-28573-9 (pbk). ▸ Combat altered social status, expectations, and character of participants with immense political and social consequences. Fascinating study of how soldiers adapted cultural resources to make sense of mass slaughter. [DSC]

22.532 Arno J. Mayer. *Political origins of the new diplomacy, 1917–1918.* 1959 ed. New York: Fertig, 1969. ▸ Sees Lenin and President Woodrow Wilson as advocates of different versions of new international order as convergence of war, revolution, and domestic and international politics smashed Europe's political order and independence. Leftist historian's influential interpretation. [DSC]

22.533 Roland N. Stromberg. *Redemption by war: the intellectuals and 1914.* Lawrence: University Press of Kansas, 1982. ISBN 0-7006-0220-8. ▸ Narrative account of how intellectuals from every country in Europe and across ideological spectrum greeted outbreak of war with frenzy of enthusiasm. [DSC]

22.534 Barbara W. Tuchman. *The guns of August.* 1962 ed. New York: Bonanza Books, 1982. ISBN 0-517-38574-0. ▸ Classic account of July and August 1914, military men, and diplomats as Europe slid into World War I. [DSC]

22.535 Barbara W. Tuchman. *The proud tower: a portrait of the world before the war, 1890–1914.* 1966 ed. New York: Bantam, 1977. ISBN 0-553-05599-2 (pbk). ▸ Vivid portrait of explosive tension in society and politics at close of long nineteenth century. [DSC]

SEE ALSO
47.451 Arno J. Mayer. *Politics and diplomacy of peacemaking.*

Politics, Economy, and Society between the Wars

22.536 Charles Bertrand, ed. *Revolutionary situations in Europe, 1917–1922: Germany, Italy, Austria-Hungary.* Montreal: Inter-University Centre for European Studies, 1977. ISBN 0-919958-03-6, ISSN 0317-5944. ▸ Essential essays, among them Maier's comparison of outcomes and Mayer's survey of connections between internal crises and war since 1870. [DSC]

22.537 Franz Borkenau. *European communism.* London: Faber & Faber, 1953. ▸ From Popular Front to liberation and Cominform. More detailed political narrative than Spriano 22.556. [DSC]

22.538 Franz Borkenau. *World communism: a history of the Communist International.* 1938 ed. Raymond Aron, Introduction. Ann Arbor: University of Michigan Press, 1962. ▸ Older work with valuable insights from former party member whose direct experiences with participants and issues sharpened his scholarly eye. Earlier title: *The Communist International.* [DSC]

22.539 Julius Braunthal. *History of the International.* Vol. 2: *1914–1943.* Vol. 3: *1943–1968.* John Clark, Peter Ford, and Kenneth Mitchell, trans. New York and Boulder: Praeger and Westview, 1967–80. ISBN 0-89158-369-6 (v. 3). ▸ Volumes cover socialism in World War I, founding of Communist International, struggles between Socialists and Communists, and continuing divisions in face of fascism, Stalinism, World War II, and cold war era. Surprisingly weak on Spanish Civil War. [DSC]

22.540 F. L. Carsten. *Revolution in Central Europe, 1918–1919.* 1972 ed. Aldershot, England: Wildwood House; distributed by Gower, 1988. ISBN 0-7045-0586-7 (cl), 0-7045-0586-X (pbk). ▸ Useful survey of events describing failure of post–World War I revolutions in Germany and Austria. [DSC]

22.541 Dieter Dowe, ed. *Jugendprotest und Generationskonflikt in Europa im zwanzigsten Jahrhundert: Deutschland, England, Frankreich, und Italien im Vergleich.* Bonn: Verlag Neue Gesellschaft, 1986. ISBN 3-87831-437-X. ▸ Essays on youth protest and intergenerational conflict in twentieth century, some in English. Notable for survey of labor-market statistics and unemployment among youth, an area needing more attention. [DSC]

22.542 Gerald D. Feldman et al., eds. *The experience of inflation: international and comparative studies.* New York: de Gruyter, 1984. (Veröffentlichungen der Historischen Kommission zu Berlin, 57. Beiträge zu Inflation und Wiederaufbau in Deutschland und Europa, 1914–1924, 2.) ISBN 3-11-009679-X. ▸ Second volume in series on inflation and reconstruction in Europe from

1914–24. Broad comparisons of banks, firms, and social conflicts in western, Central, and eastern Europe. [DSC]

22.543 Charles P. Kindleberger. *A financial history of western Europe*. London: Allen & Unwin, 1984. ISBN 0-04-332088-0. ‣ Study of money, banking, and finance from origins to twentieth century, concentrating on nineteenth and twentieth centuries. Most detailed treatment of interwar period and post–World War II. [DSC]

22.544 Charles P. Kindleberger. *The world in depression, 1929–1939*. Rev. ed. Berkeley: University of California Press, 1986. ISBN 0-520-05591-8 (cl), 0-520-05592-6 (pbk). ‣ Essential work for period, focused on Europe. See also James 31.373. [DSC]

22.545 Rudy Koshar, ed. *Splintered classes: politics and the lower middle classes in interwar Europe*. New York: Holmes & Meier, 1990. ISBN 0-8419-1124-X (cl), 0-8419-1243-2 (pbk). ‣ Case studies of and comparative introduction to rapidly changing historical picture of this group. New views of economic development stress durability and political ingenuity as well as moments of despair and authoritarianism. [DSC]

22.546 Walter Laqueur, ed. *Fascism, a reader's guide: analyses, interpretations, bibliography*. Berkeley: University of California Press, 1976. ISBN 0-520-03033-8. ‣ Collection of essays with useful and important contributions on ideology, economy, regime structure, and other aspects. Linz's long essay best introduction to comparative sociology of fascist movements and parties available anywhere. [DSC]

22.547 David Clay Large. *Between two fires: Europe's path in the 1930s*. New York: Norton, 1990. ISBN 0-393-02751-1. ‣ Uses well-chosen events, including civil war in Austria, Hitler's purge of *Sturm Abteilung* (storm troopers), Italian invasion of Ethiopia, Spanish Civil War, Munich conference, and others, to portray political atmosphere. [DSC]

22.548 Stein Ugelvik Larsen et al., eds. *Who were the Fascists? Social roots of European fascism*. Bergen: Universitetsforlaget, 1980. ISBN 82-00-05331-8. ‣ Examination of social bases of fascist movements in eastern, southern, and western Europe as well as Italy and Germany. Some chapters dated, but remains impressive as single most comprehensive survey; search for unified social explanation fails. [DSC]

22.549 Albert S. Lindemann. *The "red years": European socialism versus bolshevism, 1919–1921*. Berkeley: University of California Press, 1974. ISBN 0-520-02511-3. ‣ Comprehensive, well-written study of how the three main parties of Western socialism split along preexisting ideological, generational, and social faults as they encountered bolshevism. [DSC]

22.550 Charles S. Meier. *Recasting bourgeois Europe: stabilization in France, Germany, and Italy in the decade after World War I*. 1975 ed. Princeton: Princeton University Press, 1988. ISBN 0-691-05220-4 (cl), 0-691-10025-X (pbk). ‣ Argues replacement of parliamentary representation by corporate-interest representation helped preserve capitalism by dampening disputes over distribution of power and that this anticipated post–World War II power arrangements and contributed to rise of fascism. [DSC]

22.551 Karl J. Newman. *European democracy between the wars*. 1970 ed. Kenneth Morgan, trans. Notre Dame, Ind.: University of Notre Dame Press, 1971. ISBN 0-268-00426-9. ‣ Surveys politics and government in Germany, Austria, and across East Central Europe, 1918–38. Concentrates on how democracies destroyed themselves, rather than on their opponents. Best available comprehensive study. [DSC]

22.552 Noël O'Sullivan. *Fascism*. London: Dent, 1983. ISBN 0-460-10428-4 (cl), 0-460-11428-X (pbk). ‣ Excellent introduction to fascism in context of European intellectual and political history, examining how ideas shaped politics. Critical of search

for generic sociological explanation. Compare Sternhell 26.183 on France. [DSC]

22.553 Stanley G. Payne. *Fascism: comparison and definition*. Madison: University of Wisconsin Press, 1980. ISBN 0-299-08060-9. ‣ Balanced attempt to suggest basic categories of historical comparison, reviewing previous attempts to define fascism. [DSC]

22.554 Carl H. Pegg. *The evolution of the European idea, 1914–1932*. Chapel Hill: University of North Carolina Press, 1983. ISBN 0-8078-1559-4. ‣ Survey of pacifists and advocates of European unity and peace between world wars. Activists' idealism so distanced them from reality that story of their failure seems superficial, not tragic. [DSC]

22.555 Hans A. Schmitt, ed. *Neutral Europe between war and revolution, 1917–1923*. Charlottesville: University Press of Virginia, 1988. ISBN 0-8139-1153-2. ‣ After World War I, neutral countries experienced intense internal social and political conflict comparable to that of belligerents, yet without revolution or sustained political violence. Essays draw useful comparisons. [DSC]

22.556 Paolo Spriano. *Stalin and the European Communists*. Jon Rothschild, trans. London: Verso, 1985. ISBN 0-86091-103-9. ‣ Brief history, 1935–48; cites Winston Churchill more often than Georgi M. Dimitrov, head of Comintern. Treats Great Terror, Munich, German-Soviet pact, Communists and national unity after June 1941, and beginning of cold war. [DSC]

SEE ALSO
31.407 Pierre Ayçoberry. *The Nazi question*.
31.409 Karl Dietrich Bracher. *The German dictatorship*.
31.411 Ian Kershaw. *The Nazi dictatorship*.
48.97 Sally Marks. *The illusion of peace*.
48.124 Derek H. Aldcroft. *From Versailles to Wall Street, 1919–1929*.

Cultural and Intellectual History and Political Thought

22.557 Karl Dietrich Bracher. *The age of ideologies: a history of political thought in the twentieth century*. 1982 ed. Ewald Osers, trans. New York: St. Martin's, 1984. ISBN 0-312-01229-2. ‣ Broadly conceived, dependable introduction to and review of whole spectrum of political ideologies since turn of century, emphasizing dangers intense ideologization posed for liberal democracy. [DSC]

22.558 David Frisby. *Fragments of modernity: theories of modernity in the work of Simmel, Kracauer, and Benjamin*. 1985 ed. Cambridge, Mass.: MIT Press, 1986. ISBN 0-262-06103-1. ‣ Perceptive study presenting complex ideas with clarity. Friedrich Nietzsche and Charles Pierre Baudelaire set stage for these thinkers who provided most powerful descriptive critique of modernity. [DSC]

22.559 Martin Jay. *The dialectical imagination: a history of the Frankfurt School and the Institute of Social Research, 1923–1950*. Boston: Little, Brown, 1973. ISBN 0-316-46049-4 (cl), 0-316-45830-9 (pbk). ‣ Analysis of Weimar culture's legacy among mandarins of Left. Much admired study of background and development of some of Left's most influential intellectuals. [DSC]

22.560 Martin Jay. *Marxism and totality: the adventures of a concept from Lukács to Habermas*. Berkeley: University of California Press, 1984. ISBN 0-520-05096-7. ‣ Sympathetic, informative study of Western Marxism, pursuing concept through vicissitudes induced by tensions between Marxist intellectual and his society. [DSC]

22.561 James Joll. *Three intellectuals in politics*. 1960 ed. New York: Harper & Row, 1965. ‣ Study of French socialist Léon Blum, German industrialist Walther Rathenau, and Italian futurist and Fascist Filippo Tommaso Marinetti. Provides fine introduction to political culture in era after World War I. Earlier title: *Intellectuals in Politics: Three Biographical Essays*. [DSC]

22.562 Stephen J. Kern. *The culture of time and space, 1880–1914.* Cambridge, Mass.: Harvard University Press, 1983. ISBN 0-674-17972-2 (cl), 0-674-17973-0 (pbk). ▸ Study of transformation of categories of time and space in high and popular culture which created eternal present of twentieth century. Artful, original synthesis drawing on literature, philosophy, art, science, technology, everyday life, politics, and warfare. [DSC]

22.563 Ernst Nolte. *Three faces of fascism: Action Française, Italian fascism, national socialism.* 1965 ed. Leila Vennewitz, trans. New York: New American Library, 1969. ▸ Classic comparative account of three movements. Eccentric attempt to define fascism as revolt against transcendence. [DSC]

22.564 Anson Rabinbach. *The human motor: energy, fatigue, and the origins of modernity.* 1990 ed. Los Angeles: University of California Press, 1992. ISBN 0-520-07827-6 (pbk). ▸ Innovative, fascinating study of how sciences of labor reshaped social thought, from moral conceptions of labor in nineteenth century to twentieth-century productivism and end of work-centered society. [DSC]

22.565 Robert Wohl. *The generation of 1914.* Cambridge, Mass.: Harvard University Press, 1979. ISBN 0-674-34465-0. ▸ Study of intellectuals who identified themselves with this generation in different national cultures. Important work on how modern concept of generational identity emerging in Europe before World War I changed morality and politics. [DSC]

World War II in Europe: Origins and Impact

22.566 Sidney Aster. *1939: the making of the Second World War.* 1973 ed. New York: Simon & Schuster, 1974. ISBN 0-671-21689-9. ▸ Well-written description of climate of opinion and flow of information within governments as war approached. Draws on new documents; emphasizes Britain. [DSC]

22.567 Jørgen Hæstrup. *European resistance movements, 1939–1945: a complete history.* Westport, Conn.: Meckler, 1981. ISBN 0-930466-36-5. ▸ Survey of organization and activities, military history only. [DSC]

22.568 Tony Judt, ed. *Resistance and revolution in Mediterranean Europe, 1939–1948.* London: Routledge, 1989. ISBN 0-415-01580-4. ▸ Introduction and essays on communist role in France, Italy, Yugoslavia, and Greece. Dependable treatment of politics. [DSC]

22.569 B. H. Liddell Hart. *History of the Second World War.* 1970 ed. New York: Perigee, 1982. ISBN 0-399-50445-1 (pbk). ▸ Purely military history of World War II by great student of strategy and tactics whose own ideas and advice shaped how it was fought. [DSC]

22.570 Walter Lipgens, ed. *Documents on the history of European integration.* Vol. 1: *Continental plans for European union, 1939–1945 (including 250 documents in their original languages on 6 microfiches).* Vol. 2: *Plans for European union in Great Britain and in exile, 1939–1945 (including 107 documents in their original languages on 3 microfiches).* P. S. Falla, trans. Berlin: de Gruyter, 1985–91. (European University Institute, Series B, History, 1.) ISBN 3-11-009724-9 (v. 1), 0-89925-212-5 (v. 2). ▸ Essential collaborative reference work for history of European integration, also valuable on resistance movements. Documents plans of Nazis, Fascists, resistances in occupied and neutral countries, groups in Britain, exiles, transnational organizations, churches, and labor unions. English translations printed, original language on fiche. [DSC]

22.571 John Lukacs. *The last European war: September 1939–December 1941.* Garden City, N.Y.: Anchor, 1976. ISBN 0-385-07254-6. ▸ Study of war before it grew into world war. Treats

events and, most impressively, underlying movements and transformation of peoples, politics, state relations, national affinities, and character. Bibliographic essay. [DSC]

22.572 Ernest R. May, ed. *Knowing one's enemies: intelligence assessment before the two world wars.* Princeton: Princeton University Press, 1984. ISBN 0-691-04717-0 (cl), 0-691-00601-6 (pbk). ▸ Collection of essays on assumptions, practices, and conclusions of intelligence, topic of greater importance for World War II. Concludes end results depend on political system and on ideologies and interests of those who analyze, filter, and transmit information. [DSC]

22.573 Henri Michel. *The shadow war: resistance in Europe, 1939–1945.* Richard Barry, trans. London: Deutsch, 1972. ISBN 0-233-96350-2. ▸ Good survey and introduction to resistance movements in Europe. [DSC]

22.574 R. J. Overy. *The air war, 1939–1945.* 1980 ed. New York: Stein & Day, 1981. ISBN 0-8128-2792-9. ▸ Preparations, role of air forces in Europe and Far East, strategic bombing, organization and training, aircraft production, science, and intelligence. [DSC]

22.575 James D. Wilkinson. *The intellectual resistance in Europe.* Cambridge, Mass.: Harvard University Press, 1981. ISBN 0-674-45775-7. ▸ Examination of famed intellectuals in France, Germany, and Italy who attained greatest influence after war. Well written, insightful, but requiring more skepticism about self-images of French. [DSC]

22.576 Gordon Wright. *The ordeal of total war, 1939–1945.* Vol. 20 of *The rise of modern Europe.* New York: Harper & Row, 1968. ▸ Superb survey of impact of total war on European society, politics, and culture. Treats prelude; German expansion; broadening of scope of war in economic, scientific, and psychological terms; German occupation and responses; return of Allies; and transition to postwar period. [DSC/CKF/JSH]

22.577 Tadeusz Wyrwa. *L'idée européenne dans la résistance à travers la presse clandestine en France et en Pologne, 1933–1945.* Paris: Nouvelles Éditions Latines, 1987. ISBN 2-7233-0361-6. ▸ Notable for comparison of two movements. Argues resistances East and West united by belief that "Europe must federate or die" and that common hopes reflected spiritual unity of civilization that could not be divided. [DSC]

SEE ALSO

The Holocaust

22.578 Saul Friedlander. *Pius XII and the Third Reich: a documentation.* 1966 ed. Charles Fullman, trans. New York: Octagon Books, 1980. ISBN 0-374-92930-0. ▸ Early, incisive, and still essential interpretation of Vatican policy documented from German diplomatic documents and other correspondence. Germanophile Pius looked to Germany to defend Europe against bolshevism and was reluctant to protest genocide. [DSC]

22.579 François Furet, ed. *Unanswered questions: Nazi Germany and the genocide of the Jews.* New York: Schocken, 1989. ISBN 0-8052-4051-9 (cl), 0-8052-0908-5 (pbk). ▸ Collection of essays by important researchers on Holocaust, well chosen to reflect fundamental themes of their work and introduce their disagreements. [DSC]

22.580 Walter Laqueur. *The terrible secret: an investigation into the suppression of information about Hitler's "Final Solution."* London: Weidenfeld & Nicolson, 1980. ISBN 0-297-77835-8. ▸ Discussion of when and how news of Final Solution reached Germans, international Jewish organizations, and European Jewish communities, neutral and Allied governments, and their responses. Careful reconstruction of evidence. [DSC/JSH]

22.581 Michael R. Marrus. *The unwanted: European refugees in the twentieth century.* New York: Oxford University Press, 1985. ISBN 0-19-503615-8. ▸ Encyclopedic coverage of refugee movements and intelligent account of international institutional responses. Examination of sources and treatment of refugees in Europe since 1880s. Discusses lessons drawn from experience in Europe. Indispensable for particular events and larger patterns. [DSC/CKF/JSH]

22.582 Michael R. Marrus, ed. *The Nazi Holocaust: historical articles on the destruction of the European Jews.* 9 vols. Westport, Conn.: Meckler, 1989. ISBN 0-88736-266-4 (set). ▸ Massive collection reproducing articles on every aspect of events and on controversies in recent scholarship. [DSC]

22.583 John F. Morley. *Vatican diplomacy and the Jews during the Holocaust, 1939–1943.* New York: KTAV, 1980. ISBN 0-87068-701-8. ▸ Concludes diplomacy pursued secular institutional interests and betrayed humanitarian ideals. By Catholic scholar able to draw on documents released by Vatican. [DSC]

22.584 George L. Mosse. *Toward the Final Solution: a history of European racism.* 1978 ed. Madison: University of Wisconsin Press, 1985. ISBN 0-299-10184-3 (pbk). ▸ Very general introductory survey; last third of book treats Jewish experience in Europe from 1918 to 1945. [DSC]

SEE ALSO
21.295 Raul Hilberg. *The destruction of the European Jews.*
21.302 Michael R. Marrus. *The Holocaust in history.*
21.319 Leni Yahil. *The Holocaust.*

The Arts

22.585 H. H. Arnason. *History of modern art: painting, sculpture, architecture, photography.* 3d rev. ed. Daniel Wheeler, ed. Englewood Cliffs, N.J.: Prentice-Hall, 1986. ISBN 0-13-390360-5. ▸ Standard survey with extensive illustrations and biography. [GS]

22.586 Herschel B. Chipp, ed. *Theories of modern art: a source book by artists and critics.* Berkeley: University of California Press, 1968. ISBN 0-520-01450-2. ▸ Anthology of writings covering postimpressionism and early twentieth-century art with a few later works. Documents chosen, introduced, and annotated to give idea of how artists defined issues. [GS]

22.587 William J. R. Curtis. *Modern architecture since 1900.* 2d ed. Englewood Cliffs, N.J.: Prentice-Hall, 1987. ISBN 0-13-586694-4 (pbk). ▸ Illustrated survey of twentieth-century architecture, primarily in Europe and America. [GS]

22.588 Ann-Marie Cutul. *Twentieth-century European painting: a guide to information sources.* Detroit: Gale Research, 1980. (Art and architecture information guide series, 9.) ISBN 0-8103-1438-X. ▸ Organized by categories and countries as well as by artists, includes list of museums with important collections. [GS]

22.589 Werner Haftmann. *Painting in the twentieth century.* Rev. ed. 2 vols. Ralph Manheim and J. Seligman, trans. New York: Praeger, 1965. ▸ Standard history of European painting through 1950s. One volume of history with discussion of artists and movements; another of pictures with descriptive text. [GS]

22.590 George Heard Hamilton. *Painting and sculpture in Europe, 1880–1940.* 1983 3d ed. Harmondsworth: Penguin, 1987. ISBN 0-14-056129-3. ▸ Standard survey of postimpressionism to Second World War. [GS]

22.591 Robert Hughes. *The shock of the new.* Rev. ed. New York: Knopf, 1991. ISBN 0-679-72876-7. ▸ Growing out of television series, work is less a history of art than series of thematic treatments of visual arts in twentieth-century culture. [GS]

22.592 Robert P. Morgan. *Twentieth-century music: a history of musical styles in modern Europe and America.* New York: Norton, 1991. ISBN 0-393-95272-X. ▸ Responsible appraisal of major trends in serious or art music of Western world since 1900. Emphasis on modernist movements with much less space given to more traditional composers; little or nothing on Broadway, popular song, and jazz. [RPL]

22.593 Robert Rosenblum. *Cubism and twentieth-century art.* 1966 rev. ed. Englewood Cliffs, N.J.: Prentice-Hall, 1976. ISBN 0-13-195065-7. ▸ Most comprehensive coverage of cubism in France and elsewhere. [GS]

22.594 William S. Rubin. *Dada, surrealism, and their heritage.* 1968 ed. New York: Museum of Modern Art, 1982. ISBN 0-87070-284-X (pbk). ▸ Comprehensive treatment of movements, published in conjunction with exhibition. [GS]

22.595 Nicholas Slonimsky. *Music since 1900.* 5th ed. New York: Schirmer Books, 1993. ISBN 0-02-872418-6. ▸ Chronology pinpointing major and minor events of twentieth-century music and augmenting and diminishing reputations of various composers. Compendium of valuable information and curiosities reliably triple-checked (supplement offers corrections to the main volume), and written with wit and linguistic virtuosity. Appended documents from Soviet Union, China, and elsewhere. [RPL]

22.596 Leo Treitler. *Music and the historical imagination.* Cambridge, Mass.: Harvard University Press, 1989. ISBN 0-674-59128-3. ▸ Stimulating essays on historical understanding in music. Draws on anthropological, metahistorical, and art historical writing (Claude Lévi-Strauss, Hans-Georg Gadamer, Ernst Haus Gombrich, Erwin Panofsky). Comments on theorists of music history and on specific works from Mozart to Alban Berg. [RPL]

22.597 Hans Wingler. *The Bauhaus: Weimar, Dessau, Berlin, Chicago.* 1969 ed. Joseph Stein, ed. Wolfgang Jabs and Basil Gilbert, trans. Cambridge, Mass.: MIT Press, 1976. ISBN 0-262-23033-X. ▸ History with extensive documentation. [GS]

POSTWAR EUROPE, 1945–1989

General Studies and Political History

22.598 Michael Burgess. *Federalism and European union: political ideas, influences, and strategies in the European Community, 1972–1987.* London: Routledge, 1989. ISBN 0-415-00498-5. ▸ Contrasts visions of federalism pursued by Jean Monnet and Altiero Spinelli. Introduces some interesting issues that could be pursued in greater depth. [DSC]

22.599 Ralf Dahrendorf. *Reflections on the revolution in Europe in a letter intended to have been sent to a gentleman in Warsaw.* New York: Times Books, 1990. ISBN 0-8129-1883-5. ▸ Important intellectual interprets reunification of Europe and of Germany as victory of open society over closed system, rather than of capitalist over socialist system. [DSC]

22.600 Peter Duignan and Lewis H. Gann. *The rebirth of the West: the americanization of the democratic world, 1945–1958.*

Cambridge, Mass.: Blackwell, 1992. ISBN 1-55786-089-0. ‣ Comprehensive survey and synthesis of postwar Western Europe to 1958 within Atlantic community. Authors provide both sides of scholarly arguments about which they hold strong opinions. Very useful but poorly edited. [DSC]

22.601 Renata Fritsch-Bournazel. *Europe and German unification.* New York: Berg; distributed by St. Martin's, 1992. ISBN 0-85496-979-9 (cl), 0-85496-684-6 (pbk). ‣ Narrative account, with many well-chosen excerpts from documents, interviews, and speeches, of Germans' thoughts about Europe and other Europeans' thoughts about Germany in rush of events in 1989–90. [DSC]

22.602 Miles Kahler. *Decolonization in Britain and France: the domestic consequences of international relations.* Princeton: Princeton University Press, 1984. ISBN 0-691-07672-3 (cl), 0-691-02224-0 (pbk). ‣ Detailed comparative history of how decolonization influenced domestic politics. While France seemed colonized by its own empire and came near to civil war, England could retreat with more grace. [DSC]

22.603 Walter Laqueur. *Europe in our time: a history, 1945–1992.* New York: Viking, 1992. ISBN 0-670-83507-2. ‣ General survey of postwar era. Readable and dependable, includes Eastern as well as Western Europe. [DSC]

22.604 Walter Lipgens. *Die Anfänge der europäischen Einigungspolitik, 1945–1950.* Vol. 1: *1945–1947.* 1 vol. to date. Stuttgart: Klett, 1977. ISBN 3-12-910330-9 (v. 1). ‣ Most detailed account of pursuit of European union. Additional volumes expected. [DSC]

22.605 Richard Mayne. *The recovery of Europe, 1945–1973.* Rev. ed. Garden City, N.Y.: Anchor, 1973. ISBN 0-385-07251-1. ‣ Survey of reconstruction by British participant. Lacks hard edge of more recent scholarship, but contains valuable detail. [DSC]

22.606 Olga A. Narkiewicz. *The end of the Bolshevik dream: Western European communist parties in the late twentieth century.* London: Routledge, 1990. ISBN 0-415-02510-9. ‣ Study of origins, theories, leaders, and politics of Eurocommunism. Views of NATO and political and ideological influences at home and in East. Eurocommunism seen as paradoxical attempt to reform outdated ideology. [DSC]

22.607 Haig Simonian. *The privileged partnership: Franco-German relations in the European Community, 1969–1984.* Oxford: Clarendon, 1985. ISBN 0-19-821959-8. ‣ From improved relations in late 1960s to Kohl-Mitterrand relationship in early 1980s. Showing (as in 22.608) mutual dependency of bilateral and European Community relations. [DSC]

22.608 F. Roy Willis. *France, Germany, and the New Europe, 1945–1967.* Rev. ed. Stanford, Calif: Stanford University Press, 1968. ‣ Shows political reconciliation depended on success in building larger European Community, from occupation through Schuman plan to crisis of 1960s. [DSC]

SEE ALSO

48.389 Alan S. Milward. *The reconstruction of Western Europe, 1945–1951.*

48.428 Alfred Grosser. *The Western alliance.*

48.437 John Gillingham. *Coal, steel, and the rebirth of Europe, 1945–1955.*

48.450 A. W. DePorte. *Europe between the superpowers.*

Cultural and Intellectual History and the Arts

22.609 Peter Coleman. *The liberal conspiracy: the Congress for Cultural Freedom and the struggle for the mind of postwar Europe.* New York: Free Press, 1989. ISBN 0-02-906481-3. ‣ Essential intellectuals' cold war. Argues that Congress, which led intellectuals' anticommunist offensive, funded by Central Intelligence

Agency, and its members (Raymond Aron, Carlo Schmid, Ignazio Silone, Arthur Koestler, Michael Polanyi, Sidney Hook, Melvin Lasky, and others) were nobody's dupes. [DSC]

22.610 Saul Friedländer. *Reflections of nazism: an essay on kitsch and death.* Thomas Weyr, trans. New York: Harper & Row, 1984. ISBN 0-06-015097-1. ‣ Survey of changes in artists' and intellectuals' views of nazism since 1960s, exemplified by French writer Michel Tournier, German filmmaker Hans-Jürgen Syberberg, and others. Moral critique of postmodernism. [DSC]

22.611 H. Stuart Hughes. *Sophisticated rebels: the political culture of European dissent, 1968–1987.* Cambridge, Mass.: Harvard University Press, 1988. ISBN 0-674-82130-0. ‣ After failing in 1968, rebels accepted limits. More sophisticated culture of rebellion chose smaller, marginal worlds, defying classification as Left or Right, in which activists need not doubt the rightness of their causes. Interesting, provocative thesis. [DSC]

22.612 Gerald N. Izenberg. *The existentialist critique of Freud: the crisis of autonomy.* Princeton: Princeton University Press, 1976. ISBN 0-691-07214-0. ‣ Clear exposition of European existentialism and its influence on social theory. Existentialists remade philosophical foundations of psychology after Freud, but found concepts of selfhood and authenticity more problematic. [DSC]

22.613 Charles A. Jencks. *The language of post-modern architecture.* 6th ed. New York: Rizzoli, 1991. ISBN 0-8478-1359-2. ‣ Sometimes irreverent discussion of architecture since about 1960, including urban environments and movie sets. [GS]

22.614 Gisela Kaplan. *Contemporary Western European feminism.* New York: New York University Press, 1992. ISBN 0-8147-4622-5 (cl), 0-8147-4623-3 (pbk). ‣ Best available general history of postwar feminist movements in Scandinavian and Germanic countries, France, Netherlands, and southern Europe. Classified bibliography of English-language sources. [DSC]

22.615 John Lukacs. *Decline and rise of Europe: a study in recent history with particular emphasis on the development of a European consciousness.* 1965 ed. Westport, Conn.: Greenwood, 1976. ISBN 0-8371-8702-8. ‣ Sees decline in power of states accompanied by increasing national and cultural consciousness that can unify Europe and prevent it from merging into homogeneous world civilization postulated by liberal intellectuals. Brilliant historical interpretation. [DSC]

22.616 Allan Megill. *Prophets of extremity: Nietzsche, Heidegger, Foucault, Derrida.* Berkeley: University of California Press, 1985. ISBN 0-520-05239-0 (cl), 0-520-06028-8 (pbk). ‣ Survey of thought of four important intellectuals. Argues critics who assume radical crisis have drawn nihilistic conclusions, in part because their aestheticism allowed them to confirm unexamined prejudices. [DSC]

22.617 Quentin Skinner, ed. *The return of grand theory in the human sciences.* 1985 ed. Cambridge: Cambridge University Press, 1990. ISBN 0-521-39833-9 (pbk). ‣ Good introduction to debates of last generation. Essays on Hans-Georg Gadamer, Jacques Derrida, Michel Foucault, Jürgen Habermas, Louis Althusser, Thomas Kuhn, John Rawls, Claude Lévi-Strauss, and Annales historians. [DSC]

22.618 Marilyn Strathern. *After nature: English kinship in the late twentieth century.* Cambridge: Cambridge University Press, 1992. ISBN 0-521-40525-4 (cl), 0-521-42680-4 (pbk). ‣ Pathbreaking but difficult study contrasting images and construction of English kinship in nineteenth and twentieth centuries and changes wrought by new reproductive technologies and new cultural explicitness about relations. Presents results as general model of changes throughout West. [DSC]

22.619 Roland N. Stromberg. *After everything: Western intellectual history since 1945.* New York: St. Martin's, 1975. ‣ Wide-ranging, very informative survey to mid-seventies, capturing sense of cultural exhaustion and malaise of 1960s and 1970s particularly well. [DSC]

Social and Economic History

22.620 Peter Baldwin. *The politics of social solidarity: class bases of the European welfare state, 1875–1975.* Cambridge: Cambridge University Press, 1990. ISBN 0-521-37512-6. ‣ Comparative political history concentrating more on post-1945 period. Looks at Scandinavia, Britain, France, and Germany. Essential reading for anyone interested in history of welfare state. [DSC]

22.621 Suzanne Berger, ed. *Organizing interests in Western Europe: pluralism, corporatism, and the transformation of politics.* 1981 ed. Cambridge: Cambridge University Press, 1983. ISBN 0-521-27062-6 (pbk). ‣ Essential for interest groups in different political systems since late nineteenth century. Where older literature regarded pluralism as stabilizing because it fragmented conflicts, these essays illustrate its destabilizing effects and erosion of older political values and structures. [DSC]

22.622 Colin Crouch and Alessandro Pizzorno, eds. *The resurgence of class-conflict in Western Europe since 1968.* Vol. 1: *National studies.* Vol. 2: *Comparative analysis.* New York: Holmes & Meier, 1978. ISBN 0-8419-0355-7 (v. 1), 0-8419-0356-5 (v. 2). ‣ Essays of varying quality, providing useful coverage of labor conflicts and industrial relations. [DSC]

22.623 Geoffrey Harris. *The dark side of Europe: the extreme Right today.* Savage, Md.: Barnes & Noble, 1990. ISBN 0-389-20924-4. ‣ Survey of development of contemporary movements. For deeper historical analysis of one country, consult Betz 31.511 on postmodern politics in Germany. [DSC]

22.624 Peter J. Katzenstein. *Small states in world markets: industrial policy in Europe.* Ithaca, N.Y.: Cornell University Press, 1985. ISBN 0-8014-1729-5 (cl), 0-8014-9326-9 (pbk). ‣ Superb survey of politics and industrial planning in Scandinavia, Low Countries, and Central Europe in postwar era. [DSC]

22.625 Charles S. Maier, ed. *The changing boundaries of the political: essays on the evolving balance between state and society, public and private, in Europe.* Cambridge: Cambridge University Press, 1987. ISBN 0-521-34366-6 (cl), 0-521-34847-1 (pbk). ‣ Argument that in advanced welfare states interest group politics has blurred, even outmoded, distinction between civil society and state, creating situation in which everything is political. Mildly critical of this development. [DSC]

22.626 Arthur Marwick. *Class: image and reality in Britain, France, and the USA since 1930.* 2d ed. London: Macmillan, 1990. ISBN 0-333-51573-0 (cl), 0-333-51574-9 (pbk). ‣ Broadly documented descriptive history of colloquial images of class, class awareness, and realities of stratification through World War II. Deliberately and fruitfully eschews theory. [DSC]

22.627 Ferdinand Müller-Rommel, ed. *New politics in Western Europe: the rise and success of green parties and alternative lists.* Boulder: Westview, 1989. ISBN 0-8133-7529-0. ‣ Attempts wide, systematic coverage; useful even though essays by true believers often flawed. Consult Betz 31.511 on postmodern politics in Germany for best researched and considered discussion of single country. [DSC]

22.628 Michael Moissey Postan. *An economic history of Western Europe, 1945–1964.* London: Methuen, 1967. ‣ Useful survey emphasizing managed growth as key to robust postwar economy. [DSC]

22.629 Simon Reich. *The fruits of fascism: postwar prosperity in historical perspective.* Ithaca, N.Y.: Cornell University Press, 1990. ISBN 0-8014-2440-2 (cl), 0-8014-9729-9 (pbk). ‣ Comparative study of relations between state and individual British and German auto firms shows institutional innovations of fascist regimes survived and aided postwar prosperity. Essential reference on political history of strategies of economic competition. [DSC]

22.630 Paul White. *The West European city: a social geography.* New York: Longman, 1984. ISBN 0-582-30047-9. ‣ Introductory work whose chapters on domestic and international migration and on residential patterns and suburbs summarize important developments of recent decades. [DSC]

22.631 Elizabeth Wilson. *Women and the welfare state.* London: Tavistock, 1977. ISBN 0-422-76050-1 (cl), 0-422-76060-9 (pbk). ‣ Analysis of how welfare state shaped women's consciousness and economic function to fit perceived social needs. [BYK]

DEREK M. HIRST

British Isles, 1450–1800

During the generation since the last edition of the AHA *Guide,* the historiographic map of early modern Britain has been almost wholly redrawn. Not only have the broad contours of long familiar features of the landscape—its political and religious history—been reconfigured in the most striking fashion, but new fields aplenty have been marked out from the wilderness: the history of gender, childhood, the family, the environment, the peasantry, towns, and medicine.

In view of the dethronement of Marxist certainties in the wider world, it will come as little surprise that one significant sector of the post–World War II profession has all but disappeared. Economic history has become less a search to identify the economic underpinnings of political and social change and more a self-contained, and perhaps less popular, pursuit. Although more sophisticated in its methods, economic history is still concerned with tracing the road to modernity, but less confident that it holds the key to the whole. In their more ebullient moments, some researchers in the newer fields, anthropological historians, for example, have thought that it is they who hold the key to unlock the true meaning of the past. But two parallel developments have contrived to ensure that no one approach could shape the questions asked by the whole profession. On the one hand, with the decline of faith in external ideologies, historians in the more traditional fields have gained in self-confidence, becoming more resistant to pressures from outside. On the other hand, a growing sense of the complexity of the body social and politic has enhanced awareness of the interdependence of the whole and has expanded the definition of the political. The resulting broad field—political culture—engages historians of art and theater, gender, and family relations, as well as historians of topics more conventionally understood as political.

Some of the most striking developments in the traditional genres of historical scholarship have concerned a sense of place. For centuries, English historians have assumed the manifest destiny of English institutions and the fortunate uniqueness of English history. Imperial decline and entry into the European Community has called such faith into question; those geopolitical shifts have led scholars to recognize that they had much to learn from the experience of other parts of Europe or of the world, engendering considerable support for the comparative studies of the 1960s and 1970s. Accordingly, new topics such as the general crisis of the seventeenth century, the growth of national consciousness, the evangelization of the countryside, elite formation, agriculture, and economic development were added to revolution and state building as fashionable topics of cooperative volumes in those decades. English historians, however, were not alone in such an awakening. Historians of Scotland and Ireland—always poor relations in the family of British historians—were exposed to many of the same questions, and the self-confidence of their answers grew as the modern center of political gravity shifted away from Westminster. Indeed, the 1970s ushered in something of a renaissance of Scottish and Irish historiography, which soon passed far beyond the familiar topics of political and religious narrative. Even purblind English historians became aware that they were not alone on their island with their English sources. If the years around 1970 had seen many scholars wrestling with the lessons of European variations on common themes, two decades later the lessons taught were increasingly British, as historians came to understand that much early modern history revolved around the less than happy coming together of a British, rather than a merely English, polity.

Similar questions about integration, differentiation, and the geopolitical limits of the polity have also been asked of England itself, the best documented as well as the best endowed with researchers of the British kingdoms. The aftermath of World War II brought increased access to local and private archives, spawning a host of local studies and salutary corrections to the grand tale of national politics and national issues as told from the center. Preoccupation with the local perspective has even encouraged some historians to make the contested claim that localism—particularist unconcern with the center except insofar as it impinged on local issues—was dominant in the provinces.

The location of the early modern polity in time has been the subject of, if anything, even greater controversy than has the matter of place. In most cultures, quasi-Darwinian assumptions of the survival of the fittest and of history as a record of the winners have crept into written histories and helped underpin accounts of linear progress—toward limited monarchy and parliamentary democracy, toward tolerance and moderation, toward the scientific method, and toward "modernity" in all fields of social and economic relations. For generations these accounts dominated English historiography, but the characteristic 1960s and 1970s interest in alternatives bred challenges to the inherited narrative across a broad front. Liberal prejudices about the inexorable triumph of representative institutions—a triumph that in many versions was somehow connected with another linear progression, that of Protestant ascendancy—came to be labeled the whig version of history. Whig history was confronted by the counterculture, as studies of the thwarted radical elements in the English Revolution, of millennialism, of magic, and of witchcraft rolled off the presses. Perhaps the most effective challenge to received wisdom was mounted in the history of science, where exploration of hermeticism and the occult revealed the intellectual vitality and viability of systems and thinkers other than the experimental and mechanical, which had long been accorded heroic status. The road to the present no longer seemed quite so direct.

It was, however, the questioning from what might be called the Right that most disrupted the coherence of the dominant strands of historiography: the study of politics and the study of religion. Declining confidence in England's national significance and in its parliamentary and Protestant destiny was reflected in the abandonment of teleology. And if teleology is suspect, assumptions about long-term processes and long-term causes are vulnerable too. Without doubt the most prominent feature of the historiography of English politics and religion since the late 1970s has been a revisionism that has challenged the whig orthodoxy that held that the dynamic element in the polity was opposition to royal power, centered in Parliament, and coming to crisis in the middle and later seventeenth century. In contrast, these revisionist historians saw conservatism and consensus threatened on every hand primarily by contingent and external pressures and by personal factors such as the uncounsellability of Charles I or the Roman Catholic aspirations of James II; and they argued the widespread appeal in the eighteenth century of toryism and Jacobitism, in contrast to the whig parliamentary ascendancy celebrated by earlier scholars. The compatibility of such revisionism with the debunking of English Puritanism by historians of religion is apparent; more revealing, such iconoclasm has been pushed backward to the English Reformation itself. This, many scholars now argue, was almost wholly a matter of contingency, foisted on an unwilling people by a cynical regime, and rooting itself by a combination of police action and the force of custom. Not surprisingly, revisionist claims have been resisted, often effectively; but there is no mistaking how the central elements in what was once England's national story have been reshaped in recent years. Indeed, in one notorious version, there is not even much of a story to tell, for England is deemed to have remained an Old Regime, a society of orders dominated by crown, church, and nobility, well into the nineteenth century.

At the core of revisionism lies the denial that the early modern era saw a dynamic transition to the modern world. Although those leading the charge have primarily been concerned with the doings of elites, they have found support elsewhere; for the often exaggerated claims for transformation, which by the 1970s seemed to encompass every area of life, provoked skeptics not only among political but also among social and anthropological historians. These argued forcefully that at the most fundamental level, that of human relationships, nothing much changed from the time of the earliest medieval recordkeeping at least until industrialization; in some hands, this has become an argument for the overwhelming continuity of English society.

But it would be a mistake to assume that most work in social history has been driven by the grand polemic against whig or—that allied teleology—Marxist history. In fact, the field of social history represents one of the great historiographic successes of the last generation. If political and religious historians have been preoccupied with the challenge to received wisdom, social historians have opened whole new fields. Much of what passed in the first half of the twentieth century for social history told an unadventurous story of the conditions of life of various groups. Painstaking research in parish registers and in the records of human ills now allows us to talk more confidently of the natural and environmental constraints on human existence and of demographic responses; at the same time, vague generalizations about home and employment have become precise studies of family structure and of the social and demographic contexts of various occupations, from the physician to the criminal. More novel has been the attention to how early modern people ordered their experience of their world. Much recent work has centered on the concept of community, addressing such questions as the relative role of neighborhood and kinship in everyday relationships, the ways in which community was maintained under stress, and how change and challenge were contained.

Indeed, problems of identity and meaning have been at the heart of recent scholarship in a number of fields. If political historians have explored the mental worlds of their subjects to determine the geopolitical unit with which they identified themselves, Scottish and above all Irish historians have raised parallel questions with even greater urgency and to impressive effect. Historians of the family have tested not simply the intensity of emotional bonds but even the existence of such basic concepts as childhood, and they have asked too about the meaning of other stages and aspects of life, such as adolescence, service, courtship, and death. But it is of the history of women and gender that the most challenging of such questions have been asked. Scarcely even recognized as a subject a generation ago, the history of women in early modern Britain, as in so many other places and times, has become the focus of intense inquiry. Much of that effort has been expended on practical problems, whether in the public sphere of work and the law courts, or in the private experiences of childbirth and motherhood. Recently, however, some scholars have argued that the drama, the political rhetoric, and the popular rituals of the period betray considerable unease over matters of gender and tension over the nature of femaleness and therefore, presumably, of maleness too.

It is fair to say that there is no agreement that such tension was peculiar to the early modern period.

It may seem that the most visible outcome of the past generation of historical research has been the fragmentation of the discipline and of our sense of the British, and still more the English, past; and there are certainly those who have deplored this. Yet, although teleologies have crumbled, some comfort may be found for those who seek an uncomplicated story. The primacy of the political narrative has been challenged, but in the welter of other voices, a surprising consensus can be heard. One salutary consequence of the abandonment of teleology has been the borrowing from French scholars and from cultural anthropologists of the concept of *mentalité* or mentality—the world viewed or constructed, as nearly as possible, from within the early modern mind, rather than shaped in today's terms. The fruits have been impressive studies of the outlook and assumptions of sixteenth-century noblemen and lawyers, of seventeenth-century clergymen and craftsmen, and so on. The attempt to understand an earlier society in its own terms has necessarily given new meaning to practices and beliefs—witchcraft, popular pastimes such as football or alehouse conviviality—that whig or Marxist historians dismissed as random or irrational. These can now often be seen as firmly embedded in a system of beliefs, different perhaps from any with which we are familiar but no less real. Indeed, the supplanting of the political narrative has paradoxically been associated with an extension of the domain of the political. Growing sensitivity to the cultural and social dominance of certain groups in the modern world, and claims that their concerns represent ideology rather than absolute standards, have encouraged scholars to submit cultural schemes and programs of the past to similar questioning. Accordingly, much recent work has centered on the ideology and politics of drama and other forms of imaginative writing, of court art, of theories of commerce, and of virtue; such historicizing approaches have been most successful in complicating the traditional canon of literary and scientific achievements, which few scholars now see as the value-free and heroic endeavors once so celebrated.

The other shared feature of much recent work—or at least that on the latter part of our period, post-1650—is the prominence of aspects of commercialism. Some historians, usually of politics, still describe the aristocratic order so familiar in the historiography of a generation ago. Others, however, argue the huge economic consequences of the new patterns in private, small-scale production and consumption; the social and cultural significance of the market in clothes, in print, and in health care; the growing political impact in the eighteenth century of commercialized forms of appeal; and of the new professions that grew out of prosperity. Still more unmistakable is the way contemporaries regarded such developments. Marxist historians of political and social thought of the seventeenth century worked hard to establish an economic subtext of works whose ostensible concerns were far from economic. For many of the works of the eighteenth century no such struggle is needed, since their economic concerns are obvious. Appropriately enough, the liveliest field of intellectual history in recent years has centered on eighteenth-century theories of politeness, civility, commerce, and of the driving role of private interest and private virtue.

There is a certain irony in hearing once again celebrations of modernity, since the appeal of the new social and cultural historians owes something to the challenge to teleology mounted by revisionist political historians. There is an even greater and more salutary irony in the way such a celebration moves the focus outside England: it was a distinctively Scottish Enlightenment that fostered much of the new theorizing.

Entries are arranged under the following headings:

England
> Political History
> Political Thought
> Foreign Relations and Military History
> Economic History
> Religious History
> Intellectual History
> Social History
> Legal History
> Women, Family, and Household
> History of Science
> The Arts

Scotland

Ireland

Wales

[Contributors: BPL = Brian P. Levack, DAB = Daniel A. Baugh, DMH = Derek M. Hirst, FMLT = F.M.L. Thompson, JPG = Jack P. Greene, KSB = Karl S. Bottigheimer, KW = Kathleen Wilson, LAP = Linda A. Pollock, MHS = Michael H. Shank, MT = Margo Todd, MU = Maarten Ultee, RWK = Richard W. Kaeuper]

ENGLAND

Political History

23.1 Stanley Ayling. *The elder Pitt, earl of Chatham.* New York: McKay, 1976. ISBN 0-679-50717-5. ► Life and times of manic-depressive statesman who transformed Britain into leading imperial power. Absorbing narrative of high political intrigue in biographical genre. [KW]

23.2 G. E. Aylmer. *The king's servants: the civil service of Charles I, 1625–1642.* Rev. ed. London: Routledge & Kegan Paul, 1974. ISBN 0-7100-7894-3. ► Magisterial assessment of royal administration and character of office holding. Surveys group identity, career patterns, tenure, efficiency, corruption, and bureaucracy. Valuable comparison with more extensive (and less efficient) administration in France. [DMH]

23.3 G. E. Aylmer. *The state's servants: the civil service of the English republic, 1649–1660.* London: Routledge & Kegan Paul, 1973. ISBN 0-7100-7637-1. ► Monumental sequel to work on career patterns and competence of royal government (23.2), enlivened by suggestions on beneficial impact of ideological commitment and by prosopographies of individual officeholders. [DMH]

23.4 G. W. Bernard. *War, taxation, and rebellion in early Tudor England: Henry VIII, Wolsey, and the Amicable Grant of 1525.* New York: St. Martin's, 1986. ISBN 0-312-85611-3. ► Skillful assessment of strains imposed by opportunistic war. Nobles actively supported crown, resistance result of currency shortage in textile region not class hostility. [DMH]

23.5 John Brewer. *Party ideology and popular politics at the accession of George III.* 1976 ed. Cambridge: Cambridge University Press, 1981. ISBN 0-521-21049-6 (cl, 1976), 0-521-28701-4 (pbk). ► Reconfiguration of high and low political cultures under impact of domestic and colonial conflict, expansion of press, and radicalism around reformer John Wilkes. Major reassessment of Hanoverian political terrain. [KW]

23.6 John Brewer. *The sinews of power: war, money, and the English state, 1688–1783.* 1988 ed. Cambridge, Mass.: Harvard University Press, 1990. ISBN 0-674-80930-0 (pbk). ► Analysis of development of powerful fiscal-military complex through exigencies of continuous warfare. Discusses patterns of taxation, debt and funding, civil administration, and rise of parliamentary lobbies. Important reconceptualization of Hanoverian state. [KW]

23.7 John Brewer and John Styles, eds. *An ungovernable people: the English and their law in the seventeenth and eighteenth centuries.* New Brunswick, N.J.: Rutgers University Press, 1980. ISBN 0-8135-0891-6. ► Compelling analyses of legal and political cultures. Competing conceptions of justice and authority, rooted in shifting configurations of property and power, facilitated middling and plebeian manipulation of system. [KW]

23.8 C. D. Chandaman. *The English public revenue, 1660–1688.* Oxford: Clarendon, 1975. ISBN 0-19-828268-0. ► Magisterial financial survey of sources and yield of revenue and their political ramifications. Applause for earl of Rochester's work at Treasury in restoring crown's finances and criticism of Charles II's profligacy which wrecked them. [DMH]

23.9 S. B. Chrimes. *Henry VII.* Berkeley: University of California Press, 1972. ISBN 0-520-02266-1. ► Conventional survey but much information on administration, politics, and diplomacy, as well as on years of exile. [DMH]

23.10 J.C.D. Clark. *English society, 1688–1832: ideology, social structure, and political practice during the ancien régime.* Cambridge: Cambridge University Press, 1985. ISBN 0-521-30922-0 (cl), 0-521-31383-X (pbk). ► Study of confessional, dynastic nature of political divisions and strong mental structures of hierarchy and deference characterizing England's Old Regime. Influential conservative revisionism stressing preservative aspects of Georgian society. [KW]

23.11 Linda Colley. *In defiance of oligarchy: the Tory party, 1714–60.* Cambridge: Cambridge University Press, 1982. ISBN 0-521-23982-6 (cl), 0-521-31311-2 (pbk). ► Pathfinding revisionist challenge to established view of opposition's impotency in age of whig supremacy. Finds cohesiveness and resiliency of Hanoverian toryism, parliamentary and grass roots, in face of official proscription. [KW]

23.12 Patrick Collinson. "Puritans, men of business, and Elizabethan parliaments." *Parliamentary history* 7 (1988) 187–211. ISSN 0264-2824. ► Postrevisionist analysis of roles of partisans and placemen. Basic to any inquiry. [DMH]

23.13 Richard Cust and Ann Hughes, eds. *Conflict in early Stuart England: studies in religion and politics, 1603–1642.* New York: Longman, 1989. ISBN 0-582-03450-7 (cl), 0-582-30173-4 (pbk). ► Indispensable collection of essays, especially good for introduction to current revisionist controversy over existence and nature of opposition to crown. Also skillful analyses of religious problems and political contexts of period. [DMH]

23.14 Gary Stuart De Krey. *A fractured society: the politics of London in the first age of party, 1688–1715.* Oxford: Clarendon, 1985. ISBN 0-19-820067-6. ► Detailed political sociology of metropolitan civil life. Fissures in urban society produced by revolution, high finance, and war transformed ideological positions and social backing of parties. [KW]

23.15 David M. Dean and Norman L. Jones, eds. *The parliaments of Elizabethan England.* Oxford: Blackwell, 1990. ISBN 0-631-15267-9. ► Generally revisionist collection exploring uncontentiousness of management, taxation, moral reform, local politicking, and war needs. Some older views survive, including disruptiveness of religion and parliamentary concern with foreign policy. [DMH]

23.16 P.G.M. Dickson. *The financial revolution in England: a study in the development of public credit, 1688–1756.* New York: St. Martin's, 1967. ► Technical but important study of credit, public and private; commercial, technical, and scientific factors facilitating long-term credit in 1690s; and commercial and governmental consequences. [DMH]

23.17 Geoffrey R. Elton. *The Parliament of England, 1559–1581.* Cambridge: Cambridge University Press, 1986. ISBN 0-521-32835-7. ‣ Magisterial dissection of legislative procedures and achievements and the doing of parliamentary business under Elizabeth I. Gives short shrift to traditional assumptions of conflict and of place of Parliament. [DMH]

23.18 Geoffrey R. Elton. "Tudor government: the points of contact." In *Studies in Tudor and Stuart politics and government.* Vol. 3, pp. 3–57. Cambridge: Cambridge University Press, 1974–83. ISBN 0-521-24893-0. ‣ Brilliant revisionist analysis of workings of high politics and links between center and localities stressing consensus rather than conflict, by the leading early Tudor historian. [DMH]

23.19 Geoffrey R. Elton, ed. *The Tudor constitution: documents and commentary.* 2d ed. New York: Cambridge University Press, 1982. ISBN 0-521-24506-0 (cl), 0-521-28757-X (pbk). ‣ Fundamental work, combining documents with authoritative commentary. Stress on effective management and denial of structural problems or assertiveness of Parliament sometimes controversial. [DMH]

23.20 Anthony Fletcher. *Reform in the provinces: the government of Stuart England.* New Haven: Yale University Press, 1986. ISBN 0-300-03673-6. ‣ Excellent synthesis on local government, stressing informal controls in face-to-face communities (no towns included). Discusses periodic purges from above, increasing regularization, and seizing of initiative from central government by conscientious justices of the peace. [DMH]

23.21 Alistair Fox and John Guy. *Reassessing the Henrician age: humanism, politics, and reform, 1500–1550.* New York: Blackwell, 1986. ISBN 0-631-14614-8. ‣ Valuable essays on nonpartisan nature of humanism and on new currents in legal thought. Downplays importance of Thomas Cromwell, both in reformism and in origins of royal supremacy. [DMH]

23.22 Paul Fritz. *The English ministers and Jacobitism between the rebellions of 1715 and 1745.* Toronto: University of Toronto Press, 1975. ISBN 0-8020-5308-4. ‣ Fear of Jacobitism central element in shaping domestic and foreign policies, political careers, and British intelligence during whig ascendancy. Interesting reconstruction of obsession, delusion, and espionage in high places. [KW]

23.23 John B. Gillingham. *The Wars of the Roses: peace and conflict in fifteenth-century England.* Baton Rouge: Louisiana State University Press, 1981. ISBN 0-8071-1005-1. ‣ Best available narrative, detailed and perceptive, minimizing extent of discord. [DMH]

23.24 Michael A. R. Graves. *The Tudor parliaments: crown, Lords, and Commons, 1485–1603.* London: Longman, 1985. ISBN 0-582-49190-8 (pbk). ‣ Valuable revisionist survey stressing prominence of House of Lords and importance of procedure, management, and crown's initiative in passage of legislation. Although instability brought by religious change took time to settle, accord rather than conflict predominated. [DMH]

23.25 S. J. Gunn. *Charles Brandon, duke of Suffolk, c. 1484–1545.* New York: Blackwell, 1988. ISBN 0-631-15781-6. ‣ Careful study of major newly created nobleman, who used friendship with Henry VIII in laborious building of local power base. Sees chivalry rather than partisan ideologies as crucial. [DMH]

23.26 S. J. Gunn and P. G. Lindley, eds. *Cardinal Wolsey: church, state, and art.* Cambridge: Cambridge University Press, 1991. ISBN 0-521-37568-1. ‣ Lavishly illustrated essays on Wolsey's ambiguous role in reform and assertion of church and state and as patron over wide range of arts. [DMH]

23.27 John Guy. *Tudor England.* 1988 ed. Oxford: Oxford University Press, 1990. ISBN 0-19-873088-8 (cl), 0-19-285213-2 (pbk). ‣ Compendious survey. Main thesis, which ignores end-of-century problems, focuses on growing efficiency of Tudor state. Thorough, readable account of latest research in virtually all fields. Basic starting point. [DMH]

23.28 Christopher Haigh. *Elizabeth I.* London: Longman, 1988. ISBN 0-582-02390-4 (cl), 0-582-00534-5 (pbk). ‣ Entertaining, brisk revision of Elizabeth and Elizabethan politics, questioning her successes. Best available. [DMH]

23.29 Christopher Haigh, ed. *The reign of Elizabeth I.* Athens: University of Georgia Press, 1989. ISBN 0-8203-1131-6 (pbk). ‣ Fine revisionist essay on factions, good summaries of politics of reign, of poverty and social regulation, and of center-local relations. Provocative on Protestantism's lack of popular appeal. [DMH]

23.30 Laurence Hanson. *Government and the press, 1695–1763.* 1936 ed. Oxford: Clarendon, 1967. ‣ Well-researched narrative on early efforts to construct public opinion. Encroachment of newspapers on political process produced unsuccessful attempts to control it. Treats prosecution and its legal consequences and opposition, and government-subsidized journalism. [KW]

23.31 Tim Harris. *London crowds in the reign of Charles II: propaganda and politics from the Restoration until the Exclusion crisis.* Cambridge: Cambridge University Press, 1987. ISBN 0-521-32623-0. ‣ Insightful analysis of partisan street loyalties, reactionary as well as radical. Good on mobilization, religious and civic ideologies, and backlash. [DMH]

23.32 Caroline M. Hibbard. *Charles I and the popish plot.* Chapel Hill: University of North Carolina Press, 1983. ISBN 0-8078-1520-9. ‣ Seminal argument; detailed reconstruction and demonstration of rationality of fears of popish plot around king, crucial in onset of Civil War. [DMH]

23.33 Christopher Hill. *The world turned upside down: radical ideas during the English Revolution.* 1984 ed. Harmondsworth: Penguin, 1987. ISBN 0-14-055147-6 (pbk). ‣ Sympathetic account of radical outpouring in midst of mid-seventeenth-century revolution. Evokes outlook and excitement rather than analyzes. [DMH]

23.34 Derek Hirst. *Authority and conflict: England, 1603–1658.* Cambridge, Mass.: Harvard University Press, 1986. ISBN 0-674-05291-9 (cl), 0-674-05290-0 (pbk). ‣ Broad survey of religion, politics, and society. Reevaluates old arguments for, and revisionist denials of, inexorable conflict. Thorough account of breakdown and ensuing republic. [DMH]

23.35 Clive A. Holmes. "The county community in Stuart history and historiography." *Journal of British studies* 19.2 (1980) 54–73. ISSN 0021-9371. ‣ Demonstrates complexity of interrelationship between center and locality in politics and enforcement. Debunks localist approach to seventeenth-century crisis. [DMH]

23.36 Geoffrey Holmes. *British politics in the age of Anne.* Rev. ed. London: Hambledon, 1987. ISBN 0-907628-73-7 (cl), 0-907628-74-5 (pbk). ‣ Authoritative high political history describing contours and substance of political conflict under last Stuart monarch. Treats royal closet, Cabinet, parliamentary parties, management in Commons and Lords, and growth of electorate. [KW]

23.37 Rosemary Horrox. *Richard III: a study of service.* Cambridge: Cambridge University Press, 1989. ISBN 0-521-33428-4. ‣ Insightful assessment of troubled reign, organized around problem of feudal service and relationships and building of regional power bases. Discusses disastrous failure of this usurper to deliver promised stability. [DMH/RWK]

23.38 Henry Horwitz. *Parliament, policy, and politics in the reign of William III.* Manchester: Manchester University Press, 1977. ISBN 0-7190-0661-9. ‣ Comprehensive account of high political life in aftermath of Glorious Revolution (1688). Treats parliamentary debates and committees, progress of legislation, formation of royal Cabinet, and relations between church and state. Knowledgeable history from above. [KW]

23.39 Ann Hughes. *The causes of the English Civil War.* New York: St. Martin's, 1991. ISBN 0-312-05226-X. ▸ Invaluable synthesis, accepting revisionist stress on conjuncture, personality, and British problem (existence of multiple kingdoms), but arguing for long-term divergences in visions of English body politics. Best starting point. [DMH]

23.40 Ann Hughes. *Politics, society, and Civil War in Warwickshire, 1620–1660.* Cambridge: Cambridge University Press, 1987. ISBN 0-521-33252-4. ▸ Major antirevisionist, antilocalist, county study. Argues for importance of center and central issues, and popular partisanship even in areas outside gentry control. Discusses impact of Civil War and revolution. [DMH]

23.41 Ronald Hutton. *The Restoration: a political and religious history of England and Wales, 1658–1667.* 1985 ed. New York: Oxford University Press, 1987. ISBN 0-19-822698-5 (cl, 1985), 0-19-285183-7 (pbk). ▸ Clear narrative of collapse of republic and early years of restored monarchy. Strong interweaving of central and local crises for republic, but after Restoration central focus on king and court. [DMH]

23.42 E. W. Ives. *Anne Boleyn.* 1986 ed. Oxford: Blackwell, 1987. ISBN 0-631-14745-4. ▸ Fine biography. Argues Reformation shaped not just by king and minister but also by court faction when dangerous tensions arose with political and religious upheaval. Finds Anne's cultural sophistication was both her attraction and her doom. [DMH]

23.43 Mervyn James. *Society, politics, and culture: studies in early modern England.* 1986 ed. Cambridge: Cambridge University Press, 1988. ISBN 0-521-36877-4 (pbk). ▸ Seminal essays on aristocratic ideology, politics and reshaping of concept of honor from chivalric and feudal to civic and public, and integration of North and its nobility into central state. [DMH]

23.44 Clyve Jones, ed. *Britain in the first age of party, 1688–1750: essays presented to Geoffrey Holmes.* London: Hambledon, 1987. ISBN 0-907628-89-3 (cl), 0-907628-90-7 (pbk). ▸ Studies of political, social, and religious life which extend age of party to midcentury. Treats House of Lords, popular culture, religious and dynastic strife, and urban development. Methodologically varied. [KW]

23.45 J. R. Jones. *Country and court: England, 1658–1714.* 1978 ed. London: Arnold, 1986. ISBN 0-7131-6104-3 (pbk). ▸ Best available political survey of partisanship and revolution in later seventeenth-century England. Slightly old-fashioned but useful detail on parliamentary and court politics; strong on diplomacy and revolution of 1688. [DMH]

23.46 J. P. Kenyon. *Revolution principles: the politics of party, 1689–1720.* Cambridge: Cambridge University Press, 1977. ISBN 0-521-21542-0. ▸ Ideological battles fought over dynastic succession, religion, and popular sovereignty forged whig and tory positions. Whigs transformed from radical populists to authoritarian oligarchs. Astute conservative reading of whig myths. [KW]

23.47 J. P. Kenyon, ed. *The Stuart constitution, 1603–1688: documents and commentary.* 2d ed. Cambridge: Cambridge University Press, 1986. ISBN 0-521-30810-0 (cl), 0-521-31327-9 (pbk). ▸ Useful essays and illustrative documents on workings and problems of government, church, Parliament, and law. [DMH]

23.48 Mark A. Kishlansky. *Parliamentary selection: social and political choice in early modern England.* Cambridge: Cambridge University Press, 1986. ISBN 0-521-32231-6 (cl), 0-521-31116-0 (pbk). ▸ Lively but contentious assertion of dominance of patron-

age and deference in electoral choice until Civil War; should be read with *Albion* 19.3 (1987) 428–34. [DMH]

23.49 J. R. Lander. *Government and community: England, 1450–1509.* Cambridge, Mass.: Harvard University Press, 1980. ISBN 0-674-35793-0. ▸ Sound survey of dynastic civil wars and recovery. Strong on political history, social relations, and use crown made of habits of obedience. [DMH]

23.50 Paul Langford. *The excise crisis: society and politics in the age of Walpole.* Oxford: Clarendon, 1975. ISBN 0-19-822437-0. ▸ Discussion of administration's attempt to pass consumption tax on wine and tobacco that produced massive parliamentary and public backlash. Essential analysis of political and electoral repercussions of well-known opposition drama. [KW]

23.51 David M. Loades. *The reign of Mary Tudor: politics, government, and religion in England, 1553–1558.* 2d ed. London: Longman, 1991. ISBN 0-582-05759-0. ▸ Thorough narrative and thematic survey defending Catholic regime from many Protestant charges, then and since, of bloody mindedness and incompetence; surveys instead range of problems faced. [DMH]

23.52 Roger Lockyer. *Buckingham: the life and political career of George Villiers, first duke of Buckingham, 1592–1628.* New York: Longman, 1981. ISBN 0-582-50296-9 (cl), 0-582-49415-X (pbk). ▸ Political biography of great favorite, presenting him as less corrupt, incompetent, dictatorial, and homosexual than is commonly alleged. [DMH]

23.53 Wallace MacCaffrey. *Elizabeth I.* London: Arnold, 1993. ISBN 0-340-56167-X. ▸ Political biography distilling author's many other works on high-level politics of period; concentrates on center, in old-fashioned but entertaining and up-to-date narrative. [DMH]

23.54 Diarmaid MacCulloch. *Suffolk and the Tudors: politics and religion in an English county, 1500–1600.* New York: Oxford University Press, 1986. ISBN 0-19-822914-3. ▸ County study of replacement of aristocratic dominance not simply by gentry factionalism but also by emerging popular legalism and Protestantism. [DMH]

23.55 Paul Kleber Monod. *Jacobitism and the English people, 1688–1788.* Cambridge: Cambridge University Press, 1989. ISBN 0-521-33534-5. ▸ Methodologically innovative analysis of profound impact of pro-Stuart loyalties on social and political development and forms and content of popular political consciousness. Jacobite history at its most subtle and convincing. [KW]

23.56 John S. Morrill. *The revolt of the provinces: conservatives and radicals in the English Civil War, 1630–1650.* 1976 ed. New York: Longman, 1980. ISBN 0-582-49704-3 (pbk). ▸ Seminal if slightly overstated assertion of localism of much of discontent that led to and complicated Civil War; valuably illustrated by documents. [DMH]

23.57 John S. Morrill, ed. *Oliver Cromwell and the English Revolution.* New York: Longman, 1990. ISBN 0-582-06064-8 (cl), 0-582-01675-4 (pbk). ▸ Important essays on career and achievements, stressing humble origins, and balanced surveys of military and civil achievements. Sensitive analysis of religiosity; controversial on parliamentary activities. [DMH]

23.58 John B. Owen. *The rise of the Pelhams.* 1957 ed. New York: Barnes & Noble, 1971. ISBN 0-389-04145-9. ▸ Discussion of Henry Pelham's and his brother, duke of Newcastle's skills in handling monarch and independent backbenchers in Commons, instrumental in attainment of power after Prime Minister Walpole's fall. Based on biographical data of 686 members of Parliament. Persuasive study in tradition of Namier 24.29. [KW]

23.59 Valerie L. Pearl. *London and the outbreak of the Puritan Revolution: city government and national politics, 1625–43.* 1961 ed.

London: Oxford University Press, 1972. ▸ Influential study, part narrative, part prosopographical, of interests and politics of London's governing and clerical elite, of municipality's short-term alienation from crown, and of opposition's seizure of power. [DMH]

23.60 Linda Levy Peck. *Court patronage and corruption in early Stuart England.* Boston: Unwin Hyman, 1990. ISBN 0-04-942195-6. ▸ Important study of politics and ideology of patronage. Discusses corruption of personal tie of gratitude under pressure of commerce and other ideologies in court and local politics and in administration. [DMH]

23.61 Marie Peters. *Pitt and popularity: the patriot minister and London opinion during the Seven Years War.* Oxford: Clarendon, 1980. ISBN 0-19-822498-2. ▸ Impact of organized public opinion as represented in press on Great Commoner's standing in period of imperial wars. Thorough investigation of metropolitan political journalism. [KW]

23.62 J. H. Plumb. *The growth of political stability in England, 1675–1725.* 1967 ed. Atlantic Highlands, N.J.: Humanities, 1977. ISBN 0-391-01908-2 (pbk). ▸ Transformation of turbulent political world of Stuart period into durable and quiescent Hanoverian oligarchy through single-party government under Robert Walpole. Elegant, if adulatory analysis of high political relations in early eighteenth century. [KW]

23.63 A. J. Pollard. *Northeastern England during the Wars of the Roses: lay society, war, and politics, 1450–1500.* Oxford: Clarendon, 1990. ISBN 0-19-820087-0. ▸ Novel rooting of political turmoil in economic stress of mid-fifteenth-century Northeast. Thorough analysis of landed society and lordship. Finds political disintegration averted by Richard III's seizure of throne. [DMH]

23.64 Nicholas Rogers. *Whigs and cities: popular politics in the age of Walpole and Pitt.* Oxford: Clarendon, 1989. ISBN 0-19-821785-4. ▸ Contribution of urban radicalism to extra-parliamentary political agitations under first two Georges. Focuses on interplay of economic interest, clientage, and political loyalties. Sociology of metropolitan politics. [KW]

23.65 Conrad Russell. *The causes of the English Civil War.* New York: Oxford University Press, 1991. ISBN 0-19-822141-X. ▸ Important, entertaining revisionist lectures, arguing England ideologically incapable of resisting the king. Decisive pressures came from discontent in Scotland and Ireland and king's determination to restore his position. [DMH]

23.66 Conrad Russell. *Parliaments and English politics, 1621–1629.* 1979 ed. Oxford: Clarendon, 1982. ISBN 0-19-822691-8 (pbk). ▸ Seminal revisionist analysis arguing parliamentary behavior conciliatory, tensions not from opposition principle but wartime stresses, local pressures, and eventually religious fears. Good on governmental concerns and divisions. [DMH]

23.67 James J. Scarisbrick. *Henry VIII.* Berkeley: University of California Press, 1968. ▸ Compendious, scholarly but entertaining biography of willful king, skillfully relating high politics to diplomacy and theology. [DMH]

23.68 Roger Schofield. "Taxation and the political limits of the Tudor state." In *Law and government under the Tudors: essays presented to Sir Geoffrey Elton, Regius Professor of Modern History in the University of Cambridge, on the occasion of his retirement.* Claire Cross, David M. Loades, and J. J. Scarisbrick, eds., pp. 227–55. Cambridge: Cambridge University Press, 1988. ISBN 0-521-33510-8. ▸ Fundamental essay on reform, incidence, and administration of Tudor taxation. Includes computer demonstration of remarkably accurate assessment and yield under Henry VIII. Asserts Cardinal Wolsey's administrative skill. Discussion of politics of Elizabethan decline. [DMH]

23.69 Lois G. Schwoerer. *The Declaration of Rights, 1689.* Bal-timore: Johns Hopkins University Press, 1981. ISBN 0-8018-2430-3. ▸ Study of deliberately revolutionary nature of document that laid ground rules for William III's succession and founded England's constitutional monarchy. Radical whig reading of Glorious Revolution (1688–89) and intentions of its main actors; controversial. [KW]

23.70 Lois G. Schwoerer, ed. *The Revolution of 1688–89: changing perspectives.* Cambridge: Cambridge University Press, 1992. ISBN 0-521-39321-3. ▸ Interdisciplinary essays aimed at complicating dichotomous views of late Stuart and early Hanoverian periods. Examined from perspective of high and low political culture, press, theater, gender, and international rivalries. [KW]

23.71 Paul Seaward. *The Restoration.* New York: St. Martin's, 1991. ISBN 0-312-04929-3. ▸ Best introduction to complex period (1658–88). Argues Restoration settlement failed not only to quiet religious tensions but also to identify locus of state power. Sound narrative. [DMH]

23.72 R. Malcolm Smuts. *Court culture and the origins of a royalist tradition in early Stuart England.* Philadelphia: University of Pennsylvania Press, 1987. ISBN 0-8122-8039-3. ▸ Best study of increasingly elaborate court culture and its polemicization. Treats metropolitan and ideological contexts of art and collecting. Sees cult of monarch and role of patron under political and religious challenge. [DMH]

23.73 J. P. Sommerville. *Politics and ideology in England, 1603–1640.* London: Longman, 1986. ISBN 0-582-49432-X (pbk). ▸ Best account of pre–Civil War political thought; antirevisionist. Treats divergences over indefensible royal prerogative, subject's absolute property right, and latent tension in ideas exacerbated by political pressures, especially over church and taxation. [DMH]

23.74 David Starkey et al. *The English court: from the Wars of the Roses to the Civil War.* London: Longman, 1987. ISBN 0-582-01359-3 (cl), 0-582-429281-5 (pbk). ▸ Collection of useful essays surveying history and politics of royal court, generally arguing for continuity in this central institution of national life and politics. [DMH]

23.75 P.D.G. Thomas. *The House of Commons in the eighteenth century.* Oxford: Clarendon, 1971. ISBN 0-19-822340-4. ▸ Mechanics and evolution of lower house, from legislative and debating procedures to legal privileges and seating of members. Useful nuts-and-bolts history of ascendant institution of eighteenth century. [KW]

23.76 E. P. Thompson. *Whigs and hunters: the origins of the Black Act.* New York: Pantheon, 1975. ISBN 0-394-40011-9 (cl), 0-394-73086-0 (pbk). ▸ Stimulating, contentious neo-Marxist interpretation of Walpolean state. Class conflict context for enactment of notorious 1723 law that created fifty capital offences. Violent plebeian resistance to new property definitions. [KW]

23.77 Robert Tittler and Jennifer Loach, eds. *The mid-Tudor polity, c. 1540–1560.* Totowa, N.J.: Rowman & Littlefield, 1980. ISBN 0-8476-6257-8. ▸ Revisionist essays debunking assumptions of inevitable Protestant triumph, Catholic weakness, and Elizabethan brilliance. Strong on Parliament, towns, and diplomatic and economic crisis. [DMH]

23.78 David Underdown. *Pride's purge: politics in the Puritan Revolution.* London: Allen & Unwin, 1985. ISBN 0-04-822045-0 (pbk). ▸ Brilliant account of breakdown of parliamentarian alliance and very compromised revolution of 1648–49 and consequences for 1650s republic. Detailed political narrative integrating central, local, and army histories; prosopographical conjectures about MPs' commitment. [DMH]

23.79 David Underdown. *Revel, riot, and rebellion: popular politics and culture in England, 1603–1660.* 1985 ed. Oxford: Oxford University Press, 1987. ISBN 0-19-285193-4 (pbk). ▸ Important but controversial study of cultural and ecological roots of Civil War. Argues forms of popular ritual and celebration determined by land use, and forms of social discipline consequent on these; and thus to politics. [DMH]

23.80 Penry H. Williams. *The Tudor regime.* 1979 ed. Oxford: Clarendon, 1986. ISBN 0-19-822678-0 (pbk). ▸ Judicious thematic survey of Tudor state, its functioning, effectiveness, and assets—informal as well as formal. [DMH]

23.81 Kathleen Wilson. "Empire, trade, and popular politics in mid-Hanoverian Britain: the case of Admiral Vernon." *Past and present* 121 (1988) 74–109. ISSN 0031-2746. ▸ Analysis of role of pro-imperial and libertarian sentiments in domestic political agitation leading to Robert Walpole's fall. Also discusses commercialization of politics and political activism of "middling sort" of people. [KW]

SEE ALSO
20.569 Charles D. Ross. *Edward IV.*

Political Thought

23.82 Richard Ashcraft. *Revolutionary politics and Locke's "Two Treatises of Government."* Princeton: Princeton University Press, 1986. ISBN 0-691-07703-7 (cl), 0-691-02248-8 (pbk). ▸ Massive study of context of philosopher's thought in radical politics of restored monarchy; important but controversial claims for extent of revolutionary underground and Locke's participation. [DMH]

23.83 J. H. Burns and Mark Goldie, eds. *The Cambridge history of political thought, 1450–1700.* Cambridge: Cambridge University Press, 1991. ISBN 0-521-24716-0. ▸ Essential, monumental, starting point for any study. Contains systematic essays on main currents and thinkers from Renaissance humanism and law through religious crisis to Thomas Hobbes, John Locke, and natural law. [DMH]

23.84 J. C. Davis. *Utopia and the ideal society: a study of English utopian writing, 1516–1700.* Cambridge: Cambridge University Press, 1981. ISBN 0-521-23396-8. ▸ Schematic, wide-ranging approach stressing utopianists' pessimism about human nature and their interest in regulation as barrier against decay. Contextualizes their schemes, especially socioeconomic provision. [DMH]

23.85 H. T. Dickinson. *Liberty and property: political ideology in eighteenth-century Britain.* New York: Holmes & Meier, 1977. ISBN 0-8419-0351-4. ▸ Study of permutations and ultimate triumph of whig principles in Hanoverian discourse and of demise of tory precepts in George II's reign. Able whiggish survey of ideas about relations between court, constitution, and public. [KW]

23.86 John Dunn. *Locke.* Oxford: Oxford University Press, 1984. ISBN 0-19-287561-2 (cl), 0-19-287560-4 (pbk). ▸ Best available introduction to Locke's political philosophy. Stresses theistic rather than capitalist or partisan roots of his politics, religion, and epistemology. [DMH]

23.87 Duncan Forbes. *Hume's philosophical politics.* Cambridge: Cambridge University Press, 1975. ISBN 0-521-20754-1. ▸ Impressive location of philosopher's politics in context of Scottish Enlightenment, eighteenth-century politics, and scientific method. Focuses on Hume's theories of manners, progress, and government. [DMH]

23.88 Alistair Fox. *Thomas More: history and providence.* New Haven: Yale University Press, 1983. ISBN 0-300-02951-9. ▸ Best introduction to thought of Sir Thomas More, setting it especially in religious context. Examines all works, historical and religious, as well as *Utopia.* [DMH]

23.89 J.A.W. Gunn. *Beyond liberty and property: the process of*

self-recognition in eighteenth-century political thought. Kingston, Ont.: McGill-Queen's University Press, 1983. ISBN 0-7735-1006-0. ▸ Original history of ideas that maps ideological terrain of conservative and liberal politics. Ideas about proper relationship between subject and state key to apprehending Hanoverian society's self-image. [KW]

23.90 Thomas A. Horne. *Property rights and poverty: political argument in Britain, 1605–1834.* Chapel Hill: University of North Carolina Press, 1990. ISBN 0-8078-1912-3. ▸ Examination of natural law arguments on property, including claims to exclusive rights to ownership as against claims to inclusive economic entitlements. Shows political compromises made over practical limits on property owners and some welfare rights. [DMH]

23.91 Lisa Jardine and Anthony Grafton. "Studied for action: how Gabriel Harvey read his Livy." *Past and present* 129 (1990) 30–78. ISSN 0031-2746. ▸ Innovative essay on how intellectuals and politicians of late sixteenth century read classical political and moral thought and applied it to present. [DMH]

23.92 J.G.A. Pocock. *The Machiavellian moment: Florentine political thought and the Atlantic republican tradition.* Princeton: Princeton University Press, 1975. ISBN 0-691-07560-3. ▸ Seminal chapters on classical republicanism in revolutionary England and on argument that diffusion of landed property facilitated political activism, creating fertile tension with royal court and mercantile corruption. [DMH]

23.93 J.G.A. Pocock. *Virtue, commerce, and history: essays on political thought and history, chiefly in the eighteenth century.* Cambridge: Cambridge University Press, 1985. ISBN 0-521-25701-8 (cl), 0-521-27660-8 (pbk). ▸ Brilliant attempt to provide social history of ideas. Examines ideological ramifications of changes in property structure after 1688 revolution, which ushered in complex aristocratic, commercial, and whig-liberal order. [DMH]

23.94 G.A.J. Rogers and Alan Ryan, eds. *Perspectives on Thomas Hobbes.* 1988 ed. Oxford: Clarendon, 1990. ISBN 0-19-823914-9 (pbk). ▸ High-quality contextual and theoretical essays. Especially good on Hobbes's rhetoric and science and on problems his politics caused for acceptability of latter. [DMH]

23.95 Gordon J. Schochet. *Patriarchalism in political thought: the authoritarian family and political speculation and attitudes especially in seventeenth-century England.* New York: Basic Books, 1975. ISBN 0-465-05455-2. ▸ Survey of religious and political dogma to show dominance of scripture-derived patriarchalism in social and political thought, peaking with absolutist Sir Robert Filmer whom John Locke refuted. [DMH]

23.96 J. P. Sommerville. *Thomas Hobbes: political ideas in historical context.* New York: St. Martin's, 1992. ISBN 0-312-07966-4 (cl), 0-312-07967-2 (pbk). ▸ Best introduction to philosopher, setting his thought in variety of contexts: political, ideological, religious, and juristic. [DMH]

23.97 James Tully. *A discourse on property: John Locke and his adversaries.* Cambridge: Cambridge University Press, 1980. ISBN 0-521-22830-1. ▸ Definitive anti-Marxian account of context and character of philosopher's important property argument. Discusses religious origins of Lockean natural law. Sees property ownership and political and economic action as Christian stewardship. [DMH]

23.98 Frances A. Yates. *Astraea: the imperial theme in the sixteenth century.* London: Routledge & Kegan Paul, 1975. ISBN 0-7100-7971-0. ▸ Imaginative account of royal revivals throughout Europe of Roman imperial posture. Treats ceremony, symbol, art and architecture, and argument. [DMH]

23.99 Perez Zagorin. *A history of political thought in the English revolution.* 1954 ed. New York: Humanities, 1966. ▸ Best brief survey of political thought and thinkers during remarkably fertile period. [DMH]

SEE ALSO

22.219 Quentin Skinner. *Foundations of modern political thought.*

Foreign Relations and Military History

23.100 Simon L. Adams. "Spain or the Netherlands? The dilemmas of early Stuart foreign policy." In *Before the English Civil War: essays on early Stuart politics and government.* 1983 ed. Howard Tomlinson, ed., pp. 77–101. New York: St. Martin's, 1984. ISBN 0-312-07159-0. ▸ Important essay sketching role of strong monarchical preferences in shifting England's foreign policy during reign of James I. [DAB]

23.101 Kenneth R. Andrews. *Ships, money, and politics: seafaring and naval enterprise in the reign of Charles I.* Cambridge: Cambridge University Press, 1991. ISBN 0-521-40116-X. ▸ Collection of author's essays, constituting best study of period. Closely considers interrelation of shipping and privateering, applauds construction and use of Ship Money fleets. [DAB]

23.102 Kenneth R. Andrews. *Trade, plunder, and settlement: maritime enterprise and the genesis of the British empire, 1480–1630.* Cambridge: Cambridge University Press, 1984. ISBN 0-521-25760-3 (cl), 0-521-27698-5 (pbk). ▸ Readable Anglocentric narratives; tells story well, but lacks comparisons or assessment of meaning of empire. [DAB]

23.103 Kenneth R. Andrews, Nicholas P. Canny, and P.E.H. Hair, eds. *The westward enterprise: English activities in Ireland, the Atlantic, and America, 1480–1650.* 1979 ed. Detroit: Wayne State University Press, 1990. ▸ Lively collection with considerable focus on Ireland as stage in westward expansion. Traditional but high-quality Anglo-American essays. [DMH]

23.104 Daniel A. Baugh. *British naval administration in the age of Walpole.* Princeton: Princeton University Press, 1965. ▸ Survey of institutional context of eighteenth-century navy; administration, logistics, manning, and finance. [DMH]

23.105 Jeremy Black. *British foreign policy in the age of Walpole.* Edinburgh: Donald; distributed by Humanities, 1985. ISBN 0-85976-126-6. ▸ Best modern study of period 1715–50. [DAB]

23.106 Jeremy Black. *A system of ambition? British foreign policy, 1660–1793.* London: Longman, 1991. ISBN 0-582-08014-2 (cl), 0-582-00475-6 (pbk). ▸ Discussion of domestic and institutional context in Part 1. Very brief historical survey in Part 2, but extensive bibliography includes author's many detailed articles for further reading. [DAB]

23.107 Jeremy Black and Philip Woodfine, eds. *The British navy and the use of naval power in the eighteenth century.* 1988 ed. Atlantic Highlands, N.J.: Humanities, 1989. ISBN 0-391-03599-1. ▸ Collection of essays providing scholarly, up-to-date survey from 1689 to 1815. Includes comprehensive bibliography. [DAB]

23.108 Bernard Capp. *Cromwell's navy: the fleet and the English Revolution, 1648–1660.* Oxford: Clarendon, 1989. ISBN 0-19-820115-X. ▸ Comprehensive study of internal history—organization, administration, politics, and manpower—of republic's expanded fleet. [DAB]

23.109 John Childs. *The British army of William III, 1689–1702.* Manchester: Manchester University Press, 1987. ISBN 0-7190-1987-7. ▸ Study of organization, conditions, and performance of newly expanded army in wars against Louis XIV. Discusses problems of reconciling army with antimilitary sentiment. [DAB]

23.110 Thomas Cogswell. "Prelude to Ré: the Anglo-French struggle over La Rochelle, 1624–1627." *History* 71 (1986) 1–21.

ISSN 0018-2648. ▸ Best entry point for examining English foreign policy in later 1620s. [DAB]

23.111 Douglas Coombs. *The conduct of the Dutch: British opinion and the Dutch alliance during the War of the Spanish Succession.* The Hague: Nijhoff for University College of Ghana, Publications Board, 1958. ▸ Monograph of outstanding quality; important for study of politics, diplomacy, and grand strategy. Uses pamphlets and periodicals to show how British politicians tried to manipulate popular enmity toward Dutch. Complicated reading. [DAB/MU]

23.112 Roger Crabtree. "The idea of a Protestant foreign policy." In *Cromwell: a profile.* Ivan Roots, ed., pp. 160–89. New York: Hill & Wang, 1973. ISBN 0-8090-3715-7 (cl), 0-8090-1405-X (pbk). ▸ Useful survey of 1650s. Concludes Cromwell's motives neither anachronistic nor fanatical. [DAB]

23.113 C. G. Cruickshank. *Army royal: Henry VIII's invasion of France, 1513.* Oxford: Clarendon, 1969. ISBN 0-19-821399-9. ▸ Thorough, readable account of organization and service of Henry VIII's forces in France. Demonstrates uncertainties of postfeudal service. [DMH]

23.114 Ian Gentles. *The new model army in England, Ireland, and Scotland, 1645–1653.* Oxford: Blackwell, 1992. ISBN 0-631-15869-3. ▸ Most thorough and reliable account of formation, organization, and activity of revolutionary army. [DMH]

23.115 Gerald S. Graham. *Empire of the North Atlantic: the maritime struggle for North America.* 1958 2d ed. Toronto: University of Toronto Press, 1966. ▸ Encompasses seventeenth and eighteenth centuries. Still best general introduction. [DAB]

23.116 Vincent T. Harlow. *The founding of the second British empire, 1763–1793.* 2 vols. London: Longmans, Green, 1952–64. ▸ Classic work. Important emphasis on commerce expansion as prime motivating force, but too little attention to push for territorial dominion in India. [DAB]

23.117 John B. Hattendorf. *England in the War of the Spanish Succession: a study of the English view and conduct of grand strategy, 1702–1712.* New York: Garland, 1987. ISBN 0-8240-7813-6. ▸ Analytical approach featuring copious quantitative data. Appendix provides chronological list of international wartime agreements. Full bibliography of manuscripts and printed sources. [DAB]

23.118 G.M.D. Howat. *Stuart and Cromwellian foreign policy.* London: Black, 1974. ISBN 0-7136-1449-8. ▸ Brief, broad survey, still useful for general orientation but not as bibliographical guide to recent research. [DAB]

23.119 Jonathan I. Israel. *The Anglo-Dutch moment: essays on the Glorious Revolution and its world impact.* Cambridge: Cambridge University Press, 1991. ISBN 0-521-39075-3. ▸ Collection of essays, many examining interests of Dutch republic as well as other European countries in English Revolution of 1688. [DAB]

23.120 D. W. Jones. *War and economy in the age of William III and Marlborough.* Oxford: Blackwell, 1988. ISBN 0-631-16069-8. ▸ Technical work of unusual importance illustrating crucial role of metallic money and balance of payments in Anglo-French wars of period. [DAB]

23.121 Colin Martin and Geoffrey Parker. *The Spanish Armada.* New York: Norton, 1988. ISBN 0-393-02607-8. ▸ Multitheater essay on Armada campaign with skillful deployment of archaeological evidence on capacities of rival ships and guns. [DMH]

23.122 Richard Pares. *War and trade in the West Indies, 1739–1763.* 1936 ed. London: Cass, 1963. ▸ Pioneering work; scholarship and insights still command subject. [DAB]

23.123 J. L. Price. "Restoration England and Europe." In *The* *restored monarchy, 1660–1688.* J. R. Jones, ed., pp. 118–35. Totowa, N.J.: Rowman & Littlefield, 1979. ISBN 0-8476-6139-3. ▸ Brief overview in field lacking general synthesis of good recent research on particular aspects. [DAB]

23.124 David B. Quinn. *England and the discovery of America, 1481–1620, from the Bristol voyages of the fifteenth century to the Pilgrim settlement at Plymouth: the exploration, exploitation, and trial-and-error colonization of North America by the English.* New York: Knopf, 1974. ISBN 0-394-46673-X. ▸ Collected essays of leading scholar of British exploration. Argues plausibly for 1481 landfall by Bristol sailors in America; much on organization and conditions of voyages. [DMH]

23.125 David B. Quinn and A. N. Ryan. *England's sea empire, 1550–1642.* London: Allen & Unwin, 1983. ISBN 0-04-942179-4. ▸ Best survey available; authoritatively combines political, military, technical, and commercial factors in assessment of England's maritime expansion. [DMH]

23.126 Herbert W. Richmond. *The navy as an instrument of policy, 1558–1727.* E. A. Hughes, ed. Cambridge: Cambridge University Press, 1953. ▸ Comprehensive survey, still without equal in respect to its strategic insights. [DAB]

23.127 Karl W. Schweizer. *Frederick the Great, William Pitt, and Lord Bute: the Anglo-Prussian alliance, 1756–1763.* New York: Garland, 1991. ISBN 0-8153-0417-X. ▸ Collection of scholarly studies with continental and British perspectives. [DAB]

23.128 H. M. Scott. *British foreign policy in the age of the American Revolution.* Oxford: Clarendon, 1990. ISBN 0-19-820195-8. ▸ Unquestionably the standard work on period 1763–83; full bibliography. [DAB]

23.129 Ian K. Steele. *The English Atlantic, 1675–1740: an exploration of communication and community.* New York: Oxford University Press, 1986. ISBN 0-19-503968-8. ▸ Discussion of motifs of transatlantic communication (shipping, newspapers, etc.) between Britain and her colonies with compelling analysis of their importance for emergence of genuine transatlantic community. [DAB/JPG]

23.130 A. P. Thornton. *West-India policy under the Restoration.* Oxford: Clarendon, 1956. ▸ Detailed, scholarly, still indispensable study of emergence of coherent colonial policy, especially in respect to England's rivalry with Spain and France in this region. [DAB/JPG]

23.131 R. B. Wernham. *The making of Elizabethan foreign policy, 1558–1603.* Berkeley: University of California Press, 1980. ISBN 0-520-03966-1 (cl), 0-520-03974-2 (pbk). ▸ First-rate introduction; good on policy making in domestic and institutional as well as international context. Insists Elizabeth made valid contribution to policy making. [DMH]

23.132 C. H. Wilson. *Profit and power: a study of England and the Dutch wars.* London: Longmans, Green, 1957. ▸ Best introduction for economic context of these wars from England's standpoint. Omits third Anglo-Dutch war and needs to be read with more recent work. [DAB]

SEE ALSO
29.116 Garrett Mattingly. *The Armada.*
41.90 Robert W. Tucker and David C. Henderson. *The fall of the first British empire.*

Economic History

23.133 Robert C. Allen. *Enclosure and the yeoman: the agricultural development of the South Midlands, 1450–1850.* Oxford: Clarendon, 1992. ISBN 0-19-828296-6. ▸ Important environmentalist analysis of enclosure of common fields, and agricultural improvement. Discusses improvements of seventeenth and early eigh-

teenth centuries by small family farmers and, later, landlord-backed enclosure movement which merely extracted higher rents. [DMH]

23.134 Joyce Oldham Appleby. *Economic thought and ideology in seventeenth-century England.* Princeton: Princeton University Press, 1978. ISBN 0-691-05265-4. ▸ Survey of vast range of pamphlets, revealing growth of market society and amoralization of economic sphere. Complexity of attitudes to poor and decline of mercantilist thought. [DMH]

23.135 J. V. Beckett. *The agricultural revolution.* Oxford: Blackwell, 1990. ISBN 0-631-16287-9. ▸ Best introduction to subject whose location in time has proved contentious. Judicious on rate of adoption and economic impact of new techniques. [DMH]

23.136 Maxine Berg. *The age of manufactures: industry, innovations, and work in Britain, 1700–1820.* Totowa, N.J.: Barnes & Noble, 1985. ISBN 0-389-20584-2. ▸ Novel assertion of role of workers, especially women, in industrialization. Discusses relation between technology and community and complexity and social connections of forms of production. Incisive survey of historiography. [DMH]

23.137 C. E. Challis. *The Tudor coinage.* Manchester and New York: Manchester University Press and Barnes & Noble, 1978. ISBN 0-7190-0678-3, 0-06-491038-5. ▸ Study of legal and technological aspects of coinage, of workings of the Mint, and scale and impact of circulating currency. Partly vindicates monetarist explanations of Tudor inflation. [DMH]

23.138 J. A. Chartres. *Internal trade in England, 1500–1700.* London: Macmillan, 1977. ISBN 0-333-18358-4. ▸ Brave introduction to problems of structure, organization, and impact of internal trade. Still useful bibliography. [DMH]

23.139 K. N. Chaudhuri. *The trading world of Asia and the English East India Company, 1660–1760.* Cambridge: Cambridge University Press, 1978. ISBN 0-521-21716-4. ▸ Monumental analysis of interlocking of European and Asian markets, richly detailed on structure and organization of trade, markets, and commodities. Stresses political contexts in Europe and Asia that shaped company's remarkable history. [DMH]

23.140 L. A. Clarkson. *Proto-industrialization: the first phase of industrialization?* London: Macmillan, 1985. ISBN 0-333-34392-1 (pbk). ▸ Brief useful survey of controversy over concept of rural protoindustrialization in England. [DMH]

23.141 C.G.A. Clay. *Economic expansion and social change: England, 1500–1700.* 2 vols. Cambridge: Cambridge University Press, 1984. ISBN 0-521-25942-8 (v. 1, cl), 0-521-25943-6 (v. 2, cl), 0-521-27768-X (v. 1, pbk), 0-521-27769-8 (v. 2, pbk). ▸ Best general account of changing socioeconomic structure; especially good on commerce, agriculture, and policy. Fine bibliography. [DMH]

23.142 D. C. Coleman. *The economy of England, 1450–1750.* London: Oxford University Press, 1977. ISBN 0-19-215355-2 (cl), 0-19-289070-0 (pbk). ▸ Sound survey of slow growth on broad front, then more rapid growth in early eighteenth century. Stronger on trade and industry than on agriculture and local economies. [DMH]

23.143 D. C. Coleman. "Mercantilism revisited." *Historical journal* 23 (1980) 773–91. ISSN 0018-246X. ▸ Essential starting point for analysis of coherence of policy. Sees set of short-term responses to long-term crisis and shift in English trade and industry. [DMH]

23.144 Ralph Davis. *English overseas trade, 1500–1700.* London: Macmillan, 1973. ISBN 0-333-14419-8. ▸ Best brief introduction to patterns and organization of trade; nonquantitative. [DMH]

23.145 F. J. Fisher. *London and the English economy, 1550–1700:*

the collected essays of F.J. Fisher. P. J. Corfield and N. B. Harte, eds. London: Hambledon, 1989. ISBN 1-85285-023-X. ‣ Seminal essays of leading economic historian of London assessing impact of metropolis on national economy. [DMH]

23.146 Eleanor S. Godfrey. *The development of English glass-making, 1560–1640.* Chapel Hill: University of North Carolina Press, 1975. ISBN 0-8078-1256-0. ‣ History of typical new consumer industry. Importation of techniques and craftsmen in sixteenth century, then growing domination by courtier monopolists until Civil War. Detailed account of organization and distribution of industry. [DMH]

23.147 John Hatcher. *Plague, population, and the English economy, 1348–1530.* London: Macmillan, 1977. ISBN 0-333-21293-2. ‣ Good brief survey of short- and long-term ramifications of demographic catastrophe and slow recovery. Sees demographic change as key determinant of economy. [DMH]

23.148 R.W.K. Hinton. *The Eastland trade and the common weal in the seventeenth century.* 1959 ed. Hamden, Conn.: Archon, 1975. ISBN 0-208-01483-7. ‣ Analysis of organization, conduct, and political context of trade to Scandinavia and Baltic. Best study of single branch of trade. [DMH]

23.149 Julian Hoppit. *Risk and failure in English business, 1700–1800.* Cambridge: Cambridge University Press, 1987. ISBN 0-521-32624-9. ‣ Growing incidence of bankruptcies offsets impression of expansion associated with early Industrial Revolution. Expansion spawned risk taking and therefore bankruptcy, while waves of bankruptcies showed developing national integration of economy. [DMH]

23.150 Eric Kerridge. *The agricultural revolution.* 1967 ed. New York: Kelley, 1968. ‣ Energetically argued and documented but ultimately unconvincing case for transformation of farming methods and crops in sixteenth and seventeenth centuries rather than eighteenth; still important. [DMH]

23.151 Eric Kerridge. *Textile manufactures in early modern England.* Manchester: Manchester University Press, 1985. ISBN 0-7190-1767-X. ‣ Authoritative survey of distribution and organization of major textile industry, by agricultural historian. Considered in relation to farming regions, structure of employment, and wool types, as well as international economy. [DMH]

23.152 Eric Kerridge. *Trade and banking in early modern England.* Manchester: Manchester University Press; distributed by St. Martin's, 1988. ISBN 0-7190-2652-0. ‣ Unusual venture by agricultural historian into under-researched area. Expertise allows invaluable focus on transactions between regions and London, but downplays role of international exchange and government's lenders. [DMH]

23.153 John Langton. *Geographical change and industrial revolution: coal-mining of Southwest Lancashire, 1590–1799.* Cambridge: Cambridge University Press, 1979. ISBN 0-521-22490-X. ‣ Importance of demographic change and tenurial structure to early coal-mining industry. Treats organization of industry and changing pattern of settlement. [DMH]

23.154 Christine MacLeod. *Inventing the Industrial Revolution: the English patent system, 1660–1800.* Cambridge: Cambridge University Press, 1988. ISBN 0-521-30104-1. ‣ Analysis of economic context, technological consequences, and legal ramifications of inventions. Links patenting to consumer market, establishing status of product, rather than to labor-saving. Demolishes argument that number of patents measures economic growth. [DMH]

23.155 Edward Miller and Joan Thirsk, eds. *The agrarian history of England and Wales.* Vol. 3: *1348–1500.* Vol. 4: *1500–1640.* Vol. 5: *1640–1750.* London: Cambridge University Press, 1967–91. ISBN 0-521-20074-1 (v. 3), 0-521-20076-8 (v. 5.1), 0-521-25775-

1 (v. 5.2). ‣ Compendious, often brilliant, essays on regions and specialization, farming conditions, tenurial and economic relations, and marketing and innovation. [DMH]

23.156 W. E. Minchinton, ed. *The growth of English overseas trade in the seventeenth and eighteenth centuries.* London: Methuen; distributed by Barnes & Noble, 1969. ISBN 0-416-47970-7. ‣ Collection of fundamental articles on patterns of trade with extremely helpful introduction. Still most useful treatment. [DMH]

23.157 R. Brian Outhwaite. "Progress and backwardness in England agriculture, 1500–1650." *Economic history review,* Second series, 39.1 (1986) 1–18. ISSN 0013-0117. ‣ Best survey of relative health of agrarian economy. Concludes market pressures caused by population growth negated need for agricultural improvement and increased productivity. [DMH]

23.158 Eric Pawson. *The early Industrial Revolution: Britain in the eighteenth century.* New York: Barnes & Noble, 1979. ISBN 0-06-495464-1. ‣ Helpful, detailed account of economic change and continuity, angled toward trade, industry, demography, and agriculture. Nothing on consumerism. [DMH]

23.159 John Rule. *The experience of labour in eighteenth-century English industry.* New York: St. Martin's, 1981. ISBN 0-312-27664-8. ‣ Best survey of problem of and attitudes toward labor. Stresses overlap of putting-out (farming out) and factory systems and complexity of categories. Much custom and culture, less economics; fine introduction and bibliography. [DMH]

23.160 Margaret Spufford. *The great reclothing of rural England: petty chapmen and their wares in the seventeenth century.* London: Hambledon, 1984. ISBN 0-907628-47-8. ‣ Detailed study of group of petty chapmen (peddlers) and their activities. Argues chapmen crucial to spread of commercial and consumerist attitudes toward clothing. [DMH]

23.161 Barry E. Supple. *Commercial crisis and change in England, 1600–1642: a study in the instability of a mercantile economy.* 1959 ed. Cambridge: Cambridge University Press, 1970. ‣ Brilliant analysis of textile crisis of 1620s, causes and consequences. Attempts of contemporaries to comprehend crisis engendered preoccupation with monetary flow and balance of trade. [DMH]

23.162 Joan Thirsk. *Agricultural regions and agrarian history in England, 1500–1750.* London: Macmillan Education, 1987. ISBN 0-333-19158-7 (pbk). ‣ Best, brief synthesis of and introduction to agricultural regionalism and differentials in economic growth. Ties growth differentials to contrasts between woodland and field zones and varying impact of demography and rural industry. [DMH]

23.163 Joan Thirsk. *Economic policy and projects: the development of a consumer society in early modern England.* Oxford: Clarendon, 1978. ISBN 0-19-828274-5. ‣ Seminal study of dramatic impact of small-scale consumer industries and cash crops on employment and consumption. Also discusses role of government policy, first protective and then exploitive. [DMH]

23.164 Lorna Weatherill. *Consumer behaviour and material culture in Britain, 1660–1760.* London: Routledge, 1988. ISBN 0-415-00723-2. ‣ Imaginative attempt to quantify consumer habits, including spread of different types of goods in different sectors of populace, with estimates of relative costs. Investigates domestic function of objects and importance of display to those below gentry. [DMH]

23.165 J. R. Wordie. "The chronology of English enclosure, 1500–1914." *Economic history review,* Second series, 36.4 (1983) 483–505. ISSN 0013-0117. ‣ Best survey to date of often intractable evidence for rate of enclosure of common fields. Seventeenth century most active period. [DMH]

Religious History

23.166 Anthony Armstrong. *The Church of England, the Methodists, and society, 1700–1850.* Totowa, N.J.: Rowman & Littlefield, 1973. ISBN 0-87471-160-6 (cl), 0-87471-164-9 (pbk). ▶ Finds established church less arid, old dissent less theologically distinct, and Methodism and Evangelicalism rooted in anti-Jacobinism as well as experimental religion. Updates Sykes 23.195. [MT]

23.167 Margaret Aston. *England's iconoclasts.* Vol. 1: *Laws against images.* Oxford: Clarendon, 1988. ISBN 0-19-822438-9 (v. 1). ▶ Survey of development of conscientious objections to icons in sixteenth-century English Protestantism and resultant disestablishment of imagery. Iconoclasm treated as key to changing popular belief. [MT]

23.168 John Bossy. *The English Catholic community, 1570–1850.* 1975 ed. New York: Oxford University Press, 1976. ISBN 0-19-519847-6. ▶ Study of Catholic laity and clergy as community within English Nonconforming tradition. Focus on religious and social experience of average Catholic. Attention to domestic religion. [MT]

23.169 James E. Bradley. *Religion, revolution, and English radicalism: nonconformity in eighteenth-century politics and society.* Cambridge: Cambridge University Press, 1990. ISBN 0-521-38010-3. ▶ Quantitative study of dissenters among electorate of six open boroughs. Finds evidence for significant participatory politics and early emergence of classlike social divisions. [MT]

23.170 Paul Christianson. *Reformers and Babylon: English apocalyptic visions from the Reformation to the eve of the Civil War.* Toronto: University of Toronto Press, 1978. ISBN 0-8020-5365-3. ▶ Analysis of apocalyptic tradition related to radical political action in seventeenth century. Most exhaustive treatment to date. [MT]

23.171 Patrick Collinson. *The birthpangs of Protestant England: religious and cultural change in the sixteenth and seventeenth centuries; the third Anstey memorial lectures in the University of Kent at Canterbury, 12–15 May 1986.* New York: St. Martin's, 1988. ISBN 0-312-02366-9. ▶ Cultural history of Reformation as gradual process of changing belief and behavior. Attention to urban and domestic manifestations, religion and arts at popular level, and impact of new religion on political identity and activity. [MT]

23.172 Patrick Collinson. *The Elizabethan Puritan movement.* 1967 ed. Oxford: Clarendon, 1989. ISBN 0-19-822298-X (pbk). ▶ Still standard work on subject, although author now uses term "Puritan" very sparingly. Should be read in conjunction with author's later works (23.171, 23.173). [MT]

23.173 Patrick Collinson. *The religion of Protestants: the church in English society, 1559–1625.* 1982 ed. Oxford: Clarendon, 1985. ISBN 0-19-822685-3 (cl, 1982), 0-19-820053-6 (pbk). ▶ Survey of relationship between monarchs and bishops; magistrates and ministers; clerical activities and reputations; and popular and voluntary religion. Revisionist interpretation emphasizing consensus within church. [MT]

23.174 Claire Cross. *Church and people, 1450–1660: the triumph of the laity in the English church.* Atlantic Highlands, N.J.: Humanities, 1976. ISBN 0-391-00649-5 (cl). ▶ Synthetic and reinterpretive study showing importance of lay-clerical rivalry in church government and lay formation of religious belief. Much influenced by Dickens 23.175. [MT]

23.175 A. G. Dickens. *The English Reformation.* 2d ed. London: Batsford, 1989. ISBN 0-7134-3669-7. ▶ Slightly revised version of 1964 classic. Argues Reformation fundamentally religious rather than political, fueled by surviving Lollardy, preaching, English Bible, and popular dissatisfaction with Catholicism. [MT]

23.176 Susan Doran and Christopher Durston. *Princes, pastors, and people: the church and religion in England, 1529–1689.* London: Routledge, 1991. ISBN 0-415-05963-1 (cased), 0-415-05964-X (pbk). ▶ Best overview of recent revisionist interpretations of Reformation, spectrum of prewar Protestantism, religion and Civil War, Restoration church, and dissent. Examines both theology and popular belief and practice. [MT]

23.177 Kenneth Fincham. *Prelate as pastor: the episcopate of James I.* Oxford: Clarendon, 1990. ISBN 0-19-822921-6. ▶ Examination of activities and functions of sixty-six bishops in central politics and local society, as diocesan administrators and as moral and spiritual guides. Argues episcopate restored fortunes after 1603. Detailed analysis of doctrinal divisions. [MT]

23.178 Richard L. Greaves. *Deliver us from evil: the radical underground in Britain, 1660–1663.* New York: Oxford University Press, 1986. ISBN 0-19-503985-8. ▶ Refutes received version of Restoration Nonconformity as passive and quiescent. Examines militant Nonconformists from 1660 to second Dutch War. Daunting compendium of examples. [MT]

23.179 I. M. Green. *The re-establishment of the Church of England, 1660–1663.* Oxford: Oxford University Press, 1978. ISBN 0-19-821867-2. ▶ Revises standard view of restoration policy: strict episcopacy and severity toward dissent were not Charles II's plan, but resulted from failed attempts at moderate compromise and limited episcopate. Argues general enthusiasm for revived episcopacy. [MT]

23.180 Christopher Haigh, ed. *The English Reformation revised.* Cambridge: Cambridge University Press, 1987. ISBN 0-521-33337-7 (cl), 0-521-33631-7 (pbk). ▶ Collection of essays arguing against Dickens 23.175 that Reformation was unpopular, ineffective, unnecessary, politically imposed, and, in terms of religious passion, anemic. Important summary of recent revisionism. [MT]

23.181 Christopher Hill. *Society and Puritanism in pre-revolutionary England.* 1964 ed. Harmondsworth: Penguin, 1986. ISBN 0-14-055201-4 (pbk). ▶ Classic Marxist treatment of English Puritans as disciplined middle class that would fight the first bourgeois revolution in 1640s. [MT]

23.182 Norman L. Jones. *Faith by statute: Parliament and the settlement of religion, 1559.* London and Atlantic Highlands, N.J.: Royal Historical Society and Humanities, 1982. (Royal Historical Society studies in history, 32.) ISBN 0-901050-84-9, 0-391-02689-5. ▶ Detailed study of religious policy of Elizabeth's first parliament. Attributes more influence to Catholic members than standard view; sees more cooperation with crown by Protestant majority and more royal compromise and effective maneuvering. [MT]

23.183 Peter Lake. *Moderate Puritans and the Elizabethan church.* Cambridge: Cambridge University Press, 1982. ISBN 0-521-24010-7. ▶ Treats Elizabethan Puritans, particularly in Cambridge University, as moderate reformers defined less by Nonconformity than by zeal for godly behavior, preaching, precise doctrine, and antipopery. Self-perception as godly in conflict with world led to separatism for extremist minority. [MT]

23.184 William M. Lamont. *Godly rule: politics and religion, 1603–60.* Vol. 2 of *Puritanism and the English Revolution.* 1969 ed. Aldershot, England: Gregg Revivals; distributed by Ashgate, 1991. ISBN 0-7512-0002-6 (v. 2), 0-7512-0004-2 (set). ▶ Reinterpretation of controversies in early seventeenth-century England in terms of prophetic and eschatological beliefs of contemporaries. Intellectual history in service of political understanding. [MT]

23.185 William M. Lamont. *Richard Baxter and the millennium: Protestant imperialism and the English Revolution.* Vol. 3 of *Puritanism and the English Revolution.* 1979 ed. Aldershot, England: Gregg Revivals; distributed by Ashgate, 1991. ISBN 0-7512-0003-4 (v. 3), 0-7512-0004-2 (set). ▶ Best study of Nonconformists' religious views, especially eschatological, as they shaped his understanding of political order and monarch's role and his approach to reform of state, church, and society. [MT]

23.186 J. F. McGregor and Barry Reay, eds. *Radical religion in the English Revolution.* London: Oxford University Press, 1984. ISBN 0-19-873044-6 (cl), 0-19-873045-4 (pbk). ‣ Collection of articles on popular religious movements in fundamental conflict with established religion and theology. Examines Baptists, Levellers, Diggers, Seekers, Ranters, Quakers, and Fifth Monarchists. [MT]

23.187 Adrian Morey. *The Catholic subjects of Elizabeth I.* Totowa, N.J.: Rowman & Littlefield, 1978. ISBN 0-87471-970-4. ‣ Careful examination of lay loyalists as well as radical Jesuits against background of Elizabethan conflict with papacy and increasingly vigorous repression of recusants. [MT]

23.188 Geoffrey F. Nuttall. *Visible saints: the congregational way, 1640–1660.* Oxford: Blackwell, 1957. ‣ Still best introduction to early English and Welsh congregational theology, ecclesiology, and activity. [MT]

23.189 Rosemary O'Day. *The English clergy: the emergence and consolidation of a profession, 1558–1642.* Leicester: Leicester University Press; distributed by Humanities, 1979. ISBN 0-7185-1167-0. ‣ Development of Protestant clergy into self-conscious, coherent group committed to preaching, pastoral ministry, and to higher standard of education. First careful examination of career structure of early modern clergy. [MT]

23.190 Rosemary O'Day and Felicity Heal, eds. *Princes and paupers in the English church, 1500–1800.* Leicester: Leicester University Press; distributed by Barnes & Noble, 1981. ISBN 0-7185-1178-6. ‣ Collection of articles on finances of clergy at all levels. Focus on changing economic and social situation of post-Reformation clergy and their influence on lay society. Good use of local studies. [MT]

23.191 Kenneth L. Parker. *The English sabbath: a study of doctrine and discipline from the Reformation to the Civil War.* Cambridge: Cambridge University Press, 1988. ISBN 0-521-30535-7. ‣ Best work on subject. Argues sabbatarianism not exclusively Puritan, but perpetual concern of established church. Downplays Puritan rigor and debate over details of sabbath regulation. [MT]

23.192 Barry Reay. *The Quakers and the English Revolution.* New York: St. Martin's, 1985. ISBN 0-312-65808-7. ‣ Best study of Quaker radicalism during interregnum and descent into quietism after Restoration. [MT]

23.193 J. J. Scarisbrick. *The Reformation and the English people.* 1984 ed. Oxford: Blackwell, 1986. ISBN 0-631-13424-7 (cl, 1984), 0-631-14755-1 (pbk). ‣ Important revisionist study based on archival sources. Asserts relative popularity of pre-Reformation Catholicism and its persistence after government-imposed Reformation. Catholic perspective; dismissive of Dickens 23.175. [MT]

23.194 John Spurr. *The Restoration Church of England, 1646–1689.* New Haven: Yale University Press, 1991. ISBN 0-300-05071-2. ‣ Best account of reestablishment of state church after Civil War. Explains invention of Anglicanism and its divergence from both Roman Catholicism and reformed churches of Europe. [MT]

23.195 Norman Sykes. *Church and state in England in the eighteenth century.* 1934 ed. Hamden, Conn.: Archon, 1962. ‣ Survey of episcopal political activity, preferment, alliance with state, and doctrine (with focus on latitudinarianism). Still standard work on established church. [MT]

23.196 R. H. Tawney. *Religion and the rise of capitalism: a historical study.* 1926 ed. Harmondsworth: Penguin, 1984. ISBN 0-14-

055144-1 (pbk). ‣ Classic Marxist treatment of relationship between English Protestantism, particularly Puritanism, and demands of capitalist development. Challenging claims for economic role of religion, sees religion shaped by social and economic factors. [MT]

23.197 Keith Thomas. *Religion and the decline of magic: studies in popular beliefs in sixteenth- and seventeenth-century England.* 1971 ed. Harmondsworth: Penguin, 1978. ISBN 0-14-055150-6 (pbk). ‣ Brilliant examination of popular beliefs and practice and prosecution of magic, witchcraft, astrology, and allied beliefs after Reformation's demolition of Catholic ecclesiastical magic. Informed by cultural anthropology. [MT]

23.198 Margo Todd. *Christian humanism and the Puritan social order.* Cambridge: Cambridge University Press, 1987. ISBN 0-521-33129-3. ‣ Intellectual history of social thought placing Puritans in tradition of Erasmian humanist ideas about poor relief, domestic conduct, and social hierarchy. Reformist consensus visible in university curricula, but collapsed as religious divisions spread. [MT]

23.199 Nicholas Tyacke. *Anti-Calvinists: the rise of English Arminianism, c. 1590–1640.* 1987 ed. Oxford: Oxford University Press, 1990. ISBN 0-19-820184-2. ‣ Only full-length study of English opponents of strict predestinarianism. Contributes to understanding of Civil War as religious conflict. [MT]

23.200 Dewey D. Wallace, Jr. *Puritans and predestination: grace in English Protestant theology, 1525–1695.* Chapel Hill: University of North Carolina Press, 1982. ISBN 0-8078-1499-7. ‣ First thorough historical analysis of theological concept central to Protestantism. Finds common ground between Puritans and conformists in substance if not emphasis, until rise of Arminianism. [MT]

23.201 Tessa Watt. *Cheap print and popular piety, 1550–1640.* Cambridge: Cambridge University Press, 1991. ISBN 0-521-38255-6. ‣ Discussion of popular religious belief as reflected in cheapest printed materials—broadsides, woodcuts, and chapbooks—mixture of conservative (iconic) and Protestant (logocentric) elements. Challenges confrontational models of change. [MT]

23.202 Michael R. Watts. *The dissenters.* Vol. 1: *From the Reformation to the French Revolution.* Oxford: Clarendon, 1978. ISBN 0-19-822460-5 (v. 1). ‣ Study of shift of English and Welsh Nonconformists to quietism after Restoration. Examines laity as well as clergy, religious practice and theology, and problems with government. First full-scale treatment of subject since 1913. [MT]

23.203 S. J. Wright, ed. *Parish, church, and people: local studies in lay religion, 1350–1750.* London: Hutchinson, 1988. ISBN 0-09-173144-5. ‣ Essays by eight historians on English religious practice at parochial level, relationship between parish and civic community, and nature of popular piety and behavior. Half are local studies. [MT]

Intellectual History

23.204 J. W. Binns. *Intellectual culture in Elizabethan and Jacobean England: the Latin writings of the age.* Leeds, England: Cairns, 1990. ISBN 0-905205-73-1. ‣ Compendious examination of all English writing in Latin in two reigns when Latin was still important living language. Thematic rather than analytical or contextual arrangement. Invaluable reference work. [DMH]

23.205 Murray Cohen. *Sensible words: linguistic practice in England, 1640–1785.* Baltimore: Johns Hopkins University Press, 1977. ISBN 0-8018-1924-5. ‣ Survey of changing theories of language showing shift from preoccupation with naming things to Lockean relation of words and ideas to purely practical grammars of eighteenth century. [DMH]

23.206 Gerald R. Cragg. *Reason and authority in the eighteenth* *century.* Cambridge: Cambridge University Press, 1964. ▸ Influence of John Locke and Sir Isaac Newton on skepticism; tradition versus moral and social reform. Still impressive in range and argument. [DMH]

23.207 Maurice Cranston. *John Locke.* 1957 ed. New York: Arno, 1979. ISBN 0-405-11690-5. ▸ Best full-scale study of philosopher, surveying intellectual not political context. Treats range and coherence of his intellectual endeavors, influences on him, and his impact. [DMH]

23.208 Christopher Fox. *Locke and the Scriblerians: identity and consciousness in early eighteenth-century Britain.* Berkeley: University of California Press, 1988. ISBN 0-520- 05859-3. ▸ Sophisticated analysis of widespread unease over new philosophy of experience. Treats impact of Lockean concept of changing consciousness on Christian view of soul and moral responsibility. [DMH]

23.209 John Gascoigne. *Cambridge in the age of the Enlightenment: science, religion, and politics from the Restoration to the French Revolution.* Cambridge: Cambridge University Press, 1989. ISBN 0-521-35139-1. ▸ Account of dominance of clerical bastion by whig ideology and Newtonian orthodoxy, if not by Enlightenment ideals. [DMH]

23.210 W. Speed Hill, ed. *Studies in Richard Hooker: essays preliminary to an edition of his works.* Cleveland, Ohio: Press of Case Western Reserve University, 1972. ISBN 0-8295-0220-3. ▸ Essays assessing theologian's political and religious thought, rhetoric and style, context, and significance. Best introduction. [DMH]

23.211 Istvan Hont and Michael Ignatieff. *Wealth and virtue: the shaping of political economy in the Scottish Enlightenment.* Cambridge: Cambridge University Press, 1983. ISBN 0-521-23397-6. ▸ Important and varied essays on Scotland's civic humanist current, exploring commerce and politeness as redress for Scotland's political subordination. Also good on Samuel von Pufendorf's natural jurisprudence. [DMH]

23.212 J. W. Johnson. *The formation of English neo-classical thought.* Princeton: Princeton University Press, 1967. ▸ Extraordinarily wide-ranging study of impact of classical sources on late seventeenth- and early eighteenth-century literature and thought, emphasizing John Dryden, Jonathan Swift, and Edward Gibbon and contribution of the Dutch. [DMH]

23.213 Joseph M. Levine. *Humanism and history: the origins of modern English historiography.* Ithaca, N.Y.: Cornell University Press, 1987. ISBN 0-8014-1885-2. ▸ Assessment of humanism's historiographic contribution: textual scholarship, sense of anachronism, but preoccupation with antiquity, style, and morality; and clash of ancients and moderns. [DMH]

23.214 John MacQueen, ed. *Humanism in Renaissance Scotland.* Edinburgh: Edinburgh University Press, 1990. ISBN 0-7486-0111-2 (cl), 0-7486-0186-4 (pbk). ▸ One of most thorough and focused approaches to meaning and impact of Renaissance in national culture. Essays on law, philosophy, science, literature, visual arts, schooling, and universities. Fine illustrations. [DMH]

23.215 James K. McConica, Lucy S. Sutherland, and Leslie G. Mitchell, eds. *The history of the University of Oxford.* Vol. 3: *The collegiate university.* Vol. 5: *The eighteenth century.* Oxford: Clarendon, 1986. ISBN 0-19-951013-X (v. 3), 0-19-951015-6 (v. 5). ▸ Essays on university in its political and religious (though less on social or ideological) relations, its intellectual role, and its administration. Detailed, sometimes dazzling, sometimes dull. [DMH]

23.216 Nicholas T. Phillipson. *Hume.* New York: St. Martin's, 1989. ISBN 0-312-03076-2. ▸ Best introduction; focuses on Hume the historian, but traverses his contexts, philosophy, and political thought in order to arrive at Hume on human nature and world. [DMH]

23.217 J.G.A. Pocock. *The ancient constitution and the feudal law: a study of English historical thought in the seventeenth century, a reissue with a retrospect.* 1957 ed. Cambridge: Cambridge University Press, 1987. ISBN 0-521-30352-4 (cl), 0-521-31643-X (pbk). ▸ Influential study of discovery of feudalism by seventeenth-century historians, insularity of English law and lawyers, and politically problematic nature of concept of legal change. [DMH]

23.218 Barbara J. Shapiro. *Probability and certainty in seventeenth-century England: a study of the relationship between natural science, religion, law, and literature.* Princeton: Princeton University Press, 1983. ISBN 0-691-05279-0 (cl), 0-691-00790-X (pbk). ▸ Survey of epistemological shift wrought by science; claims to God-given absolute truths undermined by rational probabilities of demonstration and empirical evidence. [DMH]

23.219 Richard B. Sher. *Church and university in the Scottish Enlightenment: the moderate literati of Edinburgh.* Princeton: Princeton University Press, 1985. ISBN 0-691-05445-2. ▸ Establishes social and religious context for mid-eighteenth-century Scottish social and historical theorizing. Treats political subordination to England and risk of commercial corruption which bred characteristic stress on civic virtue. [DMH]

23.220 Frederick S. Siebert. *Freedom of the press in England, 1476–1776: the rise and decline of government control.* 1952 ed. Urbana: University of Illinois Press, 1965. ▸ Still most thorough survey of censorship and control. [DMH]

23.221 D. R. Woolf. *The idea of history in early Stuart England: erudition, ideology, and the "light of truth" from the accession of James I to the Civil War.* Toronto: University of Toronto Press, 1990. ISBN 0-8020-5862-0. ▸ Best study of seventeenth-century historiography, which distinguished antiquarianism from political history; latter more concerned with morals and motives, not evidence. Fine case studies, especially of John Selden, who united both strains. [DMH]

Social History

23.222 Donna T. Andrew. *Philanthropy and police: London charity in the eighteenth century.* Princeton: Princeton University Press, 1989. ISBN 0-691-05557-2. ▸ Analysis of rise of associational charities in metropolis as part of complex cluster of nationalistic ideas, values, and policies aimed at remodeling poor. Discusses ideological contexts of Hanoverian charitable initiatives. [KW]

23.223 Ian W. Archer. *The pursuit of stability: social relations in Elizabethan London.* Cambridge: Cambridge University Press, 1991. ISBN 0-521-37315-8. ▸ Best monograph on early modern London focusing on 1590s "crisis" and on community and identity. Discusses municipal, parish, and guild means by which order was maintained and extent and impact of poor relief and crime. [DMH]

23.224 Dudley W. R. Bahlman. *The moral revolution of 1688.* 1957 ed. Hamden, Conn.: Archon, 1968. ISBN 0-208-00494-7. ▸ Discussion of late seventeenth-century upheavals that produced strenuous efforts to remodel morals through reformation of manners movement, supported by Puritan strains within Church of England and emerging secular reform societies. Illuminating supplement to political accounts. [KW]

23.225 Jonathan Barry, ed. *The Tudor and Stuart town: a reader in English urban history, 1530–1688.* London: Longman, 1990. ISBN 0-582-05131-2 (cl), 0-582-05130-4 (pbk). ▸ Collection of important reprinted articles covering town's economic role, political and social control, relations with hinterland, and social structure. Invaluable introduction. [DMH]

23.226 A. L. Beier and Roger Finlay, eds. *London, 1500–1700: the making of the metropolis.* London: Longman, 1986. ISBN 0-582-

49436-2 (pbk). ▸ Essays on demographic, social, and economic development; vital contribution of political role of metropolis to its growth; diversification of manufactures and international trade; and survival of petty communities within whole. [DMH]

23.227 Peter Borsay. *The English urban renaissance: culture and society in the provincial town, 1660–1770.* 1989 ed. Oxford: Clarendon, 1991. ISBN 0-19-820002-1 (cl, 1989), 0-19-820255-5 (pbk). ▸ Lively social history of middle class. Socioeconomic and cultural resurgence of towns predicated on economic vitality, expanding middle classes, and conspicuous consumption. Bourgeois urban life as cultural differentiation. [KW]

23.228 Jeremy Boulton. *Neighbourhood and society: a London suburb in the seventeenth century.* Cambridge: Cambridge University Press, 1987. ISBN 0-521-26669-6. ▸ Fascinating, detailed analysis of small area of London. Concludes mixed residence patterns and intrusive parish authorities helped preserve social stability. Movement, and borrowing, within neighborhood preserved vital sense of community. [DMH]

23.229 John Cannon. *Aristocratic century: the peerage of eighteenth-century England.* 1984 ed. Cambridge: Cambridge University Press, 1987. ISBN 0-521-25729-8 (cl), 0-521-33566-3 (pbk). ▸ Revisionist challenge to standard view of embourgeoisement. Political dominance and social exclusivity of aristocracy from Glorious to Industrial revolutions endowed society with intellectual, political, and cultural coherence. Discusses education, recruitment, and marriage. [KW]

23.230 Peter Clark. *The English alehouse: a social history, 1200–1830.* London: Longman, 1983. ISBN 0-582-50835-5 (pbk). ▸ Well-illustrated, readable account of changing social functions of major social institution. Studies distribution, social status, architecture, reformation campaigns, and impact of growing culture of respectability. [DMH]

23.231 P. J. Corfield. *The impact of English towns, 1700–1800.* Oxford: Oxford University Press, 1982. ISBN 0-19-215830-9 (cl), 0-19-289093-X (pbk). ▸ Brief assessment of range of urban experience. Looks at rise not only of London, dockyard, and leisure towns but also industrial towns. Challenges thesis of rural proto-industrialization. [DMH]

23.232 G. A. Cranfield. *The development of the provincial newspaper, 1700–1760.* 1962 ed. Westport, Conn.: Greenwood, 1978. ISBN 0-313-20017-3. ▸ Thorough, astute assessment of local press in producing national perspective. Treats politics, production, content, and distribution of news in provinces and also dissemination of opposition political journalism. [KW]

23.233 David Cressy. *Coming over: migration and communication between England and New England in the seventeenth century.* Cambridge: Cambridge University Press, 1987. ISBN 0-521-32951-5 (cl), 0-521-33850-6 (pbk). ▸ Study of ramifications of migration, debunking Puritan exodus. Considers conditions on both sides of Atlantic and logistics of move. Concludes that searing conditions of passage shaped survivors; subsequent intercontinental communications expose importance of kin ties. [DMH]

23.234 David Cressy. *Literacy and the social order: reading and writing in Tudor and Stuart England.* Cambridge: Cambridge University Press, 1980. ISBN 0-521-22514-0. ▸ Discussion of regional, socio-occupational, and gender breakdown of literacy. Arguments for chronology of improvement challengeable and regional studies problematic, but stress on local variations in literacy irrefutable. [DMH]

23.235 Peter Earle. *The making of the English middle class: business, society, and family life in London, 1660–1730.* Berkeley: University of California Press, 1989. ISBN 0-520-06826-2. ▸ Enterprising history of middling orders of English society. Examines structures of credit, family, and social life. Concludes middle

class formed between Restoration and rise of Robert Walpole, as evinced in social, economic, and domestic life in capital. [KW]

23.236 Anthony Fletcher and John Stevenson, eds. *Order and disorder in early modern England.* Cambridge: Cambridge University Press, 1987. ISBN 0-521-34932-X (pbk). ▸ Important essays assessing informal social controls and extent of conflict. Strong on honor, rhetoric of protest, gender, and class. [DMH]

23.237 M. Dorothy George. *London life in the eighteenth century.* 1925 ed. Chicago: Academy Chicago, 1984. ISBN 0-89733-147-8 (pbk). ▸ Classic study of metropolis, unsurpassed in detail and breadth. Treats housing, poor relief, and cultures of work and sociability. Changes in attitudes and material conditions produced cleaner, healthier, and more ordered society. [KW]

23.238 Douglas Hay et al. *Albion's fatal tree: crime and society in eighteenth-century England.* New York: Pantheon, 1975. ISBN 0-394-47120-2 (cl), 0-394-73085-2 (pbk). ▸ Influential neo-Marxist social history. Concludes redefinition of property rights through legislative power of capitalist ruling class gave rise to crime as social protest. Discusses theater of the law, smuggling, poaching, and anonymity. [KW]

23.239 J. Jean Hecht. *The domestic servant class in eighteenth-century England.* 1956 ed. Westport, Conn.: Hyperion, 1981. ISBN 0-8305-0104-5. ▸ Classic social history. Treats structure, recruitment, status, living conditions, and relations with other classes. Concludes growth in numbers and prosperity of middle classes produced expanded service sector with pivotal social roles. [KW]

23.240 Derek Hirst. "The failure of godly rule in the English republic." *Past and present* 132 (1991) 33–66. ISSN 0031-2746. ▸ Examination of efforts at moral reform. Finds catechizing and discipline through local officials thwarted by inertia. New perspective on failure of English Revolution. [DMH]

23.241 Geoffrey Holmes. *Augustan England: professions, state, and society, 1680–1730.* London: Allen & Unwin, 1982. ISBN 0-04-942178-6. ▸ Detailed assertion of increasing prominence of professions, measured by numbers, wealth, and status. Sees it as major factor in increasing social and political stability, also in growth and restructuring of market. [KW]

23.242 Paul Langford. *A polite and commercial people: England, 1727–1783.* Oxford: Clarendon, 1989. ISBN 0-19-822828-7. ▸ Comprehensive survey of culture and society under impact of economic expansion. Discusses high and low politics, manners, social life, religion, and intellectual trends. Lively generalist history. [KW]

23.243 Peter Laslett. *The world we have lost: further explored.* 1983 3d ed. New York: Scribner's, 1984. ISBN 0-684-18080-4 (cl), 0-684-18079-0 (pbk). ▸ Updated classic exposition of demographic and household characteristics of early modern England arguing class analysis inappropriate. [DMH]

23.244 David Levine. *Family formation in an age of nascent capitalism.* New York: Academic Press, 1977. ISBN 0-12-445050-4. ▸ Quantifies argument for impact of lordship on household size, finding absence of manorial lord allowed demographic growth. Sees industrial bywork as crucial escape from poverty. [DMH]

23.245 David Levine and Keith Wrightson. *The making of an industrial society: Whickham, 1560–1765.* Oxford: Clarendon, 1991. ISBN 0-19-820066-8. ▸ Examination of social impact of industrialization on early coal-mining village and replacement of traditional community ties by those of capitalist economy. Partisan but learned and imaginative. [DMH]

23.246 Alan Macfarlane. *The culture of capitalism.* Oxford: Blackwell, 1987. ISBN 0-631-13626-6. ▸ Controversial attack by historical anthropologist on conventional thesis of early modern transition to modernity, whether in commercial outlook, affective personal relations, or crime; claims broad historical continuity instead. [DMH]

23.247   Robert Malcolmson. *Life and labour in England, 1700–1780.* New York: St. Martin's, 1981. ISBN 0-312-48390-2. ▸ Able investigation of plebeian experience. Examines daily life, mentalities, and protest traditions of working people, from cottagers and craftsmen to servants, and changing social relations and material standards. [KW]

23.248   Dorothy Marshall. *The English poor in the eighteenth-century: a study in social and administrative history.* 1926 ed. New York: Kelley, 1969. ISBN 0-678-06503-9. ▸ Authoritative analysis of poor relief and debate over poverty. Penalization of poverty unintentionally achieved through lack of adequate parochial machinery to administer outdoor relief. Looks at growth of workhouses and progressive initiatives. [KW]

23.249   Marjorie Keniston McIntosh. *A community transformed: the manor and liberty of Havering, 1500–1620.* Cambridge: Cambridge University Press, 1991. ISBN 0-521-38142-8. ▸ Thorough study of transformation of manor near London by immigration and socioeconomic change. Sees erosion of local community and integration into national community as educated and prosperous oligarchy emerged. [DMH]

23.250   Neil McKendrick, John Brewer, and J. H. Plumb. *The birth of a consumer society: the commercialization of eighteenth-century England.* Bloomington: Indiana University Press, 1982. ISBN 0-253-31205-1. ▸ Commodification of goods, service, and activities, from children's toys and leisure pursuits to pottery and politics, wrought through commercial expansion and middle-class prosperity. Influential bourgeois history. [KW]

23.251   Hoh-Cheung Mui and Lorna H. Mui. *Shops and shopkeeping in eighteenth-century England.* Kingston, Ont.: McGill-Queen's University Press, 1989. ISBN 0-7735-0620-9. ▸ Pioneering effort to quantify origins of consumer society, examining relationship between proliferation of retailing from London to provinces in fifty years before Industrial Revolution. Examines flow of goods, types and distribution of shops, and retail policies. [KW]

23.252   Rosemary O'Day. *Education and society, 1500–1800: the social foundations of education in early modern Britain.* London: Longman, 1982. ISBN 0-582-48917-2. ▸ Worthy synthesis, stronger on earlier than on later half of period and on England than on Scotland. Good on social function of universities, quest for patrons, changes in curriculum, and teaching methods. [DMH]

23.253   Roy Porter. *English society in the eighteenth century.* Rev. ed. London: Penguin, 1990. ISBN 0-14-013819-6. ▸ Paradox of strong and stable ruling order above and effervescent socioeconomic and political conditions below central to Hanoverian development. Stimulating assessment of culture, power, and social relations, especially of middle classes. [KW]

23.254   Wilfrid R. Prest, ed. *The professions in early modern England.* London: Croom Helm, 1987. ISBN 0-7099-2051-2. ▸ Valuable essays establishing important place of professions in preindustrial England. Discusses clergy, teachers, lawyers, medical, military, and estate stewards. [DMH]

23.255   Steve Rappaport. *Worlds within worlds: structure of life in sixteenth-century London.* Cambridge: Cambridge University Press, 1989. ISBN 0-521-35065-4. ▸ Powerfully but controversially quantifies argument for openness and stability of London society. Especially important for showing how living standards cushioned against inflation. [DMH]

23.256   Barry Reay, ed. *Popular culture in seventeenth-century England.* New York: St. Martin's, 1985. ISBN 0-312-63036-0. ▸ Diverse essays disputing case for differentiation of popular and elite cultures. Excellent on survival of local community, even in

London, in face of partisanship; on attitudes to law; and on sexuality. [DMH]

23.257   Peter Roebuck. *The Yorkshire baronets, 1640–1760: families, estates, and fortunes.* Oxford: Oxford University Press for the University of Hull, 1980. ISBN 0-19-713439-4. ▸ Case studies and prosopography showing variety of experience. Large estate favored by demography and bias of land market rather than legal expedients; landowners had little impact on economic advance. [DMH]

23.258   James M. Rosenheim. *The Townshends of Raynham: nobility in transition in Restoration and early Hanoverian England.* Middletown, Conn.: Wesleyan University Press, 1989. ISBN 0-8195-5217-8. ▸ Best account of aristocratic estate policy and politics. Argues generational shift between those born in early seventeenth century and those born in later seventeenth century; latter generation more adventurous, less localist. [DMH]

23.259   David Harris Sacks. *The widening gate: Bristol and the Atlantic economy, 1450–1700.* Berkeley: University of California Press, 1991. ISBN 0-520-07148-4. ▸ Methodologically sophisticated study of emerging culture of capitalism examining interrelation of economy, society, politics, and culture; integration of city into national political and Atlantic community; and sociocultural underpinnings of local community. [DMH]

23.260   Paul Seaver. *Wallington's world: a Puritan artisan in seventeenth-century London.* Stanford, Calif.: Stanford University Press, 1985. ISBN 0-8047-1267-0. ▸ Reconstruction of socioeconomic, religious, and political world of highly literate woodworker, whose Puritanism did not contribute to capitalist success. Invaluable for examining marginality of survival and Puritan providentialism. [DMH]

23.261   J. A. Sharpe. *Crime in early modern England, 1550–1750.* London: Longman, 1984. ISBN 0-582-48994-6 (pbk). ▸ Essential survey of patterns of crime and response, nature of criminality, role of community participation, and state direction. Highlights brief surge in quantity and severity of punishments in early seventeenth century, arguing heightened fear of crime. [DMH]

23.262   Paul Slack, ed. *Rebellion, popular protest, and the social order in early modern England.* Cambridge: Cambridge University Press, 1984. ISBN 0-521-25035-8. ▸ Reprinted essays on many aspects of popular protest, both social and religious. Stresses conservative ideology of all groups, appeals to traditional rights, and claims to be enforcers of true law of immemorial past. [DMH]

23.263   Margaret Spufford. *Contrasting communities: English villagers in the sixteenth and seventeenth centuries.* London: Cambridge University Press, 1974. ISBN 0-521-20323-6. ▸ Vivid argument for effects of demographic change and variations in land use on village social structure. Sees socioeconomic polarization with economic crisis at end of sixteenth century. Religion, however, continued to play vital role in life far down social scale. [DMH]

23.264   Margaret Spufford. *Small books and pleasant histories: popular fiction and its readership in seventeenth-century England.* 1981 ed. Athens: University of Georgia Press, 1982. ISBN 0-8203-0595-2. ▸ Sympathetic study of consumption and themes of popular literature. Finds long-term stability of popular tastes; stresses materialism, social openness, and merry sexuality of romances. Very different from France. [DMH]

23.265   Lawrence Stone. *The crisis of the aristocracy, 1558–1641.* 1965 ed. Oxford: Clarendon, 1979. ISBN 0-19-821314-X. ▸ Monumental, seminal argument for undermining of regional warlord role of nobility by economic and military change, rise of state, and changing values through humanism and Protestantism. Challenges financial arguments for rise of gentry. [DMH]

23.266   Lawrence Stone and Jeanne C. Fawtier Stone. *An open*

elite? England, 1540–1880. Oxford: Clarendon, 1984. ISBN 0-19-822645-4. ‣ Provocative reassessment of permeability of landed society. Circumscribed demographic, social, and cultural configurations of upper classes explodes myth of English social mobility. Examines patrician marriage and inheritance practices, housing, education, and socialization. [KW/FMLT]

23.267 E. P. Thompson. *Customs in common.* London: Merlin, 1991. ISBN 0-85036-411-6. ‣ Passionate, distinctive neo-Marxist reading of class relations discussing cultural complexities of plebeian existence in patrician-dominated society. Treats work, crime, protest, and survival strategies. [KW]

23.268 E. P. Thompson. "The moral economy of the English crowd in the eighteenth century." *Past and present* 50 (1971) 76–136. ISSN 0031-2746. ‣ Enormously influential reassessment of riots, stressing rationality of rioters and reciprocity of relations between rulers and ruled. Popular traditionalism toward market effective instrument of protest against encroaching capitalism. [KW]

23.269 Keith E. Wrightson. *English society, 1580–1680.* London: Hutchinson, 1982. ISBN 0-09-145170-1 (cl), 0-09-145171-X (pbk). ‣ Fine theme-driven survey focusing on emergence of more stratified, but more mobile and less local, society in which religious discipline facilitated social control. Sympathetic and convincing account of family relations. [DMH]

23.270 Keith Wrightson and David Levine. *Poverty and piety in an English village: Terling, 1525–1700.* New York: Academic Press, 1979. ISBN 0-12-765950-1. ‣ Influential study of population pressure on local resources. Growing landlessness occasioned industrial bywork to replace loss of agricultural income. Social order and moral discipline maintained by assertiveness of Puritan village oligarchy. [DMH]

23.271 E. A. Wrigley and Roger Schofield. *The population history of England, 1541–1871: a reconstruction.* Cambridge, Mass.: Harvard University Press, 1981. ISBN 0-674-69007-9. ‣ Monumental, statistically and analytically sophisticated study, of demographic trends and levels. Treats extent of illegitimacy and impact of famine, epidemic, and migration on population. [DMH]

SEE ALSO
20.394 Richard M. Smith, ed. *Land, kinship, and life-cycle.*
20.422 Charles Phythian-Adams. *Desolation of a city.*

Legal History

23.272 John H. Baker, ed. *The reports of Sir John Spelman,* Vol. 2. London: Selden Society, 1978. (Publications of the Selden Society, 94.) ‣ Brilliant account of early sixteenth-century law and legal change. Argues for revolution from within workings of law, also pressure of political and socioeconomic change. Introduction to edited documents. [DMH]

23.273 J. M. Beattie. *Crime and the courts in England, 1660–1800.* Princeton: Princeton University Press, 1986. ISBN 0-691-05437-1 (cl), 0-691-10166-3 (pbk). ‣ Essential study of working of law. Concludes law courts used by all social classes. Discusses types of crime, legal process, resolution and enforcement, economic context of crime rates, and procedural effects of increases in crime. [DMH]

23.274 C. W. Brooks. *Pettyfoggers and vipers of the commonwealth: the "lower branch" of the legal profession in early modern England.* Cambridge: Cambridge University Press, 1986. ISBN 0-521-30574-8. ‣ Study of increase of legal practitioners in variety of provincial courts. Sees growing demand for legal security in socioeconomic and legal flux, especially under Elizabeth I. Excellent on unsystematic law and practice. [DMH]

23.275 J. S. Cockburn. *A history of English assizes, 1558–1714.* Cambridge: Cambridge University Press, 1972. ISBN 0-521-

08449-0. ‣ Wide-ranging survey of changing local functions of central courts judges, hard-pressed for time and independence as religious, political, and administrative duties expanded. [DMH]

23.276 Thomas Andrew Green. *Verdict according to conscience: perspectives on the English criminal trial jury, 1200–1800.* Chicago: University of Chicago Press, 1985. ISBN 0-226-30610-0. ‣ Essays on changing role of jury. Finds development of formal prosecution in sixteenth century and of counsel in eighteenth displaced medieval assumption of self-informing jury. Juries mitigated harshness of law. [DMH]

23.277 R. H. Helmholz. *Roman canon law in Reformation England.* Cambridge: Cambridge University Press, 1990. ISBN 0-521-38191-6. ‣ Brilliant study of post-Reformation status of pre-Reformation ecclesiastical law and lawyers. Business and formalization of procedure increased, as in all courts. Common law lawyers borrowed from canonists and canon law lawyers deferred to statute. [DMH]

23.278 Cynthia B. Herrup. *The common peace: participation and the criminal law in seventeenth-century England.* Cambridge: Cambridge University Press, 1987. ISBN 0-521-33313-X. ‣ Thoughtful local study treating activity and composition of juries. Resolution of different types of cases depended on identities of victims and defendants in community. [DMH]

23.279 E. W. Ives. *The common lawyers of pre-Reformation England: Thomas Kebell, a case study.* 1983 ed. Holmes Beach, Fla.: Gaunt, 1986. ISBN 0-912004-56-8. ‣ Impressive reconstruction of career, context, outlook, and methods of leading lawyer. Discusses nature of proceedings and cases, impact of printing, and lawyers' incomes. [DMH]

23.280 W. J. Jones. *Politics and the bench: the judges and the origins of the English Civil War.* London and New York: Allen & Unwin and Barnes & Noble, 1971. ISBN 0-389-04512-8. ‣ Argues judges not sycophants but royal servants by training, ideology, and institution; politically exposed because of unpopular royal policies. Includes documents and valuable, sometimes complex commentary. [DMH]

23.281 David Lemmings. *Gentlemen and barristers: the inns of court and the English bar, 1680–1730.* Oxford: Clarendon, 1990. ISBN 0-19-822155-X. ‣ Study of legal education and career patterns. Inns of court simply social centers for gentry in London, thus legal education became individualist and successful careers were made through political contacts. [DMH]

23.282 Wilfrid R. Prest. *The rise of the barristers: a social history of the English bar, 1590–1640.* Oxford: Clarendon, 1986. ISBN 0-19-821764-1. ‣ Ambitious prosopographical and anecdotal study of formally recognized lawyers. Finds modest origins and circumstances of many in expanding profession keyed to surging local, not central, business. Stresses lawyers' education and political role. [DMH]

23.283 Donald Veall. *The popular movement for law reform: 1640–1660.* Oxford: Oxford University Press, 1970. ‣ Examination of delays, costs, and confusions of law and lawyers in early seventeenth century. Survey of arguments for simplification and reform during English Revolution. [DMH]

Women, Family, and Household

23.284 Susan Dwyer Amussen. *An ordered society: gender and class in early modern England.* Oxford: Blackwell, 1988. ISBN 0-631-15521-X. ‣ Examination of internal dynamics of family and village life, centered on structure and exercise of authority. Dissects analogy between family and state. Provocative reinterpretation of early modern society. [LAP]

23.285 Alan Bray. *Homosexuality in Renaissance England.* London: Gay Men's Press; distributed by Alyson, 1982. ISBN

0-907040-16-0 (cased), 0-907040-13-6 (pbk). ▸ Brief overview of concept of homosexuality and its place in social structure. Challenges thesis that artistic freedom accompanied by greater sexual license. [LAP]

23.286 Alice Browne. *The eighteenth-century feminist mind.* Detroit: Wayne State University Press, 1987. ISBN 0-8143-1941-6. ▸ Development of ideas about women in education, legal reform, and sexual double standard, identifying what influenced these ideas and how separate arguments became coordinated. Skillful handling of complex topic. [LAP]

23.287 Lindsey Charles and Lorna Duffin, eds. *Women and work in pre-industrial England.* London: Croom Helm, 1985. ISBN 0-7099-0814-8 (cl), 0-7099-0856-3 (pbk). ▸ Discussion of experience and representation of women's work stressing obstacles encountered by working women. Takes issue with Clark 23.289 on impact of capitalism. Quirky but informative contributions ranging from prosaic to theoretical. [LAP]

23.288 Miranda Chaytor. "Household and kinship: Ryton in the late sixteenth and early seventeenth centuries." *History workshop journal* 10 (1980) 25–60. ISSN 0309-2984. ▸ Challenging, problematic discussion stressing impermanence of domestic relationships in northern parish, diversity of arrangements, and subordinate status of women. See debate in *History Workshop Journal*, 1981 and 1982. [LAP]

23.289 Alice Clark. *Working life of women in the seventeenth century.* 1919 ed. Miranda Chaytor and Jane Lewis, Introduction. London: Routledge & Kegan Paul, 1982. ISBN 0-7100-9045-5 (pbk). ▸ Overview of female employment, stressing women's greater role in economy prior to industrialization. Now displaced, but still richly detailed work and indispensable starting point. [LAP]

23.290 Patricia Crawford. "From the woman's point of view: pre-industrial England, 1500–1750." In *Exploring women's past: essays in social history.* 1983 ed. Patricia Crawford, ed., pp. 49–85. Sydney: Allen & Unwin, 1984. ISBN 0-86861-604-4. ▸ Good introductory survey of social and economic circumstances that controlled women's lives. [LAP]

23.291 David Cressy. "Kinship and kin interaction in early modern England." *Past and present* 113 (1986) 38–69. ISSN 0031-2746. ▸ Survey of kin relations, disputing view of English kinship as narrow, shallow, and restricted. Useful corrective. [LAP]

23.292 Peter Earle. "The female labour market in London in the late seventeenth and early eighteenth centuries." *Economic history review*, Second series, 43.3 (1989) 328–53. ISSN 0013-0117. ▸ Crisp account of nature of female paid work, detailing high percentage of women in labor market. Based on depositions given to church courts. [LAP]

23.293 Amy Louise Erikson. "Common law versus common practice: the use of marriage settlements in early modern England." *Economic history review*, Second series, 43.1 (1990) 21–39. ISSN 0013-0117. ▸ Marriage settlements were intended to protect wife's property rights and were regularly employed by ordinary people. Sharp critique of previous work. Broadens understanding of complex topic. [LAP]

23.294 Valerie Fildes, ed. *Women as mothers in pre-industrial England: essays in memory of Dorothy McLaren.* London: Routledge, 1990. ISBN 0-415-02488-9. ▸ How women experienced central event of their lives. Covers pregnancy, childbirth, wet-nursing, discipline, and child abandonment, as well as concept of maternity. Much original archival research. [LAP]

23.295 Barbara J. Harris. "Property, power, and personal relations: elite mothers and sons in Yorkist and early Tudor England." *Signs* 15.3 (1990) 606–32. ISSN 0097-9740. ▸ Structural analysis of family based on assumption that family was political

as well as reproductive and affective unit. Important examination of neglected topic. [LAP]

23.296 Barbara J. Harris. "Women and politics in early Tudor England." *Historical journal* 33.2 (1990) 259–81. ISSN 0018-246X. ▸ Analysis of extent and nature of female political activity revealing importance of informal channels of power in political process. Vital switch of focus from male-dominated, formal institutions of high politics. [LAP]

23.297 Frances Harris. *A passion for government: the life of Sarah, duchess of Marlborough.* Oxford: Clarendon, 1991. ISBN 0-19-820224-5. ▸ Biography of aristocratic woman emphasizing her desire and ability to wield power in domestic and political environment. Lively portrayal of contentious woman. [LAP]

23.298 Ralph A. Houlbrooke. *The English family, 1450–1700.* London: Longman, 1984. ISBN 0-582-49045-6 (pbk). ▸ Survey of all aspects of family: marriage, parenting, adolescence, kin, death, and inheritance. Balanced synthesis and sensible introduction to topic. [LAP]

23.299 Ralph A. Houlbrooke. "Women's social life and common action in England from the fifteenth century to the eve of the Civil War." *Continuity and change* 1.2 (1986) 171–89. ISSN 0268-4160. ▸ Exploration of role of female networks in facilitating formation of independent opinion and public protest of grievances. Examines neglected aspect of women's experience. [LAP]

23.300 Martin Ingram. *Church courts, sex, and marriage in England, 1570–1640.* Cambridge: Cambridge University Press, 1987. ISBN 0-521-23285-6. ▸ Examination of church courts as important vehicles of moral reformation. Focuses on cases of marital formation and breakdown, illicit sexuality, and sexual slander, particularly in Wiltshire. Revisionist, extensively researched, elegantly critical. [LAP]

23.301 Vivienne Larminie. "Settlement and sentiment: inheritance and personal relationships among two midland gentry families in the seventeenth century." *Midland history* 12 (1987) 27–47. ISSN 0047-729X. ▸ Study of inheritance practices of Crokes and Newdigates revealing interaction between material and emotional factors. Nuanced negation of Stone's model (23.315). [LAP]

23.302 Edmund Leites. *The Puritan conscience and modern sexuality.* New Haven: Yale University Press, 1986. ISBN 0-300-03490-3. ▸ Challenges idea of Puritans as repressed individuals, hostile to sex; rather their ideal was integration of sensuality and constancy within marriage. Reflective and insightful. [LAP]

23.303 Alan Macfarlane. *The family life of Ralph Josselin, a seventeenth-century clergyman: an essay in historical anthropology.* 1970 ed. London: Norton, 1977. ISBN 0-393-00849-5. ▸ Mental and material world of Josselin, based on his diary. Innovative when it appeared and still rounded portrayal of family below level of gentry. Study influenced by anthropology. [LAP]

23.304 Alan Macfarlane. *Marriage and love in England: modes of reproduction, 1300–1840.* Oxford: Blackwell, 1986. ISBN 0-631-13992-3. ▸ Clear exposition of marital behavior and its relation to population movement. Stresses role of individual choice and importance of love. Heavy going at times but needed corrective to dominant interpretation of historiography. [LAP]

23.305 Rosalind K. Marshall. *Virgins and viragos: a history of women in Scotland from 1080 to 1980.* Chicago: Academy Chicago, 1983. ISBN 0-89733-074-9 (cl), 0-89733-075-7 (pbk). ▸ Attempt to discover what it meant to be Scottish woman in past, stressing achievement rather than subservience. Breathless overview and serviceable antidote to Anglocentric perspective. [LAP]

23.306 Margaret McCurtain and Mary O'Dowd. *Women in early modern Ireland.* Edinburgh: Edinburgh University Press;

distributed by Columbia University Press, 1991. ISBN 0-7486-0223-2 (cased). ‣ Pioneering essays on political, religious, cultural, family, and socioeconomic roles of women in British and Gaelic Ireland. [LAP]

23.307 Angus McLaren. *Reproductive rituals: the perception of fertility in England from the sixteenth to the nineteenth century.* London: Methuen, 1984. ISBN 0-416-37450-6 (cl), 0-416-37460-3 (pbk). ‣ Overview of methods by which fertility was promoted and limited, arguing family size consciously controlled. Informative survey based on anthropological research and wide range of contemporary literature. [LAP]

23.308 Susan Moller Okin. "Women and the making of the sentimental family." *Philosophy and public affairs* 11.1 (1981) 65–88. ISSN 0048-3915. ‣ Growing sentimentalization of eighteenth century worsened position of women: new ideal used to reinforce patriarchy and inferior position of women. Disputes conclusions of Stone 23.315. [LAP]

23.309 Ivy Pinchbeck and Margaret Hewitt. *Children in English society.* Vol. 1: *From Tudor times to the eighteenth century.* 1969 ed. London: Routledge & Kegan Paul, 1972. ISBN 0-7100-6499-3. ‣ Discussion of Tudor policy toward children and its failure. Alternating patterns of benevolence and indifference, seventeenth to eighteenth century. Overwhelmingly concerned with institutions and eulogizes Tudors, but still indispensable survey of state provision. [LAP]

23.310 Linda A. Pollock. *Forgotten children: parent-child relations from 1500 to 1900.* Cambridge: Cambridge University Press, 1983. ISBN 0-521-25009-9 (cl), 0-521-27133-9 (pbk). ‣ Examination of parental care based on diaries arguing for much emotional investment in children and much continuity in methods of child rearing. Spirited revision of Stone thesis (23.315). [LAP]

23.311 Linda A. Pollock. " 'Teach her to live under obedience': the making of women in the upper ranks of early modern England." *Continuity and change* 4.2 (1989) 231–58. ISSN 0268-4160. ‣ Examination of sex-role socialization of elite women, enabling them to perform dual role as adults: competent when men absent and deferential when present. Resolves paradox. [LAP]

23.312 Mary Prior, ed. *Women in English society, 1500–1800.* London: Methuen, 1985. ISBN 0-416-35700-8 (cl), 0-416-35710-5 (pbk). ‣ Intelligible and intelligent exploration of aspects of female experience: fertility, lactation, religion, mentality, widowhood, published work, and participation in urban economy. Underscores ability of women to take advantage of any opportunity. [LAP]

23.313 Lois G. Schwoerer. "Women and the Glorious Revolution." *Albion* 18.2 (1986) 195–218. ISSN 0095-1390. ‣ Study of political role of women in late seventeenth century. Activities such as petitioning, fundraising, and public protest increased awareness of political abilities of women. Highlights overlooked facet of female experience. [LAP]

23.314 Susan Staves. *Married women's separate property in England, 1660–1833.* Cambridge, Mass.: Harvard University Press, 1990. ISBN 0-674-55088-9. ‣ Analysis of relationship between law and ideology with respect to marriage. Application of contract ideals to marital relations created socially intolerable situations and led courts to reimpose patriarchal structures. Erudite, imaginative, readable. [LAP]

23.315 Lawrence Stone. *The family, sex, and marriage in England, 1500–1800.* New York: Harper & Row, 1977. ISBN 0-06-014142-5. ‣ Grand model of emergence of modern family (domesticated and nuclear) based on rise of affective individualism. Copious examples, outrageous assertions, stimulating

arguments. Fueled plethora of debates. Paperback edition (1979) heavily abridged. [LAP]

23.316 Lorna Weatherill. "A possession of one's own: women and consumer behavior in England, 1660–1740." *Journal of British studies* 25.2 (1986) 131–56. ISSN 0021-9371. ‣ Uses probate records to compare life styles of women living alone, men living alone, and women living with families. No indication of separate female subculture. Creative use of sources. [LAP]

23.317 Diane Willen. "Women in the public sphere in early modern England: the case of the urban working poor." *Sixteenth century journal* 19.4 (1988) 559–75. ISSN 0361-0160. ‣ Investigates structure and effectiveness of poor relief. Women distributed as well as received relief. Questions applicability of separate spheres model. Shrewd assessment. [LAP]

SEE ALSO

4.693 Audrey Eccles. *Obstetrics and gynaecology in Tudor and Stuart England.*

20.471 Joel T. Rosenthal. *Patriarchy and families of privilege in fifteenth-century England.*

22.203 Ian Maclean. *The Renaissance notion of woman.*

History of Science

23.318 Nicholas H. Clulee. *John Dee's natural philosophy: between science and religion.* 1988 ed. London: Routledge, 1990. ISBN 0-415-00625-2 (cl), 0-415-03122-2 (pbk). ‣ Illustrated intellectual biography of important Elizabethan magus and mathematician. Impressive on his sources and on appeal of his claims of power. [DMH]

23.319 Mordechai Feingold. *The mathematicians' apprenticeship: science, universities, and society in England, 1560–1640.* Cambridge: Cambridge University Press, 1983. ISBN 0-521-25133-8. ‣ Fine revisionist study of flexibility of universities, showing considerable provision for and interest in new mathematics and other sciences. Valuable chapter on patronage, stressing patrons' practical, not theoretical, interests. [DMH]

23.320 Mordechai Feingold, ed. *Before Newton: the life and times of Isaac Barrow.* Cambridge: Cambridge University Press, 1990. ISBN 0-521-30694-9. ‣ Discussion of relations between mathematical and religious interests of second-ranking scientist-cleric who aided Sir Isaac Newton. Excellent on Barrow's geometry and intellectual context in mid-seventeenth-century Cambridge. [DMH]

23.321 Michael Hunter. *Establishing the new science: the experience of the early Royal Society.* Woodbridge, England: Boydell, 1989. ISBN 0-85115-506-5. ‣ Detailed case studies of early Royal Society, treating concerns and meaning of Robert Boyle, relations of science and technology, and history of museums. Balanced historiographical essay. [DMH]

23.322 Michael Hunter. *Science and society in Restoration England.* Cambridge: Cambridge University Press, 1981. ISBN 0-521-22866-2 (cl), 0-521-29685-4 (pbk). ‣ Incisive study of contemporary controversy over status of science post-1660. Discusses political and religious ramifications of scientific study as well as establishment of its respectability, social appeal to gentry of fashion, and apparent promise of power and prosperity. [DMH/MHS]

23.323 Michael Hunter and Simon Schaffer, eds. *Robert Hooke: new studies.* Woodbridge, England: Boydell, 1989. ISBN 0-85115-523-5. ‣ Situates microscopist in illuminating set of intellectual and social contexts. Discusses rhetorical strategy and social ambivalence of this most "mechanical" scientist. Highly original on rhetorical force of illustrations. [DMH]

23.324 Margaret C. Jacob. *The Newtonians and the English Revolution, 1689–1720.* Ithaca, N.Y.: Cornell University Press, 1976.

ISBN 0-8014-0981-0. ‣ Seminal study of ideological status of new science. Argues Newtonian science embodied political message—stability—that served ideology of liberal Anglicanism in wake of Revolution of 1688. Examines Newtonianism's value to church leaders as check on enthusiasm, underpinning revolution settlement and role of Boyle Lectures in disseminating new cultural orthodoxy. [DMH/MHS]

23.325 Francis Maddison, Margaret Pelling, and Charles Webster, eds. *Essays on the life and work of Thomas Linacre, c. 1460–1524.* Oxford: Clarendon, 1977. ISBN 0-19-858150-5. ‣ Wideranging essays on humanist and physician, his medieval as well as European humanist context, medical interests, and significance. [DMH]

23.326 Julian Martin. *Francis Bacon, the state, and the reform of natural philosophy.* Cambridge: Cambridge University Press, 1992. ISBN 0-521-38249-1. ‣ Best contextual study of why statesman concerned himself with philosophy of nature. Analyzes impact of legal and political interests and educational reform on his philosophy. [DMH]

23.327 Antonio Perez-Ramos. *Francis Bacon's idea of science and the maker's knowledge tradition.* Oxford: Clarendon, 1988. ISBN 0-19-824979-9. ‣ Technical study of Bacon's influential protoempirical philosophy; adaptation of classical and medieval sources. Critical analysis of Bacon's method. [DMH]

23.328 Roy Porter. *The making of geology: earth science in Britain, 1660–1815.* Cambridge: Cambridge University Press, 1977. ISBN 0-521-21521-8. ‣ Model study of development of science, set in intellectual, social, and political context. [DMH]

23.329 Steven Shapin and Simon Schaffer. *Leviathan and the air-pump: Hobbes, Boyle, and the experimental life, including a translation of Thomas Hobbes, "Dialogus Physicus de Natura Aeris."* Princeton: Princeton University Press, 1985. ISBN 0-691-08393-2 (cl), 0-691-02432-4 (pbk). ‣ Innovative analysis of controversy over vacuum, Hobbes against Boyle and early Royal Society. Examines status of experiment and nature of scientific method and community. [DMH]

23.330 Charles Webster. *From Paracelsus to Newton: magic and the making of modern science.* Cambridge: Cambridge University Press, 1982. ISBN 0-521-24919-8. ‣ Essays on influence of hermeticism and millenarianism, scientists' attitudes toward witchcraft, and natural history. Asserts vitality of nonmechanist strands into age of Newton. [DMH]

23.331 Richard S. Westfall. *Never at rest: a biography of Isaac Newton.* 1980 ed. Cambridge: Cambridge University Press, 1986. ISBN 0-521-27435-4 (pbk). ‣ Huge, thorough biography of culminating figure of Scientific Revolution. Clear discussion of Newton's physics, optics, governmental service, relations with other scientists, and emergence as cultural icon. Less good on Newton's hermeticism and religion. [DMH/MHS]

SEE ALSO
4.83 I. Bernard Cohen. *The Newtonian revolution.*
4.107 Richard S. Westfall. *The construction of modern science.*

The Arts

23.332 John F. Andrews, ed. *William Shakespeare: his world, his work, his influence.* 3 vols. New York: Scribner's, 1985. ISBN 0-684-17851-6 (set). ‣ Excellent essays in volume 1 on social, political, intellectual, and cultural background, and in volume 2 on Shakespeare's method and works. Valuable starting point. [DMH]

23.333 Richard W. Bevis. *English drama: restoration and the eighteenth century, 1660–1789.* London: Longman, 1988. ISBN 0-582-49394-3 (cl), 0-582-49393-5 (pbk). ‣ Useful survey of main devel-opments in drama with attention to social and political contexts. [DMH]

23.334 A. R. Braunmuller and Michael Hattaway. *The Cambridge companion to English Renaissance drama.* Cambridge: Cambridge University Press, 1990. ISBN 0-521-34657-6 (cl), 0-521-38662-4 (pbk). ‣ Up-to-date essays on drama and its relation to society and politics before Civil War. Treats audiences, actors, venues, and genres. Valuable bibliographies and chronologies. [DMH]

23.335 Joseph Burke. *English art, 1714–1800.* Oxford: Clarendon, 1976. ISBN 0-19-817209-5. ‣ Compendious, judicious surveys with accounts of major figures and developments in visual arts. Part of series with Mercer 23.360 and Whinney and Millar 23.371. [DMH]

23.336 Martin Butler. *Theatre and crisis, 1632–1642.* Cambridge: Cambridge University Press, 1984. ISBN 0-521-24632-6. ‣ Model analysis of complex interrelations of culture and politics, stressing ambiguity of pressures on writers and audiences alike, as plays both questioned and reinforced prevailing values. [DMH]

23.337 John Caldwell. *The Oxford history of music.* Vol. 1: *From the beginnings to c. 1715.* Oxford: Clarendon, 1991. ISBN 0-19-816129-8. ‣ Superb synthesis setting main musical developments in wide variety of contexts. Essential starting point, fine bibliography. [DMH]

23.338 Rosalie L. Colie. *"My Echoing Song": Andrew Marvell's poetry of criticism.* Princeton: Princeton University Press, 1970. ISBN 0-691-06163-7. ‣ Brilliant study of epistemological and metaphysical uncertainty; Marvell approached through seventeenth-century philosophy and science rather than politics. [DMH]

23.339 Thomas N. Corns. *Uncloistered virtue: English political literature, 1640–1660.* New York: Oxford University Press, 1992. ISBN 0-19-812883-5. ‣ Sets poetry in context of other writings of revolution; careful, intelligent, and unpolemical on public engagement of arts and artists in war and revolution. Best survey. [DMH]

23.340 Leopold Damrosch, Jr. *The imaginative world of Alexander Pope.* Berkeley: University of California Press, 1987. ISBN 0-520-05975-1. ‣ Perceptive new historicist approach to Pope's poetry and its political and social context. Sees Roman Catholic poet on political margins, striving for respectability, his work reflecting those tensions. [DMH]

23.341 Christopher Dearnley. *English church music, 1650–1750, in royal chapel, cathedral, and parish church.* Oxford: Oxford University Press, 1970. ‣ Informative survey of liturgical and social settings of church music and its development. [DMH]

23.342 Jonathan Dollimore. *Radical tragedy: religion, ideology, and power in the drama of Shakespeare and his contemporaries.* Chicago: University of Chicago Press, 1984. ISBN 0-226-15538-2. ‣ Interprets tragedies, ca. 1600, as preoccupied with subversion of structures of political and religious power. Difficult to discern coherence claimed for works examined, but impressive new historicist ideological reading. [DMH]

23.343 Edward Doughtie. *English Renaissance song.* Boston: Twayne, 1986. ISBN 0-8057-6915-3. ‣ Thematic and technical analysis of linkage of music and poetry in madrigal. [DMH]

23.344 Howard Erskine-Hill. *The Augustan idea in English literature.* London: Arnold, 1983. ISBN 0-7131-6373-9. ‣ Authoritative version of conventional thesis on classical literary ideals of seventeenth and eighteenth centuries. Helpfully examines image of Augustus (Roman caesar), but depoliticizes application. [DMH]

23.345 Boris Ford, ed. *The Cambridge guide to the arts in Britain.* Vol. 3: *Renaissance and Reformation.* Vol. 4: *The seventeenth cen-*

tury. Vol. 5: *The Augustan age.* Cambridge: Cambridge University Press, 1989–91. ISBN 0-521-30976-X (v. 3), 0-521-30977-8 (v. 4), 0-521-30978-6 (v. 5). ‣ Good starting point for cultural history of each period including visual arts, music, and literature, high and low. Sometimes slight but often imaginative essays. [DMH]

23.346 Alistair Fox. *Politics and literature in the reigns of Henry VII and Henry VIII.* Oxford: Blackwell, 1989. ISBN 0-631-13566-9. ‣ Survey of wide range of early Tudor literature, set in patronage and political contexts. Strong on Sir Thomas More, John Skelton, and Thomas Wyatt. Argues political instability encouraged fictive writing. [DMH]

23.347 Mark Girouard. *Robert Smythson and the Elizabethan country house.* New Haven: Yale University Press, 1983. ISBN 0-300-03134-3. ‣ Lavishly illustrated, important study of work of England's first major architect, and prodigy houses he designed. Influences, methods, and patronage. [DMH]

23.348 Stephen Greenblatt. *Renaissance self-fashioning: from More to Shakespeare.* Chicago: University of Chicago Press, 1980. ISBN 0-226-30653-4 (cl), 0-226-30654-2 (pbk). ‣ Founding text of new historicist approach in literary studies. Argues ideological and sociopolitical determinants of writing. [DMH]

23.349 Richard Helgerson. *Forms of nationhood: the Elizabethan writing of England.* Chicago: University of Chicago Press, 1992. ISBN 0-226-32633-0. ‣ Imaginative survey of Elizabethan creation of myth of England, in vernacular literature, in common law, in maps and travel literature, in millennialist religion, and in theater, high and low. [DMH]

23.350 John Dixon Hunt. *Garden and grove: the Italian Renaissance garden in the English imagination, 1600–1750.* Princeton: Princeton University Press, 1986. ISBN 0-691-04041-9. ‣ Detailed study of prenaturalist garden design, Italian Renaissance influence on travelers drawn toward classics, and Dutch and French styles abandoned after Glorious Revolution. [DMH]

23.351 Carol Kay. *Political constructions: Defoe, Richardson, and Sterne in relation to Hobbes, Hume, and Burke.* Ithaca, N.Y.: Cornell University Press, 1988. ISBN 0-8014-2043-1. ‣ Perceptive attack on Watt's claim that novel celebrates private sphere (23.369). Argues pressure of partisan and gender politics and philosophical controversy. Fine feminist readings of texts. [DMH]

23.352 N. H. Keeble. *The literary culture of non-conformity in later seventeenth-century England.* Athens: University of Georgia Press, 1987. ISBN 0-8203-0951-6. ‣ Argues later seventeenth-century persecution drove dissenters in age of Milton and Bunyan to imaginative writing. Emphasizes spiritual experience and, after mid-century failure of Puritanism, distrust of dogma, state, and world. [DMH]

23.353 Peter Le Huray. *Music and the Reformation in England, 1549–1660.* Corr. ed. Cambridge: Cambridge University Press, 1978. ‣ Wide-ranging, compendious survey of changes worked by Reformation on musical styles at all levels. [DMH]

23.354 Richard Leppert. *Music and image: domesticity, ideology, and socio-cultural formation in eighteenth-century England.* Cambridge: Cambridge University Press, 1988. ISBN 0-521-36029-3. ‣ Imaginative gendered reading of music and performance. Discusses gender-appropriate instruments and gender and hierarchical implications of public and private performance. Integrates music with portraiture. [DMH]

23.355 Barbara Kiefer Lewalski. *Protestant poetics and the seventeenth-century religious lyric.* Princeton: Princeton University Press, 1979. ISBN 0-691-06395-8. ‣ Important study of native English Protestant devotional tradition, independent of Catholic forms, and drawing heavily on Old Testament, which shaped seventeenth-century religious lyric. [DMH]

23.356 Louis L. Martz. *Milton, poet of exile.* 2d ed. New Haven: Yale University Press, 1986. ISBN 0-300-03736-8 (pbk). ‣ Best recent introduction to John Milton's career and poetry. Seeks to reconcile Puritan and humanist, presenting him as culturally and politically estranged and his work as driven by genre and spiritual interests. [DMH]

23.357 Richard C. McCoy. *The rites of knighthood: the literature and politics of Elizabethan chivalry.* Berkeley: University of California Press, 1989. ISBN 0-520-06548-4. ‣ Best introduction, textual (especially Edmund Spenser) and contextual, to politics of Elizabethan aristocratic entertainments and chivalric display; element in power struggle at court for support of aging queen, and reverberations in literature. [DMH]

23.358 Michael McKeon. *The origins of the English novel, 1660–1740.* Baltimore: Johns Hopkins University Press, 1987. ISBN 0-8018-3291-8. ‣ Schematized but important conceptualization of impact of early modern ideological and intellectual ferment. Challenges Watt's stress on middle class (23.369) and sees novel mediating and containing conflicts. [DMH]

23.359 Joseph McMinn. *Jonathan Swift: a literary life.* New York: St. Martin's, 1991. ISBN 0-312-05275-8. ‣ Introduction to all facets of Swift's career as poet, pamphleteer, and correspondent with especial sympathy for Irish context. [DMH]

23.360 Eric Mercer. *English art, 1553–1625.* Oxford: Clarendon, 1962. ‣ Compendious, judicious surveys with accounts of major figures and developments in visual arts. Part of series with Burke 23.335 and Whinney and Millar 23.371. [DMH]

23.361 Annabel Patterson. *Censorship and interpretation: the conditions of writing and reading in early modern England.* Madison: University of Wisconsin Press, 1984. ISBN 0-299-09950-4. ‣ Innovative study of political applications of literary texts and of self-censorship and concealment that political tensions necessitated. [DMH]

23.362 Ronald Paulson. *Emblem and expression: meaning in English art of the eighteenth century.* Cambridge, Mass.: Harvard University Press, 1975. ISBN 0-674-24778-7. ‣ Innovative work on textuality of eighteenth-century art, relating images to themes and topoi of contemporary literature. Lavishly illustrated. [DMH]

23.363 Curtis Price. *Henry Purcell and the London stage.* Cambridge: Cambridge University Press, 1984. ISBN 0-521-23831-5. ‣ Definitive study of place of music in late seventeenth-century stage and vindication of agendas of Purcell and John Dryden in nondevelopment of English opera. [DMH]

23.364 David C. Price. *Patrons and musicians of the English Renaissance.* Cambridge: Cambridge University Press, 1981. ISBN 0-521-22806-9. ‣ Useful survey of patronage relationships and practices and musical tastes of great households. [DMH]

23.365 Mary Ann Radzinowicz. *Toward Samson Agonistes: the growth of Milton's mind.* Princeton: Princeton University Press, 1978. ISBN 0-691-06357-5. ‣ Superb study of one poem, locating it not only in John Milton's wider political and literary career but also in broad religious and political context. [DMH]

23.366 Kevin Sharpe. *Criticism and compliment: the politics of literature in the England of Charles I.* Cambridge: Cambridge University Press, 1987. ISBN 0-521-34239-2. ‣ Interdisciplinary revisionist defense of masques and court culture of 1630s from charges that they reveal isolation and self-delusion. Instead, finds debate and counsel on right ordering of state. Controversial. [DMH]

23.367 Roy Strong. *The cult of Elizabeth: Elizabethan portraiture and pageantry.* 1977 ed. Berkeley: University of California Press, 1986. ISBN 0-520-05840-2 (cl), 0-520-05841-0 (pbk). ‣ Fine illustrated essay on political symbolism of iconic presentation of female Protestant ruler, reconciling gender through substitution for displaced Mariolatry. [DMH]

23.368 John Summerson. *Inigo Jones.* 1964 ed. Harmondsworth: Penguin, 1983. ISBN 0-14-020839-9. ‣ Study of major Italianate architect and masque designer. Illustrations make clear why he so shaped eighteenth-century taste and what early Stuarts would have built with more money. [DMH]

23.369 Ian P. Watt. *The rise of the novel: studies in Defoe, Richardson, and Fielding.* 1957 ed. Berkeley: University of California Press, 1974. ISBN 0-520-01317-4. ‣ Authoritative, old-fashioned account of relation of novel to rise of middle class and domesticity. [DMH]

23.370 William Weber. *The rise of musical classics in eighteenth-century England: a study in canon, ritual, and ideology.* Oxford: Clarendon, 1992. ISBN 0-19-816287-1. ‣ Innovative approach to political and intellectual as well as cultural setting of music. Imaginative application of historicist method. [DMH]

23.371 M. Whinney and O. Millar. *English art, 1625–1714.* Oxford: Clarendon, 1957. ‣ Compendious, judicious surveys with accounts of major figures and developments in visual arts. Part of series with Burke 23.335 and Mercer 23.360. [DMH]

23.372 Steven N. Zwicker. *Politics and language in Dryden's poetry: the arts of disguise.* Princeton: Princeton University Press, 1984. ISBN 0-691-06618-3. ‣ Pressure of politics on period's leading public poet, who had to adjust to successive revolutions. His appointment as royal historiographer testifies to political involvement of poetry. [DMH]

SCOTLAND

23.373 Keith M. Brown. *Bloodfeud in Scotland, 1573–1625: violence, justice, and politics in an early modern society.* Edinburgh: Donald, 1986. ISBN 0-85976-134-7. ‣ Study of decline of feuding in localities and at court under pressure of clergy, crown, Parliament, and courts. Set in context of gradual growth of state power in Scotland. [BPL]

23.374 Craig Cairns et al., eds. *The history of Scottish literature.* Vol. 1: *Origins to 1660 (Mediaeval and Renaissance).* Vol. 2: *1660–1880.* 1987–88 ed. Aberdeen: Pergamon, 1989. ISBN 0-08-037725-4 (v. 1, pbk), 0-08-037726-0 (v. 2, pbk). ‣ Wide-ranging essays on learned and vernacular languages, poetry and prose, and popular and high culture. [DMH]

23.375 Ian B. Cowan. *The Scottish Covenanters, 1660–1688.* London: Gollancz, 1976. ISBN 0-575-02105-5. ‣ Traces pattern of prosecution and conciliation. Explores conflict between Cameronians and moderate Presbyterians. Mediates between nineteenth-century hagiography and negative view of Covenanters as unreasonable opponents of accommodation with episcopacy. [BPL]

23.376 T. M. Devine and David Dickson, eds. *Ireland and Scotland, 1600–1850: parallels and contrasts in economic and social development.* Edinburgh: Donald, 1983. ISBN 0-85976-089-8. ‣ Essays focus on separate countries with comparative assessments found in excellent editorial contributions. Especially good on economy. [BPL]

23.377 Gordon Donaldson. *The Scottish Reformation.* 1960 ed. Cambridge: Cambridge University Press, 1978. ISBN 0-521-08675-2. ‣ Detailed treatment of political and administrative aspects of Reformation. Challenges suddenness and completeness of Scottish movement emphasizing continuity of organization and personnel. Finds compromise between episcopacy and Presbyterianism in period after 1592. [BPL]

23.378 F. D. Dow. *Cromwellian Scotland, 1651–1660.* Edinburgh: Donald, 1979. ISBN 0-85976-049-9. ‣ Narrative study of

influence of English army on government of Scotland. Glencairn's rising of 1653–55 reveals difficulty of pacification and leads to civilizing of regime and more conciliatory government. Predominantly administrative perspective. [BPL]

23.379 John Dwyer, Roger A. Mason, and Alexander Murdoch, eds. *New perspectives on the politics and culture of early modern Scotland.* Edinburgh: Donald; distributed by Humanities, 1982. ISBN 0-85976-066-9. ‣ High-quality essays on Gaelic response to Covenanting aggression, Scottish education patronage in Scotland, eighteenth-century education, and child rearing. [BPL]

23.380 William Ferguson. *Scotland's relations with England: a survey to 1707.* Edinburgh: Donald, 1977. ISBN 0-85976-022-7. ‣ Comprehensive study of conflicts between two kingdoms and schemes for union. Minimizes ideological and economic factors in 1707 union debates emphasizing political management and bribery. Nationalistic approach to question of union. [BPL]

23.381 Michael W. Flinn et al., ed. *Scottish population history from the seventeenth century to the 1930s.* Cambridge: Cambridge University Press, 1977. ISBN 0-521-21173-5. ‣ Extensive coverage of period before first census of 1801. Assesses impact of famine, plague, and disease in seventeenth century and establishes short- and long-run movements of eighteenth century. [BPL]

23.382 R. A. Houston. *Scottish literacy and the Scottish identity: illiteracy and society in Scotland and northern England, 1600–1800.* Cambridge: Cambridge University Press, 1985. ISBN 0-521-26598-3. ‣ Quantitatively based and theoretically informed analysis with attention to reasons for literacy and political dimension of problem. Destroys myths of superior Scottish literacy and education by comparison with northern England and Europe. [BPL]

23.383 R. A. Houston and Ian D. Whyte, eds. *Scottish society, 1500–1800.* Cambridge: Cambridge University Press, 1989. ISBN 0-521-32522-6. ‣ Introduction offering valuable comprehensive survey. Innovative essays on population mobility, urban society, ideology of clans, women in economy and society, and social dislocation in highland and lowland clearances. [BPL]

23.384 James Kirk. *Patterns of reform: continuity and change in the Reformation kirk.* Edinburgh: Clark, 1989. ISBN 0-567-09505-3. ‣ Studies of church government and religious practice through reign of James VI. Focuses on conflicts between radical vision of Scottish reformers and continuation of practices of unreformed church. Reveals strength of continental influences. [BPL]

23.385 Christina Larner. *Enemies of God: the witch-hunt in Scotland.* Baltimore: Johns Hopkins University Press, 1981. ISBN 0-8018-2699-3. ‣ Examination of prosecution of witches from 1563 to early eighteenth century in comparative setting. Emphasizes social factors, state development, and belief system. Interdisciplinary study reflecting insights of sociology and anthropology. [BPL]

23.386 Maurice Lee, Jr. *Government by pen: Scotland under James VI and I.* Urbana: University of Illinois Press, 1980. ISBN 0-252-00765-4. ‣ Political history of Jacobean Scotland after 1603. Focuses on earl of Dunbar's hegemony, 1606–11, and earl of Dunfermline's less despotic methods after 1611. Finds less government by James's pen after death of Dunbar. [BPL]

23.387 Leah Leneman, ed. *Perspectives in Scottish social history: essays in honour of Rosalind Mitchison.* Aberdeen: Aberdeen University Press, 1988. ISBN 0-08-036574-4 (pbk). ‣ Includes essays on establishment of godly discipline in parish of St. Andrews, use of food to reinforce social hierarchy, geographical mobility of women, and layout of farm townships before age of improvement. [BPL]

23.388 Bruce Lenman. *The Jacobite risings in Britain, 1689–1746.* London: Methuen, 1980. ISBN 0-413-39650-9. ‣ Full account of Jacobite resistance, based on economic disillusionment and anti-unionist sentiment, fueled by royal incompetence. Rising of 1715 represented greatest challenge. Strongly anti-Hanoverian, revisionist approach. [BPL]

23.389 Michael Lynch. *Edinburgh and the Reformation.* Edinburgh: Donald; distributed by Humanities, 1981. ISBN 0-85976-069-3. ▸ Valuable contribution to urban, religious, and political history. Establishes distinctive Reformation in city. Minimizes influence of John Knox and his radical supporters, who constituted minority into 1560s. [BPL]

23.390 Michael Lynch, ed. *The early modern town in Scotland.* London: Croom Helm, 1987. ISBN 0-7099-1677-9. ▸ Political, economic, social, and religious aspects of urban history in case studies of Edinburgh, Perth, Aberdeen and Dumfries and in broader treatments of occupational structure, relations with crown, and revolution. [BPL]

23.391 S.G.E. Lythe. *The economy of Scotland in its European setting, 1550–1625.* 1960 ed. Westport, Conn.: Greenwood, 1976. ISBN 0-8371-8533-5. ▸ Balanced survey of economy in period before and after personal union of 1603. Finds subsequent significant economic growth as result of removal of English hostility. Explores trading links with England and Europe. [BPL]

23.392 Norman Macdougall. *James III: a political study.* Edinburgh: Donald, 1982. ISBN 0-85976-078-2. ▸ Interpretation of king's failures as result of character flaws rather than policies. Stresses English alliance of 1474 and efforts to centralize royal government. Challenges legend of king as recluse and poor military leader. [BPL]

23.393 Leslie J. Macfarlane. *William Elphinstone and the kingdom of Scotland, 1431–1514: the struggle for order.* Aberdeen: Aberdeen University Press, 1985. ISBN 0-08-030408-7. ▸ Biography of royal servant and bishop of Aberdeen who founded University of Aberdeen. Valuable discussion of diocesan reforms, foreign policy, and financial administration. Revisionist approach to James III and James IV. [BPL]

23.394 Allan I. Macinnes. *Charles I and the making of the Covenanting movement, 1625–1641.* Edinburgh: Donald, 1991. ISBN 0-85976-295-5. ▸ Covenanters' efforts to centralize government and reforge Scottish identity. Indictment of Charles I as architect of his own downfall. Narrative account with emphasis on royal finance, especially revocation scheme. [BPL]

23.395 Walter Makey. *The church of the Covenant, 1637–1651: revolution and social change in Scotland.* Edinburgh: Donald, 1979. ISBN 0-85976-035-9. ▸ Interpretation of revolution as product of long-term social change. Struggle between feudal magnates and ministers, leading to temporary victory of church over state. Study of ministers and elders during revolutionary period. [BPL]

23.396 Gordon Marshall. *Presbyteries and profits: Calvinism and the development of capitalism in Scotland, 1560–1707.* 1980 ed. Edinburgh: Edinburgh University Press, 1992. ISBN 0-7486-0333-6 (pbk). ▸ Anti-Marxist argument for economic impact of religion. Explores Scottish economic and financial activity to establish origins of capitalist ethos in neo-Calvinist doctrines. Relates ideological to material factors. [BPL]

23.397 Roger A. Mason, ed. *Scotland and England, 1286–1815.* Edinburgh: Donald; distributed by Humanities, 1987. ISBN 0-85976-117-0. ▸ Illuminates long-term aspects of union question. Explores James Henrisoun's proposals for union in 1540s, Covenanters and federal union, Solemn League and Covenant, Andrew Fletcher's vision of union, and anglicization of Scottish culture. [BPL]

23.398 Rosalind Mitchison. *Lordship to patronage: Scotland, 1603–1745.* 1983 ed. Edinburgh: Edinburgh University Press, 1990. ISBN 0-7486-0233-X (pbk). ▸ Concise overview of political, social, and economic development stressing improvement of

economy after 1660 and change in nature of landed aristocracy. Set in European as well as British context. [BPL]

23.399 Rosalind Mitchison and Leah Leneman. *Sexuality and social control: Scotland, 1660–1780.* Oxford: Blackwell, 1989. ISBN 0-631-15028-5. ▸ Study of regular and irregular marriage, illegitimacy, and premarital pregnancy in rural parishes. Establishes low levels of illegitimacy relative to nineteenth century and no upward trend except in Southwest. [BPL]

23.400 Nicholas T. Phillipson and Rosalind Mitchison, eds. *Scotland in the age of improvement: essays in Scottish history in the eighteenth century.* Edinburgh: Edinburgh University Press, 1970. ISBN 0-85224-183-6. ▸ Essays on aspects of Scottish social history. Studies of government and highlands 1707–45, landowner and planned village, influence of social development on education, and social origins of Enlightenment. [BPL]

23.401 Thomas I. Rae. *The administration of the Scottish frontier, 1513–1603.* Edinburgh: Edinburgh University Press, 1966. ▸ Analysis of efforts by Scots in peacetime to administer their side of border region and negotiate with English concerning frontier crime. Complex relationship of wardens of marches with local and central government. [BPL]

23.402 P.W.J. Riley. *The union of England and Scotland: a study of Anglo-Scottish politics of the eighteenth century.* Manchester and Totowa, N.J.: Manchester University Press and Rowman & Littlefield, 1978. ISBN 0-7190-0727-5, 0-8476-6155-5. ▸ Account of political maneuvers for and against union leading to Treaty of Union (1707), reflecting private interest, corruption, and short-term gain. Challenges interpretation of union as act of statesmanship. [BPL]

23.403 John Stuart Shaw. *The management of Scottish society, 1707–1764: power, nobles, lawyers, Edinburgh agents, and English influences.* Edinburgh: Donald; distributed by Humanities, 1983. ISBN 0-85976-085-5. ▸ Fine study of administration of Scotland under union. Operation of patronage machine in interests of Scottish nobles and careerists, and English political and economic stability. [DMH]

23.404 T. C. Smout. *A history of the Scottish people, 1560–1830.* 1969 ed. London: Fontana, 1987. ISBN 0-00-686027-3 (pbk). ▸ Full-scale social history with attention to economic, political, and cultural matters. Detailed studies of landowners, peasants, urban middle class, and industrial workers. Sees fundamental transformation of society in period 1690 to 1830. [BPL]

23.405 David Stevenson. *Revolution and counter-revolution in Scotland, 1644–1651.* London: Royal Historical Society, 1977. ISBN 0-901050-35-0. ▸ Political and military narrative from intervention in England to Cromwellian conquest. Extensive commentary on Covenanters' plans for union. Attributes conservatism of revolution to slow economic development and early religious settlement. [BPL]

23.406 David Stevenson. *The Scottish Revolution, 1637–1644: the triumph of the Covenanters.* 1973 ed. Newton-Abbot, England: David & Charles, 1984. ISBN 0-7153-6302-6. ▸ Authoritative, dispassionate political narrative of origins and early course of revolution, including Bishops' Wars and Solemn League and Covenant. Emphasis on conflict with Charles I with little attention to social factors. [BPL]

23.407 Christopher A. Whatley. "Economic causes and consequences of the union of 1707: a survey." *Scottish historical review* 68.2 (1989) 150–81. ISSN 0036-9241. ▸ Balanced survey of hotly debated issue. Useful summary of extensive economic literature. Deals both with economic arguments in 1707 and impact of union treaty on economic development. [BPL]

23.408 Ian D. Whyte. *Agriculture and society in seventeenth-century Scotland.* Edinburgh: Donald, 1979. ISBN 0-85976-033-2.

‣ Challenges traditional picture of agricultural development. Improvements associated with eighteenth century, including enclosures of open fields, long leases, higher crop yield, and large market shown to have been widespread after 1660, especially in lowlands. [BPL]

23.409 Arthur H. Williamson. *Scottish national consciousness in the age of James VI: the apocalypse, the union, and the shaping of Scotland's public culture.* Edinburgh: Donald, 1979. ISBN 0-85976-036-7. ‣ Examination of conflict between Scottish imperialists with British vision and Presbyterian patriots, reflecting different views of apocalypse and influencing Jacobean union debates. Explores development of historical thought. [BPL]

23.410 Jenny Wormald. *Court, kirk, and community: Scotland, 1470–1625.* London: Arnold, 1981. ISBN 0-7131-6310-0 (cl), 0-7131-6311-9 (pbk). ‣ Excellent survey with emphasis on political development, Reformation, and Renaissance culture. Challenges traditional picture of disorder and barbarism. Reveals complexity of political and religious change. [BPL]

23.411 Jenny Wormald. *Lords and men in Scotland: bonds of manrent, 1442–1603.* Edinburgh: Donald; distributed by Humanities, 1985. ISBN 0-85976-127-4. ‣ Sees proliferation of bonds of personal obligation of service to lords as reflecting desire for peace and stability, not thuggery. Reinterpretation of relationship between Scottish aristocracy and monarchy. End of bonding reflects social change. [BPL]

23.412 Jenny Wormald. *Mary Queen of Scots: a study in failure.* London: Philip, 1988. ISBN 0-540-01131-2. ‣ Harsh reevaluation of queen's rule in context of traditions of Scottish kingship. Abdication of responsibility to rule during entire reign, seeking another throne. Denies any achievements as ruler. [BPL]

23.413 Jenny Wormald, ed. *Scotland revisited.* London: Collins & Brown, 1991. ISBN 1-85585-092-3. ‣ Collection of reprinted essays providing provocative introduction to Scotland's early modern domestic history as well as to its relations with England. [DMH]

IRELAND

23.414 T. C. Barnard. *Cromwellian Ireland: English government and reform in Ireland, 1649–1660.* London: Oxford University Press, 1975. ISBN 0-19-821858-3. ‣ Avoids land question and vexed issues of colonialism to concentrate on earnest (if often unsuccessful) efforts at reform in government, finance, law, education, and religion. [KSB]

23.415 Karl S. Bottigheimer. *English money and Irish land: the "adventurers" in the Cromwellian settlement of Ireland.* Oxford: Clarendon, 1971. ISBN 0-19-822338-2. ‣ Analysis of mid-seventeenth-century expansion of Protestant landownership as outgrowth of English (and especially parliamentary) policy. [KSB]

23.416 Brendan Bradshaw. *The dissolution of the religious orders in Ireland under Henry VIII.* London: Cambridge University Press, 1974. ISBN 0-521-20342-3. ‣ Pathbreaking work concentrating on political causes, nature, and consequences of dissolution, rather than on its morality. Finds some indigenous Protestantism. [KSB]

23.417 Brendan Bradshaw. *The Irish constitutional revolution of the sixteenth century.* Cambridge: Cambridge University Press, 1979. ISBN 0-521-22206-0. ‣ Argues for importance of 1530s (and innovations of Thomas Cromwell) in establishment of rigorous direct rule over Ireland. [KSB]

23.418 Ciaran Brady and Raymond Gillespie, eds. *Natives and newcomers: essays on the making of Irish colonial society, 1534–1641.* Dublin: Irish Academic Press, 1986. ISBN 0-7165-2378-7 (cl), 0-7165-2391-4 (pbk). ‣ Essays on group identities in Irish cultural patchwork. Strong on economic pressures of 1630s on Gaelic

lords, responses of Gaelic bards to loss of patrons, and impact of Counter-Reformation. [KSB]

23.419 Nicholas P. Canny. "The formation of the Irish mind: religion, politics, and Gaelic Irish literature, 1580–1750." *Past and present* 95.2 (1982) 91–116. ISSN 0031-2746. ‣ Important attempt to study Gaelic political and religious attitudes through literary evidence. Concludes Counter-Reformation and persecution generated specifically Irish and Catholic culture. [DMH]

23.420 Nicholas P. Canny. *From Reformation to restoration: Ireland, 1534–1660.* Dublin: Helicon; distributed by Educational Company of Ireland, 1987. ISBN 0-86167-061-2. ‣ Most up-to-date survey, strongest on sixteenth-century reforms and government's-eye view; more on religion and economics than politics for seventeenth century. Balanced and subtle throughout; useful bibliography. [KSB]

23.421 Nicholas P. Canny. *Kingdom and colony: Ireland in the Atlantic world, 1560–1800.* Baltimore: Johns Hopkins University Press, 1988. ISBN 0-8018-3603-4. ‣ Argues forcefully for English colonization in Ireland as prototype for North America, justified in both cases by sense of racial superiority over pagan natives. Discusses emergence of local Protestant ruling class increasingly seeking independence from England. [KSB]

23.422 Aidan Clarke. *The Old English in Ireland, 1625–42.* Ithaca, N.Y.: Cornell University Press, 1966. ‣ Still best treatment of peculiarly complex social and political situation in Ireland of Charles I. [KSB]

23.423 Sean J. Connolly. *Religion, law, and power: the making of Protestant Ireland, 1660–1760.* New York: Oxford University Press, 1992. ISBN 0-19-820118-4. ‣ Impressive, wide-ranging analysis of consolidation of Protestant ascendancy with thoughtful and plausible address to problem of group identity. [DMH]

23.424 Patrick J. Corish. *The Catholic community in the seventeenth and eighteenth centuries.* Dublin: Helicon; distributed by Educational Company of Ireland, 1981. ‣ Best introduction to survival of Irish culture under Anglo-Scottish onslaught. [KSB]

23.425 James Stevens Curl. *The Londonderry plantation, 1609–1914: the history, architecture, and planning of the estates of the City of London and its livery companies in Ulster.* Chichester, England: Phillimore, 1986. ISBN 0-85033-577-9. ‣ Innovative study of settlement layout and building design, as well as good survey of finances, logistics, and political history of colonial venture whose roots lay in London. [DMH]

23.426 Steven G. Ellis. *Reform and revival: English government in Ireland, 1470–1534.* Woodbridge, England and New York: Boydell for Royal Historical Society and St. Martin's, 1986. ISBN 0-312-66751-5. ‣ Reexamination of lordship's claim to consideration as integral part of Tudor territories. Controversial but based on sound and extensive scholarship. [KSB]

23.427 Steven G. Ellis. *Tudor Ireland: crown, community, and the conflict of cultures, 1470–1603.* London: Longman, 1985. ISBN 0-582-49341-2 (pbk). ‣ Balanced, detailed survey; tends to see Ireland as borderland rather than as embryonic, separate nation. Recounts shift away from use of provincial magnates to forcible English rule. [KSB]

23.428 Brendan Fitzpatrick. *Seventeenth-century Ireland: the war of religions.* Totowa, N.J.: Barnes & Noble, 1989. ISBN 0-389-20814-0. ‣ Useful survey with stress on religious dimension. Good on problem of Catholic identities and initiatives; stronger on early part of century. [DMH]

23.429 Alan Ford. *The Protestant reformation in Ireland, 1590–1641.* 1985 ed. Frankfurt: Lang, 1987. ISBN 3-8204-7471-4. ‣ Illustrates and partially explains failure of Protestant church of Ireland to find substantial following. Only study of problem. [KSB]

23.430 Raymond Gillespie. *Colonial Ulster: the settlement of East Ulster, 1600–1641*. Cork, Ireland: Cork University Press for Irish Committee for Historical Sciences, 1985. ISBN 0-902561-31-6. ▸ Original study of unplanned Scots immigration which, with growing commercial pressure on land market, reshaped Ulster society in 1620s and 1630s. [KSB]

23.431 K. Theodore Hoppen. *The common scientist in the seventeenth-century: a study of the Dublin Philosophical Society, 1683–1708*. Charlottesville: University Press of Virginia, 1970. ISBN 0-8139-0292-4. ▸ Examination of efflorescence of learning in late seventeenth- and early eighteenth-century Anglo-Ireland. [KSB]

23.432 Francis G. James. *Ireland in the empire, 1688–1770: a history of Ireland from the Williamite wars to the eve of the American Revolution*. Cambridge, Mass.: Harvard University Press, 1973. ISBN 0-674-46626-8. ▸ Useful survey of Ireland's place in eighteenth-century imperial polity and economy. [KSB]

23.433 Hugh Kearney. *Strafford in Ireland, 1633–41: a study in absolutism*. 1960 ed. Cambridge: Cambridge University Press, 1989. ISBN 0-521-37822-2 (pbk). ▸ Cold-eyed view of Irish career of Thomas Wentworth, chief secular implementer of personal rule of Charles I. [KSB]

23.434 Joseph Th. Leerssen. *Mere Irish and fior-ghael: studies in the idea of Irish nationality, its development and literary expression prior to the nineteenth century*. Amsterdam: Benjamins, 1986. ISBN 90-272-2198-7. ▸ Difficult but important study based on rarely used early modern Irish-language sources. [KSB]

23.435 Colm Lennon. *The lords of Dublin in the age of the Reformation*. Dublin: Irish Academic Press, 1989. ISBN 0-7165-2419-6. ▸ Innovative study of merchant oligarchs of Ireland's capital and England's chief garrison. Shows slow spread of Protestantism from above, until ca. 1580, and increasing tensions with Whitehall and English newcomers after 1603. [DMH]

23.436 Michael MacCarthy-Morrogh. *The Munster plantation: English migration to southern Ireland, 1583–1641*. Oxford: Clarendon, 1986. ISBN 0-19-822952-6. ▸ Fullest treatment to date of Munster plantation, although native culture and sensibilities generally overlooked in work emphasizing economic development. [KSB]

23.437 T. W. Moody et al., eds. *A new history of Ireland*. Vol. 2: *Medieval Ireland, 1169–1534*. Vol. 3: *Early modern Ireland, 1534–1691*. Vol. 4: *Eighteenth-century Ireland, 1691–1800*. Edition varies ed. Oxford: Clarendon, 1976–91. ISBN 0-19-821755-2 (v. 2), 0-19-821739-0 (v. 3), 0-19-821742-0 (v. 4). ▸ Compendious, sometimes incisive, sometimes old-fashioned, essays on politics, society, religion, and culture, both Gaelic and Anglo. Essential starting point. [KSB]

23.438 Mary O'Dowd. *Power, politics, and land: early modern Sligo, 1568–1688*. Belfast: Queen's University of Belfast, Institute of Irish Studies, 1991. ISBN 0-85389-404-3. ▸ First good study of Irish locality, examining interrelations of various groups and their changing fortunes. [DMH]

23.439 Hans S. Pawlisch. *Sir John Davies and the conquest of Ireland: a study in legal imperialism*. Cambridge: Cambridge University Press, 1985. ISBN 0-521-25328-4. ▸ Revealing study of writings of leading English lawyer who demonstrated (English) legal grounds for total conquest and subjugation of Ireland. [KSB]

23.440 M. Perceval-Maxwell. *The Scottish migration to Ulster in the reign of James I*. 1973 ed. London: Routledge & Kegan Paul, 1990. ISBN 0-901905-44-5 (pbk). ▸ Account of complexity of British migration which permanently shaped intransigent Protestantism of much of Ulster. [KSB]

23.441 David B. Quinn. *The Elizabethans and the Irish*. Ithaca, N.Y.: Cornell University Press for Folger Shakespeare Library, 1966. ▸ Suggestive, pathbreaking essay on contacts between two cultures when it appeared; now classic and still useful. [KSB]

23.442 J. G. Simms. *Jacobite Ireland, 1685–91*. London: Routledge & Kegan Paul, 1969. ISBN 0-7100-6446-2. ▸ Definitive treatment of turbulent period; apportions praise and blame sparingly, yet judiciously. [KSB]

23.443 Katharine Simms. *From kings to warlords: the changing political structure of Gaelic Ireland in the later Middle Ages*. Woodbridge, England: Boydell, 1987. ISBN 0-85115-420-4. ▸ Important study of reshaping of Gaelic politics under English lordship and emergence of something like "bastard feudalism." [DMH]

WALES

23.444 David W. Howell. *Patriarchs and parasites: the gentry of South-west Wales in the eighteenth century*. Cardiff: University of Wales Press, 1986. ISBN 0-7083-0929-1. ▸ Examines varied interests, tastes, and fortunes of elite of isolated area. Demonstrates slow reception of new economic and cultural ways and absence of challenge to continued gentry dominance. [DMH]

23.445 Geraint H. Jenkins. *The foundations of modern Wales: Wales, 1642–1780*. Oxford: Clarendon, 1987. ISBN 0-19-821734-x. ▸ Rounded synthesis stressing anglicization of culture and elite and religious enthusiasm. [DMH]

23.446 Philip Jenkins. *The making of a ruling class: the Glamorgan gentry, 1640–1790*. Cambridge: Cambridge University Press, 1983. ISBN 0-521-25003-x. ▸ Balanced, persuasive sociopolitical analysis. Ascendancy of Welsh landowners based on consolidation of socioeconomic and cultural authority and political leadership. Discusses relations between high- and low-level politics and locality and state. [KW]

23.447 Glanmor Williams. *Recovery, reorientation, and Reformation: Wales, c. 1415–1642*. Oxford: Clarendon, 1987. ISBN 0-19-821733-1. ▸ Excellent survey of peaceable integration of Wales into English political and religious order; stronger on fifteenth and sixteenth centuries. Good on Welsh literary culture. [DMH]

Britain and Ireland since 1760

Apparently in the 1870s, the word "Victorian" began to appear as an adjective to signify an era. But as early as the 1830s, there was an awareness that a new age was dawning, an age to a considerable degree defined by criticism or rejection of nearly every aspect of the preceding period we now know (and generally admire) as Georgian or, more narrowly, as the Regency. To the emerging Victorians, the Regency's architecture was boring, its politics corrupt, its economy overcontrolled, its morality dubious, and its religion distressingly worldly.

In the two decades after World War I, the English turned similarly on their immediate predecessors. They found nineteenth-century architecture pompous and fussy, its art sentimental, its religion hidebound; rampant individualism virtually equated social relations with injustice, and Victorian morality was denounced as an unholy blend of repression, cant, and hypocrisy.

This hostility was brilliantly caught in the four polemical portraits—of Cardinal Manning, Florence Nightingale, Thomas Arnold, and General Gordon—that make up Lytton Strachey's *Eminent Victorians*, published in 1918. But this interpretive line had been firmly established well before the war. As a leading example, in 1911, J. L. and Barbara Hammond, admirable exemplars of the New Liberalism, had published *The Village Labourer*, demonstrating the callousness and irresponsibility of the landed classes and the government they dominated in the treatment of the rural poor in the early nineteenth century. Broadening their attack in a succession of postwar books to take in emerging industrialism and the harsh life of the growing towns, the Hammonds presented a comprehensive view of English society a century earlier that may be fairly summed up in the title of the American abridgement of one of their books, published in 1934, *The Bleak Age*.

By the time that book appeared, historians were beginning to ask if the Victorians were quite as bad as they had been made out to be, and the answer—such being the way of revisionism—was that they were not. Translations of the several volumes of *A History of the English People in the Nineteenth Century*, by the great French historian Elie Halévy (24.2), began to appear in 1924 and over the years had an influence that is still to be felt, but probably the most important signal of a reinterpretation was a two-volume collection of essays published in 1934 as *Early Victorian England, 1830–1865*. In 1936, the editor of those volumes, G. M. Young, published *Portrait of an Age: Victorian England*, an expansion of his concluding essay that brilliantly evokes a century of immense energy and creativity. Written with broad sympathy, vast learning, and a compelling fascination with out-of-the-way lore, *Portrait of an Age*, like all great conversation, is allusive, often maddeningly so; its lack of footnotes has recently been to some extent remedied (24.7). But its faults are insignificant when set against its virtues, and the book was a potent stimulus to the revival of interest in the Victorian era. No sector underwent so dramatic a recovery as architecture, heralded by Kenneth Clark's *The Gothic Revival: An Essay in the History of Taste*, which appeared in 1928 (see also below, Hitchcock 24.307); the reputations of Victorian writers, never entirely eclipsed, were extensively rehabilitated, though appreciation of most nineteenth-century painting lagged behind and still has not generated the impressive scholarly attention that has been given to continental painters.

The social revolution that took place in Britain during and immediately after World War II has now been much diminished and in some ways reversed by that ambiguous phenomenon called Thatcherism. But it is difficult to overstate the impression made on the whole Western world in the immediate postwar years, an impression not lost on historians of Britain. The tradition of interpretation that had descended from the Hammonds and quasi-socialist writers on other periods, like the distinguished economic historian and social philosopher R. H. Tawney, had seemed confirmed by the dark years of the depression-ridden thirties; the triumph of the Labour party in 1945 and the waves of social legislation and political and economic reconstruction that followed offered a further confirmation in the promise of escape through state action. From the late 1920s, however, powerful voices among economic historians, beginning with J. H. Clapham (24.110), were actively qualifying the basis for the indictment that still dominated the outlook of most historians, particularly those who concentrated on working-class history. This clash of tradition and revision meant that the nineteenth century would become a battleground contested by historians of differing political inclinations in postwar Britain, for whom two great and influential teachers may stand as types, H. L. Beales at the London School of Economics and George Kitson Clark (24.3) at Cambridge.

Understandably, historians who entered the profession in Britain in the postwar years, and even more those who flocked to Britain from other countries, were fascinated by the emergence of the welfare state and the nationalization of so much of Britain's economy, a fascination that led to the study of earlier modes of state intervention in every aspect of life in the earlier twentieth century and, more strikingly, in the nineteenth. The contours, timing, and sources of Victorian administration became matters for intense investigation, clearly establishing that the Victorian age was not an unqualified triumph for free trade, laissez-faire, and unbridled individualism. Similarly, preoccupation with other concerns of the postwar world—the dramatic British withdrawal from empire, the refashioning of the schools and the expansion of the universities, and the reinforced prestige of the professions and the intelligentsia in a time of unparalleled artistic and academic flowering—was reflected in important historical inquiry.

The postwar years also saw a striking revival of interest in Victorian religion. This development ran counter to the pronounced secularism that had characterized much of the historical profession from its nineteenth-century beginnings, but, unlike the intensive study of the welfare state or the empire, the study of religious history was seemingly not primarily in response to current preoccupations: there was no religious revival in postwar Britain worthy of the name, and while some historians of religion were committed Christians, others were not; they simply found it impossible to ignore a factor that had directly or indirectly dominated nearly every aspect of life in nineteenth-century Britain. But only recently has this remarkable and prolonged revival of religious history begun in any important way to make an impact on the awareness of historians who work outside the field; one need not agree with all the contentions of J.C.D. Clark (23.10) to recognize his accomplishment in forcing historians to confront the omnipresence of religion in the eighteenth and nineteenth centuries.

Despite disagreements in detail, by the early 1960s there was a general consensus about the shape of early and mid-Victorian history, and more and more historians were turning to the lesser-studied late nineteenth and twentieth centuries. Moreover, the latterly neglected eighteenth century was rediscovered, and emancipation was gradually won from the pall that seemed to have been cast over it by the great, once-productive influence of Sir Lewis Namier (24.28, 24.29) and his disciples. All this meant that the early nineteenth century, while so much progress had been made in the preceding twenty years, began to lapse into an agreed orthodoxy, as the publication dates of titles listed in certain sections of this chapter will indicate.

In some respects, the social and intellectual tensions and conflicts of the late 1960s, projected onward into the 1970s, confirmed that orthodoxy, for example, in giving a new appearance of relevance to a class-based historical interpretation among social historians, historians of labor, and more generally. The discovery of "history from below" (which social historians of Britain had been in fact practicing for nearly a century) brought a valuable expansion of horizons—most importantly in the belated emphasis given to the history of women (though there, again, the field was less neglected than is sometimes maintained) and in a new interest in ethnic and racial groups in a Britain becoming far less homogeneous, while neglected aspects of everyday life, such as recreation, gained new attention.

This expansion of view entailed no radically altered interpretive structure. Scholarly specialties that might have forced a "paradigm shift" failed, at least immediately, to do so. The emergence of quantitative techniques in economic and social history tended to insulate their practitioners from more ordinary historical awareness, and the same effect has been seen in the growing disjunction—at least until the last few years—between literary and historical scholars, who seem largely to be pursuing radically different questions, though recent historical interpretations drawing on linguistic and symbolic understandings are worthy of note.

Far more important than technical or interpretive methods in contributing to the isolation of historians from each other and to a degree of interpretive stagnation has been the sheer volume of published work, whether in scholarly articles or in books. Works of synthesis have become more and more difficult to write, and specialists, often organized in their own small scholarly societies, talk increasingly to themselves. It is encouraging, therefore, to be able to report that in some fields important new departures are taking place. The history of science, technology, and medicine has advanced well beyond the older triumphalist recounting of ever-broadening successes accomplished by great men. In intellectual history discarded orthodoxies and forgotten schools of thought have been disinterred; dead ends, appalling mistakes, and chicanery have found their historians; and the importance of institutions (notably provincial institutions) and of religion in shaping what is simplistically called the "nineteenth-century mind" has been demonstrated.

To the study of the provinces has been added new attention to regional development and to the constituent nations in a country whose formal name, the United Kingdom of Great Britain and Northern Ireland, has come to seem increasingly questionable. Great strides have been made in the study of Irish history, no longer a mere adjunct to the nationalist struggle, and the same is true, on a lesser scale, of the histories of Scotland and Wales. A few historians are now attempting to write a history of Britain that is not merely a history of England with appended chapters on the Celtic fringe, but that bold stroke, like the vastly different synthesis that would be required by social historians, will have to wait for a confident assessment until the next edition of this *Guide*.

It seems probable, however, that the most sweeping alteration, already in train, has once again spread outward from economic history. From the welter of detailed and often highly technical studies of regions, industries, and separate towns and villages has begun to emerge a fundamental questioning of the reality and usefulness of the very concept of the Industrial Revolution, which has been the single most important determinant of the chronological and interpretive approach of nearly all historians who work on the last two centuries. That a profound transformation took place in English— and British—society in the period covered by this chapter is undeniable. But it was a transformation whose roots go back so far and whose incidents extend so close to the present that the notion of "revolution," with its implication of crisis, may be more misleading than helpful. Moreover, the unevenness of development and the complexity of the motivation and understanding of participants in the transformation may lead to a new ordering of questions; E. A. Wrigley (24.122) has asked if, in fact, industrialism may not be a consequence of more profound anterior changes about which we know little. Thirty years ago, when E. P. Thompson's magnificent, if flawed, interpretation, *The Making of the English Working Class* (24.247), appeared, it was predicted by nearly everyone that all future work would have to begin with it. Certainly, this work inspired a generation of important research to explore (or in a few cases to rebut) its implications, and it forced its readers to consider that class was and is a far more subtle concept than most had thought. Yet, for all its virtues, Thompson's book now begins to look more like a culmination of an older understanding than the starting point of a new one.

Such radical departures have also been speeded up by the remarkable events, however ambiguous their ultimate outcome, in eastern Europe in and after 1989. Hard historical fact has now raised so many serious questions about the validity of the Marxian approach to history—that magnificent contribution to human understanding that is both a seen and unseen determinant of so much of present-day historical thinking— that an entirely new vocabulary may be needed before the historical transformation of our own time can be translated into interpretations persuasive to the audience who will read books (or perhaps not books) of history a generation or two hence.

[Contributors: AR = Alex Roland, BJCM = Brian J. C. McKercher, CSH = Christopher S. Hamlin, FMLT = F.M.L. Thompson, IM = Iain McCalman, JTS = Jon T. Sumida, JWC = John W. Cell, MD = Michael Dintenfass, PM = Patrick Manning, PSc = T. Philip Schofield, PSt = Peter Stansky, RKW = R. K. Webb, RRM = Ralph R. Menning, SEK = Sharon E. Kingsland, SH = Sandra Herbert, TD = Tom Dunne]

GENERAL STUDIES

24.1 W. L. Burn. *The age of equipoise: a study of the mid-Victorian generation.* 1964 ed. London: Allen & Unwin, 1968. ▸ Learned, idiosyncratic, and insightful study emphasizing with great verve and originality legal and social disciplines that gave stability to society priding itself on individualism. [RKW]

24.2 Elie Halévy. *A history of the English people in the nineteenth century.* Vol. 1: *England in 1815.* Vol. 2: *The liberal awakening, 1815–1830.* Vol. 3: *The triumph of reform, 1830–1841.* Vol. 4: *Victorian years, 1841–1852.* Vol. 5: *Imperialism and the rise of labour, 1895–1905.* Vol. 6: *The rule of democracy, 1905–1915.* 1947–52 2d ed. 6 vols. E. I. Watkin, trans. New York: Barnes & Noble, 1961. ▸ Published in French 1913–47 and left incomplete at Halévy's death in 1937; remains most extended, still invaluable interpretation of period 1815–1915. First volume, extraordinarily interesting retrospective analysis of England in 1815, puts forward influential but much criticized "Halévy thesis" on role of voluntary organization, especially Methodism, in avoiding revolution. Volume 1 reprinted 1987 as *A History of the English People in 1815.* [RKW]

24.3 George Kitson Clark. *The making of Victorian England.* 1972 ed. London: Macmillan, 1991. ISBN 0-689-70049-0 (pbk). ▸ Valuable synthesis looking back from mid-Victorian era to trace major elements in creation of that distinctive society. Particularly important for role of religion. [RKW]

24.4 Norman McCord. *British history, 1815–1906.* Oxford: Oxford University Press, 1991. ISBN 0-19-822857-0 (cl), 0-19-822858-9 (pbk). ▸ Surveys politics, government and administration, and (more sketchily) economy and society for each of four segments of century divided at 1830, ca. 1850, and 1880. Excellent bibliographical guide. [RKW]

24.5 Keith Robbins. *Nineteenth-century Britain: integration and diversity.* New York: Oxford University Press, 1988. ISBN 0-19-820138-9. ▸ Brief but wide-ranging and suggestive interpretation of merging (however inconclusive)—in culture, religion, politics, and recreation—of England, Wales, Scotland, and Ireland in common British nationality. [RKW]

24.6 R. K. Webb. *Modern England, from the eighteenth century to the present.* 2d ed. New York: Harper & Row, 1980. ISBN 0-06-046974-9. ▸ General introductory survey. Basic structure is political, but treats economic, social, cultural, diplomatic, and imperial matters. Useful appendixes on peerage, Church of England, law courts, and other institutions. [RKW]

24.7 G. M. Young. *Portrait of an age: Victorian England.* 1977 2d ed. George Kitson Clark, ed. New York: Oxford University Press, 1988. ISBN 0-19-212961-9 (cl, 1977), 0-19-281005-7 (pbk). ▸ As explained in section introduction, this brilliant, elliptical, and influential book was reissued with annotations supplied, though not all quotations and allusions could be traced. Remains mine of information and suggestion. Earlier title: *Victorian England: Portrait of an Age.* [RKW]

POLITICS, ca. 1760–1900

24.8 Jeremy Black, ed. *British politics and society from Walpole to Pitt, 1742–1789.* New York: St. Martin's, 1990. ISBN 0-312-04927-7. ▸ Eight concise, authoritative essays covering English society and economy, Scotland and Ireland, parliamentary and radical politics, foreign policy, empire, and religion. Useful critical bibliographies. [RKW]

24.9 Robert Blake. *Disraeli.* New York: St. Martin's, 1967.
‣ Full-scale study of striking career of political adventurer who
became bold and innovative conservative leader. [RKW]

24.10 John Brewer. *Party ideology and popular politics at the accession of George III.* 1976 ed. Cambridge: Cambridge University
Press, 1981. ISBN 0-521-21049-6 (cl, 1976), 0-521-28701-4 (pbk).
‣ Unlike Namier 24.29, emphasizes political movements outside
Parliament with notable attention to radical insurgency of John
Wilkes and his followers. [RKW]

24.11 Michael Brock. *The great Reform Act.* London: Hutchinson, 1973. ISBN 0-09-115910-5 (cl), 0-09-115911-3 (pbk).
‣ Authoritative, detailed account of genesis and passage of 1832
Reform Act which, for all its preservative intent, profoundly
transformed political system inherited from eighteenth century.
[RKW]

24.12 Richard W. Davis. *Political change and continuity, 1760–
1885: a Buckinghamshire study.* Hamden, Conn.: Archon, 1972.
ISBN 0-208-01307-5. ‣ Careful analysis of county and country-
town constituency showing independence and self-interest of
voters, the need to cultivate them, and their responsiveness to
issues. [RKW]

24.13 H. T. Dickinson, ed. *Britain and the French Revolution,
1789–1815.* New York: St. Martin's, 1989. ISBN 0-312-02840-7.
‣ Eleven essays succinctly covering aspects of British history during revolutionary period. Excellent introduction and guide to further reading. [RKW]

24.14 John Ehrman. *The younger Pitt.* Vol. 1: *The years of
acclaim.* Vol. 2: *The reluctant transition.* 2 vols. Stanford, Calif.:
Stanford University Press, 1969–83. ISBN 0-8047-1186-0 (v. 1),
0-8047-1184-4 (v. 2). ‣ Exemplary biography, on grand scale, of
William Pitt, minister who dominated period of French Revolution. Second volume covers to 1796. [RKW]

24.15 Norman Gash. *Politics in the age of Peel: a study in the
techniques of parliamentary representation, 1830–1850.* 2d ed.
Atlantic Highlands, N.J.: Humanities, 1977. ISBN 0-391-00676-2.
‣ Explanation, both general and through case studies, of working
of politics in aftermath of Reform Act of 1832. [RKW]

24.16 Norman Gash. *Reaction and reconstruction in English politics, 1832–1852.* 1965 ed. Westport, Conn.: Greenwood, 1981.
ISBN 0-313-22927-9. ‣ Lectures published in 1965 surveying
transformation of monarchy and of political parties, role of
House of Lords in reform, and church-state conflict. [RKW]

24.17 Norman Gash. *Sir Robert Peel.* Vol. 1: *Mr. Secretary Peel:
the life of Sir Robert Peel to 1830.* Vol. 2: *Sir Robert Peel: the life of
Sir Robert Peel after 1830.* 2d ed. London: Longman, 1985–86.
ISBN 0-582-49723-X (v. 1, pbk), 0-582-49722-1 (v. 2, pbk). ‣ Magisterial biography of prime minister who transformed toryism into
conservatism, instituted numerous reforms, and carried country
into free trade by repealing Corn Laws in 1846. [RKW]

24.18 H. J. Hanham. *Elections and party management: politics in
the time of Disraeli and Gladstone.* 1959 ed. Hamden, Conn.:
Archon, 1978. ISBN 0-208-01550-7. ‣ Detailed study of working
of constituencies, elections, and political parties, following
increase in electorate in 1867 which led to emergence of modern
forms of mass politics. [RKW]

24.19 Frank Hardie. *The political influence of the British monarchy, 1868–1952.* New York: Harper & Row, 1970. ‣ Brief but
useful account of political aspect of institution undergoing notable transformation in increasingly democratic country. [RKW]

24.20 Angus Hawkins. *Parliament, party, and the art of politics in
Britain, 1855–59.* Stanford: Stanford University Press, 1987. ISBN
0-8047-1317-0. ‣ Five-year narrative important to all of period
1832–67. Argues personal narrative and political categories of late

1850s conceal bipolar orientation of politics within government
and Parliament. [RKW]

24.21 Andrew Jones. *The politics of reform, 1884.* Cambridge:
Cambridge University Press, 1972. ISBN 0-521-08376-1. ‣ In contrast to 1832 and 1867, franchise reform in 1884 and redistribution in 1885 rode no wave of popular agitation, thus justifying
this high-politics account of maneuverings of politicians at center. [RKW]

24.22 Peter Mandler. *Aristocratic government in the age of reform:
Whigs and Liberals, 1830–1852.* Oxford: Clarendon, 1990. ISBN
0-19-821781-1. ‣ Argues Whig aristocracy more effective and less
anachronistic in implementing liberal program than usually
allowed in interpretations focused on commercially centered liberalism and on Peel. [RKW]

24.23 H.C.G. Matthew. *Gladstone, 1809–1874.* New York:
Oxford University Press, 1986. ISBN 0-19-822909-7. ‣ Continuing
biography, complete through first premiership, of great liberal
prime minister by editor of Gladstone's massive diaries. Based
on editor's long authoritative introductions to successive volumes
of diaries. [RKW]

24.24 H.C.G. Matthew. *The liberal imperialists: the ideas and politics of a post-Gladstonian elite.* London: Oxford University Press,
1973. ISBN 0-19-821842-7. ‣ Careful study of small, disparate, but
important group of liberal politicians who, between 1886 and
1905, tried but failed to reorient their party. [RKW]

24.25 Norman McCord. *The Anti–Corn Law League, 1838–
1846.* 2d ed. London: Allen & Unwin, 1968. ‣ Standard account
of one of most impressive and significant extra-parliamentary
campaigns of century, which was, however, peripheral to ultimate accomplishment of repeal in political sphere. [RKW]

24.26 R. T. McKenzie and Allan Silver. *Angels in marble: working-class Conservatives in urban England.* Chicago: University of
Chicago Press, 1968. ‣ Historical and sociological survey based
on small strategic samples in 1960s. Analyzes persisting electoral
phenomenon that falsified dire predictions by antireformers in
and after 1867. [RKW]

24.27 David Cresap Moore. *The politics of deference: a study of
the mid-nineteenth-century English political system.* New York:
Barnes & Noble, 1976. ISBN 0-06-494932-X. ‣ Based chiefly on
evidence in poll books—voting lists compiled prior to secret ballot in 1872—argues for critical importance of deference of electorate to social superiors. [RKW]

24.28 L. B. Namier. *England in the age of the American Revolution.* 2d ed. New York: St. Martin's, 1961. ‣ Only volume, on
1761–63, by this author of projected narrative history of this title.
Summarizes and expands on conclusions of 24.29. Assesses character and impact of George III and traces consequences of fall
of ministers Newcastle and Bute. First published 1930. [RKW]

24.29 L. B. Namier. *The structure of politics at the accession of
George III.* 1957 2d ed. New York: St. Martin's, 1970. ‣ First published in two volumes in 1929, set agenda and methodology for
research in political history for more than a generation. Narrowly
focused on electoral politics and Parliament with important analysis of use of secret service funds. [RKW]

24.30 Ian Newbould. *Whiggery and reform, 1830–41.* Stanford,
Calif.: Stanford University Press, 1990. ISBN 0-8047-1759-1.
‣ Important survey of politics and policies during "decade of
reform," demonstrating tenuous nature of whig rule arising from
party's moderate initiatives and increasingly conservative attitudes in the country. [RKW]

24.31 Avner Offer. *Property and politics, 1870–1914: landownership, law, ideology, and urban development in England.* Cambridge: Cambridge University Press, 1981. ISBN 0-521-22414-4.

▸ Detailed examination of property market—legal structures, tenure, taxation, capital raising, development, and tensions with local government authorities. Essential background for taxation of property values in 1909 budget. [RKW]

24.32 Frank O'Gorman. *Voters, patrons, and parties: the unreformed electorate of Hanoverian England, 1734–1832.* New York: Oxford University Press, 1989. ISBN 0-19-820056-0. ▸ Analysis of organization and working of political system by studying electorate rather than oligarchs, as in Namier 24.29. While mechanics of politics remain firmly local, ideology, independence, religion, and party take on much more importance. [RKW]

24.33 Cornelius O'Leary. *The elimination of corrupt practices in British elections, 1868–1911.* Oxford: Clarendon, 1962. ▸ Careful account of background and working out of Ballot Act of 1872 and Corrupt Practices Act of 1883, which transformed electoral politics. [RKW]

24.34 Richard Pares. *King George III and the politicians.* 1953 ed. New York: Oxford University Press, 1988. ISBN 0-19-821240-2 (cl), 0-19-881130-6 (pbk). ▸ Six brilliant, influential lectures, given in 1951–52, on working of monarchical government in reign of George III. Treats politicians, Parliament, parties, ministers, cabinet, and decline of personal monarchy. [RKW]

24.35 J. P. Parry. *Democracy and religion: Gladstone and the Liberal party, 1867–1875.* Cambridge: Cambridge University Press, 1986. ISBN 0-521-30948-4. ▸ Examination of politico-religious topography. Traces declining fortunes of first Gladstone administration through issues centrally involving religion. Valuable corrective for recent anti-ideological interpretations of Victorian politics. [RKW]

24.36 Henry Pelling. *Social geography of British elections, 1885–1910.* New York: St. Martin's, 1967. ▸ Thumbnail sketches, geographical and social, of constituencies within fourteen regions, correlated with electoral data. Ingenious, revealing study of first importance. [RKW]

24.37 R. T. Shannon. *Gladstone and the Bulgarian Agitation, 1876.* 2d ed. Hamden, Conn.: Archon, 1975. ISBN 0-208-01487-x. ▸ Important account of national agitation, in which Nonconformists played vital part. Sparked by Turkish massacres, episode brought Gladstone out of retirement and led eventually to Prime Minister Disraeli's defeat in 1880 elections. [RKW]

24.38 F. B. Smith. *The making of the Second Reform Bill.* Cambridge: Cambridge University Press, 1966. ▸ Superbly distilled narrative of successive bills for franchise extension, culminating in surprising passage of sweeping act in 1867 giving parliamentary vote to large proportion of urban workingmen. [RKW]

24.39 Paul Smith. *Disraelian conservatism and social reform.* Toronto: University of Toronto Press, 1967. ▸ Careful analysis of social reform legislation, 1874–80, arguing Disraelian Tory democracy destined to be minor element in landowning party whose future was linked to business. [RKW]

24.40 E. D. Steele. *Palmerston and liberalism, 1855–1865.* Cambridge: Cambridge University Press, 1991. ISBN 0-521-40045-7. ▸ Important revisionist interpretation of domestic role of longtime foreign secretary and later prime minister, arguing he contributed significantly to victory of liberalism over aristocratic power. See also Bourne 24.373. [RKW]

24.41 Robert Stewart (v.1), Richard Shannon (v. 2), and John Ramsden (v. 3). *A history of the Conservative party.* Vol. 1: *The foundation of the Conservative party, 1830–1867.* Vol. 2: *The age of Disraeli, 1868–1881.* Vol. 3: *The age of Balfour and Baldwin, 1902–1940.* 3 vols. to date. London: Longman, 1978–92. ISBN 5-582-50712-x (v. 1), 0-582-50713-8 (v. 2), 0-582-50714-6 (v. 3). ▸ Projected five-volume work, authoritatively tracing successive transformations from old toryism to modern conservatism and

from landed- to business-oriented base and party's emergence as dominant ruling group. [RKW]

24.42 J. R. Vincent. *The formation of the British Liberal party, 1857–1868.* 2d ed. New York: Barnes & Noble, 1976. ISBN 0-06-497213-5. ▸ Influential analysis of coming together of Whigs and Peelites in Liberal party, down to first Gladstone government. Considers composition of parliamentary party and rank-and-file, leadership, and (briefly) policy. [RKW]

POLITICS SINCE 1900

24.43 Samuel H. Beer. *Modern British politics: parties and pressure groups in the collectivist age.* Rev. ed. New York: Norton, 1982. ISBN 0-393-00952-1. ▸ Influential study, first published 1965, treating both ideas behind politics in contemporary Britain and role of party and interest groups in creating more collectivist politics. [PSt]

24.44 George L. Bernstein. *Liberalism and liberal politics in Edwardian England.* London: Allen & Unwin, 1986. ISBN 0-04-942198-0 (cl), 0-04-942199-9 (pbk). ▸ Detailed study of national and local liberal politics. Argues traditional aspects of liberalism provided strength, but carried danger of decreasing appeal to voters on Left. [PSt]

24.45 Robert Blake. *Unrepentant Tory: the life and times of Andrew Bonar Law, 1858–1923, prime minister of the United Kingdom.* 1955 ed. New York: St. Martin's, 1956. ▸ Masterly biography of neglected political figure giving detailed account of complex working of politics and of adaptation of Tory party to business world. British title: *The Unknown Prime Minister.* [PSt]

24.46 Neal Blewett. *The peers, the parties, and the people: the general elections of 1910.* London: Macmillan, 1972. ISBN 0-333-09811-0. ▸ Employs close analysis of Butler's studies of contemporary elections (24.47) to present compelling picture of strong Liberal party in its last two electoral victories. [PSt]

24.47 David Butler et al. *The British general election.* New York and London: Oxford University Press, St. Martin's, and Macmillan, 1945–92. ▸ Ongoing series of studies of British general election. Instant history with all its advantages and disadvantages. First book in series, by R. B. McCallum and Alison Readman, treated 1945 election; those on all elections since by David Butler, some with co-authors. [PSt]

24.48 Joseph Campbell. *Aneurin Bevan and the mirage of British socialism.* New York: Norton, 1987. ISBN 0-393-02452-0. ▸ More political essay than biography, considers Bevan as architect of National Health Service and as moral voice for socialism; points to limitations arising from his emotionalism and inconsistencies. [PSt]

24.49 P. F. Clarke. *Lancashire and the new liberalism.* Cambridge: Cambridge University Press, 1971. ISBN 0-521-08075-4. ▸ Case study of strength of Liberal party and its ideas in one county, 1906–10. Concludes collapse of party under impact of Labour party and working-class vote was not foregone conclusion. [PSt]

24.50 James E. Cronin. *The politics of state expansion: war, state, and society in twentieth-century Britain.* London: Routledge, 1991. ISBN 0-415-03623-2. ▸ Discussion of decision making and relations of politicians and civil servants in questions of finance and budget. Very helpful for understanding growth of the state. [PSt]

24.51 George Dangerfield. *The strange death of liberal England.* 1935 ed. New York: Capricorn, 1961. ▸ Vivid, still controversial and essential account of crises over House of Lords, women's suffrage, trade unions, and Ireland, demonstrating both death of old social order and vitality of political system. [PSt]

24.52 Michael Freeden. *The new liberalism: an ideology of social reform.* 1978 ed. New York: Oxford University Press, 1986. ISBN

0-19-811961-5 (pbk). ‣ Important study of intellectual and political ideas underlying new Edwardian liberalism which gave basis for many ideas that dominated twentieth-century Britain. [PSt]

24.53 Bentley B. Gilbert. *David Lloyd George: a political life.* Vol. 1: *The architect of change, 1863–1912.* Vol. 2: *Organizer of victory, 1912–1916.* Columbus: Ohio State University Press, 1987–92. ISBN 0-8142-0432-5 (v. 1), 0-8142-0597-6 (v. 2). ‣ Thorough political study of one of two most important prime ministers of century. Volume 2 covers rise to wartime leadership in 1916. Additional volumes forthcoming. [PSt]

24.54 Martin Gilbert. *Churchill: a life.* New York: Holt, 1991. ISBN 0-8050-0615-X. ‣ One-thousand-page summary of author's eight-volume biography of arguably most important politician of century. Like big series, useful as chronicle, but short on judgment and analysis. [PSt]

24.55 Sandra Stanley Holton. *Feminism and democracy: women's suffrage and reform politics in Britain, 1900–1918.* Cambridge: Cambridge University Press, 1986. ISBN 0-521-32855-1. ‣ Analysis of relationship between suffrage campaign and political radicalism. Suggestively argues women's distinctiveness gave them skills appropriate to social reform. [PSt]

24.56 Alistair Horne. *Harold Macmillan.* Vol. 1: *Politician, 1894–1956.* Vol. 2: *1957–1986.* 1987 ed. New York: Penguin, 1991. ISBN 0-14-014530-3 (v. 1), 0-14-014532-X (v. 2). ‣ Study of prime minister who combined remnants of Tory paternalism with welfare state and elements of grand style, while adapting to post-Suez limitations on British power. Useful life story of the century. [PSt]

24.57 Peter Jenkins. *Mrs. Thatcher's revolution: the ending of the socialist era.* Cambridge, Mass.: Harvard University Press, 1988. ISBN 0-674-58832-0. ‣ Analysis of prime minister's years and their background concentrating on changes in society and politics, which made society more classless but not as envisioned by Left. Includes incisive sketches of major political figures. [PSt]

24.58 Susan Kingsley Kent. *Sex and suffrage in Britain, 1860–1914.* Princeton: Princeton University Press, 1987. ISBN 0-691-05497-5. ‣ Interprets campaign for women's suffrage and attack on double standard as struggle over sexual identity and self-determination and as central to understanding of national political life. [PSt]

24.59 Richard W. Lyman. *The first Labour government, 1924.* 1957 ed. New York: Russell & Russell, 1975. ISBN 0-8462-1784-8. ‣ Full account clarifying Labour party's characteristic problem of attempting to be moderate enough to prove claim to govern and radical enough to keep true to traditions and maintain loyalty of supporters. [PSt]

24.60 David Marquand. *Ramsay MacDonald.* London: Cape, 1977. ISBN 0-224-01295-9. ‣ Definitive biography of first Labour prime minister who stood out against World War I and who, in view of many, betrayed party when he accepted leadership of national government in 1931. [PSt]

24.61 A. M. McBriar. *Fabian socialism and English politics, 1884–1918.* Cambridge: Cambridge University Press, 1962. ‣ Excellent account of powerful influence of Fabians in shaping twentieth-century state in characteristic nonideological, empirical, elitist, semi-socialist way. [PSt]

24.62 R. T. McKenzie. *British political parties: the distribution of power within the Conservative and Labour parties.* 1963 2d ed. New York: Praeger, 1964. ‣ Functional analysis of party structure. Explains how in very different ways Tory and Labour parties tried to confine control of party to party oligarchies. [PSt]

24.63 Ralph Miliband. *Parliamentary socialism: a study in the politics of Labour.* 2d ed. New York: Monthly Review Press, 1972. ‣ Powerful analysis of Labour party's failure to maintain its ide-

ology on Left and hence, according to this interpretation, limiting its effectiveness and power. [PSt]

24.64 Kenneth O. Morgan. *The people's peace: British history, 1945–1990.* Rev. ed. Oxford: Oxford University Press, 1992. ISBN 0-19-285252-3. ‣ Comprehensive account of political history since World War II, set in context of social and cultural history. Combines both detail and overview. [PSt]

24.65 Charles L. Mowat. *Britain between the wars, 1918–1940.* 1955 ed. Boston: Beacon, 1971. ISBN 0-8070-5653-7. ‣ Witty, perceptive, far-ranging account of politics in both broad terms and significant detail. Useful despite age. [PSt]

24.66 John Naylor. *Labour's international policy.* Boston: Houghton-Mifflin, 1969. ‣ Survey of Labour party's efforts, while out of office in 1930s, to remain loyal to its pacifist past while coming to terms with intervention and collective security imposed by rise of fascism. [PSt]

24.67 Peter G. J. Pulzer. *Political representation and elections in Britain.* Rev. ed. London: Allen & Unwin, 1972. ISBN 0-04-329016-7. ‣ Broad analysis of twentieth-century political process including television, opinion polls, and canvasing. [PSt]

24.68 Keith Robbins, ed. *The Blackwell biographical dictionary of British political life in the twentieth century.* Oxford: Blackwell, 1990. ISBN 0-631-15768-9. ‣ Short sketches of political figures; more concentrated for politics than relevant entries in *Dictionary of National Biography.* [PSt]

24.69 Andrew Rosen. *Rise up women! The militant campaign of the Women's Social and Political Union, 1903–1914.* London: Routledge & Kegan Paul, 1974. ISBN 0-7100-7934-6. ‣ Definitive history of militant suffrage group. [PSt]

24.70 A.J.P. Taylor. *English history, 1914–1945.* 1965 ed. New York: Oxford University Press, 1976. ISBN 0-19-821715-3 (cl), 0-19-500304-7 (pbk). ‣ With characteristic punch and lively prose, one of most important scholars of period admirably conveys excitement and color of high politics that is his primary concern. Controversial judgments, to be treated with care. [PSt]

24.71 Trevor Wilson. *The downfall of the Liberal party, 1914–1935.* Ithaca, N.Y.: Cornell University Press, 1966. ‣ Too often Liberal party written off after fall of Asquith from premiership in 1916. Vividly captures contribution of his successor, Lloyd George, to vitality and complexity of politics between wars. [PSt]

24.72 Hugo Young. *The iron lady: a biography of Margaret Thatcher.* New York: Farrar, Straus & Giroux, 1989. ISBN 0-374-22651-2 (cl), 0-374-2251-0 (pbk). ‣ Dispassionate account of three-time prime minister who broke with Tory paternalist traditions in attempt to dismantle welfare state and change Britain according to radical Right agenda. [PSt]

LAW

Legal Structures and Jurisprudence

24.73 Brian Abel-Smith and R. B. Stevens. *Lawyers and the courts: a sociological study of the English legal system.* Cambridge, Mass.: Harvard University Press, 1967. ‣ Demonstrates entrenchment of courts and legal professions in attitudes and organization of eighteenth century. Conservatism of legal education, political influence, restrictive practices, and self-satisfaction of judges and barristers precluded reform. [PSc]

24.74 P. S. Atiyah. *The rise and fall of freedom of contract.* 1979 ed. New York: Oxford University Press, 1985. ISBN 0-19-825527-6 (pbk). ‣ Set in broad context. Shows how contract increasingly interpreted as founded on free choice of parties gives way after 1870 to reassertion of collective control and greater prominence of administrative law. [PSc]

24.75 R.C.J. Cocks. *Sir Henry Maine: a study in Victorian jurisprudence.* Cambridge: Cambridge University Press, 1988. ISBN 0-521-35343-2. ▸ Traces reception of Maine's important evolutionary account of law and use of comparative method, emphasizing commitment to reform and development of jurisprudence independent of both professional tradition and Utilitarians. [PSc]

24.76 W. R. Cornish and G. N. Clark. *Law and society in England, 1750–1950.* London: Sweet & Maxwell, 1989. ISBN 0-421-311400-1 (cl), 0-421-31150-9 (pbk). ▸ Comprehensive overview of developments in legal practice, institutions, and ideas related to those in politics, economy, and society. Illustrates expansion of activities subjected to regulation, and tenacity of legal profession in defending its position. [PSc]

24.77 David Lieberman. *The province of legislation determined: legal theory in eighteenth-century Britain.* Cambridge: Cambridge University Press, 1989. ISBN 0-521-24592-3. ▸ Discussion of development of Jeremy Bentham's legal thought in response and reaction to orthodoxies of English legal theory. How Bentham came to advocate codification as means of bringing clarity and certainty to law. [PSc]

24.78 Michael Lobban. *The common law and English jurisprudence, 1760–1850.* Oxford: Clarendon, 1991. ISBN 0-19-825293-5. ▸ Nature of common-law practice misconceived by Sir William Blackstone and in Jeremy Bentham's subsequent criticism. Law remained procedure- and not rule-based, capable of responding to changing needs of society. [PSc]

Criminal Law

24.79 Margaret DeLacy. *Prison reform in Lancashire, 1700–1850: a study of local administration.* Stanford, Calif.: Stanford University Press, 1986. ISBN 0-8047-1272-7. ▸ Exemplary local study with attention to prison reforms, medical problems, and administration. Excellent critical introduction to literature. [RKW]

24.80 David J. V. Jones. *Crime, protest, community, and police in nineteenth-century Britain.* London: Routledge & Kegan Paul, 1982. ISBN 0-7100-9008-0. ▸ Case studies dealing with crime, social protest, and police in industrial and rural areas with emphasis on economic, social, and political context. Suggestive, colorful, judicious essays. [PSc]

24.81 David Philips. *Crime and authority in Victorian England: the Black Country, 1835–1860.* Totowa, N.J.: Rowman & Littlefield, 1977. ISBN 0-87471-866-X. ▸ Detailed investigation of nature of crime and identity of criminals and victims. Questions validity of distinction between ordinary and protest crimes and notion of crime as function of class conflict. [PSc]

24.82 Leon Radzinowicz. *A history of English criminal law and its administration from 1750.* Vol. 1: *The movement for reform.* Vol. 2: *The clash between private initiative and public interest in the enforcement of the law.* Vol. 3: *Cross-currents in the movement for the reform of the police.* Vol. 4: *Grappling for control.* Vol. 5: *The emergence of penal policy.* Leon Radzinowicz and Roger Hood (v. 5). London and New York: Stevens and Macmillan, 1948–86. ISBN 0-420-46280-5 (v. 5). ▸ Pioneering, exhaustive study, written from perspective of central government policy makers, using treatises and official sources. Concentrates on reform of punishment and police, assuming progress toward ever more liberal, enlightened, and successful system. Traditional legal history concerned with legal development in terms of own internal dynamic. [PSc]

24.83 Janet Semple. *Bentham's prison: a study of the Panopticon penitentiary.* Oxford: Clarendon, 1993. ISBN 0-19-827387-8. ▸ Study based on extensive archival research of Bentham's ultimately frustrated project for model prison. Conclusive contribution to debates on Panopticon's place in Bentham's political thought and on eighteenth-century penal theory. [RKW]

24.84 Martin J. Wiener. *Reconstructing the criminal: culture, law, and policy in England, 1830–1914.* Cambridge: Cambridge University Press, 1990. ISBN 0-521-35045-X. ▸ Sociologically oriented study showing how nineteenth-century paradigm of responsible individual, leading to new prison regime and certainty of punishment, was replaced in twentieth century by less punitive, more welfarist sanctions. [PSc]

ADMINISTRATION

24.85 J.E.D. Binney. *British public finance and administration, 1774–92.* Oxford: Clarendon, 1958. ▸ Detailed account of financial administration in crucial early stages of its reform from Lord Shelburne to younger Pitt. [RKW]

24.86 Emmeline W. Cohen. *The growth of the British civil service, 1780–1939.* 1941 ed. New Haven: Archon, 1965. ▸ Still only full account of creation and continuing evolution of modern civil service. [RKW]

24.87 Oliver MacDonagh. *Early Victorian government, 1830–1870.* New York: Holmes & Meier, 1977. ISBN 0-8419-0304-2. ▸ Authoritative summary of initiatives that transformed scope and structure of state in factory and mining legislation, poor law, local government, public health, public order, Ireland, and civil service reform. [RKW]

24.88 Roy M. MacLeod. "Statesmen undisguised." *American historical review* 78.5 (1973) 1386–1405. ISSN 0002-8762. ▸ Reviews controversy over "Victorian revolution in government" and its sources in ideas and practice. Principal authors in discussion were Oliver MacDonagh and Henry Parris. [RKW]

24.89 Roy M. MacLeod, ed. *Government and expertise: specialists, administrators, and professionals, 1860–1919.* Cambridge: Cambridge University Press, 1988. ISBN 0-521-30428-8. ▸ Thirteen essays examining role of experts in specific bureaucratic situations in Britain and empire in nineteenth and early twentieth centuries. [RKW]

24.90 Henry Parris. *Constitutional bureaucracy: the development of British central administration since the eighteenth century.* New York: Kelley, 1969. ▸ Effective account of uneven transition of branch of government entwined with parliamentary politics and immersed in patronage to apolitical professional civil service in place by about 1870. [RKW]

24.91 Gillian Sutherland, ed. *Studies in the growth of nineteenth-century government.* Totowa, N.J.: Rowman & Littlefield, 1972. ISBN 0-87471-080-4. ▸ Important collection of ten studies emphasizing Utilitarian influence, Trevelyan-Northcote Report, and education. [RKW]

LOCAL GOVERNMENT

24.92 William Ashworth. *The genesis of modern British town planning: a study in economic and social history of the nineteenth and twentieth centuries.* London: Routledge & Paul, 1954. ▸ Valuable survey of problems created by population growth and expanding towns, of attempts to deal with them by rebuilding and by developing new towns and suburbs, and of planning legislation from 1909 to 1947. [RKW]

24.93 Derek Fraser. *Urban politics in Victorian England: the structure of politics in Victorian cities.* Leicester: Leicester University Press; distributed by Humanities, 1976. ISBN 0-7185-1145-X. ▸ Studies of four levels of political activity in provincial towns—parochial and township administration, municipal government, parliamentary elections, and political agitations (free trade, suffrage, and education). [RKW]

24.94 E. P. Hennock. *Fit and proper persons: ideal and reality in nineteenth-century local government.* Montreal: McGill-Queens University Press, 1973. ISBN 0-7735-0154-1. ‣ Careful analysis of composition and working of municipal councils in Birmingham and Leeds between municipal reform in 1830s and 1914, with due attention to issues and ideas, often rooted in religion. [RKW]

24.95 David Owen. *The government of Victorian London, 1855-1889: the Metropolitan Board of Works, the vestries, and the City corporation.* Roy M. MacLeod, ed. Cambridge, Mass.: Belknap, 1982. ISBN 0-674-35885-6. ‣ Examination of sole metropolitan administrative agency in mid-Victorian decades and case studies of resistance of localities to centralized government. Completed by students and admirers after Owen's death in 1968. [RKW]

24.96 John Prest. *Liberty and locality: Parliament, permissive legislation, and ratepayers' democracies in the nineteenth century.* New York: Oxford University Press, 1990. ISBN 0-19-820175-3. ‣ Suggestive essay on varieties of local administration from decline of eighteenth-century private-bill legislation to mid-nineteenth century. Two localities—Ryde in Isle of Wight and Huddersfield in Yorkshire—examined in detail. [RKW]

24.97 Andrew Saint, ed. *Politics and the people of London: the London County Council, 1889-1965.* London: Hambledon, 1989. ISBN 1-85285-029-9. ‣ Essays, admittedly tentative and commendably free from triumphalism, surveying manifold activities of famous London governing body through eras of dominance by Progressives, municipal reformers, and Labour party. [RKW]

24.98 Sidney Webb and Beatrice Webb. *English local government.* Vol. 1: *The parish and the county.* Vols. 2-3: *The manor and the borough.* Vol. 4: *Statutory authorities for special purposes.* Vol. 5: *The story of the king's highway.* Vol. 6: *English prisons under local government.* Vol. 7: *English poor law history, Part 1.* Vols. 8-9: *English poor law history, Part 2: The last hundred years.* Vol. 10: *English poor law policy.* Vol. 11: *The history of liquor licensing in England.* 1903-29 ed. 11 vols. Hamden, Conn.: Archon, 1963. ‣ Magisterial study, by leaders of Fabian Socialists, of institutions of local government from earliest times to nineteenth century, originally in nine volumes (1906-22). Last two volumes of this reissue published separately from original series (1903, 1929). [RKW]

URBAN AND REGIONAL HISTORY

24.99 Asa Briggs. *Victorian cities.* 1965 ed. New York: Harper & Row, 1970. ‣ Pioneering essays, dating from 1963, on urban phenomenon generally and on Manchester, Leeds, Birmingham, London, new town of Middlesbrough, and Melbourne in Australia by dean of urban historians. [RKW]

24.100 H. J. Dyos. *Victorian suburb: a study of the growth of Camberwell.* 1961 ed. Leicester: Leicester University Press, 1966. ‣ Traces emergence of middle-class suburb south of River Thames, revealing much about speculative development; provision of infrastructure, churches, shops, and schools; and ties to growing city. [RKW]

24.101 H. J. Dyos and Michael Wolff, eds. *The Victorian city: images and realities.* 1973 ed. 2 vols. London: Routledge & Kegan Paul, 1976-78. ISBN 0-7100-7384-4 (set, 1973), 0-7100-8458-7 (v. 1), 0-7100-8812-4 (v. 2). ‣ Vast, profusely illustrated collection of essays—ranging from brilliant to dubious—embodying social, architectural, literary, and cultural perspectives. London and Manchester predominate, to neglect of other important places and subjects. [RKW]

24.102 John R. Kellett. *The impact of railways on Victorian cities.* London: Routledge & Kegan Paul, 1969. ISBN 0-7100-6315-6. ‣ Imposing, detailed study of physical impact and direct economic effects of railway. Includes five case studies on Birmingham, Manchester, Liverpool, Glasgow, and London. [RKW]

24.103 Donald J. Olsen. *The growth of Victorian London.* New York: Holmes & Meier, 1976. ISBN 0-8419-0284-4. ‣ Magnificent analysis of expansion of London from its Georgian base with attention to patterns of development, architectural styles, growth of suburbs, provision of working-class housing, and transportation networks. [RKW]

24.104 A. Temple Patterson. *Radical Leicester: a history of Leicester, 1780-1850.* Leicester: University College, 1954. ‣ Despite age, excellent example of provincial town history. Covers economic and social history of town, including effects of chartism and transformation of politics by municipal reform after 1835. [RKW]

24.105 Francis Sheppard. *London, 1808-1870: the infernal wen.* Berkeley: University of California Press, 1971. ISBN 0-520-01847-8. ‣ Sweeping account of explosive growth of world's largest city—its economic base, transport, religion and schools, public health, and radical politics—concluding with essay on living in London. [RKW]

24.106 F.M.L. Thompson. *Hampstead: building a borough, 1650-1964.* Boston: Routledge & Kegan Paul, 1974. ISBN 0-7100-7747-5. ‣ Exemplary study of development of isolated area north of London into one of most prestigious parts of metropolis. Also important, in history of Hampstead Heath, for preservation of open space. [RKW]

24.107 P. J. Waller. *Democracy and sectarianism: a political and social history of Liverpool, 1868-1939.* Liverpool: Liverpool University Press, 1981. ISBN 0-85323-074-9. ‣ Large-scale narrative history of great port city riven by ethnic and religious divisions, chiefly structured around local politics but with perceptive analysis of wider context. [RKW]

24.108 P. J. Waller. *Town, city, and nation: England, 1850-1914.* New York: Oxford University Press, 1983. ISBN 0-19-219176-4 (cl), 0-19-289163-4 (pbk). ‣ Ambitious, suggestive effort to see urban phenomenon as a whole in period of rapid growth with attention to types of towns, development, rural-urban relations, and government and services. [RKW]

ECONOMIC HISTORY

General Studies

24.109 David Cannadine. "Past and present in the English Industrial Revolution, 1880-1980." *Past and present* 103 (1984) 131-72. ISSN 0031-2746. ‣ Examination of successive analyses of late eighteenth- and early nineteenth-century economy. Argues prevailing historical assessments in each period bore close relationship to contemporary perceptions of economy. [MD]

24.110 J. H. Clapham. *An economic history of modern Britain.* Vol. 1: *The early railway age, 1830-1850.* Vol. 2: *Free trade and steel, 1850-1886.* Vol. 3: *Machines and national rivalries, 1886-1914.* 1926-39 ed. 3 vols. Cambridge: Cambridge University Press, 1967-68. ‣ Gradualist, optimistic account, stressing continuities and regional diversity. Treats demography, agriculture, industrial organization, transport, commerce, money and banking, economic policy, and standard of living. [MD]

24.111 N.F.R. Crafts. *British economic growth during the Industrial Revolution.* Oxford: Clarendon, 1985. ISBN 0-19-873066-7. ‣ Downward revision of estimates of eighteenth- and nineteenth-century growth, arguing for gradualist understanding of industrialization, noting precociousness of agricultural improvement and early transfer of resources to industry. [MD]

24.112 François Crouzet. *The Victorian economy.* New York: Columbia University Press, 1982. ISBN 0-231-05542-0 (cl), 0-231-05543-9 (pbk). ‣ Richly detailed survey, ca. 1830-1914, encompassing structure and performance of economy as whole and characteristics of individual sectors. Sees post-1870 slowdown rooted in sluggish innovation ultimately attributable to social values and attitudes. [MD]

24.113 Bernard Elbaum and William Lazonick, eds. *The decline of the British economy.* 1986 ed. Oxford: Clarendon, 1987. ISBN 0-19-828494-2 (cl, 1986), 0-19-877281-5 (pbk). ► Collection of essays elaborating institutionalist explanation of industrial decline. Emphasizes inability to transform atomistic organization of economy by mass production and corporate forms of managerial coordination. [MD]

24.114 Roderick Floud and Donald N. McCloskey, eds. *The economic history of Britain since 1700.* 2d ed. 2 vols. Cambridge: Cambridge University Press, 1993. ISBN 0-521-41498-9 (v. 1, cl), 0-521-42520-4 (v. 1, pbk). ► Essays explicitly using social scientific models and statistical methods to examine demography, technological change, supply of labor and capital, transport, agriculture, and social change in three periods dividing at 1860 and 1914. [MD]

24.115 H. J. Habakkuk. *American and British technology in the nineteenth century: the search for labour-saving inventions.* 1962 ed. Cambridge: Cambridge University Press, 1967. ► Analysis of contrasting technological responsiveness in terms of availability of resources and market opportunities. Argues against view that British entrepreneurs were ignorant of technology or irrationally indifferent to innovation. [MD]

24.116 Leslie Hannah. *The rise of the corporate economy.* 2d ed. London: Methuen, 1983. ISBN 0-416-34850-5 (cl), 0-416-34860-2 (pbk). ► Study of rise of large-scale corporations and increase in industrial concentration, noting central place of mergers and acquisitions in transition to managerial capitalism. [MD]

24.117 C. H. Lee. *The British economy since 1700: a macroeconomic perspective.* Cambridge: Cambridge University Press, 1986. ISBN 0-521-32973-6 (cl), 0-521-33861-1 (pbk). ► Broad interpretation emphasizing slow growth as enduring feature of British economic history over long term; modest contribution of manufacturing to economy; and labor-intensive nature of industry. [MD]

24.118 Paul Mantoux. *The Industrial Revolution in the eighteenth century: an outline of the beginnings of the modern factory system in England.* 1961 rev. ed. Chicago: University of Chicago Press, 1983. ISBN 0-226-50384-4 (pbk). ► Classic account of changes in farming, textile production, energy provision, and engineering culminating in factory system and its consequences. Published (French) in 1905, subsequently revised and translated. [MD]

24.119 Peter Mathias. *The first industrial nation: an economic history of Britain, 1700–1914.* 2d ed. London: Methuen, 1983. ISBN 0-416-33290-0 (cl), 0-416-33300-1 (pbk). ► Concise study of emergence of industrial economy from predominantly rural, relatively impoverished, socially stratified, but highly commercial society, noting improvement in condition of ordinary people in time of sweeping change. [MD]

24.120 R.C.O. Matthews, C. H. Feinstein, and J. C. Odling-Smee. *British economic growth, 1856–1973.* Stanford, Calif.: Stanford University Press, 1982. ISBN 0-8047-1110-0. ► Examination of short- and long-term performance of economy and its constituent sectors, employing growth-accounting framework. Vital source of quantitative information showing persistent lag in productivity. [MD]

24.121 Patrick O'Brien and Caglar Keyder. *Economic growth in Britain and France, 1780–1914: two paths to the twentieth century.* London: Allen & Unwin, 1978. ISBN 0-04-330288-2. ► Innovative study contrasting superior productivity of British agriculture, based on concentrated land ownership and capital-intensive mixed farming, with inferior productivity of unskilled, labor-

intensive British industry. Rejects Britain as paradigmatic case of industrialization. [MD]

24.122 E. A. Wrigley. *Continuity, chance, and change: the character of the Industrial Revolution in England.* Cambridge: Cambridge University Press, 1988. ISBN 0-521-35648-2. ► Reinterpretive essays questioning whether industrialization was cumulative, progressive, unitary phenomenon, emphasizing temporally coincident but accidentally related innovations in substituting mineral resources for limited organic products of land and for animate sources of energy. [MD]

Demography

24.123 Michael Anderson. *Family structure in nineteenth-century Lancashire.* Cambridge: Cambridge University Press, 1971. ISBN 0-521-08237-4. ► Pioneering sociological study of impact of industrialization and urbanization on working-class kinship system, emphasizing endurance of system when economic and normative pressure for maintenance was lacking. [MD]

24.124 Dudley Baines. *Migration in a mature economy: emigration and internal migration in England and Wales, 1861–1900.* Cambridge: Cambridge University Press, 1985. ISBN 0-521-30153-X. ► Calculates rates of emigration and return during peak period of overseas movement, finding migrants predominantly urban and decisions affected more by information about destinations than by conditions in region of origin. [MD]

24.125 J. A. Banks. *Prosperity and parenthood: a study of family planning among the Victorian middle classes.* 1954 ed. London: Routledge & Kegan Paul, 1969. ISBN 0-7100-3324-9. ► Explanation of emergence of family limitation among professional and business classes in terms of changes in incomes and living costs and of aspirations to comfort and status. See also 24.126. [MD]

24.126 J. A. Banks. *Victorian values: secularism and the size of families.* London: Routledge & Kegan Paul, 1981. ISBN 0-7100-0807-4. ► Sequel to 24.125, emphasizing mechanisms by which changes in living standards and aspirations translated into preferences for smaller families. [MD]

24.127 David Levine. *Reproducing families: the political economy of English population history.* Cambridge: Cambridge University Press, 1987. ISBN 0-521-33256-7 (cl), 0-521-33785-2 (pbk). ► Locates fundamental demographic developments in transition from feudalism to capitalism. Demise of cottage economy characterized by prudential late marriage occasioned population explosion with impoverishing effects leading in turn to fertility restraint. [MD]

24.128 Angus McLaren. *Birth control in nineteenth-century England.* New York: Holmes & Meier, 1978. ISBN 0-8419-0349-2. ► Examination of both ideological debates about family limitation and increasing resort of working-class families to traditional contraceptive practices. Especially strong on role of working-class women in restricting family size. [MD]

24.129 Robert Woods and John Woodward, eds. *Urban disease and mortality in nineteenth-century England.* New York: St. Martin's, 1984. ISBN 0-312-83434-9. ► Essays charting temporal and spatial dimensions of age-specific mortality patterns. Generally skeptical of contribution of professional medicine and sanitary revolution to decline in mortality and emphasizes improved food supply and better diet. [MD]

24.130 E. A. Wrigley and Roger Schofield. *The population history of England: a reconstruction.* 1981 ed. Cambridge: Cambridge University Press, 1989. ISBN 0-521-35688-1 (pbk). ► Exhaustive analysis of parish register data to establish patterns of mortality, fertility, and nuptiality, locating population dynamic primarily in rising marital fertility due to falling age of marriage, linked to changes in real wages. [MD]

Agriculture

24.131 J. D. Chambers and G. E. Mingay. *The agricultural revolution, 1750–1880.* 1966 ed. London: Batsford, 1969. ISBN 0-7134-1358-1 (pbk). ▸ Revisionist account of institutional and technological innovations, changing government policies, and social, economic, and political consequences. Emphasizes enclosure of common fields and changes in cropping practices, rejects idea of social catastrophe for rural population. [MD]

24.132 P. E. Dewey. *British agriculture in the First World War.* London: Routledge, 1989. ISBN 0-415-02637-7. ▸ Demonstrates relative stability of output in face of shortages of labor, feedstuffs, fertilizers, and machinery as resulting from adaptability of farming system and from milling policies rather than state policy. [MD]

24.133 B. A. Holderness. *British agriculture since 1945.* Manchester: Manchester University Press, 1985. ISBN 0-7190-1722-X. ▸ Sound description of role of farming patterns, marketing arrangements, labor supply, government policy, and Common Market in relative prosperity of agriculture, as well as social and environmental implications of farming. [MD]

24.134 G. E. Mingay, ed. *The agrarian history of England and Wales.* Vol. 6: *1750–1850.* Cambridge: Cambridge University Press, 1989. ISBN 0-521-22762-7. ▸ Essays providing encyclopedic account of farming and rural work and life in era of population growth, transport improvements, and vast expansion and diversification of markets. [MD]

24.135 P. J. Perry. *British farming in the Great Depression, 1870–1914: an historical geography.* Newton-Abbot, England: David & Charles, 1974. ISBN 0-7153-6267-4. ▸ Study of downward trend in farming after 1870. Argues period not unmitigated disaster but transition from intensive "high farming" to more diversified industry with greatly varied economic and social effects. [MD]

24.136 Michael Turner. *English parliamentary enclosure: its historical geography and economic history.* Hamden, Conn.: Archon, 1980. ISBN 0-208-01786-0. ▸ Detailed discussion of extent, distribution, and chronology of parliamentary enclosure, identifying two separate periods of intensive enclosure, ending in 1780 and 1815. Explained by inadequacy of land supply and landowner-ship patterns. [MD]

Industry

24.137 B.W.E. Alford. *W. D. and H. O. Wills and the development of the U.K. tobacco trade, 1786–1965.* London: Methuen; distributed by Barnes & Noble, 1973. ISBN 0-416-76640-4. ▸ Comprehensive history of preeminent enterprise in major consumer-goods industry. Especially good on marketing and consequences for business organization of American mass-production technology. [MD]

24.138 I.C.R. Byatt. *The British electrical industry, 1875–1914: the economic returns to a new technology.* Oxford: Clarendon, 1979. ISBN 0-19-828270-2. ▸ Survey of supply and diffusion of new American and German technology. Attributes slow utilization of electricity and modest scale of electrical manufacturing to sluggishness of economy and relative expense of electricity. [MD]

24.139 D. C. Coleman. "Gentlemen and players." *Economic history review, Second series* 26.2 (1973) 210–29. ISSN 0013-0117. ▸ Meditations on twin cults of educated amateur and practical man in nineteenth century. Traces ambiguous implications of gentlemanly ideal for business performance. [MD]

24.140 Charlotte Erickson. *British industrialists: steel and hosiery, 1850–1950.* 1959 ed. Brookfield, Vt.: Gower, 1986. ISBN 0-566-05141-9. ▸ Pioneering investigation of social origins, education, marriage choices, and career trajectories of manufacturers.

Impact of technological and organizational change on recruitment of business leaders. [MD]

24.141 D. A. Farnie. *The English cotton industry and the world market, 1815–1896.* Oxford: Clarendon, 1979. ISBN 0-19-822478-8. ▸ Analysis of trade fluctuations, business organization, and industrial structure of cotton during century of its preeminence. Critical influence of changes in American supply and Indian demand beyond control of Lancashire. [MD]

24.142 Michael W. Flinn (v. 2), Roy Church (v. 3), Barry Supple (v. 4), and William Ashworth (v. 5). *The history of the British coal industry.* Vol. 2: *1700–1830: the Industrial Revolution.* Vol. 3: *1830–1913: Victorian pre-eminence.* Vol. 4: *1913–1946: the political economy of decline.* Vol. 5: *1946–1982: the nationalized industry.* 4 vols. to date. Oxford: Clarendon, 1984–87. ISBN 0-19-828283-4 (v. 2), 0-19-828284-2 (v. 3), 0-19-828294-X (v. 4), 0-19-828295-8 (v. 5). ▸ Monumental study commissioned by National Coal Board, combining comprehensive account of industry's history with detailed analysis of mining life and thorough account of complex and contentious politics of coal. [MD]

24.143 Pat Hudson. *The genesis of industrial capital: a study of the West Riding wool textile industry, ca. 1750–1850.* Cambridge: Cambridge University Press, 1986. ISBN 0-521-25671-2. ▸ Study of financing of woolen and worsted industries during transition to factory production. Emphasizes primacy of self-financing, local and informal sources of credit, and importance of entrepreneurial respectability. [MD]

24.144 Wayne Lewchuck. *American technology and the British vehicle industry.* Cambridge: Cambridge University Press, 1987. ISBN 0-521-30269-2. ▸ Study of technological change and industrial relations using game theory. Finds managerial failure to control shop floor and concomitant restraints on technological innovation. [MD]

24.145 Peter Mathias. *The brewing industry in England, 1700–1830.* Cambridge: Cambridge University Press, 1959. ▸ Comprehensive account of agriculture-based mass-consumer industry. Charts industrialization of urban brewing, principally in London, and emergence of modern production and distributional practices. [MD]

24.146 Donald N. McCloskey. *Economic maturity and entrepreneurial decline: British iron and steel, 1870–1913.* Cambridge, Mass.: Harvard University Press, 1973. ISBN 0-674-22875-8. ▸ Employs neoclassical theory and statistical methods to assess technological responsiveness and productivity. Contends no profitable techniques neglected and efficiency maintained at internationally competitive level. [MD]

24.147 Sidney Pollard. *The genesis of modern management: a study of the Industrial Revolution in Britain.* Cambridge, Mass.: Harvard University Press, 1965. ▸ Pathbreaking study of managerial imperatives, evolving by trial and error rather than theory, and of technological and organizational innovations that created factory system. Discusses training and deployment of salaried personnel, labor recruitment and supervision, and financial controls. [MD]

24.148 Raphael Samuel. "Workshop of the world: steam power and hand technology in mid-Victorian Britain." *History workshop* 3 (1977) 6–72. ISSN 0309-2984. ▸ Examination of production techniques in wide range of industries showing slow process of mechanization and extensive reliance on hand labor, due to technical difficulties, market uncertainties, cost-benefit calculations, and customer preference. [MD]

24.149 Lars G. Sandberg. *Lancashire in decline: a study in entrepreneurship, technology, and international trade.* Columbus: Ohio State University Press, 1974. ISBN 0-8142-0199-7. ▸ Important neoclassical economic history critical of hypothesis of entrepreneurial failure. Argues cotton masters chose most effective spinning and weaving technology and that collapse in interwar years due to falling overseas demand beyond industry control. [MD]

24.150 Steven Tolliday. *Business, banking, and politics: the case of British steel, 1918–1939.* Cambridge, Mass.: Harvard University Press, 1987. ISBN 0-674-08725-9. ▸ Attributes inability of steel to reorganize for economy of scale to institutional barriers within and among firms, problems of industrial financing, and state's posture toward the industry. [MD]

24.151 Karel Williams, John Williams, and Dennis Thomas. *Why are the British bad at manufacturing?* London: Routledge & Kegan Paul, 1983. ISBN 0-7100-9561-9 (pbk). ▸ Attributes poor performance to effects of institutional environment, particularly in areas of managerial control over labor, financing, state-business relations, and composition of demand. Case studies of motor vehicles, shipbuilding, and electrical engineering. [MD]

Service Industries

24.152 Y. Cassis. "Bankers in English society in the late nineteenth century." *Economic history review, Second series* 38.2 (1985) 210–29. ISSN 0013-0117. ▸ Analysis of education, residence patterns, social activities, and marriage choices of metropolitan bankers. Argues banking elite integrated with landed aristocracy without surrendering London business. Resulting identity of outlook spared financiers from political intervention. [MD]

24.153 Stanley Chapman. *The rise of merchant banking.* London: Allen & Unwin, 1984. ISBN 0-04-332094-5. ▸ Evolution of private houses dealing in international trade, government loans, and industrial issues. Covers structure of industry, competition, changing functions, and business practices. Critical of performance in late Victorian and Edwardian periods. [MD]

24.154 Michael Collins. *Money and banking in the UK: a history.* London: Croom Helm, 1988. ISBN 0-7099-0760-5. ▸ Survey of 1826–1986 covering increasing concentration of banks, decline in deposits compared to other assets, substitution of interventionist for laissez-faire monetary policy, and enduring subordination of domestic policy to international exchange rates. [MD]

24.155 H. J. Dyos and Derek H. Aldcroft. *British transport: an economic survey from the seventeenth century to the twentieth.* Leicester: Leicester University Press, 1969. ISBN 0-7185-1081-X. ▸ Broad overview emphasizing innovations in techniques and organization of passenger and freight traffic from canals, through railroads and steamships, to internal combustion engine and civil aviation. Includes regulation and economic impact of transportational change. [MD]

24.156 W. Hamish Fraser. *The coming of the mass market, 1850–1914.* Hamden, Conn.: Archon, 1981. ISBN 0-208-01960-X. ▸ Study of significant changes in consumption and underlying innovations in production and distribution. Discusses multiple-branch firms, cooperatives, department stores, and consequent revolution in retailing. [MD]

24.157 G. R. Hawke. *Railways and economic growth in England and Wales, 1840–1870.* Oxford: Clarendon, 1970. ISBN 0-19-828249-4. ▸ Employs neoclassical theory and statistical methods to demonstrate that after thirty to forty years of investment and construction, railways saved some 10 percent of national income—about twice their contribution in United States. [MD]

24.158 Adam W. Kirkaldy. *British shipping: its history, organization, and importance.* 1914 ed. New York: Kelley, 1970. ISBN 0-678-05558-0. ▸ Comprehensive account to 1914. Treats ship design, evolution of trade routes, ownership patterns, organization, state regulation, and data on fleet size, freight carried, capital investment, costs, and profits. [MD]

24.159 R. C. Michie. *The London and New York stock exchanges,* *1850–1914.* London: Allen & Unwin, 1987. ISBN 0-04-332117-8. ▸ Comparative analysis of evolution, operations, and policies amidst technological and economic changes, linking securities markets to money and capital markets. Best account to date of City of London's role in financing domestic industry. [MD]

24.160 R. S. Sayers. *The Bank of England, 1891–1944.* 1976 ed. 3 vols. Cambridge: Cambridge University Press, 1986. ISBN 0-521-21067-4 (v. 1, cl, 1976), 0-521-21068-2 (v. 2, cl, 1976), 0-521-21066-6 (v. 3, cl, 1976), 0-521-31022-9 (pbk, set). ▸ Evolution of central banking from Baring crisis through World War II. Treats governance, policy, response to war, dislocation of world trade, mass unemployment, international monetary collapse, and domestic recovery. [MD]

24.161 Jack Simmons. *The Victorian railways.* New York: Thames & Hudson, 1991. ISBN 0-500-25110-X. ▸ Well-illustrated, panoramic study ranging from railway machinery, structures that carried it, and men who built them to impressions of railways on senses and changes in ordinary life. See also Kellet 24.102. [MD]

24.162 Oliver M. Westall, ed. *The historian and the business of insurance.* Manchester: Manchester University Press, 1984. ISBN 0-7190-0998-7. ▸ Diverse essays on fire, life, and marine insurance from mid-eighteenth century to 1960s. Discusses business organization, marketing techniques, and enterprise and innovation in a major export industry. [MD]

Standard of Living

24.163 John Burnett. *Plenty and want: a social history of food in England from 1815 to the present day.* 3d ed. London: Routledge & Kegan Paul, 1988. ISBN 0-415-00861-1. ▸ Absorbing account of food and food consumption in and outside home for every social level from palace to slum, complete with sample budgets, nutritional analysis, food preparation, and food quality. [FMLT]

24.164 Roderick Floud, Annabel Gregory, and Kenneth Wachtel. *Health, height, and history: nutritional status in the United Kingdom, 1750–1980.* Cambridge: Cambridge University Press, 1990. ISBN 0-521-30314-1. ▸ Using data on height, shows early industrialization resulted in absolute and relative improvement in working-class standard of living but urban disamenities in mid-nineteenth century caused deterioration. [MD]

24.165 Joel Mokyr. "Is there still life in the pessimist case? Consumption during the Industrial Revolution, 1790–1850." *Journal of economic history* 48.1 (1988) 69–92. ISSN 0022-0507. ▸ Econometric analysis of consumption of tea, tobacco, sugar, and coffee, showing consumption did not increase before 1850, so first decades of industrialization may not have raised standard of living. [MD]

24.166 Arthur J. Taylor, ed. *The standard of living in Britain in the Industrial Revolution.* London: Methuen, 1975. ISBN 0-416-08250-5 (cl), 0-416-08260-2 (pbk). ▸ Collection of essays including classic exchange between the pessimist Eric Hobsbawm and the optimist R. M. Hartwell and earlier work by Gilboy, Tucker, and Ashton. Lengthy introduction summarizes debate before recent innovations. [MD]

24.167 Jeffrey G. Williamson. *Did British capitalism breed inequality?* Boston: Allen & Unwin, 1985. ISBN 0-04-942186-7. ▸ Ambitious study using formal general-equilibrium analysis. Argues unusual wartime conditions slowed growth and thwarted improvement until 1820. Material conditions improved thereafter but inequality also increased. [MD]

SOCIAL HISTORY

General Studies

24.168 S. G. Checkland. *The rise of industrial society in England,* *1815–1885.* 1964 ed. London: Longman, 1971. ISBN 0-582-

48221-6 (cl), 0-582-48239-9 (pbk). ‣ Unsurpassed attempt to bring together narrative of economic development, analysis of social classes, elites, entrepreneurs, and their ideas, with some politics. Excellent introduction, slightly dated. [FMLT]

24.169 Harold J. Perkin. *The origins of modern English society, 1780–1880.* 1969 ed. London: Routledge, 1991. ISBN 0-415-05922-4. ‣ Ambitious, not unsuccessful essay in comprehensive, non-Marxist social history, portraying emergence of new class society out of Old Regime in response to modernization and through dialectic of conflicting ideals. [FMLT]

24.170 Harold J. Perkin. *The rise of professional society: England since 1880.* London: Routledge, 1989. ISBN 0-415-00890-5. ‣ Stimulating, controversial; sweeping sequel to 24.169. Argues professional ideal has taken over society, business, government, and institutions with private sector professionals routing public sector professionals after 1979. [FMLT]

24.171 John Stevenson. *British society, 1914–45.* Harmondsworth: Penguin, 1984. ISBN 0-14-022084-4 (pbk). ‣ Comprehensive account, descriptive and quantified, of social life, organization, and institutions during two world wars and interwar period. Guide to social legislation and administration, little politics. No overall thesis. [FMLT]

24.172 F.M.L. Thompson. *The rise of respectable society: a social history of Victorian Britain, 1830–1900.* Cambridge, Mass.: Harvard University Press, 1988. ISBN 0-674-77285-7. ‣ Synthesis of recent specialized studies. Argues society developed into multiplicity of groups or classes, each largely autonomous in determining its own standards of acceptable and unacceptable conduct. [FMLT]

24.173 F.M.L. Thompson, ed. *The Cambridge social history of Britain, 1750–1950.* Vol. 1: *Regions and communities.* Vol. 2: *People and their environment.* Vol. 3: *Social agencies and institutions.* 3 vols. Cambridge: Cambridge University Press, 1990. ISBN 0-521-38567-9 (set), 0-521-25788-3 (v. 1), 0-521-25789-1 (v. 2), 0-521-25790-5 (v. 3). ‣ Up-to-date accounts by leading historians of state of the art and of debate on regions, family, work, housing, diet, leisure, education, health, religion, crime, philanthropy, voluntary associations, and state and social policies. Extensive bibliographies. Indispensable. [FMLT]

Social Relations and Social Classes

24.174 Gertrude Himmelfarb. *The idea of poverty: England in the early industrial age.* 1983 ed. New York: Vintage, 1985. ISBN 0-394-53062-4 (cl, 1983), 0-394-72607-3 (pbk). ‣ Persuasive attempt to employ idea of poverty as alternative to Marxist theory of class formation and conflict and as master concept for understanding intellectual, social, and administrative changes in early industrialization. [FMLT]

24.175 Patrick Joyce. *Visions of the people: industrial England and the question of class, 1848–1914.* Cambridge: Cambridge University Press, 1991. ISBN 0-521-37152-X. ‣ Employing linguistic theory, argues class is insufficient and often misleading concept. Popular politics and popular culture analyzed by deconstructing texts from speeches and entertainment. Difficult but important book. [FMLT]

24.176 Ross McKibbin. *Ideologies of class: social relations in Britain, 1880–1950.* Oxford: Oxford University Press, 1990. ISBN 0-19-295243-4. ‣ Collection of author's essays on gambling, hobbies, and aspects of working-class culture and their challenge to concepts of class solidarity. Vigorous debunking of myths of labor history. [FMLT]

24.177 R. J. Morris. *Class and class consciousness in the Industrial Revolution, 1780–1850.* London: Macmillan, 1979. ISBN 0-333-15454-1. ‣ Critical review of historiography of class formation,

especially working class. Examines and dissects approaches of British Marxist historians. Good undergraduate text. [FMLT]

24.178 R. S. Neale. *Class in English history, 1680–1850.* Totowa, N.J.: Barnes & Noble, 1981. ISBN 0-389-20177-4. ‣ Critical account of historians' use of concepts of class and class consciousness. Sympathetic to Marxists, offers own five-class model as superior to traditional three-class structure. [FMLT]

24.179 Alistair J. Reid. *Social classes and social relations in Britain, 1850–1914.* London: Macmillan Education, 1992. ISBN 0-333-434846-9 (pbk). ‣ Critical review of historiography of class structure, moving beyond reductionists to reintegrate study of aristocracy, ruling class, bourgeoisie, and working classes. Excellent undergraduate text. [FMLT]

Aristocracy and the Upper Classes

24.180 J. V. Beckett. *The aristocracy in England, 1660–1914.* Oxford: Blackwell, 1986. ISBN 0-631-13391-7. ‣ Survey of extensive secondary literature on rural, industrial, urban, family, and political life of titled and (to lesser extent) untitled landed aristocracy. [FMLT]

24.181 David Cannadine. *The decline and fall of the British aristocracy.* 1990 ed. New York: Anchor, 1992. ISBN 0-385-42103-6 (pbk). ‣ Large, witty, anecdotal study of decline in fortune, power, and status of many aristocratic (chiefly titled) landowners, 1880–1980. Thin on survivors from Victorians and on aristocratic recruits since 1880s. Highly readable. [FMLT]

24.182 Leonore Davidoff. *The best circles: society, etiquette, and the season.* 1973 ed. London: Cresset Library, 1986. ISBN 0-09-168761-6 (pbk). ‣ Superb, very readable sociological study of development and social functions of rituals and ceremonies of Victorian high society. [FMLT]

24.183 Mark Girouard. *The Victorian country house.* Rev. ed. New Haven: Yale University Press, 1979. ISBN 0-300-02390-1. ‣ Indispensable account of physical setting of aristocratic life and developing functional specialization of country-house plans, and detailed individual treatment of new Victorian country houses. [FMLT]

24.184 W. D. Rubenstein. *Men of property: the very wealthy in Britain since the Industrial Revolution.* New Brunswick, N.J.: Rutgers University Press, 1981. ISBN 0-8135-0927-0. ‣ Pioneering, controversial study of top wealth-holders on basis of nonlanded wealth. Argues for dominance of land over other sources of wealth and dominance of commercial-financial and metropolitan wealth over industrial-manufacturing and provincial. [FMLT]

24.185 F.M.L. Thompson. *English landed society in the nineteenth century.* London: Routledge & Kegan Paul, 1963. ‣ Examination of finances, economy, social life, and political influence of landed aristocracy and gentry. Demonstrates prolongation of landed preeminence to 1914, through own wealth and capacity to absorb new blood. [FMLT]

SEE ALSO
    23.266 Lawrence Stone and Jeanne C. Fawtier Stone. *An open elite? England, 1540–1880.*

Middle and Lower Middle Classes

24.186 Gregory Anderson. *Victorian Clerks.* Manchester: Manchester University Press, 1976. ISBN 0-7190-0653-8. ‣ Study of social origins, employment, housing, religion, and politics of commercial clerks. [FMLT]

24.187 R. A. Buchanan. *The engineers: a history of the engineering profession in Britain, 1750–1914.* London: Kingsley, 1989. ISBN 1-85302-036-2. ‣ Charts rise in professional and social status, chiefly through Institution of Civil Engineers, and growing fragmentation of profession through increasing specialization in late nineteenth century. [FMLT]

24.188 Geoffrey Crossick, ed. *The lower middle class in Britain, 1870–1914.* New York: St. Martin's, 1977. ISBN 0-312-49980-9. ‣ Essays by several hands on emergence of salaried and self-employed lower middle class as distinct but not unified class. Covers religion, jobs, housing, and status of clerks, shopkeepers, and teachers. [FMLT]

24.189 Leonore Davidoff and Catherine Hall. *Family fortunes: men and women of the English middle class.* Chicago: University of Chicago Press, 1987. ISBN 0-226-13732-5 (cl), 0-226-13733-3 (pbk). ‣ Constructs large theories about nature of family firm and business middle class based largely on case studies of business and kinship networks of two families. Challenging, but not completely convincing. [FMLT]

24.190 Daniel Duman. *The English and colonial bars in the nineteenth century.* London: Croom Helm, 1983. ISBN 0-85664-468-4. ‣ Examination of social origins, education, careers, incomes, and politics of barristers and judges practicing in England and colonies. [FMLT]

24.191 Anthony Howe. *The cotton masters, 1830–1860.* Oxford: Oxford University Press, 1984. ISBN 0-19-821894-X. ‣ Major study of Lancashire industrialists who financed and managed leading early Victorian industry. Treats social origins, education, religion, politics, and life styles as well as their businesses. [FMLT]

24.192 David J. Jeremy. *Capitalists and Christians: business leaders and the churches in Britain, 1900–1960.* Oxford: Clarendon, 1990. ISBN 0-19-820121-4. ‣ Rare study of interrelationship of religion and business by quantified examination of three samples of business leaders at benchmark dates. [FMLT]

24.193 Theodore Koditschek. *Class formation and urban industrial society: Bradford, 1750–1850.* Cambridge: Cambridge University Press, 1990. ISBN 0-521-32771-7. ‣ Important exploration of class formation as a whole, bourgeois liberal class balanced against industrial working class. Full treatment of town's economy and of voluntarism; skimpy on political structures. [FMLT]

24.194 R. J. Morris. *Class, sect, and party: the making of the British middle class: Leeds, 1820–1850.* Manchester: Manchester University Press; distributed by St. Martin's, 1990. ISBN 0-7190-2225-8. ‣ Detailed study of political, philanthropic, and cultural activities. Maintains formation of urban middle class was elite-led by business and professional network, not marked by great wealth or family connections. [FMLT]

24.195 W. J. Reader. *Professional men: the rise of the professional classes in nineteenth-century England.* New York: Basic Books, 1966. ‣ Racy account of each of main professions, old and new, their functions, organization, and status. Overtaken by later research on some professions (e.g., Buchanan 24.187, Duman 24.190); still only comprehensive guide. [FMLT]

24.196 W. D. Rubenstein. *Elites and the wealthy in modern British history.* New York: St. Martin's, 1987. ISBN 0-312-00947-X. ‣ Convenient collection of author's essays (with some overlap of argument with Rubenstein 24.184) on income and wealth of upper middle class, education, and social status. Use of non-landed wealth at death as determinant can distort for large land-owners. [FMLT]

24.197 Martin J. Wiener. *English culture and the decline of the industrial spirit, 1850–1980.* 1981 ed. Cambridge: Cambridge University Press, 1988. ISBN 0-521-23418-2. ‣ Extremely influential, highly controversial, very readable essay on supposed cultural roots of apparent decline in entrepreneurial vigor as explanation of relative industrial decline. [FMLT]

24.198 Janet Wolff and John Seed, eds. *The culture of capital: art,* *power, and the nineteenth-century middle class.* Manchester: Manchester University Press; distributed by St. Martin's, 1988. ISBN 0-7190-2460-9. ‣ Seven pioneering essays on provincial middle-class culture, differing from Rubenstein 24.196 and Wiener 24.197, challenging thesis of middle-class failure to develop ideological or cultural independence and its supposed gentrification. [FMLT]

Women

24.199 Sandra Burman, ed. *Fit work for women.* New York: St. Martin's, 1979. ISBN 0-312-29417-4. ‣ Eight essays from varied perspectives of lawyers, sociologists, economists, and historians on waged and voluntary women's occupations with emphasis on domestic and quasi-domestic work. [FMLT]

24.200 Carol Dyhouse. *Girls growing up in late Victorian and Edwardian England.* London: Routledge & Kegan Paul, 1981. ISBN 0-7100-0821-X. ‣ Persuasive portrayal of education and socialization of girls in femininity, in middle and working classes, in home, and in formal schooling. [FMLT]

24.201 Pat Jalland. *Women, marriage, and politics, 1860–1914.* 1986 ed. Oxford: Oxford University Press, 1988. ISBN 0-19-822668-3 (cl, 1986), 0-19-282087-7 (pbk). ‣ Personal and private history of public women, wives, sisters, and daughters of politically prominent men. Destroys with riveting direct evidence many preconceptions about sexuality, dependence, deference, and reticence. [FMLT]

24.202 Jane Lewis. *Women in England, 1870–1950.* Bloomington: Indiana University Press, 1984. ISBN 0-253-36608-9 (cl), 0-253-28926-2 (pbk). ‣ Important survey of women's social and economic roles, covering working and middle classes and critical historiography of subject. Argues women neither free agents nor helpless victims of male power. [FMLT]

24.203 F. K. Prochaska. *Women and philanthropy in nineteenth-century England.* Oxford: Clarendon, 1980. ISBN 0-19-822627-6 (cl), 0-19-822628-4 (pbk). ‣ Reveals vast range and variety of philanthropic activity undertaken by women of all social classes from poorest to richest, far surpassing official expenditure on health, education, and poor relief. [FMLT]

24.204 Pat Thane. "Later Victorian women, 1867–1900." In *Later Victorian Britain.* T. R. Gourvish and Alan O'Day, eds., pp. 175–208. New York: St. Martin's, 1988. ISBN 0-312-01568-2. ‣ Refreshingly skeptical reappraisal of stereotypes of women's experience in society and economy. Reviews separate spheres, sexuality, family limitation, marriage, housekeeping, and work. [FMLT]

24.205 Martha Vicinus, ed. *Suffer and be still: women in the Victorian age.* 1972 ed. London: Methuen, 1980. ISBN 0-416-74340-4. ‣ Eleven essays on aspects of middle- and working-class women and their social, occupational, family, and sexual lives. Contains extensive bibliographical essay. [FMLT]

Immigrants and Ethnic Groups

24.206 Geoffrey Alderman. *Modern British Jewry.* Oxford: Clarendon, 1992. ISBN 0-19-820145-I. ‣ Authoritative, critical, readable, comprehensive social, cultural, intellectual, and political history of "old" and "new" Jewish communities in Britain since mid-nineteenth century. [FMLT]

24.207 Colin Holmes. *John Bull's island: immigration and British society, 1871–1971.* Basingstoke: Macmillan, 1988. ISBN 0-333-28209-4 (cl), 0-333-28210-8 (pbk). ‣ Survey of different immigrant groups—Irish, German, Italian, "Russian," Indian, Pakistani, West Indian, African, Jews, blacks, etc.—and their reception. Critical probing of Britain's reputation as tolerant country. [FMLT]

24.208 Lynn Hollen Lees. *Exiles of Erin: Irish migrants in Victorian London.* Ithaca, N.Y.: Cornell University Press, 1979. ISBN 0-8014-1176-9. ▸ Pioneering study of adaptation and alienation of London Irish, emphasizing development of urban Catholic culture. [FMLT]

Leisure

24.209 Peter Bailey. *Leisure and class in Victorian England: rational recreation and the contest for control, 1830–1885.* 1978 ed. London: Methuen, 1987. ISBN 0-416-02142-5 (pbk). ▸ Study of class relations, ideological and religious conflict, commercialization, and emergence of autonomous cultures. Taming of popular recreation in urban settings. [FMLT]

24.210 Hugh Cunningham. *Leisure in the Industrial Revolution, 1780–1880.* New York: St. Martin's, 1980. ISBN 0-312-47894-1. ▸ Interpretive survey of nature and uses of leisure, mainly but not exclusively by working classes, emphasizing sociocultural significance of individual and group participation in sport, entertainment, and self-improvement. [FMLT]

24.211 Cyril Ehrlich. *The piano: a history.* Rev. ed. Oxford: Clarendon, 1990. ISBN 0-19-816181-6 (cl), 0-19-816171-9 (pbk). ▸ Enchanting combination of technical, economic, social, and cultural history seen through development, manufacture, marketing, and social diffusion of piano. [FMLT]

24.212 Tony Mason, ed. *Sport in Britain: a social history.* Cambridge: Cambridge University Press, 1989. ISBN 0-521-35119-7. ▸ Essays by different hands on social history of ten popular sports, chiefly since mid-nineteenth century, focusing on organization, participation, popularity, betting, and competitions. [FMLT]

24.213 Wray Vamplew. *The turf: a social and economic history of horse racing.* London: Allen Lane, 1976. ISBN 0-7139-9730-4. ▸ Entertaining scholarly study of racing and betting from eighteenth century to 1939. Examines owners, breeders, trainers, jockeys, bookies, punters, and law. [FMLT]

24.214 J. K. Walton. *The English seaside resort: a social history, 1750–1914.* New York: St. Martin's, 1983. ISBN 0-312-25527-6. ▸ Study of supply and demand for seaside holidays, equally interesting on resort building and differentiation, and on styles of holiday-making of different classes. [FMLT]

Social Policy

24.215 John Burnett. *A social history of housing, 1815–1985.* 1986 rev. ed. London: Routledge, 1990. ISBN 0-415-05921-6. ▸ Doubly important for treatment of middle-class, suburban, and rural housing as well as of urban working classes and for its analysis of housing policies at municipal and national levels. First published in 1978. [FMLT]

24.216 Derek Fraser. *The evolution of the British welfare state: a history of social policy since the Industrial Revolution.* 2d ed. Basingstoke: Macmillan, 1973. ISBN 0-333-35999-2 (pbk). ▸ Best single-volume account of policies and institutions of state. Treats local government, poor law, factories, public health, education, old age, and unemployment. [FMLT]

24.217 Bentley B. Gilbert. *British social policy, 1914–1939.* Ithaca, N.Y.: Cornell University Press, 1970. ISBN 0-8014-0578-5. ▸ Discussion of immediate origins, in government and civil service, of policies on unemployment, health, housing, and old age. Extensive use of public records, cabinet papers, and parliamentary debates. [FMLT]

24.218 José Harris. *William Beveridge: a biography.* Oxford: Clarendon, 1977. ISBN 0-19-822459-1. ▸ Exemplary study of distinguished civil servant and university administrator whose name is associated with two reports that laid foundation for mid-twentieth-century welfare state. [RKW]

24.219 Brian Harrison. *Drink and the Victorians: the temperance question in England, 1815–1872.* Pittsburgh: University of Pittsburgh Press, 1971. ISBN 0-8229-3223-7. ▸ Excellent account of pressure-group tactics and policies of United Kingdom Alliance (antidrink), of drinking habits and alcohol consumption of Victorians, and of regulation of drink trade. [FMLT]

24.220 Anthony S. Wohl. *Endangered lives: public health in Victorian Britain.* Cambridge, Mass.: Harvard University Press, 1983. ISBN 0-674-25241-1. ▸ Survey of public health problems and achievements in Victorian Britain, including infant health, environmental pollution, housing, occupational diseases, and changes in local and central government. [CSH]

LABOR AND WORKING-CLASS HISTORY
General Studies

24.221 John Benson, ed. *The working class in England, 1875–1914.* London: Croom Helm, 1985. ISBN 0-7099-0692-7. ▸ Introductory text bringing together recent revisionist studies. Includes essays on family socialization, changing standard of health, and class consciousness as explored through strikes and industrial relations. [IM]

24.222 J.F.C. Harrison. *The common people: a history from the Norman Conquest to the present.* Totowa, N.J.: Barnes & Noble, 1984. ISBN 0-389-20470-6. ▸ Chronicle of working lives, religious beliefs, leisure pursuits, and diversity of experience of people "usually left out of history." Masterly survey aimed at general reader. [IM]

24.223 Eric Hopkins. *The rise and decline of the English working classes, 1918–1990: a social history.* New York: St. Martin's, 1991. ISBN 0-312-06156-0. ▸ Survey of changing life and labor of English working classes. Commentary on standard of living, waning of Labour party, and changing working-class image under new conservatism. [IM]

24.224 John Rule. *The labouring classes in early industrial England, 1750–1850.* London: Longman, 1986. ISBN 0-582-49172-X (pbk). ▸ Synthesis of current knowledge on material conditions, culture, and social response of working class during period of dramatic upheaval. Reviews major alternative interpretations of class. [IM]

24.225 John Stevenson. *Popular disturbances in England, 1700–1870.* 2d ed. New York: Longman, 1992. ISBN 0-582-08101-7. ▸ Detailed survey of causes, frequency, and beliefs of popular disturbances. Eschews grand general theory but explores theoretical and methodological problems. [IM]

24.226 David Vincent. *Bread, knowledge, and freedom: a study of nineteenth-century working-class autobiography.* 1981 ed. London: Methuen, 1982. ISBN 0-416-34670-7 (pbk). ▸ Dissection of main themes of 142 autobiographies covering period 1790–1850. Explores contribution autobiography makes to historical record and tackles problems of using it as primary source. [IM]

24.227 J. M. Winter, ed. *The working class in modern English history: essays in honour of Henry Pelling.* Cambridge: Cambridge University Press, 1983. ISBN 0-521-23444-1. ▸ Essays questioning whether record of organized struggle represents history of laboring people as a whole. Documents outlook, organization, and policies of labor movement while exploring broader social history. [IM]

Popular and Working-Class Movements

24.228 John Belchem. *Orator Hunt: Henry Hunt and English working-class radicalism.* New York: Oxford University Press, 1986. ISBN 0-19-822759-0. ▸ Meticulously researched biography of early nineteenth-century reformer, seeking to rescue him from reputation as vainglorious, empty demagogue, stressing pioneering working-class radicalism. [IM]

24.229 Malcolm Chase. *The people's farm: English radical agrarianism, 1775–1840.* New York: Oxford University Press, 1988. ISBN 0-19-820105-2. ▸ Traces long tradition and development of agrarian reform ideas through to Chartism. Explains why agrarianism remained integral to working-class radicalism in age of industrialization. [IM]

24.230 H. A. Clegg and A. F. Thompson, eds. *A history of British trade unions since 1889.* Vol. 1: *1889–1910.* Oxford: Clarendon, 1964. ▸ Comprehensive history of British trade unions which challenges many theories outlined in pioneering studies of trade unionism by Sidney and Beatrice Webb. Volume 2 not yet published. [IM]

24.231 James Epstein. *The lion of freedom: Feargus O'Connor and the chartist movement, 1832–1842.* London: Croom Helm, 1982. ISBN 0-85664-922-8. ▸ Novel view of controversial Irish leader challenging stereotype of egotistical demagogue and emphasizing his consistency, self-sacrifice, and leadership qualities. [IM]

24.232 Albert Goodwin. *The friends of liberty: the English democratic movement in the age of the French Revolution.* Cambridge, Mass.: Harvard University Press, 1979. ISBN 0-674-32339-4. ▸ Reassessment of complex influence of French Revolution on character and content of movement for parliamentary reform. Deals judiciously with question of revolutionary intent and evaluates government repression. [IM]

24.233 James Hinton. *Labour and socialism: a history of the British labour movement, 1867–1974.* Amherst: University of Massachusetts Press, 1983. ISBN 0-87023-393-9. ▸ Concise history and Marxist-influenced critique of labor movement from formation to 1970s. Explores relationship between organized labor and idea of socialist transformation of society. [IM]

24.234 Eric J. Hobsbawm and George Rudé. *Captain Swing: a social history of the great English agricultural uprising of 1830.* 1968 ed. New York: Norton, 1975. ISBN 0-393-00793-6. ▸ Classic Marxist analysis of social protest movement that swept English countryside. Relates economic and social structure of changing society to pattern of popular rural agitation. [IM]

24.235 Iain McCalman. *Radical underworld: prophets, revolutionaries, and pornographers in London, 1795–1840.* Cambridge: Cambridge University Press, 1988. ISBN 0-521-39755-0. ▸ Study of small band of revolutionaries between French Revolution and rise of chartism, arguing disreputable culture of tavern, blasphemous chapel, and bawdy literature must be considered alongside more respectable labor movements. [IM]

24.236 Ross McKibbin. *The evolution of the Labour party, 1910–1924.* 1974 ed. New York: Oxford University Press, 1983. ISBN 0-19-821850-8 (cl, 1974), 0-19-821899-0 (pbk). ▸ Incisive analysis of party development, illuminating character of party; explores its replacement of Liberals on Left and examines failure of party leadership to create inclusive working-class movement. [IM]

24.237 Lucy Middleton, ed. *Women in the labour movement: the British experience.* Totowa, N.J.: Rowman & Littlefield, 1977. ISBN 0-87471-942-9. ▸ Essays surveying women's contribution to British labor movement in nineteenth century. Does not fully explore tensions experienced by women in dual roles as domestic and waged workers. [IM]

24.238 Dudley Miles. *Francis Place, 1771–1854: the life of a remarkable radical.* New York: St. Martin's, 1988. ISBN 0-312-01953-X. ▸ Biography of influential moderate radical and Benthamite who helped secure repeal of Combination Acts in 1824. Understates contradictions inherent in his politics and personality. [IM]

24.239 A. E. Musson. *Trade union and social history.* Portland, Oreg.: Cass, 1974. ISBN 0-7146-3031-4. ▸ Perceptive studies in aspects of trade union history, among them industrial relations in printing trades. Illuminates some of theoretical problems encountered by labor historian. [IM]

24.240 Richard Price. *Masters, unions, and men: work control in building and the rise of labour, 1830–1914.* Cambridge: Cambridge University Press, 1980. ISBN 0-521-22882-4. ▸ Ambitious work demythologizing role of trade unionism. Situates rise of organized labor within wider social context and investigates experience of work in shaping institutional structures. [IM]

24.241 I. J. Prothero. *Artisans and politics in early nineteenth-century London: John Gast and his times.* Folkestone, England: Dawson, 1979. ISBN 0-7129-0826-9. ▸ Authoritative account of London popular radicalism prior to chartism with trade unionism as secondary theme. Argues, in defending "respectable independence," artisans no less militant or class conscious than other workers. [IM]

24.242 John Saville. *1848: the British state and the chartist movement.* Cambridge: Cambridge University Press, 1987. ISBN 0-521-33341-5. ▸ Investigates crucial moment for state and popular radicalism. Revises accepted theories on chartist strength and on links with Irish republican politics; ascribes demise of movement to state surveillance and repression. [IM]

24.243 George Spater. *William Cobbett: the poor man's friend.* 2 vols. Cambridge: Cambridge University Press, 1982. ISBN 0-521-22216-8 (v. 1), 0-521-24077-8 (v. 2). ▸ Comprehensive biography of most popular and influential nineteenth-century journalist. Portrays Cobbett as progressive as well as tory radical who enlarged language and ideology of protest. [IM]

24.244 William Stafford. *Socialism, radicalism, and nostalgia: social criticism in Britain, 1775–1830.* New York: Cambridge University Press, 1987. ISBN 0-521-32792-X (cl), 0-521-33989-8 (pbk). ▸ Summary and criticism of ten radical texts beginning with Thomas Spence's *Real Rights of Man* and ending with William Cobbett's *Rural Rides.* Lucid discussion of intellectual origins of each text. [IM]

24.245 Barbara Taylor. *Eve and the New Jerusalem: socialism and feminism in the nineteenth century.* New York: Pantheon, 1983. ISBN 0-394-52766-6 (cl), 0-394-71321-4 (pbk). ▸ Focus on women active in Owenite socialism, arguing women's rights lay at core of ideas on social progress. Reintegrates feminism into history of labor movement. [IM]

24.246 Dorothy Thompson. *The chartists: popular politics in the Industrial Revolution.* New York: Pantheon, 1984. ISBN 0-394-51140-9 (cl), 0-394-72474-7 (pbk). ▸ Scholarly account of chartism exploring why so many people believed political change could improve their situation. Assesses gains and losses without losing sight of movement's complexity. [IM]

24.247 E. P. Thompson. *The making of the English working class.* 1963 ed. London: Gollancz, 1980. ISBN 0-575-02842-4. ▸ Massive work of scholarship that forced rethinking of concepts of class. Emphasizes importance of political experience and shows workingmen as complex figures actively molding own history. [IM]

24.248 Joel H. Wiener. *Radicalism and free-thought in nineteenth-century Britain: the life of Richard Carlile.* Westport, Conn.: Greenwood, 1983. ISBN 0-313-23532-5. ▸ Study of important radical journalist, publisher, and activist. Sensitive exploration of his idiosyncratic and individualistic brand of republicanism and free thought. [IM]

Conditions of Labor

24.249 Alan Armstrong. *Farmworkers: a social and economic history, 1770–1980.* London: Batsford, 1988. ISBN 0-7134-4391-X.

▶ Survey of agricultural laborers in home, workplace, local community, and wider social environment. Charts social and economic plight while stressing shared interest between workers and employers as against Marxian class hostility. [IM]

24.250 Angela V. John, ed. *Unequal opportunities: women's employment in England, 1800–1918.* Oxford: Blackwell, 1986. ISBN 0-631-13955-9 (cl), 0-631-13956-7 (pbk). ▶ Essays exploring relationship between sex, skill, and status; women's changing employment opportunities; and participation in various facets of labor movement. Good introduction with comprehensive bibliographical note. [IM]

24.251 Patrick Joyce. *Work, society and politics: the culture of the factory in later Victorian England.* New Brunswick, N.J.: Rutgers University Press, 1980. ISBN 0-8135-0899-1 (cl), 0-8135-1083-X (pbk). ▶ Controversial argument that social order in Lancashire marked by deference and paternalism rather than class conflict. Suggests relevance of this structure of deference to other areas of labor history. [IM]

24.252 Raphael Samuel, ed. *Village life and labour.* London: Routledge, 1975. ISBN 0-7100-7499-9. ▶ Studies of "people's history," covering such topics as female rural workers, harvesting, and quarry labor in nineteenth century. Emphasizes texture and experience of laboring lives. [IM]

24.253 Gareth Stedman Jones. *Outcast London: a study in the relationship between classes in Victorian society.* 1971 ed. New York: Pantheon, 1984. ISBN 0-394-72547-6. ▶ Analysis of nineteenth-century London labor market, focusing on unskilled and underemployed workers. Challenges popular concept of urban degeneration and provides new understanding of middle-class response to "outcast London." [IM]

Working-Class Culture

24.254 Richard Hoggart. *The uses of literacy.* 1957 ed. New Brunswick, N.J.: Transaction, 1992. ISBN 0-88738-892-2. ▶ Sensitive, evocative study of changes in working-class culture during 1940s and 1950s, drawing on author's boyhood experiences. Traces replacement of traditional popular urban culture by unhealthy mass culture. [IM]

24.255 Stuart Laing. *Representations of working-class life, 1957–1964.* Basingstoke: Macmillan, 1986. ISBN 0-333-37998-5 (cl), 0-333-37999-3 (pbk). ▶ Explores paradox between apparently declining working-class culture (see Hoggart 24.254) and contemporaneous renaissance in working-class fiction, film, theater, and broadcasting. Addresses contemporary debates on high and mass culture. [IM]

24.256 Thomas Walter Laqueur. *Religion and respectability: Sunday schools and working-class culture, 1780–1850.* New Haven: Yale University Press, 1976. ISBN 0-300-01859-2. ▶ Explores interaction of class and ideology in Sunday school movement. Challenges view that schools are merely instruments of bourgeois social control, as working class ultimately made them their own. [IM]

24.257 Standish Meacham. *A life apart: English working class, 1890–1914.* Cambridge, Mass.: Harvard University Press, 1977. ISBN 0-674-53075-6. ▶ Explores fabric of working-class lives. Sees working-class culture as means of coping with economic deprivation rather than as source of labor militancy. [IM]

24.258 Ruth Richardson. *Death, dissection, and the destitute.* 1987 ed. New York: Penguin, 1989. ISBN 0-14-022862-4 (pbk). ▶ Vivid study of early nineteenth-century interaction of working class, legislators, and medical profession. Sees 1832 Anatomy Act, making pauper corpses available for medical education, as direct assault on working-class sensibilities, stimulating unity in defense of cultural norms. [IM]

24.259 Elizabeth Roberts. *A woman's place: an oral history of working-class women, 1890–1940.* Oxford: Blackwell, 1984. ISBN 0-631-13572-3. ▶ Using reminiscences of 160 subjects, stresses positive aspects of women's perception of their lives. Suggests most saw class rather than gender as key determinant. [IM]

24.260 R. K. Webb. *The British working-class reader, 1790–1848: literacy and social tension.* 1955 ed. New York: Kelley, 1971. ▶ Classic work exploring challenge presented by literate working class and showing how middle-class educationalists attempted to use cheap literature as social control. [IM]

Some Theoretical Studies

24.261 James Epstein. "Understanding the cap of liberty: symbolic practice and social conflict in early nineteenth-century England." *Past and present* 122 (1989) 75–118. ISSN 0031-2746. ▶ Study of radicals' use of symbolic gestures to reinforce and subvert meanings apparent within verbal or political discourse. Focuses on cap of liberty worn by French Jacobins to explore radical mobilization, language, and ideology. [IM]

24.262 John Foster. *Class struggle and the Industrial Revolution: early industrial capitalism in three English towns.* New York: St. Martin's, 1974. ▶ Controversial work on class and class consciousness, chiefly in factory town of Oldham. Employs Lenin's model, distinguishing between economic trade-union consciousness and political class consciousness. [IM]

24.263 Robert Glenn. *Urban workers in the early Industrial Revolution.* New York: St. Martin's, 1984. ISBN 0-312-83472-1. ▶ Detailed study of cotton town of Stockport, contesting Thompson's theory of class formation (see 24.247). Although trade organizations proliferated, they did not consolidate into class movement. [IM]

24.264 Gareth Stedman Jones. *Languages of class: studies in English working-class history, 1832–1982.* Cambridge: Cambridge University Press, 1984. ISBN 0-521-25648-8 (cl), 0-521-27631-4 (pbk). ▶ Collection of author's essays on topics ranging from chartism through recent crises in Labour party. Significant theoretical work charting thought of sophisticated Marxist historian who has assimilated sociolinguistic theory. [IM]

SEE ALSO
1.132 Perry Anderson. *Arguments within English Marxism.*
23.267 E. P. Thompson. *Customs in common.*

RELIGIOUS HISTORY

Church, State, and Politics

24.265 Walter L. Arnstein. *The Bradlaugh case: atheism, sex, and politics among the late Victorians.* 1965 ed. Columbia: University of Missouri Press, 1983. ▶ Careful account of 1880s controversy in Parliament, courts, and public opinion over seating of avowed atheist in House of Commons. [RKW]

24.266 G.F.A. Best. *Temporal pillars: Queen Anne's Bounty, the Ecclesiastical Commissioners, and the Church of England.* Cambridge: Cambridge University Press, 1964. ▶ Impressive work approaching general administrative history of Church of England. Ranges far beyond history of two organizations aimed at improving church incomes. [RKW]

24.267 Robert Hole. *Pulpits, politics, and public order in England, 1760–1832.* Cambridge: Cambridge University Press, 1989. ISBN 0-521-36486-8. ▶ Suggestive work qualifying Clark's view of consistent eighteenth-century political theology (23.10), noting denominational differences and shift from dynastic to social concerns among representative ministers (and a few laymen). [RKW]

24.268 Stephen Koss. *Nonconformity in modern British politics.* Hamden, Conn: Archon, 1975. ISBN 0-208-01553-1. ▶ Careful chronicle of decline of Nonconformist political influence, mainly centered in Liberal party, from its peak at beginning of twentieth century to 1939. [RKW]

24.269 G.I.T. Machin. *Politics and the churches in Great Britain.* Vol. 1: *1832 to 1868.* Vol. 2: *1868 to 1921.* New York: Oxford University Press, 1977–87. ISBN 0-19-826436-4 (v. 1), 0-19-820106-0 (v. 2). ▸ Authoritative, exhaustive history of church-state relations and involvement of churches in politics, first in time of redefinition and reform and then in period of consolidation and of retreat of churches from central position in British life. [RKW]

Churches and Society

24.270 Jeffrey Cox. *The English churches in a secular society: Lambeth, 1870–1930.* New York: Oxford University Press, 1982. ISBN 0-19-503019-2. ▸ Important critique of theories of secularization. Uses sociologically mixed area in South London to argue that decline in church attendance must not obscure other religious influences, e.g., social agencies, schools, and diffusive Christianity. [RKW]

24.271 Kenneth D. Brown. *A social history of the Nonconformist ministry in England and Wales, 1800–1930.* New York: Oxford University Press, 1988. ISBN 0-19-822763-9. ▸ Discussion of social origins, training, private and public lives, and career patterns, drawing on two extensive samples of Baptist, Congregationalist, and Methodist ministers. [RKW]

24.272 Alan Haig. *The Victorian clergy.* London: Croom Helm, 1984. ISBN 0-7099-1230-7. ▸ Examination of social origins and training (largely at universities but also at emerging theological colleges) of clergy of Church of England and, using sample drawn from three differing dioceses, analysis of clerical career patterns. [RKW]

24.273 Boyd Hilton. *The age of atonement: the influence of Evangelicalism on social and economic thought, 1795–1865.* 1988 ed. Oxford: Clarendon, 1991. ISBN 0-19-820107-9 (cl, 1988), 0-19-820295-4 (pbk). ▸ Important, provocative account of "Christian economics" and of stimulus of theologically based Evangelical ethical concerns on advance of government intervention in early Victorian period. [RKW]

24.274 K. S. Inglis. *Churches and the working classes in Victorian England.* 1963 ed. London: Routledge & Kegan Paul, 1974. ISBN 0-7100-4556-5. ▸ Classic analysis of working-class indifference to organized religion. Examines competing strategies of mainline churches and of insurgent ministries such as Salvation Army, settlement house movement, and labor churches. [RKW]

24.275 Edward R. Norman. *Church and society in England, 1770–1970: a historical study.* New York: Oxford University Press, 1976. ISBN 0-19-826435-6. ▸ Lively, authoritative survey of ideas about society among religious leaders, chiefly in Church of England. [RKW]

24.276 Edward R. Norman. *The Victorian Christian socialists.* Cambridge: Cambridge University Press, 1987. ISBN 0-521-32515-3. ▸ Eight essays on individuals associated with Christian socialism, arguing it was not a movement and was irrelevant to socialism as it was realized. Revisionist but concedes prophetic role in reorienting church concerns. [RKW]

24.277 James Obelkevich. *Religion and rural society: South Lindsey, 1825–1875.* New York: Oxford University Press, 1976. ISBN 0-19-822426-5. ▸ Masterful deployment of anthropological, sociological, and folkloric materials to delineate place of competing denominations in little-changing rural area. [RKW]

24.278 W. R. Ward. *Religion and society in England, 1790–1850.* London: Batsford, 1972. ISBN 0-7134-1362fl. ▸ Stimulating, controversial interpretation of churches in period of rapid social

change in terms not only of interdenominational conflict but also of tension between nondenominational religious impulses and denominational demands. [RKW]

Theology

24.279 D. W. Bebbington. *Evangelicalism in modern Britain: a history from the 1730s to the 1980s.* 1989 ed. Grand Rapids, Mich.: Baker Book House, 1992. ISBN 0-8010-1028-4 (pbk). ▸ Excellent survey defining Evangelicalism in terms of emphasis on conversion, activism, biblicism, and crucicentrism. Traces its varying forms in changing religious, intellectual, and social circumstances. [RKW]

24.280 Ieuan Ellis. *Seven against Christ: a study of "Essays and Reviews."* Leiden: Brill, 1980. ISBN 90-04-06200-9. ▸ Excellent study of genesis, publication, and reaction to volume by seven Broad churchmen, published in 1860, which created storm of controversy because of conclusions drawn from biblical criticism. [RKW]

24.281 Richard J. Helmstadter and Bernard Lightman, eds. *Victorian faith in crisis: essays on continuity and change in nineteenth-century religious belief.* Stanford, Calif.: Stanford University Press, 1990. ISBN 0-8047-1602-1. ▸ Eleven essays arguing crisis of faith far more complex than usually assumed and not tied in any simple way to emergence of Darwinian theory. [RKW]

24.282 Geoffrey Rowell. *Hell and the Victorians: a study of the nineteenth-century theological controversies concerning eternal punishment and the future life.* New York: Oxford University Press, 1974. ISBN 0-19-826638-3. ▸ Clear, revealing account of redefinition and marginalization of eschatology—concern with heaven, hell, death, and judgment—in theological debate. [RKW]

SEE ALSO
4.302 John Hedley Brooke. *Science and religion.*

Churches and Religious Movements

24.283 Clyde Binfield. *So down to prayers: studies in English Nonconformity, 1780–1920.* Totowa, N.J.: Rowman & Littlefield, 1977. ISBN 0-87471-959-3. ▸ Eleven evocative studies covering wide range of dissenting, chiefly Congregationalist, experience, emphasizing distinctive piety that informed individual and public life. [RKW]

24.284 Susan Budd. *Varieties of unbelief: atheists and agnostics in English society, 1850–1960.* London: Heinemann, 1977. ISBN 0-435-82100-8. ▸ Efficient survey with backward glance to 1800. [RKW]

24.285 Owen Chadwick. *Mackenzie's grave.* London: Hodder & Stoughton, 1959. ▸ Exception to usual parochial and celebratory work on missions. Brilliant, moving account of first Anglican mission in Central Africa, a response to call of missionary David Livingstone that went sadly awry. [RKW]

24.286 Owen Chadwick. *The spirit of the Oxford movement: tractarian essays.* Cambridge: Cambridge University Press, 1990. ISBN 0-521-37487-1. ▸ Fifteen essays, mostly pertaining to Oxford movement, which shook and then transformed Victorian Anglicanism. First essay, "The Mind of the Oxford Movement," is essential reading. [RKW]

24.287 Owen Chadwick. *The Victorian church.* 1971–72; v. 1 3d ed.; v. 2 2d ed. 2 vols. London: SCM Press, 1987. ISBN 0-334-02409-9 (v. 1, pbk), 0-334-02410-2 (v. 2, pbk). ▸ Exhaustive, imposing, personal survey of English religious scene, with Church of England predominating. Chronological narrative proceeds only to 1860, followed by thematic chapters covering whole century. [RKW]

24.288 Robert Currie, Alan D. Gilbert, and Lee Horsley.

Churches and churchgoers: patterns of church growth in the British Isles since 1700. New York: Oxford University Press, 1977. ISBN 0-19-827218-9. ▸ Exhaustive statistical compilation from various sources with commentary. Most extensive for membership and attendance but also including numbers of congregations and ministers. [RKW]

24.289 Rupert Davies and Gordon Rupp, eds. *A history of the Methodist church in Great Britain.* 4 vols. London: Epworth, 1965–88. ISBN 0-7162-0396-0 (v. 1), 0-7162-0301-4 (v. 2), 0-7162-0387-1 (v. 3), 0-7162-0444-4 (v. 4). ▸ Collaborative history, both narrative and thematic, broad in scope, objective, authoritative. Volume 1 deals with origins and eighteenth century; volume 2 with early nineteenth century; and volume 3 with subsequent history. Volume 4 contains documents and sources. [RKW]

24.290 Elizabeth Isichei. *Victorian Quakers.* Oxford: Clarendon, 1970. ISBN 0-19-821833-8. ▸ Exemplary denominational history tracing theological evolution of Friends, analyzing recruiting and loss of members and Quaker role in society, politics, philanthropy, and adult education. [RKW]

24.291 Edward R. Norman. *The English Catholic church in the nineteenth century.* 1984 ed. New York: Oxford University Press, 1985. ISBN 0-19-822689-6 (cl, 1984), 0-19-822955-0 (pbk). ▸ Useful survey of period of rapid expansion and profound transformation. Politics and ecclesiastical administration receive most attention. [RKW]

24.292 Bernard Semmel. *The Methodist revolution.* New York: Basic Books, 1973. ISBN 0-465-04570-7. ▸ Important synthesis arguing Methodist anti-Calvinist Arminianism, while politically quiescent, was fundamentally liberating. See also Davies and Rupp 24.289. [RKW]

24.293 H. L. Short. "Presbyterians under a new name." In *The English Presbyterians, from Elizabethan Puritanism to modern Unitarianism.* C. Gordon Bolam et al., eds., pp. 219–86. Boston: Beacon, 1968. ▸ Superbly compressed account of history of English Unitarianism, covering all main developments since late eighteenth century with balance and judgment. [RKW]

INTELLECTUAL AND CULTURAL HISTORY

General Studies

24.294 Noel Annan. "The intellectual aristocracy." In *Studies in social history: a tribute to G. M. Trevelyan.* 1955 ed. J. H. Plumb, ed., pp. 242–87. Freeport, N.Y.: Books for Libraries, 1969. ISBN 0-8369-1063-X. ▸ Influential, illuminating account of emergence of distinctive intellectual class marked by much intermarriage and by impact on all aspects of British life to present. [RKW]

24.295 Noel Annan. *Our age: portrait of a generation.* London: Weidenfeld & Nicolson, 1990. ISBN 0-297-81129-0. ▸ Brilliant account, carrying concept of intellectual aristocracy (24.294) into generation of opinion makers that came of age at Oxford, Cambridge, and London School of Economics between two world wars. [RKW]

24.296 Stefan Collini. *Public moralists: political thought and intellectual life in Britain, 1850–1930.* 1991 ed. New York: Oxford University Press, 1993. ISBN 0-19-820173-7 (cl, 1991), 0-19-820422-1 (pbk). ▸ Examination of context in which Victorian intellectuals worked, pervasive notions of morality and character, and public role of ethical philosophers. J. S. Mill is central figure. [RKW]

24.297 John Gross. *The rise and fall of the man of letters: English literary life since 1800.* 1969 ed. Chicago: Dee, 1992. ISBN 1-56663-000-2. ▸ Lively essay on evolution of criticism, which moved from high seriousness of early nineteenth century to quasi-priesthood

and finally channeled into academic study of English and popular journalism. [RKW]

24.298 Thomas William Heyck. *The transformation of intellectual life in Victorian England.* New York: St. Martin's, 1982. ISBN 0-312-81427-5. ▸ Useful overview, including chapters on impact of science (including history), reform of universities, and development of cultural criticism. Good bibliography. [RKW]

24.299 Walter E. Houghton. *The Victorian frame of mind, 1830–1870.* 1957 ed. New Haven: Yale University Press for Wellesley College, 1985. ISBN 0-300-00122-3. ▸ Valuable, perceptive summaries of attitudes of leading Victorian intellectuals to certain pervasive themes—optimism, anxiety, dogmatism, force, earnestness, heroes, love, hypocrisy, etc. [RKW]

24.300 Richard Jenkyns. *The Victorians and ancient Greece.* Cambridge, Mass.: Harvard University Press, 1980. ISBN 0-674-93686-8. ▸ Covers some of same ground as Turner 24.303 but complementary in its concern with attitudes toward and uses of Greek ideals among Victorian writers and artists. [RKW]

24.301 Edward Miller. *That noble cabinet: a history of the British Museum.* Athens: Ohio University Press, 1974. ISBN 0-8214-0139-4. ▸ Authoritative account of mid-eighteenth-century merging of private and royal collections and subsequent expansion in manuscripts, natural history, and printed books, to eve of administrative and physical separation of British Library. [RKW]

24.302 Janet Oppenheim. *The other world: spiritualism and psychical research in England, 1850–1914.* Cambridge: Cambridge University Press, 1985. ISBN 0-521-26505-3 (cl), 0-521-34767-X (pbk). ▸ Excellent account of broad cultural response, which drew in many prominent late Victorian scientists and intellectuals, to dissatisfaction with spiritual consequences of traditional Christianity and materialistic science. [RKW]

24.303 Frank M. Turner. *The Greek heritage in Victorian Britain.* New Haven: Yale University Press, 1981. ISBN 0-300-02480-0. ▸ Important survey of attitudes of Victorian humanists to Greek mythology, Homer, Socrates, Plato, and Athenian constitution. See also Jenkyns 24.300. [RKW]

Art and Architecture

24.304 Michael W. Brooks. *John Ruskin and Victorian architecture.* New Brunswick, N.J.: Rutgers University Press, 1987. ISBN 0-8135-1205-0. ▸ Careful examination of theoretical, rhetorical, and aesthetic elements in architectural writings of most influential Victorian critic and advocate of distinctive Gothic style. [RKW]

24.305 Paula Gillett. *Worlds of art: painters in Victorian society.* New Brunswick, N.J.: Rutgers University Press, 1990. ISBN 0-8135-1459-2. ▸ Useful survey in underserved field; examines Victorian painters, male and female, in relation to changing public and emerging professional status. [RKW]

24.306 Mark Girouard. *Sweetness and light: the "Queen Anne" movement, 1860–1900.* New York: Oxford University Press, 1977. ISBN 0-19-817330-X. ▸ Authoritative study of post-Gothic architectural enthusiasm based on Flemish and English seventeenth-century models. Style, characterized by charm and emphasis on domesticity, also found public expression in town halls and schools. [RKW]

24.307 Henry-Russell Hitchcock. *Early Victorian architecture in Britain.* 1954 ed. 2 vols. New York: Da Capo, 1972. ISBN 0-306-70195-2. ▸ Key work reevaluating architecture in thirty years after 1830, covering gothicizing influence of A.W.N. Pugin, new Houses of Parliament, railway stations, and Crystal Palace of 1851. [RKW]

24.308 Thomas Howarth. *Charles Rennie Mackintosh and the modern movement.* 2d ed. Boston: Routledge & Kegan Paul, 1977.

ISBN 0-7100-8538-9. ‣ Examination of immensely influential Scottish architect and designer in Scottish context, sources of his art, and continental impact. First published 1952. [RKW]

24.309 Nikolaus Pevsner. *High Victorian design: a study of the exhibits of 1851.* London: Architectural Press, 1951. ‣ First effort at objective assessment of long-scorned design of objects displayed at Great Exhibition—machinery, household goods, and works of art—exploring sources, virtues, and shortcomings of Victorian taste. [RKW]

24.310 Peter Stansky. *Redesigning the world: William Morris, the 1880s, and the arts and crafts.* Princeton: Princeton University Press, 1985. ISBN 0-691-06616-7. ‣ Careful study of rebellion against industrialism and bad design in internationally influential arts and crafts movement through its central figure who was also important in contemporary socialism. [RKW]

Literature, Theater, and Music

24.311 Jerome Hamilton Buckley. *The Victorian temper: a study in literary culture.* 1951 ed. Cambridge, Mass.: Harvard University Press, 1969. ISBN 0-674-93680-9. ‣ Key work, at time of publication, in reevaluation of Victorian literature. Sweeps field from early antiromanticism to late decadence, with Tennyson as central figure. [RKW]

24.312 Marilyn Butler. *Romantics, rebels, and reactionaries: English literature and its background, 1760–1830.* 1981 ed. New York: Oxford University Press, 1982. ISBN 0-19-520384-4. ‣ Influential extended essay on relation of principal Romantic writers to their historical context, ending with skeptical look at received notions of term romanticism. [RKW]

24.313 Cyril Ehrlich. *The music profession in Britain since the eighteenth century: a social history.* New York: Oxford University Press, 1985. ISBN 0-19-822665-9. ‣ Thorough, fascinating account of career patterns, training, and working conditions of musicians of all types in transition from patronage to market conditions in increasingly technological musical world. [RKW]

24.314 Martin Meisel. *Realizations: narrative, pictorial, and theatrical arts in nineteenth-century England.* Princeton: Princeton University Press, 1983. ISBN 0-691-06553-5. ‣ Impressive overview, both theoretical and thematic, of interrelations of theater with poetry, novels, and painting. Beautifully illustrated. [RKW]

24.315 Francis Mulhern. *The moment of "Scrutiny."* London: NLB, 1979. ISBN 0-86091-007-5. ‣ Study of Cambridge don F. R. Leavis, one of most influential and controversial of twentieth-century critics, and of journal *Scrutiny* (1932–53), which gave expression to his distinctive aesthetic and social views. [RKW]

24.316 John Passmore. *A hundred years of philosophy.* 1966 2d ed. Harmondsworth: Penguin, 1984. ISBN 0-14-020927-1 (pbk). ‣ Best and most authoritative introduction to course of British philosophy since J. S. Mill. First published 1957. [RKW]

24.317 Michael Sanderson. *From Irving to Olivier: a social history of the acting profession in England, 1880–1983.* New York: St. Martin's, 1984. ISBN 0-312-30768-3. ‣ Compressed but instructive survey of training, conditions, and organization of twentieth-century acting profession, in theater and in new media. [RKW]

24.318 Nicholas Temperley, ed. *The romantic age, 1800–1914.* London: Athlone; distributed by Humanities, 1981. ISBN 0-485-13005-X. ‣ Necessarily brief and often superficial essays saying little about concert organization or provincial musical activity. Still, only survey covering the many varieties of popular and art music. [RKW]

24.319 Carl Woodring. *Nature into art: cultural transformation in nineteenth-century Britain.* Cambridge, Mass.: Harvard University Press, 1989. ISBN 0-674-60465-2. ‣ General interpretation of literary history of century moving from primacy of nature to primacy of art. Like Buckley 24.311 a generation earlier, widely sensitive to historical context. [RKW]

Education and Its Uses

24.320 Asa Briggs. *The history of broadcasting in the United Kingdom.* Vol. 1: *The birth of broadcasting.* Vol. 2: *The golden age of wireless.* Vol. 3: *The war of words.* Vol. 4: *Sound and vision.* 4 vols. New York: Oxford University Press, 1961–79. ISBN 0-19-212967-8 (v. 4). ‣ Monumental history of instrument of two cultural transformations of first importance, radio and television. Most of work deals with British Broadcasting Corporation, which had monopoly until 1954 when an independent television channel was authorized. [RKW]

24.321 Lucy Brown. *Victorian news and newspapers.* New York: Oxford University Press, 1985. ISBN 0-19-822624-1. ‣ Useful overview of newspaper history with attention to handling of news, profession of journalism, distribution, and political connections. [RKW]

24.322 A. J. Engel. *From clergyman to don: the rise of the academic profession in nineteenth-century Oxford.* 1983 ed. New York: Oxford University Press, 1984. ISBN 0-19-822606-3 (cl, 1983), 0-19-820070-6 (pbk). ‣ Careful account of mid-century reforms which replaced largely temporary teaching staff of clergymen with permanent cadre of tutors and led to ambiguous ascendancy of colleges over university. [RKW]

24.323 J. R. de S. Honey. *Tom Brown's universe: the development of the English public school in the nineteenth century.* New York: Quadrangle, 1977. ISBN 0-8129-0689-6. ‣ Probably broadest introduction to system and content of reformed and rapidly expanding public schools—private boarding schools in which English elite were and are educated. [RKW]

24.324 John Hurt. *Education in evolution: church, state, society, and popular education, 1800–1870.* London: Hart-Davis, 1971. ISBN 0-246-64041-3. ‣ Reliable narrative account of evolution of mass education from voluntary societies to 1870 Education Act. Treats religious questions, teachers, pedagogy, and administration. [RKW]

24.325 Stephen Koss. *The rise and fall of the political press in Britain.* Vol. 1: *The nineteenth century.* Vol. 2: *The twentieth century.* 2 vols. Chapel Hill: University of North Carolina Press, 1981–84. ISBN 0-8078-1483-0 (v. 1), 0-8078-1598-5 (v. 2). ‣ Imposing, detailed study of changing relationship between newspapers and politics, politicians as well as political positions. [RKW]

24.326 David Newsome. *Godliness and good learning: four studies on a Victorian ideal.* Albuquerque, N.M.: Transatlantic, 1961. ISBN 0-7195-1015-5. ‣ Brilliant evocation of mid-Victorian symbiosis of Christianity and scholarship, exemplified in headmaster and schoolboy. Traces transmutation of ideal into muscular Christianity and cult of manliness. [RKW]

24.327 Sheldon Rothblatt. *The revolution of the dons: Cambridge and society in Victorian England.* 1968 ed. Cambridge: Cambridge University Press, 1981. ISBN 0-521-23958-3 (cl), 0-521-28370-1 (pbk). ‣ Broad-based study examining recruiting of students, costs, pressures for reform, ties to world of business, and victory of college dons over private coaches for control of teaching. [RKW]

24.328 Michael Sanderson. *The universities and British industry, 1850–1970.* Boston: Routledge & Kegan Paul, 1972. ISBN 0-7100-7378-X. ‣ Clear study of ties between universities and industry, in research and in placing of graduates, linkage in which Oxford and Cambridge lagged behind newer civic universities and those in Scotland and Wales. [RKW]

24.329 David Vincent. *Literacy and popular culture: England, 1750–1914.* Cambridge: Cambridge University Press, 1989. ISBN 0-521-33466-7. ▸ Commendably broad view of replacement of oral by literate culture through schools and variety of other agencies. Also good guide to other literature in vast field. [RKW]

Understanding Society

24.330 Maxine Berg. *The machinery question and the making of political economy, 1815–1848.* 1980 ed. Cambridge: Cambridge University Press, 1982. ISBN 0-521-22782-8 (cl, 1980), 0-521-28759-6 (pbk). ▸ Broad-based analysis locating origins of modern political economy in early nineteenth-century analysis of mechanization and industrialization. Identifies optimistic orthodoxy and pessimistic critique fused in Karl Marx. [MD]

24.331 Gregory Claeys. *Machinery, money, and the millennium: from moral economy to socialism, 1815–1860.* Princeton: Princeton University Press, 1987. ISBN 0-691-09430-6. ▸ Emphasizes definition of Owenite socialism embracing machine as source of progress rather than more familiar communitarian vision. [MD]

24.332 Peter Clarke. *The Keynesian revolution in the making, 1924–1936.* Oxford: Clarendon, 1988. ISBN 0-19-828304-0 (cl), 0-19-820219-9 (pbk). ▸ Stunning recovery of historical Keynes, tracing thought through overlapping arguments about administrative capacity and public policy, state intervention, and unemployment in interwar Britain. [MD]

24.333 Stefan Collini, Donald Winch, and John Burrow. *That noble science of politics: a study in nineteenth-century intellectual history.* Cambridge: Cambridge University Press, 1983. ISBN 0-521-25762-x. ▸ Related essays on nineteenth-century attempts to develop systematic account of rules and norms governing political society. Important contextual studies of J. S. Mill, Walter Bagehot, Henry Sidgwick, and others. [PSc]

24.334 Michael J. Cullen. *The statistical movement in early Victorian Britain: the foundations of empirical social research.* New York: Barnes & Noble, 1975. ISBN 0-06-491333-3. ▸ Brief summary of social statistical inquiry in seventeenth and nineteenth centuries, followed by careful examination of collection of statistical information by government departments and statistical societies. [RKW]

24.335 Joseph Hamburger. *Macaulay and the whig tradition.* Chicago: University of Chicago Press, 1976. ISBN 0-226-31472-3. ▸ Revision of traditional view of Macaulay as liberal Whig, but sees him instead as classical "trimmer," concerned with maintaining balance and stability in political system. [PSc]

24.336 T. W. Hutchison. *A review of economic doctrines, 1870–1929.* 1953 ed. Westport, Conn.: Greenwood, 1975. ISBN 0-8371-7637-9. ▸ Classic work tying leading economists to main developments in theories of markets, welfare, uncertainty, and money. Emphasizes formal analysis of maximization and equilibrium along with emerging economics of instability and unemployment. [MD]

24.337 Gerard M. Koot. *English historical economics, 1870–1926: the rise of economic history and neo-mercantilism.* Cambridge: Cambridge University Press, 1987. ISBN 0-521-32854-3. ▸ Serious reconsideration of theorists who saw economics as practical inductive discipline. Pessimistic, interventionist challenge to orthodox political economy of David Ricardo and Alfred Marshall largely neglected in whiggish histories of economic thought. [MD]

24.338 Stuart Macintyre. *A proletarian science: Marxism in Britain, 1917–1933.* 1980 ed. London: Lawrence & Wishart, 1986. ISBN 0-85315-667-0 (pbk). ▸ Examination of Marxism as distinc-

tive part of indigenous oppositional movement initially tied to larger working-class culture but then declining as its political, industrial, and cultural bases in that class eroded. [MD]

24.339 Peter P. Nicholson. *The political philosophy of the British idealists: selected studies.* Cambridge: Cambridge University Press, 1990. ISBN 0-521-37102-3. ▸ Concentrates on Thomas Hill Green, Francis Herbert Bradley, and Bernard Bosanquet, explaining attitudes toward proper end of society, justification for state, and individual freedom and rights. Sympathetic reconstruction showing unity of thought and common Hegelian influence. [PSc]

24.340 Anthony Quinton. *The politics of imperfection: the religious and secular traditions of conservative thought in England from Hooker to Oakeshott.* London: Faber & Faber, 1978. ISBN 0-571-11285-4. ▸ Brief, suggestive essays on major thinkers emphasizing intellectual imperfection as axiom of conservatism, thence attachment to traditional institutions, belief in organic society, and distrust of abstract theory. [PSc]

24.341 John M. Robson. *The improvement of mankind: the social and political thought of John Stuart Mill.* Toronto: University of Toronto Press, 1968. (University of Toronto Department of English studies and texts, 15.) ISBN 0-8020-1529-8. ▸ Study of Mill's intellectual development, through Benthamite and other influences, from mental crisis to maturity. Stresses unity and coherence in Mill's thought and practice by showing central importance of utilitarian ethic. [PSc]

24.342 F. Rosen. *Bentham, Byron, and Greece: constitutionalism, nationalism, and early liberal political thought.* Oxford: Clarendon, 1992. ISBN 0-19-820078-1. ▸ Discussion of Jeremy Bentham's constitutional theory in relation to Greek struggle for independence. Distinguishes Bentham's liberal political philosophy from emergence and application of liberalism as ideology by Bentham's followers. [PSc]

24.343 J. B. Schneewind. *Sidgwick's ethics and Victorian moral philosophy.* New York: Oxford University Press, 1977. ISBN 0-19-824552-1. ▸ Influence of Henry Sidgwick's ethical theory on debates between Utilitarians and intuitionists. His consequent synthesis, based on utilitarianism, heralded modern treatment of moral philosophy. [PSc]

24.344 T. S. Simey and M. B. Simey. *Charles Booth, social scientist.* 1960 ed. Westport, Conn.: Greenwood, 1980. ISBN 0-313-22610-5. ▸ Booth, from wealthy Liverpool ship-owning family, became pioneer social investigator. Biography in part, but primarily analysis of his great survey of London life and labor. [RKW]

24.345 Reba N. Soffer. *Ethics and society in England: the revolution in the social sciences, 1870–1914.* Berkeley: University of California Press, 1978. ISBN 0-520-03521-6. ▸ Survey of developments in economics, psychology, political science, and social psychology demonstrating distinct departure from nineteenth-century modes of thinking about society. [RKW]

24.346 William Thomas. *The philosophic radicals: nine studies in theory and practice, 1817–1841.* Oxford: Clarendon, 1979. ISBN 0-19-822490-7. ▸ Overturns view of early Utilitarians as cohesive party influencing political practice, explaining their failure by middle-class social background, lack of mass following, unattractiveness of doctrines, and diffuseness of ideas. [PSc]

SEE ALSO
23.211 Istvan Hont and Michael Ignatieff. *Wealth and virtue.*

SCIENCE AND MEDICINE

24.347 Brian Abel-Smith. *A history of the nursing profession.* New York: Springer, 1960. ▸ Discussion of politics of general hospital nursing in England and Wales. Treats structure of profession, terms and conditions of service, professional associations and unions, and public policy with twentieth-century emphasis. [RKW]

24.348 David Elliston Allen. *The naturalist in Britain: a social history.* London: Allen Lane, 1976. ISBN 0-7139-0790-8. ▸ Study interweaving politics, science, and fashion; fuller on botany and zoology than on geology. Directed toward British audience. [SH]

24.349 Olive Anderson. *Suicide in Victorian and Edwardian England.* Oxford: Clarendon, 1987. ISBN 0-19-820101-X. ▸ Impressive study of suicide patterns in London and in rural area of Sussex, popular attitudes to suicide, and range of legal, voluntary, and medical efforts at restraint. Analysis of suicide statistics. [RKW]

24.350 Susan Faye Cannon. *Science in culture: the early Victorian period.* New York: Science History Publications, 1978. ISBN 0-88202-172-9. ▸ Identifies key topics for period: Cambridge network, Broad church alliances, Humboldtian science, development of physics, professionalization, founding of British Association. Insouciant and provocatively argued; indispensable. [SH]

24.351 D.S.L. Cardwell. *The organisation of science in England.* Rev. ed. London: Heinemann Educational, 1972. ISBN 0-435-54153-6 (cl), 0-435-54154-4 (pbk). ▸ Useful chronological treatment, 1800–1918, of development of educational institutions in relation to creation of occupation of professional scientist. [SH]

24.352 Maurice P. Crosland and Crosbie Smith. "The transmission of physics from France and Britain, 1800–1840." *Historical studies in the physical sciences* 9 (1977) 1–61. ISSN 0095-9367, ISBN 0-8018-2045-6. ▸ Original treatment of national science helping to explain how physics emerged as subject in its own right by mid-nineteenth century. [SH]

24.353 James Gerald Crowther. *The Cavendish Laboratory, 1874–1974.* New York: Science History Publications, 1974. ISBN 0-88202-029-3. ▸ Celebratory, highly readable account of legendary institution and those associated with it from laboratory's founder James Clerk-Maxwell on down, including molecular biologists of mid-twentieth century. [SH]

24.354 Adrian J. Desmond. *The politics of evolution: morphology, medicine, and reform in radical London.* Chicago: University of Chicago Press, 1989. ISBN 0-226-24346-5 (cl), 0-226-14374-0 (pbk). ▸ Important new analysis of impact of evolutionary thought on early Victorian London's secular and Nonconformist colleges and conservative response. Identifies support among underpaid and dissident medical practitioners for theories favoring transmutation of species. [SH/SEK]

24.355 Gerald L. Geison. *Michael Foster and the Cambridge school of physiology: the scientific enterprise in late Victorian society.* Princeton: Princeton University Press, 1978. ISBN 0-691-08197-2. ▸ How Foster organized British physiology into laboratory-oriented research tradition, complementing work in physics at Cavendish. See Crowther 24.353. Good study of research school. [SH/SEK]

24.356 Charles Coulston Gillispie. *Genesis and geology: a study in the relations of scientific thought, natural theology, and social opinion in Great Britain.* 1951 ed. Cambridge, Mass.: Harvard University Press, 1969. ISBN 0-674-34480-4. ▸ Description of decline of natural theology. Still classic in intellectual history, despite challenges to its portrayal of history of geology. [SH]

24.357 Margaret Gowing. *Britain and atomic energy, 1939–1945.* Kenneth Jay, Introduction. New York: St. Martin's, 1964. ▸ Analysis of policy making and execution; followed by work on 1945–52 (24.358). Official history of highest quality. [RKW]

24.358 Margaret Gowing. *Independence and deterrence: Britain*

and atomic energy, 1945–1952. 2 vols. New York: St. Martin's, 1974. ▸ Continuation of 24.357. [SH]

24.359 John Henry, ed. *Cambridge physics in the thirties.* Bristol, England: Hilger, 1984. ISBN 0-85274-761-6. ▸ Useful essays by historians and scientists on practice of nuclear physics at Cavendish Laboratory in Cambridge during 1930s. [SH]

24.360 Kathleen Jones. *A history of the mental health services.* London: Routledge & Kegan Paul, 1972. ISBN 0-7100-7452-2. ▸ Useful, primarily administrative, history of treatment of mental illness and of mental hospitals from mid-eighteenth century to 1971. Part 1 originally published as *Lunacy, Law, and Conscience, 1744–1845* (1955) and part 2 as *Mental Health and Social Policy, 1845–1959* (1960). [RKW]

24.361 Roy M. MacLeod. "The Royal Society and the government grant: notes on the administration of scientific research, 1849–1914." *Historical journal* 14.2 (1971) 323–58. ISSN 0018-246X. ▸ Describes stage in development of government support of research. Useful statistics and identification of elites. [SH]

24.362 Jack Morrell and Arnold Thackray. *Gentlemen of science: early years of the British Association for the Advancement of Science.* 1981 ed. New York: Oxford University Press, 1982. ISBN 0-19-858163-7 (cl, 1981), 0-19-520396-8 (pbk). ▸ Massively documented study of origins of organization scientists used to promote their work and to gain popular support. [SH]

24.363 Janet Oppenheim. *"Shattered nerves": doctors, patients, and depression in Victorian England.* New York: Oxford University Press, 1991. ISBN 0-19-505781-3. ▸ Searching, sympathetic study of condition that baffled medical science. With alienist Sir James Crichton-Browne at center, it bridges gap between eighteenth-century "mad business" and modern psychiatry. [RKW]

24.364 M. Jeanne Peterson. *The medical profession in mid-Victorian London.* Berkeley: University of California Press, 1978. ISBN 0-520-03343-4. ▸ Social history, replete with numbers, suggesting how variety of medical practitioners consolidated themselves into elite profession. Strong on sorting out various groups of practitioners and their institutions. [SH]

24.365 Martin J. S. Rudwick. "The foundation of the Geological Society of London: its scheme for co-operative research and its struggle for independence." *British journal for the history of science* 1.4 (1963) 325–355. ISSN 0007-0874. ▸ Study of geology's break from Royal Society of London. Suggests movement toward specialization in early nineteenth century. [SH]

24.366 Colin Archibald Russell. *Science and social change in Britain and Europe, 1700–1900.* New York: St. Martin's, 1983. ISBN 0-312-10239-6. ▸ Survey with up-to-date references to literature; useful on scientific societies. [SH]

24.367 Robert E. Schofield. *The Lunar Society of Birmingham: a social history of provincial science and industry in eighteenth-century England.* Oxford: Clarendon, 1963. ▸ Portrait of influential group of fourteen men (e.g., Matthew Boulton, James Watt, Erasmus Darwin, Joseph Priestley). Stimulating study arguing for continuity between eighteenth- and nineteenth-century England and for strongly scientific foundation to Industrial Revolution. [SH]

24.368 Andrew Scull, ed. *Madhouses, mad-doctors, and madmen: the social history of psychiatry in the Victorian era.* Philadelphia: University of Pennsylvania Press, 1981. ISBN 0-8122-7801-1 (cl), 0-8122-1119-7 (pbk). ▸ Helpful essays addressing aspects of Victorian psychiatry not so fully covered in Jones 24.360. Treats profession, asylums, patient treatment, definitions of psychiatry and neurology, and legal issues. [RKW/CSH]

24.369 F. B. Smith. *The people's health, 1830–1910.* New York: Holmes & Meier, 1979. ISBN 0-8419-0448-0. ▸ Pioneering work in social history of medicine in Britain. Clear-eyed, detailed survey from patient's perspective, structured into chapters on childbirth, infancy, childhood and youth, adults, and old age. [RKW/CSH]

24.370 Rosemary Stevens. *Medical practice in modern England: the impact of specialization and state medicine.* New Haven: Yale University Press, 1966. ▸ Systematic, useful survey, treating National Health Service in depth, though well before recent changes. [SH]

24.371 David B. Wilson. "The educational matrix: physics education at early-Victorian Cambridge, Edinburgh, and Glasgow universities." In *Wranglers and physicists: studies on Cambridge physics in the nineteenth century.* P. M. Harman, ed., pp. 12–48. Manchester: Manchester University Press, 1985. ISBN 0-7190-1756-4. ▸ Comparative study of physics education. Recognizes regional and institutional variation within history of scientific ideas. [SH]

24.372 Robert M. Young. *Darwin's metaphor: nature's place in Victorian culture.* Cambridge: Cambridge University Press, 1985. ISBN 0-521-30083-5 (cl), 0-521-31742-8 (pbk). ▸ Important collection of essays arguing for common context of scientific and social thought with particular attention to Malthus as central figure. [SH]

DIPLOMATIC AND MILITARY HISTORY

Foreign Affairs

24.373 Kenneth Bourne. *Palmerston: the early years, 1784–1841.* New York: Macmillan, 1982. ISBN 0-02-903740-9. ▸ First volume of projected two concentrates on prime minister's political and diplomatic career to 1841, offering in-depth analysis of British diplomacy when Britain was sole global power. See also Steele 24.40. [BJCM]

24.374 Hedley Bull and Wm. Roger Louis, eds. *The special relationship: Anglo-American relations since 1945.* Oxford: Clarendon, 1988. ISBN 0-19-822925-9. ▸ Chapters by specialists showing basis of post–World War II foreign policy to be one of uneasy cooperation, with periodic crises, generally confirming Britain's junior status to United States. [BJCM]

24.375 John Clarke. *British diplomacy and foreign policy, 1782–1865: the national interest.* London: Unwin Hyman, 1989. ISBN 0-04-445040-0. ▸ Argues foreign policy largely successful, though changing less than has been thought, and involving more domestic influence on diplomacy and greater professionalism at all levels. [BJCM]

24.376 Michael L. Dockrill and John W. Young, eds. *British foreign policy, 1945–56.* London: Macmillan, 1989. ISBN 0-333-46042-1. ▸ In absence of any archivally based monograph, this collection of essays has particular value in looking at British diplomatic problems in various regions during first decade of cold war. [BJCM]

24.377 Erik Goldstein. *Winning the peace: British diplomatic strategy, peace planning, and the Paris Peace Conference, 1916–1920.* Oxford: Clarendon, 1991. ISBN 0-19-821584-3. ▸ Study of evolution of British war aims and peace planning from middle of World War I. Insightful conclusion that Britain achieved more than any other power at Paris Peace Conference. [BJCM]

24.378 Wendy Hinde. *Castlereagh.* London: Collins, 1981. ISBN 0-00-216308-X. ▸ Biography of early nineteenth-century foreign secretary using mix of archives and recent secondary work to offer fresh insight into diplomacy from Fourth Coalition to Britain's withdrawal from Concert of Europe. [BJCM]

24.379 Paul M. Kennedy. *The realities behind diplomacy: background influences on British external policy, 1865–1980.* London: Allen & Unwin, 1981. ISBN 0-04-902005-6. ▸ Comprehensive study by leading declinologist of link between internal and external policy to explain Britain's fall to second-rank power. Weakened by arguing back from 1980 instead of forward from 1865. [BJCM]

24.380 B.J.C. McKercher. "Wealth, power, and the new international order: Britain and the American challenge in the 1920s." *Diplomatic history* 12 (1988) 411–62. ISSN 0145-2096. ▸ Rejects World War I as explanation of Britain's fall from status as leading world power, arguing Britain retained political, strategic, and military means to resist American financial and naval challenges. [BJCM]

24.381 Charles Ronald Middleton. *The administration of British foreign policy, 1782–1846.* Durham, N.C.: Duke University Press, 1977. ISBN 0-8223-0383-3. ▸ Study of Foreign Office from founding to repeal of Corn Laws. Shows, despite some difficulties (e.g., professionalism of diplomats), firm administrative base for external policy. [BJCM]

24.382 Keith Neilson. *Strategy and supply: the Anglo-Russian alliance, 1914–1917.* London: Allen & Unwin, 1985. ISBN 0-04-940072-X. ▸ Best available case study, deftly analyzing how British foreign policy surmounted wartime crisis when military concerns and Treasury had greater influence on day-to-day diplomacy than Foreign Office. [BJCM]

24.383 Victor Rothwell. *Britain and the cold war, 1941–1947.* London: Cape, 1982. ISBN 0-224-01478-1. ▸ How Big Three cooperation to defeat Axis powers gave way to cold war, which divided Britain and United States from suspect Soviet Union. Based mainly on Foreign Office documents. [BJCM]

24.384 D. Cameron Watt. *Personalities and policies: studies in the formulation of British foreign policy in the twentieth century.* 1965 ed. Westport, Conn.: Greenwood, 1975. ISBN 0-8371-7692-1. ▸ Examination of foreign policy elite with case studies of impact of personality and of financial, strategic, and other pressures 1900–56. Best overall assessment of period. [BJCM]

SEE ALSO

Military and Naval History

24.385 Shelford Bidwell and Dominick Graham. *Fire-power: British army weapons and theories of war, 1904–1945.* 1982 ed. Boston: Allen & Unwin, 1985. ISBN 0-04-942176-X (cl, 1982), 0-04-942190-5 (pbk). ▸ Provocative study of vicissitudes of British search for correct modern military doctrine. Focus on efficient deployment of artillery, ultimately through development of complex and sensitive means of command and control. [JTS]

24.386 Brian Bond. *British military policy between the two world wars.* Oxford: Clarendon, 1980. ISBN 0-19-822464-8. ▸ Authoritative survey describing crippling of strategic planning by emphasis on imperial defense, severe financial restrictions, and lackluster military leadership. Critical assessments of army progressives and politicians. [JTS]

24.387 John D. Byrn, Jr. *Crime and punishment in the Royal Navy: discipline on the Leeward Islands station, 1784–1812.* Aldershot, England: Scolar, 1989. ISBN 0-85967-808-3. ▸ Illuminating, statistically based study of naval articles of war, courts martial, punishments, role of officers, and social and service crimes. Argues application of law at sea essentially same as on land. [JTS]

24.388 Malcolm Cooper. *The birth of independent air power: British air policy in the First World War.* London: Allen & Unwin, 1986. ISBN 0-04-942204-9. ▸ Political, economic, technical, operational, and administrative analysis of creation of world's best tactical air force. War experience did not justify creation of independent air service. Comprehensive, judicious survey. [JTS]

24.389 G.A.H. Gordon. *British seapower and procurement between the wars: a reappraisal of rearmament.* Annapolis, Md.: Naval Institute Press, 1988. ISBN 0-87021-894-8. ▸ Study of navy's leading role in creation of effective interservice system of coordinating war-industrial mobilization. Original, plausible, suggestive account of naval industrial organization, fiscal policy, and appeasement. [JTS]

24.390 Keith Grieves. *The politics of manpower, 1914–18.* New York: St. Martin's, 1987. ISBN 0-312-01320-5. ▸ Much-needed study of integration of military and industrial activity by effective control and allocation of manpower. By war's end, strict regulation of manpower by Ministry of National Service, not army command. [JTS]

24.391 Eric J. Grove. *Vanguard to Trident: British naval policy since World War II.* Annapolis, Md.: Naval Institute Press, 1987. ISBN 0-87021-552-3. ▸ Comprehensive survey of postwar British naval policy as shaped by politics and economics. Coverage of operations, technology, and strategy formulation in face of severe financial weakness and multiple threats. [JTS]

24.392 Willem Hackmann. *Seek and strike: sonar, anti-submarine warfare, and the Royal Navy, 1914–54.* London: Her Majesty's Stationery Office, 1984. ISBN 0-11-290423-8. ▸ Detailed study of Royal Navy involvement in research in underwater acoustics. Uncompromising treatment of technical subjects, administration, policy, and operations. Lavishly illustrated; indispensable source of information. [JTS]

24.393 F. H. Hinsley et al. *British intelligence in the Second World War.* Vols. 1–3: *Its influence on strategy and operations.* Vol. 4: *Security and counter-intelligence.* Vol. 5: *Strategic deception.* 5 vols. in 6. New York: Cambridge University Press, 1979–90. ISBN 0-521-22940-5 (v. 1), 0-521-24290-8 (v. 2), 0-521-35196-0 (v. 3), 0-521-39409-0 (v. 4), 0-521-40145-3 (v. 5). ▸ Official history of intelligence, counterintelligence, and deception and their influence on major operational decisions. Based on unrestricted access to secret files, credible attempt to balance accuracy, comprehensive coverage, and discretion in coordinated assessment of critically important, fascinating, but treacherous subject. [JTS]

24.394 Gerald Jordan, ed. *British military history: a supplement to Robin Higham's "Guide."* New York: Garland, 1988. ISBN 0-8240-8450-0. ▸ Coverage of works published since 1967. Topics include army, navy, air force, dominions, home front during war, science, technology, economics, medicine, law, intelligence, politics, and high command. Standard source. [JTS]

24.395 Roger Morriss. *The royal dockyards during the Revolutionary and Napoleonic wars.* Leicester: Leicester University Press, 1983. ISBN 0-7185-1215-4. ▸ Systematic, well-researched examination of yard operations, facilities, materials, labor force, officials, yard management, politics, and reform. Corrects long-established but mistaken views of shore civil departments of navy as inefficient and corrupt. [JTS]

24.396 David E. Omissi. *Air power and colonial control: the Royal Air Force, 1919–1939.* Manchester: Manchester University Press; distributed by St. Martin's, 1990. ISBN 0-7190-1960-0. ▸ Provocative, informative examination of bomber deployment against disorder in British Isles, Palestine, India, Southwest Arabia, and

Africa. Imperial police role in 1920s justified existence of air force in hostile financial environment. [JTS]

24.397 Malcolm Smith. *British air strategy between the wars.* Oxford: Clarendon, 1984. ISBN 0-19-822767-1. ▸ Standard survey of air force politics, policy, and war planning. Major policy alternatives—air deterrence, arms control and appeasement, and fighter defense—offered no panacea to Britain's fundamental defense problem of strategic overextension. [JTS]

24.398 Edward M. Spiers. *The army and society, 1815–1914.* London: Longman, 1980. ISBN 0-582-48565-7 (cl), 0-582-48566-5 (pbk). ▸ Comprehensive social history surveying Wellington's army, Crimean War, Indian Mutiny, Boer War, and army reform under Cardwell and Haldane. Chapters on officer corps and enlisted ranks. [JTS]

24.399 Hew Strachan. *Wellington's legacy: the reform of the British army, 1830–1954.* Manchester: Manchester University Press, 1984. ISBN 0-7190-0994-4. ▸ Concentrating on organization and structure, argues failure of reform arose not from army resistance but from inappropriateness of debate to circumstances that later materialized in Crimean War. [JTS]

24.400 Jon Tetsuro Sumida. *In defence of naval supremacy: finance, technology, and British naval policy, 1889–1914.* Boston: Unwin Hyman, 1989. ISBN 0-04-445104-0. ▸ Study of financial and technological context of naval policy and strategy. Radically revisionist, methodologically innovative account of Admiral Sir John Fisher's "Dreadnought revolution," Anglo-German naval rivalry, and battle of Jutland. [JTS/AR]

24.401 T.H.E. Travers. *The killing ground: the British army, the Western Front, and the emergence of modern warfare.* London: Allen & Unwin, 1987. ISBN 0-04-942205-7. ▸ Inventive, revisionist analysis of institutional character and tactical doctrines of Edwardian army, intellectual development of high command, select operations in France, and official postwar assessments. [JTS]

24.402 Myna Trustram. *Women of the regiment: marriage and the Victorian army.* Cambridge: Cambridge University Press, 1984. ISBN 0-521-26294-1. ▸ Pioneering study of social and institutional characteristics of military family life. Coverage of marriage statistics, individual and regimental responsibility for family support, prostitution and venereal disease, and governance. [JTS]

24.403 J. M. Winter. *The Great War and the British people.* Cambridge, Mass.: Harvard University Press, 1986. ISBN 0-674-36212-8. ▸ Examination of strategic demography, manpower and military service, war losses, civilian health and living standards, and demographic and cultural aftereffects. Wealth of statistical information and thorough documentation. [JTS]

SEE ALSO

47.377 David French. *British strategy and war aims, 1914–1916.*

IRELAND

General Studies

24.404 L. M. Cullen. *An economic history of Ireland since 1600.* 2d ed. London: Batsford, 1987. ISBN 0-7134-5808-9. ▸ First published in 1972 and still best survey, this edition has additional chapter on 1970s and 1980s. Framework for later work by historian who has done most to revolutionize scholarship on modern period. [TD]

24.405 L. M. Cullen. *The emergence of modern Ireland, 1600–1900.* New York: Holmes & Meier, 1981. ISBN 0-8419-0727-7. ▸ Indispensable text by leading economic and social historian, strongly influenced by Annales school. Sophisticated modernization thesis anchored in new research on population, diet, social structure, urbanization, economy, rebellion, and culture. [TD]

24.406 R. F. Foster. *Modern Ireland, 1600–1972.* London: Allen

Lane, 1989. ISBN 0-7139-9010-4. ▸ Masterful synthesis with maps, statistical tables, chronology, and excellent bibliographical essay. Best on interaction of politics and culture and on complexity of Irish historical experience. [TD]

24.407   Tom Garvin. *The evolution of Irish nationalist politics.* New York: Holmes & Meier, 1981. ISBN 0-8419-0741-2. ▸ Influential overview arguing for structural and cultural continuities in politics from late eighteenth century. Sophisticated political science approach complemented by wide-ranging, sensitive historical research. [TD]

24.408   Oliver MacDonagh. *States of mind: a study of Anglo-Irish conflict, 1780–1980.* London: Allen & Unwin, 1983. ISBN 0-04-941012-1 (cl), 0-04-941015-6 (pbk). ▸ Prize-winning, interpretive essays on *mentalité* by leading intellectual historian, uniquely combining equal expertise in Irish and British history. Original focus, dazzling insights, luminous style—already a classic. [TD]

24.409   W. E. Vaughan, ed. *Ireland under the Union, 1801–1870.* Oxford: Clarendon, 1989. ISBN 0-19-821743-9. ▸ First of three projected volumes in prestigious series covering period from 1800. Major essays on politics, economy, society, and culture by leading scholars. Black-and-white illustrations and maps, cumulative bibliography left to vol. 6. Monumental, wide-ranging, indispensable. [TD]

Society and Economy

24.410   S. J. Connolly. *Priests and people in pre-famine Ireland, 1780–1845.* New York: St. Martin's, 1982. ISBN 0-312-64411-6. ▸ Growth of modern Catholic church organization and ethos, set in contexts of clerical discipline and of conflict with traditional popular religion. New light also on marriage and sexual behavior. Scholarly, lively use of rich material. [TD]

24.411   David Dickson and P. Roebuck, eds. *Studies in Irish economic and social history.* Vol. 1: *Irish emigration, 1801–1921.* Vol. 2: *Landlords and tenants in Ireland, 1848–1904.* Vol. 3: *Religion and society in nineteenth-century Ireland.* Vol. 4: *The interwar economy in Ireland.* Vol. 5: *The modern industrialisation of Ireland, 1940–1988.* 5 vols. to date. David Fitzpatrick (v. 1), W. E. Vaughan (v. 2), S. J. Connolly (v. 3), David Johnson (v. 4), and Liam Kennedy (v. 5). Dublin: Economic & Social History Society of Ireland, 1984–89. ISBN 0-947897-00-3 (v. 1, pbk), 0-947897-01-1 (v. 2, pbk), ISSN 0790-2913. ▸ Excellent series of short introductions to modern research on selected topics. [TD]

24.412   J. M. Goldstrom and L. A. Clarkson, eds. *Irish population, economy, and society: essays in honour of Ken Connell.* Oxford: Clarendon, 1981. ISBN 0-19-822499-0. ▸ Colleagues and former students reflect and build on late Ken Connell's pioneering work in demography and social history. Particularly important are Cullen, Clarkson, and Lee on population and Goldstrom on agriculture. [TD]

24.413   Cormac O Gráda. *Ireland before and after the famine: explorations in economic history, 1800–1925.* Manchester: Manchester University Press; distributed by St. Martin's, 1988. ISBN 0-7190-1785-8. ▸ Linked essays by noted economist on key issues of demography, agricultural economy, and official policy. Framed by radical reassessment of famine historiography; puts old debates on new footing. [TD]

24.414   W. J. Smyth and K. Whelan, eds. *Common ground: essays on the historical geography of Ireland, presented to Professor T. Jones Hughes.* Cork: Cork University Press, 1988. ISBN 0-902561-53-7. ▸ Representative collection of essays by influential school of historical geographers. For modern period, see Whelan's seminal piece, "The Regional Impact of Irish Catholicism, 1700–1850." [TD]

Political History

24.415   P. Bew. *Conflict and conciliation in Ireland, 1890–1910: Parnellites and radical agrarians.* Oxford: Clarendon, 1987. ISBN 0-19-822758-2. ▸ Important study rescuing neglected period from myths of both literary revival and republican nationalism, showing continued dynamism and centrality of Home Rule party after Parnell. [TD]

24.416   Samuel Clark. *Social origins of the Irish land war.* Princeton: Princeton University Press, 1979. ISBN 0-691-05272-7 (cl), 0-691-10068-3 (pbk). ▸ Important analysis of post-famine social structure, especially emergence of ultimately dominant tenant-farmer class, who exploited problems and agitation of lower social group. Sociological approach combined with keen, cool historical judgment. [TD]

24.417   R. V. Comerford. *The Fenians in context: Irish politics and society, 1848–82.* Atlantic Highlands, N.J.: Humanities, 1985. ISBN 0-391-03312-3. ▸ Study of radical republicanism as one of several contemporary political movements fueled by aspirations of new Catholic petite bourgeoisie. Demythologizes key nationalist group and illuminates politics of formative period. [TD]

24.418   Ruth Dudley Edwards. *Patrick Pearse: the triumph of failure.* 1977 ed. New York: Taplinger, 1978. ISBN 0-8008-6267-8. ▸ Superb biography of most important leader, symbol, and retrospective interpreter of 1916 Easter Rebellion. Sympathetic demythologizing and convincing human and political portrait of classic romantic nationalist. [TD]

24.419   Ronan Fanning. *The Irish Department of Finance, 1922–58.* Dublin: Institute of Public Administration, 1978. ISBN 0-902173-82-0. ▸ Exemplary, authorized administrative history of key government department, casting new light on many aspects of politics of Irish state. [TD]

24.420   David Fitzpatrick. *Politics and Irish life, 1913–1921: provincial experience of war and revolution.* Dublin: Gill and Macmillan, 1977. ISBN 0-7171-8448-1. ▸ Brilliant local study, using wide variety of sources. Transforms understanding of every aspect of revolutionary period. Equally good on landlords, policemen, politicians, and gunmen. Classic, should be reprinted. [TD]

24.421   K. Theodore Hoppen. *Elections, politics, and society in Ireland, 1832–85.* Oxford: Clarendon, 1984. ISBN 0-19-822630-6. ▸ Scholarly, amusing tour de force weaving high and low politics into social and cultural contexts. Persuasive on franchise reform, local issues, influence, and neglected politics of liberalism and toryism. [TD]

24.422   Emmet Larkin. *The Roman Catholic church and the Home Rule movement in Ireland, 1870–1874.* Chapel Hill: University of North Carolina Press, 1990. ISBN 0-8078-1886-0. ▸ Sixth, most recently published, volume in projected eleven-volume series, authoritatively tracing, in great detail, high politics of church in nineteenth century. To be supplemented by companion volume on devotional revolution. [RKW]

24.423   Joseph J. Lee. *Ireland, 1912–1985: politics and society.* Cambridge: Cambridge University Press, 1989. ISBN 0-521-26648-3 (cl), 0-521-37741-2 (pbk). ▸ Highly original historical overview combined with trenchant critique of economic performance and cultural development. With powerful writing that earned major literary award, promises to become enduring classic. [TD]

24.424   F.S.L. Lyons. *Charles Stewart Parnell.* 1977 ed. London: Fontana, 1991. ISBN 0-00-686220-9. ▸ Masterful synthesis of author's earlier works on Parnell and Parnellism. Scholarly and urbane, but with acerbic final chapter revealing author's mixed feelings about subject that will always elude definitive biography. [TD]

24.425 Oliver MacDonagh. *Daniel O'Connell*. Vol. 1: *The hereditary bondsman, 1775–1829*. Vol. 2: *The emancipist, 1830–1847*. 2 vols. New York: St. Martin's, 1988–89. ISBN 0-312-01616-6 (v. 1), 0-312-03711-2 (v. 2). ▸ Study of life and politics of dominant Irish leader in first half of nineteenth century, making brilliant use of Maurice O'Connell's eight-volume edition of O'Connell correspondence. Classic biography, insights based on strong empathy and scholarship communicated in limpid style. [TD]

24.426 A.T.Q. Stewart. *The narrow ground: aspects of Ulster, 1609–1969*. Rev. ed. London: Faber & Faber, 1986. ISBN 0-571-15485-9 (pbk). ▸ Revision of insightful prize-winning essays setting present Northern Ireland conflict in historical context. Best on Protestant political culture. [TD]

24.427 Charles Townshend. *Political violence in Ireland: government and resistance since 1848*. Oxford: Clarendon, 1984. ISBN 0-19-821735-6 (cl), 0-19-820084-6 (pbk). ▸ Valuable overview of symbiotic relationship between Irish violence and British policy. Best on policing and use of army. [TD]

24.428 John H. Whyte. *Church and state in modern Ireland, 1923–1979*. 2d ed. Totowa, N.J.: Barnes & Noble, 1980. ISBN 0-06-497638-6. ▸ Still best analysis of relations between Catholic church and Irish state, particularly in areas of health and associated moral issues. [TD]

24.429 John H. Whyte. *Interpreting Northern Ireland*. Oxford: Clarendon, 1990. ISBN 0-19-827848-9. ▸ Authoritative guide to burgeoning research on Northern Ireland and to range of interpretations put forward, suffused by author's wide scholarship and liberal perspectives. [TD]

SCOTLAND

24.430 Robert D. Anderson. *Education and opportunity in Victorian Scotland: schools and universities*. 1983 ed. Edinburgh: Edinburgh University Press, 1989. ISBN 0-85224-617-X. ▸ Important study of whole Scottish educational system and its social implications. Variation on Saunders (24.436) and good guide to other work. [RKW]

24.431 Collum G. Brown. *The social history of religion in Scotland since 1730*. New York: Methuen, 1987. ISBN 0-416-36980-4. ▸ Valuable overview of Scottish religious situation as it evolved under challenge from denominational fragmentation, urban development, poverty, and other social problems. [RKW]

24.432 Stewart J. Brown. *Thomas Chalmers and the godly commonwealth in Scotland*. Oxford: Oxford University Press, 1982. ISBN 0-19-213114-1. ▸ Important study of influential conservative social theorist and reformer and leader of 1843 disruption that split Church of Scotland. [RKW]

24.433 George Elder Davie. *The democratic intellect: Scotland and her universities in the nineteenth century*. 1961 ed. Edinburgh: Edinburgh Unversity Press, 1981. ISBN 0-85224-435-5 (pbk). ▸ Lively, personal account of tension in philosophy, mathematics, and classics between Scottish university tradition and anglicizing pressures from England and within Scotland. [RKW]

24.434 H. J. Hanham. *Scottish nationalism*. Cambridge, Mass.: Harvard University Press, 1969. ISBN 0-674-79580-6. ▸ Concise account of movement that emerged after 1886, fueled by anglicization and failure of devolution schemes, culminating in agitation of Scottish National party from 1960s. [RKW]

24.435 Bruce Lenman. *An economic history of modern Scotland, 1660–1976*. New Haven: Archon, 1977. ISBN 0-208-01706-2. ▸ Clear, comprehensive survey of successive transformations of poor, inhospitable country by advanced agriculture, industry and commerce, and, more recently, oil. [RKW]

24.436 Laurence James Saunders. *Scottish democracy, 1815–1840: the social and intellectual background*. Edinburgh: Oliver & Boyd, 1950. ▸ Influential pioneering work interpreting early nineteenth-century Scotland in terms of erosion, through economic change and social problems, of inherited democratic ethos characterized by widespread education and opportunity. [RKW]

24.437 T. C. Smout. *A century of the Scottish people, 1830–1950*. New Haven: Yale University Press, 1986. ISBN 0-300-03774-0. ▸ General social history of working classes. [RKW]

24.438 Ronald M. Suntee. *Patronage and politics in Scotland, 1707–1832*. Edinburgh: Donald; distributed by Humanities, 1986. ISBN 0-85976-132-0. ▸ Canvases forms of patronage and offers several case studies in political arrangement in highly restrictive political society. [RKW]

WALES

24.439 P.M.H. Bell. *Disestablishment in Ireland and Wales*. London: Society for the Promotion of Christian Knowledge, 1969. (Church historical series, 90.) ISBN 0-281-02336-0. ▸ Clear account of background and passage of two acts in 1869 and 1919 that broke link between Anglican churches and state. Initiative in Wales major element in British politics. [RKW]

24.440 David W. Howell. *Land and people in nineteenth-century Wales*. London: Routledge & Kegan Paul, 1977. ISBN 0-7100-8673-3. ▸ Sympathetic, fair-minded study of landlord-tenant relations in Wales and basic Anglican-Nonconformist and Welsh divisions in countryside. Notable for giving landlords fair hearing. [FMLT]

24.441 David J. V. Jones. *Rebecca's children: a study of rural society, crime, and protest*. New York: Oxford University Press, 1989. ISBN 0-19-820099-4. ▸ Large-scale study sets highly complex form of protest in society undergoing profound displacement. Protests typically took form of attacks on tollgates by men dressed in women's clothes and series of riots that swept rural Wales in 1840s. [RKW]

24.442 Kenneth O. Morgan. *Rebirth of a nation: Wales, 1880–1980*. New York: Oxford University Press, 1981. ISBN 0-19-821736-6. ▸ Excellent general survey of last century by leading historian of Wales. Impressive bibliography. [RKW]

24.443 Kenneth O. Morgan. *Wales in British politics, 1868–1922*. 3d ed. Cardiff: University of Wales Press, 1980. ISBN 0-7083-0743-4. ▸ Authoritative study of radicalism and nationalism, which, refracted through dominating figure of David Lloyd George, made principality major factor in British politics in early twentieth century. [RKW]

THE BRITISH EMPIRE/COMMONWEALTH
General Studies

24.444 Roger Anstey. *The Atlantic slave trade and British abolition, 1760–1810*. Atlantic Highlands, N.J.: Humanities, 1975. ISBN 0-391-00371-2. ▸ Concludes humanitarian philosophic impulse of Quakers and others ended slave trade which brought only modest profit to slavers but harm to African societies. First major critique of Williams's thesis (3.212). [PM]

24.445 C. A. Bayly. *Imperial meridian: the British empire and the world, 1780–1830*. London: Longman, 1989. ISBN 0-582-04287-9 (cl), 0-582-49438-9 (pbk). ▸ Links British expansion in Canada, West Indies, Middle East, and India. Not on same large scale as earlier survey by V. T. Harlow, but largely supersedes it. [JWC]

24.446 Nupur Chaudhuri and Margaret Strobel, eds. *Western women and imperialism: complicity and resistance*. Bloomington: Indiana University Press, 1992. ISBN 0-253-31341-4 (cl), 0-253-20705-3 (pbk). ▸ Collection, with several strong articles and useful bibliographies, is probably best introduction to very active field. Argues feminism and imperialism had complex, ambiguous relationship. [JWC]

24.447 Seymour Drescher. *Econocide: British slavery in the era of abolition.* Pittsburgh: University of Pittsburgh Press, 1977. ISBN 0-8229-3344-6. ‣ Concludes British antislavery stemmed from humanitarian impulse, halting profitable slave enterprise. Critique of Williams's "decline" theory of abolition (3.212). Meticulous review of evidence, conclusion unproven. [PM]

24.448 D. K. Fieldhouse. *Economics and empire, 1830–1914.* 1973 ed. London: Macmillan, 1984. ISBN 0-333-36827-4. ‣ Thorough, painstaking critique of economic theories with wide-ranging case studies. In author's view, imperialism was indeed economic, but not simplistically so. [JWC]

24.449 Lewis H. Gann and Peter Duignan, eds. *Colonialism in Africa, 1870–1960.* 5 vols. Cambridge: Cambridge University Press, 1969–75. ISBN 0-521-07373-1 (v. 1), 0-521-07844-X (v. 3), 0-521-08641-8 (v. 4), 0-521-07859-8 (v. 5). ‣ High-quality essays, all with bibliographies. Volumes 1–2, historical; volume 3, anthropology; volume 4, economics; volume 5, bibliography. Same editors have produced several other related symposium volumes. [JWC]

24.450 William Keith Hancock. *Survey of British Commonwealth affairs.* 1937–42 ed. 3 vols. in 2. Westport, Conn.: Greenwood, 1977. ISBN 0-8371-9416-4 (v. 1), 0-8371-9417-2 (v. 2). ‣ Often called best book ever written in British imperial field. Volume 1, political: "appeasement" of colonial nationalism within the evolving commonwealth; volume 2, economic, including analysis of changing frontiers. [JWC]

24.451 Eric J. Hobsbawm. *Industry and empire: the making of modern English society, 1750 to the present day.* New York: Pantheon, 1968. ‣ One of few works linking domestic and imperial history. Argues imperialism accelerated Britain's rise to power and protracted and cushioned its decline. [JWC]

24.452 Thomas C. Holt. *The problem of freedom: race, labor, and politics in Jamaica and Britain, 1832–1938.* Baltimore: Johns Hopkins University Press, 1992. ISBN 0-8018-4216-6 (cl), 0-8018-4291-3 (pbk). ‣ Excellent comparative history linking racial and class attitudes and behavior in Jamaica and Britain. [JWC]

24.453 John M. MacKenzie. *Propaganda and empire: the manipulation of British public opinion, 1880–1960.* Manchester: Manchester University Press, 1984. ISBN 0-7190-1499-9 (cl), 0-7190-1869-2 (pbk). ‣ Argues, against Robinson and Gallagher 47.249, that imperialism had wide popular appeal. Author has also edited series on social and cultural history of imperialism. [JWC]

24.454 Nicholas Mansergh. *The commonwealth experience.* Vol. 1: *The Durham Report to the Anglo-Irish Treaty.* Vol. 2: *From British to multiracial commonwealth.* Rev. ed. 2 vols. Toronto: University of Toronto Press, 1983. ISBN 0-8020-2491-2 (v. 1, cl), 0-8020-2492-0 (v. 2, cl), 0-8020-6515-5 (v. 1, pbk), 0-8020-6516-3 (v. 2, pbk). ‣ Magisterial political survey, stressing white dominions, by author of many other works on commonwealth and Ireland. [JWC]

24.455 James Morris. *Heaven's command: an imperial progress.* 1973 ed. New York: Harcourt Brace Jovanovich, 1980. ISBN 0-15-640006-5. ‣ First volume of well-researched, entertaining trilogy, providing best popular history of British empire, from early Victorian period to 1960s. First published 1968. [JWC]

24.456 Bernard Porter. *The lion's share: a short history of British imperialism, 1850–1983.* 2d ed. London: Longman, 1984. ISBN 0-582-49387-0 (pbk). ‣ Interpretive essay arguing late nineteenth-century spread of British empire masked economic decline. New territories acquired reluctantly; need for maintenance and defense narrowed political options. Like Robinson and Gallagher 47.249, stresses inverse relationship between power and formal empire. Good undergraduate textbook, good bibliography. [JWC/RRM]

24.457 J. Holland Rose, A. P. Newton, and E. A. Benians, eds. *The Cambridge history of the British empire.* 2d ed. (v. 1) ed. 8 vols. Cambridge: Cambridge University Press, 1929–60. ‣ General survey in volumes 1–3. Additional volumes treat India, Canada, Australia, New Zealand, and South Africa. Essays dated but primary source bibliographies are still useful. [JWC]

24.458 Anil Seal. *The emergence of Indian nationalism: competition and collaboration in the later nineteenth century.* Cambridge: Cambridge University Press, 1971. ISBN 0-521-06274-8. ‣ Most important synthetic book in so-called Cambridge school, treating Indian politics largely as contest among regional power brokers. [JWC]

24.459 A. P. Thornton. *The imperial idea and its enemies: a study in British power.* 2d ed. Houndmills, England: Macmillan, 1985. ISBN 0-333-38256-0 (cl), 0-333-38257-9 (pbk). ‣ Survey, mainly of twentieth century, demonstrating that flexible and adaptive imperial ideology co-opted Labour party and democracy. [JWC]

SEE ALSO
47.241 Wm. Roger Louis, ed. *Imperialism.*
47.249 Ronald E. Robinson and John Gallagher. *Africa and the Victorians.*
48.311 Prosser Gifford and Wm. Roger Louis, eds. *Decolonization and African independence.*

Intellectual History

24.460 Philip D. Curtin. *The image of Africa: British ideas and action, 1780–1850.* Madison: University of Wisconsin Press, 1964. ‣ Argues British had more accurate image of Africa at height of slave trade in eighteenth century than at any time prior to mid-twentieth century. [JWC]

24.461 V. G. Kiernan. *The lords of human kind: black man, yellow man, and white man in an age of empire.* 1969 ed. New York: Columbia University Press, 1986. ISBN 0-231-05941-8 (pbk). ‣ Classic study of European arrogance, covering all periods and empires. [JWC]

24.462 Bernard Semmel. *Imperialism and social reform: English social-imperial thought, 1895–1914.* 1960 ed. New York: Doubleday, 1968. ‣ Classic study of intersection of imperial thought with social Darwinism, tariff reform, and Fabian socialism. [JWC]

Particular Periods

24.463 C. C. Eldridge, ed. *British imperialism in the nineteenth century.* New York: St. Martin's, 1984. ISBN 0-312-10299-2. ‣ Interpretive essays from symposium on historiographical controversies: continuity versus discontinuity, evolution of colonial self-government, stages of new imperialism, native collaboration and resistance, and role of race and social reform. Good suggestions for future reading. [JWC/RRM]

24.464 Wm. Roger Louis. *Imperialism at bay: the United States and the decolonization of the British empire, 1941–1945.* New York: Oxford University Press, 1978. ISBN 0-19-821125-2. ‣ Outstanding study based on voluminous archival research of love-hate relationship. [JWC]

24.465 D. A. Low, ed. *Congress and the raj: facets of the Indian struggle, 1917–47.* London: Heinemann, 1977. ISBN 0-435-99580-4. ‣ Essays ranging over crucial period of independence movement by authors of many important books, from both Cambridge and subaltern schools of Indian historiography. [JWC]

24.466 W. David McIntyre. *The imperial frontier in the tropics, 1865–75: a study of British colonial policy in West Africa, Malaya, and the South Pacific in the age of Gladstone and Disraeli.* New

York: St. Martin's, 1967. ▸ Analysis of how dynamics of frontier pulled British into tropics in era of comparative lack of enthusiasm at home. [JWC]

24.467 Elizabeth Monroe. *Britain's moment in the Middle East, 1914–1971*. Rev. ed. Baltimore: Johns Hopkins University Press, 1981. ISBN 0-8018-2626-0. ▸ Motivated by oil and concern over route to India, Britain steered between treacherous shoals of Zionism and Arab nationalism, from breakdown of Ottoman empire to aftermath of Suez. Classic study. [JWC]

24.468 Margery F. Perham. *Colonial sequence: a chronological commentary upon British colonial policy, especially in Africa.* 2 vols. London: Methuen; distributed by Barnes & Noble, 1967–70. ISBN 0-416-14930-0. ▸ British discourse about Africa, 1930–70, through eyes of remarkable woman, biographer and editor of great African proconsul Lord Lugard. Mainly articles from *Times* of London. [JWC]

24.469 John Manning Ward. *Colonial self-government: the British experience, 1759–1856.* Toronto: University of Toronto Press, 1976. ISBN 0-8020-2203-0. ▸ Traces constitutional development in white settlement colonies. Legalistic and somewhat dull. [JWC]

Biographies

24.470 John W. Cell. *Hailey: a study in British imperialism, 1872–1969.* Cambridge: Cambridge University Press, 1992. ISBN 0-521-41107-6. ▸ Biography of preeminent Indian civil servant who had second career as director of African Survey and adviser to Colonial Office. Examines colonialism, nationalism, and decolonization in India and Africa. [JWC]

24.471 Robert I. Rotberg. *The founder: Cecil Rhodes and the pursuit of power.* New York: Oxford University Press, 1988. ISBN 0-19-504968-3. ▸ On basis of voluminous research, demolishes myths about great imperialist (e.g., his ill health as youth) and offers good analysis of Rhodes's personality, including his sexuality. [JWC]

SEE ALSO

46.239 James Rutherford. *Sir George Grey, K.C.B., 1812–1898.*

LAWRENCE M. BRYANT

France, 1450–1789

Histories of early modern France (1450–1789) are not easily classified. For four centuries, historical interpretations and studies have supplied the foundation for the identity of France, its people, culture, and politics. Contemporary historians such as Fernand Braudel or Robert Darnton still tangle with the boundaries, groups, circumstances, and impulses that constitute "Frenchness" as a historical phenomenon, and, on this problem, they share common ground with sixteenth-century writers such as Louis Le Roy and François Hotman. Over the centuries *mutatis mutandis*, areas of research and methodologies have changed, however, along with the interests of audiences and patrons, institutions, and ideas about history.

The following bibliography is a highly selective introductory overview of influential works on the history of early modern France, primarily in English, that have been published during the past thirty years, a period described by a wide array of historians as crisis years for the discipline. The bibliography aims to reflect the issues and directions of recent research in the period as seen in the publications of practicing historians. Specialized studies in areas such as literary history, art history, emblematic history, folk history, history of mathematics, legal history, and a myriad of microhistories are not categorically included. These topics can be identified easily through the bibliographies and notations of the books included in these pages. Good sources to specialized topics are editions of collected essays that combine synthesis and monograph to offer a balance between broad patterns and new discoveries.

Many studies in this bibliography, heterogeneous in method and subject matter, are products of the blurring and crossing of traditional categories that for the last thirty years, more often than not, have enlarged our understanding of the period. The section begins with basic reference and general works. Then, studies are organized according to four broadly defined topical areas: culture and intellectual history, history of politics and government, history of religion, and history of economy and society. Each topical area has four chronological groupings: general, 1450–1610, 1610–1715, and 1715–1789. A pair of specialists in each topical area and the section editor determined a study's placement. They aimed more at producing a guide to the period than a map to specific topics.

From the 1950s to the 1980s, the journals, monographs, broader studies, and collaborative volumes of the historians associated with *Annales: économies, sociétés, civilisations* have attempted to detach social history from traditional positivist political and intellectual approaches. In following the work of Marc Bloch on rural history and the peasantry (25.322), historians J. Dupâquier (25.331), P. Goubert (25.356), and E. Le Roy Ladurie (25.337) helped to advance what is frequently tagged the Annales paradigm. In retrospect, one sees that their works and those of other *annaliste* historians are too varied and eclectic to constitute a true paradigm, but their studies share some distinctive influential features. They favor sources that can be quantified and analyzed rather than narrative as the mode of presentation; they aim for "total history" or one covering all aspects of life from basic material conditions to thought processes; they view structures and social life extended over time and inclusive of all social groups rather than according to political events and elites.

The approach leads to what is widely called "history from below" and has given impetus both to experimentation with methodologies and to a broadening of research agenda. Early modern history of the last thirty years has become rich in the study of *mentalités*, that is, the forms of thought, ways of communicating, and modes of self-identification among economically and politically marginal groups (women, servants, workers, etc.) who appear and are defined in history by accounts and records not of their own making. The history of *mentalités* is distinct from traditional history of ideas (or *idées*), that is, the writings of people conscious of their places and services in perpetuating systems like theology, law, philosophy, or politics. In the study of *mentalités*, traditional sources such as legal proceedings, tax accounts, parish records, folk rituals, or administrative reports, as well as anthropological and demographic materials have been applied to include the total social spectrum and to analyze structures and group behavior over the long term. *Annaliste* histories before the 1980s tended to draw general conclusions from local histories and the experiences of nonliterate groups. In the last two decades, historians have more carefully related the history of any particular group to relations among all groups. They have viewed group identities as a dynamic element created in the interplay between larger processes (economic, demographic, etc.) and particular strategies for survival or advantage. The elites of traditional society—the landed nobility, the officeholders, and the bourgeoisie—have become part of the evasive Annales paradigm and are now frequently studied in tandem with marginal groups and communities.

Many English-language histories of the last thirty years responded to the flow from *annaliste* France by including issues of social history in studies of religion, politics, and ideas. This more generally defined sociocultural approach was pioneered by N. Z. Davis in her influential *Society and Culture in Early Modern France* (25.326). These articles balance the emphases of the *annalistes* of the 1960s and 1970s on gradual social process, structural definitions of the object of study, and the inarticulate with traditional historical concerns for the influence of ideas and beliefs. A good sampling in English of the varieties of research within the Annales paradigm is available in the selections from *Annales* edited by R. Forster and O. Ranum (25.252, 25.333, 25.334). A leader of the most recent generation of *annalistes*, R. Chartier, reviews contemporary developments in his *Cultural History* (25.26) and particularly calls for taking care that the distinctions among the symbols and forms of different social groups not be lost in too general a cultural history. Social history still gives shadings to early modern French history among English-language historians, but it does not overshadow their subjects and methods.

Intellectual historians of the last thirty years have increasingly scrutinized the interaction of ideas and the sociopolitical status of their audiences. Studies of print culture, for example, explore the ways that particular groups received ideas and enacted them: for example, P. Beitenholz (25.41) on Basel's humanists, R. Darnton (25.101) on publishing and book trade in the production of the *Encyclopédie*, and the essays collected by R. Chartier (25.27) and by J. Censer and J. Popkin (25.95) on the role of the press in the making of political culture. John Lough's 1978 study on the cultural impact of writers (25.34) has been joined by specialized studies like D. Goodman's on new habits of reading (25.110) and E. Harth's on origins of modern literate genres (25.68). All the topics of intellectual history cannot be discussed here, but the same sort of interaction can be seen in the history of education from sixteenth-century humanist schools to the religious and new communal schools of the seventeenth and eighteenth centuries in G. Huppert's overview of education (25.47) and in Compère and Julia's massive documentation of educational foundations and curricula (25.29). Literacy has been reviewed in essays edited by F. Furet and J. Ozouf (25.32). Salons, academies, and other places for the exchange of ideas into identities or action have been widely studied, as in the essays collected by L. Hunt (25.113). For an earlier period, D. Kelley (25.50) has followed the entrance of historical-mindedness into sixteenth-century French intellectual life through its impact on legal studies. Nanner O. Keohane (25.33) traces the influence of moral philosophy on political thought. Peter Gay's *The Enlightenment* (25.107) sees the movement as the turn toward modernity, an interpretation questioned by I. Wade (25.129).

The rise of cultural history has broadened the parameters of intellectual history to include topics on popular spectacles (e.g., R. Isherwood 25.114; M. M. Bakhtin 25.40; M. Fried 25.106). The collapse of the style of Versailles in the eighteenth century has been analyzed as the making of bourgeois public space by J. Habermas (22.330). Thomas E. Crow (25.99) uses this notion to look at the ways in which artistic and salon culture gave shape to politics. In different ways, the uses of public space inform architectural studies of D. Thomson (25.58) on sixteenth-century Paris, G. Walton (25.88) on Versailles, and A. Vidler (25.128) on eighteenth-century architectural language. Rhetoric and various forms of popular narratives from the *bibliothèque bleue*, proceedings in law, and "famine plot persuasion" are included in intellectual history. Likewise, the formal culture of science and its place in thought receive attention in studies of Condorcet (Baker 25.90), mesmerism (R. Darnton 25.102), and academies (C. C. Gillispie 25.109; R. Hahn 25.112; A. Stroup 25.86). As with other topics so briefly noted here, the great effort of the last thirty years to place women into the history of the period is especially evident in intellectual and cultural histories (e.g., E. Badinter 25.89; J. DeJean 25.61). Historians of the period have necessarily had to deal with Michel Foucault's influential works and weigh the degree to which human agencies affect events and to which humans are captive of "epistemes" and, in a later work, "discursive formations" that define language and power in any set historical circumstance. The intellectual and cultural topics blend with the political history of the period in that studies of taste, art, manners, and cultural productions evaluate governmental resources for managing sociability and public life, whether in communities, towns, academies, and literary groups, or at Versailles (e.g., P. France 25.31; J. Dewald 25.62; R. Koselleck 25.117).

In political history, the recovery of France after the Hundred Years' War up to 1560 has been seen by B. Chevalier (25.149) and J. R. Major (25.177) as a period of general accord between towns, kings, and monarchical institutions. The outbreak of religious and civil wars which continued to the end of the mid-seventeenth-century revolts of the Fronde and the reign of Louis XIV (ca. 1660) covers times of collapse into near anarchy and of debates over strategies for bringing about order. In the seventeenth century, domestic revolts paled beside foreign wars that helped push France into an *état d'offices*, a government whose resources and limits were based on family interests, purchases of offices (the nobility of the robe), and agencies for tax-collecting, as discussed by R. Bonney (25.200) and J. Collins (25.203). The traditional nobility of the sword shifted their bases of operation from regional self-sufficiency to dependency on the state, the royal court, and marriage outside its ranks. Urban politics replaced traditional concerns over communal liberties with the pursuit of personal privileges and offices. Patronage, as S. Kettering (25.213) and others have shown, kept the political structure functioning.

Three great struggles dominate the period after Louis XIV's death (1715) until the Revolution of 1789: the monarchy's efforts to preserve its authority and secure income; the attempts of the nobility and high magistrates, particularly the *parlementaires*, to enlarge their role in government and deny income to the state; and the pressure of newly literate groups—resulting from education, publishing, learned societies, and commercial wealth (an example of how social, political, and intellectual history come together)—to acquire political identities. Recent political history has shown the tensions in the political system and the necessary accommodations among institutions including royal councils, provincial assemblies, town governments, nobles, Parlements, tax farmers, and other legal groups with claims to counsel the king or to be protected by the monarchy. David Parker (25.221), among others, deflates the notion that political history of the period is a simple narrative of the growth of absolute power. The point is amply illustrated in the histories on the Parlement of Paris from J. H. Shennan's survey (25.140) to many specialized studies of *parlementaire* politics (e.g., J. Dewald 25.344; A. N. Hamscher 25.206) and of urban life (P. Benedict, ed. 25.131). The same may be said for other institutions which are set forth in R. Mousnier's *The Institutions of France under the Absolute Monarchy* (25.137).

Early modern historians have factored in imagery and representations of authority with power and finance as sources for preserving the structure of state and the monarchy. Marc Bloch's *The Royal Touch* (25.132) secured royal ceremonies as a major historical topic. Since Bloch, royal funerals, coronations, entries, and *lit-de-justice* assemblies as well as royal propaganda and artistic and literary patronage have been studied as expressions of influence, power, and political institutions (e.g., F. Yates 25.194; A. M. Lecoq 25.51). Like so much in this period, decorum and ceremony took shape not according to the centralizing designs and intentions of state planners but haphazardly in performances and in response to circumstances (R. Giesey 25.133). The more the monarchy insisted on choreographing public representations of power and public taste and decorum, the more the king had to retreat into what Norbert Elias called a court society.

For religious topics, the essays in R. Briggs's *Communities of Belief* (25.249) offer an excellent introduction to the problems with which the French church grappled as both a community of believers and an ancient institution. While acknowledging other factors in religious history such as printing and lay education, he emphasizes that "religious fervour, even fanaticism, was a powerful force for change in society and politics, yet was in its turn being inflected by the very developments it helped to create." The structure of religion changed from sixteenth-century communities of belief to late seventeenth-century agencies of control. The local nature of control in witch trials gave way to zealous seventeenth-century reformers who in their imposition of impossible standards of piety lost support for religion among both traditional Christians and intellectuals. The book makes excellent use of and critiques other basic works on the extent and nature of belief in France, as well as on culture and guilt, witchcraft, magistrates, and heresy (e.g., J. Delumeau 25.250; L. Febvre 25.271). In a massive study, D. Crouzet (25.267) chronicles a France of deep anxiety over divine punishment that accounts for the violent disruption of social life, religion, and politics after 1525.

The religious and civil wars of 1560–1598 dominate sixteenth-century history. Robert Kingdon (25.276, 25.277) has followed the growth of Calvinism in France. Studies by N. M. Sutherland (25.283), M. Greengrass (25.162), and D. Nugent (25.281) explore the early status of the Huguenots. H. G. Koenigsberger (25.170) looks at the Huguenot question as both a matter of politics and religion. The writings following the massacres of St. Bartholomew's Day made this clear as seen in several studies (Kingdon 25.278; R. Descimon 25.151; J.H.M. Salmon 25.183). The responses of regions and towns to conflict during the period have been considered by B. Diefendorf (25.269), E. Le Roy Ladurie, (25.171), and others. Donald Kelley (25.166) finds Huguenot writing facilitated the leap from polemic to ideology. The demographics of the seventeenth-century Huguenot minority has been mapped by P. Benedict (25.349), and the politics of the revocation of the Edict of Nantes have been studied by J. Orcibal (25.301) and E. Labrousse (25.298), and in essays collected by M. Prestwich (25.257).

Seventeenth-century religious controversies among the Catholic majority took place in an ambience insistent on uniformity in worship and administrative order and included debates on relations with Rome and on the roles of Huguenots, Jesuits, and other religious institutions (R. Mousnier 25.219). Church histories include studies on the late sixteenth-century French episcopate, seventeenth-century Catholic reform, overviews of Louis XIV's reign, and eighteenth-century high clergy. The debates over religious practices and Catholic belief have a rich literature, including L. Goldmann's study on Pascal and the religious thought of the nobility of the robe (25.293) and A. Sedgwick (25.305) and D. Van Kley (25.127) on Jansenist controversies in religion and politics. In the eighteenth century, popular religion continued to validate beliefs through special miracles (R. Kreiser 25.313). But the excessive claims by reformers to represent all things sacred over-burdened both church and state to the breaking point, as illustrated by R. R. Palmer's classic work on "unbelief" (25.316) and by studies on atheism (A. Kors, 25.296) and desacralization (J. Merrick 25.315). Over fifteen monographs on changes in popular religious beliefs and community life are included.

Many studies analyze the impact of economic and agricultural changes on the nobility, clergy, bourgeoisie, and peasantry of early modern France. In social and economic history, three chronological benchmarks stand out: first, mid-fifteenth-century demographic growth and improved conditions in most of France; then economic stagnation and no growth in the mid-sixteenth-century until the death of Louis XIV (1715); and, finally, an upturn in population amid an unprecedented inequitable distribution of the economic and alimentary resources. Social history gives paramount importance to changes in structures and patterns of behavior. It includes very different kinds of studies: G. V. Taylor's illustration that the dynamic among the wealthy of society was to invest commercial profit into a market of social status and titles of honor (26.78), D. Garrioch's demonstration of the weakening of community life with the retreat from Parisian neighborhoods of status-seeking elites (25.383), J. Farr's depiction of master artisans' strategies for survival in Dijon (25.345), and O. Hufton's study on the ways in which society dealt with the poor (25.384).

Social, political, and intellectual historians differ on the pace and impetus leading to the sociopolitical arrangements of early modern France and over whether the arrangements were by makeshift or by design. Howell A. Lloyd (25.173) emphasizes in his overview of the sixteenth century that traditional society was transformed by the growth of the state, the growth of state finances, and the commercialization of social and political relations. Boris Porchnev (25.361, in P. J. Coreney, ed. 25.204) provoked over a decade of research with his Marxist thesis that seventeenth-century revolts were popular responses to a "Feudalo-absolutism" whereby the state collected feudal rent as taxes in order to keep support of the nobility. Many historians have persevered in a debate over the sources and nature of absolutism (e.g., R. Mousnier 25.359; A. B. Lublinskaya 25.215). According to P. Goubert (25.355), the governmental system of absolutism is best called "confusion." Alliances of interests, finds W. Beik (25.197), perpetuated arrangements that benefited the provincial ruling class, and A. N. Hamscher (25.207) shows how Parlements collaborated with the monarchy to their advantage. Yves-Marie Bercé (25.350) makes clear that peasants lost ground during the century, and S. Hanley (25.357) finds that a paternalistic family-state compact limiting women's legal status took shape. Overall, recent historical research into economics, behavior, and society has favored case studies over grand theory, whether Marxism, absolutism, mercantilism, or statism (e.g., G. Huppert 25.346; K. B. Neuschel 25.54).

Finally, over fifty biographies are listed below. These are contextual studies and excellent introductions to periods as well as persons. In intellectual history, there are among others, books on Michel de Montaigne, Jean-Jacques Rousseau, Guillaume Budé, and the comte de Boulainvilliers. In political history, recent biographies include those of kings Louis XI, Francis I, Henry II, Henry III, Henry IV, Louis XIII, and Louis XIV. Note is taken of other central political figures of a period, such as the queen of Navarre, Jeanne d'Albret; François, duke of Anjou; and Philippe, duke of Orléans. Biographies can be found in the subsection and period in which their subjects gained historical reputation. For example, those of Cardinals Richelieu, Mazarin, and de Retz are listed with political history rather than religion. Many of the most important works cannot be easily categorized, but it is hoped that users of this guide can be led to the scholarship and issues of the period in the spirit of study called for by Lucien Febvre, one informed but not preconditioned by taxonomies, categories, and definitions.

ACKNOWLEDGMENTS   *The contributors deserve acknowledgment for their exceptional professionalism and high sense of colleagueship: Dena Goodman and Henry C. Clark for intellectual and cultural history; Mack P. Holt and Jack R. Censer for political history; Barbara Diefendorf and Richard M. Golden for religion; Keith P. Luria and Philip T. Hoffman for social and economic histories. Much of the merit is theirs, what is otherwise is the responsibility of the section editor. The final work on this section took place in the ideal setting of the Folger Shakespeare Library and was made possible by a grant from the National Endowment for the Humanities. The introduction benefited from the editorial comments of Georgianna Ziegler, Nancy Klein Maguire, and Pamela Gerardi. Grace Disman, with a fellowship from the Graduate College of California State University, Chico, greatly assisted in preparing the final manuscript. Marcia Langley Bryant's help has been indispensable.*

Entries are arranged under the following headings:

Reference Works

General Studies

Cultural and Intellectual History
General Studies
1450–1610
1610–1715
1715–1789

Politics and Government
General Studies
1450–1610
1610–1715
1715–1789

Religion
General Studies
1450–1610
1610–1715
1715–1789

Economy and Society
General Studies
1450–1610
1610–1715
1715–1789

[Contributors: BBD = Barbara B. Diefendorf, DG = Dena Goodman, HCC = Henry C. Clark, JRC = Jack R. Censer, KPL = Keith P. Luria, LMB = Lawrence M. Bryant, MPH = Mack P. Holt, PTH = Philip T. Hoffman, RMG = Richard M. Golden]

REFERENCE WORKS

25.1 Louis André. *Les sources l'histoire de France: dix-septième siècle (1610–1715).* 8 vols. Paris: Picard, 1913–35. ‣ Useful for locating works published during period and scholarship up to publication of volumes. Volumes arranged topically: geographies and general histories, memoirs and letters, biographies, journals and pamphlets, political and military, maritime and colonial, religious, economic and administrative, and provincial and local. [LMB]

25.2 J. Balteau et al., eds. *Dictionnaire de biographie française.* 18 vols. to date. Paris: Letouzey & Ané, 1933–. ISBN 2-7063-0158-9 (set). ‣ Ongoing project presenting most current scholarship for French biographies. Present volumes cover to name Humann. [LMB]

25.3 *Bibliographie annuelle de l'histoire de France du cinquième siècle à 1958.* Paris: Centre National de la Recherche Scientifique, 1975–. ISSN 0067-6918. ‣ Bibliography of history of France beginning in fifteenth century. Omits literature, arts, and science. Covers books and articles and includes indexes of persons and places. Edition titles vary with date of publication. First edition appeared in 1898. [LMB]

25.4 *Bibliographie internationale de l'humanisme et de la Renaissance.* Geneva: Droz, 1965–. ISSN 0067-7000. ‣ Best source of its kind for materials on early modern France. Appears periodically; cites works in Renaissance history. [LMB]

25.5 Jacques Boussard. *Atlas historique et culturel de la France.* Jean Alazard, Preface. Paris: Elsevier, 1957. ‣ Maps, illustrations, and descriptions of regions of France. Useful standard work. [LMB]

25.6 Frances Chambers. *France.* Rev. ed. Oxford: ABC-Clio, 1990. (World bibliographical series, 13.) ISBN 1-85109-082-7. ‣ Good introduction to basic works on France in English. More for general use than for specific or recent historical information. [LMB]

25.7 Alexandre Cioranescu. *Bibliographie de la littérature française du seizième siècle.* Paris: Klincksieck, 1959. ‣ Guide to works in print of major and minor French writers and of basic scholarship to date of publication. Excellent bibliographical introductions to the historical period. [LMB]

25.8 Alexandre Cioranescu. *Bibliographie de la littérature française du dix-septième siècle.* 3 vols. Paris: Centre National de la Recherche Scientifique, 1965–66. ‣ Guide to works in print of major and minor French writers and of basic scholarship to date of volumes' publication. Excellent bibliographical introductions to the historical period. [LMB]

25.9 Alexandre Cioranescu. *Bibliographie de la littérature française du dix-huitième siècle.* 3 vols. Paris: Centre National de la Recherche Scientifique, 1969. ‣ Guide to works in print of major and minor French writers and of basic scholarship to date of publication. Excellent bibliographical introductions to the historical period. [LMB]

25.10 Alfred Franklin. *Les sources de l'histoire de France: notices bibliographiques et analytiques des inventaires et des receuils de documents relatifs à l'histoire de France.* 1877 ed. Nendeln, Liechtenstein: Kraus Reprint, 1967. ‣ Remains excellent guide to various collections of French historical writings and documents. [LMB]

25.11 *French 17.* Fort Collins, Colo.: Colorado State University for Modern Language Association, Seventeenth-Century Division. ISSN 0191-9199. ‣ Annual descriptive bibliography of French seventeenth-century studies. Helpful survey of current works. [LMB]

25.12 Henri Hauser. *Les sources de l'histoire de France, seizième siècle (1494–1610).* 1906–15 ed. 4 vols. in 2. Nendeln, Liechtenstein: Kraus Reprint, 1967. ‣ Standard guide to published documents and sources for period. [LMB]

25.13 Jean Chrétien Hoefer, ed. *Nouvelle biographie générale depuis les temps les plus réculés jusqu'à 1850–60, avec les renseignments bibliographiques et l'indication des sources à consulter.* 1852–66 ed. 46 vols. in 23. Copenhagen: Rosenkilde & Bagger, 1963–69. ‣ Rival to Michauds' *Bibliographie universelle* (25.17). [LMB]

25.14 Robert O. Lindsay and John Neu. *Mazarinades: a checklist of copies in major collections in the United States.* Metuchen, N.J.: Scarecrow, 1972. ISBN 0-8108-0369-0. ‣ Useful list of reproductions of seventeenth-century pamphlets in major American libraries from those listed in three-volume grand collection by Celestin Moreau, *Bibliographie des Mazarinades* (1850–51). [LMB]

25.15 Robert O. Lindsay and John Neu, comps. *French political pamphlets, 1547–1648: a catalog of major collections in American libraries.* Madison: University of Wisconsin Press, 1969. ISBN 0-299-04990-6. ‣ Locates copies of nearly 6,800 works of French. Most now available on microfilm from New Haven: Research Publications. [LMB]

25.16 Marcel Marion. *Dictionnaire des institutions de la France aux dix-septième et dix-huitième siècles.* 1923 ed. Paris: Picard, 1984. ISBN 2-7084-0030-4. ‣ Essential guide for historical understanding of institutions, customs, and sociopolitical practices of period. [LMB]

25.17 J. F. Michaud and L. G. Michaud. *Biographie universelle, ancienne et moderne, ou histoire, par ordre alphabetique, de la vie publique et privée de tous les hommes qui se sont fait remarquer par leurs écrits, leurs actions, leurs vertus, ou leurs crimes.* Rev. ed. 85 vols. Société de Gens de Lettres et de Savants, ed. Paris: Michaud Frères, 1811–62. ‣ Judged superior to nineteenth-century rival edition of French biographies (e.g., 25.13). [LMB]

25.18 Paul Robert. *Dictionnaire alphabetique et analogique de la langue française.* 2d rev. ed. 9 vols. Alain Rey, ed. Paris: Dictionnaires le Robert, 1985. ISBN 2-85036-099-6 (set). ▸ Standard historical dictionary with quotations from writers illustrating changes in usage and etymology. Updated version of Emile Littré's classic *Dictionaire de la langue française (1846–1872)*. [LMB]

GENERAL STUDIES

25.19 André Burguière and Jacques Revel, eds. *Histoire de France*. Vol. 1: *L'espace française*. Vol. 2: *L'état et les pouvoirs*. Vol. 3: *L'état et les conflits*. 3 vols. to date. Paris: Seuil, 1989–. ISBN 2-02-010235-8 (set), 2-02-010236-6 (v. 1), 2-02-010237-4 (v. 2), 2-02-010238-2 (v. 3). ▸ Series exploring major themes in making of French identity. Volume 1 treats how geographical space became France and how humans express being French. Volume 2 treats the state as it moves to appropriate communities. Volume 3 treats conflicts as seen in social and economic forces; in religious dissent and definitions of communities with Cathars, Protestants, and Jansenists; and in dialectic of conflict-integration of peripheral minorities. Excellent up-to-date bibliographies. [LMB]

25.20 P. E. Charvet, ed. *A literary history of France*. Vol. 2: *Renaissance France, 1470–1589*. Vol. 3: *The seventeenth century, 1600–1715*. Vol. 4: *The eighteenth century, 1715–1789*. I. D. McFarlane (v. 2), P. J. Yarrow (v. 3) and R. Niklaus (v. 4). London and New York: Benn and Barnes & Noble, 1967–74. ▸ Sound introduction to literature of each period with bibliographies. [LMB]

25.21 *Histoire de France Hachette*. 5 vols. Paris: Hachette, 1987–91. ISBN 2-01-013367-6 (set). ▸ Although framed in political narrative, volumes reflect changes of last forty years in social, economic, and cultural interpretations of French past. Volumes by leading French historians, instrumental in formulation of these interpretations. Good general bibliographies and well-selected illustrations. [LMB]

25.22 Denis Hollier, ed. *A new history of French literature*. Cambridge, Mass.: Harvard University Press, 1989. ISBN 0-674-61565-4. ▸ Self-consciously iconoclastic exploration of directions in literary study, with particular attention to impact on scholarship of Annales paradigm and Michel Foucault. [LMB]

25.23 Robert Mandrou. *Introduction to modern France, 1500–1640: an essay in historical psychology*. 1975 ed. R. E. Hallmark, trans. New York: Holmes & Meier, 1976. ISBN 0-8419-0245-3. ▸ Major *annaliste* historian's parallel histories of emergence of new French behavior, new group consciousness, and new conditions of existence during extraordinary changes of long sixteenth century. Excellent systematic bibliography. [LMB]

CULTURAL AND INTELLECTUAL HISTORY

General Studies

25.24 Anthony Blunt. *Art and architecture in France, 1500 to 1700*. 1982 4th rev. ed. London: Penguin, 1991. ISBN 0-14-56004-1 (cl), 0-14-056104-8 (pbk). ▸ Remains standard English-language introduction to arts and artists of period. Richly illustrated. [LMB]

25.25 Norman Bryson. *Word and image: French painting of the Ancien Régime*. Cambridge: Cambridge University Press, 1981. ISBN 0-521-23776-9. ▸ Engaging study of role of language in giving meaning to painting. Examines connotations of images, patterns of information, and participation of viewers in successive periods from Charles LeBrun to French Revolution. [LMB]

25.26 Roger Chartier. *Cultural history: between practices and representations*. Lydia G. Cochrane, trans. Ithaca, N.Y.: Cornell University Press, 1988. ISBN 0-8014-2223-X. ▸ Valuable essays on method and research directions for period. Four essays on issues in history of culture; four essays as models of method. [LMB]

25.27 Roger Chartier, ed. *The cultural uses of print in early mod-*

ern France. Lydia G. Cochrane, trans. Princeton: Princeton University Press, 1987. ISBN 0-691-05499-1. ▸ Essays in cultural history challenging opposition between popular and elite cultures, traditional and print cultures, and texts and human actions by exploring connections between them. Concludes culture is source for representation and meaning. [DG]

25.28 Roger Chartier, Dominique Julia, and Marie-Madeleine Compère. *L'éducation en France du dix-sixième au dix-huitième siècle*. Paris: Société d'Édition d'Enseignement Supérieur, 1976. ISBN 2-7181-5201-X. ▸ Survey of educational institutions, theories, and practices, including role of church and religious change, political and social purposes of schooling, literacy levels, and education of girls. [HCC]

25.29 Marie-Madeleine Compère and Dominique Julia. *Les collèges francais, 16e–18e siècles*. Vol. 1: *Répertoire France du Midi*. Vol. 2: *Répertoire France du Nord et l'Ouest*. 2 vols. to date. Paris: Institut National de Recherche Pédagogique and Centre National de la Recherche Scientifique, 1984–. ISBN 2-7342-0003-1 (v. 1), 2-7342-0196-8 (v. 2). ▸ Definitive guide to general education in France for period. Follows each educational establishment in stages from foundation to French Revolution. [LMB]

25.30 Lucien Febvre and Henri-Jean Martin. *The coming of the book: the impact of printing, 1450–1800*. 1976 ed. Geoffrey Nowell-Smith and David Wootton, eds. David Gerard, trans. London: Verso, 1990. ISBN 0-86091-797-5 (pbk). ▸ Examination of book and its place in social, economic, cultural, and political life by leading Annales scholars. Topics range from production of paper and invention of moveable type to influence of printing in Renaissance and Reformation. Emphasis on material base and book as object. [HCC]

25.31 Peter France. *Politeness and its discontents: problems in French classical culture*. Cambridge: Cambridge University Press, 1992. ISBN 0-521-37070-1. ▸ Broad-ranging essays on rational norms for "civilized" sociability and thought. Explores tension in politeness as ideal and oppressive force that finds re-enactment in politics from seventeenth-century court to Revolution. [DG]

25.32 François Furet and Jacques Ozouf, eds. *Reading and writing: literacy in France from Calvin to Jules Ferry*. Cambridge: Cambridge University Press, 1982. ISBN 0-521-22389-X (cl), 0-521-27402-8 (pbk). ▸ Quantitative study by Annales historians situating history of literacy within social history of France. Challenges assumptions about relationship between literacy and schooling in postrevolutionary historico-political debate between republicans and Catholics. Many maps and tables. [DG]

25.33 Nannerl O. Keohane. *Philosophy and the state in France: the Renaissance to the Enlightenment*. Princeton: Princeton University Press, 1980. ISBN 0-691-07611-1 (cl), 0-691-10078-0 (pbk). ▸ History of political thought arguing for importance of seventeenth-century moral literature in shaping that thought. Sees French discourse of interests as alternative to Anglo-Saxon discourse of rights as background to liberalism. [HCC]

25.34 John Lough. *Writer and public in France: from the Middle Ages to the present day*. Oxford: Clarendon, 1978. ISBN 0-19-815749-5. ▸ Narrative, empirical literary history with emphasis on seventeenth and eighteenth centuries. Discusses impact on writers of printing and publishing, patronage, social milieux, cultural institutions, actors and audiences, and material conditions. [DG]

25.35 Robert Mandrou. *From humanism to science, 1480–1700*. 1978 ed. Brian Pearce, trans. Harmondsworth: Penguin, 1985. ISBN 0-14-022079-8 (pbk). ▸ General study of Renaissance with emphasis on France by Annales historian. Examines ideas within context of economic and social relations, cultural institutions, political and religious authorities, and technologies of intellectual production. [DG]

25.36 Henri-Jean Martin and Roger Chartier, eds. *Histoire de l'édition française.* Vol. 1: *Le livre conquérant.* Vol. 2: *Le livre triomphant, 1660–1830.* Paris: Promodis, 1982–84. ISBN 2-903181-06-3 (v. 1), 2-903181-31-4 (v. 2). ▸ Sumptuously illustrated essay collection by leading scholars. Covers origins of printing; humanist, religious, and secular uses; elite and popular culture; book production; booksellers and printers; authors and readers; and impact of French Revolution. [DG]

25.37 Daniel Roche. *La culture des apparences: un historie du vêtement (XVIIe–XVIIIe siècle).* Paris: Fayard, 1989. ISBN 2-213-02358-1. ▸ Cultural history seen through seventeenth- and eighteenth-century manners and modes of dressing. From production of cloth to seduction of appearances, vestments as important source for understanding manners and politics of period. [LMB]

25.38 English Showalter, Jr. *The evolution of the French novel, 1641–1782.* Princeton: Princeton University Press, 1972. ISBN 0-691-06229-3. ▸ Analysis of gradual evolution of novel form within general intellectual history, especially 1700–20. Focuses on authors, literary techniques, rise of realism, and theme of individual against society. [DG]

SEE ALSO
22.330 Jürgen Habermas. *The structural transformation of the public sphere.*

1450–1610

25.39 Philippe Ariès and Georges Duby, eds. *A history of private life.* Vol. 3: *Passions of the Renaissance.* Arthur Goldhammer, trans. Cambridge, Mass.: Belknap, 1989. ISBN 0-674-39977-3 (v. 3). ▸ Collective volume in major French series. Sees origins of modernity in creation of individual and family and development of privacy out of communal social forms, practices, and spaces of Middle Ages. [DG]

25.40 Mikhail M. Bakhtin. *Rabelais and his world.* 1968 ed. Helene Iswolsky, trans. Bloomington: Indiana University Press, 1984. ISBN 0-253-34830-7 (cl), 0-253-20341-4 (pbk). ▸ Influential study by Russian literary scholar with emphasis on carnivalesque in Rabelais's work and world. Finds roots of grotesque realism in popular culture. Sees Rabelaisian laughter as foundation of democratic tradition in literature. [DG]

25.41 Peter G. Beitenholz. *Basle and France in the sixteenth century: the Basle humanists and printers in their contacts with Francophone culture.* Geneva: Droz, 1971. ISBN 0-8020-1754-1. ▸ Erudite, essential study on transmission and circulation of ideas in sixteenth century. Basle as intellectual clearinghouse for Francophone and humanist culture. [LMB]

25.42 Miriam Usher Chrisman. *Lay culture, learned culture: books and social change in Strasbourg, 1480–1599.* New Haven: Yale University Press, 1982. ISBN 0-3000-2530-0. ▸ Study of three generations of book publishing. Shows gradual divide between Latin and vernacular readers. Careful demonstration of place of books in thought and beliefs of sixteenth-century people. [LMB]

25.43 Natalie Zemon Davis. *Fiction in the archives: pardon tales and their tellers in sixteenth-century France.* Stanford, Calif.: Stanford University Press, 1987. ISBN 0-8047-1412-6 (cl), 0-8047-1799-0 (pbk). ▸ Cultural and literary analysis of letters of remission. Examines storytelling skills across classes and cultures, cultural exchange between popular and elite cultures, and relationship between legal and literary texts. [DG]

25.44 Philippe Desan, ed. *Humanism in crisis: the decline of the French Renaissance.* Ann Arbor: University of Michigan Press, 1991. ISBN 0-472-10239-7. ▸ Fourteen excellent articles on failure of humanism to transform sixteenth-century culture, politics, and

society. Sees mercantile discourse as displacing shared language and tenets of communal values. [LMB]

25.45 Werner L. Gundersheimer, ed. *French humanism, 1470–1600.* New York: Harper & Row, 1970. ▸ Excellent essays, including Augustin Renaudet and Lucien Romier on early Renaissance and Lucien Febvre on divided culture that marked end of Renaissance. Covers central issues for understanding period. [LMB]

25.46 George Huppert. *The idea of perfect history: historical erudition and historical philosophy in Renaissance France.* Urbana: University of Illinois Press, 1970. ISBN 0-252-00076-5. ▸ Argues that new ways for critiquing public life appeared in historical studies of humanists and jurists such as Étienne Pasquier, Henri Voisin de La Popelinière, and Louis Le Roy. Indispensable for rise of modern historical-mindedness among writers. [LMB]

25.47 George Huppert. *Public schools in Renaissance France.* Urbana: University of Illinois Press, 1984. ISBN 0-252-01053-1. ▸ Lucid, learned account of construction and decay of socially transforming schools of Renaissance. Concludes communal, lively humanist program subverted by state, Jesuits, Parisian influence, and economics. [LMB]

25.48 Jean Jacquot, ed. *Les fêtes de la Renaissance.* 3 vols. Paris: Centre National de la Recherche Scientifique, 1956–75. ISBN 2-222-01679-7 (v. 3). ▸ Collection of articles on all aspects of festivals, ceremonies, entries, and other public and princely celebrations in Europe; majority on early modern France. Topics include decorations, architecture, drama, program books, political propaganda, and processions. Basic to topic of festivals. [LMB]

25.49 Michel Jeanneret. *A feast of words: banquets and table talk in the Renaissance.* Jeremy Whiteley and Emma Hughes, trans. Chicago: University of Chicago Press, 1991. ISBN 0-226-39575-8 (cl), 0-226-39576-6 (pbk). ▸ Bakhtinian study (see 25.40) of Renaissance culture examining relationship between dining and discourse, body and text, codes of conduct and their transgression, self-control and excess, festivity, and play. Inventiveness of literature broadly conceived. [DG]

25.50 Donald R. Kelley. *Foundations of modern historical scholarship: language, law, and history in the French Renaissance.* New York: Columbia University Press, 1970. ISBN 0-231-03141-6. ▸ Essential study of relationship between language and historical-mindedness in Renaissance France. Concludes Lorenzo Valla and philology, legal education, humanism, and *parlementaire* culture shaped historical and antiphilosophical ways of critiquing public life. [LMB]

25.51 Anne-Marie Lecoq. *François Ier imaginaire: symbolique et politique á l'aube de la Renaissance française.* Paris: Macula, 1987. ISBN 2-86589-019-8. ▸ Richly illustrated, solidly researched; innovative study of connections between culture and politics in art and symbolism of Francis I's reign. Renaissance royal symbolism seen in process of development. [LMB]

25.52 Anthony H. T. Levi, S.J., ed. *Humanism in France at the end of the Middle Ages and in the early Renaissance.* Manchester and New York: Manchester University Press and Barnes & Noble, 1970. ISBN 0-389-03980-2. ▸ Papers from symposium on French Renaissance. Solid overview of literary and intellectual historical works on French humanism, including problems of reception of Italian humanists, of Aristotelian and Neoplatonic influence, and of roles of Budé and other humanists. [LMB]

25.53 David O. McNeil. *Guillaume Budé and humanism in the reign of Francis I.* Geneva: Droz, 1975. ▸ Major study of pivotal figure in French humanism and connections between learning and ideas in early sixteenth century. Photocopy available from Ann Arbor: University Microfilms International (1974). [LMB]

25.54 Kristen B. Neuschel. *Word of honor: interpreting noble cul-*

ture in sixteenth-century France. Ithaca, N.Y.: Cornell University Press, 1989. ISBN 0-8014-2181-0. ‣ Excellent demonstration of necessity of beginning study of late sixteenth-century politics with understanding that nobility perceived and acted according to codes of conduct and political rules very different from those of modern societies. [LMB]

25.55 Richard L. Regosin. *The matter of my book: Montaigne's "Essais" as the book of the self.* Berkeley: University of California Press, 1977. ISBN 0-520-03476-7. ‣ Study, by literary scholar, constructing Montaigne as subject and object of text through attention to language and to writing itself. Views *Essais* as about writing of books. [DG]

25.56 J.H.M. Salmon. *Renaissance and revolt: essays in the intellectual and social history of early modern France.* Cambridge: Cambridge University Press, 1987. ISBN 0-521-32769-5. ‣ Collection of essays by leading authority. Topics include stoicism, humanism, interest of state, resistance theories, and Counter-Reformation Gallicanism. [HCC]

25.57 Jean Starobinski. *Montaigne in motion.* Arthur Goldhammer, trans. Chicago: University of Chicago Press, 1985. ISBN 0-226-77129-6 (cl), 0-226-77131-8 (pbk). ‣ Subtle, indispensable reading of French essayist as reflection of sixteenth century's search for moral guidelines when appearances and force seemed to be only substance of public life. Accounts for seventeenth-century turn to mechanical certitude. [LMB]

25.58 David Thomson. *Renaissance Paris: architecture and growth, 1475–1600.* Berkeley: University of California Press, 1984. ISBN 0-520-05347-8 (cl), 0-520-05359-1 (pbk). ‣ Basic for architectural developments that shaped sixteenth-century Paris and for many years of social, cultural, and political forces behind them. Lively descriptions; generous illustrations. [LMB]

25.59 Frances A. Yates. *The French academies of the sixteenth century.* 1947 ed. London: Routledge, 1988. (Studies of the Warburg Institute, 15.) ISBN 0-415-00221-4. ‣ Cultural history of Renaissance academic movement and activities in disintegrating world of civil wars. Indispensable for context of art, literature, and thought of period. [LMB]

25.60 Frances A. Yates. *Ideas and ideals in the North European Renaissance.* London: Routledge & Kegan Paul, 1984. ISBN 0-7102-0184-2. ‣ Lucid, lively, and wide-ranging essays on cultural codes and ideas in art, politics, rituals, and elite society. Sometimes impressionistic; interpretations add to understanding of French Renaissance. [LMB]

1610–1715

25.61 Joan DeJean. *Tender geographies: women and the origins of the novel in France.* New York: Columbia University Press, 1991. ISBN 0-231-06230-3. ‣ Study of origins of French novel in seventeenth-century women's writing. Feminist rewriting of canon that places gender as major category in literary history. [DG]

25.62 Jonathan Dewald. *Aristocratic experience and the origins of modern culture: France, 1570–1715.* Berkeley: University of California Press, 1993. ISBN 0-520-07837-3. ‣ Plots major shift in aristocratic sensibilities toward freedom of self from restraints of culture, family, and monarchy. Examines literary, dramatic, and epistolary sources to show emergence of sense of being that comes closer to modern views. [LMB]

25.63 Michel Foucault. *Madness and civilization: a history of insanity in the age of reason.* 1965 ed. Richard Howard, trans. New York: Vintage, 1988. ISBN 0-679-72110-X (pbk). ‣ Study of relationship between reason and unreason as they are constituted and diverge, 1500–1800, resulting in triumph of reason and confinement of insane. Also examines relationship of madness to construction of artists and art. [DG]

25.64 Michel Foucault. *The order of things: an archaeology of the*

human sciences. 1970 ed. Alan Sheridan-Smith, trans. New York: Vintage, 1973. ISBN 0-394-71935-2 (pbk). ‣ Structuralist account of conditions of knowledge in biology, economics, and linguistics from seventeenth through nineteenth centuries, by major French theorist. [HCC]

25.65 Peter France. *Rhetoric and truth in France: Descartes to Diderot.* Oxford: Clarendon, 1972. ISBN 0-19-815709-6. ‣ Study of rhetorical education. Relates rhetoric to philosophy, reading publics, and worldliness; focuses on philosophers Descartes, Montesquieu, d'Alembert, Bossuet, Boileau, Racine, and Diderot. [DG]

25.66 Marc Fumaroli. *L'âge d'éloquence: rhétorique et "res literaria" de la Renaissance au seuil de l'époque classique.* Geneva and Paris: Droz and Champion, 1980. ‣ History of rhetoric in relation to literary, religious, and legal discourses. Discusses influence of classical models on development of Jesuit and *parlementaire* styles and impact on French Academy. [DG]

25.67 Elizabeth C. Goldsmith. *Exclusive conversations: the art of interaction in seventeenth-century France.* Philadelphia: University of Pennsylvania Press, 1988. ISBN 0-8122-8102-0. ‣ Examination of theory and practice of conversation during reign of Louis XIV; transformation of nobility into aristocracy through sociability and epistolarity. Analyzes conduct books, epistolary manuals, works of such writers as Madeleine de Scudéry; Roger, Comte de Bussy-Rabutin; and Madame de Sévigné. [DG]

25.68 Erica Harth. *Cartesian women: versions and subversions of rational discourse in the Old Regime.* Ithaca, N.Y.: Cornell University Press, 1992. ISBN 0-8014-2715-0 (cl), 0-8014-9998-4 (pbk). ‣ Analysis of implications of Cartesian universalist rationalism for educated women of seventeenth and eighteenth centuries. Discussion of particular texts as well as institutional structures such as academies and salons. [DG]

25.69 Erica Harth. *Ideology and culture in seventeenth-century France.* Ithaca, N.Y.: Cornell University Press, 1983. ISBN 0-8014-1527-6. ‣ Marxist interpretation of cultural transformations as rise of bourgeoisie over aristocracy. Examines origin of modern genres—history and novel, science and fiction—and changes in systems of representation and cultural production. [DG]

25.70 Robert M. Isherwood. *Music in the service of the king: France in the seventeenth century.* Ithaca, N.Y.: Cornell University Press, 1973. ISBN 0-8014-0734-6. ‣ Study of political and institutional significance of music in reign of Louis XIV. Examines role of music in royal ceremonics and pageantry and centralization of music under Louis XIV and his chief minister, Colbert. [HCC]

25.71 Christian Jouhaud. *Mazarinades: la Fronde des mots.* Paris: Aubier, 1985. ISBN 2-7007-0390-1. ‣ Skeptical study of pamphlets generated by abortive revolt against regency of Louis XIV. Argues political debate produced by episode was more verbal than substantive. [HCC]

25.72 Joseph Klaits. *Printed propaganda under Louis XIV: absolute monarchy and public opinion.* Princeton: Princeton University Press, 1976. ISBN 0-691-05238-7. ‣ Examination of dilemmas faced by royal ministers in their attempts to control public opinion at home and to shape image of Louis XIV abroad in age of political absolutism and rising literacy. [HCC]

25.73 Anthony H. T. Levi, S.J. *French moralists: the theory of the passions, 1585 to 1649.* Oxford: Clarendon, 1964. ‣ Learned study of schools of moral theory from Renaissance to medical theorists of mid-seventeenth century. [HCC]

25.74 Carolyn C. Lougee. *Le paradis des femmes: women, salons, and social stratification in seventeenth-century France.* Princeton: Princeton University Press, 1976. ISBN 0-691-05239-5. ‣ Analysis of salon as social institution and context of writings about women. Views *Querelle des femmes* within broader debate on social mobility and stratification. Discusses social composition of polite society and school of Saint-Cyr as counterinstitution. [DG]

25.75 Ian Maclean. *Woman triumphant: feminism in French literature, 1610–1652.* Oxford: Clarendon, 1977. ISBN 0-19-815741-x. ▸ Study of imaginative literature identifying two intense periods of "feminist" literary activity in seventeenth century. Grounds Renaissance view of women in Aristotelian thinking. Issues include family, marriage, religion, politeness, and moral and political thought. [DG]

25.76 Robert Mandrou. *Magistrats et sorciers en France au dix-septième siècle: une analyse de psychologie historique.* 1968 ed. Paris: Seuil, 1980. ISBN 2-02-005648-8. ▸ Study of mental world of witchcraft by Annales historian. Argues for role of magistrates in ending prosecutions in late seventeenth century, before belief in witchcraft had died out. [HCC]

25.77 Louis Marin. *Portrait of the king.* Martha Houle, trans. Minneapolis: University of Minnesota Press, 1988. ISBN 0-8166-1603-5 (cl), 0-8166-1604-3 (pbk). ▸ Examination of mystique of kingship under Louis XIV by French literary theorist. Discusses methods of royal representation, dynamics of flattery, and sacralization of divine-right kingship. More theory than history. [HCC]

25.78 Henri-Jean Martin. *Livre, pouvoirs, et société à Paris au dix-septième siècle (1598–1701).* 2 vols. Geneva: Droz, 1969. ▸ Examination of role of books in seventeenth-century France. Discusses changing emphasis of readers' tastes through time. Integrates statistical study of printing with social, political, and religious history of Paris. [HCC]

25.79 Michael Moriarty. *Taste and ideology in seventeenth-century France.* Cambridge: Cambridge University Press, 1988. ISBN 0-521-30686-8. ▸ Study of concept of taste within historical field of seventeenth-century discourse through close analysis of Antoine Gombauld Méré, Saint-Evremond, François La Rochefoucauld, Jean de la Bruyère, and Nicolas Boileau. Marxist analysis with attention to gender and class. [DG]

25.80 Mark Motley. *Becoming a French aristocrat: the education of the court nobility, 1580–1715.* Princeton: Princeton University Press, 1990. ISBN 0-691-05547-5. ▸ Standard work on education of male aristocrat for period. Studies education as formalized schooling in interplay with beliefs in "natural" attributes of nobles, aristocratic households, changing sociopolitical conditions, and court patronage. [LMB]

25.81 Orest A. Ranum. *Artisans of glory: writers and historical thought in seventeenth-century France.* Chapel Hill: University of North Carolina Press, 1980. ISBN 0-8078-1413-X. ▸ Study of royal historiographers from Guillaume Budé through Jean Racine, their world of thought, ambitions, historical method, networks of dependency, and relations with king. [HCC]

25.82 Leonora Cohen Rosenfield. *From beast-machine to man-machine: animal soul in French letters from Descartes to La Mettrie.* Rev. ed. New York: Octagon Books, 1968. ▸ Study of lively dispute in French scientific theory. Places René Descartes's denial of animal soul in its historical context. Illuminating for traditionalists' arguments against Descartes. [HCC]

25.83 Jeffrey K. Sawyer. *Printed poison: pamphlet propaganda, faction politics, and the public sphere in early seventeenth-century France.* Berkeley: University of California Press, 1990. ISBN 0-520-06883-1. ▸ Focused study of pamphlet literature in regency of Louis XIII (1614–17). Argues for relatively open public sphere in early seventeenth-century France. [HCC]

25.84 Howard M. Solomon. *Public welfare, science, and propaganda in seventeenth-century France: the innovations of Théophraste Renaudot.* Princeton: Princeton University Press, 1972. ISBN 0-691-05200-X. ▸ Study of physician and founder of *Gazette de France* and his attempts to use emerging resources of journalism to advance Baconian program of social improvement. [HCC]

25.85 Domna C. Stanton. *The aristocrat as art: a study of the honnête homme and the dandy in seventeenth- and nineteenth-century French literature.* New York: Columbia University Press, 1980. ISBN 0-231-03903-4. ▸ Literary study influenced by German philosopher Friedrich Nietzsche and American sociologist Thorstein Veblen. Analysis of French elites who achieved status by inventing new social criteria outside existing system. [HCC]

25.86 Alice Stroup. *A company of scientists: botany, patronage, and community at the seventeenth-century Parisian Royal Academy of Sciences.* Berkeley: University of California Press, 1990. ISBN 0-520-05949-2. ▸ Early years of premier scientific institution of early modern France. Views Academy as mercantilist company trading in knowledge for crown. Sees new form of patronage as key in development of professionalism. [DG]

25.87 Ira O. Wade. *The intellectual development of Voltaire.* Princeton: Princeton University Press, 1969. ISBN 0-691-06173-4. ▸ Intellectual biography of philosopher. Life and works as conscious results of choice and creativity. Examines intellectual origins in seventeenth-century philosophy, freethinking, poetry, classicism, and sixteenth-century prose fiction. [DG]

25.88 Guy Walton. *Louis XIV's Versailles.* Chicago: University of Chicago Press, 1986. ISBN 0-226-87254-8. ▸ Study of Versailles as architectural solution to Louis XIV's political problems. Overview of principal phases of its history and reasons behind its planning and construction into eighteenth century. [DG]

1715–1789

25.89 Elisabeth Badinter. *Emilie, Emilie: l'ambition féminine au dix-huitième siècle.* Paris: Flammarion, 1983. ISBN 2-08-210089-8. ▸ Comparative study of two eighteenth-century women writers: Madame du Châtelet and Madame d'Épinay. Argues for privileged space for ambitious women between seventeenth-century women's salon-culture, *les précieuses*, and Rousseau. [DG]

25.90 Keith Michael Baker. *Condorcet: from natural philosophy to social mathematics.* Chicago: University of Chicago Press, 1975. ISBN 0-226-03532- 8. ▸ Contextual analysis of French mathematician's thought focusing on his conception of social science. Major study that explores more general questions about scientific method, society, and politics spanning Enlightenment and French Revolution. [DG]

25.91 Keith Michael Baker. *Inventing the French Revolution: essays on French political culture in the eighteenth century.* Cambridge: Cambridge University Press, 1990. ISBN 0-521-34618-5 (cl), 0-521-38578-4 (pbk). ▸ Delineation and analysis of discourses of justice, will, and reason that defined political culture of Old Regime and ideological origins of French Revolution. Also discusses creation of public opinion. [DG]

25.92 Carol Blum. *Rousseau and the republic of virtue: the language of politics in the French Revolution.* Ithaca, N.Y.: Cornell University Press, 1986. ISBN 0-8014-1857-7. ▸ Perceptive analysis of Jean-Jacques Rousseau's works and self-image as source of cult of virtue rather than as intellectual leader. Examines influence on revolutionaries Saint-Just and Robespierre and questions of sexuality and gender. [DG]

25.93 Ernst Cassirer. *The philosophy of the Enlightenment.* 1951 ed. Fritz C. A. Koelln and James P. Pettegrove, trans. Princeton: Princeton University Press, 1979. ISBN 0-691-07150-0 (cl), 0-691-01963-0 (pbk). ▸ Classic Kantian synthesis of Enlightenment thought as moment in history of philosophy. Sees inner unity of scientific, epistemological, aesthetic, political, religious, and historical ideas, and reason as central and unifying idea. [DG]

25.94 Jack R. Censer. *The French press in the age of Enlightenment.* London: Routledge, 1994. ISBN 0-415-09730-4. ▸ Investigates contents, editors, audiences, and governmental interventions in publishing of periodicals from mid-eighteenth century to Revolution. Synthesizing work that finds monarchy more in control than most studies on topic. [LMB]

25.95 Jack R. Censer and Jeremy D. Popkin, eds. *Press and politics in pre-revolutionary France.* Berkeley: University of California Press, 1987. ISBN 0-520-05672-8. ▸ Essays in social history of ideas. Examines periodical press as political forum and major factor in construction of political culture. Topics include female readers, Jansenism, foreign and opposition press, and public opinion. [DG]

25.96 Harvey Chisick. *The limits of reform in the Enlightenment: attitudes toward the education of the lower classes in eighteenth-century France.* Princeton: Princeton University Press, 1981. ISBN 0-691-05305-7. ▸ Study of social history of ideas on popular education. Concludes Enlightenment thinkers not committed to equality or even to education for French masses beyond basic skills: Enlightenment was for the few, not the many. [DG]

25.97 Maurice Cranston. *Jean-Jacques: the early life and work of Jean-Jacques Rousseau, 1712–1754.* 1982 ed. New York: Norton, 1983. ISBN 0-393-01744-3. ▸ Sympathetic biography based on extensive scholarship in published and unpublished writings, especially correspondence. Covers childhood through early years in Paris. [DG]

25.98 Maurice Cranston. *The noble savage: Jean-Jacques Rousseau, 1754–1762.* Chicago: University of Chicago Press, 1991. ISBN 0-226-11863-0 (cl), 0-226-11864-9 (pbk). ▸ Sympathetic biography based on extensive scholarship in published and unpublished writings, especially correspondence. Covers period of major works. [DG]

25.99 Thomas E. Crow. *Painters and public life in eighteenth-century Paris.* New Haven: Yale University Press, 1985. ISBN 0-300-03354-0 (cl), 0-300-03764-3 (pbk). ▸ Art history in rich social and political context. Discusses eighteenth-century salon exhibitions and pamphlet art criticism they generated, creation of critical press and public, and art's relationship to academy and to popular culture. [DG]

25.100 Robert Darnton. *The great cat massacre and other episodes in French cultural history.* 1984 ed. New York: Vintage, 1985. ISBN 0-465-02700-8 (cl, 1984), 0-394-72927-7 (pbk). ▸ Lively essays exploring eighteenth-century culture, from peasants and printer's apprentices to townsman's description of his city, to men of letters and Jean-Jacques Rousseau's readers. Anthropological approach. [DG]

25.101 Robert Darnton. *The literary underground of the Old Regime.* Cambridge, Mass.: Harvard University Press, 1982. ISBN 0-674-53656-8 (cl), 0-674-53657-6 (pbk). ▸ Influential essays in social history of ideas challenging radicalism of Enlightenment. Maintains true radicalism lay in resentment of Grub Street writers and illicit book trade, "Rousseaus of the gutter." [DG]

25.102 Robert Darnton. *Mesmerism and the end of the Enlightenment in France.* 1968 ed. Cambridge, Mass.: Harvard University Press, 1986. ISBN 0-674-56951-2 (pbk). ▸ Mentality of literate Frenchmen in 1780s, viewed through mesmerism as radical scientific and political movement of ideas. Discusses diffusion of ideas, popular culture, radical politics, and origins of French Revolution. [DG]

25.103 Harold A. Ellis. *Boulainvilliers and the French monarchy: aristocratic politics in early eighteenth-century France.* Ithaca, N.Y.: Cornell University Press, 1988. ISBN 0-8014-2130-6. ▸ Intellectual and political biography. Erudite monograph on reactionary

nobleman and on political circles—mainly from regency period—in which he operated. [HCC]

25.104 Michel Foucault. *Discipline and punish: the birth of the prison.* 1977 ed. Alan Sheridan [-Smith], trans. New York: Vintage, 1979. ISBN 0-394-72767-3 (pbk). ▸ Highly influential study by French theorist. Genealogy of modern scientific-legal complex from which power to punish derives its bases, justifications, and rules. Modernity as age of discipline. Discusses relationship between power and knowledge, technologies of power, and history of prisons. [DG]

25.105 Elizabeth Fox-Genovese. *The origins of physiocracy: economic revolution and social order in eighteenth-century France.* Ithaca, N.Y.: Cornell University Press, 1976. ISBN 0-8014-1006-1. ▸ Intellectual history with Marxist slant. Sees Enlightenment as bourgeois ideology; physiocracy as central to it. Failure of physiocracy due to internal contradictions between market economics and feudal and statist politics. [DG]

25.106 Michael Fried. *Absorption and theatricality: painting and beholder in the age of Diderot.* 1980 ed. Chicago: University of Chicago Press, 1988. ISBN 0-226-26213-8 (pbk). ▸ Study arguing for seriousness of eighteenth-century painting from Jean Baptiste Greuze to Jacques-Louis David. Based on Denis Diderot's art criticism. Sees absorption as central concern of painters and critics redefining relationship between painter and beholder. [DG]

25.107 Peter Gay. *The Enlightenment: an interpretation.* 1966–69 ed. 2 vols. New York: Norton, 1977. ISBN 0-393-00870-3 (v. 1, pbk), 0-393-00875-4 (v. 2, pbk). ▸ Social history of ideas. Major synthesis. Triumphant view of Enlightenment as beginning of modernity; movement away from religious worldview through appeal to antiquity and toward liberal ideals of science and freedom. Bibliographic essays. [DG]

25.108 Nina Rattner Gelbart. *Feminine and opposition journalism in Old Regime France: Le Journal des Dames.* Berkeley: University of California Press, 1987. ISBN 0-520-05761-9. ▸ Lively narrative of life of eighteenth-century journal and its journalists. Window into questions of women and gender, opposition press and politics, continuities of mid-seventeenth-century forms of *frondeur* protests, and feminist traditions in French culture. [DG]

25.109 Charles Coulston Gillispie. *Science and polity in France at the end of the Old Regime.* Princeton: Princeton University Press, 1980. ISBN 0-691-08233-2. ▸ History of science through study of institutions, professions, applications, and interaction with state and society. Beginning with Turgot ministry, political neutrality of science and scientists is seen in service to the state. [DG]

25.110 Dena Goodman. *Criticism in action: Enlightenment experiments in political writing.* Ithaca, N.Y.: Cornell University Press, 1989. ISBN 0-8014-2201-9. ▸ Critical analysis of texts by philosophers Charles Montesquieu, Jean-Jacques Rousseau, and Denis Diderot. Structural approach focusing on epistolary, narrative, and dialog forms. Examines rhetorical structures and creation of enlightened, critical readers. [DG]

25.111 Lionel Gossman. *Medievalism and the ideologies of the Enlightenment: the world and work of La Curne de Sainte-Palaye.* Baltimore: Johns Hopkins University Press, 1968. ▸ Social history of ideas examining culture of medievalist in eighteenth-century Paris. Treats social milieux, academies, historiographical traditions, development of scholarly methods, and relationship to Enlightenment and medievalism. Both life and principal works. [DG]

25.112 Roger Hahn. *The anatomy of a scientific institution: the Paris Academy of Sciences, 1666–1803.* Berkeley: University of California Press, 1971. ISBN 0-520-01818-4. ▸ Study of basis of French scientific tradition in broad social, political, and intellectual context. Sees Academy of Sciences as major institution of both modernizing monarchy and Enlightenment Republic of Letters. [DG]

25.113 Lynn Hunt, ed. *The French Revolution in culture.* Berkeley: University of California Press with American Society for Eighteenth-Century Studies, 1989. (*Eighteenth-century studies*: a special issue, 22.) ISSN 0013-2586. ▸ Essays taking new approach to political culture and society primarily before 1789. Topics include conversation and public opinion, Enlightenment salons, pamphlet journalism, art criticism, festivals, royal ceremony, women and religious riots, and women and publishing. [DG]

25.114 Robert M. Isherwood. *Farce and fantasy: popular entertainment in eighteenth-century Paris.* New York: Oxford University Press, 1986. ISBN 0-19-503648-4. ▸ Examination of culture of fairs, boulevards, and Palais Royal. Challenges distinction between popular and elite culture. Popular entertainments for socially diverse audience—popular, bourgeois, noble—with roots in marketplace mockery. [DG]

25.115 Steven L. Kaplan. *The famine plot persuasion in eighteenth-century France.* Philadelphia: American Philosophical Society, 1982. (Transactions of the American Philosophical Society, 72.3.) ISBN 0-87169-723-8 (pbk). ▸ *Mentalité*-oriented study of persistent and recurring belief in famine plot across social groups. Sees it as part of collective mentality, not aberration. Based on tyranny of cereal dependence and various sociocultural factors. Analysis of political implications. [DG]

25.116 Alan Charles Kors. *D'Holbach's coterie: an Enlightenment in Paris.* Princeton: Princeton University Press, 1976. ISBN 0-691-05224-7. ▸ Social history of ideas. Model study of group of intellectuals arguing for their integration rather than marginality in relation to dominant culture of Old Regime. Discusses social composition, role in Enlightenment, and ideas. [DG]

25.117 Reinhart Koselleck. *Critique and crisis: Enlightenment and the pathogenesis of modern society.* Cambridge, Mass.: MIT Press, 1988. ISBN 0-262-11127-6. ▸ Suggestive dialectical interpretation of Enlightenment as arising from confrontation between political absolutism and Pierre Bayle's criticism. Discusses freemasonry as manifestation of Enlightenment. Argues that criticism became hypocrisy as philosophes exercised power without responsibility. [DG]

25.118 Sarah C. Maza. *Private lives and public affairs: the causes célèbres of prerevolutionary France.* Berkeley: University of California Press, 1993. ISBN 0-520-08144-7. ▸ Innovative study of political culture of Old Regime through examination of printed judicial memoires. Examines how lawyers used literary and theatrical forms to turn private matters of love and family into issues of public importance and thus to create the public. [DG]

25.119 Harry C. Payne. *The philosophes and the people.* New Haven: Yale University Press, 1976. ISBN 0-300-01907-6. ▸ Intellectual history investigating Enlightenment view of lower classes. Examines scorn of "enlightened" for "ignorant" masses, association of philosophes with elite, and conflict between elitism and social utility. [DG]

25.120 Michele Root-Bernstein. *Boulevard theater and revolution in eighteenth-century Paris.* Ann Arbor: University Microfilms International Research Press, 1984. ISBN 0-8357-1551-5. ▸ Cultural history of popular theater as microcosm of political and cultural forces behind reform and revolution. Despite mechanisms of power to marginalize boulevard theater, integration of theatrical traditions contributed to breakdown of Old Regime but not to radicalization of theater professionals. [DG]

25.121 Robert Shackleton. *Montesquieu: a critical biography.* 1961 ed. London: Oxford University Press, 1963. ▸ Standard

biography of philosopher that balances life with intelligent discussion of major works. [DG]

25.122 Mary D. Sheriff. *Fragonard: art and eroticism.* Chicago: University of Chicago Press, 1990. ISBN 0-226-75273-9. ▸ Study of major paintings. Reevaluates Jean-Honoré Fragonard and rococo as serious, rather than merely decorative. Focuses on importance of beholder and relationship between fictive and real, aesthetic and erotic, and painting and writing. [DG]

25.123 Samia I. Spencer, ed. *French women and the age of Enlightenment.* Bloomington: Indiana University Press, 1984. ISBN 0-253-32481-5. ▸ Collection of essays by historians and literary scholars. General survey that treats women and politics, society, and culture; women writers and artists; Enlightenment views of women; and portrayal of women in literature. [DG]

25.124 Jean Starobinski. *The invention of liberty, 1700–1789.* 1964 ed. Bernard C. Swift, trans. Geneva and New York: Skira and Rizzoli, 1987. ISBN 0-8478-0846-7 (pbk). ▸ Provocative interdisciplinary essay, sumptuously illustrated, on relationship of rococo and classical art to elite festive practices and Enlightenment thought. Discusses concepts of history, reason, vision, nature, and freedom and role of art. [DG]

25.125 Jean Starobinski. *Jean-Jacques Rousseau: transparency and obstruction.* Arthur Goldhammer, trans. Robert J. Morrissey, Introduction. Chicago: University of Chicago Press, 1988. ISBN 0-226-77126-1 (cl), 0-226-77128-8 (pbk). ▸ Brilliant, psychoanalytic study of Rousseau's work in its complex relation to his life and eighteenth-century culture. Discusses Rousseau's search for transparency and problem of subjectivity and self-knowledge. [DG]

25.126 Dale K. Van Kley. *The Damiens affair and the unraveling of the Ancien Régime, 1750–1770.* Princeton: Princeton University Press, 1984. ISBN 0-691-05402-9. ▸ Study of parlementary and Jansenist ideological and political origins and context of Damiens's attempted assassination of Louis XV. Concludes politico-religious disputes and desacralization of monarchy at mid-century contributed to ideological origins of French Revolution. [DG]

25.127 Dale K. Van Kley. *The Jansenists and the expulsion of the Jesuits from France, 1757–1765.* New Haven: Yale University Press, 1975. ISBN 0-300-01748-0. ▸ Original, well-substantiated thesis. Examines how small group of Jansenists in Parlement of Paris orchestrated expulsion of Jesuits from France. Argues Jansenism, because of its anticlericalism, contributed to success of Enlightenment. [RMG]

25.128 Anthony Vidler. *The writing of the walls: architectural theory in the late Enlightenment.* Princeton: Princeton Architectural Press, 1987. ISBN 0-910413-07-X (cl), 0-910413-75-4 (pbk). ▸ Wide-ranging discussion of philosophes and architects, focusing on two points of intersection between architectural thought and social change: institutional reform and historiography. Argues late eighteenth-century theorists saw architecture as functional and as language. [DG]

25.129 Ira O. Wade. *The intellectual origins of the French Enlightenment.* Princeton: Princeton University Press, 1971. ISBN 0-691-06052-5. ▸ Attempt to define Enlightenment with reference to Renaissance, baroque, and classicism. Special emphasis on Pierre Bayle and skeptical libertine tradition. [HCC]

25.130 Arthur M. Wilson. *Diderot.* 1967 ed. 2 vols. in 1. New York: Oxford University Press, 1972. ISBN 0-19-501506-1. ▸ Excellent treatment of both life and works that encompasses other important figures, such as Jean-Jacques Rousseau, Madam Johannes d'Épinay, and Grimm. Useful especially for understanding printing and political history of the *Encyclopédie* and world of encyclopedists. [DG]

SEE ALSO
22.170 Robert Darnton. *The business of enlightenment.*
26.47 Roger Chartier. *The cultural origins of the French Revolution.*

POLITICS AND GOVERNMENT

General Studies

25.131 Philip Benedict, ed. *Cities and social change in early modern France.* London: Unwin Hyman, 1989. ISBN 0-04-944017-9. ▸ Collection of articles on early modern urban life with superb overview by editor. Articles on Paris, Montpellier, Dijon, Aix-en-Provence, Toulouse, and Dauphiné. [MPH]

25.132 Marc Bloch. *The royal touch.* New York: Dorset, 1989. ISBN 0-88029-408-6. ▸ Groundbreaking study of late medieval and early modern kingship. Based on opinions about monarch's ability to heal (*scrofula*) by touching; the ceremonial presentation of the king. Original French edition, 1925. [MPH]

25.133 Ralph E. Giesey. *Cérémonial et puissance souveraine: France, XVe–XVIIe siècles.* Jeannie Carlier, trans. Paris: Colin, 1987. (Cahiers des Annales, 41.) ▸ Authoritative overview of changes in meaning of state ceremonies from fifteenth through seventeenth centuries. Politico-legal principles of king's two bodies were recast in form of embodied "royal majesty"; thought and symbolism of king's power changed from public to courtier venues. [LMB]

25.134 Sarah Hanley. *The lit de justice of the kings of France: constitutional ideology in legend, ritual, and discourse.* Princeton: Princeton University Press, 1983. (Studies presented to the International Commission for the History of Representative and Parliamentary Institutions, 65.) ISBN 0-691-05382-0. ▸ Provocative, scholarly revision of historical interpretation of events and forces that transformed descriptive phrase "*lit de justice*" into permanent and potent institution of Parlement of Paris and monarchy. Essential for constitutional history of early modern monarchy. [LMB]

25.135 Robert R. Harding. *Anatomy of a power elite: the provincial governors of early modern France.* New Haven: Yale University Press, 1978. ISBN 0-300-02202-6. ▸ Detailed study of careers, family connections, clientage networks, and wealth of provincial royal governors in period 1515–1650, showing how they worked together with robe nobility. [MPH]

25.136 Richard A. Jackson. *Vive le roi! a history of the French coronation from Charles V to Charles X.* Chapel Hill: University of North Carolina Press, 1984. ISBN 0-8078-1602-7. ▸ Analysis of French coronation ceremony, 1364–1825, showing changing nature of French kingship. Good on inalienability of royal domain, elective kingship, and imperial kingship. [MPH]

25.137 Roland Mousnier. *The institutions of France under the absolute monarchy, 1598–1789.* 2 vols. Brian Pearce and Arthur Goldhammer, trans. Chicago: University of Chicago Press, 1979–84. ISBN 0-226-54327-7 (v. 1), 0-226-54328-5 (v. 2). ▸ Most comprehensive analysis of early modern French institutions and society available. Covers crown, church, parlements, estates, etc. Outlines author's controversial view of "society of orders." [MPH]

25.138 Roland Mousnier. *La vénalité des offices sous Henri IV et Louis XIII.* 1945 ed. Geneva: Megariotis Reprints, 1979. ▸ Essential work on venality and officeholding in period. Analyzes traffic and commerce of offices as well as how venal system supplied foundations for royal government. [MPH]

25.139 Robert Muchembled. *Popular culture and elite culture in France, 1400–1750.* Lydia G. Cochrane, trans. Baton Rouge: Louisiana State University Press, 1985. ISBN 0-8071-1218-6. ▸ Highly controversial argument that advent of Catholic refor-

mation and absolutist state saw social elites ultimately suppress popular culture. Translation of 1978 French edition. [MPH]

25.140 J. H. Shennan. *The Parlement of Paris.* Ithaca, N.Y.: Cornell University Press, 1968. ▸ Shows transformation of Parlement from agent of royal will in thirteenth to fifteenth century to focus for royal opposition in sixteenth to eighteenth century. [MPH]

1450–1610

25.141 Elie Barnavi. *Le parti de Dieu: étude sociale et politique des chefs de la Ligue parisienne, 1585–1594.* Brussels: Nauwelaerts, 1980. (Travaux du Centre de Recherches sur la Civilisation de l'Europe Moderne, 20.) ISBN 2-85944-017-8. ▸ Insightful social and political study of Catholic League treating movement as forerunner to modern authoritarian and totalitarian political parties. [MPH]

25.142 Frederic J. Baumgartner. *Henry II: king of France, 1547–1559.* Durham, N.C.: Duke University Press, 1988. ISBN 0-8223-0795-2. ▸ Recent biography of Henry II. Differs from earlier studies by showing coherent foreign policy and less coherent religious policy. [MPH]

25.143 Frederic J. Baumgartner. *Radical reactionaries: the political thought of the French Catholic League.* Geneva: Droz, 1976. ▸ Most comprehensive study of League political thought in English. Emphasizes radical antimonarchical tendencies of League after 1584 couched in traditional—so-called reactionary—language. [MPH]

25.144 Jacqueline Boucher. *La cour de Henri III.* Rennes, France: Ouest-France, 1986. ISBN 2-7373-0019-3. ▸ Analytical study of Valois court under Henry III. Emphasizes role of king and royal households. Examines italianization of court life and intellectual, social, and religious natures of court. [MPH]

25.145 Lawrence M. Bryant. *The king and the city in the Parisian royal entry ceremony: politics, ritual, and art in the Renaissance.* Geneva: Droz, 1986. ISBN 0-317-65815-8. ▸ Fascinating study of how monarchs adapted and shaped rituals and art in their royal entries in order to communicate political messages about their kingship. [MPH]

25.146 David Buisseret. *Henry IV.* London: Allen & Unwin, 1984. ISBN 0-04-944012-8. ▸ Laudatory biography of king; strong on war, politics, and international diplomacy. Accentuates personal contributions of Henry to shaping of seventeenth-century French state. [MPH]

25.147 David Buisseret. *Sully and the growth of centralized government in France, 1598–1610.* London: Eyre & Spottiswoode, 1968. ▸ Best study in English of Henry IV's finance minister. Provides thorough analysis of fiscal contributions and describes his many roles outside financial sphere. [MPH]

25.148 Vittorio Caprariis. *Propaganda e pensiero politico in Francia durante le guerre di religione, 1559–1572.* Naples: Edizioni Scientifiche Italiane, 1959. (Biblioteca storica, Nuova serie, 7.) ▸ Only volume of projected two-volume study. Essential on Huguenot political ideology before St. Bartholomew's Day. [MPH]

25.149 Bernard Chevalier. *Les bonnes villes de France du quatorzième au seizième siècle.* Paris: Aubier-Montaigne, 1982. ISBN 2-7007-0291-3. ▸ Study of principal towns and role municipal privileges (especially fiscal) played in development of early modern France. [MPH]

25.150 Philippe Contamine. *Guerre, état, et société à la fin du moyen âge: études sur les armées des rois de France, 1337–1494.* Paris: Mouton, 1972. ISBN 90-279-6991-4. ▸ Social and political study of royal armies. Especially good on army's role in late medieval state-building and its interaction with civilian populations. [MPH]

25.151 Robert Descimon. *Qui étaient les Seize? Mythes et réalités de la Ligue parisienne (1585–1594)*. Paris: Mémoires de la Féderation des Sociétés Historiques et Archéologiques de Paris et de l'Ile de France and Librarie Klincksieck, 1983. ▸ Extremely valuable prosopography of 225 leading members of Paris League. Argues leaders aimed to restore medieval notion of civic community. [MPH]

25.152 Robert Descimon and Elie Barnavi. "La Ligue à Paris (1585–1594): une révision." *Annales: économies, sociétés, civilisations* 37 (1982) 72–128. ISSN 0003-441X. ▸ Debate on nature of Catholic Holy League. Descimon argues backward-looking medieval foundation; Barnavi, modern, totalitarian foundation. [MPH]

25.153 Edmund H. Dickerman. *Bellièvre and Villeroy: power in France under Henry III and Henry IV*. Providence: Brown University Press, 1971. ISBN 0-87057-131-1. ▸ Analysis of power at court through careers of two royal ministers, Pomponne de Bellièvre and Nicolas de Neufville, sieur de Villeroy. [MPH]

25.154 Barbara B. Diefendorf. *Paris city councillors in the sixteenth century: the politics of patrimony*. Princeton: Princeton University Press, 1983. ISBN 0-691-05362-6. ▸ Sociopolitical study (1535–75) of cohort of ninety city councilors who served Hôtel de Ville of Paris. Analyzes career choices, matrimonial strategies, and inheritance practices. [MPH]

25.155 Claire Dolan. *Entre tours et clochers: les gens d'élise à Aix-en-Provence au seizième siècle*. Sherbrooke, Canada, and Aix-en-Provence, France: Université de Sherbrooke and Edisud, 1981. ISBN 2-7622-0006-7. ▸ Detailed study of regular and secular clergy of Aix. Analyzes various secular and sacred roles played by clergy in municipal life of city. [MPH]

25.156 Roger Doucet. *Les institutions de la France au seizième siècle*. 2 vols. Paris: Picard, 1948. ▸ Basic information on operations of government and its offices in sixteenth-century France. Also see Zeller 25.195. [LMB]

25.157 Henri Drouot. *Mayenne et la Bourgogne: étude sur la Ligue (1587–1596)*. 2 vols. Paris: Picard, 1937. ▸ Most detailed study of League outside Paris. Argues dissatisfied magistrates, whose career advancement was blocked by sovereign courts, turned to Mayenne and League for support. [MPH]

25.158 Julian H. Franklin. *Jean Bodin and the rise of absolutist theory*. Cambridge: Cambridge University Press, 1973. ISBN 0-521-20000-8. ▸ Study of Bodin's theory of sovereignty. Strong rebuttal of Huguenot resistance theory in favor of strong royalist monarchy with indivisible sovereignty. Also discusses limits of absolutism. [MPH]

25.159 Janine Garrisson[-Estèbe]. *Tocsin pour un massacre: la saison des Saint-Barthélemy*. Paris: Centurion/Sciences Humaines, 1968. ▸ Fullest account of massacres in Paris (1572) with many useful insights, but takes old-fashioned Protestant view that social tensions and Catherine de Medici were to blame for killings. [MPH]

25.160 Ralph E. Giesey. *The juristic basis of dynastic right to the French throne*. Philadelphia: American Philosophical Society, 1961. (Transactions of the American Philosophical Society, n.s., 51.5.) ISSN 0065-9746. ▸ Demonstration of efforts to establish distinctly French notion of political legitimacy from fourteenth-century apologists for Valois monarchy to *parlementaire* claims of sixteenth century. Particular attention to Salic Law. [LMB]

25.161 Ralph E. Giesey. *The royal funeral ceremony in Renaissance France*. Geneva: Droz, 1960. ▸ Pathbreaking study showing ceremonies for royal funerals from fifteenth to seventeenth cen-

turies were major factors in shaping political theory, monarchical institutions, and ideas of state. [MPH]

25.162 Mark Greengrass. *France in the age of Henri IV: the struggle for stability*. London: Longman, 1984. ISBN 0-582-49251-3 (pbk). ▸ Analysis of how king consciously sought to create order and stability following religious wars. Though not all strategies were successful, argues that by 1610 order had been restored. [MPH]

25.163 Mack P. Holt. *The duke of Anjou and the politique struggle during the Wars of Religion*. Cambridge: Cambridge University Press, 1986. ISBN 0-521-32232-4. ▸ Insightful political study of Anjou, brother of Henry III, as more anachronism than failure in violent struggles of 1570s to 1580s. Important for understanding shaping of French monarchy. [LMB]

25.164 François Hotman. *Francogallia*. Ralph E. Giesey, ed. J.H.M. Salmon, trans. Cambridge: Cambridge University Press, 1972. ISBN 0-521-08379-6. ▸ Critical edition of *Francogallia* (1573) with Latin text and English translation on facing pages. Superb editor's introduction to period and essential statements of Huguenot resistance theory and development of historiography. [MPH]

25.165 De Lamar Jensen. *Diplomacy and dogmatism: Bernardino de Mendoza and the French Catholic League*. Cambridge, Mass.: Harvard University Press, 1964. ISBN 0-674-20800-5. ▸ Study of Spanish impact on Catholic League in France, based on deciphered correspondence of Spanish ambassador in Paris. Offers unique perspective of Paris under League occupation. [MPH]

25.166 Donald R. Kelley. *The beginning of ideology: consciousness and society in the French Reformation*. Cambridge: Cambridge University Press, 1981. ISBN 0-521-23504-9. ▸ Analysis of how Protestantism and legal writers spurred social and political protest into justifications for organized purposeful action and revolution; beginning of ideology. Essential reading for history of early modern political ideas. [LMB]

25.167 Paul Murray Kendall. *Louis XI: the universal spider*. New York: Norton, 1971. ISBN 0-393-05380-6. ▸ Biography principally focused on politics and international diplomacy. Argues Louis was largely responsible for rebuilding of France into national monarchy after Hundred Years' War. [MPH]

25.168 Raymond F. Kierstead. *Pomponne de Bellièvre: a study of the king's men in the age of Henry IV*. Evanston, Ill.: Northwestern University Press, 1968. ▸ Uses career of Pomponne de Bellièvre, chancellor of France, to illustrate problems of governing during reign of Henry IV. Good example of duties and responsibilities of royal minister. [MPH]

25.169 R. J. Knecht. *Francis I*. 1982 ed. Cambridge: Cambridge University Press, 1984. ISBN 0-521-24344-0 (cl, 1982), 0-521-27887-2 (pbk). ▸ Biography arguing Francis's personal role in shaping France of his day was considerable, to questionable point of stressing he was first "absolute" monarch in French history. [MPH]

25.170 H. G. Koenigsberger. "The organization of revolutionary parties in France and the Netherlands during the sixteenth century." *Journal of modern history* 27 (1955) 335–51. ISSN 0022-2801. ▸ Seminal article on revolutionary nature of Huguenots and Dutch rebels in second half of sixteenth century. [MPH]

25.171 Emmanuel Le Roy Ladurie. *Carnival in Romans*. Mary Feeney, trans. New York: Braziller, 1979. ISBN 0-8076-0928-5. ▸ Drama of two-week revolt in Dauphiné as basis for overview of social and political tensions inherent in much of Europe in sixteenth century. Important study of political ceremonies, folk rituals, and power struggles. [MPH]

25.172 P. S. Lewis, ed. *The recovery of France in the fifteenth cen-*

tury. 1971 ed. G. F. Martin, trans. New York: Harper & Row, 1972. ISBN 0-06-138418-6. ‣ Collection of twelve articles on recovery of France after Hundred Years' War. With one exception, translations of articles written in French. [MPH]

25.173 Howell A. Lloyd. *The state, France, and the sixteenth century.* London: Allen & Unwin, 1983. ISBN 0-04-940066-5. ‣ Argues new perception of state emerged in sixteenth century: state—not God or the people—was true source of sovereign's authority. [MPH]

25.174 J. Russell Major. "'Bastard feudalism' and the kiss: changing social mores in late medieval and early modern France." *Journal of interdisciplinary history* 17 (1987) 509–35. ISSN 0022-1953. ‣ Exploration of decline of homage in late Middle Ages when indentures replaced formal feudal exchange of homage for fief through changing social attitudes toward male kissing. [MPH]

25.175 J. Russell Major. "Bellièvre, Sully, and the assembly of notables of 1596." *Transactions of the American Philosophical Society* 64.2 (1974) 3–34. ISSN 0065-9746. ‣ This assembly as moment when Henry IV took advice of his great minister Sully to implement more absolutist policy and turned from more traditional policies advocated by Chancellor Pomponne de Bellièvre. [MPH]

25.176 J. Russell Major. "The crown and the aristocracy in Renaissance France." *American historical review* 69 (1964) 631–45. ISSN 0002-8762. ‣ Argues nobility continued to wield authority at court and provinces throughout sixteenth and seventeenth centuries, resulting in weakened monarchy. [MPH]

25.177 J. Russell Major. *Representative government in early modern France.* New Haven: Yale University Press, 1980. ISBN 0-300-02300-6. ‣ Study of superintendent of finances Michel de Marillac as architect of absolutism rather than minister of state Cardinal Richelieu, particularly in supervising creation of bureaucratic absolutism of *élections* in 1620s to supplant powers of provincial estates. [MPH]

25.178 A. Lynn Martin. *Henry III and the Jesuit politicians.* Geneva: Droz, 1973. (Travaux d'humanisme et renaissance, 134.) ‣ Study of political influence of Society of Jesus in reign of Henry III (1574–89); particular emphasis on Edmond Auger. [MPH]

25.179 Harry A. Miskimin. *Money and power in fifteenth-century France.* New Haven: Yale University Press, 1984. ISBN 0-300-03132-7. ‣ Analysis of bullion output during Hundred Years' War. Argues specie scarcity, combined with royal control of mints, played significant role in expansion of monarchy's authority. [MPH]

25.180 David Potter. *War and government in the French provinces: Picardy, 1470–1560.* Cambridge: Cambridge University Press, 1993. ISBN 0-521-43189-1. ‣ Richly detailed study of frontier province in period of Habsburg-Valois wars. French government and provincial experiences bring insight to rise of absolutist state. [MPH]

25.181 Nancy Lyman Roelker. *Queen of Navarre: Jeanne d'Albret, 1528–1572.* Cambridge, Mass.: Belknap, 1968. ISBN 0-674-74150-1. ‣ Based on Jeanne's copious correspondence, sheds light on leadership of Huguenot movement, as well as on life style of French noblewoman. [MPH]

25.182 Nancy Lyman Roelker, ed. and trans. *The Paris of Henry of Navarre as seen by Pierre de l'Estoile: selections from his "Mémoires-Journaux."* Cambridge, Mass.: Harvard University Press, 1958. ‣ English translation of selections from l'Estoile's memoirs. Especially good source for Catholic League and siege of Paris; although moderate member of Parlement, L'Estoile was enemy of both Huguenots and Leaguers. [MPH]

25.183 J.H.M. Salmon. *Society in crisis: France in the sixteenth century.* New York: St. Martin's, 1975. ‣ Most comprehensive single-volume study of Wars of Religion. Useful introductory section on society and institutions. Argues four decades of warfare resulted in social crisis in 1590s. Superb bibliography. [MPH]

25.184 N. M. Sutherland. *The French secretaries of state in the age of Catherine de Medici.* 1962 ed. Westport, Conn.: Greenwood, 1976. ISBN 0-8371-8707-9. ‣ Based on secretaries' own papers; account of civil wars through their eyes. Point of view occasionally less than objective. [MPH]

25.185 N. M. Sutherland. *The massacre of St. Bartholomew and the European conflict, 1559–1572.* New York: Barnes & Noble, 1973. ISBN 0-06-496620-8. ‣ Detailed political and diplomatic analysis of connections of international politics with St. Bartholomew's massacres in France. Resurrects reputation of Catherine de Medici. [MPH]

25.186 N. M. Sutherland. *Princes, politics, and religion, 1547–1589.* London: Hambledon, 1984. ISBN 0-907628-44-3. ‣ Revisionist articles on policies of Catherine de Medici, international dimension of Massacre of St. Bartholomew's Day, and other individuals and events. Finds religious conflicts merged into power struggles. [BBD]

25.187 M.G.A. Vale. *Charles VII.* Berkeley: University of California Press, 1974. ISBN 0-520-02787-6. ‣ Useful biographical study of Charles VII. Especially good analysis of political and socioeconomic problems facing France at close of Hundred Years' War. [MPH]

25.188 L. Scott Van Doren. "The royal *taille* in Dauphiné, 1494–1559." *Proceedings of the American Philosophical Society* 121.1 (February 1977) 70–96. ISSN 0003-049X. ‣ Detailed study of how direct tax (*taille*) was collected in Dauphiné in first half of sixteenth century. Especially good on social and economic impact of tax collection. [MPH]

25.189 L. Scott Van Doren. "The royal *taille* in Dauphiné, 1560–1610." *Western Society for French History, proceedings of the annual meeting* 3 (1976) 35–53. ISSN 0099-0329. ‣ Shows Henry III tried to destroy customary tax collection privileges of Dauphiné estates by appointing royal tax collectors. [MPH]

25.190 Richard Vaughan. *Charles the Bold: the last Valois duke of Burgundy.* 1973 ed. New York: Barnes & Noble, 1974. ISBN 0-06-497171-6. ‣ Best study, in English, of last Valois duke. Comprehensive political narrative; especially good on court. [MPH]

25.191 Martin Wolfe. *The fiscal system of Renaissance France.* New Haven: Yale University Press, 1972. ISBN 0-300-01487-2. ‣ Extremely valuable study of changes that occurred in royal tax collection system from reign of Charles VII to end of Wars of Religion. One hundred pages of appendixes. [MPH]

25.192 Michael Wolfe. *The conversion of Henri IV: politics, power, and religious belief in early modern France.* Cambridge, Mass.: Harvard University Press, 1993. ISBN 0-674-17031-8. ‣ Close study of political and religious implications of Henri IV's 1593 conversion to Catholicism. Public responses seen as sources for understanding connections between piety and social identity. [MPH]

25.193 Frances A. Yates. *Astraea: the imperial theme in the sixteenth century.* London: Routledge & Kegan Paul, 1975. ISBN 0-7100-7971-0. ‣ Analysis of royal entries, fêtes for marriage of duke of Joyeuse, and religious processions in Paris to assess imperial nature of French monarchy. Includes similar studies on English monarchy. [MPH]

25.194 Frances A. Yates. *The Valois tapestries.* 2d ed. London: Routledge & Kegan Paul, 1975. ISBN 0-7100-8244-4. ‣ Analysis of eight tapestries presented to Catherine de Medici, arguing they were symbol of religious and political conciliation offered in hopes of appealing to political moderates. Fascinating detective story. [MPH]

25.195   Gaston Zeller. *Les institutions de la France au seizième siècle.* 2d ed. Paris: Presses Universitaires de France, 1987. ISBN 2-13-040142-2. ‣ Basic information on operation of government and its offices in sixteenth-century France. See Doucet 25.156. [LMB]

SEE ALSO
20.605 P. S. Lewis. *Later medieval France.*

1610–1715

25.196   Nancy Nichols Barker. *Brother to the Sun King: Philippe, duke of Orléans.* Baltimore: Johns Hopkins University Press, 1989. ISBN 0-8018-3791-X. ‣ Biographical study of Louis XIV's brother. Focuses on how political faction and opposition traditionally fomented around person of king's brother. [MPH]

25.197   William Beik. *Absolutism and society in seventeenth-century France: state power and provincial aristocracy in Languedoc.* Cambridge: Cambridge University Press, 1985. ISBN 0-521-26309-3. ‣ Revisionist social and political study demonstrating collaboration and participation of local aristocracy of Languedoc essential to success of absolutist state of Louis XIV. [MPH]

25.198   Joseph Bergin. *Cardinal Richelieu: power and the pursuit of wealth.* New Haven: Yale University Press, 1985. ISBN 0-300-03495-4. ‣ Analysis of cardinal's wealth and fortune from inheritance, political office, land, and church. Shows how wealth was vital component of political power. [MPH]

25.199   Joseph Bergin. *The rise of Richelieu.* New Haven: Yale University Press, 1991. ISBN 0-300-04992-7. ‣ Biographical study demonstrating cardinal's political fortunes relied more on family connections and ecclesiastical patronage than political opportunism. [MPH]

25.200   Richard Bonney. *The king's debts: finance and politics in France, 1598–1661.* Oxford: Clarendon, 1981. ISBN 0-19-822563-6. ‣ Political and financial analysis of fiscal system of seventeenth-century France and its structural weaknesses which prevented any meaningful reform. Also contains useful appendixes on crown expenditure and revenue. [MPH]

25.201   Richard Bonney. *Political change in France under Richelieu and Mazarin, 1624–1661.* Oxford: Oxford University Press, 1978. ISBN 0-19-822537-7. ‣ Detailed analysis of expansion of taxation and creation of administration by royal appointees known as intendants. Emphasizes roles of two cardinals as architects of absolutism. [MPH]

25.202   William F. Church. *Richelieu and reason of state.* 1972 ed. Princeton: Princeton University Press, 1973. ISBN 0-691-05199-2. ‣ Illuminating study of cardinal's policies. Argues underlying ideology of his policies was clearly religious, limiting any secularized notion of *raison d'état.* [MPH]

25.203   James B. Collins. *Fiscal limits of absolutism: direct taxation in early seventeenth-century France.* Berkeley: University of California Press, 1988. ISBN 0-520-05911-5. ‣ Detailed examination of tax system. Argues crown's ability to enact policy limited by structural deficiencies in tax collection procedures. [MPH]

25.204   P. J. Coveney, ed. and trans. *France in crisis, 1620–1675.* Totowa, N.J.: Rowman & Littlefield, 1977. ISBN 0-87471-916-X. ‣ Valuable translations of debate between Boris Porchnev and Roland Mousnier on popular revolts; includes articles by Deyon and Méthivier. Editor's introduction weak and outdated. [MPH]

25.205   Pierre Goubert. *Louis XIV and twenty million Frenchmen.* 1970 ed. Anne Carter, trans. New York: Vintage, 1972. ISBN 0-394-71751-1 (pbk). ‣ Introduces long-term socioeconomic forces stressed by Annales school into political history of reign,

showing how they limited king's power. Translation of French edition of 1966. [MPH]

25.206   Albert N. Hamscher. *The Conseil Privé and the parlements in the age of Louis XIV: a study in French absolutism.* Philadelphia: American Philosophical Society, 1987. (Transactions of the American Philosophical Society, n.s., 77.2.) ISBN 0-87169-772-6 (pbk). ISSN 0065-9746. ‣ Study of judicial procedure in Louis XIV's reign. Shows how judicial authority of parlements interacted with royal authority in Conseil Privé to present real checks on royal absolutism. [MPH]

25.207   Albert N. Hamscher. *The Parlement of Paris after the Fronde, 1653–1673.* Pittsburgh: University of Pittsburgh Press, 1976. ISBN 0-8229-3325-X. ‣ Clear demonstration that Parlement continued to function and wield authority in opposition to crown during 1650s and was not quashed as functioning institution during revolts known as the Fronde. [MPH]

25.208   Ragnhild Hatton, ed. *Louis XIV and absolutism.* Columbus: Ohio State University Press, 1976. ISBN 0-8142-0255-1. ‣ Collection of articles offering varying interpretations of royal absolutism under Louis XIV. Eleven of thirteen articles originally published in French, first time presented in English. [MPH]

25.209   J. Michael Hayden. *France and the Estates-General of 1614.* London: Cambridge University Press, 1974. ISBN 0-521-20325-2. ‣ Presents context and background of 1614 meeting. Argues policies of regency government of Marie de Medici were not altogether dissimilar from those of Henry IV. [MPH]

25.210   Daniel Hickey. *The coming of French absolutism: the struggle for tax reform in the province of Dauphiné, 1540–1640.* Toronto: University of Toronto Press, 1986. ISBN 0-8020-5676-8. ‣ Study of tax collection in province of Dauphiné as means of demonstrating some of difficulties faced by crown in its efforts to introduce royal absolutism. [MPH]

25.211   Arlette Jouanna. *Le devoir de révolte: la noblesse française et la gestation de l'état moderne, 1559–1661.* Paris: Fayard, 1989. ISBN 2-213-02275-5. ‣ Analysis of court nobility's "duty to revolt" in order to safeguard crown, public good, etc. Argues noble rebellions of period were motivated by traditional forces of aristocratic behavior. [MPH]

25.212   Sharon Kettering. *Judicial politics and urban revolt in seventeenth-century France: the Parlement of Aix, 1629–1659.* Princeton: Princeton University Press, 1978. ISBN 0-691-05267-0. ‣ Study arguing behavior of Parlement of Aix not shaped by socioeconomic factors or hostility between crown and province, but forged around ties of clientage and factional disputes. [MPH]

25.213   Sharon Kettering. *Patrons, brokers, and clients in seventeenth-century France.* New York: Oxford University Press, 1986. ISBN 0-19-503673-5. ‣ Study of personal clientage demonstrating how, as minister of state to Louis XIII, Richelieu transformed system into permanent bureaucratic corps of powerbrokers in provinces, linking state-building and patronage as foundation of absolutism. [MPH]

25.214   Raymond F. Kierstead, ed. and trans. *State and society in seventeenth-century France.* Marilyn J. Kierstead, trans. New York: New Viewpoints, 1975. ISBN 0-531-05367-9 (cl), 0-531-05573-6 (pbk). ‣ Collection of ten articles illustrating differing interpretations of absolutism. Especially useful are articles by Russell Major on creation of elections in Guyenne and by René Pillorget on Cascaveoux Uprising. [MPH]

25.215   A. D. Lublinskaya. *French absolutism: the crucial phase, 1620–1629.* Brian Pearce, trans. Cambridge: Cambridge University Press, 1968. ISBN 0-521-07117-8. ‣ Combines analysis of so-called seventeenth-century crisis with evaluation of origins of absolutism. Argues 1620s witnessed genesis of absolute monarchy. English translation of 1965 Russian edition. [MPH]

25.216 Elizabeth Wirth Marvick. *Louis XIII: the making of a king.* New Haven: Yale University press, 1986. ISBN 0-300-03703-1. ▸ Biography of king's first sixteen years (1601–16), based on application of psychoanalytical theory to study of detailed journal of Louis's physician, Jean Héroard. [MPH]

25.217 A. Lloyd Moote. *Louis XIII, the Just.* 1989 ed. Berkeley: University of California Press, 1991. ISBN 0-520-06485-2 (cl, 1989), 0-520-07546-3 (pbk). ▸ Persuasive argument that Louis was hardly pawn of his first minister, Cardinal Richelieu, but significant figure in his own right who shaped France's destiny. [MPH]

25.218 A. Lloyd Moote. *The revolt of the judges: the Parlement of Paris and the Fronde, 1643–1652.* 1971 ed. Princeton: Princeton University Press, 1972. ISBN 0-691-05191-7. ▸ General analysis of mid-seventeenth-century crisis in France. Argues Parlement of Paris key to understanding all disparate elements involved in rebellion of the Fronde. [MPH]

25.219 Roland Mousnier. *The assassination of Henry IV: the tyrannicide problem and the consolidation of the French absolute monarchy in the early seventeenth century.* Joan Spencer, trans. New York: Scribner's, 1973. ISBN 0-684-13357-1. ▸ Especially interesting discussion of tyrannicide and its role in seventeenth-century political thought. Useful appendixes include complete text of Edict of Nantes. Translation of 1964 French edition. [MPH]

25.220 David Parker. *La Rochelle and the French monarchy: conflict and order in seventeenth-century France.* London: Royal Historical Society, 1980. (Royal Historical Society studies in history series, 19.) ISBN 0-901050-76-8. ▸ Analysis of siege of La Rochelle as microcosm of social and political tensions in society. Examines how these conflicts ultimately resolved into order by and for monarchy. [MPH]

25.221 David Parker. *The making of French absolutism.* London: Arnold, 1983. ISBN 0-7131-6382-8 (pbk). ▸ Best general statement of now generally accepted view that absolutism in practice never realized expectations of its propagandists. [MPH]

25.222 Orest A. Ranum. *The Fronde: a French revolution, 1648–1652.* New York: Norton, 1993. ISBN 0-393-03550-6. ▸ Argues, in detailed narrative, that although revolts of Fronde did not significantly alter French society and institutions, it left monarchy stronger and with standing army. [MPH]

25.223 Orest A. Ranum. *Paris in the age of absolutism.* 1968 ed. Bloomington: Indiana University Press, 1979. ISBN 0-253-19677-9 (cl), 0-253-20238-8 (pbk). ▸ Analysis of Paris, as largest city in Europe in 1600; its culture, political and social development, and failure to become commercial and economic center of expanding Europe by 1700, as London did. [MPH]

25.224 Orest A. Ranum. *Richelieu and the councillors of Louis XIII: a study of the secretaries of state and superintendents of finance in the ministry of Richelieu, 1635–1642.* 1963 ed. Westport, Conn.: Greenwood, 1976. ISBN 0-8371-8803-2. ▸ Analysis of functions of government in seventeenth century through Cardinal Richelieu's creatures. Shows how royal favor allowed Richelieu and his favorites to dominate government without opposition. [MPH]

25.225 J.H.M. Salmon. *Cardinal de Retz: the anatomy of a conspirator.* 1969 ed. New York: Macmillan, 1970. ▸ Articulates how cardinal managed to harness forces of aristocratic faction, popular discontent, ecclesiastic privilege, and constitutionalism into uprising against great minister Cardinal Mazarin, and later win favor with Louis XIV. [MPH]

25.226 Ellery Schalk. *From valor to pedigree: ideas of nobility in France in the sixteenth and seventeenth centuries.* Princeton: Princeton University Press, 1986. ISBN 0-691-05460-6. ▸ Argues contemporary emphasis on nobility changed at end of religious wars from noble virtue to birth and gentility, resulting in weaker nobilty under royal control. [MPH]

25.227 Paul Sonnino, ed. *The reign of Louis XIV: essays in celebration of Andrew Lossky.* 1990 ed. Atlantic Highlands, N.J.: Humanities, 1991. ISBN 0-391-03650-5 (cl, 1990), 0-391-03705-6 (pbk). ▸ Essays by fourteen scholars examining most aspects of reign from point of view of king and central government. Good summaries of literature and introduction to reign. [LMB]

25.228 Victor-L. Tapié. *France in the age of Louis XIII and Richelieu.* 1974 ed. D. McN. Lockie, ed. and trans. Cambridge: Cambridge University Press, 1984. ISBN 0-521-26300-X (cl), 0-521-26924-5 (pbk). ▸ Detailed political narrative of reign of Louis XIII. Comprehensive bibliography in English edition updates author's original (1952) French bibliography. [MPH]

25.229 John B. Wolf. *Louis XIV.* 1968 ed. New York: Norton, 1974. ISBN 0-393-00753-7. ▸ Most comprehensive biography of king in English. Delineates all principal personalities and all major events in Louis XIV's career, giving full coverage of his wars. [MPH]

1715–1789

25.230 Michel Antoine. *Le gouvernement et l'administration sous Louis XV: dictionnaire biographique.* Paris: Centre National de la Recherche Scientifique, 1978. ISBN 2-222-02231-2. ▸ Useful guide to minor and major figures in eighteenth-century politics. [LMB]

25.231 Keith Michael Baker, ed. *The French Revolution and the creation of modern political culture.* Vol. 1: *The political culture of the Old Regime.* Oxford: Pergamon, 1987. ISBN 0-08-034258-2. ▸ Collection of essays by leading scholars. Much variation, but main focus on intellectual developments, particularly political theory. Key portion reveals flaws in French conceptions central to development of legislative democracy. [JRC]

25.232 J. F. Bosher. *French finances, 1770–1795: from business to bureaucracy.* Cambridge: Cambridge University Press, 1970. ISBN 0-521-07764-8. ▸ Detailed evaluation of royal and revolutionary efforts to reform government and solve endemic fiscal problems. Rehabilitation of statesman and financier Jacques Necker. [JRC]

25.233 Gail Bossenga. *The politics of privilege: Old Regime and revolution in Lille.* Cambridge: Cambridge University Press, 1991. ISBN 0-521-39282-9. ▸ Analysis of complex regional politics and interrelationship between monarchy and privileged groups. Notes latter's frailty in 1789 as well as their resiliency. [JRC]

25.234 Douglas Dakin. *Turgot and the Ancien Regime in France.* 1939 ed. New York: Octagon Books, 1965. ▸ Life-and-times biography illuminating politics of period. Provides detailed picture of provincial politics through Turgot's intendancy and national politics through his time as comptroller-general of finance. Essential for period. [JRC]

25.235 William Doyle. *The Parlement of Bordeaux and the end of the Old Regime, 1771–1790.* New York: St. Martin's, 1974. ▸ Analysis of social and political world of provincial Parlement. Traces recruitment, careers, and life styles; emphasizes significance of Parlement in organizing support for Estates-General. [JRC]

25.236 Jean Egret. *The French prerevolution, 1787–1788.* Wesley D. Camp, trans. J. F. Bosher, Introduction. Chicago: University of Chicago Press, 1977. ISBN 0-226-19142-7. ▸ Narrative of conflicts leading to Revolution. Main focus on developments in Versailles among king, aristocracy, and magistracy. Provincial matters treated sparingly. Author's hostility to royal opponents now questioned. [JRC]

25.237 Peter Gay. *Voltaire's politics: the poet as realist.* 2d ed. New

Haven: Yale University Press, 1988. ISBN 0-300-04096-2 (cl), 0-300-04095-4 (pbk). ‣ Breakthrough work on Voltaire relating writings to specific political circumstances. Appears as hardheaded realist with wide array of political positions, far beyond enlightened despotism with which Voltaire is usually linked. [JRC]

25.238 Vivian R. Gruder. "Paths to political consciousness: the assembly of notables of 1787 and the 'pre-Revolution' in France." *French historical studies* 13.3 (1984) 323–55. ISSN 0016-1071. ‣ Discussion of Assembly of Notables of February–May 1787. Correction to interpretations, such as Egret 25.236, that envision group as narrowly defensive of traditional interest. [JRC]

25.239 Thomas E. Kaiser. "Money, despotism, and public opinion in early eighteenth-century France: John Law and the debate on royal credit." *Journal of modern history* 63.1 (1991) 1–28. ISSN 0022-2801. ‣ Finds early royal acceptance of legitimate public opinion. Interestingly, attracting credit inspired this change before any theories regarding popular sovereignty had effect. [JRC]

25.240 Steven L. Kaplan. *Bread, politics, and political economy in the reign of Louis XV.* 2 vols. The Hague: Nijhoff, 1976. ISBN 90-247-1873-2 (set), 90-247-1874-0 (v. 1), 90-247-1875-9 (v. 2). ‣ Greatly advances knowledge of reign of Louis XV by describing policies of free grain trade and reactions. Shows crisis of period extended beyond questions of constitutionalism. [JRC]

25.241 Joan B. Landes. *Women and the public sphere in the age of the French Revolution.* Ithaca, N.Y.: Cornell University Press, 1988. ISBN 0-8014-2141-1 (cl), 0-8014-9481-8 (pbk). ‣ Most thorough examination of gender and Revolution. Finds revolutionaries accepting antifeminist influences against courtly/salon world more favorable to feminism. [JRC]

25.242 Darline Gay Levy. *The ideas and careers of Simon-Nicolas-Henri Linguet: a study in eighteenth-century French politics.* Urbana: University of Illinois Press, 1980. ISBN 0-252-00311-X. ‣ Lawyer and publicist Linguet, a master propagandist, among first celebrities to create and sustain own persona. Flamboyant personality and ideas richly elaborated in well-written and researched work. [JRC]

25.243 Sarah C. Maza. "Le tribunal de la nation: les mémoires judiciaires et l'opinion publique à la fin de l'ancien régime." *Annales: économies, sociétés, civilisations* 42.1 (1987) 73–90. ISSN 0003-441X. ‣ Contribution to history of public opinion, revealing extraordinary power of public. Examines legal briefs, their inflammatory contents, and their broad acceptance. [JRC]

25.244 R. R. Palmer. *The age of the democratic revolution: a political history of Europe and America, 1760–1800.* Vol. 1: *The struggle.* Princeton: Princeton University Press, 1959. ISBN 0-691-00569-9 (v. 1, pbk). ‣ Magisterial study delineating particular pattern behind revolutionary outburst. Suggests three powers competing for authority: aristocracy, monarchy, and popular sovereignty. [JRC]

25.245 Jeremy D. Popkin. *News and politics in the age of revolution: Jean Luzac's "Gazette de Leyde."* Ithaca, N.Y.: Cornell University Press, 1989. ISBN 0-8014-2301-5. ‣ Comprehensive analysis of most significant French-language newspaper, *Gazette de Leyde.* Includes discussion of reportage, mechanical production, and finances. Emphasizes its important role in Old Regime and Revolution. [JRC]

25.246 Pierre Rétat, ed. *L'attentat de Damiens: discours sur l'événement au dix-huitième siècle.* Paris and Lyon: Centre National de la Recherche Scientifique and Presses Universitaires de Lyon, 1979. ISBN 2-7297-0045-5, 2-222-02598-2. ‣ Analysis of French understanding of attempt on life of Louis XV. First and most comprehensive attempt to plot reception of news. [JRC]

RELIGION
General Studies

25.247 C. J. Betts. *Early deism in France: from the so-called déistes of Lyon (1564) to Voltaire's "Lettres Philosophiques" (1734).* P. Dibon and Richard Henry Popkin, eds. The Hague: Nijhoff; distributed by Kluwer Academic, 1984. ISBN 90-247-2923-8. ‣ Study of origins of early Enlightenment thought and deism, Montesquieu and Voltaire. Corrective to works stressing long history of irreligion. [RMG]

25.248 Henri Bremond. *A literary history of religious thought in France from the Wars of Religion down to our own times.* 3 vols. to date. K. L. Montgomery, trans. New York: Macmillan, 1928–. ‣ Translation of first three volumes of Bremond's massive *Histoire littéraire du sentiment religieux en France.* Unequaled as study of early stages of Catholic Reformation, especially its humanistic and mystic currents from Saint François de Sales through *Oratoire.* [BBD]

25.249 Robin Briggs. *Communities of belief: cultural and social tension in early modern France.* Oxford: Clarendon, 1989. ISBN 0-19-821981-4. ‣ Ten essays considering local society and institutions. Particular attention to witch hunts, endemic character of popular witch beliefs, and Counter-Reformation as repressive movement with unattainable goals. Careful study of mentalities. [RMG]

25.250 Jean Delumeau. *Sin and fear: the emergence of a Western guilt culture, 13th–18th centuries.* 1990 ed. Eric Nicholson, trans. New York: St. Martin's, 1991. ISBN 0-312-03582-9 (cl, 1990), 0-312-05800-4 (pbk). ‣ Discussion of theology of sin and its diffusion in Catholic and Protestant teachings. Finds intensification of guilt as fundamental characteristic of Western society. Massive and sprawling; not exclusively French in scope. [BBD]

25.251 Lucien Febvre. "The origins of the French Reformation: a badly put question?" In *A new kind of history and other essays.* K. Folca, trans. Peter Burke, ed., pp. 44–107. New York: Harper & Row, 1973. ISBN 0-06-131784-5. ‣ Classic discussion setting aside old debate over whether evangelical reformers were "Lutherans" in favor of locating sources of Reformation in profound moral and religious crisis. [BBD]

25.252 Robert Forster and Orest A. Ranum, eds. *Ritual, religion, and the sacred: selections from "Annales: économies, sociétés, civilisations, Vol. 7."* Elborg Forster and Patricia M. Ranum, trans. Baltimore: Johns Hopkins University Press, 1982. ISBN 0-8018-2776-0 (cl), 0-8018-2778-7 (pbk). ‣ Articles on popular and ecclesiastical religious practices. Especially useful on French practices on marriage, religious conflicts in sixteenth-century Paris, and witchcraft. [BBD]

25.253 Philip T. Hoffman. *Church and community in the diocese of Lyon, 1500–1789.* New Haven: Yale University Press, 1984. ISBN 0-300-03141-6. ‣ Study of Counter-Reformation's impact on society. Argues reforming bishops, urban elites, and parish priests joined to support Tridentine Catholicism. Finds priests curtailed forms of popular religion and distanced themselves from parishioners. [RMG]

25.254 Colin Jones. *The charitable imperative: hospitals and nursing in Ancien Régime and revolutionary France.* London: Routledge, 1989. (Wellcome Institute series in the history of medicine, 9.) ISBN 0-415-02133-2. ‣ Nine essays on Christian injunction to provide charity. Considers institutions, patients, and soldiers, prostitutes, insane, and nursing orders such as Daughters of Charity. Excellent study of eighteenth-century French medicine and medical practices. [RMG]

25.255 François Lebrun, ed. *Histoire de la France religieuse.* Vol. 2: *Du christianisme flamboyant à l'aube des Lumières (XIVe–XVIIIe* *siècles).* Paris: Seuil, 1988. ISBN 2-02-010369-9 (set), 2-02-0010016-9 (v. 2). ‣ Valuable chapters on late medieval piety by Chiffoleau, sixteenth-century crisis by Venard, and Tridentine reform and era of Louis XIV by Labrousse and Sauzet. [BBD]

25.256   David Nicholls. "The social history of the French Reformation: ideology, confession, and culture." *Social history* 9.1 (1984) 25–43. ISSN 0307-1022. ‣ Historiographical survey of major themes of Protestantism and religious conflict. Covers old ideological biases and quarrels, outlining new social and cultural approaches. [BBD]

25.257   Menna Prestwich, ed. *International Calvinism, 1541–1715.* 1985 ed. Oxford: Clarendon, 1987. ISBN 0-19-821933-4 (cl, 1985), 0-19-822874-0 (pbk). ‣ Important essays by Labrousse, Yardeni, and Joutard on French Calvinism, French Calvinist political thought, and revocation of Edict of Nantes, plus essays on Calvinism outside France. [RMG]

25.258   Norman Ravitch. *Sword and mitre: government and episcopate in France and England in the age of aristocracy.* The Hague: Mouton, 1966. ISBN 0-686-22467-1. ‣ Statistical analysis of social origins and recruitment of bishops, who were increasingly drawn from sword nobility. Interesting comparisons with English and Irish bishops. [RMG]

25.259   Denis Richet. *De la réforme à la Revolution: études sur la France moderne.* Paris: Aubier, 1991. ISBN 2-7007-2232-9. ‣ Eighteen articles, some previously unpublished, underscore interrelationship between religion and politics. Of particular note are articles on Catholic League and on Séguier family. [MPH]

25.260   George A. Rothrock. *The Huguenots: a biography of a minority.* Chicago: Nelson-Hall, 1979. ISBN 0-88229-277-3. ‣ Overview of Huguenot society and politics from Reformation through revocation of Edict of Nantes. Useful introduction to broad course of events. [BBD]

25.261   Alfred Soman. *Sorcellerie et justice criminelle: le Parlement de Paris (16e–18e siècles).* Hampshire, England: Variorum, 1992. ISBN 0-86078-320-0. ‣ Collected articles, in English and French, on witch hunting, witch trials, and criminal procedure. Important articles based on extensive research in massive archives of Parlement of Paris. [BBD]

25.262   D. P. Walker. *Unclean spirits: possession and exorcism in France and England in the late sixteenth and early seventeenth centuries.* Philadelphia: University of Pennsylvania Press, 1981. ISBN 0-8122-7797-X. ‣ Brief, insightful examination of famous cases of diabolical possession and exorcism. Believes possession a combination of fraud and disease. [RMG]

1450–1610

25.263   Frederic J. Baumgartner. *Change and continuity in the French episcopate: the bishops and the Wars of Religion, 1547–1610.* Durham, N.C.: Duke University Press, 1986. ISBN 0-8223-0675-1. ‣ Discussion of episcopacy as an institution—its membership, powers, privileges, and finances—and impact of religious change and conflict on it. Incompleteness of records permits only overview of this topic. [BBD]

25.264   Philip Benedict. *Rouen during the Wars of Religion.* Cambridge: Cambridge University Press, 1981. ISBN 0-521-22818-2. ‣ Model study of interaction of social, religious, and political factors in French religious wars. Examines rise of Protestantism and impact of religious crisis in provincial capital. [BBD]

25.265   Philip Benedict. "The Saint Bartholomew's massacres in the provinces." *Historical journal* 21.2 (1978) 205–25. ISSN 0018-246X. ‣ Convincing interpretation of why violence broke out in some provincial cities and not others in 1572. Concludes Parisian rumors stimulated or assuaged unrest. [BBD]

25.266   William J. Bouwsma. *John Calvin: a sixteenth-century portrait.* 1988 ed. New York: Oxford University Press, 1989. ISBN 0-19-504394-4 (cl, 1988), 0-19-505951-4 (pbk). ‣ Interpretive study setting reformer in context of his times and stressing impact of medieval inheritance and Renaissance humanism on his thought. Depicts more human Calvin. [BBD]

25.267   Denis Crouzet. *Les guerriers de Dieu: la violence au temps des troubles de religion, vers 1525–vers 1610.* 2 vols. Seyssel, France: Champ Vallon, 1990. ISBN 2-87673-094-4 (set). ‣ Brilliant description of apocalyptic fervor and hallucinatory fears of period of religious wars. Comprehensive study of polemics of violence, both Catholic and Huguenot. [BBD]

25.268   Natalie Zemon Davis. "The sacred and the body social in sixteenth-century Lyon." *Past and present* 90 (1981) 40–70. ISSN 0031-2746. ‣ Examination of how Catholics and Protestants made use of urban space and integrative functions of their social metaphors. Pioneering attempt to explain appeal of two religions through their language and ritual. [BBD]

25.269   Barbara B. Diefendorf. *Beneath the cross: Catholics and Huguenots in sixteenth-century Paris.* New York: Oxford University Press, 1991. ISBN 0-19-506554-9 (cl), 0-19-507013-5 (pbk). ‣ Study of escalating religious conflicts from first anti-Protestant riots through Massacre of St. Bartholomew's Day. Reassesses religious dimensions of popular violence and role of Paris in civil wars. [BBD]

25.270   James K. Farge. *Orthodoxy and reform in early Reformation France: the Faculty of Theology of Paris, 1500–1543.* Leiden: Brill, 1985. ISBN 90-04-07231-4. ‣ Study of institution and organization of Paris Faculty of Theology, its members, and reaction to evangelical and Protestant trends. Sound, sympathetic treatment of misunderstood institution. [BBD]

25.271   Lucien Febvre. *The problem of unbelief in the sixteenth century: the religion of Rabelais.* Beatrice Gottlieb, trans. Cambridge, Mass.: Harvard University Press, 1982. ISBN 0-674-70825-3 (cl), 0-674-70826-1 (pbk). ‣ Classic study of sixteenth-century mentality, broader than its title. Challenges notion that Rabelais was atheist by arguing his mental world lacked tools for disbelief. [BBD]

25.272   A. N. Galpern. *The religions of the people in sixteenth-century Champagne.* Cambridge, Mass.: Harvard University Press, 1976. ISBN 0-674-75836-6. ‣ Effect of religious change and conflict on confraternal organizations, cult of saints, and other aspects of popular devotion. Pioneering study of popular piety and religious practices. [BBD]

25.273   Janine Garrisson-Estèbe. *Protestants du Midi, 1559–1598.* Rev. ed. Toulouse: Privat, 1991. ISBN 2-7089-5364-8. ‣ Sympathetic study of Huguenot culture and religious practice, politics of religious wars, and creation of independent, rebel confederation in south. Discussion of rebellion of Midi most important. [BBD]

25.274   Mark Greengrass. *The French Reformation.* Oxford: Blackwell, 1987. ISBN 0-631-14516-8 (pbk). ‣ Good, brief overview of rise of religious dissent and organization and growth of Protestant church, its social appeal, and role in France's civil wars. [BBD]

25.275   Henry Heller. *The conquest of poverty: the Calvinist revolt in sixteenth-century France.* Leiden: Brill, 1986. ISBN 90-04-07598-4 (pbk). ‣ Study of Protestantism as revolt motivated by economic crisis and social constraint. Insufficient attention to appeal of Calvinism, but useful accounts of Protestantism's spread in various cities. [BBD]

25.276   Robert M. Kingdon. *Geneva and the coming of the Wars of Religion in France, 1555–1563.* Geneva: Droz, 1956. ‣ Examination of role of Geneva in spreading Calvinist ideas and institutions. Essential on organization and politics of reformed churches through beginning of religious wars. [BBD]

25.277 Robert M. Kingdon. *Geneva and the consolidation of the French Protestant movement, 1564–1572: a contribution to the history of congregationalism, Presbyterianism, and Calvinist resistance theory.* Geneva: Droz, 1967. ▸ Key work on French Calvinism. Explores Genevan influences on doctrine, institutions, and political activities of reformed churches during first decade of Wars of Religion. [BBD]

25.278 Robert M. Kingdon. *Myths about the St. Bartholomew's Day massacres, 1572–1576.* Cambridge, Mass.: Harvard University Press, 1988. ISBN 0-674-59831-8. ▸ Key study of religious propaganda and its impact on diplomacy and political thought. Argues massacres used in international campaign to stir support for Huguenot cause. [BBD]

25.279 A. Lynn Martin. *The Jesuit mind: the mentality of an elite in early modern France.* Ithaca, N.Y.: Cornell University Press, 1988. ISBN 0-8014-2147-0. ▸ Study of Jesuit mission in sixteenth century; attitudes of members, based mainly on correspondence with Rome. Nonchronological attempt to capture mentality. [BBD]

25.280 Raymond A. Mentzer, Jr. *Heresy proceedings in Languedoc, 1500–1560.* Philadelphia: American Philosophical Society, 1984. (Transactions of the American Philosophical Society, 74.5.) ISBN 0-87169-745-9 (pbk). ▸ Examination of institutions and procedures for prosecution of religious deviance in secular and religious courts; social geography of accused heretics. Valuable for explanation of Inquisitorial procedures. [BBD]

25.281 Donald Nugent. *Ecumenism in the age of the Reformation: the Colloquy of Poissy.* Cambridge, Mass.: Harvard University Press, 1974. ISBN 0-674-23725-0. ▸ Examination of hardening of religious differences and failure of Colloquy of Poissy (1561) to achieve religious reconciliation. Explains doctrinal and political cleavages as France moved to civil war. [BBD]

25.282 Augustin Renaudet. *Préréforme et humanisme à Paris pendant les premières guerres d'Italie (1494–1517).* 2d ed. Paris: Argences, 1953. ▸ Classic work on sixteenth-century university life, early French humanism, and evangelical reformers. Attempts to renew spiritual life in Paris in context of domestic and foreign politics. [BBD]

25.283 N. M. Sutherland. *The Huguenot struggle for recognition.* New Haven: Yale University Press, 1980. ISBN 0-300-02328-6. ▸ Study of relations among Protestants, Catholics, and French crown, based largely on royal edicts and official pronouncements regarding religious practice up through 1598. Useful data despite bias in favor of Huguenots. [BBD]

25.284 Larissa Taylor. *Soldiers of Christ: preaching in late medieval and Reformation France.* New York: Oxford University Press, 1992. ISBN 0-19-506993-5. ▸ Analysis of religious values and practices as seen through sermons. Valuable insight into art of preaching, popular theology, lay piety, preachers' attitudes toward women, and early response to heresy. [BBD]

25.285 François Wendel. *Calvin: the origins and development of his religious thought.* 1963 ed. Philip Mairet, trans. Durham, N.C.: Labyrinth, 1987. ISBN 0-939464-44-6 (pbk). ▸ Brief biography, primarily oriented toward explaining Calvin's theology. Shows his independence of thought and impact of contemporary theological controversies. Relies heavily on his *Institutes of the Christian Religion.* [BBD]

SEE ALSO
27.293 E. William Monter. *Witchcraft in France and Switzerland.*

1610–1715

25.286 Joseph Bergin. *Cardinal de La Rochefoucauld: leadership and reform in the French church.* New Haven: Yale University Press, 1987. ISBN 0-300-04104-7. ▸ Instructive example of one man's role in reforming religious orders and raising clerical standards in divided and decentralized church. Good view of Counter-Reformation from above. [BBD]

25.287 Pierre Blet. *Le clergé de France, Louis XIV, et le Saint Siège de 1695 à 1715.* Vatican City: Archivio Vaticano, 1989. (Collectanea Archivi Vaticani, 25.) ISBN 88-85042-13-9. ▸ Last of three works by author tracing French church from 1615 to end of Louis XIV's reign. Profound study of church-state-papal relations. [RMG]

25.288 Emanuel Chill. "Religion and mendicity in seventeenth-century France." *International review of social history* 7 (1962) 400–25. ISSN 0020-8590. ▸ Study linking absolutism, repressive Catholicism, and desire for social control. Argues secret organization, Company of the Holy Sacrament, equated mendicity with criminality; from 1665, Paris General Hospital served as workshop for beggars and prostitutes. [RMG]

25.289 Jeanne Ferté. *La vie religieuse dans les campagnes parisiennes (1622–1695).* Paris: Librairie Philosophique J. Vrin, 1962. ISBN 2-7116-4053-1. ▸ Analytical, quantitative study of priests and religion for seventeenth-century Parisian countryside. Massive, essential regional work. [RMG]

25.290 Richard M. Golden. *The godly rebellion: Parisian curés and the religious Fronde, 1652–1662.* Chapel Hill: University of North Carolina Press, 1981. ISBN 0-8078-1466-0. ▸ Reinterpretation of period of Fronde by emphasizing ecclesiastical politics. Concludes Third Fronde followed those of *parlementaires* and princes; led by parish priests, imbued with Jansenism. [RMG]

25.291 Richard M. Golden, ed. *Church, state, and society under the Bourbon kings of France.* Lawrence, Kan.: Coronado, 1982. ISBN 0-87291-161-6. ▸ Articles on Jansenism, Jesuits, witchcraft, Huguenots, refusal of sacraments controversy, and diocesan clergy. Important for church-state and internal church conflicts and problems. [RMG]

25.292 Richard M. Golden, ed. *The Huguenot connection: the Edict of Nantes, its revocation, and early French migration to South Carolina.* Dordrecht: Kluwer Academic, 1988. ISBN 90-247-3645-5. ▸ Collection of essays; thoroughly revisionist interpretations. Sutherland argues no religious toleration and no political or Huguenot cooperation with government resulted from Edict of Nantes. Labrousse emphasizes political motives and fear of Huguenots. [RMG]

25.293 Lucien Goldmann. *The hidden god: a study of tragic vision in the "Pensées" of Pascal and the tragedies of Racine.* Philip Thody, trans. New York: Humanities, 1964. ▸ Study of Pascal and Racine as sources for understanding Jansenist sense of God as simultaneously absent and present. Marxist analysis linking tragic vision as particular mentality of nobility of the robe. [RMG]

25.294 John H. Grever. "The religious history of the reign." In *The reign of Louis XIV: essays in celebration of Andrew Lossky.* 1990 ed. Paul Sonnino, ed., pp. 159–77. Atlantic Highlands, N.J.: Humanities, 1991. ISBN 0-391-03650-5 (cl, 1990), 0-391-03705-6 (pbk). ▸ Evenhanded, brief synthesis of religious views during era of Louis XIV, with particular attention to recent scholarship. [RMG]

25.295 H. G. Judge. "Louis XIV and the church." In *Louis XIV and the craft of kingship.* 1969 ed. John C. Rule, ed., pp. 240–64. Columbus: Ohio State University Press, 1970. ▸ Summary of internal church conflicts and religious developments. Strong on ecclesiastical politics involving Gallicanism, Jansenism, and Quietism. [RMG]

25.296 Alan Charles Kors. *The orthodox sources of disbelief.* Vol. 1: *Atheism in France, 1650–1729.* Princeton: Princeton University Press, 1990. ISBN 0-691-05575-0 (v. 1). ‣ Revisionist view of origins of Enlightenment atheism. Finds origins of atheism not among freethinkers, but in debates among orthodox theologians concerning proofs of existence of God. [RMG]

25.297 Elisabeth Labrousse. *Bayle.* 1983 ed. Denys Potts, trans. Oxford: Oxford University Press, 1985. ISBN 0-19-287541-8 (cl), 0-19-287540-X (pbk). ‣ Study of Pierre Bayle as Calvinist, controversialist, and heroic figure. Unquestionably best study of philosopher and critic in English. [RMG]

25.298 Elisabeth Labrousse. *"Une foi, une loi, un roi? Essai sur la révocation de l'Édit de Nantes.* Geneva and Paris: Labor & Fides and Payot, 1985. ISBN 2-8309-0038-3, 2-228-18040-8. ‣ Indispensable work on revocation. Sees Huguenots as subversive republicans, divided among themselves in impossible political situation. Argues politics explains revocation. [RMG]

25.299 Louis J. Lekai. *The rise of the Cistercian strict observance in seventeenth-century France.* Washington, D.C.: Catholic University of America Press, 1968. ‣ Erudite account of quarrel between Strict Observance and Common Observance during Counter-Reformation. More religious politics than religion. [RMG]

25.300 Keith P. Luria. *Territories of grace: cultural change in the seventeenth-century diocese of Grenoble.* Berkeley: University of California Press, 1991. ISBN 0-520-06810-6. ‣ Examination of religion as evolving product of interaction between villagers and reforming clergy. Revises oversimplified notions of elite versus popular culture; complex and convincing interpretation of cultural interaction. [BBD]

25.301 Jean Orcibal. *Louis XIV et les Protestants: la cabale des accommodeurs de religion, la Caisse des conversions, la révocation de l'Édit de Nantes.* Paris: Vrin, 1951. ‣ Erudite account of Huguenots during reign of Louis XIV and revocation of Edict of Nantes. Attention to impact of foreign policy. [RMG]

25.302 Richard Parish. *Pascal's "Lettres Provinciales": a study in polemic.* 1989 ed. Oxford: Clarendon, 1991. ISBN 0-19-815155-1. ‣ Analysis of Pascal's polemical style against Jesuits in Lettres Provinciales and Pensées, as well as Jesuits' counterpolemic. Helpful evaluation of controversy through works of neglected Jesuit writers. [RMG]

25.303 Elisabeth Israels Perry. *From theology to history: French religious controversy and the revocation of the Edict of Nantes.* The Hague: Nijhoff, 1973. ISBN 90-247-1578-4. ‣ Study of ninety works on Catholic and Protestant controversialists of Reformation and civil wars. Concludes Protestant use of history superior to Catholic. Good analysis of major intellectuals. [RMG]

25.304 Walter Rex. *Essays on Pierre Bayle and religious controversy.* The Hague: Nijhoff, 1965. ‣ Study of Bayle as seventeenth-century Calvinist rather than precursor of Enlightenment. View of Bayle similar to that of Labrousse 25.297. [RMG]

25.305 Alexander Sedgwick. *Jansenism in seventeenth-century France: voices from the wilderness.* Charlottesville: University Press of Virginia, 1977. ISBN 0-8139-0702-0. ‣ Only broad synthesis in English on seventeenth-century Jansenism. Stresses theological aspects and opposition to government. [RMG]

25.306 Paul Sonnino. *Louis XIV's view of the papacy (1661–1667).* Berkeley: University of California Press, 1966. ‣ Study of clash between French ambassador and papal guards in Rome, its aftermath, and Louis XIV's attitudes toward papacy. Solid effort to penetrate Sun King's mind. [RMG]

25.307 René Taveneaux, ed. *Le Catholicisme dans la France classique, 1610–1715.* 2 vols. Paris: Société d'Édition d'Enseignement

Supérieur, 1980. ISBN 2-7181-2108-4 (set). ‣ Overview of religious life from end of Wars of Religion to Enlightenment. Thematically organized, from ecclesiastical structures to pastoral initiatives and currents of Catholic thought. [BBD]

25.308 Maarten Ultee. *The Abbey of St. Germain des Près in the seventeenth century.* New Haven: Yale University Press, 1981. ISBN 0-300-02562-9. ‣ Social history of Parisian monastery during first half of Maurist reform. Engaging analysis of recruitment and monastic life; particularly useful on monastery's economic activities and strategies. [BBD]

25.309 F. Ellen Weaver. *The evolution of the reform of Port-Royal: from the rule of Cîteaux to Jansenism.* Paris: Beauchesne, 1978. ‣ Institutional study considering impact of spirituality. Finds reform of Cistercian convent of Port-Royal influenced by Counter-Reformation. Also discusses impact of Jansenism through Angélique de Saint-Jean. [RMG]

25.310 Charles E. Williams. *The French Oratorians and absolutism, 1611–1641.* New York: Lang, 1989. ISBN 0-8204-0789-5. ‣ Study of Bérulle and Congregation of the Oratory in context of seventeenth-century politics and society. Locates origins of Oratory priests among bourgeois officers opposed to growing state absolutism. [BBD]

1715–1789

25.311 Geoffrey Adams. *The Huguenots and French opinion, 1685–1787: the Enlightenment debate on toleration.* Waterloo, Ont.: Wilfrid Laurier University Press for Canadian Corporation for Studies in Religion, 1991. ISBN 0-88920-217-6 (cl), 0-88920-209-5 (pbk). ‣ Solid examination of philosophes and others. Traces attitudes of intellectuals toward Huguenots which gradually increased in toleration. [RMG]

25.312 David D. Bien. *The Calas affair: persecution, toleration, and heresy in eighteenth-century Toulouse.* 1960 ed. Westport, Conn.: Greenwood, 1979. ISBN 0-313-21206-6. ‣ Refutation of Voltaire's view that Catholic bigotry of magistrates was to blame for execution of Jean Calas in 1762. Rather, war and economic depression resulted in intensification of stereotype of Huguenots as socially dangerous and politically seditious. Concludes fear of Huguenot uprising resulted in general scapegoating. [RMG]

25.313 B. Robert Kreiser. *Miracles, convulsions, and ecclesiastical politics in early eighteenth-century Paris.* Princeton: Princeton University Press, 1978. ISBN 0-691-05262-X. ‣ Study of popular religion in context of church, government, and cult of miracles at Saint-Médard cemetery. Best study of how convulsionaries and Jansenism created religious movement among lower social groups in Paris. [RMG]

25.314 John McManners. *French ecclesiastical society under the Ancien Régime: a study of Angers in the eighteenth century.* 1960 ed. Manchester: Manchester University Press, 1968. ‣ Ecclesiastical history of Angers showing pervasive role of church and clergy to early years of French Revolution. Major study of provincial religious life. [RMG]

25.315 Jeffrey W. Merrick. *The desacralization of the French monarchy in the eighteenth century.* Baton Rouge: Louisiana State University Press, 1990. ISBN 0-8071-1537-1. ‣ Study on demise of divine-right monarchy as result of public debates between Catholic church and parlements. Major issues were Jansenism and toleration of Protestants. [RMG]

25.316 R. R. Palmer. *Catholics and unbelievers in eighteenth-century France.* 1947 ed. Princeton: Princeton University press, 1970. ISBN 0-691-05108-9 (cl), 0-691-00750-0 (pbk). ‣ First major study to take account of anti-Enlightenment thinkers. Finds opponents of philosophes had recourse to history and nature but were unequal to task of successfully rebutting unbelievers. [RMG]

25.317 Timothy Tackett. *Priest and parish in eighteenth-century France: a social and political study of the curés in a diocese of Dauphiné, 1750–1791.* Princeton: Princeton University Press, 1977. ISBN 0-691-05243-3 (cl), 0-691-10199-X (pbk). ‣ Seminal examination of ecclesiastical careers and politicization of parish priests in diocese of Gap through French Revolution. [RMG]

25.318 Michel Vovelle. *Piété baroque et déchristianisation en Provence au dix-huitième siècle: les attitudes devant la mort d'après les clauses des testaments.* Abridged ed. Paris: Seuil, 1978. ISBN 2-02-004885-X. ‣ Quantitative analysis of wills showing changes in attitudes toward death in Provence. Concludes diminution of religious clauses indicates dechristianization. Influential study in collective mentalities. [RMG]

ECONOMY AND SOCIETY

General Studies

25.319 René Baehrel. *Une croissance: La Basse Provence rurale de la fin du dix-sixième siècle à 1789.* 1961 ed. Paris: École des Hautes Études en Sciences Sociales, 1988. ISBN 2-7132-0910-2. ‣ Study making controversial break with Annales paradigm of economic decline in history. Focuses on real possibility of economic growth in rural economy of seventeenth-century Provence. [PTH]

25.320 Micheline Baulant[-Duchaillut] and Jean Meuvret. *Prix des céréales extraits de la mercuriale de Paris (1520–1698).* 2 vols. Paris: S.E.V.P.E.N., 1960–62. ISBN 2-7132-0119-5. ‣ Fundamental source for grain prices in Paris. [PTH]

25.321 François Billaçois. *The duel: its rise and fall in early modern France.* Trista Selous, ed. and trans. New Haven: Yale University Press, 1990. ISBN 0-300-04028-8. ‣ Examination of practices of dueling, its sociology, religious and legal campaign against it, resistance to campaign, and cultural themes and symbols that resonated in duel. [KPL]

25.322 Marc Bloch. *French rural history: an essay on its basic characteristics.* Janet Sondheimer, trans. Berkeley: University of California Press, 1966. ISBN 0-520-00127-3 (cl), 0-520-01660-2 (pbk). ‣ Classic study by Annales-school founder of long-term evolution of rural world, including patterns of settlement, agrarian regimes, lord-peasant relations, rural communities, and agricultural revolution. Model of *longue durée* approach. [KPL]

25.323 Fernand Braudel and Ernest Labrousse. *Histoire économique et sociale de la France.* Vol. 2: *Les derniers temps de l'âge seigneurial aux préludes de l'âge industriel (1660–1789).* Paris: Presses Universitaires de France, 1970. ‣ Overview of French social and economic history. Covers countryside and cities, industry and agriculture, with emphasis on demography and rigidities of Old Regime. [PTH]

25.324 Pierre Chaunu and Richard Gascon. *De 1450 à 1660: l'état et la ville.* Paris: Presses Universitaires de France, 1977. ISSN 0035-239X. ‣ Somewhat rapid overview of state and its evolution by Chaunu, coupled with Gascon's description of sixteenth-century cities focusing on merchants, bankers, and trade. [PTH]

25.325 Natalie Zemon Davis. "Ghosts, kin, and progeny: some features of family life in early modern France." *Daedalus* 106 (1977) 87–114. ISSN 0011-5266. ‣ Important discussion of multigenerational family strategy, family identity, and strengthening of parental power over children. Illustrates interactions and tensions between family choices and political, religious, and social developments. [KPL]

25.326 Natalie Zemon Davis. *Society and culture in early modern France: eight essays.* Stanford, Calif.: Stanford University Press, 1975. ISBN 0-8047-0868-1 (cl), 0-8047-0972-6 (pbk). ‣ Pioneering collection of essays. Topics include labor relations, religious change among urban journeymen and women, youth groups and

world-turned-upside-down, meanings of religious violence, printing's impact, proverbs, and popular culture. [KPL]

25.327 Jonathan Dewald. *Pont-St-Pierre, 1398–1789: lordship, community, and capitalism in early modern France.* Berkeley: University of California Press, 1987. ISBN 0-520-05673-6. ‣ Case study of noble-village relations and economic change. Describes decline of seigneurial power, questions nobles' ability to adapt to market economy, and suggests capitalism took root instead among village elite. [KPL]

25.328 Barbara B. Diefendorf and Carla Hesse, eds. *Culture and identity in early modern Europe (1500–1800): essays in honor of Natalie Zemon Davis.* Ann Arbor: University of Michigan Press, 1993. ISBN 0-472-10470-5. ‣ Collection of essays showing Davis's influence on historical study of period. Stresses impulses and forces in creating individual and collective identities among Europeans. [MPH]

25.329 Georges Duby, ed. *Histoire de la France urbaine.* Vol. 3: *La ville classique de la Renaissance aux Révolutions.* Andre Chedeville, Jacques Le Goff, and Jacques Rossiaud. Paris: Seuil, 1981. ISBN 2-02-005591-0 (set), 2-02-005978-9 (v. 3). ‣ Multiauthored social and cultural history of French urban life. [PTH]

25.330 Georges Duby and Armand Wallon, eds. *Histoire de la France rurale.* Vol. 2: *L'âge classique.* H. Neveux, J. Jacquart, and E. Le Roy Ladurie. Paris: Seuil, 1975. ISBN 2-02-005150-8 (set), 2-02-004268-1 (v. 2). ‣ Multiauthored overview of French rural society since Middle Ages, covering demographic trends, regional differences, and social and economic developments. Convenient summary of Annales view of countryside. [PTH]

25.331 Jacques Dupâquier et al. *Histoire de la population française.* 4 vols. Paris: Presses Universitaires de France, 1988. ISBN 2-13-040109-0 (v. 1), 2-13-041383-8 (v. 2), 2-13-041928-3 (v. 3), 2-13-042070-2 (v. 4). ‣ Multiauthored review of historical demography and history of family. Covers usual demographic topics, from fertility to mortality crises, plus mobility and relationship between demography and economy. Also touches on history of mentalities. Volumes 1 and 2 cover early modern period. [PTH]

25.332 Cissie C. Fairchilds. *Poverty and charity in Aix-en-Provence, 1640–1789.* Baltimore: Johns Hopkins University Press, 1976. ISBN 0-8018-1677-7. ‣ Study of municipal poor and poor relief. Examines impact of state's supplanting of church on donations to relief institutions of Counter-Reformation, and Enlightenment, with consideration of process of dechristianization. [KPL]

25.333 Robert Forster and Orest A. Ranum, eds. *Deviants and the abandoned in French society: selections from "Annales: économies, sociétés, civilisations, Vol. 4."* Elborg Forster and Patricia M. Ranum, trans. Baltimore: Johns Hopkins University Press, 1978. ISBN 0-8018-1991-1 (cl), 0-8018-1992-X (pbk). ‣ Collection of journal articles on prostitutes, abandoned children, criminals condemned to galleys, vagrants, arsonists, insane, and prisoners. Examples of Annales approaches to social history of deviants. [KPL]

25.334 Robert Forster and Orest A. Ranum, eds. *Family and society: selections from "Annales: économies, sociétés, civilisations, Vol. 2."* Elborg Forster and Patricia M. Ranum, trans. Baltimore: Johns Hopkins University Press, 1976. ISBN 0-8018-1780-3 (cl), 0-8018-1781-1 (pbk). ‣ Articles from journal treating French inheritance customs (Le Roy Ladurie), remarriage (Baulant), illicit sexuality (Depauw), and economic effects of late marriage (Burguière). Articles also cover other periods and countries. [KPL]

25.335 Edward Whiting Fox. *History in geographic perspective: the other France.* 1971 ed. New York: Norton, 1972. ISBN 0-393-

05433-0 (cl, 1971), 0-393-00650-6 (pbk). ▸ Sweeping though not entirely supportable interpretation of enduring political divisions between commercial port cities tied to international trade and hinterland agricultural towns dominated by administrative government. [KPL]

25.336 Philip T. Hoffman. "Land rents and agricultural productivity: the Paris Basin, 1450–1789." *Journal of economic history* 51.4 (1991) 771–805. ISSN 0022-0507. ▸ Argues agriculture in Paris basin was capable of growth and was thriving on eve of Revolution. Concludes true obstacles to growth, such as small farm size, were less important than economic consequences of warfare and civil disorder. [PTH]

25.337 Emmanuel Le Roy Ladurie. *The peasants of Languedoc.* 1974 ed. John Day, trans. Urbana: University of Illinois Press, 1976. ISBN 0-252-00411-6 (cl, 1974), 0-252-00635-6 (pbk). ▸ Classic example of Annales school "total" history. Combines demographic, economic, geographic, and cultural history in description of *longue-durée* agrarian cycle, fourteenth to eighteenth centuries, in rural world. [KPL]

25.338 Jean-Marc Moriceau and Gilles Postel-Vinay. *Ferme, entreprise, famille: grande exploitation et changements agricole; les Chartier, XVIIe–XIXe siècles.* Paris: École des Hautes Études en Sciences Sociales, 1992. (Les hommes et la terre, 21.) ISBN 2-7132-0979-X. ▸ Novel case study of social and economic dealings of family of tenant farmers near Paris, from sixteenth to late nineteenth century. Casts doubt on assumption that countryside was incapable of economic growth. Useful account of effects of Revolution. [PTH]

25.339 Kathryn Norberg. *Rich and poor in Grenoble, 1600–1814.* Berkeley: University of California Press, 1985. ISBN 0-520-05260-9. ▸ Examination of social attitudes toward urban poor traced through relief efforts of Catholic institutions and statistical study of testamentary bequests. Illustrates change from paternalistic and repressive Counter-Reformation ethic to bureaucratic, impersonal Enlightenment aid. [KPL]

25.340 Robert A. Schneider. *Public life in Toulouse, 1463–1789: from municipal republic to cosmopolitan city.* Ithaca, N.Y.: Cornell University Press, 1989. ISBN 0-8014-2191-8. ▸ Study of evolution of urban society and culture. Concludes vertical ties between elite and populace persisted until late seventeenth century when dissolved under impact of absolutism, Parisian culture, and aggravated economic conditions. [KPL]

25.341 Frank C. Spooner. *The international economy and monetary movements in France, 1493–1725.* Cambridge, Mass.: Harvard University Press, 1972. ISBN 0-674-45840-0. ▸ Thorough consideration of relationship between monetary change and economy. [LMB]

25.342 David Weir. "Life under pressure: France and England, 1670–1870." *Journal of economic history* 44.1 (1984) 27–47. ISSN 0022-0507. ▸ Important comparative article relating French and English demographic variables to economic conditions. Casts grave doubt on Malthusian models common to early modern economic history. [PTH]

25.343 Robert Wheaton and Tamara K. Hareven, eds. *Family and sexuality in French history.* Philadelphia: University of Pennsylvania Press, 1980. ISBN 0-8122-7775-9. ▸ Essays combining structural and cultural approaches to family history on various topics including clandestine marriages, repression of sexuality, charivaris, interactions of extended kin and nuclear families, and decline of fertility. [KPL]

SEE ALSO

22.253 Jean-Louis Flandrin. *Families in former times.*

1450–1610

25.344 Jonathan Dewald. *The formation of a provincial nobility: the magistrates of the Parliament of Rouen, 1449–1610.* Princeton: Princeton University Press, 1980. ISBN 0-691-05283-2. ▸ Study of robe nobility and origins, sources of wealth, and economic attitudes shared with sword nobility. Underplays view of competing nobilities; argues in favor of cohesive aristocratic elite. [KPL]

25.345 James R. Farr. *Hands of honor: artisans and their world in Dijon, 1550–1650.* Ithaca, N.Y.: Cornell University Press, 1988. ISBN 0-8014-2172-1. ▸ Uses cultural theory to study master artisans. Deemphasizes corporate divisions; suggests that masters were nascent class defined by common culture, kinship networks, and shared interests vis-à-vis authorities and journeymen. [KPL]

25.346 George Huppert. *Les bourgeois gentilshommes: an essay on the definition of elites in Renaissance France.* Chicago: University of Chicago Press, 1977. ISBN 0-226-36099-7. ▸ Study arguing existence of new sixteenth-century gentry between nobility and bourgeoisie, typified by essayist Michel de Montaigne and statesman Étienne Denis, duc de Pasquier. Position based on legal careers, officeholding, and distinct outlook. [KPL]

25.347 Emmanuel Le Roy Ladurie and Michel Morineau. *De 1450 à 1660: paysannerie et croissance.* Paris: Presses Universitaires de France, 1977. ▸ Social and economic history of peasantry in sixteenth century as driven by population growth and barriers posed by mentalities and limited technology (Ladurie). Interesting picture of economy as a whole by Morineau, who has broken with Annales paradigm. [PTH]

25.348 James B. Wood. *The nobility of the "election" of Bayeux, 1463–1666: continuity through change.* Princeton: Princeton University Press, 1980. ISBN 0-691-05294-8. ▸ Challenges older view of noble economic decline vis-à-vis bourgeoisie in sixteenth and seventeenth centuries. Suggests improved economic position of nobility led to success in integrating new nobles. [KPL]

1610–1715

25.349 Philip Benedict. *The Huguenot population of France, 1600–1685: the demographic fate and customs of a religious minority.* Philadelphia: American Philosophical Society, 1991. (Transactions of the American Philosophical Society, 81.5.) ▸ Important study of Protestant population, attentive to national trends and regional variations. Demonstrates community's ability to retain majority of its members despite increasing persecution; discusses patterns of marriage and sexual relations. [KPL]

25.350 Yves-Marie Bercé. *History of peasant revolts: the social origins of rebellion in early modern France.* Amanda Whitmore, trans. Cambridge: Polity, 1990. ISBN 0-7456-0411-0. ▸ Study of causes, rhythm, organization, and mentalities of frequent large popular revolts. Argues revolts were responses of local society to increasing state intrusiveness and eventually disappeared under state repression. Translation of *Histoire des croquants: étude des soulèvements populaires au dix-septième siècle dans la sud-ouest de la France* (1974). [KPL]

25.351 Leon Bernard. *The emerging city: Paris in the age of Louis XIV.* Durham, N.C.: Duke University Press, 1970. ISBN 0-8223-0214-4. ▸ Synthesis describing seventeenth-century "modernization" of Paris, sparked by population increase. Examines topographical and architectural changes, improvements in transportation, labor, poverty, theater, and growth of city administration. [KPL]

25.352 Davis Bitton. *The French nobility in crisis, 1560–1640.* Stanford, Calif.: Stanford University Press, 1969. ISBN 0-8047-0684-0. ▸ Thesis of "identity crisis" among nobility brought on by attacks of contemporary writers on aristocratic privileges and sociopolitical function. Overstates evidence of noble economic decline. [KPL]

25.353 Jacques Dupâquier. *La population rurale du bassin Parisien à l'époque de Louis XIV.* Paris: École des Hautes Études en Sciences Sociales, 1979. ISBN 2-7132-0692-8. ‣ Reconstruction of population of Paris basin, broadly defined, using sources other than Paris registers. [PTH]

25.354 Madeleine Foisil. *La révolte des nu-pieds et les révoltes normandes de 1639.* Paris: Presses Universitaires de France, 1970. (Travaux du Centre de Recherche sur la Civilisation de l'Europe Moderne, 7, and Publications de la Faculté des Lettres et Sciences Humanes de Paris-Sorbonne, Série "Recherches," 57.) ISBN 2-13-030687-X. ‣ Study of one of most important tax revolts in early modern France. [PTH]

25.355 Pierre Goubert. *The Ancien Régime: French society, 1600–1750.* 1973 ed. Steve Cox, trans. New York: Harper & Row, 1974. ISBN 0-06-136101-1 (cl, 1973), 0-06-131822-1 (pbk). ‣ Annales school handbook, sensitive to intricacies and self-descriptions of Old Regime society. Analyzes nobility and rural and urban society with emphasis on privilege, wealth, and custom in defining social divisions. [KPL]

25.356 Pierre Goubert. *Beauvais et la Beauvaisis de 1600 à 1730: contribution à l'histoire sociale de la France du dix-septième siècle.* 1960 ed. 2 vols. Paris: École des Hautes Études en Sciences Sociales, 1982. ISBN 2-7132-0810-6 (v. 1), 2-7132-0811-4 (v. 2). ‣ Demographic, economic, and social analysis of cloth-producing town and surrounding, proto-industrialized countryside. Classic Annales study of economic evolution leading to prosperity of bourgeoisie and decline of nobles, artisans, and peasants. [KPL]

25.357 Sarah Hanley. "Engendering the state: family formation and state building in early modern France." *French historical studies* 16.1 (1989) 4–27. ISSN 0016-1071. ‣ Maintains that sixteenth and seventeenth centuries witnessed family-state compact in regard to familial law between crown and officeholders. Examines women's response to compact and conceptions of familial and political authority. [LMB]

25.358 Jean Meuvret. *Le problème des subsistances à l'époque de Louis XIV.* 3 vols. in 6. Paris: Mouton and École des Hautes Études en Sciences Sociales, 1977–88. ISBN 2-7193-0424-7 (v. 1.1), 2-7132-0034-2 (v. 1.2), 2-7132-0877-7 (v. 2), 2-7132-0886-8 (v. 3). ‣ Fundamental work on rural history, covering farm technology, organization of grain trade, and burden of privileges in countryside. Raises questions about nearly every Annales school assumption about rural society and agrarian economy from Bloch 25.322 onward. [PTH]

25.359 Roland Mousnier. "The Fronde." In *Preconditions of revolution in early modern Europe.* 1970 ed. Robert Forster and Jack P. Greene, eds., pp. 131–59. Baltimore: Johns Hopkins University Press, 1972. ISBN 0-8018-1176-7 (cl, 1970), 0-8018-1377-8 (pbk). ‣ Study of how deep-seated social and political conflicts among diverse groups in first half of seventeenth century percolated into Fronde, revolt that "cut vertically through the hierarchy of French society." [LMB]

25.360 René Pillorget. *Les mouvements insurrectionnels de Provence entre 1596 et 1715.* Paris: Pedone, 1975. ISBN 2-233-00013-7. ‣ Study of urban and rural rebellions, their causes and organization. Argues revolts were response of whole communities to state intrusion but decreased after 1660 as local elites withdrew their leadership. [KPL]

25.361 Boris Porchnev. *Les soulèvements populaires en France de dix-septième siècle.* Paris: Flammarion, 1972. ISBN 2-08-081039-1. ‣ Marxist analysis of popular revolts. Argues absolutist state served noble class by collecting feudal rent as taxes, "feudalizing"

bourgeoisie, and repressing popular rebellions resulting from noble-peasant class conflict. [KPL]

25.362 Thomas J. Schaeper. *The economy of France in the second half of the reign of Louis XIV.* Montreal: Interuniversity Centre for European Studies, 1980. (Research report, 2.) ISBN 0-919958-06-0 (pbk). ‣ Reassessment of post-1680 economic crisis as less serious than usually depicted. Deemphasizes negative impact of royal policy to argue trade and industry produced roots of later growth. [KPL]

25.363 Warren C. Scoville. *The persecution of Huguenots and French economic development, 1680–1720.* Berkeley: University of California Press, 1960. ‣ Analysis reverses contention that Protestant emigration after revocation of Edict of Nantes caused economic depression. Surveys various economic activities and argues other government policies, especially war, were more detrimental. [KPL]

25.364 Sal Alexander Westrich. *The Ormée of Bordeaux: a revolution during the Fronde.* Baltimore: Johns Hopkins University Press, 1972. ISBN 0-8018-1306-9. ‣ Description of popular uprising during revolts of the Fronde as revolutionary movement directed at monarchy and local oligarchy. Provides analysis of urban society and of class basis of uprising. [KPL]

1715–1789

25.365 P. W. Bamford. *Privilege and profit: a business family in eighteenth-century France.* Philadelphia: University of Pennsylvania Press, 1988. ISBN 0-8122-8135-7. ‣ Study of entrepreneurial de la Chaussade family. Describes early industrial revolution through family's timber and metallurgy businesses and examines role of royal privilege in economic development. [KPL]

25.366 Lenard R. Berlanstein. *The barristers of Toulouse in the eighteenth century (1740–1793).* Baltimore: Johns Hopkins University Press, 1975. ISBN 0-8018-1582-7. ‣ Examination of professionals grouped between bourgeoisie and judicial aristocracy. Finds that although imbued with Enlightenment reformism and largely obstructed from noble status, they nevertheless supported Parlement over revolutionary Jacobins. [KPL]

25.367 J. F. Bosher. *The Canada merchants, 1713–1763.* Oxford: Clarendon, 1987. ISBN 0-19-821134-1. ‣ Study of change in Canada traders from Catholic group tied to monarchy to one dominated by cosmopolitan Huguenots associated with foreign Protestants and Atlantic economy. [KPL]

25.368 J. F. Bosher. *The single-duty project: a study of the movement for a French customs union in the eighteenth century.* London: University of London and Athlone, 1964. ‣ Study of movement to replace numerous internal tolls with national customs union. Concludes reformers' programs for rational organization of tariffs and economic development succeeded only at Revolution. [KPL]

25.369 Thomas Brennan. *Public drinking and popular culture in eighteenth-century Paris.* Princeton: Princeton University Press, 1988. ISBN 0-691-05519-X. ‣ Study of taverns' role as cultural arena for reproducing laboring- and middle-class men's values and conflicts over consumption, generosity, honor, and leisure. Uncovers importance of drinking's sociability from history of elite censure. [KPL]

25.370 Iain A. Cameron. *Crime and repression in the Auvergne and Guyenne, 1720–1790.* Cambridge: Cambridge University Press, 1981. ISBN 0-521-23882-X. ‣ Study of regional *prévôtal* courts and mounted police that maintained surveillance of rural people and control of marginal groups. Argues reforms made for fair and effective if underfunded force. [KPL]

25.371 Nicole Castan. *Justice et répression en Languedoc à l'époque des Lumières.* Paris: Flammarion, 1980. ISBN 2-08-210656-X.

▸ Excellent overview of criminal court system in old regime Languedoc. [PTH]

25.372 Yves Castan. *Honnêteté et relations sociales en Languedoc (1715–1780).* Paris: Plon, 1974. ▸ Model study for examining workings of criminal court system in local history. Uses criminal records to explore social relations. [PTH]

25.373 Guy Chaussinand-Nogaret. *The French nobility in the eighteenth century: from feudalism to Enlightenment.* William Doyle, trans. Cambridge: Cambridge University Press, 1985. ISBN 0-521-25623-2 (cl), 0-521-27590-3 (pbk). ▸ Contribution to revisionist view that nobility was not conservative but varied elite, imbued with Enlightenment progessivism and renewed by wealthy middle-class entrants. Finds nobility united to spark revolt. [KPL]

25.374 John G. Clark. *La Rochelle and the Atlantic economy during the eighteenth century.* Baltimore: Johns Hopkins University Press, 1981. ISBN 0-8018-2529-6. ▸ Study of Atlantic port and its elite family networks and businesses. Traces decline to competition with better-endowed ports, isolation from rural economy, effects of government policies, and warfare. [KPL]

25.375 Adeline Daumard and François Furet. *Structures et relations sociales à Paris au milieu du dix-huitième siècle.* Paris: Colin, 1961. ▸ Analysis of Parisian social structure based on notarial documents. [PTH]

25.376 Cissie C. Fairchilds. *Domestic enemies: servants and their masters in Old Regime France.* Baltimore: Johns Hopkins University Press, 1984. ISBN 0-8018-2978-X. ▸ Examination of changing nature of service from pattern that mirrored patriarchal society and met desire for status displays to pattern characterized by wage labor, household work, and female servants. [KPL]

25.377 Arlette Farge. *La vie fragile: violence, pouvoirs, et solidarités à Paris au dix-huitième siècle.* Paris: Hachette, 1986. ISBN 2-01-011242-3. ▸ Study of street life in Paris based on criminal records. [PTH]

25.378 Franklin L. Ford. *Robe and sword: the regrouping of the French aristocracy after Louis XIV.* Cambridge, Mass.: Harvard University Press, 1953. ISBN 0-674-77415-9. ▸ Important synthesis on resurgence of aristocratic political power based on social alliance between sword and robe nobles that obstructed political reform. [KPL]

25.379 Robert Forster. *The house of Saulx-Tavannes: Versailles and Burgundy, 1700–1830.* Baltimore: Johns Hopkins University Press, 1971. ISBN 0-8018-1247-X. ▸ Case study of noble family's dependency on royal court, sinecures, and honors. Argues courtiership meant debt and thus tightfisted absentee estate management, alienating tenants and provoking rural revolution. [KPL]

25.380 Robert Forster. *Merchants, landlords, magistrates: the Depont family in eighteenth-century France.* Baltimore: Johns Hopkins University Press, 1980. ISBN 0-8018-2406-0. ▸ Study of rise to notable elite of Protestant merchant family with footholds in land, administration, and Parisian society. Family converted to Catholicism and formed alliances with nobility. [KPL]

25.381 Robert Forster. *The nobility of Toulouse in the eighteenth century: a social and economic study.* 1960 ed. New York: Octagon Books, 1971. ISBN 0-374-92817-7. ▸ Argues against thesis of decadence of country gentlemen. Concludes nobles thrived through thriftiness, estate management, investment, and ties to magistracy and administration. [KPL]

25.382 Maurice Garden. *Lyon et les lyonnais au dix-huitième siècle.* 1970 ed. Paris: Flammarion, 1975. ISBN 2-08-210642-X. ▸ Social history of eighteenth-century Lyon, with emphasis on demography, wealth, social structure, and life of city's numerous artisans and textile workers. [PTH]

25.383 David Garrioch. *Neighbourhood and community in Paris,*

1740–1790. Cambridge: Cambridge University Press, 1986. ISBN 0-521-30732-5. ▸ Analysis of self-regulating communities of Paris, formed from ties of kinship, economic dependence, and sociability. Concludes bonds weakened as elites withdrew from neighborhood life. [KPL]

25.384 Olwen H. Hufton. *The poor of eighteenth-century France, 1750–1789.* 1974 ed. Oxford: Clarendon, 1979. ISBN 0-19-822519-9 (cl, 1974), 0-19-822558-X (pbk). ▸ Important study of poverty, work, and family relations among indigents. Examines conflict among Catholic attitudes toward poor relief, anticlericalism, and social idealism of Enlightenment. [KPL]

25.385 Colin Jones. *Charity and "bienfaisance": the treatment of the poor in the Montpellier region, 1740–1815.* Cambridge: Cambridge University Press, 1982. ISBN 0-521-24593-1. ▸ Case study of forms of poor relief from religiously inspired almsgiving to pragmatic Enlightenment view of social welfare. Describes Revolution's failure to institute more successful poor-relief regime. [KPL]

25.386 Steven L. Kaplan. *Provisioning Paris: merchants and millers in the grain and flour trade during the eighteenth century.* Ithaca, N.Y.: Cornell University Press, 1984. ISBN 0-8014-1600-0. ▸ Exhaustive study of all-important bread trade. Examines business practices, commercialization of milling, myths surrounding trade, debates of philosophes, and crucial role of government regulation to maintain public order. [KPL]

25.387 Steven L. Kaplan and Cynthia J. Koepp, eds. *Work in France: representations, meaning, organization, and practice.* Ithaca, N.Y.: Cornell University Press, 1986. ISBN 0-8014-1697-3. ▸ Multiauthored collection on organization and representation of work in France, eighteenth century to present. Topics include labor relations, workshop discipline, and attempt to abolish guilds under Old Regime. [PTH]

25.388 Herbert Lüthy. *La banque protestante en France, de la révocation de l'Édit de Nantes à la Révolution.* 1959–61 ed. 2 vols. Paris: S.E.V.P.E.N., 1970. (École Practique des Hautes Études, Affaires et gens d'affaires, 19.) ▸ Study of banking families dispelling conspiratorial myth of "Protestant bank" and Weberian link between confession and capitalism. Concludes group identified through persecution, exile, international networks, business practices, and exclusion from royal privilege. [KPL]

25.389 Sarah C. Maza. *Servants and masters in eighteenth-century France: the uses of loyalty.* Princeton: Princeton University Press, 1983. ISBN 0-691-05394-4. ▸ Study of largest workers' category in Old Regime. Traces change from aristocratic service model, primarily male, based on fidelity and conspicuous display to bourgeois model, primarily female and household-centered. [KPL]

25.390 Michel Morineau. *Les faux-semblants d'un démarrage économique: agriculture et démographie en France au dix-huitième siècle.* Paris: Colin, 1971. ▸ Argues against eighteenth-century agricultural revolution by comparing yields from 1840 and Old Regime. Finds agricultural output fluctuated greatly from late Middle Ages into nineteenth century because of various forces, but not because of agricultural revolution. [PTH]

25.391 Jean Quéniart. *Culture et société urbaines dans la France de l'ouest au dix-huitième siècle.* Paris: Klincksieck, 1978. ▸ Study of sociological and geographical diffusion of literacy and book culture, based on statistical analyses of signatures and personal libraries. Demonstrates literacy increased, but book reading lagged among middle social levels. [KPL]

25.392 James C. Riley. *The Seven Years' War and the Old Regime in France: the economic and financial toll.* Princeton: Princeton University Press, 1986. ISBN 0-691-05488-6. ▸ Study arguing economic impact of war not as severe as generally assumed. Worst effect was on governmental debt, which became key political issue of declining Old Regime. [KPL]

25.393 Daniel Roche. *The people of Paris: an essay in popular culture in the eighteenth century.* Marie Evans and Gwynne Lewis, trans. Berkeley: University of California Press, 1987. ISBN 0-520-05857-7 (cl), 0-520-06031-8 (pbk). ‣ Examination of life styles and material culture of workers and poor, including housing, dress, reading habits, and economic conditions. Illustrates appropriation of cultural refinements by popular classes and increasing tensions with police. [KPL]

25.394 Hilton L. Root. *Peasants and king in Burgundy: agrarian foundations of French absolutism.* Berkeley: University of California Press, 1987. ISBN 0-520-05720-1. ‣ Reconceptualization of state-peasant relations, arguing modernizing and centralizing monarchy strengthened rather than weakened communal institutions to insure taxable communities. Maintains capitalist market production did not contradict communal viability. [KPL]

25.395 Jean-Laurent Rosenthal. *The fruits of revolution: property rights, litigation, and French agriculture, 1700–1860.* Cambridge: Cambridge University Press, 1992. ISBN 0-521-39220-9. ‣ Uses economics and case studies of irrigation and drainage to shed light on privileges, legal system, and obstacles to economic growth in Old Regime. Demonstrates that legal reforms of Revolution removed barriers to economic growth. [PTH]

25.396 Julius R. Ruff. *Crime, justice, and public order in Old Regime France: the sénéchaussées of Libourne and Bazas, 1696–1789.* London: Croom Helm, 1984. ISBN 0-7099-2256-6. ‣ Local study arguing that despite rising fear of property crime, violent crime still predominated in cases before seneschals' courts. Suggests harsh laws were moderated by inefficiency and judicial latitude. [KPL]

25.397 Robert M. Schwartz. *Policing the poor in eighteenth-century France.* Chapel Hill: University of North Carolina Press, 1988. ISBN 0-8078-1735-X. ‣ Examination of state response to growing problem of mendicity and public concern with insecurity. Argues, contrary to general view, that state repression of vagrancy was increasingly effective and welcomed. [KPL]

25.398 Michael Sonenscher. *The hatters of eighteenth-century France.* Berkeley: University of California Press, 1987. ISBN 0-520-05827-5. ‣ Discussion of work arrangements and corporate traditions resulting from interaction between artisanal practices, culture, and broader civil law and notions of civil rights. [KPL]

25.399 Michael Sonenscher. *Work and wages: natural law, politics, and the eighteenth-century French trades.* Cambridge: Cambridge University Press, 1989. ISBN 0-521-32984-1. ‣ Reconstruction of world of journeymen and artisans shedding considerable light on natural law, civil court records, and artisanal economy of Old Regime. Makes good use of court records. [PTH]

25.400 Robert Louis Stein. *The French slave trade in the eighteenth century: an Old Regime business.* Madison: University of Wisconsin Press, 1979. ISBN 0-299-07910-4. ‣ Examination of commerce founded on notions of moral superiority and traditional forms of business organization linking families as short-term investors. Argues slave trade proved very profitable for merchants and nation. [KPL]

25.401 Robert Louis Stein. *The French sugar business in the eighteenth century.* Baton Rouge: Louisiana State University Press, 1988. ISBN 0-8071-1434-0. ‣ Description of West Indian sugar production and France as sugar distributor to Europe. Finds business combined modern large plantations and refineries with traditional small-scale, merchant-family enterprises protected by privilege and patronage. [KPL]

25.402 James F. Traer. *Marriage and family in eighteenth-century France.* Ithaca, N.Y.: Cornell University Press, 1980. ISBN 0-8014-1298-6. ‣ Examination of change from patriarchal conception of family regulated by state to Enlightenment view stressing equality and sentiment. Concludes revolutionary legislation followed Enlightenment ideas, but Napoleon's Civil Code reasserted authoritarianism. [KPL]

25.403 David G. Troyansky. *Old age in the Old Regime: image and experience in eighteenth-century France.* Ithaca, N.Y.: Cornell University Press, 1989. ISBN 0-8014-2299-X. ‣ Examination of experience of and attitudes toward aging through demography, art, literature, and religious, philosophical, and social writing. Traces development of attitude combining respect for aged with recognition of social problems posed by them. [KPL]

25.404 Alan Williams. *The police of Paris, 1718–1789.* Baton Rouge: Louisiana State University Press, 1979. ISBN 0-8071-0491-4. ‣ Examination of first modern urban police force and its ability and efforts to maintain all aspects of public order. Argues professionalization of force reflected expanding definition of government responsibilities. [KPL]

SEE ALSO
26.63 T.J.A. Le Goff. *Vannes and its region.*
26.78 George V. Taylor. "Non-capitalist wealth and the origin of the French Revolution."

Section 26

L I N D A   L .   C L A R K

France since 1789

Historians of modern France, whether composing broad surveys or monographs, frequently link their subject or interpretation to the history of France's first revolutionary decade, 1789–1799. This complex event was both a rupture with the past and a perpetuator of some of the Old Regime's habits and innovations—including the monarchy's centralizing tendencies—as Alexis de Tocqueville observed in his classic, *The Old Regime and the French Revolution* (26.80). The Revolution's goals and methods, laws and institutions, achievements and failures are often the starting point for discussions of later political and institutional developments or ideologies and cultural practices. Bitter arguments about the merits of various revolutionaries' liberal and democratic ideas and innovations continued to divide politicians and citizens in national and local arenas until at least 1945 (and, to a lesser extent, still do). With the exception of the short-lived Second Republic (1848–1852), no nineteenth-century regime enthusiastically embraced most of the Revolution until the Third Republic (1870–1940) was securely in republican hands after 1879. Not surprisingly, then, France's famed revolutionary decade occupies more entries than any other ten-year bloc in this highly selective, introductory bibliography.

The focus of many studies of the Revolution and other periods has been influenced significantly during recent decades by various concerns of French academicians and intellectuals. Since the 1960s, many historians have acknowledged the profound impact on their work of the goals and methods of historians attached to the journal *Annales: Economies, Sociétés, Civilisations*, founded in 1929 by Lucien Febvre and Marc Bloch, led after 1956 by Fernand Braudel, and later joined by another generation, including Jacques Le Goff, Emmanuel Le Roy Ladurie, and, among the specialists for the post-1789 period, Maurice Agulhon, François Furet, Jacques Ozouf, Mona Ozouf, Michelle Perrot, and Michel Vovelle. The *annalistes'* emphasis on producing a comprehensive picture of past societies—incorporating geography, economic structure, and all social groups—deeply influenced not only historians of France but also specialists in many other countries' social history. *Annalistes* also legitimated the incorporation into historical study of long-neglected groups of people, frequently considered marginal to the traditional historian's concern with government leaders framing domestic and foreign policies. Deemphasizing familiar political, diplomatic, and military themes and also sharp chronological divides, *annalistes* sought continuities over long blocs of time and often underscored the limited impact of political change on popular beliefs and behavior. To recapture the history of the humble and marginal—such as peasants, artisans, industrial workers, children, women, and the old—and also to reinforce studies of the powerful, *annaliste* disciples employed a methodology resting on careful statistical study of such data as landholding patterns, censuses, marriage contracts, wills, and institutional enrollments and clients. For interpretation they drew freely on theories embraced by anthropologists, sociologists, economists, and other social scientists. Collaborative multivolume surveys of many centuries of economic, social, urban, and rural history are among the recent fruits of *annaliste* labors.

Studies of the poor and often powerless members of French society might or might not indicate their authors' political sympathies. Whether Marxist or not, many twentieth-century historians of France have employed the categories of social-class analysis utilized by Karl Marx and Friedrich Engels in *The Communist Manifesto* (1848) and later embraced not only by the European political Left but also by many social analysts representing other political stances or aspiring to ideological neutrality. Thus a Marxist paradigm has long prevailed in many twentieth-century histories of the Revolution of 1789, particularly those written in France. This paradigm—developed by Albert Mathiez, refined by G. Lefebvre (26.62), and perpetuated by A. Soboul (26.74) and Vovelle (all four, editors, in succession, of the *Annales historiques de la Révolution française*)—also had many non-French adherents. By the 1960s, however, some Anglo-American historians (such as Alfred Cobban and George Taylor) were developing a significant revisionist critique, grounded in the argument that empirical data refuted Marxist interpretation. Taylor (26.78, 26.79) demonstrated, for example, an intermingling of aristocratic and bourgeois interests in both landowning and newer capitalist endeavors and thereby challenged Lefebvre's assumptions about the underlying economic roots of class conflict between the Old Regime's aristocratic second estate and leading members of the third estate of commoners. By 1989—the year of the Revolution's bicentennial and the collapse of communist regimes in Eastern Europe—Furet, a French revisionist, also had challenged Lefebvre's classic account of the Revolution's origins and won many converts. Moreover, Furet (26.53) shifted from earlier revisionists' socioeconomic analysis and focused on the cultural and linguistic foundations of political attitudes before and during the Revolution. In the United States, L. Hunt (26.58) emphasized similar themes and added a stimulating discussion of revolutionary imagery. Thus historians of the Revolution, like those of many other periods and nations, also addressed, and sometimes embraced, the linguistic concerns of philosophers and literary critics and so questioned the accuracy of analyses grounded in documents whose language had not first been decoded or deconstructed.

The topical and methodological reorientation of studies of the Revolution has a counterpart in approaches to the history of the nineteenth century. During the 1970s and earlier 1980s, enthusiasts for the "new" social history sought to recover the experiences of the poor and powerless, often presented as historical actors able to operate independently of elites. The working classes' job experiences, ideologies, associations and labor unions, strikes, and political protest were central topics. Historians such as Charles Tilly, Yves Lequin, Bernard Moss, and Joan Scott believed that the process often termed "proletarianization"—the change from artisanal production to industrial production by nonskilled workers—supplied the root cause of mounting working-class anger. Manifestations of this anger were outbursts in the workplace, strikes, and eventually labor unions (fully legalized only in 1884) and socialist politics. William Sewell (26.374) brought linguistic concerns into the study of workers' mentalities by suggesting that vocabulary and mind-sets from Old Regime guilds were maintained and refashioned as workers coped with stressful changes once industrialization began. What Sewell interpreted as a continuation of artisanal pride was recast, however, by philosopher J. Rancière into a workers' "dream," a needed psychological defense against unpleasant work realities. Some historians also questioned or modified the emphasis on class conflict for understanding nineteenth-century social history. Lenard Berlanstein (26.348), for example, cautiously noted certain improvements in some Parisian workers' lives—including better wages and more leisure activities—and also many workers' votes for republicans, the brutal suppression of the Commune of 1871 notwithstanding.

For those no longer convinced of the centrality of social history's methodology, a return to political and cultural history has great appeal. Furthermore, if some workers and a much larger group of nineteenth-century Frenchmen, the peasantry, voted republican later in the century, then there was every reason to investigate how the French state and politicians of various stripes had reached out to an electorate, initially very limited in size during the Bourbon Restoration (1814–1830) and July Monarchy (1830–1848) but based on universal manhood suffrage after the Revolution of 1848. Indeed, not all *annalistes* had avoided political themes. Agulhon (26.115), for example, studied the development of political consciousness among ordinary people in the Var from 1789 to 1851. Recent books about liberalism, republicanism, and socialism by C. Welch (26.271), C. Nicolet (26.39), W. Logue (26.256), and T. Judt (26.161) are but four of the works (many in French and too numerous to include) focused on how various generations adjusted political convictions after the Revolutionary-Napoleonic upheaval. Representations of the "republic" and "nation" over a broad time frame also enrich an important essay collection edited by P. Nora (26.27). While important biographies of politicians and ideologists continue to appear, much recent political history differs from older versions of the genre by looking at how government policies affected the larger society. Two examples are P. Rosanvallon's survey of the development of the state (26.229) and its social and economic policies since 1789 and M. L. Stewart's case study (26.185) of the positive and negative impact of Third Republic protective legislation on women workers.

In different ways, Rosanvallon and Stewart demonstrate that studies of the political and social are not incompatible but, in fact, complementary, with each element the richer when viewed in relationship to the other. The same is true for works on other important themes. For example, the politicization of peasants as well as workers has attracted both social and political historians. Yet there is no consensus about the moment when most Frenchmen might be said to belong to the national political community. For Agulhon (26.115, 26.116), J. Merriman (26.120), and T. Margadant (26.119), the crucial moment was the Second Republic. Eugene Weber (26.383) argued, however, that peasants joined the national culture only when the Third Republic built new schools and roads and more effectively indoctrinated army conscripts. Similarly, M. Burns (26.141) emphasized rural disinterest in the political crises surrounding the Boulanger and Dreyfus affairs. For the twentieth century, as other scholars follow American historian R. Paxton's lead (26.199) in addressing the difficult issues raised by the Vichy Regime's collaboration (1940–1944) with Nazi Germany, the social and intellectual backgrounds of supporters of the antidemocratic and radical Right receive attention, along with more detail on Vichy policies and Resistance efforts.

The history of education is also a field where political and social themes meet. It has been enlarged by studies of literacy patterns, pupils' and teachers' origins, and links between schooling and social mobility. Raymond Grew and P. Harrigan's important statistical study (26.292) builds on an inquiry by Furet and Ozouf (26.290), who challenged old assumptions about the actual impact of the famous Guizot (1833) and Ferry (1881–1882) education laws by arguing that social demand for schooling (from parents, employers, and workers) did more to extend literacy than national policy. At a time of social change and mounting concern about depopulation, the Third Republic's preoccupation with gender roles has been well demonstrated in studies of girls' education and other state policies affecting children and mothers.

Religious history also draws in the state because of the major impact of the Revolution of 1789 on the Catholic church, the clergy's continuing role as village notables, and controversies surrounding formal separation of church and state in 1905. Popular religious convictions receive attention in Vovelle's important study of responses to the "radical" Revolution's dechristianization (26.81) and T. Kselman's work on the nineteenth century (26.328). The feminization of nineteenth-century religion is addressed, from different perspectives, in C. Langlois's study of women's religious orders (26.329) and B. Smith's treatment of bourgeoises (26.343).

Linguistic concerns—including variations in the meaning of key words over time, differing usages by contemporaries, and an inherent warping of meaning in some conventional usage—have entered cultural as well as political and social history. Alongside continuing interest in the famed political "engagement" of intellectuals, there is methodological novelty offered by J. Allen's (26.235) refocusing of attention from texts to readers' interpretations of texts (a theme building on work by Old Regime specialists) and by D. LaCapra's reading of Gustave Flaubert (26.255). Scott has stimulated historians to consider the positive and negative linguistic contrasts between "male" and "female" and, by noting differences between men and women workers' ideas, also provoked continuing discussion about the relative importance of gender and class for identity formation (26.372). Most recent work on women similarly emphasizes the social learning of gender roles, and, as the placement of titles concerning women in this bibliography's various subsections indicates, such research has considerably enhanced political, institutional, and social history and also made French women visible in new journals and book series devoted explicitly to women. As K. Offen (26.414) noted, the word "feminism" entered English vocabularies after the French coinage of *féminisme* during the late nineteenth century.

Many themes treated by historians of modern France fit under more than one classifying label. This bibliography's organization mirrors that dilemma, while also reflecting historians' diverse interests. The section opens with general surveys and biographical and historical dictionaries. Two large subdivisions follow, one arranged chronologically for political, diplomatic, and military history and the other a topical listing for social, economic, institutional, and cultural history. Readers will notice relatively less for foreign policy and war than for other topics because these not only overlap with this *Guide*'s multinational European section but are also, like science and Jewish history, the subjects of separate sections.

ACKNOWLEDGMENTS *The section editor gratefully acknowledges the assistance provided by all contributors who suggested appropriate titles and wrote annotations: James S. Allen, Lenard R. Berlanstein, Gordon C. Bond, Jean-Claude Caron, Jack R. Censer, Marjorie M. Farrar, Rachel G. Fuchs, Bertram M. Gordon, Patrick J. Harrigan, Steven C. Hause, Natalie Isser, Edgar L. Newman, Karen M. Offen, Harry W. Paul, Judith F. Stone, Judith Wishnia, and Robert J. Young.*

Entries are arranged under the following headings:

Reference Works

General Studies

Political History

French Revolution, 1789–1799
Napoleonic Era: Consulate and Empire, 1799–1814/15
Bourbon Restoration, 1814/15–1830
July Monarchy, 1830–1848
Second Republic, 1848–1852
Second Empire, 1852–1870
Third Republic, 1870–1940
Vichy Regime and Resistance, 1940–1944
Fourth Republic, 1944–1958
Fifth Republic, 1958–

Administration, Law, and Public Policy

Cultural and Intellectual History

Economic History: Agriculture, Commerce, and Industry

Education and Scientific Institutions

Family, Childhood, and Demography

Religion

Social Classes

General Studies
Middle Classes and Professions
Nobility
Working Classes

Rural, Regional, and Urban History

Rural and Regional
Urban

Women and Gender

[Contributors: BMG = Bertram M. Gordon, CSH = Christopher S. Hamlin, DEL = David E. Leary, ELN = Edgar L. Newman, GCB = Gordon C. Bond, HWP = Harry W. Paul, JFS = Judith F. Stone, JRC = Jack R. Censer, JSA = James Smith Allen, JSH = John S. Hill, JW = Judith Wishnia, KMO = Karen M. Offen, LLC = Linda L. Clark, LRB = Lenard R. Berlanstein, MMF = Marjorie M. Farrar, NKI = Natalie K. Isser, PJH = Patrick J. Harrigan, PWS = Paul W. Schroeder, RGF = Rachel G. Fuchs, RJY = Robert J. Young, SCH = Steven C. Hause]

REFERENCE WORKS

26.1 J. Balteau et al., eds. *Dictionnaire de biographie française.* 18 vols. to date. Paris: Letouzey et Ané, 1933–. ISBN 2-7063-0158-9 (set). ‣ Most comprehensive French biographical dictionary, covering all time periods. Some earlier volumes less likely to include important women. [LLC]

26.2 David S. Bell, Douglas W. J. Johnson, and Peter Morris, eds. *A biographical dictionary of French political leaders since 1870.* New York: Simon & Schuster, 1990. ISBN 0-13-084690-2. ‣ Entries for 419 individuals (twenty-three women) important in governments, political parties, labor organizations, press, army, wartime resistance, or for articulating political ideologies, Third Republic to present. Valuable bibliography for each entry. [LLC]

26.3 Owen Connelly et al., eds. *Historical dictionary of Napoleonic France, 1799–1815.* Westport, Conn.: Greenwood, 1985. ISBN 0-313-21321-6. ‣ Entries emphasize major individuals and events of Napoleon's French and European empire. Includes many nonmilitary topics and satellite kingdoms ruled by Napoleon's relatives. Brief bibliography for each entry. [GCB]

26.4 William E. Echard, ed. *Historical dictionary of the French Second Empire, 1852–1870.* Westport, Conn.: Greenwood, 1985. ISBN 0-313-21136-1. ‣ Reference work including comprehensive coverage of political, military, cultural, and social history; brief

bibliography for each entry. Especially noteworthy entries about press, art, and culture. Useful resource and guide. [NKI]

26.5 François Furet and Mona Ozouf, eds. *Critical dictionary of the French Revolution.* 2 vols. Arthur Goldhammer, trans. Cambridge, Mass.: Belknap, 1989. ISBN 0-674-17728-2. ‣ Massive work inspired by Furet's embrace of explanations emphasizing ideological rather than social factors. Individual pieces represent latest findings, interpretations, and also frequently modify or elaborate on Furet's positions. [JRC]

26.6 Patrick H. Hutton, ed. *Historical dictionary of the French Third Republic, 1870–1940.* 2 vols. New York: Greenwood, 1986. ISBN 0-313-22080-8 (set), 0-313-25551-2 (v. 1), 0-313-25552-0 (v. 2). ‣ 755 entries, primarily biographical (e.g., 196 political personalities; 232 writers, artists, scholars), with bibliographies. Also twenty-four valuable interpretive essays (e.g., economy, social stratification, women); numerous entries on institutions, events, and policies. [LLC]

26.7 Jean Jolly, ed. *Dictionnaire des parlementaires français: notices biographiques sur les ministres, députés et sénateurs français de 1889 à 1940.* 8 vols. Paris: Presses Universitaires de France, 1960–77. ‣ Biographical entries for all government ministers and members of Third Republic legislatures from 1 May 1889 to 1940. Extension of Robert and Cougny 26.11 with cross-references to pre-1889 legislative careers. [LLC]

26.8 Jean Maîtron, ed. *Dictionnaire biographique du mouvement ouvrier français.* Part 1: *1789–1864: de la Révolution française à la Première Internationale.* Part 2: *1864–1871: la Première Internationale et la Commune.* Part 3: *1871–1914: de la Commune à la Grande Guerre.* Part 4: *1914–1939: de la Première à la Seconde Guerre Mondiale.* 4 parts in numerous vols. to date. Paris: Ouvrières, 1964–91. ‣ Unique reference, much archival material cited. Includes bibliographies and iconographies. Sometimes sees subjects through red- or rose-colored glasses, portraying them as more socialist and revolutionary than they were. [ELN]

26.9 Edgar Leon Newman, ed. *Historical dictionary of France from the 1815 Restoration to the Second Empire.* 2 vols. Westport, Conn.: Greenwood, 1987. ISBN 0-313-22751-9 (set), 0-313-26045-1 (v. 1), 0-313-26046-X (v. 2). ‣ Starting point for period 1815–52, including various and conflicting viewpoints. Covers romanticism, conservatism, socialism, Bonapartism, republicanism, and, especially, memory of 1789 Revolution. Much social history. Bibliography for each entry; indexed. [ELN]

26.10 Wayne Northcutt, ed. *Historical dictionary of the French Fourth and Fifth Republics, 1946–1990.* New York: Greenwood, 1992. ISBN 0-313-26356-6. ‣ Over 250 entries covering political, diplomatic, military, economic, social, and cultural topics; some very broad, some specific. Short bibliography with each entry; useful chronological and political appendixes. [LLC]

26.11 Adolphe Robert and Gaston Cougny. *Dictionnaire des parlementaires français comprénant tous les membres des assemblées françaises et tous les ministres français depuis le première mai 1789 jusqu'au première mai 1889: avec leurs noms, état civil, états de services, actes politiques, votes parlementaires, etc.* 5 vols. Paris: Bourloton, 1889–91. ‣ Biographical entries for all government ministers and members of French legislatures from Estates General of 1789 through Third Republic as of April 1889. Available in photocopy from Ann Arbor: University Microfilms International, 1975. [LLC]

26.12 Samuel F. Scott and Barry Rothaus, eds. *Historical dictionary of the French Revolution, 1789–1799.* 2 vols. Westport, Conn.: Greenwood, 1985. ISBN 0-313-21141-8 (set), 0-313-24804-4 (v. 1), 0-313-24805-2 (v. 2). ‣ Compendium of relatively brief articles on revolutionary subjects. Tremendous range, including biographical sketches, events, groups, and important concepts. Helpful bibliography for each item. [JRC]

26.13 Jean Tulard, ed. *Dictionnaire Napoléon*. Rev. ed. Paris: Fayard, 1989. ISBN 2-213-02286-0. ▸ Monumental, authoritative collection of 3,228 articles by 205 contributors, comprising over 1,700 pages of text. Surveys virtually all aspects of Napoleonic France. Brief bibliography with many entries. [GCB]

26.14 Robert J. Young, ed. *French foreign policy, 1918–1945: a guide to research and research materials*. Rev. ed. Wilmington, Del.: Scholarly Resources, 1991. ISBN 0-8420-2308-9. ▸ Clear, helpful reference work including introduction to history, organization, and responsibilities of French foreign ministry. Offers practical information on French archives and libraries and extended bibliography of secondary literature. [RJY/JSH]

26.15 Benoît Yvert, ed. *Dictionnaire des ministres de 1789 à 1989*. Paris: Perrin, 1990. ISBN 2-262-007101. ▸ Brief biographical entries for all cabinet ministers since 1789 and valuable introductory sections with the composition of each cabinet. Indexed. [LLC]

GENERAL STUDIES

26.16 John Ardagh. *France today*. 1987 rev. ed. New York: Penguin, 1988. ISBN 0-14-010098-9. ▸ Introduction to contemporary France: economy, regions, farmers, urban dwellers, youth, daily life, and arts. Focus on significant shifts in social life as France became more integrated into European community. [BMG]

26.17 Fernand Braudel and Ernest Labrousse, eds. *Histoire économique et sociale de la France*. Vol. 3: *L'avènement de l'ère industrielle (1789–années 1880)*. Vol. 4: *L'ère industrielle et la société d'aujourd'hui (1880–1980)*. Paris: Presses Universitaires de France, 1976–82. ISBN 2-13-033820-8 (v. 3.1), 2-13-033821-6 (v. 3.2), 2-13-035482-3 (v. 4.1), 2-13-035956-6 (v. 4.2), 2-13-035957-4 (v. 4.3). ▸ Synthesis by leading historians treating industrial growth, transportation, demography, food prices, peasants and rural exodus, urbanization, twentieth-century state capitalism, middle-class composition and psychology, and working classes. Richly illustrated with bibliography. [LLC]

26.18 André Burguière and Jacques Revel, eds. *Histoire de la France*. Vol. 1: *L'espace français*. Vol. 2: *L'état et ses pouvoirs*. Vol. 3: *Les conflits*. 3 vols. Paris: Seuil, 1989–90. ISBN 2-02-010235-8 (set), 2-02-010236-6 (v. 1), 2-02-010237-4 (v. 2), 2-02-010238-2 (v. 3). ▸ Survey by leading historians associated with Annales school. Thematic organization deliberately shuns chronology to treat space (geography, demography, economy, culture); formation of state (religious, social, political conflicts); and French cultural uniqueness. [LLC]

26.19 Alfred Cobban. *A history of modern France*. Vol. 1: *1715–1799*. Vol. 2 : *1799–1871*. Vol. 3: *1871–1962*. 2d ed. 3 vols. Harmondsworth: Penguin, 1973–74. ISBN 0-14-020403-2 (v. 1), 0-14-020525-X (v. 2), 0-14-020711-2 (v. 3). ▸ Stimulating general history. Anti-Marxist interpretation emphasizing turning points: Revolution ended period of social transformation, paradoxically providing basis for conservative society; 1799 marks break, not 1789; and Third Republic an age of greatness. [MMF]

26.20 Jean Favier, ed. *Histoire de France*. Vol. 4: *Les révolutions de 1789 à 1851*. Vol. 5: *La France des patriotes de 1851 à 1918*. Vol. 6: *Notre siècle de 1918 à 1988*. 6 vols. Paris: Fayard, 1985–91. ISBN 2-213-01487-6 (set), 2-213-01574-0 (v. 4), 2-213-01655-0 (v. 5), 2-213-02039-6 (v. 6). ▸ Multivolume survey by leading experts in political and economic history. Emphasizes reasons for both conflicts and consensus. Traditional chronological organization with year-by-year appendixes of chronologies and bibliography. [LLC]

26.21 François Furet and Maurice Agulhon. *Histoire de France*. Vol. 4: *La révolution: de Turgot à Jules Ferry*. Vol. 5: *La République: de Jules Ferry à François Mitterrand, 1880 à nos jours*. 5 vols. Paris: Hachette, 1988–90. ISBN 2-01-013367-6 (set), 2-01-013367-6 (v.

4), 2-01-009463-8 (v. 5). ▸ Up-to-date, richly illustrated surveys by leading French historians. Political history combined with social, economic, and cultural history. Reflects changing trends in interpretation of French Revolution and aftermath. [LLC]

26.22 Stanley Hoffmann. *Decline or renewal? France since the 1930s*. New York: Viking, 1974. ISBN 0-670-26235-8. ▸ Provocative, interpretive essays (first published 1963) on politics, economy, society, and foreign policy. Emphasis on French prosperity in Common Market, recovery from debilitating effects of World War II, and Indochinese and Algerian colonial wars. [BMG]

26.23 Stanley Hoffmann et al. *In search of France: the economy, society, and political system in the twentieth century*. 1963 ed. New York: Harper & Row, 1965. ▸ Essays include Hoffmann's penetrating analysis of Third Republic political and social structures arguing that 1930s shocks destroyed political compromise of "stalemate society." Also J. Pitts on family and roots of individual and collective rebellion. [MMF]

26.24 Maurice Larkin. *France since the Popular Front: government and people*. New York: Oxford University Press, 1988. ISBN 0-19-873034-9 (cl), 0-19-873035-7 (pbk). ▸ Thorough survey of political, social, economic, and cultural institutions, 1936–86. Finds ideological divisions of 1930s becoming more muted after mid-1970s. [BMG]

26.25 Yves Lequin, ed. *Histoire des français, dix-neuvième et vingtième siècles*. Vol. 1: *Un peuple et son pays*. Vol. 2: *La société*. Vol. 3: *Les citoyens et la démocratie*. 3 vols. Paris: Colin, 1983–84. ISBN 2-200-37055-5 (v. 1), 2-200-37054-7 (v. 2), 2-200-37056-3 (v. 3). ▸ Comprehensive thematic survey of nineteenth and twentieth centuries by leading experts. Covers geography; demography; family structures; strategies for social mobility; industrialization; urbanization; place in society of peasants, businessmen, and workers; and popular culture. Richly illustrated; bibliography. [LLC]

26.26 Jean Meyer and Charles Ageron. *Histoire de la France coloniale*. Vol. 1: *Des origines à 1914*. Vol. 2: *1914–1990*. 2 vols. Paris: Colin, 1990–91. ISBN 2-200-37218-3 (v. 1), 2-200-37217-5 (v. 2). ▸ Up-to-date survey of French colonial history from seventeenth century to present. [LLC]

26.27 Pierre Nora, ed. *Les lieux de mémoire*. Vol. 1: *La République*. Vol. 2: *La nation*. 2 vols. to date. Paris: Gallimard, 1984–86. ISBN 2-07-070192-1 (v. 1), 2-07-070658-3 (v. 2.1), 2-07-070659-1 (v. 2.2), 2-07-070794-6 (v. 2.3). ▸ Stimulating, richly illustrated essays on representations of republic and nation (especially after 1789) found in officialdom's and, sometimes, society's creation of memories through patriotic symbols, books, monuments, ceremonies, and commemorative events. Projected volume 3: *Les France*. [LLC]

26.28 Charles Tilly. *The contentious French*. Cambridge, Mass.: Belknap, 1986. ISBN 0-674-16695-7 (cl), 0-674-16696-5 (pbk). ▸ Sociology and history merged in ambitious, complex discussion of 400 years of popular protest, fueled by building of state and development of capitalism. Traces changes in content and forms of protest. [LLC]

26.29 Gordon Wright. *France in modern times: from the Enlightenment to the present*. 4th ed. New York: Norton, 1987. ISBN 0-393-95582-6 (pbk). ▸ Perceptive interpretive synthesis, Enlightenment to Fifth Republic. Focus on evolution of government and society. Thematic organization within broad chronological divisions, incorporates historiographical controversies, monographs, and interpretive studies. Excellent bibliographical essays. [MMF]

26.30 Theodore Zeldin. *France, 1848–1945*. Vol. 1: *Ambition and love*. Vol. 2: *Politics and anger*. Vol. 3: *Intellect and pride*. Vol. 4: *Taste and corruption*. Vol. 5: *Anxiety and hypocrisy*. Rev. ed. 5 vols. Oxford: Clarendon, 1979–81. ISBN 0-19-285106-3 (set). ▸ Stimulating, topical reinterpretation dissects social structures, political divisions, values, behavior, and institutions. Emphasizes permanent features, not events and change; avoids causality. French society compartmentalized by ideology, region, occupation, social class, and partisan versus consensus mentalities. [MMF]

POLITICAL HISTORY

26.31 Edward Berenson. *Populist religion and left-wing politics in France, 1830–1852.* Princeton: Princeton University Press, 1984. ISBN 0-691-05396-0. ‣ Stimulating, controversial argument that popular socialism emanated from traditional, popular Christianity. In 1848, socialism attracted artisans and peasants by presenting Jesus as first socialist, trinity as Liberty-Equality-Fraternity, and salvation as 2 percent loans. [ELN]

26.32 Irene Collins. *The government and the newspaper press in France, 1814–1881.* London: Oxford University Press, 1959. ‣ Traces history of freedom of press: censored (1814–19), uncensored but controlled (1819–81), and free (1881). Newspapers helped overthrow Charles X (1830), Louis-Philippe (1848), and Napoleon III (1870). Many republicans feared power of press but supported freeing it. Best English-language work. [ELN]

26.33 Leslie Derfler. *President and parliament: a short history of the French presidency.* Boca Raton: University Presses of Florida, 1983. ISBN 0-8130-0733-X. ‣ Thoughtful general history discussing executive-legislative relations, Third to Fifth Republics, noting events shaping constitutional developments. Despite continuity in foreign and defense policies, weak presidency contributed to political instability, a central modern French problem. [MMF]

26.34 Raoul Girardet. *La société militaire dans la France contemporaine, 1815–1939.* Paris: Plon, 1953. ‣ Perceptive, exploratory analysis of army as social group. Treats daily life, recruitment, place within national consciousness, "idée militaire" varieties. Old professional and new national Third Republic armies nonpolitical, obeyed legally constituted authorities. [MMF]

26.35 André Jardin and André-Jean Tudesq. *Restoration and reaction, 1815–1848.* Elborg Forster, trans. Cambridge: Cambridge University Press, 1983. ISBN 0-521-25241-5 (cl), 0-521-35855-8 (pbk). ‣ Valuable survey. Despite appearances of revolutionary mentality and centralized government, France (1815–48) had socioeconomic stability and regional diversity thanks to dominance of local notables (especially old bourgeois families), who both delayed and prepared centralization, industrialization, parliamentary democracy, and liberalism. [ELN]

26.36 Tony Judt. *Marxism and the French Left: studies in labor and politics in France, 1830–1981.* Oxford: Clarendon, 1986. ISBN 0-19-821929-6 (cl), 0-19-821578-9 (pbk). ‣ Presents five loosely connected essays reinterpreting evolution of socialism in terms of ideology, revolutionary politics, and experiences of working people. Critiques many conventional views, especially those of labor historians. [LRB]

26.37 Michel L. Martin. *Warriors to managers: the French military establishment since 1945.* Chapel Hill: University of North Carolina Press, 1981. ISBN 0-8078-1421-0. ‣ Study of military's changing recruitment, social composition, and discipline. Relates military to foreign policy, finding Fourth Republic's colonial wars retarded modernizing military technology. General de Gaulle's nuclear force altered air force and navy more than army. [BMG]

26.38 Bernard Ménager. *Les Napoléon du peuple.* Paris: Aubier, 1988. ISBN 2-7007-2215-9. ‣ Survey of post-1815 Bonapartism: 1815–52, popular with people as bulwark against notables, priests, disorder, and poverty; 1852–70, Bonapartism a compromise between authoritarianism and democracy, preparing way for Republic. After 1870, Bonapartism turned conservative and

died. Disputes Marxist interpretation of Bonapartism as authoritarian defense of capitalist bourgeoisie. [ELN]

26.39 Claude Nicolet. *L'idée républicaine en France, 1789–1924: essai d'histoire critique.* Paris: Gallimard, 1982. ISBN 2-07-023096-1. ‣ Interaction between republicanism (its theorists and politicians) and other philosophies from Rousseau to Alain. Expert on ancient Roman republic argues that republican ideology responsible for triumph of republican regime. [LLC]

26.40 Douglas Porch. *Army and revolution: France, 1815–1848.* London: Routledge & Kegan Paul, 1974. ISBN 0-7100-7460-3. ‣ Excellent analysis of military administration. May underplay army's politicization by attributing officers' unrest to blockage of careers, not politics. During Restoration officers were promoted more slowly and paid less than British and Prussian officers. After pensions doubled in 1834, army loyal to government. [ELN]

26.41 René Rémond. *The right wing in France from 1815 to de Gaulle.* 2d ed. James M. Laux, trans. Philadelphia: University of Pennsylvania Press, 1969. ISBN 0-8122-7490-3. ‣ Classic synthetic essay dividing Right into three doctrinally different movements—legitimism, Orléanism, and Bonapartism—each with own authentic political traditions, ideas, temperament, and clientele. Interpretive, systematic presentation. Updated 1982 French edition available. [MMF]

26.42 William Serman. *Les origines des officiers français, 1848–1870.* Paris: Publications de la Sorbonne, 1979. (Publications de la Sorbonne, Serie "n.s. Recherches," 33.) ISBN 2-85944-015-1. ‣ Model social history of professional group. Analysis of army officers' backgrounds shows them far less aristocratic than English and Prussian counterparts. Recruitment more open, but promotions favored middle-class rather than lower-class officers. [LLC]

26.43 John E. Talbott. *The war without a name: France in Algeria, 1954–1962.* New York: Knopf; distributed by Random House, 1980. ISBN 0-394-50909-9. ‣ Most concise treatment in English of French response to colonial rebellion ending Fourth Republic. Contrasts de Gaulle's 1944–46 colonialism with post-1958 disengagement from empire. Faults Fourth Republic governing parties for ineptitude. [BMG]

26.44 David Thomson. *Democracy in France since 1870.* 1969 5th ed. London: Cassell, 1989. ISBN 0-304-31706-3 (pbk). ‣ Perceptive, classic conceptualization of republican history as compromise between conflicting forces. 1905 watershed between successful liquidation of past political issues and subsequent inadequate social and economic solutions. [MMF]

SEE ALSO

French Revolution, 1789–1799

26.45 Jack R. Censer. *Prelude to power: the Parisian radical press, 1789–1791.* Baltimore: Johns Hopkins University Press, 1976. ISBN 0-8018-1816-8. ‣ Pioneering examination of radical press as window on early years of revolutionaries. Emphasizes continuities between early and later radicals. [JRC]

26.46 Jack R. Censer, ed. *The French Revolution and intellectual history.* Chicago: Dorsey, 1989. ISBN 0-256-06856-9 (pbk). ‣ Places newest work on intellectual history in context of older social history paradigm. Includes Lucas's important social interpretation and highly significant ideological discussions by Furet, Darnton, Hunt, and others. [JRC]

26.47 Roger Chartier. *The cultural origins of the French Revolution.* Lydia G. Cochrane, trans. Durham, N.C.: Duke University Press, 1991. ISBN 0-8223-0981-5 (cl), 0-8223-0993-9 (pbk).

▸ Focuses on broad trends—such as loss of belief in sacrality of king—within wider culture to explain Revolution. Provides controversial contrasts with ideological and class historiography. [JRC]

26.48 Richard Cobb. *The people's armies, the armées révolutionnaires: instrument of the Terror in the departments, April 1793 to floréal year II.* Marianne Elliott, trans. New Haven: Yale University Press, 1987. ISBN 0-300-02728-1 (cl), 0-300-04042-3 (pbk). ▸ Most systematic among Cobb's many works. Here as elsewhere, envisions *menu peuple* (little people) as both deserving of sympathy and representing very disagreeable sides of human nature. [JRC]

26.49 Alfred Cobban. *Aspects of the French Revolution.* 1968 ed. London: Paladin, 1971. ISBN 0-393-00512-7 (pbk). ▸ Collection of essays detailing author's critique of class-based interpretations of Revolution. Contains other important essays, particularly two on ideas of Robespierre. [JRC]

26.50 William Doyle. *Origins of the French Revolution.* 2d ed. Oxford: Oxford University Press, 1988. ISBN 0-19-822283-1 (cl), 0-19-822284-X (pbk). ▸ Bold attack on class explanations of Revolution. Excellent historiographical essay and masterful use of recent research. Provides separate explanations for fall of Old Regime and emergence of revolutionary principles. [JRC]

26.51 William Doyle. *The Oxford history of the French Revolution.* 1989 ed. New York: Oxford University Press, 1990. ISBN 0-19-822781-7 (cl, 1989), 0-19-285221-3 (pbk). ▸ Well written and exhaustive; extensive knowledge of provincial developments. Opposed to traditional class interpretation but also to ideological explanations; emphasizes early unpopularity of Revolution. [JRC]

26.52 Alan Forrest. *The soldiers of the French Revolution.* Durham, N.C.: Duke University Press, 1990. ISBN 0-8223-0909-2 (cl), 0-8223-0935-1 (pbk). ▸ Well-written synthesis on soldiers' social circumstances. Finds that despite desire to construct idealistic revolutionary army, troops more committed to survival, and governments mainly concerned with controlling this force. [JRC]

26.53 François Furet. *Interpreting the French Revolution.* Elborg Forster, trans. Cambridge: Cambridge University Press, 1981. ISBN 0-521-23574-X (cl), 0-521-28049-4 (pbk). ▸ Sharp critique of Marxist interpretation of Revolution, followed by sweeping alternate interpretation. Helped usher in entirely new school emphasizing ideological developments. [JRC]

26.54 Jacques Léon Godechot. *The counter-revolution: doctrine and action, 1789–1804.* Salvator Attanasio, trans. Princeton: Princeton University Press, 1981. ISBN 0-691-00788-8. ▸ Classic study of counterrevolution. Thesis that counterrevolution at any given moment always appeared larger and more threatening to revolutionaries than it actually was. [LLC]

26.55 Norman Hampson. *Prelude to terror: the Constituent Assembly and the failure of consensus, 1789–1791.* Oxford: Blackwell, 1988. ISBN 0-631-15237-7. ▸ Pessimistic treatment of Revolution finding seeds of Terror present at early date. Similar to Furet 26.53 in identifying central problem as dominance of ideology of popular sovereignty. [JRC]

26.56 Olwen H. Hufton. *Women and the limits of citizenship in the French Revolution.* Toronto: University of Toronto Press, 1992. ISBN 0-8020-5898-1 (cl), 0-8020-6837-5 (pbk). ▸ Interlocking essays on activities of women and reasons for their eventual disenchantment with Revolution. Attacks historians who discuss women's condition using only discourses, but shares their view regarding Revolution's negative effect. [JRC]

26.57 Lynn Hunt. *The family romance of the French Revolution.* Berkeley: University of California Press, 1992. ISBN 0-520-07741-5 (cl), 0-520-08270-2 (pbk). ▸ Introduces novel thesis on role of

culture in making of French Revolution. Focuses on society's understanding of role of family relations, especially tension between fathers and sons. [JRC]

26.58 Lynn Hunt. *Politics, culture, and class in the French Revolution.* Berkeley: University of California Press, 1984. ISBN 0-520-05204-8 (cl), 0-520-05740-6 (pbk). ▸ General interpretation of Revolution. Concern for ideological, cultural, and social developments. Many novel views but shares much with Furet 26.53 and Ozouf 26.67. [JRC]

26.59 David P. Jordan. *The king's trial: Louis XVI vs. the French Revolution.* Berkeley: University of California Press, 1979. ISBN 0-520-03684-0. ▸ Superb narrative of critical event. Clearly shows options open to monarch as well as to Jacobin opponents. [JRC]

26.60 Gary Kates. *The Cercle social, the Girondins, and the French Revolution.* Princeton: Princeton University Press, 1985. ISBN 0-691-05440-1. ▸ Tells story of Cercle social, a political club among the most inventive in mobilizing public opinion. Makes case for club as source of Girondins. See also Sydenham 26.77. [JRC]

26.61 Michael L. Kennedy. *The Jacobin clubs in the French Revolution.* Vol. 1: *The first years.* Vol. 2: *The middle years.* 2 vols. to date. Princeton: Princeton University Press, 1982–88. ISBN 0-691-05337-5 (v. 1), 0-691-05526-2 (v. 2). ▸ First two published volumes of trilogy take history of Jacobins up to Terror. Focus mainly on provincial clubs' membership, organization, and activities. More narration and insights than particular themes. [JRC]

26.62 Georges Lefebvre. *The coming of the French Revolution.* 1947 ed. R. R. Palmer, trans. Princeton: Princeton University Press, 1989. ISBN 0-691-05112-7 (cl), 0-691-00751-9 (pbk). ▸ Account of causes of and early development of Revolution by most widely admired historian with class-based perspective. Emphasizes collusion of many classes and initial unity. [JRC]

26.63 T.J.A. Le Goff. *Vannes and its region: a study of town and country in eighteenth-century France.* Oxford: Clarendon, 1981. ISBN 0-19-822515-6. ▸ Detailed local study plumbing sources of counterrevolution in western France. Instead of pointing to lack of urban middle class, emphasizes conservative middle peasantry that Revolution inadvertently alienated. [JRC]

26.64 Colin Lucas. *The structure of the Terror: the example of Javogues and the Loire.* London: Oxford University Press, 1973. ISBN 0-19-821843-5. ▸ Exhaustive study of interaction between central government agent and local radicals and officials in order to implement Terror. Ironic that locals followed national goals better than representative from Paris. [JRC]

26.65 Martyn Lyons. *France under the Directory.* Cambridge: Cambridge University Press, 1975. ISBN 0-521-20785-1 (cl), 0-521-09950-1 (pbk). ▸ Only recent synthesis of Directory (1795–99) covering variety of social, cultural, and political issues. Substitutes political for class explanation of developments. [JRC]

26.66 Sara E. Melzer and Leslie W. Rabine, eds. *Rebel daughters: women and the French Revolution.* New York: Oxford University Press, 1992. ISBN 0-19-506886-6 (cl), 0-19-507016-X (pbk). ▸ New collection of essays by, among others, Levy and Applewhite, who emphasize political opportunities created for women during Revolution and explicitly dispute view that Revolution, through gender definitions, politically excluded women. [JRC]

26.67 Mona Ozouf. *Festivals and the French Revolution.* Alan Sheridan, trans. Cambridge, Mass.: Harvard University Press, 1988. ISBN 0-674-29883-7. ▸ Complex investigation examining many aspects of revolutionary festivals. Serious treatment of festivals as indicating more than political views. [JRC]

26.68 R. R. Palmer. *Twelve who ruled: the year of the Terror in the French Revolution.* Rev. ed. Princeton: Princeton University

Press, 1989. ISBN 0-691-05119-4 (cl), 0-691-00761-6 (pbk). ‣ Richly detailed study of Committee of Public Safety. Follows events throughout France. Finds that purpose of Terror went beyond simple retention of power and explains Robespierre's idealism. [JRC]

26.69 Candice E. Proctor. *Women, equality, and the French Revolution.* New York: Greenwood, 1990. ISBN 0-313-27245-X. ‣ Comprehensive study of ideas about women and equality during Revolution, using archives and press. Emphasizes continuities in ideas from Old Regime to postrevolutionary period. Criticizes Revolution's rejection of women's claims to equality. [KMO]

26.70 R. B. Rose. *Gracchus Babeuf: the first revolutionary Communist.* Stanford, Calif.: Stanford University Press, 1978. ISBN 0-8047-0949-1. ‣ Extraordinary biography of Babeuf casting significant light on entire era. Babeuf's communism emerges as less utopian than most historians suggest. [JRC]

26.71 George Rudé. *The crowd in the French Revolution.* 1959 ed. Westport, Conn.: Greenwood, 1986. ISBN 0-313-25168-1. ‣ Classic analysis of great revolutionary riots. Finds that revolutionary crowds, composed of wage earners, gradually developed independent political views but still acted in response to rising bread prices. [JRC]

26.72 Reynald Sécher. *Le génocide franco-français: la Vendée-Vengée.* 3d ed. Paris: Presses Universitaires de France, 1989. ISBN 2-13-042744-8. ‣ Much disputed analysis of counterrevolutionary Vendée revolt claiming that revolutionaries' repression constituted genocide. Central work in attacks on Revolution by extremely conservative historians. [JRC]

26.73 Morris Slavin. *The French Revolution in miniature: section Droits-de-l'Homme, 1789–1795.* Princeton: Princeton University Press, 1984. ISBN 0-691-05415-0. ‣ Political narrative of one Parisian neighborhood with analysis of its central institutions. Contributes to historiography by revealing interaction between national government and local activists. [JRC]

26.74 Albert Soboul. *The sans-culottes: the popular movement and revolutionary government, 1793–1794.* Remy Inglis Hall, trans. Princeton: Princeton University Press, 1980. ISBN 0-691-05320-0 (cl), 0-691-00782-9 (pbk). ‣ Valuable analysis of social and mental framework as well as politics of Parisian working men during year two of revolutionary calendar, 1793–94. Locates ultimate weakness of group in their social heterogeneity. [JRC]

26.75 Donald M. G. Sutherland. *The Chouans: the social origins of popular counter-revolution in Upper Brittany, 1770–1796.* Oxford: Clarendon, 1982. ISBN 0-19-822579-2. ‣ Relates well to Le Goff's analysis (26.63) of counterrevolution in western France. Goes beyond to add important factors, including particular vision of community. [JRC]

26.76 Donald M. G. Sutherland. *France 1789–1815: Revolution and counterrevolution.* 1985 ed. New York: Oxford Univerisity Press, 1986. ISBN 0-19-520512-X (cl), 0-19-520513-8 (pbk). ‣ Complex survey of French Revolution and Napoleonic era, emphasizing Revolution. Argument that Revolution represented rise of new political class; sympathetic view of counter-Revolution. Excellent mastery of field. [JRC]

26.77 M. J. Sydenham. *The Girondins.* London: University of London, 1961. (University of London historical studies, 8.) ‣ Political narrative of Legislative Assembly with careful analysis of Girondin party demonstrating disunity within party. Work by Kates (26.60) and others led to disputes on this matter. [JRC]

26.78 George V. Taylor. "Non-capitalist wealth and the origin of the French Revolution." *American historical review* 72.2 (1967) 469–96. ISSN 0002-8762. ‣ Textured analysis of omnipresence of landed wealth throughout elites. Contradicts notion of bourgeois

revolution in which revolutionary bourgeoisie constituted capitalist elite, isolated from other classes. Points to political explanations. [JRC]

26.79 George V. Taylor. "Revolutionary and nonrevolutionary content in the Cahiers of 1789: an interim report." *French historical studies* 7.4 (1972) 479–502. ISSN 0016-1071. ‣ Groundbreaking analysis of lists of grievances on eve of Revolution shows late radicalization of public opinion away from traditional complaints. Points to short-term developments as cause of Revolution. [JRC]

26.80 Alexis de Tocqueville. *The Old Regime and the French Revolution.* Stuart Gilbert, trans. Garden City, N.Y.: Doubleday, 1955. ISBN 0-385-09260-1. ‣ Classic interpretation emphasizing undermining of Old Regime by monarchy's policies and aristocratic responses. Focuses on philosophers as creators of revolutionary ethos. Viewpoint still exercises influence over modern scholarship, including Furet 26.53. [JRC]

26.81 Michel Vovelle. *Religion et révolution: la déchristianisation de l'an II.* Paris: Hachette, 1976. ISBN 2-01-002038-3. ‣ Companion work to author's earlier massive study of Old Regime religious values (25.318). Present study evaluates dechristianization during Revolution, finds that Terror may have stimulated only those developments already in the making. [JRC]

26.82 Isser Woloch. *Jacobin legacy: the democratic movement under the Directory.* Princeton: Princeton University Press, 1970. ISBN 0-691-06183-1. ‣ Essential study of Jacobinism after Terror charting problems, revitalization, and downfall. Tends to treat Jacobins as principled rather than opportunistic. [JRC]

Napoleonic Era: Consulate and Empire, 1799–1814/15

26.83 Eric A. Arnold, Jr. *Fouché, Napoleon, and the general police.* Washington, D.C.: University Press of America, 1979. ISBN 0-8191-0716-6. ‣ Valuable study of administration, organization, and activities of Napoleonic police in France under direction of Joseph Fouché, Anne-Jean Savary, and Marshal Adrien de Moncey. [GCB]

26.84 Louis Bergeron. *France under Napoleon.* R. R. Palmer, trans. Princeton: Princeton University Press, 1981. ISBN 0-691-05333-2 (cl), 0-691-00789-6 (pbk). ‣ Important survey of government and society under Napoleon. Examination and analysis of French institutions, economy, society, and political administration of consulate and empire. [GCB]

26.85 David G. Chandler. *The campaigns of Napoleon.* 1966 ed. 2 vols. Norwalk, Conn.: Easton, 1991. ‣ Comprehensive study of Napoleon's generalship and military campaigns. Analysis of mastery of art of war. [GCB]

26.86 David G. Chandler. *Dictionary of the Napoleonic wars.* New York: Macmillan, 1979. ISBN 0-02-523670-9. ‣ Biographical, topical entries for 1,200 individuals, battles, treaties, and other military and political themes relating to Napoleonic era. [GCB]

26.87 Guy Chaussinand-Nogaret, Louis Bergeron, and Robert Forster. "Les notables du 'Grand Empire' en 1810." *Annales: économies, sociétés, civilisations* 26.5 (1971) 1052–75. ISSN 0395-2649. ‣ Important examination of social results of Revolution. Emphasizes continued strength of property holders and residual political power of early revolutionaries. [JRC]

26.88 Irene Collins. *Napoleon and his parliaments, 1800–1815.* New York: St. Martin's, 1979. ISBN 0-312-55892-9. ‣ Best available study of workings of legislative institutions under Napoleon during consulate and empire. Examines Napoleon's changing attitude toward these bodies and his manipulation of political system he designed. [GCB]

26.89 Owen Connelly. *Napoleon's satellite kingdoms: managing conquered peoples.* 1965 ed. Malabar, Fla.: Krieger, 1990. ‣ Comprehensive look at Napoleonic empire in Europe, examining several states placed under Bonapartist rule. Treats goals and positive-negative impact of Napoleonic rule. [GCB]

26.90 Vincent Cronin. *Napoleon Bonaparte: an intimate biography.* New York: Morrow, 1972. ▸ Balanced but generally favorable biography examining private and public life. Useful introduction to man and his impact on Europe. More emphasis on Napoleon as statesman than as military leader. [GCB]

26.91 Christopher Frayling, ed. and trans. *Napoleon wrote fiction.* 1972 ed. New York: St. Martin's, 1973. ▸ Collection of youthful Napoleon's essays, short stories, political tract, and poem written between ages sixteen and twenty-six. Selections and editor's introduction provide interesting insights into character and early education. [GCB]

26.92 Pieter Geyl. *Napoleon, for and against.* Rev. ed. Olive Renier, trans. London: Cape, 1964. ▸ Classic account of French authors' and historians' positive and negative assessments of Napoleon during nineteenth and first decades of twentieth century. Written by noted Dutch historian after concentration camp experience. [LLC]

26.93 J. Christopher Herold. *The age of Napoleon.* 1963 ed. New York: American Heritage, 1989. ISBN 0-8281-0491-3 (pbk). ▸ Broad, readable introductory survey of France and Europe and impact of French revolutionary movement, including cultural developments. Somewhat critical of Napoleon the man and his influence on European history. [GCB]

26.94 Robert B. Holtman. *The Napoleonic revolution.* 1967 ed. Baton Rouge: Louisiana State University Press, 1981. ISBN 0-8071-0487-6. ▸ Topically organized examination of Napoleon's major contributions: mapmaker, lawgiver, educator, economist, and propagandist. Sympathetic assessment of his influence and legacy of his efforts. [GCB]

26.95 Donald D. Horward, ed. *Napoleonic military history: a bibliography.* New York: Garland, 1986. ISBN 0-8240-9058-6. ▸ Research tool and introduction to manuscript and printed archival materials and major published works. Collection of twenty-four articles, each surveying literature and current research on various Napoleonic campaigns and dependent states. [GCB]

26.96 Frank A. Kafker and James M. Laux, eds. *Napoleon and his times: selected interpretations.* Rev. ed. Malabar, Fla.: Krieger, 1992. ISBN 0-89464-47-8. ▸ Balanced anthology on eleven issues surrounding Napoleon's life, career, and influence on European history. Written by some thirty leading authorities in field, including Parker on Napoleon's youth and personality. [GCB]

26.97 Georges Lefebvre. *Napoleon.* 2 vols. Henry F. Stockhold and J. E. Anderson, trans. New York: Columbia University Press, 1969. ISBN 0-231-02558-0 (v. 1), 0-231-03313-3 (v. 2). ▸ Comprehensive, generally balanced study of Napoleonic era, focusing on France and Napoleon's impact rather than on Napoleon's private life. [GCB]

26.98 Felix Markham. *Napoleon.* 1963 ed. New York: New American Library, 1989. ISBN 0-451-62653-2 (pbk). ▸ Balanced biography of rise and fall of Napoleon and his European empire. Notes how Napoleon seized opportunities presented by French Revolution to secure power. Examines private and public life. [GCB]

26.99 Jean Tulard. *Napoleon: the myth of the savior.* Teresa Waugh, trans. London: Weidenfeld & Nicolson, 1984. ISBN 0-297-78439-0. ▸ Scholarly study of Napoleon's rise and fall. Sympathetic analysis of factors and circumstances contributing to his success and failure. [GCB]

26.100 Edward A. Whitcomb. *Napoleon's diplomatic service.*

Durham, N.C.: Duke University Press, 1979. ISBN 0-8223-0421-x. ▸ Detailed description and analysis of French Ministry of Foreign Affairs and diplomatic service under Napoleon. Challenges view that Napoleon's government deteriorated. [GCB]

Bourbon Restoration, 1814/15–1830

26.101 R. S. Alexander. *Bonapartism and revolutionary tradition in France: the fédérés of 1815.* Cambridge: Cambridge University Press, 1991. ISBN 0-521-36112-5. ▸ Seminal monograph on transmission of revolutionary liberalism (constitutional liberty, equal opportunity, patriotism). Federations of Hundred Days (1815), unlike 1792 federations, were narrowly bourgeois: a propertied revolutionary elite defending constitutional liberalism and France. Few links to Bonaparte or populace. [ELN]

26.102 Vincent W. Beach. *Charles X of France, his life and times.* Boulder: Pruett, 1971. ▸ Best scholarly biography of much-maligned king who desired return to "natural order of things" (absolute divine-right monarchy) after short period of constitutional government. Judges king lazy and misguided but not stupid. [ELN]

26.103 Guillaume de Bertier de Sauvigny. *The Bourbon Restoration.* Lynn M. Case, trans. Philadelphia: University of Pennsylvania Press, 1966. ▸ Indispensable survey by leading scholar of Restoration. Sympathetic to Restoration, which governed constitutionally, administered honestly, and restored France's diplomatic and economic credit. [ELN]

26.104 Sherman Kent. *The election of 1827 in France.* Cambridge, Mass.: Harvard University Press, 1975. ISBN 0-674-24321-8. ▸ Important study of royalism's strength, liberalism's weakness. Shows constitutional legalism of Restoration government and strength and stupidity of Royalist party. Stronger than liberals, Royalists lost 1827 elections when ultra-Royalists betrayed own prime minister. [ELN]

26.105 Stanley Mellon. *The political uses of history: a study of historians in the French Restoration.* Stanford, Calif.: Stanford University Press, 1958. ▸ Best study of French Revolution from perspective of Restoration historians. Liberal historians blamed Revolution on intransigent nobles and priests; royalist historians blamed Revolution on liberals destroying stable, happy society and causing Terror and irreligion. [ELN]

26.106 Nicholas J. Richardson. *The French prefectoral corps, 1814–1830.* Cambridge: Cambridge University Press, 1966. ▸ Best available study of Restoration prefectoral corps. Moderate ministries appointed mainly ex-Napoleonic officials, rightist ministries appointed nobles; no ministry replaced more than half the prefects. By contrast, July Monarchy of 1830 replaced 95 percent of prefects. [ELN]

26.107 Alan B. Spitzer. *Old hatreds and young hopes: the French Carbonari against the Bourbon Restoration.* Cambridge, Mass.: Harvard University Press, 1971. ISBN 0-674-63220-6. ▸ Best study of anti-Bourbon conspiracies of 1822 which linked generations: republican and imperial notables and reform-minded youth. Carbonari mixed Bonapartists, future Orléanists, and republicans, but failed for lack of political program and popular support. [ELN]

July Monarchy, 1830–1848

26.108 Robert J. Bezucha. *The Lyon uprising of 1834: social and political conflict in the early July Monarchy.* Cambridge, Mass.: Harvard University Press, 1974. ISBN 0-674-53965-6. ▸ Important monograph on Lyon silkweaver revolt, considered first modern workers' insurrection but actually involving traditional craftsmen whose modernity was demand for distinct rights. Seeking to restore old artisan organizations, revolts were economic, not political. [ELN]

26.109 H.A.C. Collingham. *The July Monarchy: a political history of France, 1830–1848*. London: Longman, 1988. ISBN 0-582-02186-3 (cl), 0-582-01334-8 (pbk). ‣ Elegant survey presenting new research. Revolution of 1830 destroyed old order and empowered disunited bourgeoisie who attempted to reconcile monarchy with democracy, faith with reason, and order with freedom. Failed because society polarized. Revolution of 1848 ushered in bourgeois authoritarianism. Contrast with Ménager 26.38. [ELN]

26.110 Douglas W. J. Johnson. *Guizot: aspects of French history, 1787–1874*. 1963 ed. Westport, Conn.: Greenwood, 1975. ISBN 0-8371-8566-1. ‣ Best biography of Prime Minister Guizot, sympathetically depicted as rational, eclectic man in passionate, uncompromising times. Failure and 1848 Revolution attributed to his inability to reconcile freedom with monarchy, national sovereignty with limited franchise, and Protestants with Catholics, and to lessen France's imperial ambitions. [ELN/PWS]

26.111 John M. Merriman, ed. *1830 in France*. New York: New Viewpoints, 1975. ISBN 0-531-05580-9. ‣ Seven essays on 1830 France. Sees crowd in 1830 Revolution as patriotic, Bonapartist, and traditional artisans. Addresses protests beyond 1830 and beyond Paris and cities. Artisans, inspired by 1830, organized against new July Monarchy, bourgeois in image. [ELN]

26.112 Pamela M. Pilbeam. *The 1830 Revolution in France*. New York: St. Martin's, 1991. ISBN 0-312-06178-1. ‣ Disputes revolutionary nature of 1830 Revolution. Argues that insurrectionaries were artisans and peasants opposed to capitalist restructuring (outlawing craft guilds, privatizing village commons). Many new officials had served Napoleon and now shared power with old landowning elite. Valuable local archival research; expands Pinkney's thesis (26.114). [ELN]

26.113 David H. Pinkney. *Decisive years in France, 1840–1847*. Princeton: Princeton University Press, 1986. ISBN 0-691-05467-3. ‣ Treats 1840s as crucial watershed in modern French history, marking turn from rural to industrial economy and fragmented to centralized political system. Debatable thesis, but richly documented and wonderfully expressed. [ELN]

26.114 David H. Pinkney. *The French Revolution of 1830*. Princeton: Princeton University Press, 1972. ISBN 0-691-05202-6 (cl), 0-691-10011-X (pbk). ‣ Best available study of 1830 Revolution; seen as spontaneous and muddled. Parisian and provincial revolutionary crowds were mainly Bonapartist skilled artisans, yet trusted liberals. Revolution changed little, landed gentry kept power, and new officials had earlier served empire. [ELN]

Second Republic, 1848–1852

26.115 Maurice Agulhon. *The Republic in the village: the people of the Var from the French Revolution to the Second Republic*. Janet Lloyd, trans. Cambridge: Cambridge University Press, 1982. ISBN 0-521-23693-2. ‣ Seminal study of countryside's politicization. Department of the Var legitimist-Catholic (1832) became democratic-socialist (1848). Economy not cause of shift; rather intermediaries (press, bourgeois "missionaries") infused traditional customs (charivaris, songs) with democratic ideas, linking traditional grievances with national republicanism. [ELN]

26.116 Maurice Agulhon. *The republican experiment, 1848–1852*. 1982 ed. Janet Lloyd, trans. Cambridge: Cambridge University Press, 1983. ISBN 0-521-24829-9 (cl), 0-521-28988-2 (pbk). ‣ Preeminent scholar surveys Second Republic's failure. Republicans failed to support Republic because they were legalistic (opposed June 1848 insurrection) and idealistic (anticlerical, socialist, romantic). Bonaparte's social repression and economic moderation attracted bourgeoisie, Catholics, progressive industrialists, Saint-Simonian socialists, and uneducated workers. Underestimates Bonaparte's popularity; compare Ménager 26.38. [ELN]

26.117 Peter H. Amann. *Revolution and mass democracy: the Paris club movement in 1848*. Princeton: Princeton University Press, 1975. ISBN 0-691-05223-9. ‣ Seminal study ascribing failure of *démocrates-socialistes* to electorate's conservatism. Political clubs appearing after 1848 Revolution had 100,000 members by March; only 25,000 in May. Defeated in elections and then outlawed by July, clubs were victorious even in defeat, politicizing workers. Agrees with Price 26.121. [ELN]

26.118 James Chastain. *The liberation of sovereign peoples: the French foreign policy of 1848*. Athens: Ohio University Press, 1988. ISBN 0-8214-0888-7. ‣ Thesis that French foreign policy after 1848 Revolution sought to liberate oppressed peoples outside France. Disputes Jennings's thesis (1973) that Alphonse de Lamartine and Jules Bastide pursued cautious, conservative diplomacy. [LLC]

26.119 Ted W. Margadant. *French peasants in revolt: the insurrection of 1851*. Princeton: Princeton University Press, 1979. ‣ Study of rural politicization. Finds resistance to Louis Napoleon's 1851 coup greatest where town and country closely linked. Urban Montagnard radicals recruited peasants by adapting doctrines to needs and traditions. Sees peasants as less religious than Berenson 26.31, less Bonapartist than Ménager 26.38. Agrees with Merriman 26.120 and Agulhon 26.115. [ELN]

26.120 John M. Merriman. *The agony of the Republic: the repression of the Left in revolutionary France, 1848–1851*. New Haven: Yale University Press, 1978. ISBN 0-300-02151-8. ‣ Analysis of Louis Napoleon's defeat of Second Republic. Attributes defeat to government repression and thus contests arguments of André-Jean Tudesq (people conservative), Marx (people ignorant), and Ménager (people Bonapartist [26.38]). May overestimate *démocrates-socialiste* appeal. Contrast Price 26.121 and Amann 26.117. [ELN]

26.121 Roger Price. *The French Second Republic: a social history*. Ithaca, N.Y.: Cornell University Press, 1972. ISBN 0-8014-0686-2. ‣ Useful survey arguing that 1848 Paris revolution generated conservative reaction because most Frenchmen owned property or expected to. Provinces and propertied defeated *démocrates-socialistes* (see Merriman 26.120 and Margadant 26.119) by voting for Louis Napoleon's conservative defense of property and political status quo, a conservatism seen as still triumphant. Compare Ménager 26.38. [ELN]

26.122 Mary Lynn Stewart-McDougall. *The artisan republic: revolution, reaction, and resistance in Lyon, 1848–1851*. Kingston, Ont.: McGill-Queen's University Press, 1984. ISBN 0-7735-0426-5. ‣ Important analysis of why Lyon, 1848–51, more leftist, more *démocrate-socialiste*, but calmer than Paris. After 1834 repression, Lyon silkweavers organized secret societies, paving way for dominating local government of 1848–49. Era ended when Louis Napoleon removed artisans from office and industrialization destroyed crafts. Contrast Ménager 26.38. [ELN]

Second Empire, 1852–1870

26.123 Stuart L. Campbell. *The Second Empire revisited: a study in French historiography*. New Brunswick, N.J.: Rutgers University Press, 1978. ISBN 0-8135-0856-8. ‣ Traces changing historical interpretations of Second Empire from Third Republic through post–World War II period. Gives critical evaluations and insights into French development during and after Second Empire. [NKI]

26.124 T.A.B. Corley. *Democratic despot: a life of Napoleon III*. 1969 ed. Westport, Conn.: Greenwood, 1974. ISBN 0-8371-7587-9. ‣ Brief biography of Napoleon III treating efforts as administrator, politician, and leader. Very sympathetic in assessment of emperor's contributions to French development. [NKI]

26.125 Natalie Isser. *Antisemitism during the French Second Empire*. New York: Lang, 1991. (American University studies,

Series 9, History, 100.) ISBN 0-8204-1454-9. ▸ Useful introduction to status of Jews and antisemitism in mid-nineteenth century. Examines how antimodernism and social apprehension led to increase of antisemitism among both ultramontane Catholics and Socialists. [NKI]

26.126 David I. Kulstein. *Napoleon III and the working class: a study of government propaganda under the Second Empire.* Sacramento: California State Colleges; distributed by Ward Ritchie Press, 1969. ▸ First systematic treatment of how Napoleon III's government used modern methods of propaganda to maintain control over populace, especially working class. Claims Bonapartist propaganda exaggerated government amelioration of working conditions. [NKI]

26.127 Bernard Le Clère and Vincent Wright. *Les préfets du Second Empire.* Paris: Colin, 1973. (Cahiers de la Fondation Nationale des Sciences Politiques, 187.) ▸ Excellent, detailed analysis of how French administration functioned and examination of lives, education, and proclivities of prefects. Gives insight into relationship between central government and provinces. [NKI]

26.128 Howard C. Payne. *The police state of Louis Napoleon Bonaparte, 1851–1860.* Seattle: University of Washington Press, 1966. ▸ One of the best available examinations of organization and theory of political repression. Explains how Bonapartist officials sustained support for government. Emphasizes continuity of policies from Orléanist regime. [NKI]

26.129 David H. Pinkney. *Napoleon III and the rebuilding of Paris.* 1958 ed. Princeton: Princeton University Press, 1972. ▸ Classic description of complex process of financing, directing, and designing urban redevelopment. Stresses that financial operations were more irregular than illegal. Praises beauty of Paris and argues that rebuilding met essential social needs. [NKI]

26.130 Alain Plessis. *The rise and fall of the Second Empire, 1852–1871.* 1985 ed. Jonathan Mandelbaum, trans. Cambridge: Cambridge University Press, 1987. ISBN 0-521-35856-6 (pbk). ▸ Survey, mainly discussing political, social, and economic themes. Good introduction and overview of institutions and culture, although often lacks detail. [NKI]

26.131 Roger L. Williams. *Gaslight and shadow: the world of Napoleon III, 1851–1870.* 1957 ed. Westport, Conn.: Greenwood, 1977. ISBN 0-83719821-6. ▸ Collection of biographies of important and interesting people such as Jean G.V.F. Persigny, Charles A.L.J. Morny, Charles R. F. Montalembert, Jacques Offenbach. Ten vignettes illuminating politics and culture of Second Empire. [NKI]

26.132 Theodore Zeldin. *The political system of Napoleon III.* 1963 ed. New York: Norton, 1971. ▸ Classic description of administrative practices, tracing evolution from authoritarian to liberal empire, and manipulation of politics by Bonapartists to ensure control. Claims there were liberal tendencies in regime from its beginning. [NKI]

SEE ALSO
47.131 William E. Echard. *Napoleon III and the Concert of Europe.*

Third Republic, 1870–1940

26.133 Malcolm Anderson. *Conservative politics in France.* London: Allen & Unwin, 1974. ISBN 0-04-320093-1. ▸ Introductory analysis of conservative republican politics and organizations. Surveys right-wing political organizations and behavior, but not traditions or ideologies. Focuses on development of dominating, disciplined, national conservative party from scattered, weak, transitory political associations. [MMF]

26.134 Philip C. F. Bankwitz. *Maxime Weygand and civil-military relations in modern France.* Cambridge, Mass.: Harvard Uni-

versity Press, 1967. ISBN 0-674-55701-8. ▸ Important case study for specialists of alienation of military from Republic. Conflicts between General Weygand and politicians over disarmament, length of service, and army size during 1930s initiated military disobedience to civilian leadership. [MMF]

26.135 Jean-Jacques Becker. *The Great War and the French people.* Arnold J. Pomerans, trans. Jay Winter, Introduction. New York: St. Martin's, 1986. ISBN 0-312-34679-4. ▸ Study of wartime public opinion; follows author's monumental study (in French), *1914.* Deep-rooted sense of nationhood enabled vast majority to accept war, encouraged by teachers, writers, and church; antiwar forces minimal. [MMF]

26.136 Serge Berstein. *Histoire du parti radical.* Vol. 1: *La recherche de l'âge d'or, 1919–1926.* Vol. 2: *Le temps des crises et des mutations: crises du radicalisme, 1926–1939.* 2 vols. Paris: Presses de la Fondation Nationale des Sciences Politiques, 1980–82. ISBN 2-7246-0437-7 (v. 1), 2-7246-0461-X (v. 2). ▸ Thorough analysis of Radical party ideology, structures, adherents, leaders, and responses to interwar events. Centrist governing party used turn-of-century solutions for postwar problems, thereby contributing to stability and stagnation. [MMF]

26.137 Marc L. B. Bloch. *Strange defeat: a statement of evidence written in 1940.* 1949 ed. Gerard Hopkins, trans. New York: Octagon Books, 1968. ISBN 0-374-90665-3. ▸ Leading historian's summary of deep-seated social and cultural reasons for 1940 defeat. Still one of best accounts of 1940 debacle, written by eyewitness who later died in anti-Nazi resistance. [BMG]

26.138 Georges Bonnefous and Edouard Bonnefous. *Histoire politique de la Troisième République (1906–1940).* Vol. 1: *L'avant guerre (1906–1914).* Vol. 2: *La Grande Guerre (1914–1918).* Vol. 3: *L'après-guerre (1919–1924).* Vol. 4: *Cartel des gauches et union nationale (1924–1929).* Vol. 5: *La République en danger: des ligues au Front Populaire (1930–1936).* Vol. 6: *Vers le Front Populaire à la conférence de Munich (1936–1939).* Vol. 7: *La course vers l'abîme: la fin de la Troisième République (1938–1940).* 2d rev. ed. 7 vols. plus index. Paris: Presses Universitaires de France, 1973–87. ISBN 2-13-039824-3. ▸ Detailed, chronological political history (1906–40) based primarily on parliamentary debates. Organized by legislatures; discusses elections, ministries' composition, issues, and laws. Centrist interpretation of politics as alternation between leftist and rightist inclinations; 1905, pivotal divide. [MMF]

26.139 Jean-Denis Bredin. *The affair: the case of Alfred Dreyfus.* 1986 ed. Jeffrey Mehlman, trans. Birmingham, Ala.: Notable Trials Library, 1989. ▸ Careful examination of military and civilian trials in Dreyfus affair and larger confrontation of opposing worldviews. Emphasizes strength of antisemites, nationalists, and militarists; also Republicans' slower response. Occasionally detail overwhelming. [JFS]

26.140 Henri Brunschwig. *French colonialism, 1871–1914: myths and realities.* Rev. ed. William G. Brown, trans. New York: Praeger, 1966. ▸ Discussion of expansion into Asia and Africa. Emphasizes political and nationalistic motivations of Premier Jules Ferry and successors. Concludes overseas expansion intended to divert public attention from Franco-Prussian War loss; economic motivations secondary. Revision of French original. [LLC]

26.141 Michael Burns. *Rural society and French politics: Boulangism and the Dreyfus affair, 1886–1900.* Princeton: Princeton University Press, 1984. ISBN 0-691-05423-1. ▸ Argues for distinct, complex political life of countryside. Electoral responses of four rural departments to major national crises studied in depth. Most controversial finding is that Dreyfus affair had little impact. [JFS]

26.142 Joel Colton. *Leon Blum: humanist in politics.* 1966 ed. Durham, N.C.: Duke University Press, 1987. ISBN 0-8223-0762-

6 (pbk). ▸ Balanced biography of first socialist premier portrays human virtues and political weaknesses. Emphasizes Popular Front. Blum's exercise-of-power formula let Socialists accept political responsibility within existing constitutional and economic framework. [MMF]

26.143 Jean-Baptiste Duroselle. *Clemenceau.* Paris: Fayard, 1988. ISBN 2-213-02214-3. ▸ Recent exhaustive biography incorporating previous studies. Culminates in Clemenceau's wartime leadership of Third Republic; emphasizes lifelong commitment to individual action and liberty. [JFS]

26.144 Jean-Baptiste Duroselle. *La décadence, 1932–1939.* Paris: Imprimerie Nationale, 1979. ISBN 2-11-080736-9, ISSN 0180-9563. ▸ Masterful, detailed account of French foreign policy during traumatic 1930s. Critically assesses statesmen's responses to crises; analyzes forces, interests, and attitudes shaping policy. Governing classes' collective responsibility for ultimate policy failure. [MMF]

26.145 Stewart Edwards. *The Paris Commune, 1871.* 1971 ed. Chicago: Quadrangle, 1973. ISBN 0-8129-0259-9. ▸ Careful, illustrated study places Commune in tradition of urban, patriotic sans-culotte uprisings and also identifies revolutionary innovations. Underscores intensity and extent of repression. Influenced by its centenary publication. [JFS]

26.146 Jack D. Ellis. *The physician-legislators of France: medicine and politics in the early Third Republic, 1870–1914.* Cambridge: Cambridge University Press, 1990. ISBN 0-521-38208-4. ▸ Exemplary, well-researched, collective biography traces development of new local elite and its impact on national politics. Medical training and practice influenced affiliation with republican Left and support for public health legislation. [JFS]

26.147 Sanford Elwitt. *The making of the Third Republic: class and politics in France, 1868–1884.* Baton Rouge: Louisiana State University Press, 1975. ISBN 0-8071-0077-3. ▸ Delineates development of stable bourgeois order compatible with republican state and democratic ideology. Government education and railroad policies united capitalists and petty producers. Often underestimates tensions within socially conservative alliance. [JFS]

26.148 Jean Estèbe. *Les ministres de la République, 1871–1914.* Paris: Presses de la Fondation Nationale des Sciences Politiques, 1982. ISBN 2-7246-0471-7. ▸ Very useful analysis of social, economic, educational, and professional characteristics of 320 government members; wealth of statistics. Emphasizes predominance of bourgeoisie with diplomas and increasing numbers from lower middle class. [JFS]

26.149 Marjorie Milbank Farrar. *Principled pragmatist: the political career of Alexandre Millerand.* New York: Berg; distributed by St. Martin's, 1991. ISBN 0-85496-665-X. ▸ Study of major Third Republic politician's evolution from youthful radical to parliamentary socialist leader to right-of-center war minister, premier, and president of Republic. Important but neglected, controversial republican leader. [MMF]

26.150 John F. Godfrey. *Capitalism at war: industrial policy and bureaucracy in France, 1914–1918.* Leamington Spa, England: Berg; distributed by St. Martin's, 1987. ISBN 0-85496-519-X. ▸ Analysis of wartime power struggles of bureaucrats, politicians, and industrialists over state control of industry. Successful import and production controls limited by interservice rivalries, profiteering, and inefficiency. New interpretation of total war economy and impact. [MMF]

26.151 François Goguel. *La politique des partis sous la Troisième République.* 1958 4th ed. Paris: Seuil, 1960. ▸ Penetrating, possibly too rigid, conceptual analysis of Third Republic political parties, written during author's World War II captivity. Two rival French

political temperaments: party of movement versus party of established order. [MMF]

26.152 Harvey Goldberg. *The life of Jean Jaurès.* Madison: University of Wisconsin Press, 1962. ▸ Definitive study of life and times of socialist leader. Sympathetic portrait, presenting major political issues of France and Second International with Jaurès center stage. [JFS]

26.153 Daniel Halévy. *The end of the notables.* Alain Silvera, ed. June Guicharnaud, trans. Middletown, Conn.: Wesleyan University Press, 1974. ISBN 0-8195-4066-8 (cl), 0-8195-6030-8 (pbk). ▸ Classic 1930 (French) study examining political collapse of traditional elites and their replacement by new republican leadership. Set tone for negative evaluations of radical politicians and Third Republic. [JFS]

26.154 Steven C. Hause. *Women's suffrage and social politics in the French Third Republic.* Princeton: Princeton University Press, 1984. ISBN 0-691-05427-4 (cl), 0-691-10167-1 (pbk). ▸ Comprehensive survey of political movement for women's votes. Detail on organizations and publications. Suggestive interpretations of feminism and patriarchy; suffragists' success possibly retarded by women leaders' concerns about Republic's survival. [JFS]

26.155 Ronald Chalmers Hood III. *Royal republicans: the French naval dynasties between the world wars.* Baton Rouge: Louisiana State University Press, 1985. ISBN 0-8071-1211-9. ▸ Study of social origins, professional training, and political convictions of interwar naval officers. Valuable coverage of neglected topic, but some questionable sweeping generalizations about officers' support for Action Française. [LLC]

26.156 Patrick H. Hutton. *The cult of the revolutionary tradition: the Blanquists in French politics, 1864–1893.* Berkeley: University of California Press, 1981. ISBN 0-520-04114-3. ▸ Innovative examination of complex movement of Auguste Blanqui and disciples which influenced twentieth-century Right and Left. Stresses importance of cultural and nonrational elements. Involvement with Boulangism critical turning point. [JFS]

26.157 William D. Irvine. *The Boulanger affair reconsidered: royalism, Boulangism, and the origins of the radical Right in France.* New York: Oxford University Press, 1989. ISBN 0-19-505334-6. ▸ Persuasive argument that royalist money, organization, and voters were indispensable. General Boulanger revitalized moribund traditional Right. Criticizes F. Seager (*Boulanger Affair,* 1969), Sternhell 26.182, and others who have stressed Boulanger's working-class support. [JFS]

26.158 William D. Irvine. *French conservatism in crisis: the Republican Federation of France in the 1930's.* Baton Rouge: Louisiana State University Press, 1979. ISBN 0-8071-0555-4. ▸ Impressive study of most important Third Republic conservative political party. Fills gap in literature on traditional Right. Elitist party feared social revolution in 1930s and thus supported proto-fascist leagues, appeasement, and Vichy government. [MMF]

26.159 Julian Jackson. *The politics of Depression in France, 1932–1936.* Cambridge: Cambridge University Press, 1985. ISBN 0-521-26559-2. ▸ Argues that governmental deflationary policies and all parties' opposition to devaluing franc prevented France's recovery from Depression and caused subsequent undermining of republican stability. Novel interpretation: stagnation chosen as lesser evil. [MMF]

26.160 Julian Jackson. *The Popular Front in France: defending democracy, 1934–38.* Cambridge: Cambridge University Press, 1988. ISBN 0-521-32088-7. ▸ Basic, English-language synthesis analyzing Popular Front's triple character of government, political coalition, and mass movement, reflected in debates on origins, 1936 strikes, communist tactics, and nonintervention in

Spain. Balances economic and social failures against antifascist success. [MMF]

26.161 Tony Judt. *Socialism in Provence, 1871–1914: a study in the origins of the modern French Left.* Cambridge: Cambridge University Press, 1979. ISBN 0-521-22172-2 (cl), 0-521-12598-X (pbk). ▸ Regional study of southern politics and society. Explains how and why politically astute, property-owning peasants supported socialism. Controversial conclusions reassessing French socialism and modernization. [JFS]

26.162 John F. V. Keiger. *France and the origins of the First World War.* New York: St. Martin's, 1983. ISBN 0-312-30292-4. ▸ Discussion of France's role focusing on Poincaré, Franco-Russian alliance, and French decision-making apparatus. Sees incoherent foreign policy, 1905–11, and vigorous leadership, 1912–14. Concludes system of alliances dangerously rigid; limited leaders' choices. [MMF]

26.163 Jere C. King. *Generals and politicians: conflict between France's high command, Parliament, and government, 1914–1918.* 1951 ed. Westport, Conn.: Greenwood, 1971. ISBN 0-8371-4713-1. ▸ Influential case study of wartime conflicts between civilian statesmen and professional soldiers. Civil-military relations evolved from initial military dictatorship to final civilian dominance. Sympathetic to civilians, sees wartime power dichotomy threatening democracy. [MMF]

26.164 Gerd Krumeich. *Armaments and politics in France on the eve of the First World War: the introduction of three-year conscription, 1913–1914.* Stephen Conn, trans. Dover, N.H.: Berg, 1984. ISBN 0-907582-15-X (cl), 0-907582-34-6 (pbk). ▸ Impressive, detailed analysis of domestic-foreign policy relationship, reflected in political struggles to enact three-year military service and progressive income tax. Refutes polarization thesis; sees basic interparty consensus on defense foreshadowing 1914 *union sacrée*. For specialists. [MMF]

26.165 Maurice Larkin. *Church and state after the Dreyfus affair: the separation issue in France.* London: Macmillan, 1974. ISBN 0-333-14703-0. ▸ Extensive study of church archives providing new perspective on parliamentary politics and foreign relations with Vatican. Although unsympathetic to Radicals, identifies Catholic intransigence as major factor pushing many reluctant Republicans to separation of church and state. [JFS]

26.166 Peter J. Larmour. *The French Radical party in the 1930's.* Stanford, Calif.: Stanford University Press, 1964. ISBN 0-8047-0206-3. ▸ Best available critique of Radicals' transformation into centrist party. Emphasizes politicians' inability to respond to 1930s crises, immobility, and lack of party discipline. Believes press sources convey politicians' responses to 1930s challenges better than party history. [MMF]

26.167 Herman Lebovics. *The alliance of iron and wheat in the Third French Republic, 1860–1914: origins of the new conservatism.* Baton Rouge: Louisiana State University Press, 1988. ISBN 0-8071-1350-6. ▸ Argues that industrialists and large landowners constructed republican-conservative order in response to economic depression and workers' militancy that persisted into mid-twentieth century. Book criticized for reliance on German model. [JFS]

26.168 Leo A. Loubère. *Radicalism in Mediterranean France: its rise and decline, 1848–1914.* Albany: State University of New York Press, 1974. ISBN 0-87395-094-1. ▸ Demonstrates important interaction between region and pivotal republican political movement. Peasant wine growers and their economy figure as prominent link. Sharply criticized by Judt 26.161. [JFS]

26.169 Karl Marx. *Civil war in France: the Paris Commune.* 2d ed. New York: International, 1988. ▸ Classic work portraying 1871 Commune uprising as proletarian effort to seize state power

and expropriate expropriators. While much criticized, influenced three generations of socialist and communist militants, as well as historians. Also includes Lenin's writings on Commune and Fedorovsky's "Marx's Civil War in France." [JFS]

26.170 Jean-Marie Mayeur and Madeleine Rebérioux. *The Third Republic from its origins to the Great War, 1871–1914.* J. R. Foster, trans. Cambridge: Cambridge University Press, 1984. ISBN 0-521-24931-7 (cl), 0-521-35857-4 (pbk). ▸ Combining two separate French studies, links political developments to social, cultural, and economic contexts. Useful survey of period. Evaluates extent to which moderate Republicans and then Radicals affected state and society. [JFS]

26.171 Pierre Miquel. *Poincaré.* 1961 ed. Paris: Fayard, 1984. ISBN 2-213-01513-9. ▸ Sympathetic political biography, concentrating on 1912–29 and Poincaré's savior role as wartime president and postwar premier. Study of very representative Third Republic statesman and committed republican centrist in crisis era. [MMF]

26.172 Philip G. Nord. *Paris shopkeepers and the politics of resentment.* Princeton: Princeton University Press, 1986. ISBN 0-691-05454-1. ▸ Influential reexamination of relations between petite bourgeoisie's experiences and politics in French capital. Argues against inevitable connections between class and political choice. Stresses economic and cultural dislocations and shifting political allegiances. [JFS]

26.173 Karen M. Offen. "Depopulation, nationalism, and feminism in fin-de-siècle France." *American historical review* 89 (1984) 648–77. ISSN 0002-8762. ▸ Pathbreaking argument demonstrating centrality of gender issues in Third Republic debates. Focuses on ubiquitous concerns about depopulation affecting republican politicians, nationalists, and feminists. [JFS]

26.174 Douglas Porch. *The march to the Marne: the French army, 1871–1914.* Cambridge: Cambridge University Press, 1981. ISBN 0-521-23883-8. ▸ Provocative revisionist study, attributing 1914 army shortcomings (incompetent high command, tactical errors, and armaments scarcity) to Radicals' politicization of army after Dreyfus affair. Sympathetically portrays officers as politically neutral, not antirepublican. [MMF]

26.175 Antoine Prost. *In the wake of war: les anciens combattants and French society.* Helen McPhail, trans. New York: Berg; distributed by St. Martin's, 1992. ISBN 0-85496-672-2 (cl), 0-85496-337-5 (pbk). ▸ Social and intellectual history of World War I veterans and their organizations. Disputes notion of antirepublican, profascist leanings for majority of veterans; stresses pacifist, antimilitarist war legacy. Abridgement of three-volume French study. [LLC]

26.176 David B. Ralston. *The army of the Republic: the place of the military in the political evolution of France, 1871–1914.* Cambridge, Mass.: MIT Press, 1967. ▸ Comprehensive general study of reorganization of military institutions after 1870 defeat. Republic's pragmatic entente between supportive civilian authorities and politically neutral army leaders resolved national defense problem, culminated in World War I military success. [MMF]

26.177 Theodore Ropp. *The development of a modern navy: French naval policy, 1871–1904.* Stephen S. Roberts, ed. Annapolis: Naval Institute Press, 1987. ISBN 0-87021-141-2. ▸ Slightly edited version of fifty-year-old dissertation, valuable for treating neglected field. Interesting discussion of how political differences figured in competing views of strategy and assessments of weapons and ships. [LLC]

26.178 John Rothney. *Bonapartism after Sedan.* Ithaca, N.Y.: Cornell University Press, 1969. ▸ Basic study of Bonapartist political group during formation of Third Republic in 1870s. Republicans and Orléanists joined to block their revival. Bonapartists failed to develop authoritarian democracy. [JFS]

26.179 Pierre Sorlin. *Waldeck-Rousseau.* Paris: Colin, 1966. ‣ Major biography and in-depth analysis of leader of moderate republicanism. Critical for understanding bourgeois conservatives committed to republican state and willing to recognize existence of social problems. [JFS]

26.180 Robert Soucy. *French fascism: the first wave, 1924–1933.* New Haven: Yale University Press, 1986. ISBN 0-300-03488-1. ‣ Specialized study of appeal and weaknesses of French fascism as part of middle-class backlash against liberalism and socialism, not foreign ideology. Stresses economic and social links to conservatism but tactical differences. [MMF]

26.181 Charles Sowerwine. *Sisters or citizens? Women and socialism in France since 1876.* Cambridge: Cambridge University Press, 1982. ISBN 0-521-23484-0. ‣ Stimulating examination of early feminist-socialist alliance and limits of socialist appeal to women. Concludes class identity obliterated gender issues to detriment of women, feminism, and socialist movement. Also available in photocopy from Ann Arbor: University Microfilms International, 1991. [JFS]

26.182 Zeev Sternhell. *La droite révolutionnaire, 1885–1914: les origines française du fascisme.* Paris: Seuil, 1978. ISBN 2-02-004844-2. ‣ Controversial intellectual history of New Right emerging from mass society and becoming source of fascism. Battling democracy, it adopted nationalism, antisemitism, and antiparliamentarianism from Left. [JFS]

26.183 Zeev Sternhell. *Neither Right nor Left: fascist ideology in France.* David Maisel, trans. Berkeley: University of California Press, 1986. ISBN 0-520-05207-2. ‣ Provocative study treating fascism as synthesis of organic nationalism and anti-Marxist socialism, not traditional conservatism. Refutes Rémond's thesis linking fascism and Bonapartist tradition (26.41). Emphasizes that fascist ideology of revolt appealed when democratic liberalism and socialism in crisis. [MMF]

26.184 David Stevenson. *French war aims against Germany, 1914–1919.* Oxford: Clarendon, 1982. ISBN 0-19-822574-1. ‣ Significant synthesis of French wartime diplomacy. Government's principal aim was security from Germany, reflected in Versailles Treaty's reparations and territorial clauses. Emphasizes Clemenceau's role. [MMF]

26.185 Mary Lynn Stewart. *Women, work, and the French state: labour protection and social patriarchy, 1879–1919.* Kingston, Ont.: McGill-Queen's University Press, 1989. ISBN 0-7735-0704-3. ‣ Important study of social policy and gender. Demonstrates how gender-specific legislation intensified women's disadvantages in dual labor market. Calls for reconsideration of function and consequences of protective legislation. [JFS]

26.186 Judith F. Stone. *The search for social peace: reform legislation in France, 1890–1914.* Albany: State University of New York Press, 1985. ISBN 0-88706-022-6 (cl), 0-88706-023-4 (pbk). ‣ New perspective with argument that central issue of Third Republic was containment of working class. Bourgeois politicians divided on means. Coalition of Radicals and Socialists enacted reform legislation, but lacked enough power to implement it. [JFS]

26.187 David Robin Watson. *Georges Clemenceau: a political biography.* 1974 ed. New York: McKay, 1976. ISBN 0-679-50703-5. ‣ Careful study of major political figure, providing excellent information on parliamentary politics and useful appendixes on political parties. Essentially sympathetic to this republican's liberal individualism. [JFS]

26.188 Eugen Joseph Weber. *Action Française: royalism and reaction in twentieth-century France.* Stanford, Calif.: Stanford University Press, 1962. ISBN 0-8047-0134-2. ‣ Influential analysis for

specialists of Charles Maurras's neomonarchist movement and journal, 1899–1944. Incoherent doctrine of integral nationalism sought return to pre-1789 institutions; violent tactics but not totalitarian goals. Appealed to young intellectuals but ineffective politically. [MMF]

26.189 Claude Willard. *Les Guesdistes: le mouvement socialiste en France, 1893–1905.* Paris: Éditions Sociales, 1965. ‣ Exhaustive study arguing central importance of Jules Guesde and followers in working-class politics and Marxist tradition. Guesdistes' influence explains persistent problems: dogmatism and vacillation between reformist and revolutionary programs. [JFS]

26.190 Robert Wohl. *French communism in the making, 1914–1924.* Stanford, Calif.: Stanford University Press, 1966. ISBN 0-8047-0177-6. ‣ Analyzes French and Russian Communist parties' shared antecedents in pre-1914 crisis of liberalism. French party's bolshevization due to proletariat alienation from anachronistic policies of socialist Section Française de l'Internationale Ouvrière (French Section of the Workers International) and Confédération Générale du Travail (General Federation of Labor), and to pro-Soviet revolutionary, opportunistic leadership. [MMF]

26.191 Robert J. Young. *In command of France: French foreign policy and military planning, 1933–1940.* Cambridge, Mass.: Harvard University Press, 1978. ISBN 0-674-44536-8. ‣ French diplomatic and military responses to problem of interwar security vis-à-vis Germany. Casts doubt on morally couched explanations for such responses; emphasizes certain political, economic, and strategic reasons. [RJY]

26.192 Robert J. Young. *Power and pleasure: Louis Barthou and the Third French Republic.* Montreal, Que.: McGill-Queen's University Press, 1991. ISBN 0-7735-0863-5. ‣ Biography addressed to international as well as domestic politics. Public career and private life of centrist politician; set within cultural life of upper middle class. [RJY]

SEE ALSO
48.194 Anthony Adamthwaite. *France and the coming of the Second World War, 1936–1939.*

Vichy Regime and Resistance, 1940–1944

26.193 Henri Amouroux. *La grande histoire des français sous l'occupation, 1939–1945.* 8 vols. Paris: Laffont, 1976–91. ISBN 2-221-00130-3 (set). ‣ Detailed history of politics and everyday life in Nazi-occupied France, 1940–44. Usually balanced view, treating resisters, collaborators, and majority who simply tried to muddle through. Work continued (volumes 9–) under title *La grande histoire des Français après l'occupation.* [BMG]

26.194 Jean-Pierre Azéma. *From Munich to the liberation, 1938–1944.* Janet Lloyd, trans. Cambridge: Cambridge University Press, 1984. ISBN 0-521-25237-7 (cl), 0-521-27238-6 (pbk). ‣ Detailed account from appeasement of Hitler at Munich through 1944 liberation. Argues that resistance followed Jacobin patriotic ideal that prevented Right from claiming mantle of patriotism held since Dreyfus affair. [BMG]

26.195 Jean-Pierre Azéma and François Bédarida, eds. *Le régime de Vichy et les français.* Paris: Fayard, 1992. ISBN 2-213-02683-1. ‣ Collection of fifty-three essays and two roundtable discussions introducing latest work on Vichy. Part one provides valuable historiographical overview. Topics include policies toward Jews and women, institutional responses, and departmental case studies. [LLC]

26.196 Bertram M. Gordon. *Collaborationism in France during the Second World War.* Ithaca, N.Y.: Cornell University Press, 1980. ISBN 0-8014-1263-3. ‣ Most complete study of political movements during occupation that wanted France aligned more closely to Nazi Germany than even Vichy government wished. Treats movements as phase in ongoing history of Right. [BMG]

26.197 H. R. Kedward. *Resistance in Vichy France: a study of ideas and motivation in the southern zone, 1940–1942.* Oxford: Oxford University Press, 1978. ISBN 0-19-822529-6. ▸ Specialist study of resistance in unoccupied Vichy zone from June 1940 armistice to November 1942 German occupation of southern zone. Finds many nuances of political opinion in clandestine press, even within Communist party. [BMG]

26.198 Henri Nogueres et al. *Histoire de la Résistance, de 1940 à 1945.* 5 vols. Paris: Laffont, 1967–81. ISBN 2-221-00141-9 (set). ▸ Detailed chronicle of organized French Resistance during World War II, written by journalists active in it. Treats main Resistance networks, including Communists, whose role is downplayed in some other accounts. [BMG]

26.199 Robert O. Paxton. *Vichy France: old guard and new order, 1940–1944.* 1972 ed. New York: Columbia University Press, 1982. ISBN 0-231-05426-2 (cl), 0-231-05427-0 (pbk). ▸ History of Vichy government, 1940–44, arguing leaders collaborated willingly with Nazis, sometimes offering more than Germans demanded. Controversial book setting parameters for continuing debate about extent of collaboration. [BMG]

26.200 Margaret L. Rossiter. *Women in the Resistance.* New York: Praeger, 1986. ISBN 0-03-005338-2 (cl), 0-03-005339-0 (pbk). ▸ Excavates evidence of women's participation in French Resistance activities during Vichy period, using archives and interviews. Pioneering study. [KMO]

26.201 Henry Rousso. *The Vichy syndrome: history and memory in France since 1944.* Arthur Goldhammer, trans. Cambridge, Mass.: Harvard University Press, 1991. ISBN 0-674-93538-1. ▸ Groundbreaking history of debate about Vichy, collaboration, and resistance from end of World War II to present. Finds controversies over these issues so traumatic that France has suffered collectively ever since from Vichy syndrome. [BMG]

26.202 John F. Sweets. *Choices in Vichy France: the French under Nazi occupation.* New York: Oxford University Press, 1986. ISBN 0-19-503751-0. ▸ Study of Clermont-Ferrand (locus of film *The Sorrow and the Pity*) during German occupation. Finds some truth in postwar depictions of nation of resisters; sees overstatement in histories emphasizing French collaboration. [BMG]

Fourth Republic, 1944–1958

26.203 Jean-Pierre Rioux. *The Fourth Republic, 1944–1958.* 1987 ed. Godfrey Rogers, trans. Cambridge: Cambridge University Press, 1989. ISBN 0-521-25238-5 (cl), 0-521-38916-X (pbk). ▸ Introductory political survey of 1944 liberation, interwar parties' return, de Gaulle's 1946 resignation as head of provisional government, and colonial wars (Indochina, Algeria) that doomed Fourth Republic and prompted de Gaulle's return. Basis laid for later economic prosperity. [BMG]

26.204 Andrew Shennan. *Rethinking France: plans for renewal, 1940–1946.* Oxford: Clarendon, 1989. ISBN 0-19-827520-X. ▸ Specialist study analyzing reform plans developed after 1940 defeat by Pétain's Vichy government, Gaullist Free French, and regrouped postliberation parties. Argues that de Gaulle's insistence on waiting for parliamentary elections meant France lost fleeting opportunity for reform. [BMG]

26.205 Irwin M. Wall. *The United States and the making of postwar France, 1945–1954.* Cambridge: Cambridge University Press, 1991. ISBN 0-521-40217-4. ▸ Documents American use of unprecedented post-1945 influence to prevent Communists taking power. Sometimes heavy-handed efforts produced mixed results and resentment; more durable impact from cultural influences on education, business, consumers, and popular culture. [BMG]

26.206 Philip Williams. *Crisis and compromise: politics in the Fourth Republic.* Hamden, Conn.: Anchor Books, 1964. ▸ Most detailed discussion in English of making and unmaking of governments, 1944–58. Moderate social-democratic view of politics producing collapse during Algerian crisis. Cold war Third Force coalition squeezed between Communists and nonsupportive Right. [BMG]

Fifth Republic, 1958–

26.207 Robert Aldrich and John Connell. *France's overseas frontier: Départements et Territoires d'Outre-Mer.* Cambridge: Cambridge University Press, 1992. ISBN 0-521-39061-3. ▸ Best available study of remnants of French empire, the Départements d'Outre Mer–Territoires d'Outre Mer (DOM-TOM), showing political, economic, and cultural ties of territories to France. Argues that even if some territories became independent, France would retain others, never be limited just to Europe. [BMG]

26.208 Bernard E. Brown. *Protest in Paris: anatomy of a revolt.* Morristown, N.J.: General Learning Press, 1974. ▸ Introductory study of Paris 1968 student revolt against General de Gaulle's government. Emphasizes students' opposition to political liberalism and to rapid modernization changing French society in 1960s. [BMG]

26.209 Jacques Chapsal. *La vie politique sous la Cinquième République.* Vol. 1: *1958–1974.* Vol. 2: *1974–1987.* 5th ed. 2 vols. Paris: Presses Universitaires de France, 1990. ISBN 2-13-043528-9 (v. 1), 2-13-043593-9 (v. 2). ▸ Chronologically organized survey from French viewpoint presenting major developments in political, economic, and diplomatic history of Fifth Republic since 1958. [LLC]

26.210 Jean Charlot. *The Gaullist phenomenon.* New York: Praeger, 1971. ▸ Analysis of social and political support for Gaullist movement and de Gaulle's role. Useful treatment of Gaullism as conservative movement but includes flawed prediction that Gaullist majority had made Left permanent minority. [BMG]

26.211 Michel Crozier. *Strategies for change: the future of French society.* William Beer, trans. Cambridge, Mass.: MIT Press, 1982. ISBN 0-262-03082-9. ▸ Critique of French bureaucracy, partly based on author's earlier books on stalled society and bureaucratic phenomenon. Crozier's arguments for political decentralization and democratizing elite schools influenced socialist policy after 1981 victory. [BMG]

26.212 Hervé Hamon and Patrick Rotman. *Génération.* 2 vols. Paris: Seuil, 1987–88. ISBN 2-02-009550-5 (set). ▸ Most comprehensive study available of origins, events, and results of 1968 student-worker revolt. Idealism (inspired by Mao and Sartre) of 1960s youth-fueled rebellion. Unsuccessful rebellion accelerated Communists' decline and influenced feminists, ecologists, and socialist recovery. [BMG]

26.213 James F. Hollifield and George Ross, eds. *Searching for the new France.* New York: Routledge, 1991. ISBN 0-415-90249-5 (cl), 0-415-90250-9 (pbk). ▸ Best available series of articles analyzing contemporary politics, society, trade unions, intelligentsia, and foreign policy. Concludes France now modernized consumer society, like European neighbors and United States, but somehow still searching for identity. [BMG]

26.214 Jane Jenson and George Ross. *The view from inside: a French communist cell in crisis.* Berkeley: University of California Press, 1984. ISBN 0-520-04991-8. ▸ Best study of French Communist party from inside, focusing on daily lives of Communist party cell members, largely Parisian intellectuals and white-collar workers. Notes post-1978 militants' disillusionment with leadership's anachronistic rhetoric, out of touch with economic modernization and feminism. [BMG]

26.215 Jean Lacouture. *De Gaulle.* Vol. l: *The rebel, 1890–1944.* Vol. 2: *The ruler, 1944–1970.* Abr. ed. 2 vols. Patrick O'Brian, trans. (v. 1). Alan Sheridan, trans. (v. 2). New York: Norton, 1990–92. ISBN 0-393-02699-X (v. 1), 0-393-03084-9 (v. 2). ‣ Most complete biography of General de Gaulle, emphasizing personal story and career more than evolution of surrounding social forces. Condensation of three-volume study. [BMG]

26.216 Nonna Mayer and Pascal Perrineau, eds. *Le Front National à découvert.* Paris: Presses de la Fondation Nationale des Sciences Politiques, 1989. ISBN 2-7246-0564-0. ‣ Most complete study to date of Jean-Marie Le Pen's National Front. Discusses movement's history, leaders, followers, ideas, and some local electoral campaigns. Sudden appearance in 1980s but continuities with earlier right wing. [BMG]

26.217 George Ross, Stanley Hoffmann, and Sylvia Malzacher, eds. *The Mitterrand experiment: continuity and change in modern France.* New York: Oxford University Press, 1987. ISBN 0-19-520608-8 (cl), 0-19-520312-6 (pbk). ‣ Stimulating collection of essays, from 1981 socialist victory in presidential and parliamentary elections to defeat in 1986 parliamentary elections. Socialists turned from ideology to consensual, moderate government, disappointing some supporters, mollifying some opponents, and establishing precedent for regular Left-Right alternation. [BMG]

ADMINISTRATION, LAW, AND PUBLIC POLICY

26.218 Susan Bachrach. *Dames employées: the feminization of postal work in nineteenth-century France.* New York: Institute for Research in History and Haworth Press, 1984. (Women and history, 8.) ISBN 0-86656-205-2, ISSN 0276-3885. ‣ As civil service expanded, women were hired for new postal jobs at lower pay than men, but wages and conditions better than for most women workers. Men protested feminization. Valuable case study. [JW]

26.219 Clive H. Church. *Revolution and red tape: the French ministerial bureaucracy, 1770–1850.* Oxford: Clarendon, 1981. ISBN 0-19-822562-8. ‣ Basic study of development of centralized bureaucracy in period of revolution. Slow and complex change from royal administration to paid body of civil servants. Discusses pros and cons of bureaucracy including frustrations of citizens. [JW]

26.220 William B. Cohen. *Rulers of empire: the French colonial service in Africa.* Stanford, Calif.: Hoover Institution Press, 1971. ISBN 0-8179-1951-1. ‣ Africa as case study of colonial administrators. History of training and functions of personnel and organization of administration in various colonies. Contribution to understanding of French imperialism. [JW]

26.221 Jacques Léon Godechot. *Les institutions de la France sous la Révolution et l'empire.* 3d ed. Paris: Presses Universitaires de France, 1985. ISBN 2-13-038665-2. ‣ Encyclopedic look at institutions of Revolution and Napoleonic era by leading French historian. Series of well-informed essays on myriad of subjects in areas often little known. [JRC]

26.222 Joelle Guillais. *Crimes of passion: dramas of private life in nineteenth-century France.* 1990 ed. Jane Dunnett, trans. New York: Routledge, 1991. ISBN 0-415-90390-4. ‣ Best available study of court records and press discussion concerning murder trials resulting from domestic violence and jealousy in heterosexual love relationships. Argues for placing crimes of passion within historical record. [KMO]

26.223 Ruth Harris. *Murderers and madness: medicine, law, and society in the fin de siècle.* Oxford: Clarendon, 1989. ISBN 0-19-822991-7. ‣ Original, informative combination of legal and scientific history. New medico-psychiatric approaches to crime undermined traditional attitudes toward criminal mind and changed judicial and penal strategies. Discusses courts, culture of judges, and treatment of women and poor. [JW]

26.224 Jill Harsin. *Policing prostitution in nineteenth-century Paris.* Princeton: Princeton University Press, 1985. ISBN 0-691-05439-8. ‣ Basic study of early nineteenth-century development of police regulation of Paris prostitutes, including registration and medical control. Examines administrative structure, legal base, and practical functioning of system. [KMO]

26.225 Benjamin F. Martin. *Crime and criminal justice under the Third Republic: the shame of Marianne.* Baton Rouge: Louisiana State University Press, 1990. ISBN 0-8071-1572-X. ‣ Discussion of crime statistics, famous cases, organization of police and judiciary, criminal procedures, court functions, and punishments. Strong argument that gender and class prejudices and political influence led to miscarriages of justice. [JW]

26.226 Allan Mitchell. *The divided path: the German influence on social reform in France after 1870.* Chapel Hill: University of North Carolina Press, 1991. ISBN 0-8078-1964-6. ‣ Unique comparative study of politicians' and doctors' attempts to develop social welfare for more interventionist state, allegedly on German model. Depopulation fears and competition with Germany spurred reforms, despite avowed French ideal of individual liberty. [RGF]

26.227 Patricia O'Brien. *The promise of punishment: prisons in nineteenth-century France.* Princeton: Princeton University Press, 1982. ISBN 0-691-05339-1. ‣ Pioneering study of evolution of concept of incarceration to punish crime. Discussion of prison operation, culture of prisoners, and gender differences. Treatment both in prison and after release created class of criminals, not their rehabilitation. [JW]

26.228 Frederick F. Ridley and Jean Blondel. *Public administration in France.* 2d ed. Peter Campbell, Introduction. New York: Barnes & Noble, 1969. ‣ Very informative analysis of organization and function of post–World War I central administration and major ministries (e.g., culture, finance, justice). Some historical background on administrative growth and development. [JW]

26.229 Pierre Rosanvallon. *L'état en France de 1789 à nos jours.* Paris: Seuil, 1990. ISBN 2-02-011523-9. ‣ Surveys changing relationships between state and society. Emphasis on specificity of French state's role after 1789 Revolution, development of social legislation, and economic intervention. Valuable fifty-five–page bibliography on administration and policy. [LLC]

26.230 Vivien A. Schmidt. *Democratizing France: the political and administrative history of decentralization.* Cambridge: Cambridge University Press, 1990. ISBN 0-521-39156-3. ‣ Detailed study arguing that parameters for decentralization debate set by 1789 Revolution; sees 1981–86 socialist decentralization as continuing early Third Republic efforts. Recent socialist legislation made informal patterns of decentralization into law. [BMG]

26.231 Ezra N. Suleiman. *Politics, power, and bureaucracy in France: the administrative elite.* Princeton: Princeton University Press, 1974. ISBN 0-691-07552-2 (cl), 0-691-10225 (pbk). ‣ Fascinating sociological study of postwar bureaucracy. Higher civil service as integral part of political-administrative system. Emphasizes importance of centralized state; discusses recruitment and social origins of administrators. [JW]

26.232 Guy Thuillier. *La vie quotidienne dans les ministères au dix-neuvième siècle.* Paris: Hachette, 1976. ISBN 2-01-001999-7. ‣ Readable introduction to world of government clerks by leading administrative history specialist. Addresses work conditions, decision making, recruitment, advancement, and complaints of civil servants; also women's entry into ministries. [JW]

26.233 Judith Wishnia. *The proletarianizing of the fonctionnaires:*

civil service workers and the labor movement under the Third Republic. Baton Rouge: Louisiana State University Press, 1990. ISBN 0-8071-1590-8 (cl), 0-8071-1659-9 (pbk). ▸ Only book in English treating civil servants as new working class. Shows evolution and growth of civil service and political consciousness of civil servants, including women. Relates *fonctionnaires'* unionization to other blue-collar organizations and broader political developments. [JW]

CULTURAL AND INTELLECTUAL HISTORY

26.234 Maurice Agulhon. *Marianne into battle: republican imagery and symbolism in France, 1789–1880.* Janet Lloyd, trans. Cambridge: Cambridge University Press, 1981. ISBN 0-521-23577-4 (cl), 0-521-28224-1 (pbk). ▸ Insightful essay tracing changing meaning of political symbol (Marianne) from radical to conservative republicanism, from Revolution to Third Republic, from popular to national image. Key shifts in 1793, 1848, and 1877. [JSA]

26.235 James Smith Allen. *In the public eye: a history of reading in modern France, 1800–1940.* Princeton: Princeton University Press, 1991. ISBN 0-691-03162-2. ▸ Contributes to defining new field of intellectual history: readers' interpretations of textual content. Art and act of reading as both subjects and objects of change in French economy, society, politics, and culture. [JSA]

26.236 Jacques Barzun. *Berlioz and the romantic century: an introduction to the age of romanticism.* 1969 3d ed. 2 vols. Chicago: University of Chicago Press, 1982. ISBN 0-226-03861-0 (pbk). ▸ Berlioz's life, work, and times in European culture. Reassesses reputation of and scholarship on composer since nineteenth century. Useful scholarly apparatus and appendix. Exemplary intellectual biography. [JSA]

26.237 Jonathan Beecher. *Charles Fourier: the visionary and his world.* Berkeley: University of California Press, 1986. ISBN 0-520-05600-0 (cl), 0-520-07179-4 (pbk). ▸ Massive intellectual biography of leading utopian socialist. Treats Fourier's response to collapse of Enlightenment philosophy and society as effort to create comprehensive science of nature and humanity. Fourier as prophet, not isolated madman. [LLC]

26.238 Claude Bellanger et al., eds. *Histoire générale de la presse française.* 5 vols. Paris: Presses Universitaires de France, 1969–76. ISBN 2-13-030284-X (v. 1), 2-13-030258-0 (v. 2), 2-13-032149-6 (v. 3), 2-13-033451-1 (v. 4), 2-13-033613-2 (v. 5). ▸ Collaborative history of French newspaper press from its origins to recent times. Treats newspaper's forms, contents, changes, contexts, and consequences. Well illustrated; good bibliographies. Uneven scholarship but otherwise useful reference. [JSA]

26.239 Pierre Bourdieu. *Distinction: a social critique of the judgement of taste.* Richard Nice, trans. Cambridge, Mass.: Harvard University Press, 1984. ISBN 0-674-21280-0 (cl), 0-674-21277-0 (pbk). ▸ Taste as cultural capital that reflects and legitimates social classification, status, and power in postwar France. Major theoretical study of lingering aristocratic and bourgeois ideals in French cultural discrimination. [JSA]

26.240 Robert Brécy. *Florilège de la chanson révolutionnaire de 1789 au Front Populaire.* Rev. ed. Paris: Les Éditions Ouvrières, 1990. ISBN 2-7082-2872-2. ▸ Handsomely illustrated volume by leading scholar of French songs. Includes only songs of rebellion, none of love, wine, patriotism, or contentment. Regrets present-day capture of popular music by anodyne "tubes," by Maurice Chevalier, Edith Piaf. [ELN]

26.241 Jean-Claude Caron. *Générations romantiques: les étudiants de Paris et le Quartier Latin (1814–1851).* Maurice Agulhon, Preface. Paris: Colin, 1991. ISBN 2-200-37241-8. ▸ Important study correcting view of students as radicals. Doubling of number of law and medical students (1814–51) created new meritocracy.

Bourgeois, liberal students helped politicize 1830 revolutionary crowds. Became less radical after professionals obtained vote in 1831; broke with workers and socialists. [ELN]

26.242 Christophe Charle. *Naissance des intellectuels, 1880–1900.* Paris: Éditions de Minuit, 1990. ISBN 2-7073-1331-9, 2-7073-1325-4. ▸ Empirical study of engaged intellectuals as self-conscious group: social perception and political category a function of Third Republic's stabilization. Dreyfus affair key to definition and role of contemporary cultural elite. [JSA]

26.243 Roger Chartier. "Intellectual history or sociocultural history? The French trajectories." In *Modern European intellectual history: reappraisals and new perspectives.* Dominick LaCapra and Steven L. Kaplan, eds., pp. 13–46. Ithaca, N.Y.: Cornell University Press, 1982. ISBN 0-8014-1470-9 (cl), 0-8014-9881-3 (pbk). ▸ Critique of dominant Annales tradition in French intellectual history—*mentalité*, quantification, categorization—to redefine history of culture in itself and in society. Insightful treatment of recent problems, issues, and approaches. [JSA]

26.244 Linda L. Clark. *Social Darwinism in France.* University: University of Alabama Press, 1984. ISBN 0-8173-0149-6. ▸ Comprehensive survey of French ideas about Darwinism's implications for human society. Traces critical and approving responses to Darwinism. Emphasizes prevalence of Darwinian terminology in pre-1914 discourse, but finds limited number of full-fledged social Darwinists. [LLC]

26.245 Priscilla Parkhurst Clark. *Literary France: the making of a culture.* Rev. ed. Berkeley: University of California Press, 1991. ISBN 0-520-05703-1 (cl), 0-520-07397-5 (pbk). ▸ Scholarly essay defining and tracing development of distinctly French literary culture in marketplace, public institutions, and social hierarchy. Focus on Parisian intellectual elites, especially Voltaire, Victor Hugo, and Jean-Paul Sartre. Scholarly essay. [JSA]

26.246 Terry Nichols Clark. *Prophets and patrons: the French university and the emergence of the social sciences.* Cambridge, Mass.: Harvard University Press, 1973. ISBN 0-674-71580-2. ▸ Discusses emergence of social sciences within context of intellectual climate, higher education, institutes, ministries, and prophet/patron clusters. Paradigm, talent, and structures defined intellectual activity. Tests innovative theoretical model. [JSA/DEL]

26.247 Timothy J. Clark. *The painting of modern life: Paris in the art of Manet and his followers.* 1984 ed. Princeton: Princeton University Press, 1986. ISBN 0-691-00275-4. ▸ Artistic representation as social construct. Identifies impressionism's implicit bourgeois ideology in stylistic uncertainty and modernist marginality. Model Marxist treatment of art as historical source in specific context: complex, heretical, combative. [JSA]

26.248 Alain Corbin. *The foul and the fragrant: odor and the French social imagination.* Miriam Kochan, Roy Porter, and Christopher Prendergast, trans. Cambridge, Mass.: Harvard University Press, 1986. ISBN 0-674-31175-2 (cl), 0-674-31176-0 (pbk). ▸ Provocative, illuminating study of changing conception and function of smell in physical science, urban planning, and social sensibilities and implications. Argues that modernization meant greater sensitivity to olfactory sensation. Sanitary reform and social engineering seen as aspects of social control. Annales history *par excellence.* [JSA/CSH]

26.249 Maurice Crubellier. *Histoire culturelle de la France, XIXe–XXe siècle.* Paris: Colin, 1974. ▸ Analysis of evolving national culture as lived experience, from traditional Old Regime particularisms to modern mass media and their contemporary critics. Cultural life as independent historical force. Comprehensive survey. [JSA]

26.250 Jane F. Fulcher. *The nation's image: French grand opera as politics and politicized art.* Cambridge: Cambridge University

Press, 1987. ISBN 0-521-32774-1. ▸ Stimulating but not fully convincing thesis that both direction and repertoire of Paris Opera reflected governments' political goals, Restoration through Second Empire. Composers' intentions and music's aesthetic qualities submerged in politics. [LLC]

26.251   H. Stuart Hughes. *The obstructed path: French social thought in the years of desperation, 1930–1960.* New York: Harper & Row, 1968. ▸ In response to cultural crisis, French intellectuals made deliberate political commitments and thereby redefined Cartesian tradition of moral certainty in social thought. Influential sequel to 22.403; reprinted in *Between Committment and Disillusion* (1987). [JSA]

26.252   Emmet Kennedy. *A cultural history of the French Revolution.* New Haven: Yale University Press, 1989. ISBN 0-300-04426-7 (cl), 0-300-05013-5 (pbk). ▸ *Annaliste* analysis of French Revolution as cultural event within long- and medium-term structures. Identifies most enduring change as politics derived from religion of humanity. Original research, able synthesis. [JSA]

26.253   William R. Keylor. *Academy and community: the foundation of the French historical profession.* Cambridge, Mass.: Harvard University Press, 1975. ISBN 0-674-00255-5. ▸ Scholarly monograph on establishment of history as academic profession, distinct from philosophy and literature, with claims to scientific validity despite political uses and critiques of its methods during Third Republic. [JSA]

26.254   Lloyd S. Kramer. *Threshold of a new world: intellectuals and the exile experience in Paris, 1830–1848.* Ithaca, N.Y.: Cornell University Press, 1988. ISBN 0-8014-1939-5. ▸ Comparative intellectual history centered on Parisian exile experience. Context and community of Paris as social reality and cultural perception formative in Heinrich Heine's poetry, Marx's theory, and Adam Mickiewicz's nationalism. [JSA]

26.255   Dominick LaCapra. *"Madame Bovary" on trial.* Ithaca, N.Y.: Cornell University Press, 1982. ISBN 0-8014-1477-6 (cl), 0-8014-9361-7 (pbk). ▸ Identifies subversive qualities of Gustave Flaubert's style which challenged ideological basis of fiction, society, and law. Controversial application of literary theory to intellectual history; text as historical event. [JSA]

26.256   William Logue. *From philosophy to sociology: the evolution of French liberalism, 1870–1914.* De Kalb: Northern Illinois University Press, 1983. ISBN 0-87580-088-2. ▸ Scholarly examination of mainstream political thought in Third Republic. Relations between state, society, and individual redefined by shift in liberalism's intellectual foundations from eclecticism through idealism to sociology. [JSA]

26.257   Herbert R. Lottman. *The Left Bank: writers, artists, and politics from the Popular Front to the cold war.* Boston: Houghton-Mifflin, 1982. ISBN 0-395-31322-8. ▸ Rise and fall of engaged Parisian intellectuals whose international reputation derived from conflict between communism and fascism until German occupation and Soviet de-Stalinization destroyed ideological commitments. Engaging popular history. [JSA]

26.258   Patricia Mainardi. *Art and politics of the Second Empire: the Universal Exposition of 1855 and 1867.* New Haven: Yale University Press, 1987. ISBN 0-300-03871-2. ▸ Important description of role of government of Second Empire in fostering fine arts. Imperial patronage led to end of domination by Académie des Beaux-Arts and emergence of new eclecticism in French art. [NKI]

26.259   Frank Edward Manuel. *The prophets of Paris: Turgot, Condorcet, Saint-Simon, Fourier, and Comte.* 1962 ed. New York: Harper & Row, 1965. ▸ Biographical and contextual modification of Lovejoy's history of ideas (1.434). "Spectrum of moral alternatives" from Enlightenment reflections to romantic systems of

utopian thought; 1789 the key transition. Stimulating reading. [JSA]

26.260   Robert A. Nye. *Crime, madness, and politics in modern France: the medical concept of national decline.* Princeton: Princeton University Press, 1984. ISBN 0-691-05414-2. ▸ Study of scientific ideas about physiological and social pathologies which shaped public discourse of national decline before 1914. Social science dimension to politics of nationalism and cultural crisis. Important interdisciplinary scholarship. [JSA]

26.261   Pascal Ory and Jean-François Sirinelli. *Les intellectuels en France, de l'affaire Dreyfus à nos jours.* Paris: Colin, 1986. ISBN 2-200-31223-7. ▸ Important synthesis traces intellectuals' role from 1890s to early 1980s. Twentieth-century intellectuals developed notions of generation and sociability. Post-1968 crisis for intellectuals, rise of New Left and New Right. [LLC]

26.262   Mark Poster. *Existential Marxism in postwar France: from Sartre to Althusser.* Princeton: Princeton University Press, 1975. ISBN 0-691-07212-4 (cl), 0-691-01994-0 (pbk). ▸ Marxism and existentialism converged in Jean-Paul Sartre to establish New Left social theory after May 1968 events. Existential Marxism as emerging ideology. Emphasizes intellectual history's relationship to social change. Useful survey. [JSA]

26.263   Charles Rearick. *Pleasures of the Belle Epoque: entertainment and festivity in turn-of-the-century France.* New Haven: Yale University Press, 1985. ISBN 0-300-03230-7 (cl), 0-300-04381-3 (pbk). ▸ Study of rise and failure of mass culture in public festivities, popular cabarets, world fairs, and music halls. While popular entertainment developed, modernization's problems remained. Shattuck's avant-garde redefined (26.266). Well-illustrated, passionate historical speculation. [JSA]

26.264   David L. Schalk. *The spectrum of political engagement: Mounier, Benda, Nizan, Brasillach, Sartre.* Princeton: Princeton University Press, 1979. ISBN 0-691-05275-1. ▸ Traces origin and development of political, social, and ideological positions, conflicts, and influence of five French intellectuals, 1920–45: the moral imperative of deliberate, self-conscious, yet critical, engagement. Provocative. [JSA]

26.265   Jerrold Seigel. *Bohemian Paris: culture, politics, and the boundaries of bourgeois life, 1830–1930.* New York: Viking Penguin, 1986. ISBN 0-670-80723-0 (cl), 0-14-009440-7 (pbk). ▸ Parisian bohemians as self-consciously marginal bourgeois challenging social convention and political moderation from romanticism to surrealism. Blurred identities the essence of avant-garde. Elaboration of earlier work by Shattuck (26.266). [JSA]

26.266   Roger Shattuck. *The banquet years: the origins of the avant-garde in France, 1885 to World War I; Alfred Jarry, Henri Rousseau, Erik Satie, Guillaume Apollinaire.* Rev. ed. New York: Viking, 1968. ISBN 0-394-70415-0. ▸ Witty exemplar of comparative cultural history. Avant-garde originated in life imitating art during Belle Epoque. Jarry, Rousseau, Satie, and Apollinaire self-conscious representatives of French modernism. [JSA]

26.267   Debora L. Silverman. *Art nouveau in fin-de-siècle France: politics, psychology, and style.* Berkeley: University of California Press, 1989. ISBN 0-520-06322-8. ▸ Suggestive essay on liberalism's fin-de-siècle crisis manifested in art. Political, social, and psychological factors in art nouveau's stylistic transformation from wrought-iron monuments to decorative interiors. [JSA]

26.268   Alan B. Spitzer. *The French generation of 1820.* Princeton: Princeton University Press, 1987. ISBN 0-691-05496-7. ▸ Argues that 1820 generation, innocent of Revolution's crimes, united to seek new ideals. But did these self-conscious innovators really innovate? Compare Merriman 26.120, Agulhon 26.116, and Ménager 26.38. May underestimate Revolution's hold on postrevolutionary youth. [ELN]

26.269 K. Steven Vincent. *Pierre-Joseph Proudhon and the rise of French republican socialism.* New York: Oxford University Press, 1984. ISBN 0-19-503413-9. ▸ Intellectual biography of major reformist socialist, libertarian anarchist, and rival of Marx. Relates Proudhon to emerging republican labor and cooperative movements during July Monarchy to explain appeal to artisans and peasants. [LLC]

26.270 Eugen Joseph Weber. *France, fin de siècle.* Cambridge, Mass.: Belknap, 1986. ISBN 0-674-31812-9 (cl), 0-674-31813-7 (pbk). ▸ Upper-class cultural pessimism amid pervasive material progress defined profound ambivalence in contemporary consciousness of rapid historical change. History of telling detail à la Theodore Zeldin (26.30): lively, personal, impressionistic. [JSA]

26.271 Cheryl B. Welch. *Liberty and utility: the French Idéologues and the transformation of liberalism.* New York: Columbia University Press, 1984. ISBN 0-231-05130-1. ▸ Scholarly reassessment of French liberal ideas—utility, liberty, democracy—in Ideologues' conceptions of social science, political economy, and constitutional government. Contrasts English and French radical reformism in theory and practice. [JSA]

26.272 Rosalind H. Williams. *Dream worlds: mass consumption in late nineteenth-century France.* Berkeley: University of California Press, 1982. ISBN 0-520-04355-3. ▸ Insightful essay on emergence and evolution of consumer mentality. Authority of courtly model displaced by realities and illusions of mass consumption, challenged by elitist and democratic critics. Perception and context interdependent. [JSA]

ECONOMIC HISTORY: AGRICULTURE, COMMERCE, AND INDUSTRY

26.273 Peter H. Amann. *The corncribs of Buzet: modernizing agriculture in the French southwest.* Princeton: Princeton University Press, 1990. ISBN 0-691-05563-7. ▸ Up-to-date, detailed case study of agricultural modernization in five Haute-Garonne villages since 1945. Buzet more successful than others because political leaders and younger farmers desired change. Links local concerns, state intervention, and international pressures. [LLC]

26.274 Lenard R. Berlanstein. *Big business and industrial conflict in nineteenth-century France: a social history of the Parisian Gas Company.* Berkeley: University of California Press, 1991. ISBN 0-520-07234-0. ▸ Business and labor history combined in detailed study of salaried managers, white-collar employees, and industrial laborers within one enterprise. Focuses on attitudes and protests as economic development created new social and political tensions. [LRB]

26.275 François Caron. *An economic history of modern France.* Barbara Brag, trans. New York: Columbia University Press, 1979. ISBN 0-231-03860-7. ▸ Comprehensive survey arguing against view that French economic development was peculiarly backward. [LRB]

26.276 M. C. Cleary. *Peasants, politicians, and producers: the organization of agriculture in France since 1918.* Cambridge: Cambridge University Press, 1989. ISBN 0-521-33347-4. ▸ Useful survey and analysis of origins and development of agricultural syndicates, cooperatives, and mutual associations in diverse regions. Emphasizes local and Catholic initiatives. Finds these organizations significant for rural economic change and survival of family farms. [LLC]

26.277 Hugh D. Clout. *Agriculture in France on the eve of the railway age.* London: Croom Helm, 1980. ISBN 0-85664-919-8. ▸ Suggests nineteenth-century revolutions not inspired by agrarian change. Finds no French agrarian revolution; seed-to-yield ratio same in 1790 and 1840 (1: 6.1). Only farms near cities modernized, but peasants' attitudes changed even if techniques did not; see Margadant 26.119 and Agulhon 26.115. [ELN]

26.278 Ellen Furlough. *Consumer cooperation in France: the politics of consumption, 1834–1930.* Ithaca, N.Y.: Cornell University Press, 1991. ISBN 0-8014-2512-3. ▸ Best study of consumer cooperative movement, linking it to both middle-class and working-class economic interests and politics. Example of Nord department highlights working-class component. Also explains how consumerism became increasingly associated with women. [LLC]

26.279 Richard F. Kuisel. *Capitalism and the state in modern France: renovation and economic management in the twentieth century.* Cambridge: Cambridge University Press, 1981. ISBN 0-521-23474-3 (cl), 0-521-27378-1(pbk). ▸ Important study of capitalist renovation of twentieth-century economy. Economic development characterized by modernity, defined as expansion and collaboration of private and public managerial interests. [BMG]

26.280 James M. Laux. *In first gear: the French automobile industry to 1914.* Montreal: McGill-Queen's University Press, 1976. ISBN 0-7735-0264-5. ▸ Survey of development of markets and firms within key twentieth-century industry, in which France was early leader. Focuses on entrepreneurship and factors affecting business decisions. [LRB]

26.281 Maurice Lévy-Leboyer and François Bourguignon. *The French economy in the nineteenth century: an essay in econometric analysis.* Jesse Bryan and Virginia Perotin, trans. Cambridge: Cambridge University Press, 1990. ISBN 0-521-33147-1. ▸ Survey based on sophisticated statistical methods. Emphasizes slowdown in second half of nineteenth century after Second Empire. [LRB]

26.282 Leo A. Loubère. *The wine revolution in France: the twentieth century.* Princeton: Princeton University Press, 1990. ISBN 0-691-05592-0. ▸ Interesting study extends wine industry history from author's *The Red and the White* (1978); economic, technical, legal themes, 1910s through 1980s. Stresses importance of post-1945 mechanization and greater state regulation; prosperity ended traditional village life. [LLC]

26.283 Michael B. Miller. *The Bon Marché: bourgeois culture and the department store, 1869–1920.* Princeton: Princeton University Press, 1981. ISBN 0-691-05321-9. ▸ Social and business history of important urban innovation. Case study of one store, considers both personnel and development of consumer habits. [LRB]

26.284 Guy Palmade. *French capitalism in the nineteenth century.* Graeme M. Holmes, trans. New York: Barnes & Noble, 1972. ISBN 0-389-04166-1. ▸ Chronicle of dynamic economic growth of Second Empire and retrenchment thereafter. Focuses on entrepreneurship and innovations in business organization. [LRB]

26.285 Roger Price. *The modernization of rural France: communications networks and agricultural market structures in nineteenth-century France.* New York: St. Martin's, 1983. ISBN 0-312-54302-6. ▸ Survey of agricultural production and markets before and after railroad expansion in second half of century. Examines impact of railroad on ending subsistence crises after 1850s and farmers' reorientation of production for market demand. [LLC]

EDUCATION AND SCIENTIFIC INSTITUTIONS

26.286 Robert D. Anderson. *Education in France, 1848–1870.* Oxford: Clarendon, 1975. ISBN 0-19-827311-8. ▸ Standard study integrating political, administrative, and social history, during dynamic period of educational growth and initiatives. Chronological parameters lead to exaggeration of initiatives of Second Empire. [PJH]

26.287 Donald N. Baker and Patrick J. Harrigan, eds. *The making of Frenchmen: current directions in the history of education in France, 1679–1979.* Waterloo, Ont.: Historical Reflections Press, 1980. (Historical reflections, Directions, 2.) ISBN 0-88898-024-8, ISSN 0315-7997. ▸ Thirty-four previously unpublished articles (twenty-two in French), divided by levels of schooling, teaching, and parallel education. Historiographical survey and extensive bibliography. Focuses on social history and higher education. [PJH]

26.288 Linda L. Clark. *Schooling the daughters of Marianne: textbooks and the socialization of girls in modern French primary schools.* Albany: State University of New York Press, 1984. ISBN 0-87395-787-3 (cl), 0-87395-786-5 (pbk). ▸ Pioneering analysis of images of women in schoolbooks, illustrating political and social preoccupations of French political and pedagogical leaders. Persistent sexism as pronounced as class or other distinctions, despite diminishment after World War II. [PJH]

26.289 Robert Fox and George Weisz, eds. *The organization of science and technology in France, 1808–1914.* New York: Cambridge University Press, 1980. ISBN 0-521-23234-1. ▸ Ten essays by specialists providing introduction to scholarship on scientific institutions. Contends nineteenth-century science and technology were vital, not declining and inferior to German efforts. Treats university science, medicine, research, provincial learned societies, and careers. [HWP]

26.290 François Furet and Jacques Ozouf. *Reading and writing: literacy in France from Calvin to Jules Ferry.* Cambridge: Cambridge University Press, 1982. ISBN 0-521-22389-X (cl), 0-521-27402-8 (pbk). ▸ Pathbreaking study of literacy in itself rather than as adjunct to other topics. Emphasizes private initiatives and missionary activity more than state initiatives. Northeastern departments led. Treats gender, urbanization, and social factors. [PJH]

26.291 Robert Gildea. *Education in provincial France, 1800–1914: a study of three departments.* Oxford: Clarendon, 1983. ISBN 0-19-821941-5. ▸ Compares culture and society of regions to national trends. Questions correctly importance of religion and national state, showing local initiatives' importance, but in atypical departments. Best read with national histories. [PJH]

26.292 Raymond Grew and Patrick J. Harrigan. *School, state, and society: the growth of elementary schooling in nineteenth-century France—a quantitative analysis.* Ann Arbor: University of Michigan Press, 1991. ISBN 0-472-10095-5. ▸ Examination of availability of schooling, enrollments, and teachers; compares Catholic and lay, boys and girls, public and private, and primary and secondary patterns. Early nineteenth-century schooling and literacy more developed than once believed; private initiatives often precede national ones. [PJH]

26.293 Patrick J. Harrigan. *Mobility, elites, and secondary education in French society of the Second Empire.* Waterloo, Ont.: Wilfrid Laurier University Press, 1980. ISBN 0-88920-087-4. ▸ Unique quantitative analysis of 27,700 high school graduates' career aspirations, first jobs, and fathers' occupations. Schools open to petite bourgeoisie and upward mobility possible, although father's occupation important; avenue to professional elites. [PJH]

26.294 Sandra Horvath-Peterson. *Victor Duruy and French education: liberal reform in the Second Empire.* Baton Rouge: Louisiana State University Press, 1984. ISBN 0-8071-1157-0. ▸ Sympathetic biography of France's most important mid-nineteenth-century education leader. Good on biographical detail, administration, relations with church, and innovations, but superficial on particular aspects of system. [PJH]

26.295 Jo Burr Margadant. *Madame le professeur: women educators in the Third Republic.* Princeton: Princeton University Press, 1990. ISBN 0-691-05593-9 (cl), 0-691-00864-7 (pbk). ▸ Pioneering analysis of social origins and careers of 213 women professors in first generation of women public secondary school teachers. Examines differences between male and female curricula. Women professors maintained independence in careers and private life. [PJH]

26.296 Françoise Mayeur. *L'éducation des filles en France au dix-neuvième siècle.* Paris: Hachette, 1979. ISBN 2-01-003824-X. ▸ Good introductory survey to education legislation and administrative divisions by gender. Gender stereotypes prevailed despite innovations within girls' schools. Recognizes nuns' contributions to girls' schooling. [PJH]

26.297 Françoise Mayeur. *L'enseignement secondaire des jeunes filles sous la Troisième République.* Paris: Fondation Nationale des Sciences Politiques, 1977. ISBN 2-724-60384-2 (cl), 2-724-60384-4 (pbk). ▸ Broad, introductory discussion of administrative, political, and social history of girls' public secondary schooling; less on pupils. Schools perpetuated bourgeois gender stereotypes but provided entry to teaching. Program aligned with male secondary schools after 1924. [PJH]

26.298 Joseph N. Moody. *French education since Napoleon.* Syracuse, N.Y.: Syracuse University Press, 1978. ISBN 0-8156-2193-0. ▸ Succinct cultural, political, and social history incorporating new research findings through mid-1970s. Chronological organization but attentive to longer trends. Critical of elitism and increasing centralization of public school system. [PJH]

26.299 Mary Jo Nye. *Science in the provinces: scientific communities and provincial leadership in France, 1860–1930.* Berkeley: University of California Press, 1986. ISBN 0-520-05561-6. ▸ Specialized monograph on university science faculties in Bordeaux, Grenoble, Lyon, Nancy, and Toulouse. Contends provincial scientists as productive as German and, sometimes, Parisian counterparts. Local economic and cultural factors related to scientific specializations. [HWP]

26.300 Jacques Ozouf and Mona Ozouf. *La république des instituteurs.* Paris: Gallimard, 1992. ISBN 2-02-018899-6. ▸ Important, massive study of a generation of primary school teachers, based on questionnaires completed by over two thousand teachers whose careers began before 1914. Treats family background, culture and values, politics, unionization, and gender differences. [LLC]

26.301 R. R. Palmer. *The improvement of humanity: education and the French Revolution.* Princeton: Princeton University Press, 1985. ISBN 0-691-05434-7. ▸ Modernization, nationalization, and secularization triumphed over original revolutionary democratic ideals. Sympathetic to Revolution's ultimate achievements, but revisionist in concluding that Revolution was not only immediately disruptive to education but also often consistent with prior educational trends. [PJH]

26.302 Louis Henri Parias, ed. *Histoire générale de l'enseignement et de l'éducation en France.* Vol. 3: *De la Révolution à l'école républicaine.* Vol. 4: *L'école et la famille dans une société en mutation.* Paris: Nouvelle Librairie de France, 1981. ▸ Most detailed syntheses of French educational history. Chronological, administrative, and political approach and emphasis on state more traditional than North American scholarship. Unique in examination of experiences outside classroom. [PJH]

26.303 Harry W. Paul. *From knowledge to power: the rise of the science empire in France, 1860–1939.* Cambridge: Cambridge University Press, 1985. ISBN 0-521-26504-5. ▸ Informative essays on modernization and expansion of scientific institutions. Special emphasis on university reform, partly in response to middle-class demand. Biology and agriculture discussed more extensively than other sciences. [HWP]

26.304 Antoine Prost. *Histoire de l'enseignement en France, 1800–1967.* 2d ed. Paris: Colin, 1970. ISBN 2-200-31079-X. ▸ First attempt to survey entire educational system. Topically organized, linking schooling and social-class divisions; useful tables, brief documents. Excellent introduction but superseded by Parias's volumes (26.302) and more recent monographs. [PJH]

26.305 Robert J. Smith. *The École Normale Supérieure and the Third Republic.* Albany: State University of New York Press, 1982. ISBN 0-87395-540-4 (cl), 0-87395-541-2 (pbk). ‣ Specialized study of rise and post–World War II decline of *grande école* that prepared educational elite. 3,200 graduates from middle classes pursued abstract curriculum and became intellectually conservative. [PJH]

26.306 John E. Talbott. *The politics of educational reform in France, 1918–1940.* Princeton: Princeton University Press, 1969. ‣ Survey of ideological and political divisions within post-1918 French politics and education debates. Democratic efforts to create common primary schooling failed with split between Radicals and Socialists but presaged Fifth Republic reforms. [PJH]

26.307 George Weisz. *The emergence of modern universities in France, 1863–1914.* Princeton: Princeton University Press, 1983. ISBN 0-691-05375-8 (cl), 0-691-10197-3 (pbk). ‣ Comprehensive, scholarly study of how reform after 1870–71 defeat led by 1896 to sixteen universities that were research centers rather than examining boards. Rivalries inhibited change, but successful reform challenges thesis of stalemate society. [PJH]

FAMILY, CHILDHOOD, AND DEMOGRAPHY

26.308 Maurice Crubellier. *L'enfance et la jeunesse dans la société française, 1800–1950.* Paris: Colin, 1979. ISBN 2-200-31023-4. ‣ Survey of transformation of institutions and attitudes affecting children from those of family, village, and parish to those of industry and secular republican state. Treats socialization and disciplining of youth in education, sports, hygiene, work, and leisure. [RGF]

26.309 Margaret H. Darrow. *Revolution in the house: family, class, and inheritance in southern France, 1775–1825.* Princeton: Princeton University Press, 1990. ISBN 0-691-05562-9. ‣ Detailed, technical analysis of families' choice of heir, examined by household and social origin. Family inheritance strategies were altered by changes in law, nature of work, property, and regional economies. [RGF]

26.310 Jacques Dupâquier et al. *Histoire de la population française.* Vol. 3: *De 1789 à 1914.* Vol. 4: *De 1914 à nos jours.* Paris: Presses Universitaires de France, 1988. ISBN 2-13-041928-3 (v. 3), 2-13-042070-2 (v. 4). ‣ Comprehensive overview of demographic change treating fertility, depopulation, eugenics, and geographical and social mobility. Examines changes in family structure and impact of urbanization, medicine, laws, social policies, and wartime dislocations. [RGF]

26.311 Rachel G. Fuchs. *Abandoned children: foundlings and child welfare in nineteenth-century France.* Albany: State University of New York Press, 1984. ISBN 0-87395-748-2 (cl), 0-87395-750-4 (pbk). ‣ Pioneering study of public policy and attitudes toward child abandonment. Treats foundling homes, wet-nursing, foster care of children from birth to adulthood, mortality, life prospects, and public policy's evolution and impact on mothers and children. [RGF]

26.312 Colin Heywood. *Childhood in nineteenth-century France: work, health, and education among the classes populaires.* Cambridge: Cambridge University Press, 1988. ISBN 0-521-35038-7. ‣ Best available study of changes in children's agrarian and industrial labor within and apart from family. Treats rural and urban education in school and workplace. Details reasons for 1841 and 1874 child labor legislation. [RGF]

26.313 Katherine A. Lynch. *Family, class, and ideology in early industrial France: social policy and the working-class family, 1825–1848.* Madison: University of Wisconsin Press, 1988. ISBN 0-299-11790-1 (cl), 0-299-11794-4 (pbk). ‣ Concise introduction to social Catholics' and secular economists' perspectives on working-class family, showing impact of moral attitudes on institu-

tions and charity in Lille, Mulhouse, and Rouen. Examines illegitimacy, child abandonment, and children's industrial work. [RGF]

26.314 Angus McLaren. *Sexuality and the social order: the debate over the fertility of women and workers in France, 1770–1920.* New York: Holmes & Meier, 1983. ISBN 0-8419-0744-7. ‣ Pathbreaking general study of attitudes toward sexuality and opposition to birth control expressed by Catholics, physicians, socialists, moralists. Also examines rival view of Paul Robin and other radicals advocating Malthusianism. Debate analyzed within context of fertility decline. [RGF]

26.315 Roderick Phillips. *Family breakdown in late eighteenth-century France: divorces in Rouen, 1792–1803.* Oxford: Clarendon, 1980. ISBN 0-19-822572-5. ‣ Analyzes cases of divorce (legal option newly available during Revolution) to examine nature of family conflict. Among many insights is significant role of neighbors as support system. [JRC]

26.316 Catherine Rollet-Echalier. *La politique à l'égard de la petite enfance sous la Troisième République.* 2 vols. Paris: Presses Universitaires de France, 1990. ISBN 2-7332-0127-1. ‣ Comprehensive survey of dominant Third Republic political attitudes affecting children as influenced by ideologies, medical discoveries, Pasteurian revolution. Declining birth rate prompted policies, laws, and facilities to prevent infant mortality and to protect children. [RGF]

26.317 Martine Segalen. *Love and power in the peasant family: rural France in the nineteenth century.* Sarah Matthews, trans. Chicago: University of Chicago Press, 1983. ISBN 0-226-74451-5. ‣ General study of relationships between husband and wife including rituals of marriage, baptism, and death. Reveals complementary functions for each member of rural family and relates household strategies to land and community. [RGF]

26.318 George D. Sussman. *Selling mothers' milk: the wet-nursing business in France, 1715–1914.* Urbana: University of Illinois Press, 1982. ISBN 0-252-00919-3. ‣ General study of wet-nursing as important social phenomenon. Families paid women living outside cities to wet-nurse infants. Presents economic and cultural explanations for acceptance and decline of practice. [RGF]

26.319 Etienne Van de Walle. *The female population of France in the nineteenth century: a reconstruction of eighty-two departments.* Princeton: Princeton University Press, 1974. ISBN 0-691-09360-1. ‣ Valuable statistical reference work on female population, omitting departments of the Seine (Paris) and Seine-Inférieure, correcting official census figures. Argues that decline in French birth rate appears to have preceded modernization. [KMO]

26.320 Lee Shai Weissbach. *Child labor reform in nineteenth-century France: assuring the future harvest.* Baton Rouge: Louisiana State University Press, 1989. ISBN 0-8071-1483-9. ‣ Specialized analysis of development and implementation of child labor reform legislation of 1841 and 1874 in different areas of France. Shows persistent difficulties in enactment and enforcement. [RGF]

SEE ALSO
22.457 Jacques Donzelot. *The policing of families.*

RELIGION

26.321 Odile Arnold. *Le corps et l'âme: la vie des religieuses au dix-neuvième siècle.* Paris: Seuil, 1984. ISBN 2-02-006656-4. ‣ Pioneering study of collective lives of Catholic nuns in nineteenth-century France. Unifying theme of ideas about body and separation of body and soul in nuns' thought and daily existence. [KMO]

26.322 Jean Baubérot. *Le retour des Huguenots: la vitalité Protestante, dix-neuvième–vingtième siècle.* Paris: Cerf, 1985. ISBN 2-204-02405-8. ‣ Good introduction to French Reformed church after

Napoleonic Concordat of 1802. Most important for stress on role of Calvinism in shaping laic state, individualism, and social policy. [SCH]

26.323 Gérard Cholvy and Y. M. Hilaire. *Histoire religieuse de la France contemporaine.* Vol. 1: *1800–1880.* Vol. 2: *1880–1930.* Vol. 3: *1930–1988.* 3 vols. Toulouse: Privat, 1985–88. ISBN 2-7089-5321-4 (v. 1), 2-7089-5330-3 (v. 2), 2-7089-5344-3 (v. 3). ▸ Detailed analysis of both institutions and popular belief. Within LeBras school of religious sociology and anthropology, synthesizes best of French research, adding original contributions of authors. [PJH]

26.324 Adrien Dansette. *Religious history of modern France.* 2 vols. New York: Herder & Herder, 1961. ▸ Fullest account in English. History of institutions and church-state relations from liberal Catholic perspective. Concludes that dechristianization and secularization resulted from church's failure to answer needs of modern society. [PJH]

26.325 André Encrevé. *Les Protestants en France de 1800 à nos jours: histoire d'une réintégration.* Paris: Stock, 1985. ISBN 2-234-01815-3. ▸ Survey of Calvinist and Lutheran reestablishment in France. Good basic introduction to French Protestantism, stressing nineteenth century. [SCH]

26.326 Ralph Gibson. *A social history of French Catholicism, 1789–1914.* London: Routledge, 1989. ISBN 0-415-01619-3. ▸ Survey of best secondary material regarding popular religion. Incorporates local French studies of religious anthropology for Old Regime. Stresses distance of reformed Tridentine clergy from urban masses in nineteenth century. [PJH]

26.327 John Hellman. *Emmanuel Mounier and the new Catholic Left, 1930–1950.* Toronto: University of Toronto Press, 1981. ISBN 0-8020-2399-1. ▸ Intellectual biography of founder and editor of *Esprit,* leading French Catholic leftist journal, espousing personalism as alternative to laissez-faire liberalism and communism. [PJH]

26.328 Thomas A. Kselman. *Miracles and prophecies in nineteenth-century France.* New Brunswick, N.J.: Rutgers University Press, 1983. ISBN 0-8135-0963-7. ▸ Stimulating scholarly analysis of importance and intensity of informal religion through study of shrines, miracle cults, and pilgrimages. Traditional religious fervor intensified alongside dechristianization. Hierarchy adopted Lourdes after initial skepticism because of popular worship. [PJH]

26.329 Claude Langlois. *Le Catholicisme au féminin: les congrégations françaises à supérieure générale au dix-neuvième siècle.* Paris: Cerf, 1984. ISBN 2-204-02215-2. ▸ Thorough and only account of expanding women's religious orders, especially teaching and nursing. Essential guide, more encyclopedic than interpretive. Emphasizes institution more than members. [PJH]

26.330 André Latreille et al. *Histoire du Catholicisme en France: la période contemporaine (du dix-huitième siècle à nos jours).* Paris: Spes, 1962. ▸ Survey using traditional approaches treats response of church to Revolution, dechristianization, and secularization. Decline of formal religious practice. Church more responsive to social and political trends in twentieth century than in nineteenth. [PJH]

26.331 John McManners. *Church and state in France, 1870–1914.* 1972 ed. New York: Harper & Row, 1973. ISBN 0-06-136114-3. ▸ Traditional in emphasis on political rather than social history but excellent, sensitive introduction to process of secularization. Critical of reactionary elements within Catholic church hierarchy. [PJH]

26.332 John McManners. *The French Revolution and the church.* 1969 ed. Westport, Conn.: Greenwood, 1982. ISBN 0-313-23074-9. ▸ Less sympathetic to church than recent histories of revolutionary years. Discusses dechristianization and revolutionary

cults. Revolutionary experience set church's conservative stance for nineteenth century. [PJH]

26.333 Timothy Tackett. *Religion, revolution, and regional culture in eighteenth-century France: the ecclesiastical oath of 1791.* Princeton: Princeton University Press, 1986. ISBN 0-691-05470-3 (pbk). ▸ Exhaustive study of oath required of clergy by revolutionaries' Civil Constitution of the Clergy, 1790. Important analysis of resistance to or acceptance of oath demonstrates regional patterns and similarities continuing into twentieth century. [JRC]

SOCIAL CLASSES
General Studies

26.334 Henri Mendras. *Social change in modern France: towards a cultural anthropology of the Fifth Republic.* Cambridge: Cambridge University Press, 1991. ISBN 0-521-39108-3 (cl), 0-521-39998-X (pbk). ▸ Stimulating, up-to-date survey of past thirty years, which saw transformation as revolutionary as 1789: changes in social classes, army, church, education, and relationships between sexes and generations. Post-1968 moral revolution meant more freedom to shape individual identities. [BMG]

26.335 Roger Price. *A social history of nineteenth-century France.* New York: Holmes & Meier, 1987. ISBN 0-8419-1165-7 (cl), 0-8419-1166-5 (pbk). ▸ Strong synthesis of recent literature. Emphasizes impact of economic and demographic change on political structure. Covers elites as well as lower classes. [LRB]

26.336 Barnett Singer. *Village notables in nineteenth-century France: priests, mayors, schoolmasters.* Albany: State University of New York Press, 1983. ISBN 0-87395-629-X (cl), 0-87395-630-3 (pbk). ▸ Unique survey, descriptive rather than quantitative, of background, role, and influence of rural priests, mayors, and schoolmasters. Special emphasis on conflict between priests and mayors allied with teachers during heyday of Third Republic anticlericalism. [LLC]

Middle Classes and Professions

26.337 Christophe Charle. *Les élites de la République, 1880–1900.* Paris: Fayard, 1987. ISBN 2-213-02027-2. ▸ Important, massive study documenting Third Republic's altered patterns of recruiting elites. Quantitative analysis of social origins, education, wealth, and marriages of businessmen, high-ranking civil servants, and academic intellectuals. University elites most democratized, business least. [LLC]

26.338 Adeline Daumard. *La bourgeoisie parisienne de 1815 à 1848.* Paris: Service d'Édition et de Vente des Publications de l'Éducation, 1963. (Démographie et sociétés, 8.) ▸ Bourgeois values (independence, advancement, enrichment, work) dominated after Revolution. Bourgeoisie (15 percent of the Paris population) heterogeneous yet cohesive; valued mobility, but society's rigid structure, 1815–48, led middle bourgeoisie to revolt in 1848. Classic study. [ELN]

26.339 Gerald L. Geison, ed. *Professions and the French state, 1700–1900.* Philadelphia: University of Pennsylvania Press, 1984. ISBN 0-8122-7912-3. ▸ Five essays introducing recent scholarship on state's role in history of engineering, academic science, and medical professions. Emphasizes importance of *grandes écoles* and state educational credentials and certification in contrast to Anglo-American assumptions about professional autonomy. [LLC]

26.340 David M. Gordon. *Merchants and capitalists: industrialization and provincial politics in mid-nineteenth-century France.* University: University of Alabama Press, 1985. ISBN 0-8173-0210-7. ▸ Significant monograph on how businessmen's political behavior was affected by social and economic modernization.

Indicates more wealth led to growing opposition among much of bourgeoisie, who chafed at government regulations. [NKI]

26.341 Yvonne Knibiehler et al. *Cornettes et blouses blanches: les infirmières dans la société française (1880–1980)*. Paris: Hachette, 1984. ISBN 2-01-010198-7. ▸ Pioneering inquiry into development of major women's profession in France, encompassing lay nurses and religious personnel. Draws on both documents and oral histories to dramatize changes in profession. [KMO]

26.342 Anne Martin-Fugier. *La bourgeoise: femme au temps de Paul Bourget*. Paris: Grasset et Fasquelle, 1983. ISBN 2-246-28521-6. ▸ Unique study of images of bourgeois women and their changing roles around 1900, especially as seen in fiction and memoirs of men and women writers. [LLC]

26.343 Bonnie G. Smith. *Ladies of the leisure class: the bourgeoises of northern France in the nineteenth century*. Princeton: Princeton University Press, 1981. ISBN 0-691-05330-8 (cl), 0-691-10121-3 (pbk). ▸ Striking discussion of bourgeois women's domestic culture. Treats reproduction, household management, and religion. Industrialization moved industrialists' wives from workplace to home, where they maintained preindustrial religious culture, including charity and respect for hierarchy. [RGF]

26.344 Peter N. Stearns. *Paths to authority: the middle class and the industrial labor force in France, 1820–48*. Urbana: University of Illinois Press, 1978. ISBN 0-252-00633-X. ▸ Important survey contending that French entrepreneurs were paternalistic because French labor scarcer than English. Downplays employers' fear of revolution. Industry resisted reform while liberal rhetoric encouraged discontent. After 1850, workers became restive; paternalism became discipline. [ELN]

Nobility

26.345 David Higgs. *Nobles in nineteenth-century France: the practice of inegalitarianism*. Baltimore: Johns Hopkins University Press, 1987. ISBN 0-8018-3061-3. ▸ Contends nobles did not merge with bourgeoisie to form new class of notables as Jardin and Tudesq argued (26.35). Not swept away by Revolution, nobility imposed their sociability, politics, and taste on internally divided country. Rich yet inconsistent argument. [ELN]

Working Classes

26.346 Elinor A. Accampo. *Industrialization, family life, and class relations: Saint-Chamond, 1815–1914*. Berkeley: University of California Press, 1989. ISBN 0-520-06095-4. ▸ Innovative examination of demography and labor conditions in working-class community. Brings techniques of family reconstitution to study of class formation. [LRB]

26.347 Kathryn E. Amdur. *Syndicalist legacy: trade unions and politics in two French cities in the era of World War I*. Urbana: University of Illinois Press, 1986. ISBN 0-252-01238-0. ▸ Specialist study of survival of antipolitical labor traditions in twentieth century. Blends local social history with national ideological analysis. [LRB]

26.348 Lenard R. Berlanstein. *The working people of Paris, 1871–1914*. Baltimore: Johns Hopkins University Press, 1984. ISBN 0-8018-3241-1. ▸ Comprehensive but concise survey of changes in conditions on and off the job for laborers and white-collar employees. Challenges optimistic claims about improving living standards and leisure. [LRB]

26.349 Lenard R. Berlanstein. "Working with language: the linguistic turn in French labor history." *Comparative studies in society and history* 33.2 (1991) 426–40. ISSN 0010-4175. ▸ Historiographical essay reviewing recent works that revise labor history from cultural perspective. Highlights contributions of poststructuralism and feminist theory. [LRB]

26.350 Herrick Chapman. *State capitalism and working-class radicalism in the French aircraft industry*. Berkeley: University of California Press, 1991. ISBN 0-520-05953-0 (cl), 0-520-07125-5 (pbk). ▸ Original and convincing study which accounts for strength of communism among factory laborers in twentieth century. Focus on state policy in shaping industrial relations. [LRB]

26.351 Louis Chevalier. *Laboring classes and dangerous classes in Paris during the first half of the nineteenth century*. Frank Jellinek, trans. New York: Fertig, 1973. ISBN 0-86527-114-3. ▸ Bleak picture of urban crisis pointing to importance of demographic analysis for urban history. Considers deterioration of urban conditions as influx of poor immigrants overwhelmed capital. [LRB]

26.352 Lorraine Coons. *Women homeworkers in the Parisian garment industry, 1860–1915*. New York: Garland, 1985. ISBN 0-8240-8035-1. ▸ Best available examination of Parisian women's home industrial work, focusing on female heads of households and social attitudes. Emphasizes centrality of economic, not moral, issues: male workers viewed women as competitors, employers encouraged piecework system. [KMO]

26.353 Alain Cottereau. "The distinctiveness of working-class cultures in France, 1848–1914." In *Working-class formation: nineteenth-century patterns in Western Europe and the United States*. Ira Katznelson and Aristide Zolberg, eds., pp. 111–54. Princeton: Princeton University Press, 1986. ISBN 0-691-05485-1 (cl), 0-691-10207-4 (pbk). ▸ Innovatively reconceptualizes problem of why union membership was lower in France than in England or Germany. Argues for importance of informal organization among protesting workers. [LRB]

26.354 Gary S. Cross. *Immigrant workers in industrial France: the making of a new laboring class*. Philadelphia: Temple University Press, 1983. ISBN 0-87722-300-9. ▸ Examination of influx of southern and eastern Europeans and North Africans in response to interwar labor shortages. Considers state policies and responses of political parties. [LRB]

26.355 Madeleine Guilbert. *Les fonctions des femmes dans l'industrie*. Paris: Mouton, 1966. (École Pratique des Hautes Études, Section des sciences économiques et sociales, Études européennes, 4.) ▸ Important historical and sociological study of women's roles and sexual division of labor in twentieth-century industrial production, focusing on metal industries. Long historical introduction to issue of women's work. [KMO]

26.356 Gay L. Gullickson. *Spinners and weavers of Auffay: rural industry and the sexual division of labor in a French village, 1750–1850*. Cambridge: Cambridge University Press, 1986. ISBN 0-521-32280-4. ▸ Pioneering study illuminating broad issues for proto-industrialization by focusing on gendered division of labor in a Normandy village. Discussion of women's arrival in formerly male occupations (weaving and agricultural day labor) and new opportunities for women in dressmaking. [KMO]

26.357 Michael Hanagan. *The logic of solidarity: artisans and industrial workers in three French towns, 1871–1914*. Urbana: University of Illinois Press, 1980. ISBN 0-252-00758-1 (pbk). ▸ Stimulating, detailed analysis of conditions permitting labor organization in three towns and department of Loire. Stresses importance of alliances among skilled and unskilled workers. [LRB]

26.358 Patricia J. Hilden. *Working women and socialist politics in France, 1880–1914: a regional study*. Oxford: Clarendon, 1986. ISBN 0-19-821935-0. ▸ Controversial examination of female factory workers' role in active local labor movement in department of Nord. Argues for importance of work, rather than family, in establishing political identities. [LRB]

26.359 Christopher H. Johnson. *Utopian communism in France: Cabet and the Icarians, 1839–1851*. Ithaca, N.Y.: Cornell University Press, 1974. ISBN 0-8014-0895-4. ▸ Best study of workers' movement led by Étienne Cabet. Attracting perhaps 100,000 skilled, proud, literate urban artisans, Cabet's communism awakened working-class consciousness. Authoritarian and modeled on Christianity, its class collaborationism ill-suited to reigning spirit of democracy, secularism, and class struggle. [ELN]

26.360 Steven L. Kaplan and Cynthia J. Koepp, eds. *Work in France: representations, meaning, organization, and practice.* Ithaca, N.Y.: Cornell University Press, 1986. ISBN 0-8014-1697-3. ▸ Innovative collection of essays by leading scholars covering labor from eighteenth to twentieth century. Presents wide variety of approaches. [LRB]

26.361 Yves Lequin. *Les ouvriers de la région lyonnaise, 1848–1914.* 2 vols. Lyon: Presses Universitaires de Lyon, 1977. ISBN 2-7297-0004-8 (v. 1), 2-7297-0006-4 (v. 2). ▸ Exhaustive empirical analysis of working-class development in important industrial area. Follows structural changes as industrial labor gradually replaced artisanal labor. [LRB]

26.362 Theresa M. McBride. *The domestic revolution: the modernization of household service in England and France, 1820–1920.* New York: Holmes & Meier, 1976. ISBN 0-8419-0248-8. ▸ Study of female servants with comparisons to England. Argues that domestic service enabled working-class women to acquire middle-class habits and attitudes. Implications for modernization theory and class mobility not previously considered. [KMO]

26.363 Theresa M. McBride. "French women and trade unionism: the first hundred years." In *The world of women's trade unionism: comparative historical essays.* Norbert C. Soldon, ed., pp. 35–56. Westport, Conn.: Greenwood, 1985. ISBN 0-313-22792-6. ▸ Survey of women's participation in labor agitation since 1884 legalization of unions. Argues that separate organizations of women nurtured sense of solidarity and attention to women's specific problems as workers, wives, and mothers. [KMO]

26.364 Bernard Moss. *The origins of the French labor movement, 1830–1914: the socialism of skilled workers.* 1976 ed. Berkeley: University of California Press, 1980. ISBN 0-520-04101-1. ▸ Stimulating effort to root working-class institutions and ideas in experience of artisans facing gradual industrial change. Insists on producers' associations as key to workers' aspirations. [LRB]

26.365 Gérard Noiriel. *Workers in French society in the nineteenth and twentieth centuries.* Helen McPhail, trans. Oxford: Berg; distributed by St. Martin's, 1990. ISBN 0-85496-610-2. ▸ One of few general surveys of wage earners. Stresses gradualness of class formation and fragility of class traditions. [LRB]

26.366 Michelle Perrot. *Workers on strike, France 1871–1890.* Chris Turner, trans. New Haven: Yale University Press, 1987. ISBN 0-300-03849-6. ▸ Uses profiles of thousands of job actions to analyze working-class protest. Abridgement of important French book *Les ouvriers en grève.* Sheds much light on working-class culture. [LRB]

26.367 Jacques Rancière. *The nights of labor: the workers' dream in nineteenth-century France.* John Drury, trans. Donald Reid, Introduction. Philadelphia: Temple University Press, 1989. ISBN 0-87722-625-3. ▸ Author a Platonist; argues that workers wanted to excel in thoughtplace, not workplace, because no workplace can be humanizing. Only intellectual rebels can be free. Maverick, challenging thesis. Contrast Merriman 26.120, Agulhon 26.115, 26.116, Price 26.121, and Johnson 26.359. [ELN]

26.368 William M. Reddy. *The rise of market culture: the textile trade and French society, 1750–1900.* Cambridge: Cambridge University Press, 1984. ISBN 0-521-25653-4 (cl), 0-521-34779-3 (pbk). ▸ Original but controversial analysis of evolution of work and community among factory laborers. Draws on cultural

anthropology and linguistic theory to provide non-Marxian interpretation of their protest. [LRB]

26.369 Donald Reid. *The miners of Decazeville: a genealogy of deindustrialization.* Cambridge, Mass.: Harvard University Press, 1986. ISBN 0-674-57634-9. ▸ Covers evolution of work and local politics. Stresses role of republican state in shaping miners' socialism. Study notable for its long-term perspective. [LRB]

26.370 Frederick F. Ridley. *Revolutionary syndicalism in France: the direct action of its time.* Cambridge: Cambridge University Press, 1970. ISBN 0-521-07907-1. ▸ Basic introduction to principles and practices of Confédération Générale du Travail (umbrella organization of unions), 1902–14. Insists on syndicalism as workers' union movement, but attends mainly to theories and theorists, with little on rank-and-file activities. See also Stearns 26.376. [JFS]

26.371 George Ross. *Workers and Communists in France: from the Popular Front to Eurocommunism.* Berkeley: University of California Press, 1982. ISBN 0-520-04075-9. ▸ Best available study focusing on relations between Communist party and France's largest trade union, Confédération Générale du Travail (CGT). Stresses ways party control limited success of trade union activity. [LRB]

26.372 Joan Wallach Scott. *The glassworkers of Carmaux: French craftsmen and political action in a nineteenth-century city.* Cambridge, Mass.: Harvard University Press, 1974. ISBN 0-674-35440-0 (cl), 0-674-35441-9 (pbk). ▸ Classic study of how elite group of artisans became class-conscious militants. Finds key in threat of proletarianization. [LRB]

26.373 William H. Sewell, Jr. *Structure and mobility: the men and women of Marseille, 1820–1870.* Cambridge: Cambridge University Press, 1985. ISBN 0-521-26237-2. ▸ One of the rare quantitative analyses of intergenerational change in social status for a French city. Finds immigrants were relatively more successful than native workers. [LRB]

26.374 William H. Sewell, Jr. *Work and revolution in France: the language of labor from the Revolution to 1848.* Cambridge: Cambridge University Press, 1980. ISBN 0-521-23442-5 (cl), 0-521-29951-9 (pbk). ▸ Innovative study showing how political and social changes brought workers to refashion corporate idiom into class consciousness. Draws on cultural anthropology and insists on autonomy of cultural forces in creating class. [LRB]

26.375 Edward Shorter and Charles Tilly. *Strikes in France, 1830–1968.* London: Cambridge University Press, 1974. ISBN 0-521-20293-0. ▸ Comparative quantitative study providing long-term perspective on development of workers' protest. Argues that strikes were intended to make state intervene in industrial relations. [LRB]

26.376 Peter N. Stearns. *Revolutionary syndicalism and French labor: a cause without rebels.* New Brunswick, N.J.: Rutgers University Press, 1971. ISBN 0-8135-0688-3. ▸ Controversial thesis that syndicalism was insignificant movement. Examines strike activity and insists that many French workers were more modern and less revolutionary than assumed. Ridley 26.370 offers opposing views. [JFS]

RURAL, REGIONAL, AND URBAN HISTORY
Rural and Regional

26.377 Laura Levine Frader. *Peasants and protest: agricultural workers, politics, and unions in the Aude, 1850–1914.* Berkeley: University of California Press, 1991. ISBN 0-520-06809-2. ▸ Scholarly monograph linking economic change and Mediterranean left-wing politics in a wine-producing region. Focus on village of Coursan with economy based on peasant workers, small proprietors, and agrarian capitalists. Also includes women's work and family roles. [LLC]

26.378 Peter M. Jones. *The peasantry in the French Revolution.* Cambridge: Cambridge University Press, 1988. ISBN 0-521-33070-X (cl), 0-521-33716-X (pbk). ‣ Synthetic, well-informed work covering much essential ground. Defends class-based position on peasantry, as defined by Lefebvre (26.62), including notion that cultivators were collectivists and hostile to capitalism. [JRC]

26.379 Peter M. Jones. *Politics and rural society: the southern Massif Central, c. 1750–1880.* New York: Cambridge University Press, 1985. ISBN 0-521-25797-2. ‣ Specialized monograph on society, economy, family, culture, and politics in harsh highland environment of South-Central France. Political interpretation disputes thesis of 1848 watershed; patronage and kinship retarded national politics permeating culturally backward region until Third Republic. [LLC]

26.380 Etienne Juillard et al. *Apogée et crise de la civilisation paysanne, 1789–1914* and *La fin de la France paysanne de 1914 à nos jours.* Vols. 3 and 4 of *Histoire de la France rurale.* Georges Duby and Armand Wallon, eds. Paris: Seuil, 1976–77. ISBN 2-02-004637-7. ‣ Richly illustrated, collaborative, documented survey. Treats impact on countryside of local and national politics, roads, railroads, and schools. Sees 1880–1914 as modernizing watershed. Volume 4 treats rural syndicalism, changes in family life, and labor. [LLC]

26.381 James R. Lehning. *The peasants of Marlhes: economic development and family organization in nineteenth-century France.* Chapel Hill: University of North Carolina Press, 1980. ISBN 0-8078-1441-3. ‣ Specialized, detailed analysis of rural family's economy and structure—including inheritance, life stages, family roles, migration—within framework of rural community's economic change, 1850–1900. Families adapted to economic development, maintaining their objectives. [RGF]

26.382 Jack E. Reece. *The Bretons against France: ethnic minority nationalism in twentieth-century Brittany.* Chapel Hill: University of North Carolina Press, 1977. ISBN 0-8078-1304-4. ‣ Objective study of small Breton regional autonomy movement, originating in largely right-wing, clerical, aristocratic circles; some collaborated with Nazis. More recently, emphasis on cultural goals, left-wing elements, and intellectuals' leading role. [LLC]

26.383 Eugen Joseph Weber. *Peasants into Frenchmen: the modernization of rural France, 1870–1914.* 1976 ed. London: Chatto & Windus, 1979. ISBN 0-7011-2439-3. ‣ Important, stimulating study of popular mentalities; questions assumptions about national identity. Argues Third Republic's transportation, education, and conscription policies finally integrated rural population into nation. Sometimes criticized for impressionistic evidence. [JFS]

26.384 Laurence W. Wylie. *Village in the Vaucluse.* 3d ed. Cambridge, Mass.: Harvard University Press, 1974. ISBN 0-674-93937-9 (cl), 0-674-93936-0 (pbk). ‣ Classic account of life and attitudes in mountainous village, 1950–51, with updates on changes by 1956 and late 1960s. Valuable chapters on family, school, and political views. [LLC]

Urban

26.385 Maurice Agulhon et al. *La ville de l'âge industriel: le cycle haussmannien* and *La ville aujourd'hui: croissance urbaine et crise du citadin.* Vols. 4 and 5 of *Histoire de la France urbaine.* Georges Duby, ed. Paris: Seuil, 1983–85. ISBN 2-02-006493-6 (v. 4), 2-02-008916-5 (v. 5). ‣ Collection of general essays by leading French experts. Covers many aspects of urban life and synthesizes recent research. Richly illustrated; bibliography. [LRB]

26.386 Norma Evenson. *Paris: a century of change, 1878–1978.* New Haven: Yale University Press, 1979. ISBN 0-300-02210-7 (cl), 0-300-02667-6 (pbk). ‣ General survey of physical alterations in growing metropolis. Emphasizes innovations in urban planning and architecture. [LRB]

26.387 John M. Merriman. *The margins of city life: explorations of the French urban frontier, 1815–1851.* New York: Oxford University Press, 1991. ISBN 0-19-506438-0. ‣ Provocative study evoking hard lives of people occupying unstable, denigrated, or illicit positions on fringes of working class. Argues that despised groups shared sense of not belonging. [LRB]

26.388 John M. Merriman. *The red city: Limoges and the French nineteenth century.* New York: Oxford University Press, 1985. ISBN 0-19-503590-9 (cl), 0-19-505682-5 (pbk). ‣ Comprehensive, detailed study of revolutionary social groups in context of urban and industrial change. Stresses autonomy of insurrectionary activity until turn of century. [LRB]

26.389 Leslie Page Moch. *Paths to the city: regional migration in nineteenth-century France.* Beverly Hills, Calif.: Sage, 1983. ISBN 0-8039-1985-9. ‣ Detailed, convincing study of urbanization examining why men and women migrated from villages and small towns to Nîmes. Stresses economic dislocations in hinterlands. [LRB]

26.390 Ann-Louise Shapiro. *Housing the poor of Paris, 1850–1902.* Madison: University of Wisconsin Press, 1985. ISBN 0-299-09880-x. ‣ Best available examination of bourgeois campaign to improve housing conditions for Parisian poor. Stresses how little was accomplished. [LRB]

26.391 Tyler Stovall. *The rise of the Paris red belt.* Berkeley: University of California Press, 1990. ISBN 0-520-06320-1. ‣ Innovative exploration of communist support in working-class suburbs of French capital. Stresses party's success in mobilizing aggrieved homeowners. [LRB]

26.392 Anthony Sutcliffe. *The autumn of central Paris: the defeat of town planning, 1850–1970.* London: Arnold, 1970. ISBN 0-7131-5549-3. ‣ Analysis of social and political forces determining capital's physical development. Explains why central district remained relatively unchanged while key activities shifted westward. Available as photocopy from Ann Arbor: University Microfilms International. [LRB]

WOMEN AND GENDER

26.393 Deirdre Bair. *Simone de Beauvoir: a biography.* New York: Summit, 1990. ISBN 0-671-60681-6. ‣ First contextual study of life and career of famed writer and philosopher whose work, *Second Sex*, helped revive feminism during second half of twentieth century. [KMO]

26.394 Patrick Kay Bidelman. *Pariahs stand up! The founding of the liberal feminist movement in France, 1858–1889.* Westport, Conn.: Greenwood, 1982. ISBN 0-313-23006-4. ‣ First comprehensive study of French campaign for women's rights during Second Empire and early Third Republic, focusing on Maria Deraismes, Léon Richer, and Hubertine Auclert. Sympathetic to women's rights advocates. [KMO]

26.395 Frances Ida Clark. *The position of women in contemporary France.* 1937 ed. Westport, Conn.: Hyperion, 1981. ISBN 0-8305-0101-0. ‣ Comprehensive and still unsurpassed study of women's position in 1930s France. Favors women's rights with emphasis on sexual differences. Strong on impact of Catholic feminists. [KMO]

26.396 Alain Corbin. *Women for hire: prostitution and sexuality in France after 1850.* Alan Sheridan, trans. Cambridge, Mass.: Harvard University Press, 1990. ISBN 0-674-95543-9. ‣ Pioneering, archive-based study of laws, institutions, and practices regulating French prostitution 1850–1914. Analyzes men's debate about commercialized sex as regulatory efforts shifted from prison system to improving public hygiene. Translation of *Les filles de noce: misère sexuelle et prostitution (19e et 20e siècles)* (1978). [KMO]

26.397 Cécile Dauphin et al. "Women's culture and women's power: issues in French women's history." In *Writing women's history: international perspectives.* Karen M. Offen, Ruth Roach Pierson, and Jane Rendall, eds. Camille Garnier, trans., pp. 107–33. Bloomington: Indiana University Press, 1991. ISBN 0-253-34160-4 (cl), 0-253-20651-0 (pbk). ‣ Survey of contributions (mainly French) to women's history. Critique of apolitical orientation of Annales school approach to writing women's history. Calls for inquiry into power relations between women and men. [KMO]

26.398 Claire Duchen. *Feminism in France: from May '68 to Mitterrand.* London: Routledge & Kegan Paul, 1986. ISBN 0-7102-0455-8 (pbk). ‣ Stimulating examination of development of feminist theory and movement (MLF, Mouvement pour la Libération des Femmes) from 1968 rebellion to Mitterrand presidency. Primary focus on university and literary circles. [BMG/KMO]

26.399 Sarah Fishman. *We will wait: wives of French prisoners of war, 1940–1945.* New Haven: Yale University Press, 1991. ISBN 0-300-04774-6. ‣ Groundbreaking organizational study of wives of war prisoners during German occupation of France. Contends these women displayed considerable organizational talent but retained traditional values, emphasizing roles as wives and mothers. [KMO]

26.400 Rachel G. Fuchs. *Poor and pregnant in Paris: strategies for survival in the nineteenth century.* New Brunswick, N.J.: Rutgers University Press, 1992. ISBN 0-8135-1779-6 (cl), 0-8135-1780-X (pbk). ‣ Ambitious, innovative analysis of how changing religious and political attitudes influenced women's reproductive strategies and government policy. Treats institutional childbearing, child-care options, abortion, and infanticide. Highlights personal networks, charity, and development of public welfare. [RGF]

26.401 Felicia Gordon. *The integral feminist: Madeleine Pelletier, 1874–1939.* Minneapolis: University of Minnesota Press, 1990. ISBN 0-8166-1902-6 (cl), 0-8166-1903-4 (pbk). ‣ First scholarly biography of Pelletier, woman physician and socialist-feminist advocate of suffrage and reproductive freedom for women. [KMO]

26.402 Susan K. Grogan. *French socialism and sexual difference: women and the new society, 1803–1844.* 1991 ed. New York: St. Martin's, 1992. ISBN 0-312-07250-3. ‣ Most recent reexamination of utopian socialists' attitudes toward women and gender. Argues sexual difference central to Utopians' understanding of society and social change. [KMO]

26.403 Madelyn Gutwirth. *The twilight of the goddesses: women and representation in the French revolutionary era.* New Brunswick, N.J.: Rutgers University Press, 1992. ISBN 0-8135-1799-0 (cl), 0-8135-1787-7 (pbk). ‣ Landmark study of depictions of women in prints and paintings, texts, and allegory. Argues that such cultural representations were highly political and increasingly detrimental to French women's status after the Revolution. [KMO]

26.404 Steven C. Hause. *Hubertine Auclert: the French suffragette.* New Haven: Yale University Press, 1987. ISBN 0- 300-03845-3. ‣ First scholarly biography in any language of major French campaigner for women's rights, including vote. Complements author's major study of social politics of women's suffrage (26.154). [KMO]

26.405 Laurence Klejman and Florence Rochefort. *L'égalité en marche: le féminisme sous la Troisième République.* Paris: Presses

de la Fondation Nationale des Sciences Politiques and Des Femmes, 1989. ISBN 2-7246-0567-5, 2-7210-0382-8. ‣ Offers state-of-the-art study of French feminist movement, 1870–1940. Emphasizes women's fight for equality on all fronts (education, employment, vote), rather than more recent goal of liberation. [KMO]

26.406 Yvonne Knibiehler and Catherine Fouquet. *La femme et les médecins: analyse historique.* Paris: Hachette, 1983. ISBN 2-01-008299-0. ‣ Important study of French medical attitudes toward women since eighteenth century. Examines social constructions of "feminine nature" based on reproductive physiology, and subsequent challenges to these by women and men alike. [KMO]

26.407 Yvonne Knibiehler and Régine Goutalier. *La femme au temps des colonies.* Paris: Stock, 1985. ISBN 2-234-01806-4. ‣ Pathbreaking inquiry into women's role in French colonialism, both as colonizers and colonized, with particular regard to Africa. [KMO]

26.408 Odile Krakovitch. *Les femmes bagnardes.* Paris: Orban, 1990. ISBN 2-85565-572-2. ‣ Archival study of 2,000 women criminals deported to French penal colonies in Guyana and New Caledonia during Second Empire and Third Republic. Finds these women more exploited in penal colonies than in France. [KMO]

26.409 James F. McMillan. *Housewife or harlot: the place of women in French society, 1870–1940.* New York: St. Martin's, 1981. ISBN 0-312-39347-7. ‣ Most recent survey in English of subject. Strongest chapters treat World War I and its effects on women's status. [KMO]

26.410 Claire Goldberg Moses. *French feminism in the nineteenth century.* Albany: State University of New York Press, 1984. ISBN 0-87395-859-4 (cl), 0-87395-860-8 (pbk). ‣ Comprehensive study of ideas and organizations of early French feminists. Especially strong on Saint-Simonian socialist feminists and their allies, with whose analyses and objectives author sympathizes. [KMO]

26.411 Janine Mossuz-Lavau. *Les lois de l'amour: les politiques de la sexualité en France de 1950 à nos jours.* Paris: Payot, 1991. ISBN 2-228-88388-3. ‣ Historical-legal study of sexual liberation in France since 1950. Includes laws regulating contraception and abortion; sex education; campaigns against rape and sexual harassment; and homosexual rights. [KMO]

26.412 Janine Mossuz-Lavau and Mariette Sineau. *Enquête sur les femmes et la politique en France.* Paris: Presses Universitaire de France, 1983. ISBN 2-13-037859-5. ‣ Important synthesis concerning women's political leanings since obtaining vote in 1945. Argues that as Catholic affiliations decreased, women abstained less, voted increasingly for Left and in 1981 supported socialists, and also shunned extremist factions. [KMO]

26.413 Karen M. Offen. "Body politics: women, work, and the politics of motherhood in France, 1920–1950." In *Maternity and gender policies: women and the rise of the European welfare states, 1880s–1950s.* Gisela Bock and Pat Thane, eds., pp. 138–59. London: Routledge, 1991. ISBN 0-415-04773-0. ‣ Pioneering examination of intersections of pronatalist discourse, controversies over women's work, political difficulties, and feminist agitation. Strands blended in formulating programs for state support of motherhood in post-1945 welfare state. [KMO]

26.414 Karen M. Offen. "On the French origin of the words feminism and feminist." *Feminist issues* 8.2 (1988) 45–51. ISSN 0270-6679. ‣ Survey of terms' birth in France in 1880s and spread into other languages by early twentieth century. Raises questions about multiple meanings of feminism. [KMO]

26.415 Michelle Perrot, ed. *Writing women's history.* Felicia Pheasant, trans. Oxford: Blackwell, 1992. ISBN 0-631-15632-1 (cl), 0-631-18612-3 (pbk). ‣ Pathbreaking articles asking whether women's history can be distinct field of inquiry. Consensus that sexes must be studied in relation to one another and differences examined to demonstrate centrality of gender in history. [KMO]

26.416 Yannick Ripa. *Women and madness.* Catherine du Peloux Menagé, trans. Minneapolis: University of Minnesota Press, 1990. ISBN 0-8166-1929-8. ‣ Pioneering study of women and insanity since 1838 using Salpêtrière asylum records and medical literature. Finds women severely disadvantaged in power relations with doctors and impossible medical norms for proper female behavior. [KMO]

26.417 Joan Wallach Scott. "Work identities for men and women: the politics of work and family in the Parisian garment trades in 1848" and " 'L'ouvrière!' Mot impie, sordide. . . .': Women workers in the discourse of French political economy, 1840–1860." In *Gender and the politics of history.* Joan Wallach Scott., pp. 93–112, notes: 213–17; 139–63, notes: 221–25. New York: Columbia University Press, 1988. ISBN 0-231-06554-X. ‣ Important essays on language and gender. Analyzes men and women garment workers' language concerning women, work, and family. Women's work central in political economists' debates. Contends studies of representations of family and gender differences are central for rewriting economic and labor history. [KMO]

26.418 Dorothy McBride Stetson. *Women's rights in France.* Westport, Conn.: Greenwood, 1987. ISBN 0-313-25403-6, ISSN 0147-104X. ‣ Study of immense changes in French laws and policies affecting women between 1965 and mid-1980s. Examines effects of these changes on women's lives. [KMO]

26.419 Laura S. Strumingher. *The odyssey of Flora Tristan.* New York: Lang, 1988. ISBN 0-8204-0888-3. ‣ Brief biographical study of Flora Tristan, important advocate of rights for women and workers during July Monarchy. [KMO]

26.420 Françoise Thébaud. *La femme au temps de la guerre de quatorze.* Paris: Stock, 1986. ISBN 2-234-01748-3. ‣ Comprehensive survey of French women's complicated encounter with First World War. Changes in work roles and attitudes toward women's nature and place in society. [KMO]

26.421 Françoise Thébaud. *Quand nos grand-mères donnaient la vie: la maternité en France dans l'entre-deux-guerres.* Lyon: Presses Universitaires de Lyon, 1986. ISBN 2-7297-0294-6. ‣ Pathbreaking study of social, medical, and institutional construction of childbirth in Paris during 1920s and 1930s. [KMO]

Section 27

MAARTEN ULTEE AND WILLARD ALLEN FLETCHER

Low Countries and Switzerland

During early modern times the Low Countries were loosely associated territories with fluctuating frontiers. Located in the northwest corner of Europe, they included coastal areas from Dunkirk to Delfzijl where the Dutch language was spoken, as well as inland provinces with French and German speakers. The population earned its living through fishing, farming, textile manufacturing, and shipping. These lands were part of the Burgundian inheritance of Emperor Charles V (1519–1555). Together with other territories acquired by Charles, they were known collectively as the Seventeen Provinces. There were also anomalies, such as the Prince-Bishopric of Liège, not under Habsburg rule.

During the reign of Philip II, son of Charles V and king of Spain, a monumental revolt began in the 1560s. This revolt in defense of local privileges was at first stronger in the southern provinces of Flanders and Brabant, and it coincided with the rise of Calvinism. Ultimately the seven northern provinces of Holland, Zeeland, Utrecht, Overijssel, Groningen, Guelderland, and Friesland won their independence as the United Provinces of the Netherlands, or Dutch Republic. Most of the southern provinces were reconquered by Spanish troops. The separation of North and South was recognized in the Twelve Years Truce (1609–1621), and made final by the Peace of Westphalia (1648). The Spanish Netherlands were granted to Austria in 1714. The Dutch Republic, despite the French invasion of 1672, lasted until 1795.

Since Holland became the wealthiest and most populous province, its name is often applied to the northern nation as a whole. Likewise, the word *Nederlands* is translated as *Dutch*, applying to North and South, as in Dutch art, Dutch language, Dutch Revolt, etc. The more formal *Netherlandish* is preferred by art historians, who also use Flemish to designate art and artists located south of the great rivers.

By one estimate, over 62,000 books and articles on the history of the Netherlands were published between 1940 and 1980 (Vollmuller, *Nijhoffs Geschiedenis-lexicon*, 27.10). We have tried to choose works most useful to students and teachers of history. These include surveys and standard reference works, along with outstanding monographs presenting various scholarly viewpoints. Some consideration has also been given to ease of access.

The selection of titles for English-speaking readers risks placing too much emphasis on political and diplomatic history, because these topics have received the most attention from Anglo-American historians. Nonetheless we have made a conscientious effort to include a variety of works, arranged in chronological order under various topics.

The topics covered in greatest detail prior to 1789 are the religious and political history of the Reformation and the Revolt; the economic, social, and cultural history of the Dutch Republic; and the eighteenth-century revolutions. In part, this selection reflects our interests as contributors and the limitations of space, but it also indicates directions of current historiography. There is very little repetition of the sources and works listed in the 1961 *Guide*—only seven of the titles listed are reprised. Readers who seek older references may find them in the earlier edition.

Topics that receive less attention here include the southern Netherlands in general, the eighteenth century, history of science, history of women, and biographies. The provinces that remained under Habsburg rule recently have been the subject of more study, especially by Belgian historians. As for the eighteenth century, once regarded as a period of faded glory in both North and South, scholars are now treating the themes of decline, Enlightenment, and revolution in a larger European context and identifying their specific manifestations. History of science and history of women are also flourishing in the Low Countries, and biographies have broad popular appeal.

Some of the most exciting current work is available only in Dutch. While many historians of the Low Countries are fluent in conversational English, most publish their scholarly works in Dutch or French, often with English summaries. Thanks to official encouragement and subsidies, more Dutch and Belgian books are being translated. The American reader can look forward to the appearance of many new studies in the coming years.

The post-1789 historiography of the Low Countries was of course profoundly affected by the French Revolution and its aftermath. In sudden as well as gradual manifestations of nationalism, the political unity of the Low Countries, as represented by the Kingdom of the Netherlands between 1815 and 1830, was decisively altered. The new political and economic realities imposed by that fragmentation forced Belgian, Dutch, and Luxembourg historians to create new frames of reference and formulate new approaches in the study of their separate, national histories. Their work reflects, in varying degrees, an ongoing commitment to traditional fields of study—politics or foreign relations, for example—as well as a productive interest in the "new history." No limited selection of books and articles, principally in English, can possibly convey an appreciation of the volume and, especially, the diversity of studies published on the history of the Low Countries. While methodologies borrowed from such disciplines as anthropology, psychology, and sociology, among others, have provided historians with new tools of research, Marxism, however fleeting its political influence, has also contributed important elements to frameworks of social and political analysis.

Post-1945 internal political and social developments in the three states provided additional stimuli to investigate the roots and evolution of a wide array of social conditions. Historians were faced with new challenges regarding definitions of class and status, and, above all, the articulation and integration of women's history into their depictions of the past. Contributions along such lines have been part of Belgian and Dutch historiography for a considerable length of time. Luxembourg historiography has only recently begun to reflect an interest in the "new history"; women's history especially remains woefully neglected. Post-1945 international trends toward politico-military superblocs, economic integration, and administrative centralism have, curiously enough, also fostered national introspection and placed strong emphasis on regional and ethnic diversity. The impressive list of Belgian publications on the history of Flanders and Wallonia bears witness to the new preeminence of regional history in Belgium, especially among historians committed to the "new history." Much the same may be said of their Dutch colleagues, who have centered much of their work on aspects of Dutch societal structure. Their findings on *verzuiling* and its collapse, as well as their studies of ethnic minorities, reveal a high level of sophistication in the application of the new methodologies. Luxembourg historians, so long caught up in the history of politics and diplomacy—a result of the many hidden designs and direct assaults on their independence—have responded to new trends by moving closer to the history of mentalities in order to probe the depths of a national Luxembourg consciousness.

There is of course ample indication that contemporary historical scholarship in the Low Countries, as elsewhere, has become very specialized. Individual contributions, at times illuminating even if narrowly focused, are often the product of research projects formulated and carried out by so-called working groups. Far less common are the broad, scholarly syntheses produced by individual historians who, like Henri Pirenne in earlier decades, are able to impose upon their books an overarching vision and fundamental unity of structure and purpose.

Geographically unlike the Low Countries, Switzerland presents different historiographical problems, as our colleague E. William Monter notes. A small but fiercely independent country, Switzerland has confounded students of nationalism because it lacks both linguistic and religious uniformity. Its citizens speak four official languages, although Germanophones constitute a large majority (nearly 70 percent, against 20 percent Francophone and 10 percent Italophone). This basic fact has shaped Swiss historiography in important ways. There is no truly dominant language for Swiss historical scholarship. Most Swiss scholars function in either German or French, and their most important historical works tend to appear in both languages, although not in English (which is spoken abundantly in hotels and banks, and is even the official language of Swissair, but remains unimportant for historians). Our bibliography necessarily reflects this state of affairs.

Switzerland, which has a plausible claim to being Europe's oldest functioning democracy, has been a confederation of autonomous cantons since 1291. It has expanded from its original three units to twenty-five today, managing to survive the enduring divisions resulting from the Protestant Reformation, the fall of the old confederation during the French Revolution and Napoleonic era, and the deep Franco-German rifts of world wars in the twentieth century. Swiss federalism makes its local history often more significant than its national history. Places such as Basel, Zurich, and Geneva matter more for European history than for Swiss history, while the variety of its individual units makes some cantonal histories (for example, the polyglot Alpine confederations of Grisons or Valais) appear as richly tangled and informative as that of the national federation.

The fact that the Low Countries and Switzerland form a borderland between France and Germany has left its imprint on the historiography of these regions. Despite the often brutal consequences of invasion, occupation, and annexation by their powerful neighbors, the cultural and social heritage of the Belgians, Dutch, Luxembourgers, and Swiss also gained immeasurable benefits from intellectual and cultural intercourse with these nations. Where the record of historical writing may suggest a regional focus, the analytical work of the historians cited are often informed by an impressive knowledge of comparative history. The rich history and culture of these countries have attracted a multitude of historians and enabled some of them to make magisterial contributions.

ACKNOWLEDGMENTS   *This essay was written by Maarten Ultee, Willard Allen Fletcher, and E. William Monter.*

[Contributors: ACD = Alastair C. Duke, EWM = E. William Monter, ICF = Ian C. Fletcher, JB = James Boyden, JLP = Janet L. Polasky, MU = Maarten Ultee, TAB = Thomas A. Brady, Jr., WAF = Willard Allen Fletcher]

LOW COUNTRIES, 1450–1789

Guides, Bibliographies, and Chronologies

27.1 Wybe Jappe Alberts. "Literaturbericht zur Geschichte der Niederlande (Allgemeines und Mittelalter), Veröffentlichungen 1954–1960." *Historische Zeitschrift*, Sonderheft 2 (1965) 1–57. ISSN 0440-971X. ▸ Survey (in German) of writings on general and medieval Dutch history. Now somewhat dated. [MU]

27.2 Hendrik de Buck. *Bibliografie der geschiedenis van Nederland.* Leiden: Brill, 1968. ▸ Select bibliography of works relating to prehistory and history of present kingdom of Netherlands through 1963. Lists inventories as well as literature on political, local, international, maritime, economic, legal, and ecclesiastical history. [ACD]

27.3 Alice Clare Carter et al. *Historical research in the Low Countries, 1970–1975: a critical survey.* The Hague: Nijhoff, 1981. ISBN 90-247-9094-8. ▸ Very useful comments in English on recent historical works, compiled from annual bibliographies in *Acta Historiae Neerlandicae*. [MU]

27.4 Léopold Genicot. *Vingt ans de recherche historique en Belgique, 1969–1988.* Brussels: Crédit Communal, 1990. (Collection historique, 2.) ISBN 2-87193-102-X, ISSN 0774-3122. ▸ Comprehensive, even more detailed sequel to Houtte 27.5. Together volumes provide overview of nearly fifty years of Belgian historical scholarship. [MU]

27.5 J. A. van Houtte. *Un quart de siècle de recherche historique en Belgique, 1944–1968.* Louvain: Nauwelaerts, 1970. ▸ Wide-ranging bibliography of historical works produced in Belgium in postwar period. Useful references to regional journals and local histories, arranged by subject and period; indexed by authors only. Continued by Genicot 27.4. [MU]

27.6 H.P.H. Jansen. *Prisma Kalendarium: Geschiedenis van de Lage Landen in jaartallen.* 1971 ed. Utrecht: Spectrum, 1988. ISBN 90-274-1894-2. ▸ Extremely useful chronological history of Netherlands, giving brief summaries of important events from antiquity to present; lists of rulers and index. [MU]

27.7 Horst Lademacher. "Literaturbericht über die Geschichte der Niederlande (Allgemeines und Neuzeit) Veröffentlichungen, 1945–1970." In Walther Kienast, ed. *Historische Zeitschrift*, Sonderheft 5 (1973) 9–117. ISSN 0440-971X. ▸ Lengthy, detailed, judicious bibliographic survey (in German) of history of Netherlands. Covers bibliographies, collections, political, social, economic, colonial, religious, and local history. [MU]

27.8 Wijnand W. Mijnhardt, ed. *Kantelend geschiedbeeld: Nederlandse historiografie sinds 1945.* Utrecht: Spectrum, 1983. ISBN 90-274-6239-9. ▸ Selective critical assessment of postwar monographs and articles on Dutch history since 1500. Contributors review writing on revolt, golden age, urban patriciate, socioeconomic history, intellectual history, industrialization, colonial history, etc. [ACD/WAF]

27.9 Eg. I. Strubbe and Leon Voet. *De chronologie van de middeleeuwen en de moderne tijden in de Nederlanden.* 1960 ed. Brussels: Commission Royale d'Histoire, 1991. ▸ Historical chronology for Low Countries (Belgium and Netherlands), early Middle Ages to 1960. [ACD]

27.10 H.W.J. Volmuller, ed. *Nijhoffs geschiedenis-lexikon: Nederland en Belgie.* The Hague: Nijhoff, 1981. ISBN 90-247-9078-6. ▸ Handbook for history of Belgium, Luxembourg, and Netherlands. Brief entries on events, institutions, organizations, persons, places, and politics, with bibliographies, illustrations, and cross-references. [ACD]

SEE ALSO
  16.3 W. Ph. Coolhaas. *A critical survey of studies on Dutch colonial history.*

General Studies

27.11 D. P. Blok et al., eds. *Algemene geschiedenis der Nederlanden.* 15 vols. Haarlem, Netherlands: Fibula–Van Dishoeck, 1977–83. ISBN 90-228-3800-5 (set). ▸ Most recent multivolume history of Benelux (Belgium, Netherlands, and Luxembourg) countries, Roman period through 1980. Well supplied with illustrations, tables, diagrams, maps, graphs, and up-to-date bibliographies. Some editors adopt Annales approach. [ACD]

27.12 Léopold Genicot. *Histoire de la Wallonie.* Paris: Éditions Universitaires, 1973. ▸ Survey of history of southern region of Belgium. Based on regional historiographical tradition stressing identity of separate Wallonia as distinct from artificial Belgian nation-state. [JLP]

27.13 K.H.D. Haley. *The Dutch in the seventeenth century.* New York: Harcourt Brace Jovanovich, 1972. ISBN 0-15-126855-X (cl), 0-15-518473-3 (pbk). ▸ Brief introductory text, useful for general readers. See Boxer 16.95, Price 27.137, and Wilson 27.19. [MU]

27.14 J. A. van Houtte et al. *Algemene geschiedenis der Nederlanden.* 13 vols. Utrecht: de Haan, 1949–58. ▸ Older comprehensive multivolume history of northern and southern Netherlands, now supplemented but not superseded by Blok et al., eds., 27.11. [MU]

27.15 Johan Huizinga. *Dutch civilisation in the seventeenth century and other essays.* 1968 ed. Pieter Geyl and F.W.N. Hugenholtz, eds. Arnold J. Pomerans, trans. New York: Harper & Row, 1969. ▸ Reflections on Dutch culture and nature of history. Character of Dutch civilization attributed chiefly to geographical situation of Netherlands, decentralized form of government, and precocity and preeminence of towns. [ACD]

27.16 Horst Lademacher. *Geschichte der Niederlande: Politik—Verfassung—Wirtschaft.* Darmstadt: Wissenschaftliche Buchgesellschaft, 1983. ISBN 3-534-07082-8. ▸ Overview of Dutch history from Burgundian times to present. Conscientious, competent, good bibliographic essay. [MU]

27.17 Audrey M. Lambert. *The making of the Dutch landscape: an historical geography of the Netherlands.* 2d ed. London: Academic Press, 1985. ISBN 0-12-434645-6. ▸ Beginning with physical geography of present-day Netherlands, examines settlement patterns, urban development, and land reclamation from prehistoric times to 1960s. Extensive bibliography. [ACD]

27.18 William Temple. *Observations upon the United Provinces of the Netherlands.* 1672 ed. G. N. Clark, ed. Oxford: Clarendon, 1972. ▸ Good starting point for students; lively and astute observations by English diplomat who served in Brussels and The Hague. See Haley 27.62. [MU]

27.19 Charles H. Wilson. *The Dutch republic and the civilization of the seventeenth century.* New York: McGraw-Hill, 1968. ▸ Brief introduction to golden age of Dutch republic, suitable for general readers. Special attention to economic history and intellectual life—science, arts, and letters. See also Boxer 16.95, Haley 27.13, and Price 27.137. [MU]

SEE ALSO
16.95 C. R. Boxer. *The Dutch seaborne empire, 1600–1800.*

Constitutional History

27.20 Jan Dhondt. *Estates or powers: essays in the parliamentary history of the southern Netherlands from the twelfth to the eighteenth century.* Willem Blockmans, ed. Heule, Belgium: UGA, 1977. (Anciens pays et assemblées d'états, 69.) ▸ Collection of author's major essays on estates of southern Netherlands. Important for history of representative bodies from twelfth to eighteenth century. [JLP]

27.21 S. J. Fockema Andreae. *De Nederlandse staat onder de republiek.* 1961 7th ed. Amsterdam: Noord-Hollandsche Uitgevers Maatschappij, 1975. (Verhandelingen der Koninklijke Nederlandse Akademie der Wetenschappen, Afdeling letterkunde, Nieuwe reeks, 68.3.) ▸ Description of institutions during republic, essential for legal and constitutional history. Complements work of Fruin and Colenbrander (27.22). [MU]

27.22 Robert Fruin and H. T. Colenbrander. *Geschiedenis der staatsinstellingen in Nederland tot den val der republiek.* 1922 rev. ed. The Hague: Nijhoff, 1980. ISBN 90-247-9022-0. ▸ Handbook describing powers and operation of central, provincial, and local government in northern Netherlands (United Provinces) from sixteenth century through 1795. [ACD]

27.23 Martin van Gelderen. *The political thought of the Dutch revolt, 1555–1590.* Cambridge: Cambridge University Press, 1992. ISBN 0-521-39204-7. ▸ Political writings concerned chiefly with defense of liberty, including freedom of conscience. Writers drew on traditions of medieval and Renaissance Dutch constitutionalism. Convincing argument that Dutch had major influence on European thought. [ACD/MU]

27.24 Eco O. G. Haitsma Mulier. *The myth of Venice and Dutch republican thought in the seventeenth century.* Gerard T. Moran, trans. Assen: Van Gorcum, 1980. ISBN 90-232-1781-0. ▸ Venice's constitution served as model for Dutch writers who advocated Aristotelian ideal of mixed state. Philosophical writers such as Dirk Graswinckel, De la Court brothers, and Spinoza differed in

use they made of myth of Venice. Subtle, polished account. [ACD]

27.25 E. H. Kossmann. *Politieke theorie in het zeventiende-eeuwse Nederland.* Amsterdam: Noord-Hollandsche Uitgevers Maatschappij, 1960. (Verhandelingen der Koninklijke Nederlandse Akademie van Wetenschappen, Afdeling letterkunde, Nieuwe reeks, 67.2.) ▸ Examination of discussion in legal and academic circles about nature of state provoked by emergence of Dutch republic. Both republican and monarchist traditions represented. Cartesian political theorists receive special attention. [ACD]

27.26 E. H. Kossmann. "Popular sovereignty at the beginning of the Dutch ancien régime." *Acta historiae Neerlandicae* 14 (1981) 1–29. ISSN 0065-129X, ISBN 90-247-9097-2. ▸ Calvinist resistance theory intended not simply to justify revolt, but to show how political power should be used and by whom. [ACD]

27.27 Herbert H. Rowen, ed. *The Low Countries in early modern times.* New York: Walker and Harper & Row, 1972. ISBN 0-8027-2035-8 (cl), 0-06-139310-X (pbk). ▸ Old-fashioned collection of translated selections from sources; mostly political history. [MU]

27.28 H. Wansink. "Holland and six allies: the republic of the seven United Provinces." In *Britain and the Netherlands; metropolis, dominion, and province: papers delivered to the fourth Anglo-Dutch Historical Conference.* J. S. Bromley and E. H. Kossmann, eds., pp. 133–55. The Hague: Nijhoff, 1971. ISBN 90-247-1223-8. ▸ Examination of theory and practice of government of Dutch republic. Concludes that despite major differences, Holland's predominance, Calvinism, and common respect for provincial liberty underpinned unequal alliance. Significant for understanding of regional interests. [ACD]

Burgundian and Habsburg Periods

27.29 Walter Prevenier and Willem Blockmans. *The Burgundian Netherlands.* Cambridge: Cambridge University Press, 1986. ISBN 0-521-30611-6. ▸ Examination of how Low Countries acquired distinctive character for dynastic, but especially, economic and cultural reasons, 1380–1530. Emphasizes urban contribution: wealthy burghers chiefly responsible for flowering of Burgundian art. Lavishly illustrated. [ACD]

27.30 James D. Tracy. *A financial revolution in the Habsburg Netherlands: renten and renteniers in the county of Holland, 1515–1565.* Berkeley: University of California Press, 1985. ISBN 0-520-05425-3. ▸ Carefully shows how states of Holland assumed collective responsibility for debts, secured by future subsidies. Prompt payment enhanced credit rating and encouraged growth of market in annuities. This change shifted political balance between monarch and representative assemblies in favor of latter. [ACD]

27.31 James D. Tracy. *Holland under Habsburg rule, 1506–1566: the formation of a body politic.* Berkeley: University of California Press, 1990. ISBN 0-520-06882-3. ▸ Discussion of development of Holland's political self-awareness during period. Sees enhanced fiscal responsibility of provincial states and perceived threat to provincial and municipal privileges as result of wars of Charles V, Holy Roman Emperor. [ACD]

Revolt of the Netherlands, 1568–1648

27.32 Robert S. Duplessis. *Lille and the Dutch revolt: urban stability in an era of revolution, 1500–1582.* Cambridge: Cambridge University Press, 1991. ISBN 0-521-39415-5. ▸ Nuanced account of politics, religion, economic and social conditions in important town in Walloon Flanders. Lille stayed loyal to Philip II during Dutch revolt because of political response of local ruling class. [MU]

27.33 Martin van Gelderen, ed. *The Dutch revolt.* Cambridge:

Cambridge University Press, 1992. ISBN 0-521-39122-9 (cl), 0-521-39809-6 (pbk). ‣ Edition of five important tracts from time of revolt, translated into English. See Gelderen 27.23 for commentary. [MU]

27.34 Pieter Geyl. *The Revolt of the Netherlands, 1555–1609.* 1932 ed. London: Cassell, 1988. ISBN 0-304-32249-0. ‣ Classic work arguing for artificiality of north-south division, attributed to military standoff between republic and Spain rather than to religious differences. Dutch-language edition (1931). See Parker 27.44. [MU]

27.35 C. C. Hibben. *Gouda in revolt: particularism and pacificism in the Revolt of the Netherlands, 1572–1588.* Utrecht: Hes, 1983. ISBN 90-6194-203-9 (pbk). ‣ Exemplary analysis of local politics in Holland during Dutch revolt. Gouda's magistrates cared more for town's economic interests than for William of Orange or Calvinism. Continued to hope for negotiated peace with Spain as late as 1588. [ACD]

27.36 H. G. Koenigsberger. "Why did the States General of the Netherlands become revolutionary in the sixteenth century?" In *Politicians and virtuosi: essays in early modern history*, pp. 63–76. London: Hambledon, 1986. (Studies presented to the International Commission for the History of Representative and Parliamentary Institutions, 69.) ISBN 0-907628-65-6. ‣ Argues that logic of situation after 1572 compelled first states of Holland, and later States General, to adopt revolutionary system of parliamentary government. [ACD]

27.37 E. H. Kossmann and A. F. Mellink, eds. *Texts concerning the Revolt of the Netherlands.* Cambridge: Cambridge University Press, 1974. ISBN 0-521-20014-8. ‣ Translated extracts from political literature provoked by Dutch revolt as rebels labored to justify conduct and wrestled with issue of sovereignty. Dutch political ideas discussed at length in introductory essay. [ACD]

27.38 Pasquier de Le Barre. *The time of troubles in the Low Countries: the chronicles and memoirs of Pasquier de Le Barre of Tournai, 1559–1567.* Charlie R. Steen, ed. New York: Lang, 1989. (Renaissance and Baroque, 1.) ISBN 0-8204-0852-2, ISSN 0897-7836. ‣ Translation of memoirs of public prosecutor of Tournai, who was himself executed by Spanish government in 1568. Accounts of coming of Protestantism, iconoclasm, and revolt. Good introduction. [MU]

27.39 John L. Motley. *History of the United Netherlands from the death of William the Silent to the Twelve Years' Truce, 1609.* 1860 ed. 6 vols. New York: AMS Press, 1973. ISBN 0-404-04526-X (v. 6), 0-404-04527-8 (v. 7), 0-404-04528-6 (v. 8), 0-404-04529-4 (v. 9), 0-404-04530-8 (v. 10), 0-404-04531-6 (v. 11). ‣ Continuation of author's grand nineteenth-century history (27.40); assumes division between Protestant Holland and Catholic Belgium already established. Concludes with Twelve Years' Truce in war with Spain (1609). [MU]

27.40 John L. Motley. *The rise of the Dutch republic: a history.* 1856 ed. 5 vols. New York: AMS Press, 1973. ISBN 0-404-04521-9 (v. 1), 0-404-04522-7 (v. 2), 0-404-04523-5 (v. 3), 0-404-04524-3 (v. 4), 0-404-04525-1 (v. 5). ‣ Classic nineteenth-century narrative of Dutch revolt, portrayed as heroic Protestant struggle against benighted Spanish Catholic oppression. Concludes with assassination of William of Orange (1584). See Geyl 27.34 and Parker 27.44 for more modern interpretations. [MU]

27.41 F. G. Oosterhoff. *Leicester and the Netherlands, 1586–1587.* Utrecht: Hes, 1988. ISBN 90-6194-496-1. ‣ Examination of Earl of Leicester's perception of Dutch domestic politics. Concludes that despite his grave errors of judgment, Anglo-Dutch alliance crucial to survival of revolt. Reviews constitutional debate on sovereignty. [ACD]

27.42 *Opstand en pacificatie in de lage landen; bijdrage tot de studie van de Pacificatie van Gent: verslagboek van het Tweedaags Colloquium bij vierhonderdste verjaring van de Pacificatie van Gent.* The Hague: Nijgh & Van Ditmar, 1976. ISBN 90-236-3355-5. ‣ Collection of articles on 1576 treaty (Pacification of Ghent) that united all provinces to drive out Spaniards. Argues treaty can no longer be regarded as coming together of north and south to produce revolt. Studies development of political consciousness. See articles in *Tijdschrift voor Geschiedenis* 89.3 (1976). [JLP]

27.43 Geoffrey Parker. *Army of Flanders and the Spanish road, 1567–1659: logistics of Spanish victory and defeat in the Low Countries' wars.* 1972 ed. Cambridge: Cambridge University Press, 1990. ISBN 0-521-09907-2 (pbk). ‣ Outstanding monograph on organization, mobilization, administration, and financing of Spanish army in Low Countries. Spain's achievements and resilience so far from home put alleged decline into perspective. Good discussion of mutinies and mutineers. [ACD]

27.44 Geoffrey Parker. *The Dutch revolt.* 1985 rev. ed. London: Penguin, 1990. ISBN 0-14-013712-2 (pbk). ‣ Sets Revolt of Netherlands in international context. Discerns three revolts (1565–68, 1569–76, 1576–81) defined by location, leadership, and issues. Most recent and best synthesis with full annotation. [ACD]

27.45 Geoffrey Parker. *Spain and the Netherlands, 1559–1609: ten studies.* 1978 rev. ed. London: Fontana, 1990. ISBN 0-00-686201-2 (pbk). ‣ Collection of brilliantly argued essays, published 1970–78, on political and economic aspects of revolt and early Dutch republic. [MU]

27.46 Heinz Schilling. "Der Aufstand der Niederlande: bürgerliche Revolution oder Elitenkonflikt?" In *200 Jahre amerikanische Revolution und moderne Revolutionsforschung.* Hans-Ulrich Wehler, ed., pp. 177–231. Göttingen: Vandenhoeck & Ruprecht, 1976. (Geschichte und Gesellschaft, Sonderheft, 2.) ISBN 3-525-36401-6. ‣ Interpretation of Dutch revolt as part of European-wide antagonism between absolutist *Fürstenstaat* and traditional elites. High nobility remained loyal (except William of Orange), but lesser nobility deeply divided. [ACD]

27.47 J. W. Smit. "The Netherlands revolution." In *Preconditions of revolution in early modern Europe.* Robert Forster and Jack P. Greene, eds., pp. 19–54. Baltimore: Johns Hopkins University Press, 1970. ISBN 0-8018-1176-7. ‣ Suggestive essay concluding that endemic political instability in Habsburg Netherlands aggravated by simultaneous strengthening of both central authority and representative bodies. Mercantile class well entrenched in Holland, yet too weak to impose progressive economic and religious regime on south. [ACD]

27.48 N. M. Sutherland. "William of Orange and the Revolt of the Netherlands: a missing dimension." *Archive for Reformation history* 74 (1983) 201–31. ISSN 0003-9381. ‣ Argues William of Orange important in great ideological struggle against international Catholicism. Papal and royal authority at stake; concludes William captive to events beyond his control. [MU]

27.49 K. W. Swart. *William the Silent and the Revolt of the Netherlands.* London: Historical Association, 1978. (Historical Association general series, 94.) ISBN 0-85278-197-0. ‣ Study of William of Orange's steadfast opposition to Spanish tyranny to his death. Leadership of revolt, 1572–76, was his most enduring achievement, but pro-French policy misconceived. Brief sketch of interpretation to appear in longer biography. [ACD]

27.50 C. V. Wedgwood. *William the Silent, William of Nassau, Prince of Orange, 1533–1584.* 1944 ed. New York: Norton, 1968. ‣ Concentrates on personality of prince of Orange, hero of Dutch revolt. Written before studies of other leaders, towns, and provinces; needs revision. [MU]

27.51 Herman van der Wee. "The economy as a factor in the start of the Revolt of the Netherlands." *Acta historiae Neerlandica*

5 (1972) 52–67. ISSN 0065-129X. ▸ Reconsiders role of economic factors in Dutch revolt. Growing prosperity contributed generally to spiritual emancipation of population, but crisis of early 1560s shook confidence of middle classes, who reacted by giving ear to Calvinist preachers. [ACD]

27.52 Charles H. Wilson. *Queen Elizabeth and the Revolt of the Netherlands.* 1970 ed. The Hague: Nijhoff, 1979. ISBN 90-247-2273-X. ▸ Controversial reassessment of Elizabethan foreign policy with regard to Dutch revolt. English queen's reluctance to give open support to rebels before 1585 criticized as pennywise, pound foolish. [ACD]

27.53 J. J. Woltjer. *Friesland in Hervormingstijd.* Leiden: Universitaire pers Leiden, 1962. (Leidse historische reeks van de Rijksuniversiteit te Leiden, 7.) ▸ Analysis of political-religious tensions in Friesland (ca. 1520–80). Friesland part of Habsburg Netherlands, yet provincial elite remained aloof. Religious and political polarization postponed until late sixteenth century. [ACD]

27.54 J. J. Woltjer. "De vredemakers." *Tijdschrift voor Geschiedenis* 89.3 (1976) 299–321. ISSN 0040-7518. ▸ Seminal reassessment of Dutch revolt (1559–80). Gives due weight to efforts of peace makers to resolve political-religious conflicts. [ACD]

Seventeenth Century

27.55 Stephen B. Baxter. *William III and the defense of European liberty, 1650–1702.* 1966 ed. Westport, Conn.: Greenwood, 1976. ISBN 0-8371-8161-5. ▸ Best biography of stadholder-king, prince of Orange and later king of England. Explains William's role as leader of coalitions against Louis XIV of France; uses Dutch and English sources. [MU]

27.56 J. C. Boogman. "The raison-d'état politician, John de Witt." *Acta historiae Neerlandicae* 11 (1978) 55–78. ISSN 0065-129X. ▸ Good explanation of statecraft of grand pensionary, "perfect Hollander." See Rowen 27.66, 27.67. [MU]

27.57 G. N. Clark. *The Dutch alliance and the war against French trade, 1688–1697.* 1923 ed. New York: Russell & Russell, 1971. (Publications of the University of Manchester, historical series, 42.) ▸ Narrative of Anglo-Dutch efforts to cut off trade with France, response of France and neutral powers, and mixed results. Lacks statistical data but argues that states were unable to use trade as weapon; consequence of war was economic depression. [MU]

27.58 H. A. Enno van Gelder. *Getemperde vrijheid: een verhandeling over de verhouding van Kerk en Staat in de Republiek der Verenigde Nederlanden en de vrijheid van meningsuiting in zake godsdienst, drukpers en onderwijs, gedurende de 17e eeuw.* Groningen: Wolters-Noordhoff, 1972. ISBN 90-01-39012-9. ▸ Subtle examination of church-state relations in United Provinces. Considers limited nature of freedom Dutch enjoyed in matters of religion, press, and education. [ACD]

27.59 Pieter Geyl. *The Netherlands in the seventeenth century.* Edition varies. 2 vols. London: Benn, 1961. ▸ Largely topical 1930s survey, influenced by Greater Netherlands ideas; now somewhat outmoded. Argues reunion of north and south frustrated by war, religious differences, and commercial interests. [MU]

27.60 Pieter Geyl. *Orange and Stuart, 1641–1672.* 1969 ed. Arnold J. Pomerans, trans. New York: Scribner's, 1970. ▸ Close study of relations between two aristocratic families with higher aspirations, their fortunes fluctuating with civil strife, international wars, and dynastic accidents. Dutch edition originally published 1939. [MU]

27.61 Donald Haks. *Huwelijk en gezin in Holland in de 17de en 18de eeuw: processtukken en moralisten over aspecten van het laat*

17de- en 18de-eeuwse gezinsleven. 1982 ed. Utrecht: Hes, 1985. ISBN 90-6194-015-X. ▸ Pioneering study of marriage and family through legal cases and moralist writings. Chapters on relatives and neighbors, sexual behavior, marital choices, household relations, and divorce. Dutch family fitted northwest European type, but was perhaps more modern. English summary. [MU]

27.62 K.H.D. Haley. *An English diplomat in the Low Countries: Sir William Temple and John de Witt, 1665–1672.* New York: Oxford University Press, 1986. ISBN 0-19-822917-8. ▸ Examination of Temple's diplomacy in Münster, Brussels, and The Hague; his work with de Witt for Anglo-Dutch alliance contrary to pro-French policy of Charles II. Carefully researched and documented. [MU]

27.63 Jonathan I. Israel. *The Dutch republic and the Hispanic world, 1606–1661.* New York: Oxford University Press, 1982. ISBN 0-19-826534-4. ▸ Well-documented work on Dutch-Spanish conflict. Special emphasis on economic warfare and its consequences in Europe and overseas. Shows diversity of Dutch opinion toward Spain; local interests of towns and provinces often prevailed over national points of view. [MU/JB]

27.64 Jonathan I. Israel. *Empires and entrepôts: the Dutch, the Spanish monarchy, and the Jews, 1585–1713.* London: Hambledon, 1990. ISBN 1-85285-022-1. ▸ Provocative essays on political and economic aspects of Dutch revolt and ensuing wars; Spanish and Jewish history. Challenging, often disputed, views. [MU]

27.65 D. J. Roorda. *Partij en factie: de oproeren van 1672 in de steden van Holland en Zeeland: een krachtmeting tussen partijen en fracties.* 1961 ed. Groningen: Wolters-Noordhoff, 1979. ISBN 90-01-39024-2 (pbk). ▸ Brilliant social analysis of politics in crucial year 1672, when republic was invaded by France. William III became stadholder, but no radical democratic party came to power. Summary in English. [MU]

27.66 Herbert H. Rowen. *John de Witt, grand pensionary of Holland, 1625–1672.* Princeton: Princeton University Press, 1978. ISBN 0-691-05247-6. ▸ Exhaustive, dull narrative biography of leader during stadholderless period, great emphasis on foreign policy. Stays too close to de Witt's papers, overwhelming reader with tiresome detail; students will prefer livelier abridged edition (27.67). [MU]

27.67 Herbert H. Rowen. *John de Witt, statesman of the "True Freedom."* Cambridge: Cambridge University Press, 1986. ISBN 0-521-30391-5. ▸ Abridgement of author's overly lengthy biography (27.66); more readable and preferred, unless reference notes are required. [MU]

27.68 Herbert H. Rowen. *The princes of Orange: the stadholders in the Dutch republic.* Cambridge: Cambridge University Press, 1988. ISBN 0-521-34525-1. ▸ Chronological account of stadholders as military commanders and political leaders of Dutch republic, from William the Silent to Frederick V. Discusses "stadholderless periods," 1650–72 and 1747. Good introduction with biographical summaries. [MU]

27.69 Jan den Tex. *Oldenbarnevelt.* R. B. Powell, trans. Cambridge: Cambridge University Press, 1973. ISBN 0-521-08429-6 (set). ▸ Abridged translation of definitive biography of pensionary of Holland who played leading role in revolt against Spain and sponsored Twelve Years' Truce. Victim of Orangists and contraremonstrants, executed 1619. [MU]

Eighteenth Century

27.70 Yvan van den Berghe. *Jacobijnen en traditionalisten: de reacties van de Bruggelingen in de revolutietijd, 1780–1794.* 2 vols. Brussels: Pro Civitate, 1972. (Pro Civitate, historische uitgaven, 8.32.) ▸ Study of revolutionaries in Bruges during eighteenth-century revolt against Austria and establishment of Belgian independence. Analyzes divisions separating most radical Flemish revolutionaries from defenders of traditional estates. [JLP]

27.71 Wayne Ph. te Brake. *Regents and rebels: the revolutionary world of an eighteenth-century Dutch city*. Cambridge, Mass.: Blackwell, 1989. ISBN 1-55786-040-8. ▸ Excellent local study of revolutionary period in Deventer (Overijssel), population 8,000, with social and political dimensions set in international context. [MU]

27.72 Alice Clare Carter. *The Dutch republic in Europe in the Seven Years' War*. Coral Gables, Fla.: University of Miami Press, 1971. ISBN 0-87024-203-2. ▸ Uses Dutch sources to show why republic remained neutral. Significant for discussion of Dutch eighteenth-century political decline. [MU]

27.73 Alice Clare Carter. *Neutrality or commitment: the evolution of Dutch foreign policy, 1667–1795*. London: Arnold, 1975. ISBN 0-7131-5767-4 (cl), 0-7131-5768-2 (pbk). ▸ Argues Dutch neutrality in eighteenth century was conscious diplomatic strategy, not result of political weakness. [MU]

27.74 Jan Craeybeckx. "The Brabant Revolution: a conservative revolution in a backward country?" *Acta historiae Neerlandicae* 9 (1970) 49–83. ISSN 0065-129X. ▸ Study of Belgian Revolution of 1789 that overthrew Austrian emperor Joseph II, questioning why revolution in this industrializing society was conservative. [JLP]

27.75 Roderick Geikie and Isabel A. Montgomery. *The Dutch barrier, 1705–1719*. 1930 ed. New York: Greenwood, 1968. ▸ Discussion of role of Low Countries during and after War of Spanish Succession, when Dutch republic sought to maintain line of fortresses against France in southern Netherlands. [MU]

27.76 Ragnhild Hatton. *Diplomatic relations between Great Britain and the Dutch republic, 1714–1721*. London: East & West for Anglo-Netherlands Society, 1950. ▸ Anglo-Dutch relations between treaties of Utrecht and Nystad. Makes good use of archives in The Hague, London, and Paris to show Dutch statesmen striving to preserve independent policy, as well as French efforts to separate allies. [MU]

27.77 Janet L. Polasky. *Revolution in Brussels, 1787–1793*. Brussels and Hanover, N.H.: Académie Royale de Belgique and University Press of New England for University of New Hampshire, 1987. ISBN 0-87451-385-5 (pbk). ▸ Discussion of Brabant Revolution and French occupation of Brussels at end of eighteenth century. Argues broad-based privileged groups coalesced to defend Old Regime in this industrializing society. [JLP]

27.78 Janet L. Polasky. "Traditionalists, democrats, and Jacobins in revolutionary Brussels." *Journal of modern history* 56.2 (1984) 227–62. ISSN 0022-2801. ▸ Study of three political factions that led Belgian Revolution, 1789–93. Links between economic background of revolutionaries and political philosophy of factions. [JLP]

27.79 J. W. Schulte Nordholt. *The Dutch republic and American independence*. Herbert H. Rowen, trans. Chapel Hill: University of North Carolina Press, 1982. ISBN 0-8078-1530-6. ▸ Study of influence of American Revolution on Dutch republic; accounts of John Adams's diplomacy, Dutch debates over participation in war, and Dutch visitors' impressions of America. Sympathetic and engaging, important for age of democratic revolution. [MU]

SEE ALSO
23.111 Douglas Coombs. *The conduct of the Dutch*.
30.108 Walter W. Davis. *Joseph II*.

Economic and Social History

27.80 J. Aalbers. "Holland's financial problems (1713–1733) and the wars against Louis XIV." In *Britain and the Netherlands, IV: war and society*. Alastair C. Duke and C. A. Tamse, eds., pp.

79–93. The Hague: Nijhoff, 1977. ISBN 90-247-2012-5. ▸ Shows province of Holland was exhausted financially by wars. Argues diplomatic policy of nonalignment dictated by economic decline; projects for reorganizing state finances failed. Themes expanded in author's Dutch thesis, *De Republiek en de vrede van Europa* (1980). [MU]

27.81 Violet Barbour. *Capitalism in Amsterdam in the seventeenth century*. 1950 ed. Ann Arbor: University of Michigan Press, 1963. ▸ Minor classic on examination of Dutch commercial practices, investment in trading companies and financial institutions of Amsterdam. Concludes Dutch refined traditional practices rather than innovated new ones. [ACD]

27.82 Marten G. Buist. *At Spes non Fracta: Hope and Co., 1770–1815, merchant bankers and diplomats at work*. The Hague: Nijhoff, 1974. ISBN 90-247-1629-2. ▸ Massive dissertation on influential merchant banking firm. Explores Dutch lending techniques and diplomatic implications. Bankers tried to combine loans and trading relations. [MU]

27.83 Peter Burke. *Venice and Amsterdam: a study of seventeenth-century elites*. London: Temple Smith, 1974. ISBN 0-85117-052-8. ▸ Innovative comparison of ruling elites of two early modern cities: doges and Procuratori di San Marco of Venice, and Amsterdam council. Venetians lived as nobles, while Amsterdam regents were bourgeois. [MU]

27.84 Alice Clare Carter. *Getting, spending, and investing in early modern times: essays on Dutch, English, and Huguenot economic history*. Assen: Van Gorcum, 1975. ISBN 90-232-1243-6. ▸ Collected essays by distinguished scholar of eighteenth-century Dutch and English economic history. [MU]

27.85 David W. Davies. *A primer of Dutch seventeenth-century overseas trade*. The Hague: Nijhoff, 1961. ▸ Lyrical description of Dutch trade to all parts of world, based on published sources. Illustrations; no statistical tables. Lively introductory reading. [MU]

27.86 Jan De Vries. *Barges and capitalism: passenger transportation in the Dutch economy, 1632–1839*. Utrecht: Hes, 1981. ISBN 90-6194-432-5. ▸ Ingenious, intelligent work on mass transportation system in Dutch republic. Though canal network contributed to urban growth and fostered more rational mentality, organizational structure remained firmly precapitalist. [ACD]

27.87 Jan De Vries. "The decline and rise of the Dutch economy, 1675–1900." In *Technique, spirit, and form in the making of modern economies: essays in honor of William N. Parker*. Gary Saxonhouse and Gavin Wright, eds., pp. 149–89. Greenwich, Conn.: JAI Press, 1984. (Research in economic history, Supplement, 3.) ISBN 0-89232-414-7. ▸ Seminal article on economic trends from seventeenth-century golden age to twentieth century. Carefully considers earlier writers' views of national income, wages, industrialization, and growth. Reaches remarkable and novel conclusions on Dutch economy. [MU]

27.88 Jan De Vries. *Dutch rural economy in the golden age, 1500–1700*. New Haven: Yale University Press, 1974. ISBN 0-300-01608-5. ▸ Excellent monograph showing Dutch rural economy highly specialized in late sixteenth century; contributed to expansion of entire economy. Increasingly wealthy farming community provided consumer market for industrial goods while surplus population supplied essential manpower for urban economy. [ACD]

27.89 Jan De Vries. "On the modernity of the Dutch republic." *Journal of economic history* 33.1 (1973) 191–202. ISSN 0022-0507. ▸ Alleged modernity of Dutch republic's economy attributed in part to weakness of seigneurial institutions. [ACD]

27.90 A. Th. van Deursen. *Plain lives in a golden age: popular culture, religion, and society in seventeenth-century Holland*. Maarten Ultee, trans. Cambridge: Cambridge University Press, 1991. ISBN 0-521-36606-2 (cl), 0-521-36785-9 (pbk). ‣ Description of working conditions of common people, poverty, mobility, popular culture, women, government, war, and religious attitudes of Calvinists, Catholics, and Mennonites. Standard work, based on extensive archival research. [MU]

27.91 Jan Dhondt. "The cotton industry at Ghent during the French regime." In *Essays in European economic history, 1789–1914*. François Crouzet, W. H. Chaloner, and W. M. Stern, eds., pp. 15–52. New York: St. Martin's, 1969. ISBN 0-7131-5461-6. ‣ Discussion of revolution in textile production in Flanders at end of eighteenth and beginning of nineteenth centuries. Discusses how industrialization in Ghent differed from that of England but still resulted in creation of industrial empire. [JLP]

27.92 Jan Dhondt and M. Bruwier. "The Low Countries, 1700–1914." Chapter 6 of *The emergence of industrial societies*. 1973 ed. Carlo M. Cipolla, ed. New York: Barnes & Noble, 1976. (Fontana economic history of Europe, 4.1.) ISBN 0-06-492179-4 (v. 4.1). ‣ Survey of Belgian industrialization, discussing unique features of industrial revolution in textiles and heavy industry in regions of Flanders and Liège that began in eighteenth century. [JLP]

27.93 J. A. Faber. *Drie eeuwen Friesland: economische en sociale ontwikkeling van 1500 tot 1800*. 1972 ed. Leeuwarden, Netherlands: Uitgevery De Tille, 1973. (Varia Frisica, 9.) ISBN 90-70010-23-2. ‣ Quantitative study demonstrating secular trends in economic and demographic development of Friesland. Despite significant changes, Frisian economy and society remained fairly stable. Data published in companion volume. [ACD]

27.94 Marijke Gijswijt-Hofstra and Willem Frijhoff, eds. *Witchcraft in the Netherlands: from the fourteenth to the twentieth century*. Rachel M. J. van der Wilden-Fall, trans. Rotterdam: Universitaire Pers, 1991. ISBN 90-237-1143-2. ‣ Translated collection of articles on witchcraft, first volume in series on political and social history of Low Countries. Ranges widely over time and space; useful for comparative purposes. [MU]

27.95 Myron P. Gutmann. *War and rural life in the early modern Low Countries*. Princeton: Princeton University Press, 1980. ISBN 0-691-05291-3. ‣ Although lower Maas region (Liège-Maastricht) suffered continual warfare, ca. 1620–1750, rural population proved resilient. Hard-pressed peasants benefited from prospering coal and iron industries in region. Improved military discipline reduced brutality of war for civilians. Substantial work with larger implications. [ACD]

27.96 J. A. van Houtte. *An economic history of the Low Countries, 800–1800*. New York: St. Martin's, 1977. ISBN 0-312-23320-5. ‣ Comprehensive survey of development of highly urbanized economies of Low Countries by period and by topic (population, agriculture, industry, trade, banking). Precocity attributed to conjunction of demographic pressures, specialized agriculture, weak manorialism, and growth of international trade. [ACD]

27.97 Jonathan I. Israel. *Dutch primacy in world trade, 1585–1740*. Oxford: Oxford University Press, 1989. ISBN 0-19-821139-2. ‣ Ambitious, brilliant attempt to classify Dutch trade in chronological phases. Examines Dutch activity in markets for luxury goods as well as staples, and clarifies relationships between war and commerce. [MU]

27.98 P. W. Klein. *De Trippen in de 17e eeuw: een studie over het ondernemersgedrag op de Hollandse stapelmarkt*. Assen: Van Gorcum, 1965. ‣ Careful study of Trip family in Holland and Sweden in arms trade. Confirms contribution monopolistic entrepreneurs made to Dutch commercial capitalism in seventeenth century. English summary. [ACD]

27.99 Paul M. M. Klep. *Bevolking en arbeid in transformatie: een*

onderzoek naar de ontwikkelingen in Brabant, 1700–1900. Nijmegen, Netherlands: Socialistiese Uitgeverij Nijmegen, 1981. ISBN 90-6168-771-3. ‣ Study of industrial revolution in central Belgian province of Brabant. Analysis of population explosion after 1750 and adaptation of economic structures. [JLP]

27.100 Catharina Lis. *Social change and the labouring poor: Antwerp, 1770–1860*. New Haven: Yale University Press, 1986. ISBN 0-300-03610-8. ‣ Study of economic transformation of Antwerp from textile center to port center. Argues pauperization in nineteenth century related to accelerated development of capitalism, but not necessarily to industrialization. [JLP/WAF]

27.101 Jan Lucassen. *Migrant labour in Europe, 1600–1900: the drift to the North Sea*. Donald A. Bloch, trans. London: Croom Helm, 1987. ISBN 0-7099-4117-X. ‣ Study of migration of workers to North Sea coast, ca. 1800, based on surveys taken in First French Empire. Compares migration in other areas and makes first attempt at long-term socioeconomic analysis of changes in system. [MU]

27.102 Sherrin Marshall. *Dutch gentry, 1500–1650: family, faith, and fortune*. New York: Greenwood, 1987. ISBN 0-313-25021-9. ‣ Detailed examination of over 1,000 gentry in northern Netherlands, majority of whom originated in Utrecht. Investigates marriage patterns, family relationships, life styles, and mentalities. Seeks to do justice to women. [ACD]

27.103 George Masselman. *The cradle of colonialism*. New Haven: Yale University Press, 1963. ‣ Survey of building of Dutch empire in Southeast Asia, 1595–1629, emphasizing role of Jan Pietersz Coen, buccaneering merchant of Dutch East India Company. Mostly based on published sources; debatable views on development of modern colonialism. See Boxer 16.95. [MU]

27.104 H.F.K. van Nierop. *The nobility of Holland: from knights to regents, 1500–1650*. Maarten Ultee, trans. Cambridge: Cambridge University Press, 1993. ISBN 0-521-39260-8. ‣ Elegant social and economic study of nobility of province of Holland. Nobility not impoverished and continued to play important political role during and after Dutch revolt. Useful comparative data. [MU]

27.105 N. W. Posthumus. *Inquiry into the history of prices in Holland*. 2 vols. Leiden: Brill, 1946–64. ‣ Basic data on price history, noting four phases: stability to 1550; rapid and continuous expansion, 1550–1665; stagnation, 1665–1820; and renewed rise. [MU]

27.106 G. D. Ramsay. *The queen's merchants and the Revolt of the Netherlands: the end of the Antwerp mart*, Part 2. Manchester: Manchester University Press, 1986. ISBN 0-7190-1849-8. ‣ Thorough study of decline of Antwerp market in sixteenth century, emphasizing English trade relations, based on English and continental sources. Attributes more significance to political than economic factors. See also Part 1: *The City of London*. [MU]

27.107 James C. Riley. "The Dutch economy after 1650: decline or growth?" *Journal of European economic history* 13 (1984) 521–69. ISSN 0391-5115. ‣ Careful summary of scholarly literature and statistics on Dutch decline, 1650–1860. Notes hypotheses of moderate decline, definitive decline, and growth. Concludes economic growth hypothesis most plausible. [MU]

27.108 James C. Riley. *International government finance and the Amsterdam capital market, 1740–1815*. Cambridge: Cambridge University Press, 1980. ISBN 0-521-22677-5. ‣ Technical study of finance in Dutch republic, well documented from Amsterdam banking archives. Includes description, accounting, and graphs of borrowing by European states; important comparative implications. [MU]

27.109 H. K. Roessingh. *Inlandse tabak: expansie en contractie van een handelsgewas in de 17e en 18e eeuw in Nederland*. Zutphen, Netherlands: Walburg Pers, 1976. ISBN 90-6011-283-0. ‣ Massive, widely praised statistical study of Dutch tobacco in seventeenth and eighteenth centuries. Tobacco was cash crop for farmers in Utrecht and Gelderland; towns and countryside interdependent in responding to economic change. English summary. [MU]

27.110 Ivo Schöffer. "Did Holland's golden age coincide with a period of crisis?" *Acta historiae Neerlandica* 1 (1966) 82–107. ISSN 0065-129X. ▸ Author makes skeptical contribution to debate on general crisis of seventeenth century. Draws attention to relatively favorable position enjoyed by contemporary United Provinces. [ACD]

27.111 B. H. Slicher van Bath. *Een samenleving onder spanning: geschiedenis van het platteland in Overijssel.* 1957 ed. Utrecht: Hes, 1977. ISBN 90-6194-331-0. ▸ Major work relating agricultural life in inland province to political developments, 1500–1800. Notes population increase, more gradual economic development, and high unemployment. Influential work for later studies of agriculture and economics. [MU]

27.112 C. Vandenbroeke. *Agriculture et alimentation.* Ghent: Centre Belge d'Histoire Rurale, 1975. (Publication, Centre Belge d'Histoire Rurale, 49.) ▸ Rural history of early modern Belgium. New approach to social and economic history of peasantry. First published in Dutch, 1970. [JLP]

27.113 C. Vandenbroeke. *Sociale geschiedenis van het vlaamse volk.* 1981 ed. Louvain: Kritak, 1984. ISBN 90-630-3123-8. ▸ Social history of Flanders, treating sexuality, fertility, and popular culture of common people. Study of everyday life based on statistical data, supported by charts and graphs. [JLP]

27.114 Johan de Vries. *De economische achteruitgang der republiek in de achttiende eeuw.* 1959 ed. Leiden: Stenfert Kroese, 1968. ▸ Important revisionist work arguing that, while Dutch republic suffered economic decline relative to other nations in eighteenth century, it continued to prosper in absolute terms. See Riley 27.107. [MU]

27.115 Herman van der Wee. *The growth of the Antwerp market and the European economy (XIV–XVI centuries).* 3 vols. The Hague: Nijhoff, 1963. ▸ Analysis of reasons for Antwerp's becoming chief commercial metropolis, ca. 1500, and its (mis)fortunes in sixteenth century. Covers trade, industry, and money market. Appendix with statistical data. [ACD]

27.116 Herman van der Wee and Eddy van Cauwenberghe, eds. *Productivity of land and agricultural innovation in the Low Countries (1250–1800).* Louvain: Leuven University Press, 1978. ISBN 90-6186-073-3. ▸ Collection of articles on economic history of Belgium. Studies range from exploration of tithes, to land productivity, to general question of whether there was agricultural revolution. [JLP]

27.117 Charles H. Wilson. *Anglo-Dutch commerce and finance in the eighteenth century.* 1941 ed. Cambridge: Cambridge University Press, 1966. ▸ Pioneering effort using Amsterdam sources to follow movement of Dutch capital from entrepôt trade to financing of British public debt, 1713–80; not quantitative. Readable; worthwhile. [MU]

27.118 Charles H. Wilson. *Profit and power: a study of England and the Dutch wars.* 1957 ed. The Hague: Nijhoff, 1978. ISBN 90-247-2083-4. ▸ Classic account; argues economic motives were paramount in Anglo-Dutch wars. England faced stiff competition from more internationally oriented Dutch. English Navigation Acts seen as protectionist; compromise reached with Treaty of Breda (1667). [MU]

27.119 Charles H. Wilson. "Taxation and the decline of empires, an unfashionable theme." In *Economic history and the historian, collected essays,* pp. 114–27. New York: Praeger, 1969. ▸ Argues that high taxes on food and consumer goods seriously

weakened competitiveness of Dutch industry by forcing up wages. [MU]

27.120 A. M. van der Woude. *Het noorderkwartier: een regionaal historisch onderzoek in de demografische en economische geschiedenis van westelijk Nederland van de late middeleeuwen tot het begin van de negentiende eeuw.* 1972 ed. 3 vols. Utrecht: Hes, 1983. ISBN 90-6194-243-8. ▸ Contribution to debate on expansion and decline of Dutch republic. Investigates rapid demographic and economic development of Holland north of Amsterdam, 1500–1650, and subsequent century of severe contraction. Quantitative data presented in tables and graphs. [ACD]

Cultural and Intellectual History

27.121 Christiane Berkvens-Stevelinck. *Prosper Marchand: la vie et l'oeuvre, 1678–1756.* Leiden: Brill, 1987. (Studies over de geschiedenis van de Leidse Universiteit, 4.) ISBN 90-04-08354-5, ISSN 0169-8362. ▸ Masterly study of Huguenot exile writer and publisher. Important for understanding scholarly publishing during early Enlightenment. [MU]

27.122 P. J. Buijnsters. *Justus van Effen (1684–1735): leven en werk.* Utrecht: Hes, 1992. ISBN 90-6194-058-3. ▸ Pathbreaking study of Dutch journalist who wrote *Hollandsche Spectator,* encouraging indigenous Enlightenment. Remarkable reconstruction of life of prolific writer who never published under his own name and left few surviving letters. [MU]

27.123 Gerald Cerny. *Theology, politics, and letters at the crossroads of European civilization: Jacques Basnage and the Baylean Huguenot refugees in the Dutch republic.* Dordrecht: Nijhoff; distributed by Kluwer, 1987. ISBN 90-247-3150-X. ▸ Dissertation on Basnage, Huguenot refugee theologian and historiographer to States General. Shows Basnage's learned, moderate Calvinist views close to those of Pierre Bayle, though Basnage not as skeptical. [MU]

27.124 I. H. van Eeghen. *De Amsterdamse boekhandel, 1680–1725.* 5 vols. in 6. Amsterdam: Scheltema & Holkema and Israel, 1960–78. (Publicaties van de Gemeentelijke Archiefdienst van Amsterdam, 1, 2, 4, 7, 12.) ISBN 90-6072-131-4 (v. 5). ▸ Outstanding archival work on publishing at Amsterdam on eve of Enlightenment. Contains many useful documents on Jean Louis de Lorme and other publishers and booksellers and on book trade in republic, 1572–1795. English summary. [MU]

27.125 Willem Frijhoff. *La Société Néerlandaise et ses gradués, 1575–1814: une recherche sérielle sur le statut des intellectuels.* Amsterdam: APA Holland University Press, 1981. ISBN 90-302-1232-2. ▸ Annales study of higher education in early modern Netherlands. Statistics on enrollment patterns, social origins, and professional careers of graduates. Useful comparative data. [MU]

27.126 R. G. Fuks-Mansfeld. *De Sefardim in Amsterdam tot 1795: aspecten van en joodse minderheid in een Hollandse stad.* Hilversum: Historische Vereniging Holland/Verloren, 1989. (Hollandse studiën, 23.) ISBN 90-70403-24-2. ▸ Sound study of Sefardic Jews of Amsterdam from first sixteenth-century settlement to 1795. Shows struggles to maintain community and win acceptance; notes their significant cultural influence on Huguenot refugees and Enlightenment. English summary. [MU]

27.127 Graham C. Gibbs. "The role of the Dutch republic as the intellectual entrepôt of Europe in the seventeenth and eighteenth centuries." *Bijdragen en Mededelingen betreffende de Geschiedenis der Nederlanden* 86 (1971) 323–49. ISSN 0165-0505. ▸ Because of its relatively free publishing climate, Dutch republic important in spreading philosophical and political ideas through newspapers, journals, and inexpensive books. Based on wide reading. [MU]

27.128 Graham C. Gibbs. "Some intellectual and political influences of the Huguenot émigrés in the United Provinces, c. 1680–1730." *Bijdragen en Mededelingen betreffende de Geschiedenis der Nederlanden* 90 (1975) 255–87. ISSN 0165-0505. ▸ Shows Huguenot exiles in Dutch republic leading figures in writing, printing, and bookselling in pre-Enlightenment. Exported French books and culture across Europe. Questions how much they influenced Dutch culture. [MU]

27.129   Craig E. Harline. *Pamphlets, printing, and political culture in the early Dutch republic.* Dordrecht: Nijhoff, 1987. ISBN 90-247-3511-4. ▸ First statistical study of popular pamphlets in collections at Royal Library (The Hague), at Leiden University, and at Ghent. Confirms general consensus on content, political and religious interests, and freedom of press in Dutch republic. [MU]

27.130   Margaret C. Jacob. *The radical Enlightenment: pantheists, Freemasons, and republicans.* London: Allen & Unwin, 1981. ISBN 0-04-901029-8. ▸ Much criticized work arguing for continuity of radical political and philosophical traditions from late Stuart England to Huguenot exiles in Dutch republic. See review by G. C. Gibbs, *British Journal for the History of Science* 17 (1984) 67–81. [MU]

27.131   Margaret C. Jacob and Wijnand W. Mijnhardt, eds. *The Dutch republic in the eighteenth century: decline, Enlightenment, and revolution.* Ithaca, N.Y.: Cornell University Press, 1992. ISBN 0-8014-2624-3 (cl), 0-8014-8050-7 (pbk). ▸ Collection of wide-ranging studies of neglected period of Dutch history from 1987 Washington, D.C. conference. Essential for further research; some essays, such as Mijnhardt's on Dutch Enlightenment, now best works available in English. [MU]

27.132   Elisabeth Labrousse. *Bayle.* 1983 ed. Denys Potts, trans. Oxford: Oxford University Press, 1985. ISBN 0-19-287541-8 (cl), 0-19-287540-X (pbk). ▸ Brief biography of Huguenot exile philosopher and literary critic who lived in Dutch republic for twenty-five years. Based on author's comprehensive two-volume study published in French (1963–64). [MU]

27.133   I. Leonard Leeb. *The ideological origins of the Batavian Revolution: history and politics in the Dutch republic, 1747–1800.* The Hague: Nijhoff, 1973. ISBN 90-247-5157-8. ▸ Intellectual background of Dutch revolutions of eighteenth century drawn from printed sources. Contains useful information on emerging constitutionalism, Orangist and Patriot ideology, and democratic revolution. [MU]

27.134   Th. H. Lunsingh Scheurleer and G.H.M. Posthumus Meyjes, eds. *Leiden University in the seventeenth century: an exchange of learning.* Leiden: Brill, 1975. ISBN 90-04-04267-9. ▸ Worthwhile contributions, mainly in English, on intellectual and academic developments at Leiden in seventeenth century. Areas covered include theology, anatomy, philology, experimental sciences, and printing. [ACD]

27.135   Wijnand W. Mijnhardt. *Tot heil van 't menschdom: culturele genootschappen in Nederland, 1750–1815.* Amsterdam: Rodopi, 1988. (Nieuwe Nederlandse bijdragen tot de geschiedenis der geneeskunde en der natuurwetenschappen, 24.) ISBN 90-6203-780-1, ISSN 0168-9827. ▸ Learned analysis of cultural societies; essential study of Enlightenment, not limited to bourgeois sociability. Dutch members, especially regents, wanted to put companionship and knowledge into practice as social reforms. English summary. [MU]

27.136   I.J.A. Nijenhuis. *Een joodse philosophe: Isaac de Pinto (1717–1787) en de ontwikkeling van politieke economie in de Europese Verlichting.* Amsterdam: Nederlandsch Economisch Historisch Archief, 1992. ISBN 90-71617-58-0. ▸ Good biography and intellectual analysis of Jewish economic theorist and Enlightened philosophe. English summary. [MU]

27.137   J. L. Price. *Culture and society in the Dutch republic during the seventeenth century.* New York: Scribner's, 1974. ISBN 0-684-13589-2. ▸ Sensible but colorless account of Dutch culture in context of political and social life of republic. Painters, who still worked as craftsmen, received commissions from regents of Holland towns. These circumstances help to explain distinctiveness of golden age culture. [ACD]

27.138   C.S.M. Rademaker. *Life and work of Gerardus Joannus Vossius (1577–1649).* Assen: Van Gorcum, 1981. ISBN 90-232-1785-3. ▸ Standard biography of leading Dutch humanist historian. Detailed and well documented. [MU]

27.139   Deric Regin. *Traders, artists, burghers: a cultural history of Amsterdam in the seventeenth century.* Assen: Van Gorcum, 1976. ISBN 90-232-1427-7. ▸ Impressionistic account of Amsterdam life and culture using literary and artistic evidence. Modest, unassuming; for general readers. [MU]

27.140   Simon Schama. *The embarrassment of riches: an interpretation of Dutch culture in the golden age.* 1987 ed. Berkeley: University of California Press, 1988. ISBN 0-520-06147-0 (pbk). ▸ Idiosyncratic interpretation of golden age culture, written in dazzling style. Assertions about wealth, guilt, and Calvinist society disputed by Dutch historians; should be used with caution. [MU]

27.141   Maria A. Schenkeveld. *Dutch literature in the age of Rembrandt: themes and ideas.* Amsterdam: Benjamins, 1991. (Utrecht publications in general and comparative literature, 28.) ISBN 90-272-2214-2, ISSN 0167-8175. ▸ Best English-language history of Dutch literature in golden age. Contains helpful references to texts and translations. [MU]

27.142   Leon Voet. *Antwerp, the golden age: the rise and glory of the metropolis in the sixteenth century.* Antwerp: Mercatorfonds; distributed by Schram, 1973. ISBN 0-8390-0136-3. ▸ Lavishly illustrated history of Antwerp during sixteenth century. Surveys town government, cosmopolitan population, artistic and intellectual life. Useful bibliographies. [ACD]

27.143   Leon Voet. *The golden compasses: a history and evaluation of the printing and publishing activites of the Officina Plantiniana at Antwerp.* Vol. 1: *Christophe Plantin and the Moretuses.* Vol. 2: *The management of a printing and publishing house in Renaissance and Baroque.* New York: Schram, 1969–72. ▸ Detailed account of important Antwerp publishers Plantin and Moretus, including relations with scholars. By director of Plantin Museum who made extensive use of archives. [MU]

Religion

27.144   Michel Cloet. *Het kerkelijk leven in een landelijke dekenij van Vlaanderen tijdens de zeventiende eeuw: Tielt van 1609 tot 1700.* Louvain: Universiteitsbibliotheek, 1968. (Universiteit te Leuven, werken op het gebied van de geschiedenis en de filologie, 5.4.) ▸ Religious life of village of Tielt in seventeenth century. Local history of religious ideas. [JLP]

27.145   Phyllis Mack Crew. *Calvinist preaching and iconoclasm in the Netherlands, 1544–1569.* Cambridge: Cambridge University Press, 1978. ISBN 0-521-21739-3. ▸ Demonstrates heterogeneity of Calvinist preachers in southern Low Countries who were less exponents of revolutionary ideology than guardians of order in uncertain world. Narrowly focused but sound. [ACD]

27.146   Johan Decavele. *Dageraad van de Reformatie in Vlaanderen (1520–1565).* 2 vols. Brussels: Palais des Académies, 1975. (Verhandelingen van de Koninklijke Academie voor wetenschappen, letteren, en schone kunsten van Belgie, Klasse der letteren, 37.76.) ▸ Exhaustive history of Protestant Reformation in county of Flanders with full bibliographies, maps, tables, and lists of dissidents. Demonstrates widespread support for Anabaptism and Calvinism in towns and industrialized countryside. [ACD]

27.147 A. Th. van Deursen. *Bavianen en slijkgeuzen: kerk en kerkvolk ten tijde van Maurits en Oldenbarnevelt.* 1974 ed. Franeker, Netherlands: Van Wijnen, 1991. ISBN 90-5194-067-X. ‣ Brilliant analysis of Calvinist congregations in Holland, ca. 1590–1625, during remonstrant and counter-remonstrant quarrels, using consistorial and synodal records. Major work; some material also used in Deursen 27.90. [ACD]

27.148 Solange Deyon and Alain Lottin. *Les "casseurs" de l'été 1566: l'iconoclasme dans le nord de la France.* Paris: Hachette, 1981. ISBN 2-01-004519-X. ‣ Review of Calvinist activities in French-speaking provinces of Habsburg Netherlands. Reflects on causes of religious violence, especially image breaking, and motivation of iconoclasts. Useful for comparative purposes. [ACD]

27.149 Alastair C. Duke. *Reformation and revolt in the Low Countries.* London: Hambledon, 1990. ISBN 1-85285-021-3. ‣ Collected essays on aspects of Dutch Reformation and revolt. Characterizes early Reformation as eclectic and discusses reasons for success of Calvinism in some areas and failure in others. Best recent work on sixteenth-century religious problems. [ACD/MU]

27.150 Andrew C. Fix. *Prophecy and reason: the Dutch collegiants in the early Enlightenment.* Princeton: Princeton University Press, 1991. ISBN 0-691-03141-X. ‣ Radical Dutch religious thinkers who began as spiritualist and millenarian sect, ca. 1620, gradually became rationalistic by 1690. High intellectual history of movement, related to Spinoza, John Locke, and other figures. [MU]

27.151 G. Groenhuis. "Calvinism and national consciousness: the Dutch republic as the new Israel." In *Church and state since the Reformation: papers delivered to the seventh Anglo-Dutch Historical Conference.* Alastair C. Duke and C. A. Tamse, eds., pp. 118–33. The Hague: Nijhoff, 1981. ISBN 90-247-9077-8 (pbk). ‣ Examination of mentality of orthodox Calvinist clergy whose belief in an observant and elect Dutch nation could not be realized. [ACD]

27.152 W. Nijenhuis. "Variants within Dutch Calvinism in the sixteenth century." *Acta historiae Neerlandicae* 12 (1979) 48–64. ISSN 0065-129X, ISBN 90-247-2236-5. ‣ Draws distinction between moderate and precise Calvinists. Unfortunately distinction is too crude to convey properly diversity of Dutch Calvinism before ca. 1590. [ACD]

27.153 Andrew Pettegree. *Emden and the Dutch revolt: exile and the development of reformed Protestantism.* Oxford: Clarendon, 1992. ISBN 0-19-822739-6. ‣ Persecuted Calvinists in Low Countries, ca. 1555–85, looked to Emden in Germany for safe haven, ecclesiastical advice, and books. Includes short-title catalog of books printed at Emden. Solid and useful. [ACD]

27.154 L. J. Rogier. *Geschiedenis van het katholicisme in Noord-Nederland in de 16e en 17e eeuw.* 3 vols. Amsterdam: Urbi & Orbi, 1947. ‣ Standard, though controversial, history of Catholicism in northern Netherlands during Dutch revolt and seventeenth century. Catholicism appears as natural confession of majority; northern provinces protestantized from above. First edition preferred to unannotated third, slightly revised, edition. Abridged edition available in French: *Histoire du catholicisme hollandais depuis le seizième siècle.* [ACD]

27.155 Heinz Schilling. *Religion, political culture, and the emergence of early modern society: essays in German and Dutch history.* Leiden: Brill, 1992. ISBN 90-04-09607-8. ‣ Stimulating articles, originally in German, on political culture of urban society in northern Germany and Netherlands in early modern period, confessionalization, Second Reformation and state building, and modern characteristics of Dutch republic. [ACD]

27.156 Keith L. Sprunger. *Dutch Puritanism: a history of English and Scottish churches in the Netherlands in the sixteenth and seventeenth centuries.* Leiden: Brill, 1982. ISBN 90-04-06793-0. ‣ Valu-able account of English-speaking dissenting churches in Netherlands and relations with Dutch and English governments. Activity in these refugee churches fluctuated with changes in English regimes. [MU]

27.157 James D. Tracy. "With and without the Counter-Reformation: the Catholic church in the Spanish Netherlands and the Dutch republic, 1580–1650—a review of the literature since 1945." *Catholic historical review* 81.4 (1985) 547–75. ISSN 0008-8080. ‣ Very useful bibliographic essay on religious history of Netherlands, north and south. Examines post-Tridentine reforms, practice, and piety; compares findings of local histories and raises questions for research. [MU]

Art

27.158 J. Bruyn et al. *A corpus of Rembrandt paintings.* 3 vols. to date. D. Cook-Radmore, trans. The Hague: Nijhoff; distributed by Kluwer, 1982–. ISBN 90-247-2613-1 (set), 90-247-2614-X (v. 1), 90-247-3339-1 (v. 2), 90-247-3781-8 (v. 3), 90-247-2764-2 (limited numbered edition), 90-247-2771-5 (limited numbered set). ‣ Definitive catalog of Rembrandt Research Project, team of scholars working for over twenty years to analyze artist's works. Some attributions still matter of judgment. [MU]

27.159 Georges Dogaer. *Flemish miniature painting in the fifteenth and sixteenth centuries.* Anna E. C. Simoni et al., trans. Amsterdam: Israel, 1987. ISBN 90-6078-089-2, 90-6078-078-7. ‣ Study of manuscript illustration in Renaissance Flanders. [JLP]

27.160 Bob Haak. *The golden age: Dutch painters of the seventeenth century.* Elizabeth Willems-Treeman, ed. and trans. New York: Abrams, 1984. ISBN 0-8109-0956-1. ‣ Best overview of Dutch art at its peak. Lavishly illustrated and well worth reading. [MU]

27.161 John B. Knipping. *Iconography of the Counter Reformation in the Netherlands: heaven on earth.* 2 vols. Nieuwkoop, Netherlands: de Graaf, 1974. ISBN 90-6004-342-1. ‣ Examination of subject matter of religious art that expressed elite and popular piety of Counter-Reformation in southern and northern Netherlands. Extensively revised edition of Dutch original (1939–42). Liberally illustrated. [ACD]

27.162 John Michael Montias. *Art and artisans in Delft: a socioeconomic study of the seventeenth century.* Princeton: Princeton University Press, 1982. ISBN 0-691-03986-0 (cl), 0-691-10129-9 (pbk). ‣ Thorough social history by economist, based on family archives and notarial records, showing who made and bought Dutch art in golden age. Majority of paintings bought by wealthiest third of population. [MU]

27.163 John Michael Montias. *Vermeer and his milieu: a web of social history.* Princeton: Princeton University Press, 1989. ISBN 0-691-04051-6. ‣ Meticulous exploration of Vermeer's family background with translated excerpts of many documents. Argues Vermeer had one significant patron, Pieter Claesz van Ruijven, local regent. [MU]

27.164 Peter C. Sutton et al. *Masters of seventeenth-century Dutch landscape painting.* Boston: Museum of Fine Arts; distributed by the University of Pennsylvania, 1987. ISBN 0-8122-8105-5 (cl), 0-87846-282-1 (pbk). ‣ Catalog of exhibition of landscape paintings, which were naturalistic but not always topographically exact. Painters specialized in subjects and sold works on open market. Excludes marine paintings and cityscapes; cites substantial literature. [MU]

27.165 Jane Iandola Watkins et al., eds. *Masters of seventeenth-century Dutch genre painting.* Philadelphia: Philadelphia Museum of Art; distributed by University of Pennsylvania, 1984. ISBN 0-8122-7951-4. ‣ Catalog of influential exhibition of Dutch painters of everyday life. Important for stimulating reexamination of realistic versus symbolic character of paintings. [MU]

BELGIUM SINCE 1789

General and Constitutional History

27.166 Jean Duvieusart. *La question royale, crise et dénouement: juin, juillet, août 1950.* 2d ed. Brussels: Centre de Recherche et d'Information Socio-Politiques, 1975. ▸ Prime minister's informative account of critical phase of highly charged, passionate debate over royal question. Contains hitherto unpublished documents. [WAF]

27.167 John Fitzmaurice. *The politics of Belgium: crisis and compromise in a plural society.* 2d ed. Leo Tindemans, Foreword. London: Hurst, 1988. ISBN 1-85065-038-1. ▸ Concise survey of Belgian historical, economic, and social development; administrative institutions; and parties and pressure groups. [WAF]

27.168 Hervé Hasquin, ed. *La Wallonie: le pays et les hommes.* 2d ed. 2 vols. Brussels: La Renaissance du Livre, 1979–80. ▸ Comprehensive, illustrated history of Wallonia by prominent Belgian historians. [WAF]

27.169 E. H. Kossmann. *The Low Countries, 1780–1940.* Oxford: Clarendon, 1978. ISBN 0-19-822108-8. ▸ Authoritative synthesis of political, socioeconomic, and cultural history of Belgium and Netherlands. [WAF]

27.170 Mina Martens, ed. *Histoire de Bruxelles.* Brussels: Éditions Universitaires, 1976. ISBN 2-7089-4764-8. ▸ General narrative history of Brussels by established historians and archivists, distinct from regional histories of Flanders and Wallonia. [WAF]

27.171 Robert Senelle. *The reform of the Belgian state.* 5 vols. Brussels: Ministry of Foreign Affairs, External Trade and Cooperation in Development, 1978–90. (Memo from Belgium, views and surveys, 179, 182, 189, 196, 198.) ▸ Descriptive analysis of constitutional reforms since 1967. Includes texts of amended articles and new laws, Claes-Moreau Agreement, and Community Pact. [WAF]

27.172 Jean Stengers et al. *Histoire de la Belgique contemporaine, 1914–1970.* Brussels: La Renaissance du Livre, 1975. ▸ Large, richly illustrated history by eminent Belgian historians, complementing seminal work of Henri Pirenne, 1914–70. [WAF]

27.173 Marie Rose Thelemans. "Deux institutions centrales sous le régime français en Belgique." *Revue belge de philologie et d'histoire* 41, 43, 44 (1963, 1965, 1966) 1091–1135, 1272–1323, 500–60. ISSN 0035-0818. ▸ Useful analytical description of French radical administrative reforms in occupied (annexed) Belgium, 1793 95. [WAF]

27.174 Stephen B. Wickman, ed. *Belgium, a country study.* 1984 2d ed. Washington, D.C.: The Studies: sold by United States Government Printing Office, 1985. (American University foreign area studies: area handbook series, 550–170.) ▸ Useful compilation of data organized in descriptive chapters: historical background, society and its environment, economy, and government and national security. [WAF]

27.175 Els Witte. "Le parlement belge de fonctionnaires, 1830–1848." *Parlements, états, et représentation* 4.2 (1984) 157–67. ISSN 0260-6755. ▸ Detailed analysis of significant role of administrative, judicial, and other state functionaries as members of national legislature. French summary of longer study in *Revue belge de philologie et d'histoire* 59.4 (1981) 828–82. [WAF]

27.176 Els Witte, ed. *Histoire de Flandre: des origines à nos jours.* Brussels: La Renaissance du Livre, 1983. ▸ Comprehensive history, with illustrations, of Flanders by leading Belgian historians. [WAF]

Political History

27.177 Hugues Dumont et al. *Belgitude et crise de l'état belge, actes du colloque: organisé par la Faculté de Droit des Facultés Universi-*taires Saint-Louis, le 24 novembre 1988. Brussels: Facultés Universitaires Saint-Louis, 1989. (Publications des Facultés Universitaires Saint-Louis, 48.) ISBN 2-8028-0069-8. ▸ Expert scrutiny of postwar separatist and federalist impulses affecting survival of nation and state. [WAF]

27.178 Lewis H. Gann and Peter Duignan. *The rulers of Belgian Africa, 1884–1914.* Princeton: Princeton University Press, 1979. ISBN 0-691-05277-8. ▸ Survey with tables and charts of evolution of Belgian administrative rule in Congo Free State and later. [WAF]

27.179 Roger Keyes. *Outrageous fortune: the tragedy of Leopold III of the Belgians, 1901–1941.* London: Secker & Warburg, 1984. ISBN 0-436-23320-7. ▸ Balanced reexamination of dramatic circumstances of surrender in May 1940. Refutes British and French charges of treason against King Leopold III. [WAF]

27.180 Xavier Mabille. *Histoire politique de la Belgique: facteurs et acteurs de changement.* Brussels: Centre de Recherche et d'Information Socio-Politiques, 1986. ISBN 2-87075-018-9. ▸ Survey of major phases of Wallon-Flemish and other cleavages. [WAF]

27.181 Janet L. Polasky. "Women in revolutionary Belgium: from stone throwers to hearth tenders." *History workshop* 21 (1986) 87–104. ISSN 0309-2984, ISBN 0-7102-0220-2. ▸ Examination of women's participation in Brabant Revolution of 1789 and economic and sociopolitical reasons for lack of similar participation in Belgian Revolution of 1830. [ICF]

27.182 Jean Puissant. *L'évolution du mouvement ouvrier socialiste dans le Borinage.* Brussels: Palais des Académies, 1982. (Mémoires de la classe des lettres. Collection in 8°, Deuxième série, 65.5.) ISBN 2-8031-0031-2. ▸ Impressive study of socialist labor movement in Borinage; focus on chronological and structural development. [WAF]

27.183 John W. Rooney, Jr. *Revolt in the Netherlands: Brussels, 1830.* Lawrence, Kan.: Coronado, 1982. ISBN 0-87291-156-X. ▸ Well-documented analysis of authenticity of Belgian revolution, which was decisively supported by working class in Brussels, under leadership of alienated liberal press, lawyers, and Flemish clergy. [WAF]

27.184 Els Witte and Jan Craeybeckx. *La Belgique politique de 1830 à nos jours: les tensions d'une démocratie bourgeoise.* Rev. ed. Serge Govaert, trans. Brussels: Labor, 1987. ISBN 2-8040-0269-1. ▸ Remarkable survey and interpretation of Belgian history to 1980. Insightful views on philosophical, social, and linguistic cleavages, liberal versus clerical struggle, role of middle and lower classes, and Flemish movement. [WAF]

SEE ALSO
47.27 Daniel H. Thomas. *The guarantee of Belgian independence and neutrality in European diplomacy, 1830's–1930's.*
47.30 Jonathan E. Helmreich. *Belgium and Europe.*
47.450 Sally Marks. *Innocent abroad.*

Economic History

27.185 John R. Gillingham. *Belgian business in the Nazi new order.* Ghent: Jan Dhondt Foundation, 1977. ▸ Original but contested thesis of collaboration by Belgian banking and industrial elites with Germany for purposes of profit, modernization, and increased influence on financial and economic policies. [WAF]

27.186 Ginette Kurgan-van Hentenryk. *Rail, finance, et politique: les entreprises Philippart, 1865–1890.* Brussels: Éditions de l'Université de Bruxelles, 1982. (Université Libre de Bruxelles, Faculté de Philosophie et Lettres, 84.) ISBN 2-8004-0784-0. ▸ Massive research and solid analysis of Philippart's role in interplay of market forces and politics in expansionist era. Exposes contradictory aspects of public and private goals and developments both pre-1850 and post-1870. [WAF]

27.187 Anne van Neck. *Les débuts de la machine à vapeur dans l'industrie belge, 1800–1850.* Brussels: Académie Royale de Belgique, 1979. (Histoire quantitative et développement de la Belgique, révolution industrielle, 2.2.) ▸ Detailed analytical account of impact of fixed steam engines, their construction and usage in economic sectors, production, cost, and capital resources. [WAF]

Social and Cultural History

27.188 Jeannine Bayer-Lothe. *Paupérisme et bienfaisance à Namur au dix-neuvième siècle, 1815–1914.* Brussels: Crédit Communal de Belgique, 1978. (Collection histoire pro civitate, Série in 8°, 51.) ▸ Pathbreaking model study. Urbanization and development of small shops, in combination with consumer price decline, had more positive impact than welfare programs in nineteenth-century Namur. [WAF]

27.189 J. de Belder. "Changes in the socio-economic status of the Belgian nobility in the nineteenth century." *Acta historiae Neerlandicae* 15 (1982) 1–20. ISSN 0065-129X, ISBN 90-247-9158-8. ▸ Preliminary findings on decline of nobility, its tendency to dissolve into upper-middle-class elites, its role, influence, and legacy to conservative and liberal groups. [WAF]

27.190 Eliane Gubin. "Flamingantisme et patriotisme en Belgique au dix-neuvième siècle." *Tijdschrift voor Geschiedenis* 95.4 (1982) 558–76. ISSN 0040-7518. ▸ Overview of post-1830 evolutionary trends of Flemish movement: loyal acceptance of Belgian state, quest for Flemish cultural emancipation and linguistic homogeneity, and economic strength. [WAF]

27.191 Eliane Gubin and Patrick Lefèvre. "Obligation scolaire et société en Belgique au dix-neuvième siècle: réflexions à propos du premier projet de loi sur l'enseignement obligatoire (1883)." *Revue belge de philologie et d'histoire* 63.2 (1985) 324–76. ISSN 0035-0818. ▸ Detailed analysis of political, economic, and social ramifications of legislation for obligatory schooling of children ages six to twelve. [WAF]

27.192 Patricia J. Hilden. "The rhetoric and iconography of reform: women coal miners in Belgium, 1840–1914." *The Historical journal* 34.2 (1991) 411–36. ISSN 0018-246X. ▸ Prize-winning essay based on socioeconomic, literary, and artistic sources. Examines reformers' perceptions about women coal miners, their transformation into heroic and romantic figures by writers, painters, and sculptors. [WAF]

27.193 Marcel Janssens. "The two literatures in Belgium since 1830." In *Conflict and coexistence in Belgium: the dynamics of a culturally divided society.* Arend Lijphart, ed., pp. 93–106. Berkeley: University of California, Institute of International Studies, 1981. (Research series, 46.) ISBN 0-87725-146-0 (pbk). ▸ Account of historical phases of Belgian literary diversity; assessment of thesis of Belgitude (Belgian cultural essence), and of French and Dutch literary specificity. [WAF]

27.194 Ginette Kurgan-van Hentenryk. "A forgotten class: the petite bourgeoisie in Belgium, 1850–1914." In *Shopkeepers and master artisans in nineteenth-century Europe.* Geoffrey Crossick and Heinz-Gerhard Haupt, eds., pp. 120–33. London: Methuen, 1984. ISBN 0-416-35660-5. ▸ Brief overview of economic, political, and social evolution, and role of lower middle class. [WAF]

27.195 Peter Scholliers. "L'identité des ouvriers-mécaniciens gantois au dix-neuvième siècle: une contribution au débat sur le rôle social de l'élite ouvrière." *Histoire, économie, et société* 6.1 (1987) 83–111. ISSN 0752-5702. ▸ Excellent case study of privileged status of skilled metal workers of Ghent before 1880s and subsequent decline in wake of mass production. Development of metal workers' leading role in socialist labor movement. [WAF]

27.196 Reginald de Schryver. "The Belgian Revolution and the emergence of Belgium's biculturalism." In *Conflict and coexistence*

in *Belgium: the dynamics of a culturally divided society.* Arend Lijphart, ed., pp. 13–33. Berkeley: University of California, Institute of International Studies, 1981. (Research series, 46.) ISBN 0-87725-146-0 (pbk). ▸ Account of developments in French-language predominance post-1830 and limited linguistic concessions to Flemish in 1970s and 1980s. [WAF]

27.197 Denise de Weerdt. *En de vrouwen? Vrouw, vrouwenbeweging, en feminisme in België, 1830–1960.* Ghent: Masereelfonds, 1980. ISBN 90-6417-041-X. ▸ Overview, devoid of feminist theory, based on wide variety of source materials, of history of Belgian women's movement. [WAF]

27.198 Aristide R. Zolberg. "The making of Flemings and Walloons: Belgium, 1830–1914." *Journal of interdisciplinary history* 5.2 (1974) 179–236. ISSN 0022-1953. ▸ Historical and theoretical analysis, with tables, of transformation of 1830 linguistic segmentation through fundamental socioeconomic and political developments. [WAF]

LUXEMBOURG SINCE 1789
General and Constitutional History

27.199 Albert Calmes and Christian Calmes. *Histoire contemporaine du Grand-Duché de Luxembourg.* Edition varies. 11 vols. Luxembourg: Saint-Paul, 1939–79. ▸ Synthesis of Luxembourg history since 1814, focused on politics and diplomacy. [WAF]

27.200 Carlo Hury and Jules Christophory, comps. *Luxembourg.* Santa Barbara, Calif.: ABC-Clio, 1981. ISBN 0-903450-37-2. ▸ Comprehensive, annotated bibliography. [WAF]

27.201 Pierre Majerus. *L'état luxembourgeois: manuel de droit constitutionnel et de droit administratif.* 5th ed. Luxembourg: Imprimerie Centrale, 1983. ▸ Standard historical and analytical work on constitutional and administrative law. Explication of modifications of constitutional texts and procedures. [WAF]

27.202 Pierre Majerus. *The institutions of the Grand Duchy of Luxembourg.* Rev. ed. Jean-Mathias Goerens, ed. Luxembourg: Grand Duchy of Luxembourg, Ministry of State Press and Information Service, 1989. ▸ Source book on constitutional structures, executive, legislative, and judicial branches, and public administration. [WAF]

27.203 James Newcomer. *The Grand Duchy of Luxembourg: the evolution of nationhood, 963 A.D. to 1983.* Lanham, Md. and Fort Worth: University Press of America and Texas Christian University, 1984. ISBN 0-8191-3845-2 (cl), 0-8191-3846-0 (pbk). ▸ General political history, with economic and social data, of Luxembourg during Holy Roman Empire and during periods of domination by Spain, Austria, France, and Germany. [WAF]

Politics, Diplomacy, and War

27.204 Albert Calmes and Christian Calmes. *Au fil de l'histoire.* Edition varies. 5 vols. Luxembourg: Saint-Paul, 1968–77. ▸ Popular accounts of events and individuals in Luxembourg political, economic, and social history between 1789 and 1919. [WAF]

27.205 François Decker. *La conscription militaire au département des Forêts.* 2 vols. Luxembourg: Saint-Paul, 1980. ▸ Detailed study of conscription and fate of Luxembourgers in armies of directory, consulate, and empire. [WAF]

27.206 Paul Dostert. *Luxemburg zwischen Selbstbehauptung und nationaler Selbstaufgabe: die deutsche Besatzungspolitik und die volksdeutsche Bewegung, 1940–1945.* Luxembourg: Saint-Paul, 1985. ▸ Comprehensive history of efforts by German civil administration and collaborators to achieve annexation of Grand Duchy by Third Reich. [WAF]

27.207 Willard Allen Fletcher. "The German administration in Luxembourg, 1940–1942: toward a 'de facto' annexation." *The*

Historical journal 13.3 (1970) 533–44. ISSN 0018-246X. ‣ Concise account of political and administrative changes introduced by German civil administration in occupied Luxembourg. [WAF]

27.208 Willard Allen Fletcher. "*Plan und Wirklichkeit*: German military government in Luxemburg, 1940." In *Historians and archivists: essays in modern German history and archival policy.* George O. Kent, ed., pp. 145–72. Fairfax, Va.: George Mason University Press, 1991. ISBN 0-913969-32-X. ‣ Expert analysis of pre-invasion plans and wartime operations of short-lived military government. [WAF]

27.209 Emile Haag and Emile Krier. *La Grande-Duchesse et son gouvernement pendant la Deuxième Guerre Mondiale: 1940, l'année du dilemme.* Luxembourg: Éditions RTL, 1987. ISBN 2-87951-202-6 (pbk). ‣ Perceptive scholarly study, supplemented by document texts, of political problems and uncertainties confronting government-in-exile in France and Portugal, 1940. [WAF]

27.210 Georges Heisbourg. *Le gouvernement luxembourgeois en exile.* 4 vols. Luxembourg: Saint-Paul, 1986–91. ISBN 2-87963-020-7 (v. 2), 2-87963-058-4 (v. 3), 2-87963-140-8 (v. 4). ‣ Uneven account of wartime politics of government-in-exile's shift from neutrality to active membership in Allied coalition. [WAF]

27.211 Joseph Maertz. *Luxemburg in der Ardennenoffensive, 1944/45.* 8th ed. Luxembourg: Saint-Paul, 1981. ‣ Popular account of military operations in Luxembourg Ardennes during Battle of the Bulge. [WAF]

27.212 E. T. Melchers. *Kriegsschauplatz Luxemburg: August 1914, Mai 1940.* 4th ed. Luxembourg: Saint-Paul, 1979. ‣ Expert comparative account of German military invasions of Luxembourg in both world wars. [WAF]

27.213 E. T. Melchers. *Luxemburg: Befreiung und Ardennenoffensive, 1944–1945.* Luxembourg: Saint-Paul, 1984. ‣ Well-researched history, by professional military officer, of liberation of Luxembourg and subsequent Ardennes offensive. [WAF]

27.214 Gilbert Trausch. *Le Luxembourg: émergence d'un état et d'une nation.* Antwerp: Mercatorfonds, 1989. ISBN 90-6153-206-X. ‣ Convincing interpretation by leading Luxembourg historian on emergence of national identity and consciousness in wake of repeated threats to territorial independence, 1839–1919. [WAF]

Economic History

27.215 Henri Koch. "Die Luxemburger Arbeiterklasse und ihre Gewerkschaften." *Hémecht* 29.4, 30.3, 30.4 (1977–78) 473–500, 303–42, 531–63. ISSN 0018-0270. ‣ Useful, sparsely documented survey of history of trade union movement, subject yet to receive attention of professional historians. [WAF]

27.216 Jean-Luc Mousset. *L'industrialisation du Luxembourg de 1800 à 1914.* Luxembourg: Musée d'Histoire et d'Art, 1988. ‣ Survey of development of basic industries: textile, tanning, iron, and steel. [WAF]

Social and Cultural History

27.217 Françoise Bedos et al. *Famille et structures sociales au Luxembourg.* Luxembourg: Ministère de la Famille, du Logement Social, et de la Solidarité Sociale, 1978. ‣ Pioneering, well-documented examination of relationship between family and social institutions and structures, as well as impact on family of industrialization and urbanization. [WAF]

27.218 Michael Braun. *Die luxemburgische Sozialversicherung bis zum Zweiten Weltkrieg: Entwicklung, Probleme, und Bedeutung.* Stuttgart: Klett, 1982. ISBN 3-608-91118-9. ‣ Comprehensive history of social policy, social security legislation and administration, and political party programs and objectives. Includes tables on

fiscal policies, social security contributions, population, etc. [WAF]

27.219 Pierre Grégoire. *Luxemburgs Kulturentfaltung im neunzehnten Jahrhundert: eine kritische Darstellung des Literarischen, Künstlerischen, und Wissenschaftlichen Lebens.* Luxembourg: De Frendeskrees, 1981. ‣ Historical treatise on influence of French and German intellectual and cultural currents. [WAF]

27.220 Gilbert Trausch. "Contributions à l'histoire sociale de la question du Luxembourg, 1914–1922." *Hémecht* 26.1 (1974) 7–118. ISSN 0018-0270. ‣ Insightful examination of linkage among socioeconomic issues, wartime occupation, postwar political turbulence, French and Belgian annexation schemes, and transition from *Zollverein* membership to adherence to Belgo-Luxembourg Customs Union. [WAF]

27.221 Gérard Trausch. *La croissance démographique du Grand-Duché de Luxembourg du début du dix-neuvième siècle à nos jours: les mouvements naturels de la population.* 2d ed. Esch-sur-Alzette, Luxembourg: Imprimerie Victor, 1973. ‣ Demographic study with numerous statistical tables. Focuses on impact of migratory movements on small population. [WAF]

27.222 Gilbert Trausch. "L'immigration italienne au Luxembourg des origines (1890) à la grande crise de 1929." *Hémecht* 33.4 (1981) 443–71. ISSN 0018-0270. ‣ Detailed examination, with statistical data, of impact of Italian immigration on labor and syndicalism, social mores, and integration. [WAF]

THE NETHERLANDS SINCE 1789

General and Constitutional History

27.223 Ken Gladdish. *Governing from the centre: politics and policy-making in the Netherlands.* De Kalb: Northern Illinois University Press, 1991. ISBN 0-87580-162-5. ‣ Historical and analytical study of post-1945 Dutch institutions of government, corporate reconstruction, parliamentary and executive modus operandi, public policy, and links to international organizations. [WAF]

27.224 Peter King and Michael Wintle, comps. *The Netherlands.* Santa Barbara, Calif.: ABC-Clio, 1988. ISBN 1-85109-041-X. ‣ Comprehensive, annotated bibliography. [WAF]

27.225 Margrit B. Krewson. *The Netherlands and northern Belgium: a selective bibliography of reference works.* Washington, D.C.: Library of Congress, 1989. ISBN 0-8444-0637-6. ‣ Select but unannotated bibliography of Library of Congress holdings. [WAF]

27.226 Netherlands Ministry of Home Affairs. *The constitution of the kingdom of the Netherlands.* The Hague: Ministry of Home Affairs, 1983. ‣ Integral text of the Constitution. [WAF]

27.227 Gerald Newton. *The Netherlands: an historical and cultural survey, 1795–1977.* Boulder: Westview, 1978. ISBN 0-89158-802-7. ‣ Useful survey of Dutch language and literature, history, political developments, decolonization, foreign policy, women's rights, and society. [WAF]

27.228 William Z. Shetter. *The Netherlands in perspective: the organizations of society and environment.* Leiden: Nijhoff, 1987. ISBN 90-6890070-6. ‣ General, informative introduction to Dutch constitutional structures and political, social, and cultural life. [WAF]

27.229 J. J. Woltjer. *Recent verleden: de geschiedenis van Nederland in de twintigste eeuw.* Amsterdam: Balans, 1992. ISBN 90-5018-152-X. ‣ Up-to-date interpretation of twentieth-century Dutch history. Emphasis on social and economic change since 1945, but also shows influence of long historical processes. Stimulating, challenging, essential for advanced readers. [MU]

Politics, Diplomacy, and War

27.230 Herman Bakvis. *Catholic power in the Netherlands.* Kingston, Ont.: McGill-Queen's University Press, 1981. ISBN 0-7735-0361-7. ‣ Narrowly focused account chronicling dramatic postwar decline of Catholic power after sudden collapse of Catholic subculture in 1960s and 1970s. [WAF]

27.231 Wayne Ph. te Brake et al. "Women and political culture in the Dutch revolutions." In *Women and politics in the age of the democratic revolution.* Harriet B. Applewhite and Darline Gay Levy, eds., pp. 109–46. Ann Arbor: University of Michigan Press, 1990. ISBN 0-472-09413-0. ‣ Examination of women's participation in Patriot Revolution of 1780s and Batavian Revolution of 1795, gendered nature of both aristocratic and popular politics, and emergence of feminist issues in Dutch popular culture. [ICF]

27.232 Erik Hansen. "Fascism and nazism in the Netherlands, 1929–39." *European studies review* 11 (1981) 355–85. ISSN 0014-3111. ‣ Informed analysis of ineffectiveness of fragmented fascist movement and of mass-movement potential of national socialist movement (NSB) in context of 1930s socioeconomic situation. [WAF]

27.233 Gerhard Hirschfeld. *Nazi rule and Dutch collaboration: the Netherlands under German occupation, 1940–1945.* Louise Willmot, trans. Oxford: Berg; distributed by St. Martin's, 1988. ISBN 0-85496-146-1. ‣ Perceptive study of various forms of Dutch collaboration during German occupation. [WAF]

27.234 Louis de Jong et al., eds. *Het koninkrijk der Nederlanden in de tweede wereldoorlog.* 14 vols. in 29. The Hague: Staatsdrukkerij & Uitgeverijbedrijf, 1969–91. ‣ Seminal multivolume study of Netherlands under German occupation in World War II. [WAF]

27.235 Maarten Kuitenbrouwer. *The Netherlands and the rise of modern imperialism: colonies and foreign policy, 1870–1902.* Hugh Beyer, trans. New York: Berg; distributed by St. Martin's, 1991. ISBN 0-85496-681-1. ‣ Interesting study of interaction of foreign policy and imperialism, set in comparative historical framework of British, Dutch, and Portuguese expansion. [WAF]

27.236 Arend Lijphart. *The politics of accommodation: pluralism and democracy in the Netherlands.* 2d ed. Berkeley: University of California Press, 1975. ISBN 0-520-02918-6 (cl), 0-520-02900-3 (pbk). ‣ Synthesis of Dutch politics. Second edition adds examination of disintegration of "pillarized society," concept made famous by author. [WAF]

27.237 J. Presser. *The destruction of the Dutch Jews.* 1968 ed. Arnold J. Pomerans, trans. New York: Dutton, 1969. ‣ Especially valuable history of predeportation phase of persecution of Jews by Germans and their Dutch collaborators. By professional historian who survived in hiding. [WAF]

27.238 Marinus Johannes Franciscus Robijns. "Les radicaux aux Pays-Bas (1840–1851)." *Acta historiae Neerlandica* 5 (1971) 103–34. ISSN 0065-129X. ‣ Synopsis of larger study on ineffectual role of Dutch radicals whose ideas about social justice, democracy, and freedom of press were far in advance of liberal and progressive parties. [WAF]

27.239 Simon Schama. *Patriots and liberators: revolution in the Netherlands, 1780–1813.* New York: Knopf, 1977. ISBN 0-394-48516-5. ‣ Superb examination of reverberations of Dutch and French revolutions, French rule, struggle between oligarchy and reformers (resolved in 1848), and emergence of modern bureaucratic system. [WAF]

27.240 C. A. Tamse. "The role of small countries in the international politics of the 1860s: the Netherlands and Belgium in Europe." *Acta historiae Neerlandicae* 9 (1976) 143–69. ISSN 0065-129X. ‣ Examination of Dutch and Belgian efforts to protect status of small independent states against threats from Vienna Congress diplomacy and Franco-Prussian rivalry. [WAF]

27.241 H. L. Wesseling. "Post-imperial Holland." *Journal of contemporary history* 15 (1980) 125–42. ISSN 0022-0094. ‣ Short, informed essay on impact of decolonization on Dutch politics, trade, and society. [WAF]

Economic History

27.242 Paul Deprez. "The Low Countries." In *European demography and economic growth.* W. R. Lee, ed., pp. 236–83. New York: St. Martin's, 1979. ISBN 0-312-26935-8. ‣ Succinct account of demographic history of Netherlands and Belgium, with statistical tables for each country, 1840–1949. [WAF]

27.243 Richard T. Griffiths. "The creation of a national Dutch economy, 1795–1909." *Tijdschrift voor Geschiedenis* 95.4 (1982) 513–37. ISSN 0040-7518. ‣ Expert survey of national economic integration: removal of institutional barriers, expansion of water and rail transport, unitary fiscal policies, and patterns of regional development. [WAF]

27.244 Richard T. Griffiths. *Industrial retardation in the Netherlands, 1830–1850.* The Hague: Nijhoff, 1979. ISBN 90-247-2199-7. ‣ Incisive study of industrial sector. Stagnation attributed to supply and demand imbalances, wage and transportation costs, exclusion from external markets, and foreign competition in internal markets. [WAF]

27.245 A. Heerding. *The history of N. V. Philips' gloeilampenfabrieken.* 2 vols. Derek S. Jordan, trans. Cambridge: Cambridge University Press, 1986–88. ISBN 0-521-32169-7 (v. 1), 0-521-32170-0 (v. 2). ‣ Excellent study of Dutch incandescent lamp industry. [WAF]

27.246 Jan Aart de Jonge. "Industrial growth in the Netherlands (1850–1914)." *Acta historiae Neerlandica* 5 (1971) 159–212. ISSN 0065-129X. ‣ Synopsis of dissertation on Dutch economic sectors, concluding Industrial Revolution occurred not in 1860s but in 1890s. [WAF]

27.247 J.M.M. Meere. "Long-term trends in income and wealth inequality in the Netherlands, 1808–1940." *Historical social research* 27 (1983) 8–37. ISSN 0172-6404. ‣ Very useful quantitative analysis of phases in income distribution and wealth inequality patterns. [WAF]

27.248 Joel Mokyr. *Industrialization in the Low Countries, 1795–1850.* New Haven: Yale University Press, 1976. ISBN 0-300-01892-4. ‣ Excellent comparative study combining theoretical model of early European industrialization with historical data. Identifies and analyzes causal factors in modernization of Belgium and retardation of Dutch economy, respectively. [WAF]

27.249 Johan de Vries. *The Netherlands economy in the twentieth century: an examination of the most characteristic features in the period 1900–1970.* Derek S. Jordan, trans. Assen: Van Gorcum, 1978. ISBN 90-232-1594-X. ‣ Expert analytical survey of issues and policies during distinct phases of Dutch economic cycles between 1865 and 1976. [WAF]

27.250 Charles H. Wilson. *The history of Unilever: a study in economic growth and social change.* 1954–68 ed. 3 vols. London: Cassell, 1970. ISBN 0-304-93604-9 (v. 1), 0-304-93605-7 (v. 2), 0-304-93606-5 (v. 3). ‣ Exemplary business history of giant Anglo-Dutch multinational company, producers of soap and food products. Reprint of two-volume 1954 edition and abridgement of volume 3. [MU]

Social and Cultural History

27.251 Hans van Amersfoort. *Immigration and the formation of minority groups: the Dutch experience, 1945–1975.* Robert Lyng, trans. Cambridge: Cambridge University Press, 1982. ISBN 0-521-23293-7. ▸ Sophisticated theoretical and historical analysis of post–World War II immigration and formation of Indonesian, Moluccan, Surinamese, and guest worker minorities. [WAF]

27.252 Christopher Bagley. *The Dutch plural society: a comparative study in race relations.* London: Oxford University Press for Institute of Race Relations, 1973. ISBN 0-19-218405-9. ▸ Expert historical and sociological analysis of integration of immigrants from former Dutch colonial possessions. [WAF]

27.253 Erik H. Bax. *Modernization and cleavage in Dutch society: a study of long-term economic and social change.* Aldershot, England: Avebury, 1990. ISBN 0-566-07164-9. ▸ Excellent analysis of economic modernization and its impact on post-1960 social and political process of de-pillarization. See Lijphart 27.236. [WAF]

27.254 Mineke Bosch, ed. *Politics and friendship: letters from the International Woman Suffrage Alliance, 1902–1942.* Columbus: Ohio State University Press, 1990. ISBN 0-8142-0509-7. ▸ Informative introduction and collection of letters on women's issues from International Woman Suffrage Alliance in the Internationaal Archief voor de Vrouwenbeweging (IAV), founded by Dutch feminists in 1935. [WAF]

27.255 H. Daalder. "Dutch Jews in a segmented society." *Acta historiae Neerlandicae* 10 (1978) 175–94. ISSN 0065-129X, ISBN 90-247-2021-4. ▸ Informative history on place of Jewish community in Dutch "pillarized" society. [WAF]

27.256 Henk van Dijk et al. "Regional differences in social mobility patterns in the Netherlands between 1830 and 1940." *Journal of social history* 17 (1984) 435–52. ISSN 0022-4529. ▸ Convincing study of selected Dutch towns to support hypothesis of close relationship between industrialization and social mobility. [WAF]

27.257 Maria Grever. "On the origins of Dutch women's historiography: three portraits (1840–1970)." In *Current issues in women's history.* Arina Angerman et al., eds., pp. 249–69. London: Routledge, 1989. ISBN 0-415-00361-X (cl), 0-415-00362-8 (pbk). ▸ General account of contribution of women historians; frame of reference derived from concept of women's culture. Focuses on intellectual activities and inhibiting factors. [WAF]

27.258 Francisca de Haan. *Sekse op kantoor: over vrowelijkheid, mannelijkheid en macht, Nederland, 1860–1940.* Hilversum, Netherlands: Verloren, 1992. (Publikaties Faculteit Historische en Kunstwetenschappen, 5.) ISBN 90-6550-404-4. ▸ Discussion of emancipation and reinforcement of gender roles and women's struggles to win jobs and avoid harassment, using labor statistics, questionnaires, and oral histories of office workers. [MU]

27.259 Erik Hansen and Peter A. Prosper, Jr. "Education and Dutch society: the Bond van Nederlandse Onderwijzers in the late nineteenth century." *Histoire sociale/Social history* 17.34 (1984) 335–56. ISSN 0018-2257. ▸ Well-reasoned analysis of failure of voluntary civic association to prevent, within framework of *verzuiling* (societal pillarization), divisive inroads by clerical bloc on Dutch elementary education. [WAF]

27.260 H. P. Hogeweg-De Haart. "The history of the women's movement in the Netherlands." *Netherlands journal of sociology* 14.1 (1978) 1940. ISSN 0038-0172. ▸ Overview of distinct developmental phases of movement since 1792. [WAF]

27.261 F. L. van Holthoon. "Beggary and social control: government policy and beggary, particularly in the province of Groningen between 1823 and 1870." *Economisch en sociaal-historisch jaarboek* 43 (1980) 155–93. ▸ Innovative case study of beggars' behavior and effectiveness of social control policies. [WAF]

27.262 Marco H. D. van Leeuwen. *Bijstand in Amsterdam, ca. 1800–1850: armenzorg als beheersings- en overlevingsstrategie.* Zwolle, Netherlands and Amsterdam: Waanders and Gemeentearchief, 1992. (Publikaties van het Gemeentearchief Amsterdam, 19.) ISBN 90-663-0324-7. ▸ Well-documented case study describing and analyzing Amsterdam poor relief in terms of identity and rationale of provider and recipient groups and effects of poor relief on society. [WAF]

27.263 A. J. Schuurman. *Materiële cultuur en levensstijl: een onderzoek naar de taal der dingen op het Nederlandse platteland in de negentiende eeuw, de Zaanstreek, Oost-Groningen, Oost-Brabant.* Wageningen, Netherlands: Afd. Agrarische Geschiedenis, Landbouwuniversiteit, 1989. (A.A.G. bijdragen, 30.) ISSN 0511-0726. ▸ Carefully structured comparative history of evolution of household material culture of laborers, farmers, middle and upper middle/higher classes for periods 1830–34, 1860–64, and 1890–94. Model study. [WAF]

27.264 James W. Skillen and S. W. Carlson-Thies. "Religion and political development in nineteenth-century Holland." *Publius* 12.3 (1982) 43–64. ISSN 0048-5950. ▸ Reliable refutation of hypothesis that modernization and secularism always linked in political development using evidence from historical linkage of politics and religion. [WAF]

27.265 J. M. Welcker. *Heren en arbeiders in de vroege Nederlandse arbeidersbeweging, 1870–1914.* Amsterdam: Van Gennep, 1978. ISBN 90-6012-312-3. ▸ Interesting analysis of working-class conditions, based on interviews, budgets, letters, and anarchistic and alternative ideas and activities. [WAF]

27.266 Michael Wintle. *Pillars of piety: religion in the Netherlands in the nineteenth century, 1813–1901.* Hull: Hull University Press, 1987. (Occasional papers in modern Dutch studies, 2.) ISBN 0-85958-465-8 (pbk), ISSN 0144-3070. ▸ Good synthesis of complex conflict between progressive liberals and conservatives within religious denominations. [WAF]

SWITZERLAND

General Studies

27.267 Hektor Ammann and Karl Schib. *Historischer Atlas der Schweiz/Atlas historique de la Suisse.* 2d ed. Aarau: Sauerländer, 1958. ▸ Outstanding historical atlas of federal state, combining national with cantonal historical maps. [EWM]

27.268 Edgar Bonjour, H. S. Offler, and G. R. Potter. *A short history of Switzerland.* 1952 ed. Westport, Conn.: Greenwood, 1985. ISBN 0-313-24675-0. ▸ Most reliable, although relatively brief, general history of Switzerland available in English. Emphasizes political and religious events; stops in 1939. [EWM]

27.269 Hanno Helbling et al., eds. *Handbuch der Schweizer Geschichte.* 2d ed. 2 vols. Zurich: Berichthaus, 1980. ISBN 3-85572-041-X (set), 3-85572-042-8 (v. 1), 3-85572-043-6 (v. 2). ▸ Indispensable, collectively edited, richly detailed bibliographic guide to Swiss history. [EWM]

27.270 Ulrich Im Hof et al., eds. *Geschichte der Schweiz—und der Schweizer.* 1982–83 ed. 3 vols. in 1. Basel: Helbing & Luchtenhahn, 1986. ISBN 3-7190-0943-2 (pbk). ▸ Probably best general history of Switzerland now available. Strong on social and economic history, with many maps and illustrations; rich in bibliographical notes. Also available in French as *Nouvelle histoire de la Suisse et des Suisses* (1983). [EWM]

27.271 James Murray Luck. *A history of Switzerland: the first 100,000 years: before the beginnings to the days of the present.* Palo Alto, Calif.: Society for the Promotion of Science and Scholarship, 1985. ISBN 0-930664-06-X. ▸ Dull sketch of Swiss history to

1914, followed by twenty-five topical chapters by various authors on aspects of modern Swiss civilization. [EWM]

27.272 William Martin and Pierre Béguin. *Switzerland, from Roman times to the present.* Jocasta Innes, trans. New York: Praeger, 1971. ISBN 0-236-15402-8. ‣ Old-fashioned political history to 1929 with added chapter for events to 1966. [EWM]

Political History

27.273 Benjamin R. Barber. *The death of communal liberty: a history of freedom in a Swiss mountain canton.* Princeton: Princeton University Press, 1974. ISBN 0-691-07554-9. ‣ Well-researched study of ancient and modern communalism in Swiss Alpine canton of Grisons/Graubünden. [EWM]

27.274 Edgar Bonjour. *Geschichte der schweizerischen Neutralität: vier Jahrhunderte eidgenössischer Aussenpolitik.* Rev. ed. 9 vols. Basel: Helbing & Luchtenhahn, 1965–76. ‣ Controversial but indispensable account of Swiss foreign policy to 1945. [EWM]

27.275 Edgar Bonjour. *Swiss neutrality: its history and meaning.* 2d ed. Marie D. Hottinger, trans. London: Allen & Unwin, 1952. ‣ Concise summary and reflections summarizing early work but superseded by larger study (27.274). [EWM]

27.276 John R. G. Jenkins. *Jura separatism in Switzerland.* Oxford: Clarendon, 1986. ISBN 0-19-823247-0. ‣ Painstaking historical geography of Switzerland's only new canton since 1815. [EWM]

27.277 Heinz K. Meier. *Friendship under stress: U.S.-Swiss relations, 1900–1950.* Bern: Lang, 1970. ‣ Careful, straightforward narrative of twentieth-century Swiss-American diplomacy; sequel to 27.279. [EWM]

27.278 Heinz K. Meier. "The Swiss national general strike of November 1918." In *Neutral Europe between war and revolution, 1917–1923.* Hans A. Schmitt, ed., pp. 66–86. Charlottesville: University Press of Virginia, 1988. ISBN 0-8139-1153-2. ‣ Study of lone case of Swiss flirtation with bolshevism, tempest in teapot to which federal government overreacted. [EWM]

27.279 Heinz K. Meier. *The United States and Switzerland in the nineteenth century.* The Hague: Mouton, 1963. ‣ Conventional account of early Swiss-American diplomatic relations, 1815–1900. [EWM]

27.280 William E. Rappard. *Collective security in Swiss experience, 1291–1948.* London: Allen & Unwin, 1948. ‣ Brief abridgement (about one-fourth) of author's fundamental work on domestic Swiss arbitration, *Cinq siècles de sécurité collective (1291–1798): les expériences de la Suisse sous le régime des pactes de secours mutuel* (1945). [EWM]

SEE ALSO
47.132 Ann G. Imlah. *Britain and Switzerland, 1845–60.*

Economic and Social History

27.281 Jean-François Bergier. *Histoire économique de la Suisse.* 1983 ed. Lausanne: Éditions-Diffusion Payot-Lausanne, 1984. ISBN 2-601-00441-X. ‣ Outstanding history by internationally famous expert of Swiss economy from Middle Ages to 1980, from agriculture and transport via mercenary service to industry and banking. [EWM]

27.282 Paul P. Bernard. *Rush to the Alps: the evolution of vacationing in Switzerland.* Boulder: East European Quarterly; distributed by Columbia University Press, 1978. (East European monographs, 37.) ISBN 0-914710-30-3. ‣ Well-researched history of Swiss tourist industry since eighteenth century. [EWM]

27.283 B. M. Biucchi. "The Industrial Revolution in Switzer-land, 1700–1914." Chapter 10 of *The emergence of industrial societies.* 1973 ed. Carlo M. Cipolla, ed. New York: Barnes & Noble, 1976. (Fontana economic history of Europe, 4.2.) ISBN 0-06-492180-8 (v. 4.2). ‣ Portrait of precocious Industrial Revolution in Switzerland with advanced technology, little urbanization, and no proletariat. [EWM]

27.284 E. William Monter. *Calvin's Geneva.* New York: Wiley, 1967. ‣ Standard account of newly independent city-state, Europe's first Puritan society. [EWM]

27.285 Leo Schelbert. "On becoming an emigrant: a structural view of eighteenth- and nineteenth-century Swiss data." *Perspectives in American history* 7.3 (1973) 441–95. ISSN 0079-0990. ‣ Synthetic overview of Swiss emigration to United States before 1900, using literary and demographic data. [EWM]

27.286 Lee Palmer Wandel. *Always among us: images of the poor in Zwingli's Zurich.* Cambridge: Cambridge University Press, 1990. ISBN 0-521-39096-6. ‣ Brief interdisciplinary study of poor relief in sixteenth-century Zurich, using iconography to explain Protestant reforms. [EWM]

Cultural History

27.287 Harold S. Bender. *Conrad Grebel, c. 1498–1526: founder of the Swiss Brethren sometimes called Anabaptists.* 1950 ed. Scottdale, Pa.: Herald, 1971. ISBN 0-8361-1123-0. ‣ Standard Mennonite-pacifist biography of key Swiss Anabaptist martyr, stressing ecclesiology. [EWM]

27.288 Gordon A. Craig. *The triumph of liberalism: Zurich in the golden age, 1830–1869.* New York: Scribner's, 1988. ISBN 0-684-19062-1. ‣ Magisterial survey of leading canton in mid-nineteenth-century Swiss federation, emphasizing political, economic, and cultural life. [EWM]

27.289 Hans R. Guggisberg. *Basel in the sixteenth century: aspects of the city republic before, during, and after the Reformation.* St. Louis: Center for Reformation Research, 1982. ISBN 0-910345-00-7. ‣ Brief survey of Basel during Renaissance and Reformation. [EWM]

27.290 Martin Gumpert. *Dunant, the story of the Red Cross.* 1938 ed. Garden City, N.Y.: Blue Ribbon Books, 1942. ‣ Laudatory biography of Jean-Henri Dunant (1828–1910), Genevan founder of International Red Cross. Can be supplemented by multivolume official history of organization from Crimean War to World War II. [EWM]

27.291 Leland Herder, ed. *The sources of Swiss Anabaptism: the Grebel letters and related documents.* Scottdale, Pa.: Herald, 1985. ISBN 0-8361-1251-2. ‣ Exhaustive collection of documents in English translation, supplementing Bender's biography of founder of Swiss Anabaptism (27.287). [EWM]

27.292 J. Christopher Herold. *The Swiss without halos.* 1948 ed. Westport, Conn.: Greenwood, 1979. ISBN 0-313-21268-6. ‣ Remarkably lively set of well-informed essays, strongest on cultural history, particularly in western Switzerland. [EWM]

27.293 E. William Monter. *Witchcraft in France and Switzerland: the borderlands during the Reformation.* Ithaca, N.Y.: Cornell University Press, 1976. ISBN 0-8014-0963-2. ‣ Innovative analysis of endemic witch hunts throughout sixteenth- and seventeenth-century French Switzerland. [EWM]

27.294 G. R. Potter. *Zwingli.* 1976 ed. Cambridge: Cambridge University Press, 1984. ISBN 0-521-27888-0 (pbk). ‣ Best English-language introduction to history of Swiss Reformation in form of lengthy biography of its principal leader, Ulrich Zwingli (1484–1531). [EWM/TAB]

27.295 James M. Stayer. "Reublin and Brötli, the revolutionary beginnings of Swiss Anabaptism: proceedings of the colloquium organized by the Faculty of Protestant Theology of Strasbourg, 20–22 February 1975." In *The origins and characteristics of Anabaptism*. Marc Lienhard, ed., pp. 83–102. The Hague: Nijhoff, 1977. (Archives internationales d'histoire des idées, 87.) ISBN 90-247-1896-1. ‣ Study of origins of Anabaptism through biography of two priests. Significant alternative to Mennonite-pacifist view of Swiss Anabaptists during 1525 Peasants' War. [EWM]

27.296 John M. Vincent. *Costume and conduct in the laws of Basel, Bern, and Zurich, 1370–1800*. 1935 ed. New York: Greenwood, 1969. ISBN 0-8371-2363-1. ‣ Pithy study of remarkably detailed Swiss sumptuary codes. [EWM]

PAUL F. GRENDLER AND ANTONIO SANTOSUOSSO

Italy since 1350

This section offers a bibliography of the history of Italy starting at 1350. The bibliography is divided into three major chronological blocks: the Renaissance (1350–1600), early modern Italy (1600–1789), and modern Italy (1789–1988). The last block is further divided into four phases: the Risorgimento (1789–1861), the Liberal Period (1861–1919), the Fascist Period (1919–1943), and Contemporary Italy (1943–1988).

While any date dividing the Middle Ages from the Renaissance in Italy must be somewhat arbitrary, 1350 seems more appropriate than any other. First, Francesco Petrarch wrote a number of works in the middle years of the century in which he staked out new directions; he attacked aspects of the medieval intellectual world and offered alternatives that became some of the foundation attitudes of Renaissance humanism. Fifteenth-century Italians judged him to be the father of the Renaissance, and most late twentieth-century scholars concur. Second, a number of scholars have noted changes in the politics and structure of Italian city-states in the middle of the fourteenth century which, in their view, signified the origins of that much-studied institution, the modern state. Finally, the Great Plague of 1348–1350 marked a significant demographic pause. Hence, the year 1350 seems the best date for the beginning of the bibliography of Italian history.

The first important unit of Italian history was the Renaissance, ca. 1350 to ca. 1600. The combination of Renaissance humanism, a political system of autonomous city-states of republics and principalities, and an urban commercial economy marks out Renaissance Italy as a distinct unit. An older view that the Renaissance was only a transitional period from medieval to modern times ignores a great deal of human activity that could not have happened earlier than 1350 and did not happen after 1600.

During the Renaissance, the development of humanism was probably the most distinctive and powerful influence on the period. Scholars have devoted a great deal of energy to defining, analyzing, and charting the development of Renaissance humanism in its many forms and consequences. Some of the most important research in any language has come from English-language scholars. The debates over such matters as whether the essence of humanism was a civic ethic or a series of learned disciplines have had a ripple effect over the entire field. Historical studies of politics and society often also reflect different views on humanism. Hence, the bibliography begins with humanism and related matters.

Because Rome is the location of the papacy, and because it and local churches have always been important in Italian life, religious affairs loom large in Italian history. The bibliography reflects the importance of religious history but is limited to Italian religious history. Thus, for example, studies on Italian Protestantism are listed here, while studies on such topics as relations between the papacy and the German Reformation are not.

Many historians have chosen to study individual regions or towns rather than Italy as a whole. The reason is obvious: from 1350 until political unification of most of Italy under one government in 1860, numerous independent or semi-independent political units divided the peninsula. Social, religious, economic, and other differences were the result of that political diversity. Or, perhaps, regional differences preceded and rendered impossible political unity for many centuries. Hence, the first half of our bibliography pays particular attention to regional history; it groups works by regions, proceeding generally from north to south. The bibliography for post-1789 Italy pays less attention to regional history because of the focus on unification. Nevertheless, a strong tradition of local studies continues in Italian historiography in all periods and is reflected in some of the most recent works. To cite one example, the recent multivolume *Storia d'Italia* (28.2) includes volumes on different regions of modern Italy.

The Renaissance period and nineteenth- and twentieth-century Italy have been intensively studied from the beginning of modern historical study in the nineteenth century and continued to be the major focus of historical scholarship in the past thirty years. But Italian history between 1600 and 1789 has been relatively neglected in spite of some exceptional works. Regrettably, English-language historians in particular have devoted little attention to this period. The tendency in Italian historiography to separate the seventeenth century, seen as a period of decline, from the eighteenth century, seen as the beginning of a social and intellectual renewal that ultimately produced unification, is not reflected here because there are so few works.

The larger half of the bibliography deals with modern Italy, 1789–1988. We felt that 1789 was a less controversial and more reasonable date for the origins of the Risorgimento (1789–1861) than 1713, 1748, 1815, or 1848. The beginning of the French Revolution also initiated a period in Italian history that generated the first political movement demanding radical political change in the arrangements of the Italian states. It also yielded the classic essay by Melchiorre Gioia explaining why Italy should be unified.

The post-Risorgimento period of liberal Italy (1861–1919) follows. We have chosen 1919 as the end of liberal Italy and the beginning of the fascist period, even though Mussolini did not become prime minister until 31 October 1922, after the March on Rome. The aftermath of World War I created the turmoil and unrest that enabled the fascist movement to prosper and eventually succeed. We share the views of historians such as Luigi Salvatorelli and Federico Chabod that the roots of fascism must be sought in the war period, either in the "radiant days" of May 1915 when a small minority pushed the country and Parliament into war, or in the displacement caused by the war and its immediate aftermath. The year 1943 marked the end of the fascist period even though Mussolini and his Republic of Salò did not fall until 1945. Democratic Italy, with its strengths and weaknesses, began when Mussolini handed his resignation to King Victor Emmanuel III on 25 July 1943. Although the terminus of the bibliography is 1988, we list only a few titles for contemporary Italy (post-1945), because we believe that historians emphasize events further removed from the present. The constant flux of near-current events is more properly the subject matter of political science.

There has been an enormous expansion of English-language Italian history in the past thirty years. The growth of Italian history has been so great that this third edition of the *Guide* repeats very few titles from the second edition. The field has been transformed, especially in Renaissance history. Few English-language works were written about Renaissance Italy between 1900 and 1960 because the anti-Burckhardtian reaction, "the revolt of the medievalists," as Wallace K. Ferguson called it, dominated English-language historical scholarship. But as a result of the enormously fruitful influence on English-language scholarship of emigré scholars fleeing fascist Germany and Italy, important works about Renaissance Italy have been written since 1960. There is hardly a work since 1960 that does not reflect the influence of such emigré scholars as Hans Baron, Felix Gilbert, and Paul Oskar Kristeller. They brought to the English-speaking scholarly world an intense interest in Renaissance Italy, knowledge of the sources, and methodological sophistication.

The maturation of Renaissance studies has been matched for the post-1789 period. In the first half of the last thirty years, the emphasis seems to have been on the Risorgimento period, where contributions of such historians as Denis Mack Smith, Stuart J. Woolf, Clara M. Lovett, and Paul Ginsborg have been especially significant. More recently, much of the attention has shifted to liberal Italy, to certain aspects of fascism, and to contemporary Italy. There have been a number of fine interdisciplinary studies, especially on the economy and society of the liberal period. On the other hand, except for its collapse at the eve of World War I, English-language scholars have partially neglected Giolittian Italy (1900–1914) and totally neglected Crispi's period (1887–1896). A number of good studies have appeared for the years at the eve of the Great War. The work of Adrian Lyttelton stands supreme in the English-speaking world for the fascist period, although a number of outstanding studies on provincial fascism (e.g., Paul Corner on Ferrara [28.410]) have appeared in the last few years. Finally, Paul Ginsborg's recent survey of post-1945 Italy (28.449) seems the right publication to bring together the scattered studies on contemporary Italy.

There has been so much good historical scholarship in the past thirty years that a book or two can be offered for practically every subject and chronological period in Italian history since 1350. Nevertheless, the greatest amount of scholarship on the history of Italy continues to be written in Italian. We have found it difficult to restrict the number of entries to 450 and to focus on English-language works. Inevitably, many excellent books and articles have been excluded. The largest problem has been the lack of space to include additional essential works written in Italian. We have tried to choose the most significant Italian titles, but this has not always been possible for the post-1789 period because of the need to cover the field. When there are adequate works in English on a topic, or Italian works available in English, occasionally an English work that fills a gap in coverage has been preferred and a major Italian work omitted. For the historian who reads Italian, the *Dizionario biografico degli italiani*, the leftist *Storia d'Italia* (28.2), published by Einaudi, and the centrist *Storia d'Italia* (28.3), published by UTET, are very useful for further access to Italian works. We also recommend that users study carefully the various bibliographical and historiographical works listed in each section before proceeding further in their use of Italian scholarship.

Much Italian historiography, especially that written by non-Italians, tends to be methodologically eclectic. This is especially evident for the Renaissance period, for which there has never been and certainly is not now a dominant methodological approach or interpretation. There are probably two reasons for this eclecticism. First, many historians of Italy tend to be skeptical; they doubt orthodoxies and like to focus on practical consequences. This bent seems to benefit historiography. Second, Italian historians typically welcome outside historiographical influences but fail to become fervent followers of new trends in large numbers. The result is to confirm eclecticism and to prevent the development of a dominant historiographical tradition.

On the other hand, post-1789 English scholarship reflects more closely the ideological divisions of Italian scholarship written by Italians. Italian scholars of the twentieth century have followed a number of historiographical approaches: Crocean-liberal, democratic, radical, socialist, fascist, and Catholic, sometimes with no clear-cut divisions among the various schools. The most influential approaches among these have been, without doubt, Benedetto Croce's liberal view until the post–World War II period and the appearance of the Marxist materialism of Antonio Gramsci. The Gramscian approach, which was the tool that most Italian scholars used to demolish the Crocean view of history, has found one of its best expressions in Einaudi's *Storia d'Italia*. The more recent UTET *Storia d'Italia* reflects a more eclectic and broadly based ideological premise that is consistent with the tone of Italian historiography of the last fifteen years or so. Since very few historical works about Italy written in Italian have been translated into English, the English-only reader cannot taste the full flavor of Italian scholarly debate on the history of Italy. By contrast, many historical works about Italy written in English have been translated into Italian. We hope for a more even "balance of trade" in translations in the future. Until then, the works in the following bibliography will enable the reader to learn more about a complex and stimulating people who have contributed so much to modern civilization.

[Contributors: AG = Arthur Goldschmidt, Jr., APK = Alexander P. Khazdan, AS = Antonio Santosuosso, FHS = Fiona Harris Stoertz, HEA = Howard E. Adelman, KP = Kenneth Pennington, PFG = Paul F. Grendler, PWS = Paul W. Schroeder]

REFERENCE WORKS

28.1 Alberto M. Ghisalberti, Massimiliano Pavan, and Vincenzo Capelletti, eds. *Dizionario biografico degli italiani.* 39 vols. to date. Rome: Istituto Enciclopedia Italiana, 1960–. ▸ Thousands of biographies of Italians of every epoch. Biographies are monographs of very high quality; majority are best available study of the subject. All entries include exhaustive bibliographies. Has reached "Di Falco." [PFG]

28.2 *Storia d'Italia.* 25 vols. to date. Turin: Einaudi, 1972–. ISBN 88-06-58529-0 (set), *Annali:* 88-06-05417-1 (v. 5), 88-06-05595-X (v. 6), 88-06-05680-8 (v. 7), 88-06-59341-2 (v. 9). *Le Regioni:* 88-06-05720-0 (Veneto), 88-06-58040-X (Calabria), 88-06-59725-6 (Toscana), 88-06-59349-8 (Sicilia), 88-06-11645-2 (Umbria), 88-06-59917-8, 88-06-58040-X (Marche), 88-06-11415-8 (Puglia), 88-06-11876-5 (Campania), 88-06-12637-7 (Lazio). ▸ Vast survey in two subseries, *Annali* and *Le Regioni*, of Italian history from fall of Roman empire to present. Seeks explanation of contemporary Italy in the past. Various Italian and foreign authors, some with outstanding contributions, others mediocre. Interpretations usually follow Marxist line, although not rigidly ideological. [AS]

28.3 *Storia d'Italia.* 24 vols. to date. Turin: UTET, 1978–. ISBN 88-02-03431-1 (*Introduzione*), 88-02-03510-5 (v. 1), 88-02-03871-6 (v. 3), 88-02-03568-7 (v. 4), 88-02-04036-2 (v. 5), 88-02-04039-7 (v. 7), 88-02-02539-8 (v. 9), 88-02-03906-2 (v. 10), 88-02-03829-5 (v. 11), 88-02-04026-5 (v. 12.1), 88-02-04498-8 (v. 12.2), 88-02-02451-4 (v. 13.2), 88-02-02519-3 (v. 14), 88-02-04499-6 (v. 15), 88-02-03829-5 (v. 16), 88-02-03473-7 (v. 17), 88-02-03955-0 (v. 18.1), 88-02-04043-5 (v. 18.2), 88-02-03657-8 (v. 20), 88-02-03758-2 (v. 21), 88-02-03795-7 (v. 23). ▸ Vast survey of Italian history from Longobard period (sixth century) to present. Emphasizes diversity and regionalism with volumes dedicated to preunification states, but switches to unitary view during Risorgimento period. Centrist approach; fine contributions by Italian and foreign scholars. [AS]

RENAISSANCE ITALY, 1350–1600

28.4 Jacob Burckhardt. *The civilization of the Renaissance in Italy.* Rev. ed. 2 vols. Benjamin Nelson and Charles Edward Trinkaus, eds. S.G.C. Middlemore, trans. Harmondsworth: Penguin, 1990. ISBN 0-14-044534-X (pbk). ▸ Classic study (1860). Defined Italian Renaissance as beginning of modern world and individualism as essence of Renaissance. Although no contemporary historian is strict Burckhardtian, this work remains stimulating (if infuriating to medievalists). [PFG]

28.5 Wallace K. Ferguson. *The Renaissance in historical thought: five centuries of interpretation.* 1948 ed. New York: AMS Press, 1981. ISBN 0-404-14887-5. ▸ Study of concept of Renaissance, pro and con, beginning with contemporary views of fourteenth and fifteenth centuries to date of publication. Classic work of historiography. [PFG]

28.6 John R. Hale, ed. *A concise encyclopaedia of the Italian Renaissance.* London: Thames & Hudson, 1981. ISBN 0-500-23333-0. ▸ Useful reference work with short discussions of major persons, places, events, concepts, and ideas of Italian Renaissance. [PFG]

RENAISSANCE HUMANISM

28.7 Mario Emilio Cosenza. *Biographical and bibliographical dictionary of the Italian humanists and of the world of classical scholarship in Italy, 1300–1800.* 2d ed. 6 vols. Boston: Hall, 1962–67. ‣ Much information on lives and works of humanists. Good English starting point and only place to locate some obscure figures. Based on file cards accumulated over lifetime. [PFG]

28.8 F. Edward Cranz, Paul Oskar Kristeller, and Virginia Brown, eds. *Catalogus translationum et commentariorum: mediaeval and Renaissance Latin translations and commentaries, annotated lists and guides.* 6 vols. to date. Washington, D.C.: Catholic University of America Press, 1960–. ISBN 0-8132-0400-3 (v. 2), 0-8132-0540-9 (v. 3), 0-8132-0547-6 (v. 4), 0-8132-0547-6 (v. 5), 0-8132-0618-9 (v. 6). ‣ Annotated lists of medieval and Renaissance commentaries on ancient Latin and Greek works and Latin translations of Greek works. Short descriptions of commentators and translations. Documents recovery and spread of classical tradition. European coverage with emphasis on Italy. [PFG]

28.9 Benjamin G. Kohl. *Renaissance humanism, 1300–1550: a bibliography of materials in English.* New York: Garland, 1985. ISBN 0-8240-8773-9. ‣ Lists books, journal articles, reference tools, and English translations of primary sources through 1982. European coverage with primary emphasis on Italy; begins with medieval background, followed by chronological and geographical coverage. [PFG]

SEE ALSO
22.213 Albert Rabil, Jr., ed. *Renaissance humanism.*

Humanism: Definitions and Themes

28.10 Hans Baron. *The crisis of the early Italian Renaissance: civic humanism and republican liberty in an age of classicism and tyranny.* Rev. ed. Princeton: Princeton University Press, 1966. ‣ Comprehensive study of transition from medieval thought to humanism. Argues that Milanese threat (ca. 1402) caused Florentine intellectuals to join classical studies with devotion to Florence, producing civic humanism. Much discussed thesis. [PFG]

28.11 Hans Baron. *In search of Florentine civic humanism: essays on the transition from medieval to modern thought.* 2 vols. Princeton: Princeton University Press, 1988. ISBN 0-691-05512-2 (v. 1), 0-691-05513-0 (v. 2). ‣ Collection of articles written over fifty years describing transition from late medieval classicism to Renaissance humanism. Important articles on interpretation of Cicero and civic wealth supplement author's civic humanism thesis. [PFG]

28.12 Jerry H. Bentley. *Humanists and Holy Writ: New Testament scholarship in the Renaissance.* Princeton: Princeton University Press, 1983. ISBN 0-691-05392-8. ‣ Analyzes pioneering humanistic editing of text of New Testament (including Greek version) by Valla, Erasmus, and Spanish Complutensian polyglot edition of 1520. Documents development of humanistic textual criticism. [PFG]

28.13 Eugenio Garin. *Italian humanism: philosophy and civic life in the Renaissance.* 1965 ed. Peter Munz, trans. Westport, Conn.: Greenwood, 1975. ISBN 0-8371-8578-5. ‣ History of major currents of thought of Italian Renaissance from Petrarch (ca. 1350) through early seventeenth century by distinguished Italian historian. Civic life thesis similar to Baron's civic humanism (28.10). [PFG]

28.14 Eugenio Garin. *Portraits from the quattrocento.* Victor A. Velen and Elizabeth Velen, trans. New York: Harper & Row, 1972. ISBN 0-06-138629-4. ‣ Major essay on civic life and humanist values of Florentine chancellors. Eight essays on other major fifteenth-century figures: Aeneas Silvius Piccolomini, Ficino, Politian, and Pico. Good example of author's approach. [PFG]

28.15 Eugenio Garin. *Science and civic life in the Italian Renaissance.* 1969 ed. Peter Munz, trans. Gloucester, Mass.: Smith, 1978. ISBN 0-8446-2110-2. ‣ Six articles on interpretations of the Renaissance, Leonardo da Vinci, Galileo (two), science, and astrology. [PFG]

28.16 Craig Kallendorf. *In praise of Aeneas: Virgil and epideictic rhetoric in the early Italian Renaissance.* Hanover, N.H.: University Press of New England, 1989. ISBN 0-87451-473-8. ‣ How Italian humanists (Petrarch, Boccaccio, Salutati, Vegio, and Landino) interpreted Virgil. Development of rhetoric of praise with implications for other aspects of humanism. [PFG]

28.17 Paul Oskar Kristeller. *Renaissance thought: the classic, scholastic, and humanistic strains.* New York: Harper & Row, 1961. ‣ Defines humanistic studies as grammar, rhetoric, history, poetry, and moral philosophy based on standard ancient Latin and Greek authors; humanists as teachers and scholars of same. Widely accepted definition by leading authority. Revision of 1955 *The Classics and Renaissance Thought.* [PFG]

28.18 Paul Oskar Kristeller. *Renaissance thought, II: papers on humanism and the arts.* New York: Harper & Row, 1965. ‣ Nine articles on Italian humanism, its spread to rest of Europe, Platonic academy of Florence, role of man, Paduan Averroism, Italian prose, music, and system of the arts. Pioneering work. [PFG]

28.19 George W. McClure. *Sorrow and consolation in Italian humanism.* Princeton: Princeton University Press, 1991. ISBN 0-691-05598-X. ‣ Study of consolatory treatises. Classical origins of genre, then consolatory letters and manuals of consolation by Petrarch, Salutati, Ficino et al. Part of history of emotions and psychology. [PFG]

28.20 John M. McManamon. *Funeral oratory and the cultural ideals of Italian humanism.* Chapel Hill: University of North Carolina Press, 1989. ISBN 0-8078-1783-X. ‣ Original study examining Latin funeral oratory between 1374 and 1534 to study humanistic themes and their penetration into Italian culture. Based on extensive manuscript sources. Demonstrates triumph of humanist rhetoric and values. [PFG]

28.21 John M. McManamon. "Innovation in early humanist rhetoric: the oratory of Pier Paolo Vergerio the Elder." *Rinascimento,* Serie 2, 22.2 (1982) 3–31. ISSN 0080-3073. ‣ Documents Vergerio's revival of classical rhetoric in Padua, 1393. Classical form, ancient rhetorical figures, style, attempt to move listener, and call to civic action characterize Renaissance rhetoric. Important article. [PFG]

28.22 Anthony Molho and John A. Tedeschi, eds. *Renaissance essays in honor of Hans Baron.* DeKalb: Northern Illinois University Press, 1971. ISBN 0-87580-022-X. ‣ Thirty-six articles on late medieval and Renaissance history, especially Italy, by distinguished scholars. First three essays assess contribution of Baron, others discuss Italian, German, French, and English topics. [PFG]

28.23 John W. O'Malley. *Praise and blame in Renaissance Rome: rhetoric, doctrine, and reform in the sacred orators of the papal court, ca. 1450–1521.* Durham, N.C.: Duke University Press, 1979. ISBN 0-8223-0428-7. ‣ Revival of classical epideictic rhetoric, speeches of praise and blame. Discusses differences from medieval rhetoric, effort to move and to please, and themes of dignity of man and peace among men. [PFG]

28.24 L. D. Reynolds and Nigel Guy Wilson. *Scribes and scholars: a guide to the transmission of Greek and Latin literature.* 3d ed. Oxford: Clarendon, 1991. ISBN 0-19-872145-5 (cl), 0-19-872146-3 (pbk). ‣ Good, brief history of transmission of ancient Greek and Latin texts to Western thought from Middle Ages through eighteenth century. Particularly useful for Renaissance Italy. [PFG]

28.25 Eugene F. Rice, Jr. *Saint Jerome in the Renaissance.* 1985 ed. Baltimore: Johns Hopkins University Press, 1988. ISBN 0-8018-2381-1 (cl, 1985), 0-8018-3747-2 (pbk). ‣ Traces changing image of Jerome (d. 419 or 420) between 1300 and 1600 through scholarship, literature, and art. Fascinating study of how humanists saw one of their most honored early Christian predecessors. [PFG]

28.26 Jerrold E. Siegel. *Rhetoric and philosophy in Renaissance humanism: the union of eloquence and wisdom, Petrarch to Valla.* Princeton: Princeton University Press, 1968. ‣ Rejects Baron thesis (28.10). Argues that humanists were rhetoricians not necessarily committed to civic values. Stresses importance of eloquence and links with medieval *dictatores* (letter writers). Covers Petrarch, Salutati, Bruni, and Valla. [PFG]

28.27 Charles Edward Trinkaus. *In our image and likeness: humanity and divinity in Italian humanist thought.* 2 vols. Chicago: University of Chicago Press, 1970. ISBN 0-226-81245-6. ‣ Major study of religious thought of Italian humanists centered on theme that man was created in God's image and likeness. Discusses Petrarch, Salutati, and Valla among others. Shows importance of will and rhetorical theology. [PFG]

28.28 Charles Edward Trinkaus. *The scope of Renaissance humanism.* Ann Arbor: University of Michigan Press, 1983. ISBN 0-472-10031-9. ‣ Essays by master scholar. After retrospective look at development of field in North America, emphasizes Renaissance consciousness and humanism as embracing both Italy and northern Europe, including Luther and Calvin. [PFG]

28.29 Berthold L. Ullman. *The origin and development of humanistic script.* Rome: Storia e Letteratura, 1960. ‣ Account of invention of new forms of Latin handwriting in Italy ca. 1400. New handwriting became roman and italic typefaces. [PFG]

Greek and Byzantine Influences on Italy and Humanism

28.30 Deno John Geanakoplos. *Byzantium and the Renaissance: Greek scholars in Venice, studies in the dissemination of Greek learning from Byzantium to Western Europe.* 1962 ed. Hamden, Conn.: Archon, 1973. ISBN 0-208-01311-3. ‣ Studies five representative Greek emigrant scholars from Byzantium and Crete to Venice, ca. 1400–1530. Introductory chapters on Venetian-Byzantine relations, Greek colony in Venice. First published as *Greek Scholars in Venice: Studies in the Dissemination of Greek Learning from Byzantium to Western Europe.* [PFG]

28.31 John Monfasani. *George of Trebizond: a biography and a study of his rhetoric and logic.* Leiden: Brill, 1976. ISBN 90-04-04370-5. ‣ Excellent study of George of Trebizond (1395–1472/3), Greek emigré scholar who brought Byzantine rhetoric to Italy. Important for humanism and views on Plato and Aristotle. [PFG]

28.32 Roberto Weiss. *Medieval and humanist Greek: collected essays.* Padua: Antenore, 1977. ‣ Eight English, eleven Italian studies on extent of knowledge of Greek in Western Europe in Middle Ages and early Renaissance. Articles on Italy, England, Paris, and on Petrarch and minor figures. [PFG]

SEE ALSO
8.332 Deno John Geanakoplos. *Interaction of the "sibling."*

Petrarch and Boccaccio

28.33 Thomas Goddard Bergin. *Boccaccio.* New York: Viking, 1981. ISBN 0-670-17735-0. ‣ Best English-language biography of Boccaccio (1313–75), vernacular writer, follower of Petrarch, and early enthusiast of ancient culture. Includes numerous summaries of Boccaccio's works. [PFG]

28.34 Morris Bishop. *Petrarch and his world.* Bloomington: Indiana University Press, 1963. ‣ Learned and elegantly written biography of Petrarch (1304–74) allowing poet-scholar to emerge as human being. Includes many translations from Petrarch's works. [PFG]

28.35 Vittore Branca. *Boccaccio: the man and his works.* Richard Monges and Dennis J. McAuliffe, trans. New York: New York University Press, 1976. ISBN 0-8147-0953-2. ‣ Detailed study of Boccaccio's life followed by analysis of *Decameron* in context of medieval literary forms, language, and mercantile world. Author leading Italian authority on subject. [PFG]

Florentine Humanism

28.36 Robert Black. *Benedetto Accolti and the Florentine Renaissance.* Cambridge: Cambridge University Press, 1985. ISBN 0-521-25016-1. ‣ Study of Accolti (1415–64), Florentine chancellor, and his humanistic writings and history. Sees humanism as continuum from ca. 1300 with little originality in fifteenth century. Unconvincing minority view. [PFG]

28.37 Alison Brown. *Bartolomeo Scala, 1430–1497, chancellor of Florence: the humanist as bureaucrat.* Princeton: Princeton University Press, 1979. ISBN 0-691-05270-0. ‣ Comprehensive study of life and works of important Florentine humanist. Describes development of Florentine humanism. [PFG]

28.38 Arthur Field. *The origins of the Platonic academy of Florence.* Princeton: Princeton University Press, 1988. ISBN 0-691-05533-5. ‣ Study of group of intellectuals who created neo-Platonic philosophy in mid-fifteenth century. Contrary to previous views, argues that Medici rulers of Florence played no role in founding Platonic academy. [PFG]

28.39 Gordon Griffiths, James Hankins, and David Thompson, eds. and trans. *The humanism of Leonardo Bruni: selected texts.* Binghamton, N.Y.: Medieval & Renaissance Texts & Studies with Renaissance Society of America, 1987. (Renaissance texts series, 10.) ISBN 0-86698-029-6. ‣ Translations of major works of Florentine civic humanist Bruni (1369–1444) with good general introduction, biography of Bruni, and discussions of individual works. Accepts Baron's argument (28.10) with some reservations. [PFG]

28.40 Lauro Martines. *The social world of the Florentine humanists, 1390–1460.* Princeton: Princeton University Press, 1963. ‣ Pioneering study of wealth, public lives, families, and marriages of fifty-six humanists. Argues that civic humanism was ideology of Florentine ruling class and that humanism declined when Medici took power. Marxist approach. [PFG]

28.41 Donald J. Wilcox. *The development of Florentine humanist historiography in the fifteenth century.* Cambridge, Mass.: Harvard University Press, 1969. ISBN 0-674-20026-8. ‣ Study of humanist histories of Florence by Leonardo Bruni, Poggio Bracciolini, and Bartolomeo Scala. Argues they exhibited new style emphasizing political liberty, psychological analysis, and use of rhetoric. [PFG]

28.42 Ronald G. Witt. *Hercules at the crossroads: the life, works, and thought of Coluccio Salutati.* Durham, N.C.: Duke University Press, 1983. ISBN 0-8223-0527-5. ‣ Magisterial study of Salutati (1331–1406), chancellor (chief civil servant) of Florence and link between Petrarch and fifteenth-century humanism. Explores transition from medieval thought to Renaissance. [PFG]

Humanism in Other Regions

28.43 Girolamo Arnaldi, Gianfranco Folena, and Marino Berengo, eds. *Storia della cultura veneta.* 10 vols. to date. Venice: Neri Pozza, 1976–. ‣ Excellent comprehensive account of every aspect of intellectual history broadly conceived for Venice and the Veneto from early medieval times. Series complete to World

War I with one or two volumes to come. Expert authors; some original monographs. [PFG]

28.44 Jerry H. Bentley. *Politics and culture in Renaissance Naples.* Princeton: Princeton University Press, 1987. ISBN 0-691-05498-3. ▸ Initial English overview of Neapolitan humanism, 1435–1501. Analyzes humanist works. Stresses links between humanists and monarchs. Makes comparisons with humanism elsewhere in Italy. [PFG]

28.45 William J. Bouwsma. *Venice and the defense of republican liberty: Renaissance values in the age of the Counter-Reformation.* Berkeley: University of California Press, 1968. ▸ Argues that Venice embodied republican liberty, modernity, and lay values against hierarchical, medieval, and theocratic papacy in struggle reaching climax in 1606/7. Most Venetian historians believe Bouwsma's contrast is overdrawn. [PFG]

28.46 John F. D'Amico. *Renaissance humanism in papal Rome: humanists and churchmen on the eve of the Reformation.* 1983 ed. Baltimore: Johns Hopkins University Press, 1991. ISBN 0-8018-2860-0 (cl, 1983), 0-8018-4224-7 (pbk). ▸ Excellent pioneering study on Roman humanism, ca. 1450–1527, covering classicism, Ciceronian language, theology, and employment opportunities for humanists. Points up differences from humanism elsewhere. Paolo Cortesi, Raffaele Maffei, and Adriano Castellesi key figures. [PFG]

28.47 Gary Ianziti. *Humanistic historiography under the Sforzas: politics and propaganda in fifteenth-century Milan.* Oxford: Clarendon, 1988. ISBN 0-19-822893-7. ▸ Study of writings on Milanese princes and politics by contemporary humanists. Documents emergence of realistic description of politics and propaganda to promote prince's image. Explains differences between Milanese humanism and humanism elsewhere. [PFG]

28.48 Margaret L. King. *Venetian humanism in an age of patrician dominance.* Princeton: Princeton University Press, 1986. ISBN 0-691-05465-7. ▸ Best available study of fifteenth-century Venetian humanists and patricians. Argues Venetian humanist ideology promoted unity and stability in society. Emphasizes links between humanism, society, and politics. [PFG]

28.49 Patricia H. Labalme. *Bernardo Giustiniani: a Venetian of the quattrocento.* Rome: Storia e Letteratura, 1969. ▸ Study of important Venetian patrician, statesman, humanist, and historian (1408–89). Sees Venetian humanism as more conservative than elsewhere, placing greater emphasis on state than on individual. [PFG]

28.50 Egmont Lee. *Sixtus IV and men of letters.* Rome: Storia e Letteratura, 1978. ▸ Study of careers of humanists at Rome, especially 1471–84, and role of humanists in papal bureaucracy and university. Corrects previous view that Sixtus IV did not support humanistic studies. [PFG]

28.51 Oliver Logan. *Culture and society in Venice, 1470–1790: the Renaissance and its heritage.* New York: Scribner's, 1972. ISBN 0-684-12766-0. ▸ Overview of society, myth of Venice, state, intellectual life, literature, art, and patronage with no clear thesis. Concentrates on period 1470–1630. [PFG]

28.52 Diana Maury Robin. *Filelfo in Milan: writings, 1451–1477.* Princeton: Princeton University Press, 1991. ISBN 0-691-03185-1. ▸ Analysis of Latin and Greek works (texts included) of Francesco Filelfo (1398–1481), important humanist who mainly served princes. Works described contemporary events and persons. Explores nuances and language of prince-humanist patronage exchange. [PFG]

28.53 Charles L. Stinger. *The Renaissance in Rome.* Bloomington: Indiana University Press, 1985. ISBN 0-253-35002-6. ▸ Cultural history of Rome, 1443–1527. Mood, myth, and symbol as manifested in ceremony, festival, and image. Papal ideology of Rome as renewed ancient city exercising spiritual leadership. [PFG]

TOPICS IN INTELLECTUAL HISTORY

Printing

28.54 Leonardas Vytautas Gerulaitis. *Printing and publishing in fifteenth-century Venice.* Chicago: American Library Association, 1976. ISBN 0-8389-0126-3. ▸ Statistical analysis with comments on subject matter of fifteenth-century books published in Venice. Classics and religious books dominated. Comparisons with northern European publishing. [PFG]

28.55 Martin Lowry. *Nicholas Jenson and the rise of Venetian publishing in Renaissance Europe.* Oxford: Blackwell, 1991. ISBN 0-631-17394-3. ▸ Venetian printing (1470–80) with Jenson a key figure. Small industry relying on noble patrons became large, diversified, and highly competitive commercial enterprise. Venice assumed commanding role in European publishing at this time. [PFG]

28.56 Martin Lowry. *The world of Aldus Manutius: business and scholarship in Renaissance Venice.* Ithaca, N.Y.: Cornell University Press, 1979. ISBN 0-8014-1214-5. ▸ Stimulating study of Aldine Press, 1494–1515, most important scholarly publisher of Renaissance. Emphasizes links between humanism and business. Analyzes printing of first editions of many ancient Greek and Latin texts. [PFG]

28.57 Victor Scholderer. *Fifty essays in fifteenth- and sixteenth-century bibliography.* Dennis E. Rhodes, ed. Amsterdam: Hertzberger, 1966. ▸ Good essays on early Italian and European printing by authority on incunables. "Printers and Readers in Italy in the Fifteenth Century" is excellent brief survey of beginning of printing in Italy. [PFG]

Education

28.58 Paul F. Grendler. *Schooling in Renaissance Italy: literacy and learning, 1300–1600.* 1989 ed. Baltimore: Johns Hopkins University Press, 1991. ISBN 0-8018-3725-1 (cl), 0-8018-4229-8 (pbk). ▸ Comprehensive intellectual and social history of primary and secondary education. Describes kinds of schools, schooling and literacy rates by sexes, curricula, classroom procedures, textbooks, religious education, and impact on society. [PFG]

28.59 R.G.G. Mercer. *The teaching of Gasparino Barzizza, with special reference to his place in Paduan humanism.* London: Modern Humanities Research Association, 1979. (Texts and dissertations, 10.) ISBN 0-900547-51-0. ▸ Pioneering study of Barzizza (1360–1430), humanist professor at University of Padua (1407–21), who played major role in introducing humanistic studies. Taught future humanists and nobles; key figure in transition from medieval to Renaissance learning. [PFG]

28.60 Paul Lawrence Rose. *The Italian renaissance of mathematics: studies on humanists and mathematicians from Petrarch to Galileo.* Geneva: Droz, 1976. ▸ Only English-language work on mathematical revival in context of humanism. Emphasizes recovery of ancient Greek mathematics, links with humanism, and mentality of mathematicians rather than technical history of mathematics. [PFG]

28.61 Frank J. Swetz. *Capitalism and arithmetic: the new math of the fifteenth-century including the full text of the "Treviso Arithmetic" of 1478.* 2d ed. David Eugene Smith, trans. La Salle, Ill.: Open Court, 1987. ISBN 0-87548-438-7 (cl), 0-8126-9014-1 (pbk). ▸ English translation of earliest printed mathematical book (1478), a commercial arithmetic (abbacus). Study of contents and explanation of Italian historical and commercial context. [PFG]

28.62 Warren Van Egmond. *Practical mathematics in the Italian*

Renaissance: a catalog of Italian abbacus manuscripts and printed books to 1600. Florence: Istituto e Museo di Storia della Scienza di Firenze, 1980. (Istituto e Museo di Storia della Scienza, Monografia, 4.) ‣ Introduction offers excellent brief overview of commercial mathematics, context of mathematics, and examples of problems in context of Italian commerce and business, 1300–1600. Catalog follows. Important pioneering study. [PFG]

28.63 William Harrison Woodward. *Vittorino da Feltre and other humanist educators.* 1897 ed. New York: Columbia University, Teacher's College, 1963. ISBN 0-8077-2359-2. ‣ Study of school and teaching methods of famous humanist educator Vittorino da Feltre (ca. 1378–1446/7) with translations of humanist pedagogical treatises by Vergerio, Bruni, Aeneas Sylvius Piccolomini, and Battista Guarini. Old but useful. [PFG]

SEE ALSO
22.183 Anthony Grafton and Lisa Jardine. *From humanism to the humanities.*

Philosophy

28.64 Brian P. Copenhaver and Charles B. Schmitt. *Renaissance philosophy.* Oxford: Oxford University Press, 1992. ISBN 0-19-219203-5 (cl), 0-19-289184-7 (pbk). ‣ Best one-volume survey of subject in any language; very readable. Covers all major developments, 1400–1600, with emphasis on Italy. Aristotelianism, Platonism, philosophies of nature, and key figures such as Valla, Ficino, and Bruno. [PFG]

28.65 James Hankins. *Plato in the Italian Renaissance.* 2 vols. Leiden: Brill, 1991. ISBN 90-04-09163-7 (set), 90-04-09161-0 (v. 1), 90-04-09162-9 (v. 2), 90-04-09552-7 (v. 1, pbk), ISSN 0166-1302. ‣ Reception and interpretation of Plato in fifteenth-century Italy. Assesses quality of translations and major humanist commentaries in Florence, Milan, and Rome. Argues that Plato was unacceptable until literal meaning transcended. Ambitious work. [PFG]

28.66 Paul Oskar Kristeller. *Eight philosophers of the Italian Renaissance.* 1964 ed. Stanford, Calif.: Stanford University Press, 1966. ‣ Good introductions to thought of Petrarch, Valla, Ficino, Pico della Mirandola, Pomponazzi, Telesio, Patrizi, and Giordano Bruno and their contributions to Renaissance thought. [PFG]

28.67 Paul Oskar Kristeller. *The philosophy of Marsilio Ficino.* 1943 ed. Virginia Conant, trans. Gloucester, Mass.: Smith, 1964. ‣ Standard monograph on Ficino (1433–99), translator of Plato and founder of Renaissance Platonism, who saw Platonism and Christianity as compatible. Philosophical approach emphasizing being, causality, man, and God. [PFG]

28.68 Martin L. Pine. *Pietro Pomponazzi: radical philosopher of the Renaissance.* Padua: Antenore, 1986. ‣ Life and thought of Pomponazzi (1462–1525), most important Aristotelian philosopher of Renaissance, who argued that reason could not prove soul's immortality. Only recent English monograph on Pomponazzi. [PFG]

28.69 Charles B. Schmitt et al., eds. *The Cambridge history of Renaissance philosophy.* 1988 ed. Cambridge: Cambridge University Press, 1990. ISBN 0-521-25104-4. ‣ European coverage 1350 to 1600, organized by philosophical subjects (natural philosophy, moral philosophy, etc.) and chapters on history, rhetoric, and printing. Written by international authorities. No comparable book in any language. [PFG]

28.70 Frances A. Yates. *Giordano Bruno and the hermetic tradition.* 1964 ed. Chicago: University of Chicago Press, 1991. ISBN 0-226-95007-7 (pbk). ‣ History of influence of tradition of magic coming from writings of ancient Hermes Trismegistus during

Renaissance. Studies of Ficino, Giovanni Pico, Henry Cornelius Agrippa, and especially Bruno. [PFG]

SEE ALSO
22.216 Charles B. Schmitt. *Aristotle and the Renaissance.*

Political, Historical, and Social Thought

28.71 Federico Chabod. *Machiavelli and the Renaissance.* 1958 ed. Alessandro Passerin d'Entrèves, Introduction. David Moore, trans. New York: Harper & Row, 1965. ‣ Masterful essays by distinguished Italian historian depict Machiavelli as intuitive rather than systematic thinker; places him in historical context. Essay on Renaissance affirms unity of Renaissance vision. [PFG]

28.72 Sebastian de Grazia. *Machiavelli in hell.* Princeton: Princeton University Press, 1989. ISBN 0-691-05538-6. ‣ Argues that Machiavelli invented new statecraft and moral reasoning to justify prince's evil actions for good of state. State's welfare God's greatest concern; thus any action supporting state ethically justifiable. Important work. [AS]

28.73 Felix Gilbert. *History: choice and commitment.* Cambridge, Mass.: Belknap, 1977. ISBN 0-674-39656-1. ‣ Fourteen essays on Italian Renaissance and political and historical thought in Florence and Venice. Important articles on Machiavelli; five essays on twentieth-century German historians and diplomacy. [PFG]

28.74 Felix Gilbert. *Machiavelli and Guicciardini: politics and history in sixteenth-century Florence.* 1965 ed. New York: Norton, 1984. ISBN 0-393-30123-0 (pbk). ‣ Best account of genesis of political writings of Machiavelli and historical writings of Guicciardini. Sets them in context of changing Florentine views on politics and its language during period of crisis. [PFG]

28.75 Paul F. Grendler. "Chivalric romances in the Italian Renaissance." *Studies in medieval and Renaissance history,* n.s., 10 (1988) 59–102. ISSN 0081-8224. ‣ Analysis of most widely read genre of secular popular literature. Relates content of romances to social life and values; gives evidence of readership. Only article on this topic. [PFG]

28.76 Paul F. Grendler. *Critics of the Italian world, 1530–1560: Anton Francesco Doni, Nicolò Franco, and Ortensio Lando.* Madison: University of Wisconsin Press, 1969. ISBN 0-299-05220-6. ‣ Pioneering study of writers who criticized current politics, religion, society, and learning and offered utopian alternatives. Discussion of vernacular press and authors. Contemporary critique of Renaissance values heralding end of Renaissance. [PFG]

28.77 William McCuaig. *Carlo Sigonio: the changing world of the late Renaissance.* Princeton: Princeton University Press, 1989. ISBN 0-691-05558-0. ‣ Life and works of Sigonio (1522/3–84), pioneering and very important critical historian of ancient Rome and medieval Italy who had difficulties with censors. Good study of intellectual milieu. [PFG]

28.78 Roberto Ridolfi. *The life of Francesco Guicciardini.* Cecil Grayson, trans. New York: Knopf, 1968. ‣ Standard, excellent biography of Guicciardini (1483–1540), most important Renaissance historian. Emphasizes his Florentine aristocratic views and career as governor for Medici popes despite republican sympathies. [PFG]

28.79 Roberto Ridolfi. *The life of Niccolò Machiavelli.* Cecil Grayson, trans. Chicago: University of Chicago Press, 1963. ‣ Standard, excellent biography of Machiavelli. Emphasizes his role in Florentine chancery, fervent republicanism, friendship with Guicciardini, and disappointments rather than writings. Very human and likeable Machiavelli emerges. [PFG]

28.80 Antonio Santosuosso. *Vita di Giovanni della Casa.* Rome: Bulzoni, 1979. ‣ Excellent biography of Della Casa (1503–56), author, diplomat, and churchman who wrote most famous treatise on manners in Italian language. Social behavior with emphasis on class relations. [PFG]

POLITICAL, SOCIAL, AND RELIGIOUS HISTORY
Diplomacy and War

28.81 Charles Calvert Bayley. *War and society in Renaissance Florence: the De Militia of Leonardo Bruni.* Toronto: University of Toronto Press, 1961. ‣ Discusses rise of mercenaries and decline in concept of citizen militia which Bruni attempted to revive in 1422. Tradition of militia revitalized with Machiavelli. Good discussion of Florentine war policies. [PFG]

28.82 John R. Hale. *Renaissance war studies.* London: Hambledon, 1983. ISBN 0-907628-02-8 (cl), 0-907628-17-6 (pbk). ‣ Eighteen articles, published 1960–82, dealing with fortifications, bastions, recruitment and training of officers, military literature, and reactions to war in Renaissance by leading authority in the field; emphasis on Italy. [PFG]

28.83 Michael E. Mallett. *Mercenaries and their masters: warfare in Renaissance Italy.* Totowa, N.J.: Rowman & Littlefield, 1974. ISBN 0-87471-447-8. ‣ Covers 1200–1500 with emphasis on fifteenth century. Argues against stereotype of mercenary captain as unreliable and unwilling to fight: mercenary forces were loyal, professional; evolved into standing armies. [PFG]

28.84 Michael E. Mallett and John R. Hale. *The military organization of a Renaissance state: Venice ca. 1400 to 1617.* Cambridge: Cambridge University Press, 1984. ISBN 0-521-24842-6. ‣ Detailed study of land forces of Venice. Emphasizes links between government and armies, mercenaries becoming long-term standing armies and subjects settling on borders of mainland state. [PFG]

28.85 Garrett Mattingly. *Renaissance diplomacy.* 1955 ed. New York: Dover, 1988. ISBN 0-486-25570-0 (pbk). ‣ Argues that modern diplomacy began in fifteenth century when Italian city-states established resident embassies at other capitals. Forms and techniques of diplomacy spread to North in sixteenth century. Classic study. [PFG]

28.86 Piero Pieri. *Il Rinascimento e la crisi militare italiana.* Turin: Einaudi, 1952. ‣ Fundamental work, one-third on economic, social, and political background. Soldiers and military art not inferior to invaders. States collapsed because of weak political structures and fragile balance of power. [AS]

28.87 Kenneth M. Setton. *The papacy and the Levant, 1204–1571.* Vol. 1: *The thirteenth and fourteenth centuries.* Vol. 2: *The fifteenth century.* Vols. 3 and 4: *The sixteenth century.* 4 vols. Philadelphia: American Philosophical Society, 1976–1984. (Memoirs of the American Philosophical Society, 114, 127, 161, 162.) ISBN 0-87169-114-0 (v. 1), 0-87169-127-2 (v. 2), 0-87169-161-2 (v. 3), 0-87169-162-0 (v. 4), ISSN 0065-9738. ‣ Monumental political, diplomatic, and military history of long struggle between Christian Europe and Turks culminating in battle of Lepanto in 1571. Also information on European and Venetian politics, papal conclaves, Council of Trent, and much else. Broad, narrative history (continued at 28.194). [PFG]

Florence and Tuscany

28.88 Marvin B. Becker. *Florence in transition.* Vol. 1: *The decline of the commune.* Vol. 2: *Studies in the rise of the territorial state.* 2 vols. Baltimore: Johns Hopkins University Press, 1967–68. ‣ Transformation of Florentine state (1300–1400) from decentralized medieval system, in which guilds, church, and family shared power, to centralized proto-modern state controlling lives of citizens through financial measures and stronger laws. Skyrocketing public debt and new leaders instruments of change. Brucker offers different perspective (28.91). [PFG]

28.89 John K. Brackett. *Criminal justice and crime in late Renaissance Florence, 1537–1609.* Cambridge: Cambridge University Press, 1992. ISBN 0-521-40405-3. ‣ Study of Otto di Guardia, chief criminal court. Florentine criminal justice relatively moderate and flexible, but not strictly equitable. Justice system became more centralized, but did not contribute significantly to growth of state. [PFG]

28.90 Judith C. Brown. *In the shadow of Florence: provincial society in Renaissance Pescia.* New York: Oxford University Press, 1982. ISBN 0-19-502993-3. ‣ Economic and demographic study of provincial town, ca. 1400–1600. Concludes that Pescia adapted well to international economy and perhaps profited rather than suffered from Florentine hegemony. Interesting data on public finances. [PFG]

28.91 Gene A. Brucker. *The civic world of early Renaissance Florence.* Princeton: Princeton University Press, 1977. ISBN 0-691-05244-1. ‣ Detailed political history, 1382–1434, arguing that Florentine politics changed from corporate to elitist in response to foreign threats and changing social order. Differs from Becker 28.88. Contrary to Baron 28.10, sees emergence of civic humanism ca. 1411, not 1402. [PFG]

28.92 Gene A. Brucker. *Florentine politics and society, 1343–78.* Princeton: Princeton University Press, 1962. ‣ Social analysis of Florentine merchant leaders and their belief in making public policy through group consultation and consensus. Detailed political history follows; emphasizes role of elites. [PFG]

28.93 Gene A. Brucker. *Renaissance Florence.* 1969 ed. Berkeley: University of California Press, 1983. ISBN 0-520-04915-5 (cl), 0-520-04695-1 (pbk). ‣ Good introduction to Florence, 1380–1450. Emphasizes physical city, commercial economy, social structure, political elite, church, and culture. Government became more elitist and restricted. Epilogue covers 1469–1532. [PFG]

28.94 Humfrey C. Butters. *Governors and government in early sixteenth-century Florence, 1502–1519.* Oxford: Clarendon, 1985. ISBN 0-19-822593-8. ‣ Detailed narrative of internal politics and foreign policy during turbulent period in which Florentine republic came under Medici rule again. Chronicles shifting alliances and failure of citizen militia. [PFG]

28.95 Samuel Kline Cohn, Jr. *The laboring classes in Renaissance Florence.* New York: Academic Press, 1980. ISBN 0-12-179180-7. ‣ Study of working classes (1340–1530) based on marriage contracts and criminal records. Concludes that insurrectionary workers of fourteenth century turned inward and quiescent in fifteenth century. Marxist approach emphasizing class struggle. [PFG]

28.96 Richard A. Goldthwaite. *The building of Renaissance Florence: an economic and social history.* Baltimore: Johns Hopkins University Press, 1980. ISBN 0-8018-2342-0 (cl), 0-8018-2977-1 (pbk). ‣ Broad study of construction boom in Florence, ca. 1350–1550. Economic, social, and architectural history with reasons for building. Information on patrons, workers, wages, prices, and impact on city. [PFG]

28.97 Richard A. Goldthwaite. *Private wealth in Renaissance Florence: a study of four families.* Princeton: Princeton University Press, 1968. ‣ Controversial analysis of wealth of four upper-class families, ca. 1400–1550. Argues extended cognate family or clan was dividing into individual nuclear households. See Kent 28.102 for alternative view. [PFG]

28.98 John R. Hale. *Florence and the Medici: the pattern of control.* 1977 ed. New York: Thames & Hudson, 1986. ISBN 0-500-27301-4 (pbk). ‣ Survey of Medici rulers of Florence and two Medici popes (1434–1737). Emphasizes social and political reasons for authority. Good introduction to subject although lacking detail and extensive documentation. [PFG]

28.99 David Herlihy. *Medieval and Renaissance Pistoia: the social history of an Italian town, 1200–1430.* New Haven: Yale University Press, 1967. ▸ Economic and demographic study of small urban center. Argues that plague killed children and old people, leaving young adults to revive economy. *Mezzadria* system, in which landlord and peasant shared expenses and harvest, improved lot of peasantry in fifteenth century. Available on microfilm from Ann Arbor: University Microfilms International, 1979. [PFG]

28.100 David Herlihy and Christiane Klapisch-Zuber. *Tuscans and their families: a study of the Florentine catasto of 1427.* New Haven: Yale University Press, 1985. ISBN 0-300-03056-8. ▸ Monumental demographic and economic study of 260,000 persons in Florentine state between 1340s and 1500. Treats household composition and size, ages of married couples, and distribution of wealth. Abridged from French edition (1978). [PFG]

28.101 Dale V. Kent. *The rise of the Medici: faction in Florence, 1426–1434.* Oxford: Oxford University Press, 1978. ISBN 0-19-822520-2. ▸ Detailed study identifying Medici party in its neighborhood and patronage networks. Sees Medici assumption of power in 1434 as result of conflict between elite groups rather than class struggle. [PFG]

28.102 Francis William Kent. *Household and lineage in Renaissance Florence: the family life of the Capponi, Ginori, and Rucellai.* Princeton: Princeton University Press, 1977. ISBN 0-691-05237-9. ▸ Analyzes three wealthy Florentine families, 1420–1550, focusing on social and political ties. Argues against Goldthwaite 28.97 that clan and nuclear family coexisted. [PFG]

28.103 Lauro Martines. *Lawyers and statecraft in Renaissance Florence.* Princeton: Princeton University Press, 1968. ▸ Study of social backgrounds, education, professional activities, and political roles of Florentine lawyers, 1380–1530; operations and legal ideas concerning state. Sees lawyers as extremely influential in Renaissance state. [PFG]

28.104 Christine Meek. *Lucca, 1369–1400: politics and society in an early Renaissance city-state.* Oxford: Oxford University Press, 1978. ISBN 0-19-821866-4. ▸ Detailed political history of Tuscan city-state that achieved independence in 1369; oligarchic family rule; explanation of city's commerce and finances. Useful for comparison with other Tuscan city-states. [PFG]

28.105 Anthony Molho. *Florentine public finances in the early Renaissance, 1400–1433.* Cambridge, Mass.: Harvard University Press, 1971. ISBN 0-674-30665-1. ▸ Stimulating study demonstrating prolonged financial crisis. Restricted group of Florentine entrepreneurs acquired overwhelming share of public debt by 1433, leading to Medici party ascendancy in 1434. [PFG]

28.106 John M. Najemy. *Corporatism and consensus in Florentine electoral politics, 1280–1400.* Chapel Hill: University of North Carolina Press, 1982. ISBN 0-8078-1506-3. ▸ Study of electoral conflict between merchant guilds desiring greater equality and oligarchy of elite families. Guilds won in 1292, 1343, and 1378, but elite families consolidated power at end of period, ushering in civic humanism. [PFG]

28.107 Nicolai Rubinstein. *The government of Florence under the Medici (1434 to 1494).* Oxford: Clarendon, 1966. ▸ Detailed constitutional and political study of technical means by which Medici party secured political control through adapting and manipulating electoral process. Medici consolidated power in 1458. [PFG]

28.108 John N. Stephens. *The fall of the Florentine republic, 1512–1530.* Oxford: Clarendon, 1983. ISBN 0-19-822599-7. ▸ Political and constitutional essay on fall of republic to Medici as consequence of foreign policy crises. Medici transformed institutions of republic with cooperation of leading families. [PFG]

28.109 Richard C. Trexler. *The spiritual power: republican Flor-*

ence under interdict. Leiden: Brill, 1974. ISBN 90-04-03699-7. ▸ Study of period 1376–78 when papacy put Florence under interdict, shutting down religious services; also economic and political consequences. Concludes that ecclesiastical censure is effective weapon. [PFG/KP]

Venice and the Veneto

28.110 David Chambers and Brian S. Pullan, eds. *Venice: a documentary history, 1450–1630.* Oxford: Blackwell, 1992. ISBN 0-631-16383-2 (cl), 0-631-18303-5 (pbk). ▸ Well-chosen collection of translated archival documents with connecting text. Documents every aspect of Renaissance Venice: physical description, government, corruption, crime and punishment, social life, church, class structure, poor relief, culture, and art. [PFG]

28.111 Robert Finlay. *Politics in Renaissance Venice.* New Brunswick, N.J.: Rutgers University Press, 1980. ISBN 0-8135-0888-6. ▸ Excellent analysis of how politics worked in Venice, ca. 1490–1540. Family and long apprenticeship prerequisites to power in gerontocratic system. Factionalism and electoral competition produced much-admired order and stability. [PFG]

28.112 James S. Grubb. *Firstborn of Venice: Vicenza in the early Renaissance state.* Baltimore: Johns Hopkins University Press, 1988. ISBN 0-8018-3613-1. ▸ Study of relations between subject city and capital in fifteenth century. Emphasizes administrative practice, legal institutions, fiscal policy, and ideology. Sees Venetian rule as generally benign and Vicenza as loyal. [PFG]

28.113 John R. Hale, ed. *Renaissance Venice.* 1973 ed. London: Faber & Faber, 1977. ISBN 0-571-08975-5 (cl, 1973), 0-571-10429-0 (pbk). ▸ Sixteen articles by experts on Venetian nobility, army, naval actions, ambassadorial reports, humanism, historiography, politics, painting, law, merchant psychology, investments, and church. Informative, high-quality collection. [PFG]

28.114 Frederic C. Lane. *Venice: a maritime republic.* Baltimore: Johns Hopkins University Press, 1973. ISBN 0-8018-1445-6 (cl), 0-8018-1460-X (pbk). ▸ Magisterial study of Venice to 1797 with emphasis on medieval and Renaissance periods. Underlines influence of sea on development of Venice. Trade, shipping, institutions, politics, and governing caste discussed. Best one-volume history in any language. [PFG]

28.115 Edward Muir. *Civic ritual in Renaissance Venice.* Princeton: Princeton University Press, 1981. ISBN 0-691-05325-1. ▸ Civic myths and public pageants established notion of sacred political institutions. Rituals promoted belief that Venice was founded in liberty, had right to empire, and was protected by St. Mark. Convincing study. [PFG]

28.116 Brian S. Pullan. *Rich and poor in Renaissance Venice: the social institutions of a Catholic state, to 1620.* Cambridge, Mass.: Harvard University Press, 1971. ISBN 0-674-76940-6. ▸ Study rich in information on Venetian poor relief through private lay confraternities, direct state aid, and Jewish loan banks. New poor relief by state complemented traditional efforts; common goal was stable society and salvation. Includes detailed archival study of Venetian Jewry. [PFG/HEA]

28.117 Guido Ruggiero. *Violence in early Renaissance Venice.* New Brunswick, N.J.: Rutgers University Press, 1980. ISBN 0-8135-0894-0. ▸ Study of incidence and punishment of violence in Venice, 1290–1406. Analyzes perpetrators and victims of murder, rape, assault, and crimes of speech. Generally fair justice system but social class mattered in determining punishment. Photocopy available from Ann Arbor: University Microfilms International. [PFG]

28.118 *Storia di Vicenza.* 4 vols. in 6 parts. Vicenza: Neri Pozza, 1987–. ▸ Excellent, detailed history of Vicenza written by experts.

Covers all aspects of history, literature, and art from prehistory to twentieth century. Particularly good on local religious history and Vicenza as part of Venetian empire, 1404–1797. [PFG]

Other Cities and Regions

28.119   Cecilia M. Ady. *The Bentivoglio of Bologna: a study in despotism.* 1937 ed. London: Oxford University Press, 1969. ‣ Study of ruling family and politics in fifteenth-century Bologna. In and out of power earlier, Bentivoglio ruled from 1454 until overthrown in 1506. Good account of court life. [PFG]

28.120   D. M. Bueno de Mesquita. *Giangaleazzo Visconti Duke of Milan (1351–1402): a study in the political career of an Italian despot.* Cambridge: Cambridge University Press, 1941. ‣ Only study of politics, diplomacy, and wars of ruler who nearly succeeded in creating North Italian monarchy. Failure divided Italy into numerous independent states for centuries. Available on microfilm from Ann Arbor: University Microfilms International, 1975. [PFG]

28.121   Antonio Calabria and John A. Marino, eds. and trans. *Good government in Spanish Naples.* New York: Lang, 1990. (American University studies, Series 9: history, 71.) ISBN 0-8204-0929-4, ISSN 0740-0462. ‣ Six articles by Italian scholars on kingdom of Naples, 1503–1647. Politics, agriculture, demography, poor relief, financial crisis, and revolt of 1647. Revisionist outlook presenting Naples as case study of early modern state. [PFG]

28.122   Benedetto Croce. *History of the kingdom of Naples.* 1925 ed. H. Stuart Hughes, ed. Frances Frenaye, trans. Chicago: University of Chicago Press, 1970. ISBN 0-226-12080-5 (cl), 0-226-12081-3 (pbk). ‣ Sweeping history covering period 1268–1861 by leading idealist philosopher. Focuses on governing class of Naples and contrast between intellectual vitality and political failure. Starting point for Neapolitan history. [PFG]

28.123   Werner L. Gundersheimer. *Ferrara: the style of a Renaissance despotism.* Princeton: Princeton University Press, 1973. ISBN 0-691-05210-7. ‣ Introductory survey of Ferrara in fifteenth century. Shows how personality of ruler decisively influenced art and culture; focuses on governing style and administration. Argument for studying small states. [PFG]

28.124   P. J. Jones. *The Malatesta of Rimini and the papal state: a political history.* Cambridge: Cambridge University Press, 1974. ISBN 0-521-20042-3. ‣ Thorough but unexciting political and military history of ruling family of the Marches in Central Italy, ca. 1300–1509. Study of famous Renaissance despots in action. [PFG]

28.125   H. G. Koenigsberger. *The practice of empire.* Rev. ed. Batista I. Roca, Introduction. Ithaca, N.Y.: Cornell University Press, 1969. ‣ Study of administration and policies of Spanish rule over Sicily in sixteenth century. Populace basically accepted Spanish rule. Earlier title: *The Government of Sicily under Philip II of Spain;* new foreward and bibliography. [PFG]

28.126   John Larner. *The lords of Romagna: Romagnol society and the origins of the signorie.* Ithaca, N.Y.: Cornell University Press, 1965. ‣ Guide to structure and personalities of politics and society in region ruled by competing, notorious quasi-feudal nobles. Material on life in towns and countryside covering 1200 to 1400. [PFG]

28.127   Michael E. Mallett. *The Borgias: the rise and fall of a Renaissance dynasty.* 1969 ed. Chicago: Academy Chicago, 1987. ISBN 0-89733-238-5 (pbk). ‣ Separates fact from legend in notorious family that produced two popes plus Cesare Borgia (Machiavelli's princely model) and Lucrezia Borgia, who supposedly poisoned her husbands. Concludes Borgia enemies spread dubious tales. [PFG]

28.128   *Mantova: la storia.* 3 vols. Mantua: Istituto Carlo d'Arco

per la Storia di Mantova, 1958–61. ‣ Detailed history by various authors from prehistory until Mantua incorporated into Italian state in 1866. Ruling Gonzaga family very important in Renaissance politics and religion. Only recent history of key but neglected region. [PFG]

28.129   Lauro Martines, ed. *Violence and civil disorder in Italian cities, 1200–1500.* Berkeley: University of California Press, 1972. (UCLA Center for Medieval and Renaissance Studies contributions, 5.) ISBN 0-520-01906-7. ‣ Interesting articles by experts describing violence in Milan, Ferrara, Florence, Venice, Siena, and Rome: assassination attempts, reprisals, plus demographic and family roots of male violence. [PFG]

28.130   Peter Partner. *The papal state under Martin V: the administration and government of the temporal power in the early fifteenth century.* London: British School at Rome, 1958. ‣ Background sketch followed by detailed study of administration, finances, politics, diplomacy, and justice in papal temporal state, 1417–31. Credits Martin V for bringing order out of chaos. Pioneering study. [PFG]

28.131   Peter Partner. *The pope's men: the papal civil service in the Renaissance.* Oxford: Clarendon, 1990. ISBN 0-19-821995-4. ‣ Study of offices in papal court of Rome, their duties, and the humanists and others who held them, 1417–1527. Includes material on papal finances. [PFG/KP]

28.132   A.F.C. Ryder. *The kingdom of Naples under Alfonso the Magnanimous: the making of a modern state.* Oxford: Clarendon, 1976. ISBN 0-19-822535-0. ‣ Broad study of Naples under Alfonso V of Aragon (1396, r. 1442–58). Discusses royal household, administration, politics, warfare, finances, and justice. Development of crown's power seen as prototypically modern. [PFG]

28.133   *Storia della Sicilia.* 10 vols. Naples: Società Editrice Storia di Napoli e della Sicilia, 1977–81. ‣ Superb, comprehensive survey of Sicily from prehistory to twentieth century. Covers history, economics, archaeology, literature, art, music, and folklore. Articles written by experts. Starting point for understanding a complex land. [PFG]

28.134   *Storia di Milano.* 17 vols. Milan: Fondazione Treccani degli Alfieri per la Storia di Milano, 1953–66. ‣ First of major collaborative histories of Italian cities; covers origins to 1915. Specialists discuss every aspect of city and state of Milan. Fundamental work. [PFG]

28.135   *Storia di Napoli.* 11 vols. Naples: Società Editrice Storia di Napoli, 1967–78. ‣ Superb collaborative history of Naples from origins to 1950. Covers every aspect of city and state. [PFG]

Banking and Business

28.136   Raymond Adrien De Roover. *The rise and decline of the Medici bank, 1397–1494.* 1963 ed. New York: Norton, 1966. ‣ Prize-winning study by distinguished historian of business and banking of bank's organization, operating methods, loan policies, investments, profits, and losses. Based on secret account books. [PFG]

28.137   Raymond Adrien De Roover. *San Bernardino of Siena and Sant'Antonino of Florence: the two great economic thinkers of the Middle Ages.* Boston: Harvard Graduate School of Business Administration, Baker Library, 1967. (Kress Library publications, 19.) ‣ Economic thought of famous fifteenth-century preacher and theologian who defended private property and developed utility theory. While disapproving interest-bearing loans, permitted gain on money exchange. [PFG]

28.138   Frederic C. Lane. *Andrea Barbarigo: merchant of Venice, 1418–1449.* 1944 ed. New York: Octagon Books, 1967. ‣ Business history of merchant who traded throughout Mediterranean based especially on account books. Valuable discussion of accounting and genesis of double-entry bookkeeping. [PFG]

28.139 Frederic C. Lane. *Studies in Venetian social and economic history.* Benjamin G. Kohl and Reinhold C. Mueller, eds. London: Variorum, 1987. ISBN 0-86078-202-6. ‣ Informative studies published 1963–86 on politics, double-entry bookkeeping, pepper prices, crossbow, naval actions, seaborne transportation, wages of seamen, banking, gold and silver, insurance, and galleys in medieval and Renaissance Venice. [PFG]

28.140 Frederic C. Lane. *Venice and history: the collected papers of Frederic C. Lane.* Baltimore: Johns Hopkins University Press, 1966. ‣ Studies of shipping, business partnerships, banking, funded public debt, trade fairs, naval architecture, maritime law, and wages and diet of seamen in Venice during Middle Ages and Renaissance by eminent authority. [PFG]

28.141 Frederic C. Lane and Reinhold C. Mueller. *Coins and moneys of account.* Vol. 1 of *Money and banking in medieval and Renaissance Venice.* Baltimore: Johns Hopkins University Press, 1985. ISBN 0-8018-3157-1. ‣ Monumental account of functioning of Venetian moneys before 1500. Emphasizes changes in content and ratings of coins, monetary policy, standards of value, and means of payment. Numerous tables and illustrations. [PFG]

28.142 Iris Origo. *The merchant of Prato: Francesco di Marco Datini.* Rev. ed. New York: Octagon Books, 1979. ISBN 0-374-96149-2. ‣ Study of merchant Datini (ca. 1331–1406) based on numerous surviving letters and records. Best available history of Renaissance business plus account of extended family and relations between spouses. [PFG]

Women, Family, and Social Life

28.143 Ernst Breisach. *Caterina Sforza: a Renaissance virago.* Chicago: University of Chicago Press, 1967. ‣ Biography of flamboyant Caterina Sforza (1462/3–1509), gentlewoman, then ruler of Forli and Imola in the Romagna. Gave as good as she got in brutal, treacherous political world. [PFG]

28.144 Gene A. Brucker. *Giovanni and Lusanna: love and marriage in Renaissance Florence.* 1986 ed. Berkeley: University of California Press, 1988. ISBN 0-520-05655-8 (cl, 1986), 0-520-06328-7 (pbk). ‣ Artisan Lusanna claimed in 1455 that noble Giovanni secretly married her during twelve-year love affair; he denied marriage took place and won court case. Marriage, social class, and law. Fascinating personal story. [PFG]

28.145 Philip Gavitt. *Charity and children in Renaissance Florence: the Ospedale degli Innocenti, 1410–1536.* Ann Arbor: University of Michigan Press, 1990. ISBN 0-472-10183-8. ‣ Study of foundling hospital for abandoned children. After wet-nursing, children were given foster care and placed for adoption. Comments on historiographical issues involving poor, family, and children. [PFG]

28.146 Margaret L. King. *Women of the Renaissance.* Chicago: University of Chicago Press, 1991. ISBN 0-226-43617-9 (cl), 0-226-43618-7 (pbk). ‣ Synthesis for Europe with emphasis on Italy cautiously arguing that women's sense of themselves changed a little in Renaissance. Considers women in family roles, women affected by church, and exceptional and learned women. [PFG]

28.147 Margaret L. King and Albert Rabil, Jr., eds. and trans. *Her immaculate hand: selected works by and about the women humanists of quattrocento Italy.* Binghamton, N.Y.: Medieval & Renaissance Texts & Studies, 1983. (Medieval & Renaissance Texts & Studies, 20.) ISBN 0-86698-023-7. ‣ Essay on life patterns of fifteenth-century North Italian women humanists. Translation of letters of seven women plus letters by male humanists. Contemporaries saw women humanists as prodigies. [PFG]

28.148 Christiane Klapisch-Zuber. *Women, family, and ritual in Renaissance Italy.* Lydia Cochrane, trans. Chicago: University of Chicago Press, 1985. ISBN 0-226-43925-9. ‣ Demographic and ethnographic articles on women, family, foundlings, female servants, wet-nursing, dowries, nuptial rites, dolls, charivari, and naming of children in Florence, 1300–1500. Not always convincing. [PFG]

28.149 Thomas Kuehn. *Law, family, and women: toward a legal anthropology of Renaissance Italy.* Chicago: University of Chicago Press, 1991. ISBN 0-226-45762-1. ‣ Studies in fifteenth-century Florentine legal history: arbitrations, conceptions of property, honor, legitimate marriage, dowries, female inheritance, and gender distinctions in law. Disputes Klapisch-Zuber's (28.148) contention that men legally controlled women. [PFG]

28.150 Patricia H. Labalme, ed. *Beyond their sex: learned women of the European past.* 1980 ed. New York: New York University Press, 1984. ISBN 0-8147-4998-4 (cl, 1980), 0-8147-5007-9 (pbk). ‣ Eight good studies, four on Italian Renaissance women, by experts on lives and accomplishments of learned women, obstacles they had to overcome, and limitations of their role. [PFG]

28.151 Edward Muir and Ruggiero Guido, eds. *Microhistory and the lost peoples of Europe.* Eren Branch, trans. Baltimore: Johns Hopkins University Press, 1991. ISBN 0-8018-4182-8 (cl), 0-8018-4183-6 (pbk). ‣ Eight articles on Italy (six for 1490–1650 period) from journal *Quaderni Storici* illustrating microhistory defined as studying small event in order to isolate and test abstractions of social analysis. Microhistory searches details of historical event for explanatory theory and is heavily ethnographic. Excellent introduction by Muir. [PFG]

28.152 Guido Ruggiero. *The boundaries of Eros: sex crime and sexuality in Renaissance Venice.* 1985 ed. New York: Oxford University Press, 1989. ISBN 0-19-503465-1 (cl, 1985), 0-19-505696-5 (pbk). ‣ Colorful study of sex crimes in fourteenth- and fifteenth-century Venice: fornication, adultery, rape, homosexuality, and convent scandals based on court records. Sheds light on rhetoric of sex and marriage. [PFG]

28.153 Richard C. Trexler. *Public life in Renaissance Florence.* New York: Academic Press, 1980. ISBN 0-12-699550-8. ‣ Wide-ranging, highly interpretive study of public ritual, ceremonies, street actions, executions, etc. Argues that civic rituals had political meaning and maintained relations between different parts of population. [PFG]

28.154 Ronald F. E. Weissman. *Ritual brotherhood in Renaissance Florence.* New York: Academic Press, 1982. ISBN 0-12-744480-7. ‣ Social history of confraternities, 1400–1600. Analyzes membership by occupation, neighborhood, and social network; examines internal organization, officeholding, and activities of confraternities. Concludes confraternities became more elitist. [PFG/FHS]

SEE ALSO
  20.1442 James R. Banker. *Death in the community.*

Italian Catholicism before 1500

28.155 Joseph Gill. *The Council of Florence.* Rev. ed. New York: AMS Press, 1982. ISBN 0-404-17016-1. ‣ Study of church council of 1439 which reunited Latin and Greek churches, including background, dogmatic discussion, opposition in Byzantium, and aftermath which saw Greeks reject union by 1453. [PFG/APK]

28.156 Denys Hay. *The church in Italy in the fifteenth century: the Birkbeck lectures, 1971.* Cambridge: Cambridge University Press, 1977. ISBN 0-521-21532-3. ‣ Introductory survey of Catholic church in Italy: diocesan and parochial organization, quality of religious life, effects of schism, and reform efforts. Calls attention to many gaps in research. [PFG/KP]

28.157 Iris Origo. *The world of San Bernardino.* 1962 ed. London: Reprint Society, 1964. ▸ Narrative history of San Bernardino of Siena (1380–1444), most popular and appealing preacher of his century. Many excerpts from sermons full of insights into everyday life. [PFG]

28.158 Ludwig von Pastor. *The history of the popes from the close of the Middle Ages, drawn from the secret archives of the Vatican and other original sources.* 1891–1953 ed. 40 vols. Frederick I. Antrobus et al., eds. Wilmington, N.C.: Consortium, 1978. ISBN 0-8434-0650-X (set). ▸ Monumental history of papacy, 1305–1799. Outdated ideas about pagan Renaissance but unequaled for period 1513–1667. Conclave elections, brief biographies of popes, religious and political policies, and other aspects of leadership of Catholic church. Papal sympathies do not diminish value of work. [PFG]

28.159 Roberto Ridolfi. *The life of Girolamo Savonarola.* 1959 ed. Cecil Grayson, trans. Westport, Conn.: Greenwood, 1976. ISBN 0-8371-8873-3. ▸ Standard narrative biography of Savonarola (1452–98), religious prophet and virtual ruler of Florence, 1494–98. Translation omits documentation of original Italian edition (1952). [PFG]

28.160 Donald Weinstein. *Savonarola and Florence: prophecy and patriotism in the Renaissance.* Princeton: Princeton University Press, 1970. ISBN 0-691-05184-0. ▸ Argues that Florentine civic traditions transformed Savonarola into prophet of Florentine millennialism, freedom, and glory. Valuable study of "myth of Florence" before Savonarola and latter's posthumous influence. Available in photocopy from Ann Arbor: University Microfilms International, 1987. [PFG]

Sixteenth-Century Italian Catholicism

28.161 Christopher F. Black. *Italian confraternities in the sixteenth century.* Cambridge: Cambridge University Press, 1989. ISBN 0-521-36487-6. ▸ Comprehensive study of religious brotherhoods of lay men and women who carried on charitable and social activities. Roles in hospitals and orphanages, prayers for dying, etc., studied in context of urban society. [PFG]

28.162 J. M. de Bujanda, ed. *Index des Livres Interdits.* 7 vols. to date. Sherbrooke, Que.: Centre d'Études de la Renaissance, Éditions de l'Université de Sherbrooke, 1984–. ISBN 2-7622-0029-6 (v. 1), 2-7622-0033-4 (v. 2), 2-7622-0036-9 (v. 3), 2-7622-0024-5 (v. 4), 2-7622-0024-5 (v. 5), 2-7622-0045-8 (v. 6), 2-7622-0055-5 (v. 7). ▸ Publication of all sixteenth-century *Indices of Prohibited Books* issued by papacy, Venice, Paris, Louvain, Spain, and Portugal. Each volume has historical introduction, analysis of contents of *Index*, identifications of prohibited books, lists of editions of prohibited books, photographic reproduction of original printing of *Index*, and discussion of relationship between *Indices*. Essential work. [PFG]

28.163 Samuel Kline Cohn, Jr. *Death and property in Siena, 1205–1800: strategies for the afterlife.* Baltimore: Johns Hopkins University Press, 1988. ISBN 0-8018-3594-1. ▸ Study of wills to investigate shifting attitudes toward charity, religion, and property. Finds changes at 1363 plague and in 1575–76 with Tridentine reforms. Has been criticized for uneven sampling of wills at different chronological points. [PFG]

28.164 Richard M. Douglas. *Jacopo Sadoleto, 1477–1547: humanist and reformer.* Cambridge, Mass.: Harvard University Press, 1959. ▸ Study of humanist, papal secretary, and cardinal who was part of Catholic reform circles and involved in much papal policy. Engaged in written debates with Calvin and other Protestants. [PFG]

28.165 Paul F. Grendler. *The Roman Inquisition and the Venetian press, 1540–1605.* Princeton: Princeton University Press, 1977. ISBN 0-691-05245-X. ▸ Comprehensive study of press censorship through Inquisition and *Index* in Venice, leading publisher of

Europe, in context of papal-Venetian relations. Sees censorship as joint church-state effort. [PFG]

28.166 Barbara McClung Hallman. *Italian cardinals, reform, and the church as property.* Berkeley: University of California Press, 1985. (Publications of the UCLA Center for Medieval and Renaissance Studies, 22.) ISBN 0-520-04937-3. ▸ Study of largely ineffective attempt to reform abuses in conferral, sale, and holding of ecclesiastical offices among Italian cardinals, 1492–1570. Discussion of how ecclesiastical fiscal system worked. [PFG]

28.167 John M. Headley and John B. Tomaro, eds. *San Carlo Borromeo: Catholic reform and ecclesiastical politics in the second half of the sixteenth century.* Washington, D.C. and London: Folger Shakespeare Library and Associated University Presses, 1988. ISBN 0-918016-92-4. ▸ Fifteen articles on activities and influence of Borromeo (1538–84), bishop of Milan and prototypical church reformer. Larger issues of Catholic reform raised. Only modern book in English on important topic. [PFG]

28.168 William V. Hudon. *Marcello Cervini and ecclesiastical government in Tridentine Italy.* DeKalb: Northern Illinois University Press, 1992. ISBN 0-87580-169-2. ▸ Life of Cervini (1501–55), humanist, administrator, reformer, and briefly pope (April 1555). Wanted apostolic church and strong papacy. Revisionist work rejecting standard view that church policy was conflict between moderates and intransigents and won by latter. [PFG]

28.169 Hubert Jedin. *A history of the Council of Trent.* Vol. 1: *The struggle for the Council.* Vol. 2: *The first sessions at Trent, 1545–47.* 2 vols. Ernest Graf, trans. London: Nelson, 1957–61. ▸ First two volumes of standard history of Council of Trent (1545–63) in which Catholic church formulated doctrine, reformed abuses, and answered Protestant challenge. Volume 1 discusses conciliar theory, earlier councils, and preparations (1400–1545); volume 2 early sessions. Essential work. Additional volumes (3–5) available in German and Italian. [PFG]

28.170 Hubert Jedin. *Papal legate at the Council of Trent: Cardinal Seripando.* Frederic C. Eckhoff, trans. St. Louis: Herder, 1947. ▸ Comprensive study of life and works of Girolamo Seripando (1492/3–1563), cardinal, general of Augustinian order, and major figure of Catholic reform in Italy. Lacks some documentation of German original. [PFG]

28.171 Ruth Martin. *Witchcraft and the Inquisition in Venice, 1550–1650.* Oxford: Blackwell, 1989. ISBN 0-631-16118-X. ▸ Sees attack on witchcraft as attempt to purify popular religious observances. Venice had no witchcraze because Inquisition proceeded in cautious, legal, and humane manner. But Inquisition failed to eliminate magic and superstition. [PFG]

28.172 John W. O'Malley. "Was Ignatius Loyola a church reformer? How to look at early modern Catholicism." *Catholic historical review* 77.2 (1991) 177–93. ISSN 0008-8080. ▸ Convincingly argues for terms "early modern Catholicism" and "cure of souls" as unifying force for sixteenth- and seventeenth-century Catholicism to replace older concepts of Catholic Reformation and Counter-Reformation. [PFG]

28.173 John W. O'Malley, ed. *Catholicism in early modern history: a guide to research.* St. Louis: Center for Reformation Research, 1988. (Reformation guides to research, 2.) ISBN 0-910345-02-3. ▸ Sixteen surveys of current state of research on various topics and geographical areas of Catholicism, 1500–1700: popular piety, religious orders, Council of Trent, Inquisition, education, etc. Comprehensive bibliographies. [PFG]

28.174 Paolo Prodi. *The papal prince, one body and two souls: the papal monarchy in early modern Europe.* Susan Haskins, trans. Cambridge: Cambridge University Press, 1987. ISBN 0-521-32259-6. ▸ Explores dual temporal and spiritual nature of papacy in theory and practice. Discussion of temporal and spiritual powers by contemporary canon lawyers. Difficult reading. [PFG]

28.175 Antonio Santosuosso. "The moderate inquisitor: Giovanni Della Casa's Venetian nunciature, 1544–1549." *Studi Veneziani*, n.s., 2 (1978) 119–210. ISSN 0081-6264. ‣ Della Casa as participant in activities of Venetian Inquisition in prosecution of heresy at critical period. Part of recent historiography seeing Inquisition as moderate tribunal. Good case study. [PFG]

28.176 John A. Tedeschi. *The prosecution of heresy: collected studies on the Inquisition in early modern Italy.* Binghamton, N.Y.: Medieval & Renaissance Texts & Studies, 1991. ISBN 0-86698-089-x. ‣ Eleven studies of Inquisition and *Index*, 1540–1700, emphasizing procedures and functioning, also witchcraft and printing. Objective study refuting myth of cruel tribunal held by past historiography. [PFG]

Italian Protestant Reformation

28.177 Barry Collett. *Italian Benedictine scholars and the Reformation: the congregation of Santa Giustina of Padua.* Oxford: Clarendon, 1985. ISBN 0-19-822934-8. ‣ Italian Benedictines who adopted humanistic theology and tried unsuccessfully to bridge gap between Catholic and Protestant theology through the benefit of Christ crucified, 1480–1570. Major work on Italian Protestant Reformation. [PFG]

28.178 Dermot Fenlon. *Heresy and obedience in Tridentine Italy: Cardinal Pole and the Counter-Reformation.* Cambridge: Cambridge University Press, 1972. ISBN 0-521-20005-9. ‣ Good intellectual biography of Italian career (1521–26, 1530–54) of Pole (1500–58) and of Italian Evangelism generally. Pole believed in justification by faith while remaining loyal to papacy. Nearly became pope but later suspected of heresy. [PFG]

28.179 Carlo Ginzburg. *The cheese and the worms: the cosmos of a sixteenth-century miller.* 1980 ed. John A. Tedeschi and Anne Tedeschi, trans. Harmondsworth: Penguin, 1982. ISBN 0-14-006046-4 (pbk). ‣ Account of miller from Friuli with materialistic cosmological views. Interpreted as example of peasant oral culture existing independently of learned culture; view not universally accepted. Miller executed by unknown means in 1601. [PFG]

28.180 Philip Murray Jourdan McNair. *Peter Martyr in Italy: an anatomy of apostasy.* Oxford: Clarendon, 1967. ‣ Intellectual biography and life of Italian Protestant Peter Martyr Vermigli (1499–1562) until his flight from Italy in 1542. Offers somewhat rigid scheme for classifying degrees of Italian religious dissent. [PFG]

28.181 Anne Jacobson Schutte. *Pier Paolo Vergerio: the making of an Italian reformer.* Geneva: Droz, 1977. ‣ Italian career of Vergerio (1498–1565), bishop and diplomat, who became Protestant exile in Switzerland in 1549. Chronicles development of Protestantism in Italy and Vergerio's conversion to new faith. [PFG]

EARLY MODERN ITALY, 1600–1789

Political, Economic, and Social History

28.182 Tommaso Astarita. *The continuity of feudal power: the Caracciolo of Brienza in Spanish Naples.* Cambridge: Cambridge University Press, 1992. ISBN 0-521-40474-6. ‣ Good revisionist study of feudal family which controlled several towns and 15,000 souls in kingdom of Naples, 1550–1725. Emphasizes economic organization and paternalistic rule. Concludes feudal families maintained wealth and prospered through good management. [PFG]

28.183 Dino Carpanetto and Giuseppe Ricuperati. *Italy in the age of reason, 1685–1789.* Caroline Higgitt, trans. New York: Longman, 1987. ISBN 0-582-48338-7 (cl), 0-582-49145-2 (pbk). ‣ Good general history of period addressing population, country-side, trade, classes, Enlightenment ideas, political reforms, crisis of old regime, and intellectual implications. Emphasizes distinctiveness of Italian Enlightenment within European context. [PFG]

28.184 Eric W. Cochrane. *Florence in the forgotten centuries, 1527–1800: a history of Florence and the Florentines in the age of the grand dukes.* Chicago: University of Chicago Press, 1973. ISBN 0-226-11150-4. ‣ Well-written, colorful narrative history focusing on key personalities in each epoch within historical context. Lacks notes; bibliographical essays do not always support text. [PFG]

28.185 James Cushman Davis. *The decline of the Venetian nobility as a ruling class.* Baltimore: Johns Hopkins University Press, 1962. ‣ Discusses decline in number of Venetian noble males between 1500 and 1797 as consequence of restricting marriages and economic problems. Declining numbers rendered nobility less capable of governing. [PFG]

28.186 Robert C. Davis. *Shipbuilders of the Venetian arsenal: workers and workplace in the preindustrial city.* Baltimore: Johns Hopkins University Press, 1991. ISBN 0-8018-4095-3. ‣ Mostly ethnographic study of workers of Venetian shipyard, 1621–70. Organization, wages, and discipline within shipyard; crime, disorder, magic, community, and civic role of workers outside shipyard. [PFG]

28.187 R. Burr Litchfield. *Emergence of a bureaucracy: the Florentine patricians, 1530–1790.* Princeton: Princeton University Press, 1986. ISBN 0-691-05487-8. ‣ Describes how fractious republic became bureaucratic princedom. Development of bureaucracy with transformation of Florentine patricians into state administrators. Information on careers and salaries plus economic and agricultural policy. Dull but useful. [PFG]

28.188 John A. Marino. *Pastoral economics in the kingdom of Naples.* Baltimore: Johns Hopkins University Press, 1988. ISBN 0-8018-3437-6. ‣ Economic and social history of sheep-grazing and wool trade, 1590–1780. Emphasizes interaction between market economy and social structure, private wealth and public patronage, and seventeenth-century decline and eighteenth-century growth. [PFG]

28.189 Frank McArdle. *Altopascio: a study in Tuscan rural society, 1587–1784.* Cambridge: Cambridge University Press, 1978. ISBN 0-521-21619-2. ‣ Detailed study of agrarian system in small village and Medici-controlled estate: economy, demography, family structure, and class relations. Does not find social crisis in seventeenth-century rural Tuscany. [PFG]

28.190 Laurie Nussdorfer. *Civic politics in the Rome of Urban VIII.* Princeton: Princeton University Press, 1992. ISBN 0-691-03182-7. ‣ Good analysis of civic government under absolute ruler. Concludes lay government had substantial authority. Interregnum between popes was occasion for criticizing pope. Contribution to growing literature on early modern cities. [PFG]

28.191 Brian S. Pullan, ed. *Crisis and change in the Venetian economy in the sixteenth and seventeenth centuries.* London: Methuen, 1968. ‣ Eight articles by specialists on shipping, spices, wool industry, wages, and agriculture. Sees Venetian economy shifting from sea commerce to manufacturing and agriculture rather than suffering absolute decline. [PFG]

28.192 Richard Tilden Rapp. *Industry and economic decline in seventeenth-century Venice.* Cambridge, Mass.: Harvard University Press, 1976. ISBN 0-674-44545-7. ‣ Study of employment and labor force as index of economic prosperity. Venice did not decline as employment shifted from export industries to manufacturing for domestic market. Guilds accepted technological change. [PFG]

28.193 Domenico Sella. *Crisis and continuity: the economy of Spanish Lombardy in the seventeenth century.* Cambridge, Mass.:

Harvard University Press, 1979. ISBN 0-674-17675-8. ▸ Emphasizes crisis and decay of urban economy and resilience and strength of countryside in contrast with previous studies. Sees refeudalization as fiscal measure rather than instrument of social oppression. [PFG]

28.194 Kenneth M. Setton. *Venice, Austria, and the Turks in the seventeenth century.* Philadelphia: American Philosophical Society, 1991. (Memoirs of the American Philosophical Society, 192.) ISBN 0-87169-192-2. ▸ Continuation (from 1571 to 1718) of 28.87. Detailed account of Venetian-Turkish wars, 1645–69, when Venice lost Crete, and wars of 1680s, when Venice allied with Austria to win. Discusses destruction of Parthenon. [PFG]

28.195 Geoffrey Symcox. *Victor Amadeus II: absolutism in the Savoyard state, 1675–1730.* Berkeley: University of California Press, 1983. ISBN 0-520-04974-8. ▸ Political history of ruler who built independent North Italian state which eventually became center of united Italian state. Early enlightened despot, Victor Amadeus, successfully fought wars and modernized state. [PFG]

28.196 Stuart J. Woolf. *The poor in western Europe in the eighteenth and nineteenth centuries.* London: Methuen, 1986. ISBN 0-416-39330-6. ▸ In spite of title, focus mainly on Italy around beginning of nineteenth century. Well-researched collection of essays. [AS]

Anthropological, Intellectual, and Religious History

28.197 Judith C. Brown. *Immodest acts: the life of a lesbian nun in Renaissance Italy.* New York: Oxford University Press, 1986. ISBN 0-19-503675-1. ▸ Benedetta Carlini (1590–1661), nun at Pescia, had troubling religious visions. Claimed possession by male angel and entered into lesbian relationship with nun sharing cell. Discussion of lesbianism, mysticism, and possession. [PFG]

28.198 William J. Callahan and David Higgs, eds. *Church and society in Catholic Europe of the eighteenth century.* Cambridge: Cambridge University Press, 1979. ISBN 0-521-22424-1. ▸ Articles by specialists on Italian, French, Spanish, Portuguese, German, Austrian, Hungarian, and Polish churches and popular religion. Topics include social function of church, recruitment of clergy, and poor relief. Good comparative history. [PFG]

28.199 Owen Chadwick. *The popes and European revolution.* Oxford: Clarendon, 1981. ISBN 0-19-826919-6. ▸ Description of Catholicism and papacy in eighteenth century and papal policies during revolutions of 1789–1815. Emphasis on southern Europe, especially Italy. Pulls together much useful information without polemics. [PFG]

28.200 Eric W. Cochrane. *Tradition and Enlightenment in the Tuscan academies, 1690–1800.* 1961 ed. Chicago: University of Chicago Press, 1962. ▸ Study of thirty-five academies whose membership included prominent figures and from which came ideas of reform. Argues change of attitudes led to state reforms. [PFG]

28.201 Carlo Ginzburg. *The night battles: witchcraft and agrarian cults in the sixteenth and seventeenth centuries.* 1983 ed. John A. Tedeschi and Anne Tedeschi, trans. New York: Penguin, 1985. ISBN 0-14-007688-3 (pbk). ▸ Story of fertility cult in which seventeenth-century Friulian peasants in dream state ritually battled witches to safeguard harvest. Skillful use of Inquisition records to study peasant culture. [PFG]

28.202 Hanns Gross. *Rome in the age of Enlightenment: the post-Tridentine syndrome and the ancien régime.* Cambridge: Cambridge University Press, 1990. ISBN 0-521-37211-9. ▸ History of eighteenth-century Rome with much information on demography, economy, government, charity, law enforcement, Jansenism, and arts; unreliable on education. Argues that Tridentine papacy could not adjust to Enlightenment. [PFG]

28.203 Marcello Maestro. *Cesare Beccaria and the origins of penal reform.* Philadelphia: Temple University Press, 1973. ISBN 0-87722-024-7. ▸ Only English-language biography of criminal law reformer Beccaria (1738–94) who wanted punishment to fit crime and opposed death penalty. Beccaria worked for economic and other Enlightenment reforms. [PFG]

28.204 Giorgio Tagliacozzo and Donald Phillip Verene, eds. *Giambattista Vico's science of humanity.* Baltimore: Johns Hopkins University Press, 1976. ISBN 0-8018-1720-X. ▸ Large collection of studies on Vico (1668–1744), seminal thinker in history, law, and philosophy. Includes list of modern editions of Vico's works and comprehensive bibliography of works on Vico in English. [PFG]

28.205 Franco Venturi. *Italy and the Enlightenment: studies in a cosmopolitan century.* Stuart J. Woolf, ed. Susan Corsi, trans. New York: New York University Press, 1972. ISBN 0-8147-8752-5. ▸ Essays by distinguished Italian historian of Enlightenment who places Italy in European context. Wide-ranging intellectual history of ideas in historical context as reformers tried to change institutions. [PFG]

MODERN ITALY, 1789–1988

Bibliography and Historiography

28.206 Frank J. Coppa, ed. *Dictionary of modern Italian history.* Westport, Conn.: Greenwood, 1985. ISBN 0-313-22983-X. ▸ Useful dictionary by expert American scholars; covers events and personalities of modern Italy. Entries from 100 to 900 words, usually with short bibliographical note. [AS]

28.207 Charles F. Delzell. *Italy in modern times: an introduction to the historical literature in English.* Washington, D.C.: American Historical Association, 1964. (Service center for teachers of history, 60.) ▸ Well-informed, thoughtful discussion of English-language sources on Italian history from mid-eighteenth century, but for post-1861 see Delzell's more recent work (28.300). [AS]

28.208 Roland Sarti. *A select bibliography of English-language books on modern Italian history.* Amherst: University of Massachusetts Press, 1989. (Program in Western European studies, Occasional papers series, 6.) ▸ Brief but useful bibliographical pamphlet on period 1714 to post-1945. Divides titles into sixteen groups mainly along chronological lines. Short introduction; entries listed without annotation. [AS]

28.209 Hans A. Schmitt, ed. *Historians of modern Europe.* Baton Rouge: Louisiana State University Press, 1971. ISBN 0-8071-0836-7. ▸ Articles on major Italian historians: Delzell on Omodeo, Peck on Salvemini, Salomone on Chabod, and Tannenbaum on Volpe. [AS]

General Studies

28.210 Giorgio Candeloro. *Storia dell'Italia moderna.* Edition varies. 11 vols. Milan: Feltrinelli, 1956–86. ISBN 88-07-80796-3 (v. 1). ▸ Gramscian interpretation of Italian history from 1700 to 1950. Arranged chronologically but often with extensive attention to social and economic problems. Excellent bibliographical notes; fair and balanced toward alternative views. [AS]

28.211 Shepard B. Clough. *The economic history of modern Italy.* New York: Columbia University Press, 1964. ▸ Covers period 1815 to 1960s but mainly postunification. Italy established industrial base between 1860 and late 1890s, expanded in 1890s, suffered during World War I and under fascism, and recovered well after World War II. [AS]

28.212 Frank J. Coppa, ed. *Studies in modern Italian history from the Risorgimento to the Republic.* New York: Lang, 1986. ISBN 0-8204-0180-3. ▸ Conference papers on aspects of Italian history, including reappraisals of crucial trends: Risorgimento, Giolittian Italy as democracy in the making or seedbed of fascism, rebellion and violence from 1914 to present, foreign policy, post–World War II economy, and historicism. [AS]

28.213 Ronald S. Cunsolo. *Italian nationalism: from its origins to World War II.* Malabar, Fla.: Krieger, 1990. ISBN 0-89874-938-7. ‣ Useful survey of Italian nationalism in two parts: analysis and documents. Different conceptions of nationalism and its status as ideal of minority were sources of weakness. [AS]

28.214 Denis Mack Smith. *Modern Sicily after 1713.* Vol. 3 of *History of Sicily.* Moses I. Finley, ed. New York: Viking, 1968. ISBN 0-670-46492-9 (v. 2–3). ‣ Vivid evocation of Sicilian history by major historian. Mack Smith probably at his best in understanding conditions of southern Italy. [AS]

28.215 Maurice F. Neufeld. *Italy, school for awakening countries: the Italian labor movement in its political, social, and economic setting from 1800 to 1960.* 1961 ed. Westport, Conn.: Greenwood, 1974. ISBN 0-8371-6339-0. ‣ Reliable work on Italian labor movement. History of movement divided into three main phases: 1800–90, 1890–1926, and 1926–60. Ties labor to other aspects of Italian life, especially social history. [AS]

28.216 Arthur James Beresford Whyte. *The evolution of modern Italy.* 1944 ed. New York: Norton, 1965. ISBN 0-393-00298-5. ‣ Mostly on Risorgimento. Emphasizes House of Savoy and Cavour; minimizes contribution of Garibaldi and Mazzini. Dated liberal analysis but detailed military account of period still valuable. [AS]

28.217 Stuart J. Woolf. *A history of Italy, 1700–1860: the social constraints of political change.* London: Methuen, 1979. ISBN 0-416-80880-8. ‣ Sensitive, insightful general study of Italy from period of reforms to unity. Pioneering social history of period. Revised from 1973 Italian edition. [AS]

RISORGIMENTO, 1789–1861

Bibliography and Historiography

28.218 Antonio Gramsci. *Prison notebooks.* Joseph A. Buttigieg, ed. and trans. Antonio Callari, trans. New York: Columbia University Press, 1991. ISBN 0-231-06082-3 (v. 1). ‣ Translation of volume 1 of Gramsci's notebooks based on second Italian edition (1975). Like Croce on liberal historians, Gramsci has had enormous influence on socialist scholars of modern Italy. His view of unification as a failed revolution especially important. [AS]

28.219 Raymond Grew. "How success spoiled the Risorgimento." *Journal of modern history* 34.3 (1962) 239–53. ISSN 0022-2801. ‣ Important article on how unification was achieved. Cavour made substantial mistakes. Should be read with other views: Gramsci 28.218, Lovett 28.257, and Davis 28.337. [AS]

28.220 Leopoldo Marchetti, ed. *Nuove questioni di storia del Risorgimento e dell'unità di Italia.* 1961 ed. 2 vols. Milan: Marzorati, 1969. ‣ Collection of essays on various topics from Risorgimento to 1918 with extensive bibliographical notes. Some essays important; see especially Francesco Curato on 1848 and Rosario Romeo on Cavour. [AS]

28.221 Walter Maturi. *Interpretazioni del Risorgimento: lezioni di storia della storiografia.* Turin: Einaudi, 1962. ‣ Clear, balanced analysis of writings on Risorgimento, fruit of university lectures 1945–60. Bibliographic addition by Rosario Romeo. Fundamental work. [AS]

28.222 Emilia Morelli, ed. *Bibliografia dell'età del Risorgimento in onore di Alberto M. Ghisalberti.* 4 vols. Florence: Olschki, 1971–77. ‣ International team of contributors; quality of contributions uneven. Many entries simple lists of titles, others annotated. Volume 4 contains indexes. Essential tool for scholarly investigation of period; vast bibliography. [AS]

General Studies

28.223 Harry Hearder. *Italy in the age of the Risorgimento, 1790–1870.* London: Longman, 1983. ISBN 0-582-49146-0 (pbk). ‣ Excellent general history but difficult for nonexpert. Part 1 covers situation in various Italian states; part 2 chronological history. Historiographical trends in chapter 1. Good bibliographical notes. [AS]

28.224 Bolton H. King. *A history of Italian unity: being a political history from 1814 to 1871.* 1924 rev. ed. 2 vols. New York: Russell & Russell, 1967. ‣ Straight political analysis except for chapters 3–5 and 40 on social conditions. Influential interpretation in spite of moralistic approach and antipapal bias. First published 1899. [AS]

28.225 Aurelio Lepre. *Storia del Mezzogiorno nel Risorgimento.* 1974 2d ed. Rome: Riuniti, 1977. ‣ Chronological essays on southern Italy and Risorgimento from 1700 to Garibaldi's conquest. Leftist interpretation. [AS]

28.226 Adolfo Omodeo. *Difesa del Risorgimento.* Rev. ed. Turin: Einaudi, 1955. ‣ Classic essays on Charles Albert, Cavour, and especially moderate liberal Gioberti, leader of neo-Guelphism—that is, attempt to split alliance between church and Restoration leaders and make church accept idea of liberal, united Italy. Neo-Hegelian interpretation of history by student of Croce. [AS]

28.227 Piero Pieri. *Storia militare del Risorgimento: guerre e insurrezioni.* Turin: Einaudi, 1962. ‣ Fundamental work by greatest Italian military historian of past generation. Covers conspiracies, revolutions, and wars within economic, social, intellectual, and political context. [AS]

28.228 Luigi Salvatorelli. *The Risorgimento: thought and action.* Mario Domandi, trans. Charles F. Delzell, Introduction. New York: Harper & Row, 1970. ISBN 0-06-136022-8. ‣ Ethical-political view of Risorgimento as material and spiritual process. Published in 1943 in Italian by democratic historian critical of fascist interpretation of Italian history. Fundamental work; excellent introduction. [AS]

Origins

28.229 *Atti del convegno sul tema: Napoleone e l'Italia (Roma 8–13 ottobre 1969).* 2 vols. Rome: Accademia Nazionale dei Lincei, 1973. (Problemi attuali di scienza e di cultura, Quaderno, 179.) ‣ Good collection of conference papers on diplomacy, military history, politics, economy, historiography, artistic life, and states of Napoleonic Italy, 1796–1814. [AS]

28.230 Renzo De Felice. *Italia giacobina.* Naples: Scientifiche Italiane, 1965. (L'Acropoli, 13.) ‣ Five essays, clear and well documented, by major debater on definition of Italian Jacobin. Especially interesting synthesis of Italy, 1796–99 (chapter 1). [AS]

28.231 Gaudens Megaro. *Vittorio Alfieri: forerunner of Italian nationalism.* 1930 ed. New York: Octagon Books, 1975. ISBN 0-374-95557-3. ‣ Pioneering work on Italian nationalism. Alfieri key intellectual during French revolutionary period and greatest Italian writer of tragedies. See Noether 28.232. [AS]

28.232 Emiliana P. Noether. *Seeds of Italian nationalism, 1700–1815.* 1951 ed. New York: AMS Press, 1969. ‣ Study of national awakening among literary figures in eighteenth century and its earlier roots. Argues that nineteenth-century unification owes much to this literary nationalism. Good bibliography. [PFG]

28.233 John Rosselli. *Lord William Bentinck and the British occupation of Sicily, 1811–14.* Cambridge: Cambridge University Press, 1956. ‣ Unlike other scholars, Rosselli argues that Bentinck did not play role among Italian secret societies before he reached continental Italy in 1814. [AS]

28.234 Carlo Zaghi. *La rivoluzione francese e l'Italia: studi e ri-*

cerche. Naples: Cymba, 1966. ▸ Important collection of essays and notes, written between 1934 and 1966, on first phase of French occupation, 1796–99. Especially important on Directory Italian policy and on Cisalpine Republic. See also by same author volume 18 of *Storia d'Italia* (28.3). [AS]

Restoration Italy: Order and Revolution

28.235 Harold M. Acton. *The Bourbons of Naples, 1734–1825.* 1956 ed. New York: Barnes & Noble, 1974. ISBN 0-06-470007-0. ▸ Sympathetic interpretation of often criticized rulers of Naples. Hails artistic achievements, minimizes shortcomings elsewhere, captures court life; weak on state's economic and social structure. [AS]

28.236 Harold M. Acton. *The last Bourbons of Naples, 1825–1861.* 1956 ed. New York: St. Martin's, 1962. ▸ Sympathetic portrayal of dynasty; counteracts negative judgment of other historians. Readable, interesting, but weak on economic and social structure. [AS]

28.237 George Fitz-Hardinge Berkeley and Joan Berkeley. *Italy in the making, 1815–48.* 1932–40 ed. 3 vols. Cambridge: Cambridge University Press, 1968. ISBN 0-521-07427-4 (v. 1), 0-521-07428-2 (v. 2), 0-521-07429-0 (v. 3). ▸ Volume 1, 1815–46, and volume 2, 1846–48, focus on Pius IX, and volume 3, diplomatic and military analysis of 1848. Sympathetic, conservative view of Italian quest for independence by English Catholic historians. Emphasis on moderate liberals, tolerant toward Metternich, and sympathetic toward Charles Albert and Pius IX. Investigation centered on Sardinia and Papal States. [AS]

28.238 Gaetano Cingari. *Mezzogiorno e Risorgimento: la restaurazione a Napoli dal 1821 al 1830.* Bari: Laterza, 1970. ▸ Well-researched portrayal of harsh period of repression following failure of Revolution of 1820–21. [AS]

28.239 Elizabeth L. Eisenstein. *The first professional revolutionist: Filippo Buonarroti (1761–1837), a biographical essay.* Cambridge, Mass.: Harvard University Press, 1959. ▸ Biography of most important Italian Jacobin and later head of Carboneria. Good on Buonarroti's link to Babeuf. For Italian role prefer works by Saitta 28.250 and Garrone 28.241. Excellent bibliographical essay. [AS]

28.240 Donald E. Emerson. *Metternich and the political police: security and subversion in the Hapsburg monarchy, 1815–30.* The Hague: Nijhoff, 1968. ▸ Assessment of Metternich's role in activities of Austrian secret police, maintaining that Metternich did not consider Italian secret societies a serious threat. See Reinerman 28.247 for alternative view. [AS]

28.241 Alessandro Galante Garrone. *Filippo Buonarroti e i rivoluzionari dell'ottocento, 1828–37.* Rev. ed. Turin: Einaudi, 1972. ▸ Essential in addition to Saitta on Buonarroti (28.250) because covers revolutionary's later years as head of Carboneria, often in rivalry with Mazzini's Young Italy. [AS]

28.242 Edward E. Y. Hales. *Revolution and papacy, 1769–1846.* 1960 ed. Notre Dame, Ind.: University of Notre Dame Press, 1966. ▸ Readable, sympathetic view of difficult period for papacy. Stops prior to Pius IX, subject of another book by Hales (28.270). Uses materials from Vatican archives. [AS]

28.243 Aurelio Lepre. *La Rivoluzione Napoletana del 1820–21.* Rome: Riuniti, 1967. ▸ One of Lepre's important studies on kingdom of Two Sicilies addressing Revolution of 1820–21, its initial success, and final failure. Leftist interpretation. [AS]

28.244 R. John Rath. "The Carbonari: their origins, initiation rites, and aims." *American historical review* 69 (1964) 353–70. ISSN 0002-8762. ▸ Discusses origins and ritual of most famous secret society of Risorgimento, spark of revolutions of 1820 in Napoli and of 1831 in Central Italy. See also Emerson's book on Metternich and political police (28.240). [AS]

28.245 R. John Rath. *The fall of the Napoleonic kingdom of Italy, 1814.* 1941 ed. New York: Octagon Books, 1975. ISBN 0-374-96718-0. ▸ Well-researched, balanced account of how kingdom of Italy, created by Napoleon, fell in 1814, and how Austria took control of region by June of that year. Approaches topic from Austrian viewpoint. [AS]

28.246 R. John Rath. *The provisional Austrian regime in Lombardy Venetia, 1814–1815.* Austin: University of Texas Press, 1969. ISBN 0-292-78385-X. ▸ Vital (with 28.245) for understanding of acquisition of Lombardy Venetia and Italian question. Austrian Restoration of 1814–15 set guidelines until 1848; not oppressive but insensitive toward ideological aims of Lombard bourgeoisie. Fair but critical appraisal of Austrian record. For later period, see volume 18 of *Storia d'Italia* (28.3). [AS/PWS]

28.247 Alan J. Reinerman. *Austria and the papacy in the age of Metternich.* Vol. 1: *Between conflict and cooperation, 1809–30.* Vol. 2: *Revolution and reaction, 1830–38.* Washington, D.C.: Catholic University of America Press, 1979–89. ISBN 0-8132-0548-4 (v. 1), 0-8132-0548-1 (v. 2). ▸ How Metternich's relationship with papacy was important for defense of Habsburg empire and Restoration, for shaping papacy's internal and foreign policy and its reaction to liberalism and nationalism, and for influencing key moments of Risorgimento. Excellent archival research by Catholic historian. [AS/PWS]

28.248 John M. Robinson. *Cardinal Consalvi, 1757–1824.* New York: St. Martin's, 1987. ISBN 0-312-01297-7. ▸ Engaging, popular biography of cardinal who played important role in Napoleonic Italy and who restored papacy to strong international and internal position during Restoration. Uses some manuscript sources from Vatican archives. [AS]

28.249 George T. Romani. *The Neapolitan Revolution of 1820–1821.* 1950 ed. Westport, Conn.: Greenwood, 1978. ISBN 0-313-20395-4. ▸ Reliable although dated version of first revolution of Risorgimento in kingdom of Two Sicilies in 1820; also revolution in kingdom of Sardinia the next year. Metternich and Austria crushed both in 1821. [AS]

28.250 Armando Saitta. *Filippo Buonarroti: contributo alla storia della sua vita e del suo pensiero.* 2d ed. 2 vols. Rome: Istituto Storico Italiano per l'Età Moderna e Contemporanea, 1972. ▸ Collection of essays on various aspects of life and thought of most important Italian Jacobin and later leader of Carboneria. Well researched; many important documents. [AS]

Mazzini and the Democrats

28.251 George A. Carbone. "The long detour: Italy's search for unity." In *Studies in modern European history in honor of Franklin C. Palm.* Frederick J. Cox et al., eds., pp. 49–80. New York: Bookman, 1956. ▸ Cattaneo's ideas about regional autonomy fulfilled only in 1948 constitution. Interpretation influenced by postfascist Italian historiography. See also Lovett 28.256. [AS]

28.252 Elizabeth Adams Daniels. *Jessie White Mario: Risorgimento revolutionary.* Athens: Ohio University Press, 1972. ISBN 0-8214-0103-3. ▸ Biography of English journalist, married to Italian revolutionary. Strong supporter of Mazzini and democratic movement; conspirator, journalist, and biographer in pursuit of political and social reform. [AS]

28.253 Franco Della Peruta. *Mazzini e i rivoluzionari italiani: il partito d'Azione, 1830–45.* Milan: Feltrinelli, 1974. ▸ Fundamental work on Mazzini and his Action party. Extensive documentation in support of Emilia Morelli's thesis on establishment of democratic republican groups in northern Italy by early 1840s. [AS]

28.254 Gwilym O. Griffith. *Mazzini: prophet of modern Europe.* 1932 ed. New York: Fertig, 1970. ▸ Democratic and thus favorable interpretation of Mazzini's role based mainly on Mazzini's own writings before 1836. [AS]

28.255 Edward E. Y. Hales. *Mazzini and the secret societies: the making of a myth.* London: Eyre & Spottiswoode, 1956. ‣ Readable survey of Mazzini's early life; less insightful on secret societies. Slightly hostile view of Mazzini by English Catholic historian. [AS]

28.256 Clara M. Lovett. *Carlo Cattaneo and the politics of the Risorgimento, 1820–1860.* The Hague: Nijhoff, 1972. ISBN 90-247-1283-1. ‣ Excellent study of Cattaneo as reluctant revolutionary, neither radical nor precursor of democratic federalism; ambiguous and contradictory but reformer at heart. Annotated bibliography. See Carbone 28.251. [AS]

28.257 Clara M. Lovett. *The democratic movement in Italy, 1830–1876.* Cambridge, Mass.: Harvard University Press, 1982. ISBN 0-674-19645-7. ‣ Important book advancing three hypotheses: democrats' attempts were not abstract; they had lasting impact on culture and society; and movement produced first professional politicians in Italy. Excellent bibliographical essay. [AS]

28.258 Clara M. Lovett. *Giuseppe Ferrari and the Italian revolution.* Chapel Hill: University of North Carolina Press, 1979. ISBN 0-8078-1354-0. ‣ Well-researched, thoughtful work on important ·Radical Democrat, seen as product of European radical-socialist tradition. Emphasis on Ferrari's role in unification process and activity in Parliament of united Italy. [AS]

28.259 William Roberts. *Prophet in exile: Joseph Mazzini in England, 1837–1868.* New York: Lang, 1989. ISBN 0-8204-1051-9. ‣ How Mazzini's years of exile in England influenced his thought, how he became channel for British and continental thought, and how he influenced British political life. [AS]

28.260 Gaetano Salvemini. *Mazzini.* 1957 ed. I. M. Rawson, trans. New York: Collier, 1962. ‣ Deals separately with Mazzini's thought and action. Influential although flawed work of democratic school. First published in 1905, considerably revised in 1915; also additions in first English edition of 1957. [AS]

Moderate Liberals and Neo-Guelphs

28.261 Kent Roberts Greenfield. *Economics and liberalism in the Risorgimento: a study of nationalism in Lombardy, 1814–1848.* 1965 ed. Westport, Conn.: Greenwood, 1978. ISBN 0-313-20510-8. ‣ Part 1 on economics, part 2 on liberal thought and action. Important discussion of Italian movement away from Metternich's view of state and adoption of laissez-faire conception of economy and society. [AS]

28.262 Claude Leetham. *Rosmini: priest and philosopher.* Rev. ed. New York: New City Press, 1982. ISBN 0-911782-39-7. ‣ Biography of intellectual Catholic clergyman, example of disintegration of union between church and Restoration. Rosmini moderate liberal, for a while close to Gioberti's neo-Guelphism. Earlier title: *Rosmini: Priest, Philosopher, and Patriot* (1957). [AS]

28.263 Vito Lo Curto and Mario Themelly. *Gli scrittori cattolici dalla restaurazione all'unità.* Rome: Laterza, 1976. ‣ Surveys both reactionary and reformist Catholic intellectuals during Risorgimento beginning with Napoleonic Italy. Excellent essay on Gioberti. Annotated bibliography. [AS]

28.264 Ronald Marshall. *Massimo d'Azeglio: an artist in politics, 1798–1866.* London: Oxford University Press, 1966. ‣ Well-written biography of moderate liberal leader and link between Liberals and House of Savoy. Researched in British and Italian archives. [AS]

The Revolutions of 1848

28.265 Roger Aubert. *Le pontificat de Pie IX.* Rev. ed. Paris: Bloud & Gay, 1963. ‣ Best general study of Pius IX. Very critical

of Pius's secretary of state, Antonelli. Excellent bibliography. For comprehensive survey of Pius IX see the Italian works by Giacomo Martina (1974–90). [AS]

28.266 Delio Cantimori. "Italy in 1848." In *The opening of an era: 1848: an historical symposium.* 1948 ed. F. Fejtö, ed., pp. 114–42. New York: Fertig, 1966. ‣ Thoughtful account of revolutions of 1848 and of First War of Independence against Austria in 1848–49 by major Italian historian. [AS]

28.267 Frank J. Coppa. *Cardinal Giacomo Antonelli and papal politics in European affairs.* Albany: State University of New York Press, 1990. ISBN 0-7914-0184-7 (cl), 0-7914-0185-5 (pbk). ‣ Antonelli, secretary of state under Pius IX from 1849 to 1878, shaped papacy's foreign policy and played leading role against Italian unity. Well written and researched; extensive annotated bibliography. [AS]

28.268 Frank J. Coppa. *Pope Pius IX: crusader in a secular age.* Boston: Twayne, 1979. ISBN 0-8057-7727-X. ‣ Broad but scholarly survey of Pius IX's life and impact on Risorgimento, liberal Italy, and the church. Extensive bibliography; most titles annotated. [AS]

28.269 Paul Ginsborg. *Daniele Manin and the Venetian Revolution of 1848–49.* Cambridge: Cambridge University Press, 1979. ISBN 0-521-22077-7. ‣ Detailed monograph on Venetian revolution and how Italian Democrats and Republicans failed to win leadership of Risorgimento. Examines Gramsci's view of Risorgimento; leftist view. Excellent research. [AS]

28.270 Edward E. Y. Hales. *Pio Nono: a study in European politics and religion in the nineteenth century.* 1954 ed. Garden City, N.Y.: Doubleday, 1962. ‣ First English biography of twentieth century on Pius IX based on limited research when access to Vatican archives not allowed. Sympathetic view of pope by English Catholic historian. [AS]

28.271 Alan Sked. *The survival of the Habsburg empire: Radetzky, the imperial army, and the class war, 1848.* London: Longman, 1979. ISBN 0-582-50711-1. ‣ How Radetzky held together army on brink of disintegration and went on to defeat Sardinians and revolutionaries in 1848 and 1849. Military history from sociological, political, and social-psychological viewpoint. Impressive documentation. [AS]

28.272 Howard McGaw Smyth. "The armistice of Novara: a legend of a liberal king." *Journal of modern history* 7 (1935) 141–82. ISSN 0022-2801. ‣ Invalidates claim that Victor Emmanuel II fought to keep Sardinian constitution against wish of Field Marshall Radetzky in 1849. Revisionist view in opposition to Thayer 28.288 and King 28.224. [AS]

28.273 Howard McGaw Smyth. "Piedmont and Prussia: the influence of the campaigns of 1848–49 on the constitutional development of Italy." *American historical review* 60 (1950) 479–502. ISSN 0002-8762. ‣ Sardinia's constitutional development resulted from war of 1848–49, not work of House of Savoy or of Cavour. Simplistic view according to Maturi 28.221. [AS]

28.274 George M. Trevelyan. *Garibaldi's defense of the Roman Republic.* 1907 ed. London: Cassell, 1988. ISBN 0-304-32224-5 (pbk). ‣ First (with 28.296 and 28.295) of classic trilogy on Garibaldi by whig historian. Trevelyan considered it his best; not so according to Maturi 28.221. Evocative narrative and brilliant military history. Weak on political and social structure. [AS]

28.275 George M. Trevelyan. *Manin and the Venetian Revolution of 1848.* 1923 ed. London: Longmans, Green, 1990. ‣ Concentrates on Venetian revolutionary Manin and establishment of Venetian republic in 1848. Not well researched; weakest of Trevelyan's books on Risorgimento. Whig history. [AS]

SEE ALSO
    47.100 A.J.P. Taylor. *The Italian problem in European diplomacy, 1847–1849.*

The Unification Process

28.276 *Atti del congresso di storia del Risorgimento italiano.* 2 vols. Rome: Istituto per la Storia del Risorgimento, 1961. (Biblioteca scientifica: atti dei congresso, 5.) ‣ Important collection of articles, *Atti del XXXVIII Congresso* on 1859 and *Atti del XXXIX Congresso* on Expedition of Thousand. See especially Salvatorelli, Moscati, Valsecchi, and Pieri on 1859; D'Entreves, Godechot, and Mack Smith on Thousand. [AS]

28.277 Robert C. Binkley. *Realism and nationalism, 1852–1871.* Vol. 15 of *The rise of modern Europe.* 1935 ed. New York: Harper & Row, 1963. ‣ Italian unification from European perspective. Cavour's process of unification one of several options; minimizes Cavour's role. [AS]

28.278 Frank J. Coppa. *Camillo di Cavour.* New York: Twayne, 1973. ISBN 0-8057-3018-4. ‣ Stresses aspects of career and life usually overlooked in English. Readable account sympathetic to Cavour who united Italy and strengthened parliamentary system. Based on secondary and printed primary sources. [AS]

28.279 Frank J. Coppa. *The origins of the Italian wars of independence.* New York: Longman, 1992. ISBN 0-582-04046-9 (cl), 0-582-04045-0 (pbk). ‣ Italian wars from 1848 Revolution to 1870 occupation of Rome. Unification the product of both Italian patriotism and foreign intervention and rivalries. Meticulous use of sources; university textbook. [AS]

28.280 Alberto M. Ghisalberti. *Orsini minore.* Rome: Edizioni dell'Ateneo, 1955. ‣ Excellent source on early years of Felice Orsini, Radical Democrat who tried to assassinate Napoleon III in January 1858. After revolutions of 1848–49, democratic currents split into various groups: pro-Mazzini, radical, or favoring unity under monarchy. [AS]

28.281 Raymond Grew. *A sterner plan for Italian unity: the Italian National Society in the Risorgimento.* Princeton: Princeton University Press, 1963. ISBN 0-691-05155-0. ‣ Detailed analysis of National Society founded after 1848–49 to support unification under House of Savoy. Critical of Cavourians and moderate liberals. Covers period up to 1861. [AS]

28.282 William Keith Hancock. *Ricasoli and the Risorgimento in Tuscany.* 1926 ed. New York: Fertig, 1969. ‣ Liberal interpretation of ambitious nationalist who steered Tuscany toward annexation to Italy in 1859–60 and later became prime minister of Italy. Available on microfilm from London: Faber & Gwyer, 1990. [AS]

28.283 William A. Jenks. *Francis Joseph and the Italians, 1849–1859.* Charlottesville: University Press of Virginia, 1978. ISBN 0-8139-0758-6. ‣ How Austrian emperor felt toward Lombardy-Venetia, policies toward other Italian states, attempts at conciliation in Lombardy-Venetia, and why he declared war against Sardinia in 1859. Readable but simplistic. [AS]

28.284 Denis Mack Smith. *Cavour.* New York: Knopf, 1985. ISBN 0-394-53885-4. ‣ Broad but scholarly biography. Brings together evidence presented in previous works; extensive bibliographical notes. Author more sympathetic to Cavour here than in previous writings. See Romeo 28.287 for alternative interpretation. [AS]

28.285 Denis Mack Smith. *Victor Emanuel, Cavour, and the Risorgimento.* London: Oxford University Press, 1971. ISBN 0-19-212550-8. ‣ Fundamental text on Risorgimento. Essays on controversial episodes and problems, 1840–70. Less critical of Cavour than author's earlier work (28.292), yet unification still seen as bitter struggle between opposing interests. [AS]

28.286 Michael St. John Packe. *The bombs of Orsini.* London: Secker & Warburg, 1957. ‣ Engaging but superficial account of Felice Orsini's life. Orsini saw Napoleon III as obstacle to Italian unity. Moved away from Mazzini after 1849 toward more radical view of Italian independence. [AS]

28.287 Rosario Romeo. *Cavour e il suo tempo.* (v. 2–3) 3d ed., (v. 1) 4th ed. 3 vols. Bari: Laterza, 1969–84. ISBN 88-420-2107 (v. 1), 88-420-2389-2 (v. 2), 88-420-2396-5 (v. 3). ‣ Most comprehensive study of Cavour by Crocean-trained liberal historian. More than biography, general history of period. Important sections on economy and diplomacy. Interpretation differs from Mack Smith's (28.284). [AS]

28.288 William R. Thayer. *The life and times of Cavour.* 1914 ed. 2 vols. Boston: Houghton-Mifflin, 1990. ‣ Interesting example of liberal interpretation of Cavour's life but superseded by more recent works. For most representative liberal view, see Romeo's multivolume biography (28.287). For different interpretation, see Mack Smith 28.285. [AS]

28.289 Arthur James Beresford Whyte. *The early life and letters of Cavour, 1810–1848.* 1925 ed. Westport, Conn.: Greenwood, 1976. ISBN 0-8371-8504-1. ‣ Enthusiastic interpretation of Cavour based on Francesco Ruffini's biography (1912). Cavour's European background allowed him to transcend Italian regionalistic biases. Dated liberal interpretation. [AS]

28.290 Arthur James Beresford Whyte. *The political life and letters of Cavour, 1848–1861.* 1930 ed. Westport. Conn.: Greenwood, 1975. ISBN 0-8371-7939-4. ‣ Enthusiastic interpretation, based on Cavour-Nigra correspondence and Public Record Office documents. Cavour had clear unification plan from beginning. Dated liberal interpretation. [AS]

SEE ALSO
    47.142 Derek E. D. Beales. *England and Italy, 1859–1860.*
    47.143 Arnold Blumberg. *A carefully planned accident.*

Garibaldi and the Thousand

28.291 Giuseppe Guerzoni. *Garibaldi: con documenti editi ed inediti.* 1882 ed. 2 vols. Florence: Barbera, 1977. ‣ Most complete, detailed biography of Garibaldi by Garibaldi's friend and officer during Expedition of the Thousand. [AS]

28.292 Denis Mack Smith. *Cavour and Garibaldi, 1860: a study in political conflict.* 1954 ed. Cambridge: Cambridge University Press, 1985. ISBN 0-521-30356-7 (cl), 0-521-31637-5 (pbk). ‣ Seminal work on roles of Cavour and Garibaldi during Expedition of Thousand. Critical of Cavour, seen as obstacle to Garibaldi and manipulator of plebiscitary system of annexation. See also Mack Smith 28.285. [AS]

28.293 Denis Mack Smith. *Garibaldi: a great life in brief.* 1956 ed. Westport, Conn.: Greenwood, 1982. ISBN 0-313-23618-6. ‣ Good, short biography. Mack Smith's views have developed considerably since its publication in 1956 (e.g., 28.285). [AS]

28.294 Jasper Ridley. *Garibaldi.* New York: Viking, 1974. ISBN 0-670-33548-7. ‣ Enthusiastic biography of Garibaldi, portrayed as man with warm personality and absolute integrity and sincerity. Based on published and unpublished sources. [AS]

28.295 George M. Trevelyan. *Garibaldi and the making of Italy: June-November 1860.* 1911 ed. London: Longmans, Green, 1948. ‣ Fascinating narrative history of crucial last stages of unification of Italy. Third of Trevelyan's Garibaldi trilogy (with 28.274 and 28.296). Brilliant military account. Wrong on aspects of southern social structure. Whig history. [AS]

28.296 George M. Trevelyan. *Garibaldi and the Thousand.* 1909 ed. London: Cassell, 1989. ISBN 0-304-31704-7 (pbk). ‣ Covers Garibaldi's conquest of kingdom of Two Sicilies. Brilliant military history and second of Trevelyan's Garibaldi trilogy (with 28.274 and 28.295). Weak on social structure. Accepts political myths since rejected; Whig history. [AS]

28.297   Franco Valsecchi. "European diplomacy and the Expedition of the Thousand: the conservative powers." In *A century of conflict, 1850–1950: essays for A.J.P. Taylor*. 1966 ed. Martin Gilbert, ed., pp. 47–72. New York: Atheneum, 1967. ▸ How conservative states reacted to Garibaldi's conquest of kingdom of Two Sicilies. Discusses Austria's failure to reconstitute conservative front to prevent further expansion by Piedmont during Expedition. [AS]

LIBERAL ITALY, 1861–1919
General Studies

28.298   Martin Clark. *Modern Italy, 1871–1982*. London: Longman, 1984. ISBN 0-582-48361-1 (cl), 0-582-48362-x (pbk). ▸ Balanced, well-researched general history of period. Emphasis on social topics but also thorough on ideological and political aspects. [AS]

28.299   Benedetto Croce. *A history of Italy, 1871–1915*. 1929 ed. Cecilia M. Ady, trans. New York: Russell & Russell, 1963. ▸ Classic and most influential liberal interpretation. Ethico-political approach. Liberal Italy a positive period; World War I destroyed process of evolution. Emphasis on ideas and individuals, disregards economy and society. [AS]

28.300   Charles F. Delzell. *Italy in the twentieth century*. Washington, D.C.: American Historical Association, 1980. (American Historical Association pamphlets, 428.) ISBN 0-87229-024-7 (pbk). ▸ Excellent bibliographical and historiographical discussion of mainly secondary English and Italian sources from postunification to contemporary Italy. [AS]

28.301   Margot Hentze. *Pre-fascist Italy: the rise and fall of the parliamentary regime*. 1939 ed. New York: Octagon Books, 1972. ISBN 0-374-93809-1. ▸ General scholarly survey from unity to 1919. Critical of liberal Italy and sympathetic to emergence of fascism which appealed to men weary of chaos. Very different from Croce's liberal interpretation (28.299). [AS]

28.302   Denis Mack Smith. *Italy: a modern history*. Rev. ed. Ann Arbor: University of Michigan Press, 1969. ISBN 0-472-07051-7. ▸ Unlike Croce 28.299, Mack Smith sees liberal Italy as negative and harbinger of emergence of fascism. Leader of radical school, whose targets include Liberals, Catholics, Fascists, and Communists. Influential interpretation. [AS]

28.303   Salvatore Saladino. *Italy from unification to 1919: growth and decay of a liberal regime*. Arlington Heights, Ill.: Harlan Davidson, 1970. ISBN 0-88295-762-7 (pbk). ▸ Survey of liberal Italy with focus on Giolitti. [AS]

28.304   Christopher Seton-Watson. *Italy from liberalism to fascism, 1870–1925*. New York: Barnes & Noble, 1967. ▸ Good analysis of World War I; ends with establishment of fascist dictatorship. [AS]

28.305   Cecil J. S. Sprigge. *The development of modern Italy*. 1943 ed. New York: Fertig, 1969. ▸ General survey 1848 to 1922 by *Manchester Guardian* Rome correspondent. Quite critical of liberal Italy, especially of Agostino Depretis, Crispi, and Giolitti. [AS]

28.306   Edward R. Tannenbaum and Emiliana P. Noether, eds. *Modern Italy: a topical history since 1861*. New York: New York University Press, 1974. ISBN 0-8147-8156-x. ▸ Excellent collection of articles, mostly covering 1861 to present; one on Risorgimento statecraft and ideology by Salomone. [AS]

28.307   Franco Valsecchi and Giuseppe Martini, eds. *La storiografia italiana negli ultimi vent'anni*. 2 vols. Milan: Marzorati,

1981. ▸ Collection of Italian historical scholarship published during twenty-year period following World War II. Papers address topics from antiquity to 1967. [AS]

28.308   Maurice Vaussard. *Histoire de l'Italie moderne, 1870–1970*. Paris: Hachette, 1972. ▸ Clear, balanced rendering of history of modern Italy. [AS]

The State and the Army

28.309   John A. Davis. *Conflict and control: law and order in nineteenth-century Italy*. Atlantic Highlands, N.J.: Humanities Press International, 1988. ISBN 0-391-03579-7. ▸ Duality of conflict and order in liberal Italy; how it influenced political developments and institutional change. [AS]

28.310   John Gooch. *Army, state, and society in Italy, 1870–1915*. New York: St. Martin's, 1989. ISBN 0-312-02523-8. ▸ Institutional analysis of Italian army. Focus on how politicized army was political servant of state but in reality loyal only to royal house. Short chapter on Risorgimento. [AS]

28.311   Denis Mack Smith. *Italy and its monarchy*. New Haven: Yale University Press, 1989. ISBN 0-300-04661-8. ▸ Engaging analysis of Savoy kings from 1861 to their fall in 1946. Kings played active or passive role in all major government decisions. Lack of access to some sources makes author's conclusions tentative at times. [AS]

28.312   Giorgio Rochat and Giulio Massobrio. *Breve storia dell'esercito italiano dal 1861 al 1943*. Turin: Einaudi, 1978. ▸ Army was liberal state's weapon for social repression; supported Mussolini's conquest of power. Poor performance in World War II result of both military and fascist shortsightedness. Good leftist analysis. [AS]

28.313   John Whittam. *The politics of the Italian army, 1861–1918*. Hamden, Conn.: Archon, 1977. ISBN 0-208-01597-3. ▸ Explains military policies of nonaggressive society and how military related to society. About one-third on Risorgimento. Based on secondary sources. [AS]

Southern Postunification Problems

28.314   Anton Blok. *The mafia of a Sicilian village, 1860–1960: a study of violent peasant entrepreneurs*. 1974 ed. Prospect Heights, Ill.: Waveland, 1988. ISBN 0-88133-325-5 (pbk). ▸ Unlike brigandage, mafia did not oppose unified Italy. Its presence a serious problem of southern question in Sicily. Study centers on Sicilian village. [AS]

28.315   Eric J. Hobsbawm. *Primitive rebels: studies in archaic forms of social movement in the nineteenth and twentieth centuries*. 3d ed. Manchester: Manchester University Press, 1971. ISBN 0-7190-0493-4. ▸ Pioneering work on primitive movements of social protest not included in classic socialist patterns of agitation. Model of social bandits could be applied to Italian brigands after unification. Most chapters deal with Italy. Marxist analysis. [AS]

28.316   Franco Molfese. *Storia del brigantaggio dopo l'unità*. 4th ed. Milan: Feltrinelli, 1976. ▸ Fundamental work on problem that new Italian state faced against brigands in mainland southern Italy. Brigandage seen not just as banditism, but as social and political protest against new state. Excellent bibliography. [AS]

The Roman Question: Church and State in Postunification Italy

28.317   Emile Bourgeois and E. Clermont. *Rome et Napoleon III, 1849–1870: étude sur les origines et la chute du deuxième empire*. Paris: Cohen, 1907. ▸ Classic work on Roman question from failure of Roman Republic to annexation of Papal States in 1870. [AS]

28.318 S. William Halperin. *Italy and the Vatican at war: a study of their relations from the outbreak of the Franco-Prussian War to the death of Pius IX.* 1939 ed. New York: Greenwood, 1968. ▸ Unbiased view of Roman question. How great powers finally withdrew obstacles to annexation of remaining Papal States to Italy. Title misleading; focus on international ramifications of question, not just Italy and Vatican. [AS]

28.319 Arturo Carlo Jemolo. *Church and state in Italy, 1850–1950.* 1960 ed. David Moore, trans. Philadelphia: Dufour, 1961. ▸ Abbreviated version of original work on church-state relationship from Risorgimento onward. Fundamental work. But see later revised and expanded third edition: *Chiesa e stato in Italia dalla unificazione a Giovanni XXIII.* [AS]

28.320 Ivan Scott. *The Roman question and the powers, 1848–65.* The Hague: Nijhoff, 1969. ▸ Survey of Roman question and attitude of great powers toward Italy's unification and then toward Rome's annexation. Difficult to use; poorly edited. [AS]

SEE ALSO
47.145 Lynn M. Case. *Franco-Italian relations, 1860–1865.*
47.147 S. William Halperin. *Diplomat under stress.*

Foreign Policy

28.321 R.J.B. Bosworth. *Italy, the least of the great powers: Italian foreign policy before the First World War.* Cambridge: Cambridge University Press, 1979. ISBN 0-521-22366-0. ▸ Aims and methods of Italian diplomacy from turn of century. Argues that liberal foreign policy absurd. Extensive research, but interpretation sometimes malicious, often patronizing. Emphasis on San Giuliano's foreign policy. [AS]

28.322 Federico Chabod. *Le premesse.* Vol. 1 of *Storia della politica estera italiana dal 1870 al 1896.* 1951 ed. Bari: Laterza, 1965. ▸ Classic, brilliant study of foreign policy, 1870–96. Numerous bibliographical notes, original documents, and citations. Excellent portrayal of main personalities. Volume 2 never published. [AS]

SEE ALSO
47.35 C. J. Lowe and F. Marzari. *Italian foreign policy, 1870–1940.*

Imperialism and Colonialism

28.323 William C. Askew. *Europe and Italy's acquisition of Libya, 1911–12.* Durham: University of North Carolina Press, 1942. ▸ Pioneering work on diplomatic history of Turco-Italian War, 1911–12. Most of Askew's conclusions remain acceptable, although author had no access to archives. See also Childs 28.325 and Simon 28.331. [AS]

28.324 George Fitz-Hardinge Berkeley. *The campaign of Adowa and the rise of Menelik.* 1902 ed. New York: Negro University Press, 1969. ISBN 0-8371-1132-3. ▸ Detailed military account of campaign and battle of Adowa (1896). [AS]

28.325 Timothy W. Childs. *Italo-Turkish diplomacy and the war over Libya, 1911–12.* Leiden: Brill, 1990. ISBN 90-04-09025-8. ▸ Supports Askew's views (28.323) on diplomatic aspects. Sees war from Ottoman viewpoint; brings together views of modern Italian historians on topic. Based on Italian and Turkish archives. [AS]

28.326 Angelo Del Boca. *Gli italiani in Africa Orientale.* Vol. 1: *Dall'unità alla marcia su Roma.* Vol. 2: *La conquista dell'Impero.* Vol. 3: *La caduta dell'Impero.* Vol. 4: *Nostalgia delle colonie.* 4 vols. Rome: Laterza, 1976–85. ISBN 88-420-2638-7 (v. 1), 88-420-2715-4 (v. 2), 88-420-2810-X (v. 3). ▸ Critical, often bitter, analysis of Italian colonialism, both in terms of achievement and motivation from 1870. Leftist interpretation. Excellent work. [AS]

28.327 Robert L. Hess. *Italian colonialism in Somalia.* Chicago: University of Chicago Press, 1966. ▸ Covers 1885 to World War II. Italian imperialism had no consistent colonial ideology. Rule in Somalia rather light: respected local customs and economic exploitation unsuccessful. Research mostly in Italian archives. [AS]

28.328 Francesco Malgeri. *La guerra libica, 1911–12.* Rome: Storia e Letteratura, 1970. ▸ Detailed rendering of Italy's conquest of Libya. Conquest a typical example of pre-1914 international relations; caused collapse of Giolittian system of government. Good research. [AS]

28.329 Jean Louis Miège. *L'imperialisme colonial italien de 1870 à nos jours.* Paris: Societé d'Édition d'Enseignement Superieur, 1968. (Regards sur l'histoire, Histoire generale, 3.2.) ▸ Italian imperialist aims ancient, but implementation recent. Driven by politics and ideology of demographic outlet, not economic expansion. Good survey, excellent bibliography, some documents. [AS]

28.330 Claudio G. Segré. *Fourth shore: the Italian colonization of Libya.* Chicago: University of Chicago Press, 1974. ISBN 0-226-74474-4. ▸ Balanced account of origins, achievements, and downfall of Italian colonial rule in Libya. Demographic colonization expensive and ultimately a failure: economic and political burden. Includes bibliographical essay. [AS/AG]

28.331 Rachel Simon. *Libya between Ottomanism and nationalism: the Ottoman involvement in Libya during the war with Italy, 1911–1919.* Berlin: Schwarz, 1987. ISBN 3-922968-58-9 (pbk). ▸ Revised Ph.D. thesis. Thorough research of Italian, Turkish, and other sources. Detailed but not always well organized or insightful on Italian side. Focuses on Libya. [AS]

28.332 Douglas H. Varley, comp. *A bibliography of Italian colonisation in Africa with a section on Abyssinia.* Rev. ed. Folkestone, England: Dawson, 1970. ISBN 0-7129-0421-2. ▸ Titles without annotations. Badly organized, although useful for gathering together a number of English-language sources. [AS]

28.333 Richard A. Webster. *Industrial imperialism in Italy, 1908–15.* Berkeley: University of California Press, 1975. ISBN 0-520-02724-8. ▸ Military-industrial complex forced Italy toward social repression at home and expansionism abroad. Imperialism of 1911–15 in Balkans and Asia Minor was industrial, unlike Francesco Crispi's demographic African imperialism of 1890s. [AS]

Economy and Society

28.334 Donald Howard Bell. *Sesto San Giovanni: workers, culture, and politics in an Italian town, 1880–1922.* New Brunswick, N.J.: Rutgers University Press, 1986. ISBN 0-8135-1142-9. ▸ How modern Italian working class took shape in a town. Agents of change not only factory but preexisting worker culture and working-class community life. How Socialists, Catholics, and Fascists related to workers. [AS]

28.335 Rudolph M. Bell. *Fate and honor, family and village: demographic and cultural change in rural Italy since 1800.* Chicago: University of Chicago Press, 1979. ISBN 0-226-04208-1. ▸ Sympathetic view of Italian peasantry in ethnohistorian's study of one northern and three geographically different southern towns, 1800 to 1970s. Concepts listed in title symbolize Italian peasant's worldview. [AS]

28.336 Luciano Cafagna. "Italy, 1830–1914." In *The emergence of industrial societies.* Carlo M. Cipolla, ed., vol. 4.1, pp. 279–328. New York: Barnes & Noble, 1976. ISBN 0-06- 492179-4 (v. 4.1). ▸ Eight pages on Risorgimento, rest on postunification. Industrial development concentrated in northwestern Italy, conducted with disregard for rest of country. Argues against Gerschenkron's view (28.338) of economic growth. [AS]

28.337 John A. Davis, ed. *Gramsci and Italy's passive revolution.* New York: Barnes & Noble, 1979. ISBN 0-06-491609-X. ▸ Eight fine contributions of social and economic history on Gramsci's concept of passive revolution, that is, nature and shortcomings of liberal state. Most essays on liberal Italy but also on Risorgimento and fascist Italy. [AS]

28.338 Alexander Gerschenkron. "The rate of industrial growth in Italy, 1881–1913." In *Economic backwardness in historical perspective: a book of essays.* 1962 ed., pp. 72–89. Cambridge, Mass.: Belknap, 1979. ISBN 0-674-22600-3. ▸ "Take-off" of Italian industrial revolution from 1896 to 1908 brought about mainly by banks, although rate of growth inferior to England and France. Influential article with debatable thesis. [AS]

28.339 Adrian Lyttelton. "Milan 1880–1922: the city of industrial capitalism." In *People and communities in the Western world.* Gene A. Brucker, ed., vol. 2, pp. 244–88. Homewood, Ill.: Dorsey, 1979. ISBN 0-256-02186-4 (v. 2). ▸ General but insightful survey of most important Italian industrial center from end of century to first stages of fascist hegemony. Social history; brief discussion of most aspects of Milanese life. [AS]

28.340 Roland Sarti. *Long live the strong: a history of rural society in the Apennine mountains.* Amherst: University of Massachusetts Press, 1985. ISBN 0-87023-466-8. ▸ Social study of Tuscan hilltown from liberal to postwar period. Interesting because it centers on relatively little known sector of Italian society, mountain people. [AS]

28.341 Louise Tilly. "Italy." In *The rebellious century, 1830–1930.* Charles Tilly et al., eds., pp. 87–190. Cambridge, Mass.: Harvard University Press, 1975. ISBN 0-674-74955-3. ▸ General overview of economic and social change in Italy, mostly on postunification period. How economic transformation led to collective action and mass violence. Relationship between emergence of fascism and workers' agitation. [AS]

28.342 Gianni Toniolo. *An economic history of liberal Italy, 1850–1918.* 1952 ed. Maria Rees, trans. New York: Routledge, 1990. ISBN 0-415-03500-7. ▸ Macroeconomic history of liberal Italy. Argues that 1849–1919 provided framework for remarkable post-1945 recovery. Three parts: trends and cycles, economic development, and historiography. Challenges Gerschenkron's thesis (28.338) on Italian economic development. Previous title: *The Process of Underdeveloped Areas.* [AS]

Emigration

28.343 William A. Douglass. *Emigration in a South Italian town: an anthropological history.* New Brunswick, N.J.: Rutgers University Press, 1984. ISBN 0-8135-0984-X. ▸ Causes and consequences of emigration from Molise town of Agnone, 1871–1922. Emigration result of traditional factors but also attempt by less privileged to improve their condition. Combination of anthropological and historical method. [AS]

28.344 Robert F. Foerster. *The Italian emigration of our times.* 1919 ed. New York: Arno, 1969. ▸ Pioneering work on causes of emigration: overpopulation, inadequate rainfall, deforestation and land erosion, malaria, earthquakes, unfair taxation system, exploitation by large landowners, and unemployment among landless agricultural workers. [AS]

28.345 Ercole Sori. *L'emigrazione italiana dall'unità alla seconda guerra mondiale.* Bologna: Il Mulino, 1979. ▸ Demographic study of emigration from unification to World War II. [AS]

Socialism

28.346 Spencer Di Scala. *Dilemmas of Italian socialism: the politics of Filippo Turati.* Amherst: University of Massachusetts Press, 1980. ISBN 0-87023-285-1. ▸ Clever, clear discussion of Turati's leadership from foundation of Italian Socialist party to 1912. How Turati's belief in nonviolent, gradual achievement of socialism fit within and changed Giolittian government system. [AS]

28.347 Manuel G. Gonzales. *Andrea Costa and the rise of socialism in the Romagna.* Washington, D.C.: University Press of America, 1980. ISBN 0-8191-0952-5 (pbk). ▸ Analysis of transition of Marxist movement from anarchism to socialism between 1871 and 1892 in Romagna. Most of credit, according to Gonzales, should go to Costa. Well documented. [AS]

28.348 Daniel L. Horowitz. *The Italian labor movement.* Cambridge, Mass.: Harvard University Press, 1963. ▸ History of trade unionism from late nineteeth century to 1950s. How Socialists, Communists, and Catholics competed for control of trade unions. Emphasis on postwar period. See also Neufeld 28.215. [AS]

28.349 Richard Hostetter. *The Italian socialist movement.* Vol. 1: *Origins, 1860–82.* Princeton: Van Nostrand, 1958. ▸ Scholarly, careful survey of origins of socialist movement from end of Risorgimento to defeat of anarchist movement. Discusses role of Mazzini, Pisacane, Bakunin, early anarchists, and Costa. Volume 2 never published. [AS]

28.350 Paul Piccone. *Italian Marxism.* Berkeley: University of California Press, 1983. ISBN 0-520-04798-2. ▸ Short, condensed, insightful description of development of Italian Marxism from its origins to Gramscian heritage. Probably a little too clever for nonexpert in Italian history. [AS]

28.351 Samuel J. Surace. *Ideology, economic change, and the working classes: the case of Italy.* Berkeley: University of California Press, 1966. ▸ Examines changes in working class from 1850s to 1914. Workers' dissatisfaction low in early 1800s, high later because of economic changes and desire for change within and outside working class. Sociological use of historical data. [AS]

Giolittian Italy

28.352 Alberto Aquarone. *Tre capitoli sull'Italia giolittiana.* Bologna: Il Mulino, 1987. ISBN 88-15-01396-2. ▸ Chapters from unfinished work on Giolittian Italy; lack coherence but contain many insights on Giolitti and his relationship to government, parliament, nation, citizen and state, and political forces and movements. [AS]

28.353 Frank J. Coppa. *Planning, protectionism, and politics in liberal Italy: economics and politics in the Giolittian age.* Washington, D.C.: Catholic University of America Press, 1971. ISBN 0-8132-0510-7. ▸ Good study with emphasis on Giolitti's economic policies. Argues that Giolitti's approach was positive: state should provide greater protection to people and produce greater economic wealth. [AS]

28.354 Franco De Felice. "L'età giolittiana." *Studi storici* 1 (1969) 114–90. ISSN 0039-3037. ▸ Survey of Giolittian historiography from 1949 to 1969. Emphasizes debate on whether Giolittian Italy was prelude to fascism or democracy in the making. [AS]

28.355 Serge Hughes. *The fall and rise of modern Italy.* 1967 ed. Westport, Conn.: Greenwood, 1983. ISBN 0-313-23737-9. ▸ Intellectual survey from turn of century to 1960s. In period 1890–1960, failure of Liberals, Socialists, and Catholics to work toward common goals. From 1960 onward, Socialists accepted into government by Christian Democrats, a positive step. Emphasizes Croce's influence. [AS]

28.356 A. William Salomone. *Italy in the Giolittian era: Italian democracy in the making, 1900–14.* 2d ed. Gaetano Salvemini, Introduction. Philadelphia: University of Pennsylvania Press, 1960. ▸ Giolittian Italy not prologue to fascism, but period of democracy in the making. Liberal view. Influential pioneering work, but rather dated. [AS]

28.357 A. William Salomone, ed. *Italy from the Risorgimento to fascism: an inquiry into the origins of the totalitarian state.* 1970 ed. New York: Doubleday, 1971. ▸ Excellent collection of book and article excerpts on liberal origins of fascism. Section on Risorgimento, but emphasis on debate whether Giolittian Italy was prologue to fascism or prelude to democracy. [AS]

28.358 Nino Valeri. *Giovanni Giolitti.* Turin: UTET, 1972. ▸ Best biography of Giolitti. Balanced, clear, and well researched. Extensive bibliography. [AS]

World War I

28.359 Luigi Albertini. *The origins of the war of 1914.* 1952–57 ed. 3 vols. Isabella M. Massey, trans. Westport, Conn.: Greenwood, 1980. ISBN 0-313-22401-3 (set), 0-313-22402-1 (v. 1), 0-313-22403-X (v. 2), 0-313-22404-8 (v. 3). ▸ Emphasis on diplomatic origins of war by Italian conservative liberal. Critical of Giolitti and especially San Giuliano for way Italy entered war. Somewhat dated, yet many useful insights; solid documentation. [AS]

28.360 Simon Mark Jones. *Domestic factors in Italian intervention in the First World War.* New York: Garland, 1986. ISBN 0-8240-1922-9. ▸ Sees factors drawing Italy into war as hostility against Giolitti, economic downturn, socialist insurgence, imperialism, and industrialists' eagerness to shed German economic and financial hegemony in Italy. Emphasizes economic pressures. [AS]

28.361 Piero Melograni. *Storia politica della grande guerra, 1915–18.* 1971 3d ed. 2 vols. Rome: Laterza, 1977. ▸ Balanced view of political, social, and economic impact of war; little on diplomatic and military aspects. Defeat at Caporetto result of military errors, not collapse of Italian morale. Good analysis of relationship of government with military leadership. [AS]

28.362 Piero Pieri. *L'Italia nella prima guerra mondiale, 1915–18.* 5th ed. Turin: Einaudi, 1973. ▸ Synthesis of Italy's role during World War I. Best democratic interpretation of war by interventionist historian: war a great victory, fulfilled initial aims. [AS]

28.363 William A. Renzi. *In the shadow of the sword: Italy's neutrality and entrance into the Great War, 1914–15.* New York: Lang, 1987. (American University studies, Series 9: history, 26.) ISBN 0-8204-0410-1, ISSN 0740-0462. ▸ Well-researched analysis of domestic and international factors influencing Italian diplomacy, first to remain neutral and then to enter war in 1915. Mediocre leaders and small minority imposed entry upon nation. [AS]

28.364 Giorgio Rochat. *L'Italia nella prima guerra mondiale: problemi di interpretazione e prospettive di ricerche.* Milano: Feltrinelli, 1976. ▸ Historiographical essay followed by discussion of how fascist and nationalist patriotism stifled discussion of war's class aspects; war an imperialist venture and instrument of internal oppression. See Pieri's democratic interventionist view (28.362). [AS]

Cultural Life

28.365 Richard Drake. *Byzantium for Rome: the politics of nostalgia in Umbertian Italy, 1878–1900.* Chapel Hill: University of North Carolina Press, 1980. ISBN 0-8078-1405-9. ▸ Evocative picture of end-of-century intellectuals torn between two images of Italy: decadent Byzantium and virile Rome. How politics of nostalgia were linked to anti-parliamentarianism and Corradini's nationalism. [AS]

28.366 H. Stuart Hughes. *Consciousness and society: the reorientation of European social thought, 1890–1930.* Rev. ed. New York: Vintage, 1977. ISBN 0-394-70201-8. ▸ Insightful analysis of European cultural life from end of nineteenth century. Note especially

sensitive portrayal of thought of Vilfredo Pareto, Gaetano Mosca, Benedetto Croce, and Antonio Gramsci. [AS]

28.367 Edmund E. Jacobitti. *Revolutionary humanism and historicism in modern Italy.* New Haven: Yale University Press, 1981. ISBN 0-300-02479-7. ▸ Discusses Neapolitan intellectual environment as embodied in Benedetto Croce, thinker who shaped, he argues, modern Italian mind even more than Gramsci. Intelligent intellectual analysis. [AS]

28.368 David D. Roberts. *Benedetto Croce and the uses of historicism.* Berkeley: University of California Press, 1987. ISBN 0-520-05904-2. ▸ New look at Croce's historicism. Croce, one of best known European intellectuals, confronted some of crucial challenges of his time. Looks at religion, political theory, and historiography. [AS]

28.369 John A. Thayer. *Italy and the Great War: politics and culture, 1870–1915.* Madison: University of Wisconsin Press, 1964. ▸ Emphasis on historical significance of World War I. Often brilliant analysis of post-Risorgimento period. Debates whether Great War was proper conclusion of Risorgimento or breach with political, cultural, and diplomatic traditions of past. [AS]

FASCIST ITALY, 1919–1943
Bibliography and Historiography

28.370 Alberto Aquarone. *Fascismo e antifascismo nella storiografia italiana.* Rome: Edizioni della Voce, 1986. ▸ Articles on fascist historiography. Covers, often brilliantly, most topics and events from origins of fascism to World War II. [AS]

28.371 Philip V. Cannistraro, ed. *Historical dictionary of fascist Italy.* Westport, Conn.: Greenwood, 1982. ISBN 0-313-21317-8. ▸ International contributors including number of well-known experts on fascism. Most entries with bibliographies. [AS]

28.372 Renzo De Felice. *Interpretations of fascism.* Brenda Huff Everett, trans. Cambridge, Mass.: Harvard University Press, 1977. ISBN 0-674-45962-8. ▸ Definition of European fascism, followed by historiography of Italian fascism. Presents model to understand phenomenon. Important book. Emphasizes similarities although author's more recent work underscores differences. [AS]

28.373 Renzo De Felice, ed. *Bibliografia orientativa del fascismo.* Rome: Bonacci, 1991. ISBN 88-7573-108-X. ▸ More than 10,000 titles of books, pamphlets, and articles covering period 1919–45. Extensive cross-index; essential research tool. [AS]

28.374 Guido Quazza et al. *Storiografia e fascismo.* Milan: Angeli, 1985. (Collana dell'Instituto Nazionale per la Storia Movimento di Liberazione in Italia, Nuova series, 6.) ▸ Important articles on historiography, totalitarianism, power relations, foreign policy, and social consensus. Bibliographical appendix lists 870 titles. Articles written in 1983, bibliography in 1984. [AS]

28.375 A. William Salomone. "Italy: contemporary historiography." In *International handbook of historical studies: contemporary research and theory.* Georg G. Iggers and Harold T. Parker, eds., pp. 233–51. Westport, Conn.: Greenwood, 1979. ISBN 0-313-21367-4. ▸ Contemporary Italian historiography from end of World War II to Red Brigades' assassination of Aldo Moro in 1978. Emphasis especially on influence of Marxist Gramsci. [AS]

28.376 Roberto Vivarelli. "Italy, 1919–21: the current state of research." *Journal of contemporary history* 3 (1968) 103–12. ISSN 0022-0094. ▸ Assessment of research on emergence of fascist movement by authority on this period. Argues that nationalist movement most powerful influence on fascism. Author belongs to radical democratic school. [AS]

General Studies

28.377   G. A. Borgese. *Goliath: the march of fascism.* New York: Viking, 1937. ‣ Denies that fascism was creation of one man, Mussolini. Seeks sources of fascism in Italian history, beginning with Dante. Thesis no longer accepted. [AS]

28.378   Alan Cassels. *Fascist Italy.* 2d ed. Arlington Heights, Ill.: Harlan Davidson, 1985. ISBN 0-88295-828-3 (pbk). ‣ Brief and clear although some views debatable, especially on foreign policy. Useful bibliographical note. [AS]

28.379   Federico Chabod. *History of Italian fascism.* 1963 ed. Muriel Grindrod, trans. New York: Fertig, 1975. ‣ Uneven, yet insightful short book on period 1918–48. Fascism product of dislocation caused by war. Chabod a great and very influential liberal Italian historian. Book is product of 1950 Sorbonne lectures. [AS]

28.380   Alexander J. De Grand. *Italian fascism: its origins and development.* 2d ed. Lincoln: University of Nebraska Press, 1989. ISBN 0-8032-6578-6 (pbk). ‣ Fascism a force working within existing economic and social hierarchies. Behind facade of unity, regime fragmented ideologically and politically into fiefdoms, each with own version of fascism. Excellent bibliographical essay. [AS]

28.381   H. Stuart Hughes. *The United States and Italy.* 3d rev. ed. Cambridge, Mass.: Harvard University Press, 1979. ISBN 0-674-92545-9. ‣ Excellent study of fascist and contemporary Italy. Good synthesis of economic, social, and cultural patterns. Discusses relationship between United States and Italy but emphasis on fascist period. [AS]

28.382   Eileen A. Millar, ed. *The legacy of fascism: lectures delivered at the University of Glasgow.* Glasgow: University of Glasgow, Department of Italian, 1989. ISBN 0-85261-285-0. ‣ Lectures on Giolittian system, fascism's political legacy, *squadrismo* (violence of fascist squads), the church and fascism, and Ignazio Silone. Select bibliography of English titles (C. Duggan). [AS]

28.383   Luigi Salvatorelli and Giovanni Mira. *Storia d'Italia nel periodo fascista.* 3d ed. 2 vols. Turin: Einaudi, 1972. ‣ Best synthesis of fascist Italy despite unavailability of archival material and documents in 1952 (1st ed.). Authors antifascist but interpretation very balanced. Salvatorelli a democratic historian, Mira a journalist, expert in economics. Earlier title: *Storia del fascismo: l'Italia dal 1919 al 1945.* See also Santarelli 28.384 and Tamaro 28.385. [AS]

28.384   Enzo Santarelli. *Storia del movimento e del regime fascista.* 2 vols. Rome: Riuniti, 1967. ‣ Origin and development of fascism and how it related to Italy and Europe. Emphasis on economic, ideological, institutional, and military factors that made fascism's success as movement and regime possible. Important contribution. Leftist interpretation. See also Salvatorelli and Mira 28.383 and Tamaro 28.385. [AS]

28.385   Attilio Tamaro. *Venti anni di storia, 1922–43.* 1953–54 ed. 3 vols. Rome: Volpe, 1971. ‣ Very detailed fascist interpretation of movement's hold over Italy from 1922 to 1943. See Salvatorelli and Mira's democratic rendering (28.383) and Santarelli's Marxist analysis (28.384). [AS]

28.386   Gioacchino Volpe. *History of the fascist movement.* Rome: Edizioni di Novissima, 1936. ‣ Justification of fascist movement, dealing with fascist state until early 1930s. Useful as historiographical example of fascist interpretations. [AS]

Mussolini

28.387   Renzo De Felice. *Mussolini.* Vol. 1: *Mussolini il rivoluzionario, 1883–1920.* Vol. 2: *Mussolini il fascista.* Vol. 2.1: *La conquista del potere, 1921–1929.* Vol. 2.2: *L'organizzazione dello stato fascista, 1925–1929.* Vol. 3: *Mussolini il duce.* Vol. 3.1: *Gli anni del consenso.* Vol. 3.2: *Lo stato totalitario, 1936–1940.* Vol. 4: *Mussolini l'alleato, 1940–1945.* Vol. 4.1: *L'Italia in guerra, 1940–1943.* Vol. 4.1.1: *Dalla guerra "breve" alla guerra lunga.* Vol. 4.1.2: *Crisi e agonia del regime.* 4 vols. to date. Turin: Einaudi, 1965–. ISBN 88-06-59306-4 (v. 4). ‣ Fundamental biography of Mussolini and of fascist Italy. Model for generation of scholars. One more volume planned (volume 4.2: *Mussolini l'alleato, la guerra civile*). [AS]

28.388   Laura Fermi. *Mussolini.* 1961 ed. Chicago: University of Chicago Press, 1974. ISBN 0-226-24375-3. ‣ Lively, entertaining book concentrating on crucial episodes of Mussolini's life by wife of political refugee, physicist Enrico Fermi. Good read; insightful on Mussolini's character, but weak on fascist policies. [AS]

28.389   Max Gallo. *Mussolini's Italy: twenty years of fascist era.* Charles Lam Markmann, trans. London: Abelard-Schuman, 1974. ISBN 0-200-72140-2. ‣ Popular history of fascism, treated mainly as account of Mussolini's biography. From 1964 French edition. [AS]

28.390   A. James Gregor. *Young Mussolini and the intellectual origins of fascism.* Berkeley: University of California Press, 1979. ISBN 0-520-03799-5. ‣ Revisionist thesis by political scientist of Mussolini's political makeup. Mussolini not a demagogue, but consistent thinker and Marxist heretic whose main influence came from syndicalist tradition. [AS]

28.391   Ivone Kirkpatrick. *Mussolini: a study in power.* 1964 ed. Westport, Conn.: Greenwood, 1976. ISBN 0-8371-8400-2. ‣ Good biography by British diplomat with firsthand knowledge of Mussolini. Convincing on Mussolini's character and foreign policy. Relies on Wiskemann 28.443 and Deakin 28.444 for post-1929 period. Weak on domestic policies. [AS]

28.392   Denis Mack Smith. *Mussolini.* New York: Vintage, 1983. ISBN 0-394-71658-2 (pbk). ‣ Narrative political biography; focus on public life. Mussolini a complex man, politically intelligent and recklessly ambitious. Fascism bigger than Mussolini, but Mussolini crucial to its successes and failures. Engaging narrative but some debatable interpretations; good place to start. [AS]

28.393   Gaudens Megaro. *Mussolini in the making.* 1938 ed. New York: Fertig, 1967. ‣ Pioneering work on Mussolini's socialist years. Now superseded by volume 1 of De Felice's multivolume biography (28.387). Characterizes fascism as a combination of nationalism and syndicalism. [AS]

28.394   Paolo Monelli. *Mussolini: the intimate life of a demagogue.* 1953 ed. Brigid Maxwell, trans. New York: Vanguard, 1954. ‣ Gossipy, entertaining biography concentrating on Mussolini's private life by Italian journalist. Quite useful in spite of approach. [AS]

Fascist Leaders

28.395   Harry Fornari. *Mussolini's gadfly: Roberto Farinacci.* Nashville: Vanderbilt University Press, 1971. ISBN 0-8265-1167-8. ‣ Uneven biography of one of radical leaders of fascist movement. Farinacci violent, independent-minded "ras" (fascist leader) of Cremona. [AS]

28.396   Giorgio Rochat. *Italo Balbo.* Turin: UTET, 1986. ISBN 88-02-04002-8. ‣ Biography; section on Balbo as minister of air force published earlier. Places Balbo within context of fascist period. Leftist interpretation. [AS]

28.397   Claudio G. Segré. *Italo Balbo: a fascist life.* Berkeley: University of California Press, 1987. ISBN 0-520-05866-6. ‣ Political biography depicting Balbo as intelligent, capable, and incomparable as organizer. Institutions typical of fascist regime alien to him. For early years see also Corner 28.410. [AS]

Gabriele D'Annunzio

28.398 Philippe Jullian. *D'Annunzio*. Stephen Hardmann, trans. New York: Viking, 1973. ISBN 0-670-25603-X. ‣ Engaging biography of man who best embodied cultural climate of era. Important both as cultural and nationalist leader. His march on Fiume (1919) set example for fascist march on Rome. [AS]

28.399 Michael A. Ledeen. *The first duce: D'Annunzio in Fiume*. Baltimore: Johns Hopkins University Press, 1977. ISBN 0-8018-1860-5. ‣ Argues that D'Annunzio, who forcibly occupied Fiume (1919) against wishes of great powers, was among great innovators; Fiume expedition one of watershed events of century. D'Annunzio set style, Mussolini followed. [AS]

28.400 Anthony Rhodes. *D'Annunzio: the poet as superman*. 1959 ed. New York: McDowell, 1960. ‣ Once standard English work on D'Annunzio, now dated. Ledeen 28.399 or Jullian 28.398 better. [AS]

The Postwar Period

28.401 René Albrecht-Carrié. *Italy at the Paris Peace Conference*. 1938 ed. Hamden, Conn.: Archon, 1966. ‣ Standard work on Italy at conference ending World War I. Italy's request and failure to annex Fiume a source of unrest and among causes of myth of mutilated victory—postwar fuel for fascism's success. [AS]

28.402 John M. Cammett. *Antonio Gramsci and the origins of Italian communism*. Stanford, Calif.: Stanford University Press, 1967. ISBN 0-8047-0141-5. ‣ Fine work on Gramsci during two periods of his greatest intellectual activity: 1919–20 and 1929–34. [AS]

28.403 Elisa Carrillo. *Alcide De Gasperi: the long apprenticeship*. Notre Dame, Ind.: University of Notre Dame Press, 1965. ‣ Biography covering De Gasperi's early years until his return to political life in 1944. Argues that Christian Democrat leader well suited to launch Italy as democratic republic and faithful ally of free world. [AS]

28.404 Alexander J. De Grand. *The Italian Left in the twentieth century: a history of the Socialist and Communist parties*. Bloomington: Indiana University Press, 1989. ISBN 0-253-33107-2. ‣ Parallel history of Socialist and Communist parties from origins to present-day Italy. How two parties related to each other and to governments in power. Largely focuses on post-1917 period. [AS]

28.405 John N. Molony. *The emergence of political Catholicism in Italy: partito Popolare, 1919–1926*. Totowa, N.J.: Rowman & Littlefield, 1977. ISBN 0-87471-943-7. ‣ How and why Popular party, predecessor of postwar Christian Democratic party, was rendered ineffective against fascism and eventually dismantled. Limited sources. [AS]

28.406 Paolo Spriano. *The occupation of factories: Italy, 1920*. Gwyin A. Williams, trans. London: Pluto, 1975. ISBN 0-902818-68-6 (cl), 0-902818-67-8 (pbk). ‣ Well-documented analysis of failure of socialist occupation of factories in 1920 and eventual fascist reaction and success. Fear of socialist revolution one of reasons for allegiance to fascism by certain groups of Italian society. [AS]

28.407 Richard A. Webster. *The cross and the fasces: Christian democracy and fascism in Italy*. Stanford, Calif.: Stanford University Press, 1960. ‣ Survey of Catholic political movement from postunification through foundation of Popular party in 1919, fascist regime, and emergence of Christian Democratic party. Uneven treatment. [AS]

Fascism to 1925

28.408 Alberto Aquarone. *L'organizzazione dello stato totalitario*. 1965 ed. 2 vols. Turin: Einaudi, 1978. ‣ Argues, unlike Germino 28.423, that in spite of totalitarian facade, fascist state was Catholic and dynastic. Many other sources of allegiance remained such as monarchy, church, big businessmen, and large landowners. Important work. [AS]

28.409 Anthony L. Cardoza. *Agrarian elites and Italian fascism: the province of Bologna, 1901–26*. Princeton: Princeton University Press, 1982. ISBN 0-691-05360-X. ‣ Agrarian fascism of key province of Bologna was led by big commercial farmers, risen to prominence after 1900, worried about socialist advances; emphasizes longstanding class grievances. Revisionist thesis like Corner on Ferrara (28.410). [AS]

28.410 Paul Corner. *Fascism in Ferrara, 1919–25*. Oxford: Oxford University Press, 1975. ISBN 0-19-821857-5. ‣ Excellent study of nature and methods of fascism in key area of lower Po valley around Ferrara, Balbo's city. How balance between rural leaders and lower middle classes provided basis for agrarian fascism. [AS]

28.411 Alexander J. De Grand. *The Italian Nationalist Association and the rise of fascism in Italy*. Lincoln: University of Nebraska Press, 1978. ISBN 0-8032-0949-5. ‣ Nationalist movement from early 1900s to establishment of fascist dictatorship in 1925. Argues that nationalists, unlike syndicalists, influenced fascism toward more conservative positions. Based on archival sources. [AS]

28.412 Alice A. Kelikian. *Town and country under fascism: the transformation of Brescia, 1915–26*. Oxford: Clarendon, 1986. ISBN 0-19-821970-9. ‣ Fascism a response to postwar crisis. At Brescia, fascism not a rightist petite bourgeoisie movement, but conservative reshuffling of middle and upper class. Supports views of Cardoza (28.409) and Corner (28.410) that fascist regime allied to capitalism. [AS]

28.413 Adrian Lyttelton. *The seizure of power: fascism in Italy, 1919–29*. 2d ed. Princeton: Princeton University Press, 1987. ISBN 0-691-07761-4 (cl), 0-691-02278-X (pbk). ‣ Fundamental work on fascist takeover. Emphasis on seizure of power by gradual erosion of liberal state, destruction of opposition, and creation of new institutions. Based on extensive archival research. [AS]

28.414 Antonio Repaci. *La Marcia su Roma: mito e realtà*. 2 vols. Rome: Canesi, 1963. ‣ Fine meticulous account of march on Rome. Volume 2 contains documents. [AS]

28.415 David D. Roberts. *The syndicalist tradition and Italian fascism*. Chapel Hill: University of North Carolina Press, 1979. ISBN 0-8078-1351-6. ‣ Emphasizes syndicalist origins of fascism. Role of syndicalist influence measured within political, social, economic, and psychocultural context of emergence of fascism. [AS]

28.416 Jack J. Roth. *The cult of violence: Sorel and the Sorelians*. Berkeley: University of California Press, 1980. ISBN 0-520-03772-3. ‣ Discusses ties between Sorel's views and revolutionary syndicalism, integral nationalism, bolshevism, and fascism. [AS]

28.417 Gaetano Salvemini. *The origins of fascism in Italy*. Roberto Vivarelli, ed. New York: Harper & Row, 1973. ISBN 0-06-136068-6 (cl), 0-06-131646-6 (set). ‣ Covers period from end of World War I to establishment of dictatorship in 1925. Based on Harvard course (1919–29) given by political exile and democratic historian. His best work on fascism. [AS]

28.418 Frank M. Snowden. *The fascist revolution in Tuscany, 1919–22*. Cambridge: Cambridge University Press, 1989. ISBN 0-521-36117-6. ‣ Links fascism to agricultural modernization against peasant and socialist interests. Tuscan fascism rooted in countryside but also attracted urban groups. In common: fear of bolshevism, lack of confidence in state, and willingness to use violence to defend order, property, and hierarchy. [AS]

28.419 Frank M. Snowden. *Violence and great estates in the south of Italy: Apulia, 1900–1922.* Cambridge: Cambridge University Press, 1986. ISBN 0-521-30731-7. ▸ Agrarian reaction in one of most developed areas of southern Italy. Except for Apulia, fascism did not have early success in southern Italy. [AS]

28.420 Angelo Tasca [Rossi]. *The rise of Italian fascism, 1918–1922.* 1938 ed. Peter Wait and Dorothy Wait, trans. New York: Gordon, 1976. ▸ Socialist view of rise of fascism by one of the founders of Italian Communist party. Very good on leftist response to fascism. Better to use revised edition, *Nascita e avvento del fascismo: l'Italia dal 1918 al 1922* (1950). [AS]

The Fascist State

28.421 Paolo Alatri et al. *Fascismo e capitalismo.* Milan: Feltrinelli, 1976. ▸ Important collection by leftist scholars on fascism's relationship to capitalism. Articles by Alatri, Carocci, Castronovo, Collotti, Quazza, Rochat, and Tranfaglia. [AS]

28.422 Victoria De Grazia. *The culture of consent: mass organization and leisure in fascist Italy.* Cambridge: Cambridge University Press, 1981. ISBN 0-521-23705-X. ▸ Fascists attempted to organize consent and to create nationwide political culture that transcended petty personal goals. Ideological consensus remained fragile and superficial. Well written and argued. [AS]

28.423 Dante L. Germino. *The Italian Fascist party in power: a study in totalitarian rule.* Minneapolis: University of Minnesota Press, 1959. ▸ Good description of fascist command structure. Weak on overall political context. Argues that fascism was totalitarian form of government. [AS]

28.424 Tracy H. Koon. *Believe, obey, fight: political socialization of youth in fascist Italy, 1922–43.* Chapel Hill: University of North Carolina Press, 1985. ISBN 0-8078-1652-3. ▸ Investigation of fascist youth propaganda, program, and apparatus of socialization. Fascists did not attempt to alter family structure; aimed to control secondary agents of socialization. [AS]

28.425 Luisa Passerini. *Fascism in popular memory: the cultural experience of the Turin working class.* Robert Lumley and Jude Bloomfield, trans. Cambridge: Cambridge University Press, 1987. ISBN 0-521-30290-0. ▸ Analytical study of workers' memories of fascism. Interviews conducted between 1976 and 1981; subjects born before 1922 and came to Turin in early thirties. Interviewed only male factory workers and women with working-class fathers or husbands. [AS]

28.426 John F. Pollard. *The Vatican and Italian fascism, 1929–32: a study in conflict.* Cambridge: Cambridge University Press, 1985. ISBN 0-521-26870-2. ▸ Centers on Lateran Pacts and conflict over Catholic Action. Collaboration between church and state opportunistic; normally they opposed one another because of conflicting totalitarian claims on society. Well documented and argued. [AS]

28.427 Guido Quazza et al., eds. *Fascismo e società italiana.* Turin: Einaudi, 1973. ▸ Important collection by leftist scholars on fascism's relationship to Italian history, economy, army, judiciary, church, and culture. Main theme: fascism did not represent break with past. [AS]

28.428 Ernesto Rossi. *Padroni del vapore e fascismo.* 5th rev. ed. Bari: Laterza, 1966. ▸ Uneven but insightful treatment of relationship between big business and advent of fascism and of fascist economic policies during period in power. Earlier editions under title *I padroni del vapore.* [AS]

28.429 Gaetano Salvemini. *Under the axe of fascism.* 1936 ed. New York: Citadel, 1971. ISBN 0-8065-0240-1 (pbk). ▸ Polemical but convincing discussion of fascist ruling class: party leaders, army chiefs, top bureaucrats, and big businessmen. Groups rein-

forced each other, although Fascist party kept overall control. [AS]

28.430 Roland Sarti. *Fascism and the industrial leadership in Italy, 1919–40: a study in the expansion of private power under fascism.* Berkeley: University of California Press, 1971. ISBN 0-520-01855-9. ▸ Careful, well-documented study of how industrialists kept economic control through self-organized institutions: Fascist party subordinated labor by controlling both socialist and Catholic unions. [AS]

28.431 Edward R. Tannenbaum. *The fascist experience: Italian society and culture, 1922–1945.* New York: Basic Books, 1972. ISBN 0-465-06877-4. ▸ Emphasis on fascist social context, life under fascist rule, and effect of fascism on education, group activities, and cultural enterprises. Also role of church and business in implementing fascist values in society. [AS]

28.432 Doug Thompson. *State control in fascist Italy: culture and conformity, 1925–1943.* Manchester: Manchester University Press; distributed by St. Martin's, 1991. ISBN 0-7190-3463-9. ▸ Reevaluation of means of achieving political hegemony between 1925 and 1943. Discusses cultural and ideological context as well as political basis of fascism. [AS]

Antifascism

28.433 Charles F. Delzell. *Mussolini's enemies: the Italian antifascist resistance.* 1961 ed. Princeton: Princeton University Press, 1989. ▸ Resistance to Mussolini from formation of clandestine opposition in 1926 to armed resistance, 1943–45. Well written and researched. Photocopy available from Ann Arbor: Michigan University Microfilms International, 1989. [AS]

28.434 Iris Origo. *A need to testify: portraits of Lauro De Bosis, Ruth Draper, Gaetano Salvemini, Ignazio Silone, and an essay on biography.* San Diego, Calif.: Harcourt Brace Jovanovich, 1984. ISBN 0-15-164989-8. ▸ Engaging biographical portraits of people linked by antifascism. Chapters on Salvemini and Silone especially good. [AS]

28.435 Frank Rosengarten. *The Italian anti-fascist press (1919–1945): from the legal opposition press to the underground newspapers of World War II.* Cleveland: Case Western Reserve University, 1968. ▸ How Fascists attacked press and how press went from legal opposition (1919–26) to underground press of armed resistance. One chapter discusses link between Resistance and Risorgimento and how some consider Resistance a second Risorgimento because all classes involved against fascism. [AS]

Fascist Foreign Policy

28.436 George W. Baer. *The coming of the Italian-Ethiopian War.* Cambridge, Mass.: Harvard University Press, 1967. ▸ Diplomatic background of war with Ethiopia. Italy's invasion challenged and finally discredited League of Nations. [AS]

28.437 James Barros. *The Corfu incident: Mussolini and the League of Nations.* Princeton: Princeton University Press, 1965. ▸ Reaction of League of Nations to Mussolini's invasion of Corfu in 1923; crisis solved outside League's machinery and in no way denied Mussolini fruits of his aggression. Based on some primary sources; British and French official documents unavailable. [AS]

28.438 Alan Cassels. *Italian foreign policy, 1918–1945: a guide to research and research materials.* Rev. ed. Wilmington, Del.: Scholarly Resources, 1991. ISBN 0-8420-2307-0. ▸ Covers sources on foreign policy from end of World War I to end of World War II. [AS]

28.439 Alan Cassels. *Mussolini's early diplomacy.* Princeton: Princeton University Press, 1970. ISBN 0-691-05179-8. ▸ Covers October 1922 to February 1927. Mussolini appeared to accept settlement of World War I, but in reality supported revisionism from very beginning and was spokesman for aggressive nationalism. [AS]

28.440 Angelo Del Boca. *The Ethiopian War, 1935–41.* 1965 ed. P. D. Cummings, trans. Chicago: University of Chicago Press, 1969. ISBN 0-226-14217-5. ‣ Detailed account of Italian-Ethiopian War, 1935–36, emphasizing military aspects. Very critical of Italian colonialism. Leftist interpretation; see author's recent volumes 2–3 of *Gli italiani in Africa Orientale* (28.326). [AS]

28.441 Maxwell Henry Hays Macartney and Paul Cremona. *Italy's foreign and colonial policy, 1914–1937.* 1938 ed. London: Oxford University Press, 1990. ‣ Rather overrated analysis of Italy's strength. Dated although a few conclusions still valid. Also available in microfilm from New Haven: Yale University Library, 1990. [AS]

28.442 Mario Toscano. *The origins of the Pact of Steel.* 1967 ed. Baltimore: Johns Hopkins University Press, 1968. ‣ Meticulous reconstruction of diplomatic origins of Pact of Steel. Based on Italian, British, American, and German diplomatic documents and memoirs. [AS]

28.443 Elizabeth Wiskemann. *The Rome-Berlin Axis: a history of the relations between Hitler and Mussolini.* 3d ed. London: Oxford University Press, 1969. ‣ Detailed but somewhat dated account of Mussolini's relationship to Hitler. Also available on microfilm from Ann Arbor: Michigan University Microfilms, 1969. [AS]

World War II

28.444 Frederick William D. Deakin. *The brutal friendship: Mussolini, Hitler, and the fall of Italian fascism.* New York: Harper & Row, 1962. ‣ Meticulous analysis of Italian politics and relationship of two dictators from fall of 1942 to 1945. Fundamental, detailed account of Mussolini's last stand, the Republic of Salò. [AS]

28.445 MacGregor Knox. *Mussolini unleashed, 1939–1941: politics and strategy in fascist Italy's last war.* Cambridge: Cambridge University Press, 1982. ISBN 0-521-23917-6. ‣ Well-researched, controversial thesis. Mussolini waged war against popular opinion; aimed to destroy social order at home and to remake it in his own image after quick conquest abroad. Consult volume 23 of *Storia d'Italia* (28.3). [AS]

28.446 John Joseph Timothy Sweet. *Iron arm: the mechanization of Mussolini's army, 1920–40.* Westport, Conn.: Greenwood, 1980. ISBN 0-313-22179-0, ISSN 0084-9251. ‣ Italy's undistinguished battlefield record resulted from failure to mechanize its army adequately. Based on good research and sources. [AS]

CONTEMPORARY ITALY, 1943–1988

Bibliography

28.447 Peter M. Lange and Robert Samuels. *Studies on Italy, 1943–1975: select bibliography of American and British materials in political science, economics, sociology, and anthropology.* Alessandro Bruschi, ed. Turin: Fondazione Agnelli, 1977. ‣ One hundred eighty-three pages of titles dealing with Italy from 1943 to 1975. [AS]

28.448 Clara M. Lovett. *Contemporary Italy: a selective bibliography.* Washington, D.C.: Library of Congress, 1985. ISBN 0-8444-0473-X (pbk). ‣ About 1,300 titles, without annotation, for period 1945–83 (ninety-eight in English) emphasizing social science more than history. Grouped according to topic. [AS]

General Studies

28.449 Paul Ginsborg. *A history of contemporary Italy: society and politics, 1943–1988.* London: Penguin, 1990. ISBN 0-14-012496-9. ‣ Excellent survey covering most important aspects of contemporary Italy. Emphasis on obsessive and overwhelming need for reform and failure to achieve reformist goals. [AS]

28.450 Donald Sassoon. *Contemporary Italy: politics, economy and society since 1945.* 3d ed. London: Longman, 1986. ISBN 0-582-29551-3 (pbk). ‣ Approaches political system through economic and social development, comparing it to other industrial countries. Italy in chronic state of crisis: society and economy have changed rapidly, political elites have not. [AS]

Politics, Society, and Culture

28.451 Percy A. Allum. *Politics and society in postwar Naples.* Cambridge: Cambridge University Press, 1973. ISBN 0-521-08424-5. ‣ Excellent study of structures that determined political attitudes of politicians and people and kind of politics they generated. [AS]

28.452 Zygmunt G. Baránski and Robert Lumley, eds. *Culture and conflict in postwar Italy: essays on mass and popular culture.* Houndsmill: Macmillan and University of Reading, Graduate School of European and International Studies, 1990. ISBN 0-333-45804-4 (cl), 0-333-45805-2 (pbk). ‣ Seventeen interdisciplinary essays in which various authors attempt to overcome traditional picture of culture to portray radical changes since postwar period. Covers history, language, social movements, cinema, television, intellectuals, and design. [AS]

28.453 Roy Palmer Domenico. *Italian Fascists on trial, 1943–1948.* Chapel Hill: University of North Carolina Press, 1991. ISBN 0-8078-2006-7. ‣ Investigation of democratic Italy's sanctions against Fascists and how transition to democracy affected Fascists, goals and targets of sanctions, means used to punish Fascists, and who opposed sanctions and why. [AS]

28.454 Paolo Farneti. *The Italian party system, 1945–1980.* S. E. Finer and Alfio Mastropaolo, eds. New York: St. Martin's, 1985. ISBN 0-312-43923-7. ‣ Since mid-1970s collective movements, unions, and local initiatives have challenged close identity between party system and political system. Parties have aligned along Right and Left, each distinguished in three parts: right, center, and left. [AS]

28.455 David Moss. *The politics of left-wing violence in Italy, 1969–85.* New York: St. Martin's, 1989. ISBN 0-312-02814-8. ‣ Left-wing terrorist aims not homogeneous. Practitioners divided over meaning and use of violence; few desired to go underground. Opponents had difficulty defining meaning, causes, and extent of terrorism. [AS]

RICHARD L. KAGAN AND ADRIAN SHUBERT

Spain and Portugal

When this *Guide* last appeared, in 1961, Iberian historiography was decidedly out of date. Historians of both Spain and Portugal continued to work in a traditional mode, emphasizing diplomatic, political, and intellectual history. Topics connected with the rise and eventual decline of Spain and Portugal's overseas empires were of overriding concern. The medieval and early modern periods were favored; the nineteenth and twentieth centuries, presenting a less attractive picture, were largely ignored.

Both countries were still firmly in the grip of dictatorships dating from before World War II, and this basic fact of life had a significant effect on the way history was written and even on what constituted "appropriate" topics for research. In Spain, both the centralization of funding in the Consejo Superior de Investigación Científica and the power of "politically correct" *catedráticos* who controlled university departments of history minimized new approaches and dissenting interpretations and kept them firmly on the margins.

Of special interest was what historians interpreted as Iberia's failure to modernize along European lines. Many attributed economic backwardness and a disorderly political history to national character and the notion that Iberians were by nature different from other Europeans. This idea was used by the Franco and Salazar regimes as a means of self-justification: their people were ill-suited for such "foreign" inventions as democracy and required a different political solution, more congruent with national traditions. The tendency of historians to treat Spain and Portugal in isolation, as if the Iberian experience were disconnected from broader trends in European history, only made matters worse.

Movement away from this state of affairs began slowly in the 1960s. In Spain, the impetus for change came initially from foreign scholars such as R. Carr and J. H. Elliott in Britain, F. Braudel and P. Vilar in France, and R. Herr and G. Jackson in the United States. (If one wanted to choose specific dates, the publication of Elliott's *Imperial Spain* [29.7] in 1963 and Carr's classic *Spain, 1808–1939* [29.3] in 1966 are probably the best.) These and other foreign scholars asked new questions and introduced new methodologies. They also introduced a comparative dimension to the study of the evolution of the Iberian world that led to nothing short of a revolution in the way Iberian history was conceived and written.

Gradually Iberian history as practiced by foreign scholars grew closer in orientation and subject matter to that of other European countries and in so doing attracted new attention and respect. Although research in Portugal and Spain continued to be hampered by inadequate archival and library facilities, the field attracted growing numbers of students, particularly in France, Britain, and the United States. The creation of the Society for Spanish and Portuguese Historical Studies in the United States in 1969 symbolized Iberian history's coming of age.

At the same time, a new generation of Spaniards was also beginning to renew the writing of their history, especially for the modern period. For Spaniards, the annual colloquia organized by the exiled historian Manuel Tuñon de Lara at the University of Pau (France) were of great importance. St. Anthony's College, Oxford, where Carr was master, was another focus. Topics such as labor movements, political dissent, and regionalism, earlier taboo for the regime, as well as serious study of the Spanish Civil War, became part of a more broadly defined history. The pioneering studies of A. H. Oliveira Marques on the history of the controversial First Republic (1910–1926) had a similarly catalytic effect on the historiography of twentieth-century Portugal.

Still, so long as the dictatorship remained in place, the possibilities for renovation and change were tightly constrained. The Portuguese Revolution in 1974 and the transition to democracy in Spain, which began with Franco's death in 1975, ushered in a period of dizzying change. There was more freedom to investigate the recent past as well as specific aspects of the more distant past, such as the Inquisition. New types of history, especially social history, began to be written. At the same time, these changes have resulted in a broader audience, as the publication of monthly magazines directed at the general reading public, such as *Historia 16* in Madrid and *L'Avenc* in Barcelona, seemed to suggest.

The period of Spanish history that has probably benefited most from the methodological changes outlined above has been the sixteenth and seventeenth centuries. The groundwork was laid by foreign scholars, the majority intent on analyzing the underlying causes of the "decline of Spain." Research proceeded along two major lines: the first, inspired by the Annales school of economic and social history, led to a series of local and regional studies that revealed the diversity of the peninsula's economy and called into question previous assumptions about the extent and the timing of Spain's decline; the second favored political history and especially sought to analyze Spanish decline as part of the "general crisis" of seventeenth-century Europe, a comparative approach that cast doubt on Spanish exceptionalism along with the utility of "decline" as an analytical category. Consequently, scholars have recently begun to look beyond the question of decline and attempt to examine early modern Spanish history on its own terms. This has fostered new interest in social history and has already led to a new understanding of the role of the monarchy and such monarchical institutions as the Inquisition in Spanish society. At the same time, this analytical turn has allowed for a new look at the eighteenth century, particularly insofar as it concerns the economy, the Enlightenment, and Spain's relationship with its American colonies.

Early modern Portuguese history registered similar advances, especially concerning the epoch of discoveries, Portugal's relationship with its overseas colonies, and the economic effects of empire upon the metropolis. Of crucial importance here was the work of V. M. Godinho and the French historian, F. Mauro. Meanwhile, A. M. Hespanha and other scholars attached to the Universidade Nova de Lisboa were largely responsible for a resurgence of interest in the history of early seventeenth-century Portugal, especially as it involved the Restoration of 1640.

Despite these advances, knowledge of early modern Iberia still lags behind that of other early modern states. Intellectual history remains underdeveloped and political history has only recently begun to move beyond the arena of the royal court or to address questions of political cultures and language. Similarly, despite new interest in social history, family history, and women's history, the study of the aristocracy, local oligarchies, and the clergy has been largely neglected. Biography and cultural history also remain important lacunae.

The historiography of the modern period has improved immeasurably in the last twenty-five years or so but remains much less developed than either early modern history or the modern history of such countries as Italy, France, or Germany. There have been fewer methodological innovations and the work that is done clusters around a handful of topics, such as the labor movement, Spain's Second Republic and the Civil War, and, more recently, the Salazar's *Estado Novo* and the Franco regime. (This clustering is more pronounced for foreign scholars than for the Spaniards and Portuguese themselves.) By contrast, the nineteenth century remains relatively unexplored.

With regard to themes, political, intellectual, and economic history have retained their dominance to a much greater extent in Spain and Portugal than elsewhere. Social history remains relatively weak, although the recent appearance of such scholarly journals as *Análise Social* and *Ler História* (in Portugal) and *Historia Social* (in Spain) are signs of change. Within the wide world of social history, a somewhat old-fashioned labor history is most active, the social history of the working class is only beginning, and women's and demographic history are also developing fields.

The installation of democracy in Spain has brought inestimable benefits to the writing of history. A freer intellectual climate has not only broadened the range of historical inquiry but also introduced scholars to methodological innovations arriving from abroad. Scholarship has also benefited from the programs of various nongovernmental foundations (the Gulbenkian Foundation in Portugal, established in the 1960s, is especially noteworthy in this regard) as well as the entrance of both countries into the European Community (now the European Union) in 1986. Membership in this union has promoted scholarly interchange and provided funding for art exhibitions, international conferences, and research.

Yet the coming of democracy, in Spain at least, has also had one less beneficial effect. In the decentralized, semi-federal "state of the autonomies" that was created by the Constitution of 1978, regions and localities have become more important and have come to control more resources. Some of these have been used to fund historical research and publication, and this has contributed to the emergence of an unprecedented number of journals and publishing houses with geographically limited interests and distribution. At the same time, municipal, provincial, and regional governments—not to mention local financial entities such as the Cajas de Ahorros—have also been publishing. The result has been an abundance of historical writing, but one that has led to fragmentation and weakened quality control.

Still, there can be no doubt that both Spanish and Portuguese history have blossomed in the past three decades and especially since 1975. It is more vital, more diverse, and more open to the outside world than at any other time in this century. In the future, these trends will probably continue.

The Iberianists of the English-speaking world will continue to bring the concerns and issues of their broader fields to the study of Spain and Portugal. Less happily, the spiraling expense of living in both countries and the growing scarcity of research funding in our universities will make it increasingly difficult for younger scholars to spend the extended periods of time in the archives that are essential for effective research. Perhaps our role will become one of attempting to provide synthesis, of helping put together the vast and increasingly complex jigsaw puzzle of research produced by the Spaniards and Portuguese themselves.

On balance, however, the future of both Spanish and Portuguese history in North America looks very bright. Multicultural concerns, combined with a new interest among North American latinos in their Iberian roots and a more general interest in the process of cultural contact and exchange, are placing new demands upon schools and universities to offer classes in these once neglected areas. The study of Spanish history is also benefiting from the fact that Spanish is by far the most popular "foreign" language in the United States. At the same time, exhibitions and other activities spawned by the Quincentennial celebrations of 1992 have focused new attention on the history and culture of Spain and Portugal alike. While this attention can be expected to diminish somewhat in the years ahead, it may help to enhance the heretofore marginal position of Iberian studies within North American historical scholarship.

ACKNOWLEDGMENTS   *This essay was written by Richard L. Kagan, Adrian Shubert, and Douglas R. Wheeler.*

Entries are arranged under the following headings:

General Studies

Early Modern Spain
    Catholic Monarchs, 1450–1516
    Habsburg Spain, 1516–1700
    Bourbon Monarchy, 1700–1808

Modern Spain, 1800–1992
    General Studies
    Liberal Spain, 1800–1875
    Restoration, 1876–1930
    Second Republic and Civil War, 1931–1939
    Franco's Spain, 1939–1975
    Democratic Spain, 1975–1992

Portugal
    Portuguese Empire, 1450–1806
    Constitutional Monarchy, 1807–1910
    Republican Portugal, 1910–1926
    Dictatorship, 1926–1974
    Democratic Portugal, 1974–1992

[Contributors: AS = Adrian Shubert, DW = Douglas Wheeler, JB = James Boyden, JFP = James F. Powers, JSH = John S. Hill, MAB = Mark A. Burkholder, PHF = Paul H. Freedman, RJW = Richard J. Walter, RLK = Richard L. Kagan, SHB = Suzanne H. Burkholder, TC = Thomas Cohen]

GENERAL STUDIES

29.1 Ann Bridge and Susan Lowndes. *The selective traveller in Portugal*. London: Chatto & Windus, 1978. ISBN 0-7011-0576-3. ▸ Superior guidebook to country's historic buildings, monuments, and arts with useful historical and geographical background. [DW]

29.2 Raymond Carr. *Modern Spain, 1875–1980.* 1980 ed. New York: Oxford University Press, 1988. ISBN 0-19-289090-5 (pbk). ▸ Survey of Spanish political history, Restoration to 1980. Sees search for political system that enjoyed generalized acceptance and stability as principal issue for people of period. [AS]

29.3 Raymond Carr. *Spain, 1808–1975.* 2d ed. Oxford: Clarendon, 1982. ISBN 0-19-822128-2 (cl), 0-19-822127-4 (pbk). ▸ Best available survey of history of Spain. Emphasizes failure of Spanish liberalism in twentieth century. [AS]

29.4 Richard E. Chandler and Kessel Schwartz. *A new history of Spanish literature.* Rev. ed. Baton Rouge: Louisiana State University Press, 1991. ISBN 0-8071-1699-8 (cl), 0-8071-1735-8 (pbk). ▸ Update of classic (1891) study by George Ticknor. Organized chronologically by genre: epic and narrative poetry, drama, fiction, etc. Coverage spotty and quality uneven but still useful for reference. Bibliography only in first edition of 1961. [RLK]

29.5 James W. Cortada, comp. *A bibliographic guide to Spanish diplomatic history, 1460–1977.* Westport, Conn.: Greenwood, 1977. ISBN 0-8371-9685-X. ▸ Chronologically arranged survey of existing literature pertaining to Spanish diplomacy. International guide with material listed by country. [SHB]

29.6 Antonio Domínguez Ortiz. *The golden age of Spain, 1516–1659.* James Casey, trans. New York: Basic Books, 1971. ▸ Comprehensive survey by one of Spain's leading historians. Particularly good on economy, society, *moriscos* (christianized Moors), and other marginal groups. [RLK]

29.7 John H. Elliott. *Imperial Spain, 1469–1716.* 1963 ed. New York: Penguin, 1990. ISBN 0-14-013517-0. ▸ Elegantly written survey emphasizing Spain's rise to imperial grandeur and subsequent seventeeth-century decline. Essential reading. [RLK]

29.8 John H. Elliott, ed. *The Spanish world: civilization and

empire, Europe and the Americas, past and present.* New York: Abrams, 1991. ISBN 0-8109-3409-4. ▸ Essays on Spain's contribution to world civilization in art, literature, government, religion, and society. Excellent on Spanish family. Includes chapter on Hispanic culture in United States. [RLK]

29.9 Richard Herr. *An historical essay on modern Spain.* 1971 ed. Berkeley: University of California Press, 1974. ISBN 0-520-02534-2. ▸ General history focusing on nineteenth and twentieth centuries. Emphasis on three cultural tensions: ideological conflicts, agrarian question, and geographical-regional questions. Earlier title: *Spain.* [AS]

29.10 R. O. Jones, ed. *A literary history of Spain.* New York: Barnes & Noble, 1971–73. ▸ Best general history of Spanish literature currently available. Eight volumes published. Catalogued under individual authors as follows: A. D. Deyermond (Middle Ages); R. O. Jones (prose and poetry, sixteenth to seventeenth centuries); Edward M. Wilson (golden age drama); Nigel Glendinning (eighteenth century); Donald L. Shaw (nineteenth century); G. G. Brown (twentieth century); Arthur Terry (Catalan literature); Jean Franco (Spanish-American literature since independence). Volumes unnumbered. [RLK]

29.11 Henry Kamen. *A concise history of Spain.* New York: Scribner's, 1973. ISBN 0-684-13850-6. ▸ Well-illustrated survey written for general reader. Emphasizes broad economic and political developments, late antiquity to mid-twentieth century. Coverage uneven. [RLK]

29.12 Henry Kamen. *Golden age Spain.* Atlantic Highlands, N.J.: Humanities Press International, 1988. ISBN 0-391-03584-3. ▸ Introductory manual; useful primarily as brief, up-to-date survey of historical literature and debates. Excellent bibliography. [JB]

29.13 Henry Kamen. *Spain: a society in conflict, 1479–1714.* 2d ed. London: Longman, 1991. ISBN 0-582-06723-5. ▸ Comprehensive survey. Argues Spain was backward society ill-prepared for empire. Better on economy, society, and religion than on politics, diplomacy, or royal court. [RLK]

29.14 Marion Kaplan. *The Portuguese: the land and its people.* New York: Viking, 1991. ISBN 0-670-82364-3. ▸ Popular history and contemporary affairs artfully combined with reference material in both English and Portuguese. Focus on Portugal's integration with European community. [DW]

29.15 Robert W. Kern, ed. *Historical dictionary of modern Spain, 1700–1988.* New York: Greenwood, 1990. ISBN 0-313-25971-2. ▸ Dictionary of Spanish history since 1700. Numerous entries on individuals, political and social organizations, events, and concepts. [AS]

29.16 H. V. Livermore. *A new history of Portugal.* 2d ed. Cambridge: Cambridge University Press, 1976. ISBN 0-521-21320-7 (cl), 0-521-29103-8 (pbk). ▸ Survey from twelfth century to 1974 Revolution and aftermath. Emphasis on politics. [DW]

29.17 A. W. Lovett. *Early Habsburg Spain, 1517–1598.* Oxford: Oxford University Press, 1986. ISBN 0-19-8822139-8 (cl), 0-19-822138-x (pbk). ▸ Traditional survey of reigns of Charles V (1516–59) and Philip II (1559–98). Emphasis on dynastic politics and empire; final section on social history. Good bibliography. [JB]

29.18 John Lynch. *Bourbon Spain, 1700–1808.* Cambridge, Mass.: Blackwell, 1989. ISBN 0-631-14576-1. ▸ Excellent survey focusing on classical dilemma of Old Regime: how to reform system without destroying it. Discussion of economy and society overshadowed by superbly written political history. Essential reading for Latin American colonialists. [SHB/MAB]

29.19 John Lynch. *The Hispanic world in crisis and change, 1598–

1700. Cambridge, Mass.: Blackwell, 1992. ISBN 0-631-17697-7. ‣ Masterly survey incorporating recent research. Argues Spain's decline as imperial power linked to growing independence of its American colonies. Notable attention to colonial trade and emergence of more mature and less economically dependent colonies. Required reading. Earlier title: *Spain under the Habsburgs*, vol. 2. [RLK/MAB]

29.20 John Lynch. *Spain, 1516–1598: from nation state to world empire*. Cambridge, Mass.: Blackwell, 1991. ISBN 0-631-17696-9. ‣ Thorough but dull survey of economic, social, and political developments, emphasizing Spain's emergence as world power. Useful background reading for colonialists. Revised, updated edition of *Spain under the Habsburgs*, vol. 1. [RLK/MAB]

29.21 José Calvet de Magalhães. *Breve historia diplomatica de Portugal*. 2d ed. Lisbon: Publiçãoes Europa-America, 1990. ISBN 972-1-03000-7. ‣ Concise compendium of Portugal's long diplomatic history, twelfth century to 1910. Includes outlines of principal treaties with sources. [DW]

29.22 A. H. de Oliveira Marques. *History of Portugal*. New York: Columbia University Press, 1976. ISBN 0-231-08353-X. ‣ Excellent survey, antiquity to 1976. Influenced by Annales school, underplays role of personality and *mentalités*. Includes material on Brazil. [DW/MAB]

29.23 Stanley G. Payne. *A history of Spain and Portugal*. 2 vols. Madison: University of Wisconsin Press, 1973. ISBN 0-299-06274-0 (v. 1), 0-299-06284-8 (v. 2). ‣ Major economic and political trends, survey of antiquity to 1971; little on culture and society. Most reliable on post-1800 period. [RLK]

29.24 P. E. Russell, ed. *Spain: a companion to Spanish studies*. 1973 ed. London: Methuen, 1976. ISBN 0-416-16410-2 (cl), 0-416-84110-4 (pbk). ‣ Essays designed to introduce students of literature to major periods of Spanish history starting with Middle Ages. Useful background reading. [RLK]

29.25 Joel Serrão, ed. *Dicionario de história de Portugal*. 1963–71 ed. Porto, Portugal: Livraria Figueirinhas, 1981. ‣ Historical encyclopedia of Portuguese history from ancient times to twentieth century. Best on institutions, age of discovery, and topics to 1926. [DW]

29.26 Adrian Shubert. *The land and the people of Spain*. New York: HarperCollins, 1992. ISBN 0-06-020217-3. ‣ Illustrated survey of Spanish history, antiquity to present. Intended for high school students. [AS]

29.27 Adrian Shubert. *A social history of modern Spain*. Boston: Unwin Hyman, 1990. ISBN 0-04-445458-9 (cl), 0-04-445459-7 (pbk). ‣ Synthesis of much published work on social history of Spain in both Spanish and English. Argues Spain was fully part of European mainstream. [AS]

29.28 Dan Stanislawski. *The individuality of Portugal: a study in historical-political geography*. 1959 ed. New York: Greenwood, 1969. ISBN 0-8371-2120-5. ‣ Comprehensive regional geography with strong historical base. Controversial thesis on geographical uniqueness as basis of independence from Spain. [DW]

29.29 Jaime Vicens Vives. *Approaches to the history of Spain*. 2d ed. Joan Connelly Ullman, ed. and trans. Berkeley: University of California Press, 1970. ISBN 0-520-01422-7. ‣ Short interpretive account, antiquity to twentieth century. Pioneering in its focus on general economic and social themes. [RLK]

29.30 Jaime Vicens Vives. *An economic history of Spain*. Frances A. López Morillas, trans. Princeton: Princeton University Press, 1969. ‣ Analysis of development of Spanish economy across two millennia. Emphasizes diversity of peninsular economy. Dated in parts but still useful. [RLK]

29.31 Douglas L. Wheeler, ed. *Historical dictionary of Portugal.*

Metuchen, N.J.: Scarecrow, 1993. ‣ Introduction to Portuguese history, antiquity to present. Entries include biographies, events, and concepts. [DW]

SEE ALSO
16.96 C. R. Boxer. *The Portuguese seaborne empire, 1415–1825.*

EARLY MODERN SPAIN

Catholic Monarchs, 1450–1516

29.32 William A. Christian, Jr. *Apparitions in late medieval and Renaissance Spain*. Princeton: Princeton University Press, 1981. ISBN 0-691-05326-X. ‣ Fascinating study of religious visions and visionaries in Castile and Catalonia, 1399–1523. Analyzes importance for development of local religious cults. [RLK]

29.33 John Edwards. *Christian Córdoba: the city and its region in the late Middle Ages*. New York: Cambridge University Press, 1982. ISBN 0-521-24320-3. ‣ Details economic, governmental, and religious aspects of important Andalusian city in fourteenth and fifteenth centuries. Shows domination of city and countryside by aristocracy; prefigures sixteenth-century pattern. Particularly informative on deteriorating relationship between Christians and Jews. [RLK/JFP]

29.34 Felipe Fernández-Armesto. *The Canary Islands after the conquest: the making of a colonial society in the early sixteenth century*. Oxford: Clarendon, 1982. ISBN 0-19-821888-5. ‣ Analysis of conquest and subsequent nature of Spanish settlement in Canaries during reign of Ferdinand and Isabella. Stresses importance of islands as laboratory for colonization in Americas. [RLK]

29.35 Felipe Fernández-Armesto. *Ferdinand and Isabella*. 1975 ed. New York: Dorset, 1991. ISBN 0-88029-744-1. ‣ Popular history updating Prescott's classic study (29.48). Discusses major features of monarchs' policies at home and abroad. [RLK]

29.36 Stephen Haliczer. *The comuneros of Castile: the forging of a revolution, 1475–1521*. Madison: University of Wisconsin Press, 1981. ISBN 0-299-08500-7. ‣ Analysis of *comunero* revolt (1519–21). Distinguished for emphasis on preconditions stemming from period of Catholic monarchs rather than trigger of Charles V's accession in 1516. Draws on functionalist theories of revolution. [JB]

29.37 J.R.L. Highfield, comp. *Spain in the fifteenth century, 1369–1516: essays and extracts by historians of Spain*. Frances A. López Morillas, trans. London: Macmillan, 1972. ISBN 0-333-11135-4. ‣ Collection of essays on various aspects of late medieval Spain, including economy, law, religion, and Catholic monarchs as seen by contemporaries. Fragmented but useful. [RLK]

29.38 J. N. Hillgarth. *Castilian hegemony, 1410–1516*. Vol. 2 of *The Spanish kingdoms, 1250–1516*. Oxford: Clarendon, 1978. ISBN 0-19-822530-X. ‣ Masterly survey emphasizing rise of Castile and reign of Ferdinand and Isabella. Encyclopedic, very useful for reference and bibliography. [RLK]

29.39 Richard L. Kagan. "Spain of Ferdinand and Isabella." In *Circa 1492: art in the age of exploration*. Jay A. Levenson, ed., pp. 55–62. New Haven: Yale University Press, 1991. ISBN 0-300-05167-0 (cl), 0-300-05217-0 (pbk). ‣ Brief introduction to economy, society, and religion in Spain at end of fifteenth century. Examines royal support of Columbus. Designed for students and general reader. [RLK]

29.40 Henry Kamen. "The Mediterranean and the expulsion of the Jews." *Past and present* 119 (1988) 30–55. ‣ Revisionist article reducing number of Jews expelled in 1492 and reassessing impact of expulsion on Spanish economy. Offers introduction to recent literature on polemical topic, much of which is not available in English. [RLK]

29.41 Peggy K. Liss. *Isabel the queen: life and times*. New York:

Oxford University Press, 1992. ISBN 0-19-507356-8. ‣ Best available biography of Isabella. Excellent use of contemporary sources. Offers overview of culture, politics, and religion in Isabelline Spain. [RLK]

29.42 Marvin Lunenfeld. *Keepers of the city: the corregidores of Isabella I of Castile, 1474–1504.* New York: Cambridge University Press, 1987. ISBN 0-521-32930-2. ‣ Archive-based study of crown representatives in Castile's cities. Good on municipal government and limitations imposed on centralized royal authority. Implications for governance of Spain's American colonies. [RLK]

29.43 Caro Lynn. *A college professor of the Renaissance: Lucio Marineo Siculo among the Spanish humanists.* Chicago: University of Chicago Press, 1937. ‣ Biography of Lucio Marineo Siculo (1444–1536), Italian humanist and historian at court of Ferdinand and Isabella. Important for origins of Renaissance in Spain. [RLK]

29.44 Mark D. Meyerson. *The Muslims of Valencia in the age of Ferdinand and Isabel: between coexistence and crusade.* Berkeley: University of California Press, 1992. ISBN 0-520-06888-2. ‣ Fine study analyzing character of Spain's important Muslim minority in late fifteenth and early sixteenth centuries. Contrasts toleration of Muslims to royal policy of expelling Jews. [RLK]

29.45 Helen Nader. *The Mendoza family in the Spanish Renaissance, 1350 to 1550.* New Brunswick, N.J.: Rutgers University Press, 1979. ISBN 0-8135-0876-2. ‣ Examination of multifaceted contributions of prominent aristocratic family to culture and politics of fifteenth-century Castile. Questionable hypothesis concerning start of Spanish Renaissance. Excellent on Iñigo Lopez de Mendoza, count of Tendilla, Granada's first Christian governor. [RLK]

29.46 Joseph Pérez. *Isabel y Fernando: los reyes católicos.* Madrid: Nerea, 1988. ISBN 84-86763-06-1. ‣ Best history of reign of Catholic monarchs currently in print. Available also in original French. Excellent bibliography. [RLK]

29.47 William D. Phillips, Jr. *Enrique IV and the crisis of fifteenth-century Castile, 1425–1480.* Cambridge, Mass.: Mediaeval Academy of America, 1978. (*Speculum* anniversary monographs, 3.) ISBN 0-910956-63-4. ‣ Examination of Castile's political and administrative history under Juan II (1407–54) and Enrique IV (1454–74). Skillful use of archival and chronicle sources. Discusses growing importance of jurists in royal government. [RLK]

29.48 William H. Prescott. *History of the reign of Ferdinand and Isabella.* Boston: Little, Brown, 1837. ‣ Classic treatment, in grand narrative style. Excellent use of contemporary chronicles. Still worth reading for its heroic picture of monarchs. [RLK/PHF]

Habsburg Spain, 1516–1700

29.49 Angel Alcalá Galve, ed. *The Spanish Inquisition and the Inquisitorial mind.* Boulder and Highland Lakes, N.J.: Social Science Monographs and Atlantic Research Publications; distributed by Columbia University Press, 1987. (Atlantic studies on society in change, 49.) ISBN 0-88033-952-7. ‣ Contributions to quincentenary conference on Inquisition. Provides good sense of shape and direction of research in 1980s and movement toward use of Inquisitorial records to illuminate broader sociocultural issues. [JB]

29.50 Ida Altman. *Emigrants and society: Extremadura and America in the sixteenth century.* Berkeley: University of California Press, 1989. ISBN 0-520-06494-1. ‣ Best study of characteristics of Castilian emigration to New World. Well researched, very readable; documents human links between Spain and America. [JB]

29.51 James S. Amelang. *Honored citizens of Barcelona: patrician culture and class relations, 1490–1714.* Princeton: Princeton University Press, 1986. ISBN 0-691-05461-4. ‣ Examination of formation and emerging world view of compound elite in early modern Barcelona. Shrewdly argued, places Catalan example squarely within general historiography of European cities. [JB]

29.52 Ignacio Atienza Hernández. *Aristocracia, poder y riqueza en la España moderna: la casa de Osuna, siglos XV–XIX.* Mexico City: Siglo Veintiuno de España, 1987. ISBN 84-323-0601-0. ‣ Fine case study of great Castilian house, based on thorough archival research and sophisticated quantitative analysis. No better study exists of economic basis of noble power. [JB]

29.53 Yitzhak Fritz Baer. *A history of the Jews in Christian Spain.* 1961–66 ed. 2 vols. Louis Schoffman, trans. Philadelphia: Jewish Publication Society of America, 1992. ISBN 0-8276-0431-9 (set, pbk), 0-8276-0425-4 (v. 1, pbk), 0-8276-0426-2 (v. 2, pbk). ‣ Standard study of fifteenth-century Spanish Jewry. Controversially argues many *conversos* (Jewish converts to Christianity) were judaizers; considers scale and effects of expulsion. [JB]

29.54 Marcel Bataillon. *Erasmo y España: estudios sobre la historia espiritual del siglo XVI.* 2d 1959 ed. Antonio Alatorre, trans. Mexico City: Fondo de Cultura Económica, 1966. ISBN 84-375-50158-X. ‣ Work of staggering erudition, treating Cardinal Francisco Ximenez Cisneros's reforms, multiple aspects of Spanish Erasmianism, and its ultimate condemnation. Starting point for all subsequent work on intellectual history of sixteenth-century Spanish Christianity. [JB]

29.55 Bartolomé Bennassar. *The Spanish character: attitudes and mentalities from the sixteenth to the nineteenth centuries.* Benjamin Keen, trans. Berkeley: University of California Press, 1979. ISBN 0-520-03401-5. ‣ Stimulating essay on Spanish popular culture illustrated with well-chosen anecdotes. Minimizes dynamism and diversity of Spanish culture. Qualifies but does not reject notion of national character. [JB]

29.56 Bartolomé Bennassar. *Valladolid au siècle d'or, une ville de Castille et sa campagne au seizième siècle.* Paris: Mouton, 1967. (École Practique des Haute Études, Sorbonne, Sixième section, Sciences économique et sociales, Civilisation et société, 4.) ‣ Superb study in Annales tradition. Remains best account of Castilian city and its hinterland. Society, economy, administration, and law receive detailed and interrelated coverage. Available also in Spanish translation. [JB]

29.57 Jodi Bilinkoff. *The Avila of Saint Teresa: religious reform in a sixteenth-century city.* Ithaca, N.Y.: Cornell University Press, 1989. ISBN 0-8014-2203-5. ‣ Original contribution to vast literature on Teresa, places Carmelite reform within political and religious context of Ávila and other contemporary movements. Good on female spirituality in this society. [JB]

29.58 Jonathan Brown. *The golden age of painting in Spain.* New Haven: Yale University Press, 1991. ISBN 0-300-04760-6. ‣ Beautifully illustrated survey of sixteenth- and seventeenth-century painting, placing artists and patrons in social and intellectual context. [JB]

29.59 Jonathan Brown. *Images and ideas in seventeenth-century Spanish painting.* Princeton: Princeton University Press, 1978. ISBN 0-691-03941-0 (cl), 0-691-00315-7 (pbk). ‣ Penetrating essays on Francisco de Pacheco, Diego de Velázquez, Francisco de Zurburán, and other Spanish artists. Especially valuable for recreation of intellectual world of Seville at start of seventeenth century. [RLK]

29.60 Jonathan Brown. *Velázquez, painter and courtier.* New Haven: Yale University Press, 1986. ISBN 0-300-03466-0. ‣ First-rate study of life and work of seventeenth century's greatest artist. Velázquez's career illuminates court of Philip IV as well as art world. Beautifully illustrated. [JB]

29.61 Jonathan Brown et al. *El Greco of Toledo.* Boston: Little,

Brown, 1982. ISBN 0-8212-15019 (cl), 0-8212-1506-X (pbk). ‣ Collection of beautifully illustrated essays placing El Greco and his art in historical and social context. Noteworthy study of Toledo by Kagan. [JB]

29.62 Jonathan Brown and John H. Elliott. *A palace for a king: the Buen Retiro and the court of Philip IV.* New Haven: Yale University Press, 1980. ISBN 0-300-02507-6 (cl), 0-300-03621-3 (pbk). ‣ Construction of Buen Retiro palace in 1630s provides opportunity for productive collaboration between history and art history. Analysis focuses on elaborately contrived presentation of majestic, generous kingship. Richly illustrated. [JB]

29.63 Ramón Carande. *Carlos V y sus banqueros.* 3d abr. ed. 3 vols. Barcelona: Crítica, 1987. ISBN 84-7423-326-7. ‣ Pioneering financial study. Details revenues, commitments, and borrowing of emperor. Finds expense of imperial enterprises ruinous to economy of Castile. [JB]

29.64 Julio Caro Baroja. *Las formas complejas de la vida religiosa: religión, sociedad, y carácter en la España de los siglos XVI y XVII.* Madrid: Akal, 1978. ISBN 84-73-39359-7. ‣ Sociological analysis of multiple aspects of Spanish religiosity in Habsburg period. Penetrating in parts; superficial in others. Difficult to digest. [JB]

29.65 Julio Caro Baroja. "Honour and shame: a historical account of several conflicts." In *Honour and shame: the values of Mediterranean society.* 1966 ed. J. G. Peristiany, ed. Mrs. R. Johnson, trans., pp. 79–137. Chicago: University of Chicago Press, 1974. ISBN 0-226-65714-0. ‣ Historical anthropology tracing development and deformation of Spanish notions of honor and definitions of shameful behavior. Attempts to link, not always successfully, early modern notions of honor to religious caste divisions. [JB]

29.66 James Casey. *The kingdom of Valencia in the seventeenth century.* New York: Cambridge University Press, 1979. ISBN 0-521-21939-6. ‣ Useful account of forgotten realm of crown of Aragon. Quantitative social history, especially valuable for role of *moriscos* (christianized Moors) and effect of expulsion on rural society. [JB]

29.67 James Casey. "Spain: a failed transition." In *The European crisis of the 1590s.* Peter Clark, ed., pp. 209–28. Boston: Allen & Unwin, 1985. ISBN 0-04-940074-6. ‣ Analysis of severe shocks of 1590s. Concludes Spain's seventeenth-century decline largely result of failed transition to more urbanized economy at end of sixteenth century. [JB]

29.68 William A. Christian, Jr. *Local religion in sixteenth-century Spain.* Princeton: Princeton University Press, 1981. ISBN 0-691-05306-5. ‣ Sociologically informed analysis of popular Catholic practice, based on Philip II's *Relaciones Topográficas* of 1570s. Interesting on vows, shrines, devotional trends, and local clerical compromise with somewhat unorthodox worship. [JB]

29.69 Jaime Contreras and Gustav Henningsen. "Forty-four thousand cases of the Spanish Inquisition (1540–1700): analysis of a historical data bank." In *The Inquisition in early modern Europe: studies on methods and sources.* Gustav Henningsen and John A. Tedeschi, eds. Anne Born, trans., pp. 100–29. Dekalb: Northern Illinois University Press, 1986. ISBN 0-87580-102-1. ‣ Summary of extensive statistical analysis of Inquisition cases with breakdowns by tribunal, offense, and punishment over time. [JB]

29.70 Marcelin Defourneaux. *Daily life in Spain in the golden age.* 1970 ed. Newton Branch, trans. Stanford, Calif.: Stanford University Press, 1979. ISBN 0-8047-1036-8 (cl), 0-8047-1029-5 (pbk). ‣ Literary and anecdotal social history. Perhaps too convinced of singularity of Spanish character, but provides thoughtful introduction to cultural attitudes and links literary picaresque to history. [JB]

29.71 Antonio Domínguez Ortiz. *Las clases privilegiadas en el antiguo régimen.* 1973 ed. Madrid: ISTMO, 1985. (Ciclos y temas de la história de España Colleccion Fundamentos, 31.) ISBN 84-7090-019-6 (cl), 84-7090-010-5 (pbk). ‣ Remains best introduction to two privileged orders—nobles and clergy—of Habsburg Spain. Highly readable essay based on broad research. Abridgement of *Sociedad Española en el Siglo XVII.* [JB]

29.72 Antonio Domínguez Ortiz. *Crisis y decadencia de la España de los Austrias.* 1969 ed. Barcelona: Ariel, 1984. ISBN 84-344-1020-6. ‣ Wide-ranging collection of essays including penetrating account of aristocratic conspiracy, 1640s, and anatomy of final crisis of Habsburg era. Selections from works of a master. [JB]

29.73 Antonio Domínguez Ortiz. *Orto y ocaso de Sevilla.* 3d ed. Seville: University of Seville Press, 1981. ISBN 84-7405-193-2. ‣ First major work of great historian. Provides sweeping vision of rise, decline, and recovery of key city of early modern Spain. [JB]

29.74 John H. Elliott. *The count-duke of Olivares: the statesman in an age of decline.* New Haven: Yale University Press, 1986. ISBN 0-300-03390-7. ‣ Finest biography of any figure of Habsburg era, culmination of thirty-year study of Philip IV's prime minister. Overcomes deficiencies of sources, while providing definitive political history. [JB]

29.75 John H. Elliott. *The revolt of the Catalans: a study in the decline of Spain (1598–1640).* 1963 ed. New York: Cambridge University Press, 1984. ISBN 0-521-27890-2 (pbk). ‣ Rich archival study of antecedents, course, and consequences of revolt of 1640; focuses both on internal Catalan developments and relations between principality and central government of Prime Minister Olivares. Essential reading. [JB]

29.76 John H. Elliott. "Revolts in the Spanish monarchy." In *Preconditions of revolution in early modern Europe.* Robert Forster and Jack P. Greene, eds., pp. 109–30. Baltimore: Johns Hopkins University Press, 1970. ISBN 0-8018-1176-7. ‣ Lucid, insightful examination of revolts of 1640s in constituent realms of monarchy. Concludes prospects of success depended on adherence of local elites to rebellion. [JB]

29.77 John H. Elliott. *Spain and its world, 1500–1700: selected essays.* New Haven: Yale University Press, 1989. ISBN 0-300-04217-5. ‣ Very useful collection of author's essays, including seminal analyses of Spanish decline (1961, 1977), treatment of Habsburg court (1987), and splendid examination of Catalan elite (1967). [JB]

29.78 Manuel Fernández Alvarez. *Charles V, elected emperor and hereditary ruler.* J. A. Lalaguna, trans. London: Thames & Hudson, 1975. ISBN 0-500-87001-2. ‣ Good brief biography and survey of reign with emphasis on Charles as king of Spain. [JB]

29.79 J. A. Fernández-Santamaría. *Reason of state and statecraft in Spanish political thought, 1595–1640.* Lanham, Md.: University Press of America, 1983. ISBN 0-8191-3046-X (cl), 0-8191-3047-8 (pbk). ‣ One of few English-language studies on seventeenth-century Spanish political thought. Tends to decontextualize both authors and ideas. [RLK]

29.80 J. A. Fernández-Santamaría. *The state, war, and peace: Spanish political thought in the Renaissance, 1516–1559.* New York: Cambridge University Press, 1977. ISBN 0-521-21438-6. ‣ Best survey of topic. Rigorous intellectual history, ranging widely among imperialists, anti-imperialists, school of Salamanca, Erasmians, humanists, and advisers to rulers. [JB]

29.81 Ellen G. Friedman. *Spanish captives in North Africa in the early modern age.* Madison: University of Wisconsin Press, 1983. ISBN 0-299-09380-8. ‣ Examines "little war" of hostage-taking conducted by Barbary states. Argues this "terrorism" gravely affected Spaniards, keeping them aware of long struggle with Islam. Interesting on captivity and ransoming. [JB]

29.82 David C. Goodman. *Power and penury: government, technology, and science in Philip II's Spain.* New York: Cambridge University Press, 1988. ISBN 0-521-30532-2. ‣ Ranges from occult sciences through development of military technology to medical arts, revising view of Philip II as narrow-minded and Spain as closed society. Original and very impressive. [JB]

29.83 Majorie Grice-Hutchinson. *The school of Salamanca: readings in Spanish monetary theory, 1544–1605.* Oxford: Clarendon, 1952. ‣ Examination of ideas on money, banking, and exchange pioneered by Francisco de Vitoria, Diego de Soto, and other theologians at University of Salamanca. Important for understanding Spanish mercantilism and intellectual reaction to arrival of bullion from Americas. [RLK]

29.84 Stephen Haliczer. *Inquisition and society in the kingdom of Valencia, 1478–1834.* Berkeley: University of California Press, 1990. ISBN 0-520-06729-0. ‣ Carefully researched account of regional tribunal over its long evolution. Holy Office, its goals, and bureaucratic development linked to shifts in Valencian politics and society. [JB]

29.85 Stephen Haliczer, ed. *Inquisition and society in early modern Europe.* London: Croom Helm, 1987. ISBN 0-7099-1263-3. ‣ Uneven but valuable essay collection. Contains noteworthy exploration of popular religion by Nalle and makes available to English reader selections from important work of Jaime Contreras, Virgilio Pinto Crespo, Jean-Pierre Dedieu, and other Inquisition scholars. [JB]

29.86 Alistair Hamilton. *Heresy and mysticism in sixteenth-century Spain: Alumbrados.* Toronto: University of Toronto Press, 1992. ISBN 0-8020-2143-4. ‣ Recent solid introduction to subject for English-language readers. Demonstrates that Inquisitors' definition of *alumbradismo* (illuminism) was broadly defined. [JB]

29.87 Earl J. Hamilton. *American treasure and the price revolution in Spain, 1501–1650.* 1934 ed. New York: AMS Press, 1983. ISBN 0-404-19811-2. ‣ Classic study arguing American treasure was "poison pill" for Spanish economy because of inflationary effects. Interpretations have been challenged but remains valuable for price, wage, and bullion import series. [JB]

29.88 Earl J. Hamilton. "The decline of Spain." *Economic history review,* first series 8.2 (1938) 168–79. ISSN 0013-0117. ‣ Classic statement of economic origins of decline by leading advocate of monetarist interpretation. Began modern debate on Spain's decline. [JB]

29.89 Gustav Henningsen. "The archives and the historiography of the Spanish Inquisition." In *The Inquisition in early modern Europe: studies on sources and methods.* Gustav Henningsen and John A. Tedeschi, eds. Lawrence Scott Rainey, trans., pp. 54–78. Dekalb: Northern Illinois University Press, 1986. ISBN 0-87580-102-1. ‣ Useful survey of location and extent of Inquisitorial documentation with brief analysis of historiography and projection of trends in research. [JB]

29.90 Gustav Henningsen. *The witches' advocate: Basque witchcraft and the Spanish Inquisition, 1609–1614.* Reno: University of Nevada Press, 1980. ISBN 0-87417-056-7. ‣ Interesting examination of Inquisitor's rejection of witch craze. Interpretations sometimes forced but very valuable for account of Inquisitorial procedure and notions of witchcraft. [JB]

29.91 David Howarth. *The voyage of the Armada: the Spanish story.* 1981 ed. New York: Penguin, 1982. ISBN 0-14-006315-5 (pbk). ‣ Fine popular history presenting Enterprise of England from viewpoint of vanquished. Very critical of Philip II but pioneered rehabilitation of Armada's commander Medina Sidonia. [JB]

29.92 Charles Jago. "The 'crisis of the aristocracy' in seventeenth-century Castile." *Past and present* 84 (1979) 60–90. ISSN 0031-2746. ‣ Pioneering examination of liquidity crisis of grandee houses and their strategies for recovery. Their success and state's support crucial to perpetuation of traditional aristocratic society into modern era. [JB]

29.93 Richard L. Kagan. *Lawsuits and litigants in Castile, 1500–1700.* Chapel Hill: University of North Carolina Press, 1981. ISBN 0-8078-1457-1. ‣ Thorough study of contours of litigious society, based largely on records of *chancillería* of Valladolid. Most informative account in English of early modern Spanish legal and judicial system. [JB]

29.94 Richard L. Kagan. *Lucrecia's dreams: politics and prophecy in sixteenth-century Spain.* Berkeley: University of California Press, 1990. ISBN 0-520-06655-3. ‣ Fascinating microhistory informed by psychological theory. Visions of Lucrecia de León, a young *madrileña*, marked rare female intervention in affairs of church and state and left her open to investigation by authorities. [JB]

29.95 Richard L. Kagan. *Students and society in early modern Spain.* Baltimore: Johns Hopkins University Press, 1974. ISBN 0-8018-1583-5. ‣ Education in Habsburg and Bourbon Spain with special emphasis on linkage of universities' growth and decay to changing needs of state. Well researched, fine essay on sources. [JB]

29.96 Richard L. Kagan, ed. *Spanish cities of the golden age: the views of Anton van den Wyngaerde.* Berkeley: University of California Press, 1989. ISBN 0-520-05610-8. ‣ Unique visual portrait of cities of mid-sixteenth-century Spain. Essays on artistic tastes of Philip II, urban planning, and development. Lavishly illustrated and produced. [JB]

29.97 Henry Kamen. "The decline of Spain: a historical myth?" *Past and present* 81 (1978) 24–50. ISSN 0031-2746. ‣ Original if eccentric contribution to decline debate. Spain always economically dependent and never had true rise, thus did not really decline. Problematic thesis, but retains value in demonstrating structural economic weaknesses. [JB]

29.98 Henry Kamen. *Inquisition and society in Spain in the sixteenth and seventeenth centuries.* Bloomington: Indiana University Press, 1985. ISBN 0-253-33015-7 (cl), 0-253-22775-5 (pbk). ‣ Best modern English-language survey of Holy Office. Author recants earlier Marxist interpretation and moves toward controversial idea that Inquisition enjoyed consensus support among Christian Spaniards. Readable and wide ranging. [JB]

29.99 Henry Kamen. *Spain in the later seventeenth century, 1665–1700.* New York: Longman, 1980. ISBN 0-582-49036-7 (cl), 0-582-49037-5 (pbk). ‣ Best survey of era of Charles II. Combines original research with synthesis in examination of politics, society, and economy. Argues seeds of eighteenth-century change sown in maligned era. [JB]

29.100 Hayward Keniston. *Francisco de los Cobos, secretary of the emperor Charles V.* Pittsburgh: University of Pittsburgh Press, 1960. ‣ Detailed view of mechanics of Spanish administration under Charles V, but not very analytical. Also interesting for rise and character of ambitious and talented Cobos. [JB]

29.101 Julius Klein. *The mesta: a study in Spanish economic history, 1273–1836.* 1920 ed. Port Washington, N.Y.: Kennikat, 1964. ‣ Classic study arguing royal protection of pastoral agriculture, in form of privileges accorded to shipowners' association (*mesta*), harmed arable farming and contributed to economic decline. [JB]

29.102 H. G. Koenigsberger. "National consciousness in early modern Spain." In *Politicians and virtuosi: essays in early modern history.* , pp. 121–47. Ronceverte, W.V.: Hambledon, 1986. ISBN

0-907628-65-6. ▸ Clear, concise analysis concluding Spanish nationalism per se did not emerge until Napoleonic period. Finds instead a certain kind of intellectual nationalism, unifying as well as divisive religious sentiments, and growing Castilian nationalism in Habsburg era. [JB]

29.103 H. G. Koenigsberger. *The practice of empire.* Rev. ed. Batista I. Roca, Introduction. Ithaca, N.Y.: Cornell University Press, 1969. ISBN 0-8014-0502-5. ▸ Case study of imperial administration and viceregal government. Important contribution to neglected field of Spanish Italy. Excellent introduction on Spanish system of conciliar government. Earlier title: *The Government of Sicily under Philip II of Spain.* [JB]

29.104 H. G. Koenigsberger. "The statecraft of Philip II." *European studies review* 1.1 (1971) 1–21. ISSN 0014-3111. ▸ Lucid, concise analysis of Philip's government and his priorities as ruler. Indispensable for understanding king and assessing his successes and failures. [JB]

29.105 George Kubler. *Building the Escorial.* Princeton: Princeton University Press, 1982. ISBN 0-691-03975-5. ▸ Technical narrative of design and construction of Philip II's great monument. Revealing look at construction trades and costs. Well illustrated. [JB]

29.106 Henry Charles Lea. *A history of the Inquisition of Spain.* 1906–07 ed. 4 vols. New York: AMS Press, 1988. ISBN 0-404-03920-0 (set). ▸ Remains treasury of information, despite whig-Protestant bias. Wide-ranging research presented in lively style. Conclusion to volume 4 provides classic statement of culturally stunting effects of Inquisition. [JB]

29.107 A. W. Lovett. *Philip II and Mateo Vázquez de Leca: the government of Spain (1572–1592).* Geneva: Droz, 1977. ▸ Detailed, archive-based study focusing on career of important royal secretary. Few general conclusions but insights into workings of Spanish government, formation of policy, etc. [RLK]

29.108 A. W. Lovett. "Philip II, Antonio Pérez, and the kingdom of Aragon." *European history quarterly* 18 (1988) 131–53. ISSN 0014-3111. ▸ Good brief account of conflict over regional liberties provoked by royal secretary Pérez's flight from imprisonment, 1590. Concludes Aragonese aristocracy hesitated while central government acted swiftly and surely to isolate revolt. [JB]

29.109 Nina A. Mallory. *El Greco to Murillo: Spanish painting in the golden age, 1556–1700.* New York: HarperCollins, 1990. ISBN 0-06-435531-4 (cl), 0-06-430195-8 (pbk). ▸ Good brief survey of painting; aesthetic rather than historical emphasis. Illustrated. [JB]

29.110 William S. Maltby. *Alba: a biography of Fernando Alvarez de Toledo, third duke of Alba, 1507–1582.* Berkeley: University of California Press, 1983. ISBN 0-520-04694-3. ▸ Good account of first phase of Dutch revolt and Spanish response. Strongest on duke's military career; favorable assessment restoring Alba's reputation. [JB]

29.111 Gregorio Marañon. *Antonio Pérez, "Spanish traitor."* Charles David Ley, trans. New York: Roy, 1955. ▸ Condensed English-language version of classic (1947) study of Philip II's renegade secretary. Insights into monarch's character, court society, and political uses of Inquisition. [RLK]

29.112 José Antonio Maravall. *Culture of the baroque: analysis of a historical structure.* Terry Cochran, trans. Minneapolis: University of Minnesota Press, 1986. ISBN 0-8166-1443-1. ▸ Argues Spanish and general baroque culture characterized by modernization directed toward social control and defense of traditional order. Translation exacerbates difficulty of original, but author deserves English readership. [JB]

29.113 Antonio Márquez. *Literatura e Inquisición en España.* Madrid: Taurus, 1980. ISBN 84-306-2124-5. ▸ Study of Inquisi-

torial censorship of literature with eye to resolving long debate over its cultural effects. Periodizes and clarifies extent of censorship using quantitative techniques. Valuable appendixes. [JB]

29.114 Colin Martin and Geoffrey Parker. *The Spanish Armada.* New York: Norton, 1988. ISBN 0-393-02607-8. ▸ Richly illustrated account of famous sea battle. Good on military and political context. Incorporates new and somewhat controversial archaeological information on Spanish gunnery. [RLK]

29.115 Linda Martz. *Poverty and welfare in Habsburg Spain: the example of Toledo.* New York: Cambridge University Press, 1983. ISBN 0-521-23952-4. ▸ Theory and legislation of poor relief in Castile. Discusses charitable institutions of Toledo using Pullan's model in study of Venice (28.116). Relief incapable of halting deterioration of conditions for poor. Thorough archival study. [JB]

29.116 Garrett Mattingly. *The Armada.* 1959 ed. Boston: Houghton-Mifflin, 1988. ISBN 0-395-08366-4 (pbk). ▸ Marvelous narrative history with somewhat whiggish slant. Fine explanation of interrelated conflicts in northwestern Europe, 1587–89. Supremely readable. [JB]

29.117 Malveena McKendrick. *Theatre in Spain, 1490–1700.* Cambridge: Cambridge University Press, 1989. ISBN 0-521-35592-3. ▸ Sweeping coverage of various aspects of rise of Spain's national theater: commercial theater, court drama, religious *autos*, etc. Emphasis on seventeenth-century *comedia.* Good bibliography. [RLK]

29.118 E. William Monter. *Frontiers of heresy: the Spanish Inquisition from the Basque lands to Sicily.* New York: Cambridge University Press, 1990. ISBN 0-521-37468-5. ▸ Interesting view of Holy Office operating outside Castile. Concludes Inquisition effective agent of royal authority in crown of Aragon. [JB]

29.119 Helen Nader. *Liberty in absolutist Spain: the Habsburg sale of towns, 1516–1700.* Baltimore: Johns Hopkins University Press, 1990. ISBN 0-8018-3850-9. ▸ Much broader than subtitle would indicate. Thorough examination of relations between crown and municipalities, making compelling case for decentralization as basis of Habsburg absolutism. Conclusions on significance of municipal governments important for colonialists. [JB/MAB]

29.120 Sara Nalle. *God in La Mancha: religious reform and the people of Cuenca, 1500–1650.* Baltimore: Johns Hopkins University Press, 1992. ISBN 0-8018-4384-7. ▸ Superb diocesan-level study detailing nature and progress of ecclesiastical reform during Counter-Reformation. Analyzes clerical education, devotional practices, masses, etc. [RLK]

29.121 Sara Nalle. "Literacy and culture in early modern Castile." *Past and present* 125 (1989) 65–96. ISSN 0031-2746. ▸ Analysis, based on archival sources for Cuenca, of literacy, growth of reading public, book market, attempts to control popular reading. Sees general expansion in sixteenth century and retrenchment in seventeenth. [JB]

29.122 Benzion Netanyahu. *The marranos of Spain from the late fourteenth to the early sixteenth century, according to contemporary Hebrew sources.* 1966 2d ed. Millwood, N.Y.: American Academy for Jewish Research and Kraus, 1973. ▸ Concludes, on basis of study of contemporary rabbinical responsa literature, New Christians were overwhelmingly sincere converts. Implies Inquisitorial persecution motivated by antisemitism, not fear of apostasy. Compare Baer 29.53. [JB]

29.123 Steven N. Orso. *Philip IV and the decoration of the alcázar of Madrid.* Princeton: Princeton University Press, 1986. ISBN 0-691-04036-2. ▸ Technical art history illuminates representation of Philip IV (1621–1665), known as the Planet King. Very readable and well illustrated. [JB]

29.124 Geoffrey Parker. *The army of Flanders and the Spanish road, 1567–1659: the logistics of Spanish victory and defeat in the Low Countries' wars.* Cambridge: Cambridge University Press, 1972. ISBN 0-521-08462-8. ▸ Masterly military and administrative history, focusing on difficulties of fighting long war at great distance. Concretely demonstrates that finances are sinews of war. Excellent analysis of mutinies. [JB]

29.125 Geoffrey Parker. *The Dutch revolt.* Ithaca, N.Y.: Cornell University Press, 1977. ISBN 0-8014-1136-x. ▸ Study of revolt largely from Habsburg perspective. Sound narrative; revises whig-Protestant bias of earlier English-language works. [JB]

29.126 Geoffrey Parker. *Philip II.* Boston: Little, Brown, 1978. ISBN 0-316-69080-5. ▸ Best recent biography. Generally sympathetic, takes pains to refute traditional Protestant interpretation of Philip as vicious zealot. Uneven coverage of narrative history of reign; lacks scholarly apparatus. [JB]

29.127 Geoffrey Parker. "Spain, her enemies, and the Revolt of the Netherlands, 1559–1648." *Past and present* 49 (1970) 72–95. ISSN 0031-2746. ▸ Relates progress of suppressing revolt to Habsburg finances and priorities. Fear of France and defense of Mediterranean both outweighed Netherlands in Spanish calculations. [JB]

29.128 Mary Elizabeth Perry. *Crime and society in early modern Seville.* Hanover, N.H.: University Press of New England, 1980. ISBN 0-87451-177-1. ▸ Readable depiction of Sevillian underworld, its relations with legitimate society and civil authority, drawing on archival and literary sources. Analysis of deviance informed by structuralism. [JB]

29.129 Mary Elizabeth Perry. *Gender and disorder in early modern Seville.* Princeton: Princeton University Press, 1990. ISBN 0-691-03143-6 (cl), 0-691-00854-x (pbk). ▸ Examination of broad range of female experience in Habsburg Seville; best such study available in English. Weakened by thesis asserting tightening of social control without sufficient proof. [JB]

29.130 Carla Rahn Phillips. *Ciudad Real, 1500–1750: growth, crisis, and readjustment in the Spanish economy.* Cambridge, Mass.: Harvard University Press, 1979. ISBN 0-674-13285-8. ▸ Concise quantitative study of medium-sized city, tracing its adjustments to prosperity and economic deterioration. Model local monograph. [JB]

29.131 Carla Rahn Phillips. *Six galleons for the king of Spain: imperial defense in the early seventeenth century.* Baltimore: Johns Hopkins University Press, 1986. ISBN 0-8018-3092-3. ▸ Vivid archival study of shipbuilding, logistics of naval defense, and grave problems and long-term success of effort to defend Spanish Atlantic empire. Fine grounding of general thesis in painstaking research. [JB/MAB]

29.132 Carla Rahn Phillips. "Time and duration: a model for the economy of early modern Spain." *American historical review* 92.3 (1987) 531–62. ISSN 0002-8762. ▸ Provocative neo-Malthusian analysis, synthesizing local studies, of differential regional economic evolution, ca. 1550–1700. Tends to diminish role of government in decline. [JB]

29.133 Peter Pierson. *Commander of the Armada: the seventh duke of Medina Sidonia.* New Haven: Yale University Press, 1989. ISBN 0-300-04408-9. ▸ Biography focusing on Armada campaign with positive assessment of Medina Sidonia's conduct. Includes interesting brief account of finances and strategies of aristocratic house. [JB]

29.134 Peter Pierson. *Philip II of Spain.* London: Thames & Hudson, 1975. ISBN 0-500-87003-9. ▸ Useful life-and-times study based on wide secondary reading. For context of reign, better than Parker 29.126, but lacks Parker's feel for king's character. [JB]

29.135 Ruth Pike. *Aristocrats and traders: Sevillian society in the sixteenth century.* Ithaca, N.Y.: Cornell University Press, 1972. ISBN 0-8014-0699-4. ▸ Readable survey of society highs and lows based on archival and literary sources. Emphasizes heterogeneity of Sevillian society in expansive sixteenth century. [JB]

29.136 Virgilio Pinto Crespo. *Inquisición y control ideológico en la España del siglo XVI.* Madrid: Taurus, 1983. ISBN 84-306-3509-2. ▸ Elaboration of Inquisitorial censorship during sixteenth century; apparatus carefully described on basis of extensive research. Concludes censorship key to reduced intellectual effervescence of late century. [JB]

29.137 Leopold von Ranke. *The Ottoman and the Spanish empires in the sixteenth and seventeenth centuries.* 1843 ed. Walter K. Kelly, trans. New York: AMS Press, 1975. ISBN 0-404-09266-7. ▸ Pithy, detailed account of administration and court rivalries under Charles V, Philip II, and Philip III, based on Venetian ambassadors' reports. Comparative dimension unsuccessful, but foreshadows Braudel's study of Mediterranean (22.58). [JB]

29.138 Joan Reglà. "La España de los Austrias." In *Historia de España y América, social y económica.* Vol. 3: *Los Austrias.* 1961 ed. 5 vols. Jaime Vicens Vives, ed., pp. 1–317. Barcelona: Vicens-Vives, 1982. ISBN 84-316-1864-7. ▸ Partly outdated but remains worthy introduction to social and economic history of Habsburg era. This entry and entire series a great achievement of Catalan-annalist school of Vicens. [JB]

29.139 David Sven Reher. *Town and country in pre-industrial Spain: Cuenca, 1550–1870.* New York: Cambridge University Press, 1990. ISBN 0-521-35292-4. ▸ Technical demographic study underscoring urban-rural interdependence. Provides graphic demonstration of Castilian urban economic crisis, decline, and long stagnation. [JB]

29.140 David R. Ringrose. *Madrid and the Spanish economy, 1560–1850.* Berkeley: University of California Press, 1983. ISBN 0-520-04311-1. ▸ Skillful, readable economic history examining deforming effects of Madrid's growth on Castilian and Spanish economy. Ambitious, convincing analysis of multiple variables, expertly informed by theory. [JB]

29.141 M. J. Rodríguez-Salgado. *The changing face of empire: Charles V, Philip II, and Habsburg authority, 1551–1559.* New York: Cambridge University Press, 1988. ISBN 0-521-30346-X. ▸ Detailed study of diplomatic and financial situation during transition between reigns. Difficult reading but worthwhile for grasp of causes of Philip's financial problems and Dutch revolt. [JB]

29.142 M. J. Rodríguez-Salgado. "The court of Philip II of Spain." In *Princes, patronage, and the nobility: the court at the beginning of the modern age, c. 1450–1650.* Ronald G. Asch and Adolf M. Birke, eds., pp. 205–44. New York: German Historical Institute and Oxford University Press, 1991. ISBN 0-19-920502-7. ▸ Examination of organization of court and ceremonial evolution during Philip's reign. Good on king's work habits and mechanics of transaction of business. [JB]

29.143 John C. Rule and John J. TePaske, eds. *The character of Philip II: the problem of moral judgments in history.* Boston: Heath, 1963. ▸ Excerpts, translated when necessary, from sixteenth- to twentieth-century appraisals of Philip II. Illustrates full range of opinion, from prudent king to Motley's "incarnation of evil." [JB]

29.144 Noël Salomon. *La vida rural castellana en tiempos de Felipe II.* Francesc Espinet Burunat, trans. Barcelona: Ariel, 1982. ISBN 84-344-6540-X. ▸ Study of new Castilian peasantry, seigneurial regime, and agricultural system as abstracted from Philip II's *Relaciones Topográficas* of 1570s. Laden with information and valuable tabular data. [JB]

29.145 Ernst Schafer. *El consejo real y supremo de las Indias: su historia, organización, y labor administrativa hasta la terminación* *de la casa de Austria.* Seville: Carmona, 1936. ▸ Traditional, detailed, systematic, institutional study; old but remains best account of components of Habsburg conciliar system. [JB]

29.146   Henry Seaver. *The great revolt in Castile: a study of the comunero movement of 1520–1521.* 1928 ed. New York: Houghton-Mifflin, 1966. ▸ Narrative history of old school, hardly analytical but gripping and still useful as basic account of revolt and its immediate causes. [JB]

29.147   Albert A. Sicroff. *Les controverses des statuts de pureté de sang en Espagne du quinzième au dix-septième siècle.* 1960 ed. Madrid: Taurus, 1985. ▸ Study of origins, elaboration, reform, and persistence of statutes and obsession with *limpieza de sangre* (purity of blood) in early modern Spain. Demonstrates conversion of religious differences between Christians and Jews into racial divisions. [JB]

29.148   R. A. Stradling. *Philip IV and the government of Spain, 1621–1665.* New York: Cambridge University Press, 1988. ISBN 0-521-32333-9. ▸ Important political study of entire reign, presenting favorably revised view of Philip's energies and interest in government. Does not take account of Elliott 29.74, but remains best work on reign post-1643. [JB]

29.149   R. A. Stradling. "Seventeenth-century Spain: decline or survival?" *European studies review* 9 (1979) 157–94. ISSN 0014-3111. ▸ Argues against simple equation of economic with political decline. Despite mounting structural weaknesses, Spain remained European power until 1660s. Administration effectively marshalled dwindling resources. [JB]

29.150   I.A.A. Thompson. "Crown and Córtes in Castile, 1590–1665." *Parliaments, estates, and representation* 2.1 (1982) 29–45. ISSN 0260-6755. ▸ Shrewd article, sees waning of Córtes (parliament) in late seventeenth century as indication of decentralization and municipal strength rather than of enhanced absolutism. Rare insight into mechanics of Castilian internal administration. [JB]

29.151   I.A.A. Thompson. *War and government in Habsburg Spain, 1560–1620.* London: Athlone, 1976. ISBN 0-485-11166-7. ▸ Well-crafted, underappreciated study of organization and administration of Habsburg military machine. Revealing look at more general problems of governmental administration in period. Extensively researched. [JB]

29.152   Modesto Ulloa. *La hacienda real de Castilla en el reinado de Felipe II.* 3d rev. ed. Madrid: Fundación Universitaria Española, Seminario "Cisneros," 1986. ISBN 84-7392-019-8. ▸ Monumental archival study of Castilian treasury, indispensable for understanding underpinnings and consequences of Philip's policies. Systematic, sometimes tedious, but grand accomplishment. [JB]

29.153   David Vassberg. *Land and society in golden-age Castile.* New York: Cambridge University Press, 1984. ISBN 0-521-25470-1. ▸ Original archival study of land ownership and use in sixteenth century. Argues Castilian agriculture adjusted to keep pace with growth until late sixteenth century; marginal land failures then hastened decline. [JB]

29.154   Pierre Vilar. "The age of Don Quixote." In *Essays in European economic history, 1500–1800.* Peter Earle, ed., pp. 100–12. Oxford: Clarendon, 1974. ISBN 0-19-877054-5. ▸ Vivid essay on Spain in decline. Marxist vision of empire as supreme stage of feudalism, society out of its proper time. Evocative. [JB]

29.155   Barbara Von Barghahn. *Age of gold, age of iron: Renaissance Spain and symbols of monarchy, the imperial legacy of Charles V and Philip II, royal castles, palace-monasteries, princely houses.* 2 vols. Lanham, Md.: University Press of America, 1985. ISBN 0-8191-4739-7. ▸ Technical account of royal monuments and representations of majesty within them. Greatest value lies in

plates of volume 2. Unfortunately, reproductions sometimes of poor quality. [JB]

29.156   Michael R. Weisser. *The peasants of the Montes: the roots of rural rebellion in Spain.* Chicago: University of Chicago Press, 1976. ISBN 0-226-89158-5. ▸ Fascinating, well-researched social history of peasant communities in region of Toledo. Valiant attempt to link sixteenth-century conditions to twentieth-century peasant anarchism. [JB]

29.157   Patrick Williams. "El reinado de Felipe III." In *La crisis de la hegemonía española, siglo XVII.* José Andrés-Gallego, ed., pp. 419–43. Madrid: Rialp, 1981. ISBN 84-249-1452- X. ▸ Brief but most satisfactory recent account of reign. [JB]

29.158   Frances A. Yates. "Charles V and the idea of the empire." In *Astraea: the imperial theme in the sixteenth century,* pp. 1–28. Boston: Ark, 1985. ISBN 0-7448-0025-0 (pbk). ▸ Brilliant sketch of ideas that shaped imperial aims and propaganda of Charles V with analysis of iconography and regalia of his reign. [JB]

SEE ALSO
  18.190 Andrew C. Hess. *The forgotten frontier.*
  27.63 Jonathan I. Israel. *The Dutch republic and the Hispanic world, 1606–1661.*

Bourbon Monarchy, 1700–1808

29.159   George M. Addy. *The Enlightenment in the University of Salamanca.* Durham, N.C.: Duke University Press, 1966. ▸ Charts course of Salamanca's struggle with reform in eighteenth century and measures degree of success until War of Independence. Important work on Enlightenment in Spain. [SHB]

29.160   A. Owen Aldridge, ed. *The Ibero-American Enlightenment.* Urbana: University of Illinois Press, 1971. ISBN 0-252-00122-2. ▸ Fourteen essays illustrating common trends in spread of Enlightenment in Iberian peninsula and North and South America. Suggests movement transcended national boundaries. [SHB/MAB]

29.161   Jacques A. Barbier. "The culmination of the Bourbon reforms, 1787–1792." *Hispanic American historical review* 57.1 (1977) 51–68. ISSN 0018-2168. ▸ Valuable contribution reassessing colonial administration immediately after death of imperialist minister José de Gálvez and abolition of Ministry of the Indies. Perceptive analysis. Debate follows in *Hispanic American Historical Review* 58 (1978) 33–39, 447–80. [SHB/MAB]

29.162   Jacques A. Barbier. "Peninsular finance and colonial trade: the dilemma of Charles IV's Spain." *Journal of Latin American studies* 12.1 (1980) 21–37. ISSN 0022-216X. ▸ Examination of administrative policies with respect to colonial revenues. Concludes toward end of Charles IV's reign, official policy did not consider colonies sources for peninsular economic development; surrendered imperial trade into hands of multinational interests in effort to avoid bankruptcy. Informative, persuasive analysis. [SHB/MAB]

29.163   Jacques A. Barbier and Herbert S. Klein. "Revolutionary wars and public finances: the Madrid Treasury, 1784–1807." *Journal of economic history* 41 (1981) 315–339. ISSN 0022-0507. ▸ Important study of Madrid Treasury demonstrating that during wartime, crown, unwilling to restructure tax base, relied heavily on borrowing. Provides background to changing government policies. [SHB]

29.164   J. F. Bourgoing. *The modern state of Spain.* 4 vols. London: For J. Stockdale, 1808. ▸ Observations of French diplomat. Detailed, colorful account with illustrations. [SHB]

29.165   Vera Lee Brown [Holmes]. "Studies in the history of Spain in the second half of the eighteenth century." *Smith College* *studies in history* 15.1–2 (1929–30) 3–92. ‣ Topics include diplomatic outlook of Spanish court after 1763. Good on Anglo-French rivalry for Spanish trade, 1763–83, and relations between Spain and Portugal, 1763–77. [SHB]

29.166 Michael E. Burke. *The Royal College of San Carlos: surgery and Spanish medical reform in the late eighteenth century.* Durham, N.C.: Duke University Press, 1977. ISBN 0-8223-0382-5. ‣ Important study of institution that established modern medicine and surgery in Spain. Illustrates challenges and dilemmas facing reformers during Enlightenment. [SHB]

29.167 William J. Callahan. *Honor, commerce, and industry in eighteenth-century Spain.* Boston: Harvard Graduate School of Business Administration, 1972. ‣ Argues campaign to elevate social esteem of commerce and manufactures was conservative effort and did not significantly change traditional hierarchical order. Important study challenging widely accepted interpretation. [SHB]

29.168 William J. Callahan. "A note on the Real y General Junta de Comercio." *Economic history review* 21.3 (1968) 519–28. ‣ Brief, balanced assessment of *junta's* performance. Assesses strength and weakness as government institution responsible, in part, for economic policy. Points out unjustified criticism of performance. [SHB]

29.169 William J. Callahan. "The Spanish church." In *Church and society in Catholic Europe in the eighteenth century.* William J. Callahan and David Higgs, eds., pp. 34–50. Cambridge: Cambridge University Press, 1979. ISBN 0-521-22424-1. ‣ Traces origins of Spanish church's problems in modern Spain. As position within society eroded, church became increasingly defensive and developed theocratic view of its role in society. [SHB]

29.170 Raymond Carr. "Spain." In *The European nobility in the eighteenth century: studies of the nobilities of the major European states in the pre-reform era.* Albert Goodwin, ed., pp. 43–59. New York: Harper & Row, 1967. ‣ Valuable introductory examination of political, economic, and social power and privileges of grandees, titled and untitled nobility. Includes their attitudes and those of foreigners who observed them. [SHB]

29.171 Antonio Domínguez Ortiz. *Hechos y figuras del siglo XVIII español.* 2d ed. Madrid: Siglo Ventiuno de España, 1980. ‣ Valuable collection of brief essays on end of *señorial* regime, views and efforts of some enlightened individuals, and reflections on "two Spains." [SHB]

29.172 Antonio Domínguez Ortiz. *Sociedad y estado en el siglo XVIII español.* Barcelona: Ariel, 1976. ISBN 84-344-6509-4. ‣ Superb analysis of Spanish society in eighteenth century with valuable section on geography, economy, and society of various regions. [SHB]

29.173 Iris H. W. Engstrand. "The Enlightenment in Spain: influences upon New World policy." *The Americas* 41.4 (1985) 436–44. ISSN 0003-1615. ‣ Effects of Enlightenment include changing role of missionary orders, ideas of various ministers, goals of José de Gálvez, and policies of Charles III and viceroys during California's settlement. [SHB]

29.174 John R. Fisher. *Commercial relations between Spain and Spanish America in the era of free trade, 1778–1796.* Liverpool: University of Liverpool, Centre of Latin-American Studies, 1985. (Monograph series, 13.) ISBN 0-902806-11-2 (cl), 0-902806-12-2 (pbk). ‣ Meticulous, infomative analysis of value, distribution, and nature of legal trade between Spain and Spanish America based on ships' registers. Discusses impact of free trade on respective economies: Spanish America benefited more than Spain. [SHB/MAB]

29.175 A. David Francis. *The first Peninsular War, 1702–1713.* New York: St. Martin's, 1975. ‣ Thorough military account of peninsular campaigns from British point of view. Coherent and factual with strict adherence to primary sources. [SHB]

29.176 Earl J. Hamilton. *War and prices in Spain, 1651–1800.* 1947 ed. New York: Russell & Russell, 1969. ‣ Classic study of impact of war on commodity prices and price-wage ratio's role in economic decay, recovery, and inflation. Presents fundamental statistics for students of Spanish economic history. [SHB]

29.177 Simon Harcourt-Smith. *Cardinal of Spain: the life and strange career of Alberoni.* New York: Knopf, 1944. ‣ Lively and colorful account of Giulio Alberoni, cardinal and royal favorite who directed Spanish policy from 1715 to 1719. Severely criticizes British for spurning offer of friendship. [SHB]

29.178 W. N. Hargreaves-Mawdsley, comp. *Spain under the Bourbons, 1700–1833: a collection of documents.* Columbia: University of South Carolina Press, 1973. ISBN 0-87249-289-3 (cl), 0-87249-200-7 (pbk). ‣ English translations of important state documents relating primarily to diplomatic and political matters. [RLK]

29.179 Richard Herr. *The eighteenth-century revolution in Spain.* Princeton: Princeton University Press, 1958. ‣ Excellent analysis of eighteenth-century Spain. Traces effects of Enlightenment and French Revolution on political and religious attitudes. Attributes origins of "two Spains" to opposing political ideologies, disputes over agrarian reform, and unequal economic development. [SHB]

29.180 Richard Herr. *Rural change and royal finances at the end of the Old Regime.* Berkeley: University of California Press, 1989. ISBN 0-520-05948-4. ‣ Comprehensive, superb study of disentailment during reign of Charles IV. Challenges view that disentailment spelled economic disaster and Spain was experiencing bourgeois revolution. [SHB]

29.181 Douglas Hilt. *The troubled trinity: Godoy and the Spanish monarchs.* Tuscaloosa: University of Alabama Press, 1987. ISBN 0-8173-0320-0. ‣ Manuel Godoy portrayed as enlightened minister who tried and failed to reconcile liberal reform and conservative tradition in Spain. Based on personal correspondence and Godoy's own recollections. [SHB/AS]

29.182 Anthony Hull. *Charles III and the revival of Spain.* Washington, D.C.: University Press of America, 1980. ISBN 0-8191-1021-3 (cl), 0-8191-1022-1 (pbk). ‣ Portrayal of Charles III as great king with only one defect: passion for hunting. All other aspects interpreted in positive light. Biography set in historical context. [SHB]

29.183 Henry Kamen. "Melchor de Macanaz and the foundations of Bourbon power in Spain." *English historical review* 80.317 (1965) 699–716. ISSN 0013-8266. ‣ Portrayed as Spain's first great reformer. Revolutionary changes at beginning of Bourbon era attributable to him and other Spanish ministers, not French influence. [SHB]

29.184 Henry Kamen. *The War of Succession in Spain, 1700–1715.* Bloomington: Indiana University Press, 1969. ISBN 0-253-19025-8. ‣ Best comprehensive treatment of War of Succession. Impact of war on Spain regenerative, enhancing state power; improvement over Habsburg Spain. Excellent analysis of Philip V's early years. [SHB]

29.185 Charles E. Kany. *Life and manners in Madrid, 1750–1800.* 1932 ed. New York: AMS Press, 1985. ISBN 0-404-03634-1. ‣ Lively, well-illustrated account based on plays of Don Ramón de la Cruz, travelers' accounts, and municipal records. Readable classic account of many aspects of urban life. [SHB]

29.186 James C. La Force. *The development of the Spanish textile industry, 1750–1800.* Berkeley: University of California Press, 1965. ‣ Valuable study of royal efforts to restore economic vitality to Spain by developing textile industry. Explanations of failure and Spain's geographic and systemic barriers to economic transformation. [SHB]

29.187 Massimo Livi-Bacci. "Fertility and nuptiality changes in Spain from the late eighteenth to the early twentieth century." *Population studies* 22.1,2 (1968) 83–102, 211–34. ISSN 0032-4728. ▸ Detailed, demographic study of Spanish marriage patterns and population growth, using figures drawn from eighteenth-century census. Concludes fertility rates low in this preindustrial country. [SHB]

29.188 Jean O. McLachlan. *Trade and peace with Old Spain, 1667–1750.* 1940 ed. New York: Octagon Books, 1974. ISBN 0-374-95520-4. ▸ Study of relationship between commerce and diplomacy in England and Spain. Analyzes importance of colonial trading interests compared to those of other merchants. [SHB]

29.189 C. C. Noel. "Opposition to Enlightened reform in Spain: Campomanes and the clergy, 1765–1775." *Societas* 3.1 (1973) 21–43. ▸ Argues significant opposition to Enlightened reform manifested itself in political and ecclesiastical conflicts under Charles III. Clerics, aristocrats, and bureaucrats united in opposition under church banner. [SHB]

29.190 J.H.R. Polt. *Gaspar Melchor de Jovellanos.* Gerald E. Wade, ed. New York: Twayne, 1971. ▸ Brief biographical sketch with examination of principal works and theories. First general study of Enlightenment reformer in English. Also discusses later impact of pedagogical theories and works on economics. [SHB]

29.191 David R. Ringrose. *Transportation and economic stagnation in Spain, 1750–1850.* 1970 ed. Berkeley: University of California Press, 1983. ISBN 0-520-04311-1. ▸ Focus on geographic barriers and transportation bottlenecks as causes of social and economic stagnation in Spain's interior. Economic backwardness linked to institutional failure to solve transport problems. Valuable contribution. [SHB]

29.192 Laura Rodríguez. "The Spanish riots of 1766." *Past and present* 59 (1973) 117–46. ISSN 0031-2746. ▸ Important description and analysis of riots, rare events in Spain. Good comparison with Old Regime riots elsewhere in Europe. Includes socioeconomic background of rioters and local and national response. [SHB]

29.193 Peter Sahlins. *Boundaries: the making of France and Spain in the Pyrenees.* Berkeley: University of California Press, 1989. ISBN 0-520-06538-7. ▸ Fascinating study of state building and making of political boundary between France and Spain. Focuses on Cerdanya valley, 1649–1868. Important for social history of Catalonia. Argues local villages and communities played major role, and villagers adopted national identities as part of local struggles. [RLK/AS]

29.194 Jean Sarrailh. *La España ilustrada de la segunda mitad del siglo XVIII.* Antonio Alatorre, trans. Mexico City: Fondo de Cultura Económica, 1957. ▸ Classic study of Enlightenment in Spain. Examined against panorama of social, economic, and cultural stagnation, analyzes efforts of individuals and groups (economic societies) to implement reform in their country. [SHB]

29.195 Robert Jones Shafer. *The economic societies in the Spanish world, 1763–1821.* Syracuse, N. Y.: Syracuse University Press, 1958. ▸ Although primarily concerned with America, first six chapters constitute valuable contribution on economic societies in Spain. Describes history, policies, and activities. [SHB]

29.196 Joan Sherwood. *Poverty in eighteenth-century Spain: the women and children of the Inclusa.* Toronto: University of Toronto Press, 1988. ISBN 0-8020-2662-1. ▸ Study of foundling hospital in Madrid providing outlet for poor who could not afford to feed children. Suggests institutional infanticide despite enlightened efforts to deal with abandonment of children. [SHB]

29.197 Robert S. Smith. "English economic thought in Spain, 1776–1848." *South Atlantic quarterly* 67.2 (1968) 306–37. ▸ Traces transmission of ideas through translations (especially French) of English writings, original works in Spanish indicating British influence, and texts for formal courses in economics. [SHB]

29.198 Janis A. Tomlinson. *Goya and the twilight of the Enlightenment.* New Haven: Yale University Press, 1992. ISBN 0-300-05462-9. ▸ Important revisionist study setting artist within historical and intellectual—as well as artistic—context of late eighteenth-century Madrid. Excellent bibliography. [RLK]

29.199 Joseph Townsend. *A journey through Spain and Portugal in the years 1786 and 1787.* London: Dilly, 1791. ▸ Detailed account with vivid images of towns, people, customs, buildings, agricultural practices, medical practices, etc., by minister and son of London merchant. [SHB]

29.200 Geoffrey J. Walker. *Spanish politics and imperial trade, 1700–1789.* Bloomington: Indiana University Press, 1979. ISBN 0-253-12150-7. ▸ Useful examination of Spain's struggle to maintain its monopolistic hold on New World and colonial trade and colonists' role in policy making. Unprecedented study of colonial trade, primarily 1700–40. [SHB/MAB]

MODERN SPAIN, 1800–1992

General Studies

29.201 Ruth Behar. *Santa María del Monte: the presence of the past in a Spanish village.* Princeton: Princeton University Press, 1986. ISBN 0-691-09419-5. ▸ Intellectually ambitious study of village in province of León combining historical and ethnographic approaches. Focus on persistence of longstanding patterns of family and community life. [AS]

29.202 Gerald Brenan. *The Spanish labyrinth: an account of the social and political background of the Civil War.* 1960 ed. New York: Cambridge University Press, 1990. ▸ Classic study of Spanish history from 1874 to outbreak of Civil War. Sees Spain as different from other European countries and portrays Civil War as explosion of economic and social tensions which had been building for many years. [AS]

29.203 James W. Cortada, ed. *Spain in the twentieth-century world: essays on Spanish diplomacy, 1898–1978.* Westport, Conn.: Greenwood, 1980. ISBN 0-313-21326-7. ▸ Useful collection of essays on aspects of Spain's foreign relations in twentieth century showing how Spain still influences most regions of world. [AS]

29.204 Marianne Heiberg. *The making of the Basque nation.* New York: Cambridge University Press, 1989. ISBN 0-521-36103-6. ▸ Study of Basque nationalism in nineteenth and twentieth centuries and how it created Basque nation. Argues ethnic nationalism emerged where main alternative strategy, patron-client relationships, weak. [AS]

29.205 Frances Lannon. *Privilege, persecution, and prophecy: the Catholic church in Spain, 1875–1975.* Oxford: Clarendon, 1987. ISBN 0-19-821923-7. ▸ Superb study of Catholic life and politics in Spain from Restoration to end of Franco regime. Emphasizes internal structures and tensions of Catholicism and many regional variations. [AS]

29.206 Benjamin Martin. *The agony of modernization: labor and industrialization in Spain.* Ithaca, N.Y.: ILR Press, 1990. ISBN 0-87546-165-4. ▸ Comprehensive account of Spanish labor movement and labor relations through end of Spanish Civil War. Argues large-scale labor unrest of early twentieth century reflected country's partial and uneven economic development. [AS]

29.207 Gary Wray McDonogh. *Good families of Barcelona: a* *social history of power in the industrial era.* Princeton: Princeton University Press, 1986. ISBN 0-691-09426-8. ‣ Study of Barcelona elite in nineteenth and twentieth centuries. Focus on role of family and kinship and especially on ability of elite to adapt family to new circumstances. [AS]

29.208 Jordi Nadal. "Spain, 1830–1914." In *The Fontana economic history of Europe.* Vol. 4.2: *The emergence of industrial societies.* 1973 ed. Carlo M. Cipolla, ed., pp. 532–627. New York: Barnes & Noble, 1976. ‣ Abridged version of author's classic book-length, Spanish-language study of Spain's economic development. Portrays Industrial Revolution as having failed in Spain although some progress made. [AS]

29.209 Stanley G. Payne. *Basque nationalism.* Reno: University of Nevada Press, 1975. ISBN 0-87417-042-7. ‣ Introductory study of nationalist politics in Basque country, 1890s through Franco regime. [AS]

29.210 Stanley G. Payne. *Politics and the military in modern Spain.* Stanford, Calif.: Stanford University Press, 1967. ‣ Classic account of relation of Spanish military to Spanish government and politics in nineteenth and twentieth centuries. Argues frequent military intervention in government result of breakdown of Spanish political society rather than of military ambition. [AS]

29.211 José M. Sánchez. *Reform and reaction: the politico-religious background of the Spanish Civil War.* Chapel Hill: University of North Carolina Press, 1964. ‣ Groundbreaking study of relations between Catholic church and Spanish state, beginning of nineteenth century to Spanish Civil War. Argues authoritarianism and intolerance of Spanish church derived from strength of these characteristics among Spaniards themselves. [AS]

29.212 Nicolás Sánchez-Albornoz. *The economic modernization of Spain, 1830–1930.* New York: New York University Press, 1987. ISBN 0-8147-7861-5. ‣ Important collection of essays on Spanish economy. Reveals overall picture of unbalanced process of development as cause of problems. [AS]

Liberal Spain, 1800–1875

29.213 Timothy E. Anna. *Spain and the loss of America.* Lincoln: University of Nebraska Press, 1983. ISBN 0-8032-1014-0. ‣ Best available study of Spanish policy toward revolutions for independence in Spanish America. Focuses on highest levels of power; finds there was no consensus there at any time. [AS]

29.214 Renato Barahona. *Vizcaya on the eve of Carlism: politics and society, 1800–1833.* Reno: University of Nevada Press, 1989. ISBN 0-87417-122-9. ‣ Stimulating study of politics and society in Vizcaya to determine origins of First Carlist War. Challenges usual analyses of Carlism by emphasizing role of class conflict in Vizcaya which had direct link to rise of Carlism in region. [AS]

29.215 William J. Callahan. *Church, politics, and society in Spain, 1750–1874.* Cambridge, Mass.: Harvard University Press, 1984. ISBN 0-674-13125-8. ‣ Important discussion of reactions of church to political and social change in eighteenth and nineteenth centuries and how it became focus of societal conflict. Shows Spain far from being fully Catholic society well before twentieth-century conflict. [AS/SHB]

29.216 Eric Christiansen. *The origins of military power in Spain, 1800–1854.* London: Oxford University Press, 1967. ‣ Pioneering study of political activities of military in first half of nineteenth century. Finds roots of political intervention in army's internal tensions and changing relationship between army and civil society during transition from old regime to liberalism. [AS]

29.217 Michael P. Costeloe. *Response to revolution: imperial Spain and the Spanish American revolutions, 1810–1840.* Cambridge: Cambridge University Press, 1986. ISBN 0-521-32083-6. ‣ Well-researched study of how Spaniards saw and responded to

revolution for independence in Spanish America. Argues various political groups in Spain shared common attitude to those revolutions, seeking to prevent loss of empire; underscores lack of awareness of developments and refusal to accept realities. Read with Graham 38.127 and Lynch 38.150. [AS/RJW]

29.218 Charles J. Esdaile. *The Spanish army in the Peninsular War.* New York: Manchester University Press, 1988. ISBN 0-7190-2538-9. ‣ Study of Spanish army during War of Independence against France. Argues chief legacy of war was to leave Spain with army that equated its interests with national good and frequently intervened in politics. [AS]

29.219 Michael Glover. *Legacy of glory: the Bonaparte kingdom of Spain, 1808–1813.* New York: Scribner's, 1971. ISBN 0-684-12558-7. ‣ Classic study of Spain under rule of Napoleon's brother, Joseph, and of military history of Peninsular War. Emphasizes tense relations between Joseph and Napoleon. [AS]

29.220 John T. Graham. *Donoso Cortés, utopian romanticist and political realist.* Columbia: University of Missouri Press, 1971. ISBN 0-8262-0155-5. ‣ Useful biography of nineteenth-century conservative intellectual and political figure. Portrays Cortés as many-sided figure and thinker of European stature. [AS]

29.221 Gabriel H. Lovett. *Napoleon and the birth of modern Spain.* New York: New York University Press, 1965. ‣ Study of French presence in Spain under Napoleon and its impact on Spanish development. Shows how French involvement in Spain undermined Napoleonic empire and contributed to collapse of Old Regime in Spain itself. [AS]

29.222 Carlos Marichal. *Spain (1834–1844): a new society.* London: Tamesis, 1977. ISBN 84-399-7339-X. ‣ Study of transition from absolute monarchy to parliamentary system. Emphasizes importance of National Militia, political parties, and municipal governments as well as army officers and parallels between transition in Spain and in other European countries. Best available study in English. [AS]

Restoration, 1876–1930

29.223 Earl R. Beck. *A time of triumph and of sorrow: Spanish politics during the reign of Alfonso XII, 1874–1885.* Carbondale: Southern Illinois University Press, 1979. ISBN 0-8093-0902-5. ‣ Argues neither king nor dominant political figure of period, Antonio Cánovas del Castillo, able to achieve much in modernizing and liberalizing country. Sees triumph in achievement of stability and restoration of Bourbon monarchy; sorrow in Alfonso's personal tragedies and unrealized aspirations. [AS]

29.224 Shlomo Ben-Ami. *Fascism from above: the dictatorship of Primo de Rivera in Spain, 1923–1930.* New York: Oxford University Press, 1983. ISBN 0-19-822596-2. ‣ Provocative, stimulating study of military dictatorship of General Miguel Primo de Rivera (September 1923 to January 1930). Portrays period as attempt to create form of fascism and as clear forerunner to Francisco Franco's "New State." [AS]

29.225 Shlomo Ben-Ami. *The origins of the Second Republic in Spain.* New York: Oxford University Press, 1978. ISBN 0-19-821871-0. ‣ Influential study of political transformation from Primo de Rivera dictatorship to Second Republic. Emphasizes revival of republicanism, emergence of responsible socialist movement, and modernizing processes stimulated by dictatorship. [AS]

29.226 Carolyn Boyd. *Praetorian politics in liberal Spain.* Chapel Hill: University of North Carolina Press, 1979. ISBN 0-8078-1368-0. ‣ Study of role of armed forces in breakdown of parliamentary system in Spain between 1917 and 1923. Argues Spanish praetorianism result of combination of military's disposition to intervene and insecurity of liberal state that invited intervention. [AS]

29.227 George R. Esenwein. *Anarchist ideology and the working-class movement in Spain, 1868–1898.* Berkeley: University of California Press, 1989. ISBN 0-520-06398-8. ‣ Best available description of evolution of anarchist ideology and its impact on behavior of labor movement. Rejects view that Spanish anarchism was millenarian movement. Also argues that it had following among intellectuals. [AS]

29.228 Douglas W. Foard. *The revolt of the aesthetes: Ernesto Giménez Caballero and the origins of Spanish fascism.* New York: Lang, 1989. ISBN 0-8204-0927-8. ‣ Study of writer Ernesto Giménez Caballero's career. Links emergence of fascism in Spain to developments in arts. [AS]

29.229 C.A.M. Hennessy. *The federal republic in Spain: Pi y Margall and the federal republican movement, 1868–1874.* Westport, Conn.: Greenwood, 1962. ‣ Study of federal republican movement and its leader, Francisco Pi y Margall. Portrayed as self-contained, nineteenth-century movement, related to republican movements elsewhere in Europe, but distinguished by equation of feudalism with republicanism. [AS]

29.230 Paul Heywood. "The labour movement in Spain before 1914." In *Labour and socialist movements in Europe before 1914.* Dick Geary, ed., pp. 231–65. Oxford, New York: Berg; distributed by St. Martin's, 1989. ISBN 0-85496-200-X. ‣ Brief but valuable survey of Spanish labor movement. Emphasizes relative weakness of movement, importance of regional variations, role of state, movements' organizational structures, and poverty of indigenous Marxist theory. [AS]

29.231 Paul Heywood. *Marxism and the failure of organized socialism in Spain, 1879–1936.* New York: Cambridge University Press, 1990. ‣ Specialist study of ideology and practice of Socialist party (PSOE) from foundation to outbreak of Civil War. Shows longstanding coexistence of revolutionary rhetoric and reformist practice and weakness of theoretical base which impeded wise political choices in 1930s. [AS]

29.232 Edgar Holt. *The Carlist wars in Spain.* Chester Springs, Pa.: Dufour, 1967. ‣ Classic history of First Carlist War with much attention to role of British Auxiliary Legion. [AS]

29.233 Temma Kaplan. *Anarchists of Andalucia, 1868–1903.* Princeton: Princeton University Press, 1977. ISBN 0-691-05263-0. ‣ Controversial study of anarchist movement in sherry-producing region of southern province of Cádiz. Argues against view of anarchism as millenarian or irrational movement, rather, well-organized defense of material interests of peasants and workers. [AS]

29.234 Temma Kaplan. *Red city, blue period: social movements in Picasso's Barcelona.* Berkeley: University of California Press, 1992. ISBN 0-520-07507-2. ‣ Intellectually ambitious, provocative study of social movements in Barcelona from 1880s to 1930. Focus on shared experience of civic culture and role of women in its creation and transformation. [AS]

29.235 Robert W. Kern. *Liberals, reformers, and caciques in Restoration Spain, 1875–1909.* Albuquerque: University of New Mexico Press, 1974. ISBN 0-8263-0347-1. ‣ Important study of caciquismo, system of institutionalized political bossism that characterized Spanish political life during Restoration, and of critics of system. Argues this was symptom of difficulties of instituting liberal political system in underdeveloped, largely rural society, similar to problems of contemporary Third World. [AS]

29.236 V. G. Kiernan. *The Revolution of 1854 in Spanish history.* Oxford: Clarendon, 1966. ‣ Classic study of Revolution of 1854 and *Bienio*, two-year period of progressive liberal rule to which it gave rise. Emphasizes failure of liberal political leaders to understand Spain's social and economic problems and inability of younger, more radical figures to learn from that failure. [AS]

29.237 Solomon Lipp. *Francisco Giner de los Ríos: Spanish Socrates.* Waterloo, Ont.: Wilfred Laurier University Press; distributed by Humanities Press, 1985. ISBN 0-88920-159-5. ‣ Study of leading intellectual of late nineteenth century. Describes wide-ranging influence of his thought. [AS]

29.238 Gerald H. Meaker. *The revolutionary Left in Spain, 1914–1923.* Stanford, Calif.: Stanford University Press, 1974. ISBN 0-8047-0845-2. ‣ Development of anarchist and communist movements. Locates weakness of Spanish communism in continued revolutionary vitality of anarchism and consequent absence of ideological vacuum as in France. Standard English-language work. [AS]

29.239 J. Randolph Mosher. *The birth of mass politics in Spain: Lerrouxismo in Barcelona, 1901–1909.* New York: Garland, 1991. ISBN 0-8240-2545-8. ‣ Study of Alejandro Lerroux and Radical party in Barcelona in first decade of twentieth century. Seen as political expression of modernization. [AS]

29.240 Stanley G. Payne, ed. *Politics and society in twentieth-century Spain.* New York: New Viewpoints, 1976. ISBN 0-531-05382-2 (cl), 0-531-05588-4 (pbk). ‣ Valuable but somewhat dated collection of essays on aspects of Spanish politics. Includes important articles by Spanish historian Javier Tusell not available elsewhere in English. [AS]

29.241 H. Ramsden. *The 1898 movement in Spain: towards a reinterpretation with special reference to "En Torno al Casticismo" and "Idearium Español."* Totowa, N.J.: Rowman & Littlefield, 1974. ISBN 0-87471-586-5. ‣ Study of two major works of important group of early twentieth-century writers, Generation of 1898, one by Angel Ganivet, other by Miguel de Unamuno. Finds that they contain key elements that came to characterize Spanish thought in early twentieth century. [AS]

29.242 James H. Rial. *Revolution from above: the Primo de Rivera dictatorship in Spain, 1923–1930.* Fairfax, Va.: George Mason University Press, 1986. ISBN 0-913969-01-X. ‣ Valuable study of political, economic, and social reforms of Primo de Rivera dictatorship. Despite admirable energy and ambition, reforms failed because of Primo's misconceptions of problems facing country and reliance on established elites. [AS]

29.243 Joaquín Romero Maura. "*Caciquismo* as a political system." In *Patrons and clients in Mediterranean states.* Ernest Gellner and John Waterbury, eds., pp. 53–62. Hanover, N.H.: Center for Mediterranean Studies of the American Universities Field Staff, 1977. ISBN 0-910116-99-7. ‣ Provocative analysis of *caciquismo*, system of political bossism prominent in Spain in late nineteenth and early twentieth centuries. Argues widespread political demobilization made system possible. [AS]

29.244 Adrian Shubert. *The road to revolution in Spain: the coal miners of Asturias, 1860–1934.* Urbana: University of Illinois Press, 1987. ISBN 0-252-01368-9. ‣ Study of economic and social change and labor organization in coal-mining region of northern Spain leading to insurrection of October 1934. Portrays episode as rank-and-file response to deteriorating social and political conditions. [AS]

29.245 Joan Connelly Ullman. *The tragic week: a study of anticlericalism in Spain, 1875–1912.* Cambridge, Mass.: Harvard University Press, 1968. ‣ Study of major outbreak of anticlerical violence in Barcelona in July 1909. Argues political function of anticlericalism was to divert popular radicalism away from issues that would lead to social and political change. [AS]

29.246 Colin M. Winston. *Workers and the Right in Spain, 1900–1936.* Princeton: Princeton University Press, 1985. ISBN 0-691-05433-9. ‣ Study of Sindicatos Libres, right-wing union movement that emerged in Barcelona in early twentieth century.

Argues willingness of these unions to engage in strikes allowed it to succeed where more docile Catholic unions failed. [AS]

Second Republic and Civil War, 1931–1939

29.247   Martha A. Ackelsberg. *Free women of Spain: anarchism and the struggle for the emancipation of women.* Bloomington: Indiana University Press, 1991. ISBN 0-253-301-203 (cl), 0-253-20634-0 (pbk). ▸ Account of Mujeres Libres, anarchist women's organization created during Spanish Civil War. Argues creation of organization and its difficult relations with Confederacion Nacional del Trabajo (CNT) reflected anarchism's inability to accommodate special needs and problems of women. [AS]

29.248   Anthony Aldgate. *Cinema and history: British newsreels and the Spanish Civil War.* London: Scholar, 1979. ISBN 0-85967-485-1 (cl), 0-85967-486-X (pbk). ▸ Examination of film coverage of Spanish Civil War by British newsreel companies. Stresses influence of newsreel coverage and role in impeding full understanding of events in Spain. [AS]

29.249   Martin S. Alexander and Helen Graham, eds. *The French and Spanish popular fronts: comparative perpectives.* New York: Cambridge University Press, 1989. ISBN 0-521-35081-6. ▸ Collection of essays on Popular Front in Spain and France. Views popular fronts as mass movements for social change rather than elite political alliances. [AS]

29.250   Martin Blinkhorn. *Carlism and crisis in Spain, 1931–1939.* New York: Cambridge University Press, 1975. ISBN 0-521-20729-0. ▸ Study of ideology and internal politics of Carlist movement, its relationship to other elements of Spanish Right during Second Republic, and role during Civil War. Emphasizes Carlist hostility to republic and its ambiguous relationship to Franco regime. [AS]

29.251   Martin Blinkhorn, ed. *Spain in conflict, 1931–1939: democracy and its enemies.* Beverly Hills, Calif.: Sage, 1986. ISBN 0-8039-9745-0. ▸ Collection of essays on aspects of history of Second Republic and Civil War. Focuses on fragmentation of Left, coalescence of Right, and foreign intervention. [AS]

29.252   Burnett Bolloten. *The Spanish Civil War: revolution and counterrevolution.* Chapel Hill: University of North Carolina Press, 1991. ISBN 0-8078-1906-9. ▸ Monumental study of politics of republican-held territory during Spanish Civil War based on vast primary research. Focus on Spanish Communist party and its efforts to reverse social revolution that occurred at beginning of conflict. [AS]

29.253   Vincent Brome. *The International Brigades: Spain, 1936–1939.* New York: Morrow, 1966. ▸ Account of International Brigades in Civil War emphasizing idealism of volunteers. [AS]

29.254   Pierre Broué and Emile Temime. *The revolution and the Civil War in Spain.* London: Faber & Faber, 1970. ISBN 0-571-09773-1. ▸ Study of Second Republic and Civil War by two French historians, one sympathetic to progressive Republicans, other to Communists. Presents Spanish conditions as analogous to those of contemporary Third World countries and Civil War as similar to revolutionary movements in other countries. [AS]

29.255   Tom Buchanan. *The Spanish Civil War and the British labour movement.* New York: Cambridge University Press, 1991. ISBN 0-521-39333-7. ▸ Superb study of response of British labor movement to Spanish Civil War. Argues main concern of British labor leaders was to defend labor's institutional interests, especially given lack of consensus on Spain among British workers. [AS]

29.256   E. H. Carr. *The Comintern and the Spanish Civil War.* New York: Pantheon, 1984. ISBN 0-394-53550-2 (cl), 0-394-72263-9 (pbk). ▸ Study of communist activities during Spanish

Civil War. Argues Soviet policy motivated more by need to defend Soviet national interests than to spread revolution. [AS]

29.257   Raymond Carr. *The Civil War in Spain, 1936–1939.* London: Weidenfeld & Nicolson, 1986. ISBN 0-297-78899-X (pbk). ▸ Analysis of and commentary on Spanish Civil War. Sees republican defeat as result of military and political failures of Popular Front as well as failure of democracies to support republic. [AS]

29.258   David T. Cattell. *Communism and the Spanish Civil War.* New York: Russell & Russell, 1965. ▸ Study of role of Soviet Union and Communists during Spanish Civil War. Argues Communists' activities helped extend life of republic in face of overwhelming nationalist military superiority and that Soviet Union's goal was to defend itself against fascist states. [AS]

29.259   George A. Collier. *Socialists of rural Andalucia.* Stanford, Calif.: Stanford University Press, 1987. ISBN 0-8047-1411-8. ▸ Study of social, economic, and political developments in town in province of Huelva, 1930s through 1960s. Argues socialist radicalization during Second Republic produced by success in changing local balance of power. [AS]

29.260   Robert G. Colodny. *Spain: the glory and the tragedy.* New York: Humanities Press, 1970. ISBN 0-391-00087-X. ▸ Brief account of Spanish Civil War, seen as symbol with universal relevance and as analogous to Vietnam War. [AS]

29.261   James W. Cortada. *Historical dictionary of the Spanish Civil War, 1936–1939.* Westport, Conn.: Greenwood, 1982. ISBN 0-313-22054-9. ▸ Very useful dictionary of important persons, organizations, and events of Spanish Civil War. [AS]

29.262   John F. Coverdale. *Italian intervention in the Spanish Civil War.* Princeton: Princeton University Press, 1975. ▸ Study arguing Italian intervention motivated by traditional foreign policy concerns, especially Italy's position in Europe and Mediterranean. [AS]

29.263   Jill Edwards. *The British government and the Spanish Civil War, 1936–1939.* London: Macmillan, 1979. ISBN 0-333-24260-2. ▸ Study of British government's response to Spanish Civil War. Judges anticommunism as initially most important among various factors that led Britain to support nonintervention. [AS]

29.264   Sheelagh M. Ellwood. *The Spanish Civil War.* Cambridge, Mass.: Blackwell, 1991. ISBN 0-631-18048-6 (cl), 0-631-16617-3 (pbk). ▸ Brief account of Civil War, focusing on key social and political issues and main players; chronological narrative. Excellent for students. [AS]

29.265   Ronald Fraser. *Blood of Spain: an oral history of the Spanish Civil War, 1936–1939.* 1979 ed. New York: Pantheon, 1986. ISBN 0-394-73854-3 (pbk). ▸ Brilliant oral history of Spanish Civil War emphasizing lived experience of participants. Mosaic presentation using interviews with more than 300 people. [AS]

29.266   Helen Graham. *Socialism and war: the Spanish Socialist party in power and crisis, 1936–1939.* New York: Cambridge University Press, 1991. ISBN 0-521-39257-8. ▸ Study of Socialist party (PSOE) during Civil War. Argues party's disintegration result of preexisting crisis, exacerbated by circumstances of Civil War. [AS]

29.267   Dolores Ibarruri. *They shall not pass: the autobiography of La Pasionaria.* New York: International Publishers, 1966. ▸ Autobiography of Dolores Ibarruri, woman who became major leader of Spanish Communist party; focuses on 1930s. [AS]

29.268   Gabriel Jackson. *The Spanish republic and the Civil War, 1931–1939.* Princeton: Princeton University Press, 1965. ▸ Classic study of Second Republic and Civil War emphasizing events as seen from within Spain. Sees turning point in history of republic in events of 1934, but rejects idea that Civil War was inevitable from that point. [AS]

29.269 Verle B. Johnston. *Legions of Babel: the International Brigades in the Spanish Civil War*. University Park: Pennsylvania State University Press, 1967. ‣ Account of International Brigades during Civil War, arguing that by prolonging war, volunteers helped defeat Germany in World War II. [AS]

29.270 Douglas Little. *Malevolent neutrality: the United States, Great Britain, and the origins of the Spanish Civil War*. Ithaca, N.Y.: Cornell University Press, 1985. ISBN 0-8014-1769-4. ‣ Study of relations between Spain and two democracies during 1930s. Finds roots of American and British nonintervention in fear of revolution, nourished by difficult relations with Second Republic. [AS]

29.271 Neil MacMaster. *Spanish fighters: an oral history of Civil War and exile*. New York: St. Martin's, 1990. ISBN 0-312-04738-x. ‣ Oral history of experiences of Spanish couple during Civil War and postwar exile in France. [AS]

29.272 Edward A. Malefakis. *Agrarian reform and peasant revolution in Spain: origins of the Civil War*. New Haven: Yale University Press, 1970. ISBN 0-300-01210-1. ‣ Classic study of agrarian reform policies of Second Republic and reasons for its failure. Blames failure on inability of Republicans and Socialists to develop coherent and shared program for agrarian reform. [AS]

29.273 Jerome R. Mintz. *The anarchists of Casas Viejas*. Chicago: University of Chicago Press, 1982. ISBN 0-226-53106-6. ‣ Development of anarchism in Andalucian town of Casas Viejas with focus on abortive uprising of 11 January 1933. Rejects view of anarchism as irrational, religious-type movement and shows insurrection as response to nationwide revolutionary strike called by national leadership. [AS]

29.274 Stanley G. Payne. *Falange: a history of Spanish fascism*. Stanford, Calif.: Stanford University Press, 1961. ‣ Pioneering study of Spanish fascist party, Falange Española, from foundation to late 1950s. Seen as Spanish phenomenon in which emotional tone more important than ideology. [AS]

29.275 Stanley G. Payne. *Spain's first democracy: the Second Republic, 1931–1936*. Madison: University of Wisconsin Press, 1993. ISBN 0-299-13670-1 (cl), 0-299-13674-4 (pbk). ‣ Detailed study considers Second Republic as major attempt at democratization and reform in interwar period. Blames failure primarily on moderate republican political leaders. [AS]

29.276 Stanley G. Payne. *The Spanish revolution*. New York: Norton, 1970. ISBN 0-297-00124-8. ‣ Account of revolutionary Left in Spain in 1930s with emphasis on industrial working class over rural movements. Attributes breakdown of Second Republic to Left. [AS]

29.277 Paul Preston. *The coming of the Spanish Civil War: reform, reaction, and revolution in the Second Republic*. 1978 ed. New York: Methuen, 1983. ISBN 0-416-35720-2. ‣ Stimulating study of politics of Second Republic from 1931 to 1936. Emphasizes role of Socialist party and importance of internal divisions present since 1917. [AS]

29.278 Paul Preston. *The Spanish Civil War, 1936–1939*. New York: Grove, 1986. ISBN 0-394-55565-1. ‣ Lavishly illustrated, brief interpretive account of Second Republic and Civil War. Clearly favorable to attempts of Left to legislate social reform during Second Republic and equally hostile to Nationalists, their supporters, and Franco regime. [AS]

29.279 Paul Preston, ed. *Revolution and war and Spain, 1931–1939*. New York: Methuen, 1984. ISBN 0-416-34960-9 (cl), 0-416-34970-6 (pbk). ‣ Collection of recent works on Second Republic

and Civil War. Shows variety of conflicts: regional, religious, and class that lay behind and within Civil War. [AS]

29.280 Raymond L. Proctor. *Hitler's Luftwaffe in the Spanish Civil War*. Westport, Conn.: Greenwood, 1983. ISBN 0-313-22246-0. ‣ Role of German air force in Spanish Civil War. Concludes individual airmen benefited from experience but leaders failed to learn many important lessons. [AS]

29.281 Dante A. Puzzo. *Spain and the great powers, 1936–1941*. New York: Columbia University Press, 1962. ‣ Study of involvement of European great powers in Spanish Civil War. Argues Great Britain chief architect of nonintervention and French decision not to allow arms shipments to Spain was key diplomatic event of war. [AS]

29.282 R. Dan Richardson. *Comintern army: the International Brigades and the Spanish Civil War*. Lexington: University Press of Kentucky, 1982. ISBN 0-8131-1439-X. ‣ Study of International Brigades and their participation in Spanish Civil War. Argues Brigades were intrinsically political and formed integral part of Soviet-Comintern apparatus in Spain. [AS]

29.283 Richard A. H. Robinson. *The origins of Franco's Spain: the Right, the republic, and revolution, 1931–1936*. Pittsburgh: University of Pittsburgh Press, 1970. ISBN 0-8229-1099-3. ‣ Study of Spanish Right during Second Republic with focus on Confederation Española de Derechos Autonomas. Blames Socialist party for failure of republic by abandoning democratic methods and appealing to violence. [AS]

29.284 Jesús Salas Larrázabal. *Air war over Spain*. Margaret Kelley, trans. David Mondey, ed. of translation. London: Allan, 1974. ISBN 0-7110-0521-4. ‣ Study of role of aviation in Civil War by pronationalist historian. [AS]

29.285 José M. Sánchez. *The Spanish Civil War as a religious tragedy*. Notre Dame, Ind.: University of Notre Dame Press, 1987. ISBN 0-268-01726-3. ‣ Study of religious dimension of Spanish Civil War, arguing religion was key issue of war and war was climax of long struggle between Catholicism and liberal secularism. [AS]

29.286 Frank Sedwick. *The tragedy of Manuel Azaña and the fate of the Spanish republic*. Columbus: Ohio State University Press, 1963. ‣ Study of role of Prime Minister Manuel Azaña in politics of Second Republic. Sees Azaña as Spanish Kerensky, besieged by fanatics of both Left and Right. [AS]

29.287 Herbert G. Southworth. *Guernica! Guernica! A study of journalism, diplomacy, propaganda, and history*. Berkeley: University of California Press, 1977. ISBN 0-520-02830-9. ‣ Definitive study of bombing of town of Guernica on 26 April 1937 and of international newspaper coverage of event. Argues responsibility for bombing lay with President Franco's nationalist command and officers of German Condor Legion. [AS]

29.288 Hugh Thomas. *The Spanish Civil War*. 3d rev. ed. New York: Harper & Row, 1977. ISBN 0-06-014278-2. ‣ Complex, fast-moving account; best available introduction to civil war between factions in divided Europe. Argues political disunity main cause of republican defeat. Enlarged edition of general history of Civil War, first published 1961. [AS/JSH]

29.289 Marjorie A. Valleau. *The Spanish Civil War in American and European films*. Ann Arbor: UMI Research Press, 1982. ISBN 0-8357-1312-1. ‣ Study of portrayal of Civil War in six American and six European films. Finds American films politically neutral and more oriented to entertainment while European films politically committed. [AS]

29.290 Robert H. Whealey. *Hitler and Spain: the Nazi role in the Spanish Civil War*. Lexington: University Press of Kentucky, 1989. ISBN 0-8131-1621-X. ‣ Study of German intervention in

Spanish Civil War. Argues Hitler successful in realizing objective of shifting balance of power in Europe. [AS]

SEE ALSO
38.119 Mark Falcoff and Fredrick B. Pike, eds. *The Spanish Civil War, 1936–39.*

Franco's Spain, 1939–1975

29.291 Joseph A. Aceves and William A. Douglass, eds. *The changing faces of rural Spain.* Cambridge, Mass.: Schenkman; distributed by Halsted, 1976. ISBN 0-470-00236-0 (cl), 0-470-00237-9 (pbk). ▸ Collection of essays on change in various areas of rural Spain in twentieth century. Finds improved conditions in rural world, ironically, led to depopulation. [AS]

29.292 Charles W. Anderson. *The political economy of modern Spain: policy making in an authoritarian system.* Madison: University of Wisconsin Press, 1970. ISBN 0-299-05611-2. ▸ Study of economic policy making under Franco regime. Concludes problem-solving capacities of regime not dissimilar to those of liberal democracies. [AS]

29.293 E. Ramón Arango. *The Spanish political system: Franco's legacy.* Boulder: Westview, 1978. ISBN 0-89158-177-4. ▸ Study of political system of Franco regime and of emerging post-Franco democracy. Rejects views of Spain as different from rest of Europe; sees Spain as contemporary modernizing nation. [AS]

29.294 Sebastian Balfour. *Dictatorship, workers, and the city: labour in greater Barcelona since 1939.* New York: Clarendon, 1989. ISBN 0-19-822740-X. ▸ Pioneering study of urban development and labor movement in greater Barcelona between 1939 and 1988. Argues Franco regime's vertical unions provided some real benefits to workers but legacy of those unions hampered labor's adaptation to democratic system after 1975. [AS]

29.295 Stanley H. Brandes. *Migration, kinship, and community: tradition and transition in a Spanish village.* New York: Academic Press, 1975. ISBN 0-12-125750-9. ▸ Study of impact of depopulation on village in Castile. Argues change has led to preservation and extension of traditional mechanisms of local integration and identity. [AS]

29.296 Raymond Carr and Juan Pablo Fusi Aizpurua. *Spain: dictatorship to democracy.* 2d ed. London: Allen & Unwin, 1981. ISBN 0-04-9460153 (cl), 0-04-946014-5 (pbk). ▸ Study of political, economic, and social evolution of Spain under Franco; narrative of political developments 1969–77. Emphasis on rapidity of change in 1960s and 1970s. [AS]

29.297 Robert P. Clark. *The Basques: the Franco years and beyond.* Reno: University of Nevada Press, 1979. ISBN 0-87417-057-5. ▸ Study of Basque nationalist movement during and after Franco regime. Sees conflict between ethnicity and class as major determinant of Basque politics. [AS]

29.298 Sheelagh M. Ellwood. *Spanish fascism in the Franco era.* New York: St. Martin's, 1987. ISBN 0-312-00540-7. ▸ History of Falange Española, small fascist party that became core of official party of Franco regime. Argues Falange survived by sacrificing whatever political or social ideals it had. [AS]

29.299 Josep Fontana and Jordi Nadal. "Spain, 1914–1970." In *Fontana economic history of Europe.* Vol. 6.2: *Contemporary economies.* Carlo M. Cipolla, ed., pp. 460–529. New York: Barnes & Noble, 1976. ▸ Study of economic development. Emphasizes growth in 1960s but also its fragility. [AS]

29.300 Joe Foweraker. *Making democracy in Spain: grass-roots struggle in the south, 1955–1975.* New York: Cambridge University Press, 1989. ISBN 0-521-35406-4. ▸ Important study of grass-roots political and union struggle in Jerez region of Andalucia

during Franco regime. Argues Spanish democracy product of popular struggles, emerging out of immediate problems. [AS]

29.301 Ronald Fraser. *In hiding: the life of Manuel Cortés.* New York: Pantheon, 1972. ISBN 0-394-47941-6. ▸ Oral history of republican mayor of small village who spent thirty years in hiding after end of Civil War. [AS]

29.302 Ronald Fraser. *The Pueblo: a mountain village on the Costa del Sol.* London: Lane, 1973. ISBN 0-7139-0582-4. ▸ Oral history of mountain village near Malaga in twentieth century. Emphasizes watershed represented by growth of foreign tourism after 1950 and major changes it brought to local economy and villagers' outlook. [AS]

29.303 Susan Tax Freeman. *Neighbors: the social contract in a Castilian hamlet.* Chicago: University of Chicago Press, 1970. ISBN 0-226-26169-2. ▸ Anthropological study of Castilian village emphasizing egalitarian tradition of nonhierarchical organization and use of shared ceremony to express common bonds. [AS]

29.304 Juan Pablo Fusi Aizpurua. *Franco: a biography.* Felipe Fernández-Armesto, trans. New York: Harper & Row, 1987. ISBN 0-06-433127-X. ▸ Stimulating biographical essay offering brief critical survey of life of General Francisco Franco. Portrays subject as middle-class soldier seeking to impose what he saw as unity and order Spain needed, as well as trying to deal with regime's lack of democratic legitimacy during 1960s and 1970s. [AS]

29.305 Richard Gillespie. *The Spanish Socialist party: a history of factionalism.* New York: Clarendon, 1989. ISBN 0-19-822798-1. ▸ General history of Socialist party (Partido Socialista Obrero Español) with emphasis on period since 1939. Argues persistent factionalism obstructed effective opposition to Franco but also made possible changes in outlook that contributed to its role in transition. [AS]

29.306 David D. Gilmore. *The people of the plain: class and community in lower Andalusia.* New York: Columbia University Press, 1980. ISBN 0-231-04754-1. ▸ Study of class structure of rural town in Andalusia toward end of Franco regime. Argues class fundamental principle of social organization and seen as such by locals. [AS]

29.307 Richard Gunther. *Public policy in a no-party state: Spanish planning and budgeting in the twilight of the Franquist era.* Berkeley: University of California Press, 1980. ISBN 0-520-03752-9. ▸ Study of internal dynamics of Franco regime in 1970s with regard to public expenditure. Argues policy priorities on economic questions determined through personal negotiations among ministers. [AS]

29.308 Edward C. Hansen. *Rural Catalonia under the Franco regime.* New York: Cambridge University Press, 1977. ISBN 0-521-21457-2. ▸ Study of impact of Franco regime on Alto Penedes region of Catalonia. Focus on relationship between power and cultural institutions, especially patronage and friendship. [AS]

29.309 Susan Friend Harding. *Remaking Ibieca: rural life in Aragon under Franco.* Chapel Hill: University of North Carolina Press, 1984. ISBN 0-8078-1594-2. ▸ Study of social change in Aragonese village during Franco regime. Argues villagers participated in changes willingly, unaware they would destroy way of life. [AS]

29.310 Guy Hermet. *The Communists in Spain: study of an underground movement.* S. Seago and H. Fox, trans. Westmead, England: Saxon House, 1974. ISBN 0-347-01032-6. ▸ Study of Communist party from end of Civil War. Argues virulent anticommunism of Franco regime raised party's prestige, at same time justifying regime's existence. [AS]

29.311 Hank Johnston. *Tales of nationalism: Catalonia, 1939–1979.* New Brunswick, N.J.: Rutgers University Press, 1991. ISBN 0-8135-1705-2. ▸ Study of Catalan nationalism based on interviews with eighty-two militants. Contends cultural processes at level of individual and everyday life crucial to reemergence of movement. [AS]

29.312 Sima Lieberman. *The contemporary Spanish economy: a historical perspective.* Boston: Allen & Unwin, 1982. ISBN 0-04-339026-9. ▸ Study of Spanish economic development in twentieth century with focus on causes of serious economic, social, and political problems of 1980s. Argues persistence of traditional economic institutions impeded economic development. [AS]

29.313 Carmelo Lisón-Tolosana. *Belmonte de los Caballeros: anthropology and history in an Aragonese village.* Princeton: Princeton University Press, 1983. ISBN 0-691-09402-0 (cl), 0-691-02829-x (pbk). ▸ Study of changes in village in Aragon, end of Civil War to 1960. Finds social life based on strong individualism. [AS]

29.314 Eusebio Mujal-León. *Communism and political change in Spain.* Bloomington: Indiana University Press, 1983. ISBN 0-253-31389-9. ▸ Study of Communist party from end of Civil War to transition to democracy. Argues party's failure to become major force in democratic Spain result of its association with Civil War, regional and ideological conflicts, contradictions within communist policies, and revival of Socialist party. [AS]

29.315 Stanley G. Payne. *The Franco regime, 1936–1975.* Madison: University of Wisconsin Press, 1987. ISBN 0-299-11070-2. ▸ Comprehensive political history of Franco regime from Civil War until Franco's death in 1975. Emphasizes eclecticism of Franco's ideas; argues, while changes his regime oversaw made democratic regime possible, Franco deserves no credit for transition. [AS]

29.316 Paul Preston. *Franco: a biography.* London: Harper-Collins, 1993. ISBN 0-06-215863-9. ▸ Monumental biography of Francisco Franco; very critical. Will remain definitive study until Franco archives are made available. [AS]

29.317 Paul Preston. *The politics of revenge: fascism and the military in twentieth-century Spain.* Boston: Unwin Hyman, 1990. ISBN 0-04-445463-5. ▸ Collection of essays on Spanish Right from 1930s to 1980s. Emphasizes army's changing place within Spanish society and consequent changes to its political role. [AS]

29.318 Paul Preston, ed. *Spain in crisis: the evolution and decline of the Franco regime.* New York: Barnes & Noble, 1976. ISBN 0-06-495711-X. ▸ Collection of essays describing how forces of Franco regime and opposition arrived at political crisis of mid-1970s (continuation of Franco regime). Shows coincidence of interest between opposition and part of economic elite which suggests democratization likely outcome. [AS]

29.319 Denis Smyth. *Diplomacy and strategy of survival: British policy and Franco's Spain, 1940–1941.* New York: Cambridge University Press, 1986. ISBN 0-521-22819-0. ▸ Study of British diplomatic efforts to keep Spain out of World War II. Argues goal achieved by end of 1940 although British policy makers did not realize this. [AS]

29.320 Louis Stein. *Beyond death and exile: the Spanish republicans in France, 1939–1955.* Cambridge, Mass.: Harvard University Press, 1979. ISBN 0-674-06888-2. ▸ Study of Spanish republicans exiled in France after Civil War. Shows exiles continued to struggle against fascism, both in Spain and elsewhere, in vain hope that democracies would eliminate Franco once World War II was over. [AS]

29.321 John Sullivan. *ETA and Basque nationalism: the fight for Euzkadi, 1890–1986.* New York: Routledge, 1988. ISBN 0-415-00366-0. ▸ Study of radical Basque nationalist organization, ETA,

from creation through mid-1980s. Argues ETA deeply rooted in Basque history and society, which distinguished it from terrorist groups such as Bader-Meinhoff or Red Brigades. [AS]

29.322 Cyrus Ernesto Zirkzadeh. *A rebellious people: Basques, protests, and politics.* Reno: University of Nevada Press, 1991. ISBN 0-87417-173-3. ▸ Study of Basque politics since emergence of nationalist movement in 1890s. Interprets political violence as product of choices made by political activists hoping to spark revolution. [AS]

Democratic Spain, 1975–1992

29.323 Christopher Abel and Nissa Torrents, eds. *Spain: conditional democracy.* New York: St. Martin's, 1984. ISBN 0-312-7459-7. ▸ Collection of articles on politics, culture, and society in Spain during transition to democracy after 1975. Focus on threats to Spanish democracy posed by military. [AS]

29.324 Robert P. Clark. *Negotiating with ETA: obstacles to peace in the Basque country, 1975–1988.* Reno: University of Nevada Press, 1990. ISBN 0-87417-162-8. ▸ Study of attempts by Spanish governments to negotiate with Basque separatist organization (ETA). Argues negotiations remain best way to resolve situation. [AS]

29.325 Peter J. Donaghy and Michael T. Newton. *Spain: a guide to political and economic institutions.* New York: Cambridge University Press, 1987. ISBN 0-521-30032-0 (cl), 0-521-31734-7 (pbk). ▸ Valuable guide to major political and economic institutions created after death of Francisco Franco in 1975. [AS]

29.326 Robert M. Fishman. *Working-class organization and the return to democracy in Spain.* Ithaca, N.Y.: Cornell University Press, 1990. ISBN 0-8014-2061-X. ▸ Study of role of labor movement in transition to democracy after 1975 and its adoption of policy of negotiated reform. Emphasizes role of factory-level leaders in development of union organization and in labor's response to national political issues. [AS]

29.327 David Gilmour. *The transformation of Spain: from Franco to the constitutional monarchy.* New York: Quartet, 1985. ISBN 0-7043-2461-X. ▸ Study of transition to democracy following death of Francisco Franco in 1975. Emphasizes widespread restraint and contributions of wide range of people to making transition a success, but gives King Juan Carlos most praise. [AS]

29.328 Richard Gunther, Giacomo Sani, and Goldie Shabad. *Spain after Franco: the making of a competitive party system.* Berkeley: University of California Press, 1988. ISBN 0-520-06384-8 (cl), 0-520-06336-8 (pbk). ▸ Study of process of creating competitive system of political parties following death of Franco. Argues outcome was product of decisions taken by political elites within constraints of social, political, and historical context. [AS]

29.329 Thomas D. Lancaster and Gary Prevost, eds. *Politics and change in Spain.* New York: Praeger, 1985. ISBN 0-03-000937-5. ▸ Collection of essays on transition to democracy following death of Franco in 1975 using coalitional politics as framework for analysis. [AS]

29.330 José Maria Maravall. *Transition to democracy in Spain.* New York: St. Martin's, 1982. ISBN 0-312-62632-0. ▸ Study of transition to democracy by minister in first socialist government. Sees transition as product of confluence of reformist politics from above and pressures and demands from below. [AS]

29.331 Paul Preston. *The triumph of democracy in Spain.* New York: Methuen, 1986. ISBN 0-416-36350-4. ▸ Political history of last years of Franco regime and transition to democracy up to electoral victory of Socialist party in October 1982. Emphasizes role of King Juan Carlos and moderate leaders on both Left and Right. [AS]

29.332 Paul Preston and Denis Smyth. *Spain, the EEC, and NATO*. Boston: Routledge & Kegan Paul, 1984. ISBN 0-7100-9559-7. ▸ Study of Spain's relation with European Economic Community and North Atlantic Treaty Organization and public response to membership in each. Argues Spanish membership important to other Western European countries. [AS]

29.333 Donald Share. *Dilemmas of social democracy: the Spanish Socialist Workers' party in the 1980's*. New York: Greenwood, 1989. ISBN 0-313-26074-5. ▸ Study of Socialist party (PSOE), its success and move to Right since 1975. Argues downplaying social democratic policies was precondition for coming to power in 1982, but rejection of those policies while in power result of variety of considerations. [AS]

29.334 Joseba Zulaika. *Basque violence: metaphor and sacrament*. Reno: University of Nevada Press, 1988. ISBN 0-87417-132-6. ▸ Anthropological study of political violence in Basque country. Sees violence as both myth and metaphor within Basque culture. [AS]

PORTUGAL

Portuguese Empire, 1450–1806

29.335 Fortunato de Almeida. *História da igreja em Portugal*. 2d ed. 4 vols. Damião Peres, ed. Porto, Portugal: Portugalense Editora, 1967–71. ▸ Standard work, first published 1910–21. Conservative interpretation of Catholic church and its mission in Portugal and empire. [TC]

29.336 Carlos de Azevedo and Chester E. V. Brummell. *Churches of Portugal*. New York: Scala; distributed by Harper & Row, 1985. ISBN 0-935748-66-0. ▸ Brief essays by Azevedo about major periods in Portuguese architecture, accompanied by superb color and black-and-white photographs by Brummell. [TC]

29.337 João Lúcio d'Azevedo. *A evolução do Sebastianismo*. 2d ed. Lisbon: Texeira, 1947. ▸ Study, by determined skeptic, of popular Portuguese belief in return of King Sebastian. Killed at battle of Alcacer Quibir (1578), but body never found. [TC]

29.338 Marcel Bataillon. *Études sur le Portugal au temps de l'humanisme*. Coimbra: Universidade, 1952. ▸ Studies of humanists Damião de Gois and Gil Vicente, Erasmianism in Portugal, and related subjects by author of classic study of Erasmianism in Spain. [TC]

29.339 William Beckford. *The journal of William Beckford in Portugal and Spain, 1787–1788*. Boyd Alexander, ed. London: Hart-Davis, 1954. ▸ Englishman's account of eight-month sojourn in Lisbon among Portuguese aristocracy. Widely read for vivid depictions of elite society and political intrigues in Lisbon. [TC]

29.340 Aubrey F. G. Bell. *Gil Vicente*. Oxford: Oxford University Press, 1921. ▸ Critical biography by one of pioneers of Portuguese literary studies. Vicente (ca. 1469–ca. 1536) a dramatist and court poet celebrated for lyricism and comic gifts. [TC]

29.341 Aubrey F. G. Bell. *Luis de Camões*. Oxford: Oxford University Press, 1923. ▸ Critical biography of Camões (ca. 1524–80), author of Portugal's national epic, *The Lusiads* (29.347). [TC]

29.342 Aubrey F. G. Bell. *Portuguese literature*. 1922 ed. Oxford: Clarendon, 1970. ▸ Remains best general introduction in English. Focuses on neglected corpus of pre-nineteenth-century Portuguese literature. [TC]

29.343 Harry Bernstein. *The lord mayor of Lisbon: the Portuguese tribune of the people and his twenty-four guilds*. Lanham, Md.: University Press of America, 1989. ISBN 0-8191-7235-9. ▸ Argues *juiz do povo* (tribune) and guilds constituted effective voice for working people between 1640 and abolition of guilds in 1834. Narrow but well-balanced study. [TC]

29.344 C. R. Boxer. *A great Luso-Brazilian figure: Padre Antonio Vieira, S. J., 1608–1697*. London: Hispanic and Luso-Brazilian Councils, 1957. ▸ Superior account of life and thought of Jesuit missionary, writer, and diplomat. Emphasizes Vieira's literary talent and his defense of American Indians and New Christians. [TC]

29.345 James C. Boyajian. *Portuguese bankers at the court of Spain, 1626–1650*. New Brunswick, N.J.: Rutgers University Press, 1983. ISBN 0-8135-0962-9. ▸ Documents Philip IV's controversial policy of using Portuguese bankers, many of whom were New Christians. Offers larger insights into economic activity under Habsburgs. [TC]

29.346 Mary Elizabeth Brooks. *A king for Portugal: the Madrigal conspiracy, 1594–95*. Madison: University of Wisconsin Press, 1964. ▸ Spirited retelling of strange story of arrest and execution by Spanish authorities of Gabriel de Espinosa (pastry maker of Madrigal), who claimed to be returning King Sebastian of Portugal. [TC]

29.347 Luis Vaz de Camões. *The Lusiads*. 1952 ed. William C. Atkinson, trans. New York: Penguin, 1987. ISBN 0-14-044026-7. ▸ Portuguese national epic; celebrates destiny of Portugal and Portuguese from time of first settlers to age of Vasco da Gama and his successors throughout empire. Includes useful introduction to poet and his world. [TC]

29.348 Marcus Cheke. *Dictator of Portugal: a life of the marquis of Pombal, 1699–1782*. 1938 ed. Freeport, N.Y.: Books for Libraries, 1969. ISBN 0-8369-5041-0. ▸ Only English biography of powerful minister responsible for negotiation of new commercial ties with England, rebuilding of Lisbon after 1755 earthquake, and expulsion of Jesuits from Portugal and empire. [TC]

29.349 Bailey W. Diffie and George D. Winius. *Foundations of the Portuguese empire, 1415–1580*. Minneapolis: University of Minnesota Press, 1977. ISBN 0-8166-0782-6. ▸ Covers shorter time span than Boxer 16.97 but like it stands as fundamental interpretive survey in English of Portuguese innovations in navigation and of Portuguese expansion in Asia and Africa. [TC]

29.350 T. F. Earle. *Theme and image in the poetry of Sá de Miranda*. 1984 ed. Oxford: Oxford University Press, 1989. ISBN 0-19-815754-1. ▸ Wide-ranging study of classical sources of Sá de Miranda (1481–1558), metric innovations, and his moralizing satires and eclogues. [TC]

29.351 H.E.S. Fisher. *The Portugal trade: a study of Anglo-Portuguese commerce, 1700–1770*. London: Methuen, 1971. ISBN 0-416-17650-X. ▸ Well-documented discussion focusing on Anglo-Portuguese trade in eighteenth century. Sections on export of wine to England and North American colonies. Argues trade with Portugal acted as important stimulus to English economic development, particularly during years 1700–40. [TC]

29.352 Eduardo d'Oliveira Franca. *Portugal na época da Restauração*. São Paulo: Ciências e Letras da Universidade de São Paulo, Faculdade de Filosofia, 1951. ▸ Classic, but difficult to find, study focusing on what author argues are distinctive manifestations of baroque age in Portugal. Particularly valuable for analyses of elite mentality and of historiography and literature of period. [TC]

29.353 A. David Francis. *The Methuens and Portugal, 1691–1708*. Cambridge: Cambridge University Press, 1966. ▸ Competent account of Anglo-Portuguese diplomatic and commercial relations. Focuses on treaties negotiated by John Methuen, English minister in Lisbon. [TC]

29.354 A. David Francis. *Portugal, 1715–1808: Joanine, Pombaline, and rococo Portugal as seen by British diplomats and traders*. London: Tamesis, 1985. ISBN 0-7293-0190-7. ▸ Comprehensive study of diplomatic and economic forces that reinforced patterns of Anglo-Portuguese mutual dependence from Treaty of Utrecht to Peninsular War. [TC]

29.355   A. David Francis. *The wine trade.* New York: Barnes & Noble, 1972. ISBN 0-06-492230-8. ▸ Study of English wine trade during eighteenth century focusing on traffic in port wine. Brief but intriguing passages about wine production and comparative Anglo-Portuguese consumption habits. [TC]

29.356   Vitorino Magalhães Godinho. "Portugal and her empire." In *The new Cambridge modern history.* Vol. 5: *The ascendancy of France, 1648–88.* F. L. Carsten, ed., pp. 384–97. Cambridge: Cambridge University Press, 1964. ▸ Analysis of war with Spain and threats to empire during period following Restoration (1640). Includes wide-ranging overview of economic and political structures by outstanding historian whose work is generally unavailable in English. [TC]

29.357   Vitorino Magalhães Godinho. "Portugal and her empire, 1680–1720." In *The new Cambridge modern history.* Vol. 6: *The rise of Great Britain and Russia, 1688–1715/25.* J. S. Bromley, ed., pp. 509–39. Cambridge: Cambridge University Press, 1970. ISBN 0-521-07524-6. ▸ Classic analysis of transformation of imperial economy during seventeenth and eighteenth centuries. Emphasizes increasing importance of Anglo-Portuguese trade and of Brazilian exports, particularly gold. [TC]

29.358   Thomas Richard Graham. *The Jesuit Antonio Vieira and his plans for the economic rehabilitation of seventeenth-century Portugal.* São Paulo: Seção de Publiçacôes da Divisão de Arquivo do Estado, 1978. ▸ Useful study of Vieira's preoccupation with Portuguese economy during period of decline. Argues Vieira, despite religious vocation, interested primarily in politics and economics. [TC]

29.359   Carl A. Hanson. *Economy and society in baroque Portugal, 1668–1703.* Minneapolis: University of Minnesota Press, 1981. ISBN 0-8166-0969-1. ▸ Useful study of reign of King Pedro II. Analyzes failure of Portuguese to develop domestic industries and argues relative prosperity achieved after 1690 result of stronger ties with England and influx of gold from Brazil. [TC]

29.360   Henry H. Hart. *Luis de Camões and the "Epic of the Lusiads."* Norman: University of Oklahoma Press, 1962. ▸ Sound survey of poet's life and work. Translations of poems and additional lyrics; bibliography with numerous English titles. [TC]

29.361   Alexandre Herculano. *History of the origin and establishment of the Inquisition in Portugal.* 1926 ed. New York: KTAV, 1972. ISBN 0-87068-153-2. ▸ Author, forceful critic of Inquisition, focuses on King John II's protracted struggle with pope to establish tribunal in Portugal. Valuable prolegomena by Yosef Hayim Yerushalmi. [TC]

29.362   Elisabeth Feist Hirsch. *Damião de Gois: the life and thought of a Portuguese humanist, 1502–1574.* The Hague: Nijhoff, 1967. ▸ Excellent study of historian best known for his chronicles of kings John II and Manuel I. Argues Gois's trial by Inquisition as Erasmian was symptomatic of general resurgence of Catholic orthodoxy in Portugal. [TC]

29.363   International Colloquium on Luso-Brazilian Studies. *Proceedings of the International Colloquium on Luso-Brazilian Studies.* Nashville: Vanderbilt University Press, 1953. ▸ Papers from variety of disciplines as well as guides to archives and libraries and suggestions for further research. Remains important collection because of stature of contributors. [TC]

29.364   T. D. Kendrick. *The Lisbon earthquake.* London: Methuen, 1956. ▸ Popular account of contemporary speculations (in Portugal and rest of Europe, particularly England) about meaning of events of November 1755. [TC]

29.365   George Kubler. *Portuguese plain architecture: between*

spices and diamonds, 1521–1706. Middletown, Conn.: Wesleyan University Press, 1972. ISBN 0-8195-4045-5. ▸ Analysis of development of Portuguese vernacular style during sixteenth and seventeenth centuries, emphasizing overlapping influences of European, colonial, and indigenous elements. Extensive illustrations. [TC]

29.366   George Kubler and Martin Soria. *Art and architecture in Spain and Portugal and their American dominions, 1500–1800.* Baltimore: Penguin, 1959. ▸ Survey focusing on Spain, but chapters on Portuguese architecture (Kubler) and on painting and sculpture (Soria) are comprehensive. Excellent bibliography and illustrations. [TC]

29.367   H. V. Livermore, ed. *Portugal and Brazil: an introduction.* 1953 ed. Oxford: Clarendon, 1970. ▸ Essays in honor of Aubrey Bell and Edgar Prestage. Twelve contributions addressing Portuguese history and culture. Includes bibliographies of writings of Bell and Prestage. [TC]

29.368   Rose Macaulay. *They went to Portugal.* 1946 ed. Middlesex, England: Penguin, 1985. ISBN 0-14-009537-3. ▸ Comprehensive survey of English travelers in Portugal from Crusades to nineteenth century. Vivid appreciations of William Thomas Beckford and Robert Southey as well as large cast of less celebrated writers. [TC]

29.369   A. H. de Oliveira Marques. *Daily life in Portugal in the late Middle Ages.* S. S. Wyatt, trans. Madison: University of Wisconsin Press, 1971. ISBN 0-299-05580-9. ▸ Study of work, food, dress, courtship and domesticity, religiosity, high culture, and popular culture, written with fine eye for quotations and telling details. [TC]

29.370   Edgar Prestage. *The diplomatic relations of Portugal with France, England, and Holland from 1640 to 1668.* Watford, England: Voss Michael, 1925. ▸ Focuses on key figures and events from 1640 Restoration to recognition of independence by Spain. Reliable accounts of individual diplomatic missions; lacks larger narrative focus. [TC]

29.371   I. S. Révah. *Études Portugaises.* Paris: Fundação Calouste Gulbenkian/Centro Cultural Portugues, 1975. ▸ Essays by one of leading students of marranos in Portugal. Includes classic articles about marranos (christianized Jews) and Inquisition, development of Portuguese language, and writings of dramatist Gil Vicente and historian João de Barros. [TC]

29.372   P. E. Russell. *Prince Henry the Navigator: the rise and fall of a culture hero.* New York: Clarendon, 1984. ISBN 0-19-952250-2. ▸ Publication of lecture providing suggestive look at man and his times. No adequate full-length biography of Prince Henry has yet been written. [TC]

29.373   Elaine Sanceau. *The perfect prince: a biography of the king Dom João II (who continued the work of Henry the Navigator).* Porto, Portugal: Livraria Civilização, 1959. ▸ Biography of King John (João) II (1455–95), who sponsored expedition of Bartolomeu Dias to Cape of Good Hope. Adequate introduction; lacks scholarly apparatus. [TC]

29.374   Elaine Sanceau. *The reign of the fortunate king, 1495–1521.* Hamden, Conn.: Archon, 1969. ISBN 0-208-00968-X. ▸ Biography of King Manuel I, whose reign saw apogee of Portuguese expansion overseas. Written for general audience; lacks scholarly apparatus. [TC]

29.375   Antonio José Saraiva. *Renascimento e Contra-Reforma.* Vol. 2 of *História da cultura em Portugal.* Lisbon: Jornal do Forro, 1955. 3 vols. ▸ Best general introduction to Portuguese culture prior to 1580. Studies diffusion of books, nautical innovations, advances in science, humanist thought, and literature. [TC]

29.376   Antonio José Saraiva. *A ressaca do Renascimento.* Vol. 3

of *História da cultura em Portugal*. Lisbon: Jornal do Forro, 1962. 3 vols. ▸ Best general introduction to Portuguese culture to 1580. Studies of sixteenth-century social structure, religious persecution and Inquisition, ideology of imperial expansion, and life and writings of Luis de Camões. [TC]

29.377 A. C. de C. M. Saunders. *A social history of black slaves and freedmen in Portugal, 1441–1555*. New York: Cambridge University Press, 1982. ISBN 0-521-23150-7. ▸ Solid monograph analyzing slave trade and status of blacks from arrival of first slaves to publication of first attack on treatment of blacks in Portugal. [TC]

29.378 Stuart Schwartz. "The voyage of the vassals: royal power, noble obligations, and merchant capital before the Portuguese Restoration of Independence, 1624–1660." *American historical review* 96.3 (1991) 735–62. ISSN 0002-8762. ▸ Superb study focusing on relations between crown, nobility, and merchants (primarily New Christians, or descendents of converted Jews) in loss and recovery of Bahia (Brazil) from Dutch in 1624–25. Places incident within larger context of sociopolitical change in seventeenth-century Europe. [TC]

29.379 Robert C. Smith. *The art of Portugal, 1500–1800*. New York: Meredith, 1968. ▸ Only general history in English. Masterly surveys of Portuguese architecture, painting, and sculpture. Most important contribution for attention to decorative arts, ceramics in particular. Superb illustrations. [TC]

29.380 Ronald W. Sousa. *The rediscoverers: major writers in the Portuguese literature of regeneration*. University Park: Pennsylvania State University Press, 1981. ISBN 0-271-0030-6. ▸ Literary study of prophetic elements in Portuguese literature from sixteenth to twentieth century. Individual chapters devoted to Luis Camões, Antonio Vieira, João Almeida Garrett, José Eça de Queiros, and Fernando Pessoa. [TC]

29.381 Robert Southey. *Journals of a residence in Portugal, 1800–1801, and a visit to France 1838, supplemented by extracts from his correspondence*. 1960 ed. Adolfo Cabral, ed. Westport, Conn.: Greenwood, 1978. ISBN 0-313-20590-6. ▸ Penetrating observations by English poet and historian, written when he had full command of language and history of Portugal. [TC]

29.382 George West. *A list of the writings of Charles Ralph Boxer, published between 1926 and 1984, compiled for his eightieth birthday*. London: Tamesis, 1984. ISBN 0-7293-0187-7. ▸ Comprehensive bibliography of writings of preeminent modern historian of Portuguese world. [TC]

29.383 Yosef Hayim Yerushalmi. *The Lisbon massacre of 1506 and the royal image in the "Shebet Yehudah."* Cincinnati, Ohio: Hebrew Union College, 1976. (*Hebrew Union College annual*, Supplements, 1.) ISBN 0-87820-600-0. ▸ Analysis of account of massacre of 1,000 New Christians provided in *Shebet Yehudah* of Solomon Ibn Verga. Appendixes include texts of letters and decrees as well as German account of massacre. [TC]

SEE ALSO
21.130 Yosef H. Yerushalmi. *From Spanish court to Italian ghetto*.
37.465 Kenneth Maxwell. *Conflicts and conspiracies*.

Constitutional Monarchy, 1807–1910

29.384 Marcus Cheke. *Carlota Joaquina, queen of Portugal*. 1947 ed. Freeport, N.Y.: Books for Libraries, 1969. ISBN 0-8369-5040-2. ▸ Biography, with historical background, of life and times of Spanish-born wife of King João VI. Depicted as power behind throne. [DW]

29.385 H. V. Livermore. *Portugal: a short history*. 2d ed. New York: Cambridge University Press, 1976. ISBN 0-521-21320-7 (cl), 0-521-29103-8 (pbk). ▸ Concise, clear analysis of nineteenth-

century Portugal emphasizing political and some social history. [DW]

29.386 Neill Macaulay. *Dom Pedro: the struggle for liberty in Brazil and Portugal, 1798–1834*. Durham, N.C.: Duke University Press, 1986. ISBN 0-8223-0681-6. ▸ First full biography of first emperor of Brazil and protagonist in War of the Brothers over possession of Portuguese throne. [DW]

29.387 Miriam Halpern Pereira. *Revolução, financas, dependência externa*. Lisbon: Sá da Costa, 1979. ▸ Economic history of Portugal in first half of nineteenth century with essay and anthology of principal documents. [DW]

29.388 Albert Silbert. *Do Portugal de Antigo Regime ao Portugal oitocentista*. 3d ed. Lisbon: Livros Horizonte, 1981. ▸ Social and economic history, 1780–1830, with emphasis on agrarian and financial problems. Also highlights British liberal influence on Portuguese military. [DW]

SEE ALSO
47.235 R. J. Hammond. *Portugal and Africa, 1815–1910*.

Republican Portugal, 1910–1926

29.389 Aubrey F. G. Bell. *Portugal of the Portuguese*. London: Pitman, 1915. ▸ British Hispanist's fond, rich portrait of rural Portugal in 1914 and critique of urban, republican political cliques. [DW]

29.390 A. H. de Oliveira Marques. *A Ia republica Portuguesa*. 1970 2d ed. Lisbon: Livros Horizonte, 1980. ▸ Survey of principal facts and figures stressing social and economic structures and history. [DW]

29.391 Douglas L. Wheeler. *Republican Portugal: a political history, 1910–1926*. Madison: University of Wisconsin Press, 1978. ISBN 0-299-07450-1. ▸ Political history from fall of monarchy to end of parliamentary republic. Emphasizes political and military conspiracies and political parties. [DW]

Dictatorship, 1926–1974

29.392 Caroline B. Brettell. *Men who migrate, women who wait*. Princeton: Princeton University Press, 1986. ISBN 0-691-09424-1. ▸ Artful marriage of historical and anthropological approaches by anthropologist studying emigration and social and demographic history of northern village. [DW]

29.393 Manuel Villaverde Cabral. "Agrarian structures and recent rural movements in Portugal." *Journal of peasant studies* 5.4 (1978) 411–45. ISSN 0306-6150. ▸ Analysis of agrarian structures and peasant movements region by region. [DW]

29.394 Antonio de Figuerido. *Portugal: fifty years of dictatorship*. New York: Holmes & Meier, 1975. ISBN 0-8419-0237-2. ▸ Popular history of Estado Novo regime from 1926 to 1934 emphasizing central roles of António Salazar and interested groups by exiled Socialist. [DW]

29.395 Tom Gallagher. *Portugal: a twentieth-century interpretation*. Manchester: Manchester University Press, 1983. ▸ Moderately successful history from 1910 to 1980 concentrating on period of dictatorship, 1933–74. Based largely on secondary works and British diplomatic records. [DW]

29.396 Lawrence S. Graham and Harry M. Makler, eds. *Contemporary Portugal: the revolution and its antecedents*. Austin: University of Texas Press, 1979. ISBN 0-292-71047-X. ▸ Collection of chapters of uneven quality on history, politics, and economy of Portuguese dictatorship. Includes origins of 1974 military coup which toppled regime. [DW]

29.397 Hugh Kay. *Salazar and modern Portugal*. New York: Hawthorne, 1970. ▸ Biography of Salazar emphasizing Catholic background. Based on secondary works and printed documents. Major issues and ideas thoroughly analyzed. [DW]

29.398 Herminio Martins. "Portugal." In *European fascism*. S. J. Woolf, ed., pp. 302–36. New York: Vintage, 1969. ▸ Sociologist's analysis of dictatorship into 1960s. Stresses social and economic composition of leadership and ruling groups. Also discusses institutions, including secret police. [DW]

29.399 Dawn L. Raby. *Fascism and resistance in Portugal: Communists, Liberals, and military dissidents in the opposition to Salazar, 1941–1974.* New York: Manchester University Press, 1988. ISBN 0-7190-2514-1. ▸ History of diverse and persistent but ineffectual opposition to dictatorship emphasizing period 1958–74. Original materials on role of Communist party. [DW]

29.400 Richard A. H. Robinson. *Contemporary Portugal: a history.* Boston: Allen & Unwin, 1979. ISBN 0-04-946013-7. ▸ Survey of split between dictatorship (1926–74) and democracy (1974–78). Clear explanations of complex political changes. [DW]

29.401 Douglas L. Wheeler. "António de Oliveira Salazar (1889–1970)." In *Research guide to European historical biography.* Walter Beacham, ed., pp. 1727–38. Washington, D.C.: Beacham, 1992. ISBN 1-933833-28-8. ▸ Biographical note on Salazar including activities of historical significance. Overview and evaluation of main biographical sources and primary sources; annotated critical bibliography. [DW]

Democratic Portugal, 1974–1992

29.402 Hugo Gil Ferreira and Michael W. Marshall, eds. *Portugal's revolution: ten years on.* New York: Cambridge University Press, 1986. ISBN 0-521-32204-9. ▸ History of 1974 military coup and revolutionary aftermath to 1984. Includes interviews with key figures, translated texts, and chronology. [DW]

29.403 Lawrence S. Graham and Douglas L. Wheeler, eds. *In search of modern Portugal: the revolution and its consequences.* Madison: University of Wisconsin Press, 1983. ISBN 0-299-08990-8. ▸ Essays from 1979 conference analyzing causes, course, and consequences of 1974 military coup and its impact on politics, society, and economy. Multidisciplinary and comprehensive. [DW]

29.404 Robert Harvey. *Portugal: birth of a democracy.* New York: St. Martin's, 1978. ISBN 0-312-63184-7. ▸ Journalist's clear account of 1974 Revolution and first three years of new regime with focus on government and politics. [DW]

29.405 Michael Hasgor. *Portugal in revolution.* Beverly Hills, Calif.: Sage, 1976. ISBN 0-8039-0647-1. ▸ History of Portuguese Revolution, 1974–75, by Israeli historian. Excellent, brief study for general reader. [DW]

29.406 Kenneth Maxwell, ed. *Portugal in the 1980's: dilemmas of democratic consolidation.* New York: Greenwood, 1986. ISBN 0-313-24889-3. ▸ Analyses of Portugal since 1974: foreign affairs, economics, society, and politics. Documentation somewhat dated. [DW]

29.407 Kenneth Maxwell and Michael H. Haltzel, eds. *Portugal: ancient country, young democracy.* Washington, D.C.: Woodrow Wilson Center Press, 1990. ISBN 0-943875-20-X (cl), 0-943875-19-6 (pbk). ▸ Analyses of contemporary Portugal up to 1987: economy, political culture, foreign affairs, and transition to pluralist democracy. Essays of inconsistent quality. [DW]

29.408 Douglas Porch. *The Portuguese armed forces and the revolution.* Stanford, Calif.: Hoover Institution Press, 1977. ISBN 0-85664-391-2. ▸ Military historian's analysis of origins of armed forces movement which overthrew dictatorship in 1974. [DW]

R. PO-CHIA HSIA

German States and the Habsburg Empire, 1493–1800

Compared to the state of the field as described by H. Holborn in the 1961 *Guide*, the most striking characteristic of current scholarship is simply that the historiography of German-speaking, early modern central Europe has emerged as a distinctive field. Thirty years ago, the history of the Holy Roman empire and Switzerland was subsumed under the heading Modern German History following the dominant interpretive model of German historicism. Defined by a nationalist framework, the history of central Europe from the sixteenth to the eighteenth century was interpreted primarily as different stages leading to the nationalist struggles and the emergence of a unified German state during the nineteenth century. An example of this approach was the well-known textbook in German history by Holborn, which developed the themes of German history from the Reformation to the twentieth century.

Although the nationalist perspective still informs recent historical works, primarily those of political historians in Germany, during the past thirty years the field of early modern central Europe has moved in very different directions. Three features are prominent. First, chronologically, the field has detached itself from modern German history: history chairs in German universities are now commonly designated as medieval, early modern, and modern, and a standard periodization is now generally accepted in the profession (early modern is defined as 1495 to 1789/1806 in former West Germany, and as early bourgeois [*frühbürgerlich*] 1470/1500 to 1789 in former East Germany). Second, the topics of research have vastly increased. Although political and institutional history still informs a great deal of research, historians of early modern central Europe have explored hitherto neglected topics in social, economic, and cultural history. Current publications on women, gender, minorities, ritual, and daily life are the most recent examples of this orientation, alongside established interest in the history of popular culture, the peasantry, and cities. This greater diversity of interest is closely associated with a third development in the field: its internationalization. Whereas only a handful of non-German historians were interested in early modern central Europe in 1961, scholars currently active in the field include American, Canadian, Australian, British, French, and a small number of Czech, Dutch, Belgian, Danish, Italian, Israeli, and Japanese historians, in addition of course to German-speaking historians in Germany, Austria, and Switzerland.

Outside of German-speaking countries, scholarship in the English language constitutes an important element in the field, not only in terms of the scope of research but also in terms of its methodological contributions. Whereas political and institutional history still remains perhaps one of the most important research foci of our German colleagues, English- or German-language scholarship, particularly in North America, has helped to create or invigorate new topics of research in the history of women, Jews, culture, and the peasantry. Methodologically, English-language scholarship in the field is more open to non-Germanic influences, such as the research paradigms associated with the French Annales school and the Italian approach of *microstoria*. There are, however, remarkable exceptions in Germany, such as Hans Medick's study of Laichlingen, Manfred Jakubowski-Tiessen's book on "Sturmflut 1717," and Otto Ulbricht's work on infanticide in the eighteenth century. Nevertheless, there is a greater methodological openness in non-German scholarship, liberated on the one hand from the minutiae of local history (*Landesgeschichte*), and on the other from the dominant discourse of historicism.

Differences in approaches, however, do not indicate a lack of cooperation. Several joint conferences between historians in North America and central Europe during the past eight years point to the significance and maturity of English-language historiography. The first joint conference in 1984 at Chicago emphasized the politics and institutions of the Holy Roman empire. The second joint conference in 1986 at Mainz focused on "Estates and Society in the Old Reich." A third conference in 1991 at Minneapolis was dedicated to the history of the Habsburg monarchy. Similarly, in 1991 the American Society for Reformation Research and its German counterpart, the Verein für Reformationsgeschichte held the first ever joint conference in Washington, D.C., sponsored by the German Historical Institute, which was established in 1987 in the nation's capital. With scheduled joint conferences and the regular participation of individual North American scholars in colloquia held in Europe, the future of American-European cooperation in this field seems assured.

English-language publications on early modern central Europe tend to fall into three chronological clusters: the sixteenth century, especially the early Reformation years and the problem of "confessionalization"; the seventeenth century, focusing on issues of war, famine, and pestilence; and the eighteenth century, with focus on the Enlightenment and absolutism.

The Reformation has a long-established presence in English-language scholarship, given the prominence of Protestant theology and church history in the first American universities. In the past twenty years, English-language publications on the German Reformation have made original and significant contributions, notably in the study of popular religion, women, gender, iconography, and the Reformation in the cities. Compared to German-language monographs, there is a better integration of social and religious history with political and institutional history. The compartmentalization between theology and history, still prominent in German academic publications, is less pronounced in English-language scholarship. In specific topics such as the history of Anabaptists, Jews, and women, and in particular approaches, such as the social history of the Reformation, English-language scholarship is perhaps at the cutting edge of the field today.

Another cluster of publications centers on the eighteenth century, especially on the themes of Enlightenment and absolutism. A great deal of interest focuses on the two dynasties that would compete for leadership in central Europe, the Habsburg and the Hohenzollern. Publications on eighteenth-century history are particularly strong in biographies of monarchs, ministers, and thinkers, although more recent research is turning to social, economic, and cultural themes.

An increasingly important trend points to broad thematic interests that span the early modern centuries. In Reformation research, for example, it has long been recognized that concentration on the early decades of the reform movement can be shortsighted, and that the later sixteenth and early seventeenth centuries are crucial to understanding the larger impact of the initial Reformation movement. Likewise, specialists on the eighteenth century are keenly aware of the seventeenth-century roots of Enlightenment thought and have explored the connections between cameralist policies and enlightened absolutism of the eighteenth century, pietism and constitutional thought of the late seventeenth century. More recently, there are attempts to link seventeenth- and eighteenth-century German history with colonial American history by exploring, for example, the lives of emigrants from central Europe who went to North America. These studies add a transatlantic dimension to research on early modern German history. In this regard, our German colleagues have helped to establish the agenda for future debates in advancing the concepts of confessionalization, social disciplining, christianization, and dechristianization as working hypotheses to investigate the history of early modern central Europe.

A final word about German unification in 1990 is in order. The collapse of the German Democratic Republic, the absorption of East Germany by the West, and the subsequent purge of the former East German universities have long-term consequences for early modern German historiography that are as yet unclear. The most important result has been the abandonment of Marxism and the concept of "early bourgeois revolution" in historiographical discourse. Furthermore, one can notice a renewed interest in the question of national identity during the early modern period. A period of intense self-reflection will perhaps characterize the coming years, as our German colleagues question the historical context behind the concepts and language that have shaped their understanding of German history.

Entries are arranged under the following headings:

General Studies

Revolution and Reformation, 1500–1550

Age of Confessional Conflicts, 1550–1650

Age of Absolutism, 1650–1800

Women, Gender, and Family, 1500–1800

Socioeconomic History, 1500–1700

Socioeconomic History, 1700–1800

Urban History, 1600–1800

Cultural History, 1500–1650

Cultural History, 1650–1800

[Contributors: AF = Andrea Feldman, CH = Caroline Hannaway, CRF = Christopher R. Friedrichs, CWI = Charles W. Ingrao, HLA = Hugh L. Agnew, IB = Ivo Banac, JBK = Jonathan B. Knudsen, JJS = James J. Sheehan, JLP = Janet L. Polasky, JML = Jennifer M. Lloyd, JS = Jonathan Sperber, KZ = Kristin E. S. Zapalac, MEW = Merry E. Wiesner-Hanks, ML = Mary Lindemann, PZ = Perez D. Zagorin, RH = R. Po-chia Hsia, SBV = Steven Béla Várdy, SKN = Susan C. Karant-Nunn, TAB = Thomas A. Brady, Jr., TR = Thomas Robisheaux, WJC = William J. Courtenay]

GENERAL STUDIES

30.1 Phillip N. Bebb and Sherrin Marshall, eds. *The process of change in early modern Europe: essays in honor of Miriam Usher Chrisman.* Athens: Ohio University Press, 1988. ISBN 0-8214-0900-X. ▸ Original essays on early modern Germany with focus on urban, cultural, political, and German Jewish history. [RH]

30.2 Monika Hagenmaier and Sabine Holtz, eds. *Krisenbewusstsein und Krisenbewältigung in der frühen Neuzeit—crisis in early modern Europe: Festschrift für Hans-Christoph Rublack.* Frankfurt: Lang, 1992. ISBN 3-631-43535-5. ▸ Collection of essays on early modern Germany, including six contributions in English by leading historians of sixteenth- and seventeenth-century German religious history. [RH]

30.3 Michael Hughes. *Early modern Germany, 1477–1806.* Philadelphia: University of Pennsylvania Press, 1992. ISBN 0-8122-3182-1 (cl), 0-8122-1427-7 (pbk). ▸ First textbook in English on early modern Germany with emphasis on political and institutional history. Draws on wide range of recent monographs. [RH]

30.4 *Politics and society in the Holy Roman Empire, 1500–1806.* Chicago: University of Chicago Press, 1986. (*Journal of modern history*, Supplement, 58.) ISSN 0022-2801. ▸ Eleven (seven German and four North American) papers from conference sponsored by *Journal of Modern History* at University of Chicago (April 1984). Topics range from intellectual to institutional, political, and diplomatic history. German contributions represent several major research directions. Some articles in English. [RH]

30.5 Georg Schmidt, ed. *Stände und Gesellschaft im alten Reich.* Stuttgart: Steiner, 1989. (Veröffentlichungen des Instituts für Europäische Geschichte, Mainz, Abteilung für Universalgeschichte. Beiheft, 29.) ISBN 3-515-05074-4. ▸ Fifteen research and historiographical essays, seven by American historians, from joint German-American conference on political, institutional, and social history of Holy Roman Empire. [RH]

30.6 Kyle C. Sessions and Phillip N. Bebb, eds. *Pietas et societas: new trends in Reformation social history: essays in memory of Harold J. Grimm.* Kirksville, Mo.: Sixteenth Century Journal Publications, 1985. (Sixteenth century essays and studies, 4.) ISBN 0-940474-04-2. ▸ Represents earlier trends in social history, now in part superceded by more recent research. [RH]

30.7 Jonathan W. Zophy, ed. *The Holy Roman Empire: a dictionary handbook.* Westport, Conn.: Greenwood, 1980. ISBN 0-313-21457-3. ▸ Selected, short entries on individuals and topics from medieval and early modern German history at introductory level. Volume includes chronology, genealogies, and bibliography. [RH]

REVOLUTION AND REFORMATION, 1500–1550

30.8 Roland H. Bainton. *Here I stand: a life of Martin Luther.* 1950 ed. Nashville: Abingdon, 1991. ISBN 0-687-16895-3. ▸ Most widely read biography in English; detailed account of Luther's life and beliefs. Portrays Luther as renewer of Christian religion. [TAB/PZ]

30.9 Gerhard Benecke. *Maximilian I (1459–1519): an analytical biography.* London: Routledge & Kegan Paul, 1982. ISBN 0-7100-9023-4. ▸ Only modern biography of Maximilian in English. Portrays Maximilian as neither medieval nor modern, but shrewd ruler of Austria and Germany. [TAB]

30.10 Peter Blickle. *The communal reformation: the quest for salvation in sixteenth-century Germany.* Thomas Dunlap, trans. Atlantic Highlands, N.J.: Humanities Press, 1992. ISBN 0-391-03730-7. ▸ Stimulating thesis on reformation as religious communalism of burghers and peasants and culmination of medieval communal movement. Based on South Germany and Switzerland. [TAB]

30.11 Peter Blickle. *The revolution of 1525: the German Peasants' War from a new perspective.* 1981 ed. Thomas A. Brady, Jr. and H. C. Erik Midelfort, trans. Baltimore: Johns Hopkins University Press, 1985. ISBN 0-8018-2472-9 (cl, 1981), 0-8018-3162-8 (pbk). ▸ Original and controversial interpretation of German Peasants' War as revolution of common man in response to agrarian crisis and refeudalization, based on rebels' grievance lists. [TAB]

30.12 Heinrich Bornkamm. *Luther in mid-career, 1521–1530.* Karin Bornkamm, ed. E. Theodore Bachmann, trans. Philadelphia: Fortress, 1983. ISBN 0-8006-0692-2. ▸ Biography of Luther in his most productive period as churchman. Incomplete study of larger project by representative of German "Luther renaissance." [TAB]

30.13 Thomas A. Brady, Jr. *Ruling class, regime, and Reformation at Strasbourg, 1520–1555.* Leiden: Brill, 1978. ISBN 90-04-05285-2. ▸ Pioneering and pathbreaking analysis of Strasbourg's elite and their response to Reformation movement. Sociologically oriented and based on prosopography. [TAB]

30.14 Thomas A. Brady, Jr. *Turning Swiss: cities and empire, 1450–1550.* Cambridge: Cambridge University Press, 1985. ISBN 0-521-30525-X. ▸ A synthetic narrative of South German cities' dilemma between imperial loyalty and imitation of Swiss. Based on social and political geography. [TAB]

30.15 Karl Brandi. *The emperor Charles V: the growth and destiny of a man and of a world-empire.* 1939 ed. C. V. Wedgwood, trans. London: Cape, 1968. ▸ Classic biography; one of most important studies of life, personality, career, and rule of Charles V. Sees Charles's life task as restoration of universal Christian imperium. English translation omits footnote references. [TAB]

30.16 Martin Brecht. *Martin Luther.* 2 vols. James L. Schaaf, trans. Philadelphia: Fortress, 1985–90. ISBN 0-8006-0738-4 (v. 1), 0-8006-2463-7 (v. 2). ▸ Fullest and most authoritative modern biography of Luther. [TAB]

30.17 W.D.J. Cargill Thompson. *The political thought of Martin Luther.* A. G. Dickens, Preface. Philip Broadhead, ed. Totowa, N.J.: Barnes & Noble, 1984. ISBN 0-389-20468-4. ▸ Survey of main lines of Luther's political thought. [TAB]

30.18 Miriam Usher Chrisman. *Strasbourg and the reform: a* *study in the process of change.* New Haven: Yale University Press, 1967. ‣ Early study of urban reform in one city. Interprets Reformation essentially as movement to laicize religion. [TAB]

30.19 Claus-Peter Clasen. *Anabaptism: a social history, 1525–1618, Switzerland, Austria, Moravia, South and Central Germany.* Ithaca, N.Y.: Cornell University Press, 1972. ISBN 0-8014-0696-x. ‣ Groundbreaking quantitative analysis of all known Anabaptists. Demonstrates movement's small size and shift from urban to rural predominance. [TAB]

30.20 A. G. Dickens. *The German nation and Martin Luther.* New York: Harper & Row, 1974. ISBN 0-06-136141-0. ‣ Interpretation of Reformation as urban event. First general account of German Reformation to take account of modern work on urban Reformation. [TAB]

30.21 Mark U. Edwards, Jr. *Luther's last battles: politics and polemics, 1531–46.* Ithaca, N.Y.: Cornell University Press, 1983. ISBN 0-8014-1564-0. ‣ Useful summary of scholarship on how the older Luther saw world as gripped in struggle between good and evil, but his violent polemics not sign of illness or despair. Based on pamphlet literature during era of Schmalkaldic League (1530–47). [TAB]

30.22 Friedrich Engels. "The Peasant War in Germany." In *The German revolutions, the Peasant War in Germany and Germany: revolution and counter-revolution.* Leonard Krieger, ed., pp. 19–119. Moissaye J. Olgin, trans. Chicago: University of Chicago Press, 1967. ISBN 0-226-20868-0 (cl), 0-226-20869-9 (pbk). ‣ Classic German socialist interpretation of Reformation as part of early bourgeois revolution in Germany. [TAB]

30.23 Stephen A. Fischer-Galati. *Ottoman imperialism and German Protestantism, 1521–1555.* 1959 ed. New York: Octagon Books, 1972. ISBN 0-374-92747-2. ‣ Study of role of Ottoman military pressure in imperial politics during the formative years of German Protestant movement. Emphasizes important, often neglected factor. [TAB]

30.24 Abraham Friesen. *Thomas Muentzer, a destroyer of the godless: the making of a sixteenth-century religious revolutionary.* Berkeley: University of California Press, 1990. ISBN 0-520-06761-4. ‣ Career of radical theologian and leader of Peasants' War in Thuringia. Most comprehensive recent biography in English. [TAB]

30.25 Léon-E. Halkin. *Erasmus: a critical biography.* John Tonkin, trans. Cambridge, Mass.: Blackwell, 1992. ISBN 0-631-16929-6. ‣ Useful biography of Dutch humanist by leading Belgian scholar. [TAB]

30.26 R. Po-chia Hsia. *Society and religion in Münster, 1535–1618.* New Haven: Yale University Press, 1984. ISBN 0-300-03005-3. ‣ Detailed sociocultural analysis of revival and reform of Catholic society after fall of Anabaptist kingdom based on innovative methodology. Concludes Counter-Reformation religion gradually replaced late medieval forms of Catholicism. [TAB]

30.27 R. Po-chia Hsia, ed. *The German people and the Reformation.* Ithaca, N.Y.: Cornell University Press, 1988. ISBN 0-8014-2064-4 (cl), 0-8014-9485-0 (pbk). ‣ Anthology by German and North American authors on social history of German Reformation with special reference to common people. Displays variety of current methods and themes of social history. [TAB]

30.28 Johannes Janssen. *History of the German people at the close of the Middle Ages.* 1896–1910 ed. 17 vols. M. A. Mitchell and A. M. Christie, trans. New York: AMS Press, 1966. ‣ Major statement by German Roman Catholic against Ranke's interpretation (30.38): Reformation disrupted great age of German Christian culture and introduced period of decay and fragmentation. [TAB]

30.29 Susan C. Karant-Nunn. *Zwickau in transition, 1500–1547: the Reformation as an agent of change.* Columbus: Ohio State University Press, 1987. ISBN 0-8142-0421-x. ‣ Based on government German-language archives. Extends discussion of urban reform into eastern parts of Holy Roman Empire. Coming of Lutheranism made social conflicts more manageable but promoted princely authority over this Saxony city. [TAB]

30.30 Joseph Lortz. *The Reformation in Germany.* 2 vols. Ronald Walls, trans. London: Darton, Longman & Todd, 1968. ISBN 0-232-48386-8. ‣ Early, more objective evaluation of Luther by German Catholic historian. Sees German Catholic Reformation as collision of Luther's profound, sincere, but extreme theology with church in theological confusion and religious disarray. [TAB]

30.31 Alisdair E. McGrath. *Luther's theology of the cross: Martin Luther's theological breakthrough.* Oxford: Blackwell, 1985. ISBN 0-631-13855-2. ‣ Discussion of origins and crystallization of Luther's theology. Most recent treatment of central topic of early twentieth-century "Luther renaissance." [TAB]

30.32 Alisdair E. McGrath. *Reformation thought: an introduction.* Oxford: Blackwell, 1988. ISBN 0-631-15802-2 (cl), 0-631-15803-0 (pbk). ‣ Survey of ideas of leading reformers. Best recent introduction to Reformation theology. [TAB]

30.33 Bernd Moeller. *Imperial cities and the Reformation: three essays.* H. C. Erik Midelfort and Mark U. Edwards, Jr., eds. and trans. Philadelphia: Fortress, 1972. ISBN 0-8006-0121-1. ‣ Pioneering essay (German edition, 1962) on role of free cities during Reformation and on South German origins of Reformed (Calvinist) Protestantism. [TAB]

30.34 Heiko A. Oberman. *Luther: man between God and the Devil.* Eileen Walliser-Schwarzbart, trans. New Haven: Yale University Press, 1989. ISBN 0-300-03794-5 (cl). ‣ Analysis of Luther in religious and political perspective of his age. Boldly original historicization of Luther with emphasis on his apocalyptic vision. [TAB]

30.35 Heiko A. Oberman. *Masters of the Reformation: the emergence of a new intellectual climate in Europe.* Dennis Martin, trans. Cambridge: Cambridge University Press, 1981. ISBN 0-521-23098-5. ‣ Study of vitality and social relevance of academic scholasticism, especially nominalism, in immediately pre-Reformation Germany, to such matters as tithes, usury, and witchcraft. Synthesis of master intellectual historian. [TAB]

30.36 Steven E. Ozment. *Mysticism and dissent: religious ideology and social protest in the sixteenth century.* New Haven: Yale University Press, 1973. ISBN 0-300-01576-3. ‣ Discussion of six masters of religious dissent in Reformation Germany. Sees common heritage in mystical theology of influential work, *Theologia Deutsch.* [TAB]

30.37 Steven E. Ozment. *The Reformation in the cities: the appeal of Protestantism to sixteenth-century Germany and Switzerland.* New Haven: Yale University Press, 1975. ISBN 0-300-01898-3. ‣ Brilliant but controversial interpretation of urban reform in South Germany and Switzerland. Emphasizes psychological, not social, roots and unity of urban with Lutheran reform. [TAB]

30.38 Leopold von Ranke. *History of the Reformation in Germany.* 1905 ed. 2 vols. Robert A. Johnson, ed. Sarah Austin, trans. New York: Unger, 1966. ‣ Classic German Protestant interpretation of Reformation as national experience. Movement for German national political reform merged with Luther's renewal of Christendom, only to be frustrated of its goal by Catholic resistance. Incomplete translation. [TAB]

30.39 F. Rapp. *Réformes et Réformation à Strasbourg: église et société dans le diocèse de Strasbourg (1450–1525).* Paris: Ophrys, 1974. (Collection de l'Institut des Hautes Études Alsaciennes, 23.) ISBN 2-7080-0411-5. ‣ Best social history of pre-Reformation clergy. Growing estrangement between clergy and laity resulted from clerical financial involvement and promotion of aliens, chiefly Swabians, to local benefices. [TAB]

30.40 Hans-Christoph Rublack. *Eine bürgerliche Reformation, Nördlingen.* Gütersloh: Mohn, 1982. ISBN 3-579-01677-6. ▸ Study of reformation religion and politics in mid-size Franconian free city. Illustrates limited options enjoyed by rulers of such cities. [TAB]

30.41 Heinz Schilling. *Aufbruch und Krise: Deutschland, 1517–1648.* Vol. 4 of *Die Deutschen und ihre Nation.* Berlin: Siedler, 1988. ISBN 3-88680-059-8. ▸ General interpretation of Reformation era, based on view of reformation as movement that promoted state formation and social discipline. [TAB]

30.42 Ernst Schubert. *Einführung in die Grundprobleme der deutschen Geschichte im Spätmittelalter.* Darmstadt: Wissenschaftliche Buchgesellschaft, 1992. ISBN 3-534-08823-9. ▸ Best introduction to history of pre-Reformation Germany. [TAB]

30.43 Tom Scott. *Freiburg and the Breisgau: town-country relations in the age of Reformation and Peasants' War.* Oxford: Clarendon, 1986. ISBN 0-19-821996-2. ▸ Study of Reformation and Peasants' War against background of town-land relations in southwestern Germany. Economic integration of town and hinterland as background to conflict, not cooperation, between burghers and peasants. [TAB]

30.44 Tom Scott and R. W. Scribner, eds. and trans. *The German Peasants' War: a history in documents.* Atlantic Highlands, N.J.: Humanities Press, 1991. ISBN 0-391-03681-5. ▸ Outstanding introduction to German Peasants' War. Anthology of translated original sources plus introductions and maps. [TAB]

30.45 R. W. Scribner. *For the sake of simple folk: popular propaganda for the German Reformation.* Cambridge: Cambridge University Press, 1981. ISBN 0-521-24192-8. ▸ Discussion of spreading of Reformation movement through word and image. Pioneering study in nonliterate culture and popular movements. [TAB]

30.46 R. W. Scribner. *The German Reformation.* Atlantic Highlands, N.J.: Humanities Press, 1986. ISBN 0-391-03362-X (pbk). ▸ Brief, suggestive introduction to subject. Emphasizes German Reformation as social movement. [TAB]

30.47 R. W. Scribner. *Popular culture and popular movements in Reformation Germany.* London: Hambledon, 1987. ISBN 0-907628-81-8. ▸ Collected original and stimulating essays on urban reform, communications, and ritual by leading social historian. [TAB]

30.48 R. W. Scribner and Gerhard Benecke, eds. *The German Peasant War of 1525: new viewpoints.* London: Allen & Unwin, 1979. ISBN 0-04-900031-4 (cl), 0-04-900032-2 (pbk). ▸ Indispensable anthology of articles on causes, general interpretation, prehistory, military organization, and ideas of German Peasants' War. [TAB]

30.49 Lewis W. Spitz. *The religious Renaissance of the German humanists.* Cambridge, Mass.: Harvard University Press, 1963. ▸ Individual studies of leading German humanists. Contrasts religious ideas with theology of Luther. Older but still reliable. [TAB]

30.50 James M. Stayer. *Anabaptists and the sword.* 2d ed. Lawrence, Kan.: Coronado, 1976. ISBN 0-87291-081-4. ▸ Innovative study of Anabaptist thought and practice on violence and war. Concludes pacifism not originally normative mark of movement. [TAB]

30.51 James M. Stayer. *The German Peasants' War and Anabaptist community of goods.* Montreal: McGill-Queen's University Press, 1991. ISBN 0-7735-0842-2. ▸ Anabaptist movement shared social origins with the Peasants' War. Anabaptist idea of mutual

aid comes from more general ideal of the common good in sixteenth-century communities. Continues author's previous argument. [TAB]

30.52 Gerald Strauss. *Law, resistance, and the state: the opposition to Roman law in Reformation Germany.* Princeton: Princeton University Press, 1986. ISBN 0-691-05469-X. ▸ Detailed, persuasive analysis of tradition, customary law, local liberties, and privileges of estates as elements in opposition to territorial state formation and especially to reception of Roman law. [TAB]

30.53 Gerald Strauss. *Nuremberg in the sixteenth century: city politics and life between Middle Ages and modern times.* Rev. ed. Bloomington: Indiana University Press, 1976. ISBN 0-253-34149-3 (cl), 0-253-34150-7 (pbk). ▸ Global study of city central to South German commerce, manufacturing, and culture and to Lutheran Reformation. Best study of single city in English. [TAB]

SEE ALSO

22.16 Steven E. Ozment, ed. *Reformation Europe.*
22.125 Euan Cameron. *The European Reformation.*
22.130 A. G. Dickens and John M. Tonkin. *The Reformation in historical thought.*
22.138 Joseph Lecler. *Toleration and the Reformation.* Vol. 1.
22.151 George Hunston Williams. *The radical Reformation.*
27.294 G. R. Potter. *Zwingli.*
28.169 Hubert Jedin. *A History of the Council of Trent.* Vol. 1.

AGE OF CONFESSIONAL CONFLICTS, 1550–1650

30.54 Wolfgang Behringer. *Hexenverfolgung in Bayern: Volksmagie, Glaubenseifer, und Staatsräson in der frühen Neuzeit.* 1987 ed. Munich: Oldenbourg, 1988. ISBN 3-486-53902-7. ▸ Excellent analysis of witchcraft beliefs and witch hunting in early modern Bavaria. Gives equal attention to agrarian crises in villages and high-level policy debates in ducal council and universities. [RH]

30.55 Robert Bireley. *Religion and politics in the age of the Counterreformation: Emperor Ferdinand II, William Lamormaini, S.J., and the formation of imperial policy.* Chapel Hill: University of North Carolina Press, 1981. ISBN 0-8078-1470-9. ▸ Case study in confessionalization, revealing central role of Jesuits in shaping policy in Catholic territories. [SKN]

30.56 Karlheinz Blaschke. "The Reformation and the rise of the territorial state." In *Luther and the modern state in Germany.* James D. Tracy, ed., pp. 61–75. Kirksville, Mo.: Sixteenth Century Journal Publishers, 1986. (Sixteenth century essays and studies, 7.) ISBN 0-940474-07-7. ▸ Discussion of Saxon princes' exploitation of religion for statist purposes. Little documentation; no discussion of Schilling or other theories of confessionalization. [SKN]

30.57 John Bossy. "The Counter-Reformation and the people of Catholic Europe." *Past and present* 47 (1970) 51–70. ISSN 0031-2746. ▸ Harbinger of confessionalization theories; shows determination among post-Tridentine Catholic authorities to enforce parochial observance. Notes use of catechisms and education as instruments of conformity that invaded intimacy of family. Most examples non-German but has broad applicability. [SKN]

30.58 Amy Nelson Burnett. "Church discipline and moral Reformation in the thought of Martin Bucer." *Sixteenth century journal* 22.3 (1991) 439–56. ISSN 0361-0160. ▸ Persuasive treatment of Protestant reformer as antecedent and model for later confessionalizers. [SKN]

30.59 Louis Châtellier. *The Europe of the devout: the Catholic Reformation and the formation of a new society.* Jean Birrell, trans. Cambridge and Paris: Cambridge University Press and Éditions de la Maison des Sciences de l'Homme, 1989. ISBN 0-521-36333-0. ▸ Study of transformation of society through Marian congregations. Pious lay brotherhoods, founded by Jesuits, facilitated social discipline and state control. Encompasses all of Catholic Europe from Council of Trent through eighteenth century. Part synthesis, part original research. [SKN]

30.60 Henry J. Cohn. "The territorial princes in Germany's Second Reformation, 1559–1622." In *International Calvinism, 1541–1715*. Menna Prestwich, ed., pp. 135–65. Oxford: Clarendon, 1985. ISBN 0-19-821933-4. ▸ Invaluable survey and evaluation of Second (Calvinist) Reformation. Concludes territorial rulers who adopted reformed faith and imposed it by fiat were genuinely convinced by its theological precepts, but also perceived political advantages accruing to them. [SKN]

30.61 Eileen T. Dugan. "The funeral sermon as a key to familial values in early modern Nördlingen." *Sixteenth century journal* 20.4 (1989) 631–44. ISSN 0361-0160. ▸ Analysis of sermons from 1589 to 1712. Author could well use same evidence to discuss funeral sermon as instrument of confessionalizing family. [SKN]

30.62 Marc R. Forster. *The Counter-Reformation in the villages: religion and reform in the bishopric of Speyer, 1560–1720*. Ithaca, N.Y.: Cornell University Press, 1992. ISBN 0-8014-2566-2. ▸ Revisionist discussion focusing on popular revival of Catholicism in rural Southwest Germany during eighteenth century. Denies effectiveness of Counter-Reformation due to absence of confessional early modern state in Speyer. [RH]

30.63 Richard L. Gawthrop. "The social role of seventeenth-century German territorial states." In *Germania illustrata: essays on early modern Germany presented to Gerald Strauss*. Andrew C. Fix and Susan C. Karant-Nunn, eds., pp. 243–58. Kirksville, Mo.: Sixteenth Century Journal Publishers, 1992. (Sixteenth century essays and studies, 18.) ISBN 0-940474-19-0. ▸ Sees continuity in patterns of government between sixteenth and seventeenth centuries, including methods of gaining submission of populace. Tax surge of seventeenth century fostered villages' integration into market economy, bringing major social change compatible with absolutism. [SKN]

30.64 Kaspar von Greyerz. *The late city Reformation in Germany: the case of Colmar, 1522–1628*. Wiesbaden: Steiner, 1980. (Veröffentlichungen des Instituts für Europäische Geschichte, Mainz: Abteilung für Abendländische Religionsgeschichte, 98.) ISBN 3-515-02997-4. ▸ Argues for continuity of urban Reformation into the second half of sixteenth century, although reforms were carried out by magistrates from above and not from popular pressure from below. [RH]

30.65 R. Po-chia Hsia. "Printing, censorship, and antisemitism in Reformation Germany." In *The process of change in early modern Europe: essays in honor of Miriam Usher Chrisman*. Phillip N. Bebb and Sherrin Marshall, eds. Athens: Ohio University Press, 1988. ISBN 0-8214-0900-X. ▸ Brief reminder that both printing and censorship were tools of state but censorship of antisemitic booklet proved the ineffectiveness of mandate. [SKN]

30.66 R. Po-chia Hsia. *Social discipline in the Reformation: Central Europe, 1550–1750*. 1989 ed. London: Routledge, 1992. ISBN 0-415-01148-5 (cl, 1989), 0-415-01149-3 (pbk). ▸ Indispensable English-language summary of all significant works to 1989 on confessionalization and social disciplining in Germany. Shows very similar state-enhancing processes, whether in Lutheran Württemberg, Calvinist Rhenish Palatinate, or Catholic Bavaria. [SKN]

30.67 Robert Jütte. "Poor relief and social discipline in sixteenth-century Europe." *European studies review* 11 (1981) 25–52. ISSN 0014-3111. ▸ Inspired by Oestreich 30.72, reveals discipline as common feature of legislation for poor in early modern Europe. Protestant and Catholic authorities alike mistrusted poor and instituted regulations to control behavior of poor in common interest. [SKN]

30.68 Susan C. Karant-Nunn. "Kinder, Küche, Kirche: social ideology in the sermons of Johannes Mathesius." In *Germania illustrata: essays on early modern Germany presented to Gerald Strauss*. Andrew C. Fix and Susan C. Karant-Nunn, eds., pp. 121–40. Kirksville, Mo.: Sixteenth Century Journal Publishers, 1992. (Sixteenth century essays and studies, 18.) ISBN 0-940474-19-0. ▸ Regards sermons, in this case those of Saxon preacher Mathesius, as means of inculcating ideals of familial order and obedience. Women were seen as dangerous and in need of control. [SKN]

30.69 Michael Kunze. *Highroad to the stake: a tale of witchcraft*. William E. Yuill, trans. Chicago: University of Chicago Press, 1987. ISBN 0-226-46211-0 (cl), 0-226-46212-9 (pbk). ▸ Addition to vast literature on witch trials showing fear of diabolism may be related to pursuit of order. Case study of territorial prince's use of diabolism to force confessionalization. Written by popular writer in highly readable style. [SKN]

30.70 H. C. Erik Midelfort. *Witch hunting in southwestern Germany, 1562–1684: the social and intellectual foundations*. Stanford, Calif.: Stanford University Press, 1972. ISBN 0-8047-0805-3. ▸ Classic, pioneering work on social and intellectual origins of witch hunt in southwestern Germany. [RH]

30.71 Bodo Nishan. "Reformed irenicism and the Leipzig colloquy of 1631." *Central European history* 9.1 (1976) 3–26. ISSN 0008-9389. ▸ Presents Lutheran responses to spread of Calvinism (Second Reformation) within Germany against background of Swedish advance during Thirty Years' War. For specialists. [SKN]

30.72 Gerhard Oestreich. *Geist und Gestalt des frühmodernen Staates: ausgewählte Aufsätze*. Berlin: Duncker & Humblot, 1969. ▸ Influential study (Schilling 30.82 and Reinhard 30.76), introducing concept of social disciplining: early modern ruler affected by revived Stoic principles (Neostoicism) and extended notion of individual self-discipline to all citizens in order to render them truly Christian and also smoothly governable in accordance with his wishes. [SKN]

30.73 Gerhard Oestreich. *Neostoicism and the early modern state*. Brigitta Oestreich and H. G. Koenigsberger, eds. David McLintock, trans. Cambridge: Cambridge University Press, 1982. ISBN 0-521-24202-9. ▸ In part a translation of earlier study (30.72), but some essays rewritten and others new. Important background on social disciplining and police. Social discipline, self-discipline, and self-confidence, encouraged by Neostoicism, combined with natural law and religious tradition to form foundation of modern state. Chapter 9, "'Police' and *Prudentia Civilis* in the Seventeenth Century," is crucial. [SKN/JML]

30.74 Wolfgang Reinhard. "Gegenreformation als Modernisierung? Prolegomena zu einer Theorie des konfessionellen Zeitalters." *Archive for Reformation history* 68 (1977) 226–52. ISSN 0003-9381. ▸ Relates confessionalization to process of governmental and economic modernization. [SKN]

30.75 Wolfgang Reinhard. "Konfessionen und Konfessionalisierung in Deutschland." In *Bekenntnis und Geschichte: die Confessio Augustana im historischen Zusammenhang: Ringvorlesung der Universität Augsburg im Jubiläumsjahr 1980*. Wolfgang Reinhard, ed., pp. 165–89. Munich: Vögel, 1981. (Schriften der Philosophischen Fakultäten der Universität Augsburg, 20.) ISBN 3-920896-64-5. ▸ Key theoretical work, with Schilling 30.80 and Reinhard 30.76, describing confessionalization, especially in relation to Catholic territories. [SKN]

30.76 Wolfgang Reinhard. "Zwang zur Konfessionalisierung? Prolegomena zu einer Theorie des konfessionellen Zeitalters." *Zeitschrift für historische Forschung* 10 (1983) 257–77. ISSN 0340-0174. ▸ Central exposition of confessionalization theory, noting use of compulsion by state in achieving subjects' religious conformity. [SKN]

30.77 Thomas Robisheaux. "Peasants and pastors: rural youth control and the Reformation in Hohenlohe, 1540–1680." *Social history* 6 (1981) 281–300. ISSN 0307-1022. ▸ Innovative study on how peasants supported Reformation's strengthening of patriarchal family. Motives were, however, more economic than spiritual. Youths' marital choices had to be controlled for family well being. [SKN]

30.78 Hans-Christoph Rublack, ed. *Die lutherische Konfessionalisierung in Deutschland: Wissenschaftliches Symposion des Vereins für Reformationsgeschichte, 1988.* Gütersloh: Mohn, 1992. (Schriften des Vereins für Reformationsgeschichte, 197.) ISBN 3-579-01665-2. ▸ Recent collection of symposium papers on confessionalization specifically in Lutheran territories. Represents current state of field. [SKN]

30.79 Heinz Schilling. "Between the territorial state and urban liberty: Lutheranism and Calvinism in the county of Lippe." In *The German people and the Reformation.* R. Po-chia Hsia, ed., pp. 263–83. Ithaca, N.Y.: Cornell University Press, 1988. ISBN 0-8014-2064-4 (cl), 0-8014-9485-0 (pbk). ▸ Concise summary of Schilling's interpretation of religion and state building in county of Lippe, presented in detail in *Konfessionskonflikt und Staatsbildung* (30.83); best read in German. [SKN]

30.80 Heinz Schilling. "Confessionalization in the empire: religious and societal change in Germany between 1555 and 1620." In *Religion, political culture, and the emergence of early modern society: essays in German and Dutch history*, pp. 205–45. Leiden: Brill, 1992. ISBN 90-04-09607-8. ▸ Translation of Schilling's key theoretical essay, "Die Konfessionalisierung im Reich" (30.82). Delineates four phases of confessionalization: 1540s to 1560s, preparation; 1570s, confessional polarization and confrontation; 1580s to 1620s, violent efforts to convert; and 1620s to eighteenth century, gradual irenicism. [SKN]

30.81 Heinz Schilling. " 'History of crime' or 'history of sin'? Some reflections on the social history of early modern church discipline." In *Politics and society in Reformation Europe: essays for Sir Geoffrey Elton on his sixty-fifth birthday.* E. I. Kouri and Tom Scott, eds., pp. 289–310. New York: St. Martin's, 1987. ISBN 0-312-00537-7. ▸ Building on Oestreich's concept of "social disciplining" (30.72), looks at Emden, Groningen, and Leiden to distinguish contemporary notions between crime and sin. Church, state, and congregations cooperated in imposing discipline; tried to perfect eucharistic community. Sin often criminalized. [SKN]

30.82 Heinz Schilling. "Die Konfessionalisierung im Reich: Religiöser und gesellschaftlicher Wandel in Deutschland zwischen 1555 und 1620." *Historische Zeitschrift* 246.1 (1988) 1–45. ISSN 0933-5420. ▸ Updated summary of findings described in detail in 30.83. Essential compendium of Schilling's original theory of confessionalization in setting of earldom of Lippe. Translated as "Confessionalization in the Empire" (30.80). [SKN]

30.83 Heinz Schilling. *Konfessionskonflikt und Staatsbildung: eine Fallstudie über das Verhältnis von religiösem und sozialem Wandel in der Frühneuzeit am Beispiel der Grafschaft Lippe.* Gütersloh: Mohn, 1981. ISBN 3-579-01675-X. ▸ Pioneering study of interaction of religion and politics in one territory, earldom of Lippe. Earl exploited religion to advantage, converting to reformed faith, which produced conflict with Lutheran citizens of Lemgo, a major town. [SKN]

30.84 Heinz Schilling. "The Reformation and the rise of the early modern state." In *Luther and the modern state in Germany.* James D. Tracy, ed., pp. 21–30. Kirksville, Mo.: Sixteenth Century Journal Publishers, 1986. (Sixteenth century essays and studies, 7.) ISBN 0-940474-07-7. ▸ Confessionalization theory in a

nutshell. German territorial state's monopolization of church and religion "preceded and facilitated the monopolization of military force and taxation," which were essential to absolutist rulers. [SKN]

30.85 Heinz Schilling. "The Reformation in the Hanseatic cities." *Sixteenth century journal* 14.4 (1983) 443–56. ISSN 0361-0160. ▸ Very abbreviated study, relating Hanseatic city Reformation to territorial state building. [SKN]

30.86 Heinz Schilling. "The Second Reformation: problems and issues." In *Religion, political culture, and the emergence of early modern society: essays in German and Dutch history.* , pp. 247–301. Leiden: Brill, 1992. ISBN 90-04-09607-8. ▸ Translation of controversial essay on Second Reformation, referring to adoption of reformed faith by number of princes in late sixteenth and early seventeenth centuries. Regards confessionalization and Second Reformation as conceptually inseparable. [SKN]

30.87 Heinz Schilling. "Die 'zweite Reformation' als Kategorie der Geschichtswissenschaft." In *Die reformierte Konfessionalisierung in Deutschland: das Problem der "Zweiten Reformation"; Wissenschaftliches Symposiun des Vereins für Reformationsgeschichte, 1985.* Heinz Schilling, ed., pp. 387–437. Gütersloh: Mohn, 1986. (Schriften des Vereins für Reformationsgeschichte, 195.) ISBN 3-579-01664-4. ▸ Exposition and defense of controversial theories of Second Reformation, upsurge of Calvinism associated with profound social and mental change occurring in age of state building. Represents current state of field. [SKN]

30.88 R. W. Scribner. "Police and the territorial state in sixteenth-century Württemberg." In *Politics and society in Reformation Europe: essays for Sir Geoffrey Elton on his sixty-fifth birthday.* E. I. Kouri and Tom Scott, eds., pp. 102–20. New York: St. Martin's, 1987. ISBN 0-312-00537-7. ▸ Discussion suggesting authorities made no great strides toward achieving orderly society. Law and order always precariously balanced. Uses court records from Urfehde. [SKN]

30.89 R. W. Scribner. "Social control and the possibility of an urban Reformation." In *Popular culture and popular movements in Reformation Germany.* , pp. 175–84. London: Hambledon, 1987. ISBN 0-907628-81-8 (cl), 0-907628-82-6 (pbk). ▸ English translation of German essay, defining social control in terms of Reformation movement. Useful in debate on social disciplining as aspect of confessionalization. [SKN]

30.90 Gerald Strauss. "Lutheranism and literacy: a reassessment " In *Religion and society in early modern Europe, 1500–1800.* Kaspar von Greyerz, ed., pp. 109–23. London· German Historical Institute and Allen & Unwin, 1984. ISBN 0-04-940078-9. ▸ In part, a response to criticism of his earlier study (30.91), reaffirming those findings. Lutheran authorities quickly saw literacy had to be controlled. Schools became means of producing personnel needed by state. [SKN]

30.91 Gerald Strauss. *Luther's house of learning: indoctrination of the young in the German Reformation.* Baltimore: Johns Hopkins University Press, 1978. ISBN 0-8018-2051-0. ▸ Discussion of early modern concepts of childhood and education. Assertion that initial Lutheran attempt to convert people's minds and hearts failed, set off decade-long debate. Ideas now integrated into core literature on states' methods of confessionalization and social disciplining. [SKN]

30.92 Gerald Strauss. "The social function of schools in the Lutheran Reformation in Germany." *History of education quarterly* 28.2 (1988) 191–206. ISSN 0018-2680. ▸ Amplified and reiterated views of author on Lutheran schooling as instrument of social and political control. Supplementary to 30.91. [SKN]

30.93 Joachim Whaley. "Obedient servants? Lutheran attitudes to authority and society in the first half of the seventeenth century: the case of Johann Balthasar Schupp." *Historical journal* 35.1 (1992) 27–42. ISSN 0018-246X. ‣ Examination of case of Hamburg pastor and former court preacher to determine whether clergy unquestioningly supported and promoted self-aggrandizing state. This cleric, while at least affirming duty of subjects to obey, also criticized princely misbehavior. [SKN]

30.94   William J. Wright. "Evaluating the results of sixteenth-century educational policy: some Hessian data." *Sixteenth century journal* 18.3 (1987) 411–26. ISSN 0361-0160. ‣ Landgrave Philip (d. 1567) used school and university reform to produce suitable personnel for benefit of advancing state. [SKN]

30.95   Ernst Walter Zeeden. *Die Entstehung der Konfessionen: Grundlagen und Formen der Konfessionsbildung im Zeitalter der Glaubenskämpfe.* 1964 ed. Munich: Oldenbourg, 1965. ‣ Forebear of current confessionalization theories; introduces term, "building of confessions" (*Konfessionsbildung*) and links state to deliberate use of religion for its own purposes. [SKN]

30.96   Ernst Walter Zeeden. *Konfessionsbildung: Studien zur Reformation, Gegenreformation, und katholischen Reform.* Stuttgart: Klett-Cotta, 1985. ISBN 3-608-91166-9. ‣ Collection of key essays, noting procedural and structural similarities among three dominant faiths: Catholic, Lutheran, and Calvinist (reformed). Protestantism retained number of Catholic practices. [SKN]

AGE OF ABSOLUTISM, 1650–1800

30.97   Derek E. D. Beales. *Joseph II.* Vol. 1: *In the shadow of Maria Theresa, 1741–1780.* Cambridge: Cambridge University Press, 1987. ISBN 0-521-24240-1 (v. 1). ‣ Definitive treatment of co-regency of Maria Theresa and Joseph II. Balanced yet more positive interpretation of Joseph's character and contributions, somewhat at expense of empress and Chancellor Kaunitz. [CWI]

30.98   C.B.A. Behrens. *Society, government, and the Enlightenment: the experiences of eighteenth-century France and Prussia.* New York: Harper & Row, 1985. ISBN 0-06-430386-1. ‣ Comprehensive comparison of governmental systems on eve of French Revolution. Comparison of developments in France and Prussia that led to different transitions to bourgeois societies. Demonstrates Prussian model far more effective in meeting society's needs and thus averted threat of revolution. [CWI/JML]

30.99   Gerhard Benecke. *Society and politics in Germany, 1500–1750.* London: Routledge & Kegan Paul, 1974. ISBN 0-7100-7842-0. ‣ Eccentric but brilliant examination of regional and local government in county of Lippe and Westphalia. Stress on cooperation between princes, estates, and imperial institutions reinforces thesis that Holy Roman Empire functioned at regional level. [CWI]

30.100   Jean Bérenger. *Finances et absolutisme autrichien dans la seconde moitié du dix-septième siècle.* Paris: Publications de la Sorbonne, Imprimerie Nationale, 1975. (Serie Sorbonne, 1.) ‣ Detailed profile of taxation and finance, as seen in relationship between crown and estates under Leopold I. Demonstrates Habsburgs less absolute and more dependent on reaching consensus with loyal aristocracy. [CWI/JML]

30.101   Paul P. Bernard. *From the Enlightenment to the police state: the public life of Johann Anton Pergen.* Urbana: University of Illinois Press, 1991. ISBN 0-252-01745-5. ‣ Political biography of Austrian diplomat and minister who built Austrian secret police just before and during French Revolution. Traces growing disillusionment and paranoia of "enlightened" officials and rulers at beginning of revolutionary age. [CWI]

30.102   Paul P. Bernard. *Joseph II.* New York: Twayne, 1968. ‣ Brief, balanced political biography of controversial ruler. Now somewhat outdated but still useful, readable survey. [CWI]

30.103   Paul P. Bernard. *The limits of enlightenment: Joseph II and*

the law. Urbana: University of Illinois Press, 1979. ISBN 0-252-00735-2. ‣ Short, archive-based study, drawn from finite number of surviving court records. Portrays Joseph as increasingly compulsive despot, whose intervention in criminal cases violated Enlightenment notions of separation of justice from administration. Engaging narrative. [CWI]

30.104   T.C.W. Blanning. *Joseph II and enlightened despotism.* London: Longman, 1970. ISBN 0-582-31406-2. ‣ Very short, very readable examination of Joseph II as tragically flawed but, nonetheless, enlightened ruler. Argues persuasively he was among most benevolent of those monarchs who were partly but genuinely motivated by Enlightenment values. [CWI]

30.105   T.C.W. Blanning. *Reform and revolution in Mainz, 1743–1803.* London: Cambridge University Press, 1974. ISBN 0-521-20418-6. ‣ Rich portrait of "enlightened" government in middle-sized German state. Places popular conservatism at center of opposition to government reformers; suggests widespread societal support for Old Regime against forces of French Revolution. [CWI/JJS]

30.106   F. L. Carsten. *The origins of Prussia.* 1954 ed. Westport, Conn.: Greenwood, 1981. ISBN 0-313-23220-2. ‣ Traces evolution of Prussian absolutism under Frederick William, the Great Elector (1640–88). Shows how elector achieved power to tax in exchange for permitting nobility to extend its authority over peasantry. [CWI]

30.107   F. L. Carsten. *Princes and parliaments in Germany from the fifteenth to the eighteenth century.* 1959 ed. Oxford: Clarendon, 1963. ‣ Examination of relations between princes and estates in Bavaria, Hesse, Saxony, Württemberg, and several Rhenish principalities. Sympathetic to estates' opposition to princely centralization, long before it was fashionable. [CWI]

30.108   Walter W. Davis. *Joseph II: an imperial reformer for the Austrian Netherlands.* The Hague: Nijhoff, 1974. ISBN 90-247-1593-8. ‣ Biography of Austrian emperor who precipitated Belgian revolt at end of eighteenth century. Study of how Joseph II's clerical and administrative reforms alienated all segments of Belgian society. Portrays Joseph as well-intentioned but excessively arbitrary and insensitive to regional traditions. [CWI/JLP]

30.109   P.G.M. Dickson. *Finance and government under Maria Theresa, 1740–1780.* Vol. 1: *Society and government.* Vol. 2: *Finance and credit.* Oxford: Clarendon, 1987. ISBN 0-19-822570-9 (v. 1), 0-19-822882-1 (v. 2). ‣ Comprehensive, meticulous, archive-based examination of Austrian state finance. Treats both societal and governmental foundations, as well as attempts at fiscal reform. Includes monarchy's Belgian and Italian dominions. Suggests fiscal and administrative reforms stemmed from need to confront Prussian threat more than from Enlightenment influences. [CWI]

30.110   Walter Louis Dorn. "The Prussian bureaucracy in the eighteenth century." *Political science quarterly* 46, 47 (1931, 1932) 75–94, 259–73. ISSN 0032-3195. ‣ Exceptionally lucid and concise description of Prussian administrative reform. Judges Frederick William I's General Directory inefficient, but also criticizes Frederick II's alternatives for entrenching bureaucratic opposition to crown. [CWI]

30.111   Reinhold August Dorwart. *The administrative reforms of Frederick William I of Prussia.* 1953 ed. Westport, Conn.: Greenwood, 1971. ISBN 0-8371-5578-9. ‣ Explicitly detailed description of complexities of Prussian administration. Understandably dry but definitive. [CWI]

30.112   Reinhold August Dorwart. *The Prussian welfare state before 1740.* Cambridge, Mass.: Harvard University Press, 1971. ISBN 0-674-71975-1. ‣ Examination of central government's comprehensive provision for public welfare through application of police ordinances. Excellent study of vital role played by administrative theories before advent of Enlightenment and enlightened absolutism. [CWI]

30.113 R.J.W. Evans. *The making of the Habsburg monarchy, 1550–1700: an interpretation.* 1979 ed. Oxford: Oxford University Press, 1984. ISBN 0-19-822560-1 (cl, 1979), 0-19-873085-3 (pbk). ‣ Immensely important for understanding monarchy's evolution and resilience. Study strengthened by extensive knowledge of aristocratic networks and numerous languages of Habsburg empire. Habsburg great power emerged through symbiosis of dynasty, aristocracy, and Counter-Reformation church with unique culture somewhat distinct from European rationalism. [CWI/SKN]

30.114 Sidney B. Fay. *The rise of Brandenburg-Prussia to 1786.* 1964 Rev. ed. Klaus Epstein, ed. Malabar, Fla.: Krieger, 1981. ISBN 0-89874-377-X. ‣ Very short, well-written survey of Prussia's emergence focusing on Hohenzollern accomplishments from Great Elector (1640–88) to Frederick the Great. Dated, simple great-man narrative nonetheless offers best, brief overview of subject. [CWI]

30.115 Linda Frey and Marsha Frey. *Frederick I: the man and his times.* Boulder: East European Monographs, 1984. ISBN 0-88033-058-9. ‣ First English-language biography of Prussia's first, baroque king. Pedestrian, anecdotal account short on analysis. Nonetheless, useful, well-written introduction to subject. [CWI]

30.116 Mary Fulbrook. *Piety and politics: religion and the rise of absolutism in England, Württemberg, and Prussia.* Cambridge: Cambridge University Press, 1983. ISBN 0-521-25612-7 (cl), 0-521-27633-0 (pbk). ‣ Comparative study of pietism's and Puritanism's varied role in evolution of absolutism: successfully undermining it in Stuart England, accepting it in Württemberg, while strongly reinforcing Prussia's bureaucratic *Polizeistaat.* Historical sociology. [CWI/ML]

30.117 John G. Gagliardo. *Germany under the Old Regime, 1600–1790.* London: Longman, 1991. ISBN 0-582-49105-3 (cl), 0-582-49106-1 (pbk). ‣ Comprehensive survey affording equal attention to Austria, Prussia, and smaller German states. Utilizes most recent research. Useful bibliography with excellent maps. [CWI]

30.118 Dietrich Gerhard, ed. *Ständische Vertretungen in Europa im siebzehnten und achtzehnten Jahrhundert.* 1969 ed. Göttingen: Vandenhoeck & Ruprecht, 1974. (Veröffentlichungen des Max-Planck-Instituts für Geschichte, 27.) (Studies presented to the International Commission for the History of Representative and Parliamentary Institutions, 37.) ISBN 3-525-35332-4. ‣ Case studies of individual diets by leading authorities. Focuses heavily on Central Europe with chapters on numerous German states as well as Austria and Hungary. [CWI]

30.119 Walther Hubatsch. *Frederick the Great of Prussia: absolutism and administration.* London: Thames & Hudson, 1975. ISBN 0-500-87002-0. ‣ Generally positive account; especially valuable for Frederick's early development. Detailed examination of his administrative policies. Somewhat dry, nonetheless excellent account of Frederick as domestic ruler. [CWI]

30.120 Michael Hughes. *Law and politics in eighteenth-century Germany: the Imperial Aulic Council in the reign of Charles VI.* Wolfeboro, N.H.: Boydell, 1988. (Royal Historical Society studies in history, 55.) ISBN 0-86193-212-9. ‣ Study of constitutional disputes in Mecklenburg and East Frisia at height of Habsburgs' imperial authority. Judges Aulic Council to be both professional and reasonably effective, albeit within limits imposed by intra-German political rivalries. [CWI]

30.121 Charles W. Ingrao. *The Hessian mercenary state: ideas, institutions, and reform under Frederick II, 1760–1785.* Cambridge:

Cambridge University Press, 1987. ISBN 0-521-32756-3. ‣ Examination of relationship between ideology, consultative government, and domestic reform. Interprets Enlightenment absolutism as benevolent but self-limiting hybrid of Enlightenment, cameralist, and Christian (especially pietist) values. [CWI]

30.122 Charles W. Ingrao. *In quest and crisis: Emperor Joseph I and the Habsburg monarchy.* West Lafayette, Ind.: Purdue University Press, 1979. ISBN 0-911198-53-9. ‣ Narrative attributes Austria's triumphs during War of Spanish Succession to decisive leadership and its allies' quest for balance of power. Italy conquered and Hungary pacified at cost of surrendering more remote objectives in Germany and Spain. [CWI]

30.123 Charles W. Ingrao. "The problem of 'enlightened absolutism' and the German states." In *Politics and society in the Holy Roman Empire, 1500–1806*, pp. 161–80. Chicago: University of Chicago Press, 1986. (*Journal of modern history,* Supplement, 58.) ISSN 0022-2801. ‣ Lucid analysis of differing German and Anglo-American perspectives in debate over enlightened absolutism. Special focus on German states. Sees absolutism as hybrid of Enlightenment, cameralist, and Christian values. [CWI]

30.124 Hubert C. Johnson. *Frederick the Great and his officials.* New Haven: Yale University Press, 1975. ISBN 0-300-01755-3. ‣ Silesian wars exposed flaws of Frederick William I's administrative system and prompted radical restructuring after 1763. Characterizes relationship between Frederick II and his bureaucratic nobility as one of close cooperation and mutual dependency. By Hans Rosenberg student. [CWI]

30.125 Robert A. Kann and Zdeněk V. David. *The peoples of the eastern Habsburg lands, 1526–1918.* Seattle: University of Washington Press, 1984. ISBN 0-295-96095-7. ‣ Examination of political, economic, and cultural ambience of Habsburgs' non-German dominions, along national lines. Sometimes fragmented by ethnic organization, but contains much unique material on individual provinces and nationalities. [CWI/SBV]

30.126 Grete Klingenstein. *Staatsverwaltung und kirchliche Autorität im achtzehnten Jahrhundert: das Problem der Zensur in der theresianischen Reform.* Munich: Oldenbourg, 1970. ‣ Forces of secularization and reform Catholicism coalesced under Charles VI and young Maria Theresa (1725–50). Followed by intensive assault on Jesuit control of censorship and elite education (1750–60). [CWI]

30.127 Helen P. Liebel. *Enlightened bureaucracy versus enlightened despotism in Baden, 1750–1792.* Philadelphia: American Philosophical Society, 1965. (Transactions of the American Philosophical Society, n.s., 55.5.) ‣ Credits talented, perceptive bureaucrats for enlightened reform, rather than Karl Friedrich Margrave of Baden. Profiles economic thought of Johann Jacob Reinhard and Johann Georg Schlosser. [CWI]

30.128 C. A. Macartney. *Maria Theresa and the house of Austria.* London: English Universities Press, 1969. ISBN 0-340-05253-8. ‣ Well-written, generally flattering biography in great-man tradition. Still best treatment of subject in English. [CWI]

30.129 C. A. Macartney, ed. *The Habsburg and Hohenzollern dynasties in the seventeenth and eighteenth centuries.* New York: Walker, 1970. ‣ Still most extensive collection of English-language sources on subject. Translations of key documents, sometimes uncomfortably close to original construction. [CWI]

30.130 Henrik Marczali. *Hungary in the eighteenth century.* 1910 ed. New York: Arno, 1971. ISBN 0-405-02760-5. ‣ Comprehensive survey of Hungary during first half of eighteenth century. Examines royal and local government institutions, economic conditions, religious divisions, and social groups. Despite age, still best portrait of Hungary after reconquest. [CWI]

30.131 William J. McGill. *Maria Theresa.* New York: Irvington,

1972. ISBN 0-8290-1738-0. ▸ Brief, very readable, though now somewhat dated undergraduate-level portrait. [CWI]

30.132 Derek McKay. *Prince Eugene of Savoy.* London: Thames & Hudson, 1977. ISBN 0-500-87007-1. ▸ Superbly written, balanced biography judges Eugene brilliant general, but also indifferent administrator and generally unsympathetic personality. Good resource for domestic politics under Emperor Charles VI. [CWI]

30.133 James Van Horn Melton. *Absolutism and the eighteenth-century origins of compulsory schooling in Prussia and Austria.* Cambridge: Cambridge University Press, 1988. ISBN 0-521-34668-1. ▸ Provocative, well-written account tracing governmental adoption of pietist pedagogy in Prussia, then Austria. Attributes reforms to desire for greater social control in enforcing hardworking, loyal subjects, not Enlightenment. [CWI]

30.134 Gerhard Ritter. *Frederick the Great: a historical profile.* 1968 ed. Peter Paret, trans. Berkeley: University of California Press, 1974. ISBN 0-520-02775-2 (pbk). ▸ Very readable political biography of Frederick's reign. Somewhat dated, inaccurate, and overly positive evaluation. Nevertheless, still best treatment in English, pending translation of Schieder's study (30.138). [CWI]

30.135 Hans Rosenberg. *Bureaucracy, aristocracy, and autocracy: the Prussian experience, 1660–1815.* 1958 ed. Boston: Beacon, 1966. ▸ Bureaucracy evolved from electors' palladin to autonomous institution with own *esprit de corps* and organizational ethos. Best for analysis of defiant bureaucratic absolutism under Frederick II. [CWI]

30.136 Gunther E. Rothenberg. *The Austrian military border in Croatia, 1522–1747.* Urbana: University of Illinois Press, 1960. ▸ Standard history of military frontier institution in Croatia. Austria defended Croatian border against Turkish attack with soldier-colonists. Real enemy administrative muddle between inner Austrian and Croatian estates, Counter-Reformation clergy, and weak central government. [CWI/AF/IB]

30.137 Gunther E. Rothenberg. *The military border in Croatia, 1740–1881: a study of an imperial institution.* Chicago: University of Chicago Press, 1966. ▸ Continuation of 30.136 to dissolution. Military border evolved as important arm of Austrian army. Napoleonic conquests introduced Illyrian nationalism and conflict between colonists, Habsburg military, and Croatia and Hungary. Emphasis on military and institutional affairs, less on internal development. [CWI/AF/IB]

30.138 Theodor Schieder. *Friedrich der Grosse: ein Königtum der Widersprache.* Frankfurt: Propyläen, 1983. ISBN 3-549-07638-X. ▸ Imaginatively conceived, balanced biography. Longman translation due to appear in 1993. [CWI]

30.139 H. M. Scott, ed. *Enlightened absolutism: reform and reformers in later eighteenth-century Europe.* London: Macmillan, 1990. ISBN 0-333-43960-0 (cl), 0-333-43961-9 (pbk). ▸ Generally positive, well-written interpretation, reflecting recent research trends by leading authorities. Half of book treats Central Europe, including three chapters on Habsburg monarchy. [CWI]

30.140 John P. Spielman. *Leopold I of Austria.* New Brunswick, N.J.: Rutgers University Press, 1977. ISBN 0-8135-0836-3. ▸ Balanced, well-written, undergraduate-level survey of Leopold's long reign (1657–1705). Explains reliance on Catholicism and loyal nobility as "twin pillars" that supported monarchy. [CWI]

30.141 Henry E. Strakosch. *State absolutism and the rule of law: the struggle for the codification of civil law in Austria, 1753–1811.* University Park: Pennsylvania State University Press, 1967. ▸ Analysis of limited legal reform and codification under Maria Theresa and Joseph II. Success achieved after French Revolution through triumph of Kant's notion of total obedience to rule of law. Sophisticated combination of history and philosophy. [CWI]

30.142 Keith Tribe. *Governing economy: the reformation of German economic discourse, 1750–1840.* Cambridge: Cambridge University Press, 1988. ISBN 0-521-30316-8. ▸ Examination of cameral sciences' domination of Austrian and German political economy until Adam Smith's work gained acceptance in 1790s. Considerable coverage of Justus Henning Bohmer and Joseph von Sonnenfels. [CWI]

30.143 James Allen Vann. *The making of a state: Württemberg, 1593–1793.* Ithaca, N.Y.: Cornell University Press, 1984. ISBN 0-8014-1553-5. ▸ Analysis of evolving constitutional relationship between monarch, privy council, and estates. Suggests path to absolutism neither linear nor inevitable. Remarkable profile of local political culture and opposition; but questionable whether Württemberg is typical. [CWI]

30.144 James Allen Vann. *The Swabian Kreis: institutional growth in the Holy Roman Empire, 1648–1715.* 1975 ed. New York: Lang, 1982. ▸ Examination of how system of imperial circles operated, especially in providing for defense in wars against Turks and Louis XIV's France. Strong support for notion that Holy Roman Empire functioned at regional level. [CWI]

30.145 Ernst Wangermann. *From Joseph II to the Jacobin trials: government policy and public opinion in the Habsburg dominions in the period of the French Revolution.* 2d ed. London: Oxford University Press, 1969. ISBN 0-19-821832-X. ▸ Controversial study of Austrian regime's reaction to popular unrest. Argues Joseph II repealed radical reforms because of threat of radical revolution, rather than because of conservative opposition. [CWI]

30.146 Herman Weill. *Frederick the Great and Samuel Cocceji: a study in the reform of the Prussian judicial administration, 1740–1755.* Madison: Wisconsin State Historical Society for University of Wisconsin Press, Department of History, 1961. ▸ Straightforward presentation with useful information, less analysis. Unreserved at times, exaggerated praise for emperor and his chancellor. [CWI]

30.147 William E. Wright. *Serf, seigneur, and sovereign: agrarian reform in eighteenth-century Bohemia.* Minneapolis: University of Minnesota Press, 1966. ▸ Lucid study of intensifying attempts to reform manorial system. Concentrates on Bohemia under Maria Theresa and Joseph II. Failure attributed to problems of implementation and enforcement, as well as Joseph II's lack of moderation and sensitivity. [CWI/HLA]

SEE ALSO

WOMEN, GENDER, AND FAMILY, 1500–1800

30.148 Roland H. Bainton. *Women of the Reformation in Germany and Italy.* 1971 ed. Boston: Beacon, 1974. ISBN 0-8070-5651-0 (pbk). ▸ Brief biographies of reformers' wives, noblewomen who influenced Reformation, and Anabaptist martyrs. No analysis but good information and easy to read. [MEW]

30.149 Rita Bake. *Vorindustrielle Frauenerwerbsarbeit: Arbeits- und Lebensweise von Manufakturarbeiterinnen im Deutschland des achtzehnten Jahrhunderts unter besonderer Berücksichtigung Hamburgs.* Cologne: Pahl-Rugenstein, 1984. ISBN 3-7609-5177-5. ▸ Investigation of working life and more generally social conditions of women who worked in factories and sweatshops of many industries, including cloth and metals. Relates state support of these to development of workhouses; surveys changes in ideas about gender and work. [MEW]

30.150 Barbara Becker-Cantarino, ed. *Die Frau von der Refor-*

mation zur Romantik: die Situation der Frau vor dem Hintergrund der Literatur- und Sozialgeschichte. 2d ed. Bonn: Bouvier Verlag Herbert Grundmann, 1985. ISBN 3-416-01603-3. ▸ Essays discussing women authors, scientists, and religious leaders and more general situation of women in Germany, 1500–1850. Most essays present sophisticated analysis of ideas about women and women's response to them. [MEW]

30.151 Barbara Becker-Cantarino. *Der lange Weg zur Mündigkeit: Frau und Literatur (1500–1800).* Stuttgart: Metzler, 1987. ISBN 3-476-00612-3. ▸ Discussion of many types of women authors—religious writers, poets, playwrights—situating them in legal and ideological framework. Views women as active participants in all types of intellectual life, but also marginalized. [MEW]

30.152 Gisela Brinker-Gabler. *Deutsche Dichterinnen vom sechzehnten Jahrhundert bis zur Gegenwart: Gedichte und Lebensläufe.* 1978 ed. Frankfurt: Fischer, 1990. ISBN 3-596-23701-7 (pbk). ▸ Survey of large number of female poets with introductory comments and selections from their work. First modern printing of many poems in collection; invaluable for social as well as literary history. [MEW]

30.153 Susanna Burghartz. "The equation of women and witches: a case study of witchcraft trials in Lucerne and Lausanne in the fifteenth and sixteenth centuries." In *The German underworld: deviants and outcasts in German history.* Richard J. Evans, ed., pp. 57–74. London: Routledge & Kegan Paul, 1988. ISBN 0-415-00367-9. ▸ Uses Swiss examples to test existing theories of why most accused of witchcraft were women. Calls, without overstating case, for gender to become more central category to all aspects of research on witch craze. [MEW]

30.154 Miriam Usher Chrisman. "Women and the Reformation in Strasbourg, 1490–1530." *Archive for Reformation history* 63 (1972) 143–67. ISSN 0003-9381. ▸ Discussion of women's participation in Reformation and its effects on women in Strasbourg, center of moderation. Good biographical details and attention to local issues. [MEW]

30.155 Barbara Duden. *The woman beneath the skin: a doctor's patients in eighteenth-century Germany.* Thomas Dunlap, trans. Cambridge, Mass.: Harvard University Press, 1991. ISBN 0-674-95403-3. ▸ Analysis of how German doctor and his women patients around 1730 experienced and envisioned inside of female body. Based on huge series of case histories. Fascinating cultural history at its finest. [MEW/JBK/CH]

30.156 Paula Sutter Fichtner. *Protestantism and primogeniture in early modern Germany.* New Haven: Yale University Press, 1989. ISBN 0-300-04425-9. ▸ Brief study of why primogeniture was accepted earlier and more quickly by Catholic than by Protestant princes. Careful investigation of practical effects of Reformation and changes in ideology about one small issue. [MEW]

30.157 Arlene Miller Guinsberg. "The counterthrust to sixteenth-century misogyny: the work of Agrippa and Paracelsus." *Historical reflections* 8 (1981) 3–28. ISSN 0315-7997. ▸ Discussion of sources, content, and effects of antimisogynist works of Agrippa and Paracelsus. Views works as clearly fringe ideas in sixteenth century, but with later resonance in pietism and elsewhere. [MEW]

30.158 Gunnar Heinsohn and Otto Steiger. *Die Vernichtung der weisen Frauen: Beiträge zur Theorie und Geschichte von Bevölkerung und Kindheit.* 3d rev. ed. Munich: Heyne, 1989. ISBN 3-453-302987-9. ▸ Argues witch persecutions resulted from early modern state attempts to encourage population growth by killing women who knew traditional methods of birth control. Poor scholarship and anachronistic thesis, but made great splash in German popular press. [MEW]

30.159 Ruth-Ellen B. Joeres and Mary Jo Maynes, eds. *German women in the eighteenth and nineteenth centuries: a social and literary history.* Bloomington: Indiana University Press, 1985. ISBN 0-253-32578-1. ▸ Essays from 1983 interdisciplinary meeting at University of Minnesota discussing women authors, women in literature, and women's economic role. Uneven, as all collections are, but some methodologically sophisticated essays. [MEW]

30.160 Susan C. Karant-Nunn. "Continuity and change: some effects of the Reformation on the women of Zwickau." *Sixteenth century journal* 13.2 (1982) 17–42. ISSN 0361-0160. ▸ Traces women's actions in German city of Zwickau during early years of Reformation and effects of religious and institutional change on women. Sees both positive and negative results of change to Protestantism. [MEW]

30.161 Susan C. Karant-Nunn. "The transmission of Luther's teachings on women and matrimony: the case of Zwickau." *Archive for Reformation history* 77 (1986) 31–46. ISSN 0003-9381. ▸ Part of new interest in actual impact of Reformation and its gendered content. Explores different ways Luther's ideas were communicated to urban women orally, in print, and through illustrations. [MEW]

30.162 Mary Lindemann. "Love for hire: the regulation of the wet-nursing business in eighteenth-century Hamburg." *Journal of family history* 6.4 (1981) 379–92. ISSN 0363-1990. ▸ Traces attempts in Hamburg to implement new social and medical ideas about wet-nursing as part of more general attempts at poor relief and social control. One of few investigations looking at wet nurses themselves and not simply at parents who hired them. [MEW]

30.163 Hans Medick. "Village spinning bees: sexual culture and free time among rural youth in early modern Germany." In *Interest and emotion: essays on the study of family and kinship.* Hans Medick and David Warren Sabean, eds., pp. 317–39. Cambridge and Paris: Cambridge University Press and Éditions de la Maison des Sciences de l'Homme, 1984. ISBN 0-521-24969-4. ▸ Uses visual and written evidence to explore courtship and sociability functions of village spinning bees and criticism this evoked. Fine consideration of moral economy of rural premodern people. [MEW]

30.164 Michael Mitterauer and Reinhard Sieder. *The European family: patriarchy and partnership from the Middle Ages to the present.* Karla Oosterveen and Manfred Hoerzinger, trans. Chicago: University of Chicago Press, 1982. ISBN 0-226-53240-2 (cl), 0-226-53241-0 (pbk). ▸ Analysis of family structure and function and relationships within family primarily in German-speaking lands by two Viennese scholars. Stresses impact of economic change, and elaborates Cambridge-group notion of family life cycle. [MEW]

30.165 Cornelia Niekus Moore. *The maiden's mirror: reading materials for German girls in the sixteenth and seventeenth centuries.* Wiesbaden: Harrassowitz, 1987. (Wolfenbütteler Forschungen, 36.) ISBN 3-447-02746-0. ▸ Survey of literature produced specifically for girls or that assumed girls would be among its readers. Concludes home, school, and convent were each distinct "literary clusters." Useful German parallel to many studies of English books for women. [MEW]

30.166 Steven E. Ozment. *Magdalena and Balthasar: an intimate portrait of life in sixteenth-century Europe, revealed in the letters of a Nuremberg husband and wife.* 1986 ed. New Haven: Yale University Press, 1989. ISBN 0-300-04378-3 (pbk). ▸ Translation of and extensive commentary on letters between Magdalena and Balthasar Paumgartner, written 1582–98. For general audience; based on nineteenth-century German edition. [MEW]

30.167 Steven E. Ozment. *When fathers ruled: family life in Reformation Europe.* Cambridge, Mass.: Harvard University Press, 1983. ISBN 0-674-95120-4 (cl), 0-674-95121-2 (pbk). ▸ Analysis of effects of Protestant Reformation on women's role and family life using both Protestant and Catholic sources. Sees Protestant ideas as generally positive for women. [MEW]

30.168 Hans Pohl and Wilhelm Treue, eds. *Die Frau in der deutschen Wirtschaft: Referate und Diskussionsbeiträge des achten Wissenschaftlichen Symposiums der Gesellschaft für Unternehmensgeschichte.* Wiesbaden: Steiner, 1985. (*Zeitschrift für Unternehmensgeschichte*, Beiheft, 35.) ISBN 3-515-04278-4 (pbk). ▸ Conference papers and discussions ranging from Middle Ages to twentieth century. Personal differences influence discussion, but only conference of type and level ever held in Germany whose proceedings have been published. [MEW]

30.169 Jean H. Quataert. "The shaping of women's work in manufacturing: guilds, households, and the state in Central Europe, 1648–1870." *American historical review* 90.5 (1985) 1122–48. ISSN 0002-8762. ▸ Argues crafts such as linen weaving, which continued in household production, declined in status because linked with women's work. Clearly sets gender ideology as key determinant of occupational structures. [MEW]

30.170 Lyndal Roper. " 'The common man,' 'the common good,' 'common meaning': gender and meaning in the German Reformation commune." *Social history* 12.1 (1987) 1–21. ISSN 0307-1022. ▸ Challenges unreflective use of phrase "the common man" in Reformation scholarship by showing it was clearly gendered and that "common" was pejorative when applied to women. Probing linguistic analysis. [MEW]

30.171 Lyndal Roper. *The holy household: women and morals in Reformation Augsburg.* Oxford: Clarendon, 1989. ISBN 0-19-821769-2. ▸ Analysis of women and men within context of marriage, work, sexuality, and religious and institutional changes brought by Reformation. Controversial but convincing argument that gender lies at base of Protestant ideas of sin, authority, and community. [MEW]

30.172 Lyndal Roper. "Stealing manhood: capitalism and magic in early modern Germany." *Gender and history* 3.1 (1991) 4–22. ISSN 0953-5233. ▸ Case study of Fuggers of Augsburg, arguing for links between magic, early modern capitalism, and masculine notions of honor of one's name. Highly suggestive and thought provoking. [MEW]

30.173 Lyndal Roper. "Will and honor: sex, words, and power in Augsburg criminal trials." *Radical history review* 43 (1989) 45–71. ISSN 0163-6545. ▸ Uses interrogation records to argue men used concept of will and women that of honor when talking about sexuality in sixteenth century. Careful gender analysis of language. [MEW]

30.174 Lyndal Roper. "Witchcraft and fantasy in early modern Germany." *History workshop* 32 (1991) 19–43. ISSN 0309-2984. ▸ Explores self-understanding of those who came to see themselves as witches as well as their accusers, stressing tensions of motherhood. Uses modern psychoanalytical categories in nonreductive way. [MEW]

30.175 David Warren Sabean. "Young bees in an empty hive: relations between brothers-in-law in a South German village around 1800." In *Interest and emotion: essays on the study of family and kinship.* Hans Medick and David Warren Sabean, eds., pp. 171–86. Cambridge and Paris: Cambridge University Press and Éditions de la Maison des Sciences de l'Homme, 1984. ISBN 0-521-24969-4. ▸ Study of how disputes over and cooperation in rights to land shaped relations between brothers-in-law and family. Based on single village but larger speculative conclusions. [MEW]

30.176 Thomas Max Safley. *Let no man put asunder: the control of marriage in the German Southwest, a comparative study, 1550–1600.* Kirksville, Mo.: Sixteenth Century Journal Publishers, 1984. (Sixteenth century essays and studies, 2.) ISBN 0-940474-

02-6. ▸ Archive-based comparative study of Catholic and Protestant marriage law and marital litigation in Constance, Basel, and Freiburg. Fascinating stories and conclusions about both religious similarities and differences. [MEW]

30.177 Martha Schad. *Die Frauen des Hauses Fugger von der Lilie (15.–17. Jahrhundert): Augsburg, Ortenburg, Trient.* Tübingen: Mohr, 1989. (Studien zur Fuggergeschichte und Schwabische Forschungsgemeinschaft bei der Kommission für Bayerische Landesgeschichte, Reihe 4, 31, and 22.) ISBN 3-16-545478-7. ▸ Presents women of Fugger house, both lay and religious, as active participants in re-Catholicizing of Augsburg. Somewhat old-fashioned methodology of series of individual biographies, but based on solid archival research. [MEW]

30.178 Otto Ulbricht. "Infanticide in eighteenth-century Germany." In *The German underworld: deviants and outcasts in German history.* Richard J. Evans, ed., pp. 108–40. London: Routledge & Kegan Paul, 1988. ISBN 0-415-00367-9. ▸ Analysis of social situations, personal relationships, and motives of women charged with infanticide. One of few studies based on actual court records from North Germany. [MEW]

30.179 Barbara Vogel and Ulrike Weckel, eds. *Frauen in der Ständegesellschaft: Leben und Arbeiten in der Stadt vom späten Mittelalter bis zur Neuzeit.* Hamburg: Krämer, 1991. ISBN 3-926952-25-3. ▸ Twelve essays by mostly younger German scholars about various aspects of women's economic role, legal status, and social position, 1500–1850. Good awareness of role of both social class and gender; most essays theoretically sophisticated. [MEW]

30.180 Ingeborg Weber-Kellermann. *Die deutsche Familie: Versuch einer Sozialgeschichte.* 1974 ed. Frankfurt: Suhrkamp, 1984. ISBN 3-518-36685-8. ▸ General, illustrated survey of family in Germany from prehistory to present. Balanced introduction relying on older work with some interesting longer discussions of popular literature and practices. [MEW]

30.181 Kurt Wesoly. "Der weibliche Bevölkerungsanteil in spätmittelalterlichen und frühneuzeitlichen Städten und die Betätigung von Frauen im zünftigen Handwerk (insbesondere am Mittel und Oberrhein)." *Zeitschrift für Geschichte des Oberrheins* 89 (1980) 69–117. ISSN 0044-2607. ▸ Disputes commonly held assumption that there was population imbalance in favor of women in late medieval cities and that medieval guilds were open to women. Direct refutation of golden-age-for-women ideas; based on archival evidence. [MEW]

30.182 Merry E. Wiesner. "Beyond women and the family: towards a gender analysis of the Reformation." *Sixteenth century journal* 18.3 (1987) 311–21. ISSN 0361-0160. ▸ Calls for integration of gender as category of analysis in all areas of Reformation scholarship, not just studies of women or family. Largely suggestive and bibliographic. [MEW]

30.183 Merry E. Wiesner. "Guilds, male bonding, and women's work in early modern Germany." *Gender and history* 1.2 (1989) 125–37. ISSN 0953-5233. ▸ Analysis of gendered nature of notions of honor in craft guilds and role this played in exclusion of women from craft work. Stresses ideological constraints on economic structures. [MEW]

30.184 Merry E. Wiesner. "*Wandervogels* and women: journeymen's concepts of masculinity in early modern Germany." *Journal of social history* 24.4 (1991) 767–82. ISSN 0022-4529. ▸ Analysis of development of notions of masculinity that were antifamily, antifemale, and antipatriarchal among journeymen, 1500–1800. Sees class as important determinant of gender ideology. [MEW]

30.185 Merry E. Wiesner. *Working women in Renaissance Germany.* New Brunswick, N.J.: Rutgers University Press, 1986. ISBN 0-8135-1138-0. ▸ Pioneering survey of women's work experiences in six South German cities, 1450–1650, finding similar trends despite religious, political, and economic differences. Views ideology as well as economics as determinative and sees increasing restrictions throughout period. [MEW]

30.186 Joy Wiltenburg. *Disorderly women and female power in the street literature of early modern England and Germany.* Charlottesville: University Press of Virginia, 1992. ISBN 0-8139-1350-0 (cl), 0-8139-1351-9 (pbk). ▸ Uses enormous range of popular literature to compare figure of disorderly woman in discussions of marriage, sexual relations, and crime in two countries. Fine translations, new sources, and good awareness of national differences in social background. [MEW]

30.187 Jean M. Woods and Marie Fürstenwald. *Schriftstellerinnen, Künstlerinnen, und gelehrte Frauen des deutschen Barock: ein Lexikon.* Stuttgart: Metzler, 1984. ISBN 3-476-00551-8. ▸ Lexicon of female authors, scientists, artists, and other learned women born between 1580 and 1720 in German-speaking areas. Extremely useful list of their published and unpublished works and location of these when available. [MEW]

30.188 Heide Wunder. "Frauen in der Gesellschaft Mitteleuropas im späten Mittelalter und in der frühen Neuzeit (funfzehnten bis achtzehnten Jahrhundert)." In *Hexen und Zauberer: die grosse Verfolgung—ein europäischen Phänomen in der Steiermark.* Helfried Valentinisch, ed. Graz: Leykam, 1987. ISBN 3-7011-7184-X. ▸ Survey of all aspects of women's existence, biological, cultural, economic, and social, in early modern Central Europe. One of best brief summaries in any language. [MEW]

30.189 Heide Wunder and Christina Vanja, eds. *Wandel der Geschlechterbeziehungen zu Beginn der Neuzeit.* Frankfurt: Suhrkamp, 1991. ISBN 3-518-28513-0. ▸ Collection of essays by historians, theologians, and literary critics on various aspects of gender relations, 1500–1700. Essays complement one another and are among most sophisticated to appear in German on gender issues. [MEW]

SEE ALSO
4.326 Londa L. Schiebinger. *The mind has no sex?*
22.131 Jane Dempsey Douglass. *Women, freedom, and Calvin.*
22.135 Joyce L. Irwin. *Womanhood in radical Protestantism.*
22.142 Sherrin Marshall, ed. *Women in Reformation and Counter-Reformation Europe.*

SOCIOECONOMIC HISTORY, 1500–1700

30.190 Wilhelm Abel. *Agricultural fluctuations in Europe: from the thirteenth to the twentieth centuries.* Joan Thirsk, Foreword. Olive Ordish, trans. New York: St. Martin's, 1980. ISBN 0-312-01465-1. ▸ Broad survey of agricultural trends; standard introduction to rural population and economy in early modern Central Europe. Neo-Malthusian classic stressing population change as motor of change in countryside. [TR]

30.191 Wilhelm Abel. *Geschichte der deutschen Landwirtschaft vom frühen Mittelalter bis zum neunzehnten Jahrhundert.* 3d ed. Stuttgart: Ulmer, 1978. ISBN 3-8001-3041-6. ▸ Broad overview of agriculture, technology, settlement patterns, population, and economy. Author's distinctive neo-Malthusianism provides backdrop to agricultural trends in premodern era. Voluminous references to specialized literature in German. [TR]

30.192 Wilhelm Abel. *Massenarmut und Hungerkrisen in vorindustriellen Europa: Versuch ein Synopsis.* Hamburg: Parey, 1974. ISBN 3-490-04315-4. ▸ Panoramic survey of mass impoverishment of rural and urban populations since late Middle Ages. Case study of consequences of wage-price gap of sixteenth and seventeenth centuries. [TR]

30.193 János M. Bak, ed. *The German Peasant War of 1525.* London: Cass, 1975. ISBN 0-7146-3063-2. ▸ Glimpse into diversity of

scholarly opinion about origins, dynamics, and goals of rebellion. Illustrates explosion of scholarship in early 1970s on Peasants' War and reasons why no consensus view on rebellion. [TR]

30.194 Thomas Barnett-Robisheaux. "Peasant revolts in Germany and Central Europe after the Peasants' War: comments on the literature." *Central European history* 17 (1984) 384–403. ISSN 0008-9389. ▸ Discussion of new research on German peasant revolts after 1525 with excellent guide to literature in German and English. Poses more questions than it answers. [TR]

30.195 Lutz K. Berkner. "Inheritance, land tenure, and peasant family structure: a German regional comparison." In *Family and inheritance: rural society in Western Europe, 1200–1800.* Jack Goody, Joan Thirsk, and E. P. Thompson, eds., pp. 71–95. Cambridge: Cambridge University Press, 1976. ISBN 0-521-21246-4. ▸ Pioneering study of relationship of inheritance customs to family structure in countryside. Part of generation of scholarship stressing relationship between property and family structure that isolated peasant family from culture, religion, and state power. [TR]

30.196 Karlheinz Blaschke. *Bevölkerungsgeschichte von Sachsen bis zur industriellen Revolution.* Weimar: Böhlau, 1967. ▸ One of few demographic histories of region of Germany. Shows population densities over time but not mortality, fertility, and nuptiality rates. Methods now outdated; population history before family reconstitution techniques developed. [TR]

30.197 Peter Blickle. "Peasant revolts in the German empire in the late Middle Ages." *Social history* 4 (1979) 223–39. ISSN 0307-1022. ▸ Concise overview of mounting discontent in countryside on eve of Peasants' War. [TR]

30.198 Ingomar Bog. "Wachstumsprobleme der oberdeutschen Wirtschaft, 1540–1618." *Jahrbücher für Nationalökonomie und Statistik* 179 (1966) 493–537. ISSN 0021-4027. ▸ Key contribution to debate over German economy on eve of Thirty Years' War. Focus on problems of South German international commerce overlooks trends in local economies and in town-country relationships. [TR]

30.199 Otto Brunner. *Adeliges Landleben und europäischer Geist: Leben und Werk, Wolf Helmhards von Hohberg, 1612–1688.* Salzburg: Müller, 1949. ▸ Remarkable view into world of German and Austrian nobility in seventeenth century through work of provincial man of letters. Evokes rural ethos lost as modern states and capitalist ethic developed. Romanticized view of past uninformed by modern social history. [TR]

30.200 Otto Brunner. "'Das ganze Haus' und die alteuropäische Ökonomik." In *Neue Wege der Verfassungs- und Sozialgeschichte.* 3d ed. Otto Brunner, ed., pp. 103–27. Göttingen: Vandenhoeck & Ruprecht, 1980. ISBN 3-525-36104-1. ▸ Provocative argument that premodern economies structured around subsistence needs of household. Romanticism for past shines through, but accords well with modern sociological theories about peasant economy. [TR]

30.201 Günther Franz. *Der dreissigjährige Krieg und das deutsche Volk: Untersuchungen zur Bevölkerungs und Agrargeschichte.* 4th ed. Stuttgart: Fischer, 1979. ISBN 3-437-50233-6. ▸ Meticulous survey of population losses and economic changes during Thirty Years' War, informing any discussion of seventeenth century. Narrowly links most socioeconomic change to war and neglects more recent and broader discussions of seventeenth-century crisis. [TR]

30.202 William W. Hagen. "How mighty the Junkers? Peasant rents and seigneurial profits in sixteenth-century Brandenburg." *Past and present* 108 (1985) 80–116. ISSN 0031-2746. ▸ One of first empirical studies of Junker wealth and power disproving Rosenberg's (30.214) and Wallerstein's (22.275) view that Junkers relied primarily on political coercion for economic domination. Long overdue revisionist approach to rural Brandenburg. [TR]

30.203 William W. Hagen. "Seventeenth-century crisis in Brandenburg: the Thirty Years' War, the destabilization of serfdom, and the rise of absolutism." *American historical review* 94 (1989) 302–35. ISSN 0002-8762. ▸ Revisionist approach to rural Brandenburg into seventeenth century (sequel to 30.202). Persuasive, thoroughly documented view of socioeconomic foundations of Brandenburg-Prussian absolutism. [TR]

30.204 Peter-Michael Hahn. *Fürstliche Territorialhoheit und lokale Adelsgewalt: die herrschaftliche Durchdringung des ländlichen Raumes zwischen Elbe und Aller (1300–1700).* Berlin: de Gruyter, 1989. (Veröffentlichungen der Historischen Kommission zu Berlin, 72.) ISBN 3-11-012118-2. ▸ Rise and fall of German provincial nobility told with thoroughness and revisionist vigor. Old mark nobles adjusted to agrarian advance and new opportunities of sixteenth century, but entered protracted crisis in seventeenth century. Refreshing new look at Brandenburg's nobles and rural worlds independent of state. [TR]

30.205 Arthur E. Imhof. *Die verlorenen Welten: Alltagsbewältigung durch unsere Vorfahren und weshalb wir uns heute so schwer damit tun.* Munich: Beck, 1984. ISBN 3-406-30270-X. ▸ Lively look at how famine, plague, and war shaped life cycle and world of peasant. Interdisciplinary work; begins as modern demography, ends as cultural and religious history. Modern dilemmas created by demographic transition in modern world. [TR]

30.206 Henry Kamen. "The economic and social consequences of the Thirty Years' War." *Past and present* 39 (1968) 44–61. ISSN 0031-2746. ▸ Short article defining issues on subject barely explored in Anglo-American scholarship. Moves beyond old view of war as uniform disaster for German-speaking Central Europe. [TR]

30.207 Hermann Kellenbenz. *Deutsche Wirtschaftsgeschichte.* Vol. 1: *Von den Anfangen bis zum Ende des achtzehnten Jahrhunderts.* Munich: Beck, 1977. ISBN 3-406-06987-8 (v. 1). ▸ Thorough, descriptive survey of German economic history in premodern period. Sets discussions of commerce, agriculture, industry, and finance in context of contemporary population and political and social trends. Handy, essential reference. [TR]

30.208 Hermann Kellenbenz. "Rural industries in the West from the end of the Middle Ages to the eighteenth century." In *Essays in European economic history, 1500–1800.* Peter Earle, ed., pp. 45–88. Oxford: Clarendon, 1974. ISBN 0-19-877054-5. ▸ Sound empirical overview of development of rural industries in early modern Germany. Careful descriptive account without theoretical flourishes. [TR]

30.209 Peter Kriedte, Hans Medick, and Jürgen Schlumbohm. *Industrialization before industrialization: rural industry in the genesis of capitalism.* Beate Schempp, trans. Cambridge: Cambridge University Press, 1981. ISBN 0-521-23809-9 (cl), 0-521-28228-4 (pbk). ▸ Theoretically informed approach to development of rural industry. Abstract sociological analysis fuses Franklin F. Mendel's model of protoindustry with Alexander Chayanov's theory of peasant economy in suggestive way. [TR]

30.210 Friedrich Lütge. *Geschichte der deutschen Agrarverfassung vom frühen Mittelalter bis zum neunzehnten Jahrhundert.* 2d ed. Stuttgart: Ulmer, 1967. ▸ Primer in premodern German agrarian systems. Distinctions between different seigneurial regimes are described with legal and "constitutional" rigor but not with the eye of a social historian. Dry and tedious but an essential starting point for understanding regional complexity. [TR]

30.211 Friedrich Lütge. "Die wirtschaftliche Lage Deutschlands vor Ausbruch des Dreissigjährigen Krieges." In *Studien zur Sozial und Wirtschaftsgeschichte: gesammelte Abhandlungen,* pp.

336–95. Stuttgart: Fischer, 1963. ▸ Survey of decline and adjustment of German economy after halcyon days of commercial expansion in early sixteenth century. Suggests stagnation and decline set in before Thirty Years' War. [TR]

30.212 Herman Rebel. *Peasant classes: the bureaucratization of property and family relations under early Habsburg absolutism, 1511–1636.* Princeton: Princeton University Press, 1983. ISBN 0-691-05366-9. ▸ Innovative study of growth of state power in Austrian countryside and "house communities" that Austria fostered among peasantry. Cogent Weberian sociological analysis of peasant revolts of 1596, 1626, and 1636. [TR/TAB/SKN]

30.213 Thomas Robisheaux. *Rural society and the search for order in early modern Germany.* Cambridge: Cambridge University Press, 1989. ISBN 0-521-35626-1. ▸ Probing study of village society during long agrarian advance and decline in sixteenth and seventeenth centuries. Focuses on complex interplay of population, social stratification, family, and state power in small patrimonial state. Richly, meticulously documented. [TR]

30.214 Hans Rosenberg. "The rise of the Junkers in Brandenburg-Prussia, 1410–1653." *American historical review* 49 (1943–44) 1–22, 228–40. ISSN 0002-8762. ▸ Classic study of rise of Prussian Junkers as lords and allies of Hohenzollerns. Overstates close political ties of nobility to Brandenburg-Prussian state. [TR]

30.215 Helmut Rössler, ed. *Deutscher Adel.* 2 vols. Darmstadt: Wissenschaftliche Buchgesellschaft, 1965. ▸ Standard overview of German nobility. Increasingly outdated but remains starting point. [TR]

30.216 David Warren Sabean. "Family and land tenure: a case study of conflict in the German Peasants' War (1525)." *Peasant studies newsletter* 3 (1974) 1–15. ISSN 0162-203X. ▸ Case study of Upper Swabia showing how peasant conflicts over land and resources increased on eve of Peasants' War. Rare glimpse into internal dynamics of German peasant family and village before 1525. [TR]

30.217 David Warren Sabean. *Power in the blood: popular culture and village discourse in early modern Germany.* Ph.D. dissertation. Cambridge: Cambridge University Press, 1984. ISBN 0-521-26455-3. ▸ Six lively, colorful stories about how villagers came to terms with overbearing bureaucrats, arrogant pastors, witches, the poor, and relatives. Explorations of power and society at intersection of history and anthropology. [TR]

30.218 David Warren Sabean. *The social background to the Peasants' War of 1525 in southern Upper Swabia.* Madison: University of Wisconsin Press, 1969. ▸ Pioneering study of social and economic origins of rural discontent before 1525 that now informs every discussion of Peasants' War. Shows how population pressures and increasing pressures on peasant resources set stage for massive rising. Unsurpassed in explaining village society before 1525. Also available in photocopy from Ann Arbor: University Microfilms International. [TR]

30.219 Rudolf Schlögl. *Bauern, Krieg, und Staat: Oberbayerische Bauernwirtschaft und frühmoderner Staat im siebzehnten Jahrhundert.* Göttingen: Vandenhoeck & Ruprecht, 1988. (Veröffentlichungen des Max-Planck-Instituts für Geschichte, 89.) ISBN 3-525-35625-0. ▸ Theoretically informed analysis of crisis of German peasant economy in seventeenth century. Regional monograph with broader implications. [TR]

30.220 Winfried Schulze. "Peasant resistance in sixteenth- and seventeenth-century Germany in a European context." In *Religion, politics, and social protest: three studies on early modern Germany.* Kaspar von Greyerz, ed., pp. 61–98. London and Boston: German Historical Institute and Allen & Unwin, 1984. ISBN 0-04-940077-0. ▸ Brief overview of peasant revolts in Germany in light of historiography on European peasant rebellions. Illustrates continuing impact of peasant resistance to authority long after Peasants' War. [TR]

30.221 Tom Scott. "Economic conflict and co-operation on the Upper Rhine, 1450–1600." In *Politics and society in Reformation Europe: essays for Sir Geoffrey Elton on his sixty-fifth birthday.* E. I. Kouri and Tom Scott, eds., pp. 210–31. London: Macmillan, 1987. ISBN 0-333-41737-2. ‣ Model case study of development of German regional economy. Lively and vital Upper Rhine economy revolved around local town-country relationships, not international commerce that fascinates most economic historians. [TR]

30.222 B. H. Slicher van Bath. *The agrarian history of western Europe, A.D. 500–1850.* Olive Ordish, trans. London: Arnold, 1963. ‣ Broad overview of premodern European agriculture remains best survey of agricultural technology and productivity for period. Pivots on introduction of new intensive agriculture in Low Countries as key to economic change away from subsistence agriculture. Technical and detailed; illustrated with numerous case studies. [TR]

30.223 Heide Wunder. *Die bäuerliche Gemeinde in Deutschland.* Göttingen: Vandenhoeck & Ruprecht, 1986. ISBN 3-525-33473-7. ‣ Remarkably concise study of development of village as communal institution and community. Transition from relatively autonomous late medieval commune to state-dominated village of early modern era is nowhere better summed up. Superb bibliography. [TR]

SOCIOECONOMIC HISTORY, 1700–1800

30.224 Ute Frevert. *Women in German history: from bourgeois emancipation to sexual liberation.* 1988 ed. Stuart McKinnon-Evans, Terry Bond, and Barbara Norden, trans. New York: Berg, 1989. ISBN 0-85496-233-6. ‣ Good short treatment of women in eighteenth-century Germany society in opening chapters. Discusses historical background to creation of separate spheres in nineteenth century. [ML]

30.225 John G. Gagliardo. *From pariah to patriot: the changing image of the German peasant, 1770–1840.* Lexington: University Press of Kentucky, 1969. ISBN 0-8131-1187-0. ‣ Discussion of how estimation of German peasant was transformed in literature and in mostly elite perceptions after 1770. Based on literary sources, journal articles, and publicists' writings. [ML]

30.226 John G. Gagliardo. *Reich and nation: the Holy Roman Empire as idea and reality, 1763–1806.* Bloomington: Indiana University Press, 1980. ISBN 0-253-16773-6. ‣ Examination of perception of empire by surveying political pamphlets and other writings. Traces desire for preserving empire as guarantor of order in several spheres, including social and economic. [ML]

30.227 Farley Grubb. "Morbidity and mortality on the North Atlantic passage: eighteenth-century German immigration." *Journal of interdisciplinary history* 17.3 (1977) 565–86. ISSN 0022-1953. ‣ Examination of first wave of German immigrants to Pennsylvania. Quantitative study of voyage mortality and immediate postvoyage mortality. [ML]

30.228 Arno Herzig, Dieter Langewiesche, and Arnold Sywotteck, eds. *Arbeiter in Hamburg: Unterschichten, Arbeiter, und Arbeiterbewegung seit dem ausgehenden achtzehnten Jahrhundert.* Hamburg: Erziehung & Wissenschaft, 1983. ISBN 3-8103-0807-2. ‣ Useful collection of articles on labor and lower classes in major German city. Several articles treat topics in eighteenth century, including useful contributions to history of poor relief, labor policies, and Hamburg's economy. Articles based overwhelmingly on archival research. [ML]

30.229 Steve Hochstadt. "Migration in preindustrial Germany." *Central European history* 16.3 (1983) 195–224. ISSN 0008-9389.

‣ Offers significant evidence to counterbalance prevailing image of stable, immobile German society in seventeenth and eighteenth centuries. [ML]

30.230 Ulrich Im Hof. *Das gesellige Jahrhundert: Gesellschaft und Gesellschaften im Zeitalter der Aufklärung.* Munich: Beck, 1982. ISBN 3-406-08708-6. ‣ Investigation of series of societies founded for various purposes—economic, social, cultural—in eighteenth century. Societies, to large extent, focal points of Enlightenment in German cities and territories. [ML]

30.231 John E. Knodel. *Demographic behavior in the past: a study of fourteen German village populations in the eighteenth and nineteenth centuries.* Cambridge: Cambridge University Press, 1988. ISBN 0-521-32715-6. ‣ Detailed meticulous survey of demography of rural German villages in southern Germany. Employs technique of family reconstruction to survey age of marriage, mortality, fertility, and contraception. One of few solidly researched demographic studies available on early modern Germany. [ML/JJS]

30.232 John Komlos. *Nutrition and economic development in the eighteenth-century Habsburg monarchy: an anthropometric history.* Princeton: Princeton University Press, 1989. ISBN 0-691-04257-8. ‣ Original anthropometric approach to study of mortality and longevity. Evaluates statistics on body size, including height and weight, to gauge mortality and life span; relevant to both halves of empire. Original and provocative. [ML/SBV]

30.233 Franklin Kopitzsch, ed. *Aufklärung, Absolutismus, und Bürgertum in Deutschland: zwölf Aufsätze.* Munich: Nymphenburger Verlagshandlung, 1976. (Nymphenburger Texte zur Wissenschaft, 24.) ISBN 3-485-03224-7. ‣ Excellent introductory essay sketching historiography of Enlightenment, absolutism, and civil society in eighteenth-century Germany. Includes evaluation of needs for further research. Other essays treat poor relief and poverty, urban development, character of middle-class society, and enlightened absolutism. [ML]

30.234 Anthony J. La Vopa. *Grace, talent, and merit: poor students, clerical careers, and professional ideology in eighteenth-century Germany.* Cambridge: Cambridge University Press, 1988. ISBN 0-521-35041-7. ‣ Contribution to burgeoning literature on history of professions in Germany; subtle analysis of prosopography of those involved in education. Also significant contribution to understanding of intellectual content of German Enlightenment. [ML]

30.235 Anthony J. La Vopa. *Prussian schoolteachers: profession and office, 1763–1848.* Chapel Hill: University of North Carolina Press, 1980. ISBN 0-8078-1426-1. ‣ Study of history of education intersecting with study of history of professions. Discusses mostly primary schoolmasters in rural (less in city) schools. [ML]

30.236 W. R. Lee. "Bastardy and socioeconomic structure of South Germany." *Journal of interdisciplinary history* 7.3 (1977) 403–25. ISSN 0022-1953. ‣ Examination of history of illegitimacy in Bavaria. Describes reasons for changing perceptions of bastardy from insignificant social problem to significant barometer of moral decay. [ML]

30.237 Mary Lindemann. *Patriots and paupers: Hamburg, 1712–1830.* New York: Oxford University Press, 1990. ISBN 0-19-506140-3. ‣ Urban history of Germany's major port. Considers social, economic, and demographic history of city through lens of poor relief reform. [ML]

30.238 Hans Mauersberg. *Wirtschafts- und Sozialgeschichte zentraleuropäischer Städte in neuerer Zeit: dargestellt an den Beispielen von Basel, Frankfurt am M[ain], Hamburg, Hannover, und München.* Göttingen: Vandenhoeck & Ruprecht, 1960. ‣ Pioneering comparative study of five major cities. Detailed analyses of tax systems, social structures, economics, and administration. Early but remarkable achievement reflecting extensive primary research in many municipal archives. [ML]

30.239 Charles E. McClelland. *State, society, and university in Germany, 1700–1914*. Cambridge: Cambridge University Press, 1980. ISBN 0-521-22742-9. ▸ Well-balanced introduction to development of universities in context of rise of bureaucratic state and within social context of eighteenth-century German society. Especially good on rise of scholarly ideal and institutional tensions caused by expansion after turn of century. Major synthetic work on history of German higher education. [ML/JJS]

30.240 Hans Medick and David Warren Sabean, eds. *Interest and emotion: essays on the study of family and kinship*. Cambridge and Paris: Cambridge University Press and Maison des Sciences de l'Homme, 1984. ISBN 0-521-24969-4. ▸ Application of ethnographic and anthropological methods to study of family and family relations. Several articles on German topics, including kinship and family in village and rural society, on infanticide in Bavaria, and on sexual culture and leisure time. [ML]

30.241 James Van Horn Melton and Douglas A. Unfug, eds. *The French Revolution in Germany and Austria*. Atlanta: Emory University, 1989. (*Central European history*, 22.2.) ISSN 0008-9389. ▸ Series of articles evaluating impact of French Revolution. Important essays on politics with some major implications for social and economic life. [ML]

30.242 Peter Petschauer. "Eighteenth-century opinions about education for women." *Central European history* 19.3 (1986) 262–92. ISSN 0008-9389. ▸ Study of works of early advocates for women's education in Germany. Draws heavily on writings of Germany's first female medical doctor, Dorothea Christiane Leporin. [ML]

30.243 Theodore K. Rabb. "The effect of the Thirty Years' War on the German economy." *Journal of modern history* 34.1 (1962) 40–51. ISSN 0022-2801. ▸ Outline of main features of debate on Thirty Years' War. Presents now-questioned argument that war started long period of general decline in Germanies, replacing prosperity with disaster at least in immediate postwar era. [ML]

30.244 David Warren Sabean. *Property, production, and family in Neckerhausen, 1700–1870*. Cambridge: Cambridge University Press, 1990. ISBN 0-521-38538-5 (cl), 0-521-38692-6 (pbk). ▸ Finely researched study of small village in Württemberg. Important discussions of landholding patterns, family life, village social and economic structures, and demography. [ML]

30.245 James J. Sheehan. *German history, 1770–1866*. New York: Oxford University Press, 1989. ISBN 0-19-822120-7. ▸ Lucid and elegant synthesis of eighteenth-century politics, society, culture, and economy. Moves away from Prussocentric history, giving considerable attention to other territories and cities in Germanies. [ML]

30.246 Keith Tribe. "Cameralism and the science of government." *Journal of modern history* 56.2 (1984) 263–84. ISSN 0022-2801. ▸ Examination of role of *Polizei* and development of internal administration. Important implications for programs attempting to implement major social and economic reforms. [ML]

30.247 Keith Tribe. *Governing economy: the reformation of German economic discourse, 1750–1840*. New York: Cambridge University Press, 1988. ISBN 0-521-30316-8. ▸ Modern treatment of rise of German cameralism and its development as academic discipline in eighteenth century. Stresses contributions of cameralism to economic thought. [ML]

30.248 Otto Ulbricht. "The debate about foundling hospitals in Enlightenment Germany: infanticide, illegitimacy, and infant mortality rates." *Central European history* 18.3/4 (1985) 211–57. ISSN 0008-9389. ▸ Detailed, careful study of foundling hospitals

as they fit into wider pattern of enlightened reforms. Explains why advocates of foundling hospitals gradually lost support. [ML]

30.249 Mack Walker. "Rights and functions: the social categories of eighteenth-century German jurists and cameralists." *Journal of modern history* 50.1 (1978) 234–51. ISSN 0022-2801. ▸ Discussion of how German jurists and cameralists constructed social structure and social categories by leading expert on period. Explores relationships between social and constitutional history. [ML]

SEE ALSO
31.95 Hans-Ulrich Wehler. *Deutsche Gesellschaftsgeschichte*. Vol. 1.
31.97 T.C.W. Blanning. *The French Revolution in Germany*.

URBAN HISTORY, 1600–1800

30.250 Alexander Francis Cowan. *The urban patriciate: Lübeck and Venice, 1580–1700*. Cologne: Böhlau, 1986. (Quellen und Darstellungen zur Hansischen Geschichte, n.F., 30.) ISBN 3-412-06084-0. ▸ Comparison of urban elites in two great European commercial cities. Membership in patriciate more open to newcomers in Lübeck than in Venice, but both groups showed capacity to adapt to new economic conditions. [CRF]

30.251 Franklin L. Ford. *Strasbourg in transition, 1648–1789*. 1958 ed. New York: Norton, 1966. ▸ An introductory summary of the political, social, and cultural transformation of major German city after annexation by France (1681). Persistence of German culture despite growing French influence illustrates special character of border communities. [CRF]

30.252 Étienne François. *Koblenz im achtzehnten Jahrhundert: zur Sozial- und Bevölkerungsstruktur einer deutschen Residenzstadt*. Göttingen: Vandenhoeck & Ruprecht, 1982. (Veröffentlichungen des Max-Planck-Instituts für Geschichte, 72.) ISBN 3-525-35386-3. ▸ Exemplary case study of social conditions in medium-sized German city of eighteenth century. Demonstrates persistence of traditional demographic norms, economic structures, and social values to end of Old Regime. [CRF]

30.253 Christopher R. Friedrichs. "Capitalism, mobility, and class formation in the early modern German city." *Past and present* 69 (1975) 24–49. ISSN 0031-2746. ▸ Uses data from Nördlingen to argue as upward mobility declined and economic dependence on capitalist merchants increased, craftsmen came to form distinct lower middle class. [CRF]

30.254 Christopher R. Friedrichs. "Urban conflicts and the imperial constitution in seventeenth-century Germany." *Journal of modern history* 58, Supplement (1986) 98–123. ISSN 0022-2801. ▸ Rival parties in urban conflicts appealed to different institutions of Holy Roman Empire to uphold their claims. Struggle between magistrates and citizens in Wetzlar illustrates strategies for using imperial constitution to promote local aims. [CRF]

30.255 Christopher R. Friedrichs. *Urban society in an age of war: Nördlingen, 1580–1720*. Princeton: Princeton University Press, 1979. ISBN 0-691-05278-6. ▸ Model analysis of social structure, social mobility, and economic change in one city. Recovery from devastation of Thirty Years' War reversed by onset of new wars in late seventeenth century. As artisans lost wealth, capitalist merchants gained power. [CRF]

30.256 Klaus Gerteis. *Die deutschen Städte in der frühen Neuzeit: zur Vorgeschichte der "bürgerlichen Welt."* Darmstadt: Wissenschaftliche Buchgesellschaft, 1986. ISBN 3-534-01683-1. ▸ Comprehensive overview of political, administrative, social, and economic developments in early modern German city, stressing resistance to change in some sectors and adaptability in others. Useful bibliography. [CRF]

30.257 Helen P. Liebel. "Laissez-faire vs. mercantilism: the rise of Hamburg and the Hamburg bourgeoisie vs. Frederick the Great in the crisis of 1763." *Vierteljahrschrift für Sozial- und Wirtschaftsgeschichte* 52.2 (1965) 207–38. ISSN 0340-8728. ‣ Opposition to mercantilist policies of Prussia following Seven Years' War stimulated Hamburg's merchant elite to formulate laissez-faire doctrines anticipating ideas of Adam Smith. [CRF]

30.258 Karin Newman. "Hamburg in the European economy, 1660–1750." *Journal of European economic history* 14.1 (1985) 57–93. ISSN 0391-5115. ‣ Explains Hamburg's increasing importance as center for transfer of goods to and from Central Europe. City's location gave it advantages over rival ports in Germany and Netherlands. [CRF]

30.259 Bernd Roeck. *Als wollt die Welt schier brechen: eine Stadt im Zeitalter des Dreissigjährigen Krieges.* Munich: Beck, 1991. ISBN 3-406-35500-5. ‣ Exhaustive, imaginative study of Augsburg from 1580s to end of Thirty Years' War. Detailed analysis of social structure; demography; and political, cultural, and religious life of great imperial city. Classic adaptation of author's two-volume *Habilitationsschrift.* [RH]

30.260 Gerald Lyman Soliday. *A community in conflict: Frankfurt society in the seventeeth and early eighteenth centuries.* Hanover, N.H.: University Press of New England for Brandeis University Press, 1974. ISBN 0-87451-092-9. ‣ Constitutional struggle in Frankfurt from 1705 to 1732 pitted citizens first against magistrates, then against noncitizens and Jews. Conflict in this corporate society initially disruptive but eventually integrative as hostility shifted to "outsiders." [CRF]

30.261 Gerhard Taddey, ed. *Lexicon der deutschen Geschichte: Personen, Ereignisse, Institutionen von der Zeitwende bis zum Ausgang des Zweiten Weltkrieges.* 2d ed. Stuttgart: Kröner, 1983. ISBN 3-520-81302-5. ‣ Outstanding one-volume reference work for all aspects of German history, especially political. In addition to information on major events and individuals, covers each territory and free city of Holy Roman Empire and each German state after 1806. [CRF]

30.262 Mack Walker. *German home towns: community, state, and general estate, 1648–1871.* Ithaca, N.Y.: Cornell University Press, 1971. ISBN 0-8014-0670-6. ‣ Outstanding, influential interpretation linking local history to fundamental themes in German history. Distinctive guild-centered character of small, semiautonomous towns continued to shape German values deep into nineteenth century. Holy Roman Empire insulated townspeople from strong central government. [CRF/CWI/JS/JJS]

30.263 Joachim Whaley. *Religious toleration and social change in Hamburg, 1529–1819.* Cambridge: Cambridge University Press, 1985. ISBN 0-521-26189-9. ‣ Discussion of growing acceptance of Catholic, Calvinist, and Jewish minorities in major German commercial center despite objections by Lutheran clergy based on exhaustive archival research. Toleration seen as resulting from pragmatic rather than philosophical concerns. [CRF]

30.264 Gerd Wunder. *Die Bürger von Hall: Sozialgeschichte einer Reichsstadt, 1216–1802.* Sigmaringen: Thorbecke, 1980. (Forschungen aus Württembergisch Franken, 16.) ISBN 3-7995-7613-4. ‣ Comprehensive survey of social history of Schwäbisch Hall in Middle Ages and early modern period. Sophisticated methodology and analysis underpin lively treatment of city's various social and occupational groups. [CRF]

CULTURAL HISTORY, 1500–1650

30.265 Dorothy Alexander. *The German single-leaf woodcut, 1600–1700: a pictorial catalogue.* 2 vols. New York: Abaris, 1977. ISBN 0-913870-05-0. ‣ Illustrated catalog of German broadsheet woodcuts by anonymous as well as known artists. Short biographies of artists. [KZ]

30.266 Christiane Andersson and Charles Talbot, eds. *From a mighty fortress: prints, drawings, and books in the age of Luther, 1483–1546.* Detroit: Detroit Institute of Arts, 1983. ISBN 0-89558-091-8 (pbk). ‣ Catalog of exhibition of material from Kunstsammlungen der Veste Coburg and Landesbibliothek Coburg with essays by historians as well as art historians and detailed entries. [KZ]

30.267 Rosemarie Aulinger. *Das Bild des Reichstages im sechzehnten Jahrhundert: Beiträge zu einer typologischen Analyse schriftlicher und bildlicher Quellen.* Göttingen: Vandenhoeck & Ruprecht, 1980. (Schriftenreihe der Historischen Kommision bei der Bayerischen Akademie der Wissenschaften, 18.) ISBN 3-525-35915-2. ‣ Detailed analysis of day-to-day activities and rituals of imperial diets based on visual as well as written sources. [KZ]

30.268 Roland H. Bainton. "Dürer and Luther as the Man of Sorrows." *Art bulletin* 29 (1947) 269–72. ISSN 0004-3079. ‣ Analysis of Dürer's self-portraits as form of *imitatio Christi* and history of such images. See Koerner 30.295. [KZ]

30.269 Michael Baxandall. *The limewood sculptors of Renaissance Germany.* New Haven: Yale University Press, 1980. ISBN 0-300-02423-1. ‣ Lavishly illustrated examination of German limewood sculptures. Viewed primarily in terms of material and material aspects of their creation—function in society, markets, and guilds—rather than in terms of their creators. No new material on guilds, markets, or religious context but unusual to find art historian taking material, social, and religious context this seriously. [KZ]

30.270 Frank L. Borchardt. *German antiquity in Renaissance myth.* Baltimore: Johns Hopkins University Press, 1971. ISBN 0-8018-1268-2. ‣ Survey of medieval narratives of mythic German past as revived by German Renaissance writers. Emphasis on vigor of vernacular and on revitalization of medieval material by writers who failed to find suitable material in classical authors to whom they had turned under influence of Italian humanists. [KZ]

30.271 Thomas A. Brady, Jr. "The social place of a German Renaissance artist: Hans Baldung Grien (1484/85–1545) at Strasbourg." *Central European history* 8 (1975) 295–315. ISSN 0008-9389. ‣ Argues against trend, at least in case of Baldung, a social, economic, and political success, that Reformation did not diminish artist's position. Baldung simply turned to other genres. [KZ]

30.272 Miriam Usher Chrisman. "From polemic to propaganda: the development of mass persuasion in the late sixteenth century." *Archive for Reformation history* 73 (1982) 175–95. ISSN 0003-9381. ‣ Examination of impact of final split between religious camps on rhetorical developments in illustrated pamphlets and broadsheets. Illuminates medium and method essential to state builders. [KZ/SKN]

30.273 Miriam Usher Chrisman. *Lay culture, learned culture: books and social change in Strasbourg, 1480–1599.* New Haven: Yale University Press, 1982. ISBN 0-300-02530-0. ‣ Important study ranging from printing process itself to printers and their diverse products to different cultures they defined. Although 40 percent of citizenry may have owned books, book ownership was fragmented by social classes and by divide between vernacular and Latin cultures. [KZ]

30.274 Carl C. Christensen. *Art and the Reformation in Germany.* Athens: Ohio University Press, 1979. ISBN 0-8214-0388-5. ‣ General overview of impact of Reformation on German art, treating iconoclasm, Luther on images, and iconographical developments. [KZ]

30.275 Richard van Dülmen. *Theatre of horror: crime and punishment in early modern Germany.* 1985 ed. Elisabeth Neu, trans. Cambridge: Polity, 1990. ISBN 0-7456-0616-4. ‣ Analysis of meaning and eventual disappearance of legal rituals of execution in early modern Germany. Using visual as well as more usual legal sources, argues increasing dramatization of public punishment was (generally unsuccessful) attempt to reduce crime and popularity of criminals by disgracing honor and body of criminal. [KZ]

30.276 Carlos M. N. Eire. *War against the idols: the reformation of worship from Erasmus to Calvin.* Cambridge: Cambridge University Press, 1986. ISBN 0-521-30685-X. ▸ Examination of theological and theoretical underpinnings of Protestant attack on Catholic use of visual images in worship. [KZ]

30.277 Norbert Elias. *The civilizing process.* 1978 ed. 2 vols. Edmund Jephcott, trans. New York: Pantheon, 1982. ISBN 0-394-71133-5 (v. 1, pbk), 0-394-71134-3 (v. 2, pbk). ▸ Deservedly famous analysis arguing for connection between civilizing process and development of absolutist state: ruling classes trained by royal courts to restrain physical urges. Only a sociologist could imagine connection between development of fork and development of state; only a brilliant sociologist could prove it. [KZ]

30.278 Robert John Weston Evans. "Culture and anarchy in the empire, 1540–1680." In *Special issue: the culture of the Holy Roman Empire, 1540–1680*, pp. 14–30. Atlanta: Emory University, 1985. (*Central European history*, 18.) ISSN 0008-9389. ▸ Symposium essay surveying attempts to create unity through universalizing imperial occultism. [KZ]

30.279 Robert John Weston Evans. *Rudolf II and his world: a study in intellectual history, 1576–1612.* Oxford: Clarendon, 1973. ISBN 0-19-822516-4. ▸ Pathbreaking study of intellectual and cultural milieu of Rudolf II. Argues for vibrancy of imperialist vision. Astonishing command of Czech sources. [KZ]

30.280 Charles Garside, Jr. *Zwingli and the arts.* 1966 ed. New York: Da Capo, 1981. ISBN 0-306-76018-5. ▸ Analysis of Zwingli's attitude toward arts construed more broadly than usual. Treats Swiss reformer's iconoclasm in relation to Erasmus's position, but also his attitude toward music. [KZ]

30.281 Richard L. Gawthrop and Gerald Strauss. "Protestantism and literacy in early modern Germany." *Past and present* 104 (1984) 31–55. ISSN 0031-2746. ▸ Discussion of evidence against assumption of widespread Bible reading among laity in sixteenth century. [KZ]

30.282 Max Geisberg. *The German single-leaf woodcut, 1500–1550.* 4 vols. Walter L. Strauss, ed. New York: Hacker, 1974. ISBN 0-87817-125-8. ▸ Illustrated catalog of woodcuts distributed as broadsheets in first half of century. Brief bio-bibliography for each known artist. [KZ]

30.283 Anthony Grafton. "The world of the polyhistors: humanism and encyclopedism." In *Special issue: the culture of the Holy Roman Empire, 1540–1680*, pp. 31–47. Atlanta: Emory University, 1985. (*Central European history*, 18.) ISSN 0008-9389. ▸ Brief symposium essay viewing seventeenth-century encyclopedic organization of universal knowledge in terms of humanism and rhetorical concerns with eloquence. [KZ]

30.284 Maria Grossmann. *Humanism in Wittenberg, 1485–1517.* Nieuwkoop, Netherlands: De Graaf, 1975. ISBN 90-600-4333-2. ▸ Brief survey of humanism in Wittenberg before Reformation emphasizing role of Frederick the Wise and other individuals. Includes discussion of printing and arts as well as history of university. [KZ]

30.285 Michael Hackenberg. "Books in artisan homes of sixteenth-century Germany." *Journal of library history* 21.1 (1986) 72–91. ISSN 0022-2259. ▸ Study based on property inventories taken at testator's death shows midcentury growth in artisans' reading interests beyond confines of craft concerns and religious devotion. [KZ]

30.286 Andrée Hayum. *The Isenheim altarpiece: God's medicine and the painter's vision.* Princeton: Princeton University Press, 1989. ISBN 0-691-04070-2. ▸ Iconographic analysis of function of famous altarpiece in its social and religious culture, in terms of liturgical and therapeutic action. For audiences lay and clerical. [KZ]

30.287 Henry-Russell Hitchcock. *German Renaissance architecture.* Princeton: Princeton University Press, 1981. ISBN 0-691-03959-3. ▸ Traditional survey of German Renaissance architecture arranged topically. [KZ]

30.288 R. Po-chia Hsia. *The myth of ritual murder: Jews and magic in Reformation Germany.* New Haven: Yale University Press, 1988. ISBN 0-300-04120-9. ▸ Examination of intertwined discourses (theological, legal, medical) of ritual murder in popular and learned culture as manifestation of specifically Christian (eucharistic) concerns as well as of anti-Jewish sentiment. Situates discourse in specific contexts of disputes between emperor and municipalities, ideological conflicts between religious parties, etc. [KZ]

30.289 Jane Campbell Hutchison. *Albrecht Dürer: a biography.* Princeton: Princeton University Press, 1990. ISBN 0-691-03978-X. ▸ Biography of the Nuremberg artist as *homo economicus* as well as Renaissance man. Particularly useful for extensive quotations included from letters and other primary sources. [KZ]

30.290 Oliver Impey and Arthur MacGregor, eds. *The origins of museums: the cabinet of curiosities in sixteenth- and seventeenth-century Europe.* Oxford: Clarendon, 1985. ISBN 0-19-952108-5. ▸ Important collection of essays on collecting: analyses of origins, and evolution of diverse collections (some encyclopedic, some devoted to art, to scientific instruments, and to natural phenomena) assembled by bourgeois citizens as well as nobles and princes. [KZ]

30.291 Thomas DaCosta Kaufmann. *Art and architecture in Central Europe, 1550–1620: an annotated bibliography.* Boston: Hall, 1988. ISBN 0-8161-8594-8. ▸ Useful annotated bibliography arranged by geographical area, media, and individual artists. Employing primary as well as secondary sources. Includes material on patronage and collecting. [KZ]

30.292 Thomas DaCosta Kaufmann. *Variations on the imperial theme in the age of Maximilian II and Rudolf II.* New York: Garland, 1978. ISBN 0-8240-3231-4. ▸ Examination of tournaments, paintings, and contents and disposition of objects in Rudolf II's encyclopedic *Kunstkammer* as symbolic claims to universal empire. [KZ]

30.293 Samuel Kinser. "Presentation and representation: Carnival at Nuremberg, 1450–1550." *Representations* 13 (1986) 1–33. ISSN 0734-6018. ▸ Analysis of carnival parades, plays, and pranks as cultural politics, enactments of short-term political conflicts, and also as intercommunal negotiations between high and low culture. Carnival became static representation as it lost calendrical, customary place. [KZ]

30.294 Dieter Koepplin and Tilman Falk. *Lukas Cranach, Gemälde, Zeichnungen, Druckgraphik: Austellung in Kunstmuseum Basel, 15. Juni–8. September 1974.* 2 vols. Basel: Birkhäuser, 1974–76. ISBN 3-7643-0708-0. ▸ Extensive catalog for exhibition held in Kunstmuseum, Basel in 1974. Draws interesting, problematic connections between art and Reformation, social issues, gender, politics. [KZ]

30.295 Joseph Leo Koerner. "Albrecht Dürer and the moment of self-portraiture." In *Literatur und Kosmos: Innen- und Aussenwelten in der deutschen Literatur des fünfzehnten bis siebzehnten Jahrhunderts.* Gerhild Scholz Williams and Lynn Tatlock, eds., pp. 409–39. Amsterdam: Rodopi, 1986. (*Daphnis: Zeitschrift für mittlere deutsche Literatur*, 15.) ISBN 90-6203-859-X (pbk), ISSN

0300-693X. ‣ Refines topos of Dürer-as-Christ in self-portraits (see Bainton 30.268) with discussion of relationship to Veronica's veil (Vera Icon), the "image not made with human hands." [KZ]

30.296 Joseph Leo Koerner. "The mortification of the image: death as hermeneutic in Hans Baldung Grien." *Representations* 10 (1985) 52–101. ISSN 0734-6018. ‣ Stunning analysis of problems of nudity and voyeurism in artist's work not simply as misogyny, but as postlapsarian hermeneutics. [KZ]

30.297 Hans-Joachim Köhler. *Bibliographie der Flugschriften des sechzehnten Jahrhunderts.* Tübingen: Bibliotheca Academica Verlag, 1991–. ISBN 3-928471-01-5. ‣ Bibliography of sixteenth-century German pamphlet literature and published guide to microfiche collection compiled by same author. [KZ]

30.298 *Martin Luther und die Reformation in Deutschland: Ausstellung zum fünfhundert. Geburtstag Martin Luthers.* Frankfurt: Insel, 1983. ISBN 3-458-14081-6. ‣ Illustrated catalog of exhibit at Germanisches Nationalmuseum, Nuremberg, 1983, in honor of five-hundreth anniversary of Luther's birth. Exhaustive survey, with sections arranged topically and introduced by leading scholars. [KZ]

30.299 Metropolitan Museum of Art and Germanisches Nationalmuseum. *Gothic and Renaissance art in Nuremberg, 1300–1550.* Munich and New York: Prestel and Metropolitan Museum of Art, 1986. ISBN 0-87099-465-4 (cl), 0-87099-466-2 (pbk). ‣ Illustrated catalog of exhibition at Metropolitan Museum of Art and Germanisches Nationalmuseum, Nuremberg. Essays on city, craft organization, and works in different media, as well as biographies of artists. [KZ]

30.300 Keith Moxey. *Peasants, warriors, and wives: popular imagery in the Reformation.* Chicago: University of Chicago Press, 1989. ISBN 0-226-54391-9. ‣ Provocative argument that art, like gender and social class (also subjects of analysis), entirely socially constructed. Well-argued thesis, based on woodcuts that were clearly part of semiotic of social control. Thesis nonetheless controversial when extended to other types of images. [KZ]

30.301 James H. Overfield. *Humanism and scholasticism in late medieval Germany.* Princeton: Princeton University Press, 1984. ISBN 0-691-07292-2. ‣ Study of introduction of humanist reading into German universities and its clash with traditional scholastic curriculum and masters. Argues against notion of sharp scholastic-humanist divide in universities. Humanists present in all universities and neither particularly critical of academic practice nor sharply attacked by established scholastics. [KZ/WJC]

30.302 Steven E. Ozment, ed. *Religion and culture in the Renaissance and Reformation.* Kirksville, Mo.: Sixteenth Century Journal Publishers, 1989. (Sixteenth century essays and studies, 11.) ISBN 0-940474-11-5. ‣ Papers from 1987 Harvard symposium ranging from Jewish magic and Christian demon possession to civic rituals of autonomy and dependence. [KZ]

30.303 Erwin Panofsky. *Albrecht Dürer.* 3d ed. 2 vols. Princeton: Princeton University Press, 1948. ‣ Still standard intellectual and cultural biography of quintessential German Renaissance artist. Includes catalog of works. [KZ]

30.304 Erwin Panofsky. "Erasmus and the visual arts." *Journal of the Warburg and Courtauld Institutes* 32 (1969) 200–27. ISSN 0075-4390. ‣ Extensive discussion of Erasmus's position on use of images in worship. [KZ]

30.305 James A. Parente, Jr. *Religious drama and the humanist tradition: Christian theater in Germany and in the Netherlands, 1500–1680.* Leiden: Brill, 1987. ISBN 90-04-08094-5. ‣ Comprehensive analysis of impact of religious and ethical concerns on humanist drama. Analyzes texts in neo-Latin, German, and Dutch. [KZ]

30.306 James A. Parente, Jr. "The seventeenth-century literary text: aesthetic problems and perspectives." In *Special issue: the culture of the Holy Roman Empire, 1540–1680,* pp. 48–69. Atlanta: Emory University, 1985. (*Central European history,* 18.) ISSN 0008-9389. ‣ Argues seventeenth-century German vernacular literature derived force from struggle to achieve new creativity against previous genres, struggle displayed in texts as "didacticism, bombast, and stasis." [KZ]

30.307 Linda B. Parshall and Peter W. Parshall. *Art and the Reformation: an annotated bibliography.* Boston: Hall, 1986. ISBN 0-8161-8602-2. ‣ Useful bibliography arranged topically. Includes reformers as well as artists; employs primary as well as secondary sources. Brief descriptions of works listed. [KZ]

30.308 Hans Preuss. *Martin Luther, der Künstler.* Gütersloh: Bertelsmann, 1931. ‣ Old but standard work on Wittenberg reformer's relation to visual, musical, and poetic arts. [KZ]

30.309 David Price. *The political dramaturgy of Nicodemus Frischlin: essays on humanist drama in Germany.* Chapel Hill: University of North Carolina Press, 1990. ISBN 0-8078-8111-2. ‣ Study of complex interaction between humanism, politics, theology, and development of dramatic genres on basis of life and work of most important German playwright of latter sixteenth century. [KZ]

30.310 Lionel Rothkrug. *Religious practices and collective perceptions: hidden homologies in the Renaissance and Reformation.* Waterloo, Ont.: University of Waterloo, Department of History, 1980. (Historical reflections/Réflexions historiques, 7.1.) ISSN 0315-7997. ‣ Controversial reevaluation of success or failure of German Reformation. Links pre-Christian cults, witchcraft, pogroms, Mariology, and pilgrimages. Concludes grafting Christian cult onto preexisting roots prevents cult's uprooting centuries later. [KZ]

30.311 Gunter Schade, ed. *Kunst der Reformationszeit, Staatliche Museen zu Berlin, Hauptstadt der DDR: Ausstellung im Alten Museum vom 20. August bis 13. November 1983.* Berlin: Elefanten, 1983. ISBN 3-88520-113-5. ‣ Illustrated catalog of East Berlin exhibition for "Year of Luther." Good example of state of East German art history before Wall fell: early bourgeois revolutionary Marxism together with humanism and Reformation ideology. [KZ]

30.312 Werner Schade. *Cranach, a family of master painters.* Helen Sebba, trans. New York: Putnam, 1980. ISBN 0-399-11831-4. ‣ Collective biography of three Cranach artists in economic, political, cultural, and religious milieu. Profusely illustrated; includes documents in translation. [KZ]

30.313 R. W. Scribner. "Images of the peasant, 1514–1525." *Journal of peasant studies* 3 (1975–76) 29–48. ISSN 0306-6150. ‣ Contrasts Lutheran images showing "common sense" of peasant (versus cleric) with hostile satires to interpret diverse attitudes toward peasants at time of Peasants' War. [KZ]

30.314 Larry Silver. "The state of research in northern European art of the Renaissance era." *Art bulletin* 68.4 (1986) 518–35. ISSN 0004-3079. ‣ Balanced summary of directions in art historical research on northern Renaissance since works of Panofsky (30.303, 30.304, 20.1438, 22.297, 22.298). [KZ]

30.315 Jeffrey Chipps Smith, ed. *Nuremberg, a Renaissance city, 1500–1618.* Austin: University of Texas Press for Archer M. Huntington Art Gallery, University of Texas at Austin, 1983. ISBN 0-292-75527-9. ‣ One of few exhibition catalogs focusing more on art in artistic and economic contexts than on art as expression of Reformation ideology. Particularly useful on fine metalwork for which Nuremberg was famous. [KZ]

30.316 Margarete Stirm. *Die Bilderfrage in der Reformation.* Gütersloh: Mohn, 1977. ISBN 3-579-04302-1. ‣ Detailed albeit somewhat anachronistic survey of problem of image in sixteenth-century theology. Treats major reformers as well as some radicals (Karlstadt). [KZ]

30.317   Gerald Strauss. *Historian in an age of crisis: the life and work of Johannes Aventinus, 1477–1534*. Cambridge, Mass.: Harvard University Press, 1963. ‣ Model intellectual biography of Bavarian humanist historiographer writing at time of political and religious crisis. Couched as portrait of individual experiencing waning of Middle Ages. [KZ]

30.318   Walter L. Strauss. *The German single-leaf woodcut, 1550–1600: a pictorial catalogue*. 3 vols. New York: Abaris, 1975. ‣ Illustrated catalog of woodcuts produced as broadsheets. Brief biobibliographies of known artists, but works by anonymous masters also included. [KZ]

30.319   Kristin E. S. Zapalac. *"In his image and likeness": political iconography and religious change in Regensburg, 1500–1600*. Ithaca, N.Y.: Cornell University Press, 1990. ISBN 0-8014-2269-8. ‣ Analysis of impact of Lutheranism on political language in German city. Unusual source material (wills, bookbindings, frescoes, woodcuts) used to trace spread of paternal language from theological to political thought (in latter case, language attributed first to citizens, then to city council). [KZ]

30.320   Herbert Zschelletzschky. *Die "drei gottlosen Maler" von Nürnberg: Sebald Beham, Berthel Beham, und Georg Pencz: historische Grundlagen und ikonologische Probleme ihrer Graphik zu Reformations- und Bauernkriegszeit*. Leipzig: Seemann, 1975. ‣ Discussion of graphics by three artists exiled from Nuremberg in social, political, and religious milieu. Detailed Marxist analysis of lives as well as works of three fascinating artists. [KZ]

SEE ALSO

21.94 Jerome Friedman. *The most ancient testimony.*
22.159 Peter Burke. *Popular culture in early modern Europe.*
22.172 Elizabeth L. Eisenstein. *The printing press as an agent of change.*
27.286 Lee Palmer Wandel. *Always among us.*

CULTURAL HISTORY, 1650–1800

30.321   Henry E. Allison. *Lessing and the Enlightenment: his philosophy of religion and its relation to eighteenth-century thought*. Ann Arbor: University of Michigan Press, 1966. ‣ Intellectual biography from perspective of religious development. Special focus on religious debates of later years and on Leibnizian roots of religious position. [JBK]

30.322   F. M. Barnard. *Herder's social and political thought: from Enlightenment to nationalism*. Oxford: Clarendon, 1965. ‣ Analytical treatment of Johann Gottfried Herder's thought: particularly organicism, *Volk*, nation, and humanity. Ideas treated within context of late Enlightenment and early romanticism. [JBK]

30.323   Karl Barth. *Protestant theology in the nineteenth century: its background and history*. 1972 ed. Valley Forge, Pa.: Judson, 1973. ISBN 0-8170-0572-2. ‣ Classic study of German thought. Original studies of theological views of Gotthold Ephriam Lessing, Immanuel Kant, Johann Gottfried Herder, Novalis, and Georg Wilhelm Friedrich Hegel. [JBK/PZ]

30.324   Lewis White Beck. *Early German philosophy: Kant and his predecessors*. Cambridge, Mass.: Belknap, 1969. ISBN 0-674-22125-7. ‣ Comprehensive account of German philosophy in cultural context from Middle Ages through Kant's critical period. Individual chapters on chief figures and useful bibliographical introductions. [JBK]

30.325   Frederick C. Beiser. *The fate of reason: German philosophy from Kant to Fichte*. Cambridge, Mass.: Harvard University Press, 1987. ISBN 0-674-29502-1. ‣ Study of reorientation of German cultural life in decade after publication of Immanuel Kant's first

critique. Emphasizes depth and breadth of debates over Kant's philosophy. [JBK]

30.326   Paul P. Bernard. *Jesuits and Jacobins: Enlightenment and enlightened despotism in Austria*. Urbana: University of Illinois Press, 1971. ISBN 0-252-00180-X. ‣ Study of Josephenism and relations to Jesuit order from perspective of writers of Austrian Enlightenment. Treats censorship, freemasonry, and literary underground. [JBK]

30.327   Eric A. Blackall. *The emergence of German as a literary language, 1700–1775*. 2d ed. Ithaca, N.Y.: Cornell University Press, 1978. ISBN 0-8014-1170-X. ‣ Rich examination of German language in seventeenth and eighteenth centuries. Extensive quotations and valuable bibliographical essay. [JBK]

30.328   Hans Erich Bödeker et al., eds. *Aufklärung und Geschichte: Studien zur deutschen Geschichtswissenschaft im achtzehnten Jahrhundert*. Göttingen: Vandenhoeck & Ruprecht, 1986. (Veröffentlichungen des Max-Planck-Instituts für Geschichte, 81.) ISBN 3-525-35397-9. ‣ Essays, half in English, exploring sense of history and historicizing of life in various dimensions of academic and public culture. Revises traditional view of ahistorical Enlightenment. [JBK]

30.329   Nicholas Boyle. *Goethe: the poet and his age*. Vol. 1: *The poetry of desire, 1749–1790*. Oxford: Oxford University Press, 1991. ISBN 0-19-815866-1 (v. 1, cl), 0-19-282981-5 (v. 1, pbk). ‣ Traces Goethe's life up to 1790 in rich social and cultural detail. Mixture of literary and historical analysis. [JBK]

30.330   Volkmar Braunbehrens. *Mozart in Vienna, 1781–1791*. 1989 ed. Timothy Bell, trans. New York: Grove Weidenfeld, 1990. ISBN 0-8021-1009-6. ‣ Broadly conceived cultural study of Mozart's last decade. Historical interpolations link biography to important problems of Austrian Enlightenment. [JBK]

30.331   Walter H. Bruford. *Culture and society in classical Weimar, 1775–1806*. 1962 ed. Cambridge: Cambridge University Press, 1975. ISBN 0-521-09910-2 (pbk). ‣ Describes court in Weimar and resident intellectuals (Christoph Martin Wieland, Goethe, Herder). Contributes to understanding of classical doctrine of self-cultivation (*Bildung*). [JBK]

30.332   Henri Brunschwig. *Enlightenment and romanticism in eighteenth-century Prussia*. Frank Jellinek, trans. Chicago: University of Chicago Press, 1974. ISBN 0-226-07768-3. ‣ Description of Prussian Enlightenment in literary and social terms after death of Frederick II. Significant sections on moral crisis and emancipation of Prussian Jewry. [JBK]

30.333   Hans W. Frei. *The eclipse of biblical narrative: a study in eighteenth- and nineteenth-century hermeneutics*. New Haven: Yale University Press, 1974. ISBN 0-300-01623-9 (cl), 0-300-02602-1 (pbk). ‣ Transformation in biblical interpretation from perspective of Protestant theological tradition. Places loss of realism in reading of Bible and resulting crisis of interpretation within wider context of German and European letters. [JBK]

30.334   Arsenii Gulyga. *Immanuel Kant: his life and thought*. Marijan Despalatovic, trans. Boston: Birkhauser, 1987. ISBN 0-8176-3195-X. ‣ Biography of Kant emphasizing cultural and social context of his thought. Arguments written from perspective of future developments of German idealism. [JBK]

30.335   H. S. Harris. *Hegel's development: toward the sunlight, 1770–1801*. Oxford: Clarendon, 1972. ISBN 0-19-824358-8. ‣ Careful reconstruction of Hegel's intellectual development and philosophical views within his age. Important treatment of idealism and neohumanist classicism. [JBK]

30.336   Eckhart Hellmuth, ed. *The transformation of political culture: England and Germany in the late eighteenth century*. Oxford:

Oxford University Press, 1990. ISBN 0-19-920501-9. ‣ Studies of political culture among various orders and classes in Germany and England: peasantry, clergy, provincial associations, and journals. Essays directly and indirectly compare cultural differences and confront issues of exceptionalism in each society. [JBK]

30.337 Eberhard Hempel. *Baroque art and architecture in Central Europe: Germany, Austria, Switzerland, Hungary, Czechoslovakia, Poland.* Elisabeth Hempel and Marguerite Kay, trans. Baltimore: Penguin, 1965. ‣ Extended treatment of painting, sculpture, and architecture in Germany and Habsburg lands from sixteenth to eighteenth century. Lengthy discussions of social conditions and careful stylistic analyses. [JBK]

30.338 Friedrich Otto Hertz. *The development of the German public mind: a social history of German political sentiments, aspirations, and ideas.* Vol. 2: *The age of Enlightenment.* New York: Macmillan, 1962. ‣ History of public law as idea and social practice from seventeenth century to dissolution of empire. Treats large and small states, and impact of religion, politics, and economics on public life. [JBK]

30.339 Robert A. Kann. *A study in Austrian intellectual history: from late baroque to romanticism.* 1960 ed. New York: Octagon Books, 1973. ISBN 0-374-94504-7. ‣ Study of Austrian intellectual life through biographies of Abraham-a-Sancta-Clara (Ulrich Megerle) and Joseph von Sonnenfels. Develops general view of cycles of Austrian cultural history. [JBK]

30.340 Heinz D. Kittsteiner. *Die Entstehung des modernen Gewissens.* Frankfurt: Insel, 1991. ISBN 3-458-16148-1. ‣ Description of genesis and transformation of idea of conscience within Protestant theology, philosophy, and society from Reformation to end of seventeenth century. Cultural history of disciplining of lower orders. [JBK]

30.341 Jonathan B. Knudsen. *Justus Möser and the German Enlightenment.* New York: Cambridge University Press, 1986. ISBN 0-521-32011-9. ‣ Biographical study of administrator, historian, and man of letters from small ecclesiastical state. Examines practical efforts at reform and statist component within German Enlightenment. [JBK]

30.342 Leonard Krieger. *The German idea of freedom: history of a political tradition.* 1957 ed. Chicago: University of Chicago Press, 1972. ISBN 0-226-45347-2. ‣ Social and philosophical interpretation of German political ideas, seventeenth to nineteenth century. Classic statement of origins of German exceptionalism in early modern period. Subtle, complex, difficult study. [JBK/JS]

30.343 Leonard Krieger. *The politics of discretion: Pufendorf and the acceptance of natural law.* Chicago: University of Chicago Press, 1965. ‣ Intellectual biography of Samuel Pufendorf, systematically treating various aspects of his life. Contribution to understanding of seventeenth-century natural law tradition. [JBK]

30.344 Rudolf W. Meyer. *Leibnitz and the seventeenth-century revolution.* J. P. Stern, trans. Cambridge: Bowes & Bowes, 1952. ‣ Intellectual biography of Leibniz in context of general crisis of seventeenth century. Also examines continuing importance of Leibniz's views on human freedom and humanity's existential condition. [JBK]

30.345 Hans Joachim Moser. *Heinrich Schütz: his life and work.* Carl F. Pfatteicher, trans. Saint Louis: Concordia, 1959. ‣ Standard, older biography of the campanist Schütz. Valuable detailed exploration of music and cultural life of sixteenth and seventeenth centuries. [JBK]

30.346 Günter Niggl. *Geschichte der deutschen Autobiographie im achtzehnten Jahrhundert: theoretische Grundlegung und literarische Entfaltung.* Stuttgart: Metzler, 1977. ISBN 3-476-00318-3.

‣ Traces development of autobiography from seventeenth-century pietism through German classicism. Wealth of examples and careful distinctions. [JBK]

30.347 James C. O'Flaherty. *Hamann's "Socratic Memorabilia": a translation and commentary.* Baltimore: Johns Hopkins University Press, 1967. ‣ Lengthy introduction to Johann Georg Hamann's life and work, his relationship to Immanuel Kant and Königsberg, and Hamann's philosophic effort to emancipate himself from rationalist tradition. Important figure for study of counter-Enlightenment. [JBK]

30.348 Roy Pascal. *The German Sturm und Drang.* 1953 ed. Manchester: Manchester University Press, 1967. ISBN 0-7190-0194-3. ‣ Thematic analysis of late eighteenth-century generational revolt. Careful attention to social historical questions and to philosophical underpinnings of movement. [JBK]

30.349 Peter Hanns Reill. *The German Enlightenment and the rise of historicism.* Berkeley: University of California Press, 1975. ISBN 0-520-02594-6. ‣ Description of historical thought, patterns of causality, explanation, and development in German Enlightenment. Intellectual history focusing on important individuals recovers richness of historical speculation and research in period. [JBK]

30.350 Friedrich von Schiller. *On the aesthetic education of man: in a series of letters.* 1967 ed. Elizabeth M. Wilkinson and L. A. Willoughby, eds. and trans. Oxford: Clarendon, 1982. ISBN 0-19-815786-X. ‣ Includes lengthy introduction to late eighteenth-century aesthetics, politics, and educational theory. Schiller's views central to new ideal of self-cultivation or *Bildung.* Copies of original letters provided. [JBK]

30.351 Maynard Solomon. *Beethoven.* New York: Schirmer, 1977. ISBN 0-02-872460-7 (cl), 0-02-872240-X (pbk). ‣ Psychoanalytical biography of Beethoven paying careful attention to cultural and intellectual settings in Bonn and Vienna in last quarter of century. [JBK]

30.352 F. Ernest Stoeffler. *German pietism during the eighteenth century.* Leiden: Brill, 1973. ISBN 90-04-03668-7. ‣ Synthesis of varieties of pietism: August Hermann Francke and Halle, Swabia, and Württemberg, Count Nicolaus Ludvig von Zinzendorf and Moravians, and radical neopietism. Balanced treatment of theology and biography. [JBK]

30.353 John Stroup. *The struggle for identity in the clerical estate: Northwest German Protestant opposition to absolutist policy in the eighteenth century.* Leiden: Brill, 1984. ISBN 90-04-07009-5. ‣ Analysis of Lutheran clergy, its social status, values, resistance, and adaption to secular pressures during Enlightenment. Stresses resistance to secular absolutism and importance of regionalism for Lutheran clergy. [JBK]

30.354 Paul R. Sweet. *Wilhelm von Humboldt: a biography.* 2 vols. Columbus: Ohio State University Press, 1978–80. ISBN 0-8142-0274-8 (v. 1), 0-8142-0279-9 (v. 2). ‣ Detailed, balanced biography of statesman's life and thought. [JBK]

30.355 Rudolf Vierhaus. *Germany in the age of absolutism, 1648–1763.* Jonathan B. Knudsen, trans. New York: Cambridge University Press, 1988. ISBN 0-521-32686-9 (cl), 0-521-33936-7 (pbk). ‣ Chapter on cultural life describing transition from baroque to Enlightenment. Emphasizes varieties of secular and religious culture, role of princes and their courts, and gradual reemergence of particular ethical and cultural vision with burgher class. [JBK]

30.356 Mack Walker. *Johann Jakob Moser and the Holy Roman Empire of the German nation.* Chapel Hill: University of North Carolina Press, 1981. ISBN 0-8078-1441-5. ‣ Biographical study of important jurist, councillor, and scholar of imperial law. Recreates world of estates and corporate bodies in eighteenth century. [JBK]

30.357 Albert Ward. *Book production, fiction, and the German reading public, 1740–1800.* Oxford: Clarendon, 1974. ISBN 0-19-818157-4. ▸ Analysis of emergence of German literary public, its changing intellectual interests, and evolution of book trade. Makes use of eighteenth-century book fair catalogs and quantifies changes in taste. [JBK]

SEE ALSO
21.97 Jonathan I. Israel. *European Jewry in the age of mercantilism, 1550–1750.*
21.132 Alexander Altmann. *Moses Mendelssohn.*
21.145 Deborah Hertz. *Jewish high society in Old Regime Berlin.*
22.282 Manfred F. Bukofzer. *Music in the baroque era.*
31.121 Klaus Epstein. *The genesis of German conservatism.*

JAMES J. SHEEHAN

German States and the Habsburg Empire since 1789

At the center of modern German history and historiography is the problem of national identity: what does it mean to be a German? Is German nationality a matter of language, culture, religion, biology, or some elusive combination of acquired and inherited traits? And what is Germany? Does it have a clearly defined shape, set apart from its neighbors by natural geographical boundaries? Where is its center? Is there a political form especially appropriate for the German character? These questions were first posed in the eighteenth century, when some Germans insisted that nationality was the source and foundation of cultural achievement. In the nineteenth century, the question of national identity became increasingly politicized when Germans, like many other Europeans, began to regard the nation-state as the natural unit around which public life should be organized.

In theory, of course, there was no one clear and compelling answer to the problem of German identity. Even such an apparently straightforward characteristic as language quickly dissolves into a complex set of questions about dialects and linguistic divisions. To identify nationality with culture is merely to pose the same question in a different way, since one could easily ask where German culture began and that of its neighbors ended? In the heartland of the Reformation, religion was hardly a source of national unity. Racial definitions were no more than mythical projections, which made little sense in an area long inhabited by diverse ethnic groups. Geographically, German Europe was internally divided by rivers and mountain ranges and, on its eastern frontier, completely open to the movement of people and cultures. German political life had always been decentralized, institutionally diverse, and regionally distinctive. Thus by the time the national question took political form, there were several contending versions of what the new nation was, where its center should be, and how it should be governed. None of these was, in and of itself, necessarily more plausible than its competitors.

In the end, the question of German identity was not solved by debates over theoretical plausibility and personal preference but rather, in Otto von Bismarck's famous phrase, "by blood and iron." Prussia's military victories in 1866 and 1870 enabled it to define a nation that excluded Austria and to gather the smaller German states into an empire governed from Berlin. This Germany became the basis of German politics and the focus of German historiography.

Even before 1866, historians played an important part in the cultural and political struggle to define German national identity. Some of them were among the most effective advocates of a *kleindeutsch* (little Germany) solution, that is, a Germany without Austria, dominated by Prussia. After 1866, these historians and their students turned the narrative of Prussia's triumph into German national history. Like all national histories, this was the story of how the nation realized and attained its true identity, the story of the inevitable, natural triumph of the only true Germany. Alternative visions of the national past were pushed aside and largely forgotten. Austria, which for centuries had been enmeshed in German politics and remained a vital element in German culture, suddenly stopped being part of German history. As so often happens, the price of political defeat was historical invisibility.

The German empire did not last very long. Defeated in 1918, it lost the territory taken from France in 1870 and the monarchical constitution imposed by Bismarck. The republic founded amid the wreckage of defeat and revolution was destroyed by Hitler in 1933. His foreign political successes after 1938 once again altered the geographical shape of Germany by absorbing a number of new territories, including the Austrian republic, which, like its German counterpart, had been created in 1918. This *Anschluss* of the two German states did not survive Hitler's defeat in 1945. Moreover, a substantial amount of formerly German land in the east was taken by Poland and the Soviet Union. In 1949, the failure of the Soviet Union and the Western Allies to agree on a common German policy resulted in the creation of two German states, the Federal Republic in the west, the German Democratic Republic in the east. Forty-one years later, the GDR disappeared when its citizens voted to join the Federal Republic.

It is remarkable that despite the frequency with which Germany's geographical shape and institutional character changed, the basic definition of German history has remained constant. Indeed when the two postwar states merged in 1990, many called it a "reunification" even though the new Germany had never existed in its present form and had only the most problematic connections to earlier versions of a united German nation-state. But if the subject of German history has not much changed since 1866, its shape and purpose certainly have. To the founders of the *kleindeutsch* school, German history was the triumphant record of the nation's birth. To their successors after 1918, most of whom were never reconciled with the republic, it became a tragic story of betrayal and defeat. Under national socialism, German history again was seen in a triumphant mode, although this time the hero was not the Prussian state but the German *Volk*, led and personified by Adolf Hitler.

The destruction of Hitler's Reich in 1945 and the subsequent division of the country disrupted the continuity of German national history. But at the same time, the memory of the crimes committed in Germany's name during the Nazi era gave German history a persistent and pervasive power. Paradoxically, the same historical process that destroyed the political existence of the German nation, ensured its continued historical significance as a burden to be born by both the successor states to Hitler's Reich. How, Germans had to ask themselves, did nazism fit into their national history? Some tried to argue that it was an aberration, merely the result of a series of unfortunate, even fortuitous events that enabled Hitler to seize power. Others claimed that the sources of nazism were European rather than German, to be found in the rise of totalitarian democracy after 1789 or in the crisis of international capitalism. But such efforts to disassociate nazism from its German roots were never successful: the German question —the question of Germany's historical identity—was now inseparable from the question of national socialism's causes and consequences.

Between the early 1960s and the late 1980s, the most powerful set of answers to this question rested on a belief in what some historians called Germany's *Sonderweg*, its "special path" into modernity. There are many different versions of the *Sonderweg*, but all of them emphasize two things about the German past. First, nazism must be understood in the light of powerful institutional and cultural continuities in the German experience, which reach back well before 1914, perhaps even before 1866. Second, the most significant of these continuities are those that separated Germany from the West, thus inhibiting the development of liberal institutions and encouraging the growth of right-wing radicalism. Proponents of the *Sonderweg*, therefore, regard German history as a deviation from the healthy evolution of the West, a deeply rooted pathology of which nazism was only the last and most destructive manifestation. Various formulations of this view can be found in the works of émigré historians such as H. Rosenberg and H. Holborn, Americans such as L. Krieger and F. Stern, and Germans such as F. Fischer, R. Dahrendorf, and many others. Perhaps the most coherent and influential version of the *Sonderweg* analysis is the one identified with the work of H.-U. Wehler and his colleagues and students at the University of Bielefeld.

The advocates of the *Sonderweg* have never been without their critics. Many scholars (31.320, 47.339, 47.375), for example, bitterly attacked Fischer for blaming the outbreak of World War I on the German government and for suggesting that Germany's expansionist war aims after 1914 anticipated the Nazis' racial imperialism after 1933. More recently, T. Nipperdey (31.179, 31.180) has argued that historians too often have presented a distorted view of the German empire that omits its positive features and thus charts an overly deterministic course from 1866 to 1933. Other scholars, led by D. Blackbourn and G. Eley (31.174), have questioned the assumption that German modernization was so clearly different from the West's; because there is no reason to view the Western brand of modernization as normal, it is better to recognize both difference and commonalities across Europe. In Blackbourn and Eley's view, the German bourgeoisie, who are usually blamed for being weaker and less effective than their Western counterparts, in fact merely exercised power through different institutions than in Britain or France.

In addition to these persistent debates over the *Sonderweg*, a number of other new developments can be seen in recent German historiography. There has been, for example, new interest in the role of religion and particularly of political Catholicism in German public life. Regional history, never as strong in Germany as in France or Britain, has become increasingly vital, as has a concern for what Germans call the history of everyday life, an anthropologically based examination of social groups and practices. Grassroots politics, voting behavior, and other forms of popular political action have begun to attract more scholarly attention. At the same time, new work on the history of women and family life has opened up these important and too often neglected areas. There is every reason to believe that in the years ahead we will learn more about how the lives of ordinary men and women shaped and were shaped by the major political forces that have always had the major claim on German historians' attention.

Although we cannot be sure what its effects will be, the formation of a new German state in 1990 will certainly have a powerful impact on German historiography. Scholars will now have access to a vast storehouse of previously unavailable information, mainly but not only about the postwar period. Moreover, the disappearance of the German Democratic Republic has posed a series of questions about its origins and nature, as well as about its relationship to the West. Was there a chance for national unification in the early postwar period? Did the GDR have to take the path it did? Who is to blame for its demise? Were there alternatives to unification? After 1990, as after 1866, the redefinition of German political life will require a redefinition of questions about German historical identity. In other words, because Germans now have a new nation, they will have to find a new national history.

[Contributors: AS = Antonio Santosuosso, CSA = Celia S. Applegate, DSC = Donald Stephen Cloyd, JJS = James J. Sheehan, JS = Jonathan Sperber, JWB = John W. Boyer, NDC = Noel D. Cary, PH = Peter Hayes, RFW = Richard F. Wetzell]

REFERENCE WORKS

31.1 Hermann Aubin and Wolfgang Zorn, eds. *Handbuch der deutschen Wirtschafts- und Sozialgeschichte.* 1971–76 ed. 2 vols. Stuttgart: Klett-Cotta, 1976–78. ISBN 3-12-900130-1 (v. 1), 3-12-900140-9 (v. 2). ▸ Survey of economic and social history, prehistory to post-1945. Uneven and outdated but still useful for bibliographical references and information. [JJS]

31.2 Christa Berg et al., eds. *Handbuch der deutschen Bildungsgeschichte.* 3 vols. to date. Munich: Beck, 1987–. ISBN 3-406-32468-1 (set). ▸ Projected six-volume work covering 1500 to present. High-quality essays by various authors on educational institutions and their social significance. [JJS]

31.3 Otto Brunner, Werner Conze, and Reinhart Koselleck, eds. *Geschichtliche Grundbegriffe: historisches Lexikon zur politisch-sozialen Sprache in Deutschland.* 7 vols. Stuttgart: Klett, 1972–92. ISBN 3-12-903850-7 (v. 1), 3-12-903860-4 (v. 2), 3-12-903870-1 (v. 3), 3-12-903880-9 (v. 4), 3-12-903890-6 (v. 5), 3-12-903900-7 (v. 6), 3-12-903912-0 (v. 7). ▸ Uneven collection of articles on key concepts; some summarize leading thinkers, others relate changing patterns of meaning to structural changes in German politics and society. See review by James Sheehan, *Journal of Modern History* 50.2 (1978) 312–19. [JJS]

31.4 Helena Cole, Jane Caplan, and Hanna Schissler, eds. *The history of women in Germany from medieval times to the present: bibliography of English-language publications.* Washington, D.C.: German Historical Institute, 1990. (Reference guides of the German Historical Institute, 3.) ▸ Valuable guide to English-language materials on women's history. Splendid teaching aid. [JJS]

31.5 F. C. Dahlmann et al., eds. *Dahlmann-Waitz Quellenkunde der deutschen Geschichte: Bibliographie der Quellen und der Literatur zur deutschen Geschichte.* 8 vols. Stuttgart: Hiersemann, 1965–88. ISBN 3-7772-6511-X (set). ▸ Recent edition of nineteenth-century classic; most complete handbook for German history. Parts out of date but still useful as source of information and guide to older publications. [JJS]

31.6 Winfried Dotzauer et al., eds. *Quellenkunde zur deutschen Geschichte der Neuzeit: von 1500 bis zur Gegenwart.* 5 vols. in 6. Darmstadt, Germany: Wissenschaftliche Buchgesellschaft, 1977–87. ISBN 3-534-07477-7 (v. 1), 3-534-07328-2 (v. 3) 3-534-07247-2 (v. 4), 3-534-07084-4 (v. 5.1), 3-534-07633-8 (v. 5.2). ▸ Extremely useful annotated guide to sources on periods, problems, and individuals. Best place to begin any new research project. [JJS]

31.7 Dieter Fricke et al., eds. *Lexikon zur Parteiengeschichte: die bürgerlichen und kleinbürgerlichen Parteien und Verbände in Deutschland (1789–1945).* 4 vols. Cologne and Leipzig: Pahl-Rugenstein and VEB Bibliographisches Institut, 1983–86. ISBN 3-7609-0782-2 (v. 1), 3-7609-0877-2 (v. 2), 3-7609-0878-0 (v. 3), 3-7609-0879-9 (v. 4). ▸ One of most important collaborative projects from former German Democratic Republic. Combines heavy-handed Marxist interpretations with accurate information about parties, interest groups, and other political organizations. Includes guide to sources and bibliography. [JJS]

31.8 Bruno Gebhardt. *Handbuch der deutschen Geschichte.* 10th ed. 4 vols. in 5. Herbert Grundmann, ed. Stuttgart: Klett-Cotta, 1991. ISBN 3-12-902510-3 (v. 1), 3-12-902520-4 (v. 2), 3-12-902530-8 (v. 3), 3-12-902540-5 (v. 4.1), 3-12-902550-2 (v. 4.2). ▸ Shorter and easier to use than *Dahlmann-Waitz* 31.5. Entries uneven in quality but provide reliable information and useful guide to sources. [JJS]

31.9 *Grosser historischer Weltatlas.* Edition varies. 3 vols. Munich: Bayerischer Schulbuch, 1978–81. ISBN 3-7627-6150-7 (set). ▸ Best historical atlas. Particular emphasis on European and especially German history. [JJS]

31.10 Carl Haase. *The records of German history in German and certain other record offices with short notes on libraries and other collections.* Boppard, Germany: Boldt, 1975. ISBN 3-7646-1638-5. ▸ Short guide to German archives with brief descriptions of content and location. Will need revision in light of reorganization of archives following German unification (1990). [JJS]

31.11 Günther Hödl et al., eds. *Österreichische historische Bibliographie/Austrian historical bibliography.* Salzburg: Neugebauer, 1967–. ISBN 3-85376-100-3 (set), 3-85376-092-9 (v. 1–3, set). ▸ Comprehensive annual bibliography of essays, dissertations, books, and other works of historical scholarship published in Austria since 1945. [JWB]

31.12 Jürgen Kocka and Gerhard Albert Ritter, eds. *Statistische Arbeitsbücher zur neueren deutschen Geschichte.* 9 vols. to date. Munich: Beck, 1975–87. ISBN 3-406-04023-3 (v. 1), 3-406-05406-4 (v. 2), 3-406-04509-X (v. 3), 3-406-31836-3 (v. 4), 3-406-07610-6 (v. 5), 3-406-08518-0 (v. 6), 3-406-04024-1 (v. 7), 3-406-32055-4 (v. 8), 3-406-31583-6 (v. 9). ▸ Useful collection of data on range of social and economic issues. Helpful for teaching and as introduction to major developments. Unnumbered volumes cover 1815 to present. [JJS]

31.13 Hellmuth Rossler et al., eds. *Biographisches Wörterbuch zur deutschen Geschichte.* 2d ed. 3 vols. Munich: Francke, 1973–75. ISBN 3-7720-1053-9 (v. 1), 3-7720-1082-2 (v. 2), 3-7720-1104-7 (v. 3). ▸ Biographical sketches of most important historical figures with brief references to additional sources of information. Useful introductions. [JJS]

31.14 Georg Wilhelm Sante, ed. *Geschichte der deutschen Länder: "Territorien Ploetz."* 2 vols. Würzburg: Ploetz, 1964–71. ISBN 3-87640-033-3 (set). ▸ Institutional history of individual regions from Middle Ages to 1950s. By following changing political map of German Europe, provides fascinating picture of regional diversity and institutional variety. [JJS]

GENERAL STUDIES

The Problem of National Identity

31.15 Celia Applegate. *A nation of provincials: The German idea of Heimat.* Berkeley: University of California Press, 1990. ISBN 0-520-06394-5. ▸ Innovative study of local and national identity in Palatinate. Uses records and publications of local organizations to reconstruct idea of *Heimat* (homeland) that is at once part of and deeper than larger nation. [JJS]

31.16 John W. Boyer. "Some reflections on the problem of Austria, Germany, and Mitteleuropa." *Central European history* 22.3–4 (1989) 301–15. ISSN 0008-9389. ▸ Concise, thoughtful introduction to relationship of Austria to German history and historiography. [JJS]

31.17 John Breuilly, ed. *The state of Germany: the national idea in the making, unmaking, and remaking of a modern nation-state.* London: Longman, 1992. ISBN 0-582-07864-4 (cl), 0-582-07865-

2 (pbk). ▸ Useful introduction to recent research on nationalism and nation building. Discusses idea of nation from eighteenth century to present, especially good on period since 1945, including unification of 1990. [JJS]

31.18 Otto Büsch and James J. Sheehan, eds. *Die Rolle der Nation in der deutschen Geschichte und Gegenwart: Beiträge zu einer internationalen Konferenz in Berlin (West) vom 16. bis 18. Juni 1983.* Berlin: Colloquium, 1985. (Einzelveröffentlichungen der Historischen Kommission zu Berlin, 50.) ISBN 3-7678-0651-7. ▸ Essays on nation and state from eighteenth century to postwar era reflecting divided thinking about German problem in mid-1980s. Especially good on forces promoting and inhibiting national unification. [JJS]

31.19 David Calleo. *The German problem reconsidered: Germany and the world order, 1870 to the present.* Cambridge: Cambridge University Press, 1978. ISBN 0-521-22309-1. ▸ Anti-Wehler and Bielefeld school (31.185), finds Germany's problems not from some inherent flaw in culture or society but from international position and timing of economic development. Stimulating but not totally convincing. [JJS]

31.20 Gordon A. Craig. *The Germans.* 1982 ed. New York: Meridian, 1991. ISBN 0-452-01085-3 (cl), 0-452-00968-5 (pbk). ▸ Topically organized reflections on German history based on fifty years of experience. Graceful, literate, especially good on culture. [JJS]

31.21 Ralf Dahrendorf. *Society and democracy in Germany.* 1967 ed. Westport, Conn.: Greenwood, 1979. ISBN 0-313-22027-1. ▸ Combines sociology and history to explore why Germany failed to create liberal society. Somewhat dated but still worth reading; one of most influential books written about Germany since 1945. [JJS]

31.22 Harold James. *A German identity, 1770–1990.* New York: Routledge, 1989. ISBN 0-415-90180-4. ▸ Traces cycles of national idea from culture, to politics, to economics. Usefully engages recent thinking about nationalism; reflects attitudes about nation on eve of unification of 1990. Controversial and stimulating. [JJS]

31.23 Friedrich Meinecke. *Cosmopolitanism and the national state.* Robert Kimber, trans. Felix Gilbert, Introduction. Princeton: Princeton University Press, 1970. ISBN 0-691-05177-1. ▸ Celebration of nation created in 1871 by viewing ideas about German nationhood. Classic, more of interest as example of national thought than as historical analysis. First published as *Weltbürgertum und Nationalstaat* (1907). [JJS]

31.24 James J. Sheehan. "What is German history? Reflections on the role of the nation in German history and historiography." *Journal of modern history* 53.1 (1981) 1–23. ISSN 0022-2801. ▸ Sustained critique of idea that Germany created in 1871 was natural or inevitable. Reflects growing uncertainty about German nationalism and nationhood in early 1980s. [JJS]

31.25 J. P. Stern. *Heart of Europe: essays on literature and ideology.* Oxford: Blackwell, 1992. ISBN 0-631-15849-9 (cl), 0-631-18473-2 (pbk). ▸ Reflections on problem of political and cultural identity by leading literary critic. Especially good on German issues in Central European context. [JJS]

Historiography

31.26 Andreas Dorpalen. *German history in Marxist perspective: the East German approach.* 1985 ed. Detroit: Wayne State University Press, 1988. ISBN 0-8143-2076-7 (pbk). ▸ Learned assessment of East German historical writing strongly emphasizing political history. Focuses on discerning official or consensual view of each period in Germany's past rather than variations in outlook since 1949. [NDC]

31.27 Georg G. Iggers. *The German conception of history: the* national tradition of historical thought from Herder to the present. Rev. ed. Middletown, Conn.: Wesleyan University Press; distributed by Harper & Row, 1983. ISBN 0-8195-6080-4 (pbk). ‣ Interpretation of assumptions and political values of German historical thought from Wilhelm von Humboldt to Friedrich Meinecke. Finds idealist position static in face of societal change and predisposed to look upon state as benevolent. [CSA]

31.28 Georg G. Iggers, ed. *Marxist historiography in transformation: East German social history in the 1980s.* Bruce Little, trans. New York: Berg; distributed by St. Martin's, 1991. ISBN 0-85496-228-X. ‣ Extends account in Dorpalen 31.26. Introduction analyzes role of history in East Germany; selected essays include some of best social history from East Germany. Especially interesting is Zwahr's account of class formation in Leipzig. [JJS]

31.29 Hans Kohn, ed. *German history: some new German views.* Herbert H. Rowen, trans. Boston: Beacon, 1954. ‣ Reflections on German history in light of Nazi catastrophe by ten German historians. One of earliest, most influential efforts at historiographical rethinking and renewal after 1945. [JJS]

31.30 Hartmut Lehmann and James J. Sheehan, eds. *An interrupted past: German-speaking refugee historians in the United States after 1933.* Washington, D.C. and Cambridge: German Historical Institute and Cambridge University Press, 1991. ISBN 0-521-40326-X. ‣ Discussion of impact of German refugee historians on American historiography and impact of America on historians and their families. Good introduction to major trends in American views of Germany after 1945. [JJS]

31.31 Hans-Ulrich Wehler. "Historiography in Germany today." In *Observations on "The Spiritual Situation of the Age": contemporary German perspectives.* Jürgen Habermas, ed. Andrew Buchwalter, trans., pp. 221–59. Cambridge, Mass.: MIT Press, 1984. ISBN 0-262-08132-6 (cl), 0-262-58074-8 (pbk). ‣ Leading participant describes revolution in historical studies in 1960s, especially its relationship to changes in political climate and institutional character of German universities. Partisan but powerful analysis. [JJS]

31.32 Hans-Ulrich Wehler, ed. *Deutsche Historiker.* 9 vols. Göttingen: Vandenhoeck & Ruprecht, 1971–82. ISBN 3-525-33309-9 (v. 1), 3-525-33310-2 (v. 2), 3-525-33314-5 (v. 3), 3-525-33315-3 (v. 4), 3-525-33316-1 (v. 5), 3-525-33443-5 (v. 6), 3-525-33449-4 (v. 7), 3-525-33467-2 (v. 8), 3-525-33474-5 (v. 9). ‣ Series of biographical sketches of leading nineteenth- and twentieth-century historians with guide to their most important works. Excellent introduction to modern German historiography. [JJS]

Surveys

31.33 Volker R. Berghahn. *Modern Germany: society, economy, and politics in the twentieth century.* 2d ed. Cambridge: Cambridge University Press, 1987. ISBN 0-521-34505-7 (cl), 0-521-34748-3 (pbk). ‣ Clear, well-balanced textbook account; particularly good on post-1945 period and on economic developments. [JJS]

31.34 F. Roy Bridge. *The Habsburg monarchy among the great powers, 1815–1918.* New York: Berg; distributed by St. Martin's, 1990. ISBN 0-85496-307-3. ‣ Authoritative survey focusing most heavily on second half of century. Minimizes impact of domestic political influences in conduct of foreign policy, while emphasizing gap between reality and appearance marking Austria-Hungary's putative status as great power. [JWB]

31.35 William Carr. *A history of Germany, 1815–1990.* 4th ed. London: Arnold; distributed by Routledge Chapman & Hall, 1991. ISBN 0-340-55930-6. ‣ Best brief, one-volume survey in English. Especially good on political and diplomatic history. [JJS]

31.36 Gordon A. Craig. *Germany, 1866–1945.* New York: Oxford University Press, 1978. ISBN 0-19-822113-4. ‣ Brilliantly

written narrative of German nation-state from victorious beginnings to destruction. Particularly good on political developments and high culture. [JJS]

31.37 Mary Fulbrook. *The divided nation: a history of Germany, 1918–1990.* 1991 ed. New York: Oxford University Press, 1992. ISBN 0-19-507570-6 (cl), 0-19-507571-4 (pbk). ‣ Well-balanced textbook account; unusually full treatment of post-1945 period in context of recurrent problems of German history. [JJS]

31.38 Barbara Jelavich. *Modern Austria: empire and republic, 1815–1986.* Cambridge: Cambridge University Press, 1987. ISBN 0-521-30320-6 (cl), 0-521-31625-1 (pbk). ‣ General narrative survey, especially useful for nonspecialist readers. Clearly and intelligently written with minimum of controversial or otherwise unsupportable judgments. [JWB]

31.39 Robert A. Kann. *A history of the Habsburg empire, 1526–1918.* 1974 ed. Berkeley: University of California Press, 1980. ISBN 0-520-02408-7 (cl, 1974), 0-520-04206-9 (pbk). ‣ General history of Habsburg empire, written with sensitivity for events in Vienna, in regions, and among various nationalities. Carefully combines narrative of domestic forces with overview of foreign policy. Best history of monarchy in English. [JWB]

31.40 C. A. Macartney. *The Habsburg empire, 1790–1918.* 1968 ed. London: Weidenfeld & Nicolson, 1971. ISBN 0-297-00400-X. ‣ Detailed narrative history of empire. One of few general histories of monarchy to take history of Hungary seriously. Wrong in many particulars and partisan on behalf of Hungarian state rights, but still best general introduction to nineteenth-century Austrian history in any language. [JWB]

31.41 Thomas Nipperdey. *Deutsche Geschichte, 1800–1866: Bürgerwelt und starker Staat.* Munich: Beck, 1983. ISBN 3-406-09354-X. ‣ Broad-based, richly textured synthesis of German history from Napoleon to Bismarck. In Prussian tradition but emphasizes open-endedness of future political developments. English translation expected. [JJS]

31.42 Franz Schnabel. *Deutsche Geschichte im neunzehnten Jahrhundert.* Edition varies. 4 vols. in 8. Freiburg: Herder, 1964–65. ‣ Fragmentary but brilliant synthesis by one of twentieth century's finest historians. Especially good on intellectual and religious history; corrective to Protestant, pro-Prussian orientation of most traditional historiography. [JJS]

31.43 James J. Sheehan. *German history, 1770–1866.* New York: Oxford University Press, 1989. ISBN 0-19-822120-7. ‣ General survey emphasizing state building, economic development, and spread of print-based culture. Questions inevitability of German unification under Prussian domination. [JJS]

31.44 Alan Sked. *The decline and fall of the Habsburg empire, 1815–1918.* London: Longman, 1989. ISBN 0-582-02530-3 (cl), 0-582-02531-1 (pbk). ‣ Discussion of whether decline of empire was inevitable, rejecting simplistic arguments about necessity of its collapse. Intelligent, helpful overview based on selective engagement with latest scholarship. [JWB]

31.45 A.J.P. Taylor. *The Habsburg monarchy, 1809–1918: a history of the Austrian empire and Austria-Hungary.* 1948 2d ed. Chicago: University of Chicago Press, 1976. ISBN 0-226-79145-9. ‣ Insightful, entertaining survey of last century of empire. Most pungent and stylish general history Austria has ever merited. [JWB]

31.46 Heinrich von Treitschke. *History of Germany in the nineteenth century.* 1915–19 ed. 7 vols. Eden Paul and Cedar Paul, trans. William Harbutt Dawson, Introduction. New York: AMS Press, 1968. ‣ Incomplete masterwork by founder of Prussian school, covering period from Thirty Years' War to eve of Revolution of 1848. Interesting as example of nationalist historiography but also has some great if heavily biased historical writing; still worth reading. [JJS]

31.47 Adam Wandruszka. *The House of Habsburg: six hundred years of a European dynasty.* 1964 ed. Cathleen Epstein and Hans Epstein, trans. Garden City, N.Y.: Doubleday, 1965. ▸ Concise history of dynasty, balancing attention to personalities of individual monarchs with broader appreciation of role of crown as political, religious, and moral institution. [JWB]

Political Movements and Institutions

31.48 Margaret Lavinia Anderson. "Piety and politics: recent work on German Catholicism." *Journal of modern history* 63.4 (1991) 681–716. ISSN 0022-2801. ▸ Guide to recent work on German religious history and agenda for future research. Excellent introduction to vital but too often ignored set of issues. [JJS]

31.49 Gordon A. Craig. *The politics of the Prussian army, 1640–1945.* 1955 ed. New York: Oxford University Press, 1964. ISBN 0-19-500257-1. ▸ Analysis of German history as series of constitutional struggles in which army played crucial and usually reactionary role. Military institutions seen in long historical perspective. Particular emphasis on twentieth century. [JJS]

31.50 István Deák. *Beyond nationalism: a social and political history of the Habsburg officer corps, 1848–1918.* 1990 ed. New York: Oxford University Press, 1992. ISBN 0-19-504505-X (cl, 1990), 0-19-504506-8 (pbk). ▸ Sympathetic portrait of Austrian officer corps, based on substantial statistical data, on archival and printed sources, and on author's own shrewd assessments. Stresses role of corps as collective agent that helped maintain imperial unity amid multiethnic diversity and conflict. [JWB]

31.51 Georg Franz. *Liberalismus: die deutschliberale Bewegung in der habsburgischen Monarchie.* Munich: Callwey, 1955. ▸ Older survey of much neglected but supremely important topic. Shows various ideological and social components of liberal movement in Austria. Dated but still useful account. [JWB]

31.52 Ernst Rudolf Huber. *Deutsche Verfassungsgeschichte seit 1789.* Edition varies. 8 vols. Stuttgart: Kohlhammer, 1978–91. ISBN 3-17-002501-5 (v. 1), 3-17-009741-5 (v. 2), 3-17-010099-8 (v. 3), 3-17-007471-7 (v. 4), 3-17-001055-7 (v. 5), 3-17-001056-5 (v. 6), 3-17-008378-3 (v. 7), 3-17-010835-2 (v. 8). ▸ Extraordinary work, much broader than constitutional history. Treats political institutions and developments, 1789–1933, from conservative perspective. Goldmine of valuable biographical and bibliographical information. [JJS]

31.53 Ernst Rudolf Huber, ed. *Dokumente zur deutschen Verfassungsgeschichte.* 3d ed. 4 vols. Stuttgart: Kohlhammer, 1978–91. ISBN 3-17-001844-2 (v. 1), 3-17-001845-0 (v. 2), 3-17-005060-5 (v. 3), 3-17-011718-1 (v. 4). ▸ Companion to 31.52; well-selected documents on German political developments, including constitutions, party programs, and important legislation. [JJS]

31.54 Ernst Rudolf Huber and Wolfgang Huber, eds. *Staat und Kirche im neunzehnten und zwanzigsten Jahrhundert: Dokumente zur Geschichte des deutschen Staatskirchenrechts.* 4 vols. Berlin: Duncker & Humblot, 1973–88. ISBN 3-428-02988-7 (v. 1), 3-428-03630-1 (v. 2), 3-428-05268-4 (v. 3), 3-428-06362-7 (v. 4). ▸ Wide variety of primary sources on church-state relations from end of Holy Roman Empire to Weimar republic. Basic source for critically important issue. [JJS]

31.55 Michael Hughes. *Nationalism and society: Germany, 1800–1945.* London: Arnold, 1988. ISBN 0-7131-6522-7. ▸ Useful, up-to-date introduction emphasizing nationalism's changing character with healthy skepticism about nationalist myths and power of nationalism as source of cohesion. [JJS]

31.56 Georg G. Iggers, ed. *The social history of politics: critical perspectives in West German historical writing since 1945.* Leam-

ington Spa: Berg, 1985. ISBN 0-907582-35-4 (cased), 0-907582-78-8 (pbk). ▸ Collected essays on nineteenth-century politics and society by ten leading historians. Good introduction to Bielefeld school. [JJS]

31.57 Kurt G. A. Jeserich, Hans Pohl, and Georg-Christoph von Unruh, eds. *Deutsche Verwaltungsgeschichte.* 6 vols. Stuttgart: Deutsche Verlags-Anstalt, 1983–88. ISBN 3-421-06117-3 (v. 1), 3-421-06118-1 (v. 2), 3-421-06133-5 (v. 3), 3-421-06134-3 (v. 4), 3-421-06135-1 (v. 5), 3-421-06136-X (v. 6). ▸ Examination of administrative institutions from Middle Ages to Federal Republic. Great deal of information and references; uneven and sometimes difficult to use. [JJS]

31.58 Larry Eugene Jones and James Retallack, eds. *Elections, mass politics, and social change in modern Germany.* Washington, D.C. and Cambridge: German Historical Institute and Cambridge University Press, 1992. ISBN 0-521-41846-1 (cl), 0-521-42912-9 (pbk). ▸ Essays on national and local elections, 1871–1933; includes discussions of gender, class, and region. Good introduction to recent research on popular politics. [JJS]

31.59 Eckart Kehr. *Economic interest, militarism, and foreign policy: essays on German history.* Gordon A. Craig, ed. Grete Heinz, trans. Berkeley: University of California Press, 1977. ISBN 0-520-02880-5. ▸ Stimulating, critical, but often overstated articles of interwar German historian now widely celebrated as father of modern German historical revisionism; influential for German historians of 1960s and 1970s. Attention to domestic political forces that shaped German militarism and pre–World War I foreign policy. [CSA/JJS]

31.60 Leonard Krieger. *The German idea of freedom: history of a political tradition.* 1957 ed. Chicago: University of Chicago Press, 1972. ISBN 0-226-45347-2. ▸ Ideas and actions of liberalism in Germany, Enlightenment through era of Bismarck. Subtle, complex, difficult study emphasizing long-term intellectual traditions but connecting them to social and political developments. [JS]

31.61 George L. Mosse. *The nationalization of the masses: political symbolism and mass movements in Germany from the Napoleonic wars through the Third Reich.* 1975 ed. Ithaca, N.Y.: Cornell University Press, 1991. ISBN 0-8014-9978-X (pbk). ▸ Imaginative, risky, not always convincing, but unfailingly interesting attempt to trace origins and development of German nationalism, especially in art and aesthetics. [JJS]

31.62 Gerhard Ritter. *The sword and the scepter: the problem of militarism in Germany.* 1969–73 ed. 4 vols. Heinz Norden, trans. Princeton: Scholar's Bookshelf, 1988. ISBN 0-945726-22-8 (set, cl), 0-945726-17-1 (set, pbk). ▸ Examination of late eighteenth century to 1918 emphasizing modern rather than traditional origins of militarism. Vilifies Quartermaster General Ludendorff and sees 1917 as watershed. Volume 3 especially good on social origins of militarism. [JJS]

31.63 Gunther E. Rothenberg. *The army of Francis Joseph.* West Lafayette: Purdue University Press, 1976. ISBN 0-911198-41-5. ▸ Careful survey of institutionalist policies and practices with appreciation of larger domestic and foreign contexts. Concludes army functioned well as institution and outlived dynasty it swore to defend. [JWB]

31.64 Theodor Schieder. *The state and society in our times: studies in the history of the nineteenth and twentieth centuries.* C.A.M. Sym, trans. London: Nelson, 1962. ▸ Essays by influential postwar historian whose major works not available in English. Collection includes important studies of liberal political ideas and organizations. [JJS]

31.65 Hagen Schulze. *The course of German nationalism: from Frederick the Great to Bismarck, 1763–1867.* Sarah Hanbury-Tenison, trans. Cambridge: Cambridge University Press, 1991. ISBN

0-521-37379-4 (cl), 0-521-37759-5 (pbk). ‣ Emphasizes social basis of nationalism with particularly good account of Revolution of 1848. Contains number of documents useful for teaching; valuable introduction. [JJS]

31.66 James J. Sheehan. *German liberalism in the nineteenth century.* Chicago: University of Chicago Press, 1978. ISBN 0-226-75207-0. ‣ Survey emphasizing structural inhibitions to development of liberalism in Germany, seen as illiberal society. Still useful when read with critics like Blackbourn and Eley 31.174. [JJS]

31.67 Jonathan Sperber. *Popular Catholicism in nineteenth-century Germany.* Princeton: Princeton University Press, 1984. ISBN 0-691-05432-0. ‣ Social, political, and cultural history of German Catholics in Rhineland-Westphalia, 1830–80, from social disruption and cultural decay to successful consolidation of distinctive Catholic milieu. [CSA]

31.68 Mack Walker. *German home towns: community, state, and general estate, 1648–1871.* Ithaca, N.Y.: Cornell University Press, 1971. ISBN 0-8014-0670-6. ‣ Classic study providing deep insight into social relations and political development in modern Germany. Finds guild burghers and their small, semi-autonomous towns under assault by forces of market and state. [JS/JJS]

Social and Economic Developments

31.69 Klaus J. Bade, ed. *Population, labour, and migration in nineteenth- and twentieth-century Germany.* Leamington Spa: Berg; distributed by St. Martin's, 1987. ISBN 0-85496-503-3. ‣ Important articles on what has become central issue in contemporary German politics. Good introduction to work of Germany's leading historian of emigration. [JJS]

31.70 Knut Borchardt. *Perspectives on modern German economic history and policy.* Peter Lambert, trans. Cambridge: Cambridge University Press, 1991. ISBN 0-521-36310-1 (cl), 0-521-36858-8 (pbk). ‣ Collected essays by one of Germany's leading economic historians. Discussions of regional variations in growth and economic collapse of Weimar republic especially important. Good introduction to recent work on economic history. [JJS]

31.71 Geoffrey Cocks and Konrad H. Jarausch, eds. *German professions, 1800–1950.* New York: Oxford University Press, 1990. ISBN 0-19-505596-9. ‣ Essays on various professional groups including teachers, engineers, and civil servants; most based on authors' previously published monographs. Good survey of recent research on professions and professionalization. [JJS]

31.72 Richard J. Evans and W. R. Lee, eds. *The German family: essays on the social history of the family in nineteenth-and twentieth-century Germany.* Totowa, N.J.: Barnes & Noble, 1981. ISBN 0-389-20101-4. ‣ Good essays on working women and demography, as well as Hausen's important article on separation of gender roles. Excellent introduction to historiography. [JJS]

31.73 Richard J. Evans and W. R. Lee, eds. *The German peasantry: conflict and community in rural society from the eighteenth to the twentieth centuries.* 1985 ed. Ian Farr, Introduction. New York: St. Martin's, 1986. ISBN 0-312-32597-5. ‣ Excellent historiographical introduction and several good local studies including important essay by William Hagen on Prussian peasantry. Overall, questions conventional picture of peasants as passive victims of historical change. [JJS]

31.74 John C. Fout, ed. *German women in the nineteenth century: a social history.* New York: Holmes & Meier, 1984. ISBN 0-8419-0843-5 (cl), 0-8419-0844-3 (pbk). ‣ Uneven collection of essays, most emphasizing repression of women. Good introduction by author and excellent bibliography. [JJS]

31.75 Ute Frevert. *Women in German history: from bourgeois*

emancipation to sexual liberation. Stuart McKinnon-Evans, Terry Bond, and Barbara Norden, trans. New York: Berg, 1989. ISBN 0-85496-233-6. ‣ Critical, generally pessimistic survey of women's struggle for political, social, and sexual equality; emphasizes persistence of restrictions on true liberation. Best introduction to subject by leading German scholar. [JJS]

31.76 Alexander Gerschenkron. *An economic spurt that failed: four lectures in Austrian history.* Princeton: Princeton University Press, 1977. ISBN 0-691-04216-0. ‣ Insightful but controversial interpretation of state-sponsored railway and canal building proposed by Ernest von Koerber, Austrian minister-president (1900–04) which, if implemented, could have launched great spurt of economic development. Identifies political forces and individuals responsible for undercutting reforms. [JWB]

31.77 David F. Good. *The economic rise of the Habsburg empire, 1750–1914.* Berkeley: University of California Press, 1984. ISBN 0-520-05094-0. ‣ Excellent analytic survey based on latest scholarship. Rejects older arguments about economic failure of Hapsburg empire, insisting Austria enjoyed vigorous economic development. [JWB]

31.78 Karl Hardach. *The political economy of Germany in the twentieth century.* Berkeley: University of California Press, 1980. ISBN 0-520-03809-6. ‣ Clear, concise survey, useful statistical data, and sensitive to theoretical issues; but mainly concerned with political causes and impact of economic developments. Fine introduction now somewhat out of date. [JJS]

31.79 W. O. Henderson. *The rise of German industrial power, 1834–1914.* Berkeley: University of California Press, 1975. ISBN 0-520-03073-7 (cl), 0-520-03120-2 (pbk). ‣ Discussion of broad lines of German economic development, as well as differences among regions. Charts political, economic, and commercial aspects of industrial success, and role of individuals. [CSA]

31.80 Alfred Kelly, ed. and trans. *The German worker: working-class autobiographies from the age of industrialization.* Berkeley: University of California Press, 1987. ISBN 0-520-05972-7 (cl), 0-520-06124-1 (pbk). ‣ Selections from nineteen autobiographies illuminating political, social, and cultural life among German working people, including factory workers, servants, farm workers, and craftsmen. Splendid, accessible portrait of everyday life. [JJS]

31.81 Martin Kitchen. *The political economy of Germany, 1815–1914.* London: Croom Helm, 1978. ISBN 0-85664-610-5. ‣ Study focusing on reciprocal interaction between economic development and social structure with attention to disjunction between exceptional economic growth and stubbornly unchanging political and social formations. [CSA]

31.82 Jürgen Kocka. *Arbeitsverhältnisse und Arbeiterexistenzen: Grundlagen der Klassenbildung im neunzehnten Jahrhundert.* Bonn: Dietz, 1990. ISBN 3-8012-0153-8. ‣ Monumental synthesis, splendid bibliography. Emphasizes modernization and class formation; designed to introduce future volumes on political developments. [JJS]

31.83 Jürgen Kocka. *Weder Stand noch Klasse: Unterschichten um 1800.* Bonn: Dietz, 1990. ISBN 3-8012-0152-X. ‣ Brief introduction to social history of lower orders at beginning of nineteenth century. Theoretical blending of Marx and Weber, methodological blending of quantitative and qualitative materials. Excellent guide to most recent research. [JJS]

31.84 Jürgen Kocka, ed. *Bürgertum im neunzehnten Jahrhundert: Deutschland im europäischen Vergleich.* 3 vols. Munich: Deutscher Taschenbuch, 1988. ISBN 3-423-04482-9 (set). ‣ Result of large collective research project on wide range of social, economic, political, and cultural issues. Not cohesive analysis but rich array of special studies, many with comparative dimension. [JJS]

31.85 John Komlos. *The Habsburg monarchy as a customs union: economic development in Austria-Hungary in the nineteenth century.* Princeton: Princeton University Press, 1983. ISBN 0-691-04239-x. ‣ Soundly researched exploration of dynamics behind monarchy's economic development in nineteenth century with special attention to interaction between Austria and Hungary. While Austria might have done as well without Hungary, Hungary received considerable benefits from her connection with Austrian economy after 1850. [JWB]

31.86 W. R. Lee, ed. *German industry and German industrialisation: essays in German economic and business history in the nineteenth and twentieth centuries.* London: Routledge, 1991. ISBN 0-415-02155-3. ‣ Introduction provides excellent guide to recent historiography. Essays reflect new economic history using economic theory and quantitative data. Skeptical of political explanations of economic phenomena. [JJS]

31.87 Charles E. McClelland. *State, society, and university in Germany, 1700–1914.* Cambridge: Cambridge University Press, 1980. ISBN 0-521-22742-9. ‣ Useful general survey using Göttingen as example of new type of university. Especially good on rise of scholarly ideal and institutional tensions caused by expansion after turn of century. Well-balanced introduction. [JJS]

31.88 Robert G. Moeller, ed. *Peasants and lords in modern Germany: recent studies in agricultural history.* Boston: Allen & Unwin, 1986. ISBN 0-04-943037-8. ‣ Eight studies covering period from empire through national socialism, very much in Bielefeld tradition. Includes good introduction to historiography. [JJS]

31.89 Gregory W. Pedlow. *The survival of the Hessian nobility, 1770–1870.* Princeton: Princeton University Press, 1988. ISBN 0-691-05503-3. ‣ Study of economic, social, and political development of landed nobility in poor region of western Germany. Shows how landed aristocracy adapted to liberal and capitalist society. [JS]

31.90 Heinz Reif. *Westfälischer Adel, 1770–1860: vom Herrschaftsstand zur regionalen Elite.* Göttingen: Vandenhoeck & Ruprecht, 1979. (Kritische Studien zur Geschichtswissenschaft, 35.) ISBN 3-525-35991-8. ‣ Long, careful study of provincial nobility emphasizing adaption to modern society, especially in political behavior. Best local study of German aristocracy. [JJS]

31.91 James S. Roberts. *Drink, temperance, and the working class in nineteenth-century Germany.* Boston: Allen & Unwin, 1984. ISBN 0-04-943029-7. ‣ Innovative study of everyday life among working people. Examines drinking both as social problem evoking temperance movements and as source of nutrition and sociability. [JJS]

31.92 Eda Sagarra. *A social history of Germany, 1648–1914.* New York: Holmes & Meier, 1977. ISBN 0-8419-0332-8. ‣ Thoughtful survey of social groups in modern Germany based on printed sources and covering broad range of topics. Especially useful for beginning students. [JJS]

31.93 Frank B. Tipton. "The national consensus in German economic history." *Central European history* 7.3 (1974) 195–224. ISSN 0008-9389. ‣ Critical of use of nation as basic unit for economic history. Emphasizes limited economic impact of political developments and significance of regional variation. Important corrective to established historiography. [JJS]

31.94 Mack Walker. *Germany and the emigration, 1816–1885.* Cambridge, Mass.: Harvard University Press, 1964. ‣ Study of forces driving emigration, especially demography and social changes, and excellent regional analysis. Stimulating if sometimes fragmentary analysis. [JJS]

31.95 Hans-Ulrich Wehler. *Deutsche Gesellschaftsgeschichte.* 2 vols. to date. Munich: Beck, 1987–. ISBN 3-406-32490-8 (set). ‣ One of most ambitious scholarly projects of postwar period (see

review by John Breuilly in *German History* 9.2 [1991] 211–30). First two volumes (covering 1700–1849) ordered according to Weberian concept of modernization and critically concerned with inequality. Extraordinary bibliographical guides to range of social, economic, and political problems. [JJS]

31.96 Peter-Christian Witt, ed. *Wealth and taxation in Central Europe: the history and sociology of public finance.* Leamington Spa: Berg; distributed by St. Martin's, 1987. ISBN 0-85496-523-8. ‣ Essays on taxes and finance from end of Middle Ages to twentieth century. Especially valuable as introduction to author who has done much important work on these problems. [JJS]

SEE ALSO
  30.231 John E. Knodel. *Demographic behavior in the past.*
  30.244 David Warren Sabean. *Property, production, and family in Neckarhausen, 1700–1870.*

REVOLUTIONARY ERA, 1789–1815

Impact of the French Revolution

31.97 T.C.W. Blanning. *The French Revolution in Germany: occupation and resistance in the Rhineland, 1792–1802.* Oxford: Clarendon, 1983. ISBN 0-19-822564-4. ‣ Vigorously argued, anti-French, antirevolutionary account. Military exploitation, heavy taxation, and forced secularization produced widespread hostility to French rule throughout Rhineland. [JJS]

31.98 T.C.W. Blanning. "German Jacobins and the French Revolution." *Historical journal* 23.4 (1980) 985–1002. ISSN 0018-246x. ‣ Sustained attack on those who see German Jacobinism as important element in German democratic tradition. Supporters of Jacobinism few in number and politically isolated. [JJS]

31.99 T.C.W. Blanning. *Reform and revolution in Mainz, 1743–1803.* Cambridge: Cambridge University Press, 1974. ISBN 0-521-20418-6. ‣ Fine account of city and electorate at end of Old Regime and of Revolution's impact. Downplays indigenous sympathy for Revolution. [JJS]

31.100 Jeffry Diefendorf. *Businessmen and politics in the Rhineland, 1789–1834.* Princeton: Princeton University Press, 1980. ISBN 0-691-05298-0. ‣ Outline of political education of Rhenish businessmen from revolution to Customs Union. More positive account of French influence than Blanning 31.97; emphasizes businessmen's adaptability as they sought control over local affairs and defended own interests. [JJS]

31.101 G. P. Gooch. *Germany and the French Revolution.* 1920 ed. New York: Russell & Russell, 1966. ‣ Account of revolution's impact on German philosophy and literature by one of Britain's then leading historians. Out of date but still worthwhile for information and quotations. [JJS]

31.102 Karl A. Roider, Jr. *Baron Thugut and Austria's response to the French Revolution.* Princeton: Princeton University Press, 1987. ISBN 0-691-05135-6. ‣ Carefully researched study arguing principal motive behind Director of Foreign Affairs Thugut's foreign policy was hostility to French Revolution and desire to impede spread to rest of Europe. Excellent biography with useful discussion of Austrian diplomatic strategy at end of eighteenth century. [JWB]

Reform and Reorganization of the German States

31.103 Helmut Berding and Hans-Peter Ullmann, eds. *Deutschland zwischen Revolution und Restauration.* Königstein im Taunus, Germany: Athenäum, 1981. ISBN 3-7610-7240-6. ‣ Essays on reform in various German states with emphasis on economic developments and fiscal policy. Departure from heroic, Prusso-centric views that once dominated history of reform era. [JJS]

31.104 Carl von Clausewitz. *Historical and political writings.*

Peter Paret and Daniel Moran, eds. and trans. Princeton: Princeton University Press, 1992. ISBN 0-691-03192-4. ▸ Collection of essays providing unique insights into contemporary scene by one of greatest military theorists of all time. Especially valuable essay on causes of Prussia's defeat in 1806. [JJS]

31.105 Werner Conze. "The effects of nineteenth-century liberal agrarian reforms on social structure in Central Europe." In *Essays in European economic history, 1789–1914.* 1970 ed. François Crouzet, W. H. Chaloner, and W. M. Stern, eds., pp. 53–81. New York: St. Martin's, 1970. ▸ Translation of 1948 article summarizing author's research on agrarian social structure. Extraordinary synthesis of local developments, emphasizing variety and complexity. [JJS]

31.106 Reinhart Koselleck. *Preussen zwischen Reform und Revolution: allgemeines Landrecht, Verwaltung, und soziale Bewegung von 1791 bis 1848.* 2d ed. Stuttgart: Klett-Cotta im Deutschen Taschenbuch, 1989. ISBN 3-423-04496-9. ▸ Subtle, powerful analysis of reform in Prussia before and after French Revolution. Emphasizes state's difficulty in changing system on which it depended; see J. Sperber's review article in *Journal of Modern History* 57.2 (1985) 278–96. [JJS]

31.107 Friedrich Meinecke. *The age of German liberation, 1795–1815.* Peter Paret, ed. Peter Paret and Helmuth Fischer, trans. Berkeley: University of California Press, 1977. ISBN 0-520-02792-2. ▸ Classic statement of patriotic version of reform era. Pro-Prussian and anti-French, emphasizes heroic resistance of Prussia and victory of national idea. Originally published as *Das Zeitalter der deutschen Erhebung, 1795–1815* (1906). [JJS]

31.108 James van Horn Melton and Douglas A. Unfug, eds. *The French Revolution in Germany and Austria.* Atlanta: Emory University, 1989. (Central European history, 22.2.) ISSN 0008-9389. ▸ Recent research on aspects of revolutionary period. Blanning's analysis of historiography on French Revolution and modernization in Germany especially valuable. [JJS]

31.109 Peter Paret. *Clausewitz and the state: the man, his theories, and his times.* 1976 ed. Princeton: Princeton University Press, 1985. ISBN 0-691-05448-7 (cl), 0-691-00806-x (pbk). ▸ Best book on Prussian general and military theorist; provides bibliographical information and well-balanced account of historical context for strategic theories and political values. [JJS]

31.110 Peter Paret. *Yorck and the era of Prussian reform, 1807–1815.* Princeton: Princeton University Press, 1966. ▸ Sympathetic, revisionist portrait of Prussian soldier often dismissed as reactionary. Excellent on historical background, particularly military tactics, strategy, and institutions before and after reform. [JJS]

31.111 Gerhard Ritter. *Stein: eine politische Biographie.* 3d rev. ed. Stuttgart: Deutsche Verlags-Anstalt, 1958. ▸ Remains best one-volume treatment of great reformer. Sympathetic account emphasizing patriotic achievements in struggle against Napoleon. [JJS]

31.112 Hans Rosenberg. *Bureaucracy, aristocracy, and autocracy: the Prussian experience, 1660–1815.* 1958 ed. Cambridge, Mass.: Harvard University Press, 1966. ▸ Critical account of Prussian bureaucracy viewed in harsh light of twentieth-century German history: reformers interested in increasing own power, not in progress or patriotism; they share responsibility for liberal democracy's failure. On Rosenberg, see special issue of *Central European History* 24.1 (1991). [JJS]

31.113 Hans A. Schmitt. "Germany without Prussia: a closer look at the Confederation of the Rhine." *German studies review* 6.1 (1983) 9–39. ISSN 0149-7952. ▸ Revisionist assessment of confederation, traditionally viewed as alien institution imposed on

Germans by French. Seen here as potentially positive federal solution to German question. [JJS]

31.114 Walter M. Simon. *The failure of the Prussian reform movement, 1807–1819.* 1955 ed. New York: Fertig, 1971. ▸ Discussion emphasizing agrarian, constitutional, and military reform. Failure of reform had unfortunate, long-range consequences. Especially critical of Chancellor Hardenberg's unwillingness to press for change and inability to cooperate with potential allies. [JJS]

31.115 Ernst Wangermann. *From Joseph II to the Jacobin trials: government policy and public opinion in the Habsburg dominions in the period of the French Revolution.* 2d ed. London: Oxford University Press, 1969. ISBN 0-19-821832-x. ▸ Description of ambivalent impact of Emperor Joseph II's reforms and unraveling of many initiatives under his successors Leopold II and especially Francis II. Special focus on repression in 1792 and on putative Jacobin conspiracy that preoccupied government in 1794–95. [JWB]

31.116 Eberhard Weis, ed. *Reformen im rheinbündischen Deutschland.* Munich: Oldenbourg, 1984. ISBN 3-486-51671-x. ▸ Specialized studies on aspects of Rhenish confederation; synthesis by Vierhaus especially valuable. Departure from Prussocentric picture of reform era. See also Berding and Ullmann 31.103. [JJS]

SEE ALSO
30.354 Paul R. Sweet. *Wilhelm von Humboldt.*

Revolutionary Culture

31.117 Eugene N. Anderson. *Nationalism and the cultural crisis in Prussia, 1806–1815.* 1939 ed. New York: Octagon Books, 1976. ISBN 0-374-90228-3. ▸ Biographically arranged studies of leading theorists of German nationalism. Clear account of ideas but no analysis of relationship to popular movements. Tends to overemphasize contemporary importance of national enthusiasm. [JJS]

31.118 Reinhold Aris. *History of political thought in Germany from 1789 to 1815.* 1936 ed. New York: Russell & Russell, 1965. ▸ Biographically organized study of major theorists. Clear, well-balanced accounts of Immanuel Kant, J. G. Fichte, Joseph Görres, and others; lacks Epstein's capacity to weave together ideas and context (31.121). Solid but not exciting. [JJS]

31.119 Nicholas Boyle. *The poetry of desire (1749–1790).* Vol. 1 of *Goethe: the poet and the age.* Oxford: Oxford University Press, 1991. ISBN 0-19-815866-1 (v. 1). ▸ First volume of what will be best modern biography of Germany's greatest writer. Combines astute readings of works with excellent account of historical context. Splendid introduction to German literary culture at end of eighteenth century. [JJS]

31.120 Laurence Dickey. *Hegel: religion, economics, and the politics of the spirit, 1770–1807.* Cambridge: Cambridge University Press, 1987. ISBN 0-521-33035-1. ▸ Brilliant account of philosopher's intellectual development in historical context. Especially good on lasting influence of youthful experiences in Württemberg and religious sources of his thought. [JJS]

31.121 Klaus Epstein. *The genesis of German conservatism.* 1966 ed. Princeton: Princeton University Press, 1975. ISBN 0-691-10030-6 (pbk). ▸ Analysis of ideas of important conservative theorists against well-drawn historical background. Sees conservatism as response to Enlightenment, capitalism, and rise of bourgeoisie. Especially good on reform before and during French Revolution. [JJS]

31.122 Daniel Moran. *Toward the century of words: Johann Cotta and the politics of the public realm in Germany, 1795–1832.* Berkeley: University of California Press, 1990. ISBN 0-520-06640-5. ▸ Examination of history of press and its public through career of important publisher. Especially good for origins of political opinions under impact of French Revolution and restoration. [JJS]

31.123 H. S. Reiss, ed. *The political thought of the German romantics, 1793–1815.* New York: Macmillan, 1955. ‣ Series of biographically oriented essays on leading romantic poets and theorists. Sound account of political ideas, little analysis of origins and significance. [JJS]

31.124 Theodore Ziolkowski. *German romanticism and its institutions.* Princeton: Princeton University Press, 1990. ISBN 0-691-06801-1. ‣ Examination of institutions important for careers and work of leading romantics; chapters on mining, law, asylums, universities, and museums. Excellent on social and cultural institutions in early nineteenth century; not always convincing on connections between institutions and ideas. [JJS]

POST–CONGRESS OF VIENNA: RESTORATION AND REVOLUTION, 1815–1850

Politics

31.125 Hartwig Brandt. *Parlamentarismus in Württemberg, 1819–1870: Anatomie eines deutschen Landtags.* Düsseldorf: Droste, 1987. ISBN 3-7700-5142-4. ‣ Exhaustive study, important for analysis of development of parliamentary and political institutions. Examines monarchy, parliament, elections, and organized politics in medium-sized German state, 1815–1870. [JS]

31.126 Donald E. Emerson. *Metternich and the political police: security and subversion in the Habsburg monarchy (1815–1830).* 1968 ed. The Hague: Nijhoff, 1969. ‣ Useful survey of possibilities and limitations of censorship and other controls. Discussion of Metternich's role in activity of Austrian secret police; did not consider Italian secret societies a threat. (See also Reinerman 28.247.) Lacks general conclusions on Metternich's regime. [JWB/AS]

31.127 John R. Gillis. *The Prussian bureaucracy in crisis, 1840–1860: origins of an administrative ethos.* Stanford, Calif.: Stanford University Press, 1971. ISBN 0-8047-0756-1. ‣ Examination of career patterns and job opportunities in Prussian bureaucracy and their political consequences. Interesting incorporation of generational perspective to understand shaping of important social group. [JS]

31.128 Theodore S. Hamerow. *Restoration, revolution, reaction: economics and politics in Germany, 1815–1871.* 1958 ed. Princeton: Princeton University Press, 1966. ‣ Broad study of German Revolution of 1848, pointing to social conflicts to explain its outbreak and failure. Classic account; not entirely supported by latest scholarship but still challenging interpretation. [JS]

31.129 Loyd E. Lee. *The politics of harmony: civil service, liberalism, and social reform in Baden, 1800–1850.* Newark: University of Delaware Press, 1980. ISBN 0-87413-143-X. ‣ Analysis of bureaucracy and politics in small German state, long center of liberal and radical ideas. Emphasizes unintended political consequences of governmental action. [JS]

31.130 Alf Lüdtke. *Police and state in Prussia, 1815–1850.* Pete Burgess, trans. Cambridge and Paris: Cambridge University Press and Éditions de la Maison des Sciences de l'Homme, 1989. ISBN 0-521-30164-5. ‣ Application of structuralist Marxism to classic historical problem of nature and action of state in Germany. Looks at exercise of police and state power in Prussia. [JS]

31.131 Herbert Obenaus. *Anfänge des Parlamentarismus in Preussen bis 1848.* Düsseldorf: Droste, 1984. ISBN 3-7700-5116-5 (cl), 3-7700-5090-8 (pbk). ‣ Definitive study and acute analysis of politics, including origins of 1848 Revolution. Monarch, bureaucracy, feudal provincial legislatures (Diets), and movement for constitution and parliament in Prussia, 1815–48. [JS]

31.132 James J. Sheehan. "Liberalism and society in Germany, 1815–1848." *Journal of modern history* 45.4 (1973) 583–604. ISSN 0022-2801. ‣ Social basis and social ideas of liberalism in Germany before Revolution of 1848. Important work, showing liberalism not just *laissez-faire* movement of bourgeoisie. [JS]

31.133 Heinrich Ritter von Srbik. *Metternich: der Staatsmann und der Mensch.* 1925–54 ed. 3 vols. Graz: Akademische Druck- und Verlagsanstalt, 1979–84. ISBN 3-201-01264-5 (set). ‣ Important, serious study of Austrian diplomat. Smooths evident contradictions in Metternich's thought and practice by subsuming his tactics into presumed realm of coherent and constructive principles. History on grand, if not always convincing, scale. [JWB]

31.134 Carl Wegert. "The genesis of youthful radicalism: Hessen-Nassau, 1806–19." *Central European history* 10.3 (1977) 183–205. ISSN 0008-9389. ‣ Case study of origins and development of student radicalism in Germany during Napoleonic era and Restoration. Emphasizes generational conflict. [JS]

31.135 George S. Werner. *Bavaria in the German confederation, 1820–1848.* Rutherford, N.J.: Fairleigh Dickinson University Press, 1977. ISBN 0-8386-1932-0. ‣ Discussion of relations between Bavaria, German great powers, and German confederation. Interesting study of possibilities and limitations of federal polity in Central Europe. [JS]

31.136 Stanley Zucker. "Female political opposition in pre-1848 Germany: the role of Kathinka Zitz-Halein." In *German women in the nineteenth century: a social history.* John C. Fout, ed., pp. 133–50. New York: Holmes & Meier, 1984. ISBN 0-8419-0843-5 (cl), 0-8419-0844-3 (pbk). ‣ Study of one woman's role in religious and political opposition before 1848 Revolution. Good discussion of interaction between personal history, early feminist perspectives, and political life. [JS]

SEE ALSO
  28.247 Alan J. Reinerman. *Austria and the papacy in the age of Metternich.*
  47.42 Alan W. Palmer. *Metternich.*
  47.71 Robert D. Billinger, Jr. *Metternich and the German question.*

Society and Economics

31.137 Pierre Ayçoberry. *Cologne entre Napoléon et Bismarck: la croissance d'une ville rhénane.* Paris: Aubier-Montaigne, 1981. ISBN 2-7007-0261-1. ‣ Social, economic, political, and cultural development of Cologne in first two-thirds of nineteenth century. Revealing, insightful local study, in best Annales tradition. [JS]

31.138 Robert M. Berdahl. *The politics of the Prussian nobility: the development of a conservative ideology, 1770–1848.* Princeton: Princeton University Press, 1988. ISBN 0-691-05536-X. ‣ Development of Junker class and its relationship to origins of conservatism in Germany. Strong on interaction between social group's position and ideas it espoused. [JS]

31.139 Jerome Blum. *Noble landowners and agriculture in Austria, 1815–1848: a study in the origins of the peasant emancipation of 1848.* Baltimore: Johns Hopkins University Press, 1948. ‣ Dated in particulars and lacking archival-source base, but still useful as introduction to Austrian agrarian history. Argues that, long before emancipation of peasantry in 1848, noble landowners sought to modernize estates and increase profitability, many actually favored abolition of robot (compulsory work) system. [JWB]

31.140 Rolf Dumke. "Intra-German trade in 1837 and regional economic development." *Vierteljahrsschrift für Sozial- und Wirtschaftsgeschichte* 64.4 (1977) 468–96. ISSN 0340-8728. ‣ Discussion of economic benefits of German Customs Union. Destroys myths of its popularity and of its relation to national unity. Points to importance of fiscal motivations. [JS]

31.141 Josef Ehmer. *Familienstruktur und Arbeitsorganization im frühindustriellen Wien.* Munich: Oldenbourg, 1980. ISBN 3-486-50171-2. ▸ Careful, probing analysis of labor in Vienna between 1800 and 1870. Shows consequences of transformation of Vienna's economy in nineteenth century from handwork to factory-based production to working-class family structures. [JWB]

31.142 Frederick Marquardt. "A working class in Berlin in the 1840s?" In *Sozialgeschichte heute: Festschrift für Hans Rosenberg zum siebzigsten Geburtstag.* Hans-Ulrich Wehler, ed., pp. 191–210. Göttingen: Vandenhoeck & Ruprecht, 1974. ISBN 3-525-35962-4. ▸ Analysis of social conditions and political consciousness of working people in Berlin on eve of 1848 Revolution. Argues common consciousness of class was developing among disparate groups of laborers. [JS]

31.143 Josef Mooser. "Property and wood theft: agrarian capitalism and social conflict in rural society, a Westphalian case study." In *Peasants and lords in modern Germany: recent studies in agricultural history.* Robert G. Moeller, ed., pp. 52–80. Boston: Allen & Unwin, 1986. ISBN 0-04-943037-8. ▸ Penetrating analysis of key source of social tensions in early nineteenth-century Germany: conflict between peasants and landholding nobility over forest use. [JS]

31.144 Michael J. Neufeld. *The skilled metalworkers of Nuremberg: craft and class in the industrial revolution.* New Brunswick, N.J.: Rutgers University Press, 1989. ISBN 0-8135-1394-4. ▸ Study of social and political development of industrial labor force in German city. Shows complementary rather than contradictory nature of craft and class consciousness. [JS]

31.145 Hanna Schissler. "The Junkers: notes on the social and historical significance of the agrarian elite in Prussia." In *Peasants and lords in modern Germany: recent studies in agricultural history.* Robert G. Moeller, ed., pp. 24–51. Boston: Allen & Unwin, 1986. ISBN 0-04-943037-8. ▸ Brief discussion of political and economic fortunes of East Elbian landed aristocracy, particularly during age of Prussian agrarian reforms. Useful summary. [JS]

31.146 Richard Tilly. *Financial institutions and industrialization in the Rhineland, 1815–1870.* Madison: University of Wisconsin Press, 1966. ISBN 0-299-03920-X. ▸ Pioneering study of German industrialization and of Prussian state economic policy. Treats public finance, banking, and economic development in western Germany in early industrial era. [JS]

31.147 Frank B. Tipton. *Regional variations in the economic development of Germany during the nineteenth century.* Middletown, Conn.: Wesleyan University Press, 1976. ISBN 0-8195-4096-X. ▸ Discussion of regional differences and specialization in German economic life. Downplays idea of national market and influence of government policy on economy, emphasizing importance of region. [JS]

Culture

31.148 Robert M. Bigler. *The politics of German Protestantism: the rise of the Protestant church elite in Prussia, 1815–1848.* Berkeley: University of California Press, 1972. ISBN 0-520-01881-8. ▸ Examination of organizational and theological developments and conflicts among Prussian Protestants. Good explanation of interaction of religion and politics. [JS]

31.149 Eric Dorn Brose. *The politics of technological change in Prussia: out of the shadow of antiquity, 1809–1848.* Princeton: Princeton University Press, 1992. ISBN 0-691-05685-4. ▸ Analysis of attitude of different branches of Prussian government toward technology, industrialization, economic growth, and their politi-

cal implications. Challenges long-held assumptions; highlights influence of neoclassicist thought. [JS]

31.150 Alice M. Hanson. *Musical life in Biedermeier Vienna.* London: Cambridge University Press, 1985. ISBN 0-521-25799-9. ▸ Fine study of music in social and political context and as aesthetic and sensual experience. Treats musicians, living they earned, patrons, and public in Restoration era Vienna. [JS/JWB]

31.151 Peter Uwe Hohendahl. *Building a national literature: the case of Germany, 1830–1870.* Renate Baron Franciscono, trans. Ithaca, N.Y.: Cornell University Press, 1989. ISBN 0-8014-1862-3 (cl), 0-8014-9622-5 (pbk). ▸ Discussion of creation of national literary culture and establishment of standard classics of German literature. Heavy use of literary theory, at times very abstract, but interesting insights into cultural development. [JS]

31.152 Christa Jungnickel and Russell McCormmach. *The torch of mathematics, 1800–1870.* Vol. 1 of *Intellectual mastery of nature: theoretical physics from Ohm to Einstein.* Chicago: University of Chicago Press, 1986. ISBN 0-226-41581-3. ▸ Examination of intellectual and institutional rise and triumph of theoretical physics in nineteenth-century Germany. Empirically detailed study, combining internalist and institutionalist perspectives in history of science. [JS]

31.153 Leonard Krieger. *Ranke: the meaning of history.* Chicago: University of Chicago Press, 1977. ISBN 0-226-45349-9. ▸ Penetrating study, valuable both as contribution to intellectual history and to historical theory. Examines historian's overall conception of history as embodied in his works. [JS]

31.154 Anthony J. La Vopa. *Prussian schoolteachers: profession and office, 1763–1848.* Chapel Hill: University of North Carolina Press, 1980. ISBN 0-8078-1426-1. ▸ Uses concept of professionalization to delineate teachers' efforts at self-improvement and difficulties they encountered. Treats education, social standing, and economic prospects of primary-school teachers in kingdom of Prussia. [JS]

31.155 Helen Waddy Lepovitz. *Images of faith: expressionism, Catholic folk art, and the Industrial Revolution.* Athens: University of Georgia Press, 1991. ISBN 0-8203-1256-8. ▸ Rise and fall of Bavarian folk art of painting religious pictures on glass. Study in interrelationship of popular piety, artistic traditions, and economic change. [JS]

31.156 Catherine M. Prelinger. *Charity, challenge, and change: religious dimensions of the mid-nineteenth-century women's movement in Germany.* New York: Greenwood, 1987. ISBN 0-313-25401-X. ▸ Detailed study of women's organizations and origins of feminism centering on city of Hamburg. Emphasizes role of religious dissent. [JS]

31.157 Eda Sagarra. *Tradition and revolution: German literature and society, 1830–1890.* New York: Basic Books, 1971. ISBN 0-465-08682-9. ▸ Useful introduction to and survey of major works of literature and literary movements in Germany from late romanticism to early expressionism. [JS]

31.158 Joanne Schneider. "Enlightened reforms and Bavarian girls' education: tradition through innovation." In *German women in the nineteenth century: a social history.* John C. Fout, ed., pp. 55–71. New York: Holmes & Meier, 1984. ISBN 0-8419-0843-5 (cl) 0-8419-0844-3 (pbk). ▸ Theory and practice of girls' education in early nineteenth-century Bavaria. Concentrates on secondary schooling. [JS]

31.159 John Edward Toews. *Hegelianism: the path toward dialectical humanism, 1805–1841.* Cambridge: Cambridge University Press, 1980. ISBN 0-521-23048-9. ▸ Discussion of philosopher and his ideas, their institutional setting, development of Hegelian philosophical school, and its political ramifications. Excellent account of emotional impact of Hegel's philosophy and its political role. [JS]

31.160 R. Steven Turner. "The growth of professorial research in Prussia, 1818–1848: causes and context." *Historical studies in the physical sciences* 3 (1971) 137–82. ISSN 0073-2672, ISBN 0-8122-7646-9. ▸ Analysis of institutional, intellectual, and political trends leading toward definition of research as basic activity of Prussian university professor. Convincing if somewhat schematic argument. [JS]

SEE ALSO
  21.166 David J. Sorkin. *The transformation of German Jewry, 1780–1840.*
  22.429 Bernard M. G. Reardon. *Religion in the age of romanticism.*

Revolution of 1848–1849

31.161 Manfred Botzenhart. *Deutscher Parlamentarismus in der Revolutionszeit: 1848–1850.* Düsseldorf: Droste, 1977. ISBN 3-7700-5090-8. ▸ Analysis of parliaments, their internal workings, authority, actions, and relation to executive power and extra-parliamentary politics in German Revolution of 1848. Thorough, detailed study with broad implications. [JS]

31.162 Frank Eyck. *The Frankfurt parliament, 1848–49.* London and New York: Macmillan and St. Martin's, 1968. ISBN 0-312-30343-9. ▸ Good critical account of German National Assembly's unsuccessful effort to create unified national state during Revolution of 1848. Emphasizes obstacles to nationalism. Perhaps overly sympathetic to conservatives. [JS]

31.163 Oscar J. Hammen. *The red '48ers: Karl Marx and Friedrich Engels.* New York: Scribner's, 1969. ISBN 0-684-05708-3. ▸ Biographical treatment of two founders of modern communism as practitioners and not just theorists of Revolution in 1848. Places Marx and Engels, at times a little harshly, in contemporary context. [JS]

31.164 Dieter Langewiesche. "Republik, Monarchie, und soziale Frage: Grundprobleme der deutschen Revolution von 1848." *Historische Zeitschrift* 230.3 (1980) 529–48. ISSN 0018-2613. ▸ Delineation of basic social and political conflicts underlying German Revolution of 1848. Indispensable introduction to modern scholarship on topic. [JS]

31.165 Andrew Lees. *Revolution and reflection: intellectual change in Germany during the 1850s.* The Hague: Nijhoff, 1974. ISBN 90-247-1638-1. ▸ Intellectual ferment during quiet interlude, period in German politics after failure of Revolution of 1848. Finds extensive debates on national unity, political reform, and social question not simply supine deference to authority. Refreshing corrective to conventional wisdom. [CSA]

31.166 Donald J. Mattheisen. "History as current events: recent works on the German Revolution of 1848." *American historical review* 88.5 (1983) 1219–37. ISSN 0002-8762. ▸ Helpful English-language summary of studies, published in 1960s and 1970s, on German Revolution of 1848 with attention to present-day political implications. [JS]

31.167 Donald J. Mattheisen. "Voters and parliaments in the German Revolution of 1848: an analysis of the Prussian Constituent Assembly." *Central European history* 5.1 (1972) 3–22. ISSN 0008-9389. ▸ Quantitative study of parliamentary alignments in German 1848 Revolution. Good introduction to quantitative historical study of legislative decisions and to parliamentary politics in 1848. [JS]

31.168 P. H. Noyes. *Organization and revolution: working-class associations in the German revolutions of 1848–1849.* Princeton: Princeton University Press, 1966. ISBN 0-691-05140-2. ▸ Origins

of German labor movement in 1848 Revolution. Useful as introductory, English-language survey. [JS]

31.169 R. John Rath. *The Viennese Revolution of 1848.* 1957 ed. New York: Greenwood, 1969. ISBN 0-8371-2465-4. ▸ Careful narrative account of revolution in Vienna, relying heavily on contemporary printed materials and focusing on voices recorded in or exemplified by those tracts. Still useful survey, although now somewhat dated interpretive framework. [JWB]

31.170 Wolfram Siemann. *Die deutsche Revolution von 1848/49.* Frankfurt: Suhrkamp, 1985. ISBN 3-518-11266-X. ▸ General history of 1848 Revolution. Best introduction to topic; particularly good on political organization, collective violence, and everyday life, but not neglectful of diplomacy, parliamentarism, or nationalism. [JS]

31.171 Alan Sked. *The survival of the Habsburg empire: Radetzky, the imperial army, and the class war, 1848.* London: Longman, 1979. ISBN 0-582-50711-1. ▸ Explores role of army in revolutionary events of 1848, focusing on field marshal's defeats and victories in Italy. Powerfully argues that army mirrored Austrian civil society in experiencing political divisions that paralyzed monarchy as whole. [JWB/AS]

31.172 Jonathan Sperber. *Rhineland radicals: the democratic movement and the Revolution of 1848–1849.* Princeton: Princeton University Press, 1991. ISBN 0-691-03172-X. ▸ Preconditions of, precursors to, and course of 1848 Revolution in region of western Germany. Detailed work emphasizing importance of political exploitation of social and confessional conflict. [JS]

31.173 Stanley Zucker. "German women and the Revolution of 1848–49: Kathinka Zitz-Halein and the Humania Association." *Central European history* 13.3 (1980) 237–54. ISSN 0008-9389. ▸ Discussion of political activity of women in German 1848 Revolution, as exemplified by activities of radical and feminist Kathinka Zitz and women's group she founded in Mainz. Important contribution to history of women in revolution. [JS]

SEE ALSO
  21.160 Werner E. Mosse, Arnold Paucker, and Reinhard Rürup, eds. *Revolution and evolution.*
  22.352 Lewis B. Namier. *1848.*

GERMAN STATES AND GERMAN EMPIRE, 1850–1914

Surveys and Interpretations

31.174 David Blackbourn and Geoff Eley. *The peculiarities of German history: bourgeois society and politics in nineteenth-century Germany.* Oxford: Oxford University Press, 1984. ISBN 0-19-873058-6 (cl), 0-19-873057-8 (pbk). ▸ Most important challenge to key concepts of postwar revisionist view of German history. Seeks instead to interpret German developments on own terms and in full European perspective. [CSA]

31.175 Jack Dukes and Joachim Remak, eds. *Another Germany: a reconsideration of the imperial era.* Boulder: Westview, 1988. ISBN 0-8133-7265-8. ▸ Useful corrective to historiographical fashions of 1960s and 1970s. Emphasizes reform and democratic currents in kaisers' Germany. [CSA]

31.176 Richard J. Evans, ed. *Society and politics in Wilhelmine Germany.* New York and London: Barnes & Noble and Croom Helm, 1978. ISBN 0-06-492036-4 (cl), 0-7099-0429-0 (pbk). ▸ Original essays by British historians on heretofore neglected aspects of German society under Kaiser Wilhelm II. Sociohistorical emphasis, ranging from peasant populism, to military-industrial relations, to women. [CSA]

31.177 Jürgen Kocka. "German history before Hitler: the debate about the German *Sonderweg*." *Journal of contemporary history* 23.1 (1988) 3–16. ISSN 0022-0094. ▸ Vigorous defense of concept of Germany's special path (*Sonderweg*) against main critics. Reasserts importance of late nationhood, class conflict, weak liberalism, and continuity of bureaucratic state. [CSA]

31.178   Robert G. Moeller. "The *Kaiserreich* recast? Continuity and change in modern German historiography." *Journal of social history* 17.4 (1984) 655–84. ISSN 0022-4529. ▸ Critical appraisal of debate among historians over nature of imperial German state and society. Finds broad common ground in fascination with continuity and comparative perspectives. [CSA]

31.179   Thomas Nipperdey. *Deutsche Geschichte, 1866–1918.* Vol. 1: *Arbeitswelt und Bürgergeist.* Munich: Beck, 1990. ISBN 3-406-34453-4. ▸ Comprehensive, synthetic examination of structures and ways of life that shaped history of Germany after 1866. Magisterial last work from, arguably, postwar Germany's greatest historian. [CSA]

31.180   Thomas Nipperdey. *Deutsche Geschichte, 1866–1918.* Vol. 2: *Machtstaat vor der Demokratie.* Munich: Beck, 1992. ISBN 3-406-34801-7. ▸ Concluding volume of author's great historical synthesis (with 31.179). Emphasis on foreign and domestic politics, parties, interest groups, diplomacy, and institutional structure. Well balanced, beautifully written. [JJS]

31.181   James Retallack. "Social history with vengeance? Reactions to H.-U. Wehler's *Deutsche Kaiserreich.*" *German studies review* 7.3 (1984) 423–50. ISSN 0149-7952. ▸ Clear, even-handed analysis of controversy provoked by Wehler's *German Empire* (31.185). [CSA]

31.182   James J. Sheehan, ed. *Imperial Germany.* New York: New Viewpoints, 1976. ISBN 0-531-05374-1 (cl), 0-531-05581-7 (pbk). ▸ Articles on social and economic developments, elites, and foreign policy in imperial Germany with representation of revisionist emphasis on primacy of domestic politics. Includes such important milestones as Wehler's account of Bismarck's imperialism. [CSA]

31.183   Michael Stürmer. *Das ruhelose Reich: Deutschland, 1866–1918.* Berlin: Severin & Siedler, 1983. ISBN 3-88680-051-2. ▸ Structural and narrative account of Germany. Development of highly industrialized world power with emphasis on instability in internal affairs and foreign relations—restless empire of title. Stimulating, controversial synthesis. [CSA]

31.184   Michael Stürmer, ed. *Das kaiserliche Deutschland: Politik und Gesellschaft, 1870–1918.* 1970 ed. Düsseldorf: Droste, 1984. ISBN 3-7700-0905-3. ▸ Wide-ranging articles by leading German historians on politics and society of Bismarck's Germany. Attention to immediate legacy and long-term consequences. Represents most distinguished practitioners of structural-societal approach to politics, as well as their more conservative colleagues. [CSA]

31.185   Hans-Ulrich Wehler. *The German empire, 1871–1918.* 1985 ed. Kim Traynor, trans. Leamington Spa: Berg, 1989. ISBN 0-907582-22-2 (cl), 0-907582-32-X (pbk). ▸ Critical revisionist view of Bismarckian empire and Hohenzollern monarchy against background of social and economic power structures. Emphasis on ruling system and strategies of control. For analysis of controversy it provoked, see Retallack 31.181. [CSA]

Chancellor Otto von Bismarck and the Formation of Empire

31.186   Eugene N. Anderson. *The social and political conflict in Prussia, 1858–1864.* 1954 ed. New York: Octagon Books, 1968. ▸ Discussion of basic political configurations in Prussia on eve of German unification. Important though dated account of liberals and conservatives in constitutional conflicts of Prussian New Era. [CSA]

31.187   Helmut Böhme. *Deutschlands Weg zur Großmacht: Stu-*

dien zum Verhältnis von Wirtschaft und Staat während der Reichsgründungszeit, 1848–1881. 1966 ed. Cologne: Kiepenheuer & Witsch, 1974. ISBN 3-462-00874-9. ▸ Classic account of German chancellor's unification of Germany from perspective of economic and commercial policy. Austrian exclusion from German empire seen largely as matter of calculated Prussian economic moves. Argument can be found in English in Böhme, ed. 31.188. [CSA]

31.188   Helmut Böhme, ed. *The foundation of German empire: select documents.* Agatha Ramm, trans. London: Oxford University Press, 1971. ISBN 0-19-873012-8. ▸ Summarizes and illustrates arguments of Böhme (31.187). [JJS]

31.189   William Carr. *The origins of the wars of German unification.* London: Longman, 1991. ISBN 0-582-49147-9 (cased), 0-582-49148-7 (pbk). ▸ Origins and impact of three major wars fought by Prussia in creating German empire of 1871. Accounts for ideological and domestic political factors. Best account in English. [CSA]

31.190   Gordon A. Craig. *The battle of Königgrätz: Prussia's victory over Austria, 1866.* 1964 ed. Westport, Conn.: Greenwood, 1975. ISBN 0-8371-8563-7. ▸ Classic account of battle that decided future shape of unified Germany. Emphasis on political aspects with good explanation of technological and military significance. [CSA]

31.191   Ernst Engelberg. *Bismarck: das Reich in der Mitte Europas.* Berlin: Siedler, 1990. ISBN 3-88680-385-6. ▸ Continuation of author's biography of German chancellor (31.192). Takes story to his fall from power with interpretation of Bismarck as historical opponent of rising forces of socialism. [CSA]

31.192   Ernst Engelberg. *Bismarck: Urpreusse und Reichsgründer.* Berlin: Siedler, 1985. ISBN 3-88680-121-7. ▸ Major biography of German chancellor by East German historian. Effort to cast new light on origins and milieu, but largely argument about Bismarck as agent of bourgeois revolution from above. [CSA]

31.193   Heinrich Friedjung. *The struggle for supremacy in Germany, 1859–1866.* 1935 ed. A.J.P. Taylor and W. L. McElwee, trans. New York: Russell & Russell, 1966. ▸ English-language abridgement of account first published in 1897 by one of Austria's most intelligent and passionate German-liberal historians. Critical perspective on Austrian policy makers of 1850s and 1860s bespoke author's frustrations with Austrian politics in his own time, as well as with results of 1866. [JWB]

31.194   Lothar Gall. *Bismarck, the white revolutionary.* Vol. 1: *1815–1871.* J. A. Underwood, trans. Boston: Allen & Unwin, 1986. ISBN 0-04-943040-8 (v. 1). ▸ Major postwar biography (with 31.195) of German chancellor with emphasis on radical character of his transformation of German state. Neo-Hegelian portrait of man not quite transcending limitations of his times. [CSA]

31.195   Lothar Gall. *Bismarck, the white revolutionary.* Vol. 2: *1871–1898.* J. A. Underwood, trans. Boston: Allen & Unwin, 1986. ISBN 0-04-943053-X (v. 2). ▸ Concluding volume of Bismarck biography (with 31.194), covering his postunification years relatively briefly. Depicts Bismarck as accelerating historical process despite his conservative convictions. [CSA]

31.196   Theodore S. Hamerow. *The social foundations of German unification, 1858–1871.* Vol. 1: *Ideas and institutions.* Princeton: Princeton University Press, 1969. ISBN 0-691-05174-7 (set). ▸ Broad-based study of social, ideological, and political-institutional forces at work in Germany in decades surrounding formal unification. Emphasis on growth of industrial capitalism and its bourgeoisie as context for new nationalism. Especially useful for translations from contemporary sources. [CSA]

31.197   Theodore S. Hamerow. *The social foundations of German unification, 1858–1871.* Vol. 2: *Struggles and accomplishments.*

Princeton: Princeton University Press, 1972. ISBN 0-691-05174-7 (set). ▸ Chronological unfolding of German unification against broad social, ideological, and institutional background. Sees unification as triumph of nationalism. [CSA]

31.198 Nicholas M. Hope. *The alternative to German unification: the anti-Prussian party, Frankfurt, Nassau, and the two Hessen, 1859–1867*. Wiesbaden: Steiner, 1973. (Veröffentlichungen des Instituts für Europäische Geschichte, Mainz, 65.) ISBN 3-515-01036-X. ▸ Analysis of opposition to Prussian-led small Germany in some smaller German states. Emphasizes extent of disagreement among Germans on eventual size and nature of unified Germany. Valuable corrective to Prussocentric view. [CSA]

31.199 Otto Pflanze. *Bismarck and the development of Germany*. Vol. 1: *The period of unification, 1815–1871*. 2d ed. Princeton: Princeton University Press, 1990. ISBN 0-691-05587-4. ▸ Magisterial study of unification as revolutionizing of German state and society with Bismarck as latest and last in long series of conservatives who transformed state in order to maintain its authority. [CSA]

31.200 Otto Pflanze. *Bismarck and the development of Germany*. Vol. 2: *The period of consolidation, 1871–1880*. 2d ed. Princeton: Princeton University Press, 1990. ISBN 0-691-05588-2. ▸ Study of Bismarck's domination of German political life in decade of liberal influence on national agenda, especially in struggle against German Catholicism. [CSA]

31.201 Otto Pflanze. *Bismarck and the development of Germany*. Vol. 3: *The period of fortification, 1880–1898*. 2d ed. Princeton: Princeton University Press, 1990. ISBN 0-691-05589-0. ▸ Study of Bismarck's increasing turn toward counterrevolution and conservatism in last years of his rule. Sees Bismarckian era as dead end for Germany that exhausted possibilities of democratization from above. [CSA]

31.202 Hans A. Schmitt. "From sovereign states to Prussian provinces: Hanover and Hesse-Nassau, 1866–1871." *Journal of modern history* 57.1 (1985) 24–56. ISSN 0022-2801. ▸ Discussion of annexations in 1866 of Nassau, Hanover, and Hesse-Cassel to Prussia as prelude to German unification. Vigorously argues Prussian policy marked by flexibility and pragmatic toleration of provincial diversity. [CSA]

31.203 Franz Schnabel. "The Bismarck problem." In *German history: some new German views*. Hans Kohn, ed. Herbert H. Rowen, trans., pp. 65–93. Boston: Beacon, 1954. ▸ Influential postwar look at problem posed by Bismarck, that is, question of responsibility for subsequent German development and disaster. Finds him limited by contradictions of his age and without moral purpose. [CSA]

31.204 Dennis E. Showalter. *Railroads and rifles: soldiers, technology, and the unification of Germany*. 1975 ed. Hamden, Conn.: Shoe String, 1986. ISBN 0-208-02137-X (pbk). ▸ Study of how Prussian army met technological challenge of Industrial Revolution and thereby became military instrument strong enough to unite Germany by force. Important study of technology and strategy. [CSA]

Political Parties and Organizations

31.205 David Blackbourn. *Class, religion, and local politics in Wilhelmine Germany: the Center party in Württemberg before 1914*. New Haven: Yale University Press, 1980. ISBN 0-300-02464-9. ▸ Analysis of political significance of Center party within local and national context. Emphasizes volatile nature of imperial German politics. Important as examination of regional diversity. [CSA]

31.206 Roger Chickering. *Imperial Germany and a world without war: the peace movement and German society, 1892–1914*. Princeton: Princeton University Press, 1975. ISBN 0-691-05228-X (cl), 0-691-10036-5 (pbk). ▸ Study of German pacifism in political and social context, its members and its groups. Reveals crucial connection between German internal politics and differing views on international relations. [CSA]

31.207 Roger Chickering. *We men who feel most German: a cultural study of the Pan-German League, 1886–1914*. Boston: Allen & Unwin, 1984. ISBN 0-04-943030-0. ▸ Analysis of attitudes and influence of Pan-German League, most radical of patriotic pressure groups in imperial Germany. Important attempt to illuminate mental world of Protestant nationalism. [CSA]

31.208 Geoff Eley. *Reshaping the German Right: radical nationalism and political change after Bismarck*. 1980 ed. Ann Arbor: University of Michigan Press, 1991. ISBN 0-472-08132-2. ▸ Discussion of new pressure groups of 1890s as arena for nationalist activists of new variety. Covers, among other issues, their conflicts with establishment over colonial policy and naval expansion to uncover character of popular politics and German state. Controversial, argumentative, and stimulating. [CSA]

31.209 Ellen Lovell Evans. *The German Center party, 1870–1933: a study in political Catholicism*. Carbondale: Southern Illinois University Press, 1981. ISBN 0-8093-0997-1. ▸ Survey of entire history of Catholic Center party to delineate Catholic influence on policies and actions. Emphasizes issues party confronted more than institutional developments. [CSA]

31.210 Richard S. Levy. *The downfall of the antisemitic political parties in imperial Germany*. New Haven: Yale University Press, 1975. ISBN 0-300-01803-7. ▸ Questions assumption of direct continuity between late nineteenth-century antisemitism and nazism. Points to complete failure, disgrace, and collapse of antisemitic parties in imperial Germany; history overshadowed by subsequent events. [CSA]

31.211 Vernon L. Lidtke. *The alternative culture: socialist labor in imperial Germany*. New York: Oxford University Press, 1985. ISBN 0-19-503507-0. ▸ Richly textured account of what it meant to be Social Democrat in imperial Germany. Emphasis on distinctive communities of song, sport, and education that flourished alongside but rarely intersected with bourgeois counterparts. [CSA]

31.212 Vernon L. Lidtke. *The outlawed party: social democracy in Germany, 1878–1890*. Princeton: Princeton University Press, 1966. ISBN 0-691-05141-0. ▸ Thorough account of German Social Democratic party during period of its semi-suppression under Bismarck's Socialist Law. Emphasis on achievement of holding party together under adversity. Also available from Ann Arbor: University Microfilms International. [CSA]

31.213 Shlomo Na'aman. *Der deutsche Nationalverein: die politische Konstituierung des deutschen Bürgertums, 1859–1867*. Düsseldorf: Droste, 1987. ISBN 3-7700-5139-4. ▸ Exhaustive account of workings and program of German National Association in decade before unification. Finds origins of late nineteenth-century political alignments and key to elusive politics of German middle class. [CSA]

31.214 Mary Nolan. *Social democracy and society: working-class radicalism in Düsseldorf, 1890–1920*. Cambridge: Cambridge University Press, 1981. ISBN 0-521-23473-5. ▸ Account of work, culture, and community among Düsseldorf workers. Considers how their political radicalism was genuine reflection of mobilized class consciousness. Important case study. [CSA]

31.215 Jean H. Quataert. *Reluctant feminists in German social democracy, 1885–1917*. Princeton: Princeton University Press, 1979. ISBN 0-691-05276-X. ▸ Charts convergence of socialism and feminism in German labor movement around turn of century with attention to competing identities and loyalties of class and sex. [CSA]

31.216 James Retallack. *Notables of the Right: the Conservative party and political mobilization in Germany, 1876–1918.* Boston: Unwin Hyman, 1988. ISBN 0-04-900038-1. ▸ Political history of German conservatism, institutional development, ideological foundation, and legislative record. Focus on unresolved tensions between political exclusivity and mass inclusion. Best English-language account. [CSA]

31.217 Ronald J. Ross. *Beleaguered tower: the dilemma of political Catholicism in Wilhelmine Germany.* Notre Dame, Ind.: University of Notre Dame Press, 1976. ISBN 0-268-00547-8. ▸ Account of Catholic Center party emphasizing isolation in German society as whole and resulting internal strife over secularity or religiosity of party. [CSA]

31.218 Carl E. Schorske. *German social democracy, 1905–1917: the development of the great schism.* 1955 ed. Cambridge, Mass.: Harvard University Press, 1983. ISBN 0-674-35125-8 (pbk). ▸ Powerfully argued analysis of German Social Democratic party in years of electoral success and internal tension following rejection of revisionism. Explains origins of fateful divide between revolutionary communism and social democracy. [CSA]

31.219 James J. Sheehan. "Liberalism and the city in nineteenth-century Germany." *Past and present* 51 (1971) 116–37. ISSN 0031-2746. ▸ General problem of liberalism's decline in latter half of nineteenth century illuminated by role of Liberals in urban government. City councils as refuge of Liberals' elitist nonpolitical politics against hurly-burly of democracy. [CSA]

31.220 Dan S. White. *The splintered party: national liberalism in Hessen and the Reich, 1867–1918.* Cambridge, Mass.: Harvard University Press, 1976. ISBN 0-674-83320-1. ▸ Explores tensions within regionally based party struggling to express national program and elite party struggling with dilemmas of representation. Sees weakness of German liberalism in discord of National Liberal party. Pioneering study of regional politics. [CSA]

31.221 George G. Windell. *The Catholics and German unity, 1866–1871.* Minneapolis: University of Minnesota Press, 1954. ▸ Discussion of role of Catholicism in politics of unification between defeat of Catholic Austria in 1866 and foundation of Bismarck's dominantly Protestant empire in 1871. Disputes notion of Catholic apathy and emphasizes smaller German states. Useful study of neglected topic. [CSA]

31.222 Heinrich August Winkler. *Preussischer Liberalismus und deutscher Nationalstaat: Studien zur Geschichte der deutschen Fortschrittspartei, 1861–1866.* Tübingen: Mohr, 1964. ▸ Standard discussion of politics of liberalism and nationalism, as embodied in German Progressive party in years of Prussian constitutional conflict. Analyzes tensions and affinities between desire for national unity and drive toward bourgeois emancipation. [CSA]

Political Issues and Personalities

31.223 Margaret Lavinia Anderson. *Windthorst: a political biography.* Oxford: Clarendon, 1981. ISBN 0-19-822578-4. ▸ Public career of Chancellor Bismarck's main foe, leader of Catholic Center party. Important study of German parliamentarianism in its heroic age with Windthorst's political Catholicism as Germany's version of Gladstone's Liberal party. [CSA]

31.224 Margaret Lavinia Anderson and Kenneth D. Barkin. "The myth of the Puttkamer purge and the reality of the *Kulturkampf*: some reflections on the historiography of imperial Germany." *Journal of modern history* 54.4 (1982) 647–86. ISSN 0022-2801. ▸ Questions unresearched assumption of major shift to Right in German politics in 1878. Finds, instead, broadening and even liberalizing of public opinion that Bismarck was quick to contain. Powerful challenge to important source of Bielefeld school (see Iggers, ed. 31.56). [CSA]

31.225 Lamar Cecil. *Albert Ballin: business and politics in imperial Germany, 1888–1918.* Princeton: Princeton University Press, 1967. ▸ Biography of managing director of Hamburg-American Line, world's largest shipping line. Sheds light on wealthy bourgeoisie of Wilhelmine Germany and its general lack of support for political reform. [CSA]

31.226 Lamar Cecil. *Wilhelm II: prince and emperor, 1859–1900.* 1 vol. to date. Chapel Hill: University of North Carolina Press, 1989–. ISBN 0-8078-1828-3 (v. 1). ▸ First of proposed two-volume biography of self-centered, isolated, and exceedingly foolish man and last German kaiser. Effort to explain nature of his influence while acknowledging his almost complete separation from other Germans. [CSA]

31.227 Geoff Eley. "Defining social imperialism: use and abuse of an idea." *Social history* 1.3 (1976) 265–90. ISSN 0307-1022. ▸ Sustained attack on concept shaping much recent interpretation of imperial Germany. Argues for political importance of grass-roots mobilization through right-wing pressure groups. [CSA]

31.228 Isabel V. Hull. *The entourage of Kaiser Wilhelm II, 1888–1918.* Cambridge: Cambridge University Press, 1982. ISBN 0-521-23665-7. ▸ Well-written, carefully researched account of how last kaiser ruled, through and with whom. Personal and structural analysis of civilian and, later, military advisers, caste mentality, and support for semi-autocratic rule of monarch. [CSA]

31.229 Konrad H. Jarausch. *The enigmatic chancellor: Bethmann Hollweg and the hubris of imperial Germany.* New Haven: Yale University Press, 1973. ISBN 0-300-01295-0. ▸ Political biography of last chancellor of imperial Germany. Emphasis on riddle of his personality, as well as mirages, illusions, shadows, and enigmas that marked final years of Wilhelmine empire. [CSA]

31.230 Michael John. *Politics and the law in late nineteenth-century Germany: the origins of the Civil Code.* Oxford: Clarendon, 1989. ISBN 0-19-822748-5. ▸ View of Germany's great work of legal unification, Civil Code of 1899, from perspective of century of legal and political developments. Attention to evolution of attitudes toward law, nation, and society. Pioneering study of important subject. [CSA]

31.231 Katharine Anne Lerman. *The chancellor as courtier: Bernhard von Bülow and the governance of Germany, 1900–1909.* Cambridge: Cambridge University Press, 1990. ISBN 0-521-38155-X. ▸ New look at critical period in history of imperial Germany. Emphasizes Bülow's dependence on his special relationship to emperor and ultimately unsuccessful efforts to develop coherent foreign and domestic policy. Somewhat limited but highly useful study. [JJS]

31.232 Klaus Erich Pollmann. *Parlamentarismus im Norddeutschen Bund, 1867–1870.* Düsseldorf: Droste, 1985. ISBN 3-7700-5130-0. ▸ Study of impressive constitutional and legislative achievements of North German Confederation in years immediately preceding German unification. Discussion of debates and decisions that decisively shaped future German law and political practice. [CSA]

31.233 John C. G. Röhl. *Germany without Bismarck: the crisis of government in the Second Reich, 1890–1900.* Berkeley: University of California Press, 1967. ▸ Survey of decade of confusion and disunity that followed Bismarck's fall from power. Charts growth of kaiser's power, which in turn made possible disastrous and irresponsible policies leading to world war. [CSA]

31.234 David Schoenbaum. *Zabern 1913: consensus politics in imperial Germany.* London: Allen & Unwin, 1982. ISBN 0-04-943025-4. ▸ Detailed reconstruction of Zabern affair (military's arrest of civilians) in Alsace and of its complex aftermath. Illuminates military-political relations in imperial Germany through single incident and intense outcry it provoked. [CSA]

31.235 Fritz Stern. *Gold and iron: Bismarck, Bleichröder, and the building of the German empire.* 1977 ed. New York: Random House, 1979. ISBN 0-394-49545-4 (cl, 1977), 0-394-74034-3 (pbk). ‣ Richly textured, broad-ranging life and times of Chancellor Bismarck's banker and collaborator. Window into terrible ambiguity of Jewish wealth and success in imperial Germany. Also available, Ann Arbor: University Microfilms International. [CSA]

31.236 Stanley Suval. *Electoral politics in Wilhelmine Germany.* Chapel Hill: University of North Carolina Press, 1985. ISBN 0-8078-1631-0. ‣ Important, innovative analysis of workings of German electoral system between Bismarck and World War I. Argues, against conventional wisdom, for vitality and viability of electoral politics; sees voting as expression of fundamental social relationships. [CSA]

Society and Economics

31.237 Kenneth D. Barkin. *The controversy over German industrialization, 1890–1902.* Chicago: University of Chicago Press, 1970. ISBN 0-226-03712-6. ‣ Useful analysis of late-century debates over consequences of German industrialization on society and community. Characterized by comparisons between stable, beneficent social order of agriculture and cutthroat, crisis-ridden world of industrialization. [CSA]

31.238 David Blackbourn. "The *Mittelstand* in German society and politics, 1871–1914." *Social history* 2.4 (1977) 409–34. ISSN 0307-1022. ‣ Examination of idea that lower middle class was preyed upon by extreme Right. Seen instead as group with little cohesion and little in common, but nevertheless active agent in imperial German politics. [CSA]

31.239 Nicholas Bullock and James Read. *The movement for housing reform in Germany and France, 1840–1914.* Cambridge: Cambridge University Press, 1985. ISBN 0-521-22537-X. ‣ Study of ideas and accomplishments of housing reform movement in Germany and France, covering wide range of issues and national differences. Attention to interplay of ideal and possible in housing legislation. Important introduction to subject. [CSA]

31.240 David F. Crew. *Town in the Ruhr: a social history of Bochum, 1860–1914.* New York: Columbia University Press, 1979. ISBN 0-231-04300-7 (cl), 0-231-04301-5 (pbk). ‣ Pioneering social history of industrial city in its years of transformation. Examines such characteristics as migration patterns, class relations, militance, and occupational mobility. [CSA]

31.241 Geoff Eley. "Labor history, social history, *Alltagsgeschichte*: experience, culture, and the politics of the everyday—a new direction for German social history?" *Journal of modern history* 61.2 (1989) 297–343. ISSN 0022-2801. ‣ Overview of enormous amount of recent literature on everyday life, particularly among working classes, in contemporary political and intellectual context. [CSA]

31.242 Richard J. Evans. *Death in Hamburg: society and politics in the cholera years, 1830–1910.* 1987 ed. Harmondsworth: Penguin, 1990. ISBN 0-14-012473-X (pbk). ‣ Wide-ranging, important history of cholera and public health policy in nineteenth-century Hamburg as window on German political and social history. Highlights deep class divisions that allegedly shaped city's inept response to epidemic of 1892. [CSA]

31.243 Richard J. Evans, ed. *The German working class, 1888–1933: the politics of everyday life.* London and Totowa, N.J.: Croom Helm and Barnes & Noble, 1982. ISBN 0-7099-0431-2, 0-389-20118-9. ‣ Leaves aside socialist politics and ideology and respectable working class in favor of pilferage, drink, industrial sabotage, prostitution, illegitimacy, and other aspects of rougher side of working-class life. Useful introduction to new research. [CSA]

31.244 Barbara Franzoi. *At the very least she pays the rent: women and German industrialization, 1871–1914.* Westport, Conn.: Greenwood, 1985. ISBN 0-313-24487-1. ‣ Pioneering examination of impact of industrialization on working women. Attention to women's work choices, how they made them, and how this affected private and public lives. [CSA]

31.245 Robert Gellately. *The politics of economic despair: shopkeepers and German politics, 1890–1914.* London: Sage, 1974. ISBN 0-8039-9917-8. ‣ Discussion of economic position of retailers at close of nineteenth century and frustrations leading to political mobilization and demands for state help. Argues against view they were manipulated from above and writes implicitly to explain later turn to nazism. Best English-language study of these groups. [CSA]

31.246 Marion A. Kaplan. "Tradition and transition: the acculturation, assimilation, and integration of Jews in imperial Germany—a gender analysis." *Yearbook (Leo Baeck Institute)* 27 (1982) 3–36. ISSN 0075-8744. ‣ Pressures for and against assimilation within Jewish community with particular attention to role of women, either as agents of assimilation or as preservers of culture. Significant contribution to Jewish and women's history. [CSA]

31.247 John E. Knodel. *The decline of fertility in Germany, 1871–1939.* Princeton: Princeton University Press, 1974. ISBN 0-691-09359-8. ‣ Study of demographic transition and modernization in Germany with particular attention to declining fertility rates. Examines all provinces and voluminous demographic data, as well as wide range of possible explanations. [CSA]

31.248 Jürgen Kocka. *Unternehmer in der deutschen Industrialisierung.* Göttingen: Vandenhoeck & Ruprecht, 1975. ISBN 3-525-33381-1. ‣ Profile of men and developing organizational forms that led German industrialization, particularly in latter part of nineteenth century. Attention to various types of businessmen, from salesmen to engineers to financiers. Summarizes some of author's pathbreaking research. [CSA]

31.249 Brian Ladd. *Urban planning and civic order in Germany, 1860–1914.* Cambridge, Mass.: Harvard University Press, 1990. ISBN 0-674-93115-7. ‣ Examines pioneering work of city planners, who sought to impose order on increasingly chaotic urban spaces of nineteenth-century Germany. Attention to political and social circumstances that shaped work and academic discipline of city planning. Important contribution to urban history. [CSA]

31.250 Alf Lüdtke. "Cash, coffee breaks, horseplay: *Eigensinn* and politics among factory workers in Germany c. 1900." In *Confrontation, class consciousness, and the labor process: studies in proletarian class formation.* Michael Hanagan and Charles Stephenson, eds., pp. 65–95. Westport, Conn.: Greenwood, 1986. ISBN 0-313-25140-1. ‣ Discovers true politics of working-class life in give and take of life on and off shop floor. Example of everyday-life approach to social history (Eley 31.241). [CSA]

31.251 Alf Lüdtke. "Organizational order or *Eigensinn?* Workers' privacy and workers' politics in imperial Germany." In *Rites of power: symbolism, ritual, and politics since the Middle Ages.* Sean Wilentz, ed., pp. 303–33. Philadelphia: University of Pennsylvania Press, 1985. ISBN 0-8122-7948-4. ‣ Examination of everyday experience of working lives to find real arena of working-class politics. Concept of *Eigensinn* (willfulness) used to identify actions that reflect authentic self-consciousness of workers. [CSA]

31.252 Charles E. McClelland. *The German experience of professionalization: modern learned professions and their organizations from the early nineteenth century to the Hitler era.* Cambridge: Cambridge University Press, 1991. ISBN 0-521-39457-0. ‣ Analysis of development of modern learned professions (medicine, law, teaching, engineering), especially in close relationship to state power. Shows how they eventually achieved degree of autonomy from state, along with own professional standards. [CSA]

31.253 J. A. Perkins. "The agricultural revolution in Germany, 1850–1914." *Journal of European economic history* 10.1 (1981) 71–118. ISSN 0391-5115. ‣ Study of agricultural development in Germany, especially intensification of production and increasing labor efficiency. Departs from single-minded attention to agricultural policies in explaining social and political decline of Prussian Junkerdom. [CSA]

31.254 Hans-Jürgen Puhle. "Lords and peasants in the *Kaiserreich*." In *Peasants and lords in modern Germany: recent studies in agricultural history*. Robert G. Moeller, ed., pp. 81–109. Boston: Allen & Unwin, 1986. ISBN 0-04-943037-8. ‣ Agrarian social conditions and politics as key to German developments from 1871 to 1914. Makes accessible in English some of themes from his classic work in German on agrarian interests and Prussian conservatism. [CSA]

31.255 Klaus Tenfelde. *Die Sozialgeschichte der Bergarbeiterschaft an der Ruhr im neunzehnten Jahrhundert*. 2d ed. Bonn: Verlag Neue Gesellschaft, 1981. ISBN 3-87831-344-6. ‣ Thorough social history of workers in mining industry from early days through mature industry and fully formed working class. [CSA]

31.256 Shulamit Volkov. *The rise of popular antimodernism in Germany: the urban master artisans, 1873–1896*. Princeton: Princeton University Press, 1978. ISBN 0-691-05264-6. ‣ Plots increasingly strident discontents of segment of Germany's lower middle classes. Controversial effort to give substance to thesis of late century great depression and subsequent rise of proto-fascist political sentiments. [CSA]

SEE ALSO
   21.167 Uriel Tal. *Christians and Jews in Germany*.
   21.168 Jack Wertheimer. *Unwelcome strangers*.

Culture

31.257 James C. Albisetti. *Secondary school reform in imperial Germany*. Princeton: Princeton University Press, 1983. ISBN 0-691-05373-1. ‣ Educational history as window on cultural and political values. Culture and institution of *Gymnasium* and of late century efforts at reform to meet changing demands of German society. Best English-language study. [CSA]

31.258 David Cahan. *An institute for an empire: the Physikalisch-Technische Reichsanstalt, 1871–1918*. Cambridge: Cambridge University Press, 1988. ISBN 0-521-33057-2. ‣ Important study of Physikalisch-Technische Reichsanstalt, leading scientific institution in imperial Germany. Emphasis on links between scientific innovation, technology, state, and industry. [CSA]

31.259 Andreas Dorpalen. *Heinrich von Treitschke*. 1957 ed. Port Washington, N.Y.: Kennikat, 1973. ISBN 0-8046-1693-0. ‣ Full-length biography (1834–96) of one of most influential teachers and publicists of Bismarckian Germany, as well as premier spokesman of Prusso-German nationalist position. [CSA]

31.260 Frederick Gregory. *Scientific materialism in nineteenth-century Germany*. Dordrecht: Reidel, 1977. ISBN 90-277-0760-X (cl), 90-277-0763-4 (pbk). ‣ Comprehensive account of German materialism in second half of nineteenth century and its immense influence on public opinion. Treats key figures (Vogt, Moleschott, Büchner, Czolbe), their ideas and claims to scientific validity, their revolt against idealism. [CSA]

31.261 Konrad H. Jarausch. *Students, society, and politics in imperial Germany: the rise of academic illiberalism*. Princeton: Princeton University Press, 1982. ISBN 0-691-05345-6 (cl), 0-691-10131-0 (pbk). ‣ Useful analysis of social structure of German university and mentality of its students during imperial period. Finds high

professional standards accompanied by erosion of liberal education, combination with ultimately tragic consequences. [CSA]

31.262 Alfred Kelly. *The descent of Darwin: the popularization of Darwinism in Germany, 1860–1914*. Chapel Hill: University of North Carolina Press, 1981. ISBN 0-8078-1460-1. ‣ Social history of Darwinian ideas in late nineteenth-century Germany. Finds German Darwinists mostly on Left and argues popular Darwinism reinforced moderate strains within German socialism. Best account in English. [CSA]

31.263 David B. King et al. *Essays on culture and society in modern Germany*. Gary D. Stark and Bede Karl Lackner, eds. Leonard Krieger, Introduction. College Station: Texas A&M University Press for University of Texas at Arlington, 1982. ISBN 0-89096-137-9. ‣ Examination of interactions between cultural values and social institutions in modern Germany with attention to divergence from Western Europe, cultural elites, cultural criticism, social realism, film, and music. [CSA]

31.264 Marjorie Lamberti. *State, society, and the elementary school in imperial Germany*. New York: Oxford University Press, 1989. ISBN 0-19-505611-6. ‣ Study of politics of school reform in Germany from 1870 to enactment of important reform in 1906. Depicts continuing hold of confessional and local loyalties on German minds and reluctance of state to pursue policy of secularization. Particularly good on religious issues. [CSA]

31.265 Walter Laqueur. *Young Germany: a history of the German youth movement*. 1962 ed. R.H.S. Crossman, Introduction. New Brunswick, N.J.: Transaction, 1984. ISBN 0-88738-002-6 (cl), 0-87855-960-4 (pbk). ‣ Study of early twentieth-century youth movement as microcosm of modern Germany. Explains romantic ideas, mass organization, and broad influence on generation of future leaders. [CSA]

31.266 Andrew Lees. "Debates about the big city in Germany, 1890–1914." *Societas: a review of social history* 5.1 (1975) 1–29. ISSN 0037-8879. ‣ Focus on range of opinions in Germany about cities at time of tremendous urban growth. Balances usual emphasis on antiurban antimodernism with attention to long-standing role of cities and urbanism in German life. [CSA]

31.267 Charles E. McClelland. *The German historians and England: a study in nineteenth-century views*. Cambridge: Cambridge University Press, 1971. ISBN 0-521-08063-0. ‣ Thorough examination of attitudes toward and about England among succeeding generations of nineteenth-century German historians. Image of country used to chart changing political culture, in particular rising antiliberalism. [CSA]

31.268 Wolfgang J. Mommsen. *Max Weber and German politics, 1890–1920*. Michael S. Steinberg, trans. Chicago: University of Chicago Press, 1984. ISBN 0-226-53397-2. ‣ Challenging, critical account of sociologist's political ideas and activities. Focus on his ambivalent attitudes toward democracy, his nationalism, and his elitism. [CSA]

31.269 George L. Mosse. *The crisis of German ideology: intellectual origins of the Third Reich*. 1964 ed. New York: Schocken, 1981. ISBN 0-8052-0669-8. ‣ Shows how ideas of national socialism were deeply embedded in German history. Attention to late nineteenth-century racial thought, Germanic Christianity, mysticism, and other antiliberal ideas in their institutional and cultural setting. Challenging, controversial attempt to fuse social and intellectual history. [CSA]

31.270 Fritz K. Ringer. *The decline of the German mandarins: the German academic community, 1890–1933*. 1969 ed. Hanover, N.H.: University Press of New England, 1990. ISBN 0-8195-6235-1. ‣ Classic account of influential elite in crisis. Charts deepening cultural pessimism of German professoriate, against background of institutional development, traditions, stature, influence, and ideas of culture, rationality, and politics. [CSA]

31.271 Peter D. Stachura. *The German youth movement, 1900–1945: an interpretative and documentary history.* New York: St. Martin's, 1981. ISBN 0-312-32624-6. ▸ Study of youth organizations from *Wandervogel* to Hitler Youth. Attention to lines of continuity and signs of generational stress. Includes useful documentary evidence. [CSA]

31.272 Gary D. Stark. *Entrepreneurs of ideology: neoconservative publishers in Germany, 1890–1933.* Chapel Hill: University of North Carolina Press, 1981. ISBN 0-8078-1452-0. ▸ Sociological and intellectual history of important institutions—leading conservative publishing houses—in dissemination of antimodernist, racist, and nationalist ideas in late nineteenth- and early twentieth-century Germany. [CSA]

31.273 Fritz Stern. *The politics of cultural despair: a study in the rise of the Germanic ideology.* 1961 ed. Berkeley: University of California Press, 1974. ISBN 0-520-02626-8 (cl), 0-520-02643-8 (pbk). ▸ Thought of Paul de Lagarde, Julius Langbehn, and Moeller van der Bruck as measure of German intellectual descent into nihilism and pathological cultural criticism. Prophets of nazism's false utopia of national rebirth. Classic study of antimodernism. [CSA]

HABSBURG MONARCHY, 1850–1914

Reference Works and General Studies

31.274 Gustav Kolmer. *Parlament und Verfassung in Österreich.* 1902–14 ed. 8 vols. Graz: Akademische Druck- und Verlagsanstalt, 1972. ISBN 3-201-00787-0 (set). ▸ Massive multivolume history of parliamentary politics in Austria, 1861–1904, by Austro-German liberal journalist. Extremely detailed, containing wealth of information presented with eager and sometimes unreflective partisanship. [JWB]

31.275 Arthur J. May. *The Hapsburg monarchy, 1867–1914.* Cambridge, Mass.: Harvard University Press, 1951. ▸ Older narrative, broadly sympathetic to empire, that retains utility. Outline of political trends and social and cultural developments in both halves of monarchy, as well as evolution of Austro-Hungarian foreign policy. Also available from Ann Arbor: University Microfilms International. [JWB]

31.276 Adam Wandruszka and Peter Urbanitsch, eds. *Die Habsburgermonarchie, 1848 bis 1918.* Vol. 1: *Die wirtschaftliche Entwicklung.* Vol. 2: *Verwaltung und Rechtswesen.* Vol. 3: *Die Völker des Reiches.* Vol. 4: *Die Konfessionen.* Vol. 5: *Die bewaffnete Macht.* Vol. 6: *Die Habsburgermonarchie im System der internationalen Beziehungen.* 6 vols. to date. Vienna: Verlag der Österreichischen Akademie der Wissenschaften, 1973–. ISBN 3-7001-0030-2 (v. 1), 3-7001-0081-7 (v. 2), 3-7001-0217-8 (v. 3), 3-7001-0658-0 (v. 4), 3-7001-1122-3 (v. 5), 3-7001-1682-9 (v. 6.1). ▸ Massive study of Austria-Hungary since 1848, organized in separate volumes on public administration and civil service; people of empire; religion and confessions; armed forces; and economy. Several volumes yet to appear. Indispensable reference work. [JWB]

31.277 Solomon Wank et al., eds. *The mirror of history: essays in honor of Fritz Fellner.* Santa Barbara, Calif.: ABC-Clio, 1988. ISBN 0-87436-468-X. ▸ Essays on various aspects of modern Austrian or Hungarian history, in honor of senior scholar who has worked to facilitate cooperation between Austrian and American historians. [JWB]

The Problem of Nationalism

31.278 Oszkár Jászi. *The dissolution of the Habsburg monarchy.* 1929 ed. Chicago: University of Chicago Press, 1961. ▸ Brilliant analysis of last decades of empire arguing long-term national par-

ticularism wrecked monarchy. Classic text, dated in many particulars, but still worth reading. [JWB]

31.279 Robert A. Kann. *The multinational empire: nationalism and national reform in the Habsburg monarchy, 1848–1918.* 1950 ed. 2 vols. New York: Octagon Books, 1964. ▸ Massive, turgidly written survey of theory and practice of nationalism, national reform, and national conflict in Austria. Combines detailed knowledge of Austrian legal and constitutional systems with interest in political and social forces that shaped and exploited those systems. Dated in particulars but fairminded, useful introduction. [JWB]

31.280 Hans Mommsen. *Die Sozialdemokratie und die Nationalitätenfrage im habsburgischen Vielvölkerstaat.* Vienna: Europa, 1963. ▸ Survey of Austrian Social Democratic party's efforts as agent of supranationalism to appeal to diverse ethnic constituents on basis of shared, working-class interest. Slow progress of political reform ultimately intensified destructive national conflicts within party itself. Still major book on prewar Austrian social democracy. [JWB]

31.281 Gerald Stourzh. *Die Gleichberechtigung der Nationalitäten in der Verfassung und Verwaltung Österreichs, 1848–1918.* 1980 ed. Vienna: Verlag der Österreichischen Akademie der Wissenschaften, 1985. ISBN 3-7001-0680-7. ▸ Thoughtful, intelligent investigation of legal and political consequences of rights granted to nationalities in Austria by December 1867 legislation. Special focus on role of high courts in guaranteeing and protecting individual and collective rights. Important work on late imperial political culture. [JWB]

SEE ALSO
33.153 Gary B. Cohen. *The politics of ethnic survival.*
33.160 Bruce M. Garver. *The Young Czech party, 1874–1901, and the emergence of a multi-party system.*

Political Movements

31.282 Roy A. Austensen. "Austria and the 'struggle for supremacy in Germany,' 1848–64." *Journal of modern history* 52 (1980) 195–225. ISSN 0022-2801. ▸ Controversial critique of previous historiographical assumptions. Argues ministers Felix Schwarzenberg, Karl Buol-Schauenstein, and Johann Rechberg continued basic features of Metternich's German policy. [JWB]

31.283 John W. Boyer. "The end of an old regime: visions of political reform in late imperial Austria." *Journal of modern history* 58 (1986) 159–93. ISSN 0022-2801. ▸ Discussion of three different strategies for political reform in Austria at beginning of twentieth century. Shows ambitions behind and ultimate failure of all three; suggests reasons for collapse of empire must be sought in decade of political crisis preceding war in 1914. [JWB]

31.284 John W. Boyer. *Political radicalism in late imperial Vienna: origins of the Christian social movement 1848 to 1897.* Chicago: University of Chicago Press, 1981. ISBN 0-226-06957-5. ▸ First of two-volume interpretation of radical bourgeois politics in Vienna, 1848–1918. Stresses continuities in political action and discourse in Vienna, while emphasizing fundamental role of Austrian social democracy as radical antagonist of all forms of middle-class politics. [JWB]

31.285 Harm-Hinrich Brandt. *Der österreichische Neoabsolutismus: Staatsfinanzen und Politik, 1848–1860.* 2 vols. Göttingen: Vandenhoeck & Ruprecht, 1978. (Schriftenreihe der Historischen Kommission bei der Bayerischen Akademie der Wissenschaften, 15.) ISBN 3-525-35910-1. ▸ Massive investigation of policies and politics of neo-absolutist regime, placing special emphasis on state finances. Particularly effective in demonstrating powerful currents for change embedded in regime, and inexorable limits and ultimate failure regime confronted. Excellent if ponderous work. [JWB]

31.286 Fritz Fellner. "Das 'Februarpatent' von 1861: Entstehung und Bedeutung." *Mitteilungen des Instituts für Österreichische Geschichtsforschung* 63 (1955) 549–64. ISSN 0073-8484. ‣ Important essay on origins of February 1861 Patent, basis for liberal-constitutionalist state in Austria, finally established in 1867. Argues Patent built and expanded on provisions contained in Diploma of October 1860, rather than repudiating that document. [JWB]

31.287 Leopold Kammerhofer, ed. *Studien zum Deutschliberalismus in Zisleithanien, 1873–1879: Herrschaftsfundierung und Organisationsformen des politischen Liberalismus.* Vienna: Verlag der Österreichischen Akademie der Wissenschaften, 1992. (Studien zur Geschichte der österreichisch-ungarischen Monarchie, 25.) ISBN 3-7001-1921-6. ‣ Collectively authored volume presenting latest scholarship on internal history of liberal regime in Austria in 1870s. Essays on party organizations and elections, state and church, civil service, oppositional movements, liberalism and economy, social question, and foreign affairs. Important synthetic work. [JWB]

31.288 Bruce F. Pauley. *From prejudice to persecution: a history of Austrian anti-Semitism.* Chapel Hill: University of North Carolina Press, 1992. ISBN 0-8078-1995-6. ‣ Explores various antisemitic ideological categories and political movements in interwar Austria. Balanced, sensible study of very controversial subject. [JWB]

31.289 Peter G. J. Pulzer. *The rise of political antisemitism in Germany and Austria.* Rev. ed. Cambridge, Mass.: Harvard University Press, 1988. ISBN 0-674-77166-4. ‣ Examination of political and social manifestations of antisemitism, 1867–1918. Sees this period of cultural despair and social conflict as seedbed for Nazi ideology and demonstration of failure of nineteenth-century liberalism. [CSA]

31.290 Josef Redlich. *Das österreichische Staats- und Reichsproblem: geschichtliche Darstellung der inneren Politik der habsburgischen Monarchie von 1848 bis zum Untergang des Reiches.* 1920–26 ed. 2 vols. Leipzig: Reinhold, 1983. ‣ Magisterial analysis of problem of imperial governance in Austria, 1848–67, with important implications for last decades of empire's history. Book's rationale and emotional hue reflect crisis of interwar period, but offers tribute to great political community that author and others had lost. Also available as photocopy from University of California Bindery. [JWB]

31.291 Andrew G. Whiteside. *The socialism of fools: Georg Ritter von Schönerer and Austrian pan-Germanism.* Berkeley: University of California Press, 1975. ISBN 0-520-02434-6. ‣ Argues Schönerer's pan-Germanism was form of rightist radicalism dedicated to extremism and total solutions. Intelligent appreciation of dangerous and historically important, but third-rate politician. [JWB]

SEE ALSO

47.360 Samuel R. Williamson, Jr. *Austria-Hungary and the origins of the First World War.*

Issues and Personalities

31.292 Jean-Paul Bled. *Franz Joseph.* Teresa Bridgeman, trans. Cambridge, Mass.: Blackwell, 1992. ISBN 0-631-16778-1. ‣ Most recent biography of monarch whose reign spanned almost seventy years and who came to symbolize state he conscientiously, if not always successfully, governed. Fairminded, up-to-date, sympathetic book. [JWB]

31.293 Fritz Fellner. "Kaiser Franz Josef und das Parlament: Materialien zur Geschichte der Innenpolitik Österreichs in den Jahren 1867–1873." *Mitteilungen des Österreichischen Staatsarchivs* 9 (1956) 287–347. ‣ Classic essay on relationship of crown to liberal regime in Austria in first decade of constitutionalism. Argues emperor sought to establish strict limits to competencies

of new parliament and gained considerable facility in managing often unruly parliamentary regime. [JWB]

31.294 Brigitte Hamann. *The reluctant empress.* Ruth Hein, trans. New York: Knopf, 1986. ISBN 0-394-53717-3. ‣ Intelligent, well-researched biography of Elisabeth of Austria. Illuminates private side of imperial house as well as privilege, power, and occasional dilettantism of Austrian high aristocracy. [JWB]

31.295 William A. Jenks. *Austria under the iron ring, 1879–1893.* Charlottesville: University Press of Virginia, 1965. ‣ Favorable, revisionist portrait of regime of Count Eduard Taaffe, emphasizing Taaffe's accomplishments in face of extreme difficulties. Best available treatment of one of most important Austrian cabinets. [JWB]

31.296 William A. Jenks. *The Austrian electoral reform of 1907.* 1950 ed. New York: Octagon Books, 1974. ISBN 0-374-94205-6. ‣ Standard survey of most important electoral reform project in monarchy's history. Still useful as introduction to subject, although author did not utilize archival sources. [JWB]

31.297 Heinrich Lutz. *Österreich-Ungarn und die Gründung des deutschen Reiches: europäische Entscheidungen, 1867–1871.* Frankfurt: Propyläen, 1979. ISBN 3-549-07392-5. ‣ Authoritative analysis of Austrian diplomatic options and initiatives manifesting quiet sympathy for Count Friedrich Beust's vision of post-German Confederation of Central Europe in which Austria would enjoy role of moral and political prominence. Especially sensitive to effect on Austria's foreign policy of dualistic structure of state governance imposed in 1867. [JWB]

SEE ALSO

33.684 Vladmir Dedijer. *The road to Sarajevo.*

Society and Economics

31.298 Harriet Anderson. *Utopian feminism: women's movements in fin-de-siècle Vienna.* New Haven: Yale University Press, 1992. ISBN 0-300-05736-9. ‣ Argues Viennese feminism was autonomous and visionary project with important and positive impact on position of women in civil society. Important contribution. [JWB]

31.299 Erna Appelt. *Von Ladenmädchen, Schreibfräulein, und Gouvernanten: die weiblichen Angestellten Wiens zwischen 1900 und 1934.* Vienna: Verlag für Gesellschaftskritik, 1985. ISBN 3-900351-41-4. ‣ Examination of history of women's employment in Vienna focusing on growth of service-sector jobs. Utilizes interesting interview data as well as more conventional sources. Valuable monograph on development of professional opportunities for women. [JWB]

31.300 Ilsa Barea. *Vienna.* 1966 ed. New York: Knopf, 1967. ‣ Narrative account of historical and cultural ethos of Hapsburg capital. Genially written, combining intelligence and insight about city with personal reflections based on author's past. [JWB]

31.301 Steven Beller. *Vienna and the Jews, 1867–1938: a cultural history.* Cambridge: Cambridge University Press, 1989. ISBN 0-521-35180-4. ‣ Argues Jews held preponderant place among Viennese cultural elites, and gave Viennese culture special intellectuality. Important contribution to understanding of cultural impact of Jews in *fin-de-siècle* Vienna. [JWB]

31.302 Evan Burr Bukey. *Hitler's hometown: Linz, Austria, 1908–1945.* Bloomington: Indiana University Press, 1986. ISBN 0-253-32833-0. ‣ Fine, careful monograph arguing tradition of interelite collaboration and collusion on political and economic matters evolved in Linz in late nineteenth and early twentieth centuries and endured into First Republic. Decisive social and economic change only came to city with German occupation of 1938. [JWB]

31.303 Scott M. Eddie. "Economic policy and economic development in Austria-Hungary, 1867–1913." In *The industrial economies: the development of economic and social policies.* Vol. 8 of *The Cambridge economic history of Europe.* Peter Mathias and Sidney Pollard, eds., pp. 814–86. Cambridge: Cambridge University Press, 1989. ISBN 0-521-22504-3. ▸ Argues considerations of nationality question were basis for Austria's redistributive policies, while Hungary pursued far more coherent strategy of economic development. [JWB]

31.304 Hubert Ch. Ehalt, Gernot Heiss, and Hannes Stekl, eds. *Glücklich ist, wer vergisst . . . ? Das andere Wien um 1900.* Vienna: Böhlau, 1986. ISBN 3-205-08857-3. ▸ Corrective to nostalgic, overly stylized accounts of artistic culture and high bourgeois and aristocratic society in turn-of-century Vienna. Contributers include important younger Austrian historians. [JWB]

31.305 William H. Hubbard. *Auf dem Weg zur Grossstadt: eine Sozialgeschichte der Stadt Graz, 1850–1914.* Eleonore Krabicka, trans. Vienna: Verlag für Geschichte und Politik, 1984. ISBN 3-7028-0230-4. ▸ Highly competent monograph examining population growth, social stratification, economic development, and local politics in German Austria's second largest city. [JWB]

31.306 Dieter Langewiesche. *Zur Freizeit des Arbeiters: Bildungsbestrebungen und Freizeitgestaltung österreichischer Arbeiter im Kaiserreich und in der ersten Republik.* Stuttgart: Klett-Cotta, 1980. ISBN 3-12-911960-4. ▸ Exploration of educational aspirations and cultural activities of Social Democratic party. Special attention to reading choices of workers, based on library loans. Argues workers much preferred belletristic works to those espousing socialist or even social scientific themes. [JWB]

31.307 Eduard März. *Austrian banking and financial policy: Creditanstalt at a turning point, 1913–1923.* Charles Kessler, trans. New York: St. Martin's, 1984. ISBN 0-312-06124-2. ▸ Simultaneously explores history of Austria's greatest bank during transition from empire to republic and economic and political contexts in which it operated. Broad, institutionally oriented history of banking and finance. [JWB]

31.308 J. Robert Wegs. *Growing up working class: continuity and change among Viennese youth, 1890–1938.* University Park: Pennsylvania State University Press, 1989. ISBN 0-271-00637-4. ▸ Combines extensive oral history interviews with printed sources to argue conventional divisions within and between working class and lower middle classes fluid and more complex than commonly appreciated. Important revisionist analysis. [JWB]

SEE ALSO
  21.162 Marsha L. Rozenblit. *The Jews of Vienna, 1867–1914.*
  21.170 Robert S. Wistrich. *The Jews of Vienna in the age of Franz Joseph.*

Culture

31.309 Hermann Broch. *Hugo von Hofmannsthal and his time: the European imagination, 1860–1920.* Michael P. Steinberg, ed. and trans. Chicago: University of Chicago Press, 1984. ISBN 0-226-07514-1 (cl), 0-226-07516-8 (pbk). ▸ Uses writer's life and thought to explore major issues in *fin-de-siècle* Austrian culture. Penetrating exploration of relationship between ethics and aesthetics; also contains subtle interpretation of late nineteenth-century European intellectual history more generally. [JWB]

31.310 Allan Janik and Stephen Toulmin. *Wittgenstein's Vienna.* 1973 ed. New York: Simon & Schuster, 1974. ISBN 0-671-21360-1 (cl, 1973), 0-671-21725-9 (pbk). ▸ Argues philosopher was exposed to paradoxical divergences between appearance and reality in many sectors of Viennese life and that his thought reflected contemporary crises in art, morality, and sociability. [JWB]

31.311 William M. Johnston. *The Austrian mind: an intellectual and social history, 1848–1938.* 1972 ed. Berkeley: University of California Press, 1976. ISBN 0-520-03182-2 (cl), 0-520-04955-1 (pbk). ▸ Encyclopedic review of major and secondary intellectuals and public figures with attention to social and political contexts. Demonstrates broad range of creative forces monarchy nurtured in its last decades. Footnotes particularly useful for follow-up reading. [JWB]

31.312 David S. Luft. *Robert Musil and the crisis of European culture, 1880–1942.* Berkeley: University of California Press, 1980. ISBN 0-520-03852-5 (cl), 0-520-05328-1 (pbk). ▸ Presents Musil as representative writer who explored collapse of liberal ideologies in early twentieth century. Extremely sensitive to context of Musil's life, as well as to ambivalence and complexity of his thought. [JWB]

31.313 William J. McGrath. *Dionysian art and populist politics in Austria.* New Haven: Yale University Press, 1974. ISBN 0-300-01656-5. ▸ History of circle of young Viennese intellectuals in 1870s and 1880s who found inspiration to rebel against liberal politics and culture in work of Arthur Schopenhauer, Friedrich Nietzsche, and Richard Wagner. [JWB]

31.314 William J. McGrath. *Freud's discovery of psychoanalysis: the politics of hysteria.* Ithaca, N.Y.: Cornell University Press, 1986. ISBN 0-8014-1770-8. ▸ Sensitive, subtle account of cultural context within which Freud worked. Extremely insightful discussion of influence of Brentano and Schopenhauer on Freud's philosophical thinking. [JWB]

31.315 Carl E. Schorske. *Fin-de-siècle Vienna: politics and culture.* 1979 ed. New York: Vintage, 1981. ISBN 0-394-74478-0 (pbk). ▸ Powerful, elegant analysis of Viennese cultural history, focusing on crisis of liberals and liberalism. Exemplary, influential model of how to integrate practices of social and intellectual history. One of most important contributions to study of modern Central European history in any language since 1945. [JWB]

31.316 Michael P. Steinberg. *The meaning of the Salzburg Festival: Austria as theater and ideology, 1890–1938.* Ithaca, N.Y.: Cornell University Press, 1989. ISBN 0-8014-2362-7. ▸ Argues founders saw festival as way of reconstituting and asserting renewed Austrian identity; festival sought to meld contradictory elements of pan-European cosmopolitanism and baroque nationalism. Stresses prominent role of assimilated Austrian Jews in festival's refashioning of Catholic culture. [JWB]

31.317 Edward Timms. *Karl Kraus, apocalyptic satirist: culture and catastrophe in Habsburg Vienna.* New Haven: Yale University Press, 1986. ISBN 0-300-03611-6. ▸ Shrewd appreciation of Kraus's work up to 1918, setting it in cultural and political context of upheavals through which he lived and to which he mightily contributed. Especially acute analysis of Kraus during war and of ambivalence undergirding his play: *The Last Days of Mankind.* [JWB]

31.318 C. E. Williams. *The broken eagle: the politics of Austrian literature from empire to Anschluss.* New York: Barnes & Noble, 1974. ISBN 0-06-497713-7. ▸ Essays on nine modern Austrian writers—from Hugo von Hofmannsthal to Karl Kraus—exploring reaction to political challenges, 1914–38. Argues pre-1914 Austrian literature lacked overt political awareness; war triggered new appreciation of political themes and concerns among leading literary figures. [JWB]

WAR AND REVOLUTION, 1914–1919

Strategy and Politics

31.319 Klaus Epstein. *Matthias Erzberger and the dilemma of German democracy.* 1959 ed. New York: Fertig, 1971. ▸ Sympathetic biography of Center party parliamentarian who played crucial role in passing Reichstag's Peace Resolution, negotiating German armistice, and achieving ratification of Versailles treaty. Fell victim to political assassination in 1921. [RFW]

31.320 Fritz Fischer. *Germany's aims in the First World War.* New York: Norton, 1967. ISBN 0-393-05347-4 (cl), 0-393-09798-6 (pbk). ‣ Abridged translation of *Griff nach der Weltmacht* (1961). Challenges notion that German government sought to restrain annexationist demands of military and industrial leaders by arguing that Chancellor Bethmann Hollweg himself endorsed far-reaching annexations from beginning of war. Controversy following publication focused on introductory chapters which argue that Bethmann deliberately risked war and therefore bears substantial share of responsibility for its outbreak. [RFW]

31.321 Hans W. Gatzke. *Germany's drive to the west (Drang nach Westen): a study of Germany's western war aims during the First World War.* 1950 ed. Westport, Conn.: Greenwood, 1978. ISBN 0-313-20507-8. ‣ Imperial Chancellor Bethmann Hollweg made crucial mistake of leaving war aims vague, but primary responsibility for propagating expansionist war aims (preventing peace of understanding) rests with annexationist minority of industrialists, pan-Germans, and Supreme Command. Based on published materials. Dated but still useful introduction. [RFW]

31.322 Martin Kitchen. *The silent dictatorship: the politics of the German High Command under Hindenburg and Ludendorff, 1916–1918.* New York: Holmes & Meier, 1976. ISBN 0-8419-0277-1. ‣ How High Command gained ascendancy over civilian government and largely determined domestic and foreign policy. Forcefully argues politics of High Command represented militarized form of Bonapartism, standing halfway between Bismarck's Bonapartism and Nazi dictatorship. [RFW]

31.323 H. W. Koch, ed. *The origins of the First World War: great power rivalry and German war aims.* 2d ed. London: Macmillan, 1984. ISBN 0-333-37298-0 (pbk). ‣ Reprint of ten contributions to controversy provoked by Fischer's assertion that German statesmen deliberately accepted risk of war in July 1914 (31.320). Includes articles by Fischer, Geiss, Joll, Zechlin, Erdmann, and others. Helpful introduction to debate. [RFW]

SEE ALSO
47.333 Volker R. Berghahn. *Germany and the approach of war in 1914.*
47.340 Imanuel Geiss. *July 1914, the outbreak of the First World War.*

Society and Economics

31.324 Gerald D. Feldman. *Army, industry, and labor in Germany, 1914–1918.* 1966 ed. Providence: Berg; distributed by St. Martin's, 1992. ISBN 0-85496-764-8 (pbk). ‣ Argues wartime mobilization was crucial to development of collective bargaining. Examines how military's desire to ensure social cohesion necessary for economic mobilization led to recognition of unions as legitimate representatives of labor. Classic account of wartime politics and economy. [RFW]

31.325 Jürgen Kocka. *Facing total war: German society, 1914–1918.* Barbara Weinberger, trans. Cambridge, Mass.: Harvard University Press, 1984. ISBN 0-674-29031-3. ‣ Using model of class society, argues class antagonisms became sharper during war, but state became more autonomous and less instrument of ruling class. Translation of *Klassengesellschaft im Krieg* (1973). Useful synthesis. [RFW]

31.326 Albrecht Mendelssohn Bartholdy. *The war and German society: the testament of a Liberal.* 1937 ed. New York: Fertig, 1971. ‣ Highly idiosyncratic but illuminating account of material and moral impact of war by distinguished German lawyer. Lively picture of the times. [RFW]

31.327 Richard Wall and Jay Winter, eds. *The upheaval of war:*

family, work, and welfare in Europe, 1914–1918. Cambridge: Cambridge University Press, 1988. ISBN 0-521-32345-2. ‣ Contributions on Germany include essays on changing consumption patterns, women's work, pronatalism, social hygiene, and youth movements as well as comparative essay on German and British families. Important new research. [RFW]

31.328 Robert Weldon Whalen. *Bitter wounds: German victims of the Great War, 1914–1939.* Ithaca, N.Y.: Cornell University Press, 1984. ISBN 0-8014-1653-1. ‣ Innovative examination of experience of war victims, concentrating on interaction between war victims' organizations and welfare system. Stresses democratic potential of war victims' movement and failure of welfare bureaucracy. [RFW]

SEE ALSO
22.530 Gerd Hardach. *The First World War, 1914–1918.*

Revolution of 1918–1919

31.329 Charles B. Burdick and Ralph H. Lutz, eds. *The political institutions of the German revolution, 1918–1919.* New York: Praeger for the Hoover Institution on War, Revolution, and Peace, Stanford University, 1966. ‣ Collection of translated documents: first public announcements of Vollzugsrat of Berlin Workers' and Soldiers' Council; minutes of First Congress of Workers' and Soldiers' Councils; and minutes of Rat der Volksbeauftragten and of subsequent Reich Ministry until autumn 1919. [RFW]

31.330 F. L. Carsten. *Revolution in Central Europe, 1918–1919.* Berkeley: University of California Press, 1972. ISBN 0-520-02084-7. ‣ Broad survey emphasizing spontaneous spread of soldiers' and workers' councils throughout Germany and Austria. Interpretive focus on missed opportunities; revisionist interpretation. Mainly based on primary sources, little engagement with historiography. [RFW]

31.331 Richard A. Comfort. *Revolutionary Hamburg: labor politics in the early Weimar republic.* Stanford, Calif.: Stanford University Press, 1966. ‣ Seeks to explain how powerful labor movement that mounted Revolution of 1918 became deeply split by 1924. Argues Social Democratic party (SPD) and Free Trade Unions alienated large portion of new political force, industrial workers, who turned to Communists as "vehicle of protest." [RFW]

31.332 Daniel Horn. *The German naval mutinies of World War I.* New Brunswick, N.J.: Rutgers University Press, 1969. ISBN 0-8135-0598-4. ‣ Convincing argument that mutinies not due to subversion of navy by socialist groups. Instead, mutiny of August 1917 resulted from bad treatment of enlisted men by officers, and mutinies of fall 1918 were reaction to illegal orders that amounted to admirals' rebellion against government. [RFW]

31.333 Georg P. Meyer. *Bibliographie zur deutschen Revolution 1918/19.* Göttingen: Vandenhoeck & Ruprecht, 1977. ISBN 3-525-35481-9. ‣ Over 1,500 titles, including bibliographies, review articles, memoirs, and document collections; secondary literature (including local studies) on First World War, council movement, political parties, military, bureaucracy, economy and society, Weimar constitution, and Versailles treaty. [RFW]

31.334 Allan Mitchell. *Revolution in Bavaria, 1918–1919: the Eisner regime and the Soviet republic.* Princeton: Princeton University Press, 1965. ‣ Well-written account of role of independent socialist leader, Kurt Eisner. Eisner himself sought compromise between parliamentary and council systems, but was unable to prevent polarization of political forces that led to civil war between two factions after his death. [RFW]

31.335 Wolfgang J. Mommsen. "The German revolution, 1918–1920: political revolution and social protest movement." In *Social change and political development in Weimar Germany.* Richard

Bessel and E. J. Feuchtwanger, eds., pp. 21–54. London and Totowa, N.J.: Croom Helm and Barnes & Noble, 1981. ISBN 0-389-20176-6. ‣ Critique of revisionists. Government's main error was not that it failed to recognize democratic potential of councils but that it misread strikes and protests as signs of Spartacist rebellion rather than manifestations of widespread social protest. [RFW]

31.336 David W. Morgan. *The socialist Left and the German revolution: a history of the German Independent Social Democratic party, 1917–1922.* Ithaca, N.Y.: Cornell University Press, 1975. ISBN 0-8014-0851-2. ‣ Detailed history of Independent Social Democratic party (USPD) with emphasis on role in Revolution of 1918. Argues party's ideology of class struggle hampered commitment to democracy and helped prevent consolidation of republic. Critical of revisionist interpretation of revolution. [RFW]

31.337 Reinhard Rürup. "Problems of the German revolution, 1918–19." *Journal of contemporary history* 4 (1968) 109–35. ISSN 0022-0094. ‣ Revisionist interpretation arguing majority of workers' and soldiers' councils were not socialist, but radical democrat. Hence revolution did not pose bolshevik threat, but created fluid situation in which leaders could have achieved greater democratization than they did. [RFW]

World War I and the Dissolution of the Habsburg Monarchy

31.338 Otto Bauer. *The Austrian revolution.* 1925 abr. ed. H. J. Stenning, trans. New York: Franklin, 1970. ‣ Combination of author's own brilliant partisanship on behalf of Austro-Marxists with acute insights into early history of republic. Abridged English translation of original work (1923) elaborating author's theory of balance of class forces. [JWB]

31.339 Mark Cornwall, ed. *The last years of Austria-Hungary: essays in political and military history, 1908–1918.* Exeter: University of Exeter Press, 1990. ISBN 0-85989-306-5. ‣ Seven essays on classic issue of whether internal or external forces were more responsible for collapse of monarchy. Evaluates role of First World War in state's dissolution. Especially useful in charting continuities in government policies before and after 1914. [JWB]

31.340 Edmund Glaise von Horstenau. *The collapse of the Austro-Hungarian empire.* Ian F. D. Morrow, trans. London: Dent, 1930. ‣ Important early study by director of Austrian War Archive and former general staff officer attached to High Command during World War I. [JWB]

31.341 Arthur J. May. *The passing of the Habsburg monarchy.* 2 vols. Philadelphia: University of Pennsylvania Press, 1966. ‣ Based on wide reading and control of sources, but also disjointed in presentation and dated or questionable in some interpretations. Especially useful for survey of press opinion during war. [JWB]

31.342 Josef Redlich. *Austrian war government.* New Haven: Yale University Press, 1929. (Carnegie Endowment for International Peace, Division of Economics and History: economic and social history of the world war, translated and abridged series, 6.) ‣ Still one of best analyses of domestic and administrative politics of monarchy during First World War. Sensitive to structural as well as personal and ideological factors behind loss of legitimacy and effectiveness experienced by imperial civil service. [JWB]

31.343 Gary W. Shanafelt. *The secret enemy: Austria-Hungary and the German alliance, 1914–1918.* Boulder: East European Monographs; distributed by Columbia University Press, 1985. (East European monographs, 187.) ISBN 0-88033-080-5. ‣ Excellent discussion of Austria's wartime collaboration with Germany. Based on extensive archival research, demonstrating alliance helped polarize imperial political system and contributed to collapse. [JWB]

31.344 Reinhard Sieder. "Behind the lines: working-class family life in wartime Vienna." In *The upheaval of war: family, work, and welfare in Europe, 1914–1918.* Richard Wall and Jay Winter, eds., pp. 109–38. Cambridge: Cambridge University Press, 1988. ISBN 0-521-32345-2. ‣ Analysis of massive social and economic dislocations caused by mobilization, enlistment, war deaths, and war wounded. Ultimately invested new Social Democratic municipal regime with authority to restabilize nuclear family and reinvent traditions of patriarchy. [JWB]

31.345 Z.A.B. Zeman. *The break-up of the Habsburg empire, 1914–1918: a study in national and social revolution.* 1961 ed. New York: Octagon Books, 1977. ISBN 0-374-98847-1. ‣ Study of now traditional question of whether empire was destroyed from within during war, or whether collapse caused by Allied decisions from without, culminating in peace conferences. Argues final responsibility for destruction of Austria-Hungary lay with ruling elites. [JWB]

SEE ALSO
  47.374 Wilfried Fest. *Peace or partition.*
  47.419 Leo Valiani. *The end of Austria-Hungary.*

WEIMAR REPUBLIC, 1919–1933

Reference Works and General Studies

31.346 Wolfgang Benz and Hermann Graml, eds. *Biographisches Lexikon zur Weimarer Republik.* Munich: Beck, 1988. ISBN 3-406-32988-8. ‣ Best source for brief biographical information on major figures in Weimar's political, economic, and cultural life. About 500 entries; articles include bibliographical references. [RFW]

31.347 Richard Bessel and E. J. Feuchtwanger, eds. *Social change and political development in Weimar Germany.* London and Totowa, N.J.: Croom Helm and Barnes & Noble, 1981. ISBN 0-389-20176-6. ‣ Important collection of essays on Revolution of 1918, inflation, politics of rearmament, agriculture, women's question, politics of corporatism, Nazi-communist street battles, German-Russian relations, and dissolution of bourgeois party system. [RFW]

31.348 Erich Eyck. *A history of the Weimar republic.* 1962–63 ed. 2 vols. Harlan P. Hanson and Robert G. L. Waite, trans. New York: Atheneum, 1970. ‣ Detailed narrative of Weimar politics by liberal who participated in Weimar's public life as lawyer, journalist, and Berlin city councillor. Still worth reading for richness of detail. Translation of *Geschichte der Weimarer Republik* (1954–56). [RFW]

31.349 Eberhard Kolb. *The Weimar republic.* P. S. Falla, trans. London: Unwin Hyman, 1988. ISBN 0-04-943049-1 (cased), 0-04-943050-5 (pbk). ‣ Brief narrative survey with emphasis on political history, followed by thematic review of historiography with references to bibliography of over 650 titles. Includes chronology. Ideal as introduction. [RFW]

31.350 Detlev J. K. Peukert. *The Weimar republic: the crisis of classical modernity.* Richard Deveson, trans. New York: Hill & Wang, 1992. ISBN 0-8090-9674-9. ‣ Comprehensive interpretive survey emphasizing social history. Argues Weimar's stagnant economy and segmentation of its political culture reduced ability to reconcile different interests within framework of social and political compromise reached in 1918–19. Translation of *Die Weimarer Republik* (1987). [RFW]

31.351 Peter D. Stachura. *The Weimar era and Hitler, 1918–1933: a critical bibliography.* Oxford: Clio, 1977. ISBN 0-903450-08-9. ‣ Comprehensive annotated bibliography of books and articles in German, English, and French, including primary and secondary sources. Over 3,500 titles arranged by topic; coverage includes rise of national socialism. [RFW]

Political Parties

31.352 Werner T. Angress. *Stillborn revolution: the communist bid for power in Germany, 1921–1923.* 1963 ed. 2 vols. Port Washington, N.Y.: Kennikat, 1972. ISBN 0-8046-1622-1 (set). ‣ History of Communist party (KPD) arguing that, after Rosa Luxemburg's death, founders' vision of spontaneous revolution degenerated into irresponsible putschism, party democracy was destroyed, and bolshevik influence increased. These trends perpetuated party's isolation from masses and doomed uprisings to failure. Somewhat dated but still best account. [RFW]

31.353 Richard Breitman. *German socialism and Weimar democracy.* Chapel Hill: University of North Carolina Press, 1981. ISBN 0-8078-1462-8. ‣ Useful introduction examining Social Democratic party (SPD) leadership's interaction with parliamentary system. Argues SPD's attempt to preserve parliamentary democracy through integration with bourgeois forces failed as result of unfavorable political and economic circumstances and party's ideological determinism. [RFW]

31.354 Ben Fowkes. *Communism in Germany under the Weimar republic.* London: Macmillan, 1984. ISBN 0-333-27270-6 (cl), 0-333-27271-4 (pbk). ‣ Narrative history of Communist party (KPD), focusing on leadership, with brief analysis of membership and organization. Argues after brief period of failed uprisings, party became home to discontented masses and instrument of Soviet foreign policy. [RFW]

31.355 Lewis Hertzmann. *DNVP: right-wing opposition in the Weimar republic, 1918–1924.* Lincoln: University of Nebraska Press, 1963. ‣ History of German National People's party (DNVP) concentrating on intra-party struggles between Old Conservatives, Free Conservatives, antisemites, and Christian-Socialists. Although Old Conservatives achieved predominance by 1924, internal tensions posed continued threat of disintegration. Still useful as introduction. [RFW]

31.356 Larry Eugene Jones. *German liberalism and the dissolution of the Weimar party system, 1918–1933.* Chapel Hill: University of North Carolina Press, 1988. ISBN 0-8078-1764-3. ‣ Comprehensive history focusing on German Democratic party and German People's party. Argues failure not predetermined by problems within liberal tradition but mainly due to socioeconomic developments that destroyed social base. [RFW]

31.357 Rudolf Morsey. *Die Deutsche Zentrumspartei, 1917–1923.* Düsseldorf: Droste, 1966. ‣ Comprehensive account arguing Center party's existence depended on its mediating function as party of coalition and compromise. As resulting compromises reduced credibility, party maintained electoral support by appealing to confessional interests. [RFW]

31.358 Heinrich August Winkler. *Von der Revolution zur Stabilisierung: Arbeiter und Arbeiterbewegung in der Weimarer Republik, 1918 bis 1924* [v. 1]. *Der Schein der Normalität: Arbeiter und Arbeiterbewegung in der Weimarer Republik, 1924 bis 1930* [v. 2]. *Der Weg in die Katastrophe: Arbeiter und Arbeiterbewegung in der Weimarer Republik, 1930 bis 1933* [v. 3]. 3 vols. Berlin: Dietz, 1984–87. ISBN 3-8012-0093-0 (v. 1), 3-8012-0094-9 (v. 2), 3-8012-0095-7 (v. 3). ‣ Comprehensive account of labor movement (socialist and communist parties, trade unions) and role in Weimar politics, combined with social history of working class. Broadly conceived, large sections can be read as political history of Weimar. [RFW]

Political Issues and Personalities

31.359 F. L. Carsten. *The Reichswehr and politics, 1918–1933.* 1966 ed. Berkeley: University of California Press, 1973. ISBN 0-520-02492-3. ‣ Examination of how antirepublican officers won out over those willing to build republican army, made army into autonomous entity, organized Reichswehr's secret cooperation

with paramilitary groups and Red Army, and contributed to fall of republic. Valuable synthesis. [RFW]

31.360 James M. Diehl. *Paramilitary politics in Weimar Germany.* Bloomington: Indiana University Press, 1977. ISBN 0-253-34292-9. ‣ Thorough examination of militarization of German political life, 1918–30, by tracing development of paramilitary organizations from formation of Free Corps to activities of Political Combat Leagues which helped prepare ground for NSDAP (National-Sozialistische Deutsche Arbeiterpartei) and SA (Sturmabteilung). [RFW]

31.361 Andreas Dorpalen. *Hindenburg and the Weimar republic.* Princeton: Princeton University Press, 1964. ‣ Comprehensive account of Field Marshal Hindenburg's role as president of Weimar republic. Special attention to intrigues around him that helped destroy parliamentary democracy. [RFW]

31.362 Modris Eksteins. *The limits of reason: the German democratic press and the collapse of Weimar democracy.* London: Oxford University Press, 1975. ISBN 0-19-821862-1. ‣ Examination of three democratic newspaper concerns. Argues political independence and self-confidence of democratic press were eroded by journalists' alienation from Weimar politics and by economic difficulties making newspapers susceptible to outside interference. Important contribution to understanding liberalism's failure. [RFW]

31.363 Peter Fritzsche. *Rehearsals for fascism: populism and political mobilization in Weimar Germany.* New York: Oxford University Press, 1990. ISBN 0-19-505780-5. ‣ Argues fragmentation of bourgeois electoral politics in 1920s was accompanied by populist political mobilization of bourgeoisie on local level. Based on examination of local politics in several Lower Saxon towns. Innovative and stimulating. [RFW]

31.364 Harry Kessler. *In the twenties: the diaries of Harry Kessler.* Charles Kessler, trans. Otto Friedrich, Introduction. New York: Holt Rinehart & Winston, 1971. ISBN 0-03-072630-1. ‣ Remarkable diaries (1918–37) of diplomat, writer, pacifist, and arts patron, whose close connections with many political and artistic figures made him uniquely qualified to chronicle political and cultural life of Weimar republic. Translation of *Tagebücher* (1961). [RFW]

31.365 John A. Leopold. *Alfred Hugenberg: the radical nationalist campaign against the Weimar republic.* New Haven: Yale University Press, 1977. ISBN 0-300-02068-6. ‣ Thorough biographical examination of how, between 1928 and 1933, German National People's party (DNVP) chairman's pan-German convictions led him to overrule party moderates and attempt to build radical nationalist front against republic by cooperating with Nazis. [RFW]

31.366 J. P. Nettl. *Rosa Luxemburg.* 2 vols. London: Oxford University Press, 1966. ‣ Comprehensive, sympathetic biography covering German leftist's public and private life, including Polish, Russian, and German activities. Argues her most important contribution to Marxism was emphasis on action and participation. [RFW]

31.367 Henry Ashby Turner, Jr. *Stresemann and the politics of the Weimar republic.* 1963 ed. Westport, Conn.: Greenwood, 1979. ISBN 0-313-20900-6. ‣ Interprets role of leader of German People's party in domestic politics as that of pragmatic conservative. Crucial in winning bourgeois support for republic, he failed to provide his political course with firm institutional party base. Classic account of domestic dimensions of Stresemann's policies. [RFW]

31.368 Robert G. L. Waite. *Vanguard of nazism: the Free Corps movement in postwar Germany, 1918–1923.* 1952 ed. Cambridge, Mass.: Harvard University Press, 1970. ISBN 0-674-93142-4.

▶ Detailed narrative of movement's activities, arguing that although political beliefs inchoate and most members did not support Hitler in early years, their violent hostility to liberal democracy and brutality of spirit made important contribution to rise of nazism. [RFW]

Society and Economics

31.369 Renate Bridenthal, Atina Grossmann, and Marion A. Kaplan, eds. *When biology became destiny: women in Weimar and Nazi Germany.* New York: Monthly Review Press, 1984. ISBN 0-85345-642-9 (cl), 0-85345-643-7 (pbk). ▶ Important collection of articles on women in politics and work, women's organizations, politics of reproduction, women in Nazi party, and effects of Nazi policies on women. Presents differing interpretations of relationship between German feminism and Nazi rule. [RFW]

31.370 Jane Caplan. *Government without administration: state and civil service in Weimar and Nazi Germany.* Oxford: Clarendon, 1988. ISBN 0-19-822993-3. ▶ Attributes failure of civil service reform under Nazis to clash of claims about political representation. While civil service sought to create administration that eliminated political process of government, Nazis aimed at building government without administration. [RFW]

31.371 Gerald D. Feldman et al., eds. *The German inflation reconsidered: a preliminary balance.* Berlin: de Gruyter, 1982. (Veröffentlichungen der Historischen Kommission zu Berlin, 54. Beiträge zu Inflation und Wiederaufbau in Deutschland und Europa, 1914–1924, 1.) ISBN 3-11-008721-9. ▶ Fourteen essays (in English and German) on economic analysis of inflation, history of German economic policy, 1914–24, and political and social consequences of inflation for various social groups. Summarizes important research. [RFW]

31.372 Carl-Ludwig Holtfrerich. *The German inflation, 1914–1923: causes and effects in international perspective.* Theo Balderston, trans. Berlin: de Gruyter, 1986. ISBN 0-89925-206-0. ▶ Best, brief account of inflation; economic history with strong interest in political factors. Finds inflation facilitated adjustment of economy to war and then peace, equalized wealth, and allowed postwar Germany to finance imports and reparations with foreign resources. [RFW]

31.373 Harold James. *The German slump: politics and economics, 1924–1936.* Oxford: Clarendon, 1986. ISBN 0-19-821972-5. ▶ Detailed examination of public finance, industrial organization, labor politics, agriculture, and banking. Argues German interwar depression was result of structural problems of industrial rigidification which even Nazi recovery did not overcome. [RFW]

31.374 Robert G. Moeller. *German peasants and agrarian politics, 1914–1924: the Rhineland and Westphalia.* Chapel Hill: University of North Carolina Press, 1986. ISBN 0-8078-1676-0. ▶ Useful analysis of rural society. Argues rural hostility toward Weimar not primarily result of antidemocratic attitudes dating back to imperial Germany or of agrarian crisis of late twenties, but of economic grievances originating in war economy and postwar recovery. [RFW]

31.375 Peter D. Stachura, ed. *Unemployment and the Great Depression in Weimar Germany.* New York: St. Martin's, 1986. ISBN 0-312-83267-2. ▶ Useful collection of essays on causes of unemployment; impact on women, youth, and physicians; trade union policy; development of work-creation programs; and effect of unemployment on right- and left-wing radicalism. [RFW]

Culture

31.376 Istvan Deák. *Weimar Germany's left-wing intellectuals: a political history of the "Weltbühne" and its circle.* Berkeley: University of California Press, 1968. ▶ Weltbühne's dreams of socialist society were utopian, but its relentless criticism of republican

politics (including crusade for socialist unity) often to the point; cannot be held responsible for republic's destruction. Best introduction in English. [RFW]

31.377 Peter Gay. *Weimar culture: the outsider as insider.* 1968 ed. Westport, Conn.: Greenwood, 1981. ISBN 0-313-22972-4. ▶ Brief overview examining expressionist drama and painting; New Objectivity in architecture and literature; George circle and poetry; fear of modernity in philosophy, history, and literature; and cartelization of culture. Excellent annotated bibliography. [RFW]

31.378 W. L. Guttsman. *Workers' culture in Weimar Germany: between tradition and commitment.* Oxford: Berg; distributed by St. Martin's, 1990. ISBN 0-907582-59-1. ▶ Focuses on cultural organizations of socialist labor movement (workers' sport, music, visual arts, theater), but also examines interaction with culture of everyday life and commercial culture of new media. [RFW]

31.379 Jeffrey Herf. *Reactionary modernism: technology, culture, and politics in Weimar and the Third Reich.* 1984 ed. Cambridge: Cambridge University Press, 1986. ISBN 0-521-26566-5 (cl, 1984), 0-521-33833-6 (pbk). ▶ Controversial but stimulating examination of paradoxical combination of political irrationalism and modern technology first advocated by German engineers and Weimar's conservative revolutionaries that became crucial component of Nazi ideology. [RFW]

31.380 Walter Laqueur. *Weimar: a cultural history, 1918–1933.* 1974 ed. New York: Perigee, 1980. ISBN 0-399-50346-3. ▶ Encyclopedic survey of republic's left- and right-wing intellectuals, literature, theater, music, visual arts, architecture, academic disciplines, popular culture, and cinema; thumbnail sketches of major figures and their works. Bibliography. [RFW]

31.381 John Willett. *Art and politics in the Weimar period: the new sobriety, 1917–1933.* 1978 ed. New York: Pantheon, 1980. ISBN 0-394-49628-0 (cl, 1978), 0-394-73991-4 (pbk). ▶ Examination of particular constructive vision (New Sobriety) that provided modern movement in arts with audience, function, and unity and allowed it to penetrate entire society. Not general survey; excellent illustrations and tables. [RFW]

Collapse of the Republic

31.382 David Abraham. *The collapse of the Weimar republic: political economy and crisis.* 2d ed. New York: Holmes & Meier, 1986. ISBN 0-8419-1083-9 (cl), 0-8419-1084-7 (pbk). ▶ Controversial analysis of economic sector examining system of cooperation between export-oriented industrialists and organized labor and its collapse during Depression. On charges of inaccuracy leveled against first edition and ensuing controversy, see exchange in *Central European History* 17 (1984) 159–293. [RFW]

31.383 Knut Borchardt. "Constraints and room for manoeuvre in the Great Depression of the early thirties: towards a revision of the received historical picture." In *Perspectives on modern German economic history and policy.* Peter Lambert, trans., pp. 143–60. Cambridge: Cambridge University Press, 1991. ISBN 0-521-36310-1 (cl), 0-521-36858-8 (pbk). ▶ Argues Weimar economy crippled by excessive wages prior to Great Depression; neither unions nor government could accept reductions. When Depression hit, no plan of deficit spending could have solved problem. Article sparked vigorous debate when originally published in 1979. [RFW]

31.384 Karl Dietrich Bracher. *Die Auflösung der Weimarer Republik: eine Studie zum Problem des Machtverfalls in der Demokratie.* 1955 ed. Düsseldorf: Droste, 1984. ISBN 3-7700-0908-8 (pbk). ▶ Seminal work; systematic analysis of Weimar's power structure followed by detailed examination of dissolution of parliamentary democracy after 1930. Argues fateful transition to presidential regime in 1930 not result of failure of parliamentary democracy but of President Hindenburg's and Chancellor Brüning's preference for authoritarian solution. [RFW]

31.385 Martin Broszat. *Hitler and the collapse of Weimar Germany.* Volker R. Berghahn, trans. Leamington Spa: Berg; distributed by St. Martin's, 1987. ISBN 0-85496-509-2 (cl), 0-85496-517-3 (pbk). ‣ Survey of National Socialists' rise to power with emphasis on period 1929–33. Stresses openness of situation up to Chancellor Brüning's fall and "logic of development" underlying subsequent intrigues that led to Hitler's appointment as chancellor. Translation of *Die Machtergreifung* (1984). [RFW]

31.386 Theodor Eschenburg et al. *The path to dictatorship, 1918–1933: ten essays.* 1966 ed. Fritz Stern, Introduction. J. S. Conway, trans. New York: Praeger, 1967. ‣ Ten essays by German scholars, originally broadcast on German radio, examining problems of Weimar democracy, Weimar's political parties, National Socialists' seizure of power, resistance, and lessons for future. Good, brief introduction to important issues. [RFW]

31.387 Ian Kershaw, ed. *Weimar: why did German democracy fail?* New York: St. Martin's, 1990. ISBN 0-312-04470-4. ‣ Two contrasting assessments of Weimar's economic viability and Borchardt thesis (31.383): study of role of employers and workers in Weimar's collapse and comprehensive examination of causes of collapse. Helpful historiographical introduction and bibliography. [RFW]

31.388 Jürgen Baron von Kruedener, ed. *Economic crisis and political collapse: the Weimar republic, 1924–1933.* New York: Berg; distributed by St. Martin's, 1990. ISBN 0-85496-232-8. ‣ Contributions to debate over Chancellor Brüning's economic policy and viability of Weimar economy generated by Borchardt's articles (31.383). [RFW]

31.389 Erich Matthias and Rudolf Morsey, eds. *Das Ende der Parteien 1933: Darstellungen und Dokumente.* 1960 ed. Düsseldorf: Droste, 1984. ‣ Classic study examining behavior of major German parties during crisis of parliamentary system, 1930–33, and their dissolution after Hitler's appointment as chancellor. Separate chapters for each party with documentary appendixes. [RFW]

31.390 Eve Rosenhaft. *Beating the Fascists? The German Communists and political violence, 1929–1933.* Cambridge: Cambridge University Press, 1983. ISBN 0-521-23638-X. ‣ Analysis of communist gang warfare against Nazis as part of migration of political activity from workplace to neighborhood. Convincing examination of Communist party's failure to transform violence into offensive revolutionary movement. [RFW]

31.391 Henry Ashby Turner, Jr. *German big business and the rise of Hitler.* New York: Oxford University Press, 1985. ISBN 0-19-503492-9. ‣ Argues big business did not play major role in disintegration of republic after 1930, had no part in Hitler's appointment as chancellor, and its financial contributions to NSDAP (National-Sozialistische Deutsche Arbeiterpartei) were of marginal significance. Important contribution to longstanding debate. [RFW]

AUSTRIA, 1919–1945

Austrian Republic, 1918–1938

31.392 Heinrich Benedikt, ed. *Geschichte der Republik Österreich.* 1954 ed. Munich: Oldenbourg, 1977. ISBN 3-486-48371-4. ‣ Collection of essays. Especially important contributions by Goldinger and Wandruszka on political developments between 1918 and 1945. First serious articulation of theory that Austrian politics in twentieth century profoundly shaped and defined by three independent but interconnected camps. [JWB]

31.393 Gerhard Botz. *Gewalt in der Politik: Attentäte, Zusammenstösse, Putschversuche, Unruhen in Österreich, 1918 bis 1938.* 2d

ed. Munich: Fink, 1983. ISBN 3-7705-1295-2. ‣ Excellent, probing examination of patterns of political violence, providing statistical information on perpetrators and victims, as well as detailed narrations of particular events. Connects incidence of violence to levels of wider social and economic dislocation and political instability. [JWB]

31.394 F. L. Carsten. *The first Austrian republic, 1918–1938: a study based on British and Austrian documents.* Aldershot, England: Gower, 1986. ISBN 0-566-05162-1. ‣ Summary of British diplomatic commentaries on Austrian public affairs set in loose chronological framework. Useful information, but lacks strong analytic perspective. [JWB]

31.395 C. Earl Edmondson. *The Heimwehr and Austrian politics, 1918–1936.* Athens: University of Georgia Press, 1978. ISBN 0-8203-0437-9. ‣ Charts Heimwehr's attempts to influence government policy, but also shows limits of success, resulting from fragmentary national identity, dependence on outside support, and inconsistent leadership. [JWB]

31.396 Harriet Pass Freidenreich. *Jewish politics in Vienna, 1918–1938.* Bloomington: Indiana University Press, 1991. ISBN 0-253-32475-0. ‣ Explores political factions within Viennese Jewish community in Austrian First Republic, arguing Jewish political behavior reflected dilemmas experienced by Jewish communal groups elsewhere in twentieth-century Europe. Especially insightful on response of Viennese Jews to Austro-fascist corporate state, 1934–38. [JWB]

31.397 Helmut Gruber. *Red Vienna: experiment in working-class culture, 1919–1934.* New York: Oxford University Press, 1991. ISBN 0-19-506914-5. ‣ Important, vigorously argued discussion of municipal socialist attempt to create workers' utopia. Examines obstacles and limits faced by party leadership in imposing its cultural ideas on existing worker subcultures. [JWB]

31.398 Charles A. Gulick. *Austria from Habsburg to Hitler.* 1948 ed. 2 vols. Walther Federn, Foreword. Berkeley: University of California Press, 1980. ISBN 0-520-04211-5. ‣ Magisterial survey of political history of First Republic, researched and written between 1934 and 1947. Vigorous defence of Austrian socialist politics, notable as example of limits and opportunities of early cold war historiography on Austria. [JWB]

31.399 Klemens von Klemperer. *Ignaz Seipel: Christian statesman in a time of crisis.* Princeton: Princeton University Press, 1972. ISBN 0-691-05197-6. ‣ Careful, sensitive portrait of extremely controversial Austrian priest-politician. Valuable for history of First Republic more generally. [JWB]

31.400 Ulrich Kluge. *Der österreichische Ständestaat, 1934–1938: Entstehung und Scheitern.* Munich: Oldenbourg, 1984. ISBN 3-7028-0225-8. ‣ Provocative analysis of origins and structure of Austro-fascist state, stressing long-term genesis within terrain of interwar politics. Downplays influence of external forces in its creation. Strong arguments for negative continuities in interwar Austrian history. [JWB]

31.401 Jill Lewis. *Fascism and the working class in Austria, 1918–1934: the failure of labour in the First Republic.* New York: Berg; distributed by St. Martin's, 1991. ISBN 0-85496-581-5. ‣ History of Styrian labor movement exploring impact of mass unemployment, political violence, and rise of fascism on key socialist sector outside of Vienna. Useful corrective to Austrian socialist histories that focus primarily on capital city. [JWB]

31.402 Alfred D. Low. *The Anschluss movement, 1931–1938, and the great powers.* Boulder: East European Monographs; distributed by Columbia University Press, 1985. (East European Monographs, 185.) ISBN 0-88033-078-3. ‣ Sequel to author's earlier study (47.447), arguing *Anschluss* question (merging of Austria and Germany) a European rather than merely Austrian or German problem in 1930s. Sound contribution to interwar Central European diplomacy. [JWB]

31.403 Anson Rabinbach. *The crisis of Austrian socialism: from Red Vienna to civil war, 1927–1934.* Chicago: University of Chicago Press, 1983. ISBN 0-226-70121-2. ▸ Demonstrates interwar Social Democrats caught between oppositionalism and institutionalism, leading to dangerous illusions within party elite itself. Vigorous, if sympathetic, critique of socialist assumptions in February 1934. [JWB]

SEE ALSO
47.447 Alfred D. Low. *The Anschluss movement, 1918–1919, and the Paris Peace Conference.*

National Socialism in Austria

31.404 Radomír V. Luža. *The resistance in Austria, 1938–1945.* Minneapolis: University of Minnesota Press, 1984. ISBN 0-8166-1226-9. ▸ Excellent examination of resistance's political isolation from Austrian exile community, fragmented leadership, administrative structure, motives, and values. Unique in Europe, resistance fighters received virtually no recognition in postwar Austria. Informed by author's personal experiences with Czech resistance, 1938–45. [JWB]

31.405 Bruce F. Pauley. *Hitler and the forgotten Nazis: a history of Austrian national socialism.* Chapel Hill: University of North Carolina Press, 1981. ISBN 0-8078-1456-3. ▸ History of Austrian Nazi movement from beginnings through March 1938, demonstrating complex web of competing rivalries and loyalties from which party constituted itself. Important for understanding immediate background to *Anschluss* (merging of Austria and Germany). [JWB]

31.406 Emmerich Tálos, Ernst Hanisch, and Wolfgang Neugebauer, eds. *NS-Herrschaft in Österreich, 1938–1945.* Vienna: Verlag für Gesellschaftskritik, 1988. ISBN 3-900351-84-8. ▸ Essays on various aspects of political, cultural, and economic life in Austria during national socialist period. Insists Austria and its people not merely passive victims of Nazi occupation. Contributions uneven in quality, but best current work on wartime Austria. [JWB]

NATIONAL SOCIALISM AND ITS AFTERMATH

General Studies and Interpretations

31.407 Pierre Ayçoberry. *The Nazi question: an essay on the interpretations of national socialism, 1922–1975.* Robert Hurley, trans. New York: Pantheon, 1981. ISBN 0-394-50948-X (cl), 0-394-74841-7 (pbk). ▸ Penetrating, chronologically organized summary and analysis of evolving interpretations of Nazi Germany since 1930s. Stresses close relationship to political preconceptions of their authors. [PH]

31.408 Richard Bessel, ed. *Life in the Third Reich.* Oxford: Oxford University Press, 1987. ISBN 0-19-215892-9 (cl), 0-19-285184-5 (pbk). ▸ Compilation of clear, up-to-date, expert essays for nonspecialist on specific themes and topics, including village life, youth, state, and antisemitic policy. [PH]

31.409 Karl Dietrich Bracher. *The German dictatorship: the origins, structure, and effects of national socialism.* 1970 ed. Peter Gay, Introduction. Jean Steinberg, trans. Harmondsworth: Penguin, 1980. ISBN 0-14-055155-7. ▸ Most profound, thorough single-volume treatment of rise and of nazism, interpreted as form of totalitarianism. Neither easy to read nor free of error, but magisterial classic. [PH]

31.410 Gerhard Hirschfeld and Lothar Kettenacker, eds. *Der "Führerstaat," Mythos und Realität: Studien zur Struktur und Politik des Dritten Reiches/The "Führer State," myth and reality: studies on the structure and politics of the Third Reich.* Stuttgart: Klett-Cotta, 1981. (Publications of the German Historical Institute, London, 8.) ISBN 3-12-915350-0. ▸ Collection of conference papers (half in English, half in German) providing fundamental point of access to important differences between intentionalist and functionalist interpretations of Nazi regime. Fine discussions of Hitler's role, key political and social groups, and aspects of economic policy. [PH]

31.411 Ian Kershaw. *The Nazi dictatorship: problems and perspectives of interpretation.* 2d ed. New York: Arnold; distributed by Routledge, Chapman & Hall, 1989. ISBN 0-340-49008-X (pbk). ▸ Up-to-date analytical summary of controversial issues in historiography. Weak on relationship between politics and economics, but otherwise comprehensive and thoughtful. [PH]

31.412 J. Noakes and Geoffrey Pridham, eds. *Nazism: 1919–1945, a history in documents and eyewitness accounts.* 1983–88 ed. 2 vols. New York: Schocken; distributed by Pantheon, 1990. ISBN 0-8052-0973-5 (v. 1), 0-8052-0972-7 (v. 2). ▸ Excellent collection of contemporary sources on nearly all aspects of Hitlerian *Reich* with helpful, informed introductory and connecting comments by editors. [PH]

The Nazi Party and Its Rise to Power

31.413 William Sheridan Allen. *The Nazi seizure of power: the experience of a single German town, 1922–1945.* Rev. ed. New York: Watts, 1984. ISBN 0-531-09935-0 (cl), 0-531-05633-3 (pbk). ▸ Unsurpassed examination of nazism's rise and rule through prism of small, North German town. Stresses roles of class antagonism and Nazi grassroots organization in helping party to power, then decline of initial enthusiasm after 1933. Engaging and perceptive. [PH]

31.414 Thomas Childers. *The Nazi voter: the social foundations of fascism in Germany, 1919–1933.* Chapel Hill: University of North Carolina Press, 1983. ISBN 0-8078-1570-5 (cl), 0-8078-4147-1 (pbk). ▸ Careful computer analysis of changes in Nazi electorate over time. Concludes that on eve of takeover, Hitler presided over broad-based but fragile catch-all protest party. [PH]

31.415 Harold J. Gordon, Jr. *Hitler and the Beer Hall Putsch.* Princeton: Princeton University Press, 1972. ISBN 0-691-05189-5 (cl), 0-691-10000-4 (pbk). ▸ Definitive dissection of first Nazi attempt to seize power, stressing responsibility of Bavarian conservatives for encouraging coup and importance of its failure in both galvanizing Hitler and partially immunizing Bavaria to him. Vigorously written. [PH]

31.416 Michael H. Kater. *The Nazi party: a social profile of members and leaders, 1919–1945.* 1983 ed. Cambridge, Mass.: Harvard University Press, 1985. ISBN 0-674-60655-8 (cl, 1983), 0-674-60656-6 (pbk). ▸ Detailed social profile of members and leaders of National Socialist German Workers' party (NSDAP, Nazi party) from inception to 1945, based on statistical samples from party records. Vital reference work, although figures and interpretations do not always mesh. [PH]

31.417 Barbara Miller Lane and Leila J. Rupp, eds. and trans. *Nazi ideology before 1933: a documentation.* Austin: University of Texas Press, 1978. ISBN 0-292-75512-0. ▸ Collection of speeches and pronouncements by leading Nazis (other than Hitler). Very illuminating on contributions to party's socioeconomic and racial doctrines. [PH]

31.418 Dietrich Orlow. *The history of the Nazi party.* Vol. 1: *1919–1933.* Pittsburgh: University of Pittsburgh Press, 1969. ISBN 0-8229-3183-4. ▸ Thorough study of party internal organization and power struggles from origins to its takeover. Overtaken by later research in some respects, but still essential starting point. [PH]

31.419 Dietrich Orlow. *The history of the Nazi party.* Vol. 2:

1933–45. Pittsburgh: University of Pittsburgh Press, 1973. ISBN 0-8229-3253-9. ▸ Meticulous examination of party's role and development once in power with emphasis on internal infighting and tension between aspirations to elitism and mass membership. [PH]

Adolf Hitler

31.420 Rudolph Binion. *Hitler among the Germans*. 1976 ed. De Kalb: Northern Illinois University Press, 1984. ISBN 0-87580-531-0 (pbk). ▸ Psychohistorical examination emphasizing interlocking impulses to relive traumas behind Hitler's and German people's self-destructive drive toward Auschwitz and Stalingrad. Imaginative and clearly reasoned. [PH]

31.421 Sebastian Haffner. *The meaning of Hitler*. 1979 ed. Ewald Osers, trans. Cambridge, Mass.: Harvard University Press, 1983. ISBN 0-674-55775-1 (pbk). ▸ Perceptive, fluent examination of Hitler's psychology and career by German journalist who observed both firsthand. Under such headings as achievements, mistakes, crimes, and betrayal offers brilliant insights, occasionally at price of strict accuracy. [PH]

31.422 Eberhard Jäckel. *Hitler's worldview: a blueprint for power*. Herbert Arnold, trans. Cambridge, Mass.: Harvard University Press, 1981. ISBN 0-674-40425-4. ▸ Revealing analysis of development of Hitler's ideology into logically coherent system centered on two goals: eastward expansion and annihilation of Jews. Admirably concise, sharp, and lucid. [PH]

31.423 Ian Kershaw. *Hitler*. London: Longman, 1991. ISBN 0-582-08053-3 (cased), 0-582-55277-x (pbk). ▸ Deft, reliable, and concise exploration of sources and extent of Hitler's power from charisma and consensus to repression and disorganization of government. [PH]

31.424 Gerhard Schreiber. *Hitler: Interpretationen, 1923–1983: Ergebnisse, Methoden, und Probleme der Forschung*. 1984 ed. Darmstadt: Wissenschaftliche Buchgesellschaft, 1988. ISBN 3-534-07081-x. ▸ Highly intelligent, comprehensive guide to evaluations of and sources concerning Hitler both before and after 1945. [PH]

31.425 Rainer Zitelmann. *Hitler: Selbstverständnis eines Revolutionärs*. 1989 rev. ed. Stuttgart: Klett-Cotta, 1991. ISBN 3-608-95779-0. ▸ Provocative, original study presenting Hitler's domestic goals and foreign policies as logical outcomes of his revolutionary social and economic intentions. [PH]

Armaments and Aggression

31.426 Omer Bartov. *Hitler's army: soldiers, Nazis, and war in the Third Reich*. New York: Oxford University Press, 1991. ISBN 0-19-506-879-3. ▸ Refutes claim that German soldiers remained relatively professional in conduct by demonstrating barbarizing effects of Nazi ideology, material shortages, harsh discipline, and brutal fighting on Eastern Front. Well written, based on numerous private eyewitness accounts as well as official sources. [PH]

31.427 Wilhelm Deist et al. *The build-up of German aggression*. P. S. Falla, Dean S. McMurry, and Ewald Osers, trans. Oxford: Clarendon, 1990. ISBN 0-19-822866-x. ▸ Multidimensional study of German war preparations covering not only rearmament, foreign policy, and economics, but also Nazi propaganda and social organization. Essential reference work, exhaustive and generally authoritative with excellent bibliography. [PH]

31.428 Klaus A. Meier et al. *Germany's initial conquests in Europe*. Dean S. McMurry and Ewald Osers, trans. Oxford: Clarendon, 1991. ISBN 0-19-822885-6. ▸ Detailed examination of German army, navy, and air strategy and operations from Polish campaign to Battle of Britain. Briefer sections on occupation pol-

icy and tactics of Germany's adversaries. Military history in broad sense. [PH]

31.429 Klaus-Jürgen Müller. *The army, politics, and society in Germany, 1933–1945: studies in the army's relation to nazism*. New York: St. Martin's, 1987. ISBN 0-312-00918-6. ▸ Three lectures placing uneven progress from cooperation to opposition between Nazi regime and higher reaches of German military in historical context. Focus on decisive aspirations to privilege and professionalism among generals. Concise, highly critical judgments of leading German expert. [PH]

31.430 Williamson Murray. *Luftwaffe*. Baltimore: Nautical & Aviation Publishing, 1985. ISBN 0-933852-45-2. ▸ Analysis of German air strategy, reasons for failure, and contribution of Allied bombing to German defeat. Beautifully written, broad-based military history. [PH]

31.431 R. J. Overy et al. "Germany, 'domestic crisis,' and war in 1939." *Past and present* 116, 122 (1987, 1989) 138–68, 200–40. ISSN 0031-2746. ▸ Illuminating essay and rejoinders over relative importance of military and strategic opportunities created by Britain and France or economic pressures within Germany in setting off World War II in Europe. [PH]

31.432 Norman Rich. *Hitler's war aims*. Vol. 1: *Ideology, the Nazi state, and the course of expansion*. 1973 ed. New York: Norton, 1976. ISBN 0-393-05454-3 (cl, 1973), 0-393-00802-9 (pbk). ▸ Study of Third Reich's goals, means, and measures in pursuit of conquest through December 1941. Skillful narrative integrating diplomatic, military, economic, and political events and concerns. [PH]

31.433 Norman Rich. *Hitler's war aims*. Vol. 2: *The establishment of the new order*. New York: Norton, 1974. ISBN 0-393-05509-4 (cl). ▸ Focus on implementation of Nazi goals in occupied and Allied lands, 1941–45, with emphasis on extent of collaboration and difficulties and ineffectiveness of resistance. Valuable work of research and synthesis. [PH]

31.434 Charles S. Thomas. *The German navy in the Nazi era*. Annapolis, Md.: Naval Institute Press, 1990. ISBN 0-87021-791-7. ▸ Straightforward, well-researched study of political attitudes and behavior of naval officer corps. Stresses roles of bureaucratic self-interest, devotion to Hitler, and force of ideology in keeping commanders loyal. [PH]

31.435 Gerhard L. Weinberg. *The foreign policy of Hitler's Germany*. Vol. 1: *Diplomatic revolution in Europe, 1933–36*. 1970 ed. Chicago: University of Chicago Press, 1983. ISBN 0-226-88509-7 (cl, 1970), 0-226-88513-5 (pbk). ▸ Definitive account of how Hitler reset international stage in order to begin turning foreign policy ideas into practice. Traditional, archive-based diplomatic history of very high order. [PH]

31.436 Gerhard L. Weinberg. *The foreign policy of Hitler's Germany*. Vol. 2: *Starting World War II, 1937–1939*. Chicago: University of Chicago Press, 1980. ISBN 0-226-88511-9. ▸ Monumental depiction of Hitler's determination to unleash aggressive war and of circumstances that dictated its timing. Centered on Germany, but actually comprehensive analysis of European diplomacy. [PH]

Society and Economics

31.437 Avraham Barkai. *Nazi economics: ideology, theory, and policy*. Ruth Hadass-Vashitz, trans. New Haven: Yale University Press, 1990. ISBN 0-300-04466-6. ▸ Close examination of formative period, 1933–36, stressing distinctness of Nazi economic ideology and party's consistency and autonomy in enacting it. Clear, perceptive, and vigorously argued. [PH]

31.438 Gustavo Corni. *Hitler and the peasants: agrarian policy of the Third Reich, 1930–1939*. David Kerr, trans. New York: Berg;

distributed by St. Martin's, 1990. ISBN 0-85496-620-X. ▸ Well-researched, revisionist study of rural support, ideology, policy, and production of Nazi regime, 1930–39. Shows party leaders assumed and merely sought to soften decline of German agriculture. [PH]

31.439 Peter Hayes. *Industry and ideology: I.G. Farben in the Nazi era.* 1987 ed. Cambridge: Cambridge University Press, 1988. ISBN 0-521-32948-5 (cl, 1987), 0-521-36823-5 (pbk). ▸ Definitive study of relations between I.G. Farben, largest private enterprise in Germany, and Nazi regime. Traces firm's infamous role in Nazi crimes to interaction of largely defensive corporate strategy with ideologically defined context. [PH]

31.440 Edward L. Homze. *Foreign labor in Nazi Germany.* Princeton: Princeton University Press, 1967. ▸ Survey of why and how Third Reich enlisted millions of foreign workers, emphasizing characteristically Nazi combination of administrative confusion and ruthlessness. Limited attention to living and working conditions. [PH]

31.441 Michael H. Kater. *Doctors under Hitler.* Chapel Hill: University of North Carolina Press, 1989. ISBN 0-8078-1842-9. ▸ Wide-ranging history of medical profession in Third Reich, mixing quantitative analysis and narrative. Details exceptional degree of support for nazism among physicians. Special attention to problems of female, and persecution of Jewish, practitioners. [PH]

31.442 Claudia Koonz. *Mothers in the Fatherland: women, the family, and Nazi politics.* 1987 ed. New York: St. Martin's, 1988. ISBN 0-312-54933-4 (cl, 1987), 0-312-02256-5 (pbk). ▸ Study of extent of and reasons for collaboration and resistance among mostly middle-class women in Nazi Germany, emphasizing impact of widespread acceptance of separate male and female spheres in life. Marred by factual errors and inconsistencies, but unflinching and thought provoking. [PH]

31.443 Timothy W. Mason. "Women in Germany, 1925–40." *History workshop* 1, 2 (1976) 74–113, 1–32. ISSN 0309-2984. ▸ Wide-ranging analysis of social reality of German women under headings of family, welfare, and work. Stresses limited extent of emancipation in Weimar republic, internal contradictions of Nazi policy, and reconciling function of family life under adverse economic circumstances. Inconclusive but pathbreaking study. [PH]

31.444 David Schoenbaum. *Hitler's social revolution: class and status in Nazi Germany, 1933–1939.* 1966 ed. New York: Norton, 1980. ISBN 0-393-00993-9 (pbk). ▸ Classic study of content and consequences of Nazi social ideology, 1933–39. Chapters on labor, business, agriculture, women, state, and social mobility. Argues Hitler's regime remade (in part unintentionally) German notions of class and status. Fluent, fundamental work. [PH]

31.445 Jill Stephenson. *Women in Nazi society.* New York: Barnes & Noble, 1975. ISBN 0-06-496528-7. ▸ Roles in family, education, work, and professions, 1930–40. Stresses ironic and ambiguous outcomes of policies that reflected clashing ideological, economic, and political considerations. [PH]

Popular Opinion and Resistance

31.446 Jay W. Baird. *To die for Germany: heroes in the Nazi pantheon.* Bloomington: Indiana University Press, 1990. ISBN 0-253-31125-X. ▸ Study of representative forms, makers, and heroes of Nazi political mythology, emphasizing persistent glorification of death. Fascinating, readable glimpse into mental world of nazism. [PH]

31.447 J. S. Conway. *The Nazi persecution of the churches, 1933–45.* New York: Basic Books, 1968. ▸ Sober, balanced, and well-grounded study of church-state relations tracing policy disputes on both sides, steady radicalization of regime's stance, and overall failure of main denominations to act on beliefs. [PH]

31.448 Peter Hoffmann. *The history of the German Resistance, 1933–1945.* 1977 ed. Richard Barry, trans. Cambridge, Mass.: MIT Press, 1979. ISBN 0-262-08088-5 (cl, 1977), 0-262-58038-1 (pbk). ▸ Definitive study of opposition within military and government circles, assassination attempt of 1944, fates of conspirators and their families, and reasons for repeated failure. Exhaustive and sympathetic. [PH]

31.449 Ian Kershaw. *The "Hitler myth": image and reality in the Third Reich.* Oxford: Clarendon, 1987. ISBN 0-19-821964-4 (cl), 0-19-282234-9 (pbk). ▸ Fine explanation of breadth and basis of Nazi leader's popularity in Germany and Nazis' skill in exploiting it. Companion piece to 31.450 on other aspects of popular opinion. [PH]

31.450 Ian Kershaw. *Popular opinion and political dissent in the Third Reich: Bavaria, 1933–45.* Oxford: Clarendon, 1983. ISBN 0-19-821922-9 (cl), 0-19-821971-7 (pbk). ▸ Description of limits of Nazi success in changing attitudes of confused majority of Germans through case study of Bavaria. Concentrates on occupational issues, religious matters, and antisemitism. [PH]

31.451 George L. Mosse, ed. *Nazi culture: intellectual, cultural, and social life in the Third Reich.* 1966 ed. Salvator Attanasio et al., trans. New York: Schocken, 1981. ISBN 0-8052-0668-X (pbk). ▸ Fine collection of contemporary materials on life and thought in Third Reich, especially on women and families, education, religion, myths and heroes, and racial science. Excellent point of access to Nazi worldview and propaganda. [PH]

31.452 Detlev J. K. Peukert. *Inside Nazi Germany: conformity, opposition, and rascism in everyday life.* 1987 ed. Richard Deveson, trans. New Haven: Yale University Press, 1989. ISBN 0-300-03863-1 (cl, 1987), 0-300-04480-1 (pbk). ▸ Study of ambivalent attitudes and behavior of ordinary Germans under Nazi rule with attention to continuities between Nazi social policies and those that preceded and followed. Sees Third Reich as one pathological response to modernity rather than specifically German phenomenon. [PH]

31.453 Robert R. Taylor. *The word in stone: the role of architecture in the national socialist ideology.* Berkeley: University of California Press, 1974. ISBN 0-520-02193-2. ▸ Thorough examination of Nazi architectural preferences and practice, outlining variety of styles favored for particular purposes and ideological message embodied in each. Skillful blend of intellectual-cultural and political history. [PH]

31.454 David Welch. *Propaganda and the German cinema, 1933–1945.* 1983 ed. New York: Oxford University Press, 1985. ISBN 0-19-822598-9 (cl, 1983), 0-19-821974-1 (pbk). ▸ Combines history of movie industry in Third Reich with thematically organized analysis of principal films designed to mold public opinion and behavior. Skillful analysis of written and visual record. [PH]

Racial Policy and Practice

31.455 Hannah Arendt. *Eichmann in Jerusalem: a report on the banality of evil.* 1964 rev. ed. New York: Penguin, 1987. ISBN 0-14-004450-7. ▸ Classic statement of "banality of evil," presenting Holocaust as carried out by small-minded bureaucrats hungry for approval and advancement. Contains controversial critiques of Jewish leaders in Nazi-occupied lands and of Israeli prosecutors of SS officer Adolf Eichmann. Sometimes unfair and inaccurate but indispensable. [PH]

31.456 Avraham Barkai. *From boycott to annihilation: the economic struggle of German Jews, 1933–1943.* William Templer, trans. Hanover, N.H.: University Press of New England for Brandeis University Press, 1989. (Tauber Institute for the Study of European Jewry series, 11.) ISBN 0-87451-490-8. ▸ Study of continuous Nazi assault on livelihoods of Jewish Germans, resulting self-help measures, and beginnings of forced labor. Admirably clear, forceful corrective to several historical legends. [PH]

31.457 Richard Breitman. *Architect of genocide: Himmler and the Final Solution.* 1991 ed. Hanover, N.H.: University Press of New England, 1992. (Tauber Institute for the Study of European Jewry series, 14.) ISBN 0-394-56841-9 (cl, 1991), 0-87451-596-3 (pbk). ▸ Argues Heinrich Himmler played decisive role in translating Nazi antisemitism into mass murder and that SS intent on that solution to Jewish problem even before World War II began. Well researched and revealing but not conclusive. [PH]

31.458 Christopher R. Browning. *Ordinary men: Reserve Police Battalion 101 and the final solution in Poland.* New York: HarperCollins, 1992. ISBN 0-06-019013-2. ▸ Dispassionate and disturbing exposé of mundane motives that made average Germans of Police Battalion 101 into mass murderers. Noteworthy use of postwar German court records. [PH]

31.459 Michael Burleigh and Wolfgang Wippermann. *The racial state: Germany, 1933–1945.* Cambridge: Cambridge University Press, 1991. ISBN 0-521-39114-8 (cl), 0-521-39802-9 (pbk). ▸ Informative study placing racial policy at core of Nazi theory and practice. Traces ruthless persecution of Jews, gypsies, "asocial" individuals, homosexuals, and mentally handicapped. Excellent work of both synthesis and interpretation. [PH]

31.460 Robert Gellately. *The Gestapo and German society: enforcing racial policy, 1933–1945.* 1990 ed. Oxford: Clarendon, 1991. ISBN 0-19-822869-4 (cl, 1990), 0-19-820297-0 (pbk). ▸ Demonstration of reliance of understaffed machinery of racial persecution on tip-offs and denunciations by average German citizens. Valuable contribution to assessing extent and forms of terror in Third Reich and relationship between rulers and ruled. [PH]

31.461 Karl A. Schleunes. *The twisted road to Auschwitz: Nazi policy toward German Jews, 1933–1939.* 1970 ed. Urbana: University of Illinois Press, 1990. ISBN 0-252-06147-0 (pbk). ▸ Recounts improvised, ill-coordinated, and gradual escalation of Nazi assault on German Jews. Distinguished by original perspective and calm, lucid writing. [PH]

SEE ALSO
21.295 Raul Hilberg. *The destruction of the European Jews.*

Coming to Terms with the Past

31.462 Peter Baldwin, ed. *Reworking the past: Hitler, the Holocaust, and the historians' debate.* Boston: Beacon, 1990. ISBN 0-8070-4302-8. ▸ Collection of essays occasioned by West German historians' debate of 1980s over interpreting nazism, Holocaust, and their place in German and world history. Good introductory and bibliographical guides to controversy. [PH]

31.463 Richard J. Evans. *In Hitler's shadow: West German historians and the attempt to escape from the Nazi past.* New York: Pantheon, 1989. ISBN 0-394-57686-1. ▸ Makes empirical case against recent historical writings that explicitly or implicitly exculpate Hitler and those who followed him. Pointed, vigorous extended essay. [PH]

31.464 Charles S. Maier. *The unmasterable past: history, Holocaust, and German national identity.* Cambridge, Mass.: Harvard University Press, 1988. ISBN 0-674-92975-6 (cl), 0-674-92976-4 (pbk). ▸ Meditation on contemporary forms and problems of recalling and writing about Nazi era and Holocaust. Sometimes too elegant, but full of sharp, sound reflections. [PH]

Origins of the Postwar Era

31.465 John E. Farquharson. *The Western Allies and the politics of food: agrarian management in postwar Germany.* Leamington Spa: Berg, 1985. ISBN 0-907582-24-9. ▸ Treatment of role of food supply as shaper of policy, disrupter of inter-Allied cooperation,

and political instrument during occupation of Germany. Important, long-overdue contribution. [PH]

31.466 John Gimbel. *The American occupation of Germany: politics and the military, 1945–1949.* Stanford, Calif.: Stanford University Press, 1968. ISBN 0-8047-0667-0. ▸ Administrative history centering on range of interests that gave United States policy fundamental unity beneath superficial discontinuities and on importance of French as much as Soviet actions in shaping events. Rests exclusively on American and German sources. [PH]

31.467 John Gimbel. *Science, technology, and reparations: exploitation and plunder in postwar Germany.* Stanford, Calif.: Stanford University Press, 1990. ISBN 0-8047-1761-3. ▸ Study of American extraction of militarily and commercially useful personnel, patents, and know-how from Germany after World War II. Judicious, concise, well researched and written. [PH]

31.468 Linda Hunt. *Secret agenda: the United States government, Nazi scientists, and Project Paperclip, 1945 to 1990.* New York: St. Martin's, 1991. ISBN 0-312-05510-2. ▸ Well-researched, highly critical account of Project Paperclip, under which United States officials brought numerous German scientists, some deeply implicated in Nazi war crimes, to work for American space and defense programs after World War II. [PH]

31.469 Lutz Niethammer. *Die Mitläuferfabrik: die Entnazifizierung am Beispiel Bayerns.* Berlin: Dietz, 1982. ISBN 3-8012-0082-5. ▸ Examination of contradictory purposes and practice of denazification in Bavaria, especially process by which indigenous authorities redefined former active Nazis into simple fellow-travelers. Groundbreaking work of archival research. Reprint of *Entnazifizierung in Bayern* (1972). [PH]

31.470 Edward N. Peterson. *The American occupation of Germany: retreat to victory.* Detroit: Wayne State University Press, 1977. ISBN 0-8143-1588-7. ▸ Soundly researched, soberly argued examination of United States policy making and implementation at upper and local levels. Concludes that only by retreating from initially harsh directives did military government achieve some of its purposes. [PH]

31.471 Edward N. Peterson. *The many faces of defeat: the German people's experience in 1945.* New York: Lang, 1990. ISBN 0-8204-1351-8. ▸ Plight of "ordinary" Germans and prisoners of war in 1945 under occupiers whose behavior varied only in degree, not in kind. One sided and badly printed, but provides essential, often forgotten perspective. [PH]

31.472 Gregory W. Sandford. *From Hitler to Ulbricht: the communist reconstruction of East Germany, 1945–46.* Princeton: Princeton University Press, 1983. ISBN 0-691-05367-7. ▸ Study of means and ends of Soviet program of socioeconomic democratization in eastern Germany. Temperate and open minded, but stresses poisonous effects of Communist party's insistence on control. [PH]

31.473 Raymond G. Stokes. *Divide and prosper: the heirs of I.G. Farben under Allied authority, 1945–1951.* Berkeley: University of California Press, 1988. ISBN 0-520-06248-5. ▸ Study of Allied decartellization policy and German economic recovery as exemplified by postwar fate of I.G. Farben companies and its successors. Clear, judicious, illuminating account, based on extensive archival research. [PH]

31.474 James F. Tent. *Mission on the Rhine: reeducation and denazification in American-occupied Germany.* Chicago: University of Chicago Press, 1982. ISBN 0-226-79357-5 (cl), 0-226-79358-3 (pbk). ▸ Model study of reeducation and denazification in American occupation zone and effectiveness of local efforts to stymie these programs. [PH]

SEE ALSO
48.398 Thomas Alan Schwartz. *America's Germany.*

SECOND AUSTRIAN REPUBLIC

Origins

31.475 William B. Bader. *Austria between East and West, 1945–1955.* Stanford, Calif.: Stanford University Press, 1966. ▸ Austrian question after 1945 in context of larger postwar dilemmas. Thoughtful survey of Austrian politics as it developed in context of four power tensions. [JWB]

31.476 Fritz Fellner. "The problem of the Austrian nation after 1945." *Journal of modern history* 60 (1988) 264–89. ISSN 0022-2801. ▸ Examination of often contested construction of specifically Austrian national identity after World War II, focusing on political figures, historians, and other writers. Argues Austrian history cannot be divorced from larger history of Central Europe and too emphatic preoccupation with Austrian nationalist ideology in age of transnational order dangerously anachronistic. [JWB]

31.477 Robert H. Keyserlingk. *Austria in World War II: an Anglo-American dilemma.* Kingston: McGill-Queen's University Press, 1988. ISBN 0-7735-0644-6. ▸ Revisionist argument that Western Allies' eventual recognition of Austria's independence and victimization by Germany resulted only from exigencies of late wartime diplomacy, further enhanced by pressures of cold war. [JWB]

31.478 Oliver Rathkolb, ed. *Gesellschaft und Politik am Beginn der Zweiten Republik: vertrauliche Berichte der US-Militäradministration aus Österreich, 1945, in englischer Originalfassung.* Vienna: Böhlau, 1985. ISBN 3-205-05005-3. ▸ Valuable collection of materials (in English original) relating to immediate postwar Austria generated by intelligence officials in United States military administration. Reports and letters by University of Chicago-trained historians Paul R. Sweet and Edgar N. Johnson are of special interpretive and analytic utility. Documents show continuities as well as discontinuities embedded within Austrian civil society between 1937 and 1945/46. [JWB]

31.479 Gerald Stourzh. *Geschichte des Staatsvertrages, 1945–1955: Österreichs Weg zur Neutralität.* 3d ed. Graz: Styria, 1985. ISBN 3-222-11621-0. ▸ Careful survey of Austrian efforts to secure full independence after 1945, showing complicated path Austrian leaders trod as unwilling hostages of Four Power politics. Authoritative work on history of Austrian State Treaty. [JWB]

31.480 Reinhold Wagnleitner. *Coca-colonisation und Kalter Krieg: die Kulturmission der USA in Österreich nach dem Zweiten Weltkrieg.* Vienna: Verlag für Gesellschaftskritik, 1991. ISBN 3-85115-131-3. ▸ Explores impact of American popular culture, media, and aesthetic values on Austrian society after 1945, considering both official and market-driven cultural interventions. Shows extent of penetration of American cultural artifacts, programs, and trends into all areas of private and public life. [JWB]

SEE ALSO
48.427 Audrey Kurth Cronin. *Great power politics and the struggle over Austria, 1945–1955.*

Politics and Society

31.481 Peter J. Katzenstein. *Corporatism and change: Austria, Switzerland, and the politics of industry.* Ithaca, N.Y.: Cornell University Press, 1984. ISBN 0-8014-1716-3. ▸ Analysis of political economy of Austria and Switzerland showing how each economic model profoundly influenced by history and politics. Especially good in describing and explaining genesis and operations of Austrian social corporatism. [JWB]

31.482 Anton Pelinka and Fritz Plasser, eds. *Das österreichische Parteiensystem.* Vienna: Böhlau, 1988. ISBN 3-205-08910-3. ▸ Critical essays on state of Austrian party system in later 1980s illuminating state of discipline of political science in Austria. Covers

wide range of important topics including electoral behavior, party finances and organizational structure, and Austrian parties and parliamentary system in comparative perspective. Detailed, useful research tool. [JWB]

31.483 G. Bingham Powell, Jr. *Social fragmentation and political hostility: an Austrian case study.* Stanford, Calif.: Stanford University Press, 1970. ISBN 0-8047-0715-4. ▸ Analysis of politics in small Salzburg town of Hallein, using variety of comparative theoretical perspectives. Argues Hallein's political culture characterized by high degree of fragmentation and polarization among party activists, creating serious governance problems for city political elites. [JWB]

31.484 Karl R. Stadler. *Austria.* New York: Praeger, 1971. ▸ Insists Austrian history has own internal dynamic apart from that of Germany; Austrian nation as *sui generis.* Part of larger body of historical work advocating separate and special Austrian identity in modern world. [JWB]

31.485 Kurt Steiner, Fritz Fellner, and Hubert Feichtlbauer, eds. *Modern Austria.* Palo Alto, Calif.: Society for the Promotion of Science & Scholarship, 1981. ISBN 0-930664-03-5. ▸ Collection of essays on major components of Austrian society, politics, and culture, stressing reconstitution of republic out of ruins of 1945. Contributions by professional politicians and other public figures complement those by university-based scholars. Useful, if slightly dated, survey of second republic at mid-career. [JWB]

31.486 Melanie A. Sully. *A contemporary history of Austria.* London: Routledge, 1990. ISBN 0-415-01928-1. ▸ Informative, thoughtful review of modern Austrian politics focusing mainly on events and ideas of 1980s. Stresses challenges faced by established political parties and corporatist system. Useful discussion of election of Kurt Waldheim and political aftermath. [JWB]

31.487 Melanie A. Sully. *Political parties and elections in Austria.* New York: St. Martin's, 1981. ISBN 0-312-62325-9. ▸ Brief, but intelligent overview of political system of second republic. Written at high point of Bruno Kreisky's regime and thus slightly dated in imputation of stability and longevity to then socialist leadership. [JWB]

FEDERAL REPUBLIC

Reference Works and General Studies

31.488 Dennis L. Bark and David R. Gress. *A history of West Germany.* Vol. 1: *From shadow to substance, 1945–1963.* Vol. 2: *Democracy and its discontents, 1963–1991.* Oxford: Blackwell, 1989. ISBN 0-631-16924-5 (set), 0-631-16787-0 (v. 1), 0-631-16788-9 (v. 2). ▸ Comprehensive narrative history, emphasizing politics and based on published sources; fullest synthetic account in English. Authors, unabashed admirers of West Germany's postwar democratic transformation, view customary emphasis on debilitated German psyche as reflection of debilitations of Federal Republic's left-wing domestic critics. [NDC]

31.489 Karl Dietrich Bracher et al., eds. *Geschichte der Bundesrepublik Deutschland.* 6 vols. Stuttgart and Wiesbaden: Deutsche Verlags-Anstalt and Brockhaus, 1981–87. ISBN 3-7653-0328-3 (set). ▸ Illustrated, chronologically ordered general history, each portion by distinguished senior historian. Authoritative, encyclopedic in scope, frequently original, yet accessible and lively. Partly based on newly available primary sources. [NDC]

31.490 David P. Conradt. *The German polity.* 4th ed. New York: Longman, 1989. ISBN 0-8013-0125-4. ▸ Survey of development of regional and federal institutions (political, governmental, social) in framework of mature, liberal, late capitalist society; eschews notion of German exceptionalism. Intended for students but more broadly useful. [NDC]

31.491 *The German Tribune: a weekly review of the German press.*

Hamburg: Reinecke, 1962–. ISSN 0016-8858. ▸ Translations of significant articles (from both Germanies) on politics, economics, society, and arts. Vital source (e.g., on reunification). [NDC]

31.492 Alfred Grosser. *Germany in our time: a political history of the postwar years.* Paul Stephenson, trans. New York: Praeger, 1971. ▸ Eclectic classic; topical coverage of occupation era and formative decades for both German states (strongly emphasizing West). Evolution of political and economic institutions and popular moral climate, often via striking anecdotes. [NDC]

31.493 Elizabeth Harvey. "The two Germanies: recent publications on the Federal Republic, the German Democratic Republic, and the German question." *The historical journal* 33.4 (1990) 953–70. ISSN 0018-246X. ▸ Review of important political and economic literature, including some in German. Cogent discussion of central historiographical issues: continuity and change after 1945, periodization, and relationship between histories of two Germanies. [NDC]

31.494 Peter J. Katzenstein. *Policy and politics in West Germany: the growth of a semisovereign state.* Philadelphia: Temple University Press, 1987. ISBN 0-87722-263-0 (cl), 0-87722-264-9 (pbk). ▸ Study of policy formation in 1970s and 1980s and interface of state, economy, and citizenry. Topics include state institutions, economic management, industrial relations, social welfare, guest workers, and administrative and university reform. Analysis, original documents, tables, extensive topical bibliography. [NDC]

31.495 Peter H. Merkl, ed. *The Federal Republic of Germany at forty.* New York: New York University Press, 1989. ISBN 0-8147-5445-7 (cl), 0-8147-5446-5 (pbk). ▸ Twenty-one essays of varying quality by political scientists and historians treating constitution, parties, trade unions, feminism, Protestant church (East and West), and relations with United States, Israel, and European community. [NDC]

31.496 Anna J. Merritt and Richard L. Merritt, comps. *Politics, economics, and society in the two Germanies, 1945–75: a bibliography of English-language works.* Urbana: University of Illinois Press, 1978. ISBN 0-252-00684-4. ▸ List of 8,548 items treating demography, occupation era, politics, economics, social and cultural structure, and foreign policies. Excludes items in popular press on art, science and technology, fiction, and individual articles in German-focused periodicals (conveniently listed). [NDC]

31.497 Elisabeth Noelle-Neumann. *The Germans: public opinion polls, 1967–1980.* Westport, Conn.: Greenwood, 1981. ISBN 0-313-22490-9. ▸ Allensbach polls, extensively covering political and social attitudes, personal life styles, national and historical consciousness. [NDC]

31.498 Gerhard Albert Ritter and Merith Niehuss. *Wahlen in Deutschland, 1946–1991: ein Handbuch.* Munich: Beck, 1991. ISBN 3-406-35207-3. ▸ Results and extensive demographic analysis of all free elections (East and West) to state, national, and European parliaments. Numerous graphs, maps, and electoral and demographic tables—latter also useful to social historians. [NDC]

31.499 Carl-Christoph Schweitzer et al., eds. *Politics and government in the Federal Republic of Germany: basic documents.* New York: St. Martin's, 1984. ISBN 0-312-62622-3. ▸ Excerpted documents with clear explanatory introductions and annotations, covering origins of Federal Republic, Basic Law (constitution), parliamentary procedure, judicial review, speeches, party programs, federalism, churches, interest groups, military service, economic policy, foreign policy, and German policy. [NDC]

31.500 Henry Ashby Turner, Jr. *Germany from partition to reunification.* Rev. ed. New Haven: Yale University Press, 1992. ISBN 0-300-05345-2 (cl), 0-300-05347-9 (pbk). ▸ Concise political histories of East and West German states with some attention to effect of each upon other. Useful primer for students and non-

specialists. Previously published as *The Two Germanies since 1945, East and West* (1987). [NDC]

SEE ALSO

48.437 John Gillingham. *Coal, steel, and the rebirth of Europe, 1945–1955.*

Political Parties

31.501 Gerard Braunthal. *The West German Social Democrats, 1969–1982: profile of a party in power.* Boulder: Westview, 1983. ISBN 0-86531-958-8 (pbk). ▸ Political scientist's informative profile of party's organization, demographics, factions, leadership, electioneering (national, state, and local), policy discussions, and relationship with women, labor, and churches during its governmental years. [NDC]

31.502 Rob Burns and Wilfried van der Will. *Protest and democracy in West Germany: extra-parliamentary opposition and the democratic agenda.* New York: St. Martin's, 1988. ISBN 0-312-01681-6. ▸ Sympathetic, yet judicious study of persistence, evolution, impact, and democratic significance of leftist intellectual and countercultural civic activism. Treats rearmament debate (1950s), student movement (1960s), feminism, and antinuclear and environmental Green movement (1980s). Includes chronology. [NDC]

31.503 Clay Clemens. *Reluctant realists: the Christian Democrats and West German Ostpolitik.* Durham, N.C.: Duke University Press, 1989. ISBN 0-8223-0900-9. ▸ Discussion of Christian Democrats' (CDU/CSU) path from opposition (1969–82) to ambivalent continuation (1982–89) of Brandt-Schmidt *Ostpolitik.* Internal, domestic, and foreign constraints on policy making in CDU/CSU. Clearer than Griffith 48.453 but more specialized. [NDC]

31.504 Gordon D. Drummond. *The German Social Democrats in opposition, 1949–1960: the case against rearmament.* Norman: University of Oklahoma Press, 1982. ISBN 0-8061-1730-3. ▸ Lucid history of rearmament question (defining domestic issue in early Federal Republic) and evolution of Socialist Party of Germany (SPD) away from its official Marxist program. Overly reliant on published sources. [NDC]

31.505 Dietrich Orlow. "West German parties since 1945: continuity and change." *Central European history* 18.2 (1985) 188–201. ISSN 0008-9389. ▸ Links postwar party system to partisan traditions it transcended. Useful conceptual overview, pending forthcoming longer works by author, Christian Soe, and Noel D. Cary on individual parties. [NDC]

31.506 Geoffrey Pridham. *Christian democracy in Western Germany: the CDU/CSU in government and opposition, 1945–1976.* New York: St. Martin's, 1977. ISBN 0-312-13396-0. ▸ Factional, organizational, and conceptual development and sources of unity in diverse catch-all party. [NDC]

31.507 Gordon Smith. *Democracy in Western Germany: parties and politics in the Federal Republic.* 3d ed. New York: Holmes & Meier, 1986. ISBN 0-8419-1096-0 (pbk). ▸ Historical genesis and postwar evolution of constitutional framework, party system, and patterns of coalition and opposition. How and why democracy, despite difficulties, proved politically integrative after 1945. [NDC]

Political Issues and Personalities

31.508 Donald Abenheim. *Reforging the iron cross: the search for tradition in the West German armed forces.* Princeton: Princeton University Press, 1988. ISBN 0-691-05534-3. ▸ Analysis of continuity and change in postwar German military. Interplay of military heritage, democratic anxiety, historical consciousness, pragmatic defense needs, and soldierly morale in defining institutional identity of new army (1950s to 1980s). [NDC]

31.509 Konrad Adenauer. *Memoirs, 1945–1953.* Beate Ruhm von Oppen, trans. Chicago: Regnery, 1966. ‣ Unusually systematic, well-documented memoirs illuminating conditions in occupation era, emergence of Christian Democratic party, creation of West German state, road to sovereignty, and European integration. Three subsequent volumes (*Erinnerungen*) not translated. [NDC]

31.510 Arnulf Baring. *Machtwechsel: die Àra Brandt-Scheel.* Stuttgart: Deutsche Verlags-Anstalt, 1982. ISBN 3-421-06095-9. ‣ Eventful political history of first social-liberal government (German Socialist party/Free Democratic party). Treats origins, *Ostpolitik*, controversies, and Chancellor Willy Brandt's fall (1974). Lively, informative book profits from author's unusual access to chief political figures and to confidential documents (facilitated by President Scheel). [NDC]

31.511 Hans-Georg Betz. *Postmodern politics in Germany: the politics of resentment.* New York: St. Martin's, 1991. ISBN 0-312-04881-5. ‣ Superb study of emergence of Greens and of right-wing radicalism in Germany. Illuminates social, economic, and demographic foundations of postmodern politics. [DSC]

31.512 Willy Brandt. *People and politics: the years 1960–1975.* J. Maxwell Brownjohn, trans. Boston: Little, Brown, 1978. ISBN 0-316-10640-2. ‣ One of several memoirs by West Berlin's mayor, Social Democratic party chairman, West Germany's foreign minister, chancellor, and architect of *Ostpolitik*. Heavy emphasis on foreign relations; intriguing insights on foreign and domestic personalities. [NDC]

31.513 Mark Cioc. *Pax atomica: the nuclear defense debate in West Germany during the Adenauer era.* New York: Columbia University Press, 1988. ISBN 0-231-06590-6. ‣ Key parliamentary and extra-parliamentary debate (church, scientists, labor) with implications for identity formation in Federal Republic. [NDC]

31.514 Lewis J. Edinger. *Kurt Schumacher: a study in personality and political behavior.* Stanford, Calif.: Stanford University Press, 1965. ‣ Why dynamic, obdurate, self-righteous social democratic leader could not exploit seemingly advantageous postwar situation in order to win power. Classic biography but with controversial psychohistorical dimension. [NDC]

31.515 Ilya I. Levkov, ed. *Bitburg and beyond: encounters in American, German, and Jewish history.* New York: Shapolsky, 1987. ISBN 0-933503-52-0 (jacket), 0-933503-94-6 (cl). ‣ Contemporary comment, including statements by principals, regarding controversial Reagan-Kohl 1985 visit to cemetery containing SS graves. Includes text of President von Weiszäcker's celebrated speech on fortieth anniversary of end of World War II. [NDC]

31.516 Jack M. Schick. *The Berlin crisis, 1958–1962.* Philadelphia: University of Pennsylvania Press, 1971. ISBN 0-8122-7633-7. ‣ Good overview of entire crisis. [NDC]

31.517 Franz Josef Strauss. *Die Erinnerungen.* Berlin: Goldmann, 1991. ISBN 3-442-12823-4. ‣ Memoirs of Christian Socialist party (CSU) chieftain, Bavarian minister president, federal defense and finance minister, chancellor candidate, and king-maker. Larger-than-life personality with controversial career intersecting nearly every significant political event in West Germany's history. [NDC]

SEE ALSO
48.415 Jeffrey Herf. *War by other means.*
48.453 William E. Griffith. *The Ostpolitik of the Federal Republic of Germany.*
48.455 Wolfram F. Hanrieder. *Germany, America, Europe.*

Society and Economics

31.518 Volker R. Berghahn. *The Americanisation of West German industry, 1945–1973.* Cambridge: Cambridge University Press, 1986. ISBN 0-521-32990-6. ‣ Examination of industry's complex and uneven adaptation (political, economic, psychological, managerial) to liberal and democratic ethos. Analysis of roles of United States, German governmental policies, shifting sectoral dominance, and generational change. [NDC]

31.519 Hans-Joachim Braun. *The German economy in the twentieth century.* London: Routledge, 1990. ISBN 0-415-02101-4. ‣ Most recent, adequate overview. Treats origins of economic miracle, concept of social market economy, postwar policy development, capital and labor, structural change, and foreign trade. Also treats earlier periods, but shuns continuity issue. [NDC]

31.520 Ulrich Herbert. *A history of foreign labor in Germany, 1880–1980: seasonal workers/forced laborers/guest workers.* William Templer, trans. Ann Arbor: University of Michigan Press, 1990. ISBN 0-472-10159-5. ‣ Popular unwillingness to assimilate 4.5 million non-German guest workers (*de facto* immigrants to West Germany) historically contextualized in important cross-period study. Includes discussion of Nazi slave labor and postwar integration of German refugees. [NDC]

31.521 Eva Kolinsky. *Women in West Germany: life, work, and politics.* Oxford: Berg; distributed by St. Martin's, 1989. ISBN 0-85496-238-7. ‣ Conceptually modest but informative introductory survey, examining changes in legal rights, public and private attitudes, family roles, schooling, careers and employment, and political opportunities. Many statistical tables; topical bibliographies. [NDC]

Culture

31.522 Peter Demetz. *After the fires: recent writing in the Germanies, Austria, and Switzerland.* San Diego, Calif.: Harcourt Brace Jovanovich, 1986. ISBN 0-15-103958-5. ‣ Chapters on postwar cultural trends in each country, alternating chapters on particular themes, genres, or writers (including Group 47, Heinrich Böll, Günter Grass, Max Frisch, Christa Wolf). Accessible but idiosyncratic cultural tour. [NDC]

31.523 Anton Kaes. *From Hitler to Heimat: the return of history as film.* Cambridge, Mass.: Harvard University Press, 1989. ISBN 0-674-32455-2. ‣ Critical analysis of New German Cinema of 1970s and 1980s. Explores moral and psychological ambiguities of varied attempts to reconstruct memory or to engage or elicit vision of past. [NDC]

31.524 Charles E. McClelland and Steven P. Scher, eds. *Postwar German culture: an anthology.* New York: Dutton, 1974. ISBN 0-525-47365-3. ‣ Excellent sampler of postwar intellectual discourse. Excerpts from historians, philosophers, scientists, poets, novelists, critics, musicians, artists, and architects. Editorial introductions describe historical context, educational systems, media, and cultural trends in German-speaking countries. Illustrated. [NDC]

31.525 James F. Tent. *The Free University of Berlin: a political history.* Bloomington: Indiana University Press, 1988. ISBN 0-253-32666-4. ‣ History of West Berlin's university, from cold war origins to central role in university reforms and generational rebellion of 1960s and beyond. Illuminating political and cultural case study. [NDC]

GERMAN DEMOCRATIC REPUBLIC

Reference Works and General Studies

31.526 Stephen R. Burant, ed. *East Germany: a country study.* 3d ed. Washington, D.C.: United States Government Printing Office, 1988. (Area handbook series, DA pam, 550–155.) ‣ Historical development and 1987 status of demographics, governmental and party institutions, armed forces, popular attitudes, social structure, economy, COMECON, and Warsaw Pact. Extensive topical bibliography; tables. Efficient, informative source. [NDC]

31.527 David Childs. *The GDR: Moscow's German ally.* 2d ed. Boston: Unwin Hyman, 1988. ISBN 0-04-445095-8 (pbk). ▸ Comprehensive, yet accessible discussion of history, constitutional changes, economy, education, churches, Socialist Unity Party of Germany (SED), block parties, intellectuals, mass media, women, foreign relations, impact of Gorbachev, discontent, and tour-de-horizon just before collapse. [NDC]

31.528 Mike Dennis. *German Democratic Republic: politics, economics, and society.* London: Pinter, 1988. ISBN 0-86187-412-9 (cl), 0-86187-413-7 (pbk). ▸ Concise history and topical analysis (economy, social issues, political culture, institutions, dissent) with numerous tables. Also traces shifting analyses by republic's own historians and sociologists. Especially illuminating overview, despite premise of state's stability. [NDC]

31.529 Henry Krisch. *The German Democratic Republic: the search for identity.* Boulder: Westview, 1985. ISBN 0-89158-850-7. ▸ Concise overview of East Germany as "product of a thousand years of German and European history." Discusses politics, economy, identity, international position, women, education, sports, and dissent, especially in 1970s and early 1980s. [NDC]

31.530 Hermann Weber. *Die DDR, 1945–1986.* Munich: Oldenbourg, 1988. ISBN 3-486-52191-8 (cl), 3-486-52361-9 (pbk). ▸ History of Sozialistische Einheitspartei Deutschlands (SED) state. Shifts in regime's repressiveness and domestic standing connected to conflicting needs for demarcation from West and for Western economic aid. Includes invaluable extended historiographical essay. [NDC]

Politics and Society

31.531 Bruce Allen. *Germany east: dissent and opposition.* Montreal: Black Rose, 1989. ISBN 0-921689-33-0 (cl), 0-921689-32-2 (pbk). ▸ Origins of civic movements of 1989 can be gleaned from this short history of leftist and Christian dissent. Structured thematically around Eastern Bloc's crises: 1953, 1956, 1961, 1968, 1980, and Gorbachev era. [NDC]

31.532 Arnulf Baring. *Uprising in East Germany: June 17, 1953.* David Schoenbaum, Introduction. Gerald Onn, trans. Ithaca, N.Y.: Cornell University Press, 1972. ISBN 0-8014-0703-6. ▸ Controversial semipopular account linking East's repressive course after uprising to West's inflexible "policy of strength." German edition (1965) thus was calling for new *Ostpolitik.* Includes documents. [NDC]

31.533 Thomas A. Baylis. *The technical intelligentsia and the East German elite: legitimacy and social change in mature communism.* Berkeley: University of California Press, 1974. ISBN 0-520-02395-1. ▸ Examination of dialectical interaction between industrial and social engineers. Ideological socialization of former, recruitment into political elite, and impact on evolution of communist society. Intelligent, enduring study of technocratic adaptation. [NDC]

31.534 Margy Gerber et al., eds. *Selected papers from the fifteenth New Hampshire symposium on the German Democratic Republic.* Lanham, Md.: University Press of America, 1991. ISBN 0-8191-8094-7. ▸ Broad panorama of expert studies, covering such topics as media, writers, and film makers; gender, sex, and social issues; music and popular culture; technology and environmental issues; national identity; and foreign perceptions. [NDC]

31.535 Robert F. Goeckel. *The Lutheran church and the East German state: political conflict and change under Ulbricht and Honecker.* Ithaca, N.Y.: Cornell University Press, 1990. ISBN 0-8014-2259-0. ▸ Probing history of church's ambiguous place as agent of both change and adaptation. Treats early church-state confrontations, ties to West, generational change, connection to peace movement, and shifting *modus vivendi* of Honecker years (1971–89). [NDC]

31.536 Erich Honecker. *From my life.* Oxford: Pergamon, 1981. ISBN 0-08-024532-3. ▸ Tendentious but interesting early chapters (communist youth, anti-Nazi activities, imprisonment) followed by ritual recitations of East German viewpoint on two Germanies, Berlin Wall (whose construction he supervised), détente, achievements of socialism (celebrated via tables), Olympics, and Third World. [NDC]

31.537 Marilyn Rueschemeyer and Christiane Lemke. *The quality of life in the German Democratic Republic: changes and developments in a state socialist society.* 2 vols. in 1. Armonk, N.Y.: Sharpe, 1989. ISBN 0-87332-484-6. ▸ Thirteen scholarly essays (four by East Germans) on everyday life in mature East Germany. Useful on housing, workplace, impact of technology, environmental damage, and church. Less satisfying on gender roles, leisure time, media, family, and school. [NDC]

31.538 Carola Stern. *Ulbricht: a political biography.* New York: Praeger, 1965. ▸ Very rudimentary popular biography (only one in English) of leader of German Communist party, East German deputy premier, and builder of Berlin Wall. Published six years before his fall (1971). [NDC]

31.539 J.K.A. Thomaneck and James Mellis, eds. *Politics, society, and government in the German Democratic Republic: basic documents.* Oxford: Berg; distributed by St. Martin's, 1989. ISBN 0-85496-247-6. ▸ Excerpted documents with explanatory introductions. Covers origins, constitutional changes, parties, trade unions, judiciary, military, youth, women, church, dissent, economic policy, foreign policy, and German policy. Less organized and annotated than Schweitzer's comparable volume (31.499). [NDC]

Revolution and Unification

31.540 John Bornemann. *After the Wall: East meets West in the new Berlin.* New York: Basic Books, 1991. ISBN 0-465-00083-5. ▸ From revolution to reunification: vignettes and voices from the East. Cultural disorientation and impact on individual and group identity and self-respect. [NDC]

31.541 Jeffrey Gedmin. *The hidden hand: Gorbachev and the collapse of East Germany.* Washington, D.C.: American Enterprise Institute Press; distributed by University Press of America and National Book Network, 1992. (American Enterprise Institute studies, 554.) ISBN 0-8447-3794-1 (cl), 0-8447-3815-8 (pbk). ▸ History of East German and Soviet policy on German unity, followed by top-down descriptive analysis of East German communism's last-minute reform discussion and slide under popular pressure toward "inadvertent revolution." [NDC]

31.542 Constantine C. Menges. *The future of Germany and the Atlantic Alliance.* Washington, D.C.: American Enterprise Institute Press; distributed by National Book Network, 1991. (American Enterprise Institute studies, 512.) ISBN 0-8447-3731-3. ▸ Useful early attempt to place reunification into context of West German parties' past positions (not always fair to Social Democrats). Includes texts of Two-Plus-Four and German-Soviet treaties. Discussion of future alternatives already dated. [NDC]

31.543 Elizabeth Pond. *After the Wall: American policy toward Germany.* New York: Priority; distributed by Brookings Institution, 1990. ISBN 0-87078-323-8. ▸ Concise, lively, intelligent contemporary account, in international context, of German events of 1989–90. [NDC]

Section 32

MICHAEL F. METCALF

Scandinavia and the Baltic States

Historical research across Scandinavia and the Baltic states is and has been pursued under dramatically different circumstances since the development of the field as a professional discipline during the nineteenth century. The subjective need to mobilize historical scholarship in the service of nation-building was long dominant in Finland and Norway as Finland struggled to maintain its autonomy in the increasingly hostile tsarist empire of which it was a part and as Norway worked to reestablish its national identity while finding ways to increase its autonomy within the Union monarchy with Sweden. Moreover, both nations became independent states during the early twentieth century, and both found themselves at war to preserve their sovereignty at the outbreak of World War II. For historians in Denmark and Sweden, well-established states since the sixteenth century, this need was muted, although Denmark's loss of Schleswig-Holstein in 1864 did lead to a great interest in redefining the state and emphasizing Danish social institutions.

The situation for the Baltic nations, of course, has been much more precarious throughout the nineteenth and twentieth centuries. Not only were these countries under Russian imperial rule until 1917, but the social and economic structure—as well as the inheritance of the past—meant that resident elites were largely recruited from among resident Germans rather than Estonians, Latvians, or Lithuanians. Following independence at the end of World War I, the Baltic states required time to build their institutions of higher education and their capacity for historical research. Progress was difficult under the trying economic and political conditions of the 1920s and 1930s, and subsequent Soviet and German occupation in the years after 1940 put a significant damper on historical research even before the Soviets returned to stay until the early 1990s. During the post–World War II period, the bulk of publications on the history of the Baltic states that appeared in the West was written by exiles from the communist regimes and their offspring.

The external circumstances facing historians in these countries have naturally affected the type and quality of research and writing they have undertaken, as have the archival resources at hand and the extent to which they have been accessible. In the Scandinavian states and Finland, historians have generally found conditions comparable to those in Germany in terms of support for universities and outlets for publication. Unlike their German colleagues, historians in the Nordic countries—with the exception of the German occupation of Denmark and Norway during World War II—have been spared periods of censorship and extended fiscal crisis. For historians in the

Baltic states, however, the investigation of political and intellectual history has been extremely difficult for most of the past half-century. Historians in exile, too, long found their working conditions severely constrained by the barriers to archival access posed both by their status as exiles and by the political sensitivities of the Soviet authorities.

Of special significance is the official status of history and a number of related disciplines in Finland as so-called "national disciplines," which are clearly viewed in the context of fostering national identity and a sense of belonging to a very specific community. While this has not hampered critical research, it has joined with the particular historical circumstances of emergent statehood, Civil War, and international conflict to focus more attention on diplomatic and military history in Finland than in any other state treated in this section.

Characteristic of many of the efforts of Baltic historians-in-exile during the post–World War II period was a level of political diatribe concerning post-1940 political events and issues of Baltic-Russian relations that clearly revealed their intellectual and political agendas. Nevertheless, serious work has appeared, especially in West Germany, the United States, and Sweden, and professional Baltic studies organizations were founded in each of those countries in the 1970s. These arranged professional meetings and generally raised the professional standards of the field. Historians in these organizations, now a generation distant from their parents' bitterness and polemics, brought about a new standard of professionalism in the study of Baltic history in the West.

In the Nordic states, but not in the Baltic states, a number of joint research projects and special issues of journals have been devoted since the 1970s to comparing and contrasting the experiences of the five countries. In this guide, examples of these efforts include special issues of the *Scandinavian Journal of History* and the *Scandinavian Economic History Review* as well as collections of essays published in book form on topics ranging from the standard of living in the five countries to banking, the demographic transition, literacy, and religious revivalism. Thus, the Scandinavian historians' tradition of writing primarily about problems in the history of their own individual countries has in the past twenty years been challenged by efforts to look at the region as a whole and to interject a comparative approach into the research process. At times these efforts have fallen short of their laudable comparative goals, with contributors from the individual countries utilizing methodologies that differ to such an extent as to make comparison difficult.

Areas of strength in Scandinavian historical research in recent decades have included demographic, economic, family, labor, migration, and social history. The excellent vital statistics maintained since the seventeenth century, first by parish clergy in the state church and then by civil authorities, have provided a wealth of data for demographers and family and emigration historians. Likewise, computing facilities and the funds to utilize them have been readily available since the mid-1960s, with the Swedes—then the wealthiest of the Scandinavians—taking the lead. Scandinavian historians in these fields have been much more active in international historical circles than their colleagues in other specialties, thus making their work more accessible than the work of many of their compatriots to speakers of English. Likewise, the methodological sophistication of these historians—stemming from their early access to the requisite hardware and software—has been noted internationally.

Historical interest in Denmark, Iceland, Norway, and Sweden in recent decades has been dominated by social history and its various subfields, with economic history, too, playing a prominent role. On balance, the stepchild of the profession has been political history, with two exceptions: the political aspects of labor history and the "power-state" (military state or absolutist state) of the seventeenth century. This second topic has been particularly prominent in the last decade or so, especially in Denmark and Sweden. An inter-Nordic project on this theme is now producing very interesting results that should have an international audience when made available in languages other than those of the Nordic countries themselves.

This comment on language of publication requires some elaboration. Publication of historical research in the Nordic countries is largely supported by public funds through the universities and the research councils, and in some of the countries stipulations require that publication subsidies largely be restricted to publications in the national language. Thus there are structural as well as practical barriers to the publication of more historical research in the major European languages, and this tends to skew what is available in English, to name but the most obvious language. Users of this guide will therefore find a large number of entries concerned with Sweden in the seventeenth century, in large measure the result of the prodigious publication record of Professor Michael Roberts and the discussions his work has prompted. Readers will also note a large number of entries concerning Finland in international politics in the twentieth century, although in this case the reasons lie more in the translation of a number of Finnish works for publication in the English-speaking world, with its abiding interest in East-West relations during the Cold War period.

Historical research in the Scandinavian countries has been rich and sophisticated in most areas of inquiry, with a fair number of books and articles available to readers of English and German. Yet, there are many areas of inquiry in which a great deal remains to be done to inform international readers of the results of research conducted by historians in these countries, but published in their own languages. Especially rewarding would be greater access to social history research in Denmark and Sweden and to early modern Dano-Norwegian political and economic history. In general, historians of Europe writing in English would find much to gain from using a comparative approach that includes the Scandinavian case in their examination of cultural, economic, political, and social phenomena.

In the Baltic states of Estonia, Latvia, and Lithuania, their very brief histories as independent states, the political rigidity of the Soviet authorities throughout the period of the Cold War, and the extreme constraints on research in their archives have all combined to limit severely the amount and range of historical scholarship available to readers of English. Scholars in the post–Cold War era will find no difficulty in identifying important topics in Baltic political and social history that will provide fruitful, nearly untouched avenues for inquiry.

The complexity of presenting the historical literature on eight separate states that have varying histories of independence or incorporation in larger states over the early modern and modern periods has influenced the organization of this section. The section opens with subsections on reference works and national histories; the urban world, commerce, and industry; and demography, family, and household. Following these subsections are major subsections on the early modern and modern periods, which in turn are divided into general, Scandinavian, and Baltic sections. Finally, the early modern section on Scandinavia is divided into sections on the two extant monarchies of Denmark-Norway and Sweden (including Finland), and the modern sections are divided into national subdivisions.

Entries are arranged under the following headings:

[Contributors: MFM = Michael F. Metcalf]

REFERENCE WORKS

Bibliographies

32.1　Marianne Bagge Hansen and Gerd Callesen, eds. *Foreign-language literature on the Nordic labour movements/Fremdsprachige Literatur über die nordischen Arbeiterbewegungen.* Copenhagen: Arbejderbevægelsens Bibliotek og Arkiv, 1992. (Arbejderbevægelsens Bibliotek og Arkivs bibliografiske serie, 7.) ISSN 0107-4628. ‣ Important bibliography of titles in major world languages on history, politics, and activities of labor movements in five Nordic countries: Denmark, Finland, Iceland, Norway, and Sweden. [MFM]

32.2　*Finnish and Baltic history and literatures.* Cambridge, Mass.: Widener Library; distributed by Harvard University Press, 1972. (Widener Library shelflist, 40.) ISBN 0-674-30205-2. ‣ Comprehensive listing of Harvard University's Widener Library holdings on Finland and Baltic states as of early 1970s. Very useful bibliographical tool, widely available in research libraries. [MFM]

32.3　Erik Gøbel et al. "Select bibliography of contributions to economic and social history appearing in Scandinavian books, periodicals, and yearbooks, 1990." *Scandinavian economic history review* 39.3 (1991) 95–119. ISSN 0358-5522. ‣ Latest annual bibliography of literature on economic and social history published in five Nordic countries. Inaugurated in 1968 and currently arranged by theme. Some English-language works cited. [MFM]

32.4　Richard D. Hacken. "Scandinavian social economics since 1930: a bibliographic note." *Review of social economy* 44.2 (1986) 159–77. ISSN 0034-6764. ‣ Select bibliography of works (many in English), emphasizing Scandinavian "middle way" between capitalism and socialism. [MFM]

32.5　Kristina Nyman, comp. *Finland's war years, 1939–1945: a list of books and articles concerning the Winter War and the contin-*uation war, excluding literature in Finnish and Russian. Helsinki: Society of Military History, 1973. (Sotahistoriallisen Seuran Julkaisuja, 4.) ‣ Very useful bibliography of titles in English, German, French, Swedish, and other languages on Finland during Second World War. [MFM]

32.6　Stewart P. Oakley, comp. *Scandinavian history, 1520–1970: a list of books and articles in English.* London: Historical Association, 1984. ISBN 0-85278-268-3 (pbk). ‣ Thorough inventory of English-language works with annotations on content, coverage, and usefulness. Lists secondary works published 1880–1980, as well as some important studies and travelers' accounts published earlier. [MFM]

32.7　Salme Pruuden, comp. *Catalogue of books and periodicals on Estonia in the British Library Reference Division.* Dalibor B. Chrástek and Christine G. Thomas, eds. New York: Garland, 1981. ISBN 0-8240-9553-7. ‣ Comprehensive bibliography of titles in all languages. Includes 800 titles under rubric "history" and has many other rubrics of direct relevance to historians. [MFM]

32.8　Trygve R. Skarsten, comp. *The Scandinavian Reformation: a bibliographic guide.* St. Louis: Center for Reformation Research, 1985. (Sixteenth-century bibliography, 25.) ‣ Comprehensive bibliography of over 1,600 books and articles on all aspects of Reformation in Nordic countries. [MFM]

Dictionaries, Atlases, and Research Aids

32.9　Eino Jutikkala. *Suomen historian kartasto: Atlas of Finnish history.* Porvoo, Finland: Werner Söderström Osakeyhtiö, 1959. ‣ Seventy-four historical maps covering all periods. Special attention to language distribution, military actions, post roads, administrative districts, and settlement patterns. Finnish and English text. [MFM]

32.10　Timothy P. Mulligan. "New keys for old doors: new finding aids to records concerning the Baltic states during World War 2." *Journal of Baltic studies* 21.1 (1990) 53–58. ISSN 0162-9778. ‣ Review of recent finding guides to German and Russian archives as they relate to German policies in occupied Estonia, Latvia, and Lithuania, 1941–44. [MFM]

32.11　Byron J. Nordstrom, ed. *Dictionary of Scandinavian history.* Westport, Conn.: Greenwood, 1986. ISBN 0-313-22887-6. ‣ Useful, selective reference work stressing depth rather than breadth of coverage. Signed entries accompanied by bibliographical references. [MFM]

32.12　Stewart P. Oakley. "Reconstructing Scandinavian farms, 1660–1860: sources in Denmark, Iceland, Norway, and Sweden." *Scandinavian economic history review* 34.3 (1986) 181–203. ISSN 0358-5522. ‣ Description of rich archival sources available for reconstructing peasant households, tracing farm ownership, and following economic and cultural development of peasant villages from 1660s (for Iceland from 1690s). [MFM]

32.13　Ulf Sporrong and Hans-Fredrik Wennström, eds. *Maps and mapping.* [Stockholm]: National Atlas of Sweden, 1990. ISBN 91-87760-02-9. ‣ Discussion of development of maps in Sweden since 1532. Special attention to early mapping done by Land Survey and to uses of those maps as historical sources. [MFM]

HISTORIOGRAPHY

32.14　Rolf Adamson. "Economic history research in Sweden since the mid-1970s." *Scandinavian economic history review* 36.3 (1988) 51–66. ISSN 0358-5522. ‣ Critical historiographical presentation of economic history as practiced at Swedish universities in 1970s and 1980s, pointing to strength of very specific studies and absence of comprehensive ones. [MFM]

32.15　H. Arnold Barton. "The Danish agrarian reforms, 1784–1814, and the historians." *Scandinavian economic history review*

36.1 (1988) 46–61. ISSN 0358-5522. ‣ Well-researched examination of historiography of late eighteenth-century Danish agrarian reforms, analyzing contexts in which Danish historians have interpreted these reforms. [MFM]

32.16 Tatiana Brustin-Berenstein. "The historiographic treatment of the abortive attempt to deport the Danish Jews." *Yad Vashem studies* 17 (1986) 181–218. ISSN 0084-3296. ‣ Highly critical, revisionist appraisal of extant studies of rescue of Danish Jews and their acceptance of accounts of assistance by two Germans, Georg Ferdinand Duckwitz and Werner Best. [MFM]

32.17 Lars Edgren and Lars Olsson. "Swedish working-class history." *International labor and working-class history* 35 (1989) 69–80. ISSN 0147-5479. ‣ Descriptive analysis of Swedish labor historians coming out of 1960s who have studied changing power relations between employers and workers; gender bias one of remaining gaps, as most studies deal only with skilled male workers. [MFM]

32.18 Bernhard Paul Falk. *Geschichtsschreibung und nationale Ideologie: der norwegische Historiker Johan Ernst Sars.* Heidelberg: Winter Universitätsverlag, 1991. ISBN 3-533-04397-5 (cl), 3-533-04396-7 (pbk). ‣ Useful analysis of historical argument, thought, and writing of one of Norway's most influential nineteenth-century historians and his contributions to creation of Norwegian national ideology. [MFM]

32.19 Carl-Johan Gadd and Ulf Jonsson. "Agrarian history as a sub-field of Swedish economic history." *Scandinavian economic history review* 38.2 (1990) 18–30. ISSN 0358-5522. ‣ Fine overview showing complete revision of traditional notions as result of internationally stimulated research in postwar period. Swedish agricultural development kept pace with European; freehold peasants, not large estates, spearheaded agricultural reform. [MFM]

32.20 Carl-Axel Gemzell. "Scandinavian history in international research." *Scandinavian journal of history* 5.4 (1980) 239–56. ISSN 0346-8755. ‣ Discussion of treatment of issues in Scandinavian history by non-Scandinavian scholars to ascertain breadth and quality of coverage. Useful insights and observations from Scandinavian perspective. [MFM]

32.21 Kjell Haarstad. "A historiographical survey of *det store hamskiftet* in Norwegian agriculture." *Scandinavian journal of history* 8.3 (1983) 151–70. ISSN 0346-8755. ‣ Very useful study presenting last century's research on transformation of Norwegian agriculture and pointing out remaining directions for inquiry, not least of all into history of mentalities. [MFM]

32.22 Karl-Gustaf Hildebrand. "Swedish economic history before the 1980s." *Scandinavian economic history review* 38.2 (1990) 31–40. ISSN 0358-5522. ‣ Description of economic history departments established in all Swedish universities in 1947. Early practitioners empiricists who studied commercial and industrial firms. In 1960s and 1970s, alternative approaches introduced by nondogmatic Marxists. [MFM]

32.23 Hans Christian Johansen. "Trends in modern and early modern social history writing in Denmark after 1970." *Social history* 8.3 (1983) 375–81. ISSN 0307-1022. ‣ Very useful guide to Danish social history written in 1970s and early 1980s. Treats working-class history, historical demography, education and literacy, history of women, and everyday life. [MFM]

32.24 Niels Kærgaard. "The earliest history of econometrics: some neglected Danish contributions." *History of political economy* 16.3 (1984) 437–44. ISSN 0018-2702. ‣ Convincing study arguing first work in econometrics appeared with Danish economist E. P. Mackeprang's dissertation in 1906, not with later work of American economist Henry L. Moore on aspects of World War I. [MFM]

32.25 Thorkild Kjærgaard. "The farmer interpretation of Dan-

ish history." *Scandinavian journal of history* 10.2 (1985) 97–118. ISSN 0346-8755. ‣ Analysis of historiographical presentation of farmers as progressives and landowners as reactionaries in eighteenth-century Denmark. Questions this and standard portrayal of economic and social conditions calling for major reinterpretation of rural society. [MFM]

32.26 Olle Krantz. "Macroecomic history in Sweden." *Scandinavian economic history review* 38.2 (1990) 41–51. ISSN 0358-5522. ‣ Divides field into five areas and indicates major research projects in each, including trade cycles, price history for period since 1700, sectoral studies, and analysis of growth and structure of economy. Descriptive in nature. [MFM]

32.27 Helen Liebel-Weckowicz. "Nations and peoples: Baltic-Russian history and the development of Herder's theory of culture." *Canadian journal of history* 21.1 (1986) 1–23. ISSN 0008-4107. ‣ Interesting argument that Johann Herder's five years in Riga and study of Baltic history, language, and folklore contributed to his rejection of rational nation-state in favor of national identity based on culture and environment. [MFM]

32.28 Håkan Lindgren. "Swedish historical research on banking during the 1980's: tradition and renewal." *Scandinavian economic history review* 39.3 (1991) 5–19. ISSN 0358-5522. ‣ Critical discussion of developments in writing of banking history in Sweden during 1980s. In issue devoted to research on banking history in Scandinavia. [MFM]

32.29 Lars Magnusson. "Social history as economic history in Sweden: some remarks." *Scandinavian economic history review* 38.2 (1990) 52–58. ISSN 0358-5522. ‣ Broad portrayal of social history as practiced in Sweden as subdiscipline of economic history. Presents major avenues of research, including standard of living and social issues in preindustrial society. [MFM]

32.30 Ohto Manninen. "Red, white, and blue in Finland, 1918: a survey of interpretations of the Civil War." *Scandinavian journal of history* 3.3 (1978) 229–49. ISSN 0346-8755. ‣ Overview of literature to date, summarizing state of knowledge. Points to need for further work concerning motivations of those who remained neutral throughout war. [MFM]

32.31 Tapani Mauranen. "Review of research in economic and social history in Finland in the 1970s and 1980s." *Scandinavian economic history review* 36.3 (1988) 23–41. ISSN 0358-5522. ‣ Broad review of research on macroeconomics; nature, energy, and technology; agriculture; industrial processing; public economic policy; business history; local history; demography; and social history. Contrasts recent quantitative approaches with older, descriptive ones. [MFM]

32.32 Jan Eivind Myhre. "Research into Norwegian living conditions in the period 1750–1914." *Scandinavian economic history review* 34.2 (1986) 159–66. ISSN 0358-5522. ‣ Survey of various interpretations over last twenty years, noting new ground broken since 1975 thanks to comprehensive price, wage, and consumption data and utilization of business archives. [MFM]

32.33 Ulf Olsson. "Business history as economic history." *Scandinavian economic history review* 38.2 (1990) 59–64. ISSN 0358-5522. ‣ Descriptive study concluding business history in Sweden facilitated by opening of archives by many leading companies. Characterizes work to date, including studies of whole industries and cross-sectional studies of such phenomena as working conditions. [MFM]

32.34 Ulf Olsson. "Recent research in Sweden on the standard of living during the eighteenth and nineteenth centuries." *Scandinavian economic history review* 34.2 (1986) 153–58. ISSN 0358-5522. ‣ Survey of broad range of studies that have produced converging picture of worsening material conditions, 1780–1820, followed by steady improvement during transformation of agriculture and process of industrialization. [MFM]

32.35   Tönu Parming. " 'Baltic studies': the emergence, development, and problematics of an area studies' specialization." *Journal of Baltic studies* 18.2 (1987) 133–66. ISSN 0162-9778. ▸ Well-documented examination of development of Baltic studies as field following World War II, role of émigrés, and field's active expansion since 1970 with creation of Baltic studies associations. [MFM]

32.36   Krystyna Piechura. "Voltaire's interpretation of the international rivalry in the eastern Baltic region." *Journal of Baltic studies* 16.4 (1985) 357–72. ISSN 0162-9778. ▸ Convincing analysis of Voltaire's interpretation of struggle for Baltic provinces among Sweden, Polish-Lithuanian Commonwealth, and Muscovy-Russia since sixteenth century. Comments on Voltaire's attitude that Baltic region unworthy of independence. [MFM]

32.37   Gert von Pistohlkors. "Regionalism as a concept of Baltic historiography: some introductory remarks." *Journal of Baltic studies* 18.2 (1987) 125–32. ISSN 0162-9778. ▸ Insightful discussion of historical development of Baltic countries as geographic region whose inhabitants have never shared common sense of historical identity thanks to national, religious, and social differences. [MFM]

32.38   Georg von Rauch, ed. *Geschichte der deutschbaltischen Geschichtsschreibung.* Cologne: Böhlau for Baltisches Historische Kommission, 1986. ISBN 3-412-05085-7. ▸ Useful examinations by fifteen contributors of German historical writing in Baltic provinces from medieval chronicles to modern era, emphasizing nineteenth and first eighteen years of twentieth centuries. [MFM]

32.39   Hain Rebas. " 'Baltic regionalism'??" *Journal of Baltic studies* 19.2 (1988) 101–16. ISSN 0162-9778. ▸ Lively essay disputing concept of Baltic regionalism. Concludes indigenous populations never understood themselves in regional context; points out denotation of Baltic region first made in nineteenth century by German minority and Russians. [MFM]

32.40   Mauricio Rojas. "The 'Swedish model' in historical perspective." *Scandinavian economic history review* 39.2 (1991) 64–74. ISSN 0358-5522. ▸ Stimulating essay looks at historical roots of model, emphasizing need to take history into account and viewing model as rearticulation of ancestral values typical of Swedish peasant society. [MFM]

32.41   Francis Sejersted. "The development of economic history in Norway." *Scandinavian economic history review* 36.3 (1988) 42–50. ISSN 0358-5522. ▸ Insightful description of Norwegian economic history as dominated by researchers trained as historians whose main fields of research are in business history, preindustrial economic history, premodern agrarian history, and history of technology. [MFM]

32.42   Alfred Erich Senn. "Perestroika in Lithuanian historiography: the Molotov-Ribbentrop Pact." *Russian review* 49.1 (1990) 43–56. ISSN 0036-0341. ▸ Useful discussion of shifting Soviet stances on existence of secret protocols concerning Baltic states attached to Molotov-Ribbentrop Pact of 1939, culminating in 1989 admission and condemnation of their existence. [MFM]

32.43   Hannu Soikkanen. "Finnish research on changes in the standard of living." *Scandinavian economic history review* 34.2 (1986) 167–70. ISSN 0358-5522. ▸ Useful historiographic introduction to Finnish research on standard of living in Finland between 1850 and 1965. [MFM]

32.44   Edward Thaden. "Ivan IV in Baltic German historiography." *Russian history* 14.1–4 (1987) 377–94. ISSN 0094-288X. ▸ Analysis of Livonian policy of Ivan IV using four sixteenth-century chronicles and studies published by three modern historians. Suggests much work remains before clear picture can emerge. [MFM]

32.45   Rolf Torstendahl. "Minimum demands and optimum norms in Swedish historical research, 1920–1960: the 'Weibull school' in Swedish historiography." *Scandinavian journal of history* 6.2 (1981) 117–41. ISSN 0346-8755. ▸ Examination of growth of Weibullian tradition of radical source criticism and prominence of its practitioners in mid-twentieth century. Best available introduction in English to history of Swedish historiography. [MFM]

32.46   Ulla Wikander. "On women's history and economic history." *Scandinavian economic history review* 38.2 (1990) 65–71. ISSN 0358-5522. ▸ Useful examination of growing interest in women's history within discipline of economic history. Most research to date concerned with gender division of labor during period of industrialization. [MFM]

GENERAL STUDIES

32.47   Alfred S. Bilmanis. *A history of Latvia.* Westport, Conn.: Greenwood, 1951. ISBN 0-8371-1446-2. ▸ Dated yet useful overview of Latvian history from ancient times to World War II. Focuses on early modern and modern periods. [MFM]

32.48   Sten Carlsson and Jerker Rosén. *Svensk historia.* 2d ed. 2 vols. Stockholm: Svenska Bokförlaget, 1964. ▸ Standard scholarly work in its time; still very useful as guide to Swedish historical research prior to 1960. Each narrative/analytical section followed by comprehensive discussion of previous historiography. [MFM]

32.49   Aksel E. Christensen et al., eds. *Danmarks historie.* 10 vols. Copenhagen: Gyldendal, 1977–92. ISBN 87-01-53441-6 (v. 1). ▸ Best comprehensive scholarly history of Denmark and of Danish historiography (volume 10) currently available. Contains comprehensive bibliographical references and discussions of past research. [MFM]

32.50   Thomas Kingston Derry. *A history of Scandinavia: Norway, Sweden, Denmark, Finland, and Iceland.* Minneapolis: University of Minnesota Press, 1979. ISBN 0-8166-0835-0. ▸ Best comprehensive history of Scandinavia available in English. Covers prehistory to mid-1970s, but much stronger on nineteenth and twentieth centuries than on earlier periods. [MFM]

32.51   Ole Feldbæk, ed. *Dansk identitetshistorie.* 4 vols. Copenhagen: Reitzels, 1991–92. ISBN 87-7421-696-1 (set). ▸ Multiauthored, multivolume work presenting first comprehensive attempt to capture shifting history of national mentalities in Denmark from Reformation to present. [MFM]

32.52   Finn Gad. *The history of Greenland.* 2 vols. Ernst Dupont, trans. London: Hurst, 1970, 1973. ISBN 0-900966-23-8 (v. 1), 0-900966-91-2 (v. 2). ▸ Comprehensive history of Greenland as Norse and then Danish colony. [MFM]

32.53   Eli F. Heckscher. *An economic history of Sweden.* Göran Ohlin, trans. Gunnar Heckscher, Supplement. Cambridge, Mass.: Harvard University Press, 1954. ▸ Dated but still very useful history of Swedish economy by one of giants in field of economic history. Especially useful for early modern period. [MFM]

32.54   Jørgen Jensen et al. *Dansk socialhistorie.* 7 vols. and index. Copenhagen: Gyldendal with Statens Humanistiske Forskningsråd, 1979–82. ISBN 87-01-82331-0 (set). ▸ Volumes 3 through 7 of this excellent study of Danish social history cover early modern and modern periods. Leading experts author or coauthor each volume; many useful tables and graphs; extensive bibliographies. [MFM]

32.55   Eino Jutikkala and Kauko Pirinen. *A history of Finland.* Rev. ed. Paul Sjöblom, trans. London: Heinemann, 1979. ISBN 0-434-37760-0. ▸ Best history of Finland available in English for early modern period and first decades of nineteenth century. [MFM]

32.56 Karen Larsen. *A history of Norway.* Princeton: Princeton University Press for American-Scandinavian Foundation, 1948. ▸ Dated but still very best history of Norway available in English for early modern period; surpassed by Derry 32.323 for nineteenth and twentieth centuries. [MFM]

32.57 W. R. Mead. *An historical geography of Scandinavia.* New York: Academic Press, 1981. ISBN 0-12-487420-7. ▸ Very useful snapshots of historical geography of Scandinavia at several periods, mostly early modern and modern. Includes bibliographies, tables, and maps. [MFM]

32.58 Knut Mykland, ed. *Norges historie.* 15 vols. Oslo: Cappelen, 1976–79. ISBN 82-02-03453-1 (set). ▸ Very best comprehensive history of Norway published to date. Multivolume work accompanied by rich array of illustrations; volume 15 devoted to maps, tables, and index. [MFM]

32.59 Stewart P. Oakley. *A short history of Denmark.* New York: Praeger, 1972. ▸ Best of available histories of Denmark in English that cover early modern as well as modern period. [MFM]

32.60 Helge Pohjolan-Pirhonen and Veikko Huttunen. *Kansakunnan historia.* 7 vols. Porvoo, Finland: Werner Söderström Osakeyhtiö, 1967–74. ISBN 951-0-02049-4 (cl), 951-0-02048-6 (pbk). ▸ Most comprehensive multivolume history of Finland available. Accompanied by numerous illustrations and political cartoons; lacks comprehensive bibliography or index. [MFM]

32.61 Toivo U. Raun. *Estonia and the Estonians.* 2d ed. Stanford, Calif.: Hoover Institution Press for Stanford University, 1991. (Studies of nationalities in the USSR, Hoover Press publication, 405.) ISBN 0-817-99131-X (cl), 0-817-99132-8 (pbk). ▸ Carefully documented overview of Estonian history from Middle Ages to 1991. Only volume of its kind. [MFM]

32.62 Kurt Samuelsson. *From great power to welfare state: 300 years of Swedish social development.* London: Allen & Unwin, 1968. ISBN 0-04-948002-2. ▸ Comprehensive essay on social and economic aspects of development of Swedish state from seventeenth century through mid-1960s by leading Swedish economic historian. Of historiographic interest. [MFM]

32.63 Franklin D. Scott. *Sweden, the nation's history.* Rev. ed. Steven Koblik, Epilog. Carbondale, Ill.: Southern Illinois University Press, 1988. ISBN 0-8093-1513-0 (cl), 0-8093-1489-4 (pbk). ▸ Most recent, comprehensive survey of Swedish history from Viking age to mid-1980s, with special strengths in sections on nineteenth and twentieth centuries. [MFM]

32.64 Fred Singleton. *A short history of Finland.* New York: Cambridge University Press, 1989. ISBN 0-521-32275-8 (cl), 0-521-31136-5 (pbk). ▸ Best brief survey of Finland's history available in English. [MFM]

32.65 Richard F. Tomasson. *Iceland: the first new society.* Minneapolis: University of Minnesota Press, 1980. ISBN 0-8166-0913-6. ▸ Best survey of history of Iceland available in English; especially strong on twentieth century. Written by sociologist. [MFM]

URBAN WORLD, COMMERCE, AND INDUSTRY

32.66 Jorma Ahvenainen. "The competitive position of the Finnish sawmill industry in the 1920s and 1930s." *Scandinavian economic history review* 33.3 (1985) 173–92. ISSN 0358-5522. ▸ Outline of major developments in Finland's most important export sector in interwar period, demonstrating effects of Soviet Union's exit from and reentry into international lumber market. [MFM]

32.67 Sven-Erik Åström. "Northeastern Europe's timber trade between the Napoleonic and Crimean wars: a preliminary

study." *Scandinavian economic history review* 35.2 (1987) 170–77. ISSN 0358-5522. ▸ Useful examination of growing importance of timber exports from Finland to western Europe between 1815 and 1855, in comparison to exports from St. Petersburg and Baltic littoral. [MFM]

32.68 Dan Bäcklund. "Continuous transformation: the leading cities of Sweden, 1820–1970." *Scandinavian economic history review* 39.2 (1991) 3–28. ISSN 0358-5522. ▸ Critical test of hypothesis that leading cities are stable in retaining their positions at top of hierarchy. Finds hypothesis somewhat empty; argues demographic and administrative factors as important as technological and economic ones. [MFM]

32.69 Kristine Bruland. *British technology and European industrialization: the Norwegian textile industry in the mid-nineteenth century.* New York: Cambridge University Press, 1989. ISBN 0-521-35083-2. ▸ Excellent study of technology transfer in period of industrialization, especially open export of "technological packages" including equipment, advice, and British workers to oversee their installation and operation. [MFM]

32.70 Kristine Bruland, ed. *Technology transfer and Scandinavian industrialisation.* New York: Berg; distributed by St. Martin's, 1991. ISBN 0-85496-605-6. ▸ Important collection of fifteen contributions dealing with development of Scandinavian industry and shipping in nineteenth century. Emphasizes transfer of foreign technology to Scandinavian countries. [MFM]

32.71 Ole Feldbæk. "The Danish Asia trade, 1620–1807: trade and volume." *Scandinavian economic history review* 39.1 (1991) 3–27. ISSN 0358-5522. ▸ Thoroughly researched study concentrating on stable trading system established with China and India after 1732, growth of trade (especially 1772–1807), and its contributions to social, cultural, political, and economic change in Denmark. [MFM]

32.72 Ole Feldbæk. "The Danish trading companies of the seventeenth and eighteenth centuries." *Scandinavian economic history review* 34.3 (1986) 204–18. ISSN 0358-5522. ▸ Thoughtful study of twenty companies that operated between 1616 and 1843. Places companies in mercantilist context and emphasizes need of company organization to meet demands of trade to Asia. [MFM]

32.73 David R. Goldfield. "Metropolitan planning in Sweden, 1890–1945: the European context." *History of European ideas* 7.4 (1986) 335–51. ISSN 0191-6599. ▸ Useful examination of development and expansion of metropolitan housing policy from 1930. Traces practices in Swedish capital in European context. [MFM]

32.74 Gísli Gunnarsson. *Monopoly trade and economic stagnation: studies in the foreign trade of Iceland, 1602–1787.* Lund: Ekonomisk-Historiska Föreningen, 1983. (Skrifter utgivna av Ekonomisk-Historiska Föreningen i Lund, 38.) ISBN 91-85611-06-9 (pbk). ▸ Penetrating exploration of effects of Danish royal monopoly of commerce to Iceland on island's economic health and development. [MFM]

32.75 Carl G. Gustavson. *The small giant: Sweden enters the industrial era.* Athens: Ohio University Press, 1986. ISBN 0-8214-0825-9. ▸ Comprehensive history of Swedish manufacturing sector and its concomitant capital markets from late eighteenth century to outbreak of World War I. [MFM]

32.76 Sakari Heikkinen and Riitta Hjerppe. "The growth of Finnish industry in 1860–1913: causes and linkages." *Journal of European economic history* 16.2 (1987) 227–44. ISSN 0391-5115. ▸ Survey and analysis of growth of industrial and handicraft output. Argues growth initially driven by foreign demand through 1880s, then by foreign and domestic demand together from mid-1890s to 1913. [MFM]

32.77 Merja-Liisa Hinkkanen-Lievonen. *British trade and enter-*

prise in the Baltic states, 1919–1925. Helsinki: Suomen Historiallinen Seura, 1984. (Studia historica, 14.) ISBN 951-9254-54-4, ISSN 0081-6493. ▸ Comprehensive analysis of Anglo-Baltic economic and political relations in 1920s, casting light on problems of Baltic economies and role of foreign capital in them. [MFM]

32.78 Maths Isacson and Lars Magnusson. *Proto-industrialisation in Scandinavia: craft skills in the industrial revolution.* New York: Berg; distributed by St. Martin's, 1987. ISBN 0-85496-514-9. ▸ Carefully researched study of crafts and their contribution to and role in industrialization of Scandinavia. Special attention to Swedish case. [MFM]

32.79 Hans Christian Johansen and Per Boje. "Working-class housing in Odense, 1750–1914." *Scandinavian economic history review* 34.2 (1986) 135–52. ISSN 0358-5522. ▸ Outline of changes and expansion of working-class housing in large Danish provincial town. Exemplifies uses of rich Scandinavian source materials for social and architectural history. [MFM]

32.80 Jens Chr. V. Johansen. "Falster and Elsinore, 1680–1705: a comparative study of rural and urban crime." *Social history* 15.1 (1990) 97–109. ISSN 0307-1022. ▸ Important study utilizing large number of court cases in one rural and one urban jurisdiction to raise questions about differences in resolving conflict and exercising social control. [MFM]

32.81 Lennart Jörberg. "The industrial revolution in the Nordic countries." In *The Fontana economic history of Europe.* Carlo M. Cipolla, ed. Paul Britten Austin, trans., vol. 4.2, pp. 375–485. London: Fontana/Collins, 1973. ISBN 0-06-492180-8. ▸ Best available introduction to history of industrialization in Nordic countries. Deals with all sectors of economy; contains useful statistical tables. [MFM]

32.82 Niels Buus Kristensen. "Industrial growth in Denmark, 1872–1913—in relation to the debate on an industrial breakthrough." *Scandinavian economic history review* 37.1 (1989) 3–22. ISSN 0358-5522. ▸ Sophisticated mobilization of new statistics on industrial value to bolster argument that Denmark achieved its industrial breakthrough over period 1872–1913. [MFM]

32.83 Sima Lieberman. *The industrialization of Norway, 1800–1920.* Oslo: Universitetsforlaget, 1970. ▸ Now somewhat dated but still very serviceable history of industrial development of Norway. [MFM]

32.84 Ole Markussen. "Danish industry, 1920–1939: technology, rationalization, and modernization." *Scandinavian journal of history* 13.2–3 (1988) 233–56. ISSN 0346-8755. ▸ Useful description of Danish industry between world wars. Argues these were years of transition, but that Danish industry still burdened by outmoded production methods. [MFM]

32.85 Timo Myllyntaus. *Electrifying Finland: the transfer of a new technology into a late industrialising economy.* Houndmills: Macmillan Academic and Professional, 1991. (ETLA-The Research Institute of the Finnish Economy Series, Series A, 15.) ISBN 0-333-53132-9. ▸ Fascinating study tracing diffusion and economic impact of electricity and role of electrification as catalyst for modernization. [MFM]

32.86 Timo Myllyntaus. "The Finnish model of technology transfer." *Economic development and cultural change* 38.3 (1990) 625–43. ISSN 0013-0079. ▸ Innovative exploration of examples of technology transfer to Finland, 1809–80. Discusses licensing, import of patents and machinery, as well as impact of Finns traveling abroad and of immigration to Finland. [MFM]

32.87 Eva Österberg and Dag Lindström. *Crime and social control in medieval and early modern Swedish towns.* Stockholm: Almqvist & Wiksell, 1988. ISBN 91-55-42246-2 (pbk). ▸ Systematic analysis of crime and its social regulation in Stockholm and

two provincial towns, utilizing court and fine-payment records. [MFM]

32.88 Anders Skonhoft. "Home-led or export-led growth? The growth of the Norwegian electronics industry in the postwar period." *Scandinavian economic history review* 38.1 (1990) 50–73. ISSN 0358-5522. ▸ Technically sophisticated study of transformation of industry from one based on domestic market demand, bolstered by government purchases for defense and telecommunications, to important export sector. [MFM]

32.89 Johan Söderberg, Ulf Jonsson, and Christer Persson. *A stagnating metropolis: the economy and demography of Stockholm, 1750–1850.* New York: Cambridge University Press, 1991. ISBN 0-521-39046-X. ▸ Comprehensive study of Stockholm's declining fortunes after 1750. Focuses on high rates of poverty and death among men as contributing to Stockholm's low rate of marriage and high rate of illegitimacy. [MFM]

32.90 Sanjay Subrahmanyam. "The Coromandel trade of the Danish East India Company, 1618–1649." *Scandinavian economic history review* 37.1 (1989) 41–56. ISSN 0358-5522. ▸ Excellent examination of Danish company founded by Dutch merchants who were backed by Christian IV. Company concentrated successfully on intra-Asian trade, but ultimately was driven out by Dutch. [MFM]

SEE ALSO
4.483 Svante Lindqvist. *Technology on trial.*

DEMOGRAPHY, FAMILY, AND HOUSEHOLD

32.91 Tommy Bengtsson, Gunnar Fridlizius, and Rolf Ohlsson, eds. *Pre-industrial population change: the mortality decline and short-term population movements.* Stockholm: Almqvist & Wiksell, 1984. ISBN 91-22-00741-5. ▸ Stimulating collection of technical as well as qualitative studies, including works by leading scholars in field. Eight of sixteen contributions deal with factors contributing to mortality decline in Denmark, Finland, Norway, and Sweden. [MFM]

32.92 Anders Brändström and Lars-Göran Tedebrand, eds. *Society, health, and population during the demographic transition.* Stockholm: Almqvist & Wiksell, 1988. (Report from the Demographic Data Base, Umeå University, 4.) ISBN 91-22-01216-8. ▸ Eighteen of twenty-eight contributions on Denmark, Finland, Norway, and Sweden. Important issues include patterns of mortality, effects of vaccination, childcare, nursing, health conditions, and health profession. Focuses on eighteenth to twentieth centuries. [MFM]

32.93 Michael Drake. *Population and society in Norway, 1735–1865.* London: Cambridge University Press, 1969. ISBN 0-521-07319-7. ▸ Examination of writings of Thomas Malthus and Eilert Sundt and high rate of population growth in half century following 1815. Concludes fertility changed little over period, but mortality dropped after 1815, explaining growth. Excellent tables. [MFM]

32.94 Inez Egerbladh. "From complex to simple family households: peasant households in northern coastal Sweden, 1700–1900." *Journal of family history* 14.3 (1989) 241–64. ISSN 0363-1990. ▸ Methodologically sophisticated examination of landed peasants in northern coastal Sweden revealing simplification of family households from eighteenth to nineteenth centuries. Explanation based on demographic, economic, ecological, and geographic factors. [MFM]

32.95 Tom Ericsson. "Kinship and sociability: urban shopkeepers in nineteenth-century Sweden." *Journal of family history* 14.3 (1989) 229–39. ISSN 0363-1990. ▸ Useful study utilizing listings of godparents of urban shopkeepers' children to demonstrate that godparents were drawn from same or higher, but not lower, social circles. Refutes idea that *petite bourgeoisie* mingled with working class. [MFM]

32.96 Ingrid Eriksson and John Rogers. *Rural labor and population change: social and demographic developments in East-Central Sweden during the nineteenth century.* Uppsala and Stockholm: University of Uppsala and Almqvist & Wiksell, 1978. (Studia historica Upsaliensia, 100.) ISBN 91-554-0740-4. ▸ Study of growth of class of landless laborers known as *statare* and of its effect on demographic developments by means of cohort analysis. Painstaking presentation of methodology. [MFM]

32.97 Mats Essemyr. "Food, fare, and nutrition: some reflections on the historical development of food consumption." *Scandinavian economic history review* 34.2 (1986) 76–89. ISSN 0358-5522. ▸ Excellent utilization of ironworks records to study food supplies and consumption patterns of workers, 1730–1880. Finds diet rich in proteins and calories, with rye a staple and meat plentiful. [MFM]

32.98 Gunnar Fridlizius. "The deformation of cohorts: nineteenth-century mortality decline in a general perspective." *Scandinavian economic history review* 37.3 (1989) 3–17. ISSN 0358-5522. ▸ Sophisticated discussion of factors influencing decline in mortality, arguing that cohort-specific factors more important than regional epidemics or personal behavior and that improved sanitation more important than better nutrition. [MFM]

32.99 David Gaunt. "Rural household organization and inheritance in northern Europe." *Journal of family history* 12.1–3 (1987) 121–41. ISSN 0363-1990. ▸ Use of early modern evidence from Scandinavia to argue that family historians must attend to qualitative sources to avoid missing long-term changes not revealed by quantitative data. [MFM]

32.100 Gísli Ágúst Gunnlaugsson. *Family and household in Iceland, 1801–1930: studies in the relationship between demographic and socio-economic development, social legislation, and family and household structures.* Uppsala: Uppsala University; distributed by Almqvist & Wiksell, 1988. (Studia historica Upsaliensia, 154.) ISBN 91-554-2278-8, ISSN 0081-6531. ▸ Useful description of Icelandic population growth, its impact, and government efforts to control reproduction. Traces settlement of coastal communities, development of commercial fishing, and subsequent demise of pauperism. [MFM]

32.101 Hans Christian Johansen. "Growing old in an urban environment." *Continuity and change* 2.2 (1987) 297–305. ISSN 0268-4160. ▸ Compelling reconstruction of individual life histories in eighteenth-century Odense. Reveals little social contact between generations and confirms impression from early census materials that elderly did not live with children. [MFM]

32.102 Juhan Kahk, Heldur Palli, and Halliki Uibu. "Peasant family and household in Estonia in the eighteenth and the first half of the nineteenth centuries." *Journal of family history* 7.1 (1982) 76–88. ISSN 0363-1990. ▸ Sophisticated examination of household structure, social mobility, patterns of property transfer from original heads of household, and other topics. Concludes forms of households depended more on social than demographic factors. [MFM]

32.103 Ulla-Britt Lithell. *Breast-feeding and reproduction: studies in marital fertility and infant mortality in nineteenth-century Finland and Sweden.* Uppsala: University of Uppsala; distributed by Almqvist & Wiksell, 1981. (Studia historica Upsaliensia, 120.) ISBN 91-554-1164-9 (pbk), ISSN 0081-6531. ▸ Innovative analysis of influence of nursing customs and standards of living. Suggests nursing had considerable preventive effect against pregnancy and that determinants of practice were cultural as well as economic. [MFM]

32.104 Ulla-Britt Lithell. "Premium weaving in the nineteenth-century parish of Nätra: women, production, and reproduction." *Historisk tidskrift* 105.4 (1985) 471–90. ISSN 0345-469X. ▸ Well-documented analysis linking surprisingly high infant mortality rate in nineteenth-century Swedish parish to female premium weavers' early discontinuation of breast-feeding. [MFM]

32.105 Kenneth A. Lockridge. *The fertility transition in Sweden: a preliminary look at smaller geographic units, 1855–1890.* Umeå: Umeå University, Demographic Data Base, 1983. (Report from the Demographic Data Base, Umeå University, 3.) ISSN 0349-5132. ▸ Useful examination of early trend of modern family limitation in three rural districts to find commonalities. Finds no common social structure or dynamic; suggests relative secularization of cultural climate as likely key. [MFM]

32.106 Bobbi S. Low and Alice L. Clarke. "Family patterns in nineteenth-century Sweden: impact of occupational status and landownership." *Journal of family history* 16.2 (1991) 117–38. ISSN 0363-1990. ▸ Methodologically sophisticated comparison of data from four parishes to demonstrate that occupational status and ownership of land affected men's reproductive lives and that legitimacy and birth order influenced their access to resources. [MFM]

32.107 Wolfgang Lutz. "Factors associated with the Finnish fertility decline since 1776." *Population studies* 41.3 (1987) 463–82. ISSN 0032-4728. ▸ Useful contribution to international discussions of demographic transition utilizing sophisticated quantitative modeling. Finds significant early fertility decline at end of eighteenth century; secular decline starting ca. 1910. [MFM]

32.108 Margareta R. Matovic. "The Stockholm marriage: extra-legal family formation in Stockholm, 1860–1890." *Continuity and change* 1.3 (1986) 385–413. ISSN 0268-4160. ▸ Excellent study arguing high rate of illegitimacy in Stockholm is deceptive as many children born into marriage-like settings and later legitimized by parents' wedding. Concludes women made choices on basis of economic resources available. [MFM]

32.109 Thorvald Moe. *Demographic developments and economic growth in Norway, 1740–1940.* New York: Arno, 1977. ISBN 0-405-10802-8. ▸ Important econometric analysis of determinants of fertility and nuptiality to 1865 and explanation of long- and short-term variations in Norwegian emigration after 1865. [MFM]

32.110 Marie Clark Nelson. *Bitter bread: the famine in Norrbotten, 1867–1868.* Uppsala and Stockholm: University of Uppsala and Almqvist & Wiksell, 1988. (Studia historica Upsaliensia, 153.) ISBN 91-554-2264-0. ▸ Well-documented study of food shortages, 1867–68, that led to first mass emigration from Sweden and Norway. Concentrates on particular circumstances in Sweden's northernmost county. [MFM]

32.111 Andrejs Plakans. "The demographic transition in the Baltic provinces and Finland: prospects for a comparative study." *Journal of Baltic studies* 15.2–3 (1984) 171–84. ISSN 0162-9778. ▸ Useful comparison of state of research on demography of Finland and Baltic states both there and abroad. Suggests need to disaggregate data by ethnic groupings in Baltic states. [MFM]

32.112 Andrejs Plakans and Charles Wetherell. "The kinship domain in an East European peasant community: Pinkenhof, 1833–1850." *American historical review* 93.2 (1988) 359–87. ISSN 0002-8762. ▸ Use of records of estate near Riga to provide material for study of long-term changes in peasant kinship relations. Examines kinship networks and ties of individuals; discusses methodological difficulties. [MFM]

32.113 Lars G. Sandberg and Richard H. Steckel. "Overpopulation and malnutrition rediscovered: hard times in nineteenth-century Sweden." *Explorations in economic history* 25 (1988) 1–19. ISSN 0014-4983. ▸ Convincing study linking sharp rise in child mortality (late 1840s) and decline in height of average draftee born around 1840 to increased percentage of children living in households at or below subsistence level. [MFM]

32.114 Wilfried Schlau. "An assessment of demographic development in the Baltic states." *Journal of Baltic studies* 19.3 (1988) 219–34. ISSN 0162-9778. ▸ Methodologically sophisticated study attributing decreasing fertility in two Estonian and Latvian districts since 1850 primarily to individualization of farm ownership and farm families' desire to avoid subdividing farms among many heirs. [MFM]

32.115 T. Paul Schultz. "Changing world prices, women's wages, and the fertility transition: Sweden, 1860–1910." *Journal of political economy* 93.6 (1985) 1126–54. ISSN 0022-3808. ▸ Creative use of world market prices and women's wages to study fertility transition. Argues that improvements in women's wages relative to those of men contributed to decline in fertility. [MFM]

32.116 Jan Sundin. "Family building in paternalistic proto-industries: a cohort study from nineteenth-century iron foundries." *Journal of family history* 14.3 (1989) 265–89. ISSN 0363-1990. ▸ Excellent comparison of Swedes born at ironworks and in rural area to study social and demographic patterns at ironworks. Concludes latter clearly influenced by organization and demands of work, economic fluctuations, and paternalism. [MFM]

32.117 Oiva Turpeinen. "Infant mortality in Finland, 1749–1865." *Scandinavian economic history review* 27.1 (1979) 1–21. ISSN 0358-5522. ▸ Useful discussion of temporal, regional, and social variations across Finland. Shows fluctuations had little correlation with harvest yields; highest rates not in poorest, but rather in relatively wealthy areas. [MFM]

32.118 Joseph Zitomersky. "Ecology, class, or culture? Explaining family residence and support of the elderly in the Swedish agrarian past." *Scandinavian journal of history* 12.2 (1987) 117–60. ISSN 0346-8755. ▸ Critical and useful review of principal methods used by Swedish researchers to study elderly. Applies those methods to multigenerational residential patterns in rural Sweden, 1780–1910. [MFM]

EARLY MODERN PERIOD TO 1815

General Studies

32.119 Artur Attman. *The struggle for Baltic markets: powers in conflict, 1558–1618.* Gothenburg, Sweden: Kungl. Vetenskaps-och Vitterhets-Samhället, 1979. (Acta Regiae Societatis Scientiarum et Litterarum Gothoburgensis, Humaniora, 14.) ISBN 91-85252-15-8, ISSN 0072-4823. ▸ Important study arguing primacy of desire to dominate Baltic trade as motive force in late sixteenth- and early seventeenth-century struggle among Poland, Russia, and Sweden for control of Baltic littoral. [MFM]

32.120 D. G. Kirby. *Northern Europe in the early modern period: the Baltic world, 1492–1772.* London: Longman, 1990. ISBN 0-582-00410-1 (cl), 0-582-00411-X (pbk). ▸ Comprehensive essay with considerable attention paid to Livonian wars, role of Sweden as imperial power, and rise of Russia. Best overview of early modern Baltic history. [MFM]

32.121 Walther Kirchner. *The rise of the Baltic question.* 1954 ed. Westport, Conn.: Greenwood, 1970. ISBN 0-8371-3009-3. ▸ Broad survey of German, Danish, Polish, Russian, and Swedish interests in and attempts to gain control over Baltic littoral during late sixteenth century. Well documented. [MFM]

Scandinavia

32.122 H. Arnold Barton. *Scandinavia in the revolutionary era, 1760–1815.* Minneapolis: University of Minnesota Press, 1986. ISBN 0-8166-1392-3 (cl), 0-8166-1392-1 (pbk). ▸ Innovative, comprehensive treatment of intellectual, social, and political

developments cast in spirit of R. R. Palmer 22.353. Especially strong on Sweden and Denmark. Considerable attention to historiography. [MFM]

32.123 Loftur Guttormsson. "The development of popular religious literacy in the seventeenth and eighteenth centuries." *Scandinavian journal of history* 15.1 (1990) 7–35. ISSN 0346-8755. ▸ Fascinating study concluding home instruction instrumental in producing high degree of reading ability in Scandinavia by end of period. Finds religious context of assuring literacy soon surpassed by secular applications. [MFM]

32.124 B. J. Hovde. *The Scandinavian countries, 1720–1865.* 2 vols. Boston: Chapman & Grimes, 1943. ▸ Dated, but remains best introduction available in English to overall structure of Scandinavian societies in eighteenth and first half of nineteenth centuries. [MFM]

32.125 Ingrid Markussen. "The development of writing ability in the Nordic countries in the eighteenth and nineteenth centuries." *Scandinavian journal of history* 15.1 (1990) 37–63. ISSN 0346-8755. ▸ Interesting examination of commonalities throughout region. Concludes determining factors in spread of mass writing ability were political and economic growth, increased public schooling, and growing perception of utility of being able to write. [MFM]

32.126 Stewart P. Oakley. "The peasantry of Scandinavia on the eve of the French Revolution." *History of European ideas* 12.3 (1990) 363–75. ISSN 0191-6599. ▸ Useful study concluding reforms in Scandinavia during last two decades of eighteenth century released many peasants from dependence on landlords, allowing them to secure tenure of their land. Sees farmers becoming middle class. [MFM]

32.127 Trygve R. Skarsten. "The reception of the Augsburg Confession in Scandinavia." *Sixteenth century journal* 11.3 (1980) 87–98. ISSN 0361-0160. ▸ Broad treatment of Lutheran Reformation in Nordic countries. Compares and contrasts its introduction and consolidation in individual kingdoms. Also deals with failed attempts to diverge from Confession. [MFM]

32.128 Vagn Skovgaard-Petersen. "Literacy in the Nordic countries, 1550–1900: a comparative study." *Scandinavian journal of history* 15.1 (1990) 1–5. ISSN 0346-8755. ▸ Introductory survey of joint Nordic research project. Stresses that reading and understanding Bible were viewed as duty of every Lutheran Scandinavian, but that diffusion of writing skills closely linked to occupation. [MFM]

32.129 Kåre Tønnesson. "Tenancy, freehold, and enclosure in Scandinavia from the seventeenth to the nineteenth century." *Scandinavian journal of history* 6.3 (1981) 191–206. ISSN 0346-8755. ▸ Useful explanation of various, divergent Scandinavian paths toward agriculture dominated by peasant freeholds. Demonstrates impact of differences in political structure for development of patterns of landownership. [MFM]

Denmark-Norway

32.130 Jens Christian Beyer. "King in exile: Christian II and the Netherlands, 1523–1531." *Scandinavian journal of history* 11.3 (1986) 205–28. ISSN 0346-8755. ▸ Useful study dealing with Danish king's exile from perspective of Dutch-Hanseatic conflict. Treats his unsuccessful efforts to secure aid from Margaret of Austria and Charles V to regain his throne. [MFM]

32.131 K. E. Christopherson. "Lady Inger and her family: Norway's exemplar of mixed motives in the Reformation." *Church history* 55.1 (1986) 21–38. ISSN 0009-6407. ▸ Interesting examination of role played by Norwegian noblewoman and her two sons-in-law in Norwegian Reformation. Concludes conflict with church over monastery lands added to calls for humanistic reform. [MFM]

32.132 Inger Dübeck. "European law concerning *privilegia* and a Danish industrial joint-stock company." *Scandinavian journal of history* 7.3 (1982) 177–93. ISSN 0346-8755. ‣ Excellent study of granting of special privileges in mid-eighteenth century to iron-monger's factory. Investigates process by which privileges were conferred and contemporary arguments pro and con. [MFM]

32.133 Ole Feldbæk. *Denmark and the armed neutrality, 1800–1801: small power policy in a world war.* Copenhagen: Akademisk, 1980. (Københavns Universitet, Institut for Økonomiskhistorie, 16.) ISBN 87-500-1913-9. ‣ Elegant study of proactive diplomacy by small European state courting self-interest of great and small powers alike to maximize its freedom of action in time of crisis. [MFM]

32.134 Karen J. Friedmann. "Fencing, herding, and tethering in Denmark, from open-field agriculture to enclosure." *Agricultural history* 58.4 (1984) 584–97. ISSN 0002-1482. ‣ Informative examination of shifting responsibilities for protecting crops from livestock. Argues that, prior to enclosure, crop growers responsible; after enclosure, livestock owners. Discusses collective responsibility for enforcement. [MFM]

32.135 Ole Peter Grell. "The city of Malmö and the Danish Reformation." *Archiv für Reformationsgeschichte* 79 (1988) 311–39. ISSN 0003-9381. ‣ Extensive study of official pronouncement of Danish Reformation in 1536 preceded by accomplished fact in Malmö. Traces early beginnings of Reformation, reactions of Catholic church, and attitudes toward secular authority. [MFM]

32.136 Gísli Ágúst Gunnlaugsson. "The granting of privileges to industry in eighteenth-century Iceland." *Scandinavian journal of history* 7.3 (1982) 195–204. ISSN 0346-8755. ‣ Useful examination of who applied for royal privileges and financial support, how government dealt with requests, how decisions were made, to whom decisions were made known, and how affected parties reacted. [MFM]

32.137 Ingrid Henriksen. "Peasants and the market." *Scandinavian economic history review* 38.3 (1990) 3–21. ISSN 0358-5522. ‣ Useful review of research argues eighteenth-century agrarian reforms, and possibly monetary and credit policy, more important than favorable development of agricultural terms of trade in orienting Danish peasant households to commodities market. [MFM]

32.138 Knud J. V. Jespersen. "Absolute monarchy in Denmark: change and continuity." *Scandinavian journal of history* 12.4 (1987) 307–16. ISSN 0346-8755. ‣ Disputes earlier interpretations of transition to absolutism, arguing it was much smoother than previously thought. Argues taxation required to support incessant warfare gradually gave monarch increasing power over time. [MFM]

32.139 Knud J. V. Jespersen. "Social change and military revolution in early modern Europe: some Danish evidence." *Historical journal* 26.1 (1983) 1–13. ISSN 0018-246X. ‣ Important study of survival of knight service in Denmark until 1679 from military, social, and political angles. Argues it was dictated primarily by political need of nobility to justify its privileges. [MFM]

32.140 Leon Jespersen. "The *Machtstaat* in seventeenth-century Denmark." *Scandinavian journal of history* 10.4 (1985) 271–304. ISSN 0346-8755. ‣ Excellent outline of development of militarized tax state. Argues interrelationship of military policy and taxation practices necessitated centralization of power to meet external threats and greatly expand military capacity. [MFM]

32.141 Thorkild Kjærgaard. "Origins of economic growth in European societies since the sixteenth century: the case of agriculture." *Journal of European economic history* 15.3 (1986) 591–

98. ISSN 0391-5115. ‣ Innovative analysis of published agricultural treatises in Denmark and Schleswig-Holstein, 1590–1814, suggesting that growth and dissemination of printed information greatly affected European economic development. [MFM]

32.142 Thorkild Kjærgaard. "The rise of press and public opinion in eighteenth-century Denmark-Norway." *Scandinavian journal of history* 14.3 (1989) 215–30. ISSN 0346-8755. ‣ Thoroughly documented examination of proposition that new mass-circulation publications represented public opinion, as they claimed. Finds publications created by intellectuals and civil servants who stood to benefit directly from reforms they advocated. [MFM]

32.143 Gunner Lind. "Military and absolutism: the army officers of Denmark-Norway as a social group and political factor, 1660–1848." *Scandinavian journal of history* 12.3 (1987) 221–43. ISSN 0346-8755. ‣ Intriguing social and political profile of officers' corps. Analysis shows half of officers in seventeenth century were foreigners, but majority were Danes or Norwegians by 1710, and only 20 percent were noblemen. [MFM]

32.144 Thomas Munck. *The peasantry and the early absolute monarchy in Denmark, 1660–1708.* Copenhagen: Landbohistorisk Selskab, 1979. ISBN 87-7526-061-1. ‣ Comprehensive analysis of forms and conditions of land tenure, seigneurial authority, military service, and estate management. Discusses changes brought by introduction of absolutism and relations between peasantry and crown. [MFM]

32.145 Anne-Hilde Nagel. "The decision-making process and the granting of privileges to Froland Works." *Scandinavian journal of history* 7.3 (1982) 205–31. ISSN 0346-8755. ‣ Well-documented study of issuance of privileges to Norwegian foundry through bureaucracy of Danish monarchy to ascertain and evaluate decision-making process. Finds ability of private parties to influence outcome was marginal. [MFM]

32.146 E. Ladewig Petersen. "Defence, war, and finance: Christian IV and the Council of the Realm, 1596–1629." *Scandinavian journal of history* 7.4 (1982) 277–313. ISSN 0346-8755. ‣ Important study tracing erosion of Danish constitutional constraints on royal power with explosive growth of state. Presents Council's 1628 attempt to impose complete financial control over crown. [MFM]

32.147 Agnete Raaschou-Nielsen. "Danish agrarian reform and economic theory." *Scandinavian economic history review* 38.3 (1990) 44–61. ISSN 0358-5522. ‣ Stimulating essay argues that replacement of open-field system by enclosure largely initiated by peasants in freeholding and tenant villages following socially differentiated participation in cash economy and breakdown of village social network. [MFM]

32.148 Øystein Rian. "State and society in seventeenth-century Norway." *Scandinavian journal of history* 10.4 (1985) 337–63. ISSN 0346-8755. ‣ Excellent outline of increasing regulation of society through higher levels of taxation that helped create new administrative elite. Concludes taxes raised in time of war did not return to prewar levels once peace was restored. [MFM]

32.149 Thomas Riis. *Should auld acquaintance be forgot ... : Scottish-Danish relations, c. 1450–1707.* 2 vols. Odense: Odense University Press, 1988. ISBN 87-7492-693-4 (v. 1), 87-7492-694-2 (v. 2), 87-7492-695-0 (set). ‣ Comprehensive description of permanent migration of Scots to Denmark, their experience in Denmark, and temporary stays of Danes in Scotland, concentrating on military service, trade, crafts, and university life. [MFM]

32.150 Leland B. Sather. "The proper prince: the rearing of Christian August." *Scandinavian studies* 54.2 (1982) 103–22. ISSN 0036-5637. ‣ Well-documented discussion of how education of Prince Christian August may have influenced his conduct as viceroy in Norway and crown prince of Sweden during crucial years between 1807 and 1810. [MFM]

32.151 Lee Soltow. "The life cycle of ownership in Norway, 1664–1930." *Journal of European economic history* 18.2 (1989) 433–46. ISSN 0391-5115. ▸ Useful study of patterns of wealth, landownership, and land occupancy across life cycle at intervals over three centuries. Shows individual well-being rising from age twenty to about fifty before falling off somewhat. [MFM]

32.152 Poul Thestrup. *The standard of living in Copenhagen, 1730–1800: some methods of measurement.* Copenhagen: Københavns Universitets Fond til Tilvejebringelse af Læremidler; distributed by Gads, 1971. (Københavns Universitet, Institut for Økonomisk Historie, Publikation, 5.) ISBN 87-505-0145-3. ▸ Thorough analytical and statistical study of pattern of consumption, movement of wages, and standard of living in Danish capital. [MFM]

32.153 Victor E. Thoren. *The lord of Uraniborg: a biography of Tycho Brahe.* New York: Cambridge University Press, 1991. ISBN 0-521-35158-8. ▸ New perspectives on Tycho's life and new analyses of nearly all aspects of his scientific work. [MFM]

32.154 Ole Tuxen. "Principle and priorities: the Danish view of neutrality during the colonial war of 1755–63." *Scandinavian journal of history* 13.2–3 (1988) 207–32. ISSN 0346-8755. ▸ Outline of principles of neutrality Danes observed and general European view of rights and duties of neutrals held at mid-century. Follows Danish application and deployment of principles during Seven Years' War (1756–63). [MFM]

Sweden (including Finland)

32.155 Sven-Erik Åström. "The role of Finland in the Swedish national and war economies during Sweden's period as a great power." *Scandinavian journal of history* 11.2 (1986) 135–47. ISSN 0346-8755. ▸ Uses statistics on taxation, conscription, and composition of Swedish cavalry units to establish Finland's disproportionately large manpower and small financial contributions to Sweden's war efforts in seventeenth century. [MFM]

32.156 Sven-Erik Åström. "Swedish imperialism under the microscope [rev. art.]." *Scandinavian economic history review* 30.3 (1982) 227–33. ISSN 0358-5522. ▸ Critical review of Roberts 32.188 on Swedish imperial experience. Represents alternative interpretation of Swedish expansionism. [MFM]

32.157 Artur Attman. *Swedish aspirations and the Russian market during the seventeenth century.* Eva Green and Allen Green, trans. Gothenburg, Sweden: Kungl. Vetenskaps- och Vitterhets-Samhället, 1985. (Acta Regiae Societatis Scientiarum et Litterarum Gothoburgensis, Humaniora, 24.) ISBN 91-85252-35-2, ISSN 0072-4823. ▸ Discussion of impact of Swedish hopes for domination of Russian market on formulation of seventeenth-century Swedish foreign policy. Important argument that economic aspirations were decisive. [MFM]

32.158 E. Baigent. "Swedish cadastral mapping, 1628–1700: a neglected legacy." *Geographical journal* 156.1 (1990) 62–69. ISSN 0016-7398. ▸ Important introduction to unsurpassed cadastral maps from seventeenth-century Sweden and its possessions, their history, and theories concerning purposes for which they were commissioned. [MFM]

32.159 Günter Barudio. *Gustav Adolf, der Große: eine politische Biographie.* Frankfurt: Fischer, 1982. ISBN 3-10-004205-0. ▸ Important political biography of Sweden's Gustavus Adolphus by German historian with flair for writing. [MFM]

32.160 Göran Behre. "Scots in 'Little London': Scots settlers and cultural development in Gothenburg in the eighteenth century." *Northern Scotland* 7.2 (1987) 133–50. ISSN 0306-5278. ▸ Broad discussion of role played by Scots in eighteenth-century

Gothenburg, emphasizing community's cultural life, its role in commerce, and its service as conduit for British cultural phenomena into Sweden. [MFM]

32.161 Stellan Dahlgren and Hans Norman. *The rise and fall of New Sweden: Governor Johan Risingh's journal, 1654–1655, in its historical context.* Marie Clark Nelson, trans. Uppsala: Uppsala University; distributed by Almqvist & Wiksell, 1988. (Acta Bibliothecae r. Universitatis Upsaliensis, 27.) ISBN 91-554-2137-7, ISSN 0346-7465. ▸ Well-researched articles on Swedish state's involvement in New Sweden Company and on Swedish colonial venture in Delaware, 1638–55, with annotated translation of Risingh's informative journal. [MFM]

32.162 Birgitta Ericsson. "Central power and local community: joint Nordic research on the granting of *privilegia* to industrial enterprises in Scandinavia during the eighteenth century." *Scandinavian journal of history* 7.3 (1982) 173–76. ISSN 0346-8755. ▸ Introduces Nordic project conducted in 1970s and early 1980s and places accompanying articles by Dübeck, Gunnlaugsson, Nagel, and Kuisma in context. [MFM]

32.163 R. M. Hatton. *Charles XII of Sweden.* London: Weidenfeld & Nicolson, 1968. ISBN 0-297-74826-2. ▸ Excellent study of life and times of Charles XII, whose reign was marked by eighteen years of war with Peter I of Russia and ultimate weakening of Swedish empire. [MFM]

32.164 Kurt Johannesson. *The renaissance of the Goths in sixteenth-century Sweden: Johannes and Olaus Magnus as politicians and historians.* James Larson, ed. and trans. Berkeley: University of California Press, 1991. ISBN 0-520-07013-5. ▸ Study analyzing uses of past made by sixteenth-century Swedish churchmen and politicians in midst of Reformation and Counter-Reformation. Important insights into intellectual world and role of rhetoric and history in politics. [MFM]

32.165 Lennart Jörberg. *A history of prices in Sweden, 1732–1914.* 2 vols. Lund: Gleerup, 1972. ▸ Analytical history of prices, discussing monetary system, weights and measures, market price scales, and price fluctuations. Concentrates on grain, livestock, and iron-industry prices. [MFM]

32.166 Eino Jutikkala. "Tenancy, freehold, and enclosure in Finland from the seventeenth to the nineteenth century." *Scandinavian journal of history* 7.4 (1982) 339–44. ISSN 0346-8755. ▸ Survey of evolving patterns of land tenure and ownership in Finland in comparison and contrast to other parts of Scandinavia. Supplements article by Tønnesson on Scandinavia (32.129). [MFM]

32.167 Iiro Kajanto. *Porthan and classical scholarship: a study of classical influences in eighteenth-century Finland.* Helsinki: Suomalainen Tiedeakatemia; distributed by Akateeminen Kirjakauppa, 1984. (Annales Academiae Scientiarum Fennicae, Series B, 225.) ISBN 951-41-0488-9. ▸ Useful analysis of work and thinking of noted professor of eloquence and influential representative of Enlightenment within eighteenth-century Finnish society. [MFM]

32.168 Per-Arne Karlsson. "Housekeeping ideology and equilibrium policy in eighteenth-century Sweden: socio-economic theory and practice prior to the market economy." *Scandinavian economic history review* 37.2 (1989) 51–77. ISSN 0358-5522. ▸ Insightful study argues philosophy underlying Swedish economic thinking based on concept of balance among various functional units and proper division of labor. When iron export industry threatened equilibrium, action was taken to control it. [MFM]

32.169 Markku Kuisma. "When country dwellers became staple town burghers: the establishment of the first export sawmill in eastern Finnish hinterland and the granting of privileges to the export sawmill industry of Savo in the 1760's and 1770's." *Scan-*

dinavian journal of history 7.3 (1982) 233–54. ISSN 0346-8755.
▸ Thorough study of successful efforts of Finnish officials, landowners, and peasants to obtain sawmill privileges stubbornly opposed by town merchants. Shows responsiveness of Swedish Riksdag to political pressure from interested parties. [MFM]

32.170 Jan Lindegren. "The Swedish 'military state,' 1560–1720." *Scandinavian journal of history* 10.4 (1985) 305–66. ISSN 0346-8755. ▸ Historical materialist's interesting interpretation of factors producing military state in early modern Sweden. Argues redistribution of social surplus through institutional changes in control and administration created basis for absolutism. [MFM]

32.171 Sten Lindroth. *A history of Uppsala University, 1477–1977.* Uppsala: Uppsala University; distributed by Almqvist & Wiksell, 1976. ISBN 91-506-0081-8. ▸ History of Sweden's oldest university from its uneven beginnings in waning days of Catholicism through its blossoming as first-class university in twentieth century by leading intellectual historian. [MFM]

32.172 Arne Losman, Agneta Lundström, and Margareta Revera, eds. *The age of New Sweden.* Stockholm: Livrustkammaren, 1988. ISBN 91-8759400-5. ▸ Five essays on mid-seventeenth-century Swedish culture, politics, and society. See especially those by Nilsson on war and social change and by Revera on aristocratic culture and social change. [MFM]

32.173 Lars Magnusson. "Corruption and civic order: natural law and economic discourse in Sweden during the age of freedom." *Scandinavian economic history review* 37.2 (1989) 78–105. ISSN 0358-5522. ▸ Excellent demonstration of how discourse on natural rights influenced thought of Anders Nordencrantz, who argued that Sweden could maximize economic development only if its social and political base were broadened. [MFM]

32.174 Lars Magnusson. "Mercantilism and 'reform' mercantilism: the rise of economic discourse in Sweden during the eighteenth century." *History of political economy* 19.3 (1987) 415–33. ISSN 0018-2702. ▸ Important review of promotion of economic growth supported by the state. Argues creation and promotion of strong manufacturing sector viewed as critical to maintenance of favorable balance of trade and economic expansion. [MFM]

32.175 Michael F. Metcalf. "Conflict as catalyst: parliamentary innovation in eighteenth-century Sweden." *Parliaments, estates, and representation* 8.1 (1988) 63–76. ISSN 0260-6755. ▸ Study of political conflict within Sweden's four-estate Parliament and between monarch and Parliament that suggests theoretical framework for analyzing role of conflict in process of political innovation. [MFM]

32.176 Michael F. Metcalf. *Goods, ideas, and values: the East Indies trade as an agent of change in eighteenth-century Sweden.* Minneapolis: University of Minnesota, The Associates of the James Ford Bell Library, 1988. ▸ Comprehensive description of roles of Swedish East India Company in eighteenth-century Swedish economy and society, suggesting ways it served to introduce new concepts and practices into Swedish life. [MFM]

32.177 Michael F. Metcalf. "Parliamentary sovereignty and royal reaction, 1719–1809." In *The Riksdag: a history of the Swedish Parliament.* Michael F. Metcalf, ed., pp. 109–64. New York: St. Martin's, 1987. ISBN 0-312-00784-1. ▸ Comprehensive description of development of Riksdag's supreme power after 1718, refinement of parliamentary procedures and party politics, and dismantling of regime by Gustav III and his son. [MFM]

32.178 Michael F. Metcalf. *Russia, England, and Swedish party politics, 1762–1766: the interplay between great power diplomacy and domestic politics during Sweden's age of liberty.* Totowa, N.J.: Rowman and Littlefield, 1977. (Studies presented to the International Commission for the History of Representative and Parliamentary Institutions, 51.) ISBN 0-87471-904-6. ▸ Investigation of attempts

of foreign powers to influence decisions of Sweden's four-estate Riksdag, manipulation of foreign aid by one Swedish political party, and mechanics of party system. Based on extensive archival research. [MFM]

32.179 Eva Österberg. *Mentalities and other realities: essays in medieval and early modern Scandinavian history.* Alan Crozier, trans. Lund: Lund University Press, 1991. ISBN 91-7966-176-9. ▸ Study concentrating on beliefs and behaviors of peasants and patterns of interaction between state and local society. Heavier treatment of early modern than of medieval society. Uses Swedish data. [MFM]

32.180 Panu Pulma. "The Riksdag, the state bureaucracy, and the administration of hospitals in eighteenth-century Sweden." *Scandinavian journal of history* 10.2 (1985) 119–41. ISSN 0346-8755. ▸ Thoroughly documented review of role of Riksdag and bureaucracy in providing hospitals for poor. Suggests policies reflected differences between central government and local authorities and that this contest superseded concern about delivering services. [MFM]

32.181 Michael Roberts. *The age of liberty: Sweden, 1719–1772.* Cambridge: Cambridge University Press, 1986. ISBN 0-521-32092-5. ▸ Important essay presenting central issues in eighteenth-century Swedish political and parliamentary history during period of parliamentary sovereignty, diminished foreign ambition, and economic and social change. [MFM]

32.182 Michael Roberts. *British diplomacy and Swedish politics, 1758–1773.* Minneapolis: University of Minnesota Press, 1980. ISBN 0-8166-0910-1. ▸ Penetrating analysis of conduct of British diplomacy toward Sweden (and Russia) and of Swedish party politics during diplomatic mission of British minister to Sweden, Sir John Goodricke, 1763–73. [MFM]

32.183 Michael Roberts. *The early Vasas: a history of Sweden, 1523–1611.* 1968 ed. Cambridge: Cambridge University Press, 1986. ISBN 0-521-06930-0 (cl), 0-521-31182-9 (pbk). ▸ Magnificent treatment of cultural, economic, military, political, religious, and social history of Sweden during reigns of Gustav Vasa, his three sons, and one of his grandsons. [MFM]

32.184 Michael Roberts. *Essays in Swedish history.* Minneapolis: University of Minnesota Press, 1967. ▸ Important essays on constitutional, diplomatic, military, political, and social history of early modern Sweden; emphasis on seventeenth century. [MFM]

32.185 Michael Roberts. *From Oxenstierna to Charles XII: four studies.* New York: Cambridge University Press, 1991. ISBN 0-521-40014-7. ▸ Two studies of Charles X Gustav's policies, bringing new insights to study of his reign. Essays on Axel Oxenstierna in Germany and on Charles XII's death at Fredrikshald are useful. [MFM]

32.186 Michael Roberts. *Gustavus Adolphus: a history of Sweden, 1611–1632.* 2 vols. London: Longmans, Green, 1953–58. ▸ Classic treatment of great monarch portraying how his partnership with Swedish aristocracy and his administrative, political, and military reforms catapulted Sweden onto European stage as great power. [MFM]

32.187 Michael Roberts. *Gustavus Adolphus and the rise of Sweden.* London: English Universities Press, 1973. ISBN 0-340-12414-8. ▸ Useful introduction to reign of Gustavus Adolphus and Sweden's participation in Thirty Years' War by leading authority on subject. [MFM]

32.188 Michael Roberts. *The Swedish imperial experience, 1560–1718.* Cambridge: Cambridge University Press, 1979. ISBN 0-521-22502-7. ▸ Major essay on rise and fall of Sweden's short-lived Baltic empire, exploring historiographical debate concerning Swedish aims in empire building. [MFM]

32.189 Michael Roberts, ed. *Sweden as a great power, 1611–1697: government-society-foreign policy.* New York: St. Martin's, 1968. ▸ Collection of translated documents containing very useful constitutional, parliamentary, diplomatic, and other selected papers, illustrating major points in seventeenth-century Swedish political history. [MFM]

32.190 Michael Roberts, ed. *Sweden's age of greatness, 1632–1718.* New York: St. Martin's, 1973. ISBN 0-333-09354-1. ▸ Several outstanding essays on aspects of seventeenth-century Sweden's church, economic, commercial, military, political, and social history. Contributions by leading Swedish historians and editor. [MFM]

32.191 Göran Rystad. "The estates of the realm, the monarchy, and empire, 1611–1718." In *The Riksdag: a history of the Swedish Parliament.* Michael F. Metcalf, ed., pp. 61–108. New York: St. Martin's, 1987. ISBN 0-312-00784-1. ▸ Excellent study contextualizing shifting fortunes of parliamentary institutions in Sweden. Highlights uses to which they were put by successive regimes and how Riksdag's stature was solidified. [MFM]

32.192 Bengt Sandin. "Education, popular culture, and the surveillance of the population in Stockholm between 1600 and the 1840s." *Continuity and change* 3.3 (1988) 357–90. ISSN 0268-4160. ▸ Reassessment of roles of schooling in early modern period and elaboration of educational system for lower classes in larger Swedish towns between 1600 and 1850. Questions earlier interpretations. [MFM]

32.193 Herman Schück. "Sweden's early parliamentary institutions from the thirteenth century to 1611." In *The Riksdag: a history of the Swedish Parliament.* Michael F. Metcalf, ed., pp. 5–60. New York: St. Martin's, 1987. ISBN 0-312-00784-1. ▸ Seminal discussion of development of representative institutions in Sweden in broad political context attributing prime responsibility for institutionalization of quadricameral Riksdag to reign of Gustav Vasa. [MFM]

32.194 Johan Söderberg. "Real wage trends in urban Europe, 1730–1850: Stockholm in a comparative perspective." *Social history* 12.2 (1987) 155–76. ISSN 0307-1022. ▸ Important comparison of wage data for unskilled agricultural laborers with data for unskilled urban construction workers. Finds common decline in real wages, 1732–1800; improvement, 1800–20; downturn, 1825–50; and sustained upward trend, 1850–1900. [MFM]

32.195 Johan Söderberg and Arne Jansson. "Corn price rises and equalisation: real wages in Stockholm, 1650–1719." *Scandinavian economic history review* 36.2 (1988) 42–67. ISSN 0358-5522. ▸ Excellent study assessing city's economic development during period of European depression, using price, wage, and cost-of-living indexes. Finds general increase, suggesting overestimation of presumed seventeenth-century European crisis. [MFM]

32.196 Sven G. Trulsson. *British and Swedish policies and strategies in the Baltic after the Peace of Tilsit in 1807: a study of decision-making.* Lund: Liber Läromedel and Gleerup, 1976. ISBN 91-40-04250-2. ▸ Analysis of Sweden's and Great Britain's strategic decision making concerning Russia and Baltic region following agreement between Napoleon and Alexander I that led to Russia's invasion of Finland in 1808. [MFM]

32.197 Carl J. Uhr. "Anders Chydenius, 1729–1803: a Finnish predecessor to Adam Smith." *Western economic journal* 2.2 (1964) 85–116. ISSN 0715-4577. ▸ Important presentation of Finnish pastor's approach to philosophy of economic liberalism, his career, and his unique contributions to economic thought, especially his general theory of liberal economy. [MFM]

32.198 Anthony F. Upton. "Absolutism and the rule of law: the case of Karl XI of Sweden." *Parliaments, estates, and representation* 8.1 (1988) 31–46. ISSN 0260-6755. ▸ Detailed investigation of monarch's adherence to laws, noting infringements on theoretical constitutional constraints, but pointing out absence of clearly formulated constitutional law or mechanisms by which to enact it. [MFM]

32.199 Anthony F. Upton. "The Riksdag of 1680 and the establishment of royal absolutism in Sweden." *English historical review* 52.403 (1987) 281–308. ISSN 0013-8266. ▸ Convincing refutation of idea of prior plan to introduce royal absolutism. Argues constitutional change grew from procedural problems during meetings summoned to finance military reorganization; nonetheless, absolutism fell on fertile soil. [MFM]

32.200 Pentti Virrankoski. "Anders Chydenius and the government of Gustavus III of Sweden in the 1770s." *Scandinavian journal of history* 13.2–3 (1988) 107–19. ISSN 0346-8755. ▸ Useful study follows thinking of Finnish pastor, economic thinker, and member of Riksdag toward new, antiparliamentarian regime of Gustav III. Finds he remained royalist in hopes of promoting desired reforms and private ambitions. [MFM]

32.201 Voltaire. *Lion of the North, Charles XII of Sweden.* M.F.O. Jenkins, trans. Rutherford, N.J.: Fairleigh Dickinson University Press, 1981. ISBN 0-8386-3077-4. ▸ Classic eighteenth-century biography of Sweden's prominent warrior-king by an even more prominent admirer. [MFM]

Baltic Provinces

32.202 Alexander V. Berkis. *The history of the duchy of Courland (1561–1795).* Towson, Md.: Harrod, 1969. ▸ Thoroughly documented, comprehensive history of duchy of Courland in early modern period, emphasizing political developments, abilities of ducal regime, and constraints on continued autonomy. [MFM]

32.203 Edgars Dunsdorfs. *The Livonian estates of Axel Oxenstierna.* Stockholm: Almqvist & Wiksell, 1981. ISBN 91-22-00363-0 (pbk). ▸ Study of Livonian estate society during period of Swedish rule. Concentrates on land acquisitions of Gustavus Adolphus's chancellor and history of his estates to end of Swedish period. [MFM]

32.204 Vytautas Kavolis. "The devil's invasion: cultural changes in early modern Lithuania." *Lituanus* 35.4 (1989) 5–26. ISSN 0024-5089. ▸ Innovative analysis of cultural modernization against background of Reformation. Argues cultural modernization superseded by cultural decline following union with Poland in 1569, subsequent religious repression, wars, and economic stagnation. [MFM]

32.205 Jerzy Lukowski. *Liberty's folly: the Polish-Lithuanian commonwealth in the eighteenth century, 1697–1795.* New York: Routledge, 1991. ISBN 0-415-03228-8. ▸ Comprehensive history of commonwealth from late seventeenth century until its final demise and partition in 1795. [MFM]

32.206 Antanas Musteikis. *The Reformation in Lithuania: religious fluctuations in the sixteenth century.* Boulder: East European Monographs, distributed by Columbia University Press, 1988. (East European monographs, 246.) ISBN 0-88033-143-7. ▸ Analysis of rapid rise and decline of Protestantism in Grand Duchy of Lithuania in sixteenth century. Weberian approach. [MFM]

32.207 Jerzy Ochmanski. "The national idea in Lithuania from the sixteenth to the first half of the nineteenth century: the problem of cultural-linguistic differentiation." *Harvard Ukrainian studies* 10.3–4 (1986) 301–15. ISSN 0363-5570. ▸ Traces evolution of concept of Lithuanian nation up to mid-sixteenth century and subsequent polonization as most pervasive foreign influence. Finds evidence for early loss of national identity separate from Poland. [MFM]

MODERN PERIOD SINCE 1815

General Studies

32.208 Edgar Anderson. "The Crimean War in the Baltic area." *Journal of Baltic studies* 5.4 (1974) 339–61. ISSN 0162-9778. ▸ Well-documented examination of British military operations in Baltic provinces as part of allied blockade of Russia. Touches on British political thinking concerning possible alliance with oppressed Baltic peoples. [MFM]

32.209 Edgar Anderson. "Finnish-Baltic relations, 1918–1940: an appraisal." *Scandinavian studies* 54.1 (1982) 51–72. ISSN 0036-5637. ▸ Useful examination of attempts and failure of newly independent Finland and newly formed Baltic states to forge common policy bloc in interwar period. Lacks footnotes. [MFM]

32.210 Osmo Jussila. "The presentation of Baltic and Finnish affairs within the tsarist government in the eighteenth and nineteenth centuries." *Journal of Baltic studies* 16.4 (1985) 373–82. ISSN 0162-9778. ▸ Useful description of legislative procedures concerning Baltic and Finnish affairs and development of Finland's autonomy. Argues Finnish affairs presented to tsar directly by minister for Finland, but Baltic affairs through usual Russian system. [MFM]

32.211 Pertti Luntinen. *The Baltic question, 1903–1908.* Helsinki: Suomalainen Tiedeakatemia, 1975. ISBN 951-41-0250-9. ▸ Detailed study of British, Danish, German, Norwegian, and Russian diplomacy concerning question of continued British access to Baltic Sea following breakup of Swedish-Norwegian Union in 1905. [MFM]

32.212 Temira Pachmuss. "Russian culture in the Baltic states and Finland, 1920–1940." *Journal of Baltic studies* 16.4 (1985) 383–402. ISSN 0162-9778. ▸ Useful study concludes Russian cultural life vigorous, although less so in Lithuania than elsewhere. Russian minorities enjoyed cultural autonomy, own publications, theaters, schools. [MFM]

32.213 Toivo U. Raun. "Finland and Estonia: cultural and political relations, 1917–1940." *Journal of Baltic studies* 18.1 (1987) 5–20. ISSN 0162-9778. ▸ Study of development of close cultural ties between newly independent and linguistically related states unaccompanied by close political relations. Argues Finland chose Scandinavian orientation and was alienated by establishment of authoritarian regime in Estonia (1934). [MFM]

32.214 Toivo U. Raun. "The Latvian and Estonian national movements, 1860–1914." *Slavonic and East European review* 64.1 (1986) 66–80. ISSN 0037-6795. ▸ Comparative study concluding national revival movements among Latvians and Estonians confronted similar situations in face of German upper class and intensified attempts at russification. Finds Latvian middle-class intelligentsia took lead in mid-nineteenth century. [MFM]

32.215 Toivo U. Raun. "The Revolution of 1905 in the Baltic provinces and Finland." *Slavic review* 43.3 (1984) 453–67. ISSN 0037-6779. ▸ Incisive examination of dissimilar experiences of and outcomes for Baltic provinces and Finland in 1905. Revolutionary violence in Baltic brought suppression; Finnish restraint brought restoration of political rights. [MFM]

SEE ALSO
34.305 Edward C. Thaden, ed. *Russification in the Baltic provinces and Finland, 1855–1914.*

Scandinavia

32.216 Gerard Aalders. "The failure of the Scandinavian Defence Union, 1948–1949." *Scandinavian journal of history* 15.2 (1990) 125–53. ISSN 0346-8755. ▸ Most recent attempt to explain failure of negotiations among Denmark, Norway, and Sweden for postwar defensive alliance; this failure led to Denmark and Norway's membership in NATO. [MFM]

32.217 Peter Baldwin. "The Scandinavian origins of the social interpretation of the welfare state." *Comparative studies in society and history* 31.1 (1989) 3–24. ISSN 0010-4175. ▸ Study of origins of welfare systems of Denmark and Sweden, stressing initiatives of nonsocialist parties in promoting tax financing of social benefits and their universal availability. [MFM]

32.218 Solveig Halvorsen. "Scandinavian trade unions in the 1890s, with special reference to the Scandinavian stonemasons' union." *Scandinavian journal of history* 13.1 (1988) 3–21. ISSN 0346-8755. ▸ Exploration of role of Scandinavian workers' congresses in establishing pan-Scandinavian and national trade union. Emphasizes leadership role of Danish trade unions in Scandinavian cooperation. Presents one union's experience. [MFM]

32.219 Torkel Jansson. "The age of associations: principles and forms of organization between corporations and mass organizations—a comparative Nordic study from a Swedish viewpoint." *Scandinavian journal of history* 13.4 (1988) 321–43. ISSN 0346-8755. ▸ Comparative research project arguing that voluntary associations served as bridge from earlier corporatist social structures to modern societies based on liberal principles and individual membership. [MFM]

32.220 Raymond E. Lindgren. *Norway-Sweden: union, disunion, and Scandinavian integration.* Princeton: Princeton University Press, 1959. ▸ Still useful study of complex issues surrounding formation and dissolution of union between Sweden and Norway (1814–1905), as well as formulation of cooperative relationship at Norwegian independence. [MFM]

32.221 Ulf Lindström. *Fascism in Scandinavia, 1920–1940.* Stockholm: Almqvist & Wiksell, 1985. ISBN 91-22-00742-3. ▸ Best available comparative study of proto-fascist and fascist political parties in Scandinavian countries. Analyzes success of Conservative and Social Democratic parties in containing challenge from Far Right. [MFM]

32.222 Klaus Misgeld. "As the iron curtain descended: the coordinating committee of the Nordic labour movement and the Socialist International between Potsdam and Geneva (1945–55)." *Scandinavian journal of history* 13.1 (1988) 49–63. ISSN 0346-8755. ▸ Insightful study of situation of Scandinavian Social Democrats in postwar international politics. Finds common caution regarding Communists only point of full consensus; practical applications of membership in Socialist International remained unclear. [MFM]

32.223 Henrik S. Nissen, ed. *Scandinavia during the Second World War.* Thomas Munch-Petersen, trans. Minneapolis: University of Minnesota Press, 1983. ISBN 0-8166-1110-6. ▸ Collection of essays by Scandinavian and Finnish researchers on many aspects of World War II, including domestic politics. [MFM]

32.224 Hans Norman and Harald Runblom. *Transatlantic connections: Nordic migration to the New World after 1800.* Oslo: Norwegian University Press; distributed by Oxford University Press, 1988. ISBN 82-00-06988-5. ▸ Comprehensive survey of twenty years of research on Scandinavian emigration to North America and Scandinavian immigrant experience in America by two leading scholars in field. [MFM]

32.225 Øyvind Østerud. *Agrarian structure and peasant politics in Scandinavia: a comparative study of rural response to economic change.* Oslo: Universitetsforlaget, 1978. ISBN 82-00-01702-8. ▸ Comparative sociological investigation into rural politics and political mobilization in context of late nineteenth-century economic and political change in Scandinavian countries. [MFM]

32.226 Richard Petrow. *The bitter years: the invasion and occu-*

pation of Denmark and Norway, April 1940–May 1945. New York: Morrow, 1974. ISBN 0-688-00275-7. ▸ Dated but still very useful treatment of German invasion of Denmark and Norway and subsequent German occupation of both states. [MFM]

32.227 Nils Roll-Hansen. "Geneticists and the eugenics movement in Scandinavia." *British journal for the history of science* 22.3 (1989) 335–46. ISSN 0007-0874. ▸ Important description of individuals and groups in movement, as well as their ideas. Finds spectrum included nearly racist views in decades prior to 1920s. Movement's popularity declined dramatically following World War II. [MFM]

32.228 Ger van Roon. "Great Britain and the Oslo states." *Journal of contemporary history* 24.4 (1989) 657–64. ISSN 0022-0094. ▸ Critical examination of sporadic economic cooperation among Belgium, Denmark, Finland, Luxembourg, Netherlands, Norway, and Sweden following trade agreement of December 1930 and tensions created by England's devaluation of pound in 1931. [MFM]

32.229 T.J.T. Rooth. "Tariffs and trade bargaining: Anglo-Scandinavian economic relations in the 1930s." *Scandinavian economic history review* 34.1 (1986) 54–71. ISSN 0358-5522. ▸ Well-documented study of Britain's trade policies with Scandinavian states and their implications. Finds Norway and Sweden treated better than Denmark and Finland; British leverage great at time of restrictive trading practices and underconsumption. [MFM]

Denmark

32.230 Henning Søby Andersen. "Denmark between the wars with Britain, 1801–7." *Scandinavian journal of history* 14.3 (1989) 231–38. ISSN 0346-8755. ▸ Useful examination of precarious situation of a Denmark caught between French and British diplomacy, 1801–1807, culminating in Britain's seizure of Danish navy, which forced Denmark into arms of France. [MFM]

32.231 Bent Blüdnikow. "Denmark during the First World War." *Journal of contemporary history* 24.4 (1989) 683–703. ISSN 0022-0094. ▸ Innovative examination of highly visible activities of Danish Red Cross serving prisoners of war abroad and gaining political prestige for Denmark. Suggests neutrality equivocal and tending to favor Germany. [MFM]

32.232 Per Boje. "The standard of living in Denmark, 1750–1914." *Scandinavian economic history review* 34.2 (1986) 171–79. ISSN 0358-5522. ▸ Examination of various research approaches used to establish reliable knowledge of improved living standards during period in question. [MFM]

32.233 Steven M. Borish. *The land of the living: the Danish folk high schools and Denmark's non-violent path to modernization.* Nevada City, Calif.: Blue Dolphin, 1991. ISBN 0-931892-62-7. ▸ Anthropologist's history of Danish folk high schools from their origins in 1840s to present, emphasizing their role in facilitating democratic transformation and overall modernization. [MFM]

32.234 Niels Finn Christiansen. "Reformism within Danish social democracy until the 1930s." *Scandinavian journal of history* 3.4 (1978) 297–322. ISSN 0346-8755. ▸ Useful study of development of party's ideology from its early beginnings. Emphasizes predominance of revisionism and suggests one reason was party's persistent need to ally with *petite bourgeoisie.* [MFM]

32.235 Niels Clemmensen. "The development and structure of associations in Denmark, c. 1750–1880." *Scandinavian journal of history* 13.4 (1988) 355–70. ISSN 0346-8755. ▸ Examination of association movement from scientific and aesthetic groups of eighteenth century through their politicization after 1825. Argues urban associations sought to promote bourgeois interests; rural ones, to provide help for poor. [MFM]

32.236 Richard Cornell. "K. K. Steincke's notion of *personlig*

kultur and the moral basis of Danish social democracy." *Scandinavian studies* 54.3 (1982) 220–38. ISSN 0036-5637. ▸ Sensitive description of moral and political philosophy of Karl Kristian Steincke and how his insistence on moral content of social democracy influenced social legislation he introduced as minister for social affairs, 1929–35. [MFM]

32.237 Henrik Dethlefsen. "Denmark and the German occupation: cooperation, negotiation, or collaboration?" *Scandinavian journal of history* 15.3 (1990) 193–206. ISSN 0346-8755. ▸ Sophisticated analysis of response to occupation after 1940. Suggests overriding policy of collaboration to maintain power and independence of Danish elites went through two stages before collapsing in 1943. [MFM]

32.238 Carsten Due-Nielsen. "Denmark and the First World War." *Scandinavian journal of history* 10.1 (1985) 1–18. ISSN 0346-8755. ▸ Useful reconsideration of foreign policy and subsequent domestic change. Traces effects of neutral policy and geopolitical situation on trade, government intervention in economy, and ideological conflict. [MFM]

32.239 Eric S. Einhorn. *National security and domestic politics in post-war Denmark: some principle issues, 1945–1961.* Odense: Odense University Press, 1975. ISBN 87-7492-151-7. ▸ Analysis of interface between security policy and domestic politics in Denmark in postwar period, emphasizing complexities of alliance politics and mixed public opinion concerning North Atlantic Treaty Organization. [MFM]

32.240 Jørgen Hæstrup. *Secret alliance: a study of the Danish Resistance Movement, 1940–1945.* 3 vols. Alison Borch-Johansen, trans. New York: New York University Press, 1976–77. ISBN 0-8147-3431-6 (set), 0-8147-3428-6 (v. 1), 0-8147-3429-4 (v. 2), 0-8147-3430-8 (v. 3). ▸ Uses full panoply of sources available for research at time of publication and remains best study of Danish Resistance Movement available in English. [MFM]

32.241 Per H. Hansen. "From growth to crisis: the Danish banking system from 1850 to the interwar years." *Scandinavian economic history review* 39.3 (1991) 20–40. ISSN 0358-5522. ▸ Discussion of legal setting within which banks functioned, structure of system and its relative importance for economy as a whole, crises system faced, and possible directions for research. [MFM]

32.242 Holger Hjelholt. *Great Britain, the Danish-German conflict, and the Danish succession, 1850–1852: from the London Protocol to the Treaty of London (the 2nd of August 1850 and the 8th of May 1852).* Copenhagen: Munksgaard, 1971. (Kongelige Danske Videnskabernesselskab: historisk-filosofiske meddelelser, 45.1.) ISSN 0106-0481. ▸ Careful analysis of Anglo-Danish relations in connection with Dano-German dispute over Schleswig-Holstein and Danish succession. [MFM]

32.243 Carsten Holbraad. *Danish neutrality: a study in the foreign policy of a small state.* New York: Oxford University Press, 1991. ISBN 0-19-827356-8. ▸ Comprehensive study of Danish foreign relations in context of small state politics, tracing development of Danish policy stances from eighteenth century to postwar period. [MFM]

32.244 Leon Dalgas Jensen. "Denmark and the Marshall Plan, 1947–48: the decision to participate." *Scandinavian journal of history* 14.1 (1989) 57–83. ISSN 0346-8755. ▸ Well-documented study of decision-making process and Danes' balancing of economic and political interests. Finds tensions in negotiations and concessions to United States matched by steps to preserve as much freedom of action as possible. [MFM]

32.245 Hans Christian Johansen. *The Danish economy in the twentieth century.* New York: St. Martin's, 1987. ISBN 0-312-00373-0. ▸ Best treatment of twentieth-century Danish economic history available in English; many tables accompany text. [MFM]

32.246 W. Glyn Jones. *Denmark.* Rev. ed. London: Croom Helm, 1986. ISBN 0-7099-1468-7. ▸ Best available English-language treatment of nineteenth- and twentieth-century Danish history. [MFM]

32.247 Bruce H. Kirmmse. *Kirkegaard in golden age Denmark.* Bloomington: Indiana University Press, 1990. ISBN 0-253-33044-0. ▸ Comprehensive study and reinterpretation of social and political thinking of Søren Kierkegaard, as well as social, political, and cultural history of Denmark during its so-called golden age (1800–50). [MFM]

32.248 Hans Kuhn. "Romantic myths, student agitation, and international politics: the Danish intellectuals and Slesvig-Holsten." *Scandinavica* 27.1 (1988) 5–19. ISSN 0036-5653. ▸ Useful examination of roots of romantic Scandinavianism in nineteenth-century Denmark, student pressure to abandon Holstein and incorporate Duchy of Schleswig, and government's adoption of that program in 1848. [MFM]

32.249 Paul D. Lockhart. "Danish interwar politics and the Defence Law of 1937." *War and society* 7.1 (1989) 54–70. ISSN 0729-2473. ▸ Well-researched study showing that Danish armed forces actually weakened during late 1930s, despite growing threat from Germany. Neutrality unquestioned, but role of armed forces heavily debated; 1937 reorganization provided no strategic answers. [MFM]

32.250 Vadis O. Lumans. "The Nordic destiny: the peculiar role of the German minority in North Schleswig in Hitler's plans and policies for Denmark." *Scandinavian journal of history* 15.2 (1990) 109–23. ISSN 0346-8755. ▸ Thoroughly researched study rejecting notion of fifth column. Maintains Hitler stressed common Nordic destiny of Danes and Germans, rejecting pro-Nazi activists; Danes and North Schleswig Germans found common destiny, but one different from that envisioned by Hitler. [MFM]

32.251 Bengt Nilson. "Butter, bacon, and coal: Anglo-Danish commercial relations, 1947–51." *Scandinavian journal of history* 13.2–3 (1988) 257–77. ISSN 0346-8755. ▸ Thoroughly documented examination of Danish conundrum of how to resist British intimidation in area of trade relations while lacking alternative markets. Focuses heavily on goals and implementation of British Labour government's policy. [MFM]

32.252 Christian D. Nøkkentved. "Migration in nineteenth-century rural Denmark: the case of Magleby parish." *Scandinavian studies* 59.4 (1987) 389–403. ISSN 0036-5637. ▸ Thoroughly researched examination of shifting patterns from short- to long-distance migration after 1850 and to increasing migration of men to towns after 1875. Finds one resident in four born outside parish by 1900. [MFM]

32.253 Bente Rosenbeck. "The boundaries of femininity: the Danish experience, 1880–1980." *Scandinavian journal of history* 12.1 (1987) 47–62. ISSN 0346-8755. ▸ Examination of concept of femininity and resulting social roles and ideological assumptions. Early marriage and better health meant women had more years without children later in life. Discusses growing influence of gynecology. [MFM]

32.254 Susan Seymour. *Anglo-Danish relations and Germany, 1933–1945.* Odense: Odense University Press, 1982. ISBN 87-7492-399-4 (pbk). ▸ Monographic study of Anglo-Danish relations in trade policy and diplomacy from rise of Hitler to end of World War II, with special reference to Germany. [MFM]

32.255 Signild Vallgårda. "Hospitals and the poor in Denmark, 1750–1880." *Scandinavian journal of history* 13.2–3 (1988) 95–105. ISSN 0346-8755. ▸ Examination of growth of hospitals as means to save money on poor relief through health care and to improve workers' morale. Shows hospitals had positive effect in improving health environment. [MFM]

32.256 Poul Villaume. "Neither appeasement nor servility: Denmark and the Atlantic Alliance, 1949–55." *Scandinavian journal of history* 14.2 (1989) 155–79. ISSN 0346-8755. ▸ Closely argued study concluding pro-NATO parties viewed economic stability as best defense. Governments wary of United States policy but accepted presence of airbases and nuclear weapons; Danish political cooperation with North Atlantic Treaty Organization greater than military participation. [MFM]

32.257 Vagn Wåhlin. "Popular revivalism in Denmark: recent research trends and results." *Scandinavian journal of history* 11.4 (1986) 363–87. ISSN 0346-8755. ▸ Discussion of research on Grundtvigian and Home Mission revival movements that arose after 1860. Challenges adequacy of analyses that attempt to explain movements solely in terms of social and economic trends. [MFM]

SEE ALSO
42.227 Kristian Hvidt. *Flight to America.*

Finland

32.258 Risto Alapuro. *State and revolution in Finland.* Berkeley: University of California Press, 1988. ISBN 0-520-05813-5. ▸ Controversial sociological examination of state making, class structure, national and class integration, and Civil War in early twentieth-century Finland. Also examines interwar years. [MFM]

32.259 Roy Allison. *Finland's relations with the Soviet Union, 1944–84.* New York: St. Martin's, 1985. ISBN 0-312-29066-7. ▸ Important study concentrating on Finnish perspective and exploring economic relations as well as Finnish security policy and neutrality, Soviet strategy, and impact of Soviet influence on Finland. [MFM]

32.260 Lawrence Backlund. "Rudolf Holsti in Moscow: an episode in Fenno-Soviet relations." *Journal of Baltic studies* 19.3 (1988) 249–66. ISSN 0162-9778. ▸ Well-documented investigation into confidence-building measures undertaken by Finland to allay Soviet fears of Finnish collusion with Nazi Germany. Finns emphasized their Scandinavian identity and support for League of Nations. [MFM]

32.261 William R. Copeland. *The uneasy alliance: collaboration between the Finnish opposition and the Russian underground, 1899–1904.* Helsinki: Suomalainen Tiedeakatemia, 1973. (Annales Academiæ Scientiarum Fennicæ, Series B, 179.) ISBN 951-41-0085-9. ▸ Penetrating examination of growth of Finnish resistance to russification from 1898 and development of cooperation—and then uneasy alliance—between Finnish resistance and Russian liberals until 1903. [MFM]

32.262 Max Engman. "Migration from Finland to Russia during the nineteenth century." *Scandinavian journal of history* 3.2 (1978) 155–77. ISSN 0346-8755. ▸ Excellent discussion of labor migration from Finland to Russian metropolis of St. Petersburg in context of Russian empire's annexation of Finland and its economy in nineteenth century. [MFM]

32.263 Max Engman and David Kirby, eds. *Finland: people, nation, state.* Bloomington: Indiana University Press, 1989. ISBN 0-253-32067-4. ▸ Fourteen articles by leading scholars covering topics ranging from labor movement to women's movement, from role of Ostrobothnia in Finland's history to Finland as successor state. [MFM]

32.264 Basil Greenhill and Ann Giffard. *The British assault on Finland, 1854–1855: a forgotten naval war.* Annapolis, Md.: Naval Institute Press, 1988. ISBN 0-87021-057-2. ▸ Well-written, thoroughly researched study of construction of Russian fortress of Bomarsund in the Åland Islands and of British destruction of fortress during Crimean War. [MFM]

32.265 Pertti Haapala. "How was the working class formed?

The case of Finland, 1850–1920." *Scandinavian journal of history* 12.3 (1987) 179–97. ISSN 0346-8755. ▸ Study concluding late Finnish industrialization delayed labor-capital struggle and its influence on formation of working class. Challenges Marxist interpretations by suggesting that independence struggle and fight for democracy very influential. [MFM]

32.266 Pekka Kalevi Hamalainen. *In time of storm: revolution, Civil War, and the ethnolinguistic issue in Finland.* Albany: State University of New York Press, 1979. ISBN 0-8739-5375-4. ▸ Comprehensive study of language issue in Finnish politics at time—and in wake—of revolution in Russia and Civil War in Finland. Very well researched and documented. [MFM]

32.267 Sakari Heikkinen. "On private consumption and the standard of living in Finland, 1860–1912." *Scandinavian economic history review* 34.2 (1986) 122–34. ISSN 0358-5522. ▸ Useful study of how private consumption used to indicate standard of living. Shows significant increases, 1860–70 and 1890–1912, closely related to increases in real wages and gross domestic product per capita. [MFM]

32.268 John H. Hodgson. *Communism in Finland: a history and an interpretation.* Princeton: Princeton University Press, 1967. ▸ Dated but still important study of left-wing politics in Finland from 1918 through 1966 elections, with special emphasis on Finnish Communist party and its internal development. [MFM]

32.269 Nils G. Holm. "Recent research into revivalist movements in Finland." *Scandinavian journal of history* 11.4 (1986) 317–33. ISSN 0346-8755. ▸ Catalogs movements and suggests how various aspects of Finnish history have influenced its religious life. Numerous references to recent research on revivalist groups within and outside of state Lutheran church. [MFM]

32.270 Steven Duncan Huxley. *Constitutionalist insurgency in Finland: Finnish "passive resistance" against russification as a case of nonmilitary struggle in the European resistance tradition.* Helsinki: Finnish Historical Society, 1990. (Studia historica, 38.) ISBN 951-8915-40-7, ISSN 0081-6493. ▸ Analysis in peace studies tradition of "active-passive resistance" in Finland, 1898–1905, contrasting its efficacy for constitutionalist cause with 1904 assassinations and Revolution of 1905. [MFM]

32.271 Travis Beal Jacobs. *America and the Winter War, 1939–1940.* New York: Garland, 1981. ISBN 0-8240-4857-1. ▸ Study of Russo-Finnish Winter War with emphasis on role of United States and American diplomacy in playing out of crisis. [MFM]

32.272 Max Jacobson. *The diplomacy of the Winter War.* 2d ed. Helsinki: Otava University Press, 1984. ISBN 951-1-08060-1 (pbk). ▸ Quasi-official interpretation of Finnish diplomacy during Russo-Finnish Winter War of 1939–40, written at height of cold war by leading Finnish diplomat. Still well worth reading. [MFM]

32.273 Stig Jägerskiöld. *Mannerheim: marshal of Finland.* Minneapolis: University of Minnesota Press, 1986. ISBN 0-8166-1527-6. ▸ Abbreviated English-language version of author's monumental, eight-volume biography of towering figure in history of Finland, from independence in 1917 to end of World War II. [MFM]

32.274 Osmo Jussila. "Finland and the Russian Duma." *Journal of Baltic studies* 19.3 (1988) 241–48. ISSN 0162-9778. ▸ Well-documented study of unsuccessful attempts to demand parallel status with imperial legislature for Finland's Eduskunta (parliament). To Russian authorities, unity of empire required that Duma's functions extend to Finland. [MFM]

32.275 Lauri Karvonen. *From white to blue-and-black: Finnish fascism in the inter-war era.* Helsinki: Finnish Society of Sciences and Letters, 1988. (Commentationes scientiarum socialium, 36.) ISBN 951-653-152-0, ISSN 0355-256X. ▸ Comprehensive study of

rise and development of radical Right and proto-fascist political movements in Finland during interwar period. [MFM]

32.276 Reino Kero. *Migration from Finland to North America in the years between the United States Civil War and the First World War.* Turku, Finland: Turun Yliopisto, 1974. (Annales Universitatis Turkuensis, Series B, 130.) ISBN 951-641-124-X. ▸ Remains standard history of Finnish emigration to United States. Statistical and qualitative data form basis for this impressive study. [MFM]

32.277 D. G. Kirby. *Finland in the twentieth century.* Minneapolis: University of Minnesota Press, 1979. ISBN 0-8166-0895-4. ▸ Lively, culturally informed political history of Finland, dealing critically and intelligently with such topics as 1918 Civil War and Finland's co-belligerency with Germany, 1941–44. [MFM]

32.278 D. G. Kirby. "New wine in old vessels? The Finnish Socialist Workers' party, 1919–1923." *Slavonic and East European review* 66.3 (1988) 426–45. ISSN 0037-6795. ▸ Leading authority argues Finnish Socialist Workers' party (SSTP), more syndicalist than Bolshevik, displaced discredited Social Democrats in wake of Civil War. Following arrest of leaders in 1923, remaining activists joined Communist party. [MFM]

32.279 D. G. Kirby. "'The worker's cause': rank-and-file attitudes in the Finnish Social Democratic party, 1905–1918." *Past and present* 111 (1986) 130–64. ISSN 0031-2746. ▸ Excellent study showing party, dominated by older artisans and young intellectuals, allied with rural crofters after revolutionary events of 1905–1906. Stresses loyalty and solidarity of labor movement and forging of class consciousness. [MFM]

32.280 D. G. Kirby, ed. and trans. *Finland and Russia, 1808–1920: from autonomy to independence, a selection of documents.* London: Macmillan, 1975. ISBN 0-333-16905-0. ▸ Useful collection of sources key to understanding Russo-Finnish relations during Finland's period as autonomous grand duchy in Russian empire. [MFM]

32.281 Keijo Korhonen. *Autonomous Finland in the political thought of nineteenth-century Russia.* Turku, Finland: Turun Yliopisto, 1967. (Annales Universitatis Turkuensis, Series B, 105.) ▸ Compelling examination of evolution of autonomous Finland as political ideal for Russian liberals and strained relations between pan-Slavists and Russian liberals over "Finnish question," 1870–90. [MFM]

32.282 H. Peter Krosby. *Finland, Germany, and the Soviet Union, 1940–1941: the Petsamo dispute.* Madison: University of Wisconsin Press, 1968. ISBN 0-299-05140-4. ▸ Careful analysis of major dispute following Russo-Finnish Winter War, 1939–40, concerning rich nickel deposits in Petsamo region on Finland's Arctic coast. [MFM]

32.283 Matti Lackman. "The Finnish secret police and political intelligence: their methods and collaborators in the 1920s and 30s." *Scandinavian journal of history* 12.3 (1987) 199–219. ISSN 0346-8755. ▸ Closely argued study of national secret police formed in 1918 as temporary organ to follow movements of defeated Red activists. Continually infiltrated Finnish Communist party in 1930s, leading to retaliatory killings. [MFM]

32.284 Maria Lähteenmäki. "The foreign contacts of the Finnish working women's movement (c. 1900–18)." *Scandinavian journal of history* 13.1 (1988) 29–37. ISSN 0346-8755. ▸ Well-documented study of how women's labor movement in late nineteenth century was internationalized through work of Hilja Pärssinen, socialist teacher, poet, and translator. Argues movement maintained contacts with Russian and Scandinavian activists. [MFM]

32.285 Esa Lahtinen. "Finnish participation in cooperation within the Nordic labour movement, 1880–1918." *Scandinavian* *journal of history* 13.1 (1988) 23–28. ISSN 0346-8755. ▸ Useful introduction to development of Finnish labor movement, its acquisition of socialist attributes in 1890s, cooperation with Scandinavian labor movements, and realignment in 1913 with Russian anti-tsarists. [MFM]

32.286 Ilkka Liikanen. "Light to our people: educational organization and the mobilization of Fennomania in the 1870s." *Scandinavian journal of history* 13.4 (1988) 421–38. ISSN 0346-8755. ▸ Examination of first organized national mobilization of Finns in support of any cause. Modeled new forms of social interaction involving different classes; important impact on later organizational efforts by others. [MFM]

32.287 Pertti Luntinen. *F. A. Seyn: a political biography of a tsarist imperialist as administrator of Finland.* Helsinki: Finnish Historical Society, 1985. (Studia historica, 19.) ISBN 951-9254-72-2 (pbk), ISSN 0081-6493. ▸ Highly criticized for lacking depth and historical feel, but serves as one of few studies on Russian administration of Finland in early twentieth century. [MFM]

32.288 Eino Lyytinen. *Finland in British politics in the First World War.* Helsinki: Suomalainen Tiedeakatemia; distributed by Akateeminen Kirjakauppa, 1980. (Annales Academiæ Scientiarum Fennicæ, Series B, 207.) ISBN 951-41-0364-5 (pbk), ISSN 0066-2011. ▸ Informative study of tensions between London and Helsinki in light of German aid to Whites in Finnish Civil War and British cooperation with Finnish Reds while intervening in northern Russia. [MFM]

32.289 Jukka Nevakivi. *The appeal that was never made: the Allies, Scandinavia, and the Finnish Winter War, 1939–1940.* Marjatta Nevakivi, trans. Montreal: McGill-Queen's University Press, 1976. ISBN 0-7735-0262-9. ▸ Penetrating analysis of relations among Finland, Scandinavian powers, and Western Allies during Russo-Finnish Winter War, focusing on issue of possible Allied military aid to Finland. [MFM]

32.290 Ilkka Nummela and Erkki K. Laitinen. "Distribution of income in Kuopio, 1880–1910." *Scandinavian economic history review* 35.3 (1987) 237–53. ISSN 0358-5522. ▸ Sophisticated statistical examination of effects of industrialization on Finnish town. Shows increased employment, but also increase of economic inequalities through growth of business and real estate incomes. [MFM]

32.291 Juhani Paasivirta. *Finland and Europe: international crises in the period of autonomy, 1808–1914.* David G. Kirby, ed. and abridgement. Anthony F. Upton and Sirkka R. Upton, trans. Minneapolis: University of Minnesota Press, 1981. ISBN 0-8166-1046-0. ▸ Extensive study of Finland's position in European diplomacy, opinion, and politics during its 110-year history as autonomous duchy in Russian empire. Based on extensive archival and press research. [MFM]

32.292 Juhani Paasivirta. *The victors in World War I and Finland.* Helsinki: Finnish Historical Society, 1965. (Studia historica, 7.) ▸ Critical study of Finland's situation at independence and role of triumphant Western Allies in shaping parameters of that independence. [MFM]

32.293 Tapani Paavonen. "Neutrality, protectionism, and the international community: Finnish foreign economic policy in the period of reconstruction of the international economy, 1945–1950." *Scandinavian economic history review* 37.1 (1989) 23–40. ISSN 0358-5522. ▸ Useful examination of halting Finnish participation in international economic integration following 1945. Finds unwillingness to remove protections for import-substitution industries despite efforts of wood-processing industry and consumers to open up trade. [MFM]

32.294 Matti Peltonen. "Agrarian world market and Finnish farm economy: the agrarian transition in Finland in late nine-

teenth and early twentieth centuries." *Scandinavian economic history review* 36.1 (1988) 26–45. ISSN 0358-5522. ▸ Well-researched analysis of impact of developing world trade in grain, dairy, and forest products on social conditions and land distribution in rural Finland. Concludes economic realignments led to political alliance between crofters and labor. [MFM]

32.295 Risto E. J. Penttilä. *Finland's search for security through defence, 1944–89.* New York: St. Martin's, 1991. ISBN 0-312-04895-5. ▸ Comprehensive study of Finnish defense and security policy during nearly half century following Finland's capitulation to Soviets in 1944. [MFM]

32.296 Juhani Piilonen. "Women's contribution to 'Red Finland,' 1918." *Scandinavian journal of history* 13.1 (1988) 39–48. ISSN 0346-8755. ▸ Closely argued examination of feminist advances on Red side during Finland's Civil War, including equal rights with men, inclusion on municipal councils, appointment of female ministers, and controversial service of females in Red Guard. [MFM]

32.297 Tuomo Polvinen. *Between East and West: Finland in international politics, 1944–1947.* D. G. Kirby and Peter Herring, eds. and trans. Minneapolis: University of Minnesota Press, 1986. ISBN 0-8166-1459-8. ▸ Comprehensive outline of parameters of and constraints on Finnish foreign policy choices, first as co-belligerent of Germany, then as defeated nation under Russian-dominated supervision of Allied Control Commission. [MFM]

32.298 Hannu Rautkallio. *Finland and the Holocaust: the rescue of Finland's Jews.* Paul Sjöblom, trans. New York: Holocaust Library, 1987. ISBN 0-89604-120-4 (cl), 0-89604-121-2 (pbk). ▸ Controversial, heavily criticized study of Finland's policies toward Finnish and other Jews during and after Finland's co-belligerency with Germany, 1941–44. [MFM]

32.299 Marvin Rintala. "Finnish students in politics: the Academic Karelia Society." *East European quarterly* 6.2 (1972) 192–205. ISSN 0012-8449. ▸ Excellent description of activities of Finnish student politicians in context of Academic Karelia Society (student organization) and in wake of Civil War and independence. Emphasizes expansionist ambitions. [MFM]

32.300 Marvin Rintala. *Four Finns: political profiles.* Berkeley: University of California Press, 1969. ▸ Insightful biographical essays treating political contributions of four prominent Finns who helped shape political history of their country between 1918 and 1956. [MFM]

32.301 Marvin Rintala. *Three generations: the extreme right wing in Finnish politics.* Bloomington: Indiana University Press, 1962. ▸ Important study of radical right-wing influences in Finnish politics from 1918 through interwar period, with special attention to Academic Karelia Society (student organization) and proto-fascist Lapua movement. [MFM]

32.302 C. Jay Smith, Jr. *Finland and the Russian Revolution, 1917–1922.* Athens: University of Georgia Press, 1958. ▸ Straightforward but well-documented study of Finnish Civil War of 1918 and its aftermath in context of Bolshevik Revolution and subsequent Russian Civil War. [MFM]

32.303 Henrik Stenius. "The adoption of the principle of association in Finland." *Scandinavian journal of history* 13.4 (1988) 345–54. ISSN 0346-8755. ▸ Useful overview of attitudes toward and development of self-help associations in first half of nineteenth century. Finds initial debate concerned whether people should address issues beyond their individual sphere. [MFM]

32.304 Wolodymyr Stojko. "Finland's relations with the Russian provisional government." *East European quarterly* 19.4 (1985) 439–57. ISSN 0012-8449. ▸ Useful study revealing imperial thinking of Kerensky government, which accepted autonomous Finnish government but refused recognition of sovereignty legislated by Eduskunta in July 1917, in Law of Supreme Power. [MFM]

32.305 Marianne Tallberg. "Nursing and medical care in Finland from the eighteenth to the late nineteenth century: the background for the introduction of nurses' training in Finland in 1889 with some comparisons with developments in Sweden." *Scandinavian journal of history* 14.4 (1989) 269–83. ISSN 0346-8755. ▸ Examination of development of training and standards. Finds Finland compared unfavorably with Sweden in level of training for nurses. Detailed discussion of developments in work organization and duties of nurses. [MFM]

32.306 Anthony F. Upton. *Finland in crisis, 1940–1941: a study in small-power politics.* Ithaca, N.Y.: Cornell University Press, 1965. ▸ Best English-language study of Finland's handling of diplomatic crisis following its defeat in Winter War and Germany's occupation of Denmark, Norway, Low Countries, and France. [MFM]

32.307 Anthony F. Upton. *Finland, 1939–1940.* 1974 ed. Newark: University of Delaware Press, 1979. ISBN 0-87413-156-1. ▸ Very good study of Finland's response to Soviet pressures for territorial concessions following Molotov-Ribbentrop Pact and of subsequent Russo-Finnish Winter War (1939–40). [MFM]

32.308 Anthony F. Upton. *The Finnish Revolution, 1917–1918.* Minneapolis: University of Minnesota Press, 1980. ISBN 0-8166-0905-5. ▸ Monumental political history of Finland's emergence as independent state and its brutal Civil War. Narrative rather than explicitly analytical, with many quotations. [MFM]

32.309 Olli Vehviläinen. "German armed forces and the Finnish civilian population, 1941–1944." *Scandinavian journal of history* 12.4 (1987) 345–58. ISSN 0346-8755. ▸ Interesting examination of relations between German troops operating in northern Finland and Finnish civilians. Concludes relations were generally good despite anti-Nazi stance of workers and leftists, but sees breakdown following Finnish armistice with Soviet army. [MFM]

32.310 William A. Wilson. *Folklore and nationalism in modern Finland.* Bloomington: Indiana University Press, 1976. ISBN 0-253-32327-4. ▸ Monographic study of use of folklore in construction of nationalism in nineteenth- and twentieth-century Finland. [MFM]

Iceland

32.311 Ingimar Einarsson. *Patterns of societal development in Iceland.* Uppsala: Uppsala University; distributed by Almqvist & Wiksell, 1987. (Acta Universitatis Upsaliensis, Studia sociologica Upsaliensia, 26.) ISBN 91-554-2015-X, ISSN 0585-5551. ▸ Investigation of patterns of societal development in Iceland, 1930–80, in context of Wallerstein's semi-periphery (22.275). Heavily sociological, yet useful in absence of accessible works on Icelandic social history. [MFM]

32.312 þorleifur Friðriksson. "Economic assistance from the Nordic Social Democratic parties to Icelandic social democracy, 1918–1939: internationalism or manipulation?" *Scandinavian journal of history* 13.2–3 (1988) 141–65. ISSN 0346-8755. ▸ Well-documented study of financial support for Icelandic Social Democratic party from sister parties in Scandinavia. Argues strings included requirement not to fuse with Communist party. Concludes Social Democrats found cooperation possible throughout period. [MFM]

32.313 Sigfus Jonsson. "International saltfish markets and the Icelandic economy, ca. 1900–1940." *Scandinavian economic history review* 34.1 (1986) 20–40. ISSN 0358-5522. ▸ Statistically sophisticated study showing export of saltfish led growth in economy. Real export income fluctuated 22.5 percent per year on

average, but rose steadily over period. Finds considerable dependence on Italian and Spanish markets. [MFM]

32.314 Finnur Magnússon. *The hidden class: culture and class in a maritime setting, Iceland, 1880–1942.* Aarhus, Denmark: Aarhus University Press, 1990. ISBN 87-7288-279-4. ▸ Anthropological analysis of development of class structure in Icelandic fishing and farming community in late nineteenth and early twentieth centuries. [MFM]

32.315 Magnús S. Magnússon. *Iceland in transition: labour and socio-economic change before 1940.* Lund: Ekonomisk-Historiska Föreningen, 1985. (Skrifter utgivna av Ekonomisk-Historiska Föreningen i Lund, 45.) ISBN 91-85611-14-X (pbk). ▸ Useful examination of economic and social transformation of Iceland brought about by its integration into broader European commercial economy in late nineteenth and first decades of twentieth centuries. [MFM]

32.316 Pétur Pétursson. *Church and social change: a study in the secularization process in Iceland, 1830–1930.* Helsingborg, Sweden: Plus Ultra, 1983. ISBN 91-97035-59-9 (pbk). ▸ Monographic study of transformation of Icelandic church in face of revivalism and secularization during period of economic transformation. [MFM]

32.317 Pétur Pétursson. "Revivalism and lay religious movements on Iceland: a survey and an account of the current state of research." *Scandinavian journal of history* 11.4 (1986) 335–44. ISSN 0346-8755. ▸ Useful overview suggesting little success for revival movements in either nineteenth or twentieth centuries. Personal and family nature of Lutheranism in Iceland and efforts to gain national independence accommodated Icelanders' emotional needs. [MFM]

32.318 Hrefna Róbertsdóttir. "Icelandic societies in the nineteenth century: the founding of societies before the advent of mass movements." *Scandinavian journal of history* 13.4 (1988) 371–84. ISSN 0346-8755. ▸ Useful study showing early associations in Iceland, late 1700s to mid-1800s, predominantly involved government officials. Farmers and Reykjavik patriciate became active mid-century, followed by *petite bourgeoisie* and laborers in late 1800s. [MFM]

Norway

32.319 Samuel Abrahamsen. *Norway's response to the Holocaust.* New York: Holocaust Library, 1991. ISBN 0-89604-116-6 (cl), 0-89604-117-4 (pbk). ▸ Best treatment in English of experience of Norway's Jews during World War II; also discusses what was known in Norway about Hitler's Final Solution. [MFM]

32.320 Ida Blom. "Changing gender identities in an industrializing society: the case of Norway, c. 1870–c. 1914." *Gender and history* 2.2 (1990) 131–47. ISSN 0953-5233. ▸ Broad examination of generational changes in Norwegian middle-class women's perceptions of womanhood and equality between sexes as reflected in late nineteenth-century women's magazines. Proposes new contextual explanations for these changes. [MFM]

32.321 Ida Blom. "Women's politics and women in politics in Norway since the end of the nineteenth century." *Scandinavian journal of history* 12.1 (1987) 17–33. ISSN 0346-8755. ▸ Sweeping survey of shifting successes of Norwegian women in gaining political office since passage of female suffrage in 1913. Stresses underrepresentation prior to 1970s and great strides since. [MFM]

32.322 Svein Dahl. "The attitude of the Norwegian Conservative party towards state intervention in economic life during the interwar period." *Scandinavian journal of history* 12.4 (1987) 297–305. ISSN 0346-8755. ▸ Useful study of how conservatives participated in expansion of government authority in economy in response to Depression. First favored indirect state intervention, but later advocated protectionism and regulation of competition. [MFM]

32.323 Thomas Kingston Derry. *A history of modern Norway, 1814–1972.* Oxford: Oxford University Press, 1973. ISBN 0-19-822503-2. ▸ Most comprehensive English-language treatment of modern Norwegian history available to date. Considerable attention to economic and cultural issues within overall political framework. [MFM]

32.324 Aage Engesæter. "Poverty, overpopulation, and the early emigration from Sogn." C. A. Clausen, trans. *Norwegian-American studies* 32 (1989) 31–51. ISSN 0078-1983. ▸ Analysis suggests neither population pressure nor overpopulation provide full explanation. Instead, finds disproportionate share of emigration from area of least population pressure. [MFM]

32.325 John T. Flint. *Historical role analysis in the study of religious change: mass educational development in Norway, 1740–1891.* New York: Cambridge University Press, 1990. ISBN 0-521-37099-X. ▸ Historical sociological analysis of reinforcing interplay of lay mobilization, secularization, and educational development in Norway in eighteenth and nineteenth centuries, leading, among other things, to religious diversity. [MFM]

32.326 Tore Gjelsvik. *Norwegian Resistance, 1940–1945.* Thomas Kingston Derry, trans. Montreal: McGill-Queen's University Press, 1979. ISBN 0-7735-0507-5. ▸ Best, most comprehensive study of Norwegian Resistance Movement (1940–45) available in English. [MFM]

32.327 Frederick Hale. "British and American millenarianism in Norway during the breakthrough of modernity." *Fides et historia* 19.1 (1987) 35–50. ISSN 0884-5379. ▸ Broad study concluding Church of Norway opposed millenarianism, 1875–1900, but movement cut broadly across denominational lines and influenced Methodist, Baptist, and Lutheran Free churches. [MFM]

32.328 Frederick Hale. "The development of religious freedom in Norway." *Journal of church and state* 23.1 (1981) 47–68. ISSN 0021-969X. ▸ Reviews rise of Christian Nonconformity in nineteenth century and growth of denominationalism. Surveys current discussions and prospects for disestablishment of state church. [MFM]

32.329 Arne Hassing. "The churches of Norway and the Jews, 1933–1943." *Journal of ecumenical studies* 26.3 (1989) 496–522. ISSN 0022-0558. ▸ Penetrating examination of Church of Norway's stance on antisemitism following German occupation. Shows how prior policy of silence nullified practical effect of public protests over deportation of Jews in 1942. [MFM]

32.330 Arne Hassing. *Religion and power: the case of Methodism in Norway.* Lake Junaluska, N.C., and Waynesville, N.C.: United Methodist Church and The Mountaineer, General Commission on Archives and History, 1980. ▸ History of Methodism in Norway to 1914, emphasizing its role in Norway's democratization along with roles of liberal, labor, abstinence, and prohibition movements. [MFM]

32.331 Fritz Hodne. *The Norwegian economy, 1920–1980.* New York: St. Martin's, 1983. ISBN 0-312-57938-1. ▸ Skillful overview of Norwegian economy in interwar and postwar periods, with special attention to problems of Depression, war economy, and postwar reconstruction. [MFM]

32.332 Fritz Hodne and Bjørn Basberg. "Public infrastructure, its indispensability for economic growth: the case of Norwegian public health measures, 1850–1940." *Scandinavian economic history review* 35.2 (1987) 145–69. ISSN 0358-5522. ▸ Methodologically sophisticated study using demographic data to link improved health of Norwegians in nineteenth and twentieth centuries to better diet and other material factors. Attributes secondary influence to development of public-sector health infrastructure. [MFM]

32.333 Oddvar K. Hoidal. *Quisling: a study in treason.* Oslo and New York: Norwegian University Press; distributed by Oxford University Press, 1989. ISBN 82-00-18400-5. ▸ Exhaustive political biography of leader of Norwegian Nazi party (Nasjonal Samling), his political background and development, failed quest for leadership under German tutelage, and demise. [MFM]

32.334 Sven G. Holtsmark. "Atlantic orientation or regional groupings: elements of Norwegian foreign policy discussions during the Second World War." *Scandinavian journal of history* 14.4 (1989) 311–24. ISSN 0346-8755. ▸ Well-documented study concluding foreign policy debates about alliances, starting in 1942, included challenges to Atlantic strategy from Poland and Sweden that raised questions about small states participating in Scandinavian or European framework. [MFM]

32.335 François Kersaudy. *Norway, 1940.* New York: St. Martin's, 1990. ISBN 0-312-06427-6. ▸ Useful study of military campaigns in Norway during spring and early summer of 1940, with special attention to policies of British and French governments. [MFM]

32.336 Arne Kiel and Lars Mjøset. "Wage formation in the Norwegian industry, 1840–1985." *Scandinavian economic history review* 38.1 (1990) 19–49. ISSN 0358-5522. ▸ Excellent analysis of wage formation in industrial sector, noting differences between largely competitive labor market in nineteenth century and more organized patterns during twentieth century. [MFM]

32.337 Jan Tore Klovland. "A chronology of cycles in real economic activity for Norway, 1867–1914." *Scandinavian economic history review* 37.3 (1989) 18–38. ISSN 0358-5522. ▸ Technically sophisticated study finding cycles in Norway generally quite similar to those in major European countries. Analysis based on gross domestic product indicator employing monthly data on foreign trade, shipping activity, and railway receipts. [MFM]

32.338 Sverre Knutsen. "From expansion to panic and crash: the Norwegian banking system and its customers, 1913–1924." *Scandinavian economic history review* 39.3 (1991) 41–71. ISSN 0358-5522. ▸ Thorough examination of development of system with aim of explaining why postwar slump of 1920–21 produced major banking crisis. Finds weakness of credit institutions too great to withstand pressure from depression. [MFM]

32.339 Terje I. Leiren. "The role of kingship in the monarchist-republican debate in Norway, 1905." *Historian* 48.2 (1986) 268–78. ISSN 0018-2370. ▸ Useful examination of 1905 debate—at dissolution of union with Sweden—over choice between monarchy or republic. Both positions argued, but plebiscite overwhelmingly favored monarchy. [MFM]

32.340 B. Lindsay Lowell. "Sociological theories and the great emigration." *Norwegian-American studies* 32 (1989) 53–69. ISSN 0078-1983. ▸ Exploration of applicability of three sociological theories to Norwegian emigration in late nineteenth century. Rejects overpopulation theory; suggests social networking most important since emigrants left to join acquaintances who emigrated earlier. [MFM]

32.341 Kari Melby. "The housewife ideology in Norway between the two world wars." *Scandinavian journal of history* 14.2 (1989) 181–93. ISSN 0346-8755. ▸ Stimulating examination of history of Norwegian Housewives' Union (1915), middle-class organization that advocated professionalizing housework and requiring formal training in order to secure its status. [MFM]

32.342 Alan S. Milward. *The fascist economy in Norway.* Oxford: Clarendon, 1972. ISBN 0198214960. ▸ Careful study of economic policies pursued by German authorities in occupied Norway and their impact on Norwegian economy. [MFM]

32.343 Kjell Bjørn Minde and Jan Ramstad. "The development of real wages in Norway about 1730–1910." *Scandinavian economic history review* 34.2 (1986) 90–121. ISSN 0358-5522. ▸ Study showing real wages grew in most branches of economy, 1720–60, and in some branches, 1820–70; then cheap food accelerated growth of real wages in general. Recounts research by others. [MFM]

32.344 Sten Sparre Nilson. "Factional strife in the Norwegian Labour party, 1918–1924." *Journal of contemporary history* 16.4 (1981) 691–704. ISSN 0022-0094. ‣ Important discussion of split within Labor party over membership in Comintern that led to formation of a right splinter party (Social Democrats) and—after withdrawal—a left splinter party (Communists). [MFM]

32.345 Olav Riste. "Norway in exile, 1940–1945: the formation of an alliance relationship." *Scandinavian journal of history* 12.4 (1987) 317–29. ISSN 0346-8755. ‣ Stimulating essay on government-in-exile's efforts to forge working relationship with British government, which had helped drag Norway into war and then left it in the lurch once Germany invaded. [MFM]

32.346 Val D. Rust. *The democratic tradition and the evolution of schooling in Norway.* New York: Greenwood, 1989. ISBN 0-313-26849-5. ‣ Comprehensive examination of development of public education in Norway from Norway's separation from Denmark in 1814 to 1980s through four reform cycles (two each in nineteenth and twentieth centuries). [MFM]

32.347 Anne-Lise Seip. "Eilert Sundt: a founding father of the social sciences in Norway." *Scandinavian journal of history* 11.3 (1986) 229–42. ISSN 0346-8755. ‣ Useful study of strong advocate of education to bridge gaps among classes and student of poverty and social relations. Sundt sought social peace through elimination of poverty. [MFM]

32.348 Anne-Lise Seip. "Who cares? Child, family, and social policy in twentieth-century Norway." *Scandinavian journal of history* 12.4 (1987) 331–43. ISSN 0346-8755. ‣ Useful study of shift in Norwegian society from "family state" with parents dominating child care to "welfare state" with large share of responsibility transferred to state. [MFM]

32.349 Ingrid Semmingsen. *Norway to America: a history of the migration.* Einar Haugen, trans. Minneapolis: University of Minnesota Press, 1978. ISBN 0-8166-0842-3. ‣ Informed, comprehensive survey of Norwegian emigration to United States in nineteenth century, covering economic and political background as well as experience of Norwegian emigrants. [MFM]

32.350 Bjørn Slettan. "Religious movements in Norway: attitudes and trends in recent research." *Scandinavian journal of history* 11.4 (1986) 345–61. ISSN 0346-8755. ‣ Sketch of Norwegian religious history, discussing relevant research on revivalism and religion in general. Deals with such topics as growth of organizations, social class, women, and such lay movements as counterculture. [MFM]

32.351 Harald Thuen. "Education or punishment? Reformatory schools in Norway, 1840–1950." *History of education* 20.1 (1991) 49–60. ISSN 0046-760X. ‣ Useful survey of creation and development of these institutions, which were viewed as appropriate alternatives to prison. Criticism developed in 1930s that they were neither educating nor reforming those incarcerated. [MFM]

32.352 Kåre Tønnesson. "Popular protest and organization: the Thrane movement in preindustrial Norway, 1849–1855." *Scandinavian journal of history* 13.2–3 (1988) 121–39. ISSN 0346-8755. ‣ Interesting description of Marcus Thrane's Drammen Workers Association, Norway's first mass political movement which mobilized some 30,000 members across country between 1849 and 1851, but was repressed when movement became radicalized after 1851. [MFM]

32.353 Hans Try. "Dualism in the early history of Norwegian associations." *Scandinavian journal of history* 13.4 (1988) 385–98. ISSN 0346-8755. ‣ Useful study of Norwegian popular associations in temperance, labor, agriculture, etc., which were decen-

tralized, democratic, and critical of status quo; other associations hierarchical, elite led, and based in capital. [MFM]

32.354 Nils Morten Udgaard. *Great power politics and Norwegian foreign policy: a study of Norway's foreign relations, November 1940–February 1948.* Oslo: Universitetsforlaget, 1973. ISBN 82-00-01258-1 (cl), 82-00-01256-5 (pbk). ‣ Still useful analysis of development and implementation of Norwegian foreign policy during years of Norway's government-in-exile and during immediate postwar period. [MFM]

SEE ALSO
42.226 Jon Gjerde. *From peasants to farmers.*
47.402 Olav Riste. *The neutral ally.*

Sweden

32.355 Gerard Aalders and Cees Wiebes. "Stockholms Enskilda Bank, German Bosch, and I. G. Farben: a short history of cloaking." *Scandinavian economic history review* 33.1 (1985) 25–50. ISSN 0358-5522. ‣ Thoroughly researched study of major Swedish bank's pretended ownership during interwar period of pre-1914 subsidiaries of two major German firms and post-1945 consequences of this subterfuge. [MFM]

32.356 Ingrid Åberg. "Revivalism, philanthropy, and emancipation: women's liberation and organization in the early nineteenth century." *Scandinavian journal of history* 13.4 (1988) 399–420. ISSN 0346-8755. ‣ Insightful study of Swedish women's utilization of early nineteenth-century voluntary associations as vehicles to increase their involvement in society without crossing still-forbidden boundary into public sphere. [MFM]

32.357 Ronny Ambjörnsson. "The conscientious worker: ideas and ideals in a Swedish working-class culture." *History of European ideas* 10.1 (1989) 59–67. ISSN 0191-6599. ‣ Useful examination of concepts helping to shape Swedish working-class culture around 1900 and values helping to shape working-class ideology that contributed to Swedish social democracy. [MFM]

32.358 Peter Baldwin. "How socialist is solidaristic social policy? Swedish postwar reform as a case in point." *International review of social history* 33.2 (1988) 121–47. ISSN 0020-8590. ‣ Study challenging received notions about exclusive link between Social Democrats and development of Swedish welfare state, emphasizing liberal and conservative initiatives to remove means testing. [MFM]

32.359 Klaus-Richard Böhme. "The principal features of Swedish defence policy, 1925–1945." *Revue internationale d'histoire militaire* 57 (1984) 119–34. ISSN 0254-8186. ‣ Thorough analysis of changes and developments from Disarmament Resolution of 1925 through Defense Resolution of 1936 and World War II. Finds that by 1945, Swedish military qualitatively and quantitatively strong by international comparison. [MFM]

32.360 W. M. Carlgren. *Swedish foreign policy during the Second World War.* Arthur Spencer, trans. New York: St. Martin's, 1977. ISBN 0-312-78058-3. ‣ First history of Swedish diplomacy between 1939 and 1945 by scholar with full access to Swedish foreign ministry archives. Only such work available in English. [MFM]

32.361 Allan Carlson. *The Swedish experiment in family politics: the Myrdals and the interwar population crisis.* New Brunswick, N.J.: Transaction, 1990. ISBN 0-88738-299-1. ‣ Unsympathetic yet informative study of formulation of Swedish pronatalist population policy in 1930s, tracing Gunnar and Alva Myrdal's contributions to concept of public responsibility for maternal and child health. [MFM]

32.362 Sten Carlsson. "From four estates to two chambers: the Riksdag in a period of transition, 1809–1921." In *The Riksdag: a history of the Swedish Parliament.* Michael F. Metcalf, ed., pp. 165–222. New York: St. Martin's, 1987. ISBN 0-312-00784-1.

▸ Useful examination of political history of Sweden in nineteenth and early twentieth centuries though limited to issues of constitutional change and cameral reform. Close attention to democratization of representation. [MFM]

32.363 S. Cho and Nils Runeby, eds. *Traditional thought and ideological change: Sweden and Japan in the age of industrialisation.* Stockholm: University of Stockholm, Department of Japanese and Korean, 1988. (Japanological studies, 8.) ISBN 91-7540-063-4. ▸ Includes useful essays on Swedish historical thought around 1900, history of Swedish higher education, concept of family in twentieth-century Sweden, and economic thought in Swedish trade union movement. Contains similar studies on Japan. [MFM]

32.364 Arvid Cronenberg. "The armed forces as instruments of security policy: some guidelines in modern Swedish war planning before 1945 against the background of contemporary security policy thinking." *Revue internationale d'histoire militaire* 57 (1984) 135–86. ISSN 0254-8186. ▸ Comprehensive analysis of formulation of strategic doctrine in nineteenth century; defense plan of 1906; war planning, 1910–14; disarmament debate, 1920–25; defense plans of 1927 and 1939; and wartime thinking, 1939–45. [MFM]

32.365 Lars Edgren. "Crafts in transformation? Masters, journeymen, and apprentices in a Swedish town, 1800–1850." *Continuity and change* 1.3 (1986) 363–83. ISSN 0268-4160. ▸ Penetrating investigation of structure of crafts in Malmö. Finds small workshops and workers domiciled with masters. Concludes career prospects for journeymen good, but very poor for apprentices, who were little more than cheap labor. [MFM]

32.366 Tom Ericsson. "The *Mittelstand* in Swedish class society, 1870–1914." *Scandinavian journal of history* 9.4 (1984) 313–28. ISSN 0346-8755. ▸ Useful study of organizations representing shopkeepers and artisans, finding demands raised by both groups remarkably similar. Views activity as part of broader European mobilization of lower middle class. [MFM]

32.367 Martin Fritz. "A question of practical politics: economic neutrality during the Second World War." *Revue internationale d'histoire militaire* 57 (1984) 95–118. ISSN 0254-8186. ▸ Very useful discussion of trade through Skaggerak blockade, formal control of Swedish-German trade, and neutrality issues around iron-ore and ball-bearing exports. Argues Sweden's precarious economic position required maximizing trade with Germany. [MFM]

32.368 Martin Fritz et al. *The adaptable nation: essays in Swedish economy during the Second World War.* Stockholm: Almqvist & Wiksell, 1982. (Publications of the Institute of Economic History of Gothenburg University, 50.) ISBN 91-85196-22-3, ISSN 0072-5080. ▸ Very good essays on Swedish wartime economy, 1939–45, Swedish trade with Germany in iron ore and ball bearings, and interaction of state, industry, and credit market in Sweden's rearmament. [MFM]

32.369 Jonas Frykman and Orvar Löfgren. *Culture builders: a historical anthropology of middle-class life.* Alan Crozier, trans. New Brunswick, N.J.: Rutgers University Press, 1987. ISBN 0-8135-1209-3 (cl), 0-8135-1239-5 (pbk). ▸ Fascinating ethnographic study of developing middle-class worldview and life style in nineteenth- and early twentieth-century Sweden. Follows emergence of family-centered life style. Ignores religion. [MFM]

32.370 Anders Gustavsson. "New trends in recent Swedish research into revivalism." *Scandinavian journal of history* 11.4 (1986) 301–07. ISSN 0346-8755. ▸ Useful overview relating revivalism to basic patterns of human behavior and studying it as cult process. Success apparently inhibited by presence of competing movements (religious and secular) in same region. [MFM]

32.371 Bo K. A. Huldt. "Swedish disarmament and security policy from the 1920s to the 1980s." *Revue internationale d'histoire*

militaire 57 (1984) 35–57. ISSN 0254-8186. ▸ Detailed examination of disarmament as security policy and tension between disarmament and rearmament in Swedish policy debate and formulation at different points over six decades, including discussion of Nordic nuclear-free zone. [MFM]

32.372 Alf W. Johansson and Torbjörn Norman. "The Swedish policy of neutrality in a historical perspective." *Revue internationale d'histoire militaire* 57 (1984) 69–94. ISSN 0254-8186. ▸ Excellent study tracing development and implications of policy from its inception in post-Napoleonic period through 1960s. Examines economic considerations and choices between neutrality and collective security. [MFM]

32.373 Ann-Sofic Kälvemark. *More children of better quality? Aspects on Swedish population policy in the 1930s.* Stockholm: Almqvist & Wiksell, 1980. (Acta Universitatis Upsaliensis, Studia historica Upsaliensia, 115.) ISBN 91-554-1094-4. ▸ Study of lively debates over population policy at time when nativity rates had reached all-time lows and regrowing population was matter of keen political concern. [MFM]

32.374 Steven Koblik. *The stones cry out: Sweden's response to the persecution of the Jews, 1933–1945.* David Mel Paul and Margareta Paul, documents trans. New York: Holocaust Library, 1988. ISBN 0-89604-118-2 (cl), 0-89604-119-0 (pbk). ▸ Critical study of reactions of Swedish government, church, and humanitarian agencies to plight of Jews in Nazi Germany and to early news of Holocaust. [MFM]

32.375 Steven Koblik. *Sweden, the neutral victor: Sweden and the Western powers, 1917–1918; a study of Anglo-American–Swedish relations.* Stockholm: Läromedelsförlagen, 1972. ISBN 91-24-22677-7. ▸ Well-documented study of how technical assistance to Germany's foreign ministry by Sweden's conservative cabinet was used by Allies and Swedish liberals to change Sweden's government and liberalize its electoral process. [MFM]

32.376 Steven Koblik. "Sweden's attempts to aid Jews, 1939–1945." *Scandinavian studies* 56.2 (1984) 89–113. ISSN 0036 5637. ▸ Description of Sweden's policy toward Scandinavian and European Jews, 1939–45, and important aid and asylum efforts begun in 1942. Reevaluates Bernadotte mission of 1945 and negotiations leading to it. [MFM]

32.377 Leif Lewin. *Ideology and strategy: a century of Swedish politics.* Victor Kayfetz, trans. New York: Cambridge University Press, 1988. ISBN 0-521-34330-5. ▸ Description and analysis of eight major political crises in Swedish parliamentary politics from 1880s to 1980s, by prominent Swedish political scientist. [MFM]

32.378 Sven-Eric Liedman. "Civil servants close to the people: Swedish university intellectuals and society at the turn of the century." *History of European ideas* 8.2 (1987) 155–66. ISSN 0191-6599. ▸ Innovative analysis of adaptation of higher education degrees to practical needs of society in fields of law, medicine, and teaching in 1902. Finds professors participated actively in public discourse and thus broad-based education. [MFM]

32.379 Marika Lindholm. "Swedish feminism, 1835–1945: a conservative revolution." *Journal of historical sociology* 4.2 (1991) 121–42. ISSN 0952-1909. ▸ Important study of how achievements of early Swedish feminists were shaped more by contemporary structural and political changes than by particular feminist demands. Concludes many successes stemmed from efforts of established politicians to expand their electoral base. [MFM]

32.380 Emory Lindquist. "Sweden's search for answers: the emigration survey, then and now." *Swedish-American historical quarterly* 37.4 (1986) 159–73. ISSN 0730-028X. ▸ Very useful description of massive survey, authorized by Swedish Parliament in 1904, to discover causes of emigration, producing wealth of data for historians. [MFM]

32.381 Torborg Lundell. "Ellen Key and Swedish feminist views on motherhood." *Scandinavian studies* 56.4 (1984) 351–69. ISSN 0036-5637. ▸ Useful discussion of radical views on motherhood in turn-of-century writings of Swedish philosopher in context of later twentieth-century feminist views on social definitions of motherhood. [MFM]

32.382 Lars Magnusson. "Drinking and the *verlag* system, 1820–1850: the significance of taverns and drink in Eskilstuna before industrialisation." *Scandinavian economic history review* 34.1 (1986) 1–19. ISSN 0358-5522. ▸ Innovative study finding taverns played important cultural and business role. Buying drinks important investment in community building for artisans and workers in context of securing work and favors in putting-out (*verlag*) system. [MFM]

32.383 Sture Martinius. "Capitalism: a threat against freehold farms around the middle of nineteenth century?" *Scandinavian economic history review* 35.2 (1987) 178–90. ISSN 0358-5522. ▸ Fine essay which answers question in the negative. Finds economic progress of Swedish freeholders more capitalistic than that of large landowners; freeholders also better off socially and politically. [MFM]

32.384 C. G. McKay. "Iron ore and Section D: the Oxelösund operation." *Historical journal* 29.4 (1986) 975–78. ISSN 0018-246X. ▸ Thoroughly researched story of bungled British covert operation in Sweden (1939–40) targeted at sabotaging iron-ore exports to Germany and swaying Swedish public opinion against Hitler. Agent arrested and imprisoned by Swedish government. [MFM]

32.385 Donald Meyer. *Sex and power: the rise of women in America, Russia, Sweden, and Italy.* 2d ed. Middletown, Conn.: Wesleyan University Press, 1989. ISBN 0-8195-5153-8 (cl), 0-8195-6214-9 (pbk). ▸ Excellent examination of Swedish attitudes toward women in late eighteenth and nineteenth centuries. Follows rise and history of feminism in cultural, economic, and political spheres. [MFM]

32.386 Roger Miller and Torvald Gerger. *Social change in nineteenth-century Swedish agrarian society.* Stockholm: Almqvist & Wiksell, 1985. (Acta Universitatis Stockholmiensis, Stockholm studies in human geography, 5.) ISBN 91-22-00781-4 (pbk). ▸ Study utilizing time-geographic model to portray society and economy of rural Locknevi estate and Vrångfall village in period of change from precapitalist to market economy. Excellent use of multiple historical sources. [MFM]

32.387 Jens Möller. "The landed estate and the railway: the introduction of a new means of transport in southern Sweden." *Journal of transport history* 8.2 (1987) 147–63. ISSN 0022-5266. ▸ Useful examination of changes in agricultural and settlement patterns as evidenced by accounts and ledgers of large estate. Finds railway facilitated transition from grains to animal products in Swedish agricultural exports. [MFM]

32.388 Magnus Mörner. " 'The Swedish model': historical perspectives." *Scandinavian journal of history* 14.3 (1989) 245–67. ISSN 0346-8755. ▸ Excellent study finding Swedish welfare state historically unique thanks to near steady growth of income since mid-seventeenth century and sociopolitical attitudes toward consensus and compromise found in Swedish agrarian society and nation's political tradition. [MFM]

32.389 Ingemar Nygren. "The transformation of bank structures in the industrial period: the case of Sweden, 1820–1913." *Journal of European economic history* 12.1 (1983) 29–68. ISSN 0391-5115. ▸ Important examination of structural evolution of banks to 1870; consolidation of institutional credit market, 1875–95; establishment of modern national bank by mid-1890s; and role of banks as suppliers of credit to industry. [MFM]

32.390 Christer Persson. "Freehold farmers and land ownership structure in a parish of southeastern Sweden during the nineteenth century." *Journal of historical geography* 14.3 (1988) 245–59. ISSN 0305-7488. ▸ Detailed study contrasting market integration of Swedish freehold farmers in grain-producing areas with more traditional practices of farmers in Locknevi parish. Finds that farmers in Locknevi, with its marginal agricultural land, maintained traditional peasant society, purchasing only their farmsteads. [MFM]

32.391 Allan Pred. *Place, practice, and structure: social and spatial transformation in southern Sweden, 1750–1850.* Totowa, N.J.: Barnes & Noble, 1986. ISBN 0-389-20615-6. ▸ Prominent cultural geographer's study of implementation of enclosure reforms in Scania within context of developing markets and population growth, highlighting impact of social change at local level. [MFM]

32.392 John G. Rice. "Indicators of social change in rural Sweden in the late nineteenth century." *Journal of historical geography* 4.1 (1978) 23–34. ISSN 0305-7488. ▸ Fascinating examination of process of social change through increased range of first names given to children born in rural parish following coming of railroad and regular access to national periodicals. [MFM]

32.393 Olof Ruin. *Tage Erlander: serving the welfare state, 1946–1969.* Michael F. Metcalf, trans. Pittsburgh: University of Pittsburgh Press, 1990. ISBN 0-8229-3631-3. ▸ Biography of Sweden's long-serving postwar social democratic prime minister written as study of political leadership and governance in modern welfare state. [MFM]

32.394 Harald Runblom and Hans Norman, eds. *From Sweden to America: a history of the migration; collective work of the Uppsala Migration Research Project.* Minneapolis: University of Minnesota Press, 1976. (Studia historica Upsaliensia, 74.) ISBN 0-8166-0776-1. ▸ Landmark collection of essays by Uppsala historians on Swedish emigration to North and South America and how to study it. Examines Swedish emigration policy, causes of emigration, and remigration phenomenon. [MFM]

32.395 Hans Sjögren. "The financial contracts of large firms: a longitudinal study of Swedish firms and commercial banks, 1919–1947." *Scandinavian economic history review* 39.3 (1991) 72–94. ISSN 0358-5522. ▸ Study demonstrating that most Swedish commercial banks enjoyed long-term, complex relationships with large firms based on concerns of economic security and sustained by mutual dependency. Suggests new directions for research. [MFM]

32.396 Lee Soltow. "Inequalities on the eve of mass migration: agricultural holdings in Sweden and the United States in 1845–1850." *Scandinavian economic history review* 35.3 (1987) 219–36. ISSN 0358-5522. ▸ Sophisticated statistical study comparing cross-national distribution of wealth suggests 20 percent of Swedes migrated to United States in search of land during second half of century because landowning prospects much better in United States. [MFM]

32.397 Lee Soltow. "The rich and the destitute in Sweden, 1805–1855: a test of Tocqueville's inequality hypotheses." *Economic history review* 42.1 (1989) 43–63. ISSN 0013-0117. ▸ Using quinquennial Swedish censuses listing households as destitute, poor, moderately rich, or rich, tests and generally substantiates Tocqueville's hypothesis of declining levels of inequality with economic improvement for rich; methodologically sophisticated. [MFM]

32.398 Johan Söderberg. "Causes of poverty in Sweden in the nineteenth century." *Journal of European economic history* 11.2 (1982) 369–402. ISSN 0391-5115. ▸ Penetrating analysis suggesting that commercialization of agriculture brought decline in poverty, while industrialization brought significant reductions. Concludes poverty trends unfavorable where these developments slow or late. [MFM]

32.399 Nils Stjernquist. "From bicameralism to unicameralism: the democratic Riksdag, 1921–1986." In *The Riksdag: a history of the Swedish Parliament.* Michael F. Metcalf, ed., pp. 223–303. New York: St. Martin's, 1987. ISBN 0-312-00784-1. ▸ Broad institutional analysis of evolving Riksdag as well as historical coverage of Swedish politics since introduction of universal suffrage and parliamentary government. Special attention to party politics. [MFM]

32.400 Lennart G. Svensson. *Higher education and the state in Swedish history.* Stockholm: Almqvist & Wiksell, 1987. ISBN 91-22-00893-4. ▸ Study of development of higher education in Sweden from seventeenth to late twentieth century, concentrating on evolution of government-university relations, changes in organization, and professionalization. [MFM]

32.401 Timothy Alan Tilton. *The political theory of Swedish social democracy: through the welfare state to socialism.* New York: Oxford University Press, 1990. ISBN 0-19-827496-3 (cl), 0-19-827874-8 (pbk). ▸ Major study in history of ideas of Swedish Social Democrats and their leaders in twentieth century concerning reformation of society and economy. [MFM]

SEE ALSO
42.247 Robert Clifford Ostergren. *A community transplanted.*

Baltic Provinces to 1918

32.402 Andrew Ezergailis and Gert von Pistohlkors, eds. *Die baltischen Provinzen Russlands zwischen den Revolutionen von 1905 und 1917.* Cologne: Böhlau, 1982. ISBN 3-412-01582-2. ▸ Collection of well-researched essays illuminating economic, social, and political changes in Baltic provinces of Russian empire between Russian revolutions of 1905 and 1917. [MFM]

32.403 Michael Haltzel. *Der Abbau der deutschen ständischen Selbstverwaltung in den Ostseeprovinzen Rußlands: ein Beitrag zur Geschichte der russischen Unifizierungspolitik, 1855–1905.* Marburg: Herder-Institut, 1977. ISBN 3-87969-143-6. ▸ Careful analysis of Russian attempts to integrate Baltic provinces into empire in years following Crimean War through russification of administration, education, and judicial system. [MFM]

32.404 Juhan Kahk. *Peasant and lord in the process of transition from feudalism to capitalism in the Baltics: an attempt of interdisciplinary history.* Tallinn, Estonia: Eesti Raamat, 1982. ▸ Very useful study of economic and social changes accompanying introduction of capitalist economic practices in Baltic provinces. [MFM]

32.405 Juhan Kahk. "The spread of agricultural machines in Estonia from 1860–1880." *Agricultural history* 62.3 (1988) 33–44. ISSN 0002-1482. ▸ Penetrating examination of changes in Estonian agriculture and their social and economic background. Shows dearth of skilled labor, inadequacy of agricultural science, and landlords' reluctance to invest in technology slowed introduction of machinery. [MFM]

32.406 Edward C. Thaden. "Baltic national movements during the nineteenth century." *Journal of Baltic studies* 16.4 (1985) 411–21. ISSN 0162-9778. ▸ Important, critical review article of collections of essays on national movements in Baltic countries. Useful introduction to state of scholarship. [MFM]

32.407 Edward C. Thaden. "Iurii Fedorovich Samarin and Baltic history." *Journal of Baltic studies* 17.4 (1986) 321–28. ISSN 0162-9778. ▸ Introduction to Russian historian (1819–76) in Riga, who studied socioeconomic conditions in Baltic provinces and championed interests of peasants and workers by promoting need for Russian government intervention in Baltic affairs. [MFM]

Baltic States

32.408 Itzchok Adirim. "Realities of economic growth and distribution in the Baltic states." *Journal of Baltic studies* 19.1 (1988) 49–59. ISSN 0162-9778. ▸ Comparative analysis of economic development in Baltic states, 1961–84, as compared with Soviet Union as whole; offers explanation of more rapid growth of Baltic economies. [MFM]

32.409 Rolf Ahmann. "The German treaties with Estonia and Latvia of 7 June 1939: bargaining ploy or an alternative for German-Soviet understanding?" *Journal of Baltic studies* 20.4 (1989) 337–64. ISSN 0162-9778. ▸ Thoroughly researched study placing Germany's nonaggression treaties with Estonia and Latvia in June 1939 in broader diplomatic context of German-Soviet relations. Illustrates relative impotence of Baltic states. [MFM]

32.410 Walter C. Clemens, Jr. *Baltic independence and Russian empire.* New York: St. Martin's, 1991. ISBN 0-312-04806-8. ▸ Study of relations between Baltic states and Russian/Soviet empire throughout century. Devotes bulk of attention to 1985–90 period; very useful footnotes. [MFM]

32.411 John Hiden. "From war to peace: Britain, Germany, and the Baltic states, 1918–1921." *Journal of Baltic studies* 19.4 (1988) 371–82. ISSN 0162-9778. ▸ Proposes new approaches to study of Baltic states in interwar period. Brief, well-documented case study reexamining commercial competition between England and Germany in years immediately following World War I. [MFM]

32.412 John Hiden and Patrick Salmon. *The Baltic nations and Europe: Estonia, Latvia, and Lithuania in the twentieth century.* New York: Longman, 1991. ISBN 0-582-08246-3 (cl), 0-582-08245-5 (pbk). ▸ Good introduction to histories of Baltic nations from around 1900 to 1940. Better on Estonia, Latvia, and pre-1940 period than on Lithuania and post-1940 period. [MFM]

32.413 John Hiden and Thomas Lane, eds. *The Baltic and the outbreak of the Second World War.* New York: Cambridge University Press, 1992. ISBN 0-521-40467-3. ▸ Very good essays concerning complicated situation of Baltic states on eve of World War II, caught as they were between interests of Germany and Soviet Union. [MFM]

32.414 John Hiden and Aleksander Loit, eds. *The Baltic in international relations between the two world wars: symposium organized by the Centre for Baltic Studies, November 11–13, 1986, University of Stockholm, Frescati.* Stockholm: University of Stockholm, Centre for Baltic Studies; distributed by Almqvist & Wiksell, 1988. (Acta Universitatis Stockholmiensis, Studia Baltica Stockholmiensia, 3.) ISBN 91-22-01194-3. ▸ Eighteen articles on regional alliance systems in Baltic, Baltic powers' relations with great powers, and transnational aspects of foreign relations in Baltic, 1918–39, some of which are very good. [MFM]

32.415 Dietrich Ander Loeber, Vytas Stanley Vardys, and Laurence P. A. Kitching, eds. *Regional identity under Soviet rule: the case of the Baltic states.* Hackettstown, N.J.: Institute for the Study of Law, Politics, and Society of Socialist States, 1990. (Publications of the Association for the Advancement of Baltic Studies, 6.) ISBN 0-9624906-0-1. ▸ One of last Soviet era analyses of situation of Baltic states of Estonia, Latvia, and Lithuania within Soviet Union and how they manifested and preserved their identity. [MFM]

32.416 Vincent E. McHale. "The party systems of the Baltic states: a comparative European perspective." *Journal of Baltic studies* 17.4 (1986) 295–312. ISSN 0162-9778. ▸ Useful structural analysis of origins and roles of rightist, centrist, and leftist political parties in Estonia, Latvia, and Lithuania, 1918–40. Stresses influence of needed land reforms, presence of ethnic minorities, and nationalist movements. [MFM]

32.417 Romuald J. Misiunas and Rein Taagepera. *The Baltic states: years of dependence, 1940–1990.* Rev. ed. Berkeley: University of California Press, 1993. ISBN 0-520-08227-3 (cl), 0-520-08228-1 (pbk). ▸ Well-documented history of Baltic states under Soviet occupation, designed as sequel to von Rauch 32.419. [MFM]

32.418 Stanley W. Page. *The formation of the Baltic states: a study of the effects of great power politics upon the emergence of Lithuania, Latvia, and Estonia.* Cambridge, Mass.: Harvard University Press, 1959. ▸ Very good analysis of various forces—including German military supremacy, nationalism, and bolshevism—contributing to and shaping emergence of three Baltic republics as independent states in 1918. [MFM]

32.419 Georg von Rauch. *The Baltic states, the years of independence: Estonia, Latvia, Lithuania, 1917–1940.* Gerald Onn, trans. Berkeley: University of California Press, 1974. ISBN 0-520-02600-4. ▸ Best general history of Baltic states during interwar period. First published in German in 1970. [MFM]

32.420 Zvi Segal. "Jewish minorities in the Baltic republics in the postwar years." *Journal of Baltic studies* 19.1 (1988) 60–66. ISSN 0162-9778. ▸ Preliminary description of efforts of Jews to preserve identity in face of Soviet oppression. Finds more success in Lithuania than in Estonia and Latvia, but ultimately Jewish cultural presence disappeared. [MFM]

32.421 Vytas Stanley Vardys and Romuald J. Misiunas, eds. *The Baltic states in peace and war, 1917–1945.* University Park: Pennsylvania State University Press, 1978. ISBN 0-271-00534-3. ▸ Excellent collection of essays on Baltic states during years of Russian Revolution, independence, annexation to Soviet Union, and World War II. [MFM]

32.422 Izidors Vizulis. *The Molotov-Ribbentrop Pact of 1939: the Baltic case.* New York: Praeger, 1990. ISBN 0-275-93456-X. ▸ Interesting analysis of effects of Molotov-Ribbentrop Pact on Baltic states, concentrating on subsequent Soviet pressures for territorial concessions and ultimate Soviet annexation of Estonia, Latvia, and Lithuania. [MFM]

SEE ALSO
    48.113 John Hiden. *The Baltic states and Weimar Ostpolitik.*

Estonia

32.423 Tönu Parming. *The collapse of liberal democracy and the rise of authoritarianism in Estonia.* Beverly Hills, Calif.: Sage, 1975. ISBN 0-8039-9913-5. ▸ Very good analysis of collapse of democratic institutions and their displacement by authoritarian rule in Estonia during interwar period, using electoral, labor market, and other economic data to illustrate arguments. [MFM]

32.424 Tönu Parming. "The electoral achievements of the Communist party in Estonia, 1920–1940." *Slavic review* 42.3 (1983) 426–47. ISSN 0037-6779. ▸ Useful presentation of electoral data for parties during interwar years. Attributes Communist party's poor showing after 1923 to its attempted coup in 1924. [MFM]

32.425 Toivo U. Raun. "Estonian emigration within the Russian empire, 1860–1917." *Journal of Baltic studies* 17.4 (1986) 350–63. ISSN 0162-9778. ▸ Excellent study showing that high rents and land hunger in Estonia, and availability of land in Russia, produced broad emigration of Estonians to other parts of Russian empire (1860–1917), mostly to neighboring regions. [MFM]

32.426 Ants Viires. "Discovering Estonian folk art at the beginning of the twentieth century." *Journal of Baltic studies* 17.2 (1986) 79–97. ISSN 0162-9778. ▸ Well-documented study of revival of Estonian folk art as new source of national identity, joining folklore; women's handicrafts featured at annual agricul-

tural exhibitions from 1900; folk art museum established as Estonian National Museum. [MFM]

Latvia

32.427 Andrew Ezergailis. *The 1917 Revolution in Latvia.* Boulder: East European Quarterly; distributed by Columbia University Press, 1974. (East European monographs, 8.) ISBN 0-914710-01-X. ▸ Detailed study of political history of 1917 Revolution in Latvia, concentrating on Latvian Social Democratic party, Bolshevik takeover, and establishment of first Latvian Socialist Republic. [MFM]

32.428 Adolfs Silde. "The role of Russian-Latvians in the sovietization of Latvia." *Journal of Baltic studies* 18.2 (1987) 191–208. ISSN 0162-9778. ▸ Study arguing dearth of local Communists led Soviets to bring Latvians from Russia. Those born and raised in Russia promoted complete sovietization; native-born Latvians who emigrated to Russia opposed it. Useful appendixes. [MFM]

32.429 Zigurds L. Zile. "Origin and development of the Latvian legal profession: the century before independence." *Journal of Baltic studies* 20.1 (1989) 3–64. ISSN 0162-9778. ▸ Thorough, well-documented examination of development of legal profession among speakers of Latvian through examination of matriculants at legal faculties and study of nature and parameters of legal practice between 1819 and 1918. [MFM]

Lithuania

32.430 Alfonsas Eidintas. "The emigration policy of the *Tautininkai* regime in Lithuania, 1926–1940." Alfred Erich Senn, trans. *Journal of Baltic studies* 16.1 (1985) 64–72. ISSN 0162-9778. ▸ Well-documented study of Lithuanian Nationalist party efforts to increase control of emigration bureaus and provide penalties for fraud to stem heavy emigration. Argues emigration unrestricted until economic crisis of 1929–30. [MFM]

32.431 Yaacov Iram. "The persistence of Jewish ethnic identity: the educational experience in interwar Poland and Lithuania, 1919–1939." *History of education* 14.4 (1985) 273–82. ISSN 0046-760X. ▸ Useful discussion of major Zionist and non-Zionist educational programs of interwar years. Poland and Lithuania abandoned commitments to minority rights made in 1919; Jewish efforts then concentrated on education to preserve cultural identity. [MFM]

32.432 Thomas A. Oleszczuk. *Political justice in the USSR: dissent and repression in Lithuania, 1969–1987.* Boulder: East European Monographs; distributed by Columbia University Press, 1988. (East European monographs, 247.) ISBN 0-88033-144-5. ▸ Very useful exploration of dynamics of protest and repression in Lithuanian SSR in context of Soviet administration of justice. [MFM]

32.433 Leonas Sabaliunas. "Adaptive behavior in foreign policy crisis situations: Lithuania, 1938–1940." *East European quarterly* 21.2 (1987) 165–81. ISSN 0012-8449. ▸ Very good study of nature and strengths of interwar Lithuanian government tracing its reactions to—and means of addressing—foreign policy crises with Poland (1938), Germany (1939), and Soviet Union (1940). [MFM]

32.434 Leonas Sabaliunas. *Lithuania in crisis: nationalism to communism, 1939–1940.* Bloomington: Indiana University Press, 1972. ISBN 0-253-33600-7. ▸ Useful monographic study of interwar politics and economic development in Lithuania, with special emphasis on crisis of 1939–40 brought on by German seizure of Klaipeda (Memel). [MFM]

32.435 Leonas Sabaliunas. *Lithuanian social democracy in perspective, 1893–1914.* Durham, N.C.: Duke University Press, 1990. ISBN 0-8223-1015-5. ▸ Rare study of Lithuanian political party prior to independence. Traces beginnings of Lithuanian social democracy with its early nationalist bent from founding to World War I. [MFM]

32.436 Alfred Erich Senn. *The emergence of modern Lithuania.* 1959 ed. Westport, Conn.: Greenwood, 1975. ISBN 0-8371-7780-4. ▸ Dated but still very useful study of Lithuania's modern history, with emphasis on years to World War II. [MFM]

32.437 Alfred Erich Senn. *The great powers, Lithuania, and the Vilna question, 1920–1928.* Leiden: Brill, 1966. ▸ Still useful monographic treatment of one of most enduring territorial disputes among newly independent nations of eastern and central Europe following World War I. [MFM]

32.438 Saulius Sužiedėlis. "The military mobilization campaigns of 1943 and 1944 in German-occupied Lithuania: contrasts in resistance and collaboration." *Journal of Baltic studies* 21.1 (1990) 33–52. ISSN 0162-9778. ▸ Thoroughly researched study arguing Lithuanians maintained independence as primary goal during German occupation and thus resisted military recruitment to Lithuanian SS legion in 1943 because independent Lithuania opposed by Germany. [MFM]

32.439 George Urbaniak. "French involvement in the Polish-Lithuanian dispute, 1918–1920." *Journal of Baltic studies* 16.1 (1985) 52–63. ISSN 0162-9778. ▸ Well-documented study showing that France, as part of policy to promote *cordon sanitaire* between Russia and Germany, favored peaceful union between Poland and Lithuania over independent and weak Lithuania. Counseled Poland against use of force against Lithuania, but ultimately countenanced Poland's annexation of Vilna region. [MFM]

32.440 George Urbaniak. "Lithomania versus panpolonism: the roots of the Polish-Lithuanian conflict before 1914." *Canadian Slavonic papers* 31.2 (1989) 107–27. ISSN 0008-5006. ▸ Useful study concluding peasant emancipation and defeat of January Insurrection in 1860s dismantled social order and elevated new classes lacking attachments to Polish-Lithuanian commonwealth. Argues conflicting attitudes of new and old political elites remained unreconciled. [MFM]

32.441 Vytas Stanley Vardys, ed. *Lithuania under the Soviets: portrait of a nation, 1940–65.* New York: Praeger, 1965. ▸ Comprehensive, responsible study of Lithuania under Soviet rule, written at time when access to sources was severely limited. [MFM]

32.442 Robert A. Vitas. *The United States and Lithuania: the Stimson doctrine of nonrecognition.* New York: Praeger, 1990. ISBN 0-275-93412-8. ▸ Study concentrating on United States policy formation during and after World War II, and on United States support for Lithuanian and other Baltic diplomatic missions in Washington during cold war. Excellent bibliography. [MFM]